S0-BDI-138

PRESENTED TO

on this day of ,

From

on the occasion of

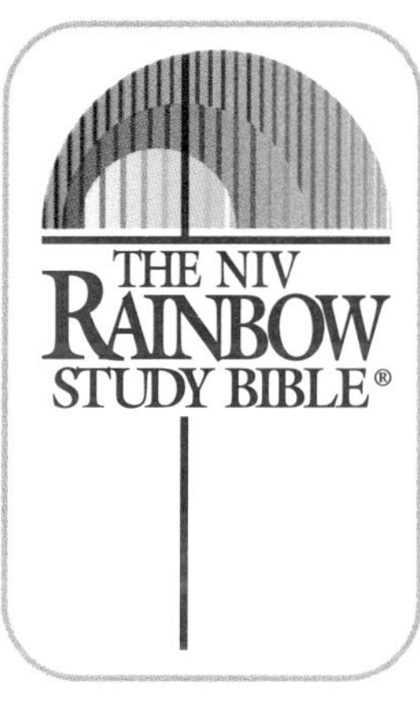

HOLY BIBLE

New International Version

THE NIV RAINBOW STUDY BIBLE®

Every Verse Color-Coded
Bold Line® Edition

Words of God (*the Father, the Son, and the Holy Spirit*) distinguished with Bold Underlining,
Book Introductions and Outlines, Center Column Cross-References,
Sectional Headings, In-Text Maps, Bookmarker with Color-Code System,
Subject Guide, Concordance and Other Special Study Aids.

CARMEL • NEW YORK 10512

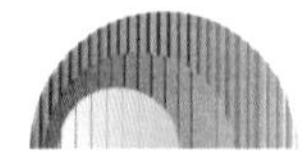

THE RAINBOW STUDY BIBLE®

This Guideposts edition is published by special arrangement with Rainbow Studies, Inc.

The NIV Rainbow Study Bible (New International Version):

ISBN 0-933657-17-X Burgundy Cloth; Indexed 0-933657-20-X
ISBN 0-933657-18-8 Burgundy Imitation Leather; Indexed 0-933657-21-8
ISBN 0-933657-19-6 Burgundy Bonded Leather; Indexed 0-933657-22-6
ISBN 0-933657-31-5 Burgundy Genuine Leather; Indexed 0-933657-35-8
ISBN 0-933657-23-4 Gospel of John, Paperback

Library of Congress Catalog Card Number 92-61901

Scriptural Promise for The NIV Rainbow Study Bible

Then God said to Noah and to his sons with him:
"I now establish my covenant with you and with your descendants after
you and with every living creature that was with you — the birds,
the livestock and all the wild animals, all those that came out of the ark
with you — every living creature on earth. I establish my covenant with
you: Never again will all life be cut off by the waters of a flood;
never again will there be a flood to destroy the earth."
And God said, "This is the sign of the covenant I am making
between me and you and every living creature with you,
a covenant for all generations to come:

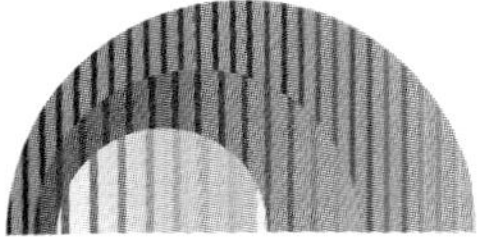

I have set my rainbow in the clouds, and it will be the sign
of the covenant between me and the earth. Whenever I bring clouds
over the earth and the rainbow appears in the clouds, I will remember
my covenant between me and you and all living creatures of every kind.
Never again will the waters become a flood to destroy all life.
Whenever the rainbow appears in the clouds, I will see it and
remember the everlasting covenant between God
and all living creatures of every kind on the earth."
So God said to Noah, "This is the sign of the covenant I have
established between me and all life on the earth."

GENESIS 9:8-17

TO THE READER

The NIV Rainbow Study Bible IS JOYFULLY PRESENTED to the Christian community and to all those seeking to know their Creator in a closer way. This is the first and only Bible to aid the reader by color-coding *every* verse of the *entire* Bible and by distinguishing with Bold Underlining all spoken Words of God (the Father, the Son, and the Holy Spirit) throughout the text.

This project has required countless hours and even years of dedicated work in areas of expertise including research, writing, proof-editing, art design, composition, and financial planning. But it is not the desire of Rainbow Studies Int'l. to take any credit... rather we give all credit to the One that made this work possible. We hereby acknowledge that this work is not available because of man's efforts, but because of God's grace, mercy, and faithfulness to further the Gospel through unworthy, yet willing, people.

Our prayer is that you may grow in sensitivity and obedience to the prompting of the Holy Spirit as you read and meditate upon the Word of God and that you will mirror the life of Jesus Christ in your own walk.

To God the Father, God the Son, and God the Holy Spirit be given all glory and praise, now and forevermore.

The Publisher

TABLE OF CONTENTS

WORDS OF EXPLANATION

THE TITLE

The Rainbow Study Bible may seem an obvious title for a Bible of many colors, but there are several significant reasons for this choice.

First, as our Scriptural Promise from the opening book of the Bible (Genesis 9:8-17) points out, the rainbow is a gift from God and the seal of his covenant with mankind. In the closing book of the Bible (Revelation 4:3), a rainbow encircles the very throne of God. A true example of the beauty of God's color which reveals Biblical significance as well, the *Rainbow* in ***The Rainbow Study Bible*** has special meaning.

The Rainbow Study Bible has been designated a *Study* Bible because it has new study features found in no other Bible. These features include color-coding of *every* verse of the Bible and distinguishing all spoken Words of God (the Father, the Son, and the Holy Spirit). *Study* is indeed simplified in ***The Rainbow Study Bible.***

WHY ANOTHER STUDY BIBLE?

With the increase and renewal of studying the Bible, Rainbow Studies Int'l. saw a need for a study Bible easy enough for the young, new, or relatively inexperienced reader to understand, yet comprehensive enough to satisfy the more serious and mature Bible student. Thus...***The Rainbow Study Bible!***

Absolutely nothing could be more simple or basic than color-coding the *entire* Bible. No turning of pages or looking up corresponding information. Verses on any subject given can be found by simply looking for a certain *color.*

Our 20th-century world is color-oriented. Colors are easily identifiable, universal, and exciting, which is why this Bible is so enjoyable to read. But, the acute simplicity of ***The Rainbow Study Bible*** does not end with merely encouraging each person to have a copy he can call his own...this Bible is uniquely designed to actually encourage more and more *reading* and *meditating* upon the Word of God. The easy-to-use format will aid those desiring to witness, teach, preach, give devotionals, memorize scriptures, or to better understand Scripture for their personal insight.

The Rainbow Study Bible has been developed under the conviction that the Holy Spirit of God is directing this complete effort.

DESIGN OF COLOR-CODING SYSTEM

The Rainbow Study Bible is a simple, yet thorough, study Bible based upon the premise that *every* verse of the *entire* Bible falls under one of twelve thematic headings. Each of these twelve headings is assigned a different color; then each verse of the Bible is color-coded to the heading to which it is most closely related.

Identification charts help to categorize all the subjects and breakdowns under each of the twelve thematic headings. These charts are designed by a common sense approach so as to doctrinally and spiritually tie together the related items listed under each heading.

The Rainbow Study Bible allows the serious Bible student the opportunity to study and teach the great Bible themes, while avoiding a time-consuming or complicated system. It has been designed so as to provide both the average layman and the mature pastor help in an alternative Bible that is enjoyable to read and easily understood and shared with others.

PHILOSOPHY OF COLOR-CODING SYSTEM

The Rainbow Study Bible, a sixteen-year effort of its developer, Rainbow Studies, Inc., has utilized the expertise of a devout team of top Christian educators and theologians of diverse backgrounds. We have painstakingly sought precision and accuracy, but we recognize that only the Word of God is totally without error. Any imperfections attributed to our human limitations shall, therefore, be corrected in future publications as we are so enlightened.

- The design is according to a layman's perspective (to make teaching, studying, and categorizing as *simple* as possible).

- Generally, verses are marked as they make up a major passage containing an overall *collective* thought.
- For emphasis, verses are often color-coded individually.
- Many times more than one color is applicable. When this is the case, the color believed to be the most strongly related is used.
- The important factor, when a scripture has two or more subjects thought to be equally strong, is not so much to which color the reader is directed as that he is indeed directed to one of them.
- The same basic verse in two different places of the Bible may be marked in different colors depending upon how lead-up and subsequent verses affect its most strongly related color.

SIGNIFICANCE OF NUMBERS AND COLORS

Numbers and colors were studied as to their significance to Biblical teachings. Not all numbers, nor all colors, have Biblical significance, but assignments were made to correspond where pertinent. This aids the reader in committing the 12 divisions and colors to memory. Consider the following:

- *Twelve* subject divisions selected because 12 is a number of completeness in the Bible, as evidenced by the 12 tribes of Israel in the Old Testament and the 12 apostles in the New Testament.
- *God* in the *first* position because there is one God.
- *Satan* in the *sixth* position because of the significance of 666 and the mark of the beast in the book of Revelation.
- *Salvation* in *seventh* position because 7 signifies holiness and perfection.
- *Commandments* in *tenth* position because of their relationship with the 10 Commandments given to Moses.
- *Purple* assigned to *God* because it is a color of royalty.
- *Blue* assigned to *Salvation* because it has a heavenly or eternal connotation.
- *Silver* assigned to *History* because it signifies age or experience.

DESIGN OF BOLD LINE® EDITION

The Words of God (the Father, the Son, and the Holy Spirit) are distinguished with Bold Underlining. This method, which provides immediate identification, spans the entire Bible, regardless of the color under which the quote may be found.

Examples:

(The Father)	The LORD God said, "It is not good for the man to be alone. I will make a helper suitable for him." Genesis 2:18
(The Son)	Then Jesus said to the centurion, "Go! It will be done just as you believed it would." And his servant was healed at that very hour. Matthew 8:13
(The Holy Spirit)	While they were worshiping the Lord and fasting, the Holy Spirit said, "Set apart for me Barnabas and Saul for the work to which I have called them." Acts 13:2

CRITERIA FOR BOLD LINE® EDITION

The compilers of ***The NIV Rainbow Study Bible*** believe that the *whole* Bible is the inspired Word of God. The decision to mark certain passages with Bold Underlining emphasizes those selections where God was speaking as the Father, Son, or Holy Spirit. These include the instances where either Biblical characters or writers repeated words they believed were quotations from God and therefore deserved special attention. For example, this often occurred when prophets ended their declarations with phrases, such as "says the Lord."

Most Bible versions have used quotation marks or similar devices to separate such quotes. A related practice has been used to emphasize the words of Jesus in Red

Letter editions of the New Testament. ***The NIV Rainbow Study Bible*** offers an expansion of these practices by distinguishing all quotes from God with Bold Underlining.

Every effort has been made to include all occasions where God was speaking or where Biblical writers or characters were quoting such words. When these occasions were not identified clearly in the text, the compilers studied the context of the passage and its relationship to comparable verses throughout the Bible.

This process recognizes both the integrity of the individual books of the Bible and the essential unity of Scripture. It also permits attention to the matter of a reader's understanding of passages. Such concerns guided all decisions regarding the marking of verses. In addition, the following guidelines were applied when they did not contradict the principles defined above.

Passages were marked when:

- "The Angel of the Lord" spoke unless he was speaking to God. (See Zech. 1:12.)
- A voice from heaven spoke words revealing God's authority. (See Dan. 4:31, 32.)
- Subsequent passages offered additional understanding.
- New Testament writers or speakers used phrases clearly associated with the words of God. (See Rom. 1:17 and Hab. 2:4.)

The following were not marked as quotes from God unless they met other criteria:

- Messianic passages.
- The Wisdom passages in Proverbs.
- Statements of false prophets or teachers.
- Typological verses.
- The words of angels or other heavenly beings other than "the Angel of the Lord."
- Speakers who were "filled with the Spirit."
- Phrases such as "says the Lord."

Additional Study Features

Although ***The NIV Rainbow Study Bible*** has been developed with two primary study features (the color-code system and bold underlining format), there are many other outstanding features as well. The study aids listed below are designed to especially benefit those desiring a more disciplined Christian walk.

- Detailed Introduction Preceding Each of the 66 Books of the Bible
- Study Outline Preceding Each of the 66 Books of the Bible
- Sectional Headings Throughout the 1,189 Chapters of the Bible
  Note: The standard New International Version sectional headings have been altered for this particular edition.
- Center Column Cross-Reference System
- Unique Page Composition
- Bookmarker with Color-Code System
- In-Text Maps
- Presentation Page
- 100 Popular Bible Passages
- 365 Popular Bible Quotations for Memorization and Meditation
- Outline of Old Testament History
- Daily Bible Reading Calendars
- Where to Find It
- Subject Guide
- Concordance
- Table of Weights and Measures
- Special Bible Maps with Index
- New International Version

Goals of *The Rainbow Study Bible*

1. To paint a picture of colors on every page and thereby make reading more enjoyable.
2. To help every reader attain a further understanding of the message in each scripture.
3. To provide easy access for studying, giving devotionals, and teaching.
4. To provide an accurate breakdown of topics.
5. To help every reader remember by color association where significant verses are located.
6. To provide an easily recognizable format distinguishing the Words of God throughout the Bible.
7. To actually encourage more and more reading of God's Word.

CONTENTS
Arranged in Biblical Order

CONTENTS
Arranged in Alphabetical Order

TABLE OF CONTENTS
In-Text and Back Maps

INTRODUCTION TO THE CROSS-REFERENCE SYSTEM

The New International Version has one of the most thorough, accurate and best organized cross-reference systems available. It began with the vision of one individual more than a decade ago and by the time it was completed involved more than forty people and a half-dozen computers.

The cross references link words or phrases in the NIV text with counterpart Biblical references listed in a center column on each page. The raised letters indicating these cross references are set in a light italic typeface to distinguish them from the NIV text note letters, which use a roman typeface. When a single word is addressed by both, the roman NIV text note comes first, as in Matthew 1:21, "Jesus[c*i*]."

The lists of references are in Biblical order with one exception: If reference is made to a verse within the same chapter, that verse (indicated by "ver") is listed first.

In the Old Testament some references are marked with an asterisk (*), which means that the Old Testament verse or phrase is quoted in the New Testament (see, for example, Genesis 1:3). The corresponding information is provided in the New Testament by the NIV text note (see 2 Corinthians 4:6).

An important feature of this cross-reference system is in its notation of parallel and reference passages. When two or more sections of Scripture are nearly identical or deal with the same event, "parallel passage" ("pp") is noted at the sectional heading (see Matthew 21:33-46). These parallel passages are especially common in the Gospels and in Samuel, Kings, and Chronicles. When the passages are similar but do not deal with the same event, they are noted with "Ref" at the sectional headings (see Matthew 22:2-14).

To conserve space and avoid repetition, parallel passages or references that are noted at sectional headings are not repeated in the reference column.

PREFACE

THE NEW INTERNATIONAL VERSION is a completely new translation of the Holy Bible made by over a hundred scholars working directly from the best available Hebrew, Aramaic and Greek texts. It had its beginning in 1965 when, after several years of exploratory study by committees from the Christian Reformed Church and the National Association of Evangelicals, a group of scholars met at Palos Heights, Illinois, and concurred in the need for a new translation of the Bible in contemporary English. This group, though not made up of official church representatives, was transdenominational. Its conclusion was endorsed by a large number of leaders from many denominations who met in Chicago in 1966.

Responsibility for the new version was delegated by the Palos Heights group to a self-governing body of fifteen, the Committee on Bible Translation, composed for the most part of biblical scholars from colleges, universities and seminaries. In 1967 the New York Bible Society (now the International Bible Society) generously undertook the financial sponsorship of the project—a sponsorship that made it possible to enlist the help of many distinguished scholars. The fact that participants from the United States, Great Britain, Canada, Australia and New Zealand worked together gave the project its international scope. That they were from many denominations—including Anglican, Assemblies of God, Baptist, Brethren, Christian Reformed, Church of Christ, Evangelical Free, Lutheran, Mennonite, Methodist, Nazarene, Presbyterian, Wesleyan and other churches—helped to safeguard the translation from sectarian bias.

How it was made helps to give the New International Version its distinctiveness. The translation of each book was assigned to a team of scholars. Next, one of the Intermediate Editorial Committees revised the initial translation, with constant reference to the Hebrew, Aramaic or Greek. Their work then went to one of the General Editorial Committees, which checked it in detail and made another thorough revision. This revision in turn was carefully reviewed by the Committee on Bible Translation, which made further changes and then released the final version for publication. In this way the entire Bible underwent three revisions, during each of which the translation was examined for its faithfulness to the original languages and for its English style. All this involved many thousands of hours of research and discussion regarding the meaning of the texts and the precise way of putting them into English. It may well be that no other translation has been made by a more thorough process of review and revision from committee to committee than this one.

From the beginning of the project, the Committee on Bible Translation held to certain goals for the New International Version: that it would be an accurate translation and one that would have clarity and literary quality and so prove suitable for public and private reading, teaching, preaching, memorizing and liturgical use. The Committee also sought to preserve some measure of continuity with the long tradition of translating the Scriptures into English.

In working toward these goals, the translators were united in their commitment to the authority and infallibility of the Bible as God's Word in written form. They believe that it contains the divine answer to the deepest needs of humanity, that it sheds unique light on our path in a dark world, and that it sets forth the way to our eternal well-being.

The first concern of the translators has been the accuracy of the translation and its fidelity to the thought of the biblical writers. They have weighed the significance of the lexical and grammatical details of the Hebrew, Aramaic and Greek texts. At the same time, they have striven for more than a word-for-word translation. Because thought patterns and syntax differ from language to language, faithful communication of the meaning of the writers of the Bible demands frequent modifications in sentence structure and constant regard for the contextual meanings of words.

A sensitive feeling for style does not always accompany scholarship. Accordingly the Committee on Bible Translation submitted the developing version to a number of stylistic consultants. Two of them read every book of both Old and New Testaments twice—once before and once after the last major revision—and made invaluable suggestions. Samples of the translation were tested for clarity and ease of reading by various kinds of people—young and old, highly educated and less well educated, ministers and laymen.

Concern for clear and natural English—that the New International Version should be idiomatic but not idiosyncratic, contemporary but not dated—motivated the translators and consultants. At the same time, they tried to reflect the differing styles of the biblical writers. In view of the international use of English, the translators sought to avoid obvious Americanisms on the one hand and obvious Anglicisms on the other. A British edition reflects the comparatively few differences of significant idiom and of spelling.

As for the traditional pronouns "thou," "thee" and "thine" in reference to the Deity, the translators judged that to use these archaisms (along with the old verb forms such as "doest," "wouldest" and "hadst") would violate accuracy in translation. Neither Hebrew, Aramaic nor Greek uses special pronouns for the persons of the Godhead. A present-day translation is not enhanced by forms that in the time of the King James Version were used in everyday speech, whether referring to God or man.

For the Old Testament the standard Hebrew text, the Masoretic Text as published in the latest editions of *Biblia Hebraica*, was used throughout. The Dead Sea Scrolls contain material bearing on an earlier stage of the Hebrew text. They were consulted, as were the Samaritan Pentateuch and the ancient scribal traditions relating to textual changes. Sometimes a variant Hebrew reading in the margin of the Masoretic Text was followed instead of the text itself. Such instances, being variants within the Masoretic tradition, are not specified by footnotes. In rare cases, words in the consonantal text were divided differently from the way they appear in the Masoretic Text. Footnotes indicate this. The translators also consulted the more important early versions—the Septuagint; Aquila, Symmachus and Theodotion; the Vulgate; the Syriac Peshitta; the Targums; and for the Psalms the *Juxta Hebraica* of Jerome. Readings from these versions were occasionally followed where the Masoretic Text seemed doubtful and where accepted principles of textual criticism showed that one or more of these textual witnesses appeared to provide the correct reading. Such instances are footnoted. Sometimes vowel letters and vowel signs did not, in the judgment of the translators, represent the correct vowels for the original consonantal text. Accordingly some words were read with a different set of vowels. These instances are usually not indicated by footnotes.

The Greek text used in translating the New Testament was an eclectic one. No other piece of ancient literature has such an abundance of manuscript witnesses as does the New Testament. Where existing manuscripts differ, the translators made their choice of readings according to accepted principles of New Testament textual criticism. Footnotes call attention to places where there was uncertainty about what the original text was. The best current printed texts of the Greek New Testament were used.

There is a sense in which the work of translation is never wholly finished. This applies to all great literature and uniquely so to the Bible. In 1973 the New Testament in the New International Version was published. Since then, suggestions for corrections and revisions have been received from various sources. The Committee on Bible Translation carefully considered the suggestions and adopted a number of them. These were incorporated in the first printing of the entire Bible in 1978. Additional revisions were made by the Committee on Bible Translation in 1983 and appear in printings after that date.

As in other ancient documents, the precise meaning of the biblical texts is sometimes uncertain. This is more often the case with the Hebrew and Aramaic texts than with the Greek text. Although archaeological and linguistic discoveries in this century aid in understanding difficult passages, some uncertainties remain. The more significant of these have been called to the reader's attention in the footnotes.

In regard to the divine name *YHWH*, commonly referred to as the *Tetragrammaton*, the translators adopted the device used in most English versions of rendering that name as "LORD" in capital letters to distinguish it from *Adonai*, another Hebrew word rendered "Lord," for which small letters are used. Wherever the two names stand together in the Old Testament as a compound name of God, they are rendered "Sovereign LORD."

Because for most readers today the phrases "the LORD of hosts" and "God of hosts" have little meaning, this version renders them "the LORD Almighty" and "God Almighty." These renderings convey the sense of the Hebrew, namely, "he who is sovereign over all the 'hosts' (powers) in heaven and on earth, especially over the 'hosts' (armies) of Israel." For readers unacquainted with Hebrew this does not make clear the distinction between *Sabaoth* ("hosts" or "Almighty") and *Shaddai* (which can also be translated "Almighty"), but the latter occurs infrequently and is always footnoted. When *Adonai* and *YHWH Sabaoth* occur together, they are rendered "the Lord, the LORD Almighty."

As for other proper nouns, the familiar spellings of the King James Version are generally retained. Names traditionally spelled with "ch," except where it is final, are usually spelled in this translation with "k" or "c," since the biblical languages do not have the sound that "ch" frequently indicates in English—for example, in *chant*. For well-known names such as Zechariah, however, the traditional spelling has been retained. Variation in the spelling of names in the original languages has usually not been indicated. Where a person or place has two or more different names in the Hebrew, Aramaic or Greek texts, the more familiar one has generally been used, with footnotes where needed.

To achieve clarity the translators sometimes supplied words not in the original texts but required by the context. If there was uncertainty about such material, it is enclosed in brackets. Also for the sake of clarity or style, nouns, including some proper nouns, are sometimes substituted for pronouns, and vice versa. And though the Hebrew writers often shifted back and forth between first, second and third personal pronouns without change of antecedent, this translation often makes them uniform, in accordance with English style and without the use of footnotes.

Poetical passages are printed as poetry, that is, with indentation of lines and with separate stanzas. These are generally designed to reflect the structure of Hebrew poetry. This poetry is normally characterized by parallelism in balanced lines. Most of the poetry in the Bible is in the Old Testament, and scholars differ regarding the scansion of Hebrew lines. The translators determined the stanza divisions for the most part by analysis of the subject matter. The stanzas therefore serve as poetic paragraphs.

As an aid to the reader, italicized sectional headings are inserted in most of the books. They are not to be regarded as part of the NIV text, are not for oral reading, and are not intended to dictate the interpretation of the sections they head.

The footnotes in this version are of several kinds, most of which need no explanation. Those giving alternative translations begin with "Or" and generally introduce the alternative with the last word preceding it in the text, except when it is a single-word alternative; in poetry quoted in a footnote a slant mark indicates a line division. Footnotes introduced by "Or" do not have uniform significance. In some cases two possible translations were considered to have about equal validity. In other cases, though the translators were convinced that the translation in the text was correct, they judged that another interpretation was possible and of sufficient importance to be represented in a footnote.

In the New Testament, footnotes that refer to uncertainty regarding the original text are introduced by "Some manuscripts" or similar expressions. In the Old Testament, evidence for the reading chosen is given first and evidence for the alternative is added after a semicolon (for example: Septuagint; Hebrew *father*). In such notes the term "Hebrew" refers to the Masoretic Text.

It should be noted that minerals, flora and fauna, architectural details, articles of clothing and jewelry, musical instruments and other articles cannot always be identified with precision. Also measures of capacity in the biblical period are particularly uncertain (see the table of weights and measures following the text).

Like all translations of the Bible, made as they are by imperfect man, this one undoubtedly falls short of its goals. Yet we are grateful to God for the extent to which he has enabled us to realize these goals and for the strength he has given us and our colleagues to complete our task. We offer this version of the Bible to him in whose name and for whose glory it has been made. We pray that it will lead many into a better understanding of the Holy Scriptures and a fuller knowledge of Jesus Christ the incarnate Word, of whom the Scriptures so faithfully testify.

The Committee on Bible Translation

June 1978
(Revised August 1983)

Names of the translators and editors may be secured
from the International Bible Society,
translation sponsors of the New International Version,
P.O. Box 62970, Colorado Springs, Colorado, 80962-2970 U.S.A.

Color-Coded Guide for SUBJECT HEADINGS

GOD

DISCIPLESHIP

LOVE

FAITH

SIN

SATAN

SALVATION

FAMILY

WITNESSING

COMMANDMENTS

HISTORY

PROPHECY

Color-Coded Guide for SUBJECT CATEGORIES

GOD	the Father; the Son, Jesus Christ; the Holy Spirit
DISCIPLESHIP	obedience; praise
LOVE	joy; kindness
FAITH	prayer; miracles
SIN	evil; judgment of the ungodly
SATAN	false teachers; idolatry
SALVATION	blessings; deliverance
FAMILY	genealogies; marriage
WITNESSING	teaching; counseling
COMMANDMENTS	offerings; law
HISTORY	creation; war
PROPHECY	promises; covenants

Color-Coded Guide for SUBJECT BREAKDOWNS

GOD	the Father; the Son, Jesus Christ; the Holy Spirit; the Word of God; Savior; Lord; Messiah; I AM; Lamb of God; King of Kings; Alpha & Omega
DISCIPLESHIP	obedience; praise; service; worship; wisdom; works; commitment; fellowship; follower; spiritual gifts; fruit
LOVE	joy; kindness; mercy; mourning; lament; comfort; compassion; peace; sympathy; humility; charity
FAITH	prayer; miracles; courage; confession; repentance; fasting; healing; hope; confidence; conviction; belief
SIN	evil; judgment of the ungodly; death; hell; curses; condemnation; temptation; unbelief; hatred; hypocrisy; apostasy
SATAN	false teachers; idolatry; destruction of idols; demons; devil; serpent; evil spirits; false prophets; false worship; witchcraft; antichrist
SALVATION	blessings; deliverance; holiness; heaven; the tabernacle; angels; eternity; resurrection; second coming; judgment of the godly; grace
FAMILY	genealogies; marriage; sexual concerns; children; parenthood; home; adultery; fornication; divorce; friendships; relationships
WITNESSING	teaching; counseling; questioning; instruction; testimony; ministry; preaching; evangelism; gospel; doctrine; sayings
COMMANDMENTS	offerings; law; priesthood; feasts; Sabbath; tithing; baptism; the Lord's Supper; church; deacon; growth
HISTORY	creation; war; times; places; journeys; narration; chronological record of events; vocations; kings; earth; mankind
PROPHECY	promises; covenants; revelations; vows; visions; dreams; oaths; pledges; inspiration; fulfillment; future

Examples of Color-Coded Verses in THE NIV RAINBOW STUDY BIBLE®

GOD	PSALM 95:3 • For the LORD is the great God, the great King above all gods.
DISCIPLESHIP	JOHN 12:26 • Whoever serves me must follow me; and where I am, my servant also will be...
LOVE	1 JOHN 4:7 • Dear friends, let us love one another, for love comes from God. Everyone who loves has been born of God and knows God.
FAITH	HEBREWS 11:1 • Now faith is being sure of what we hope for and certain of what we do not see.
SIN	JAMES 1:15 • Then, after desire has conceived, it gives birth to sin; and sin, when it is full-grown, gives birth to death.
SATAN	1 PETER 5:8 • ...Your enemy the devil prowls around like a roaring lion looking for someone to devour.
SALVATION	ACTS 4:12 • Salvation is found in no one else, for there is no other name under heaven given to men by which we must be saved.
FAMILY	EPHESIANS 5:31 • For this reason a man will leave his father and mother and be united to his wife, and the two will become one flesh.
WITNESSING	PROVERBS 14:25 • A truthful witness saves lives, but a false witness is deceitful.
COMMANDMENTS	EXODUS 20:8-10 • Remember the Sabbath day by keeping it holy. Six days you shall labor and do all your work, but the seventh day...
HISTORY	1 SAMUEL 17:4 • A champion named Goliath, who was from Gath, came out of the Philistine camp. He was over nine feet tall.
PROPHECY	2 PETER 1:21 • For prophecy never had its origin in the will of man, but men spoke from God as they were carried along by the Holy Spirit.

THE OLD TESTAMENT

New International Version

Every Verse Color-Coded

Bold Line® Edition

GENESIS

Author: Moses.

Date Written: Between 1450 and 1400 B.C.

Time Span: Chapters 1-11 record the first years of man's history from the creation to the tower of Babel. Chapters 12-50 cover about 300 years, centering around the lives of 4 men: Abraham, Isaac, Jacob and Joseph. Genesis spans more time than the other 65 books of the Bible combined.

Title: The word "genesis" means "beginning" or "origin." *Bereshith*, the first word in the Hebrew text, means "in the beginning."

Background: Genesis is the first of the 5 books of Moses, called the Pentateuch. Genesis deals with the history of the human race dwelling in the lands from Eden to Ur in the first 11 chapters, and from Canaan to Egypt in the remaining 39 chapters. This first book forms the basis for all further revelation about God and his plan for man.

Where Written: The general belief is that Moses received this revelation while on Mount Sinai in the desert.

To Whom: Genesis is written for the benefit of the Israelites, but the messages contained herein are timeless...as the promises God made to the patriarchs are made known and the foundation is set for the revelation of God's love and the redemption of mankind through Jesus Christ.

Content: God uses his Word to speak all of creation into being. This creation is perfect until man sins by listening to Satan instead of trusting God and obeying his plan. This sin of Adam and Eve results in spiritual death and eventually leads to filling the world with hate, violence and disobedience. Finally, sin prevails until God uses a flood to destroy mankind, except righteous Noah and his family. Even after this, sin sweeps the land, and the people build the huge tower of Babel in defiance of God. God never stops loving man, however, and the last 39 chapters of Genesis reveal how God—through the family of Abraham—directs history to establish the early stages in his plan to save the people and mend their fellowship with him. The book closes with God's chosen people in Egypt.

Key Words: "Beginning"; "Man"; "Covenant." Genesis accounts for the "beginning" of the heavens and earth, plant and animal life, "man" and woman, sin and civilization, and God's work of redemption. God's eternal plan of salvation for mankind is revealed through the "covenant" he establishes with Abraham.

Themes: • God creates man in his own image for fellowship with him. • Man is created with a body, a soul, a spirit and a free will to make decisions for or against God. • Though we sin, God will not give up on us or abandon us. • In spite of our failures, God loves us and sees our value and worth. • The Lord has a plan for every life...and it includes salvation and total obedience to his Word. • God has the love and the power to protect and provide for us as we place our faith in him.

Outline:
1. The story of creation. 1:1-2:25
2. The beginning of sin and death. 3:1-5:32
3. The story of Noah. 6:1-10:32
4. The tower of Babel. 11:1-11:9
5. The life of Abraham. 11:10-25:18
6. The life of Isaac. 25:19-26:35
7. The life of Jacob. 27:1-36:43
8. The life of Joseph. 37:1-50:26

GENESIS

God's six days of creation.

1 In the beginning[a] God created the
heavens and the earth.[b] 2Now the
earth was[a] formless and empty,[c]
darkness was over the surface of
the deep, and the Spirit of God[d]
was hovering over the waters.

3And God said,[e] "Let there be light,"
and there was light.[f] 4God saw that
the light was good, and he separated the light from the darkness. 5God
called the light "day," and the darkness he called "night."[g] And there
was evening, and there was morning—the first day.
6And God said, "Let there be an expanse[h] between the waters to separate water from water." 7So God
made the expanse and separated
the water under the expanse from
the water above it.[i] And it was so.
8God called the expanse "sky." And
there was evening, and there was
morning—the second day.
9And God said, "Let the water under
the sky be gathered to one place,[j]
and let dry ground appear." And it
was so. 10God called the dry ground
"land," and the gathered waters he
called "seas." And God saw that it
was good.
11Then God said, "Let the land
produce vegetation:[k] seed-bearing
plants and trees on the land that
bear fruit with seed in it, according to their various kinds." And it
was so. 12The land produced vegetation: plants bearing seed according to their kinds and trees bearing
fruit with seed in it according to
their kinds. And God saw that it was
good. 13And there was evening, and
there was morning—the third day.
14And God said, "Let there be lights[l] in
the expanse of the sky to separate
the day from the night, and let
them serve as signs[m] to mark seasons[n] and days and years, 15and let
them be lights in the expanse of
the sky to give light on the earth."
And it was so. 16God made two
great lights—the greater light to
govern[o] the day and the lesser
light to govern[p] the night. He also
made the stars.[q] 17God set them in
the expanse of the sky to give light
on the earth, 18to govern the day
and the night,[r] and to separate
light from darkness. And God saw
that it was good. 19And there was
evening, and there was morning—the fourth day.
20And God said, "Let the water teem
with living creatures, and let birds
fly above the earth across the expanse of the sky." 21So God created
the great creatures of the sea and
every living and moving thing with
which the water teems,[s] according
to their kinds, and every winged
bird according to its kind. And God
saw that it was good. 22God blessed
them and said, "Be fruitful and increase in number and fill the water
in the seas, and let the birds increase on the earth."[t] 23And there
was evening, and there was morning—the fifth day.
24And God said, "Let the land produce
living creatures according to their
kinds: livestock, creatures that move
along the ground, and wild animals,
each according to its kind." And it
was so. 25God made the wild animals[u] according to their kinds, the
livestock according to their kinds,
and all the creatures that move
along the ground according to their
kinds. And God saw that it was
good.
26Then God said, "Let us[v] make
man in our image,[w] in our likeness,
and let them rule[x] over the fish of
the sea and the birds of the air, over
the livestock, over all the earth,[b]
and over all the creatures that move
along the ground."

1:1 [a]Jn 1:1-2 [b]Ps 90:2; Isa 42:5; Ac 17:24; Heb 11:3; Rev 4:11
1:2 [c]Jer 4:23 [d]Ps 104:30
1:3 [e]Ps 33:6,9; [f]2Co 4:6*
1:5 [g]Ps 74:16
1:6 [h]Jer 10:12
1:7 [i]Job 38:8-11,16; Ps 148:4
1:9 [j]Job 38:8-11; Ps 104:6-9; Pr 8:29; Jer 5:22; 2Pe 3:5
1:11 [k]Ps 65:9-13; 104:14
1:14 [l]Ps 74:16 [m]Jer 10:2 [n]Ps 104:19
1:16 [o]Ps 136:8 [p]Ps 136:9 [q]Job 38:7, 31-32; Ps 8:3; Isa 40:26
1:18 [r]Jer 33:20,25
1:21 [s]Ps 104:25-26
1:22 [t]ver 28; Ge 8:17
1:25 [u]Jer 27:5
1:26 [v]Ps 100:3 [w]Ge 9:6; Jas 3:9 [x]Ps 8:6-8

a*2* Or possibly *became* b*26* Hebrew; Syriac *all the wild animals*

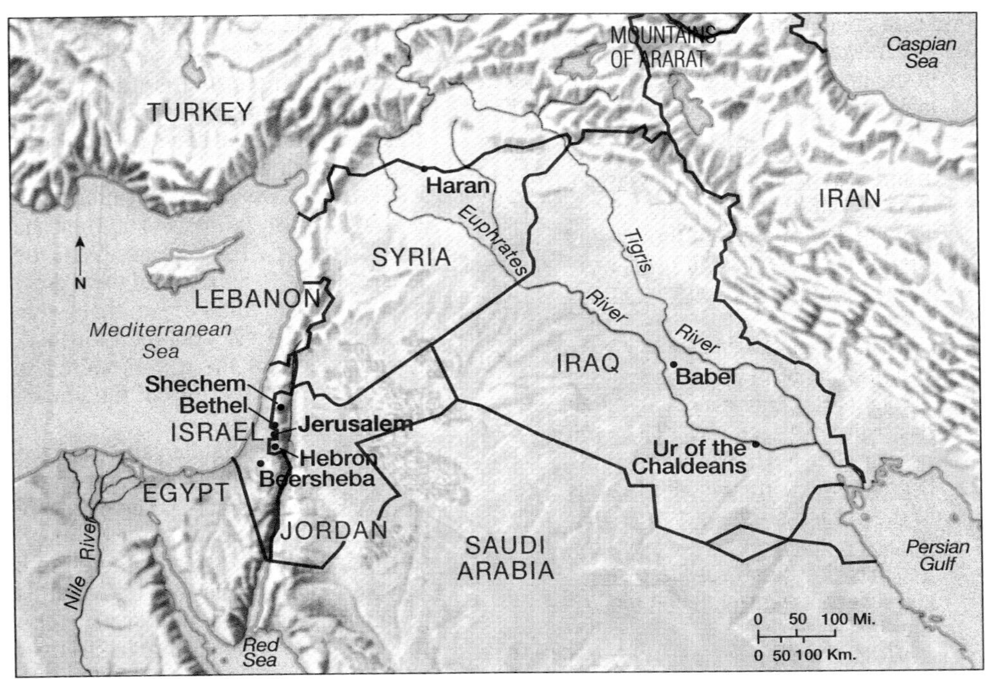

KEY PLACES IN GENESIS

God created the universe and the earth. Then he made man and woman, giving them a home in a beautiful garden. Unfortunately, Adam and Eve disobeyed God and were expelled from the garden (3:24).

Mountains of Ararat Adam and Eve's sin brought sin into the human race. Years later, sin had run rampant and God decided to destroy the earth with a great flood. But Noah, his family, and two of each animal were safe in the ark. When the floods receded, the ark rested on the mountains of Ararat (8:4).

Babel People never learn. Again sin abounded and the pride of the people led them to build a huge tower as a monument to their own greatness—obviously they had no thought of God. As punishment, God scattered the people by giving them different languages (11:8,9).

Ur of the Chaldeans Abram, a descendant of Shem and father of the Hebrew nation, was born in this great city (11:28).

Haran Terah, Lot, Abram, and Sarai left Ur and, following the fertile crescent of the Euphrates River, headed toward the land of Canaan. Along the way, they settled in the city of Haran for a while (11:31).

Shechem God urged Abram to leave Haran and go to a place where he would become the father of a great nation (12:1,2). So Abram, Lot, and Sarai traveled to the land of Canaan and settled near a city called Shechem (12:6).

Hebron Abraham moved on to Hebron where he put down his deepest roots (13:18). Abraham, Isaac, and Jacob all lived and were buried here.

Beersheba A well was dug here as a sign of an oath between Abraham and the army of King Abimelech (21:31). Years later, as Isaac was moving from place to place, God appeared to him here and passed on to him the covenant he had made with his father, Abraham (26:23-25).

Bethel After deceiving his brother, Jacob left Beersheba and fled to Haran. Along the way, God revealed himself to Jacob in a dream and passed on the covenant he had made with Abraham and Isaac (28:10-22). Jacob lived in Haran, worked for Laban, and married Leah and Rachel (29:15-28). After a tense meeting with his brother Esau, Jacob returned to Bethel (35:1).

Egypt Jacob had 12 sons, including Joseph, Jacob's favorite. Joseph's ten older brothers grew jealous, until one day the brothers sold him to Midianite merchants going to Egypt. Eventually, Joseph rose from Egyptian slave to Pharaoh's "right-hand man," saving Egypt from famine. His entire family moved from Canaan to Egypt and settled there (46:3,4).

27So God created man in his own
image,[a]
in the image of God he created him;
male and female[b] he created them.

28God blessed them and said to them, "Be fruitful and increase in number; fill the earth[c] and subdue it. Rule over the fish of the sea and the birds of the air and over every living creature that moves on the ground."

29Then God said, "I give you every seed-bearing plant on the face of the whole earth and every tree that has fruit with seed in it. They will be yours for food.[d] 30And to all the beasts of the earth and all the birds of the air and all the creatures that move on the ground—everything that has the breath of life in it—I give every green plant for food.[e]" And it was so.

31God saw all that he had made,[f] and it was very good.[g] And there was evening, and there was morning—the sixth day.

God's seventh day of rest.

2 Thus the heavens and the earth were completed in all their vast array.

2By the seventh day God had finished the work he had been doing; so on the seventh day he rested[c] from all his work.[h] 3And God blessed the seventh day and made it holy,[i] because on it he rested from all the work of creating that he had done.

Adam and Eve in the Garden of Eden.

4This is the account of the heavens and the earth when they were created.

When the LORD God made the earth and the heavens— 5and no shrub of the field had yet appeared on the earth[d] and no plant of the field had yet sprung up,[j] for the LORD God had not sent rain on the earth[dk] and there was no man to work the ground, 6but streams[e] came up from the earth and watered the whole surface of the ground— 7the LORD God formed the man[f] from the dust[l] of the ground[m] and breathed into his nostrils the breath[n] of life,[o] and the man became a living being.[p]

8Now the LORD God had planted a garden in the east, in Eden;[q] and there he put the man he had formed. 9And the LORD God made all kinds of trees grow out of the ground—trees that were pleasing to the eye and good for food. In the middle of the garden were the tree of life[r] and the tree of the knowledge of good and evil.[s]

10A river watering the garden flowed from Eden; from there it was separated into four headwaters. 11The name of the first is the Pishon; it winds through the entire land of Havilah, where there is gold. 12(The gold of that land is good; aromatic resin[g] and onyx are also there.) 13The name of the second river is the Gihon; it winds through the entire land of Cush.[h] 14The name of the third river is the Tigris;[t] it runs along the east side of Asshur. And the fourth river is the Euphrates.

15The LORD God took the man and put him in the Garden of Eden to work it and take care of it. 16And the LORD God commanded the man, "You are free to eat from any tree in the garden; 17but you must not eat from the tree of the knowledge of good and evil, for when you eat of it you will surely die."[u]

18The LORD God said, "It is not good for the man to be alone. I will make a helper suitable for him."[v]

19Now the LORD God had formed out of the ground all the beasts of the field[w] and all the birds of the air. He brought them to the man to see what he would name them; and whatever the man called each living creature,[x] that was its name. 20So the man gave names to

1:27 [a]1Co 11:7 [b]Ge 5:2; Mt 19:4*; Mk 10:6*
1:28 [c]Ge 9:1,7; Lev 26:9
1:29 [d]Ps 104:14
1:30 [e]Ps 104:14, 27; 145:15
1:31 [f]Ps 104:24 [g]1Ti 4:4
2:2 [h]Ex 20:11; 31:17; Heb 4:4*
2:3 [i]Lev 23:3; Isa 58:13
2:5 [j]Ge 1:11 [k]Ps 65:9-10
2:7 [l]Ge 3:19 [m]Ps 103:14 [n]Job 33:4 [o]Ac 17:25 [p]1Co 15:45*
2:8 [q]Ge 3:23,24; Isa 51:3
2:9 [r]Ge 3:22,24; Rev 2:7; 22:2,14,19 [s]Eze 47:12
2:14 [t]Da 10:4
2:17 [u]Dt 30:15,19; Ro 5:12; 6:23; Jas 1:15
2:18 [v]1Co 11:9
2:19 [w]Ps 8:7 [x]Ge 1:24

c*2* Or *ceased*; also in verse 3 d*5* Or *land*; also in verse 6 e*6* Or *mist* f*7* The Hebrew for *man (adam)* sounds like and may be related to the Hebrew for *ground (adamah)*; it is also the name *Adam* (see Gen. 2:20). g*12* Or *good; pearls* h*13* Possibly southeast Mesopotamia

all the livestock, the birds of the air
and all the beasts of the field.
But for Adam[i] no suitable helper was
found. 21So the LORD God caused the
man to fall into a deep sleep; and while
he was sleeping, he took one of the
man's ribs[j] and closed up the place
with flesh. 22Then the LORD God made
a woman from the rib[k][a] he had taken
out of the man, and he brought her to
the man.
23The man said,

"This is now bone of my bones
and flesh of my flesh;[b]
she shall be called 'woman,[l]'
for she was taken out of man."

24For this reason a man will leave his
father and mother and be united[c] to his
wife, and they will become one flesh.[d]
25The man and his wife were both
naked,[e] and they felt no shame.

The serpent's deceit leads to the fall of Adam and Eve.

3 Now the serpent[f] was more crafty
than any of the wild animals the
LORD God had made. He said to the
woman, "Did God really say, 'You must
not eat from any tree in the garden'?"
2The woman said to the serpent,
"We may eat fruit from the trees in the
garden, 3but God did say, 'You must
not eat fruit from the tree that is in the
middle of the garden, and you must
not touch it, or you will die.'"
4"You will not surely die," the serpent
said to the woman.[g] 5"For God knows
that when you eat of it your eyes will
be opened, and you will be like God,[h]
knowing good and evil."
6When the woman saw that the fruit
of the tree was good for food and pleasing to the eye, and also desirable[i] for
gaining wisdom, she took some and ate
it. She also gave some to her husband,
who was with her, and he ate it.[j] 7Then
the eyes of both of them were opened,
and they realized they were naked; so
they sewed fig leaves together and made
coverings for themselves.

8Then the man and his wife heard the
sound of the LORD God as he was walking[k] in the garden in the cool of the
day, and they hid[l] from the LORD God
among the trees of the garden. 9But the
LORD God called to the man, "Where
are you?"
10He answered, "I heard you in the
garden, and I was afraid because I was
naked; so I hid."
11And he said, "Who told you that
you were naked? Have you eaten from
the tree that I commanded you not to
eat from?"
12The man said, "The woman you put
here with me—she gave me some fruit
from the tree, and I ate it."
13Then the LORD God said to the
woman, "What is this you have done?"
The woman said, "The serpent deceived me,[m] and I ate."
14So the LORD God said to the serpent,
"Because you have done this,

"Cursed[n] are you above all the livestock
and all the wild animals!
You will crawl on your belly
and you will eat dust[o]
all the days of your life.
15And I will put enmity
between you and the woman,
and between your offspring[m][p] and hers;[q]
he will crush[n] your head,[r]
and you will strike his heel."

16To the woman he said,

"I will greatly increase your pains in childbearing;
with pain you will give birth to children.
Your desire will be for your husband,
and he will rule over you.[s]"

17To Adam he said, "Because you listened to your wife and ate from the
tree about which I commanded you,
'You must not eat of it,'

2:22 [a]1Co 11:8,9,12
2:23 [b]Ge 29:14; Eph 5:28-30
2:24 [c]Mal 2:15 [d]Mt 19:5*; Mk 10:7-8*; 1Co 6:16*; Eph 5:31*
2:25 [e]Ge 3:7,10-11
3:1 [f]2Co 11:3; Rev 12:9; 20:2
3:4 [g]Jn 8:44; 2Co 11:3
3:5 [h]Isa 14:14; Eze 28:2
3:6 [i]Jas 1:14-15; 1Jn 2:16 [j]1Ti 2:14
3:8 [k]Dt 23:14 [l]Job 31:33; Ps 139:7-12; Jer 23:24
3:13 [m]2Co 11:3; 1Ti 2:14
3:14 [n]Dt 28:15-20 [o]Isa 65:25; Mic 7:17
3:15 [p]Jn 8:44; Ac 13:10; 1Jn 3:8 [q]Isa 7:14; Mt 1:23; Rev 12:17 [r]Ro 16:20; Heb 2:14
3:16 [s]1Co 11:3; Eph 5:22

[i]*20* Or *the man* [j]*21* Or *took part of the man's side* [k]*22* Or *part* [l]*23* The Hebrew for *woman* sounds like the Hebrew for *man.* [m]*15* Or *seed* [n]*15* Or *strike*

"Cursed[a] is the ground because of you;
through painful toil you will eat of it
all the days of your life.[b]
18 It will produce thorns and thistles for
you,
and you will eat the plants of the
field.[c]
19 By the sweat of your brow
you will eat your food[d]
until you return to the ground,
since from it you were taken;
for dust you are
and to dust you will return."[e]

20 Adam[o] named his wife Eve,[p] because
she would become the mother of all the
living.
21 The LORD God made garments of
skin for Adam and his wife and clothed
them. 22 And the LORD God said, "The
man has now become like one of us,
knowing good and evil. He must not be
allowed to reach out his hand and take
also from the tree of life[f] and eat, and
live forever." 23 So the LORD God banished him from the Garden of Eden[g] to
work the ground[h] from which he had
been taken. 24 After he drove the man
out, he placed on the east side[q] of the
Garden of Eden cherubim[i] and a flaming sword[j] flashing back and forth to
guard the way to the tree of life.[k]

Cain kills his brother Abel and is punished by God.

4 Adam[o] lay with his wife Eve, and
she became pregnant and gave birth
to Cain.[r] She said, "With the help of
the LORD I have brought forth[s] a man."
2 Later she gave birth to his brother
Abel.[l]
Now Abel kept flocks, and Cain
worked the soil. 3 In the course of time
Cain brought some of the fruits of the
soil as an offering to the LORD.[m] 4 But
Abel brought fat portions[n] from some
of the firstborn of his flock.[o] The LORD
looked with favor on Abel and his offering,[p] 5 but on Cain and his offering he
did not look with favor. So Cain was
very angry, and his face was downcast.
6 Then the LORD said to Cain, "Why
are you angry? Why is your face downcast? 7 If you do what is right, will you
not be accepted? But if you do not do
what is right, sin is crouching at your
door;[q] it desires to have you, but you
must master it.[r]"
8 Now Cain said to his brother Abel,
"Let's go out to the field."[t] And while
they were in the field, Cain attacked
his brother Abel and killed him.[s]
9 Then the LORD said to Cain, "Where
is your brother Abel?"
"I don't know," he replied. "Am I my
brother's keeper?"
10 The LORD said, "What have you
done? Listen! Your brother's blood cries
out to me from the ground.[t] 11 Now you
are under a curse and driven from the
ground, which opened its mouth to receive your brother's blood from your
hand. 12 When you work the ground, it
will no longer yield its crops for you. You
will be a restless wanderer on the earth."
13 Cain said to the LORD, "My punishment is more than I can bear. 14 Today
you are driving me from the land, and
I will be hidden from your presence;[u] I
will be a restless wanderer on the earth,
and whoever finds me will kill me."[v]
15 But the LORD said to him, "Not so[u];
if anyone kills Cain[w], he will suffer vengeance seven times over.[x]" Then the
LORD put a mark on Cain so that no one
who found him would kill him. 16 So Cain
went out from the LORD's presence and
lived in the land of Nod,[v] east of Eden.[y]
17 Cain lay with his wife, and she became pregnant and gave birth to Enoch.
Cain was then building a city, and he
named it after his son[z] Enoch. 18 To
Enoch was born Irad, and Irad was the
father of Mehujael, and Mehujael was
the father of Methushael, and Methushael was the father of Lamech.
19 Lamech married two women, one

3:17 [a]Ge 5:29; Ro 8:20-22 [b]Job 5:7; 14:1; Ecc 2:23
3:18 [c]Ps 104:14
3:19 [d]2Th 3:10 [e]Ge 2:7; Ps 90:3; 104:29; Ecc 12:7
3:22 [f]Rev 22:14
3:23 [g]Ge 2:8 [h]Ge 4:2
3:24 [i]Ex 25:18-22 [j]Ps 104:4 [k]Ge 2:9
4:2 [l]Lk 11:51
4:3 [m]Nu 18:12
4:4 [n]Lev 3:16 [o]Ex 13:2,12 [p]Heb 11:4
4:7 [q]Nu 32:23 [r]Ro 6:16
4:8 [s]Mt 23:35; 1Jn 3:12
4:10 [t]Ge 9:5; Nu 35:33; Heb 12:24; Rev 6:9-10
4:14 [u]2Ki 17:18; Ps 51:11; 139:7-12; Jer 7:15; 52:3 [v]Ge 9:6; Nu 35:19,21, 27,33
4:15 [w]Eze 9:4,6 [x]ver 24; Ps 79:12
4:16 [y]Ge 2:8
4:17 [z]Ps 49:11

[o]*20, 1* Or *The man* [p]*20* *Eve* probably means *living.* [q]*24* Or *placed in front* [r]*1* *Cain* sounds like the Hebrew for *brought forth* or *acquired.* [s]*1* Or *have acquired* [t]*8* Samaritan Pentateuch, Septuagint, Vulgate and Syriac; Masoretic Text does not have *"Let's go out to the field."* [u]*15* Septuagint, Vulgate and Syriac; Hebrew *Very well* [v]*16* *Nod* means *wandering* (see verses 12 and 14).

named Adah and the other Zillah.
20Adah gave birth to Jabal; he was the
father of those who live in tents and
raise livestock. **21**His brother's name was
Jubal; he was the father of all who play
the harp and flute. **22**Zillah also had a
son, Tubal-Cain, who forged all kinds
of tools out of[w] bronze and iron. Tubal-
Cain's sister was Naamah.
23Lamech said to his wives,

"Adah and Zillah, listen to me;
wives of Lamech, hear my words.
I have killed[x][a] a man for wounding
me,
a young man for injuring me.
24If Cain is avenged[b] seven times,[c]
then Lamech seventy-seven times."

25Adam lay with his wife again, and
she gave birth to a son and named him
Seth,[y][d] saying, "God has granted me
another child in place of Abel, since
Cain killed him."[e] **26**Seth also had a
son, and he named him Enosh.
At that time men began to call on[z]
the name of the LORD.[f]

Adam's family line to Noah.

5 This is the written account of
Adam's line.

When God created man, he made
him in the likeness of God.[g] **2**He created them male and female[h] and blessed
them. And when they were created, he
called them "man.[a]"
3When Adam had lived 130 years, he
had a son in his own likeness, in his
own image;[i] and he named him Seth.
4After Seth was born, Adam lived 800
years and had other sons and daughters. **5**Altogether, Adam lived 930 years,
and then he died.[j]
6When Seth had lived 105 years, he
became the father[b] of Enosh. **7**And after
he became the father of Enosh, Seth
lived 807 years and had other sons
and daughters. **8**Altogether, Seth lived
912 years, and then he died.
9When Enosh had lived 90 years, he
became the father of Kenan. **10**And after
he became the father of Kenan, Enosh
lived 815 years and had other sons
and daughters. **11**Altogether, Enosh lived
905 years, and then he died.
12When Kenan had lived 70 years,
he became the father of Mahalalel.
13And after he became the father of
Mahalalel, Kenan lived 840 years and
had other sons and daughters. **14**Altogether, Kenan lived 910 years, and then
he died.
15When Mahalalel had lived 65 years,
he became the father of Jared. **16**And
after he became the father of Jared,
Mahalalel lived 830 years and had other sons and daughters. **17**Altogether, Mahalalel lived 895 years, and then he
died.
18When Jared had lived 162 years,
he became the father of Enoch.[k] **19**And
after he became the father of Enoch,
Jared lived 800 years and had other
sons and daughters. **20**Altogether, Jared
lived 962 years, and then he died.
21When Enoch had lived 65 years,
he became the father of Methuselah.
22And after he became the father of Methuselah, Enoch walked with God[l] 300
years and had other sons and daughters. **23**Altogether, Enoch lived 365 years.
24Enoch walked with God;[m] then he was
no more, because God took him away.[n]
25When Methuselah had lived 187
years, he became the father of Lamech.
26And after he became the father of
Lamech, Methuselah lived 782 years
and had other sons and daughters.
27Altogether, Methuselah lived 969
years, and then he died.
28When Lamech had lived 182 years,
he had a son. **29**He named him Noah[c]
and said, "He will comfort us in the labor and painful toil of our hands caused
by the ground the LORD has cursed.[o]"
30After Noah was born, Lamech lived
595 years and had other sons and
daughters. **31**Altogether, Lamech lived
777 years, and then he died.

4:23 [a]Ex 20:13; Lev 19:18
4:24 [b]Dt 32:35 [c]ver 15
4:25 [d]Ge 5:3 [e]ver 8
4:26 [f]Ge 12:8; 1Ki 18:24; Ps 116:17; Joel 2:32; Zep 3:9; Ac 2:21; 1Co 1:2
5:1 [g]Ge 1:27; Eph 4:24; Col 3:10
5:2 [h]Ge 1:27; Mt 19:4; Mk 10:6; Gal 3:28
5:3 [i]Ge 1:26; 1Co 15:49
5:5 [j]Ge 3:19
5:18 [k]Jude 14
5:22 [l]ver 24; Ge 6:9; 17:1; 48:15; Mic 6:8; Mal 2:6
5:24 [m]ver 22 [n]2Ki 2:1,11; Heb 11:5
5:29 [o]Ge 3:17; Ro 8:20

[w] *22* Or *who instructed all who work in* [x] *23* Or *I will kill* [y] *25* *Seth* probably means *granted.*
[z] *26* Or *to proclaim* [a] *2* Hebrew *adam*
[b] *6* *Father* may mean *ancestor*; also in verses 7-26.
[c] *29* *Noah* sounds like the Hebrew for *comfort.*

32 After Noah was 500 years old, he became the father of Shem, Ham and Japheth.

The wickedness of man grieves God.

6 When men began to increase in number on the earth[a] and daughters were born to them, 2 the sons of God saw that the daughters of men were beautiful, and they married any of them they chose. 3 Then the LORD said, "My Spirit will not contend with[d] man forever,[b] for he is mortal[e];[c] his days will be a hundred and twenty years."

4 The Nephilim[d] were on the earth in those days—and also afterward—when the sons of God went to the daughters of men and had children by them. They were the heroes of old, men of renown.

5 The LORD saw how great man's wickedness on the earth had become, and that every inclination of the thoughts of his heart was only evil all the time.[e] 6 The LORD was grieved[f] that he had made man on the earth, and his heart was filled with pain. 7 So the LORD said, "I will wipe mankind, whom I have created, from the face of the earth—men and animals, and creatures that move along the ground, and birds of the air—for I am grieved that I have made them." 8 But Noah found favor in the eyes of the LORD.[g]

Righteous Noah is commanded to build the ark.

9 This is the account of Noah.

Noah was a righteous man, blameless among the people of his time,[h] and he walked with God.[i] 10 Noah had three sons: Shem, Ham and Japheth.[j]

11 Now the earth was corrupt in God's sight and was full of violence.[k] 12 God saw how corrupt the earth had become, for all the people on earth had corrupted their ways.[l] 13 So God said to Noah, "I am going to put an end to all people, for the earth is filled with violence because of them. I am surely going to destroy both them and the earth.[m] 14 So make yourself an ark of cypress[f] wood;[n] make rooms in it and coat it with pitch[o] inside and out. 15 This is how you are to build it: The ark is to be 450 feet long, 75 feet wide and 45 feet high.[g] 16 Make a roof for it and finish[h] the ark to within 18 inches[i] of the top. Put a door in the side of the ark and make lower, middle and upper decks. 17 I am going to bring floodwaters on the earth to destroy all life under the heavens, every creature that has the breath of life in it. Everything on earth will perish.[p] 18 But I will establish my covenant with you,[q] and you will enter the ark[r]—you and your sons and your wife and your sons' wives with you. 19 You are to bring into the ark two of all living creatures, male and female, to keep them alive with you. 20 Two[s] of every kind of bird, of every kind of animal and of every kind of creature that moves along the ground will come to you to be kept alive. 21 You are to take every kind of food that is to be eaten and store it away as food for you and for them."

22 Noah did everything just as God commanded him.[t]

Noah, his family and the animals enter the ark.

7 The LORD then said to Noah, "Go into the ark, you and your whole family,[u] because I have found you righteous[v] in this generation. 2 Take with you seven[j] of every kind of clean[w] animal, a male and its mate, and two of every kind of unclean animal, a male and its mate, 3 and also seven of every kind of bird, male and female, to keep their various kinds alive throughout the earth. 4 Seven days from now I will send rain on the earth for forty days and forty nights, and I will wipe from

6:1 *a* Ge 1:28
6:3 *b* Isa 57:16 *c* Ps 78:39
6:4 *d* Nu 13:33
6:5 *e* Ge 8:21; Ps 14:1-3
6:6 *f* 1Sa 15:11,35; Isa 63:10
6:8 *g* Ge 19:19; Ex 33:12,13, 17; Lk 1:30; Ac 7:46
6:9 *h* Ge 7:1; Eze 14:14,20; Heb 11:7; 2Pe 2:5 *i* Ge 5:22
6:10 *j* Ge 5:32
6:11 *k* Eze 7:23; 8:17
6:12 *l* Ps 14:1-3
6:13 *m* ver 17; Eze 7:2-3
6:14 *n* Heb 11:7; 1Pe 3:20 *o* Ex 2:3
6:17 *p* Ge 7:4,21-23; 2Pe 2:5
6:18 *q* Ge 9:9-16 *r* Ge 7:1,7,13
6:20 *s* Ge 7:15
6:22 *t* Ge 7:5,9,16
7:1 *u* Mt 24:38 *v* Ge 6:9; Eze 14:14
7:2 *w* ver 8; Ge 8:20; Lev 10:10; 11:1-47

d *3* Or *My spirit will not remain in* e *3* Or *corrupt* f *14* The meaning of the Hebrew for this word is uncertain. g *15* Hebrew *300 cubits long, 50 cubits wide and 30 cubits high* (about 140 meters long, 23 meters wide and 13.5 meters high) h *16* Or *Make an opening for light by finishing* i *16* Hebrew *a cubit* (about 0.5 meter) j *2* Or *seven pairs*; also in verse 3

the face of the earth every living creature I have made."

5And Noah did all that the LORD commanded him.[a]

6Noah was six hundred years old when the floodwaters came on the earth. 7And Noah and his sons and his wife and his sons' wives entered the ark to escape the waters of the flood. 8Pairs of clean and unclean animals, of birds and of all creatures that move along the ground, 9male and female, came to Noah and entered the ark, as God had commanded Noah. 10And after the seven days the floodwaters came on the earth.

The flood lasts forty days and forty nights.

11In the six hundredth year of Noah's life, on the seventeenth day of the second month—on that day all the springs of the great deep[b] burst forth, and the floodgates of the heavens[c] were opened. 12And rain fell on the earth forty days and forty nights.[d]

13On that very day Noah and his sons, Shem, Ham and Japheth, together with his wife and the wives of his three sons, entered the ark. 14They had with them every wild animal according to its kind, all livestock according to their kinds, every creature that moves along the ground according to its kind and every bird according to its kind, everything with wings. 15Pairs of all creatures that have the breath of life in them came to Noah and entered the ark.[e] 16The animals going in were male and female of every living thing, as God had commanded Noah. Then the LORD shut him in.

17For forty days[f] the flood kept coming on the earth, and as the waters increased they lifted the ark high above the earth. 18The waters rose and increased greatly on the earth, and the ark floated on the surface of the water. 19They rose greatly on the earth, and all the high mountains under the entire heavens were covered.[g] 20The waters rose and covered the mountains to a depth of more than twenty feet.[k,l] 21Every living thing that moved on the earth perished—birds, livestock, wild animals, all the creatures that swarm over the earth, and all mankind.[h] 22Everything on dry land that had the breath of life[i] in its nostrils died. 23Every living thing on the face of the earth was wiped out; men and animals and the creatures that move along the ground and the birds of the air were wiped from the earth.[j] Only Noah was left, and those with him in the ark.[k]

24The waters flooded the earth for a hundred and fifty days.[l]

Receding waters leave the ark resting on the mountains of Ararat.

8 But God remembered[m] Noah and all the wild animals and the livestock that were with him in the ark, and he sent a wind over the earth,[n] and the waters receded. 2Now the springs of the deep and the floodgates of the heavens[o] had been closed, and the rain had stopped falling from the sky. 3The water receded steadily from the earth. At the end of the hundred and fifty days the water had gone down, 4and on the seventeenth day of the seventh month the ark came to rest on the mountains of Ararat. 5The waters continued to recede until the tenth month, and on the first day of the tenth month the tops of the mountains became visible.

6After forty days Noah opened the window he had made in the ark 7and sent out a raven, and it kept flying back and forth until the water had dried up from the earth. 8Then he sent out a dove to see if the water had receded from the surface of the ground. 9But the dove could find no place to set its feet because there was water over all the surface of the earth; so it returned to Noah in the ark. He

7:5 [a]Ge 6:22
7:11 [b]Eze 26:19 [c]Ge 8:2
7:12 [d]ver 4
7:15 [e]Ge 6:19
7:17 [f]ver 4
7:19 [g]Ps 104:6
7:21 [h]Ge 6:7,13
7:22 [i]Ge 1:30
7:23 [j]Mt 24:39; Lk 17:27; 1Pe 3:20; 2Pe 2:5 [k]Heb 11:7
7:24 [l]Ge 8:3
8:1 [m]Ge 9:15; 19:29; Ex 2:24; 1Sa 1:11,19 [n]Ex 14:21
8:2 [o]Ge 7:11

k*20* Hebrew *fifteen cubits* (about 6.9 meters)
l*20* Or *rose more than twenty feet, and the mountains were covered*

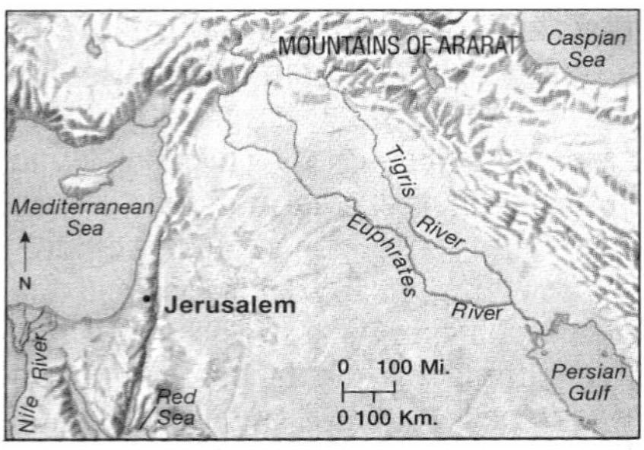

Mountains of Ararat

The boat touched land in the mountains of Ararat, located in present-day Turkey. There it rested for almost eight months before Noah, his family, and the animals stepped onto dry land.

reached out his hand and took the
dove and brought it back to himself in
the ark. 10He waited seven more days
and again sent out the dove from the
ark. 11When the dove returned to him
in the evening, there in its beak was a
freshly plucked olive leaf! Then Noah
knew that the water had receded from
the earth. 12He waited seven more days
and sent the dove out again, but this
time it did not return to him.
13By the first day of the first month
of Noah's six hundred and first year,
the water had dried up from the earth.
Noah then removed the covering from
the ark and saw that the surface of the
ground was dry. 14By the twenty-seventh
day of the second month the earth was
completely dry.

Noah and his family come out of the ark.

15Then God said to Noah, 16"Come
out of the ark, you and your wife and
your sons and their wives.[a] 17Bring out
every kind of living creature that is
with you—the birds, the animals, and
all the creatures that move along the
ground—so they can multiply on the
earth and be fruitful and increase in
number upon it."[b]
18So Noah came out, together with
his sons and his wife and his sons'
wives. 19All the animals and all the
creatures that move along the ground
and all the birds—everything that moves
on the earth—came out of the ark, one
kind after another.
20Then Noah built an altar to the
LORD[c] and, taking some of all the clean
animals and clean[d] birds, he sacrificed
burnt offerings[e] on it. 21The LORD
smelled the pleasing aroma[f] and said
in his heart: "Never again will I curse
the ground[g] because of man, even
though[m] every inclination of his heart
is evil from childhood.[h] And never
again will I destroy all living creatures,[i]
as I have done.

22"As long as the earth endures,
seedtime and harvest,
cold and heat,
summer and winter,
day and night
will never cease."[j]

The rainbow is the sign of God's covenant.

9 Then God blessed Noah and his
sons, saying to them, "Be fruitful
and increase in number and fill the
earth.[k] 2The fear and dread of you will
fall upon all the beasts of the earth and
all the birds of the air, upon every creature that moves along the ground, and
upon all the fish of the sea; they are
given into your hands. 3Everything that
lives and moves will be food for you.[l]
Just as I gave you the green plants, I now
give you everything.
4"But you must not eat meat that has
its lifeblood still in it.[m] 5And for your
lifeblood I will surely demand an accounting. I will demand an accounting
from every animal.[n] And from each man,
too, I will demand an accounting for
the life of his fellow man.[o]

6"Whoever sheds the blood of man,
by man shall his blood be shed;[p]
for in the image of God[q]
has God made man.

7As for you, be fruitful and increase in

8:16 [a]Ge 7:13
8:17 [b]Ge 1:22
8:20 [c]Ge 12:7-8; 13:18; 22:9 [d]Ge 7:8; Lev 11:1-47 [e]Ge 22:2,13; Ex 10:25
8:21 [f]Lev 1:9,13; 2Co 2:15 [g]Ge 3:17 [h]Ge 6:5; Ps 51:5; Jer 17:9 [i]Ge 9:11,15; Isa 54:9
8:22 [j]Ge 1:14; Jer 33:20,25
9:1 [k]Ge 1:22
9:3 [l]Ge 1:29
9:4 [m]Lev 3:17; 17:10-14; Dt 12:16, 23-25; 1Sa 14:33
9:5 [n]Ex 21:28-32 [o]Ge 4:10
9:6 [p]Ge 4:14; Ex 21:12,14; Lev 24:17; Mt 26:52 [q]Ge 1:26

m21 Or *man, for*

number; multiply on the earth and increase upon it."[a]
8 Then God said to Noah and to his
sons with him: 9 "I now establish my
covenant with you[b] and with your descendants after you 10 and with every
living creature that was with you—the
birds, the livestock and all the wild
animals, all those that came out of the
ark with you—every living creature on
earth. 11 I establish my covenant[c] with
you: Never again will all life be cut off by
the waters of a flood; never again will
there be a flood to destroy the earth."[d]
12 And God said, "This is the sign of
the covenant[e] I am making between me
and you and every living creature with
you, a covenant for all generations to
come: 13 I have set my rainbow in the
clouds, and it will be the sign of the
covenant between me and the earth.
14 Whenever I bring clouds over the
earth and the rainbow appears in the
clouds, 15 I will remember my covenant[f]
between me and you and all living creatures of every kind. Never again will
the waters become a flood to destroy all
life. 16 Whenever the rainbow appears
in the clouds, I will see it and remember the everlasting covenant[g] between
God and all living creatures of every
kind on the earth."
17 So God said to Noah, "This is the
sign of the covenant[h] I have established
between me and all life on the earth."

Noah curses Canaan but blesses Shem and Japheth.

18 The sons of Noah who came out of
the ark were Shem, Ham and Japheth.
(Ham was the father of Canaan.)[i]
19 These were the three sons of Noah,
and from them came the people who
were scattered over the earth.[j]
20 Noah, a man of the soil, proceeded[n]
to plant a vineyard. 21 When he drank
some of its wine, he became drunk and
lay uncovered inside his tent. 22 Ham,
the father of Canaan, saw his father's
nakedness and told his two brothers
outside. 23 But Shem and Japheth took
a garment and laid it across their shoulders; then they walked in backward
and covered their father's nakedness.
Their faces were turned the other way
so that they would not see their father's
nakedness.
24 When Noah awoke from his wine
and found out what his youngest son
had done to him, 25 he said,

"Cursed be Canaan![k]
The lowest of slaves
will he be to his brothers.[l]"

26 He also said,

"Blessed be the LORD, the God of
Shem!
May Canaan be the slave of Shem.[o]
27 May God extend the territory of
Japheth[p];
may Japheth live in the tents of
Shem,
and may Canaan be his[q] slave."

Noah's age and death.

28 After the flood Noah lived 350 years.
29 Altogether, Noah lived 950 years, and
then he died.

10 This is the account[m] of Shem,
Ham and Japheth, Noah's sons,
who themselves had sons after the
flood.

The Japhethites.

10:2-5pp— 1Ch 1:5-7

2 The sons[r] of Japheth:
Gomer,[n] Magog,[o] Madai, Javan,
Tubal,[p] Meshech and Tiras.
3 The sons of Gomer:
Ashkenaz,[q] Riphath and Togarmah.[r]
4 The sons of Javan:
Elishah, Tarshish,[s] the Kittim
and the Rodanim.[s] 5 (From these

9:7 [a]Ge 1:22
9:9 [b]Ge 6:18
9:11 [c]ver 16; Isa 24:5 [d]Ge 8:21; Isa 54:9
9:12 [e]ver 17; Ge 17:11
9:15 [f]Ex 2:24; Lev 26:42,45; Dt 7:9; Eze 16:60
9:16 [g]ver 11; Ge 17:7,13, 19; 2Sa 7:13; 23:5
9:17 [h]ver 12; Ge 17:11
9:18 [i]ver 25-27; Ge 10:6,15
9:19 [j]Ge 10:32
9:25 [k]ver 18 [l]Ge 25:23; Jos 9:23
10:1 [m]Ge 2:4
10:2 [n]Eze 38:6 [o]Eze 38:2; Rev 20:8 [p]Isa 66:19
10:3 [q]Jer 51:27 [r]Eze 27:14; 38:6
10:4 [s]Eze 27:12, 25; Jnh 1:3

n*20* Or *soil, was the first* o*26* Or *be his slave*
p*27* *Japheth* sounds like the Hebrew for *extend.*
q*27* Or *their* r*2* *Sons* may mean *descendants* or *successors* or *nations*; also in verses 3, 4, 6, 7, 20-23, 29 and 31. s*4* Some manuscripts of the Masoretic Text and Samaritan Pentateuch (see also Septuagint and 1 Chron. 1:7); most manuscripts of the Masoretic Text *Dodanim*

the maritime peoples spread out
into their territories by their clans
within their nations, each with
its own language.)

The Hamites.

10:6-20pp— 1Ch 1:8-16

6The sons of Ham:
Cush, Mizraim,[t] Put and Canaan.[a]
7The sons of Cush:
Seba, Havilah, Sabtah, Raamah
and Sabteca.
The sons of Raamah:
Sheba and Dedan.

8Cush was the father[u] of Nimrod, who
grew to be a mighty warrior on the
earth. 9He was a mighty hunter before
the LORD; that is why it is said, "Like
Nimrod, a mighty hunter before the
LORD." 10The first centers of his kingdom
were Babylon,[b] Erech, Akkad and Calneh, in[v] Shinar.[wc] 11From that land he
went to Assyria,[d] where he built Nineveh,[e] Rehoboth Ir,[x] Calah 12and Resen,
which is between Nineveh and Calah;
that is the great city.

13Mizraim was the father of
the Ludites, Anamites, Lehabites,
Naphtuhites, 14Pathrusites, Casluhites (from whom the Philistines[f]
came) and Caphtorites.
15Canaan[g] was the father of
Sidon[h] his firstborn,[y] and of the
Hittites,[i] 16Jebusites,[j] Amorites,
Girgashites, 17Hivites, Arkites, Sinites, 18Arvadites, Zemarites and
Hamathites.

Later the Canaanite[k] clans scattered
19and the borders of Canaan[l] reached
from Sidon[m] toward Gerar as far as Gaza,
and then toward Sodom, Gomorrah, Admah and Zeboiim, as far as Lasha.
20These are the sons of Ham by their
clans and languages, in their territories
and nations.

The Semites.

10:21-31pp— Ge 11:10-27; 1Ch 1:17-27

21Sons were also born to Shem, whose
older brother was[z] Japheth; Shem was
the ancestor of all the sons of Eber.[n]

22The sons of Shem:
Elam,[o] Asshur, Arphaxad,[p] Lud
and Aram.
23The sons of Aram:
Uz,[q] Hul, Gether and Meshech.[a]
24Arphaxad was the father of[b] Shelah,
and Shelah the father of Eber.[r]
25Two sons were born to Eber:
One was named Peleg,[c] because
in his time the earth was divided;
his brother was named Joktan.
26Joktan was the father of
Almodad, Sheleph, Hazarmaveth,
Jerah, 27Hadoram, Uzal, Diklah,
28Obal, Abimael, Sheba, 29Ophir,
Havilah and Jobab. All these were
sons of Joktan.

30The region where they lived stretched
from Mesha toward Sephar, in the eastern hill country.
31These are the sons of Shem by their
clans and languages, in their territories
and nations.

32These are the clans of Noah's sons,[s]
according to their lines of descent,
within their nations. From these the
nations spread out over the earth[t] after
the flood.

Tower of Babel.

11 Now the whole world had one
language and a common speech.
2As men moved eastward,[d] they found
a plain in Shinar[wu] and settled there.
3They said to each other, "Come, let's
make bricks[v] and bake them thoroughly." They used brick instead of stone,
and tar[w] for mortar. 4Then they said,
"Come, let us build ourselves a city, with
a tower that reaches to the heavens,[x]

10:6 [a]ver 15; Ge 9:18
10:10 [b]Ge 11:9 [c]Ge 11:2
10:11 [d]Ps 83:8; Mic 5:6 [e]Jnh 1:2; 4:11; Na 1:1
10:14 [f]Ge 21:32,34; 26:1,8
10:15 [g]ver 6; Ge 9:18 [h]Eze 28:21 [i]Ge 23:3,20
10:16 [j]1Ch 11:4
10:18 [k]Ge 12:6; Ex 13:11
10:19 [l]Ge 11:31; 13:12; 17:8 [m]ver 15
10:21 [n]ver 24; Nu 24:24
10:22 [o]Jer 49:34 [p]Lk 3:36
10:23 [q]Job 1:1
10:24 [r]ver 21
10:32 [s]ver 1 [t]Ge 9:19
11:2 [u]Ge 10:10
11:3 [v]Ex 1:14 [w]Ge 14:10
11:4 [x]Dt 1:28; 9:1

t*6* That is, Egypt; also in verse 13 u*8* *Father* may mean *ancestor* or *predecessor* or *founder*; also in verses 13, 15, 24 and 26. v*10* Or *Erech and Akkad—all of them in* w*10, 2* That is, Babylonia x*11* Or *Nineveh with its city squares* y*15* Or *of the Sidonians, the foremost* z*21* Or *Shem, the older brother of* a*23* See Septuagint and 1 Chron. 1:17; Hebrew *Mash* b*24* Hebrew; Septuagint *father of Cainan, and Cainan was the father of* c*25* *Peleg* means *division.* d*2* Or *from the east*; or *in the east*

so that we may make a name[a] for ourselves and not be scattered over the face of the whole earth."[b]

5But the LORD came down[c] to see the city and the tower that the men were building. 6The LORD said, "If as one people speaking the same language they have begun to do this, then nothing they plan to do will be impossible for them. 7Come, let us[d] go down and confuse their language so they will not understand each other."[e]

8So the LORD scattered them from there over all the earth,[f] and they stopped building the city. 9That is why it was called Babel[e][g]—because there the LORD confused the language of the whole world. From there the LORD scattered them over the face of the whole earth.

Account of Shem.

11:10-27pp— Ge 10:21-31; 1Ch 1:17-27

10This is the account of Shem.

Two years after the flood, when Shem was 100 years old, he became the father[f] of Arphaxad. 11And after he became the father of Arphaxad, Shem lived 500 years and had other sons and daughters.

12When Arphaxad had lived 35 years, he became the father of Shelah.[h] 13And after he became the father of Shelah, Arphaxad lived 403 years and had other sons and daughters.[g]

14When Shelah had lived 30 years, he became the father of Eber. 15And after he became the father of Eber, Shelah lived 403 years and had other sons and daughters.

16When Eber had lived 34 years, he became the father of Peleg. 17And after he became the father of Peleg, Eber lived 430 years and had other sons and daughters.

18When Peleg had lived 30 years, he became the father of Reu. 19And after he became the father of Reu, Peleg lived 209 years and had other sons and daughters.

20When Reu had lived 32 years, he became the father of Serug.[i] 21And after he became the father of Serug, Reu lived 207 years and had other sons and daughters.

22When Serug had lived 30 years, he became the father of Nahor. 23And after he became the father of Nahor, Serug lived 200 years and had other sons and daughters.

24When Nahor had lived 29 years, he became the father of Terah.[j] 25And after he became the father of Terah, Nahor lived 119 years and had other sons and daughters.

26After Terah had lived 70 years, he became the father of Abram,[k] Nahor[l] and Haran.

Account of Terah.

27This is the account of Terah.

Terah became the father of Abram, Nahor and Haran. And Haran became the father of Lot.[m] 28While his father Terah was still alive, Haran died in Ur of the Chaldeans,[n] in the land of his birth. 29Abram and Nahor both married. The name of Abram's wife was Sarai,[o] and the name of Nahor's wife was Milcah;[p] she was the daughter of Haran, the father of both Milcah and Iscah. 30Now Sarai was barren; she had no children.[q]

31Terah took his son Abram, his grandson Lot son of Haran, and his daughter-in-law Sarai, the wife of his son Abram, and together they set out from Ur of the Chaldeans[r] to go to Canaan.[s] But when they came to Haran, they settled there.

32Terah lived 205 years, and he died in Haran.

11:4 [a]Ge 6:4 [b]Dt 4:27
11:5 [c]ver 7; Ge 18:21; Ex 3:8; 19:11,18,20
11:7 [d]Ge 1:26 [e]Ge 42:23
11:8 [f]Ge 9:19; Lk 1:51
11:9 [g]Ge 10:10
11:12 [h]Lk 3:35
11:20 [i]Lk 3:35
11:24 [j]Lk 3:34
11:26 [k]Lk 3:34 [l]Jos 24:2
11:27 [m]ver 31; Ge 12:4; 14:12; 19:1; 2Pe 2:7
11:28 [n]ver 31; Ge 15:7
11:29 [o]Ge 17:15 [p]Ge 22:20
11:30 [q]Ge 16:1; 18:11
11:31 [r]Ge 15:7; Ne 9:7; Ac 7:4 [s]Ge 10:19

e *9* That is, Babylon; *Babel* sounds like the Hebrew for *confused*. f *10* *Father* may mean *ancestor*; also in verses 11-25. g *12,13* Hebrew; Septuagint (see also Luke 3:35, 36 and note at Gen. 10:24) *35 years, he became the father of Cainan. 13And after he became the father of Cainan, Arphaxad lived 430 years and had other sons and daughters, and then he died. When Cainan had lived 130 years, he became the father of Shelah. And after he became the father of Shelah, Cainan lived 330 years and had other sons and daughters*

God calls Abram and promises him blessings.

12 The LORD had said to Abram,
"Leave your country, your people and your father's household and go
to the land I will show you.[a]

2"I will make you into a great nation[b]
and I will bless you;[c]
I will make your name great,
and you will be a blessing.
3I will bless those who bless you,
and whoever curses you I will
curse;[d]
and all peoples on earth
will be blessed through you.[e]"

4So Abram left, as the LORD had told
him; and Lot went with him. Abram
was seventy-five years old when he set
out from Haran.[f] 5He took his wife
Sarai, his nephew Lot, all the possessions they had accumulated and the
people[g] they had acquired in Haran, and
they set out for the land of Canaan, and
they arrived there.
6Abram traveled through the land[h] as
far as the site of the great tree of
Moreh[i] at Shechem. At that time the
Canaanites[j] were in the land. 7The
LORD appeared to Abram[k] and said, "To
your offspring[h] I will give this land."[l] So
he built an altar there to the LORD,[m]
who had appeared to him.
8From there he went on toward the
hills east of Bethel[n] and pitched his tent,
with Bethel on the west and Ai on the
east. There he built an altar to the LORD
and called on the name of the LORD.
9Then Abram set out and continued
toward the Negev.[o]

Abram and Sarai deceive the Pharaoh of Egypt.

12:10-20Ref— Ge 20:1-18; 26:1-11

10Now there was a famine in the
land, and Abram went down to Egypt
to live there for a while because the
famine was severe. 11As he was about to
enter Egypt, he said to his wife Sarai,
"I know what a beautiful woman you
are. 12When the Egyptians see you, they
will say, 'This is his wife.' Then they
will kill me but will let you live. 13Say
you are my sister,[p] so that I will be
treated well for your sake and my life
will be spared because of you."
14When Abram came to Egypt, the
Egyptians saw that she was a very beautiful woman. 15And when Pharaoh's
officials saw her, they praised her to
Pharaoh, and she was taken into his
palace. 16He treated Abram well for her
sake, and Abram acquired sheep and
cattle, male and female donkeys, menservants and maidservants, and camels.
17But the LORD inflicted serious diseases on Pharaoh and his household[q]
because of Abram's wife Sarai. 18So
Pharaoh summoned Abram. "What have
you done to me?"[r] he said. "Why didn't
you tell me she was your wife? 19Why
did you say, 'She is my sister,' so that I
took her to be my wife? Now then, here
is your wife. Take her and go!" 20Then
Pharaoh gave orders about Abram to
his men, and they sent him on his way,
with his wife and everything he had.

Quarreling causes Abram and Lot to separate.

13 So Abram went up from Egypt
to the Negev,[s] with his wife and
everything he had, and Lot went with
him. 2Abram had become very wealthy
in livestock and in silver and gold.
3From the Negev he went from place
to place until he came to Bethel,[t] to
the place between Bethel and Ai where
his tent had been earlier 4and where
he had first built an altar.[u] There Abram
called on the name of the LORD.
5Now Lot, who was moving about
with Abram, also had flocks and herds
and tents. 6But the land could not support them while they stayed together,
for their possessions were so great that
they were not able to stay together.[v]
7And quarreling[w] arose between Abram's
herdsmen and the herdsmen of Lot.
The Canaanites and Perizzites were also
living in the land[x] at that time.

12:1 [a]Ac 7:3*; Heb 11:8
12:2 [b]Ge 15:5; 17:2,4; 18:18; 22:17; Dt 26:5 [c]Ge 24:1,35
12:3 [d]Ge 27:29; Ex 23:22; Nu 24:9 [e]Ge 18:18; 22:18; 26:4; Ac 3:25; Gal 3:8*
12:4 [f]Ge 11:31
12:5 [g]Ge 14:14; 17:23
12:6 [h]Heb 11:9 [i]Ge 35:4; Dt 11:30 [j]Ge 10:18
12:7 [k]Ge 17:1; 18:1; Ex 6:3 [l]Ge 13:15,17; 15:18; 17:8; Ps 105:9-11 [m]Ge 13:4
12:8 [n]Ge 13:3
12:9 [o]Ge 13:1,3
12:13 [p]Ge 20:2; 26:7
12:17 [q]1Ch 16:21
12:18 [r]Ge 20:9; 26:10
13:1 [s]Ge 12:9
13:3 [t]Ge 12:8
13:4 [u]Ge 12:7
13:6 [v]Ge 36:7
13:7 [w]Ge 26:20,21 [x]Ge 12:6

h*7* Or *seed*

8 So Abram said to Lot, "Let's not have any quarreling between you and me,[a] or between your herdsmen and mine, for we are brothers.[b] 9 Is not the whole land before you? Let's part company. If you go to the left, I'll go to the right; if you go to the right, I'll go to the left."

Lot moves to wicked Sodom.

10 Lot looked up and saw that the whole plain of the Jordan was well watered, like the garden of the LORD,[c] like the land of Egypt, toward Zoar.[d] (This was before the LORD destroyed Sodom and Gomorrah.)[e] 11 So Lot chose for himself the whole plain of the Jordan and set out toward the east. The two men parted company: 12 Abram lived in the land of Canaan, while Lot lived among the cities of the plain[f] and pitched his tents near Sodom.[g] 13 Now the men of Sodom were wicked and were sinning greatly against the LORD.[h]

God's covenant with Abram is renewed.

14 The LORD said to Abram after Lot had parted from him, "Lift up your eyes from where you are and look north and south, east and west.[i] 15 All the land that you see I will give to you and your offspring[i] forever.[j] 16 I will make your offspring like the dust of the earth, so that if anyone could count the dust, then your offspring could be counted. 17 Go, walk through the length and breadth of the land,[k] for I am giving it to you."

18 So Abram moved his tents and went to live near the great trees of Mamre[l] at Hebron,[m] where he built an altar to the LORD.[n]

Abram rescues Lot from captivity.

14 At this time Amraphel king of Shinar,[j][o] Arioch king of Ellasar, Kedorlaomer king of Elam and Tidal king of Goiim 2 went to war against Bera king of Sodom, Birsha king of Gomorrah, Shinab king of Admah, Shemeber king of Zeboiim,[p] and the king of Bela (that is, Zoar).[q] 3 All these latter kings joined forces in the Valley of Siddim (the Salt Sea[k][r]). 4 For twelve years they had been subject to Kedorlaomer, but in the thirteenth year they rebelled.

5 In the fourteenth year, Kedorlaomer and the kings allied with him went out and defeated the Rephaites[s] in Ashteroth Karnaim, the Zuzites in Ham, the Emites[t] in Shaveh Kiriathaim 6 and the Horites[u] in the hill country of Seir,[v] as far as El Paran[w] near the desert. 7 Then they turned back and went to En Mishpat (that is, Kadesh), and they conquered the whole territory of the Amalekites, as well as the Amorites who were living in Hazazon Tamar.[x]

8 Then the king of Sodom, the king of Gomorrah,[y] the king of Admah, the king of Zeboiim[z] and the king of Bela (that is, Zoar) marched out and drew up their battle lines in the Valley of Siddim 9 against Kedorlaomer king of Elam, Tidal king of Goiim, Amraphel king of Shinar and Arioch king of Ellasar—four kings against five. 10 Now the Valley of Siddim was full of tar pits, and when the kings of Sodom and Gomorrah fled, some of the men fell into them and the rest fled to the hills.[a] 11 The four kings seized all the goods of Sodom and Gomorrah and all their food; then they went away. 12 They also carried off Abram's nephew Lot and his possessions, since he was living in Sodom.

13 One who had escaped came and reported this to Abram the Hebrew. Now Abram was living near the great trees of Mamre[b] the Amorite, a brother[l] of Eshcol and Aner, all of whom were allied with Abram. 14 When Abram heard that his relative had been taken captive, he called out the 318 trained men born in his household[c] and went in pursuit as far as Dan.[d] 15 During the night Abram divided his men to attack them and he routed them, pursuing them as far as Hobah, north of Damascus. 16 He

13:8 [a]Pr 15:18; 20:3 [b]Ps 133:1
13:10 [c]Ge 2:8-10; Isa 51:3 [d]Ge 19:22,30 [e]Ge 14:8; 19:17-29
13:12 [f]Ge 19:17, 25,29 [g]Ge 14:12
13:13 [h]Ge 18:20; Eze 16:49-50; 2Pe 2:8
13:14 [i]Ge 28:14; Dt 3:27
13:15 [j]Ge 12:7; Gal 3:16*
13:17 [k]ver 15; Nu 13:17-25
13:18 [l]Ge 14:13, 24; 18:1 [m]Ge 35:27 [n]Ge 8:20
14:1 [o]Ge 10:10
14:2 [p]Ge 10:19 [q]Ge 13:10
14:3 [r]Nu 34:3,12; Dt 3:17; Jos 3:16; 15:2,5
14:5 [s]Ge 15:20; Dt 2:11,20 [t]Dt 2:10
14:6 [u]Dt 2:12,22 [v]Dt 2:1,5,22 [w]Ge 21:21; Nu 10:12
14:7 [x]2Ch 20:2
14:8 [y]Ge 13:10; 19:17-29 [z]Dt 29:23
14:10 [a]Ge 19:17,30
14:13 [b]ver 24; Ge 13:18
14:14 [c]Ge 15:3 [d]Dt 34:1; Jdg 18:29

i *15* Or *seed*; also in verse 16 j *1* That is, Babylonia; also in verse 9 k *3* That is, the Dead Sea
l *13* Or *a relative*; or *an ally*

recovered all the goods and brought back
his relative Lot and his possessions, together with the women and the other
people.

Abram gives a tenth to Melchizedek.

17 After Abram returned from defeating Kedorlaomer and the kings allied
with him, the king of Sodom came out
to meet him in the Valley of Shaveh
(that is, the King's Valley).[a]
18 Then Melchizedek[b] king of Salem[m][c]
brought out bread and wine. He was
priest of God Most High, 19 and he
blessed Abram,[d] saying,

"Blessed be Abram by God Most
High,
Creator[n] of heaven and earth.[e]
20 And blessed be[o] God Most High,[f]
who delivered your enemies into
your hand."

Then Abram gave him a tenth of everything.[g]
21 The king of Sodom said to Abram,
"Give me the people and keep the goods
for yourself."
22 But Abram said to the king of
Sodom, "I have raised my hand[h] to the
LORD, God Most High, Creator of heav-
en and earth,[i] and have taken an oath
23 that I will accept nothing belonging
to you,[j] not even a thread or the thong
of a sandal, so that you will never be
able to say, 'I made Abram rich.' 24 I
will accept nothing but what my men
have eaten and the share that belongs
to the men who went with me—to
Aner, Eshcol and Mamre. Let them
have their share."

God promises an heir and a land to Abram.

15 After this, the word of the LORD
came to Abram[k] in a vision:

"Do not be afraid,[l] Abram.
I am your shield,[p][m]
your very great reward.[q]"

2 But Abram said, "O Sovereign LORD,
what can you give me since I remain
childless[n] and the one who will inherit[r]
my estate is Eliezer of Damascus?"
3 And Abram said, "You have given me
no children; so a servant[o] in my household will be my heir."
4 Then the word of the LORD came to
him: "This man will not be your heir,
but a son coming from your own body
will be your heir.[p]" 5 He took him outside and said, "Look up at the heavens
and count the stars[q]—if indeed you
can count them." Then he said to him,
"So shall your offspring be."[r]
6 Abram believed the LORD, and he
credited it to him as righteousness.[s]
7 He also said to him, "I am the LORD,
who brought you out of Ur of the
Chaldeans to give you this land to take
possession of it."
8 But Abram said, "O Sovereign LORD,
how can I know[t] that I will gain possession of it?"
9 So the LORD said to him, "Bring me
a heifer, a goat and a ram, each three
years old, along with a dove and a
young pigeon."
10 Abram brought all these to him, cut
them in two and arranged the halves
opposite each other;[u] the birds, however, he did not cut in half.[v] 11 Then
birds of prey came down on the carcasses, but Abram drove them away.
12 As the sun was setting, Abram fell
into a deep sleep,[w] and a thick and
dreadful darkness came over him.
13 Then the LORD said to him, "Know
for certain that your descendants will
be strangers in a country not their
own, and they will be enslaved[x] and
mistreated four hundred years.[y] 14 But I
will punish the nation they serve as
slaves, and afterward they will come
out[z] with great possessions.[a] 15 You,
however, will go to your fathers in
peace and be buried at a good old
age.[b] 16 In the fourth generation your

14:17 [a] 2Sa 18:18
14:18 [b] Ps 110:4; Heb 5:6 [c] Ps 76:2; Heb 7:2
14:19 [d] Heb 7:6 [e] ver 22
14:20 [f] Ge 24:27 [g] Ge 28:22; Dt 26:12; Heb 7:4
14:22 [h] Ex 6:8; Da 12:7; Rev 10:5-6 [i] ver 19
14:23 [j] 2Ki 5:16
15:1 [k] Da 10:1 [l] Ge 21:17; 26:24; 46:3; 2Ki 6:16; Ps 27:1; Isa 41:10,13-14 [m] Dt 33:29; 2Sa 22:3,31; Ps 3:3
15:2 [n] Ac 7:5
15:3 [o] Ge 24:2,34
15:4 [p] Gal 4:28
15:5 [q] Ps 147:4; Jer 33:22 [r] Ge 12:2; 22:17; Ex 32:13; Ro 4:18*; Heb 11:12
15:6 [s] Ps 106:31; Ro 4:3*, 20-24*; Gal 3:6*; Jas 2:23*
15:8 [t] Lk 1:18
15:10 [u] ver 17; Jer 34:18 [v] Lev 1:17
15:12 [w] Ge 2:21
15:13 [x] Ex 1:11 [y] ver 16; Ex 12:40; Ac 7:6,17
15:14 [z] Ac 7:7* [a] Ex 12:32-38
15:15 [b] Ge 25:8

[m] *18* That is, Jerusalem [n] *19* Or *Possessor*; also in verse 22 [o] *20* Or *And praise be to* [p] *1* Or *sovereign* [q] *1* Or *shield; / your reward will be very great* [r] *2* The meaning of the Hebrew for this phrase is uncertain.

descendants will come back here, for the sin of the Amorites[a] has not yet reached its full measure."

17When the sun had set and darkness had fallen, a smoking firepot with a blazing torch appeared and passed between the pieces.[b] 18On that day the LORD made a covenant with Abram and said, "To your descendants I give this land,[c] from the river[s] of Egypt[d] to the great river, the Euphrates— 19the land of the Kenites, Kenizzites, Kadmonites, 20Hittites, Perizzites, Rephaites, 21Amorites, Canaanites, Girgashites and Jebusites."

Sarai gives her maidservant, Hagar, to Abram.

16 Now Sarai, Abram's wife, had borne him no children.[e] But she had an Egyptian maidservant[f] named Hagar; 2so she said to Abram, "The LORD has kept me from having children. Go, sleep with my maidservant; perhaps I can build a family through her."[g]

Abram agreed to what Sarai said. 3So after Abram had been living in Canaan[h] ten years, Sarai his wife took her Egyptian maidservant Hagar and gave her to her husband to be his wife. 4He slept with Hagar, and she conceived.

When she knew she was pregnant, she began to despise her mistress. 5Then Sarai said to Abram, "You are responsible for the wrong I am suffering. I put my servant in your arms, and now that she knows she is pregnant, she despises me. May the LORD judge between you and me."[i]

6"Your servant is in your hands," Abram said. "Do with her whatever you think best." Then Sarai mistreated Hagar; so she fled from her.

7The angel of the LORD[j] found Hagar near a spring in the desert; it was the spring that is beside the road to Shur.[k] 8And he said, "Hagar, servant of Sarai, where have you come from, and where are you going?"

"I'm running away from my mistress Sarai," she answered.

9Then the angel of the LORD told her, "Go back to your mistress and submit to her." 10The angel added, "I will so increase your descendants that they will be too numerous to count."[l]

11The angel of the LORD also said to her:

"You are now with child
  and you will have a son.
You shall name him Ishmael,[t]
  for the LORD has heard of your
    misery.[m]
12He will be a wild donkey of a man;
  his hand will be against everyone
  and everyone's hand against him,
and he will live in hostility
  toward[u] all his brothers.[n]"

13She gave this name to the LORD who spoke to her: "You are the God who sees me," for she said, "I have now seen[v] the One who sees me."[o] 14That is why the well was called Beer Lahai Roi[w]; it is still there, between Kadesh and Bered.

Ishmael is born to Hagar.

15So Hagar bore Abram a son,[p] and Abram gave the name Ishmael to the son she had borne. 16Abram was eighty-six years old when Hagar bore him Ishmael.

Abram's name is changed to Abraham.

17 When Abram was ninety-nine years old, the LORD appeared to him and said, "I am God Almighty[x];[q] walk before me and be blameless.[r] 2I will confirm my covenant between me and you[s] and will greatly increase your numbers."

3Abram fell facedown, and God said to him, 4"As for me, this is my covenant with you:[t] You will be the father of many nations.[u] 5No longer will you be called Abram[y]; your name will be

15:16 [a]1Ki 21:26
15:17 [b]ver 10
15:18 [c]Ge 12:7 [d]Nu 34:5
16:1 [e]Ge 11:30; Gal 4:24-25 [f]Ge 21:9
16:2 [g]Ge 30:3-4, 9-10
16:3 [h]Ge 12:5
16:5 [i]Ge 31:53
16:7 [j]Ge 21:17; 22:11,15; 31:11 [k]Ge 20:1
16:10 [l]Ge 13:16; 17:20
16:11 [m]Ex 2:24; 3:7,9
16:12 [n]Ge 25:18
16:13 [o]Ge 32:30
16:15 [p]Gal 4:22
17:1 [q]Ge 28:3; Ex 6:3 [r]Dt 18:13
17:2 [s]Ge 15:18
17:4 [t]Ge 15:18 [u]ver 16; Ge 12:2; 35:11; 48:19

s *18* Or *Wadi* t *11* *Ishmael* means *God hears.* u *12* Or *live to the east / of* v *13* Or *seen the back of* w *14* *Beer Lahai Roi* means *well of the Living One who sees me.* x *1* Hebrew *El-Shaddai* y *5* *Abram* means *exalted father.*

Abraham,[z][a] for I have made you a father of many nations.[b] 6I will make you very fruitful;[c] I will make nations of you, and kings will come from you.[d] 7I will establish my covenant as an everlasting covenant between me and you and your descendants after you for the generations to come, to be your God[e] and the God of your descendants after you.[f] 8The whole land of Canaan,[g] where you are now an alien,[h] I will give as an everlasting possession to you and your descendants after you;[i] and I will be their God."

A covenant of circumcision is established.

9Then God said to Abraham, "As for you, you must keep my covenant, you and your descendants after you for the generations to come. 10This is my covenant with you and your descendants after you, the covenant you are to keep: Every male among you shall be circumcised.[j] 11You are to undergo circumcision,[k] and it will be the sign of the covenant[l] between me and you. 12For the generations to come every male among you who is eight days old must be circumcised,[m] including those born in your household or bought with money from a foreigner—those who are not your offspring. 13Whether born in your household or bought with your money, they must be circumcised. My covenant in your flesh is to be an everlasting covenant. 14Any uncircumcised male, who has not been circumcised in the flesh, will be cut off from his people;[n] he has broken my covenant."

Sarai's name is changed to Sarah.

15God also said to Abraham, "As for Sarai your wife, you are no longer to call her Sarai; her name will be Sarah. 16I will bless her and will surely give you a son by her.[o] I will bless her so that she will be the mother of nations;[p] kings of peoples will come from her."

17Abraham fell facedown; he laughed[q] and said to himself, "Will a son be born to a man a hundred years old? Will Sarah bear a child at the age of ninety?" 18And Abraham said to God, "If only Ishmael might live under your blessing!"

19Then God said, "Yes, but your wife Sarah will bear you a son,[r] and you will call him Isaac.[a] I will establish my covenant with him[s] as an everlasting covenant for his descendants after him. 20And as for Ishmael, I have heard you: I will surely bless him; I will make him fruitful and will greatly increase his numbers.[t] He will be the father of twelve rulers,[u] and I will make him into a great nation.[v] 21But my covenant I will establish with Isaac, whom Sarah will bear to you by this time next year."[w] 22When he had finished speaking with Abraham, God went up from him.

23On that very day Abraham took his son Ishmael and all those born in his household or bought with his money, every male in his household, and circumcised them, as God told him. 24Abraham was ninety-nine years old when he was circumcised,[x] 25and his son Ishmael was thirteen; 26Abraham and his son Ishmael were both circumcised on that same day. 27And every male in Abraham's household, including those born in his household or bought from a foreigner, was circumcised with him.

Abraham welcomes three visitors.

18 The LORD appeared to Abraham near the great trees of Mamre[y] while he was sitting at the entrance to his tent in the heat of the day. 2Abraham looked up and saw three men[z] standing nearby. When he saw them, he hurried from the entrance of his tent to meet them and bowed low to the ground.

3He said, "If I have found favor in your eyes, my lord,[b] do not pass your servant by. 4Let a little water be brought, and then you may all wash your feet[a]

17:5 [a]ver 15; Ne 9:7 [b]Ro 4:17*
17:6 [c]Ge 35:11 [d]Mt 1:6
17:7 [e]Ex 29:45,46 [f]Ro 9:8; Gal 3:16
17:8 [g]Ps 105:9,11 [h]Ge 23:4; 28:4; Ex 6:4 [i]Ge 12:7
17:10 [j]ver 23; Ge 21:4; Jn 7:22; Ac 7:8; Ro 4:11
17:11 [k]Ex 12:48; Dt 10:16 [l]Ro 4:11
17:12 [m]Lev 12:3; Lk 2:21
17:14 [n]Ex 4:24-26
17:16 [o]Ge 18:10 [p]Ge 35:11; Gal 4:31
17:17 [q]Ge 18:12; 21:6
17:19 [r]Ge 18:14; 21:2 [s]Ge 26:3
17:20 [t]Ge 16:10 [u]Ge 25:12-16 [v]Ge 21:18
17:21 [w]Ge 21:2
17:24 [x]Ro 4:11
18:1 [y]Ge 13:18; 14:13
18:2 [z]ver 16,22; Ge 32:24; Jos 5:13; Jdg 13:6-11; Heb 13:2
18:4 [a]Ge 19:2; 43:24

[z]5 *Abraham* means *father of many.* [a]19 *Isaac* means *he laughs.* [b]3 Or *O Lord*

and rest under this tree. 5Let me get you something to eat,[a] so you can be refreshed and then go on your way—now that you have come to your servant."

"Very well," they answered, "do as you say."

6So Abraham hurried into the tent to Sarah. "Quick," he said, "get three seahs[c] of fine flour and knead it and bake some bread."

7Then he ran to the herd and selected a choice, tender calf and gave it to a servant, who hurried to prepare it. 8He then brought some curds and milk and the calf that had been prepared, and set these before them.[b] While they ate, he stood near them under a tree.

Sarah laughs at the promise of a son.

9"Where is your wife Sarah?" they asked him.

"There, in the tent," he said.

10Then the LORD[d] said, "I will surely return to you about this time next year, and Sarah your wife will have a son."[c]

Now Sarah was listening at the entrance to the tent, which was behind him. 11Abraham and Sarah were already old and well advanced in years,[d] and Sarah was past the age of childbearing.[e] 12So Sarah laughed[f] to herself as she thought, "After I am worn out and my master[e][g] is old, will I now have this pleasure?"

13Then the LORD said to Abraham, "Why did Sarah laugh and say, 'Will I really have a child, now that I am old?' 14Is anything too hard for the LORD?[h] I will return to you at the appointed time next year and Sarah will have a son."

15Sarah was afraid, so she lied and said, "I did not laugh."

But he said, "Yes, you did laugh."

Abraham intercedes for Sodom.

16When the men got up to leave, they looked down toward Sodom, and Abraham walked along with them to see them on their way. 17Then the LORD said, "Shall I hide from Abraham[i] what I am about to do?[j] 18Abraham will surely become a great and powerful nation,[k] and all nations on earth will be blessed through him. 19For I have chosen him, so that he will direct his children[l] and his household after him to keep the way of the LORD[m] by doing what is right and just, so that the LORD will bring about for Abraham what he has promised him."

20Then the LORD said, "The outcry against Sodom and Gomorrah is so great and their sin so grievous 21that I will go down[n] and see if what they have done is as bad as the outcry that has reached me. If not, I will know."

22The men turned away and went toward Sodom,[o] but Abraham remained standing before the LORD.[f] 23Then Abraham approached him and said: "Will you sweep away the righteous with the wicked?[p] 24What if there are fifty righteous people in the city? Will you really sweep it away and not spare[g] the place for the sake of the fifty righteous people in it?[q] 25Far be it from you to do such a thing—to kill the righteous with the wicked, treating the righteous and the wicked alike. Far be it from you! Will not the Judge[h] of all the earth do right?"[r]

26The LORD said, "If I find fifty righteous people in the city of Sodom, I will spare the whole place for their sake.[s]"

27Then Abraham spoke up again: "Now that I have been so bold as to speak to the Lord, though I am nothing but dust and ashes,[t] 28what if the number of the righteous is five less than fifty? Will you destroy the whole city because of five people?"

"If I find forty-five there," he said, "I will not destroy it."

29Once again he spoke to him, "What if only forty are found there?"

18:5 [a]Jdg 13:15
18:8 [b]Ge 19:3
18:10 [c]Ro 9:9*
18:11 [d]Ge 17:17 [e]Ro 4:19
18:12 [f]Ge 17:17; 21:6 [g]1Pe 3:6
18:14 [h]Jer 32:17, 27; Zec 8:6; Mt 19:26; Lk 1:37; Ro 4:21
18:17 [i]Am 3:7 [j]Ge 19:24
18:18 [k]Gal 3:8*
18:19 [l]Dt 4:9-10; 6:7 [m]Jos 24:15; Eph 6:4
18:21 [n]Ge 11:5
18:22 [o]Ge 19:1
18:23 [p]Nu 16:22
18:24 [q]Jer 5:1
18:25 [r]Job 8:3,20; Ps 58:11; 94:2; Isa 3:10-11; Ro 3:6
18:26 [s]Jer 5:1
18:27 [t]Ge 2:7; 3:19; Job 30:19; 42:6

c*6* That is, probably about 20 quarts (about 22 liters)
d*10* Hebrew *Then he* e*12* Or *husband*
f*22* Masoretic Text; an ancient Hebrew scribal tradition *but the LORD remained standing before Abraham*
g*24* Or *forgive*; also in verse 26 h*25* Or *Ruler*

He said, "For the sake of forty, I will
not do it."
30Then he said, "May the Lord not
be angry, but let me speak. What if
only thirty can be found there?"
He answered, "I will not do it if I find
thirty there."
31Abraham said, "Now that I have
been so bold as to speak to the Lord,
what if only twenty can be found
there?"
He said, "For the sake of twenty, I will
not destroy it."
32Then he said, "May the Lord not be
angry, but let me speak just once
more.[a] What if only ten can be found
there?"
He answered, "For the sake of ten,[b] I
will not destroy it."
33When the LORD had finished speaking with Abraham, he left, and Abraham returned home.

Two angels visit Lot.

19 The two angels arrived at Sodom[c]
in the evening, and Lot was sitting in the gateway of the city.[d] When
he saw them, he got up to meet them
and bowed down with his face to the
ground. 2"My lords," he said, "please
turn aside to your servant's house. You
can wash your feet[e] and spend the
night and then go on your way early in
the morning."
"No," they answered, "we will spend
the night in the square."
3But he insisted so strongly that they
did go with him and entered his house.
He prepared a meal for them, baking
bread without yeast, and they ate.[f]
4Before they had gone to bed, all the
men from every part of the city of
Sodom—both young and old—surrounded the house. 5They called to
Lot, "Where are the men who came to
you tonight? Bring them out to us so
that we can have sex with them."[g]
6Lot went outside to meet them[h] and
shut the door behind him 7and said,
"No, my friends. Don't do this wicked
thing. 8Look, I have two daughters

18:32 [a]Jdg 6:39 [b]Jer 5:1
19:1 [c]Ge 18:22 [d]Ge 18:1
19:2 [e]Ge 18:4; Lk 7:44
19:3 [f]Ge 18:6
19:5 [g]Jdg 19:22; Isa 3:9; Ro 1:24-27
19:6 [h]Jdg 19:23
19:8 [i]Jdg 19:24
19:9 [j]Ex 2:14; Ac 7:27
19:11 [k]Dt 28:28-29; 2Ki 6:18; Ac 13:11
19:12 [l]Ge 7:1
19:13 [m]1Ch 21:15
19:14 [n]Nu 16:21 [o]Ex 9:21; Lk 17:28
19:15 [p]Nu 16:26 [q]Rev 18:4
19:17 [r]Jer 48:6 [s]ver 26

who have never slept with a man. Let
me bring them out to you, and you can
do what you like with them. But don't do
anything to these men, for they have
come under the protection of my roof."[i]
9"Get out of our way," they replied.
And they said, "This fellow came here
as an alien, and now he wants to play
the judge![j] We'll treat you worse than
them." They kept bringing pressure on
Lot and moved forward to break down
the door.
10But the men inside reached out and
pulled Lot back into the house and
shut the door. 11Then they struck the
men who were at the door of the house,
young and old, with blindness[k] so that
they could not find the door.

Sodom and Gomorrah are destroyed.

12The two men said to Lot, "Do you
have anyone else here—sons-in-law,
sons or daughters, or anyone else in
the city who belongs to you?[l] Get them
out of here, 13because we are going to
destroy this place. The outcry to the
LORD against its people is so great that
he has sent us to destroy it."[m]
14So Lot went out and spoke to his
sons-in-law, who were pledged to marry[1] his daughters. He said, "Hurry and
get out of this place, because the LORD
is about to destroy the city![n]" But his
sons-in-law thought he was joking.[o]
15With the coming of dawn, the
angels urged Lot, saying, "Hurry! Take
your wife and your two daughters who
are here, or you will be swept away[p]
when the city is punished.[q]"
16When he hesitated, the men grasped
his hand and the hands of his wife and
of his two daughters and led them
safely out of the city, for the LORD was
merciful to them. 17As soon as they
had brought them out, one of them
said, "Flee for your lives![r] Don't look
back,[s] and don't stop anywhere in the
plain! Flee to the mountains or you will
be swept away!"

[1] *14* Or *were married to*

18But Lot said to them, "No, my lords,[j] please! 19Your[k] servant has found favor in your[k] eyes, and you[k] have shown great kindness to me in sparing my life. But I can't flee to the mountains; this disaster will overtake me, and I'll die. 20Look, here is a town near enough to run to, and it is small. Let me flee to it—it is very small, isn't it? Then my life will be spared."

21He said to him, "Very well, I will grant this request too; I will not overthrow the town you speak of. 22But flee there quickly, because I cannot do anything until you reach it." (That is why the town was called Zoar.[l])

23By the time Lot reached Zoar, the sun had risen over the land. 24Then the LORD rained down burning sulfur on Sodom and Gomorrah[a]—from the LORD out of the heavens.[b] 25Thus he overthrew those cities and the entire plain, including all those living in the cities—and also the vegetation in the land.[c] 26But Lot's wife looked back,[d] and she became a pillar of salt.[e]

27Early the next morning Abraham got up and returned to the place where he had stood before the LORD.[f] 28He looked down toward Sodom and Gomorrah, toward all the land of the plain, and he saw dense smoke rising from the land, like smoke from a furnace.[g]

29So when God destroyed the cities of the plain, he remembered Abraham, and he brought Lot out of the catastrophe[h] that overthrew the cities where Lot had lived.

Lot's descendants are conceived in sin.

30Lot and his two daughters left Zoar and settled in the mountains,[i] for he was afraid to stay in Zoar. He and his two daughters lived in a cave. 31One day the older daughter said to the younger, "Our father is old, and there is no man around here to lie with us, as is the custom all over the earth. 32Let's get our father to drink wine and then lie with him and preserve our family line through our father."

33That night they got their father to drink wine, and the older daughter went in and lay with him. He was not aware of it when she lay down or when she got up.

34The next day the older daughter said to the younger, "Last night I lay with my father. Let's get him to drink wine again tonight, and you go in and lie with him so we can preserve our family line through our father." 35So they got their father to drink wine that night also, and the younger daughter went and lay with him. Again he was not aware of it when she lay down or when she got up.

36So both of Lot's daughters became pregnant by their father. 37The older daughter had a son, and she named him Moab[m]; he is the father of the Moabites[j] of today. 38The younger daughter also had a son, and she named him Ben-Ammi[n]; he is the father of the Ammonites[k] of today.

Abraham lies about Sarah to deceive Abimelech.

20:1-18Ref— Ge 12:10-20; 26:1-11

20 Now Abraham moved on from there[l] into the region of the Negev and lived between Kadesh and Shur. For a while he stayed in Gerar,[m] 2and there Abraham said of his wife Sarah, "She is my sister.[n]" Then Abimelech king of Gerar sent for Sarah and took her.[o]

3But God came to Abimelech in a dream[p] one night and said to him, "You are as good as dead because of the woman you have taken; she is a married woman."[q]

4Now Abimelech had not gone near her, so he said, "Lord, will you destroy an innocent nation?[r] 5Did he not say to me, 'She is my sister,' and didn't she

19:24 [a]Dt 29:23; Isa 1:9; 13:19 [b]Lk 17:29; 2Pe 2:6; Jude 7
19:25 [c]Ps 107:34; Eze 16:48
19:26 [d]ver 17 [e]Lk 17:32
19:27 [f]Ge 18:22
19:28 [g]Rev 9:2; 18:9
19:29 [h]2Pe 2:7
19:30 [i]ver 19
19:37 [j]Dt 2:9
19:38 [k]Dt 2:19
20:1 [l]Ge 18:1 [m]Ge 26:1,6,17
20:2 [n]ver 12; Ge 12:13; 26:7 [o]Ge 12:15
20:3 [p]Job 33:15; Mt 27:19 [q]Ps 105:14
20:4 [r]Ge 18:25

j *18* Or *No, Lord*; or *No, my lord* k *19* The Hebrew is singular. l *22 Zoar* means *small.* m *37 Moab* sounds like the Hebrew for *from father.* n *38 Ben-Ammi* means *son of my people.*

also say, 'He is my brother'? I have done this with a clear conscience and clean hands."

6Then God said to him in the dream, "Yes, I know you did this with a clear conscience, and so I have kept[a] you from sinning against me. That is why I did not let you touch her. 7Now return the man's wife, for he is a prophet, and he will pray for you[b] and you will live. But if you do not return her, you may be sure that you and all yours will die."

8Early the next morning Abimelech summoned all his officials, and when he told them all that had happened, they were very much afraid. 9Then Abimelech called Abraham in and said, "What have you done to us? How have I wronged you that you have brought such great guilt upon me and my kingdom? You have done things to me that should not be done.[c]" 10And Abimelech asked Abraham, "What was your reason for doing this?"

11Abraham replied, "I said to myself, 'There is surely no fear of God[d] in this place, and they will kill me because of my wife.'[e] 12Besides, she really is my sister, the daughter of my father though not of my mother; and she became my wife. 13And when God had me wander from my father's household, I said to her, 'This is how you can show your love to me: Everywhere we go, say of me, "He is my brother." ' "

14Then Abimelech brought sheep and cattle and male and female slaves and gave them to Abraham,[f] and he returned Sarah his wife to him. 15And Abimelech said, "My land is before you; live wherever you like."[g]

16To Sarah he said, "I am giving your brother a thousand shekels[o] of silver. This is to cover the offense against you before all who are with you; you are completely vindicated."

17Then Abraham prayed to God,[h] and God healed Abimelech, his wife and his slave girls so they could have children again, 18for the LORD had closed up every womb in Abimelech's household because of Abraham's wife Sarah.[i]

Isaac is born to Sarah.

21 Now the LORD was gracious to Sarah[j] as he had said, and the LORD did for Sarah what he had promised.[k] 2Sarah became pregnant and bore a son[l] to Abraham in his old age,[m] at the very time God had promised him. 3Abraham gave the name Isaac[p][n] to the son Sarah bore him. 4When his son Isaac was eight days old, Abraham circumcised him,[o] as God commanded him. 5Abraham was a hundred years old when his son Isaac was born to him.

6Sarah said, "God has brought me laughter,[p] and everyone who hears about this will laugh with me." 7And she added, "Who would have said to Abraham that Sarah would nurse children? Yet I have borne him a son in his old age."

Hagar and Ishmael are sent away.

8The child grew and was weaned, and on the day Isaac was weaned Abraham held a great feast. 9But Sarah saw that the son whom Hagar the Egyptian had borne to Abraham[q] was mocking,[r] 10and she said to Abraham, "Get rid of that slave woman and her son, for that slave woman's son will never share in the inheritance with my son Isaac."[s]

11The matter distressed Abraham greatly because it concerned his son.[t] 12But God said to him, "Do not be so distressed about the boy and your maidservant. Listen to whatever Sarah tells you, because it is through Isaac that your offspring[q] will be reckoned.[u] 13I will make the son of the maidservant into a nation[v] also, because he is your offspring."

14Early the next morning Abraham took some food and a skin of water and gave them to Hagar. He set them on her shoulders and then sent her off with the boy. She went on her way and wandered in the desert of Beersheba.[w]

15When the water in the skin was gone, she put the boy under one of the

20:6 [a] 1Sa 25:26,34
20:7 [b] ver 17; 1Sa 7:5; Job 42:8
20:9 [c] Ge 12:18; 26:10; 34:7
20:11 [d] Ge 42:18; Ps 36:1 [e] Ge 12:12; 26:7
20:14 [f] Ge 12:16
20:15 [g] Ge 13:9
20:17 [h] Job 42:9
20:18 [i] Ge 12:17
21:1 [j] 1Sa 2:21 [k] Ge 8:1; 17:16,21; Gal 4:23
21:2 [l] Ge 17:19 [m] Gal 4:22; Heb 11:11
21:3 [n] Ge 17:19
21:4 [o] Ge 17:10,12; Ac 7:8
21:6 [p] Ge 17:17; Isa 54:1
21:9 [q] Ge 16:15 [r] Gal 4:29
21:10 [s] Gal 4:30*
21:11 [t] Ge 17:18
21:12 [u] Ro 9:7*; Heb 11:18*
21:13 [v] ver 18
21:14 [w] ver 31,32

o *16* That is, about 25 pounds (about 11.5 kilograms)
p *3* *Isaac* means *he laughs.* q *12* Or *seed*

bushes. 16 Then she went off and sat
down nearby, about a bowshot away,
for she thought, "I cannot watch the
boy die." And as she sat there nearby,
she[r] began to sob.
17 God heard the boy crying,[a] and the
angel of God called to Hagar from heav-
en and said to her, "What is the matter, Hagar? Do not be afraid; God has
heard the boy crying as he lies there.
18 Lift the boy up and take him by the
hand, for I will make him into a great
nation.[b]"
19 Then God opened her eyes[c] and
she saw a well of water. So she went
and filled the skin with water and gave
the boy a drink.
20 God was with the boy[d] as he grew
up. He lived in the desert and became
an archer. 21 While he was living in the
Desert of Paran, his mother got a wife
for him[e] from Egypt.

Abraham makes a treaty with Abimelech.

22 At that time Abimelech and Phicol
the commander of his forces said to
Abraham, "God is with you in everything you do. 23 Now swear[f] to me here
before God that you will not deal falsely
with me or my children or my descendants. Show to me and the country
where you are living as an alien the
same kindness I have shown to you."
24 Abraham said, "I swear it."
25 Then Abraham complained to
Abimelech about a well of water that
Abimelech's servants had seized.[g] 26 But
Abimelech said, "I don't know who
has done this. You did not tell me, and
I heard about it only today."
27 So Abraham brought sheep and cattle and gave them to Abimelech, and the
two men made a treaty.[h] 28 Abraham set
apart seven ewe lambs from the flock,
29 and Abimelech asked Abraham, "What
is the meaning of these seven ewe lambs
you have set apart by themselves?"
30 He replied, "Accept these seven
lambs from my hand as a witness[i] that
I dug this well."

21:17 [a]Ex 3:7
21:18 [b]ver 13
21:19 [c]Nu 22:31
21:20 [d]Ge 26:3,24; 28:15; 39:2,21,23
21:21 [e]Ge 24:4,38
21:23 [f]ver 31; Jos 2:12
21:25 [g]Ge 26:15,18, 20-22
21:27 [h]Ge 26:28,31
21:30 [i]Ge 31:44,47, 48,50,52
21:31 [j]Ge 26:33
21:33 [k]Ge 4:26 [l]Dt 33:27
22:1 [m]Dt 8:2,16; Heb 11:17; Jas 1:12-13
22:2 [n]ver 12,16; Jn 3:16; Heb 11:17; 1Jn 4:9 [o]2Ch 3:1
22:6 [p]Jn 19:17
22:7 [q]Lev 1:10

31 So that place was called Beersheba,[s][j]
because the two men swore an oath
there.
32 After the treaty had been made at
Beersheba, Abimelech and Phicol the
commander of his forces returned to
the land of the Philistines. 33 Abraham
planted a tamarisk tree in Beersheba,
and there he called upon the name of
the LORD,[k] the Eternal God.[l] 34 And Abraham stayed in the land of the Philistines for a long time.

Abraham's willingness to offer Isaac.

22 Some time later God tested[m]
Abraham. He said to him, "Abraham!"
"Here I am," he replied.
2 Then God said, "Take your son[n],
your only son, Isaac, whom you love,
and go to the region of Moriah.[o] Sacrifice him there as a burnt offering on
one of the mountains I will tell you
about."
3 Early the next morning Abraham got
up and saddled his donkey. He took with
him two of his servants and his son
Isaac. When he had cut enough wood
for the burnt offering, he set out for
the place God had told him about. 4 On
the third day Abraham looked up and
saw the place in the distance. 5 He said
to his servants, "Stay here with the
donkey while I and the boy go over
there. We will worship and then we
will come back to you."
6 Abraham took the wood for the
burnt offering and placed it on his son
Isaac,[p] and he himself carried the fire
and the knife. As the two of them went
on together, 7 Isaac spoke up and said
to his father Abraham, "Father?"
"Yes, my son?" Abraham replied.
"The fire and wood are here," Isaac
said, "but where is the lamb[q] for the
burnt offering?"
8 Abraham answered, "God himself will
provide the lamb for the burnt offering,

[r] *16* Hebrew; Septuagint *the child* [s] *31 Beersheba* can mean *well of seven* or *well of the oath.*

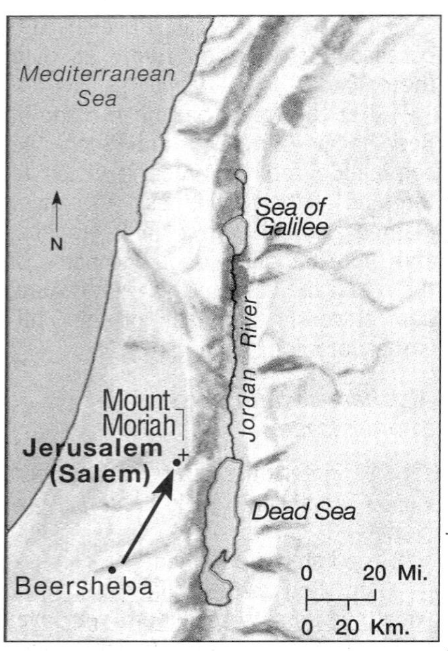

Abraham's Trip to Mount Moriah

Abraham and Isaac traveled the 50 or 60 miles from Beersheba to Mount Moriah in about three days. This was a very difficult time for Abraham, who was on his way to sacrifice his beloved son, Isaac.

my son." And the two of them went on
together.
9When they reached the place God
had told him about, Abraham built an
altar there and arranged the wood on
it. He bound his son Isaac and laid him
on the altar,[a] on top of the wood. 10Then
he reached out his hand and took the
knife to slay his son. 11But the angel of
the LORD called out to him from heav-
en, "Abraham! Abraham!"
"Here I am," he replied.
12"Do not lay a hand on the boy," he
said. "Do not do anything to him. Now
I know that you fear God,[b] because you
have not withheld from me your son,
your only son.[c]"
13Abraham looked up and there in a
thicket he saw a ram[t] caught by its
horns. He went over and took the ram
and sacrificed it as a burnt offering
instead of his son.[d] 14So Abraham called
that place The LORD Will Provide. And
to this day it is said, "On the mountain
of the LORD it will be provided.[e]"

22:9 [a]Heb 11:17-19; Jas 2:21
22:12 [b]1Sa 15:22; Jas 2:21-22 [c]ver 2; Jn 3:16
22:13 [d]Ro 8:32
22:14 [e]ver 8
22:16 [f]Lk 1:73; Heb 6:13
22:17 [g]Heb 6:14* [h]Ge 15:5 [i]Ge 26:24; 32:12 [j]Ge 24:60
22:18 [k]Ge 12:2,3; Ac 3:25*; Gal 3:8* [l]ver 10
22:20 [m]Ge 11:29
22:23 [n]Ge 24:15
23:2 [o]Jos 14:15 [p]ver 19; Ge 13:18
23:4 [q]Ge 17:8; 1Ch 29:15; Ps 105:12; Heb 11:9,13
23:6 [r]Ge 14:14-16; 24:35

15The angel of the LORD called to Abraham from heaven a second time 16and
said, "I swear by myself,[f] declares the
LORD, that because you have done this
and have not withheld your son, your
only son, 17I will surely bless you and
make your descendants[g] as numerous
as the stars in the sky[h] and as the sand
on the seashore.[i] Your descendants will
take possession of the cities of their
enemies,[j] 18and through your offspring[u]
all nations on earth will be blessed,[k]
because you have obeyed me."[l]
19Then Abraham returned to his servants, and they set off together for
Beersheba. And Abraham stayed in
Beersheba.
20Some time later Abraham was told,
"Milcah is also a mother; she has borne
sons to your brother Nahor:[m] 21Uz the
firstborn, Buz his brother, Kemuel (the
father of Aram), 22Kesed, Hazo, Pildash,
Jidlaph and Bethuel." 23Bethuel became
the father of Rebekah.[n] Milcah bore these
eight sons to Abraham's brother Nahor.
24His concubine, whose name was
Reumah, also had sons: Tebah, Gaham,
Tahash and Maacah.

Sarah's death and burial.

23 Sarah lived to be a hundred and
twenty-seven years old. 2She
died at Kiriath Arba[o] (that is, Hebron)[p]
in the land of Canaan, and Abraham
went to mourn for Sarah and to weep
over her.
3Then Abraham rose from beside his
dead wife and spoke to the Hittites.[v] He
said, 4"I am an alien and a stranger[q]
among you. Sell me some property for
a burial site here so I can bury my dead."
5The Hittites replied to Abraham,
6"Sir, listen to us. You are a mighty
prince[r] among us. Bury your dead in
the choicest of our tombs. None of us
will refuse you his tomb for burying
your dead."

[t]*13* Many manuscripts of the Masoretic Text, Samaritan Pentateuch, Septuagint and Syriac; most manuscripts of the Masoretic Text *a ram behind* ⌊*him*⌋
[u]*18* Or *seed*
[v]*3* Or *the sons of Heth*; also in verses 5, 7, 10, 16, 18 and 20

7 Then Abraham rose and bowed down before the people of the land, the Hittites. 8 He said to them, "If you are willing to let me bury my dead, then listen to me and intercede with Ephron son of Zohar[a] on my behalf 9 so he will sell me the cave of Machpelah, which belongs to him and is at the end of his field. Ask him to sell it to me for the full price as a burial site among you."

10 Ephron the Hittite was sitting among his people and he replied to Abraham in the hearing of all the Hittites who had come to the gate[b] of his city. 11 "No, my lord," he said. "Listen to me; I give[w][c] you the field, and I give[w] you the cave that is in it. I give[w] it to you in the presence of my people. Bury your dead."

12 Again Abraham bowed down before the people of the land 13 and he said to Ephron in their hearing, "Listen to me, if you will. I will pay the price of the field. Accept it from me so I can bury my dead there."

14 Ephron answered Abraham, 15 "Listen to me, my lord; the land is worth four hundred shekels[x] of silver,[d] but what is that between me and you? Bury your dead."

16 Abraham agreed to Ephron's terms and weighed out for him the price he had named in the hearing of the Hittites: four hundred shekels of silver,[e] according to the weight current among the merchants.

17 So Ephron's field in Machpelah near Mamre[f]—both the field and the cave in it, and all the trees within the borders of the field—was deeded 18 to Abraham as his property in the presence of all the Hittites who had come to the gate of the city. 19 Afterward Abraham buried his wife Sarah in the cave in the field of Machpelah near Mamre (which is at Hebron) in the land of Canaan. 20 So the field and the cave in it were deeded[g] to Abraham by the Hittites as a burial site.

Rebekah becomes Isaac's wife by the efforts of Abraham's servant.

24 Abraham was now old and well advanced in years, and the LORD had blessed him in every way.[h] 2 He said to the chief[y] servant in his household, the one in charge of all that he had,[i] "Put your hand under my thigh.[j] 3 I want you to swear by the LORD, the God of heaven and the God of earth,[k] that you will not get a wife for my son[l] from the daughters of the Canaanites,[m] among whom I am living, 4 but will go to my country and my own relatives[n] and get a wife for my son Isaac."

5 The servant asked him, "What if the woman is unwilling to come back with me to this land? Shall I then take your son back to the country you came from?"

6 "Make sure that you do not take my son back there," Abraham said. 7 "The LORD, the God of heaven, who brought me out of my father's household and my native land and who spoke to me and promised me on oath, saying, '<u>To your offspring</u>[z][o] <u>I will give this land</u>'[p]—he will send his angel before you[q] so that you can get a wife for my son from there. 8 If the woman is unwilling to come back with you, then you will be released from this oath of mine. Only do not take my son back there." 9 So the servant put his hand under the thigh[r] of his master Abraham and swore an oath to him concerning this matter.

10 Then the servant took ten of his master's camels and left, taking with him all kinds of good things from his master. He set out for Aram Naharaim[a] and made his way to the town of Nahor. 11 He had the camels kneel down near the well[s] outside the town; it was toward evening, the time the women go out to draw water.[t]

12 Then he prayed, "O LORD, God of my master Abraham,[u] give me success today, and show kindness to my master Abraham. 13 See, I am standing beside this spring, and the daughters of the townspeople are coming out to draw water. 14 May it be that when I say to a

23:8 [a]Ge 25:9
23:10 [b]Ge 34:20-24; Ru 4:4
23:11 [c]2Sa 24:23
23:15 [d]Eze 45:12
23:16 [e]Jer 32:9; Zec 11:12
23:17 [f]Ge 25:9; 49:30-32; 50:13; Ac 7:16
23:20 [g]Jer 32:10
24:1 [h]ver 35
24:2 [i]Ge 39:4-6 [j]ver 9; Ge 47:29
24:3 [k]Ge 14:19 [l]Ge 28:1; Dt 7:3 [m]Ge 10:15-19
24:4 [n]Ge 12:1; 28:2
24:7 [o]Gal 3:16* [p]Ge 12:7; 13:15 [q]Ex 23:20,23
24:9 [r]ver 2
24:11 [s]Ex 2:15 [t]ver 13; 1Sa 9:11
24:12 [u]ver 27,42, 48; Ge 26:24; Ex 3:6,15,16

[w] *11* Or *sell* [x] *15* That is, about 10 pounds (about 4.5 kilograms) [y] *2* Or *oldest* [z] *7* Or *seed*
[a] *10* That is, Northwest Mesopotamia

girl, 'Please let down your jar that I may
have a drink,' and she says, 'Drink, and
I'll water your camels too'—let her be
the one you have chosen for your servant Isaac. By this I will know[a] that you
have shown kindness to my master."
15 Before he had finished praying,[b]
Rebekah[c] came out with her jar on her
shoulder. She was the daughter of
Bethuel son of Milcah,[d] who was the
wife of Abraham's brother Nahor.[e]
16 The girl was very beautiful,[f] a virgin;
no man had ever lain with her. She went
down to the spring, filled her jar and
came up again.
17 The servant hurried to meet her
and said, "Please give me a little water
from your jar."
18 "Drink,[g] my lord," she said, and
quickly lowered the jar to her hands and
gave him a drink.
19 After she had given him a drink,
she said, "I'll draw water for your camels
too,[h] until they have finished drinking."
20 So she quickly emptied her jar into the
trough, ran back to the well to draw
more water, and drew enough for all his
camels. 21 Without saying a word, the
man watched her closely to learn
whether or not the LORD had made his
journey successful.[i]
22 When the camels had finished drinking, the man took out a gold nose ring[j]
weighing a beka[b] and two gold bracelets
weighing ten shekels.[c] 23 Then he asked,
"Whose daughter are you? Please tell
me, is there room in your father's house
for us to spend the night?"
24 She answered him, "I am the daughter of Bethuel, the son that Milcah bore
to Nahor.[k]" 25 And she added, "We have
plenty of straw and fodder, as well as
room for you to spend the night."
26 Then the man bowed down and
worshiped the LORD,[l] 27 saying, "Praise
be to the LORD,[m] the God of my master
Abraham, who has not abandoned his
kindness and faithfulness[n] to my master. As for me, the LORD has led me on
the journey[o] to the house of my master's relatives."[p]
28 The girl ran and told her mother's
household about these things. 29 Now Rebekah had a brother named Laban,[q]
and he hurried out to the man at the
spring. 30 As soon as he had seen the
nose ring, and the bracelets on his sister's arms, and had heard Rebekah tell
what the man said to her, he went out
to the man and found him standing by
the camels near the spring. 31 "Come,
you who are blessed by the LORD,"[r] he
said. "Why are you standing out here?
I have prepared the house and a place
for the camels."
32 So the man went to the house, and
the camels were unloaded. Straw and
fodder were brought for the camels, and
water for him and his men to wash
their feet.[s] 33 Then food was set before
him, but he said, "I will not eat until I
have told you what I have to say."
"Then tell us," ⌊Laban⌋ said.
34 So he said, "I am Abraham's servant.
35 The LORD has blessed my master abundantly,[t] and he has become wealthy. He
has given him sheep and cattle, silver
and gold, menservants and maidservants,
and camels and donkeys.[u] 36 My master's
wife Sarah has borne him a son in her[d]
old age,[v] and he has given him everything he owns.[w] 37 And my master made
me swear an oath, and said, 'You must
not get a wife for my son from the daughters of the Canaanites, in whose land
I live,[x] 38 but go to my father's family and
to my own clan, and get a wife for my
son.'[y]
39 "Then I asked my master, 'What if
the woman will not come back with
me?'[z]
40 "He replied, 'The LORD, before
whom I have walked, will send his angel
with you[a] and make your journey a success, so that you can get a wife for my
son from my own clan and from my father's family. 41 Then, when you go to my
clan, you will be released from my oath
even if they refuse to give her to you—
you will be released from my oath.'[b]
42 "When I came to the spring today,

24:14 [a]Jdg 6:17,37
24:15 [b]ver 45 [c]Ge 22:23 [d]Ge 22:20 [e]Ge 11:29
24:16 [f]Ge 26:7
24:18 [g]ver 14
24:19 [h]ver 14
24:21 [i]ver 12
24:22 [j]ver 47
24:24 [k]ver 15
24:26 [l]ver 48,52; Ex 4:31
24:27 [m]Ex 18:10; Ru 4:14; 1Sa 25:32 [n]ver 49; Ge 32:10; Ps 98:3 [o]ver 21 [p]ver 12,48
24:29 [q]ver 4; Ge 29:5,12,13
24:31 [r]Ge 26:29; Ru 3:10; Ps 115:15
24:32 [s]Ge 43:24; Jdg 19:21
24:35 [t]ver 1 [u]Ge 13:2
24:36 [v]Ge 21:2,10 [w]Ge 25:5
24:37 [x]ver 3
24:38 [y]ver 4
24:39 [z]ver 5
24:40 [a]ver 7
24:41 [b]ver 8

b*22* That is, about 1/5 ounce (about 5.5 grams)
c*22* That is, about 4 ounces (about 110 grams)
d*36* Or *his*

I said. 'O LORD, God of my master Abraham, if you will, please grant success[a]
to the journey on which I have come.
43See, I am standing beside this spring;[b]
if a maiden comes out to draw water and
I say to her, "Please let me drink a little
water from your jar,"[c] 44and if she says to
me, "Drink, and I'll draw water for your
camels too," let her be the one the LORD
has chosen for my master's son.'

45"Before I finished praying in my
heart,[d] Rebekah came out, with her jar
on her shoulder.[e] She went down to the
spring and drew water, and I said to
her, 'Please give me a drink.'[f]

46"She quickly lowered her jar from
her shoulder and said, 'Drink, and I'll
water your camels too.'[g] So I drank, and
she watered the camels also.

47"I asked her, 'Whose daughter are
you?'[h]

"She said, 'The daughter of Bethuel son
of Nahor, whom Milcah bore to him.'[i]

"Then I put the ring in her nose and
the bracelets on her arms,[j] 48and I
bowed down and worshiped the
LORD.[k] I praised the LORD, the God of
my master Abraham, who had led me
on the right road to get the granddaughter of my master's brother for his
son.[l] 49Now if you will show kindness
and faithfulness[m] to my master, tell me;
and if not, tell me, so I may know which
way to turn."

50Laban and Bethuel answered, "This
is from the LORD;[n] we can say nothing
to you one way or the other.[o] 51Here is
Rebekah; take her and go, and let her
become the wife of your master's son,
as the LORD has directed."

52When Abraham's servant heard
what they said, he bowed down to the
ground before the LORD.[p] 53Then the
servant brought out gold and silver
jewelry and articles of clothing and
gave them to Rebekah; he also gave
costly gifts[q] to her brother and to her
mother. 54Then he and the men who
were with him ate and drank and spent
the night there.

When they got up the next morning, he
said, "Send me on my way[r] to my master."

55But her brother and her mother
replied, "Let the girl remain with us ten
days or so; then you[e] may go."

56But he said to them, "Do not detain
me, now that the LORD has granted
success to my journey. Send me on my
way so I may go to my master."

57Then they said, "Let's call the girl
and ask her about it." 58So they called
Rebekah and asked her, "Will you go
with this man?"

"I will go," she said.

59So they sent their sister Rebekah
on her way, along with her nurse[s] and
Abraham's servant and his men. 60And
they blessed Rebekah and said to her,

> "Our sister, may you increase
> to thousands upon thousands;[t]
> may your offspring possess
> the gates of their enemies."[u]

61Then Rebekah and her maids got
ready and mounted their camels and
went back with the man. So the servant took Rebekah and left.

62Now Isaac had come from Beer
Lahai Roi,[v] for he was living in the
Negev.[w] 63He went out to the field one
evening to meditate,[f][x] and as he
looked up, he saw camels approaching.
64Rebekah also looked up and saw
Isaac. She got down from her camel
65and asked the servant, "Who is that
man in the field coming to meet us?"

"He is my master," the servant
answered. So she took her veil and
covered herself.

66Then the servant told Isaac all he
had done. 67Isaac brought her into the
tent of his mother Sarah, and he married Rebekah.[y] So she became his wife,
and he loved her;[z] and Isaac was comforted after his mother's death.[a]

Abraham's death and burial.

25:1-4pp— 1Ch 1:32-33

25 Abraham took[g] another wife,
whose name was Keturah. 2She
bore him Zimran, Jokshan, Medan,

24:42 [a]ver 12
24:43 [b]ver 13 [c]ver 14
24:45 [d]1Sa 1:13 [e]ver 15 [f]ver 17
24:46 [g]ver 18-19
24:47 [h]ver 23 [i]ver 24 [j]Eze 16:11-12
24:48 [k]ver 26 [l]ver 27
24:49 [m]Ge 47:29; Jos 2:14
24:50 [n]Ps 118:23 [o]Ge 31:7,24, 29,42
24:52 [p]ver 26
24:53 [q]ver 10,22
24:54 [r]ver 56,59
24:59 [s]Ge 35:8
24:60 [t]Ge 17:16 [u]Ge 22:17
24:62 [v]Ge 16:14; 25:11 [w]Ge 20:1
24:63 [x]Ps 1:2; 77:12; 119:15,27,48, 97,148; 143:5; 145:5
24:67 [y]Ge 25:20 [z]Ge 29:18,20 [a]Ge 23:1-2

[e]55 Or *she* [f]63 The meaning of the Hebrew for this word is uncertain. [g]1 Or *had taken*

Midian, Ishbak and Shuah.[a] 3Jokshan was
the father of Sheba and Dedan; the descendants of Dedan were the Asshurites,
the Letushites and the Leummites. 4The
sons of Midian were Ephah, Epher,
Hanoch, Abida and Eldaah. All these
were descendants of Keturah.

5Abraham left everything he owned to
Isaac.[b] 6But while he was still living, he
gave gifts to the sons of his concubines[c]
and sent them away from his son Isaac[d]
to the land of the east.

7Altogether, Abraham lived a hundred
and seventy-five years. 8Then Abraham
breathed his last and died at a good old
age,[e] an old man and full of years; and
he was gathered to his people.[f] 9His
sons Isaac and Ishmael buried him[g] in
the cave of Machpelah near Mamre, in
the field of Ephron son of Zohar the
Hittite,[h] 10the field Abraham had bought
from the Hittites.[h][i] There Abraham was
buried with his wife Sarah. 11After
Abraham's death, God blessed his son
Isaac, who then lived near Beer Lahai
Roi.[j]

Account of Ishmael.

25:12-16pp— 1Ch 1:29-31

12This is the account of Abraham's
son Ishmael, whom Sarah's maidservant, Hagar[k] the Egyptian, bore to
Abraham.[l]

13These are the names of the sons of
Ishmael, listed in the order of their
birth: Nebaioth the firstborn of Ishmael,
Kedar, Adbeel, Mibsam, 14Mishma,
Dumah, Massa, 15Hadad, Tema, Jetur,
Naphish and Kedemah. 16These were
the sons of Ishmael, and these are the
names of the twelve tribal rulers[m]
according to their settlements and
camps. 17Altogether, Ishmael lived a
hundred and thirty-seven years. He
breathed his last and died, and he was
gathered to his people.[n] 18His descendants settled in the area from Havilah
to Shur, near the border of Egypt, as
you go toward Asshur. And they lived
in hostility toward[i] all their brothers.[o]

Account of Isaac.

19This is the account of Abraham's
son Isaac.

Abraham became the father of Isaac,
20and Isaac was forty years old[p] when
he married Rebekah[q] daughter of Bethuel the Aramean from Paddan Aram[j] and
sister of Laban[r] the Aramean.

21Isaac prayed to the LORD on behalf
of his wife, because she was barren.
The LORD answered his prayer,[s] and his
wife Rebekah became pregnant. 22The
babies jostled each other within her,
and she said, "Why is this happening
to me?" So she went to inquire of the
LORD.[t]

23The LORD said to her,

"Two nations[u] are in your womb,
and two peoples from within you
will be separated;
one people will be stronger than the
other,
and the older will serve the
younger.[v]"

24When the time came for her to
give birth, there were twin boys in her
womb. 25The first to come out was red,
and his whole body was like a hairy
garment;[w] so they named him Esau.[k]
26After this, his brother came out, with
his hand grasping Esau's heel;[x] so he
was named Jacob.[l][y] Isaac was sixty
years old when Rebekah gave birth to
them.

Sale of Esau's birthright to Jacob.

27The boys grew up, and Esau became
a skillful hunter, a man of the open
country,[z] while Jacob was a quiet man,
staying among the tents. 28Isaac, who
had a taste for wild game,[a] loved Esau,
but Rebekah loved Jacob.[b]

29Once when Jacob was cooking some
stew, Esau came in from the open
country, famished. 30He said to Jacob,

25:2 [a]1Ch 1:32,33
25:5 [b]Ge 24:36
25:6 [c]Ge 22:24 [d]Ge 21:10,14
25:8 [e]Ge 15:15 [f]ver 17; Ge 35:29; 49:29,33
25:9 [g]Ge 35:29 [h]Ge 50:13
25:10 [i]Ge 23:16
25:11 [j]Ge 16:14
25:12 [k]Ge 16:1 [l]Ge 16:15
25:16 [m]Ge 17:20
25:17 [n]ver 8
25:18 [o]Ge 16:12
25:20 [p]ver 26; Ge 26:34 [q]Ge 24:67 [r]Ge 24:29
25:21 [s]1Ch 5:20; 2Ch 33:13; Ezr 8:23; Ps 127:3; Ro 9:10
25:22 [t]1Sa 9:9; 10:22
25:23 [u]Ge 17:4 [v]Ge 27:29,40; Mal 1:3; Ro 9:11-12*
25:25 [w]Ge 27:11
25:26 [x]Hos 12:3 [y]Ge 27:36
25:27 [z]Ge 27:3,5
25:28 [a]Ge 27: 19 [b]Ge 27:6

[h]*10* Or *the sons of Heth* [i]*18* Or *lived to the east of* [j]*20* That is, Northwest Mesopotamia
[k]*25 Esau* may mean *hairy*; he was also called Edom, which means *red.* [l]*26 Jacob* means *he grasps the heel* (figuratively, *he deceives*).

"Quick, let me have some of that red
stew! I'm famished!" (That is why he
was also called Edom.[m])
31 Jacob replied, "First sell me your
birthright."
32 "Look, I am about to die," Esau said.
"What good is the birthright to me?"
33 But Jacob said, "Swear to me first."
So he swore an oath to him, selling his
birthright[a] to Jacob.
34 Then Jacob gave Esau some bread
and some lentil stew. He ate and drank,
and then got up and left.
So Esau despised his birthright.

God's promise to Abraham continues through Isaac.

26:1-11Ref— Ge 12:10-20; 20:1-18

26 Now there was a famine in the
land[b]—besides the earlier famine
of Abraham's time—and Isaac went to
Abimelech king of the Philistines in
Gerar.[c] 2 The LORD appeared[d] to Isaac
and said, "Do not go down to Egypt; live
in the land where I tell you to live.[e]
3 Stay in this land for a while,[f] and I
will be with you and will bless you.[g]
For to you and your descendants I will
give all these lands[h] and will confirm the
oath I swore to your father Abraham.
4 I will make your descendants as numerous as the stars in the sky[i] and will give
them all these lands, and through your
offspring[n] all nations on earth will be
blessed,[j] 5 because Abraham obeyed me[k]
and kept my requirements, my commands, my decrees and my laws." 6 So
Isaac stayed in Gerar.

Isaac deceives Abimelech concerning Rebekah.

7 When the men of that place asked
him about his wife, he said, "She is my
sister,[l]" because he was afraid to say,
"She is my wife." He thought, "The men
of this place might kill me on account
of Rebekah, because she is beautiful."
8 When Isaac had been there a long
time, Abimelech king of the Philistines
looked down from a window and saw
Isaac caressing his wife Rebekah. 9 So

25:33 [a]Ge 27:36; Heb 12:16
26:1 [b]Ge 12:10 [c]Ge 20:1
26:2 [d]Ge 12:7; 17:1; 18:1 [e]Ge 12:1
26:3 [f]Ge 20:1; 28:15 [g]Ge 12:2; 22:16-18 [h]Ge 12:7; 13:15; 15:18
26:4 [i]Ge 15:5; 22:17; Ex 32:13 [j]Ge 12:3; 22:18; Gal 3:8
26:5 [k]Ge 22:16
26:7 [l]Ge 12:13; 20:2,12; Pr 29:25
26:10 [m]Ge 20:9
26:11 [n]Ps 105:15
26:12 [o]ver 3; Job 42:12
26:13 [p]Pr 10:22
26:14 [q]Ge 24:36 [r]Ge 37:11
26:15 [s]Ge 21:30 [t]Ge 21:25
26:16 [u]Ex 1:9
26:18 [v]Ge 21:30
26:20 [w]Ge 21:25

Abimelech summoned Isaac and said,
"She is really your wife! Why did you
say, 'She is my sister'?"
Isaac answered him, "Because I
thought I might lose my life on account
of her."
10 Then Abimelech said, "What is this
you have done to us?[m] One of the men
might well have slept with your wife,
and you would have brought guilt upon
us."
11 So Abimelech gave orders to all
the people: "Anyone who molests[n] this
man or his wife shall surely be put to
death."

Isaac is blessed with great wealth.

12 Isaac planted crops in that land
and the same year reaped a hundred-
fold, because the LORD blessed him.[o]
13 The man became rich, and his wealth
continued to grow until he became
very wealthy.[p] 14 He had so many flocks
and herds and servants[q] that the Philistines envied him.[r] 15 So all the wells[s]
that his father's servants had dug in the
time of his father Abraham, the Philistines stopped up,[t] filling them with
earth.
16 Then Abimelech said to Isaac,
"Move away from us; you have become
too powerful for us.[u]"
17 So Isaac moved away from there
and encamped in the Valley of Gerar
and settled there. 18 Isaac reopened the
wells[v] that had been dug in the time of
his father Abraham, which the Philistines had stopped up after Abraham
died, and he gave them the same names
his father had given them.
19 Isaac's servants dug in the valley
and discovered a well of fresh water
there. 20 But the herdsmen of Gerar
quarreled with Isaac's herdsmen and
said, "The water is ours!"[w] So he named
the well Esek,[o] because they disputed
with him. 21 Then they dug another
well, but they quarreled over that one
also; so he named it Sitnah.[p] 22 He

[m] 30 *Edom* means *red.* [n] 4 Or *seed* [o] 20 *Esek* means *dispute.* [p] 21 *Sitnah* means *opposition.*

moved on from there and dug another
well, and no one quarreled over it. He
named it Rehoboth,[q] saying, "Now the
LORD has given us room and we will
flourish[a] in the land."
23 From there he went up to Beersheba.
24 That night the LORD appeared to him
and said, "I am the God of your father
Abraham.[b] Do not be afraid,[c] for I am
with you; I will bless you and will increase the number of your descendants[d]
for the sake of my servant Abraham."[e]
25 Isaac built an altar[f] there and called
on the name of the LORD. There he
pitched his tent, and there his servants
dug a well.
26 Meanwhile, Abimelech had come
to him from Gerar, with Ahuzzath his
personal adviser and Phicol the commander of his forces.[g] 27 Isaac asked them,
"Why have you come to me, since you
were hostile to me and sent me away?[h]"
28 They answered, "We saw clearly that
the LORD was with you;[i] so we said,
'There ought to be a sworn agreement
between us'—between us and you. Let
us make a treaty with you 29 that you
will do us no harm, just as we did not
molest you but always treated you well
and sent you away in peace. And now
you are blessed by the LORD."[j]
30 Isaac then made a feast[k] for them,
and they ate and drank. 31 Early the next
morning the men swore an oath[l] to each
other. Then Isaac sent them on their way,
and they left him in peace.
32 That day Isaac's servants came and
told him about the well they had dug.
They said, "We've found water!" 33 He
called it Shibah,[r] and to this day the name
of the town has been Beersheba.[s][m]
34 When Esau was forty years old,[n] he
married Judith daughter of Beeri the
Hittite, and also Basemath daughter of
Elon the Hittite.[o] 35 They were a source
of grief to Isaac and Rebekah.[p]

Isaac gives Jacob the blessing intended for Esau.

27 When Isaac was old and his
eyes were so weak that he
could no longer see,[q] he called for
Esau his older son[r] and said to him,
"My son."
"Here I am," he answered.
2 Isaac said, "I am now an old man
and don't know the day of my death.[s]
3 Now then, get your weapons—your
quiver and bow—and go out to the open
country[t] to hunt some wild game for
me. 4 Prepare me the kind of tasty food
I like and bring it to me to eat, so that I
may give you my blessing[u] before I die."
5 Now Rebekah was listening as Isaac
spoke to his son Esau. When Esau left
for the open country to hunt game and
bring it back, 6 Rebekah said to her son
Jacob,[v] "Look, I overheard your father say
to your brother Esau, 7 'Bring me some
game and prepare me some tasty food to
eat, so that I may give you my blessing
in the presence of the LORD before I die.'
8 Now, my son, listen carefully and do
what I tell you:[w] 9 Go out to the flock
and bring me two choice young goats,
so I can prepare some tasty food for
your father, just the way he likes it.
10 Then take it to your father to eat, so
that he may give you his blessing before
he dies."
11 Jacob said to Rebekah his mother,
"But my brother Esau is a hairy man,[x]
and I'm a man with smooth skin. 12 What
if my father touches me?[y] I would appear
to be tricking him and would bring down
a curse on myself rather than a blessing."
13 His mother said to him, "My son,
let the curse fall on me.[z] Just do what I
say;[a] go and get them for me."
14 So he went and got them and
brought them to his mother, and she
prepared some tasty food, just the way
his father liked it. 15 Then Rebekah took
the best clothes[b] of Esau her older son,
which she had in the house, and put
them on her younger son Jacob. 16 She
also covered his hands and the smooth
part of his neck with the goatskins.
17 Then she handed to her son Jacob the
tasty food and the bread she had made.

26:22 [a] Ge 17:6; Ex 1:7
26:24 [b] Ge 24:12; Ex 3:6 [c] Ge 15:1 [d] ver 4 [e] Ge 17:7
26:25 [f] Ge 12:7,8; 13:4,18; Ps 116:17
26:26 [g] Ge 21:22
26:27 [h] ver 16
26:28 [i] Ge 21:22
26:29 [j] Ge 24:31; Ps 115:15
26:30 [k] Ge 19:3
26:31 [l] Ge 21:31
26:33 [m] Ge 21:14
26:34 [n] Ge 25:20 [o] Ge 28:9; 36:2
26:35 [p] Ge 27:46
27:1 [q] Ge 48:10; 1Sa 3:2 [r] Ge 25:25
27:2 [s] Ge 47:29
27:3 [t] Ge 25:27
27:4 [u] ver 10,25,31; Ge 49:28; Dt 33:1; Heb 11:20
27:6 [v] Ge 25:28
27:8 [w] ver 13,43
27:11 [x] Ge 25:25
27:12 [y] ver 22
27:13 [z] Mt 27:25 [a] ver 8
27:15 [b] ver 27

q 22 *Rehoboth* means *room.* r 33 *Shibah* can mean *oath* or *seven.* s 33 *Beersheba* can mean *well of the oath* or *well of seven.*

18He went to his father and said, "My
father."
"Yes, my son," he answered. "Who
is it?"
19Jacob said to his father, "I am Esau
your firstborn. I have done as you told
me. Please sit up and eat some of my
game so that you may give me your
blessing."[a]
20Isaac asked his son, "How did you
find it so quickly, my son?"
"The LORD your God gave me success,[b]" he replied.
21Then Isaac said to Jacob, "Come
near so I can touch you,[c] my son, to
know whether you really are my son
Esau or not."
22Jacob went close to his father Isaac,
who touched him and said, "The voice
is the voice of Jacob, but the hands are
the hands of Esau." 23He did not recognize him, for his hands were hairy like
those of his brother Esau;[d] so he
blessed him. 24"Are you really my son
Esau?" he asked.
"I am," he replied.
25Then he said, "My son, bring me
some of your game to eat, so that I may
give you my blessing."[e]
Jacob brought it to him and he ate;
and he brought some wine and he
drank. 26Then his father Isaac said to
him, "Come here, my son, and kiss me."
27So he went to him and kissed
him[f]. When Isaac caught the smell of
his clothes,[g] he blessed him and said,

"Ah, the smell of my son
is like the smell of a field
that the LORD has blessed.[h]
28May God give you of heaven's dew[i]
and of earth's richness[j]—
an abundance of grain and new
wine.[k]
29May nations serve you
and peoples bow down to you.[l]
Be lord over your brothers,
and may the sons of your mother
bow down to you.[m]
May those who curse you be cursed
and those who bless you be
blessed.[n]"

27:19 [a] ver 4
27:20 [b] Ge 24:12
27:21 [c] ver 12
27:23 [d] ver 16
27:25 [e] ver 4
27:27 [f] Heb 11:20 [g] SS 4:11 [h] Ps 65:9-13
27:28 [i] Dt 33:13 [j] ver 39 [k] Ge 45:18; Nu 18:12; Dt 33:28
27:29 [l] Isa 45:14,23; 49:7,23 [m] Ge 9:25; 25:23; 37:7 [n] Ge 12:3; Nu 24:9; Zep 2:8
27:31 [o] ver 4
27:32 [p] ver 18
27:33 [q] ver 29; Ge 28:3,4; Ro 11:29
27:34 [r] Heb 12:17
27:35 [s] Jer 9:4; 12:6
27:36 [t] Ge 25:26 [u] Ge 25:33
27:37 [v] ver 28
27:38 [w] Heb 12:17
27:39 [x] ver 28
27:40 [y] 2Sa 8:14 [z] Ge 25:23 [a] 2Ki 8:20-22

30After Isaac finished blessing him
and Jacob had scarcely left his father's
presence, his brother Esau came in from
hunting. 31He too prepared some tasty
food and brought it to his father. Then
he said to him, "My father, sit up and
eat some of my game, so that you may
give me your blessing."[o]
32His father Isaac asked him, "Who
are you?"[p]
"I am your son," he answered, "your
firstborn, Esau."
33Isaac trembled violently and said,
"Who was it, then, that hunted game
and brought it to me? I ate it just before
you came and I blessed him—and indeed he will be blessed![q]"
34When Esau heard his father's words,
he burst out with a loud and bitter cry[r]
and said to his father, "Bless me—me
too, my father!"
35But he said, "Your brother came
deceitfully[s] and took your blessing."
36Esau said, "Isn't he rightly named
Jacob[t]?[t] He has deceived me these two
times: He took my birthright,[u] and now
he's taken my blessing!" Then he asked,
"Haven't you reserved any blessing for
me?"
37Isaac answered Esau, "I have made
him lord over you and have made all
his relatives his servants, and I have sustained him with grain and new wine.[v]
So what can I possibly do for you, my
son?"
38Esau said to his father, "Do you have
only one blessing, my father? Bless me
too, my father!" Then Esau wept aloud.[w]
39His father Isaac answered him,

"Your dwelling will be
away from the earth's richness,
away from the dew[x] of heaven
above.
40You will live by the sword
and you will serve[y] your brother.[z]
But when you grow restless,
you will throw his yoke
from off your neck.[a]"

t36 *Jacob* means *he grasps the heel* (figuratively, *he deceives*).

Jacob flees from Esau to Laban.

41Esau held a grudge[a] against Jacob[b] because of the blessing his father had given him. He said to himself, "The days of mourning[c] for my father are near; then I will kill my brother Jacob."[d]

42When Rebekah was told what her older son Esau had said, she sent for her younger son Jacob and said to him, "Your brother Esau is consoling himself with the thought of killing you. 43Now then, my son, do what I say:[e] Flee at once to my brother Laban[f] in Haran.[g] 44Stay with him for a while[h] until your brother's fury subsides. 45When your brother is no longer angry with you and forgets what you did to him,[i] I'll send word for you to come back from there. Why should I lose both of you in one day?"

46Then Rebekah said to Isaac, "I'm disgusted with living because of these Hittite women. If Jacob takes a wife from among the women of this land, from Hittite women like these, my life will not be worth living."[j]

28 So Isaac called for Jacob and blessed[u] him and commanded him: "Do not marry a Canaanite woman.[k] 2Go at once to Paddan Aram,[v] to the house of your mother's father Bethuel.[l] Take a wife for yourself there, from among the daughters of Laban, your mother's brother. 3May God Almighty[w][m] bless you and make you fruitful[n] and increase your numbers until you become a community of peoples. 4May he give you and your descendants the blessing given to Abraham,[o] so that you may take possession of the land where you now live as an alien,[p] the land God gave to Abraham." 5Then Isaac sent Jacob on his way, and he went to Paddan Aram,[q] to Laban son of Bethuel the Aramean, the brother of Rebekah,[r] who was the mother of Jacob and Esau.

6Now Esau learned that Isaac had blessed Jacob and had sent him to Paddan Aram to take a wife from there, and that when he blessed him he commanded him, "Do not marry a Canaanite woman,"[s] 7and that Jacob had obeyed his father and mother and had gone to Paddan Aram. 8Esau then realized how displeasing the Canaanite women[t] were to his father Isaac;[u] 9so he went to Ishmael and married Mahalath, the sister of Nebaioth[v] and daughter of Ishmael son of Abraham, in addition to the wives he already had.[w]

Jacob dreams of a stairway reaching to heaven.

10Jacob left Beersheba and set out for Haran.[x] 11When he reached a certain place, he stopped for the night because the sun had set. Taking one of the stones there, he put it under his head and lay down to sleep. 12He had a dream[y] in which he saw a stairway[x] resting on the earth, with its top reaching to heaven, and the angels of God were ascending and descending on it.[z] 13There above it[y] stood the LORD,[a] and he said: "I am the LORD, the God of your father Abraham and the God of Isaac.[b] I will give you and your descendants the land[c] on which you are lying. 14Your descendants will be like the dust of the earth, and you[d] will spread out to the west and to the east, to the north and to the south.[e] All peoples on earth will be blessed through you and your offspring.[f] 15I am with you[g] and will watch over you[h] wherever you go, and I will bring you back to this land. I will not leave you[i] until I have done what I have promised you."[j]

16When Jacob awoke from his sleep, he thought, "Surely the LORD is in this place, and I was not aware of it." 17He was afraid and said, "How awesome is this place![k] This is none other than the house of God; this is the gate of heaven."

18Early the next morning Jacob took the stone he had placed under his head and set it up as a pillar[l] and poured oil on top of it.[m] 19He called that place Bethel,[z] though the city used to be called Luz.[n]

27:41 [a]Ge 37:4 [b]Ge 32:11 [c]Ge 50:4,10 [d]Ob 1:10
27:43 [e]ver 8 [f]Ge 24:29 [g]Ge 11:31
27:44 [h]Ge 31:38,41
27:45 [i]ver 35
27:46 [j]Ge 26:35
28:1 [k]Ge 24:3
28:2 [l]Ge 25:20
28:3 [m]Ge 17:1 [n]Ge 17:6
28:4 [o]Ge 12:2,3 [p]Ge 17:8
28:5 [q]Hos 12:12 [r]Ge 24:29
28:6 [s]ver 1
28:8 [t]Ge 24:3 [u]Ge 26:35
28:9 [v]Ge 25:13 [w]Ge 26:34
28:10 [x]Ge 11:31
28:12 [y]Ge 20:3 [z]Jn 1:51
28:13 [a]Ge 12:7; 35:7,9; 48:3 [b]Ge 26:24 [c]Ge 13:15; 35:12
28:14 [d]Ge 26:4 [e]Ge 13:14 [f]Ge 12:3; 18:18; 22:18; Gal 3:8
28:15 [g]Ge 26:3; 48:21 [h]Nu 6:24; Ps 121:5,7-8 [i]Dt 31:6,8 [j]Nu 23:19
28:17 [k]Ex 3:5; Jos 5:15
28:18 [l]Ge 35:14 [m]Lev 8:11
28:19 [n]Jdg 1:23,26

u *1* Or *greeted* v *2* That is, Northwest Mesopotamia; also in verses 5, 6 and 7 w *3* Hebrew *El-Shaddai*
x *12* Or *ladder* y *13* Or *There beside him*
z *19* *Bethel* means *house of God.*

20Then Jacob made a vow,[a] saying, "If
God will be with me and will watch over
me[b] on this journey I am taking and
will give me food to eat and clothes to
wear 21so that I return safely[c] to my father's house, then the LORD[a] will be
my God[d] 22and[b] this stone that I have
set up as a pillar will be God's house,[e]
and of all that you give me I will give
you a tenth.[f]"

Jacob marries Laban's daughters, Leah and Rachel.

29 Then Jacob continued on his
journey and came to the land
of the eastern peoples.[g] 2There he saw
a well in the field, with three flocks of
sheep lying near it because the flocks
were watered from that well. The stone
over the mouth of the well was large.
3When all the flocks were gathered there,
the shepherds would roll the stone
away from the well's mouth and water
the sheep. Then they would return the
stone to its place over the mouth of the
well.
4Jacob asked the shepherds, "My
brothers, where are you from?"
"We're from Haran,[h]" they replied.
5He said to them, "Do you know
Laban, Nahor's grandson?"
"Yes, we know him," they answered.
6Then Jacob asked them, "Is he
well?"
"Yes, he is," they said, "and here
comes his daughter Rachel with the
sheep."
7"Look," he said, "the sun is still high;
it is not time for the flocks to be gathered. Water the sheep and take them
back to pasture."
8"We can't," they replied, "until all
the flocks are gathered and the stone
has been rolled away from the mouth
of the well. Then we will water the
sheep."
9While he was still talking with them,
Rachel came with her father's sheep,[i]
for she was a shepherdess. 10When Jacob
saw Rachel daughter of Laban, his mother's brother, and Laban's sheep, he went

28:20 [a]Ge 31:13; Jdg 11:30; 2Sa 15:8 [b]ver 15
28:21 [c]Jdg 11:31 [d]Dt 26:17
28:22 [e]Ge 35:7,14 [f]Ge 14:20; Lev 27:30
29:1 [g]Jdg 6:3,33
29:4 [h]Ge 28:10
29:9 [i]Ex 2:16
29:10 [j]Ex 2:17
29:11 [k]Ge 33:4
29:12 [l]Ge 13:8; 14:14,16 [m]Ge 24:28
29:13 [n]Ge 24:29
29:14 [o]Ge 2:23; Jdg 9:2; 2Sa 19:12-13
29:18 [p]Hos 12:12
29:20 [q]SS 8:7; Hos 12:12
29:21 [r]Jdg 15:1
29:22 [s]Jdg 14:10; Jn 2:1-2
29:25 [t]Ge 12:18 [u]Ge 27:36

over and rolled the stone away from
the mouth of the well and watered his
uncle's sheep.[j] 11Then Jacob kissed
Rachel and began to weep aloud.[k] 12He
had told Rachel that he was a relative[l] of
her father and a son of Rebekah. So she
ran and told her father.[m]
13As soon as Laban[n] heard the news
about Jacob, his sister's son, he hurried
to meet him. He embraced him and
kissed him and brought him to his
home, and there Jacob told him all these
things. 14Then Laban said to him, "You
are my own flesh and blood."[o]
After Jacob had stayed with him for
a whole month, 15Laban said to him,
"Just because you are a relative of mine,
should you work for me for nothing?
Tell me what your wages should be."
16Now Laban had two daughters; the
name of the older was Leah, and the
name of the younger was Rachel. 17Leah
had weak[c] eyes, but Rachel was lovely
in form, and beautiful. 18Jacob was in
love with Rachel and said, "I'll work
for you seven years in return for your
younger daughter Rachel."[p]
19Laban said, "It's better that I give
her to you than to some other man. Stay
here with me." 20So Jacob served sev-
en years to get Rachel, but they seemed
like only a few days to him because of
his love for her.[q]
21Then Jacob said to Laban, "Give me
my wife. My time is completed, and I
want to lie with her.[r]"
22So Laban brought together all the
people of the place and gave a feast.[s]
23But when evening came, he took his
daughter Leah and gave her to Jacob,
and Jacob lay with her. 24And Laban
gave his servant girl Zilpah to his daughter as her maidservant.
25When morning came, there was
Leah! So Jacob said to Laban, "What is
this you have done to me?[t] I served
you for Rachel, didn't I? Why have you
deceived me?[u]"

[a] *20,21* Or *Since God . . . father's house, the LORD*
[b] *21,22* Or *house, and the LORD will be my God, 22then*
[c] *17* Or *delicate*

26 Laban replied, "It is not our custom
here to give the younger daughter in
marriage before the older one. 27 Finish
this daughter's bridal week;[a] then we
will give you the younger one also, in return for another seven years of work."
28 And Jacob did so. He finished the
week with Leah, and then Laban gave
him his daughter Rachel to be his wife.
29 Laban gave his servant girl Bilhah[b] to
his daughter Rachel as her maidservant.[c] 30 Jacob lay with Rachel also, and
he loved Rachel more than Leah.[d] And
he worked for Laban another seven
years.[e]

Leah gives birth to Reuben, Simeon, Levi and Judah.

31 When the LORD saw that Leah was
not loved,[f] he opened her womb,[g] but
Rachel was barren. 32 Leah became pregnant and gave birth to a son. She named
him Reuben,[d] for she said, "It is because
the LORD has seen my misery.[h] Surely
my husband will love me now."
33 She conceived again, and when she
gave birth to a son she said, "Because
the LORD heard that I am not loved, he
gave me this one too." So she named
him Simeon.[e][i]
34 Again she conceived, and when she
gave birth to a son she said, "Now at
last my husband will become attached
to me,[j] because I have borne him three
sons." So he was named Levi.[f][k]
35 She conceived again, and when she
gave birth to a son she said, "This time
I will praise the LORD." So she named
him Judah.[g][l] Then she stopped having
children.

Dan and Naphtali born to Bilhah.

30 When Rachel saw that she was
not bearing Jacob any children,[m]
she became jealous of her sister.[n] So she
said to Jacob, "Give me children, or I'll
die!"
2 Jacob became angry with her and
said, "Am I in the place of God, who has
kept you from having children?"[o]
3 Then she said, "Here is Bilhah, my
maidservant. Sleep with her so that she
can bear children for me and that through
her I too can build a family."[p]
4 So she gave him her servant Bilhah
as a wife.[q] Jacob slept with her,[r] 5 and
she became pregnant and bore him a
son. 6 Then Rachel said, "God has vindicated me;[s] he has listened to my plea
and given me a son." Because of this
she named him Dan.[h][t]
7 Rachel's servant Bilhah conceived
again and bore Jacob a second son.
8 Then Rachel said, "I have had a great
struggle with my sister, and I have
won."[u] So she named him Naphtali.[i][v]

Gad and Asher born to Zilpah.

9 When Leah saw that she had
stopped having children, she took her
maidservant Zilpah and gave her to
Jacob as a wife.[w] 10 Leah's servant Zilpah bore Jacob a son. 11 Then Leah said,
"What good fortune!"[j] So she named
him Gad.[k][x]
12 Leah's servant Zilpah bore Jacob a
second son. 13 Then Leah said, "How
happy I am! The women will call me[y]
happy."[z] So she named him Asher.[l][a]

Issachar, Zebulun and Dinah born to Leah.

14 During wheat harvest, Reuben went
out into the fields and found some man-
drake plants,[b] which he brought to
his mother Leah. Rachel said to Leah,
"Please give me some of your son's mandrakes."
15 But she said to her, "Wasn't it
enough[c] that you took away my husband? Will you take my son's mandrakes too?"
"Very well," Rachel said, "he can sleep

29:27 [a]Jdg 14:12
29:29 [b]Ge 30:3 [c]Ge 16:1
29:30 [d]ver 16 [e]Ge 31:41
29:31 [f]Dt 21:15-17 [g]Ge 11:30; 30:1; Ps 127:3
29:32 [h]Ge 16:11; 31:42; Ex 4:31; Dt 26:7; Ps 25:18
29:33 [i]Ge 34:25; 49:5
29:34 [j]Ge 30:20; 1Sa 1:2-4 [k]Ge 49:5-7
29:35 [l]Ge 49:8; Mt 1:2-3
30:1 [m]Ge 29:31; 1Sa 1:5-6 [n]Lev 18:18
30:2 [o]Ge 16:2; 20:18; 29:31
30:3 [p]Ge 16:2
30:4 [q]ver 9,18 [r]Ge 16:3-4
30:6 [s]Ps 35:24; 43:1; La 3:59 [t]Ge 49:16-17
30:8 [u]Hos 12:3-4 [v]Ge 49:21
30:9 [w]ver 4
30:11 [x]Ge 49:19
30:13 [y]Ps 127:3 [z]Pr 31:28; Lk 1:48 [a]Ge 49:20
30:14 [b]SS 7:13
30:15 [c]Nu 16:9,13

[d]32 *Reuben* sounds like the Hebrew for *he has seen my misery*; the name means *see, a son*.
[e]33 *Simeon* probably means *one who hears*.
[f]34 *Levi* sounds like and may be derived from the Hebrew for *attached*. [g]35 *Judah* sounds like and may be derived from the Hebrew for *praise*.
[h]6 *Dan* here means *he has vindicated*. [i]8 *Naphtali* means *my struggle*. [j]11 Or *"A troop is coming!"*
[k]11 *Gad* can mean *good fortune* or *a troop*.
[l]13 *Asher* means *happy*.

with you tonight in return for your son's
mandrakes."
16So when Jacob came in from the
fields that evening, Leah went out to
meet him. "You must sleep with me,"
she said. "I have hired you with my
son's mandrakes." So he slept with her
that night.
17God listened to Leah,[a] and she became pregnant and bore Jacob a fifth
son. 18Then Leah said, "God has rewarded me for giving my maidservant
to my husband." So she named him
Issachar.[m b]
19Leah conceived again and bore Jacob a sixth son. 20Then Leah said, "God
has presented me with a precious gift.
This time my husband will treat me
with honor, because I have borne him
six sons." So she named him Zebulun.[n c]
21Some time later she gave birth to a
daughter and named her Dinah.

Joseph born to Rachel.

22Then God remembered Rachel;[d] he
listened to her and opened her womb.[e]
23She became pregnant and gave birth
to a son[f] and said, "God has taken
away my disgrace."[g] 24She named him
Joseph,[o h] and said, "May the LORD add
to me another son."[i]

Jacob is made wealthy by agreement with Laban.

25After Rachel gave birth to Joseph,
Jacob said to Laban, "Send me on my
way[j] so I can go back to my own homeland. 26Give me my wives and children,
for whom I have served you,[k] and I will
be on my way. You know how much
work I've done for you."
27But Laban said to him, "If I have
found favor in your eyes, please stay. I
have learned by divination that[p] the LORD
has blessed me because of you."[l] 28He
added, "Name your wages,[m] and I will
pay them."
29Jacob said to him, "You know how
I have worked for you[n] and how your
livestock has fared under my care.[o]

30:17 [a]Ge 25:21
30:18 [b]Ge 49:14
30:20 [c]Ge 35:23; 49:13; Mt 4:13
30:22 [d]Ge 8:1; 1Sa 1:19-20 [e]Ge 29:31
30:23 [f]ver 6 [g]Isa 4:1; Lk 1:25
30:24 [h]Ge 35:24; 37:2; 39:1; 49:22-26 [i]Ge 35:17
30:25 [j]Ge 24:54
30:26 [k]Ge 29:20,30; Hos 12:12
30:27 [l]Ge 26:24; 39:3,5
30:28 [m]Ge 29:15
30:29 [n]Ge 31:6 [o]Ge 31:38-40
30:30 [p]1Ti 5:8
30:32 [q]Ge 31:8,12
30:35 [r]Ge 31:1

30The little you had before I came has
increased greatly, and the LORD has
blessed you wherever I have been. But
now, when may I do something for my
own household?[p]"
31"What shall I give you?" he asked.
"Don't give me anything," Jacob replied. "But if you will do this one thing
for me, I will go on tending your flocks
and watching over them: 32Let me go
through all your flocks today and remove from them every speckled or
spotted sheep, every dark-colored lamb
and every spotted or speckled goat.[q]
They will be my wages. 33And my honesty will testify for me in the future,
whenever you check on the wages you
have paid me. Any goat in my possession that is not speckled or spotted, or
any lamb that is not dark-colored, will
be considered stolen."
34"Agreed," said Laban. "Let it be as
you have said." 35That same day he removed all the male goats that were
streaked or spotted, and all the speckled or spotted female goats (all that
had white on them) and all the dark-
colored lambs, and he placed them in
the care of his sons.[r] 36Then he put a
three-day journey between himself and
Jacob, while Jacob continued to tend
the rest of Laban's flocks.
37Jacob, however, took fresh-cut
branches from poplar, almond and plane
trees and made white stripes on them
by peeling the bark and exposing the
white inner wood of the branches.
38Then he placed the peeled branches
in all the watering troughs, so that they
would be directly in front of the flocks
when they came to drink. When the
flocks were in heat and came to drink,
39they mated in front of the branches.
And they bore young that were streaked
or speckled or spotted. 40Jacob set apart
the young of the flock by themselves,
but made the rest face the streaked and
dark-colored animals that belonged to

[m]*18 Issachar* sounds like the Hebrew for *reward.* [n]*20 Zebulun* probably means *honor.* [o]*24 Joseph* means *may he add.* [p]*27* Or possibly *have become rich and*

Laban. Thus he made separate flocks for himself and did not put them with Laban's animals. [41]Whenever the stronger females were in heat, Jacob would place the branches in the troughs in front of the animals so they would mate near the branches, [42]but if the animals were weak, he would not place them there. So the weak animals went to Laban and the strong ones to Jacob. [43]In this way the man grew exceedingly prosperous and came to own large flocks, and maidservants and menservants, and camels and donkeys.[a]

Jacob flees from Laban.

31 Jacob heard that Laban's sons were saying, "Jacob has taken everything our father owned and has gained all this wealth from what belonged to our father." [2]And Jacob noticed that Laban's attitude toward him was not what it had been.

[3]Then the LORD said to Jacob, "Go back[b] to the land of your fathers and to your relatives, and I will be with you."[c]

[4]So Jacob sent word to Rachel and Leah to come out to the fields where his flocks were. [5]He said to them, "I see that your father's attitude toward me is not what it was before, but the God of my father has been with me.[d] [6]You know that I've worked for your father with all my strength,[e] [7]yet your father has cheated me by changing my wages ten times.[f] However, God has not allowed him to harm me.[g] [8]If he said, 'The speckled ones will be your wages,' then all the flocks gave birth to speckled young; and if he said, 'The streaked ones will be your wages,'[h] then all the flocks bore streaked young. [9]So God has taken away your father's livestock and has given them to me.[i]

[10]"In breeding season I once had a dream in which I looked up and saw that the male goats mating with the flock were streaked, speckled or spotted. [11]The angel of God[j] said to me in the dream, 'Jacob.' I answered, 'Here I am.' [12]And he said, 'Look up and see that all the male goats mating with the flock are streaked, speckled or spotted, for I have seen all that Laban has been doing to you.[k] [13]I am the God of Bethel,[l] where you anointed a pillar and where you made a vow to me. Now leave this land at once and go back to your native land.[m]'"

[14]Then Rachel and Leah replied, "Do we still have any share in the inheritance of our father's estate? [15]Does he not regard us as foreigners? Not only has he sold us, but he has used up what was paid for us.[n] [16]Surely all the wealth that God took away from our father belongs to us and our children. So do whatever God has told you."

[17]Then Jacob put his children and his wives on camels, [18]and he drove all his livestock ahead of him, along with all the goods he had accumulated in Paddan Aram,[q] to go to his father Isaac[o] in the land of Canaan.[p]

[19]When Laban had gone to shear his sheep, Rachel stole her father's household gods.[q] [20]Moreover, Jacob deceived[r] Laban the Aramean by not telling him he was running away.[s] [21]So he fled with all he had, and crossing the River,[r] he headed for the hill country of Gilead.[t]

Laban pursues Jacob.

[22]On the third day Laban was told that Jacob had fled. [23]Taking his relatives with him, he pursued Jacob for seven days and caught up with him in the hill country of Gilead. [24]Then God came to Laban the Aramean in a dream at night and said to him,[u] "Be careful not to say anything to Jacob, either good or bad."[v]

[25]Jacob had pitched his tent in the hill country of Gilead when Laban overtook him, and Laban and his relatives camped there too. [26]Then Laban said to Jacob, "What have you done? You've deceived me,[w] and you've carried off

q *18* That is, Northwest Mesopotamia r *21* That is, the Euphrates

30:43 [a]ver 30; Ge 12:16; 13:2; 24:35; 26:13-14
31:3 [b]ver 13; Ge 32:9 [c]Ge 21:22; 26:3; 28:15
31:5 [d]Ge 21:22; 26:3
31:6 [e]Ge 30:29
31:7 [f]ver 41; Job 19:3 [g]ver 52; Ps 37:28; 105:14
31:8 [h]Ge 30:32
31:9 [i]ver 1,16; Ge 30:42
31:11 [j]Ge 16:7; 48:16
31:12 [k]Ex 3:7
31:13 [l]Ge 28:10-22 [m]ver 3; Ge 32:9
31:15 [n]Ge 29:20
31:18 [o]Ge 35:27 [p]Ge 10:19
31:19 [q]ver 30,32, 34-35; Ge 35:2; Jdg 17:5; 1Sa 19:13; Hos 3:4
31:20 [r]Ge 27:36 [s]ver 27
31:21 [t]Ge 37:25
31:24 [u]Ge 20:3; Job 33:15 [v]Ge 24:50
31:26 [w]Ge 27:36

my daughters like captives in war.[a]
27 Why did you run off secretly and deceive me? Why didn't you tell me, so I
could send you away with joy and
singing to the music of tambourines[b]
and harps?[c] 28 You didn't even let me
kiss my grandchildren and my daughters good-by.[d] You have done a foolish
thing. 29 I have the power to harm
you;[e] but last night the God of your
father[f] said to me, 'Be careful not to say
anything to Jacob, either good or bad.'
30 Now you have gone off because you
longed to return to your father's house.
But why did you steal my gods?[g]"

31 Jacob answered Laban, "I was afraid,
because I thought you would take your
daughters away from me by force. 32 But
if you find anyone who has your gods,
he shall not live.[h] In the presence of
our relatives, see for yourself whether
there is anything of yours here with me;
and if so, take it." Now Jacob did not
know that Rachel had stolen the gods.

33 So Laban went into Jacob's tent
and into Leah's tent and into the tent
of the two maidservants, but he found
nothing. After he came out of Leah's
tent, he entered Rachel's tent. 34 Now
Rachel had taken the household gods
and put them inside her camel's saddle and was sitting on them. Laban
searched[i] through everything in the
tent but found nothing.

35 Rachel said to her father, "Don't be
angry, my lord, that I cannot stand up
in your presence;[j] I'm having my period." So he searched but could not find
the household gods.

36 Jacob was angry and took Laban to
task. "What is my crime?" he asked
Laban. "What sin have I committed that
you hunt me down? 37 Now that you have
searched through all my goods, what
have you found that belongs to your
household? Put it here in front of your
relatives[k] and mine, and let them judge
between the two of us.

38 "I have been with you for twenty
years now. Your sheep and goats have
not miscarried, nor have I eaten rams
from your flocks. 39 I did not bring you
animals torn by wild beasts; I bore the
loss myself. And you demanded payment from me for whatever was stolen
by day or night.[l] 40 This was my situation: The heat consumed me in the
daytime and the cold at night, and sleep
fled from my eyes. 41 It was like this for
the twenty years I was in your household. I worked for you fourteen years
for your two daughters[m] and six years
for your flocks, and you changed my
wages ten times.[n] 42 If the God of my
father,[o] the God of Abraham and the
Fear of Isaac,[p] had not been with me,[q]
you would surely have sent me away
empty-handed. But God has seen my
hardship and the toil of my hands,[r] and
last night he rebuked you."

Laban leaves after covenant with Jacob.

43 Laban answered Jacob, "The wom-
en are my daughters, the children are
my children, and the flocks are my
flocks. All you see is mine. Yet what can
I do today about these daughters of
mine, or about the children they have
borne? 44 Come now, let's make a covenant,[s] you and I, and let it serve as a
witness between us."[t]

45 So Jacob took a stone and set it up
as a pillar.[u] 46 He said to his relatives,
"Gather some stones." So they took
stones and piled them in a heap, and
they ate there by the heap. 47 Laban
called it Jegar Sahadutha,[s] and Jacob
called it Galeed.[t]

48 Laban said, "This heap is a witness
between you and me today." That is
why it was called Galeed. 49 It was also
called Mizpah,[u][v] because he said, "May
the LORD keep watch between you and
me when we are away from each other. 50 If you mistreat my daughters or if
you take any wives besides my daughters, even though no one is with us,
remember that God is a witness[w] between you and me."

s47 The Aramaic *Jegar Sahadutha* means *witness heap.* t47 The Hebrew *Galeed* means *witness heap.* u49 *Mizpah* means *watchtower.*

31:26 [a] 1Sa 30:2-3
31:27 [b] Ex 15:20 [c] Ge 4:21
31:28 [d] ver 55
31:29 [e] ver 7 [f] ver 53
31:30 [g] ver 19; Jdg 18:24
31:32 [h] Ge 44:9
31:34 [i] ver 37; Ge 44:12
31:35 [j] Ex 20:12; Lev 19:3,32
31:37 [k] ver 23
31:39 [l] Ex 22:13
31:41 [m] Ge 29:30 [n] ver 7
31:42 [o] ver 5; Ex 3:15; 1Ch 12:17 [p] ver 53; Isa 8:13 [q] Ps 124:1-2 [r] Ge 29:32
31:44 [s] Ge 21:27; 26:28 [t] Jos 24:27
31:45 [u] Ge 28:18
31:49 [v] Jdg 11:29; 1Sa 7:5-6
31:50 [w] Jer 29:23; 42:5

51Laban also said to Jacob, "Here is this heap, and here is this pillar[a] I have set up between you and me. 52This heap is a witness, and this pillar is a witness,[b] that I will not go past this heap to your side to harm you and that you will not go past this heap and pillar to my side to harm me.[c] 53May the God of Abraham[d] and the God of Nahor, the God of their father, judge between us."[e]

So Jacob took an oath[f] in the name of the Fear of his father Isaac.[g] 54He offered a sacrifice there in the hill country and invited his relatives to a meal. After they had eaten, they spent the night there.

55Early the next morning Laban kissed his grandchildren and his daughters[h] and blessed them. Then he left and returned home.[i]

Jacob prepares for a meeting with Esau.

32 Jacob also went on his way, and the angels of God[j] met him. 2When Jacob saw them, he said, "This is the camp of God!"[k] So he named that place Mahanaim.[v][l]

3Jacob sent messengers ahead of him to his brother Esau[m] in the land of Seir, the country of Edom.[n] 4He instructed them: "This is what you are to say to my master Esau: 'Your servant Jacob says, I have been staying with Laban and have remained there till now. 5I have cattle and donkeys, sheep and goats, menservants and maidservants.[o] Now I am sending this message to my lord, that I may find favor in your eyes.[p]'"

6When the messengers returned to Jacob, they said, "We went to your brother Esau, and now he is coming to meet you, and four hundred men are with him."[q]

7In great fear[r] and distress Jacob divided the people who were with him into two groups,[w] and the flocks and herds and camels as well. 8He thought, "If Esau comes and attacks one group,[x] the group[x] that is left may escape."

9Then Jacob prayed, "O God of my father Abraham, God of my father Isaac,[s] O LORD, who said to me, 'Go back to your country and your relatives, and I will make you prosper,'[t] 10I am unworthy of all the kindness and faithfulness[u] you have shown your servant. I had only my staff when I crossed this Jordan, but now I have become two groups. 11Save me, I pray, from the hand of my brother Esau, for I am afraid he will come and attack me,[v] and also the mothers with their children.[w] 12But you have said, 'I will surely make you prosper and will make your descendants like the sand[x] of the sea, which cannot be counted.[y]'"

13He spent the night there, and from what he had with him he selected a gift[z] for his brother Esau: 14two hundred female goats and twenty male goats, two hundred ewes and twenty rams, 15thirty female camels with their young, forty cows and ten bulls, and twenty female donkeys and ten male donkeys. 16He put them in the care of his servants, each herd by itself, and said to his servants, "Go ahead of me, and keep some space between the herds."

17He instructed the one in the lead: "When my brother Esau meets you and asks, 'To whom do you belong, and where are you going, and who owns all these animals in front of you?' 18then you are to say, 'They belong to your servant[a] Jacob. They are a gift sent to my lord Esau, and he is coming behind us.'"

19He also instructed the second, the third and all the others who followed the herds: "You are to say the same thing to Esau when you meet him. 20And be sure to say, 'Your servant Jacob is coming behind us.'" For he thought, "I will pacify him with these gifts I am sending on ahead; later, when I see him, perhaps he will receive me."[b] 21So Jacob's gifts went on ahead of him, but he himself spent the night in the camp.

31:51 [a]Ge 28:18
31:52 [b]Ge 21:30 [c]ver 7; Ge 26:29
31:53 [d]Ge 28:13 [e]Ge 16:5 [f]Ge 21:23,27 [g]ver 42
31:55 [h]ver 28 [i]Ge 18:33; 30:25
32:1 [j]Ge 16:11; 2Ki 6:16-17; Ps 34:7; 91:11; Heb 1:14
32:2 [k]Ge 28:17 [l]2Sa 2:8,29
32:3 [m]Ge 27:41-42 [n]Ge 25:30; 36:8,9
32:5 [o]Ge 12:16; 30:43 [p]Ge 33:8, 10,15
32:6 [q]Ge 33:1
32:7 [r]ver 11
32:9 [s]Ge 28:13; 31:42 [t]Ge 31:13
32:10 [u]Ge 24:27
32:11 [v]Ps 59:2 [w]Ge 27:41
32:12 [x]Ge 22:17 [y]Ge 28:13-15; Hos 1:10; Ro 9:27
32:13 [z]Ge 43:11, 15,25,26; Pr 18:16
32:18 [a]Ge 18:3
32:20 [b]Ge 33:10; Pr 21:14

v2 *Mahanaim* means *two camps.* w7 Or *camps;* also in verse 10 x8 Or *camp*

Jacob wrestles all night, and his name is changed to Israel.

22 That night Jacob got up and took his two wives, his two maidservants and his eleven sons and crossed the ford of the Jabbok.[a] 23 After he had sent them across the stream, he sent over all his possessions. 24 So Jacob was left alone, and a man[b] wrestled with him till daybreak. 25 When the man saw that he could not overpower him, he touched the socket of Jacob's hip[c] so that his hip was wrenched as he wrestled with the man. 26 Then the man said, "Let me go, for it is daybreak."

But Jacob replied, "I will not let you go unless you bless me."[d]

27 The man asked him, "What is your name?"

"Jacob," he answered.

28 Then the man said, "Your name will no longer be Jacob, but Israel,[y][e] because you have struggled with God and with men and have overcome."

29 Jacob said, "Please tell me your name."[f]

But he replied, "Why do you ask my name?"[g] Then he blessed[h] him there.

30 So Jacob called the place Peniel,[z] saying, "It is because I saw God face to face,[i] and yet my life was spared."

31 The sun rose above him as he passed Peniel,[a] and he was limping because of his hip. 32 Therefore to this day the Israelites do not eat the tendon attached to the socket of the hip, because the socket of Jacob's hip was touched near the tendon.

Jacob and Esau reconcile.

33 Jacob looked up and there was Esau, coming with his four hundred men;[j] so he divided the children among Leah, Rachel and the two maidservants. 2 He put the maidservants and their children in front, Leah and her children next, and Rachel and Joseph in the rear. 3 He himself went on ahead and bowed down to the ground[k] seven times as he approached his brother.

4 But Esau ran to meet Jacob and embraced him; he threw his arms around his neck and kissed him. And they wept.[l] 5 Then Esau looked up and saw the women and children. "Who are these with you?" he asked.

Jacob answered, "They are the children God has graciously given your servant.[m]"

6 Then the maidservants and their children approached and bowed down. 7 Next, Leah and her children came and bowed down. Last of all came Joseph and Rachel, and they too bowed down.

8 Esau asked, "What do you mean by all these droves I met?"[n]

"To find favor in your eyes, my lord,"[o] he said.

9 But Esau said, "I already have plenty, my brother. Keep what you have for yourself."

10 "No, please!" said Jacob. "If I have found favor in your eyes, accept this gift from me. For to see your face is like seeing the face of God,[p] now that you have received me favorably.[q] 11 Please accept the present[r] that was brought to you, for God has been gracious to me[s] and I have all I need." And because Jacob insisted, Esau accepted it.

12 Then Esau said, "Let us be on our way; I'll accompany you."

13 But Jacob said to him, "My lord knows that the children are tender and that I must care for the ewes and cows that are nursing their young. If they are driven hard just one day, all the animals will die. 14 So let my lord go on ahead of his servant, while I move along slowly at the pace of the droves before me and that of the children, until I come to my lord in Seir.[t]"

15 Esau said, "Then let me leave some of my men with you."

"But why do that?" Jacob asked. "Just let me find favor in the eyes of my lord."[u]

16 So that day Esau started on his way back to Seir. 17 Jacob, however, went to Succoth,[v] where he built a place for

32:22 [a]Dt 2:37; 3:16; Jos 12:2
32:24 [b]Ge 18:2
32:25 [c]ver 32
32:26 [d]Hos 12:4
32:28 [e]Ge 17:5; 35:10; 1Ki 18:31
32:29 [f]Jdg 13:17 [g]Jdg 13:18 [h]Ge 35:9
32:30 [i]Ge 16:13; Ex 24:11; Nu 12:8; Jdg 6:22; 13:22
33:1 [j]Ge 32:6
33:3 [k]Ge 18:2; 42:6
33:4 [l]Ge 45:14-15
33:5 [m]Ge 48:9; Ps 127:3; Isa 8:18
33:8 [n]Ge 32:14-16 [o]Ge 24:9; 32:5
33:10 [p]Ge 16:13 [q]Ge 32:20
33:11 [r]1Sa 25:27 [s]Ge 30:43
33:14 [t]Ge 32:3
33:15 [u]Ge 34:11; 47:25; Ru 2:13
33:17 [v]Jos 13:27; Jdg 8:5,6,8, 14-16, Ps 60:6

[y] *28 Israel* means *he struggles with God.*
[z] *30 Peniel* means *face of God.*
[a] *31* Hebrew *Penuel,* a variant of *Peniel*

himself and made shelters for his livestock. That is why the place is called
Succoth.[b]
18After Jacob came from Paddan
Aram,[c][a] he arrived safely at the[d] city of
Shechem[b] in Canaan and camped within
sight of the city. **19**For a hundred pieces
of silver,[e] he bought from the sons of
Hamor, the father of Shechem,[c] the plot
of ground[d] where he pitched his tent.
20There he set up an altar and called it
El Elohe Israel.[f]

Dinah is defiled by Shechem.

34 Now Dinah,[e] the daughter Leah
had borne to Jacob, went out
to visit the women of the land. **2**When
Shechem son of Hamor the Hivite, the
ruler of that area, saw her, he took her
and violated her. **3**His heart was drawn
to Dinah daughter of Jacob, and he loved
the girl and spoke tenderly to her. **4**And
Shechem said to his father Hamor, "Get
me this girl as my wife."
5When Jacob heard that his daughter
Dinah had been defiled, his sons were in
the fields with his livestock; so he kept
quiet about it until they came home.
6Then Shechem's father Hamor went
out to talk with Jacob.[f] **7**Now Jacob's
sons had come in from the fields as soon
as they heard what had happened. They
were filled with grief and fury, because
Shechem had done a disgraceful thing
in[g] Israel[g] by lying with Jacob's daughter—a thing that should not be done.[h]
8But Hamor said to them, "My son
Shechem has his heart set on your
daughter. Please give her to him as his
wife. **9**Intermarry with us; give us your
daughters and take our daughters for
yourselves. **10**You can settle among us;[i]
the land is open to you.[j] Live in it,
trade[h] in it,[k] and acquire property in it."
11Then Shechem said to Dinah's father
and brothers, "Let me find favor in your
eyes, and I will give you whatever you
ask. **12**Make the price for the bride[l] and
the gift I am to bring as great as you
like, and I'll pay whatever you ask me.
Only give me the girl as my wife."

33:18 [a]Ge 25:20; 28:2 [b]Jos 24:1; Jdg 9:1
33:19 [c]Jos 24:32 [d]Jn 4:5
34:1 [e]Ge 30:21
34:6 [f]Jdg 14:2-5
34:7 [g]Dt 22:21; Jdg 20:6; 2Sa 13:12 [h]Jos 7:15
34:10 [i]Ge 47:6,27 [j]Ge 13:9; 20:15 [k]Ge 42:34
34:12 [l]Ex 22:16; Dt 22:29; 1Sa 18:25
34:14 [m]Ge 17:14; Jdg 14:3
34:15 [n]Ex 12:48
34:19 [o]ver 3
34:20 [p]Ru 4:1; 2Sa 15:2
34:24 [q]Ge 23:10

The sons of Jacob take revenge.

13Because their sister Dinah had been
defiled, Jacob's sons replied deceitfully
as they spoke to Shechem and his father
Hamor. **14**They said to them, "We can't
do such a thing; we can't give our sister to a man who is not circumcised.[m]
That would be a disgrace to us. **15**We
will give our consent to you on one
condition only: that you become like
us by circumcising all your males.[n]
16Then we will give you our daughters
and take your daughters for ourselves.
We'll settle among you and become
one people with you. **17**But if you will
not agree to be circumcised, we'll take
our sister[i] and go."
18Their proposal seemed good to Hamor and his son Shechem. **19**The young
man, who was the most honored of all
his father's household, lost no time in
doing what they said, because he was
delighted with Jacob's daughter.[o] **20**So
Hamor and his son Shechem went to
the gate of their city[p] to speak to their
fellow townsmen. **21**"These men are
friendly toward us," they said. "Let them
live in our land and trade in it; the land
has plenty of room for them. We can
marry their daughters and they can
marry ours. **22**But the men will consent
to live with us as one people only on the
condition that our males be circumcised,
as they themselves are. **23**Won't their
livestock, their property and all their
other animals become ours? So let us
give our consent to them, and they will
settle among us."
24All the men who went out of the
city gate[q] agreed with Hamor and his son
Shechem, and every male in the city was
circumcised.
25Three days later, while all of them
were still in pain, two of Jacob's sons,

b *17 Succoth* means *shelters.* c *18* That is, Northwest Mesopotamia d *18* Or *arrived at Shalem, a* e *19* Hebrew *hundred kesitahs*; a kesitah was a unit of money of unknown weight and value.
f *20 El Elohe Israel* can mean *God, the God of Israel* or *mighty is the God of Israel.* g *7* Or *against*
h *10* Or *move about freely*; also in verse 21
i *17* Hebrew *daughter*

Simeon and Levi, Dinah's brothers, took their swords[a] and attacked the unsuspecting city, killing every male.[b] 26 They put Hamor and his son Shechem to the sword and took Dinah from Shechem's house and left. 27 The sons of Jacob came upon the dead bodies and looted the city where[j] their sister had been defiled. 28 They seized their flocks and herds and donkeys and everything else of theirs in the city and out in the fields. 29 They carried off all their wealth and all their women and children, taking as plunder everything in the houses.

30 Then Jacob said to Simeon and Levi, "You have brought trouble on me by making me a stench[c] to the Canaanites and Perizzites, the people living in this land.[d] We are few in number,[e] and if they join forces against me and attack me, I and my household will be destroyed."

31 But they replied, "Should he have treated our sister like a prostitute?"

Jacob builds an altar at Bethel.

35 Then God said to Jacob, "Go up to Bethel[f] and settle there, and build an altar there to God, who appeared to you when you were fleeing from your brother Esau."[g]

2 So Jacob said to his household[h] and to all who were with him, "Get rid of the foreign gods[i] you have with you, and purify yourselves and change your clothes.[j] 3 Then come, let us go up to Bethel, where I will build an altar to God, who answered me in the day of my distress[k] and who has been with me wherever I have gone.[l]" 4 So they gave Jacob all the foreign gods they had and the rings in their ears, and Jacob buried them under the oak at Shechem.[m] 5 Then they set out, and the terror of God[n] fell upon the towns all around them so that no one pursued them.

6 Jacob and all the people with him came to Luz[o] (that is, Bethel) in the land of Canaan. 7 There he built an altar, and he called the place El Bethel,[k] because it was there that God revealed himself to him[p] when he was fleeing from his brother.

8 Now Deborah, Rebekah's nurse,[q] died and was buried under the oak below Bethel. So it was named Allon Bacuth.[l]

9 After Jacob returned from Paddan Aram,[m] God appeared to him again and blessed him.[r] 10 God said to him, "Your name is Jacob,[n] but you will no longer be called Jacob; your name will be Israel.[o]"[s] So he named him Israel.

11 And God said to him, "I am God Almighty[p];[t] be fruitful and increase in number. A nation[u] and a community of nations will come from you, and kings will come from your body.[v] 12 The land I gave to Abraham and Isaac I also give to you, and I will give this land to your descendants after you.[w]"[x] 13 Then God went up from him[y] at the place where he had talked with him.

14 Jacob set up a stone pillar at the place where God had talked with him, and he poured out a drink offering on it; he also poured oil on it.[z] 15 Jacob called the place where God had talked with him Bethel.[q][a]

Rachel dies after giving birth to Benjamin.

16 Then they moved on from Bethel. While they were still some distance from Ephrath, Rachel began to give birth and had great difficulty. 17 And as she was having great difficulty in childbirth, the midwife said to her, "Don't be afraid, for you have another son."[b] 18 As she breathed her last—for she was dying—she named her son Ben-Oni.[r] But his father named him Benjamin.[s]

19 So Rachel died and was buried on the way to Ephrath (that is, Bethlehem[c]). 20 Over her tomb Jacob set up a pillar,

34:25 [a]Ge 49:5 [b]Ge 49:7
34:30 [c]Ex 5:21; 1Sa 13:4 [d]Ge 13:7 [e]Ge 46:27; 1Ch 16:19; Ps 105:12
35:1 [f]Ge 28:19 [g]Ge 27:43
35:2 [h]Ge 18:19; Jos 24:15 [i]Ge 31:19 [j]Ex 19:10,14
35:3 [k]Ge 32:7 [l]Ge 28:15, 20-22; 31:3,42
35:4 [m]Jos 24:25-26
35:5 [n]Ex 15:16; 23:27; Jos 2:9
35:6 [o]Ge 28:19; 48:3
35:7 [p]Ge 28:13
35:8 [q]Ge 24:59
35:9 [r]Ge 32:29
35:10 [s]Ge 17:5
35:11 [t]Ge 17:1; Ex 6:3 [u]Ge 28:3; 48:4 [v]Ge 17:6
35:12 [w]Ge 13:15; 28:13 [x]Ge 12:7; 26:3
35:13 [y]Ge 17:22
35:14 [z]Ge 28:18
35:15 [a]Ge 28:19
35:17 [b]Ge 30:24
35:19 [c]Ge 48:7; Ru 1:1,19; Mic 5:2; Mt 2:16

j 27 Or *because* k 7 *El Bethel* means *God of Bethel.* l 8 *Allon Bacuth* means *oak of weeping.* m 9 That is, Northwest Mesopotamia; also in verse 26 n 10 *Jacob* means *he grasps the heel* (figuratively, *he deceives*). o 10 *Israel* means *he struggles with God.* p 11 Hebrew *El-Shaddai* q 15 *Bethel* means *house of God.* r 18 *Ben-Oni* means *son of my trouble.* s 18 *Benjamin* means *son of my right hand.*

and to this day that pillar marks Rachel's tomb.[a]

The twelve sons of Jacob.

35:23-26pp— 1Ch 2:1-2

[21]Israel moved on again and pitched
his tent beyond Migdal Eder. [22]While
Israel was living in that region, Reuben
went in and slept with his father's concubine[b] Bilhah,[c] and Israel heard of it.

Jacob had twelve sons:
[23]The sons of Leah:
Reuben the firstborn[d] of Jacob, Simeon, Levi, Judah,[e] Issachar and Zebulun.[f]
[24]The sons of Rachel:
Joseph[g] and Benjamin.[h]
[25]The sons of Rachel's maidservant Bilhah:
Dan and Naphtali.[i]
[26]The sons of Leah's maidservant Zilpah:
Gad[j] and Asher.[k]
These were the sons of Jacob, who were born to him in Paddan Aram.

Isaac's death and burial.

[27]Jacob came home to his father Isaac
in Mamre,[l] near Kiriath Arba[m] (that is,
Hebron), where Abraham and Isaac
had stayed. [28]Isaac lived a hundred
and eighty years.[n] [29]Then he breathed
his last and died and was gathered to
his people,[o] old and full of years.[p] And
his sons Esau and Jacob buried him.[q]

Descendants of Esau.

36:10-14pp— 1Ch 1:35-37
36:20-28pp— 1Ch 1:38-42

36 This is the account of Esau (that is, Edom).[r]

[2]Esau took his wives from the
women of Canaan:[s] Adah daughter
of Elon the Hittite,[t] and Oholibamah daughter of Anah[u] and granddaughter of Zibeon the Hivite—
[3]also Basemath daughter of Ishmael
and sister of Nebaioth.
[4]Adah bore Eliphaz to Esau, Basemath bore Reuel,[v] [5]and Oholibamah bore Jeush, Jalam and Korah.
These were the sons of Esau, who
were born to him in Canaan.
[6]Esau took his wives and sons
and daughters and all the members of his household, as well as
his livestock and all his other animals and all the goods he had acquired in Canaan,[w] and moved to
a land some distance from his brother Jacob. [7]Their possessions were
too great for them to remain together; the land where they were
staying could not support them both
because of their livestock.[x] [8]So
Esau[y] (that is, Edom) settled in the
hill country of Seir.[z]

[9]This is the account of Esau the father of the Edomites in the hill country of Seir.

[10]These are the names of Esau's sons:
Eliphaz, the son of Esau's wife Adah, and Reuel, the son of Esau's wife Basemath.
[11]The sons of Eliphaz:[a]
Teman,[b] Omar, Zepho, Gatam and Kenaz.
[12]Esau's son Eliphaz also had a concubine named Timna, who bore him Amalek.[c] These were grandsons of Esau's wife Adah.[d]
[13]The sons of Reuel:
Nahath, Zerah, Shammah and Mizzah. These were grandsons of Esau's wife Basemath.
[14]The sons of Esau's wife Oholibamah daughter of Anah and granddaughter of Zibeon, whom she bore to Esau:
Jeush, Jalam and Korah.

[15]These were the chiefs[e] among Esau's descendants:
The sons of Eliphaz the firstborn of Esau:
Chiefs Teman,[f] Omar, Zepho,
Kenaz, [16]Korah,[t] Gatam and
Amalek. These were the chiefs descended from Eliphaz in Edom; they were grandsons of Adah.[g]

35:20 [a]1Sa 10:2
35:22 [b]Ge 49:4; 1Ch 5:1 [c]Ge 29:29; Lev 18:8
35:23 [d]Ge 46:8 [e]Ge 29:35 [f]Ge 30:20
35:24 [g]Ge 30:24 [h]ver 18
35:25 [i]Ge 30:8
35:26 [j]Ge 30:11 [k]Ge 30:13
35:27 [l]Ge 13:18; 18:1 [m]Jos 14:15
35:28 [n]Ge 25:7,20
35:29 [o]Ge 25:8; 49:33 [p]Ge 15:15 [q]Ge 25:9
36:1 [r]Ge 25:30
36:2 [s]Ge 28:8-9 [t]Ge 26:34 [u]ver 25
36:4 [v]1Ch 1:35
36:6 [w]Ge 12:5
36:7 [x]Ge 13:6; 17:8; 28:4
36:8 [y]Dt 2:4 [z]Ge 32:3
36:11 [a]ver 15-16; Job 2:11 [b]Am 1:12; Hab 3:3
36:12 [c]Ex 17:8,16; Nu 24:20; 1Sa 15:2 [d]ver 16
36:15 [e]Ex 15:15 [f]Job 2:11
36:16 [g]ver 12

[t]*16* Masoretic Text; Samaritan Pentateuch (see also Gen. 36:11 and 1Chron. 1:36) does not have *Korah*.

[17]The sons of Esau's son Reuel:[a]
Chiefs Nahath, Zerah, Shammah and Mizzah. These were the chiefs descended from Reuel in Edom; they were grandsons of Esau's wife Basemath.
[18]The sons of Esau's wife Oholibamah:
Chiefs Jeush, Jalam and Korah. These were the chiefs descended from Esau's wife Oholibamah daughter of Anah.
[19]These were the sons of Esau (that is, Edom),[b] and these were their chiefs.

[20]These were the sons of Seir the Horite,[c] who were living in the region:
Lotan, Shobal, Zibeon, Anah, [21]Dishon, Ezer and Dishan. These sons of Seir in Edom were Horite chiefs.
[22]The sons of Lotan:
Hori and Homam.[u] Timna was Lotan's sister.
[23]The sons of Shobal:
Alvan, Manahath, Ebal, Shepho and Onam.
[24]The sons of Zibeon:
Aiah and Anah. This is the Anah who discovered the hot springs[v] in the desert while he was grazing the donkeys of his father Zibeon.
[25]The children of Anah:
Dishon and Oholibamah daughter of Anah.
[26]The sons of Dishon[w]:
Hemdan, Eshban, Ithran and Keran.
[27]The sons of Ezer:
Bilhan, Zaavan and Akan.
[28]The sons of Dishan:
Uz and Aran.
[29]These were the Horite chiefs:
Lotan, Shobal, Zibeon, Anah, [30]Dishon, Ezer and Dishan. These were the Horite chiefs, according to their divisions, in the land of Seir.

Kings who reigned in Edom.

36:31-43pp— 1Ch 1:43-54

[31]These were the kings who reigned in Edom before any Israelite king[d] reigned[x]:
[32]Bela son of Beor became king of Edom. His city was named Dinhabah.
[33]When Bela died, Jobab son of Zerah from Bozrah[e] succeeded him as king.
[34]When Jobab died, Husham from the land of the Temanites[f] succeeded him as king.
[35]When Husham died, Hadad son of Bedad, who defeated Midian in the country of Moab,[g] succeeded him as king. His city was named Avith.
[36]When Hadad died, Samlah from Masrekah succeeded him as king.
[37]When Samlah died, Shaul from Rehoboth on the river[y] succeeded him as king.
[38]When Shaul died, Baal-Hanan son of Acbor succeeded him as king.
[39]When Baal-Hanan son of Acbor died, Hadad[z] succeeded him as king. His city was named Pau, and his wife's name was Mehetabel daughter of Matred, the daughter of Me-Zahab.

[40]These were the chiefs descended from Esau, by name, according to their clans and regions:
Timna, Alvah, Jetheth, [41]Oholibamah, Elah, Pinon, [42]Kenaz, Teman, Mibzar, [43]Magdiel and Iram. These were the chiefs of Edom, according to their settlements in the land they occupied.

This was Esau the father of the Edomites.

36:17 [a]1Ch 1:37
36:19 [b]Ge 25:30
36:20 [c]Ge 14:6; Dt 2:12,22; 1Ch 1:38
36:31 [d]Ge 17:6; 1Ch 1:43
36:33 [e]Jer 49:13,22
36:34 [f]Eze 25:13
36:35 [g]Ge 19:37; Nu 22:1; Dt 1:5; Ru 1:1,6

[u]*22* Hebrew *Hemam,* a variant of *Homam* (see 1 Chron. 1:39) [v]*24* Vulgate; Syriac *discovered water;* the meaning of the Hebrew for this word is uncertain. [w]*26* Hebrew *Dishan,* a variant of *Dishon* [x]*31* Or *before an Israelite king reigned over them* [y]*37* Possibly the Euphrates [z]*39* Many manuscripts of the Masoretic Text, Samaritan Pentateuch and Syriac (see also 1 Chron. 1:50); most manuscripts of the Masoretic Text *Hadar*

Joseph's dreams cause his brothers to hate him.

37 Jacob lived in the land where
his father had stayed,[a] the land
of Canaan.[b]

2This is the account of Jacob.

Joseph, a young man of seventeen, was
tending the flocks[c] with his brothers,
the sons of Bilhah[d] and the sons of Zilpah,[e] his father's wives, and he brought
their father a bad report[f] about them.
3Now Israel loved Joseph more than
any of his other sons,[g] because he had
been born to him in his old age;[h] and
he made a richly ornamented[a] robe[i] for
him. 4When his brothers saw that
their father loved him more than any
of them, they hated him[j] and could not
speak a kind word to him.
5Joseph had a dream,[k] and when he
told it to his brothers, they hated him
all the more. 6He said to them, "Listen
to this dream I had: 7We were binding
sheaves of grain out in the field when
suddenly my sheaf rose and stood
upright, while your sheaves gathered
around mine and bowed down to it."[l]
8His brothers said to him, "Do you
intend to reign over us? Will you actually rule us?"[m] And they hated him all
the more because of his dream and what
he had said.
9Then he had another dream, and
he told it to his brothers. "Listen," he
said, "I had another dream, and this
time the sun and moon and eleven stars
were bowing down to me."
10When he told his father as well as
his brothers,[n] his father rebuked him
and said, "What is this dream you had?
Will your mother and I and your brothers actually come and bow down to the
ground before you?"[o] 11His brothers were
jealous of him,[p] but his father kept the
matter in mind.[q]

Joseph is sold by his brothers and taken to Egypt.

12Now his brothers had gone to graze

37:1 [a]Ge 17:8 [b]Ge 10:19
37:2 [c]Ps 78:71 [d]Ge 35:25 [e]Ge 35:26 [f]1Sa 2:24
37:3 [g]Ge 25:28 [h]Ge 44:20 [i]2Sa 13:18-19
37:4 [j]Ge 27:41; 49:22-23; Ac 7:9
37:5 [k]Ge 20:3; 28:12
37:7 [l]Ge 42:6,9; 43:26,28; 44:14; 50:18
37:8 [m]Ge 49:26
37:10 [n]ver 5 [o]ver 7; Ge 27:29
37:11 [p]Ac 7:9 [q]Lk 2:19,51
37:14 [r]Ge 13:18; 35:27
37:17 [s]2Ki 6:13

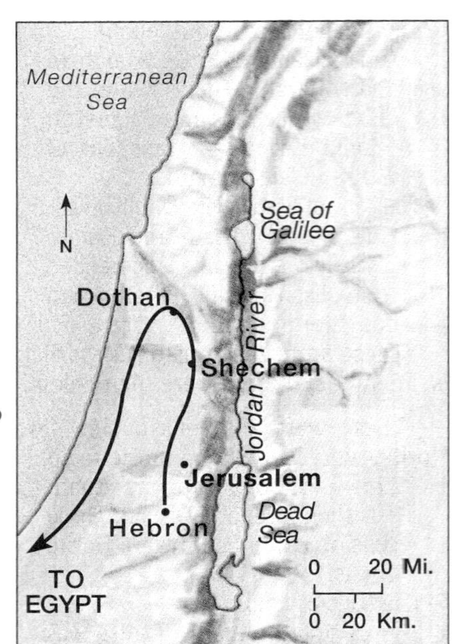

Joseph Goes to Meet His Brothers

Jacob asked Joseph to go find his brothers, who were grazing their flocks near Shechem. When Joseph arrived, he learned that his brothers had gone on to Dothan, which lay along a major trade route to Egypt. There the jealous brothers sold Joseph as a slave to a group of Midianite merchants on their way to Egypt.

their father's flocks near Shechem, 13and
Israel said to Joseph, "As you know, your
brothers are grazing the flocks near
Shechem. Come, I am going to send you
to them."
"Very well," he replied.
14So he said to him, "Go and see if
all is well with your brothers and with
the flocks, and bring word back to
me." Then he sent him off from the
Valley of Hebron.[r]
When Joseph arrived at Shechem,
15a man found him wandering around
in the fields and asked him, "What are
you looking for?"
16He replied, "I'm looking for my
brothers. Can you tell me where they
are grazing their flocks?"
17"They have moved on from here,"
the man answered. "I heard them say,
'Let's go to Dothan.[s]'"

a3 The meaning of the Hebrew for *richly ornamented* is uncertain; also in verses 23 and 32.

So Joseph went after his brothers and found them near Dothan. 18But they saw him in the distance, and before he reached them, they plotted to kill him.[a]

19"Here comes that dreamer!" they said to each other. 20"Come now, let's kill him and throw him into one of these cisterns[b] and say that a ferocious animal devoured him. Then we'll see what comes of his dreams."[c]

21When Reuben heard this, he tried to rescue him from their hands. "Let's not take his life," he said.[d] 22"Don't shed any blood. Throw him into this cistern here in the desert, but don't lay a hand on him." Reuben said this to rescue him from them and take him back to his father.

23So when Joseph came to his brothers, they stripped him of his robe—the richly ornamented robe he was wearing— 24and they took him and threw him into the cistern.[e] Now the cistern was empty; there was no water in it.

25As they sat down to eat their meal, they looked up and saw a caravan of Ishmaelites coming from Gilead. Their camels were loaded with spices, balm and myrrh,[f] and they were on their way to take them down to Egypt.[g]

26Judah said to his brothers, "What will we gain if we kill our brother and cover up his blood?[h] 27Come, let's sell him to the Ishmaelites and not lay our hands on him; after all, he is our brother,[i] our own flesh and blood." His brothers agreed.

28So when the Midianite[j] merchants came by, his brothers pulled Joseph up out of the cistern and sold him for twenty shekels[b] of silver to the Ishmaelites, who took him to Egypt.[k]

29When Reuben returned to the cistern and saw that Joseph was not there, he tore his clothes.[l] 30He went back to his brothers and said, "The boy isn't there! Where can I turn now?"[m]

31Then they got Joseph's robe,[n] slaughtered a goat and dipped the robe in the blood. 32They took the ornamented robe back to their father and said, "We found this. Examine it to see whether it is your son's robe."

33He recognized it and said, "It is my son's robe! Some ferocious animal[o] has devoured him. Joseph has surely been torn to pieces."[p]

34Then Jacob tore his clothes,[q] put on sackcloth[r] and mourned for his son many days.[s] 35All his sons and daughters came to comfort him, but he refused to be comforted. "No," he said, "in mourning will I go down to the grave[c][t] to my son." So his father wept for him.

36Meanwhile, the Midianites[d] sold Joseph in Egypt to Potiphar, one of Pharaoh's officials, the captain of the guard.[u]

37:18 [a]1Sa 19:1; Mk 14:1; Ac 23:12
37:20 [b]Jer 38:6,9 [c]Ge 50:20
37:21 [d]Ge 42:22
37:24 [e]Jer 41:7
37:25 [f]Ge 43:11 [g]ver 28
37:26 [h]ver 20; Ge 4:10
37:27 [i]Ge 42:21
37:28 [j]Ge 25:2; Jdg 6:1-3 [k]Ge 45:4-5; Ps 105:17; Ac 7:9
37:29 [l]ver 34; Ge 44:13; Job 1:20
37:30 [m]ver 22; Ge 42:13,36
37:31 [n]ver 3,23
37:33 [o]ver 20 [p]Ge 44:20,28
37:34 [q]ver 29 [r]2Sa 3:31 [s]Ge 50:3, 10,11
37:35 [t]Ge 42:38; 44:22,29,31
37:36 [u]Ge 39:1
38:2 [v]1Ch 2:3
38:3 [w]ver 6; Ge 46:12; Nu 26:19
38:7 [x]ver 10; Ge 46:12; 1Ch 2:3
38:8 [y]Dt 25:5-6; Mt 22:24-28
38:10 [z]Ge 46:12; Dt 25:7-10

Tamar gives birth to twins by her father-in-law, Judah.

38 At that time, Judah left his brothers and went down to stay with a man of Adullam named Hirah. 2There Judah met the daughter of a Canaanite man named Shua.[v] He married her and lay with her; 3she became pregnant and gave birth to a son, who was named Er.[w] 4She conceived again and gave birth to a son and named him Onan. 5She gave birth to still another son and named him Shelah. It was at Kezib that she gave birth to him.

6Judah got a wife for Er, his firstborn, and her name was Tamar. 7But Er, Judah's firstborn, was wicked in the LORD's sight; so the LORD put him to death.[x]

8Then Judah said to Onan, "Lie with your brother's wife and fulfill your duty to her as a brother-in-law to produce offspring for your brother."[y] 9But Onan knew that the offspring would not be his; so whenever he lay with his brother's wife, he spilled his semen on the ground to keep from producing offspring for his brother. 10What he did was wicked in the LORD's sight; so he put him to death also.[z]

b*28* That is, about 8 ounces (about 0.2 kilogram)
c*35* Hebrew *Sheol* d*36* Samaritan Pentateuch, Septuagint, Vulgate and Syriac (see also verse 28); Masoretic Text *Medanites*

11Judah then said to his daughter-in-
law Tamar, "Live as a widow in your
father's house until my son Shelah
grows up."[a] For he thought, "He may
die too, just like his brothers." So Tamar
went to live in her father's house.
12After a long time Judah's wife, the
daughter of Shua, died. When Judah had
recovered from his grief, he went up to
Timnah,[b] to the men who were shearing his sheep, and his friend Hirah the
Adullamite went with him.
13When Tamar was told, "Your father-
in-law is on his way to Timnah to shear
his sheep," 14she took off her widow's
clothes, covered herself with a veil to
disguise herself, and then sat down at
the entrance to Enaim, which is on
the road to Timnah. For she saw that,
though Shelah[c] had now grown up, she
had not been given to him as his wife.
15When Judah saw her, he thought
she was a prostitute, for she had covered her face. 16Not realizing that she
was his daughter-in-law,[d] he went over
to her by the roadside and said, "Come
now, let me sleep with you."
"And what will you give me to sleep
with you?" she asked.
17"I'll send you a young goat[e] from
my flock," he said.
"Will you give me something as a
pledge[f] until you send it?" she asked.
18He said, "What pledge should I give
you?"
"Your seal[g] and its cord, and the staff
in your hand," she answered. So he
gave them to her and slept with her,
and she became pregnant by him. 19After
she left, she took off her veil and put
on her widow's clothes[h] again.
20Meanwhile Judah sent the young
goat by his friend the Adullamite in
order to get his pledge back from the
woman, but he did not find her. 21He
asked the men who lived there, "Where
is the shrine prostitute[i] who was beside
the road at Enaim?"
"There hasn't been any shrine prostitute here," they said.
22So he went back to Judah and said,
"I didn't find her. Besides, the men who
lived there said, 'There hasn't been any
shrine prostitute here.'"
23Then Judah said, "Let her keep what
she has, or we will become a laughingstock. After all, I did send her this
young goat, but you didn't find her."
24About three months later Judah was
told, "Your daughter-in-law Tamar is
guilty of prostitution, and as a result she
is now pregnant."
Judah said, "Bring her out and have
her burned to death!"[j]
25As she was being brought out, she
sent a message to her father-in-law. "I am
pregnant by the man who owns these,"
she said. And she added, "See if you recognize whose seal and cord and staff
these are."[k]
26Judah recognized them and said,
"She is more righteous than I,[l] since I
wouldn't give her to my son Shelah.[m]"
And he did not sleep with her again.
27When the time came for her to give
birth, there were twin boys in her
womb.[n] 28As she was giving birth, one
of them put out his hand; so the midwife
took a scarlet thread and tied it on his
wrist and said, "This one came out first."
29But when he drew back his hand, his
brother came out, and she said, "So this
is how you have broken out!" And he
was named Perez.[e][o] 30Then his brother,
who had the scarlet thread on his wrist,
came out and he was given the name
Zerah.[f][p]

Joseph prospers in Potiphar's house.

39 Now Joseph had been taken
down to Egypt. Potiphar, an
Egyptian who was one of Pharaoh's officials, the captain of the guard,[q] bought
him from the Ishmaelites who had tak-
en him there.[r]
2The LORD was with Joseph[s] and he
prospered, and he lived in the house
of his Egyptian master. 3When his master saw that the LORD was with him[t]
and that the LORD gave him success in
everything he did,[u] 4Joseph found favor

38:11 [a]Ru 1:13
38:12 [b]ver 14; Jos 15:10,57
38:14 [c]ver 11
38:16 [d]Lev 18:15; 20:12
38:17 [e]Eze 16:33 [f]ver 20
38:18 [g]ver 25
38:19 [h]ver 14
38:21 [i]Lev 19:29; Hos 4:14
38:24 [j]Lev 21:9; Dt 22:21,22
38:25 [k]ver 18
38:26 [l]1Sa 24:17 [m]ver 11
38:27 [n]Ge 25:24
38:29 [o]Ge 46:12; Nu 26:20,21; Ru 4:12,18; 1Ch 2:4; Mt 1:3
38:30 [p]1Ch 2:4
39:1 [q]Ge 37:36 [r]Ge 37:25; Ps 105:17
39:2 [s]Ge 21:20,22; Ac 7:9
39:3 [t]Ge 21:22; 26:28 [u]Ps 1:3

[e] *29 Perez* means *breaking out.* [f] *30 Zerah* can mean *scarlet* or *brightness.*

in his eyes and became his attendant.
Potiphar put him in charge of his
household, and he entrusted to his care
everything he owned.[a] 5From the time
he put him in charge of his household
and of all that he owned, the LORD
blessed the household of the Egyptian
because of Joseph.[b] The blessing of the
LORD was on everything Potiphar had,
both in the house and in the field. 6So
he left in Joseph's care everything he
had; with Joseph in charge, he did not
concern himself with anything except
the food he ate.

Potiphar's wife falsely accuses Joseph.

Now Joseph was well-built and handsome,[c] 7and after a while his master's
wife took notice of Joseph and said,
"Come to bed with me!"[d]

8But he refused.[e] "With me in charge,"
he told her, "my master does not concern himself with anything in the house;
everything he owns he has entrusted
to my care. 9No one is greater in this
house than I am.[f] My master has withheld nothing from me except you, because you are his wife. How then could
I do such a wicked thing and sin against
God?"[g] 10And though she spoke to Joseph day after day, he refused to go to
bed with her or even be with her.

11One day he went into the house to
attend to his duties, and none of the
household servants was inside. 12She
caught him by his cloak[h] and said, "Come
to bed with me!" But he left his cloak
in her hand and ran out of the house.

13When she saw that he had left his
cloak in her hand and had run out of
the house, 14she called her household
servants. "Look," she said to them,
"this Hebrew has been brought to us
to make sport of us! He came in here
to sleep with me, but I screamed.[i]
15When he heard me scream for help,
he left his cloak beside me and ran out
of the house."

16She kept his cloak beside her until
his master came home. 17Then she told
him this story:[j] "That Hebrew slave you
brought us came to me to make sport
of me. 18But as soon as I screamed for
help, he left his cloak beside me and
ran out of the house."

19When his master heard the story
his wife told him, saying, "This is how
your slave treated me," he burned with
anger.[k] 20Joseph's master took him and
put him in prison,[l] the place where the
king's prisoners were confined.

But while Joseph was there in the
prison, 21the LORD was with him; he
showed him kindness and granted him
favor in the eyes of the prison warden.[m]
22So the warden put Joseph in charge of
all those held in the prison, and he was
made responsible for all that was done
there.[n] 23The warden paid no attention
to anything under Joseph's care, because
the LORD was with Joseph and gave him
success in whatever he did.[o]

Joseph interprets dreams of the cupbearer and the baker.

40 Some time later, the cupbearer[p] and the baker of the king of
Egypt offended their master, the king of
Egypt. 2Pharaoh was angry[q] with his two
officials, the chief cupbearer and the
chief baker, 3and put them in custody in
the house of the captain of the guard,[r]
in the same prison where Joseph was
confined. 4The captain of the guard
assigned them to Joseph,[s] and he attended them.

After they had been in custody for
some time, 5each of the two men—the
cupbearer and the baker of the king of
Egypt, who were being held in prison—
had a dream the same night, and each
dream had a meaning of its own.[t]

6When Joseph came to them the next
morning, he saw that they were dejected. 7So he asked Pharaoh's officials who
were in custody with him in his master's house, "Why are your faces so sad
today?"[u]

8"We both had dreams," they answered, "but there is no one to interpret
them."[v]

39:4 [a]ver 8,22; Ge 24:2
39:5 [b]Ge 26:24; 30:27
39:6 [c]1Sa 16:12
39:7 [d]2Sa 13:11; Pr 7:15-18
39:8 [e]Pr 6:23-24
39:9 [f]Ge 41:33,40 [g]Ge 20:6; 42:18; 2Sa 12:13
39:12 [h]Pr 7:13
39:14 [i]Dt 22:24,27
39:17 [j]Ex 23:1,7; Ps 101:5
39:19 [k]Pr 6:34
39:20 [l]Ge 40:3; Ps 105:18
39:21 [m]Ex 3:21
39:22 [n]ver 4
39:23 [o]ver 3
40:1 [p]Ne 1:11
40:2 [q]Pr 16:14,15
40:3 [r]Ge 39:20
40:4 [s]Ge 39:4
40:5 [t]Ge 41:11
40:7 [u]Ne 2:2
40:8 [v]Ge 41:8,15

Then Joseph said to them, "Do not
interpretations belong to God?[a] Tell me
your dreams."
9So the chief cupbearer told Joseph
his dream. He said to him, "In my dream
I saw a vine in front of me, 10and on
the vine were three branches. As soon
as it budded, it blossomed, and its clusters ripened into grapes. 11Pharaoh's cup
was in my hand, and I took the grapes,
squeezed them into Pharaoh's cup and
put the cup in his hand."
12"This is what it means,[b]" Joseph
said to him. "The three branches are
three days. 13Within three days Pharaoh
will lift up your head and restore you
to your position, and you will put
Pharaoh's cup in his hand, just as you
used to do when you were his cupbearer. 14But when all goes well with
you, remember me[c] and show me kindness;[d] mention me to Pharaoh and get
me out of this prison. 15For I was forcibly carried off from the land of the
Hebrews,[e] and even here I have done
nothing to deserve being put in a dungeon."
16When the chief baker saw that
Joseph had given a favorable interpretation, he said to Joseph, "I too had a
dream: On my head were three baskets
of bread.[g] 17In the top basket were all
kinds of baked goods for Pharaoh, but
the birds were eating them out of the
basket on my head."
18"This is what it means," Joseph
said. "The three baskets are three days.[f]
19Within three days Pharaoh will lift off
your head[g] and hang you on a tree.[h] And
the birds will eat away your flesh."
20Now the third day was Pharaoh's
birthday,[h] and he gave a feast for all his
officials.[i] He lifted up the heads of the
chief cupbearer and the chief baker in
the presence of his officials: 21He restored the chief cupbearer to his position, so that he once again put the cup
into Pharaoh's hand,[j] 22but he hanged[i]
the chief baker,[k] just as Joseph had
said to them in his interpretation.[l]
23The chief cupbearer, however, did
not remember Joseph; he forgot him.[m]

Joseph interprets Pharaoh's dreams.

41 When two full years had passed,
Pharaoh had a dream:[n] He was
standing by the Nile, 2when out of the
river there came up seven cows, sleek
and fat,[o] and they grazed among the
reeds.[p] 3After them, seven other cows,
ugly and gaunt, came up out of the
Nile and stood beside those on the
riverbank. 4And the cows that were
ugly and gaunt ate up the seven sleek,
fat cows. Then Pharaoh woke up.
5He fell asleep again and had a second
dream: Seven heads of grain, healthy
and good, were growing on a single
stalk. 6After them, seven other heads
of grain sprouted—thin and scorched
by the east wind. 7The thin heads of
grain swallowed up the seven healthy,
full heads. Then Pharaoh woke up; it
had been a dream.
8In the morning his mind was troubled,[q] so he sent for all the magicians[r]
and wise men of Egypt. Pharaoh told
them his dreams, but no one could
interpret them for him.
9Then the chief cupbearer said to
Pharaoh, "Today I am reminded of my
shortcomings. 10Pharaoh was once angry
with his servants,[s] and he imprisoned
me and the chief baker in the house of
the captain of the guard.[t] 11Each of us
had a dream the same night, and each
dream had a meaning of its own.[u] 12Now
a young Hebrew was there with us, a
servant of the captain of the guard. We
told him our dreams, and he interpreted them for us, giving each man the interpretation of his dream.[v] 13And things
turned out exactly as he interpreted them
to us: I was restored to my position, and
the other man was hanged.[i][w]"
14So Pharaoh sent for Joseph, and he
was quickly brought from the dungeon.[x]
When he had shaved and changed his
clothes, he came before Pharaoh.
15Pharaoh said to Joseph, "I had a
dream, and no one can interpret it. But I

40:8 [a]Ge 41:16; Da 2:22, 28,47
40:12 [b]Ge 41:12,15, 25; Da 2:36; 4:19
40:14 [c]Lk 23:42 [d]Jos 2:12; 1Sa 20:14,42; 1Ki 2:7
40:15 [e]Ge 37:26-28
40:18 [f]ver 12
40:19 [g]ver 13
40:20 [h]Mt 14:6-10 [i]Mk 6:21
40:21 [j]ver 13
40:22 [k]ver 19 [l]Ps 105:19
40:23 [m]Job 19:14; Ecc 9:15
41:1 [n]Ge 20:3
41:2 [o]ver 26 [p]Isa 19:6
41:8 [q]Da 2:1,3; 4:5,19 [r]Ex 7:11,22; Da 1:20; 2:2,27; 4:7
41:10 [s]Ge 40:2 [t]Ge 39:20
41:11 [u]Ge 40:5
41:12 [v]Ge 40:12
41:13 [w]Ge 40:22
41:14 [x]Ps 105:20; Da 2:25

[g] *16* Or *three wicker baskets* [h] *19* Or *and impale you on a pole* [i] *22, 13* Or *impaled*

have heard it said of you that when you hear a dream you can interpret it."[a]

16"I cannot do it," Joseph replied to Pharaoh, "but God will give Pharaoh the answer he desires."[b]

17Then Pharaoh said to Joseph, "In my dream I was standing on the bank of the Nile, 18when out of the river there came up seven cows, fat and sleek, and they grazed among the reeds. 19After them, seven other cows came up—scrawny and very ugly and lean. I had never seen such ugly cows in all the land of Egypt. 20The lean, ugly cows ate up the seven fat cows that came up first. 21But even after they ate them, no one could tell that they had done so; they looked just as ugly as before. Then I woke up.

22"In my dreams I also saw seven heads of grain, full and good, growing on a single stalk. 23After them, seven other heads sprouted—withered and thin and scorched by the east wind. 24The thin heads of grain swallowed up the seven good heads. I told this to the magicians, but none could explain it to me.[c]"

25Then Joseph said to Pharaoh, "The dreams of Pharaoh are one and the same. God has revealed to Pharaoh what he is about to do.[d] 26The seven good cows[e] are seven years, and the seven good heads of grain are seven years; it is one and the same dream. 27The seven lean, ugly cows that came up afterward are seven years, and so are the seven worthless heads of grain scorched by the east wind: They are seven years of famine.[f]

28"It is just as I said to Pharaoh: God has shown Pharaoh what he is about to do. 29Seven years of great abundance[g] are coming throughout the land of Egypt, 30but seven years of famine[h] will follow them. Then all the abundance in Egypt will be forgotten, and the famine will ravage the land.[i] 31The abundance in the land will not be remembered, because the famine that follows it will be so severe. 32The reason the dream was given to Pharaoh in two forms is that the matter has been firmly decided[j] by God, and God will do it soon.

33"And now let Pharaoh look for a discerning and wise man[k] and put him in charge of the land of Egypt. 34Let Pharaoh appoint commissioners over the land to take a fifth[l] of the harvest of Egypt during the seven years of abundance.[m] 35They should collect all the food of these good years that are coming and store up the grain under the authority of Pharaoh, to be kept in the cities for food.[n] 36This food should be held in reserve for the country, to be used during the seven years of famine that will come upon Egypt,[o] so that the country may not be ruined by the famine."

37The plan seemed good to Pharaoh and to all his officials.[p] 38So Pharaoh asked them, "Can we find anyone like this man, one in whom is the spirit of God[j]?"[q]

39Then Pharaoh said to Joseph, "Since God has made all this known to you, there is no one so discerning and wise as you. 40You shall be in charge of my palace, and all my people are to submit to your orders.[r] Only with respect to the throne will I be greater than you."

Joseph is set over all the land of Egypt.

41So Pharaoh said to Joseph, "I hereby put you in charge of the whole land of Egypt."[s] 42Then Pharaoh took his signet ring[t] from his finger and put it on Joseph's finger. He dressed him in robes of fine linen and put a gold chain around his neck.[u] 43He had him ride in a chariot as his second-in-command,[k] and men shouted before him, "Make way[l]!"[v] Thus he put him in charge of the whole land of Egypt.

44Then Pharaoh said to Joseph, "I am Pharaoh, but without your word no one will lift hand or foot in all Egypt."[w] 45Pharaoh gave Joseph the name Zaphenath-Paneah and gave him Asenath

j38 Or *of the gods* k43 Or *in the chariot of his second-in-command*; or *in his second chariot*
l43 Or *Bow down*

41:15 [a]Da 5:16
41:16 [b]Ge 40:8; Da 2:30; Ac 3:12; 2Co 3:5
41:24 [c]ver 8
41:25 [d]Da 2:45
41:26 [e]ver 2
41:27 [f]Ge 12:10; 2Ki 8:1
41:29 [g]ver 47
41:30 [h]ver 54; Ge 47:13 [i]ver 56
41:32 [j]Nu 23:19; Isa 46:10-11
41:33 [k]ver 39
41:34 [l]1Sa 8:15 [m]ver 48
41:35 [n]ver 48
41:36 [o]ver 56
41:37 [p]Ge 45:16
41:38 [q]Nu 27:18; Job 32:8; Da 4:8,8-9,18; 5:11,14
41:40 [r]Ps 105:21-22; Ac 7:10
41:41 [s]Ge 42:6; Da 6:3
41:42 [t]Est 3:10 [u]Da 5:7,16,29
41:43 [v]Est 6:9
41:44 [w]Ps 105:22

daughter of Potiphera, priest of On,[m] to be his wife.[a] And Joseph went throughout the land of Egypt.

46Joseph was thirty years old[b] when he entered the service[c] of Pharaoh king of Egypt. And Joseph went out from Pharaoh's presence and traveled throughout Egypt. **47**During the seven years of abundance the land produced plentifully. **48**Joseph collected all the food produced in those seven years of abundance in Egypt and stored it in the cities. In each city he put the food grown in the fields surrounding it. **49**Joseph stored up huge quantities of grain, like the sand of the sea; it was so much that he stopped keeping records because it was beyond measure.

Manasseh and Ephraim are born.

50Before the years of famine came, two sons were born to Joseph by Asenath daughter of Potiphera, priest of On.[d] **51**Joseph named his firstborn[e] Manasseh[n] and said, "It is because God has made me forget all my trouble and all my father's household." **52**The second son he named Ephraim[o][f] and said, "It is because God has made me fruitful[g] in the land of my suffering."

Seven years of famine begin.

53The seven years of abundance in Egypt came to an end, **54**and the seven years of famine began,[h] just as Joseph had said. There was famine in all the other lands, but in the whole land of Egypt there was food. **55**When all Egypt began to feel the famine,[i] the people cried to Pharaoh for food. Then Pharaoh told all the Egyptians, "Go to Joseph and do what he tells you."[j]

56When the famine had spread over the whole country, Joseph opened the storehouses and sold grain to the Egyptians, for the famine[k] was severe throughout Egypt. **57**And all the countries came to Egypt to buy grain from Joseph,[l] because the famine was severe in all the world.

41:45 [a]ver 50; Ge 46:20,27
41:46 [b]Ge 37:2 [c]1Sa 16:21; Da 1:19
41:50 [d]Ge 46:20; 48:5
41:51 [e]Ge 48:14, 18,20
41:52 [f]Ge 48:1,5; 50:23 [g]Ge 17:6; 28:3; 49:22
41:54 [h]ver 30; Ps 105:11; Ac 7:11
41:55 [i]Dt 32:24 [j]ver 41
41:56 [k]Ge 12:10
41:57 [l]Ge 42:5; 47:15
42:1 [m]Ac 7:12
42:2 [n]Ge 43:8
42:4 [o]ver 38
42:5 [p]Ge 41:57 [q]Ge 12:10; Ac 7:11
42:6 [r]Ge 41:41 [s]Ge 37:7-10
42:7 [t]ver 30
42:8 [u]Ge 37:2
42:9 [v]Ge 37:7
42:13 [w]Ge 37:30, 33; 44:20

Jacob sends his ten sons to Egypt to buy grain.

42 When Jacob learned that there was grain in Egypt,[m] he said to his sons, "Why do you just keep looking at each other?" **2**He continued, "I have heard that there is grain in Egypt. Go down there and buy some for us, so that we may live and not die."[n]

3Then ten of Joseph's brothers went down to buy grain from Egypt. **4**But Jacob did not send Benjamin, Joseph's brother, with the others, because he was afraid that harm might come to him.[o] **5**So Israel's sons were among those who went to buy grain,[p] for the famine was in the land of Canaan also.[q]

6Now Joseph was the governor of the land,[r] the one who sold grain to all its people. So when Joseph's brothers arrived, they bowed down to him with their faces to the ground.[s] **7**As soon as Joseph saw his brothers, he recognized them, but he pretended to be a stranger and spoke harshly to them.[t] "Where do you come from?" he asked.

"From the land of Canaan," they replied, "to buy food."

8Although Joseph recognized his brothers, they did not recognize him.[u] **9**Then he remembered his dreams[v] about them and said to them, "You are spies! You have come to see where our land is unprotected."

10"No, my lord," they answered. "Your servants have come to buy food. **11**We are all the sons of one man. Your servants are honest men, not spies."

12"No!" he said to them. "You have come to see where our land is unprotected."

13But they replied, "Your servants were twelve brothers, the sons of one man, who lives in the land of Canaan. The youngest is now with our father, and one is no more."[w]

14Joseph said to them, "It is just as I

[m]*45* That is, Heliopolis; also in verse 50
[n]*51* *Manasseh* sounds like and may be derived from the Hebrew for *forget.* [o]*52* *Ephraim* sounds like the Hebrew for *twice fruitful.*

told you: You are spies! **15**And this is how you will be tested: As surely as Pharaoh lives,[a] you will not leave this place unless your youngest brother comes here. **16**Send one of your number to get your brother; the rest of you will be kept in prison, so that your words may be tested to see if you are telling the truth.[b] If you are not, then as surely as Pharaoh lives, you are spies!" **17**And he put them all in custody[c] for three days.

18On the third day, Joseph said to them, "Do this and you will live, for I fear God:[d] **19**If you are honest men, let one of your brothers stay here in prison, while the rest of you go and take grain back for your starving households. **20**But you must bring your youngest brother to me,[e] so that your words may be verified and that you may not die." This they proceeded to do.

21They said to one another, "Surely we are being punished because of our brother.[f] We saw how distressed he was when he pleaded with us for his life, but we would not listen; that's why this distress[g] has come upon us."

22Reuben replied, "Didn't I tell you not to sin against the boy?[h] But you wouldn't listen! Now we must give an accounting[i] for his blood."[j] **23**They did not realize that Joseph could understand them, since he was using an interpreter.

24He turned away from them and began to weep, but then turned back and spoke to them again. He had Simeon taken from them and bound before their eyes.[k]

Joseph sends his brothers home with grain and their silver.

25Joseph gave orders to fill their bags with grain,[l] to put each man's silver back in his sack,[m] and to give them provisions for their journey.[n] After this was done for them, **26**they loaded their grain on their donkeys and left.

27At the place where they stopped for the night one of them opened his sack to get feed for his donkey, and he saw his silver in the mouth of his sack.[o] **28**"My silver has been returned," he said to his brothers. "Here it is in my sack."

Their hearts sank and they turned to each other trembling and said, "What is this that God has done to us?"[p]

29When they came to their father Jacob in the land of Canaan, they told him all that had happened to them. They said, **30**"The man who is lord over the land spoke harshly to us[q] and treated us as though we were spying on the land. **31**But we said to him, 'We are honest men; we are not spies.[r] **32**We were twelve brothers, sons of one father. One is no more, and the youngest is now with our father in Canaan.'

33"Then the man who is lord over the land said to us, 'This is how I will know whether you are honest men: Leave one of your brothers here with me, and take food for your starving households and go.[s] **34**But bring your youngest brother to me so I will know that you are not spies but honest men. Then I will give your brother back to you, and you can trade[p] in the land.[t]'"

35As they were emptying their sacks, there in each man's sack was his pouch of silver! When they and their father saw the money pouches, they were frightened.[u] **36**Their father Jacob said to them, "You have deprived me of my children. Joseph is no more and Simeon is no more, and now you want to take Benjamin.[v] Everything is against me!"

37Then Reuben said to his father, "You may put both of my sons to death if I do not bring him back to you. Entrust him to my care, and I will bring him back."

38But Jacob said, "My son will not go down there with you; his brother is dead[w] and he is the only one left. If harm comes to him[x] on the journey you are taking, you will bring my gray head down to the grave[q][y] in sorrow.[z]"

Benjamin returns with his brothers to Egypt.

43 Now the famine was still severe in the land.[a] **2**So when they had eaten all the grain they had brought

42:15 [a]1Sa 17:55
42:16 [b]ver 11
42:17 [c]Ge 40:4
42:18 [d]Ge 20:11; Lev 25:43
42:20 [e]ver 15,34; Ge 43:5; 44:23
42:21 [f]Ge 37:26-28 [g]Hos 5:15
42:22 [h]Ge 37:21-22 [i]Ge 9:5 [j]1Ki 2:32; 2Ch 24:22; Ps 9:12
42:24 [k]ver 13; Ge 43:14,23; 45:14-15
42:25 [l]Ge 43:2 [m]Ge 44:1,8 [n]Ro 12:17, 20-21
42:27 [o]Ge 43:21-22
42:28 [p]Ge 43:23
42:30 [q]ver 7
42:31 [r]ver 11
42:33 [s]ver 19,20
42:34 [t]Ge 34:10
42:35 [u]Ge 43:12, 15,18
42:36 [v]Ge 43:14
42:38 [w]Ge 37:33 [x]ver 4 [y]Ge 37:35 [z]Ge 44:29,34
43:1 [a]Ge 12:10; 41:56-57

p34 Or *move about freely* q38 Hebrew *Sheol*

from Egypt, their father said to them,
"Go back and buy us a little more food."
3But Judah said to him, "The man
warned us solemnly, 'You will not see
my face again unless your brother is
with you.'[a] 4If you will send our brother along with us, we will go down and
buy food for you. 5But if you will not
send him, we will not go down, because the man said to us, 'You will not
see my face again unless your brother
is with you.[b]'"
6Israel asked, "Why did you bring this
trouble on me by telling the man you
had another brother?"
7They replied, "The man questioned
us closely about ourselves and our family. 'Is your father still living?'[c] he asked
us. 'Do you have another brother?'[d] We
simply answered his questions. How
were we to know he would say, 'Bring
your brother down here'?"
8Then Judah said to Israel his father,
"Send the boy along with me and we
will go at once, so that we and you and
our children may live and not die.[e] 9I
myself will guarantee his safety; you
can hold me personally responsible for
him. If I do not bring him back to you
and set him here before you, I will
bear the blame before you all my life.[f]
10As it is, if we had not delayed, we
could have gone and returned twice."
11Then their father Israel said to them,
"If it must be, then do this: Put some
of the best products of the land in your
bags and take them down to the man
as a gift[g]—a little balm[h] and a little
honey, some spices[i] and myrrh, some
pistachio nuts and almonds. 12Take double the amount of silver with you, for
you must return the silver that was put
back into the mouths of your sacks.[j]
Perhaps it was a mistake. 13Take your
brother also and go back to the man at
once. 14And may God Almighty[r][k] grant
you mercy before the man so that he
will let your other brother and Benjamin come back with you.[l] As for me,
if I am bereaved, I am bereaved."[m]
15So the men took the gifts and double the amount of silver, and Benjamin
also. They hurried[n] down to Egypt and
presented themselves[o] to Joseph. 16When
Joseph saw Benjamin with them, he said
to the steward of his house,[p] "Take these
men to my house, slaughter an animal
and prepare dinner;[q] they are to eat
with me at noon."
17The man did as Joseph told him and
took the men to Joseph's house. 18Now
the men were frightened[r] when they
were taken to his house. They thought,
"We were brought here because of the
silver that was put back into our sacks
the first time. He wants to attack us and
overpower us and seize us as slaves and
take our donkeys."
19So they went up to Joseph's steward and spoke to him at the entrance
to the house. 20"Please, sir," they said,
"we came down here the first time to
buy food.[s] 21But at the place where we
stopped for the night we opened our
sacks and each of us found his silver—
the exact weight—in the mouth of his
sack. So we have brought it back with
us.[t] 22We have also brought additional
silver with us to buy food. We don't
know who put our silver in our sacks."
23"It's all right," he said. "Don't be
afraid. Your God, the God of your father,
has given you treasure in your sacks;[u] I
received your silver." Then he brought
Simeon out to them.[v]
24The steward took the men into Joseph's house,[w] gave them water to wash
their feet[x] and provided fodder for their
donkeys. 25They prepared their gifts for
Joseph's arrival at noon, because they
had heard that they were to eat there.
26When Joseph came home, they presented to him the gifts[y] they had brought
into the house, and they bowed down
before him to the ground.[z] 27He asked
them how they were, and then he said,
"How is your aged father you told me
about? Is he still living?"[a]
28They replied, "Your servant our
father is still alive and well." And they
bowed low to pay him honor.[b]
29As he looked about and saw his

43:3 [a]Ge 42:15; 44:23
43:5 [b]Ge 42:15; 2Sa 3:13
43:7 [c]ver 27 [d]Ge 42:13
43:8 [e]Ge 42:2; Ps 33:18-19
43:9 [f]Ge 42:37; 44:32; Phm 1:18-19
43:11 [g]Ge 32:20; Pr 18:16 [h]Ge 37:25; Jer 8:22 [i]1Ki 10:2
43:12 [j]Ge 42:25
43:14 [k]Ge 17:1; 28:3; 35:11 [l]Ge 42:24 [m]Est 4:16
43:15 [n]Ge 45:9,13 [o]Ge 47:2,7
43:16 [p]Ge 44:1,4,12 [q]ver 31; Lk 15:23
43:18 [r]Ge 42:35
43:20 [s]Ge 42:3
43:21 [t]ver 15; Ge 42:27,35
43:23 [u]Ge 42:28 [v]Ge 42:24
43:24 [w]ver 16 [x]Ge 18:4; 24:32
43:26 [y]Mt 2:11 [z]Ge 37:7,10
43:27 [a]ver 7
43:28 [b]Ge 37:7

[r]14 Hebrew *El-Shaddai*

brother Benjamin, his own mother's son, he asked, "Is this your youngest brother, the one you told me about?"[a] And he said, "God be gracious to you,[b] my son." 30 Deeply moved[c] at the sight of his brother, Joseph hurried out and looked for a place to weep. He went into his private room and wept[d] there.

31 After he had washed his face, he came out and, controlling himself,[e] said, "Serve the food."

32 They served him by himself, the brothers by themselves, and the Egyptians who ate with him by themselves, because Egyptians could not eat with Hebrews,[f] for that is detestable to Egyptians.[g] 33 The men had been seated before him in the order of their ages, from the firstborn to the youngest; and they looked at each other in astonishment. 34 When portions were served to them from Joseph's table, Benjamin's portion was five times as much as anyone else's.[h] So they feasted and drank freely with him.

Joseph's silver cup is found in Benjamin's sack.

44 Now Joseph gave these instructions to the steward of his house: "Fill the men's sacks with as much food as they can carry, and put each man's silver in the mouth of his sack.[i] 2 Then put my cup, the silver one, in the mouth of the youngest one's sack, along with the silver for his grain." And he did as Joseph said.

3 As morning dawned, the men were sent on their way with their donkeys. 4 They had not gone far from the city when Joseph said to his steward, "Go after those men at once, and when you catch up with them, say to them, 'Why have you repaid good with evil?[j] 5 Isn't this the cup my master drinks from and also uses for divination?[k] This is a wicked thing you have done.'"

6 When he caught up with them, he repeated these words to them. 7 But they said to him, "Why does my lord say such things? Far be it from your servants to do anything like that! 8 We even brought back to you from the land of Canaan the silver we found inside the mouths of our sacks.[l] So why would we steal silver or gold from your master's house? 9 If any of your servants is found to have it, he will die;[m] and the rest of us will become my lord's slaves."

10 "Very well, then," he said, "let it be as you say. Whoever is found to have it will become my slave; the rest of you will be free from blame."

11 Each of them quickly lowered his sack to the ground and opened it. 12 Then the steward proceeded to search, beginning with the oldest and ending with the youngest. And the cup was found in Benjamin's sack.[n] 13 At this, they tore their clothes.[o] Then they all loaded their donkeys and returned to the city.

Judah pleads with Joseph for Benjamin's freedom.

14 Joseph was still in the house when Judah and his brothers came in, and they threw themselves to the ground before him.[p] 15 Joseph said to them, "What is this you have done? Don't you know that a man like me can find things out by divination?[q]"

16 "What can we say to my lord?" Judah replied. "What can we say? How can we prove our innocence? God has uncovered your servants' guilt. We are now my lord's slaves[r]—we ourselves and the one who was found to have the cup.[s]"

17 But Joseph said, "Far be it from me to do such a thing! Only the man who was found to have the cup will become my slave. The rest of you, go back to your father in peace."

18 Then Judah went up to him and said: "Please, my lord, let your servant speak a word to my lord. Do not be angry[t] with your servant, though you are equal to Pharaoh himself. 19 My lord asked his servants, 'Do you have a father or a brother?'[u] 20 And we answered, 'We have an aged father, and there is a young son born to him in his

43:29 [a] Ge 42:13 [b] Nu 6:25; Ps 67:1
43:30 [c] Jn 11:33,38 [d] Ge 42:24; 45:2,14,15; 46:29
43:31 [e] Ge 45:1
43:32 [f] Gal 2:12 [g] Ge 46:34; Ex 8:26
43:34 [h] Ge 37:3; 45:22
44:1 [i] Ge 42:25
44:4 [j] Ps 35:12
44:5 [k] Ge 30:27; Dt 18:10-14
44:8 [l] Ge 42:25; 43:21
44:9 [m] Ge 31:32
44:12 [n] ver 2
44:13 [o] Ge 37:29; Nu 14:6; 2Sa 1:11
44:14 [p] Ge 37:7,10
44:15 [q] ver 5; Ge 30:27
44:16 [r] ver 9; Ge 43:18 [s] ver 2
44:18 [t] Ge 18:30; Ex 32:22
44:19 [u] Ge 43:7

old age.[a] His brother is dead,[b] and he
is the only one of his mother's sons left,
and his father loves him.'[c]
21"Then you said to your servants,
'Bring him down to me so I can see him
for myself.'[d] 22And we said to my lord,
'The boy cannot leave his father; if he
leaves him, his father will die.'[e] 23But
you told your servants, 'Unless your
youngest brother comes down with you,
you will not see my face again.'[f] 24When
we went back to your servant my father,
we told him what my lord had said.
25"Then our father said, 'Go back and
buy a little more food.'[g] 26But we said,
'We cannot go down. Only if our youngest brother is with us will we go. We
cannot see the man's face unless our
youngest brother is with us.'
27"Your servant my father said to us,
'You know that my wife bore me two
sons.[h] 28One of them went away from
me, and I said, "He has surely been torn
to pieces."[i] And I have not seen him
since. 29If you take this one from me too
and harm comes to him, you will bring
my gray head down to the grave[s] in
misery.'[j]
30"So now, if the boy is not with us
when I go back to your servant my father
and if my father, whose life is closely
bound up with the boy's life,[k] 31sees that
the boy isn't there, he will die. Your
servants will bring the gray head of our
father down to the grave in sorrow.
32Your servant guaranteed the boy's safety to my father. I said, 'If I do not bring
him back to you, I will bear the blame
before you, my father, all my life!'[l]
33"Now then, please let your servant
remain here as my lord's slave[m] in place
of the boy,[n] and let the boy return with
his brothers. 34How can I go back to my
father if the boy is not with me? No! Do
not let me see the misery that would
come upon my father."[o]

Joseph makes himself known to his brothers.

45 Then Joseph could no longer
control himself[p] before all his
attendants, and he cried out, "Have
everyone leave my presence!" So there
was no one with Joseph when he made
himself known to his brothers. 2And
he wept[q] so loudly that the Egyptians
heard him, and Pharaoh's household
heard about it.[r]
3Joseph said to his brothers, "I am
Joseph! Is my father still living?"[s] But
his brothers were not able to answer
him,[t] because they were terrified at his
presence.
4Then Joseph said to his brothers,
"Come close to me." When they had
done so, he said, "I am your brother
Joseph, the one you sold into Egypt![u]
5And now, do not be distressed[v] and
do not be angry with yourselves for selling me here,[w] because it was to save
lives that God sent me ahead of you.[x]
6For two years now there has been
famine in the land, and for the next five
years there will not be plowing and
reaping. 7But God sent me ahead of
you to preserve for you a remnant[y] on
earth and to save your lives by a great
deliverance.[t][z]

Joseph instructs his brothers to return for Jacob.

8"So then, it was not you who sent me
here, but God. He made me father[a] to
Pharaoh, lord of his entire household and
ruler of all Egypt.[b] 9Now hurry back to
my father and say to him, 'This is what
your son Joseph says: God has made me
lord of all Egypt. Come down to me; don't
delay.[c] 10You shall live in the region of
Goshen[d] and be near me—you, your
children and grandchildren, your flocks
and herds, and all you have. 11I will provide for you there,[e] because five years
of famine are still to come. Otherwise
you and your household and all who
belong to you will become destitute.'
12"You can see for yourselves, and so
can my brother Benjamin, that it is
really I who am speaking to you. 13Tell
my father about all the honor accorded

44:20 [a]Ge 37:3 [b]Ge 37:33 [c]Ge 42:13
44:21 [d]Ge 42:15
44:22 [e]Ge 37:35
44:23 [f]Ge 43:5
44:25 [g]Ge 43:2
44:27 [h]Ge 46:19
44:28 [i]Ge 37:33
44:29 [j]Ge 42:38
44:30 [k]1Sa 18:1
44:32 [l]Ge 43:9
44:33 [m]Ge 43:18 [n]Jn 15:13
44:34 [o]Est 8:6
45:1 [p]Ge 43:31
45:2 [q]Ge 29:11 [r]ver 16; Ge 46:29
45:3 [s]Ac 7:13 [t]ver 15
45:4 [u]Ge 37:28
45:5 [v]Ge 42:21 [w]Ge 42:22 [x]ver 7-8; Ge 50:20; Ps 105:17
45:7 [y]2Ki 19:4, 30,31; Isa 10:20,21; Mic 4:7; Zep 2:7 [z]Ex 15:2; Est 4:14; Isa 25:9
45:8 [a]Jdg 17:10 [b]Ge 41:41
45:9 [c]Ge 43:10
45:10 [d]Ge 46:28,34; 47:1
45:11 [e]Ge 47:12

[s]*29* Hebrew *Sheol*; also in verse 31 [t]*7* Or *save you as a great band of survivors*

me in Egypt and about everything you have seen. And bring my father down here quickly.[a]"

14 Then he threw his arms around his brother Benjamin and wept, and Benjamin embraced him, weeping. 15 And he kissed[b] all his brothers and wept over them. Afterward his brothers talked with him.[c]

16 When the news reached Pharaoh's palace that Joseph's brothers had come,[d] Pharaoh and all his officials were pleased. 17 Pharaoh said to Joseph, "Tell your brothers, 'Do this: Load your animals and return to the land of Canaan, 18 and bring your father and your families back to me. I will give you the best of the land of Egypt[e] and you can enjoy the fat of the land.'[f]

19 "You are also directed to tell them, 'Do this: Take some carts[g] from Egypt for your children and your wives, and get your father and come. 20 Never mind about your belongings, because the best of all Egypt will be yours.'"

21 So the sons of Israel did this. Joseph gave them carts, as Pharaoh had commanded, and he also gave them provisions for their journey.[h] 22 To each of them he gave new clothing, but to Benjamin he gave three hundred shekels[u] of silver and five sets of clothes.[i] 23 And this is what he sent to his father: ten donkeys loaded with the best things of Egypt, and ten female donkeys loaded with grain and bread and other provisions for his journey. 24 Then he sent his brothers away, and as they were leaving he said to them, "Don't quarrel on the way!"[j]

25 So they went up out of Egypt and came to their father Jacob in the land of Canaan. 26 They told him, "Joseph is still alive! In fact, he is ruler of all Egypt." Jacob was stunned; he did not believe them.[k] 27 But when they told him everything Joseph had said to them, and when he saw the carts[l] Joseph had sent to carry him back, the spirit of their father Jacob revived. 28 And Israel said, "I'm convinced! My son Joseph is still alive. I will go and see him before I die."

45:13 [a]Ac 7:14
45:15 [b]Lk 15:20 [c]ver 3
45:16 [d]Ac 7:13
45:18 [e]Ge 27:28; 46:34; 47:6,11,27; Nu 18:12,29 [f]Ps 37:19
45:19 [g]Ge 46:5
45:21 [h]Ge 42:25
45:22 [i]Ge 37:3; 43:34
45:24 [j]Ge 42:21-22
45:26 [k]Ge 44:28
45:27 [l]ver 19
46:1 [m]Ge 21:14; 28:10 [n]Ge 26:24; 28:13; 31:42
46:2 [o]Ge 15:1; Job 33:14-15 [p]Ge 22:1; 31:11
46:3 [q]Ge 28:13 [r]Ge 12:2; Dt 26:5 [s]Ex 1:7
46:4 [t]Ge 28:15; 48:21; Ex 3:8 [u]Ge 50:1,24
46:5 [v]Ge 45:19
46:6 [w]Dt 26:5; Jos 24:4; Ps 105:23; Isa 52:4; Ac 7:15
46:7 [x]Ge 45:10
46:8 [y]Ex 1:1; Nu 26:4
46:9 [z]1Ch 5:3
46:10 [a]Ge 29:33; Nu 26:14 [b]Ex 6:15
46:11 [c]Ge 29:34; Nu 3:17

Jacob and his family move to Egypt.

46 So Israel set out with all that was his, and when he reached Beersheba,[m] he offered sacrifices to the God of his father Isaac.[n]

2 And God spoke to Israel in a vision at night[o] and said, "Jacob! Jacob!"

"Here I am,"[p] he replied.

3 "I am God, the God of your father,"[q] he said. "Do not be afraid to go down to Egypt, for I will make you into a great nation[r] there.[s] 4 I will go down to Egypt with you, and I will surely bring you back again.[t] And Joseph's own hand will close your eyes.[u]"

5 Then Jacob left Beersheba, and Israel's sons took their father Jacob and their children and their wives in the carts[v] that Pharaoh had sent to transport him. 6 They also took with them their livestock and the possessions they had acquired in Canaan, and Jacob and all his offspring went to Egypt.[w] 7 He took with him to Egypt his sons and grandsons and his daughters and granddaughters—all his offspring.[x]

Names of those moving are listed.

8 These are the names of the sons of Israel[y] (Jacob and his descendants) who went to Egypt:

Reuben the firstborn of Jacob.
9 The sons of Reuben:[z]
Hanoch, Pallu, Hezron and Carmi.
10 The sons of Simeon:[a]
Jemuel,[b] Jamin, Ohad, Jakin, Zohar and Shaul the son of a Canaanite woman.
11 The sons of Levi:[c]
Gershon, Kohath and Merari.
12 The sons of Judah:[d]
Er, Onan, Shelah, Perez and Zerah (but Er and Onan had died in the land of Canaan).
The sons of Perez:[e]
Hezron and Hamul.

46:12 [d]Ge 29:35 [e]1Ch 2:5; Mt 1:3

u22 That is, about 7 1/2 pounds (about 3.5 kilograms)

13 The sons of Issachar:[a]
Tola, Puah,[v][b] Jashub[w] and Shimron.
14 The sons of Zebulun:[c]
Sered, Elon and Jahleel.
15 These were the sons Leah bore to Jacob in Paddan Aram,[x] besides his daughter Dinah. These sons and daughters of his were thirty-three in all.

16 The sons of Gad:[d]
Zephon,[y][e] Haggi, Shuni, Ezbon, Eri, Arodi and Areli.
17 The sons of Asher:[f]
Imnah, Ishvah, Ishvi and Beriah.
Their sister was Serah.
The sons of Beriah:
Heber and Malkiel.
18 These were the children born to Jacob by Zilpah,[g] whom Laban had given to his daughter Leah[h]—sixteen in all.

19 The sons of Jacob's wife Rachel:
Joseph and Benjamin.[i] 20 In Egypt, Manasseh[j] and Ephraim[k] were born to Joseph by Asenath daughter of Potiphera, priest of On.[z]
21 The sons of Benjamin:[l]
Bela, Beker, Ashbel, Gera, Naaman, Ehi, Rosh, Muppim, Huppim and Ard.
22 These were the sons of Rachel who were born to Jacob—fourteen in all.

23 The son of Dan:
Hushim.
24 The sons of Naphtali:
Jahziel, Guni, Jezer and Shillem.
25 These were the sons born to Jacob by Bilhah,[m] whom Laban had given to his daughter Rachel[n]—seven in all.

26 All those who went to Egypt with Jacob—those who were his direct descendants, not counting his sons' wives—numbered sixty-six persons.[o] 27 With the two sons[a] who had been born to Joseph in Egypt, the members of Jacob's family, which went to Egypt, were seventy[b] in all.[p]

Joseph and Jacob meet at Goshen.

28 Now Jacob sent Judah ahead of him to Joseph to get directions to Goshen.[q] When they arrived in the region of Goshen, 29 Joseph had his chariot made ready and went to Goshen to meet his father Israel. As soon as Joseph appeared before him, he threw his arms around his father[c] and wept for a long time.[r]

30 Israel said to Joseph, "Now I am ready to die, since I have seen for myself that you are still alive."

31 Then Joseph said to his brothers and to his father's household, "I will go up and speak to Pharaoh and will say to him, 'My brothers and my father's household, who were living in the land of Canaan, have come to me.[s] 32 The men are shepherds; they tend livestock, and they have brought along their flocks and herds and everything they own.' 33 When Pharaoh calls you in and asks, 'What is your occupation?'[t] 34 you should answer, 'Your servants have tended livestock from our boyhood on, just as our fathers did.' Then you will be allowed to settle in the region of Goshen,[u] for all shepherds are detestable to the Egyptians.[v]"

Pharaoh welcomes Jacob and his family.

47 Joseph went and told Pharaoh, "My father and brothers, with their flocks and herds and everything they own, have come from the land of Canaan and are now in Goshen."[w] 2 He chose five of his brothers and presented them before Pharaoh.

3 Pharaoh asked the brothers, "What is your occupation?"[x]

"Your servants are shepherds," they replied to Pharaoh, "just as our fathers were." 4 They also said to him, "We have come to live here awhile,[y] because the

46:13 [a]Ge 30:18 [b]1Ch 7:1
46:14 [c]Ge 30:20
46:16 [d]Ge 30:11 [e]Nu 26:15
46:17 [f]Ge 30:13; 1Ch 7:30-31
46:18 [g]Ge 30:10 [h]Ge 29:24
46:19 [i]Ge 44:27
46:20 [j]Ge 41:51 [k]Ge 41:52
46:21 [l]Nu 26:38-41; 1Ch 7:6-12; 8:1
46:25 [m]Ge 30:8 [n]Ge 29:29
46:26 [o]ver 5-7; Ex 1:5; Dt 10:22
46:27 [p]Ac 7:14
46:28 [q]Ge 45:10
46:29 [r]Ge 45:14-15; Lk 15:20
46:31 [s]Ge 47:1
46:33 [t]Ge 47:3
46:34 [u]Ge 45:10 [v]Ge 43:32; Ex 8:26
47:1 [w]Ge 46:31
47:3 [x]Ge 46:33
47:4 [y]Ge 15:13; Dt 26:5

v *13* Samaritan Pentateuch and Syriac (see also 1 Chron. 7:1); Masoretic Text *Puvah* w *13* Samaritan Pentateuch and some Septuagint manuscripts (see also Num. 26:24 and 1 Chron. 7:1); Masoretic Text *Iob* x *15* That is, Northwest Mesopotamia y *16* Samaritan Pentateuch and Septuagint (see also Num. 26:15); Masoretic Text *Ziphion* z *20* That is, Heliopolis a *27* Hebrew; Septuagint *the nine children* b *27* Hebrew (see also Exodus 1:5 and footnote); Septuagint (see also Acts 7:14) *seventy-five* c *29* Hebrew *around him*

famine is severe in Canaan[a] and your
servants' flocks have no pasture. So
now, please let your servants settle in
Goshen."[b]
5Pharaoh said to Joseph, "Your father
and your brothers have come to you,
6and the land of Egypt is before you;
settle your father and your brothers in
the best part of the land.[c] Let them
live in Goshen. And if you know of any
among them with special ability,[d] put
them in charge of my own livestock."
7Then Joseph brought his father Jacob
in and presented him before Pharaoh.
After Jacob blessed[d] Pharaoh,[e] 8Phar-
aoh asked him, "How old are you?"
9And Jacob said to Pharaoh, "The years
of my pilgrimage are a hundred and thirty.[f] My years have been few and difficult,[g] and they do not equal the years
of the pilgrimage of my fathers.[h]" 10Then
Jacob blessed[e] Pharaoh[i] and went out
from his presence.
11So Joseph settled his father and his
brothers in Egypt and gave them property in the best part of the land, the
district of Rameses,[j] as Pharaoh directed. 12Joseph also provided his father and
his brothers and all his father's household with food, according to the number of their children.[k]

Joseph's famine program benefits Pharaoh.

13There was no food, however, in the
whole region because the famine was
severe; both Egypt and Canaan wasted
away because of the famine.[l] 14Joseph
collected all the money that was to be
found in Egypt and Canaan in payment
for the grain they were buying, and he
brought it to Pharaoh's palace.[m] 15When
the money of the people of Egypt and
Canaan was gone, all Egypt came to Joseph and said, "Give us food. Why should
we die before your eyes?[n] Our money is
used up."
16"Then bring your livestock," said Joseph. "I will sell you food in exchange
for your livestock, since your money is
gone." 17So they brought their livestock
to Joseph, and he gave them food in
exchange for their horses,[o] their sheep
and goats, their cattle and donkeys. And
he brought them through that year
with food in exchange for all their livestock.
18When that year was over, they came
to him the following year and said, "We
cannot hide from our lord the fact that
since our money is gone and our livestock belongs to you, there is nothing
left for our lord except our bodies and
our land. 19Why should we perish before your eyes—we and our land as
well? Buy us and our land in exchange
for food, and we with our land will be
in bondage to Pharaoh. Give us seed so
that we may live and not die, and that
the land may not become desolate."
20So Joseph bought all the land in
Egypt for Pharaoh. The Egyptians, one
and all, sold their fields, because the
famine was too severe for them. The
land became Pharaoh's, 21and Joseph
reduced the people to servitude,[f] from
one end of Egypt to the other. 22Howev-
er, he did not buy the land of the priests,
because they received a regular allotment
from Pharaoh and had food enough from
the allotment[p] Pharaoh gave them. That
is why they did not sell their land.
23Joseph said to the people, "Now that
I have bought you and your land today
for Pharaoh, here is seed for you so you
can plant the ground. 24But when the
crop comes in, give a fifth[q] of it to Pharaoh. The other four-fifths you may keep
as seed for the fields and as food for
yourselves and your households and
your children."
25"You have saved our lives," they
said. "May we find favor in the eyes of
our lord;[r] we will be in bondage to Pharaoh."
26So Joseph established it as a law
concerning land in Egypt—still in force
today—that a fifth of the produce belongs to Pharaoh. It was only the land of

47:4 [a]Ge 43:1 [b]Ge 46:34
47:6 [c]Ge 45:18 [d]Ex 18:21,25
47:7 [e]ver 10; 2Sa 14:22
47:9 [f]Ge 25:7 [g]Heb 11:9,13 [h]Ge 35:28
47:10 [i]ver 7
47:11 [j]Ex 1:11; 12:37
47:12 [k]Ge 45:11
47:13 [l]Ge 41:30; Ac 7:11
47:14 [m]Ge 41:56
47:15 [n]ver 19; Ex 16:3
47:17 [o]Ex 14:9
47:22 [p]Dt 14:28-29; Ezr 7:24
47:24 [q]Ge 41:34
47:25 [r]Ge 32:5

[d]*7* Or *greeted* [e]*10* Or *said farewell to*
[f]*21* Samaritan Pentateuch and Septuagint (see also Vulgate); Masoretic Text *and he moved the people into the cities*

the priests that did not become Pharaoh's.[a]
27Now the Israelites settled in Egypt
in the region of Goshen. They acquired
property there and were fruitful and
increased greatly in number.[b]

Joseph vows to bury Jacob in Canaan.

28Jacob lived in Egypt[c] seventeen
years, and the years of his life were a
hundred and forty-seven. 29When the
time drew near for Israel to die,[d] he
called for his son Joseph and said to him,
"If I have found favor in your eyes, put
your hand under my thigh[e] and promise
that you will show me kindness and
faithfulness.[f] Do not bury me in Egypt,
30but when I rest with my fathers, carry me out of Egypt and bury me where
they are buried."[g]
"I will do as you say," he said.
31"Swear to me,"[h] he said. Then Joseph swore to him,[i] and Israel worshiped
as he leaned on the top of his staff.[g][j]

Jacob blesses Joseph's sons, Ephraim and Manasseh.

48 Some time later Joseph was told,
"Your father is ill." So he took
his two sons Manasseh and Ephraim[k]
along with him. 2When Jacob was told,
"Your son Joseph has come to you," Israel
rallied his strength and sat up on the bed.
3Jacob said to Joseph, "God Almighty[h]
appeared to me at Luz[l] in the land of Canaan, and there he blessed me[m] 4and
said to me, 'I am going to make you fruitful and will increase your numbers.[n] I
will make you a community of peoples,
and I will give this land as an everlasting
possession to your descendants after you.'
5"Now then, your two sons born to
you in Egypt[o] before I came to you here
will be reckoned as mine; Ephraim and
Manasseh will be mine,[p] just as Reuben and Simeon are mine. 6Any children born to you after them will be
yours; in the territory they inherit they
will be reckoned under the names of
their brothers. 7As I was returning from
Paddan,[i] to my sorrow Rachel died in
the land of Canaan while we were still
on the way, a little distance from Ephrath. So I buried her there beside the
road to Ephrath" (that is, Bethlehem).[q]
8When Israel saw the sons of Joseph,
he asked, "Who are these?"
9"They are the sons God has given
me here,"[r] Joseph said to his father.
Then Israel said, "Bring them to me
so I may bless[s] them."
10Now Israel's eyes were failing because of old age, and he could hardly
see.[t] So Joseph brought his sons close to
him, and his father kissed them[u] and embraced them.
11Israel said to Joseph, "I never expected to see your face again, and now
God has allowed me to see your children too."[v]
12Then Joseph removed them from
Israel's knees and bowed down with his
face to the ground. 13And Joseph took
both of them, Ephraim on his right
toward Israel's left hand and Manasseh
on his left toward Israel's right hand,[w]
and brought them close to him. 14But
Israel reached out his right hand and put
it on Ephraim's head, though he was
the younger, and crossing his arms, he
put his left hand on Manasseh's head,
even though Manasseh was the firstborn.[x]
15Then he blessed[y] Joseph and said,

"May the God before whom my
fathers
Abraham and Isaac walked,
the God who has been my shepherd[z]
all my life to this day,
16the Angel who has delivered me
from all harm
—may he bless these boys.[a]
May they be called by my name
and the names of my fathers
Abraham and Isaac,[b]
and may they increase greatly
upon the earth."

47:26 [a]ver 22
47:27 [b]Ge 17:6; 46:3; Ex 1:7
47:28 [c]Ps 105:23
47:29 [d]Dt 31:14 [e]Ge 24:2 [f]Ge 24:49
47:30 [g]Ge 49:29-32; 50:5,13; Ac 7:15-16
47:31 [h]Ge 21:23 [i]Ge 24:3 [j]Heb 11:21 *fn* 1Ki 1:47
48:1 [k]Ge 41:52
48:3 [l]Ge 28:19 [m]Ge 28:13; 35:9-12
48:4 [n]Ge 17:6
48:5 [o]Ge 41:50-52; 46:20 [p]1Ch 5:1; Jos 14:4
48:7 [q]Ge 35:19
48:9 [r]Ge 33:5 [s]Ge 27:4
48:10 [t]Ge 27:1 [u]Ge 27:27
48:11 [v]Ge 50:23; Ps 128:6
48:13 [w]Ps 110:1
48:14 [x]Ge 41:51
48:15 [y]Ge 17:1 [z]Ge 49:24
48:16 [a]Heb 11:21 [b]Ge 28:13

[g]*31* Or *Israel bowed down at the head of his bed*
[h]*3* Hebrew *El-Shaddai* [i]*7* That is, Northwest Mesopotamia

17When Joseph saw his father placing his right hand on Ephraim's head[a]
he was displeased; so he took hold of his
father's hand to move it from Ephraim's
head to Manasseh's head. 18Joseph said
to him, "No, my father, this one is the
firstborn; put your right hand on his
head."
19But his father refused and said, "I
know, my son, I know. He too will become a people, and he too will become
great.[b] Nevertheless, his younger brother will be greater than he,[c] and his
descendants will become a group of
nations." 20He blessed them that day
and said,

"In your[j] name will Israel pronounce
this blessing:
'May God make you like Ephraim[d]
and Manasseh.[e]'"

So he put Ephraim ahead of Manasseh.
21Then Israel said to Joseph, "I am
about to die, but God will be with you[k][f]
and take you[k] back to the land of your[k]
fathers.[g] 22And to you, as one who is
over your brothers,[h] I give the ridge of
land[l][i] I took from the Amorites with
my sword and my bow."

48:17 [a]ver 14
48:19 [b]Ge 17:20 [c]Ge 25:23
48:20 [d]Nu 2:18 [e]Nu 2:20; Ru 4:11
48:21 [f]Ge 26:3; 46:4 [g]Ge 28:13; 50:24
48:22 [h]Ge 37:8 [i]Jos 24:32; Jn 4:5
49:1 [j]Nu 24:14; Jer 23:20
49:2 [k]Ps 34:11
49:3 [l]Ge 29:32 [m]Dt 21:17; Ps 78:51
49:4 [n]Isa 57:20 [o]Ge 35:22; Dt 27:20
49:5 [p]Ge 34:25; Pr 4:17
49:6 [q]Pr 1:15; Eph 5:11 [r]Ge 34:26
49:7 [s]Jos 19:1,9; 21:1-42
49:8 [t]Dt 33:7; 1Ch 5:2
49:9 [u]Nu 24:9; Eze 19:5; Mic 5:8 [v]Rev 5:5
49:10 [w]Nu 24:17, 19; Ps 60:7 [x]Ps 2:9; Isa 42:1,4
49:13 [y]Ge 30:20; Dt 33:18-19; Jos 19:10-11
49:14 [z]Ge 30:18

Jacob's final words to his sons.

49:1-28Ref— Dt 33:1-29

49 Then Jacob called for his sons
and said: "Gather around so I
can tell you what will happen to you in
days to come.[j]

2"Assemble and listen, sons of Jacob;
listen to your father Israel.[k]

3"Reuben, you are my firstborn,[l]
my might, the first sign of my
strength,[m]
excelling in honor, excelling in
power.
4Turbulent as the waters,[n] you will no
longer excel,
for you went up onto your father's
bed,
onto my couch and defiled it.[o]

5"Simeon and Levi are brothers—
their swords[m] are weapons of
violence.[p]
6Let me not enter their council,
let me not join their assembly,[q]
for they have killed men in their
anger[r]
and hamstrung oxen as they pleased.
7Cursed be their anger, so fierce,
and their fury, so cruel!
I will scatter them in Jacob
and disperse them in Israel.[s]

8"Judah,[n] your brothers will praise you;
your hand will be on the neck of
your enemies;
your father's sons will bow down
to you.[t]
9You are a lion[u]'s cub, O Judah;[v]
you return from the prey, my son.
Like a lion he crouches and lies
down,
like a lioness—who dares to rouse
him?
10The scepter will not depart from
Judah,[w]
nor the ruler's staff from between
his feet,
until he comes to whom it belongs[o]
and the obedience of the nations is
his.[x]
11He will tether his donkey to a vine,
his colt to the choicest branch;
he will wash his garments in wine,
his robes in the blood of grapes.
12His eyes will be darker than wine,
his teeth whiter than milk.[p]

13"Zebulun[y] will live by the seashore
and become a haven for ships;
his border will extend toward
Sidon.

14"Issachar[z] is a rawboned[q] donkey
lying down between two
saddlebags.[r]

[j]*20* The Hebrew is singular. [k]*21* The Hebrew is plural. [l]*22* Or *And to you I give one portion more than to your brothers—the portion* [m]*5* The meaning of the Hebrew for this word is uncertain. [n]*8* *Judah* sounds like and may be derived from the Hebrew for *praise.* [o]*10* Or *until Shiloh comes*; or *until he comes to whom tribute belongs* [p]*12* Or *will be dull from wine, / his teeth white from milk* [q]*14* Or *strong* [r]*14* Or *campfires*

15When he sees how good is his
resting place
and how pleasant is his land,
he will bend his shoulder to the
burden
and submit to forced labor.

16"Dan[s][a] will provide justice for his
people
as one of the tribes of Israel.
17Dan[b] will be a serpent by the roadside,
a viper along the path,
that bites the horse's heels
so that its rider tumbles backward.

18"I look for your deliverance,
O LORD.[c]

19"Gad[t][d] will be attacked by a band of
raiders,
but he will attack them at their
heels.

20"Asher's[e] food will be rich;
he will provide delicacies fit for a
king.

21"Naphtali[f] is a doe set free
that bears beautiful fawns.[u]

22"Joseph[g] is a fruitful vine,
a fruitful vine near a spring,
whose branches climb over a wall.[v]
23With bitterness archers attacked
him;
they shot at him with hostility.[h]
24But his bow remained steady,
his strong arms[i] stayed[w] limber,
because of the hand of the Mighty
One of Jacob,[j]
because of the Shepherd, the Rock
of Israel,[k]
25because of your father's God,[l] who
helps you,
because of the Almighty,[x] who
blesses you
with blessings of the heavens above,
blessings of the deep that lies
below,[m]
blessings of the breast and womb.
26Your father's blessings are greater
than the blessings of the ancient
mountains,
than[y] the bounty of the age-old hills.
Let all these rest on the head of Joseph,
on the brow of the prince among[z]
his brothers.[n]

27"Benjamin[o] is a ravenous wolf;
in the morning he devours the
prey,
in the evening he divides the
plunder."

28All these are the twelve tribes of
Israel, and this is what their father said
to them when he blessed them, giving
each the blessing appropriate to him.

Jacob's death.

29Then he gave them these instructions:[p] "I am about to be gathered to
my people.[q] Bury me with my fathers[r]
in the cave in the field of Ephron the
Hittite, 30the cave in the field of Machpelah,[s] near Mamre in Canaan, which
Abraham bought as a burial place from
Ephron the Hittite, along with the field.[t]
31There Abraham[u] and his wife Sarah[v]
were buried, there Isaac and his wife
Rebekah[w] were buried, and there I
buried Leah. 32The field and the cave
in it were bought from the Hittites.[a]"
33When Jacob had finished giving instructions to his sons, he drew his feet
up into the bed, breathed his last and
was gathered to his people.[x]

Jacob's burial in Canaan.

50 Joseph threw himself upon his
father and wept over him and
kissed him.[y] 2Then Joseph directed the
physicians in his service to embalm his
father Israel. So the physicians embalmed
him,[z] 3taking a full forty days, for that
was the time required for embalming.
And the Egyptians mourned for him seventy days.[a]

49:16 [a]Ge 30:6; Dt 33:22; Jdg 18:26-27
49:17 [b]Jdg 18:27
49:18 [c]Ps 119:166, 174
49:19 [d]Ge 30:11; Dt 33:20; 1Ch 5:18
49:20 [e]Ge 30:13; Dt 33:24
49:21 [f]Ge 30:8; Dt 33:23
49:22 [g]Ge 30:24; Dt 33:13-17
49:23 [h]Ge 37:24
49:24 [i]Ps 18:34 [j]Ps 132:2,5; Isa 1:24; 41:10 [k]Isa 28:16
49:25 [l]Ge 28:13 [m]Ge 27:28
49:26 [n]Dt 33:15-16
49:27 [o]Ge 35:18; Jdg 20:12-13
49:29 [p]Ge 50:16 [q]Ge 25:8 [r]Ge 15:15; 47:30; 50:13
49:30 [s]Ge 23:9 [t]Ge 23:20
49:31 [u]Ge 25:9 [v]Ge 23:19 [w]Ge 35:29
49:33 [x]ver 29; Ge 25:8; Ac 7:15
50:1 [y]Ge 46:4
50:2 [z]ver 26; 2Ch 16:14
50:3 [a]Ge 37:34; Nu 20:29; Dt 34:8

s *16 Dan* here means *he provides justice.* t *19 Gad* can mean *attack* and *band of raiders.* u *21* Or *free; / he utters beautiful words* v *22* Or *Joseph is a wild colt, / a wild colt near a spring, / a wild donkey on a terraced hill* w *23,24* Or *archers will attack . . . will shoot . . . will remain . . . will stay* x *25* Hebrew *Shaddai* y *26* Or *of my progenitors, / as great as* z *26* Or *the one separated from* a *32* Or *the sons of Heth*

4When the days of mourning had passed, Joseph said to Pharaoh's court, "If I have found favor in your eyes, speak to Pharaoh for me. Tell him, 5'My father made me swear an oath[a] and said, "I am about to die; bury me in the tomb I dug for myself[b] in the land of Canaan."[c] Now let me go up and bury my father; then I will return.'"

6Pharaoh said, "Go up and bury your father, as he made you swear to do."

7So Joseph went up to bury his father. All Pharaoh's officials accompanied him—the dignitaries of his court and all the dignitaries of Egypt— 8besides all the members of Joseph's household and his brothers and those belonging to his father's household. Only their children and their flocks and herds were left in Goshen. 9Chariots and horsemen[b] also went up with him. It was a very large company.

10When they reached the threshing floor of Atad, near the Jordan, they lamented loudly and bitterly;[d] and there Joseph observed a seven-day period[e] of mourning for his father. 11When the Canaanites who lived there saw the mourning at the threshing floor of Atad, they said, "The Egyptians are holding a solemn ceremony of mourning." That is why that place near the Jordan is called Abel Mizraim.[c]

12So Jacob's sons did as he had commanded them: 13They carried him to the land of Canaan and buried him in the cave in the field of Machpelah, near Mamre, which Abraham had bought as a burial place from Ephron the Hittite, along with the field.[f] 14After burying his father, Joseph returned to Egypt, together with his brothers and all the others who had gone with him to bury his father.

Joseph's promise of continued provision for his brothers.

15When Joseph's brothers saw that their father was dead, they said, "What if Joseph holds a grudge against us and pays us back for all the wrongs we did to him?"[g] 16So they sent word to Joseph, saying, "Your father left these instructions before he died: 17'This is what you are to say to Joseph: I ask you to forgive your brothers the sins and the wrongs they committed in treating you so badly.' Now please forgive the sins of the servants of the God of your father." When their message came to him, Joseph wept.

18His brothers then came and threw themselves down before him.[h] "We are your slaves,"[i] they said.

19But Joseph said to them, "Don't be afraid. Am I in the place of God?[j] 20You intended to harm me,[k] but God intended[l] it for good[m] to accomplish what is now being done, the saving of many lives.[n] 21So then, don't be afraid. I will provide for you and your children.[o]" And he reassured them and spoke kindly to them.

Joseph's death in Egypt.

22Joseph stayed in Egypt, along with all his father's family. He lived a hundred and ten years[p] 23and saw the third generation[q] of Ephraim's children. Also the children of Makir[r] son of Manasseh were placed at birth on Joseph's knees.[d]

24Then Joseph said to his brothers, "I am about to die.[s] But God will surely come to your aid[t] and take you up out of this land to the land[u] he promised on oath to Abraham, Isaac and Jacob."[v] 25And Joseph made the sons of Israel swear an oath and said, "God will surely come to your aid, and then you must carry my bones up from this place."[w]

26So Joseph died at the age of a hundred and ten. And after they embalmed him,[x] he was placed in a coffin in Egypt.

50:5 [a]Ge 47:31 [b]2Ch 16:14; Isa 22:16 [c]Ge 47:31
50:10 [d]2Sa 1:17; Ac 8:2 [e]1Sa 31:13; Job 2:13
50:13 [f]Ge 23:20; Ac 7:16
50:15 [g]Ge 37:28; 42:21-22
50:18 [h]Ge 37:7 [i]Ge 43:18
50:19 [j]Ro 12:19; Heb 10:30
50:20 [k]Ge 37:20 [l]Mic 4:11-12 [m]Ro 8:28 [n]Ge 45:5
50:21 [o]Ge 45:11; 47:12
50:22 [p]Ge 25:7; Jos 24:29
50:23 [q]Job 42:16 [r]Nu 32:39,40
50:24 [s]Ge 48:21 [t]Ex 3:16-17 [u]Ge 15:14 [v]Ge 12:7; 26:3; 28:13; 35:12
50:25 [w]Ge 47:29-30; Ex 13:19; Jos 24:32; Heb 11:22
50:26 [x]ver 2

b*9* Or *charioteers* c*11* *Abel Mizraim* means *mourning of the Egyptians.* d*23* That is, were counted as his

EXODUS

Author: Moses.

Date Written: Between 1450 and 1400 B.C.

Time Span: Approximately 431 years (the period of time from the arrival of Jacob in Egypt to the construction of the tabernacle in the desert).

Title: The word "exodus" means "exit" or "departure."

Background: The second book of the Pentateuch, Exodus, is a continuation of the story in the book of Genesis. Only 70 descendants of Jacob journeyed to Egypt, but after increasing abundantly in number they became oppressed as slaves to Egyptian leaders who did not remember Joseph (Jacob's son). During the preceding 4 centuries the people have grown to a nation of some 3 million before their exodus from Egypt begins.

Where Written: The general belief is that Moses received this revelation while on Mount Sinai in the desert.

To Whom: To the Israelites.

Content: Exodus begins with the descendants of Jacob living in slavery to the Egyptians. Moses is called and directed by God to lead the Israelites out of this bondage. Israel is finally permitted to leave Egypt after God directs Moses to pronounce a series of plagues upon Egypt and the pharaoh. The Passover is instituted, emphasizing that blood redemption is always necessary (chapter 12), and the resulting covenant between God and the Israelites identifies them as God's chosen people. God then delivers Israel miraculously through the Red Sea. At Mount Sinai God gives the Ten Commandments, but later has to judge the people for their apostasy and worship of the golden calf (chapter 32). A few months after this, the tabernacle is constructed.

Key Words: "Deliverance"; "Redemption"; "Commandments." The "deliverance" of the people of Israel from their oppression as slaves is just one of the many miraculous acts performed by God for the complete "redemption" of his chosen people. The Ten "Commandments" and other laws give the people the instruction needed to live as God desires.

Themes: • God's protection and provision are available to his children in times of need. • Obedience to the Word of God brings prosperity and blessings...disobedience brings failure and punishment. • Part of our covenant agreement with God is that we trust and obey him in return for his deliverance and salvation. • God's promises can be depended upon totally and uncompromisingly.

Outline:

1. Israel's bondage and Moses' preparation. 1:1-4:31
2. God's redemption of Israel from Egypt. 5:1-15:21
3. Israel's wilderness journey to Mount Sinai. 15:22-18:27
4. God's covenant and the Ten Commandments. 19:1-24:18
5. The tabernacle and related regulations. 25:1-31:18
6. Israel's apostasy. 32:1-32:35
7. Renewal of God's covenant. 33:1-40:38

EXODUS

A new king oppresses
the growing number of Israelites.

1 These are the names of the sons of
Israel[a] who went to Egypt with Jacob, each with his family: 2Reuben,
Simeon, Levi and Judah; 3Issachar, Zebulun and Benjamin; 4Dan and Naphtali;
Gad and Asher. 5The descendants of
Jacob numbered seventy[a] in all;[b] Joseph
was already in Egypt.
6Now Joseph and all his brothers and
all that generation died,[c] 7but the Israelites were fruitful and multiplied greatly and became exceedingly numerous,[d]
so that the land was filled with them.
8Then a new king, who did not know
about Joseph, came to power in Egypt.
9"Look," he said to his people, "the
Israelites have become much too numerous[e] for us. 10Come, we must deal
shrewdly[f] with them or they will become even more numerous and, if war
breaks out, will join our enemies, fight
against us and leave the country."[g]
11So they put slave masters[h] over
them to oppress them with forced labor,[i]
and they built Pithom and Rameses[j]
as store cities[k] for Pharaoh. 12But the
more they were oppressed, the more
they multiplied and spread; so the Egyptians came to dread the Israelites 13and
worked them ruthlessly.[l] 14They made
their lives bitter with hard labor in
brick and mortar and with all kinds of
work in the fields; in all their hard labor
the Egyptians used them ruthlessly.[m]

Pharaoh commands that Hebrew
boys be killed at birth.

15The king of Egypt said to the Hebrew
midwives, whose names were Shiph-
rah and Puah, 16"When you help the
Hebrew women in childbirth and observe them on the delivery stool, if it
is a boy, kill him; but if it is a girl, let
her live." 17The midwives, however,
feared[n] God and did not do what the
king of Egypt had told them to do;[o]
they let the boys live. 18Then the king of
Egypt summoned the midwives and
asked them, "Why have you done this?
Why have you let the boys live?"
19The midwives answered Pharaoh,
"Hebrew women are not like Egyptian
women; they are vigorous and give birth
before the midwives arrive."[p]
20So God was kind to the midwives[q]
and the people increased and became
even more numerous. 21And because
the midwives feared God, he gave them
families[r] of their own.
22Then Pharaoh gave this order to all
his people: "Every boy that is born[b]
you must throw into the Nile, but let
every girl live."[s]

Baby Moses is taken from the Nile
and raised by Pharaoh's daughter.

2 Now a man of the house of Levi
married a Levite woman,[t] 2and she
became pregnant and gave birth to a
son. When she saw that he was a fine
child, she hid him for three months.[u]
3But when she could hide him no longer,
she got a papyrus basket for him and
coated it with tar and pitch. Then she
placed the child in it and put it among
the reeds along the bank of the Nile.
4His sister[v] stood at a distance to see
what would happen to him.
5Then Pharaoh's daughter went
down to the Nile to bathe, and her
attendants were walking along the river bank.[w] She saw the basket among
the reeds and sent her slave girl to get
it. 6She opened it and saw the baby.
He was crying, and she felt sorry for
him. "This is one of the Hebrew babies,"
she said.
7Then his sister asked Pharaoh's
daughter, "Shall I go and get one of the
Hebrew women to nurse the baby for
you?"

1:1 [a]Ge 46:8
1:5 [b]Ge 46:26
1:6 [c]Ge 50:26
1:7 [d]Ge 46:3; Dt 26:5; Ac 7:17
1:9 [e]Ps 105:24-25
1:10 [f]Ps 83:3 [g]Ac 7:17-19
1:11 [h]Ex 3:7 [i]Ge 15:13; Ex 2:11; 5:4; 6:6-7 [j]Ge 47:11 [k]1Ki 9:19; 2Ch 8:4
1:13 [l]Dt 4:20
1:14 [m]Ex 2:23; 6:9; Nu 20:15; Ps 81:6; Ac 7:19
1:17 [n]ver 21; Pr 16:6 [o]Da 3:16-18; Ac 4:18-20; 5:29
1:19 [p]Jos 2:4-6; 2Sa 17:20
1:20 [q]ver 12; Pr 11:18; Isa 3:10
1:21 [r]1Sa 2:35; 2Sa 7:11,27-29; 1Ki 11:38
1:22 [s]Ac 7:19
2:1 [t]Ex 6:20; Nu 26:59
2:2 [u]Ac 7:20; Heb 11:23
2:4 [v]Ex 15:20; Nu 26:59
2:5 [w]Ex 7:15; 8:20

a*5* Masoretic Text (see also Gen. 46:27); Dead Sea Scrolls and Septuagint (see also Acts 7:14 and note at Gen. 46:27) *seventy-five* b*22* Masoretic Text; Samaritan Pentateuch, Septuagint and Targums *born to the Hebrews*

KEY PLACES IN EXODUS

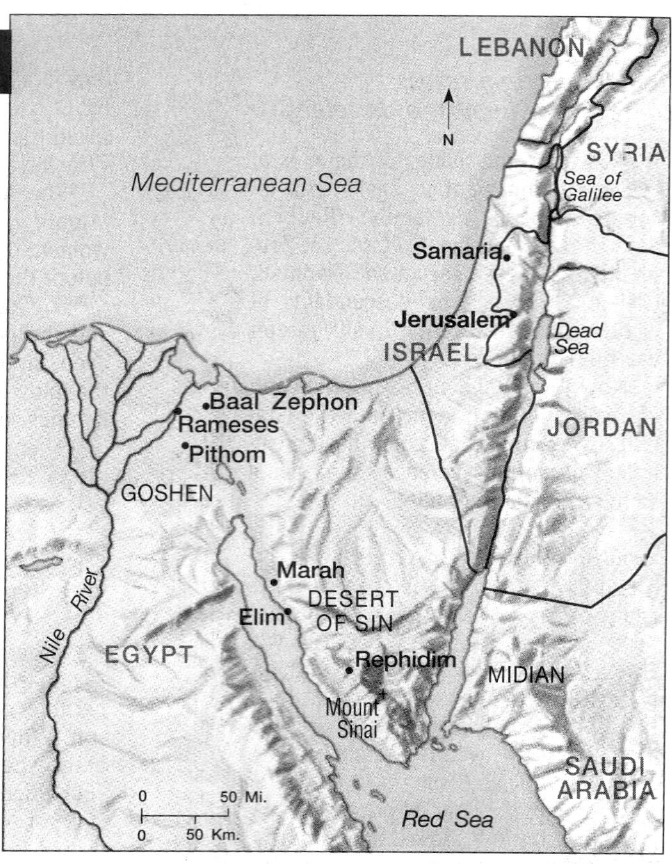

Goshen This area was given to Jacob and his family when they moved to Egypt (Genesis 47:5,6). It became the Hebrews' homeland for 400 years and remained separate from the main Egyptian centers, for Egyptian culture looked down upon shepherds and nomads. As the years passed, Jacob's family grew into a large nation (1:7).

Pithom and Rameses After 400 years, a Pharaoh came to the throne who had no respect for these descendants of Joseph and feared their large numbers. He forced them into slavery in order to oppress and subdue them. Out of their slave labor, the supply cities of Pithom and Rameses were built (1:11).

Midian Moses, an Egyptian prince who was born a Hebrew, killed an Egyptian and fled for his life to Midian. Here he became a shepherd and married a woman named Zipporah. It was while he was here that God commissioned him for the job of leading the Hebrew people out of Egypt (2:15–4:31).

Baal Zephon Slavery was not to last because God planned to deliver his people. After choosing Moses and Aaron to be his spokesmen to Pharaoh, God worked a series of dramatic miracles in the land of Egypt to convince Pharaoh to let the Hebrews go (5:1–12:33). When finally freed, the entire nation set out with the riches of Egypt (12:34-36). One of their first stops was at Baal Zephon (14:1), where Pharaoh, who had changed his mind, chased the Hebrews and trapped them against the Red Sea. But God parted the waters and led the people through the sea on dry land. When Pharaoh's army tried to pursue, the waters collapsed around them, and they were drowned (14:5-31).

Marah Moses now led the people southward. The long trek across the desert brought hot tempers and parched throats for this mass of people. At Marah, the water they found was bitter, but God sweetened it (15:22-25).

Elim As they continued their journey, the Hebrews (now called Israelites) came to Elim, an oasis with 12 springs (15:27).

Desert of Sin Leaving Elim, the people headed into the Desert of Sin. Here the people became hungry, so God provided them with manna that came from heaven and covered the ground each morning (16:1, 13-15). The people ate this manna until they entered the promised land.

Rephidim Moses led the people to Rephidim where they found no water. But God miraculously provided water from a rock (17:1,5,6). Here the Israelites encountered their first test in battle: the Amalekites attacked and were defeated (17:9-13). Moses' father-in-law, Jethro, then arrived on the scene with some sound advice on delegating responsibilities (18).

Mount Sinai God had previously appeared to Moses on this mountain and commissioned him to lead Israel (3:1,2). Now Moses returned with the people God had asked him to lead. For almost a year the people had camped at the foot of Mount Sinai. During this time God gave them his Ten Commandments as well as other laws for right living. He also provided the blueprint for building the tabernacle (19–40).

God was forging a holy nation, prepared to live for and serve him alone.

8“Yes, go,” she answered. And the girl went and got the baby’s mother. 9Pharaoh’s daughter said to her, “Take this baby and nurse him for me, and I will pay you.” So the woman took the baby and nursed him. 10When the child grew older, she took him to Pharaoh’s daughter and he became her son. She named him Moses,[c] saying, “I drew him out of the water.”

Moses kills an Egyptian and flees to Midian.

11One day, after Moses had grown up, he went out to where his own people[a] were and watched them at their hard labor. He saw an Egyptian beating a Hebrew, one of his own people. 12Glancing this way and that and seeing no one, he killed the Egyptian and hid him in the sand. 13The next day he went out and saw two Hebrews fighting. He asked the one in the wrong, “Why are you hitting your fellow Hebrew?”[b]

14The man said, “Who made you ruler and judge over us?[c] Are you thinking of killing me as you killed the Egyptian?” Then Moses was afraid and thought, “What I did must have become known.”

15When Pharaoh heard of this, he tried to kill Moses, but Moses fled from Pharaoh and went to live in Midian,[d] where he sat down by a well. 16Now a priest of Midian[e] had seven daughters, and they came to draw water[f] and fill the troughs to water their father’s flock. 17Some shepherds came along and drove them away, but Moses got up and came to their rescue and watered their flock.[g]

18When the girls returned to Reuel[h] their father, he asked them, “Why have you returned so early today?”

19They answered, “An Egyptian rescued us from the shepherds. He even drew water for us and watered the flock.”

20“And where is he?” he asked his daughters. “Why did you leave him? Invite him to have something to eat.”[i]

Moses marries Zipporah.

21Moses agreed to stay with the man, who gave his daughter Zipporah[j] to Moses in marriage. 22Zipporah gave birth to a son, and Moses named him Gershom,[d] saying, “I have become an alien[k] in a foreign land.”

23During that long period,[l] the king of Egypt died. The Israelites groaned in their slavery and cried out, and their cry[m] for help because of their slavery went up to God. 24God heard their groaning and he remembered his covenant[n] with Abraham, with Isaac and with Jacob. 25So God looked on the Israelites and was concerned[o] about them.

From within a burning bush God calls Moses.

3 Now Moses was tending the flock of Jethro[p] his father-in-law, the priest of Midian, and he led the flock to the far side of the desert and came to Horeb,[q] the mountain[r] of God. 2There the angel of the LORD[s] appeared to him in flames of fire from within a bush.[t] Moses saw that though the bush was on fire it did not burn up. 3So Moses thought, “I will go over and see this strange sight—why the bush does not burn up.”

4When the LORD saw that he had gone over to look, God called to him from within the bush, “Moses! Moses!”

And Moses said, “Here I am.”

5“Do not come any closer,” God said. “Take off your sandals, for the place where you are standing is holy ground.”[u] 6Then he said, “I am the God of your father, the God of Abraham, the God of Isaac and the God of Jacob.”[v] At this, Moses hid his face, because he was afraid to look at God.

7The LORD said, “I have indeed seen the misery of my people in Egypt. I have heard them crying out because of their slave drivers, and I am concerned[w]

2:11 [a]Ac 7:23; Heb 11:24-26
2:13 [b]Ac 7:26
2:14 [c]Ac 7:27*
2:15 [d]Ac 7:29; Heb 11:27
2:16 [e]Ex 3:1 [f]Ge 24:11
2:17 [g]Ge 29:10
2:18 [h]Nu 10:29
2:20 [i]Ge 31:54
2:21 [j]Ex 18:2
2:22 [k]Ex 18:3-4; Heb 11:13
2:23 [l]Ac 7:30 [m]Ex 3:7,9; Dt 26:7; Jas 5:4
2:24 [n]Ex 6:5; Ps 105:10,42
2:25 [o]Ex 3:7; 4:31
3:1 [p]Ex 2:18 [q]1Ki 19:8 [r]Ex 18:5
3:2 [s]Ge 16:7 [t]Dt 33:16; Mk 12:26; Ac 7:30
3:5 [u]Ge 28:17; Jos 5:15; Ac 7:33*
3:6 [v]Ex 4:5; Mt 22:32*; Mk 12:26*; Lk 20:37*; Ac 7:32*
3:7 [w]Ex 2:25

c *10* *Moses* sounds like the Hebrew for *draw out.*
d *22* *Gershom* sounds like the Hebrew for *an alien there.*

about their suffering. 8So I have come
down[a] to rescue them from the hand
of the Egyptians and to bring them up
out of that land into a good and spacious
land, a land flowing with milk and
honey[b]—the home of the Canaanites,
Hittites, Amorites, Perizzites, Hivites
and Jebusites.[c] 9And now the cry of the
Israelites has reached me, and I have
seen the way the Egyptians are
oppressing[d] them. 10So now, go. I am
sending you to Pharaoh to bring my
people the Israelites out of Egypt."[e]
11But Moses said to God, "Who am
I,[f] that I should go to Pharaoh and
bring the Israelites out of Egypt?"
12And God said, "I will be with you.[g]
And this will be the sign to you that it is
I who have sent you: When you have
brought the people out of Egypt, you[e]
will worship God on this mountain."
13Moses said to God, "Suppose I go
to the Israelites and say to them, 'The
God of your fathers has sent me to
you,' and they ask me, 'What is his
name?' Then what shall I tell them?"
14God said to Moses, "I AM WHO I
AM.[f] This is what you are to say to the
Israelites: 'I AM[h] has sent me to you.'"
15God also said to Moses, "Say to the
Israelites, 'The LORD,[g] the God of your
fathers—the God of Abraham, the God
of Isaac and the God of Jacob—has sent
me to you.' This is my name[i] forever,
the name by which I am to be remembered from generation to generation.
16"Go, assemble the elders[j] of Israel
and say to them, 'The LORD, the God
of your fathers—the God of Abraham,
Isaac and Jacob—appeared to me and
said: I have watched over you and have
seen what has been done to you in
Egypt. 17And I have promised to bring
you up out of your misery in Egypt[k] into
the land of the Canaanites, Hittites,
Amorites, Perizzites, Hivites and
Jebusites—a land flowing with milk
and honey.'
18"The elders of Israel will listen[l] to
you. Then you and the elders are to go
to the king of Egypt and say to him,
'The LORD, the God of the Hebrews,

3:8 [a]Ge 50:24 [b]ver 17; Ex 13:5; Dt 1:25 [c]Ge 15:18-21
3:9 [d]Ex 1:14; 2:23
3:10 [e]Mic 6:4
3:11 [f]Ex 6:12,30; 1Sa 18:18
3:12 [g]Ge 31:3; Jos 1:5; Ro 8:31
3:14 [h]Ex 6:2-3; Jn 8:58; Heb 13:8
3:15 [i]Ps 135:13; Hos 12:5
3:16 [j]Ex 4:29
3:17 [k]Ge 15:16; Jos 24:11
3:18 [l]Ex 4:1,8,31 [m]Ex 5:1,3
3:19 [n]Ex 4:21; 5:2
3:20 [o]Ex 6:1,6; 9:15 [p]Dt 6:22; Ne 9:10; Ac 7:36 [q]Ex 12:31-33
3:21 [r]Ex 12:36 [s]Ps 105:37
3:22 [t]Ex 11:2 [u]Eze 39:10
4:1 [v]Ex 3:18; 6:30
4:2 [w]ver 17,20
4:5 [x]Ex 19:9
4:6 [y]Nu 12:10; 2Ki 5:1,27

has met with us. Let us take a three-
day journey into the desert to offer sacrifices[m] to the LORD our God.' 19But I
know that the king of Egypt will not
let you go unless a mighty hand[n] compels him. 20So I will stretch out my
hand[o] and strike the Egyptians with all
the wonders[p] that I will perform among
them. After that, he will let you go.[q]
21"And I will make the Egyptians
favorably disposed[r] toward this people,
so that when you leave you will not go
empty-handed.[s] 22Every woman is to
ask her neighbor and any woman living in her house for articles of silver
and gold[t] and for clothing, which you
will put on your sons and daughters.
And so you will plunder[u] the Egyptians."

Moses' staff becomes a snake.

4 Moses answered, "What if they do
not believe me or listen[v] to me and
say, 'The LORD did not appear to you'?"
2Then the LORD said to him, "What
is that in your hand?"
"A staff,"[w] he replied.
3The LORD said, "Throw it on the
ground."
Moses threw it on the ground and it
became a snake, and he ran from it.
4Then the LORD said to him, "Reach out
your hand and take it by the tail." So
Moses reached out and took hold of the
snake and it turned back into a staff in
his hand. 5"This," said the LORD, "is so
that they may believe[x] that the LORD,
the God of their fathers—the God of
Abraham, the God of Isaac and the
God of Jacob—has appeared to you."

Moses' hand becomes leprous.

6Then the LORD said, "Put your hand
inside your cloak." So Moses put his
hand into his cloak, and when he took
it out, it was leprous,[h] like snow.[y]

[e] *12* The Hebrew is plural. [f] *14* Or *I WILL BE WHAT I WILL BE* [g] *15* The Hebrew for *LORD* sounds like and may be derived from the Hebrew for *I AM* in verse 14. [h] *6* The Hebrew word was used for various diseases affecting the skin—not necessarily leprosy.

7“Now put it back into your cloak,”
he said. So Moses put his hand back
into his cloak, and when he took it out,
it was restored,[a] like the rest of his flesh.
8Then the LORD said, “If they do not
believe you or pay attention to the first
miraculous sign, they may believe the
second. 9But if they do not believe
these two signs or listen to you, take
some water from the Nile and pour it
on the dry ground. The water you take
from the river will become blood[b] on
the ground.”
10Moses said to the LORD, “O Lord, I
have never been eloquent, neither in
the past nor since you have spoken to
your servant. I am slow of speech and
tongue.”[c]
11The LORD said to him, “Who gave
man his mouth? Who makes him deaf
or mute? Who gives him sight or makes
him blind?[d] Is it not I, the LORD? 12Now
go; I will help you speak and will teach
you what to say.”[e]
13But Moses said, “O Lord, please
send someone else to do it.”

Aaron is appointed as Moses' spokesman.

14Then the LORD's anger burned
against Moses and he said, “What
about your brother, Aaron the Levite?
I know he can speak well. He is already on his way to meet[f] you, and his
heart will be glad when he sees you.
15You shall speak to him and put words
in his mouth;[g] I will help both of you
speak and will teach you what to do.
16He will speak to the people for you,
and it will be as if he were your mouth[h]
and as if you were God to him. 17But
take this staff[i] in your hand so you can
perform miraculous signs[j] with it.”

Moses leaves Jethro and returns to Egypt.

18Then Moses went back to Jethro
his father-in-law and said to him, “Let
me go back to my own people in Egypt
to see if any of them are still alive.”

4:7 [a]Nu 12:13-15; Dt 32:39; 2Ki 5:14; Mt 8:3
4:9 [b]Ex 7:17-21
4:10 [c]Ex 6:12; Jer 1:6
4:11 [d]Ps 94:9; Mt 11:5
4:12 [e]Isa 50:4; Jer 1:9; Mt 10:19-20; Mk 13:11; Lk 12:12; 21:14-15
4:14 [f]ver 27
4:15 [g]Nu 23:5,12,16
4:16 [h]Ex 7:1-2
4:17 [i]ver 2 [j]Ex 7:9-21
4:19 [k]Ex 2:15 [l]Ex 2:23
4:20 [m]Ex 17:9; Nu 20:8-9,11
4:21 [n]Ex 3:19,20 [o]Ex 7:3,13; 9:12,35;14:4,8; Dt 2:30; Isa 63:17; Jn 12:40; Ro 9:18
4:22 [p]Isa 63:16; 64:8; Jer 31:9; Hos 11:1; Ro 9:4
4:23 [q]Ex 5:1; 7:16 [r]Ex 11:5; 12:12,29
4:24 [s]Nu 22:22
4:25 [t]Ge 17:14; Jos 5:2,3
4:27 [u]Ex 3:1 [v]ver 14
4:28 [w]ver 8-9,16
4:29 [x]Ex 3:16
4:31 [y]ver 8; Ex 3:18 [z]Ex 2:25

Jethro said, “Go, and I wish you well.”
19Now the LORD had said to Moses
in Midian, “Go back to Egypt, for all
the men who wanted to kill[k] you are
dead.[l]” 20So Moses took his wife and
sons, put them on a donkey and started
back to Egypt. And he took the staff[m]
of God in his hand.
21The LORD said to Moses, “When you
return to Egypt, see that you perform
before Pharaoh all the wonders[n] I have
given you the power to do. But I will
harden his heart[o] so that he will not
let the people go. 22Then say to Pharaoh, ‘This is what the LORD says: Israel
is my firstborn son,[p] 23and I told you,
“Let my son go,[q] so he may worship
me.” But you refused to let him go; so
I will kill your firstborn son.’ ”[r]
24At a lodging place on the way, the
LORD met ⌊Moses⌋[i] and was about to
kill[s] him. 25But Zipporah took a flint
knife, cut off her son's foreskin[t] and
touched ⌊Moses'⌋ feet with it.[j] “Surely
you are a bridegroom of blood to me,”
she said. 26So the LORD let him alone.
(At that time she said “bridegroom of
blood,” referring to circumcision.)
27The LORD said to Aaron, “Go into the
desert to meet Moses.” So he met Moses
at the mountain[u] of God and kissed[v]
him. 28Then Moses told Aaron everything the LORD had sent him to say,[w]
and also about all the miraculous signs
he had commanded him to perform.
29Moses and Aaron brought together
all the elders[x] of the Israelites, 30and
Aaron told them everything the LORD
had said to Moses. He also performed
the signs before the people, 31and they
believed.[y] And when they heard that
the LORD was concerned[z] about them
and had seen their misery, they bowed
down and worshiped.

Pharaoh commands the Israelites to make bricks without straw.

5 Afterward Moses and Aaron went
to Pharaoh and said, “This is what

[i]*24* Or ⌊*Moses' son*⌋; Hebrew *him* [j]*25* Or *and drew near* ⌊*Moses'*⌋ *feet*

the LORD, the God of Israel, says: 'Let
my people go, so that they may hold a
festival[a] to me in the desert.'"
2Pharaoh said, "Who is the LORD,[b]
that I should obey him and let Israel go?
I do not know the LORD and I will not let
Israel go."[c]
3Then they said, "The God of the
Hebrews has met with us. Now let us
take a three-day journey into the desert
to offer sacrifices to the LORD our God,
or he may strike us with plagues[d] or
with the sword."
4But the king of Egypt said, "Moses
and Aaron, why are you taking the
people away from their labor?[e] Get back
to your work!" 5Then Pharaoh said,
"Look, the people of the land are now
numerous,[f] and you are stopping them
from working."
6That same day Pharaoh gave this
order to the slave drivers and foremen
in charge of the people: 7"You are no
longer to supply the people with straw
for making bricks; let them go and
gather their own straw. 8But require
them to make the same number of
bricks as before; don't reduce the quota.
They are lazy; that is why they are crying out, 'Let us go and sacrifice to our
God.' 9Make the work harder for the
men so that they keep working and pay
no attention to lies."
10Then the slave drivers and the foremen went out and said to the people,
"This is what Pharaoh says: 'I will not
give you any more straw. 11Go and get
your own straw wherever you can find
it, but your work will not be reduced at
all.'" 12So the people scattered all over
Egypt to gather stubble to use for straw.
13The slave drivers kept pressing them,
saying, "Complete the work required
of you for each day, just as when you
had straw." 14The Israelite foremen
appointed by Pharaoh's slave drivers
were beaten[g] and were asked, "Why
didn't you meet your quota of bricks
yesterday or today, as before?"
15Then the Israelite foremen went
and appealed to Pharaoh: "Why have
you treated your servants this way?
16Your servants are given no straw, yet
we are told, 'Make bricks!' Your servants are being beaten, but the fault is
with your own people."
17Pharaoh said, "Lazy, that's what you
are—lazy![h] That is why you keep saying, 'Let us go and sacrifice to the LORD.'
18Now get to work. You will not be
given any straw, yet you must produce
your full quota of bricks."
19The Israelite foremen realized they
were in trouble when they were told,
"You are not to reduce the number of
bricks required of you for each day."
20When they left Pharaoh, they found
Moses and Aaron waiting to meet them,
21and they said, "May the LORD look
upon you and judge you! You have made
us a stench[i] to Pharaoh and his officials
and have put a sword in their hand to
kill us."[j]
22Moses returned to the LORD and
said, "O Lord, why have you brought
trouble upon this people?[k] Is this why
you sent me? 23Ever since I went to
Pharaoh to speak in your name, he has
brought trouble upon this people, and
you have not rescued[l] your people at
all."

Renewal of God's covenant.

6 Then the LORD said to Moses,
"Now you will see what I will do
to Pharaoh: Because of my mighty
hand[m] he will let them go;[n] because of
my mighty hand he will drive them
out of his country."[o]
2God also said to Moses, "I am the
LORD. 3I appeared to Abraham, to Isaac
and to Jacob as God Almighty,[k][p] but by
my name[q] the LORD[l][r] I did not make
myself known to them.[m] 4I also established my covenant[s] with them to give
them the land of Canaan, where they
lived as aliens.[t] 5Moreover, I have
heard the groaning[u] of the Israelites,
whom the Egyptians are enslaving,
and I have remembered my covenant.

5:1 [a]Ex 3:18
5:2 [b]2Ki 18:35; Job 21:15 [c]Ex 3:19
5:3 [d]Ex 3:18
5:4 [e]Ex 1:11
5:5 [f]Ex 1:7,9
5:14 [g]Isa 10:24
5:17 [h]ver 8
5:21 [i]Ge 34:30 [j]Ex 14:11
5:22 [k]Nu 11:11
5:23 [l]Jer 4:10
6:1 [m]Ex 3:19 [n]Ex 3:20 [o]Ex 12:31, 33,39
6:3 [p]Ge 17:1 [q]Ps 68:4; 83:18; Isa 52:6 [r]Ex 3:14
6:4 [s]Ge 15:18 [t]Ge 28:4,13
6:5 [u]Ex 2:23

k3 Hebrew *El-Shaddai* l3 See note at Exodus 3:15.
m3 Or *Almighty, and by my name the LORD did I not let myself be known to them?*

6"Therefore, say to the Israelites: 'I am the LORD, and I will bring you out from under the yoke of the Egyptians. I will free you from being slaves to them, and I will redeem[a] you with an outstretched arm[b] and with mighty acts of judgment. 7I will take you as my own people, and I will be your God.[c] Then you will know[d] that I am the LORD your God, who brought you out from under the yoke of the Egyptians. 8And I will bring you to the land[e] I swore with uplifted hand[f] to give to Abraham, to Isaac and to Jacob.[g] I will give it to you as a possession. I am the LORD.'"

9Moses reported this to the Israelites, but they did not listen to him because of their discouragement and cruel bondage.

10Then the LORD said to Moses, 11"Go, tell Pharaoh king of Egypt to let the Israelites go out of his country."

12But Moses said to the LORD, "If the Israelites will not listen to me, why would Pharaoh listen to me, since I speak with faltering lips[n]?"[h]

Family records of Reuben, Simeon and Levi.

13Now the LORD spoke to Moses and Aaron about the Israelites and Pharaoh king of Egypt, and he commanded them to bring the Israelites out of Egypt.

14These were the heads of their families[o]:[i]

The sons of Reuben the firstborn son of Israel were Hanoch and Pallu, Hezron and Carmi. These were the clans of Reuben.

15The sons of Simeon[j] were Jemuel, Jamin, Ohad, Jakin, Zohar and Shaul the son of a Canaanite woman. These were the clans of Simeon.

16These were the names of the sons of Levi according to their records: Gershon,[k] Kohath and Merari.[l] Levi lived 137 years.

17The sons of Gershon, by clans, were Libni and Shimei.[m]

18The sons of Kohath were Amram, Izhar, Hebron and Uzziel.[n] Kohath lived 133 years.

19The sons of Merari were Mahli and Mushi.[o]

These were the clans of Levi according to their records.

20Amram married his father's sister Jochebed, who bore him Aaron and Moses.[p] Amram lived 137 years.

21The sons of Izhar[q] were Korah, Nepheg and Zicri.

22The sons of Uzziel were Mishael, Elzaphan[r] and Sithri.

23Aaron married Elisheba, daughter of Amminadab[s] and sister of Nahshon, and she bore him Nadab and Abihu,[t] Eleazar[u] and Ithamar.[v]

24The sons of Korah[w] were Assir, Elkanah and Abiasaph. These were the Korahite clans.

25Eleazar son of Aaron married one of the daughters of Putiel, and she bore him Phinehas.[x]

These were the heads of the Levite families, clan by clan.

26It was this same Aaron and Moses to whom the LORD said, "Bring the Israelites out of Egypt by their divisions."[y] 27They were the ones who spoke to Pharaoh king of Egypt about bringing the Israelites out of Egypt. It was the same Moses and Aaron.

God encourages Moses.

28Now when the LORD spoke to Moses in Egypt, 29he said to him, "I am the LORD.[z] Tell Pharaoh king of Egypt everything I tell you."

30But Moses said to the LORD, "Since I speak with faltering lips,[a] why would Pharaoh listen to me?"

7 Then the LORD said to Moses, "See, I have made you like God[b] to Pharaoh, and your brother Aaron will be your prophet. 2You are to say

6:6 [a]Dt 7:8; 1Ch 17:21 [b]Dt 26:8
6:7 [c]Dt 4:20; 2Sa 7:24 [d]Ex 16:12; Isa 41:20
6:8 [e]Ge 15:18; 26:3 [f]Ge 14:22 [g]Ps 136:21-22
6:12 [h]ver 30; Ex 4:10; Jer 1:6
6:14 [i]Ge 46:9
6:15 [j]Ge 46:10; 1Ch 4:24
6:16 [k]Ge 46:11 [l]Nu 3:17
6:17 [m]1Ch 6:17
6:18 [n]1Ch 6:2,18
6:19 [o]1Ch 6:19; 23:21
6:20 [p]Ex 2:1-2; Nu 26:59
6:21 [q]1Ch 6:38
6:22 [r]Lev 10:4; Nu 3:30
6:23 [s]Ru 4:19,20 [t]Lev 10:1 [u]Nu 3:2,32 [v]Nu 26:60
6:24 [w]Nu 26:11
6:25 [x]Nu 25:7,11; Jos 24:33; Ps 106:30
6:26 [y]Ex 7:4; 12:17,41,51
6:29 [z]ver 11; Ex 7:2
6:30 [a]ver 12; Ex 4:10
7:1 [b]Ex 4:16

n *12* Hebrew *I am uncircumcised of lips*; also in verse 30 o *14* The Hebrew for *families* here and in verse 25 refers to units larger than clans.

everything I command you, and your
brother Aaron is to tell Pharaoh to let
the Israelites go out of his country.
3But I will harden Pharaoh's heart,[a] and
though I multiply my miraculous signs
and wonders in Egypt, 4he will not listen[b] to you. Then I will lay my hand
on Egypt and with mighty acts of judgment[c] I will bring out my divisions, my
people the Israelites. 5And the Egyptians
will know that I am the LORD[d] when I
stretch out my hand[e] against Egypt and
bring the Israelites out of it."
6Moses and Aaron did just as the
LORD commanded[f] them. 7Moses was
eighty years old[g] and Aaron eighty-three
when they spoke to Pharaoh.

Aaron's staff becomes a snake.

8The LORD said to Moses and Aaron,
9"When Pharaoh says to you, 'Perform a
miracle,[h]' then say to Aaron, 'Take your
staff and throw it down before Pharaoh,'
and it will become a snake."[i]
10So Moses and Aaron went to
Pharaoh and did just as the LORD commanded. Aaron threw his staff down
in front of Pharaoh and his officials,
and it became a snake. 11Pharaoh then
summoned wise men and sorcerers,
and the Egyptian magicians[j] also did the
same things by their secret arts:[k] 12Each
one threw down his staff and it became
a snake. But Aaron's staff swallowed
up their staffs. 13Yet Pharaoh's heart[l]
became hard and he would not listen to
them, just as the LORD had said.

First plague: Waters become blood.

14Then the LORD said to Moses,
"Pharaoh's heart is unyielding;[m] he
refuses to let the people go. 15Go to
Pharaoh in the morning as he goes out
to the water. Wait on the bank of the
Nile to meet him, and take in your
hand the staff that was changed into a
snake. 16Then say to him, 'The LORD,
the God of the Hebrews, has sent me to
say to you: Let my people go, so that
they may worship[n] me in the desert.
But until now you have not listened.

7:3 [a]Ex 4:21; 11:9
7:4 [b]Ex 11:9 [c]Ex 3:20; 6:6
7:5 [d]ver 17; Ex 8:19,22 [e]Ex 3:20
7:6 [f]ver 2
7:7 [g]Dt 31:2; 34:7; Ac 7:23,30
7:9 [h]Isa 7:11; Jn 2:18 [i]Ex 4:2-5
7:11 [j]Ge 41:8; 2Ti 3:8 [k]ver 22; Ex 8:7,18
7:13 [l]Ex 4:21
7:14 [m]Ex 8:15,32; 10:1,20,27
7:16 [n]Ex 3:18; 5:1,3
7:17 [o]Ex 5:2 [p]Ex 4:9; Rev 11:6; 16:4
7:18 [q]ver 21,24
7:19 [r]Ex 8:5-6,16; 9:22; 10:12,21; 14:21
7:20 [s]Ex 17:5 [t]Ps 78:44; 105:29
7:22 [u]ver 11
8:1 [v]Ex 3:12,18; 4:23
8:3 [w]Ex 10:6

17This is what the LORD says: By this
you will know that I am the LORD:[o]
With the staff that is in my hand I will
strike the water of the Nile, and it will
be changed into blood.[p] 18The fish in
the Nile will die, and the river will
stink; the Egyptians will not be able to
drink its water.'"[q]
19The LORD said to Moses, "Tell Aaron,
'Take your staff and stretch out your
hand[r] over the waters of Egypt—over
the streams and canals, over the ponds
and all the reservoirs'—and they will
turn to blood. Blood will be everywhere in Egypt, even in the wooden
buckets and stone jars."
20Moses and Aaron did just as the
LORD had commanded. He raised his
staff in the presence of Pharaoh and
his officials and struck the water of the
Nile,[s] and all the water was changed
into blood.[t] 21The fish in the Nile died,
and the river smelled so bad that the
Egyptians could not drink its water.
Blood was everywhere in Egypt.
22But the Egyptian magicians did the
same things by their secret arts,[u] and
Pharaoh's heart became hard; he would
not listen to Moses and Aaron, just as
the LORD had said. 23Instead, he turned
and went into his palace, and did not
take even this to heart. 24And all the
Egyptians dug along the Nile to get
drinking water, because they could not
drink the water of the river.

Second plague: Frogs.

8 25Seven days passed after the LORD
struck the Nile. 1Then the LORD said
to Moses, "Go to Pharaoh and say to
him, 'This is what the LORD says: Let my
people go, so that they may worship[v]
me. 2If you refuse to let them go, I will
plague your whole country with frogs.
3The Nile will teem with frogs. They
will come up into your palace and your
bedroom and onto your bed, into the
houses of your officials and on your people,[w] and into your ovens and kneading
troughs. 4The frogs will go up on you
and your people and all your officials.'"

5Then the LORD said to Moses, "Tell Aaron, 'Stretch out your hand with your staff[a] over the streams and canals and ponds, and make frogs come up on the land of Egypt.'"

6So Aaron stretched out his hand over the waters of Egypt, and the frogs[b] came up and covered the land. 7But the magicians did the same things by their secret arts;[c] they also made frogs come up on the land of Egypt.

8Pharaoh summoned Moses and Aaron and said, "Pray[d] to the LORD to take the frogs away from me and my people, and I will let your people go to offer sacrifices[e] to the LORD."

9Moses said to Pharaoh, "I leave to you the honor of setting the time for me to pray for you and your officials and your people that you and your houses may be rid of the frogs, except for those that remain in the Nile."

10"Tomorrow," Pharaoh said.

Moses replied, "It will be as you say, so that you may know there is no one like the LORD our God.[f] 11The frogs will leave you and your houses, your officials and your people; they will remain only in the Nile."

12After Moses and Aaron left Pharaoh, Moses cried out to the LORD about the frogs he had brought on Pharaoh. 13And the LORD did what Moses asked. The frogs died in the houses, in the courtyards and in the fields. 14They were piled into heaps, and the land reeked of them. 15But when Pharaoh saw that there was relief, he hardened his heart[g] and would not listen to Moses and Aaron, just as the LORD had said.

Third plague: Gnats.

16Then the LORD said to Moses, "Tell Aaron, 'Stretch out your staff and strike the dust of the ground,' and throughout the land of Egypt the dust will become gnats." 17They did this, and when Aaron stretched out his hand with the staff and struck the dust of the ground, gnats[h] came upon men and animals. All the dust throughout the land of Egypt became gnats. 18But when the magicians[i] tried to produce gnats by their secret arts,[j] they could not. And the gnats were on men and animals.

19The magicians said to Pharaoh, "This is the finger[k] of God." But Pharaoh's heart was hard and he would not listen, just as the LORD had said.

Fourth plague: Flies.

20Then the LORD said to Moses, "Get up early in the morning[l] and confront Pharaoh as he goes to the water and say to him, 'This is what the LORD says: Let my people go, so that they may worship[m] me. 21If you do not let my people go, I will send swarms of flies on you and your officials, on your people and into your houses. The houses of the Egyptians will be full of flies, and even the ground where they are.

22"'But on that day I will deal differently with the land of Goshen, where my people live;[n] no swarms of flies will be there, so that you will know[o] that I, the LORD, am in this land. 23I will make a distinction[p] between my people and your people. This miraculous sign will occur tomorrow.'"

24And the LORD did this. Dense swarms of flies poured into Pharaoh's palace and into the houses of his officials, and throughout Egypt the land was ruined by the flies.[p]

25Then Pharaoh summoned[q] Moses and Aaron and said, "Go, sacrifice to your God here in the land."

26But Moses said, "That would not be right. The sacrifices we offer the LORD our God would be detestable to the Egyptians.[r] And if we offer sacrifices that are detestable in their eyes, will they not stone us? 27We must take a three-day journey into the desert to offer sacrifices[s] to the LORD our God, as he commands us."

28Pharaoh said, "I will let you go to offer sacrifices to the LORD your God in

8:5 [a]Ex 7:19
8:6 [b]Ps 78:45; 105:30
8:7 [c]Ex 7:11
8:8 [d]ver 28; Ex 9:28; 10:17 [e]ver 25
8:10 [f]Ex 9:14; Dt 4:35; 33:26; 2Sa 7:22; 1Ch 17:20; Ps 86:8; Isa 46:9; Jer 10:6
8:15 [g]Ex 7:14
8:17 [h]Ps 105:31
8:18 [i]Ex 9:11; Da 5:8 [j]Ex 7:11
8:19 [k]Ex 7:5; 10:7; Ps 8:3; Lk 11:20
8:20 [l]Ex 7:15; 9:13 [m]ver 1; Ex 3:18
8:22 [n]Ex 9:4,6,26; 10:23; 11:7 [o]Ex 7:5; 9:29
8:24 [p]Ps 78:45; 105:31
8:25 [q]ver 8; Ex 9:27
8:26 [r]Ge 43:32; 46:34
8:27 [s]Ex 3:18

p23 Septuagint and Vulgate; Hebrew *will put a deliverance*

the desert, but you must not go very
far. Now pray[a] for me."
29 Moses answered, "As soon as I
leave you, I will pray to the LORD, and
tomorrow the flies will leave Pharaoh
and his officials and his people. Only be
sure that Pharaoh does not act deceitfully[b] again by not letting the people go
to offer sacrifices to the LORD."
30 Then Moses left Pharaoh and prayed
to the LORD,[c] 31 and the LORD did what
Moses asked: The flies left Pharaoh
and his officials and his people; not a fly
remained. 32 But this time also Pharaoh
hardened his heart[d] and would not let
the people go.

Fifth plague: Death of livestock.

9 Then the LORD said to Moses, "Go
to Pharaoh and say to him, 'This is
what the LORD, the God of the Hebrews,
says: "Let my people go, so that they
may worship[e] me." 2 If you refuse to let
them go and continue to hold them
back, 3 the hand[f] of the LORD will bring a
terrible plague on your livestock in the
field—on your horses and donkeys and
camels and on your cattle and sheep
and goats. 4 But the LORD will make a
distinction between the livestock of
Israel and that of Egypt,[g] so that no
animal belonging to the Israelites will
die.'"
5 The LORD set a time and said,
"Tomorrow the LORD will do this in the
land." 6 And the next day the LORD did
it: All the livestock[h] of the Egyptians
died,[i] but not one animal belonging to
the Israelites died. 7 Pharaoh sent men
to investigate and found that not even
one of the animals of the Israelites had
died. Yet his heart was unyielding and
he would not let the people go.[j]

Sixth plague: Boils.

8 Then the LORD said to Moses and
Aaron, "Take handfuls of soot from a
furnace and have Moses toss it into
the air in the presence of Pharaoh. 9 It
will become fine dust over the whole
land of Egypt, and festering boils[k] will
break out on men and animals throughout the land."
10 So they took soot from a furnace
and stood before Pharaoh. Moses tossed
it into the air, and festering boils broke
out on men and animals. 11 The magicians[l] could not stand before Moses
because of the boils that were on them
and on all the Egyptians. 12 But the
LORD hardened Pharaoh's heart[m] and he
would not listen to Moses and Aaron,
just as the LORD had said to Moses.

Seventh plague: Hail.

13 Then the LORD said to Moses, "Get
up early in the morning, confront Pharaoh and say to him, 'This is what the
LORD, the God of the Hebrews, says:
Let my people go, so that they may
worship[n] me, 14 or this time I will send
the full force of my plagues against you
and against your officials and your people, so you may know[o] that there is no
one like[p] me in all the earth. 15 For by
now I could have stretched out my
hand and struck you and your people[q]
with a plague that would have wiped
you off the earth. 16 But I have raised
you up[q] for this very purpose,[r] that I
might show you my power[s] and that
my name might be proclaimed in all
the earth. 17 You still set yourself against
my people and will not let them go.
18 Therefore, at this time tomorrow I
will send the worst hailstorm[t] that has
ever fallen on Egypt, from the day it
was founded till now.[u] 19 Give an order
now to bring your livestock and everything you have in the field to a place of
shelter, because the hail will fall on
every man and animal that has not
been brought in and is still out in the
field, and they will die.'"
20 Those officials of Pharaoh who
feared[v] the word of the LORD hurried
to bring their slaves and their livestock
inside. 21 But those who ignored the
word of the LORD left their slaves and
livestock in the field.

8:28 [a]ver 8; Ex 9:28; 1Ki 13:6
8:29 [b]ver 15
8:30 [c]ver 12
8:32 [d]ver 8,15; Ex 4:21
9:1 [e]Ex 8:1
9:3 [f]Ex 7:4
9:4 [g]ver 26; Ex 8:22
9:6 [h]ver 19-21; Ex 11:5 [i]Ps 78:48-50
9:7 [j]Ex 7:14; 8:32
9:9 [k]Dt 28:27,35; Rev 16:2
9:11 [l]Ex 8:18
9:12 [m]Ex 4:21
9:13 [n]Ex 8:20
9:14 [o]Ex 8:10 [p]2Sa 7:22; 1Ch 17:20; Ps 86:8; Isa 46:9; Jer 10:6
9:15 [q]Ex 3:20
9:16 [r]Pr 16:4 [s]Ro 9:17*
9:18 [t]ver 23 [u]ver 24
9:20 [v]Pr 13:13

q16 Or *have spared you*

22 Then the LORD said to Moses,
"Stretch out your hand toward the sky
so that hail will fall all over Egypt—
on men and animals and on everything growing in the fields of Egypt."
23 When Moses stretched out his staff
toward the sky, the LORD sent thunder[a]
and hail,[b] and lightning flashed down
to the ground. So the LORD rained hail
on the land of Egypt; 24 hail fell and
lightning flashed back and forth. It was
the worst storm in all the land of Egypt
since it had become a nation.
25 Throughout Egypt hail struck everything in the fields—both men and animals; it beat down everything growing
in the fields and stripped every tree.[c]
26 The only place it did not hail was the
land of Goshen,[d] where the Israelites
were.[e]

27 Then Pharaoh summoned Moses
and Aaron. "This time I have sinned,"[f]
he said to them. "The LORD is in the
right,[g] and I and my people are in the
wrong. 28 Pray[h] to the LORD, for we have
had enough thunder and hail. I will let
you go;[i] you don't have to stay any
longer."

29 Moses replied, "When I have gone
out of the city, I will spread out my
hands[j] in prayer to the LORD. The thunder will stop and there will be no more
hail, so you may know that the earth[k] is
the LORD's. 30 But I know that you and
your officials still do not fear the LORD
God."

31 (The flax and barley[l] were destroyed, since the barley had headed and the
flax was in bloom. 32 The wheat and
spelt, however, were not destroyed,
because they ripen later.)

33 Then Moses left Pharaoh and went
out of the city. He spread out his hands
toward the LORD; the thunder and hail
stopped, and the rain no longer poured
down on the land. 34 When Pharaoh
saw that the rain and hail and thunder
had stopped, he sinned again: He and
his officials hardened their hearts. 35 So
Pharaoh's heart[m] was hard and he
would not let the Israelites go, just as
the LORD had said through Moses.

9:23 [a]Ps 18:13 [b]Jos 10:11; Ps 78:47; 105:32; Isa 30:30; Eze 38:22; Rev 8:7; 16:21
9:25 [c]Ps 105:32-33
9:26 [d]ver 4 [e]Ex 8:22; 10:23; 11:7; 12:13
9:27 [f]Ex 10:16 [g]2Ch 12:6; Ps 129:4; La 1:18
9:28 [h]Ex 10:17 [i]Ex 8:8
9:29 [j]1Ki 8:22,38; Ps 143:6; Isa 1:15 [k]Ex 19:5; Ps 24:1; 1Co 10:26
9:31 [l]Ru 1:22; 2:23
9:35 [m]Ex 4:21
10:1 [n]Ex 4:21 [o]Ex 7:3
10:2 [p]Ex 12:26-27; 13:8,14; Dt 4:9; Ps 44:1; 78:4,5; Joel 1:3
10:3 [q]1Ki 21:29; Jas 4:10; 1Pe 5:6
10:4 [r]Rev 9:3
10:5 [s]Ex 9:32; Joel 1:4
10:7 [t]Ex 23:33; Jos 23:7-13; 1Sa 18:21; Ecc 7:26 [u]Ex 8:19
10:8 [v]Ex 8:8

Eighth plague: Locusts.

10 Then the LORD said to Moses,
"Go to Pharaoh, for I have hardened his heart[n] and the hearts of his
officials so that I may perform these
miraculous signs[o] of mine among them
2 that you may tell your children[p] and
grandchildren how I dealt harshly with
the Egyptians and how I performed my
signs among them, and that you may
know that I am the LORD."

3 So Moses and Aaron went to
Pharaoh and said to him, "This is what
the LORD, the God of the Hebrews, says:
'How long will you refuse to humble[q]
yourself before me? Let my people go,
so that they may worship me. 4 If you
refuse to let them go, I will bring locusts[r] into your country tomorrow.
5 They will cover the face of the ground
so that it cannot be seen. They will
devour what little you have left[s] after
the hail, including every tree that is
growing in your fields. 6 They will fill
your houses and those of all your officials and all the Egyptians—something
neither your fathers nor your forefathers
have ever seen from the day they settled
in this land till now.'" Then Moses
turned and left Pharaoh.

7 Pharaoh's officials said to him, "How
long will this man be a snare[t] to us? Let
the people go, so that they may worship
the LORD their God. Do you not yet
realize that Egypt is ruined?"[u]

8 Then Moses and Aaron were brought
back to Pharaoh. "Go, worship[v] the LORD
your God," he said. "But just who will
be going?"

9 Moses answered, "We will go with
our young and old, with our sons and
daughters, and with our flocks and
herds, because we are to celebrate a
festival to the LORD."

10 Pharaoh said, "The LORD be with
you—if I let you go, along with your
women and children! Clearly you are
bent on evil.[r] 11 No! Have only the men
go; and worship the LORD, since that's
what you have been asking for." Then

[r] *10* Or *Be careful, trouble is in store for you!*

Moses and Aaron were driven out of
Pharaoh's presence.
12And the LORD said to Moses,
"Stretch out your hand[a] over Egypt so
that locusts will swarm over the land
and devour everything growing in the
fields, everything left by the hail."
13So Moses stretched out his staff over
Egypt, and the LORD made an east wind
blow across the land all that day and
all that night. By morning the wind had
brought the locusts;[b] 14they invaded all
Egypt and settled down in every area
of the country in great numbers. Never
before had there been such a plague of
locusts,[c] nor will there ever be again.
15They covered all the ground until it
was black. They devoured[d] all that was
left after the hail—everything growing
in the fields and the fruit on the trees.
Nothing green remained on tree or
plant in all the land of Egypt.
16Pharaoh quickly summoned Moses
and Aaron and said, "I have sinned[e]
against the LORD your God and against
you. 17Now forgive my sin once more
and pray[f] to the LORD your God to take
this deadly plague away from me."
18Moses then left Pharaoh and prayed
to the LORD.[g] 19And the LORD changed
the wind to a very strong west wind,
which caught up the locusts and carried
them into the Red Sea.[s] Not a locust
was left anywhere in Egypt. 20But the
LORD hardened Pharaoh's heart,[h] and he
would not let the Israelites go.

Ninth plague: Darkness.

21Then the LORD said to Moses,
"Stretch out your hand toward the sky
so that darkness[i] will spread over
Egypt—darkness that can be felt." 22So
Moses stretched out his hand toward
the sky, and total darkness[j] covered all
Egypt for three days. 23No one could see
anyone else or leave his place for three
days. Yet all the Israelites had light in
the places where they lived.[k]
24Then Pharaoh summoned Moses
and said, "Go, worship the LORD. Even
your women and children[l] may go with
you; only leave your flocks and herds
behind."
25But Moses said, "You must allow
us to have sacrifices and burnt offerings
to present to the LORD our God. 26Our
livestock too must go with us; not a hoof
is to be left behind. We have to use
some of them in worshiping the LORD
our God, and until we get there we will
not know what we are to use to worship the LORD."
27But the LORD hardened Pharaoh's
heart,[m] and he was not willing to let
them go. 28Pharaoh said to Moses, "Get
out of my sight! Make sure you do not
appear before me again! The day you
see my face you will die."
29"Just as you say," Moses replied, "I
will never appear[n] before you again."

Tenth plague: Firstborn sons will die.

11 Now the LORD had said to Moses,
"I will bring one more plague on
Pharaoh and on Egypt. After that, he
will let you go from here, and when he
does, he will drive you out completely.
2Tell the people that men and women
alike are to ask their neighbors for articles of silver and gold."[o] 3(The LORD
made the Egyptians favorably disposed
toward the people, and Moses himself
was highly regarded[p] in Egypt by Pharaoh's officials and by the people.)
4So Moses said, "This is what the
LORD says: 'About midnight[q] I will go
throughout Egypt. 5Every firstborn[r] son
in Egypt will die, from the firstborn son
of Pharaoh, who sits on the throne, to
the firstborn son of the slave girl, who
is at her hand mill, and all the firstborn
of the cattle as well. 6There will be
loud wailing[s] throughout Egypt—worse
than there has ever been or ever will
be again. 7But among the Israelites not
a dog will bark at any man or animal.'
Then you will know that the LORD
makes a distinction[t] between Egypt
and Israel. 8All these officials of yours
will come to me, bowing down before

10:12 [a]Ex 7:19
10:13 [b]Ps 105:34
10:14 [c]Ps 78:46; Joel 2:1-11,25
10:15 [d]ver 5; Ps 105:34-35
10:16 [e]Ex 9:27
10:17 [f]Ex 8:8
10:18 [g]Ex 8:30
10:20 [h]Ex 4:21; 11:10
10:21 [i]Dt 28:29
10:22 [j]Ps 105:28; Rev 16:10
10:23 [k]Ex 8:22
10:24 [l]ver 8-10
10:27 [m]ver 20; Ex 4:21
10:29 [n]Heb 11:27
11:2 [o]Ex 3:21,22
11:3 [p]Dt 34:11
11:4 [q]Ex 12:29
11:5 [r]Ex 4:23; Ps 78:51
11:6 [s]Ex 12:30
11:7 [t]Ex 8:22

s *19* Hebrew *Yam Suph*; that is, Sea of Reeds

me and saying, 'Go,[a] you and all the people who follow you!' After that I will leave." Then Moses, hot with anger, left Pharaoh.

9 The LORD had said to Moses, "Pharaoh will refuse to listen[b] to you—so that my wonders may be multiplied in Egypt." 10 Moses and Aaron performed all these wonders before Pharaoh, but the LORD hardened Pharaoh's heart,[c] and he would not let the Israelites go out of his country.

The Passover

12:14-20pp— Lev 23:4-8; Nu 28:16-25; Dt 16:1-8

12 The LORD said to Moses and Aaron in Egypt, 2 "This month is to be for you the first month,[d] the first month of your year. 3 Tell the whole community of Israel that on the tenth day of this month each man is to take a lamb[t] for his family, one for each household. 4 If any household is too small for a whole lamb, they must share one with their nearest neighbor, having taken into account the number of people there are. You are to determine the amount of lamb needed in accordance with what each person will eat. 5 The animals you choose must be year-old males without defect,[e] and you may take them from the sheep or the goats. 6 Take care of them until the fourteenth day of the month,[f] when all the people of the community of Israel must slaughter them at twilight.[g] 7 Then they are to take some of the blood and put it on the sides and tops of the doorframes of the houses where they eat the lambs. 8 That same night[h] they are to eat the meat roasted[i] over the fire, along with bitter herbs,[j] and bread made without yeast.[k] 9 Do not eat the meat raw or cooked in water, but roast it over the fire—head, legs and inner parts. 10 Do not leave any of it till morning;[l] if some is left till morning, you must burn it. 11 This is how you are to eat it: with your cloak tucked into your belt, your sandals on your feet and your staff in your hand. Eat it in haste;[m] it is the LORD's Passover.[n]

12 "On that same night I will pass through[o] Egypt and strike down every firstborn—both men and animals—and I will bring judgment on all the gods[p] of Egypt. I am the LORD.[q] 13 The blood will be a sign for you on the houses where you are; and when I see the blood, I will pass over you. No destructive plague will touch you when I strike Egypt.

14 "This is a day you are to commemorate;[r] for the generations to come you shall celebrate it as a festival to the LORD—a lasting ordinance.[s] 15 For seven days you are to eat bread made without yeast.[t] On the first day remove the yeast from your houses, for whoever eats anything with yeast in it from the first day through the seventh must be cut off[u] from Israel. 16 On the first day hold a sacred assembly, and another one on the seventh day. Do no work at all on these days, except to prepare food for everyone to eat—that is all you may do.

17 "Celebrate the Feast of Unleavened Bread, because it was on this very day that I brought your divisions out of Egypt.[v] Celebrate this day as a lasting ordinance for the generations to come. 18 In the first month[w] you are to eat bread made without yeast, from the evening of the fourteenth day until the evening of the twenty-first day. 19 For seven days no yeast is to be found in your houses. And whoever eats anything with yeast in it must be cut off from the community of Israel, whether he is an alien or native-born. 20 Eat nothing made with yeast. Wherever you live, you must eat unleavened bread."

21 Then Moses summoned all the elders of Israel and said to them, "Go at once and select the animals for your families and slaughter the Passover[x] lamb. 22 Take a bunch of hyssop, dip it into the blood in the basin and put some of the blood[y] on the top and on

11:8 [a]Ex 12:31-33
11:9 [b]Ex 7:4
11:10 [c]Ex 4:21; 10:20,27
12:2 [d]Ex 13:4; Dt 16:1
12:5 [e]Lev 22:18-21; Heb 9:14
12:6 [f]Lev 23:5; Nu 9:1-3,5,11 [g]Ex 16:12; Dt 16:4,6
12:8 [h]Ex 34:25; Nu 9:12 [i]Dt 16:7 [j]Nu 9:11 [k]Dt 16:3-4; 1Co 5:8
12:10 [l]Ex 23:18; 34:25
12:11 [m]Dt 16:3 [n]ver 13,21,27, 43; Dt 16:1
12:12 [o]Ex 11:4; Am 5:17 [p]Nu 33:4 [q]Ex 6:2
12:14 [r]Ex 13:9 [s]ver 17,24; Ex 13:5,10; 2Ki 23:21
12:15 [t]Ex 13:6-7; 23:15; 34:18; Lev 23:6; Dt 16:3 [u]Ge 17:14; Nu 9:13
12:17 [v]ver 41; Ex 13:3
12:18 [w]ver 2; Lev 23:5-8; Nu 28:16-25
12:21 [x]ver 11; Mk 14:12-16
12:22 [y]ver 7; Heb 11:28

t3 The Hebrew word can mean *lamb* or *kid*; also in verse 4.

both sides of the doorframe. Not one of
you shall go out the door of his house
until morning. 23When the LORD goes
through the land to strike down the
Egyptians, he will see the blood[a] on the
top and sides of the doorframe and will
pass over[b] that doorway, and he will not
permit the destroyer[c] to enter your houses and strike you down.

24"Obey these instructions as a lasting
ordinance for you and your descendants.
25When you enter the land that the
LORD will give you as he promised,
observe this ceremony. 26And when
your children[d] ask you, 'What does this
ceremony mean to you?' 27then tell
them, 'It is the Passover[e] sacrifice to the
LORD, who passed over the houses of
the Israelites in Egypt and spared our
homes when he struck down the Egyptians.'" Then the people bowed down
and worshiped.[f] 28The Israelites did
just what the LORD commanded Moses
and Aaron.

29At midnight[g] the LORD struck down
all the firstborn[h] in Egypt, from the
firstborn of Pharaoh, who sat on the
throne, to the firstborn of the prisoner,
who was in the dungeon, and the firstborn of all the livestock[i] as well. 30Phar-
aoh and all his officials and all the
Egyptians got up during the night, and
there was loud wailing[j] in Egypt, for
there was not a house without someone dead.

The Exodus.

31During the night Pharaoh summoned Moses and Aaron and said, "Up!
Leave my people, you and the Israelites! Go, worship[k] the LORD as you
have requested. 32Take your flocks and
herds,[l] as you have said, and go. And
also bless me."

33The Egyptians urged the people to
hurry and leave[m] the country. "For otherwise," they said, "we will all die!"
34So the people took their dough before
the yeast was added, and carried it on
their shoulders in kneading troughs
wrapped in clothing. 35The Israelites
did as Moses instructed and asked the
Egyptians for articles of silver and gold[n]
and for clothing. 36The LORD had made
the Egyptians favorably disposed
toward the people, and they gave them
what they asked for; so they plundered[o]
the Egyptians.

37The Israelites journeyed from Rameses to Succoth.[p] There were about six
hundred thousand men[q] on foot, besides
women and children. 38Many other
people[r] went up with them, as well as
large droves of livestock, both flocks
and herds. 39With the dough they had
brought from Egypt, they baked cakes
of unleavened bread. The dough was
without yeast because they had been
driven out[s] of Egypt and did not have
time to prepare food for themselves.

40Now the length of time the Israelite
people lived in Egypt[u] was 430 years.[t]
41At the end of the 430 years, to the
very day, all the LORD's divisions[u] left
Egypt.[v] 42Because the LORD kept vigil
that night to bring them out of Egypt, on
this night all the Israelites are to keep
vigil to honor the LORD for the generations to come.[w]

The Passover regulations.

43The LORD said to Moses and Aaron,
"These are the regulations for the
Passover:[x]

"No foreigner[y] is to eat of it. 44Any
slave you have bought may eat of it
after you have circumcised[z] him, 45but
a temporary resident and a hired worker[a] may not eat of it.

46"It must be eaten inside one house;
take none of the meat outside the house.
Do not break any of the bones.[b] 47The
whole community of Israel must celebrate it.

48"An alien living among you who
wants to celebrate the LORD's Passover
must have all the males in his household circumcised; then he may take part
like one born in the land.[c] No uncircumcised male may eat of it. 49The

12:23 [a]Rev 7:3 [b]ver 13 [c]1Co 10:10; Heb 11:28
12:26 [d]Ex 10:2; 13:8,14-15; Jos 4:6
12:27 [e]ver 11 [f]Ex 4:31
12:29 [g]Ex 11:4 [h]Ex 4:23; Ps 78:51 [i]Ex 9:6
12:30 [j]Ex 11:6
12:31 [k]Ex 8:8
12:32 [l]Ex 10:9,26
12:33 [m]Ps 105:38
12:35 [n]Ex 3:22
12:36 [o]Ex 3:22
12:37 [p]Nu 33:3-5 [q]Ex 38:26; Nu 1:46; 11:13,21
12:38 [r]Nu 11:4
12:39 [s]ver 31-33; Ex 6:1; 11:1
12:40 [t]Ge 15:13; Ac 7:6; Gal 3:17
12:41 [u]ver 17; Ex 6:26 [v]Ex 3:10
12:42 [w]Ex 13:10; Dt 16:1,6
12:43 [x]ver 11 [y]ver 48; Nu 9:14
12:44 [z]Ge 17:12-13
12:45 [a]Lev 22:10
12:46 [b]Nu 9:12; Jn 19:36*
12:48 [c]Nu 9:14

u*40* Masoretic Text; Samaritan Pentateuch and Septuagint *Egypt and Canaan*

same law applies to the native-born and
to the alien[a] living among you."
50All the Israelites did just what the
LORD had commanded Moses and Aaron.
51And on that very day the LORD
brought the Israelites out of Egypt by
their divisions.[b]

Consecration of firstborn males.

13 The LORD said to Moses, 2"Consecrate to me every firstborn
male.[c] The first offspring of every womb
among the Israelites belongs to me,
whether man or animal."
3Then Moses said to the people,
"Commemorate this day, the day you
came out of Egypt, out of the land of
slavery, because the LORD brought you
out of it with a mighty hand.[d] Eat nothing containing yeast.[e] 4Today, in the
month of Abib,[f] you are leaving. 5When
the LORD brings you into the land of the
Canaanites, Hittites, Amorites, Hivites
and Jebusites[g]—the land he swore to
your forefathers to give you, a land
flowing with milk and honey—you are
to observe this ceremony[h] in this month:
6For seven days eat bread made without yeast and on the seventh day hold
a festival[i] to the LORD. 7Eat unleavened
bread during those seven days; nothing with yeast in it is to be seen
among you, nor shall any yeast be seen
anywhere within your borders. 8On that
day tell your son,[j] 'I do this because of
what the LORD did for me when I came
out of Egypt.' 9This observance will be
for you like a sign on your hand and a
reminder on your forehead[k] that the
law of the LORD is to be on your lips.
For the LORD brought you out of Egypt
with his mighty hand. 10You must
keep this ordinance[l] at the appointed
time year after year.
11"After the LORD brings you into
the land of the Canaanites and gives it
to you, as he promised on oath to you
and your forefathers, 12you are to give
over to the LORD the first offspring of
every womb. All the firstborn males of
your livestock belong to the LORD.[m]
13Redeem with a lamb every firstborn
donkey, but if you do not redeem it,
break its neck.[n] Redeem every firstborn
among your sons.[o]
14"In days to come, when your son[p]
asks you, 'What does this mean?' say
to him, 'With a mighty hand the LORD
brought us out of Egypt, out of the
land of slavery.[q] 15When Pharaoh stubbornly refused to let us go, the LORD
killed every firstborn in Egypt, both
man and animal. This is why I sacrifice
to the LORD the first male offspring of
every womb and redeem each of my
firstborn sons.'[r] 16And it will be like a
sign on your hand and a symbol on your
forehead[s] that the LORD brought us out
of Egypt with his mighty hand."

A pillar of cloud and a pillar of fire.

17When Pharaoh let the people go,
God did not lead them on the road
through the Philistine country, though
that was shorter. For God said, "If they
face war, they might change their minds
and return to Egypt."[t] 18So God led[u]
the people around by the desert road
toward the Red Sea.[v] The Israelites went
up out of Egypt armed for battle.[v]
19Moses took the bones of Joseph[w]
with him because Joseph had made the
sons of Israel swear an oath. He had
said, "God will surely come to your
aid, and then you must carry my bones
up with you from this place."[wx]
20After leaving Succoth they camped
at Etham on the edge of the desert.[y]
21By day the LORD went ahead of them
in a pillar of cloud[z] to guide them on
their way and by night in a pillar of
fire to give them light, so that they
could travel by day or night. 22Neither
the pillar of cloud by day nor the pillar
of fire by night left its place in front of
the people.

12:49 [a]Nu 15:15-16, 29; Gal 3:28
12:51 [b]ver 41; Ex 6:26
13:2 [c]ver 12,13,15; Ex 22:29; Nu 3:13; Dt 15:19; Lk 2:23*
13:3 [d]Ex 3:20; 6:1 [e]Ex 12:19
13:4 [f]Ex 12:2
13:5 [g]Ex 3:8 [h]Ex 12:25-26
13:6 [i]Ex 12:15-20
13:8 [j]ver 14; Ex 10:2; Ps 78:5-6
13:9 [k]ver 16; Dt 6:8; 11:18
13:10 [l]Ex 12:24-25
13:12 [m]Lev 27:26; Lk 2:23*
13:13 [n]Ex 34:20 [o]Nu 18:15
13:14 [p]Ex 10:2; 12:26-27; Dt 6:20 [q]ver 3,9
13:15 [r]Ex 12:29
13:16 [s]ver 9
13:17 [t]Ex 14:11; Nu 14:1-4; Dt 17:16
13:18 [u]Ps 136:16 [v]Jos 1:14
13:19 [w]Jos 24:32; Ac 7:16 [x]Ge 50:24-25
13:20 [y]Nu 33:6
13:21 [z]Ex 14:19,24; 33:9-10; Nu 9:16; Dt 1:33; Ne 9:12,19; Ps 78:14; 99:7; 105:39; Isa 4:5; 1Co 10:1

v *18* Hebrew *Yam Suph*; that is, Sea of Reeds
w *19* See Gen. 50:25.

Pharaoh pursues the Israelites.

14 Then the LORD said to Moses, [2]"Tell the Israelites to turn back and encamp near Pi Hahiroth, between Migdol[a] and the sea. They are to encamp by the sea, directly opposite Baal Zephon. [3]Pharaoh will think, 'The Israelites are wandering around the land in confusion, hemmed in by the desert.' [4]And I will harden Pharaoh's heart,[b] and he will pursue them. But I will gain glory[c] for myself through Pharaoh and all his army, and the Egyptians will know that I am the LORD."[d] So the Israelites did this.

[5]When the king of Egypt was told that the people had fled, Pharaoh and his officials changed their minds about them and said, "What have we done? We have let the Israelites go and have lost their services!" [6]So he had his chariot made ready and took his army with him. [7]He took six hundred of the best chariots, along with all the other chariots of Egypt, with officers over all of them. [8]The LORD hardened the heart[e] of Pharaoh king of Egypt, so that he pursued the Israelites, who were marching out boldly.[f] [9]The Egyptians—all Pharaoh's horses and chariots, horsemen[x] and troops—pursued the Israelites and overtook[g] them as they camped by the sea near Pi Hahiroth, opposite Baal Zephon.

[10]As Pharaoh approached, the Israelites looked up, and there were the Egyptians, marching after them. They were terrified and cried[h] out to the LORD. [11]They said to Moses, "Was it because there were no graves in Egypt that you brought us to the desert to die?[i] What have you done to us by bringing us out of Egypt? [12]Didn't we say to you in Egypt, 'Leave us alone; let us serve the Egyptians'? It would have been better for us to serve the Egyptians than to die in the desert!"

Israelites cross the Red Sea on dry ground.

[13]Moses answered the people, "Do not be afraid.[j] Stand firm and you will see[k] the deliverance the LORD will bring you today. The Egyptians you see today you will never see[l] again. [14]The LORD will fight[m] for you; you need only to be still."[n]

[15]Then the LORD said to Moses, "Why are you crying out to me? Tell the Israelites to move on. [16]Raise your staff[o] and stretch out your hand over the sea to divide the water[p] so that the Israelites can go through the sea on dry ground. [17]I will harden the hearts of the Egyptians so that they will go in after them.[q] And I will gain glory through Pharaoh and all his army, through his chariots and his horsemen. [18]The Egyptians will know that I am the LORD when I gain glory through Pharaoh, his chariots and his horsemen."

[19]Then the angel of God, who had been traveling in front of Israel's army, withdrew and went behind them. The pillar of cloud[r] also moved from in front and stood behind them, [20]coming between the armies of Egypt and Israel. Throughout the night the cloud brought darkness to the one side and light to the other side; so neither went near the other all night long.

[21]Then Moses stretched out his hand over the sea, and all that night the LORD drove the sea back with a strong east wind[s] and turned it into dry land. The waters were divided,[t] [22]and the Israelites went through the sea on dry ground,[u] with a wall of water on their right and on their left.

[23]The Egyptians pursued them, and all Pharaoh's horses and chariots and horsemen followed them into the sea. [24]During the last watch of the night the LORD looked down from the pillar of fire and cloud[v] at the Egyptian army and threw it into confusion. [25]He made the wheels of their chariots come off[y] so that they had difficulty driving. And the Egyptians said, "Let's get away from the Israelites! The LORD is fighting[w] for them against Egypt."

14:2 [a]Nu 33:7; Jer 44:1
14:4 [b]Ex 4:21 [c]Ro 9:17, 22-23 [d]Ex 7:5
14:8 [e]ver 4; Ex 11:10 [f]Nu 33:3; Ac 13:17
14:9 [g]Ex 15:9
14:10 [h]Jos 24:7; Ne 9:9; Ps 34:17
14:11 [i]Ps 106:7-8
14:13 [j]Ge 15:1 [k]2Ch 20:17; Isa 41:10, 13-14 [l]ver 30
14:14 [m]ver 25; Ex 15:3; Dt 1:30; 3:22; 2Ch 20:29 [n]Ps 37:7; 46:10; Isa 30:15
14:16 [o]Ex 4:17; Nu 20:8-9,11 [p]Isa 10:26
14:17 [q]ver 4
14:19 [r]Ex 13:21
14:21 [s]Ex 15:8 [t]Ps 74:13; 114:5; Isa 63:12
14:22 [u]Ex 15:19; Ne 9:11; Ps 66:6; Heb 11:29
14:24 [v]Ex 13:21
14:25 [w]ver 14

[x]*9* Or *charioteers*; also in verses 17, 18, 23, 26 and 28 [y]*25* Or *He jammed the wheels of their chariots* (see Samaritan Pentateuch, Septuagint and Syriac)

26Then the LORD said to Moses,
"Stretch out your hand over the sea so
that the waters may flow back over the
Egyptians and their chariots and horsemen." 27Moses stretched out his hand
over the sea, and at daybreak the sea
went back to its place.[a] The Egyptians
were fleeing toward[z] it, and the LORD
swept them into the sea.[b] 28The water
flowed back and covered the chariots
and horsemen—the entire army of
Pharaoh that had followed the Israelites into the sea. Not one of them
survived.
29But the Israelites went through the
sea on dry ground,[c] with a wall of water
on their right and on their left. 30That
day the LORD saved[d] Israel from the
hands of the Egyptians, and Israel saw
the Egyptians lying dead on the shore.
31And when the Israelites saw the great
power the LORD displayed against the
Egyptians, the people feared the LORD
and put their trust[e] in him and in
Moses his servant.

Moses' song to the LORD.

15 Then Moses and the Israelites sang this song[f] to the LORD:

"I will sing[g] to the LORD,
for he is highly exalted.
The horse and its rider
he has hurled into the sea.
2The LORD is my strength[h] and my song;
he has become my salvation.[i]
He is my God,[j] and I will praise him,
my father's God, and I will exalt[k] him.
3The LORD is a warrior;[l]
the LORD is his name.[m]
4Pharaoh's chariots and his army[n]
he has hurled into the sea.
The best of Pharaoh's officers
are drowned in the Red Sea.[a]
5The deep waters have covered them;
they sank to the depths like a stone.[o]
6"Your right hand,[p] O LORD,
was majestic in power.
Your right hand, O LORD,
shattered the enemy.
7In the greatness of your majesty
you threw down those who opposed you.
You unleashed your burning anger;[q]
it consumed them like stubble.
8By the blast of your nostrils[r]
the waters piled up.[s]
The surging waters stood firm like a wall;[t]
the deep waters congealed in the heart of the sea.

9"The enemy boasted,
'I will pursue,[u] I will overtake them.
I will divide the spoils;[v]
I will gorge myself on them.
I will draw my sword
and my hand will destroy them.'
10But you blew with your breath,
and the sea covered them.
They sank like lead
in the mighty waters.[w]

11"Who among the gods is like you,[x] O LORD?
Who is like you—
majestic in holiness,[y]
awesome in glory,[z]
working wonders?
12You stretched out your right hand
and the earth swallowed them.

13"In your unfailing love you will lead[a]
the people you have redeemed.
In your strength you will guide them
to your holy dwelling.[b]
14The nations will hear and tremble;[c]
anguish will grip the people of Philistia.
15The chiefs[d] of Edom will be terrified,
the leaders of Moab will be seized with trembling,[e]
the people[b] of Canaan will melt[f] away;
16 terror[g] and dread will fall upon them.

14:27 [a]Jos 4:18 [b]Ex 15:1,21; Ps 78:53; 106:11
14:29 [c]ver 22
14:30 [d]Ps 106:8,10,21
14:31 [e]Ps 106:12; Jn 2:11
15:1 [f]Rev 15:3 [g]Ps 106:12
15:2 [h]Ps 59:17 [i]Ps 18:2,46; Isa 12:2; Hab 3:18 [j]Ge 28:21 [k]Ex 3:6,15-16; Isa 25:1
15:3 [l]Ex 14:14; Ps 24:8; Rev 19:11 [m]Ex 6:2-3,7-8; Ps 83:18
15:4 [n]Ex 14:6-7
15:5 [o]ver 10; Ne 9:11
15:6 [p]Ps 118:15
15:7 [q]Ps 78:49-50
15:8 [r]Ex 14:21 [s]Ps 78:13 [t]Ex 14:22
15:9 [u]Ex 14:5-9 [v]Jdg 5:30; Isa 53:12
15:10 [w]ver 5; Ex 14:27-28
15:11 [x]Ex 8:10; Dt 3:24; Ps 77:13 [y]Isa 6:3; Rev 4:8 [z]Ps 8:1
15:13 [a]Ne 9:12; Ps 77:20 [b]Ps 78:54
15:14 [c]Dt 2:25
15:15 [d]Ge 36:15 [e]Nu 22:3 [f]Jos 5:1
15:16 [g]Ex 23:27; Jos 2:9

z *27* Or *from* a *4* Hebrew *Yam Suph*; that is, Sea of Reeds; also in verse 22 b *15* Or *rulers*

By the power of your arm
they will be as still as a stone[a]—
until your people pass by, O LORD,
until the people you bought[c][b] pass by.
17You will bring them in and plant[c] them
on the mountain[d] of your inheritance—
the place, O LORD, you made for your dwelling,
the sanctuary, O Lord, your hands established.
18The LORD will reign
for ever and ever."

19When Pharaoh's horses, chariots and horsemen[d] went into the sea,[e] the LORD brought the waters of the sea back over them, but the Israelites walked through the sea on dry ground.[f] 20Then Miriam[g] the prophetess,[h] Aaron's sister, took a tambourine in her hand, and all the women followed her, with tambourines and dancing.[i] 21Miriam sang to them:

"Sing to the LORD,
for he is highly exalted.
The horse and its rider
he has hurled into the sea."[j]

Bitter waters at Marah are made sweet.

22Then Moses led Israel from the Red Sea and they went into the Desert of Shur. For three days they traveled in the desert without finding water. 23When they came to Marah, they could not drink its water because it was bitter. (That is why the place is called Marah.[e][k]) 24So the people grumbled[l] against Moses, saying, "What are we to drink?"

25Then Moses cried out[m] to the LORD, and the LORD showed him a piece of wood. He threw it into the water, and the water became sweet.

There the LORD made a decree and a law for them, and there he tested[n] them. 26He said, "If you listen carefully to the voice of the LORD your God and do what is right in his eyes, if you pay attention to his commands and keep all his decrees,[o] I will not bring on you any of the diseases[p] I brought on the Egyptians, for I am the LORD, who heals[q] you."

27Then they came to Elim, where there were twelve springs and seventy palm trees, and they camped[r] there near the water.

God feeds his people with quail and manna.

16 The whole Israelite community set out from Elim and came to the Desert of Sin,[s] which is between Elim and Sinai, on the fifteenth day of the second month after they had come out of Egypt. 2In the desert the whole community grumbled[t] against Moses and Aaron. 3The Israelites said to them, "If only we had died by the LORD's hand in Egypt![u] There we sat around pots of meat and ate all the food[v] we wanted, but you have brought us out into this desert to starve this entire assembly to death."

4Then the LORD said to Moses, "I will rain down bread from heaven[w] for you. The people are to go out each day and gather enough for that day. In this way I will test them and see whether they will follow my instructions. 5On the sixth day they are to prepare what they bring in, and that is to be twice[x] as much as they gather on the other days."

6So Moses and Aaron said to all the Israelites, "In the evening you will know that it was the LORD who brought you out of Egypt,[y] 7and in the morning you will see the glory[z] of the LORD, because he has heard your grumbling[a] against him. Who are we, that you should grumble against us?"[b] 8Moses also said, "You will know that it was the LORD when he gives you meat to eat in the evening and all the bread you want in the morning, because he has heard your grumbling against him

15:16 [a]1Sa 25:37 [b]Ps 74:2
15:17 [c]Ps 44:2 [d]Ps 78:54,68
15:19 [e]Ex 14:28 [f]Ex 14:22
15:20 [g]Nu 26:59 [h]Jdg 4:4 [i]Jdg 11:34; 1Sa 18:6; Ps 30:11; 150:4
15:21 [j]ver 1; Ex 14:27
15:23 [k]Nu 33:8
15:24 [l]Ex 14:12; 16:2
15:25 [m]Ex 14:10 [n]Jdg 3:4
15:26 [o]Dt 7:12 [p]Dt 28:27, 58-60 [q]Ex 23:25-26
15:27 [r]Nu 33:9
16:1 [s]Nu 33:11,12
16:2 [t]Ex 14:11; 15:24; 1Co 10:10
16:3 [u]Ex 17:3 [v]Nu 11:4,34
16:4 [w]Dt 8:3; Jn 6:31*
16:5 [x]ver 22
16:6 [y]Ex 6:6
16:7 [z]ver 10; Isa 35:2; 40:5 [a]ver 12; Nu 14:2, 27,28 [b]Nu 16:11

c*16* Or *created* d*19* Or *charioteers* e*23* *Marah* means *bitter.*

Who are we? You are not grumbling
against us, but against the LORD."[a]
9Then Moses told Aaron, "Say to the
entire Israelite community, 'Come before the LORD, for he has heard your
grumbling.'"
10While Aaron was speaking to the
whole Israelite community, they looked
toward the desert, and there was the
glory[b] of the LORD appearing in the
cloud.[c]
11The LORD said to Moses, 12"I have
heard the grumbling[d] of the Israelites.
Tell them, 'At twilight you will eat meat,
and in the morning you will be filled
with bread. Then you will know that I
am the LORD your God.'"
13That evening quail[e] came and covered the camp, and in the morning
there was a layer of dew[f] around the
camp. 14When the dew was gone, thin
flakes like frost[g] on the ground appeared
on the desert floor. 15When the Israelites saw it, they said to each other,
"What is it?" For they did not know
what it was.
Moses said to them, "It is the bread[h]
the LORD has given you to eat. 16This is
what the LORD has commanded: 'Each
one is to gather as much as he needs.
Take an omer[f][i] for each person you
have in your tent.'"
17The Israelites did as they were told;
some gathered much, some little. 18And
when they measured it by the omer, he
who gathered much did not have too
much, and he who gathered little did
not have too little.[j] Each one gathered
as much as he needed.
19Then Moses said to them, "No one
is to keep any of it until morning."[k]
20However, some of them paid no
attention to Moses; they kept part of it
until morning, but it was full of maggots
and began to smell. So Moses was angry
with them.
21Each morning everyone gathered as
much as he needed, and when the sun
grew hot, it melted away. 22On the sixth
day, they gathered twice[l] as much—
two omers[g] for each person—and the
leaders of the community[m] came and
reported this to Moses. 23He said to
them, "This is what the LORD commanded: 'Tomorrow is to be a day of
rest, a holy Sabbath[n] to the LORD. So
bake what you want to bake and boil
what you want to boil. Save whatever
is left and keep it until morning.'"
24So they saved it until morning, as
Moses commanded, and it did not stink
or get maggots in it. 25"Eat it today,"
Moses said, "because today is a Sabbath to the LORD. You will not find any
of it on the ground today. 26Six days you
are to gather it, but on the seventh day,
the Sabbath,[o] there will not be any."
27Nevertheless, some of the people
went out on the seventh day to gather
it, but they found none. 28Then the LORD
said to Moses, "How long will you[h]
refuse to keep my commands[p] and my
instructions? 29Bear in mind that the
LORD has given you the Sabbath; that is
why on the sixth day he gives you
bread for two days. Everyone is to stay
where he is on the seventh day; no
one is to go out." 30So the people rested
on the seventh day.

An omer of manna is kept for future generations.

31The people of Israel called the
bread manna.[i][q] It was white like
coriander seed and tasted like wafers
made with honey. 32Moses said, "This
is what the LORD has commanded:
'Take an omer of manna and keep it
for the generations to come, so they
can see the bread I gave you to eat in
the desert when I brought you out of
Egypt.'"
33So Moses said to Aaron, "Take a
jar and put an omer of manna[r] in it.
Then place it before the LORD to be
kept for the generations to come."
34As the LORD commanded Moses,
Aaron put the manna in front of the
Testimony,[s] that it might be kept.

16:8 [a] 1Sa 8:7; Ro 13:2
16:10 [b] ver 7; Nu 16:19 [c] Ex 13:21; 1Ki 8:10
16:12 [d] ver 7
16:13 [e] Nu 11:31; Ps 78:27-28; 105:40 [f] Nu 11:9
16:14 [g] ver 31; Nu 11:7-9; Ps 105:40
16:15 [h] ver 4; Jn 6:31
16:16 [i] ver 32,36
16:18 [j] 2Co 8:15*
16:19 [k] ver 23; Ex 12:10; 23:18
16:22 [l] ver 5 [m] Ex 34:31
16:23 [n] Ge 2:3; Ex 20:8; 23:12; Lev 23:3
16:26 [o] Ex 20:9-10
16:28 [p] 2Ki 17:14; Ps 78:10; 106:13
16:31 [q] Nu 11:7-9
16:33 [r] Heb 9:4
16:34 [s] Ex 25:16,21,22; 40:20; Nu 17:4,10

f *16* That is, probably about 2 quarts (about 2 liters); also in verses 18, 32, 33 and 36 g *22* That is, probably about 4 quarts (about 4.5 liters) h *28* The Hebrew is plural. i *31* *Manna* means *What is it?* (see verse 15).

[35]The Israelites ate manna[a] forty years,[b]
until they came to a land that was settled; they ate manna until they reached
the border of Canaan.[c]
[36](An omer is one tenth of an ephah.)

Moses strikes a rock at Horeb and water comes out.

17 The whole Israelite community
set out from the Desert of Sin,[d]
traveling from place to place as the LORD
commanded. They camped at Rephidim,
but there was no water[e] for the people
to drink. [2]So they quarreled with Moses
and said, "Give us water[f] to drink."
Moses replied, "Why do you quarrel
with me? Why do you put the LORD to
the test?"[g]
[3]But the people were thirsty for water
there, and they grumbled[h] against Moses.
They said, "Why did you bring us up
out of Egypt to make us and our children and livestock die of thirst?"
[4]Then Moses cried out to the LORD,
"What am I to do with these people?
They are almost ready to stone[i] me."
[5]The LORD answered Moses, "Walk
on ahead of the people. Take with you
some of the elders of Israel and take in
your hand the staff with which you
struck the Nile,[j] and go. [6]I will stand
there before you by the rock at Horeb.
Strike the rock, and water[k] will come
out of it for the people to drink." So
Moses did this in the sight of the elders
of Israel. [7]And he called the place Massah[j] and Meribah[k][l] because the Israelites quarreled and because they tested
the LORD saying, "Is the LORD among
us or not?"

Moses' hands are held up and the Amalekites are defeated.

[8]The Amalekites[m] came and attacked
the Israelites at Rephidim. [9]Moses said
to Joshua, "Choose some of our men
and go out to fight the Amalekites.
Tomorrow I will stand on top of the hill
with the staff[n] of God in my hands."
[10]So Joshua fought the Amalekites as
Moses had ordered, and Moses, Aaron
and Hur[o] went to the top of the hill.
[11]As long as Moses held up his hands,
the Israelites were winning,[p] but whenever he lowered his hands, the Amalekites were winning. [12]When Moses'
hands grew tired, they took a stone
and put it under him and he sat on it.
Aaron and Hur held his hands up—one
on one side, one on the other—so that
his hands remained steady till sunset.
[13]So Joshua overcame the Amalekite
army with the sword.
[14]Then the LORD said to Moses,
"Write[q] this on a scroll as something
to be remembered and make sure that
Joshua hears it, because I will completely blot out the memory of Amalek[r]
from under heaven."
[15]Moses built an altar and called it
The LORD is my Banner. [16]He said, "For
hands were lifted up to the throne of

j7 *Massah* means *testing*. k7 *Meribah* means *quarreling*.

16:35 [a]Jn 6:31,49 [b]Ne 9:21 [c]Jos 5:12
17:1 [d]Ex 16:1 [e]Nu 33:14
17:2 [f]Nu 20:2 [g]Dt 6:16; Ps 78:18,41; 1Co 10:9
17:3 [h]Ex 15:24; 16:2-3
17:4 [i]Nu 14:10; 1Sa 30:6
17:5 [j]Ex 7:20
17:6 [k]Nu 20:11; Ps 114:8; 1Co 10:4
17:7 [l]Nu 20:13,24; Ps 81:7
17:8 [m]Ge 36:12; Dt 25:17-19
17:9 [n]Ex 4:17
17:10 [o]Ex 24:14
17:11 [p]Jas 5:16
17:14 [q]Ex 24:4; 34:27; Nu 33:2 [r]1Sa 15:3; 30:17-18

Journey to Mount Sinai

God miraculously supplied food and water in the desert for the Israelites. In the Desert of Sin, he provided manna (16). At Rephidim, he provided water from a rock (17:1-7). Finally God brought them to the foot of Mount Sinai, where he gave them his holy laws.

the LORD. The[l] LORD will be at war against the Amalekites from generation to generation."

Jethro brings Zipporah and her two sons to Moses.

18 Now Jethro, the priest of Midian[a] and father-in-law of Moses, heard of everything God had done for Moses and for his people Israel, and how the LORD had brought Israel out of Egypt.

2After Moses had sent away his wife Zipporah,[b] his father-in-law Jethro received her 3and her two sons.[c] One son was named Gershom,[m] for Moses said, "I have become an alien in a foreign land";[d] 4and the other was named Eliezer,[n][e] for he said, "My father's God was my helper; he saved me from the sword of Pharaoh."

5Jethro, Moses' father-in-law, together with Moses' sons and wife, came to him in the desert, where he was camped near the mountain[f] of God. 6Jethro had sent word to him, "I, your father-in-law Jethro, am coming to you with your wife and her two sons."

7So Moses went out to meet his father-in-law and bowed down[g] and kissed[h] him. They greeted each other and then went into the tent. 8Moses told his father-in-law about everything the LORD had done to Pharaoh and the Egyptians for Israel's sake and about all the hardships they had met along the way and how the LORD had saved[i] them.

9Jethro was delighted to hear about all the good things the LORD had done for Israel in rescuing them from the hand of the Egyptians. 10He said, "Praise be to the LORD,[j] who rescued you from the hand of the Egyptians and of Pharaoh, and who rescued the people from the hand of the Egyptians. 11Now I know that the LORD is greater than all other gods,[k] for he did this to those who had treated Israel arrogantly."[l] 12Then Jethro, Moses' father-in-law, brought a burnt offering and other sacrifices to God, and Aaron came with all the elders of

18:1 [a]Ex 2:16; 3:1
18:2 [b]Ex 2:21; 4:25
18:3 [c]Ex 4:20; Ac 7:29 [d]Ex 2:22
18:4 [e]1Ch 23:15
18:5 [f]Ex 3:1
18:7 [g]Ge 43:28 [h]Ge 29:13
18:8 [i]Ex 15:6,16; Ps 81:7
18:10 [j]Ge 14:20; Ps 68:19-20
18:11 [k]Ex 12:12; 15:11; 2Ch 2:5 [l]Lk 1:51
18:12 [m]Dt 12:7
18:15 [n]Nu 9:6,8; Dt 17:8-13
18:16 [o]Lev 24:12
18:18 [p]Nu 11:11, 14,17
18:19 [q]Ex 3:12 [r]Nu 27:5
18:20 [s]Dt 5:1 [t]Ps 143:8 [u]Dt 1:18
18:21 [v]Ac 6:3 [w]Dt 16:19; Ps 15:5; Eze 18:8 [x]Dt 1:13,15; 2Ch 19:5-10
18:22 [y]Dt 1:17-18 [z]Nu 11:17

Israel to eat bread with Moses' father-in-law in the presence[m] of God.

Jethro advises Moses to appoint judges.

13The next day Moses took his seat to serve as judge for the people, and they stood around him from morning till evening. 14When his father-in-law saw all that Moses was doing for the people, he said, "What is this you are doing for the people? Why do you alone sit as judge, while all these people stand around you from morning till evening?"

15Moses answered him, "Because the people come to me to seek God's will.[n] 16Whenever they have a dispute, it is brought to me, and I decide between the parties and inform them of God's decrees and laws."[o]

17Moses' father-in-law replied, "What you are doing is not good. 18You and these people who come to you will only wear yourselves out. The work is too heavy for you; you cannot handle it alone.[p] 19Listen now to me and I will give you some advice, and may God be with you.[q] You must be the people's representative before God and bring their disputes[r] to him. 20Teach them the decrees and laws,[s] and show them the way to live[t] and the duties they are to perform.[u] 21But select capable men[v] from all the people—men who fear God, trustworthy men who hate dishonest gain[w]—and appoint them as officials[x] over thousands, hundreds, fifties and tens. 22Have them serve as judges for the people at all times, but have them bring every difficult case[y] to you; the simple cases they can decide themselves. That will make your load lighter, because they will share[z] it with you. 23If you do this and God so commands, you will be able to stand the strain, and all these people will go home satisfied."

24Moses listened to his father-in-law

[l]16 Or *"Because a hand was against the throne of the* LORD, *the* [m]3 *Gershom* sounds like the Hebrew for *an alien there.* [n]4 *Eliezer* means *my God is helper.*

and did everything he said. 25 He chose capable men from all Israel and made them leaders of the people, officials over thousands, hundreds, fifties and tens.[a] 26 They served as judges for the people at all times. The difficult cases they brought to Moses, but the simple ones they decided themselves.[b]

27 Then Moses sent his father-in-law on his way, and Jethro returned to his own country.[c]

Moses' encounter with God at Mount Sinai.

19 In the third month after the Israelites left Egypt—on the very day—they came to the Desert of Sinai. 2 After they set out from Rephidim,[d] they entered the Desert of Sinai, and Israel camped there in the desert in front of the mountain.[e]

3 Then Moses went up to God, and the LORD called[f] to him from the mountain and said, "This is what you are to say to the house of Jacob and what you are to tell the people of Israel: 4 'You yourselves have seen what I did to Egypt,[g] and how I carried you on eagles' wings[h] and brought you to myself. 5 Now if you obey me fully[i] and keep my covenant,[j] then out of all nations you will be my treasured possession.[k] Although the whole earth[l] is mine, 6 you[o] will be for me a kingdom of priests[m] and a holy nation.'[n] These are the words you are to speak to the Israelites."

7 So Moses went back and summoned the elders of the people and set before them all the words the LORD had commanded him to speak. 8 The people all responded together, "We will do everything the LORD has said."[o] So Moses brought their answer back to the LORD.

9 The LORD said to Moses, "I am going to come to you in a dense cloud,[p] so that the people will hear me speaking[q] with you and will always put their trust in you." Then Moses told the LORD what the people had said.

10 And the LORD said to Moses, "Go to the people and consecrate[r] them today and tomorrow. Have them wash their clothes[s] 11 and be ready by the third day,[t] because on that day the LORD will come down on Mount Sinai in the sight of all the people. 12 Put limits for the people around the mountain and tell them, 'Be careful that you do not go up the mountain or touch the foot of it. Whoever touches the mountain shall surely be put to death. 13 He shall surely be stoned[u] or shot with arrows; not a hand is to be laid on him. Whether man or animal, he shall not be permitted to live.' Only when the ram's horn sounds a long blast may they go up to the mountain."

14 After Moses had gone down the mountain to the people, he consecrated them, and they washed their clothes. 15 Then he said to the people, "Prepare yourselves for the third day. Abstain from sexual relations."

16 On the morning of the third day there was thunder and lightning, with a thick cloud over the mountain, and a very loud trumpet blast.[v] Everyone in the camp trembled.[w] 17 Then Moses led the people out of the camp to meet with God, and they stood at the foot of the mountain. 18 Mount Sinai was covered with smoke,[x] because the LORD descended on it in fire.[y] The smoke billowed up from it like smoke from a furnace,[z] the whole mountain[p] trembled[a] violently, 19 and the sound of the trumpet grew louder and louder. Then Moses spoke and the voice[b] of God answered[c] him.[q]

20 The LORD descended to the top of Mount Sinai and called Moses to the top of the mountain. So Moses went up 21 and the LORD said to him, "Go down and warn the people so they do not force their way through to see[d] the LORD and many of them perish. 22 Even the priests, who approach[e] the LORD, must consecrate themselves, or the LORD will break out against them."[f]

18:25 [a]Dt 1:13-15
18:26 [b]ver 22
18:27 [c]Nu 10:29-30
19:2 [d]Ex 17:1 [e]Ex 3:1
19:3 [f]Ex 3:4; Ac 7:38
19:4 [g]Dt 29:2 [h]Isa 63:9
19:5 [i]Ex 15:26 [j]Dt 5:2 [k]Dt 14:2; Ps 135:4 [l]Ex 9:29; Dt 10:14
19:6 [m]1Pe 2:5 [n]Dt 7:6; 26:19; Isa 62:12
19:8 [o]Ex 24:3,7; Dt 5:27
19:9 [p]ver 16; Ex 24:15-16 [q]Dt 4:12,36
19:10 [r]Lev 11:44; Heb 10:22 [s]Ge 35:2
19:11 [t]ver 16
19:13 [u]Heb 12:20*
19:16 [v]Heb 12:18-19; Rev 4:1 [w]Heb 12:21
19:18 [x]Ps 104:32 [y]Ex 3:2; 24:17; Dt 4:11; 2Ch 7:1; Ps 18:8; Heb 12:18 [z]Ge 19:28 [a]Jdg 5:5; Ps 68:8; Jer 4:24
19:19 [b]Ne 9:13 [c]Ps 81:7
19:21 [d]Ex 3:5; 1Sa 6:19
19:22 [e]Lev 10:3 [f]2Sa 6:7

[o] *5,6* Or *possession, for the whole earth is mine.* [6] *You*
[p] *18* Most Hebrew manuscripts; a few Hebrew manuscripts and Septuagint *all the people*
[q] *19* Or *and God answered him with thunder*

[23]Moses said to the LORD, "The people
cannot come up Mount Sinai, because
you yourself warned us, 'Put limits[a]
around the mountain and set it apart as
holy.'"
[24]The LORD replied, "Go down and
bring Aaron[b] up with you. But the
priests and the people must not force
their way through to come up to the
LORD, or he will break out against them."
[25]So Moses went down to the people
and told them.

The Ten Commandments.

20:1-17pp— Dt 5:6-21

20 And God spoke all these
words:

[2]"I am the LORD your God, who
brought you out of Egypt,
out of the land of slavery.[c]
[3]"You shall have no other gods
before[r] me.[d]
[4]"You shall not make for yourself
an idol[e] in the form of anything in heaven above or on
the earth beneath or in the
waters below. [5]You shall not
bow down to them or wor-
ship[f] them; for I, the LORD
your God, am a jealous God,[g]
punishing the children for
the sin of the fathers to the
third and fourth generation[h]
of those who hate me, [6]but
showing love to a thousand[i]
⌊generations⌋ of those who
love me and keep my com-
mandments.
[7]"You shall not misuse the name of
the LORD your God, for the
LORD will not hold anyone
guiltless who misuses his
name.[j]
[8]"Remember the Sabbath[k] day by
keeping it holy. [9]Six days you
shall labor and do all your
work,[l] [10]but the seventh day
is a Sabbath to the LORD your
God. On it you shall not do
any work, neither you, nor
your son or daughter, nor
your manservant or maidservant, nor your animals, nor
the alien within your gates.
[11]For in six days the LORD
made the heavens and the
earth, the sea, and all that is
in them, but he rested[m] on
the seventh day. Therefore
the LORD blessed the Sabbath
day and made it holy.
[12]"Honor your father and your
mother,[n] so that you may live
long in the land the LORD
your God is giving you.
[13]"You shall not murder.[o]
[14]"You shall not commit adultery.[p]
[15]"You shall not steal.[q]
[16]"You shall not give false testimony
against your neighbor.[r]
[17]"You shall not covet[s] your neighbor's house. You shall not
covet your neighbor's wife,
or his manservant or maidservant, his ox or donkey,
or anything that belongs to
your neighbor."

[18]When the people saw the thunder
and lightning and heard the trumpet[t]
and saw the mountain in smoke, they
trembled with fear. They stayed at a distance [19]and said to Moses, "Speak to us
yourself and we will listen. But do not
have God speak to us or we will die."[u]
[20]Moses said to the people, "Do not
be afraid. God has come to test you, so
that the fear[v] of God will be with you
to keep you from sinning."[w]
[21]The people remained at a distance,
while Moses approached the thick darkness[x] where God was.
[22]Then the LORD said to Moses, "Tell
the Israelites this: 'You have seen for
yourselves that I have spoken to you
from heaven:[y] [23]Do not make any gods
to be alongside me;[z] do not make for
yourselves gods of silver or gods of
gold.[a]
[24]"'Make an altar of earth for me

19:23 [a]ver 12
19:24 [b]Ex 24:1,9
20:2 [c]Ex 13:3
20:3 [d]Dt 6:14; Jer 35:15
20:4 [e]Lev 26:1; Dt 4:15-19, 23; 27:15
20:5 [f]Isa 44:15, 17,19 [g]Ex 34:14; Dt 4:24 [h]Nu 14:18; Jer 32:18
20:6 [i]Dt 7:9
20:7 [j]Lev 19:12; Mt 5:33
20:8 [k]Ex 31:13-16; Lev 26:2
20:9 [l]Ex 34:21; Lk 13:14
20:11 [m]Ge 2:2
20:12 [n]Mt 15:4*; Mk 7:10*; Eph 6:2
20:13 [o]Mt 5:21*; Ro 13:9*
20:14 [p]Mt 19:18*
20:15 [q]Lev 19:11,13; Mt 19:18*
20:16 [r]Ex 23:1,7; Mt 19:18*
20:17 [s]Ro 7:7*; 13:9*; Eph 5:3
20:18 [t]Ex 19:16-19; Heb 12:18-19
20:19 [u]Dt 5:5,23-27; Gal 3:19
20:20 [v]Dt 4:10; Isa 8:13 [w]Pr 16:6
20:21 [x]Dt 5:22
20:22 [y]Ne 9:13
20:23 [z]ver 3 [a]Ex 32:4,8,31

[r]3 Or *besides*

and sacrifice on it your burnt offerings
and fellowship offerings,[s] your sheep and
goats and your cattle. Wherever I cause
my name[a] to be honored, I will come to
you and bless[b] you. 25If you make an
altar of stones for me, do not build it
with dressed stones, for you will defile
it if you use a tool[c] on it. 26And do not
go up to my altar on steps, lest your
nakedness be exposed on it.'

21 "These are the laws[d] you are to
set before them:

Laws of God: Judgments.

21:2-6pp— Dt 15:12-18
21:2-11Ref— Lev 25:39-55

2"If you buy a Hebrew servant, he is
to serve you for six years. But in the seventh year, he shall go free,[e] without paying anything. 3If he comes alone, he is
to go free alone; but if he has a wife
when he comes, she is to go with him.
4If his master gives him a wife and she
bears him sons or daughters, the woman and her children shall belong to her
master, and only the man shall go free.
5"But if the servant declares, 'I love
my master and my wife and children and
do not want to go free,'[f] 6then his master must take him before the judges.[t][g]
He shall take him to the door or the
doorpost and pierce his ear with an awl.
Then he will be his servant for life.[h]
7"If a man sells his daughter as a servant, she is not to go free as menservants do. 8If she does not please the
master who has selected her for himself,[u] he must let her be redeemed. He
has no right to sell her to foreigners,
because he has broken faith with her.
9If he selects her for his son, he must
grant her the rights of a daughter. 10If
he marries another woman, he must
not deprive the first one of her food,
clothing and marital rights.[i] 11If he does
not provide her with these three things,
she is to go free, without any payment
of money.
12"Anyone who strikes a man and
kills him shall surely be put to death.[j]
13However, if he does not do it intentionally, but God lets it happen, he is to
flee to a place[k] I will designate. 14But if
a man schemes and kills another man
deliberately,[l] take him away from my
altar and put him to death.[m]
15"Anyone who attacks[v] his father
or his mother must be put to death.
16"Anyone who kidnaps another and
either sells[n] him or still has him when
he is caught must be put to death.[o]
17"Anyone who curses his father or
mother must be put to death.[p]
18"If men quarrel and one hits the
other with a stone or with his fist[w] and
he does not die but is confined to bed,
19the one who struck the blow will not
be held responsible if the other gets up
and walks around outside with his staff;
however, he must pay the injured man
for the loss of his time and see that he
is completely healed.
20"If a man beats his male or female
slave with a rod and the slave dies as a
direct result, he must be punished, 21but
he is not to be punished if the slave gets
up after a day or two, since the slave is
his property.[q]
22"If men who are fighting hit a pregnant woman and she gives birth pre-
maturely[x] but there is no serious injury,
the offender must be fined whatever
the woman's husband demands[r] and
the court allows. 23But if there is serious injury, you are to take life for life,[s]
24eye for eye, tooth for tooth,[t] hand for
hand, foot for foot, 25burn for burn,
wound for wound, bruise for bruise.
26"If a man hits a manservant or
maidservant in the eye and destroys it,
he must let the servant go free to compensate for the eye. 27And if he knocks
out the tooth of a manservant or maidservant, he must let the servant go
free to compensate for the tooth.
28"If a bull gores a man or a woman
to death, the bull must be stoned to
death,[u] and its meat must not be eaten.

20:24 [a]Dt 12:5; 16:6,11; 2Ch 6:6 [b]Ge 12:2
20:25 [c]Dt 27:5-6
21:1 [d]Dt 4:14
21:2 [e]Jer 34:8,14
21:5 [f]Dt 15:16
21:6 [g]Ex 22:8-9 [h]Ne 5:5
21:10 [i]1Co 7:3-5
21:12 [j]Ge 9:6; Mt 26:52
21:13 [k]Nu 35:10-34; Dt 19:2-13; Jos 20:9; 1Sa 24:4, 10,18
21:14 [l]Heb 10:26 [m]Dt 19:11-12; 1Ki 2:28-34
21:16 [n]Ge 37:28 [o]Ex 22:4; Dt 24:7
21:17 [p]Lev 20:9-10; Mt 15:4*; Mk 7:10*
21:21 [q]Lev 25:44-46
21:22 [r]ver 30; Dt 22:18-19
21:23 [s]Lev 24:19; Dt 19:21
21:24 [t]Mt 5:38*
21:28 [u]ver 32; Ge 9:5

s*24* Traditionally *peace offerings* t*6* Or *before God* u*8* Or *master so that he does not choose her* v*15* Or *kills* w*18* Or *with a tool* x*22* Or *she has a miscarriage*

But the owner of the bull will not be
held responsible. 29If, however, the bull
has had the habit of goring and the owner has been warned but has not kept it
penned up and it kills a man or woman,
the bull must be stoned and the owner
also must be put to death. 30However, if
payment is demanded of him, he may
redeem his life by paying whatever is
demanded.[a] 31This law also applies if the
bull gores a son or daughter. 32If the bull
gores a male or female slave, the owner must pay thirty shekels[y][b] of silver to
the master of the slave, and the bull must
be stoned.

33"If a man uncovers a pit or digs one
and fails to cover it and an ox or a donkey falls into it, 34the owner of the pit
must pay for the loss; he must pay its
owner, and the dead animal will be his.

35"If a man's bull injures the bull of
another and it dies, they are to sell the
live one and divide both the money
and the dead animal equally. 36However,
if it was known that the bull had the
habit of goring, yet the owner did not
keep it penned up, the owner must pay,
animal for animal, and the dead animal
will be his.

Laws of God: Personal property.

22 "If a man steals an ox or a
sheep and slaughters it or sells
it, he must pay back[c] five head of cattle
for the ox and four sheep for the sheep.

2"If a thief is caught breaking in[d] and
is struck so that he dies, the defender is
not guilty of bloodshed;[e] 3but if it happens[z] after sunrise, he is guilty of bloodshed.

"A thief must certainly make restitution, but if he has nothing, he must be
sold[f] to pay for his theft.

4"If the stolen animal is found alive in
his possession—whether ox or donkey
or sheep—he must pay back double.[g]

5"If a man grazes his livestock in a
field or vineyard and lets them stray and
they graze in another man's field, he
must make restitution from the best of
his own field or vineyard.

6"If a fire breaks out and spreads into
thornbushes so that it burns shocks of
grain or standing grain or the whole
field, the one who started the fire must
make restitution.

7"If a man gives his neighbor silver
or goods for safekeeping and they are
stolen from the neighbor's house, the
thief, if he is caught, must pay back
double.[h] 8But if the thief is not found,
the owner of the house must appear before the judges[a][i] to determine whether
he has laid his hands on the other
man's property. 9In all cases of illegal
possession of an ox, a donkey, a sheep,
a garment, or any other lost property
about which somebody says, 'This is
mine,' both parties are to bring their
cases before the judges.[j] The one whom
the judges declare[b] guilty must pay
back double to his neighbor.

10"If a man gives a donkey, an ox, a
sheep or any other animal to his neighbor for safekeeping and it dies or is
injured or is taken away while no one is
looking, 11the issue between them will
be settled by the taking of an oath[k]
before the LORD that the neighbor did
not lay hands on the other person's
property. The owner is to accept this,
and no restitution is required. 12But if
the animal was stolen from the neighbor, he must make restitution to the
owner. 13If it was torn to pieces by a
wild animal, he shall bring in the remains as evidence and he will not be
required to pay for the torn animal.[l]

14"If a man borrows an animal from
his neighbor and it is injured or dies
while the owner is not present, he must
make restitution. 15But if the owner is
with the animal, the borrower will not
have to pay. If the animal was hired, the
money paid for the hire covers the loss.

Laws of God: Personal relationships.

16"If a man seduces a virgin[m] who is
not pledged to be married and sleeps

21:30 [a]ver 22; Nu 35:31
21:32 [b]Zec 11:12-13; Mt 26:15; 27:3,9
22:1 [c]2Sa 12:6; Pr 6:31; Lk 19:8
22:2 [d]Mt 6:19-20; 24:43 [e]Nu 35:27
22:3 [f]Ex 21:2; Mt 18:25
22:4 [g]Ge 43:12
22:7 [h]ver 4
22:8 [i]Ex 21:6; Dt 17:8-9; 19:17
22:9 [j]ver 28; Dt 25:1
22:11 [k]Heb 6:16
22:13 [l]Ge 31:39
22:16 [m]Dt 22:28

y*32* That is, about 12 ounces (about 0.3 kilogram)
z*3* Or *if he strikes him* a*8* Or *before God*; also in verse 9 b*9* Or *whom God declares*

with her, he must pay the bride-price, and she shall be his wife. 17 If her father absolutely refuses to give her to him, he must still pay the bride-price for virgins.

18 "Do not allow a sorceress[a] to live.

19 "Anyone who has sexual relations with an animal[b] must be put to death.

20 "Whoever sacrifices to any god other than the LORD must be destroyed.[c c]

21 "Do not mistreat an alien[d] or oppress him, for you were aliens[e] in Egypt.

22 "Do not take advantage of a widow or an orphan.[f] 23 If you do and they cry out[g] to me, I will certainly hear their cry.[h] 24 My anger will be aroused, and I will kill you with the sword; your wives will become widows and your children fatherless.[i]

25 "If you lend money to one of my people among you who is needy, do not be like a moneylender; charge him no interest.[d j] 26 If you take your neighbor's cloak as a pledge,[k] return it to him by sunset, 27 because his cloak is the only covering he has for his body. What else will he sleep in? When he cries out to me, I will hear, for I am compassionate.[l]

28 "Do not blaspheme God[e m] or curse the ruler of your people.[n]

29 "Do not hold back offerings[o] from your granaries or your vats.[f]

"You must give me the firstborn of your sons.[p] 30 Do the same with your cattle and your sheep.[q] Let them stay with their mothers for seven days, but give them to me on the eighth day.[r]

31 "You are to be my holy people.[s] So do not eat the meat of an animal torn by wild beasts;[t] throw it to the dogs.

Laws of God: Justice.

23 "Do not spread false reports.[u] Do not help a wicked man by being a malicious witness.[v]

2 "Do not follow the crowd in doing wrong. When you give testimony in a lawsuit, do not pervert justice[w] by siding with the crowd, 3 and do not show favoritism to a poor man in his lawsuit.

4 "If you come across your enemy's ox or donkey wandering off, be sure to take it back to him.[x] 5 If you see the donkey[y] of someone who hates you fallen down under its load, do not leave it there; be sure you help him with it.

6 "Do not deny justice[z] to your poor people in their lawsuits. 7 Have nothing to do with a false charge[a] and do not put an innocent or honest person to death, for I will not acquit the guilty.

8 "Do not accept a bribe,[b] for a bribe blinds those who see and twists the words of the righteous.

9 "Do not oppress an alien;[c] you yourselves know how it feels to be aliens, because you were aliens in Egypt.

Laws of God: Rest.

10 "For six years you are to sow your fields and harvest the crops, 11 but during the seventh year let the land lie unplowed and unused. Then the poor among your people may get food from it, and the wild animals may eat what they leave. Do the same with your vineyard and your olive grove.

12 "Six days do your work,[d] but on the seventh day do not work, so that your ox and your donkey may rest and the slave born in your household, and the alien as well, may be refreshed.

13 "Be careful[e] to do everything I have said to you. Do not invoke the names of other gods; do not let them be heard on your lips.

Laws of God: Three annual festivals.

14 "Three times[f] a year you are to celebrate a festival to me.

15 "Celebrate the Feast of Unleavened Bread;[g] for seven days eat bread made without yeast, as I commanded you. Do this at the appointed time in the month

22:18 [a]Lev 20:27; Dt 18:11; 1Sa 28:3 **22:19** [b]Lev 18:23; Dt 27:21 **22:20** [c]Dt 17:2-5 **22:21** [d]Lev 19:33 [e]Dt 10:19 **22:22** [f]Dt 24:6, 10,12,17 **22:23** [g]Lk 18:7 [h]Dt 15:9; Ps 18:6 **22:24** [i]Ps 69:24; 109:9 **22:25** [j]Lev 25:35-37; Dt 23:20; Ps 15:5 **22:26** [k]Dt 24:6 **22:27** [l]Ex 34:6 **22:28** [m]Lev 24:11, 16 [n]Ecc 10:20; Ac 23:5* **22:29** [o]Ex 23:15,16, 19 [p]Ex 13:2 **22:30** [q]Ex 13:12; Dt 15:19 [r]Lev 22:27 **22:31** [s]Lev 19:2 [t]Eze 4:14 **23:1** [u]Ex 20:16; Ps 101:5 [v]Ps 35:11; Ac 6:11 **23:2** [w]Dt 16:19 **23:4** [x]Dt 22:1-3 **23:5** [y]Dt 22:4 **23:6** [z]ver 2 **23:7** [a]Eph 4:25 **23:8** [b]Dt 10:17; 16:19; Pr 15:27 **23:9** [c]Ex 22:21

23:12 [d]Ex 20:9 **23:13** [e]1Ti 4:16 **23:14** [f]Ex 34:23,24 **23:15** [g]Ex 12:17

c *20* The Hebrew term refers to the irrevocable giving over of things or persons to the LORD, often by totally destroying them. d *25* Or *excessive interest* e *28* Or *Do not revile the judges* f *29* The meaning of the Hebrew for this phrase is uncertain.

of Abib, for in that month you came out
of Egypt.
"No one is to appear before me empty-
handed.[a]
16"Celebrate the Feast of Harvest
with the firstfruits[b] of the crops you sow
in your field.
"Celebrate the Feast of Ingathering at
the end of the year, when you gather in
your crops from the field.[c]
17"Three times[d] a year all the men are
to appear before the Sovereign LORD.
18"Do not offer the blood of a sacrifice
to me along with anything containing
yeast.[e]
"The fat of my festival offerings must
not be kept until morning.[f]
19"Bring the best of the firstfruits[g] of
your soil to the house of the LORD your
God.
"Do not cook a young goat in its
mother's milk.[h]

An angel is sent by God to prepare the way.

20"See, I am sending an angel[i] ahead
of you to guard you along the way and
to bring you to the place I have prepared.[j] 21Pay attention to him and listen[k] to what he says. Do not rebel
against him; he will not forgive your
rebellion,[l] since my Name is in him.
22If you listen carefully to what he says
and do all that I say, I will be an enemy[m]
to your enemies and will oppose those
who oppose you. 23My angel will go
ahead of you and bring you into the
land of the Amorites, Hittites, Perizzites,
Canaanites, Hivites and Jebusites,[n] and I
will wipe them out. 24Do not bow down
before their gods or worship[o] them or
follow their practices.[p] You must demolish[q] them and break their sacred stones
to pieces. 25Worship the LORD your
God,[r] and his blessing[s] will be on your
food and water. I will take away sickness[t] from among you, 26and none will
miscarry or be barren[u] in your land. I
will give you a full life span.[v]
27"I will send my terror[w] ahead of you
and throw into confusion[x] every nation
you encounter. I will make all your enemies turn their backs and run. 28I will
send the hornet[y] ahead of you to drive
the Hivites, Canaanites and Hittites out
of your way. 29But I will not drive them
out in a single year, because the land
would become desolate and the wild
animals[z] too numerous for you. 30Little
by little I will drive them out before you,
until you have increased enough to take
possession of the land.
31"I will establish your borders from
the Red Sea[g] to the Sea of the Philistines,[h] and from the desert to the River.[i][a] I will hand over to you the people
who live in the land and you will drive
them out[b] before you. 32Do not make a
covenant[c] with them or with their
gods. 33Do not let them live in your
land, or they will cause you to sin
against me, because the worship of their
gods will certainly be a snare[d] to you."

God calls Moses to meet with him on Mount Sinai.

24 Then he said to Moses, "Come
up to the LORD, you and Aaron,
Nadab and Abihu,[e] and seventy of the
elders[f] of Israel. You are to worship at a
distance, 2but Moses alone is to approach the LORD; the others must not
come near. And the people may not
come up with him."
3When Moses went and told the
people all the LORD's words and laws,
they responded with one voice, "Everything the LORD has said we will do."[g]
4Moses then wrote[h] down everything
the LORD had said.
He got up early the next morning
and built an altar at the foot of the
mountain and set up twelve stone pillars[i] representing the twelve tribes of
Israel. 5Then he sent young Israelite
men, and they offered burnt offerings
and sacrificed young bulls as fellowship

23:15 [a]Ex 34:20 **23:16** [b]Ex 34:22 [c]Dt 16:13 **23:17** [d]Dt 16:16 **23:18** [e]Ex 34:25 [f]Dt 16:4 **23:19** [g]Ex 22:29; Dt 26:2,10 [h]Dt 14:21 **23:20** [i]Ex 14:19; 32:34 [j]Ex 15:17 **23:21** [k]Nu 14:11; Dt 18:19 [l]Ps 78:8,40,56 **23:22** [m]Ge 12:3; Dt 30:7 **23:23** [n]ver 20; Jos 24:8,11 **23:24** [o]Ex 20:5 [p]Dt 12:30-31 [q]Ex 34:13; Nu 33:52 **23:25** [r]Dt 6:13; Mt 4:10 [s]Dt 7:12-15; 28:1-14 [t]Ex 15:26 **23:26** [u]Dt 7:14; Mal 3:11 [v]Job 5:26 **23:27** [w]Ex 15:14; Dt 2:25 [x]Dt 7:23 **23:28** [y]Dt 7:20; Jos 24:12 **23:29** [z]Dt 7:22 **23:31** [a]Ge 15:18 [b]Jos 21:44; 24:12,18 **23:32** [c]Ex 34:12; Dt 7:2 **23:33** [d]Dt 7:16; Ps 106:36 **24:1** [e]Ex 6:23; Lev 10:1-2 [f]Nu 11:16

24:3 [g]Ex 19:8; Dt 5:27 **24:4** [h]Dt 31:9 [i]Ge 28:18

g*31* Hebrew *Yam Suph*; that is, Sea of Reeds
h*31* That is, the Mediterranean i*31* That is, the Euphrates

offerings[j] to the LORD. 6Moses took
half of the blood[a] and put it in bowls,
and the other half he sprinkled on the
altar. 7Then he took the Book of the
Covenant[b] and read it to the people.
They responded, "We will do everything
the LORD has said; we will obey."
8Moses then took the blood, sprinkled
it on the people and said, "This is the
blood of the covenant[c] that the LORD has
made with you in accordance with all
these words."
9Moses and Aaron, Nadab and Abihu,
and the seventy elders[d] of Israel went
up 10and saw[e] the God of Israel. Under
his feet was something like a pavement
made of sapphire,[k][f] clear as the sky[g]
itself. 11But God did not raise his hand
against these leaders of the Israelites;
they saw[h] God, and they ate and drank.
12The LORD said to Moses, "Come
up to me on the mountain and stay
here, and I will give you the tablets of
stone,[i] with the law and commands I
have written for their instruction."
13Then Moses set out with Joshua[j]
his aide, and Moses went up on the
mountain[k] of God. 14He said to the
elders, "Wait here for us until we come
back to you. Aaron and Hur are with
you, and anyone involved in a dispute
can go to them."
15When Moses went up on the
mountain, the cloud[l] covered it, 16and
the glory[m] of the LORD settled on Mount
Sinai. For six days the cloud covered
the mountain, and on the seventh day
the LORD called to Moses from within
the cloud.[n] 17To the Israelites the glory
of the LORD looked like a consuming
fire[o] on top of the mountain. 18Then
Moses entered the cloud as he went on
up the mountain. And he stayed on the
mountain forty[p] days and forty nights.[q]

The tabernacle offerings.

25:1-7pp— Ex 35:4-9

25 The LORD said to Moses, 2"Tell
the Israelites to bring me an
offering. You are to receive the offering for me from each man whose heart
prompts[r] him to give. 3These are the
offerings you are to receive from them:
gold, silver and bronze; 4blue, purple
and scarlet yarn and fine linen; goat
hair; 5ram skins dyed red and hides of
sea cows[l]; acacia wood; 6olive oil[s] for
the light; spices for the anointing oil
and for the fragrant incense; 7and onyx
stones and other gems to be mounted
on the ephod[t] and breastpiece.[u]
8"Then have them make a sanctuary[v] for me, and I will dwell[w] among
them. 9Make this tabernacle and all its
furnishings exactly like the pattern[x] I
will show you.

The ark of the Testimony.

25:10-20pp— Ex 37:1-9

10"Have them make a chest[y] of acacia
wood—two and a half cubits long, a
cubit and a half wide, and a cubit and
a half high.[m] 11Overlay it with pure
gold, both inside and out, and make a
gold molding around it. 12Cast four gold
rings for it and fasten them to its four
feet, with two rings on one side and
two rings on the other. 13Then make
poles of acacia wood and overlay them
with gold. 14Insert the poles into the
rings on the sides of the chest to carry
it. 15The poles are to remain in the rings
of this ark; they are not to be removed.[z] 16Then put in the ark the Testimony,[a] which I will give you.
17"Make an atonement cover[n][b] of pure
gold—two and a half cubits long and a
cubit and a half wide.[o] 18And make two
cherubim out of hammered gold at the
ends of the cover. 19Make one cherub
on one end and the second cherub on
the other; make the cherubim of one
piece with the cover, at the two ends.
20The cherubim are to have their wings
spread upward, overshadowing[c] the

24:6 [a]Heb 9:18
24:7 [b]Heb 9:19
24:8 [c]Heb 9:20*; 1Pe 1:2
24:9 [d]ver 1
24:10 [e]Mt 17:2; Jn 1:18; 6:46 [f]Eze 1:26 [g]Rev 4:3
24:11 [h]Ge 32:30; Ex 19:21
24:12 [i]Ex 32:15-16
24:13 [j]Ex 17:9 [k]Ex 3:1
24:15 [l]Ex 19:9
24:16 [m]Ex 16:10 [n]Ps 99:7
24:17 [o]Ex 3:2; Dt 4:36; Heb 12:18,29
24:18 [p]Dt 9:9 [q]Ex 34:28
25:2 [r]Ex 35:21; 1Ch 29:5,7,9; Ezr 2:68; 2Co 8:11-12; 9:7
25:6 [s]Ex 27:20; 30:22-32
25:7 [t]Ex 28:4,6-14 [u]Ex 28:15-30
25:8 [v]Ex 36:1-5; Heb 9:1-2 [w]Ex 29:45; 1Ki 6:13; 2Co 6:16; Rev 21:3
25:9 [x]ver 40; Ac 7:44; Heb 8:5
25:10 [y]Dt 10:1-5; Heb 9:4
25:15 [z]1Ki 8:8
25:16 [a]Dt 31:26; Heb 9:4
25:17 [b]Ro 3:25
25:20 [c]1Ki 8:7; 1Ch 28:18; Heb 9:5

j *5* Traditionally *peace offerings* k *10* Or *lapis lazuli* l *5* That is, dugongs m *10* That is, about 3 3/4 feet (about 1.1 meters) long and 2 1/4 feet (about 0.7 meter) wide and high n *17* Traditionally *a mercy seat* o *17* That is, about 3 3/4 feet (about 1.1 meters) long and 2 1/4 feet (about 0.7 meter) wide

cover with them. The cherubim are to face each other, looking toward the cover. 21 Place the cover on top of the ark[a] and put in the ark the Testimony,[b] which I will give you. 22 There, above the cover between the two cherubim[c] that are over the ark of the Testimony, I will meet[d] with you and give you all my commands for the Israelites.

The table.

25:23-29pp— Ex 37:10-16

23 "Make a table[e] of acacia wood—two cubits long, a cubit wide and a cubit and a half high.[p] 24 Overlay it with pure gold and make a gold molding around it. 25 Also make around it a rim a handbreadth[q] wide and put a gold molding on the rim. 26 Make four gold rings for the table and fasten them to the four corners, where the four legs are. 27 The rings are to be close to the rim to hold the poles used in carrying the table. 28 Make the poles of acacia wood, overlay them with gold and carry the table with them. 29 And make its plates and dishes of pure gold, as well as its pitchers and bowls for the pouring out of offerings.[f] 30 Put the bread of the Presence[g] on this table to be before me at all times.

The lampstand.

25:31-39pp— Ex 37:17-24

31 "Make a lampstand[h] of pure gold and hammer it out, base and shaft; its flowerlike cups, buds and blossoms shall be of one piece with it. 32 Six branches are to extend from the sides of the lampstand—three on one side and three on the other. 33 Three cups shaped like almond flowers with buds and blossoms are to be on one branch, three on the next branch, and the same for all six branches extending from the lampstand. 34 And on the lampstand there are to be four cups shaped like almond flowers with buds and blossoms. 35 One bud shall be under the first pair of branches extending from the lampstand, a second bud under the second pair, and a third bud under the third pair—six branches in all. 36 The buds and branches shall all be of one piece with the lampstand, hammered out of pure gold.

37 "Then make its seven lamps[i] and set them up on it so that they light the space in front of it. 38 Its wick trimmers and trays are to be of pure gold. 39 A talent[r] of pure gold is to be used for the lampstand and all these accessories. 40 See that you make them according to the pattern[j] shown you on the mountain.

25:21 [a]Ex 26:34 [b]ver 16
25:22 [c]Nu 7:89; 1Sa 4:4; 2Sa 6:2; 2Ki 19:15; Ps 80:1; Isa 37:16 [d]Ex 29:42-43
25:23 [e]Heb 9:2
25:29 [f]Nu 4:7
25:30 [g]Lev 24:5-9
25:31 [h]1Ki 7:49; Zec 4:2; Heb 9:2; Rev 1:12
25:37 [i]Ex 27:21; Lev 24:3-4; Nu 8:2
25:40 [j]Ex 26:30; Nu 8:4; Ac 7:44; Heb 8:5*

The curtains.

26:1-37pp— Ex 36:8-38

26 "Make the tabernacle with ten curtains of finely twisted linen and blue, purple and scarlet yarn, with cherubim worked into them by a skilled craftsman. 2 All the curtains are to be the same size—twenty-eight cubits long and four cubits wide.[s] 3 Join five of the curtains together, and do the same with the other five. 4 Make loops of blue material along the edge of the end curtain in one set, and do the same with the end curtain in the other set. 5 Make fifty loops on one curtain and fifty loops on the end curtain of the other set, with the loops opposite each other. 6 Then make fifty gold clasps and use them to fasten the curtains together so that the tabernacle is a unit.

7 "Make curtains of goat hair for the tent over the tabernacle—eleven altogether. 8 All eleven curtains are to be the same size—thirty cubits long and four cubits wide.[t] 9 Join five of the curtains together into one set and the other six into another set. Fold the sixth curtain double at the front of the tent. 10 Make

p *23* That is, about 3 feet (about 0.9 meter) long and 1 1/2 feet (about 0.5 meter) wide and 2 1/4 feet (about 0.7 meter) high q *25* That is, about 3 inches (about 8 centimeters) r *39* That is, about 75 pounds (about 34 kilograms) s *2* That is, about 42 feet (about 12.5 meters) long and 6 feet (about 1.8 meters) wide t *8* That is, about 45 feet (about 13.5 meters) long and 6 feet (about 1.8 meters) wide

fifty loops along the edge of the end curtain in one set and also along the edge of the end curtain in the other set. **11**Then make fifty bronze clasps and put them in the loops to fasten the tent together as a unit. **12**As for the additional length of the tent curtains, the half curtain that is left over is to hang down at the rear of the tabernacle. **13**The tent curtains will be a cubit[u] longer on both sides; what is left will hang over the sides of the tabernacle so as to cover it. **14**Make for the tent a covering of ram skins dyed red, and over that a covering of hides of sea cows.[v][a]

15"Make upright frames of acacia wood for the tabernacle. **16**Each frame is to be ten cubits long and a cubit and a half wide,[w] **17**with two projections set parallel to each other. Make all the frames of the tabernacle in this way. **18**Make twenty frames for the south side of the tabernacle **19**and make forty silver bases to go under them—two bases for each frame, one under each projection. **20**For the other side, the north side of the tabernacle, make twenty frames **21**and forty silver bases—two under each frame. **22**Make six frames for the far end, that is, the west end of the tabernacle, **23**and make two frames for the corners at the far end. **24**At these two corners they must be double from the bottom all the way to the top, and fitted into a single ring; both shall be like that. **25**So there will be eight frames and sixteen silver bases—two under each frame.

26"Also make crossbars of acacia wood: five for the frames on one side of the tabernacle, **27**five for those on the other side, and five for the frames on the west, at the far end of the tabernacle. **28**The center crossbar is to extend from end to end at the middle of the frames. **29**Overlay the frames with gold and make gold rings to hold the crossbars. Also overlay the crossbars with gold.

30"Set up the tabernacle according to the plan[b] shown you on the mountain.

26:14 [a]Ex 36:19; Nu 4:25
26:30 [b]Ex 25:9,40; Ac 7:44; Heb 8:5
26:31 [c]2Ch 3:14; Mt 27:51; Heb 9:3 [d]Ex 36:35
26:33 [e]Ex 40:3,21; Lev 16:2 [f]Heb 9:2-3
26:34 [g]Ex 25:21; 40:20; Heb 9:5
26:35 [h]Heb 9:2 [i]Ex 40:22,24
27:1 [j]Eze 43:13
27:2 [k]Ps 118:27

31"Make a curtain[c] of blue, purple and scarlet yarn and finely twisted linen, with cherubim[d] worked into it by a skilled craftsman. **32**Hang it with gold hooks on four posts of acacia wood overlaid with gold and standing on four silver bases. **33**Hang the curtain from the clasps and place the ark of the Testimony behind the curtain.[e] The curtain will separate the Holy Place from the Most Holy Place.[f] **34**Put the atonement cover[g] on the ark of the Testimony in the Most Holy Place. **35**Place the table[h] outside the curtain on the north side of the tabernacle and put the lampstand[i] opposite it on the south side.

36"For the entrance to the tent make a curtain of blue, purple and scarlet yarn and finely twisted linen—the work of an embroiderer. **37**Make gold hooks for this curtain and five posts of acacia wood overlaid with gold. And cast five bronze bases for them.

The altar.

27:1-8pp— Ex 38:1-7

27 "Build an altar[j] of acacia wood, three cubits[x] high; it is to be square, five cubits long and five cubits wide.[y] **2**Make a horn[k] at each of the four corners, so that the horns and the altar are of one piece, and overlay the altar with bronze. **3**Make all its utensils of bronze—its pots to remove the ashes, and its shovels, sprinkling bowls, meat forks and firepans. **4**Make a grating for it, a bronze network, and make a bronze ring at each of the four corners of the network. **5**Put it under the ledge of the altar so that it is halfway up the altar. **6**Make poles of acacia wood for the altar and overlay them with bronze. **7**The poles are to be inserted into the rings so they will be on two sides of the altar when it is carried. **8**Make the altar hollow,

[u] *13* That is, about 1 1/2 feet (about 0.5 meter)
[v] *14* That is, dugongs
[w] *16* That is, about 15 feet (about 4.5 meters) long and 2 1/4 feet (about 0.7 meter) wide
[x] *1* That is, about 4 1/2 feet (about 1.3 meters)
[y] *1* That is, about 7 1/2 feet (about 2.3 meters) long and wide

out of boards. It is to be made just as you were shown[a] on the mountain.

27:8
[a]Ex 25:9,40

The courtyard.

27:9-19pp— Ex 38:9-20

9"Make a courtyard for the tabernacle. The south side shall be a hundred cubits[z] long and is to have curtains of finely twisted linen, 10with twenty posts and twenty bronze bases and with silver hooks and bands on the posts. 11The north side shall also be a hundred cubits long and is to have curtains, with twenty posts and twenty bronze bases and with silver hooks and bands on the posts.

12"The west end of the courtyard shall be fifty cubits[a] wide and have curtains, with ten posts and ten bases. 13On the east end, toward the sunrise, the courtyard shall also be fifty cubits wide. 14Curtains fifteen cubits[b] long are to be on one side of the entrance, with three posts and three bases, 15and curtains fifteen cubits long are to be on the other side, with three posts and three bases.

16"For the entrance to the courtyard, provide a curtain twenty cubits[c] long, of blue, purple and scarlet yarn and finely twisted linen—the work of an embroiderer—with four posts and four bases. 17All the posts around the courtyard are to have silver bands and hooks, and bronze bases. 18The courtyard shall be a hundred cubits long and fifty cubits wide,[d] with curtains of finely twisted linen five cubits[e] high, and with bronze bases. 19All the other articles used in the service of the tabernacle, whatever their function, including all the tent pegs for it and those for the courtyard, are to be of bronze.

Oil for the lamps.

27:20-21pp— Lev 24:1-3

20"Command the Israelites to bring you clear oil of pressed olives for the light so that the lamps may be kept burning. 21In the Tent of Meeting,[b] outside the curtain that is in front of the Testimony,[c] Aaron and his sons are to keep the lamps[d] burning before the LORD from evening till morning. This is to be a lasting ordinance[e] among the Israelites for the generations to come.

27:21
[b]Ex 28:43
[c]Ex 26:31,33
[d]Ex 25:37; 30:8; 1Sa 3:3; 2Ch 13:11
[e]Ex 29:9; Lev 3:17; 16:34; Nu 18:23; 19:21

Sacred garments for Aaron and his sons.

28 "Have Aaron[f] your brother brought to you from among the Israelites, along with his sons Nadab and Abihu, Eleazar and Ithamar, so they may serve me as priests.[g] 2Make sacred garments[h] for your brother Aaron, to give him dignity and honor. 3Tell all the skilled men[i] to whom I have given wisdom[j] in such matters that they are to make garments for Aaron, for his consecration, so he may serve me as priest. 4These are the garments they are to make: a breastpiece,[k] an ephod, a robe,[l] a woven tunic,[m] a turban and a sash. They are to make these sacred garments for your brother Aaron and his sons, so they may serve me as priests. 5Have them use gold, and blue, purple and scarlet yarn, and fine linen.

28:1
[f]Heb 5:4
[g]Nu 18:1-7; Heb 5:1

28:2
[h]Ex 29:5,29; 31:10; 39:1; Lev 8:7-9,30

28:3
[i]Ex 31:6; 36:1
[j]Ex 31:3

28:4
[k]ver 15-30
[l]ver 31-35
[m]ver 39

The ephod.

28:6-14pp— Ex 39:2-7

6"Make the ephod of gold, and of blue, purple and scarlet yarn, and of finely twisted linen—the work of a skilled craftsman. 7It is to have two shoulder pieces attached to two of its corners, so it can be fastened. 8Its skillfully woven waistband is to be like it—of one piece with the ephod and made with gold, and with blue, purple and scarlet yarn, and with finely twisted linen.

9"Take two onyx stones and engrave on them the names of the sons of Israel
10in the order of their birth—six names

z *9* That is, about 150 feet (about 46 meters); also in verse 11 a *12* That is, about 75 feet (about 23 meters); also in verse 13 b *14* That is, about 22 1/2 feet (about 6.9 meters); also in verse 15 c *16* That is, about 30 feet (about 9 meters) d *18* That is, about 150 feet (about 46 meters) long and 75 feet (about 23 meters) wide e *18* That is, about 7 1/2 feet (about 2.3 meters)

on one stone and the remaining six on
the other. 11Engrave the names of the
sons of Israel on the two stones the way
a gem cutter engraves a seal. Then
mount the stones in gold filigree settings
12and fasten them on the shoulder pieces
of the ephod as memorial stones for the
sons of Israel. Aaron is to bear the names
on his shoulders as a memorial before the
LORD. 13Make gold filigree settings 14and
two braided chains of pure gold, like a
rope, and attach the chains to the settings.

The breastpiece.

28:15-28pp— Ex 39:8-21

15"Fashion a breastpiece for making
decisions—the work of a skilled craftsman. Make it like the ephod: of gold,
and of blue, purple and scarlet yarn, and
of finely twisted linen. 16It is to be
square—a span[f] long and a span wide—
and folded double. 17Then mount four
rows of precious stones on it. In the first
row there shall be a ruby, a topaz and a
beryl; 18in the second row a turquoise,
a sapphire[g] and an emerald; 19in the
third row a jacinth, an agate and an
amethyst; 20in the fourth row a chrysolite, an onyx and a jasper.[h] Mount them
in gold filigree settings. 21There are to
be twelve stones, one for each of the
names of the sons of Israel, each engraved like a seal with the name of one
of the twelve tribes.

22"For the breastpiece make braided
chains of pure gold, like a rope. 23Make
two gold rings for it and fasten them to
two corners of the breastpiece. 24Fasten
the two gold chains to the rings at the
corners of the breastpiece, 25and the
other ends of the chains to the two settings, attaching them to the shoulder
pieces of the ephod at the front. 26Make
two gold rings and attach them to the
other two corners of the breastpiece
on the inside edge next to the ephod.
27Make two more gold rings and attach
them to the bottom of the shoulder
pieces on the front of the ephod, close
to the seam just above the waistband
of the ephod. 28The rings of the breastpiece are to be tied to the rings of the
ephod with blue cord, connecting it to
the waistband, so that the breastpiece
will not swing out from the ephod.

29"Whenever Aaron enters the Holy
Place,[a] he will bear the names of the
sons of Israel over his heart on the
breastpiece of decision as a continuing
memorial before the LORD. 30Also put
the Urim and the Thummim[b] in the
breastpiece, so they may be over Aaron's
heart whenever he enters the presence
of the LORD. Thus Aaron will always
bear the means of making decisions for
the Israelites over his heart before the
LORD.

Other sacred garments.

28:31-43pp— Ex 39:22-31

31"Make the robe of the ephod entirely of blue cloth, 32with an opening for
the head in its center. There shall be a
woven edge like a collar[i] around this
opening, so that it will not tear. 33Make
pomegranates of blue, purple and scarlet yarn around the hem of the robe,
with gold bells between them. 34The
gold bells and the pomegranates are to
alternate around the hem of the robe.
35Aaron must wear it when he ministers. The sound of the bells will be heard
when he enters the Holy Place before
the LORD and when he comes out, so
that he will not die.

36"Make a plate of pure gold and
engrave on it as on a seal: HOLY TO THE
LORD.[c] 37Fasten a blue cord to it to attach
it to the turban; it is to be on the front
of the turban. 38It will be on Aaron's
forehead, and he will bear the guilt[d]
involved in the sacred gifts the Israelites consecrate, whatever their gifts
may be. It will be on Aaron's forehead
continually so that they will be acceptable to the LORD.

39"Weave the tunic of fine linen and
make the turban of fine linen. The sash

28:29 [a]ver 12

28:30 [b]Lev 8:8; Nu 27:21; Dt 33:8; Ezr 2:63; Ne 7:65

28:36 [c]Zec 14:20

28:38 [d]Lev 10:17; 22:9,16; Nu 18:1; Heb 9:28; 1Pe 2:24

[f]*16* That is, about 9 inches (about 22 centimeters)
[g]*18* Or *lapis lazuli* [h]*20* The precise identification of some of these precious stones is uncertain. [i]*32* The meaning of the Hebrew for this word is uncertain.

is to be the work of an embroiderer.
40 Make tunics, sashes and headbands
for Aaron's sons,[a] to give them dignity
and honor. 41 After you put these clothes
on your brother Aaron and his sons,
anoint[b] and ordain them. Consecrate
them so they may serve me as priests.[c]
42 "Make linen undergarments[d] as a
covering for the body, reaching from
the waist to the thigh. 43 Aaron and his
sons must wear them whenever they
enter the Tent of Meeting[e] or approach
the altar to minister in the Holy Place, so
that they will not incur guilt and die.[f]
"This is to be a lasting ordinance[g] for
Aaron and his descendants.

The consecration of the priests.

29:1-37pp— Lev 8:1-36

29 "This is what you are to do to
consecrate them, so they may
serve me as priests: Take a young bull
and two rams without defect. 2 And from
fine wheat flour, without yeast, make
bread, and cakes mixed with oil, and
wafers spread with oil.[h] 3 Put them in a
basket and present them in it—along
with the bull and the two rams. 4 Then
bring Aaron and his sons to the entrance
to the Tent of Meeting and wash them
with water.[i] 5 Take the garments[j] and
dress Aaron with the tunic, the robe of
the ephod, the ephod itself and the
breastpiece. Fasten the ephod on him
by its skillfully woven waistband.[k] 6 Put
the turban on his head and attach the
sacred diadem[l] to the turban. 7 Take the
anointing oil[m] and anoint him by pouring it on his head. 8 Bring his sons and
dress them in tunics 9 and put headbands
on them. Then tie sashes on Aaron
and his sons.[j][n] The priesthood is theirs
by a lasting ordinance.[o] In this way
you shall ordain Aaron and his sons.
10 "Bring the bull to the front of the
Tent of Meeting, and Aaron and his
sons shall lay their hands on its head.
11 Slaughter it in the LORD's presence at
the entrance to the Tent of Meeting.
12 Take some of the bull's blood and put
it on the horns[p] of the altar with your
finger, and pour out the rest of it at the
base of the altar. 13 Then take all the
fat[q] around the inner parts, the covering of the liver, and both kidneys with
the fat on them, and burn them on the
altar. 14 But burn the bull's flesh and its
hide and its offal outside the camp.[r] It is
a sin offering.
15 "Take one of the rams, and Aaron
and his sons shall lay their hands on its
head. 16 Slaughter it and take the blood
and sprinkle it against the altar on all
sides. 17 Cut the ram into pieces and
wash the inner parts and the legs, putting them with the head and the other
pieces. 18 Then burn the entire ram on
the altar. It is a burnt offering to the
LORD, a pleasing aroma,[s] an offering
made to the LORD by fire.
19 "Take the other ram,[t] and Aaron
and his sons shall lay their hands on its
head. 20 Slaughter it, take some of its
blood and put it on the lobes of the right
ears of Aaron and his sons, on the
thumbs of their right hands, and on the
big toes of their right feet. Then sprinkle blood against the altar on all sides.
21 And take some of the blood[u] on the
altar and some of the anointing oil[v] and
sprinkle it on Aaron and his garments
and on his sons and their garments.
Then he and his sons and their garments will be consecrated.[w]
22 "Take from this ram the fat, the fat
tail, the fat around the inner parts, the
covering of the liver, both kidneys with
the fat on them, and the right thigh.
(This is the ram for the ordination.)
23 From the basket of bread made without yeast, which is before the LORD,
take a loaf, and a cake made with oil,
and a wafer. 24 Put all these in the hands
of Aaron and his sons and wave them
before the LORD as a wave offering.[x]
25 Then take them from their hands
and burn them on the altar along with
the burnt offering for a pleasing aroma
to the LORD, an offering made to the
LORD by fire. 26 After you take the breast
of the ram for Aaron's ordination, wave

28:40 [a]ver 4; Ex 39:41
28:41 [b]Ex 29:7; Lev 10:7 [c]Ex 29:7-9; 30:30; 40:15; Lev 8:1-36; Heb 7:28
28:42 [d]Lev 6:10; 16:4,23; Eze 44:18
28:43 [e]Ex 27:21 [f]Ex 20:26 [g]Lev 17:7
29:2 [h]Lev 2:1,4; 6:19-23
29:4 [i]Ex 40:12; Heb 10:22
29:5 [j]Ex 28:2; Lev 8:7 [k]Ex 28:8
29:6 [l]Lev 8:9
29:7 [m]Ex 30:25, 30,31; Lev 8:12; 21:10; Nu 35:25; Ps 133:2
29:9 [n]Ex 28:40 [o]Ex 40:15; Nu 3:10; 18:7; 25:13; Dt 18:5
29:12 [p]Ex 27:2
29:13 [q]Lev 3:3,5,9
29:14 [r]Lev 4:11-12, 21; Heb 13:11
29:18 [s]Ge 8:21
29:19 [t]ver 3
29:21 [u]Heb 9:22 [v]Ex 30:25,31 [w]ver 1
29:24 [x]Lev 7:30

j9 Hebrew; Septuagint *on them*

it before the LORD as a wave offering,
and it will be your share.[a]
27“Consecrate those parts of the ordination ram that belong to Aaron and
his sons:[b] the breast that was waved and
the thigh that was presented. 28This is
always to be the regular share from the
Israelites for Aaron and his sons. It is
the contribution the Israelites are to
make to the LORD from their fellowship
offerings.[k][c]
29“Aaron's sacred garments will belong to his descendants so that they can
be anointed and ordained in them.[d]
30The son[e] who succeeds him as priest
and comes to the Tent of Meeting to
minister in the Holy Place is to wear
them seven days.
31“Take the ram for the ordination and
cook the meat in a sacred place. 32At
the entrance to the Tent of Meeting,
Aaron and his sons are to eat the meat
of the ram and the bread[f] that is in the
basket. 33They are to eat these offerings
by which atonement was made for their
ordination and consecration. But no one
else may eat[g] them, because they are
sacred. 34And if any of the meat of the
ordination ram or any bread is left over
till morning,[h] burn it up. It must not be
eaten, because it is sacred.
35“Do for Aaron and his sons everything I have commanded you, taking
seven days to ordain them. 36Sacrifice a
bull each day[i] as a sin offering to make
atonement. Purify the altar by making
atonement for it, and anoint it to consecrate[j] it. 37For seven days make atonement for the altar and consecrate it.
Then the altar will be most holy, and
whatever touches it will be holy.[k]

The daily offering.

38“This is what you are to offer on the
altar regularly each day:[l] two lambs a
year old. 39Offer one in the morning
and the other at twilight.[m] 40With the
first lamb offer a tenth of an ephah[l] of
fine flour mixed with a quarter of a hin[m]
of oil from pressed olives, and a quarter of a hin of wine as a drink offering.
41Sacrifice the other lamb at twilight
with the same grain offering and its
drink offering as in the morning—a
pleasing aroma, an offering made to the
LORD by fire.
42“For the generations to come[n] this
burnt offering is to be made regularly at
the entrance to the Tent of Meeting before the LORD. There I will meet you and
speak to you;[o] 43there also I will meet
with the Israelites, and the place will be
consecrated by my glory.[p]
44“So I will consecrate the Tent of
Meeting and the altar and will consecrate Aaron and his sons to serve me as
priests.[q] 45Then I will dwell[r] among the
Israelites and be their God.[s] 46They will
know that I am the LORD their God, who
brought them out of Egypt so that I
might dwell among them. I am the LORD
their God.[t]

The altar of incense.

30:1-5pp— Ex 37:25-28

30 “Make an altar[u] of acacia wood
for burning incense.[v] 2It is to be
square, a cubit long and a cubit wide,
and two cubits high[n]—its horns[w] of one
piece with it. 3Overlay the top and all
the sides and the horns with pure gold,
and make a gold molding around it.
4Make two gold rings for the altar below
the molding—two on opposite sides—
to hold the poles used to carry it. 5Make
the poles of acacia wood and overlay
them with gold. 6Put the altar in front of
the curtain that is before the ark of the
Testimony—before the atonement cover[x] that is over the Testimony—where
I will meet with you.
7“Aaron must burn fragrant incense[y]
on the altar every morning when he
tends the lamps. 8He must burn incense
again when he lights the lamps at twilight so incense will burn regularly before the LORD for the generations to
come. 9Do not offer on this altar any

29:26 [a]Lev 7:31-34
29:27 [b]Lev 7:31,34; Dt 18:3
29:28 [c]Lev 10:15
29:29 [d]Nu 20:26,28
29:30 [e]Nu 20:28
29:32 [f]Mt 12:4
29:33 [g]Lev 10:14; 22:10,13
29:34 [h]Ex 12:10
29:36 [i]Heb 10:11 [j]Ex 40:10
29:37 [k]Ex 30:28-29; 40:10; Mt 23:19
29:38 [l]Nu 28:3-8; 1Ch 16:40; Da 12:11
29:39 [m]Eze 46:13-15
29:42 [n]Ex 30:8 [o]Ex 25:22
29:43 [p]1Ki 8:11
29:44 [q]Lev 21:15
29:45 [r]Ex 25:8; Lev 26:12; Zec 2:10; Jn 14:17 [s]2Co 6:16; Rev 21:3
29:46 [t]Ex 20:2
30:1 [u]Ex 37:25 [v]Rev 8:3
30:2 [w]Ex 27:2
30:6 [x]Ex 25:22; 26:34
30:7 [y]ver 34-35; Ex 27:21; 1Sa 2:28

[k]*28* Traditionally *peace offerings* [l]*40* That is, probably about 2 quarts (about 2 liters) [m]*40* That is, probably about 1 quart (about 1 liter) [n]*2* That is, about 1 1/2 feet (about 0.5 meter) long and wide and about 3 feet (about 0.9 meter) high

other incense[a] or any burnt offering or
grain offering, and do not pour a drink
offering on it. 10 Once a year Aaron shall
make atonement[b] on its horns. This
annual atonement must be made with
the blood of the atoning sin offering for
the generations to come. It is most holy
to the LORD."

The atonement money.

11 Then the LORD said to Moses,
12 "When you take a census[c] of the
Israelites to count them, each one must
pay the LORD a ransom[d] for his life
at the time he is counted. Then no
plague[e] will come on them when you
number them. 13 Each one who crosses
over to those already counted is to
give a half shekel,[o] according to the
sanctuary shekel,[f] which weighs twenty gerahs. This half shekel is an offering to the LORD. 14 All who cross over,
those twenty years old or more, are to
give an offering to the LORD. 15 The rich
are not to give more than a half shekel
and the poor are not to give less[g] when
you make the offering to the LORD to
atone for your lives. 16 Receive the atonement money from the Israelites and
use it for the service of the Tent of
Meeting.[h] It will be a memorial for the
Israelites before the LORD, making atonement for your lives."

The bronze basin.

17 Then the LORD said to Moses,
18 "Make a bronze basin,[i] with its bronze
stand, for washing. Place it between the
Tent of Meeting and the altar, and put
water in it. 19 Aaron and his sons are to
wash their hands and feet[j] with water[k]
from it. 20 Whenever they enter the Tent
of Meeting, they shall wash with water
so that they will not die. Also, when
they approach the altar to minister by
presenting an offering made to the LORD
by fire, 21 they shall wash their hands
and feet so that they will not die. This is
to be a lasting ordinance[l] for Aaron and
his descendants for the generations to
come."

The sacred anointing oil.

22 Then the LORD said to Moses,
23 "Take the following fine spices: 500
shekels[p] of liquid myrrh,[m] half as much
(that is, 250 shekels) of fragrant cinnamon, 250 shekels of fragrant cane,
24 500 shekels of cassia[n]—all according
to the sanctuary shekel—and a hin[q] of
olive oil. 25 Make these into a sacred
anointing oil, a fragrant blend, the work
of a perfumer.[o] It will be the sacred
anointing oil.[p] 26 Then use it to anoint[q]
the Tent of Meeting, the ark of the Testimony, 27 the table and all its articles,
the lampstand and its accessories, the
altar of incense, 28 the altar of burnt offering and all its utensils, and the basin
with its stand. 29 You shall consecrate
them so they will be most holy, and
whatever touches them will be holy.[r]
30 "Anoint Aaron and his sons and
consecrate[s] them so they may serve me
as priests. 31 Say to the Israelites, 'This
is to be my sacred anointing oil for the
generations to come. 32 Do not pour it
on men's bodies and do not make any
oil with the same formula. It is sacred,
and you are to consider it sacred.[t]
33 Whoever makes perfume like it and
whoever puts it on anyone other than a
priest must be cut off[u] from his people.'"

The holy incense.

34 Then the LORD said to Moses,
"Take fragrant spices—gum resin, ony-
cha and galbanum—and pure frankincense, all in equal amounts, 35 and
make a fragrant blend of incense, the
work of a perfumer.[v] It is to be salted
and pure and sacred. 36 Grind some of
it to powder and place it in front of the
Testimony in the Tent of Meeting,
where I will meet with you. It shall be
most holy[w] to you. 37 Do not make any
incense with this formula for yourselves; consider it holy[x] to the LORD.
38 Whoever makes any like it to enjoy

30:9 [a]Lev 10:1
30:10 [b]Lev 16:18-19, 30
30:12 [c]Ex 38:25; Nu 1:2,49; 2Sa 24:1 [d]Nu 31:50; Mt 20:28 [e]2Sa 24:13
30:13 [f]Nu 3:47; Mt 17:24
30:15 [g]Pr 22:2; Eph 6:9
30:16 [h]Ex 38:25-28
30:18 [i]Ex 38:8; 40:7,30
30:19 [j]Ex 40:31-32; Isa 52:11 [k]Ps 26:6
30:21 [l]Ex 27:21; 28:43
30:23 [m]Ge 37:25
30:24 [n]Ps 45:8
30:25 [o]Ex 37:29 [p]Ex 40:9
30:26 [q]Ex 40:9; Lev 8:10; Nu 7:1
30:29 [r]Ex 29:37
30:30 [s]Ex 29:7; Lev 8:2,12,30
30:32 [t]ver 25,37
30:33 [u]ver 38; Ge 17:14
30:35 [v]ver 25
30:36 [w]ver 32; Ex 29:37; Lev 2:3
30:37 [x]ver 32

[o] *13* That is, about 1/5 ounce (about 6 grams); also in verse 15 [p] *23* That is, about 12 1/2 pounds (about 6 kilograms) [q] *24* That is, probably about 4 quarts (about 4 liters)

its fragrance must be cut off[a] from his people."

Call of Bezalel and Oholiab to construct the tabernacle.

31:2-6pp— Ex 35:30-35

31 Then the LORD said to Moses, 2"See, I have chosen Bezalel[b] son of Uri, the son of Hur, of the tribe of Judah, 3and I have filled him with the Spirit of God, with skill, ability and knowledge in all kinds of crafts[c]— 4to make artistic designs for work in gold, silver and bronze, 5to cut and set stones, to work in wood, and to engage in all kinds of craftsmanship. 6Moreover, I have appointed Oholiab son of Ahisamach, of the tribe of Dan, to help him. Also I have given skill to all the craftsmen to make everything I have commanded you: 7the Tent of Meeting,[d] the ark of the Testimony[e] with the atonement cover[f] on it, and all the other furnishings of the tent— 8the table[g] and its articles, the pure gold lampstand[h] and all its accessories, the altar of incense, 9the altar of burnt offering and all its utensils, the basin with its stand— 10and also the woven garments[i], both the sacred garments for Aaron the priest and the garments for his sons when they serve as priests, 11and the anointing oil[j] and fragrant incense for the Holy Place. They are to make them just as I commanded you."

Sign of the Sabbath.

12Then the LORD said to Moses, 13"Say to the Israelites, 'You must observe my Sabbaths.[k] This will be a sign[l] between me and you for the generations to come, so you may know that I am the LORD, who makes you holy.[r][m]

14"'Observe the Sabbath, because it is holy to you. Anyone who desecrates it must be put to death;[n] whoever does any work on that day must be cut off from his people. 15For six days, work[o] is to be done, but the seventh day is a Sabbath of rest,[p] holy to the LORD. Whoever does any work on the Sabbath day must be put to death. 16The Israelites are to observe the Sabbath, celebrating it for the generations to come as a lasting covenant. 17It will be a sign[q] between me and the Israelites forever, for in six days the LORD made the heavens and the earth, and on the seventh day he abstained from work and rested.[r]'"

18When the LORD finished speaking to Moses on Mount Sinai, he gave him the two tablets of the Testimony, the tablets of stone[s] inscribed by the finger of God.[t]

Aaron makes a golden calf.

32 When the people saw that Moses was so long in coming down from the mountain,[u] they gathered around Aaron and said, "Come, make us gods[s] who will go before us. As for this fellow Moses who brought us up out of Egypt, we don't know what has happened to him."[v]

2Aaron answered them, "Take off the gold earrings[w] that your wives, your sons and your daughters are wearing, and bring them to me." 3So all the people took off their earrings and brought them to Aaron. 4He took what they handed him and made it into an idol cast in the shape of a calf,[x] fashioning it with a tool. Then they said, "These are your gods,[t] O Israel, who brought you up out of Egypt."

5When Aaron saw this, he built an altar in front of the calf and announced, "Tomorrow there will be a festival[y] to the LORD." 6So the next day the people rose early and sacrificed burnt offerings and presented fellowship offerings.[u][z] Afterward they sat down to eat and drink and got up to indulge in revelry.[a]

7Then the LORD said to Moses, "Go down, because your people, whom you brought up out of Egypt,[b] have become corrupt.[c] 8They have been quick to turn

30:38 [a]ver 33
31:2 [b]Ex 36:1,2; 1Ch 2:20
31:3 [c]1Ki 7:14
31:7 [d]Ex 36:8-38 [e]Ex 37:1-5 [f]Ex 37:6
31:8 [g]Ex 37:10-16 [h]Ex 37:17-24
31:10 [i]Ex 28:2; 39:1,41
31:11 [j]Ex 30:22-32
31:13 [k]Ex 20:8; Lev 19:3,30 [l]Eze 20:12,20 [m]Lev 11:44
31:14 [n]Nu 15:32-36
31:15 [o]Ex 20:8-11 [p]Ge 2:3; Ex 16:23
31:17 [q]ver 13 [r]Ge 2:2-3
31:18 [s]Ex 24:12 [t]Ex 32:15-16; 34:1,28; Dt 4:13; 5:22
32:1 [u]Ex 24:18; Dt 9:9-12 [v]Ac 7:40*
32:2 [w]Ex 35:22
32:4 [x]Dt 9:16; Ne 9:18; Ps 106:19; Ac 7:41
32:5 [y]Lev 23:2,37; 2Ki 10:20
32:6 [z]Nu 25:2; Ac 7:41 [a]ver 17-19; 1Co 10:7*
32:7 [b]ver 4,11 [c]Ge 6:11-12; Dt 9:12

[r]13 Or *who sanctifies you*; or *who sets you apart as holy* [s]1 Or *a god*; also in verses 23 and 31 [t]4 Or *This is your god*; also in verse 8 [u]6 Traditionally *peace offerings*

away from what I commanded them and
have made themselves an idol[a] cast in
the shape of a calf. They have bowed
down to it and sacrificed[b] to it and have
said, 'These are your gods, O Israel,
who brought you up out of Egypt.'[c]
9 "I have seen these people," the LORD
said to Moses, "and they are a stiff-
necked[d] people. 10 Now leave me alone
so that my anger may burn against them
and that I may destroy them. Then I will
make you into a great nation."[e]
11 But Moses sought the favor[f] of the
LORD his God. "O LORD," he said, "why
should your anger burn against your
people, whom you brought out of Egypt
with great power and a mighty hand?[g]
12 Why should the Egyptians say, 'It was
with evil intent that he brought them
out, to kill them in the mountains and to
wipe them off the face of the earth'?[h]
Turn from your fierce anger; relent and
do not bring disaster on your people.
13 Remember[i] your servants Abraham,
Isaac and Israel, to whom you swore
by your own self:[j] 'I will make your
descendants as numerous as the stars[k]
in the sky and I will give your descendants all this land[l] I promised them,
and it will be their inheritance forever.'"
14 Then the LORD relented[m] and did not
bring on his people the disaster he had
threatened.

Moses breaks the tablets and burns the golden calf.

15 Moses turned and went down the
mountain with the two tablets of the
Testimony[n] in his hands.[o] They were
inscribed on both sides, front and back.
16 The tablets were the work of God;
the writing was the writing of God,
engraved on the tablets.[p]
17 When Joshua heard the noise of
the people shouting, he said to Moses,
"There is the sound of war in the camp."
18 Moses replied:

"It is not the sound of victory,
it is not the sound of defeat;
it is the sound of singing that I
hear."

32:8 [a]Ex 20:4 [b]Ex 22:20 [c]1Ki 12:28
32:9 [d]Ex 33:3,5; 34:9; Isa 48:4; Ac 7:51
32:10 [e]Nu 14:12; Dt 9:14
32:11 [f]Dt 9:18 [g]Dt 9:26
32:12 [h]Nu 14:13-16; Dt 9:28
32:13 [i]Ex 2:24 [j]Ge 22:16; Heb 6:13 [k]Ge 15:5; 26:4 [l]Ge 12:7
32:14 [m]2Sa 24:16; Ps 106:45
32:15 [n]Ex 31:18 [o]Dt 9:15
32:16 [p]Ex 31:18
32:19 [q]Dt 9:16 [r]Dt 9:17
32:20 [s]Dt 9:21
32:22 [t]Dt 9:24
32:23 [u]ver 1
32:24 [v]ver 4
32:27 [w]Nu 25:3,5; Dt 33:9
32:30 [x]1Sa 12:20 [y]Lev 1:4; Nu 25:13

19 When Moses approached the camp
and saw the calf[q] and the dancing, his
anger burned and he threw the tablets
out of his hands, breaking them to
pieces[r] at the foot of the mountain.
20 And he took the calf they had made
and burned it in the fire; then he ground
it to powder, scattered it on the water[s]
and made the Israelites drink it.
21 He said to Aaron, "What did these
people do to you, that you led them into
such great sin?"
22 "Do not be angry, my lord," Aaron
answered. "You know how prone these
people are to evil.[t] 23 They said to me,
'Make us gods who will go before us.
As for this fellow Moses who brought
us up out of Egypt, we don't know what
has happened to him.'[u] 24 So I told them,
'Whoever has any gold jewelry, take it
off.' Then they gave me the gold, and I
threw it into the fire, and out came this
calf!"[v]

God uses the Levites to kill 3,000 idolaters.

25 Moses saw that the people were
running wild and that Aaron had let
them get out of control and so become a
laughingstock to their enemies. 26 So he
stood at the entrance to the camp and
said, "Whoever is for the LORD, come to
me." And all the Levites rallied to him.
27 Then he said to them, "This is
what the LORD, the God of Israel, says:
'Each man strap a sword to his side.
Go back and forth through the camp
from one end to the other, each killing
his brother and friend and neighbor.'"[w]
28 The Levites did as Moses commanded,
and that day about three thousand of
the people died. 29 Then Moses said,
"You have been set apart to the LORD
today, for you were against your own
sons and brothers, and he has blessed
you this day."
30 The next day Moses said to the
people, "You have committed a great
sin.[x] But now I will go up to the LORD;
perhaps I can make atonement[y] for
your sin."

31So Moses went back to the LORD and said, "Oh, what a great sin these people have committed![a] They have made themselves gods of gold.[b] 32But now, please forgive their sin—but if not, then blot me[c] out of the book[d] you have written."

33The LORD replied to Moses, "Whoever has sinned against me I will blot out[e] of my book. 34Now go, lead the people to the place[f] I spoke of, and my angel[g] will go before you. However, when the time comes for me to punish,[h] I will punish them for their sin."

35And the LORD struck the people with a plague because of what they did with the calf[i] Aaron had made.

The LORD talks to Moses face to face.

33 Then the LORD said to Moses, "Leave this place, you and the people you brought up out of Egypt, and go up to the land I promised on oath to Abraham, Isaac and Jacob, saying, 'I will give it to your descendants.'[j] 2I will send an angel[k] before you and drive out the Canaanites, Amorites, Hittites, Perizzites, Hivites and Jebusites.[l] 3Go up to the land flowing with milk and honey.[m] But I will not go with you, because you are a stiff-necked[n] people and I might destroy[o] you on the way."

4When the people heard these distressing words, they began to mourn[p] and no one put on any ornaments. 5For the LORD had said to Moses, "Tell the Israelites, 'You are a stiff-necked people. If I were to go with you even for a moment, I might destroy you. Now take off your ornaments and I will decide what to do with you.'" 6So the Israelites stripped off their ornaments at Mount Horeb.

7Now Moses used to take a tent and pitch it outside the camp some distance away, calling it the "tent of meeting."[q] Anyone inquiring of the LORD would go to the tent of meeting outside the camp. 8And whenever Moses went out to the tent, all the people rose and stood at the entrances to their tents,[r] watching Moses until he entered the tent. 9As Moses went into the tent, the pillar of cloud[s] would come down and stay at the entrance, while the LORD spoke[t] with Moses. 10Whenever the people saw the pillar of cloud standing at the entrance to the tent, they all stood and worshiped, each at the entrance to his tent. 11The LORD would speak to Moses face to face,[u] as a man speaks with his friend. Then Moses would return to the camp, but his young aide Joshua son of Nun did not leave the tent.

Moses prays for the presence of God.

12Moses said to the LORD, "You have been telling me, 'Lead these people,'[v] but you have not let me know whom you will send with me. You have said, 'I know you by name[w] and you have found favor with me.' 13If you are pleased with me, teach me your ways[x] so I may know you and continue to find favor with you. Remember that this nation is your people."[y]

14The LORD replied, "My Presence[z] will go with you, and I will give you rest."[a]

15Then Moses said to him, "If your Presence does not go with us, do not send us up from here. 16How will anyone know that you are pleased with me and with your people unless you go with us?[b] What else will distinguish me and your people from all the other people on the face of the earth?"[c]

17And the LORD said to Moses, "I will do the very thing you have asked, because I am pleased with you and I know you by name."

18Then Moses said, "Now show me your glory."

19And the LORD said, "I will cause all my goodness to pass in front of you, and I will proclaim my name, the LORD, in your presence. I will have mercy on whom I will have mercy, and I will have compassion on whom I will have com-

32:31 [a]Dt 9:18 [b]Ex 20:23
32:32 [c]Ro 9:3 [d]Ps 69:28; Da 12:1; Php 4:3; Rev 3:5; 21:27
32:33 [e]Dt 29:20; Ps 9:5
32:34 [f]Ex 3:17 [g]Ex 23:20 [h]Dt 32:35; Ps 99:8; Ro 2:5-6
32:35 [i]ver 4
33:1 [j]Ge 12:7
33:2 [k]Ex 32:34 [l]Ex 23:27-31; Jos 24:11
33:3 [m]Ex 3:8 [n]Ex 32:9 [o]Ex 32:10
33:4 [p]Nu 14:39
33:7 [q]Ex 29:42-43
33:8 [r]Nu 16:27
33:9 [s]Ex 13:21 [t]Ex 31:18; Ps 99:7
33:11 [u]Nu 12:8; Dt 34:10
33:12 [v]Ex 3:10 [w]ver 17; Jn 10:14-15; 2Ti 2:19
33:13 [x]Ps 25:4; 86:11; 119:33 [y]Ex 34:9; Dt 9:26,29
33:14 [z]Isa 63:9 [a]Jos 21:44; 22:4
33:16 [b]Nu 14:14 [c]Ex 34:10

passion.[a] 20But," he said, "you cannot
see my face, for no one may see[b] me
and live."
21Then the LORD said, "There is a
place near me where you may stand on
a rock. 22When my glory passes by, I
will put you in a cleft in the rock and
cover you with my hand[c] until I have
passed by. 23Then I will remove my
hand and you will see my back; but my
face must not be seen."

Two new tablets of stone.

34 The LORD said to Moses,
"Chisel out two stone tablets
like the first ones, and I will write on
them the words that were on the first
tablets,[d] which you broke.[e] 2Be ready
in the morning, and then come up on
Mount Sinai.[f] Present yourself to me
there on top of the mountain. 3No one
is to come with you or be seen anywhere on the mountain;[g] not even the
flocks and herds may graze in front of
the mountain."
4So Moses chiseled out two stone
tablets like the first ones and went up
Mount Sinai early in the morning, as
the LORD had commanded him; and he
carried the two stone tablets in his
hands. 5Then the LORD came down in
the cloud and stood there with him
and proclaimed his name, the LORD.[h]
6And he passed in front of Moses, proclaiming, "The LORD, the LORD, the
compassionate[i] and gracious God, slow to
anger,[j] abounding in love[k] and faithfulness,[l] 7maintaining love to thousands,[m]
and forgiving wickedness, rebellion
and sin.[n] Yet he does not leave the
guilty unpunished;[o] he punishes the
children and their children for the sin
of the fathers to the third and fourth
generation."
8Moses bowed to the ground at once
and worshiped. 9"O Lord, if I have found
favor in your eyes," he said, "then let
the Lord go with us.[p] Although this is a
stiff-necked people, forgive our wickedness and our sin, and take us as your
inheritance."[q]

Renewal of God's covenant.

10Then the LORD said: "I am making
a covenant[r] with you. Before all your
people I will do wonders never before
done in any nation in all the world.[s] The
people you live among will see how
awesome is the work that I, the LORD,
will do for you. 11Obey what I command you today. I will drive out before
you the Amorites, Canaanites, Hittites,
Perizzites, Hivites and Jebusites.[t] 12Be
careful not to make a treaty with those
who live in the land where you are
going, or they will be a snare[u] among
you. 13Break down their altars, smash
their sacred stones and cut down their
Asherah poles.[v][v] 14Do not worship any
other god,[w] for the LORD, whose name
is Jealous, is a jealous God.[x]
15"Be careful not to make a treaty
with those who live in the land; for
when they prostitute[y] themselves to
their gods and sacrifice to them, they
will invite you and you will eat their
sacrifices.[z] 16And when you choose
some of their daughters as wives[a] for
your sons and those daughters prostitute
themselves to their gods,[b] they will
lead your sons to do the same.
17"Do not make cast idols.[c]
18"Celebrate the Feast of Unleavened Bread.[d] For seven days eat bread
made without yeast,[e] as I commanded
you. Do this at the appointed time in
the month of Abib,[f] for in that month
you came out of Egypt.
19"The first offspring[g] of every womb
belongs to me, including all the firstborn males of your livestock, whether
from herd or flock. 20Redeem the firstborn donkey with a lamb, but if you do
not redeem it, break its neck.[h] Redeem
all your firstborn sons.
"No one is to appear before me empty-handed.[i]
21"Six days you shall labor, but on
the seventh day you shall rest;[j] even

33:19 [a]Ro 9:15*
33:20 [b]Ge 32:30; Isa 6:5
33:22 [c]Ps 91:4
34:1 [d]Dt 10:2,4 [e]Ex 32:19
34:2 [f]Ex 19:11
34:3 [g]Ex 19:12-13, 21
34:5 [h]Ex 33:19
34:6 [i]Ps 86:15 [j]Nu 14:18; Ro 2:4 [k]Ne 9:17; Ps 103:8; Joel 2:13 [l]Ps 108:4
34:7 [m]Ex 20:6 [n]Ps 103:3; 130:4,8; Da 9:9; 1Jn 1:9 [o]Job 10:14; Na 1:3
34:9 [p]Ex 33:15 [q]Ps 33:12
34:10 [r]Dt 5:2-3 [s]Ex 33:16; Dt 4:32
34:11 [t]Ex 33:2
34:12 [u]Ex 23:32-33
34:13 [v]Ex 23:24; Dt 12:3; 2Ki 18:4
34:14 [w]Ex 20:3 [x]Ex 20:5; Dt 4:24
34:15 [y]Jdg 2:17 [z]Nu 25:2; 1Co 8:4
34:16 [a]Dt 7:3 [b]1Ki 11:4
34:17 [c]Ex 32:8
34:18 [d]Ex 12:17 [e]Ex 12:15 [f]Ex 12:2
34:19 [g]Ex 13:2
34:20 [h]Ex 13:13,15 [i]Ex 23:15; Dt 16:16
34:21 [j]Ex 20:9; Lk 13:14

[v] *13* That is, symbols of the goddess Asherah

during the plowing season and harvest
you must rest.
22“Celebrate the Feast of Weeks
with the firstfruits of the wheat harvest,
and the Feast of Ingathering[a] at the turn
of the year.[w] 23Three times[b] a year all
your men are to appear before the
Sovereign LORD, the God of Israel. 24I
will drive out nations[c] before you and
enlarge your territory, and no one will
covet your land when you go up three
times each year to appear before the
LORD your God.
25“Do not offer the blood of a sacrifice
to me along with anything containing
yeast,[d] and do not let any of the sacrifice from the Passover Feast remain
until morning.[e]
26“Bring the best of the firstfruits of
your soil to the house of the LORD your
God.
“Do not cook a young goat in its
mother's milk.”[f]
27Then the LORD said to Moses,
“Write[g] down these words, for in accordance with these words I have made a
covenant with you and with Israel.”
28Moses was there with the LORD forty
days and forty nights[h] without eating
bread or drinking water. And he wrote
on the tablets[i] the words of the covenant—the Ten Commandments.[j]

Moses' face is radiant after being with God.

29When Moses came down from
Mount Sinai with the two tablets of the
Testimony in his hands,[k] he was not
aware that his face was radiant[l] because
he had spoken with the LORD. 30When
Aaron and all the Israelites saw Moses,
his face was radiant, and they were
afraid to come near him. 31But Moses
called to them; so Aaron and all the
leaders of the community came back to
him, and he spoke to them. 32Afterward
all the Israelites came near him, and
he gave them all the commands[m] the
LORD had given him on Mount Sinai.
33When Moses finished speaking to
them, he put a veil[n] over his face. 34But
whenever he entered the LORD's pres-

34:22 [a]Ex 23:16
34:23 [b]Ex 23:14
34:24 [c]Ex 23:28; 33:2; Ps 78:55
34:25 [d]Ex 23:18 [e]Ex 12:8,10
34:26 [f]Ex 23:19
34:27 [g]Ex 17:14; 24:4
34:28 [h]Ge 7:4; Ex 24:18; Mt 4:2 [i]ver 1; Ex 31:18 [j]Dt 4:13; 10:4
34:29 [k]Ex 32:15 [l]Ps 34:5; Mt 17:2; 2Co 3:7,13
34:32 [m]Ex 24:3
34:33 [n]2Co 3:13
35:1 [o]Ex 34:32
35:2 [p]Ex 20:9-10 34:21; Lev 23:3
35:3 [q]Ex 16:23
35:10 [r]Ex 31:6
35:11 [s]Ex 26:1-37
35:12 [t]Ex 25:10-22
35:13 [u]Ex 25:23-30; Lev 24:5-6
35:14 [v]Ex 25:31

ence to speak with him, he removed
the veil until he came out. And when
he came out and told the Israelites
what he had been commanded, 35they
saw that his face was radiant. Then
Moses would put the veil back over
his face until he went in to speak with
the LORD.

The Sabbath rest.

35 Moses assembled the whole
Israelite community and said
to them, “These are the things the
LORD has commanded[o] you to do: 2For
six days, work is to be done, but the
seventh day shall be your holy day, a
Sabbath[p] of rest to the LORD. Whoever
does any work on it must be put to
death. 3Do not light a fire in any of your
dwellings on the Sabbath day.[q]”

Offerings for the tabernacle.

35:4-9pp— Ex 25:1-7
35:10-19pp— Ex 39:32-41

4Moses said to the whole Israelite
community, “This is what the LORD has
commanded: 5From what you have,
take an offering for the LORD. Everyone
who is willing is to bring to the LORD
an offering of gold, silver and bronze;
6blue, purple and scarlet yarn and fine
linen; goat hair; 7ram skins dyed red
and hides of sea cows[x]; acacia wood;
8olive oil for the light; spices for the
anointing oil and for the fragrant
incense; 9and onyx stones and other
gems to be mounted on the ephod and
breastpiece.
10“All who are skilled among you
are to come and make everything the
LORD has commanded:[r] 11the tabernacle[s] with its tent and its covering, clasps,
frames, crossbars, posts and bases; 12the
ark[t] with its poles and the atonement
cover and the curtain that shields it;
13the table[u] with its poles and all its
articles and the bread of the Presence;
14the lampstand[v] that is for light with
its accessories, lamps and oil for the

w *22* That is, in the fall x *7* That is, dugongs; also in verse 23

light; **15**the altar[a] of incense with its
poles, the anointing oil[b] and the fragrant
incense;[c] the curtain for the doorway
at the entrance to the tabernacle; **16**the
altar[d] of burnt offering with its bronze
grating, its poles and all its utensils; the
bronze basin with its stand; **17**the curtains of the courtyard with its posts and
bases, and the curtain for the entrance
to the courtyard;[e] **18**the tent pegs for
the tabernacle and for the courtyard,
and their ropes; **19**the woven garments
worn for ministering in the sanctuary—
both the sacred garments[f] for Aaron
the priest and the garments for his sons
when they serve as priests."
20Then the whole Israelite community withdrew from Moses' presence,
21and everyone who was willing and
whose heart moved him came and
brought an offering to the LORD for
the work on the Tent of Meeting, for
all its service, and for the sacred garments. **22**All who were willing, men
and women alike, came and brought
gold jewelry of all kinds: brooches,
earrings, rings and ornaments. They all
presented their gold as a wave offering
to the LORD. **23**Everyone who had blue,
purple or scarlet yarn[g] or fine linen, or
goat hair, ram skins dyed red or hides
of sea cows brought them. **24**Those
presenting an offering of silver or
bronze brought it as an offering to the
LORD, and everyone who had acacia
wood for any part of the work brought
it. **25**Every skilled woman[h] spun with
her hands and brought what she had
spun—blue, purple or scarlet yarn or
fine linen. **26**And all the women who
were willing and had the skill spun the
goat hair. **27**The leaders[i] brought onyx
stones and other gems to be mounted
on the ephod and breastpiece. **28**They
also brought spices and olive oil for
the light and for the anointing oil and
for the fragrant incense.[j] **29**All the
Israelite men and women who were
willing[k] brought to the LORD freewill
offerings[l] for all the work the LORD
through Moses had commanded them
to do.

35:15 [a]Ex 30:1-6 [b]Ex 30:25 [c]Ex 30:34-38
35:16 [d]Ex 27:1-8
35:17 [e]Ex 27:9
35:19 [f]Ex 28:2; 31:10; 39:1
35:23 [g]1Ch 29:8
35:25 [h]Ex 28:3
35:27 [i]1Ch 29:6; Ezr 2:68
35:28 [j]Ex 25:6
35:29 [k]ver 21; 1Ch 29:9 [l]ver 4-9; Ex 25:1-7; 36:3; 2Ki 12:4
35:31 [m]ver 35; 2Ch 2:7,14
35:34 [n]Ex 31:6 [o]2Ch 2:14
35:35 [p]ver 31; Ex 31:3,6; 1Ki 7:14
36:1 [q]Ex 28:3 [r]Ex 25:8
36:2 [s]Ex 31:2 [t]Ex 31:6 [u]Ex 25:2; 35:21,26; 1Ch 29:5
36:3 [v]Ex 35:29
36:5 [w]2Ch 24:14; 31:10; 2Co 8:2-3

The call of God upon Bezalel and Oholiab.

35:30-35pp— Ex 31:2-6

30Then Moses said to the Israelites,
"See, the LORD has chosen Bezalel son
of Uri, the son of Hur, of the tribe of
Judah, **31**and he has filled him with the
Spirit of God, with skill, ability and
knowledge in all kinds of crafts[m]—
32to make artistic designs for work in
gold, silver and bronze, **33**to cut and set
stones, to work in wood and to engage
in all kinds of artistic craftsmanship.
34And he has given both him and Oholiab[n] son of Ahisamach, of the tribe of
Dan, the ability to teach[o] others. **35**He
has filled them with skill to do all kinds
of work[p] as craftsmen, designers, embroi-
derers in blue, purple and scarlet yarn
and fine linen, and weavers—all of
them master craftsmen and designers.

36 **1**So Bezalel, Oholiab and every
skilled person[q] to whom the
LORD has given skill and ability to
know how to carry out all the work of
constructing the sanctuary[r] are to do
the work just as the Lord has commanded."

The people are restrained after much giving.

2Then Moses summoned Bezalel[s]
and Oholiab[t] and every skilled person
to whom the LORD had given ability
and who was willing[u] to come and do
the work. **3**They received from Moses
all the offerings[v] the Israelites had
brought to carry out the work of constructing the sanctuary. And the people continued to bring freewill offerings
morning after morning. **4**So all the
skilled craftsmen who were doing all
the work on the sanctuary left their
work **5**and said to Moses, "The people
are bringing more than enough[w] for
doing the work the LORD commanded
to be done."
6Then Moses gave an order and they
sent this word throughout the camp:
"No man or woman is to make anything
else as an offering for the sanctuary."

And so the people were restrained from bringing more, [7]because what they already had was more[a] than enough to do all the work.

The tabernacle is constructed.

36:8-38pp— Ex 26:1-37

[8]All the skilled men among the workmen made the tabernacle with ten curtains of finely twisted linen and blue, purple and scarlet yarn, with cherubim worked into them by a skilled craftsman. [9]All the curtains were the same size—twenty-eight cubits long and four cubits wide.[y] [10]They joined five of the curtains together and did the same with the other five. [11]Then they made loops of blue material along the edge of the end curtain in one set, and the same was done with the end curtain in the other set. [12]They also made fifty loops on one curtain and fifty loops on the end curtain of the other set, with the loops opposite each other. [13]Then they made fifty gold clasps and used them to fasten the two sets of curtains together so that the tabernacle was a unit.[b]

[14]They made curtains of goat hair for the tent over the tabernacle—eleven altogether. [15]All eleven curtains were the same size—thirty cubits long and four cubits wide.[z] [16]They joined five of the curtains into one set and the other six into another set. [17]Then they made fifty loops along the edge of the end curtain in one set and also along the edge of the end curtain in the other set. [18]They made fifty bronze clasps to fasten the tent together as a unit.[c] [19]Then they made for the tent a covering of ram skins dyed red, and over that a covering of hides of sea cows.[a]

[20]They made upright frames of acacia wood for the tabernacle. [21]Each frame was ten cubits long and a cubit and a half wide,[b] [22]with two projections set parallel to each other. They made all the frames of the tabernacle in this way. [23]They made twenty frames for the south side of the tabernacle [24]and made forty silver bases to go under them—two bases for each frame, one under each projection. [25]For the other side, the north side of the tabernacle, they made twenty frames [26]and forty silver bases—two under each frame. [27]They made six frames for the far end, that is, the west end of the tabernacle, [28]and two frames were made for the corners of the tabernacle at the far end. [29]At these two corners the frames were double from the bottom all the way to the top and fitted into a single ring; both were made alike. [30]So there were eight frames and sixteen silver bases—two under each frame.

[31]They also made crossbars of acacia wood: five for the frames on one side of the tabernacle, [32]five for those on the other side, and five for the frames on the west, at the far end of the tabernacle. [33]They made the center crossbar so that it extended from end to end at the middle of the frames. [34]They overlaid the frames with gold and made gold rings to hold the crossbars. They also overlaid the crossbars with gold.

[35]They made the curtain[d] of blue, purple and scarlet yarn and finely twisted linen, with cherubim worked into it by a skilled craftsman. [36]They made four posts of acacia wood for it and overlaid them with gold. They made gold hooks for them and cast their four silver bases. [37]For the entrance to the tent they made a curtain of blue, purple and scarlet yarn and finely twisted linen—the work of an embroiderer;[e] [38]and they made five posts with hooks for them. They overlaid the tops of the posts and their bands with gold and made their five bases of bronze.

The tabernacle's ark.

37:1-9pp— Ex 25:10-20

37 Bezalel[f] made the ark[g] of acacia wood—two and a half cubits

36:7 [a]1Ki 7:47
36:13 [b]ver 18
36:18 [c]ver 13
36:35 [d]Ex 39:38; Mt 27:51; Lk 23:45; Heb 9:3
36:37 [e]Ex 27:16
37:1 [f]Ex 31:2 [g]Ex 30:6; 39:35; Dt 10:3

[y]*9* That is, about 42 feet (about 12.5 meters) long and 6 feet (about 1.8 meters) wide [z]*15* That is, about 45 feet (about 13.5 meters) long and 6 feet (about 1.8 meters) wide [a]*19* That is, dugongs [b]*21* That is, about 15 feet (about 4.5 meters) long and 2 1/4 feet (about 0.7 meter) wide

long, a cubit and a half wide, and a cubit
and a half high.[c] 2He overlaid it with
pure gold,[a] both inside and out, and
made a gold molding around it. 3He
cast four gold rings for it and fastened
them to its four feet, with two rings on
one side and two rings on the other.
4Then he made poles of acacia wood
and overlaid them with gold. 5And he
inserted the poles into the rings on the
sides of the ark to carry it.
6He made the atonement cover[b] of
pure gold—two and a half cubits long
and a cubit and a half wide.[d] 7Then he
made two cherubim[c] out of hammered
gold at the ends of the cover. 8He made
one cherub on one end and the second
cherub on the other; at the two ends he
made them of one piece with the cover.
9The cherubim had their wings spread
upward, overshadowing[d] the cover with
them. The cherubim faced each other,
looking toward the cover.[e]

The table.

37:10-16pp— Ex 25:23-29

10They[e] made the table[f] of acacia
wood—two cubits long, a cubit wide,
and a cubit and a half high.[f] 11Then they
overlaid it with pure gold[g] and made a
gold molding around it. 12They also
made around it a rim a handbreadth[g]
wide and put a gold molding on the rim.
13They cast four gold rings for the table
and fastened them to the four corners,
where the four legs were. 14The rings[h]
were put close to the rim to hold the
poles used in carrying the table. 15The
poles for carrying the table were made
of acacia wood and were overlaid with
gold. 16And they made from pure gold
the articles for the table—its plates
and dishes and bowls and its pitchers
for the pouring out of drink offerings.

The lampstand.

37:17-24pp— Ex 25:31-39

17They made the lampstand[i] of pure
gold and hammered it out, base and
shaft; its flowerlike cups, buds and
blossoms were of one piece with it.
18Six branches extended from the sides
of the lampstand—three on one side
and three on the other. 19Three cups
shaped like almond flowers with buds
and blossoms were on one branch, three
on the next branch and the same for
all six branches extending from the
lampstand. 20And on the lampstand were
four cups shaped like almond flowers
with buds and blossoms. 21One bud was
under the first pair of branches extending from the lampstand, a second bud
under the second pair, and a third bud
under the third pair—six branches in
all. 22The buds and the branches were
all of one piece with the lampstand,
hammered out of pure gold.[j]
23They made its seven lamps,[k] as well
as its wick trimmers and trays, of pure
gold. 24They made the lampstand and
all its accessories from one talent[h] of
pure gold.

The altar of incense.

37:25-28pp— Ex 30:1-5

25They made the altar of incense[l] out
of acacia wood. It was square, a cubit
long and a cubit wide, and two cubits
high[i]—its horns[m] of one piece with it.
26They overlaid the top and all the sides
and the horns with pure gold, and
made a gold molding around it. 27They
made two gold rings[n] below the molding—two on opposite sides—to hold
the poles used to carry it. 28They made
the poles of acacia wood and overlaid
them with gold.[o]
29They also made the sacred anointing
oil[p] and the pure, fragrant incense[q]—
the work of a perfumer.

37:2 [a]ver 11,26
37:6 [b]Ex 26:34; 31:7; Heb 9:5
37:7 [c]Eze 41:18
37:9 [d]Heb 9:5 [e]Dt 10:3
37:10 [f]Heb 9:2
37:11 [g]ver 2
37:14 [h]ver 27
37:17 [i]Heb 9:2; Rev 1:12
37:22 [j]ver 17; Nu 8:4
37:23 [k]Ex 40:4,25
37:25 [l]Ex 30:34-36; Lk 1:11; Heb 9:4; Rev 8:3 [m]Ex 27:2; Rev 9:13
37:27 [n]ver 14
37:28 [o]Ex 25:13
37:29 [p]Ex 31:11 [q]Ex 30:1,25; 39:38

[c] *1* That is, about 3 3/4 feet (about 1.1 meters) long and 2 1/4 feet (about 0.7 meter) wide and high
[d] *6* That is, about 3 3/4 feet (about 1.1 meters) long and 2 1/4 feet (about 0.7 meter) wide [e] *10* Or *He;* also in verses 11-29 [f] *10* That is, about 3 feet (about 0.9 meter) long, 1 1/2 feet (about 0.5 meter) wide, and 2 1/4 feet (about 0.7 meter) high [g] *12* That is, about 3 inches (about 8 centimeters) [h] *24* That is, about 75 pounds (about 34 kilograms) [i] *25* That is, about 1 1/2 feet (about 0.5 meter) long and wide, and about 3 feet (about 0.9 meter) high

The altar of burnt offering.

38:1-7pp— Ex 27:1-8

38 They[j] built the altar of burnt offering of acacia wood, three cubits[k] high; it was square, five cubits long and five cubits wide.[l] 2 They made a horn at each of the four corners, so that the horns and the altar were of one piece, and they overlaid the altar with bronze.[a] 3 They made all its utensils[b] of bronze—its pots, shovels, sprinkling bowls, meat forks and firepans. 4 They made a grating for the altar, a bronze network, to be under its ledge, halfway up the altar. 5 They cast bronze rings to hold the poles for the four corners of the bronze grating. 6 They made the poles of acacia wood and overlaid them with bronze. 7 They inserted the poles into the rings so they would be on the sides of the altar for carrying it. They made it hollow, out of boards.

The bronze basin.

8 They made the bronze basin[c] and its bronze stand from the mirrors of the women[d] who served at the entrance to the Tent of Meeting.

The courtyard.

38:9-20pp— Ex 27:9-19

9 Next they made the courtyard. The south side was a hundred cubits[m] long and had curtains of finely twisted linen, 10 with twenty posts and twenty bronze bases, and with silver hooks and bands on the posts. 11 The north side was also a hundred cubits long and had twenty posts and twenty bronze bases, with silver hooks and bands on the posts.

12 The west end was fifty cubits[n] wide and had curtains, with ten posts and ten bases, with silver hooks and bands on the posts. 13 The east end, toward the sunrise, was also fifty cubits wide. 14 Curtains fifteen cubits[o] long were on one side of the entrance, with three posts and three bases, 15 and curtains fifteen cubits long were on the other side of the entrance to the courtyard, with three posts and three bases. 16 All the curtains around the courtyard were of finely twisted linen. 17 The bases for the posts were bronze. The hooks and bands on the posts were silver, and their tops were overlaid with silver; so all the posts of the courtyard had silver bands.

18 The curtain for the entrance to the courtyard was of blue, purple and scarlet yarn and finely twisted linen—the work of an embroiderer. It was twenty cubits[p] long and, like the curtains of the courtyard, five cubits[q] high, 19 with four posts and four bronze bases. Their hooks and bands were silver, and their tops were overlaid with silver. 20 All the tent pegs[e] of the tabernacle and of the surrounding courtyard were bronze.

Materials for the tabernacle.

21 These are the amounts of the materials used for the tabernacle, the tabernacle of the Testimony,[f] which were recorded at Moses' command by the Levites under the direction of Ithamar[g] son of Aaron, the priest. 22 (Bezalel[h] son of Uri, the son of Hur, of the tribe of Judah, made everything the LORD commanded Moses; 23 with him was Oholiab[i] son of Ahisamach, of the tribe of Dan—a craftsman and designer, and an embroiderer in blue, purple and scarlet yarn and fine linen.) 24 The total amount of the gold from the wave offering used for all the work on the sanctuary[j] was 29 talents and 730 shekels,[r] according to the sanctuary shekel.[k]

25 The silver obtained from those of the community who were counted in the census[l] was 100 talents and 1,775 shekels,[s] according to the sanctuary

38:2 [a]2Ch 1:5
38:3 [b]Ex 31:9
38:8 [c]Ex 30:18; 40:7 [d]Dt 23:17; 1Sa 2:22; 1Ki 14:24
38:20 [e]Ex 35:18
38:21 [f]Nu 1:50,53; 8:24; 9:15; 10:11; 17:7; 1Ch 23:32; 2Ch 24:6; Ac 7:44; Rev 15:5 [g]Nu 4:28,33
38:22 [h]Ex 31:2
38:23 [i]Ex 31:6
38:24 [j]Ex 30:16 [k]Ex 30:13; Lev 27:25; Nu 3:47; 18:16
38:25 [l]Ex 30:12

[j] *1* Or *He*; also in verses 2-9 [k] *1* That is, about 4 1/2 feet (about 1.3 meters) [l] *1* That is, about 7 1/2 feet (about 2.3 meters) long and wide [m] *9* That is, about 150 feet (about 46 meters) [n] *12* That is, about 75 feet (about 23 meters) [o] *14* That is, about 22 1/2 feet (about 6.9 meters) [p] *18* That is, about 30 feet (about 9 meters) [q] *18* That is, about 7 1/2 feet (about 2.3 meters) [r] *24* The weight of the gold was a little over one ton (about 1 metric ton). [s] *25* The weight of the silver was a little over 3 3/4 tons (about 3.4 metric tons).

shekel— 26one beka per person,[a] that is, half a shekel,[t] according to the sanctuary shekel,[b] from everyone who had crossed over to those counted, twenty years old or more,[c] a total of 603,550 men.[d] 27The 100 talents[u] of silver were used to cast the bases[e] for the sanctuary and for the curtain—100 bases from the 100 talents, one talent for each base. 28They used the 1,775 shekels[v] to make the hooks for the posts, to overlay the tops of the posts, and to make their bands.

29The bronze from the wave offering was 70 talents and 2,400 shekels.[w] 30They used it to make the bases for the entrance to the Tent of Meeting, the bronze altar with its bronze grating and all its utensils, 31the bases for the surrounding courtyard and those for its entrance and all the tent pegs for the tabernacle and those for the surrounding courtyard.

Sacred garments.

39 From the blue, purple and scarlet yarn[f] they made woven garments for ministering in the sanctuary.[g] They also made sacred garments[h] for Aaron, as the LORD commanded Moses.

The ephod.

39:2-7pp— Ex 28:6-14

2They[x] made the ephod of gold, and of blue, purple and scarlet yarn, and of finely twisted linen. 3They hammered out thin sheets of gold and cut strands to be worked into the blue, purple and scarlet yarn and fine linen—the work of a skilled craftsman. 4They made shoulder pieces for the ephod, which were attached to two of its corners, so it could be fastened. 5Its skillfully woven waistband was like it—of one piece with the ephod and made with gold, and with blue, purple and scarlet yarn, and with finely twisted linen, as the LORD commanded Moses.

6They mounted the onyx stones in gold filigree settings and engraved them like a seal with the names of the sons of Israel. 7Then they fastened them on the shoulder pieces of the ephod as memorial[i] stones for the sons of Israel, as the LORD commanded Moses.

The breastpiece.

39:8-21pp— Ex 28:15-28

8They fashioned the breastpiece[j]—the work of a skilled craftsman. They made it like the ephod: of gold, and of blue, purple and scarlet yarn, and of finely twisted linen. 9It was square—a span[y] long and a span wide—and folded double. 10Then they mounted four rows of precious stones on it. In the first row there was a ruby, a topaz and a beryl; 11in the second row a turquoise, a sapphire[z] and an emerald; 12in the third row a jacinth, an agate and an amethyst; 13in the fourth row a chrysolite, an onyx and a jasper.[a] They were mounted in gold filigree settings. 14There were twelve stones, one for each of the names of the sons of Israel, each engraved like a seal with the name of one of the twelve tribes.[k]

15For the breastpiece they made braided chains of pure gold, like a rope. 16They made two gold filigree settings and two gold rings, and fastened the rings to two of the corners of the breastpiece. 17They fastened the two gold chains to the rings at the corners of the breastpiece, 18and the other ends of the chains to the two settings, attaching them to the shoulder pieces of the ephod at the front. 19They made two gold rings and attached them to the other two corners of the breastpiece on the inside edge next to the ephod. 20Then they made two more gold rings and attached them to the bottom of the shoulder pieces on the front of the ephod, close

38:26 [a]Ex 30:12 [b]Ex 30:13 [c]Ex 30:14 [d]Ex 12:37; Nu 1:46

38:27 [e]Ex 26:19

39:1 [f]Ex 35:23 [g]Ex 35:19 [h]ver 41; Ex 28:2

39:7 [i]Lev 24:7; Jos 4:7

39:8 [j]Lev 8:8

39:14 [k]Rev 21:12

[t]*26* That is, about 1/5ounce (about 5.5 grams)
[u]*27* That is, about 3 3/4 tons (about 3.4 metric tons)
[v]*28* That is, about 45pounds (about 20 kilograms)
[w]*29* The weight of the bronze was about 2 1/2 tons (about 2.4 metric tons). [x]*2* Or *He*; also in verses 7, 8 and 22 [y]*9* That is, about 9 inches (about 22 centimeters) [z]*11* Or *lapis lazuli* [a]*13* The precise identification of some of these precious stones is uncertain.

to the seam just above the waistband of
the ephod. 21They tied the rings of the
breastpiece to the rings of the ephod
with blue cord, connecting it to the
waistband so that the breastpiece would
not swing out from the ephod—as the
LORD commanded Moses.

Other sacred garments.

39:22-31pp— Ex 28:31-43

22They made the robe of the ephod
entirely of blue cloth—the work of a
weaver— 23with an opening in the center of the robe like the opening of a
collar,[b] and a band around this opening,
so that it would not tear. 24They made
pomegranates of blue, purple and scarlet
yarn and finely twisted linen around the
hem of the robe. 25And they made bells
of pure gold and attached them around
the hem between the pomegranates.
26The bells and pomegranates alternated
around the hem of the robe to be worn
for ministering, as the LORD commanded
Moses.

27For Aaron and his sons, they made
tunics of fine linen[a]—the work of a
weaver— 28and the turban[b] of fine linen,
the linen headbands and the undergarments of finely twisted linen. 29The
sash was of finely twisted linen and
blue, purple and scarlet yarn—the
work of an embroiderer—as the LORD
commanded Moses.

30They made the plate, the sacred diadem, out of pure gold and engraved on
it, like an inscription on a seal: HOLY TO
THE LORD. 31Then they fastened a blue
cord to it to attach it to the turban, as
the LORD commanded Moses.

Moses inspects and approves all the work.

39:32-41pp— Ex 35:10-19

32So all the work on the tabernacle,
the Tent of Meeting, was completed.
The Israelites did everything just as the
LORD commanded Moses.[c] 33Then they
brought the tabernacle to Moses: the
tent and all its furnishings, its clasps,
frames, crossbars, posts and bases; 34the
covering of ram skins dyed red, the
covering of hides of sea cows[c] and the
shielding curtain; 35the ark of the Testimony[d] with its poles and the atonement cover; 36the table with all its
articles and the bread of the Presence;
37the pure gold lampstand[e] with its row
of lamps and all its accessories, and the
oil for the light; 38the gold altar,[f] the
anointing oil, the fragrant incense, and
the curtain[g] for the entrance to the tent;
39the bronze altar with its bronze grating, its poles and all its utensils; the
basin with its stand; 40the curtains of
the courtyard with its posts and bases,
and the curtain for the entrance to the
courtyard;[h] the ropes and tent pegs for
the courtyard; all the furnishings for the
tabernacle, the Tent of Meeting; 41and
the woven garments worn for ministering in the sanctuary, both the sacred
garments for Aaron the priest and the
garments for his sons when serving as
priests.

42The Israelites had done all the work
just as the LORD had commanded Moses.[i]
43Moses inspected the work and saw
that they had done it just as the LORD
had commanded. So Moses blessed[j]
them.

The LORD instructs Moses to set up the tabernacle.

40 Then the LORD said to Moses:
2"Set up the tabernacle, the
Tent of Meeting,[k] on the first day of the
first month.[l] 3Place the ark[m] of the Testimony in it and shield the ark with
the curtain. 4Bring in the table and set
out what belongs on it.[n] Then bring in
the lampstand[o] and set up its lamps.
5Place the gold altar[p] of incense in front
of the ark of the Testimony and put the
curtain at the entrance to the tabernacle.
6"Place the altar of burnt offering in
front of the entrance to the tabernacle,
the Tent of Meeting; 7place the basin[q]
between the Tent of Meeting and the

39:27 [a]Lev 6:10
39:28 [b]Ex 28:4
39:32 [c]ver 42-43; Ex 25:9
39:35 [d]Ex 30:6
39:37 [e]Ex 25:31
39:38 [f]Ex 30:1-10 [g]Ex 36:35
39:40 [h]Ex 27:9-19
39:42 [i]Ex 25:9
39:43 [j]Lev 9:22,23; Nu 6:23-27; 2Sa 6:18; 1Ki 8:14,55; 2Ch 30:27
40:2 [k]Nu 1:1 [l]ver 17; Ex 12:2
40:3 [m]ver 21; Nu 4:5; Ex 26:33
40:4 [n]Ex 25:30 [o]ver 22-25; Ex 26:35
40:5 [p]ver 26; Ex 30:1
40:7 [q]ver 30; Ex 30:18

b*23* The meaning of the Hebrew for this word is uncertain. c*34* That is, dugongs

altar and put water in it. **8**Set up the
courtyard around it and put the curtain
at the entrance to the courtyard.
9"Take the anointing oil and anoint[a]
the tabernacle and everything in it; consecrate it and all its furnishings, and it
will be holy. **10**Then anoint the altar of
burnt offering and all its utensils; consecrate[b] the altar, and it will be most
holy. **11**Anoint the basin and its stand
and consecrate them.
12"Bring Aaron and his sons to the
entrance to the Tent of Meeting and
wash them with water.[c] **13**Then dress
Aaron in the sacred garments,[d] anoint
him and consecrate[e] him so he may
serve me as priest. **14**Bring his sons and
dress them in tunics. **15**Anoint them just
as you anointed their father, so they may
serve me as priests. Their anointing will
be to a priesthood that will continue for
all generations to come.[f]" **16**Moses did
everything just as the LORD commanded
him.
17So the tabernacle[g] was set up on the
first day of the first month[h] in the second
year. **18**When Moses set up the tabernacle, he put the bases in place, erected
the frames, inserted the crossbars and
set up the posts. **19**Then he spread the
tent over the tabernacle and put the
covering over the tent, as the LORD
commanded him.
20He took the Testimony[i] and placed
it in the ark, attached the poles to the
ark and put the atonement cover over it.
21Then he brought the ark into the tabernacle and hung the shielding curtain[j]
and shielded the ark of the Testimony,
as the LORD commanded him.
22Moses placed the table[k] in the Tent
of Meeting on the north side of the tabernacle outside the curtain **23**and set out
the bread[l] on it before the LORD, as the
LORD commanded him.
24He placed the lampstand[m] in the
Tent of Meeting opposite the table on
the south side of the tabernacle **25**and
set up the lamps[n] before the LORD, as
the LORD commanded him.
26Moses placed the gold altar[o] in the
Tent of Meeting in front of the curtain
27and burned fragrant incense on it, as
the LORD commanded[p] him. **28**Then he
put up the curtain[q] at the entrance to the
tabernacle.
29He set the altar of burnt offering
near the entrance to the tabernacle, the
Tent of Meeting, and offered on it burnt
offerings and grain offerings,[r] as the
LORD commanded him.
30He placed the basin[s] between the
Tent of Meeting and the altar and put
water in it for washing, **31**and Moses
and Aaron and his sons used it to wash
their hands and feet. **32**They washed
whenever they entered the Tent of
Meeting or approached the altar,[t] as the
LORD commanded Moses.
33Then Moses set up the courtyard[u]
around the tabernacle and altar and put
up the curtain[v] at the entrance to the
courtyard. And so Moses finished the
work.

The glory of the LORD fills the tabernacle.

34Then the cloud[w] covered the Tent of
Meeting, and the glory of the LORD filled
the tabernacle. **35**Moses could not enter
the Tent of Meeting because the cloud
had settled upon it, and the glory of the
LORD filled the tabernacle.[x]
36In all the travels of the Israelites,
whenever the cloud lifted from above
the tabernacle, they would set out;[y]
37but if the cloud did not lift, they did
not set out—until the day it lifted. **38**So
the cloud[z] of the LORD was over the tabernacle by day, and fire was in the cloud
by night, in the sight of all the house of
Israel during all their travels.

40:9 [a]Ex 30:26; Lev 8:10
40:10 [b]Ex 29:36
40:12 [c]Lev 8:1-13
40:13 [d]Ex 28:41 [e]Lev 8:12
40:15 [f]Ex 29:9; Nu 25:13
40:17 [g]Nu 7:1 [h]ver 2
40:20 [i]Ex 16:34; 25:16; Dt 10:5; 1Ki 8:9; Heb 9:4
40:21 [j]Ex 26:33
40:22 [k]Ex 26:35
40:23 [l]ver 4
40:24 [m]Ex 26:35
40:25 [n]ver 4; Ex 25:37
40:26 [o]ver 5; Ex 30:6
40:27 [p]Ex 30:7
40:28 [q]Ex 26:36
40:29 [r]ver 6; Ex 29:38-42
40:30 [s]ver 7
40:32 [t]Ex 30:20
40:33 [u]Ex 27:9 [v]ver 8
40:34 [w]Nu 9:15-23; 1Ki 8:12
40:35 [x]1Ki 8:11; 2Ch 5:13-14
40:36 [y]Nu 9:17-23; 10:13; Ne 9:19
40:38 [z]Ex 13:21; Nu 9:15; 1Co 10:1

LEVITICUS

Author: Moses.

Date Written: Between 1450 and 1400 B.C.

Time Span: 1 month.

Title: The word "Leviticus" means "pertaining to the Levites." The title is appropriate since the Israelite priests were Levites, and the ministry of these priests is discussed.

Background: The third book of the Pentateuch, Leviticus, is a continuation of the story in the book of Exodus. The book begins with Israel having completed construction of the tabernacle. This handbook of instructions for the priests is given during Israel's one-year encampment at Mount Sinai.

Where Written: The general belief is that Moses received this revelation while on Mount Sinai in the desert.

To Whom: To the Israelites.

Content: Leviticus sets down regulations to preserve the spiritual, moral and physical purity of the people. Instructions are provided on how to live holy lives through sacrifice and worship. Also discussed are the 5 major offerings: 1) burnt offering, 2) grain offering, 3) fellowship offering, 4) sin offering and 5) guilt offering. Other concerns of Leviticus include: Aaron's role as priest; laws for the priesthood; cleanliness; the Day of Atonement; laws to regulate holiness in all of life; and the appointed feasts of the Lord.

Key Words: "Sanctified"; "Holiness." The Levites and, more specifically, the priests are set aside for service or "sanctified" to live as examples of "holiness" before all the people in all that they do.

Themes: • Sin is always detestable in God's sight. • God's plan is that all sin must be atoned for by the offering of sacrificial blood (as fulfilled in Christ's atonement). • God is totally holy, and he requires our holiness and dedication. • God is not the author of confusion, but of orderliness in worship. • We keep God's laws not to become acceptable to him, but as an expression of our love for and trust in him. • Faithfulness to God's Word allows his peace and presence to fill our lives.

Outline:

1. Laws concerning offerings. 1:1-7:38
2. Laws concerning the priesthood. 8:1-10:20
3. Laws concerning personal purity. 11:1-15:33
4. The Day of Atonement. 16:1-16:34
5. Laws for sanctification of the people. 17:1-20:27
6. Laws for sanctification of the priests. 21:1-22:33
7. Laws concerning the Sabbath and other appointed feasts. 23:1-25:55
8. Blessings versus curses set before the people. 26:1-26:46
9. Laws concerning vows. 27:1-27:34

LEVITICUS

Regulations: Burnt offerings.

1 The LORD called to Moses[a] and spoke
to him from the Tent of Meeting.[b]
He said, 2"Speak to the Israelites and
say to them: 'When any of you brings an
offering to the LORD, bring as your offering an animal from either the herd or
the flock.[c]

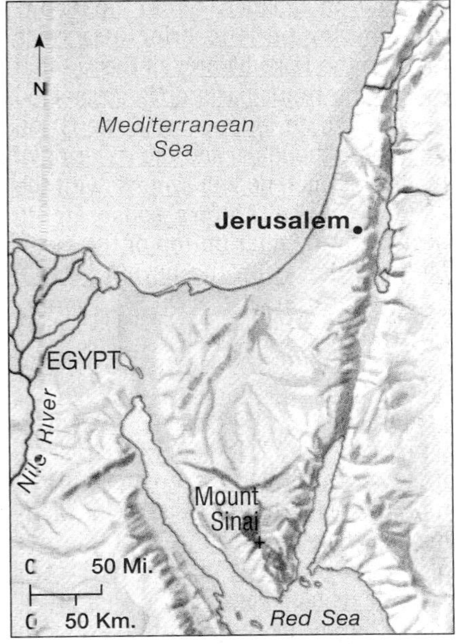

The Israelites at Mount Sinai

Throughout the book of Leviticus, the Israelites were camped at the foot of Mount Sinai. It was time to regroup as a nation and learn the importance of following God as they prepared to march toward the promised land.

3" 'If the offering is a burnt offering
from the herd, he is to offer a male without defect.[d] He must present it at the
entrance to the Tent[e] of Meeting so that
it[a] will be acceptable to the LORD. 4He
is to lay his hand on the head[f] of the
burnt offering, and it will be accepted
on his behalf to make atonement[g] for
him. 5He is to slaughter[h] the young bull
before the LORD, and then Aaron's sons
the priests shall bring the blood and
sprinkle it against the altar on all sides[i]
at the entrance to the Tent of Meeting.
6He is to skin[j] the burnt offering and
cut it into pieces. 7The sons of Aaron
the priest are to put fire on the altar
and arrange wood[k] on the fire. 8Then
Aaron's sons the priests shall arrange
the pieces, including the head and the
fat,[l] on the burning wood that is on
the altar. 9He is to wash the inner parts
and the legs with water, and the priest
is to burn all of it on the altar.[m] It is a
burnt offering, an offering made by fire,
an aroma pleasing to the LORD.[n]
10" 'If the offering is a burnt offering
from the flock, from either the sheep or
the goats,[o] he is to offer a male without
defect. 11He is to slaughter it at the
north side of the altar before the LORD,
and Aaron's sons the priests shall sprinkle its blood against the altar on all
sides.[p] 12He is to cut it into pieces, and
the priest shall arrange them, including
the head and the fat, on the burning
wood that is on the altar. 13He is to
wash the inner parts and the legs with
water, and the priest is to bring all of it
and burn it on the altar. It is a burnt
offering, an offering made by fire, an
aroma pleasing to the LORD.
14" 'If the offering to the LORD is a
burnt offering of birds, he is to offer a
dove or a young pigeon.[q] 15The priest
shall bring it to the altar, wring off the
head and burn it on the altar; its blood
shall be drained out on the side of the
altar.[r] 16He is to remove the crop with
its contents[b] and throw it to the east
side of the altar, where the ashes[s] are.
17He shall tear it open by the wings,
not severing it completely,[t] and then
the priest shall burn it on the wood[u]
that is on the fire on the altar. It is a
burnt offering, an offering made by fire,
an aroma pleasing to the LORD.

Regulations: Grain offerings.

2 " 'When someone brings a grain
offering[v] to the LORD, his offering is

1:1 [a]Ex 19:3; 25:22 [b]Nu 7:89
1:2 [c]Lev 22:18-19
1:3 [d]Ex 12:5; Dt 15:21; Heb 9:14; 1Pe 1:19 [e]Lev 17:9
1:4 [f]Ex 29:10,15; Lev 3:2 [g]2Ch 29:23-24
1:5 [h]Lev 3:2,8 [i]Heb 12:24; 1Pe 1:2
1:6 [j]Lev 7:8
1:7 [k]Lev 6:12
1:8 [l]ver 12
1:9 [m]Ex 29:18 [n]ver 13; Ge 8:21; Nu 15:8-10; Eph 5:2
1:10 [o]ver 3; Ex 12:5
1:11 [p]ver 5
1:14 [q]Ge 15:9; Lev 5:7; Lk 2:24
1:15 [r]Lev 5:9
1:16 [s]Lev 6:10
1:17 [t]Ge 15:10 [u]Lev 5:8
2:1 [v]Lev 6:14-18

a*3* Or *he* b*16* Or *crop and the feathers*; the meaning of the Hebrew for this word is uncertain.

to be of fine flour. He is to pour oil[a] on it, put incense on it 2 and take it to Aaron's sons the priests. The priest shall take a handful of the fine flour[b] and oil, together with all the incense,[c] and burn this as a memorial portion[d] on the altar, an offering made by fire, an aroma pleasing to the LORD. 3 The rest of the grain offering belongs to Aaron and his sons;[e] it is a most holy part of the offerings made to the LORD by fire.

4 " 'If you bring a grain offering baked in an oven, it is to consist of fine flour: cakes made without yeast and mixed with oil, or[c] wafers made without yeast and spread with oil.[f] 5 If your grain offering is prepared on a griddle, it is to be made of fine flour mixed with oil, and without yeast. 6 Crumble it and pour oil on it; it is a grain offering. 7 If your grain offering is cooked in a pan,[g] it is to be made of fine flour and oil. 8 Bring the grain offering made of these things to the LORD; present it to the priest, who shall take it to the altar. 9 He shall take out the memorial portion[h] from the grain offering and burn it on the altar as an offering made by fire, an aroma pleasing to the LORD.[i] 10 The rest of the grain offering belongs to Aaron and his sons;[j] it is a most holy part of the offerings made to the LORD by fire.

11 " 'Every grain offering you bring to the LORD must be made without yeast,[k] for you are not to burn any yeast or honey in an offering made to the LORD by fire. 12 You may bring them to the LORD as an offering of the firstfruits,[l] but they are not to be offered on the altar as a pleasing aroma. 13 Season all your grain offerings with salt. Do not leave the salt of the covenant[m] of your God out of your grain offerings; add salt to all your offerings.

14 " 'If you bring a grain offering of firstfruits[n] to the LORD, offer crushed heads of new grain roasted in the fire. 15 Put oil and incense on it; it is a grain offering. 16 The priest shall burn the memorial portion[o] of the crushed grain and the oil, together with all the incense, as an offering made to the LORD by fire.

2:1 [a]Nu 15:4
2:2 [b]Lev 5:11 [c]Lev 6:15; Isa 66:3 [d]ver 9,16; Lev 5:12; 6:15; 24:7; Ac 10:4
2:3 [e]ver 10; Lev 6:16; 10:12,13
2:4 [f]Ex 29:2
2:7 [g]Lev 7:9
2:9 [h]ver 2 [i]Ex 29:18; Lev 6:15
2:10 [j]ver 3
2:11 [k]Ex 23:18; 34:25; Lev 6:16
2:12 [l]Lev 7:13; 23:10
2:13 [m]Nu 18:19; Eze 43:24
2:14 [n]Lev 23:10
2:16 [o]ver 2
3:1 [p]Lev 7:11-34 [q]Lev 1:3; 22:21
3:2 [r]Ex 29:10,15 [s]Lev 1:5
3:3 [t]Ex 29:13
3:5 [u]Lev 7:29-34 [v]Ex 29:13, 38-42
3:6 [w]ver 1
3:7 [x]Lev 17:8-9
3:8 [y]ver 2; Lev 1:5
3:11 [z]ver 5 [a]ver 16; Lev 21:6,17
3:13 [b]Ex 24:6

Regulations: Fellowship offerings.

3 " 'If someone's offering is a fellowship offering,[d][p] and he offers an animal from the herd, whether male or female, he is to present before the LORD an animal without defect.[q] 2 He is to lay his hand on the head[r] of his offering and slaughter it[s] at the entrance to the Tent of Meeting. Then Aaron's sons the priests shall sprinkle the blood against the altar on all sides. 3 From the fellowship offering he is to bring a sacrifice made to the LORD by fire: all the fat[t] that covers the inner parts or is connected to them, 4 both kidneys with the fat on them near the loins, and the covering of the liver, which he will remove with the kidneys. 5 Then Aaron's sons[u] are to burn it on the altar on top of the burnt offering[v] that is on the burning wood, as an offering made by fire, an aroma pleasing to the LORD.

6 " 'If he offers an animal from the flock as a fellowship offering[w] to the LORD, he is to offer a male or female without defect. 7 If he offers a lamb, he is to present it before the LORD.[x] 8 He is to lay his hand on the head of his offering and slaughter it[y] in front of the Tent of Meeting. Then Aaron's sons shall sprinkle its blood against the altar on all sides. 9 From the fellowship offering he is to bring a sacrifice made to the LORD by fire: its fat, the entire fat tail cut off close to the backbone, all the fat that covers the inner parts or is connected to them, 10 both kidneys with the fat on them near the loins, and the covering of the liver, which he will remove with the kidneys. 11 The priest shall burn them on the altar[z] as food,[a] an offering made to the LORD by fire.

12 " 'If his offering is a goat, he is to present it before the LORD. 13 He is to lay his hand on its head and slaughter it in front of the Tent of Meeting. Then Aaron's sons shall sprinkle[b] its blood against the altar on all sides. 14 From what he offers he is to make this offering to the

c*4* Or *and* d*1* Traditionally *peace offering*; also in verses 3, 6 and 9

LORD by fire: all the fat that covers the inner parts or is connected to them, 15both kidneys with the fat on them near the loins, and the covering of the liver, which he will remove with the kidneys. 16The priest shall burn them on the altar as food, an offering made by fire, a pleasing aroma. All the fat is the LORD's.[a]

17" 'This is a lasting ordinance for the generations to come,[b] wherever you live: You must not eat any fat or any blood.[c]' "

Regulations: Sin offerings.

4 The LORD said to Moses, 2"Say to the Israelites: 'When anyone sins unintentionally[d] and does what is forbidden in any of the LORD's commands—

3" 'If the anointed priest sins, bringing guilt on the people, he must bring to the LORD a young bull[e] without defect as a sin offering[f] for the sin he has committed. 4He is to present the bull at the entrance to the Tent of Meeting before the LORD.[g] He is to lay his hand on its head and slaughter it before the LORD. 5Then the anointed priest shall take some of the bull's blood[h] and carry it into the Tent of Meeting. 6He is to dip his finger into the blood and sprinkle some of it seven times before the LORD, in front of the curtain of the sanctuary. 7The priest shall then put some of the blood on the horns of the altar of fragrant incense that is before the LORD in the Tent of Meeting. The rest of the bull's blood he shall pour out at the base of the altar[i] of burnt offering[j] at the entrance to the Tent of Meeting. 8He shall remove all the fat[k] from the bull of the sin offering—the fat that covers the inner parts or is connected to them, 9both kidneys with the fat on them near the loins, and the covering of the liver, which he will remove with the kidneys[l]— 10just as the fat is removed from the ox[e] sacrificed as a fellowship offering.[f] Then the priest shall burn them on the altar of burnt offering. 11But the hide of the bull and all its flesh, as well as the head and legs, the inner parts and offal[m]— 12that is, all the rest of the bull—he must take outside the camp[n] to a place ceremonially clean,[o] where the ashes are thrown, and burn it in a wood fire on the ash heap.

13" 'If the whole Israelite community sins unintentionally[p] and does what is forbidden in any of the LORD's commands, even though the community is unaware of the matter, they are guilty. 14When they become aware of the sin they committed, the assembly must bring a young bull[q] as a sin offering[r] and present it before the Tent of Meeting. 15The elders of the community are to lay their hands on the bull's head[s] before the LORD, and the bull shall be slaughtered before the LORD. 16Then the anointed priest is to take some of the bull's blood[t] into the Tent of Meeting. 17He shall dip his finger into the blood and sprinkle it before the LORD[u] seven times in front of the curtain. 18He is to put some of the blood on the horns of the altar that is before the LORD[v] in the Tent of Meeting. The rest of the blood he shall pour out at the base of the altar of burnt offering at the entrance to the Tent of Meeting. 19He shall remove all the fat[w] from it and burn it on the altar, 20and do with this bull just as he did with the bull for the sin offering. In this way the priest will make atonement[x] for them, and they will be forgiven.[y] 21Then he shall take the bull outside the camp and burn it as he burned the first bull. This is the sin offering for the community.[z]

22" 'When a leader[a] sins unintentionally[b] and does what is forbidden in any of the commands of the LORD his God, he is guilty. 23When he is made aware of the sin he committed, he must bring as his offering a male goat without defect. 24He is to lay his hand on the goat's head and slaughter it at the place

3:16 [a]1Sa 2:16
3:17 [b]Lev 6:18; 17:7 [c]Ge 9:4; Lev 7:25-26; 17:10-16; Dt 12:16; Ac 15:20
4:2 [d]Lev 5:15-18; Ps 19:12; Heb 9:7
4:3 [e]ver 14; Ps 66:15 [f]Lev 9:2-22; Heb 9:13-14
4:4 [g]Lev 1:3
4:5 [h]Lev 16:14
4:7 [i]ver 34; Lev 8:15 [j]ver 18,30; Lev 5:9; 9:9; 16:18
4:8 [k]Lev 3:3-5
4:9 [l]Lev 3:4
4:11 [m]Ex 29:14; Lev 9:11; Nu 19:5
4:12 [n]Heb 13:11 [o]Lev 6:11
4:13 [p]ver 2; Lev 5:2-4,17; Nu 15:24-26
4:14 [q]ver 3 [r]ver 23,28
4:15 [s]Lev 1:4; 8:14,22; Nu 8:10
4:16 [t]ver 5
4:17 [u]ver 6
4:18 [v]ver 7
4:19 [w]ver 8
4:20 [x]Heb 10:10-12 [y]Nu 15:25
4:21 [z]Lev 16:5,15
4:22 [a]Nu 31:13 [b]ver 2

e *10* The Hebrew word can include both male and female. f *10* Traditionally *peace offering*; also in verses 26, 31 and 35 where the burnt offering is slaughtered before the LORD. It is a sin offering. 25 Then the priest shall take some of the blood of the sin offering with his finger and put it on the horns of the altar of burnt offering and pour out the rest of the blood at the base of the altar.[a] 26 He shall burn all the fat on the altar as he burned the fat of the fellowship offering. In this way the priest will make atonement for the man's sin, and he will be forgiven.[b]

27 " 'If a member of the community sins unintentionally[c] and does what is forbidden in any of the LORD's commands, he is guilty. 28 When he is made aware of the sin he committed, he must bring as his offering[d] for the sin he committed a female goat[e] without defect. 29 He is to lay his hand on the head[f] of the sin offering[g] and slaughter it at the place of the burnt offering. 30 Then the priest is to take some of the blood with his finger and put it on the horns of the altar of burnt offering[h] and pour out the rest of the blood at the base of the altar. 31 He shall remove all the fat, just as the fat is removed from the fellowship offering, and the priest shall burn it on the altar as an aroma pleasing to the LORD.[i] In this way the priest will make atonement for him, and he will be forgiven.

32 " 'If he brings a lamb as his sin offering, he is to bring a female without defect.[j] 33 He is to lay his hand on its head and slaughter it for a sin offering at the place where the burnt offering is slaughtered.[k] 34 Then the priest shall take some of the blood of the sin offering with his finger and put it on the horns of the altar of burnt offering and pour out the rest of the blood at the base of the altar.[l] 35 He shall remove all the fat, just as the fat is removed from the lamb of the fellowship offering, and the priest shall burn it on the altar[m] on top of the offerings made to the LORD by fire. In this way the priest will make atonement for him for the sin he has committed, and he will be forgiven.

5 " 'If a person sins because he does not speak up when he hears a public charge to testify[n] regarding something he has seen or learned about, he will be held responsible.[o]

2 " 'Or if a person touches anything ceremonially unclean—whether the carcasses of unclean wild animals or of unclean livestock or of unclean creatures that move along the ground[p]—even though he is unaware of it, he has become unclean and is guilty.

3 " 'Or if he touches human uncleanness[q]—anything that would make him unclean—even though he is unaware of it, when he learns of it he will be guilty.

4 " 'Or if a person thoughtlessly takes an oath[r] to do anything, whether good or evil—in any matter one might carelessly swear about—even though he is unaware of it, in any case when he learns of it he will be guilty.

5 " 'When anyone is guilty in any of these ways, he must confess[s] in what way he has sinned 6 and, as a penalty for the sin he has committed, he must bring to the LORD a female lamb or goat from the flock as a sin offering;[t] and the priest shall make atonement for him for his sin.

7 " 'If he cannot afford[u] a lamb, he is to bring two doves or two young pigeons to the LORD as a penalty for his sin—one for a sin offering and the other for a burnt offering. 8 He is to bring them to the priest, who shall first offer the one for the sin offering. He is to wring its head from its neck,[v] not severing it completely,[w] 9 and is to sprinkle some of the blood of the sin offering against the side of the altar; the rest of the blood must be drained out at the base of the altar.[x] It is a sin offering. 10 The priest shall then offer the other as a burnt offering in the prescribed way[y] and make atonement for him for the sin he has committed, and he will be forgiven.[z]

11 " 'If, however, he cannot afford two doves or two young pigeons, he is to bring as an offering for his sin a tenth of

4:25 [a] ver 7,18,30, 34; Lev 9:9
4:26 [b] Lev 5:10
4:27 [c] ver 2; Nu 15:27
4:28 [d] ver 23 [e] ver 3
4:29 [f] ver 4,24 [g] Lev 1:4
4:30 [h] ver 7
4:31 [i] Ge 8:21
4:32 [j] ver 28
4:33 [k] ver 29
4:34 [l] ver 7
4:35 [m] ver 26,31
5:1 [n] Pr 29:24 [o] ver 17
5:2 [p] Lev 11:11, 24-40; Dt 14:8
5:3 [q] Nu 19:11-16
5:4 [r] Nu 30:6,8
5:5 [s] Lev 16:21; 26:40; Nu 5:7; Pr 28:13
5:6 [t] Lev 4:28
5:7 [u] Lev 12:8; 14:21
5:8 [v] Lev 1:15 [w] Lev 1:17
5:9 [x] Lev 4:7,18
5:10 [y] Lev 1:14-17 [z] Lev 4:26

an ephah[g] of fine flour[a] for a sin offering. He must not put oil or incense on
it, because it is a sin offering. 12He is to
bring it to the priest, who shall take a
handful of it as a memorial portion and
burn it on the altar on top of the offerings made to the LORD by fire. It is a sin
offering. 13In this way the priest will
make atonement[b] for him for any of
these sins he has committed, and he
will be forgiven. The rest of the offering
will belong to the priest,[c] as in the case
of the grain offering.' "

Regulations: Guilt offerings.

14The LORD said to Moses: 15"When a
person commits a violation and sins
unintentionally in regard to any of the
LORD's holy things, he is to bring to the
LORD as a penalty[d] a ram[e] from the flock,
one without defect and of the proper
value in silver, according to the sanctuary shekel.[h f] It is a guilt offering. 16He
must make restitution[g] for what he has
failed to do in regard to the holy things,
add a fifth of the value[h] to that and give
it all to the priest, who will make atonement for him with the ram as a guilt
offering, and he will be forgiven.

17"If a person sins and does what is
forbidden in any of the LORD's commands, even though he does not know
it,[i] he is guilty and will be held responsible. 18He is to bring to the priest as a
guilt offering a ram from the flock, one
without defect and of the proper value.
In this way the priest will make atonement for him for the wrong he has committed unintentionally, and he will be
forgiven.[j] 19It is a guilt offering; he has
been guilty of[i] wrongdoing against the
LORD."

6 The LORD said to Moses: 2"If anyone sins and is unfaithful to the
LORD[k] by deceiving his neighbor[l] about
something entrusted to him or left in his
care[m] or stolen, or if he cheats him, 3or
if he finds lost property and lies about
it,[n] or if he swears falsely, or if he commits any such sin that people may do—
4when he thus sins and becomes guilty,
he must return[o] what he has stolen or
taken by extortion, or what was entrusted to him, or the lost property he found,
5or whatever it was he swore falsely
about. He must make restitution[p] in full,
add a fifth of the value to it and give it
all to the owner on the day he presents
his guilt offering.[q] 6And as a penalty he
must bring to the priest, that is, to the
LORD, his guilt offering,[r] a ram from the
flock, one without defect and of the
proper value. 7In this way the priest
will make atonement[s] for him before the
LORD, and he will be forgiven for any
of these things he did that made him
guilty."

Additional regulations
for the various offerings.

8The LORD said to Moses: 9"Give
Aaron and his sons this command:
'These are the regulations for the burnt
offering: The burnt offering is to remain
on the altar hearth throughout the
night, till morning, and the fire must be
kept burning on the altar. 10The priest
shall then put on his linen clothes, with
linen undergarments next to his body,[t]
and shall remove the ashes of the burnt
offering that the fire has consumed on
the altar and place them beside the altar. 11Then he is to take off these clothes
and put on others, and carry the ashes
outside the camp to a place that is ceremonially clean.[u] 12The fire on the altar
must be kept burning; it must not go
out. Every morning the priest is to add
firewood and arrange the burnt offering
on the fire and burn the fat of the fellowship offerings[j] on it. 13The fire must
be kept burning on the altar continu-
ously; it must not go out.

14" 'These are the regulations for the
grain offering:[v] Aaron's sons are to bring
it before the LORD, in front of the altar.
15The priest is to take a handful of fine
flour and oil, together with all the

5:11 [a]Lev 2:1
5:13 [b]Lev 4:26 [c]Lev 2:3
5:15 [d]Lev 22:14 [e]Nu 5:8 [f]Ex 30:13
5:16 [g]Lev 6:4 [h]Lev 22:14; Nu 5:7
5:17 [i]ver 15; Lev 4:2
5:18 [j]ver 15
6:2 [k]Nu 5:6; Ac 5:4; Col 3:9 [l]Pr 24:28 [m]Ex 22:7
6:3 [n]Dt 22:1-3
6:4 [o]Lk 19:8
6:5 [p]Nu 5:7 [q]Lev 5:15
6:6 [r]Lev 5:15
6:7 [s]Lev 4:26
6:10 [t]Ex 28:39-42, 43; 39:28
6:11 [u]Lev 4:12
6:14 [v]Lev 2:1; 15:4

g *11* That is, probably about 2 quarts (about 2 liters)
h *15* That is, about 2/5 ounce (about 11.5 grams)
i *19* Or *has made full expiation for his*
j *12* Traditionally *peace offerings*

incense on the grain offering,[a] and burn the memorial portion[b] on the altar as an aroma pleasing to the LORD. **16**Aaron and his sons[c] shall eat the rest[d] of it, but it is to be eaten without yeast[e] in a holy place;[f] they are to eat it in the courtyard of the Tent of Meeting. **17**It must not be baked with yeast; I have given it as their share of the offerings made to me by fire. Like the sin offering and the guilt offering, it is most holy.[g] **18**Any male descendant of Aaron may eat it.[h] It is his regular share of the offerings made to the LORD by fire for the generations to come. Whatever touches them will become holy.[k][i] ’”

19The LORD also said to Moses, **20**“This is the offering Aaron and his sons are to bring to the LORD on the day he[l] is anointed: a tenth of an ephah[m][j] of fine flour as a regular grain offering,[k] half of it in the morning and half in the evening. **21**Prepare it with oil on a griddle;[l] bring it well-mixed and present the grain offering broken[n] in pieces as an aroma pleasing to the LORD. **22**The son who is to succeed him as anointed priest shall prepare it. It is the LORD’s regular share and is to be burned completely. **23**Every grain offering of a priest shall be burned completely; it must not be eaten.”

24The LORD said to Moses, **25**“Say to Aaron and his sons: ‘These are the regulations for the sin offering: The sin offering is to be slaughtered before the LORD[m] in the place[n] the burnt offering is slaughtered; it is most holy. **26**The priest who offers it shall eat it; it is to be eaten in a holy place,[o] in the courtyard[p] of the Tent of Meeting. **27**Whatever touches any of the flesh will become holy,[q] and if any of the blood is spattered on a garment, you must wash it in a holy place. **28**The clay pot[r] the meat is cooked in must be broken; but if it is cooked in a bronze pot, the pot is to be scoured and rinsed with water. **29**Any male in a priest’s family may eat it;[s] it is most holy.[t] **30**But any sin offering whose blood is brought into the Tent of Meeting to make atonement in the Holy Place[u] must not be eaten; it must be burned.[v]

7 “ ‘These are the regulations for the guilt offering,[w] which is most holy: **2**The guilt offering is to be slaughtered in the place where the burnt offering is slaughtered, and its blood is to be sprinkled against the altar on all sides. **3**All its fat[x] shall be offered: the fat tail and the fat that covers the inner parts, **4**both kidneys with the fat on them near the loins, and the covering of the liver, which is to be removed with the kidneys. **5**The priest shall burn them on the altar as an offering made to the LORD by fire. It is a guilt offering. **6**Any male in a priest’s family may eat it,[y] but it must be eaten in a holy place; it is most holy.[z]

7“ ‘The same law applies to both the sin offering and the guilt offering: They belong to the priest[a] who makes atonement with them. **8**The priest who offers a burnt offering for anyone may keep its hide for himself. **9**Every grain offering baked in an oven or cooked in a pan or on a griddle[b] belongs to the priest who offers it, **10**and every grain offering, whether mixed with oil or dry, belongs equally to all the sons of Aaron.

11“ ‘These are the regulations for the fellowship offering[o] a person may present to the LORD:

12“ ‘If he offers it as an expression of thankfulness, then along with this thank offering[c] he is to offer cakes of bread made without yeast and mixed with oil, wafers[d] made without yeast and spread with oil, and cakes of fine flour well-kneaded and mixed with oil. **13**Along with his fellowship offering of thanksgiving he is to present an offering with cakes of bread made with yeast.[e] **14**He is to bring one of each kind as an offering, a contribution to the LORD; it belongs to the priest who sprinkles the blood of the fellowship offerings. **15**The meat of his fellowship offering of thanksgiving

6:15 [a]Lev 2:9 [b]Lev 2:2
6:16 [c]Lev 2:3 [d]Eze 44:29 [e]Lev 2:11 [f]Lev 10:13
6:17 [g]ver 29; Ex 40:10; Nu 18:9,10
6:18 [h]ver 29; Nu 18:9-10 [i]ver 27
6:20 [j]Ex 16:36 [k]Ex 29:2
6:21 [l]Lev 2:5
6:25 [m]Lev 1:3 [n]Lev 1:5,11
6:26 [o]ver 16 [p]Lev 10:17-18
6:27 [q]Ex 29:37
6:28 [r]Lev 11:33; 15:12
6:29 [s]ver 18 [t]ver 17
6:30 [u]Lev 4:18 [v]Lev 4:12
7:1 [w]Lev 5:14-6:7
7:3 [x]Ex 29:13; Lev 3:4,9
7:6 [y]Lev 6:18; Nu 18:9-10 [z]Lev 2:3
7:7 [a]Lev 6:17,26; 1Co 9:13
7:9 [b]Lev 2:5
7:12 [c]ver 13,15 [d]Lev 2:4; Nu 6:15
7:13 [e]Lev 23:17; Am 4:5

[k]*18* Or *Whoever touches them must be holy*; similarly in verse 27 [l]*20* Or *each* [m]*20* That is, probably about 2 quarts (about 2 liters) [n]*21* The meaning of the Hebrew for this word is uncertain.
[o]*11* Traditionally *peace offering*; also in verses 13-37

must be eaten on the day it is offered; he must leave none of it till morning.[a]

16"'If, however, his offering is the result of a vow or is a freewill offering, the sacrifice shall be eaten on the day he offers it, but anything left over may be eaten on the next day.[b] 17Any meat of the sacrifice left over till the third day must be burned up. 18If any meat of the fellowship offering is eaten on the third day, it will not be accepted.[c] It will not be credited[d] to the one who offered it, for it is impure; the person who eats any of it will be held responsible.

19"'Meat that touches anything ceremonially unclean must not be eaten; it must be burned up. As for other meat, anyone ceremonially clean may eat it. 20But if anyone who is unclean eats any meat of the fellowship offering belonging to the LORD, that person must be cut off from his people.[e] 21If anyone touches something unclean[f]—whether human uncleanness or an unclean animal or any unclean, detestable thing—and then eats any of the meat of the fellowship offering belonging to the LORD, that person must be cut off from his people.'"

Eating of the fat and blood forbidden.

22The LORD said to Moses, 23"Say to the Israelites: 'Do not eat any of the fat of cattle, sheep or goats.[g] 24The fat of an animal found dead or torn by wild animals[h] may be used for any other purpose, but you must not eat it. 25Anyone who eats the fat of an animal from which an offering by fire may be[p] made to the LORD must be cut off from his people. 26And wherever you live, you must not eat the blood[i] of any bird or animal. 27If anyone eats blood,[j] that person must be cut off from his people.'"

The priest's portion of the offerings.

28The LORD said to Moses, 29"Say to the Israelites: 'Anyone who brings a fellowship offering to the LORD is to bring part of it as his sacrifice to the LORD. 30With his own hands he is to bring the offering made to the LORD by fire; he is to bring the fat, together with the breast, and wave the breast before the LORD as a wave offering.[k] 31The priest shall burn the fat on the altar, but the breast belongs to Aaron and his sons.[l] 32You are to give the right thigh of your fellowship offerings to the priest as a contribution.[m] 33The son of Aaron who offers the blood and the fat of the fellowship offering shall have the right thigh as his share. 34From the fellowship offerings of the Israelites, I have taken the breast that is waved and the thigh[n] that is presented and have given them to Aaron the priest and his sons[o] as their regular share from the Israelites.'"

35This is the portion of the offerings made to the LORD by fire that were allotted to Aaron and his sons on the day they were presented to serve the LORD as priests. 36On the day they were anointed,[p] the LORD commanded that the Israelites give this to them as their regular share for the generations to come.

37These, then, are the regulations for the burnt offering,[q] the grain offering,[r] the sin offering, the guilt offering, the ordination offering[s] and the fellowship offering, 38which the LORD gave Moses on Mount Sinai on the day he commanded the Israelites to bring their offerings to the LORD,[t] in the Desert of Sinai.

The ordination of Aaron and his sons.

8:1-36pp— Ex 29:1-37

8 The LORD said to Moses, 2"Bring Aaron and his sons, their garments, the anointing oil,[u] the bull for the sin offering, the two rams and the basket containing bread made without yeast,[v] 3and gather the entire assembly[w] at the entrance to the Tent of Meeting." 4Moses did as the LORD commanded him, and the assembly gathered at the

7:15 [a]Lev 22:30
7:16 [b]Lev 19:5-8
7:18 [c]Lev 19:7 [d]Nu 18:27
7:20 [e]Lev 22:3-7
7:21 [f]Lev 5:2; 11:24,28
7:23 [g]Lev 3:17; 17:13-14
7:24 [h]Ex 22:31
7:26 [i]Ge 9:4
7:27 [j]Lev 17:10-24; Ac 15:20,29
7:30 [k]Ex 29:24; Nu 6:20
7:31 [l]ver 34
7:32 [m]ver 34; Lev 9:21; Nu 6:20
7:34 [n]Lev 10:15 [o]Ex 29:27; Nu 18:18-19
7:36 [p]Ex 40:13,15; Lev 8:12,30
7:37 [q]Lev 6:9 [r]Lev 6:14 [s]ver 1,11
7:38 [t]Lev 1:2
8:2 [u]Ex 30:23-25, 30 [v]Ex 29:2-3
8:3 [w]Nu 8:9

p25 Or *fire is*

entrance to the Tent of Meeting.
5Moses said to the assembly, "This is
what the LORD has commanded to be
done." 6Then Moses brought Aaron
and his sons forward and washed them
with water.[a] 7He put the tunic on Aaron,
tied the sash around him, clothed him
with the robe and put the ephod on
him. He also tied the ephod to him by
its skillfully woven waistband; so it was
fastened on him.[b] 8He placed the breastpiece on him and put the Urim and
Thummim[c] in the breastpiece. 9Then he
placed the turban on Aaron's head and
set the gold plate, the sacred diadem,[d]
on the front of it, as the LORD commanded Moses.
10Then Moses took the anointing oil[e]
and anointed[f] the tabernacle and everything in it, and so consecrated them.
11He sprinkled some of the oil on the
altar seven times, anointing the altar
and all its utensils and the basin with its
stand, to consecrate them.[g] 12He poured
some of the anointing oil on Aaron's
head and anointed[h] him to consecrate
him.[i] 13Then he brought Aaron's sons
forward, put tunics on them, tied sashes
around them and put headbands on
them, as the LORD commanded Moses.
14He then presented the bull[j] for the
sin offering,[k] and Aaron and his sons
laid their hands on its head. 15Moses
slaughtered the bull and took some of
the blood, and with his finger he put it
on all the horns of the altar[l] to purify
the altar.[m] He poured out the rest of
the blood at the base of the altar. So he
consecrated it to make atonement for
it.[n] 16Moses also took all the fat around
the inner parts, the covering of the liver, and both kidneys and their fat, and
burned it on the altar. 17But the bull
with its hide and its flesh and its offal[o]
he burned up outside the camp,[p] as the
LORD commanded Moses.
18He then presented the ram[q] for the
burnt offering, and Aaron and his sons
laid their hands on its head. 19Then
Moses slaughtered the ram and sprinkled the blood against the altar on all
sides. 20He cut the ram into pieces and

8:6 [a]Ex 29:4; 30:19; Ps 26:6; Ac 22:16; 1Co 6:11; Eph 5:26
8:7 [b]Ex 28:4
8:8 [c]Ex 28:30
8:9 [d]Ex 28:36
8:10 [e]ver 2 [f]Ex 30:26
8:11 [g]Ex 30:29
8:12 [h]Lev 21:10,12 [i]Ex 30:30
8:14 [j]Lev 4:3 [k]Ps 66:15; Eze 43:19
8:15 [l]Lev 4:7 [m]Heb 9:22 [n]Eze 43:20
8:17 [o]Lev 4:11 [p]Lev 4:12
8:18 [q]ver 2
8:22 [r]ver 2
8:24 [s]Heb 9:18-22
8:29 [t]Lev 7:31-34
8:30 [u]Ex 28:2 [v]Nu 3:3

burned the head, the pieces and the fat.
21He washed the inner parts and the
legs with water and burned the whole
ram on the altar as a burnt offering, a
pleasing aroma, an offering made to the
LORD by fire, as the LORD commanded
Moses.
22He then presented the other ram,
the ram for the ordination,[r] and Aaron
and his sons laid their hands on its
head. 23Moses slaughtered the ram and
took some of its blood and put it on the
lobe of Aaron's right ear, on the thumb
of his right hand and on the big toe of
his right foot. 24Moses also brought
Aaron's sons forward and put some of
the blood on the lobes of their right
ears, on the thumbs of their right hands
and on the big toes of their right feet.
Then he sprinkled blood against the
altar on all sides.[s] 25He took the fat, the
fat tail, all the fat around the inner parts,
the covering of the liver, both kidneys
and their fat and the right thigh. 26Then
from the basket of bread made without
yeast, which was before the LORD, he
took a cake of bread, and one made with
oil, and a wafer; he put these on the
fat portions and on the right thigh.
27He put all these in the hands of Aaron and his sons and waved them before the LORD as a wave offering. 28Then
Moses took them from their hands and
burned them on the altar on top of the
burnt offering as an ordination offering,
a pleasing aroma, an offering made to
the LORD by fire. 29He also took the
breast—Moses' share of the ordination
ram[t]—and waved it before the LORD as
a wave offering, as the LORD commanded Moses.
30Then Moses took some of the
anointing oil and some of the blood
from the altar and sprinkled them on
Aaron and his garments[u] and on his
sons and their garments. So he consecrated[v] Aaron and his garments and his
sons and their garments.
31Moses then said to Aaron and his
sons, "Cook the meat at the entrance to
the Tent of Meeting and eat it there
with the bread from the basket of ordi-

nation offerings, as I commanded, saying,[q] 'Aaron and his sons are to eat it.' 32Then burn up the rest of the meat and the bread. 33Do not leave the entrance to the Tent of Meeting for seven days, until the days of your ordination are completed, for your ordination will last seven days. 34What has been done today was commanded by the LORD[a] to make atonement for you. 35You must stay at the entrance to the Tent of Meeting day and night for seven days and do what the LORD requires,[b] so you will not die; for that is what I have been commanded." 36So Aaron and his sons did everything the LORD commanded through Moses.

Aaron's offerings for himself and the people.

9 On the eighth day[c] Moses summoned Aaron and his sons and the elders of Israel. 2He said to Aaron, "Take a bull calf for your sin offering and a ram for your burnt offering, both without defect, and present them before the LORD. 3Then say to the Israelites: 'Take a male goat for a sin offering, a calf and a lamb—both a year old and without defect—for a burnt offering, 4and an ox[r] and a ram for a fellowship offering[s] to sacrifice before the LORD, together with a grain offering mixed with oil. For today the LORD will appear to you.[d]'"

5They took the things Moses commanded to the front of the Tent of Meeting, and the entire assembly came near and stood before the LORD. 6Then Moses said, "This is what the LORD has commanded you to do, so that the glory of the LORD[e] may appear to you."

7Moses said to Aaron, "Come to the altar and sacrifice your sin offering and your burnt offering and make atonement for yourself and the people; sacrifice the offering that is for the people and make atonement for them, as the LORD has commanded.[f]"

8So Aaron came to the altar and slaughtered the calf as a sin offering[g] for himself. 9His sons brought the blood to him,[h] and he dipped his finger into the blood and put it on the horns of the altar; the rest of the blood he poured out at the base of the altar.[i] 10On the altar he burned the fat, the kidneys and the covering of the liver from the sin offering, as the LORD commanded Moses; 11the flesh and the hide[j] he burned up outside the camp.[k]

12Then he slaughtered the burnt offering. His sons handed him the blood, and he sprinkled it against the altar on all sides. 13They handed him the burnt offering piece by piece, including the head, and he burned them on the altar.[l] 14He washed the inner parts and the legs and burned them on top of the burnt offering on the altar.

15Aaron then brought the offering that was for the people.[m] He took the goat for the people's sin offering and slaughtered it and offered it for a sin offering as he did with the first one.

16He brought the burnt offering and offered it in the prescribed way.[n] 17He also brought the grain offering, took a handful of it and burned it on the altar in addition to the morning's burnt offering.[o]

18He slaughtered the ox and the ram as the fellowship offering for the people.[p] His sons handed him the blood, and he sprinkled it against the altar on all sides. 19But the fat portions of the ox and the ram—the fat tail, the layer of fat, the kidneys and the covering of the liver— 20these they laid on the breasts, and then Aaron burned the fat on the altar. 21Aaron waved the breasts and the right thigh before the LORD as a wave offering,[q] as Moses commanded.

22Then Aaron lifted his hands toward the people and blessed them.[r] And having sacrificed the sin offering, the burnt offering and the fellowship offering, he stepped down.

23Moses and Aaron then went into the Tent of Meeting. When they came

8:34 [a]Heb 7:16
8:35 [b]Nu 3:7; 9:19; Dt 11:1; 1Ki 2:3; Eze 48:11
9:1 [c]Eze 43:27
9:4 [d]Ex 29:43
9:6 [e]ver 23; Ex 24:16
9:7 [f]Heb 5:1,3; 7:27
9:8 [g]Lev 4:1-12
9:9 [h]ver 12,18 [i]Lev 4:7
9:11 [j]Lev 4:11 [k]Lev 4:12; 8:17
9:13 [l]Lev 1:8
9:15 [m]Lev 4:27-31
9:16 [n]Lev 1:1-13
9:17 [o]Lev 2:1-2; 3:5
9:18 [p]Lev 3:1-11
9:21 [q]Ex 29:24,26; Lev 7:30-34
9:22 [r]Nu 6:23; Dt 21:5; Lk 24:50

q*31* Or *I was commanded:* r*4* The Hebrew word can include both male and female; also in verses 18 and 19. s*4* Traditionally *peace offering*; also in verses 18 and 22

out, they blessed the people; and the glory of the LORD[a] appeared to all the people. 24Fire[b] came out from the presence of the LORD and consumed the burnt offering and the fat portions on the altar. And when all the people saw it, they shouted for joy and fell facedown.[c]

Nadab and Abihu are consumed by fire.

10 Aaron's sons Nadab and Abihu[d] took their censers, put fire in them[e] and added incense; and they offered unauthorized fire before the LORD, contrary to his command.[f] 2So fire came out from the presence of the LORD and consumed them,[g] and they died before the LORD. 3Moses then said to Aaron, "This is what the LORD spoke of when he said:

"'Among those who approach me[h]
I will show myself holy;[i]
in the sight of all the people
I will be honored.[j]'"

Aaron remained silent.

4Moses summoned Mishael and Elzaphan,[k] sons of Aaron's uncle Uzziel,[l] and said to them, "Come here; carry your cousins outside the camp,[m] away from the front of the sanctuary." 5So they came and carried them, still in their tunics,[n] outside the camp, as Moses ordered.

6Then Moses said to Aaron and his sons Eleazar and Ithamar, "Do not let your hair become unkempt,[t][o] and do not tear your clothes, or you will die and the LORD will be angry with the whole community.[p] But your relatives, all the house of Israel, may mourn for those the LORD has destroyed by fire. 7Do not leave the entrance to the Tent of Meeting or you will die, because the LORD's anointing oil[q] is on you." So they did as Moses said.

Decrees from the LORD.

8Then the LORD said to Aaron, 9"You and your sons are not to drink wine[r] or other fermented drink[s] whenever you go into the Tent of Meeting, or you will die. This is a lasting ordinance for the generations to come. 10You must distinguish between the holy and the common, between the unclean and the clean,[t] 11and you must teach[u] the Israelites all the decrees the LORD has given them through Moses.[v]"

12Moses said to Aaron and his remaining sons, Eleazar and Ithamar, "Take the grain offering left over from the offerings made to the LORD by fire and eat it prepared without yeast beside the altar,[w] for it is most holy. 13Eat it in a holy place, because it is your share and your sons' share of the offerings made to the LORD by fire; for so I have been commanded. 14But you and your sons and your daughters may eat the breast that was waved and the thigh that was presented. Eat them in a ceremonially clean place;[x] they have been given to you and your children as your share of the Israelites' fellowship offerings.[u] 15The thigh[y] that was presented and the breast that was waved must be brought with the fat portions of the offerings made by fire, to be waved before the LORD as a wave offering. This will be the regular share for you and your children, as the LORD has commanded."

16When Moses inquired about the goat of the sin offering[z] and found that it had been burned up, he was angry with Eleazar and Ithamar, Aaron's remaining sons, and asked, 17"Why didn't you eat the sin offering[a] in the sanctuary area? It is most holy; it was given to you to take away the guilt of the community by making atonement for them before the LORD. 18Since its blood was not taken into the Holy Place,[b] you should have eaten the goat in the sanctuary area, as I commanded."

19Aaron replied to Moses, "Today they sacrificed their sin offering and their burnt offering[c] before the LORD, but such things as this have happened to me. Would the LORD have been pleased if I

9:23 [a]ver 6
9:24 [b]Jdg 6:21; 2Ch 7:1 [c]1Ki 18:39
10:1 [d]Ex 24:1; Nu 3:2-4; 26:61 [e]Lev 16:12 [f]Ex 30:9
10:2 [g]Nu 3:4; 16:35; 26:61
10:3 [h]Ex 19:22 [i]Ex 30:29; Lev 21:6; Eze 28:22 [j]Isa 49:3
10:4 [k]Ex 6:22 [l]Ex 6:18 [m]Ac 5:6,9,10
10:5 [n]Lev 8:13
10:6 [o]Lev 21:10 [p]Nu 1:53; 16:22; Jos 7:1; 22:18; 2Sa 24:1
10:7 [q]Ex 28:41; Lev 21:12
10:9 [r]Hos 4:11 [s]Pr 20:1; Isa 28:7; Eze 44:21; Lk 1:15; Eph 5:18; 1Ti 3:3; Tit 1:7
10:10 [t]Lev 11:47; 20:25; Eze 22:26
10:11 [u]Mal 2:7 [v]Dt 24:8
10:12 [w]Lev 6:14-18; 21:22
10:14 [x]Ex 29:24, 26-27; Lev 7:31,34; Nu 18:11
10:15 [y]Lev 7:34
10:16 [z]Lev 9:3
10:17 [a]Lev 6:24-30
10:18 [b]Lev 6:26,30
10:19 [c]Lev 9:12

t *6* Or *Do not uncover your heads* u *14* Traditionally *peace offerings*

had eaten the sin offering today?”
20 When Moses heard this, he was satisfied.

Clean and unclean food.

11:1-23pp— Dt 14:3-20

11 The LORD said to Moses and
Aaron, 2 “Say to the Israelites: ‘Of
all the animals that live on land, these
are the ones you may eat:[a] 3 You may eat
any animal that has a split hoof completely divided and that chews the cud.
4 “ ‘There are some that only chew the
cud or only have a split hoof, but you
must not eat them. The camel, though it
chews the cud, does not have a split
hoof; it is ceremonially unclean for you.
5 The coney,[v] though it chews the cud,
does not have a split hoof; it is unclean
for you. 6 The rabbit, though it chews the
cud, does not have a split hoof; it is unclean for you. 7 And the pig,[b] though it
has a split hoof completely divided, does
not chew the cud; it is unclean for you.
8 You must not eat their meat or touch
their carcasses; they are unclean for you.[c]
9 “ ‘Of all the creatures living in the
water of the seas and the streams, you
may eat any that have fins and scales.
10 But all creatures in the seas or streams
that do not have fins and scales—
whether among all the swarming things
or among all the other living creatures
in the water—you are to detest.[d] 11 And
since you are to detest them, you must
not eat their meat and you must detest
their carcasses. 12 Anything living in the
water that does not have fins and scales
is to be detestable to you.
13 “ ‘These are the birds you are to
detest and not eat because they are
detestable: the eagle, the vulture, the
black vulture, 14 the red kite, any kind of
black kite, 15 any kind of raven, 16 the
horned owl, the screech owl, the gull,
any kind of hawk, 17 the little owl, the
cormorant, the great owl, 18 the white
owl, the desert owl, the osprey, 19 the
stork, any kind of heron, the hoopoe
and the bat.[w]
20 “ ‘All flying insects that walk on all
fours are to be detestable to you.[e]
21 There are, however, some winged
creatures that walk on all fours that you
may eat: those that have jointed legs for
hopping on the ground. 22 Of these you
may eat any kind of locust,[f] katydid,
cricket or grasshopper. 23 But all other
winged creatures that have four legs you
are to detest.
24 “ ‘You will make yourselves unclean
by these; whoever touches their carcasses will be unclean till evening. 25 Whoever picks up one of their carcasses
must wash his clothes,[g] and he will be
unclean till evening.[h]
26 “ ‘Every animal that has a split hoof
not completely divided or that does not
chew the cud is unclean for you; whoever touches ⌊the carcass of⌋ any of them
will be unclean. 27 Of all the animals that
walk on all fours, those that walk on
their paws are unclean for you; whoever
touches their carcasses will be unclean
till evening. 28 Anyone who picks up
their carcasses must wash his clothes,
and he will be unclean till evening.
They are unclean for you.
29 “ ‘Of the animals that move about
on the ground, these are unclean for
you: the weasel, the rat,[i] any kind of
great lizard, 30 the gecko, the monitor
lizard, the wall lizard, the skink and the
chameleon. 31 Of all those that move
along the ground, these are unclean for
you. Whoever touches them when they
are dead will be unclean till evening.
32 When one of them dies and falls on
something, that article, whatever its
use, will be unclean, whether it is made
of wood, cloth, hide or sackcloth.[j] Put it
in water; it will be unclean till evening,
and then it will be clean. 33 If one of
them falls into a clay pot, everything in
it will be unclean, and you must break
the pot.[k] 34 Any food that could be eat-
en but has water on it from such a pot
is unclean, and any liquid that could be
drunk from it is unclean. 35 Anything
that one of their carcasses falls on

11:2 [a]Ac 10:12-14
11:7 [b]Isa 65:4; 66:3,17
11:8 [c]Isa 52:11; Heb 9:10
11:10 [d]Lev 7:18
11:20 [e]Ac 10:14
11:22 [f]Mt 3:4; Mk 1:6
11:25 [g]Lev 14:8,47; 15:5 [h]ver 40; Nu 31:24
11:29 [i]Isa 66:17
11:32 [j]Lev 15:12
11:33 [k]Lev 6:28; 15:12

[v] *5* That is, the hyrax or rock badger [w] *19* The precise identification of some of the birds, insects and animals in this chapter is uncertain.

becomes unclean; an oven or cooking
pot must be broken up. They are unclean, and you are to regard them as
unclean. 36A spring, however, or a cistern for collecting water remains clean,
but anyone who touches one of these
carcasses is unclean. 37If a carcass falls
on any seeds that are to be planted, they
remain clean. 38But if water has been
put on the seed and a carcass falls on it,
it is unclean for you.

39" 'If an animal that you are allowed
to eat dies, anyone who touches the
carcass will be unclean till evening.
40Anyone who eats some of the carcass
must wash his clothes, and he will be
unclean till evening.[a] Anyone who picks
up the carcass must wash his clothes,
and he will be unclean till evening.

41" 'Every creature that moves about
on the ground is detestable; it is not to
be eaten. 42You are not to eat any creature that moves about on the ground,
whether it moves on its belly or walks
on all fours or on many feet; it is
detestable. 43Do not defile yourselves
by any of these creatures.[b] Do not make
yourselves unclean by means of them
or be made unclean by them. 44I am the
LORD your God;[c] consecrate yourselves[d]
and be holy,[e] because I am holy.[f] Do not
make yourselves unclean by any creature that moves about on the ground.
45I am the LORD who brought you up out
of Egypt[g] to be your God;[h] therefore be
holy, because I am holy.[i]

46" 'These are the regulations concerning animals, birds, every living
thing that moves in the water and every
creature that moves about on the
ground. 47You must distinguish between
the unclean and the clean, between living creatures that may be eaten and
those that may not be eaten.[j]' "

Purification of a woman after childbirth.

12 The LORD said to Moses, 2"Say
to the Israelites: 'A woman who
becomes pregnant and gives birth to a
son will be ceremonially unclean for
seven days, just as she is unclean during
her monthly period.[k] 3On the eighth day
the boy is to be circumcised.[l] 4Then
the woman must wait thirty-three days
to be purified from her bleeding. She
must not touch anything sacred or go
to the sanctuary until the days of her
purification are over. 5If she gives birth
to a daughter, for two weeks the woman
will be unclean, as during her period.
Then she must wait sixty-six days to be
purified from her bleeding.

6" 'When the days of her purification
for a son or daughter are over,[m] she is
to bring to the priest at the entrance to
the Tent of Meeting a year-old lamb[n] for
a burnt offering and a young pigeon or a
dove for a sin offering.[o] 7He shall offer
them before the LORD to make atonement for her, and then she will be ceremonially clean from her flow of blood.

" 'These are the regulations for the
woman who gives birth to a boy or a
girl. 8If she cannot afford a lamb, she is
to bring two doves or two young
pigeons,[p] one for a burnt offering and
the other for a sin offering.[q] In this way
the priest will make atonement for her,
and she will be clean.[r]' "

Examining and treating infectious skin diseases.

13 The LORD said to Moses and
Aaron, 2"When anyone has a
swelling[s] or a rash or a bright spot[t] on
his skin that may become an infectious
skin disease,[x][u] he must be brought to
Aaron the priest[v] or to one of his sons[y]
who is a priest. 3The priest is to examine the sore on his skin, and if the hair
in the sore has turned white and the
sore appears to be more than skin
deep,[z] it is an infectious skin disease.
When the priest examines him, he shall
pronounce him ceremonially unclean.[w]
4If the spot[x] on his skin is white but
does not appear to be more than skin

11:40 [a]Lev 17:15; 22:8; Eze 44:31
11:43 [b]Lev 20:25
11:44 [c]Ex 6:2,7; Isa 43:3; 51:15 [d]Lev 20:7 [e]Ex 19:6 [f]Lev 19:2; Ps 99:3; Eph 1:4; 1Th 4:7; 1Pe 1:15,16*
11:45 [g]Lev 25:38,55; Ex 6:7; 20:2 [h]Ge 17:7 [i]Ex 19:6; 1Pe 1:16*
11:47 [j]Lev 10:10
12:2 [k]Lev 15:19; 18:19
12:3 [l]Ge 17:12; Lk 1:59; 2:21
12:6 [m]Lk 2:22 [n]Ex 29:38; Lev 23:12; Nu 6:12,14; 7:15 [o]Lev 5:7
12:8 [p]Ge 15:9; Lev 14:22 [q]Lev 5:7; Lk 2:22-24* [r]Lev 4:26
13:2 [s]ver 10,19, 28,43 [t]ver 4,38,39; Lev 14:56 [u]ver 3,9,15; Ex 4:6; Lev 14:3,32; Nu 5:2; Dt 24:8 [v]Dt 24:8
13:3 [w]ver 8,11,20, 30; Lev 21:1; Nu 9:6
13:4 [x]ver 2

x2 Traditionally *leprosy*; the Hebrew word was used for various diseases affecting the skin—not necessarily leprosy; also elsewhere in this chapter. y2 Or *descendants* z3 Or *be lower than the rest of the skin*; also elsewhere in this chapter

deep and the hair in it has not turned
white, the priest is to put the infected
person in isolation for seven days.[a] **5**On
the seventh day[b] the priest is to examine him,[c] and if he sees that the sore is
unchanged and has not spread in the
skin, he is to keep him in isolation
another seven days. **6**On the seventh
day the priest is to examine him again,
and if the sore has faded and has not
spread in the skin, the priest shall pronounce him clean;[d] it is only a rash. The
man must wash his clothes,[e] and he will
be clean.[f] **7**But if the rash does spread in
his skin after he has shown himself to
the priest to be pronounced clean, he
must appear before the priest again.[g]
8The priest is to examine him, and if
the rash has spread in the skin, he shall
pronounce him unclean; it is an infectious disease.

9"When anyone has an infectious skin
disease, he must be brought to the
priest. **10**The priest is to examine him,
and if there is a white swelling in the
skin that has turned the hair white and
if there is raw flesh in the swelling, **11**it
is a chronic skin disease[h] and the priest
shall pronounce him unclean. He is not
to put him in isolation, because he is
already unclean.

12"If the disease breaks out all over
his skin and, so far as the priest can see,
it covers all the skin of the infected person from head to foot, **13**the priest is to
examine him, and if the disease has covered his whole body, he shall pronounce
that person clean. Since it has all turned
white, he is clean. **14**But whenever raw
flesh appears on him, he will be unclean. **15**When the priest sees the raw
flesh, he shall pronounce him unclean.
The raw flesh is unclean; he has an
infectious disease.[i] **16**Should the raw
flesh change and turn white, he must go
to the priest. **17**The priest is to examine
him, and if the sores have turned white,
the priest shall pronounce the infected
person clean;[j] then he will be clean.

18"When someone has a boil[k] on his
skin and it heals, **19**and in the place
where the boil was, a white swelling or
reddish-white[l] spot[m] appears, he must
present himself to the priest. **20**The
priest is to examine it, and if it appears
to be more than skin deep and the hair
in it has turned white, the priest shall
pronounce him unclean. It is an infectious skin disease[n] that has broken out
where the boil was. **21**But if, when the
priest examines it, there is no white
hair in it and it is not more than skin
deep and has faded, then the priest is
to put him in isolation for seven days.
22If it is spreading in the skin, the priest
shall pronounce him unclean; it is infectious. **23**But if the spot is unchanged and
has not spread, it is only a scar from the
boil, and the priest shall pronounce him
clean.[o]

24"When someone has a burn on his
skin and a reddish-white or white spot
appears in the raw flesh of the burn,
25the priest is to examine the spot, and
if the hair in it has turned white, and it
appears to be more than skin deep, it
is an infectious disease that has broken
out in the burn. The priest shall pronounce him unclean; it is an infectious
skin disease.[p] **26**But if the priest examines it and there is no white hair in the
spot and if it is not more than skin deep
and has faded, then the priest is to put
him in isolation for seven days.[q] **27**On
the seventh day the priest is to examine
him,[r] and if it is spreading in the skin,
the priest shall pronounce him unclean;
it is an infectious skin disease. **28**If, however, the spot is unchanged and has not
spread in the skin but has faded, it is a
swelling from the burn, and the priest
shall pronounce him clean; it is only a
scar from the burn.[s]

29"If a man or woman has a sore on
the head[t] or on the chin, **30**the priest is
to examine the sore, and if it appears to
be more than skin deep and the hair in
it is yellow and thin, the priest shall pronounce that person unclean; it is an
itch, an infectious disease of the head or
chin. **31**But if, when the priest examines
this kind of sore, it does not seem to be
more than skin deep and there is no
black hair in it, then the priest is to put

13:4 [a]ver 5,21,26, 33,46; Lev 14:38; Nu 12:14,15; Dt 24:9
13:5 [b]Lev 14:9 [c]ver 27,32, 34,51
13:6 [d]ver 13,17, 23,28,34; Mt 8:3; Lk 5:12-14 [e]Lev 11:25 [f]Lev 11:25; 14:8,9,20,48; 15:8; Nu 8:7
13:7 [g]Lk 5:14
13:11 [h]Ex 4:6; Lev 14:8; Nu 12:10; Mt 8:2
13:15 [i]ver 2
13:17 [j]ver 6
13:18 [k]Ex 9:9
13:19 [l]ver 24,42; Lev 14:37 [m]ver 2
13:20 [n]ver 2
13:23 [o]ver 6
13:25 [p]ver 11
13:26 [q]ver 4
13:27 [r]ver 5
13:28 [s]ver 2
13:29 [t]ver 43,44

the infected person in isolation for sev-
en days.[a] **32**On the seventh day the
priest is to examine the sore,[b] and if the
itch has not spread and there is no yellow hair in it and it does not appear to
be more than skin deep, **33**he must be
shaved except for the diseased area, and
the priest is to keep him in isolation
another seven days. **34**On the seventh
day the priest is to examine the itch,[c]
and if it has not spread in the skin and
appears to be no more than skin deep,
the priest shall pronounce him clean.
He must wash his clothes, and he will
be clean.[d] **35**But if the itch does spread
in the skin after he is pronounced clean,
36the priest is to examine him, and if
the itch has spread in the skin, the
priest does not need to look for yellow
hair; the person is unclean.[e] **37**If, however, in his judgment it is unchanged and
black hair has grown in it, the itch is
healed. He is clean, and the priest shall
pronounce him clean.

38"When a man or woman has white
spots on the skin, **39**the priest is to
examine them, and if the spots are dull
white, it is a harmless rash that has broken out on the skin; that person is
clean.

40"When a man has lost his hair and
is bald,[f] he is clean. **41**If he has lost his
hair from the front of his scalp and has a
bald forehead, he is clean. **42**But if he
has a reddish-white sore on his bald
head or forehead, it is an infectious disease breaking out on his head or forehead. **43**The priest is to examine him,
and if the swollen sore on his head or
forehead is reddish-white like an infectious skin disease, **44**the man is diseased
and is unclean. The priest shall pronounce him unclean because of the sore
on his head.

45"The person with such an infectious disease must wear torn clothes,[g]
let his hair be unkempt,[a] cover the lower part of his face[h] and cry out, 'Unclean! Unclean!'[i] **46**As long as he has
the infection he remains unclean. He
must live alone; he must live outside
the camp.[j]

Cleansing from mildew in clothing.

47"If any clothing is contaminated
with mildew—any woolen or linen
clothing, **48**any woven or knitted material of linen or wool, any leather or
anything made of leather— **49**and if
the contamination in the clothing, or
leather, or woven or knitted material,
or any leather article, is greenish or reddish, it is a spreading mildew and must
be shown to the priest.[k] **50**The priest is
to examine the mildew[l] and isolate the
affected article for seven days. **51**On the
seventh day he is to examine it,[m] and if
the mildew has spread in the clothing,
or the woven or knitted material, or the
leather, whatever its use, it is a destructive mildew; the article is unclean.[n]
52He must burn up the clothing, or the
woven or knitted material of wool or
linen, or any leather article that has the
contamination in it, because the mildew
is destructive; the article must be
burned up.[o]

53"But if, when the priest examines it,
the mildew has not spread in the clothing, or the woven or knitted material, or
the leather article, **54**he shall order that
the contaminated article be washed.
Then he is to isolate it for another seven
days. **55**After the affected article has
been washed, the priest is to examine
it, and if the mildew has not changed its
appearance, even though it has not
spread, it is unclean. Burn it with fire,
whether the mildew has affected one
side or the other. **56**If, when the priest
examines it, the mildew has faded after
the article has been washed, he is to
tear the contaminated part out of the
clothing, or the leather, or the woven or
knitted material. **57**But if it reappears in
the clothing, or in the woven or knitted
material, or in the leather article, it is
spreading, and whatever has the mildew
must be burned with fire. **58**The clothing, or the woven or knitted material, or
any leather article that has been washed
and is rid of the mildew, must be
washed again, and it will be clean."

a45 Or *clothes, uncover his head*

13:31 [a]ver 4
13:32 [b]ver 5
13:34 [c]ver 5 [d]Lev 11:25
13:36 [e]ver 30
13:40 [f]Lev 21:5; 2Ki 2:23; Isa 3:24; 15:2; 22:12; Eze 27:31; 29:18; Am 8:10; Mic 1:16
13:45 [g]Lev 10:6 [h]Eze 24:17, 22; Mic 3:7 [i]Lev 5:2; La 4:15; Lk 17:12
13:46 [j]Nu 5:1-4; 12:14; 2Ki 7:3; 15:5; Lk 17:12
13:49 [k]Mk 1:44
13:50 [l]Eze 44:23
13:51 [m]ver 5 [n]Lev 14:44
13:52 [o]ver 55,57

[57]These are the regulations concerning contamination by mildew in woolen or linen clothing, woven or knitted material, or any leather article, for pronouncing them clean or unclean.

Cleansing from infectious skin diseases.

14 The LORD said to Moses, [2]"These are the regulations for the diseased person at the time of his ceremonial cleansing, when he is brought to the priest:[a] [3]The priest is to go outside the camp and examine him.[b] If the person has been healed of his infectious skin disease,[b] [4]the priest shall order that two live clean birds and some cedar wood, scarlet yarn and hyssop be brought for the one to be cleansed.[c] [5]Then the priest shall order that one of the birds be killed over fresh water in a clay pot. [6]He is then to take the live bird and dip it, together with the cedar wood, the scarlet yarn and the hyssop, into the blood of the bird that was killed over the fresh water.[d] [7]Seven times he shall sprinkle[e] the one to be cleansed of the infectious disease and pronounce him clean. Then he is to release the live bird in the open fields.

[8]"The person to be cleansed must wash his clothes,[f] shave off all his hair and bathe with water;[g] then he will be ceremonially clean.[h] After this he may come into the camp,[i] but he must stay outside his tent for seven days. [9]On the seventh day he must shave off all his hair; he must shave his head, his beard, his eyebrows and the rest of his hair. He must wash his clothes and bathe himself with water, and he will be clean.

[10]"On the eighth day[j] he must bring two male lambs and one ewe lamb a year old, each without defect, along with three-tenths of an ephah[c] of fine flour mixed with oil for a grain offering,[k] and one log[d] of oil.[l] [11]The priest who pronounces him clean shall present both the one to be cleansed and his offerings before the LORD at the entrance to the Tent of Meeting.

[12]"Then the priest is to take one of the male lambs and offer it as a guilt offering,[m] along with the log of oil; he shall wave them before the LORD as a wave offering.[n] [13]He is to slaughter the lamb in the holy place[o] where the sin offering and the burnt offering are slaughtered. Like the sin offering, the guilt offering belongs to the priest;[p] it is most holy. [14]The priest is to take some of the blood of the guilt offering and put it on the lobe of the right ear of the one to be cleansed, on the thumb of his right hand and on the big toe of his right foot.[q] [15]The priest shall then take some of the log of oil, pour it in the palm of his own left hand, [16]dip his right forefinger into the oil in his palm, and with his finger sprinkle some of it before the LORD seven times. [17]The priest is to put some of the oil remaining in his palm on the lobe of the right ear of the one to be cleansed, on the thumb of his right hand and on the big toe of his right foot, on top of the blood of the guilt offering. [18]The rest of the oil in his palm the priest shall put on the head of the one to be cleansed and make atonement for him before the LORD.

[19]"Then the priest is to sacrifice the sin offering and make atonement for the one to be cleansed from his uncleanness. After that, the priest shall slaughter the burnt offering [20]and offer it on the altar, together with the grain offering, and make atonement for him, and he will be clean.[r]

[21]"If, however, he is poor[s] and cannot afford these,[t] he must take one male lamb as a guilt offering to be waved to make atonement for him, together with a tenth of an ephah[e] of fine flour mixed with oil for a grain offering, a log of oil, [22]and two doves or two young pigeons,[u] which he can afford, one for a sin offering and the other for a burnt offering.

14:2 [a]Mt 8:2-4; Mk 1:40-44; Lk 5:12-14; 17:14
14:3 [b]Lev 13:46
14:4 [c]ver 6,49,51, 52; Nu 19:6; Ps 51:7
14:6 [d]ver 4
14:7 [e]2Ki 5:10,14; Isa 52:15; Eze 36:25
14:8 [f]Lev 11:25; 13:6 [g]ver 9 [h]ver 20 [i]Nu 5:2,3; 12:14,15; 2Ch 26:21
14:10 [j]Mt 8:4; Mk 1:44; Lk 5:14 [k]Lev 2:1 [l]ver 12,15,21, 24
14:12 [m]Lev 5:18; 6:6-7 [n]Ex 29:24
14:13 [o]Ex 29:11 [p]Lev 6:24-30; 7:7
14:14 [q]Ex 29:20; Lev 8:23
14:20 [r]ver 8
14:21 [s]Lev 5:7; 12:8 [t]ver 22,32
14:22 [u]Lev 5:7

b *3* Traditionally *leprosy*; the Hebrew word was used for various diseases affecting the skin—not necessarily leprosy; also elsewhere in this chapter. c *10* That is, probably about 6 quarts (about 6.5 liters) d *10* That is, probably about 2/3 pint (about 0.3 liter); also in verses 12, 15, 21 and 24 e *21* That is, probably about 2 quarts (about 2 liters)

23 "On the eighth day he must bring them for his cleansing to the priest at the entrance to the Tent of Meeting, before the LORD.[a] 24 The priest is to take the lamb for the guilt offering,[b] together with the log of oil,[c] and wave them before the LORD as a wave offering.[d] 25 He shall slaughter the lamb for the guilt offering and take some of its blood and put it on the lobe of the right ear of the one to be cleansed, on the thumb of his right hand and on the big toe of his right foot.[e] 26 The priest is to pour some of the oil into the palm of his own left hand,[f] 27 and with his right forefinger sprinkle some of the oil from his palm seven times before the LORD. 28 Some of the oil in his palm he is to put on the same places he put the blood of the guilt offering—on the lobe of the right ear of the one to be cleansed, on the thumb of his right hand and on the big toe of his right foot. 29 The rest of the oil in his palm the priest shall put on the head of the one to be cleansed, to make atonement for him before the LORD.[g] 30 Then he shall sacrifice the doves or the young pigeons, which the person can afford,[h] 31 one[f] as a sin offering and the other as a burnt offering,[i] together with the grain offering. In this way the priest will make atonement before the LORD on behalf of the one to be cleansed.[j]"

32 These are the regulations for anyone who has an infectious skin disease[k] and who cannot afford the regular offerings[l] for his cleansing.

Cleansing from mildew in a house.

33 The LORD said to Moses and Aaron, 34 "When you enter the land of Canaan,[m] which I am giving you as your possession,[n] and I put a spreading mildew in a house in that land, 35 the owner of the house must go and tell the priest, 'I have seen something that looks like mildew in my house.' 36 The priest is to order the house to be emptied before he goes in to examine the mildew, so that nothing in the house will be pronounced unclean. After this the priest is to go in and inspect the house. 37 He is to examine the mildew on the walls, and if it has greenish or reddish[o] depressions that appear to be deeper than the surface of the wall, 38 the priest shall go out the doorway of the house and close it up for seven days.[p] 39 On the seventh day[q] the priest shall return to inspect the house. If the mildew has spread on the walls, 40 he is to order that the contaminated stones be torn out and thrown into an unclean place outside the town.[r] 41 He must have all the inside walls of the house scraped and the material that is scraped off dumped into an unclean place outside the town. 42 Then they are to take other stones to replace these and take new clay and plaster the house.

43 "If the mildew reappears in the house after the stones have been torn out and the house scraped and plastered, 44 the priest is to go and examine it and, if the mildew has spread in the house, it is a destructive mildew; the house is unclean.[s] 45 It must be torn down—its stones, timbers and all the plaster—and taken out of the town to an unclean place.

46 "Anyone who goes into the house while it is closed up will be unclean till evening.[t] 47 Anyone who sleeps or eats in the house must wash his clothes.[u]

48 "But if the priest comes to examine it and the mildew has not spread after the house has been plastered, he shall pronounce the house clean,[v] because the mildew is gone. 49 To purify the house he is to take two birds and some cedar wood, scarlet yarn and hyssop.[w] 50 He shall kill one of the birds over fresh water in a clay pot.[x] 51 Then he is to take the cedar wood, the hyssop,[y] the scarlet yarn and the live bird, dip them into the blood of the dead bird and the fresh water, and sprinkle the house seven times.[z] 52 He shall purify the house with the bird's blood, the fresh water, the live bird, the cedar wood, the hyssop

14:23 [a] ver 10,11
14:24 [b] Nu 6:14 [c] ver 10 [d] ver 12
14:25 [e] ver 14; Ex 29:20
14:26 [f] ver 15
14:29 [g] ver 18
14:30 [h] Lev 5:7
14:31 [i] ver 22; Lev 5:7; 15:15,30 [j] ver 18,19
14:32 [k] Lev 13:2 [l] ver 21
14:34 [m] Ge 12:5; Ex 6:4; Nu 13:2 [n] Ge 17:8; 48:4; Nu 27:12; 32:22; Dt 3:27; 7:1; 32:49
14:37 [o] Lev 13:19
14:38 [p] Lev 13:4
14:39 [q] Lev 13:5
14:40 [r] ver 45
14:44 [s] Lev 13:51
14:46 [t] Lev 11:24
14:47 [u] Lev 11:25
14:48 [v] Lev 13:6
14:49 [w] ver 4; 1Ki 4:33; ver 4
14:50 [x] ver 5
14:51 [y] ver 6; Ps 51:7 [z] ver 4,7

[f] *31* Septuagint and Syriac; Hebrew *31 such as the person can afford, one*

and the scarlet yarn. 53Then he is to
release the live bird in the open fields[a]
outside the town. In this way he will
make atonement for the house, and it
will be clean.[b]"
54These are the regulations for any
infectious skin disease,[c] for an itch, 55for
mildew[d] in clothing or in a house, 56and
for a swelling, a rash or a bright spot,[e]
57to determine when something is clean
or unclean.
These are the regulations for infectious skin diseases and mildew.[f]

Cleansing of the man's bodily discharges.

15 The LORD said to Moses and
Aaron, 2"Speak to the Israelites
and say to them: 'When any man has a
bodily discharge,[g] the discharge is unclean. 3Whether it continues flowing
from his body or is blocked, it will make
him unclean. This is how his discharge
will bring about uncleanness:
4" 'Any bed the man with a discharge
lies on will be unclean, and anything he
sits on will be unclean. 5Anyone who
touches his bed must wash his clothes[h]
and bathe with water,[i] and he will be
unclean till evening.[j] 6Whoever sits on
anything that the man with a discharge
sat on must wash his clothes and bathe
with water, and he will be unclean till
evening.
7" 'Whoever touches the man[k] who
has a discharge[l] must wash his clothes
and bathe with water, and he will be
unclean till evening.
8" 'If the man with the discharge
spits[m] on someone who is clean, that
person must wash his clothes and bathe
with water, and he will be unclean till
evening.
9" 'Everything the man sits on when
riding will be unclean, 10and whoever
touches any of the things that were
under him will be unclean till evening;
whoever picks up those things[n] must
wash his clothes and bathe with water,
and he will be unclean till evening.
11" 'Anyone the man with a discharge

14:53 [a]ver 7 [b]ver 20
14:54 [c]Lev 13:2,30
14:55 [d]Lev 13:47-52
14:56 [e]Lev 13:2
14:57 [f]Lev 10:10
15:2 [g]ver 16,32; Lev 22:4; Nu 5:2; 2Sa 3:29; Mt 9:20
15:5 [h]Lev 11:25 [i]Lev 14:8 [j]Lev 11:24
15:7 [k]ver 19; Lev 22:5 [l]ver 16; Lev 22:4
15:8 [m]Nu 12:14
15:10 [n]Nu 19:10
15:12 [o]Lev 6:28 [p]Lev 11:32
15:13 [q]Lev 8:33 [r]ver 5
15:14 [s]Lev 14:22
15:15 [t]Lev 5:7 [u]Lev 14:31 [v]Lev 14:18,19
15:16 [w]ver 2; Lev 22:4; Dt 23:10 [x]ver 5; Dt 23:11
15:18 [y]1Sa 21:4
15:19 [z]ver 24; Lev 12:2
15:21 [a]ver 27

touches without rinsing his hands with
water must wash his clothes and bathe
with water, and he will be unclean till
evening.
12" 'A clay pot[o] that the man touches
must be broken, and any wooden article[p] is to be rinsed with water.
13" 'When a man is cleansed from his
discharge, he is to count off seven days[q]
for his ceremonial cleansing; he must
wash his clothes and bathe himself with
fresh water, and he will be clean.[r] 14On
the eighth day he must take two doves
or two young pigeons[s] and come before
the LORD to the entrance to the Tent of
Meeting and give them to the priest.
15The priest is to sacrifice them, the one
for a sin offering[t] and the other for a
burnt offering.[u] In this way he will make
atonement before the LORD for the
man because of his discharge.[v]
16" 'When a man has an emission of
semen,[w] he must bathe his whole body
with water, and he will be unclean till
evening.[x] 17Any clothing or leather that
has semen on it must be washed with
water, and it will be unclean till evening.
18When a man lies with a woman and
there is an emission of semen,[y] both
must bathe with water, and they will be
unclean till evening.

Cleansing of the woman's bodily discharges.

19" 'When a woman has her regular
flow of blood, the impurity of her monthly period[z] will last seven days, and anyone who touches her will be unclean
till evening.
20" 'Anything she lies on during her
period will be unclean, and anything
she sits on will be unclean. 21Whoever
touches her bed must wash his clothes
and bathe with water, and he will be
unclean till evening.[a] 22Whoever touches anything she sits on must wash his
clothes and bathe with water, and he
will be unclean till evening. 23Whether
it is the bed or anything she was sitting
on, when anyone touches it, he will be
unclean till evening.

24"'If a man lies with her and her
monthly flow[a] touches him, he will be
unclean for seven days; any bed he lies
on will be unclean.

25"'When a woman has a discharge of
blood for many days at a time other than
her monthly period[b] or has a discharge
that continues beyond her period, she
will be unclean as long as she has the
discharge, just as in the days of her period. 26Any bed she lies on while her
discharge continues will be unclean, as
is her bed during her monthly period,
and anything she sits on will be unclean,
as during her period. 27Whoever touches them will be unclean; he must wash
his clothes and bathe with water, and he
will be unclean till evening.

28"'When she is cleansed from her
discharge, she must count off seven
days, and after that she will be ceremonially clean. 29On the eighth day she
must take two doves or two young
pigeons[c] and bring them to the priest at
the entrance to the Tent of Meeting.
30The priest is to sacrifice one for a sin
offering and the other for a burnt offering. In this way he will make atonement
for her before the LORD for the uncleanness of her discharge.[d]

31"'You must keep the Israelites separate from things that make them unclean, so they will not die in their
uncleanness for defiling my dwelling
place,[g][e] which is among them.'"

32These are the regulations for a man
with a discharge, for anyone made
unclean by an emission of semen,[f] 33for
a woman in her monthly period, for a
man or a woman with a discharge, and
for a man who lies with a woman who
is ceremonially unclean.[g]

Instructions for entering the Most Holy Place.

16:2-34pp— Lev 23:26-32; Nu 29:7-11

16 The LORD spoke to Moses after
the death of the two sons of
Aaron who died when they approached
the LORD.[h] 2The LORD said to Moses:
"Tell your brother Aaron not to come
whenever he chooses[i] into the Most
Holy Place[j] behind the curtain in front
of the atonement cover on the ark, or
else he will die, because I appear[k] in the
cloud[l] over the atonement cover.

3"This is how Aaron is to enter the
sanctuary area:[m] with a young bull for a
sin offering and a ram for a burnt offering. 4He is to put on the sacred linen
tunic, with linen undergarments next to
his body; he is to tie the linen sash
around him and put on the linen turban.[n] These are sacred garments;[o] so he
must bathe himself with water[p] before
he puts them on. 5From the Israelite
community[q] he is to take two male
goats[r] for a sin offering and a ram for a
burnt offering.

6"Aaron is to offer the bull for his
own sin offering to make atonement for
himself and his household.[s] 7Then he
is to take the two goats and present
them before the LORD at the entrance
to the Tent of Meeting. 8He is to cast
lots for the two goats—one lot for the
LORD and the other for the scapegoat.[h]
9Aaron shall bring the goat whose lot
falls to the LORD and sacrifice it for a sin
offering. 10But the goat chosen by lot as
the scapegoat shall be presented alive
before the LORD to be used for making
atonement[t] by sending it into the desert
as a scapegoat.

11"Aaron shall bring the bull for his
own sin offering to make atonement
for himself and his household,[u] and he
is to slaughter the bull for his own sin
offering. 12He is to take a censer full of
burning coals[v] from the altar before the
LORD and two handfuls of finely ground
fragrant incense[w] and take them behind
the curtain. 13He is to put the incense
on the fire before the LORD, and the
smoke of the incense will conceal the
atonement cover above the Testimony,
so that he will not die.[x] 14He is to take
some of the bull's blood[y] and with his
finger sprinkle it on the front of the

15:24 [a]ver 19; Lev 12:2; 18:19; 20:18; Eze 18:6
15:25 [b]Mt 9:20; Mk 5:25; Lk 8:43
15:29 [c]Lev 14:22
15:30 [d]Lev 5:10; 14:20,31; 18:19; 2Sa 11:4; Mk 5:25; Lk 8:43
15:31 [e]Lev 20:3; Nu 5:3; 19:13,20; 2Sa 15:25; 2Ki 21:7; Ps 33:14; 74:7; 76:2; Eze 5:11; 23:38
15:32 [f]ver 2
15:33 [g]ver 19,24,25
16:1 [h]Lev 10:1
16:2 [i]Ex 30:10; Heb 9:7 [j]Heb 9:25; 10:19 [k]Ex 25:22 [l]Ex 40:34
16:3 [m]Heb 9:24,25
16:4 [n]Ex 28:39 [o]Ex 28:42 [p]ver 24; Heb 10:22
16:5 [q]Lev 4:13-21 [r]2Ch 29:23
16:6 [s]Lev 9:7; Heb 5:3; 7:27; 9:7,12
16:10 [t]Isa 53:4-10; Ro 3:25; 1Jn 2:2
16:11 [u]Heb 7:27; 9:7
16:12 [v]Lev 10:1 [w]Ex 30:34-38
16:13 [x]Ex 28:43; Lev 22:9
16:14 [y]Lev 4:5; Heb 9:7,13,25

g*31* Or *my tabernacle* h*8* That is, the goat of removal; Hebrew *azazel*; also in verses 10 and 26

atonement cover; then he shall sprinkle
some of it with his finger seven times
before the atonement cover.[a]
15"He shall then slaughter the goat for
the sin offering for the people[b] and take
its blood behind the curtain[c] and do
with it as he did with the bull's blood:
He shall sprinkle it on the atonement
cover and in front of it. 16In this way he
will make atonement[d] for the Most Holy
Place because of the uncleanness and
rebellion of the Israelites, whatever
their sins have been. He is to do the
same for the Tent of Meeting, which is
among them in the midst of their
uncleanness. 17No one is to be in the
Tent of Meeting from the time Aaron
goes in to make atonement in the Most
Holy Place until he comes out, having
made atonement for himself, his household and the whole community of Israel.
18"Then he shall come out to the
altar[e] that is before the LORD and make
atonement for it. He shall take some of
the bull's blood and some of the goat's
blood and put it on all the horns of the
altar.[f] 19He shall sprinkle some of the
blood on it with his finger seven times
to cleanse it and to consecrate it from
the uncleanness of the Israelites.[g]

The scapegoat.

20"When Aaron has finished making
atonement for the Most Holy Place, the
Tent of Meeting and the altar, he shall
bring forward the live goat. 21He is to
lay both hands on the head of the live
goat and confess[h] over it all the wickedness and rebellion of the Israelites—all
their sins—and put them on the goat's
head. He shall send the goat away into
the desert in the care of a man appointed
for the task. 22The goat will carry on itself all their sins[i] to a solitary place; and
the man shall release it in the desert.
23"Then Aaron is to go into the Tent
of Meeting and take off the linen garments he put on before he entered the
Most Holy Place, and he is to leave
them there.[j] 24He shall bathe himself
with water in a holy place and put on
his regular garments.[k] Then he shall
come out and sacrifice the burnt offering for himself and the burnt offering
for the people, to make atonement for
himself and for the people. 25He shall
also burn the fat of the sin offering on
the altar.
26"The man who releases the goat as
a scapegoat must wash his clothes[l] and
bathe himself with water; afterward he
may come into the camp. 27The bull and
the goat for the sin offerings, whose
blood was brought into the Most Holy
Place to make atonement, must be tak-
en outside the camp;[m] their hides, flesh
and offal are to be burned up. 28The
man who burns them must wash his
clothes and bathe himself with water;
afterward he may come into the camp.

The Day of Atonement.

29"This is to be a lasting ordinance for
you: On the tenth day of the seventh
month you must deny yourselves[i][n] and
not do any work—whether native-born
or an alien living among you— 30because
on this day atonement will be made for
you, to cleanse you. Then, before the
LORD, you will be clean from all your
sins.[o] 31It is a sabbath of rest, and you
must deny yourselves;[p] it is a lasting
ordinance. 32The priest who is anointed
and ordained to succeed his father as
high priest is to make atonement. He is
to put on the sacred linen garments[q]
33and make atonement for the Most
Holy Place, for the Tent of Meeting and
the altar, and for the priests and all the
people of the community.[r]
34"This is to be a lasting ordinance for
you: Atonement is to be made once a
year[s] for all the sins of the Israelites."
And it was done, as the LORD commanded Moses.

Sacrifices are to be made only at the tabernacle.

17 The LORD said to Moses, 2"Speak
to Aaron and his sons and to all
the Israelites and say to them: 'This is

16:14 [a]Lev 4:6
16:15 [b]Heb 9:7,12 [c]Heb 9:3
16:16 [d]Ex 29:36
16:18 [e]Lev 4:7 [f]Lev 4:25
16:19 [g]Eze 43:20
16:21 [h]Lev 5:5
16:22 [i]Isa 53:12
16:23 [j]Eze 42:14; 44:19
16:24 [k]ver 3-5
16:26 [l]Lev 11:25
16:27 [m]Lev 4:12,21; Heb 13:11
16:29 [n]Lev 23:27, 32; Nu 29:7; Isa 58:3
16:30 [o]Jer 33:8; Eph 5:26
16:31 [p]Isa 58:3,5
16:32 [q]ver 4; Nu 20:26,28
16:33 [r]ver 11,16-18
16:34 [s]Heb 9:7,25

[i]29 Or *must fast*; also in verse 31

what the LORD has commanded: 3 Any Israelite who sacrifices an ox,[j] a lamb or a goat in the camp or outside of it 4 instead of bringing it to the entrance to the Tent of Meeting to present it as an offering to the LORD in front of the tabernacle of the LORD[a]—that man shall be considered guilty of bloodshed; he has shed blood and must be cut off from his people.[b] 5 This is so the Israelites will bring to the LORD the sacrifices they are now making in the open fields. They must bring them to the priest, that is, to the LORD, at the entrance to the Tent of Meeting and sacrifice them as fellowship offerings.[k] 6 The priest is to sprinkle the blood against the altar of the LORD[c] at the entrance to the Tent of Meeting and burn the fat as an aroma pleasing to the LORD.[d] 7 They must no longer offer any of their sacrifices to the goat idols[l][e] to whom they prostitute themselves.[f] This is to be a lasting ordinance for them and for the generations to come.'

8 "Say to them: 'Any Israelite or any alien living among them who offers a burnt offering or sacrifice 9 and does not bring it to the entrance to the Tent of Meeting[g] to sacrifice it to the LORD—that man must be cut off from his people.

All eating of blood is forbidden.

10 " 'Any Israelite or any alien living among them who eats any blood—I will set my face against that person who eats blood[h] and will cut him off from his people. 11 For the life of a creature is in the blood,[i] and I have given it to you to make atonement for yourselves on the altar; it is the blood that makes atonement for one's life.[j] 12 Therefore I say to the Israelites, "None of you may eat blood, nor may an alien living among you eat blood."

13 " 'Any Israelite or any alien living among you who hunts any animal or bird that may be eaten must drain out the blood and cover it with earth,[k] 14 because the life of every creature is its blood. That is why I have said to the Israelites, "You must not eat the blood of any creature, because the life of every creature is its blood; anyone who eats it must be cut off."[l]

15 " 'Anyone, whether native-born or alien, who eats anything found dead or torn by wild animals[m] must wash his clothes and bathe with water, and he will be ceremonially unclean till evening; then he will be clean. 16 But if he does not wash his clothes and bathe himself, he will be held responsible.' "

Instructions on sexual morality.

18 The LORD said to Moses, 2 "Speak to the Israelites and say to them: 'I am the LORD your God.[n] 3 You must not do as they do in Egypt, where you used to live, and you must not do as they do in the land of Canaan, where I am bringing you. Do not follow their practices.[o] 4 You must obey my laws and be careful to follow my decrees. I am the LORD your God.[p] 5 Keep my decrees and laws, for the man who obeys them will live by them.[q] I am the LORD.

6 " 'No one is to approach any close relative to have sexual relations. I am the LORD.

7 " 'Do not dishonor your father[r] by having sexual relations with your mother.[s] She is your mother; do not have relations with her.

8 " 'Do not have sexual relations with your father's wife;[t] that would dishonor your father.[u]

9 " 'Do not have sexual relations with your sister,[v] either your father's daughter or your mother's daughter, whether she was born in the same home or elsewhere.

10 " 'Do not have sexual relations with your son's daughter or your daughter's daughter; that would dishonor you.

11 " 'Do not have sexual relations with the daughter of your father's wife, born to your father; she is your sister.

12 " 'Do not have sexual relations with

17:4 [a]Dt 12:5-21 [b]Ge 17:14
17:6 [c]Lev 3:2 [d]Nu 18:17
17:7 [e]Ex 22:20; 2Ch 11:15 [f]Ex 32:8; 34:15; Dt 32:17; 1Co 10:20
17:9 [g]ver 4
17:10 [h]Ge 9:4; Lev 3:17; Dt 12:16,23; 1Sa 14:33
17:11 [i]ver 14; Ge 9:4 [j]Heb 9:22
17:13 [k]Lev 7:26; Dt 12:16
17:14 [l]ver 11; Ge 9:4
17:15 [m]Ex 22:31; Dt 14:21
18:2 [n]Ex 6:7; Lev 11:44; Eze 20:5
18:3 [o]ver 24-30; Ex 23:24; Lev 20:23
18:4 [p]ver 2
18:5 [q]Eze 20:11; Ro 10:5*; Gal 3:12*
18:7 [r]Lev 20:11 [s]Eze 22:10
18:8 [t]1Co 5:1 [u]Lev 20:11
18:9 [v]Lev 20:17

j3 The Hebrew word can include both male and female. k5 Traditionally *peace offerings*
l7 Or *demons*

your father's sister;[a] she is your father's
close relative.
13"'Do not have sexual relations
with your mother's sister, because she
is your mother's close relative.
14"'Do not dishonor your father's
brother by approaching his wife to have
sexual relations; she is your aunt.[b]
15"'Do not have sexual relations with
your daughter-in-law.[c] She is your son's
wife; do not have relations with her.
16"'Do not have sexual relations with
your brother's wife;[d] that would dishon-
or your brother.
17"'Do not have sexual relations with
both a woman and her daughter.[e] Do
not have sexual relations with either
her son's daughter or her daughter's
daughter; they are her close relatives.
That is wickedness.
18"'Do not take your wife's sister as a
rival wife and have sexual relations with
her while your wife is living.
19"'Do not approach a woman to have
sexual relations during the uncleanness
of her monthly period.[f]
20"'Do not have sexual relations with
your neighbor's wife[g] and defile yourself
with her.
21"'Do not give any of your children[h]
to be sacrificed[m] to Molech,[i] for you
must not profane the name of your
God.[j] I am the LORD.
22"'Do not lie with a man as one lies
with a woman;[k] that is detestable.
23"'Do not have sexual relations with
an animal and defile yourself with it. A
woman must not present herself to an
animal to have sexual relations with it;
that is a perversion.[l]
24"'Do not defile yourselves in any of
these ways, because this is how the
nations that I am going to drive out
before you[m] became defiled.[n] 25Even the
land was defiled; so I punished it for its
sin,[o] and the land vomited out its inhabitants.[p] 26But you must keep my decrees
and my laws. The native-born and the
aliens living among you must not do any
of these detestable things, 27for all these
things were done by the people who
lived in the land before you, and the
land became defiled. 28And if you defile
the land, it will vomit you out as it vomited out the nations that were before you.
29"'Everyone who does any of these
detestable things—such persons must
be cut off from their people. 30Keep my
requirements[q] and do not follow any of
the detestable customs that were practiced before you came and do not defile
yourselves with them. I am the LORD
your God.[r]'"

Instructions for holy living.

19 The LORD said to Moses, 2"Speak
to the entire assembly of Israel
and say to them: 'Be holy because I, the
LORD your God, am holy.[s]
3"'Each of you must respect his mother and father,[t] and you must observe my
Sabbaths. I am the LORD your God.[u]
4"'Do not turn to idols or make gods
of cast metal for yourselves.[v] I am the
LORD your God.
5"'When you sacrifice a fellowship
offering[n] to the LORD, sacrifice it in such
a way that it will be accepted on your
behalf. 6It shall be eaten on the day you
sacrifice it or on the next day; anything
left over until the third day must be
burned up. 7If any of it is eaten on the
third day, it is impure and will not be
accepted. 8Whoever eats it will be held
responsible because he has desecrated
what is holy to the LORD; that person
must be cut off from his people.
9"'When you reap the harvest of your
land, do not reap to the very edges of
your field or gather the gleanings of your
harvest.[w] 10Do not go over your vineyard a second time or pick up the grapes
that have fallen. Leave them for the
poor and the alien. I am the LORD your
God.
11"'Do not steal.[x]
"'Do not lie.[y]
"'Do not deceive one another.
12"'Do not swear falsely by my name[z]
and so profane the name of your God. I
am the LORD.

18:12 [a]Lev 20:19
18:14 [b]Lev 20:20
18:15 [c]Lev 20:12
18:16 [d]Lev 20:21
18:17 [e]Lev 20:14
18:19 [f]Lev 15:24; 20:18
18:20 [g]Ex 20:14; Lev 20:10; Mt 5:27,28; 1Co 6:9; Heb 13:4
18:21 [h]Dt 12:31 [i]Lev 20:2-5 [j]Lev 19:12; 21:6; Eze 36:20
18:22 [k]Lev 20:13; Dt 23:18; Ro 1:27
18:23 [l]Ex 22:19; Lev 20:15; Dt 27:21
18:24 [m]ver 3,27,30 [n]Dt 18:12
18:25 [o]Lev 20:23; Dt 9:5; 18:12 [p]ver 28; Lev 20:22
18:30 [q]Dt 11:1 [r]ver 2
19:2 [s]1Pe 1:16*; Lev 11:44
19:3 [t]Ex 20:12 [u]Lev 11:44
19:4 [v]Ex 20:4,23; 34:17; Lev 26:1; Ps 96:5; 115:4-7
19:9 [w]Lev 23:10, 22; Dt 24:19-22
19:11 [x]Ex 20:15 [y]Eph 4:25
19:12 [z]Ex 20:7; Mt 5:33

m *21* Or *to be passed through* ⌊*the fire*⌋
n *5* Traditionally *peace offering*

13“ ‘Do not defraud your neighbor or rob him.[a]

“ ‘Do not hold back the wages of a hired man overnight.[b]

14“ ‘Do not curse the deaf or put a stumbling block in front of the blind,[c] but fear your God. I am the LORD.

15“ ‘Do not pervert justice;[d] do not show partiality[e] to the poor or favoritism to the great, but judge your neighbor fairly.

16“ ‘Do not go about spreading slander[f] among your people.

“ ‘Do not do anything that endangers your neighbor’s life.[g] I am the LORD.

17“ ‘Do not hate your brother in your heart.[h] Rebuke your neighbor frankly[i] so you will not share in his guilt.

18“ ‘Do not seek revenge[j] or bear a grudge[k] against one of your people, but love your neighbor as yourself.[l] I am the LORD.

19“ ‘Keep my decrees.

“ ‘Do not mate different kinds of animals.

“ ‘Do not plant your field with two kinds of seed.[m]

“ ‘Do not wear clothing woven of two kinds of material.[n]

20“ ‘If a man sleeps with a woman who is a slave girl promised to another man but who has not been ransomed or given her freedom, there must be due punishment. Yet they are not to be put to death, because she had not been freed. 21The man, however, must bring a ram to the entrance to the Tent of Meeting for a guilt offering to the LORD.[o] 22With the ram of the guilt offering the priest is to make atonement for him before the LORD for the sin he has committed, and his sin will be forgiven.

23“ ‘When you enter the land and plant any kind of fruit tree, regard its fruit as forbidden.[o] For three years you are to consider it forbidden[o]; it must not be eaten. 24In the fourth year all its fruit will be holy,[p] an offering of praise to the LORD. 25But in the fifth year you may eat its fruit. In this way your harvest will be increased. I am the LORD your God.

26“ ‘Do not eat any meat with the blood still in it.[q]

“ ‘Do not practice divination or sorcery.[r]

27“ ‘Do not cut the hair at the sides of your head or clip off the edges of your beard.[s]

28“ ‘Do not cut your bodies for the dead or put tattoo marks on yourselves. I am the LORD.

29“ ‘Do not degrade your daughter by making her a prostitute,[t] or the land will turn to prostitution and be filled with wickedness.

30“ ‘Observe my Sabbaths and have reverence for my sanctuary. I am the LORD.[u]

31“ ‘Do not turn to mediums or seek out spiritists,[v] for you will be defiled by them. I am the LORD your God.

32“ ‘Rise in the presence of the aged, show respect for the elderly[w] and revere your God. I am the LORD.

33“ ‘When an alien lives with you in your land, do not mistreat him. 34The alien living with you must be treated as one of your native-born.[x] Love him as yourself, for you were aliens in Egypt.[y] I am the LORD your God.

35“ ‘Do not use dishonest standards when measuring length, weight or quantity. 36Use honest scales and honest weights, an honest ephah[p] and an honest hin.[q][z] I am the LORD your God, who brought you out of Egypt.

37“ ‘Keep all my decrees and all my laws and follow them. I am the LORD.’ ”

Punishment awaiting various sins.

20 The LORD said to Moses, 2“Say to the Israelites: ‘Any Israelite or any alien living in Israel who gives[r] any of his children to Molech must be put to death. The people of the community are to stone him. 3I will set my face against that man and I will cut him off from his people; for by giving his children to Molech, he has defiled my sanctuary[a] and profaned my holy name.[b] 4If

19:13 [a]Ex 22:15, 25-27 [b]Dt 24:15; Jas 5:4
19:14 [c]Dt 27:18
19:15 [d]Ex 23:2,6 [e]Dt 1:17
19:16 [f]Ps 15:3; Eze 22:9 [g]Ex 23:7
19:17 [h]1Jn 2:9; 3:15 [i]Mt 18:15; Lk 17:3
19:18 [j]Ro 12:19 [k]Ps 103:9 [l]Mt 5:43*; 19:16*; 22:39*; Mk 12:31*; Lk 10:27*; Jn 13:34; Ro 13:9*; Gal 5:14*; Jas 2:8*
19:19 [m]Dt 22:9 [n]Dt 22:11
19:21 [o]Lev 5:15
19:24 [p]Pr 3:9
19:26 [q]Lev 17:10 [r]Dt 18:10
19:27 [s]Lev 21:5
19:29 [t]Dt 23:18
19:30 [u]Lev 26:2
19:31 [v]Lev 20:6; Isa 8:19
19:32 [w]1Ti 5:1
19:34 [x]Ex 12:48 [y]Dt 10:19
19:36 [z]Dt 25:13-15
20:3 [a]Lev 15:31 [b]Lev 18:21

o23 Hebrew *uncircumcised* p36 An ephah was a dry measure. q36 A hin was a liquid measure.
r2 Or *sacrifices*; also in verses 3 and 4

the people of the community close their eyes when that man gives one of his children to Molech and they fail to put him to death,[a] 5I will set my face against that man and his family and will cut off from their people both him and all who follow him in prostituting themselves to Molech.

6"'I will set my face against the person who turns to mediums and spiritists to prostitute himself by following them, and I will cut him off from his people.[b]

7"'Consecrate yourselves and be holy,[c] because I am the LORD your God. 8Keep my decrees and follow them. I am the LORD, who makes you holy.[s][d]

9"'If anyone curses his father or mother,[e] he must be put to death.[f] He has cursed his father or his mother, and his blood will be on his own head.[g]

10"'If a man commits adultery with another man's wife[h]—with the wife of his neighbor—both the adulterer and the adulteress must be put to death.

11"'If a man sleeps with his father's wife, he has dishonored his father.[i] Both the man and the woman must be put to death; their blood will be on their own heads.

12"'If a man sleeps with his daughter-in-law,[j] both of them must be put to death. What they have done is a perversion; their blood will be on their own heads.

13"'If a man lies with a man as one lies with a woman, both of them have done what is detestable.[k] They must be put to death; their blood will be on their own heads.

14"'If a man marries both a woman and her mother,[l] it is wicked. Both he and they must be burned in the fire, so that no wickedness will be among you.[m]

15"'If a man has sexual relations with an animal,[n] he must be put to death, and you must kill the animal.

16"'If a woman approaches an animal to have sexual relations with it, kill both the woman and the animal. They must be put to death; their blood will be on their own heads.

17"'If a man marries his sister[o], the daughter of either his father or his mother, and they have sexual relations, it is a disgrace. They must be cut off before the eyes of their people. He has dishonored his sister and will be held responsible.

18"'If a man lies with a woman during her monthly period[p] and has sexual relations with her, he has exposed the source of her flow, and she has also uncovered it. Both of them must be cut off from their people.

19"'Do not have sexual relations with the sister of either your mother or your father,[q] for that would dishonor a close relative; both of you would be held responsible.

20"'If a man sleeps with his aunt,[r] he has dishonored his uncle. They will be held responsible; they will die childless.

21"'If a man marries his brother's wife,[s] it is an act of impurity; he has dishonored his brother. They will be childless.

22"'Keep all my decrees and laws and follow them, so that the land[t] where I am bringing you to live may not vomit you out. 23You must not live according to the customs of the nations[u] I am going to drive out before you.[v] Because they did all these things, I abhorred them. 24But I said to you, "You will possess their land; I will give it to you as an inheritance, a land flowing with milk and honey."[w] I am the LORD your God, who has set you apart from the nations.[x]

25"'You must therefore make a distinction between clean and unclean animals and between unclean and clean birds.[y] Do not defile yourselves by any animal or bird or anything that moves along the ground—those which I have set apart as unclean for you. 26You are to be holy to me[t] because I, the LORD, am holy,[z] and I have set you apart from the nations to be my own.

27"'A man or woman who is a medium or spiritist among you must be put

20:4 [a]Dt 17:2-5
20:6 [b]Lev 19:31
20:7 [c]Eph 1:4; 1Pe 1:16*
20:8 [d]Ex 31:13
20:9 [e]Dt 27:16 [f]Ex 21:17; Mt 15:4*; Mk 7:10* [g]ver 11; 2Sa 1:16
20:10 [h]Ex 20:14; Dt 5:18; 22:22
20:11 [i]Lev 18:7; Dt 27:23
20:12 [j]Lev 18:15
20:13 [k]Lev 18:22
20:14 [l]Lev 18:17 [m]Dt 27:23
20:15 [n]Lev 18:23
20:17 [o]Lev 18:9
20:18 [p]Lev 15:24; 18:19
20:19 [q]Lev 18:12-13
20:20 [r]Lev 18:14
20:21 [s]Lev 18:16
20:22 [t]Lev 18:25-28
20:23 [u]Lev 18:3 [v]Lev 18:24, 27,30
20:24 [w]Ex 3:8; 13:5; 33:3 [x]Ex 33:16
20:25 [y]Lev 11:1-47; Dt 14:3-21
20:26 [z]Lev 19:2

s *8* Or *who sanctifies you*; or *who sets you apart as holy* t *26* Or *be my holy ones*

to death.[a] You are to stone them; their
blood will be on their own heads.'"

Instructions concerning priests.

21 The LORD said to Moses, "Speak
to the priests, the sons of Aaron,
and say to them: 'A priest must not
make himself ceremonially unclean for
any of his people who die,[b] 2except for a
close relative, such as his mother or
father, his son or daughter, his brother,
3or an unmarried sister who is dependent on him since she has no husband—
for her he may make himself unclean.
4He must not make himself unclean for
people related to him by marriage,[u] and
so defile himself.
5" 'Priests must not shave their heads
or shave off the edges of their beards[c] or
cut their bodies.[d] 6They must be holy to
their God and must not profane the
name of their God.[e] Because they present the offerings made to the LORD by
fire,[f] the food of their God, they are to
be holy.
7" 'They must not marry women
defiled by prostitution or divorced from
their husbands,[g] because priests are
holy to their God.[h] 8Regard them as
holy,[i] because they offer up the food of
your God. Consider them holy, because
I the LORD am holy—I who make you
holy.[v]
9" 'If a priest's daughter defiles herself
by becoming a prostitute, she disgraces
her father; she must be burned in the
fire.[j]
10" 'The high priest, the one among
his brothers who has had the anointing
oil poured on his head and who has
been ordained to wear the priestly garments,[k] must not let his hair become
unkempt[w] or tear his clothes.[l] 11He must
not enter a place where there is a dead
body.[m] He must not make himself
unclean,[n] even for his father or mother,
12nor leave the sanctuary of his God or
desecrate it, because he has been dedicated by the anointing oil[o] of his God. I
am the LORD.
13" 'The woman he marries must be
a virgin.[p] 14He must not marry a widow,
a divorced woman, or a woman defiled
by prostitution, but only a virgin from
his own people, 15so he will not defile
his offspring among his people. I am the
LORD, who makes him holy.[x]' "
16The LORD said to Moses, 17"Say to
Aaron: 'For the generations to come
none of your descendants who has a
defect may come near to offer the food
of his God.[q] 18No man who has any
defect[r] may come near: no man who is
blind or lame, disfigured or deformed;
19no man with a crippled foot or hand,
20or who is hunchbacked or dwarfed, or
who has any eye defect, or who has festering or running sores or damaged testicles.[s] 21No descendant of Aaron the
priest who has any defect is to come
near to present the offerings made to
the LORD by fire. He has a defect; he
must not come near to offer the food
of his God. 22He may eat the most holy
food of his God,[t] as well as the holy food;
23yet because of his defect, he must not
go near the curtain or approach the
altar, and so desecrate my sanctuary. I
am the LORD, who makes them holy.[y]' "
24So Moses told this to Aaron and his
sons and to all the Israelites.

22 The LORD said to Moses, 2"Tell
Aaron and his sons to treat with
respect the sacred offerings the Israelites consecrate to me, so they will not
profane my holy name. I am the LORD.
3"Say to them: 'For the generations to
come, if any of your descendants is
ceremonially unclean and yet comes
near the sacred offerings that the Israelites consecrate to the LORD, that person must be cut off from my presence.[u]
I am the LORD.
4" 'If a descendant of Aaron has an
infectious skin disease[z] or a bodily discharge,[v] he may not eat the sacred

20:27 [a]Lev 19:31
21:1 [b]Eze 44:25
21:5 [c]Eze 44:20 [d]Lev 19:28; Dt 14:1
21:6 [e]Lev 18:21 [f]Lev 3:11
21:7 [g]ver 13,14 [h]Eze 44:22
21:8 [i]ver 6
21:9 [j]Ge 38:24; Lev 19:29
21:10 [k]Lev 16:32 [l]Lev 10:6
21:11 [m]Nu 19:11, 13,14 [n]Lev 19:28
21:12 [o]Ex 29:6-7; Lev 10:7
21:13 [p]Eze 44:22
21:17 [q]ver 6
21:18 [r]Lev 22:19-25
21:20 [s]Dt 23:1; Isa 56:3
21:22 [t]1Co 9:13
22:3 [u]Lev 7:20,21; Nu 19:13
22:4 [v]Lev 14:1-32; 15:2-15

[u]*4* Or *unclean as a leader among his people*
[v]*8* Or *who sanctify you*; or *who set you apart as holy*
[w]*10* Or *not uncover his head* [x]*15* Or *who sanctifies him*; or *who sets him apart as holy*
[y]*23* Or *who sanctifies them*; or *who sets them apart as holy* [z]*4* Traditionally *leprosy*; the Hebrew word was used for various diseases affecting the skin—not necessarily leprosy.

offerings until he is cleansed. He will
also be unclean if he touches something
defiled by a corpse[a] or by anyone who
has an emission of semen, 5or if he
touches any crawling thing[b] that makes
him unclean, or any person[c] who makes
him unclean, whatever the uncleanness
may be. 6The one who touches any such
thing will be unclean till evening. He
must not eat any of the sacred offerings
unless he has bathed himself with water.
7When the sun goes down, he will be
clean, and after that he may eat the
sacred offerings, for they are his food.[d]
8He must not eat anything found dead[e]
or torn by wild animals,[f] and so become
unclean[g] through it. I am the LORD.

9"'The priests are to keep my requirements so that they do not become guilty
and die[h] for treating them with contempt. I am the LORD, who makes them
holy.[a]

10"'No one outside a priest's family
may eat the sacred offering, nor may the
guest of a priest or his hired worker eat
it. 11But if a priest buys a slave with
money, or if a slave is born in his household, that slave may eat his food.[i] 12If a
priest's daughter marries anyone other
than a priest, she may not eat any of the
sacred contributions. 13But if a priest's
daughter becomes a widow or is divorced, yet has no children, and she
returns to live in her father's house as in
her youth, she may eat of her father's
food. No unauthorized person, however,
may eat any of it.

14"'If anyone eats a sacred offering by
mistake, he must make restitution to
the priest for the offering and add a fifth
of the value[j] to it. 15The priests must
not desecrate the sacred offerings the
Israelites present to the LORD[k] 16by
allowing them to eat the sacred offerings
and so bring upon them guilt requiring
payment.[l] I am the LORD, who makes
them holy.'"

Only sacrifices of animals without defect are acceptable.

17The LORD said to Moses, 18"Speak to
Aaron and his sons and to all the Israelites and say to them: 'If any of you—
either an Israelite or an alien living in
Israel—presents a gift[m] for a burnt offering to the LORD, either to fulfill a vow or
as a freewill offering, 19you must present a male without defect[n] from the
cattle, sheep or goats in order that it
may be accepted on your behalf. 20Do
not bring anything with a defect,[o]
because it will not be accepted on your
behalf. 21When anyone brings from the
herd or flock a fellowship offering[b][p] to
the LORD to fulfill a special vow or as a
freewill offering, it must be without
defect or blemish to be acceptable. 22Do
not offer to the LORD the blind, the
injured or the maimed, or anything with
warts or festering or running sores. Do
not place any of these on the altar as
an offering made to the LORD by fire.
23You may, however, present as a freewill offering an ox[c] or a sheep that is
deformed or stunted, but it will not be
accepted in fulfillment of a vow. 24You
must not offer to the LORD an animal
whose testicles are bruised, crushed,
torn or cut.[q] You must not do this in
your own land, 25and you must not
accept such animals from the hand of a
foreigner and offer them as the food of
your God.[r] They will not be accepted on
your behalf, because they are deformed
and have defects.'"

26The LORD said to Moses, 27"When a
calf, a lamb or a goat is born, it is to
remain with its mother for seven days.[s]
From the eighth day on, it will be
acceptable as an offering made to the
LORD by fire. 28Do not slaughter a cow
or a sheep and its young on the same
day.[t]

29"When you sacrifice a thank offering[u] to the LORD, sacrifice it in such a
way that it will be accepted on your
behalf. 30It must be eaten that same day;
leave none of it till morning.[v] I am the
LORD.

22:4 [a]Lev 11:24-28, 39
22:5 [b]Lev 11:24-28, 43 [c]Lev 15:7
22:7 [d]Nu 18:11
22:8 [e]Lev 11:39 [f]Ex 22:31; Lev 17:15 [g]Lev 11:40
22:9 [h]ver 16; Ex 28:43
22:11 [i]Ge 17:13; Ex 12:44
22:14 [j]Lev 5:15
22:15 [k]Nu 18:32
22:16 [l]ver 9
22:18 [m]Lev 1:2
22:19 [n]Lev 1:3
22:20 [o]Dt 15:21; 17:1; Mal 1:8,14; Heb 9:14; 1Pe 1:19
22:21 [p]Lev 3:6; Nu 15:3,8
22:24 [q]Lev 21:20
22:25 [r]Lev 21:6
22:27 [s]Ex 22:30
22:28 [t]Dt 22:6,7
22:29 [u]Lev 7:12; Ps 107:22
22:30 [v]Lev 7:15

a*9* Or *who sanctifies them*; or *who sets them apart as holy*; also in verse 16 b*21* Traditionally *peace offering* c*23* The Hebrew word can include both male and female.

31“Keep[a] my commands and follow
them. I am the LORD. 32Do not profane
my holy name.[b] I must be acknowledged
as holy by the Israelites.[c] I am the LORD,
who makes[d] you holy[e] 33and who
brought you out of Egypt to be your
God.[d] I am the LORD.”

23 The LORD said to Moses, 2“Speak
to the Israelites and say to
them: ‘These are my appointed feasts,[e]
the appointed feasts of the LORD, which
you are to proclaim as sacred assemblies.[f]

The Sabbath.

3“ ‘There are six days when you may
work,[g] but the seventh day is a Sabbath
of rest,[h] a day of sacred assembly. You
are not to do any work; wherever you
live, it is a Sabbath to the LORD.

The Passover and the Feast of Unleavened Bread.

23:4-8pp— Ex 12:14-20; Nu 28:16-25; Dt 16:1-8

4“ ‘These are the LORD’s appointed
feasts, the sacred assemblies you are to
proclaim at their appointed times: 5The
LORD’s Passover begins at twilight on
the fourteenth day of the first month.[i]
6On the fifteenth day of that month the
LORD’s Feast of Unleavened Bread
begins; for seven days you must eat
bread made without yeast. 7On the first
day hold a sacred assembly[j] and do no
regular work. 8For seven days present
an offering made to the LORD by fire.
And on the seventh day hold a sacred
assembly and do no regular work.’ ”

Feast of Firstfruits.

9The LORD said to Moses, 10“Speak to
the Israelites and say to them: ‘When
you enter the land I am going to give
you and you reap its harvest, bring to
the priest a sheaf[k] of the first grain you
harvest. 11He is to wave the sheaf before
the LORD[l] so it will be accepted on your
behalf; the priest is to wave it on the
day after the Sabbath. 12On the day you
wave the sheaf, you must sacrifice as a
burnt offering to the LORD a lamb a year
old without defect, 13together with its
grain offering[m] of two-tenths of an
ephah[f] of fine flour mixed with oil—an
offering made to the LORD by fire, a
pleasing aroma—and its drink offering
of a quarter of a hin[g] of wine. 14You
must not eat any bread, or roasted or
new grain, until the very day you bring
this offering to your God.[n] This is to be a
lasting ordinance for the generations to
come,[o] wherever you live.

Feast of Weeks.

23:15-22pp— Nu 28:26-31; Dt 16:9-12

15“ ‘From the day after the Sabbath,
the day you brought the sheaf of the
wave offering, count off seven full weeks.
16Count off fifty days up to the day after
the seventh Sabbath,[p] and then present
an offering of new grain to the LORD.
17From wherever you live, bring two
loaves made of two-tenths of an ephah
of fine flour, baked with yeast, as a wave
offering of firstfruits[q] to the LORD. 18Pre-
sent with this bread seven male lambs,
each a year old and without defect, one
young bull and two rams. They will be
a burnt offering to the LORD, together
with their grain offerings and drink
offerings—an offering made by fire, an
aroma pleasing to the LORD. 19Then
sacrifice one male goat for a sin offering and two lambs, each a year old, for
a fellowship offering.[h] 20The priest is to
wave the two lambs before the LORD as
a wave offering, together with the bread
of the firstfruits. They are a sacred offering to the LORD for the priest. 21On that
same day you are to proclaim a sacred
assembly[r] and do no regular work.[s]
This is to be a lasting ordinance for the
generations to come, wherever you live.
22“ ‘When you reap the harvest[t] of
your land, do not reap to the very edges
of your field or gather the gleanings of

22:31 [a]Dt 4:2,40; Ps 105:45
22:32 [b]Lev 18:21 [c]Lev 10:3
22:33 [d]Lev 11:45
23:2 [e]ver 4,37,44; Nu 29:39 [f]ver 21,27
23:3 [g]Ex 20:9 [h]Ex 20:10; 31:13-17; Lev 19:3; Dt 5:13; Heb 4:9,10
23:5 [i]Ex 12:18-19; Nu 28:16-17; Dt 16:1-8
23:7 [j]ver 3,8
23:10 [k]Ex 23:16,19; 34:26
23:11 [l]Ex 29:24
23:13 [m]Lev 2:14-16; 6:20
23:14 [n]Ex 34:26 [o]Nu 15:21
23:16 [p]Nu 28:26; Ac 2:1
23:17 [q]Ex 34:22; Lev 2:12
23:21 [r]ver 2 [s]ver 3
23:22 [t]Lev 19:9

d *32* Or *made* e *32* Or *who sanctifies you*; or *who sets you apart as holy* f *13* That is, probably about 4 quarts (about 4.5 liters); also in verse 17
g *13* That is, probably about 1 quart (about 1 liter)
h *19* Traditionally *peace offering*

your harvest.[a] Leave them for the poor
and the alien. I am the LORD your God.'"

Feast of Trumpets.

23:23-25pp— Nu 29:1-6

23The LORD said to Moses, **24**"Say to
the Israelites: 'On the first day of the
seventh month you are to have a day of
rest, a sacred assembly commemorated
with trumpet blasts.[b] **25**Do no regular
work,[c] but present an offering made to
the LORD by fire.'"

Day of Atonement.

23:26-32pp— Lev 16:2-34; Nu 29:7-11

26The LORD said to Moses, **27**"The
tenth day of this seventh month[d] is the
Day of Atonement.[e] Hold a sacred
assembly[f] and deny yourselves,[i] and
present an offering made to the LORD by
fire. **28**Do no work on that day, because
it is the Day of Atonement, when atonement is made for you before the LORD
your God. **29**Anyone who does not deny
himself on that day must be cut off from
his people.[g] **30**I will destroy from among
his people[h] anyone who does any work
on that day. **31**You shall do no work at
all. This is to be a lasting ordinance for
the generations to come, wherever you
live. **32**It is a sabbath of rest for you, and
you must deny yourselves. From the
evening of the ninth day of the month
until the following evening you are to
observe your sabbath."

Feast of Tabernacles.

23:33-43pp— Nu 29:12-39; Dt 16:13-17

33The LORD said to Moses, **34**"Say to
the Israelites: 'On the fifteenth day of
the seventh month the LORD's Feast of
Tabernacles[i] begins, and it lasts for
seven days. **35**The first day is a sacred
assembly; do no regular work. **36**For sev-
en days present offerings made to the
LORD by fire, and on the eighth day hold
a sacred assembly[j] and present an offering made to the LORD by fire. It is the
closing assembly; do no regular work.
37("'These are the LORD's appointed
feasts, which you are to proclaim as
sacred assemblies for bringing offerings
made to the LORD by fire—the burnt
offerings and grain offerings, sacrifices
and drink offerings[k] required for each
day. **38**These offerings are in addition to
those for the LORD's Sabbaths[l] and[j] in
addition to your gifts and whatever you
have vowed and all the freewill offerings
you give to the LORD.)
39"'So beginning with the fifteenth
day of the seventh month, after you
have gathered the crops of the land, celebrate the festival to the LORD for seven
days;[m] the first day is a day of rest, and
the eighth day also is a day of rest. **40**On
the first day you are to take choice fruit
from the trees, and palm fronds, leafy
branches and poplars,[n] and rejoice
before the LORD your God for seven
days. **41**Celebrate this as a festival to the
LORD for seven days each year. This is
to be a lasting ordinance for the generations to come; celebrate it in the seventh month. **42**Live in booths[o] for seven
days: All native-born Israelites are to live
in booths **43**so your descendants will
know[p] that I had the Israelites live in
booths when I brought them out of
Egypt. I am the LORD your God.'"
44So Moses announced to the Israelites the appointed feasts of the LORD.

Oil and bread are set before the LORD.

24:1-3pp— Ex 27:20-21

24 The LORD said to Moses, **2**"Command the Israelites to bring you
clear oil of pressed olives for the light so
that the lamps may be kept burning continually. **3**Outside the curtain of the Testimony in the Tent of Meeting, Aaron is
to tend the lamps before the LORD from
evening till morning, continually. This
is to be a lasting ordinance for the generations to come. **4**The lamps on the
pure gold lampstand[q] before the LORD
must be tended continually.

23:22 [a]Lev 19:10; Dt 24:19-21; Ru 2:15
23:24 [b]Lev 25:9; Nu 10:9,10; 29:1
23:25 [c]ver 21
23:27 [d]Lev 16:29 [e]Ex 30:10 [f]Nu 29:7
23:29 [g]Ge 17:14; Nu 5:2
23:30 [h]Lev 20:3
23:34 [i]Ex 23:16; Dt 16:13; Ezr 3:4; Ne 8:14; Zec 14:16; Jn 7:2
23:36 [j]2Ch 7:9; Ne 8:18; Jn 7:37
23:37 [k]ver 2,4
23:38 [l]Eze 45:17
23:39 [m]Ex 23:16; Dt 16:13
23:40 [n]Ne 8:14-17
23:42 [o]Ne 8:14-16
23:43 [p]Dt 31:13; Ps 78:5
24:4 [q]Ex 25:31; 31:8

[i]*27* Or *and fast*; also in verses 29 and 32
[j]*38* Or *These feasts are in addition to the LORD's Sabbaths, and these offerings are*

5"Take fine flour and bake twelve
loaves of bread,[a] using two-tenths of an
ephah[k] for each loaf. 6Set them in two
rows, six in each row, on the table of
pure gold[b] before the LORD. 7Along each
row put some pure incense as a memorial portion[c] to represent the bread and
to be an offering made to the LORD by
fire. 8This bread is to be set out before
the LORD regularly,[d] Sabbath after Sabbath,[e] on behalf of the Israelites, as a
lasting covenant. 9It belongs to Aaron
and his sons,[f] who are to eat it in a holy
place, because it is a most holy part of
their regular share of the offerings made
to the LORD by fire."

Shelomith's son is stoned.

10Now the son of an Israelite mother
and an Egyptian father went out among
the Israelites, and a fight broke out in
the camp between him and an Israelite.
11The son of the Israelite woman blasphemed the Name[g] with a curse; so
they brought him to Moses. (His mother's name was Shelomith, the daughter
of Dibri the Danite.) 12They put him in
custody until the will of the LORD should
be made clear to them.[h]
13Then the LORD said to Moses:
14"Take the blasphemer outside the
camp. All those who heard him are to
lay their hands on his head, and the
entire assembly is to stone him.[i] 15Say to
the Israelites: 'If anyone curses his God,[j]
he will be held responsible; 16anyone
who blasphemes the name of the LORD
must be put to death.[k] The entire assembly must stone him. Whether an alien
or native-born, when he blasphemes the
Name, he must be put to death.
17" 'If anyone takes the life of a
human being, he must be put to death.[l]
18Anyone who takes the life of someone's animal must make restitution[m]—
life for life. 19If anyone injures his neighbor, whatever he has done must be
done to him: 20fracture for fracture, eye
for eye, tooth for tooth.[n] As he has
injured the other, so he is to be injured.
21Whoever kills an animal must make
restitution, but whoever kills a man
must be put to death.[o] 22You are to have
the same law for the alien[p] and the
native-born.[q] I am the LORD your God.' "
23Then Moses spoke to the Israelites,
and they took the blasphemer outside
the camp and stoned him. The Israelites
did as the LORD commanded Moses.

The sabbath year.

25 The LORD said to Moses on
Mount Sinai, 2"Speak to the
Israelites and say to them: 'When you
enter the land I am going to give you,
the land itself must observe a sabbath to
the LORD. 3For six years sow your fields,
and for six years prune your vineyards
and gather their crops.[r] 4But in the seventh year the land is to have a sabbath
of rest, a sabbath to the LORD. Do not
sow your fields or prune your vineyards.
5Do not reap what grows of itself or harvest the grapes of your untended vines.
The land is to have a year of rest.
6Whatever the land yields during the
sabbath year[s] will be food for you—for
yourself, your manservant and maidservant, and the hired worker and temporary resident who live among you, 7as
well as for your livestock and the wild
animals in your land. Whatever the land
produces may be eaten.

The Year of Jubilee.

25:8-38Ref— Dt 15:1-11
25:39-55Ref— Ex 21:2-11; Dt 15:12-18

8" 'Count off seven sabbaths of
years—seven times seven years—so
that the seven sabbaths of years amount
to a period of forty-nine years. 9Then
have the trumpet[t] sounded everywhere
on the tenth day of the seventh month;
on the Day of Atonement sound the
trumpet throughout your land. 10Con-
secrate the fiftieth year and proclaim liberty[u] throughout the land to all its
inhabitants. It shall be a jubilee[v] for you;
each one of you is to return to his family
property and each to his own clan.

24:5 [a]Ex 25:30
24:6 [b]Ex 25:23-30; 1Ki 7:48
24:7 [c]Lev 2:2
24:8 [d]Nu 4:7; 1Ch 9:32; 2Ch 2:4 [e]Mt 12:5
24:9 [f]Lev 8:31; Mt 12:4; Mk 2:26; Lk 6:4
24:11 [g]Ex 3:15
24:12 [h]Ex 18:16; Nu 15:34
24:14 [i]Lev 20:27; Dt 13:9; 17:5,7; 21:21
24:15 [j]Ex 22:28
24:16 [k]1Ki 21:10, 13; Mt 26:66
24:17 [l]Ge 9:6; Ex 21:12; Nu 35:30-31; Dt 27:24
24:18 [m]ver 21
24:20 [n]Ex 21:24; Mt 5:38*
24:21 [o]ver 17
24:22 [p]Ex 12:49 [q]Nu 9:14; 15:16
25:3 [r]Ex 23:10
25:6 [s]ver 20
25:9 [t]Lev 23:24
25:10 [u]Isa 61:1; Jer 34:8,15, 17; Lk 4:19 [v]Nu 36:4

[k]5 That is, probably about 4 quarts (about 4.5 liters)

11 The fiftieth year shall be a jubilee for you; do not sow and do not reap what grows of itself or harvest the untended vines. 12 For it is a jubilee and is to be holy for you; eat only what is taken directly from the fields.

13 " 'In this Year of Jubilee[a] everyone is to return to his own property.

14 " 'If you sell land to one of your countrymen or buy any from him, do not take advantage of each other.[b] 15 You are to buy from your countryman on the basis of the number of years[c] since the Jubilee. And he is to sell to you on the basis of the number of years left for harvesting crops. 16 When the years are many, you are to increase the price, and when the years are few, you are to decrease the price,[d] because what he is really selling you is the number of crops. 17 Do not take advantage of each other,[e] but fear your God.[f] I am the LORD your God.[g]

18 " 'Follow my decrees and be careful to obey my laws, and you will live safely in the land.[h] 19 Then the land will yield its fruit,[i] and you will eat your fill and live there in safety. 20 You may ask, "What will we eat in the seventh year[j] if we do not plant or harvest our crops?" 21 I will send you such a blessing[k] in the sixth year that the land will yield enough for three years. 22 While you plant during the eighth year, you will eat from the old crop and will continue to eat from it until the harvest of the ninth year comes in.[l]

23 " 'The land must not be sold permanently, because the land is mine[m] and you are but aliens[n] and my tenants. 24 Throughout the country that you hold as a possession, you must provide for the redemption of the land.

25 " 'If one of your countrymen becomes poor and sells some of his property, his nearest relative[o] is to come and redeem[p] what his countryman has sold. 26 If, however, a man has no one to redeem it for him but he himself prospers and acquires sufficient means to redeem it, 27 he is to determine the value for the years since he sold it and refund the balance to the man to whom he sold it; he can then go back to his own property. 28 But if he does not acquire the means to repay him, what he sold will remain in the possession of the buyer until the Year of Jubilee. It will be returned in the Jubilee, and he can then go back to his property.[q]

29 " 'If a man sells a house in a walled city, he retains the right of redemption a full year after its sale. During that time he may redeem it. 30 If it is not redeemed before a full year has passed, the house in the walled city shall belong permanently to the buyer and his descendants. It is not to be returned in the Jubilee. 31 But houses in villages without walls around them are to be considered as open country. They can be redeemed, and they are to be returned in the Jubilee.

32 " 'The Levites always have the right to redeem their houses in the Levitical towns,[r] which they possess. 33 So the property of the Levites is redeemable—that is, a house sold in any town they hold—and is to be returned in the Jubilee, because the houses in the towns of the Levites are their property among the Israelites. 34 But the pastureland belonging to their towns must not be sold; it is their permanent possession.[s]

35 " 'If one of your countrymen becomes poor[t] and is unable to support himself among you, help him[u] as you would an alien or a temporary resident, so he can continue to live among you. 36 Do not take interest[v] of any kind[1] from him, but fear your God, so that your countryman may continue to live among you. 37 You must not lend him money at interest or sell him food at a profit. 38 I am the LORD your God, who brought you out of Egypt to give you the land of Canaan and to be your God.[w]

39 " 'If one of your countrymen becomes poor among you and sells himself to you, do not make him work as a slave.[x] 40 He is to be treated as a hired

25:13 [a] ver 10
25:14 [b] Lev 19:13; 1Sa 12:3,4
25:15 [c] Lev 27:18,23
25:16 [d] ver 27,51,52
25:17 [e] Pr 22:22; Jer 7:5,6; 1Th 4:6 [f] Lev 19:14 [g] Lev 19:32
25:18 [h] Lev 26:4,5; Dt 12:10; Ps 4:8; Jer 23:6
25:19 [i] Lev 26:4
25:20 [j] ver 4
25:21 [k] Dt 28:8,12; Hag 2:19; Mal 3:10
25:22 [l] Lev 26:10
25:23 [m] Ex 19:5 [n] Ge 23:4; 1Ch 29:15; Ps 39:12; Heb 11:13; 1Pe 2:11
25:25 [o] Ru 2:20; Jer 32:7 [p] Lev 27:13, 19,31; Ru 4:4
25:28 [q] ver 10
25:32 [r] Nu 35:1-8; Jos 21:2
25:34 [s] Nu 35:2-5
25:35 [t] Dt 24:14,15 [u] Dt 15:8; Ps 37:21,26; Lk 6:35
25:36 [v] Ex 22:25; Dt 23:19-20
25:38 [w] Ge 17:7; Lev 11:45
25:39 [x] Ex 21:2; Dt 15:12; 1Ki 9:22

[1] 36 Or *take excessive interest*; similarly in verse 37

worker or a temporary resident among
you; he is to work for you until the Year
of Jubilee. 41 Then he and his children
are to be released, and he will go back
to his own clan and to the property[a] of
his forefathers. 42 Because the Israelites
are my servants, whom I brought out of
Egypt, they must not be sold as slaves.
43 Do not rule over them ruthlessly,[b] but
fear your God.
44 " 'Your male and female slaves are to
come from the nations around you; from
them you may buy slaves. 45 You may
also buy some of the temporary residents living among you and members
of their clans born in your country, and
they will become your property. 46 You
can will them to your children as inherited property and can make them slaves
for life, but you must not rule over your
fellow Israelites ruthlessly.
47 " 'If an alien or a temporary resident
among you becomes rich and one of
your countrymen becomes poor and
sells himself to the alien living among
you or to a member of the alien's clan,
48 he retains the right of redemption
after he has sold himself. One of his relatives[c] may redeem him: 49 An uncle or
a cousin or any blood relative in his clan
may redeem him. Or if he prospers,[d] he
may redeem himself. 50 He and his buyer
are to count the time from the year he
sold himself up to the Year of Jubilee.
The price for his release is to be based
on the rate paid to a hired man[e] for
that number of years. 51 If many years
remain, he must pay for his redemption
a larger share of the price paid for him.
52 If only a few years remain until the
Year of Jubilee, he is to compute that
and pay for his redemption accordingly.
53 He is to be treated as a man hired
from year to year; you must see to it
that his owner does not rule over him
ruthlessly.
54 " 'Even if he is not redeemed in any
of these ways, he and his children are to
be released in the Year of Jubilee, 55 for
the Israelites belong to me as servants.
They are my servants, whom I brought
out of Egypt. I am the LORD your God.

Blessings promised to the obedient.

26 " 'Do not make idols[f] or set up
an image or a sacred stone[g] for
yourselves, and do not place a carved
stone[h] in your land to bow down before
it. I am the LORD your God.
2 " 'Observe my Sabbaths and have
reverence for my sanctuary.[i] I am the
LORD.
3 " 'If you follow my decrees and are
careful to obey[j] my commands, 4 I will
send you rain[k] in its season, and the
ground will yield its crops and the trees
of the field their fruit.[l] 5 Your threshing
will continue until grape harvest and the
grape harvest will continue until planting, and you will eat all the food you
want[m] and live in safety in your land.[n]
6 " 'I will grant peace in the land,[o] and
you will lie down[p] and no one will make
you afraid.[q] I will remove savage beasts[r]
from the land, and the sword will not
pass through your country. 7 You will
pursue your enemies, and they will fall
by the sword before you. 8 Five of you
will chase a hundred, and a hundred of
you will chase ten thousand, and your
enemies will fall by the sword before
you.[s]
9 " 'I will look on you with favor and
make you fruitful and increase your
numbers,[t] and I will keep my covenant[u]
with you. 10 You will still be eating last
year's harvest when you will have to
move it out to make room for the new.[v]
11 I will put my dwelling place[m][w] among
you, and I will not abhor you. 12 I will
walk[x] among you and be your God, and
you will be my people.[y] 13 I am the LORD
your God, who brought you out of Egypt
so that you would no longer be slaves to
the Egyptians; I broke the bars of your
yoke[z] and enabled you to walk with
heads held high.

Curses promised to the disobedient.

14 " 'But if you will not listen to me and
carry out all these commands,[a] 15 and if
you reject my decrees and abhor my

25:41 [a]ver 28
25:43 [b]Ex 1:13; Eze 34:4; Col 4:1
25:48 [c]Ne 5:5
25:49 [d]ver 26
25:50 [e]Job 7:1; Isa 16:14; 21:16
26:1 [f]Ex 20:4; Lev 19:4; Dt 5:8 [g]Ex 23:24 [h]Nu 33:52
26:2 [i]Lev 19:30
26:3 [j]Dt 7:12; 11:13,22; 28:1,9
26:4 [k]Dt 11:14 [l]Ps 67:6
26:5 [m]Dt 11:15; Joel 2:19,26; Am 9:13 [n]Lev 25:18
26:6 [o]Ps 29:11; 85:8; 147:14 [p]Ps 4:8 [q]Zep 3:13 [r]ver 22
26:8 [s]Dt 32:30; Jos 23:10
26:9 [t]Ge 17:6; Ne 9:23 [u]Ge 17:7
26:10 [v]Lev 25:22
26:11 [w]Ex 25:8; Ps 76:2; Eze 37:27
26:12 [x]Ge 3:8 [y]2Co 6:16*
26:13 [z]Eze 34:27
26:14 [a]Dt 28:15-68; Mal 2:2

[m]11 Or *my tabernacle*

laws and fail to carry out all my commands and so violate my covenant, **16**then I will do this to you: I will bring upon you sudden terror, wasting diseases and fever[a] that will destroy your sight and drain away your life.[b] You will plant seed in vain, because your enemies will eat it.[c] **17**I will set my face[d] against you so that you will be defeated by your enemies; those who hate you will rule over you,[e] and you will flee even when no one is pursuing you.[f]

18"'If after all this you will not listen to me, I will punish you for your sins seven times over.[g] **19**I will break down your stubborn pride[h] and make the sky above you like iron and the ground beneath you like bronze.[i] **20**Your strength will be spent in vain,[j] because your soil will not yield its crops, nor will the trees of the land yield their fruit.[k]

21"'If you remain hostile toward me and refuse to listen to me, I will multiply your afflictions seven times over,[l] as your sins deserve. **22**I will send wild animals[m] against you, and they will rob you of your children, destroy your cattle and make you so few in number that your roads will be deserted.

23"'If in spite of these things you do not accept my correction[n] but continue to be hostile toward me, **24**I myself will be hostile toward you and will afflict you for your sins seven times over. **25**And I will bring the sword upon you to avenge the breaking of the covenant. When you withdraw into your cities, I will send a plague[o] among you, and you will be given into enemy hands. **26**When I cut off your supply of bread,[p] ten women will be able to bake your bread in one oven, and they will dole out the bread by weight. You will eat, but you will not be satisfied.

27"'If in spite of this you still do not listen to me but continue to be hostile toward me, **28**then in my anger I will be hostile toward you, and I myself will punish you for your sins seven times over. **29**You will eat the flesh of your sons and the flesh of your daughters.[q] **30**I will destroy your high places,[r] cut down your incense altars[s] and pile your dead bodies on the lifeless forms of your idols,[t] and I will abhor you. **31**I will turn your cities into ruins and lay waste your sanctuaries,[u] and I will take no delight in the pleasing aroma of your offerings. **32**I will lay waste the land,[v] so that your enemies who live there will be appalled. **33**I will scatter you among the nations[w] and will draw out my sword and pursue you. Your land will be laid waste, and your cities will lie in ruins. **34**Then the land will enjoy its sabbath years all the time that it lies desolate and you are in the country of your enemies;[x] then the land will rest and enjoy its sabbaths. **35**All the time that it lies desolate, the land will have the rest it did not have during the sabbaths you lived in it.

36"'As for those of you who are left, I will make their hearts so fearful in the lands of their enemies that the sound of a windblown leaf will put them to flight.[y] They will run as though fleeing from the sword, and they will fall, even though no one is pursuing them. **37**They will stumble over one another as though fleeing from the sword, even though no one is pursuing them. So you will not be able to stand before your enemies.[z] **38**You will perish among the nations; the land of your enemies will devour you.[a] **39**Those of you who are left will waste away in the lands of their enemies because of their sins; also because of their fathers' sins they will waste away.[b]

40"'But if they will confess their sins and the sins of their fathers[c]—their treachery against me and their hostility toward me, **41**which made me hostile toward them so that I sent them into the land of their enemies—then when their uncircumcised hearts[d] are humbled and they pay for their sin, **42**I will remember my covenant with Jacob[e] and my covenant with Isaac[f] and my covenant with Abraham, and I will remember the land. **43**For the land will be deserted by them and will enjoy its sabbaths while it lies desolate without them. They will pay for their sins

26:16 [a]Dt 28:22,35 [b]1Sa 2:33 [c]Job 31:8
26:17 [d]Lev 17:10 [e]Ps 106:41 [f]ver 36,37; Dt 28:7,25; Ps 53:5
26:18 [g]ver 21
26:19 [h]Isa 25:11 [i]Dt 28:23
26:20 [j]Ps 127:1; Isa 17:11 [k]Dt 11:17
26:21 [l]ver 18
26:22 [m]Dt 32:24
26:23 [n]Jer 2:30; 5:3
26:25 [o]Nu 14:12; Eze 5:17
26:26 [p]Ps 105:16; Isa 3:1; Mic 6:14
26:29 [q]Dt 28:53
26:30 [r]2Ch 34:3; Eze 6:3 [s]Eze 6:6 [t]Eze 6:13
26:31 [u]Ps 74:3-7
26:32 [v]Jer 9:11
26:33 [w]Dt 4:27; Eze 12:15;20:23; Zec 7:14
26:34 [x]ver 43; 2Ch 36:21
26:36 [y]Eze 21:7
26:37 [z]Jos 7:12
26:38 [a]Dt 4:26
26:39 [b]Eze 4:17
26:40 [c]Jer 3:12-15; Lk 15:18; 1Jn 1:9
26:41 [d]Eze 44:7,9; Ac 7:51
26:42 [e]Ge 22:15-18; 28:15; [f]Ge 26:5

because they rejected my laws and
abhorred my decrees. 44Yet in spite of
this, when they are in the land of their
enemies, I will not reject them or
abhor[a] them so as to destroy them completely,[b] breaking my covenant[c] with
them. I am the LORD their God. 45But for
their sake I will remember[d] the covenant with their ancestors whom I
brought out of Egypt[e] in the sight of the
nations to be their God. I am the LORD.'"
46These are the decrees, the laws and
the regulations that the LORD established
on Mount Sinai between himself and
the Israelites through Moses.[f]

Commandments concerning vows made to God.

27 The LORD said to Moses,
2"Speak to the Israelites and
say to them: 'If anyone makes a special
vow[g] to dedicate persons to the LORD by
giving equivalent values, 3set the value
of a male between the ages of twenty
and sixty at fifty shekels[n] of silver,
according to the sanctuary shekel[o];[h] 4and
if it is a female, set her value at thirty
shekels.[p] 5If it is a person between the
ages of five and twenty, set the value of
a male at twenty shekels[q] and of a
female at ten shekels.[r] 6If it is a person
between one month and five years, set
the value of a male at five shekels[s][i] of
silver and that of a female at three
shekels[t] of silver. 7If it is a person sixty
years old or more, set the value of a
male at fifteen shekels[u] and of a female
at ten shekels. 8If anyone making the
vow is too poor to pay[j] the specified
amount, he is to present the person to
the priest, who will set the value[k] for
him according to what the man making
the vow can afford.
9"'If what he vowed is an animal that
is acceptable as an offering to the LORD,
such an animal given to the LORD
becomes holy. 10He must not exchange
it or substitute a good one for a bad one,
or a bad one for a good one;[l] if he
should substitute one animal for another, both it and the substitute become
holy. 11If what he vowed is a ceremonially unclean animal—one that is not
acceptable as an offering to the LORD—
the animal must be presented to the
priest, 12who will judge its quality as
good or bad. Whatever value the priest
then sets, that is what it will be. 13If the
owner wishes to redeem[m] the animal,
he must add a fifth to its value.
14"'If a man dedicates his house as
something holy to the LORD, the priest
will judge its quality as good or bad.
Whatever value the priest then sets, so
it will remain. 15If the man who dedicates his house redeems it,[n] he must
add a fifth to its value, and the house
will again become his.
16"'If a man dedicates to the LORD
part of his family land, its value is to be
set according to the amount of seed
required for it—fifty shekels of silver to
a homer[v] of barley seed. 17If he dedicates his field during the Year of Jubilee,
the value that has been set remains.
18But if he dedicates his field after the
Jubilee, the priest will determine the
value according to the number of years
that remain[o] until the next Year of Jubilee, and its set value will be reduced.
19If the man who dedicates the field
wishes to redeem it, he must add a fifth
to its value, and the field will again
become his. 20If, however, he does not
redeem the field, or if he has sold it to
someone else, it can never be redeemed.
21When the field is released in the
Jubilee,[p] it will become holy, like a field
devoted to the LORD;[q] it will become the
property of the priests.[w]
22"'If a man dedicates to the LORD a
field he has bought, which is not part of
his family land, 23the priest will determine its value up to the Year of Jubilee,

26:44 [a]Ro 11:2 [b]Dt 4:31; Jer 30:11 [c]Jer 33:26
26:45 [d]Ge 17:7 [e]Ex 6:8; Lev 25:38
26:46 [f]Lev 7:38; 27:34
27:2 [g]Nu 6:2
27:3 [h]Ex 30:13; Nu 3:47; 18:16
27:6 [i]Nu 18:16
27:8 [j]Lev 5:11 [k]ver 12,14
27:10 [l]ver 33
27:13 [m]ver 15,19; Lev 25:25
27:15 [n]ver 13,20
27:18 [o]Lev 25:15
27:21 [p]Lev 25:10 [q]ver 28; Nu 18:14; Eze 44:29

[n]*3* That is, about 1 1/4 pounds (about 0.6 kilogram); also in verse 16 [o]*3* That is, about 2/5 ounce (about 11.5 grams); also in verse 25 [p]*4* That is, about 12 ounces (about 0.3 kilogram) [q]*5* That is, about 8 ounces (about 0.2 kilogram) [r]*5* That is, about 4 ounces (about 110 grams); also in verse 7 [s]*6* That is, about 2 ounces (about 55 grams) [t]*6* That is, about 1 1/4 ounces (about 35 grams) [u]*7* That is, about 6 ounces (about 170 grams) [v]*16* That is, probably about 6 bushels (about 220 liters) [w]*21* Or *priest*

and the man must pay its value on that
day as something holy to the LORD. 24In
the Year of Jubilee the field will revert to
the person from whom he bought it,[a]
the one whose land it was. 25Every value
is to be set according to the sanctuary
shekel,[b] twenty gerahs[c] to the shekel.
26"'No one, however, may dedicate
the firstborn of an animal, since the
firstborn already belongs to the LORD;[d]
whether an ox[x] or a sheep, it is the
LORD's. 27If it is one of the unclean animals,[e] he may buy it back at its set value, adding a fifth of the value to it. If he
does not redeem it, it is to be sold at its
set value.
28"'But nothing that a man owns and
devotes[y][f] to the LORD—whether man or
animal or family land—may be sold or
redeemed; everything so devoted is most
holy to the LORD.
29"'No person devoted to destruction[z]
may be ransomed; he must be put to
death.

27:24 [a]Lev 25:28
27:25 [b]Ex 30:13; Nu 18:16 [c]Nu 3:47; Eze 45:12
27:26 [d]Ex 13:2,12
27:27 [e]ver 11
27:28 [f]Nu 18:14; Jos 6:17-19
27:30 [g]Ge 28:22; 2Ch 31:6; Mal 3:8
27:32 [h]Jer 33:13; Eze 20:37
27:33 [i]ver 10
27:34 [j]Lev 26:46; Dt 4:5

30"'A tithe[g] of everything from the
land, whether grain from the soil or fruit
from the trees, belongs to the LORD; it
is holy to the LORD. 31If a man redeems
any of his tithe, he must add a fifth of
the value to it. 32The entire tithe of the
herd and flock—every tenth animal that
passes under the shepherd's rod[h]—will
be holy to the LORD. 33He must not pick
out the good from the bad or make any
substitution.[i] If he does make a substitution, both the animal and its substitute
become holy and cannot be redeemed.'"

34These are the commands the LORD
gave Moses on Mount Sinai for the
Israelites.[j]

[x]*26* The Hebrew word can include both male and female. [y]*28* The Hebrew term refers to the irrevocable giving over of things or persons to the LORD. [z]*29* The Hebrew term refers to the irrevocable giving over of things or persons to the LORD, often by totally destroying them.

NUMBERS

Author: Moses.

Date Written: Between 1450 and 1400B.C.

Time Span: About 39 years (the period of Israel's history from the second year after the exodus to just prior to the conquest of Canaan).

Title: The book of Numbers gets its name from the 2 censuses (numberings) of Israel.

Background: The fourth book of the Pentateuch, Numbers, is a continuation of the story in the book of Leviticus. Approximately one month elapses from the time the tabernacle is constructed at the end of Exodus to the time of the census at the beginning of Numbers. During that month the instructions in the book of Leviticus are given.

Where Written: Mount Sinai and the desert, as Moses leads the people to the promised land.

To Whom: To the Israelites.

Content: Numbers is the story of nearly 40 years of wilderness wandering by the Israelites between the times of 2 separate censuses of the people. The first census is of the old generation, the generation that came up out of Egypt. It takes place at Mount Sinai in the second year of the exodus. The second census is of the new generation. It takes place on the plains of Moab, opposite Jericho, 38 years later just prior to the nation's entering of Canaan. Even though the old generation (with the exception of Joshua and Caleb) is not allowed to enter the promised land, God still provides for and sustains the people through these wanderings.

Key Words: "Wanderings"; "Census." The emphasis of Numbers is on the "wanderings" of the Israelites in the desert during the time between the "census" taken of the old generation of Israelites and later the "census" of the new generation.

Themes: • Our discipline from God is sometimes stern, but he ultimately rewards those who are obedient to his Word. • Believers will never have to live in the desert...but may have to walk through it. • Just as God's punishment of disobedience is sure...so is God's pardon and restoration for repentance. • We can progress as children of God only as we allow him to nurture our growth. • Murmuring and complaining are offensive to the God we serve (chapter 11).

Outline:
1. The first census of the Israelites is taken. 1:1-4:49
2. The old generation prepares to inherit the promised land. 5:1-10:10
3. The old generation fails to inherit the promised land. 10:11-21:35
4. Israel encounters the Moabites and Balaam. 22:1-25:18
5. The second census of the Israelites is taken. 26:1-26:65
6. The new generation prepares to inherit the promised land. 27:1-36:13

NUMBERS

God commands Moses to take a census.

1 The LORD spoke to Moses in the
Tent of Meeting[a] in the Desert of
Sinai[b] on the first day of the second
month[c] of the second year after the Israelites came out of Egypt. He said: 2 “Take
a census[d] of the whole Israelite community by their clans and families, listing
every man by name, one by one. 3 You
and Aaron are to number by their divisions all the men in Israel twenty years
old or more[e] who are able to serve in the
army. 4 One man from each tribe, each
the head of his family,[f] is to help you.[g]
5 These are the names of the men who
are to assist you:

from Reuben,[h] Elizur son of Shedeur;
6 from Simeon, Shelumiel son of Zurishaddai;
7 from Judah,[i] Nahshon son of Amminadab;[j]
8 from Issachar,[k] Nethanel son of Zuar;
9 from Zebulun,[l] Eliab son of Helon;
10 from the sons of Joseph:
from Ephraim,[m] Elishama son of Ammihud;
from Manasseh, Gamaliel son of Pedahzur;
11 from Benjamin, Abidan son of Gideoni;
12 from Dan,[n] Ahiezer son of Ammishaddai;
13 from Asher,[o] Pagiel son of Ocran;
14 from Gad, Eliasaph son of Deuel;[p]
15 from Naphtali,[q] Ahira son of Enan.”

16 These were the men appointed from
the community, the leaders[r] of their ancestral tribes. They were the heads of
the clans of Israel.[s]

17 Moses and Aaron took these men
whose names had been given, 18 and
they called the whole community together on the first day of the second month.[t]
The people indicated their ancestry[u] by
their clans and families, and the men
twenty years old or more were listed by
name, one by one, 19 as the LORD commanded Moses. And so he counted
them in the Desert of Sinai:

20 From the descendants of Reuben[v] the firstborn son of Israel:
All the men twenty years old or more who were able to serve in the army were listed by name, one by one, according to the records of their clans and families.
21 The number from the tribe of Reuben was 46,500.

22 From the descendants of Simeon:[w]
All the men twenty years old or more who were able to serve in the army were counted and listed by name, one by one, according to the records of their clans
and families. 23 The number from
the tribe of Simeon was 59,300.

24 From the descendants of Gad:[x]
All the men twenty years old or more who were able to serve in the army were listed by name, according to the records of their
clans and families. 25 The number
from the tribe of Gad was 45,650.

26 From the descendants of Judah:[y]
All the men twenty years old or more who were able to serve in the army were listed by name, according to the records of their
clans and families. 27 The number
from the tribe of Judah was 74,600.

28 From the descendants of Issachar:[z]
All the men twenty years old or more who were able to serve in the army were listed by name, according to the records of their
clans and families. 29 The num-
ber from the tribe of Issachar was 54,400.

30 From the descendants of Zebulun:[a]
All the men twenty years old or more who were able to serve in

1:1 [a]Ex 40:2 [b]Ex 19:1 [c]Ex 40:17
1:2 [d]Ex 30:11-16; Nu 26:2
1:3 [e]Ex 30:14
1:4 [f]ver 16 [g]Ex 18:21; Dt 1:15
1:5 [h]Ge 29:32; Dt 33:6; Rev 7:5
1:7 [i]Ge 29:35; Ps 78:68 [j]Ru 4:20; 1Ch 2:10; Lk 3:32
1:8 [k]Ge 30:18
1:9 [l]ver 30
1:10 [m]ver 32
1:12 [n]ver 38
1:13 [o]ver 40
1:14 [p]Nu 2:14
1:15 [q]ver 42
1:16 [r]Ex 18:25 [s]ver 4; Ex 18:21; Nu 7:2
1:18 [t]ver 1 [u]Ezr 2:59; Heb 7:3
1:20 [v]Nu 26:5-11; Rev 7:5
1:22 [w]Nu 26:12-14; Rev 7:7
1:24 [x]Ge 30:11; Nu 26:15-18; Rev 7:5
1:26 [y]Ge 29:35; Nu 26:19-22; Mt 1:2; Rev 7:5
1:28 [z]Nu 26:23-25; Rev 7:7
1:30 [a]Nu 26:26-27; Rev 7:8

KEY PLACES IN NUMBERS

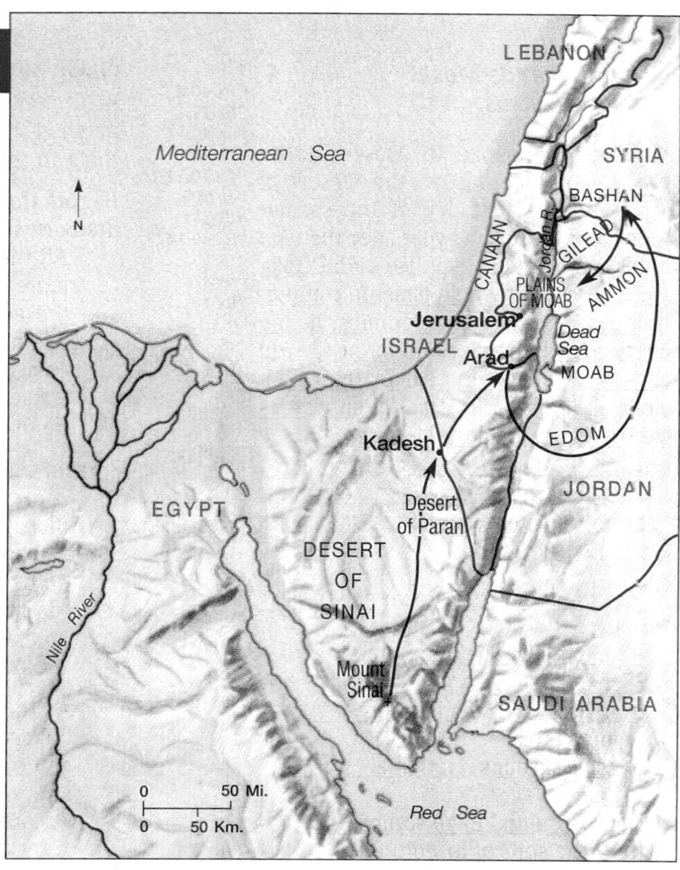

Mount Sinai Numbers begins at Mount Sinai in the Desert of Sinai with Moses taking a census of the men eligible for battle. As the battle preparations began, the people also prepared for the spiritual warfare they would face. The promised land was full of wicked people who would try to entice the Israelites to sin. God, therefore, taught Moses and the Israelites how to live rightly (1:1–12:15).

Desert of Paran After a full year at Mount Sinai, the Israelites broke camp and began their march toward the promised land by moving into the Desert of Paran. From there, one leader from each tribe was sent to spy out the new land. After 40 days they returned, and all but Joshua and Caleb were too afraid to enter. Because of their lack of faith, the Israelites were made to wander in the desert for 40 years (12:16–19:22).

Kadesh With the years of wandering nearing an end, the Israelites set their sights once again on the promised land. Kadesh was the oasis where they spent most of their desert years. Miriam died here. And it was here that Moses angrily struck the rock, which kept him from entering the promised land (20).

Arad When the king there heard that Israel was on the move, he attacked, but he was soundly defeated. Moses then led the people southward and eastward around the Dead Sea (21:1-3).

Edom The Israelites wanted to travel through Edom, but the king of Edom refused them passage (20:14-22). So they traveled around Edom and became very discouraged. The people complained, and God sent venomous snakes to punish them. Only by looking at a bronze snake on a pole could those bitten be healed (21:4-9).

Ammon Next, King Sihon of the Amorites refused Israel passage. When he attacked, Israel defeated his army and conquered the territory as far as the border of Ammon (21:21-32).

Bashan Moses sent spies to Bashan. King Og attacked, but he was also defeated (21:33-35).

Plains of Moab The people camped on the plains of Moab, east of the Jordan River across from Jericho. They were on the verge of entering the promised land (22:1).

Moab King Balak of Moab, terrified of the Israelites, called upon Balaam, a famous sorcerer, to curse Israel from the mountains above where the Israelites camped. But the Lord caused Balaam to bless them instead (22:2–24:25).

Gilead The tribes of Reuben and Gad decided to settle in the fertile country of Gilead east of the Jordan River because it was a good land for their sheep. But first they promised to help the other tribes conquer the land west of the Jordan River (32).

the army were listed by name,
according to the records of their
clans and families. 31The number
from the tribe of Zebulun was
57,400.

32From the sons of Joseph:
From the descendants of Ephraim:[a]
All the men twenty years old or
more who were able to serve in
the army were listed by name,
according to the records of their
clans and families. 33The number
from the tribe of Ephraim was
40,500.
34From the descendants of Manasseh:[b]
All the men twenty years old or
more who were able to serve in
the army were listed by name,
according to the records of their
clans and families. 35The number
from the tribe of Manasseh was
32,200.

36From the descendants of Benjamin:[c]
All the men twenty years old or
more who were able to serve in
the army were listed by name,
according to the records of their
clans and families. 37The number
from the tribe of Benjamin was
35,400.

38From the descendants of Dan:[d]
All the men twenty years old or
more who were able to serve in
the army were listed by name,
according to the records of their
clans and families. 39The number
from the tribe of Dan was
62,700.

40From the descendants of Asher:[e]
All the men twenty years old or
more who were able to serve in
the army were listed by name,
according to the records of their
clans and families. 41The number
from the tribe of Asher was
41,500.

42From the descendants of Naphtali:[f]
All the men twenty years old or
more who were able to serve in
the army were listed by name,
according to the records of their
clans and families. 43The number
from the tribe of Naphtali was
53,400.

44These were the men counted by
Moses and Aaron[g] and the twelve leaders of Israel, each one representing his
family. 45All the Israelites twenty years
old or more who were able to serve in
Israel's army were counted according
to their families. 46The total number was
603,550.[h]

The Levites are reserved for tabernacle service.

47The families of the tribe of Levi,[i]
however, were not counted[j] along with
the others. 48The LORD had said to Moses: 49"You must not count the tribe of
Levi or include them in the census of
the other Israelites. 50Instead, appoint
the Levites to be in charge of the tabernacle of the Testimony[k]—over all its
furnishings and everything belonging to
it. They are to carry the tabernacle and
all its furnishings; they are to take care
of it and encamp around it. 51Whenever
the tabernacle is to move, the Levites
are to take it down, and whenever the
tabernacle is to be set up, the Levites
shall do it.[l] Anyone else who goes near
it shall be put to death. 52The Israelites
are to set up their tents by divisions,
each man in his own camp under his
own standard.[m] 53The Levites, however,
are to set up their tents around the
tabernacle of the Testimony so that
wrath will not fall[n] on the Israelite community. The Levites are to be responsible for the care of the tabernacle of the
Testimony.[o]"

54The Israelites did all this just as
the LORD commanded Moses.

Arrangement of the tribal camps around the Tent of Meeting.

2 The LORD said to Moses and Aaron:
2"The Israelites are to camp around
the Tent of Meeting some distance

1:32 [a]Nu 26:35-37
1:34 [b]Nu 26:28-34; Rev 7:6
1:36 [c]Nu 26:38-41; 2Ch 17:17; Rev 7:8
1:38 [d]Ge 30:6; Nu 26:42-43
1:40 [e]Nu 26:44-47; Rev 7:6
1:42 [f]Nu 26:48-50; Rev 7:6
1:44 [g]Nu 26:64
1:46 [h]Ex 12:37; 38:26; Nu 2:32; 26:51
1:47 [i]Nu 2:33; 26:57 [j]Nu 4:3,49
1:50 [k]Ex 38:21; Ac 7:44
1:51 [l]Nu 3:38; 4:1-33
1:52 [m]Nu 2:2; Ps 20:5
1:53 [n]Lev 10:6; Nu 16:46; 18:5 [o]Nu 18:2-4

from it, each man under his standard[a] with the banners of his family."

3On the east, toward the sunrise, the divisions of the camp of Judah are to encamp under their standard. The leader of the people of Judah is Nahshon son of Amminadab.[b] 4His division numbers 74,600.

5The tribe of Issachar will camp next to them. The leader of the people of Issachar is Nethanel son of Zuar.[c] 6His division numbers 54,400.

7The tribe of Zebulun will be next. The leader of the people of Zebulun is Eliab son of Helon.[d] 8His division numbers 57,400.

9All the men assigned to the camp of Judah, according to their divisions, number 186,400. They will set out first.[e]

10On the south will be the divisions of the camp of Reuben under their standard. The leader of the people of Reuben is Elizur son of Shedeur.[f] 11His division numbers 46,500.

12The tribe of Simeon will camp next to them. The leader of the people of Simeon is Shelumiel son of Zurishaddai.[g] 13His division numbers 59,300.

14The tribe of Gad will be next. The leader of the people of Gad is Eliasaph son of Deuel.[a][h] 15His division numbers 45,650.

16All the men assigned to the camp of Reuben,[i] according to their divisions, number 151,450. They will set out second.

17Then the Tent of Meeting and the camp of the Levites[j] will set out in the middle of the camps. They will set out in the same order as they encamp, each in his own place under his standard.

18On the west will be the divisions of the camp of Ephraim[k] under their standard. The leader of the people of Ephraim is Elishama son of Ammihud.[l] 19His division numbers 40,500.

20The tribe of Manasseh will be next to them. The leader of the people of Manasseh is Gamaliel son of Pedahzur.[m] 21His division numbers 32,200.

22The tribe of Benjamin will be next. The leader of the people of Benjamin is Abidan son of Gideoni.[n] 23His division numbers 35,400.

24All the men assigned to the camp of Ephraim,[o] according to their divisions, number 108,100. They will set out third.[p]

25On the north will be the divisions of the camp of Dan, under their standard. The leader of the people of Dan is Ahiezer son of Ammishaddai.[q] 26His division numbers 62,700.

27The tribe of Asher will camp next to them. The leader of the people of Asher is Pagiel son of Ocran.[r] 28His division numbers 41,500.

29The tribe of Naphtali will be next. The leader of the people of Naphtali is Ahira son of Enan.[s] 30His division numbers 53,400.

31All the men assigned to the camp of Dan number 157,600. They will set out last,[t] under their standards.

32These are the Israelites, counted according to their families. All those in the camps, by their divisions, number 603,550.[u] 33The Levites, however, were not counted[v] along with the other Israelites, as the LORD commanded Moses.

34So the Israelites did everything the LORD commanded Moses; that is the way they encamped under their standards, and that is the way they set out, each with his clan and family.

2:2 [a]Nu 1:52; Ps 74:4; Isa 31:9
2:3 [b]Nu 10:14; Ru 4:20; 1Ch 2:10
2:5 [c]Nu 1:8
2:7 [d]Nu 1:9
2:9 [e]Nu 10:14
2:10 [f]Nu 1:5
2:12 [g]Nu 1:6
2:14 [h]Nu 1:14
2:16 [i]Nu 10:18
2:17 [j]Nu 1:53; 10:21
2:18 [k]Ge 48:20; Jer 31:18-20 [l]Nu 1:10
2:20 [m]Nu 1:10
2:22 [n]Nu 1:11; Ps 68:27
2:24 [o]Nu 10:22 [p]Ps 80:2
2:25 [q]Nu 1:12
2:27 [r]Nu 1:13
2:29 [s]Nu 1:15
2:31 [t]Nu 10:25
2:32 [u]Ex 38:26; Nu 1:46
2:33 [v]Nu 1:47; 26:57-62

a *14* Many manuscripts of the Masoretic Text, Samaritan Pentateuch and Vulgate (see also Num. 1:14); most manuscripts of the Masoretic Text *Reuel*

Names of Aaron's sons.

3 This is the account of the family of Aaron and Moses[a] at the time the LORD talked with Moses on Mount Sinai.

2 The names of the sons of Aaron were Nadab the firstborn and Abihu, Eleazar and Ithamar.[b] 3 Those were the names of Aaron's sons, the anointed priests,[c] who were ordained to serve as priests. 4 Nadab and Abihu, however, fell dead before the LORD[d] when they made an offering with unauthorized fire before him in the Desert of Sinai.[e] They had no sons; so only Eleazar and Ithamar served as priests during the lifetime of their father Aaron.[f]

5 The LORD said to Moses, 6 "Bring the tribe of Levi[g] and present them to Aaron the priest to assist him.[h] 7 They are to perform duties for him and for the whole community at the Tent of Meeting by doing the work[i] of the tabernacle. 8 They are to take care of all the furnishings of the Tent of Meeting, fulfilling the obligations of the Israelites by doing the work of the tabernacle. 9 Give the Levites to Aaron and his sons;[j] they are the Israelites who are to be given wholly to him.[b] 10 Appoint Aaron and his sons to serve as priests;[k] anyone else who approaches the sanctuary must be put to death."[l]

11 The LORD also said to Moses, 12 "I have taken the Levites[m] from among the Israelites in place of the first male offspring[n] of every Israelite woman. The Levites are mine,[o] 13 for all the firstborn are mine.[p] When I struck down all the firstborn in Egypt, I set apart for myself every firstborn in Israel, whether man or animal. They are to be mine. I am the LORD."

Moses' counting of the Levites.

14 The LORD said to Moses in the Desert of Sinai, 15 "Count[q] the Levites by their families and clans. Count every male a month old or more."[r] 16 So Moses counted them, as he was commanded by the word of the LORD.

3:1 [a]Ex 6:27
3:2 [b]Ex 6:23; Nu 26:60
3:3 [c]Ex 28:41
3:4 [d]Lev 10:2 [e]Lev 10:1 [f]1Ch 24:1
3:6 [g]Dt 10:8; 31:9; 1Ch 15:2 [h]Nu 8:6-22; 18:1-7; 2Ch 29:11
3:7 [i]Lev 8:35; Nu 1:50
3:9 [j]Nu 8:19; 18:6
3:10 [k]Ex 29:9 [l]Nu 1:51
3:12 [m]Mal 2:4 [n]ver 41; Nu 8:16,18 [o]Ex 13:2
3:13 [p]Ex 13:12
3:15 [q]ver 39 [r]Nu 26:62
3:17 [s]Ge 46:11 [t]Ex 6:16
3:18 [u]Ex 6:17
3:19 [v]Ex 6:18
3:20 [w]Ge 46:11 [x]Ex 6:19
3:21 [y]Ex 6:17
3:25 [z]Ex 25:9 [a]Ex 26:14 [b]Ex 26:36; Nu 4:25
3:26 [c]Ex 27:9 [d]Ex 35:18
3:27 [e]1Ch 26:23
3:29 [f]Nu 1:53
3:31 [g]Ex 25:10-22 [h]Ex 25:23 [i]Ex 25:31 [j]Ex 27:1; 30:1 [k]Ex 26:33

17 These were the names of the sons of Levi:[s]
Gershon, Kohath and Merari.[t]
18 These were the names of the Gershonite clans:
Libni and Shimei.[u]
19 The Kohathite clans:
Amram, Izhar, Hebron and Uzziel.[v]
20 The Merarite clans:[w]
Mahli and Mushi.[x]
These were the Levite clans, according to their families.

21 To Gershon belonged the clans of the Libnites and Shimeites;[y] these were the Gershonite clans. 22 The number of all the males a month old or more who were counted was 7,500. 23 The Gershonite clans were to camp on the west, behind the tabernacle. 24 The leader of the families of the Gershonites was Eliasaph son of Lael. 25 At the Tent of Meeting the Gershonites were responsible for the care of the tabernacle[z] and tent, its coverings,[a] the curtain at the entrance[b] to the Tent of Meeting, 26 the curtains of the courtyard[c], the curtain at the entrance to the courtyard surrounding the tabernacle and altar, and the ropes[d]—and everything related to their use.

27 To Kohath belonged the clans of the Amramites, Izharites, Hebronites and Uzzielites;[e] these were the Kohathite clans. 28 The number of all the males a month old or more was 8,600.[c] The Kohathites were responsible for the care of the sanctuary. 29 The Kohathite clans were to camp on the south side[f] of the tabernacle. 30 The leader of the families of the Kohathite clans was Elizaphan son of Uzziel. 31 They were responsible for the care of the ark,[g] the table,[h] the lampstand,[i] the altars,[j] the articles of the sanctuary used in ministering, the curtain,[k] and everything related to their

b *9* Most manuscripts of the Masoretic Text; some manuscripts of the Masoretic Text, Samaritan Pentateuch and Septuagint (see also Num. 8:16) *to me*
c *28* Hebrew; some Septuagint manuscripts *8,300*

use.[a] 32The chief leader of the Levites
was Eleazar son of Aaron, the priest. He
was appointed over those who were
responsible for the care of the sanctuary.

33To Merari belonged the clans of the
Mahlites and the Mushites;[b] these were
the Merarite clans. 34The number of all
the males a month old or more who
were counted was 6,200. 35The leader
of the families of the Merarite clans
was Zuriel son of Abihail; they were to
camp on the north side of the tabernacle.[c] 36The Merarites were appointed[d]
to take care of the frames of the tabernacle, its crossbars, posts, bases, all its
equipment, and everything related to
their use, 37as well as the posts of the
surrounding courtyard with their bases,
tent pegs and ropes.

38Moses and Aaron and his sons were
to camp to the east[e] of the tabernacle,
toward the sunrise, in front of the Tent
of Meeting.[f] They were responsible for
the care of the sanctuary[g] on behalf of
the Israelites. Anyone else who approached the sanctuary was to be put
to death.[h]

39The total number of Levites counted
at the LORD's command by Moses and
Aaron according to their clans, including
every male a month old or more, was
22,000.[i]

Substitution of the Levites for firstborn of the Israelites.

40The LORD said to Moses, "Count all
the firstborn Israelite males who are a
month old or more[j] and make a list of
their names. 41Take the Levites for me
in place of all the firstborn of the Israelites,[k] and the livestock of the Levites
in place of all the firstborn of the livestock of the Israelites. I am the LORD."
42So Moses counted all the firstborn
of the Israelites, as the LORD commanded
him. 43The total number of firstborn
males a month old or more, listed by
name, was 22,273.[l]

3:31 [a]Nu 4:15
3:33 [b]Ex 6:19
3:35 [c]Nu 1:53; 2:25
3:36 [d]Nu 4:32
3:38 [e]Nu 2:3 [f]Nu 1:53 [g]ver 7; Nu 18:5 [h]ver 10; Nu 1:51
3:39 [i]Nu 26:62
3:40 [j]ver 15
3:41 [k]ver 12
3:43 [l]ver 39
3:46 [m]Ex 13:13; Nu 18:15
3:47 [n]Lev 27:6 [o]Ex 30:13 [p]Lev 27:25
3:50 [q]ver 46-48
4:2 [r]Ex 30:12
4:3 [s]ver 23; Nu 8:25; 1Ch 23:3,24, 27; Ezr 3:8
4:4 [t]ver 19
4:5 [u]Ex 26:31,33 [v]Ex 25:10,16
4:6 [w]Ex 25:13-15; 1Ki 8:7; 2Ch 5:8
4:7 [x]Ex 25:23,29; Lev 24:6 [y]Ex 25:30

44The LORD also said to Moses,
45"Take the Levites in place of all the
firstborn of Israel, and the livestock of
the Levites in place of their livestock.
The Levites are to be mine. I am the
LORD. 46To redeem[m] the 273 firstborn
Israelites who exceed the number of the
Levites, 47collect five shekels[d][n] for each
one, according to the sanctuary shekel,[o]
which weighs twenty gerahs.[p] 48Give
the money for the redemption of the
additional Israelites to Aaron and his
sons."

49So Moses collected the redemption
money from those who exceeded the
number redeemed by the Levites.
50From the firstborn of the Israelites he
collected silver weighing 1,365 shekels,[e][q] according to the sanctuary shekel.
51Moses gave the redemption money
to Aaron and his sons, as he was commanded by the word of the LORD.

Service of the Kohathites.

4 The LORD said to Moses and Aaron:
2"Take a census[r] of the Kohathite
branch of the Levites by their clans and
families. 3Count all the men from thirty
to fifty years of age[s] who come to serve
in the work in the Tent of Meeting.

4"This is the work of the Kohathites
in the Tent of Meeting: the care of the
most holy things.[t] 5When the camp is
to move, Aaron and his sons are to go in
and take down the shielding curtain[u]
and cover the ark of the Testimony with
it.[v] 6Then they are to cover this with
hides of sea cows,[f] spread a cloth of solid blue over that and put the poles[w] in
place.

7"Over the table of the Presence[x]
they are to spread a blue cloth and put
on it the plates, dishes and bowls, and
the jars for drink offerings; the bread
that is continually there[y] is to remain
on it. 8Over these they are to spread a
scarlet cloth, cover that with hides of
sea cows and put its poles in place.

[d]*47* That is, about 2 ounces (about 55 grams)
[e]*50* That is, about 35 pounds (about 15.5 kilograms)
[f]*6* That is, dugongs; also in verses 8, 10, 11, 12, 14 and 25

9"They are to take a blue cloth and
cover the lampstand that is for light,
together with its lamps, its wick trimmers and trays,[a] and all its jars for the
oil used to supply it. **10**Then they are to
wrap it and all its accessories in a covering of hides of sea cows and put it
on a carrying frame.
11"Over the gold altar[b] they are to
spread a blue cloth and cover that with
hides of sea cows and put its poles in
place.
12"They are to take all the articles
used for ministering in the sanctuary,
wrap them in a blue cloth, cover that
with hides of sea cows and put them on
a carrying frame.
13"They are to remove the ashes from
the bronze altar[c] and spread a purple
cloth over it. **14**Then they are to place
on it all the utensils used for ministering
at the altar, including the firepans, meat
forks,[d] shovels and sprinkling bowls.[e]
Over it they are to spread a covering of
hides of sea cows and put its poles[f] in
place.
15"After Aaron and his sons have finished covering the holy furnishings and
all the holy articles, and when the camp
is ready to move, the Kohathites are to
come to do the carrying.[g] But they must
not touch the holy things or they will
die.[h] The Kohathites are to carry those
things that are in the Tent of Meeting.
16"Eleazar[i] son of Aaron, the priest, is
to have charge of the oil for the light,[j]
the fragrant incense, the regular grain
offering[k] and the anointing oil. He is to
be in charge of the entire tabernacle
and everything in it, including its holy
furnishings and articles."
17The LORD said to Moses and Aaron,
18"See that the Kohathite tribal clans
are not cut off from the Levites. **19**So
that they may live and not die when
they come near the most holy things,[l]
do this for them: Aaron and his sons are
to go into the sanctuary and assign to
each man his work and what he is to
carry. **20**But the Kohathites must not go
in to look[m] at the holy things, even for
a moment, or they will die."

Service of the Gershonites.

21The LORD said to Moses, **22**"Take a
census also of the Gershonites by their
families and clans. **23**Count all the men
from thirty to fifty years of age[n] who
come to serve in the work at the Tent
of Meeting.
24"This is the service of the Gershonite clans as they work and carry burdens: **25**They are to carry the curtains
of the tabernacle,[o] the Tent of Meeting,[p] its covering[q] and the outer covering of hides of sea cows, the curtains
for the entrance to the Tent of Meeting,
26the curtains of the courtyard surrounding the tabernacle and altar, the
curtain for the entrance, the ropes and
all the equipment used in its service.
The Gershonites are to do all that needs
to be done with these things. **27**All their
service, whether carrying or doing other
work, is to be done under the direction
of Aaron and his sons. You shall assign
to them as their responsibility all they
are to carry. **28**This is the service of the
Gershonite clans[r] at the Tent of Meeting. Their duties are to be under the
direction of Ithamar son of Aaron, the
priest.

Service of the Merarites.

29"Count the Merarites by their clans
and families.[s] **30**Count all the men from
thirty to fifty years of age who come to
serve in the work at the Tent of Meeting.
31This is their duty as they perform
service at the Tent of Meeting: to carry
the frames of the tabernacle, its crossbars, posts and bases,[t] **32**as well as the
posts of the surrounding courtyard with
their bases, tent pegs, ropes, all their
equipment and everything related to
their use. Assign to each man the specific things he is to carry. **33**This is the service of the Merarite clans as they work
at the Tent of Meeting under the direction of Ithamar son of Aaron, the priest."

Numbering of the Levites.

34Moses, Aaron and the leaders of the
community counted the Kohathites[u] by

4:9 [a]Ex 25:31, 37,38
4:11 [b]Ex 30:1
4:13 [c]Ex 27:1-8
4:14 [d]2Ch 4:16 [e]Jer 52:18 [f]Ex 27:6
4:15 [g]Nu 7:9 [h]Nu 1:51; 2Sa 6:6,7
4:16 [i]Lev 10:6 [j]Ex 25:6 [k]Ex 29:41; Lev 6:14-23
4:19 [l]ver 15
4:20 [m]Ex 19:21; 1Sa 6:19
4:23 [n]ver 3; 1Ch 23:3,24, 27
4:25 [o]Ex 27:10-18; Nu 3:26 [p]Nu 3:25 [q]Ex 26:14
4:28 [r]Nu 7:7
4:29 [s]Ge 46:11
4:31 [t]Nu 3:36
4:34 [u]ver 2

their clans and families. **35**All the men from thirty to fifty years of age who came to serve in the work in the Tent of Meeting, **36**counted by clans, were 2,750. **37**This was the total of all those in the Kohathite clans[a] who served in the Tent of Meeting. Moses and Aaron counted them according to the LORD's command through Moses.

38The Gershonites[b] were counted by their clans and families. **39**All the men from thirty to fifty years of age who came to serve in the work at the Tent of Meeting, **40**counted by their clans and families, were 2,630. **41**This was the total of those in the Gershonite clans who served at the Tent of Meeting. Moses and Aaron counted them according to the LORD's command.

42The Merarites were counted by their clans and families. **43**All the men from thirty to fifty years of age who came to serve in the work at the Tent of Meeting, **44**counted by their clans, were 3,200. **45**This was the total of those in the Merarite clans.[c] Moses and Aaron counted them according to the LORD's command through Moses.

46So Moses, Aaron and the leaders of Israel counted all the Levites by their clans and families. **47**All the men from thirty to fifty years of age[d] who came to do the work of serving and carrying the Tent of Meeting **48**numbered 8,580.[e] **49**At the LORD's command through Moses, each was assigned his work and told what to carry.

Thus they were counted,[f] as the LORD commanded Moses.

Command to send away unclean persons from the camp.

5 The LORD said to Moses, **2**"Command the Israelites to send away from the camp anyone who has an infectious skin disease[g][g] or a discharge[h] of any kind, or who is ceremonially unclean[i] because of a dead body. **3**Send away male and female alike; send them outside the camp so they will not defile their camp, where I dwell among them.[j]" **4**The Israelites did this; they sent them outside the camp. They did just as the LORD had instructed Moses.

5The LORD said to Moses, **6**"Say to the Israelites: 'When a man or woman wrongs another in any way[h] and so is unfaithful[k] to the LORD, that person is guilty[l] **7**and must confess[m] the sin he has committed. He must make full restitution[n] for his wrong, add one fifth to it and give it all to the person he has wronged. **8**But if that person has no close relative to whom restitution can be made for the wrong, the restitution belongs to the LORD and must be given to the priest, along with the ram with which atonement is made for him.[o] **9**All the sacred contributions the Israelites bring to a priest will belong to him.[p] **10**Each man's sacred gifts are his own, but what he gives to the priest will belong to the priest.[q] ' "

Test for a wife suspected of being unfaithful.

11Then the LORD said to Moses, **12**"Speak to the Israelites and say to them: 'If a man's wife goes astray[r] and is unfaithful to him **13**by sleeping with another man,[s] and this is hidden from her husband and her impurity is undetected (since there is no witness against her and she has not been caught in the act), **14**and if feelings of jealousy[t] come over her husband and he suspects his wife and she is impure—or if he is jealous and suspects her even though she is not impure— **15**then he is to take his wife to the priest. He must also take an offering of a tenth of an ephah[i][u] of barley flour[v] on her behalf. He must not pour oil on it or put incense on it, because it is a grain offering for jealousy, a reminder[w] offering to draw attention to guilt.

16" 'The priest shall bring her and

4:37 [a]Nu 3:27
4:38 [b]Ge 46:11
4:45 [c]ver 29
4:47 [d]ver 3
4:48 [e]Nu 3:39
4:49 [f]Nu 1:47
5:2 [g]Lev 13:46 [h]Lev 15:2; Mt 9:20 [i]Lev 13:3; Nu 9:6-10
5:3 [j]Lev 26:12; Nu 35:34; 2Co 6:16
5:6 [k]Lev 6:2 [l]Lev 5:14–6:7
5:7 [m]Lev 5:5; 26:40; Jos 7:19; Lk 19:8 [n]Lev 6:5
5:8 [o]Lev 6:6,7; 7:7
5:9 [p]Lev 6:17; 7:6-14
5:10 [q]Lev 10:13
5:12 [r]Ex 20:14
5:13 [s]Lev 18:20; 20:10
5:14 [t]Pr 6:34; SS 8:6
5:15 [u]Ex 16:36 [v]Lev 6:20 [w]Eze 29:16

[g]*2* Traditionally *leprosy*; the Hebrew word was used for various diseases affecting the skin—not necessarily leprosy. [h]*6* Or *woman commits any wrong common to mankind* [i]*15* That is, probably about 2 quarts (about 2 liters)

have her stand before the LORD. [17]Then he shall take some holy water in a clay jar and put some dust from the tabernacle floor into the water. [18]After the priest has had the woman stand before the LORD, he shall loosen her hair[a] and place in her hands the reminder offering, the grain offering for jealousy, while he himself holds the bitter water that brings a curse. [19]Then the priest shall put the woman under oath and say to her, "If no other man has slept with you and you have not gone astray[b] and become impure while married to your husband, may this bitter water that brings a curse not harm you. [20]But if you have gone astray[c] while married to your husband and you have defiled yourself by sleeping with a man other than your husband"— [21]here the priest is to put the woman under this curse of the oath[d]—"may the LORD cause your people to curse and denounce you when he causes your thigh to waste away and your abdomen to swell.[j] [22]May this water[e] that brings a curse[f] enter your body so that your abdomen swells and your thigh wastes away.[k]"

"'Then the woman is to say, "Amen. So be it.[g]"

[23]"'The priest is to write these curses on a scroll[h] and then wash them off into the bitter water. [24]He shall have the woman drink the bitter water that brings a curse, and this water will enter her and cause bitter suffering. [25]The priest is to take from her hands the grain offering for jealousy, wave it before the LORD[i] and bring it to the altar. [26]The priest is then to take a handful of the grain offering as a memorial offering and burn it on the altar; after that, he is to have the woman drink the water. [27]If she has defiled herself and been unfaithful to her husband, then when she is made to drink the water that brings a curse, it will go into her and cause bitter suffering; her abdomen will swell and her thigh waste away,[l] and she will become accursed[j] among her people. [28]If, however, the woman has not defiled herself and is free from impurity, she will be cleared of guilt and will be able to have children.

[29]"'This, then, is the law of jealousy when a woman goes astray[k] and defiles herself while married to her husband, [30]or when feelings of jealousy come over a man because he suspects his wife. The priest is to have her stand before the LORD and is to apply this entire law to her. [31]The husband will be innocent of any wrongdoing, but the woman will bear the consequences[l] of her sin.'"

Laws and vows of the Nazirites.

6 The LORD said to Moses, [2]"Speak to the Israelites and say to them: 'If a man or woman wants to make a special vow[m], a vow of separation to the LORD as a Nazirite,[n] [3]he must abstain from wine[o] and other fermented drink and must not drink vinegar[p] made from wine or from other fermented drink. He must not drink grape juice or eat grapes or raisins. [4]As long as he is a Nazirite, he must not eat anything that comes from the grapevine, not even the seeds or skins.

[5]"'During the entire period of his vow of separation no razor[q] may be used on his head.[r] He must be holy until the period of his separation to the LORD is over; he must let the hair of his head grow long. [6]Throughout the period of his separation to the LORD he must not go near a dead body.[s] [7]Even if his own father or mother or brother or sister dies, he must not make himself ceremonially unclean[t] on account of them, because the symbol of his separation to God is on his head. [8]Throughout the period of his separation he is consecrated to the LORD.

[9]"'If someone dies suddenly in his presence, thus defiling the hair he has dedicated,[u] he must shave his head on the day of his cleansing[v]—the seventh day. [10]Then on the eighth day he must

5:18 [a]Lev 10:6; 1Co 11:6
5:19 [b]ver 12,29
5:20 [c]ver 12
5:21 [d]Jos 6:26; 1Sa 14:24; Ne 10:29
5:22 [e]Ps 109:18 [f]ver 18 [g]Dt 27:15
5:23 [h]Jer 45:1
5:25 [i]Lev 8:27
5:27 [j]Isa 43:28; 65:15; Jer 26:6; 29:18; 42:18; 44:12,22; Zec 8:13
5:29 [k]ver 19
5:31 [l]Lev 5:1; 20:17
6:2 [m]Ge 28:20; Ac 21:23 [n]Jdg 13:5; 16:17; Am 2:11,12
6:3 [o]Lk 1:15 [p]Ru 2:14; Ps 69:21; Pr 10:26
6:5 [q]Ps 52:2; 57:4; 59:7; Isa 7:20; Eze 5:1 [r]1Sa 1:11
6:6 [s]Lev 21:1-3; Nu 19:11-22
6:7 [t]Nu 9:6
6:9 [u]ver 18 [v]Lev 14:9

j21 Or *causes you to have a miscarrying womb and barrenness* k22 Or *body and cause you to be barren and have a miscarrying womb* l27 Or *suffering; she will have barrenness and a miscarrying womb*

bring two doves or two young pigeons[a]
to the priest at the entrance to the Tent
of Meeting. 11The priest is to offer one
as a sin offering and the other as a burnt
offering[b] to make atonement[c] for him
because he sinned by being in the presence of the dead body. That same day
he is to consecrate his head. 12He must
dedicate himself to the LORD for the
period of his separation and must bring
a year-old male lamb as a guilt offering.
The previous days do not count, because he became defiled during his separation.

13"'Now this is the law for the
Nazirite when the period of his separation is over.[d] He is to be brought to the
entrance to the Tent of Meeting.
14There he is to present his offerings to
the LORD: a year-old male lamb without
defect for a burnt offering, a year-old
ewe lamb without defect for a sin offering,[e] a ram without defect for a fellowship offering,[m] 15together with their
grain offerings and drink offerings,[f] and
a basket of bread made without yeast—
cakes made of fine flour mixed with oil,
and wafers spread with oil.[g]

16"'The priest is to present them
before the LORD and make the sin offering and the burnt offering. 17He is to
present the basket of unleavened bread
and is to sacrifice the ram as a fellowship offering to the LORD, together with
its grain offering and drink offering.

18"'Then at the entrance to the Tent of
Meeting, the Nazirite must shave off
the hair that he dedicated.[h] He is to take
the hair and put it in the fire that is
under the sacrifice of the fellowship
offering.

19"'After the Nazirite has shaved off
the hair of his dedication, the priest is
to place in his hands a boiled shoulder
of the ram, and a cake and a wafer from
the basket, both made without yeast.
20The priest shall then wave them
before the LORD as a wave offering; they
are holy and belong to the priest,
together with the breast that was waved
and the thigh that was presented. After
that, the Nazirite may drink wine.[i]

21"'This is the law of the Nazirite
who vows his offering to the LORD in
accordance with his separation, in addition to whatever else he can afford. He
must fulfill the vow he has made, according to the law of the Nazirite.'"

22The LORD said to Moses, 23"Tell
Aaron and his sons, 'This is how you
are to bless[j] the Israelites. Say to them:

24"'"The LORD bless you[k]
and keep you;[l]
25the LORD make his face shine upon
you[m]
and be gracious to you;[n]
26the LORD turn his face[o] toward you
and give you peace."[p]'

27"So they will put my name[q] on the
Israelites, and I will bless them."

Offerings at the dedication of the tabernacle

7 When Moses finished setting up
the tabernacle,[r] he anointed it and
consecrated it and all its furnishings.[s]
He also anointed and consecrated the
altar and all its utensils.[t] 2Then the leaders of Israel,[u] the heads of families who
were the tribal leaders in charge of
those who were counted, made offerings. 3They brought as their gifts before
the LORD six covered carts and twelve
oxen—an ox from each leader and a cart
from every two. These they presented
before the tabernacle.

4The LORD said to Moses, 5"Accept
these from them, that they may be used
in the work at the Tent of Meeting. Give
them to the Levites as each man's work
requires."

6So Moses took the carts and oxen
and gave them to the Levites. 7He gave
two carts and four oxen to the Gershonites,[v] as their work required, 8and he
gave four carts and eight oxen to the
Merarites,[w] as their work required. They
were all under the direction of Ithamar
son of Aaron, the priest. 9But Moses did
not give any to the Kohathites, because

6:10 [a]Lev 5:7; 14:22
6:11 [b]Ge 8:20 [c]Ex 29:36
6:13 [d]Ac 21:26
6:14 [e]Lev 14:10; Nu 15:27
6:15 [f]Nu 15:1-7 [g]Ex 29:2; Lev 2:4
6:18 [h]ver 9; Ac 21:24
6:20 [i]Ecc 9:7
6:23 [j]Dt 21:5; 1Ch 23:13
6:24 [k]Dt 28:3-6; Ps 28:9 [l]1Sa 2:9; Ps 17:8
6:25 [m]Job 29:24; Ps 31:16; 80:3; 119:135 [n]Ge 43:29; Ps 25:16; 86:16
6:26 [o]Ps 4:6; 44:3 [p]Ps 29:11; 37:11,37; Jn 14:27
6:27 [q]Dt 28:10; 2Sa 7:23; 2Ch 7:14; Ne 9:10; Jer 25:29
7:1 [r]Ex 40:17 [s]Ex 40:9 [t]ver 84,88; Ex 40:10
7:2 [u]Nu 1:5-16
7:7 [v]Nu 4:24-26, 28
7:8 [w]Nu 4:31-33

m *14* Traditionally *peace offering*; also in verses 17 and 18

they were to carry on their shoulders[a]
the holy things, for which they were
responsible.
10When the altar was anointed,[b] the
leaders brought their offerings for its
dedication[c] and presented them before
the altar. 11For the LORD had said to Moses, "Each day one leader is to bring his
offering for the dedication of the altar."

12The one who brought his offering on
the first day was Nahshon son of Amminadab of the tribe of Judah.
13His offering was one silver plate
weighing a hundred and thirty
shekels,[n] and one silver sprinkling
bowl weighing seventy shekels,[o]
both according to the sanctuary
shekel,[d] each filled with fine flour
mixed with oil as a grain offering;[e]
14one gold dish weighing ten shekels,[p] filled with incense;[f] 15one
young bull,[g] one ram and one male
lamb a year old, for a burnt offering;[h] 16one male goat for a sin offering;[i] 17and two oxen, five rams, five
male goats and five male lambs a
year old, to be sacrificed as a fellowship offering.[q][j] This was the
offering of Nahshon son of Amminadab.[k]

18On the second day Nethanel son of
Zuar,[l] the leader of Issachar, brought his
offering.
19The offering he brought was one
silver plate weighing a hundred and
thirty shekels, and one silver sprinkling bowl weighing seventy shekels, both according to the sanctuary
shekel, each filled with fine flour
mixed with oil as a grain offering;
20one gold dish[m] weighing ten shekels, filled with incense; 21one
young bull, one ram and one male
lamb a year old, for a burnt offering;
22one male goat for a sin offering;
23and two oxen, five rams, five
male goats and five male lambs a
year old, to be sacrificed as a fellowship offering. This was the offering
of Nethanel son of Zuar.

24On the third day, Eliab son of Helon,[n]

7:9 [a]Nu 4:15
7:10 [b]ver 1 [c]2Ch 7:9
7:13 [d]Ex 30:13; Nu 3:47 [e]Lev 2:1
7:14 [f]Ex 30:34
7:15 [g]Ex 24:5; 29:3; Nu 28:11 [h]Lev 1:3
7:16 [i]Lev 4:3,23
7:17 [j]Lev 3:1 [k]Nu 1:7
7:18 [l]Nu 1:8
7:20 [m]ver 14
7:24 [n]Nu 1:9
7:30 [o]Nu 1:5
7:36 [p]Nu 1:6

the leader of the people of Zebulun,
brought his offering.
25His offering was one silver plate
weighing a hundred and thirty shekels, and one silver sprinkling bowl
weighing seventy shekels, both according to the sanctuary shekel,
each filled with fine flour mixed
with oil as a grain offering; 26one
gold dish weighing ten shekels,
filled with incense; 27one young
bull, one ram and one male lamb a
year old, for a burnt offering; 28one
male goat for a sin offering; 29and
two oxen, five rams, five male goats
and five male lambs a year old, to
be sacrificed as a fellowship offering. This was the offering of Eliab
son of Helon.

30On the fourth day Elizur son of
Shedeur,[o] the leader of the people of
Reuben, brought his offering.
31His offering was one silver plate
weighing a hundred and thirty
shekels, and one silver sprinkling
bowl weighing seventy shekels,
both according to the sanctuary
shekel, each filled with fine flour
mixed with oil as a grain offering;
32one gold dish weighing ten
shekels, filled with incense; 33one
young bull, one ram and one male
lamb a year old, for a burnt offering;
34one male goat for a sin offering;
35and two oxen, five rams, five
male goats and five male lambs a
year old, to be sacrificed as a fellowship offering. This was the offering
of Elizur son of Shedeur.

36On the fifth day Shelumiel son of
Zurishaddai,[p] the leader of the people
of Simeon, brought his offering.
37His offering was one silver plate
weighing a hundred and thirty
shekels, and one silver sprinkling

[n] *13* That is, about 3 1/4 pounds (about 1.5 kilograms); also elsewhere in this chapter [o] *13* That is, about 1 3/4 pounds (about 0.8 kilogram); also elsewhere in this chapter [p] *14* That is, about 4 ounces (about 110 grams); also elsewhere in this chapter [q] *17* Traditionally *peace offering*; also elsewhere in this chapter

bowl weighing seventy shekels,
both according to the sanctuary
shekel, each filled with fine flour
mixed with oil as a grain offering;
38one gold dish weighing ten shekels, filled with incense; 39one young
bull, one ram and one male lamb a
year old, for a burnt offering; 40one
male goat for a sin offering; 41and
two oxen, five rams, five male goats
and five male lambs a year old, to be
sacrificed as a fellowship offering.
This was the offering of Shelumiel
son of Zurishaddai.

42On the sixth day Eliasaph son of
Deuel,[a] the leader of the people of Gad,
brought his offering.

43His offering was one silver plate
weighing a hundred and thirty shekels, and one silver sprinkling bowl
weighing seventy shekels, both
according to the sanctuary shekel,
each filled with fine flour mixed
with oil as a grain offering; 44one
gold dish weighing ten shekels,
filled with incense; 45one young
bull, one ram and one male lamb a
year old, for a burnt offering; 46one
male goat for a sin offering; 47and
two oxen, five rams, five male goats
and five male lambs a year old, to
be sacrificed as a fellowship offering. This was the offering of Eliasaph son of Deuel.

48On the seventh day Elishama son of
Ammihud,[b] the leader of the people of
Ephraim, brought his offering.

49His offering was one silver plate
weighing a hundred and thirty shekels, and one silver sprinkling bowl
weighing seventy shekels, both according to the sanctuary shekel,
each filled with fine flour mixed
with oil as a grain offering; 50one
gold dish weighing ten shekels, filled
with incense; 51one young bull, one
ram and one male lamb a year old,
for a burnt offering; 52one male goat
for a *sin offering*; 53and two oxen,
five rams, five male goats and five
male lambs a year old, to be sacri-

7:42 [a]Nu 1:14
7:48 [b]Nu 1:10
7:53 [c]Nu 1:10
7:54 [d]Nu 1:10; 2:20
7:60 [e]Nu 1:11
7:66 [f]Nu 1:12; 2:25

ficed as a fellowship offering. This
was the offering of Elishama son of
Ammihud.[c]

54On the eighth day Gamaliel son of
Pedahzur,[d] the leader of the people of
Manasseh, brought his offering.

55His offering was one silver plate
weighing a hundred and thirty shekels, and one silver sprinkling bowl
weighing seventy shekels, both according to the sanctuary shekel,
each filled with fine flour mixed
with oil as a grain offering; 56one
gold dish weighing ten shekels,
filled with incense; 57one young
bull, one ram and one male lamb a
year old, for a burnt offering; 58one
male goat for a sin offering; 59and
two oxen, five rams, five male goats
and five male lambs a year old, to
be sacrificed as a fellowship offering.
This was the offering of Gamaliel
son of Pedahzur.

60On the ninth day Abidan son of
Gideoni,[e] the leader of the people of
Benjamin, brought his offering.

61His offering was one silver plate
weighing a hundred and thirty shekels, and one silver sprinkling bowl
weighing seventy shekels, both
according to the sanctuary shekel,
each filled with fine flour mixed
with oil as a grain offering; 62one
gold dish weighing ten shekels,
filled with incense; 63one young
bull, one ram and one male lamb a
year old, for a burnt offering; 64one
male goat for a sin offering; 65and
two oxen, five rams, five male
goats and five male lambs a year
old, to be sacrificed as a fellowship
offering. This was the offering of
Abidan son of Gideoni.

66On the tenth day Ahiezer son of
Ammishaddai,[f] the leader of the people
of Dan, brought his offering.

67His offering was one silver plate
weighing a hundred and thirty shekels, and one silver sprinkling bowl
weighing seventy shekels, both

according to the sanctuary shekel,
each filled with fine flour mixed
with oil as a grain offering; **68**one
gold dish weighing ten shekels,
filled with incense; **69**one young
bull, one ram and one male lamb a
year old, for a burnt offering; **70**one
male goat for a sin offering; **71**and
two oxen, five rams, five male goats
and five male lambs a year old, to
be sacrificed as a fellowship offering.
This was the offering of Ahiezer
son of Ammishaddai.

72On the eleventh day Pagiel son of
Ocran,[a] the leader of the people of
Asher, brought his offering.
73His offering was one silver plate
weighing a hundred and thirty shekels, and one silver sprinkling bowl
weighing seventy shekels, both according to the sanctuary shekel,
each filled with fine flour mixed
with oil as a grain offering; **74**one
gold dish weighing ten shekels,
filled with incense; **75**one young
bull, one ram and one male lamb a
year old, for a burnt offering; **76**one
male goat for a sin offering; **77**and
two oxen, five rams, five male goats
and five male lambs a year old, to
be sacrificed as a fellowship offering.
This was the offering of Pagiel son
of Ocran.

78On the twelfth day Ahira son of Enan,[b]
the leader of the people of Naphtali,
brought his offering.
79His offering was one silver plate
weighing a hundred and thirty shekels, and one silver sprinkling bowl
weighing seventy shekels, both
according to the sanctuary shekel,
each filled with fine flour mixed
with oil as a grain offering; **80**one
gold dish weighing ten shekels,
filled with incense; **81**one young
bull, one ram and one male lamb a
year old, for a burnt offering; **82**one
male goat for a sin offering; **83**and
two oxen, five rams, five male goats
and five male lambs a year old, to
be sacrificed as a fellowship offering.
This was the offering of Ahira son
of Enan.

84These were the offerings of the
Israelite leaders for the dedication of
the altar when it was anointed:[c] twelve
silver plates, twelve silver sprinkling
bowls[d] and twelve gold dishes.[e] **85**Each
silver plate weighed a hundred and
thirty shekels, and each sprinkling bowl
seventy shekels. Altogether, the silver
dishes weighed two thousand four hundred shekels,[r] according to the sanctuary shekel. **86**The twelve gold dishes
filled with incense weighed ten shekels
each, according to the sanctuary shekel.
Altogether, the gold dishes weighed a
hundred and twenty shekels.[s] **87**The
total number of animals for the burnt
offering came to twelve young bulls,
twelve rams and twelve male lambs a
year old, together with their grain offering. Twelve male goats were used for
the sin offering. **88**The total number of
animals for the sacrifice of the fellowship
offering came to twenty-four oxen, sixty
rams, sixty male goats and sixty male
lambs a year old. These were the offerings for the dedication of the altar after
it was anointed.[f]
89When Moses entered the Tent of
Meeting to speak with the LORD,[g] he
heard the voice speaking to him from
between the two cherubim above the
atonement cover[h] on the ark of the
Testimony. And he spoke with him.

Setting up the lamps.

8 The LORD said to Moses, **2**"Speak
to Aaron and say to him, 'When
you set up the seven lamps, they are to
light the area in front of the lampstand.[i] '"
3Aaron did so; he set up the lamps so
that they faced forward on the lampstand, just as the LORD commanded
Moses. **4**This is how the lampstand
was made: It was made of hammered
gold[j]—from its base to its blossoms.

7:72 [a]Nu 1:13
7:78 [b]Nu 1:15; 2:29
7:84 [c]ver 1,10 [d]Nu 4:14 [e]ver 14
7:88 [f]ver 1,10
7:89 [g]Ex 25:21,22; 33:9,11 [h]Ps 80:1; 99:1
8:2 [i]Ex 25:37; Lev 24:2,4
8:4 [j]Ex 25:18,36; 25:18

[r]*85* That is, about 60 pounds (about 28 kilograms)
[s]*86* That is, about 3 pounds (about 1.4 kilograms)

The lampstand was made exactly like
the pattern[a] the LORD had shown Moses.

Cleansing and setting apart of the Levites.

5The LORD said to Moses: 6"Take the
Levites from among the other Israelites
and make them ceremonially clean.[b]
7To purify them, do this: Sprinkle the
water of cleansing[c] on them; then have
them shave their whole bodies[d] and
wash their clothes,[e] and so purify themselves. 8Have them take a young bull
with its grain offering of fine flour
mixed with oil;[f] then you are to take a
second young bull for a sin offering.
9Bring the Levites to the front of the
Tent of Meeting[g] and assemble the
whole Israelite community.[h] 10You are
to bring the Levites before the LORD,
and the Israelites are to lay their hands
on them.[i] 11Aaron is to present the Levites before the LORD as a wave offering[j]
from the Israelites, so that they may be
ready to do the work of the LORD.
12"After the Levites lay their hands
on the heads of the bulls,[k] use the one
for a sin offering to the LORD and the
other for a burnt offering, to make
atonement[l] for the Levites. 13Have the
Levites stand in front of Aaron and his
sons and then present them as a wave
offering to the LORD. 14In this way you
are to set the Levites apart from the
other Israelites, and the Levites will be
mine.[m]
15"After you have purified the Levites
and presented them as a wave offering,[n] they are to come to do their work
at the Tent of Meeting. 16They are the
Israelites who are to be given wholly to
me. I have taken them as my own in
place of the firstborn, the first male offspring[o] from every Israelite woman.
17Every firstborn male in Israel, whether
man or animal,[p] is mine. When I struck
down all the firstborn in Egypt, I set
them apart for myself.[q] 18And I have
taken the Levites in place of all the firstborn sons in Israel.[r] 19Of all the Israelites, I have given the Levites as gifts to
Aaron and his sons[s] to do the work at
the Tent of Meeting on behalf of the
Israelites[t] and to make atonement for
them[u] so that no plague will strike the
Israelites when they go near the sanctuary."
20Moses, Aaron and the whole Israelite community did with the Levites
just as the LORD commanded Moses.
21The Levites purified themselves and
washed their clothes.[v] Then Aaron presented them as a wave offering before
the LORD and made atonement for them
to purify them.[w] 22After that, the Levites came to do their work at the Tent
of Meeting under the supervision of
Aaron and his sons. They did with the
Levites just as the LORD commanded
Moses.
23The LORD said to Moses, 24"This
applies to the Levites: Men twenty-five
years old or more[x] shall come to take
part in the work at the Tent of Meeting,[y] 25but at the age of fifty, they must
retire from their regular service and
work no longer. 26They may assist their
brothers in performing their duties at
the Tent of Meeting, but they themselves must not do the work. This, then,
is how you are to assign the responsibilities of the Levites."

Celebration of the Passover.

9 The LORD spoke to Moses in the
Desert of Sinai in the first month[z]
of the second year after they came out of
Egypt.[a] He said, 2"Have the Israelites
celebrate the Passover at the appointed time. 3Celebrate it at the appointed
time, at twilight on the fourteenth day
of this month, in accordance with all
its rules and regulations.[b]"
4So Moses told the Israelites to celebrate the Passover, 5and they did so in
the Desert of Sinai at twilight on the
fourteenth day of the first month.[c] The
Israelites did everything just as the
LORD commanded Moses.
6But some of them could not celebrate
the Passover on that day because they
were ceremonially unclean[d] on account

8:4 [a]Ex 25:9
8:6 [b]Lev 22:2; Isa 1:16; 52:11
8:7 [c]Nu 19:9,17 [d]Lev 14:9; Dt 21:12 [e]Lev 14:8
8:8 [f]Lev 2:1; Nu 15:8-10
8:9 [g]Ex 40:12 [h]Lev 8:3
8:10 [i]Ac 6:6
8:11 [j]Lev 7:30
8:12 [k]Ex 29:10 [l]Ex 29:36
8:14 [m]Nu 3:12
8:15 [n]Ex 29:24
8:16 [o]Nu 3:12
8:17 [p]Ex 4:23 [q]Ex 13:2; Lk 2:23
8:18 [r]Nu 3:12
8:19 [s]Nu 3:9 [t]Nu 1:53 [u]Nu 16:46
8:21 [v]ver 7 [w]ver 12
8:24 [x]1Ch 23:3 [y]Ex 38:21; Nu 4:3
9:1 [z]Ex 40:2 [a]Nu 1:1
9:3 [b]Ex 12:2-11, 43-49; Lev 23:5-8; Dt 16:1-8
9:5 [c]Ex 12:1-13; Jos 5:10
9:6 [d]Lev 5:3

of a dead body. So they came to Moses
and Aaron[a] that same day 7and said to
Moses, "We have become unclean because of a dead body, but why should
we be kept from presenting the LORD's
offering with the other Israelites at the
appointed time?"
8Moses answered them, "Wait until
I find out what the LORD commands
concerning you."[b]
9Then the LORD said to Moses, 10"Tell
the Israelites: 'When any of you or your
descendants are unclean because of a
dead body or are away on a journey,
they may still celebrate[c] the LORD's
Passover. 11They are to celebrate it on
the fourteenth day of the second month
at twilight. They are to eat the lamb,
together with unleavened bread and bitter herbs.[d] 12They must not leave any
of it till morning[e] or break any of its
bones.[f] When they celebrate the Passover, they must follow all the regulations. 13But if a man who is ceremonially
clean and not on a journey fails to celebrate the Passover, that person must be
cut off from his people[g] because he did
not present the LORD's offering at the
appointed time. That man will bear the
consequences of his sin.
14" 'An alien[h] living among you who
wants to celebrate the LORD's Passover
must do so in accordance with its rules
and regulations. You must have the same
regulations for the alien and the native-
born.' "

The Israelites are guided by the cloud.

15On the day the tabernacle, the Tent
of the Testimony, was set up, the cloud[i]
covered it. From evening till morning
the cloud above the tabernacle looked
like fire.[j] 16That is how it continued to
be; the cloud covered it, and at night it
looked like fire. 17Whenever the cloud
lifted from above the Tent, the Israelites set out; wherever the cloud settled, the Israelites encamped.[k] 18At the
LORD's command the Israelites set out,
and at his command they encamped. As
long as the cloud stayed over the tabernacle, they remained in camp. 19When
the cloud remained over the tabernacle
a long time, the Israelites obeyed the
LORD's order and did not set out. 20Some-
times the cloud was over the tabernacle
only a few days; at the LORD's command
they would encamp, and then at his
command they would set out. 21Some-
times the cloud stayed only from evening
till morning, and when it lifted in the
morning, they set out. Whether by day
or by night, whenever the cloud lifted,
they set out. 22Whether the cloud stayed
over the tabernacle for two days or a
month or a year, the Israelites would
remain in camp and not set out; but
when it lifted, they would set out. 23At
the LORD's command they encamped,
and at the LORD's command they set
out. They obeyed the LORD's order, in
accordance with his command through
Moses.

Two silver trumpets.

10 The LORD said to Moses:
2"Make two trumpets[l] of hammered silver, and use them for calling
the community[m] together and for having the camps set out. 3When both are
sounded, the whole community is to assemble before you at the entrance to the
Tent of Meeting. 4If only one is sounded,
the leaders[n]—the heads of the clans of
Israel—are to assemble before you.
5When a trumpet blast is sounded, the
tribes camping on the east are to set
out.[o] 6At the sounding of a second
blast, the camps on the south are to set
out.[p] The blast will be the signal for
setting out. 7To gather the assembly,
blow the trumpets,[q] but not with the
same signal.[r]
8"The sons of Aaron, the priests, are
to blow the trumpets. This is to be a
lasting ordinance for you and the generations to come.[s] 9When you go into
battle in your own land against an enemy who is oppressing you,[t] sound a
blast on the trumpets. Then you will
be remembered[u] by the LORD your God

9:6 [a]Ex 18:15; Nu 27:2
9:8 [b]Ex 18:15; Nu 27:5,21; Ps 85:8
9:10 [c]2Ch 30:2
9:11 [d]Ex 12:8
9:12 [e]Ex 12:10,43 [f]Ex 12:46; Jn 19:36*
9:13 [g]Ge 17:14; Ex 12:15
9:14 [h]Ex 12:48,49
9:15 [i]Ex 40:34 [j]Ex 13:21
9:17 [k]Ex 40:36-38; Nu 10:11,12; 1Co 10:1
10:2 [l]Ne 12:35; Ps 47:5 [m]Jer 4:5,19; 6:1; Hos 5:8; Joel 2:1,15; Am 3:6
10:4 [n]Ex 18:21; Nu 1:16; 7:2
10:5 [o]ver 14
10:6 [p]ver 18
10:7 [q]Eze 33:3; Joel 2:1 [r]1Co 14:8
10:8 [s]Nu 31:6
10:9 [t]Jdg 2:18; 6:9; 1Sa 10:18; Ps 106:42 [u]Ge 8:1

and rescued from your enemies.[a] 10Also at your times of rejoicing—your appointed feasts and New Moon festivals[b]—you are to sound the trumpets[c] over your burnt offerings and fellowship offerings,[t] and they will be a memorial for you before your God. I am the LORD your God."

The Israelites' departure from Sinai.

11On the twentieth day of the second month of the second year,[d] the cloud lifted[e] from above the tabernacle of the Testimony. 12Then the Israelites set out from the Desert of Sinai and traveled from place to place until the cloud came to rest in the Desert of Paran. 13They set out, this first time, at the LORD's command through Moses.[f]

14The divisions of the camp of Judah went first, under their standard.[g] Nahshon son of Amminadab[h] was in command. 15Nethanel son of Zuar was over the division of the tribe of Issachar, 16and Eliab son of Helon was over the division of the tribe of Zebulun. 17Then the tabernacle was taken down, and the Gershonites and Merarites, who carried it, set out.[i]

18The divisions of the camp of Reuben went next, under their standard.[j] Elizur son of Shedeur was in command. 19Shelumiel son of Zurishaddai was over the division of the tribe of Simeon, 20and Eliasaph son of Deuel was over the division of the tribe of Gad. 21Then the Kohathites set out, carrying the holy things.[k] The tabernacle was to be set up before they arrived.[l]

22The divisions of the camp of Ephraim[m] went next, under their standard. Elishama son of Ammihud was in command. 23Gamaliel son of Pedahzur was over the division of the tribe of Manasseh, 24and Abidan son of Gideoni was over the division of the tribe of Benjamin.

25Finally, as the rear guard[n] for all the units, the divisions of the camp of Dan set out, under their standard. Ahiezer son of Ammishaddai was in command. 26Pagiel son of Ocran was over the division of the tribe of Asher, 27and Ahira son of Enan was over the division of the tribe of Naphtali. 28This was the order of march for the Israelite divisions as they set out.

29Now Moses said to Hobab[o] son of Reuel[p] the Midianite, Moses' father-in-law,[q] "We are setting out for the place about which the LORD said, 'I will give it to you.'[r] Come with us and we will treat you well, for the LORD has promised good things to Israel."

30He answered, "No, I will not go;[s] I am going back to my own land and my own people."

31But Moses said, "Please do not leave us. You know where we should camp in the desert, and you can be our eyes.[t] 32If you come with us, we will share with you[u] whatever good things the LORD gives us.[v]"

33So they set out[w] from the mountain of the LORD and traveled for three days. The ark of the covenant of the LORD[x] went before them during those three days to find them a place to rest. 34The cloud of the LORD was over them by day when they set out from the camp.[y]

35Whenever the ark set out, Moses said,

"Rise up, O LORD!
May your enemies be scattered;[z]
may your foes flee before you.[a]"

36Whenever it came to rest, he said,

"Return,[b] O LORD,
to the countless thousands of
Israel.[c]"

The people complain about their hardships.

11 Now the people complained about their hardships in the hearing of the LORD, and when he heard them his anger was aroused. Then fire from the LORD burned among them[d] and consumed some of the outskirts of the

10:9 [a]Ps 106:4
10:10 [b]Ps 81:3 [c]Lev 23:24
10:11 [d]Ex 40:17 [e]Nu 9:17
10:13 [f]Dt 1:6
10:14 [g]Nu 2:3-9 [h]Nu 1:7
10:17 [i]Nu 4:21-32
10:18 [j]Nu 2:10-16
10:21 [k]Nu 4:20 [l]ver 17
10:22 [m]Nu 2:24
10:25 [n]Nu 2:31; Jos 6:9
10:29 [o]Jdg 4:11 [p]Ex 2:18 [q]Ex 3:1 [r]Ge 12:7
10:30 [s]Mt 21:29
10:31 [t]Job 29:15
10:32 [u]Dt 10:18 [v]Ps 22:27-31; 67:5-7
10:33 [w]ver 12; Dt 1:33 [x]Jos 3:3
10:34 [y]Nu 9:15-23
10:35 [z]Ps 68:1 [a]Dt 7:10; 32:41; Ps 68:2; Isa 17:12-14
10:36 [b]Isa 63:17 [c]Dt 1:10
11:1 [d]Lev 10:2

[t]10 Traditionally *peace offerings*

camp. 2 When the people cried out to Moses, he prayed to the LORD[a] and the fire died down. 3 So that place was called Taberah,[u][b] because fire from the LORD had burned among them.

4 The rabble with them began to crave other food,[c] and again the Israelites started wailing[d] and said, "If only we had meat to eat! 5 We remember the fish we ate in Egypt at no cost—also the cucumbers, melons, leeks, onions and garlic.[e] 6 But now we have lost our appetite; we never see anything but this manna!"

7 The manna was like coriander seed[f] and looked like resin.[g] 8 The people went around gathering it, and then ground it in a handmill or crushed it in a mortar. They cooked it in a pot or made it into cakes. And it tasted like something made with olive oil. 9 When the dew[h] settled on the camp at night, the manna also came down.

10 Moses heard the people of every family wailing, each at the entrance to his tent. The LORD became exceedingly angry, and Moses was troubled. 11 He asked the LORD, "Why have you brought this trouble on your servant? What have I done to displease you that you put the burden of all these people on me?[i] 12 Did I conceive all these people? Did I give them birth? Why do you tell me to carry them in my arms, as a nurse carries an infant,[j] to the land you promised on oath to their forefathers?[k] 13 Where can I get meat for all these people?[l] They keep wailing to me, 'Give us meat to eat!' 14 I cannot carry all these people by myself; the burden is too heavy for me.[m] 15 If this is how you are going to treat me, put me to death[n] right now[o]—if I have found favor in your eyes—and do not let me face my own ruin."

Seventy elders are appointed to help Moses.

16 The LORD said to Moses: "Bring me seventy of Israel's elders who are known to you as leaders and officials among the people. Have them come to the Tent of Meeting, that they may stand there with you. 17 I will come down and speak with you there, and I will take of the Spirit that is on you and put the Spirit on them.[p] They will help you carry the burden of the people so that you will not have to carry it alone.[q]

18 "Tell the people: 'Consecrate yourselves[r] in preparation for tomorrow, when you will eat meat. The LORD heard you when you wailed,[s] "If only we had meat to eat! We were better off in Egypt!"[t] Now the LORD will give you meat, and you will eat it. 19 You will not eat it for just one day, or two days, or five, ten or twenty days, 20 but for a whole month—until it comes out of your nostrils and you loathe it[u]—because you have rejected the LORD,[v] who is among you, and have wailed before him, saying, "Why did we ever leave Egypt?"'"

21 But Moses said, "Here I am among six hundred thousand men[w] on foot, and you say, 'I will give them meat to eat for a whole month!' 22 Would they have enough if flocks and herds were slaughtered for them? Would they have enough if all the fish in the sea were caught for them?"[x]

23 The LORD answered Moses, "Is the LORD's arm too short?[y] You will now see whether or not what I say will come true for you.[z]"

24 So Moses went out and told the people what the LORD had said. He brought together seventy of their elders and had them stand around the Tent. 25 Then the LORD came down in the cloud[a] and spoke with him,[b] and he took of the Spirit[c] that was on him and put the Spirit on the seventy elders.[d] When the Spirit rested on them, they prophesied,[e] but they did not do so again.[v]

26 However, two men, whose names were Eldad and Medad, had remained in the camp. They were listed among the elders, but did not go out to the Tent. Yet the Spirit also rested on them,

11:2 [a] Nu 21:7
11:3 [b] Dt 9:22
11:4 [c] Ex 12:38 [d] Ps 78:18; 1Co 10:6
11:5 [e] Ex 16:3
11:7 [f] Ex 16:31 [g] Ge 2:12
11:9 [h] Ex 16:13
11:11 [i] Ex 5:22
11:12 [j] Isa 40:11; 49:23 [k] Ex 13:5
11:13 [l] Jn 6:5-9
11:14 [m] Ex 18:18
11:15 [n] Ex 32:32 [o] 1Ki 19:4; Jnh 4:3
11:17 [p] ver 25,29; 1Sa 10:6; 2Ki 2:9,15; Joel 2:28 [q] Ex 18:18
11:18 [r] Ex 19:10 [s] Ex 16:7 [t] ver 5; Ac 7:39
11:20 [u] Ps 78:29; 106:14,15 [v] Jos 24:27; 1Sa 10:19
11:21 [w] Ex 12:37
11:22 [x] Mt 15:33
11:23 [y] Isa 50:2; 59:1 [z] Nu 23:19; Eze 12:25; 24:14
11:25 [a] Nu 12:5 [b] ver 17 [c] 1Sa 10:6 [d] Ac 2:17 [e] 1Sa 10:10

[u] 3 *Taberah* means *burning*. [v] 25 Or *prophesied and continued to do so*

and they prophesied in the camp. 27A young man ran and told Moses, "Eldad and Medad are prophesying in the camp."

28Joshua son of Nun, who had been Moses' aide[a] since youth, spoke up and said, "Moses, my lord, stop them!"[b]

29But Moses replied, "Are you jealous for my sake? I wish that all the LORD's people were prophets[c] and that the LORD would put his Spirit on them!" 30Then Moses and the elders of Israel returned to the camp.

God supplies the people with quail.

31Now a wind went out from the LORD and drove quail[d] in from the sea. It brought them[w] down all around the camp to about three feet[x] above the ground, as far as a day's walk in any direction. 32All that day and night and all the next day the people went out and gathered quail. No one gathered less than ten homers.[y] Then they spread them out all around the camp. 33But while the meat was still between their teeth[e] and before it could be consumed, the anger of the LORD burned against the people, and he struck them with a severe plague.[f] 34Therefore the place was named Kibroth Hattaavah,[z][g] because there they buried the people who had craved other food.

35From Kibroth Hattaavah the people traveled to Hazeroth[h] and stayed there.

Miriam and Aaron oppose Moses.

12 Miriam and Aaron began to talk against Moses because of his Cushite wife,[i] for he had married a Cushite. 2"Has the LORD spoken only through Moses?" they asked. "Hasn't he also spoken through us?"[j] And the LORD heard this.[k]

3(Now Moses was a very humble man,[l] more humble than anyone else on the face of the earth.)

4At once the LORD said to Moses, Aaron and Miriam, "Come out to the Tent of Meeting, all three of you." So

11:28 [a]Ex 33:11; Jos 1:1 [b]Mk 9:38-40
11:29 [c]1Co 14:5
11:31 [d]Ex 16:13; Ps 78:26-28
11:33 [e]Ps 78:30 [f]Ps 106:15
11:34 [g]Dt 9:22
11:35 [h]Nu 33:17
12:1 [i]Ex 2:21
12:2 [j]Nu 16:3 [k]Nu 11:1
12:3 [l]Mt 11:29
12:5 [m]Nu 11:25
12:6 [n]Ge 15:1; 46:2 [o]Ge 31:10; 1Ki 3:5; Heb 1:1
12:7 [p]Jos 1:1-2; Ps 105:26 [q]Heb 3:2,5
12:8 [r]Dt 34:10 [s]Ex 20:4; Ps 17:15
12:9 [t]Ge 17:22
12:10 [u]Ex 4:6; Dt 24:9 [v]2Ki 5:1,27
12:11 [w]2Sa 19:19; 24:10
12:13 [x]Isa 30:26; Jer 17:14
12:14 [y]Dt 25:9; Job 17:6; 30:9-10; Isa 50:6 [z]Lev 13:46; Nu 5:2-3

the three of them came out. 5Then the LORD came down in a pillar of cloud;[m] he stood at the entrance to the Tent and summoned Aaron and Miriam. When both of them stepped forward, 6he said, "Listen to my words:

"When a prophet of the LORD is
among you,
I reveal myself to him in visions,[n]
I speak to him in dreams.[o]
7But this is not true of my servant
Moses;[p]
he is faithful in all my house.[q]
8With him I speak face to face,
clearly and not in riddles;[r]
he sees the form of the LORD.[s]
Why then were you not afraid
to speak against my servant
Moses?"

9The anger of the LORD burned against them, and he left them.[t]

Miriam is punished with leprosy.

10When the cloud lifted from above the Tent, there stood Miriam—leprous,[a] like snow.[u] Aaron turned toward her and saw that she had leprosy;[v] 11and he said to Moses, "Please, my lord, do not hold against us the sin we have so foolishly committed.[w] 12Do not let her be like a stillborn infant coming from its mother's womb with its flesh half eaten away."

13So Moses cried out to the LORD, "O God, please heal her![x]"

14The LORD replied to Moses, "If her father had spit in her face,[y] would she not have been in disgrace for seven days? Confine her outside the camp[z] for seven days; after that she can be brought back." 15So Miriam was confined outside the camp for seven days, and the people did not move on till she was brought back.

w*31* Or *They flew* x*31* Hebrew *two cubits* (about 1 meter) y*32* That is, probably about 60 bushels (about 2.2 kiloliters) z*34* *Kibroth Hattaavah* means *graves of craving*. a*10* The Hebrew word was used for various diseases affecting the skin—not necessarily leprosy.

[1]6After that, the people left Hazeroth[a]
and encamped in the Desert of Paran.

Men explore the land of Canaan.

13 The LORD said to Moses, 2"Send
some men to explore[b] the land of
Canaan, which I am giving to the Israelites. From each ancestral tribe send
one of its leaders."
3So at the LORD's command Moses
sent them out from the Desert of Paran.
All of them were leaders of the Israelites. 4These are their names:

from the tribe of Reuben, Shammua
son of Zaccur;
5from the tribe of Simeon, Shaphat
son of Hori;
6from the tribe of Judah, Caleb son
of Jephunneh;[c]
7from the tribe of Issachar, Igal son
of Joseph;
8from the tribe of Ephraim, Hoshea
son of Nun;
9from the tribe of Benjamin, Palti
son of Raphu;
10from the tribe of Zebulun, Gaddiel
son of Sodi;
11from the tribe of Manasseh (a tribe
of Joseph), Gaddi son of Susi;
12from the tribe of Dan, Ammiel son
of Gemalli;
13from the tribe of Asher, Sethur son
of Michael;
14from the tribe of Naphtali, Nahbi
son of Vophsi;
15from the tribe of Gad, Geuel son of
Maki.

16These are the names of the men
Moses sent to explore the land. (Moses
gave Hoshea son of Nun[d] the name
Joshua.)[e]
17When Moses sent them to explore
Canaan, he said, "Go up through the
Negev[f] and on into the hill country.[g]
18See what the land is like and whether
the people who live there are strong or
weak, few or many. 19What kind of
land do they live in? Is it good or bad?
What kind of towns do they live in?
Are they unwalled or fortified? 20How is

12:16 [a]Nu 11:35
13:2 [b]Dt 1:22
13:6 [c]ver 30; Nu 14:6,24; 34:19; Jdg 1:12-15
13:16 [d]ver 8 [e]Dt 32:44
13:17 [f]Ge 12:9 [g]Jdg 1:9
13:20 [h]Dt 1:25
13:21 [i]Nu 20:1; 27:14; 33:36; Jos 15:1 [j]Jos 19:28 [k]Jos 13:5
13:22 [l]Jos 15:14 [m]Jos 15:13 [n]Ps 78:12,43; Isa 19:11,13
13:26 [o]Nu 32:8

the soil? Is it fertile or poor? Are there
trees on it or not? Do your best to bring
back some of the fruit of the land.[h]" (It
was the season for the first ripe grapes.)
21So they went up and explored the
land from the Desert of Zin[i] as far as
Rehob,[j] toward Lebo[b] Hamath.[k] 22They
went up through the Negev and came to
Hebron, where Ahiman, Sheshai and
Talmai,[l] the descendants of Anak,[m] lived.
(Hebron had been built seven years
before Zoan in Egypt.)[n] 23When they
reached the Valley of Eshcol,[c] they cut
off a branch bearing a single cluster of
grapes. Two of them carried it on a pole
between them, along with some pomegranates and figs. 24That place was
called the Valley of Eshcol because of
the cluster of grapes the Israelites cut
off there. 25At the end of forty days they
returned from exploring the land.

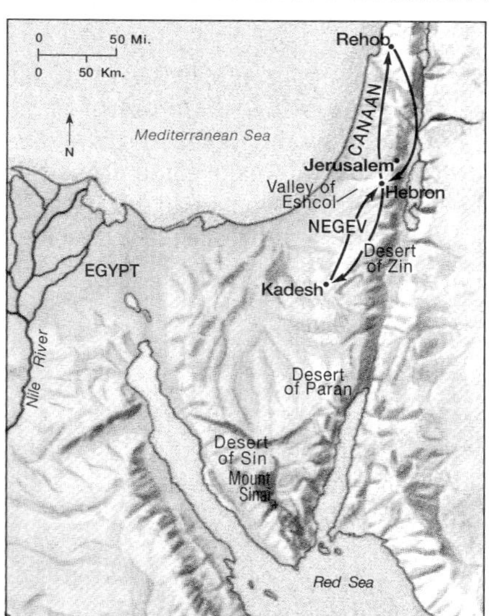

Route of the Spies

The spies traveled from Kadesh at the southernmost edge of the Desert of Zin to Rehob at the northernmost edge and back, a round trip of about 500 miles.

26They came back to Moses and
Aaron and the whole Israelite commu-
nity at Kadesh in the Desert of Paran.
There they reported to them[o] and to the

b *21* Or *toward the entrance to* c *23* *Eshcol* means *cluster*; also in verse 24.

whole assembly and showed them the fruit of the land. 27They gave Moses this account: "We went into the land to which you sent us, and it does flow with milk and honey![a] Here is its fruit.[b] 28But the people who live there are powerful, and the cities are fortified and very large.[c] We even saw descendants of Anak there. 29The Amalekites live in the Negev; the Hittites, Jebusites and Amorites live in the hill country; and the Canaanites live near the sea and along the Jordan."

30Then Caleb silenced the people before Moses and said, "We should go up and take possession of the land, for we can certainly do it."

31But the men who had gone up with him said, "We can't attack those people; they are stronger than we are."[d] 32And they spread among the Israelites a bad report[e] about the land they had explored. They said, "The land we explored devours[f] those living in it. All the people we saw there are of great size.[g] 33We saw the Nephilim[h] there (the descendants of Anak[i] come from the Nephilim). We seemed like grasshoppers in our own eyes, and we looked the same to them."

The Israelites refuse to enter Canaan.

14 That night all the people of the community raised their voices and wept aloud. 2All the Israelites grumbled against Moses and Aaron, and the whole assembly said to them, "If only we had died in Egypt! Or in this desert![j] 3Why is the LORD bringing us to this land only to let us fall by the sword? Our wives and children will be taken as plunder. Wouldn't it be better for us to go back to Egypt?" 4And they said to each other, "We should choose a leader and go back to Egypt.[k]"

Moses intercedes for the people.

5Then Moses and Aaron fell facedown[l] in front of the whole Israelite assembly gathered there. 6Joshua son of Nun and Caleb son of Jephunneh, who were among those who had explored the land, tore their clothes 7and said to the entire Israelite assembly, "The land we passed through and explored is exceedingly good.[m] 8If the LORD is pleased with us,[n] he will lead us into that land, a land flowing with milk and honey,[o] and will give it to us. 9Only do not rebel[p] against the LORD. And do not be afraid of the people of the land,[q] because we will swallow them up. Their protection is gone, but the LORD is with us. Do not be afraid of them."

10But the whole assembly talked about stoning[r] them. Then the glory of the LORD[s] appeared at the Tent of Meeting to all the Israelites. 11The LORD said to Moses, "How long will these people treat me with contempt? How long will they refuse to believe in me,[t] in spite of all the miraculous signs I have performed among them? 12I will strike them down with a plague and destroy them, but I will make you into a nation[u] greater and stronger than they."

13Moses said to the LORD, "Then the Egyptians will hear about it! By your power you brought these people up from among them.[v] 14And they will tell the inhabitants of this land about it. They have already heard[w] that you, O LORD, are with these people and that you, O LORD, have been seen face to face, that your cloud stays over them, and that you go before them in a pillar of cloud by day and a pillar of fire by night.[x] 15If you put these people to death all at one time, the nations who have heard this report about you will say, 16'The LORD was not able to bring these people into the land he promised them on oath; so he slaughtered them in the desert.'[y]

17"Now may the Lord's strength be displayed, just as you have declared: 18'The LORD is slow to anger, abounding in love and forgiving sin and rebellion.[z] Yet he does not leave the guilty unpunished; he punishes the children for the sin of the fathers to the third and fourth generation.'[a] 19In accordance with your

13:27 [a]Ex 3:8 [b]Dt 1:25
13:28 [c]Dt 1:28; 9:1,2
13:31 [d]Dt 1:28; 9:1; Jos 14:8
13:32 [e]Nu 14:36,37 [f]Eze 36:13,14 [g]Am 2:9
13:33 [h]Ge 6:4 [i]Dt 1:28
14:2 [j]Nu 11:1
14:4 [k]Ne 9:17
14:5 [l]Nu 16:4,22, 45
14:7 [m]Nu 13:27; Dt 1:25
14:8 [n]Dt 10:15 [o]Nu 13:27
14:9 [p]Dt 1:26; 9:7,23,24 [q]Dt 1:21; 7:18; 20:1
14:10 [r]Ex 17:4 [s]Lev 9:23
14:11 [t]Ps 78:22; 106:24
14:12 [u]Ex 32:10
14:13 [v]Ex 32:11-14; Ps 106:23
14:14 [w]Ex 15:14 [x]Ex 13:21
14:16 [y]Jos 7:7
14:18 [z]Ex 34:6; Ps 145:8; Jnh 4:2 [a]Ex 20:5

great love, forgive[a] the sin of these people,[b] just as you have pardoned them
from the time they left Egypt until
now."[c]

The Israelites' punishment is forty years in the desert.

20The LORD replied, "I have forgiven
them,[d] as you asked. 21Nevertheless, as
surely as I live[e] and as surely as the glory
of the LORD fills the whole earth,[f] 22not
one of the men who saw my glory and
the miraculous signs I performed in
Egypt and in the desert but who disobeyed me and tested me ten times[g]—
23not one of them will ever see the land
I promised on oath[h] to their forefathers.
No one who has treated me with contempt will ever see it.[i] 24But because
my servant Caleb has a different spirit
and follows me wholeheartedly,[j] I will
bring him into the land he went to, and
his descendants will inherit it.[k] 25Since
the Amalekites and Canaanites are living in the valleys, turn[l] back tomorrow
and set out toward the desert along the
route to the Red Sea.[d]"
26The LORD said to Moses and Aaron:
27"How long will this wicked community grumble against me? I have heard
the complaints of these grumbling Israelites.[m] 28So tell them, 'As surely as I
live,[n] declares the LORD, I will do to you
the very things I heard you say: 29In this
desert your bodies will fall[o]—every one
of you twenty years old or more[p] who
was counted in the census and who has
grumbled against me. 30Not one of you
will enter the land I swore with uplifted
hand to make your home, except Caleb
son of Jephunneh and Joshua son of
Nun. 31As for your children that you
said would be taken as plunder, I will
bring them in to enjoy the land you
have rejected.[q] 32But you—your bodies
will fall[r] in this desert. 33Your children
will be shepherds here for forty years,
suffering for your unfaithfulness, until
the last of your bodies lies in the desert.
34For forty years—one year for each of
the forty days you explored the land[s]—
you will suffer for your sins and know
what it is like to have me against you.'
35I, the LORD, have spoken, and I will
surely do these things[t] to this whole
wicked community, which has banded
together against me. They will meet
their end in this desert; here they will
die."
36So the men Moses had sent[u] to
explore the land, who returned and
made the whole community grumble
against him by spreading a bad report[v]
about it— 37these men responsible for
spreading the bad report[w] about the
land were struck down and died of a
plague[x] before the LORD. 38Of the men
who went to explore the land, only Joshua son of Nun and Caleb son of Jephunneh survived.[y]
39When Moses reported this to all
the Israelites, they mourned[z] bitterly.
40Early the next morning they went up
toward the high hill country. "We have
sinned[a]," they said. "We will go up to
the place the LORD promised."
41But Moses said, "Why are you disobeying the LORD's command? This will
not succeed![b] 42Do not go up, because
the LORD is not with you. You will be
defeated by your enemies,[c] 43for the
Amalekites and Canaanites will face you
there. Because you have turned away
from the LORD, he will not be with you
and you will fall by the sword."
44Nevertheless, in their presumption
they went up[d] toward the high hill country, though neither Moses nor the ark
of the LORD's covenant moved from the
camp.[e] 45Then the Amalekites and Canaanites who lived in that hill country
came down and attacked them and beat
them down all the way to Hormah.[f]

Regulations: Supplementary offerings.

15 The LORD said to Moses,
2"Speak to the Israelites and say
to them: 'After you enter the land I am
giving you[g] as a home 3and you present
to the LORD offerings made by fire, from

14:19 [a]Ex 34:9 [b]Ps 106:45 [c]Ps 78:38
14:20 [d]Ps 106:23; Mic 7:18-20
14:21 [e]Dt 32:40; Isa 49:18 [f]Ps 72:19; Isa 6:3; Hab 2:14
14:22 [g]Ex 14:11; 32:1; 1Co 10:5
14:23 [h]Nu 32:11 [i]Heb 3:18
14:24 [j]ver 6-9; Jos 14:8,14 [k]Nu 32:12
14:25 [l]Dt 1:40
14:27 [m]Ex 16:12
14:28 [n]ver 21
14:29 [o]Nu 26:65 [p]Nu 1:45
14:31 [q]Ps 106:24
14:32 [r]1Co 10:5
14:34 [s]Nu 13:25
14:35 [t]Nu 23:19
14:36 [u]Nu 13:4-16 [v]Nu 13:32
14:37 [w]1Co 10:10 [x]Nu 16:49
14:38 [y]Jos 14:6
14:39 [z]Ex 33:4
14:40 [a]Dt 1:41
14:41 [b]2Ch 24:20
14:42 [c]Dt 1:42
14:44 [d]Dt 1:43 [e]Nu 31:6
14:45 [f]Nu 21:3; Dt 1:44; Jdg 1:17
15:2 [g]Lev 23:10

[d]25 Hebrew *Yam Suph*; that is, Sea of Reeds

the herd or the flock,[a] as an aroma
pleasing to the LORD[b]—whether burnt
offerings[c] or sacrifices, for special vows
or freewill offerings[d] or festival offerings[e]— 4then the one who brings his
offering shall present to the LORD a
grain offering[f] of a tenth of an ephah[e] of
fine flour mixed with a quarter of a hin[f]
of oil. 5With each lamb for the burnt offering or the sacrifice, prepare a quarter
of a hin of wine[g] as a drink offering.
6"'With a ram[h] prepare a grain offering[i] of two-tenths of an ephah[g] of fine
flour mixed with a third of a hin[h] of
oil,[j] 7and a third of a hin of wine as a
drink offering. Offer it as an aroma
pleasing to the LORD.
8"'When you prepare a young bull as
a burnt offering or sacrifice, for a special vow or a fellowship offering[i][k] to the
LORD, 9bring with the bull a grain offering of three-tenths of an ephah[j][l] of fine
flour mixed with half a hin[k] of oil. 10Also
bring half a hin of wine as a drink offering. It will be an offering made by fire,
an aroma pleasing to the LORD. 11Each
bull or ram, each lamb or young goat,
is to be prepared in this manner. 12Do
this for each one, for as many as you
prepare.
13"'Everyone who is native-born[m]
must do these things in this way when
he brings an offering made by fire as
an aroma pleasing to the LORD. 14For
the generations to come, whenever an
alien or anyone else living among you
presents an offering made by fire as an
aroma pleasing to the LORD, he must do
exactly as you do. 15The community is
to have the same rules for you and for
the alien living among you; this is a
lasting ordinance for the generations
to come.[n] You and the alien shall be
the same before the LORD: 16The same
laws and regulations will apply both to
you and to the alien living among
you.[o]'"
17The LORD said to Moses, 18"Speak to
the Israelites and say to them: 'When
you enter the land to which I am taking
you 19and you eat the food of the land,[p]
present a portion as an offering to the
LORD. 20Present a cake from the first of
your ground meal[q] and present it as an
offering from the threshing floor.[r]
21Throughout the generations to come
you are to give this offering to the LORD
from the first of your ground meal.[s]

Regulations: Sin offerings.

22"'Now if you unintentionally fail to
keep any of these commands the LORD
gave Moses[t]— 23any of the LORD's commands to you through him, from the
day the LORD gave them and continuing
through the generations to come— 24and
if this is done unintentionally without
the community being aware of it,[u] then
the whole community is to offer a young
bull for a burnt offering[v] as an aroma
pleasing to the LORD, along with its
prescribed grain offering and drink offering, and a male goat for a sin offering.[w] 25The priest is to make atonement
for the whole Israelite community, and
they will be forgiven,[x] for it was not
intentional and they have brought to
the LORD for their wrong an offering
made by fire and a sin offering. 26The
whole Israelite community and the
aliens living among them will be forgiv-
en, because all the people were involved in the unintentional wrong.[y]
27"'But if just one person sins unintentionally,[z] he must bring a year-old
female goat for a sin offering. 28The
priest is to make atonement before the
LORD for the one who erred by sinning
unintentionally, and when atonement
has been made for him, he will be forgiven.[a] 29One and the same law applies
to everyone who sins unintentionally,
whether he is a native-born Israelite or
an alien.
30"'But anyone who sins defiantly,[b]
whether native-born or alien,[c] blasphemes the LORD, and that person must

15:3 [a]Lev 1:2 [b]ver 24; Ge 8:21; Ex 29:18 [c]Nu 28:19,27 [d]Lev 22:18, 21; Ezr 1:4 [e]Lev 23:1-44
15:4 [f]Lev 2:1; 6:14
15:5 [g]Nu 28:7,14
15:6 [h]Lev 5:15 [i]Nu 28:12 [j]Eze 46:14
15:8 [k]Lev 1:3; 3:1
15:9 [l]Lev 14:10
15:13 [m]Lev 16:29
15:15 [n]ver 29; Nu 9:14
15:16 [o]Nu 9:14
15:19 [p]Jos 5:11,12
15:20 [q]Ex 34:26; Lev 23:14; Dt 26:2,10 [r]Lev 2:14
15:21 [s]Ro 11:16
15:22 [t]Lev 4:2
15:24 [u]Lev 5:15 [v]Lev 4:14 [w]Lev 4:3
15:25 [x]Lev 4:20; Ro 3:25; Heb 2:17
15:26 [y]ver 24
15:27 [z]Lev 4:27
15:28 [a]Lev 4:35
15:30 [b]Nu 14:40-44; Dt 1:43; 17:13; Ps 19:13 [c]ver 14

[e]*4* That is, probably about 2 quarts (about 2 liters) [f]*4* That is, probably about 1 quart (about 1 liter); also in verse 5 [g]*6* That is, probably about 4 quarts (about 4.5 liters) [h]*6* That is, probably about 1 1/4 quarts (about 1.2 liters); also in verse 7 [i]*8* Traditionally *peace offering* [j]*9* That is, probably about 6 quarts (about 6.5 liters) [k]*9* That is, probably about 2 quarts (about 2 liters); also in verse 10

be cut off from his people. 31Because he has despised the LORD's word and broken his commands,[a] that person must surely be cut off; his guilt remains on him.[b]'"

Stoning a man for breaking the Sabbath.

32While the Israelites were in the desert, a man was found gathering wood on the Sabbath day.[c] 33Those who found him gathering wood brought him to Moses and Aaron and the whole assembly, 34and they kept him in custody, because it was not clear what should be done to him.[d] 35Then the LORD said to Moses, "The man must die.[e] The whole assembly must stone him outside the camp.[f]" 36So the assembly took him outside the camp and stoned him to death, as the LORD commanded Moses.

Tassels on corners of garments.

37The LORD said to Moses, 38"Speak to the Israelites and say to them: 'Throughout the generations to come you are to make tassels on the corners of your garments,[g] with a blue cord on each tassel. 39You will have these tassels to look at and so you will remember[h] all the commands of the LORD, that you may obey them and not prostitute yourselves by going after the lusts of your own hearts and eyes. 40Then you will remember to obey all my commands and will be consecrated to your God.[i] 41I am the LORD your God, who brought you out of Egypt to be your God. I am the LORD your God.'"

Korah, Dathan and Abiram lead a rebellion.

16 Korah[j] son of Izhar, the son of Kohath, the son of Levi, and certain Reubenites—Dathan and Abiram, sons of Eliab,[k] and On son of Peleth—became insolent[l] 2and rose up against Moses. With them were 250 Israelite men, well-known community leaders who had been appointed members of the council.[l] 3They came as a group to oppose Moses and Aaron[m] and said to them, "You have gone too far! The whole community is holy,[n] every one of them, and the LORD is with them.[o] Why then do you set yourselves above the LORD's assembly?"[p]

4When Moses heard this, he fell facedown.[q] 5Then he said to Korah and all his followers: "In the morning the LORD will show who belongs to him and who is holy,[r] and he will have that person come near him. The man he chooses[s] he will cause to come near him. 6You, Korah, and all your followers are to do this: Take censers 7and tomorrow put fire and incense in them before the LORD. The man the LORD chooses will be the one who is holy. You Levites have gone too far!"

8Moses also said to Korah, "Now listen, you Levites! 9Isn't it enough for you that the God of Israel has separated you from the rest of the Israelite community and brought you near himself to do the work at the LORD's tabernacle and to stand before the community and minister to them?[t] 10He has brought you and all your fellow Levites near himself, but now you are trying to get the priesthood too.[u] 11It is against the LORD that you and all your followers have banded together. Who is Aaron that you should grumble[v] against him?[w]"

12Then Moses summoned Dathan and Abiram, the sons of Eliab. But they said, "We will not come! 13Isn't it enough that you have brought us up out of a land flowing with milk and honey to kill us in the desert?[x] And now you also want to lord it over us?[y] 14Moreover, you haven't brought us into a land flowing with milk and honey[z] or given us an inheritance of fields and vineyards.[a] Will you gouge out the eyes of[m] these men?[b] No, we will not come!"

15Then Moses became very angry and said to the LORD, "Do not accept their

15:31 [a]2Sa 12:9; Ps 119:126; Pr 13:13 [b]Lev 5:1; Eze 18:20
15:32 [c]Ex 31:14,15; 35:2,3
15:34 [d]Nu 9:8
15:35 [e]Ex 31:14,15; Dt 21:21 [f]Lev 20:2; 24:14; Ac 7:58
15:38 [g]Dt 22:12; Mt 23:5
15:39 [h]Dt 4:23; 6:12; Ps 73:27
15:40 [i]Lev 11:44; Ro 12:1; Col 1:22; 1Pe 1:15
16:1 [j]Jude 1:11 [k]Nu 26:8; Dt 11:6
16:2 [l]Nu 1:16; 26:9
16:3 [m]ver 7; Ps 106:16 [n]Ex 19:6 [o]Nu 14:14 [p]Nu 12:2
16:4 [q]Nu 14:5
16:5 [r]Lev 10:3; 2Ti 2:19* [s]Nu 17:5; Ps 65:4
16:9 [t]Nu 3:6; Dt 10:8
16:10 [u]Nu 3:10; 18:7
16:11 [v]1Co 10:10 [w]Ex 16:7
16:13 [x]Nu 14:2 [y]Ac 7:27,35
16:14 [z]Lev 20:24 [a]Ex 22:5; 23:11; Nu 20:5 [b]Jdg 16:21; 1Sa 11:2

[l] *1* Or *Peleth—took* ⌊*men*⌋ [m] *14* Or *you make slaves of*; or *you deceive*

offering. I have not taken so much as a
donkey[a] from them, nor have I wronged
any of them."
16 Moses said to Korah, "You and all
your followers are to appear before the
LORD tomorrow—you and they and
Aaron.[b] 17 Each man is to take his censer
and put incense in it—250 censers in
all—and present it before the LORD. You
and Aaron are to present your censers
also." 18 So each man took his censer,
put fire and incense in it, and stood
with Moses and Aaron at the entrance
to the Tent of Meeting. 19 When Korah
had gathered all his followers in opposition to them[c] at the entrance to the
Tent of Meeting, the glory of the LORD[d]
appeared to the entire assembly. 20 The
LORD said to Moses and Aaron, 21 "Separate yourselves from this assembly so I
can put an end to them at once."[e]
22 But Moses and Aaron fell facedown[f] and cried out, "O God, God of
the spirits of all mankind,[g] will you be
angry with the entire assembly when
only one man sins?"[h]

God destroys the rebels.

23 Then the LORD said to Moses, 24 "Say
to the assembly, 'Move away from the
tents of Korah, Dathan and Abiram.'"
25 Moses got up and went to Dathan
and Abiram, and the elders of Israel followed him. 26 He warned the assembly,
"Move back from the tents of these
wicked men![i] Do not touch anything
belonging to them, or you will be swept
away[j] because of all their sins." 27 So
they moved away from the tents of
Korah, Dathan and Abiram. Dathan and
Abiram had come out and were standing with their wives, children and little
ones at the entrances to their tents.
28 Then Moses said, "This is how you
will know that the LORD has sent me[k] to
do all these things and that it was not
my idea: 29 If these men die a natural
death and experience only what usually
happens to men, then the LORD has not
sent me.[l] 30 But if the LORD brings about
something totally new, and the earth
opens its mouth and swallows them,
with everything that belongs to them,
and they go down alive into the grave,[n][m]
then you will know that these men
have treated the LORD with contempt."
31 As soon as he finished saying all
this, the ground under them split apart[n]
32 and the earth opened its mouth and
swallowed them,[o] with their households
and all Korah's men and all their possessions. 33 They went down alive into the
grave, with everything they owned; the
earth closed over them, and they perished and were gone from the community. 34 At their cries, all the Israelites
around them fled, shouting, "The earth
is going to swallow us too!"
35 And fire came out from the LORD[p]
and consumed[q] the 250 men who were
offering the incense.
36 The LORD said to Moses, 37 "Tell
Eleazar son of Aaron, the priest, to take
the censers out of the smoldering remains and scatter the coals some distance away, for the censers are holy—
38 the censers of the men who sinned at
the cost of their lives.[r] Hammer the
censers into sheets to overlay the altar,
for they were presented before the LORD
and have become holy. Let them be a
sign[s] to the Israelites."
39 So Eleazar the priest collected the
bronze censers brought by those who
had been burned up, and he had them
hammered out to overlay the altar, 40 as
the LORD directed him through Moses.
This was to remind the Israelites that
no one except a descendant of Aaron
should come to burn incense[t] before
the LORD,[u] or he would become like
Korah and his followers.[v]

A plague kills 14,700 people.

41 The next day the whole Israelite
community grumbled against Moses and
Aaron. "You have killed the LORD's people," they said.
42 But when the assembly gathered
in opposition[w] to Moses and Aaron and
turned toward the Tent of Meeting, suddenly the cloud covered it and the glory

16:15 [a] 1Sa 12:3
16:16 [b] ver 6
16:19 [c] ver 42 [d] Ex 16:7; Nu 14:10; 20:6
16:21 [e] Ex 32:10
16:22 [f] Nu 14:5 [g] Nu 27:16; Job 12:10; Heb 12:9 [h] Ge 18:23
16:26 [i] Isa 52:11 [j] Ge 19:15
16:28 [k] Ex 3:12; Jn 5:36; 6:38
16:29 [l] Ecc 3:19
16:30 [m] ver 33; Ps 55:15
16:31 [n] Mic 1:3-4
16:32 [o] Nu 26:11; Dt 11:6; Ps 106:17
16:35 [p] Nu 11:1-3; 26:10 [q] Lev 10:2
16:38 [r] Pr 20:2 [s] Nu 26:10; Eze 14:8; 2Pe 2:6
16:40 [t] Ex 30:7-10; Nu 1:51 [u] 2Ch 26:18 [v] Nu 3:10
16:42 [w] ver 19; Nu 20:6

[n] *30* Hebrew *Sheol*; also in verse 33

of the LORD appeared. 43 Then Moses
and Aaron went to the front of the Tent
of Meeting, 44 and the LORD said to
Moses, 45 "Get away from this assembly
so I can put an end to them at once."
And they fell facedown.
46 Then Moses said to Aaron, "Take
your censer and put incense in it, along
with fire from the altar, and hurry to the
assembly[a] to make atonement[b] for them.
Wrath has come out from the LORD; the
plague[c] has started." 47 So Aaron did as
Moses said, and ran into the midst of
the assembly. The plague had already
started among the people,[d] but Aaron
offered the incense and made atonement for them. 48 He stood between the
living and the dead, and the plague stopped.[e] 49 But 14,700 people died from the
plague, in addition to those who had
died because of Korah.[f] 50 Then Aaron
returned to Moses at the entrance to
the Tent of Meeting, for the plague had
stopped.

The budding of Aaron's staff.

17 The LORD said to Moses,
2 "Speak to the Israelites and get
twelve staffs from them, one from the
leader of each of their ancestral tribes.
Write the name of each man on his staff.
3 On the staff of Levi write Aaron's
name,[g] for there must be one staff for
the head of each ancestral tribe. 4 Place
them in the Tent of Meeting in front of
the Testimony,[h] where I meet with you.[i]
5 The staff belonging to the man I
choose[j] will sprout, and I will rid myself
of this constant grumbling against you
by the Israelites."
6 So Moses spoke to the Israelites, and
their leaders gave him twelve staffs, one
for the leader of each of their ancestral
tribes, and Aaron's staff was among
them. 7 Moses placed the staffs before
the LORD in the Tent of the Testimony.[k]
8 The next day Moses entered the Tent
of the Testimony and saw that Aaron's
staff, which represented the house of
Levi, had not only sprouted but had budded, blossomed and produced almonds.[l]
9 Then Moses brought out all the staffs
from the LORD's presence to all the Israelites. They looked at them, and each
man took his own staff.
10 The LORD said to Moses, "Put back
Aaron's staff in front of the Testimony, to
be kept as a sign to the rebellious.[m] This
will put an end to their grumbling against
me, so that they will not die." 11 Moses
did just as the LORD commanded him.
12 The Israelites said to Moses, "We
will die! We are lost, we are all lost![n]
13 Anyone who even comes near the
tabernacle of the LORD will die.[o] Are we
all going to die?"

*Instructions for the priests
and Levites.*

18 The LORD said to Aaron, "You,
your sons and your father's family
are to bear the responsibility for offenses
against the sanctuary,[p] and you and
your sons alone are to bear the responsibility for offenses against the priesthood. 2 Bring your fellow Levites from
your ancestral tribe to join you and
assist you when you and your sons
minister[q] before the Tent of the Testimony. 3 They are to be responsible to
you and are to perform all the duties of
the Tent,[r] but they must not go near
the furnishings of the sanctuary or the
altar, or both they and you will die.[s]
4 They are to join you and be responsible
for the care of the Tent of Meeting—
all the work at the Tent—and no one
else may come near where you are.
5 "You are to be responsible for the
care of the sanctuary and the altar,[t] so
that wrath will not fall on the Israelites
again. 6 I myself have selected your fellow Levites from among the Israelites
as a gift to you,[u] dedicated to the LORD
to do the work at the Tent of Meeting.
7 But only you and your sons may serve
as priests in connection with everything
at the altar and inside the curtain.[v] I am
giving you the service of the priesthood
as a gift.[w] Anyone else who comes near
the sanctuary must be put to death.[x]"
8 Then the LORD said to Aaron, "I

16:46 [a]Lev 10:6 [b]Nu 18:5; 25:13; Dt 9:22 [c]Nu 8:19; Ps 106:29
16:47 [d]Nu 25:6-8
16:48 [e]Nu 25:8; Ps 106:30
16:49 [f]ver 32
17:3 [g]Nu 1:3
17:4 [h]ver 7 [i]Ex 25:22
17:5 [j]Nu 16:5
17:7 [k]Ex 38:21; Ac 7:44
17:8 [l]Eze 17:24; Heb 9:4
17:10 [m]Dt 9:24
17:12 [n]Isa 6:5
17:13 [o]Nu 1:51
18:1 [p]Ex 28:38
18:2 [q]Nu 3:10
18:3 [r]Nu 1:51 [s]ver 7; Nu 4:15
18:5 [t]Nu 16:46
18:6 [u]Nu 3:9
18:7 [v]Heb 9:3,6 [w]ver 20; Ex 29:9 [x]Nu 3:10

myself have put you in charge of the
offerings presented to me; all the holy
offerings the Israelites give me I give
to you and your sons as your portion
and regular share.[a] **9**You are to have the
part of the most holy offerings that is kept
from the fire. From all the gifts they bring
me as most holy offerings, whether
grain[b] or sin[c] or guilt offerings,[d] that part
belongs to you and your sons. **10**Eat it
as something most holy; every male
shall eat it.[e] You must regard it as holy.
11"This also is yours: whatever is set
aside from the gifts of all the wave offerings[f] of the Israelites. I give this to you
and your sons and daughters as your
regular share. Everyone in your household who is ceremonially clean[g] may
eat it.
12"I give you all the finest olive oil
and all the finest new wine and grain
they give the LORD as the firstfruits of
their harvest.[h] **13**All the land's firstfruits that they bring to the LORD will
be yours.[i] Everyone in your household
who is ceremonially clean may eat it.
14"Everything in Israel that is devoted[o]
to the LORD[j] is yours. **15**The first offspring of every womb, both man and
animal, that is offered to the LORD is
yours.[k] But you must redeem[l] every firstborn son and every firstborn male of
unclean animals.[m] **16**When they are a
month old, you must redeem them at
the redemption price set at five shekels[p][n] of silver, according to the sanctuary
shekel,[o] which weighs twenty gerahs.
17"But you must not redeem the firstborn of an ox, a sheep or a goat; they
are holy.[p] Sprinkle their blood[q] on the
altar and burn their fat as an offering
made by fire, an aroma pleasing to the
LORD. **18**Their meat is to be yours, just as
the breast of the wave offering[r] and the
right thigh are yours. **19**Whatever is set
aside from the holy offerings the Israelites present to the LORD I give to you
and your sons and daughters as your regular share. It is an everlasting covenant
of salt[s] before the LORD for both you and
your offspring."
20The LORD said to Aaron, "You will
have no inheritance in their land, nor
will you have any share among them;[t] I
am your share and your inheritance[u]
among the Israelites.
21"I give to the Levites all the tithes[v]
in Israel as their inheritance[w] in return
for the work they do while serving at
the Tent of Meeting. **22**From now on the
Israelites must not go near the Tent of
Meeting, or they will bear the consequences of their sin and will die.[x] **23**It is
the Levites who are to do the work at the
Tent of Meeting and bear the responsibility for offenses against it. This is a
lasting ordinance for the generations to
come. They will receive no inheritance[y]
among the Israelites. **24**Instead, I give to
the Levites as their inheritance the
tithes that the Israelites present as an
offering to the LORD. That is why I said
concerning them: 'They will have no
inheritance among the Israelites.'"
25The LORD said to Moses, **26**"Speak to
the Levites and say to them: 'When you
receive from the Israelites the tithe I
give you[z] as your inheritance, you must
present a tenth of that tithe as the
LORD's offering.[a] **27**Your offering will be
reckoned to you as grain from the
threshing floor or juice from the winepress. **28**In this way you also will present
an offering to the LORD from all the
tithes[b] you receive from the Israelites.
From these tithes you must give the
LORD's portion to Aaron the priest. **29**You
must present as the LORD's portion the
best and holiest part of everything given
to you.'
30"Say to the Levites: 'When you
present the best part, it will be reckoned to you as the product of the
threshing floor or the winepress.[c] **31**You
and your households may eat the rest
of it anywhere, for it is your wages for
your work at the Tent of Meeting. **32**By
presenting the best part[d] of it you will
not be guilty in this matter; then you
will not defile the holy offerings[e] of the
Israelites, and you will not die.'"

18:8 [a]Lev 6:16; 7:6,31-34,36
18:9 [b]Lev 2:1 [c]Lev 6:25 [d]Lev 5:15; 7:7
18:10 [e]Lev 6:16
18:11 [f]Ex 29:26 [g]Lev 22:1-16
18:12 [h]Ex 23:19; Ne 10:35
18:13 [i]Ex 22:29; 23:19
18:14 [j]Lev 27:28
18:15 [k]Ex 13:2 [l]Nu 3:46 [m]Ex 13:13
18:16 [n]Lev 27:6 [o]Ex 30:13
18:17 [p]Dt 15:19 [q]Lev 3:2
18:18 [r]Lev 7:30
18:19 [s]Lev 2:13; 2Ch 13:5
18:20 [t]Dt 12:12 [u]Dt 10:9; 14:27; 18:1-2; Jos 13:33; Eze 44:28
18:21 [v]Dt 14:22; Mal 3:8 [w]Lev 27:30-33; Heb 7:5
18:22 [x]Lev 22:9; Nu 1:51
18:23 [y]ver 20
18:26 [z]ver 21 [a]Ne 10:38
18:28 [b]Mal 3:8
18:30 [c]ver 27
18:32 [d]Lev 22:15 [e]Lev 19:8

o *14* The Hebrew term refers to the irrevocable giving over of things or persons to the LORD. p *16* That is, about 2 ounces (about 55 grams)

The red heifer sacrifice and the water of purification.

19 The LORD said to Moses and
Aaron: 2"This is a requirement of
the law that the LORD has commanded:
Tell the Israelites to bring you a red
heifer[a] without defect or blemish[b] and
that has never been under a yoke.[c]
3Give it to Eleazar[d] the priest; it is to
be taken outside the camp[e] and slaughtered in his presence. 4Then Eleazar the
priest is to take some of its blood on
his finger and sprinkle[f] it seven times
toward the front of the Tent of Meeting.
5While he watches, the heifer is to be
burned—its hide, flesh, blood and
offal.[g] 6The priest is to take some cedar
wood, hyssop[h] and scarlet wool[i] and
throw them onto the burning heifer.
7After that, the priest must wash his
clothes and bathe himself with water.[j]
He may then come into the camp, but
he will be ceremonially unclean till
evening. 8The man who burns it must
also wash his clothes and bathe with
water, and he too will be unclean till
evening.
9"A man who is clean shall gather up
the ashes of the heifer[k] and put them
in a ceremonially clean place outside the
camp. They shall be kept by the Israelite community for use in the water of
cleansing;[l] it is for purification from sin.
10The man who gathers up the ashes of
the heifer must also wash his clothes,
and he too will be unclean till evening.
This will be a lasting ordinance both
for the Israelites and for the aliens living
among them.
11"Whoever touches the dead body[m]
of anyone will be unclean for seven
days.[n] 12He must purify himself with the
water on the third day and on the seventh day;[o] then he will be clean. But if
he does not purify himself on the third
and seventh days, he will not be clean.
13Whoever touches the dead body[p] of
anyone and fails to purify himself defiles
the LORD's tabernacle.[q] That person
must be cut off from Israel.[r] Because the
water of cleansing has not been sprinkled on him, he is unclean;[s] his uncleanness remains on him.
14"This is the law that applies when a
person dies in a tent: Anyone who
enters the tent and anyone who is in it
will be unclean for seven days, 15and
every open container without a lid fastened on it will be unclean.
16"Anyone out in the open who
touches someone who has been killed
with a sword or someone who has died
a natural death,[t] or anyone who touches
a human bone or a grave,[u] will be unclean for seven days.
17"For the unclean person, put some
ashes[v] from the burned purification offering into a jar and pour fresh water over
them. 18Then a man who is ceremonially clean is to take some hyssop,[w] dip it
in the water and sprinkle the tent and
all the furnishings and the people who
were there. He must also sprinkle anyone who has touched a human bone or a
grave or someone who has been killed
or someone who has died a natural
death. 19The man who is clean is to
sprinkle the unclean person on the third
and seventh days, and on the seventh
day he is to purify him.[x] The person
being cleansed must wash his clothes
and bathe with water, and that evening
he will be clean. 20But if a person who is
unclean does not purify himself, he must
be cut off from the community, because
he has defiled the sanctuary of the LORD.
The water of cleansing has not been
sprinkled on him, and he is unclean.
21This is a lasting ordinance for them.
"The man who sprinkles the water of
cleansing must also wash his clothes,
and anyone who touches the water of
cleansing will be unclean till evening.
22Anything that an unclean[y] person
touches becomes unclean, and anyone
who touches it becomes unclean till
evening."

Miriam's death.

20 In the first month the whole
Israelite community arrived at
the Desert of Zin,[z] and they stayed at

19:2 [a]Ge 15:9; Heb 9:13 [b]Lev 22:19-25 [c]Dt 21:3; 1Sa 6:7
19:3 [d]Nu 3:4 [e]Lev 4:12,21; Heb 13:11
19:4 [f]Lev 4:17
19:5 [g]Ex 29:14
19:6 [h]ver 18; Ps 51:7 [i]Lev 14:4
19:7 [j]Lev 11:25; 16:26,28; 22:6
19:9 [k]Heb 9:13 [l]ver 13; Nu 8:7
19:11 [m]Lev 21:1; Nu 5:2 [n]Nu 31:19
19:12 [o]ver 19; Nu 31:19
19:13 [p]Lev 20:3 [q]Lev 15:31; 2Ch 36:14 [r]Lev 7:20; 22:3 [s]Hag 2:13
19:16 [t]Nu 31:19 [u]Mt 23:27
19:17 [v]ver 9
19:18 [w]ver 6
19:19 [x]Eze 36:25; Heb 10:22
19:22 [y]Lev 5:2; Hag 2:13,14
20:1 [z]Nu 13:21

Kadesh.[a] There Miriam[b] died and was buried.

Moses strikes the rock for water.

2Now there was no water for the community,[c] and the people gathered in opposition[d] to Moses and Aaron. 3They quarreled[e] with Moses and said, "If only we had died when our brothers fell dead before the LORD![f] 4Why did you bring the LORD's community into this desert, that we and our livestock should die here?[g] 5Why did you bring us up out of Egypt to this terrible place? It has no grain or figs, grapevines or pomegranates.[h] And there is no water to drink!"

6Moses and Aaron went from the assembly to the entrance to the Tent of Meeting and fell facedown,[i] and the glory of the LORD[j] appeared to them. 7The LORD said to Moses, 8"Take the staff,[k] and you and your brother Aaron gather the assembly together. Speak to that rock before their eyes and it will pour out its water.[l] You will bring water out of the rock for the community so they and their livestock can drink."

9So Moses took the staff from the LORD's presence,[m] just as he commanded him. 10He and Aaron gathered the assembly together in front of the rock and Moses said to them, "Listen, you rebels, must we bring you water out of this rock?"[n] 11Then Moses raised his arm and struck the rock twice with his staff. Water[o] gushed out, and the community and their livestock drank.

12But the LORD said to Moses and Aaron, "Because you did not trust in me enough to honor me as holy[p] in the sight of the Israelites, you will not bring this community into the land I give them."[q]

13These were the waters of Meribah,[q][r] where the Israelites quarreled[s] with the LORD and where he showed himself holy among them.

Edom denies Israel passage.

14Moses sent messengers from Kadesh[t] to the king of Edom,[u] saying:

"This is what your brother Israel says: You know[v] about all the hardships that have come upon us. 15Our forefathers went down into Egypt,[w] and we lived there many years.[x] The Egyptians mistreated[y] us and our fathers, 16but when we cried out to the LORD, he heard our cry[z] and sent an angel[a] and brought us out of Egypt.

"Now we are here at Kadesh, a town on the edge of your territory. 17Please let us pass through your country. We will not go through any field or vineyard, or drink water from any well. We will travel along the king's highway and not turn to the right or to the left until we have passed through your territory.[b]"

18But Edom answered:

"You may not pass through here; if you try, we will march out and attack you with the sword."

19The Israelites replied:

"We will go along the main road, and if we or our livestock[c] drink any of your water, we will pay for it.[d] We only want to pass through on foot—nothing else."

20Again they answered:

"You may not pass through."

Then Edom came out against them with a large and powerful army. 21Since Edom refused to let them go through their territory, Israel turned away from them.[e]

Aaron's death.

22The whole Israelite community set out from Kadesh and came to Mount Hor.[f] 23At Mount Hor, near the border of Edom,[g] the LORD said to Moses and Aaron, 24"Aaron will be gathered to his people.[h] He will not enter the land I give the Israelites, because both of you

20:1 [a]Nu 33:36 [b]Ex 15:20
20:2 [c]Ex 17:1 [d]Nu 16:19
20:3 [e]Ex 17:2 [f]Nu 14:2; 16:31-35
20:4 [g]Ex 14:11; 17:3; Nu 14:3; 16:13
20:5 [h]Nu 16:14
20:6 [i]Nu 14:5 [j]Nu 16:19
20:8 [k]Ex 4:17,20 [l]Ex 17:6; Isa 43:20
20:9 [m]Nu 17:10
20:10 [n]Ps 106:32,33
20:11 [o]Ex 17:6; Dt 8:15; Ps 78:16; Isa 48:2; 1Co 10:4
20:12 [p]Nu 27:14 [q]ver 24; Dt 1:37; 3:27
20:13 [r]Ex 17:7 [s]Dt 33:8; Ps 95:8; 106:32
20:14 [t]Jdg 11:16-17 [u]Dt 2:4 [v]Jos 2:11; 9:9
20:15 [w]Ge 46:6 [x]Ge 15:13; Ex 12:40 [y]Ex 1:11; Dt 26:6
20:16 [z]Ex 2:23; 3:7 [a]Ex 14:19
20:17 [b]Nu 21:22
20:19 [c]Ex 12:38 [d]Dt 2:6,28
20:21 [e]Dt 2:8; Jdg 11:18
20:22 [f]Nu 33:37
20:23 [g]Nu 33:37 **20:24** [h]Ge 25:8

q *13 Meribah* means *quarreling.*

rebelled against my command[a] at the
waters of Meribah. 25 Get Aaron and his
son Eleazar and take them up Mount
Hor.[b] 26 Remove Aaron's garments and
put them on his son Eleazar, for Aaron
will be gathered to his people;[c] he will
die there."
27 Moses did as the LORD commanded:
They went up Mount Hor in the sight of
the whole community. 28 Moses removed
Aaron's garments and put them on his
son Eleazar.[d] And Aaron died there[e] on
top of the mountain. Then Moses and
Eleazar came down from the mountain,
29 and when the whole community
learned that Aaron had died, the entire
house of Israel mourned for him[f] thirty
days.

Moses makes a bronze snake.

21 When the Canaanite king of
Arad,[g] who lived in the Negev,[h]
heard that Israel was coming along the
road to Atharim, he attacked the Israelites and captured some of them. 2 Then
Israel made this vow to the LORD: "If
you will deliver these people into our
hands, we will totally destroy[r] their cities." 3 The LORD listened to Israel's plea
and gave the Canaanites over to them.
They completely destroyed them and
their towns; so the place was named
Hormah.[s]
4 They traveled from Mount Hor[i] along
the route to the Red Sea,[t] to go around
Edom. But the people grew impatient
on the way;[j] 5 they spoke against God[k]
and against Moses, and said, "Why have
you brought us up out of Egypt to die in
the desert?[l] There is no bread! There
is no water! And we detest this miserable food!"[m]
6 Then the LORD sent venomous
snakes[n] among them; they bit the people
and many Israelites died.[o] 7 The people
came to Moses[p] and said, "We sinned
when we spoke against the LORD and
against you. Pray that the LORD[q] will
take the snakes away from us." So Moses
prayed[r] for the people.
8 The LORD said to Moses, "Make a
snake and put it up on a pole;[s] anyone
who is bitten can look at it and live."
9 So Moses made a bronze snake[t] and
put it up on a pole. Then when anyone
was bitten by a snake and looked at the
bronze snake, he lived.[u]
10 The Israelites moved on and camped
at Oboth.[v] 11 Then they set out from
Oboth and camped in Iye Abarim, in
the desert that faces Moab[w] toward the
sunrise. 12 From there they moved on
and camped in the Zered Valley.[x] 13 They
set out from there and camped alongside the Arnon[y], which is in the desert
extending into Amorite territory. The
Arnon is the border of Moab, between
Moab and the Amorites. 14 That is why
the Book of the Wars of the LORD says:

". . .Waheb in Suphah[u] and the
ravines,
the Arnon 15 and[v] the slopes of the
ravines
that lead to the site of Ar[z]
and lie along the border of Moab."

16 From there they continued on to
Beer,[a] the well where the LORD said to
Moses, "Gather the people together and
I will give them water."
17 Then Israel sang this song:[b]

"Spring up, O well!
Sing about it,
18 about the well that the princes dug,
that the nobles of the people sank—
the nobles with scepters and staffs."

Then they went from the desert to
Mattanah, 19 from Mattanah to Nahaliel,
from Nahaliel to Bamoth, 20 and from
Bamoth to the valley in Moab where the
top of Pisgah overlooks the wasteland.

Sihon and Og are defeated.

21 Israel sent messengers to say to
Sihon[c] king of the Amorites:

20:24 [a]ver 10
20:25 [b]Nu 33:38
20:26 [c]ver 24
20:28 [d]Ex 29:29 [e]Nu 33:38; Dt 10:6; 32:50
20:29 [f]Dt 34:8
21:1 [g]Nu 33:40; Jos 12:14 [h]Jdg 1:9,16
21:4 [i]Nu 20:22 [j]Dt 2:8; Jdg 11:18
21:5 [k]Ps 78:19 [l]Nu 14:2,3 [m]Nu 11:6
21:6 [n]Dt 8:15; Jer 8:17 [o]1Co 10:9
21:7 [p]Ps 78:34; Hos 5:15 [q]Ex 8:8; Ac 8:24 [r]Nu 11:2
21:8 [s]Jn 3:14
21:9 [t]2Ki 18:4 [u]Jn 3:14-15
21:10 [v]Nu 33:43
21:11 [w]Nu 33:44
21:12 [x]Dt 2:13,14
21:13 [y]Nu 22:36; Jdg 11:13,18
21:15 [z]ver 28; Dt 2:9,18
21:16 [a]Jdg 9:21
21:17 [b]Ex 15:1
21:21 [c]Dt 1:4; 2:26-27; Jdg 11:19-21

r *2* The Hebrew term refers to the irrevocable giving over of things or persons to the LORD, often by totally destroying them; also in verse 3. s *3* *Hormah* means *destruction.* t *4* Hebrew *Yam Suph*; that is, Sea of Reeds u *14* The meaning of the Hebrew for this phrase is uncertain. v *14,15* Or *"I have been given from Suphah and the ravines / of the Arnon* [15]*to*

[22]"Let us pass through your country. We will not turn aside into any field or vineyard, or drink water from any well. We will travel along the king's highway until we have passed through your territory.[a]"

[23]But Sihon would not let Israel pass through his territory.[b] He mustered his entire army and marched out into the desert against Israel. When he reached Jahaz,[c] he fought with Israel. [24]Israel, however, put him to the sword[d] and took over his land from the Arnon to the Jabbok, but only as far as the Ammonites,[e] because their border was fortified. [25]Israel captured all the cities of the Amorites[f] and occupied them, including Heshbon and all its surrounding settlements. [26]Heshbon was the city of Sihon[g] king of the Amorites, who had fought against the former king of Moab and had taken from him all his land as far as the Arnon.

[27]That is why the poets say:

"Come to Heshbon and let it be
rebuilt;
let Sihon's city be restored.

[28]"Fire went out from Heshbon,
a blaze from the city of Sihon.[h]
It consumed Ar[i] of Moab,
the citizens of Arnon's heights.[j]
[29]Woe to you, O Moab![k]
You are destroyed, O people of
Chemosh![l]
He has given up his sons as
fugitives[m]
and his daughters as captives[n]
to Sihon king of the Amorites.

[30]"But we have overthrown them;
Heshbon is destroyed all the way
to Dibon.[o]
We have demolished them as far as
Nophah,
which extends to Medeba."

[31]So Israel settled in the land of the Amorites.

[32]After Moses had sent spies to Jazer,[p] the Israelites captured its surrounding settlements and drove out the Amorites who were there. [33]Then they turned and went up along the road toward Bashan[q,r] and Og king of Bashan and his whole army marched out to meet them in battle at Edrei.[s]

[34]The LORD said to Moses, "Do not be afraid of him, for I have handed him over to you, with his whole army and his land. Do to him what you did to Sihon king of the Amorites, who reigned in Heshbon.[t]"

[35]So they struck him down, together with his sons and his whole army, leaving them no survivors. And they took possession of his land.

Balak sends for Balaam to curse Israel.

22 Then the Israelites traveled to the plains of Moab and camped along the Jordan across from Jericho.[w][u]

[2]Now Balak son of Zippor[v] saw all that Israel had done to the Amorites, [3]and Moab was terrified because there were so many people. Indeed, Moab was filled with dread[w] because of the Israelites.

[4]The Moabites said to the elders of Midian, "This horde is going to lick up everything around us, as an ox licks up the grass of the field."

So Balak son of Zippor, who was king of Moab at that time, [5]sent messengers to summon Balaam son of Beor,[x] who was at Pethor, near the River,[x] in his native land. Balak said:

"A people has come out of Egypt; they cover the face of the land and have settled next to me. [6]Now come and put a curse[y] on these people, because they are too powerful for me. Perhaps then I will be able to defeat them and drive them out of the country. For I know that those you bless are blessed, and those you curse are cursed."

[7]The elders of Moab and Midian left, taking with them the fee for divination.[z]

21:22 [a]Nu 20:17
21:23 [b]Nu 20:21 [c]Dt 2:32; Jdg 11:20
21:24 [d]Dt 2:33; Ps 135:10-11; Am 2:9 [e]Dt 2:37
21:25 [f]Nu 13:29; Jdg 10:11; Am 2:10
21:26 [g]Dt 29:7; Ps 135:11
21:28 [h]Jer 48:45 [i]ver 15 [j]Nu 22:41; Isa 15:2
21:29 [k]Isa 25:10; Jer 48:46 [l]Jdg 11:24; 1Ki 11:7,33; 2Ki 23:13; Jer 48:7,46 [m]Isa 15:5 [n]Isa 16:2
21:30 [o]Nu 32:3; Isa 15:2; Jer 48:18,22
21:32 [p]Nu 32:1,3, 35; Jer 48:32
21:33 [q]Dt 3:3 [r]Dt 3:4 [s]Dt 1:4; 3:1,10; Jos 13:12,31
21:34 [t]Dt 3:2
22:1 [u]Nu 33:48
22:2 [v]Jdg 11:25
22:3 [w]Ex 15:15
22:5 [x]Dt 23:4; Jos 13:22; 24:9; Ne 13:2; Mic 6:5; 2Pe 2:15
22:6 [y]ver 12,17; Nu 23:7,11, 13
22:7 [z]Nu 23:23; 24:1

w *1* Hebrew *Jordan of Jericho*; possibly an ancient name for the Jordan River   x *5* That is, the Euphrates

When they came to Balaam, they told
him what Balak had said.
8"Spend the night here," Balaam said
to them, "and I will bring you back the
answer the LORD gives me.[a]" So the
Moabite princes stayed with him.
9God came to Balaam[b] and asked,[c]
"Who are these men with you?"
10Balaam said to God, "Balak son of
Zippor, king of Moab, sent me this message: 11'A people that has come out of
Egypt covers the face of the land. Now
come and put a curse on them for me.
Perhaps then I will be able to fight them
and drive them away.'"
12But God said to Balaam, "Do not go
with them. You must not put a curse on
those people, because they are blessed.[d]"
13The next morning Balaam got up
and said to Balak's princes, "Go back to
your own country, for the LORD has
refused to let me go with you."

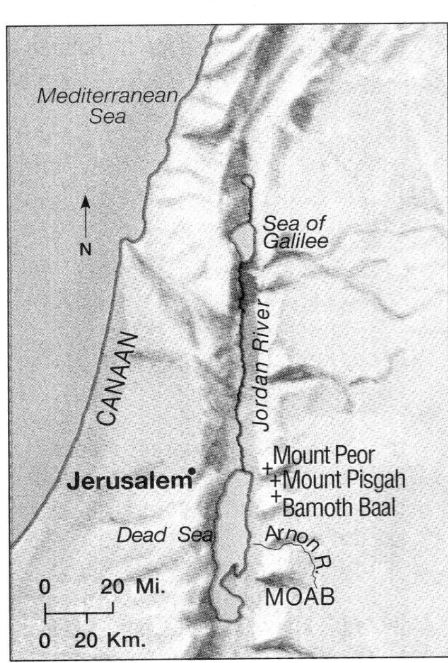

The Story of Balaam

At King Balak's request Balaam traveled nearly 400 miles to curse Israel. Balak took Balaam to Bamoth Baal ("the high places of Baal"), then to Mount Pisgah, and finally to Mount Peor. Each place looked over the plains of Moab where the Israelites were camped. But to the king's dismay, Balaam blessed, not cursed, Israel.

22:8 [a]ver 19
22:9 [b]Ge 20:3 [c]ver 20
22:12 [d]Ge 12:2; 22:17; Nu 23:20
22:17 [e]ver 37; Nu 24:11 [f]ver 6
22:18 [g]ver 38; Nu 23:12,26; 24:13; 1Ki 22:14; 2Ch 18:13; Jer 42:4
22:19 [h]ver 8
22:20 [i]Ge 20:3 [j]ver 35,38; Nu 23:5,12, 16,26; 24:13; 2Ch 18:13
22:22 [k]Ex 4:14 [l]Ge 16:7; Ex 23:20; Jdg 13:3,6,13
22:23 [m]Jos 5:13 [n]ver 25,27

14So the Moabite princes returned to
Balak and said, "Balaam refused to come
with us."
15Then Balak sent other princes, more
numerous and more distinguished than
the first. 16They came to Balaam and
said:

> "This is what Balak son of Zip-
> por says: Do not let anything keep
> you from coming to me, 17because
> I will reward you handsomely[e] and
> do whatever you say. Come and put
> a curse[f] on these people for me."

18But Balaam answered them, "Even
if Balak gave me his palace filled with silver and gold, I could not do anything
great or small to go beyond the command of the LORD my God.[g] 19Now stay
here tonight as the others did, and I
will find out what else the LORD will
tell me.[h]"
20That night God came to Balaam[i] and
said, "Since these men have come to
summon you, go with them, but do only
what I tell you."[j]

Balaam's donkey speaks.

21Balaam got up in the morning, saddled his donkey and went with the
princes of Moab. 22But God was very
angry[k] when he went, and the angel of
the LORD[l] stood in the road to oppose
him. Balaam was riding on his donkey,
and his two servants were with him.
23When the donkey saw the angel of the
LORD standing in the road with a drawn
sword[m] in his hand, she turned off the
road into a field. Balaam beat her[n] to get
her back on the road.
24Then the angel of the LORD stood in
a narrow path between two vineyards,
with walls on both sides. 25When the
donkey saw the angel of the LORD, she
pressed close to the wall, crushing Balaam's foot against it. So he beat her
again.
26Then the angel of the LORD moved
on ahead and stood in a narrow place
where there was no room to turn, either
to the right or to the left. 27When the

donkey saw the angel of the LORD, she
lay down under Balaam, and he was
angry[a] and beat her with his staff.
28Then the LORD opened the donkey's
mouth,[b] and she said to Balaam, "What
have I done to you to make you beat me
these three times?[c]"
29Balaam answered the donkey, "You
have made a fool of me! If I had a sword
in my hand, I would kill you right
now.[d]"
30The donkey said to Balaam, "Am I
not your own donkey, which you have
always ridden, to this day? Have I been
in the habit of doing this to you?"
"No," he said.
31Then the LORD opened Balaam's
eyes,[e] and he saw the angel of the LORD
standing in the road with his sword
drawn. So he bowed low and fell facedown.
32The angel of the LORD asked him,
"Why have you beaten your donkey
these three times? I have come here to
oppose you because your path is a reckless one before me.[y] 33The donkey saw
me and turned away from me these
three times. If she had not turned away,
I would certainly have killed you by
now,[f] but I would have spared her."
34Balaam said to the angel of the LORD,
"I have sinned.[g] I did not realize you
were standing in the road to oppose
me. Now if you are displeased, I will
go back."
35The angel of the LORD said to Balaam, "Go with the men, but speak
only what I tell you." So Balaam went
with the princes of Balak.
36When Balak heard that Balaam was
coming, he went out to meet him at
the Moabite town on the Arnon[h] border,
at the edge of his territory. 37Balak said to
Balaam, "Did I not send you an urgent
summons? Why didn't you come to me?
Am I really not able to reward you?"
38"Well, I have come to you now,"
Balaam replied. "But can I say just anything? I must speak only what God puts
in my mouth."[i]
39Then Balaam went with Balak to
Kiriath Huzoth. 40Balak sacrificed cattle
and sheep,[j] and gave some to Balaam
and the princes who were with him.
41The next morning Balak took Balaam
up to Bamoth Baal,[k] and from there he
saw part of the people.[l]

Balaam blesses Israel with messages from the LORD.

23 Balaam said, "Build me seven
altars here, and prepare seven
bulls and seven rams[m] for me." 2Balak
did as Balaam said, and the two of them
offered a bull and a ram on each altar.[n]
3Then Balaam said to Balak, "Stay
here beside your offering while I go
aside. Perhaps the LORD will come to
meet with me.[o] Whatever he reveals to
me I will tell you." Then he went off to
a barren height.
4God met with him,[p] and Balaam said,
"I have prepared seven altars, and on
each altar I have offered a bull and a
ram."
5The LORD put a message in Balaam's
mouth[q] and said, "Go back to Balak and
give him this message."[r]
6So he went back to him and found
him standing beside his offering, with
all the princes of Moab.[s] 7Then Balaam[t]
uttered his oracle:[u]

"Balak brought me from Aram,
the king of Moab from the eastern
mountains.
'Come,' he said, 'curse Jacob for me;
come, denounce Israel.'[v]
8How can I curse
those whom God has not cursed?[w]
How can I denounce
those whom the LORD has not
denounced?
9From the rocky peaks I see them,
from the heights I view them.
I see a people who live apart
and do not consider themselves
one of the nations.[x]
10Who can count the dust of Jacob[y]
or number the fourth part of Israel?
Let me die the death of the righteous,[z]
and may my end be like theirs![a]"

22:27 [a]Nu 11:1; Jas 1:19
22:28 [b]2Pe 2:16 [c]ver 32
22:29 [d]Dt 25:4; Pr 12:10; 27:23-27; Mt 15:19
22:31 [e]Ge 21:19
22:33 [f]ver 29
22:34 [g]Ge 39:9; Nu 14:40; 1Sa 15:24,30; 2Sa 12:13; 24:10; Job 33:27; Ps 51:4
22:36 [h]Nu 21:13
22:38 [i]Nu 23:5,16, 26
22:40 [j]Nu 23:1,14, 29; Eze 45:23
22:41 [k]Nu 21:28 [l]Nu 23:13
23:1 [m]Nu 22:40
23:2 [n]ver 14,30
23:3 [o]ver 15
23:4 [p]ver 16
23:5 [q]Dt 18:18; Jer 1:9 [r]Nu 22:20
23:6 [s]ver 17
23:7 [t]Nu 22:5 [u]ver 18; Nu 24:3,21 [v]Nu 22:6; Dt 23:4
23:8 [w]Nu 22:12
23:9 [x]Ex 33:16; Dt 32:8; 33:28
23:10 [y]Ge 13:16 [z]Ps 116:15; Isa 57:1 [a]Ps 37:37

y32 The meaning of the Hebrew for this clause is uncertain.

11Balak said to Balaam, "What have you done to me? I brought you to curse my enemies, but you have done nothing but bless them!"[a]

12He answered, "Must I not speak what the LORD puts in my mouth?"[b]

13Then Balak said to him, "Come with me to another place where you can see them; you will see only a part but not all of them. And from there, curse them for me." 14So he took him to the field of Zophim on the top of Pisgah, and there he built seven altars and offered a bull and a ram on each altar.[c]

15Balaam said to Balak, "Stay here beside your offering while I meet with him over there."

16The LORD met with Balaam and put a message in his mouth[d] and said, "Go back to Balak and give him this message."

17So he went to him and found him standing beside his offering, with the princes of Moab. Balak asked him, "What did the LORD say?"

18Then he uttered his oracle:

"Arise, Balak, and listen;
hear me, son of Zippor.
19God is not a man,[e] that he should lie,
nor a son of man, that he should change his mind.[f]
Does he speak and then not act?
Does he promise and not fulfill?
20I have received a command to bless;
he has blessed,[g] and I cannot change it.[h]

21"No misfortune is seen in Jacob,[i]
no misery observed in Israel.[z][j]
The LORD their God is with them;[k]
the shout of the King[l] is among them.
22God brought them out of Egypt;[m]
they have the strength of a wild ox.[n]
23There is no sorcery against Jacob,
no divination[o] against Israel.
It will now be said of Jacob
and of Israel, 'See what God has done!'
24The people rise like a lioness;[p]
they rouse themselves like a lion[q]
that does not rest till he devours his prey
and drinks the blood of his victims."

25Then Balak said to Balaam, "Neither curse them at all nor bless them at all!"

26Balaam answered, "Did I not tell you I must do whatever the LORD says?"

27Then Balak said to Balaam, "Come, let me take you to another place.[r] Perhaps it will please God to let you curse them for me from there." 28And Balak took Balaam to the top of Peor,[s] overlooking the wasteland.

29Balaam said, "Build me seven altars here, and prepare seven bulls and seven rams for me." 30Balak did as Balaam had said, and offered a bull and a ram on each altar.

24

Now when Balaam saw that it pleased the LORD to bless Israel, he did not resort to sorcery[t] as at other times, but turned his face toward the desert.[u] 2When Balaam looked out and saw Israel encamped tribe by tribe, the Spirit of God came upon him[v] 3and he uttered his oracle:

"The oracle of Balaam son of Beor,
the oracle of one whose eye sees clearly,
4the oracle of one who hears the words of God,[w]
who sees a vision from the Almighty,[a][x]
who falls prostrate, and whose eyes are opened:

5"How beautiful are your tents, O Jacob,
your dwelling places, O Israel!

6"Like valleys they spread out,
like gardens beside a river,
like aloes[y] planted by the LORD,
like cedars beside the waters.[z]
7Water will flow from their buckets;
their seed will have abundant water.

23:11 [a]Nu 24:10; Ne 13:2
23:12 [b]Nu 22:20,38
23:14 [c]ver 2
23:16 [d]Nu 22:38
23:19 [e]Isa 55:9; Hos 11:9 [f]1Sa 15:29; Mal 3:6; Tit 1:2; Jas 1:17
23:20 [g]Ge 22:17; Nu 22:12 [h]Isa 43:13
23:21 [i]Ps 32:2,5; Ro 4:7-8 [j]Isa 40:2; Jer 50:20 [k]Ex 29:45,46; Ps 145:18 [l]Dt 33:5; Ps 89:15-18
23:22 [m]Nu 24:8 [n]Dt 33:17; Job 39:9
23:23 [o]Nu 24:1; Jos 13:22
23:24 [p]Na 2:11 [q]Ge 49:9
23:27 [r]ver 13
23:28 [s]Ps 106:28
24:1 [t]Nu 23:23 [u]Nu 23:28
24:2 [v]Nu 11:25,26; 1Sa 10:10; 19:20; 2Ch 15:1
24:4 [w]Nu 22:20 [x]Ge 15:1
24:6 [y]Ps 45:8 [z]Ps 1:3; 104:16

z21 Or *He has not looked on Jacob's offenses / or on the wrongs found in Israel.* a4 Hebrew *Shaddai*; also in verse 16

"Their king will be greater than
Agag;[a]
their kingdom will be exalted.[b]

8"God brought them out of Egypt;
they have the strength of a wild
ox.
They devour hostile nations
and break their bones in pieces;[c]
with their arrows they pierce
them.[d]
9Like a lion they crouch and lie down,
like a lioness[e]—who dares to rouse
them?

"May those who bless you be
blessed
and those who curse you be
cursed!"[f]

10Then Balak's anger burned against
Balaam. He struck his hands together[g]
and said to him, "I summoned you to
curse my enemies, but you have blessed
them[h] these three times.[i] 11Now leave
at once and go home! I said I would
reward you handsomely,[j] but the LORD
has kept you from being rewarded."
12Balaam answered Balak, "Did I not
tell the messengers you sent me,[k]
13'Even if Balak gave me his palace filled
with silver and gold, I could not do anything of my own accord, good or bad, to
go beyond the command of the LORD[l]—
and I must say only what the LORD
says'?[m] 14Now I am going back to my
people, but come, let me warn you of
what this people will do to your people
in days to come."[n]
15Then he uttered his oracle:

"The oracle of Balaam son of Beor,
the oracle of one whose eye sees
clearly,
16the oracle of one who hears the
words of God,
who has knowledge from the Most
High,
who sees a vision from the Almighty,
who falls prostrate, and whose
eyes are opened:

17"I see him, but not now;
I behold him, but not near.[o]
A star will come out of Jacob;[p]
a scepter will rise out of Israel.[q]
He will crush the foreheads of Moab,[r]
the skulls[b] of[c] all the sons of Sheth.[d]
18Edom[s] will be conquered;
Seir, his enemy, will be conquered,
but Israel will grow strong.
19A ruler will come out of Jacob[t]
and destroy the survivors of the
city."

20Then Balaam saw Amalek[u] and uttered his oracle:

"Amalek was first among the nations,
but he will come to ruin at last."

21Then he saw the Kenites[v] and uttered his oracle:

"Your dwelling place is secure,
your nest is set in a rock;
22yet you Kenites will be destroyed
when Asshur[w] takes you captive."

23Then he uttered his oracle:

"Ah, who can live when God does
this?[e]
24 Ships will come from the shores of
Kittim;[x]
they will subdue Asshur and Eber,[y]
but they too will come to ruin.[z]"

25Then Balaam[a] got up and returned
home and Balak went his own way.

Israel joins Moab in worshiping Baal.

25 While Israel was staying in Shittim,[b] the men began to indulge
in sexual immorality[c] with Moabite wom-
en,[d] 2who invited them to the sacrifices[e]
to their gods.[f] The people ate and
bowed down before these gods. 3So
Israel joined in worshiping the Baal of
Peor.[g] And the LORD's anger burned
against them.
4The LORD said to Moses, "Take all
the leaders of these people, kill them

24:7 [a]2Sa 15:8 [b]2Sa 5:12; 1Ch 14:2; Ps 145:11-13
24:8 [c]Ps 2:9; Jer 50:17 [d]Ps 45:5
24:9 [e]Ge 49:9; Nu 23:24 [f]Ge 12:3
24:10 [g]Eze 21:14 [h]Nu 23:11 [i]Ne 13:2
24:11 [j]Nu 22:17
24:12 [k]Nu 22:18
24:13 [l]Nu 22:18 [m]Nu 22:20
24:14 [n]Ge 49:1; Nu 31:8,16; Da 2:28; Mic 6:5
24:17 [o]Rev 1:7 [p]Mt 2:2 [q]Ge 49:10 [r]Nu 21:29; Isa 15:1–16:14
24:18 [s]Am 9:12
24:19 [t]Ge 49:10; Mic 5:2
24:20 [u]Ex 17:14
24:21 [v]Ge 15:19
24:22 [w]Ge 10:22
24:24 [x]Ge 10:4 [y]Ge 10:21 [z]ver 20
24:25 [a]Nu 31:8
25:1 [b]Jos 2:1; Mic 6:5 [c]1Co 10:8; Rev 2:14 [d]Nu 31:16
25:2 [e]Ex 34:15 [f]Ex 20:5; Dt 32:38; 1Co 10:20
25:3 [g]Ps 106:28; Hos 9:10

b *17* Samaritan Pentateuch (see also Jer. 48:45); the meaning of the word in the Masoretic Text is uncertain. c *17* Or possibly *Moab, / batter* d *17* Or *all the noisy boasters* e *23* Masoretic Text; with a different word division of the Hebrew *A people will gather from the north.*

and expose them in broad daylight before the LORD,[a] so that the LORD's fierce
anger[b] may turn away from Israel."
5So Moses said to Israel's judges,
"Each of you must put to death[c] those of
your men who have joined in worshiping the Baal of Peor."

A plague is stopped when Phinehas slays Zimri and Cozbi.

6Then an Israelite man brought to his
family a Midianite woman right before
the eyes of Moses and the whole assembly of Israel while they were weeping
at the entrance to the Tent of Meeting.
7When Phinehas son of Eleazar, the son
of Aaron, the priest, saw this, he left
the assembly, took a spear in his hand
8and followed the Israelite into the tent.
He drove the spear through both of
them—through the Israelite and into
the woman's body. Then the plague
against the Israelites was stopped;[d] 9but
those who died in the plague[e] numbered
24,000.[f]
10The LORD said to Moses, 11"Phinehas son of Eleazar, the son of Aaron,
the priest, has turned my anger away
from the Israelites;[g] for he was as zealous as I am for my honor[h] among them,
so that in my zeal I did not put an end
to them. 12Therefore tell him I am making my covenant of peace[i] with him.
13He and his descendants will have a
covenant of a lasting priesthood,[j] because he was zealous for the honor of
his God and made atonement[k] for the
Israelites."
14The name of the Israelite who was
killed with the Midianite woman was
Zimri son of Salu, the leader of a Sime-
onite family. 15And the name of the
Midianite woman who was put to death
was Cozbi[l] daughter of Zur, a tribal chief
of a Midianite family.[m]
16The LORD said to Moses, 17"Treat the
Midianites[n] as enemies and kill them,
18because they treated you as enemies
when they deceived you in the affair of
Peor[o] and their sister Cozbi, the daughter of a Midianite leader, the woman
who was killed when the plague came
as a result of Peor."

25:4 [a]Dt 4:3 [b]Dt 13:17
25:5 [c]Ex 32:27
25:8 [d]Nu 16:46-48; Ps 106:30
25:9 [e]Nu 14:37; 1Co 10:8 [f]Nu 31:16
25:11 [g]Ps 106:30 [h]Ex 20:5; Dt 32:16,21; Ps 78:58
25:12 [i]Isa 54:10; Eze 34:25; Mal 2:4,5
25:13 [j]Ex 29:9 [k]Nu 16:46
25:15 [l]ver 18 [m]Nu 31:8; Jos 13:21
25:17 [n]Nu 31:1-3
25:18 [o]Nu 31:16
26:2 [p]Ex 30:11-16; 38:25-26; Nu 1:2 [q]Nu 1:3
26:3 [r]Nu 33:48 [s]Nu 22:1
26:5 [t]Ge 46:9 [u]1Ch 5:3
26:9 [v]Nu 16:1 [w]Nu 1:16 [x]Nu 16:2
26:10 [y]Nu 16:35,38
26:11 [z]Ex 6:24 [a]Nu 16:33; Dt 24:16
26:12 [b]1Ch 4:24
26:13 [c]Ge 46:10

Moses' second census of Israel.

26 After the plague the LORD said
to Moses and Eleazar son of
Aaron, the priest, 2"Take a census[p] of
the whole Israelite community by families—all those twenty years old or more
who are able to serve in the army[q] of
Israel." 3So on the plains of Moab[r] by the
Jordan across from Jericho,[f3][s] Moses and
Eleazar the priest spoke with them and
said, 4"Take a census of the men twenty
years old or more, as the LORD commanded Moses."

These were the Israelites who came
out of Egypt:

5The descendants of Reuben, the firstborn son of Israel, were:
through Hanoch,[t] the Hanochite clan;
through Pallu,[u] the Palluite clan;
6through Hezron, the Hezronite clan;
through Carmi, the Carmite clan.
7These were the clans of Reuben;
those numbered were 43,730.
8The son of Pallu was Eliab, 9and the
sons of Eliab[v] were Nemuel, Dathan
and Abiram. The same Dathan and Abiram were the community[w] officials who
rebelled against Moses and Aaron and
were among Korah's followers when
they rebelled against the LORD.[x] 10The
earth opened its mouth and swallowed
them along with Korah, whose followers died when the fire devoured the
250 men. And they served as a warning
sign.[y] 11The line of Korah,[z] however, did
not die out.[a]

12The descendants of Simeon by their
clans were:
through Nemuel, the Nemuelite clan;
through Jamin,[b] the Jaminite clan;
through Jakin, the Jakinite clan;
13through Zerah,[c] the Zerahite clan;

f3 Hebrew *Jordan of Jericho*; possibly an ancient name for the Jordan River; also in verse 63

through Shaul, the Shaulite clan.
14These were the clans of Simeon; there
were 22,200 men.[a]

15The descendants of Gad by their clans
were:
through Zephon,[b] the Zephonite
clan;
through Haggi, the Haggite clan;
through Shuni, the Shunite clan;
16through Ozni, the Oznite clan;
through Eri, the Erite clan;
17through Arodi,[g] the Arodite clan;
through Areli, the Arelite clan.
18These were the clans of Gad;[c] those
numbered were 40,500.

19Er and Onan were sons of Judah, but
they died[d] in Canaan.
20The descendants of Judah by their
clans were:
through Shelah,[e] the Shelanite clan;
through Perez, the Perezite clan;
through Zerah, the Zerahite clan.[f]
21The descendants of Perez were:
through Hezron,[g] the Hezronite
clan;
through Hamul, the Hamulite
clan.
22These were the clans of Judah;[h] those
numbered were 76,500.

23The descendants of Issachar by their
clans were:
through Tola,[i] the Tolaite clan;
through Puah, the Puite[h] clan;
24through Jashub,[j] the Jashubite clan;
through Shimron, the Shimronite
clan.
25These were the clans of Issachar;[k]
those numbered were 64,300.

26The descendants of Zebulun by their
clans were:
through Sered, the Seredite clan;
through Elon, the Elonite clan;
through Jahleel, the Jahleelite clan.
27These were the clans of Zebulun;[l]
those numbered were 60,500.

28The descendants of Joseph by their
clans through Manasseh and Ephraim
were:

26:14 [a]Nu 1:23
26:15 [b]Ge 46:16
26:18 [c]Nu 1:25; Jos 13:24-28
26:19 [d]Ge 38:2-10; 46:12
26:20 [e]1Ch 2:3 [f]Jos 7:17
26:21 [g]Ru 4:19; 1Ch 2:9
26:22 [h]Nu 1:27
26:23 [i]Ge 46:13; 1Ch 7:1
26:24 [j]Ge 46:13
26:25 [k]Nu 1:29
26:27 [l]Nu 1:31
26:29 [m]Jos 17:1 [n]Jdg 11:1
26:30 [o]Jos 17:2; Jdg 6:11
26:33 [p]Nu 27:1 [q]Nu 36:11
26:34 [r]Nu 1:35
26:37 [s]Nu 1:33
26:38 [t]Ge 46:21; 1Ch 7:6

29The descendants of Manasseh:
through Makir,[m] the Makirite clan
(Makir was the father of Gilead[n]);
through Gilead, the Gileadite clan.
30These were the descendants of
Gilead:
through Iezer,[o] the Iezerite clan;
through Helek, the Helekite clan;
31through Asriel, the Asrielite clan;
through Shechem, the Shechem-
ite clan;
32through Shemida, the Shemida-
ite clan;
through Hepher, the Hepherite
clan.
33(Zelophehad[p] son of Hepher had
no sons; he had only daughters,
whose names were Mahlah, Noah, Hoglah, Milcah and Tirzah.)[q]
34These were the clans of Manasseh;
those numbered were 52,700.[r]

35These were the descendants of Ephraim by their clans:
through Shuthelah, the Shuthela-
hite clan;
through Beker, the Bekerite clan;
through Tahan, the Tahanite clan.
36These were the descendants of
Shuthelah:
through Eran, the Eranite clan.
37These were the clans of Ephraim;[s]
those numbered were 32,500.

These were the descendants of Joseph
by their clans.

38The descendants of Benjamin[t] by their
clans were:
through Bela, the Belaite clan;
through Ashbel, the Ashbelite clan;
through Ahiram, the Ahiramite clan;
39through Shupham,[i] the Shuphamite
clan;
through Hupham, the Huphamite
clan.

g*17* Samaritan Pentateuch and Syriac (see also Gen. 46:16); Masoretic Text *Arod* h*23* Samaritan Pentateuch, Septuagint, Vulgate and Syriac (see also 1 Chron. 7:1); Masoretic Text *through Puvah, the Punite* i*39* A few manuscripts of the Masoretic Text, Samaritan Pentateuch, Vulgate and Syriac (see also Septuagint); most manuscripts of the Masoretic Text *Shephupham*

40The descendants of Bela through
Ard[a] and Naaman were:
through Ard,[j] the Ardite clan;
through Naaman, the Naamite
clan.
41These were the clans of Benjamin;[b]
those numbered were 45,600.

42These were the descendants of Dan
by their clans:
through Shuham,[c] the Shuhamite
clan.
These were the clans of Dan: 43All of
them were Shuhamite clans; and those
numbered were 64,400.

44The descendants of Asher by their
clans were:
through Imnah, the Imnite clan;
through Ishvi, the Ishvite clan;
through Beriah, the Beriite clan;
45and through the descendants of
Beriah:
through Heber, the Heberite clan;
through Malkiel, the Malkielite
clan.
46(Asher had a daughter named Serah.)
47These were the clans of Asher;[d]
those numbered were 53,400.

48The descendants of Naphtali[e] by their
clans were:
through Jahzeel, the Jahzeelite clan;
through Guni, the Gunite clan;
49through Jezer, the Jezerite clan;
through Shillem, the Shillemite
clan.
50These were the clans of Naphtali;[f]
those numbered were 45,400.

51The total number of the men of Israel
was 601,730.[g]

Distribution of the land by lot.

52The LORD said to Moses, 53"The
land is to be allotted to them as an
inheritance based on the number of
names.[h] 54To a larger group give a larger inheritance, and to a smaller group
a smaller one; each is to receive its
inheritance according to the number[i]
of those listed. 55Be sure that the land
is distributed by lot.[j] What each group
inherits will be according to the names
for its ancestral tribe. 56Each inheritance
is to be distributed by lot among the
larger and smaller groups."

Census of the Levites.

57These were the Levites[k] who were
counted by their clans:
through Gershon, the Gershonite
clan;
through Kohath, the Kohathite clan;
through Merari, the Merarite clan.
58These also were Levite clans:
the Libnite clan,
the Hebronite clan,
the Mahlite clan,
the Mushite clan,
the Korahite clan.
(Kohath was the forefather of Amram;[l] 59the name of Amram's wife
was Jochebed,[m] a descendant of
Levi, who was born to the Levites[k]
in Egypt. To Amram she bore Aaron,
Moses[n] and their sister Miriam.
60Aaron was the father of Nadab
and Abihu, Eleazar and Ithamar.[o]
61But Nadab and Abihu[p] died when
they made an offering before the
LORD with unauthorized fire.)[q]

62All the male Levites a month old or
more numbered 23,000.[r] They were
not counted[s] along with the other Israelites because they received no inheritance[t] among them.[u]

Only Caleb and Joshua remain from the first census.

63These are the ones counted by
Moses and Eleazar the priest when they
counted the Israelites on the plains of
Moab[v] by the Jordan across from Jericho. 64Not one of them was among
those counted[w] by Moses and Aaron the
priest when they counted the Israelites
in the Desert of Sinai. 65For the LORD

26:40 [a]Ge 46:21; 1Ch 8:3
26:41 [b]Nu 1:37
26:42 [c]Ge 46:23
26:47 [d]Nu 1:41
26:48 [e]Ge 46:24; 1Ch 7:13
26:50 [f]Nu 1:43
26:51 [g]Ex 12:37; 38:26; Nu 1:46; 11:21
26:53 [h]Jos 11:23; 14:1; Eze 45:8
26:54 [i]Nu 33:54
26:55 [j]Nu 34:14
26:57 [k]Ge 46:11; Ex 6:16-19
26:58 [l]Ex 6:20
26:59 [m]Ex 2:1 [n]Ex 6:20
26:60 [o]Nu 3:2
26:61 [p]Lev 10:1-2 [q]Nu 3:4
26:62 [r]Nu 3:39 [s]Nu 1:47 [t]Nu 18:23 [u]Nu 2:33; Dt 10:9
26:63 [v]ver 3
26:64 [w]Nu 14:29; Dt 2:14-15; Heb 3:17

j*40* Samaritan Pentateuch and Vulgate (see also Septuagint); Masoretic Text does not have *through Ard.*
k*59* Or *Jochebed, a daughter of Levi, who was born to Levi*

had told those Israelites they would surely die in the desert,[a] and not one of them was left except Caleb son of Jephunneh and Joshua son of Nun.[b]

Inheritance of Zelophehad's daughters.

27:1-11pp— Nu 36:1-12

27 The daughters of Zelophehad[c] son of Hepher,[d] the son of Gilead, the son of Makir,[e] the son of Manasseh, belonged to the clans of Manasseh son of Joseph. The names of the daughters were Mahlah, Noah, Hoglah, Milcah and Tirzah. They approached
2the entrance to the Tent of Meeting and stood before Moses, Eleazar the priest, the leaders and the whole assembly, and said,
3"Our father died in the desert.[f] He was not among Korah's followers, who banded together against the LORD,[g] but he died for his own sin and left no sons.[h]
4Why should our father's name disappear from his clan because he had no son? Give us property among our father's relatives."
5So Moses brought their case[i] before the LORD[j]
6and the LORD said to him,
7"What Zelophehad's daughters are saying is right. You must certainly give them property as an inheritance[k] among their father's relatives and turn their father's inheritance over to them.[l]
8"Say to the Israelites, 'If a man dies and leaves no son, turn his inheritance over to his daughter.
9If he has no daughter, give his inheritance to his brothers.
10If he has no brothers, give his inheritance to his father's brothers.
11If his father had no brothers, give his inheritance to the nearest relative in his clan, that he may possess it. This is to be a legal requirement[m] for the Israelites, as the LORD commanded Moses.'"

Selection of Joshua as Moses' successor.

12Then the LORD said to Moses, "Go up this mountain in the Abarim range[n] and see the land[o] I have given the Israelites.
13After you have seen it, you too will be gathered to your people,[p] as your brother Aaron[q] was,
14for when the community rebelled at the waters in the Desert of Zin, both of you disobeyed my command to honor me as holy[r] before their eyes." (These were the waters of Meribah[s] Kadesh, in the Desert of Zin.)
15Moses said to the LORD,
16"May the LORD, the God of the spirits of all mankind,[t] appoint a man over this community
17to go out and come in before them, one who will lead them out and bring them in, so the LORD's people will not be like sheep without a shepherd."[u]
18So the LORD said to Moses, "Take Joshua son of Nun, a man in whom is the spirit,[1][v] and lay your hand on him.[w]
19Have him stand before Eleazar the priest and the entire assembly and commission him[x] in their presence.[y]
20Give him some of your authority so the whole Israelite community will obey him.[z]
21He is to stand before Eleazar the priest, who will obtain decisions for him by inquiring[a] of the Urim[b] before the LORD. At his command he and the entire community of the Israelites will go out, and at his command they will come in."
22Moses did as the LORD commanded him. He took Joshua and had him stand before Eleazar the priest and the whole assembly.
23Then he laid his hands on him and commissioned him, as the LORD instructed through Moses.

Regulations: Daily offerings.

28 The LORD said to Moses,
2"Give this command to the Israelites and say to them: 'See that you present to me at the appointed time the food[c] for my offerings made by fire, as an aroma pleasing to me.'
3Say to them: 'This is the offering made by fire that you are to present to the LORD: two lambs a year old without defect, as a regular burnt offering each day.[d]
4Prepare one lamb in the morning and the other at twilight,
5together with a grain

26:65 [a]Nu 14:28; 1Co 10:5 [b]Jos 14:6-10
27:1 [c]Nu 26:33 [d]Jos 17:2,3 [e]Nu 36:1
27:3 [f]Nu 26:65 [g]Nu 16:2 [h]Nu 26:33
27:5 [i]Ex 18:19 [j]Nu 9:8
27:7 [k]Job 42:15 [l]Jos 17:4
27:11 [m]Nu 35:29
27:12 [n]Nu 33:47; Jer 22:20 [o]Dt 3:23-27; 32:48-52
27:13 [p]Nu 31:2 [q]Nu 20:28
27:14 [r]Nu 20:12 [s]Ex 17:7; Dt 32:51; Ps 106:32
27:16 [t]Nu 16:22
27:17 [u]Dt 31:2; 1Ki 22:17; Eze 34:5; Zec 10:2; Mt 9:36; Mk 6:34
27:18 [v]Ge 41:38; Nu 11:25-29 [w]ver 23; Dt 34:9
27:19 [x]Dt 3:28; 31:14,23 [y]Dt 31:7
27:20 [z]Jos 1:16,17
27:21 [a]Jos 9:14 [b]Ex 28:30
28:2 [c]Lev 3:11
28:3 [d]Ex 29:38

[1] *18* Or *Spirit*

offering of a tenth of an ephah[m] of fine
flour mixed with a quarter of a hin[n] of
oil[a] from pressed olives. 6This is the regular burnt offering instituted at Mount
Sinai[b] as a pleasing aroma, an offering
made to the LORD by fire. 7The accom-
panying drink offering[c] is to be a quarter
of a hin of fermented drink with each
lamb. Pour out the drink offering to the
LORD at the sanctuary.[d] 8Prepare the second lamb at twilight, along with the
same kind of grain offering and drink
offering that you prepare in the morning. This is an offering made by fire, an
aroma pleasing to the LORD.[e]

Regulations: Sabbath offerings.

9" 'On the Sabbath[f] day, make an offering of two lambs a year old without
defect, together with its drink offering
and a grain offering of two-tenths of an
ephah[o][g] of fine flour mixed with oil.
10This is the burnt offering for every
Sabbath, in addition to the regular burnt
offering[h] and its drink offering.

Regulations: Monthly offerings.

11" 'On the first of every month,[i] present to the LORD a burnt offering of two
young bulls, one ram and seven male
lambs a year old, all without defect.[j]
12With each bull there is to be a grain
offering[k] of three-tenths of an ephah[p][l] of
fine flour mixed with oil; with the ram,
a grain offering of two-tenths of an
ephah of fine flour mixed with oil; 13and
with each lamb, a grain offering[m] of a
tenth of an ephah of fine flour mixed
with oil. This is for a burnt offering, a
pleasing aroma, an offering made to the
LORD by fire. 14With each bull there is
to be a drink offering[n] of half a hin[q] of
wine; with the ram, a third of a hin[r];
and with each lamb, a quarter of a hin.
This is the monthly burnt offering to be
made at each new moon[o] during the
year. 15Besides the regular burnt offering[p] with its drink offering, one male
goat is to be presented to the LORD as a
sin offering.[q]

28:5 [a]Lev 2:1; Nu 15:4
28:6 [b]Ex 19:3
28:7 [c]Ex 29:41 [d]Lev 3:7
28:8 [e]Lev 1:9
28:9 [f]Ex 20:10 [g]Lev 23:13
28:10 [h]ver 3
28:11 [i]Nu 10:10 [j]Lev 1:3
28:12 [k]Nu 15:6 [l]Nu 15:9
28:13 [m]Lev 6:14
28:14 [n]Nu 15:7 [o]Ezr 3:5
28:15 [p]ver 3,23,24 [q]Lev 4:3
28:16 [r]Ex 12:6,18; Lev 23:5; Dt 16:1
28:17 [s]Ex 12:19 [t]Ex 23:15; 34:18; Lev 23:6; Dt 16:3-8
28:18 [u]Ex 12:16; Lev 23:7
28:20 [v]Lev 14:10
28:22 [w]Ro 8:3 [x]Nu 15:28
28:26 [y]Ex 34:22 [z]Ex 23:16 [a]ver 18; Dt 16:10

Regulations: The Passover.

28:16-25pp— Ex 12:14-20; Lev 23:4-8; Dt 16:1-8

16" 'On the fourteenth day of the first
month the LORD's Passover[r] is to be held.
17On the fifteenth day of this month
there is to be a festival; for seven days[s]
eat bread made without yeast.[t] 18On the
first day hold a sacred assembly and do
no regular work.[u] 19Present to the LORD
an offering made by fire, a burnt offering
of two young bulls, one ram and seven
male lambs a year old, all without defect. 20With each bull prepare a grain
offering of three-tenths of an ephah[v] of
fine flour mixed with oil; with the ram,
two-tenths; 21and with each of the sev-
en lambs, one-tenth. 22Include one male
goat as a sin offering[w] to make atonement for you.[x] 23Prepare these in addition to the regular morning burnt
offering. 24In this way prepare the food
for the offering made by fire every day
for seven days as an aroma pleasing to
the LORD; it is to be prepared in addition to the regular burnt offering and its
drink offering. 25On the seventh day
hold a sacred assembly and do no regular
work.

Regulations: Feast of Weeks.

28:26-31pp— Lev 23:15-22; Dt 16:9-12

26" 'On the day of firstfruits,[y] when
you present to the LORD an offering of
new grain during the Feast of Weeks,[z]
hold a sacred assembly and do no regular work.[a] 27Present a burnt offering of
two young bulls, one ram and seven
male lambs a year old as an aroma
pleasing to the LORD. 28With each bull
there is to be a grain offering of three-
tenths of an ephah of fine flour mixed
with oil; with the ram, two-tenths;
29and with each of the seven lambs,

m *5* That is, probably about 2 quarts (about 2 liters); also in verses 13, 21 and 29 n *5* That is, probably about 1 quart (about 1 liter); also in verses 7 and 14 o *9* That is, probably about 4 quarts (about 4.5 liters); also in verses 12, 20 and 28 p *12* That is, probably about 6 quarts (about 6.5 liters); also in verses 20 and 28 q *14* That is, probably about 2 quarts (about 2 liters) r *14* That is, probably about 1 1/4 quarts (about 1.2 liters)

one-tenth.[a] 30 Include one male goat to make atonement for you. 31 Prepare these together with their drink offerings, in addition to the regular burnt offering[b] and its grain offering. Be sure the animals are without defect.

Regulations: Feast of Trumpets.

29:1-6pp— Lev 23:23-25

29 "'On the first day of the seventh month hold a sacred assembly and do no regular work.[c] It is a day for you to sound the trumpets. 2 As an aroma pleasing to the LORD,[d] prepare a burnt offering of one young bull, one ram and seven male lambs a year old, all without defect.[e] 3 With the bull prepare a grain offering of three-tenths of an ephah[s] of fine flour mixed with oil; with the ram, two-tenths[t]; 4 and with each of the seven lambs, one-tenth.[u] 5 Include one male goat[f] as a sin offering to make atonement for you. 6 These are in addition to the monthly[g] and daily burnt offerings[h] with their grain offerings and drink offerings as specified. They are offerings made to the LORD by fire—a pleasing aroma.

Regulations: Day of Atonement.

29:7-11pp— Lev 16:2-34; 23:26-32

7 "'On the tenth day of this seventh month hold a sacred assembly. You must deny yourselves[v][i] and do no work.[j] 8 Present as an aroma pleasing to the LORD a burnt offering of one young bull, one ram and seven male lambs a year old, all without defect. 9 With the bull prepare a grain offering[k] of three-tenths of an ephah of fine flour mixed with oil; with the ram, two-tenths; 10 and with each of the seven lambs, one-tenth.[l] 11 Include one male goat as a sin offering, in addition to the sin offering for atonement and the regular burnt offering[m] with its grain offering, and their drink offerings.

Regulations: Feast of Tabernacles.

29:12-39pp— Lev 23:33-43; Dt 16:13-17

12 "'On the fifteenth day of the seventh[n] month,[o] hold a sacred assembly and do no regular work. Celebrate a festival to the LORD for seven days. 13 Present an offering made by fire as an aroma pleasing to the LORD, a burnt offering of thirteen young bulls, two rams and fourteen male lambs a year old, all without defect. 14 With each of the thirteen bulls prepare a grain offering[p] of three-tenths of an ephah of fine flour mixed with oil; with each of the two rams, two-tenths; 15 and with each of the fourteen lambs, one-tenth. 16 Include one male goat as a sin offering, in addition to the regular burnt offering with its grain offering and drink offering.[q]

17 "'On the second day[r] prepare twelve young bulls, two rams and fourteen male lambs a year old, all without defect.[s] 18 With the bulls, rams and lambs, prepare their grain offerings[t] and drink offerings[u] according to the number specified.[v] 19 Include one male goat as a sin offering,[w] in addition to the regular burnt offering with its grain offering, and their drink offerings.

20 "'On the third day prepare eleven bulls, two rams and fourteen male lambs a year old, all without defect.[x] 21 With the bulls, rams and lambs, prepare their grain offerings and drink offerings according to the number specified.[y] 22 Include one male goat as a sin offering, in addition to the regular burnt offering with its grain offering and drink offering.

23 "'On the fourth day prepare ten bulls, two rams and fourteen male lambs a year old, all without defect. 24 With the bulls, rams and lambs, prepare their grain offerings and drink offerings according to the number specified. 25 Include one male goat as a sin offering, in addition to the regular burnt offering with its grain offering and drink offering.

26 "'On the fifth day prepare nine bulls, two rams and fourteen male lambs

28:29 [a]ver 13
28:31 [b]ver 3,19
29:1 [c]Lev 23:24
29:2 [d]Nu 28:2 [e]Nu 28:3
29:5 [f]Nu 28:15
29:6 [g]Nu 28:11 [h]Nu 28:3
29:7 [i]Ac 27:9 [j]Ex 31:15; Lev 16:29; 23:26-32
29:9 [k]ver 3,18
29:10 [l]Nu 28:13
29:11 [m]Lev 16:3; Nu 28:3
29:12 [n]1Ki 8:2 [o]Lev 23:24
29:14 [p]ver 3
29:16 [q]ver 6
29:17 [r]Lev 23:36 [s]Nu 28:3
29:18 [t]ver 9 [u]Nu 28:7 [v]Nu 15:4-12
29:19 [w]Nu 28:15
29:20 [x]ver 17
29:21 [y]ver 18

[s]3 That is, probably about 6 quarts (about 6.5 liters); also in verses 9 and 14 [t]3 That is, probably about 4 quarts (about 4.5 liters); also in verses 9 and 14 [u]4 That is, probably about 2 quarts (about 2 liters); also in verses 10 and 15 [v]7 Or *must fast*

a year old, all without defect. 27With the bulls, rams and lambs, prepare their grain offerings and drink offerings according to the number specified. 28Include one male goat as a sin offering, in addition to the regular burnt offering with its grain offering and drink offering.

29" 'On the sixth day prepare eight bulls, two rams and fourteen male lambs a year old, all without defect. 30With the bulls, rams and lambs, prepare their grain offerings and drink offerings according to the number specified. 31Include one male goat as a sin offering, in addition to the regular burnt offering with its grain offering and drink offering.

32" 'On the seventh day prepare seven bulls, two rams and fourteen male lambs a year old, all without defect. 33With the bulls, rams and lambs, prepare their grain offerings and drink offerings according to the number specified. 34Include one male goat as a sin offering, in addition to the regular burnt offering with its grain offering and drink offering.

35" 'On the eighth day hold an assembly[a] and do no regular work. 36Present an offering made by fire as an aroma pleasing to the LORD,[b] a burnt offering of one bull, one ram and seven male lambs a year old,[c] all without defect. 37With the bull, the ram and the lambs, prepare their grain offerings and drink offerings according to the number specified. 38Include one male goat as a sin offering, in addition to the regular burnt offering with its grain offering and drink offering.

39" 'In addition to what you vow[d] and your freewill offerings, prepare these for the LORD at your appointed feasts:[e] your burnt offerings,[f] grain offerings, drink offerings and fellowship offerings.[w]' "

40Moses told the Israelites all that the LORD commanded him.

The binding nature of vows and pledges.

30 Moses said to the heads of the tribes of Israel:[g] "This is what the LORD commands: 2When a man makes a vow to the LORD or takes an oath to obligate himself by a pledge, he must not break his word but must do everything he said.[h]

3"When a young woman still living in her father's house makes a vow to the LORD or obligates herself by a pledge 4and her father hears about her vow or pledge but says nothing to her, then all her vows and every pledge by which she obligated herself will stand.[i] 5But if her father forbids her when he hears about it, none of her vows or the pledges by which she obligated herself will stand; the LORD will release her because her father has forbidden her.

6"If she marries after she makes a vow[j] or after her lips utter a rash promise by which she obligates herself 7and her husband hears about it but says nothing to her, then her vows or the pledges by which she obligated herself will stand. 8But if her husband[k] forbids her when he hears about it, he nullifies the vow that obligates her or the rash promise by which she obligates herself, and the LORD will release her.

9"Any vow or obligation taken by a widow or divorced woman will be binding on her.

10"If a woman living with her husband makes a vow or obligates herself by a pledge under oath 11and her husband hears about it but says nothing to her and does not forbid her, then all her vows or the pledges by which she obligated herself will stand. 12But if her husband nullifies them when he hears about them, then none of the vows or pledges that came from her lips will stand.[l] Her husband has nullified them, and the LORD will release her. 13Her husband may confirm or nullify any vow she makes or any sworn pledge to deny herself. 14But if her husband says nothing to her about it from day to day, then he confirms all her vows or the pledges binding on her. He confirms them by saying nothing to her when he hears about them. 15If, however, he nullifies them some time after he hears

29:35 [a]Lev 23:36
29:36 [b]Lev 1:9 [c]ver 2
29:39 [d]Nu 6:2 [e]Lev 23:2 [f]Lev 1:3; 1Ch 23:31; 2Ch 31:3
30:1 [g]Nu 1:4
30:2 [h]Dt 23:21-23; Jdg 11:35; Job 22:27; Ps 22:25; 50:14; 116:14; Pr 20:25; Ecc 5:4,5; Jnh 1:16
30:4 [i]ver 7
30:6 [j]Lev 5:4
30:8 [k]Ge 3:16
30:12 [l]Eph 5:22; Col 3:18

w39 Traditionally *peace offerings*

about them, then he is responsible for
her guilt."
16These are the regulations the LORD
gave Moses concerning relationships
between a man and his wife, and between a father and his young daughter
still living in his house.

God's vengeance on the Midianites.

31 The LORD said to Moses, 2"Take
vengeance on the Midianites[a] for
the Israelites. After that, you will be
gathered to your people.[b]"
3So Moses said to the people, "Arm
some of your men to go to war against
the Midianites and to carry out the
LORD's vengeance[c] on them. 4Send into
battle a thousand men from each of the
tribes of Israel." 5So twelve thousand
men armed for battle, a thousand from
each tribe, were supplied from the clans
of Israel. 6Moses sent them into battle,
a thousand from each tribe, along with
Phinehas son of Eleazar, the priest, who
took with him articles from the sanctuary[d] and the trumpets[e] for signaling.
7They fought against Midian, as the
LORD commanded Moses, and killed
every man.[f] 8Among their victims were
Evi, Rekem, Zur, Hur and Reba[g]—the
five kings of Midian.[h] They also killed Balaam son of Beor with the sword.[i] 9The
Israelites captured the Midianite women
and children and took all the Midianite
herds, flocks and goods as plunder.
10They burned all the towns where the
Midianites had settled, as well as all
their camps.[j] 11They took all the plunder and spoils, including the people and
animals,[k] 12and brought the captives,
spoils and plunder to Moses and Eleazar
the priest and the Israelite assembly[l] at
their camp on the plains of Moab, by
the Jordan across from Jericho.[x]
13Moses, Eleazar the priest and all the
leaders of the community went to meet
them outside the camp. 14Moses was
angry with the officers of the army[m]—
the commanders of thousands and commanders of hundreds—who returned
from the battle.
15"Have you allowed all the women
to live?" he asked them. 16"They were
the ones who followed Balaam's advice[n]
and were the means of turning the Israelites away from the LORD in what happened at Peor,[o] so that a plague struck
the LORD's people. 17Now kill all the
boys. And kill every woman who has
slept with a man,[p] 18but save for yourselves every girl who has never slept
with a man.

Purification of the soldiers.

19"All of you who have killed anyone
or touched anyone who was killed[q]
must stay outside the camp seven days.
On the third and seventh days you must
purify yourselves[r] and your captives.
20Purify every garment[s] as well as
everything made of leather, goat hair
or wood."
21Then Eleazar the priest said to the
soldiers who had gone into battle, "This
is the requirement of the law that the
LORD gave Moses: 22Gold, silver, bronze,
iron,[t] tin, lead 23and anything else that
can withstand fire must be put through
the fire,[u] and then it will be clean. But
it must also be purified with the water
of cleansing.[v] And whatever cannot
withstand fire must be put through that
water. 24On the seventh day wash your
clothes and you will be clean.[w] Then
you may come into the camp."

Division of the spoils.

25The LORD said to Moses, 26"You and
Eleazar the priest and the family heads
of the community are to count all the
people[x] and animals that were captured.
27Divide[y] the spoils between the soldiers who took part in the battle and the
rest of the community. 28From the soldiers who fought in the battle, set apart
as tribute for the LORD[z] one out of every
five hundred, whether persons, cattle,
donkeys, sheep or goats. 29Take this tribute from their half share and give it to
Eleazar the priest as the LORD's part.

31:2 [a]Ge 25:2 [b]Nu 20:26; 27:13
31:3 [c]Jdg 11:36; 1Sa 24:12; 2Sa 4:8; 22:48; Ps 94:1; 149:7
31:6 [d]Nu 14:44 [e]Nu 10:9
31:7 [f]Dt 20:13; Jdg 21:11; 1Ki 11:15,16
31:8 [g]Jos 13:21 [h]Nu 25:15 [i]Jos 13:22
31:10 [j]Ge 25:16; 1Ch 6:54; Ps 69:25; Eze 25:4
31:11 [k]Dt 20:14
31:12 [l]Nu 27:2
31:14 [m]ver 48; Ex 18:21; Dt 1:15
31:16 [n]2Pe 2:15; Rev 2:14 [o]Nu 25:1-9
31:17 [p]Dt 7:2; 20:16-18; Jdg 21:11
31:19 [q]Nu 19:16 [r]Nu 19:12
31:20 [s]Nu 19:19
31:22 [t]Jos 6:19; 22:8
31:23 [u]1Co 3:13 [v]Nu 19:9,17
31:24 [w]Lev 11:25
31:26 [x]Nu 1:19
31:27 [y]Jos 22:8; 1Sa 30:24
31:28 [z]Nu 18:21

[x] *12* Hebrew *Jordan of Jericho*; possibly an ancient name for the Jordan River

30From the Israelites' half, select one out
of every fifty, whether persons, cattle,
donkeys, sheep, goats or other animals.
Give them to the Levites, who are responsible for the care of the LORD's tabernacle.[a]" 31So Moses and Eleazar the
priest did as the LORD commanded
Moses.
32The plunder remaining from the
spoils that the soldiers took was 675,000
sheep, 3372,000 cattle, 3461,000 donkeys 35and 32,000 women who had
never slept with a man.
36The half share of those who fought
in the battle was:

337,500 sheep, 37of which the tribute for the LORD[b] was 675;
3836,000 cattle, of which the tribute
for the LORD was 72;
3930,500 donkeys, of which the tribute for the LORD was 61;
4016,000 people, of which the tribute
for the LORD was 32.

41Moses gave the tribute to Eleazar
the priest as the LORD's part,[c] as the
LORD commanded Moses.
42The half belonging to the Israelites,
which Moses set apart from that of the
fighting men— 43the community's half—
was 337,500 sheep, 4436,000 cattle,
4530,500 donkeys 46and 16,000 people.
47From the Israelites' half, Moses selected one out of every fifty persons and
animals, as the LORD commanded him,
and gave them to the Levites, who were
responsible for the care of the LORD's
tabernacle.
48Then the officers who were over
the units of the army—the commanders of thousands and commanders of
hundreds—went to Moses 49and said
to him, "Your servants have counted the
soldiers under our command, and not
one is missing.[d] 50So we have brought
as an offering to the LORD the gold articles each of us acquired—armlets,
bracelets, signet rings, earrings and
necklaces—to make atonement for ourselves[e] before the LORD."
51Moses and Eleazar the priest accepted from them the gold—all the
crafted articles. 52All the gold from the
commanders of thousands and commanders of hundreds that Moses and
Eleazar presented as a gift to the LORD
weighed 16,750 shekels.[y] 53Each soldier had taken plunder[f] for himself.
54Moses and Eleazar the priest accepted
the gold from the commanders of thousands and commanders of hundreds and
brought it into the Tent of Meeting as
a memorial[g] for the Israelites before the
LORD.

31:30 [a]Nu 3:7; 18:3
31:37 [b]ver 38-41
31:41 [c]Nu 5:9; 18:8
31:49 [d]Jer 23:4
31:50 [e]Ex 30:16
31:53 [f]Dt 20:14
31:54 [g]Ex 28:12
32:1 [h]Nu 21:32 [i]Ex 12:38
32:3 [j]ver 34 [k]ver 36 [l]ver 37; Isa 15:4; 16:9; Jer 48:34 [m]ver 38; Jos 13:17; Eze 25:9
32:4 [n]Nu 21:34 [o]Ex 12:38
32:7 [p]Nu 13:27–14:4
32:8 [q]Nu 13:3,26; Dt 1:19-25
32:9 [r]Nu 13:23; Dt 1:24
32:10 [s]Nu 11:1
32:11 [t]Ex 30:14

Land east of the Jordan for Reuben, Gad and the half-tribe of Manasseh.

32 The Reubenites and Gadites,
who had very large herds and
flocks, saw that the lands of Jazer[h] and
Gilead were suitable for livestock.[i] 2So
they came to Moses and Eleazar the
priest and to the leaders of the community, and said, 3"Ataroth,[j] Dibon, Jazer,
Nimrah,[k] Heshbon, Elealeh,[l] Sebam,
Nebo and Beon[m]— 4the land the LORD
subdued[n] before the people of Israel—
are suitable for livestock,[o] and your servants have livestock. 5If we have found
favor in your eyes," they said, "let this
land be given to your servants as our
possession. Do not make us cross the
Jordan."
6Moses said to the Gadites and Reubenites, "Shall your countrymen go to
war while you sit here? 7Why do you discourage the Israelites from going over
into the land the LORD has given them?[p]
8This is what your fathers did when I
sent them from Kadesh Barnea to look
over the land.[q] 9After they went up to
the Valley of Eshcol[r] and viewed the
land, they discouraged the Israelites from
entering the land the LORD had given
them. 10The LORD's anger was aroused[s]
that day and he swore this oath: 11'Because they have not followed me wholeheartedly, not one of the men twenty
years old or more[t] who came up out of
Egypt will see the land I promised on

[y]52 That is, about 420 pounds (about 190 kilograms)

oath[a] to Abraham, Isaac and Jacob[b]— **12**not one except Caleb son of Jephunneh the Kenizzite and Joshua son of Nun, for they followed the LORD wholeheartedly.'[c] **13**The LORD's anger burned against Israel[d] and he made them wander in the desert forty years, until the whole generation of those who had done evil in his sight was gone.[e]

14"And here you are, a brood of sinners, standing in the place of your fathers and making the LORD even more angry with Israel.[f] **15**If you turn away from following him, he will again leave all this people in the desert, and you will be the cause of their destruction.[g]"

16Then they came up to him and said, "We would like to build pens here for our livestock[h] and cities for our women and children. **17**But we are ready to arm ourselves and go ahead of the Israelites[i] until we have brought them to their place.[j] Meanwhile our women and children will live in fortified cities, for protection from the inhabitants of the land. **18**We will not return to our homes until every Israelite has received his inheritance.[k] **19**We will not receive any inheritance with them on the other side of the Jordan, because our inheritance has come to us on the east side of the Jordan."[l]

20Then Moses said to them, "If you will do this—if you will arm yourselves before the LORD for battle,[m] **21**and if all of you will go armed over the Jordan before the LORD until he has driven his enemies out before him— **22**then when the land is subdued before the LORD, you may return[n] and be free from your obligation to the LORD and to Israel. And this land will be your possession before the LORD.[o]

23"But if you fail to do this, you will be sinning against the LORD; and you may be sure that your sin will find you out.[p] **24**Build cities for your women and children, and pens for your flocks,[q] but do what you have promised.[r]"

25The Gadites and Reubenites said to Moses, "We your servants will do as our lord commands. **26**Our children and wives, our flocks and herds will remain here in the cities of Gilead.[s] **27**But your servants, every man armed for battle, will cross over to fight before the LORD, just as our lord says."

28Then Moses gave orders about them[t] to Eleazar the priest and Joshua son of Nun and to the family heads of the Israelite tribes. **29**He said to them, "If the Gadites and Reubenites, every man armed for battle, cross over the Jordan with you before the LORD, then when the land is subdued before you, give them the land of Gilead as their possession. **30**But if they do not cross over with you armed, they must accept their possession with you in Canaan."

31The Gadites and Reubenites answered, "Your servants will do what the LORD has said.[u] **32**We will cross over before the LORD into Canaan armed, but the property we inherit will be on this side of the Jordan."

33Then Moses gave to the Gadites,[v] the Reubenites and the half-tribe of Manasseh son of Joseph the kingdom of Sihon king of the Amorites[w] and the kingdom of Og king of Bashan—the whole land with its cities and the territory around them.[x]

34The Gadites built up Dibon, Ataroth, Aroer,[y] **35**Atroth Shophan, Jazer,[z] Jogbehah, **36**Beth Nimrah[a] and Beth Haran as fortified cities, and built pens for their flocks. **37**And the Reubenites rebuilt Heshbon, Elealeh and Kiriathaim, **38**as well as Nebo[b] and Baal Meon (these names were changed) and Sibmah. They gave names to the cities they rebuilt.

39The descendants of Makir[c] son of Manasseh went to Gilead, captured it and drove out the Amorites who were there. **40**So Moses gave Gilead to the Makirites,[d] the descendants of Manasseh, and they settled there. **41**Jair, a descendant of Manasseh, captured their settlements and called them Havvoth Jair.[z][e] **42**And Nobah captured Kenath and

32:11 [a]Nu 14:23 [b]Nu 14:28-30
32:12 [c]Nu 14:24,30; Dt 1:36; Ps 63:8
32:13 [d]Ex 4:14 [e]Nu 14:28-35; 26:64,65
32:14 [f]ver 10; Dt 1:34; Ps 78:59
32:15 [g]Dt 30:17-18; 2Ch 7:20
32:16 [h]Ex 12:38; Dt 3:19
32:17 [i]Jos 4:12,13 [j]Nu 22:4; Dt 3:20
32:18 [k]Jos 22:1-4
32:19 [l]Jos 12:1
32:20 [m]Dt 3:18
32:22 [n]Jos 22:4 [o]Dt 3:18-20
32:23 [p]Ge 4:7; 44:16; Isa 59:12
32:24 [q]ver 1,16 [r]Nu 30:2
32:26 [s]Jos 1:14
32:28 [t]Dt 3:18-20; Jos 1:13
32:31 [u]ver 29
32:33 [v]Jos 13:24-28; 1Sa 13:7 [w]Dt 2:26 [x]Nu 21:24; Jos 12:6
32:34 [y]Dt 2:36; Jdg 11:26
32:35 [z]ver 3
32:36 [a]ver 3
32:38 [b]ver 3; Isa 15:2; Jer 48:1,22
32:39 [c]Ge 50:23

32:40 [d]Dt 3:15; Jos 17:1 **32:41** [e]Dt 3:14; Jos 13:30; Jdg 10:4; 1Ch 2:23

[z]41 Or *them the settlements of Jair*

its surrounding settlements and called it
Nobah after himself.[a]

Israel's journey from Egypt is summarized.

33 Here are the stages in the journey of the Israelites when they
came out of Egypt[b] by divisions under
the leadership of Moses and Aaron.[c] 2 At
the LORD's command Moses recorded the
stages in their journey. This is their
journey by stages:

3 The Israelites set out from Rameses on the fifteenth day of the first
month, the day after the Passover.[d]
They marched out boldly[e] in full
view of all the Egyptians, 4 who
were burying all their firstborn,
whom the LORD had struck down
among them; for the LORD had
brought judgment on their gods.[f]
5 The Israelites left Rameses and
camped at Succoth.[g]
6 They left Succoth and camped at
Etham, on the edge of the desert.[h]
7 They left Etham, turned back to
Pi Hahiroth, to the east of Baal Zephon,[i] and camped near Migdol.[j]
8 They left Pi Hahiroth[a] and
passed through the sea[k] into the
desert, and when they had traveled
for three days in the Desert of
Etham, they camped at Marah.[l]
9 They left Marah and went to
Elim, where there were twelve
springs and seventy palm trees, and
they camped[m] there.
10 They left Elim and camped by
the Red Sea.[b]
11 They left the Red Sea and
camped in the Desert of Sin.[n]
12 They left the Desert of Sin and
camped at Dophkah.
13 They left Dophkah and camped
at Alush.
14 They left Alush and camped at
Rephidim, where there was no
water for the people to drink.
15 They left Rephidim[o] and
camped in the Desert of Sinai.[p]
16 They left the Desert of Sinai
and camped at Kibroth Hattaavah.[q]
17 They left Kibroth Hattaavah and
camped at Hazeroth.[r]
18 They left Hazeroth and camped
at Rithmah.
19 They left Rithmah and camped
at Rimmon Perez.
20 They left Rimmon Perez and
camped at Libnah.[s]
21 They left Libnah and camped
at Rissah.
22 They left Rissah and camped
at Kehelathah.
23 They left Kehelathah and
camped at Mount Shepher.
24 They left Mount Shepher and
camped at Haradah.
25 They left Haradah and camped
at Makheloth.
26 They left Makheloth and
camped at Tahath.
27 They left Tahath and camped
at Terah.
28 They left Terah and camped at
Mithcah.
29 They left Mithcah and camped
at Hashmonah.
30 They left Hashmonah and
camped at Moseroth.[t]
31 They left Moseroth and camped
at Bene Jaakan.
32 They left Bene Jaakan and
camped at Hor Haggidgad.
33 They left Hor Haggidgad and
camped at Jotbathah.[u]
34 They left Jotbathah and camped
at Abronah.
35 They left Abronah and camped
at Ezion Geber.[v]
36 They left Ezion Geber and
camped at Kadesh, in the Desert of
Zin.[w]
37 They left Kadesh and camped
at Mount Hor,[x] on the border of
Edom.[y] 38 At the LORD's command
Aaron the priest went up Mount
Hor, where he died[z] on the first

32:42 [a] 2Sa 18:18; Ps 49:11
33:1 [b] Mic 6:4 [c] Ps 77:20
33:3 [d] Ex 13:4 [e] Ex 14:8
33:4 [f] Ex 12:12
33:5 [g] Ex 12:37
33:6 [h] Ex 13:20
33:7 [i] Ex 14:9 [j] Ex 14:2
33:8 [k] Ex 14:22 [l] Ex 15:23
33:9 [m] Ex 15:27
33:11 [n] Ex 16:1
33:15 [o] Ex 17:1 [p] Ex 19:1
33:16 [q] Nu 11:34
33:17 [r] Nu 11:35
33:20 [s] Jos 10:29
33:30 [t] Dt 10:6
33:33 [u] Dt 10:7
33:35 [v] Dt 2:8; 1Ki 9:26; 22:48
33:36 [w] Nu 20:1
33:37 [x] Nu 20:22 [y] Nu 20:16; 21:4
33:38 [z] Dt 10:6

a *8* Many manuscripts of the Masoretic Text, Samaritan Pentateuch and Vulgate; most manuscripts of the Masoretic Text *left from before Hahiroth*
b *10* Hebrew *Yam Suph*; that is, Sea of Reeds; also in verse 11

day of the fifth month of the fortieth
year after the Israelites came out of
Egypt.[a] 39 Aaron was a hundred and
twenty-three years old when he
died on Mount Hor.
40 The Canaanite king of Arad,[b]
who lived in the Negev of Canaan,
heard that the Israelites were
coming.
41 They left Mount Hor and
camped at Zalmonah.
42 They left Zalmonah and camped
at Punon.
43 They left Punon and camped
at Oboth.[c]
44 They left Oboth and camped
at Iye Abarim, on the border of
Moab.[d]
45 They left Iyim[c] and camped at
Dibon Gad.
46 They left Dibon Gad and
camped at Almon Diblathaim.
47 They left Almon Diblathaim
and camped in the mountains of
Abarim,[e] near Nebo.
48 They left the mountains of
Abarim and camped on the plains
of Moab by the Jordan across from
Jericho.[d][f] 49 There on the plains of
Moab they camped along the Jordan from Beth Jeshimoth to Abel
Shittim.[g]

God orders Canaan's idols to be destroyed.

50 On the plains of Moab by the Jordan across from Jericho the LORD said to
Moses, 51 "Speak to the Israelites and say
to them: 'When you cross the Jordan
into Canaan,[h] 52 drive out all the inhabitants of the land before you. Destroy all
their carved images and their cast idols,
and demolish all their high places.[i]
53 Take possession of the land and settle
in it, for I have given you the land to possess.[j] 54 Distribute the land by lot, according to your clans.[k] To a larger group
give a larger inheritance, and to a smaller group a smaller one. Whatever falls to
them by lot will be theirs. Distribute it
according to your ancestral tribes.

33:38 [a]Nu 20:25-28
33:40 [b]Nu 21:1
33:43 [c]Nu 21:10
33:44 [d]Nu 21:11
33:47 [e]Nu 27:12
33:48 [f]Nu 22:1
33:49 [g]Nu 25:1
33:51 [h]Jos 3:17
33:52 [i]Ex 23:24; 34:13; Lev 26:1; Dt 7:2,5; 12:3; Jos 11:12; Ps 106:34-36
33:53 [j]Dt 11:31; Jos 21:43
33:54 [k]Nu 26:54
33:55 [l]Jos 23:13; Jdg 2:3; Ps 106:36
34:2 [m]Ge 17:8; Dt 1:7-8; Ps 78:54-55 [n]Eze 47:15
34:3 [o]Jos 15:1-3 [p]Ge 14:3
34:4 [q]Jos 15:3 [r]Nu 32:8
34:5 [s]Ge 15:18; Jos 15:4
34:7 [t]Eze 47:15-17
34:8 [u]Nu 13:21; Jos 13:5
34:11 [v]2Ki 23:33; Jer 39:5 [w]Dt 3:17; Jos 11:2; 13:27

55 " 'But if you do not drive out the
inhabitants of the land, those you allow
to remain will become barbs in your
eyes and thorns[l] in your sides. They
will give you trouble in the land where
you will live. 56 And then I will do to you
what I plan to do to them.' "

Boundaries of Canaan.

34 The LORD said to Moses,
2 "Command the Israelites and
say to them: 'When you enter Canaan,
the land that will be allotted to you as
an inheritance[m] will have these boundaries:[n]

3 " 'Your southern side will include
some of the Desert of Zin[o] along the
border of Edom. On the east, your
southern boundary will start from the
end of the Salt Sea,[e][p] 4 cross south of
Scorpion[f] Pass,[q] continue on to Zin and
go south of Kadesh Barnea.[r] Then it will
go to Hazar Addar and over to Azmon,
5 where it will turn, join the Wadi of
Egypt[s] and end at the Sea.[g]
6 " 'Your western boundary will be the
coast of the Great Sea. This will be your
boundary on the west.
7 " 'For your northern boundary,[t] run a
line from the Great Sea to Mount Hor
8 and from Mount Hor to Lebo[h] Hamath.[u] Then the boundary will go to
Zedad, 9 continue to Ziphron and end at
Hazar Enan. This will be your boundary
on the north.
10 " 'For your eastern boundary, run a
line from Hazar Enan to Shepham. 11 The
boundary will go down from Shepham
to Riblah[v] on the east side of Ain and
continue along the slopes east of the Sea
of Kinnereth.[i][w] 12 Then the boundary will
go down along the Jordan and end at
the Salt Sea.
" 'This will be your land, with its
boundaries on every side.' "

[c]45 That is, Iye Abarim [d]48 Hebrew *Jordan of Jericho*; possibly an ancient name for the Jordan River; also in verse 50 [e]3 That is, the Dead Sea; also in verse 12 [f]4 Hebrew *Akrabbim* [g]5 That is, the Mediterranean; also in verses 6 and 7 [h]8 Or *to the entrance to* [i]11 That is, Galilee

13 Moses commanded the Israelites:
"Assign this land by lot as an inheritance.[a] The LORD has ordered that it be
given to the nine and a half tribes,
14 because the families of the tribe of
Reuben, the tribe of Gad and the half-
tribe of Manasseh have received their
inheritance.[b] 15 These two and a half
tribes have received their inheritance
on the east side of the Jordan of Jericho,[j]
toward the sunrise."

Names of men assigned to divide the land.

16 The LORD said to Moses, 17 "These
are the names of the men who are to
assign the land for you as an inheritance:
Eleazar the priest and Joshua[c] son of
Nun. 18 And appoint one leader from
each tribe to help[d] assign the land.
19 These are their names:

Caleb[e] son of Jephunneh,
from the tribe of Judah;[f]
20 Shemuel son of Ammihud,
from the tribe of Simeon;[g]
21 Elidad son of Kislon,
from the tribe of Benjamin;[h]
22 Bukki son of Jogli,
the leader from the tribe of Dan;
23 Hanniel son of Ephod,
the leader from the tribe of Manasseh son of Joseph;
24 Kemuel son of Shiphtan,
the leader from the tribe of
Ephraim son of Joseph;
25 Elizaphan son of Parnach,
the leader from the tribe of Zebulun;
26 Paltiel son of Azzan,
the leader from the tribe of Issachar;
27 Ahihud son of Shelomi,
the leader from the tribe of Asher;[i]
28 Pedahel son of Ammihud,
the leader from the tribe of
Naphtali."

29 These are the men the LORD commanded to assign the inheritance to the
Israelites in the land of Canaan.

34:13 [a] Jos 14:1-5
34:14 [b] Nu 32:33; Jos 14:3
34:17 [c] Jos 14:1
34:18 [d] Nu 1:4,16
34:19 [e] Nu 26:65 [f] Ge 29:35; Dt 33:7
34:20 [g] Ge 49:5
34:21 [h] Ge 49:27; Ps 68:27
34:27 [i] Nu 1:40
35:2 [j] Lev 25:32-34; Jos 14:3,4
35:6 [k] Jos 20:7-9; 21:3,13
35:8 [l] Nu 26:54; 33:54; Jos 21:1-42
35:10 [m] Jos 20:2
35:11 [n] ver 22-25 [o] Ex 21:13; Dt 19:1-13
35:12 [p] Dt 19:6; Jos 20:3

Forty-eight towns for the Levites.

35 On the plains of Moab by the
Jordan across from Jericho,[k]
the LORD said to Moses, 2 "Command the
Israelites to give the Levites towns to
live in[j] from the inheritance the Israelites will possess. And give them pasturelands around the towns. 3 Then they
will have towns to live in and pasturelands for their cattle, flocks and all their
other livestock.
4 "The pasturelands around the towns
that you give the Levites will extend out
fifteen hundred feet[l] from the town wall.
5 Outside the town, measure three thousand feet[m] on the east side, three thousand on the south side, three thousand
on the west and three thousand on the
north, with the town in the center.
They will have this area as pastureland
for the towns.

Six cities of refuge.

35:6-34Ref— Dt 4:41-43; 19:1-14; Jos 20:1-9

6 "Six of the towns you give the
Levites will be cities of refuge, to which
a person who has killed someone may
flee.[k] In addition, give them forty-two
other towns. 7 In all you must give the
Levites forty-eight towns, together with
their pasturelands. 8 The towns you give
the Levites from the land the Israelites
possess are to be given in proportion
to the inheritance of each tribe: Take
many towns from a tribe that has many,
but few from one that has few."[l]
9 Then the LORD said to Moses:
10 "Speak to the Israelites and say to
them: 'When you cross the Jordan into
Canaan,[m] 11 select some towns to be
your cities of refuge, to which a person
who has killed someone[n] accidentally[o]
may flee. 12 They will be places of refuge
from the avenger,[p] so that a person
accused of murder may not die before he

j *15* *Jordan of Jericho* was possibly an ancient name for the Jordan River.
k *1* Hebrew *Jordan of Jericho*; possibly an ancient name for the Jordan River
l *4* Hebrew *a thousand cubits* (about 450 meters)
m *5* Hebrew *two thousand cubits* (about 900 meters)

stands trial before the assembly. 13 These
six towns you give will be your cities of
refuge. 14 Give three on this side of the
Jordan and three in Canaan as cities of
refuge. 15 These six towns will be a place
of refuge for Israelites, aliens and any
other people living among them, so that
anyone who has killed another accidentally can flee there.
16 "'If a man strikes someone with an
iron object so that he dies, he is a murderer; the murderer shall be put to
death.[a] 17 Or if anyone has a stone in his
hand that could kill, and he strikes
someone so that he dies, he is a murderer; the murderer shall be put to
death. 18 Or if anyone has a wooden
object in his hand that could kill, and he
hits someone so that he dies, he is a
murderer; the murderer shall be put to
death. 19 The avenger of blood shall put
the murderer to death; when he meets
him, he shall put him to death.[b] 20 If
anyone with malice aforethought shoves
another or throws something at him
intentionally[c] so that he dies 21 or if in
hostility he hits him with his fist so
that he dies, that person shall be put to
death; he is a murderer. The avenger
of blood shall put the murderer to death
when he meets him.
22 "'But if without hostility someone
suddenly shoves another or throws
something at him unintentionally[d] 23 or,
without seeing him, drops a stone on
him that could kill him, and he dies,
then since he was not his enemy and he
did not intend to harm him, 24 the assembly[e] must judge between him and the
avenger of blood according to these
regulations. 25 The assembly must protect the one accused of murder from the
avenger of blood and send him back to
the city of refuge to which he fled. He
must stay there until the death of the
high priest, who was anointed with the
holy oil.[f]
26 "'But if the accused ever goes outside the limits of the city of refuge to
which he has fled 27 and the avenger of
blood finds him outside the city, the
avenger of blood may kill the accused

35:16 [a]Ex 21:12; Lev 24:17
35:19 [b]ver 21
35:20 [c]Ge 4:8; Ex 21:14; Dt 19:11; 2Sa 3:27; 20:10
35:22 [d]ver 11; Ex 21:13
35:24 [e]ver 12; Jos 20:6
35:25 [f]Ex 29:7
35:29 [g]Nu 27:11
35:30 [h]ver 16; Dt 17:6; 19:15; Mt 18:16; Jn 7:51; 2Co 13:1; Heb 10:28
35:33 [i]Ge 9:6; Ps 106:38; Mic 4:11
35:34 [j]Lev 18:24, 25 [k]Ex 29:45
36:1 [l]Nu 26:29 [m]Nu 27:2
36:2 [n]Nu 26:33; 27:1,7

without being guilty of murder. 28 The
accused must stay in his city of refuge
until the death of the high priest; only
after the death of the high priest may he
return to his own property.
29 "'These are to be legal requirements[g] for you throughout the generations to come, wherever you live.
30 "'Anyone who kills a person is to be
put to death as a murderer only on the
testimony of witnesses. But no one is to
be put to death on the testimony of only
one witness.[h]
31 "'Do not accept a ransom for the
life of a murderer, who deserves to die.
He must surely be put to death.
32 "'Do not accept a ransom for anyone who has fled to a city of refuge and
so allow him to go back and live on his
own land before the death of the high
priest.
33 "'Do not pollute the land where
you are. Bloodshed pollutes the land,[i]
and atonement cannot be made for the
land on which blood has been shed,
except by the blood of the one who
shed it. 34 Do not defile the land[j] where
you live and where I dwell,[k] for I, the
LORD, dwell among the Israelites.'"

Problems resolved concerning the inheritance of Zelophehad's daughters.

36:1-12pp— Nu 27:1-11

36 The family heads of the clan of
Gilead[l] son of Makir, the son of
Manasseh, who were from the clans of
the descendants of Joseph, came and
spoke before Moses and the leaders,[m]
the heads of the Israelite families. 2 They
said, "When the LORD commanded my
lord to give the land as an inheritance
to the Israelites by lot, he ordered you to
give the inheritance of our brother
Zelophehad[n] to his daughters. 3 Now
suppose they marry men from other
Israelite tribes; then their inheritance
will be taken from our ancestral inheritance and added to that of the tribe
they marry into. And so part of the
inheritance allotted to us will be taken

away. 4When the Year of Jubilee[a] for
the Israelites comes, their inheritance
will be added to that of the tribe into
which they marry, and their property
will be taken from the tribal inheritance
of our forefathers."
5Then at the LORD's command Moses
gave this order to the Israelites: "What
the tribe of the descendants of Joseph is
saying is right. 6This is what the LORD
commands for Zelophehad's daughters:
They may marry anyone they please as
long as they marry within the tribal
clan of their father. 7No inheritance[b] in
Israel is to pass from tribe to tribe, for
every Israelite shall keep the tribal land
inherited from his forefathers. 8Every
daughter who inherits land in any Israelite tribe must marry someone in her
father's tribal clan,[c] so that every Israelite will possess the inheritance of his
fathers. 9No inheritance may pass from
tribe to tribe, for each Israelite tribe is
to keep the land it inherits."
10So Zelophehad's daughters did as
the LORD commanded Moses. 11Zelophe-
had's daughters—Mahlah, Tirzah, Hoglah, Milcah and Noah[d]—married their
cousins on their father's side. 12They
married within the clans of the descendants of Manasseh son of Joseph, and
their inheritance remained in their father's clan and tribe.
13These are the commands and regulations the LORD gave through Moses[e] to
the Israelites on the plains of Moab by
the Jordan across from Jericho.[n][f]

36:4 [a]Lev 25:10
36:7 [b]1Ki 21:3
36:8 [c]1Ch 23:22
36:11 [d]Nu 26:33; 27:1
36:13 [e]Lev 26:46; 27:34 [f]Nu 22:1

[n]*13* Hebrew *Jordan of Jericho*; possibly an ancient name for the Jordan River

DEUTERONOMY

Author: Moses. (However, Joshua probably recorded Moses' death in chapter 34.)

Date Written: Between 1410 and 1395 B.C.

Time Span: 1-2 months.

Title: It is derived from the Greek word, *Deuteronomion,* which means "second law-giving."

Background: The Pentateuch concludes with this fifth and final book of Moses. Deuteronomy begins at the end of Israel's 40-year period in the desert when the new generation is preparing to enter the promised land (Canaan).

Where Written: On the plains near the Jordan River in Moab (due east of Jericho).

To Whom: To the new generation of Israelites.

Content: A number of years have passed since the law was given at Mount Sinai to the parents of these Israelites. But that generation has since died in the desert (except Caleb and Joshua), and this new generation needs to learn how to develop a proper relationship with God. Thus, 3 farewell sermons to Israel are given by the 120-year-old Moses just prior to his death, and the appointment of Joshua as Moses' successor takes place. These addresses challenge the people to live their future in faith and obedience as they review their past. Moral and legal regulations are expanded upon, and the Ten Commandments are repeated.

Key Words: "Remember"; "Covenant"; "Obedience." Moses gives constant encouragement to the Israelites to "remember" their original "covenant" with the God of the patriarchs, who has freed them from Egyptian bondage and sustained them through the desert. The only proper response from such an undeserving people is "obedience" to God without reservation.

Themes: • There is but one true God. • Obedience brings blessings...disobedience brings punishment. • Genuine love for God is evidenced by holy living and by love for others. • God's power and faithfulness can be depended on during our times of need. • We must teach our children to fear the Lord and keep his commandments (chapter 6).

Outline:

1. Moses' first sermon: Review of Israel's history. 1:1-4:43
2. Moses' second sermon: Review of the law. 4:44-11:32
   Application of the law. 12:1-26:19
   Blessings and curses. 27:1-28:68
3. Moses' third sermon: Renewal of Israel's covenant. 29:1-30:20
4. The appointment of Joshua as Moses' successor. 31:1-32:43
5. Moses' final words and death. 32:44-34:12

DEUTERONOMY

Moses begins his speech to the Israelites: The promise of God.

1 These are the words Moses spoke to all Israel in the desert east of the Jordan—that is, in the Arabah—opposite Suph, between Paran and Tophel, Laban, Hazeroth and Dizahab. 2(It takes eleven days to go from Horeb[a] to Kadesh Barnea[b] by the Mount Seir road.)

3In the fortieth year,[c] on the first day of the eleventh month, Moses proclaimed[d] to the Israelites all that the LORD had commanded him concerning them. 4This was after he had defeated Sihon[e] king of the Amorites, who reigned in Heshbon,[f] and at Edrei had defeated Og[g] king of Bashan, who reigned in Ashtaroth.

5East of the Jordan in the territory of Moab, Moses began to expound this law, saying:

6The LORD our God said to us[h] at Horeb,[i] "You have stayed long enough at this mountain. 7Break camp and advance into the hill country of the Amorites; go to all the neighboring peoples in the Arabah, in the mountains, in the western foothills, in the Negev[j] and along the coast, to the land of the Canaanites and to Lebanon,[k] as far as the great river, the Euphrates. 8See, I have given you this land. Go in and take possession of the land that the LORD swore[l] he would give to your fathers—to Abraham, Isaac and Jacob—and to their descendants after them."

9At that time I said to you, "You are too heavy a burden for me to carry alone.[m] 10The LORD your God has increased your numbers so that today you are as many[n] as the stars in the sky.[o] 11May the LORD, the God of your fathers, increase you a thousand times and bless you as he has promised![p] 12But how can I bear your problems and your burdens and your disputes all by myself? 13Choose some wise, understanding and respected men[q] from each of your tribes, and I will set them over you."

14You answered me, "What you propose to do is good."

15So I took[r] the leading men of your tribes, wise and respected men, and appointed them to have authority over you—as commanders of thousands, of hundreds, of fifties and of tens and as tribal officials. 16And I charged your judges at that time: Hear the disputes between your brothers and judge fairly,[s] whether the case is between brother Israelites or between one of them and an alien.[t] 17Do not show partiality[u] in judging; hear both small and great alike. Do not be afraid of any man,[v] for judgment belongs to God. Bring me any case too hard for you, and I will hear it.[w] 18And at that time I told you everything you were to do.

The Israelites in their rebellion refuse to take the land.

19Then, as the LORD our God commanded us, we set out from Horeb and went toward the hill country of the Amorites through all that vast and dreadful desert[x] that you have seen, and so we reached Kadesh Barnea.[y] 20Then I said to you, "You have reached the hill country of the Amorites, which the LORD our God is giving us. 21See, the LORD your God has given you the land. Go up and take possession of it as the LORD, the God of your fathers, told you. Do not be afraid;[z] do not be discouraged."

22Then all of you came to me and said, "Let us send men ahead to spy out the land for us and bring back a report about the route we are to take and the towns we will come to."

23The idea seemed good to me; so I selected[a] twelve of you, one man from each tribe. 24They left and went up into the hill country, and came to the Valley of Eshcol[b] and explored it. 25Taking with them some of the fruit of the land, they brought it down to us and reported,[c] "It is a good land that the LORD our God is giving us."

1:2 [a]Ex 3:1 [b]Nu 13:26; Dt 9:23
1:3 [c]Nu 33:38 [d]Dt 4:1-2
1:4 [e]Nu 21:21-26 [f]Nu 21:25 [g]Nu 21:33-35; Jos 13:12
1:6 [h]Nu 10:13 [i]Ex 3:1
1:7 [j]Jos 10:40 [k]Dt 11:24
1:8 [l]Ge 12:7; 15:18; 17:7-8; 26:4; 28:13
1:9 [m]Ex 18:18
1:10 [n]Ge 15:5 [o]Dt 10:22; 28:62
1:11 [p]Ge 22:17; Ex 32:13
1:13 [q]Ex 18:21
1:15 [r]Ex 18:25
1:16 [s]Dt 16:18; Jn 7:24 [t]Lev 24:22
1:17 [u]Lev 19:15; Dt 16:19; Pr 24:23; Jas 2:1 [v]2Ch 19:6 [w]Ex 18:26
1:19 [x]Dt 8:15; Jer 2:2,6 [y]ver 2; Nu 13:26
1:21 [z]Jos 1:6,9,18
1:23 [a]Nu 13:1-3
1:24 [b]Nu 13:21-25
1:25 [c]Nu 13:27

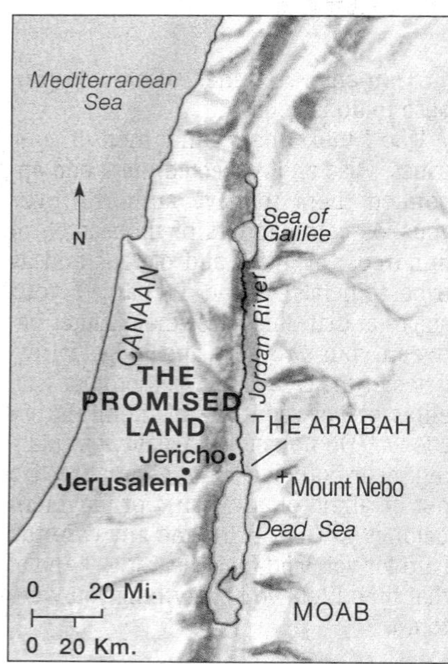

Events in Deuteronomy

The book of Deuteronomy opens with Israel camped east of the Jordan River in the Arabah in the land of Moab. Just before the people crossed the river into the promised land, Moses delivered an inspirational speech indicating how they were to live.

26But you were unwilling to go up;[a]
you rebelled against the command of the
LORD your God. 27You grumbled[b] in your
tents and said, "The LORD hates us; so he
brought us out of Egypt to deliver us
into the hands of the Amorites to destroy
us. 28Where can we go? Our brothers
have made us lose heart. They say, 'The
people are stronger and taller[c] than we
are; the cities are large, with walls up to
the sky. We even saw the Anakites[d]
there.'"

29Then I said to you, "Do not be terrified; do not be afraid of them. 30The
LORD your God, who is going before you,
will fight[e] for you, as he did for you in
Egypt, before your very eyes, 31and in
the desert. There you saw how the LORD
your God carried[f] you, as a father carries his son, all the way you went until
you reached this place."

32In spite of this, you did not trust[g]
in the LORD your God, 33who went ahead
of you on your journey, in fire by night
and in a cloud by day,[h] to search[i] out
places for you to camp and to show you
the way you should go.

34When the LORD heard what you said,
he was angry and solemnly swore:[j]
35"Not a man of this evil generation
shall see the good land[k] I swore to give
your forefathers, 36except Caleb son of
Jephunneh. He will see it, and I will
give him and his descendants the land
he set his feet on, because he followed
the LORD wholeheartedly.[l]"

37Because of you the LORD became
angry[m] with me also and said, "You shall
not enter[n] it, either. 38But your assistant, Joshua[o] son of Nun, will enter it.
Encourage[p] him, because he will lead[q]
Israel to inherit it. 39And the little ones
that you said would be taken captive,[r]
your children who do not yet know[s]
good from bad—they will enter the land.
I will give it to them and they will take
possession of it. 40But as for you, turn
around and set out toward the desert
along the route to the Red Sea.[a][t]"

41Then you replied, "We have sinned
against the LORD. We will go up and
fight, as the LORD our God commanded
us." So every one of you put on his
weapons, thinking it easy to go up into
the hill country.

42But the LORD said to me, "Tell them,
'Do not go up and fight, because I will
not be with you. You will be defeated
by your enemies.'"[u]

43So I told you, but you would not
listen. You rebelled against the LORD's
command and in your arrogance you
marched up into the hill country. 44The
Amorites who lived in those hills came
out against you; they chased you like a
swarm of bees[v] and beat you down
from Seir all the way to Hormah. 45You
came back and wept before the LORD,
but he paid no attention to your weeping and turned a deaf ear to you.
46And so you stayed in Kadesh[w] many
days—all the time you spent there.

1:26 [a]Nu 14:1-4
1:27 [b]Dt 9:28; Ps 106:25
1:28 [c]Nu 13:32 [d]Nu 13:33; Dt 9:1-3
1:30 [e]Ex 14:14; Dt 3:22; Ne 4:20
1:31 [f]Dt 32:10-12; Isa 46:3-4; 63:9; Hos 11:3; Ac 13:18
1:32 [g]Ps 106:24; Jude 1:5
1:33 [h]Ex 13:21; Ps 78:14 [i]Nu 10:33
1:34 [j]Nu 14:23, 28-30
1:35 [k]Ps 95:11
1:36 [l]Nu 14:24; Jos 14:9
1:37 [m]Dt 3:26; 4:21 [n]Nu 20:12
1:38 [o]Nu 14:30 [p]Dt 31:7 [q]Dt 3:28
1:39 [r]Nu 14:3 [s]Isa 7:15-16
1:40 [t]Nu 14:25
1:42 [u]Nu 14:41-43
1:44 [v]Ps 118:12
1:46 [w]Nu 20:1; Jdg 11:17

a*40* Hebrew *Yam Suph*; that is, Sea of Reeds

The forty years of wandering.

2 Then we turned back and set out toward the desert along the route to the Red Sea,[b][a] as the LORD had directed me. For a long time we made our way around the hill country of Seir.

2 Then the LORD said to me, 3 "You have made your way around this hill country long enough; now turn north. 4 Give the people these orders:[b] 'You are about to pass through the territory of your brothers the descendants of Esau, who live in Seir. They will be afraid of you, but be very careful. 5 Do not provoke them to war, for I will not give you any of their land, not even enough to put your foot on. I have given Esau the hill country of Seir as his own.[c] 6 You are to pay them in silver for the food you eat and the water you drink.' "

7 The LORD your God has blessed you in all the work of your hands. He has watched[d] over your journey through this vast desert. These forty years the LORD your God has been with you, and you have not lacked anything.

8 So we went on past our brothers the descendants of Esau, who live in Seir. We turned from the Arabah road, which comes up from Elath and Ezion Geber,[e] and traveled along the desert road of Moab.[f]

9 Then the LORD said to me, "Do not harass the Moabites or provoke them to war, for I will not give you any part of their land. I have given Ar[g] to the descendants of Lot[h] as a possession."

10 (The Emites[i] used to live there—a people strong and numerous, and as tall as the Anakites.[j] 11 Like the Anakites, they too were considered Rephaites, but the Moabites called them Emites. 12 Horites used to live in Seir, but the descendants of Esau drove them out. They destroyed the Horites from before them and settled in their place, just as Israel did[k] in the land the LORD gave them as their possession.)

13 And the LORD said, "Now get up and cross the Zered Valley." So we crossed the valley.

14 Thirty-eight years passed from the time we left Kadesh Barnea[l] until we crossed the Zered Valley. By then, that entire generation[m] of fighting men had perished from the camp, as the LORD had sworn to them.[n] 15 The LORD's hand was against them until he had completely eliminated[o] them from the camp.

16 Now when the last of these fighting men among the people had died, 17 the LORD said to me, 18 "Today you are to pass by the region of Moab at Ar. 19 When you come to the Ammonites,[p] do not harass them or provoke them to war, for I will not give you possession of any land belonging to the Ammonites. I have given it as a possession to the descendants of Lot.[q]"

20 (That too was considered a land of the Rephaites, who used to live there; but the Ammonites called them Zamzummites. 21 They were a people strong and numerous, and as tall as the Anakites.[r] The LORD destroyed them from before the Ammonites, who drove them out and settled in their place. 22 The LORD had done the same for the descendants of Esau, who lived in Seir,[s] when he destroyed the Horites from before them. They drove them out and have lived in their place to this day. 23 And as for the Avvites[t] who lived in villages as far as Gaza, the Caphtorites[u] coming out from Caphtor[c][v] destroyed them and settled in their place.)

24 "Set out now and cross the Arnon Gorge.[w] See, I have given into your hand Sihon the Amorite, king of Heshbon, and his country. Begin to take possession of it and engage him in battle. 25 This very day I will begin to put the terror[x] and fear[y] of you on all the nations under heaven. They will hear reports of you and will tremble[z] and be in anguish because of you."

26 From the desert of Kedemoth I sent messengers to Sihon king of Heshbon offering peace and saying, 27 "Let us pass through your country. We will stay on

2:1 [a]Nu 21:4
2:4 [b]Nu 20:14-21
2:5 [c]Ge 36:8; Jos 24:4
2:7 [d]Dt 8:2-4
2:8 [e]1Ki 9:26 [f]Jdg 11:18
2:9 [g]Nu 21:15 [h]Ge 19:36-38
2:10 [i]Ge 14:5 [j]Nu 13:22,33
2:12 [k]ver 22
2:14 [l]Nu 13:26 [m]Nu 14:29-35 [n]Dt 1:34-35
2:15 [o]Ps 106:26
2:19 [p]Ge 19:38 [q]ver 9
2:21 [r]ver 10
2:22 [s]Ge 36:8
2:23 [t]Jos 13:3 [u]Ge 10:14 [v]Am 9:7
2:24 [w]Nu 21:13-14; Jdg 11:13,18
2:25 [x]Dt 11:25 [y]Jos 2:9,11 [z]Ex 15:14-16

b *1* Hebrew *Yam Suph*; that is, Sea of Reeds
c *23* That is, Crete

the main road; we will not turn aside to the right or to the left.[a] **28**Sell us food to eat and water to drink for their price in silver. Only let us pass through on foot[b]— **29**as the descendants of Esau, who live in Seir, and the Moabites, who live in Ar, did for us—until we cross the Jordan into the land the LORD our God is giving us." **30**But Sihon king of Heshbon refused to let us pass through. For the LORD[c] your God had made his spirit stubborn[d] and his heart obstinate in order to give him into your hands, as he has now done.

31The LORD said to me, "See, I have begun to deliver Sihon and his country over to you. Now begin to conquer and possess his land."[e]

32When Sihon and all his army came out to meet us in battle[f] at Jahaz, **33**the LORD our God delivered him over to us and we struck him down,[g] together with his sons and his whole army. **34**At that time we took all his towns and completely destroyed[d][h] them—men, women and children. We left no survivors. **35**But the livestock and the plunder from the towns we had captured we carried off for ourselves. **36**From Aroer[i] on the rim of the Arnon Gorge, and from the town in the gorge, even as far as Gilead, not one town was too strong for us. The LORD our God gave[j] us all of them. **37**But in accordance with the command of the LORD our God,[k] you did not encroach on any of the land of the Ammonites,[l] neither the land along the course of the Jabbok[m] nor that around the towns in the hills.

The Israelites' battles.

3 Next we turned and went up along the road toward Bashan, and Og king of Bashan with his whole army marched out to meet us in battle at Edrei.[n] **2**The LORD said to me, "Do not be afraid[o] of him, for I have handed him over to you with his whole army and his land. Do to him what you did to Sihon king of the Amorites, who reigned in Heshbon."

3So the LORD our God also gave into our hands Og king of Bashan and all his army. We struck them down, leaving no survivors.[p] **4**At that time we took all his cities. There was not one of the sixty cities that we did not take from them—the whole region of Argob, Og's kingdom in Bashan.[q] **5**All these cities were fortified with high walls and with gates and bars, and there were also a great many unwalled villages. **6**We completely destroyed[d] them, as we had done with Sihon king of Heshbon, destroying[d][r] every city—men, women and children. **7**But all the livestock and the plunder from their cities we carried off for ourselves.

8So at that time we took from these two kings of the Amorites the territory east of the Jordan, from the Arnon Gorge as far as Mount Hermon. **9**(Hermon is called Sirion[s] by the Sidonians; the Amorites call it Senir.)[t] **10**We took all the towns on the plateau, and all Gilead, and all Bashan as far as Salecah[u] and Edrei, towns of Og's kingdom in Bashan. **11**(Only Og king of Bashan was left of the remnant of the Rephaites.[v] His bed[e] was made of iron and was more than thirteen feet long and six feet wide.[f] It is still in Rabbah[w] of the Ammonites.)

Distribution of the land east of the Jordan.

12Of the land that we took over at that time, I gave the Reubenites and the Gadites the territory north of Aroer[x] by the Arnon Gorge, including half the hill country of Gilead, together with its towns. **13**The rest of Gilead and also all of Bashan, the kingdom of Og, I gave to the half tribe of Manasseh. (The whole region of Argob in Bashan used to be known as a land of the Rephaites. **14**Jair,[y] a descendant of Manasseh, took the

2:27 [a]Nu 21:21-22
2:28 [b]Nu 20:19
2:30 [c]Jos 11:20 [d]Ex 4:21; Nu 21:23; Ro 9:18
2:31 [e]Dt 1:8
2:32 [f]Nu 21:23
2:33 [g]Dt 29:7
2:34 [h]Dt 3:6; 7:2
2:36 [i]Dt 3:12; 4:48; Jos 13:9 [j]Ps 44:3
2:37 [k]ver 18-19 [l]Nu 21:24 [m]Ge 32:22; Dt 3:16
3:1 [n]Nu 21:33
3:2 [o]Nu 21:34
3:3 [p]Nu 21:35
3:4 [q]1Ki 4:13
3:6 [r]Dt 2:24,34
3:9 [s]Dt 4:48; Ps 29:6 [t]1Ch 5:23
3:10 [u]Jos 13:11
3:11 [v]Ge 14:5 [w]2Sa 12:26; Jer 49:2
3:12 [x]Nu 32:32-38; Dt 2:36; Jos 13:8-13
3:14 [y]Nu 32:41; 1Ch 2:22

[d] *34,6* The Hebrew term refers to the irrevocable giving over of things or persons to the LORD, often by totally destroying them. [e] *11* Or *sarcophagus* [f] *11* Hebrew *nine cubits long and four cubits wide* (about 4 meters long and 1.8 meters wide)

whole region of Argob as far as the border of the Geshurites and the Maacathites; it was named after him, so that to this day Bashan is called Havvoth Jair.[g]) 15And I gave Gilead to Makir.[a] 16But to the Reubenites and the Gadites I gave the territory extending from Gilead down to the Arnon Gorge (the middle of the gorge being the border) and out to the Jabbok River,[b] which is the border of the Ammonites. 17Its western border was the Jordan in the Arabah, from Kinnereth[c] to the Sea of the Arabah (the Salt Sea[h][d]), below the slopes of Pisgah.

18I commanded you at that time: "The LORD your God has given you this land to take possession of it. But all your able-bodied men, armed for battle, must cross over ahead of your brother Israelites.[e] 19However, your wives, your children and your livestock (I know you have much livestock) may stay in the towns I have given you, 20until the LORD gives rest to your brothers as he has to you, and they too have taken over the land that the LORD your God is giving them, across the Jordan. After that, each of you may go back to the possession I have given you."

God forbids Moses to cross the Jordan.

21At that time I commanded Joshua: "You have seen with your own eyes all that the LORD your God has done to these two kings. The LORD will do the same to all the kingdoms over there where you are going. 22Do not be afraid[f] of them; the LORD your God himself will fight[g] for you."

23At that time I pleaded with the LORD: 24"O Sovereign LORD, you have begun to show to your servant your greatness[h] and your strong hand. For what god[i] is there in heaven or on earth who can do the deeds and mighty works[j] you do?[k] 25Let me go over and see the good land[l] beyond the Jordan—that fine hill country and Lebanon."

26But because of you the LORD was angry[m] with me and would not listen to me. "That is enough," the LORD said. "Do not speak to me anymore about this matter. 27Go up to the top of Pisgah and look west and north and south and east. Look at the land with your own eyes, since you are not going to cross this Jordan.[n] 28But commission[o] Joshua, and encourage and strengthen him, for he will lead this people across[p] and will cause them to inherit the land that you will see." 29So we stayed in the valley near Beth Peor.[q]

Moses exhorts the people to keep God's commands.

4 Hear now, O Israel, the decrees and laws I am about to teach you. Follow them so that you may live[r] and may go in and take possession of the land that the LORD, the God of your fathers, is giving you. 2Do not add[s] to what I command you and do not subtract from it, but keep the commands of the LORD your God that I give you.

3You saw with your own eyes what the LORD did at Baal Peor.[t] The LORD your God destroyed from among you everyone who followed the Baal of Peor, 4but all of you who held fast to the LORD your God are still alive today.

5See, I have taught you decrees and laws as the LORD my God commanded me, so that you may follow them in the land you are entering to take possession of it. 6Observe them carefully, for this will show your wisdom[u] and understanding to the nations, who will hear about all these decrees and say, "Surely this great nation is a wise and understanding people."[v] 7What other nation is so great[w] as to have their gods near[x] them the way the LORD our God is near us whenever we pray to him? 8And what other nation is so great as to have such righteous decrees and laws as this body of laws I am setting before you today?

9Only be careful,[y] and watch yourselves closely so that you do not forget

3:15 [a]Nu 32:39-40
3:16 [b]Nu 21:24
3:17 [c]Nu 34:11; Jos 13:27 [d]Ge 14:3; Jos 12:3
3:18 [e]Nu 32:17
3:22 [f]Dt 1:29 [g]Ex 14:14; Dt 20:4
3:24 [h]Dt 11:2 [i]Ex 15:11; Ps 86:8 [j]Ps 71:16,19 [k]2Sa 7:22
3:25 [l]Dt 4:22
3:26 [m]Dt 1:37; 31:2
3:27 [n]Nu 27:12
3:28 [o]Nu 27:18-23 [p]Dt 31:3,23
3:29 [q]Dt 4:46; 34:6
4:1 [r]Dt 5:33; 8:1; 16:20; 30:15-20; Eze 20:11; Ro 10:5
4:2 [s]Dt 12:32; Jos 1:7; Rev 22:18-19
4:3 [t]Nu 25:1-9; Ps 106:28
4:6 [u]Dt 30:19-20; Ps 19:7; Pr 1:7 [v]Job 28:28
4:7 [w]2Sa 7:23 [x]Ps 46:1; Isa 55:6
4:9 [y]Pr 4:23

g *14* Or *called the settlements of Jair* h *17* That is, the Dead Sea

the things your eyes have seen or let
them slip from your heart as long as you
live. Teach[a] them to your children[b] and
to their children after them. 10Remem-
ber the day you stood before the LORD
your God at Horeb,[c] when he said to me,
"Assemble the people before me to hear
my words so that they may learn to
revere me as long as they live in the land
and may teach them to their children."
11You came near and stood at the foot of
the mountain while it blazed with fire[d]
to the very heavens, with black clouds
and deep darkness. 12Then the LORD
spoke[e] to you out of the fire. You heard
the sound of words but saw no form;
there was only a voice. 13He declared to
you his covenant,[f] the Ten Commandments,[g] which he commanded you to
follow and then wrote them on two
stone tablets. 14And the LORD directed
me at that time to teach you the decrees and laws you are to follow in the
land that you are crossing the Jordan to
possess.

Idolatry is forbidden.

15You saw no form[h] of any kind the
day the LORD spoke to you at Horeb out
of the fire. Therefore watch yourselves
very carefully,[i] 16so that you do not become corrupt and make for yourselves an
idol,[j] an image of any shape, whether
formed like a man or a woman, 17or like
any animal on earth or any bird that flies
in the air, 18or like any creature that
moves along the ground or any fish in
the waters below. 19And when you look
up to the sky and see the sun,[k] the moon
and the stars—all the heavenly array[l]—
do not be enticed into bowing down to
them and worshiping things the LORD
your God has apportioned to all the
nations under heaven. 20But as for you,
the LORD took you and brought you out
of the iron-smelting furnace,[m] out of
Egypt, to be the people of his inheritance,[n] as you now are.

21The LORD was angry with me[o] because of you, and he solemnly swore that
I would not cross the Jordan and enter
the good land the LORD your God is
giving you as your inheritance. 22I will
die in this land; I will not cross the Jordan; but you are about to cross over
and take possession of that good land.[p]
23Be careful not to forget the covenant[q]
of the LORD your God that he made with
you; do not make for yourselves an idol[r]
in the form of anything the LORD your
God has forbidden. 24For the LORD your
God is a consuming fire,[s] a jealous God.

25After you have had children and
grandchildren and have lived in the land
a long time—if you then become corrupt and make any kind of idol, doing
evil[t] in the eyes of the LORD your God
and provoking him to anger, 26I call heav-
en and earth as witnesses against you[u]
this day that you will quickly perish
from the land that you are crossing the
Jordan to possess. You will not live there
long but will certainly be destroyed.
27The LORD will scatter[v] you among the
peoples, and only a few of you will survive among the nations to which the
LORD will drive you. 28There you will
worship man-made gods[w] of wood and
stone, which cannot see or hear or eat
or smell.[x] 29But if from there you seek[y]
the LORD your God, you will find him
if you look for him with all your heart[z]
and with all your soul.[a] 30When you are
in distress and all these things have
happened to you, then in later days[b]
you will return to the LORD your God and
obey him. 31For the LORD your God is
a merciful[c] God; he will not abandon
or destroy you or forget the covenant
with your forefathers, which he confirmed to them by oath.

32Ask[d] now about the former days,
long before your time, from the day God
created man on the earth;[e] ask from one
end of the heavens to the other.[f] Has
anything so great as this ever happened,
or has anything like it ever been heard
of? 33Has any other people heard the
voice of God[i] speaking out of fire, as

4:9 [a]Ge 18:19; Eph 6:4 [b]Ps 78:5-6
4:10 [c]Ex 19:9,16
4:11 [d]Ex 19:18; Heb 12:18-19
4:12 [e]Ex 20:22; Dt 5:4,22
4:13 [f]Dt 9:9,11 [g]Ex 24:12; 31:18; 34:28
4:15 [h]Isa 40:18 [i]Jos 23:11
4:16 [j]Ex 20:4-5; 32:7; Dt 5:8; Ro 1:23
4:19 [k]Dt 17:3; Job 31:26 [l]2Ki 17:16; 21:3; Ro 1:25
4:20 [m]1Ki 8:51; Jer 11:4 [n]Ex 19:5; Dt 9:29
4:21 [o]Nu 20:12; Dt 1:37
4:22 [p]Dt 3:25
4:23 [q]ver 9,16 [r]Ex 20:4
4:24 [s]Ex 24:17; Dt 9:3; Heb 12:29
4:25 [t]2Ki 17:2,17
4:26 [u]Dt 30:18-19; Isa 1:2; Mic 6:2
4:27 [v]Lev 26:33; Dt 28:36,64; Ne 1:8
4:28 [w]Dt 28:36,64; 1Sa 26:19; Jer 16:13 [x]Ps 115:4-8; 135:15-18
4:29 [y]2Ch 15:4; Isa 55:6 [z]Jer 29:13 [a]Dt 30:1-3,10
4:30 [b]Dt 31:29; Jer 23:20; Hos 3:5
4:31 [c]2Ch 30:9; Ne 9:31; Ps 116:5; Jnh 4:2
4:32 [d]Dt 32:7; Job 8:8 [e]Ge 1:27 [f]Mt 24:31

[i]33 Or *of a god*

you have, and lived?[a] 34 Has any god ever
tried to take for himself one nation out of
another nation,[b] by testings, by miraculous signs[c] and wonders,[d] by war, by
a mighty hand and an outstretched arm,[e]
or by great and awesome deeds,[f] like
all the things the LORD your God did for
you in Egypt before your very eyes?
35 You were shown these things so that
you might know that the LORD is God;
besides him there is no other.[g] 36 From
heaven he made you hear his voice[h] to
discipline you. On earth he showed you
his great fire, and you heard his words
from out of the fire. 37 Because he loved[i]
your forefathers and chose their descendants after them, he brought you out of
Egypt by his Presence and his great
strength,[j] 38 to drive out before you nations greater and stronger than you and
to bring you into their land to give it to
you for your inheritance,[k] as it is today.
39 Acknowledge and take to heart this
day that the LORD is God in heaven above
and on the earth below. There is no
other.[l] 40 Keep[m] his decrees and commands, which I am giving you today, so
that it may go well[n] with you and your
children after you and that you may live
long[o] in the land the LORD your God gives
you for all time.

Moses sets aside three cities of refuge.

4:41-43Ref— Nu 35:6-34; Dt 19:1-14; Jos 20:1-9

41 Then Moses set aside three cities
east of the Jordan, 42 to which anyone
who had killed a person could flee if he
had unintentionally killed his neighbor
without malice aforethought. He could
flee into one of these cities and save
his life. 43 The cities were these: Bezer
in the desert plateau, for the Reubenites;
Ramoth in Gilead, for the Gadites; and
Golan in Bashan, for the Manassites.
44 This is the law Moses set before the
Israelites. 45 These are the stipulations,
decrees and laws Moses gave them when
they came out of Egypt 46 and were in
the valley near Beth Peor east of the Jordan, in the land of Sihon[p] king of the
Amorites, who reigned in Heshbon and
was defeated by Moses and the Israelites as they came out of Egypt. 47 They
took possession of his land and the land
of Og king of Bashan, the two Amorite
kings east of the Jordan. 48 This land extended from Aroer[q] on the rim of the
Arnon Gorge to Mount Siyon[j][r] (that is,
Hermon), 49 and included all the Arabah
east of the Jordan, as far as the Sea of
the Arabah,[k] below the slopes of Pisgah.

Moses reviews the Ten Commandments.

5:6-21pp— Ex 20:1-17

5 Moses summoned all Israel and
said:
Hear, O Israel, the decrees and laws I
declare in your hearing today. Learn them
and be sure to follow them. 2 The LORD
our God made a covenant[s] with us at
Horeb. 3 It was not with our fathers that
the LORD made this covenant, but with
us, with all of us who are alive here
today.[t] 4 The LORD spoke[u] to you face to
face out of the fire on the mountain. 5 (At
that time I stood between[v] the LORD and
you to declare to you the word of the
LORD, because you were afraid[w] of the
fire and did not go up the mountain.)
And he said:

6 "I am the LORD your God,
who brought you out of
Egypt, out of the land of
slavery.
7 "You shall have no other gods before[l] me.
8 "You shall not make for yourself an
idol in the form of anything in
heaven above or on the earth
beneath or in the waters below. 9 You shall not bow down
to them or worship them; for
I, the LORD your God, am a
jealous God, punishing the
children for the sin of the
fathers to the third and fourth
generation of those who hate

4:33 [a]Ex 20:22; Dt 5:24-26
4:34 [b]Ex 6:6 [c]Ex 7:3 [d]Dt 7:19; 26:8 [e]Ex 13:3 [f]Dt 34:12
4:35 [g]Dt 32:39; 1Sa 2:2; Isa 45:5,18
4:36 [h]Ex 19:9,19
4:37 [i]Dt 10:15 [j]Ex 13:3,9,14
4:38 [k]Dt 7:1; 9:5
4:39 [l]ver 35; Jos 2:11
4:40 [m]Lev 22:31; Dt 5:33 [n]Dt 5:16 [o]Dt 6:3,18; Eph 6:2-3
4:46 [p]Nu 21:26; Dt 3:29
4:48 [q]Dt 2:36 [r]Dt 3:9
5:2 [s]Ex 19:5
5:3 [t]Heb 8:9
5:4 [u]Dt 4:12, 33,36
5:5 [v]Gal 3:19 [w]Ex 20:18,21

j48 Hebrew; Syriac (see also Deut. 3:9) *Sirion*
k49 That is, the Dead Sea
l7 Or *besides*

me,[a] 10 but showing love to a
thousand ⌊generations⌋ of
those who love me and keep
my commandments.[b]
11 "You shall not misuse the name of
the LORD your God, for the
LORD will not hold anyone
guiltless who misuses his
name.[c]
12 "Observe the Sabbath day by keeping it holy,[d] as the LORD your
God has commanded you.
13 Six days you shall labor and
do all your work, 14 but the
seventh day[e] is a Sabbath to
the LORD your God. On it you
shall not do any work, neither
you, nor your son or daughter,
nor your manservant or maidservant, nor your ox, your
donkey or any of your animals, nor the alien within
your gates, so that your manservant and maidservant may
rest, as you do. 15 Remember
that you were slaves in Egypt
and that the LORD your God
brought you out of there with
a mighty hand and an out-
stretched arm.[f] Therefore the
LORD your God has commanded you to observe the Sabbath day.
16 "Honor your father and your mother,[g] as the LORD your God has
commanded you, so that you
may live long[h] and that it may
go well with you in the land
the LORD your God is giving
you.
17 "You shall not murder.[i]
18 "You shall not commit adultery.[j]
19 "You shall not steal.
20 "You shall not give false testimony
against your neighbor.
21 "You shall not covet your neighbor's
wife. You shall not set your
desire on your neighbor's
house or land, his manservant or maidservant, his ox
or donkey, or anything that
belongs to your neighbor."[k]

22 These are the commandments the
LORD proclaimed in a loud voice to your
whole assembly there on the mountain
from out of the fire, the cloud and the
deep darkness; and he added nothing
more. Then he wrote them on two stone
tablets[l] and gave them to me.
23 When you heard the voice out of the
darkness, while the mountain was ablaze
with fire, all the leading men of your
tribes and your elders came to me. 24 And
you said, "The LORD our God has shown
us his glory and his majesty, and we have
heard his voice from the fire. Today
we have seen that a man can live even
if God speaks with him.[m] 25 But now,
why should we die? This great fire will
consume us, and we will die if we hear
the voice of the LORD our God any longer.[n] 26 For what mortal man has ever
heard the voice of the living God speaking out of fire, as we have, and survived?[o] 27 Go near and listen to all that
the LORD our God says. Then tell us
whatever the LORD our God tells you.
We will listen and obey."
28 The LORD heard you when you spoke
to me and the LORD said to me, "I have
heard what this people said to you.
Everything they said was good.[p] 29 Oh,
that their hearts would be inclined to
fear me[q] and keep all my commands[r]
always, so that it might go well with
them and their children forever![s]
30 "Go, tell them to return to their
tents. 31 But you stay here[t] with me so
that I may give you all the commands,
decrees and laws you are to teach them
to follow in the land I am giving them
to possess."
32 So be careful to do what the LORD
your God has commanded you; do not
turn aside to the right or to the left.[u]
33 Walk in all the way that the LORD your
God has commanded you,[v] so that you
may live and prosper and prolong your
days[w] in the land that you will possess.

Israel is exhorted to obey God.

6 These are the commands, decrees
and laws the LORD your God

5:9 [a]Ex 34:7
5:10 [b]Jer 32:18
5:11 [c]Lev 19:12; Mt 5:33-37
5:12 [d]Ex 20:8
5:14 [e]Ge 2:2; Heb 4:4
5:15 [f]Dt 4:34
5:16 [g]Ex 20:12; Lev 19:3; Dt 27:16; Eph 6:2-3*; Col 3:20 [h]Dt 4:40
5:17 [i]Mt 5:21-22*
5:18 [j]Mt 5:27-30; Lk 18:20*; Jas 2:11*
5:21 [k]Ro 7:7*; 13:9*
5:22 [l]Ex 24:12; 31:18; Dt 4:13
5:24 [m]Ex 19:19
5:25 [n]Dt 18:16
5:26 [o]Dt 4:33
5:28 [p]Dt 18:17
5:29 [q]Ps 81:8,13 [r]Dt 11:1; Isa 48:18 [s]Dt 4:1,40
5:31 [t]Ex 24:12
5:32 [u]Dt 17:11,20; 28:14; Jos 1:7; 23:6; Pr 4:27
5:33 [v]Jer 7:23 [w]Dt 4:40

directed me to teach you to observe in the land that you are crossing the Jordan to possess, 2so that you, your children and their children after them may fear[a] the LORD your God as long as you live by keeping all his decrees and commands that I give you, and so that you may enjoy long life. 3Hear, O Israel, and be careful to obey so that it may go well with you and that you may increase greatly[b] in a land flowing with milk and honey,[c] just as the LORD, the God of your fathers, promised you.

4Hear, O Israel: The LORD our God, the LORD is one.[m][d] 5Love[e] the LORD your God with all your heart and with all your soul and with all your strength.[f] 6These commandments that I give you today are to be upon your hearts.[g] 7Impress them on your children. Talk about them when you sit at home and when you walk along the road, when you lie down and when you get up.[h] 8Tie them as symbols on your hands and bind them on your foreheads.[i] 9Write them on the doorframes of your houses and on your gates.[j]

10When the LORD your God brings you into the land he swore to your fathers, to Abraham, Isaac and Jacob, to give you—a land with large, flourishing cities you did not build,[k] 11houses filled with all kinds of good things you did not provide, wells you did not dig, and vineyards and olive groves you did not plant—then when you eat and are satisfied,[l] 12be careful that you do not forget the LORD, who brought you out of Egypt, out of the land of slavery.

13Fear the LORD[m] your God, serve him only[n] and take your oaths in his name. 14Do not follow other gods, the gods of the peoples around you; 15for the LORD your God[o], who is among you, is a jealous God and his anger will burn against you, and he will destroy you from the face of the land. 16Do not test the LORD your God[p] as you did at Massah. 17Be sure to keep the commands of the LORD your God and the stipulations and decrees he has given you.[q] 18Do what is right and good in the LORD's sight, so that it may go well[r] with you and you may go in and take over the good land that the LORD promised on oath to your forefathers, 19thrusting out all your enemies before you, as the LORD said.

The Israelites are instructed to teach their children.

20In the future, when your son asks you,[s] "What is the meaning of the stipulations, decrees and laws the LORD our God has commanded you?" 21tell him: "We were slaves of Pharaoh in Egypt, but the LORD brought us out of Egypt with a mighty hand. 22Before our eyes the LORD sent miraculous signs and wonders—great and terrible—upon Egypt and Pharaoh and his whole household. 23But he brought us out from there to bring us in and give us the land that he promised on oath to our forefathers. 24The LORD commanded us to obey all these decrees and to fear the LORD our God,[t] so that we might always prosper and be kept alive, as is the case today.[u] 25And if we are careful to obey all this law before the LORD our God, as he has commanded us, that will be our righteousness.[v]"

No treaties are to be made with the nations of Canaan.

7 When the LORD your God brings you into the land you are entering to possess and drives out before you many nations[w]—the Hittites, Girgashites, Amorites, Canaanites, Perizzites, Hivites and Jebusites, seven nations larger and stronger than you— 2and when the LORD your God has delivered them over to you and you have defeated them, then you must destroy them totally.[n] Make no treaty[x] with them, and show them no mercy.[y] 3Do not intermarry with them.[z] Do not give your daughters to their sons or take their daughters for your sons, 4for they will turn your sons away from following me to serve other gods,

6:2 [a]Ex 20:20; Dt 10:12-13
6:3 [b]Dt 5:33 [c]Ex 3:8
6:4 [d]Mk 12:29*; 1Co 8:4
6:5 [e]Mt 22:37*; Mk 12:30*; Lk 10:27* [f]Dt 10:12
6:6 [g]Dt 11:18
6:7 [h]Dt 4:9; 11:19; Eph 6:4
6:8 [i]Ex 13:9,16; Dt 11:18
6:9 [j]Dt 11:20
6:10 [k]Jos 24:13
6:11 [l]Dt 8:10
6:13 [m]Dt 10:20 [n]Mt 4:10*; Lk 4:8*
6:15 [o]Dt 4:24
6:16 [p]Ex 17:7; Mt 4:7*; Lk 4:12*
6:17 [q]Dt 11:22; Ps 119:4
6:18 [r]Dt 4:40
6:20 [s]Ex 13:14
6:24 [t]Dt 10:12; Jer 32:39 [u]Ps 41:2
6:25 [v]Dt 24:13; Ro 10:3,5
7:1 [w]Dt 31:3; Ac 13:19
7:2 [x]Ex 23:32 [y]Dt 13:8
7:3 [z]Ex 34:15-16; Ezr 9:2

m4 Or *The LORD our God is one LORD*; or *The LORD is our God, the LORD is one*; or *The LORD is our God, the LORD alone* n2 The Hebrew term refers to the irrevocable giving over of things or persons to the LORD, often by totally destroying them; also in verse 26.

and the LORD's anger will burn against
you and will quickly destroy[a] you. 5This
is what you are to do to them: Break
down their altars, smash their sacred
stones, cut down their Asherah poles[o]
and burn their idols in the fire.[b] 6For you
are a people holy[c] to the LORD your
God.[d] The LORD your God has chosen[e]
you out of all the peoples on the face
of the earth to be his people, his treasured possession.

7The LORD did not set his affection on
you and choose you because you were
more numerous than other peoples, for
you were the fewest of all peoples.[f] 8But
it was because the LORD loved[g] you and
kept the oath he swore[h] to your forefathers that he brought you out with a
mighty hand and redeemed you from
the land of slavery,[i] from the power of
Pharaoh king of Egypt. 9Know therefore
that the LORD your God is God;[j] he is the
faithful God,[k] keeping his covenant of
love[l] to a thousand generations of those
who love him and keep his commands.
10But

> those who hate him he will repay to
> their face by destruction;
> he will not be slow to repay to
> their face those who hate him.

11Therefore, take care to follow the commands, decrees and laws I give you
today.

12If you pay attention to these laws
and are careful to follow them, then the
LORD your God will keep his covenant
of love with you, as he swore to your
forefathers.[m] 13He will love you and bless
you[n] and increase your numbers. He
will bless the fruit of your womb, the
crops of your land—your grain, new
wine and oil—the calves of your herds
and the lambs of your flocks in the land
that he swore to your forefathers to give
you.[o] 14You will be blessed more than
any other people; none of your men or
women will be childless, nor any of your
livestock without young.[p] 15The LORD
will keep you free from every disease.[q]
He will not inflict on you the horrible
diseases you knew in Egypt, but he will
inflict them on all who hate you. 16You
must destroy all the peoples the LORD
your God gives over to you. Do not look
on them with pity[r] and do not serve their
gods, for that will be a snare[s] to you.

17You may say to yourselves, "These
nations are stronger than we are. How
can we drive them out?[t]" 18But do not
be afraid[u] of them; remember well what
the LORD your God did to Pharaoh and
to all Egypt.[v] 19You saw with your own
eyes the great trials, the miraculous signs
and wonders, the mighty hand and outstretched arm, with which the LORD your
God brought you out. The LORD your God
will do the same to all the peoples you
now fear.[w] 20Moreover, the LORD your
God will send the hornet[x] among them
until even the survivors who hide from
you have perished. 21Do not be terrified
by them, for the LORD your God, who is
among you,[y] is a great and awesome
God.[z] 22The LORD your God will drive
out those nations before you, little by little.[a] You will not be allowed to eliminate
them all at once, or the wild animals will
multiply around you. 23But the LORD your
God will deliver them over to you, throwing them into great confusion until they
are destroyed. 24He will give their kings
into your hand, and you will wipe out
their names from under heaven. No one
will be able to stand up against you;[b]
you will destroy them. 25The images of
their gods you are to burn[c] in the fire. Do
not covet[d] the silver and gold on them,
and do not take it for yourselves, or you
will be ensnared[e] by it, for it is detestable[f] to the LORD your God. 26Do not
bring a detestable thing into your house
or you, like it, will be set apart for destruction.[g] Utterly abhor and detest it,
for it is set apart for destruction.

Israel is exhorted to remember the LORD.

8 Be careful to follow every command
I am giving you today, so that you
may live[h] and increase and may enter

7:4 [a]Dt 6:15
7:5 [b]Ex 23:24; Dt 12:2-3
7:6 [c]Ex 19:5-6; 1Pe 2:9 [d]Ps 50:5; Jer 2:3 [e]Dt 14:2
7:7 [f]Dt 10:22
7:8 [g]Dt 10:15 [h]Ex 32:13 [i]Ex 13:14
7:9 [j]Dt 4:35 [k]1Co 1:9; 2Ti 2:13 [l]Ne 1:5; Da 9:4
7:12 [m]Lev 26:3-13; Dt 28:1-14; Ps 105:8-9
7:13 [n]Jn 14:21 [o]Dt 28:4
7:14 [p]Ex 23:26
7:15 [q]Ex 15:26
7:16 [r]ver 2; Ex 23:33 [s]Jdg 8:27
7:17 [t]Nu 33:53
7:18 [u]Dt 31:6 [v]Ps 105:5
7:19 [w]Dt 4:34
7:20 [x]Ex 23:28; Jos 24:12
7:21 [y]Jos 3:10 [z]Dt 10:17; Ne 9:32
7:22 [a]Ex 23:28-30
7:24 [b]Jos 23:9
7:25 [c]Ex 32:20; 1Ch 14:12 [d]Jos 7:21 [e]Jdg 8:27 [f]Dt 17:1
7:26 [g]Lev 27:28-29
8:1 [h]Dt 4:1

[o]5 That is, symbols of the goddess Asherah; here and elsewhere in Deuteronomy

and possess the land that the LORD
promised on oath to your forefathers.
2Remember how the LORD your God
led[a] you all the way in the desert these
forty years, to humble you and to test
you in order to know what was in your
heart, whether or not you would keep
his commands. 3He humbled you, causing you to hunger and then feeding you
with manna,[b] which neither you nor
your fathers had known, to teach you
that man does not live on bread alone
but on every word that comes from the
mouth of the LORD.[c] 4Your clothes did
not wear out and your feet did not swell
during these forty years.[d] 5Know then
in your heart that as a man disciplines
his son, so the LORD your God disciplines
you.[e]

6Observe the commands of the LORD
your God, walking in his ways and revering him.[f] 7For the LORD your God is
bringing you into a good land—a land
with streams and pools of water, with
springs flowing in the valleys and hills;[g]
8a land with wheat and barley, vines
and fig trees, pomegranates, olive oil and
honey; 9a land where bread will not be
scarce and you will lack nothing; a land
where the rocks are iron and you can
dig copper out of the hills.

10When you have eaten and are satisfied,[h] praise the LORD your God for the
good land he has given you. 11Be careful that you do not forget the LORD your
God, failing to observe his commands,
his laws and his decrees that I am giving you this day. 12Otherwise, when you
eat and are satisfied, when you build fine
houses and settle down,[i] 13and when
your herds and flocks grow large and
your silver and gold increase and all you
have is multiplied, 14then your heart
will become proud and you will forget[j]
the LORD your God, who brought you
out of Egypt, out of the land of slavery.
15He led you through the vast and dreadful desert,[k] that thirsty and waterless
land, with its venomous snakes[l] and
scorpions. He brought you water out of
hard rock.[m] 16He gave you manna to
eat in the desert, something your fathers
had never known,[n] to humble and to
test you so that in the end it might go
well with you. 17You may say to yourself,[o] "My power and the strength of
my hands have produced this wealth for
me." 18But remember the LORD your
God, for it is he who gives you the ability to produce wealth,[p] and so confirms
his covenant, which he swore to your
forefathers, as it is today.

19If you ever forget the LORD your God
and follow other gods and worship and
bow down to them, I testify against you
today that you will surely be destroyed.[q]
20Like the nations the LORD destroyed
before you, so you will be destroyed
for not obeying the LORD your God.

Moses reminds Israel of her rebelliousness.

9 Hear, O Israel. You are now about
to cross the Jordan to go in and dispossess nations greater and stronger
than you,[r] with large cities that have
walls up to the sky.[s] 2The people are
strong and tall—Anakites! You know
about them and have heard it said: "Who
can stand up against the Anakites?"[t]
3But be assured today that the LORD your
God is the one who goes across ahead
of you[u] like a devouring fire.[v] He will destroy them; he will subdue them before
you. And you will drive them out and
annihilate them quickly,[w] as the LORD
has promised you.

4After the LORD your God has driven
them out before you, do not say to yourself,[x] "The LORD has brought me here
to take possession of this land because
of my righteousness." No, it is on account
of the wickedness of these nations[y] that
the LORD is going to drive them out before you. 5It is not because of your righteousness or your integrity[z] that you
are going in to take possession of their
land; but on account of the wickedness
of these nations, the LORD your God will
drive them out before you, to accomplish what he swore[a] to your fathers,
to Abraham, Isaac and Jacob. 6Under-
stand, then, that it is not because of your

8:2 [a]Am 2:10
8:3 [b]Ex 16:12,14, 35 [c]Ex 16:2-3; Mt 4:4*; Lk 4:4*
8:4 [d]Dt 29:5; Ne 9:21
8:5 [e]2Sa 7:14; Pr 3:11-12; Heb 12:5-11; Rev 3:19
8:6 [f]Dt 5:33
8:7 [g]Dt 11:9-12
8:10 [h]Dt 6:10-12
8:12 [i]Hos 13:6
8:14 [j]Ps 106:21
8:15 [k]Jer 2:6 [l]Nu 21:6 [m]Nu 20:11; Ps 78:15; 114:8
8:16 [n]Ex 16:15
8:17 [o]Dt 9:4,7,24
8:18 [p]Pr 10:22; Hos 2:8
8:19 [q]Dt 4:26; 30:18
9:1 [r]Dt 4:38; 11:23,31 [s]Dt 1:28
9:2 [t]Nu 13:22,28, 32-33
9:3 [u]Dt 31:3; Jos 3:11 [v]Dt 4:24; Heb 12:29 [w]Ex 23:31; Dt 7:23-24
9:4 [x]Dt 8:17 [y]Lev 18:21, 24-30; Dt 18:9-14
9:5 [z]Tit 3:5 [a]Ge 12:7; 13:15; 15:7; 17:8; 26:4

righteousness that the LORD your God
is giving you this good land to possess,
for you are a stiff-necked people.[a]
7Remember this and never forget how
you provoked the LORD your God to
anger in the desert. From the day you left
Egypt until you arrived here, you have
been rebellious against the LORD. 8At
Horeb you aroused the LORD's wrath so
that he was angry enough to destroy
you.[b] 9When I went up on the mountain to receive the tablets of stone, the
tablets of the covenant that the LORD had
made with you, I stayed on the mountain forty days and forty nights; I ate
no bread and drank no water.[c] 10The
LORD gave me two stone tablets inscribed
by the finger of God.[d] On them were
all the commandments the LORD proclaimed to you on the mountain out of
the fire, on the day of the assembly.
11At the end of the forty days and
forty nights, the LORD gave me the two
stone tablets, the tablets of the covenant.
12Then the LORD told me, "Go down
from here at once, because your people
whom you brought out of Egypt have
become corrupt.[e] They have turned away
quickly[f] from what I commanded them
and have made a cast idol for themselves."
13And the LORD said to me, "I have
seen this people[g], and they are a stiff-
necked people indeed! 14Let me alone,[h]
so that I may destroy them and blot out[i]
their name from under heaven. And I
will make you into a nation stronger and
more numerous than they."
15So I turned and went down from the
mountain while it was ablaze with fire.
And the two tablets of the covenant
were in my hands.[p][j] 16When I looked, I
saw that you had sinned against the LORD
your God; you had made for yourselves
an idol cast in the shape of a calf.[k] You
had turned aside quickly from the way
that the LORD had commanded you. 17So
I took the two tablets and threw them
out of my hands, breaking them to pieces
before your eyes.
18Then once again I fell[l] prostrate before the LORD for forty days and forty
nights; I ate no bread and drank no
water, because of all the sin you had
committed, doing what was evil in the
LORD's sight and so provoking him to
anger. 19I feared the anger and wrath
of the LORD, for he was angry enough
with you to destroy you.[m] But again the
LORD listened to me.[n] 20And the LORD
was angry enough with Aaron to destroy
him, but at that time I prayed for Aaron
too. 21Also I took that sinful thing of
yours, the calf you had made, and burned
it in the fire. Then I crushed it and
ground it to powder as fine as dust and
threw the dust into a stream that flowed
down the mountain.[o]
22You also made the LORD angry at
Taberah,[p] at Massah[q] and at Kibroth
Hattaavah.[r]
23And when the LORD sent you out
from Kadesh Barnea, he said, "Go up
and take possession of the land I have
given you." But you rebelled against the
command of the LORD your God. You did
not trust[s] him or obey him. 24You have
been rebellious against the LORD ever
since I have known you.[t]
25I lay prostrate before the LORD those
forty days and forty nights because the
LORD had said he would destroy you.[u]
26I prayed to the LORD and said, "O
Sovereign LORD, do not destroy your
people, your own inheritance that you
redeemed by your great power and
brought out of Egypt with a mighty
hand.[v] 27Remember your servants Abraham, Isaac and Jacob. Overlook the stubbornness of this people, their wickedness and their sin. 28Otherwise, the
country from which you brought us will
say, 'Because the LORD was not able to
take them into the land he had promised
them, and because he hated them, he
brought them out to put them to death
in the desert.'[w] 29But they are your people, your inheritance[x] that you brought
out by your great power and your outstretched arm.[y]"

9:6 [a]ver 13; Ex 32:9; Dt 31:27
9:8 [b]Ex 32:7-10; Ps 106:19
9:9 [c]Ex 24:12,15, 18; 34:28
9:10 [d]Ex 31:18; Dt 4:13
9:12 [e]Ex 32:7-8; Dt 31:29 [f]Jdg 2:17
9:13 [g]ver 6; Ex 32:9; Dt 10:16
9:14 [h]Ex 32:10 [i]Nu 14:12; Dt 29:20
9:15 [j]Ex 19:18; 32:15
9:16 [k]Ex 32:19
9:18 [l]Ex 34:28
9:19 [m]Ex 32:10-11, 14 [n]Dt 10:10
9:21 [o]Ex 32:20
9:22 [p]Nu 11:3 [q]Ex 17:7 [r]Nu 11:34
9:23 [s]Ps 106:24
9:24 [t]ver 7; Dt 31:27
9:25 [u]ver 18
9:26 [v]Ex 32:11
9:28 [w]Ex 32:12; Nu 14:16
9:29 [x]Dt 4:20; 1Ki 8:51 [y]Dt 4:34; Ne 1:10

p *15* Or *And I had the two tablets of the covenant with me, one in each hand*

Two new tablets.

10 At that time the LORD said to me,
"Chisel out two stone tablets[a]
like the first ones and come up to me
on the mountain. Also make a wooden
chest.[q] 2I will write on the tablets the
words that were on the first tablets,
which you broke. Then you are to put
them in the chest."[b]
3So I made the ark out of acacia wood[c]
and chiseled[d] out two stone tablets like
the first ones, and I went up on the
mountain with the two tablets in my
hands. 4The LORD wrote on these tablets
what he had written before, the Ten
Commandments he had proclaimed[e] to
you on the mountain, out of the fire, on
the day of the assembly. And the LORD
gave them to me. 5Then I came back
down the mountain[f] and put the tablets
in the ark[g] I had made, as the LORD commanded me, and they are there now.[h]
6(The Israelites traveled from the wells
of the Jaakanites to Moserah.[i] There Aaron died and was buried, and Eleazar his
son succeeded him as priest.[j] 7From
there they traveled to Gudgodah and on
to Jotbathah, a land with streams of
water.[k] 8At that time the LORD set apart
the tribe of Levi[l] to carry the ark of the
covenant of the LORD, to stand before the
LORD to minister[m] and to pronounce
blessings[n] in his name, as they still do
today. 9That is why the Levites have no
share or inheritance among their brothers; the LORD is their inheritance,[o] as
the LORD your God told them.)
10Now I had stayed on the mountain
forty days and nights, as I did the first
time, and the LORD listened to me at this
time also. It was not his will to destroy
you.[p] 11"Go," the LORD said to me, "and
lead the people on their way, so that they
may enter and possess the land that I
swore to their fathers to give them."

Exhortation to walk in the ways of God.

12And now, O Israel, what does the
LORD your God ask of you[q] but to fear the
LORD your God, to walk in all his ways,
to love him,[r] to serve the LORD your God
with all your heart[s] and with all your
soul, 13and to observe the LORD's commands and decrees that I am giving you
today for your own good?
14To the LORD your God belong the
heavens, even the highest heavens,[t] the
earth and everything in it.[u] 15Yet the
LORD set his affection on your forefathers and loved[v] them, and he chose you,
their descendants, above all the nations,
as it is today. 16Circumcise[w] your hearts,
therefore, and do not be stiff-necked[x]
any longer. 17For the LORD your God is
God of gods[y] and Lord of lords, the great
God, mighty and awesome, who shows
no partiality[z] and accepts no bribes. 18He
defends the cause of the fatherless and
the widow,[a] and loves the alien, giving
him food and clothing. 19And you are to
love those who are aliens, for you yourselves were aliens in Egypt.[b] 20Fear the
LORD your God and serve him.[c] Hold
fast[d] to him and take your oaths in his
name.[e] 21He is your praise;[f] he is your
God, who performed for you those great
and awesome wonders[g] you saw with
your own eyes. 22Your forefathers who
went down into Egypt were seventy in
all,[h] and now the LORD your God has
made you as numerous as the stars in
the sky.[i]

A choice of God's blessing or curse.

11 Love[j] the LORD your God and keep
his requirements, his decrees, his
laws and his commands always.[k] 2Re-
member today that your children were
not the ones who saw and experienced
the discipline of the LORD your God:[l]
his majesty, his mighty hand, his outstretched arm; 3the signs he performed
and the things he did in the heart of
Egypt, both to Pharaoh king of Egypt
and to his whole country; 4what he did
to the Egyptian army, to its horses and
chariots, how he overwhelmed them

10:1 [a]Ex 25:10; 34:1-2 **10:2** [b]Ex 25:16,21; Dt 4:13 **10:3** [c]Ex 25:5,10; 37:1-9 [d]Ex 34:4 **10:4** [e]Ex 20:1 **10:5** [f]Ex 34:29 [g]Ex 40:20 [h]1Ki 8:9 **10:6** [i]Nu 33:30-31, 38 [j]Nu 20:25-28 **10:7** [k]Nu 33:32-34 **10:8** [l]Nu 3:6 [m]Dt 18:5 [n]Dt 21:5 **10:9** [o]Nu 18:20; Dt 18:1-2; Eze 44:28 **10:10** [p]Ex 33:17; 34:28; Dt 9:18-19,25 **10:12** [q]Mic 6:8 [r]Dt 5:33; 6:13; Mt 22:37 [s]Dt 6:5 **10:14** [t]1Ki 8:27 [u]Ex 19:5 **10:15** [v]Dt 4:37 **10:16** [w]Jer 4:4 [x]Dt 9:6 **10:17** [y]Jos 22:22; Da 2:47 [z]Ac 10:34; Ro 2:11; Eph 6:9 **10:18** [a]Ps 68:5 **10:19** [b]Lev 19:34 **10:20** [c]Mt 4:10 [d]Dt 11:22 [e]Ps 63:11 **10:21** [f]Ex 15:2; Jer 17:14 [g]Ps 106:21-22 **10:22** [h]Ge 46:26-27 [i]Ge 15:5; Dt 1:10 **11:1** [j]Dt 10:12 [k]Zec 3:7 **11:2** [l]Dt 5:24; 8:5

q*1* That is, an ark

with the waters of the Red Sea[r][a] as they were pursuing you, and how the LORD brought lasting ruin on them. 5It was not your children who saw what he did for you in the desert until you arrived at this place, 6and what he did[b] to Dathan and Abiram, sons of Eliab the Reubenite, when the earth opened its mouth right in the middle of all Israel and swallowed them up with their households, their tents and every living thing that belonged to them. 7But it was your own eyes that saw all these great things the LORD has done.

8Observe therefore all the commands I am giving you today, so that you may have the strength to go in and take over the land that you are crossing the Jordan to possess,[c] 9and so that you may live long[d] in the land that the LORD swore[e] to your forefathers to give to them and their descendants, a land flowing with milk and honey.[f] 10The land you are entering to take over is not like the land of Egypt, from which you have come, where you planted your seed and irrigated it by foot as in a vegetable garden. 11But the land you are crossing the Jordan to take possession of is a land of mountains and valleys that drinks rain from heaven.[g] 12It is a land the LORD your God cares for; the eyes[h] of the LORD your God are continually on it from the beginning of the year to its end.

13So if you faithfully obey[i] the commands I am giving you today—to love[j] the LORD your God and to serve him with all your heart and with all your soul— 14then I will send rain[k] on your land in its season, both autumn and spring rains,[l] so that you may gather in your grain, new wine and oil. 15I will provide grass[m] in the fields for your cattle, and you will eat and be satisfied.[n]

16Be careful, or you will be enticed to turn away and worship other gods and bow down to them.[o] 17Then the LORD's anger[p] will burn against you, and he will shut[q] the heavens so that it will not rain and the ground will yield no produce, and you will soon perish[r] from the good land the LORD is giving you. 18Fix these words of mine in your hearts and minds; tie them as symbols on your hands and bind them on your foreheads.[s] 19Teach them to your children,[t] talking about them when you sit at home and when you walk along the road, when you lie down and when you get up.[u] 20Write them on the doorframes of your houses and on your gates,[v] 21so that your days and the days of your children may be many[w] in the land that the LORD swore to give your forefathers, as many as the days that the heavens are above the earth.[x]

22If you carefully observe[y] all these commands I am giving you to follow—to love the LORD your God, to walk in all his ways and to hold fast[z] to him— 23then the LORD will drive out all these nations before you, and you will dispossess nations larger and stronger than you.[a] 24Every place where you set your foot will be yours:[b] Your territory will extend from the desert to Lebanon, and from the Euphrates River to the western sea.[s] 25No man will be able to stand against you. The LORD your God, as he promised you, will put the terror and fear of you on the whole land, wherever you go.[c]

26See, I am setting before you today a blessing and a curse[d]— 27the blessing[e] if you obey the commands of the LORD your God that I am giving you today; 28the curse if you disobey[f] the commands of the LORD your God and turn from the way that I command you today by following other gods, which you have not known. 29When the LORD your God has brought you into the land you are entering to possess, you are to proclaim on Mount Gerizim the blessings, and on Mount Ebal the curses.[g] 30As you know, these mountains are across the Jordan, west of the road,[t] toward the setting sun, near the great trees of Moreh,[h] in the territory of those Canaanites living in the Arabah in the vicinity of Gilgal.[i] 31You are about to cross the Jordan to enter

11:4 [a]Ex 14:27
11:6 [b]Nu 16:1-35
11:8 [c]Jos 1:7
11:9 [d]Dt 4:40; Pr 10:27 [e]Dt 9:5 [f]Ex 3:8
11:11 [g]Dt 8:7
11:12 [h]1Ki 9:3
11:13 [i]Dt 6:17 [j]Dt 10:12
11:14 [k]Lev 26:4; Dt 28:12 [l]Joel 2:23; Jas 5:7
11:15 [m]Ps 104:14 [n]Dt 6:11
11:16 [o]Dt 8:19; 29:18; Job 31:9,27
11:17 [p]Dt 6:15 [q]1Ki 8:35; 2Ch 6:26 [r]Dt 4:26
11:18 [s]Dt 6:6-8
11:19 [t]Dt 6:7 [u]Dt 4:9-10
11:20 [v]Dt 6:9
11:21 [w]Pr 3:2; 4:10 [x]Ps 72:5
11:22 [y]Dt 6:17 [z]Dt 10:20
11:23 [a]Dt 4:38; 9:1
11:24 [b]Ge 15:18; Ex 23:31; Jos 1:3; 14:9
11:25 [c]Ex 23:27; Dt 7:24
11:26 [d]Dt 30:1, 15,19
11:27 [e]Dt 28:1-14
11:28 [f]Dt 28:15
11:29 [g]Dt 27:12-13; Jos 8:33
11:30 [h]Ge 12:6 [i]Jos 4:19

r4 Hebrew *Yam Suph*; that is, Sea of Reeds
s24 That is, the Mediterranean
t30 Or *Jordan, westward*

and take possession[a] of the land the LORD your God is giving you. When you have taken it over and are living there, 32 be sure that you obey all the decrees and laws I am setting before you today.

Instructions concerning worship and offerings.

12 These are the decrees and laws you must be careful to follow in the land that the LORD, the God of your fathers, has given you to possess—as long as you live in the land.[b] 2 Destroy completely all the places on the high mountains and on the hills and under every spreading tree[c] where the nations you are dispossessing worship their gods. 3 Break down their altars, smash[d] their sacred stones and burn their Asherah poles in the fire; cut down the idols of their gods and wipe out their names from those places.

4 You must not worship the LORD your God in their way. 5 But you are to seek the place the LORD your God will choose from among all your tribes to put his Name there for his dwelling.[e] To that place you must go; 6 there bring your burnt offerings and sacrifices, your tithes[f] and special gifts, what you have vowed to give and your freewill offerings, and the firstborn of your herds and flocks. 7 There, in the presence of the LORD your God, you and your families shall eat and shall rejoice[g] in everything you have put your hand to, because the LORD your God has blessed you.

8 You are not to do as we do here today, everyone as he sees fit, 9 since you have not yet reached the resting place and the inheritance the LORD your God is giving you. 10 But you will cross the Jordan and settle in the land the LORD your God is giving[h] you as an inheritance, and he will give you rest from all your enemies around you so that you will live in safety. 11 Then to the place the LORD your God will choose as a dwelling for his Name[i]—there you are to bring everything I command you: your burnt offerings and sacrifices, your tithes and special gifts, and all the choice possessions you have vowed to the LORD. 12 And there rejoice[j] before the LORD your God, you, your sons and daughters, your menservants and maidservants, and the Levites from your towns, who have no allotment or inheritance[k] of their own. 13 Be careful not to sacrifice your burnt offerings anywhere you please. 14 Offer them only at the place the LORD will choose[l] in one of your tribes, and there observe everything I command you.

15 Nevertheless, you may slaughter your animals in any of your towns and eat as much of the meat as you want, as if it were gazelle or deer,[m] according to the blessing the LORD your God gives you. Both the ceremonially unclean and the clean may eat it. 16 But you must not eat the blood;[n] pour it out on the ground like water.[o] 17 You must not eat in your own towns the tithe of your grain and new wine and oil, or the firstborn of your herds and flocks, or whatever you have vowed to give, or your freewill offerings or special gifts. 18 Instead, you are to eat[p] them in the presence of the LORD your God at the place the LORD your God will choose[q]—you, your sons and daughters, your menservants and maidservants, and the Levites from your towns—and you are to rejoice[r] before the LORD your God in everything you put your hand to. 19 Be careful not to neglect the Levites[s] as long as you live in your land.

20 When the LORD your God has enlarged your territory[t] as he promised[u] you, and you crave meat and say, "I would like some meat," then you may eat as much of it as you want. 21 If the place where the LORD your God chooses to put his Name is too far away from you, you may slaughter animals from the herds and flocks the LORD has given you, as I have commanded you, and in your own towns you may eat as much of them as you want. 22 Eat them as you would gazelle or deer.[v] Both the ceremonially unclean and the clean may eat. 23 But be sure you do not eat the blood,[w] because the blood is the life, and you must not eat the life with the meat.

11:31 [a] Dt 9:1; Jos 1:11
12:1 [b] Dt 4:9-10; 1Ki 8:40
12:2 [c] 2Ki 16:4; 17:10
12:3 [d] Nu 33:52; Dt 7:5; Jdg 2:2
12:5 [e] ver 11,13; 2Ch 7:12,16
12:6 [f] Dt 14:22-23
12:7 [g] ver 12,18; Lev 23:40; Dt 14:26
12:10 [h] Dt 11:31
12:11 [i] ver 5; Dt 15:20; 16:2
12:12 [j] ver 7 [k] Dt 10:9; 14:29
12:14 [l] ver 11
12:15 [m] ver 20-23; Dt 14:5; 15:22
12:16 [n] Ge 9:4; Lev 7:26; 17:10-12 [o] Dt 15:23
12:18 [p] Dt 14:23 [q] ver 5 [r] ver 7,12
12:19 [s] Dt 14:27
12:20 [t] Dt 19:8 [u] Ge 15:18; Dt 11:24
12:22 [v] ver 15
12:23 [w] ver 16; Ge 9:4; Lev 17:11,14

24 You must not eat the blood; pour it out on the ground like water. 25 Do not eat it, so that it may go well[a] with you and your children after you, because you will be doing what is right[b] in the eyes of the LORD.

26 But take your consecrated things and whatever you have vowed to give,[c] and go to the place the LORD will choose. 27 Present your burnt offerings[d] on the altar of the LORD your God, both the meat and the blood. The blood of your sacrifices must be poured beside the altar of the LORD your God, but you may eat the meat. 28 Be careful to obey all these regulations I am giving you, so that it may always go well[e] with you and your children after you, because you will be doing what is good and right in the eyes of the LORD your God.

29 The LORD your God will cut off[f] before you the nations you are about to invade and dispossess. But when you have driven them out and settled in their land, 30 and after they have been destroyed before you, be careful not to be ensnared by inquiring about their gods, saying, "How do these nations serve their gods? We will do the same." 31 You must not worship the LORD your God in their way, because in worshiping their gods, they do all kinds of detestable things the LORD hates.[g] They even burn their sons[h] and daughters in the fire as sacrifices to their gods.

32 See that you do all I command you; do not add[i] to it or take away from it.

Idolaters must be stoned to death.

13 If a prophet,[j] or one who foretells by dreams, appears among you and announces to you a miraculous sign or wonder, 2 and if the sign or wonder of which he has spoken takes place, and he says, "Let us follow other gods"[k] (gods you have not known) "and let us worship them," 3 you must not listen to the words of that prophet or dreamer. The LORD your God is testing[l] you to find out whether you love him with all your heart and with all your soul. 4 It is the LORD your God you must follow,[m] and him you must revere. Keep his commands and obey him; serve him and hold fast[n] to him. 5 That prophet or dreamer must be put to death, because he preached rebellion against the LORD your God, who brought you out of Egypt and redeemed you from the land of slavery; he has tried to turn you from the way the LORD your God commanded you to follow. You must purge the evil[o] from among you.

6 If your very own brother, or your son or daughter, or the wife you love, or your closest friend secretly entices[p] you, saying, "Let us go and worship other gods" (gods that neither you nor your fathers have known, 7 gods of the peoples around you, whether near or far, from one end of the land to the other), 8 do not yield[q] to him or listen to him. Show him no pity. Do not spare him or shield him. 9 You must certainly put him to death.[r] Your hand must be the first in putting him to death, and then the hands of all the people. 10 Stone him to death, because he tried to turn you away from the LORD your God, who brought you out of Egypt, out of the land of slavery. 11 Then all Israel will hear and be afraid,[s] and no one among you will do such an evil thing again.

12 If you hear it said about one of the towns the LORD your God is giving you to live in 13 that wicked men[t] have arisen among you and have led the people of their town astray, saying, "Let us go and worship other gods" (gods you have not known), 14 then you must inquire, probe and investigate it thoroughly. And if it is true and it has been proved that this detestable thing has been done among you, 15 you must certainly put to the sword all who live in that town. Destroy it completely,[u] both its people and its livestock. 16 Gather all the plunder of the town into the middle of the public square and completely burn the town and all its plunder as a whole burnt offering to the LORD

12:25 [a]Dt 4:40; Isa 3:10 [b]Ex 15:26; Dt 13:18; 1Ki 11:38
12:26 [c]ver 17; Nu 5:9-10
12:27 [d]Lev 1:5,9,13
12:28 [e]ver 25; Dt 4:40
12:29 [f]Jos 23:4
12:31 [g]Dt 9:5 [h]Dt 18:10; Jer 32:35
12:32 [i]Dt 4:2; Jos 1:7; Rev 22:18-19
13:1 [j]Mt 24:24; Mk 13:22; 2Th 2:9
13:2 [k]ver 6,13
13:3 [l]Dt 8:2,16
13:4 [m]2Ki 23:3; 2Ch 34:31 [n]Dt 10:20
13:5 [o]Dt 17:7,12; 1Co 5:13
13:6 [p]Dt 17:2-7; 29:18
13:8 [q]Pr 1:10
13:9 [r]Dt 17:5,7
13:11 [s]Dt 19:20
13:13 [t]ver 2,6; 1Jn 2:19

[u] *15* The Hebrew term refers to the irrevocable giving over of things or persons to the LORD, often by totally destroying them.

your God.[a] It is to remain a ruin[b] forever, never to be rebuilt. 17None of those
condemned things[v] shall be found in
your hands, so that the LORD will turn
from his fierce anger;[c] he will show you
mercy, have compassion[d] on you, and increase your numbers,[e] as he promised[f]
on oath to your forefathers, 18because you
obey the LORD your God, keeping all his
commands that I am giving you today
and doing what is right[g] in his eyes.

Clean and unclean food.

14:3-20pp— Lev 11:1-23

14 You are the children[h] of the LORD
your God. Do not cut yourselves
or shave the front of your heads for the
dead, 2for you are a people holy to the
LORD your God.[i] Out of all the peoples on
the face of the earth, the LORD has chosen you to be his treasured possession.[j]
3Do not eat any detestable thing.[k]
4These are the animals you may eat:[l] the
ox, the sheep, the goat, 5the deer, the gazelle, the roe deer, the wild goat, the
ibex, the antelope and the mountain
sheep.[w] 6You may eat any animal that has
a split hoof divided in two and that
chews the cud. 7However, of those that
chew the cud or that have a split hoof
completely divided you may not eat the
camel, the rabbit or the coney.[x] Although they chew the cud, they do not
have a split hoof; they are ceremonially
unclean for you. 8The pig is also unclean;
although it has a split hoof, it does not
chew the cud. You are not to eat their
meat or touch their carcasses.[m]
9Of all the creatures living in the water,
you may eat any that has fins and scales.
10But anything that does not have fins
and scales you may not eat; for you it is
unclean.
11You may eat any clean bird. 12But
these you may not eat: the eagle, the vulture, the black vulture, 13the red kite, the
black kite, any kind of falcon, 14any kind
of raven, 15the horned owl, the screech
owl, the gull, any kind of hawk, 16the
little owl, the great owl, the white owl,
17the desert owl, the osprey, the cormorant, 18the stork, any kind of heron,
the hoopoe and the bat.
19All flying insects that swarm are unclean to you; do not eat them. 20But any
winged creature that is clean you may
eat.
21Do not eat anything you find already
dead.[n] You may give it to an alien living
in any of your towns, and he may eat it,
or you may sell it to a foreigner. But you
are a people holy to the LORD your God.[o]
Do not cook a young goat in its mother's milk.[p]

Tithing.

22Be sure to set aside a tenth[q] of all that
your fields produce each year. 23Eat the
tithe of your grain, new wine and oil,
and the firstborn of your herds and flocks
in the presence of the LORD your God at
the place he will choose as a dwelling
for his Name,[r] so that you may learn[s] to
revere the LORD your God always. 24But
if that place is too distant and you have
been blessed by the LORD your God and
cannot carry your tithe (because the place
where the LORD will choose to put his
Name is so far away), 25then exchange
your tithe for silver, and take the silver
with you and go to the place the LORD
your God will choose. 26Use the silver to
buy whatever you like: cattle, sheep,
wine or other fermented drink, or anything you wish. Then you and your
household shall eat there in the presence of the LORD your God and rejoice.[t]
27And do not neglect the Levites[u] living
in your towns, for they have no allotment
or inheritance of their own.[v]
28At the end of every three years,
bring all the tithes of that year's produce
and store it in your towns,[w] 29so that the
Levites (who have no allotment[x] or inheritance of their own) and the aliens,[y]
the fatherless and the widows who live
in your towns may come and eat and

13:16 [a]Jos 6:24 [b]Jos 8:28; Jer 49:2
13:17 [c]Nu 25:4 [d]Dt 30:3 [e]Dt 7:13 [f]Ge 22:17; 26:4,24; 28:14
13:18 [g]Dt 12:25,28
14:1 [h]Lev 19:28; 21:5; Jer 16:6; 41:5; Ro 8:14; 9:8; Gal 3:26
14:2 [i]Lev 20:26 [j]Dt 7:6; 26:18-19
14:3 [k]Eze 4:14
14:4 [l]Lev 11:2-45; Ac 10:14
14:8 [m]Lev 11:26-27
14:21 [n]Lev 17:15; 22:8 [o]ver 2 [p]Ex 23:19; 34:26
14:22 [q]Lev 27:30; Dt 12:6,17; Ne 10:37
14:23 [r]Dt 12:5 [s]Dt 4:10
14:26 [t]Dt 12:7-8
14:27 [u]Dt 12:19 [v]Nu 18:20
14:28 [w]Dt 26:12
14:29 [x]ver 27 [y]Dt 26:12

v *17* The Hebrew term refers to the irrevocable giving over of things or persons to the LORD, often by totally destroying them. w *5* The precise identification of some of the birds and animals in this chapter is uncertain. x *7* That is, the hyrax or rock badger

be satisfied, and so that the LORD your God may bless[a] you in all the work of your hands.

Canceling of debts every seven years.

15:1-11Ref— Lev 25:8-38

15 At the end of every seven years you must cancel debts.[b] 2This is how it is to be done: Every creditor shall cancel the loan he has made to his fellow Israelite. He shall not require payment from his fellow Israelite or brother, because the LORD's time for canceling debts has been proclaimed. 3You may require payment from a foreigner,[c] but you must cancel any debt your brother owes you. 4However, there should be no poor among you, for in the land the LORD your God is giving you to possess as your inheritance, he will richly bless[d] you, 5if only you fully obey the LORD your God and are careful to follow[e] all these commands I am giving you today. 6For the LORD your God will bless you as he has promised, and you will lend to many nations but will borrow from none. You will rule over many nations but none will rule over you.[f]

7If there is a poor man among your brothers in any of the towns of the land that the LORD your God is giving you, do not be hardhearted or tightfisted[g] toward your poor brother. 8Rather be openhanded[h] and freely lend him whatever he needs. 9Be careful not to harbor this wicked thought: "The seventh year, the year for canceling debts,[i] is near," so that you do not show ill will[j] toward your needy brother and give him nothing. He may then appeal to the LORD against you, and you will be found guilty of sin.[k] 10Give generously to him and do so without a grudging heart;[l] then because of this the LORD your God will bless[m] you in all your work and in everything you put your hand to. 11There will always be poor people in the land. Therefore I command you to be openhanded toward your brothers and toward the poor and needy in your land.[n]

14:29 [a]Dt 15:10; Mal 3:10
15:1 [b]Dt 31:10
15:3 [c]Dt 23:20
15:4 [d]Dt 28:8
15:5 [e]Dt 28:1
15:6 [f]Dt 28:12-13, 44
15:7 [g]1Jn 3:17
15:8 [h]Mt 5:42; Lk 6:34
15:9 [i]ver 1 [j]Mt 20:15 [k]Dt 24:15
15:10 [l]2Co 9:5 [m]Dt 14:29; 24:19
15:11 [n]Mt 26:11; Mk 14:7; Jn 12:8
15:12 [o]Ex 21:2; Lev 25:39; Jer 34:14
15:15 [p]Dt 5:15 [q]Dt 16:12
15:19 [r]Ex 13:2
15:20 [s]Dt 12:5-7, 17,18; 14:23
15:21 [t]Lev 22:19-25
15:22 [u]Dt 12:15,22
15:23 [v]Dt 12:16
16:1 [w]Ex 12:2; 13:4

Freeing Hebrew servants.

15:12-18pp— Ex 21:2-6
15:12-18Ref— Lev 25:38-55

12If a fellow Hebrew, a man or a woman, sells himself to you and serves you six years, in the seventh year you must let him go free.[o] 13And when you release him, do not send him away empty-handed. 14Supply him liberally from your flock, your threshing floor and your winepress. Give to him as the LORD your God has blessed you. 15Remember that you were slaves[p] in Egypt and the LORD your God redeemed you.[q] That is why I give you this command today.

16But if your servant says to you, "I do not want to leave you," because he loves you and your family and is well off with you, 17then take an awl and push it through his ear lobe into the door, and he will become your servant for life. Do the same for your maidservant.

18Do not consider it a hardship to set your servant free, because his service to you these six years has been worth twice as much as that of a hired hand. And the LORD your God will bless you in everything you do.

Sacrificing firstborn animals.

19Set apart for the LORD your God every firstborn male[r] of your herds and flocks. Do not put the firstborn of your oxen to work, and do not shear the firstborn of your sheep. 20Each year you and your family are to eat them in the presence of the LORD your God at the place he will choose.[s] 21If an animal has a defect, is lame or blind, or has any serious flaw, you must not sacrifice it to the LORD your God.[t] 22You are to eat it in your own towns. Both the ceremonially unclean and the clean may eat it, as if it were gazelle or deer.[u] 23But you must not eat the blood; pour it out on the ground like water.[v]

The Passover.

16:1-8pp— Ex 12:14-20; Lev 23:4-8; Nu 28:16-25

16 Observe the month of Abib[w] and celebrate the Passover of the LORD

your God, because in the month of Abib
he brought you out of Egypt by night.
2Sacrifice as the Passover to the LORD
your God an animal from your flock or
herd at the place the LORD will choose as
a dwelling for his Name.[a] 3Do not eat it
with bread made with yeast, but for sev-
en days eat unleavened bread, the bread
of affliction,[b] because you left Egypt in
haste[c]—so that all the days of your life
you may remember the time of your departure from Egypt.[d] 4Let no yeast be
found in your possession in all your land
for seven days. Do not let any of the
meat you sacrifice on the evening of the
first day remain until morning.[e]
5You must not sacrifice the Passover in
any town the LORD your God gives you
6except in the place he will choose as a
dwelling for his Name. There you must
sacrifice the Passover in the evening,
when the sun goes down, on the anniver-
sary[y][f] of your departure from Egypt.
7Roast[g] it and eat it at the place the LORD
your God will choose. Then in the morning return to your tents. 8For six days
eat unleavened bread and on the seventh day hold an assembly[h] to the LORD
your God and do no work.

Feast of Weeks

16:9-12pp— Lev 23:15-22; Nu 28:26-31

9Count off seven weeks[i] from the time
you begin to put the sickle to the standing grain.[j] 10Then celebrate the Feast of
Weeks to the LORD your God by giving
a freewill offering in proportion to the
blessings the LORD your God has given
you. 11And rejoice[k] before the LORD your
God at the place he will choose as a
dwelling for his Name—you, your sons
and daughters, your menservants and
maidservants, the Levites[l] in your towns,
and the aliens, the fatherless and the
widows living among you. 12Remember
that you were slaves in Egypt,[m] and follow carefully these decrees.

Feast of Tabernacles

16:13-17pp— Lev 23:33-43; Nu 29:12-39

13Celebrate the Feast of Tabernacles
for seven days after you have gathered
the produce of your threshing floor[n] and
your winepress.[o] 14Be joyful[p] at your
Feast—you, your sons and daughters,
your menservants and maidservants, and
the Levites, the aliens, the fatherless and
the widows who live in your towns.
15For seven days celebrate the Feast to
the LORD your God at the place the LORD
will choose. For the LORD your God will
bless you in all your harvest and in all
the work of your hands, and your joy[q]
will be complete.
16Three times a year all your men
must appear before the LORD your God
at the place he will choose: at the Feast
of Unleavened Bread, the Feast of Weeks
and the Feast of Tabernacles.[r] No man
should appear before the LORD empty-
handed:[s] 17Each of you must bring a gift
in proportion to the way the LORD your
God has blessed you.
18Appoint judges[t] and officials for each
of your tribes in every town the LORD
your God is giving you, and they shall
judge the people fairly. 19Do not pervert
justice[u] or show partiality.[v] Do not accept
a bribe,[w] for a bribe blinds the eyes of
the wise and twists the words of the righteous. 20Follow justice and justice alone,
so that you may live and possess the land
the LORD your God is giving you.

Worshiping other gods

21Do not set up any wooden Asherah
pole[z][x] beside the altar you build to the
LORD your God,[y] 22and do not erect a
sacred stone,[z] for these the LORD your
God hates.

17 Do not sacrifice to the LORD your
God an ox or a sheep that has
any defect[a] or flaw in it, for that would
be detestable to him.[b]
2If a man or woman living among
you in one of the towns the LORD gives
you is found doing evil in the eyes of the
LORD your God in violation of his covenant,[c] 3and contrary to my command[d]
has worshiped other gods, bowing down

16:2 [a]Dt 12:5,26
16:3 [b]Ex 12:8,39; 34:18 [c]Ex 12:11, 15,19 [d]Ex 13:3,6-7
16:4 [e]Ex 12:10; 34:25
16:6 [f]Ex 12:6; Dt 12:5
16:7 [g]Ex 12:8; 2Ch 35:13
16:8 [h]Ex 12:16; 13:6; Lev 23:8
16:9 [i]Ex 34:22; Lev 23:15 [j]Ex 23:16; Nu 28:26
16:11 [k]Dt 12:7 [l]Dt 12:12
16:12 [m]Dt 15:15
16:13 [n]Lev 23:34 [o]Ex 23:16
16:14 [p]ver 11
16:15 [q]Lev 23:39
16:16 [r]Ex 23:14,16 [s]Ex 34:20
16:18 [t]Dt 1:16
16:19 [u]Ex 23:2,8 [v]Lev 19:15; Dt 1:17 [w]Ecc 7:7
16:21 [x]Dt 7:5 [y]Ex 34:13; 2Ki 17:16; 21:3; 2Ch 33:3
16:22 [z]Lev 26:1
17:1 [a]Mal 1:8,13 [b]Dt 15:21
17:2 [c]Dt 13:6-11
17:3 [d]Jer 7:22-23

y6 Or *down, at the time of day* z21 Or *Do not plant any tree dedicated to Asherah*

to them or to the sun[a] or the moon or the stars of the sky, 4and this has been brought to your attention, then you must investigate it thoroughly. If it is true and it has been proved that this detestable thing has been done in Israel,[b] 5take the man or woman who has done this evil deed to your city gate and stone that person to death.[c] 6On the testimony of two or three witnesses a man shall be put to death, but no one shall be put to death on the testimony of only one witness.[d] 7The hands of the witnesses must be the first in putting him to death, and then the hands of all the people. You must purge the evil[e] from among you.

Verdicts from priests and judges.

8If cases come before your courts that are too difficult for you to judge—whether bloodshed, lawsuits or assaults[f]— take them to the place the LORD your God will choose.[g] 9Go to the priests, who are Levites, and to the judge who is in office at that time. Inquire of them and they will give you the verdict.[h] 10You must act according to the decisions they give you at the place the LORD will choose. Be careful to do everything they direct you to do. 11Act according to the law they teach you and the decisions they give you. Do not turn aside from what they tell you, to the right or to the left.[i] 12The man who shows contempt[j] for the judge or for the priest who stands ministering there to the LORD your God must be put to death. You must purge the evil from Israel. 13All the people will hear and be afraid, and will not be contemptuous again.[k]

The chosen king.

14When you enter the land the LORD your God is giving you and have taken possession of it and settled in it, and you say, "Let us set a king over us like all the nations around us,"[l] 15be sure to appoint over you the king the LORD your God chooses. He must be from among your own brothers.[m] Do not place a foreigner over you, one who is not a brother Israelite. 16The king, moreover, must not acquire great numbers of horses for himself[n] or make the people return to Egypt[o] to get more of them,[p] for the LORD has told you, "You are not to go back that way again."[q] 17He must not take many wives,[r] or his heart will be led astray. He must not accumulate large amounts of silver and gold.

18When he takes the throne of his kingdom, he is to write[s] for himself on a scroll a copy of this law, taken from that of the priests, who are Levites. 19It is to be with him, and he is to read it all the days of his life[t] so that he may learn to revere the LORD his God and follow carefully all the words of this law and these decrees 20and not consider himself better than his brothers and turn from the law[u] to the right or to the left.[v] Then he and his descendants will reign a long time over his kingdom in Israel.

The LORD is the inheritance of the priests and Levites.

18 The priests, who are Levites—indeed the whole tribe of Levi—are to have no allotment or inheritance with Israel. They shall live on the offerings made to the LORD by fire, for that is their inheritance.[w] 2They shall have no inheritance among their brothers; the LORD is their inheritance, as he promised them.

3This is the share due the priests from the people who sacrifice a bull or a sheep: the shoulder, the jowls and the inner parts.[x] 4You are to give them the firstfruits of your grain, new wine and oil, and the first wool from the shearing of your sheep,[y] 5for the LORD your God has chosen them[z] and their descendants out of all your tribes to stand and minister[a] in the LORD's name always.

6If a Levite moves from one of your towns anywhere in Israel where he is living, and comes in all earnestness to the place the LORD will choose,[b] 7he may minister in the name of the LORD his God like all his fellow Levites who serve there in the presence of the LORD. 8He

17:3 [a]Job 31:26
17:4 [b]Dt 13:12-14
17:5 [c]Lev 24:14
17:6 [d]Nu 35:30; Dt 19:15; Jos 7:25; Mt 18:16; Jn 8:17; 2Co 13:1; 1Ti 5:19; Heb 10:28
17:7 [e]Dt 13:5,9
17:8 [f]2Ch 19:10 [g]Dt 12:5; Hag 2:11
17:9 [h]Dt 19:17; Eze 44:24
17:11 [i]Dt 25:1
17:12 [j]Nu 15:30
17:13 [k]Dt 13:11; 19:20
17:14 [l]Dt 11:31; 1Sa 8:5,19-20
17:15 [m]Jer 30:21
17:16 [n]1Ki 4:26; 10:26 [o]Isa 31:1; Hos 11:5 [p]1Ki 10:28; Eze 17:15 [q]Ex 13:17
17:17 [r]1Ki 11:3
17:18 [s]Dt 31:22,24
17:19 [t]Jos 1:8
17:20 [u]1Ki 15:5 [v]Dt 5:32
18:1 [w]Dt 10:9; 1Co 9:13
18:3 [x]Lev 7:28-34
18:4 [y]Ex 22:29; Nu 18:12
18:5 [z]Ex 28:1 [a]Dt 10:8
18:6 [b]Nu 35:2-3

is to share equally in their benefits, even
though he has received money from the
sale of family possessions.[a]

Detestable practices against the LORD.

9When you enter the land the LORD
your God is giving you, do not learn to
imitate[b] the detestable ways of the
nations there. 10Let no one be found
among you who sacrifices his son or
daughter in[a] the fire, who practices divination[c] or sorcery, interprets omens, engages in witchcraft,[d] 11or casts spells, or
who is a medium or spiritist or who consults the dead. 12Anyone who does these
things is detestable to the LORD, and
because of these detestable practices the
LORD your God will drive out those nations before you.[e] 13You must be blameless before the LORD your God.

God's promise to raise up a prophet.

14The nations you will dispossess listen to those who practice sorcery or divination. But as for you, the LORD your
God has not permitted you to do so.
15The LORD your God will raise up for you
a prophet like me from among your own
brothers.[f] You must listen to him. 16For
this is what you asked of the LORD your
God at Horeb on the day of the assembly when you said, "Let us not hear the
voice of the LORD our God nor see this
great fire anymore, or we will die."[g]
17The LORD said to me: "What they say
is good. 18I will raise up for them a
prophet like you from among their brothers; I will put my words[h] in his mouth,
and he will tell them everything I command him.[i] 19If anyone does not listen
to my words that the prophet speaks in
my name, I myself will call him to account.[j] 20But a prophet who presumes
to speak in my name anything I have not
commanded him to say, or a prophet
who speaks in the name of other gods,[k]
must be put to death."[l]
21You may say to yourselves, "How can
we know when a message has not been
spoken by the LORD?" 22If what a prophet
proclaims in the name of the LORD does
not take place or come true, that is a
message the LORD has not spoken.[m] That
prophet has spoken presumptuously.[n]
Do not be afraid of him.

18:8 [a]2Ch 31:4; Ne 12:44,47
18:9 [b]Dt 12:29-31
18:10 [c]Dt 12:31 [d]Lev 19:31
18:12 [e]Lev 18:24; Dt 9:4
18:15 [f]Jn 1:21; Ac 3:22*; 7:37*
18:16 [g]Ex 20:19; Dt 5:23-27
18:18 [h]Isa 51:16; Jn 17:8 [i]Jn 4:25-26; 8:28; 12:49-50
18:19 [j]Ac 3:23*
18:20 [k]Jer 14:14 [l]Dt 13:1-5
18:22 [m]Jer 28:9 [n]ver 20
19:1 [o]Dt 12:29
19:6 [p]Nu 35:12
19:9 [q]Jos 20:7-8

Cities of refuge are set aside.

19:1-14Ref— Nu 35:6-34; Dt 4:41-43; Jos 20:1-9

19 When the LORD your God has destroyed the nations whose land
he is giving you, and when you have
driven them out and settled in their
towns and houses,[o] 2then set aside for
yourselves three cities centrally located in
the land the LORD your God is giving you
to possess. 3Build roads to them and divide into three parts the land the LORD
your God is giving you as an inheritance,
so that anyone who kills a man may flee
there.
4This is the rule concerning the man
who kills another and flees there to save
his life—one who kills his neighbor
unintentionally, without malice aforethought. 5For instance, a man may go
into the forest with his neighbor to cut
wood, and as he swings his ax to fell a
tree, the head may fly off and hit his
neighbor and kill him. That man may
flee to one of these cities and save his
life. 6Otherwise, the avenger of blood[p]
might pursue him in a rage, overtake
him if the distance is too great, and kill
him even though he is not deserving of
death, since he did it to his neighbor
without malice aforethought. 7This is
why I command you to set aside for
yourselves three cities.
8If the LORD your God enlarges your
territory, as he promised on oath to your
forefathers, and gives you the whole land
he promised them, 9because you carefully follow all these laws I command
you today—to love the LORD your God
and to walk always in his ways[q]—then
you are to set aside three more cities.
10Do this so that innocent blood will
not be shed in your land, which the
LORD your God is giving you as your

a *10* Or *who makes his son or daughter pass through*

inheritance, and so that you will not be guilty of bloodshed.[a]

11But if a man hates his neighbor and lies in wait for him, assaults and kills him,[b] and then flees to one of these cities, 12the elders of his town shall send for him, bring him back from the city, and hand him over to the avenger of blood to die. 13Show him no pity.[c] You must purge from Israel the guilt of shedding innocent blood,[d] so that it may go well with you.

14Do not move your neighbor's boundary stone set up by your predecessors in the inheritance you receive in the land the LORD your God is giving you to possess.[e]

At least two witnesses are required.

15One witness is not enough to convict a man accused of any crime or offense he may have committed. A matter must be established by the testimony of two or three witnesses.[f]

16If a malicious witness[g] takes the stand to accuse a man of a crime, 17the two men involved in the dispute must stand in the presence of the LORD before the priests and the judges[h] who are in office at the time. 18The judges must make a thorough investigation, and if the witness proves to be a liar, giving false testimony against his brother, 19then do to him as he intended to do to his brother.[i] You must purge the evil from among you. 20The rest of the people will hear of this and be afraid,[j] and never again will such an evil thing be done among you. 21Show no pity:[k] life for life, eye for eye, tooth for tooth, hand for hand, foot for foot.[l]

Instructions concerning principles of war.

20 When you go to war against your enemies and see horses and chariots and an army greater than yours,[m] do not be afraid[n] of them,[o] because the LORD your God, who brought you up out of Egypt, will be with you.

19:10 [a]Nu 35:33; Dt 21:1-9
19:11 [b]Nu 35:16
19:13 [c]Dt 7:2 [d]1Ki 2:31
19:14 [e]Dt 27:17; Pr 22:28; Hos 5:10
19:15 [f]Nu 35:30; Dt 17:6; Mt 18:16*; Jn 8:17; 2Co 13:1*; 1Ti 5:19; Heb 10:28
19:16 [g]Ex 23:1; Ps 27:12
19:17 [h]Dt 17:9
19:19 [i]Pr 19:5,9
19:20 [j]Dt 17:13; 21:21
19:21 [k]ver 13 [l]Ex 21:24; Lev 24:20; Mt 5:38*
20:1 [m]Ps 20:7; Isa 31:1 [n]Dt 31:6,8 [o]2Ch 32:7-8
20:3 [p]Jos 23:10
20:4 [q]Dt 1:30; 3:22; Jos 23:10
20:5 [r]Ne 12:27
20:7 [s]Dt 24:5
20:8 [t]Jdg 7:3
20:10 [u]Lk 14:31-32
20:11 [v]1Ki 9:21
20:13 [w]Nu 31:7
20:14 [x]Jos 8:2; 22:8
20:16 [y]Ex 23:31-33; Nu 21:2-3; Dt 7:2; Jos 11:14

2When you are about to go into battle, the priest shall come forward and address the army. 3He shall say: "Hear, O Israel, today you are going into battle against your enemies. Do not be fainthearted[p] or afraid; do not be terrified or give way to panic before them. 4For the LORD your God is the one who goes with you to fight[q] for you against your enemies to give you victory."

5The officers shall say to the army: "Has anyone built a new house and not dedicated[r] it? Let him go home, or he may die in battle and someone else may dedicate it. 6Has anyone planted a vineyard and not begun to enjoy it? Let him go home, or he may die in battle and someone else enjoy it. 7Has anyone become pledged to a woman and not married her? Let him go home, or he may die in battle and someone else marry her.[s]" 8Then the officers shall add, "Is any man afraid or fainthearted? Let him go home so that his brothers will not become disheartened too."[t] 9When the officers have finished speaking to the army, they shall appoint commanders over it.

10When you march up to attack a city, make its people an offer of peace.[u] 11If they accept and open their gates, all the people in it shall be subject to forced labor[v] and shall work for you. 12If they refuse to make peace and they engage you in battle, lay siege to that city. 13When the LORD your God delivers it into your hand, put to the sword all the men in it.[w] 14As for the women, the children, the livestock[x] and everything else in the city, you may take these as plunder for yourselves. And you may use the plunder the LORD your God gives you from your enemies. 15This is how you are to treat all the cities that are at a distance from you and do not belong to the nations nearby.

16However, in the cities of the nations the LORD your God is giving you as an inheritance, do not leave alive anything that breathes.[y] 17Completely destroy[b]

[b] *17* The Hebrew term refers to the irrevocable giving over of things or persons to the LORD, often by totally destroying them.

them—the Hittites, Amorites, Canaanites, Perizzites, Hivites and Jebusites—as the LORD your God has commanded you. 18 Otherwise, they will teach you to follow all the detestable things they do in worshiping their gods,[a] and you will sin[b] against the LORD your God.

19 When you lay siege to a city for a long time, fighting against it to capture it, do not destroy its trees by putting an ax to them, because you can eat their fruit. Do not cut them down. Are the trees of the field people, that you should besiege them?[c] 20 However, you may cut down trees that you know are not fruit trees and use them to build siege works until the city at war with you falls.

Atonement for unsolved murder.

21 If a man is found slain, lying in a field in the land the LORD your God is giving you to possess, and it is not known who killed him, 2 your elders and judges shall go out and measure the distance from the body to the neighboring towns. 3 Then the elders of the town nearest the body shall take a heifer that has never been worked and has never worn a yoke 4 and lead her down to a valley that has not been plowed or planted and where there is a flowing stream. There in the valley they are to break the heifer's neck. 5 The priests, the sons of Levi, shall step forward, for the LORD your God has chosen them to minister and to pronounce blessings[c] in the name of the LORD and to decide all cases of dispute and assault.[d] 6 Then all the elders of the town nearest the body shall wash their hands[e] over the heifer whose neck was broken in the valley, 7 and they shall declare: "Our hands did not shed this blood, nor did our eyes see it done. 8 Accept this atonement for your people Israel, whom you have redeemed, O LORD, and do not hold your people guilty of the blood of an innocent man." And the bloodshed will be atoned for.[f] 9 So you will purge[g] from yourselves the guilt of shedding innocent blood, since you have done what is right in the eyes of the LORD.

20:18 [a]Ex 34:16; Dt 7:4; 12:30-31 [b]Ex 23:33
21:5 [c]1Ch 23:13 [d]Dt 17:8-11
21:6 [e]Mt 27:24
21:8 [f]Nu 35:33-34
21:9 [g]Dt 19:13
21:10 [h]Jos 21:44
21:12 [i]Lev 14:9; Nu 6:9
21:13 [j]Ps 45:10
21:14 [k]Ge 34:2
21:15 [l]Ge 29:33
21:16 [m]1Ch 26:10
21:17 [n]Ge 49:3 [o]Ge 25:31
21:18 [p]Pr 1:8; Isa 30:1; Eph 6:1-3
21:21 [q]Dt 19:19

Marriage to a female captive.

10 When you go to war against your enemies and the LORD your God delivers them into your hands[h] and you take captives, 11 if you notice among the captives a beautiful woman and are attracted to her, you may take her as your wife. 12 Bring her into your home and have her shave her head,[i] trim her nails 13 and put aside the clothes she was wearing when captured. After she has lived in your house and mourned her father and mother for a full month,[j] then you may go to her and be her husband and she shall be your wife. 14 If you are not pleased with her, let her go wherever she wishes. You must not sell her or treat her as a slave, since you have dishonored her.[k]

Inheritance rights of the firstborn.

15 If a man has two wives, and he loves one but not the other, and both bear him sons but the firstborn is the son of the wife he does not love,[l] 16 when he wills his property to his sons, he must not give the rights of the firstborn to the son of the wife he loves in preference to his actual firstborn, the son of the wife he does not love.[m] 17 He must acknowledge the son of his unloved wife as the firstborn by giving him a double share of all he has. That son is the first sign of his father's strength.[n] The right of the firstborn belongs to him.[o]

Stoning of rebellious sons.

18 If a man has a stubborn and rebellious son who does not obey his father and mother[p] and will not listen to them when they discipline him, 19 his father and mother shall take hold of him and bring him to the elders at the gate of his town. 20 They shall say to the elders, "This son of ours is stubborn and rebellious. He will not obey us. He is a profligate and a drunkard." 21 Then all the men of his town shall stone him to death. You must purge the evil[q] from among

c *19* Or *down to use in the siege, for the fruit trees are for the benefit of man.*

you. All Israel will hear of it and be afraid.[a]

Miscellaneous laws.

22If a man guilty of a capital offense[b] is put to death and his body is hung on a tree, **23**you must not leave his body on the tree overnight.[c] Be sure to bury him that same day, because anyone who is hung on a tree is under God's curse.[d] You must not desecrate[e] the land the LORD your God is giving you as an inheritance.

22 If you see your brother's ox or sheep straying, do not ignore it but be sure to take it back to him.[f] **2**If the brother does not live near you or if you do not know who he is, take it home with you and keep it until he comes looking for it. Then give it back to him. **3**Do the same if you find your brother's donkey or his cloak or anything he loses. Do not ignore it.

4If you see your brother's donkey[g] or his ox fallen on the road, do not ignore it. Help him get it to its feet.

5A woman must not wear men's clothing, nor a man wear women's clothing, for the LORD your God detests anyone who does this.

6If you come across a bird's nest beside the road, either in a tree or on the ground, and the mother is sitting on the young or on the eggs, do not take the mother with the young.[h] **7**You may take the young, but be sure to let the mother go, so that it may go well with you and you may have a long life.[i]

8When you build a new house, make a parapet around your roof so that you may not bring the guilt of bloodshed on your house if someone falls from the roof.

9Do not plant two kinds of seed in your vineyard;[j] if you do, not only the crops you plant but also the fruit of the vineyard will be defiled.[d]

10Do not plow with an ox and a donkey yoked together.[k]

11Do not wear clothes of wool and linen woven together.[l]

21:21 [a]Dt 13:11
21:22 [b]Dt 22:26; Mk 14:64; Ac 23:29
21:23 [c]Jos 8:29; 10:27; Jn 19:31 [d]Gal 3:13* [e]Lev 18:25; Nu 35:34
22:1 [f]Ex 23:4-5
22:4 [g]Ex 23:5
22:6 [h]Lev 22:28
22:7 [i]Dt 4:40
22:9 [j]Lev 19:19
22:10 [k]2Co 6:14
22:11 [l]Lev 19:19
22:12 [m]Nu 15:37-41; Mt 23:5
22:13 [n]Dt 24:1
22:18 [o]Ex 18:21
22:21 [p]Ge 34:7; Dt 13:5; 23:17-18; Jdg 20:6; 2Sa 13:12
22:22 [q]Lev 20:10; Jn 8:5

12Make tassels on the four corners of the cloak you wear.[m]

Laws concerning sexual morality.

13If a man takes a wife and, after lying with her[n], dislikes her **14**and slanders her and gives her a bad name, saying, "I married this woman, but when I approached her, I did not find proof of her virginity," **15**then the girl's father and mother shall bring proof that she was a virgin to the town elders at the gate. **16**The girl's father will say to the elders, "I gave my daughter in marriage to this man, but he dislikes her. **17**Now he has slandered her and said, 'I did not find your daughter to be a virgin.' But here is the proof of my daughter's virginity." Then her parents shall display the cloth before the elders of the town, **18**and the elders[o] shall take the man and punish him. **19**They shall fine him a hundred shekels of silver[e] and give them to the girl's father, because this man has given an Israelite virgin a bad name. She shall continue to be his wife; he must not divorce her as long as he lives.

20If, however, the charge is true and no proof of the girl's virginity can be found, **21**she shall be brought to the door of her father's house and there the men of her town shall stone her to death. She has done a disgraceful thing[p] in Israel by being promiscuous while still in her father's house. You must purge the evil from among you.

22If a man is found sleeping with another man's wife, both the man who slept with her and the woman must die.[q] You must purge the evil from Israel.

23If a man happens to meet in a town a virgin pledged to be married and he sleeps with her, **24**you shall take both of them to the gate of that town and stone them to death—the girl because she was in a town and did not scream for help, and the man because he violated

d *9* Or *be forfeited to the sanctuary* e *19* That is, about 2 1/2 pounds (about 1 kilogram)

another man's wife. You must purge the
evil from among you.[a]
25But if out in the country a man happens to meet a girl pledged to be married
and rapes her, only the man who has
done this shall die. 26Do nothing to the
girl; she has committed no sin deserving death. This case is like that of someone who attacks and murders his
neighbor, 27for the man found the girl
out in the country, and though the betrothed girl screamed, there was no one
to rescue her.
28If a man happens to meet a virgin
who is not pledged to be married and
rapes her and they are discovered,[b] 29he
shall pay the girl's father fifty shekels
of silver.[f] He must marry the girl, for he
has violated her. He can never divorce
her as long as he lives.
30A man is not to marry his father's
wife; he must not dishonor his father's
bed.[c]

Instructions concerning exclusion from the assembly.

23 No one who has been emasculat-
ed by crushing or cutting may
enter the assembly of the LORD.
2No one born of a forbidden marriage[g] nor any of his descendants may
enter the assembly of the LORD, even
down to the tenth generation.
3No Ammonite or Moabite or any of
his descendants may enter the assembly of the LORD, even down to the tenth
generation.[d] 4For they did not come to
meet you with bread and water on your
way when you came out of Egypt, and
they hired Balaam[e] son of Beor from
Pethor in Aram Naharaim[h] to pronounce
a curse on you. 5However, the LORD your
God would not listen to Balaam but
turned the curse[f] into a blessing for you,
because the LORD your God loves you.
6Do not seek a treaty of friendship with
them as long as you live.[g]
7Do not abhor an Edomite, for he is
your brother.[h] Do not abhor an Egyptian,
because you lived as an alien in his country.[i] 8The third generation of children
born to them may enter the assembly of
the LORD.

Cleanliness exhorted in the camp.

9When you are encamped against your
enemies, keep away from everything impure. 10If one of your men is unclean
because of a nocturnal emission, he is
to go outside the camp and stay there.[j]
11But as evening approaches he is to
wash himself, and at sunset he may return to the camp.
12Designate a place outside the camp
where you can go to relieve yourself.
13As part of your equipment have something to dig with, and when you relieve
yourself, dig a hole and cover up your
excrement. 14For the LORD your God
moves[k] about in your camp to protect
you and to deliver your enemies to you.
Your camp must be holy,[l] so that he
will not see among you anything indecent and turn away from you.

Miscellaneous laws.

15If a slave has taken refuge with you,
do not hand him over to his master.[m]
16Let him live among you wherever he
likes and in whatever town he chooses.
Do not oppress[n] him.
17No Israelite man[o] or woman is to become a shrine prostitute.[p] 18You must
not bring the earnings of a female prostitute or of a male prostitute[i] into the
house of the LORD your God to pay any
vow, because the LORD your God detests
them both.
19Do not charge your brother interest,
whether on money or food or anything
else that may earn interest.[q] 20You may
charge a foreigner interest, but not a
brother Israelite, so that the LORD your
God may bless[r] you in everything you
put your hand to in the land you are
entering to possess.
21If you make a vow to the LORD your
God, do not be slow to pay it, for the
LORD your God will certainly demand

22:24 [a]ver 21-22; 1Co 5:13*
22:28 [b]Ex 22:16
22:30 [c]Lev 18:8; 20:11; 18:8; Dt 27:20; 1Co 5:1
23:3 [d]Ne 13:2
23:4 [e]Nu 22:5-6; 23:7; 2Pe 2:15
23:5 [f]Pr 26:2
23:6 [g]Ezr 9:12
23:7 [h]Ge 25:26; Ob 1:10,12 [i]Ex 22:21; 23:9; Lev 19:34; Dt 10:19
23:10 [j]Lev 15:16
23:14 [k]Lev 26:12 [l]Ex 3:5
23:15 [m]1Sa 30:15
23:16 [n]Ex 22:21
23:17 [o]Ge 19:25; 2Ki 23:7 [p]Lev 19:29; Dt 22:21
23:19 [q]Ex 22:25; Lev 25:35-37
23:20 [r]Dt 15:10; 28:12

f29 That is, about 1 1/4 pounds (about 0.6 kilogram)
g2 Or *one of illegitimate birth* h4 That is, Northwest Mesopotamia i18 Hebrew *of a dog*

it of you and you will be guilty of sin.[a]
22But if you refrain from making a vow,
you will not be guilty. 23Whatever your
lips utter you must be sure to do, because you made your vow freely to the
LORD your God with your own mouth.
24If you enter your neighbor's vineyard, you may eat all the grapes you
want, but do not put any in your basket.
25If you enter your neighbor's grainfield,
you may pick kernels with your hands,
but you must not put a sickle to his
standing grain.[b]

24 If a man marries a woman who
becomes displeasing to him[c] because he finds something indecent about
her, and he writes her a certificate of
divorce,[d] gives it to her and sends her
from his house, 2and if after she leaves
his house she becomes the wife of another man, 3and her second husband dislikes her and writes her a certificate of
divorce, gives it to her and sends her
from his house, or if he dies, 4then her
first husband, who divorced her, is not
allowed to marry her again after she
has been defiled. That would be detestable in the eyes of the LORD. Do not
bring sin upon the land the LORD[e] your
God is giving you as an inheritance.
5If a man has recently married, he
must not be sent to war or have any other duty laid on him. For one year he is
to be free to stay at home and bring
happiness to the wife he has married.[f]
6Do not take a pair of millstones—
not even the upper one—as security for
a debt, because that would be taking a
man's livelihood as security.
7If a man is caught kidnapping one of
his brother Israelites and treats him as a
slave or sells him, the kidnapper must
die.[g] You must purge the evil from
among you.
8In cases of leprous[j] diseases be very
careful to do exactly as the priests, who
are Levites, instruct you. You must follow carefully what I have commanded
them.[h] 9Remember what the LORD your
God did to Miriam along the way after
you came out of Egypt.[i]
10When you make a loan of any kind
to your neighbor, do not go into his
house to get what he is offering as a
pledge. 11Stay outside and let the man to
whom you are making the loan bring the
pledge out to you. 12If the man is poor,
do not go to sleep with his pledge in
your possession. 13Return his cloak to
him by sunset[j] so that he may sleep in
it. Then he will thank you, and it will be
regarded as a righteous act in the sight
of the LORD your God.[k]
14Do not take advantage of a hired man
who is poor and needy, whether he is a
brother Israelite or an alien living in one
of your towns.[l] 15Pay him his wages each
day before sunset, because he is poor[m]
and is counting on it.[n] Otherwise he may
cry to the LORD against you, and you will
be guilty of sin.[o]
16Fathers shall not be put to death for
their children, nor children put to death
for their fathers; each is to die for his
own sin.[p]
17Do not deprive the alien or the
fatherless of justice,[q] or take the cloak of
the widow as a pledge. 18Remember that
you were slaves in Egypt and the LORD
your God redeemed you from there. That
is why I command you to do this.
19When you are harvesting in your
field and you overlook a sheaf, do not
go back to get it.[r] Leave it for the alien,
the fatherless and the widow, so that the
LORD your God may bless[s] you in all the
work of your hands. 20When you beat
the olives from your trees, do not go over
the branches a second time.[t] Leave what
remains for the alien, the fatherless and
the widow. 21When you harvest the
grapes in your vineyard, do not go over
the vines again. Leave what remains for
the alien, the fatherless and the widow.
22Remember that you were slaves in
Egypt. That is why I command you to
do this.[u]

25 When men have a dispute, they
are to take it to court and the
judges will decide the case,[v] acquitting
the innocent and condemning the
guilty.[w] 2If the guilty man deserves to

23:21 [a]Nu 30:1-2; Ecc 5:4-5; Mt 5:33
23:25 [b]Mt 12:1; Mk 2:23; Lk 6:1
24:1 [c]Dt 22:13 [d]Mt 5:31*; 19:7-9; Mk 10:4-5
24:4 [e]Jer 3:1
24:5 [f]Dt 20:7
24:7 [g]Ex 21:16
24:8 [h]Lev 13:1-46; 14:2
24:9 [i]Nu 12:10
24:13 [j]Ex 22:26 [k]Dt 6:25; Da 4:27
24:14 [l]Lev 25:35-43; Dt 15:12-18
24:15 [m]Jer 22:13 [n]Lev 19:13 [o]Dt 15:9; Jas 5:4
24:16 [p]2Ki 14:6; 2Ch 25:4; Jer 31:29-30; Eze 18:20
24:17 [q]Dt 1:17; 10:17-18; 16:19
24:19 [r]Lev 19:9; 23:22 [s]Pr 19:17
24:20 [t]Lev 19:10
24:22 [u]ver 18
25:1 [v]Dt 19:17 [w]Dt 1:16-17

j8 The Hebrew word was used for various diseases affecting the skin—not necessarily leprosy.

be beaten,[a] the judge shall make him lie down and have him flogged in his presence with the number of lashes his crime deserves, 3but he must not give him more than forty lashes.[b] If he is flogged more than that, your brother will be degraded in your eyes.[c]

4Do not muzzle an ox while it is treading out the grain.[d]

5If brothers are living together and one of them dies without a son, his widow must not marry outside the family. Her husband's brother shall take her and marry her and fulfill the duty of a brother-in-law to her.[e] 6The first son she bears shall carry on the name of the dead brother so that his name will not be blotted out from Israel.[f]

7However, if a man does not want to marry his brother's wife, she shall go to the elders at the town gate and say, "My husband's brother refuses to carry on his brother's name in Israel. He will not fulfill the duty of a brother-in-law to me."[g] 8Then the elders of his town shall summon him and talk to him. If he persists in saying, "I do not want to marry her," 9his brother's widow shall go up to him in the presence of the elders, take off one of his sandals,[h] spit in his face and say, "This is what is done to the man who will not build up his brother's family line." 10That man's line shall be known in Israel as The Family of the Unsandaled.

11If two men are fighting and the wife of one of them comes to rescue her husband from his assailant, and she reaches out and seizes him by his private parts, 12you shall cut off her hand. Show her no pity.[i]

13Do not have two differing weights in your bag—one heavy, one light.[j] 14Do not have two differing measures in your house—one large, one small. 15You must have accurate and honest weights and measures, so that you may live long[k] in the land the LORD your God is giving you. 16For the LORD your God detests anyone who does these things, anyone who deals dishonestly.[l]

17Remember what the Amalekites[m] did to you along the way when you came out of Egypt. 18When you were weary and worn out, they met you on your journey and cut off all who were lagging behind; they had no fear of God.[n] 19When the LORD your God gives you rest from all the enemies around you in the land he is giving you to possess as an inheritance, you shall blot out the memory of Amalek[o] from under heaven. Do not forget!

Firstfruits and tithes.

26 When you have entered the land the LORD your God is giving you as an inheritance and have taken possession of it and settled in it, 2take some of the firstfruits[p] of all that you produce from the soil of the land the LORD your God is giving you and put them in a basket. Then go to the place the LORD your God will choose as a dwelling for his Name[q] 3and say to the priest in office at the time, "I declare today to the LORD your God that I have come to the land the LORD swore to our forefathers to give us." 4The priest shall take the basket from your hands and set it down in front of the altar of the LORD your God. 5Then you shall declare before the LORD your God: "My father was a wandering Aramean,[r] and he went down into Egypt with a few people[s] and lived there and became a great nation, powerful and numerous. 6But the Egyptians mistreated us and made us suffer,[t] putting us to hard labor. 7Then we cried out to the LORD, the God of our fathers, and the LORD heard our voice[u] and saw[v] our misery, toil and oppression. 8So the LORD brought us out of Egypt with a mighty hand and an outstretched arm, with great terror and with miraculous signs and wonders.[w] 9He brought us to this place and gave us this land, a land flowing with milk and honey;[x] 10and now I bring the firstfruits of the soil that you, O LORD, have given me." Place the basket before the LORD your God and bow down before him. 11And you and the Levites[y] and the aliens among you shall

25:2 [a]Lk 12:47-48
25:3 [b]2Co 11:24 [c]Job 18:3
25:4 [d]Pr 12:10; 1Co 9:9*; 1Ti 5:18*
25:5 [e]Mt 22:24; Mk 12:19; Lk 20:28
25:6 [f]Ge 38:9; Ru 4:5,10
25:7 [g]Ru 4:1-2,5-6
25:9 [h]Ru 4:7-8,11
25:12 [i]Dt 19:13
25:13 [j]Lev 19:35-37; Pr 11:1; Eze 45:10; Mic 6:11
25:15 [k]Ex 20:12
25:16 [l]Pr 11:1
25:17 [m]Ex 17:8
25:18 [n]Ps 36:1; Ro 3:18
25:19 [o]1Sa 15:2-3
26:2 [p]Ex 22:29; 23:16,19; Nu 18:13; Pr 3:9 [q]Dt 12:5
26:5 [r]Hos 12:12 [s]Ge 43:1-2; 45:7,11; 46:27; Dt 10:22
26:6 [t]Ex 1:11,14
26:7 [u]Ex 2:23-25 [v]Ex 3:9
26:8 [w]Dt 4:34
26:9 [x]Ex 3:8
26:11 [y]Dt 12:7

rejoice[a] in all the good things the LORD
your God has given to you and your
household.
12When you have finished setting
aside a tenth[b] of all your produce in the
third year, the year of the tithe,[c] you shall
give it to the Levite, the alien, the fatherless and the widow, so that they may eat
in your towns and be satisfied. 13Then
say to the LORD your God: "I have
removed from my house the sacred
portion and have given it to the Levite,
the alien, the fatherless and the widow,
according to all you commanded. I have
not turned aside from your commands
nor have I forgotten any of them.[d] 14I
have not eaten any of the sacred portion
while I was in mourning, nor have I
removed any of it while I was unclean,[e]
nor have I offered any of it to the dead.
I have obeyed the LORD my God; I have
done everything you commanded me.
15Look down from heaven,[f] your holy
dwelling place, and bless your people
Israel and the land you have given us as
you promised on oath to our forefathers,
a land flowing with milk and honey."

Covenant between God and Israel.

16The LORD your God commands you
this day to follow these decrees and laws;
carefully observe them with all your
heart and with all your soul.[g] 17You have
declared this day that the LORD is your
God and that you will walk in his ways,
that you will keep his decrees, commands and laws, and that you will obey
him. 18And the LORD has declared this
day that you are his people, his treasured possession[h] as he promised, and
that you are to keep all his commands.
19He has declared that he will set you in
praise, fame and honor high above all
the nations[i] he has made and that you
will be a people holy[j] to the LORD your
God, as he promised.

Words of the law to be written on stones.

27 Moses and the elders of Israel
commanded the people: "Keep
all these commands that I give you today.
2When you have crossed the Jordan into
the land the LORD your God is giving you,
set up some large stones and coat them
with plaster.[k] 3Write on them all the
words of this law when you have crossed
over to enter the land the LORD your
God is giving you, a land flowing with
milk and honey,[l] just as the LORD, the
God of your fathers, promised you. 4And
when you have crossed the Jordan, set
up these stones on Mount Ebal,[m] as I
command you today, and coat them
with plaster. 5Build there an altar[n] to the
LORD your God, an altar of stones. Do not
use any iron tool[o] upon them. 6Build the
altar of the LORD your God with field-
stones and offer burnt offerings on it to
the LORD your God. 7Sacrifice fellowship offerings[k] there, eating them and
rejoicing in the presence of the LORD
your God. 8And you shall write very
clearly all the words of this law on these
stones you have set up."

Curses pronounced by the Levites.

9Then Moses and the priests, who are
Levites, said to all Israel, "Be silent, O
Israel, and listen! You have now become
the people of the LORD your God.[p] 10Obey
the LORD your God and follow his commands and decrees that I give you today."
11On the same day Moses commanded
the people:
12When you have crossed the Jordan,
these tribes shall stand on Mount Gerizim[q] to bless the people: Simeon, Levi,
Judah, Issachar, Joseph and Benjamin.[r]
13And these tribes shall stand on Mount
Ebal to pronounce curses: Reuben, Gad,
Asher, Zebulun, Dan and Naphtali.
14The Levites shall recite to all the
people of Israel in a loud voice:

15"Cursed is the man who carves
an image or casts an idol[s]—a thing
detestable to the LORD, the work of
the craftsman's hands—and sets it
up in secret."
Then all the people shall say,
"Amen!"

26:11 [a]Dt 16:11
26:12 [b]Lev 27:30 [c]Nu 18:24; Dt 14:28-29; Heb 7:5,9
26:13 [d]Ps 119:141, 153,176
26:14 [e]Lev 7:20; Hos 9:4
26:15 [f]Isa 63:15; Zec 2:13
26:16 [g]Dt 4:29
26:18 [h]Ex 6:7; 19:5; Dt 7:6; 14:2; 28:9
26:19 [i]Dt 4:7-8; 28:1,13,44 [j]Ex 19:6; Dt 7:6; 1Pe 2:9
27:2 [k]Jos 8:31
27:3 [l]Dt 26:9
27:4 [m]Dt 11:29
27:5 [n]Jos 8:31 [o]Ex 20:25
27:9 [p]Dt 26:18
27:12 [q]Dt 11:29 [r]Jos 8:35
27:15 [s]Ex 20:4; 34:17; Lev 19:4; 26:1; Dt 4:16,23; 5:8; Isa 44:9

k7 Traditionally *peace offerings*

16“Cursed is the man who dishonors his father or his mother.”[a]
Then all the people shall say,
“Amen!”
17“Cursed is the man who moves
his neighbor’s boundary stone.”[b]
Then all the people shall say,
“Amen!”
18“Cursed is the man who leads
the blind astray on the road.”[c]
Then all the people shall say,
“Amen!”
19“Cursed is the man who withholds justice from the alien,[d] the
fatherless or the widow.”[e]
Then all the people shall say,
“Amen!”
20“Cursed is the man who sleeps
with his father’s wife, for he dishonors his father’s bed.”[f]
Then all the people shall say,
“Amen!”
21“Cursed is the man who has
sexual relations with any animal.”[g]
Then all the people shall say,
“Amen!”
22“Cursed is the man who sleeps
with his sister, the daughter of his father or the daughter of his mother.”[h]
Then all the people shall say,
“Amen!”
23“Cursed is the man who sleeps
with his mother-in-law.”[i]
Then all the people shall say,
“Amen!”
24“Cursed is the man who kills[j]
his neighbor secretly.”
Then all the people shall say,
“Amen!”
25“Cursed is the man who accepts
a bribe to kill an innocent person.”[k]
Then all the people shall say,
“Amen!”
26“Cursed is the man who does
not uphold the words of this law
by carrying them out.”[l]
Then all the people shall say,
“Amen!”

Promise of blessings for obedience.

28 If you fully obey the LORD your
God and carefully follow all his
commands[m] I give you today, the LORD
your God will set you high above all
the nations on earth.[n] 2All these blessings will come upon you[o] and accompany
you if you obey the LORD your God:

3You will be blessed[p] in the city
and blessed in the country.[q]
4The fruit of your womb will be
blessed, and the crops of your land
and the young of your livestock—
the calves of your herds and the
lambs of your flocks.[r]
5Your basket and your kneading
trough will be blessed.
6You will be blessed when you
come in and blessed when you go
out.[s]

7The LORD will grant that the enemies
who rise up against you will be defeated
before you. They will come at you from
one direction but flee from you in seven.[t]
8The LORD will send a blessing on your
barns and on everything you put your
hand to. The LORD your God will bless
you in the land he is giving you.
9The LORD will establish you as his
holy people,[u] as he promised you on
oath, if you keep the commands of the
LORD your God and walk in his ways.
10Then all the peoples on earth will see
that you are called by the name[v] of the
LORD, and they will fear you. 11The LORD
will grant you abundant prosperity—in
the fruit of your womb, the young of
your livestock and the crops of your
ground—in the land he swore to your
forefathers to give you.[w]
12The LORD will open the heavens, the
storehouse of his bounty, to send rain[x]
on your land in season and to bless all
the work of your hands. You will lend
to many nations but will borrow from
none.[y] 13The LORD will make you the
head, not the tail. If you pay attention
to the commands of the LORD your God
that I give you this day and carefully
follow them, you will always be at the
top, never at the bottom. 14Do not turn
aside from any of the commands I give
you today, to the right or to the left,[z]
following other gods and serving them.

27:16 [a]Ex 20:12; 21:17; Lev 19:3; 20:9
27:17 [b]Dt 19:14; Pr 22:28
27:18 [c]Lev 19:14
27:19 [d]Ex 22:21; Dt 24:19 [e]Dt 10:18
27:20 [f]Lev 18:7; Dt 22:30
27:21 [g]Lev 18:23
27:22 [h]Lev 18:9; 20:17
27:23 [i]Lev 20:14
27:24 [j]Lev 24:17; Nu 35:31
27:25 [k]Ex 23:7-8; Dt 10:17; Eze 22:12
27:26 [l]Jer 11:3; Gal 3:10*
28:1 [m]Ex 15:26; Lev 26:3; Dt 7:12-26 [n]Dt 26:19
28:2 [o]Zec 1:6
28:3 [p]Ps 128:1,4 [q]Ge 39:5
28:4 [r]Ge 49:25; Pr 10:22
28:6 [s]Ps 121:8
28:7 [t]Lev 26:8,17
28:9 [u]Ex 19:6; Dt 7:6
28:10 [v]2Ch 7:14
28:11 [w]Dt 30:9; Pr 10:22
28:12 [x]Lev 26:4 [y]Dt 15:3,6
28:14 [z]Dt 5:32

Promise of curses for disobedience.

15 However, if you do not obey[a] the
LORD your God and do not carefully follow all his commands and decrees I am
giving you today, all these curses will
come upon you and overtake you:[b]

16 You will be cursed in the city
and cursed in the country.
17 Your basket and your kneading
trough will be cursed.
18 The fruit of your womb will be
cursed, and the crops of your land,
and the calves of your herds and
the lambs of your flocks.
19 You will be cursed when you
come in and cursed when you go
out.

20 The LORD will send on you curses,[c]
confusion and rebuke[d] in everything you
put your hand to, until you are destroyed
and come to sudden ruin[e] because of the
evil you have done in forsaking him.[1]
21 The LORD will plague you with diseases
until he has destroyed you from the land
you are entering to possess.[f] 22 The LORD
will strike you with wasting disease, with
fever and inflammation, with scorching
heat and drought,[g] with blight and mildew, which will plague you until you
perish.[h] 23 The sky over your head will be
bronze, the ground beneath you iron.[i]
24 The LORD will turn the rain of your
country into dust and powder; it will
come down from the skies until you are
destroyed.

25 The LORD will cause you to be defeated before your enemies. You will
come at them from one direction but
flee from them in seven,[j] and you will
become a thing of horror to all the kingdoms on earth.[k] 26 Your carcasses will be
food for all the birds of the air and the
beasts of the earth, and there will be no
one to frighten them away.[l] 27 The LORD
will afflict you with the boils of Egypt[m]
and with tumors, festering sores and the
itch, from which you cannot be cured.
28 The LORD will afflict you with madness, blindness and confusion of mind.
29 At midday you will grope[n] about like
a blind man in the dark. You will be un-
successful in everything you do; day after
day you will be oppressed and robbed,
with no one to rescue you.

30 You will be pledged to be married to
a woman, but another will take her and
ravish her.[o] You will build a house, but
you will not live in it.[p] You will plant a
vineyard, but you will not even begin to
enjoy its fruit.[q] 31 Your ox will be slaughtered before your eyes, but you will eat
none of it. Your donkey will be forcibly
taken from you and will not be returned.
Your sheep will be given to your enemies, and no one will rescue them.
32 Your sons and daughters will be given
to another nation,[r] and you will wear out
your eyes watching for them day after
day, powerless to lift a hand. 33 A people that you do not know will eat what
your land and labor produce, and you
will have nothing but cruel oppression
all your days.[s] 34 The sights you see will
drive you mad. 35 The LORD will afflict
your knees and legs with painful boils[t]
that cannot be cured, spreading from
the soles of your feet to the top of your
head.

36 The LORD will drive you and the
king[u] you set over you to a nation unknown to you or your fathers.[v] There
you will worship other gods, gods of
wood and stone.[w] 37 You will become a
thing of horror and an object of scorn
and ridicule to all the nations where
the LORD will drive you.[x]

38 You will sow much seed in the field
but you will harvest little,[y] because
locusts will devour[z] it. 39 You will plant
vineyards and cultivate them but you will
not drink the wine or gather the grapes,
because worms will eat them.[a] 40 You
will have olive trees throughout your
country but you will not use the oil, because the olives will drop off.[b] 41 You will
have sons and daughters but you will
not keep them, because they will go
into captivity.[c] 42 Swarms of locusts will
take over all your trees and the crops
of your land.

28:15 [a]Lev 26:14 [b]Jos 23:15; Da 9:11; Mal 2:2
28:20 [c]Mal 2:2 [d]Isa 51:20; 66:15 [e]Dt 4:26
28:21 [f]Lev 26:25; Jer 24:10
28:22 [g]Lev 26:16 [h]Am 4:9
28:23 [i]Lev 26:19
28:25 [j]Isa 30:17 [k]Jer 15:4; 24:9; Eze 23:46
28:26 [l]Jer 7:33; 16:4; 34:20
28:27 [m]ver 60-61; 1Sa 5:6
28:29 [n]Job 5:14; Isa 59:10
28:30 [o]Job 31:10; Jer 8:10 [p]Am 5:11 [q]Jer 12:13
28:32 [r]ver 41
28:33 [s]Jer 5:15-17
28:35 [t]ver 27
28:36 [u]2Ki 17:4,6; 24:12,14; 25:7,11 [v]Jer 16:13 [w]Dt 4:28
28:37 [x]Jer 24:9
28:38 [y]Mic 6:15; Hag 1:6,9 [z]Joel 1:4
28:39 [a]Isa 5:10; 17:10-11
28:40 [b]Mic 6:15
28:41 [c]ver 32

[1]20 Hebrew *me*

43The alien who lives among you will rise above you higher and higher, but you will sink lower and lower.[a] 44He will lend to you, but you will not lend to him.[b] He will be the head, but you will be the tail.[c]

45All these curses will come upon you. They will pursue you and overtake you until you are destroyed,[d] because you did not obey the LORD your God and observe the commands and decrees he gave you. 46They will be a sign and a wonder to you and your descendants forever.[e] 47Because you did not serve[f] the LORD your God joyfully and gladly[g] in the time of prosperity, 48therefore in hunger and thirst, in nakedness and dire poverty, you will serve the enemies the LORD sends against you. He will put an iron yoke[h] on your neck until he has destroyed you.

49The LORD will bring a nation against you from far away, from the ends of the earth,[i] like an eagle[j] swooping down, a nation whose language you will not understand, 50a fierce-looking nation without respect for the old[k] or pity for the young. 51They will devour the young of your livestock and the crops of your land until you are destroyed. They will leave you no grain, new wine or oil, nor any calves of your herds or lambs of your flocks until you are ruined.[l] 52They will lay siege to all the cities throughout your land until the high fortified walls in which you trust fall down. They will besiege all the cities throughout the land the LORD your God is giving you.[m]

53Because of the suffering that your enemy will inflict on you during the siege, you will eat the fruit of the womb, the flesh of the sons and daughters the LORD your God has given you.[n] 54Even the most gentle and sensitive man among you will have no compassion on his own brother or the wife he loves or his surviving children, 55and he will not give to one of them any of the flesh of his children that he is eating. It will be all he has left because of the suffering your enemy will inflict on you during the siege of all your cities. 56The most gentle and sensitive[o] woman among you—so sensitive and gentle that she would not venture to touch the ground with the sole of her foot—will begrudge the husband she loves and her own son or daughter 57the afterbirth from her womb and the children she bears. For she intends to eat them secretly during the siege and in the distress that your enemy will inflict on you in your cities.

58If you do not carefully follow all the words of this law, which are written in this book, and do not revere[p] this glorious and awesome name[q]—the LORD your God— 59the LORD will send fearful plagues on you and your descendants, harsh and prolonged disasters, and severe and lingering illnesses. 60He will bring upon you all the diseases of Egypt[r] that you dreaded, and they will cling to you. 61The LORD will also bring on you every kind of sickness and disaster not recorded in this Book of the Law, until you are destroyed.[s] 62You who were as numerous as the stars in the sky[t] will be left but few in number, because you did not obey the LORD your God. 63Just as it pleased[u] the LORD to make you prosper and increase in number, so it will please[v] him to ruin and destroy you. You will be uprooted[w] from the land you are entering to possess.

64Then the LORD will scatter[x] you among all nations,[y] from one end of the earth to the other. There you will worship other gods—gods of wood and stone, which neither you nor your fathers have known. 65Among those nations you will find no repose, no resting place for the sole of your foot. There the LORD will give you an anxious mind, eyes weary with longing, and a despairing heart.[z] 66You will live in constant suspense, filled with dread both night and day, never sure of your life. 67In the morning you will say, "If only it were evening!" and in the evening, "If only it were morning!"—because of the terror that will fill your hearts and the sights that your eyes will see.[a] 68The LORD will send you back in ships to Egypt on a journey I said you should

28:43 [a]ver 13
28:44 [b]ver 12 [c]ver 13
28:45 [d]ver 15
28:46 [e]Isa 8:18; Eze 14:8
28:47 [f]Dt 32:15 [g]Ne 9:35
28:48 [h]Jer 28:13-14
28:49 [i]Jer 5:15; 6:22 [j]La 4:19; Hos 8:1
28:50 [k]Isa 47:6
28:51 [l]ver 33
28:52 [m]Jer 10:18; Zep 1:14-16,17
28:53 [n]Lev 26:29; 2Ki 6:28-29; Jer 19:9; La 2:20; 4:10
28:56 [o]ver 54
28:58 [p]Mal 1:14 [q]Ex 6:3
28:60 [r]ver 27
28:61 [s]Dt 4:25-26
28:62 [t]Dt 4:27; 10:22; Ne 9:23
28:63 [u]Jer 32:41 [v]Pr 1:26 [w]Jer 12:14; 45:4
28:64 [x]Lev 26:33; Dt 4:27 [y]Ne 1:8
28:65 [z]Lev 26:16,36
28:67 [a]ver 34; Job 7:4

never make again. There you will offer yourselves for sale to your enemies as male and female slaves, but no one will buy you.

Renewal of God's covenant with Israel.

29 These are the terms of the covenant the LORD commanded Moses to make with the Israelites in Moab, in addition to the covenant he had made with them at Horeb.[a]

2Moses summoned all the Israelites and said to them:

Your eyes have seen all that the LORD did in Egypt to Pharaoh, to all his officials and to all his land.[b] 3With your own eyes you saw those great trials, those miraculous signs and great wonders.[c] 4But to this day the LORD has not given you a mind that understands or eyes that see or ears that hear.[d] 5During the forty years that I led you through the desert, your clothes did not wear out, nor did the sandals on your feet.[e] 6You ate no bread and drank no wine or other fermented drink. I did this so that you might know that I am the LORD your God.[f]

7When you reached this place, Sihon[g] king of Heshbon and Og king of Bashan came out to fight against us, but we defeated them.[h] 8We took their land and gave it as an inheritance to the Reubenites, the Gadites and the half-tribe of Manasseh.[i]

9Carefully follow[j] the terms of this covenant, so that you may prosper in everything you do.[k] 10All of you are standing today in the presence of the LORD your God—your leaders and chief men, your elders and officials, and all the other men of Israel, 11together with your children and your wives, and the aliens living in your camps who chop your wood and carry your water.[l] 12You are standing here in order to enter into a covenant with the LORD your God, a covenant the LORD is making with you this day and sealing with an oath, 13to confirm you this day as his people,[m] that he may be your God[n] as he promised you and as he swore to your fathers, Abraham, Isaac and Jacob. 14I am making this covenant,[o] with its oath, not only with you 15who are standing here with us today in the presence of the LORD our God but also with those who are not here today.[p]

16You yourselves know how we lived in Egypt and how we passed through the countries on the way here. 17You saw among them their detestable images and idols of wood and stone, of silver and gold.[q] 18Make sure there is no man or woman, clan or tribe among you today whose heart turns away from the LORD our God to go and worship the gods of those nations; make sure there is no root among you that produces such bitter poison.[r]

19When such a person hears the words of this oath, he invokes a blessing on himself and therefore thinks, "I will be safe, even though I persist in going my own way." This will bring disaster on the watered land as well as the dry.[m] 20The LORD will never be willing to forgive him; his wrath and zeal[s] will burn[t] against that man. All the curses written in this book will fall upon him, and the LORD will blot[u] out his name from under heaven. 21The LORD will single him out from all the tribes of Israel for disaster, according to all the curses of the covenant written in this Book of the Law.

22Your children who follow you in later generations and foreigners who come from distant lands will see the calamities that have fallen on the land and the diseases with which the LORD has afflicted it.[v] 23The whole land will be a burning waste[w] of salt[x] and sulfur—nothing planted, nothing sprouting, no vegetation growing on it. It will be like the destruction of Sodom and Gomorrah,[y] Admah and Zeboiim, which the LORD overthrew in fierce anger. 24All the nations will ask: "Why has the LORD done this to this land?[z] Why this fierce, burning anger?"

25And the answer will be: "It is

29:1 [a]Dt 5:2-3
29:2 [b]Ex 19:4
29:3 [c]Dt 4:34; 7:19
29:4 [d]Isa 6:10; Ac 28:26-27; Ro 11:8*; Eph 4:18
29:5 [e]Dt 8:4
29:6 [f]Dt 8:3
29:7 [g]Dt 2:32; 3:1 [h]Nu 21:21-24, 33-35
29:8 [i]Nu 32:33; Dt 3:12-13
29:9 [j]Dt 4:6; Jos 1:7 [k]1Ki 2:3
29:11 [l]Jos 9:21, 23,27
29:13 [m]Dt 28:9 [n]Ge 17:7; Ex 6:7
29:14 [o]Jer 31:31
29:15 [p]Ac 2:39
29:17 [q]Dt 28:36
29:18 [r]Dt 11:16; Heb 12:15
29:20 [s]Eze 23:25 [t]Ps 74:1; 79:5 [u]Ex 32:33; Dt 9:14
29:22 [v]Jer 19:8
29:23 [w]Isa 34:9 [x]Jer 17:6 [y]Ge 19:24,25; Zep 2:9
29:24 [z]1Ki 9:8; Jer 22:8-9

m *19* Or *way, in order to add drunkenness to thirst."*

because this people abandoned the covenant of the LORD, the God of their fathers, the covenant he made with them when he brought them out of Egypt. 26They went off and worshiped other gods and bowed down to them, gods they did not know, gods he had not given them. 27Therefore the LORD's anger burned against this land, so that he brought on it all the curses written in this book.[a] 28In furious anger and in great wrath the LORD uprooted[b] them from their land and thrust them into another land, as it is now."

29The secret things belong to the LORD our God, but the things revealed belong to us and to our children forever, that we may follow all the words of this law.

Compassion is promised to those who return to God.

30 When all these blessings and curses[c] I have set before you come upon you and you take them to heart wherever the LORD your God disperses you among the nations,[d] 2and when you and your children return[e] to the LORD your God and obey him with all your heart and with all your soul according to everything I command you today, 3then the LORD your God will restore your fortunes[n,f] and have compassion on you and gather[g] you again from all the nations where he scattered you.[h] 4Even if you have been banished to the most distant land under the heavens, from there the LORD your God will gather you and bring you back.[i] 5He will bring[j] you to the land that belonged to your fathers, and you will take possession of it. He will make you more prosperous and numerous than your fathers. 6The LORD your God will circumcise your hearts and the hearts of your descendants,[k] so that you may love him with all your heart and with all your soul, and live. 7The LORD your God will put all these curses on your enemies who hate and persecute you.[l] 8You will again obey the LORD and follow all his commands I am giving you today. 9Then the LORD your God will make you most prosperous in all the work of your hands and in the fruit of your womb, the young of your livestock and the crops of your land.[m] The LORD will again delight in you and make you prosperous, just as he delighted in your fathers, 10if you obey the LORD your God and keep his commands and decrees that are written in this Book of the Law and turn to the LORD your God with all your heart and with all your soul.[n]

Life and death choices are set before the people.

11Now what I am commanding you today is not too difficult for you or beyond your reach.[o] 12It is not up in heaven, so that you have to ask, "Who will ascend into heaven to get it and proclaim it to us so we may obey it?"[p] 13Nor is it beyond the sea, so that you have to ask, "Who will cross the sea to get it and proclaim it to us so we may obey it?" 14No, the word is very near you; it is in your mouth and in your heart so you may obey it.

15See, I set before you today life and prosperity, death and destruction.[q] 16For I command you today to love the LORD your God, to walk in his ways, and to keep his commands, decrees and laws; then you will live and increase, and the LORD your God will bless you in the land you are entering to possess.

17But if your heart turns away and you are not obedient, and if you are drawn away to bow down to other gods and worship them, 18I declare to you this day that you will certainly be destroyed.[r] You will not live long in the land you are crossing the Jordan to enter and possess.

19This day I call heaven and earth as witnesses against you[s] that I have set before you life and death, blessings and curses.[t] Now choose life, so that you and your children may live 20and that you may love[u] the LORD your God, listen to his voice, and hold fast to him. For the LORD is your life,[v] and he will give you

29:27 [a]Da 9:11, 13,14
29:28 [b]1Ki 14:15; 2Ch 7:20; Ps 52:5; Pr 2:22
30:1 [c]ver 15,19; Dt 11:26 [d]Lev 26:40-45; Dt 28:64; 29:28; 1Ki 8:47
30:2 [e]Dt 4:30; Ne 1:9
30:3 [f]Ps 126:4 [g]Ps 147:2; Jer 32:37; Eze 34:13 [h]Jer 29:14
30:4 [i]Ne 1:8-9; Isa 43:6
30:5 [j]Jer 29:14
30:6 [k]Dt 10:16; Jer 32:39
30:7 [l]Dt 7:15
30:9 [m]Dt 28:11; Jer 31:28; 32:41
30:10 [n]Dt 4:29
30:11 [o]Isa 45:19,23
30:12 [p]Ro 10:6*
30:15 [q]Dt 11:26
30:18 [r]Dt 8:19
30:19 [s]Dt 4:26 [t]ver 1
30:20 [u]Dt 6:5; 10:20 [v]Ps 27:1; Jn 11:25

n3 Or *will bring you back from captivity*

many years in the land he swore to give to your fathers, Abraham, Isaac and Jacob.

Moses' charge to Joshua.

31 Then Moses went out and spoke these words to all Israel: 2"I am now a hundred and twenty years old[a] and I am no longer able to lead you.[b] The LORD has said to me, 'You shall not cross the Jordan.'[c] 3The LORD your God himself will cross[d] over ahead of you.[e] He will destroy these nations before you, and you will take possession of their land. Joshua also will cross[f] over ahead of you, as the LORD said. 4And the LORD will do to them what he did to Sihon and Og, the kings of the Amorites, whom he destroyed along with their land. 5The LORD will deliver[g] them to you, and you must do to them all that I have commanded you. 6Be strong and courageous.[h] Do not be afraid or terrified[i] because of them, for the LORD your God goes with you;[j] he will never leave you[k] nor forsake[l] you."

7Then Moses summoned Joshua and said[m] to him in the presence of all Israel, "Be strong and courageous, for you must go with this people into the land that the LORD swore to their forefathers to give them, and you must divide it among them as their inheritance. 8The LORD himself goes before you and will be with you;[n] he will never leave you nor forsake you. Do not be afraid; do not be discouraged."

Reading of the law every seventh year.

9So Moses wrote down this law and gave it to the priests, the sons of Levi, who carried[o] the ark of the covenant of the LORD, and to all the elders of Israel. 10Then Moses commanded them: "At the end of every seven years, in the year for canceling debts,[p] during the Feast of Tabernacles,[q] 11when all Israel comes to appear[r] before the LORD your God at the place he will choose, you shall read this law[s] before them in their hearing. 12Assemble the people—men, women and children, and the aliens living in your towns—so they can listen and learn[t] to fear the LORD your God and follow carefully all the words of this law. 13Their children,[u] who do not know this law, must hear it and learn to fear the LORD your God as long as you live in the land you are crossing the Jordan to possess."

God's charge to Moses and Joshua.

14The LORD said to Moses, "Now the day of your death[v] is near. Call Joshua and present yourselves at the Tent of Meeting, where I will commission him." So Moses and Joshua came and presented themselves at the Tent of Meeting.

15Then the LORD appeared at the Tent in a pillar of cloud, and the cloud stood over the entrance to the Tent.[w] 16And the LORD said to Moses: "You are going to rest with your fathers, and these people will soon prostitute[x] themselves to the foreign gods of the land they are entering. They will forsake[y] me and break the covenant I made with them. 17On that day I will become angry[z] with them and forsake[a] them; I will hide[b] my face from them, and they will be destroyed. Many disasters and difficulties will come upon them, and on that day they will ask, 'Have not these disasters come upon us because our God is not with us?'[c] 18And I will certainly hide my face on that day because of all their wickedness in turning to other gods.

19"Now write down for yourselves this song and teach it to the Israelites and have them sing it, so that it may be a witness for me against them. 20When I have brought them into the land flowing with milk and honey, the land I promised on oath to their forefathers,[d] and when they eat their fill and thrive, they will turn to other gods[e] and worship them, rejecting me and breaking my covenant.[f] 21And when many disasters and difficulties come upon them,[g] this song will testify against them, because it will not be forgotten by their descendants. I know what they

31:2 [a]Dt 34:7 [b]Nu 27:17; 1Ki 3:7 [c]Dt 3:23,26
31:3 [d]Nu 27:18 [e]Dt 9:3 [f]Dt 3:28
31:5 [g]Dt 7:2
31:6 [h]Jos 10:25; 1Ch 22:13 [i]Dt 7:18 [j]Dt 1:29; 20:4 [k]Jos 1:5 [l]Heb 13:5*
31:7 [m]Dt 1:38; 3:28
31:8 [n]Ex 13:21; 33:14
31:9 [o]ver 25; Nu 4:15; Jos 3:3
31:10 [p]Dt 15:1 [q]Lev 23:34
31:11 [r]Dt 16:16 [s]Jos 8:34-35; 2Ki 23:2
31:12 [t]Dt 4:10
31:13 [u]Dt 11:2; Ps 78:6-7
31:14 [v]Nu 27:13; Dt 32:49-50
31:15 [w]Ex 33:9
31:16 [x]Jdg 2:12 [y]Jdg 10:6,13
31:17 [z]Jdg 2:14,20 [a]Jdg 6:13; 2Ch 15:2 [b]Dt 32:20; Isa 1:15; 8:17 [c]Nu 14:42
31:20 [d]Dt 6:10-12 [e]Dt 32:15-17 [f]ver 16
31:21 [g]ver 17

are disposed to do,[a] even before I bring
them into the land I promised them on
oath." 22So Moses wrote[b] down this song
that day and taught it to the Israelites.
23The LORD gave this command[c] to
Joshua son of Nun: "Be strong and courageous,[d] for you will bring the Israelites
into the land I promised them on oath,
and I myself will be with you."
24After Moses finished writing in a
book the words of this law from beginning to end, 25he gave this command to
the Levites who carried the ark of the
covenant of the LORD: 26"Take this Book
of the Law and place it beside the ark
of the covenant of the LORD your God.
There it will remain as a witness against
you.[e] 27For I know how rebellious and
stiff-necked[f] you are. If you have been
rebellious against the LORD while I am
still alive and with you, how much more
will you rebel after I die! 28Assemble
before me all the elders of your tribes
and all your officials, so that I can speak
these words in their hearing and call
heaven and earth to testify against
them.[g] 29For I know that after my death
you are sure to become utterly corrupt[h]
and to turn from the way I have commanded you. In days to come, disaster[i]
will fall upon you because you will do
evil in the sight of the LORD and provoke
him to anger by what your hands have
made."

The song of Moses.

30And Moses recited the words of this
song from beginning to end in the hearing of the whole assembly of Israel:

32 Listen, O heavens,[j] and I will
speak;
hear, O earth, the words of my
mouth.
2Let my teaching fall like rain
and my words descend like dew,[k]
like showers[l] on new grass,
like abundant rain on tender
plants.

3I will proclaim the name of the
LORD.[m]
Oh, praise the greatness[n] of our
God!
4He is the Rock,[o] his works are
perfect,[p]
and all his ways are just.
A faithful God[q] who does no wrong,
upright and just is he.

5They have acted corruptly toward
him;
to their shame they are no longer
his children,
but a warped and crooked
generation.[o][r]
6Is this the way you repay[s] the LORD,
O foolish and unwise people?[t]
Is he not your Father,[u] your Creator,[p]
who made you and formed you?[v]

7Remember the days of old;
consider the generations long past.
Ask your father and he will tell you,
your elders, and they will explain
to you.[w]
8When the Most High gave the
nations their inheritance,
when he divided all mankind,[x]
he set up boundaries for the peoples
according to the number of the
sons of Israel.[q]
9For the LORD's portion[y] is his people,
Jacob his allotted inheritance.[z]

10In a desert[a] land he found him,
in a barren and howling waste.
He shielded him and cared for him;
he guarded him as the apple of his
eye,[b]
11like an eagle that stirs up its nest
and hovers over its young,[c]
that spreads its wings to catch them
and carries them on its pinions.
12The LORD alone led him;
no foreign god was with him.[d]

13He made him ride on the heights[e] of
the land
and fed him with the fruit of the
fields.

31:21 [a]Hos 5:3
31:22 [b]ver 19
31:23 [c]ver 7 [d]Jos 1:6
31:26 [e]ver 19
31:27 [f]Ex 32:9; Dt 9:6,24
31:28 [g]Dt 4:26; 30:19; 32:1
31:29 [h]Dt 32:5; Jdg 2:19 [i]Dt 28:15
32:1 [j]Isa 1:2
32:2 [k]Isa 55:11 [l]Ps 72:6
32:3 [m]Ex 33:19 [n]Dt 3:24
32:4 [o]ver 15,18,30 [p]2Sa 22:31 [q]Dt 7:9
32:5 [r]Dt 31:29
32:6 [s]Ps 116:12 [t]Ps 74:2 [u]Dt 1:31; Isa 63:16 [v]ver 15
32:7 [w]Ex 13:14
32:8 [x]Ge 11:8; Ac 17:26
32:9 [y]Jer 10:16 [z]1Ki 8:51,53
32:10 [a]Jer 2:6 [b]Ps 17:8; Zec 2:8
32:11 [c]Ex 19:4
32:12 [d]ver 39
32:13 [e]Isa 58:14

[o]*5* Or *Corrupt are they and not his children, / a generation warped and twisted to their shame*
[p]*6* Or *Father, who bought you* [q]*8* Masoretic Text; Dead Sea Scrolls (see also Septuagint) *sons of God*

He nourished him with honey from the rock,
and with oil[a] from the flinty crag,
14with curds and milk from herd and flock
and with fattened lambs and goats,
with choice rams of Bashan
and the finest kernels of wheat.[b]
You drank the foaming blood of the grape.[c]

15Jeshurun[r] grew fat[d] and kicked;
filled with food, he became heavy and sleek.
He abandoned[e] the God who made him
and rejected the Rock[f] his Savior.
16They made him jealous[g] with their foreign gods
and angered[h] him with their detestable idols.
17They sacrificed to demons, which are not God—
gods they had not known,[i]
gods that recently appeared,[j]
gods your fathers did not fear.
18You deserted the Rock, who fathered you;
you forgot[k] the God who gave you birth.

19The LORD saw this and rejected them[l]
because he was angered by his sons and daughters.[m]
20"I will hide my face[n] from them," he said,
"and see what their end will be;
for they are a perverse generation,[o]
children who are unfaithful.
21They made me jealous[p] by what is no god
and angered me with their worthless idols.[q]
I will make them envious by those who are not a people;
I will make them angry by a nation that has no understanding.[r]
22For a fire has been kindled by my wrath,
one that burns to the realm of death[s] below.[s]
It will devour the earth and its harvests
and set afire the foundations of the mountains.

23"I will heap calamities[t] upon them
and spend my arrows[u] against them.
24I will send wasting famine against them,
consuming pestilence[v] and deadly plague;[w]
I will send against them the fangs of wild beasts,[x]
the venom of vipers[y] that glide in the dust.
25In the street the sword will make them childless;
in their homes terror will reign.[z]
Young men and young women will perish,
infants and gray-haired men.[a]
26I said I would scatter[b] them
and blot out their memory from mankind,[c]
27but I dreaded the taunt of the enemy,
lest the adversary misunderstand
and say, 'Our hand has triumphed;
the LORD has not done all this.'"[d]

28They are a nation without sense,
there is no discernment in them.
29If only they were wise and would understand this[e]
and discern what their end will be!
30How could one man chase a thousand,
or two put ten thousand to flight,[f]
unless their Rock had sold them,
unless the LORD had given them up?[g]
31For their rock is not like our Rock,
as even our enemies concede.
32Their vine comes from the vine of Sodom
and from the fields of Gomorrah.
Their grapes are filled with poison
and their clusters with bitterness.

32:13 [a]Job 29:6
32:14 [b]Ps 81:16; 147:14 [c]Ge 49:11
32:15 [d]Dt 31:20 [e]ver 6; Isa 1:4,28 [f]ver 4
32:16 [g]1Co 10:22 [h]Ps 78:58
32:17 [i]Dt 28:64 [j]Jdg 5:8
32:18 [k]Isa 17:10
32:19 [l]Jer 44:21-23 [m]Ps 106:40
32:20 [n]Dt 31:17,29 [o]ver 5
32:21 [p]1Co 10:22 [q]1Ki 16:13,26 [r]Ro 10:19*
32:22 [s]Ps 18:7-8; Jer 15:14; La 4:11
32:23 [t]Dt 29:21 [u]Ps 7:13; Eze 5:16
32:24 [v]Dt 28:22 [w]Ps 91:6 [x]Lev 26:22 [y]Am 5:18-19
32:25 [z]Eze 7:15 [a]2Ch 36:17; La 2:21
32:26 [b]Dt 4:27 [c]Ps 34:16
32:27 [d]Isa 10:13
32:29 [e]Dt 5:29; Ps 81:13
32:30 [f]Lev 26:8 [g]Ps 44:12

[r]15 *Jeshurun* means *the upright one*, that is, Israel.
[s]22 Hebrew *to Sheol*

33Their wine is the venom of serpents,
the deadly poison of cobras.[a]

34"Have I not kept this in reserve
and sealed it in my vaults?[b]
35It is mine to avenge; I will repay.[c]
In due time their foot will slip;[d]
their day of disaster is near
and their doom rushes upon
them.[e]"

36The LORD will judge his people
and have compassion on his
servants[f]
when he sees their strength is gone
and no one is left, slave or free.
37He will say: "Now where are their
gods,
the rock they took refuge in,[g]
38the gods who ate the fat of their
sacrifices
and drank the wine of their drink
offerings?
Let them rise up to help you!
Let them give you shelter!

39"See now that I myself am He![h]
There is no god besides me.[i]
I put to death and I bring to life,[j]
I have wounded and I will heal,[k]
and no one can deliver out of my
hand.[l]
40I lift my hand to heaven and declare:
As surely as I live forever,
41when I sharpen my flashing sword[m]
and my hand grasps it in judgment,
I will take vengeance on my
adversaries
and repay those who hate me.[n]
42I will make my arrows drunk with
blood,[o]
while my sword devours flesh:[p]
the blood of the slain and the
captives,
the heads of the enemy leaders."

43Rejoice,[q] O nations, with his
people,[t,u]
for he will avenge the blood of his
servants;[r]
he will take vengeance on his
enemies
and make atonement for his land
and people.[s]

32:33 [a]Ps 58:4
32:34 [b]Jer 2:22; Hos 13:12
32:35 [c]Ro 12:19*; Heb 10:30* [d]Jer 23:12 [e]Eze 7:8-9
32:36 [f]Dt 30:1-3; Ps 135:14; Joel 2:14
32:37 [g]Jdg 10:14; Jer 2:28
32:39 [h]Isa 41:4 [i]Isa 45:5 [j]1Sa 2:6; Ps 68:20 [k]Hos 6:1 [l]Ps 50:22
32:41 [m]Isa 34:6; 66:16; Eze 21:9-10 [n]Jer 50:29
32:42 [o]ver 23 [p]Jer 46:10,14
32:43 [q]Ro 15:10* [r]2Ki 9:7 [s]Ps 65:3; 85:1; Rev 19:2
32:44 [t]Nu 13:8,16
32:46 [u]Eze 40:4
32:47 [v]Dt 30:20
32:49 [w]Nu 27:12
32:50 [x]Ge 25:8
32:51 [y]Nu 20:11-13 [z]Nu 27:14
32:52 [a]Dt 34:1-3 [b]Dt 1:37
33:1 [c]Jos 14:6
33:2 [d]Ex 19:18; Ps 68:8 [e]Jdg 5:4 [f]Hab 3:3

44Moses came with Joshua[v,t] son of
Nun and spoke all the words of this song
in the hearing of the people. 45When
Moses finished reciting all these words
to all Israel, 46he said to them, "Take to
heart all the words I have solemnly declared to you this day,[u] so that you may
command your children to obey carefully all the words of this law. 47They
are not just idle words for you—they are
your life.[v] By them you will live long in
the land you are crossing the Jordan to
possess."

God sends Moses to Mount Nebo, where he will die.

48On that same day the LORD told
Moses, 49"Go up into the Abarim[w] Range
to Mount Nebo in Moab, across from
Jericho, and view Canaan, the land I am
giving the Israelites as their own possession. 50There on the mountain that you
have climbed you will die[x] and be gathered to your people, just as your brother Aaron died on Mount Hor and was
gathered to his people. 51This is because
both of you broke faith with me in the
presence of the Israelites at the waters
of Meribah Kadesh in the Desert of Zin[y]
and because you did not uphold my holiness among the Israelites.[z] 52Therefore,
you will see the land only from a distance;[a] you will not enter[b] the land I
am giving to the people of Israel."

Moses' final blessings to the twelve tribes of Israel.

33:1-29Ref— Ge 49:1-28

33 This is the blessing that Moses
the man of God[c] pronounced on
the Israelites before his death. 2He said:

"The LORD came from Sinai[d]
and dawned over them from Seir;[e]
he shone forth from Mount Paran.[f]

[t]43 Or *Make his people rejoice, O nations*
[u]43 Masoretic Text; Dead Sea Scrolls (see also Septuagint) *people, / and let all the angels worship him /*
[v]44 Hebrew *Hoshea*, a variant of *Joshua*

He came with[w] myriads of holy ones[a]
from the south, from his mountain slopes.[x]
3Surely it is you who love[b] the people;
all the holy ones are in your hand.[c]
At your feet they all bow down,[d]
and from you receive instruction,
4the law that Moses gave us,[e]
the possession of the assembly of Jacob.[f]
5He was king over Jeshurun[y]
when the leaders of the people assembled,
along with the tribes of Israel.

6"Let Reuben live and not die,
nor[z] his men be few."

7And this he said about Judah:[g]

"Hear, O LORD, the cry of Judah;
bring him to his people.
With his own hands he defends his cause.
Oh, be his help against his foes!"

8About Levi he said:

"Your Thummim and Urim[h] belong
to the man you favored.
You tested him at Massah;
you contended with him at the waters of Meribah.[i]
9He said of his father and mother,[j]
'I have no regard for them.'
He did not recognize his brothers
or acknowledge his own children,
but he watched over your word
and guarded your covenant.[k]
10He teaches your precepts to Jacob
and your law to Israel.[l]
He offers incense before you
and whole burnt offerings on your altar.[m]
11Bless all his skills, O LORD,
and be pleased with the work of his hands.[n]
Smite the loins of those who rise up against him;
strike his foes till they rise no more."

12About Benjamin he said:

"Let the beloved of the LORD rest
secure in him,[o]
for he shields him all day long,
and the one the LORD loves rests
between his shoulders.[p]"

13About Joseph[q] he said:

"May the LORD bless his land
with the precious dew from heaven above
and with the deep waters that lie below;[r]
14with the best the sun brings forth
and the finest the moon can yield;
15with the choicest gifts of the ancient mountains[s]
and the fruitfulness of the everlasting hills;
16with the best gifts of the earth and its fullness
and the favor of him who dwelt in the burning bush.[t]
Let all these rest on the head of Joseph,
on the brow of the prince among[a] his brothers.
17In majesty he is like a firstborn bull;
his horns are the horns of a wild ox.[u]
With them he will gore[v] the nations,
even those at the ends of the earth.
Such are the ten thousands of Ephraim;
such are the thousands of Manasseh."

18About Zebulun[w] he said:

"Rejoice, Zebulun, in your going out,
and you, Issachar, in your tents.
19They will summon peoples to the mountain[x]
and there offer sacrifices of righteousness;[y]
they will feast on the abundance of the seas,[z]
on the treasures hidden in the sand."

20About Gad[a] he said:

"Blessed is he who enlarges Gad's domain!

33:2 [a]Da 7:10; Ac 7:53; Rev 5:11
33:3 [b]Hos 11:1 [c]Dt 14:2 [d]Lk 10:39
33:4 [e]Jn 1:17 [f]Ps 119:111
33:7 [g]Ge 49:10
33:8 [h]Ex 28:30 [i]Ex 17:7
33:9 [j]Ex 32:26-29 [k]Mal 2:5
33:10 [l]Lev 10:11; Dt 31:9-13 [m]Ps 51:19
33:11 [n]2Sa 24:23
33:12 [o]Dt 12:10 [p]Ex 28:12
33:13 [q]Ge 49:25 [r]Ge 27:28
33:15 [s]Hab 3:6
33:16 [t]Ex 3:2
33:17 [u]Nu 23:22 [v]1Ki 22:11; Ps 44:5
33:18 [w]Ge 49:13-15
33:19 [x]Ex 15:17; Isa 2:3 [y]Ps 4:5 [z]Isa 60:5,11
33:20 [a]Ge 49:19

w2 Or *from* x2 The meaning of the Hebrew for this phrase is uncertain. y5 *Jeshurun* means *the upright one,* that is, Israel; also in verse 26. z6 Or *but let* a16 Or *of the one separated from*

Gad lives there like a lion,
tearing at arm or head.
21 He chose the best land for himself;[a]
the leader's portion was kept for him.
When the heads of the people
assembled,
he carried out the LORD's righteous
will,[b]
and his judgments concerning
Israel."

22 About Dan[c] he said:

"Dan is a lion's cub,
springing out of Bashan."

23 About Naphtali he said:

"Naphtali is abounding with the
favor of the LORD
and is full of his blessing;
he will inherit southward to the
lake."

24 About Asher[d] he said:

"Most blessed of sons is Asher;
let him be favored by his brothers,
and let him bathe his feet in oil.[e]
25 The bolts of your gates will be iron
and bronze,
and your strength will equal your
days.[f]

26 "There is no one like the God of
Jeshurun,[g]
who rides on the heavens to help
you[h]
and on the clouds in his majesty.
27 The eternal God is your refuge,[i]
and underneath are the everlasting
arms.
He will drive out your enemy before
you,[j]
saying, 'Destroy him!'[k]
28 So Israel will live in safety alone;[l]
Jacob's spring is secure
in a land of grain and new wine,
where the heavens drop dew.[m]
29 Blessed are you, O Israel![n]
Who is like you,[o]
a people saved by the LORD?[p]
He is your shield and helper[q]
and your glorious sword.
Your enemies will cower before you,
and you will trample down their
high places.[b][r]"

33:21 [a]Nu 32:1-5, 31-32 [b]Jos 4:12; 22:1-3
33:22 [c]Ge 49:16
33:24 [d]Ge 49:21 [e]Ge 49:20; Job 29:6
33:25 [f]Dt 4:40; 32:47
33:26 [g]Ex 15:11 [h]Ps 104:3
33:27 [i]Ps 90:1 [j]Jos 24:18 [k]Dt 7:2
33:28 [l]Nu 23:9; Jer 23:6 [m]Ge 27:28
33:29 [n]Ps 144:15 [o]Ps 18:44 [p]2Sa 7:23 [q]Ps 115:9-11 [r]Dt 32:13
34:1 [s]Dt 32:49 [t]Dt 32:52
34:2 [u]Dt 11:24
34:3 [v]Jdg 1:16; 3:13; 2Ch 28:15
34:4 [w]Ge 28:13 [x]Ge 12:7 [y]Dt 3:27
34:5 [z]Nu 12:7 [a]Dt 32:50; Jos 1:1-2
34:6 [b]Dt 3:29 [c]Jude 1:9
34:7 [d]Dt 31:2 [e]Ge 27:1
34:8 [f]Ge 50:3,10; 2Sa 11:27
34:9 [g]Ge 41:38; Isa 11:2; Da 6:3 [h]Nu 27:18,23
34:10 [i]Dt 18:15,18 [j]Ex 33:11; Nu 12:6,8; Dt 5:4

Moses' death and burial.

34 Then Moses climbed Mount
Nebo from the plains of Moab
to the top of Pisgah, across from Jericho.[s] There the LORD showed[t] him the
whole land—from Gilead to Dan, 2 all of
Naphtali, the territory of Ephraim and
Manasseh, all the land of Judah as far as
the western sea,[c][u] 3 the Negev and the
whole region from the Valley of Jericho,
the City of Palms,[v] as far as Zoar. 4 Then
the LORD said to him, "This is the land I
promised on oath[w] to Abraham, Isaac and
Jacob when I said, 'I will give it[x] to your
descendants.' I have let you see it with
your eyes, but you will not cross[y] over
into it."
5 And Moses the servant of the LORD[z]
died[a] there in Moab, as the LORD had
said. 6 He buried him[d] in Moab, in the
valley opposite Beth Peor,[b] but to this
day no one knows where his grave is.[c]
7 Moses was a hundred and twenty years
old[d] when he died, yet his eyes were not
weak[e] nor his strength gone. 8 The Israelites grieved for Moses in the plains
of Moab thirty days, until the time of
weeping and mourning[f] was over.
9 Now Joshua son of Nun was filled
with the spirit[e] of wisdom[g] because Moses had laid his hands on him.[h] So the
Israelites listened to him and did what
the LORD had commanded Moses.
10 Since then, no prophet has risen in
Israel like Moses,[i] whom the LORD knew
face to face,[j] 11 who did all those miraculous signs and wonders[k] the LORD sent
him to do in Egypt—to Pharaoh and to
all his officials[l] and to his whole land.
12 For no one has ever shown the mighty
power or performed the awesome deeds
that Moses did in the sight of all Israel.

34:11 [k]Dt 4:34 [l]Dt 7:19

b29 Or *will tread upon their bodies* c2 That is, the Mediterranean d6 Or *He was buried* e9 Or *Spirit*

JOSHUA

Author: Joshua. However, some "elders who outlived him" (24:31) probably added portions to the book after his death.

Date Written: Between 1410 and 1350 B.C.

Time Span: 15-26 years.

Title: From the book's chief character: Joshua.

Background: Joshua is almost stoned to death by his own people (Numbers 14:6-10) nearly 40 years before the book of Joshua begins...because out of 12 spies to Canaan only he and Caleb determine to obey God's directions to conquer the land. Because of their unbelief to accept God's covenant, the children of Israel spend 40 years in the desert. But now Joshua, Moses' successor, is preparing to lead the Israelites from the desert in their conquest of the promised land.

Where Written: East of the Jordan River (the desert) before the conquest, and west of the Jordan River (Canaan) thereafter.

To Whom: To the Israelites.

Content: The book of Joshua is primarily the history of Joshua's leadership of Israel. Under divine guidance, Joshua engages in 3 strategic, military operations using brilliant divide-and-conquer tactics, insuring victory over the enemy armies in Canaan. God's miraculous interventions, including the crossing of the Jordan River and the conquest of Jericho, prove to Israel that God is aiding their efforts. The division of the promised land among the tribes of Israel and their subsequent settlement in the new land take place. Finally, Joshua exhorts the people before his death to renew their covenant and to devote themselves to serve and love God wholeheartedly.

Key Words: "Choose"; "Serve." Joshua emphasizes that we must do both by his admonition to "choose for yourselves this day whom you will serve...But as for me and my household, we will serve the LORD" (24:15).

Themes: • Our greatest asset is not our physical ability or cleverness...it is our faith in God's ability to overcome in our behalf. • Victory comes through faith in God and obedience to his Word. • Sin must be dealt with at once because it brings severe consequences. • God is always true to his promises. • All things are possible...if we have faith in him who made all things. • It is our responsibility to be obedient and faithful to the covenant of God. • God punishes sinful nations as well as sinful individuals.

Outline:

1. Israel's preparation for the conquest of Canaan. 1:1-5:15
2. The conquest of Canaan. 6:1-12:24
3. The allotments of the land of Canaan by tribe. 13:1-21:45
4. Joshua's farewell and death. 22:1-24:33

JOSHUA

God appoints Joshua to succeed Moses.

1 After the death of Moses the servant of the LORD,[a] the LORD said to Joshua[b] son of Nun, Moses' aide: 2"Moses my servant is dead. Now then, you and all these people, get ready to cross the Jordan River[c] into the land I am about to give to them—to the Israelites. 3I will give you every place where you set your foot,[d] as I promised Moses. 4Your territory will extend from the desert to Lebanon, and from the great river, the Euphrates[e]—all the Hittite country—to the Great Sea[a] on the west.[f] 5No one will be able to stand up against you[g] all the days of your life. As I was with[h] Moses, so I will be with you; I will never leave you nor forsake[i] you.

6"Be strong and courageous, because you will lead these people to inherit the land I swore to their forefathers[j] to give them. 7Be strong and very courageous. Be careful to obey all the law my servant Moses gave you; do not turn from it to the right or to the left,[k] that you may be successful wherever you go.[l] 8Do not let this Book of the Law depart from your mouth; meditate on it day and night, so that you may be careful to do everything written in it. Then you will be prosperous and successful.[m] 9Have I not commanded you? Be strong and courageous. Do not be terrified;[n] do not be discouraged, for the LORD your God will be with you wherever you go."[o]

Joshua prepares the people to cross the Jordan.

10So Joshua ordered the officers of the people: 11"Go through the camp and tell the people, 'Get your supplies ready. Three days from now you will cross the Jordan here to go in and take possession[p] of the land the LORD your God is giving you for your own.'"

12But to the Reubenites, the Gadites and the half-tribe of Manasseh,[q] Joshua said, 13"Remember the command that Moses the servant of the LORD gave you: 'The LORD your God is giving you rest[r] and has granted you this land.' 14Your wives, your children and your livestock may stay in the land that Moses gave you east of the Jordan, but all your fighting men, fully armed, must cross over ahead of your brothers. You are to help your brothers 15until the LORD gives them rest, as he has done for you, and until they too have taken possession of the land that the LORD your God is giving them. After that, you may go back and occupy your own land, which Moses the servant of the LORD gave you east of the Jordan toward the sunrise."[s]

16Then they answered Joshua, "Whatever you have commanded us we will do, and wherever you send us we will go. 17Just as we fully obeyed Moses, so we will obey you.[t] Only may the LORD your God be with you as he was with Moses. 18Whoever rebels against your word and does not obey your words, whatever you may command them, will be put to death. Only be strong and courageous!"

Rahab protects Israel's spies.

2 Then Joshua son of Nun secretly sent two spies[u] from Shittim.[v] "Go, look over the land," he said, "especially Jericho." So they went and entered the house of a prostitute[b] named Rahab[w] and stayed there.

2The king of Jericho was told, "Look! Some of the Israelites have come here tonight to spy out the land." 3So the king of Jericho sent this message to Rahab: "Bring out the men who came to you and entered your house, because they have come to spy out the whole land."

4But the woman had taken the two men and hidden them.[x] She said, "Yes, the men came to me, but I did not know where they had come from. 5At dusk, when it was time to close the city gate,

1:1 [a]Nu 12:7; Dt 34:5 [b]Ex 24:13; Dt 1:38
1:2 [c]ver 11
1:3 [d]Dt 11:24
1:4 [e]Ge 15:18 [f]Nu 34:2-12
1:5 [g]Dt 7:24 [h]Jos 3:7; 6:27 [i]Dt 31:6-8
1:6 [j]Dt 31:23
1:7 [k]Dt 5:32; 28:14 [l]Jos 11:15
1:8 [m]Dt 29:9; Ps 1:1-3
1:9 [n]Ps 27:1 [o]ver 7; Dt 31:7-8; Jer 1:8
1:11 [p]Joel 3:2
1:12 [q]Nu 32:20-22
1:13 [r]Dt 3:18-20
1:15 [s]Jos 22:1-4
1:17 [t]ver 5,9
2:1 [u]Jas 2:25 [v]Nu 25:1; Jos 3:1 [w]Heb 11:31
2:4 [x]2Sa 17:19-20

a4 That is, the Mediterranean b1 Or possibly *an innkeeper*

KEY PLACES IN JOSHUA

Shittim The story of Joshua begins with the Israelites camping at Shittim. The Israelites under Joshua were ready to enter and conquer Canaan. But before the nation moved out, Joshua received instructions from God (1:1-18).

Jordan River The entire nation prepared to cross this river, which was swollen from spring rains. After the spies returned from Jericho with a positive report, Joshua prepared the priests and people for a miracle. As the priests carried the ark into the Jordan River, the water stopped flowing and the entire nation crossed on dry ground into the promised land (2:1–4:24).

Gilgal After crossing the Jordan River, the Israelites camped at Gilgal, where they renewed their commitment to God and celebrated the Passover, the feast commemorating their deliverance from Egypt (see Exodus). As Joshua made plans for the attack on Jericho, an angel appeared to him (5:1-15).

Jericho The walled city of Jericho seemed a formidable enemy. But when Joshua followed God's plans, the great walls were no obstacle. The city was conquered with only the obedient marching of the people (6:1-27).

Ai Victory could not continue without obedience to God. That is why the disobedience of one man, Achan, brought defeat to the entire nation in the first battle against Ai. But once the sin was recognized and punished, God told Joshua to take heart and try Ai once again. This time the city was taken (7:1–8:29).

The Mountains of Ebal and Gerizim After the defeat of Ai, Joshua built an altar at Mount Ebal. Then the people divided themselves, half at the foot of Mount Ebal, half at the foot of Mount Gerizim. The priests stood between the mountains holding the ark of the covenant as Joshua read God's law to all the people (8:30-35).

Gibeon It was just after the Israelites reaffirmed their covenant with God that their leaders made a major mistake in judgment: they were tricked into making a peace treaty with the city of Gibeon. The Gibeonites pretended that they had traveled a long distance and asked the Israelites for a treaty. The leaders made the agreement without consulting God. The trick was soon discovered, but because the treaty had been made, Israel could not go back on its word. As a result, the Gibeonites saved their own lives, but they were forced to become Israel's slaves (9:1-27).

Valley of Aijalon The king of Jerusalem was very angry at Gibeon for making a peace treaty with the Israelites. He gathered armies from four other cities to attack the city. Gibeon summoned Joshua for help. Joshua took immediate action. Leaving Gilgal, he attacked the coalition by surprise. As the battle waged on and moved into the Valley of Aijalon, Joshua prayed for the sun to stand still until the enemy could be destroyed (10:1-43).

Hazor Up north in Hazor, King Jabin mobilized the kings of the surrounding cities to unite and crush Israel. But God gave Joshua and Israel victory (11:1-23).

Shiloh After the armies of Canaan were conquered, Israel gathered at Shiloh to set up the tabernacle. This movable building had been the nation's center of worship during their years of wandering. The seven tribes who had not received their land were given their allotments (18:1–19:51).

Shechem Before Joshua died he called the entire nation together at Shechem to remind them that it was God who had given them their land and that only with God's help could they keep it. The people vowed to follow God. As long as Joshua was alive, the land was at rest from war and trouble (24:1-33).

the men left. I don't know which way they went. Go after them quickly. You may catch up with them." 6(But she had taken them up to the roof and hidden them under the stalks of flax[a] she had laid out on the roof.)[b] 7So the men set out in pursuit of the spies on the road that leads to the fords of the Jordan, and as soon as the pursuers had gone out, the gate was shut.

8Before the spies lay down for the night, she went up on the roof 9and said to them, "I know that the LORD has given this land to you and that a great fear[c] of you has fallen on us, so that all who live in this country are melting in fear because of you. 10We have heard how the LORD dried up[d] the water of the Red Sea[c] for you when you came out of Egypt,[e] and what you did to Sihon and Og,[f] the two kings of the Amorites east of the Jordan, whom you completely destroyed.[d] 11When we heard of it, our hearts melted and everyone's courage failed because of you,[g] for the LORD your God is God in heaven above and on the earth[h] below. 12Now then, please swear to me by the LORD that you will show kindness to my family, because I have shown kindness to you. Give me a sure sign[i] 13that you will spare the lives of my father and mother, my brothers and sisters, and all who belong to them, and that you will save us from death."

14"Our lives for your lives!" the men assured her. "If you don't tell what we are doing, we will treat you kindly and faithfully[j] when the LORD gives us the land."

15So she let them down by a rope through the window,[k] for the house she lived in was part of the city wall. 16Now she had said to them, "Go to the hills so the pursuers will not find you. Hide yourselves there three days[l] until they return, and then go on your way."[m]

17The men said to her, "This oath[n] you made us swear will not be binding on us 18unless, when we enter the land, you have tied this scarlet cord in the window through which you let us down, and unless you have brought your father and mother, your brothers and all your family[o] into your house. 19If anyone goes outside your house into the street, his blood will be on his own head;[p] we will not be responsible. As for anyone who is in the house with you, his blood will be on our head[q] if a hand is laid on him. 20But if you tell what we are doing, we will be released from the oath you made us swear."

21"Agreed," she replied. "Let it be as you say." So she sent them away and they departed. And she tied the scarlet cord in the window.

22When they left, they went into the hills and stayed there three days, until the pursuers had searched all along the road and returned without finding them. 23Then the two men started back. They went down out of the hills, forded the river and came to Joshua son of Nun and told him everything that had happened to them. 24They said to Joshua, "The LORD has surely given the whole land into our hands;[r] all the people are melting in fear because of us."

Israel crosses the Jordan on dry ground.

3 Early in the morning Joshua and all the Israelites set out from Shittim[s] and went to the Jordan, where they camped before crossing over. 2After three days the officers went throughout the camp,[t] 3giving orders to the people: "When you see the ark of the covenant[u] of the LORD your God, and the priests,[v] who are Levites, carrying it, you are to move out from your positions and follow it. 4Then you will know which way to go, since you have never been this way before. But keep a distance of about a thousand yards[e] between you and the ark; do not go near it."

5Joshua told the people, "Consecrate yourselves,[w] for tomorrow the LORD will do amazing things among you."

6Joshua said to the priests, "Take up

2:6 [a]Jas 2:25 [b]Ex 1:17,19; 2Sa 17:19
2:9 [c]Ge 35:5; Ex 23:27; Dt 2:25
2:10 [d]Ex 14:21 [e]Nu 23:22 [f]Nu 21:21,24, 34-35
2:11 [g]Ex 15:14; Jos 5:1; 7:5; Ps 22:14; Isa 13:7 [h]Dt 4:39
2:12 [i]ver 18
2:14 [j]Jdg 1:24; Mt 5:7
2:15 [k]Ac 9:25
2:16 [l]Jas 2:25 [m]Heb 11:31
2:17 [n]Ge 24:8
2:18 [o]ver 12; Jos 6:23
2:19 [p]Eze 33:4 [q]Mt 27:25
2:24 [r]ver 9; Jos 6:2
3:1 [s]Jos 2:1
3:2 [t]Jos 1:11
3:3 [u]Nu 10:33 [v]Dt 31:9
3:5 [w]Ex 19:10,14; Lev 20:7; Jos 7:13; 1Sa 16:5; Joel 2:16

c *10* Hebrew *Yam Suph*; that is, Sea of Reeds
d *10* The Hebrew term refers to the irrevocable giving over of things or persons to the LORD, often by totally destroying them. e *4* Hebrew *about two thousand cubits* (about 900 meters)

the ark of the covenant and pass on ahead of the people." So they took it up and went ahead of them.

7And the LORD said to Joshua, "Today I will begin to exalt you[a] in the eyes of all Israel, so they may know that I am with you as I was with Moses.[b] 8Tell the priests[c] who carry the ark of the covenant: 'When you reach the edge of the Jordan's waters, go and stand in the river.' "

9Joshua said to the Israelites, "Come here and listen to the words of the LORD your God. 10This is how you will know that the living God[d] is among you and that he will certainly drive out before you the Canaanites, Hittites, Hivites, Perizzites, Girgashites, Amorites and Jebusites.[e] 11See, the ark of the covenant of the Lord of all the earth[f] will go into the Jordan ahead of you. 12Now then, choose twelve men[g] from the tribes of Israel, one from each tribe. 13And as soon as the priests who carry the ark of the LORD—the Lord of all the earth[h]—set foot in the Jordan, its waters flowing downstream[i] will be cut off and stand up in a heap.[j]"

14So when the people broke camp to cross the Jordan, the priests carrying the ark of the covenant[k] went ahead[l] of them. 15Now the Jordan is at flood stage[m] all during harvest. Yet as soon as the priests who carried the ark reached the Jordan and their feet touched the water's edge, 16the water from upstream stopped flowing.[n] It piled up in a heap a great distance away, at a town called Adam in the vicinity of Zarethan,[o] while the water flowing down[p] to the Sea of the Arabah[q] (the Salt Sea[f][r]) was completely cut off. So the people crossed over opposite Jericho. 17The priests who carried the ark of the covenant of the LORD stood firm on dry ground in the middle of the Jordan, while all Israel passed by until the whole nation had completed the crossing on dry ground.[s]

Israel builds a twelve-stone memorial.

4 When the whole nation had finished crossing the Jordan,[t] the LORD said to Joshua, 2"Choose twelve men[u] from among the people, one from each tribe, 3and tell them to take up twelve stones[v] from the middle of the Jordan from right where the priests stood and to carry them over with you and put them down at the place where you stay tonight.[w]"

4So Joshua called together the twelve men he had appointed from the Israelites, one from each tribe, 5and said to them, "Go over before the ark of the LORD your God into the middle of the Jordan. Each of you is to take up a stone on his shoulder, according to the number of the tribes of the Israelites, 6to serve as a sign among you. In the future, when your children ask you, 'What do these stones mean?'[x] 7tell them that the flow of the Jordan was cut off[y] before the ark of the covenant of the LORD. When it crossed the Jordan, the waters of the Jordan were cut off. These stones are to be a memorial[z] to the people of Israel forever."

8So the Israelites did as Joshua commanded them. They took twelve stones from the middle of the Jordan, according to the number of the tribes of the Israelites, as the LORD had told Joshua;[a] and they carried them over with them to their camp, where they put them down. 9Joshua set up the twelve stones[b] that had been[g] in the middle of the Jordan at the spot where the priests who carried the ark of the covenant had stood. And they are there to this day.

10Now the priests who carried the ark remained standing in the middle of the Jordan until everything the LORD had commanded Joshua was done by the people, just as Moses had directed Joshua. The people hurried over, 11and as soon as all of them had crossed, the ark of the LORD and the priests came to the other side while the people watched. 12The men of Reuben, Gad and the half-tribe of Manasseh crossed over, armed, in front of the Israelites,[c] as Moses had directed them. 13About forty thousand

3:7 [a]Jos 4:14; 1Ch 29:25 [b]Jos 1:5
3:8 [c]ver 3
3:10 [d]Dt 5:26; 1Sa 17:26,36; 2Ki 19:4,16; Hos 1:10; Mt 16:16; 1Th 1:9 [e]Ex 33:2; Dt 7:1
3:11 [f]ver 13; Job 41:11; Zec 6:5
3:12 [g]Jos 4:2,4
3:13 [h]ver 11 [i]ver 16 [j]Ex 15:8; Ps 78:13
3:14 [k]Ps 132:8 [l]Ac 7:44-45
3:15 [m]Jos 4:18; 1Ch 12:15
3:16 [n]Ps 66:6; 74:15 [o]1Ki 4:12; 7:46 [p]ver 13 [q]Dt 1:1 [r]Ge 14:3
3:17 [s]Ex 14:22,29
4:1 [t]Dt 27:2
4:2 [u]Jos 3:12
4:3 [v]ver 20 [w]ver 19
4:6 [x]ver 21; Ex 12:26; 13:14
4:7 [y]Jos 3:13 [z]Ex 12:14
4:8 [a]ver 20
4:9 [b]Ge 28:18; Jos 24:26; 1Sa 7:12
4:12 [c]Nu 32:27

f *16* That is, the Dead Sea g *9* Or *Joshua also set up twelve stones*

armed for battle crossed over before the LORD to the plains of Jericho for war.

14 That day the LORD exalted[a] Joshua in the sight of all Israel; and they revered him all the days of his life, just as they had revered Moses.

15 Then the LORD said to Joshua, 16 "Command the priests carrying the ark of the Testimony[b] to come up out of the Jordan."

17 So Joshua commanded the priests, "Come up out of the Jordan."

18 And the priests came up out of the river carrying the ark of the covenant of the LORD. No sooner had they set their feet on the dry ground than the waters of the Jordan returned to their place and ran at flood stage[c] as before.

19 On the tenth day of the first month the people went up from the Jordan and camped at Gilgal[d] on the eastern border of Jericho. 20 And Joshua set up at Gilgal the twelve stones[e] they had taken out of the Jordan. 21 He said to the Israelites, "In the future when your descendants ask their fathers, 'What do these stones mean?'[f] 22 tell them, 'Israel crossed the Jordan on dry ground.'[g] 23 For the LORD your God dried up the Jordan before you until you had crossed over. The LORD your God did to the Jordan just what he had done to the Red Sea[h] when he dried it up before us until we had crossed over.[h] 24 He did this so that all the peoples of the earth might know[i] that the hand of the LORD is powerful[j] and so that you might always fear the LORD your God.[k]"

The people are circumcised.

5 Now when all the Amorite kings west of the Jordan and all the Canaanite kings along the coast[l] heard how the LORD had dried up the Jordan before the Israelites until we had crossed over, their hearts melted[m] and they no longer had the courage to face the Israelites.

2 At that time the LORD said to Joshua, "Make flint knives[n] and circumcise the Israelites again." 3 So Joshua made flint knives and circumcised the Israelites at Gibeath Haaraloth.[i]

4 Now this is why he did so: All those who came out of Egypt—all the men of military age—died in the desert on the way after leaving Egypt.[o] 5 All the people that came out had been circumcised, but all the people born in the desert during the journey from Egypt had not. 6 The Israelites had moved about in the desert forty years[p] until all the men who were of military age when they left Egypt had died, since they had not obeyed the LORD. For the LORD had sworn to them that they would not see the land that he had solemnly promised their fathers to give us,[q] a land flowing with milk and honey.[r] 7 So he raised up their sons in their place, and these were the ones Joshua circumcised. They were still uncircumcised because they had not been circumcised on the way. 8 And after the whole nation had been circumcised, they remained where they were in camp until they were healed.[s]

9 Then the LORD said to Joshua, "Today I have rolled away the reproach of Egypt from you." So the place has been called Gilgal[j] to this day.

The manna stops.

10 On the evening of the fourteenth day of the month,[t] while camped at Gilgal on the plains of Jericho, the Israelites celebrated the Passover. 11 The day after the Passover, that very day, they ate some of the produce of the land:[u] unleavened bread and roasted grain.[v] 12 The manna stopped the day after[k] they ate this food from the land; there was no longer any manna for the Israelites, but that year they ate of the produce of Canaan.[w]

Jericho is destroyed.

13 Now when Joshua was near Jericho, he looked up and saw a man[x] standing in front of him with a drawn sword[y] in his hand. Joshua went up to him and asked, "Are you for us or for our enemies?"

4:14 [a]Jos 3:7
4:16 [b]Ex 25:22
4:18 [c]Jos 3:15
4:19 [d]Jos 5:9
4:20 [e]ver 3,8
4:21 [f]ver 6
4:22 [g]Jos 3:17
4:23 [h]Ex 14:21
4:24 [i]1Ki 8:42-43; 2Ki 19:19; Ps 106:8; Jer 10:7 [j]Ex 15:16; 1Ch 29:12; Ps 89:13 [k]Ex 14:31
5:1 [l]Nu 13:29 [m]Jos 2:9-11
5:2 [n]Ex 4:25
5:4 [o]Dt 2:14
5:6 [p]Dt 2:7 [q]Nu 14:23, 29-35; Dt 2:14 [r]Ex 3:8
5:8 [s]Ge 34:25
5:10 [t]Ex 12:6
5:11 [u]Nu 15:19 [v]Lev 23:14
5:12 [w]Ex 16:35
5:13 [x]Ge 18:2; 32:24 [y]Nu 22:23

h *23* Hebrew *Yam Suph*; that is, Sea of Reeds
i *3 Gibeath Haaraloth* means *hill of foreskins.* j *9 Gilgal* sounds like the Hebrew for *roll.* k *12* Or *the day*

[14]“Neither,” he replied, “but as commander of the army of the LORD I have now come.” Then Joshua fell facedown[a] to the ground in reverence, and asked him, “What message does my Lord[l] have for his servant?”

[15]The commander of the LORD’s army replied, “Take off your sandals, for the place where you are standing is holy.”[b] And Joshua did so.

6 Now Jericho[c] was tightly shut up because of the Israelites. No one went out and no one came in.

[2]Then the LORD said to Joshua, “See, I have delivered[d] Jericho into your hands, along with its king and its fighting men. [3]March around the city once with all the armed men. Do this for six days. [4]Have seven priests carry trumpets of rams’ horns in front of the ark. On the seventh day, march around the city seven times, with the priests blowing the trumpets.[e] [5]When you hear them sound a long blast[f] on the trumpets, have all the people give a loud shout;[g] then the wall of the city will collapse and the people will go up, every man straight in.”

[6]So Joshua son of Nun called the priests and said to them, “Take up the ark of the covenant of the LORD and have seven priests carry trumpets in front of it.” [7]And he ordered the people, “Advance[h]! March around the city, with the armed guard going ahead of the ark of the LORD.”

[8]When Joshua had spoken to the people, the seven priests carrying the seven trumpets before the LORD went forward, blowing their trumpets, and the ark of the LORD’s covenant followed them. [9]The armed guard marched ahead of the priests who blew the trumpets, and the rear guard[i] followed the ark. All this time the trumpets were sounding. [10]But Joshua had commanded the people, “Do not give a war cry, do not raise your voices, do not say a word until the day I tell you to shout. Then shout![j]” [11]So he had the ark of the LORD carried around the city, circling it once. Then the people returned to camp and spent the night there.

[12]Joshua got up early the next morning and the priests took up the ark of the LORD. [13]The seven priests carrying the seven trumpets went forward, marching before the ark of the LORD and blowing the trumpets. The armed men went ahead of them and the rear guard followed the ark of the LORD, while the trumpets kept sounding. [14]So on the second day they marched around the city once and returned to the camp. They did this for six days.

[15]On the seventh day, they got up at daybreak and marched around the city seven times in the same manner, except that on that day they circled the city seven times.[k] [16]The seventh time around, when the priests sounded the trumpet blast, Joshua commanded the people, “Shout! For the LORD has given you the city! [17]The city and all that is in it are to be devoted[m][l] to the LORD. Only Rahab the prostitute[n] and all who are with her in her house shall be spared, because she hid[m] the spies we sent. [18]But keep away from the devoted things,[n] so that you will not bring about your own destruction by taking any of them. Otherwise you will make the camp of Israel liable to destruction[o] and bring trouble[p] on it. [19]All the silver and gold and the articles of bronze and iron[q] are sacred to the LORD and must go into his treasury.”

[20]When the trumpets sounded,[r] the people shouted, and at the sound of the trumpet, when the people gave a loud shout,[s] the wall collapsed; so every man charged straight in, and they took the city.[t] [21]They devoted the city to the LORD and destroyed[u] with the sword every living thing in it—men and women, young and old, cattle, sheep and donkeys.

[22]Joshua said to the two men who had spied out the land, “Go into the prostitute’s house and bring her out and all who belong to her, in accordance with your oath to her.[v]” [23]So the young men

5:14 [a]Ge 17:3
5:15 [b]Ex 3:5; Ac 7:33
6:1 [c]Jos 24:11
6:2 [d]Dt 7:24; Jos 2:9,24; 8:1
6:4 [e]Lev 25:9; Nu 10:8
6:5 [f]Ex 19:13 [g]ver 20; 1Sa 4:5; Ps 42:4; Isa 42:13
6:7 [h]Ex 14:15
6:9 [i]ver 13; Isa 52:12
6:10 [j]ver 20
6:15 [k]1Ki 18:44
6:17 [l]Lev 27:28; Dt 20:17 [m]Jos 2:4
6:18 [n]Jos 7:1 [o]Jos 7:12 [p]Jos 7:25,26
6:19 [q]ver 24; Nu 31:22
6:20 [r]Jdg 6:34; Jer 4:21; Am 2:2 [s]ver 5 [t]Heb 11:30
6:21 [u]Dt 20:16
6:22 [v]Jos 2:14; Heb 11:31

[l] *14* Or *lord* [m] *17* The Hebrew term refers to the irrevocable giving over of things or persons to the LORD, often by totally destroying them; also in verses 18 and 21. [n] *17* Or possibly *innkeeper*; also in verses 22 and 25

who had done the spying went in and
brought out Rahab, her father and mother and brothers and all who belonged
to her.[a] They brought out her entire family and put them in a place outside the
camp of Israel.
24Then they burned the whole city and
everything in it, but they put the silver
and gold and the articles of bronze and
iron[b] into the treasury of the LORD's
house. **25**But Joshua spared Rahab the
prostitute,[c] with her family and all who
belonged to her, because she hid the
men Joshua had sent as spies to Jericho[d]—and she lives among the Israelites to this day.
26At that time Joshua pronounced this
solemn oath: "Cursed before the LORD
is the man who undertakes to rebuild
this city, Jericho:

"At the cost of his firstborn son
will he lay its foundations;
at the cost of his youngest
will he set up its gates."[e]

27So the LORD was with Joshua,[f] and
his fame spread[g] throughout the land.

Achan's sin and the resulting punishment.

7 But the Israelites acted unfaithfully
in regard to the devoted things[o];[h]
Achan son of Carmi, the son of Zimri,[p]
the son of Zerah,[i] of the tribe of Judah,
took some of them. So the LORD's anger
burned against Israel.
2Now Joshua sent men from Jericho
to Ai, which is near Beth Aven[j] to the
east of Bethel, and told them, "Go up and
spy out the region." So the men went
up and spied out Ai.
3When they returned to Joshua, they
said, "Not all the people will have to go
up against Ai. Send two or three thousand men to take it and do not weary
all the people, for only a few men are
there." **4**So about three thousand men
went up; but they were routed by the
men of Ai,[k] **5**who killed about thirty-six
of them. They chased the Israelites from
the city gate as far as the stone quarries[q]
and struck them down on the slopes.
At this the hearts of the people melted[l]
and became like water.
6Then Joshua tore his clothes[m] and
fell facedown to the ground before the
ark of the LORD, remaining there till evening. The elders of Israel did the same,
and sprinkled dust[n] on their heads. **7**And
Joshua said, "Ah, Sovereign LORD, why
did you ever bring this people across
the Jordan to deliver us into the hands
of the Amorites to destroy us?[o] If only
we had been content to stay on the
other side of the Jordan! **8**O Lord, what
can I say, now that Israel has been routed by its enemies? **9**The Canaanites and
the other people of the country will
hear about this and they will surround
us and wipe out our name from the
earth.[p] What then will you do for your
own great name?"
10The LORD said to Joshua, "Stand up!
What are you doing down on your face?
11Israel has sinned; they have violated
my covenant,[q] which I commanded them
to keep. They have taken some of the
devoted things; they have stolen, they
have lied,[r] they have put them with
their own possessions. **12**That is why
the Israelites cannot stand against their
enemies;[s] they turn their backs and
run because they have been made liable
to destruction.[t] I will not be with you
anymore unless you destroy whatever
among you is devoted to destruction.
13"Go, consecrate the people. Tell
them, 'Consecrate yourselves[u] in preparation for tomorrow; for this is what
the LORD, the God of Israel, says: That
which is devoted is among you, O Israel. You cannot stand against your enemies until you remove it.
14" 'In the morning, present yourselves tribe by tribe. The tribe that the
LORD takes[v] shall come forward clan by
clan; the clan that the LORD takes shall
come forward family by family; and the

6:23 [a]Jos 2:13
6:24 [b]ver 19
6:25 [c]Heb 11:31 [d]Jos 2:6
6:26 [e]1Ki 16:34
6:27 [f]Ge 39:2; Jos 1:5 [g]Jos 9:1
7:1 [h]Jos 6:18 [i]Jos 22:20
7:2 [j]Jos 18:12; 1Sa 13:5; 14:23
7:4 [k]Lev 26:17; Dt 28:25
7:5 [l]Lev 26:36; Jos 2:9,11; Eze 21:7; Na 2:10
7:6 [m]Ge 37:29 [n]1Sa 4:12; 2Sa 13:19; Ne 9:1; Job 2:12; La 2:10; Rev 18:19
7:7 [o]Ex 5:22
7:9 [p]Ex 32:12; Dt 9:28
7:11 [q]Jos 6:17-19 [r]Ac 5:1-2
7:12 [s]Nu 14:45; Jdg 2:14 [t]Jos 6:18
7:13 [u]Jos 3:5; 6:18
7:14 [v]Pr 16:33

o *1* The Hebrew term refers to the irrevocable giving over of things or persons to the LORD, often by totally destroying them; also in verses 11, 12, 13 and 15.
p *1* See Septuagint and 1 Chron. 2:6; Hebrew *Zabdi*; also in verses 17 and 18.
q *5* Or *as far as Shebarim*

family that the LORD takes shall come forward man by man. 15 He who is caught
with the devoted things shall be destroyed by fire, along with all that
belongs to him.[a] He has violated the
covenant[b] of the LORD and has done a
disgraceful thing in Israel!' "[c]
16 Early the next morning Joshua had
Israel come forward by tribes, and Judah was taken. 17 The clans of Judah came
forward, and he took the Zerahites.[d]
He had the clan of the Zerahites come
forward by families, and Zimri was tak-
en. 18 Joshua had his family come forward man by man, and Achan son of
Carmi, the son of Zimri, the son of Zerah, of the tribe of Judah, was taken.
19 Then Joshua said to Achan, "My son,
give glory[e] to the LORD,[r] the God of Israel, and give him the praise.[s] Tell[f] me
what you have done; do not hide it
from me."
20 Achan replied, "It is true! I have
sinned against the LORD, the God of Israel. This is what I have done: 21 When I
saw in the plunder a beautiful robe from
Babylonia,[t] two hundred shekels[u] of silver and a wedge of gold weighing fifty
shekels,[v] I coveted[g] them and took them.
They are hidden in the ground inside
my tent, with the silver underneath."
22 So Joshua sent messengers, and they
ran to the tent, and there it was, hidden
in his tent, with the silver underneath.
23 They took the things from the tent,
brought them to Joshua and all the Israelites and spread them out before the
LORD.
24 Then Joshua, together with all Israel, took Achan son of Zerah, the silver, the robe, the gold wedge, his sons
and daughters, his cattle, donkeys and
sheep, his tent and all that he had, to
the Valley of Achor.[h] 25 Joshua said,
"Why have you brought this trouble[i]
on us? The LORD will bring trouble on
you today."
Then all Israel stoned him,[j] and after
they had stoned the rest, they burned
them. 26 Over Achan they heaped up a
large pile of rocks, which remains to this
day. Then the LORD turned from his fierce
anger.[k] Therefore that place has been
called the Valley of Achor[w][l] ever since.

Israel kills all who live in Ai.

8 Then the LORD said to Joshua, "Do
not be afraid;[m] do not be discouraged.[n] Take the whole army[o] with you,
and go up and attack Ai. For I have delivered[p] into your hands the king of
Ai, his people, his city and his land.
2 You shall do to Ai and its king as you
did to Jericho and its king, except that
you may carry off their plunder and
livestock for yourselves.[q] Set an ambush behind the city."
3 So Joshua and the whole army moved
out to attack Ai. He chose thirty thousand of his best fighting men and sent
them out at night 4 with these orders:
"Listen carefully. You are to set an ambush behind the city. Don't go very far
from it. All of you be on the alert. 5 I
and all those with me will advance on
the city, and when the men come out
against us, as they did before, we will
flee from them. 6 They will pursue us
until we have lured them away from
the city, for they will say, 'They are
running away from us as they did before.' So when we flee from them, 7 you
are to rise up from ambush and take
the city. The LORD your God will give
it into your hand.[r] 8 When you have
taken the city, set it on fire.[s] Do what
the LORD has commanded.[t] See to it;
you have my orders."
9 Then Joshua sent them off, and they
went to the place of ambush[u] and lay
in wait between Bethel and Ai, to the
west of Ai—but Joshua spent that night
with the people.
10 Early the next morning[v] Joshua mustered his men, and he and the leaders
of Israel[w] marched before them to Ai.
11 The entire force that was with him
marched up and approached the city

7:15 [a] 1Sa 14:39 [b] ver 11 [c] Ge 34:7
7:17 [d] Nu 26:20
7:19 [e] 1Sa 6:5; Jer 13:16; Jn 9:24* [f] 1Sa 14:43
7:21 [g] Dt 7:25; Eph 5:5; 1Ti 6:10
7:24 [h] ver 26; Jos 15:7
7:25 [i] Jos 6:18 [j] Dt 17:5
7:26 [k] Nu 25:4; Dt 13:17 [l] ver 24; Isa 65:10; Hos 2:15
8:1 [m] Dt 31:6 [n] Dt 1:21; 7:18; Jos 1:9 [o] Jos 10:7 [p] Jos 6:2
8:2 [q] ver 27; Dt 20:14
8:7 [r] Jdg 7:7; 1Sa 23:4
8:8 [s] Jdg 20:29-38 [t] ver 19
8:9 [u] 2Ch 13:13
8:10 [v] Ge 22:3 [w] Jos 7:6

[r] *19* A solemn charge to tell the truth [s] *19* Or *and confess to him* [t] *21* Hebrew *Shinar*
[u] *21* That is, about 5 pounds (about 2.3 kilograms)
[v] *21* That is, about 1 1/4 pounds (about 0.6 kilogram)
[w] *26* *Achor* means *trouble.*

and arrived in front of it. They set up
camp north of Ai, with the valley between them and the city. 12Joshua had
taken about five thousand men and set
them in ambush between Bethel and
Ai, to the west of the city. 13They had
the soldiers take up their positions—all
those in the camp to the north of the
city and the ambush to the west of it.
That night Joshua went into the valley.
14When the king of Ai saw this, he
and all the men of the city hurried out
early in the morning to meet Israel in
battle at a certain place overlooking the
Arabah.[a] But he did not know[b] that an
ambush had been set against him behind the city. 15Joshua and all Israel let
themselves be driven back[c] before them,
and they fled toward the desert.[d] 16All
the men of Ai were called to pursue
them, and they pursued Joshua and were
lured away[e] from the city. 17Not a man
remained in Ai or Bethel who did not
go after Israel. They left the city open
and went in pursuit of Israel.
18Then the LORD said to Joshua, "Hold
out toward Ai the javelin[f] that is in your
hand,[g] for into your hand I will deliver
the city." So Joshua held out his javelin[h] toward Ai. 19As soon as he did this,
the men in the ambush rose quickly[i]
from their position and rushed forward.
They entered the city and captured it
and quickly set it on fire.[j]
20The men of Ai looked back and saw
the smoke of the city rising against the
sky,[k] but they had no chance to escape
in any direction, for the Israelites who
had been fleeing toward the desert had
turned back against their pursuers. 21For
when Joshua and all Israel saw that the
ambush had taken the city and that
smoke was going up from the city,
they turned around and attacked the
men of Ai. 22The men of the ambush also
came out of the city against them, so
that they were caught in the middle,
with Israelites on both sides. Israel cut
them down, leaving them neither survivors nor fugitives.[l] 23But they took the
king of Ai alive[m] and brought him to
Joshua.

8:14 [a]Dt 1:1 [b]Jdg 20:34
8:15 [c]Jdg 20:36 [d]Jos 15:61; 16:1; 18:12
8:16 [e]Jdg 20:31
8:18 [f]Job 41:26; Ps 35:3 [g]Ex 4:2; 14:16; 17:9-12 [h]ver 26
8:19 [i]Jdg 20:33 [j]ver 8
8:20 [k]Jdg 20:40
8:22 [l]Dt 7:2; Jos 10:1
8:23 [m]1Sa 15:8
8:25 [n]Dt 20:16-18
8:26 [o]Nu 21:2 [p]Ex 17:12
8:27 [q]ver 2
8:28 [r]Nu 31:10 [s]Jos 7:2; Jer 49:3 [t]Dt 13:16; Jos 10:1 [u]Ge 35:20
8:29 [v]Dt 21:23; Jn 19:31 [w]2Sa 18:17
8:30 [x]Dt 11:29 [y]Ex 20:24
8:31 [z]Ex 20:25 [a]Dt 27:6-7
8:32 [b]Dt 27:8
8:33 [c]Lev 16:29 [d]Dt 31:12 [e]Dt 11:29; 27:11-14

24When Israel had finished killing all
the men of Ai in the fields and in the
desert where they had chased them,
and when every one of them had been
put to the sword, all the Israelites returned to Ai and killed those who were
in it. 25Twelve thousand men and wom-
en fell that day—all the people of Ai.[n]
26For Joshua did not draw back the
hand that held out his javelin until he
had destroyed[x][o] all who lived in Ai.[p]
27But Israel did carry off for themselves
the livestock and plunder of this city,
as the LORD had instructed Joshua.[q]
28So Joshua burned[r] Ai[s] and made it
a permanent heap of ruins,[t] a desolate
place to this day.[u] 29He hung the king
of Ai on a tree and left him there until
evening. At sunset,[v] Joshua ordered them
to take his body from the tree and throw
it down at the entrance of the city gate.
And they raised a large pile of rocks[w]
over it, which remains to this day.

Israel renews covenant with God.

30Then Joshua built on Mount Ebal[x]
an altar[y] to the LORD, the God of Israel,
31as Moses the servant of the LORD had
commanded the Israelites. He built it
according to what is written in the Book
of the Law of Moses—an altar of uncut
stones, on which no iron tool[z] had been
used. On it they offered to the LORD
burnt offerings and sacrificed fellowship
offerings.[y][a] 32There, in the presence of
the Israelites, Joshua copied on stones the
law of Moses, which he had written.[b]
33All Israel, aliens and citizens[c] alike,
with their elders, officials and judges,
were standing on both sides of the ark
of the covenant of the LORD, facing
those who carried it—the priests, who
were Levites.[d] Half of the people stood
in front of Mount Gerizim and half of
them in front of Mount Ebal,[e] as Moses
the servant of the LORD had formerly
commanded when he gave instructions
to bless the people of Israel.

[x]*26* The Hebrew term refers to the irrevocable giving over of things or persons to the LORD, often by totally destroying them. [y]*31* Traditionally *peace offerings*

34Afterward, Joshua read all the words of the law—the blessings and the curses—just as it is written in the Book of the Law.[a] 35There was not a word of all that Moses had commanded that Joshua did not read to the whole assembly of Israel, including the women and children, and the aliens who lived among them.[b]

The Gibeonites' deceptive treaty with Joshua.

9 Now when all the kings west of the Jordan heard about these things—those in the hill country, in the western foothills, and along the entire coast of the Great Sea[z][c] as far as Lebanon (the kings of the Hittites, Amorites, Canaanites, Perizzites, Hivites and Jebusites)[d]—2they came together to make war against Joshua and Israel.

3However, when the people of Gibeon[e] heard what Joshua had done to Jericho and Ai, 4they resorted to a ruse: They went as a delegation whose donkeys were loaded[a] with worn-out sacks and old wineskins, cracked and mended. 5The men put worn and patched sandals on their feet and wore old clothes. All the bread of their food supply was dry and moldy. 6Then they went to Joshua in the camp at Gilgal[f] and said to him and the men of Israel, "We have come from a distant country; make a treaty with us."

7The men of Israel said to the Hivites,[g] "But perhaps you live near us. How then can we make a treaty[h] with you?"

8"We are your servants,[i]" they said to Joshua.

But Joshua asked, "Who are you and where do you come from?"

9They answered: "Your servants have come from a very distant country[j] because of the fame of the LORD your God. For we have heard reports[k] of him: all that he did in Egypt, 10and all that he did to the two kings of the Amorites east of the Jordan—Sihon king of Heshbon, and Og king of Bashan,[l] who reigned in Ashtaroth.[m] 11And our elders and all those living in our country said to us, 'Take provisions for your journey; go and meet them and say to them, "We are your servants; make a treaty with us."' 12This bread of ours was warm when we packed it at home on the day we left to come to you. But now see how dry and moldy it is. 13And these wineskins that we filled were new, but see how cracked they are. And our clothes and sandals are worn out by the very long journey."

14The men of Israel sampled their provisions but did not inquire[n] of the LORD. 15Then Joshua made a treaty of peace[o] with them to let them live, and the leaders of the assembly ratified it by oath.

16Three days after they made the treaty with the Gibeonites, the Israelites heard that they were neighbors, living near them. 17So the Israelites set out and on the third day came to their cities: Gibeon, Kephirah, Beeroth[p] and Kiriath Jearim.[q] 18But the Israelites did not attack them, because the leaders of the assembly had sworn an oath[r] to them by the LORD, the God of Israel.

The whole assembly grumbled[s] against the leaders, 19but all the leaders answered, "We have given them our oath by the LORD, the God of Israel, and we cannot touch them now. 20This is what we will do to them: We will let them live, so that wrath will not fall on us for breaking the oath we swore to them." 21They continued, "Let them live,[t] but let them be woodcutters and water carriers[u] for the entire community." So the leaders' promise to them was kept.

22Then Joshua summoned the Gibeonites and said, "Why did you deceive us by saying, 'We live a long way[v] from you,' while actually you live near[w] us? 23You are now under a curse:[x] You will never cease to serve as woodcutters and water carriers for the house of my God."

24They answered Joshua, "Your servants were clearly told[y] how the LORD

8:34 [a]Dt 28:61; 31:11; Jos 1:8
8:35 [b]Ex 12:38; Dt 31:12
9:1 [c]Nu 34:6 [d]Ex 3:17; Jos 3:10
9:3 [e]ver 17; Jos 10:2; 2Sa 2:12; 2Ch 1:3; Isa 28:21
9:6 [f]Jos 5:10
9:7 [g]ver 1; Jos 11:19 [h]Ex 23:32; Dt 7:2
9:8 [i]Dt 20:11; 2Ki 10:5
9:9 [j]Dt 20:15 [k]ver 24; Jos 2:9
9:10 [l]Nu 21:33 [m]Nu 21:24,35
9:14 [n]Nu 27:21
9:15 [o]Ex 23:32; Jos 11:19; 2Sa 21:2
9:17 [p]Jos 18:25 [q]1Sa 7:1-2
9:18 [r]Ps 15:4 [s]Ex 15:24
9:21 [t]ver 15 [u]Dt 29:11
9:22 [v]ver 6 [w]ver 16
9:23 [x]Ge 9:25
9:24 [y]ver 9

z *1* That is, the Mediterranean a *4* Most Hebrew manuscripts; some Hebrew manuscripts, Vulgate and Syriac (see also Septuagint) *They prepared provisions and loaded their donkeys*

your God had commanded his servant
Moses to give you the whole land and
to wipe out all its inhabitants from
before you. So we feared for our lives
because of you, and that is why we did
this. 25 We are now in your hands.[a] Do
to us whatever seems good and right
to you."
26 So Joshua saved them from the Israelites, and they did not kill them. 27 That
day he made the Gibeonites woodcutters
and water carriers for the community
and for the altar of the LORD at the place
the LORD would choose.[b] And that is what
they are to this day.

The sun stands still.

10 Now Adoni-Zedek king of Jerusalem[c] heard that Joshua had
taken Ai[d] and totally destroyed[b][e] it, doing to Ai and its king as he had done
to Jericho and its king, and that the
people of Gibeon had made a treaty of
peace[f] with Israel and were living near
them. 2 He and his people were very
much alarmed at this, because Gibeon
was an important city, like one of the
royal cities; it was larger than Ai, and
all its men were good fighters. 3 So Adoni-
Zedek king of Jerusalem appealed to
Hoham king of Hebron,[g] Piram king of
Jarmuth, Japhia king of Lachish[h] and
Debir king of Eglon. 4 "Come up and help
me attack Gibeon," he said, "because it
has made peace[i] with Joshua and the
Israelites."
5 Then the five kings of the Amorites[j]—the kings of Jerusalem, Hebron,
Jarmuth, Lachish and Eglon—joined
forces. They moved up with all their
troops and took up positions against Gibeon and attacked it.
6 The Gibeonites then sent word to
Joshua in the camp at Gilgal: "Do not
abandon your servants. Come up to us
quickly and save us! Help us, because
all the Amorite kings from the hill country have joined forces against us."
7 So Joshua marched up from Gilgal
with his entire army,[k] including all the
best fighting men. 8 The LORD said to
Joshua, "Do not be afraid[l] of them; I
have given them into your hand. Not one
of them will be able to withstand you."
9 After an all-night march from Gilgal,
Joshua took them by surprise. 10 The
LORD threw them into confusion before
Israel,[m] who defeated them in a great
victory at Gibeon. Israel pursued them
along the road going up to Beth Horon[n] and cut them down all the way
to Azekah[o] and Makkedah. 11 As they fled
before Israel on the road down from
Beth Horon to Azekah, the LORD hurled
large hailstones[p] down on them from
the sky, and more of them died from the
hailstones than were killed by the swords
of the Israelites.
12 On the day the LORD gave the Amorites[q] over to Israel, Joshua said to the
LORD in the presence of Israel:

"O sun, stand still over Gibeon,
O moon, over the Valley of
Aijalon.[r]"
13 So the sun stood still,[s]
and the moon stopped,
till the nation avenged itself on[c] its
enemies,

as it is written in the Book of Jashar.[t]
The sun stopped[u] in the middle of
the sky and delayed going down about
a full day. 14 There has never been a
day like it before or since, a day when
the LORD listened to a man. Surely the
LORD was fighting[v] for Israel!
15 Then Joshua returned with all Israel
to the camp at Gilgal.[w]

Five enemy kings are killed and then hung on trees.

16 Now the five kings had fled and hidden in the cave at Makkedah. 17 When
Joshua was told that the five kings had
been found hiding in the cave at Makkedah, 18 he said, "Roll large rocks up to
the mouth of the cave, and post some
men there to guard it. 19 But don't stop!

9:25 [a]Ge 16:6
9:27 [b]Dt 12:5
10:1 [c]Jdg 1:7 [d]Jos 8:1 [e]Dt 20:16; Jos 8:22 [f]Jos 9:15
10:3 [g]Ge 13:18 [h]2Ch 11:9; 25:27; Ne 11:30; Isa 36:2; 37:8; Jer 34:7; Mic 1:13
10:4 [i]Jos 9:15
10:5 [j]Nu 13:29
10:7 [k]Jos 8:1
10:8 [l]Dt 3:2; Jos 1:9
10:10 [m]Dt 7:23 [n]Jos 16:3,5 [o]Jos 15:35
10:11 [p]Ps 18:12; Isa 28:2,17
10:12 [q]Am 2:9 [r]Jdg 1:35; 12:12
10:13 [s]Hab 3:11 [t]2Sa 1:18 [u]Isa 38:8
10:14 [v]ver 42; Ex 14:14; Dt 1:30; Ps 106:43; 136:24
10:15 [w]ver 43

b *1* The Hebrew term refers to the irrevocable giving over of things or persons to the LORD, often by totally destroying them; also in verses 28, 35, 37, 39 and 40.
c *13* Or *nation triumphed over*

Pursue your enemies, attack them from the rear and don't let them reach their cities, for the LORD your God has given them into your hand."

20So Joshua and the Israelites destroyed them completely[a]—almost to a man—but the few who were left reached their fortified cities. 21The whole army then returned safely to Joshua in the camp at Makkedah, and no one uttered a word against the Israelites.

22Joshua said, "Open the mouth of the cave and bring those five kings out to me." 23So they brought the five kings out of the cave—the kings of Jerusalem, Hebron, Jarmuth, Lachish and Eglon. 24When they had brought these kings to Joshua, he summoned all the men of Israel and said to the army commanders who had come with him, "Come here and put your feet[b] on the necks of these kings." So they came forward and placed their feet[c] on their necks.

25Joshua said to them, "Do not be afraid; do not be discouraged. Be strong and courageous.[d] This is what the LORD will do to all the enemies you are going to fight." 26Then Joshua struck and killed the kings and hung them on five trees, and they were left hanging on the trees until evening.

27At sunset[e] Joshua gave the order and they took them down from the trees and threw them into the cave where they had been hiding. At the mouth of the cave they placed large rocks, which are there to this day.

28That day Joshua took Makkedah. He put the city and its king to the sword and totally destroyed everyone in it. He left no survivors.[f] And he did to the king of Makkedah as he had done to the king of Jericho.[g]

Southern Palestine is conquered.

29Then Joshua and all Israel with him moved on from Makkedah to Libnah and attacked it. 30The LORD also gave that city and its king into Israel's hand. The city and everyone in it Joshua put to the sword. He left no survivors there. And he did to its king as he had done to the king of Jericho.

31Then Joshua and all Israel with him moved on from Libnah to Lachish; he took up positions against it and attacked it. 32The LORD handed Lachish over to Israel, and Joshua took it on the second day. The city and everyone in it he put to the sword, just as he had done to Libnah. 33Meanwhile, Horam king of Gezer[h] had come up to help Lachish, but Joshua defeated him and his army—until no survivors were left.

34Then Joshua and all Israel with him moved on from Lachish to Eglon; they took up positions against it and attacked it. 35They captured it that same day and put it to the sword and totally destroyed everyone in it, just as they had done to Lachish.

36Then Joshua and all Israel with him went up from Eglon to Hebron[i] and attacked it. 37They took the city and put it to the sword, together with its king, its villages and everyone in it. They left no survivors. Just as at Eglon, they totally destroyed it and everyone in it.

38Then Joshua and all Israel with him turned around and attacked Debir.[j] 39They took the city, its king and its villages, and put them to the sword. Everyone in it they totally destroyed. They left no survivors. They did to Debir and its king as they had done to Libnah and its king and to Hebron.

40So Joshua subdued the whole region, including the hill country, the Negev,[k] the western foothills and the mountain slopes,[l] together with all their kings.[m] He left no survivors. He totally destroyed all who breathed, just as the LORD, the God of Israel, had commanded.[n] 41Joshua subdued them from Kadesh Barnea[o] to Gaza[p] and from the whole region of Goshen[q] to Gibeon. 42All these kings and their lands Joshua conquered in one campaign, because the LORD, the God of Israel, fought[r] for Israel.

43Then Joshua returned with all Israel to the camp at Gilgal.[s]

10:20 [a]Dt 20:16
10:24 [b]Mal 4:3 [c]Ps 110:1
10:25 [d]Dt 31:6
10:27 [e]Dt 21:23; Jos 8:9,29
10:28 [f]Dt 20:16 [g]Jos 6:21
10:33 [h]Jos 16:3,10; Jdg 1:29; 1Ki 9:15
10:36 [i]Jos 14:13; 15:13; Jdg 1:10
10:38 [j]Jos 15:15; Jdg 1:11
10:40 [k]Ge 12:9; Jos 12:8 [l]Dt 1:7 [m]Dt 7:24 [n]Dt 20:16-17
10:41 [o]Ge 14:7 [p]Ge 10:19 [q]Jos 11:16; 15:51
10:42 [r]ver 14
10:43 [s]ver 15; Jos 5:9

Israel defeats the northern coalition of kings.

11 When Jabin[a] king of Hazor[b] heard
of this, he sent word to Jobab
king of Madon, to the kings of Shimron[c] and Acshaph, 2and to the northern kings who were in the mountains,
in the Arabah[d] south of Kinnereth,[e] in
the western foothills and in Naphoth
Dor[d][f] on the west; 3to the Canaanites
in the east and west; to the Amorites,
Hittites, Perizzites and Jebusites in the
hill country; and to the Hivites[g] below Hermon in the region of Mizpah.[h]
4They came out with all their troops
and a large number of horses and chariots—a huge army, as numerous as the
sand on the seashore.[i] 5All these kings
joined forces[j] and made camp together
at the Waters of Merom, to fight against
Israel.

6The LORD said to Joshua, "Do not
be afraid of them, because by this time
tomorrow I will hand all of them over[k]
to Israel, slain. You are to hamstring[l]
their horses and burn their chariots."

7So Joshua and his whole army came
against them suddenly at the Waters of
Merom and attacked them, 8and the
LORD gave them into the hand of Israel.
They defeated them and pursued them
all the way to Greater Sidon, to Misrephoth Maim,[m] and to the Valley of Mizpah on the east, until no survivors were
left. 9Joshua did to them as the LORD had
directed: He hamstrung their horses
and burned their chariots.

10At that time Joshua turned back
and captured Hazor and put its king to
the sword. (Hazor had been the head
of all these kingdoms.) 11Everyone in it
they put to the sword. They totally
destroyed[e] them, not sparing anything
that breathed,[n] and he burned up Hazor
itself.

12Joshua took all these royal cities and
their kings and put them to the sword.
He totally destroyed them, as Moses
the servant of the LORD had commanded.[o] 13Yet Israel did not burn any of the
cities built on their mounds—except
Hazor, which Joshua burned. 14The Israelites carried off for themselves all
the plunder and livestock of these
cities, but all the people they put to
the sword until they completely destroyed them, not sparing anyone that
breathed.[p] 15As the LORD commanded
his servant Moses, so Moses commanded Joshua, and Joshua did it; he left
nothing undone of all that the LORD
commanded Moses.[q]

Joshua's conquests are summarized.

16So Joshua took this entire land: the
hill country, all the Negev, the whole
region of Goshen, the western foothills,[r] the Arabah and the mountains of
Israel with their foothills, 17from Mount
Halak, which rises toward Seir, to Baal
Gad in the Valley of Lebanon[s] below
Mount Hermon. He captured all their
kings and struck them down, putting
them to death.[t] 18Joshua waged war
against all these kings for a long time.
19Except for the Hivites living in Gibeon,[u] not one city made a treaty of peace
with the Israelites, who took them all
in battle. 20For it was the LORD himself
who hardened their hearts[v] to wage
war against Israel, so that he might destroy them totally, exterminating them
without mercy, as the LORD had commanded Moses.[w]

21At that time Joshua went and destroyed the Anakites[x] from the hill
country: from Hebron, Debir and Anab,
from all the hill country of Judah, and
from all the hill country of Israel. Joshua totally destroyed them and their
towns. 22No Anakites were left in Israelite territory; only in Gaza, Gath[y] and
Ashdod[z] did any survive. 23So Joshua
took the entire land,[a] just as the LORD
had directed Moses, and he gave it as
an inheritance[b] to Israel according to
their tribal divisions.[c]

Then the land had rest from war.[d]

11:1 [a]Jdg 4:2,7,23 [b]ver 10; 1Sa 12:9 [c]Jos 19:15
11:2 [d]Jos 12:3 [e]Nu 34:11 [f]Jos 17:11; Jdg 1:27; 1Ki 4:11
11:3 [g]Dt 7:1; Jdg 3:3,5; 1Ki 9:20 [h]Ge 31:49; Jos 15:38; 18:26
11:4 [i]Jdg 7:12; 1Sa 13:5
11:5 [j]Jdg 5:19
11:6 [k]Jos 10:8 [l]2Sa 8:4
11:8 [m]Jos 13:6
11:11 [n]Dt 20:16-17
11:12 [o]Nu 33:50-52; Dt 7:2
11:14 [p]Nu 31:11-12
11:15 [q]Ex 34:11; Jos 1:7
11:16 [r]Jos 10:41
11:17 [s]Jos 12:7 [t]Dt 7:24
11:19 [u]Jos 9:3
11:20 [v]Ex 14:17; Ro 9:18 [w]Dt 7:16; Jdg 14:4
11:21 [x]Nu 13:22,33; Dt 9:2
11:22 [y]1Sa 17:4; 1Ki 2:39; 1Ch 8:13 [z]1Sa 5:1; Isa 20:1
11:23 [a]Jos 21:43-45 [b]Dt 1:38; 12:9-10; 25:19 [c]Nu 26:53 [d]Jos 14:15

d *2* Or *in the heights of Dor* e *11* The Hebrew term refers to the irrevocable giving over of things or persons to the LORD, often by totally destroying them; also in verses 12, 20 and 21.

The Conquered Land

Joshua displayed brilliant military strategy in the way he went about conquering the land of Canaan. He first captured the well-fortified Jericho to gain a foothold in Canaan and to demonstrate the awesome might of the God of Israel. Then he gained the hill country around Bethel and Gibeon. From there he subdued towns in the lowlands. Then his army conquered important cities in the north, such as Hazor. In all, Israel conquered land both east (12:1-6) and west (12:7-24) of the Jordan River; from Mount Hermon in the north to beyond the Negev to Mount Halak in the south. Thirty-one kings and their cities had been defeated. The Israelites had overpowered the Hittites, the Amorites, the Canaanites, the Perizzites, the Hivites, and the Jebusites. Other peoples living in Canaan were yet to be conquered.

Kings defeated by Moses.

12 These are the kings of the land
whom the Israelites had defeated
and whose territory they took over east
of the Jordan, from the Arnon Gorge to
Mount Hermon,[a] including all the eastern side of the Arabah:

2Sihon king of the Amorites,
who reigned in Heshbon. He ruled
from Aroer on the rim of the Arnon Gorge—from the middle of the
gorge—to the Jabbok River, which
is the border of the Ammonites. This
included half of Gilead.[b] 3He also
ruled over the eastern Arabah from
the Sea of Kinnereth[fc] to the Sea
of the Arabah (the Salt Sea[g]), to
Beth Jeshimoth,[d] and then southward below the slopes of Pisgah.

4And the territory of Og king of Bashan,[e]
one of the last of the Rephaites, who
reigned in Ashtaroth[f] and Edrei.
5He ruled over Mount Hermon, Salecah,[g] all of Bashan to the border
of the people of Geshur[h] and Maacah,[i] and half of Gilead to the border of Sihon king of Heshbon.

6Moses, the servant of the LORD, and
the Israelites conquered them. And Moses the servant of the LORD gave their

12:1 [a]Dt 3:8
12:2 [b]Dt 2:36
12:3 [c]Jos 11:2 [d]Jos 13:20
12:4 [e]Nu 21:21,33; Dt 3:11 [f]Dt 1:4
12:5 [g]Dt 3:10 [h]1Sa 27:8 [i]Dt 3:14

f3 That is, Galilee g3 That is, the Dead Sea

land to the Reubenites, the Gadites and
the half-tribe of Manasseh to be their
possession.[a]

Kings defeated by Joshua.

7These are the kings of the land that
Joshua and the Israelites conquered on
the west side of the Jordan, from Baal Gad
in the Valley of Lebanon[b] to Mount Halak, which rises toward Seir (their lands
Joshua gave as an inheritance to the
tribes of Israel according to their tribal
divisions— 8the hill country, the western foothills, the Arabah, the mountain
slopes, the desert and the Negev[c]—the
lands of the Hittites, Amorites, Canaanites, Perizzites, Hivites and Jebusites):

9the king of Jericho[d] one
the king of Ai[e] (near Bethel) one
10the king of Jerusalem[f] one
the king of Hebron one
11the king of Jarmuth one
the king of Lachish one
12the king of Eglon one
the king of Gezer[g] one
13the king of Debir one
the king of Geder one
14the king of Hormah one
the king of Arad[h] one
15the king of Libnah one
the king of Adullam one
16the king of Makkedah one
the king of Bethel[i] one
17the king of Tappuah one
the king of Hepher[j] one
18the king of Aphek[k] one
the king of Lasharon one
19the king of Madon one
the king of Hazor one
20the king of Shimron Meron one
the king of Acshaph[l] one
21the king of Taanach one
the king of Megiddo one
22the king of Kedesh[m] one
the king of Jokneam in Carmel[n] one
23the king of Dor (in Naphoth Dor[h][o]) one
the king of Goyim in Gilgal one
24the king of Tirzah one
thirty-one kings in all.[p]

Remaining lands yet unconquered.

13 When Joshua was old and well
advanced in years,[q] the LORD said
to him, "You are very old, and there are
still very large areas of land to be taken
over.

2"This is the land that remains: all
the regions of the Philistines and
Geshurites: 3from the Shihor River[r]
on the east of Egypt to the territory of Ekron[s] on the north, all of it
counted as Canaanite (the territory of the five Philistine rulers[t] in
Gaza, Ashdod, Ashkelon, Gath and
Ekron—that of the Avvites);[u] 4from
the south, all the land of the Canaanites, from Arah of the Sidonians as far as Aphek,[v] the region
of the Amorites,[w] 5the area of the
Gebalites[i];[x] and all Lebanon[y] to the
east, from Baal Gad below Mount
Hermon to Lebo[j] Hamath.

6"As for all the inhabitants of the
mountain regions from Lebanon to
Misrephoth Maim,[z] that is, all the Sidonians, I myself will drive them out
before the Israelites. Be sure to allo-
cate this land to Israel for an inheritance, as I have instructed you,[a] 7and
divide it as an inheritance[b] among the
nine tribes and half of the tribe of
Manasseh."

Division of the land east of the Jordan.

8The other half of Manasseh,[k] the Reubenites and the Gadites had received
the inheritance that Moses had given
them east of the Jordan, as he, the servant of the LORD, had assigned[c] it to
them.

9It extended from Aroer[d] on the
rim of the Arnon Gorge, and from
the town in the middle of the gorge,
and included the whole plateau[e]
of Medeba as far as Dibon,[f] 10and

12:6 [a]Nu 32:29,33; Jos 13:8
12:7 [b]Jos 11:17
12:8 [c]Jos 11:16
12:9 [d]Jos 6:2 [e]Jos 8:29
12:10 [f]Jos 10:23
12:12 [g]Jos 10:33
12:14 [h]Nu 21:1
12:16 [i]Jos 7:2
12:17 [j]1Ki 4:10
12:18 [k]Jos 13:4
12:20 [l]Jos 11:1
12:22 [m]Jos 19:37; 20:7; 21:32 [n]1Sa 15:12
12:23 [o]Jos 11:2
12:24 [p]Ps 135:11; Dt 7:24
13:1 [q]Ge 24:1; Jos 14:10
13:3 [r]Jer 2:18 [s]Jdg 1:18 [t]Jdg 3:3 [u]Dt 2:23
13:4 [v]Jos 12:18; 19:30 [w]Am 2:10
13:5 [x]1Ki 5:18; Ps 83:7; Eze 27:9 [y]Jos 12:7
13:6 [z]Jos 11:8 [a]Nu 33:54
13:7 [b]Jos 11:23; Ps 78:55
13:8 [c]Jos 12:6
13:9 [d]ver 16; Jdg 11:26 [e]Jer 48:8,21 [f]Nu 21:30

h*23* Or *in the heights of Dor* i*5* That is, the area of Byblos j*5* Or *to the entrance to* k*8* Hebrew *With it* (that is, with the other half of Manasseh) all the towns of Sihon king of the Amorites, who ruled in Heshbon, out to the border of the Ammonites.[a] 11It also included Gilead, the territory of the people of Geshur and Maacah, all of Mount Hermon and all Bashan as far as Salecah[b]— 12that is, the whole kingdom of Og in Bashan,[c] who had reigned in Ashtaroth[d] and Edrei and had survived as one of the last of the Rephaites.[e] Moses had defeated them and taken over their land. 13But the Israelites did not drive out the people of Geshur[f] and Maacah,[g] so they continue to live among the Israelites to this day.

14But to the tribe of Levi he gave no inheritance, since the offerings made by fire to the LORD, the God of Israel, are their inheritance, as he promised them.[h]

15This is what Moses had given to the tribe of Reuben, clan by clan:

16The territory from Aroer[i] on the rim of the Arnon Gorge, and from the town in the middle of the gorge, and the whole plateau past Medeba[j] 17to Heshbon and all its towns on the plateau, including Dibon,[k] Bamoth Baal, Beth Baal Meon,[l] 18Jahaz,[m] Kedemoth, Mephaath,[n] 19Kiriathaim,[o] Sibmah, Zereth Shahar on the hill in the valley, 20Beth Peor,[p] the slopes of Pisgah, and Beth Jeshimoth 21—all the towns on the plateau and the entire realm of Sihon king of the Amorites, who ruled at Heshbon. Moses had defeated him and the Midianite chiefs,[q] Evi, Rekem, Zur, Hur and Reba[r]—princes allied with Sihon—who lived in that country. 22In addition to those slain in battle, the Israelites had put to the sword Balaam son of Beor,[s] who practiced divination. 23The boundary of the Reubenites was the bank of the Jordan. These towns and their villages were the inheritance of the Reubenites, clan by clan.

24This is what Moses had given to the tribe of Gad, clan by clan:

25The territory of Jazer,[t] all the towns of Gilead and half the Ammonite country as far as Aroer, near Rabbah; 26and from Heshbon[u] to Ramath Mizpah and Betonim, and from Mahanaim to the territory of Debir;[v] 27and in the valley, Beth Haram, Beth Nimrah, Succoth[w] and Zaphon with the rest of the realm of Sihon king of Heshbon (the east side of the Jordan, the territory up to the end of the Sea of Kinnereth[l][x]). 28These towns and their villages were the inheritance of the Gadites,[y] clan by clan.

29This is what Moses had given to the half-tribe of Manasseh, that is, to half the family of the descendants of Manasseh, clan by clan:

30The territory extending from Mahanaim[z] and including all of Bashan, the entire realm of Og king of Bashan—all the settlements of Jair[a] in Bashan, sixty towns, 31half of Gilead, and Ashtaroth and Edrei (the royal cities of Og in Bashan). This was for the descendants of Makir[b] son of Manasseh—for half of the sons of Makir, clan by clan.

32This is the inheritance Moses had given when he was in the plains of Moab across the Jordan east of Jericho. 33But to the tribe of Levi, Moses had given no inheritance; the LORD, the God of Israel, is their inheritance,[c] as he promised them.[d]

Division of the land west of the Jordan.

14 Now these are the areas the Israelites received as an inheritance in the land of Canaan, which Eleazar the priest, Joshua son of Nun and the heads of the tribal clans of Israel allotted to them.[e] 2Their inheritances

13:10 [a]Nu 21:24
13:11 [b]Jos 12:5
13:12 [c]Dt 3:11 [d]Jos 12:4 [e]Ge 14:5
13:13 [f]Jos 12:5 [g]Dt 3:14
13:14 [h]ver 33; Dt 18:1-2
13:16 [i]ver 9; Jos 12:2 [j]Nu 21:30
13:17 [k]Nu 32:3 [l]1Ch 5:8
13:18 [m]Nu 21:23 [n]Jer 48:21
13:19 [o]Nu 32:37
13:20 [p]Dt 3:29
13:21 [q]Nu 25:15 [r]Nu 31:8
13:22 [s]Nu 22:5; 31:8
13:25 [t]Nu 21:32; Jos 21:39
13:26 [u]Nu 21:25; Jer 49:3 [v]Jos 10:3
13:27 [w]Ge 33:17 [x]Nu 34:11
13:28 [y]Nu 32:33
13:30 [z]Ge 32:2 [a]Nu 32:41
13:31 [b]Ge 50:23
13:33 [c]Nu 18:20 [d]ver 14; Jos 18:7
14:1 [e]Nu 34:17-18

[l]27 That is, Galilee

were assigned by lot[a] to the nine-and-a-half tribes, as the LORD had commanded through Moses. 3 Moses had granted the two-and-a-half tribes their inheritance east of the Jordan[b] but had not granted the Levites an inheritance among the rest,[c] 4 for the sons of Joseph had become two tribes—Manasseh and Ephraim.[d] The Levites received no share of the land but only towns to live in, with pasturelands for their flocks and herds. 5 So the Israelites divided the land, just as the LORD had commanded Moses.[e]

Caleb's inheritance of Hebron.

6 Now the men of Judah approached Joshua at Gilgal, and Caleb son of Jephunneh[f] the Kenizzite said to him, "You know what the LORD said to Moses the man of God at Kadesh Barnea[g] about you and me. 7 I was forty years old when Moses the servant of the LORD sent me from Kadesh Barnea to explore the land.[h] And I brought him back a report according to my convictions,[i] 8 but my brothers who went up with me made the hearts of the people melt with fear.[j] I, however, followed the LORD my God wholeheartedly.[k] 9 So on that day Moses swore to me, 'The land on which your feet have walked will be your inheritance and that of your children[l] forever, because you have followed the LORD my God wholeheartedly.'[m]

10 "Now then, just as the LORD promised,[m] he has kept me alive for forty-five years since the time he said this to Moses, while Israel moved about in the desert. So here I am today, eighty-five years old! 11 I am still as strong[n] today as the day Moses sent me out; I'm just as vigorous to go out to battle now as I was then. 12 Now give me this hill country that the LORD promised me that day. You yourself heard then that the Anakites[o] were there and their cities were large and fortified,[p] but, the LORD helping me, I will drive them out just as he said."

13 Then Joshua blessed[q] Caleb son of Jephunneh and gave him Hebron[r] as his inheritance.[s] 14 So Hebron has belonged to Caleb son of Jephunneh the Kenizzite ever since, because he followed the LORD, the God of Israel, wholeheartedly. 15 (Hebron used to be called Kiriath Arba[t] after Arba,[u] who was the greatest man among the Anakites.)

Then the land had rest[v] from war.

Judah's allotment.

15:15-19pp—Jdg 1:11-15

15 The allotment for the tribe of Judah, clan by clan, extended down to the territory of Edom,[w] to the Desert of Zin[x] in the extreme south.

2 Their southern boundary started from the bay at the southern end of the Salt Sea,[n] 3 crossed south of Scorpion[o] Pass,[y] continued on to Zin and went over to the south of Kadesh Barnea. Then it ran past Hezron up to Addar and curved around to Karka. 4 It then passed along to Azmon[z] and joined the Wadi of Egypt,[a] ending at the sea. This is their[p] southern boundary.

5 The eastern boundary[b] is the Salt Sea as far as the mouth of the Jordan.

The northern boundary[c] started from the bay of the sea at the mouth of the Jordan, 6 went up to Beth Hoglah[d] and continued north of Beth Arabah to the Stone of Bohan[e] son of Reuben. 7 The boundary then went up to Debir from the Valley of Achor[f] and turned north to Gilgal, which faces the Pass of Adummim south of the gorge. It continued along to the waters of En Shemesh and came out at En Rogel.[g] 8 Then it ran up the Valley of Ben Hinnom along the southern slope of the Jebusite[h] city (that is, Jerusalem). From there it climbed to the top of the hill west of the Hinnom Valley at the northern end of the Valley of Rephaim. 9 From the hilltop

14:2 [a]Nu 26:55
14:3 [b]Nu 32:33 [c]Jos 13:14
14:4 [d]Ge 41:52; 48:5
14:5 [e]Nu 34:13; 35:2; Jos 21:2
14:6 [f]Nu 13:6; 14:30 [g]Nu 13:26
14:7 [h]Nu 13:17 [i]Nu 13:30; 14:6-9
14:8 [j]Nu 13:31 [k]Nu 14:24
14:9 [l]Nu 14:24; Dt 1:36
14:10 [m]Nu 14:30
14:11 [n]Dt 34:7
14:12 [o]Nu 13:33 [p]Nu 13:28
14:13 [q]Jos 22:6,7 [r]Jos 10:36 [s]Jdg 1:20; 1Ch 6:56
14:15 [t]Ge 23:2 [u]Jos 15:13 [v]Jos 11:23
15:1 [w]Nu 34:3 [x]Nu 33:36
15:3 [y]Nu 34:4
15:4 [z]Nu 34:5 [a]Ge 15:18
15:5 [b]Nu 34:10 [c]Jos 18:15-19
15:6 [d]Jos 18:19,21 [e]Jos 18:17
15:7 [f]Jos 7:24 [g]2Sa 17:17; 1Ki 1:9
15:8 [h]ver 63; Jos 18:16,28; Jdg 1:21; 19:10

m *9* Deut. 1:36 n *2* That is, the Dead Sea; also in verse 5 o *3* Hebrew *Akrabbim* p *4* Hebrew *your*

the boundary headed toward the
spring of the waters of Nephtoah,[a]
came out at the towns of Mount
Ephron and went down toward Baalah[b] (that is, Kiriath Jearim). 10Then
it curved westward from Baalah to
Mount Seir, ran along the northern
slope of Mount Jearim (that is, Kes-
alon), continued down to Beth Shemesh and crossed to Timnah.[c] 11It
went to the northern slope of Ekron,
turned toward Shikkeron, passed
along to Mount Baalah and reached
Jabneel.[d] The boundary ended at
the sea.
12The western boundary is the
coastline of the Great Sea.[q][e]
These are the boundaries around the
people of Judah by their clans.

13In accordance with the LORD's command to him, Joshua gave to Caleb son
of Jephunneh a portion in Judah—Kiriath Arba, that is, Hebron. (Arba was
the forefather of Anak.)[f] 14From Hebron
Caleb drove out the three Anakites[g]—
Sheshai, Ahiman and Talmai[h]—descendants of Anak.[i] 15From there he marched
against the people living in Debir (formerly called Kiriath Sepher). 16And Caleb said, "I will give my daughter Acsah[j]
in marriage to the man who attacks and
captures Kiriath Sepher." 17Othniel[k] son
of Kenaz, Caleb's brother, took it; so
Caleb gave his daughter Acsah to him
in marriage.
18One day when she came to Othniel,
she urged him[r] to ask her father for a
field. When she got off her donkey, Caleb
asked her, "What can I do for you?"
19She replied, "Do me a special favor.
Since you have given me land in the
Negev, give me also springs of water."
So Caleb gave her the upper and lower
springs.

20This is the inheritance of the tribe
of Judah, clan by clan:

21The southernmost towns of the tribe
of Judah in the Negev toward the
boundary of Edom were:
Kabzeel, Eder,[l] Jagur, 22Kinah,
Dimonah, Adadah, 23Kedesh, Ha-
zor, Ithnan, 24Ziph,[m] Telem, Bea-
loth, 25Hazor Hadattah, Kerioth
Hezron (that is, Hazor), 26Amam,
Shema, Moladah,[n] 27Hazar Gaddah,
Heshmon, Beth Pelet, 28Hazar
Shual, Beersheba,[o] Biziothiah, 29Ba-
alah,[p] Iim, Ezem, 30Eltolad,[q] Kesil,
Hormah, 31Ziklag,[r] Madmannah,
Sansannah, 32Lebaoth, Shilhim,
Ain and Rimmon[s]—a total of twen-
ty-nine towns and their villages.

33In the western foothills:
Eshtaol,[t] Zorah, Ashnah, 34Zano-
ah,[u] En Gannim, Tappuah, Enam,
35Jarmuth,[v] Adullam,[w] Socoh, Azekah, 36Shaaraim, Adithaim and Gederah[x] (or Gederothaim)[s]—fourteen
towns and their villages.
37Zenan, Hadashah, Migdal Gad,
38Dilean, Mizpah, Joktheel,[y] 39La-
chish,[z] Bozkath,[a] Eglon, 40Cabbon,
Lahmas, Kitlish, 41Gederoth, Beth
Dagon, Naamah and Makkedah[b]—
sixteen towns and their villages.
42Libnah, Ether, Ashan,[c] 43Iph-
tah, Ashnah, Nezib, 44Keilah, Aczib[d] and Mareshah[e]—nine towns
and their villages.
45Ekron, with its surrounding settlements and villages; 46west of
Ekron, all that were in the vicinity
of Ashdod, together with their villages; 47Ashdod,[f] its surrounding
settlements and villages; and Gaza,
its settlements and villages, as far as
the Wadi of Egypt[g] and the coastline of the Great Sea.[h]

48In the hill country:
Shamir, Jattir,[i] Socoh, 49Dannah,
Kiriath Sannah (that is, Debir[j]),
50Anab, Eshtemoh,[k] Anim, 51Go-
shen,[l] Holon and Giloh—eleven
towns and their villages.

15:9 [a]Jos 18:15 [b]1Ch 13:6 **15:10** [c]Ge 38:12; Jdg 14:1 **15:11** [d]Jos 19:33 **15:12** [e]Nu 34:6 **15:13** [f]Jos 14:13-15 **15:14** [g]Nu 13:33 [h]Nu 13:22 [i]Jdg 1:10,20 **15:16** [j]Jdg 1:12 **15:17** [k]Jdg 3:9,11 **15:21** [l]Ge 35:21 **15:24** [m]1Sa 23:14 **15:26** [n]1Ch 4:28 **15:28** [o]Ge 21:31 **15:29** [p]ver 9 **15:30** [q]Jos 19:4 **15:31** [r]1Sa 27:6 **15:32** [s]Jdg 20:45 **15:33** [t]Jdg 13:25; 16:31 **15:34** [u]1Ch 4:18; Ne 3:13 **15:35** [v]Jos 10:3 [w]1Sa 22:1 **15:36** [x]1Ch 12:4 **15:38** [y]2Ki 14:7 **15:39** [z]Jos 10:3; 2Ki 14:19 [a]2Ki 22:1 **15:41** [b]Jos 10:10 **15:42** [c]1Sa 30:30 **15:44** [d]Jdg 1:31 [e]Mic 1:15 **15:47** [f]Jos 11:22 [g]ver 4 [h]Nu 34:6 **15:48** [i]1Sa 30:27 **15:49** [j]Jos 10:3 **15:50** [k]Jos 21:14 **15:51** [l]Jos 10:41; 11:16

[q] *12* That is, the Mediterranean; also in verse 47
[r] *18* Hebrew and some Septuagint manuscripts; other Septuagint manuscripts (see also note at Judges 1:14) *Othniel, he urged her*
[s] *36* Or *Gederah and Gederothaim*

52 Arab, Dumah,[a] Eshan, 53 Janim, Beth Tappuah, Aphekah, 54 Humtah, Kiriath Arba (that is, Hebron) and Zior—nine towns and their villages.

55 Maon, Carmel,[b] Ziph, Juttah, 56 Jezreel,[c] Jokdeam, Zanoah, 57 Kain, Gibeah[d] and Timnah—ten towns and their villages.

58 Halhul, Beth Zur,[e] Gedor, 59 Maarath, Beth Anoth and Eltekon—six towns and their villages.

60 Kiriath Baal (that is, Kiriath Jearim[f]) and Rabbah[g]—two towns and their villages.

61 In the desert:

Beth Arabah, Middin, Secacah, 62 Nibshan, the City of Salt and En Gedi[h]—six towns and their villages.

63 Judah could not[i] dislodge the Jebusites[j], who were living in Jerusalem; to this day the Jebusites live there with the people of Judah.

Ephraim and (west) Manasseh's allotment.

16 The allotment for Joseph began at the Jordan of Jericho,[t] east of the waters of Jericho, and went up from there through the desert[k] into the hill country of Bethel. 2 It went on from Bethel (that is, Luz[l]),[u] crossed over to the territory of the Arkites in Ataroth, 3 descended westward to the territory of the Japhletites as far as the region of Lower Beth Horon[m] and on to Gezer,[n] ending at the sea.

4 So Manasseh and Ephraim, the descendants of Joseph, received their inheritance.[o]

5 This was the territory of Ephraim, clan by clan:

The boundary of their inheritance went from Ataroth Addar[p] in the east to Upper Beth Horon 6 and continued to the sea. From Micmethath[q] on the north it curved eastward to Taanath Shiloh, passing by it to Janoah on the east. 7 Then it went down from Janoah to Ataroth[r] and Naarah, touched Jericho and came out at the Jordan. 8 From Tappuah the border went west to the Kanah Ravine[s] and ended at the sea. This was the inheritance of the tribe of the Ephraimites, clan by clan. 9 It also included all the towns and their villages that were set aside for the Ephraimites within the inheritance of the Manassites.

10 They did not dislodge the Canaanites living in Gezer; to this day the Canaanites live among the people of Ephraim but are required to do forced labor.[t]

(East) Manasseh's allotment.

17 This was the allotment for the tribe of Manasseh as Joseph's firstborn,[u] that is, for Makir,[v] Manasseh's firstborn. Makir was the ancestor of the Gileadites, who had received Gilead and Bashan because the Makirites were great soldiers. 2 So this allotment was for the rest of the people of Manasseh—the clans of Abiezer,[w] Helek, Asriel, Shechem, Hepher and Shemida. These are the other male descendants of Manasseh son of Joseph by their clans.

3 Now Zelophehad son of Hepher,[x] the son of Gilead, the son of Makir, the son of Manasseh, had no sons but only daughters,[y] whose names were Mahlah, Noah, Hoglah, Milcah and Tirzah. 4 They went to Eleazar the priest, Joshua son of Nun, and the leaders and said, "The LORD commanded Moses to give us an inheritance among our brothers." So Joshua gave them an inheritance along with the brothers of their father, according to the LORD's command.[z] 5 Manasseh's share consisted of ten tracts of land besides Gilead and Bashan east of the Jordan, 6 because the daughters of the tribe of Manasseh received an inheritance among the sons. The land of Gilead belonged to

15:52 [a] Ge 25:14
15:55 [b] Jos 12:22
15:56 [c] Jos 17:16
15:57 [d] Jos 18:28; Jdg 19:12
15:58 [e] 1Ch 2:45
15:60 [f] Jos 18:14 [g] Dt 3:11
15:62 [h] 1Sa 23:29
15:63 [i] Jdg 1:21 [j] 2Sa 5:6
16:1 [k] Jos 8:15; 18:12
16:2 [l] Jos 18:13
16:3 [m] 2Ch 8:5 [n] Jos 10:33; 1Ki 9:15
16:4 [o] Jos 17:14
16:5 [p] Jos 18:13
16:6 [q] Jos 17:7
16:7 [r] 1Ch 7:28
16:8 [s] Jos 17:9
16:10 [t] Jos 17:13; Jdg 1:28-29; 1Ki 9:16
17:1 [u] Ge 41:51 [v] Ge 50:23
17:2 [w] Nu 26:30; 1Ch 7:18
17:3 [x] Nu 27:1 [y] Nu 26:33
17:4 [z] Nu 27:5-7

[t] 1 *Jordan of Jericho* was possibly an ancient name for the Jordan River. [u] 2 Septuagint; Hebrew *Bethel to Luz*

the rest of the descendants of Manasseh.
7The territory of Manasseh extended from Asher to Micmethath[a] east
of Shechem.[b] The boundary ran
southward from there to include
the people living at En Tappuah.
8(Manasseh had the land of Tappuah, but Tappuah[c] itself, on the
boundary of Manasseh, belonged
to the Ephraimites.) 9Then the
boundary continued south to the
Kanah Ravine.[d] There were towns
belonging to Ephraim lying among
the towns of Manasseh, but the
boundary of Manasseh was the
northern side of the ravine and
ended at the sea. 10On the south
the land belonged to Ephraim, on
the north to Manasseh. The territory of Manasseh reached the sea
and bordered Asher on the north
and Issachar[e] on the east.
11Within Issachar and Asher, Manasseh also had Beth Shan,[f] Ibleam
and the people of Dor,[g] Endor,[h] Taanach and Megiddo,[i] together with
their surrounding settlements (the
third in the list is Naphoth[v]).
12Yet the Manassites were not able[j] to
occupy these towns, for the Canaanites
were determined to live in that region.
13However, when the Israelites grew
stronger, they subjected the Canaanites
to forced labor but did not drive them
out completely.[k]
14The people of Joseph said to Joshua,
"Why have you given us only one allotment and one portion for an inheritance? We are a numerous people and
the LORD has blessed us abundantly."[l]
15"If you are so numerous," Joshua
answered, "and if the hill country of
Ephraim is too small for you, go up
into the forest and clear land for yourselves there in the land of the Perizzites and Rephaites.[m]"
16The people of Joseph replied, "The
hill country is not enough for us, and
all the Canaanites who live in the
plain have iron chariots,[n] both those in
Beth Shan and its settlements and
those in the Valley of Jezreel."
17But Joshua said to the house of Joseph—to Ephraim and Manasseh—
"You are numerous and very powerful.
You will have not only one allotment
18but the forested hill country as well.
Clear it, and its farthest limits will be
yours; though the Canaanites have iron
chariots[o] and though they are strong,
you can drive them out."

Remainder of the land divided by casting lots.

18 The whole assembly of the Israelites gathered at Shiloh[p] and
set up the Tent of Meeting[q] there.
The country was brought under their
control, 2but there were still seven Israelite tribes who had not yet received
their inheritance.
3So Joshua said to the Israelites: "How
long will you wait before you begin to
take possession of the land that the
LORD, the God of your fathers, has giv-
en you? 4Appoint three men from each
tribe. I will send them out to make a survey of the land and to write a description of it, according to the inheritance
of each.[r] Then they will return to me.
5You are to divide the land into seven
parts. Judah is to remain in its territory
on the south[s] and the house of Joseph
in its territory on the north.[t] 6After you
have written descriptions of the seven
parts of the land, bring them here to
me and I will cast lots[u] for you in the
presence of the LORD our God. 7The
Levites, however, do not get a portion
among you, because the priestly service of the LORD is their inheritance.[v]
And Gad, Reuben and the half-tribe of
Manasseh have already received their
inheritance on the east side of the Jordan. Moses the servant of the LORD
gave it to them.[w]"
8As the men started on their way to
map out the land, Joshua instructed
them, "Go and make a survey of the
land and write a description of it. Then
return to me, and I will cast lots for
you here at Shiloh[x] in the presence of

17:7 [a]Jos 16:6 [b]Ge 12:6; Jos 21:21
17:8 [c]Jos 16:8
17:9 [d]Jos 16:8
17:10 [e]Ge 30:18
17:11 [f]1Sa 31:10; 1Ki 4:12; 1Ch 7:29 [g]Jos 11:2 [h]1Sa 28:7; Ps 83:10 [i]1Ki 9:15
17:12 [j]Jdg 1:27
17:13 [k]Jos 16:10
17:14 [l]Nu 26:28-37
17:15 [m]Ge 14:5
17:16 [n]Jdg 1:19; 4:3,13
17:18 [o]ver 16
18:1 [p]Jos 19:51; 21:2; Jdg 18:31; 21:12,19; 1Sa 1:3; 4:3; Jer 7:12; 26:6 [q]Ex 27:21
18:4 [r]Mic 2:5
18:5 [s]Jos 15:1 [t]Jos 16:1-4
18:6 [u]Jos 14:2
18:7 [v]Jos 13:33 [w]Jos 13:8
18:8 [x]ver 1

[v] *11* That is, Naphoth Dor

the LORD." 9So the men left and went through the land. They wrote its description on a scroll, town by town, in seven parts, and returned to Joshua in the camp at Shiloh. 10Joshua then cast lots[a] for them in Shiloh in the presence[b] of the LORD, and there he distributed the land to the Israelites according to their tribal divisions.[c]

Benjamin's allotment.

11The lot came up for the tribe of Benjamin, clan by clan. Their allotted territory lay between the tribes of Judah and Joseph:

12On the north side their boundary began at the Jordan, passed the northern slope of Jericho and headed west into the hill country, coming out at the desert[d] of Beth Aven.[e] 13From there it crossed to the south slope of Luz[f] (that is, Bethel[g]) and went down to Ataroth Addar[h] on the hill south of Lower Beth Horon.

14From the hill facing Beth Horon[i] on the south the boundary turned south along the western side and came out at Kiriath Baal (that is, Kiriath Jearim), a town of the people of Judah. This was the western side.

15The southern side began at the outskirts of Kiriath Jearim on the west, and the boundary came out at the spring of the waters of Nephtoah.[j] 16The boundary went down to the foot of the hill facing the Valley of Ben Hinnom, north of the Valley of Rephaim. It continued down the Hinnom Valley[k] along the southern slope of the Jebusite city and so to En Rogel.[l] 17It then curved north, went to En Shemesh, continued to Geliloth, which faces the Pass of Adummim, and ran down to the Stone of Bohan[m] son of Reuben. 18It continued to the northern slope of Beth Arabah[w][n] and on down into the Arabah. 19It then went to the northern slope of Beth Hoglah and came out at the northern bay of the Salt Sea,[x][o] at the mouth of the Jordan in the south. This was the southern boundary.

20The Jordan formed the boundary on the eastern side.

These were the boundaries that marked out the inheritance of the clans of Benjamin on all sides.[p]

21The tribe of Benjamin, clan by clan, had the following cities:

Jericho, Beth Hoglah, Emek Keziz, 22Beth Arabah, Zemaraim, Bethel,[q] 23Avvim, Parah, Ophrah, 24Kephar Ammoni, Ophni and Geba[r]—twelve towns and their villages.

25Gibeon,[s] Ramah,[t] Beeroth,[u] 26Mizpah,[v] Kephirah, Mozah, 27Rekem, Irpeel, Taralah, 28Zelah,[w] Haeleph, the Jebusite city[x] (that is, Jerusalem[y]), Gibeah[z] and Kiriath—fourteen towns and their villages.

This was the inheritance of Benjamin for its clans.

Simeon's allotment.

19:2-10pp— 1Ch 4:28-33

19 The second lot came out for the tribe of Simeon, clan by clan. Their inheritance lay within the territory of Judah.[a] 2It included:

Beersheba[b] (or Sheba),[y] Moladah, 3Hazar Shual, Balah, Ezem, 4Eltolad, Bethul, Hormah, 5Ziklag, Beth Marcaboth, Hazar Susah, 6Beth Lebaoth and Sharuhen—thirteen towns and their villages;

7Ain, Rimmon, Ether and Ashan[c]—four towns and their villages— 8and all the villages around these towns as far as Baalath Beer (Ramah in the Negev).[d]

This was the inheritance of the tribe of the Simeonites, clan by clan. 9The inheritance of the Simeonites was taken from the share of Judah,[e] because Judah's portion was more than they needed. So the

18:10 [a]Nu 34:13 [b]ver 1; Jer 7:12 [c]Nu 33:54; Jos 19:51
18:12 [d]Jos 16:1 [e]Jos 7:2
18:13 [f]Ge 28:19 [g]Jdg 1:23 [h]Jos 16:5
18:14 [i]Jos 10:10
18:15 [j]Jos 15:9
18:16 [k]Jos 15:8; 2Ki 23:10 [l]Jos 15:7
18:17 [m]Jos 15:6
18:18 [n]Jos 15:6
18:19 [o]Ge 14:3
18:20 [p]Jos 21:4,17; 1Sa 9:1
18:22 [q]Jos 16:1
18:24 [r]Isa 10:29
18:25 [s]Jos 9:3 [t]Jdg 4:5 [u]Jos 9:17
18:26 [v]Jos 11:3
18:28 [w]2Sa 21:14 [x]Jos 15:8 [y]Jos 10:1 [z]Jos 15:57
19:1 [a]ver 9; Ge 49:7
19:2 [b]Ge 21:14; 1Ki 19:3
19:7 [c]Jos 15:42
19:8 [d]Jos 10:40
19:9 [e]Ge 49:7

w *18* Septuagint; Hebrew *slope facing the Arabah*
x *19* That is, the Dead Sea y *2* Or *Beersheba, Sheba*; 1Chron. 4:28 does not have *Sheba*.

Simeonites received their inheritance
within the territory of Judah.[a]

Zebulun's allotment.

10The third lot came up for Zebulun,[b]
clan by clan:
The boundary of their inheritance went as far as Sarid. 11Going
west it ran to Maralah, touched Dab-
besheth, and extended to the ravine
near Jokneam.[c] 12It turned east from
Sarid toward the sunrise to the territory of Kisloth Tabor and went on
to Daberath and up to Japhia. 13Then
it continued eastward to Gath Hepher and Eth Kazin; it came out at
Rimmon[d] and turned toward Neah.
14There the boundary went around
on the north to Hannathon and
ended at the Valley of Iphtah El.
15Included were Kattath, Nahalal,
Shimron, Idalah and Bethlehem.[e]
There were twelve towns and their
villages.
16These towns and their villages were
the inheritance of Zebulun,[f] clan by
clan.[g]

Issachar's allotment.

17The fourth lot came out for Issachar,[h]
clan by clan. 18Their territory included:
Jezreel,[i] Kesulloth, Shunem,[j]
19Hapharaim, Shion, Anaharath,
20Rabbith, Kishion, Ebez, 21Re-
meth, En Gannim, En Haddah and
Beth Pazzez. 22The boundary touched
Tabor,[k] Shahazumah and Beth Shemesh,[l] and ended at the Jordan.
There were sixteen towns and their
villages.
23These towns and their villages were
the inheritance of the tribe of Issachar,[m] clan by clan.[n]

Asher's allotment.

24The fifth lot came out for the tribe of
Asher,[o] clan by clan. 25Their territory
included:
Helkath, Hali, Beten, Acshaph,
26Allammelech, Amad and Mishal.
On the west the boundary touched
Carmel[p] and Shihor Libnath. 27It
then turned east toward Beth Dagon, touched Zebulun[q] and the
Valley of Iphtah El, and went north
to Beth Emek and Neiel, passing
Cabul[r] on the left. 28It went to Abdon,[z] Rehob,[s] Hammon[t] and Kanah,
as far as Greater Sidon.[u] 29The
boundary then turned back toward
Ramah[v] and went to the fortified
city of Tyre,[w] turned toward Hosah
and came out at the sea in the
region of Aczib,[x] 30Ummah, Aphek
and Rehob. There were twenty-two
towns and their villages.
31These towns and their villages were
the inheritance of the tribe of Asher,[y]
clan by clan.

Naphtali's allotment.

32The sixth lot came out for Naphtali,
clan by clan:
33Their boundary went from He-
leph and the large tree in Zaanannim, passing Adami Nekeb and
Jabneel to Lakkum and ending at
the Jordan. 34The boundary ran west
through Aznoth Tabor and came out
at Hukkok. It touched Zebulun on
the south, Asher on the west and
the Jordan[a] on the east. 35The fortified cities were Ziddim, Zer,
Hammath, Rakkath, Kinnereth,[z]
36Adamah, Ramah,[a] Hazor,[b] 37Ke-
desh, Edrei,[c] En Hazor, 38Iron,
Migdal El, Horem, Beth Anath and
Beth Shemesh. There were nineteen towns and their villages.
39These towns and their villages were
the inheritance of the tribe of Naphtali,
clan by clan.[d]

Dan's allotment.

40The seventh lot came out for the tribe
of Dan, clan by clan. 41The territory of
their inheritance included:
Zorah, Eshtaol, Ir Shemesh, 42Sha-
alabbin, Aijalon,[e] Ithlah, 43Elon,

19:9 [a]Eze 48:24
19:10 [b]Jos 21:7,34
19:11 [c]Jos 12:22
19:13 [d]Jos 15:32
19:15 [e]Ge 35:19
19:16 [f]ver 10; Jos 21:7 [g]Eze 48:26
19:17 [h]Ge 30:18
19:18 [i]Jos 15:56 [j]1Sa 28:4; 2Ki 4:8
19:22 [k]Jdg 4:6,12; Ps 89:12 [l]Jos 15:10
19:23 [m]Jos 17:10 [n]Ge 49:15; Eze 48:25
19:24 [o]Jos 17:7
19:26 [p]Jos 12:22
19:27 [q]ver 10 [r]1Ki 9:13
19:28 [s]Jdg 1:31 [t]1Ch 6:76 [u]Ge 10:19; Jos 11:8
19:29 [v]Jos 18:25 [w]2Sa 5:11; 24:7; Isa 23:1; Jer 25:22; Eze 26:2 [x]Jdg 1:31
19:31 [y]Ge 30:13; Eze 48:2
19:35 [z]Jos 11:2
19:36 [a]Jos 18:25 [b]Jos 11:1
19:37 [c]Nu 21:33
19:39 [d]Dt 33:23; Eze 48:3
19:42 [e]Jdg 1:35

z *28* Some Hebrew manuscripts (see also Joshua 21:30); most Hebrew manuscripts *Ebron*
a *34* Septuagint; Hebrew *west, and Judah, the Jordan,*

Timnah,[a] Ekron, 44Eltekeh, Gibbethon, Baalath, 45Jehud, Bene Berak, Gath Rimmon,[b] 46Me Jarkon and Rakkon, with the area facing Joppa.[c]

47(But the Danites had difficulty taking possession of their territory,[d] so they went up and attacked Leshem[e], took it, put it to the sword and occupied it. They settled in Leshem and named it Dan after their forefather.)[f] 48These towns and their villages were the inheritance of the tribe of Dan,[g] clan by clan.

Joshua's allotment.

49When they had finished dividing the land into its allotted portions, the Israelites gave Joshua son of Nun an inheritance among them, 50as the LORD had commanded. They gave him the town he asked for—Timnath Serah[b][h] in the hill country of Ephraim. And he built up the town and settled there.

51These are the territories that Eleazar the priest, Joshua son of Nun and the heads of the tribal clans of Israel assigned by lot at Shiloh in the presence of the LORD at the entrance to the Tent of Meeting. And so they finished dividing the land.[i]

Cities of refuge.

20:1-9Ref— Nu 35:9-34; Dt 4:41-43; 19:1-14

20 Then the LORD said to Joshua: 2"Tell the Israelites to designate the cities of refuge, as I instructed you through Moses, 3so that anyone who kills a person accidentally and unintentionally[j] may flee there and find protection from the avenger of blood.[k]

4"When he flees to one of these cities, he is to stand in the entrance of the city gate[l] and state his case before the elders[m] of that city. Then they are to admit him into their city and give him a place to live with them. 5If the avenger of blood pursues him, they must not surrender the one accused, because he killed his neighbor unintentionally and without malice aforethought. 6He is to stay in that city until he has stood trial before the assembly[n] and until the death of the high priest who is serving at that time. Then he may go back to his own home in the town from which he fled."

7So they set apart Kedesh[o] in Galilee in the hill country of Naphtali, Shechem[p] in the hill country of Ephraim, and Kiriath Arba (that is, Hebron[q]) in the hill country of Judah.[r] 8On the east side of the Jordan of Jericho[c] they designated Bezer[s] in the desert on the plateau in the tribe of Reuben, Ramoth in Gilead[t] in the tribe of Gad, and Golan in Bashan in the tribe of Manasseh. 9Any of the Israelites or any alien living among them who killed someone accidentally could flee to these designated cities and not be killed by the avenger of blood prior to standing trial before the assembly.[u]

Towns allotted to the Levites.

21:4-39pp— 1Ch 6:54-80

21 Now the family heads of the Levites approached Eleazar the priest, Joshua son of Nun, and the heads of the other tribal families of Israel[v] 2at Shiloh[w] in Canaan and said to them, "The LORD commanded through Moses that you give us towns to live in, with pasturelands for our livestock."[x] 3So, as the LORD had commanded, the Israelites gave the Levites the following towns and pasturelands out of their own inheritance:

4The first lot came out for the Kohathites, clan by clan. The Levites who were descendants of Aaron the priest were allotted thirteen towns from the tribes of Judah, Simeon and Benjamin.[y] 5The rest of Kohath's descendants were allotted ten towns from the clans of the tribes of Ephraim, Dan and half of Manasseh.[z]

6The descendants of Gershon were allotted thirteen towns from the clans of the tribes of Issachar,[a] Asher, Naphtali

19:43 [a]Ge 38:12
19:45 [b]Jos 21:24; 1Ch 6:69
19:46 [c]2Ch 2:16; Jnh 1:3
19:47 [d]Jdg 18:1 [e]Jdg 18:7,14 [f]Jdg 18:27,29
19:48 [g]Ge 30:6
19:50 [h]Jos 24:30
19:51 [i]Jos 14:1; 18:10; Ac 13:19
20:3 [j]Lev 4:2 [k]Nu 35:12
20:4 [l]Ru 4:1; Jer 38:7 [m]Jos 7:6
20:6 [n]Nu 35:12
20:7 [o]Jos 21:32; 1Ch 6:76 [p]Ge 12:6 [q]Jos 10:36; 21:11 [r]Lk 1:39
20:8 [s]Jos 21:36; 1Ch 6:78 [t]Jos 12:2
20:9 [u]Ex 21:13; Nu 35:15
21:1 [v]Jos 14:1
21:2 [w]Jos 18:1 [x]Nu 35:2-3
21:4 [y]ver 19
21:5 [z]ver 26
21:6 [a]Ge 30:18

b *50* Also known as *Timnath Heres* (see Judges 2:9)
c *8* *Jordan of Jericho* was possibly an ancient name for the Jordan River.

and the half-tribe of Manasseh in Bashan.
7The descendants of Merari,[a] clan by clan,
received twelve towns from the tribes
of Reuben, Gad and Zebulun.[b]

8So the Israelites allotted to the Levites these towns and their pasturelands,
as the LORD had commanded through
Moses.

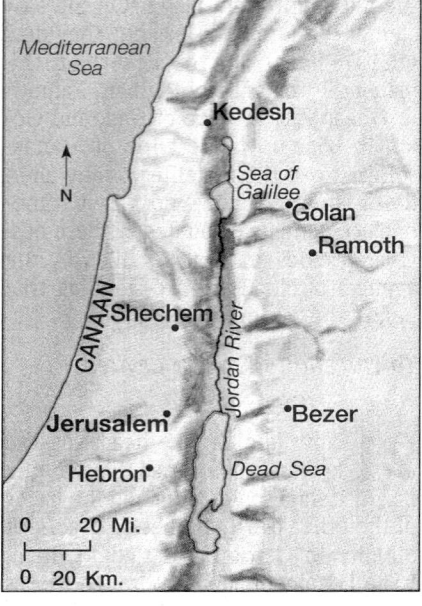

The Cities of Refuge

A city of refuge was just that–refuge for someone who committed an unintentional murder that would evoke revenge from the victim's friends and relatives. The six cities of refuge were spaced throughout the land so that a person was never too far from one.

9From the tribes of Judah and Simeon
they allotted the following towns by
name 10(these towns were assigned to
the descendants of Aaron who were
from the Kohathite clans of the Levites,
because the first lot fell to them):

11They gave them Kiriath Arba
(that is, Hebron[c]), with its surrounding pastureland, in the hill
country of Judah. (Arba was the
forefather of Anak.) 12But the fields
and villages around the city they
had given to Caleb son of Jephunneh as his possession.

13So to the descendants of Aaron
the priest they gave Hebron (a city
of refuge for one accused of murder), Libnah,[d] 14Jattir,[e] Eshtemoa,[f]
15Holon,[g] Debir, 16Ain, Juttah[h] and
Beth Shemesh,[i] together with their
pasturelands—nine towns from these
two tribes.

17And from the tribe of Benjamin
they gave them Gibeon, Geba,[j] 18An-
athoth and Almon, together with
their pasturelands—four towns.
19All the towns for the priests, the descendants of Aaron, were thirteen, together with their pasturelands.

20The rest of the Kohathite clans of the
Levites were allotted towns from the
tribe of Ephraim:

21In the hill country of Ephraim
they were given Shechem[k] (a city
of refuge for one accused of murder) and Gezer, 22Kibzaim and Beth
Horon,[l] together with their pasturelands—four towns.[m]

23Also from the tribe of Dan they
received Eltekeh, Gibbethon, 24Aija-
lon and Gath Rimmon,[n] together
with their pasturelands—four towns.

25From half the tribe of Manasseh they received Taanach and Gath
Rimmon, together with their pasturelands—two towns.
26All these ten towns and their pasturelands were given to the rest of the Kohathite clans.

27The Levite clans of the Gershonites
were given:
from the half-tribe of Manasseh,
Golan in Bashan[o] (a city of refuge
for one accused of murder[p]) and
Be Eshtarah, together with their pasturelands—two towns;
28from the tribe of Issachar,[q]
Kishion, Daberath, 29Jarmuth and
En Gannim, together with their pasturelands—four towns;
30from the tribe of Asher,[r]
Mishal, Abdon, 31Helkath and Rehob, together with their pasturelands—four towns;

21:7 [a]Ex 6:16 [b]Jos 19:10
21:11 [c]Jos 15:13; 1Ch 6:55
21:13 [d]Jos 15:42; 1Ch 6:57
21:14 [e]Jos 15:48 [f]Jos 15:50
21:15 [g]Jos 15:51
21:16 [h]Jos 15:55 [i]Jos 15:10
21:17 [j]Jos 18:24
21:21 [k]Jos 17:7; 20:7
21:22 [l]Jos 10:10 [m]1Sa 1:1
21:24 [n]Jos 19:45
21:27 [o]Jos 12:5 [p]Nu 35:6
21:28 [q]Ge 30:18
21:30 [r]Jos 17:7

32from the tribe of Naphtali,
Kedesh[a] in Galilee (a city of refuge
for one accused of murder[b]), Ham-
moth Dor and Kartan, together with
their pasturelands—three towns.
33All the towns of the Gershonite[c]
clans were thirteen, together with their
pasturelands.

34The Merarite clans (the rest of the
Levites) were given:
from the tribe of Zebulun,[d]
Jokneam, Kartah, 35Dimnah and Nahalal, together with their pasturelands—four towns;
36from the tribe of Reuben,
Bezer,[e] Jahaz, 37Kedemoth and Mephaath, together with their pasturelands—four towns;
38from the tribe of Gad,
Ramoth[f] in Gilead (a city of refuge
for one accused of murder), Mahanaim,[g] 39Heshbon and Jazer, together with their pasturelands—
four towns in all.
40All the towns allotted to the Merarite
clans, who were the rest of the Levites, were twelve.
41The towns of the Levites in the
territory held by the Israelites were
forty-eight in all, together with their pasturelands.[h] 42Each of these towns had
pasturelands surrounding it; this was
true for all these towns.

43So the LORD gave Israel all the land
he had sworn to give their forefathers,[i] and they took possession[j] of it
and settled there.[k] 44The LORD gave
them rest[l] on every side, just as he had
sworn to their forefathers. Not one of
their enemies[m] withstood them; the
LORD handed all their enemies[n] over to
them.[o] 45Not one of all the LORD's good
promises[p] to the house of Israel failed;
every one was fulfilled.

The two-and-a-half eastern tribes return home.

22 Then Joshua summoned the
Reubenites, the Gadites and the
half-tribe of Manasseh 2and said to them,

21:32 [a]Jos 12:22 [b]Nu 35:6; Jos 20:7
21:33 [c]ver 6
21:34 [d]Jos 19:10; 1Ch 6:77
21:36 [e]Jos 20:8
21:38 [f]Dt 4:43 [g]Ge 32:2
21:41 [h]Nu 35:7
21:43 [i]Dt 34:4 [j]Dt 11:31 [k]Dt 17:14
21:44 [l]Ex 33:14; Jos 1:13 [m]Dt 6:19 [n]Ex 23:31 [o]Dt 7:24; 21:10
21:45 [p]Jos 23:14; Ne 9:8
22:2 [q]Nu 32:25
22:4 [r]Nu 32:22; Dt 3:20 [s]Nu 32:18; Jos 1:13-15
22:5 [t]Isa 43:22 [u]Dt 5:29 [v]Dt 6:6,17
22:6 [w]Ex 39:43
22:7 [x]Nu 32:33; Jos 12:5 [y]Jos 17:2,5
22:8 [z]Dt 20:14 [a]Nu 31:27 [b]Ge 49:27; 1Sa 30:16; Isa 9:3
22:9 [c]Nu 32:26,29
22:12 [d]Jos 18:1

"You have done all that Moses the servant of the LORD commanded,[q] and you
have obeyed me in everything I commanded. 3For a long time now—to this
very day—you have not deserted your
brothers but have carried out the mission the LORD your God gave you. 4Now
that the LORD your God has given your
brothers rest as he promised, return to
your homes[r] in the land that Moses
the servant of the LORD gave you on the
other side of the Jordan.[s] 5But be very
careful to keep the commandment[t] and
the law that Moses the servant of the
LORD gave you: to love the LORD your
God, to walk in all his ways, to obey
his commands,[u] to hold fast to him and
to serve him with all your heart and all
your soul.[v]"
6Then Joshua blessed[w] them and sent
them away, and they went to their
homes. 7(To the half-tribe of Manasseh
Moses had given land in Bashan,[x] and
to the other half of the tribe Joshua gave
land on the west side[y] of the Jordan
with their brothers.) When Joshua sent
them home, he blessed them, 8saying,
"Return to your homes with your great
wealth—with large herds of livestock,[z]
with silver, gold, bronze and iron, and
a great quantity of clothing—and divide[a]
with your brothers the plunder[b] from
your enemies."
9So the Reubenites, the Gadites and
the half-tribe of Manasseh left the Israelites at Shiloh in Canaan to return
to Gilead,[c] their own land, which they
had acquired in accordance with the
command of the LORD through Moses.

A memorial altar is misunderstood.

10When they came to Geliloth near
the Jordan in the land of Canaan, the
Reubenites, the Gadites and the half-
tribe of Manasseh built an imposing
altar there by the Jordan. 11And when
the Israelites heard that they had built
the altar on the border of Canaan at Geliloth near the Jordan on the Israelite
side, 12the whole assembly of Israel
gathered at Shiloh[d] to go to war against
them.

13 So the Israelites sent Phinehas[a] son
of Eleazar,[b] the priest, to the land of
Gilead—to Reuben, Gad and the half-
tribe of Manasseh. 14 With him they sent
ten of the chief men, one for each of the
tribes of Israel, each the head of a family division among the Israelite clans.[c]

15 When they went to Gilead—to Reuben, Gad and the half-tribe of Manasseh—they said to them: 16 "The whole
assembly of the LORD says: 'How could
you break faith[d] with the God of Israel
like this? How could you turn away
from the LORD and build yourselves an
altar in rebellion[e] against him now?
17 Was not the sin of Peor[f] enough for
us? Up to this very day we have not
cleansed ourselves from that sin, even
though a plague fell on the community
of the LORD! 18 And are you now turning away from the LORD?

"'If you rebel against the LORD today,
tomorrow he will be angry with the
whole community[g] of Israel. 19 If the
land you possess is defiled, come over
to the LORD's land, where the LORD's tabernacle stands, and share the land with
us. But do not rebel against the LORD
or against us by building an altar for
yourselves, other than the altar of the
LORD our God. 20 When Achan son of
Zerah acted unfaithfully regarding the
devoted things,[d][h] did not wrath[i] come
upon the whole community of Israel?
He was not the only one who died for
his sin.'"[j]

21 Then Reuben, Gad and the half-
tribe of Manasseh replied to the heads
of the clans of Israel: 22 "The Mighty
One, God, the LORD! The Mighty One,
God,[k] the LORD![l] He knows![m] And let
Israel know! If this has been in rebellion or disobedience to the LORD, do
not spare us this day. 23 If we have built
our own altar to turn away from the
LORD and to offer burnt offerings and
grain offerings,[n] or to sacrifice fellowship
offerings[e] on it, may the LORD himself
call us to account.[o]

24 "No! We did it for fear that some
day your descendants might say to ours,
'What do you have to do with the LORD,
the God of Israel? 25 The LORD has made
the Jordan a boundary between us and
you—you Reubenites and Gadites! You
have no share in the LORD.' So your descendants might cause ours to stop fearing the LORD.

26 "That is why we said, 'Let us get
ready and build an altar—but not for
burnt offerings or sacrifices.' 27 On the
contrary, it is to be a witness[p] between
us and you and the generations that
follow, that we will worship the LORD
at his sanctuary with our burnt offerings, sacrifices and fellowship offerings.[q]
Then in the future your descendants will
not be able to say to ours, 'You have no
share in the LORD.'

28 "And we said, 'If they ever say this
to us, or to our descendants, we will answer: Look at the replica of the LORD's
altar, which our fathers built, not for
burnt offerings and sacrifices, but as a
witness between us and you.'

29 "Far be it from us to rebel[r] against
the LORD and turn away from him today by building an altar for burnt offerings, grain offerings and sacrifices, other
than the altar of the LORD our God that
stands before his tabernacle.[s]"

30 When Phinehas the priest and the
leaders of the community—the heads
of the clans of the Israelites—heard
what Reuben, Gad and Manasseh had
to say, they were pleased. 31 And Phinehas son of Eleazar, the priest, said to
Reuben, Gad and Manasseh, "Today we
know that the LORD is with us,[t] because you have not acted unfaithfully
toward the LORD in this matter. Now
you have rescued the Israelites from
the LORD's hand."

32 Then Phinehas son of Eleazar, the
priest, and the leaders returned to
Canaan from their meeting with the
Reubenites and Gadites in Gilead and
reported to the Israelites. 33 They were
glad to hear the report and praised
God.[u] And they talked no more about

22:13 [a]Nu 25:7 [b]Nu 3:32; Jos 24:33
22:14 [c]Nu 1:4
22:16 [d]Dt 13:14 [e]Dt 12:13-14
22:17 [f]Nu 25:1-9
22:18 [g]Lev 10:6; Nu 16:22
22:20 [h]Jos 7:1 [i]Ps 7:11 [j]Jos 7:5
22:22 [k]Dt 10:17 [l]Ps 50:1 [m]1Ki 8:39; Job 10:7; Ps 44:21; Jer 17:10
22:23 [n]Jer 41:5 [o]Dt 12:11; 18:19; 1Sa 20:16
22:27 [p]Ge 21:30; Jos 24:27 [q]Dt 12:6
22:29 [r]Jos 24:16 [s]Dt 12:13-14
22:31 [t]Lev 26:11-12; 2Ch 15:2
22:33 [u]1Ch 29:20; Da 2:19; Lk 2:28

d *20* The Hebrew term refers to the irrevocable giving over of things or persons to the LORD, often by totally destroying them. e *23* Traditionally *peace offerings*; also in verse 27

going to war against them to devastate the country where the Reubenites and the Gadites lived.

34And the Reubenites and the Gadites gave the altar this name: A Witness[a] Between Us that the LORD is God.

Joshua's farewell exhortation to the leaders.

23 After a long time had passed and the LORD had given Israel rest[b] from all their enemies around them, Joshua, by then old and well advanced in years,[c] 2summoned all Israel—their elders,[d] leaders, judges and officials[e]—and said to them: "I am old and well advanced in years. 3You yourselves have seen everything the LORD your God has done to all these nations for your sake; it was the LORD your God who fought for you.[f] 4Remember how I have allotted[g] as an inheritance for your tribes all the land of the nations that remain—the nations I conquered—between the Jordan and the Great Sea[f][h] in the west. 5The LORD your God himself will drive them out of your way. He will push them out before you, and you will take possession of their land, as the LORD your God promised you.[i]

6"Be very strong; be careful to obey all that is written in the Book of the Law of Moses, without turning aside to the right or to the left.[j] 7Do not associate with these nations that remain among you; do not invoke the names of their gods or swear[k] by them. You must not serve them or bow down[l] to them. 8But you are to hold fast to the LORD[m] your God, as you have until now.

9"The LORD has driven out before you great and powerful nations;[n] to this day no one has been able to withstand you.[o] 10One of you routs a thousand,[p] because the LORD your God fights for you,[q] just as he promised. 11So be very careful to love the LORD[r] your God.

12"But if you turn away and ally yourselves with the survivors of these nations that remain among you and if you intermarry with them[s] and associate with them,[t] 13then you may be sure that the LORD your God will no longer drive out these nations before you. Instead, they will become snares[u] and traps for you, whips on your backs and thorns in your eyes,[v] until you perish from this good land, which the LORD your God has given you.

14"Now I am about to go the way of all the earth.[w] You know with all your heart and soul that not one of all the good promises the LORD your God gave you has failed. Every promise has been fulfilled; not one has failed.[x] 15But just as every good promise of the LORD your God has come true, so the LORD will bring on you all the evil he has threatened, until he has destroyed you from this good land he has given you.[y] 16If you violate the covenant of the LORD your God, which he commanded you, and go and serve other gods and bow down to them, the LORD's anger will burn against you, and you will quickly perish from the good land he has given you.[z]"

Joshua's review of Israel's history.

24 Then Joshua assembled all the tribes of Israel at Shechem. He summoned the elders, leaders, judges and officials of Israel,[a] and they presented themselves before God.

2Joshua said to all the people, "This is what the LORD, the God of Israel, says: 'Long ago your forefathers, including Terah the father of Abraham and Nahor, lived beyond the River[g] and worshiped other gods.[b] 3But I took your father Abraham from the land beyond the River and led him throughout Canaan[c] and gave him many descendants.[d] I gave him Isaac,[e] 4and to Isaac I gave Jacob and Esau.[f] I assigned the hill country of Seir[g] to Esau, but Jacob and his sons went down to Egypt.[h]

5" 'Then I sent Moses and Aaron,[i] and I afflicted the Egyptians by what I did there, and I brought you out. 6When

22:34 [a]Ge 21:30
23:1 [b]Dt 12:9; Jos 21:44 [c]Jos 13:1
23:2 [d]Jos 7:6 [e]Jos 24:1
23:3 [f]Ex 14:14
23:4 [g]Jos 19:51 [h]Nu 34:6
23:5 [i]Ex 23:30; Nu 33:53
23:6 [j]Dt 5:32; Jos 1:7
23:7 [k]Ex 23:13; Ps 16:4; Jer 5:7 [l]Ex 20:5
23:8 [m]Dt 10:20
23:9 [n]Dt 11:23 [o]Dt 7:24
23:10 [p]Lev 26:8 [q]Ex 14:14; Dt 3:22
23:11 [r]Jos 22:5
23:12 [s]Dt 7:3 [t]Ex 34:16; Ps 106:34-35
23:13 [u]Ex 23:33 [v]Nu 33:55
23:14 [w]1Ki 2:2 [x]Jos 21:45
23:15 [y]Lev 26:17; Dt 28:15
23:16 [z]Dt 4:25-26
24:1 [a]Jos 23:2
24:2 [b]Ge 11:32
24:3 [c]Ge 12:1 [d]Ge 15:5 [e]Ge 21:3
24:4 [f]Ge 25:26 [g]Dt 2:5 [h]Ge 46:5-6
24:5 [i]Ex 3:10

f*4* That is, the Mediterranean g*2* That is, the Euphrates; also in verses 3, 14 and 15

I brought your fathers out of Egypt, you
came to the sea, and the Egyptians pursued them with chariots and horsemen[h][a] as far as the Red Sea.[i] 7But they
cried to the LORD for help, and he put
darkness[b] between you and the Egyptians; he brought the sea over them
and covered them.[c] You saw with your
own eyes what I did to the Egyptians.
Then you lived in the desert for a long
time.[d]
8"'I brought you to the land of the
Amorites who lived east of the Jordan.
They fought against you, but I gave them
into your hands. I destroyed them from
before you, and you took possession of
their land.[e] 9When Balak son of Zippor,[f] the king of Moab, prepared to
fight against Israel, he sent for Balaam
son of Beor to put a curse on you.[g]
10But I would not listen to Balaam, so
he blessed you[h] again and again, and I
delivered you out of his hand.
11"'Then you crossed the Jordan[i] and
came to Jericho.[j] The citizens of Jericho fought against you, as did also the
Amorites, Perizzites, Canaanites, Hittites, Girgashites, Hivites and Jebusites,
but I gave them into your hands.[k] 12I sent
the hornet[l] ahead of you, which drove
them out before you—also the two Amorite kings. You did not do it with your
own sword and bow. 13So I gave you a
land on which you did not toil and
cities you did not build; and you live in
them and eat from vineyards and olive
groves that you did not plant.'[m]
14"Now fear the LORD and serve him
with all faithfulness.[n] Throw away the
gods[o] your forefathers worshiped beyond the River and in Egypt,[p] and
serve the LORD. 15But if serving the LORD
seems undesirable to you, then choose
for yourselves this day whom you will
serve, whether the gods your forefathers served beyond the River, or the
gods of the Amorites,[q] in whose land
you are living. But as for me and my
household, we will serve the LORD."[r]
16Then the people answered, "Far
be it from us to forsake the LORD to serve
other gods! 17It was the LORD our God

24:6 [a]Ex 14:9
24:7 [b]Ex 14:20 [c]Ex 14:28 [d]Dt 1:46
24:8 [e]Nu 21:31
24:9 [f]Nu 22:2 [g]Nu 22:6
24:10 [h]Nu 23:11; Dt 23:5
24:11 [i]Jos 3:16-17 [j]Jos 6:1 [k]Ex 23:23; Dt 7:1
24:12 [l]Ex 23:28; Dt 7:20; Ps 44:3,6-7
24:13 [m]Dt 6:10-11
24:14 [n]Dt 10:12; 18:13; 1Sa 12:24; 2Co 1:12 [o]ver 23 [p]Eze 23:3
24:15 [q]Jdg 6:10; Ru 1:15 [r]Ru 1:16; 1Ki 18:21
24:19 [s]Lev 19:2; 20:26 [t]Ex 20:5 [u]Ex 23:21
24:20 [v]1Ch 28:9,20 [w]Ac 7:42 [x]Jos 23:15
24:22 [y]Ps 119:30,173
24:23 [z]ver 14 [a]1Ki 8:58; Ps 119:36; 141:4
24:24 [b]Ex 19:8; 24:3,7; Dt 5:27
24:25 [c]Ex 24:8 [d]Ex 15:25
24:26 [e]Dt 31:24 [f]Ge 28:18
24:27 [g]Jos 22:27

himself who brought us and our fathers
up out of Egypt, from that land of slavery, and performed those great signs
before our eyes. He protected us on
our entire journey and among all the
nations through which we traveled.
18And the LORD drove out before us all
the nations, including the Amorites,
who lived in the land. We too will serve
the LORD, because he is our God."
19Joshua said to the people, "You are
not able to serve the LORD. He is a holy
God;[s] he is a jealous God.[t] He will not
forgive your rebellion[u] and your sins.
20If you forsake the LORD[v] and serve foreign gods, he will turn[w] and bring disaster on you and make an end of you,[x]
after he has been good to you."
21But the people said to Joshua, "No!
We will serve the LORD."
22Then Joshua said, "You are witnesses against yourselves that you have
chosen[y] to serve the LORD."
"Yes, we are witnesses," they replied.
23"Now then," said Joshua, "throw
away the foreign gods[z] that are among
you and yield your hearts[a] to the LORD,
the God of Israel."
24And the people said to Joshua, "We
will serve the LORD our God and obey
him."[b]
25On that day Joshua made a covenant[c] for the people, and there at Shechem he drew up for them decrees and
laws.[d] 26And Joshua recorded these
things in the Book of the Law of God.[e]
Then he took a large stone[f] and set it
up there under the oak near the holy
place of the LORD.
27"See!" he said to all the people. "This
stone will be a witness[g] against us. It
has heard all the words the LORD has
said to us. It will be a witness against
you if you are untrue to your God."

Joshua's death and burial.

24:29-31pp—Jdg 2:6-9

28Then Joshua sent the people away,
each to his own inheritance.

[h]6 Or *charioteers* [i]6 Hebrew *Yam Suph*; that is, Sea of Reeds

29After these things, Joshua son of Nun,
the servant of the LORD, died at the age
of a hundred and ten.[a] 30And they buried him in the land of his inheritance,
at Timnath Serah[j][b] in the hill country
of Ephraim, north of Mount Gaash.
31Israel served the LORD throughout
the lifetime of Joshua and of the elders[c]
who outlived him and who had experienced everything the LORD had done
for Israel.
32And Joseph's bones, which the Israelites had brought up from Egypt,[d] were
buried at Shechem in the tract of land[e]
that Jacob bought for a hundred pieces
of silver[k] from the sons of Hamor, the
father of Shechem. This became the
inheritance of Joseph's descendants.
33And Eleazar son of Aaron[f] died and
was buried at Gibeah, which had been
allotted to his son Phinehas[g] in the hill
country of Ephraim.

24:29 [a]Jdg 2:8
24:30 [b]Jos 19:50
24:31 [c]Jdg 2:7
24:32 [d]Ge 50:25; Ex 13:19 [e]Ge 33:19; Jn 4:5; Ac 7:16
24:33 [f]Jos 22:13 [g]Ex 6:25

[j]*30* Also known as *Timnath Heres* (see Judges 2:9)
[k]*32* Hebrew *hundred kesitahs*; a kesitah was a unit of money of unknown weight and value.

JUDGES

Author: Unknown (possibly Samuel).

Date Written: Between 1043 and 1004 B.C.

Time Span: Approximately 350 years (period of time from the death of Joshua to the birth of Samuel).

Title: The book derives its title from its content about the judges of Israel, who were leaders during tribal or national emergencies at a time when there was no central government. The Hebrew title for this book, *Shopetim,* means "ruling leaders" or "judges."

Background: This book covers the period following the death of Joshua and the Israelites' initial conquest of Canaan. During this time the people, wavering between apostasy and repentance, are ruled by individual leaders called judges. The book of Judges records this era of disobedience and defeat.

Where Written: The promised land (Canaan).

To Whom: To the Israelites.

Content: Because they have not completed the conquest and occupation of the promised land, the Israelites begin to adopt the sinful ways of the surrounding nations. A tragic cycle develops: Israel falls into sin; God disciplines with foreign oppression; the people cry to God for his help; God raises up a deliverer (judge); peace is restored. This cycle of rebellion is repeated 7 times in the book, emphasizing God's love and forgiveness and the penalty for lack of faith and obedience. The stories of 3 significant judges are discussed in detail: Deborah (chapter 4); Gideon (chapters 6-8); and Samson (chapters 13-16).

Key Words: "Apostasy"; "Judgment"; "Repentance"; "Mercy." The Israelites continually fail to learn their lesson. Their "apostasy" means they will have to pay the price of "judgment" from God. But when they finally show "repentance," God will then in his "mercy" raise up a judge to lead the people to restoration and rest.

Themes: • There is always a price to be paid for our sins. • The price for sin is destruction and death. • We all need proper leadership in our lives. (The most important leader and judge for each of us today is Jesus Christ.) • Without strong leaders we are more inclined to be influenced by damaging circumstances or deceptive people. • God in his mercy will deliver us when we repent wholeheartedly of our sins and obey him. • Doing right in our own eyes is not necessarily doing right in God's eyes.

Outline:

1. Israel's failure to complete the conquest of Canaan. 1:1-3:6
2. The cycle of apostasy and deliverances. 3:7-16:31
3. Israel's fall into idolatry, immorality and civil war. 17:1-21:25

JUDGES

Israel fights the Canaanites for their land.

1:11-15pp—Jos 15:15-19

1 After the death[a] of Joshua, the Israelites asked the LORD, "Who will be the first[b] to go up and fight for us against the Canaanites?[c]"

2 The LORD answered, "Judah[d] is to go; I have given the land into their hands.[e]"

3 Then the men of Judah said to the Simeonites their brothers, "Come up with us into the territory allotted to us, to fight against the Canaanites. We in turn will go with you into yours." So the Simeonites[f] went with them.

4 When Judah attacked, the LORD gave the Canaanites and Perizzites[g] into their hands and they struck down ten thousand men at Bezek.[h] 5 It was there that they found Adoni-Bezek and fought against him, putting to rout the Canaanites and Perizzites. 6 Adoni-Bezek fled, but they chased him and caught him, and cut off his thumbs and big toes.

7 Then Adoni-Bezek said, "Seventy kings with their thumbs and big toes cut off have picked up scraps under my table. Now God has paid me back[i] for what I did to them." They brought him to Jerusalem, and he died there.

8 The men of Judah attacked Jerusalem[j] also and took it. They put the city to the sword and set it on fire.

9 After that, the men of Judah went down to fight against the Canaanites living in the hill country,[k] the Negev[l] and the western foothills. 10 They advanced against the Canaanites living in Hebron[m] (formerly called Kiriath Arba[n]) and defeated Sheshai, Ahiman and Talmai.[o]

11 From there they advanced against the people living in Debir[p] (formerly called Kiriath Sepher). 12 And Caleb said, "I will give my daughter Acsah in marriage to the man who attacks and captures Kiriath Sepher." 13 Othniel son of Kenaz, Caleb's younger brother, took it; so Caleb gave his daughter Acsah to him in marriage.

14 One day when she came to Othniel, she urged him[a] to ask her father for a field. When she got off her donkey, Caleb asked her, "What can I do for you?"

15 She replied, "Do me a special favor. Since you have given me land in the Negev, give me also springs of water." Then Caleb gave her the upper and lower springs.

16 The descendants of Moses' father-in-law,[q] the Kenite,[r] went up from the City of Palms[b][s] with the men of Judah to live among the people of the Desert of Judah in the Negev near Arad.[t]

17 Then the men of Judah went with the Simeonites[u] their brothers and attacked the Canaanites living in Zephath, and they totally destroyed[c] the city. Therefore it was called Hormah.[d][v] 18 The men of Judah also took[e] Gaza,[w] Ashkelon and Ekron—each city with its territory.

19 The LORD was with[x] the men of Judah. They took possession of the hill country, but they were unable to drive the people from the plains, because they had iron chariots.[y] 20 As Moses had promised, Hebron[z] was given to Caleb, who drove from it the three sons of Anak.[a] 21 The Benjamites, however, failed[b] to dislodge the Jebusites, who were living in Jerusalem;[c] to this day the Jebusites live there with the Benjamites.

Israel fails to take the land.

22 Now the house of Joseph attacked Bethel, and the LORD was with them. 23 When they sent men to spy out Bethel (formerly called Luz),[d] 24 the spies saw a man coming out of the city and they said to him, "Show us how to get into the city and we will see that you are treated well.[e]" 25 So he showed them, and they put the city to the sword but spared[f] the man and his whole family. 26 He then went to the land of the Hittites, where he

1:1 [a]Jos 24:29 [b]Nu 27:21 [c]ver 27; Jdg 3:1-6
1:2 [d]Ge 49:8 [e]ver 4; Jdg 3:28
1:3 [f]ver 17
1:4 [g]Ge 13:7; Jos 3:10 [h]1Sa 11:8
1:7 [i]Lev 24:19
1:8 [j]ver 21; Jos 15:63
1:9 [k]Nu 13:17 [l]Nu 21:1
1:10 [m]Ge 13:18 [n]Ge 35:27 [o]Jos 15:14
1:11 [p]Jos 15:15
1:16 [q]Nu 10:29 [r]Ge 15:19; Jdg 4:11 [s]Dt 34:3; Jdg 3:13 [t]Nu 21:1
1:17 [u]ver 3 [v]Nu 21:3
1:18 [w]Jos 11:22
1:19 [x]ver 2 [y]Jos 17:16
1:20 [z]Jos 14:9; 15:13-14 [a]ver 10; Jos 14:13
1:21 [b]Jos 15:63 [c]ver 8
1:23 [d]Ge 28:19
1:24 [e]Jos 2:12,14
1:25 [f]Jos 6:25

a *14* Hebrew; Septuagint and Vulgate *Othniel, he urged her* b *16* That is, Jericho c *17* The Hebrew term refers to the irrevocable giving over of things or persons to the LORD, often by totally destroying them. d *17* *Hormah* means *destruction.* e *18* Hebrew; Septuagint *Judah did not take*

KEY PLACES IN JUDGES

Bokim The book of Judges opens with the Israelites continuing their conquest of the promised land. Their failure to obey God and destroy all the evil inhabitants soon comes back to haunt them in two ways: (1) the enemies reorganized and counterattacked, and (2) Israel turned away from God, adopting the evil and idolatrous practices of the inhabitants of the land. The angel of the Lord appeared at Bokim to inform the Israelites that their sin and disobedience had broken their agreement with God and would result in punishment through oppression (1:1–3:11).

Jericho The nation of Moab was one of the first to oppress Israel. Moab's King Eglon conquered much of Israel–including the city of Jericho ("the City of Palms")—and forced the people to pay unreasonable taxes. The messenger chosen to deliver this tax money to King Eglon was named Ehud. But he had more than money to deliver, for he drew his hidden sword and killed the Moabite king. Ehud then escaped, only to return with an army that chased out the Moabites and freed Israel from its oppressors (3:12-31).

Hazor After Ehud's death, King Jabin of Hazor conquered Israel and oppressed the people for 20 years. Then Deborah became Israel's leader. She summoned Barak to fight Commander Sisera, the leader of King Jabin's army. Together Deborah and Barak led their army into battle against Jabin's forces in the land between Mount Tabor and the Kishon River and conquered them (4:1–5:31).

Hill of Moreh After 40 years of peace, the Midianites began to harass the Israelites by destroying their flocks and crops. When the Israelites finally cried out to God, he chose Gideon, a poor and humble farmer, to be their deliverer. After struggling with doubt and feelings of inferiority, Gideon took courage and knocked down his town's altar to Baal, causing a great uproar among the citizens. Filled with the Spirit of God, he attacked the vast army of Midian, which was camped near the hill of Moreh. With just a handful of men he sent the enemy running away in confusion (6:1–7:25).

Shechem Even great leaders make mistakes. Gideon's relations with a concubine in Shechem resulted in the birth of a son named Abimelech. Abimelech turned out to be treacherous and power hungry–stirring up the people to proclaim him king. To carry out his plan, he went so far as to kill 69 of his 70 half brothers. Eventually, some men of Shechem rebelled against Abimelech, but he gathered together an army and defeated them. His lust for power led him to ransack two other cities, but he was killed by a woman who dropped a millstone onto his head (8:28–9:57).

Land of Ammon Again Israel turned completely from God; so God turned from them. But when the Ammonites mobilized their army to attack, Israel threw away her idols and called upon God once again. Jephthah, a prostitute's son who had been run out of Israel, was asked to return and lead Israel's forces against the enemy. After defeating the Ammonites, Jephthah became involved in a war with the tribe of Ephraim over a misunderstanding (10:1–12:15).

Timnah Israel's next judge, Samson, was a miracle child promised by God to a barren couple. He was the one who would begin to free Israel from their next and most powerful oppressor, the Philistines. According to God's command, Samson was to be a Nazirite–one who took a vow to be set apart for special service to God. One of the stipulations of the vow was that Samson's hair could never be cut. But when Samson grew up, he did not always take his responsibility to God seriously. He even fell in love with a Philistine girl in Timnah and asked to marry her. Before the wedding, Samson held a party for some men in the city, using a riddle to place a bet with them. The men, however, forced Samson's fiancée into giving the answer. Furious at being tricked, Samson paid his bet with the lives of 30 Philistines who lived in the nearby city of Ashkelon (13:1–14:20).

Valley of Sorek Samson killed thousands of Philistines with his incredible strength. The nation's leaders looked for a way to stop him. They got their chance when another Philistine woman stole Samson's heart. Her name was Delilah, and she lived in the Valley of Sorek. In exchange for a great sum of money, Delilah deceived Samson into confiding in her the secret of his strength. One night while he slept, Delilah cut off his hair. As a result, Samson fell helplessly into the hands of the enemy (15:1–16:20).

Gaza Samson was blinded and led captive to a prison in Gaza. There his hair began to grow again. After a while, the Philistines held a great festival to celebrate Samson's imprisonment and to humiliate him before the crowds.When he was brought out as the entertainment, he literally brought down the house when he pushed on the main pillars of the banquet hall and killed thousands trapped inside. The prophecy that he would begin to free Israel from the Philistines had come true (16:21-31).

Hill Country of Ephraim In the hill country of Ephraim lived a man named Micah. Micah hired his own priest to perform priestly duties in the shrine which housed his collection of idols. He thought he was pleasing God with all his religiosity! Like many of the Israelites, Micah assumed that his own opinions of what was right would agree with God's (17:1-13).

Dan The tribe of Dan migrated north in order to find new territory. They sent spies ahead of them to scout out the land. One night the spies stopped at Micah's home. Looking for some assurance of victory, the spies stole Micah's idols and priest. Rejoining the tribe, they came upon the city of Laish and slaughtered the unarmed and innocent citizens, renaming the conquered city Dan. Micah's idols were then set up in the city and became the focal point of the tribe's worship for many years (18:1-31).

Gibeah The extent to which many people had fallen away from God became clear in Gibeah, a village in the territory of Benjamin. A man and his concubine were traveling north toward the hill country of Ephraim. They stopped for the night in Gibeah, thinking they would be safe. But some perverts in the city gathered around the home where they were staying and demanded that the man come out and have sexual relations with them. Instead, the man and his host pushed the concubine out the door. She was raped and abused all night. When the man found her lifeless body the next morning, he cut it into 12 pieces and sent the parts to each tribe of Israel. This tragic event demonstrated that the nation had sunk to its lowest spiritual level (19:1-30).

Mizpah The leaders of Israel came to Mizpah to decide how to punish the wicked men from the city of Gibeah. When the city leaders refused to turn the criminals over, the whole nation of Israel took vengeance upon both Gibeah and the tribe of Benjamin where the city was located. When the battle ended, the entire tribe had been destroyed except for a handful of men who took refuge in the hills. Israel had become morally depraved. The stage was now set for the much-needed spiritual renewal that would come under the prophet Samuel (20:1–21:25).

built a city and called it Luz, which is its
name to this day.
27But Manasseh did not drive out the
people of Beth Shan or Taanach or Dor or
Ibleam[a] or Megiddo and their surrounding
settlements, for the Canaanites[b] were
determined to live in that land. 28When
Israel became strong, they pressed the
Canaanites into forced labor but never
drove them out completely. 29Nor did
Ephraim drive out the Canaanites living
in Gezer,[c] but the Canaanites continued
to live there among them.[d] 30Neither did
Zebulun drive out the Canaanites living
in Kitron or Nahalol, who remained
among them; but they did subject them
to forced labor. 31Nor did Asher drive out
those living in Acco or Sidon or Ahlab
or Aczib[e] or Helbah or Aphek or Rehob,
32and because of this the people of Asher
lived among the Canaanite inhabitants of
the land. 33Neither did Naphtali drive out
those living in Beth Shemesh or Beth
Anath[f]; but the Naphtalites too lived
among the Canaanite inhabitants of the
land, and those living in Beth Shemesh
and Beth Anath became forced laborers
for them. 34The Amorites[g] confined the
Danites to the hill country, not allowing
them to come down into the plain. 35And
the Amorites were determined also to
hold out in Mount Heres, Aijalon[h] and
Shaalbim, but when the power of the
house of Joseph increased, they too were
pressed into forced labor. 36The boundary of the Amorites was from Scorpion[f]
Pass[i] to Sela and beyond.

The angel's rebuke of Israel.

2 The angel of the LORD[j] went up from
Gilgal to Bokim[k] and said, "I brought
you up out of Egypt[l] and led you into the
land that I swore to give to your forefathers.[m] I said, 'I will never break my covenant with you,[n] 2and you shall not make
a covenant with the people of this land,[o]
but you shall break down their altars.[p]'
Yet you have disobeyed me. Why have
you done this? 3Now therefore I tell you
that I will not drive them out before
you;[q] they will be ⌊thorns⌋[r] in your sides
and their gods will be a snare[s] to you."

1:27 [a]Jos 17:11 [b]ver 1
1:29 [c]1Ki 9:16 [d]Jos 16:10
1:31 [e]Jdg 10:6
1:33 [f]Jos 19:38
1:34 [g]Ex 3:17
1:35 [h]Jos 19:42
1:36 [i]Jos 15:3
2:1 [j]Jdg 6:11 [k]ver 5 [l]Ex 20:2 [m]Ge 17:8 [n]Lev 26:42-44; Dt 7:9
2:2 [o]Ex 23:32; 34:12; Dt 7:2 [p]Ex 34:13
2:3 [q]Jos 23:13 [r]Nu 33:55 [s]Dt 7:16; Jdg 3:6; Ps 106:36

[f]36 Hebrew *Akrabbim*

4When the angel of the LORD had spoken these things to all the Israelites, the people wept aloud, 5and they called that place Bokim.[g] There they offered sacrifices to the LORD.

Joshua's death and burial.

2:6-9pp—Jos 24:29-31

6After Joshua had dismissed the Israelites, they went to take possession of the land, each to his own inheritance. 7The people served the LORD throughout the lifetime of Joshua and of the elders who outlived him and who had seen all the great things the LORD had done for Israel.

8Joshua son of Nun, the servant of the LORD, died at the age of a hundred and ten. 9And they buried him in the land of his inheritance, at Timnath Heres[h] [a] in the hill country of Ephraim, north of Mount Gaash.

Israel's judgment.

10After that whole generation had been gathered to their fathers, another generation grew up, who knew neither the LORD nor what he had done for Israel.[b] 11Then the Israelites did evil in the eyes of the LORD[c] and served the Baals.[d] 12They forsook the LORD, the God of their fathers, who had brought them out of Egypt. They followed and worshiped various gods[e] of the peoples around them.[f] They provoked the LORD to anger 13because they forsook him and served Baal and the Ashtoreths.[g] 14In his anger[h] against Israel the LORD handed them over[i] to raiders who plundered them. He sold them[j] to their enemies all around, whom they were no longer able to resist.[k] 15Whenever Israel went out to fight, the hand of the LORD was against them to defeat them, just as he had sworn to them. They were in great distress.

16Then the LORD raised up judges,[i] [l] who saved[m] them out of the hands of these raiders. 17Yet they would not listen to their judges but prostituted[n] themselves to other gods and worshiped them. Unlike their fathers, they quickly turned from the way in which their fathers had walked, the way of obedience to the LORD's commands.[o] 18Whenever the LORD raised up a judge for them, he was with the judge and saved them out of the hands of their enemies as long as the judge lived; for the LORD had compassion[p] on them as they groaned[q] under those who oppressed and afflicted them. 19But when the judge died, the people returned to ways even more corrupt[r] than those of their fathers, following other gods and serving and worshiping them.[s] They refused to give up their evil practices and stubborn ways.

20Therefore the LORD was very angry[t] with Israel and said, "Because this nation has violated the covenant that I laid down for their forefathers and has not listened to me, 21I will no longer drive out[u] before them any of the nations Joshua left when he died. 22I will use them to test[v] Israel and see whether they will keep the way of the LORD and walk in it as their forefathers did." 23The LORD had allowed those nations to remain; he did not drive them out at once by giving them into the hands of Joshua.

God leaves nations to test the Israelites.

3 These are the nations the LORD left to test[w] all those Israelites who had not experienced any of the wars in Canaan 2(he did this only to teach warfare to the descendants of the Israelites who had not had previous battle experience): 3the five[x] rulers of the Philistines, all the Canaanites, the Sidonians, and the Hivites living in the Lebanon mountains from Mount Baal Hermon to Lebo[j] Hamath. 4They were left to test[y] the Israelites to see whether they would obey the LORD's commands, which he had given their forefathers through Moses.

5The Israelites lived[z] among the Canaanites, Hittites, Amorites, Perizzites, Hivites and Jebusites. 6They took their

2:9 [a]Jos 19:50
2:10 [b]Ex 5:2; 1Sa 2:12; 1Ch 28:9; Gal 4:8
2:11 [c]Jdg 3:12; 4:1; 6:1; 10:6 [d]Jdg 3:7; 8:33
2:12 [e]Ps 106:36 [f]Dt 31:16; Jdg 10:6
2:13 [g]Jdg 10:6
2:14 [h]Dt 31:17 [i]Ps 106:41 [j]Dt 32:30; Jdg 3:8 [k]Dt 28:25
2:16 [l]Ac 13:20 [m]Ps 106:43
2:17 [n]Ex 34:15 [o]ver 7
2:18 [p]Dt 32:36; Jos 1:5 [q]Ps 106:44
2:19 [r]Jdg 3:12 [s]Jdg 4:1; 8:33
2:20 [t]ver 14; Jos 23:16
2:21 [u]Jos 23:13
2:22 [v]Dt 8:2,16; Jdg 3:1,14
3:1 [w]Jdg 2:21-22
3:3 [x]Jos 13:3
3:4 [y]Dt 8:2; Jdg 2:22
3:5 [z]Ps 106:35

g5 *Bokim* means *weepers.* h9 Also known as *Timnath Serah* (see Joshua 19:50 and 24:30) i16 Or *leaders*; similarly in verses 17-19 j3 Or *to the entrance to*

daughters in marriage and gave their own
daughters to their sons, and served their
gods.[a]

Othniel delivers Israel from Aram.

7The Israelites did evil in the eyes of
the LORD; they forgot the LORD[b] their God
and served the Baals and the Asherahs.[c]
8The anger of the LORD burned against Israel so that he sold[d] them into the hands
of Cushan-Rishathaim king of Aram
Naharaim,[k] to whom the Israelites were
subject for eight years. 9But when they
cried out[e] to the LORD, he raised up for
them a deliverer, Othniel[f] son of Kenaz,
Caleb's younger brother, who saved
them. 10The Spirit of the LORD came upon
him,[g] so that he became Israel's judge[l]
and went to war. The LORD gave Cushan-
Rishathaim king of Aram into the hands
of Othniel, who overpowered him. 11So
the land had peace for forty years, until
Othniel son of Kenaz died.

Ehud delivers Israel from Moab.

12Once again the Israelites did evil in
the eyes of the LORD,[h] and because they
did this evil the LORD gave Eglon king of
Moab[i] power over Israel. 13Getting the
Ammonites and Amalekites to join him,
Eglon came and attacked Israel, and they
took possession of the City of Palms.[m][j]
14The Israelites were subject to Eglon
king of Moab for eighteen years.
15Again the Israelites cried out to the
LORD, and he gave them a deliverer[k]—
Ehud, a left-handed man, the son of Gera
the Benjamite. The Israelites sent him
with tribute to Eglon king of Moab.
16Now Ehud had made a double-edged
sword about a foot and a half[n] long,
which he strapped to his right thigh under his clothing. 17He presented the tribute to Eglon king of Moab, who was a
very fat man.[l] 18After Ehud had presented the tribute, he sent on their way the
men who had carried it. 19At the idols[o]
near Gilgal he himself turned back and
said, "I have a secret message for you,
O king."
The king said, "Quiet!" And all his
attendants left him.
20Ehud then approached him while
he was sitting alone in the upper room of
his summer palace[p] and said, "I have a
message from God for you." As the king
rose from his seat, 21Ehud reached with
his left hand, drew the sword from his
right thigh and plunged it into the king's
belly. 22Even the handle sank in after the
blade, which came out his back. Ehud did
not pull the sword out, and the fat closed
in over it. 23Then Ehud went out to the
porch[q]; he shut the doors of the upper
room behind him and locked them.
24After he had gone, the servants came
and found the doors of the upper room
locked. They said, "He must be relieving
himself[m] in the inner room of the
house." 25They waited to the point of
embarrassment,[n] but when he did not
open the doors of the room, they took a
key and unlocked them. There they saw
their lord fallen to the floor, dead.
26While they waited, Ehud got away.
He passed by the idols and escaped to
Seirah. 27When he arrived there, he blew
a trumpet[o] in the hill country of Ephraim,
and the Israelites went down with him
from the hills, with him leading them.
28"Follow me," he ordered, "for the
LORD has given Moab, your enemy, into
your hands.[p]" So they followed him
down and, taking possession of the fords
of the Jordan[q] that led to Moab, they
allowed no one to cross over. 29At that
time they struck down about ten thousand Moabites, all vigorous and strong;
not a man escaped. 30That day Moab was
made subject to Israel, and the land had
peace[r] for eighty years.

Shamgar delivers Israel from 600 Philistines.

31After Ehud came Shamgar son of
Anath,[s] who struck down six hundred[t]

3:6 [a]Ex 34:16; Dt 7:3-4
3:7 [b]Dt 4:9 [c]Ex 34:13; Jdg 2:11,13
3:8 [d]Jdg 2:14
3:9 [e]ver 15; Jdg 6:6,7; 10:10; Ps 106:44 [f]Jdg 1:13
3:10 [g]Nu 11:25,29; 24:2; Jdg 6:34; 11:29; 13:25; 14:6,19; 1Sa 11:6
3:12 [h]Jdg 2:11,14 [i]1Sa 12:9
3:13 [j]Jdg 1:16
3:15 [k]ver 9; Ps 78:34; 107:13
3:17 [l]ver 12
3:24 [m]1Sa 24:3
3:25 [n]2Ki 2:17; 8:11
3:27 [o]Jdg 6:34; 1Sa 13:3
3:28 [p]Jdg 7:9,15 [q]Jos 2:7; Jdg 7:24; 12:5
3:30 [r]ver 11
3:31 [s]Jdg 5:6 [t]Jos 23:10

[k]*8* That is, Northwest Mesopotamia [l]*10* Or *leader* [m]*13* That is, Jericho [n]*16* Hebrew *a cubit* (about 0.5 meter) [o]*19* Or *the stone quarries*; also in verse 26 [p]*20* The meaning of the Hebrew for this phrase is uncertain. [q]*23* The meaning of the Hebrew for this word is uncertain.

Philistines with an oxgoad. He too saved Israel.

Deborah and Barak's victory over Jabin and Sisera.

4 After Ehud died, the Israelites once again did evil[a] in the eyes of the LORD. 2So the LORD sold them into the hands of Jabin, a king of Canaan, who reigned in Hazor.[b] The commander of his army was Sisera,[c] who lived in Harosheth Haggoyim. 3Because he had nine hundred iron chariots[d] and had cruelly oppressed[e] the Israelites for twenty years, they cried to the LORD for help.

4Deborah, a prophetess, the wife of Lappidoth, was leading[r] Israel at that time. 5She held court under the Palm of Deborah between Ramah and Bethel[f] in the hill country of Ephraim, and the Israelites came to her to have their disputes decided. 6She sent for Barak son of Abinoam[g] from Kedesh in Naphtali and said to him, "The LORD, the God of Israel, commands you: 'Go, take with you ten thousand men of Naphtali and Zebulun and lead the way to Mount Tabor. 7I will lure Sisera, the commander of Jabin's army, with his chariots and his troops to the Kishon River[h] and give him into your hands.' "

8Barak said to her, "If you go with me, I will go; but if you don't go with me, I won't go."

9"Very well," Deborah said, "I will go with you. But because of the way you are going about this,[s] the honor will not be yours, for the LORD will hand Sisera over to a woman." So Deborah went with Barak to Kedesh,[i] 10where he summoned[j] Zebulun and Naphtali. Ten thousand men followed him, and Deborah also went with him.

11Now Heber the Kenite had left the other Kenites,[k] the descendants of Hobab,[l] Moses' brother-in-law,[t] and pitched his tent by the great tree in Zaanannim[m] near Kedesh.

12When they told Sisera that Barak son of Abinoam had gone up to Mount Tabor, 13Sisera gathered together his nine hundred iron chariots[n] and all the men with him, from Harosheth Haggoyim to the Kishon River.

14Then Deborah said to Barak, "Go! This is the day the LORD has given Sisera into your hands. Has not the LORD gone ahead[o] of you?" So Barak went down Mount Tabor, followed by ten thousand men. 15At Barak's advance, the LORD routed[p] Sisera and all his chariots and army by the sword, and Sisera abandoned his chariot and fled on foot. 16But Barak pursued the chariots and army as far as Harosheth Haggoyim. All the troops of Sisera fell by the sword; not a man was left.[q]

17Sisera, however, fled on foot to the tent of Jael, the wife of Heber the Kenite, because there were friendly relations between Jabin king of Hazor and the clan of Heber the Kenite.

18Jael went out to meet Sisera and said to him, "Come, my lord, come right in. Don't be afraid." So he entered her tent, and she put a covering over him.

19"I'm thirsty," he said. "Please give me some water." She opened a skin of milk,[r] gave him a drink, and covered him up.

20"Stand in the doorway of the tent," he told her. "If someone comes by and asks you, 'Is anyone here?' say 'No.' "

21But Jael, Heber's wife, picked up a tent peg and a hammer and went quietly to him while he lay fast asleep, exhausted. She drove the peg through his temple into the ground, and he died.[s]

22Barak came by in pursuit of Sisera, and Jael went out to meet him. "Come," she said, "I will show you the man you're looking for." So he went in with her, and there lay Sisera with the tent peg through his temple—dead.

23On that day God subdued[t] Jabin, the Canaanite king, before the Israelites. 24And the hand of the Israelites grew stronger and stronger against Jabin, the Canaanite king, until they destroyed him.

4:1 [a]Jdg 2:19
4:2 [b]Jos 11:1 [c]ver 13,16; 1Sa 12:9; Ps 83:9
4:3 [d]Jdg 1:19 [e]Ps 106:42
4:5 [f]Ge 35:8
4:6 [g]Heb 11:32
4:7 [h]Ps 83:9
4:9 [i]ver 21; Jdg 2:14
4:10 [j]ver 14; Jdg 5:15,18
4:11 [k]Jdg 1:16 [l]Nu 10:29 [m]Jos 19:33
4:13 [n]ver 3
4:14 [o]Dt 9:3; 2Sa 5:24; Ps 68:7
4:15 [p]Jos 10:10; Ps 83:9-10
4:16 [q]Ex 14:28; Ps 83:9
4:19 [r]Jdg 5:25
4:21 [s]Jdg 5:26
4:23 [t]Ne 9:24; Ps 18:47

r4 Traditionally *judging* s9 Or *But on the expedition you are undertaking* t11 Or *father-in-law*

The song of Deborah and Barak.

5 On that day Deborah and Barak son of Abinoam sang this song:[a]

[2]"When the princes in Israel take the
lead,
when the people willingly offer[b]
themselves—
praise the LORD![c]

[3]"Hear this, you kings! Listen, you
rulers!
I will sing to[u] the LORD, I will sing;
I will make music to[v] the LORD,
the God of Israel.[d]

[4]"O LORD, when you went out from
Seir,[e]
when you marched from the land
of Edom,
the earth shook, the heavens poured,
the clouds poured down water.[f]
[5]The mountains quaked[g] before the
LORD, the One of Sinai,
before the LORD, the God of Israel.

[6]"In the days of Shamgar son of Anath,[h]
in the days of Jael,[i] the roads[j] were
abandoned;
travelers took to winding paths.
[7]Village life[w] in Israel ceased,
ceased until I,[x] Deborah, arose,
arose a mother in Israel.
[8]When they chose new gods,[k]
war came to the city gates,
and not a shield or spear was seen
among forty thousand in Israel.
[9]My heart is with Israel's princes,
with the willing volunteers[l] among
the people.
Praise the LORD!

[10]"You who ride on white donkeys,[m]
sitting on your saddle blankets,
and you who walk along the road,
consider [11]the voice of the singers[y]
at the watering places.
They recite the righteous acts[n] of
the LORD,
the righteous acts of his warriors[z]
in Israel.

"Then the people of the LORD
went down to the city gates.[o]

[12]'Wake up,[p] wake up, Deborah!
Wake up, wake up, break out in
song!
Arise, O Barak!
Take captive your captives,[q] O son
of Abinoam.'

[13]"Then the men who were left
came down to the nobles;
the people of the LORD
came to me with the mighty.
[14]Some came from Ephraim, whose
roots were in Amalek;[r]
Benjamin was with the people who
followed you.
From Makir captains came down,
from Zebulun those who bear a
commander's staff.
[15]The princes of Issachar were with
Deborah;[s]
yes, Issachar was with Barak,
rushing after him into the valley.
In the districts of Reuben
there was much searching of heart.
[16]Why did you stay among the
campfires[a]
to hear the whistling for the flocks?[t]
In the districts of Reuben
there was much searching of heart.
[17]Gilead stayed beyond the Jordan.
And Dan, why did he linger by the
ships?
Asher remained on the coast[u]
and stayed in his coves.
[18]The people of Zebulun risked their
very lives;
so did Naphtali on the heights of
the field.[v]

[19]"Kings came[w], they fought;
the kings of Canaan fought
at Taanach by the waters of
Megiddo,[x]
but they carried off no silver, no
plunder.[y]
[20]From the heavens[z] the stars fought,
from their courses they fought
against Sisera.

5:1 [a]Ex 15:1
5:2 [b]2Ch 17:16; Ps 110:3 [c]ver 9
5:3 [d]Ps 27:6
5:4 [e]Dt 33:2 [f]Ps 68:8
5:5 [g]Ex 19:18; Ps 68:8; 97:5; Isa 64:3
5:6 [h]Jdg 3:31 [i]Jdg 4:17 [j]Isa 33:8
5:8 [k]Dt 32:17
5:9 [l]ver 2
5:10 [m]Jdg 10:4; 12:14
5:11 [n]1Sa 12:7; Mic 6:5 [o]ver 8
5:12 [p]Ps 57:8 [q]Ps 68:18; Eph 4:8
5:14 [r]Jdg 3:13
5:15 [s]Jdg 4:10
5:16 [t]Nu 32:1
5:17 [u]Jos 19:29
5:18 [v]Jdg 4:6,10
5:19 [w]Jos 11:5; Jdg 4:13 [x]Jdg 1:27 [y]ver 30
5:20 [z]Jos 10:11

[u]*3* Or *of* [v]*3* Or / *with song I will praise* [w]*7* Or *Warriors* [x]*7* Or *you* [y]*11* Or *archers*; the meaning of the Hebrew for this word is uncertain. [z]*11* Or *villagers* [a]*16* Or *saddlebags*

21The river Kishon[a] swept them away,
the age-old river, the river Kishon.
March on, my soul; be strong!
22Then thundered the horses' hoofs—
galloping, galloping go his mighty steeds.
23'Curse Meroz,' said the angel of the LORD.
'Curse its people bitterly,
because they did not come to help the LORD,
to help the LORD against the mighty.'

24"Most blessed of women be Jael,[b]
the wife of Heber the Kenite,
most blessed of tent-dwelling women.
25He asked for water, and she gave him milk;[c]
in a bowl fit for nobles she brought him curdled milk.
26Her hand reached for the tent peg,
her right hand for the workman's hammer.
She struck Sisera, she crushed his head,
she shattered and pierced his temple.[d]
27At her feet he sank,
he fell; there he lay.
At her feet he sank, he fell;
where he sank, there he fell—dead.

28"Through the window peered Sisera's mother;
behind the lattice she cried out,[e]
'Why is his chariot so long in coming?
Why is the clatter of his chariots delayed?'
29The wisest of her ladies answer her;
indeed, she keeps saying to herself,
30'Are they not finding and dividing the spoils:[f]
a girl or two for each man,
colorful garments as plunder for Sisera,
colorful garments embroidered,
highly embroidered garments for my neck—
all this as plunder?'

31"So may all your enemies perish, O LORD!
But may they who love you be like the sun[g]
when it rises in its strength."

Then the land had peace[h] forty years.

Midian oppresses Israel.

6 Again the Israelites did evil in the
eyes of the LORD,[i] and for seven
years he gave them into the hands of
the Midianites.[j] 2Because the power of
Midian was so oppressive,[k] the Israelites
prepared shelters for themselves in
mountain clefts, caves and strongholds.[l]
3Whenever the Israelites planted their
crops, the Midianites, Amalekites[m] and
other eastern peoples invaded the country. 4They camped on the land and ruined
the crops[n] all the way to Gaza and did
not spare a living thing for Israel, neither
sheep nor cattle nor donkeys. 5They
came up with their livestock and their
tents like swarms of locusts.[o] It was
impossible to count the men and their
camels;[p] they invaded the land to ravage
it. 6Midian so impoverished the Israelites
that they cried out[q] to the LORD for help.
7When the Israelites cried to the LORD
because of Midian, 8he sent them a
prophet, who said, "This is what the
LORD, the God of Israel, says: I brought
you up out of Egypt,[r] out of the land of
slavery. 9I snatched you from the power of Egypt and from the hand of all your
oppressors. I drove them from before you
and gave you their land.[s] 10I said to you,
'I am the LORD your God; do not worship[t] the gods of the Amorites,[u] in whose
land you live.' But you have not listened
to me."

The angel sends Gideon to deliver Israel.

11The angel of the LORD[v] came and sat
down under the oak in Ophrah that belonged to Joash the Abiezrite,[w] where his
son Gideon[x] was threshing wheat in a
winepress to keep it from the Midianites.
12When the angel of the LORD appeared to
Gideon, he said, "The LORD is with you,[y]
mighty warrior."

5:21 [a]Jdg 4:7
5:24 [b]Jdg 4:17
5:25 [c]Jdg 4:19
5:26 [d]Jdg 4:21
5:28 [e]Pr 7:6
5:30 [f]Ex 15:9; 1Sa 30:24
5:31 [g]2Sa 23:4; Ps 19:4; 89:36 [h]Jdg 3:11
6:1 [i]Jdg 2:11 [j]Nu 25:15-18; 31:1-3
6:2 [k]1Sa 13:6; Isa 8:21 [l]Heb 11:38
6:3 [m]Jdg 3:13
6:4 [n]Lev 26:16; Dt 28:30,51
6:5 [o]Jdg 7:12 [p]Jdg 8:10
6:6 [q]Jdg 3:9
6:8 [r]Jdg 2:1
6:9 [s]Ps 44:2
6:10 [t]2Ki 17:35 [u]Jer 10:2
6:11 [v]Ge 16:7 [w]Jos 17:2 [x]Heb 11:32
6:12 [y]Jos 1:5; Jdg 13:3; Lk 1:11,28

13“But sir,” Gideon replied, “if the LORD is with us, why has all this happened to us? Where are all his wonders that our fathers told[a] us about when they said, ‘Did not the LORD bring us up out of Egypt?’ But now the LORD has abandoned[b] us and put us into the hand of Midian.”

14The LORD turned to him and said, “Go in the strength you have[c] and save Israel out of Midian’s hand. Am I not sending you?”

15“But Lord,[b]” Gideon asked, “how can I save Israel? My clan is the weakest in Manasseh, and I am the least in my family.[d]”

16The LORD answered, “I will be with you[e], and you will strike down all the Midianites together.”

17Gideon replied, “If now I have found favor in your eyes, give me a sign[f] that it is really you talking to me. 18Please do not go away until I come back and bring my offering and set it before you.”

And the LORD said, “I will wait until you return.”

19Gideon went in, prepared a young goat, and from an ephah[c] of flour he made bread without yeast. Putting the meat in a basket and its broth in a pot, he brought them out and offered them to him under the oak.[g]

20The angel of God said to him, “Take the meat and the unleavened bread, place them on this rock,[h] and pour out the broth.” And Gideon did so. 21With the tip of the staff that was in his hand, the angel of the LORD touched the meat and the unleavened bread.[i] Fire flared from the rock, consuming the meat and the bread. And the angel of the LORD disappeared.

22When Gideon realized[j] that it was the angel of the LORD, he exclaimed, “Ah, Sovereign LORD! I have seen the angel of the LORD face to face!”[k]

23But the LORD said to him, “Peace! Do not be afraid.[l] You are not going to die.”

24So Gideon built an altar to the LORD there and called[m] it The LORD is Peace. To this day it stands in Ophrah[n] of the Abiezrites.

6:13 [a]Ps 44:1 [b]2Ch 15:2
6:14 [c]Heb 11:34
6:15 [d]Ex 3:11; 1Sa 9:21
6:16 [e]Ex 3:12; Jos 1:5
6:17 [f]ver 36-37; Ge 24:14; Isa 38:7-8
6:19 [g]Ge 18:7-8
6:20 [h]Jdg 13:19
6:21 [i]Lev 9:24
6:22 [j]Jdg 13:16,21 [k]Ge 32:30; Ex 33:20; Jdg 13:22
6:23 [l]Da 10:19
6:24 [m]Ge 22:14 [n]Jdg 8:32
6:25 [o]Ex 34:13; Dt 7:5
6:28 [p]1Ki 16:32
6:32 [q]Jdg 7:1; 8:29,35; 1Sa 12:11
6:33 [r]ver 3 [s]Jos 17:16
6:34 [t]Jdg 3:10; 1Ch 12:18; 2Ch 24:20

Gideon destroys Baal’s altar.

25That same night the LORD said to him, “Take the second bull from your father’s herd, the one seven years old.[d] Tear down your father’s altar to Baal and cut down the Asherah pole[e][o] beside it. 26Then build a proper kind of[f] altar to the LORD your God on the top of this height. Using the wood of the Asherah pole that you cut down, offer the second[g] bull as a burnt offering.”

27So Gideon took ten of his servants and did as the LORD told him. But because he was afraid of his family and the men of the town, he did it at night rather than in the daytime.

28In the morning when the men of the town got up, there was Baal’s altar,[p] demolished, with the Asherah pole beside it cut down and the second bull sacrificed on the newly built altar!

29They asked each other, “Who did this?”

When they carefully investigated, they were told, “Gideon son of Joash did it.”

30The men of the town demanded of Joash, “Bring out your son. He must die, because he has broken down Baal’s altar and cut down the Asherah pole beside it.”

31But Joash replied to the hostile crowd around him, “Are you going to plead Baal’s cause? Are you trying to save him? Whoever fights for him shall be put to death by morning! If Baal really is a god, he can defend himself when someone breaks down his altar.” 32So that day they called Gideon “Jerub-Baal,[h][q]” saying, “Let Baal contend with him,” because he broke down Baal’s altar.

33Now all the Midianites, Amalekites and other eastern peoples[r] joined forces and crossed over the Jordan and camped in the Valley of Jezreel.[s] 34Then the Spirit of the LORD came upon[t] Gideon, and he

b *15* Or *sir* c *19* That is, probably about 3/5 bushel (about 22 liters) d *25* Or *Take a full-grown, mature bull from your father’s herd* e *25* That is, a symbol of the goddess Asherah; here and elsewhere in Judges f *26* Or *build with layers of stone an* g *26* Or *full-grown*; also in verse 28 h *32* *Jerub-Baal* means *let Baal contend.*

blew a trumpet,[a] summoning the Abiezrites to follow him. 35He sent messengers
throughout Manasseh, calling them to
arms, and also into Asher, Zebulun and
Naphtali,[b] so that they too went up to
meet them.

Gideon tests God with a fleece.

36Gideon said to God, "If you will
save[c] Israel by my hand as you have
promised— 37look, I will place a wool
fleece on the threshing floor.[d] If there is
dew only on the fleece and all the ground
is dry, then I will know[e] that you will
save Israel by my hand, as you said."
38And that is what happened. Gideon
rose early the next day; he squeezed the
fleece and wrung out the dew—a bowlful
of water.
39Then Gideon said to God, "Do not be
angry with me. Let me make just one
more request.[f] Allow me one more test
with the fleece. This time make the
fleece dry and the ground covered with
dew." 40That night God did so. Only the
fleece was dry; all the ground was covered with dew.

Gideon selects an army of 300 men.

7 Early in the morning, Jerub-Baal[g]
(that is, Gideon) and all his men
camped at the spring of Harod. The camp
of Midian was north of them in the valley
near the hill of Moreh.[h] 2The LORD said
to Gideon, "You have too many men for
me to deliver Midian into their hands. In
order that Israel may not boast against
me that her own strength[i] has saved her,
3announce now to the people, 'Anyone
who trembles with fear may turn back
and leave Mount Gilead.[j]'" So twenty-
two thousand men left, while ten thousand remained.
4But the LORD said to Gideon, "There
are still too many[k] men. Take them down
to the water, and I will sift them for you
there. If I say, 'This one shall go with
you,' he shall go; but if I say, 'This one
shall not go with you,' he shall not go."
5So Gideon took the men down to the
water. There the LORD told him, "Separate those who lap the water with their
tongues like a dog from those who kneel
down to drink." 6Three hundred men
lapped with their hands to their mouths.
All the rest got down on their knees to
drink.
7The LORD said to Gideon, "With the
three hundred men that lapped I will
save you and give the Midianites into
your hands. Let all the other men go,
each to his own place."[l] 8So Gideon sent
the rest of the Israelites to their tents but
kept the three hundred, who took over
the provisions and trumpets of the others.
Now the camp of Midian lay below
him in the valley. 9During that night the
LORD said to Gideon, "Get up, go down
against the camp, because I am going to
give it into your hands.[m] 10If you are
afraid to attack, go down to the camp
with your servant Purah 11and listen to
what they are saying. Afterward, you will
be encouraged to attack the camp." So
he and Purah his servant went down to
the outposts of the camp. 12The Midianites, the Amalekites[n] and all the other
eastern peoples had settled in the valley,
thick as locusts.[o] Their camels[p] could no
more be counted than the sand on the
seashore.[q]
13Gideon arrived just as a man was
telling a friend his dream. "I had a
dream," he was saying. "A round loaf of
barley bread came tumbling into the
Midianite camp. It struck the tent with
such force that the tent overturned and
collapsed."
14His friend responded, "This can be
nothing other than the sword of Gideon
son of Joash, the Israelite. God has given
the Midianites and the whole camp into
his hands."

Gideon defeats Midian using trumpets and torches.

15When Gideon heard the dream and
its interpretation, he worshiped God.[r] He
returned to the camp of Israel and called
out, "Get up! The LORD has given the
Midianite camp into your hands."
16Dividing the three hundred men[s] into

6:34 [a]Jdg 3:27
6:35 [b]Jdg 4:6
6:36 [c]ver 14
6:37 [d]Ex 4:3-7 [e]Ge 24:14
6:39 [f]Ge 18:32
7:1 [g]Jdg 6:32 [h]Ge 12:6
7:2 [i]Dt 8:17; 2Co 4:7
7:3 [j]Dt 20:8
7:4 [k]1Sa 14:6
7:7 [l]1Sa 14:6
7:9 [m]Jos 2:24; 10:8; 11:6
7:12 [n]Jdg 8:10 [o]Jdg 6:5 [p]Jer 49:29 [q]Jos 11:4
7:15 [r]1Sa 15:31
7:16 [s]Ge 14:15

three companies,[a] he placed trumpets
and empty jars in the hands of all of
them, with torches inside.
17“Watch me,” he told them. “Follow
my lead. When I get to the edge of the
camp, do exactly as I do. 18When I and all
who are with me blow our trumpets,[b]
then from all around the camp blow
yours and shout, ‘For the LORD and for
Gideon.’ ”
19Gideon and the hundred men with
him reached the edge of the camp at the
beginning of the middle watch, just after
they had changed the guard. They blew
their trumpets and broke the jars that
were in their hands. 20The three companies blew the trumpets and smashed
the jars. Grasping the torches in their left
hands and holding in their right hands
the trumpets they were to blow, they
shouted, “A sword[c] for the LORD and for
Gideon!” 21While each man held his position around the camp, all the Midianites
ran, crying out as they fled.[d]
22When the three hundred trumpets
sounded,[e] the LORD caused the men
throughout the camp to turn on each other[f] with their swords. The army fled to
Beth Shittah toward Zererah as far as the
border of Abel Meholah[g] near Tabbath.
23Israelites from Naphtali, Asher and all
Manasseh were called out,[h] and they
pursued the Midianites. 24Gideon sent
messengers throughout the hill country
of Ephraim, saying, “Come down against
the Midianites and seize the waters of the
Jordan[i] ahead of them as far as Beth
Barah.”
So all the men of Ephraim were called
out and they took the waters of the Jordan as far as Beth Barah. 25They also captured two of the Midianite leaders, Oreb
and Zeeb[j]. They killed Oreb at the rock
of Oreb,[k] and Zeeb at the winepress of
Zeeb. They pursued the Midianites and
brought the heads of Oreb and Zeeb to
Gideon, who was by the Jordan.[l]

Gideon kills two kings of Midian.

8 Now the Ephraimites asked Gideon,
“Why have you treated us like this?
Why didn’t you call us when you went
to fight Midian?”[m] And they criticized
him sharply.[n]
2But he answered them, “What have I
accomplished compared to you? Aren’t
the gleanings of Ephraim’s grapes better
than the full grape harvest of Abiezer?
3God gave Oreb and Zeeb,[o] the Midianite
leaders, into your hands. What was I able
to do compared to you?” At this, their
resentment against him subsided.
4Gideon and his three hundred men,
exhausted yet keeping up the pursuit,
came to the Jordan[p] and crossed it. 5He
said to the men of Succoth,[q] “Give my
troops some bread; they are worn out,
and I am still pursuing Zebah and Zalmunna,[r] the kings of Midian.”
6But the officials of Succoth said, “Do
you already have the hands of Zebah and
Zalmunna in your possession? Why
should we give bread[s] to your troops?”[t]
7Then Gideon replied, “Just for that,
when the LORD has given Zebah and Zalmunna[u] into my hand, I will tear your
flesh with desert thorns and briers.”
8From there he went up to Peniel[i][v]
and made the same request of them, but
they answered as the men of Succoth
had. 9So he said to the men of Peniel,
“When I return in triumph, I will tear
down this tower.”[w]
10Now Zebah and Zalmunna were in
Karkor with a force of about fifteen thousand men, all that were left of the armies
of the eastern peoples; a hundred and
twenty thousand swordsmen had fallen.[x]
11Gideon went up by the route of the
nomads east of Nobah[y] and Jogbehah[z]
and fell upon the unsuspecting army.
12Zebah and Zalmunna, the two kings of
Midian, fled, but he pursued them and
captured them, routing their entire army.
13Gideon son of Joash then returned
from the battle by the Pass of Heres. 14He
caught a young man of Succoth and questioned him, and the young man wrote
down for him the names of the seventy-
seven officials of Succoth, the elders of

7:16 [a]2Sa 18:2
7:18 [b]Jdg 3:27
7:20 [c]ver 14
7:21 [d]2Ki 7:7
7:22 [e]Jos 6:20 [f]1Sa 14:20; 2Ch 20:23 [g]1Ki 4:12; 19:16
7:23 [h]Jdg 6:35
7:24 [i]Jdg 3:28
7:25 [j]Jdg 8:3; Ps 83:11 [k]Isa 10:26 [l]Jdg 8:4
8:1 [m]Jdg 12:1 [n]2Sa 19:41
8:3 [o]Jdg 7:25; Pr 15:1
8:4 [p]Jdg 7:25
8:5 [q]Ge 33:17 [r]Ps 83:11
8:6 [s]1Sa 25:11 [t]ver 15
8:7 [u]Jdg 7:15
8:8 [v]Ge 32:30; 1Ki 12:25
8:9 [w]ver 17
8:10 [x]Jdg 6:5; 7:12; Isa 9:4
8:11 [y]Nu 32:42 [z]Nu 32:35

[i]8 Hebrew *Penuel,* a variant of *Peniel*; also in verses 9 and 17

the town. 15 Then Gideon came and said to the men of Succoth, "Here are Zebah and Zalmunna, about whom you taunted me by saying, 'Do you already have the hands of Zebah and Zalmunna in your possession? Why should we give bread to your exhausted men?[a]'" 16 He took the elders of the town and taught the men of Succoth a lesson[b] by punishing them with desert thorns and briers. 17 He also pulled down the tower of Peniel and killed the men of the town.[c]

18 Then he asked Zebah and Zalmunna, "What kind of men did you kill at Tabor?[d]"

"Men like you," they answered, "each one with the bearing of a prince."

19 Gideon replied, "Those were my brothers, the sons of my own mother. As surely as the LORD lives, if you had spared their lives, I would not kill you." 20 Turning to Jether, his oldest son, he said, "Kill them!" But Jether did not draw his sword, because he was only a boy and was afraid.

21 Zebah and Zalmunna said, "Come, do it yourself. 'As is the man, so is his strength.'" So Gideon stepped forward and killed them, and took the ornaments[e] off their camels' necks.

Gideon refuses to be ruler.

22 The Israelites said to Gideon, "Rule over us—you, your son and your grandson—because you have saved us out of the hand of Midian."

23 But Gideon told them, "I will not rule over you, nor will my son rule over you. The LORD will rule[f] over you." 24 And he said, "I do have one request, that each of you give me an earring from your share of the plunder." (It was the custom of the Ishmaelites[g] to wear gold earrings.)

25 They answered, "We'll be glad to give them." So they spread out a garment, and each man threw a ring from his plunder onto it. 26 The weight of the gold rings he asked for came to seventeen hundred shekels,[j] not counting the ornaments, the pendants and the purple garments worn by the kings of Midian or the chains that were on their camels' necks. 27 Gideon made the gold into an ephod,[h] which he placed in Ophrah, his town. All Israel prostituted themselves by worshiping it there, and it became a snare[i] to Gideon and his family.

Gideon's death and burial.

28 Thus Midian was subdued before the Israelites and did not raise its head again. During Gideon's lifetime, the land enjoyed peace[j] forty years.

29 Jerub-Baal[k] son of Joash went back home to live. 30 He had seventy sons[l] of his own, for he had many wives. 31 His concubine, who lived in Shechem, also bore him a son, whom he named Abimelech.[m] 32 Gideon son of Joash died at a good old age[n] and was buried in the tomb of his father Joash in Ophrah of the Abiezrites.

33 No sooner had Gideon died than the Israelites again prostituted themselves to the Baals.[o] They set up Baal-Berith[p] as their god[q] and 34 did not remember[r] the LORD their God, who had rescued them from the hands of all their enemies on every side. 35 They also failed to show kindness to the family of Jerub-Baal (that is, Gideon) for all the good things he had done for them.[s]

Abimelech's conspiracy against seventy of his brothers.

9 Abimelech[t] son of Jerub-Baal went to his mother's brothers in Shechem and said to them and to all his mother's clan, 2 "Ask all the citizens of Shechem, 'Which is better for you: to have all seventy of Jerub-Baal's sons rule over you, or just one man?' Remember, I am your flesh and blood.[u]"

3 When the brothers repeated all this to the citizens of Shechem, they were inclined to follow Abimelech, for they said, "He is our brother." 4 They gave him seventy shekels[k] of silver from the temple of Baal-Berith,[v] and Abimelech used it to hire reckless adventurers,[w] who

8:15 [a]ver 6
8:16 [b]ver 7
8:17 [c]ver 9
8:18 [d]Jos 19:22; Jdg 4:6
8:21 [e]ver 26; Ps 83:11
8:23 [f]Ex 16:8; 1Sa 8:7; 10:19; 12:12
8:24 [g]Ge 25:13
8:27 [h]Jdg 17:5; 18:14 [i]Dt 7:16; Ps 106:39
8:28 [j]Jdg 5:31
8:29 [k]Jdg 7:1
8:30 [l]Jdg 9:2,5, 18,24
8:31 [m]Jdg 9:1
8:32 [n]Ge 25:8
8:33 [o]Jdg 2:11, 13,19 [p]Jdg 9:4 [q]Jdg 9:27,46
8:34 [r]Jdg 3:7; Dt 4:9; Ps 78:11,42
8:35 [s]Jdg 9:16
9:1 [t]Jdg 8:31
9:2 [u]Ge 29:14; Jdg 8:30
9:4 [v]Jdg 8:33 [w]Jdg 11:3; 2Ch 13:7

j*26* That is, about 43 pounds (about 19.5 kilograms)
k*4* That is, about 1 3/4 pounds (about 0.8 kilogram)

became his followers. 5He went to his
father's home in Ophrah and on one
stone murdered his seventy brothers,[a]
the sons of Jerub-Baal. But Jotham, the
youngest son of Jerub-Baal, escaped by
hiding.[b] 6Then all the citizens of Shechem and Beth Millo gathered beside the
great tree at the pillar in Shechem to
crown Abimelech king.

Jotham's illustration of the trees.

7When Jotham was told about this, he
climbed up on the top of Mount Gerizim[c] and shouted to them, "Listen to
me, citizens of Shechem, so that God
may listen to you. 8One day the trees
went out to anoint a king for themselves.
They said to the olive tree, 'Be our king.'
9"But the olive tree answered, 'Should
I give up my oil, by which both gods and
men are honored, to hold sway over the
trees?'
10"Next, the trees said to the fig tree,
'Come and be our king.'
11"But the fig tree replied, 'Should I
give up my fruit, so good and sweet, to
hold sway over the trees?'
12"Then the trees said to the vine,
'Come and be our king.'
13"But the vine answered, 'Should I
give up my wine,[d] which cheers both
gods and men, to hold sway over the
trees?'
14"Finally all the trees said to the
thornbush, 'Come and be our king.'
15"The thornbush said to the trees, 'If
you really want to anoint me king over
you, come and take refuge in my shade;[e]
but if not, then let fire come out[f] of the
thornbush and consume the cedars of
Lebanon!'[g]
16"Now if you have acted honorably
and in good faith when you made Abimelech king, and if you have been fair to
Jerub-Baal and his family, and if you have
treated him as he deserves— 17and to
think that my father fought for you,
risked his life to rescue you from the
hand of Midian 18(but today you have
revolted against my father's family, murdered his seventy sons[h] on a single stone,

9:5 [a]ver 2; Jdg 8:30 [b]2Ki 11:2
9:7 [c]Dt 11:29; 27:12; Jn 4:20
9:13 [d]Ecc 2:3
9:15 [e]Isa 30:2 [f]ver 20 [g]Isa 2:13
9:18 [h]ver 5-6; Jdg 8:30
9:20 [i]ver 15
9:23 [j]1Sa 16:14,23; 18:10; 1Ki 22:22; Isa 19:14; 33:1
9:24 [k]Nu 35:33; 1Ki 2:32 [l]ver 56-57 [m]Dt 27:25
9:27 [n]Am 9:13 [o]Jdg 8:33
9:28 [p]1Sa 25:10; 1Ki 12:16 [q]Ge 34:2,6
9:29 [r]2Sa 15:4

and made Abimelech, the son of his slave
girl, king over the citizens of Shechem
because he is your brother)— 19if then
you have acted honorably and in good
faith toward Jerub-Baal and his family
today, may Abimelech be your joy, and
may you be his, too! 20But if you have
not, let fire come out[i] from Abimelech
and consume you, citizens of Shechem
and Beth Millo, and let fire come out
from you, citizens of Shechem and Beth
Millo, and consume Abimelech!"
21Then Jotham fled, escaping to Beer,
and he lived there because he was afraid
of his brother Abimelech.

Gaal's conspiracy.

22After Abimelech had governed Israel
three years, 23God sent an evil spirit[j]
between Abimelech and the citizens of
Shechem, who acted treacherously
against Abimelech. 24God did this in
order that the crime against Jerub-Baal's
seventy sons, the shedding[k] of their
blood, might be avenged[l] on their brother Abimelech and on the citizens of Shechem, who had helped him[m] murder his
brothers. 25In opposition to him these citizens of Shechem set men on the hilltops
to ambush and rob everyone who passed
by, and this was reported to Abimelech.
26Now Gaal son of Ebed moved with
his brothers into Shechem, and its citizens put their confidence in him. 27Af-
ter they had gone out into the fields and
gathered the grapes and trodden[n] them,
they held a festival in the temple of their
god.[o] While they were eating and drinking, they cursed Abimelech. 28Then Gaal
son of Ebed said, "Who[p] is Abimelech,
and who is Shechem, that we should be
subject to him? Isn't he Jerub-Baal's son,
and isn't Zebul his deputy? Serve the men
of Hamor,[q] Shechem's father! Why should
we serve Abimelech? 29If only this people
were under my command![r] Then I would
get rid of him. I would say to Abimelech,
'Call out your whole army!'"[1]
30When Zebul the governor of the city

[1]*29* Septuagint; Hebrew *him." Then he said to Abimelech, "Call out your whole army!"*

heard what Gaal son of Ebed said, he was very angry. 31Under cover he sent messengers to Abimelech, saying, "Gaal son of Ebed and his brothers have come to Shechem and are stirring up the city against you. 32Now then, during the night you and your men should come and lie in wait[a] in the fields. 33In the morning at sunrise, advance against the city. When Gaal and his men come out against you, do whatever your hand finds to do.[b]"

34So Abimelech and all his troops set out by night and took up concealed positions near Shechem in four companies. 35Now Gaal son of Ebed had gone out and was standing at the entrance to the city gate just as Abimelech and his soldiers came out from their hiding place.[c]

36When Gaal saw them, he said to Zebul, "Look, people are coming down from the tops of the mountains!"

Zebul replied, "You mistake the shadows of the mountains for men."

37But Gaal spoke up again: "Look, people are coming down from the center of the land, and a company is coming from the direction of the soothsayers' tree."

38Then Zebul said to him, "Where is your big talk now, you who said, 'Who is Abimelech that we should be subject to him?' Aren't these the men you ridiculed?[d] Go out and fight them!"

39So Gaal led out[m] the citizens of Shechem and fought Abimelech. 40Abimelech chased him, and many fell wounded in the flight—all the way to the entrance to the gate. 41Abimelech stayed in Arumah, and Zebul drove Gaal and his brothers out of Shechem.

42The next day the people of Shechem went out to the fields, and this was reported to Abimelech. 43So he took his men, divided them into three companies[e] and set an ambush in the fields. When he saw the people coming out of the city, he rose to attack them. 44Abimelech and the companies with him rushed forward to a position at the entrance to the city gate. Then two companies rushed upon those in the fields and struck them down. 45All that day Abimelech pressed his attack against the city until he had captured it and killed its people. Then he destroyed the city[f] and scattered salt[g] over it.

46On hearing this, the citizens in the tower of Shechem went into the stronghold of the temple[h] of El-Berith. 47When Abimelech heard that they had assembled there, 48he and all his men went up Mount Zalmon.[i] He took an ax and cut off some branches, which he lifted to his shoulders. He ordered the men with him, "Quick! Do what you have seen me do!" 49So all the men cut branches and followed Abimelech. They piled them against the stronghold and set it on fire over the people inside. So all the people in the tower of Shechem, about a thousand men and women, also died.

Abimelech's death.

50Next Abimelech went to Thebez[j] and besieged it and captured it. 51Inside the city, however, was a strong tower, to which all the men and women—all the people of the city—fled. They locked themselves in and climbed up on the tower roof. 52Abimelech went to the tower and stormed it. But as he approached the entrance to the tower to set it on fire, 53a woman dropped an upper millstone on his head and cracked his skull.[k]

54Hurriedly he called to his armor-bearer, "Draw your sword and kill me,[l] so that they can't say, 'A woman killed him.'" So his servant ran him through, and he died. 55When the Israelites saw that Abimelech was dead, they went home.

56Thus God repaid the wickedness that Abimelech had done to his father by murdering his seventy brothers. 57God also made the men of Shechem pay for all their wickedness.[m] The curse of Jotham son of Jerub-Baal came on them.

Tola, then Jair, leads Israel.

10 After the time of Abimelech a man of Issachar,[n] Tola son of Puah,[o] the son of Dodo, rose to save[p] Israel. He lived in Shamir, in the hill

9:32 [a]Jos 8:2
9:33 [b]1Sa 10:7
9:35 [c]Ps 32:7; Jer 49:10
9:38 [d]ver 28-29
9:43 [e]Jdg 7:16
9:45 [f]ver 20; 2Ki 3:25 [g]Dt 29:23
9:46 [h]Jdg 8:33
9:48 [i]Ps 68:14
9:50 [j]2Sa 11:21
9:53 [k]2Sa 11:21
9:54 [l]1Sa 31:4; 2Sa 1:9
9:57 [m]ver 20
10:1 [n]Ge 30:18 [o]Ge 46:13 [p]Jdg 2:16; 6:14

m39 Or *Gaal went out in the sight of*

country of Ephraim. 2He led[n] Israel twenty-three years; then he died, and was
buried in Shamir.
3He was followed by Jair of Gilead,
who led Israel twenty-two years. 4He had
thirty sons, who rode thirty donkeys.
They controlled thirty towns in Gilead,
which to this day are called Havvoth
Jair.[o][a] 5When Jair died, he was buried in
Kamon.

Ammon and Philistia oppress Israel.

6Again the Israelites did evil in the eyes
of the LORD.[b] They served the Baals and
the Ashtoreths,[c] and the gods of Aram,
the gods of Sidon, the gods of Moab, the
gods of the Ammonites and the gods of
the Philistines.[d] And because the Israelites forsook the LORD[e] and no longer
served him, 7he became angry[f] with
them. He sold them[g] into the hands of
the Philistines and the Ammonites, 8who
that year shattered and crushed them.
For eighteen years they oppressed all the
Israelites on the east side of the Jordan in
Gilead, the land of the Amorites. 9The
Ammonites also crossed the Jordan to
fight against Judah, Benjamin and the
house of Ephraim; and Israel was in
great distress. 10Then the Israelites cried
out to the LORD, "We have sinned against
you, forsaking our God and serving the
Baals."[h]
11The LORD replied, "When the Egyptians,[i] the Amorites, the Ammonites,[j]
the Philistines,[k] 12the Sidonians, the Amalekites and the Maonites[p] oppressed
you[l] and you cried to me for help, did I
not save you from their hands? 13But you
have forsaken me and served other gods,
so I will no longer save you. 14Go and cry
out to the gods you have chosen. Let
them save you when you are in trouble![m]"
15But the Israelites said to the LORD,
"We have sinned. Do with us whatever
you think best,[n] but please rescue us
now." 16Then they got rid of the foreign
gods among them and served the LORD.[o]
And he could bear Israel's misery[p] no
longer.[q]

10:4 [a]Nu 32:41
10:6 [b]Jdg 2:11 [c]Jdg 2:13 [d]Jdg 2:12 [e]Dt 32:15
10:7 [f]Dt 31:17 [g]Dt 32:30; Jdg 2:14; 1Sa 12:9
10:10 [h]1Sa 12:10
10:11 [i]Ex 14:30 [j]Nu 21:21; Jdg 3:13 [k]Jdg 3:31
10:12 [l]Ps 106:42
10:14 [m]Dt 32:37
10:15 [n]1Sa 3:18; 2Sa 15:26
10:16 [o]Jos 24:23; Jer 18:8 [p]Isa 63:9 [q]Dt 32:36; Ps 106:44-45
10:17 [r]Ge 31:49; Jdg 11:29
10:18 [s]Jdg 11:8,9
11:1 [t]Heb 11:32 [u]Jdg 6:12
11:3 [v]2Sa 10:6,8 [w]Jdg 9:4
11:4 [x]Jdg 10:9
11:7 [y]Ge 26:27
11:8 [z]Jdg 10:18
11:10 [a]Ge 31:50; Jer 42:5
11:11 [b]Jos 11:3; Jdg 10:17; 20:1; 1Sa 10:17

17When the Ammonites were called to
arms and camped in Gilead, the Israelites
assembled and camped at Mizpah.[r] 18The
leaders of the people of Gilead said to
each other, "Whoever will launch the
attack against the Ammonites will be the
head[s] of all those living in Gilead."

Jephthah's conquest of the Ammonites.

11 Jephthah[t] the Gileadite was a
mighty warrior.[u] His father was
Gilead; his mother was a prostitute. 2Gil-
ead's wife also bore him sons, and when
they were grown up, they drove Jephthah
away. "You are not going to get any inheritance in our family," they said, "because
you are the son of another woman." 3So
Jephthah fled from his brothers and settled in the land of Tob,[v] where a group of
adventurers[w] gathered around him and
followed him.
4Some time later, when the Ammonites[x] made war on Israel, 5the elders of
Gilead went to get Jephthah from the
land of Tob. 6"Come," they said, "be our
commander, so we can fight the Ammonites."
7Jephthah said to them, "Didn't you
hate me and drive me from my father's
house?[y] Why do you come to me now,
when you're in trouble?"
8The elders of Gilead said to him,
"Nevertheless, we are turning to you
now; come with us to fight the Ammonites, and you will be our head[z] over all
who live in Gilead."
9Jephthah answered, "Suppose you
take me back to fight the Ammonites and
the LORD gives them to me—will I really
be your head?"
10The elders of Gilead replied, "The
LORD is our witness;[a] we will certainly
do as you say." 11So Jephthah went with
the elders of Gilead, and the people made
him head and commander over them.
And he repeated all his words before the
LORD in Mizpah.[b]
12Then Jephthah sent messengers to

[n]2 Traditionally *judged*; also in verse 3 [o]4 Or *called the settlements of Jair* [p]12 Hebrew; some Septuagint manuscripts *Midianites*

the Ammonite king with the question: "What do you have against us that you have attacked our country?"

13The king of the Ammonites answered Jephthah's messengers, "When Israel came up out of Egypt, they took away my land from the Arnon to the Jabbok,[a] all the way to the Jordan. Now give it back peaceably."

14Jephthah sent back messengers to the Ammonite king, 15saying:

"This is what Jephthah says: Israel did not take the land of Moab[b] or the land of the Ammonites.[c] 16But when they came up out of Egypt, Israel went through the desert to the Red Sea[q][d] and on to Kadesh.[e] 17Then Israel sent messengers[f] to the king of Edom, saying, 'Give us permission to go through your country,'[g] but the king of Edom would not listen. They sent also to the king of Moab, and he refused.[h] So Israel stayed at Kadesh.

18"Next they traveled through the desert, skirted the lands of Edom[i] and Moab, passed along the eastern side[j] of the country of Moab, and camped on the other side of the Arnon.[k] They did not enter the territory of Moab, for the Arnon was its border.

19"Then Israel sent messengers to Sihon king of the Amorites, who ruled in Heshbon, and said to him, 'Let us pass through your country to our own place.'[l] 20Sihon, however, did not trust Israel[r] to pass through his territory. He mustered all his men and encamped at Jahaz and fought with Israel.[m]

21"Then the LORD, the God of Israel, gave Sihon and all his men into Israel's hands, and they defeated them. Israel took over all the land of the Amorites who lived in that country, 22capturing all of it from the Arnon to the Jabbok and from the desert to the Jordan.[n]

23"Now since the LORD, the God of Israel, has driven the Amorites out before his people Israel, what right have you to take it over? 24Will you not take what your god Chemosh[o] gives you? Likewise, whatever the LORD our God has given us, we will possess. 25Are you better than Balak son of Zippor,[p] king of Moab? Did he ever quarrel with Israel or fight with them?[q] 26For three hundred years Israel occupied[r] Heshbon, Aroer, the surrounding settlements and all the towns along the Arnon. Why didn't you retake them during that time? 27I have not wronged you, but you are doing me wrong by waging war against me. Let the LORD, the Judge,[s][s] decide[t] the dispute this day between the Israelites and the Ammonites."

28The king of Ammon, however, paid no attention to the message Jephthah sent him.

Jephthah's vow.

29Then the Spirit[u] of the LORD came upon Jephthah. He crossed Gilead and Manasseh, passed through Mizpah of Gilead, and from there he advanced against the Ammonites. 30And Jephthah made a vow[v] to the LORD: "If you give the Ammonites into my hands, 31whatever comes out of the door of my house to meet me when I return in triumph from the Ammonites will be the LORD's, and I will sacrifice it as a burnt offering."

32Then Jephthah went over to fight the Ammonites, and the LORD gave them into his hands. 33He devastated twenty towns from Aroer to the vicinity of Minnith,[w] as far as Abel Keramim. Thus Israel subdued Ammon.

34When Jephthah returned to his home in Mizpah, who should come out to meet him but his daughter, dancing to the sound of tambourines![x] She was an only child. Except for her he had neither son nor daughter. 35When he saw her, he tore his clothes and cried, "Oh! My daughter! You have made me miserable and

11:13 [a]Ge 32:22; Nu 21:24
11:15 [b]Dt 2:9 [c]Dt 2:19
11:16 [d]Nu 14:25; Dt 1:40 [e]Nu 20:1
11:17 [f]Nu 20:14 [g]Nu 20:18,21 [h]Jos 24:9
11:18 [i]Nu 21:4 [j]Dt 2:8 [k]Nu 21:13
11:19 [l]Nu 21:21-22; Dt 2:26-27
11:20 [m]Nu 21:23; Dt 2:32
11:22 [n]Dt 2:36
11:24 [o]Nu 21:29; Jos 3:10; 1Ki 11:7
11:25 [p]Nu 22:2 [q]Jos 24:9
11:26 [r]Nu 21:25
11:27 [s]Ge 18:25 [t]Ge 16:5; 31:53; 1Sa 24:12,15
11:29 [u]Nu 11:25; Jdg 3:10; 6:34; 14:6,19; 15:14; 1Sa 11:6; 16:13; Isa 11:2
11:30 [v]Ge 28:20
11:33 [w]Eze 27:17
11:34 [x]Ex 15:20; Jer 31:4

q *16* Hebrew *Yam Suph*; that is, Sea of Reeds
r *20* Or *however, would not make an agreement for Israel*
s *27* Or *Ruler*

wretched, because I have made a vow to
the LORD that I cannot break.[a] ”
36“My father,” she replied, “you have
given your word to the LORD. Do to me
just as you promised,[b] now that the LORD
has avenged you of your enemies,[c] the
Ammonites. 37But grant me this one request,” she said. “Give me two months
to roam the hills and weep with my
friends, because I will never marry.”
38“You may go,” he said. And he let
her go for two months. She and the girls
went into the hills and wept because
she would never marry. 39After the two
months, she returned to her father and
he did to her as he had vowed. And she
was a virgin.
From this comes the Israelite custom
40that each year the young women of Israel go out for four days to commemorate
the daughter of Jephthah the Gileadite.

Jephthah battles Ephraim.

12 The men of Ephraim called out
their forces, crossed over to Zaphon and said to Jephthah, “Why did you
go to fight the Ammonites without calling
us to go with you?[d] We’re going to burn
down your house over your head.”
2Jephthah answered, “I and my people
were engaged in a great struggle with the
Ammonites, and although I called, you
didn’t save me out of their hands. 3When
I saw that you wouldn’t help, I took my
life in my hands[e] and crossed over to
fight the Ammonites, and the LORD gave
me the victory over them. Now why have
you come up today to fight me?”
4Jephthah then called together the men
of Gilead and fought against Ephraim.
The Gileadites struck them down because
the Ephraimites had said, “You Gileadites
are renegades from Ephraim and Manasseh.” 5The Gileadites captured the
fords of the Jordan[f] leading to Ephraim,
and whenever a survivor of Ephraim said,
“Let me cross over,” the men of Gilead
asked him, “Are you an Ephraimite?” If
he replied, “No,” 6they said, “All right,
say ‘Shibboleth.’ ” If he said, “Sibboleth,”
because he could not pronounce the

11:35 [a]Nu 30:2; Ecc 5:2,4,5
11:36 [b]Lk 1:38 [c]2Sa 18:19
12:1 [d]Jdg 8:1
12:3 [e]1Sa 19:5; 28:21; Job 13:14
12:5 [f]Jos 22:11; Jdg 3:28
12:14 [g]Jdg 10:4 [h]Jdg 5:10
12:15 [i]Jdg 5:14
13:1 [j]Jdg 2:11; 1Sa 12:9
13:2 [k]Jos 15:33; 19:41
13:3 [l]ver 6,8; Jdg 6:12 [m]ver 10 [n]Lk 1:13
13:4 [o]ver 14; Nu 6:2-4; Lk 1:15
13:5 [p]Nu 6:5; 1Sa 1:11 [q]Nu 6:2,13 [r]1Sa 7:13

word correctly, they seized him and killed
him at the fords of the Jordan. Forty-two
thousand Ephraimites were killed at that
time.
7Jephthah led[t] Israel six years. Then
Jephthah the Gileadite died, and was buried in a town in Gilead.

Ibzan, Elon and Abdon successively lead Israel.

8After him, Ibzan of Bethlehem led
Israel. 9He had thirty sons and thirty
daughters. He gave his daughters away
in marriage to those outside his clan, and
for his sons he brought in thirty young
women as wives from outside his clan.
Ibzan led Israel seven years. 10Then Ibzan
died, and was buried in Bethlehem.
11After him, Elon the Zebulunite led Israel ten years. 12Then Elon died, and was
buried in Aijalon in the land of Zebulun.
13After him, Abdon son of Hillel, from
Pirathon, led Israel. 14He had forty sons
and thirty grandsons,[g] who rode on seventy donkeys.[h] He led Israel eight years.
15Then Abdon son of Hillel died, and was
buried at Pirathon in Ephraim, in the hill
country of the Amalekites.[i]

Promise of a son to Manoah and his barren wife.

13 Again the Israelites did evil in the
eyes of the LORD, so the LORD delivered them into the hands of the Philistines[j] for forty years.
2A certain man of Zorah,[k] named Manoah, from the clan of the Danites, had a
wife who was sterile and remained childless. 3The angel of the LORD[l] appeared to
her[m] and said, “You are sterile and childless, but you are going to conceive and
have a son.[n] 4Now see to it that you drink
no wine or other fermented drink and
that you do not eat anything unclean,[o]
5because you will conceive and give birth
to a son. No razor[p] may be used on his
head, because the boy is to be a Nazirite,[q] set apart to God from birth, and he
will begin[r] the deliverance of Israel from
the hands of the Philistines.”

[t]7 Traditionally *judged*; also in verses 8-14

6Then the woman went to her husband and told him, "A man of God[a] came to me. He looked like an angel of God,[b] very awesome. I didn't ask him where he came from, and he didn't tell me his name. 7But he said to me, 'You will conceive and give birth to a son. Now then, drink no wine or other fermented drink and do not eat anything unclean, because the boy will be a Nazirite of God from birth until the day of his death.' "

8Then Manoah prayed to the LORD: "O Lord, I beg you, let the man of God you sent to us come again to teach us how to bring up the boy who is to be born."

9God heard Manoah, and the angel of God came again to the woman while she was out in the field; but her husband Manoah was not with her. 10The woman hurried to tell her husband, "He's here! The man who appeared to me the other day!"

11Manoah got up and followed his wife. When he came to the man, he said, "Are you the one who talked to my wife?"

"I am," he said.

12So Manoah asked him, "When your words are fulfilled, what is to be the rule for the boy's life and work?"

13The angel of the LORD answered, "Your wife must do all that I have told her. 14She must not eat anything that comes from the grapevine, nor drink any wine or other fermented drink[c] nor eat anything unclean.[d] She must do everything I have commanded her."

15Manoah said to the angel of the LORD, "We would like you to stay until we prepare a young goat[e] for you."

16The angel of the LORD replied, "Even though you detain me, I will not eat any of your food. But if you prepare a burnt offering,[f] offer it to the LORD." (Manoah did not realize that it was the angel of the LORD.)

17Then Manoah inquired of the angel of the LORD, "What is your name,[g] so that we may honor you when your word comes true?"

18He replied, "Why do you ask my name?[h] It is beyond understanding.[u]" 19Then Manoah took a young goat, together with the grain offering, and sacrificed it on a rock[i] to the LORD. And the LORD did an amazing thing while Manoah and his wife watched: 20As the flame[j] blazed up from the altar toward heaven, the angel of the LORD ascended in the flame. Seeing this, Manoah and his wife fell with their faces to the ground.[k] 21When the angel of the LORD did not show himself again to Manoah and his wife, Manoah realized[l] that it was the angel of the LORD.

22"We are doomed[m] to die!" he said to his wife. "We have seen[n] God!"

23But his wife answered, "If the LORD had meant to kill us, he would not have accepted a burnt offering and grain offering from our hands, nor shown us all these things or now told us this."[o]

Samson's birth.

24The woman gave birth to a boy and named him Samson.[p] He grew[q] and the LORD blessed him,[r] 25and the Spirit of the LORD began to stir[s] him while he was in Mahaneh Dan,[t] between Zorah and Eshtaol.

Samson tells a riddle at his marriage feast.

14 Samson went down to Timnah[u] and saw there a young Philistine woman. 2When he returned, he said to his father and mother, "I have seen a Philistine woman in Timnah; now get her for me as my wife."[v]

3His father and mother replied, "Isn't there an acceptable woman among your relatives or among all our people?[w] Must you go to the uncircumcised[x] Philistines to get a wife?[y] "

But Samson said to his father, "Get her for me. She's the right one for me." 4(His parents did not know that this was from the LORD, who was seeking an occasion to confront the Philistines;[z] for at that time they were ruling over Israel.)[a] 5Samson went down to Timnah together with his father and mother. As they

13:6 [a]ver 8; 1Sa 2:27; 9:6 [b]ver 17-18; Mt 28:3
13:14 [c]Nu 6:4 [d]ver 4
13:15 [e]ver 3; Jdg 6:19
13:16 [f]Jdg 6:20
13:17 [g]Ge 32:29
13:18 [h]Isa 9:6
13:19 [i]Jdg 6:20
13:20 [j]Lev 9:24 [k]1Ch 21:16; Eze 1:28; Mt 17:6
13:21 [l]ver 16; Jdg 6:22
13:22 [m]Dt 5:26 [n]Ge 32:30; Jdg 6:22
13:23 [o]Ps 25:14
13:24 [p]Heb 11:32 [q]1Sa 3:19 [r]Lk 1:80
13:25 [s]Jdg 3:10 [t]Jdg 18:12
14:1 [u]Ge 38:12
14:2 [v]Ge 21:21; 34:4
14:3 [w]Ge 24:4 [x]Dt 7:3 [y]Ex 34:16
14:4 [z]Jos 11:20 [a]Jdg 13:1

u *18* Or *is wonderful*

approached the vineyards of Timnah,
suddenly a young lion came roaring
toward him. 6The Spirit of the LORD came
upon him in power[a] so that he tore the
lion apart with his bare hands as he
might have torn a young goat. But he
told neither his father nor his mother
what he had done. 7Then he went down
and talked with the woman, and he liked
her.
8Some time later, when he went back
to marry her, he turned aside to look at
the lion's carcass. In it was a swarm of
bees and some honey, 9which he scooped
out with his hands and ate as he went
along. When he rejoined his parents, he
gave them some, and they too ate it. But
he did not tell them that he had taken the
honey from the lion's carcass.
10Now his father went down to see the
woman. And Samson made a feast there,
as was customary for bridegrooms.
11When he appeared, he was given thirty companions.
12"Let me tell you a riddle,[b]" Samson
said to them. "If you can give me the answer within the seven days of the feast,[c]
I will give you thirty linen garments and
thirty sets of clothes.[d] 13If you can't tell
me the answer, you must give me thirty
linen garments and thirty sets of clothes."
"Tell us your riddle," they said. "Let's
hear it."
14He replied,

"Out of the eater, something to eat;
out of the strong, something sweet."

For three days they could not give the
answer.
15On the fourth[v] day, they said to Samson's wife, "Coax[e] your husband into
explaining the riddle for us, or we will
burn you and your father's household to
death.[f] Did you invite us here to rob us?"
16Then Samson's wife threw herself on
him, sobbing, "You hate me! You don't
really love me.[g] You've given my people
a riddle, but you haven't told me the answer."
"I haven't even explained it to my
father or mother," he replied, "so why
should I explain it to you?" 17She cried

14:6 [a]Jdg 3:10; 13:25
14:12 [b]1Ki 10:1; Eze 17:2 [c]Ge 29:27 [d]Ge 45:22; 2Ki 5:5
14:15 [e]Jdg 16:5; Ecc 7:26 [f]Jdg 15:6
14:16 [g]Jdg 16:15
14:17 [h]Est 1:5
14:18 [i]ver 14
14:19 [j]Nu 11:25; Jdg 3:10; 6:34; 11:29; 13:25; 15:14; 1Sa 11:6; 16:13; 1Ki 18:46; 2Ch 24:20; Isa 11:2 [k]1Sa 11:6
14:20 [l]Jdg 15:2,6; Jn 3:29
15:1 [m]Ge 38:17
15:2 [n]Jdg 14:20

the whole seven days[h] of the feast. So on
the seventh day he finally told her, because she continued to press him. She in
turn explained the riddle to her people.
18Before sunset on the seventh day the
men of the town said to him,

"What is sweeter than honey?
What is stronger than a lion?"[i]

Samson said to them,

"If you had not plowed with my heifer,
you would not have solved my
riddle."

19Then the Spirit of the LORD came upon him in power.[j] He went down to Ashkelon, struck down thirty of their men,
stripped them of their belongings and
gave their clothes to those who had explained the riddle. Burning with anger,[k]
he went up to his father's house. 20And
Samson's wife was given to the friend[l]
who had attended him at his wedding.

Samson burns the Philistines' grain.

15 Later on, at the time of wheat harvest, Samson took a young goat[m]
and went to visit his wife. He said, "I'm
going to my wife's room." But her father
would not let him go in.
2"I was so sure you thoroughly hated
her," he said, "that I gave her to your
friend.[n] Isn't her younger sister more
attractive? Take her instead."
3Samson said to them, "This time I
have a right to get even with the Philistines; I will really harm them." 4So he
went out and caught three hundred foxes
and tied them tail to tail in pairs. He then
fastened a torch to every pair of tails, 5lit
the torches and let the foxes loose in the
standing grain of the Philistines. He
burned up the shocks and standing grain,
together with the vineyards and olive
groves.
6When the Philistines asked, "Who did
this?" they were told, "Samson, the Tim-
nite's son-in-law, because his wife was
given to his friend."

[v] *15* Some Septuagint manuscripts and Syriac; Hebrew *seventh*

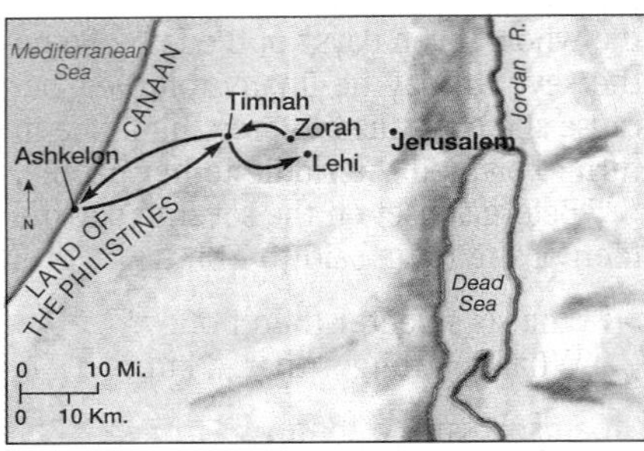

Samson's Ventures

Samson grew up in Zorah and wanted to marry a Philistine girl from Timnah. Tricked at his own wedding feast, he went to Ashkelon and killed some Philistine men and stole their clothes to pay off a bet. Samson then let himself be captured and brought to Lehi where he snapped his ropes and killed 1,000 people.

So the Philistines went up and burned her and her father to death.[a] 7Samson said to them, "Since you've acted like this, I won't stop until I get my revenge on you." 8He attacked them viciously and slaughtered many of them. Then he went down and stayed in a cave in the rock of Etam.

9The Philistines went up and camped in Judah, spreading out near Lehi.[b] 10The men of Judah asked, "Why have you come to fight us?"

"We have come to take Samson prisoner," they answered, "to do to him as he did to us."

11Then three thousand men from Judah went down to the cave in the rock of Etam and said to Samson, "Don't you realize that the Philistines are rulers over us?[c] What have you done to us?"

He answered, "I merely did to them what they did to me."

Samson kills 1,000 Philistines.

12They said to him, "We've come to tie you up and hand you over to the Philistines."

Samson said, "Swear to me that you won't kill me yourselves."

13"Agreed," they answered. "We will only tie you up and hand you over to them. We will not kill you." So they bound him with two new ropes and led him up from the rock. 14As he approached Lehi, the Philistines came toward him shouting. The Spirit of the LORD came upon him in power.[d] The ropes on his arms became like charred flax, and the bindings dropped from his hands. 15Finding a fresh jawbone of a donkey, he grabbed it and struck down a thousand men.[e]

16Then Samson said,

"With a donkey's jawbone
I have made donkeys of them.[w]
With a donkey's jawbone
I have killed a thousand men."

17When he finished speaking, he threw away the jawbone; and the place was called Ramath Lehi.[x]

18Because he was very thirsty, he cried out to the LORD,[f] "You have given your servant this great victory. Must I now die of thirst and fall into the hands of the uncircumcised?" 19Then God opened up the hollow place in Lehi, and water came out of it. When Samson drank, his strength returned and he revived.[g] So the spring was called En Hakkore,[y] and it is still there in Lehi.

20Samson led[z] Israel for twenty years[h] in the days of the Philistines.

Secret of Samson's strength revealed to Delilah.

16 One day Samson went to Gaza, where he saw a prostitute. He went in to spend the night with her. 2The people of Gaza were told, "Samson is here!" So they surrounded the place and lay in wait for him all night at the city gate.[i] They made no move during the night, saying, "At dawn we'll kill him."

3But Samson lay there only until the middle of the night. Then he got up and took hold of the doors of the city gate, together with the two posts, and tore them loose, bar and all. He lifted them to his shoulders and carried them to the top of the hill that faces Hebron.[j]

15:6 [a]Jdg 14:15
15:9 [b]ver 14,17,19
15:11 [c]Jdg 13:1; 14:4; Ps 106:40-42
15:14 [d]Jdg 3:10; 14:19; 1Sa 11:6
15:15 [e]Lev 26:8; Jos 23:10; Jdg 3:31
15:18 [f]Jdg 16:28
15:19 [g]Ge 45:27; Isa 40:29
15:20 [h]Jdg 13:1; 16:31; Heb 11:32
16:2 [i]1Sa 23:26; Ps 118:10-12; Ac 9:24
16:3 [j]Jos 10:36

[w]*16* Or *made a heap or two*; the Hebrew for *donkey* sounds like the Hebrew for *heap.* [x]*17* *Ramath Lehi* means *jawbone hill.* [y]*19* *En Hakkore* means *caller's spring.* [z]*20* Traditionally *judged*

4Some time later, he fell in love[a] with
a woman in the Valley of Sorek whose
name was Delilah. 5The rulers of the
Philistines[b] went to her and said, "See if
you can lure[c] him into showing you the
secret of his great strength and how we
can overpower him so we may tie him up
and subdue him. Each one of us will give
you eleven hundred shekels[a] of silver."[d]
6So Delilah said to Samson, "Tell me
the secret of your great strength and how
you can be tied up and subdued."
7Samson answered her, "If anyone ties
me with seven fresh thongs[b] that have
not been dried, I'll become as weak as
any other man."
8Then the rulers of the Philistines
brought her seven fresh thongs that had
not been dried, and she tied him with
them. 9With men hidden in the room,[e]
she called to him, "Samson, the Philistines are upon you!" But he snapped the
thongs as easily as a piece of string snaps
when it comes close to a flame. So the
secret of his strength was not discovered.
10Then Delilah said to Samson, "You
have made a fool of me;[f] you lied to me.
Come now, tell me how you can be tied."
11He said, "If anyone ties me securely
with new ropes[g] that have never been
used, I'll become as weak as any other
man."
12So Delilah took new ropes and tied
him with them. Then, with men hidden
in the room, she called to him, "Samson,
the Philistines are upon you!" But he
snapped the ropes off his arms as if they
were threads.
13Delilah then said to Samson, "Until
now, you have been making a fool of me
and lying to me. Tell me how you can be
tied."
He replied, "If you weave the seven
braids of my head into the fabric ⌊on the
loom⌋ and tighten it with the pin, I'll become as weak as any other man." So
while he was sleeping, Delilah took the
seven braids of his head, wove them into
the fabric 14and[c] tightened it with the
pin.
Again she called to him, "Samson, the
Philistines are upon you!"[h] He awoke
from his sleep and pulled up the pin and
the loom, with the fabric.
15Then she said to him, "How can you
say, 'I love you,'[i] when you won't confide
in me? This is the third time[j] you have
made a fool of me and haven't told me
the secret of your great strength.[k]"
16With such nagging she prodded him
day after day until he was tired to death.
17So he told her everything.[l] "No razor
has ever been used on my head," he said,
"because I have been a Nazirite[m] set
apart to God since birth. If my head were
shaved, my strength would leave me, and
I would become as weak as any other
man."
18When Delilah saw that he had told
her everything, she sent word to the rulers of the Philistines[n], "Come back once
more; he has told me everything." So
the rulers of the Philistines returned with
the silver in their hands. 19Having put
him to sleep on her lap, she called a man
to shave off the seven braids of his hair,
and so began to subdue him.[d] And his
strength left him.[o]
20Then she called, "Samson, the Philistines are upon you!"
He awoke from his sleep and thought,
"I'll go out as before and shake myself
free." But he did not know that the LORD
had left him.[p]
21Then the Philistines[q] seized him,
gouged out his eyes[r] and took him down
to Gaza. Binding him with bronze shackles, they set him to grinding[s] in the
prison. 22But the hair on his head began
to grow again after it had been shaved.

Samson's death
at the temple of Dagon.

23Now the rulers of the Philistines
assembled to offer a great sacrifice to
Dagon[t] their god and to celebrate, saying, "Our god has delivered Samson, our
enemy, into our hands."

16:4 [a]Ge 24:67
16:5 [b]Jos 13:3 [c]Ex 10:7; Jdg 14:15 [d]ver 18
16:9 [e]ver 12
16:10 [f]ver 13
16:11 [g]Jdg 15:13
16:14 [h]ver 9,20
16:15 [i]Jdg 14:16 [j]Nu 24:10 [k]ver 5
16:17 [l]Mic 7:5 [m]Nu 6:2,5; Jdg 13:5
16:18 [n]Jos 13:3; 1Sa 5:8
16:19 [o]Pr 7:26-27
16:20 [p]Nu 14:42; Jos 7:12; 1Sa 16:14; 18:12; 28:15
16:21 [q]Jer 47:1 [r]Nu 16:14 [s]Job 31:10; Isa 47:2
16:23 [t]1Sa 5:2; 1Ch 10:10

[a] *5* That is, about 28 pounds (about 13 kilograms)
[b] *7* Or *bowstrings*; also in verses 8 and 9
[c] *13,14* Some Septuagint manuscripts; Hebrew *"⌊I can⌋ if you weave the seven braids of my head into the fabric ⌊on the loom⌋." 14So she*
[d] *19* Hebrew; some Septuagint manuscripts *and he began to weaken*

24 When the people saw him, they praised their god,[a] saying,

"Our god has delivered our enemy
 into our hands,[b]
the one who laid waste our land
 and multiplied our slain."

25 While they were in high spirits,[c] they shouted, "Bring out Samson to entertain us." So they called Samson out of the prison, and he performed for them.

When they stood him among the pillars, 26 Samson said to the servant who held his hand, "Put me where I can feel the pillars that support the temple, so that I may lean against them." 27 Now the temple was crowded with men and women; all the rulers of the Philistines were there, and on the roof[d] were about three thousand men and women watching Samson perform. 28 Then Samson prayed to the LORD,[e] "O Sovereign LORD, remember me. O God, please strengthen me just once more, and let me with one blow get revenge[f] on the Philistines for my two eyes." 29 Then Samson reached toward the two central pillars on which the temple stood. Bracing himself against them, his right hand on the one and his left hand on the other, 30 Samson said, "Let me die with the Philistines!" Then he pushed with all his might, and down came the temple on the rulers and all the people in it. Thus he killed many more when he died than while he lived.

31 Then his brothers and his father's whole family went down to get him. They brought him back and buried him between Zorah and Eshtaol in the tomb of Manoah[g] his father. He had led[e][h] Israel twenty years.[i]

Idolatry of Micah and his mother.

17 Now a man named Micah[j] from the hill country of Ephraim 2 said to his mother, "The eleven hundred shekels[f] of silver that were taken from you and about which I heard you utter a curse—I have that silver with me; I took it."

Then his mother said, "The LORD bless you,[k] my son!"

3 When he returned the eleven hundred shekels of silver to his mother, she said, "I solemnly consecrate my silver to the LORD for my son to make a carved image and a cast idol.[l] I will give it back to you."

4 So he returned the silver to his mother, and she took two hundred shekels[g] of silver and gave them to a silversmith, who made them into the image and the idol.[m] And they were put in Micah's house.

5 Now this man Micah had a shrine,[n] and he made an ephod[o] and some idols[p] and installed[q] one of his sons as his priest.[r] 6 In those days Israel had no king;[s] everyone did as he saw fit.[t]

7 A young Levite from Bethlehem in Judah,[u] who had been living within the clan of Judah, 8 left that town in search of some other place to stay. On his way[h] he came to Micah's house in the hill country of Ephraim.

9 Micah asked him, "Where are you from?"

"I'm a Levite from Bethlehem in Judah," he said, "and I'm looking for a place to stay."

10 Then Micah said to him, "Live with me and be my father and priest,[v] and I'll give you ten shekels[i] of silver a year, your clothes and your food." 11 So the Levite agreed to live with him, and the young man was to him like one of his sons. 12 Then Micah installed[w] the Levite, and the young man became his priest and lived in his house. 13 And Micah said, "Now I know that the LORD will be good to me, since this Levite has become my priest."

The Danites steal Micah's idols and priest.

18 In those days Israel had no king.[x]

And in those days the tribe of the Danites was seeking a place of their own

16:24 [a]Da 5:4 [b]1Sa 31:9; 1Ch 10:9
16:25 [c]Jdg 9:27; Ru 3:7; Est 1:10
16:27 [d]Dt 22:8; Jos 2:8
16:28 [e]Jdg 15:18 [f]Jer 15:15
16:31 [g]Jdg 13:2 [h]Ru 1:1; 1Sa 4:18 [i]Jdg 15:20
17:1 [j]Jdg 18:2,13
17:2 [k]Ru 2:20; 1Sa 15:13; 2Sa 2:5
17:3 [l]Ex 20:4,23; 34:17; Lev 19:4
17:4 [m]Ex 32:4; Isa 17:8
17:5 [n]Isa 44:13; Eze 8:10 [o]Jdg 8:27 [p]Ge 31:19; Jdg 18:14 [q]Nu 16:10 [r]Ex 29:9; Jdg 18:24
17:6 [s]Jdg 18:1; 19:1; 21:25 [t]Dt 12:8
17:7 [u]Jdg 19:1; Ru 1:1-2; Mic 5:2; Mt 2:1
17:10 [v]Jdg 18:19
17:12 [w]Nu 16:10
18:1 [x]Jdg 17:6; 19:1

[e]*31* Traditionally *judged* [f]*2* That is, about 28 pounds (about 13 kilograms) [g]*4* That is, about 5 pounds (about 2.3 kilograms) [h]*8* Or *To carry on his profession* [i]*10* That is, about 4 ounces (about 110 grams)

where they might settle, because they
had not yet come into an inheritance
among the tribes of Israel.[a] 2So the Danites[b] sent five warriors from Zorah and
Eshtaol to spy out the land and explore it.
These men represented all their clans.
They told them, "Go, explore the land."[c]
The men entered the hill country of
Ephraim and came to the house of Micah,[d] where they spent the night. 3When
they were near Micah's house, they recognized the voice of the young Levite; so
they turned in there and asked him,
"Who brought you here? What are you
doing in this place? Why are you here?"
4He told them what Micah had done
for him, and said, "He has hired me and
I am his priest.[e]"
5Then they said to him, "Please inquire
of God[f] to learn whether our journey
will be successful."
6The priest answered them, "Go in
peace[g]. Your journey has the LORD's approval."
7So the five men left and came to
Laish,[h] where they saw that the people
were living in safety, like the Sidonians,
unsuspecting and secure. And since their
land lacked nothing, they were prosperous.[j] Also, they lived a long way from the
Sidonians[i] and had no relationship with
anyone else.[k]
8When they returned to Zorah and Eshtaol, their brothers asked them, "How did
you find things?"
9They answered, "Come on, let's attack
them! We have seen that the land is very
good. Aren't you going to do something?
Don't hesitate to go there and take it
over.[j] 10When you get there, you will find
an unsuspecting people and a spacious
land that God has put into your hands, a
land that lacks nothing[k] whatever.[l]"
11Then six hundred men[m] from the
clan of the Danites,[n] armed for battle, set
out from Zorah and Eshtaol. 12On their
way they set up camp near Kiriath Jearim
in Judah. This is why the place west of
Kiriath Jearim is called Mahaneh Dan[l][o]
to this day. 13From there they went on to
the hill country of Ephraim and came to
Micah's house.

18:1 [a]Jos 19:47
18:2 [b]Jdg 13:25 [c]Jos 2:1 [d]Jdg 17:1
18:4 [e]Jdg 17:12
18:5 [f]1Ki 22:5
18:6 [g]1Ki 22:6
18:7 [h]Jos 19:47 [i]ver 28
18:9 [j]Nu 13:30; 1Ki 22:3
18:10 [k]ver 7,27; Dt 8:9 [l]1Ch 4:40
18:11 [m]ver 16,17 [n]Jdg 13:2
18:12 [o]Jdg 13:25
18:14 [p]Ge 31:19; Jdg 17:5
18:16 [q]ver 11
18:17 [r]Ge 31:19; Mic 5:13
18:18 [s]Isa 46:2; Jer 43:11; Hos 10:5
18:19 [t]Job 21:5; 29:9; 40:4; Mic 7:16 [u]Jdg 17:10

14Then the five men who had spied out
the land of Laish said to their brothers,
"Do you know that one of these houses
has an ephod, other household gods, a
carved image and a cast idol?[p] Now you
know what to do." 15So they turned in
there and went to the house of the young
Levite at Micah's place and greeted him.
16The six hundred Danites,[q] armed for
battle, stood at the entrance to the gate.
17The five men who had spied out the
land went inside and took the carved
image, the ephod, the other household
gods[r] and the cast idol while the priest
and the six hundred armed men stood at
the entrance to the gate.
18When these men went into Micah's
house and took[s] the carved image, the
ephod, the other household gods and the
cast idol, the priest said to them, "What
are you doing?"
19They answered him, "Be quiet![t]
Don't say a word. Come with us, and be
our father and priest.[u] Isn't it better that
you serve a tribe and clan in Israel as
priest rather than just one man's household?" 20Then the priest was glad. He
took the ephod, the other household gods
and the carved image and went along
with the people. 21Putting their little children, their livestock and their possessions in front of them, they turned away
and left.
22When they had gone some distance
from Micah's house, the men who lived
near Micah were called together and
overtook the Danites. 23As they shouted
after them, the Danites turned and said
to Micah, "What's the matter with you
that you called out your men to fight?"
24He replied, "You took the gods I
made, and my priest, and went away.
What else do I have? How can you ask,
'What's the matter with you?'"
25The Danites answered, "Don't argue
with us, or some hot-tempered men will
attack you, and you and your family will
lose your lives." 26So the Danites went

j*7* The meaning of the Hebrew for this clause is uncertain. k*7* Hebrew; some Septuagint manuscripts *with the Arameans* l*12* *Mahaneh Dan* means *Dan's camp.*

their way, and Micah, seeing that they
were too strong for him,[a] turned around
and went back home.

Laish is renamed Dan.

27Then they took what Micah had
made, and his priest, and went on to Laish, against a peaceful and unsuspecting
people.[b] They attacked them with the
sword and burned down their city.[c]
28There was no one to rescue them because they lived a long way from Sidon[d]
and had no relationship with anyone else.
The city was in a valley near Beth Rehob.[e]
The Danites rebuilt the city and settled
there. 29They named it Dan[f] after their
forefather Dan, who was born to Israel—
though the city used to be called Laish.[g]
30There the Danites set up for themselves
the idols, and Jonathan son of Gershom,[h]
the son of Moses,[m] and his sons were
priests for the tribe of Dan until the time
of the captivity of the land. 31They continued to use the idols Micah had made,
all the time the house of God[i] was in
Shiloh.[j]

Departure of the Levite's concubine.

19 In those days Israel had no
king.
Now a Levite who lived in a remote
area in the hill country of Ephraim[k] took
a concubine from Bethlehem in Judah.[l]
2But she was unfaithful to him. She left
him and went back to her father's house
in Bethlehem, Judah. After she had been
there four months, 3her husband went to
her to persuade her to return. He had
with him his servant and two donkeys.
She took him into her father's house, and
when her father saw him, he gladly welcomed him. 4His father-in-law, the girl's
father, prevailed upon him to stay; so he
remained with him three days, eating and
drinking,[m] and sleeping there.
5On the fourth day they got up early
and he prepared to leave, but the girl's
father said to his son-in-law, "Refresh
yourself[n] with something to eat; then you
can go." 6So the two of them sat down to
eat and drink together. Afterward the
girl's father said, "Please stay tonight and
enjoy yourself.[o]" 7And when the man
got up to go, his father-in-law persuaded
him, so he stayed there that night. 8On
the morning of the fifth day, when he
rose to go, the girl's father said, "Refresh
yourself. Wait till afternoon!" So the two
of them ate together.
9Then when the man, with his concubine and his servant, got up to leave, his
father-in-law, the girl's father, said, "Now
look, it's almost evening. Spend the night
here; the day is nearly over. Stay and enjoy yourself. Early tomorrow morning you
can get up and be on your way home."
10But, unwilling to stay another night, the
man left and went toward Jebus[p] (that is,
Jerusalem), with his two saddled donkeys
and his concubine.
11When they were near Jebus and the
day was almost gone, the servant said to
his master, "Come, let's stop at this city
of the Jebusites[q] and spend the night."
12His master replied, "No. We won't go
into an alien city, whose people are not
Israelites. We will go on to Gibeah." 13He
added, "Come, let's try to reach Gibeah
or Ramah[r] and spend the night in one of
those places." 14So they went on, and the
sun set as they neared Gibeah in Benjamin.[s] 15There they stopped to spend
the night. They went and sat in the city
square,[t] but no one took them into his
home for the night.
16That evening[u] an old man from the
hill country of Ephraim,[v] who was living
in Gibeah (the men of the place were
Benjamites), came in from his work in
the fields. 17When he looked and saw the
traveler in the city square, the old man
asked, "Where are you going? Where did
you come from?"[w]
18He answered, "We are on our way
from Bethlehem in Judah to a remote
area in the hill country of Ephraim where
I live. I have been to Bethlehem in Judah
and now I am going to the house of the
LORD.[x] No one has taken me into his

18:26 [a]Ps 18:17; 35:10
18:27 [b]ver 7,10 [c]Ge 49:17; Jos 19:47
18:28 [d]ver 7 [e]Nu 13:21; 2Sa 10:6
18:29 [f]Ge 14:14 [g]Jos 19:47; 1Ki 15:20
18:30 [h]Ex 2:22; Jdg 17:3,5
18:31 [i]Jdg 19:18 [j]Jos 18:1; Jer 7:14
19:1 [k]Jdg 18:1 [l]Ru 1:1
19:4 [m]Ex 32:6
19:5 [n]ver 8; Ge 18:5
19:6 [o]ver 9,22; Jdg 16:25
19:10 [p]Ge 10:16; Jos 15:8; 1Ch 11:4-5
19:11 [q]Jos 3:10
19:13 [r]Jos 18:25
19:14 [s]1Sa 10:26; Isa 10:29
19:15 [t]Ge 19:2
19:16 [u]Ps 104:23 [v]ver 1
19:17 [w]Ge 29:4
19:18 [x]Jdg 18:31

m*30* An ancient Hebrew scribal tradition, some Septuagint manuscripts and Vulgate; Masoretic Text *Manasseh*

house. 19We have both straw and fodder[a] for our donkeys and bread and wine[b] for ourselves your servants—me, your maidservant, and the young man with us. We don't need anything."

20"You are welcome at my house," the old man said. "Let me supply whatever you need. Only don't spend the night in the square." 21So he took him into his house and fed his donkeys. After they had washed their feet, they had something to eat and drink.[c]

Hideous death of the concubine.

22While they were enjoying themselves,[d] some of the wicked men[e] of the city surrounded the house. Pounding on the door, they shouted to the old man who owned the house, "Bring out the man who came to your house so we can have sex with him.[f]"

23The owner of the house went outside[g] and said to them, "No, my friends, don't be so vile. Since this man is my guest, don't do this disgraceful thing.[h] 24Look, here is my virgin daughter,[i] and his concubine. I will bring them out to you now, and you can use them and do to them whatever you wish. But to this man, don't do such a disgraceful thing."

25But the men would not listen to him. So the man took his concubine and sent her outside to them, and they raped her and abused her[j] throughout the night, and at dawn they let her go. 26At daybreak the woman went back to the house where her master was staying, fell down at the door and lay there until daylight.

27When her master got up in the morning and opened the door of the house and stepped out to continue on his way, there lay his concubine, fallen in the doorway of the house, with her hands on the threshold. 28He said to her, "Get up; let's go." But there was no answer. Then the man put her on his donkey and set out for home.

29When he reached home, he took a knife[k] and cut up his concubine, limb by limb, into twelve parts and sent them into all the areas of Israel.[l] 30Everyone who saw it said, "Such a thing has never been seen or done, not since the day the Israelites came up out of Egypt.[m] Think about it! Consider it! Tell us what to do![n]"

War between Israel and the Benjamites.

20 Then all the Israelites[o] from Dan to Beersheba[p] and from the land of Gilead came out as one man[q] and assembled[r] before the LORD in Mizpah. 2The leaders of all the people of the tribes of Israel took their places in the assembly of the people of God, four hundred thousand soldiers[s] armed with swords. 3(The Benjamites heard that the Israelites had gone up to Mizpah.) Then the Israelites said, "Tell us how this awful thing happened."

4So the Levite, the husband of the murdered woman, said, "I and my concubine came to Gibeah[t] in Benjamin to spend the night.[u] 5During the night the men of Gibeah came after me and surrounded the house, intending to kill me.[v] They raped my concubine, and she died.[w] 6I took my concubine, cut her into pieces and sent one piece to each region of Israel's inheritance,[x] because they committed this lewd and disgraceful act[y] in Israel. 7Now, all you Israelites, speak up and give your verdict.[z]"

8All the people rose as one man, saying, "None of us will go home. No, not one of us will return to his house. 9But now this is what we'll do to Gibeah: We'll go up against it as the lot directs.[a] 10We'll take ten men out of every hundred from all the tribes of Israel, and a hundred from a thousand, and a thousand from ten thousand, to get provisions for the army. Then, when the army arrives at Gibeah[n] in Benjamin, it can give them what they deserve for all this vileness done in Israel." 11So all the men of Israel got together and united as one man[b] against the city.

19:19 [a]Ge 24:25 [b]Ge 14:18
19:21 [c]Ge 24:32-33; Lk 7:44
19:22 [d]Jdg 16:25 [e]Dt 13:13 [f]Ge 19:4-5; Jdg 20:5; Ro 1:26-27
19:23 [g]Ge 19:6 [h]Ge 34:7; Lev 19:29; Dt 22:21; Jdg 20:6; 2Sa 13:12; Ro 1:27
19:24 [i]Ge 19:8; Dt 21:14
19:25 [j]1Sa 31:4
19:29 [k]Ge 22:6 [l]Jdg 20:6; 1Sa 11:7
19:30 [m]Hos 9:9 [n]Jdg 20:7; Pr 13:10
20:1 [o]Jdg 21:5 [p]1Sa 3:20; 2Sa 3:10; 1Ki 4:25 [q]1Sa 11:7 [r]1Sa 7:5
20:2 [s]Jdg 8:10
20:4 [t]Jos 15:57 [u]Jdg 19:15
20:5 [v]Jdg 19:22 [w]Jdg 19:25-26
20:6 [x]Jdg 19:29 [y]Jos 7:15; Jdg 19:23
20:7 [z]Jdg 19:30
20:9 [a]Lev 16:8
20:11 [b]ver 1

[n] *10* One Hebrew manuscript; most Hebrew manuscripts *Geba,* a variant of *Gibeah*

12 The tribes of Israel sent men throughout the tribe of Benjamin, saying, "What about this awful crime that was committed among you? 13 Now surrender those wicked men[a] of Gibeah so that we may put them to death and purge the evil from Israel.[b]"

But the Benjamites would not listen to their fellow Israelites. 14 From their towns they came together at Gibeah to fight against the Israelites. 15 At once the Benjamites mobilized twenty-six thousand swordsmen from their towns, in addition to seven hundred chosen men from those living in Gibeah. 16 Among all these soldiers there were seven hundred chosen men who were left-handed,[c] each of whom could sling a stone at a hair and not miss.

17 Israel, apart from Benjamin, mustered four hundred thousand swordsmen, all of them fighting men.

18 The Israelites went up to Bethel[o] and inquired of God.[d] They said, "Who of us shall go first to fight[e] against the Benjamites?"

The LORD replied, "Judah shall go first."

19 The next morning the Israelites got up and pitched camp near Gibeah. 20 The men of Israel went out to fight the Benjamites and took up battle positions against them at Gibeah. 21 The Benjamites came out of Gibeah and cut down twenty-two thousand Israelites[f] on the battlefield that day. 22 But the men of Israel encouraged one another and again took up their positions where they had stationed themselves the first day. 23 The Israelites went up and wept before the LORD until evening,[g] and they inquired of the LORD. They said, "Shall we go up again to battle[h] against the Benjamites, our brothers?"

The LORD answered, "Go up against them."

24 Then the Israelites drew near to Benjamin the second day. 25 This time, when the Benjamites came out from Gibeah to oppose them, they cut down another eighteen thousand Israelites,[i] all of them armed with swords.

26 Then the Israelites, all the people, went up to Bethel, and there they sat weeping before the LORD.[j] They fasted that day until evening and presented burnt offerings and fellowship offerings[p] to the LORD.[k] 27 And the Israelites inquired of the LORD. (In those days the ark of the covenant of God[l] was there, 28 with Phinehas son of Eleazar,[m] the son of Aaron, ministering before it.)[n] They asked, "Shall we go up again to battle with Benjamin our brother, or not?"

The LORD responded, "Go, for tomorrow I will give them into your hands.[o]"

29 Then Israel set an ambush[p] around Gibeah. 30 They went up against the Benjamites on the third day and took up positions against Gibeah as they had done before. 31 The Benjamites came out to meet them and were drawn away[q] from the city. They began to inflict casualties on the Israelites as before, so that about thirty men fell in the open field and on the roads—the one leading to Bethel and the other to Gibeah.

32 While the Benjamites were saying, "We are defeating them as before,"[r] the Israelites were saying, "Let's retreat and draw them away from the city to the roads."

33 All the men of Israel moved from their places and took up positions at Baal Tamar, and the Israelite ambush charged out of its place[s] on the west[q] of Gibeah.[r] 34 Then ten thousand of Israel's finest men made a frontal attack on Gibeah. The fighting was so heavy that the Benjamites did not realize[t] how near disaster was.[u] 35 The LORD defeated Benjamin[v] before Israel, and on that day the Israelites struck down 25,100 Benjamites, all armed with swords. 36 Then the Benjamites saw that they were beaten.

Now the men of Israel had given way[w] before Benjamin, because they relied on the ambush they had set near Gibeah. 37 The men who had been in ambush made a sudden dash into Gibeah, spread

20:13 [a]Dt 13:13; Jdg 19:22 [b]Dt 17:12
20:16 [c]Jdg 3:15; 1Ch 12:2
20:18 [d]ver 26-27; Nu 27:21 [e]ver 23,28
20:21 [f]ver 25
20:23 [g]Jos 7:6 [h]ver 18
20:25 [i]ver 21
20:26 [j]ver 23 [k]Jdg 21:4
20:27 [l]Jos 18:1
20:28 [m]Jos 24:33 [n]Dt 18:5 [o]Jdg 7:9
20:29 [p]Jos 8:2,4
20:31 [q]Jos 8:16
20:32 [r]ver 39
20:33 [s]Jos 8:19
20:34 [t]Jos 8:14 [u]Isa 47:11
20:35 [v]1Sa 9:21
20:36 [w]Jos 8:15

[o] *18* Or *to the house of God*; also in verse 26
[p] *26* Traditionally *peace offerings*
[q] *33* Some Septuagint manuscripts and Vulgate; the meaning of the Hebrew for this word is uncertain.
[r] *33* Hebrew *Geba,* a variant of *Gibeah*

out and put the whole city to the sword.[a]
38The men of Israel had arranged with
the ambush that they should send up a
great cloud of smoke[b] from the city, 39and
then the men of Israel would turn in the
battle.
The Benjamites had begun to inflict
casualties on the men of Israel (about
thirty), and they said, "We are defeating
them as in the first battle."[c] 40But when
the column of smoke began to rise
from the city, the Benjamites turned and
saw the smoke of the whole city going up
into the sky.[d] 41Then the men of Israel
turned on them, and the men of Benjamin
were terrified, because they realized
that disaster had come upon them. 42So
they fled before the Israelites in the
direction of the desert, but they could
not escape the battle. And the men of
Israel who came out of the towns cut
them down there. 43They surrounded
the Benjamites, chased them and easily[s]
overran them in the vicinity of Gibeah
on the east. 44Eighteen thousand Benjamites fell, all of them valiant fighters.[e]
45As they turned and fled toward the
desert to the rock of Rimmon,[f] the
Israelites cut down five thousand men
along the roads. They kept pressing
after the Benjamites as far as Gidom
and struck down two thousand more.
46On that day twenty-five thousand
Benjamite swordsmen fell, all of them
valiant fighters. 47But six hundred men
turned and fled into the desert to the
rock of Rimmon, where they stayed four
months. 48The men of Israel went back
to Benjamin and put all the towns to the
sword, including the animals and everything else they found. All the towns they
came across they set on fire.[g]

Wives for the Benjamites are provided for in two ways.

21 The men of Israel had taken an
oath[h] at Mizpah:[i] "Not one of us
will give[j] his daughter in marriage to a
Benjamite."
2The people went to Bethel,[t] where
they sat before God until evening, raising
their voices and weeping bitterly. 3"O
LORD, the God of Israel," they cried,
"why has this happened to Israel? Why
should one tribe be missing from Israel
today?"
4Early the next day the people built an
altar and presented burnt offerings and
fellowship offerings.[u][k]
5Then the Israelites asked, "Who from
all the tribes of Israel[l] has failed to assemble before the LORD?" For they had taken
a solemn oath that anyone who failed to
assemble before the LORD at Mizpah
should certainly be put to death.
6Now the Israelites grieved for their
brothers, the Benjamites. "Today one
tribe is cut off from Israel," they said.
7"How can we provide wives for those
who are left, since we have taken an
oath[m] by the LORD not to give them any
of our daughters in marriage?" 8Then
they asked, "Which one of the tribes of
Israel failed to assemble before the LORD
at Mizpah?" They discovered that no one
from Jabesh Gilead[n] had come to the
camp for the assembly. 9For when they
counted the people, they found that none
of the people of Jabesh Gilead were there.
10So the assembly sent twelve thousand fighting men with instructions to go
to Jabesh Gilead and put to the sword
those living there, including the women
and children. 11"This is what you are to
do," they said. "Kill every male and every
woman who is not a virgin.[o]" 12They
found among the people living in Jabesh
Gilead four hundred young women who
had never slept with a man, and they
took them to the camp at Shiloh[p] in
Canaan.
13Then the whole assembly sent an
offer of peace[q] to the Benjamites at the
rock of Rimmon.[r] 14So the Benjamites
returned at that time and were given the
women of Jabesh Gilead who had been
spared. But there were not enough for all
of them.
15The people grieved for Benjamin,[s]

20:37 [a]Jos 8:19
20:38 [b]Jos 8:20
20:39 [c]ver 32
20:40 [d]Jos 8:20
20:44 [e]Ps 76:5
20:45 [f]Jos 15:32; Jdg 21:13
20:48 [g]Jdg 21:23
21:1 [h]Jos 9:18 [i]Jdg 20:1 [j]ver 7,18
21:4 [k]Jdg 20:26; 2Sa 24:25
21:5 [l]Jdg 5:23; 20:1
21:7 [m]ver 1
21:8 [n]1Sa 11:1; 31:11
21:11 [o]Nu 31:17-18
21:12 [p]Jos 18:1
21:13 [q]Dt 20:10 [r]Jdg 20:47
21:15 [s]ver 6

s*43* The meaning of the Hebrew for this word is uncertain. t*2* Or *to the house of God*
u*4* Traditionally *peace offerings*

because the LORD had made a gap in the
tribes of Israel. 16And the elders of the
assembly said, "With the women of Benjamin destroyed, how shall we provide
wives for the men who are left? 17The
Benjamite survivors must have heirs,"
they said, "so that a tribe of Israel will not
be wiped out. 18We can't give them our
daughters as wives, since we Israelites
have taken this oath: 'Cursed be anyone
who gives[a] a wife to a Benjamite.' 19But
look, there is the annual festival of the
LORD in Shiloh,[b] to the north of Bethel,
and east of the road that goes from
Bethel to Shechem, and to the south of
Lebonah."
20So they instructed the Benjamites,
saying, "Go and hide in the vineyards
21and watch. When the girls of Shiloh
come out to join in the dancing,[c] then
rush from the vineyards and each of you
seize a wife from the girls of Shiloh and
go to the land of Benjamin. 22When their
fathers or brothers complain to us, we
will say to them, 'Do us a kindness by
helping them, because we did not get
wives for them during the war, and you
are innocent, since you did not give[d]
your daughters to them.'"
23So that is what the Benjamites did.
While the girls were dancing, each man
caught one and carried her off to be his
wife. Then they returned to their inheritance and rebuilt the towns and settled
in them.[e]
24At that time the Israelites left that
place and went home to their tribes and
clans, each to his own inheritance.
25In those days Israel had no king;
everyone did as he saw fit.[f]

21:18 [a]ver 1
21:19 [b]Jos 18:1; Jdg 18:31; 1Sa 1:3
21:21 [c]Ex 15:20; Jdg 11:34
21:22 [d]ver 1,18
21:23 [e]Jdg 20:48
21:25 [f]Dt 12:8; Jdg 17:6; 18:1; 19:1

RUTH

Author: Unknown. (Tradition has suggested Samuel.)

Date Written: Uncertain. (However, the prevalent view ascribes a date between 1011 and 931 B.C.)

Time Span: 12 years (during the time of the judges).

Title: The book is named after its principal character: Ruth. Her biography is outlined in this short story.

Background: The setting for the book of Ruth begins in the country of Moab, a region northeast of the Dead Sea, but then moves to Bethlehem. This true account takes place during the dismal days of failure and rebellion of the Israelites, called the period of judges.

Where Written: Unknown (probably in Judah).

To Whom: To the Israelites.

Content: A famine forces Elimelech and his wife Naomi from their Israelite home to the country of Moab. Elimelech dies and Naomi is left with her 2 sons, who soon marry 2 Moabite girls, Orpah and Ruth. Later both of the sons die, and Naomi is left alone with Orpah and Ruth in a strange land. Orpah returns to her parents, but Ruth determines to stay with Naomi as they journey to Bethlehem. This is a beautiful story of love, commitment and devotion as Ruth tells Naomi, "Where you go I will go, and where you stay I will stay" (1:16). Ruth eventually marries a wealthy man named Boaz, by whom she bears a son, Obed, who is the grandfather of David. Ruth's proven devotion has been rewarded with a new husband, a son and a privileged position in the royal lineage of Jesus Christ.

Key Words: "Kinsman-redeemer"; "Ancestor." Boaz graphically fulfills the role of "kinsman-redeemer." As a relative, he willingly obtains the right to claim the land of Naomi and thus the right to marry Ruth, thereby fathering a son to keep the family line alive. This is only one of several relationships between "ancestors" in the story, which ends with the family tree listing Ruth and Boaz as the great-grandparents of King David.

Themes: • Genuine love at times may require uncompromising sacrifice. • Regardless of our lot in life, we can live according to the precepts of God. • Genuine love and kindness will be rewarded. • God abundantly blesses those who seek to live obedient lives. • Obedient living does not allow for "accidents" in the eternal plan of God. • God extends mercy to the merciful.

Outline:

1. Ruth determines to stay with Naomi. 1:1-1:22
2. Ruth cares for Naomi and meets Boaz. 2:1-2:23
3. Naomi plans for Boaz to redeem Ruth. 3:1-3:18
4. Ruth is rewarded for her love. 4:1-4:22

RUTH

Elimelech and his two sons die.

1 In the days when the judges ruled,[a][a]
there was a famine in the land,[b] and
a man from Bethlehem in Judah, together with his wife and two sons, went to
live for a while in the country of Moab.[c]
2The man's name was Elimelech, his
wife's name Naomi, and the names of
his two sons were Mahlon and Kilion.
They were Ephrathites from Bethlehem,[d]
Judah. And they went to Moab and lived
there.
3Now Elimelech, Naomi's husband,
died, and she was left with her two
sons. 4They married Moabite women,
one named Orpah and the other Ruth.[e]
After they had lived there about ten
years, 5both Mahlon and Kilion also
died, and Naomi was left without her
two sons and her husband.

Ruth returns with Naomi to Bethlehem.

6When she heard in Moab that the
LORD had come to the aid of his people[f]
by providing food[g] for them, Naomi
and her daughters-in-law prepared to
return home from there. 7With her two
daughters-in-law she left the place where
she had been living and set out on the
road that would take them back to the
land of Judah.
8Then Naomi said to her two daughters-in-law, "Go back, each of you, to
your mother's home. May the LORD show
kindness[h] to you, as you have shown to
your dead[i] and to me. 9May the LORD
grant that each of you will find rest[j] in
the home of another husband."
Then she kissed them and they wept
aloud 10and said to her, "We will go back
with you to your people."
11But Naomi said, "Return home, my
daughters. Why would you come with
me? Am I going to have any more sons,
who could become your husbands?[k]
12Return home, my daughters; I am too
old to have another husband. Even if I
thought there was still hope for me—
even if I had a husband tonight and then
gave birth to sons— 13would you wait
until they grew up? Would you remain
unmarried for them? No, my daughters.
It is more bitter for me than for you,
because the LORD's hand has gone out
against me![l]"

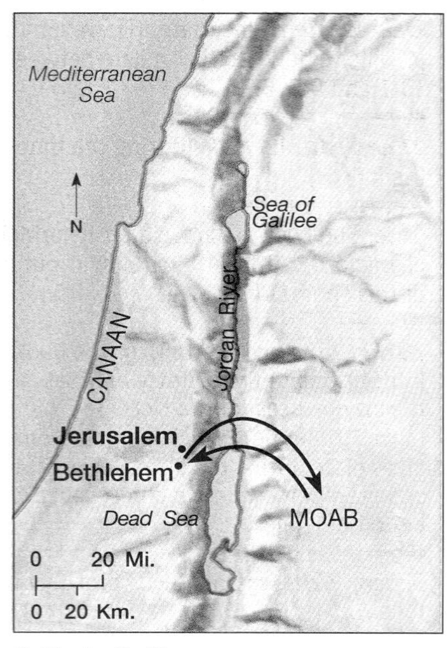

Setting for the Story

Elimelech, Naomi, and their sons traveled from Bethlehem to Moab because of a famine. After her husband and sons died, Naomi returned to Bethlehem with her daughter-in-law Ruth.

14At this they wept again. Then
Orpah kissed her mother-in-law[m] good-
by, but Ruth clung to her.[n]
15"Look," said Naomi, "your sister-in-
law is going back to her people and her
gods.[o] Go back with her."
16But Ruth replied, "Don't urge me
to leave you[p] or to turn back from you.
Where you go I will go, and where you
stay I will stay. Your people will be my
people and your God my God.[q] 17Where
you die I will die, and there I will be
buried. May the LORD deal with me, be

1:1 [a]Jdg 2:16-18 [b]Ge 12:10; Ps 105:16 [c]Jdg 3:30
1:2 [d]Ge 35:19
1:4 [e]Mt 1:5
1:6 [f]Ex 4:31; Jer 29:10; Zep 2:7 [g]Ps 132:15; Mt 6:11
1:8 [h]Ru 2:20; 2Ti 1:16 [i]ver 5
1:9 [j]Ru 3:1
1:11 [k]Ge 38:11; Dt 25:5
1:13 [l]Jdg 2:15; Job 4:5; 19:21; Ps 32:4
1:14 [m]Ru 2:11 [n]Pr 17:17; 18:24
1:15 [o]Jos 24:14; Jdg 11:24
1:16 [p]2Ki 2:2 [q]Ru 2:11,12

a *1* Traditionally *judged*

it ever so severely,[a] if anything but death
separates you and me." 18When Naomi
realized that Ruth was determined to
go with her, she stopped urging her.[b]
19So the two women went on until
they came to Bethlehem. When they arrived in Bethlehem, the whole town was
stirred[c] because of them, and the wom-
en exclaimed, "Can this be Naomi?"
20"Don't call me Naomi,[b]" she told
them. "Call me Mara,[c] because the
Almighty[d][d] has made my life very bitter.[e] 21I went away full, but the LORD
has brought me back empty.[f] Why call
me Naomi? The LORD has afflicted[e] me;
the Almighty has brought misfortune
upon me."
22So Naomi returned from Moab accompanied by Ruth the Moabitess, her
daughter-in-law, arriving in Bethlehem
as the barley harvest[g] was beginning.[h]

Ruth meets Boaz and gleans his fields.

2 Now Naomi had a relative[i] on her
husband's side, from the clan of
Elimelech,[j] a man of standing, whose
name was Boaz.[k]
2And Ruth the Moabitess said to
Naomi, "Let me go to the fields and pick
up the leftover grain[l] behind anyone in
whose eyes I find favor."
Naomi said to her, "Go ahead, my
daughter." 3So she went out and began
to glean in the fields behind the harvesters. As it turned out, she found herself working in a field belonging to
Boaz, who was from the clan of Elimelech.
4Just then Boaz arrived from Bethlehem and greeted the harvesters, "The
LORD be with you![m]"
"The LORD bless you![n]" they called
back.
5Boaz asked the foreman of his harvesters, "Whose young woman is that?"
6The foreman replied, "She is the
Moabitess[o] who came back from Moab
with Naomi. 7She said, 'Please let me
glean and gather among the sheaves
behind the harvesters.' She went into
the field and has worked steadily from
morning till now, except for a short rest
in the shelter."

Boaz protects and provides for Ruth.

8So Boaz said to Ruth, "My daughter,
listen to me. Don't go and glean in another field and don't go away from
here. Stay here with my servant girls.
9Watch the field where the men are
harvesting, and follow along after the
girls. I have told the men not to touch
you. And whenever you are thirsty, go
and get a drink from the water jars the
men have filled."
10At this, she bowed down with her
face to the ground.[p] She exclaimed,
"Why have I found such favor in your
eyes that you notice me[q]—a foreigner?[r]"
11Boaz replied, "I've been told all
about what you have done for your
mother-in-law[s] since the death of your
husband—how you left your father
and mother and your homeland and
came to live with a people you did not
know before.[t] 12May the LORD repay
you for what you have done. May you
be richly rewarded by the LORD,[u] the
God of Israel, under whose wings[v] you
have come to take refuge.[w]"
13"May I continue to find favor in
your eyes, my lord," she said. "You have
given me comfort and have spoken
kindly to your servant—though I do not
have the standing of one of your servant
girls."
14At mealtime Boaz said to her,
"Come over here. Have some bread and
dip it in the wine vinegar."
When she sat down with the harvesters, he offered her some roasted
grain. She ate all she wanted and had
some left over.[x] 15As she got up to glean,
Boaz gave orders to his men, "Even if
she gathers among the sheaves, don't
embarrass her. 16Rather, pull out some
stalks for her from the bundles and

1:17 [a]1Sa 3:17; 25:22; 2Sa 19:13; 2Ki 6:31
1:18 [b]Ac 21:14
1:19 [c]Mt 21:10
1:20 [d]Ex 6:3 [e]ver 13; Job 6:4
1:21 [f]Job 1:21
1:22 [g]Ex 9:31; Ru 2:23 [h]2Sa 21:9
2:1 [i]Ru 3:2,12 [j]Ru 1:2 [k]Ru 4:21
2:2 [l]ver 7; Lev 19:9; 23:22; Dt 24:19
2:4 [m]Jdg 6:12; Lk 1:28; 2Th 3:16 [n]Ps 129:7-8
2:6 [o]Ru 1:22
2:10 [p]1Sa 25:23 [q]Ps 41:1 [r]Dt 15:3
2:11 [s]Ru 1:14 [t]Ru 1:16-17
2:12 [u]1Sa 24:19 [v]Ps 17:8; 36:7; 57:1; 61:4; 63:7; 91:4 [w]Ru 1:16
2:14 [x]ver 18

b20 *Naomi* means *pleasant*; also in verse21.
c20 *Mara* means *bitter.* d20 Hebrew *Shaddai*; also in verse 21 e21 Or *has testified against*

leave them for her to pick up, and don't rebuke her."

[17]So Ruth gleaned in the field until evening. Then she threshed the barley she had gathered, and it amounted to about an ephah.[f] [18]She carried it back to town, and her mother-in-law saw how much she had gathered. Ruth also brought out and gave her what she had left over[a] after she had eaten enough.

[19]Her mother-in-law asked her, "Where did you glean today? Where did you work? Blessed be the man who took notice of you![b]"

Then Ruth told her mother-in-law about the one at whose place she had been working. "The name of the man I worked with today is Boaz," she said.

[20]"The LORD bless him!" Naomi said to her daughter-in-law. "He has not stopped showing his kindness[c] to the living and the dead." She added, "That man is our close relative; he is one of our kinsman-redeemers.[d]"

[21]Then Ruth the Moabitess said, "He even said to me, 'Stay with my workers until they finish harvesting all my grain.'"

[22]Naomi said to Ruth her daughter-in-law, "It will be good for you, my daughter, to go with his girls, because in someone else's field you might be harmed."

[23]So Ruth stayed close to the servant girls of Boaz to glean until the barley and wheat harvests[e] were finished. And she lived with her mother-in-law.

Ruth follows Naomi's advice.

3 One day Naomi her mother-in-law said to her, "My daughter, should I not try to find a home[g][f] for you, where you will be well provided for? [2]Is not Boaz, with whose servant girls you have been, a kinsman[g] of ours? Tonight he will be winnowing barley on the threshing floor. [3]Wash and perfume yourself,[h] and put on your best clothes. Then go down to the threshing floor, but don't let him know you are there until he has finished eating and drinking. [4]When he lies down, note the place where he is lying. Then go and uncover his feet and lie down. He will tell you what to do."

[5]"I will do whatever you say,"[i] Ruth answered. [6]So she went down to the threshing floor and did everything her mother-in-law told her to do.

Boaz is a kinsman-redeemer.

[7]When Boaz had finished eating and drinking and was in good spirits,[j] he went over to lie down at the far end of the grain pile. Ruth approached quietly, uncovered his feet and lay down. [8]In the middle of the night something startled the man, and he turned and discovered a woman lying at his feet.

[9]"Who are you?" he asked.

"I am your servant Ruth," she said. "Spread the corner of your garment[k] over me, since you are a kinsman-redeemer.[l]"

[10]"The LORD bless you, my daughter," he replied. "This kindness is greater than that which you showed earlier: You have not run after the younger men, whether rich or poor. [11]And now, my daughter, don't be afraid. I will do for you all you ask. All my fellow townsmen know that you are a woman of noble character.[m] [12]Although it is true that I am near of kin, there is a kinsman-redeemer[n] nearer than[o] I. [13]Stay here for the night, and in the morning if he wants to redeem,[p] good; let him redeem. But if he is not willing, as surely as the LORD lives[q] I will do it. Lie here until morning."

[14]So she lay at his feet until morning, but got up before anyone could be recognized; and he said, "Don't let it be known that a woman came to the threshing floor."[r]

[15]He also said, "Bring me the shawl you are wearing and hold it out." When she did so, he poured into it six measures of barley and put it on her. Then he[h] went back to town.

2:18 [a]ver 14
2:19 [b]ver 10; Ps 41:1
2:20 [c]Ru 3:10; 2Sa 2:5; Pr 17:17 [d]Ru 3:9,12; 4:1,14
2:23 [e]Dt 16:9
3:1 [f]Ru 1:9
3:2 [g]Dt 25:5-10; Ru 2:1
3:3 [h]2Sa 14:2
3:5 [i]Eph 6:1; Col 3:20
3:7 [j]Jdg 19:6,9,22; 2Sa 13:28; 1Ki 21:7; Est 1:10
3:9 [k]Eze 16:8 [l]ver 12; Ru 2:20
3:11 [m]Pr 12:4; 31:10
3:12 [n]ver 9 [o]Ru 4:1
3:13 [p]Dt 25:5; Ru 4:5; Mt 22:24 [q]Jdg 8:19; Jer 4:2
3:14 [r]Ro 14:16; 2Co 8:21

[f] *17* That is, probably about 3/5 bushel (about 22 liters) [g] *1* Hebrew *find rest* (see Ruth 1:9)
[h] *15* Most Hebrew manuscripts; many Hebrew manuscripts, Vulgate and Syriac *she*

16 When Ruth came to her mother-in-
law, Naomi asked, "How did it go, my
daughter?"
Then she told her everything Boaz
had done for her 17 and added, "He gave
me these six measures of barley, saying,
'Don't go back to your mother-in-law
empty-handed.'"
18 Then Naomi said, "Wait, my daughter, until you find out what happens. For
the man will not rest until the matter is
settled today."[a]

The marriage of Boaz and Ruth.

4 Meanwhile Boaz went up to the
town gate and sat there. When the
kinsman-redeemer he had mentioned[b]
came along, Boaz said, "Come over here,
my friend, and sit down." So he went
over and sat down.
2 Boaz took ten of the elders[c] of the
town and said, "Sit here," and they did
so. 3 Then he said to the kinsman-redeemer, "Naomi, who has come back
from Moab, is selling the piece of land
that belonged to our brother Elimelech.
4 I thought I should bring the matter to
your attention and suggest that you buy
it in the presence of these seated here
and in the presence of the elders of my
people. If you will redeem it, do so. But
if you[i] will not, tell me, so I will know.
For no one has the right to do it except
you,[d] and I am next in line."
"I will redeem it," he said.
5 Then Boaz said, "On the day you buy
the land from Naomi and from Ruth the
Moabitess, you acquire[j] the dead man's
widow, in order to maintain the name of
the dead with his property."[e]
6 At this, the kinsman-redeemer said,
"Then I cannot redeem[f] it because I
might endanger my own estate. You
redeem it yourself. I cannot do it."
7 (Now in earlier times in Israel, for
the redemption and transfer of property
to become final, one party took off his
sandal and gave it to the other. This was
the method of legalizing transactions in
Israel.)[g]
8 So the kinsman-redeemer said to
Boaz, "Buy it yourself." And he removed
his sandal.
9 Then Boaz announced to the elders
and all the people, "Today you are witnesses that I have bought from Naomi
all the property of Elimelech, Kilion and
Mahlon. 10 I have also acquired Ruth the
Moabitess, Mahlon's widow, as my wife,
in order to maintain the name of the
dead with his property, so that his name
will not disappear from among his family or from the town records.[h] Today you
are witnesses!"
11 Then the elders and all those at the
gate said, "We are witnesses.[i] May the
LORD make the woman who is coming
into your home like Rachel and Leah,[j]
who together built up the house of
Israel. May you have standing in Ephrathah[k] and be famous in Bethlehem.
12 Through the offspring the LORD gives
you by this young woman, may your
family be like that of Perez,[l] whom Tamar bore to Judah."

The genealogy of David.

4:18-22pp— 1Ch 2:5-15; Mt 1:3-6; Lk 3:31-33

13 So Boaz took Ruth and she became
his wife. Then he went to her, and the
LORD enabled her to conceive,[m] and she
gave birth to a son. 14 The women[n] said
to Naomi: "Praise be to the LORD, who
this day has not left you without a kinsman-redeemer. May he become famous
throughout Israel! 15 He will renew
your life and sustain you in your old
age. For your daughter-in-law, who loves
you and who is better to you than sev-
en sons,[o] has given him birth."
16 Then Naomi took the child, laid him
in her lap and cared for him. 17 The
women living there said, "Naomi has a
son." And they named him Obed. He
was the father of Jesse,[p] the father of
David.

3:18 [a]Ps 37:3-5
4:1 [b]Ru 3:12
4:2 [c]1Ki 21:8; Pr 31:23
4:4 [d]Lev 25:25; Jer 32:7-8
4:5 [e]Ge 38:8; Dt 25:5-6; Ru 3:13; Mt 22:24
4:6 [f]Lev 25:25; Ru 3:13
4:7 [g]Dt 25:7-9
4:10 [h]Dt 25:6
4:11 [i]Dt 25:9 [j]Ps 127:3; 128:3 [k]Ge 35:16
4:12 [l]ver 18; Ge 38:29
4:13 [m]Ge 29:31; 33:5; Ru 3:11
4:14 [n]Lk 1:58
4:15 [o]Ru 1:16-17; 2:11-12; 1Sa 1:8
4:17 [p]ver 22; 1Sa 16:1,18; 1Ch 2:12,13

[i]4 Many Hebrew manuscripts, Septuagint, Vulgate and Syriac; most Hebrew manuscripts *he* [j]5 Hebrew; Vulgate and Syriac *Naomi, you acquire Ruth the Moabitess,*

[18]This, then, is the family line of
Perez[a]:

Perez was the father of Hezron,
[19]Hezron the father of Ram,
Ram the father of Amminadab,[b]
[20]Amminadab the father of Nahshon,
Nahshon the father of Salmon,[k]
[21]Salmon the father of Boaz,[c]
Boaz the father of Obed,
[22]Obed the father of Jesse,
and Jesse the father of David.

4:18 [a]Mt 1:3-6
4:19 [b]Ex 6:23
4:21 [c]Ru 2:1

[k]*20* A few Hebrew manuscripts, some Septuagint manuscripts and Vulgate (see also verse 21 and Septuagint of 1 Chron. 2:11); most Hebrew manuscripts *Salma*

1 SAMUEL

Author: Unknown (possibly Samuel, with excerpts from the memoirs of Gad and Nathan).

Date Written: Probably between 1050 and 931 B.C. However, the book was not put into its final form until some years later, possibly between 930 and 722 B.C.

Time Span: About 94 years (period of time from the birth of Samuel to the death of Saul).

Title: This book is named after Samuel, not only because he is the principal figure in the first part, but also because he anoints Saul and David, the chief characters in the latter portion of the book.

Background: 1 Samuel is a continuation of the story in the book of Judges. It begins late in the turbulent time of the judges, when Eli is the judge-priest and Israel is being oppressed by the Philistines. 1 and 2 Samuel consist of one book in the Hebrew Bible since they cover the continuous story of their 3 main characters: Samuel, Saul and David.

Where Written: Unknown (probably in Israel).

To Whom: To the Israelites.

Content: The Israelites are insisting on a king like the pagan nations have; they no longer want God's placement of a judge over them. 1 Samuel is the story of Israel's last judge and first prophet (Samuel), her first king (Saul), and the early years of her anointed king-elect (David). Saul lacks a heart for God, so God rejects him as king. Young David then enters the picture by slaying Goliath with a sling and a stone (chapter 17) and developing a strong friendship with Saul's son, Jonathan (chapter 18). God selects David to replace Saul as king, but David has to flee to the desert to escape Saul's raging jealousy. David lives in exile until Saul and his sons die in battle at Mount Gilboa. The stage is now set for the golden age with David reigning as king of Israel.

Key Words: "Jealousy"; "Heart." The book is full of "jealousy": Israel for a king like her neighbors, and Saul for his successor David. Thus, God looks at the "heart," and his selections are not always what are expected.

Themes: • God is bigger than any problem we will ever have. • With God's help our emotions can be kept under his control. • Even God's children can fail and fall into sin. • Any life full of sin and defeat can have victory and accomplishment...if repentance and obedience are begun. • Sin in our lives may encourage God to take away our blessings and give them to others. • Our ultimate leadership should be of God, not man. • Obedience is much more important to God than sacrifice. • We, like David, should be men after God's own heart (13:14).

Outline:

1. The service of Eli as priest and judge. 1:1-4:22
2. The ministry of Samuel, the last judge of Israel. 5:1-7:17
3. The ministry of Saul, the first king of Israel. 8:1-15:35
4. David and Saul. 16:1-27:12
5. The decline and death of Saul. 28:1-31:13

1 SAMUEL

Hannah's vow and prayer for a son.

1 There was a certain man from Ramathaim, a Zuphite[a] from the hill
country[a] of Ephraim, whose name was
Elkanah[b] son of Jeroham, the son of
Elihu, the son of Tohu, the son of Zuph,
an Ephraimite. 2He had two wives;[c] one
was called Hannah and the other Peninnah. Peninnah had children, but Hannah had none.
3Year after year[d] this man went up
from his town to worship[e] and sacrifice
to the LORD Almighty at Shiloh,[f] where
Hophni and Phinehas, the two sons of
Eli, were priests of the LORD. 4When-
ever the day came for Elkanah to sacrifice,[g] he would give portions of the
meat to his wife Peninnah and to all
her sons and daughters. 5But to Hannah
he gave a double portion because he
loved her, and the LORD had closed her
womb.[h] 6And because the LORD had
closed her womb, her rival kept provoking her in order to irritate her.[i] 7This
went on year after year. Whenever Hannah went up to the house of the LORD,
her rival provoked her till she wept and
would not eat. 8Elkanah her husband
would say to her, "Hannah, why are you
weeping? Why don't you eat? Why are
you downhearted? Don't I mean more
to you than ten sons?[j]"
9Once when they had finished eating
and drinking in Shiloh, Hannah stood
up. Now Eli the priest was sitting on a
chair by the doorpost of the LORD's
temple.[b][k] 10In bitterness of soul[l] Hannah wept much and prayed to the LORD.
11And she made a vow, saying, "O LORD
Almighty, if you will only look upon
your servant's misery and remember[m]
me, and not forget your servant but
give her a son, then I will give him to
the LORD for all the days of his life, and
no razor[n] will ever be used on his
head."
12As she kept on praying to the LORD,
Eli observed her mouth. 13Hannah was
praying in her heart, and her lips were
moving but her voice was not heard.
Eli thought she was drunk 14and said to
her, "How long will you keep on getting
drunk? Get rid of your wine."
15"Not so, my lord," Hannah replied,
"I am a woman who is deeply troubled.
I have not been drinking wine or beer;
I was pouring[o] out my soul to the LORD.
16Do not take your servant for a wicked
woman; I have been praying here out of
my great anguish and grief."
17Eli answered, "Go in peace,[p] and
may the God of Israel grant you what
you have asked of him.[q]"
18She said, "May your servant find
favor in your eyes.[r]" Then she went her
way and ate something, and her face
was no longer downcast.[s]

Samuel's birth and dedication to the LORD.

19Early the next morning they arose
and worshiped before the LORD and then
went back to their home at Ramah.
Elkanah lay with Hannah his wife, and
the LORD remembered[t] her. 20So in the
course of time Hannah conceived and
gave birth to a son. She named[u] him
Samuel,[c] saying, "Because I asked the
LORD for him."
21When the man Elkanah went up
with all his family to offer the annual[v]
sacrifice to the LORD and to fulfill his
vow,[w] 22Hannah did not go. She said to
her husband, "After the boy is weaned,
I will take him and present[x] him before
the LORD, and he will live there always."
23"Do what seems best to you," Elkanah her husband told her. "Stay here
until you have weaned him; only may
the LORD make good[y] his[d] word." So the
woman stayed at home and nursed her
son until she had weaned him.
24After he was weaned, she took the
boy with her, young as he was, along

1:1 [a]Jos 17:17-18 [b]1Ch 6:27,34
1:2 [c]Dt 21:15-17; Lk 2:36
1:3 [d]ver 21; Ex 23:14; 34:23; Lk 2:41 [e]Dt 12:5-7 [f]Jos 18:1
1:4 [g]Dt 12:17-18
1:5 [h]Ge 16:1; 30:2
1:6 [i]Job 24:21
1:8 [j]Ru 4:15
1:9 [k]1Sa 3:3
1:10 [l]Job 7:11
1:11 [m]Ge 8:1; 28:20; 29:32 [n]Nu 6:1-21; Jdg 13:5
1:15 [o]Ps 42:4; 62:8; La 2:19
1:17 [p]Jdg 18:6; 1Sa 25:35; 2Ki 5:19; Mk 5:34 [q]Ps 20:3-5
1:18 [r]Ru 2:13 [s]Ecc 9:7; Ro 15:13
1:19 [t]Ge 4:1; 30:22
1:20 [u]Ge 41:51-52; Ex 2:10,22; Mt 1:21
1:21 [v]ver 3 [w]Dt 12:11
1:22 [x]ver 11,28; Lk 2:22
1:23 [y]ver 17; Nu 30:7

a *1* Or *from Ramathaim Zuphim* b *9* That is, tabernacle c *20* *Samuel* sounds like the Hebrew for *heard of God.* d *23* Masoretic Text; Dead Sea Scrolls, Septuagint and Syriac *your*

KEY PLACES IN 1 SAMUEL

Ramah Samuel was born in Ramah. Before his birth, Samuel's mother Hannah made a promise to God that she would dedicate her son to serve God alongside the priests in the tabernacle at Shiloh (1:1–2:11).

Shiloh The focal point of Israel's worship was at Shiloh, where the tabernacle and the ark of the covenant resided. Eli was the high priest, but his sons, Hophni and Phinehas, were evil men who took advantage of the people. Samuel, however, served God faithfully, and God blessed him as he grew (2:12–3:21).

Kiriath Jearim Israel was constantly at odds with the Philistines, and another battle was brewing. Hophni and Phinehas brought the ark of the covenant from Shiloh to the battlefield, believing that its mere presence would bring the Israelites victory. The Israelites were defeated by the Philistines at Ebenezer, and the ark was captured. However, the Philistines soon found out that the ark was not quite the great battle trophy they expected. For God sent plagues upon every Philistine city into which the ark was brought. Finally, the Philistines sent it back to Kiriath Jearim in Israel (4:1–7:1).

Mizpah The Israelites' defeat made them realize that God was no longer blessing them. Samuel called the people together at Mizpah and asked them to fast and pray in sorrow for their sins. The assembly at Mizpah was a tempting target for the confident Philistines who advanced for an attack. But God intervened and routed their mighty army. Meanwhile, Samuel was judging cases throughout Israel. But as Samuel grew old, the people came to him at Ramah (his home base) demanding a king in order to be like the other nations. At Mizpah, Saul was chosen by sacred appointment to be Israel's first king with the blessing, but not the approval, of God and Samuel (7:2–10:27).

Gilgal A battle with the Ammonites proved Saul's leadership abilities to the people of Israel. He protected the people of Jabesh Gilead and scattered the Ammonite army. Samuel and the people crowned Saul as king of Israel at Gilgal (11:1-15).

Valley of Elah Saul won many other battles, but over time he proved to be arrogant, sinful, and rebellious until God finally rejected him as king. Unknown to Saul, a young shepherd and musician named David was anointed to be Israel's next king. But it would be many years before David sat upon the throne. Ironically, Saul hired David to play the harp in his palace. Saul grew to like David so much that he made him his personal armor-bearer. In one particular battle with the Philistines in the Valley of Elah, David killed Goliath, the Philistines' mightiest soldier. But this victory was the beginning of the end of Saul's love for David. The Israelites praised David more than Saul, causing Saul to become so jealous that he plotted to kill David (12:1–22:23).

The Desert Even anointed kings are not exempt from troubles. David literally ran for his life from King Saul, hiding with his band of followers in the Desert of Ziph (where the men of Ziph constantly betrayed him), the Desert of Maon, and the Desert of En Gedi. Though he had opportunities to kill Saul, David refused to do so because Saul was God's anointed king (23:1–26:25).

Gath David moved his men and family to Gath, the Philistine city where King Achish lived. Saul then stopped chasing him. The Philistines seemed to welcome this famous fugitive from Israel (27:1-4).

Ziklag Desiring privacy in return for his pretended loyalty to King Achish, David asked for a city in which to house his men and family. Achish gave him Ziklag. From there David conducted raids against the cities of the Geshurites, Girzites, and Amalekites, making sure no one escaped to tell the tale (27:5-12). David later conquered the Amalekites after they raided Ziklag (30:1-31).

Mount Gilboa War with the Philistines broke out again in the north, near Mount Gilboa. Saul, who no longer relied on God, consulted a witch in a desperate attempt to contact Samuel for help. In the meantime, David was sent back to Ziklag because the Philistine commanders did not trust his loyalty in battle against Israel. The Philistines slaughtered the Israelites on Mount Gilboa, killing King Saul and his three sons, including David's loyal friend, Jonathan. Without God, Saul led a bitter and misguided life. The consequences of his sinful actions affected not only him, but hurt his family and the entire nation as well (28:1–31:13).

with a three-year-old bull,[e][a] an ephah[f] of
flour and a skin of wine, and brought
him to the house of the LORD at Shiloh.
25When they had slaughtered the bull,
they brought the boy to Eli, 26and she
said to him, "As surely as you live, my
lord, I am the woman who stood here
beside you praying to the LORD. 27I
prayed[b] for this child, and the LORD has
granted me what I asked of him. 28So
now I give him to the LORD. For his
whole life[c] he will be given over to the
LORD." And he worshiped the LORD
there.

Hannah's prayer of joy.

2 Then Hannah prayed and said:[d]

"My heart rejoices[e] in the LORD;
  in the LORD my horn[g][f] is lifted high.
My mouth boasts over my enemies,
  for I delight in your deliverance.

2"There is no one holy[h][g] like the LORD;
  there is no one besides you;
  there is no Rock[h] like our God.

3"Do not keep talking so proudly
  or let your mouth speak such
    arrogance,[i]
for the LORD is a God who knows,
  and by him deeds[j] are weighed.[k]

4"The bows of the warriors are
    broken,[l]
  but those who stumbled are armed
    with strength.
5Those who were full hire themselves
    out for food,
  but those who were hungry
    hunger no more.
She who was barren[m] has borne
    seven children,
  but she who has had many sons
    pines away.

6"The LORD brings death and makes
    alive;[n]
  he brings down to the grave[i] and
    raises up.[o]
7The LORD sends poverty and wealth;[p]
  he humbles and he exalts.[q]
8He raises[r] the poor from the dust
  and lifts the needy from the ash
    heap;
he seats them with princes
  and has them inherit a throne of
    honor.[s]

"For the foundations[t] of the earth
    are the LORD's;
  upon them he has set the world.
9He will guard the feet[u] of his saints,
  but the wicked will be silenced in
    darkness.[v]

"It is not by strength[w] that one
    prevails;
10 those who oppose the LORD will be
    shattered.[x]
He will thunder[y] against them from
    heaven;
  the LORD will judge[z] the ends of
    the earth.

"He will give strength[a] to his king
  and exalt the horn[b] of his anointed."

11Then Elkanah went home to Ramah,
but the boy ministered[c] before the LORD
under Eli the priest.

Wickedness of Eli's sons.

12Eli's sons were wicked men; they
had no regard[d] for the LORD. 13Now it
was the practice of the priests with the
people that whenever anyone offered a
sacrifice and while the meat[e] was being
boiled, the servant of the priest would
come with a three-pronged fork in his
hand. 14He would plunge it into the
pan or kettle or caldron or pot, and the
priest would take for himself whatever
the fork brought up. This is how they
treated all the Israelites who came to
Shiloh. 15But even before the fat was
burned, the servant of the priest would
come and say to the man who was sacrificing, "Give the priest some meat to
roast; he won't accept boiled meat from
you, but only raw."
16If the man said to him, "Let the fat

1:24 [a]Nu 15:8-10; Dt 12:5; Jos 18:1
1:27 [b]ver 11-13; Ps 66:19-20
1:28 [c]ver 11,22; Ge 24:26,52
2:1 [d]Lk 1:46-55 [e]Ps 9:14; 13:5 [f]Ps 89:17,24; 92:10; Isa 12:2-3
2:2 [g]Ex 15:11; Lev 19:2 [h]Dt 32:30-31; 2Sa 22:2,32
2:3 [i]Pr 8:13 [j]1Sa 16:7; 1Ki 8:39 [k]Pr 16:2; 24:11-12
2:4 [l]Ps 37:15
2:5 [m]Ps 113:9; Jer 15:9
2:6 [n]Dt 32:39 [o]Isa 26:19
2:7 [p]Dt 8:18 [q]Job 5:11; Ps 75:7
2:8 [r]Ps 113:7-8 [s]Job 36:7 [t]Job 38:4
2:9 [u]Ps 91:12 [v]Mt 8:12 [w]Ps 33:16-17
2:10 [x]Ps 2:9 [y]Ps 18:13 [z]Ps 96:13 [a]Ps 21:1 [b]Ps 89:24
2:11 [c]ver 18; 1Sa 3:1
2:12 [d]Jer 2:8; 9:6
2:13 [e]Lev 7:29-34

e*24* Dead Sea Scrolls, Septuagint and Syriac; Masoretic Text *with three bulls* f*24* That is, probably about 3/5 bushel (about 22 liters) g*1* *Horn* here symbolizes strength; also in verse 10. h*2* Or *no Holy One* i*6* Hebrew *Sheol*

be burned up first, and then take whatever you want," the servant would then answer, "No, hand it over now; if you don't, I'll take it by force."

17 This sin of the young men was very great in the LORD's sight, for they[j] were treating the LORD's offering with contempt.[a]

Samuel's childhood ministry.

18 But Samuel was ministering[b] before the LORD—a boy wearing a linen ephod.[c] 19 Each year his mother made him a little robe and took it to him when she went up with her husband to offer the annual[d] sacrifice. 20 Eli would bless Elkanah and his wife, saying, "May the LORD give you children by this woman to take the place of the one she prayed[e] for and gave to the LORD." Then they would go home. 21 And the LORD was gracious to Hannah;[f] she conceived and gave birth to three sons and two daughters. Meanwhile, the boy Samuel grew[g] up in the presence of the LORD.

22 Now Eli, who was very old, heard about everything his sons were doing to all Israel and how they slept with the women[h] who served at the entrance to the Tent of Meeting. 23 So he said to them, "Why do you do such things? I hear from all the people about these wicked deeds of yours. 24 No, my sons; it is not a good report that I hear spreading among the LORD's people. 25 If a man sins against another man, God[k] may mediate for him; but if a man sins against the LORD, who will[i] intercede[j] for him?" His sons, however, did not listen to their father's rebuke, for it was the LORD's will to put them to death.

26 And the boy Samuel continued to grow[k] in stature and in favor with the LORD and with men.

Prophecy against Eli's house.

27 Now a man of God[l] came to Eli and said to him, "This is what the LORD says: 'Did I not clearly reveal myself to your father's house when they were in Egypt under Pharaoh? 28 I chose[m] your father out of all the tribes of Israel to be my priest, to go up to my altar, to burn incense, and to wear an ephod[n] in my presence. I also gave your father's house all the offerings made with fire by the Israelites. 29 Why do you[l] scorn my sacrifice and offering[o] that I prescribed for my dwelling?[p] Why do you honor your sons more than me by fattening yourselves on the choice parts of every offering made by my people Israel?'

30 "Therefore the LORD, the God of Israel, declares: 'I promised that your house and your father's house would minister before me forever.[q]' 'Far be it from me! Those who honor me I will honor,[r] but those who despise[s] me will be disdained. 31 The time is coming when I will cut short your strength and the strength of your father's house, so that there will not be an old man in your family line[t] 32 and you will see distress in my dwelling. Although good will be done to Israel, in your family line there will never be an old man.[u] 33 Every one of you that I do not cut off from my altar will be spared only to blind your eyes with tears and to grieve your heart, and all your descendants will die in the prime of life.

34 "'And what happens to your two sons, Hophni and Phinehas, will be a sign to you—they will both die[v] on the same day.[w] 35 I will raise up for myself a faithful priest,[x] who will do according to what is in my heart and mind. I will firmly establish his house, and he will minister before my anointed[y] one always. 36 Then everyone left in your family line will come and bow down before him for a piece of silver and a crust of bread and plead, "Appoint me to some priestly office so I can have food to eat.[z]"'"

Samuel is called by the LORD.

3 The boy Samuel ministered[a] before the LORD under Eli. In those days the word of the LORD was rare;[b] there were not many visions.[c]

2:17 [a]Mal 2:7-9
2:18 [b]ver 11; 1Sa 3:1 [c]ver 28
2:19 [d]1Sa 1:3
2:20 [e]1Sa 1:11, 27-28; Lk 2:34
2:21 [f]Ge 21:1 [g]ver 26; Jdg 13:24; 1Sa 3:19; Lk 2:40
2:22 [h]Ex 38:8
2:25 [i]Nu 15:30; Jos 11:20 [j]Dt 1:17; 1Sa 3:14; Heb 10:26
2:26 [k]ver 21; Lk 2:52
2:27 [l]Ex 4:14-16; 1Ki 13:1
2:28 [m]Ex 28:1 [n]Lev 8:7-8
2:29 [o]ver 12-17 [p]Dt 12:5; Mt 10:37
2:30 [q]Ex 29:9 [r]Ps 50:23; 91:15 [s]Mal 2:9
2:31 [t]1Sa 4:11-18; 22:16-20
2:32 [u]1Ki 2:26-27; Zec 8:4
2:34 [v]1Sa 4:11 [w]1Ki 13:3
2:35 [x]1Sa 12:3; 1Ki 2:35 [y]1Sa 16:13; 2Sa 7:11,27; 1Ki 11:38
2:36 [z]1Ki 2:27
3:1 [a]1Sa 2:11 [b]Ps 74:9 [c]Am 8:11

j17 Or *men* k25 Or *the judges* l29 The Hebrew is plural.

2One night Eli, whose eyes[a] were becoming so weak that he could barely
see, was lying down in his usual place.
3The lamp[b] of God had not yet gone out,
and Samuel was lying down in the temple[m] of the LORD, where the ark of God
was. 4Then the LORD called Samuel.
Samuel answered, "Here I am.[c]" 5And
he ran to Eli and said, "Here I am; you
called me."
But Eli said, "I did not call; go back and
lie down." So he went and lay down.
6Again the LORD called, "Samuel!"
And Samuel got up and went to Eli and
said, "Here I am; you called me."
"My son," Eli said, "I did not call; go
back and lie down."
7Now Samuel did not yet know the
LORD: The word of the LORD had not yet
been revealed[d] to him.
8The LORD called Samuel a third time,
and Samuel got up and went to Eli and
said, "Here I am; you called me."
Then Eli realized that the LORD was
calling the boy. 9So Eli told Samuel, "Go
and lie down, and if he calls you, say,
'Speak, LORD, for your servant is listening.'" So Samuel went and lay down in
his place.
10The LORD came and stood there,
calling as at the other times, "Samuel!
Samuel!"
Then Samuel said, "Speak, for your
servant is listening."
11And the LORD said to Samuel: "See,
I am about to do something in Israel
that will make the ears of everyone who
hears of it tingle.[e] 12At that time I will
carry out against Eli everything[f] I spoke
against his family—from beginning to
end. 13For I told him that I would judge
his family forever because of the sin he
knew about; his sons made themselves
contemptible,[n] and he failed to restrain[g]
them. 14Therefore, I swore to the house
of Eli, 'The guilt of Eli's house will never
be atoned[h] for by sacrifice or offering.'"
15Samuel lay down until morning and
then opened the doors of the house of
the LORD. He was afraid to tell Eli the
vision, 16but Eli called him and said,
"Samuel, my son."

3:2 [a]1Sa 4:15
3:3 [b]Lev 24:1-4
3:4 [c]Isa 6:8
3:7 [d]Ac 19:12
3:11 [e]2Ki 21:12; Jer 19:3
3:12 [f]1Sa 2:27-36
3:13 [g]1Sa 2:12,17, 22,29-31
3:14 [h]Lev 15:30-31; 1Sa 2:25; Isa 22:14
3:17 [i]Ru 1:17; 2Sa 3:35
3:18 [j]Job 2:10; Isa 39:8
3:19 [k]Ge 21:22; 39:2 [l]1Sa 2:21 [m]1Sa 9:6
3:20 [n]Jdg 20:1
3:21 [o]ver 10
4:1 [p]1Sa 7:12 [q]Jos 12:18; 1Sa 29:1
4:3 [r]Jos 7:7 [s]Nu 10:35; Jos 6:7
4:4 [t]Ex 25:22; 2Sa 6:2

Samuel answered, "Here I am."
17"What was it he said to you?" Eli
asked. "Do not hide it from me. May
God deal with you, be it ever so severely,[i] if you hide from me anything he told
you." 18So Samuel told him everything,
hiding nothing from him. Then Eli said,
"He is the LORD; let him do what is good
in his eyes."[j]

Samuel is recognized as a prophet of the LORD.

19The LORD was with[k] Samuel as he
grew[l] up, and he let none[m] of his words
fall to the ground. 20And all Israel from
Dan to Beersheba[n] recognized that Samuel was attested as a prophet of the
LORD. 21The LORD continued to appear at
Shiloh, and there he revealed[o] himself
to Samuel through his word.

4 And Samuel's word came to all
Israel.

Philistines' capture of the ark of the covenant.

Now the Israelites went out to fight
against the Philistines. The Israelites
camped at Ebenezer,[p] and the Philistines
at Aphek.[q] 2The Philistines deployed
their forces to meet Israel, and as the
battle spread, Israel was defeated by the
Philistines, who killed about four thousand of them on the battlefield. 3When
the soldiers returned to camp, the elders
of Israel asked, "Why[r] did the LORD bring
defeat upon us today before the Philistines? Let us bring the ark[s] of the LORD's
covenant from Shiloh, so that it[o] may go
with us and save us from the hand of
our enemies."
4So the people sent men to Shiloh,
and they brought back the ark of the
covenant of the LORD Almighty, who is
enthroned between the cherubim.[t] And
Eli's two sons, Hophni and Phinehas,
were there with the ark of the covenant
of God.
5When the ark of the LORD's covenant

[m]*3* That is, tabernacle [n]*13* Masoretic Text; an ancient Hebrew scribal tradition and Septuagint *sons blasphemed God* [o]*3* Or *he*

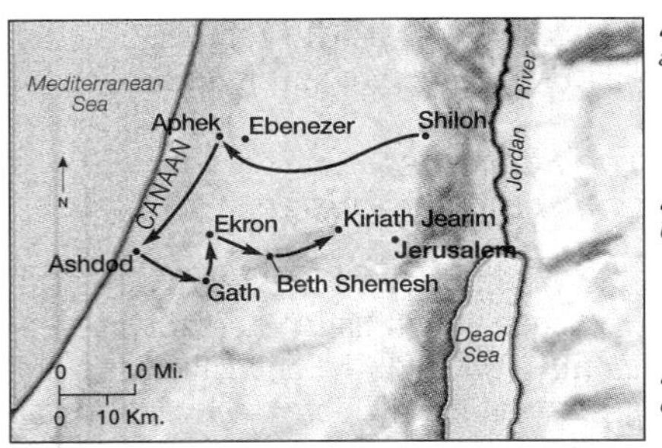

The Ark's Travels

Eli's sons took the ark from Shiloh to the battlefield on the lower plains at Ebenezer and Aphek. The Philistines captured the ark and took it to Ashdod, Gath, and Ekron. Plagues forced the people to send the ark back to Israel, where it finally was taken by cattle-driven carts to Beth Shemesh and on to the home of Eleazar in Kiriath Jearim.

came into the camp, all Israel raised
such a great shout[a] that the ground
shook. 6Hearing the uproar, the Philistines asked, "What's all this shouting in
the Hebrew camp?"
When they learned that the ark of the
LORD had come into the camp, 7the Philistines were afraid.[b] "A god has come
into the camp," they said. "We're in
trouble! Nothing like this has happened
before. 8Woe to us! Who will deliver us
from the hand of these mighty gods?
They are the gods who struck the Egyptians with all kinds of plagues in the
desert. 9Be strong, Philistines! Be men,
or you will be subject to the Hebrews,
as they[c] have been to you. Be men, and
fight!"
10So the Philistines fought, and the
Israelites were defeated[d] and every man
fled to his tent. The slaughter was very
great; Israel lost thirty thousand foot
soldiers. 11The ark of God was captured,
and Eli's two sons, Hophni and Phinehas, died.[e]

Eli's death.

12That same day a Benjamite ran from
the battle line and went to Shiloh, his
clothes torn and dust[f] on his head.
13When he arrived, there was Eli[g] sitting on his chair by the side of the
road, watching, because his heart feared
for the ark of God. When the man entered the town and told what had happened, the whole town sent up a cry.
14Eli heard the outcry and asked,
"What is the meaning of this uproar?"
The man hurried over to Eli, 15who
was ninety-eight years old and whose
eyes[h] were set so that he could not see.
16He told Eli, "I have just come from the
battle line; I fled from it this very day."
Eli asked, "What happened, my son?"
17The man who brought the news
replied, "Israel fled before the Philistines, and the army has suffered heavy
losses. Also your two sons, Hophni and
Phinehas, are dead, and the ark of God
has been captured."
18When he mentioned the ark of God,
Eli fell backward off his chair by the side
of the gate. His neck was broken and he
died, for he was an old man and heavy.
He had led[p][i] Israel forty years.

Ichabod's birth.

19His daughter-in-law, the wife of
Phinehas, was pregnant and near the
time of delivery. When she heard the
news that the ark of God had been captured and that her father-in-law and her
husband were dead, she went into labor
and gave birth, but was overcome by her
labor pains. 20As she was dying, the
women attending her said, "Don't despair; you have given birth to a son." But
she did not respond or pay any attention.
21She named the boy Ichabod,[q][j] saying, "The glory[k] has departed from
Israel"—because of the capture of the
ark of God and the deaths of her father-
in-law and her husband. 22She said,
"The glory has departed from Israel, for
the ark of God has been captured."

The Philistines place the ark in the temple of Dagon.

5 After the Philistines had captured
the ark of God, they took it from Ebenezer[l] to Ashdod.[m] 2Then they carried

4:5 [a]Jos 6:5,10
4:7 [b]Ex 15:14
4:9 [c]Jdg 13:1; 1Co 16:13
4:10 [d]ver 2; Dt 28:25; 2Sa 18:17; 2Ki 14:12
4:11 [e]1Sa 2:34; Ps 78:61,64
4:12 [f]Jos 7:6; 2Sa 1:2; 15:32; Ne 9:1; Job 2:12
4:13 [g]ver 18; 1Sa 1:9
4:15 [h]1Sa 3:2
4:18 [i]ver 13
4:21 [j]Ge 35:18 [k]Ps 26:8; Jer 2:11
5:1 [l]1Sa 4:1; 7:12 [m]Jos 13:3

p *18* Traditionally *judged* q *21* *Ichabod* means *no glory.*

the ark into Dagon's temple and set it beside Dagon.[a] 3When the people of Ashdod rose early the next day, there was Dagon, fallen[b] on his face on the ground before the ark of the LORD! They took Dagon and put him back in his place. 4But the following morning when they rose, there was Dagon, fallen on his face on the ground before the ark of the LORD! His head and hands had been broken[c] off and were lying on the threshold; only his body remained. 5That is why to this day neither the priests of Dagon nor any others who enter Dagon's temple at Ashdod step on the threshold.[d]

The Philistines are afflicted with tumors.

6The LORD's hand[e] was heavy upon the people of Ashdod and its vicinity; he brought devastation[f] upon them and afflicted them with tumors.[r][g] 7When the men of Ashdod saw what was happening, they said, "The ark of the god of Israel must not stay here with us, because his hand is heavy upon us and upon Dagon our god." 8So they called together all the rulers of the Philistines and asked them, "What shall we do with the ark of the god of Israel?"

They answered, "Have the ark of the god of Israel moved to Gath.[h]" So they moved the ark of the God of Israel.

9But after they had moved it, the LORD's hand was against that city, throwing it into a great panic.[i] He afflicted the people of the city, both young and old, with an outbreak of tumors.[s] 10So they sent the ark of God to Ekron.

As the ark of God was entering Ekron, the people of Ekron cried out, "They have brought the ark of the god of Israel around to us to kill us and our people." 11So they called together all the rulers[j] of the Philistines and said, "Send the ark of the god of Israel away; let it go back to its own place, or it[t] will kill us and our people." For death had filled the city with panic; God's hand was very heavy upon it. 12Those who did not die were afflicted with tumors, and the outcry of the city went up to heaven.

5:2 [a]Jdg 16:23
5:3 [b]Isa 19:1; 46:7
5:4 [c]Eze 6:6; Mic 1:7
5:5 [d]Zep 1:9
5:6 [e]ver 7; Ex 9:3; Ps 32:4; Ac 13:11 [f]ver 11; Ps 78:66 [g]Dt 28:27; 1Sa 6:5
5:8 [h]ver 11
5:9 [i]ver 6,11; Dt 2:15; 1Sa 7:13; Ps 78:66
5:11 [j]ver 6,8-9
6:2 [k]Ge 41:8; Ex 7:11; Isa 2:6
6:3 [l]Ex 23:15; Dt 16:16 [m]Lev 5:15 [n]ver 9
6:4 [o]ver 17-18; Jos 13:3; Jdg 3:3
6:5 [p]1Sa 5:6-11 [q]Jos 7:19; Isa 42:12; Jn 9:24; Rev 14:7
6:6 [r]Ex 7:13; 8:15; 9:34; 14:17 [s]Ex 12:31,33
6:7 [t]2Sa 6:3 [u]Nu 19:2
6:9 [v]ver 3; Jos 15:10; 21:16

The Philistines return the ark to Israel.

6 When the ark of the LORD had been in Philistine territory seven months, 2the Philistines called for the priests and the diviners[k] and said, "What shall we do with the ark of the LORD? Tell us how we should send it back to its place."

3They answered, "If you return the ark of the god of Israel, do not send it away empty,[l] but by all means send a guilt offering[m] to him. Then you will be healed, and you will know why his hand[n] has not been lifted from you."

4The Philistines asked, "What guilt offering should we send to him?"

They replied, "Five gold tumors and five gold rats, according to the number[o] of the Philistine rulers, because the same plague has struck both you and your rulers. 5Make models of the tumors[p] and of the rats that are destroying the country, and pay honor[q] to Israel's god. Perhaps he will lift his hand from you and your gods and your land. 6Why do you harden[r] your hearts as the Egyptians and Pharaoh did? When he[u] treated them harshly, did they[s] not send the Israelites out so they could go on their way?

7"Now then, get a new cart[t] ready, with two cows that have calved and have never been yoked.[u] Hitch the cows to the cart, but take their calves away and pen them up. 8Take the ark of the LORD and put it on the cart, and in a chest beside it put the gold objects you are sending back to him as a guilt offering. Send it on its way, 9but keep watching it. If it goes up to its own territory, toward Beth Shemesh,[v] then the LORD has brought this great disaster on us. But if it does not, then we will know

r*6* Hebrew; Septuagint and Vulgate *tumors. And rats appeared in their land, and death and destruction were throughout the city* s*9* Or *with tumors in the groin* (see Septuagint) t*11* Or *he* u*6* That is, God

that it was not his hand that struck us
and that it happened to us by chance."
10So they did this. They took two
such cows and hitched them to the cart
and penned up their calves. 11They
placed the ark of the LORD on the cart
and along with it the chest containing
the gold rats and the models of the
tumors. 12Then the cows went straight
up toward Beth Shemesh, keeping on
the road and lowing all the way; they
did not turn to the right or to the left.
The rulers of the Philistines followed
them as far as the border of Beth Shemesh.
13Now the people of Beth Shemesh
were harvesting their wheat in the valley, and when they looked up and saw
the ark, they rejoiced at the sight.
14The cart came to the field of Joshua
of Beth Shemesh, and there it stopped
beside a large rock. The people chopped
up the wood of the cart and sacrificed
the cows as a burnt offering[a] to the
LORD. 15The Levites[b] took down the ark
of the LORD, together with the chest
containing the gold objects, and placed
them on the large rock. On that day the
people of Beth Shemesh offered burnt
offerings and made sacrifices to the
LORD. 16The five rulers of the Philistines saw all this and then returned that
same day to Ekron.
17These are the gold tumors the Philistines sent as a guilt offering to the
LORD—one each[c] for Ashdod, Gaza,
Ashkelon, Gath and Ekron. 18And the
number of the gold rats was according
to the number of Philistine towns belonging to the five rulers—the fortified
towns with their country villages. The
large rock, on which[v] they set the ark of
the LORD, is a witness to this day in
the field of Joshua of Beth Shemesh.
19But God struck down[d] some of the
men of Beth Shemesh, putting seventy[w]
of them to death because they had
looked[e] into the ark of the LORD. The
people mourned because of the heavy
blow the LORD had dealt them, 20and
the men of Beth Shemesh asked, "Who
can stand[f] in the presence of the LORD,
this holy[g] God? To whom will the ark
go up from here?"
21Then they sent messengers to the
people of Kiriath Jearim,[h] saying, "The
Philistines have returned the ark of
the LORD. Come down and take it up to
7 your place." 1So the men of Kiriath
Jearim came and took up the ark
of the LORD. They took it to Abinadab's[i]
house on the hill and consecrated
Eleazar his son to guard the ark of the
LORD.

Samuel exhorts Israel to victory.

2It was a long time, twenty years in
all, that the ark remained at Kiriath
Jearim, and all the people of Israel
mourned and sought after the LORD.
3And Samuel said to the whole house of
Israel, "If you are returning[j] to the LORD
with all your hearts, then rid[k] yourselves of the foreign gods and the Ashtoreths[l] and commit[m] yourselves to the
LORD and serve him only,[n] and he will
deliver you out of the hand of the
Philistines." 4So the Israelites put away
their Baals and Ashtoreths, and served
the LORD only.
5Then Samuel said, "Assemble all
Israel at Mizpah[o] and I will intercede
with the LORD for you." 6When they had
assembled at Mizpah, they drew water
and poured[p] it out before the LORD. On
that day they fasted and there they
confessed, "We have sinned against the
LORD." And Samuel was leader[x][q] of Israel
at Mizpah.
7When the Philistines heard that
Israel had assembled at Mizpah, the rulers of the Philistines came up to attack
them. And when the Israelites heard
of it, they were afraid[r] because of the
Philistines. 8They said to Samuel, "Do
not stop crying[s] out to the LORD our God
for us, that he may rescue us from the
hand of the Philistines." 9Then Samuel[t]
took a suckling lamb and offered it up as

6:14 [a]2Sa 24:22; 1Ki 19:21
6:15 [b]Jos 3:3
6:17 [c]ver 4
6:19 [d]2Sa 6:7 [e]Ex 19:21; Nu 4:5,15,20
6:20 [f]2Sa 6:9; Mal 3:2; Rev 6:17 [g]Lev 11:45
6:21 [h]Jos 9:17; 15:9,60; 1Ch 13:5-6
7:1 [i]2Sa 6:3
7:3 [j]Dt 30:10; Isa 55:7; Hos 6:1 [k]Ge 35:2; Jos 24:14 [l]Jdg 2:12-13; 1Sa 31:10 [m]Joel 2:12 [n]Dt 6:13; Mt 4:10; Lk 4:8
7:5 [o]Jdg 20:1
7:6 [p]Ps 62:8; La 2:19 [q]Jdg 10:10; Ne 9:1; Ps 106:6
7:7 [r]1Sa 17:11
7:8 [s]1Sa 12:19,23; Isa 37:4; Jer 15:1
7:9 [t]Ps 99:6

v *18* A few Hebrew manuscripts (see also Septuagint); most Hebrew manuscripts *villages as far as Greater Abel, where* w *19* A few Hebrew manuscripts; most Hebrew manuscripts and Septuagint *50,070*
x *6* Traditionally *judge*

a whole burnt offering to the LORD. He
cried out to the LORD on Israel's behalf,
and the LORD answered him.[a]
10While Samuel was sacrificing the
burnt offering, the Philistines drew near
to engage Israel in battle. But that day
the LORD thundered[b] with loud thunder
against the Philistines and threw them
into such a panic[c] that they were routed
before the Israelites. 11The men of Israel
rushed out of Mizpah and pursued the
Philistines, slaughtering them along the
way to a point below Beth Car.
12Then Samuel took a stone[d] and set
it up between Mizpah and Shen. He
named it Ebenezer,[y] saying, "Thus far
has the LORD helped us." 13So the
Philistines were subdued[e] and did not
invade Israelite territory again.
Throughout Samuel's lifetime, the
hand of the LORD was against the Philistines. 14The towns from Ekron to Gath
that the Philistines had captured from
Israel were restored to her, and Israel
delivered the neighboring territory from
the power of the Philistines. And there
was peace between Israel and the Amorites.

Samuel judges Israel.

15Samuel[f] continued as judge over
Israel all the days of his life. 16From year
to year he went on a circuit from Bethel
to Gilgal to Mizpah, judging Israel in all
those places. 17But he always went back
to Ramah,[g] where his home was, and
there he also judged Israel. And he built
an altar[h] there to the LORD.

Israel rejects Samuel's sons and requests a king.

8 When Samuel grew old, he appointed[i] his sons as judges for
Israel. 2The name of his firstborn was
Joel and the name of his second was
Abijah, and they served at Beersheba.[j]
3But his sons did not walk in his ways.
They turned aside after dishonest gain
and accepted bribes[k] and perverted justice.
4So all the elders of Israel gathered
together and came to Samuel at Ramah.[l]
5They said to him, "You are old, and
your sons do not walk in your ways;
now appoint a king[m] to lead[z] us, such
as all the other nations have."
6But when they said, "Give us a king
to lead us," this displeased[n] Samuel; so
he prayed to the LORD. 7And the LORD
told him: "Listen to all that the people
are saying to you; it is not you they have
rejected, but they have rejected me as
their king.[o] 8As they have done from
the day I brought them up out of Egypt
until this day, forsaking me and serving
other gods, so they are doing to you.
9Now listen to them; but warn them
solemnly and let them know[p] what the
king who will reign over them will
do."
10Samuel told all the words of the
LORD to the people who were asking
him for a king. 11He said, "This is what
the king who will reign over you will
do: He will take[q] your sons and make
them serve with his chariots and horses,
and they will run in front of his chariots.[r] 12Some he will assign to be commanders[s] of thousands and commanders
of fifties, and others to plow his ground
and reap his harvest, and still others to
make weapons of war and equipment
for his chariots. 13He will take your
daughters to be perfumers and cooks
and bakers. 14He will take the best of
your[t] fields and vineyards[u] and olive
groves and give them to his attendants.
15He will take a tenth of your grain and
of your vintage and give it to his officials and attendants. 16Your menservants
and maidservants and the best of your
cattle[a] and donkeys he will take for his
own use. 17He will take a tenth of your
flocks, and you yourselves will become
his slaves. 18When that day comes, you
will cry out for relief from the king you
have chosen, and the LORD will not
answer[v] you in that day."
19But the people refused[w] to listen to
Samuel. "No!" they said. "We want a

7:9 [a]Jer 15:1
7:10 [b]1Sa 2:10; 2Sa 22:14-15 [c]Jos 10:10
7:12 [d]Ge 35:14; Jos 4:9
7:13 [e]Jdg 13:1,5; 1Sa 13:5
7:15 [f]ver 6; 1Sa 12:11
7:17 [g]1Sa 1:19; 8:4 [h]Jdg 21:4
8:1 [i]Dt 16:18-19
8:2 [j]Ge 22:19; 1Ki 19:3; Am 5:4-5
8:3 [k]Ex 23:8; Dt 16:19; Ps 15:5
8:4 [l]1Sa 7:17
8:5 [m]Dt 17:14-20
8:6 [n]1Sa 15:11
8:7 [o]Ex 16:8; 1Sa 10:19
8:9 [p]ver 11-18; 1Sa 10:25
8:11 [q]1Sa 10:25; 14:52 [r]Dt 17:16; 2Sa 15:1
8:12 [s]1Sa 22:7
8:14 [t]Eze 46:18 [u]1Ki 21:7,15
8:18 [v]Pr 1:28; Isa 1:15; Mic 3:4
8:19 [w]Isa 66:4; Jer 44:16

y*12 Ebenezer* means *stone of help.* z*5* Traditionally *judge*; also in verses 6 and 20 a*16* Septuagint; Hebrew *young men*

king over us. 20Then we will be like all
the other nations,[a] with a king to lead us
and to go out before us and fight our
battles."
21When Samuel heard all that the
people said, he repeated[b] it before the
LORD. 22The LORD answered, "Listen[c] to
them and give them a king."
Then Samuel said to the men of Israel, "Everyone go back to his town."

God tells Samuel that Saul will be king.

9 There was a Benjamite, a man of
standing, whose name was Kish[d]
son of Abiel, the son of Zeror, the son of
Becorath, the son of Aphiah of Benjamin.
2He had a son named Saul, an impres-
sive young man without equal[e] among
the Israelites—a head taller[f] than any of
the others.
3Now the donkeys belonging to Saul's
father Kish were lost, and Kish said to
his son Saul, "Take one of the servants
with you and go and look for the donkeys." 4So he passed through the hill[g]
country of Ephraim and through the
area around Shalisha,[h] but they did not
find them. They went on into the district of Shaalim, but the donkeys were
not there. Then he passed through the
territory of Benjamin, but they did not
find them.
5When they reached the district of
Zuph,[i] Saul said to the servant who was
with him, "Come, let's go back, or my
father will stop thinking about the donkeys and start worrying[j] about us."
6But the servant replied, "Look, in
this town there is a man of God;[k] he is
highly respected, and everything[l] he says
comes true. Let's go there now. Perhaps
he will tell us what way to take."
7Saul said to his servant, "If we go,
what can we give the man? The food in
our sacks is gone. We have no gift[m] to
take to the man of God. What do we
have?"
8The servant answered him again.
"Look," he said, "I have a quarter of a
shekel[b] of silver. I will give it to the man

8:20 [a]ver 5
8:21 [b]Jdg 11:11
8:22 [c]ver 7
9:1 [d]1Sa 14:51; 1Ch 8:33; 9:39
9:2 [e]1Sa 10:24 [f]1Sa 10:23
9:4 [g]Jos 24:33 [h]2Ki 4:42
9:5 [i]1Sa 1:1 [j]1Sa 10:2
9:6 [k]Dt 33:1; 1Ki 13:1 [l]1Sa 3:19
9:7 [m]1Ki 14:3; 2Ki 5:5,15; 8:8
9:9 [n]2Sa 24:11; 2Ki 17:13; 1Ch 9:22; 26:28; 29:29; Isa 30:10; Am 7:12
9:11 [o]Ge 24:11,13
9:12 [p]Nu 28:11-15; 1Sa 7:17 [q]Ge 31:54; 1Sa 10:5; 1Ki 3:2
9:16 [r]1Sa 10:1 [s]Ex 3:7-9
9:17 [t]1Sa 16:12
9:20 [u]ver 3

of God so that he will tell us what way
to take." 9(Formerly in Israel, if a man
went to inquire of God, he would say,
"Come, let us go to the seer," because
the prophet of today used to be called a
seer.)[n]
10"Good," Saul said to his servant.
"Come, let's go." So they set out for the
town where the man of God was.
11As they were going up the hill to
the town, they met some girls coming
out to draw[o] water, and they asked
them, "Is the seer here?"
12"He is," they answered. "He's ahead
of you. Hurry now; he has just come to
our town today, for the people have a
sacrifice[p] at the high place.[q] 13As soon
as you enter the town, you will find him
before he goes up to the high place to
eat. The people will not begin eating
until he comes, because he must bless
the sacrifice; afterward, those who are
invited will eat. Go up now; you should
find him about this time."
14They went up to the town, and as
they were entering it, there was Samuel,
coming toward them on his way up to
the high place.
15Now the day before Saul came, the
LORD had revealed this to Samuel:
16"About this time tomorrow I will send
you a man from the land of Benjamin.
Anoint[r] him leader over my people
Israel; he will deliver[s] my people from
the hand of the Philistines. I have
looked upon my people, for their cry has
reached me."
17When Samuel caught sight of Saul,
the LORD said to him, "This[t] is the man
I spoke to you about; he will govern my
people."
18Saul approached Samuel in the gateway and asked, "Would you please tell
me where the seer's house is?"
19"I am the seer," Samuel replied.
"Go up ahead of me to the high place,
for today you are to eat with me, and in
the morning I will let you go and will
tell you all that is in your heart. 20As for
the donkeys[u] you lost three days ago,

[b]*8* That is, about 1/10 ounce (about 3 grams)

do not worry about them; they have been found. And to whom is all the desire[a] of Israel turned, if not to you and all your father's family?"

21Saul answered, "But am I not a Benjamite, from the smallest tribe[b] of Israel, and is not my clan the least of all the clans of the tribe of Benjamin?[c] Why do you say such a thing to me?"

22Then Samuel brought Saul and his servant into the hall and seated them at the head of those who were invited—about thirty in number. 23Samuel said to the cook, "Bring the piece of meat I gave you, the one I told you to lay aside."

24So the cook took up the leg[d] with what was on it and set it in front of Saul. Samuel said, "Here is what has been kept for you. Eat, because it was set aside for you for this occasion, from the time I said, 'I have invited guests.'" And Saul dined with Samuel that day.

25After they came down from the high place to the town, Samuel talked with Saul on the roof[e] of his house. 26They rose about daybreak and Samuel called to Saul on the roof, "Get ready, and I will send you on your way." When Saul got ready, he and Samuel went outside together. 27As they were going down to the edge of the town, Samuel said to Saul, "Tell the servant to go on ahead of us"—and the servant did so—"but you stay here awhile, so that I may give you a message from God."

Samuel anoints Saul as king of Israel.

10 Then Samuel took a flask[f] of oil and poured it on Saul's head and kissed him, saying, "Has not the LORD anointed[g] you leader over his inheritance?[c][h] 2When you leave me today, you will meet two men near Rachel's tomb,[i] at Zelzah on the border of Benjamin. They will say to you, 'The donkeys[j] you set out to look for have been found. And now your father has stopped thinking about them and is worried[k] about you. He is asking, "What shall I do about my son?"'

3"Then you will go on from there until you reach the great tree of Tabor. Three men going up to God at Bethel[l] will meet you there. One will be carrying three young goats, another three loaves of bread, and another a skin of wine. 4They will greet you and offer you two loaves of bread, which you will accept from them.

5"After that you will go to Gibeah of God, where there is a Philistine outpost.[m] As you approach the town, you will meet a procession of prophets coming down from the high place[n] with lyres, tambourines, flutes and harps[o] being played before them, and they will be prophesying.[p] 6The Spirit[q] of the LORD will come upon you in power, and you will prophesy with them; and you will be changed into a different person. 7Once these signs are fulfilled, do whatever[r] your hand finds to do, for God is with[s] you.

8"Go down ahead of me to Gilgal.[t] I will surely come down to you to sacrifice burnt offerings and fellowship offerings,[d] but you must wait seven days until I come to you and tell you what you are to do."

9As Saul turned to leave Samuel, God changed[u] Saul's heart, and all these signs were fulfilled that day. 10When they arrived at Gibeah, a procession of prophets met him; the Spirit of God came upon him in power, and he joined in their prophesying.[v] 11When all those who had formerly known him saw him prophesying with the prophets, they asked each other, "What is this[w] that has happened to the son of Kish? Is Saul also among the prophets?"[x]

12A man who lived there answered, "And who is their father?" So it became a saying: "Is Saul also among the prophets?" 13After Saul stopped prophesying, he went to the high place.

9:20 [a]1Sa 8:5; 12:13
9:21 [b]1Sa 15:17 [c]Jdg 20:35,46
9:24 [d]Lev 7:32-34; Nu 18:18
9:25 [e]Dt 22:8; Ac 10:9
10:1 [f]1Sa 16:13; 2Ki 9:1,3,6 [g]Ps 2:12 [h]Dt 32:9; Ps 78:62,71
10:2 [i]Ge 35:20 [j]1Sa 9:4 [k]1Sa 9:5
10:3 [l]Ge 28:22; 35:7-8
10:5 [m]1Sa 13:3 [n]1Sa 9:12 [o]2Ki 3:15 [p]1Sa 19:20; 1Co 14:1
10:6 [q]ver 10; Nu 11:25; 1Sa 19:23-24
10:7 [r]Ecc 9:10 [s]Jos 1:5; Jdg 6:12; Heb 13:5
10:8 [t]1Sa 11:14-15
10:9 [u]ver 6
10:10 [v]ver 5-6; 1Sa 19:20
10:11 [w]Mt 13:54; Jn 7:15 [x]1Sa 19:24

c *1* Hebrew; Septuagint and Vulgate *over his people Israel? You will reign over the LORD's people and save them from the power of their enemies round about. And this will be a sign to you that the LORD has anointed you leader over his inheritance:*
d *8* Traditionally *peace offerings*

14Now Saul's uncle[a] asked him and
his servant, "Where have you been?"
"Looking for the donkeys," he said.
"But when we saw they were not to be
found, we went to Samuel."
15Saul's uncle said, "Tell me what
Samuel said to you."
16Saul replied, "He assured us that the
donkeys[b] had been found." But he did
not tell his uncle what Samuel had said
about the kingship.
17Samuel summoned the people of
Israel to the LORD at Mizpah[c] 18and said
to them, "This is what the LORD, the
God of Israel, says: 'I brought Israel up
out of Egypt, and I delivered you from
the power of Egypt and all the kingdoms
that oppressed[d] you.' 19But you have
now rejected your God, who saves you
out of all your calamities and distresses.
And you have said, 'No, set a king[e] over
us.' So now present[f] yourselves before
the LORD by your tribes and clans."
20When Samuel brought all the tribes
of Israel near, the tribe of Benjamin was
chosen. 21Then he brought forward the
tribe of Benjamin, clan by clan, and
Matri's clan was chosen. Finally Saul son
of Kish was chosen. But when they
looked for him, he was not to be found.
22So they inquired[g] further of the LORD,
"Has the man come here yet?"
And the LORD said, "Yes, he has hidden himself among the baggage."
23They ran and brought him out, and
as he stood among the people he was a
head taller[h] than any of the others.
24Samuel said to all the people, "Do you
see the man the LORD has chosen?[i]
There is no one like him among all the
people."
Then the people shouted, "Long live[j]
the king!"
25Samuel explained to the people the
regulations[k] of the kingship. He wrote
them down on a scroll and deposited it
before the LORD. Then Samuel dismissed
the people, each to his own home.
26Saul also went to his home in
Gibeah,[l] accompanied by valiant men
whose hearts God had touched. 27But
some troublemakers[m] said, "How can
this fellow save us?" They despised him
and brought him no gifts.[n] But Saul kept
silent.

Saul rescues Jabesh Gilead from the Ammonites.

11 Nahash[o] the Ammonite went up
and besieged Jabesh Gilead.[p] And
all the men of Jabesh said to him, "Make
a treaty[q] with us, and we will be subject
to you."
2But Nahash the Ammonite replied,
"I will make a treaty with you only on
the condition that I gouge[r] out the right
eye of every one of you and so bring disgrace[s] on all Israel."
3The elders of Jabesh said to him,
"Give us seven days so we can send
messengers throughout Israel; if no one
comes to rescue us, we will surrender
to you."
4When the messengers came to Gibeah[t] of Saul and reported these terms to
the people, they all wept[u] aloud. 5Just
then Saul was returning from the
fields, behind his oxen, and he asked,
"What is wrong with the people? Why
are they weeping?" Then they repeated
to him what the men of Jabesh had
said.
6When Saul heard their words, the
Spirit[v] of God came upon him in power,
and he burned with anger. 7He took a
pair of oxen, cut them into pieces, and
sent the pieces by messengers throughout Israel,[w] proclaiming, "This is what
will be done to the oxen of anyone[x]
who does not follow Saul and Samuel."
Then the terror of the LORD fell on the
people, and they turned out as one man.
8When Saul mustered[y] them at Bezek,[z]
the men of Israel numbered three hundred thousand and the men of Judah
thirty thousand.
9They told the messengers who had
come, "Say to the men of Jabesh Gilead,
'By the time the sun is hot tomorrow,
you will be delivered.'" When the messengers went and reported this to the
men of Jabesh, they were elated. 10They
said to the Ammonites, "Tomorrow we

10:14 [a] 1Sa 14:50
10:16 [b] 1Sa 9:20
10:17 [c] Jdg 20:1; 1Sa 7:5
10:18 [d] Jdg 6:8-9
10:19 [e] 1Sa 8:5-7; 12:12 [f] Jos 7:14; 24:1
10:22 [g] 1Sa 23:2,4, 9-11
10:23 [h] 1Sa 9:2
10:24 [i] Dt 17:15; 2Sa 21:6 [j] 1Ki 1:25,34, 39
10:25 [k] Dt 17:14-20; 1Sa 8:11-18
10:26 [l] 1Sa 11:4
10:27 [m] Dt 13:13 [n] 1Ki 10:25; 2Ch 17:5
11:1 [o] 1Sa 12:12 [p] Jdg 21:8 [q] 1Ki 20:34; Eze 17:13
11:2 [r] Nu 16:14 [s] 1Sa 17:26
11:4 [t] 1Sa 10:5,26; 15:34 [u] Jdg 2:4; 1Sa 30:4
11:6 [v] Jdg 3:10; 6:34; 13:25; 14:6; 1Sa 10:10; 16:13
11:7 [w] Jdg 19:29 [x] Jdg 21:5
11:8 [y] Jdg 20:2 [z] Jdg 1:4

will surrender[a] to you, and you can do
to us whatever seems good to you."
11The next day Saul separated his men
into three divisions;[b] during the last
watch of the night they broke into the
camp of the Ammonites and slaughtered
them until the heat of the day. Those
who survived were scattered, so that no
two of them were left together.
12The people then said to Samuel,
"Who[c] was it that asked, 'Shall Saul
reign over us?' Bring these men to us
and we will put them to death."
13But Saul said, "No one shall be put
to death today,[d] for this day the LORD has
rescued[e] Israel."
14Then Samuel said to the people,
"Come, let us go to Gilgal[f] and there reaffirm the kingship.[g]" 15So all the people
went to Gilgal[h] and confirmed Saul as
king in the presence of the LORD. There
they sacrificed fellowship offerings[e] before the LORD, and Saul and all the Israelites held a great celebration.

Samuel rebukes Israel for asking for a king.

12 Samuel said to all Israel, "I have
listened[i] to everything you said to
me and have set a king[j] over you. 2Now
you have a king as your leader.[k] As for
me, I am old and gray, and my sons are
here with you. I have been your leader
from my youth until this day. 3Here I
stand. Testify against me in the presence
of the LORD and his anointed.[l] Whose
ox have I taken? Whose donkey[m] have I
taken? Whom have I cheated? Whom
have I oppressed? From whose hand
have I accepted a bribe[n] to make me
shut my eyes? If I have done[o] any of
these, I will make it right."
4"You have not cheated or oppressed
us," they replied. "You have not taken
anything from anyone's hand."
5Samuel said to them, "The LORD is
witness against you, and also his anointed is witness this day, that you have
not found anything[p] in my hand.[q]"
"He is witness," they said.
6Then Samuel said to the people, "It
is the LORD who appointed Moses and
Aaron and brought[r] your forefathers up
out of Egypt. 7Now then, stand here,
because I am going to confront[s] you
with evidence before the LORD as to all
the righteous acts performed by the
LORD for you and your fathers.
8"After Jacob entered Egypt, they
cried[t] to the LORD for help, and the LORD
sent[u] Moses and Aaron, who brought
your forefathers out of Egypt and settled
them in this place.
9"But they forgot[v] the LORD their
God; so he sold them into the hand of
Sisera,[w] the commander of the army of
Hazor, and into the hands of the Philistines[x] and the king of Moab,[y] who
fought against them. 10They cried out to
the LORD and said, 'We have sinned; we
have forsaken[z] the LORD and served the
Baals and the Ashtoreths.[a] But now
deliver us from the hands of our enemies, and we will serve you.' 11Then the
LORD sent Jerub-Baal,[f][b] Barak,[g][c] Jephthah[d] and Samuel,[h] and he delivered
you from the hands of your enemies on
every side, so that you lived securely.
12"But when you saw that Nahash[e]
king[f] of the Ammonites was moving
against you, you said to me, 'No, we
want a king to rule[g] over us'—even
though the LORD your God was your
king. 13Now here is the king[h] you have
chosen, the one you asked[i] for; see,
the LORD has set a king over you. 14If
you fear[j] the LORD and serve and obey
him and do not rebel against his commands, and if both you and the king
who reigns over you follow the LORD
your God—good! 15But if you do not
obey the LORD, and if you rebel against[k]
his commands, his hand will be against
you, as it was against your fathers.
16"Now then, stand still and see[l] this
great thing the LORD is about to do

11:10 [a]ver 3
11:11 [b]Jdg 7:16
11:12 [c]1Sa 10:27; Lk 19:27
11:13 [d]2Sa 19:22 [e]Ex 14:13; 1Sa 19:5
11:14 [f]1Sa 10:8 [g]1Sa 10:25
11:15 [h]1Sa 10:8,17
12:1 [i]1Sa 8:7 [j]1Sa 10:24; 11:15
12:2 [k]1Sa 8:5
12:3 [l]1Sa 10:1; 24:6; 2Sa 1:14 [m]Nu 16:15 [n]Dt 16:19 [o]Ac 20:33
12:5 [p]Ac 23:9; 24:20 [q]Ex 22:4
12:6 [r]Ex 6:26; Mic 6:4
12:7 [s]Isa 1:18; Mic 6:1-5
12:8 [t]Ex 2:23 [u]Ex 3:10; 4:16
12:9 [v]Jdg 3:7 [w]Jdg 4:2 [x]Jdg 10:7; 13:1 [y]Jdg 3:12
12:10 [z]Jdg 10:10,15 [a]Jdg 2:13
12:11 [b]Jdg 6:14,32 [c]Jdg 4:6 [d]Jdg 11:1
12:12 [e]1Sa 11:1 [f]1Sa 8:5 [g]Jdg 8:23; 1Sa 8:6,19
12:13 [h]1Sa 8:5; Hos 13:11 [i]1Sa 10:24
12:14 [j]Jos 24:14
12:15 [k]ver 9; Jos 24:20; Isa 1:20
12:16 [l]Ex 14:13

[e] *15* Traditionally *peace offerings* [f] *11* Also called *Gideon* [g] *11* Some Septuagint manuscripts and Syriac; Hebrew *Bedan* [h] *11* Hebrew; some Septuagint manuscripts and Syriac *Samson*

before your eyes! 17 Is it not wheat harvest[a] now? I will call[b] upon the LORD
to send thunder and rain.[c] And you will
realize what an evil[d] thing you did in
the eyes of the LORD when you asked
for a king."
18 Then Samuel called upon the LORD,
and that same day the LORD sent thunder and rain. So all the people stood in
awe[e] of the LORD and of Samuel.
19 The people all said to Samuel,
"Pray[f] to the LORD your God for your
servants so that we will not die, for we
have added to all our other sins the evil
of asking for a king."
20 "Do not be afraid," Samuel replied.
"You have done all this evil; yet do not
turn away from the LORD, but serve
the LORD with all your heart. 21 Do not
turn away after useless[g] idols.[h] They
can do you no good, nor can they rescue
you, because they are useless. 22 For
the sake[i] of his great name[j] the LORD
will not reject[k] his people, because the
LORD was pleased to make[l] you his own.
23 As for me, far be it from me that I
should sin against the LORD by failing to
pray[m] for you. And I will teach[n] you the
way that is good and right. 24 But be
sure to fear[o] the LORD and serve him
faithfully with all your heart; consider[p]
what great[q] things he has done for you.
25 Yet if you persist[r] in doing evil, both
you and your king will be swept[s] away."

Saul's sinful offering.

13 Saul was ⌊thirty⌋[i] years old when
he became king, and he reigned
over Israel ⌊forty-⌋[j] two years.
2 Saul[k] chose three thousand men
from Israel; two thousand were with
him at Micmash and in the hill country
of Bethel, and a thousand were with
Jonathan at Gibeah[t] in Benjamin. The
rest of the men he sent back to their
homes.
3 Jonathan attacked the Philistine outpost[u] at Geba, and the Philistines heard
about it. Then Saul had the trumpet
blown throughout the land and said,
"Let the Hebrews hear!" 4 So all Israel
heard the news: "Saul has attacked the
Philistine outpost, and now Israel has
become a stench[v] to the Philistines."
And the people were summoned to join
Saul at Gilgal.
5 The Philistines assembled to fight
Israel, with three thousand[l] chariots, six
thousand charioteers, and soldiers as
numerous as the sand[w] on the seashore.
They went up and camped at Micmash,
east of Beth Aven. 6 When the men of
Israel saw that their situation was criti-
cal and that their army was hard
pressed, they hid in caves and thickets,
among the rocks, and in pits and cisterns.[x] 7 Some Hebrews even crossed the
Jordan to the land of Gad[y] and Gilead.
Saul remained at Gilgal, and all the
troops with him were quaking with fear.
8 He waited seven[z] days, the time set by
Samuel; but Samuel did not come to
Gilgal, and Saul's men began to scatter.
9 So he said, "Bring me the burnt offering and the fellowship offerings.[m]" And
Saul offered[a] up the burnt offering.
10 Just as he finished making the offering, Samuel[b] arrived, and Saul went out
to greet him.
11 "What have you done?" asked
Samuel.
Saul replied, "When I saw that the
men were scattering, and that you did
not come at the set time, and that the
Philistines were assembling at Micmash,[c] 12 I thought, 'Now the Philistines will come down against me at
Gilgal, and I have not sought the LORD's
favor.[d]' So I felt compelled to offer the
burnt offering."
13 "You acted foolishly,[e]" Samuel said.
"You have not kept[f] the command the
LORD your God gave you; if you had, he
would have established your kingdom
over Israel for all time. 14 But now your
kingdom[g] will not endure; the LORD has

12:17 [a] 1Sa 7:9-10 [b] Jas 5:18 [c] Pr 26:1 [d] 1Sa 8:6-7
12:18 [e] Ex 14:31
12:19 [f] ver 23; Ex 9:28; Jas 5:18; 1Jn 5:16
12:21 [g] Isa 41:24,29; Jer 16:19; Hab 2:18 [h] Dt 11:16
12:22 [i] Ps 106:8 [j] Jos 7:9 [k] 1Ki 6:13 [l] Dt 7:7; 1Pe 2:9
12:23 [m] Ro 1:9-10; Col 1:9; 2Ti 1:3 [n] 1Ki 8:36; Ps 34:11; Pr 4:11
12:24 [o] Ecc 12:13 [p] Isa 5:12 [q] Dt 10:21
12:25 [r] 1Sa 31:1-5 [s] Jos 24:20
13:2 [t] 1Sa 10:26
13:3 [u] 1Sa 10:5
13:4 [v] Ge 34:30
13:5 [w] Jos 11:4
13:6 [x] Jdg 6:2
13:7 [y] Nu 32:33
13:8 [z] 1Sa 10:8
13:9 [a] 2Sa 24:25; 1Ki 3:4
13:10 [b] 1Sa 15:13
13:11 [c] ver 2,5,16, 23
13:12 [d] Jer 26:19
13:13 [e] 2Ch 16:9 [f] 1Sa 15:23,24
13:14 [g] 1Sa 15:28

[i] *1* A few late manuscripts of the Septuagint; Hebrew does not have *thirty.* [j] *1* See the round number in Acts 13:21; Hebrew does not have *forty-.* [k] *1,2* Or *and when he had reigned over Israel two years, 2he* [l] *5* Some Septuagint manuscripts and Syriac; Hebrew *thirty thousand* [m] *9* Traditionally *peace offerings*

sought out a man after his own heart[a] and appointed[b] him leader of his people, because you have not kept the LORD's command."

15 Then Samuel left Gilgal[n] and went up to Gibeah[c] in Benjamin, and Saul counted the men who were with him. They numbered about six hundred.

Israel's lack of weapons.

16 Saul and his son Jonathan and the men with them were staying in Gibeah[o] in Benjamin, while the Philistines camped at Micmash. 17 Raiding[d] parties went out from the Philistine camp in three detachments. One turned toward Ophrah[e] in the vicinity of Shual, 18 another toward Beth Horon,[f] and the third toward the borderland overlooking the Valley of Zeboim[g] facing the desert.

19 Not a blacksmith[h] could be found in the whole land of Israel, because the Philistines had said, "Otherwise the Hebrews will make swords or spears!" 20 So all Israel went down to the Philistines to have their plowshares, mattocks, axes and sickles[p] sharpened. 21 The price was two thirds of a shekel[q] for sharpening plowshares and mattocks, and a third of a shekel[r] for sharpening forks and axes and for repointing goads.

22 So on the day of the battle not a soldier with Saul and Jonathan[i] had a sword or spear[j] in his hand; only Saul and his son Jonathan had them.

Jonathan's attack on the Philistines.

23 Now a detachment of Philistines had gone out to the pass[k] at Micmash.

14 1 One day Jonathan son of Saul said to the young man bearing his armor, "Come, let's go over to the Philistine outpost on the other side." But he did not tell his father.

2 Saul was staying on the outskirts of Gibeah[l] under a pomegranate tree in Migron.[m] With him were about six hundred men, 3 among whom was Ahijah, who was wearing an ephod. He was a son of Ichabod's[n] brother Ahitub[o] son of Phinehas, the son of Eli,[p] the LORD's priest in Shiloh. No one was aware that Jonathan had left.

4 On each side of the pass[q] that Jonathan intended to cross to reach the Philistine outpost was a cliff; one was called Bozez, and the other Seneh. 5 One cliff stood to the north toward Micmash, the other to the south toward Geba.

6 Jonathan said to his young armor-bearer, "Come, let's go over to the outpost of those uncircumcised[r] fellows. Perhaps the LORD will act in our behalf. Nothing[s] can hinder the LORD from saving, whether by many[t] or by few.[u]"

7 "Do all that you have in mind," his armor-bearer said. "Go ahead; I am with you heart and soul."

8 Jonathan said, "Come, then; we will cross over toward the men and let them see us. 9 If they say to us, 'Wait there until we come to you,' we will stay where we are and not go up to them. 10 But if they say, 'Come up to us,' we will climb up, because that will be our sign[v] that the LORD has given them into our hands."

11 So both of them showed themselves to the Philistine outpost. "Look!" said the Philistines. "The Hebrews are crawling out of the holes they were hiding[w] in." 12 The men of the outpost shouted to Jonathan and his armor-bearer, "Come up to us and we'll teach you a lesson.[x]"

So Jonathan said to his armor-bearer, "Climb up after me; the LORD has given them into the hand[y] of Israel."

13 Jonathan climbed up, using his hands and feet, with his armor-bearer right behind him. The Philistines fell before Jonathan, and his armor-bearer followed and killed behind him. 14 In that first attack Jonathan and his armor-bearer killed some twenty men in an area of about half an acre.[s]

13:14 [a]Ac 7:46; 13:22 [b]2Sa 6:21
13:15 [c]1Sa 14:2
13:17 [d]1Sa 14:15 [e]Jos 18:23
13:18 [f]Jos 18:13-14 [g]Ne 11:34
13:19 [h]2Ki 24:14; Jer 24:1
13:22 [i]1Ch 9:39 [j]Jdg 5:8
13:23 [k]1Sa 14:4
14:2 [l]1Sa 13:15 [m]Isa 10:28
14:3 [n]1Sa 4:21 [o]1Sa 22:11,20 [p]1Sa 2:28
14:4 [q]1Sa 13:23
14:6 [r]1Sa 17:26,36; Jer 9:26 [s]Heb 11:34 [t]Jdg 7:4 [u]1Sa 17:46-47
14:10 [v]Ge 24:14; Jdg 6:36-37
14:11 [w]1Sa 13:6
14:12 [x]1Sa 17:43-44 [y]2Sa 5:24

[n] *15* Hebrew; Septuagint *Gilgal and went his way; the rest of the people went after Saul to meet the army, and they went out of Gilgal* [o] *16* Two Hebrew manuscripts; most Hebrew manuscripts *Geba,* a variant of *Gibeah* [p] *20* Septuagint; Hebrew *plowshares* [q] *21* Hebrew *pim;* that is, about 1/4 ounce (about 8 grams) [r] *21* That is, about 1/8 ounce (about 4 grams) [s] *14* Hebrew *half a yoke;* a "yoke" was the land plowed by a yoke of oxen in one day.

15Then panic[a] struck the whole army—
those in the camp and field, and those
in the outposts and raiding[b] parties—
and the ground shook. It was a panic
sent by God.[t]
16Saul's lookouts[c] at Gibeah in Benjamin saw the army melting away in all
directions. 17Then Saul said to the men
who were with him, "Muster the forces
and see who has left us." When they
did, it was Jonathan and his armor-
bearer who were not there.
18Saul said to Ahijah, "Bring[d] the ark
of God." (At that time it was with the
Israelites.)[u] 19While Saul was talking to
the priest, the tumult in the Philistine
camp increased more and more. So Saul
said to the priest,[e] "Withdraw your
hand."
20Then Saul and all his men assembled and went to the battle. They found
the Philistines in total confusion, striking[f] each other with their swords.
21Those Hebrews who had previously
been with the Philistines and had gone
up with them to their camp went[g] over
to the Israelites who were with Saul and
Jonathan. 22When all the Israelites who
had hidden[h] in the hill country of
Ephraim heard that the Philistines were
on the run, they joined the battle in hot
pursuit. 23So the LORD rescued[i] Israel
that day, and the battle moved on beyond Beth Aven.[j]

Jonathan eats honey.

24Now the men of Israel were in distress that day, because Saul had bound
the people under an oath,[k] saying,
"Cursed be any man who eats food
before evening comes, before I have
avenged myself on my enemies!" So
none of the troops tasted food.
25The entire army[v] entered the
woods, and there was honey on the
ground. 26When they went into the
woods, they saw the honey oozing out,
yet no one put his hand to his mouth,
because they feared the oath. 27But
Jonathan had not heard that his father
had bound the people with the oath,
so he reached out the end of the staff
that was in his hand and dipped it into
the honeycomb.[l] He raised his hand to
his mouth, and his eyes brightened.[w]
28Then one of the soldiers told him,
"Your father bound the army under a
strict oath, saying, 'Cursed be any man
who eats food today!' That is why the
men are faint."
29Jonathan said, "My father has made
trouble[m] for the country. See how my
eyes brightened[x] when I tasted a little of
this honey. 30How much better it would
have been if the men had eaten today
some of the plunder they took from their
enemies. Would not the slaughter of the
Philistines have been even greater?"
31That day, after the Israelites had
struck down the Philistines from Micmash to Aijalon,[n] they were exhausted.
32They pounced on the plunder[o] and,
taking sheep, cattle and calves, they
butchered them on the ground and ate
them, together with the blood.[p] 33Then
someone said to Saul, "Look, the men
are sinning against the LORD by eating
meat that has blood in it."
"You have broken faith," he said.
"Roll a large stone over here at once."
34Then he said, "Go out among the men
and tell them, 'Each of you bring me
your cattle and sheep, and slaughter
them here and eat them. Do not sin
against the LORD by eating meat with
blood still in it.'"
So everyone brought his ox that night
and slaughtered it there. 35Then Saul
built an altar[q] to the LORD; it was the
first time he had done this.
36Saul said, "Let us go down after the
Philistines by night and plunder them
till dawn, and let us not leave one of
them alive."
"Do whatever seems best to you,"
they replied.
But the priest said, "Let us inquire
of God here."

14:15 [a]Ge 35:5; 2Ki 7:5-7 [b]1Sa 13:17
14:16 [c]2Sa 18:24
14:18 [d]1Sa 30:7
14:19 [e]Nu 27:21
14:20 [f]Jdg 7:22; 2Ch 20:23
14:21 [g]1Sa 29:4
14:22 [h]1Sa 13:6
14:23 [i]Ex 14:30; Ps 44:6-7 [j]1Sa 13:5
14:24 [k]Jos 6:26
14:27 [l]ver 43; 1Sa 30:12
14:29 [m]Jos 7:25; 1Ki 18:18
14:31 [n]Jos 10:12
14:32 [o]1Sa 15:19 [p]Ge 9:4; Lev 3:17; 7:26; 17:10-14; 19:26; Dt 12:16, 23-24
14:35 [q]1Sa 7:17

[t]*15* Or *a terrible panic* [u]*18* Hebrew; Septuagint *"Bring the ephod." (At that time he wore the ephod before the Israelites.)* [v]*25* Or *Now all the people of the land* [w]*27* Or *his strength was renewed* [x]*29* Or *my strength was renewed*

37 So Saul asked God, "Shall I go down after the Philistines? Will you give them into Israel's hand?" But God did not answer[a] him that day.

38 Saul therefore said, "Come here, all you who are leaders of the army, and let us find out what sin has been committed[b] today. 39 As surely as the LORD who rescues Israel lives,[c] even if it lies with my son Jonathan, he must die." But not one of the men said a word.

40 Saul then said to all the Israelites, "You stand over there; I and Jonathan my son will stand over here."

"Do what seems best to you," the men replied.

41 Then Saul prayed to the LORD, the God of Israel, "Give[d] me the right[e] answer."[y] And Jonathan and Saul were taken by lot, and the men were cleared. 42 Saul said, "Cast the lot between me and Jonathan my son." And Jonathan was taken.

43 Then Saul said to Jonathan, "Tell me what you have done."[f]

So Jonathan told him, "I merely tasted a little honey[g] with the end of my staff. And now must I die?"

44 Saul said, "May God deal with me, be it ever so severely,[h] if you do not die, Jonathan.[i]"

45 But the men said to Saul, "Should Jonathan die—he who has brought about this great deliverance in Israel? Never! As surely as the LORD lives, not a hair[j] of his head will fall to the ground, for he did this today with God's help." So the men rescued[k] Jonathan, and he was not put to death.

46 Then Saul stopped pursuing the Philistines, and they withdrew to their own land.

Saul leads Israel into war.

47 After Saul had assumed rule over Israel, he fought against their enemies on every side: Moab, the Ammonites,[l] Edom, the kings[z] of Zobah,[m] and the Philistines. Wherever he turned, he inflicted punishment on them.[a] 48 He fought valiantly and defeated the Amalekites,[n] delivering Israel from the hands of those who had plundered them.

Saul's family.

49 Saul's sons were Jonathan, Ishvi and Malki-Shua.[o] The name of his older daughter was Merab, and that of the younger was Michal.[p] 50 His wife's name was Ahinoam daughter of Ahimaaz. The name of the commander of Saul's army was Abner son of Ner, and Ner was Saul's uncle. 51 Saul's father Kish[q] and Abner's father Ner were sons of Abiel.

52 All the days of Saul there was bitter war with the Philistines, and whenever Saul saw a mighty or brave man, he took[r] him into his service.

Saul disobeys God by sparing Agag.

15 Samuel said to Saul, "I am the one the LORD sent to anoint[s] you king over his people Israel; so listen now to the message from the LORD. 2 This is what the LORD Almighty says: 'I will punish the Amalekites[t] for what they did to Israel when they waylaid them as they came up from Egypt. 3 Now go, attack the Amalekites and totally[u] destroy[b] everything that belongs to them. Do not spare them; put to death men and women, children and infants, cattle and sheep, camels and donkeys.'"

4 So Saul summoned the men and mustered them at Telaim—two hundred thousand foot soldiers and ten thousand men from Judah. 5 Saul went to the city of Amalek and set an ambush in the ravine. 6 Then he said to the Kenites,[v] "Go away, leave the Amalekites so that I do not destroy you along with them; for you showed kindness to all the Israelites when they came up out of Egypt." So the Kenites moved away from the Amalekites.

14:37 [a] 1Sa 10:22; 28:6,15
14:38 [b] Jos 7:11; 1Sa 10:19
14:39 [c] 2Sa 12:5
14:41 [d] Ac 1:24 [e] Pr 16:33
14:43 [f] Jos 7:19 [g] ver 27
14:44 [h] Ru 1:17 [i] ver 39
14:45 [j] 1Ki 1:52; Lk 21:18; Ac 27:34 [k] 2Sa 14:11
14:47 [l] 1Sa 11:1-13 [m] ver 52; 2Sa 10:6
14:48 [n] 1Sa 15:2,7
14:49 [o] 1Sa 31:2; 1Ch 8:33 [p] 1Sa 18:17-20
14:51 [q] 1Sa 9:1
14:52 [r] 1Sa 8:11
15:1 [s] 1Sa 9:16
15:2 [t] Ex 17:8-14; Nu 24:20; Dt 25:17-19
15:3 [u] Nu 24:20; Dt 20:16-18; Jos 6:17; 1Sa 22:19
15:6 [v] Ex 18:10,19; Nu 10:29-32; 24:22; Jdg 1:16; 4:1

[y] *41* Hebrew; Septuagint *"Why have you not answered your servant today? If the fault is in me or my son Jonathan, respond with Urim, but if the men of Israel are at fault, respond with Thummim."*
[z] *47* Masoretic Text; Dead Sea Scrolls and Septuagint *king*
[a] *47* Hebrew; Septuagint *he was victorious*
[b] *3* The Hebrew term refers to the irrevocable giving over of things or persons to the LORD, often by totally destroying them; also in verses 8,9,15,18,20 and 21.

7 Then Saul attacked the Amalekites[a]
all the way from Havilah to Shur,[b] to the
east of Egypt. 8 He took Agag king of the
Amalekites alive,[c] and all his people he
totally destroyed with the sword. 9 But
Saul and the army spared[d] Agag and
the best of the sheep and cattle, the fat
calves[c] and lambs—everything that was
good. These they were unwilling to
destroy completely, but everything that
was despised and weak they totally
destroyed.

Samuel announces the LORD's rejection of Saul.

10 Then the word of the LORD came to
Samuel: 11 "I am grieved[e] that I have
made Saul king, because he has turned[f]
away from me and has not carried out
my instructions."[g] Samuel was troubled,[h] and he cried out to the LORD all
that night.
12 Early in the morning Samuel got up
and went to meet Saul, but he was told,
"Saul has gone to Carmel.[i] There he has
set up a monument in his own honor
and has turned and gone on down to
Gilgal."
13 When Samuel reached him, Saul
said, "The LORD bless you! I have carried
out the LORD's instructions."
14 But Samuel said, "What then is this
bleating of sheep in my ears? What is
this lowing of cattle that I hear?"
15 Saul answered, "The soldiers
brought them from the Amalekites; they
spared the best of the sheep and cattle
to sacrifice to the LORD your God, but
we totally destroyed the rest."
16 "Stop!" Samuel said to Saul. "Let
me tell you what the LORD said to me
last night."
"Tell me," Saul replied.
17 Samuel said, "Although you were
once small[j] in your own eyes, did you
not become the head of the tribes of
Israel? The LORD anointed you king over
Israel. 18 And he sent you on a mission,
saying, 'Go and completely destroy those
wicked people, the Amalekites; make
war on them until you have wiped them
out.' 19 Why did you not obey the LORD?
Why did you pounce on the plunder[k]
and do evil in the eyes of the LORD?"
20 "But I did obey[l] the LORD," Saul
said. "I went on the mission the LORD
assigned me. I completely destroyed the
Amalekites and brought back Agag their
king. 21 The soldiers took sheep and cattle from the plunder, the best of what
was devoted to God, in order to sacrifice
them to the LORD your God at Gilgal."
22 But Samuel replied:

"Does the LORD delight in burnt
offerings and sacrifices
as much as in obeying the voice of
the LORD?
To obey is better than sacrifice,[m]
and to heed is better than the fat of
rams.
23 For rebellion is like the sin of
divination,[n]
and arrogance like the evil of
idolatry.
Because you have rejected[o] the word
of the LORD,
he has rejected you as king."

24 Then Saul said to Samuel, "I have
sinned.[p] I violated the LORD's command
and your instructions. I was afraid[q] of
the people and so I gave in to them.
25 Now I beg you, forgive[r] my sin and
come back with me, so that I may worship the LORD."
26 But Samuel said to him, "I will not
go back with you. You have rejected[s]
the word of the LORD, and the LORD has
rejected you as king over Israel!"
27 As Samuel turned to leave, Saul
caught hold of the hem of his robe, and
it tore.[t] 28 Samuel said to him, "The LORD
has torn[u] the kingdom of Israel from
you today and has given it to one of your
neighbors—to one better than you. 29 He
who is the Glory of Israel does not lie[v]
or change[w] his mind; for he is not a man,
that he should change his mind."

15:7 [a] 1Sa 14:48 [b] Ge 16:7; 25:17-18; Ex 15:22
15:8 [c] 1Sa 30:1
15:9 [d] ver 3,15
15:11 [e] Ge 6:6; 2Sa 24:16 [f] Jos 22:16 [g] 1Sa 13:13; 1Ki 9:6-7 [h] ver 35
15:12 [i] Jos 15:55
15:17 [j] 1Sa 9:21
15:19 [k] 1Sa 14:32
15:20 [l] ver 13
15:22 [m] Ps 40:6-8; 51:16; Isa 1:11-15; Jer 7:22; Hos 6:6; Mic 6:6-8; Mt 12:7; Mk 12:33; Heb 10:6-9
15:23 [n] Dt 18:10 [o] 1Sa 13:13
15:24 [p] 2Sa 12:13 [q] Pr 29:25; Isa 51:12-13
15:25 [r] Ex 10:17
15:26 [s] 1Sa 13:14
15:27 [t] 1Ki 11:11,31
15:28 [u] 1Sa 28:17; 1Ki 11:31
15:29 [v] 1Ch 29:11; Tit 1:2 [w] Nu 23:19; Eze 24:14

c9 Or *the grown bulls;* the meaning of the Hebrew for this phrase is uncertain.

30Saul replied, "I have sinned. But please honor[a] me before the elders of my people and before Israel; come back with me, so that I may worship the LORD your God." 31So Samuel went back with Saul, and Saul worshiped the LORD.

Samuel puts Agag to death.

32Then Samuel said, "Bring me Agag king of the Amalekites."

Agag came to him confidently,[d] thinking, "Surely the bitterness of death is past."

33But Samuel said,

"As your sword has made women
  childless,
so will your mother be childless
  among women."[b]

And Samuel put Agag to death before the LORD at Gilgal.

34Then Samuel left for Ramah,[c] but Saul went up to his home in Gibeah[d] of Saul. 35Until the day Samuel[e] died, he did not go to see Saul again, though Samuel mourned[f] for him. And the LORD was grieved that he had made Saul king over Israel.

David is anointed by Samuel.

16 The LORD said to Samuel, "How long will you mourn[g] for Saul, since I have rejected[h] him as king over Israel? Fill your horn with oil[i] and be on your way; I am sending you to Jesse[j] of Bethlehem. I have chosen[k] one of his sons to be king."

2But Samuel said, "How can I go? Saul will hear about it and kill me."

The LORD said, "Take a heifer with you and say, 'I have come to sacrifice to the LORD.' 3Invite Jesse to the sacrifice, and I will show[l] you what to do. You are to anoint[m] for me the one I indicate."

4Samuel did what the LORD said. When he arrived at Bethlehem,[n] the elders of the town trembled when they met him. They asked, "Do you come in peace?[o]"

5Samuel replied, "Yes, in peace; I have come to sacrifice to the LORD. Consecrate[p] yourselves and come to the sacrifice with me." Then he consecrated Jesse and his sons and invited them to the sacrifice.

6When they arrived, Samuel saw Eliab[q] and thought, "Surely the LORD's anointed stands here before the LORD."

7But the LORD said to Samuel, "Do not consider his appearance or his height, for I have rejected him. The LORD does not look at the things man looks at. Man looks at the outward appearance,[r] but the LORD looks at the heart."[s]

8Then Jesse called Abinadab[t] and had him pass in front of Samuel. But Samuel said, "The LORD has not chosen this one either." 9Jesse then had Shammah pass by, but Samuel said, "Nor has the LORD chosen this one." 10Jesse had seven of his sons pass before Samuel, but Samuel said to him, "The LORD has not chosen these." 11So he asked Jesse, "Are these all[u] the sons you have?"

"There is still the youngest," Jesse answered, "but he is tending the sheep."

Samuel said, "Send for him; we will not sit down[e] until he arrives."

12So he[v] sent and had him brought in. He was ruddy, with a fine appearance and handsome[w] features.

Then the LORD said, "Rise and anoint him; he is the one."

13So Samuel took the horn of oil and anointed him in the presence of his brothers, and from that day on the Spirit of the LORD[x] came upon David in power.[y] Samuel then went to Ramah.

David plays the harp for Saul.

14Now the Spirit of the LORD had departed[z] from Saul, and an evil[f] spirit[a] from the LORD tormented him.

15Saul's attendants said to him, "See, an evil spirit from God is tormenting you. 16Let our lord command his servants here to search for someone who can play the harp.[b] He will play when

15:30 [a]Isa 29:13; Jn 5:44; 12:43
15:33 [b]Ge 9:6; Jdg 1:7
15:34 [c]1Sa 7:17 [d]1Sa 11:4
15:35 [e]1Sa 19:24 [f]1Sa 16:1
16:1 [g]1Sa 15:35 [h]1Sa 15:23 [i]2Ki 9:1 [j]Ru 4:17; 1Sa 9:16 [k]Ps 78:70; Ac 13:22
16:3 [l]Ex 4:15 [m]Dt 17:15; 1Sa 9:16
16:4 [n]Ge 48:7; Lk 2:4 [o]1Ki 2:13; 2Ki 9:17
16:5 [p]Ex 19:10,22
16:6 [q]1Sa 17:13
16:7 [r]Ps 147:10 [s]1Ki 8:39; 1Ch 28:9; Isa 55:8
16:8 [t]1Sa 17:13
16:11 [u]1Sa 17:12
16:12 [v]1Sa 9:17 [w]Ge 39:6; 1Sa 17:42
16:13 [x]Nu 27:18; Jdg 11:29 [y]1Sa 10:1,6, 9-10; 11:6
16:14 [z]Jdg 16:20 [a]Jdg 9:23; 1Sa 18:10
16:16 [b]ver 23; 1Sa 18:10; 19:9; 2Ki 3:15

d*32* Or *him trembling, yet* e*11* Some Septuagint manuscripts; Hebrew *not gather around* f*14* Or *injurious*; also in verses 15, 16 and 23

the evil spirit from God comes upon
you, and you will feel better."
17So Saul said to his attendants, "Find
someone who plays well and bring him
to me."
18One of the servants answered, "I
have seen a son of Jesse of Bethlehem
who knows how to play the harp. He is a
brave man and a warrior. He speaks well
and is a fine-looking man. And the LORD
is with[a] him."
19Then Saul sent messengers to Jesse
and said, "Send me your son David,
who is with the sheep." 20So Jesse took
a donkey loaded with bread,[b] a skin of
wine and a young goat and sent them
with his son David to Saul.
21David came to Saul and entered his
service.[c] Saul liked him very much, and
David became one of his armor-bearers.
22Then Saul sent word to Jesse, saying,
"Allow David to remain in my service,
for I am pleased with him."
23Whenever the spirit from God came
upon Saul, David would take his harp
and play. Then relief would come to
Saul; he would feel better, and the evil
spirit[d] would leave him.

Goliath challenges the Israelites.

17 Now the Philistines gathered their
forces for war and assembled[e] at
Socoh in Judah. They pitched camp at
Ephes Dammim, between Socoh[f] and
Azekah. 2Saul and the Israelites assembled and camped in the Valley of Elah[g]
and drew up their battle line to meet the
Philistines. 3The Philistines occupied one
hill and the Israelites another, with the
valley between them.
4A champion named Goliath,[h] who
was from Gath, came out of the Philistine camp. He was over nine feet[g] tall.
5He had a bronze helmet on his head
and wore a coat of scale armor of bronze
weighing five thousand shekels[h]; 6on
his legs he wore bronze greaves, and a
bronze javelin[i] was slung on his back.
7His spear shaft was like a weaver's
rod,[j] and its iron point weighed six hundred shekels.[i] His shield bearer[k] went
ahead of him.
8Goliath stood and shouted to the
ranks of Israel, "Why do you come out
and line up for battle? Am I not a Philistine, and are you not the servants of
Saul? Choose[l] a man and have him come
down to me. 9If he is able to fight and
kill me, we will become your subjects;
but if I overcome him and kill him, you
will become our subjects and serve
us." 10Then the Philistine said, "This day
I defy[m] the ranks of Israel! Give me a
man and let us fight each other." 11On
hearing the Philistine's words, Saul and
all the Israelites were dismayed and terrified.

David kills Goliath with a sling and a stone.

12Now David was the son of an Eph-
rathite named Jesse,[n] who was from
Bethlehem[o] in Judah. Jesse had eight[p]
sons, and in Saul's time he was old and
well advanced in years. 13Jesse's three
oldest sons had followed Saul to the
war: The firstborn was Eliab;[q] the second, Abinadab; and the third, Shammah.[r] 14David was the youngest. The
three oldest followed Saul, 15but David
went back and forth from Saul to tend
his father's sheep[s] at Bethlehem.

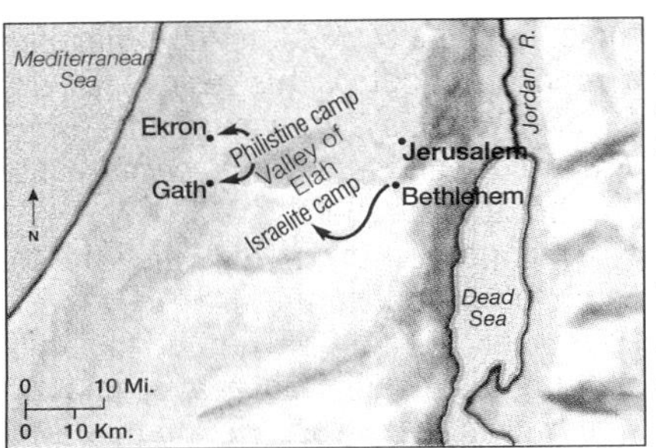

David and Goliath

The armies of Israel and Philistia faced each other across the Valley of Elah. David arrived from Bethlehem and offered to fight the giant Goliath. After David defeated Goliath, the Israelite army chased the Philistines to Ekron and Gath (Goliath's hometown).

16:18 [a]1Sa 3:19; 17:32-37
16:20 [b]1Sa 10:27; Pr 18:16
16:21 [c]Ge 41:46; Pr 22:29
16:23 [d]ver 14-16
17:1 [e]1Sa 13:5 [f]Jos 15:35; 2Ch 28:18
17:2 [g]1Sa 21:9
17:4 [h]Jos 11:21-22; 2Sa 21:19
17:6 [i]ver 45
17:7 [j]2Sa 21:19 [k]ver 41
17:8 [l]1Sa 8:17
17:10 [m]ver 26,45; 2Sa 21:21
17:12 [n]Ru 4:17; 1Ch 2:13-15 [o]Ge 35:19 [p]1Sa 16:11
17:13 [q]1Sa 16:6 [r]1Sa 16:9
17:15 [s]1Sa 16:19

g4 Hebrew *was six cubits and a span* (about 3 meters)
h5 That is, about 125 pounds (about 57 kilograms)
i7 That is, about 15 pounds (about 7 kilograms)

16For forty days the Philistine came
forward every morning and evening and
took his stand.

17Now Jesse said to his son David,
"Take this ephah[j] of roasted grain[a] and
these ten loaves of bread for your brothers and hurry to their camp. 18Take
along these ten cheeses to the commander of their unit.[k] See how your brothers[b] are and bring back some assurance[l]
from them. 19They are with Saul and all
the men of Israel in the Valley of Elah,
fighting against the Philistines."

20Early in the morning David left the
flock with a shepherd, loaded up and set
out, as Jesse had directed. He reached
the camp as the army was going out to
its battle positions, shouting the war cry.
21Israel and the Philistines were drawing up their lines facing each other.
22David left his things with the keeper
of supplies, ran to the battle lines and
greeted his brothers. 23As he was talking with them, Goliath, the Philistine
champion from Gath, stepped out from
his lines and shouted his usual[c] defiance, and David heard it. 24When the
Israelites saw the man, they all ran from
him in great fear.

25Now the Israelites had been saying,
"Do you see how this man keeps coming out? He comes out to defy Israel.
The king will give great wealth to the
man who kills him. He will also give
him his daughter[d] in marriage and will
exempt his father's family from taxes in
Israel."

26David asked the men standing near
him, "What will be done for the man
who kills this Philistine and removes
this disgrace[e] from Israel? Who is this
uncircumcised[f] Philistine that he should
defy[g] the armies of the living[h] God?"

27They repeated to him what they had
been saying and told him, "This is what
will be done for the man who kills
him."

28When Eliab, David's oldest brother,
heard him speaking with the men, he
burned with anger[i] at him and asked,
"Why have you come down here? And
with whom did you leave those few
sheep in the desert? I know how conceited you are and how wicked your
heart is; you came down only to watch
the battle."

29"Now what have I done?" said
David. "Can't I even speak?" 30He then
turned away to someone else and
brought up the same matter, and the
men answered him as before. 31What
David said was overheard and reported
to Saul, and Saul sent for him.

32David said to Saul, "Let no one lose
heart[j] on account of this Philistine; your
servant will go and fight him."

33Saul replied,[k] "You are not able to
go out against this Philistine and fight
him; you are only a boy, and he has
been a fighting man from his youth."

34But David said to Saul, "Your servant has been keeping his father's sheep.
When a lion[l] or a bear came and carried
off a sheep from the flock, 35I went after
it, struck it and rescued the sheep from
its mouth. When it turned on me, I
seized it by its hair, struck it and killed
it. 36Your servant has killed both the lion
and the bear; this uncircumcised Philistine will be like one of them, because
he has defied the armies of the living
God. 37The LORD who delivered[m] me
from the paw of the lion[n] and the paw of
the bear will deliver me from the hand
of this Philistine."

Saul said to David, "Go, and the LORD
be with[o] you."

38Then Saul dressed David in his own
tunic. He put a coat of armor on him and
a bronze helmet on his head. 39David
fastened on his sword over the tunic
and tried walking around, because he
was not used to them.

"I cannot go in these," he said to
Saul, "because I am not used to them."
So he took them off. 40Then he took his
staff in his hand, chose five smooth
stones from the stream, put them in the
pouch of his shepherd's bag and, with
his sling in his hand, approached the
Philistine.

17:17 [a]1Sa 25:18
17:18 [b]Ge 37:14
17:23 [c]ver 8-10
17:25 [d]Jos 15:16; 1Sa 18:17
17:26 [e]1Sa 11:2 [f]1Sa 14:6 [g]ver 10 [h]Dt 5:26
17:28 [i]Ge 37:4,8,11; Pr 18:19; Mt 10:36
17:32 [j]Dt 20:3; 1Sa 16:18
17:33 [k]Nu 13:31
17:34 [l]Jer 49:19; Am 3:12
17:37 [m]2Co 1:10 [n]2Ti 4:17 [o]1Sa 20:13; 1Ch 22:11,16

j *17* That is, probably about 3/5 bushel (about 22 liters)
k *18* Hebrew *thousand*
l *18* Or *some token*; or *some pledge of spoils*

41Meanwhile, the Philistine, with his
shield bearer in front of him, kept coming closer to David. 42He looked David
over and saw that he was only a boy,
ruddy and handsome,[a] and he despised[b]
him. 43He said to David, "Am I a dog,[c]
that you come at me with sticks?" And
the Philistine cursed David by his gods.
44"Come here," he said, "and I'll give
your flesh to the birds of the air and the
beasts of the field![d]"
45David said to the Philistine, "You
come against me with sword and spear
and javelin, but I come against you in
the name[e] of the LORD Almighty, the
God of the armies of Israel, whom you
have defied.[f] 46This day the LORD will
hand you over to me, and I'll strike you
down and cut off your head. Today I will
give the carcasses[g] of the Philistine army
to the birds of the air and the beasts of
the earth, and the whole world[h] will
know that there is a God in Israel.[i]
47All those gathered here will know that
it is not by sword[j] or spear that the
LORD saves;[k] for the battle[l] is the LORD's,
and he will give all of you into our
hands."
48As the Philistine moved closer to
attack him, David ran quickly toward
the battle line to meet him. 49Reaching
into his bag and taking out a stone, he
slung it and struck the Philistine on the
forehead. The stone sank into his forehead, and he fell facedown on the
ground.
50So David triumphed over the Philistine with a sling[m] and a stone; without
a sword in his hand he struck down the
Philistine and killed him.
51David ran and stood over him. He
took hold of the Philistine's sword and
drew it from the scabbard. After he
killed him, he cut[n] off his head with the
sword.[o]
When the Philistines saw that their
hero was dead, they turned and ran.
52Then the men of Israel and Judah
surged forward with a shout and pursued the Philistines to the entrance of
Gath[m] and to the gates of Ekron.[p] Their
dead were strewn along the Shaaraim[q]
road to Gath and Ekron. 53When the
Israelites returned from chasing the
Philistines, they plundered their camp.
54David took the Philistine's head and
brought it to Jerusalem, and he put the
Philistine's weapons in his own tent.
55As Saul watched David[r] going out to
meet the Philistine, he said to Abner,
commander of the army, "Abner, whose
son is that young man?"
Abner replied, "As surely as you live,
O king, I don't know."
56The king said, "Find out whose son
this young man is."
57As soon as David returned from
killing the Philistine, Abner took him
and brought him before Saul, with David
still holding the Philistine's head.
58"Whose son are you, young man?"
Saul asked him.
David said, "I am the son of your servant Jesse[s] of Bethlehem."

The friendship of Jonathan and David.

18 After David had finished talking
with Saul, Jonathan became one
in spirit with David, and he loved[t] him
as himself.[u] 2From that day Saul kept
David with him and did not let him
return to his father's house. 3And Jonathan made a covenant[v] with David because he loved him as himself. 4Jonathan
took off the robe[w] he was wearing and
gave it to David, along with his tunic,
and even his sword, his bow and his
belt.

Saul's jealousy of David.

5Whatever Saul sent him to do, David
did it so successfully[n] that Saul gave him
a high rank in the army. This pleased all
the people, and Saul's officers as well.
6When the men were returning home
after David had killed the Philistine, the
women came out from all the towns of
Israel to meet King Saul with singing
and dancing,[x] with joyful songs and with

17:42 [a]1Sa 16:12 [b]Ps 123:3-4; Pr 16:18
17:43 [c]1Sa 24:14; 2Sa 3:8; 9:8; 2Ki 8:13
17:44 [d]1Ki 20:10-11
17:45 [e]2Sa 22:33, 35; 2Ch 32:8; Ps 124:8; Heb 11:32-34 [f]ver 10
17:46 [g]Dt 28:26 [h]Jos 4:24; 1Ki 8:43; Isa 52:10 [i]1Ki 18:36; 2Ki 19:19; Isa 37:20
17:47 [j]Hos 1:7; Zec 4:6 [k]1Sa 14:6; 2Ch 14:11 [l]2Ch 20:15; Ps 44:6-7
17:50 [m]2Sa 23:21
17:51 [n]Heb 11:34 [o]1Sa 21:9
17:52 [p]Jos 15:11 [q]Jos 15:36
17:55 [r]1Sa 16:21
17:58 [s]ver 12
18:1 [t]2Sa 1:26 [u]Ge 44:30
18:3 [v]1Sa 20:8,16, 17,42
18:4 [w]Ge 41:42
18:6 [x]Ex 15:20

m52 Some Septuagint manuscripts; Hebrew *a valley*
n5 Or *wisely*

tambourines[a] and lutes. 7As they danced,
they sang:[b]

"Saul has slain his thousands,
and David his tens[c] of thousands."

8Saul was very angry; this refrain
galled him. "They have credited David
with tens of thousands," he thought,
"but me with only thousands. What
more can he get but the kingdom?[d]"
9And from that time on Saul kept a jealous eye on David.
10The next day an evil[o] spirit[e] from
God came forcefully upon Saul. He was
prophesying in his house, while David
was playing the harp, as he usually[f] did.
Saul had a spear in his hand 11and he
hurled it, saying to himself,[g] "I'll pin
David to the wall." But David eluded[h]
him twice.
12Saul was afraid[i] of David, because
the LORD[j] was with[k] David but had left
Saul. 13So he sent David away from him
and gave him command over a thousand
men, and David led[l] the troops in their
campaigns.[m] 14In everything he did he
had great success,[p][n] because the LORD
was with[o] him. 15When Saul saw how
successful[q] he was, he was afraid of him.
16But all Israel and Judah loved David,
because he led them in their campaigns.[p]

David's marriage to Saul's daughter, Michal.

17Saul said to David, "Here is my older daughter[q] Merab. I will give her to
you in marriage; only serve me bravely
and fight the battles[r] of the LORD." For
Saul said to himself,[s] "I will not raise a
hand against him. Let the Philistines do
that!"
18But David said to Saul, "Who am I,[t]
and what is my family or my father's
clan in Israel, that I should become the
king's son-in-law?[u]" 19So[r] when the
time came for Merab,[v] Saul's daughter,
to be given to David, she was given in
marriage to Adriel of Meholah.[w]
20Now Saul's daughter Michal[x] was in
love with David, and when they told

18:6 [a]Jdg 11:34; Ps 68:25
18:7 [b]Ex 15:21 [c]1Sa 21:11; 29:5
18:8 [d]1Sa 15:8
18:10 [e]1Sa 16:14 [f]1Sa 19:7
18:11 [g]1Sa 20:7,33 [h]1Sa 19:10
18:12 [i]ver 15,29 [j]1Sa 16:13 [k]1Sa 28:15
18:13 [l]ver 16; Nu 27:17 [m]2Sa 5:2
18:14 [n]Ge 39:3 [o]Ge 39:2,23; Jos 6:27; 1Sa 16:18
18:16 [p]ver 5
18:17 [q]1Sa 17:25 [r]Nu 21:14; 1Sa 25:28 [s]ver 25
18:18 [t]1Sa 9:21; 2Sa 7:18 [u]ver 23
18:19 [v]2Sa 21:8 [w]Jdg 7:22
18:20 [x]ver 28
18:21 [y]ver 17,26
18:25 [z]Ge 34:12; Ex 22:17; 1Sa 14:24 [a]ver 17
18:27 [b]ver 13; 2Sa 3:14
18:30 [c]ver 5; 2Sa 11:1
19:1 [d]1Sa 18:1 [e]1Sa 18:9

Saul about it, he was pleased. 21"I will
give her to him," he thought, "so that
she may be a snare[y] to him and so that
the hand of the Philistines may be
against him." So Saul said to David,
"Now you have a second opportunity to
become my son-in-law."
22Then Saul ordered his attendants:
"Speak to David privately and say, 'Look,
the king is pleased with you, and his
attendants all like you; now become his
son-in-law.'"
23They repeated these words to David.
But David said, "Do you think it is a
small matter to become the king's son-
in-law? I'm only a poor man and little
known."
24When Saul's servants told him what
David had said, 25Saul replied, "Say to
David, 'The king wants no other price[z]
for the bride than a hundred Philistine
foreskins, to take revenge on his enemies.'" Saul's plan[a] was to have David
fall by the hands of the Philistines.
26When the attendants told David
these things, he was pleased to become
the king's son-in-law. So before the
allotted time elapsed, 27David and his
men went out and killed two hundred
Philistines. He brought their foreskins
and presented the full number to the
king so that he might become the king's
son-in-law. Then Saul gave him his
daughter Michal[b] in marriage.
28When Saul realized that the LORD
was with David and that his daughter
Michal loved David, 29Saul became still
more afraid of him, and he remained his
enemy the rest of his days.
30The Philistine commanders continued to go out to battle, and as often as
they did, David met with more suc-
cess[s][c] than the rest of Saul's officers, and
his name became well known.

An enraged Saul seeks to kill David.

19 Saul told his son Jonathan[d] and
all the attendants to kill[e] David.

[o]*10* Or *injurious* [p]*14* Or *he was very wise* [q]*15* Or *wise* [r]*19* Or *However,* [s]*30* Or *David acted more wisely*

But Jonathan was very fond of David
2and warned him, "My father Saul is
looking for a chance to kill you. Be on
your guard tomorrow morning; go into
hiding and stay there. 3I will go out and
stand with my father in the field where
you are. I'll speak[a] to him about you and
will tell you what I find out."
4Jonathan spoke[b] well of David to Saul
his father and said to him, "Let not the
king do wrong[c] to his servant David; he
has not wronged you, and what he has
done has benefited you greatly. 5He took
his life in his hands when he killed the
Philistine. The LORD won a great victory[d] for all Israel, and you saw it and
were glad. Why then would you do
wrong to an innocent[e] man like David
by killing him for no reason?"
6Saul listened to Jonathan and took
this oath: "As surely as the LORD lives,
David will not be put to death."
7So Jonathan called David and told
him the whole conversation. He brought
him to Saul, and David was with Saul
as before.[f]
8Once more war broke out, and David
went out and fought the Philistines. He
struck them with such force that they
fled before him.
9But an evil[t] spirit[g] from the LORD
came upon Saul as he was sitting in his
house with his spear in his hand. While
David was playing the harp, 10Saul tried
to pin him to the wall with his spear,
but David eluded[h] him as Saul drove the
spear into the wall. That night David
made good his escape.
11Saul sent men to David's house to
watch[i] it and to kill him in the morning.
But Michal, David's wife, warned him,
"If you don't run for your life tonight,
tomorrow you'll be killed." 12So Michal
let David down through a window,[j] and
he fled and escaped. 13Then Michal took
an idol[u] and laid it on the bed, covering
it with a garment and putting some
goats' hair at the head.
14When Saul sent the men to capture
David, Michal said,[k] "He is ill."
15Then Saul sent the men back to see
David and told them, "Bring him up to
me in his bed so that I may kill him."
16But when the men entered, there was
the idol in the bed, and at the head was
some goats' hair.
17Saul said to Michal, "Why did you
deceive me like this and send my enemy
away so that he escaped?"
Michal told him, "He said to me, 'Let
me get away. Why should I kill you?'"

David flees to Samuel.

18When David had fled and made his
escape, he went to Samuel at Ramah[l]
and told him all that Saul had done to
him. Then he and Samuel went to
Naioth and stayed there. 19Word came
to Saul: "David is in Naioth at Ramah";
20so he sent men to capture him. But
when they saw a group of prophets[m]
prophesying, with Samuel standing there
as their leader, the Spirit of God came
upon[n] Saul's men and they also prophesied.[o] 21Saul was told about it, and he
sent more men, and they prophesied
too. Saul sent men a third time, and
they also prophesied. 22Finally, he himself left for Ramah and went to the great
cistern at Secu. And he asked, "Where
are Samuel and David?"
"Over in Naioth at Ramah," they said.
23So Saul went to Naioth at Ramah.
But the Spirit of God came even upon
him, and he walked along prophesying[p]
until he came to Naioth. 24He stripped[q]
off his robes and also prophesied in
Samuel's presence. He lay that way all
that day and night. This is why people
say, "Is Saul also among the prophets?"[r]

Jonathan helps David escape from Saul.

20 Then David fled from Naioth at
Ramah and went to Jonathan
and asked, "What have I done? What is
my crime? How have I wronged[s] your
father, that he is trying to take my life?"
2"Never!" Jonathan replied. "You are
not going to die! Look, my father doesn't

19:3 [a] 1Sa 20:12
19:4 [b] 1Sa 20:32; Pr 31:8,9; Jer 18:20 [c] Ge 42:22; Pr 17:13
19:5 [d] 1Sa 11:13; 17:49-50; 1Ch 11:14 [e] Dt 19:10-13; 1Sa 20:32; Mt 27:4
19:7 [f] 1Sa 16:21; 18:2,13
19:9 [g] 1Sa 16:14; 18:10-11
19:10 [h] 1Sa 18:11
19:11 [i] Ps 59 Title
19:12 [j] Jos 2:15; Ac 9:25
19:14 [k] Jos 2:4
19:18 [l] 1Sa 7:17
19:20 [m] ver 11,14; Jn 7:32,45 [n] Nu 11:25 [o] 1Sa 10:5; Joel 2:28
19:23 [p] 1Sa 10:13
19:24 [q] 2Sa 6:20; Isa 20:2; Mic 1:8 [r] 1Sa 10:11
20:1 [s] 1Sa 24:9

t 9 Or *injurious*   u 13 Hebrew *teraphim;* also in verse 16

do anything, great or small, without confiding in me. Why would he hide this
from me? It's not so!"
3But David took an oath[a] and said,
"Your father knows very well that I have
found favor in your eyes, and he has
said to himself, 'Jonathan must not know
this or he will be grieved.' Yet as surely
as the LORD lives and as you live, there
is only a step between me and death."
4Jonathan said to David, "Whatever
you want me to do, I'll do for you."
5So David said, "Look, tomorrow is
the New Moon festival,[b] and I am sup-
posed to dine with the king; but let me
go and hide[c] in the field until the evening of the day after tomorrow. 6If
your father misses me at all, tell him,
'David earnestly asked my permission to
hurry to Bethlehem,[d] his hometown,
because an annual[e] sacrifice is being
made there for his whole clan.' 7If he
says, 'Very well,' then your servant is
safe. But if he loses his temper,[f] you can
be sure that he is determined to harm
me. 8As for you, show kindness to your
servant, for you have brought him into
a covenant[g] with you before the LORD. If
I am guilty, then kill[h] me yourself! Why
hand me over to your father?"
9"Never!" Jonathan said. "If I had the
least inkling that my father was determined to harm you, wouldn't I tell you?"
10David asked, "Who will tell me if
your father answers you harshly?"
11"Come," Jonathan said, "let's go out
into the field." So they went there together.
12Then Jonathan said to David: "By
the LORD, the God of Israel, I will surely
sound out my father by this time the day
after tomorrow! If he is favorably disposed toward you, will I not send you
word and let you know? 13But if my
father is inclined to harm you, may the
LORD deal with me, be it ever so severely,[i] if I do not let you know and send
you away safely. May the LORD be with[j]
you as he has been with my father.
14But show me unfailing kindness like
that of the LORD as long as I live, so that
I may not be killed, 15and do not ever
cut off your kindness from my family[k]—
not even when the LORD has cut off
every one of David's enemies from the
face of the earth."
16So Jonathan made a covenant[l] with
the house of David, saying, "May the
LORD call David's enemies to account."
17And Jonathan had David reaffirm his
oath[m] out of love for him, because he
loved him as he loved himself.
18Then Jonathan said to David: "Tomorrow is the New Moon festival. You
will be missed, because your seat will
be empty.[n] 19The day after tomorrow,
toward evening, go to the place where
you hid[o] when this trouble began, and
wait by the stone Ezel. 20I will shoot
three arrows to the side of it, as though
I were shooting at a target. 21Then I
will send a boy and say, 'Go, find the
arrows.' If I say to him, 'Look, the arrows are on this side of you; bring them
here,' then come, because, as surely as
the LORD lives, you are safe; there is
no danger. 22But if I say to the boy,
'Look, the arrows are beyond[p] you,'
then you must go, because the LORD has
sent you away. 23And about the matter
you and I discussed—remember, the
LORD is witness[q] between you and me
forever."
24So David hid in the field, and when
the New Moon festival came, the king
sat down to eat. 25He sat in his customary place by the wall, opposite Jonathan,[v] and Abner sat next to Saul, but
David's place was empty.[r] 26Saul said
nothing that day, for he thought, "Something must have happened to David to
make him ceremonially unclean—surely he is unclean.[s]" 27But the next day,
the second day of the month, David's
place was empty again. Then Saul said
to his son Jonathan, "Why hasn't the
son of Jesse come to the meal, either
yesterday or today?"
28Jonathan answered, "David earnestly asked me for permission[t] to go to
Bethlehem. 29He said, 'Let me go, because our family is observing a sacrifice

20:3 [a]Dt 6:13
20:5 [b]Nu 10:10; 28:11 [c]1Sa 19:2
20:6 [d]1Sa 17:58 [e]Dt 12:5
20:7 [f]1Sa 25:17
20:8 [g]1Sa 18:3; 23:18 [h]2Sa 14:32
20:13 [i]Ru 1:17; 1Sa 3:17 [j]Jos 1:5; 1Sa 17:37; 18:12; 1Ch 22:11,16
20:15 [k]2Sa 9:7
20:16 [l]1Sa 25:22
20:17 [m]1Sa 18:3
20:18 [n]ver 5,25
20:19 [o]1Sa 19:2
20:22 [p]ver 37
20:23 [q]ver 14-15; Ge 31:50
20:25 [r]ver 18
20:26 [s]Lev 7:20-21; 15:5; 1Sa 16:5
20:28 [t]ver 6

[v]*25* Septuagint; Hebrew *wall. Jonathan arose*

in the town and my brother has ordered
me to be there. If I have found favor in
your eyes, let me get away to see my
brothers.' That is why he has not come
to the king's table."
30Saul's anger flared up at Jonathan
and he said to him, "You son of a perverse and rebellious woman! Don't I
know that you have sided with the son
of Jesse to your own shame and to the
shame of the mother who bore you?
31As long as the son of Jesse lives on
this earth, neither you nor your kingdom will be established. Now send and
bring him to me, for he must die!"
32"Why[a] should he be put to death?
What[b] has he done?" Jonathan asked his
father. 33But Saul hurled his spear at
him to kill him. Then Jonathan knew
that his father intended[c] to kill David.
34Jonathan got up from the table in
fierce anger; on that second day of the
month he did not eat, because he was
grieved at his father's shameful treatment of David.
35In the morning Jonathan went out
to the field for his meeting with David.
He had a small boy with him, 36and he
said to the boy, "Run and find the
arrows I shoot." As the boy ran, he
shot an arrow beyond him. 37When the
boy came to the place where Jonathan's
arrow had fallen, Jonathan called out
after him, "Isn't the arrow beyond[d]
you?" 38Then he shouted, "Hurry! Go
quickly! Don't stop!" The boy picked
up the arrow and returned to his master.
39(The boy knew nothing of all this;
only Jonathan and David knew.) 40Then
Jonathan gave his weapons to the boy
and said, "Go, carry them back to
town."
41After the boy had gone, David got up
from the south side ⌞of the stone⌟ and
bowed down before Jonathan three
times, with his face to the ground. Then
they kissed each other and wept together—but David wept the most.
42Jonathan said to David, "Go in
peace,[e] for we have sworn friendship[f]
with each other in the name of the LORD,
saying, 'The LORD is witness between
you and me, and between your descendants and my descendants forever.'"
Then David left, and Jonathan went
back to the town.

20:32 [a]1Sa 19:4; Mt 27:23 [b]Ge 31:36; Lk 23:22
20:33 [c]ver 7; 1Sa 18:11,17
20:37 [d]ver 22
20:42 [e]ver 22; 1Sa 1:17 [f]2Sa 1:26; Pr 18:24
21:1 [g]1Sa 14:3; 22:9,19; Ne 11:32; Isa 10:32 [h]1Sa 16:4
21:4 [i]Lev 24:8-9 [j]Ex 25:30; Mt 12:4 [k]Ex 19:15
21:5 [l]1Th 4:4
21:6 [m]Lev 24:8-9; Mt 12:3-4; Mk 2:25-28; Lk 6:1-5
21:7 [n]1Sa 22:9,22 [o]1Sa 14:47; Ps 52 Title
21:9 [p]1Sa 17:51 [q]1Sa 17:2

David takes consecrated bread and Goliath's sword.

21 David went to Nob,[g] to Ahimelech the priest. Ahimelech trembled[h] when he met him, and asked,
"Why are you alone? Why is no one
with you?"
2David answered Ahimelech the
priest, "The king charged me with a certain matter and said to me, 'No one is
to know anything about your mission
and your instructions.' As for my men, I
have told them to meet me at a certain
place. 3Now then, what do you have on
hand? Give me five loaves of bread, or
whatever you can find."
4But the priest answered David, "I
don't have any ordinary bread[i] on hand;
however, there is some consecrated[j]
bread here—provided the men have
kept[k] themselves from women."
5David replied, "Indeed women have
been kept from us, as usual whenever[w]
I set out. The men's things[x] are holy[l]
even on missions that are not holy. How
much more so today!" 6So the priest
gave him the consecrated bread,[m] since
there was no bread there except the
bread of the Presence that had been removed from before the LORD and replaced by hot bread on the day it was
taken away.
7Now one of Saul's servants was there
that day, detained before the LORD; he
was Doeg[n] the Edomite,[o] Saul's head
shepherd.
8David asked Ahimelech, "Don't you
have a spear or a sword here? I haven't
brought my sword or any other weapon,
because the king's business was urgent."
9The priest replied, "The sword[p] of
Goliath the Philistine, whom you killed
in the Valley of Elah,[q] is here; it is
wrapped in a cloth behind the ephod. If

[w]5 Or *from us in the past few days since* [x]5 Or *bodies*

you want it, take it; there is no sword here but that one."

David said, "There is none like it; give it to me."

David pretends to be insane.

10 That day David fled from Saul and went[a] to Achish king of Gath. 11 But the servants of Achish said to him, "Isn't this David, the king of the land? Isn't he the one they sing about in their dances:

"'Saul has slain his thousands,
and David his tens of
thousands'?"[b]

12 David took these words to heart and was very much afraid of Achish king of Gath. 13 So he pretended to be insane[c] in their presence; and while he was in their hands he acted like a madman, making marks on the doors of the gate and letting saliva run down his beard.

14 Achish said to his servants, "Look at the man! He is insane! Why bring him to me? 15 Am I so short of madmen that you have to bring this fellow here to carry on like this in front of me? Must this man come into my house?"

David leads 400 men.

22 David left Gath and escaped to the cave[d] of Adullam. When his brothers and his father's household heard about it, they went down to him there. 2 All those who were in distress or in debt or discontented gathered[e] around him, and he became their leader. About four hundred men were with him.

3 From there David went to Mizpah in Moab and said to the king of Moab, "Would you let my father and mother come and stay with you until I learn what God will do for me?" 4 So he left them with the king of Moab, and they stayed with him as long as David was in the stronghold.

5 But the prophet Gad[f] said to David, "Do not stay in the stronghold. Go into the land of Judah." So David left and went to the forest of Hereth.

21:10 [a] 1Sa 27:2
21:11 [b] 1Sa 18:7; 29:5; Ps 56 Title
21:13 [c] Ps 34 Title
22:1 [d] 2Sa 23:13; Ps 57 Title; 142 Title
22:2 [e] 1Sa 23:13; 25:13; 2Sa 15:20
22:5 [f] 2Sa 24:11; 1Ch 21:9; 29:29; 2Ch 29:25
22:6 [g] Jdg 4:5 [h] Ge 21:33
22:7 [i] 1Sa 8:14
22:8 [j] 1Sa 18:3; 20:16 [k] 1Sa 23:21
22:9 [l] 1Sa 21:7; Ps 52 Title [m] 1Sa 21:1
22:10 [n] Nu 27:21; 1Sa 10:22 [o] 1Sa 21:6
22:13 [p] ver 8
22:14 [q] 1Sa 19:4

Saul orders Ahimelech and the priests to be killed.

6 Now Saul heard that David and his men had been discovered. And Saul, spear in hand, was seated[g] under the tamarisk[h] tree on the hill at Gibeah, with all his officials standing around him. 7 Saul said to them, "Listen, men of Benjamin! Will the son of Jesse give all of you fields and vineyards? Will he make all of you commanders[i] of thousands and commanders of hundreds? 8 Is that why you have all conspired against me? No one tells me when my son makes a covenant[j] with the son of Jesse. None of you is concerned[k] about me or tells me that my son has incited my servant to lie in wait for me, as he does today."

9 But Doeg[l] the Edomite, who was standing with Saul's officials, said, "I saw the son of Jesse come to Ahimelech son of Ahitub at Nob.[m] 10 Ahimelech inquired[n] of the LORD for him; he also gave him provisions[o] and the sword of Goliath the Philistine."

11 Then the king sent for the priest Ahimelech son of Ahitub and his father's whole family, who were the priests at Nob, and they all came to the king. 12 Saul said, "Listen now, son of Ahitub."

"Yes, my lord," he answered.

13 Saul said to him, "Why have you conspired[p] against me, you and the son of Jesse, giving him bread and a sword and inquiring of God for him, so that he has rebelled against me and lies in wait for me, as he does today?"

14 Ahimelech answered the king, "Who[q] of all your servants is as loyal as David, the king's son-in-law, captain of your bodyguard and highly respected in your household? 15 Was that day the first time I inquired of God for him? Of course not! Let not the king accuse your servant or any of his father's family, for your servant knows nothing at all about this whole affair."

16 But the king said, "You will surely die, Ahimelech, you and your father's whole family."

17 Then the king ordered the guards at
his side: "Turn and kill the priests of the
LORD, because they too have sided with
David. They knew he was fleeing, yet
they did not tell me."
But the king's officials were not willing[a] to raise a hand to strike the priests
of the LORD.
18 The king then ordered Doeg, "You
turn and strike down the priests." So
Doeg the Edomite turned and struck
them down. That day he killed eighty-
five men who wore the linen ephod.[b]
19 He also put to the sword[c] Nob, the
town of the priests, with its men and
women, its children and infants, and its
cattle, donkeys and sheep.
20 But Abiathar,[d] a son of Ahimelech
son of Ahitub, escaped and fled to join
David.[e] 21 He told David that Saul had
killed the priests of the LORD. 22 Then
David said to Abiathar: "That day, when
Doeg[f] the Edomite was there, I knew he
would be sure to tell Saul. I am responsible for the death of your father's whole
family. 23 Stay with me; don't be afraid;
the man who is seeking your life[g] is
seeking mine also. You will be safe
with me."

Saul continues to pursue David.

23 When David was told, "Look,
the Philistines are fighting
against Keilah[h] and are looting the
threshing floors," 2 he inquired[i] of the
LORD, saying, "Shall I go and attack these
Philistines?"
The LORD answered him, "Go, attack
the Philistines and save Keilah."
3 But David's men said to him, "Here
in Judah we are afraid. How much
more, then, if we go to Keilah against
the Philistine forces!"
4 Once again David inquired of the
LORD, and the LORD answered him, "Go
down to Keilah, for I am going to give
the Philistines into your hand.[j]" 5 So
David and his men went to Keilah,
fought the Philistines and carried off
their livestock. He inflicted heavy losses
on the Philistines and saved the people
of Keilah. 6 (Now Abiathar[k] son of Ahimelech had brought the ephod down with
him when he fled to David at Keilah.)
7 Saul was told that David had gone to
Keilah, and he said, "God has handed
him over to me, for David has imprisoned himself by entering a town with
gates and bars." 8 And Saul called up all
his forces for battle, to go down to Keilah to besiege David and his men.
9 When David learned that Saul was
plotting against him, he said to Abiathar[l]
the priest, "Bring the ephod." 10 David
said, "O LORD, God of Israel, your servant has heard definitely that Saul plans
to come to Keilah and destroy the town
on account of me. 11 Will the citizens of
Keilah surrender me to him? Will Saul
come down, as your servant has heard?
O LORD, God of Israel, tell your servant."
And the LORD said, "He will."
12 Again David asked, "Will the citizens of Keilah surrender[m] me and my
men to Saul?"
And the LORD said, "They will."
13 So David and his men,[n] about six
hundred in number, left Keilah and kept
moving from place to place. When Saul
was told that David had escaped from
Keilah, he did not go there.
14 David stayed in the desert strongholds and in the hills of the Desert of
Ziph.[o] Day after day Saul searched[p] for
him, but God did not[q] give David into
his hands.
15 While David was at Horesh in the
Desert of Ziph, he learned that Saul had
come out to take his life. 16 And Saul's
son Jonathan went to David at Horesh
and helped him find strength[r] in God.
17 "Don't be afraid," he said. "My father
Saul will not lay a hand on you. You will
be king[s] over Israel, and I will be second
to you. Even my father Saul knows
this." 18 The two of them made a covenant[t] before the LORD. Then Jonathan
went home, but David remained at
Horesh.

The Ziphites betray David.

19 The Ziphites[u] went up to Saul at

22:17 [a] Ex 1:17
22:18 [b] 1Sa 2:18,31
22:19 [c] 1Sa 15:3
22:20 [d] 1Sa 23:6,9; 30:7; 1Ki 2:22, 26,27 [e] 1Sa 2:32
22:22 [f] 1Sa 21:7
22:23 [g] 1Ki 2:26
23:1 [h] Jos 15:44
23:2 [i] ver 4,12; 1Sa 30:8; 2Sa 5:19,23
23:4 [j] Jos 8:7; Jdg 7:7
23:6 [k] 1Sa 22:20
23:9 [l] ver 6; 1Sa 22:20; 30:7
23:12 [m] ver 20
23:13 [n] 1Sa 22:2; 25:13
23:14 [o] Jos 15:24,55 [p] Ps 54:3-4 [q] Ps 32:7
23:16 [r] 1Sa 30:6
23:17 [s] 1Sa 20:31; 24:20
23:18 [t] 1Sa 18:3; 20:16,42; 2Sa 9:1; 21:7
23:19 [u] 1Sa 26:1

Gibeah and said, "Is not David hiding
among us[a] in the strongholds at Horesh,
on the hill of Hakilah,[b] south of Jeshimon? 20Now, O king, come down whenever it pleases you to do so, and we will
be responsible for handing[c] him over to
the king."
21Saul replied, "The LORD bless you
for your concern[d] for me. 22Go and
make further preparation. Find out
where David usually goes and who has
seen him there. They tell me he is very
crafty. 23Find out about all the hiding
places he uses and come back to me
with definite information.[y] Then I will
go with you; if he is in the area, I will
track him down among all the clans of
Judah."
24So they set out and went to Ziph
ahead of Saul. Now David and his men
were in the Desert of Maon,[e] in the
Arabah south of Jeshimon. 25Saul and
his men began the search, and when
David was told about it, he went down
to the rock and stayed in the Desert of
Maon. When Saul heard this, he went
into the Desert of Maon in pursuit of
David.
26Saul[f] was going along one side of
the mountain, and David and his men
were on the other side, hurrying to get
away from Saul. As Saul and his forces
were closing in on David and his men
to capture them, 27a messenger came
to Saul, saying, "Come quickly! The
Philistines are raiding the land." 28Then
Saul broke off his pursuit of David and
went to meet the Philistines. That is
why they call this place Sela Hammahlekoth.[z] 29And David went up from
there and lived in the strongholds of
En Gedi.[g]

David spares Saul's life.

24 After Saul returned from pursuing the Philistines, he was told,
"David is in the Desert of En Gedi.[h]"
2So Saul took three thousand chosen
men from all Israel and set out to look[i]
for David and his men near the Crags of
the Wild Goats.
3He came to the sheep pens along the
way; a cave[j] was there, and Saul went
in to relieve[k] himself. David and his
men were far back in the cave. 4The
men said, "This is the day the LORD
spoke[l] of when he said[a] to you, 'I will
give your enemy into your hands for you
to deal with as you wish.'"[m] Then David
crept up unnoticed and cut off a corner
of Saul's robe.
5Afterward, David was conscience-
stricken[n] for having cut off a corner of
his robe. 6He said to his men, "The
LORD forbid that I should do such a thing
to my master, the LORD's anointed,[o] or
lift my hand against him; for he is the
anointed of the LORD." 7With these
words David rebuked his men and did
not allow them to attack Saul. And Saul
left the cave and went his way.
8Then David went out of the cave and
called out to Saul, "My lord the king!"
When Saul looked behind him, David
bowed down and prostrated himself
with his face to the ground.[p] 9He said to
Saul, "Why do you listen when men say,
'David is bent on harming you'? 10This
day you have seen with your own eyes
how the LORD delivered you into my
hands in the cave. Some urged me to
kill you, but I spared you; I said, 'I will
not lift my hand against my master, because he is the LORD's anointed.' 11See,
my father, look at this piece of your robe
in my hand! I cut off the corner of your
robe but did not kill you. Now understand and recognize that I am not
guilty[q] of wrongdoing or rebellion. I
have not wronged you, but you are
hunting[r] me down to take my life.
12May the LORD judge[s] between you
and me. And may the LORD avenge[t] the
wrongs you have done to me, but my
hand will not touch you. 13As the old
saying goes, 'From evildoers come evil
deeds,[u]' so my hand will not touch you.
14"Against whom has the king of
Israel come out? Whom are you pursuing? A dead dog?[v] A flea?[w] 15May the

23:19 [a]Ps 54 Title [b]1Sa 26:3
23:20 [c]ver 12
23:21 [d]1Sa 22:8
23:24 [e]Jos 15:55; 1Sa 25:2
23:26 [f]Ps 17:9
23:29 [g]2Ch 20:2
24:1 [h]1Sa 23:28-29
24:2 [i]1Sa 26:2
24:3 [j]Ps 57 Title; 142 Title [k]Jdg 3:24
24:4 [l]1Sa 25:28-30 [m]1Sa 23:17; 26:8
24:5 [n]2Sa 24:10
24:6 [o]1Sa 26:11
24:8 [p]1Sa 25:23-24
24:11 [q]Ps 7:3 [r]1Sa 23:14,23; 1Sa 26:20
24:12 [s]Ge 16:5; 31:53; Job 5:8 [t]Jdg 11:27; 1Sa 26:10
24:13 [u]Mt 7:20
24:14 [v]1Sa 17:43; 2Sa 9:8 [w]1Sa 26:20

[y]23 Or *me at Nacon* [z]28 *Sela Hammahlekoth* means *rock of parting.* [a]4 Or *"Today the LORD is saying*

LORD be our judge[a] and decide between
us. May he consider my cause and uphold[b] it; may he vindicate[c] me by delivering[d] me from your hand."

Saul weeps before the more righteous David.

[16]When David finished saying this,
Saul asked, "Is that your voice,[e] David
my son?" And he wept aloud. [17]"You
are more righteous than I,"[f] he said.
"You have treated me well,[g] but I have
treated you badly. [18]You have just now
told me of the good you did to me; the
LORD delivered[h] me into your hands, but
you did not kill me. [19]When a man finds
his enemy, does he let him get away
unharmed? May the LORD reward you
well for the way you treated me today.
[20]I know that you will surely be king[i]
and that the kingdom[j] of Israel will be
established in your hands. [21]Now
swear[k] to me by the LORD that you will
not cut off my descendants or wipe out
my name from my father's family.[l]"
[22]So David gave his oath to Saul. Then
Saul returned home, but David and his
men went up to the stronghold.[m]

Samuel's death.

25 Now Samuel died,[n] and all Israel
assembled and mourned[o] for
him; and they buried him at his home
in Ramah.[p]

Abigail's pleas to David to spare Nabal.

Then David moved down into the
Desert of Maon.[b] [2]A certain man in
Maon,[q] who had property there at Carmel, was very wealthy. He had a thousand goats and three thousand sheep,
which he was shearing in Carmel. [3]His
name was Nabal and his wife's name
was Abigail.[r] She was an intelligent and
beautiful woman, but her husband, a
Calebite,[s] was surly and mean in his
dealings.
[4]While David was in the desert, he
heard that Nabal was shearing sheep.
[5]So he sent ten young men and said to
them, "Go up to Nabal at Carmel and
greet him in my name. [6]Say to him:
'Long life to you! Good health[t] to you
and your household! And good health
to all that is yours![u]
[7]"'Now I hear that it is sheep-shearing
time. When your shepherds were with
us, we did not mistreat[v] them, and the
whole time they were at Carmel nothing of theirs was missing. [8]Ask your
own servants and they will tell you.
Therefore be favorable toward my young
men, since we come at a festive time.
Please give your servants and your son
David whatever[w] you can find for
them.'"
[9]When David's men arrived, they
gave Nabal this message in David's
name. Then they waited.
[10]Nabal answered David's servants,
"Who[x] is this David? Who is this son of
Jesse? Many servants are breaking away
from their masters these days. [11]Why
should I take my bread[y] and water, and
the meat I have slaughtered for my
shearers, and give it to men coming
from who knows where?"
[12]David's men turned around and
went back. When they arrived, they
reported every word. [13]David said to his
men, "Put on your swords!" So they put
on their swords, and David put on his.
About four hundred men went[z] up with
David, while two hundred stayed with
the supplies.[a]
[14]One of the servants told Nabal's
wife Abigail: "David sent messengers
from the desert to give our master his
greetings,[b] but he hurled insults at
them. [15]Yet these men were very good
to us. They did not mistreat[c] us, and the
whole time we were out in the fields
near them nothing was missing.[d]
[16]Night and day they were a wall[e]
around us all the time we were herding
our sheep near them. [17]Now think it
over and see what you can do, because
disaster is hanging over our master and
his whole household. He is such a wicked[f] man that no one can talk to him."

24:15 [a]ver 12 [b]Ps 35:1,23; Mic 7:9 [c]Ps 43:1 [d]Ps 119:134, 154
24:16 [e]1Sa 26:17
24:17 [f]Ge 38:26; 1Sa 26:21 [g]Mt 5:44
24:18 [h]1Sa 26:23
24:20 [i]1Sa 23:17 [j]1Sa 13:14
24:21 [k]Ge 21:23; 2Sa 21:1-9 [l]1Sa 20:14-15
24:22 [m]1Sa 23:29
25:1 [n]1Sa 28:3 [o]Nu 20:29; Dt 34:8 [p]Ge 21:21; 2Ch 33:20
25:2 [q]Jos 15:55; 1Sa 23:24
25:3 [r]Pr 31:10 [s]Jos 15:13
25:6 [t]Ps 122:7; Lk 10:5 [u]1Ch 12:18
25:7 [v]ver 15
25:8 [w]Ne 8:10
25:10 [x]Jdg 9:28
25:11 [y]Jdg 8:6
25:13 [z]1Sa 23:13 [a]1Sa 30:24
25:14 [b]1Sa 13:10
25:15 [c]ver 7 [d]ver 21
25:16 [e]Ex 14:22; Job 1:10
25:17 [f]1Sa 20:7

[b] *1* Some Septuagint manuscripts; Hebrew *Paran*

18Abigail lost no time. She took two
hundred loaves of bread, two skins of
wine, five dressed sheep, five seahs[c] of
roasted grain, a hundred cakes of raisins[a] and two hundred cakes of pressed
figs, and loaded them on donkeys.[b]
19Then she told her servants, "Go on
ahead;[c] I'll follow you." But she did not
tell her husband Nabal.

20As she came riding her donkey into
a mountain ravine, there were David
and his men descending toward her,
and she met them. 21David had just
said, "It's been useless—all my watching over this fellow's property in the
desert so that nothing of his was missing. He has paid[d] me back evil for good.
22May God deal with David,[d] be it ever
so severely,[e] if by morning I leave alive
one male[f] of all who belong to him!"

23When Abigail saw David, she quickly got off her donkey and bowed down
before David with her face to the
ground.[g] 24She fell at his feet and said:
"My lord, let the blame be on me alone.
Please let your servant speak to you;
hear what your servant has to say.
25May my lord pay no attention to that
wicked man Nabal. He is just like his
name—his name is Fool,[h] and folly goes
with him. But as for me, your servant,
I did not see the men my master sent.

26"Now since the LORD has kept you,
my master, from bloodshed[i] and from
avenging[j] yourself with your own
hands, as surely as the LORD lives and as
you live, may your enemies and all who
intend to harm my master be like
Nabal.[k] 27And let this gift,[l] which your
servant has brought to my master, be
given to the men who follow you.
28Please forgive[m] your servant's offense,
for the LORD will certainly make a lasting[n] dynasty for my master, because he
fights the LORD's battles.[o] Let no wrongdoing[p] be found in you as long as you
live. 29Even though someone is pursuing you to take your life, the life of my
master will be bound securely in the
bundle of the living by the LORD your
God. But the lives of your enemies he
will hurl[q] away as from the pocket of a

25:18 [a]1Ch 12:40 [b]2Sa 16:1
25:19 [c]Ge 32:20
25:21 [d]Ps 109:5
25:22 [e]1Sa 3:17; 20:13 [f]1Ki 14:10; 21:21; 2Ki 9:8
25:23 [g]1Sa 20:41
25:25 [h]Pr 14:16
25:26 [i]ver 33 [j]Heb 10:30 [k]2Sa 18:32
25:27 [l]Ge 33:11; 1Sa 30:26
25:28 [m]ver 24 [n]2Sa 7:11,26 [o]1Sa 18:17 [p]1Sa 24:11
25:29 [q]Jer 10:18
25:30 [r]1Sa 13:14
25:31 [s]Ge 40:14
25:32 [t]Ge 24:27; Ex 18:10; Lk 1:68
25:33 [u]ver 26
25:35 [v]Ge 19:21; 1Sa 20:42; 2Ki 5:19
25:36 [w]2Sa 13:23 [x]Pr 20:1; Isa 5:11,22; Hos 4:11 [y]ver 19
25:38 [z]1Sa 26:10; 2Sa 6:7

sling. 30When the LORD has done for my
master every good thing he promised
concerning him and has appointed him
leader[r] over Israel, 31my master will not
have on his conscience the staggering
burden of needless bloodshed or of having avenged himself. And when the
LORD has brought my master success,
remember[s] your servant."

32David said to Abigail, "Praise[t] be to
the LORD, the God of Israel, who has
sent you today to meet me. 33May you
be blessed for your good judgment and
for keeping me from bloodshed[u] this
day and from avenging myself with my
own hands. 34Otherwise, as surely as
the LORD, the God of Israel, lives, who
has kept me from harming you, if you
had not come quickly to meet me, not
one male belonging to Nabal would have
been left alive by daybreak."

35Then David accepted from her hand
what she had brought him and said,
"Go home in peace. I have heard your
words and granted[v] your request."

David's marriage to Abigail.

36When Abigail went to Nabal, he
was in the house holding a banquet like
that of a king. He was in high[w] spirits
and very drunk.[x] So she told[y] him nothing until daybreak. 37Then in the morning, when Nabal was sober, his wife
told him all these things, and his heart
failed him and he became like a stone.
38About ten days later, the LORD struck[z]
Nabal and he died.

39When David heard that Nabal was
dead, he said, "Praise be to the LORD,
who has upheld my cause against Nabal
for treating me with contempt. He has
kept his servant from doing wrong and
has brought Nabal's wrongdoing down
on his own head."

Then David sent word to Abigail, asking her to become his wife. 40His servants went to Carmel and said to
Abigail, "David has sent us to you to
take you to become his wife."

c *18* That is, probably about a bushel (about 37 liters)
d *22* Some Septuagint manuscripts; Hebrew *with David's enemies*

41She bowed down with her face to
the ground and said, "Here is your
maidservant, ready to serve you and
wash the feet of my master's servants."
42Abigail[a] quickly got on a donkey and,
attended by her five maids, went with
David's messengers and became his
wife. 43David had also married Ahinoam[b] of Jezreel, and they both were
his wives.[c] 44But Saul had given his
daughter Michal, David's wife, to
Paltiel[e][d] son of Laish, who was from
Gallim.[e]

David again spares Saul's life.

26 The Ziphites[f] went to Saul at
Gibeah and said, "Is not David
hiding[g] on the hill of Hakilah, which
faces Jeshimon?"
2So Saul went down to the Desert of
Ziph, with his three thousand chosen
men of Israel, to search[h] there for David.
3Saul made his camp beside the road
on the hill of Hakilah facing Jeshimon,
but David stayed in the desert. When
he saw that Saul had followed him
there, 4he sent out scouts and learned
that Saul had definitely arrived.[f]
5Then David set out and went to the
place where Saul had camped. He saw
where Saul and Abner[i] son of Ner, the
commander of the army, had lain down.
Saul was lying inside the camp, with
the army encamped around him.
6David then asked Ahimelech the
Hittite and Abishai son of Zeruiah,[j]
Joab's brother, "Who will go down into
the camp with me to Saul?"
"I'll go with you," said Abishai.
7So David and Abishai went to the
army by night, and there was Saul, lying
asleep inside the camp with his spear
stuck in the ground near his head. Abner and the soldiers were lying around
him.
8Abishai said to David, "Today God
has delivered your enemy into your
hands. Now let me pin him to the
ground with one thrust of my spear; I
won't strike him twice."
9But David said to Abishai, "Don't
destroy him! Who can lay a hand on
the LORD's anointed[k] and be guiltless?[l]
10As surely as the LORD lives," he said,
"the LORD himself will strike[m] him;
either his time[n] will come and he will
die,[o] or he will go into battle and perish. 11But the LORD forbid that I should
lay a hand on the LORD's anointed. Now
get the spear and water jug that are
near his head, and let's go."
12So David took the spear and water
jug near Saul's head, and they left. No
one saw or knew about it, nor did anyone wake up. They were all sleeping,
because the LORD had put them into a
deep sleep.[p]
13Then David crossed over to the
other side and stood on top of the hill
some distance away; there was a wide
space between them. 14He called out
to the army and to Abner son of Ner,
"Aren't you going to answer me, Abner?"
Abner replied, "Who are you who
calls to the king?"
15David said, "You're a man, aren't
you? And who is like you in Israel?
Why didn't you guard your lord the
king? Someone came to destroy your
lord the king. 16What you have done is
not good. As surely as the LORD lives,
you and your men deserve to die, because you did not guard your master,
the LORD's anointed. Look around you.
Where are the king's spear and water
jug that were near his head?"
17Saul recognized David's voice and
said, "Is that your voice,[q] David my
son?"
David replied, "Yes it is, my lord the
king." 18And he added, "Why is my lord
pursuing his servant? What have I done,
and what wrong[r] am I guilty of? 19Now
let my lord the king listen to his servant's words. If the LORD has incited
you against me, then may he accept an
offering.[s] If, however, men have done it,
may they be cursed before the LORD!
They have now driven me from my

25:42 [a]Ge 24:61-67
25:43 [b]Jos 15:56 [c]1Sa 27:3; 30:5
25:44 [d]2Sa 3:15 [e]Isa 10:30
26:1 [f]1Sa 23:19 [g]Ps 54 Title
26:2 [h]1Sa 13:2; 24:2
26:5 [i]1Sa 14:50; 17:55
26:6 [j]Jdg 7:10-11; 1Ch 2:16
26:9 [k]2Sa 1:14 [l]1Sa 24:5
26:10 [m]1Sa 25:38; Ro 12:19 [n]Ge 47:29; Dt 31:14; Ps 37:13 [o]1Sa 31:6; 2Sa 1:1
26:12 [p]Ge 2:21; 15:12
26:17 [q]1Sa 24:16
26:18 [r]1Sa 24:9, 11-14
26:19 [s]2Sa 16:11

e *44* Hebrew *Palti*, a variant of *Paltiel*
f *4* Or *had come to Nacon*

share in the LORD's inheritance[a] and
have said, 'Go, serve other gods.' 20Now
do not let my blood fall to the ground
far from the presence of the LORD. The
king of Israel has come out to look for a
flea[b]—as one hunts a partridge in the
mountains."
21Then Saul said, "I have sinned.[c]
Come back, David my son. Because you
considered my life precious[d] today, I will
not try to harm you again. Surely I have
acted like a fool and have erred greatly."
22"Here is the king's spear," David
answered. "Let one of your young men
come over and get it. 23The LORD rewards[e] every man for his righteousness[f]
and faithfulness. The LORD delivered you
into my hands today, but I would not lay
a hand on the LORD's anointed. 24As
surely as I valued your life today, so may
the LORD value my life and deliver[g] me
from all trouble."
25Then Saul said to David, "May you
be blessed, my son David; you will do
great things and surely triumph."
So David went on his way, and Saul
returned home.

David escapes to the land of the Philistines.

27 But David thought to himself,
"One of these days I will be
destroyed by the hand of Saul. The best
thing I can do is to escape to the land of
the Philistines. Then Saul will give up
searching for me anywhere in Israel,
and I will slip out of his hand."
2So David and the six hundred men[h]
with him left and went[i] over to Achish[j]
son of Maoch king of Gath. 3David and
his men settled in Gath with Achish.
Each man had his family with him, and
David had his two wives:[k] Ahinoam of
Jezreel and Abigail of Carmel, the widow of Nabal. 4When Saul was told that
David had fled to Gath, he no longer
searched for him.

Achish gives David the city of Ziklag.

5Then David said to Achish, "If I have
found favor in your eyes, let a place be
assigned to me in one of the country
towns, that I may live there. Why should
your servant live in the royal city with
you?"
6So on that day Achish gave him Ziklag,[l] and it has belonged to the kings of
Judah ever since. 7David lived[m] in Philistine territory a year and four months.
8Now David and his men went up
and raided the Geshurites,[n] the Girzites
and the Amalekites.[o] (From ancient
times these peoples had lived in the land
extending to Shur[p] and Egypt.) 9When-
ever David attacked an area, he did not
leave a man or woman alive,[q] but took
sheep and cattle, donkeys and camels,
and clothes. Then he returned to Achish.
10When Achish asked, "Where did
you go raiding today?" David would
say, "Against the Negev of Judah" or
"Against the Negev of Jerahmeel[r]" or
"Against the Negev of the Kenites.[s]"
11He did not leave a man or woman
alive to be brought to Gath, for he
thought, "They might inform on us and
say, 'This is what David did.'" And such
was his practice as long as he lived in
Philistine territory. 12Achish trusted
David and said to himself, "He has become so odious to his people, the Israelites, that he will be my servant
forever."

Saul consults the witch of Endor.

28 In those days the Philistines
gathered[t] their forces to fight
against Israel. Achish said to David,
"You must understand that you and your
men will accompany me in the army."
2David said, "Then you will see for
yourself what your servant can do."
Achish replied, "Very well, I will
make you my bodyguard for life."
3Now Samuel was dead,[u] and all Israel
had mourned for him and buried him in
his own town of Ramah.[v] Saul had expelled the mediums and spiritists[w] from
the land.
4The Philistines assembled and came
and set up camp at Shunem,[x] while Saul

26:19 [a] 2Sa 14:16
26:20 [b] 1Sa 24:14
26:21 [c] Ex 9:27; 1Sa 15:24 [d] 1Sa 24:17
26:23 [e] Ps 62:12 [f] Ps 7:8; 18:20,24
26:24 [g] Ps 54:7
27:2 [h] 1Sa 25:13 [i] 1Sa 21:10 [j] 1Ki 2:39
27:3 [k] 1Sa 25:43; 30:3
27:6 [l] Jos 15:31; 19:5; Ne 11:28
27:7 [m] 1Sa 29:3
27:8 [n] Jos 13:2,13 [o] Ex 17:8; 1Sa 15:7-8 [p] Ex 15:22
27:9 [q] 1Sa 15:3
27:10 [r] 1Sa 30:29; 1Ch 2:9,25 [s] Jdg 1:16
28:1 [t] 1Sa 29:1
28:3 [u] 1Sa 25:1 [v] 1Sa 7:17 [w] Ex 22:18; Lev 19:31; 20:27; Dt 18:10-11; 1Sa 15:23
28:4 [x] Jos 19:18; 2Ki 4:8

gathered all the Israelites and set up camp at Gilboa.[a] 5When Saul saw the Philistine army, he was afraid; terror filled his heart. 6He inquired[b] of the LORD, but the LORD did not answer him by dreams[c] or Urim[d] or prophets. 7Saul then said to his attendants, "Find me a woman who is a medium,[e] so I may go and inquire of her."

"There is one in Endor,[f]" they said.

8So Saul disguised[g] himself, putting on other clothes, and at night he and two men went to the woman. "Consult[h] a spirit for me," he said, "and bring up for me the one I name."

9But the woman said to him, "Surely you know what Saul has done. He has cut off[i] the mediums and spiritists from the land. Why have you set a trap for my life to bring about my death?"

10Saul swore to her by the LORD, "As surely as the LORD lives, you will not be punished for this."

Samuel appears and announces Saul's certain downfall.

11Then the woman asked, "Whom shall I bring up for you?"

"Bring up Samuel," he said.

12When the woman saw Samuel, she cried out at the top of her voice and said to Saul, "Why have you deceived me? You are Saul!"

13The king said to her, "Don't be afraid. What do you see?"

The woman said, "I see a spirit[g] coming up out of the ground."

14"What does he look like?" he asked.

"An old man wearing a robe[j] is coming up," she said.

Then Saul knew it was Samuel, and he bowed down and prostrated himself with his face to the ground.

15Samuel said to Saul, "Why have you disturbed me by bringing me up?"

"I am in great distress," Saul said. "The Philistines are fighting against me, and God has turned[k] away from me. He no longer answers me, either by prophets or by dreams. So I have called on you to tell me what to do."

28:4 [a]1Sa 31:1,3
28:6 [b]1Sa 14:37; 1Ch 10:13-14; Pr 1:28 [c]Nu 12:6 [d]Ex 28:30; Nu 27:21
28:7 [e]Ac 16:16 [f]Jos 17:11
28:8 [g]2Ch 18:29; 35:22 [h]Dt 18:10-11; 1Ch 10:13; Isa 8:19
28:9 [i]ver 3
28:14 [j]1Sa 15:27; 24:8
28:15 [k]ver 6; 1Sa 18:12
28:17 [l]1Sa 15:28
28:18 [m]1Sa 15:20 [n]1Ki 20:42
28:19 [o]1Sa 31:2
28:21 [p]Jdg 12:3; 1Sa 19:5; Job 13:14
28:23 [q]2Ki 5:13
29:1 [r]1Sa 28:1 [s]Jos 12:18; 1Sa 4:1 [t]2Ki 9:30

16Samuel said, "Why do you consult me, now that the LORD has turned away from you and become your enemy? 17The LORD has done what he predicted through me. The LORD has torn[l] the kingdom out of your hands and given it to one of your neighbors—to David. 18Because you did not obey[m] the LORD or carry out his fierce wrath[n] against the Amalekites, the LORD has done this to you today. 19The LORD will hand over both Israel and you to the Philistines, and tomorrow you and your sons[o] will be with me. The LORD will also hand over the army of Israel to the Philistines."

20Immediately Saul fell full length on the ground, filled with fear because of Samuel's words. His strength was gone, for he had eaten nothing all that day and night.

21When the woman came to Saul and saw that he was greatly shaken, she said, "Look, your maidservant has obeyed you. I took my life[p] in my hands and did what you told me to do. 22Now please listen to your servant and let me give you some food so you may eat and have the strength to go on your way."

23He refused[q] and said, "I will not eat."

But his men joined the woman in urging him, and he listened to them. He got up from the ground and sat on the couch.

24The woman had a fattened calf at the house, which she butchered at once. She took some flour, kneaded it and baked bread without yeast. 25Then she set it before Saul and his men, and they ate. That same night they got up and left.

The Philistines refuse David's help.

29 The Philistines gathered[r] all their forces at Aphek,[s] and Israel camped by the spring in Jezreel.[t] 2As the Philistine rulers marched with their units of hundreds and thousands, David

g13 Or *see spirits*; or *see gods*

and his men were marching at the rear[a]
with Achish. 3The commanders of the
Philistines asked, "What about these
Hebrews?"
Achish replied, "Is this not David,
who was an officer of Saul king of Israel?
He has already been with me for over
a year,[b] and from the day he left Saul
until now, I have found no fault in
him."
4But the Philistine commanders were
angry with him and said, "Send[c] the
man back, that he may return to the
place you assigned him. He must not go
with us into battle, or he will turn[d]
against us during the fighting. How better could he regain his master's favor
than by taking the heads of our own
men? 5Isn't this the David they sang
about in their dances:

"'Saul has slain his thousands,
and David his tens of thousands'?"[e]

6So Achish called David and said to
him, "As surely as the LORD lives, you
have been reliable, and I would be
pleased to have you serve with me in
the army. From the day[f] you came to
me until now, I have found no fault in
you, but the rulers[g] don't approve of you.
7Turn back and go in peace; do nothing
to displease the Philistine rulers."
8"But what have I done?" asked
David. "What have you found against
your servant from the day I came to you
until now? Why can't I go and fight
against the enemies of my lord the
king?"
9Achish answered, "I know that you
have been as pleasing in my eyes as an
angel[h] of God; nevertheless, the Philistine commanders[i] have said, 'He must
not go up with us into battle.' 10Now get
up early, along with your master's servants who have come with you, and
leave[j] in the morning as soon as it is
light."
11So David and his men got up early
in the morning to go back to the land of
the Philistines, and the Philistines went
up to Jezreel.

The Amalekites burn Ziklag.

30 David and his men reached
Ziklag[k] on the third day. Now
the Amalekites[l] had raided the Negev
and Ziklag. They had attacked Ziklag
and burned it, 2and had taken captive
the women and all who were in it, both
young and old. They killed none of
them, but carried them off as they went
on their way.

David overtakes the Amalekites and recovers his two wives.

3When David and his men came to
Ziklag, they found it destroyed by fire
and their wives and sons and daughters
taken captive. 4So David and his men
wept aloud until they had no strength
left to weep. 5David's two wives[m] had
been captured—Ahinoam of Jezreel and
Abigail, the widow of Nabal of Carmel.
6David was greatly distressed because
the men were talking of stoning[n] him;
each one was bitter in spirit because of
his sons and daughters. But David found
strength[o] in the LORD his God.
7Then David said to Abiathar[p] the
priest, the son of Ahimelech, "Bring me
the ephod.[q]" Abiathar brought it to
him, 8and David inquired[r] of the LORD,
"Shall I pursue this raiding party? Will I
overtake them?"
"Pursue them," he answered. "You
will certainly overtake them and succeed[s] in the rescue."
9David and the six hundred men[t] with
him came to the Besor Ravine, where
some stayed behind, 10for two hundred
men were too exhausted[u] to cross the
ravine. But David and four hundred men
continued the pursuit.
11They found an Egyptian in a field
and brought him to David. They gave
him water to drink and food to eat—
12part of a cake of pressed figs and two
cakes of raisins. He ate and was revived,[v] for he had not eaten any food
or drunk any water for three days and
three nights.
13David asked him, "To whom do you
belong, and where do you come from?"

29:2 [a]1Sa 28:2
29:3 [b]1Sa 27:7; Da 6:5
29:4 [c]1Ch 12:19 [d]1Sa 14:21
29:5 [e]1Sa 18:7; 21:11
29:6 [f]1Sa 27:8-12 [g]ver 3
29:9 [h]2Sa 14:17, 20; 19:27 [i]ver 4
29:10 [j]1Ch 12:19
30:1 [k]1Sa 29:4,11 [l]1Sa 15:7; 27:8
30:5 [m]1Sa 25:43; 2Sa 2:2
30:6 [n]Ex 17:4; Jn 8:59 [o]Ps 27:14; 56:3-4,11; Ro 4:20
30:7 [p]1Sa 22:20 [q]1Sa 23:9
30:8 [r]1Sa 23:2 [s]ver 18
30:9 [t]1Sa 27:2
30:10 [u]ver 9,21
30:12 [v]Jdg 15:19

He said, "I am an Egyptian, the slave
of an Amalekite. My master abandoned
me when I became ill three days ago.
14We raided the Negev of the Kerethites[a] and the territory belonging to
Judah and the Negev of Caleb.[b] And we
burned[c] Ziklag."
15David asked him, "Can you lead me
down to this raiding party?"
He answered, "Swear to me before
God that you will not kill me or hand
me over to my master, and I will take
you down to them."
16He led David down, and there they
were, scattered over the countryside,
eating, drinking and reveling[d] because
of the great amount of plunder[e] they had
taken from the land of the Philistines
and from Judah. 17David fought[f] them
from dusk until the evening of the next
day, and none of them got away, except
four hundred young men who rode off
on camels and fled.[g] 18David recovered[h]
everything the Amalekites had taken,
including his two wives. 19Nothing was
missing: young or old, boy or girl, plunder or anything else they had taken.
David brought everything back. 20He
took all the flocks and herds, and his
men drove them ahead of the other livestock, saying, "This is David's plunder."
21Then David came to the two hundred men who had been too exhausted[i]
to follow him and who were left behind
at the Besor Ravine. They came out to
meet David and the people with him.
As David and his men approached, he
greeted them. 22But all the evil men
and troublemakers among David's followers said, "Because they did not go
out with us, we will not share with
them the plunder we recovered. However, each man may take his wife and
children and go."
23David replied, "No, my brothers,
you must not do that with what the LORD
has given us. He has protected us and
handed over to us the forces that came
against us. 24Who will listen to what
you say? The share of the man who
stayed with the supplies is to be the
same as that of him who went down to

30:14 [a]2Sa 8:18; 1Ki 1:38,44; Eze 25:16; Zep 2:5 [b]ver 16; Jos 14:13; 15:13 [c]ver 1
30:16 [d]Lk 12:19 [e]ver 14
30:17 [f]1Sa 11:11 [g]1Sa 15:3
30:18 [h]Ge 14:16
30:21 [i]ver 10
30:24 [j]Nu 31:27; Jos 22:8
30:27 [k]Jos 7:2 [l]Jos 19:8 [m]Jos 15:48
30:28 [n]Jos 13:16 [o]Jos 15:50
30:29 [p]1Sa 27:10 [q]Jdg 1:16; 1Sa 15:6
30:30 [r]Nu 14:45; Jdg 1:17 [s]Jos 15:42
30:31 [t]Jos 14:13; 2Sa 2:1,4
31:1 [u]1Sa 28:4; 1Ch 10:1-12
31:3 [v]2Sa 1:6
31:4 [w]Jdg 9:54; 2Sa 1:6,10 [x]1Sa 14:6

the battle. All will share alike.[j]" 25David
made this a statute and ordinance for
Israel from that day to this.
26When David arrived in Ziklag, he
sent some of the plunder to the elders
of Judah, who were his friends, saying,
"Here is a present for you from the
plunder of the LORD's enemies."
27He sent it to those who were in
Bethel,[k] Ramoth[l] Negev and Jattir;[m] 28to
those in Aroer,[n] Siphmoth, Eshtemoa[o]
29and Racal; to those in the towns of the
Jerahmeelites[p] and the Kenites;[q] 30to
those in Hormah,[r] Bor Ashan,[s] Athach
31and Hebron;[t] and to those in all the
other places where David and his men
had roamed.

Deaths of Saul and his sons.

31:1-13pp— 2Sa 1:4-12; 1Ch 10:1-12

31 Now the Philistines fought against
Israel; the Israelites fled before
them, and many fell slain on Mount
Gilboa.[u] 2The Philistines pressed hard
after Saul and his sons, and they killed
his sons Jonathan, Abinadab and Malki-
Shua. 3The fighting grew fierce around
Saul, and when the archers overtook
him, they wounded[v] him critically.
4Saul said to his armor-bearer, "Draw
your sword and run me through,[w] or
these uncircumcised[x] fellows will come
and run me through and abuse me."
But his armor-bearer was terrified and
would not do it; so Saul took his own
sword and fell on it. 5When the armor-
bearer saw that Saul was dead, he too
fell on his sword and died with him. 6So
Saul and his three sons and his armor-
bearer and all his men died together that
same day.
7When the Israelites along the valley
and those across the Jordan saw that the
Israelite army had fled and that Saul and
his sons had died, they abandoned their
towns and fled. And the Philistines came
and occupied them.
8The next day, when the Philistines
came to strip the dead, they found Saul
and his three sons fallen on Mount Gilboa. 9They cut off his head and stripped

off his armor, and they sent messengers
throughout the land of the Philistines
to proclaim the news[a] in the temple of
their idols and among their people.[b]
10They put his armor in the temple of
the Ashtoreths[c] and fastened his body to
the wall of Beth Shan.[d]
11When the people of Jabesh Gilead[e]
heard of what the Philistines had done
to Saul, 12all their valiant men journeyed
through the night to Beth Shan. They
took down the bodies of Saul and his
sons from the wall of Beth Shan and
went to Jabesh, where they burned[f]
them. 13Then they took their bones[g] and
buried them under a tamarisk[h] tree at Jabesh, and they fasted[i] seven days.[j]

31:9 [a]2Sa 1:20 [b]Jdg 16:24
31:10 [c]Jdg 2:12-13; 1Sa 7:3 [d]Jos 17:11; 2Sa 21:12
31:11 [e]1Sa 11:1
31:12 [f]2Sa 2:4-7; 2Ch 16:14; Am 6:10
31:13 [g]2Sa 21:12-14 [h]1Sa 22:6 [i]2Sa 1:12 [j]Ge 50:10

2 SAMUEL

Author: Unknown (possibly Gad and Nathan).

Date Written: Probably between 1010 and 931 B.C. However, the book was not put into its final form until some years later, possibly between 930 and 722 B.C.

Time Span: About 40 years (during the reign of King David).

Title: Although Samuel is not living during the time this book takes place, it is named after him because he is the one who anointed David, the chief character of 2 Samuel.

Background: 2 Samuel is a sequel to the book of 1 Samuel. This narrative of the life of David continues with his being crowned king of Israel at the death of Saul. 2 Samuel covers the majority of David's 40-year reign in Hebron and Jerusalem. (Saul also reigned 40 years.) 1 and 2 Samuel consist of one book in the Hebrew Bible since they cover the continuous story of 3 main characters: Samuel, Saul and David.

Where Written: Unknown (probably in Israel).

To Whom: To the Israelites.

Content: The life of King David dominates the book of 2 Samuel. First, David rules over Judah for about 7 years. Then, his kingship is recognized by a unified Israel over which he reigns for 33 years. During this transition the capital is changed from Hebron to Jerusalem, where the ark of the covenant is located. David's military victories expand the borders of the promised land as his triumphs bring the nation to the very zenith of her power. David's triumphs quickly turn to tragedy in the middle of his reign, however, when his lust toward Bathsheba ultimately leads to adultery and the murder of her husband, Uriah (chapter 11). The prophet Nathan rebukes David for his sins, and David earnestly repents and is restored to God. But the price of sin still has to be paid: his son Absalom's revolt, civil war and unrest in the nation. Although the fame and glory of David has now diminished, never to be the same again, God still blesses...for to David and Bathsheba is born Solomon, who will succeed David as king and become part of the royal ancestry of Jesus Christ.

Key Words: "Anointed"; "David." The entire book revolves around the "anointed" life of "David." His victories and his failures are given in light of his position, which could only have been given to him by God.

Themes: • God can accomplish extraordinary things through the lives of ordinary people. • Our total trust should be only in God...not in men. • Though forgiven, we still must pay the consequences of our sins. • God is ready to forgive us and use us, if only we will repent and place our faith in him. • There is no sin so great that God will not forgive us if we sincerely forsake the sin and turn to him. • Obedience brings victory...disobedience brings defeat. • As a ruler thrives, so thrives the nation...as a ruler stumbles, so stumbles the nation.

Outline:

1. David's reign over Judah begins. 1:1-4:12
2. David's reign extends over Israel. 5:1-10:19
3. David sins. 11:1-11:27
4. Troubles result for David's house. 12:1-18:33
5. David is restored as king. 19:1-20:26
6. Commentary on David's latter years. 21:1-24:25

2 SAMUEL

David learns that Saul and Jonathan are dead.

1:4-12pp— 1Sa 31:1-13; 1Ch 10:1-12

1 After the death[a] of Saul, David returned from defeating[b] the Amalekites and stayed in Ziklag two days. 2On
the third day a man[c] arrived from Saul's
camp, with his clothes torn and with
dust on his head.[d] When he came to
David, he fell to the ground to pay him
honor.
3"Where have you come from?" David
asked him.
He answered, "I have escaped from
the Israelite camp."
4"What happened?" David asked.
"Tell me."
He said, "The men fled from the battle. Many of them fell and died. And
Saul and his son Jonathan are dead."
5Then David said to the young man
who brought him the report, "How do
you know that Saul and his son Jonathan are dead?"
6"I happened to be on Mount Gilboa,[e]" the young man said, "and there
was Saul, leaning on his spear, with the
chariots and riders almost upon him.
7When he turned around and saw me,
he called out to me, and I said, 'What
can I do?'
8"He asked me, 'Who are you?'
"'An Amalekite,[f]' I answered.
9"Then he said to me, 'Stand over me
and kill me! I am in the throes of death,
but I'm still alive.'
10"So I stood over him and killed him,
because I knew that after he had fallen
he could not survive. And I took the
crown[g] that was on his head and the
band on his arm and have brought them
here to my lord."
11Then David and all the men with
him took hold of their clothes and tore[h]
them. 12They mourned and wept and
fasted till evening for Saul and his son
Jonathan, and for the army of the LORD
and the house of Israel, because they
had fallen by the sword.

1:1 [a]1Sa 31:6 [b]1Sa 30:17
1:2 [c]2Sa 4:10 [d]1Sa 4:12
1:6 [e]1Sa 28:4; 31:2-4
1:8 [f]1Sa 15:2; 30:13,17
1:10 [g]Jdg 9:54; 2Ki 11:12
1:11 [h]Ge 37:29; 2Sa 3:31; 13:31
1:13 [i]ver 8
1:14 [j]1Sa 24:6; 26:9
1:15 [k]2Sa 4:12 [l]2Sa 4:10
1:16 [m]Lev 20:9; 2Sa 3:28-29; 1Ki 2:32; Mt 27:24-25; Ac 18:6
1:17 [n]2Ch 35:25
1:18 [o]Jos 10:13; 1Sa 31:3
1:19 [p]ver 27
1:20 [q]Mic 1:10 [r]1Sa 31:8 [s]Ex 15:20; 1Sa 18:6
1:21 [t]ver 6; 1Sa 31:1 [u]Eze 31:15 [v]Isa 21:5
1:22 [w]Isa 34:3,7 [x]Dt 32:42; 1Sa 18:4

13David said to the young man who
brought him the report, "Where are you
from?"
"I am the son of an alien, an Amalekite,[i]" he answered.
14David asked him, "Why were you
not afraid to lift your hand to destroy
the LORD's anointed?[j]"
15Then David called one of his men
and said, "Go, strike him down!"[k] So he
struck him down, and he died.[l] 16For
David had said to him, "Your blood be
on your own head.[m] Your own mouth
testified against you when you said, 'I
killed the LORD's anointed.'"

David laments for Saul and Jonathan.

17David took up this lament[n] concerning Saul and his son Jonathan, 18and ordered that the men of Judah be taught
this lament of the bow (it is written in
the Book of Jashar):[o]

19"Your glory, O Israel, lies slain on
your heights.
How the mighty have fallen![p]

20"Tell it not in Gath,[q]
proclaim it not in the streets of
Ashkelon,
lest the daughters of the Philistines[r]
be glad,
lest the daughters of the
uncircumcised rejoice.[s]

21"O mountains of Gilboa,[t]
may you have neither dew nor rain,
nor fields that yield offerings[u] ⌊of
grain⌋.
For there the shield of the mighty
was defiled,
the shield of Saul—no longer
rubbed with oil.[v]
22From the blood[w] of the slain,
from the flesh of the mighty,
the bow[x] of Jonathan did not turn
back,
the sword of Saul did not return
unsatisfied.

KEY PLACES IN 2 SAMUEL

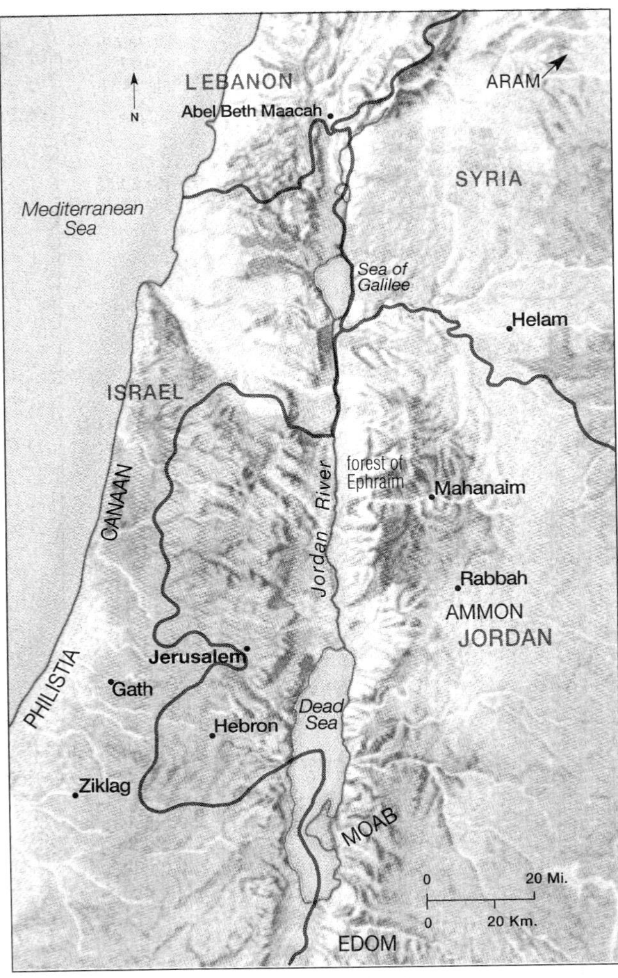

Hebron After Saul's death, David moved from the Philistine city of Ziklag to Hebron, where the tribe of Judah crowned him king. But the rest of Israel's tribes backed Saul's son Ish-Bosheth and crowned him king at Mahanaim. As a result, there was war between Judah and the rest of the tribes of Israel until Ish-Bosheth was assassinated. Then all of Israel pledged loyalty to David as their king (1:1–5:5).

Jerusalem One of David's first battles as king occurred at the fortress city of Jerusalem. David and his troops took the city by surprise, and it became his capital. It was here that David brought the ark of the covenant and made a special agreement with God (5:6–7:29).

Gath The Philistines were Israel's constant enemy, though they did give David sanctuary when he was hiding from Saul (1 Samuel 27). But when Saul died and David became king, the Philistines planned to defeat him. In a battle near Jerusalem, David and his troops routed the Philistines (5:17-25), but they were not completely subdued until David conquered Metheg Ammah (possibly near Gath) (8:1).

Moab During the time of the judges, Moab controlled many cities in Israel and demanded heavy taxes (Judges 3:12-30). David conquered Moab and, in turn, levied tribute from them (8:2).

Edom Though the Edomites and the Israelites traced their ancestry back to the same man, Isaac (Genesis 25:19-23), they were long-standing enemies. David defeated Edom and forced them to pay tribute also (8:14).

Rabbah The Ammonites insulted David's delegation and turned a peacemaking mission into angry warfare. The Ammonites called troops from Aram, but David defeated this alliance first at Helam, then at Rabbah, the capital city (9:1–12:31).

Mahanaim David had victory in the field, but problems at home. His son, Absalom, incited a rebellion and crowned himself king at Hebron. David and his men fled to Mahanaim. Acting on bad advice, Absalom mobilized his army to fight David (13:1–17:29).

Forest of Ephraim The armies of Absalom and David fought in the forest of Ephraim. Absalom's hair got caught in a tree, and Joab, David's general, found and killed him. With Absalom's death, the rebellion died and David was welcomed back to Jerusalem (18:1-19:43).

Abel Beth Maacah A man named Sheba also incited a rebellion against David. He fled to Abel Beth Maacah, but Joab and a small troop besieged the city. The citizens of Abel Beth Maacah killed Sheba themselves (20:1-26). David's victories laid the foundation for the peaceful reign of his son, Solomon.

23"Saul and Jonathan—
in life they were loved and
gracious,
and in death they were not parted.
They were swifter than eagles,[a]
they were stronger than lions.[b]

24"O daughters of Israel,
weep for Saul,
who clothed you in scarlet and
finery,
who adorned your garments with
ornaments of gold.

25"How the mighty have fallen in
battle!
Jonathan lies slain on your heights.
26I grieve for you, Jonathan my
brother;[c]
you were very dear to me.
Your love for me was wonderful,[d]
more wonderful than that of
women.

27"How the mighty have fallen!
The weapons of war have
perished!"[e]

David is anointed king over Judah.

2 In the course of time, David inquired[f] of the LORD. "Shall I go up to
one of the towns of Judah?" he asked.
The LORD said, "Go up."
David asked, "Where shall I go?"
"To Hebron,"[g] the LORD answered.
2So David went up there with his two
wives,[h] Ahinoam of Jezreel and Abigail,[i]
the widow of Nabal of Carmel. 3David
also took the men who were with him,[j]
each with his family, and they settled in
Hebron and its towns. 4Then the men of
Judah came to Hebron[k] and there they
anointed[l] David king over the house of
Judah.
When David was told that it was the
men of Jabesh Gilead[m] who had buried
Saul, 5he sent messengers to the men of
Jabesh Gilead to say to them, "The LORD
bless[n] you for showing this kindness to
Saul your master by burying him. 6May
the LORD now show you kindness and
faithfulness,[o] and I too will show you
the same favor because you have done
this. 7Now then, be strong and brave,
for Saul your master is dead, and the
house of Judah has anointed me king
over them."

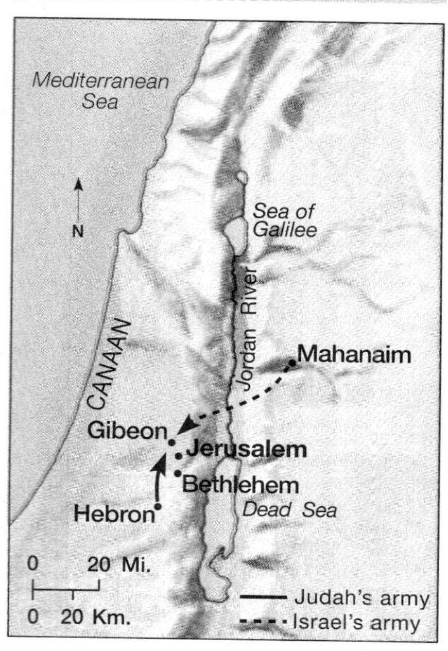

Joab Versus Abner

David was crowned king of Judah in Hebron; Ish-Bosheth was crowned king of Israel in Mahanaim. The opposing armies of Judah and Israel met at Gibeon for battle—Judah under Joab, Israel under Abner.

Ish-Bosheth is made king over Israel.

8Meanwhile, Abner[p] son of Ner, the
commander of Saul's army, had taken
Ish-Bosheth son of Saul and brought him
over to Mahanaim.[q] 9He made him king
over Gilead,[r] Ashuri[a][s] and Jezreel, and
also over Ephraim, Benjamin and all
Israel.[t]
10Ish-Bosheth son of Saul was forty
years old when he became king over
Israel, and he reigned two years. The
house of Judah, however, followed
David. 11The length of time David was
king in Hebron over the house of Judah
was seven years and six months.[u]

1:23 [a]Dt 28:49; Jer 4:13 [b]Jdg 14:18
1:26 [c]1Sa 20:42 [d]1Sa 18:1
1:27 [e]ver 19,25; 1Sa 2:4
2:1 [f]1Sa 23:2,11-12 [g]Ge 13:18; 1Sa 30:31
2:2 [h]1Sa 25:43; 30:5 [i]1Sa 25:42
2:3 [j]1Sa 27:2; 30:9
2:4 [k]1Sa 30:31 [l]1Sa 2:35; 2Sa 5:3-5 [m]1Sa 31:11-13
2:5 [n]1Sa 23:21
2:6 [o]Ex 34:6; 1Ti 1:16
2:8 [p]1Sa 14:50 [q]Ge 32:2
2:9 [r]Nu 32:26 [s]Jdg 1:32 [t]1Ch 12:29
2:11 [u]2Sa 5:5

[a]9 Or *Asher*

Israel and Judah battle.

3:2-5pp— 1Ch 3:1-4

12 Abner son of Ner, together with the
men of Ish-Bosheth son of Saul, left Mahanaim and went to Gibeon.[a] 13 Joab[b]
son of Zeruiah and David's men went
out and met them at the pool of Gibeon.
One group sat down on one side of the
pool and one group on the other side.
14 Then Abner said to Joab, "Let's have
some of the young men get up and fight
hand to hand in front of us."
"All right, let them do it," Joab said.
15 So they stood up and were counted
off—twelve men for Benjamin and Ish-
Bosheth son of Saul, and twelve for
David. 16 Then each man grabbed his opponent by the head and thrust his dagger into his opponent's side, and they
fell down together. So that place in
Gibeon was called Helkath Hazzurim.[b]
17 The battle that day was very fierce,
and Abner and the men of Israel were
defeated[c] by David's men.
18 The three sons of Zeruiah[d] were
there: Joab,[e] Abishai[f] and Asahel.[g] Now
Asahel was as fleet-footed as a wild
gazelle.[h] 19 He chased Abner, turning
neither to the right nor to the left as he
pursued him. 20 Abner looked behind
him and asked, "Is that you, Asahel?"
"It is," he answered.
21 Then Abner said to him, "Turn aside
to the right or to the left; take on one of
the young men and strip him of his
weapons." But Asahel would not stop
chasing him.
22 Again Abner warned Asahel, "Stop
chasing me! Why should I strike you
down? How could I look your brother
Joab in the face?"[i]
23 But Asahel refused to give up the
pursuit; so Abner thrust the butt of his
spear into Asahel's stomach,[j] and the
spear came out through his back. He fell
there and died on the spot. And every
man stopped when he came to the place
where Asahel had fallen and died.[k]
24 But Joab and Abishai pursued Abner, and as the sun was setting, they
came to the hill of Ammah, near Giah
on the way to the wasteland of Gibeon.
25 Then the men of Benjamin rallied behind Abner. They formed themselves
into a group and took their stand on top
of a hill.
26 Abner called out to Joab, "Must the
sword devour[l] forever? Don't you realize
that this will end in bitterness? How
long before you order your men to stop
pursuing their brothers?"
27 Joab answered, "As surely as God
lives, if you had not spoken, the men
would have continued the pursuit of
their brothers until morning.[c]"
28 So Joab[m] blew the trumpet,[n] and all
the men came to a halt; they no longer
pursued Israel, nor did they fight anymore.
29 All that night Abner and his men
marched through the Arabah. They
crossed the Jordan, continued through
the whole Bithron[d] and came to Mahanaim.[o]
30 Then Joab returned from pursuing
Abner and assembled all his men. Besides Asahel, nineteen of David's men
were found missing. 31 But David's men
had killed three hundred and sixty Benjamites who were with Abner. 32 They
took Asahel and buried him in his
father's tomb[p] at Bethlehem. Then Joab
and his men marched all night and arrived at Hebron by daybreak.

3

The war between the house of Saul
and the house of David lasted a
long time.[q] David grew stronger and
stronger,[r] while the house of Saul grew
weaker and weaker.[s]
2 Sons were born to David in Hebron:
His firstborn was Amnon the
son of Ahinoam[t] of Jezreel;
3 his second, Kileab the son of
Abigail[u] the widow of Nabal of
Carmel;
the third, Absalom[v] the son of
Maacah daughter of Talmai king
of Geshur;[w]

2:12 [a] Jos 18:25
2:13 [b] 2Sa 8:16; 1Ch 2:16; 11:6
2:17 [c] 2Sa 3:1
2:18 [d] 2Sa 3:39 [e] 2Sa 3:30 [f] 1Sa 26:6 [g] 1Ch 2:16 [h] 1Ch 12:8
2:22 [i] 2Sa 3:27
2:23 [j] 2Sa 3:27; 4:6 [k] 2Sa 20:12
2:26 [l] Dt 32:42; Jer 46:10,14
2:28 [m] 2Sa 18:16 [n] Jdg 3:27
2:29 [o] ver 8
2:32 [p] Ge 49:29
3:1 [q] 1Ki 14:30 [r] 2Sa 5:10 [s] 2Sa 2:17
3:2 [t] 1Sa 25:43; 1Ch 3:1-3
3:3 [u] 1Sa 25:42 [v] 2Sa 13:1,28 [w] 1Sa 27:8; 2Sa 13:37; 14:32; 15:8

[b] 16 *Helkath Hazzurim* means *field of daggers* or *field of hostilities.* [c] 27 Or *spoken this morning, the men would not have taken up the pursuit of their brothers*; or *spoken, the men would have given up the pursuit of their brothers by morning* [d] 29 Or *morning*; or *ravine*; the meaning of the Hebrew for this word is uncertain.

4 the fourth, Adonijah[a] the son of
Haggith;
the fifth, Shephatiah the son of
Abital;
5 and the sixth, Ithream the son of
David's wife Eglah.
These were born to David in
Hebron.

Abner unites forces with David.

6 During the war between the house
of Saul and the house of David, Abner
had been strengthening his own position in the house of Saul. 7 Now Saul
had had a concubine[b] named Rizpah[c]
daughter of Aiah. And Ish-Bosheth said
to Abner, "Why did you sleep with my
father's concubine?"
8 Abner was very angry because of
what Ish-Bosheth said and he answered,
"Am I a dog's head[d]—on Judah's side?
This very day I am loyal to the house
of your father Saul and to his family
and friends. I haven't handed you over
to David. Yet now you accuse me of an
offense involving this woman! 9 May
God deal with Abner, be it ever so severely, if I do not do for David what
the LORD promised[e] him on oath 10 and
transfer the kingdom from the house of
Saul and establish David's throne over
Israel and Judah from Dan to Beersheba."[f] 11 Ish-Bosheth did not dare to say
another word to Abner, because he was
afraid of him.
12 Then Abner sent messengers on his
behalf to say to David, "Whose land is
it? Make an agreement with me, and I
will help you bring all Israel over to
you."
13 "Good," said David. "I will make an
agreement with you. But I demand one
thing of you: Do not come into my presence unless you bring Michal daughter
of Saul when you come to see me."[g]
14 Then David sent messengers to Ish-
Bosheth son of Saul, demanding, "Give
me my wife Michal,[h] whom I betrothed
to myself for the price of a hundred
Philistine foreskins."
15 So Ish-Bosheth gave orders and had
her taken away from her husband[i] Paltiel[j] son of Laish. 16 Her husband, however, went with her, weeping behind
her all the way to Bahurim.[k] Then Abner said to him, "Go back home!" So he
went back.
17 Abner conferred with the elders[l] of
Israel and said, "For some time you have
wanted to make David your king. 18 Now
do it! For the LORD promised David, 'By
my servant David I will rescue my people Israel from the hand of the Philistines[m] and from the hand of all their
enemies.[n]'"
19 Abner also spoke to the Benjamites
in person. Then he went to Hebron to
tell David everything that Israel and the
whole house of Benjamin[o] wanted to do.
20 When Abner, who had twenty men
with him, came to David at Hebron,
David prepared a feast for him and his
men. 21 Then Abner said to David, "Let
me go at once and assemble all Israel
for my lord the king, so that they may
make a compact[p] with you, and that
you may rule over all that your heart
desires."[q] So David sent Abner away,
and he went in peace.

Joab murders Abner.

22 Just then David's men and Joab
returned from a raid and brought with
them a great deal of plunder. But Abner
was no longer with David in Hebron,
because David had sent him away, and
he had gone in peace. 23 When Joab and
all the soldiers with him arrived, he was
told that Abner son of Ner had come to
the king and that the king had sent him
away and that he had gone in peace.
24 So Joab went to the king and said,
"What have you done? Look, Abner
came to you. Why did you let him go?
Now he is gone! 25 You know Abner son
of Ner; he came to deceive you and observe your movements and find out
everything you are doing."
26 Joab then left David and sent messengers after Abner, and they brought
him back from the well of Sirah. But
David did not know it. 27 Now when

3:4 [a] 1Ki 1:5,11
3:7 [b] 2Sa 16:21-22 [c] 2Sa 21:8-11
3:8 [d] 1Sa 24:14; 2Sa 9:8; 16:9
3:9 [e] 1Sa 15:28; 1Ki 19:2
3:10 [f] Jdg 20:1; 1Sa 3:20
3:13 [g] Ge 43:5; 1Sa 18:20
3:14 [h] 1Sa 18:27
3:15 [i] Dt 24:1-4 [j] 1Sa 25:44
3:16 [k] 2Sa 16:5; 19:16
3:17 [l] Jdg 11:11
3:18 [m] 1Sa 9:16 [n] 1Sa 15:28; 2Sa 8:6
3:19 [o] 1Sa 10:20-21; 1Ch 12:2,16, 29
3:21 [p] ver 10,12 [q] 1Ki 11:37

Abner[a] returned to Hebron, Joab took
him aside into the gateway, as though
to speak with him privately. And there,
to avenge the blood of his brother Asahel, Joab stabbed him in the stomach,
and he died.[b]
28Later, when David heard about this,
he said, "I and my kingdom are forever
innocent[c] before the LORD concerning
the blood of Abner son of Ner. 29May
his blood[d] fall upon the head of Joab and
upon all his father's house![e] May Joab's
house never be without someone who
has a running sore[f] or leprosy[e] or who
leans on a crutch or who falls by the
sword or who lacks food."
30(Joab and his brother Abishai murdered Abner because he had killed their
brother Asahel in the battle at Gibeon.)
31Then David said to Joab and all the
people with him, "Tear your clothes and
put on sackcloth[g] and walk in mourning[h] in front of Abner." King David
himself walked behind the bier. 32They
buried Abner in Hebron, and the king
wept[i] aloud at Abner's tomb. All the
people wept also.
33The king sang this lament[j] for
Abner:

"Should Abner have died as the
lawless die?
34 Your hands were not bound,
your feet were not fettered.
You fell as one falls before wicked
men."

And all the people wept over him
again.
35Then they all came and urged David
to eat something while it was still day;
but David took an oath, saying, "May
God deal with me, be it ever so severely,[k] if I taste bread[l] or anything else
before the sun sets!"
36All the people took note and were
pleased; indeed, everything the king did
pleased them. 37So on that day all the
people and all Israel knew that the king
had no part[m] in the murder of Abner
son of Ner.
38Then the king said to his men,

3:27 [a]2Sa 2:8 [b]2Sa 2:22; 20:9-10; 1Ki 2:5
3:28 [c]ver 37; Dt 21:9
3:29 [d]Lev 20:9 [e]1Ki 2:31-33 [f]Lev 15:2
3:31 [g]2Sa 1:2,11; Ps 30:11; Isa 20:2 [h]Ge 37:34
3:32 [i]Nu 14:1; Pr 24:17
3:33 [j]2Sa 1:17
3:35 [k]Ru 1:17; 1Sa 3:17 [l]1Sa 31:13; 2Sa 1:12; 12:17; Jer 16:7
3:37 [m]ver 28
3:38 [n]2Sa 1:19
3:39 [o]2Sa 2:18 [p]2Sa 19:5-7 [q]1Ki 2:5-6, 33-34; Ps 41:10; 101:8
4:1 [r]2Sa 3:27; Ezr 4:4
4:2 [s]Jos 9:17; 18:25
4:3 [t]Ne 11:33
4:4 [u]1Sa 18:1 [v]1Sa 31:1-4 [w]Lev 21:18 [x]2Sa 9:3,6; 1Ch 8:34; 9:40
4:5 [y]2Sa 2:8
4:6 [z]2Sa 2:23
4:8 [a]1Sa 24:4; 25:29

"Do you not realize that a prince and a
great man has fallen[n] in Israel this day?
39And today, though I am the anointed
king, I am weak, and these sons of Zeruiah[o] are too strong for me.[p] May the
LORD repay[q] the evildoer according to
his evil deeds!"

Ish-Bosheth is beheaded.

4 When Ish-Bosheth son of Saul heard
that Abner[r] had died in Hebron,
he lost courage, and all Israel became
alarmed. 2Now Saul's son had two men
who were leaders of raiding bands.
One was named Baanah and the other
Recab; they were sons of Rimmon the
Beerothite from the tribe of Benjamin—
Beeroth[s] is considered part of Benjamin,
3because the people of Beeroth fled to
Gittaim[t] and have lived there as aliens
to this day.
4(Jonathan[u] son of Saul had a son who
was lame in both feet. He was five years
old when the news[v] about Saul and Jonathan came from Jezreel. His nurse
picked him up and fled, but as she hurried to leave, he fell and became crippled.[w] His name was Mephibosheth.)[x]
5Now Recab and Baanah, the sons of
Rimmon the Beerothite, set out for the
house of Ish-Bosheth,[y] and they arrived
there in the heat of the day while he was
taking his noonday rest. 6They went into
the inner part of the house as if to get
some wheat, and they stabbed[z] him in
the stomach. Then Recab and his brother Baanah slipped away.
7They had gone into the house while
he was lying on the bed in his bedroom.
After they stabbed and killed him, they
cut off his head. Taking it with them,
they traveled all night by way of the
Arabah. 8They brought the head of Ish-
Bosheth to David at Hebron and said
to the king, "Here is the head of Ish-
Bosheth son of Saul,[a] your enemy, who
tried to take your life. This day the LORD
has avenged my lord the king against
Saul and his offspring."

e *29* The Hebrew word was used for various diseases affecting the skin—not necessarily leprosy.

David avenges the murder of Ish-Bosheth.

9David answered Recab and his brother Baanah, the sons of Rimmon the Beerothite, "As surely as the LORD lives,
who has delivered[a] me out of all trouble,
10when a man told me, 'Saul is dead,'
and thought he was bringing good news,
I seized him and put him to death in Ziklag.[b] That was the reward I gave him for
his news! 11How much more—when
wicked men have killed an innocent
man in his own house and on his own
bed—should I not now demand his
blood[c] from your hand and rid the earth
of you!"
12So David gave an order to his men,
and they killed them.[d] They cut off their
hands and feet and hung the bodies by
the pool in Hebron. But they took the
head of Ish-Bosheth and buried it in
Abner's tomb at Hebron.

David is anointed king over Israel.

5:1-3pp— 1Ch 11:1-3

5 All the tribes of Israel[e] came to
David at Hebron and said, "We are
your own flesh and blood.[f] 2In the past,
while Saul was king over us, you were
the one who led Israel on their military
campaigns.[g] And the LORD said to you,
'You will shepherd[h] my people Israel,
and you will become their ruler.[i]'"
3When all the elders of Israel had
come to King David at Hebron, the king
made a compact[j] with them at Hebron
before the LORD, and they anointed[k]
David king over Israel.
4David was thirty years old[l] when he
became king, and he reigned[m] forty[n]
years. 5In Hebron he reigned over Judah
seven years and six months,[o] and in
Jerusalem he reigned over all Israel and
Judah thirty-three years.

David conquers Jerusalem and makes it his home.

5:6-10pp— 1Ch 11:4-9
5:11-16pp— 1Ch 3:5-9; 14:1-7

6The king and his men marched to
Jerusalem[p] to attack the Jebusites,[q] who
lived there. The Jebusites said to David,
"You will not get in here; even the blind
and the lame can ward you off." They
thought, "David cannot get in here."
7Nevertheless, David captured the fortress of Zion, the City of David.[r]
8On that day, David said, "Anyone
who conquers the Jebusites will have to
use the water shaft[f] to reach those 'lame
and blind' who are David's enemies.[g]"
That is why they say, "The 'blind and
lame' will not enter the palace."
9David then took up residence in the
fortress and called it the City of David.
He built up the area around it, from the
supporting terraces[h][s] inward. 10And he
became more and more powerful,[t] because the LORD God Almighty was with
him.
11Now Hiram[u] king of Tyre sent messengers to David, along with cedar logs
and carpenters and stonemasons, and
they built a palace for David. 12And
David knew that the LORD had established him as king over Israel and had
exalted his kingdom for the sake of his
people Israel.

Eleven sons are born to David at Jerusalem.

13After he left Hebron, David took
more concubines and wives[v] in Jerusalem, and more sons and daughters
were born to him. 14These are the
names of the children born to him
there:[w] Shammua, Shobab, Nathan, Solomon, 15Ibhar, Elishua, Nepheg, Japhia,
16Elishama, Eliada and Eliphelet.

David defeats the Philistines.

5:17-25pp— 1Ch 14:8-17

17When the Philistines heard that
David had been anointed king over
Israel, they went up in full force to
search for him, but David heard about it
and went down to the stronghold.[x]
18Now the Philistines had come and
spread out in the Valley of Rephaim;[y]

4:9 [a]Ge 48:16; 1Ki 1:29
4:10 [b]2Sa 1:2-16
4:11 [c]Ge 9:5; Ps 9:12
4:12 [d]2Sa 1:15
5:1 [e]2Sa 19:43 [f]1Ch 11:1
5:2 [g]1Sa 18:5,13, 16 [h]1Sa 16:1; 2Sa 7:7 [i]1Sa 25:30
5:3 [j]2Sa 3:21 [k]2Sa 2:4
5:4 [l]Lk 3:23 [m]1Ki 2:11; 1Ch 3:4 [n]1Ch 26:31; 29:27
5:5 [o]2Sa 2:11; 1Ch 3:4
5:6 [p]Jdg 1:8 [q]Jos 15:8
5:7 [r]2Sa 6:12,16; 1Ki 2:10
5:9 [s]ver 7; 1Ki 9:15,24
5:10 [t]2Sa 3:1
5:11 [u]1Ki 5:1,18; 1Ch 14:1
5:13 [v]Dt 17:17; 1Ch 3:9
5:14 [w]1Ch 3:5
5:17 [x]2Sa 23:14; 1Ch 11:16
5:18 [y]Jos 15:8; 17:15; 18:16

f8 Or *use scaling hooks* g8 Or *are hated by David*
h9 Or *the Millo*

19 So David inquired[a] of the LORD, "Shall
I go and attack the Philistines? Will you
hand them over to me?"
The LORD answered him, "Go, for I
will surely hand the Philistines over to
you."
20 So David went to Baal Perazim, and
there he defeated them. He said, "As
waters break out, the LORD has broken
out against my enemies before me." So
that place was called Baal Perazim.[i][b]
21 The Philistines abandoned their idols
there, and David and his men carried
them off.[c]
22 Once more the Philistines came up
and spread out in the Valley of Rephaim;
23 so David inquired of the LORD, and he
answered, "Do not go straight up, but
circle around behind them and attack
them in front of the balsam trees. 24 As
soon as you hear the sound[d] of marching in the tops of the balsam trees, move
quickly, because that will mean the
LORD has gone out in front[e] of you to
strike the Philistine army." 25 So David
did as the LORD commanded him, and he
struck down the Philistines all the way
from Gibeon[j][f] to Gezer.[g]

Uzzah is struck down for touching the ark.

6:1-11pp— 1Ch 13:1-14
6:12-19pp— 1Ch 15:25–16:3

6 David again brought together out of
Israel chosen men, thirty thousand
in all. 2 He and all his men set out from
Baalah[h] of Judah[k] to bring up from there
the ark[i] of God, which is called by the
Name,[l][j] the name of the LORD Almighty,
who is enthroned[k] between the cherubim[l] that are on the ark. 3 They set the
ark of God on a new cart[m] and brought
it from the house of Abinadab, which
was on the hill. Uzzah and Ahio, sons
of Abinadab, were guiding the new cart
4 with the ark of God on it,[m] and Ahio
was walking in front of it. 5 David and
the whole house of Israel were celebrating with all their might before the LORD,
with songs[n] and with harps, lyres, tambourines, sistrums and cymbals.[n]

6 When they came to the threshing
floor of Nacon, Uzzah reached out and
took hold of[o] the ark of God, because
the oxen stumbled. 7 The LORD's anger
burned against Uzzah because of his
irreverent act;[p] therefore God struck
him down[q] and he died there beside the
ark of God.
8 Then David was angry because the
LORD's wrath[r] had broken out against
Uzzah, and to this day that place is called
Perez Uzzah.[o][s]
9 David was afraid of the LORD that day
and said, "How[t] can the ark of the LORD
ever come to me?" 10 He was not willing
to take the ark of the LORD to be with
him in the City of David. Instead, he
took it aside to the house of Obed-
Edom[u] the Gittite. 11 The ark of the LORD
remained in the house of Obed-Edom
the Gittite for three months, and the
LORD blessed him and his entire household.[v]
12 Now King David[w] was told, "The
LORD has blessed the household of Obed-
Edom and everything he has, because of
the ark of God." So David went down
and brought up the ark of God from the
house of Obed-Edom to the City of David
with rejoicing. 13 When those who were
carrying the ark of the LORD had taken
six steps, he sacrificed[x] a bull and a fattened calf. 14 David, wearing a linen
ephod,[y] danced[z] before the LORD with
all his might, 15 while he and the entire
house of Israel brought up the ark of the
LORD with shouts and the sound of
trumpets.[a]
16 As the ark of the LORD was entering
the City of David,[b] Michal daughter of
Saul watched from a window. And when
she saw King David leaping and dancing

5:19 [a] 1Sa 23:2; 2Sa 2:1
5:20 [b] Isa 28:21
5:21 [c] Dt 7:5; 1Ch 14:12; Isa 46:2
5:24 [d] 2Ki 7:6 [e] Jdg 4:14
5:25 [f] Isa 28:21 [g] 1Ch 14:16
6:2 [h] Jos 15:9 [i] 1Sa 4:4; 7:1 [j] Lev 24:16; Isa 63:14 [k] Ps 99:1 [l] Ex 25:22; 1Ch 13:5-6
6:3 [m] Nu 7:4-9; 1Sa 6:7
6:5 [n] 1Sa 18:6-7; Ezr 3:10; Ps 150:5
6:6 [o] Nu 4:15, 19-20; 1Ch 13:9
6:7 [p] 1Ch 15:13-15 [q] Ex 19:22; 1Sa 6:19
6:8 [r] Ps 7:11 [s] Ge 38:29
6:9 [t] Ps 119:120
6:10 [u] 1Ch 13:13; 26:4-5
6:11 [v] Ge 30:27; 39:5
6:12 [w] 1Ki 8:1; 1Ch 15:25
6:13 [x] 1Ki 8:5,62
6:14 [y] Ex 19:6; 1Sa 2:18 [z] Ex 15:20
6:15 [a] Ps 47:5; 98:6
6:16 [b] 2Sa 5:7

[i] *20* Baal Perazim means *the lord who breaks out.* [j] *25* Septuagint (see also 1 Chron. 14:16); Hebrew *Geba* [k] *2* That is, Kiriath Jearim; Hebrew *Baale Judah,* a variant of *Baalah of Judah* [l] *2* Hebrew; Septuagint and Vulgate do not have *the Name.* [m] *3,4* Dead Sea Scrolls and some Septuagint manuscripts; Masoretic Text *cart* *4and they brought it with the ark of God from the house of Abinadab, which was on the hill* [n] *5* See Dead Sea Scrolls, Septuagint and 1 Chronicles 13:8; Masoretic Text *celebrating before the LORD with all kinds of instruments made of pine.* [o] *8* Perez Uzzah means *outbreak against Uzzah.*

before the LORD, she despised him in
her heart.
17They brought the ark of the LORD
and set it in its place inside the tent that
David had pitched for it,[a] and David
sacrificed burnt offerings[b] and fellowship offerings[p] before the LORD. 18After
he had finished sacrificing[c] the burnt
offerings and fellowship offerings, he
blessed the people in the name of the
LORD Almighty. 19Then he gave a loaf of
bread, a cake of dates and a cake of
raisins[d] to each person in the whole
crowd of Israelites, both men and wom-
en.[e] And all the people went to their
homes.

Michal remains childless.

20When David returned home to bless
his household, Michal daughter of Saul
came out to meet him and said, "How
the king of Israel has distinguished himself today, disrobing[f] in the sight of the
slave girls of his servants as any vulgar
fellow would!"
21David said to Michal, "It was before
the LORD, who chose me rather than
your father or anyone from his house
when he appointed[g] me ruler over the
LORD's people Israel—I will celebrate
before the LORD. 22I will become even
more undignified than this, and I will
be humiliated in my own eyes. But by
these slave girls you spoke of, I will be
held in honor."
23And Michal daughter of Saul had no
children to the day of her death.

David's offspring will build a house for the LORD.

7:1-17pp— 1Ch 17:1-15

7 After the king was settled in his
palace[h] and the LORD had given him
rest from all his enemies around him,
2he said to Nathan the prophet, "Here
I am, living in a palace[i] of cedar, while
the ark of God remains in a tent."[j]
3Nathan replied to the king, "Whatever you have in mind, go ahead and do
it, for the LORD is with you."

6:17 [a]1Ch 15:1; 2Ch 1:4 [b]Lev 1:1-17; 1Ki 8:62-64
6:18 [c]1Ki 8:22
6:19 [d]Hos 3:1 [e]Ne 8:10
6:20 [f]ver 14,16
6:21 [g]1Sa 13:14; 15:28
7:1 [h]1Ch 17:1
7:2 [i]2Sa 5:11 [j]Ex 26:1; Ac 7:45-46
7:5 [k]1Ki 8:19; 1Ch 22:8 [l]1Ki 5:3-5
7:6 [m]Ex 40:18,34 [n]1Ki 8:16
7:7 [o]Dt 23:14 [p]2Sa 5:2 [q]Lev 26:11-12
7:8 [r]1Sa 16:11 [s]2Sa 6:21 [t]Ps 78:70-72; 2Co 6:18*
7:9 [u]2Sa 5:10 [v]Ps 18:37-42
7:10 [w]Ex 15:17; Isa 5:1-7 [x]Ps 89:22-23 [y]Isa 60:18
7:11 [z]Jdg 2:16; 1Sa 12:9-11 [a]ver 1 [b]1Sa 25:28 [c]ver 27
7:12 [d]1Ki 2:1 [e]Ps 132:11-12
7:13 [f]1Ki 5:5; 8:19,29 [g]Isa 9:7
7:14 [h]Ps 89:26; Heb 1:5*

4That night the word of the LORD came
to Nathan, saying:
5"Go and tell my servant David,
'This is what the LORD says: Are
you[k] the one to build me a house
to dwell in?[l] 6I have not dwelt in a
house from the day I brought the
Israelites up out of Egypt to this day.
I have been moving from place to
place with a tent[m] as my dwelling.[n]
7Wherever I have moved with all
the Israelites,[o] did I ever say to any
of their rulers whom I commanded
to shepherd[p] my people Israel,
"Why have you not built me a
house of cedar?[q]"'
8"Now then, tell my servant
David, 'This is what the LORD Almighty says: I took you from the pasture and from following the flock[r] to
be ruler[s] over my people Israel.[t] 9I
have been with you wherever you
have gone,[u] and I have cut off all
your enemies from before you.[v] Now
I will make your name great, like
the names of the greatest men of the
earth. 10And I will provide a place
for my people Israel and will plant[w]
them so that they can have a home
of their own and no longer be disturbed. Wicked[x] people will not
oppress them anymore,[y] as they did
at the beginning 11and have done
ever since the time I appointed
leaders[q][z] over my people Israel. I
will also give you rest from all your
enemies.[a]
"'The LORD declares to you that
the LORD himself will establish[b] a
house[c] for you: 12When your days
are over and you rest[d] with your
fathers, I will raise up your offspring
to succeed you, who will come from
your own body,[e] and I will establish
his kingdom. 13He is the one who
will build a house for my Name,[f]
and I will establish the throne of his
kingdom forever.[g] 14I will be his
father, and he will be my son.[h]

p *17* Traditionally *peace offerings*; also in verse 18
q *11* Traditionally *judges*

When he does wrong, I will punish him with the rod[a] of men,
with floggings inflicted by men.
15But my love will never be taken
away from him, as I took it away
from Saul,[b] whom I removed from
before you. 16Your house and your
kingdom will endure forever before
me[r]; your throne[c] will be established forever.[d]' "

17Nathan reported to David all the
words of this entire revelation.

David's prayer of thanksgiving.

7:18-29pp— 1Ch 17:16-27

18Then King David went in and sat
before the LORD, and he said:

"Who am I,[e] O Sovereign LORD,
and what is my family, that you
have brought me this far? 19And as
if this were not enough in your
sight, O Sovereign LORD, you have
also spoken about the future of the
house of your servant. Is this your
usual way of dealing with man,[f] O
Sovereign LORD?

20"What more can David say to
you? For you know[g] your servant,[h]
O Sovereign LORD. 21For the sake of
your word and according to your
will, you have done this great thing
and made it known to your servant.

22"How great[i] you are,[j] O Sovereign LORD! There is no one like you,
and there is no God[k] but you, as we
have heard with our own ears.[l]
23And who is like your people
Israel[m]—the one nation on earth
that God went out to redeem as a
people for himself, and to make a
name for himself, and to perform
great and awesome wonders[n] by
driving out nations and their gods
from before your people, whom you
redeemed[o] from Egypt?[s] 24You have
established your people Israel as
your very own[p] forever, and you,
O LORD, have become their God.[q]

25"And now, LORD God, keep forever the promise you have made
concerning your servant and his
house. Do as you promised, 26so
that your name will be great forever. Then men will say, 'The LORD
Almighty is God over Israel!' And
the house of your servant David
will be established before you.

27"O LORD Almighty, God of Israel, you have revealed this to your
servant, saying, 'I will build a house
for you.' So your servant has found
courage to offer you this prayer. 28O
Sovereign LORD, you are God! Your
words are trustworthy,[r] and you
have promised these good things to
your servant. 29Now be pleased to
bless the house of your servant, that
it may continue forever in your
sight; for you, O Sovereign LORD,
have spoken, and with your blessing[s] the house of your servant will
be blessed forever."

David's battle victories.

8:1-14pp— 1Ch 18:1-13

8 In the course of time, David defeated
the Philistines and subdued them,
and he took Metheg Ammah from the
control of the Philistines.

2David also defeated the Moabites.[t]
He made them lie down on the ground
and measured them off with a length of
cord. Every two lengths of them were
put to death, and the third length was
allowed to live. So the Moabites became
subject to David and brought tribute.

3Moreover, David fought Hadadezer[u]
son of Rehob, king of Zobah,[v] when he
went to restore his control along the
Euphrates River. 4David captured a thousand of his chariots, seven thousand
charioteers[t] and twenty thousand foot
soldiers. He hamstrung[w] all but a hundred of the chariot horses.

5When the Arameans of Damascus[x]

7:14 [a]Ps 89:30-33
7:15 [b]1Sa 15:23, 28
7:16 [c]Ps 89:36-37 [d]ver 13
7:18 [e]Ex 3:11; 1Sa 18:18
7:19 [f]Isa 55:8-9
7:20 [g]Jn 21:17 [h]1Sa 16:7
7:22 [i]Ps 48:1; 86:10; Jer 10:6 [j]Dt 3:24 [k]Ex 15:11 [l]Ex 10:2; Ps 44:1
7:23 [m]Dt 4:32-38 [n]Dt 10:21 [o]Dt 9:26; 15:15
7:24 [p]Dt 26:18 [q]Ex 6:6-7; Ps 48:14
7:28 [r]Ex 34:6; Jn 17:17
7:29 [s]Nu 6:23-27
8:2 [t]Ge 19:37; Nu 24:17
8:3 [u]2Sa 10:16, 19 [v]1Sa 14:47
8:4 [w]Jos 11:9
8:5 [x]1Ki 11:24

r *16* Some Hebrew manuscripts and Septuagint; most Hebrew manuscripts *you* s *23* See Septuagint and 1 Chron. 17:21; Hebrew *wonders for your land and before your people, whom you redeemed from Egypt, from the nations and their gods.* t *4* Septuagint (see also Dead Sea Scrolls and 1 Chron. 18:4); Masoretic Text *captured seventeen hundred of his charioteers*

came to help Hadadezer king of Zobah,
David struck down twenty-two thousand of them. 6He put garrisons in the
Aramean kingdom of Damascus, and the
Arameans became subject to him and
brought tribute. The LORD gave David
victory wherever he went.[a]
7David took the gold shields[b] that belonged to the officers of Hadadezer and
brought them to Jerusalem. 8From Tebah[u] and Berothai,[c] towns that belonged
to Hadadezer, King David took a great
quantity of bronze.
9When Tou[v] king of Hamath[d] heard
that David had defeated the entire army
of Hadadezer, 10he sent his son Joram[w]
to King David to greet him and congratulate him on his victory in battle over
Hadadezer, who had been at war with
Tou. Joram brought with him articles of
silver and gold and bronze.
11King David dedicated[e] these articles
to the LORD, as he had done with the
silver and gold from all the nations he
had subdued: 12Edom[x] and Moab,[f] the
Ammonites[g] and the Philistines,[h] and
Amalek.[i] He also dedicated the plunder
taken from Hadadezer son of Rehob,
king of Zobah.
13And David became famous[j] after he
returned from striking down eighteen
thousand Edomites[y] in the Valley of
Salt.[k]
14He put garrisons throughout Edom,
and all the Edomites[l] became subject to
David.[m] The LORD gave David victory
wherever he went.[n]

David's officials.

8:15-18pp— 1Ch 18:14-17

15David reigned over all Israel, doing
what was just and right for all his people. 16Joab[o] son of Zeruiah was over the
army; Jehoshaphat[p] son of Ahilud was
recorder; 17Zadok[q] son of Ahitub and
Ahimelech son of Abiathar were priests;
Seraiah was secretary;[r] 18Benaiah[s] son
of Jehoiada was over the Kerethites[t]
and Pelethites; and David's sons were
royal advisers.[z]

8:6 [a]ver 14; 2Sa 3:18; 7:9
8:7 [b]1Ki 10:16
8:8 [c]Eze 47:16
8:9 [d]1Ki 8:65; 2Ch 8:4
8:11 [e]1Ki 7:51; 1Ch 26:26
8:12 [f]ver 2 [g]2Sa 10:14 [h]2Sa 5:25 [i]1Sa 27:8
8:13 [j]2Sa 7:9 [k]2Ki 14:7; 1Ch 18:12
8:14 [l]Nu 24:17-18 [m]Ge 27:29, 37-40 [n]ver 6
8:16 [o]2Sa 19:13; 1Ch 11:6 [p]2Sa 20:24; 1Ki 4:3
8:17 [q]2Sa 15:24, 29; 1Ch 16:39; 24:3 [r]1Ki 4:3; 2Ki 12:10
8:18 [s]2Sa 20:23; 1Ki 1:8,38; 1Ch 18:17 [t]1Sa 30:14
9:1 [u]1Sa 20:14-17, 42
9:2 [v]2Sa 16:1-4; 19:17,26,29
9:3 [w]1Sa 20:14 [x]2Sa 4:4
9:4 [y]2Sa 17:27-29
9:6 [z]2Sa 16:4; 19:24-30
9:7 [a]ver 1,3; 2Sa 12:8; 19:28; 1Ki 2:7; 2Ki 25:29
9:8 [b]2Sa 16:9

David restores land to Mephibosheth.

9 David asked, "Is there anyone still
left of the house of Saul to whom I
can show kindness for Jonathan's sake?"[u]
2Now there was a servant of Saul's
household named Ziba.[v] They called
him to appear before David, and the
king said to him, "Are you Ziba?"
"Your servant," he replied.
3The king asked, "Is there no one still
left of the house of Saul to whom I can
show God's kindness?"
Ziba answered the king, "There is
still a son of Jonathan;[w] he is crippled[x]
in both feet."
4"Where is he?" the king asked.
Ziba answered, "He is at the house of
Makir[y] son of Ammiel in Lo Debar."
5So King David had him brought from
Lo Debar, from the house of Makir son
of Ammiel.
6When Mephibosheth son of Jonathan, the son of Saul, came to David, he
bowed down to pay him honor.[z]
David said, "Mephibosheth!"
"Your servant," he replied.
7"Don't be afraid," David said to him,
"for I will surely show you kindness for
the sake of your father Jonathan. I will
restore to you all the land that belonged
to your grandfather Saul, and you will
always eat at my table.[a]"
8Mephibosheth bowed down and
said, "What is your servant, that you
should notice a dead dog[b] like me?"
9Then the king summoned Ziba,
Saul's servant, and said to him, "I have
given your master's grandson everything
that belonged to Saul and his family.
10You and your sons and your servants
are to farm the land for him and bring
in the crops, so that your master's

u*8* See some Septuagint manuscripts (see also 1Chron. 18:8); Hebrew *Betah.* v*9* Hebrew *Toi*, a variant of *Tou*; also in verse 10 w*10* A variant of *Hadoram* x*12* Some Hebrew manuscripts, Septuagint and Syriac (see also 1Chron. 18:11); most Hebrew manuscripts *Aram* y*13* A few Hebrew manuscripts, Septuagint and Syriac (see also 1Chron. 18:12); most Hebrew manuscripts *Aram* (that is, Arameans) z*18* Or *were priests*

grandson[a] may be provided for. And Mephibosheth, grandson of your master, will always eat at my table." (Now Ziba had fifteen sons and twenty servants.)

11 Then Ziba said to the king, "Your servant will do whatever my lord the king commands his servant to do." So Mephibosheth ate at David's[a] table like one of the king's sons.[b]

12 Mephibosheth had a young son named Mica, and all the members of Ziba's household were servants of Mephibosheth.[c] 13 And Mephibosheth lived in Jerusalem, because he always ate at the king's table, and he was crippled in both feet.

The Ammonites humiliate David's men.

10:1-19pp— 1Ch 19:1-19

10 In the course of time, the king of the Ammonites died, and his son Hanun succeeded him as king. 2 David thought, "I will show kindness to Hanun son of Nahash,[d] just as his father showed kindness to me." So David sent a delegation to express his sympathy to Hanun concerning his father.

When David's men came to the land of the Ammonites, 3 the Ammonite nobles said to Hanun their lord, "Do you think David is honoring your father by sending men to you to express sympathy? Hasn't David sent them to you to explore the city and spy it out and overthrow it?" 4 So Hanun seized David's men, shaved off half of each man's beard,[e] cut off their garments in the middle at the buttocks,[f] and sent them away.

5 When David was told about this, he sent messengers to meet the men, for they were greatly humiliated. The king said, "Stay at Jericho till your beards have grown, and then come back."

The Ammonites and Arameans are defeated.

6 When the Ammonites realized that they had become a stench[g] in David's nostrils, they hired twenty thousand Aramean[h] foot soldiers from Beth Rehob[i] and Zobah, as well as the king of Maacah[j] with a thousand men, and also twelve thousand men from Tob.

7 On hearing this, David sent Joab out with the entire army of fighting men. 8 The Ammonites came out and drew up in battle formation at the entrance to their city gate, while the Arameans of Zobah and Rehob and the men of Tob and Maacah were by themselves in the open country.

9 Joab saw that there were battle lines in front of him and behind him; so he selected some of the best troops in Israel and deployed them against the Arameans. 10 He put the rest of the men under the command of Abishai his brother and deployed them against the Ammonites. 11 Joab said, "If the Arameans are too strong for me, then you are to come to my rescue; but if the Ammonites are too strong for you, then I will come to rescue you. 12 Be strong[k] and let us fight bravely for our people and the cities of our God. The LORD will do what is good in his sight."[l]

13 Then Joab and the troops with him advanced to fight the Arameans, and they fled before him. 14 When the Ammonites saw that the Arameans were fleeing, they fled before Abishai and went inside the city. So Joab returned from fighting the Ammonites and came to Jerusalem.

15 After the Arameans saw that they had been routed by Israel, they regrouped. 16 Hadadezer had Arameans brought from beyond the River[b]; they went to Helam, with Shobach the commander of Hadadezer's army leading them.

17 When David was told of this, he gathered all Israel, crossed the Jordan and went to Helam. The Arameans formed their battle lines to meet David and fought against him. 18 But they fled before Israel, and David killed seven hundred of their charioteers and forty

9:10 [a]ver 7,11,13; 2Sa 19:28
9:11 [b]Job 36:7; Ps 113:8
9:12 [c]1Ch 8:34
10:2 [d]1Sa 11:1
10:4 [e]Lev 19:27; Isa 15:2; Jer 48:37 [f]Isa 20:4
10:6 [g]Ge 34:30 [h]2Sa 8:5 [i]Jdg 18:28 [j]Dt 3:14
10:12 [k]Dt 31:6; 1Co 16:13; Eph 6:10 [l]Jdg 10:15; 1Sa 3:18; Ne 4:14

a *11* Septuagint; Hebrew *my* b *16* That is, the Euphrates

thousand of their foot soldiers.[c] He also
struck down Shobach the commander of
their army, and he died there. 19When
all the kings who were vassals of Hadadezer saw that they had been defeated by Israel, they made peace with the
Israelites and became subject[a] to them.
So the Arameans[b] were afraid to help
the Ammonites anymore.

David sins with Bathsheba.

11 In the spring,[c] at the time when
kings go off to war, David sent
Joab[d] out with the king's men and the
whole Israelite army.[e] They destroyed
the Ammonites and besieged Rabbah.[f]
But David remained in Jerusalem.
2One evening David got up from his
bed and walked around on the roof[g] of
the palace. From the roof he saw[h] a
woman bathing. The woman was very
beautiful, 3and David sent someone to
find out about her. The man said, "Isn't
this Bathsheba,[i] the daughter of Eliam[j]
and the wife of Uriah[k] the Hittite?"
4Then David sent messengers to get
her.[l] She came to him, and he slept[m]
with her. (She had purified herself from
her uncleanness.)[n] Then[d] she went back
home. 5The woman conceived and sent
word to David, saying, "I am pregnant."

David arranges the murder of Uriah.

6So David sent this word to Joab:
"Send me Uriah[o] the Hittite." And Joab
sent him to David. 7When Uriah came
to him, David asked him how Joab was,
how the soldiers were and how the war
was going. 8Then David said to Uriah,
"Go down to your house and wash your
feet."[p] So Uriah left the palace, and a
gift from the king was sent after him.
9But Uriah slept at the entrance to the
palace with all his master's servants and
did not go down to his house.
10When David was told, "Uriah did
not go home," he asked him, "Haven't
you just come from a distance? Why
didn't you go home?"
11Uriah said to David, "The ark[q] and
Israel and Judah are staying in tents,
and my master Joab and my lord's men
are camped in the open fields. How
could I go to my house to eat and drink
and lie with my wife? As surely as you
live, I will not do such a thing!"
12Then David said to him, "Stay here
one more day, and tomorrow I will send
you back." So Uriah remained in Jerusalem that day and the next. 13At David's
invitation, he ate and drank with him,
and David made him drunk. But in the
evening Uriah went out to sleep on his
mat among his master's servants; he did
not go home.
14In the morning David wrote a letter[r] to Joab and sent it with Uriah. 15In
it he wrote, "Put Uriah in the front line
where the fighting is fiercest. Then
withdraw from him so he will be struck
down[s] and die.[t]"
16So while Joab had the city under
siege, he put Uriah at a place where he
knew the strongest defenders were.
17When the men of the city came out
and fought against Joab, some of the
men in David's army fell; moreover,
Uriah the Hittite died.
18Joab sent David a full account of the
battle. 19He instructed the messenger:
"When you have finished giving the
king this account of the battle, 20the
king's anger may flare up, and he may
ask you, 'Why did you get so close to
the city to fight? Didn't you know they
would shoot arrows from the wall?
21Who killed Abimelech[u] son of Jerub-
Besheth[e]? Didn't a woman throw an
upper millstone on him from the wall,[v]
so that he died in Thebez? Why did you
get so close to the wall?' If he asks you
this, then say to him, 'Also, your servant Uriah the Hittite is dead.'"
22The messenger set out, and when
he arrived he told David everything Joab
had sent him to say. 23The messenger
said to David, "The men overpowered
us and came out against us in the open,

10:19 [a]2Sa 8:6 [b]1Ki 11:25; 2Ki 5:1
11:1 [c]1Ki 20:22,26 [d]2Sa 2:18 [e]1Ch 20:1 [f]2Sa 12:26-28
11:2 [g]Dt 22:8; Jos 2:8 [h]Mt 5:28
11:3 [i]1Ch 3:5 [j]2Sa 23:34 [k]2Sa 23:39
11:4 [l]Lev 20:10; Ps 51 Title; Jas 1:14-15 [m]Dt 22:22 [n]Lev 15:25-30; 18:19
11:6 [o]1Ch 11:41
11:8 [p]Ge 18:4; 43:24; Lk 7:44
11:11 [q]2Sa 7:2
11:14 [r]1Ki 21:8
11:15 [s]2Sa 12:9 [t]2Sa 12:12
11:21 [u]Jdg 8:31 [v]Jdg 9:50-54

c *18* Some Septuagint manuscripts (see also 1 Chron. 19:18); Hebrew *horsemen* d *4* Or *with her. When she purified herself from her uncleanness,* e *21* Also known as *Jerub-Baal* (that is, Gideon)

but we drove them back to the entrance
to the city gate. 24 Then the archers shot
arrows at your servants from the wall,
and some of the king's men died. Moreover, your servant Uriah the Hittite is
dead."
25 David told the messenger, "Say this
to Joab: 'Don't let this upset you; the
sword devours one as well as another.
Press the attack against the city and
destroy it.' Say this to encourage Joab."

David marries Bathsheba.

26 When Uriah's wife heard that her
husband was dead, she mourned for
him. 27 After the time of mourning was
over, David had her brought to his
house, and she became his wife and
bore him a son. But the thing David had
done displeased[a] the LORD.

Nathan uses a parable to rebuke David.

12 The LORD sent Nathan[b] to
David.[c] When he came to him,[d]
he said, "There were two men in a certain town, one rich and the other poor.
2 The rich man had a very large number
of sheep and cattle, 3 but the poor man
had nothing except one little ewe lamb
he had bought. He raised it, and it grew
up with him and his children. It shared
his food, drank from his cup and even
slept in his arms. It was like a daughter
to him.
4 "Now a traveler came to the rich
man, but the rich man refrained from
taking one of his own sheep or cattle to
prepare a meal for the traveler who had
come to him. Instead, he took the ewe
lamb that belonged to the poor man and
prepared it for the one who had come to
him."
5 David[e] burned with anger against the
man and said to Nathan, "As surely as
the LORD lives, the man who did this
deserves to die! 6 He must pay for that
lamb four times over,[f] because he did
such a thing and had no pity."
7 Then Nathan said to David, "You are
the man! This is what the LORD, the God
of Israel, says: 'I anointed[g] you[h] king
over Israel, and I delivered you from
the hand of Saul. 8 I gave your master's
house to you,[i] and your master's wives
into your arms. I gave you the house of
Israel and Judah. And if all this had been
too little, I would have given you even
more. 9 Why did you despise[j] the word
of the LORD by doing what is evil in his
eyes? You struck down[k] Uriah the Hittite with the sword and took his wife to
be your own. You killed him with the
sword of the Ammonites. 10 Now, therefore, the sword[l] will never depart from
your house, because you despised me
and took the wife of Uriah the Hittite to
be your own.'
11 "This is what the LORD says: 'Out of
your own household I am going to bring
calamity upon you.[m] Before your very
eyes I will take your wives and give
them to one who is close to you, and he
will lie with your wives in broad daylight. 12 You did it in secret,[n] but I will
do this thing in broad daylight[o] before
all Israel.'"
13 Then David said to Nathan, "I have
sinned[p] against the LORD."
Nathan replied, "The LORD has taken
away[q] your sin.[r] You are not going to
die.[s] 14 But because by doing this you
have made the enemies of the LORD
show utter contempt,[f][t] the son born to
you will die."
15 After Nathan had gone home, the
LORD struck[u] the child that Uriah's wife
had borne to David, and he became ill.
16 David pleaded with God for the child.
He fasted and went into his house and
spent the nights lying[v] on the ground.
17 The elders of his household stood
beside him to get him up from the
ground, but he refused, and he would
not eat any food with them.[w]
18 On the seventh day the child died.
David's servants were afraid to tell him
that the child was dead, for they
thought, "While the child was still living, we spoke to David but he would not

11:27 [a]2Sa 12:9; Ps 51:4-5
12:1 [b]2Sa 7:2; 1Ki 20:35-41 [c]Ps 51 Title [d]2Sa 14:4
12:5 [e]1Ki 20:40
12:6 [f]Ex 22:1; Lk 19:8
12:7 [g]1Sa 16:13 [h]1Ki 20:42
12:8 [i]2Sa 9:7
12:9 [j]Nu 15:31; 1Sa 15:19 [k]2Sa 11:15
12:10 [l]2Sa 13:28; 18:14-15; 1Ki 2:25
12:11 [m]Dt 28:30; 2Sa 16:21-22
12:12 [n]2Sa 11:4-15 [o]2Sa 16:22
12:13 [p]Ge 13:13; Nu 22:34; 1Sa 15:24; 2Sa 24:10 [q]Ps 32:1-5; 51:1,9; 103:12; Zec 3:4,9 [r]Pr 28:13; Mic 7:18-19 [s]Lev 20:10; 24:17
12:14 [t]Isa 52:5; Ro 2:24
12:15 [u]1Sa 25:38
12:16 [v]2Sa 13:31; Ps 5:7
12:17 [w]2Sa 3:35

[f] *14* Masoretic Text; an ancient Hebrew scribal tradition *this you have shown utter contempt for the LORD*

listen to us. How can we tell him the child is dead? He may do something desperate."

19David noticed that his servants were whispering among themselves and he realized the child was dead. "Is the child dead?" he asked.

"Yes," they replied, "he is dead."

20Then David got up from the ground. After he had washed,[a] put on lotions and changed his clothes,[b] he went into the house of the LORD and worshiped. Then he went to his own house, and at his request they served him food, and he ate.

21His servants asked him, "Why are you acting this way? While the child was alive, you fasted and wept,[c] but now that the child is dead, you get up and eat!"

22He answered, "While the child was still alive, I fasted and wept. I thought, 'Who knows?[d] The LORD may be gracious to me and let the child live.'[e] 23But now that he is dead, why should I fast? Can I bring him back again? I will go to him,[f] but he will not return to me."[g]

Solomon is born.

24Then David comforted his wife Bathsheba,[h] and he went to her and lay with her. She gave birth to a son, and they named him Solomon.[i] The LORD loved him; 25and because the LORD loved him, he sent word through Nathan the prophet to name him Jedidiah.[g][j]

David conquers Rabbah.

11:1; 12:29-31pp— 1Ch 20:1-3

26Meanwhile Joab fought against Rabbah[k] of the Ammonites and captured the royal citadel. 27Joab then sent messengers to David, saying, "I have fought against Rabbah and taken its water supply. 28Now muster the rest of the troops and besiege the city and capture it. Otherwise I will take the city, and it will be named after me."

29So David mustered the entire army and went to Rabbah, and attacked and captured it. 30He took the crown[l] from the head of their king[h]—its weight was a talent[i] of gold, and it was set with precious stones—and it was placed on David's head. He took a great quantity of plunder from the city 31and brought out the people who were there, consigning them to labor with saws and with iron picks and axes, and he made them work at brickmaking.[j] He did this to all the Ammonite[m] towns. Then David and his entire army returned to Jerusalem.

Amnon rapes Tamar.

13 In the course of time, Amnon[n] son of David fell in love with Tamar,[o] the beautiful sister of Absalom[p] son of David.

2Amnon became frustrated to the point of illness on account of his sister Tamar, for she was a virgin, and it seemed impossible for him to do anything to her.

3Now Amnon had a friend named Jonadab son of Shimeah,[q] David's brother. Jonadab was a very shrewd man. 4He asked Amnon, "Why do you, the king's son, look so haggard morning after morning? Won't you tell me?"

Amnon said to him, "I'm in love with Tamar, my brother Absalom's sister."

5"Go to bed and pretend to be ill," Jonadab said. "When your father comes to see you, say to him, 'I would like my sister Tamar to come and give me something to eat. Let her prepare the food in my sight so I may watch her and then eat it from her hand.'"

6So Amnon lay down and pretended to be ill. When the king came to see him, Amnon said to him, "I would like my sister Tamar to come and make some special bread in my sight, so I may eat from her hand."

7David sent word to Tamar at the palace: "Go to the house of your brother

12:20 [a]Mt 6:17 [b]Job 1:20
12:21 [c]Jdg 20:26
12:22 [d]Jnh 3:9 [e]Isa 38:1-5
12:23 [f]Ge 37:35 [g]1Sa 31:13; 2Sa 13:39; Job 7:10; 10:21
12:24 [h]1Ki 1:11 [i]1Ki 1:10; 1Ch 22:9; 28:5; Mt 1:6
12:25 [j]Ne 13:26
12:26 [k]Dt 3:11; 1Ch 20:1-3
12:30 [l]1Ch 20:2; Est 8:15; Ps 21:3; 132:18
12:31 [m]1Sa 14:47
13:1 [n]2Sa 3:2 [o]2Sa 14:27; 1Ch 3:9 [p]2Sa 3:3
13:3 [q]1Sa 16:9

g*25 Jedidiah* means *loved by the LORD.* h*30* Or *of Milcom* (that is, Molech) i*30* That is, about 75 pounds (about 34 kilograms) j*31* The meaning of the Hebrew for this clause is uncertain.

Amnon and prepare some food for him."
8So Tamar went to the house of her
brother Amnon, who was lying down.
She took some dough, kneaded it, made
the bread in his sight and baked it.
9Then she took the pan and served him
the bread, but he refused to eat.
"Send everyone out of here,"[a] Amnon
said. So everyone left him. 10Then Amnon said to Tamar, "Bring the food here
into my bedroom so I may eat from your
hand." And Tamar took the bread she
had prepared and brought it to her
brother Amnon in his bedroom. 11But
when she took it to him to eat, he grabbed[b] her and said, "Come to bed with
me, my sister."[c]
12"Don't, my brother!" she said to
him. "Don't force me. Such a thing
should not be done in Israel![d] Don't do
this wicked thing.[e] 13What about me?[f]
Where could I get rid of my disgrace?
And what about you? You would be like
one of the wicked fools in Israel. Please
speak to the king; he will not keep me
from being married to you." 14But he
refused to listen to her, and since he
was stronger than she, he raped her.[g]
15Then Amnon hated her with intense
hatred. In fact, he hated her more than
he had loved her. Amnon said to her,
"Get up and get out!"
16"No!" she said to him. "Sending me
away would be a greater wrong than
what you have already done to me."
But he refused to listen to her. 17He
called his personal servant and said,
"Get this woman out of here and bolt
the door after her." 18So his servant put
her out and bolted the door after her.
She was wearing a richly ornamented[k]
robe,[h] for this was the kind of garment
the virgin daughters of the king wore.
19Tamar put ashes[i] on her head and tore
the ornamented[l] robe she was wearing.
She put her hand on her head and went
away, weeping aloud as she went.
20Her brother Absalom said to her,
"Has that Amnon, your brother, been
with you? Be quiet now, my sister; he
is your brother. Don't take this thing
to heart." And Tamar lived in her

13:9 [a]Ge 45:1
13:11 [b]Ge 39:12 [c]Ge 38:16
13:12 [d]Lev 20:17; Jdg 20:6 [e]Ge 34:7; Jdg 19:23
13:13 [f]Ge 20:12; Lev 18:9; Dt 22:21, 23-24
13:14 [g]Ge 34:2; Dt 22:25; Eze 22:11
13:18 [h]Ge 37:23; Jdg 5:30
13:19 [i]Jos 7:6; 1Sa 4:12; 2Sa 1:2; Est 4:1; Da 9:3
13:21 [j]Ge 34:7
13:22 [k]Ge 31:24 [l]Lev 19:17-18; 1Jn 2:9-11
13:23 [m]1Sa 25:7
13:28 [n]2Sa 3:3 [o]Jdg 19:6,9, 22; Ru 3:7; 1Sa 25:36 [p]2Sa 12:10
13:31 [q]Nu 14:6; 2Sa 1:11; 12:16

brother Absalom's house, a desolate
woman.
21When King David heard all this, he
was furious.[j] 22Absalom never said a
word to Amnon, either good or bad;[k] he
hated[l] Amnon because he had disgraced
his sister Tamar.

Absalom's men kill Amnon.

23Two years later, when Absalom's
sheepshearers[m] were at Baal Hazor near
the border of Ephraim, he invited all
the king's sons to come there. 24Absa-
lom went to the king and said, "Your
servant has had shearers come. Will the
king and his officials please join me?"
25"No, my son," the king replied. "All
of us should not go; we would only be
a burden to you." Although Absalom
urged him, he still refused to go, but
gave him his blessing.
26Then Absalom said, "If not, please
let my brother Amnon come with us."
The king asked him, "Why should he
go with you?" 27But Absalom urged him,
so he sent with him Amnon and the rest
of the king's sons.
28Absalom[n] ordered his men, "Listen!
When Amnon is in high[o] spirits from
drinking wine and I say to you, 'Strike
Amnon down,' then kill him. Don't be
afraid. Have not I given you this order?
Be strong and brave.[p]" 29So Absalom's
men did to Amnon what Absalom had
ordered. Then all the king's sons got up,
mounted their mules and fled.
30While they were on their way, the
report came to David: "Absalom has
struck down all the king's sons; not one
of them is left." 31The king stood up,
tore[q] his clothes and lay down on the
ground; and all his servants stood by
with their clothes torn.
32But Jonadab son of Shimeah, David's
brother, said, "My lord should not think
that they killed all the princes; only
Amnon is dead. This has been Absalom's expressed intention ever since
the day Amnon raped his sister Tamar.

[k] *18* The meaning of the Hebrew for this phrase is uncertain. [l] *19* The meaning of the Hebrew for this word is uncertain.

33My lord the king should not be concerned about the report that all the
king's sons are dead. Only Amnon is
dead."

Absalom flees.

34Meanwhile, Absalom had fled.
Now the man standing watch looked
up and saw many people on the road
west of him, coming down the side of
the hill. The watchman went and told
the king, "I see men in the direction of
Horonaim, on the side of the hill."[m]
35Jonadab said to the king, "See, the
king's sons are here; it has happened
just as your servant said."
36As he finished speaking, the king's
sons came in, wailing loudly. The king,
too, and all his servants wept very bitterly.
37Absalom fled and went to Talmai[a]
son of Ammihud, the king of Geshur.
But King David mourned for his son
every day.
38After Absalom fled and went to Geshur, he stayed there three years. 39And
the spirit of the king[n] longed to go to Absalom,[b] for he was consoled[c] concerning
Amnon's death.

Joab finds a woman to intercede for Absalom.

14 Joab[d] son of Zeruiah knew that
the king's heart longed for Absalom. 2So Joab sent someone to Tekoa[e]
and had a wise woman[f] brought from
there. He said to her, "Pretend you are
in mourning. Dress in mourning clothes,
and don't use any cosmetic lotions.[g] Act
like a woman who has spent many days
grieving for the dead. 3Then go to the
king and speak these words to him."
And Joab[h] put the words in her mouth.
4When the woman from Tekoa went[o]
to the king, she fell with her face to the
ground to pay him honor, and she said,
"Help me, O king!"
5The king asked her, "What is troubling you?"
She said, "I am indeed a widow; my
husband is dead. 6I your servant had
two sons. They got into a fight with each
other in the field, and no one was there
to separate them. One struck the other
and killed him. 7Now the whole clan has
risen up against your servant; they say,
'Hand over the one who struck his
brother down, so that we may put him
to death[i] for the life of his brother whom
he killed; then we will get rid of the
heir[j] as well.' They would put out the
only burning coal I have left,[k] leaving my
husband neither name nor descendant
on the face of the earth."
8The king said to the woman, "Go
home,[l] and I will issue an order in your
behalf."
9But the woman from Tekoa said to
him, "My lord the king, let the blame[m]
rest on me and on my father's family,[n]
and let the king and his throne be without guilt.[o]"
10The king replied, "If anyone says
anything to you, bring him to me, and
he will not bother you again."
11She said, "Then let the king invoke
the LORD his God to prevent the avenger[p] of blood from adding to the destruction, so that my son will not be destroyed."
"As surely as the LORD lives," he said,
"not one hair[q] of your son's head will
fall to the ground.[r]"
12Then the woman said, "Let your
servant speak a word to my lord the
king."
"Speak," he replied.
13The woman said, "Why then have
you devised a thing like this against the
people of God? When the king says
this, does he not convict himself,[s] for
the king has not brought back his banished son?[t] 14Like water[u] spilled on the
ground, which cannot be recovered, so
we must die.[v] But God does not take
away life; instead, he devises ways so
that a banished person[w] may not remain
estranged from him.

13:37 [a]ver 34; 2Sa 3:3; 14:23,32
13:39 [b]2Sa 14:13 [c]2Sa 12:19-23
14:1 [d]2Sa 2:18
14:2 [e]2Ch 11:6; Ne 3:5; Jer 6:1; Am 1:1 [f]2Sa 20:16 [g]Ru 3:3; 2Sa 12:20; Isa 1:6
14:3 [h]ver 19
14:7 [i]Nu 35:19 [j]Mt 21:38 [k]Dt 19:10-13
14:8 [l]1Sa 25:35
14:9 [m]1Sa 25:24 [n]Mt 27:25 [o]1Sa 25:28; 1Ki 2:33
14:11 [p]Nu 35:12,21 [q]Mt 10:30 [r]1Sa 14:45
14:13 [s]2Sa 12:7; 1Ki 20:40 [t]2Sa 13:38-39
14:14 [u]Job 14:11; Ps 58:7; Isa 19:5 [v]Job 10:8; 17:13; 30:23; Ps 22:15; Heb 9:27 [w]Nu 35:15, 25-28; Job 34:15

m*34* Septuagint; Hebrew does not have this sentence.
n*39* Dead Sea Scrolls and some Septuagint manuscripts; Masoretic Text *But* ⌊*the spirit of*⌋ *David the king* o*4* Many Hebrew manuscripts, Septuagint, Vulgate and Syriac; most Hebrew manuscripts *spoke*

15"And now I have come to say this
to my lord the king because the people
have made me afraid. Your servant
thought, 'I will speak to the king; perhaps he will do what his servant asks.
16Perhaps the king will agree to deliver
his servant from the hand of the man
who is trying to cut off both me and my
son from the inheritance[a] God gave us.'
17"And now your servant says, 'May
the word of my lord the king bring me
rest, for my lord the king is like an
angel[b] of God in discerning[c] good and
evil. May the LORD your God be with
you.'"
18Then the king said to the woman,
"Do not keep from me the answer to
what I am going to ask you."
"Let my lord the king speak," the
woman said.
19The king asked, "Isn't the hand of
Joab[d] with you in all this?"
The woman answered, "As surely as
you live, my lord the king, no one can
turn to the right or to the left from anything my lord the king says. Yes, it was
your servant Joab who instructed me to
do this and who put all these words into
the mouth of your servant. 20Your servant Joab did this to change the present
situation. My lord has wisdom[e] like that
of an angel of God—he knows everything that happens in the land.[f]"
21The king said to Joab, "Very well, I
will do it. Go, bring back the young man
Absalom."
22Joab fell with his face to the ground
to pay him honor, and he blessed the
king.[g] Joab said, "Today your servant
knows that he has found favor in your
eyes, my lord the king, because the king
has granted his servant's request."
23Then Joab went to Geshur and
brought Absalom back to Jerusalem.
24But the king said, "He must go to his
own house; he must not see my face."
So Absalom went to his own house and
did not see the face of the king.

David permits Absalom to return.

25In all Israel there was not a man so
highly praised for his handsome appearance as Absalom. From the top of his
head to the sole of his foot there was
no blemish in him. 26Whenever he cut
the hair of his head[h]—he used to cut his
hair from time to time when it became
too heavy for him—he would weigh it,
and its weight was two hundred shekels[p] by the royal standard.
27Three sons[i] and a daughter were
born to Absalom. The daughter's name
was Tamar,[j] and she became a beautiful
woman.
28Absalom lived two years in Jerusalem without seeing the king's face.
29Then Absalom sent for Joab in order
to send him to the king, but Joab refused to come to him. So he sent a second time, but he refused to come.
30Then he said to his servants, "Look,
Joab's field is next to mine, and he has
barley[k] there. Go and set it on fire." So
Absalom's servants set the field on fire.
31Then Joab did go to Absalom's house
and he said to him, "Why have your servants set my field on fire?[l]"
32Absalom said to Joab, "Look, I sent
word to you and said, 'Come here so I
can send you to the king to ask, "Why
have I come from Geshur?[m] It would
be better for me if I were still there!"'
Now then, I want to see the king's face,
and if I am guilty of anything, let him
put me to death."[n]
33So Joab went to the king and told
him this. Then the king summoned Absalom, and he came in and bowed down
with his face to the ground before the
king. And the king kissed[o] Absalom.

Absalom conspires to overthrow David.

15 In the course of time,[p] Absalom
provided himself with a chariot[q]
and horses and with fifty men to run
ahead of him. 2He would get up early
and stand by the side of the road leading to the city gate.[r] Whenever anyone
came with a complaint to be placed
before the king for a decision, Absalom

14:16 [a]Ex 34:9; 1Sa 26:19
14:17 [b]ver 20; 1Sa 29:9; 2Sa 19:27 [c]1Ki 3:9; Da 2:21
14:19 [d]ver 3
14:20 [e]1Ki 3:12,28; Isa 28:6 [f]ver 17; 2Sa 18:13; 19:27
14:22 [g]Ge 47:7
14:26 [h]2Sa 18:9; Eze 44:20
14:27 [i]2Sa 18:18 [j]2Sa 13:1
14:30 [k]Ex 9:31
14:31 [l]Jdg 15:5
14:32 [m]2Sa 3:3 [n]1Sa 20:8
14:33 [o]Ge 33:4; Lk 15:20
15:1 [p]2Sa 12:11 [q]1Sa 8:11; 1Ki 1:5
15:2 [r]Ge 23:10; 2Sa 19:8

p26 That is, about 5 pounds (about 2.3 kilograms)

would call out to him, "What town are you from?" He would answer, "Your servant is from one of the tribes of Israel." 3Then Absalom would say to him, "Look, your claims are valid and proper, but there is no representative of the king to hear you."[a] 4And Absalom would add, "If only I were appointed judge in the land![b] Then everyone who has a complaint or case could come to me and I would see that he gets justice."

5Also, whenever anyone approached him to bow down before him, Absalom would reach out his hand, take hold of him and kiss him. 6Absalom behaved in this way toward all the Israelites who came to the king asking for justice, and so he stole the hearts[c] of the men of Israel.

7At the end of four[q] years, Absalom said to the king, "Let me go to Hebron and fulfill a vow I made to the LORD. 8While your servant was living at Geshur[d] in Aram, I made this vow:[e] 'If the LORD takes me back to Jerusalem, I will worship the LORD in Hebron.[r]'"

9The king said to him, "Go in peace." So he went to Hebron.

10Then Absalom sent secret messengers throughout the tribes of Israel to say, "As soon as you hear the sound of the trumpets,[f] then say, 'Absalom is king in Hebron.'" 11Two hundred men from Jerusalem had accompanied Absalom. They had been invited as guests and went quite innocently, knowing nothing about the matter. 12While Absalom was offering sacrifices, he also sent for Ahithophel[g] the Gilonite, David's counselor,[h] to come from Giloh,[i] his hometown. And so the conspiracy gained strength, and Absalom's following kept on increasing.[j]

David flees Jerusalem.

13A messenger came and told David, "The hearts of the men of Israel are with Absalom."

14Then David said to all his officials who were with him in Jerusalem, "Come! We must flee,[k] or none of us will escape from Absalom.[l] We must leave immediately, or he will move quickly to overtake us and bring ruin upon us and put the city to the sword."

15The king's officials answered him, "Your servants are ready to do whatever our lord the king chooses."

16The king set out, with his entire household following him; but he left ten concubines[m] to take care of the palace. 17So the king set out, with all the people following him, and they halted at a place some distance away. 18All his men marched past him, along with all the Kerethites[n] and Pelethites; and all the six hundred Gittites who had accompanied him from Gath marched before the king.

19The king said to Ittai[o] the Gittite, "Why should you come along with us? Go back and stay with King Absalom. You are a foreigner,[p] an exile from your homeland. 20You came only yesterday. And today shall I make you wander[q] about with us, when I do not know where I am going? Go back, and take your countrymen. May kindness and faithfulness[r] be with you."

21But Ittai replied to the king, "As surely as the LORD lives, and as my lord the king lives, wherever my lord the king may be, whether it means life or death, there will your servant be."[s]

22David said to Ittai, "Go ahead, march on." So Ittai the Gittite marched on with all his men and the families that were with him.

23The whole countryside wept aloud as all the people passed by. The king also crossed the Kidron Valley,[t] and all the people moved on toward the desert.

The ark is returned to Jerusalem.

24Zadok[u] was there, too, and all the Levites who were with him were carrying the ark[v] of the covenant of God. They set down the ark of God, and Abiathar[w] offered sacrifices[s] until all the people had finished leaving the city.

25Then the king said to Zadok, "Take the ark of God back into the city. If I find

15:3 [a]Pr 12:2
15:4 [b]Jdg 9:29
15:6 [c]Ro 16:18
15:8 [d]2Sa 3:3; 13:37-38 [e]Ge 28:20
15:10 [f]1Ki 1:34,39; 2Ki 9:13
15:12 [g]ver 31,34; 2Sa 16:15,23; 1Ch 27:33 [h]Job 19:14; Ps 41:9; 55:13; Jer 9:4 [i]Jos 15:51 [j]Ps 3:1
15:14 [k]2Sa 12:11; 1Ki 2:26; Ps 132:1; Ps 3 Title [l]2Sa 19:9
15:16 [m]2Sa 16:21-22; 20:3
15:18 [n]1Sa 30:14; 2Sa 8:18; 20:7,23; 1Ki 1:38,44; 1Ch 18:17
15:19 [o]2Sa 18:2 [p]Ge 31:15
15:20 [q]1Sa 23:13 [r]2Sa 2:6
15:21 [s]Ru 1:16-17; Pr 17:17
15:23 [t]2Ch 29:16
15:24 [u]2Sa 8:17 [v]Nu 4:15 [w]1Sa 22:20

q *7* Some Septuagint manuscripts, Syriac and Josephus; Hebrew *forty* r *8* Some Septuagint manuscripts; Hebrew does not have *in Hebron.* s *24* Or *Abiathar went up*

favor in the LORD's eyes, he will bring me
back and let me see it and his dwelling
place[a] again. 26But if he says, 'I am not
pleased with you,' then I am ready; let
him do to me whatever seems good to
him.[b]"
27The king also said to Zadok the
priest, "Aren't you a seer?[c] Go back to
the city in peace, with your son Ahimaaz
and Jonathan[d] son of Abiathar. You and
Abiathar take your two sons with you. 28I
will wait at the fords[e] in the desert until
word comes from you to inform me."
29So Zadok and Abiathar took the ark of
God back to Jerusalem and stayed there.
30But David continued up the Mount
of Olives, weeping[f] as he went; his
head[g] was covered and he was barefoot.
All the people with him covered their
heads too and were weeping as they
went up. 31Now David had been told,
"Ahithophel[h] is among the conspirators
with Absalom." So David prayed, "O
LORD, turn Ahithophel's counsel into
foolishness."
32When David arrived at the summit,
where people used to worship God,
Hushai the Arkite[i] was there to meet
him, his robe torn and dust[j] on his head.
33David said to him, "If you go with me,
you will be a burden[k] to me. 34But if you
return to the city and say to Absalom, 'I
will be your servant, O king; I was your
father's servant in the past, but now I
will be your servant,'[l] then you can help
me by frustrating Ahithophel's advice.
35Won't the priests Zadok and Abiathar
be there with you? Tell them anything
you hear in the king's palace.[m] 36Their
two sons, Ahimaaz son of Zadok and
Jonathan[n] son of Abiathar, are there with
them. Send them to me with anything
you hear."
37So David's friend Hushai[o] arrived at
Jerusalem as Absalom[p] was entering the
city.

Ziba deceitfully obtains Mephibosheth's inheritance.

16 When David had gone a short distance beyond the summit, there
was Ziba,[q] the steward of Mephibosheth,
waiting to meet him. He had a string of
donkeys saddled and loaded with two
hundred loaves of bread, a hundred
cakes of raisins, a hundred cakes of figs
and a skin of wine.[r]
2The king asked Ziba, "Why have you
brought these?"
Ziba answered, "The donkeys are for
the king's household to ride on, the
bread and fruit are for the men to eat,
and the wine is to refresh[s] those who
become exhausted in the desert."
3The king then asked, "Where is your
master's grandson?"[t]
Ziba said to him, "He is staying in Jerusalem, because he thinks, 'Today the
house of Israel will give me back my
grandfather's kingdom.'"
4Then the king said to Ziba, "All that
belonged to Mephibosheth is now
yours."
"I humbly bow," Ziba said. "May I find
favor in your eyes, my lord the king."

Shimei curses David.

5As King David approached Bahurim,[u]
a man from the same clan as Saul's family came out from there. His name was
Shimei[v] son of Gera, and he cursed[w] as
he came out. 6He pelted David and all
the king's officials with stones, though
all the troops and the special guard were
on David's right and left. 7As he cursed,
Shimei said, "Get out, get out, you man
of blood, you scoundrel! 8The LORD has
repaid you for all the blood you shed in
the household of Saul, in whose place
you have reigned.[x] The LORD has handed
the kingdom over to your son Absalom.
You have come to ruin because you are a
man of blood!"
9Then Abishai[y] son of Zeruiah said to
the king, "Why should this dead dog
curse my lord the king? Let me go over
and cut off his head."[z]
10But the king said, "What do you and
I have in common, you sons of Zeruiah?[a] If he is cursing because the LORD
said to him, 'Curse David,' who can ask,
'Why do you do this?'"[b]

15:25 [a]Ex 15:13; Ps 43:3; Jer 25:30
15:26 [b]1Sa 3:18; 2Sa 22:20; 1Ki 10:9
15:27 [c]1Sa 9:9 [d]2Sa 17:17
15:28 [e]2Sa 17:16
15:30 [f]2Sa 19:4; Ps 126:6 [g]Est 6:12; Isa 20:2-4
15:31 [h]ver 12; 2Sa 16:23; 17:14,23
15:32 [i]Jos 16:2 [j]2Sa 1:2
15:33 [k]2Sa 19:35
15:34 [l]2Sa 16:19
15:35 [m]2Sa 17:15-16
15:36 [n]ver 27; 2Sa 17:17
15:37 [o]2Sa 16:16-17; 1Ch 27:33 [p]2Sa 16:15
16:1 [q]2Sa 9:1-13 [r]1Sa 25:18
16:2 [s]2Sa 17:27-29
16:3 [t]2Sa 9:9-10; 19:26-27
16:5 [u]2Sa 3:16 [v]2Sa 19:16-23; 1Ki 2:8-9, 36,44 [w]Ex 22:28
16:8 [x]2Sa 21:9
16:9 [y]2Sa 9:8 [z]Ex 22:28; Lk 9:54
16:10 [a]2Sa 19:22 [b]Ro 9:20

11 David then said to Abishai and all his officials, "My son,[a] who is of my own flesh, is trying to take my life. How much more, then, this Benjamite! Leave him alone; let him curse, for the LORD has told him to.[b] 12 It may be that the LORD will see my distress[c] and repay me with good[d] for the cursing I am receiving today.[e]"

13 So David and his men continued along the road while Shimei was going along the hillside opposite him, cursing as he went and throwing stones at him and showering him with dirt. 14 The king and all the people with him arrived at their destination exhausted.[f] And there he refreshed himself.

Ahithophel counsels Absalom.

15 Meanwhile, Absalom[g] and all the men of Israel came to Jerusalem, and Ahithophel[h] was with him. 16 Then Hushai[i] the Arkite, David's friend, went to Absalom and said to him, "Long live the king! Long live the king!"

17 Absalom asked Hushai, "Is this the love you show your friend? Why didn't you go with your friend?"[j]

18 Hushai said to Absalom, "No, the one chosen by the LORD, by these people, and by all the men of Israel—his I will be, and I will remain with him. 19 Furthermore, whom should I serve? Should I not serve the son? Just as I served your father, so I will serve you."[k]

20 Absalom said to Ahithophel, "Give us your advice. What should we do?"

21 Ahithophel answered, "Lie with your father's concubines whom he left to take care of the palace. Then all Israel will hear that you have made yourself a stench in your father's nostrils, and the hands of everyone with you will be strengthened." 22 So they pitched a tent for Absalom on the roof, and he lay with his father's concubines in the sight of all Israel.[l]

23 Now in those days the advice[m] Ahithophel gave was like that of one who inquires of God. That was how both David[n] and Absalom regarded all of Ahithophel's advice.

17 Ahithophel said to Absalom, "I would[t] choose twelve thousand men and set out tonight in pursuit of David. 2 I would[u] attack him while he is weary and weak.[o] I would[u] strike him with terror, and then all the people with him will flee. I would[u] strike down only the king[p] 3 and bring all the people back to you. The death of the man you seek will mean the return of all; all the people will be unharmed." 4 This plan seemed good to Absalom and to all the elders of Israel.

Hushai's advice is accepted over Ahithophel's.

5 But Absalom said, "Summon also Hushai[q] the Arkite, so we can hear what he has to say." 6 When Hushai came to him, Absalom said, "Ahithophel has given this advice. Should we do what he says? If not, give us your opinion."

7 Hushai replied to Absalom, "The advice Ahithophel has given is not good this time. 8 You know your father and his men; they are fighters, and as fierce as a wild bear robbed of her cubs.[r] Besides, your father is an experienced fighter;[s] he will not spend the night with the troops. 9 Even now, he is hidden in a cave or some other place.[t] If he should attack your troops first,[v] whoever hears about it will say, 'There has been a slaughter among the troops who follow Absalom.' 10 Then even the bravest soldier, whose heart is like the heart of a lion,[u] will melt[v] with fear, for all Israel knows that your father is a fighter and that those with him are brave.[w]

11 "So I advise you: Let all Israel, from Dan to Beersheba[x]—as numerous as the sand[y] on the seashore—be gathered to you, with you yourself leading them into battle. 12 Then we will attack him wherever he may be found, and we will fall on him as dew settles on the ground.

16:11 [a] 2Sa 12:11 [b] Ge 45:5
16:12 [c] Ps 4:1; 25:18 [d] Dt 23:5; Ro 8:28 [e] Ps 109:28
16:14 [f] 2Sa 17:2
16:15 [g] 2Sa 15:37 [h] 2Sa 15:12
16:16 [i] 2Sa 15:37
16:17 [j] 2Sa 19:25
16:19 [k] 2Sa 15:34
16:22 [l] 2Sa 12:11-12; 15:16
16:23 [m] 2Sa 17:14, 23 [n] 2Sa 15:12
17:2 [o] 2Sa 16:14 [p] 1Ki 22:31; Zec 13:7
17:5 [q] 2Sa 15:32
17:8 [r] Hos 13:8 [s] 1Sa 16:18
17:9 [t] Jer 41:9
17:10 [u] 1Ch 12:8 [v] Jos 2:9,11; Eze 21:15 [w] 2Sa 23:8; 1Ch 11:11
17:11 [x] Jdg 20:1 [y] Ge 12:2; 22:17; Jos 11:4

t *1* Or *Let me* u *2* Or *will* v *9* Or *When some of the men fall at the first attack*

Neither he nor any of his men will be
left alive. 13If he withdraws into a city,
then all Israel will bring ropes to that
city, and we will drag it down to the
valley[a] until not even a piece of it can
be found."
14Absalom and all the men of Israel
said, "The advice[b] of Hushai the Arkite
is better than that of Ahithophel."[c] For
the LORD had determined to frustrate[d]
the good advice of Ahithophel in order
to bring disaster[e] on Absalom.[f]
15Hushai told Zadok and Abiathar, the
priests, "Ahithophel has advised Absalom and the elders of Israel to do such
and such, but I have advised them to do
so and so. 16Now send a message immediately and tell David, 'Do not spend the
night at the fords in the desert;[g] cross
over without fail, or the king and all
the people with him will be swallowed
up.[h]'"
17Jonathan[i] and Ahimaaz were staying
at En Rogel.[j] A servant girl was to go
and inform them, and they were to go
and tell King David, for they could not
risk being seen entering the city. 18But
a young man saw them and told Absalom. So the two of them left quickly and
went to the house of a man in Bahurim.[k] He had a well in his courtyard, and
they climbed down into it. 19His wife
took a covering and spread it out over
the opening of the well and scattered
grain over it. No one knew anything
about it.[l]
20When Absalom's men came to the
woman[m] at the house, they asked,
"Where are Ahimaaz and Jonathan?"
The woman answered them, "They
crossed over the brook."[w] The men
searched but found no one, so they
returned to Jerusalem.
21After the men had gone, the two
climbed out of the well and went to
inform King David. They said to him,
"Set out and cross the river at once;
Ahithophel has advised such and such
against you." 22So David and all the people with him set out and crossed the Jordan. By daybreak, no one was left who
had not crossed the Jordan.

17:13 [a]Mic 1:6
17:14 [b]2Sa 16:23 [c]2Sa 15:12 [d]2Sa 15:34; Ne 4:15 [e]Ps 9:16 [f]2Ch 10:8
17:16 [g]2Sa 15:28 [h]2Sa 15:35
17:17 [i]2Sa 15:27,36 [j]Jos 15:7; 18:16
17:18 [k]2Sa 3:16; 16:5
17:19 [l]Jos 2:6
17:20 [m]Ex 1:19; Jos 2:3-5; 1Sa 19:12-17
17:23 [n]2Sa 15:12; 16:23 [o]2Ki 20:1; Mt 27:5
17:24 [p]Ge 32:2; 2Sa 2:8
17:25 [q]2Sa 19:13; 20:4,9-12; 1Ki 2:5,32; 1Ch 12:18 [r]1Ch 2:13-17
17:27 [s]1Sa 11:1 [t]Dt 3:11; 2Sa 10:1-2; 12:26,29 [u]2Sa 9:4 [v]2Sa 19:31-39; 1Ki 2:7 [w]2Sa 19:31; Ezr 2:61
17:29 [x]1Ch 12:40 [y]2Sa 16:2; Ro 12:13
18:2 [z]Jdg 7:16; 1Sa 11:11 [a]1Sa 26:6 [b]2Sa 15:19

Ahithophel hangs himself.

23When Ahithophel saw that his advice[n] had not been followed, he saddled
his donkey and set out for his house in
his hometown. He put his house in
order[o] and then hanged himself. So he
died and was buried in his father's tomb.
24David went to Mahanaim,[p] and Absalom crossed the Jordan with all the
men of Israel. 25Absalom had appointed
Amasa[q] over the army in place of Joab.
Amasa was the son of a man named
Jether,[x][r] an Israelite[y] who had married
Abigail,[z] the daughter of Nahash and sister of Zeruiah the mother of Joab. 26The
Israelites and Absalom camped in the
land of Gilead.
27When David came to Mahanaim,
Shobi son of Nahash[s] from Rabbah[t] of
the Ammonites, and Makir[u] son of Ammiel from Lo Debar, and Barzillai[v] the
Gileadite[w] from Rogelim 28brought bed-
ding and bowls and articles of pottery.
They also brought wheat and barley,
flour and roasted grain, beans and lentils,[a] 29honey and curds, sheep, and
cheese from cows' milk for David and
his people to eat.[x] For they said, "The
people have become hungry and tired
and thirsty in the desert.[y]"

Joab slays Absalom, whose head is caught in a tree.

18 David mustered the men who
were with him and appointed
over them commanders of thousands
and commanders of hundreds. 2David
sent the troops out[z]—a third under the
command of Joab, a third under Joab's
brother Abishai[a] son of Zeruiah, and a
third under Ittai[b] the Gittite. The king
told the troops, "I myself will surely
march out with you."
3But the men said, "You must not go

w20 Or *"They passed by the sheep pen toward the water."* x25 Hebrew *Ithra*, a variant of *Jether* y25 Hebrew and some Septuagint manuscripts; other Septuagint manuscripts (see also 1 Chron. 2:17) *Ishmaelite* or *Jezreelite* z25 Hebrew *Abigal*, a variant of *Abigail* a28 Most Septuagint manuscripts and Syriac; Hebrew *lentils, and roasted grain*

out; if we are forced to flee, they won't care about us. Even if half of us die, they won't care; but you are worth ten[a] thousand of us.[b] It would be better now for you to give us support from the city."[b]

4 The king answered, "I will do whatever seems best to you."

So the king stood beside the gate while all the men marched out in units of hundreds and of thousands. 5 The king commanded Joab, Abishai and Ittai, "Be gentle with the young man Absalom for my sake." And all the troops heard the king giving orders concerning Absalom to each of the commanders.

6 The army marched into the field to fight Israel, and the battle took place in the forest[c] of Ephraim. 7 There the army of Israel was defeated by David's men, and the casualties that day were great—twenty thousand men. 8 The battle spread out over the whole countryside, and the forest claimed more lives that day than the sword.

9 Now Absalom happened to meet David's men. He was riding his mule, and as the mule went under the thick branches of a large oak, Absalom's head[d] got caught in the tree. He was left hanging in midair, while the mule he was riding kept on going.

10 When one of the men saw this, he told Joab, "I just saw Absalom hanging in an oak tree."

11 Joab said to the man who had told him this, "What! You saw him? Why didn't you strike[e] him to the ground right there? Then I would have had to give you ten shekels[c] of silver and a warrior's belt.[f]"

12 But the man replied, "Even if a thousand shekels[d] were weighed out into my hands, I would not lift my hand against the king's son. In our hearing the king commanded you and Abishai and Ittai, 'Protect the young man Absalom for my sake.[e]' 13 And if I had put my life in jeopardy[f]—and nothing is hidden from the king[g]—you would have kept your distance from me."

14 Joab[h] said, "I'm not going to wait like this for you." So he took three javelins in his hand and plunged them into Absalom's heart while Absalom was still alive in the oak tree. 15 And ten of Joab's armor-bearers surrounded Absalom, struck him and killed him.[i]

16 Then Joab[j] sounded the trumpet, and the troops stopped pursuing Israel, for Joab halted them. 17 They took Absalom, threw him into a big pit in the forest and piled up[k] a large heap of rocks[l] over him. Meanwhile, all the Israelites fled to their homes.

18 During his lifetime Absalom had taken a pillar and erected it in the King's Valley[m] as a monument[n] to himself, for he thought, "I have no son[o] to carry on the memory of my name." He named the pillar after himself, and it is called Absalom's Monument to this day.

David mourns for his son Absalom.

19 Now Ahimaaz[p] son of Zadok said, "Let me run and take the news to the king that the LORD has delivered him from the hand of his enemies.[q]"

20 "You are not the one to take the news today," Joab told him. "You may take the news another time, but you must not do so today, because the king's son is dead."

21 Then Joab said to a Cushite, "Go, tell the king what you have seen." The Cushite bowed down before Joab and ran off.

22 Ahimaaz son of Zadok again said to Joab, "Come what may, please let me run behind the Cushite."

But Joab replied, "My son, why do you want to go? You don't have any news that will bring you a reward."

23 He said, "Come what may, I want to run."

So Joab said, "Run!" Then Ahimaaz

18:3 *a* 1Sa 18:7 *b* 2Sa 21:17
18:6 *c* Jos 17:18
18:9 *d* 2Sa 14:26
18:11 *e* 2Sa 3:39 *f* 1Sa 18:4
18:13 *g* 2Sa 14:19-20
18:14 *h* 2Sa 2:18; 14:30
18:15 *i* 2Sa 12:10
18:16 *j* 2Sa 2:28; 20:22
18:17 *k* Jos 7:26 *l* Jos 8:29
18:18 *m* Ge 14:17 *n* Ge 50:5; Nu 32:42; 1Sa 15:12 *o* 2Sa 14:27
18:19 *p* 2Sa 15:36 *q* ver 31; Jdg 11:36

b *3* Two Hebrew manuscripts, some Septuagint manuscripts and Vulgate; most Hebrew manuscripts *care; for now there are ten thousand like us*
c *11* That is, about 4 ounces (about 115 grams)
d *12* That is, about 25 pounds (about 11 kilograms)
e *12* A few Hebrew manuscripts, Septuagint, Vulgate and Syriac; most Hebrew manuscripts may be translated *Absalom, whoever you may be.*
f *13* Or *Otherwise, if I had acted treacherously toward him*

ran by way of the plain[g] and outran the
Cushite.
24While David was sitting between
the inner and outer gates, the watchman[a] went up to the roof of the gateway
by the wall. As he looked out, he saw a
man running alone. 25The watchman
called out to the king and reported it.
The king said, "If he is alone, he must
have good news." And the man came
closer and closer.
26Then the watchman saw another
man running, and he called down to the
gatekeeper, "Look, another man running
alone!"
The king said, "He must be bringing
good news,[b] too."
27The watchman said, "It seems to
me that the first one runs like[c] Ahimaaz
son of Zadok."
"He's a good man," the king said. "He
comes with good news."
28Then Ahimaaz called out to the
king, "All is well!" He bowed down before the king with his face to the ground
and said, "Praise be to the LORD your
God! He has delivered up the men who
lifted their hands against my lord the
king."
29The king asked, "Is the young man
Absalom safe?"
Ahimaaz answered, "I saw great confusion just as Joab was about to send the
king's servant and me, your servant, but
I don't know what it was."
30The king said, "Stand aside and wait
here." So he stepped aside and stood
there.
31Then the Cushite arrived and said,
"My lord the king, hear the good news!
The LORD has delivered you today from
all who rose up against you."
32The king asked the Cushite, "Is the
young man Absalom safe?"
The Cushite replied, "May the enemies of my lord the king and all who
rise up to harm you be like that young
man."[d]
33The king was shaken. He went up
to the room over the gateway and wept.
As he went, he said: "O my son Absalom! My son, my son Absalom! If only I
had died[e] instead of you—O Absalom,
my son, my son!"[f]

18:24 [a] 1Sa 14:16; 2Sa 19:8; 2Ki 9:17; Jer 51:12
18:26 [b] 1Ki 1:42; Isa 52:7; 61:1
18:27 [c] 2Ki 9:20
18:32 [d] Jdg 5:31; 1Sa 25:26
18:33 [e] Ex 32:32 [f] Ge 43:14; 2Sa 19:4; Ro 9:3
19:7 [g] Pr 14:28
19:8 [h] 2Sa 15:2
19:9 [i] 2Sa 8:1-14 [j] 2Sa 15:14

The men of Judah make plans to restore David to the throne.

19 Joab was told, "The king is weeping and mourning for Absalom."
2And for the whole army the victory
that day was turned into mourning,
because on that day the troops heard it
said, "The king is grieving for his son."
3The men stole into the city that day as
men steal in who are ashamed when
they flee from battle. 4The king covered
his face and cried aloud, "O my son
Absalom! O Absalom, my son, my son!"
5Then Joab went into the house to the
king and said, "Today you have humiliated all your men, who have just saved
your life and the lives of your sons and
daughters and the lives of your wives
and concubines. 6You love those who
hate you and hate those who love you.
You have made it clear today that the
commanders and their men mean nothing to you. I see that you would be
pleased if Absalom were alive today
and all of us were dead. 7Now go out
and encourage your men. I swear by the
LORD that if you don't go out, not a man
will be left with you by nightfall. This
will be worse for you than all the calamities that have come upon you from your
youth till now."[g]
8So the king got up and took his seat
in the gateway. When the men were
told, "The king is sitting in the gateway,[h]" they all came before him.
Meanwhile, the Israelites had fled to
their homes. 9Throughout the tribes of
Israel, the people were all arguing with
each other, saying, "The king delivered
us from the hand of our enemies; he is
the one who rescued us from the hand
of the Philistines.[i] But now he has fled
the country because of Absalom;[j] 10and
Absalom, whom we anointed to rule over
us, has died in battle. So why do you say
nothing about bringing the king back?"

g *23* That is, the plain of the Jordan

11King David sent this message to
Zadok[a] and Abiathar, the priests: "Ask
the elders of Judah, 'Why should you be
the last to bring the king back to his
palace, since what is being said throughout Israel has reached the king at his
quarters? 12You are my brothers, my
own flesh and blood. So why should you
be the last to bring back the king?'
13And say to Amasa,[b] 'Are you not my
own flesh and blood?[c] May God deal
with me, be it ever so severely,[d] if from
now on you are not the commander of
my army in place of Joab.[e]'"

14He won over the hearts of all the
men of Judah as though they were one
man. They sent word to the king, "Return, you and all your men." 15Then the
king returned and went as far as the
Jordan.

David pardons Shimei.

Now the men of Judah had come to
Gilgal[f] to go out and meet the king and
bring him across the Jordan. 16Shimei[g]
son of Gera, the Benjamite from Bahurim, hurried down with the men of
Judah to meet King David. 17With him
were a thousand Benjamites, along with
Ziba,[h] the steward of Saul's household,[i]
and his fifteen sons and twenty servants.
They rushed to the Jordan, where the
king was. 18They crossed at the ford to
take the king's household over and to
do whatever he wished.

When Shimei son of Gera crossed the
Jordan, he fell prostrate before the king
19and said to him, "May my lord not hold
me guilty. Do not remember how your
servant did wrong on the day my lord
the king left Jerusalem.[j] May the king
put it out of his mind. 20For I your servant know that I have sinned, but today
I have come here as the first of the whole
house of Joseph to come down and meet
my lord the king."

21Then Abishai[k] son of Zeruiah said,
"Shouldn't Shimei be put to death for
this? He cursed[l] the LORD's anointed."[m]

22David replied, "What do you and I
have in common, you sons of Zeruiah?[n]
This day you have become my adversaries! Should anyone be put to death in
Israel today?[o] Do I not know that today
I am king over Israel?" 23So the king
said to Shimei, "You shall not die." And
the king promised him on oath.[p]

Mephibosheth meets the king.

24Mephibosheth,[q] Saul's grandson,
also went down to meet the king. He
had not taken care of his feet or trimmed his mustache or washed his clothes
from the day the king left until the day
he returned safely. 25When he came
from Jerusalem to meet the king, the
king asked him, "Why didn't you go with
me,[r] Mephibosheth?"

26He said, "My lord the king, since I
your servant am lame,[s] I said, 'I will
have my donkey saddled and will ride
on it, so I can go with the king.' But
Ziba[t] my servant betrayed me. 27And he
has slandered your servant to my lord
the king. My lord the king is like an
angel[u] of God; so do whatever pleases
you. 28All my grandfather's descendants
deserved nothing but death[v] from my
lord the king, but you gave your servant
a place among those who eat at your
table.[w] So what right do I have to make
any more appeals to the king?"

29The king said to him, "Why say
more? I order you and Ziba to divide the
fields."

30Mephibosheth said to the king, "Let
him take everything, now that my lord
the king has arrived home safely."

Barzillai encounters the king.

31Barzillai[x] the Gileadite also came
down from Rogelim to cross the Jordan
with the king and to send him on his
way from there. 32Now Barzillai was a
very old man, eighty years of age. He had
provided for the king during his stay in
Mahanaim, for he was a very wealthy[y]
man. 33The king said to Barzillai, "Cross
over with me and stay with me in Jerusalem, and I will provide for you."

34But Barzillai answered the king,

19:11 [a] 2Sa 15:24
19:13 [b] 2Sa 17:25 [c] Ge 29:14 [d] Ru 1:17; 1Ki 19:2; 8:16 [e] 2Sa 2:13
19:15 [f] Jos 5:9; 1Sa 11:15
19:16 [g] 2Sa 16:5-13; 1Ki 2:8
19:17 [h] 2Sa 9:2; 16:1-2 [i] Ge 43:16
19:19 [j] 1Sa 22:15; 2Sa 16:6-8
19:21 [k] 1Sa 26:6 [l] Ex 22:28 [m] 1Sa 12:3; 26:9; 2Sa 16:7-8
19:22 [n] 2Sa 2:18; 16:10 [o] 1Sa 11:13
19:23 [p] 1Ki 2:8,42
19:24 [q] 2Sa 4:4; 9:6-10
19:25 [r] 2Sa 16:17
19:26 [s] Lev 21:18 [t] 2Sa 9:2
19:27 [u] 1Sa 29:9; 2Sa 14:17,20
19:28 [v] 2Sa 16:8; 21:6-9 [w] 2Sa 9:7,13
19:31 [x] 2Sa 17:27-29, 27; 1Ki 2:7
19:32 [y] 1Sa 25:2; 2Sa 17:27

"How many more years will I live, that I should go up to Jerusalem with the king? 35 I am now eighty[a] years old. Can I tell the difference between what is good and what is not? Can your servant taste what he eats and drinks? Can I still hear the voices of men and women singers?[b] Why should your servant be an added[c] burden to my lord the king? 36 Your servant will cross over the Jordan with the king for a short distance, but why should the king reward me in this way? 37 Let your servant return, that I may die in my own town near the tomb of my father[d] and mother. But here is your servant Kimham.[e] Let him cross over with my lord the king. Do for him whatever pleases you."

38 The king said, "Kimham shall cross over with me, and I will do for him whatever pleases you. And anything you desire from me I will do for you."

39 So all the people crossed the Jordan, and then the king crossed over. The king kissed Barzillai and gave him his blessing,[f] and Barzillai returned to his home.

40 When the king crossed over to Gilgal, Kimham crossed with him. All the troops of Judah and half the troops of Israel had taken the king over.

41 Soon all the men of Israel were coming to the king and saying to him, "Why did our brothers, the men of Judah, steal the king away and bring him and his household across the Jordan, together with all his men?"[g]

42 All the men of Judah answered the men of Israel, "We did this because the king is closely related to us. Why are you angry about it? Have we eaten any of the king's provisions? Have we taken anything for ourselves?"

43 Then the men of Israel[h] answered the men of Judah, "We have ten shares in the king; and besides, we have a greater claim on David than you have. So why do you treat us with contempt? Were we not the first to speak of bringing back our king?"

But the men of Judah responded even more harshly than the men of Israel.

Sheba leads a rebellion.

20 Now a troublemaker named Sheba son of Bicri, a Benjamite, happened to be there. He sounded the trumpet and shouted,

> "We have no share[i] in David,[j]
> no part in Jesse's son![k]
> Every man to his tent, O Israel!"

2 So all the men of Israel deserted David to follow Sheba son of Bicri. But the men of Judah stayed by their king all the way from the Jordan to Jerusalem.

3 When David returned to his palace in Jerusalem, he took the ten concubines[l] he had left to take care of the palace and put them in a house under guard. He provided for them, but did not lie with them. They were kept in confinement till the day of their death, living as widows.

Joab murders Amasa.

4 Then the king said to Amasa,[m] "Summon the men of Judah to come to me within three days, and be here yourself." 5 But when Amasa went to summon Judah, he took longer than the time the king had set for him.

6 David said to Abishai,[n] "Now Sheba son of Bicri will do us more harm than Absalom did. Take your master's men and pursue him, or he will find fortified cities and escape from us." 7 So Joab's men and the Kerethites[o] and Pelethites and all the mighty warriors went out under the command of Abishai. They marched out from Jerusalem to pursue Sheba son of Bicri.

8 While they were at the great rock in Gibeon,[p] Amasa came to meet them. Joab[q] was wearing his military tunic, and strapped over it at his waist was a belt with a dagger in its sheath. As he stepped forward, it dropped out of its sheath.

9 Joab said to Amasa, "How are you, my brother?" Then Joab took Amasa by the beard with his right hand to kiss him. 10 Amasa was not on his guard against the dagger[r] in Joab[s]'s hand, and

19:35 [a]Ps 90:10 [b]2Ch 35:25; Ezr 2:65; Ecc 2:8; 12:1; Isa 5:11-12 [c]2Sa 15:33

19:37 [d]Ge 49:29; 1Ki 2:7 [e]ver 40; Jer 41:17

19:39 [f]Ge 31:55; Ge 47:7

19:41 [g]Jdg 8:1; 12:1

19:43 [h]2Sa 5:1

20:1 [i]Ge 31:14 [j]Ge 29:14; 1Ki 12:16 [k]1Sa 22:7-8; 2Ch 10:16

20:3 [l]2Sa 15:16; 16:21-22

20:4 [m]2Sa 17:25; 19:13

20:6 [n]2Sa 21:17

20:7 [o]1Sa 30:14; 2Sa 8:18; 15:18; 1Ki 1:38

20:8 [p]Jos 9:3 [q]2Sa 2:18

20:10 [r]Jdg 3:21; 2Sa 2:23; 3:27 [s]1Ki 2:5

Joab plunged it into his belly, and his
intestines spilled out on the ground.
Without being stabbed again, Amasa
died. Then Joab and his brother Abishai
pursued Sheba son of Bicri.
11One of Joab's men stood beside
Amasa and said, "Whoever favors Joab,
and whoever is for David, let him follow
Joab!" 12Amasa lay wallowing in his
blood in the middle of the road, and the
man saw that all the troops came to a
halt[a] there. When he realized that everyone who came up to Amasa stopped, he
dragged him from the road into a field
and threw a garment over him. 13After
Amasa had been removed from the road,
all the men went on with Joab to pursue
Sheba son of Bicri.

Sheba is beheaded.

14Sheba passed through all the tribes
of Israel to Abel Beth Maacah[h] and
through the entire region of the Be-
rites,[b] who gathered together and followed him. 15All the troops with Joab
came and besieged Sheba in Abel Beth
Maacah.[c] They built a siege ramp[d] up
to the city, and it stood against the outer
fortifications. While they were battering
the wall to bring it down, 16a wise woman[e] called from the city, "Listen! Listen!
Tell Joab to come here so I can speak to
him." 17He went toward her, and she
asked, "Are you Joab?"
"I am," he answered.
She said, "Listen to what your servant
has to say."
"I'm listening," he said.
18She continued, "Long ago they used
to say, 'Get your answer at Abel,' and
that settled it. 19We are the peaceful[f]
and faithful in Israel. You are trying to
destroy a city that is a mother in Israel.
Why do you want to swallow up the
LORD's inheritance?"[g]
20"Far be it from me!" Joab replied,
"Far be it from me to swallow up or
destroy! 21That is not the case. A man
named Sheba son of Bicri, from the hill
country of Ephraim, has lifted up his
hand against the king, against David.
Hand over this one man, and I'll withdraw from the city."
The woman said to Joab, "His head[h]
will be thrown to you from the wall."
22Then the woman went to all the
people with her wise advice,[i] and they
cut off the head of Sheba son of Bicri
and threw it to Joab. So he sounded the
trumpet, and his men dispersed from the
city, each returning to his home. And
Joab went back to the king in Jerusalem.

David's royal officials.

23Joab[j] was over Israel's entire army;
Benaiah son of Jehoiada was over the
Kerethites and Pelethites; 24Adoniram[i][k]
was in charge of forced labor; Jehoshaphat[l] son of Ahilud was recorder;
25Sheva was secretary; Zadok[m] and Abiathar were priests; 26and Ira the Jairite
was David's priest.

Saul's sons are killed.

21 During the reign of David, there
was a famine[n] for three successive years; so David sought[o] the face of
the LORD. The LORD said, "It is on account of Saul and his blood-stained
house; it is because he put the Gibeonites to death."
2The king summoned the Gibeonites[p]
and spoke to them. (Now the Gibeonites were not a part of Israel but were
survivors of the Amorites; the Israelites
had sworn to ⌊spare⌋ them, but Saul in
his zeal for Israel and Judah had tried to
annihilate them.) 3David asked the Gibeonites, "What shall I do for you? How
shall I make amends so that you will
bless the LORD's inheritance?"[q]
4The Gibeonites answered him, "We
have no right to demand silver or gold
from Saul or his family, nor do we have
the right to put anyone in Israel to
death."[r]
"What do you want me to do for you?"
David asked.

20:12 [a]2Sa 2:23
20:14 [b]Nu 21:16
20:15 [c]1Ki 15:20; 2Ki 15:29 [d]2Ki 19:32; Isa 37:33; Jer 6:6; 32:24
20:16 [e]2Sa 14:2
20:19 [f]Dt 2:26 [g]1Sa 26:19; 2Sa 21:3
20:21 [h]2Sa 4:8
20:22 [i]Ecc 9:13
20:23 [j]2Sa 2:28; 8:16-18; 24:2
20:24 [k]1Ki 4:6; 5:14; 12:18; 2Ch 10:18 [l]2Sa 8:16; 1Ki 4:3
20:25 [m]1Sa 2:35; 2Sa 8:17
21:1 [n]Ge 12:10; Dt 32:24 [o]Ex 32:11
21:2 [p]Jos 9:15
21:3 [q]1Sa 26:19; 2Sa 20:19
21:4 [r]Nu 35:33-34

h *14* Or *Abel, even Beth Maacah*; also in verse 15
i *24* Some Septuagint manuscripts (see also 1 Kings 4:6 and 5:14); Hebrew *Adoram*

5They answered the king, "As for the
man who destroyed us and plotted
against us so that we have been decimat-
ed and have no place anywhere in Israel,
6let seven of his male descendants be
given to us to be killed and exposed[a]
before the LORD at Gibeah of Saul—the
LORD's chosen[b] one."
So the king said, "I will give them to
you."
7The king spared Mephibosheth[c] son
of Jonathan, the son of Saul, because of
the oath[d] before the LORD between David
and Jonathan son of Saul. **8**But the king
took Armoni and Mephibosheth, the two
sons of Aiah's daughter Rizpah,[e] whom
she had borne to Saul, together with the
five sons of Saul's daughter Merab,[j]
whom she had borne to Adriel son of
Barzillai the Meholathite.[f] **9**He handed
them over to the Gibeonites, who killed
and exposed them on a hill before the
LORD. All seven of them fell together;
they were put to death[g] during the first
days of the harvest, just as the barley
harvest was beginning.[h]

David buries the bones of Saul and Jonathan.

10Rizpah daughter of Aiah took sackcloth and spread it out for herself on a
rock. From the beginning of the harvest
till the rain poured down from the heavens on the bodies, she did not let the
birds of the air touch them by day or the
wild animals by night.[i] **11**When David
was told what Aiah's daughter Rizpah,
Saul's concubine, had done, **12**he went
and took the bones of Saul[j] and his son
Jonathan from the citizens of Jabesh
Gilead. (They had taken them secretly
from the public square at Beth Shan,[k]
where the Philistines had hung[l] them
after they struck Saul down on Gilboa.)
13David brought the bones of Saul and
his son Jonathan from there, and the
bones of those who had been killed and
exposed were gathered up.
14They buried the bones of Saul and
his son Jonathan in the tomb of Saul's
father Kish, at Zela[m] in Benjamin, and
did everything the king commanded.
After that,[n] God answered prayer[o] in
behalf of the land.

Battles between Israel and the Philistines.

21:15-22pp— 1Ch 20:4-8

15Once again there was a battle between the Philistines[p] and Israel. David
went down with his men to fight against
the Philistines, and he became exhausted. **16**And Ishbi-Benob, one of the descendants of Rapha, whose bronze
spearhead weighed three hundred shekels[k] and who was armed with a new
⌞sword⌟, said he would kill David. **17**But
Abishai[q] son of Zeruiah came to David's
rescue; he struck the Philistine down
and killed him. Then David's men swore
to him, saying, "Never again will you go
out with us to battle, so that the lamp[r]
of Israel will not be extinguished.[s]"
18In the course of time, there was another battle with the Philistines, at Gob.
At that time Sibbecai[t] the Hushathite
killed Saph, one of the descendants of
Rapha.
19In another battle with the Philistines
at Gob, Elhanan son of Jaare-Oregim[l] the
Bethlehemite killed Goliath[m] the Gittite,
who had a spear with a shaft like a
weaver's rod.[u]
20In still another battle, which took
place at Gath, there was a huge man
with six fingers on each hand and six
toes on each foot—twenty-four in all.
He also was descended from Rapha.
21When he taunted Israel, Jonathan son
of Shimeah,[v] David's brother, killed him.
22These four were descendants of
Rapha in Gath, and they fell at the hands
of David and his men.

21:6 [a]Nu 25:4 [b]1Sa 10:24
21:7 [c]2Sa 4:4 [d]1Sa 18:3; 20:8,15; 2Sa 9:7
21:8 [e]2Sa 3:7 [f]1Sa 18:19
21:9 [g]2Sa 16:8 [h]Ru 1:22
21:10 [i]ver 8; Dt 21:23; 1Sa 17:44
21:12 [j]1Sa 31:11-13 [k]Jos 17:11 [l]1Sa 31:10
21:14 [m]Jos 18:28 [n]Jos 7:26 [o]2Sa 24:25
21:15 [p]2Sa 5:25
21:17 [q]2Sa 20:6 [r]1Ki 11:36 [s]2Sa 18:3
21:18 [t]1Ch 11:29; 20:4; 27:11
21:19 [u]1Sa 17:7
21:21 [v]1Sa 16:9

[j]*8* Two Hebrew manuscripts, some Septuagint manuscripts and Syriac (see also 1 Samuel 18:19); most Hebrew and Septuagint manuscripts *Michal*
[k]*16* That is, about 7 1/2 pounds (about 3.5 kilograms)
[l]*19* Or *son of Jair the weaver* [m]*19* Hebrew and Septuagint; 1 Chron. 20:5 *son of Jair killed Lahmi the brother of Goliath*

David's song of praise to God.

22:1-51pp— Ps 18:1-50

22 David sang[a] to the LORD the words of this song when the LORD delivered him from the hand of all his enemies and from the hand of Saul.
[2]He said:

"The LORD is my rock,[b] my fortress[c]
and my deliverer;[d]
[3] my God is my rock, in whom I take refuge,[e]
my shield[f] and the horn[n][g] of my salvation.
He is my stronghold,[h] my refuge and my savior—
from violent men you save me.
[4]I call to the LORD, who is worthy[i] of praise,
and I am saved from my enemies.

[5]"The waves[j] of death swirled about me;
the torrents of destruction overwhelmed me.
[6]The cords of the grave[o][k] coiled around me;
the snares of death confronted me.
[7]In my distress[l] I called[m] to the LORD;
I called out to my God.
From his temple he heard my voice;
my cry came to his ears.

[8]"The earth[n] trembled and quaked,[o]
the foundations[p] of the heavens[p] shook;
they trembled because he was angry.
[9]Smoke rose from his nostrils;
consuming fire[q] came from his mouth,
burning coals blazed out of it.
[10]He parted the heavens and came down;
dark clouds[r] were under his feet.
[11]He mounted the cherubim and flew;
he soared[q] on the wings of the wind.[s]
[12]He made darkness his canopy around him—
the dark[r] rain clouds of the sky.
[13]Out of the brightness of his presence
bolts of lightning[t] blazed forth.
[14]The LORD thundered[u] from heaven;
the voice of the Most High resounded.
[15]He shot arrows[v] and scattered ⌊the enemies⌋,
bolts of lightning and routed them.
[16]The valleys of the sea were exposed
and the foundations of the earth laid bare
at the rebuke[w] of the LORD,
at the blast of breath from his nostrils.

[17]"He reached down from on high[x]
and took hold of me;
he drew[y] me out of deep waters.
[18]He rescued me from my powerful enemy,
from my foes, who were too strong for me.
[19]They confronted me in the day of my disaster,
but the LORD was my support.[z]
[20]He brought me out into a spacious[a] place;
he rescued[b] me because he delighted[c] in me.[d]

[21]"The LORD has dealt with me
according to my righteousness;[e]
according to the cleanness of my
hands[f] he has rewarded me.
[22]For I have kept[g] the ways of the LORD;
I have not done evil by turning from my God.
[23]All his laws are before me;[h]
I have not turned[i] away from his decrees.
[24]I have been blameless[j] before him
and have kept myself from sin.
[25]The LORD has rewarded me
according to my righteousness,[k]

22:1 [a]Ex 15:1; Jdg 5:1; Ps 18:2-50
22:2 [b]Dt 32:4; Ps 71:3 [c]Ps 31:3; 91:2 [d]Ps 144:2
22:3 [e]Dt 32:37; Jer 16:19 [f]Ge 15:1 [g]Lk 1:69 [h]Ps 9:9
22:4 [i]Ps 48:1; 96:4
22:5 [j]Ps 69:14-15; 93:4; Jnh 2:3
22:6 [k]Ps 116:3
22:7 [l]Ps 120:1 [m]Ps 34:6,15; 116:4
22:8 [n]Jdg 5:4; Ps 97:4 [o]Ps 77:18 [p]Job 26:11
22:9 [q]Ps 97:3; Heb 12:29
22:10 [r]1Ki 8:12; Na 1:3
22:11 [s]Ps 104:3
22:13 [t]ver 9
22:14 [u]1Sa 2:10
22:15 [v]Dt 32:23
22:16 [w]Na 1:4
22:17 [x]Ps 144:7 [y]Ex 2:10
22:19 [z]Ps 23:4
22:20 [a]Ps 31:8 [b]Ps 118:5 [c]Ps 22:8 [d]2Sa 15:26
22:21 [e]1Sa 26:23 [f]Ps 24:4
22:22 [g]Ge 18:19; Ps 128:1; Pr 8:32
22:23 [h]Dt 6:4-9; Ps 119:30-32 [i]Ps 119:102
22:24 [j]Ge 6:9; Eph 1:4 **22:25** [k]ver 21

[n]3 *Horn* here symbolizes strength. [o]6 Hebrew *Sheol* [p]8 Hebrew; Vulgate and Syriac (see also Psalm 18:7) *mountains* [q]11 Many Hebrew manuscripts (see also Psalm 18:10); most Hebrew manuscripts *appeared* [r]12 Septuagint and Vulgate (see also Psalm 18:11); Hebrew *massed*

according to my cleanness[s] in his
sight.

26"To the faithful you show yourself
faithful,
to the blameless you show yourself
blameless,
27to the pure[a] you show yourself pure,
but to the crooked you show
yourself shrewd.[b]
28You save the humble,[c]
but your eyes are on the haughty
to bring them low.[d]
29You are my lamp,[e] O LORD;
the LORD turns my darkness into
light.
30With your help I can advance against
a troop[t];
with my God I can scale a wall.

31"As for God, his way is perfect;[f]
the word of the LORD is flawless.[g]
He is a shield
for all who take refuge in him.
32For who is God besides the LORD?
And who is the Rock[h] except our
God?
33It is God who arms me with strength[u]
and makes my way perfect.
34He makes my feet like the feet of a
deer;[i]
he enables me to stand on the
heights.[j]
35He trains my hands[k] for battle;
my arms can bend a bow of bronze.
36You give me your shield[l] of victory;
you stoop down to make me great.
37You broaden the path[m] beneath me,
so that my ankles do not turn.

38"I pursued my enemies and crushed
them;
I did not turn back till they were
destroyed.
39I crushed[n] them completely, and
they could not rise;
they fell beneath my feet.
40You armed me with strength for battle;
you made my adversaries bow at
my feet.[o]
41You made my enemies turn their
backs[p] in flight,
and I destroyed my foes.

22:27 [a]Mt 5:8 [b]Lev 26:23-24
22:28 [c]Ex 3:8; Ps 72:12-13 [d]Isa 2:12,17; 5:15
22:29 [e]Ps 27:1
22:31 [f]Dt 32:4; Mt 5:48 [g]Ps 12:6; 119:140; Pr 30:5-6
22:32 [h]1Sa 2:2
22:34 [i]Hab 3:19 [j]Dt 32:13
22:35 [k]Ps 144:1
22:36 [l]Eph 6:16
22:37 [m]Pr 4:11
22:39 [n]Mal 4:3
22:40 [o]Ps 44:5
22:41 [p]Ex 23:27
22:42 [q]Isa 1:15 [r]Ps 50:22
22:43 [s]Mic 7:10 [t]Isa 10:6; Mic 7:10
22:44 [u]2Sa 3:1 [v]Dt 28:13 [w]2Sa 8:1-14; Isa 55:3-5
22:45 [x]Ps 66:3; 81:15
22:46 [y]Mic 7:17
22:47 [z]Ps 89:26
22:48 [a]Ps 94:1; 144:2; 1Sa 25:39
22:49 [b]Ps 140:1,4
22:50 [c]Ro 15:9*
22:51 [d]Ps 144:9-10 [e]Ps 89:20 [f]2Sa 7:13 [g]Ps 89:24,29
23:1 [h]2Sa 7:8-9; Ps 78:70-71; 89:27

42They cried for help,[q] but there was
no one to save them—[r]
to the LORD, but he did not answer.
43I beat them as fine as the dust of the
earth;
I pounded and trampled[s] them like
mud[t] in the streets.

44"You have delivered[u] me from the
attacks of my people;
you have preserved[v] me as the
head of nations.
People[w] I did not know are subject
to me,
45 and foreigners come cringing[x] to me;
as soon as they hear me, they obey
me.
46They all lose heart;
they come trembling[v][y] from their
strongholds.

47"The LORD lives! Praise be to my Rock!
Exalted be God, the Rock, my
Savior![z]
48He is the God who avenges me,[a]
who puts the nations under me,
49 who sets me free from my enemies.[b]
You exalted me above my foes;
from violent men you rescued me.
50Therefore I will praise you, O LORD,
among the nations;
I will sing praises to your name.[c]
51He gives his king great victories;[d]
he shows unfailing kindness to his
anointed,[e]
to David[f] and his descendants
forever."[g]

David's last words.

23 These are the last words of
David:

"The oracle of David son of Jesse,
the oracle of the man exalted[h] by
the Most High,

s *25* Hebrew; Septuagint and Vulgate (see also Psalm 18:24) *to the cleanness of my hands* t *30* Or *can run through a barricade* u *33* Dead Sea Scrolls, some Septuagint manuscripts, Vulgate and Syriac (see also Psalm 18:32); Masoretic Text *who is my strong refuge* v *46* Some Septuagint manuscripts and Vulgate (see also Psalm 18:45); Masoretic Text *they arm themselves.*

the man anointed[a] by the God of
Jacob,
Israel's singer of songs[w]:

2"The Spirit[b] of the LORD spoke
through me;
his word was on my tongue.
3The God of Israel spoke,
the Rock[c] of Israel said to me:
'When one rules over men in
righteousness,[d]
when he rules in the fear of God,[e]
4he is like the light of morning at
sunrise[f]
on a cloudless morning,
like the brightness after rain
that brings the grass from the
earth.'

5"Is not my house right with God?
Has he not made with me an
everlasting covenant,[g]
arranged and secured in every
part?
Will he not bring to fruition my
salvation
and grant me my every desire?
6But evil men are all to be cast aside
like thorns,[h]
which are not gathered with the
hand.
7Whoever touches thorns
uses a tool of iron or the shaft of a
spear;
they are burned up where they lie."

David's mighty men.

23:8-39pp— 1Ch 11:10-41

8These are the names of David's
mighty men:
Josheb-Basshebeth,[x] a Tahkemonite,[y]
was chief of the Three; he raised his
spear against eight hundred men, whom
he killed[z] in one encounter.
9Next to him was Eleazar son of
Dodai[i] the Ahohite.[j] As one of the three
mighty men, he was with David when
they taunted the Philistines gathered ⌊at
Pas Dammim⌋[a] for battle. Then the men
of Israel retreated, 10but he stood his
ground and struck down the Philistines
till his hand grew tired and froze to the
sword. The LORD brought about a great
victory that day. The troops returned to
Eleazar, but only to strip the dead.
11Next to him was Shammah son of
Agee the Hararite. When the Philistines
banded together at a place where there
was a field full of lentils, Israel's troops
fled from them. 12But Shammah took
his stand in the middle of the field. He
defended it and struck the Philistines
down, and the LORD brought about a
great victory.
13During harvest time, three of the
thirty chief men came down to David at
the cave of Adullam,[k] while a band of
Philistines was encamped in the Valley
of Rephaim.[l] 14At that time David was
in the stronghold,[m] and the Philistine
garrison was at Bethlehem.[n] 15David
longed for water and said, "Oh, that
someone would get me a drink of water
from the well near the gate of Bethlehem!" 16So the three mighty men broke
through the Philistine lines, drew water
from the well near the gate of Bethlehem and carried it back to David. But he
refused to drink it; instead, he poured[o]
it out before the LORD. 17"Far be it from
me, O LORD, to do this!" he said. "Is it
not the blood[p] of men who went at the
risk of their lives?" And David would
not drink it.
Such were the exploits of the three
mighty men.
18Abishai[q] the brother of Joab son of
Zeruiah was chief of the Three.[b] He
raised his spear against three hundred
men, whom he killed, and so he became
as famous as the Three. 19Was he not
held in greater honor than the Three?
He became their commander, even
though he was not included among
them.

23:1 [a]1Sa 16:12-13; Ps 89:20
23:2 [b]Mt 22:43; 2Pe 1:21
23:3 [c]Dt 32:4; 2Sa 22:2,32 [d]Ps 72:3 [e]2Ch 19:7,9; Isa 11:1-5
23:4 [f]Jdg 5:31; Ps 89:36
23:5 [g]Ps 89:29; Isa 55:3
23:6 [h]Mt 13:40-41
23:9 [i]1Ch 27:4 [j]1Ch 8:4
23:13 [k]1Sa 22:1 [l]2Sa 5:18
23:14 [m]1Sa 22:4-5 [n]Ru 1:19
23:16 [o]Ge 35:14
23:17 [p]Lev 17:10-12
23:18 [q]2Sa 10:10, 14; 1Ch 11:20

w*1* Or *Israel's beloved singer* x*8* Hebrew; some Septuagint manuscripts suggest *Ish-Bosheth,* that is, *Esh-Baal* (see also 1Chron. 11:11 *Jashobeam*). y*8* Probably a variant of *Hacmonite* (see 1Chron. 11:11) z*8* Some Septuagint manuscripts (see also 1Chron. 11:11); Hebrew and other Septuagint manuscripts *Three; it was Adino the Eznite who killed eight hundred men* a*9* See 1Chron. 11:13; Hebrew *gathered there.* b*18* Most Hebrew manuscripts (see also 1Chron. 11:20); two Hebrew manuscripts and Syriac *Thirty*

[20]Benaiah[a] son of Jehoiada was a
valiant fighter from Kabzeel,[b] who performed great exploits. He struck down
two of Moab's best men. He also went
down into a pit on a snowy day and
killed a lion. [21]And he struck down a
huge Egyptian. Although the Egyptian
had a spear in his hand, Benaiah went
against him with a club. He snatched
the spear from the Egyptian's hand and
killed him with his own spear. [22]Such
were the exploits of Benaiah son of
Jehoiada; he too was as famous as the
three mighty men. [23]He was held in
greater honor than any of the Thirty,
but he was not included among the
Three. And David put him in charge of
his bodyguard.

[24]Among the Thirty were:
Asahel[c] the brother of Joab,
Elhanan son of Dodo from Bethlehem,
[25]Shammah the Harodite,[d]
Elika the Harodite,
[26]Helez[e] the Paltite,
Ira son of Ikkesh from Tekoa,
[27]Abiezer from Anathoth,[f]
Mebunnai[c] the Hushathite,
[28]Zalmon the Ahohite,
Maharai[g] the Netophathite,[h]
[29]Heled[d] son of Baanah the Netophathite,
Ithai son of Ribai from Gibeah[i]
in Benjamin,
[30]Benaiah the Pirathonite,[j]
Hiddai[e] from the ravines of
Gaash,[k]
[31]Abi-Albon the Arbathite,
Azmaveth the Barhumite,[l]
[32]Eliahba the Shaalbonite,
the sons of Jashen,
Jonathan [33]son of[f] Shammah the
Hararite,
Ahiam son of Sharar[g] the Hararite,
[34]Eliphelet son of Ahasbai the Maacathite,
Eliam[m] son of Ahithophel[n] the
Gilonite,
[35]Hezro the Carmelite,[o]
Paarai the Arbite,

23:20 [a]2Sa 8:18; 20:23 [b]Jos 15:21
23:24 [c]2Sa 2:18
23:25 [d]Jdg 7:1; 1Ch 11:27
23:26 [e]1Ch 27:10
23:27 [f]Jos 21:18
23:28 [g]1Ch 27:13 [h]2Ki 25:23; Ne 7:26
23:29 [i]Jos 15:57
23:30 [j]Jdg 12:13 [k]Jos 24:30
23:31 [l]2Sa 3:16
23:34 [m]2Sa 11:3 [n]2Sa 15:12
23:35 [o]Jos 12:22
23:36 [p]1Sa 14:47
23:38 [q]2Sa 20:26; 1Ch 2:53
23:39 [r]2Sa 11:3
24:1 [s]Jos 9:15 [t]1Ch 27:23
24:2 [u]2Sa 20:23 [v]Jdg 20:1; 2Sa 3:10
24:3 [w]Dt 1:11
24:5 [x]Dt 2:36; Jos 13:9 [y]Nu 21:32
24:6 [z]Ge 10:19; Jos 19:28; Jdg 1:31
24:7 [a]Jos 19:29

[36]Igal son of Nathan from Zobah,[p]
the son of Hagri,[h]
[37]Zelek the Ammonite,
Naharai the Beerothite, the armor-
bearer of Joab son of Zeruiah,
[38]Ira the Ithrite,[q]
Gareb the Ithrite
[39]and Uriah[r] the Hittite.
There were thirty-seven in all.

David sins by taking a census of the fighting men.

24:1-17pp— 1Ch 21:1-17

24 Again[s] the anger of the LORD
burned against Israel, and he
incited David against them, saying, "Go
and take a census of[t] Israel and Judah."
[2]So the king said to Joab[u] and the army
commanders[i] with him, "Go throughout
the tribes of Israel from Dan to Beersheba[v] and enroll the fighting men, so that I
may know how many there are."
[3]But Joab replied to the king, "May
the LORD your God multiply the troops a
hundred times over,[w] and may the eyes
of my lord the king see it. But why does
my lord the king want to do such a
thing?"
[4]The king's word, however, overruled
Joab and the army commanders; so they
left the presence of the king to enroll
the fighting men of Israel.
[5]After crossing the Jordan, they
camped near Aroer,[x] south of the town
in the gorge, and then went through
Gad and on to Jazer.[y] [6]They went to
Gilead and the region of Tahtim Hodshi,
and on to Dan Jaan and around toward
Sidon.[z] [7]Then they went toward the fortress of Tyre[a] and all the towns of the
Hivites and Canaanites. Finally, they

[c]*27* Hebrew; some Septuagint manuscripts (see also 1 Chron. 11:29) *Sibbecai* [d]*29* Some Hebrew manuscripts and Vulgate (see also 1 Chron. 11:30); most Hebrew manuscripts *Heleb* [e]*30* Hebrew; some Septuagint manuscripts (see also 1 Chron. 11:32) *Hurai* [f]*33* Some Septuagint manuscripts (see also 1 Chron. 11:34); Hebrew does not have *son of.* [g]*33* Hebrew; some Septuagint manuscripts (see also 1 Chron. 11:35) *Sacar* [h]*36* Some Septuagint manuscripts (see also 1 Chron. 11:38); Hebrew *Haggadi* [i]*2* Septuagint (see also verse 4 and 1 Chron. 21:2); Hebrew *Joab the army commander*

went on to Beersheba[a] in the Negev[b] of Judah.

8After they had gone through the entire land, they came back to Jerusalem at the end of nine months and twenty days.

9Joab reported the number of the fighting men to the king: In Israel there were eight hundred thousand able-bodied men who could handle a sword, and in Judah five hundred thousand.[c]

David chooses a plague as his punishment.

10David was conscience-stricken[d] after he had counted the fighting men, and he said to the LORD, "I have sinned[e] greatly in what I have done. Now, O LORD, I beg you, take away the guilt of your servant. I have done a very foolish thing.[f]"

11Before David got up the next morning, the word of the LORD had come to Gad[g] the prophet, David's seer:[h] 12"Go and tell David, 'This is what the LORD says: I am giving you three options. Choose one of them for me to carry out against you.'"

13So Gad went to David and said to him, "Shall there come upon you three[j] years of famine[i] in your land? Or three months of fleeing from your enemies while they pursue you? Or three days of plague[j] in your land? Now then, think it over and decide how I should answer the one who sent me."

14David said to Gad, "I am in deep distress. Let us fall into the hands of the LORD, for his mercy[k] is great; but do not let me fall into the hands of men."

15So the LORD sent a plague on Israel from that morning until the end of the time designated, and seventy thousand of the people from Dan to Beersheba died.[l] 16When the angel stretched out his hand to destroy Jerusalem, the LORD was grieved[m] because of the calamity and said to the angel who was afflicting the people, "Enough! Withdraw your hand." The angel of the LORD[n] was then at the threshing floor of Araunah the Jebusite.

17When David saw the angel who was striking down the people, he said to the LORD, "I am the one who has sinned and done wrong. These are but sheep.[o] What have they done? Let your hand fall upon me and my family."[p]

David builds an altar to the LORD.

24:18-25pp— 1Ch 21:18-26

18On that day Gad went to David and said to him, "Go up and build an altar to the LORD on the threshing floor of Araunah the Jebusite." 19So David went up, as the LORD had commanded through Gad. 20When Araunah looked and saw the king and his men coming toward him, he went out and bowed down before the king with his face to the ground.

21Araunah said, "Why has my lord the king come to his servant?"

"To buy your threshing floor," David answered, "so I can build an altar to the LORD, that the plague on the people may be stopped."[q]

22Araunah said to David, "Let my lord the king take whatever pleases him and offer it up. Here are oxen[r] for the burnt offering, and here are threshing sledges and ox yokes for the wood. 23O king, Araunah gives[s] all this to the king." Araunah also said to him, "May the LORD your God accept you."

24But the king replied to Araunah, "No, I insist on paying you for it. I will not sacrifice to the LORD my God burnt offerings that cost me nothing."[t]

So David bought the threshing floor and the oxen and paid fifty shekels[k] of silver for them. 25David built an altar[u] to the LORD there and sacrificed burnt offerings and fellowship offerings.[l] Then the LORD answered prayer[v] in behalf of the land, and the plague on Israel was stopped.

24:7 [a]Ge 21:22-33 [b]Dt 1:7; Jos 11:3
24:9 [c]Nu 1:44-46; 1Ch 21:5
24:10 [d]1Sa 24:5 [e]2Sa 12:13 [f]Nu 12:11; 1Sa 13:13
24:11 [g]1Sa 22:5 [h]1Sa 9:9; 1Ch 29:29
24:13 [i]Dt 28:38-42, 48; Eze 14:21 [j]Lev 26:25
24:14 [k]Ne 9:28; Ps 51:1; 103:8,13; 130:4
24:15 [l]1Ch 27:24
24:16 [m]Ge 6:6; 1Sa 15:11 [n]Ex 12:23; Ac 12:23
24:17 [o]Ps 74:1 [p]Jnh 1:12
24:21 [q]Nu 16:44-50
24:22 [r]1Sa 6:14; 1Ki 19:21
24:23 [s]Eze 20:40-41
24:24 [t]Mal 1:13-14
24:25 [u]1Sa 7:17 [v]2Sa 21:14

j *13* Septuagint (see also 1 Chron. 21:12); Hebrew *seven* k *24* That is, about 1 1/4 pounds (about 0.6 kilogram) l *25* Traditionally *peace offerings*

1 KINGS

Author: Unknown (possibly Jeremiah).

Date Written: Between 640 and 550 B.C. (compiled from earlier sources).

Time Span: About 130 years (period of time from the rise of Solomon to the death of Ahab).

Title: This book is so named because it is a history of the kings who ruled Israel and Judah.

Background: This sequel to 1 and 2 Samuel begins by tracing Solomon's rise to kingship after the death of David. The story begins in a united kingdom, but ends in a nation divided into 2 kingdoms, known as Judah and Israel. 1 and 2 Kings together consist of one book in the Hebrew Bible.

Where Written: Unknown (possibly in Judah and Egypt).

To Whom: To the Israelites.

Content: 1 Kings describes Solomon's reign, wealth and wisdom. The golden age of Solomon is highlighted with construction of the temple. After his death there is division in the kingdom with his son Rehoboam ruling over Judah (southern kingdom) and Jeroboam ruling over Israel (northern kingdom). The capital of Judah at this time is Jerusalem, and the capital of Israel is Samaria. This divided situation continues for over 300 years with each nation having its own king. The book ends recounting the miracles and ministry of the prophet Elijah, especially in contrast to Israel's most wicked king, Ahab.

Key Words: "Wisdom"; "Division." Solomon's rise is directly attributable to the fact that he seeks "wisdom" from God instead of fame or fortune. But unhealthy influences from foreign wives lead to his divided heart...which, in turn, leads to "division" in the nation.

Themes: • God uses history to set before us examples of successful and of defeated lives. • We must follow godly leadership and be godly leaders for others. • God is more concerned that we have wisdom and a heart for him than in our personal accomplishments. • The consistent company we keep in family and friends can affect us positively or negatively.

Outline:

1. Reign of Solomon. 1:1-11:43
2. Divisions of Rehoboam and Jeroboam. 12:1-14:31
3. Reigns of Judah's kings. 15:1-15:24
4. Reigns of Israel's kings. 15:25-16:34
5. Elijah and Ahab. 17:1-22:53

1 KINGS

Adonijah proclaims himself king.

1 When King David was old and well advanced in years, he could not keep warm even when they put covers over him. 2So his servants said to him, "Let us look for a young virgin to attend the king and take care of him. She can lie beside him so that our lord the king may keep warm."

3Then they searched throughout Israel for a beautiful girl and found Abishag, a Shunammite,[a] and brought her to the king. 4The girl was very beautiful; she took care of the king and waited on him, but the king had no intimate relations with her.

5Now Adonijah,[b] whose mother was Haggith, put himself forward and said, "I will be king." So he got chariots[c] and horses[a] ready, with fifty men to run ahead of him. 6(His father had never interfered[d] with him by asking, "Why do you behave as you do?" He was also very handsome and was born next after Absalom.)

7Adonijah conferred with Joab[e] son of Zeruiah and with Abiathar[f] the priest, and they gave him their support. 8But Zadok[g] the priest, Benaiah[h] son of Jehoiada, Nathan[i] the prophet, Shimei[j] and Rei[b] and David's special guard[k] did not join Adonijah.

9Adonijah then sacrificed sheep, cattle and fattened calves at the Stone of Zoheleth near En Rogel.[l] He invited all his brothers, the king's sons, and all the men of Judah who were royal officials, 10but he did not invite Nathan the prophet or Benaiah or the special guard or his brother Solomon.[m]

11Then Nathan asked Bathsheba,[n] Solomon's mother, "Have you not heard that Adonijah,[o] the son of Haggith, has become king without our lord David's knowing it? 12Now then, let me advise[p] you how you can save your own life and the life of your son Solomon. 13Go in to King David and say to him, 'My lord the king, did you not swear[q] to me your servant: "Surely Solomon your son shall be king after me, and he will sit on my throne"? Why then has Adonijah become king?' 14While you are still there talking to the king, I will come in and confirm what you have said."

15So Bathsheba went to see the aged king in his room, where Abishag[r] the Shunammite was attending him. 16Bathsheba bowed low and knelt before the king.

"What is it you want?" the king asked.

17She said to him, "My lord, you yourself swore[s] to me your servant by the LORD your God: 'Solomon your son shall be king after me, and he will sit on my throne.' 18But now Adonijah has become king, and you, my lord the king, do not know about it. 19He has sacrificed[t] great numbers of cattle, fattened calves, and sheep, and has invited all the king's sons, Abiathar the priest and Joab the commander of the army, but he has not invited Solomon your servant. 20My lord the king, the eyes of all Israel are on you, to learn from you who will sit on the throne of my lord the king after him. 21Otherwise, as soon as my lord the king is laid to rest[u] with his fathers, I and my son Solomon will be treated as criminals."

22While she was still speaking with the king, Nathan the prophet arrived. 23And they told the king, "Nathan the prophet is here." So he went before the king and bowed with his face to the ground.

24Nathan said, "Have you, my lord the king, declared that Adonijah shall be king after you, and that he will sit on your throne? 25Today he has gone down and sacrificed great numbers of cattle, fattened calves, and sheep. He has invited all the king's sons, the commanders of the army and Abiathar the priest. Right now they are eating and drinking with him and saying, 'Long live King Adonijah!' 26But me your servant, and Zadok the priest, and Benaiah son of Jehoiada, and your servant Solomon he did not invite.[v] 27Is this something my lord the

1:3 [a]Jos 19:18
1:5 [b]2Sa 3:4 [c]2Sa 15:1
1:6 [d]2Sa 3:3-4
1:7 [e]1Ki 2:22,28; 1Ch 11:6 [f]1Sa 22:20; 2Sa 20:25
1:8 [g]2Sa 20:25 [h]2Sa 8:18 [i]2Sa 12:1 [j]1Ki 4:18 [k]2Sa 23:8
1:9 [l]2Sa 17:17
1:10 [m]2Sa 12:24
1:11 [n]2Sa 12:24 [o]2Sa 3:4
1:12 [p]Pr 15:22
1:13 [q]ver 30; 1Ch 22:9-13
1:15 [r]ver 1
1:17 [s]ver 13,30
1:19 [t]ver 9
1:21 [u]Dt 31:16; 1Ki 2:10
1:26 [v]ver 8,10

a5 Or *charioteers* b8 Or *and his friends*

KEY PLACES IN 1 KINGS

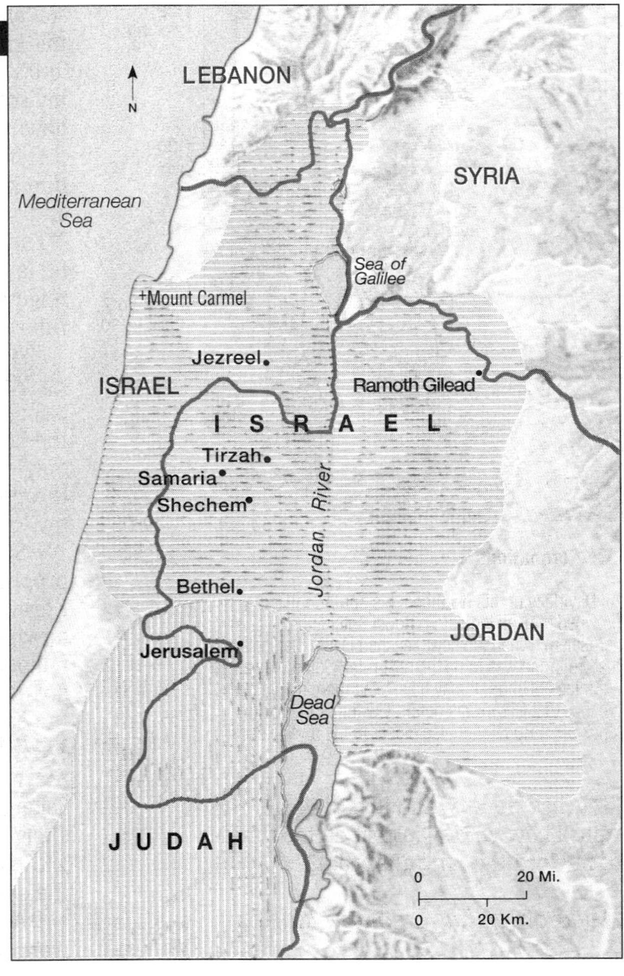

Solomon, David's son, brought Israel into its golden age. His wealth and wisdom were acclaimed worldwide. But he ignored God in his later years (1:1–11:25).

Shechem After Solomon's death, Israel assembled at Shechem to inaugurate his son Rehoboam. However, Rehoboam foolishly angered the people by threatening even heavier burdens, causing a revolt (11:26–12:19).

Israel Jeroboam, leader of the rebels, was made king of Israel, now called the northern kingdom. Jeroboam made Shechem his capital city (12:20, 25).

Judah Only the tribes of Judah and part of Benjamin remained loyal to Rehoboam. These two tribes became the southern kingdom. Rehoboam returned to Judah from Shechem and prepared to force the rebels into submission, but a prophet's message halted these plans (12:21-24).

Jerusalem Jerusalem was the capital city of Judah. Its temple, built by Solomon, was the focal point of Jewish worship. This worried Jeroboam. How could he keep his people loyal if they were constantly going to Rehoboam's capital to worship (12:26,27)?

Dan Jeroboam's solution was to set up his own worship centers. Two golden calves were made and proclaimed to be Israel's gods. One was placed in Dan, and the people were told that they could go there instead of to Jerusalem to worship (12:28, 29).

Bethel The other golden calf was placed in Bethel. The people of the northern kingdom had two convenient locations for worship in their own country, but their sin displeased God. In Jerusalem, meanwhile, Rehoboam was also allowing idolatry to creep in. The two nations were constantly at war (12:29–15:26).

Tirzah Jeroboam had moved the capital city to Tirzah (1 Kings 14:17). Next, Baasha became king of Israel after assassinating Nadab (15:27–16:22).

Samaria Israel continued to gain and lose kings through plots, assassinations, and warfare. When Omri became king, he bought a hill on which he built a new capital city, Samaria. Omri's son, Ahab, became the most wicked king in Israel. His wife Jezebel worshiped Baal. Ahab erected a temple to Baal in Samaria (16:23-34).

Mount Carmel Great evil often brings great people who oppose it. Elijah challenged the prophets of Baal and Asherah at Mount Carmel, where he would prove that they were false prophets. There Elijah humiliated these prophets and then executed them (17:1–18:46).

Jezreel Elijah returned to Jezreel. But Queen Jezebel, furious at the execution of her prophets, vowed to kill Elijah. He ran for his life, but God cared for and encouraged him. During his travels he anointed the future kings of Aram and Israel, as well as Elisha, his own replacement (19:1-21).

Ramoth Gilead The king of Aram declared war on Israel and was defeated in two battles. But the Arameans occupied Ramoth Gilead. Ahab and Jehoshaphat joined forces to recover the city. In this battle, Ahab was killed. Jehoshaphat later died (20:1–22:53).

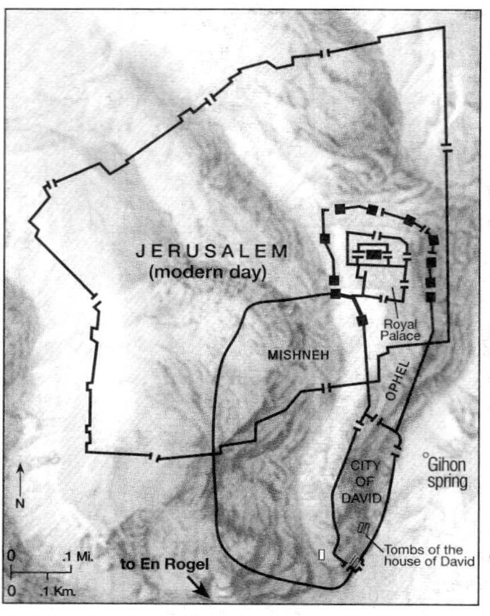

Two Coronations

As David lay on his deathbed, his son Adonijah crowned himself king at En Rogel outside of Jerusalem. When the news reached David, he declared that Solomon was to be the next ruler. Solomon was anointed at Gihon. It may have been more than a coincidence that Gihon was not only within shouting distance of En Rogel, but also closer to the royal palace.

king has done without letting his servants know who should sit on the throne
of my lord the king after him?"

David proclaims Solomon king.

1:28-53pp— 1Ch 29:21-25

28Then King David said, "Call in Bathsheba." So she came into the king's presence and stood before him.
29The king then took an oath: "As
surely as the LORD lives, who has delivered me out of every trouble,[a] 30I will
surely carry out today what I swore[b] to
you by the LORD, the God of Israel:
Solomon your son shall be king after
me, and he will sit on my throne in my
place."
31Then Bathsheba bowed low with
her face to the ground and, kneeling before the king, said, "May my lord King
David live forever!"
32King David said, "Call in Zadok the
priest, Nathan the prophet and Benaiah
son of Jehoiada." When they came before
the king, 33he said to them: "Take your
lord's servants with you and set Solomon
my son on my own mule[c] and take him
down to Gihon.[d] 34There have Zadok the
priest and Nathan the prophet anoint[e]
him king over Israel. Blow the trumpet[f]
and shout, 'Long live King Solomon!'
35Then you are to go up with him, and
he is to come and sit on my throne and
reign in my place. I have appointed him
ruler over Israel and Judah."
36Benaiah son of Jehoiada answered
the king, "Amen! May the LORD, the God
of my lord the king, so declare it. 37As
the LORD was with my lord the king, so
may he be with[g] Solomon to make his
throne even greater[h] than the throne of
my lord King David!"
38So Zadok[i] the priest, Nathan the
prophet, Benaiah son of Jehoiada, the
Kerethites[j] and the Pelethites went
down and put Solomon on King David's
mule and escorted him to Gihon.[k] 39Za-
dok the priest took the horn of oil[l] from
the sacred tent and anointed Solomon.
Then they sounded the trumpet and all
the people shouted,[m] "Long live King
Solomon!" 40And all the people went up
after him, playing flutes and rejoicing
greatly, so that the ground shook with
the sound.
41Adonijah and all the guests who
were with him heard it as they were finishing their feast. On hearing the sound
of the trumpet, Joab asked, "What's the
meaning of all the noise in the city?"
42Even as he was speaking, Jonathan[n]
son of Abiathar the priest arrived. Adonijah said, "Come in. A worthy man like
you must be bringing good news."[o]
43"Not at all!" Jonathan answered.
"Our lord King David has made Solomon king. 44The king has sent with him
Zadok the priest, Nathan the prophet,
Benaiah son of Jehoiada, the Kerethites
and the Pelethites, and they have put
him on the king's mule, 45and Zadok the
priest and Nathan the prophet have
anointed him king at Gihon. From there
they have gone up cheering, and the
city resounds[p] with it. That's the noise

1:29 [a]2Sa 4:9
1:30 [b]ver 13,17
1:33 [c]2Sa 20:6-7 [d]2Ch 32:30; 33:14
1:34 [e]1Sa 10:1; 16:3,12; 1Ki 19:16; 2Ki 9:3,13 [f]ver 25; 2Sa 5:3; 15:10
1:37 [g]Jos 1:5,17; 1Sa 20:13 [h]ver 47
1:38 [i]ver 8 [j]2Sa 8:18 [k]ver 33
1:39 [l]Ex 30:23-32; Ps 89:20 [m]ver 34; 1Sa 10:24
1:42 [n]2Sa 15:27,36 [o]2Sa 18:26
1:45 [p]ver 40

you hear. 46Moreover, Solomon has tak-
en his seat on the royal throne. 47Also,
the royal officials have come to congratulate our lord King David, saying, 'May
your God make Solomon's name more famous than yours and his throne greater[a]
than yours!' And the king bowed in worship on his bed 48and said, 'Praise be to
the LORD, the God of Israel, who has allowed my eyes to see a successor[b] on
my throne today.' "
49At this, all Adonijah's guests rose in
alarm and dispersed. 50But Adonijah, in
fear of Solomon, went and took hold of
the horns[c] of the altar. 51Then Solomon
was told, "Adonijah is afraid of King Solomon and is clinging to the horns of the
altar. He says, 'Let King Solomon swear
to me today that he will not put his servant to death with the sword.' "
52Solomon replied, "If he shows himself to be a worthy man, not a hair[d] of
his head will fall to the ground; but if evil
is found in him, he will die." 53Then King
Solomon sent men, and they brought
him down from the altar. And Adonijah
came and bowed down to King Solomon,
and Solomon said, "Go to your home."

David's charge to Solomon.

2 When the time drew near for David
to die,[e] he gave a charge to Solomon
his son.
2"I am about to go the way of all the
earth,"[f] he said. "So be strong,[g] show
yourself a man, 3and observe[h] what the
LORD your God requires: Walk in his
ways, and keep his decrees and commands, his laws and requirements, as
written in the Law of Moses, so that you
may prosper[i] in all you do and wherever
you go, 4and that the LORD may keep his
promise[j] to me: 'If your descendants
watch how they live, and if they walk
faithfully[k] before me with all their heart
and soul, you will never fail to have a
man on the throne of Israel.'
5"Now you yourself know what Joab[l]
son of Zeruiah did to me—what he did to
the two commanders of Israel's armies,
Abner[m] son of Ner and Amasa[n] son of
Jether. He killed them, shedding their
blood in peacetime as if in battle, and
with that blood stained the belt around
his waist and the sandals on his feet.
6Deal with him according to your wisdom,[o] but do not let his gray head go
down to the grave[c] in peace.
7"But show kindness to the sons of
Barzillai[p] of Gilead and let them be
among those who eat at your table.[q]
They stood by me when I fled from your
brother Absalom.
8"And remember, you have with you
Shimei[r] son of Gera, the Benjamite from
Bahurim, who called down bitter curses
on me the day I went to Mahanaim.
When he came down to meet me at the
Jordan, I swore[s] to him by the LORD: 'I
will not put you to death by the sword.'
9But now, do not consider him innocent.
You are a man of wisdom;[t] you will know
what to do to him. Bring his gray head
down to the grave in blood."

David's death.

2:10-12pp— 1Ch 29:26-28

10Then David rested with his fathers
and was buried[u] in the City of David.[v]
11He had reigned[w] forty years over Israel—seven years in Hebron and thirty-
three in Jerusalem. 12So Solomon sat on
the throne[x] of his father David, and his
rule was firmly established.[y]

Adonijah is slain.

13Now Adonijah, the son of Haggith,
went to Bathsheba, Solomon's mother.
Bathsheba asked him, "Do you come
peacefully?"[z]
He answered, "Yes, peacefully." 14Then
he added, "I have something to say to
you."
"You may say it," she replied.
15"As you know," he said, "the kingdom was mine. All Israel looked to me
as their king. But things changed, and
the kingdom has gone to my brother; for
it has come to him from the LORD. 16Now
I have one request to make of you. Do
not refuse me."

1:47 [a]ver 37; Ge 47:31
1:48 [b]2Sa 7:12; 1Ki 3:6
1:50 [c]1Ki 2:28
1:52 [d]1Sa 14:45; 2Sa 14:11
2:1 [e]Ge 47:29; Dt 31:14
2:2 [f]Jos 23:14 [g]Dt 31:7,23; Jos 1:6
2:3 [h]Dt 17:14-20; Jos 1:7 [i]1Ch 22:13
2:4 [j]2Sa 7:13,25; 1Ki 8:25 [k]2Ki 20:3; Ps 132:12
2:5 [l]2Sa 2:18; 18:5,12,14 [m]2Sa 3:27 [n]2Sa 20:10
2:6 [o]ver 9
2:7 [p]2Sa 17:27; 19:31-39 [q]2Sa 9:7
2:8 [r]2Sa 16:5-13 [s]2Sa 19:18-23
2:9 [t]ver 6
2:10 [u]Ac 2:29; 13:36 [v]2Sa 5:7
2:11 [w]2Sa 5:4,5
2:12 [x]1Ch 29:23 [y]2Ch 1:1
2:13 [z]1Sa 16:4

c*6* Hebrew *Sheol*; also in verse 9

"You may make it," she said.

17 So he continued, "Please ask King Solomon—he will not refuse you—to give me Abishag[a] the Shunammite as my wife."

18 "Very well," Bathsheba replied, "I will speak to the king for you."

19 When Bathsheba went to King Solomon to speak to him for Adonijah, the king stood up to meet her, bowed down to her and sat down on his throne. He had a throne brought for the king's mother,[b] and she sat down at his right hand.[c]

20 "I have one small request to make of you," she said. "Do not refuse me."

The king replied, "Make it, my mother; I will not refuse you."

21 So she said, "Let Abishag[d] the Shunammite be given in marriage to your brother Adonijah."

22 King Solomon answered his mother, "Why do you request Abishag[e] the Shunammite for Adonijah? You might as well request the kingdom for him—after all, he is my older brother[f]—yes, for him and for Abiathar the priest and Joab son of Zeruiah!"

23 Then King Solomon swore by the LORD: "May God deal with me, be it ever so severely,[g] if Adonijah does not pay with his life for this request! 24 And now, as surely as the LORD lives—he who has established me securely on the throne of my father David and has founded a dynasty for me as he promised[h]—Adonijah shall be put to death today!" 25 So King Solomon gave orders to Benaiah[i] son of Jehoiada, and he struck down Adonijah and he died.

Joab is slain.

26 To Abiathar[j] the priest the king said, "Go back to your fields in Anathoth.[k] You deserve to die, but I will not put you to death now, because you carried the ark[l] of the Sovereign LORD before my father David and shared all my father's hardships."[m] 27 So Solomon removed Abiathar from the priesthood of the LORD, fulfilling[n] the word the LORD had spoken at Shiloh about the house of Eli.

28 When the news reached Joab, who had conspired with Adonijah though not with Absalom, he fled to the tent of the LORD and took hold of the horns[o] of the altar. 29 King Solomon was told that Joab had fled to the tent of the LORD and was beside the altar. Then Solomon ordered Benaiah[p] son of Jehoiada, "Go, strike him down!"

30 So Benaiah entered the tent of the LORD and said to Joab, "The king says, 'Come out![q]'"

But he answered, "No, I will die here."

Benaiah reported to the king, "This is how Joab answered me."

31 Then the king commanded Benaiah, "Do as he says. Strike him down and bury him, and so clear me and my father's house of the guilt of the innocent blood[r] that Joab shed. 32 The LORD will repay[s] him for the blood he shed,[t] because without the knowledge of my father David he attacked two men and killed them with the sword. Both of them—Abner son of Ner, commander of Israel's army, and Amasa[u] son of Jether, commander of Judah's army—were better[v] men and more upright than he. 33 May the guilt of their blood rest on the head of Joab and his descendants forever. But on David and his descendants, his house and his throne, may there be the LORD's peace forever."

34 So Benaiah son of Jehoiada went up and struck down Joab and killed him, and he was buried on his own land[d] in the desert. 35 The king put Benaiah[w] son of Jehoiada over the army in Joab's position and replaced Abiathar with Zadok[x] the priest.

Shimei is slain.

36 Then the king sent for Shimei[y] and said to him, "Build yourself a house in Jerusalem and live there, but do not go anywhere else. 37 The day you leave and cross the Kidron Valley,[z] you can be sure you will die; your blood will be on your own head."[a]

2:17 [a] 1Ki 1:3
2:19 [b] 1Ki 15:13 [c] Ps 45:9
2:21 [d] 1Ki 1:3
2:22 [e] 2Sa 12:8; 1Ki 1:3 [f] 1Ch 3:2
2:23 [g] Ru 1:17
2:24 [h] 2Sa 7:11; 1Ch 22:10
2:25 [i] 2Sa 8:18
2:26 [j] 1Sa 22:20 [k] Jos 21:18 [l] 2Sa 15:24 [m] 1Sa 23:6
2:27 [n] 1Sa 2:27-36
2:28 [o] 1Ki 1:7,50
2:29 [p] ver 25
2:30 [q] Ex 21:14
2:31 [r] Nu 35:33; Dt 19:13; 21:8-9
2:32 [s] Jdg 9:57; Ps 7:16 [t] Jdg 9:24 [u] 2Sa 3:27; 20:10 [v] 2Ch 21:13
2:35 [w] 1Ki 4:4 [x] ver 27; 1Ch 29:22
2:36 [y] ver 8; 2Sa 16:5
2:37 [z] 2Sa 15:23 [a] Lev 20:9; Jos 2:19; 2Sa 1:16

d34 Or *buried in his tomb*

38Shimei answered the king, "What you say is good. Your servant will do as my lord the king has said." And Shimei stayed in Jerusalem for a long time.

39But three years later, two of Shimei's slaves ran off to Achish[a] son of Maacah, king of Gath, and Shimei was told, "Your slaves are in Gath." 40At this, he saddled his donkey and went to Achish at Gath in search of his slaves. So Shimei went away and brought the slaves back from Gath.

41When Solomon was told that Shimei had gone from Jerusalem to Gath and had returned, 42the king summoned Shimei and said to him, "Did I not make you swear by the LORD and warn you, 'On the day you leave to go anywhere else, you can be sure you will die'? At that time you said to me, 'What you say is good. I will obey.' 43Why then did you not keep your oath to the LORD and obey the command I gave you?"

44The king also said to Shimei, "You know in your heart all the wrong[b] you did to my father David. Now the LORD will repay you for your wrongdoing. 45But King Solomon will be blessed, and David's throne will remain secure[c] before the LORD forever."

46Then the king gave the order to Benaiah son of Jehoiada, and he went out and struck Shimei down and killed him.

The kingdom was now firmly established[d] in Solomon's hands.

Solomon asks for wisdom.

3:4-15pp— 2Ch 1:2-13

3 Solomon made an alliance with Pharaoh king of Egypt and married[e] his daughter.[f] He brought her to the City of David[g] until he finished building his palace[h] and the temple of the LORD, and the wall around Jerusalem. 2The people, however, were still sacrificing at the high places,[i] because a temple had not yet been built for the Name of the LORD. 3Solomon showed his love[j] for the LORD by walking according to the statutes[k] of his father David, except that he offered sacrifices and burned incense on the high places.

2:39 [a]1Sa 27:2
2:44 [b]1Sa 25:39; 2Sa 16:5-13; Eze 17:19
2:45 [c]2Sa 7:13; Pr 25:5
2:46 [d]ver 12; 2Ch 1:1
3:1 [e]1Ki 7:8 [f]1Ki 9:24 [g]2Sa 5:7 [h]1Ki 7:1; 9:15,19
3:2 [i]Lev 17:3-5; Dt 12:2,4-5; 1Ki 22:43
3:3 [j]Dt 6:5; Ps 31:23; 1Co 8:3 [k]1Ki 2:3; 9:4; 11:4,6,38
3:4 [l]1Ch 16:39
3:5 [m]1Ki 9:2 [n]Nu 12:6; Mt 1:20
3:6 [o]1Ki 2:4; 9:4 [p]1Ki 1:48
3:7 [q]Nu 27:17; 1Ch 29:1
3:8 [r]Dt 7:6 [s]Ge 15:5
3:9 [t]2Sa 14:17; Jas 1:5 [u]Pr 2:3-9; Heb 5:14 [v]Ps 72:1-2
3:11 [w]Jas 4:3
3:12 [x]1Jn 5:14-15 [y]1Ki 4:29,30, 31; 5:12; 10:23; Ecc 1:16
3:13 [z]Mt 6:33; Eph 3:20 [a]1Ki 4:21-24; Pr 3:1-2,16 [b]1Ki 10:23
3:14 [c]ver 6; Pr 3:1-2,16 [d]Ps 61:6; 91:16

4The king went to Gibeon[l] to offer sacrifices, for that was the most important high place, and Solomon offered a thousand burnt offerings on that altar. 5At Gibeon the LORD appeared[m] to Solomon during the night in a dream,[n] and God said, "Ask for whatever you want me to give you."

6Solomon answered, "You have shown great kindness to your servant, my father David, because he was faithful[o] to you and righteous and upright in heart. You have continued this great kindness to him and have given him a son[p] to sit on his throne this very day.

7"Now, O LORD my God, you have made your servant king in place of my father David. But I am only a little child[q] and do not know how to carry out my duties. 8Your servant is here among the people you have chosen,[r] a great people, too numerous to count or number.[s] 9So give your servant a discerning[t] heart to govern your people and to distinguish[u] between right and wrong. For who is able[v] to govern this great people of yours?"

10The Lord was pleased that Solomon had asked for this. 11So God said to him, "Since you have asked[w] for this and not for long life or wealth for yourself, nor have asked for the death of your enemies but for discernment in administering justice, 12I will do what you have asked.[x] I will give you a wise[y] and discerning heart, so that there will never have been anyone like you, nor will there ever be. 13Moreover, I will give you what you have not[z] asked for—both riches and honor[a]—so that in your lifetime you will have no equal[b] among kings. 14And if you walk[c] in my ways and obey my statutes and commands as David your father did, I will give you a long life."[d] 15Then Solomon awoke[e]—and he realized it had been a dream.

He returned to Jerusalem, stood before the ark of the Lord's covenant and sacrificed burnt offerings[f] and fellowship

3:15 [e]Ge 41:7 [f]1Ki 8:65

offerings.[e][a] Then he gave a feast[b] for
all his court.

Two women claim the same child.

16Now two prostitutes came to the
king and stood before him. 17One of
them said, "My lord, this woman and I
live in the same house. I had a baby
while she was there with me. 18The
third day after my child was born, this
woman also had a baby. We were alone;
there was no one in the house but the
two of us.
19"During the night this woman's son
died because she lay on him. 20So she got
up in the middle of the night and took my
son from my side while I your servant
was asleep. She put him by her breast
and put her dead son by my breast.
21The next morning, I got up to nurse
my son—and he was dead! But when I
looked at him closely in the morning
light, I saw that it wasn't the son I had
borne."
22The other woman said, "No! The
living one is my son; the dead one is
yours."
But the first one insisted, "No! The
dead one is yours; the living one is
mine." And so they argued before the
king.
23The king said, "This one says, 'My
son is alive and your son is dead,' while
that one says, 'No! Your son is dead and
mine is alive.'"
24Then the king said, "Bring me a
sword." So they brought a sword for the
king. 25He then gave an order: "Cut the
living child in two and give half to one
and half to the other."
26The woman whose son was alive was
filled with compassion[c] for her son and
said to the king, "Please, my lord, give
her the living baby! Don't kill him!"
But the other said, "Neither I nor you
shall have him. Cut him in two!"
27Then the king gave his ruling: "Give
the living baby to the first woman. Do
not kill him; she is his mother."
28When all Israel heard the verdict
the king had given, they held the king
in awe, because they saw that he had
wisdom[d] from God to administer justice.

3:15 [a]Mk 6:21 [b]Est 1:3,9; Da 5:1
3:26 [c]Ge 43:30; Isa 49:15; Jer 31:20; Hos 11:8
3:28 [d]ver 9,11-12; Col 2:3
4:2 [e]1Ch 6:10
4:3 [f]2Sa 8:16
4:4 [g]1Ki 2:35 [h]1Ki 2:27
4:8 [i]Jos 24:33
4:9 [j]Jdg 1:35 [k]Jos 21:16
4:10 [l]Jos 15:35 [m]Jos 12:17
4:11 [n]Jos 11:2
4:12 [o]Jos 17:11; Jdg 5:19 [p]Jos 3:16 [q]1Ki 19:16 [r]1Ch 6:68
4:13 [s]Nu 32:41

Solomon's officials.

4 So King Solomon ruled over all
Israel. 2And these were his chief
officials:

Azariah[e] son of Zadok—the priest;
3Elihoreph and Ahijah, sons of Shisha—secretaries;
Jehoshaphat[f] son of Ahilud—recorder;
4Benaiah[g] son of Jehoiada—commander in chief;
Zadok[h] and Abiathar—priests;
5Azariah son of Nathan—in charge of the district officers;
Zabud son of Nathan—a priest and personal adviser to the king;
6Ahishar—in charge of the palace;
Adoniram son of Abda—in charge of forced labor.

7Solomon also had twelve district governors over all Israel, who supplied
provisions for the king and the royal
household. Each one had to provide supplies for one month in the year. 8These
are their names:

Ben-Hur—in the hill country[i] of Ephraim;
9Ben-Deker—in Makaz, Shaalbim,[j] Beth Shemesh[k] and Elon Bethhanan;
10Ben-Hesed—in Arubboth (Socoh[l] and all the land of Hepher[m] were his);
11Ben-Abinadab—in Naphoth Dor[f][n] (he was married to Taphath daughter of Solomon);
12Baana son of Ahilud—in Taanach and Megiddo, and in all of Beth Shan[o] next to Zarethan[p] below Jezreel, from Beth Shan to Abel Meholah[q] across to Jokmeam;[r]
13Ben-Geber—in Ramoth Gilead (the settlements of Jair[s] son of Manasseh in Gilead were his, as well

e *15* Traditionally *peace offerings* f *11* Or *in the heights of Dor*

as the district of Argob in Bashan
and its sixty large walled cities[a]
with bronze gate bars);
14Ahinadab son of Iddo—in Mahanaim;[b]
15Ahimaaz[c]—in Naphtali (he had married Basemath daughter of Solomon);
16Baana son of Hushai[d]—in Asher and in Aloth;
17Jehoshaphat son of Paruah—in Issachar;
18Shimei[e] son of Ela—in Benjamin;
19Geber son of Uri—in Gilead (the
country of Sihon king of the
Amorites and the country of Og[f]
king of Bashan). He was the only
governor over the district.

Solomon's reign of prosperity and wisdom.

20The people of Judah and Israel were
as numerous as the sand[g] on the seashore; they ate, they drank and they
were happy. 21And Solomon ruled[h] over
all the kingdoms from the River[g][i] to the
land of the Philistines, as far as the border of Egypt.[j] These countries brought
tribute[k] and were Solomon's subjects all
his life.
22Solomon's daily provisions were thirty cors[h] of fine flour and sixty cors[i] of
meal, 23ten head of stall-fed cattle, twenty of pasture-fed cattle and a hundred
sheep and goats, as well as deer, gazelles,
roebucks and choice fowl. 24For he ruled
over all the kingdoms west of the River,
from Tiphsah[l] to Gaza, and had peace[m]
on all sides. 25During Solomon's lifetime
Judah and Israel, from Dan to Beersheba,[n] lived in safety,[o] each man under his
own vine and fig tree.[p]
26Solomon had four[j] thousand stalls for
chariot horses,[q] and twelve thousand
horses.[k]
27The district officers,[r] each in his
month, supplied provisions for King Solomon and all who came to the king's
table. They saw to it that nothing was
lacking. 28They also brought to the proper place their quotas of barley and straw
for the chariot horses and the other
horses.
29God gave Solomon wisdom[s] and very
great insight, and a breadth of understanding as measureless as the sand on
the seashore. 30Solomon's wisdom was
greater than the wisdom of all the men
of the East,[t] and greater than all the wisdom of Egypt.[u] 31He was wiser[v] than any
other man, including Ethan the Ezrahite—wiser than Heman, Calcol and Darda, the sons of Mahol. And his fame
spread to all the surrounding nations.
32He spoke three thousand proverbs[w]
and his songs[x] numbered a thousand and
five. 33He described plant life, from the
cedar of Lebanon to the hyssop that
grows out of walls. He also taught about
animals and birds, reptiles and fish.
34Men of all nations came to listen to Solomon's wisdom, sent by all the kings[y] of
the world, who had heard of his wisdom.

Hiram supplies timber for building the temple.

5:1-16pp— 2Ch 2:1-18

5 When Hiram[z] king of Tyre heard that
Solomon had been anointed king to
succeed his father David, he sent his envoys to Solomon, because he had always
been on friendly terms with David. 2Solomon sent back this message to Hiram:

3"You know that because of the
wars[a] waged against my father
David from all sides, he could not
build a temple for the Name of the
LORD his God until the LORD put his
enemies under his feet. 4But now
the LORD my God has given me
rest[b] on every side, and there is
no adversary or disaster. 5I intend,
therefore, to build a temple[c] for the
Name of the LORD my God, as the
LORD told my father David, when he
said, 'Your son whom I will put on

4:13 [a]Dt 3:4
4:14 [b]Jos 13:26
4:15 [c]2Sa 15:27
4:16 [d]2Sa 15:32
4:18 [e]1Ki 1:8
4:19 [f]Dt 3:8-10
4:20 [g]Ge 22:17; 32:12; 1Ki 3:8
4:21 [h]2Ch 9:26; Ps 72:11 [i]Jos 1:4; Ps 72:8 [j]Ge 15:18 [k]Ps 68:29
4:24 [l]Ps 72:11 [m]1Ch 22:9
4:25 [n]Jdg 20:1 [o]Jer 23:6 [p]Mic 4:4; Zec 3:10
4:26 [q]1Ki 10:26; 2Ch 1:14
4:27 [r]ver 7
4:29 [s]1Ki 3:12
4:30 [t]Ge 25:6 [u]Ac 7:22
4:31 [v]1Ki 3:12; 1Ch 2:6; 6:33; 15:19; Ps 89 Title
4:32 [w]Pr 1:1; Ecc 12:9 [x]SS 1:1
4:34 [y]1Ki 10:1; 2Ch 9:23
5:1 [z]ver 10,18; 2Sa 5:11; 1Ch 14:1
5:3 [a]1Ch 22:8; 28:3
5:4 [b]1Ki 4:24; 1Ch 22:9
5:5 [c]1Ch 17:12

g*21* That is, the Euphrates; also in verse 24
h*22* That is, probably about 185 bushels (about 6.6 kiloliters) i*22* That is, probably about 375 bushels (about 13.2 kiloliters) j*26* Some Septuagint manuscripts (see also 2 Chron. 9:25); Hebrew *forty*
k*26* Or *charioteers*

the throne in your place will build
the temple for my Name.’[a]
6“So give orders that cedars of
Lebanon be cut for me. My men will
work with yours, and I will pay you
for your men whatever wages you
set. You know that we have no one
so skilled in felling timber as the
Sidonians.”

7When Hiram heard Solomon’s message, he was greatly pleased and said,
“Praise be to the LORD today, for he has
given David a wise son to rule over this
great nation.”
8So Hiram sent word to Solomon:

“I have received the message you
sent me and will do all you want in
providing the cedar and pine logs.
9My men will haul them down from
Lebanon to the sea[b], and I will float
them in rafts by sea to the place you
specify. There I will separate them
and you can take them away. And
you are to grant my wish by providing food[c] for my royal household.”

10In this way Hiram kept Solomon supplied with all the cedar and pine logs
he wanted, 11and Solomon gave Hiram
twenty thousand cors[l] of wheat as food
for his household, in addition to twenty
thousand baths[m,n] of pressed olive oil.
Solomon continued to do this for Hiram
year after year. 12The LORD gave Solomon wisdom,[d] just as he had promised
him. There were peaceful relations between Hiram and Solomon, and the two
of them made a treaty.[e]

Solomon conscripts laborers.

13King Solomon conscripted laborers[f]
from all Israel—thirty thousand men.
14He sent them off to Lebanon in shifts
of ten thousand a month, so that they
spent one month in Lebanon and two
months at home. Adoniram[g] was in
charge of the forced labor. 15Solomon had
seventy thousand carriers and eighty
thousand stonecutters in the hills, 16as
well as thirty-three hundred[o] foremen[h]
who supervised the project and directed
the workmen. 17At the king’s command
they removed from the quarry[i] large
blocks of quality stone[j] to provide a
foundation of dressed stone for the
temple. 18The craftsmen of Solomon
and Hiram and the men of Gebal[p][k] cut
and prepared the timber and stone for
the building of the temple.

Solomon directs the temple construction.

6:1-29pp— 2Ch 3:1-14

6 In the four hundred and eightieth[q]
year after the Israelites had come
out of Egypt, in the fourth year of Solomon’s reign over Israel, in the month
of Ziv, the second month, he began to
build the temple of the LORD.[l]
2The temple[m] that King Solomon built
for the LORD was sixty cubits long, twenty wide and thirty high.[r] 3The portico at
the front of the main hall of the temple
extended the width of the temple, that is
twenty cubits,[s] and projected ten cubits[t]
from the front of the temple. 4He made
narrow clerestory windows[n] in the temple. 5Against the walls of the main hall
and inner sanctuary he built a structure
around the building, in which there were
side rooms.[o] 6The lowest floor was five
cubits[u] wide, the middle floor six cubits[v]
and the third floor seven.[w] He made off-
set ledges around the outside of the temple so that nothing would be inserted
into the temple walls.
7In building the temple, only blocks
dressed[p] at the quarry were used, and no
hammer, chisel or any other iron tool[q]
was heard at the temple site while it was
being built.

5:5 [a]2Sa 7:13; 1Ch 22:10
5:9 [b]Ezr 3:7 [c]Eze 27:17; Ac 12:20
5:12 [d]1Ki 3:12 [e]Am 1:9
5:13 [f]1Ki 9:15
5:14 [g]1Ki 4:6; 2Ch 10:18
5:16 [h]1Ki 9:23
5:17 [i]1Ki 6:7 [j]1Ch 22:2
5:18 [k]Jos 13:5
6:1 [l]Ac 7:47
6:2 [m]Eze 41:1
6:4 [n]Eze 40:16; 41:16
6:5 [o]ver 16,19-21; Eze 41:5-6
6:7 [p]Ex 20:25 [q]Dt 27:5

[l]*11* That is, probably about 125,000 bushels (about 4,400 kiloliters) [m]*11* Septuagint (see also 2 Chron. 2:10); Hebrew *twenty cors* [n]*11* That is, about 115,000 gallons (about 440 kiloliters) [o]*16* Hebrew; some Septuagint manuscripts (see also 2 Chron. 2:2, 18) *thirty-six hundred* [p]*18* That is, Byblos [q]*1* Hebrew; Septuagint *four hundred and fortieth* [r]*2* That is, about 90 feet (about 27 meters) long and 30 feet (about 9 meters) wide and 45 feet (about 13.5 meters) high [s]*3* That is, about 30 feet (about 9 meters) [t]*3* That is, about 15 feet (about 4.5 meters) [u]*6* That is, about 7 1/2 feet (about 2.3 meters); also in verses 10 and 24 [v]*6* That is, about 9 feet (about 2.7 meters) [w]*6* That is, about 10 1/2 feet (about 3.1 meters)

8The entrance to the lowest[x] floor was
on the south side of the temple; a stairway led up to the middle level and from
there to the third. 9So he built the temple
and completed it, roofing it with beams
and cedar[a] planks. 10And he built the side
rooms all along the temple. The height of
each was five cubits, and they were attached to the temple by beams of cedar.
11The word of the LORD came to Solomon: 12"As for this temple you are building, if you follow my decrees, carry out
my regulations and keep all my commands and obey them, I will fulfill
through you the promise[b] I gave to David
your father. 13And I will live among the
Israelites and will not abandon[c] my people Israel."
14So Solomon built the temple and
completed[d] it. 15He lined its interior
walls with cedar boards, paneling them
from the floor of the temple to the ceiling,[e] and covered the floor of the temple
with planks of pine. 16He partitioned off
twenty cubits[y] at the rear of the temple
with cedar boards from floor to ceiling
to form within the temple an inner sanctuary, the Most Holy Place.[f] 17The main
hall in front of this room was forty
cubits[z] long. 18The inside of the temple
was cedar,[g] carved with gourds and open
flowers. Everything was cedar; no stone
was to be seen.
19He prepared the inner sanctuary[h]
within the temple to set the ark of the
covenant[i] of the LORD there. 20The inner
sanctuary[j] was twenty cubits long, twenty wide and twenty high.[a] He overlaid
the inside with pure gold, and he also
overlaid the altar of cedar. 21Solomon
covered the inside of the temple with
pure gold, and he extended gold chains
across the front of the inner sanctuary,
which was overlaid with gold. 22So he
overlaid the whole interior with gold. He
also overlaid with gold the altar that belonged to the inner sanctuary.
23In the inner sanctuary he made a
pair of cherubim[k] of olive wood, each ten
cubits[b] high. 24One wing of the first
cherub was five cubits long, and the
other wing five cubits—ten cubits from
wing tip to wing tip. 25The second
cherub also measured ten cubits, for the
two cherubim were identical in size and
shape. 26The height of each cherub was
ten cubits. 27He placed the cherubim[l]
inside the innermost room of the temple,
with their wings spread out. The wing of
one cherub touched one wall, while the
wing of the other touched the other wall,
and their wings touched each other in
the middle of the room. 28He overlaid
the cherubim with gold.
29On the walls all around the temple,
in both the inner and outer rooms, he
carved cherubim,[m] palm trees and open
flowers. 30He also covered the floors of
both the inner and outer rooms of the
temple with gold.
31For the entrance of the inner sanctuary he made doors of olive wood with
five-sided jambs. 32And on the two olive
wood doors he carved cherubim, palm
trees and open flowers, and overlaid the
cherubim and palm trees with beaten
gold. 33In the same way he made four-
sided jambs of olive wood for the entrance to the main hall. 34He also made
two pine doors, each having two leaves
that turned in sockets. 35He carved cherubim, palm trees and open flowers on
them and overlaid them with gold hammered evenly over the carvings.
36And he built the inner courtyard of
three courses[n] of dressed stone and one
course of trimmed cedar beams.
37The foundation of the temple of the
LORD was laid in the fourth year, in the
month of Ziv. 38In the eleventh year in
the month of Bul, the eighth month, the
temple was finished in all its details
according to its specifications.[o] He had
spent seven years building it.

Solomon builds himself a palace.

7 It took Solomon thirteen years, however, to complete the construction of
his palace.[p] 2He built the Palace[q] of the

6:9 [a]ver 14,38
6:12 [b]2Sa 7:12-16; 1Ki 2:4; 9:5
6:13 [c]Ex 25:8; Lev 26:11; Dt 31:6; Heb 13:5
6:14 [d]ver 9,38
6:15 [e]1Ki 7:7
6:16 [f]Ex 26:33; Lev 16:2; 1Ki 8:6
6:18 [g]1Ki 7:24; Ps 74:6
6:19 [h]1Ki 8:6 [i]1Sa 3:3
6:20 [j]Eze 41:3-4
6:23 [k]Ex 37:1-9
6:27 [l]Ex 25:20; 37:9; 1Ki 8:7; 2Ch 5:8
6:29 [m]ver 32,35
6:36 [n]1Ki 7:12; Ezr 6:4
6:38 [o]Heb 8:5
7:1 [p]1Ki 9:10; 2Ch 8:1
7:2 [q]2Sa 7:2

x*8* Septuagint; Hebrew *middle* y*16* That is, about 30 feet (about 9 meters) z*17* That is, about 60 feet (about 18 meters) a*20* That is, about 30 feet (about 9 meters) long, wide and high b*23* That is, about 15 feet (about 4.5 meters)

Forest of Lebanon[a] a hundred cubits long, fifty wide and thirty high,[c] with four rows of cedar columns supporting trimmed cedar beams. **3**It was roofed with cedar above the beams that rested on the columns—forty-five beams, fifteen to a row. **4**Its windows were placed high in sets of three, facing each other. **5**All the doorways had rectangular frames; they were in the front part in sets of three, facing each other.[d]

6He made a colonnade fifty cubits long and thirty wide.[e] In front of it was a portico, and in front of that were pillars and an overhanging roof.

7He built the throne hall, the Hall of Justice, where he was to judge,[b] and he covered it with cedar from floor to ceiling.[f][c] **8**And the palace in which he was to live, set farther back, was similar in design. Solomon also made a palace like this hall for Pharaoh's daughter, whom he had married.[d]

9All these structures, from the outside to the great courtyard and from foundation to eaves, were made of blocks of high-grade stone cut to size and trimmed with a saw on their inner and outer faces. **10**The foundations were laid with large stones of good quality, some measuring ten cubits[g] and some eight.[h] **11**Above were high-grade stones, cut to size, and cedar beams. **12**The great courtyard was surrounded by a wall of three courses[e] of dressed stone and one course of trimmed cedar beams, as was the inner courtyard of the temple of the LORD with its portico.

Huram crafts the temple furnishings.

7:23-26pp— 2Ch 4:2-5
7:38-51pp— 2Ch 4:6,10–5:1

13King Solomon sent to Tyre and brought Huram,[i][f] **14**whose mother was a widow from the tribe of Naphtali and whose father was a man of Tyre and a craftsman in bronze. Huram was highly skilled[g] and experienced in all kinds of bronze work. He came to King Solomon and did all[h] the work assigned to him.

15He cast two bronze pillars,[i] each eighteen cubits high and twelve cubits around,[j] by line. **16**He also made two capitals[j] of cast bronze to set on the tops of the pillars; each capital was five cubits[k] high. **17**A network of interwoven chains festooned the capitals on top of the pillars, seven for each capital. **18**He made pomegranates in two rows[l] encircling each network to decorate the capitals on top of the pillars.[m] He did the same for each capital. **19**The capitals on top of the pillars in the portico were in the shape of lilies, four cubits[n] high. **20**On the capitals of both pillars, above the bowl-shaped part next to the network, were the two hundred pomegranates[k] in rows all around. **21**He erected the pillars at the portico of the temple. The pillar to the south he named Jakin[o] and the one to the north Boaz.[p][l] **22**The capitals on top were in the shape of lilies. And so the work on the pillars was completed.

23He made the Sea[m] of cast metal, circular in shape, measuring ten cubits[g] from rim to rim and five cubits high. It took a line of thirty cubits[q] to measure around it. **24**Below the rim, gourds encircled it—ten to a cubit. The gourds were cast in two rows in one piece with the Sea.

25The Sea stood on twelve bulls,[n] three facing north, three facing west, three facing south and three facing east. The Sea rested on top of them, and their hindquarters were toward the center. **26**It was a handbreadth[r] in thickness, and

7:2 *a* 1Ki 10:17; 2Ch 9:16
7:7 *b* Ps 122:5; Pr 20:8 *c* 1Ki 6:15
7:8 *d* 1Ki 3:1; 2Ch 8:11
7:12 *e* 1Ki 6:36
7:13 *f* 2Ch 2:13
7:14 *g* Ex 31:2-5; 35:31; 36:1; 2Ch 2:14 *h* 2Ch 4:11,16
7:15 *i* 2Ki 25:17; 2Ch 3:15; 4:12; 52:17,21
7:16 *j* 2Ki 25:17
7:20 *k* 2Ch 3:16; 4:13; Jer 52:23
7:21 *l* 1Ki 6:3; 2Ch 3:17
7:23 *m* 2Ki 25:13; 1Ch 18:8; Jer 52:17
7:25 *n* 2Ch 4:4-5; Jer 52:20

c *2* That is, about 150 feet (about 46 meters) long, 75 feet (about 23 meters) wide and 45 feet (about 13.5 meters) high d *5* The meaning of the Hebrew for this verse is uncertain. e *6* That is, about 75 feet (about 23 meters) long and 45 feet (about 13.5 meters) wide f *7* Vulgate and Syriac; Hebrew *floor* g *10, 23* That is, about 15 feet (about 4.5 meters) h *10* That is, about 12 feet (about 3.6 meters) i *13* Hebrew *Hiram,* a variant of *Huram*; also in verses 40 and 45 j *15* That is, about 27 feet (about 8.1 meters) high and 18 feet (about 5.4 meters) around k *16* That is, about 7 1/2 feet (about 2.3 meters); also in verse 23 l *18* Two Hebrew manuscripts and Septuagint; most Hebrew manuscripts *made the pillars, and there were two rows* m *18* Many Hebrew manuscripts and Syriac; most Hebrew manuscripts *pomegranates* n *19* That is, about 6 feet (about 1.8 meters); also in verse 38 o *21* *Jakin* probably means *he establishes.* p *21* *Boaz* probably means *in him is strength.* q *23* That is, about 45 feet (about 13.5 meters) r *26* That is, about 3 inches (about 8 centimeters)

its rim was like the rim of a cup, like a
lily blossom. It held two thousand baths.[s]
27He also made ten movable stands[a] of
bronze; each was four cubits long, four
wide and three high.[t] 28This is how the
stands were made: They had side panels
attached to uprights. 29On the panels between the uprights were lions, bulls and
cherubim—and on the uprights as well.
Above and below the lions and bulls
were wreaths of hammered work. 30Each
stand[b] had four bronze wheels with
bronze axles, and each had a basin resting on four supports, cast with wreaths
on each side. 31On the inside of the stand
there was an opening that had a circular frame one cubit[u] deep. This opening
was round, and with its basework it
measured a cubit and a half.[v] Around its
opening there was engraving. The panels
of the stands were square, not round.
32The four wheels were under the panels, and the axles of the wheels were
attached to the stand. The diameter of
each wheel was a cubit and a half. 33The
wheels were made like chariot wheels;
the axles, rims, spokes and hubs were
all of cast metal.
34Each stand had four handles, one on
each corner, projecting from the stand.
35At the top of the stand there was a
circular band half a cubit[w] deep. The supports and panels were attached to the
top of the stand. 36He engraved cherubim, lions and palm trees on the surfaces
of the supports and on the panels, in
every available space, with wreaths all
around. 37This is the way he made the
ten stands. They were all cast in the
same molds and were identical in size
and shape.
38He then made ten bronze basins,[c]
each holding forty baths[x] and measuring
four cubits across, one basin to go on
each of the ten stands. 39He placed five of
the stands on the south side of the temple and five on the north. He placed the
Sea on the south side, at the southeast
corner of the temple. 40He also made
the basins and shovels and sprinkling
bowls.
So Huram finished all the work he
had undertaken for King Solomon in the
temple of the LORD:

41the two pillars;
the two bowl-shaped capitals on
top of the pillars;
the two sets of network decorating
the two bowl-shaped capitals on
top of the pillars;
42the four hundred pomegranates for
the two sets of network (two
rows of pomegranates for each
network, decorating the bowl-
shaped capitals[d] on top of the pillars);
43the ten stands with their ten basins;
44the Sea and the twelve bulls under it;
45the pots, shovels and sprinkling
bowls.[e]

All these objects that Huram made
for King Solomon for the temple of the
LORD were of burnished bronze. 46The
king had them cast in clay molds in the
plain[f] of the Jordan between Succoth[g]
and Zarethan.[h] 47Solomon left all these
things unweighed,[i] because there were
so many; the weight of the bronze was
not determined.
48Solomon also made all the furnishings that were in the LORD's temple:

the golden altar;
the golden table[j] on which was the
bread of the Presence;[k]
49the lampstands[l] of pure gold (five on
the right and five on the left, in
front of the inner sanctuary);
the gold floral work and lamps and
tongs;
50the pure gold basins, wick trimmers,
sprinkling bowls, dishes and
censers;[m]

7:27 [a] ver 38; 2Ch 4:14
7:30 [b] 2Ki 16:17
7:38 [c] Ex 30:18; 2Ch 4:6
7:42 [d] ver 20
7:45 [e] Ex 27:3
7:46 [f] 2Ch 4:17 [g] Ge 33:17; Jos 13:27 [h] Jos 3:16
7:47 [i] 1Ch 22:3
7:48 [j] Ex 37:10 [k] Ex 25:30
7:49 [l] Ex 25:31-38
7:50 [m] 2Ki 25:13

[s] *26* That is, probably about 11,500 gallons (about 44 kiloliters); the Septuagint does not have this sentence. [t] *27* That is, about 6 feet (about 1.8 meters) long and wide and about 4 1/2 feet (about 1.3 meters) high [u] *31* That is, about 1 1/2 feet (about 0.5 meter) [v] *31* That is, about 2 1/4 feet (about 0.7 meter); also in verse 32 [w] *35* That is, about 3/4 foot (about 0.2 meter) [x] *38* That is, about 230 gallons (about 880 liters)

and the gold sockets for the doors
of the innermost room, the Most
Holy Place, and also for the doors
of the main hall of the temple.

51When all the work King Solomon
had done for the temple of the LORD was
finished, he brought in the things his
father David had dedicated[a]—the silver
and gold and the furnishings—and he
placed them in the treasuries of the
LORD's temple.

The ark is brought to the temple.

8:1-21pp— 2Ch 5:2–6:11

8 Then King Solomon summoned into
his presence at Jerusalem the elders
of Israel, all the heads of the tribes and
the chiefs[b] of the Israelite families, to
bring up the ark[c] of the LORD's covenant
from Zion, the City of David.[d] 2All the
men of Israel came together to King Solomon at the time of the festival[e] in the
month of Ethanim, the seventh month.[f]
3When all the elders of Israel had arrived, the priests[g] took up the ark, 4and
they brought up the ark of the LORD and
the Tent of Meeting[h] and all the sacred
furnishings in it. The priests and Levites
carried them up, 5and King Solomon and
the entire assembly of Israel that had
gathered about him were before the ark,
sacrificing[i] so many sheep and cattle that
they could not be recorded or counted.
6The priests then brought the ark of
the LORD's covenant[j] to its place in the
inner sanctuary of the temple, the Most
Holy Place, and put it beneath the wings
of the cherubim.[k] 7The cherubim spread
their wings over the place of the ark and
overshadowed the ark and its carrying
poles. 8These poles were so long that
their ends could be seen from the Holy
Place in front of the inner sanctuary, but
not from outside the Holy Place; and they
are still there today.[l] 9There was nothing
in the ark except the two stone tablets[m]
that Moses had placed in it at Horeb,
where the LORD made a covenant with
the Israelites after they came out of
Egypt.

10When the priests withdrew from
the Holy Place, the cloud[n] filled the temple of the LORD. 11And the priests could
not perform their service because of the
cloud, for the glory of the LORD filled his
temple.

Solomon gives a blessing.

12Then Solomon said, "The LORD has
said that he would dwell in a dark
cloud;[o] 13I have indeed built a magnificent temple for you, a place for you to
dwell[p] forever."
14While the whole assembly of Israel
was standing there, the king turned
around and blessed[q] them. 15Then he
said:

"Praise be to the LORD,[r] the God of
Israel, who with his own hand has
fulfilled what he promised with his
own mouth to my father David. For
he said, 16'Since the day I brought
my people Israel out of Egypt, I have
not chosen a city in any tribe of
Israel to have a temple built for my
Name[s] to be there, but I have chosen[t] David[u] to rule my people Israel.'
17"My father David had it in his
heart to build a temple[v] for the
Name of the LORD, the God of Israel. 18But the LORD said to my father
David, 'Because it was in your heart
to build a temple for my Name, you
did well to have this in your heart.
19Nevertheless, you[w] are not the one
to build the temple, but your son,
who is your own flesh and blood—
he is the one who will build the
temple for my Name.'[x]
20"The LORD has kept the promise he made: I have succeeded David
my father and now I sit on the
throne of Israel, just as the LORD
promised, and I have built[y] the
temple for the Name of the LORD,
the God of Israel. 21I have provided a place there for the ark, in
which is the covenant of the LORD
that he made with our fathers when
he brought them out of Egypt."

7:51 [a] 2Sa 8:11
8:1 [b] Nu 7:2 [c] 2Sa 6:17 [d] 2Sa 5:7
8:2 [e] 2Ch 7:8 [f] Lev 23:34
8:3 [g] Nu 7:9; Jos 3:3
8:4 [h] 1Ki 3:4; 2Ch 1:3
8:5 [i] 2Sa 6:13
8:6 [j] 2Sa 6:17 [k] 1Ki 6:19,27
8:8 [l] Ex 25:13-15
8:9 [m] Ex 24:7-8; 25:21; 40:20; Dt 10:2-5; Heb 9:4
8:10 [n] Ex 40:34-35; 2Ch 7:1-2
8:12 [o] Ps 18:11; 97:2
8:13 [p] Ex 15:17; 2Sa 7:13; Ps 132:13
8:14 [q] 2Sa 6:18
8:15 [r] 2Sa 7:12-13; 1Ch 29:10,20; Ne 9:5; Lk 1:68
8:16 [s] Dt 12:5 [t] 1Sa 16:1 [u] 2Sa 7:4-6,8
8:17 [v] 2Sa 7:2; 1Ch 17:1
8:19 [w] 2Sa 7:5 [x] 2Sa 7:13; 1Ki 5:3,5
8:20 [y] 1Ch 28:6

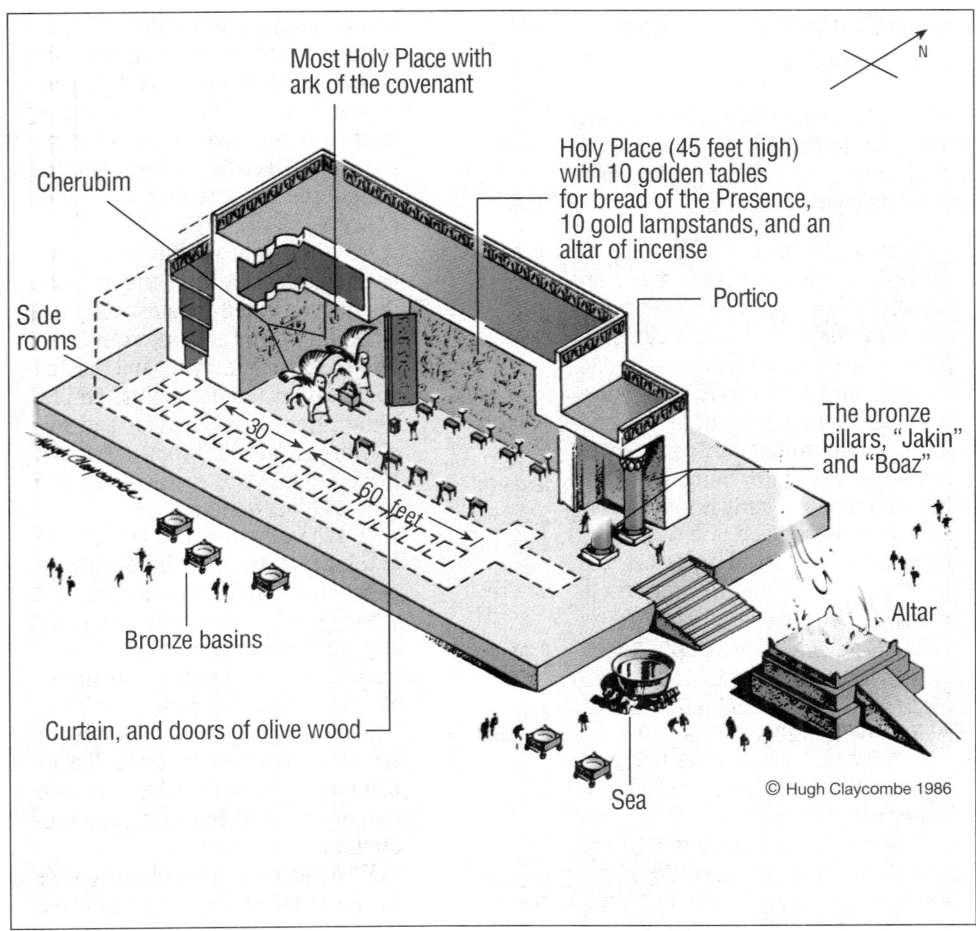

Solomon's Temple
960-586 B.C.

Solomon's temple was a beautiful sight. It took over seven years to build and was a magnificent building containing gold, silver, bronze, and cedar. This house for God was without equal. The description is found in 2 Chronicles 2–4.

FURNISHINGS

Cherubim: represented heavenly beings, symbolized God's presence and holiness (gold-plated, 15 feet wide)

Ark of the covenant: contained the law written on two tablets, symbolized God's presence with Israel (wood overlaid with gold)

Curtain: separated the Holy Place from the Most Holy Place (blue, purple, and crimson yarn and fine linen, with cherubim worked into it)

Doors: between Holy Place and Most Holy Place (wood overlaid with gold)

Golden tables (wood overlaid with gold), *gold lampstands* (with seven lamps on each stand), and *altar of incense* (wood overlaid with gold): instruments for priestly functions in the Holy Place

Bronze pillars: named Jakin (meaning "he establishes") and Boaz (meaning "in him is strength")— taken together they could mean "God provides the strength"

Altar: for burning of sacrifices (bronze)

Sea: for priests' washing (had 12,000 gallon capacity)

Bronze basins: for washing the sacrifices (water basins on wheeled bases)

Solomon's prayer of dedication.

8:22-53pp— 2Ch 6:12-40

22Then Solomon stood before the altar
of the LORD in front of the whole assembly of Israel, spread out his hands[a]
toward heaven 23and said:

"O LORD, God of Israel, there is
no God like[b] you in heaven above or
on earth below—you who keep your
covenant of love[c] with your servants who continue wholeheartedly
in your way. 24You have kept your
promise to your servant David my
father; with your mouth you have
promised and with your hand you
have fulfilled it—as it is today.
25"Now LORD, God of Israel, keep
for your servant David my father the
promises[d] you made to him when
you said, 'You shall never fail to have
a man to sit before me on the throne
of Israel, if only your sons are careful in all they do to walk before me
as you have done.' 26And now, O
God of Israel, let your word that you
promised[e] your servant David my
father come true.
27"But will God really dwell[f] on
earth? The heavens, even the highest heaven, cannot contain[g] you.
How much less this temple I have
built! 28Yet give attention to your
servant's prayer and his plea for mercy, O LORD my God. Hear the cry
and the prayer that your servant is
praying in your presence this day.
29May your eyes be open[h] toward[i]
this temple night and day, this place
of which you said, 'My Name[j]
shall be there,' so that you will hear
the prayer your servant prays toward
this place. 30Hear the supplication
of your servant and of your people
Israel when they pray toward this
place. Hear from heaven, your dwelling place, and when you hear, forgive.[k]
31"When a man wrongs his neighbor and is required to take an oath
and he comes and swears the oath[l]
before your altar in this temple,
32then hear from heaven and act.
Judge between your servants, condemning the guilty and bringing
down on his own head what he
has done. Declare the innocent not
guilty, and so establish his innocence.[m]
33"When your people Israel have
been defeated[n] by an enemy because
they have sinned[o] against you, and
when they turn back to you and confess your name, praying and making
supplication to you in this temple,
34then hear from heaven and forgive the sin of your people Israel and
bring them back to the land you
gave to their fathers.
35"When the heavens are shut up
and there is no rain[p] because your
people have sinned against you, and
when they pray toward this place
and confess your name and turn
from their sin because you have
afflicted them, 36then hear from
heaven and forgive the sin of your
servants, your people Israel. Teach[q]
them the right way[r] to live, and send
rain on the land you gave your people for an inheritance.
37"When famine[s] or plague comes
to the land, or blight[t] or mildew,
locusts or grasshoppers, or when an
enemy besieges them in any of their
cities, whatever disaster or disease
may come, 38and when a prayer or
plea is made by any of your people
Israel—each one aware of the afflictions of his own heart, and
spreading out his hands toward this
temple— 39then hear from heav-
en, your dwelling place. Forgive and
act; deal with each man according
to all he does, since you know[u] his
heart (for you alone know the
hearts of all men), 40so that they
will fear[v] you all the time they live
in the land you gave our fathers.
41"As for the foreigner who does
not belong to your people Israel
but has come from a distant land
because of your name— 42for men

8:22 [a]Ex 9:29; Ezr 9:5
8:23 [b]1Sa 2:2; 2Sa 7:22 [c]Dt 7:9,12; Ne 1:5; 9:32; Da 9:4
8:25 [d]1Ki 2:4
8:26 [e]2Sa 7:25
8:27 [f]Ac 7:48 [g]2Ch 2:6; Ps 139:7-16; Isa 66:1; Jer 23:24
8:29 [h]2Ch 7:15; Ne 1:6 [i]Da 6:10 [j]Dt 12:11
8:30 [k]Ps 85:2
8:31 [l]Ex 22:11
8:32 [m]Dt 25:1
8:33 [n]Lev 26:17; Dt 28:25 [o]Lev 26:39
8:35 [p]Lev 26:19; Dt 28:24
8:36 [q]1Sa 12:23; Ps 25:4; 94:12 [r]Ps 5:8; 27:11; Jer 6:16
8:37 [s]Lev 26:26 [t]Dt 28:22
8:39 [u]1Sa 16:7; 1Ch 28:9; Ps 11:4; Jer 17:10; Jn 2:24; Ac 1:24
8:40 [v]Ps 130:4

will hear of your great name and
your mighty hand[a] and your outstretched arm—when he comes and
prays toward this temple, 43then
hear from heaven, your dwelling
place, and do whatever the foreigner asks of you, so that all the peoples of the earth may know[b] your
name and fear[c] you, as do your own
people Israel, and may know that
this house I have built bears your
Name.

44"When your people go to war
against their enemies, wherever you
send them, and when they pray to
the LORD toward the city you have
chosen and the temple I have built
for your Name, 45then hear from
heaven their prayer and their plea,
and uphold their cause.

46"When they sin against you—
for there is no one who does not
sin[d]—and you become angry with
them and give them over to the enemy, who takes them captive[e] to his
own land, far away or near; 47and
if they have a change of heart in
the land where they are held captive, and repent and plead[f] with you
in the land of their conquerors and
say, 'We have sinned, we have done
wrong, we have acted wickedly';[g]
48and if they turn back to you with
all their heart[h] and soul in the land
of their enemies who took them
captive, and pray[i] to you toward the
land you gave their fathers, toward
the city you have chosen and the
temple[j] I have built for your Name;
49then from heaven, your dwelling
place, hear their prayer and their
plea, and uphold their cause. 50And
forgive your people, who have
sinned against you; forgive all the
offenses they have committed
against you, and cause their conquerors to show them mercy;[k] 51for
they are your people and your inheritance,[l] whom you brought out
of Egypt, out of that iron-smelting
furnace.[m]

52"May your eyes be open to your
servant's plea and to the plea of your
people Israel, and may you listen to
them whenever they cry out to you.
53For you singled them out from
all the nations of the world to be
your own inheritance,[n] just as you
declared through your servant Moses when you, O Sovereign LORD,
brought our fathers out of Egypt."

54When Solomon had finished all these
prayers and supplications to the LORD,
he rose from before the altar of the LORD,
where he had been kneeling with his
hands spread out toward heaven. 55He
stood and blessed[o] the whole assembly
of Israel in a loud voice, saying:

56"Praise be to the LORD, who has
given rest[p] to his people Israel just
as he promised. Not one word has
failed of all the good promises[q] he
gave through his servant Moses.
57May the LORD our God be with us
as he was with our fathers; may he
never leave us nor forsake[r] us. 58May
he turn our hearts[s] to him, to walk
in all his ways and to keep the commands, decrees and regulations he
gave our fathers. 59And may these
words of mine, which I have prayed
before the LORD, be near to the LORD
our God day and night, that he may
uphold the cause of his servant and
the cause of his people Israel according to each day's need, 60so that
all the peoples[t] of the earth may
know that the LORD is God and that
there is no other.[u] 61But your hearts
must be fully committed[v] to the
LORD our God, to live by his decrees
and obey his commands, as at this
time."

The temple dedication.

8:62-66pp— 2Ch 7:1-10

62Then the king and all Israel with
him offered sacrifices before the LORD.
63Solomon offered a sacrifice of fellowship offerings[y] to the LORD: twenty-two
thousand cattle and a hundred and

8:42 [a]Dt 3:24
8:43 [b]1Sa 17:46; 2Ki 19:19 [c]Ps 102:15
8:46 [d]Pr 20:9; Ecc 7:20; Ro 3:9; 1Jn 1:8-10 [e]Lev 26:33-39; Dt 28:64
8:47 [f]Lev 26:40; Ne 1:6 [g]Ps 106:6; Da 9:5
8:48 [h]Dt 4:29; Jer 29:12-14 [i]Da 6:10 [j]Jnh 2:4
8:50 [k]2Ch 30:9; Ps 106:46
8:51 [l]Dt 4:20; 9:29; Ne 1:10 [m]Jer 11:4
8:53 [n]Ex 19:5; Dt 9:26-29
8:55 [o]ver 14; 2Sa 6:18
8:56 [p]Dt 12:10 [q]Jos 21:45; 23:15
8:57 [r]Dt 31:6; Jos 1:5; Heb 13:5
8:58 [s]Ps 119:36
8:60 [t]Jos 4:24; 1Sa 17:46 [u]Dt 4:35; 1Ki 18:39; Jer 10:10-12
8:61 [v]1Ki 11:4; 15:3,14; 2Ki 20:3

y63 Traditionally *peace offerings*; also in verse 64

twenty thousand sheep and goats. So
the king and all the Israelites dedicated the temple of the LORD.
64 On that same day the king consecrated the middle part of the courtyard
in front of the temple of the LORD, and
there he offered burnt offerings, grain
offerings and the fat of the fellowship
offerings, because the bronze altar[a] before the LORD was too small to hold the
burnt offerings, the grain offerings and
the fat of the fellowship offerings.
65 So Solomon observed the festival[b] at
that time, and all Israel with him—a vast
assembly, people from Lebo[z] Hamath[c]
to the Wadi of Egypt.[d] They celebrated it
before the LORD our God for seven days
and seven days more, fourteen days in
all. 66 On the following day he sent the
people away. They blessed the king and
then went home, joyful and glad in heart
for all the good things the LORD had
done for his servant David and his people Israel.

God's covenant with Solomon.

9:1-9pp— 2Ch 7:11-22

9 When Solomon had finished[e] building the temple of the LORD and the
royal palace, and had achieved all he
had desired to do, 2 the LORD appeared[f]
to him a second time, as he had appeared to him at Gibeon. 3 The LORD said
to him:

"I have heard[g] the prayer and plea
you have made before me; I have
consecrated this temple, which you
have built, by putting my Name
there forever. My eyes[h] and my
heart will always be there.
4 "As for you, if you walk before
me in integrity of heart[i] and uprightness, as David[j] your father did,
and do all I command and observe
my decrees and laws, 5 I will establish[k] your royal throne over Israel
forever, as I promised David your
father when I said, 'You shall never
fail[l] to have a man on the throne
of Israel.'
6 "But if you[a] or your sons turn
away[m] from me and do not observe
the commands and decrees I have
given you[a] and go off to serve other gods and worship them, 7 then I
will cut off Israel from the land[n] I
have given them and will reject this
temple I have consecrated for my
Name.[o] Israel will then become a
byword[p] and an object of ridicule[q]
among all peoples. 8 And though this
temple is now imposing, all who
pass by will be appalled and will
scoff and say, 'Why has the LORD
done such a thing to this land and to
this temple?'[r] 9 People will answer,
'Because they have forsaken the
LORD their God, who brought their
fathers out of Egypt, and have embraced other gods, worshiping and
serving them—that is why the LORD
brought all this disaster on them.'"

Various details of Solomon's life.

9:10-28pp— 2Ch 8:1-18

10 At the end of twenty years, during
which Solomon built these two buildings—the temple of the LORD and the
royal palace— 11 King Solomon gave
twenty towns in Galilee to Hiram king of
Tyre, because Hiram had supplied him
with all the cedar and pine and gold[s] he
wanted. 12 But when Hiram went from
Tyre to see the towns that Solomon had
given him, he was not pleased with
them. 13 "What kind of towns are these
you have given me, my brother?" he
asked. And he called them the Land of
Cabul,[b][t] a name they have to this day.
14 Now Hiram had sent to the king 120
talents[c] of gold.
15 Here is the account of the forced
labor King Solomon conscripted[u] to build
the LORD's temple, his own palace, the
supporting terraces,[d][v] the wall of Jerusalem, and Hazor,[w] Megiddo and Gezer.[x]
16 (Pharaoh king of Egypt had attacked
and captured Gezer. He had set it on

8:64 [a]2Ch 4:1
8:65 [b]ver 2; Lev 23:34 [c]Nu 34:8; Jos 13:5; Jdg 3:3; 2Ki 14:25 [d]Ge 15:18
9:1 [e]1Ki 7:1; 2Ch 8:6
9:2 [f]1Ki 3:5
9:3 [g]2Ki 20:5; Ps 10:17 [h]Dt 11:12; 1Ki 8:29
9:4 [i]Ge 17:1 [j]1Ki 15:5
9:5 [k]1Ch 22:10 [l]2Sa 7:15; 1Ki 2:4
9:6 [m]2Sa 7:14
9:7 [n]2Ki 17:23; 25:21 [o]Jer 7:14 [p]Ps 44:14 [q]Dt 28:37
9:8 [r]Dt 29:24; Jer 22:8-9
9:11 [s]2Ch 8:2
9:13 [t]Jos 19:27
9:15 [u]Jos 16:10; 1Ki 5:13 [v]ver 24; 2Sa 5:9 [w]Jos 19:36 [x]Jos 17:11

[z]*65* Or *from the entrance to* [a]*6* The Hebrew is plural. [b]*13* *Cabul* sounds like the Hebrew for *good-for-nothing.* [c]*14* That is, about 4 1/2 tons (about 4 metric tons) [d]*15* Or *the Millo*; also in verse 24

fire. He killed its Canaanite inhabitants and then gave it as a wedding gift to his daughter, Solomon's wife. **17**And Solomon rebuilt Gezer.) He built up Lower Beth Horon,[a] **18**Baalath,[b] and Tadmor[e] in the desert, within his land, **19**as well as all his store cities[c] and the towns for his chariots[d] and for his horses[f]—whatever he desired to build in Jerusalem, in Lebanon and throughout all the territory he ruled.

20All the people left from the Amorites, Hittites, Perizzites, Hivites and Jebusites (these peoples were not Israelites), **21**that is, their descendants[e] remaining in the land, whom the Israelites could not exterminate[g][f]—these Solomon conscripted for his slave labor force,[g] as it is to this day. **22**But Solomon did not make slaves[h] of any of the Israelites; they were his fighting men, his government officials, his officers, his captains, and the commanders of his chariots and charioteers. **23**They were also the chief officials[i] in charge of Solomon's projects—550 officials supervising the men who did the work.

24After Pharaoh's daughter[j] had come up from the City of David to the palace Solomon had built for her, he constructed the supporting terraces.[k]

25Three[l] times a year Solomon sacrificed burnt offerings and fellowship offerings[h] on the altar he had built for the LORD, burning incense before the LORD along with them, and so fulfilled the temple obligations.

26King Solomon also built ships[m] at Ezion Geber,[n] which is near Elath in Edom, on the shore of the Red Sea.[i] **27**And Hiram sent his men—sailors[o] who knew the sea—to serve in the fleet with Solomon's men. **28**They sailed to Ophir[p] and brought back 420 talents[j] of gold, which they delivered to King Solomon.

The queen of Sheba visits Solomon.

10:1-13pp— 2Ch 9:1-12

10 When the queen of Sheba[q] heard about the fame of Solomon and his relation to the name of the LORD, she came to test him with hard questions.[r] **2**Arriving at Jerusalem with a very great caravan—with camels carrying spices, large quantities of gold, and precious stones—she came to Solomon and talked with him about all that she had on her mind. **3**Solomon answered all her questions; nothing was too hard for the king to explain to her. **4**When the queen of Sheba saw all the wisdom of Solomon and the palace he had built, **5**the food on his table,[s] the seating of his officials, the attending servants in their robes, his cupbearers, and the burnt offerings he made at[k] the temple of the LORD, she was overwhelmed.

6She said to the king, "The report I heard in my own country about your achievements and your wisdom is true. **7**But I did not believe these things until I came and saw with my own eyes. Indeed, not even half was told me; in wisdom and wealth[t] you have far exceeded the report I heard. **8**How happy your men must be! How happy your officials, who continually stand before you and hear[u] your wisdom! **9**Praise[v] be to the LORD your God, who has delighted in you and placed you on the throne of Israel. Because of the LORD's eternal love for Israel, he has made you king, to maintain justice[w] and righteousness."

10And she gave the king 120 talents[l] of gold,[x] large quantities of spices, and precious stones. Never again were so many spices brought in as those the queen of Sheba gave to King Solomon.

11(Hiram's ships brought gold from Ophir;[y] and from there they brought great cargoes of almugwood[m] and precious stones. **12**The king used the almugwood to make supports for the temple of the LORD and for the royal palace,

9:17 [a]Jos 16:3; 2Ch 8:5
9:18 [b]Jos 19:44
9:19 [c]ver 1 [d]1Ki 4:26
9:21 [e]Ge 9:25-26 [f]Jos 15:63; 17:12; Jdg 1:21,27,29 [g]Ezr 2:55,58
9:22 [h]Lev 25:39
9:23 [i]1Ki 5:16
9:24 [j]1Ki 3:1; 7:8 [k]2Sa 5:9; 1Ki 11:27; 2Ch 32:5
9:25 [l]Ex 23:14; 2Ch 8:12-13,16
9:26 [m]1Ki 22:48 [n]Nu 33:35; Dt 2:8
9:27 [o]1Ki 10:11; Eze 27:8
9:28 [p]1Ch 29:4
10:1 [q]Ge 10:7,28; Mt 12:42; Lk 11:31 [r]Jdg 14:12
10:5 [s]1Ch 26:16
10:7 [t]1Ch 29:25
10:8 [u]Pr 8:34
10:9 [v]1Ki 5:7 [w]2Sa 8:15; Ps 33:5; 72:2
10:10 [x]ver 2
10:11 [y]Ge 10:29; 1Ki 9:27-28

e *18* The Hebrew may also be read *Tamar.*
f *19* Or *charioteers* g *21* The Hebrew term refers to the irrevocable giving over of things or persons to the LORD, often by totally destroying them.
h *25* Traditionally *peace offerings* i *26* Hebrew *Yam Suph*; that is, Sea of Reeds j *28* That is, about 16 tons (about 14.5 metric tons) k *5* Or *the ascent by which he went up to* l *10* That is, about 4 1/2 tons (about 4 metric tons) m *11* Probably a variant of *algumwood*; also in verse 12

and to make harps and lyres for the musicians. So much almugwood has never been imported or seen since that day.)

13 King Solomon gave the queen of Sheba all she desired and asked for, besides what he had given her out of his royal bounty. Then she left and returned with her retinue to her own country.

Solomon's wisdom and wealth are described.

10:14-29pp— 2Ch 1:14-17; 9:13-28

14 The weight of the gold[a] that Solomon received yearly was 666 talents,[n] 15 not including the revenues from merchants and traders and from all the Arabian kings and the governors of the land.

16 King Solomon made two hundred large shields[b] of hammered gold; six hundred bekas[o] of gold went into each shield. 17 He also made three hundred small shields of hammered gold, with three minas[p] of gold in each shield. The king put them in the Palace of the Forest of Lebanon.[c]

18 Then the king made a great throne inlaid with ivory and overlaid with fine gold. 19 The throne had six steps, and its back had a rounded top. On both sides of the seat were armrests, with a lion standing beside each of them. 20 Twelve lions stood on the six steps, one at either end of each step. Nothing like it had ever been made for any other kingdom. 21 All King Solomon's goblets were gold, and all the household articles in the Palace of the Forest of Lebanon were pure gold. Nothing was made of silver, because silver was considered of little value in Solomon's days. 22 The king had a fleet of trading ships[q][d] at sea along with the ships of Hiram. Once every three years it returned, carrying gold, silver and ivory, and apes and baboons.

23 King Solomon was greater in riches[e] and wisdom[f] than all the other kings of the earth. 24 The whole world sought audience with Solomon to hear the wisdom[g] God had put in his heart. 25 Year after year, everyone who came brought a gift—articles of silver and gold, robes, weapons and spices, and horses and mules.

26 Solomon accumulated chariots and horses;[h] he had fourteen hundred chariots and twelve thousand horses,[r] which he kept in the chariot cities and also with him in Jerusalem. 27 The king made silver as common[i] in Jerusalem as stones, and cedar as plentiful as sycamore-fig trees in the foothills. 28 Solomon's horses were imported from Egypt[s] and from Kue[t]—the royal merchants purchased them from Kue. 29 They imported a chariot from Egypt for six hundred shekels[u] of silver, and a horse for a hundred and fifty.[v] They also exported them to all the kings of the Hittites[j] and of the Arameans.

Solomon's idolatrous wives.

11 King Solomon, however, loved many foreign women[k] besides Pharaoh's daughter—Moabites, Ammonites, Edomites, Sidonians and Hittites. 2 They were from nations about which the LORD had told the Israelites, "You must not intermarry[l] with them, because they will surely turn your hearts after their gods." Nevertheless, Solomon held fast to them in love. 3 He had seven hundred wives of royal birth and three hundred concubines, and his wives led him astray. 4 As Solomon grew old, his wives turned his heart after other gods, and his heart was not fully devoted[m] to the LORD his God, as the heart of David his father had been. 5 He followed Ashtoreth[n] the goddess of the Sidonians, and Molech[w][o] the detestable god of the Ammonites. 6 So Solomon did evil in the eyes of the LORD; he did not follow the LORD completely, as David his father had done.

7 On a hill east[p] of Jerusalem, Solomon

10:14 [a] 1Ki 9:28
10:16 [b] 1Ki 14:26-28
10:17 [c] 1Ki 7:2
10:22 [d] 1Ki 9:26
10:23 [e] 1Ki 3:13 [f] 1Ki 4:30
10:24 [g] 1Ki 3:9,12,28
10:26 [h] Dt 17:16; 1Ki 4:26; 9:19; 2Ch 1:14; 9:25
10:27 [i] Dt 17:17
10:29 [j] 2Ki 7:6-7
11:1 [k] Dt 17:17; Ne 13:26
11:2 [l] Ex 34:16; Dt 7:3-4
11:4 [m] 1Ki 8:61; 9:4
11:5 [n] ver 33; Jdg 2:13; 2Ki 23:13 [o] ver 7
11:7 [p] 2Ki 23:13

[n] *14* That is, about 25 tons (about 23 metric tons)
[o] *16* That is, about 7 1/2 pounds (about 3.5 kilograms)
[p] *17* That is, about 3 3/4 pounds (about 1.7 kilograms)
[q] *22* Hebrew *of ships of Tarshish* [r] *26* Or *charioteers* [s] *28* Or possibly *Muzur*, a region in Cilicia; also in verse 29 [t] *28* Probably *Cilicia*
[u] *29* That is, about 15 pounds (about 7 kilograms)
[v] *29* That is, about 3 3/4 pounds (about 1.7 kilograms)
[w] *5* Hebrew *Milcom*; also in verse 33

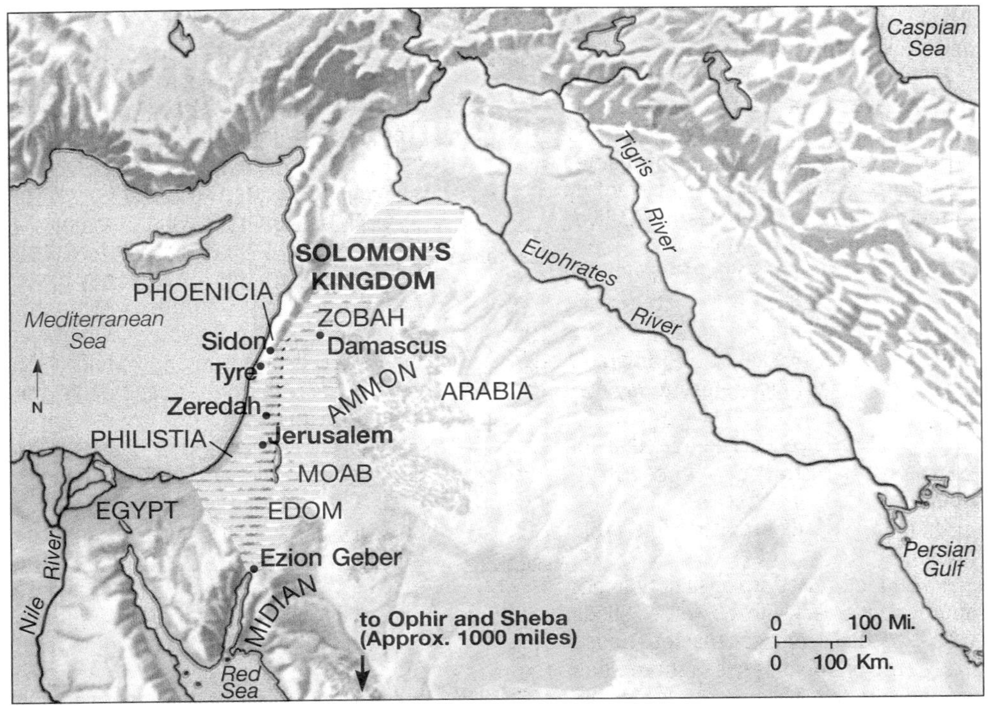

Friends and Enemies

Solomon's reputation brought acclaim and riches from many nations, but he disobeyed God, marrying pagan women and worshiping their gods. So God raised up enemies like Hadad from Edom and Rezon from Zobah (modern-day Syria). Jeroboam from Zeredah was another enemy who would eventually divide this mighty kingdom.

built a high place for Chemosh[a] the detestable god of Moab, and for Molech[b]
the detestable god of the Ammonites.
8He did the same for all his foreign wives,
who burned incense and offered sacrifices to their gods.
9The LORD became angry with Solomon because his heart had turned away
from the LORD, the God of Israel, who
had appeared[c] to him twice. 10Although
he had forbidden Solomon to follow other gods,[d] Solomon did not keep the
LORD's command.[e] 11So the LORD said to
Solomon, "Since this is your attitude and
you have not kept my covenant and my
decrees, which I commanded you, I will
most certainly tear[f] the kingdom away
from you and give it to one of your sub-
ordinates. 12Nevertheless, for the sake of
David your father, I will not do it during
your lifetime. I will tear it out of the hand
of your son. 13Yet I will not tear the

11:7 [a]Nu 21:29; Jdg 11:24 [b]Lev 20:2-5; Ac 7:43
11:9 [c]ver 2-3; 1Ki 3:5; 9:2
11:10 [d]1Ki 9:6 [e]1Ki 6:12
11:11 [f]ver 31; 1Ki 12:15-16; 2Ki 17:21
11:13 [g]1Ki 12:20 [h]2Sa 7:15 [i]Dt 12:11
11:15 [j]Dt 20:13; 2Sa 8:14; 1Ch 18:12
11:18 [k]Nu 10:12

whole kingdom from him, but will give
him one tribe[g] for the sake[h] of David my
servant and for the sake of Jerusalem,
which I have chosen."[i]

Solomon's adversaries.

14Then the LORD raised up against Solomon an adversary, Hadad the Edomite,
from the royal line of Edom. 15Earlier
when David was fighting with Edom,
Joab the commander of the army, who
had gone up to bury the dead, had struck
down all the men in Edom.[j] 16Joab and
all the Israelites stayed there for six
months, until they had destroyed all the
men in Edom. 17But Hadad, still only a
boy, fled to Egypt with some Edomite officials who had served his father. 18They
set out from Midian and went to Paran.[k]
Then taking men from Paran with them,
they went to Egypt, to Pharaoh king of

Egypt, who gave Hadad a house and land and provided him with food.

19 Pharaoh was so pleased with Hadad that he gave him a sister of his own wife, Queen Tahpenes, in marriage. 20 The sister of Tahpenes bore him a son named Genubath, whom Tahpenes brought up in the royal palace. There Genubath lived with Pharaoh's own children.

21 While he was in Egypt, Hadad heard that David rested with his fathers and that Joab the commander of the army was also dead. Then Hadad said to Pharaoh, "Let me go, that I may return to my own country."

22 "What have you lacked here that you want to go back to your own country?" Pharaoh asked.

"Nothing," Hadad replied, "but do let me go!"

23 And God raised up against Solomon another adversary,[a] Rezon son of Eliada, who had fled from his master, Hadadezer[b] king of Zobah. 24 He gathered men around him and became the leader of a band of rebels when David destroyed the forces[x] ⌊of Zobah⌋; the rebels went to Damascus,[c] where they settled and took control. 25 Rezon was Israel's adversary as long as Solomon lived, adding to the trouble caused by Hadad. So Rezon ruled in Aram[d] and was hostile toward Israel.

26 Also, Jeroboam son of Nebat rebelled[e] against the king. He was one of Solomon's officials, an Ephraimite from Zeredah, and his mother was a widow named Zeruah.

27 Here is the account of how he rebelled against the king: Solomon had built the supporting terraces[y][f] and had filled in the gap in the wall of the city of David his father. 28 Now Jeroboam was a man of standing,[g] and when Solomon saw how well[h] the young man did his work, he put him in charge of the whole labor force of the house of Joseph.

29 About that time Jeroboam was going out of Jerusalem, and Ahijah[i] the prophet of Shiloh met him on the way, wearing a new cloak. The two of them were alone out in the country, 30 and Ahijah took hold of the new cloak he was wearing and tore[j] it into twelve pieces. 31 Then he said to Jeroboam, "Take ten pieces for yourself, for this is what the LORD, the God of Israel, says: 'See, I am going to tear[k] the kingdom out of Solomon's hand and give you ten tribes. 32 But for the sake of my servant David and the city of Jerusalem, which I have chosen out of all the tribes of Israel, he will have one tribe. 33 I will do this because they have[z] forsaken me and worshiped[l] Ashtoreth the goddess of the Sidonians, Chemosh the god of the Moabites, and Molech the god of the Ammonites, and have not walked in my ways, nor done what is right in my eyes, nor kept my statutes[m] and laws as David, Solomon's father, did.

34 " 'But I will not take the whole kingdom out of Solomon's hand; I have made him ruler all the days of his life for the sake of David my servant, whom I chose and who observed my commands and statutes. 35 I will take the kingdom from his son's hands and give you ten tribes. 36 I will give one tribe[n] to his son so that David my servant may always have a lamp[o] before me in Jerusalem, the city where I chose to put my Name. 37 However, as for you, I will take you, and you will rule over all that your heart desires;[p] you will be king over Israel. 38 If you do whatever I command you and walk in my ways and do what is right in my eyes by keeping my statutes[q] and commands, as David my servant did, I will be with you. I will build you a dynasty[r] as enduring as the one I built for David and will give Israel to you. 39 I will humble David's descendants because of this, but not forever.' "

40 Solomon tried to kill Jeroboam, but Jeroboam fled to Egypt, to Shishak[s] the king, and stayed there until Solomon's death.

Solomon's death.

11:41-43pp— 2Ch 9:29-31

41 As for the other events of Solomon's

11:23 [a]ver 14 [b]2Sa 8:3
11:24 [c]2Sa 8:5; 10:8,18
11:25 [d]2Sa 10:19
11:26 [e]2Sa 20:21; 1Ki 12:2; 2Ch 13:6
11:27 [f]1Ki 9:24
11:28 [g]Ru 2:1 [h]Pr 22:29
11:29 [i]1Ki 12:15; 14:2; 2Ch 9:29
11:30 [j]1Sa 15:27
11:31 [k]ver 11
11:33 [l]ver 5-7 [m]1Ki 3:3
11:36 [n]ver 13; 1Ki 12:17 [o]1Ki 15:4; 2Ki 8:19
11:37 [p]2Sa 3:21
11:38 [q]Dt 17:19 [r]Jos 1:5; 2Sa 7:11,27
11:40 [s]2Ch 12:2

x24 Hebrew *destroyed them* y27 Or *the Millo*
z33 Hebrew; Septuagint, Vulgate and Syriac *because he has*

reign—all he did and the wisdom he displayed—are they not written in the book
of the annals of Solomon? 42Solomon
reigned in Jerusalem over all Israel forty
years. 43Then he rested with his fathers
and was buried in the city of David his
father. And Rehoboam[a] his son succeeded him as king.

Rehoboam rejects the elders' advice.

12:1-24pp— 2Ch 10:1–11:4

12 Rehoboam went to Shechem, for
all the Israelites had gone there
to make him king. 2When Jeroboam son
of Nebat heard this (he was still in Egypt,
where he had fled[b] from King Solomon),
he returned from[a] Egypt. 3So they sent
for Jeroboam, and he and the whole assembly of Israel went to Rehoboam and
said to him: 4"Your father put a heavy
yoke[c] on us, but now lighten the harsh
labor and the heavy yoke he put on us,
and we will serve you."
5Rehoboam answered, "Go away for
three days and then come back to me."
So the people went away.
6Then King Rehoboam consulted the
elders[d] who had served his father Solomon during his lifetime. "How would you
advise me to answer these people?" he
asked.
7They replied, "If today you will be a
servant to these people and serve them
and give them a favorable answer,[e] they
will always be your servants."
8But Rehoboam rejected the advice the
elders gave him and consulted the young
men who had grown up with him and
were serving him. 9He asked them,
"What is your advice? How should we answer these people who say to me, 'Light-
en the yoke your father put on us'?"
10The young men who had grown up
with him replied, "Tell these people who
have said to you, 'Your father put a heavy
yoke on us, but make our yoke lighter'—
tell them, 'My little finger is thicker than
my father's waist. 11My father laid on you
a heavy yoke; I will make it even heavier. My father scourged you with whips;
I will scourge you with scorpions.'"

11:43 [a]1Ki 14:21; Mt 1:7
12:2 [b]1Ki 11:40
12:4 [c]1Sa 8:11-18; 1Ki 4:20-28
12:6 [d]1Ki 4:2
12:7 [e]Pr 15:1
12:14 [f]Ex 1:14; 5:5-9, 16-18
12:15 [g]ver 24; Dt 2:30; Jdg 14:4; 2Ch 22:7; 25:20 [h]1Ki 11:29

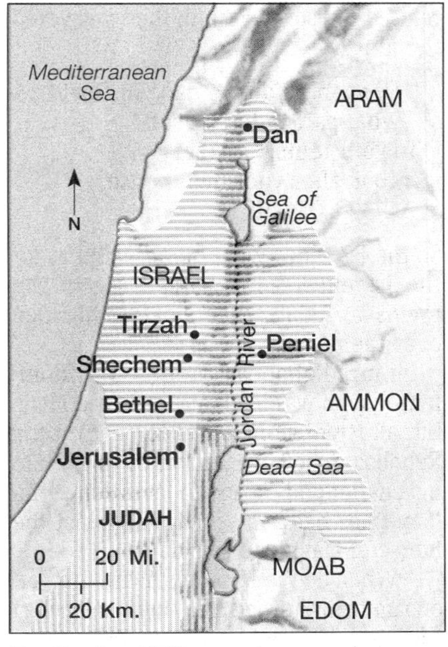

The Kingdom Divides

Rehoboam's threat of heavier burdens caused a rebellion and divided the nation. Rehoboam ruled the southern kingdom; Jeroboam ruled the northern kingdom. Jeroboam set up idols in Dan and Bethel to discourage worship in Jerusalem. At the same time, Aram, Ammon, Moab, and Edom claimed independence from the divided nation.

12Three days later Jeroboam and all the
people returned to Rehoboam, as the king
had said, "Come back to me in three
days." 13The king answered the people
harshly. Rejecting the advice given him
by the elders, 14he followed the advice
of the young men and said, "My father
made your yoke heavy; I will make it
even heavier. My father scourged[f] you
with whips; I will scourge you with scorpions." 15So the king did not listen to the
people, for this turn of events was from
the LORD,[g] to fulfill the word the LORD
had spoken to Jeroboam son of Nebat
through Ahijah[h] the Shilonite.

Ten tribes of Israel revolt to Jeroboam.

16When all Israel saw that the king

[a]2 Or *he remained in*

refused to listen to them, they answered the king:

"What share do we have in David,
what part in Jesse's son?
To your tents, O Israel![a]
Look after your own house,
O David!"

So the Israelites went home. 17But as for the Israelites who were living in the towns of Judah,[b] Rehoboam still ruled over them.

18King Rehoboam sent out Adoniram,[b][c] who was in charge of forced labor, but all Israel stoned him to death. King Rehoboam, however, managed to get into his chariot and escape to Jerusalem. 19So Israel has been in rebellion against the house of David[d] to this day.

20When all the Israelites heard that Jeroboam had returned, they sent and called him to the assembly and made him king over all Israel. Only the tribe of Judah remained loyal to the house of David.[e]

21When Rehoboam arrived in Jerusalem, he mustered the whole house of Judah and the tribe of Benjamin—a hundred and eighty thousand fighting men—to make war[f] against the house of Israel and to regain the kingdom for Rehoboam son of Solomon.

22But this word of God came to Shemaiah[g] the man of God: 23"Say to Rehoboam son of Solomon king of Judah, to the whole house of Judah and Benjamin, and to the rest of the people, 24'This is what the LORD says: Do not go up to fight against your brothers, the Israelites. Go home, every one of you, for this is my doing.'" So they obeyed the word of the LORD and went home again, as the LORD had ordered.

Jeroboam makes two golden calves.

25Then Jeroboam fortified Shechem[h] in the hill country of Ephraim and lived there. From there he went out and built up Peniel.[c][i]

26Jeroboam thought to himself, "The kingdom will now likely revert to the house of David. 27If these people go up to offer sacrifices at the temple of the LORD in Jerusalem,[j] they will again give their allegiance to their lord, Rehoboam king of Judah. They will kill me and return to King Rehoboam."

28After seeking advice, the king made two golden calves.[k] He said to the people, "It is too much for you to go up to Jerusalem. Here are your gods, O Israel, who brought you up out of Egypt."[l] 29One he set up in Bethel,[m] and the other in Dan.[n] 30And this thing became a sin;[o] the people went even as far as Dan to worship the one there.

31Jeroboam built shrines[p] on high places and appointed priests[q] from all sorts of people, even though they were not Levites. 32He instituted a festival on the fifteenth day of the eighth[r] month, like the festival held in Judah, and offered sacrifices on the altar. This he did in Bethel, sacrificing to the calves he had made. And at Bethel he also installed priests at the high places he had made. 33On the fifteenth day of the eighth month, a month of his own choosing, he offered sacrifices on the altar he had built at Bethel.[s] So he instituted the festival for the Israelites and went up to the altar to make offerings.

A man of God from Judah prophesies Josiah's birth.

13 By the word of the LORD a man of God[t] came from Judah to Bethel,[u] as Jeroboam was standing by the altar to make an offering. 2He cried out against the altar by the word of the LORD: "O altar, altar! This is what the LORD says: 'A son named Josiah[v] will be born to the house of David. On you he will sacrifice the priests of the high places who now make offerings here, and human bones will be burned on you.'" 3That same day the man of God gave a sign:[w] "This is the sign the LORD has declared: The altar will be split apart and the ashes on it will be poured out."

12:16 [a]2Sa 20:1
12:17 [b]1Ki 11:13,36
12:18 [c]2Sa 20:24; 1Ki 4:6; 5:14
12:19 [d]2Ki 17:21
12:20 [e]1Ki 11:13,32
12:21 [f]2Ch 11:1
12:22 [g]2Ch 12:5-7
12:25 [h]Jdg 9:45 [i]Jdg 8:8,17
12:27 [j]Dt 12:5-6
12:28 [k]Ex 32:4; 2Ki 10:29; 17:16 [l]Ex 32:8
12:29 [m]Ge 28:19 [n]Jdg 18:27-31
12:30 [o]1Ki 13:34; 2Ki 17:21
12:31 [p]1Ki 13:32 [q]Nu 3:10; 1Ki 13:33; 2Ki 17:32; 2Ch 11:14-15; 13:9
12:32 [r]Lev 23:33-34; Nu 29:12
12:33 [s]Nu 15:39; 1Ki 13:1; Am 7:13
13:1 [t]2Ki 23:17 [u]1Ki 12:32-33
13:2 [v]2Ki 23:15-16, 20
13:3 [w]Jdg 6:17; Isa 7:14; Jn 2:11; 1Co 1:22

b *18* Some Septuagint manuscripts and Syriac (see also 1 Kings 4:6 and 5:14); Hebrew *Adoram* c *25* Hebrew *Penuel,* a variant of *Peniel*

4When King Jeroboam heard what the
man of God cried out against the altar at
Bethel, he stretched out his hand from
the altar and said, "Seize him!" But the
hand he stretched out toward the man
shriveled up, so that he could not pull
it back. 5Also, the altar was split apart
and its ashes poured out according to
the sign given by the man of God by the
word of the LORD.

6Then the king said to the man of God,
"Intercede[a] with the LORD your God and
pray for me that my hand may be restored." So the man of God interceded
with the LORD, and the king's hand was
restored and became as it was before.

7The king said to the man of God,
"Come home with me and have something to eat, and I will give you a gift."[b]

8But the man of God answered the
king, "Even if you were to give me half
your possessions,[c] I would not go with
you, nor would I eat bread[d] or drink
water here. 9For I was commanded by
the word of the LORD: 'You must not eat
bread or drink water or return by the
way you came.'" 10So he took another
road and did not return by the way he
had come to Bethel.

An old prophet lies to the man of God.

11Now there was a certain old prophet
living in Bethel, whose sons came and
told him all that the man of God had
done there that day. They also told their
father what he had said to the king.
12Their father asked them, "Which
way did he go?" And his sons showed
him which road the man of God from
Judah had taken. 13So he said to his sons,
"Saddle the donkey for me." And when
they had saddled the donkey for him, he
mounted it 14and rode after the man of
God. He found him sitting under an
oak tree and asked, "Are you the man of
God who came from Judah?"

"I am," he replied.

15So the prophet said to him, "Come
home with me and eat."

16The man of God said, "I cannot turn
back and go with you, nor can I eat
bread[e] or drink water with you in this
place. 17I have been told by the word of
the LORD: 'You must not eat bread or
drink water there or return by the way
you came.'"

18The old prophet answered, "I too am
a prophet, as you are. And an angel said
to me by the word of the LORD: 'Bring
him back with you to your house so that
he may eat bread and drink water.'" (But
he was lying[f] to him.) 19So the man of
God returned with him and ate and
drank in his house.

A lion kills the man of God.

20While they were sitting at the table,
the word of the LORD came to the old
prophet who had brought him back.
21He cried out to the man of God who
had come from Judah, "This is what the
LORD says: 'You have defied[g] the word of
the LORD and have not kept the command the LORD your God gave you. 22You
came back and ate bread and drank water
in the place where he told you not to eat
or drink. Therefore your body will not be
buried in the tomb of your fathers.'"

23When the man of God had finished
eating and drinking, the prophet who
had brought him back saddled his donkey for him. 24As he went on his way, a
lion[h] met him on the road and killed him,
and his body was thrown down on the
road, with both the donkey and the lion
standing beside it. 25Some people who
passed by saw the body thrown down
there, with the lion standing beside the
body, and they went and reported it in
the city where the old prophet lived.

26When the prophet who had brought
him back from his journey heard of it, he
said, "It is the man of God who defied
the word of the LORD. The LORD has given
him over to the lion, which has mauled
him and killed him, as the word of the
LORD had warned him."

27The prophet said to his sons, "Saddle
the donkey for me," and they did so.
28Then he went out and found the body
thrown down on the road, with the don-

13:6 [a]Ex 8:8; 9:28; 10:17; Lk 6:27-28; Ac 8:24; Jas 5:16
13:7 [b]1Sa 9:7; 2Ki 5:15
13:8 [c]Nu 22:18; 24:13 [d]ver 16
13:16 [e]ver 8
13:18 [f]Dt 13:3
13:21 [g]ver 26
13:24 [h]1Ki 20:36

key and the lion standing beside it. The
lion had neither eaten the body nor
mauled the donkey. 29So the prophet
picked up the body of the man of God,
laid it on the donkey, and brought it
back to his own city to mourn for him
and bury him. 30Then he laid the body
in his own tomb, and they mourned over
him and said, "Oh, my brother!"[a]

31After burying him, he said to his
sons, "When I die, bury me in the grave
where the man of God is buried; lay my
bones[b] beside his bones. 32For the message he declared by the word of the LORD
against the altar in Bethel and against
all the shrines on the high places[c] in the
towns of Samaria[d] will certainly come
true."[e]

33Even after this, Jeroboam did not
change his evil ways, but once more appointed priests for the high places from
all sorts[f] of people. Anyone who wanted
to become a priest he consecrated for the
high places. 34This was the sin[g] of the
house of Jeroboam that led to its downfall and to its destruction[h] from the face
of the earth.

Ahijah's prophecy against Jeroboam.

14 At that time Abijah son of Jeroboam became ill, 2and Jeroboam
said to his wife, "Go, disguise yourself,
so you won't be recognized as the wife
of Jeroboam. Then go to Shiloh. Ahijah[i]
the prophet is there—the one who told
me I would be king over this people.
3Take ten loaves of bread[j] with you,
some cakes and a jar of honey, and go
to him. He will tell you what will happen to the boy." 4So Jeroboam's wife did
what he said and went to Ahijah's house
in Shiloh.

Now Ahijah could not see; his sight
was gone because of his age. 5But the
LORD had told Ahijah, "Jeroboam's wife
is coming to ask you about her son, for
he is ill, and you are to give her such
and such an answer. When she arrives,
she will pretend to be someone else."

6So when Ahijah heard the sound of
her footsteps at the door, he said, "Come
in, wife of Jeroboam. Why this pretense?
I have been sent to you with bad news.
7Go, tell Jeroboam that this is what the
LORD, the God of Israel, says: 'I raised you
up from among the people and made you
a leader[k] over my people Israel. 8I tore[l]
the kingdom away from the house of
David and gave it to you, but you have
not been like my servant David, who
kept my commands and followed me
with all his heart, doing only what was
right[m] in my eyes. 9You have done more
evil than all who lived before you. You
have made for yourself other gods, idols[n]
made of metal; you have provoked me to
anger and thrust me behind your back.[o]

10"'Because of this, I am going to bring
disaster on the house of Jeroboam. I will
cut off from Jeroboam every last male
in Israel—slave or free.[p] I will burn up
the house of Jeroboam as one burns
dung, until it is all gone.[q] 11Dogs[r] will
eat those belonging to Jeroboam who die
in the city, and the birds of the air will
feed on those who die in the country.
The LORD has spoken!'

12"As for you, go back home. When
you set foot in your city, the boy will die.
13All Israel will mourn for him and bury
him. He is the only one belonging to Jeroboam who will be buried, because he
is the only one in the house of Jeroboam
in whom the LORD, the God of Israel, has
found anything good.[s]

14"The LORD will raise up for himself a
king over Israel who will cut off the family of Jeroboam. This is the day! What?
Yes, even now.[d] 15And the LORD will
strike Israel, so that it will be like a reed
swaying in the water. He will uproot[t]
Israel from this good land that he gave
to their forefathers and scatter them beyond the River,[e] because they provoked[u]
the LORD to anger by making Asherah[v]
poles.[f] 16And he will give Israel up because of the sins[w] Jeroboam has committed and has caused Israel to commit."

13:30 [a]Jer 22:18
13:31 [b]2Ki 23:18
13:32 [c]ver 2; Lev 26:30 [d]1Ki 16:24,28 [e]2Ki 23:16
13:33 [f]1Ki 12:31; 2Ch 11:15; 13:9
13:34 [g]1Ki 12:30 [h]1Ki 14:10
14:2 [i]1Sa 28:8; 2Sa 14:2; 1Ki 11:29
14:3 [j]1Sa 9:7
14:7 [k]2Sa 12:7-8; 1Ki 16:2
14:8 [l]1Ki 11:31, 33,38 [m]1Ki 15:5
14:9 [n]Ex 34:17; 1Ki 12:28; 2Ch 11:15 [o]Ne 9:26; Ps 50:17; Eze 23:35
14:10 [p]Dt 32:36; 1Ki 21:21; 2Ki 9:8-9; 14:26 [q]1Ki 15:29
14:11 [r]1Ki 16:4; 21:24
14:13 [s]2Ch 12:12; 19:3
14:15 [t]Dt 29:28; 2Ki 15:29; 17:6; Ps 52:5 [u]Jos 23:15-16 [v]Ex 34:13; Dt 12:3
14:16 [w]1Ki 12:30; 13:34; 15:30,34; 16:2

[d]*14* The meaning of the Hebrew for this sentence is uncertain. [e]*15* That is, the Euphrates [f]*15* That is, symbols of the goddess Asherah; here and elsewhere in 1 Kings

The death of Jeroboam's son, Abijah.

17 Then Jeroboam's wife got up and left
and went to Tirzah.[a] As soon as she
stepped over the threshold of the house,
the boy died. 18 They buried him, and
all Israel mourned for him, as the LORD
had said through his servant the prophet Ahijah.
19 The other events of Jeroboam's reign,
his wars and how he ruled, are written
in the book of the annals of the kings
of Israel. 20 He reigned for twenty-two
years and then rested with his fathers.
And Nadab his son succeeded him as
king.

Rehoboam's evil reign in Judah.

14:21,25-31pp— 2Ch 12:9-16

21 Rehoboam son of Solomon was king
in Judah. He was forty-one years old
when he became king, and he reigned
seventeen years in Jerusalem, the city the
LORD had chosen out of all the tribes of
Israel in which to put his Name. His
mother's name was Naamah; she was an
Ammonite.[b]
22 Judah[c] did evil in the eyes of the
LORD. By the sins they committed they
stirred up his jealous anger[d] more than
their fathers had done. 23 They also set
up for themselves high places, sacred
stones[e] and Asherah poles on every high
hill and under every spreading tree.[f]
24 There were even male shrine prostitutes[g] in the land; the people engaged
in all the detestable practices of the nations the LORD had driven out before
the Israelites.
25 In the fifth year of King Rehoboam,
Shishak king of Egypt attacked[h] Jerusalem. 26 He carried off the treasures of
the temple[i] of the LORD and the treasures of the royal palace. He took everything, including all the gold shields[j]
Solomon had made. 27 So King Rehoboam made bronze shields to replace
them and assigned these to the commanders of the guard on duty at the
entrance to the royal palace. 28 Whenever the king went to the LORD's temple, the guards bore the shields, and
afterward they returned them to the
guardroom.
29 As for the other events of Rehoboam's reign, and all he did, are they not
written in the book of the annals of the
kings of Judah? 30 There was continual
warfare[k] between Rehoboam and Jeroboam. 31 And Rehoboam rested with his
fathers and was buried with them in
the City of David. His mother's name
was Naamah; she was an Ammonite.[l]
And Abijah[g] his son succeeded him as
king.

Abijah reigns in Judah.

15:1-2,6-8pp—2Ch 13:1-2,22–14:1

15 In the eighteenth year of the reign
of Jeroboam son of Nebat, Abijah[h]
became king of Judah, 2 and he reigned in
Jerusalem three years. His mother's name
was Maacah[m] daughter of Abishalom.[i]
3 He committed all the sins his father
had done before him; his heart was
not fully devoted[n] to the LORD his God,
as the heart of David his forefather had
been. 4 Nevertheless, for David's sake the
LORD his God gave him a lamp[o] in Jerusalem by raising up a son to succeed
him and by making Jerusalem strong.
5 For David had done what was right in
the eyes of the LORD and had not failed
to keep[p] any of the LORD's commands all
the days of his life—except in the case
of Uriah[q] the Hittite.
6 There was war[r] between Rehoboam[j] and Jeroboam throughout ⌊Abijah's⌋
lifetime. 7 As for the other events of Abijah's reign, and all he did, are they not
written in the book of the annals of the
kings of Judah? There was war between
Abijah and Jeroboam. 8 And Abijah rested
with his fathers and was buried in the
City of David. And Asa his son succeeded him as king.

14:17 [a]ver 12; 1Ki 15:33; 16:6-9
14:21 [b]ver 31; 1Ki 11:1; 2Ch 12:13
14:22 [c]2Ch 12:1 [d]Dt 32:21; Ps 78:58; 1Co 10:22
14:23 [e]Dt 16:22; 2Ki 17:9-10; Eze 16:24-25 [f]Dt 12:2; Isa 57:5
14:24 [g]Dt 23:17; 1Ki 15:12; 2Ki 23:7
14:25 [h]1Ki 11:40; 2Ch 12:2
14:26 [i]1Ki 15:15,18 [j]1Ki 10:17
14:30 [k]1Ki 12:21; 15:6
14:31 [l]ver 21; 2Ch 12:16
15:2 [m]2Ch 11:20; 13:2
15:3 [n]1Ki 11:4; Ps 119:80
15:4 [o]2Sa 21:17; 1Ki 11:36; 2Ch 21:7
15:5 [p]1Ki 9:4; 14:8 [q]2Sa 11:2-27; 12:9
15:6 [r]1Ki 14:30

g *31* Some Hebrew manuscripts and Septuagint (see also 2 Chron. 12:16); most Hebrew manuscripts *Abijam* h *1* Some Hebrew manuscripts and Septuagint (see also 2 Chron. 12:16); most Hebrew manuscripts *Abijam*; also in verses 7 and 8
i *2* A variant of *Absalom*; also in verse 10
j *6* Most Hebrew manuscripts; some Hebrew manuscripts and Syriac *Abijam* (that is, Abijah)

Asa reigns in Judah.

15:9-22pp— 2Ch 14:2-3; 15:16–16:6
15:23-24pp— 2Ch 16:11–17:1

9In the twentieth year of Jeroboam
king of Israel, Asa became king of Judah,
10and he reigned in Jerusalem forty-one
years. His grandmother's name was Maacah[a] daughter of Abishalom.
11Asa did what was right in the eyes
of the LORD, as his father David had done.
12He expelled the male shrine prostitutes[b] from the land and got rid of all the
idols his fathers had made. 13He even deposed his grandmother Maacah from her
position as queen mother, because she
had made a repulsive Asherah pole. Asa
cut the pole down[c] and burned it in
the Kidron Valley. 14Although he did not
remove the high places, Asa's heart was
fully committed[d] to the LORD all his life.
15He brought into the temple of the LORD
the silver and gold and the articles that
he and his father had dedicated.[e]
16There was war[f] between Asa and
Baasha king of Israel throughout their
reigns. 17Baasha king of Israel went up
against Judah and fortified Ramah[g] to prevent anyone from leaving or entering the
territory of Asa king of Judah.
18Asa then took all the silver and gold
that was left in the treasuries of the
LORD's temple[h] and of his own palace. He
entrusted it to his officials and sent[i]
them to Ben-Hadad[j] son of Tabrimmon,
the son of Hezion, the king of Aram, who
was ruling in Damascus. 19"Let there be
a treaty between me and you," he said,
"as there was between my father and
your father. See, I am sending you a gift
of silver and gold. Now break your treaty
with Baasha king of Israel so he will
withdraw from me."
20Ben-Hadad agreed with King Asa and
sent the commanders of his forces against
the towns of Israel. He conquered[k] Ijon,
Dan, Abel Beth Maacah and all Kinnereth in addition to Naphtali. 21When
Baasha heard this, he stopped building
Ramah and withdrew to Tirzah. 22Then
King Asa issued an order to all Judah—
no one was exempt—and they carried
away from Ramah the stones and timber
Baasha had been using there. With them
King Asa built up Geba[l] in Benjamin, and
also Mizpah.
23As for all the other events of Asa's
reign, all his achievements, all he did and
the cities he built, are they not written
in the book of the annals of the kings of
Judah? In his old age, however, his feet
became diseased. 24Then Asa rested with
his fathers and was buried with them in
the city of his father David. And Jehoshaphat[m] his son succeeded him as king.

Nadab reigns in Israel.

25Nadab son of Jeroboam became king
of Israel in the second year of Asa king
of Judah, and he reigned over Israel two
years. 26He did evil in the eyes of the
LORD, walking in the ways of his father[n]
and in his sin, which he had caused Israel to commit.
27Baasha son of Ahijah of the house
of Issachar plotted against him, and he
struck him down[o] at Gibbethon,[p] a Philistine town, while Nadab and all Israel
were besieging it. 28Baasha killed Nadab
in the third year of Asa king of Judah and
succeeded him as king.
29As soon as he began to reign, he
killed Jeroboam's whole family.[q] He did
not leave Jeroboam anyone that breathed,
but destroyed them all, according to the
word of the LORD given through his servant Ahijah the Shilonite— 30because
of the sins[r] Jeroboam had committed and
had caused Israel to commit, and because
he provoked the LORD, the God of Israel,
to anger.
31As for the other events of Nadab's
reign, and all he did, are they not written in the book of the annals of the kings
of Israel? 32There was war[s] between Asa
and Baasha king of Israel throughout
their reigns.

Baasha reigns in Israel.

33In the third year of Asa king of Judah,
Baasha son of Ahijah became king of all
Israel in Tirzah, and he reigned twenty-
four years. 34He did evil[t] in the eyes of

15:10 [a] ver 2
15:12 [b] 1Ki 14:24; 22:46
15:13 [c] Ex 32:20
15:14 [d] ver 3; 1Ki 8:61; 22:43
15:15 [e] 1Ki 7:51
15:16 [f] ver 32
15:17 [g] Jos 18:25; 1Ki 12:27
15:18 [h] ver 15; 1Ki 14:26 [i] 2Ki 12:18 [j] 1Ki 11:23-24
15:20 [k] Jdg 18:29; 2Sa 20:14; 2Ki 15:29
15:22 [l] Jos 18:24; 21:17
15:24 [m] Mt 1:8
15:26 [n] 1Ki 12:30; 14:16
15:27 [o] 1Ki 14:14 [p] Jos 19:44; 21:23
15:29 [q] 1Ki 14:10,14
15:30 [r] 1Ki 14:9,16
15:32 [s] ver 16
15:34 [t] ver 26; 1Ki 12:28-29; 13:33; 14:16

the LORD, walking in the ways of Jeroboam and in his sin, which he had caused Israel to commit.

Jehu's prophecy against Baasha.

16 Then the word of the LORD came to Jehu[a] son of Hanani[b] against Baasha: [2]"I lifted you up from the dust[c] and made you leader[d] of my people Israel, but you walked in the ways of Jeroboam and caused[e] my people Israel to sin and to provoke me to anger by their sins. [3]So I am about to consume Baasha and his house,[f] and I will make your house like that of Jeroboam son of Nebat. [4]Dogs[g] will eat those belonging to Baasha who die in the city, and the birds of the air will feed on those who die in the country."

[5]As for the other events of Baasha's reign, what he did and his achievements, are they not written in the book of the annals[h] of the kings of Israel? [6]Baasha rested with his fathers and was buried in Tirzah.[i] And Elah his son succeeded him as king.

[7]Moreover, the word of the LORD came[j] through the prophet Jehu[k] son of Hanani to Baasha and his house, because of all the evil he had done in the eyes of the LORD, provoking him to anger by the things he did, and becoming like the house of Jeroboam—and also because he destroyed it.

Elah reigns in Israel.

[8]In the twenty-sixth year of Asa king of Judah, Elah son of Baasha became king of Israel, and he reigned in Tirzah two years.

[9]Zimri, one of his officials, who had command of half his chariots, plotted against him. Elah was in Tirzah at the time, getting drunk[l] in the home of Arza, the man in charge[m] of the palace at Tirzah. [10]Zimri came in, struck him down and killed him in the twenty-seventh year of Asa king of Judah. Then he succeeded him as king.

[11]As soon as he began to reign and was seated on the throne, he killed off Baasha's whole family.[n] He did not spare a single male, whether relative or friend. [12]So Zimri destroyed the whole family of Baasha, in accordance with the word of the LORD spoken against Baasha through the prophet Jehu— [13]because of all the sins Baasha and his son Elah had committed and had caused Israel to commit, so that they provoked the LORD, the God of Israel, to anger by their worthless idols.[o]

[14]As for the other events of Elah's reign, and all he did, are they not written in the book of the annals of the kings of Israel?

Zimri reigns in Israel.

[15]In the twenty-seventh year of Asa king of Judah, Zimri reigned in Tirzah seven days. The army was encamped near Gibbethon,[p] a Philistine town. [16]When the Israelites in the camp heard that Zimri had plotted against the king and murdered him, they proclaimed Omri, the commander of the army, king over Israel that very day there in the camp. [17]Then Omri and all the Israelites with him withdrew from Gibbethon and laid siege to Tirzah. [18]When Zimri saw that the city was taken, he went into the citadel of the royal palace and set the palace on fire around him. So he died, [19]because of the sins he had committed, doing evil in the eyes of the LORD and walking in the ways of Jeroboam and in the sin he had committed and had caused Israel to commit.

[20]As for the other events of Zimri's reign, and the rebellion he carried out, are they not written in the book of the annals of the kings of Israel?

Omri reigns in Israel.

[21]Then the people of Israel were split into two factions; half supported Tibni son of Ginath for king, and the other half supported Omri. [22]But Omri's followers proved stronger than those of Tibni son of Ginath. So Tibni died and Omri became king.

[23]In the thirty-first year of Asa king

16:1 [a]ver 7; 2Ch 19:2; 20:34 [b]2Ch 16:7
16:2 [c]1Sa 2:8 [d]1Ki 14:7-9 [e]1Ki 15:34
16:3 [f]ver 11; 1Ki 14:10; 15:29; 21:22
16:4 [g]1Ki 14:11
16:5 [h]1Ki 14:19; 15:31
16:6 [i]1Ki 14:17; 15:33
16:7 [j]1Ki 15:27,29 [k]ver 1
16:9 [l]2Ki 9:30-33 [m]1Ki 18:3
16:11 [n]ver 3
16:13 [o]Dt 32:21; 1Sa 12:21; Isa 41:29
16:15 [p]Jos 19:44; 1Ki 15:27

of Judah, Omri became king of Israel, and he reigned twelve years, six of them in Tirzah.[a] 24He bought the hill of Samaria from Shemer for two talents[k] of silver and built a city on the hill, calling it Samaria,[b] after Shemer, the name of the former owner of the hill.

25But Omri did evil[c] in the eyes of the LORD and sinned more than all those before him. 26He walked in all the ways of Jeroboam son of Nebat and in his sin, which he had caused[d] Israel to commit, so that they provoked the LORD, the God of Israel, to anger by their worthless idols.[e]

27As for the other events of Omri's reign, what he did and the things he achieved, are they not written in the book of the annals of the kings of Israel? 28Omri rested with his fathers and was buried in Samaria. And Ahab his son succeeded him as king.

Ahab reigns in Israel.

29In the thirty-eighth year of Asa king of Judah, Ahab son of Omri became king of Israel, and he reigned in Samaria over Israel twenty-two years. 30Ahab son of Omri did more[f] evil in the eyes of the LORD than any of those before him. 31He not only considered it trivial to commit the sins of Jeroboam son of Nebat, but he also married[g] Jezebel daughter[h] of Ethbaal king of the Sidonians, and began to serve Baal[i] and worship him. 32He set up an altar for Baal in the temple[j] of Baal that he built in Samaria. 33Ahab also made an Asherah pole[k] and did more[l] to provoke the LORD, the God of Israel, to anger than did all the kings of Israel before him.

34In Ahab's time, Hiel of Bethel rebuilt Jericho. He laid its foundations at the cost of his firstborn son Abiram, and he set up its gates at the cost of his youngest son Segub, in accordance with the word of the LORD spoken by Joshua son of Nun.[m]

Elijah is fed by ravens.

17 Now Elijah[n] the Tishbite, from Tishbe[l] in Gilead,[o] said to Ahab, "As the LORD, the God of Israel, lives, whom I serve, there will be neither dew nor rain[p] in the next few years except at my word."

2Then the word of the LORD came to Elijah: 3"Leave here, turn eastward and hide in the Kerith Ravine, east of the Jordan. 4You will drink from the brook, and I have ordered the ravens[q] to feed you there."

5So he did what the LORD had told him. He went to the Kerith Ravine, east of the Jordan, and stayed there. 6The ravens brought him bread and meat in the morning[r] and bread and meat in the evening, and he drank from the brook.

God sends Elijah to the widow of Zarephath.

7Some time later the brook dried up because there had been no rain in the land. 8Then the word of the LORD came to him: 9"Go at once to Zarephath[s] of Sidon and stay there. I have commanded a widow[t] in that place to supply you with food." 10So he went to Zarephath. When he came to the town gate, a widow was there gathering sticks. He called to her and asked, "Would you bring me a little water in a jar so I may have a drink?"[u] 11As she was going to get it, he called, "And bring me, please, a piece of bread."

12"As surely as the LORD your God lives," she replied, "I don't have any bread—only a handful of flour in a jar and a little oil[v] in a jug. I am gathering a few sticks to take home and make a meal for myself and my son, that we may eat it—and die."

13Elijah said to her, "Don't be afraid. Go home and do as you have said. But first make a small cake of bread for me from what you have and bring it to me, and then make something for yourself and your son. 14For this is what the LORD, the God of Israel, says: 'The jar of flour will not be used up and the jug of oil will not run dry until the day the LORD gives rain on the land.'"

16:23 [a] 1Ki 15:21
16:24 [b] 1Ki 13:32; Jn 4:4
16:25 [c] Dt 4:25; Mic 6:16
16:26 [d] ver 19 [e] Dt 32:21
16:30 [f] ver 25; 1Ki 14:9
16:31 [g] Dt 7:3; 1Ki 11:2 [h] Jdg 18:7; 2Ki 9:34 [i] 2Ki 10:18; 17:16
16:32 [j] 2Ki 10:21,27; 11:18
16:33 [k] 2Ki 13:6 [l] ver 29,30; 1Ki 14:9; 21:25
16:34 [m] Jos 6:26
17:1 [n] Mal 4:5; Jas 5:17 [o] Jdg 12:4 [p] Dt 10:8; 1Ki 18:1; 2Ki 3:14; Lk 4:25
17:4 [q] Ge 8:7
17:6 [r] Ex 16:8
17:9 [s] Ob 1:20 [t] Lk 4:26
17:10 [u] Ge 24:17; Jn 4:7
17:12 [v] ver 1; 2Ki 4:2

[k] *24* That is, about 150 pounds (about 70 kilograms)
[l] *1* Or *Tishbite, of the settlers*

15 She went away and did as Elijah had
told her. So there was food every day for
Elijah and for the woman and her family. 16 For the jar of flour was not used up
and the jug of oil did not run dry, in
keeping with the word of the LORD spoken by Elijah.

17 Some time later the son of the woman who owned the house became ill.
He grew worse and worse, and finally
stopped breathing. 18 She said to Elijah,
"What do you have against me, man of
God? Did you come to remind me of my
sin[a] and kill my son?"

19 "Give me your son," Elijah replied.
He took him from her arms, carried him
to the upper room where he was staying,
and laid him on his bed. 20 Then he cried
out to the LORD, "O LORD my God, have
you brought tragedy also upon this widow I am staying with, by causing her son
to die?" 21 Then he stretched[b] himself
out on the boy three times and cried to
the LORD, "O LORD my God, let this boy's
life return to him!"

22 The LORD heard Elijah's cry, and the
boy's life returned to him, and he lived.
23 Elijah picked up the child and carried
him down from the room into the house.
He gave him to his mother and said,
"Look, your son is alive!"

24 Then the woman said to Elijah,
"Now I know[c] that you are a man of
God and that the word of the LORD from
your mouth is the truth."[d]

Elijah defeats Baal's prophets at Mount Carmel.

18 After a long time, in the third[e]
year, the word of the LORD came
to Elijah: "Go and present yourself to
Ahab, and I will send rain[f] on the land."
2 So Elijah went to present himself to
Ahab.

Now the famine was severe in Samaria, 3 and Ahab had summoned Obadiah,
who was in charge[g] of his palace. (Obadiah was a devout believer[h] in the LORD.
4 While Jezebel[i] was killing off the LORD's
prophets, Obadiah had taken a hundred
prophets and hidden[j] them in two caves,
fifty in each, and had supplied them with
food and water.) 5 Ahab had said to Obadiah, "Go through the land to all the
springs and valleys. Maybe we can find
some grass to keep the horses and mules
alive so we will not have to kill any of
our animals." 6 So they divided the land
they were to cover, Ahab going in one
direction and Obadiah in another.

7 As Obadiah was walking along, Elijah met him. Obadiah recognized[k] him,
bowed down to the ground, and said, "Is
it really you, my lord Elijah?"

8 "Yes," he replied. "Go tell your master, 'Elijah is here.'"

9 "What have I done wrong," asked
Obadiah, "that you are handing your servant over to Ahab to be put to death?
10 As surely as the LORD your God lives,
there is not a nation or kingdom where
my master has not sent someone to look[l]
for you. And whenever a nation or kingdom claimed you were not there, he
made them swear they could not find
you. 11 But now you tell me to go to my
master and say, 'Elijah is here.' 12 I don't
know where the Spirit[m] of the LORD may
carry you when I leave you. If I go and
tell Ahab and he doesn't find you, he
will kill me. Yet I your servant have
worshiped the LORD since my youth.
13 Haven't you heard, my lord, what I
did while Jezebel was killing the prophets of the LORD? I hid a hundred of the
LORD's prophets in two caves, fifty in
each, and supplied them with food and
water. 14 And now you tell me to go to
my master and say, 'Elijah is here.' He
will kill me!"

15 Elijah said, "As the LORD Almighty
lives, whom I serve, I will surely present[n] myself to Ahab today."

16 So Obadiah went to meet Ahab and
told him, and Ahab went to meet Elijah.
17 When he saw Elijah, he said to him,
"Is that you, you troubler[o] of Israel?"

18 "I have not made trouble for Israel,"
Elijah replied. "But you[p] and your father's
family have. You have abandoned[q] the
LORD's commands and have followed the
Baals. 19 Now summon the people from
all over Israel to meet me on Mount

17:18 [a]2Ki 3:13; Lk 5:8
17:21 [b]2Ki 4:34; Ac 20:10
17:24 [c]Jn 3:2; 16:30 [d]Ps 119:43; Jn 17:17
18:1 [e]1Ki 17:1; Lk 4:25; Jas 5:17 [f]Dt 28:12
18:3 [g]1Ki 16:9 [h]Ne 7:2
18:4 [i]2Ki 9:7 [j]ver 13; Isa 16:3
18:7 [k]2Ki 1:8
18:10 [l]1Ki 17:3
18:12 [m]2Ki 2:16; Eze 3:14; Ac 8:39
18:15 [n]1Ki 17:1
18:17 [o]Jos 7:25; 1Ki 21:20; Ac 16:20
18:18 [p]1Ki 16:31,33; 21:25 [q]2Ch 15:2

Carmel.[a] And bring the four hundred and fifty prophets of Baal and the four hundred prophets of Asherah, who eat at Jezebel's table."

20So Ahab sent word throughout all Israel and assembled the prophets on Mount Carmel. 21Elijah went before the people and said, "How long will you waver[b] between two opinions? If the LORD is God, follow him; but if Baal is God, follow him."

But the people said nothing.

22Then Elijah said to them, "I am the only one of the LORD's prophets left,[c] but Baal has four hundred and fifty prophets.[d] 23Get two bulls for us. Let them choose one for themselves, and let them cut it into pieces and put it on the wood but not set fire to it. I will prepare the other bull and put it on the wood but not set fire to it. 24Then you call on the name of your god, and I will call on the name of the LORD. The god who answers by fire[e]—he is God."

Then all the people said, "What you say is good."

25Elijah said to the prophets of Baal, "Choose one of the bulls and prepare it first, since there are so many of you. Call on the name of your god, but do not light the fire." 26So they took the bull given them and prepared it.

Then they called on the name of Baal from morning till noon. "O Baal, answer us!" they shouted. But there was no response;[f] no one answered. And they danced around the altar they had made.

27At noon Elijah began to taunt them. "Shout louder!" he said. "Surely he is a god! Perhaps he is deep in thought, or busy, or traveling. Maybe he is sleeping and must be awakened."[g] 28So they shouted louder and slashed[h] themselves with swords and spears, as was their custom, until their blood flowed. 29Midday passed, and they continued their frantic prophesying until the time for the evening sacrifice.[i] But there was no response, no one answered, no one paid attention.[j]

30Then Elijah said to all the people, "Come here to me." They came to him, and he repaired the altar[k] of the LORD, which was in ruins. 31Elijah took twelve stones, one for each of the tribes descended from Jacob, to whom the word of the LORD had come, saying, "Your name shall be Israel."[l] 32With the stones he built an altar in the name[m] of the LORD, and he dug a trench around it large enough to hold two seahs[m] of seed. 33He arranged[n] the wood, cut the bull into pieces and laid it on the wood. Then he said to them, "Fill four large jars with water and pour it on the offering and on the wood."

34"Do it again," he said, and they did it again.

"Do it a third time," he ordered, and they did it the third time. 35The water ran down around the altar and even filled the trench.

36At the time of sacrifice, the prophet Elijah stepped forward and prayed: "O LORD, God of Abraham,[o] Isaac and Israel, let it be known[p] today that you are God in Israel and that I am your servant and have done all these things at your command.[q] 37Answer me, O LORD, answer me, so these people will know that you, O LORD, are God, and that you are turning their hearts back again."

38Then the fire[r] of the LORD fell and burned up the sacrifice, the wood, the stones and the soil, and also licked up the water in the trench.

39When all the people saw this, they fell prostrate and cried, "The LORD—he is God! The LORD—he is God!"[s]

40Then Elijah commanded them, "Seize the prophets of Baal. Don't let anyone get away!" They seized them, and Elijah had them brought down to the Kishon Valley[t] and slaughtered[u] there.

Elijah prays and the drought ends.

41And Elijah said to Ahab, "Go, eat and drink, for there is the sound of a heavy rain." 42So Ahab went off to eat and drink, but Elijah climbed to the top of Carmel, bent down to the ground and put his face between his knees.[v]

18:19 [a]Jos 19:26
18:21 [b]Jos 24:15; 2Ki 17:41; Mt 6:24
18:22 [c]1Ki 19:10 [d]ver 19
18:24 [e]ver 38; 1Ch 21:26
18:26 [f]Ps 115:4-5; Jer 10:5; 1Co 8:4; 12:2
18:27 [g]Hab 2:19
18:28 [h]Lev 19:28; Dt 14:1
18:29 [i]Ex 29:41 [j]ver 26
18:30 [k]1Ki 19:10
18:31 [l]Ge 32:28; 35:10; 2Ki 17:34
18:32 [m]Col 3:17
18:33 [n]Ge 22:9; Lev 1:6-8
18:36 [o]Ex 3:6; Mt 22:32 [p]1Ki 8:43; 2Ki 19:19 [q]Nu 16:28
18:38 [r]Lev 9:24; Jdg 6:21; 1Ch 21:26; 2Ch 7:1; Job 1:16
18:39 [s]ver 24
18:40 [t]Jdg 4:7 [u]Dt 13:5; 18:20; 2Ki 10:24-25
18:42 [v]ver 19-20; Jas 5:18

m32 That is, probably about 13 quarts (about 15 liters)

43"Go and look toward the sea," he told
his servant. And he went up and looked.
"There is nothing there," he said.
Seven times Elijah said, "Go back."
44The seventh time the servant reported, "A cloud[a] as small as a man's hand is
rising from the sea."
So Elijah said, "Go and tell Ahab,
'Hitch up your chariot and go down before the rain stops you.'"
45Meanwhile, the sky grew black with
clouds, the wind rose, a heavy rain came
on and Ahab rode off to Jezreel. 46The
power[b] of the LORD came upon Elijah and,
tucking his cloak into his belt,[c] he ran
ahead of Ahab all the way to Jezreel.

Jezebel threatens to kill Elijah.

19 Now Ahab told Jezebel everything
Elijah had done and how he had
killed[d] all the prophets with the sword.
2So Jezebel sent a messenger to Elijah
to say, "May the gods deal with me, be it
ever so severely,[e] if by this time tomorrow I do not make your life like that of
one of them."
3Elijah was afraid[n] and ran[f] for his life.
When he came to Beersheba in Judah,
he left his servant there, 4while he himself went a day's journey into the desert.
He came to a broom tree, sat down under
it and prayed that he might die. "I have
had enough, LORD," he said. "Take my
life;[g] I am no better than my ancestors."
5Then he lay down under the tree and
fell asleep.[h]
All at once an angel touched him and
said, "Get up and eat." 6He looked around,
and there by his head was a cake of
bread baked over hot coals, and a jar of
water. He ate and drank and then lay
down again.
7The angel of the LORD came back a
second time and touched him and said,
"Get up and eat, for the journey is too
much for you." 8So he got up and ate
and drank. Strengthened by that food,
he traveled forty[i] days and forty nights
until he reached Horeb,[j] the mountain of
God. 9There he went into a cave[k] and
spent the night.
And the word of the LORD came to him:
"What are you doing here, Elijah?"
10He replied, "I have been very zealous[l] for the LORD God Almighty. The
Israelites have rejected your covenant,
broken down your altars, and put your
prophets to death with the sword. I am
the only one left,[m] and now they are trying to kill me too."
11The LORD said, "Go out and stand on
the mountain[n] in the presence of the
LORD, for the LORD is about to pass by."
Then a great and powerful wind[o] tore
the mountains apart and shattered the
rocks before the LORD, but the LORD was
not in the wind. After the wind there
was an earthquake, but the LORD was
not in the earthquake. 12After the earthquake came a fire, but the LORD was
not in the fire. And after the fire came a
gentle whisper.[p] 13When Elijah heard it,
he pulled his cloak over his face[q] and
went out and stood at the mouth of the
cave.
Then a voice said to him, "What are
you doing here, Elijah?"
14He replied, "I have been very zealous for the LORD God Almighty. The
Israelites have rejected your covenant,
broken down your altars, and put your
prophets to death with the sword. I am
the only one left,[r] and now they are trying to kill me too."
15The LORD said to him, "Go back the
way you came, and go to the Desert of
Damascus. When you get there, anoint
Hazael[s] king over Aram. 16Also, anoint[t]
Jehu son of Nimshi king over Israel, and
anoint Elisha[u] son of Shaphat from Abel
Meholah to succeed you as prophet.
17Jehu will put to death any who escape
the sword of Hazael,[v] and Elisha will put
to death any who escape the sword of
Jehu. 18Yet I reserve[w] seven thousand in
Israel—all whose knees have not bowed
down to Baal and all whose mouths have
not kissed[x] him."

Elisha's call.

19So Elijah went from there and found

18:44 [a]Lk 12:54
18:46 [b]2Ki 3:15 [c]2Ki 4:29; 9:1
19:1 [d]1Ki 18:40
19:2 [e]1Ki 20:10; 2Ki 6:31; Ru 1:17
19:3 [f]Ge 31:21
19:4 [g]Nu 11:15; Jer 20:18; Jnh 4:8
19:5 [h]Ge 28:11
19:8 [i]Ex 24:18; 34:28; Dt 9:9-11,18; Mt 4:2 [j]Ex 3:1
19:9 [k]Ex 33:22
19:10 [l]Nu 25:13 [m]1Ki 18:4,22; Ro 11:3*
19:11 [n]Ex 24:12 [o]Eze 1:4; 37:7
19:12 [p]Job 4:16; Zec 4:6
19:13 [q]ver 9; Ex 3:6
19:14 [r]ver 10
19:15 [s]2Ki 8:7-15
19:16 [t]2Ki 9:1-3,6 [u]ver 21; 2Ki 2:9,15
19:17 [v]2Ki 8:12,29; 9:14; 13:3,7,22
19:18 [w]Ro 11:4* [x]Hos 13:2

n3 Or *Elijah saw*

Elisha son of Shaphat. He was plowing
with twelve yoke of oxen, and he himself was driving the twelfth pair. Elijah
went up to him and threw his cloak[a]
around him. 20Elisha then left his oxen
and ran after Elijah. "Let me kiss my father and mother good-by,"[b] he said, "and
then I will come with you."
"Go back," Elijah replied. "What have
I done to you?"
21So Elisha left him and went back. He
took his yoke of oxen[c] and slaughtered
them. He burned the plowing equipment
to cook the meat and gave it to the people, and they ate. Then he set out to follow Elijah and became his attendant.[d]

Samaria is attacked.

20 Now Ben-Hadad[e] king of Aram
mustered his entire army. Accompanied by thirty-two kings with their
horses and chariots, he went up and besieged Samaria and attacked it. 2He sent
messengers into the city to Ahab king
of Israel, saying, "This is what Ben-Hadad
says: 3'Your silver and gold are mine, and
the best of your wives and children are
mine.'"
4The king of Israel answered, "Just as
you say, my lord the king. I and all I have
are yours."
5The messengers came again and said,
"This is what Ben-Hadad says: 'I sent to
demand your silver and gold, your wives
and your children. 6But about this time
tomorrow I am going to send my officials to search your palace and the houses of your officials. They will seize everything you value and carry it away.'"
7The king of Israel summoned all the
elders of the land and said to them, "See
how this man is looking for trouble![f]
When he sent for my wives and my children, my silver and my gold, I did not
refuse him."
8The elders and the people all answered, "Don't listen to him or agree to
his demands."
9So he replied to Ben-Hadad's messengers, "Tell my lord the king, 'Your servant will do all you demanded the first
time, but this demand I cannot meet.'"
They left and took the answer back to
Ben-Hadad.
10Then Ben-Hadad sent another message to Ahab: "May the gods deal with
me, be it ever so severely, if enough
dust[g] remains in Samaria to give each of
my men a handful."
11The king of Israel answered, "Tell
him: 'One who puts on his armor should
not boast[h] like one who takes it off.'"
12Ben-Hadad heard this message while
he and the kings were drinking[i] in their
tents,[o] and he ordered his men: "Prepare
to attack." So they prepared to attack the
city.
13Meanwhile a prophet came to Ahab
king of Israel and announced, "This is
what the LORD says: 'Do you see this vast
army? I will give it into your hand today, and then you will know[j] that I am
the LORD.'"
14"But who will do this?" asked Ahab.
The prophet replied, "This is what
the LORD says: 'The young officers of the
provincial commanders will do it.'"
"And who will start[k] the battle?" he
asked.
The prophet answered, "You will."
15So Ahab summoned the young officers of the provincial commanders, 232
men. Then he assembled the rest of the
Israelites, 7,000 in all. 16They set out at
noon while Ben-Hadad and the 32 kings
allied with him were in their tents getting drunk.[l] 17The young officers of the
provincial commanders went out first.
Now Ben-Hadad had dispatched scouts,
who reported, "Men are advancing from
Samaria."
18He said, "If they have come out for
peace, take them alive; if they have come
out for war, take them alive."
19The young officers of the provincial commanders marched out of the city
with the army behind them 20and each
one struck down his opponent. At that,
the Arameans fled, with the Israelites
in pursuit. But Ben-Hadad king of Aram
escaped on horseback with some of his

19:19 [a]2Ki 2:8,14
19:20 [b]Mt 8:21-22; Lk 9:61
19:21 [c]2Sa 24:22 [d]ver 16
20:1 [e]1Ki 15:18; 22:31; 2Ki 6:24
20:7 [f]2Ki 5:7
20:10 [g]2Sa 22:43; 1Ki 19:2
20:11 [h]Pr 27:1; Jer 9:23
20:12 [i]ver 16; 1Ki 16:9
20:13 [j]ver 28; Ex 6:7
20:14 [k]Jdg 1:1
20:16 [l]ver 12; 1Ki 16:9

[o]*12* Or *in Succoth*; also in verse 16

horsemen. 21 The king of Israel advanced and overpowered the horses and chariots and inflicted heavy losses on the Arameans.

22 Afterward, the prophet[a] came to the king of Israel and said, "Strengthen your position and see what must be done, because next spring[b] the king of Aram will attack you again."

23 Meanwhile, the officials of the king of Aram advised him, "Their gods are gods[c] of the hills. That is why they were too strong for us. But if we fight them on the plains, surely we will be stronger than they. 24 Do this: Remove all the kings from their commands and replace them with other officers. 25 You must also raise an army like the one you lost—horse for horse and chariot for chariot—so we can fight Israel on the plains. Then surely we will be stronger than they." He agreed with them and acted accordingly.

26 The next spring[d] Ben-Hadad mustered the Arameans and went up to Aphek[e] to fight against Israel. 27 When the Israelites were also mustered and given provisions, they marched out to meet them. The Israelites camped opposite them like two small flocks of goats, while the Arameans covered the countryside.[f]

28 The man of God came up and told the king of Israel, "This is what the LORD says: 'Because the Arameans think the LORD is a god of the hills and not a god[g] of the valleys, I will deliver this vast army into your hands, and you will know[h] that I am the LORD.'"

29 For seven days they camped opposite each other, and on the seventh day the battle was joined. The Israelites inflicted a hundred thousand casualties on the Aramean foot soldiers in one day. 30 The rest of them escaped to the city of Aphek,[i] where the wall collapsed on twenty-seven thousand of them. And Ben-Hadad fled to the city and hid[j] in an inner room.

Ahab makes a treaty with Ben-Hadad.

31 His officials said to him, "Look, we have heard that the kings of the house of Israel are merciful. Let us go to the king of Israel with sackcloth[k] around our waists and ropes around our heads. Perhaps he will spare your life."

32 Wearing sackcloth around their waists and ropes around their heads, they went to the king of Israel and said, "Your servant Ben-Hadad says: 'Please let me live.'"

The king answered, "Is he still alive? He is my brother."

33 The men took this as a good sign and were quick to pick up his word. "Yes, your brother Ben-Hadad!" they said.

"Go and get him," the king said. When Ben-Hadad came out, Ahab had him come up into his chariot.

34 "I will return the cities[l] my father took from your father," Ben-Hadad offered. "You may set up your own market areas in Damascus,[m] as my father did in Samaria."

⌊Ahab said,⌋ "On the basis of a treaty[n] I will set you free." So he made a treaty with him, and let him go.

Ahab is condemned for disobedience.

35 By the word of the LORD one of the sons of the prophets said to his companion, "Strike me with your weapon," but the man refused.[o]

36 So the prophet said, "Because you have not obeyed the LORD, as soon as you leave me a lion[p] will kill you." And after the man went away, a lion found him and killed him.

37 The prophet found another man and said, "Strike me, please." So the man struck him and wounded him. 38 Then the prophet went and stood by the road waiting for the king. He disguised himself with his headband down over his eyes. 39 As the king passed by, the prophet called out to him, "Your servant went into the thick of the battle, and someone came to me with a captive and said, 'Guard this man. If he is missing, it will be your life for his life,[q] or you must

20:22 [a] ver 13 [b] ver 26; 2Sa 11:1
20:23 [c] 1Ki 14:23; Ro 1:21-23
20:26 [d] ver 22 [e] 2Ki 13:17
20:27 [f] Jdg 6:6; 1Sa 13:6
20:28 [g] ver 23 [h] ver 13
20:30 [i] ver 26 [j] 1Ki 22:25; 2Ch 18:24
20:31 [k] Ge 37:34
20:34 [l] 1Ki 15:20 [m] Jer 49:23-27 [n] Ex 23:32
20:35 [o] 1Ki 13:21; 2Ki 2:3-7
20:36 [p] 1Ki 13:24
20:39 [q] 2Ki 10:24

pay a talent[p] of silver.' 40While your servant was busy here and there, the man
disappeared."
"That is your sentence," the king of
Israel said. "You have pronounced it
yourself."
41Then the prophet quickly removed
the headband from his eyes, and the king
of Israel recognized him as one of the
prophets. 42He said to the king, "This is
what the LORD says: 'You have set free
a man I had determined should die.[q][a]
Therefore it is your life for his life,[b] your
people for his people.'" 43Sullen and angry,[c] the king of Israel went to his palace
in Samaria.

Jezebel has Naboth stoned to obtain his vineyard.

21 Some time later there was an in-
cident involving a vineyard belonging to Naboth[d] the Jezreelite. The
vineyard was in Jezreel,[e] close to the
palace of Ahab king of Samaria. 2Ahab
said to Naboth, "Let me have your vineyard to use for a vegetable garden, since
it is close to my palace. In exchange I
will give you a better vineyard or, if you
prefer, I will pay you whatever it is
worth."
3But Naboth replied, "The LORD forbid
that I should give you the inheritance[f]
of my fathers."
4So Ahab went home, sullen and angry[g] because Naboth the Jezreelite had
said, "I will not give you the inheritance
of my fathers." He lay on his bed sulking
and refused to eat.
5His wife Jezebel came in and asked
him, "Why are you so sullen? Why won't
you eat?"
6He answered her, "Because I said to
Naboth the Jezreelite, 'Sell me your vineyard; or if you prefer, I will give you
another vineyard in its place.' But he
said, 'I will not give you my vineyard.'"
7Jezebel his wife said, "Is this how you
act as king over Israel? Get up and eat!
Cheer up. I'll get you the vineyard[h] of
Naboth the Jezreelite."
8So she wrote letters in Ahab's name,

20:42 [a]Jer 48:10 [b]ver 39; Jos 2:14; 1Ki 22:31-37
20:43 [c]1Ki 21:4
21:1 [d]2Ki 9:21 [e]1Ki 18:45-46
21:3 [f]Lev 25:23; Nu 36:7; Eze 46:18
21:4 [g]1Ki 20:43
21:7 [h]1Sa 8:14
21:8 [i]Ge 38:18; Est 3:12; 8:8,10
21:10 [j]Ac 6:11 [k]Ex 22:28; Lev 24:15-16
21:12 [l]Isa 58:4
21:13 [m]2Ki 9:26
21:15 [n]1Sa 8:14
21:19 [o]2Ki 9:26; Ps 9:12; Isa 14:20 [p]1Ki 22:38

placed his seal[i] on them, and sent them
to the elders and nobles who lived in
Naboth's city with him. 9In those letters she wrote:

"Proclaim a day of fasting and seat
Naboth in a prominent place among
the people. 10But seat two scoundrels[j] opposite him and have them
testify that he has cursed[k] both God
and the king. Then take him out and
stone him to death."

11So the elders and nobles who lived
in Naboth's city did as Jezebel directed
in the letters she had written to them.
12They proclaimed a fast[l] and seated
Naboth in a prominent place among the
people. 13Then two scoundrels came and
sat opposite him and brought charges
against Naboth before the people, saying, "Naboth has cursed both God and
the king." So they took him outside the
city and stoned him to death.[m] 14Then
they sent word to Jezebel: "Naboth has
been stoned and is dead."
15As soon as Jezebel heard that Naboth
had been stoned to death, she said to
Ahab, "Get up and take possession of
the vineyard[n] of Naboth the Jezreelite
that he refused to sell you. He is no
longer alive, but dead." 16When Ahab
heard that Naboth was dead, he got up
and went down to take possession of
Naboth's vineyard.

Elijah prophesies against Ahab and Jezebel.

17Then the word of the LORD came to
Elijah the Tishbite: 18"Go down to meet
Ahab king of Israel, who rules in Samaria.
He is now in Naboth's vineyard, where
he has gone to take possession of it. 19Say
to him, 'This is what the LORD says: Have
you not murdered a man and seized his
property?' Then say to him, 'This is what
the LORD says: In the place where dogs
licked up Naboth's blood,[o] dogs[p] will lick
up your blood—yes, yours!'"

p*39* That is, about 75 pounds (about 34 kilograms)
q*42* The Hebrew term refers to the irrevocable giving over of things or persons to the LORD, often by totally destroying them.

20 Ahab said to Elijah, "So you have
found me, my enemy!"[a]
"I have found you," he answered, "because you have sold[b] yourself to do evil
in the eyes of the LORD. 21 'I am going to
bring disaster on you. I will consume
your descendants and cut off from Ahab
every last male[c] in Israel—slave or free.
22 I will make your house[d] like that of Jeroboam son of Nebat and that of Baasha
son of Ahijah, because you have provoked
me to anger and have caused Israel to
sin.'[e]
23 "And also concerning Jezebel the
LORD says: 'Dogs[f] will devour Jezebel by
the wall of[r] Jezreel.'
24 "Dogs[g] will eat those belonging to
Ahab who die in the city, and the birds of
the air will feed on those who die in the
country."
25 (There was never[h] a man like Ahab,
who sold himself to do evil in the eyes
of the LORD, urged on by Jezebel his wife.
26 He behaved in the vilest manner by
going after idols, like the Amorites[i] the
LORD drove out before Israel.)
27 When Ahab heard these words, he
tore his clothes, put on sackcloth[j] and
fasted. He lay in sackcloth and went
around meekly.
28 Then the word of the LORD came to
Elijah the Tishbite: 29 "Have you noticed
how Ahab has humbled himself before
me? Because he has humbled himself, I
will not bring this disaster in his day, but
I will bring it on his house in the days
of his son."[k]

Ahab listens to false prophets instead of Micaiah.

22:1-28pp— 2Ch 18:1-27

22 For three years there was no war
between Aram and Israel. 2 But
in the third year Jehoshaphat king of
Judah went down to see the king of
Israel. 3 The king of Israel had said to his
officials, "Don't you know that Ramoth
Gilead[l] belongs to us and yet we are doing nothing to retake it from the king of
Aram?"
4 So he asked Jehoshaphat, "Will you
go with me to fight[m] against Ramoth
Gilead?"
Jehoshaphat replied to the king of Israel, "I am as you are, my people as your
people, my horses as your horses." 5 But
Jehoshaphat also said to the king of Israel,
"First seek the counsel[n] of the LORD."
6 So the king of Israel brought together the prophets—about four hundred
men—and asked them, "Shall I go to
war against Ramoth Gilead, or shall I
refrain?"
"Go,"[o] they answered, "for the Lord
will give it into the king's hand."
7 But Jehoshaphat asked, "Is there not
a prophet[p] of the LORD here whom we
can inquire of?"
8 The king of Israel answered Jehoshaphat, "There is still one man through
whom we can inquire of the LORD, but
I hate[q] him because he never prophesies
anything good[r] about me, but always
bad. He is Micaiah son of Imlah."
"The king should not say that," Jehoshaphat replied.
9 So the king of Israel called one of his
officials and said, "Bring Micaiah son of
Imlah at once."
10 Dressed in their royal robes, the king
of Israel and Jehoshaphat king of Judah
were sitting on their thrones at the
threshing floor[s] by the entrance of the
gate of Samaria, with all the prophets
prophesying before them. 11 Now Zedekiah son of Kenaanah had made iron
horns[t] and he declared, "This is what the
LORD says: 'With these you will gore the
Arameans until they are destroyed.'"
12 All the other prophets were prophesying the same thing. "Attack Ramoth
Gilead and be victorious," they said, "for
the LORD will give it into the king's
hand."
13 The messenger who had gone to
summon Micaiah said to him, "Look, as
one man the other prophets are predicting success for the king. Let your word
agree with theirs, and speak favorably."
14 But Micaiah said, "As surely as the

21:20 [a] 1Ki 18:17 [b] ver 25; 2Ki 17:17; Ro 7:14
21:21 [c] 1Ki 14:10; 2Ki 9:8
21:22 [d] 1Ki 15:29; 16:3 [e] 1Ki 12:30
21:23 [f] 2Ki 9:10,34-36
21:24 [g] 1Ki 14:11; 16:4
21:25 [h] ver 20; 1Ki 16:33
21:26 [i] Ge 15:16; Lev 18:25-30; 2Ki 21:11
21:27 [j] Ge 37:34; 2Sa 3:31; 2Ki 6:30
21:29 [k] 2Ki 9:26
22:3 [l] Dt 4:43; Jos 21:38
22:4 [m] 2Ki 3:7
22:5 [n] Ex 33:7; 2Ki 3:11
22:6 [o] 1Ki 18:19
22:7 [p] 2Ki 3:11
22:8 [q] Am 5:10 [r] Isa 5:20
22:10 [s] ver 6
22:11 [t] Dt 33:17; Zec 1:18-21

[r] *23* Most Hebrew manuscripts; a few Hebrew manuscripts, Vulgate and Syriac (see also 2 Kings 9:26) *the plot of ground at*

LORD lives, I can tell him only what the
LORD tells me."[a]
15When he arrived, the king asked him,
"Micaiah, shall we go to war against Ramoth Gilead, or shall I refrain?"
"Attack and be victorious," he answered,
"for the LORD will give it into the king's
hand."
16The king said to him, "How many
times must I make you swear to tell me
nothing but the truth in the name of the
LORD?"
17Then Micaiah answered, "I saw all
Israel scattered on the hills like sheep
without a shepherd,[b] and the LORD said,
'These people have no master. Let each
one go home in peace.'"
18The king of Israel said to Jehoshaphat, "Didn't I tell you that he never
prophesies anything good about me, but
only bad?"
19Micaiah continued, "Therefore hear
the word of the LORD: I saw the LORD
sitting on his throne[c] with all the host[d]
of heaven standing around him on his
right and on his left. 20And the LORD said,
'Who will entice Ahab into attacking
Ramoth Gilead and going to his death
there?'
"One suggested this, and another that.
21Finally, a spirit came forward, stood
before the LORD and said, 'I will entice
him.'
22"'By what means?' the LORD asked.
"'I will go out and be a lying[e] spirit in
the mouths of all his prophets,' he said.
"'You will succeed in enticing him,'
said the LORD. 'Go and do it.'
23"So now the LORD has put a lying
spirit in the mouths of all these prophets[f] of yours. The LORD has decreed disaster for you."
24Then Zedekiah[g] son of Kenaanah
went up and slapped[h] Micaiah in the
face. "Which way did the spirit from[s] the
LORD go when he went from me to speak
to you?" he asked.
25Micaiah replied, "You will find out
on the day you go to hide[i] in an inner
room."
26The king of Israel then ordered,
"Take Micaiah and send him back to
Amon the ruler of the city and to Joash
the king's son 27and say, 'This is what the
king says: Put this fellow in prison[j] and
give him nothing but bread and water
until I return safely.'"
28Micaiah declared, "If you ever return
safely, the LORD has not spoken[k] through
me." Then he added, "Mark my words,
all you people!"

22:14 [a]Nu 22:18; 24:13; 1Ki 18:10,15
22:17 [b]ver 34-36; Nu 27:17; Mt 9:36
22:19 [c]Isa 6:1; Eze 1:26; Da 7:9 [d]Job 1:6; 2:1; Ps 103:20-21; Mt 18:10; Heb 1:7,14
22:22 [e]Jdg 9:23; 1Sa 16:14; 18:10; 19:9; Eze 14:9; 2Th 2:11
22:23 [f]Eze 14:9
22:24 [g]ver 11 [h]Ac 23:2
22:25 [i]1Ki 20:30
22:27 [j]2Ch 16:10
22:28 [k]Dt 18:22
22:30 [l]2Ch 35:32
22:31 [m]2Sa 17:2
22:34 [n]2Ch 35:23
22:36 [o]2Ki 14:12
22:38 [p]1Ki 21:19

Israel is defeated, and Ahab is slain.

22:29-36pp— 2Ch 18:28-34

29So the king of Israel and Jehoshaphat king of Judah went up to Ramoth
Gilead. 30The king of Israel said to Jehoshaphat, "I will enter the battle in
disguise,[l] but you wear your royal
robes." So the king of Israel disguised
himself and went into battle.
31Now the king of Aram had ordered
his thirty-two chariot commanders, "Do
not fight with anyone, small or great,
except the king[m] of Israel." 32When the
chariot commanders saw Jehoshaphat,
they thought, "Surely this is the king of
Israel." So they turned to attack him, but
when Jehoshaphat cried out, 33the chariot commanders saw that he was not the
king of Israel and stopped pursuing him.
34But someone drew his bow[n] at random and hit the king of Israel between
the sections of his armor. The king told
his chariot driver, "Wheel around and
get me out of the fighting. I've been
wounded." 35All day long the battle
raged, and the king was propped up in
his chariot facing the Arameans. The
blood from his wound ran onto the floor
of the chariot, and that evening he died.
36As the sun was setting, a cry spread
through the army: "Every man to his
town; everyone to his land!"[o]
37So the king died and was brought to
Samaria, and they buried him there.
38They washed the chariot at a pool in
Samaria (where the prostitutes bathed),[t]
and the dogs[p] licked up his blood, as the
word of the LORD had declared.

s24 Or *Spirit of*   t38 Or *Samaria and cleaned the weapons*

39 As for the other events of Ahab's reign,
including all he did, the palace he built
and inlaid with ivory,[a] and the cities he
fortified, are they not written in the
book of the annals of the kings of Israel?
40 Ahab rested with his fathers. And Ahaziah his son succeeded him as king.

Jehoshaphat reigns in Judah.

22:41-50pp— 2Ch 20:31–21:1

41 Jehoshaphat son of Asa became king
of Judah in the fourth year of Ahab king
of Israel. 42 Jehoshaphat was thirty-five
years old when he became king, and he
reigned in Jerusalem twenty-five years.
His mother's name was Azubah daughter of Shilhi. 43 In everything he walked
in the ways of his father Asa[b] and did not
stray from them; he did what was right
in the eyes of the LORD. The high places,[c]
however, were not removed, and the people continued to offer sacrifices and burn
incense there. 44 Jehoshaphat was also at
peace with the king of Israel.
45 As for the other events of Jehoshaphat's reign, the things he achieved and
his military exploits, are they not written in the book of the annals of the kings
of Judah? 46 He rid the land of the rest of
the male shrine prostitutes[d] who remained there even after the reign of his
father Asa. 47 There was then no king[e] in
Edom; a deputy ruled.
48 Now Jehoshaphat built a fleet of trading ships[u][f] to go to Ophir for gold, but
they never set sail—they were wrecked
at Ezion Geber. 49 At that time Ahaziah
son of Ahab said to Jehoshaphat, "Let my
men sail with your men," but Jehoshaphat refused.

Jehoram reigns in Judah.

50 Then Jehoshaphat rested with his fathers and was buried with them in the
city of David his father. And Jehoram his
son succeeded him.

Ahaziah reigns in Israel.

51 Ahaziah son of Ahab became king of
Israel in Samaria in the seventeenth year
of Jehoshaphat king of Judah, and he
reigned over Israel two years. 52 He did
evil[g] in the eyes of the LORD, because he
walked in the ways of his father and
mother and in the ways of Jeroboam son
of Nebat, who caused Israel to sin. 53 He
served and worshiped Baal[h] and provoked
the LORD, the God of Israel, to anger, just
as his father[i] had done.

22:39 [a] 2Ch 9:17; Am 3:15
22:43 [b] 2Ch 17:3 [c] 1Ki 3:2; 15:14; 2Ki 12:3
22:46 [d] Dt 23:17; 1Ki 14:24; 15:12
22:47 [e] 2Sa 8:14; 2Ki 3:9; 8:20
22:48 [f] 1Ki 9:26; 10:22
22:52 [g] 1Ki 15:26; 21:25
22:53 [h] Jdg 2:11 [i] 1Ki 16:30-32

[u] *48* Hebrew *of ships of Tarshish*

2 KINGS

Author: Unknown, possibly Jeremiah. (However, it has been suggested that chapter 25 was written by an exile after the Babylonian captivity.)

Date Written: Between 640 and 550 B.C. (compiled from earlier sources).

Time Span: About 293 years (period from the time of the prophet Elisha to the captivity of Judah).

Title: This book is so named because it is a history of the kings who ruled Israel and Judah.

Background: 2 Kings is a sequel to the book of 1 Kings. The 2 books form one book in the Hebrew Bible. 2 Kings continues the story of kings over the divided kingdom, leading to the final overthrow and deportation of both Israel and Judah's people.

Where Written: Unknown (possibly from Judah and Egypt).

To Whom: To the Israelites.

Content: 2 Kings depicts the downfall of the divided kingdom. Prophets continue to warn the people that the judgment of God is at hand, but they will not repent. The kingdom of Israel is repeatedly ruled by wicked kings, and even though a few of Judah's kings are good, the majority are bad. These few good rulers, along with Elisha and other prophets, cannot stop the nation's decline. The northern kingdom of Israel is eventually destroyed by the Assyrians (chapter 17), and about 136 years later the southern kingdom of Judah is destroyed by the Babylonians (chapter 25). Though the people of God are in captivity, God stays true to his covenant, preserving a remnant for himself.

Key Words: "Appraisal"; "Captivity." The general idea of 2 Kings is to give an "appraisal" of each king, especially in his relationship to God and the covenant. The majority are appraised as evil in God's sight, which leads Israel and Judah into separate "captivity."

Themes: • God hates sin and he will not allow it to continue indefinitely. • God may at times use pagans to bring correction to his people. • God loves us so much that he sometimes has to discipline us. • God gives us warning before delivering his judgment. • We can have total confidence that God will never leave us or forsake us.

Outline:

1. Elijah's replacement by Elisha. 1:1-8:15
2. Israel's decline and fall. 8:16-17:6
3. Israel's exile to Assyria because of sin. 17:7-17:41
4. Judah's survival. 18:1-23:30
5. Judah's exile to Babylon. 23:31-25:30

2 KINGS

Fire from heaven consumes Ahaziah's messengers.

1 After Ahab's death, Moab[a] rebelled
against Israel. 2 Now Ahaziah had
fallen through the lattice of his upper
room in Samaria and injured himself.
So he sent messengers,[b] saying to them,
"Go and consult Baal-Zebub,[c] the god
of Ekron,[d] to see if I will recover[e] from
this injury."
3 But the angel[f] of the LORD said to
Elijah[g] the Tishbite, "Go up and meet
the messengers of the king of Samaria
and ask them, 'Is it because there is no
God in Israel[h] that you are going off to
consult Baal-Zebub, the god of Ekron?'
4 Therefore this is what the LORD says:
'You will not leave[i] the bed you are lying
on. You will certainly die!'" So Elijah
went.
5 When the messengers returned to the
king, he asked them, "Why have you
come back?"
6 "A man came to meet us," they
replied. "And he said to us, 'Go back to
the king who sent you and tell him,
"This is what the LORD says: Is it because
there is no God in Israel that you are
sending men to consult Baal-Zebub, the
god of Ekron? Therefore you will not
leave the bed you are lying on. You will
certainly die!"'"
7 The king asked them, "What kind of
man was it who came to meet you and
told you this?"
8 They replied, "He was a man with a
garment of hair[j] and with a leather belt
around his waist."
The king said, "That was Elijah the
Tishbite."
9 Then he sent[k] to Elijah a captain[l]
with his company of fifty men. The captain went up to Elijah, who was sitting
on the top of a hill, and said to him,
"Man of God, the king says, 'Come
down!'"
10 Elijah answered the captain, "If I am
a man of God, may fire come down from
heaven and consume you and your fifty
men!" Then fire[m] fell from heaven and
consumed the captain and his men.
11 At this the king sent to Elijah another captain with his fifty men. The captain said to him, "Man of God, this is
what the king says, 'Come down at
once!'"
12 "If I am a man of God," Elijah
replied, "may fire come down from heav-
en and consume you and your fifty
men!" Then the fire of God fell from
heaven and consumed him and his fifty
men.
13 So the king sent a third captain with
his fifty men. This third captain went
up and fell on his knees before Elijah.
"Man of God," he begged, "please have
respect for my life[n] and the lives of these
fifty men, your servants! 14 See, fire has
fallen from heaven and consumed the
first two captains and all their men. But
now have respect for my life!"
15 The angel[o] of the LORD said to Elijah,
"Go down with him; do not be afraid[p] of
him." So Elijah got up and went down
with him to the king.
16 He told the king, "This is what the
LORD says: Is it because there is no God
in Israel for you to consult that you have
sent messengers[q] to consult Baal-Zebub,
the god of Ekron? Because you have done
this, you will never leave[r] the bed you
are lying on. You will certainly die!"
17 So he died,[s] according to the word of
the LORD that Elijah had spoken.

Joram succeeds Ahaziah.

Because Ahaziah had no son, Joram[a][t]
succeeded him as king in the second
year of Jehoram son of Jehoshaphat king
of Judah. 18 As for all the other events
of Ahaziah's reign, and what he did, are
they not written in the book of the annals
of the kings of Israel?

Elijah divides the Jordan.

2 When the LORD was about to take[u]
Elijah up to heaven in a whirlwind,[v]

a *17* Hebrew *Jehoram,* a variant of *Joram*

1:1 [a]Ge 19:37; 2Sa 8:2; 2Ki 3:5
1:2 [b]ver 16 [c]Mk 3:22 [d]1Sa 6:2; Isa 2:6; 14:29; Mt 10:25 [e]Jdg 18:5; 2Ki 8:7-10
1:3 [f]ver 15; Ge 16:7 [g]1Ki 17:1 [h]1Sa 28:8
1:4 [i]ver 6,16; Ps 41:8
1:8 [j]1Ki 18:7; Zec 13:4; Mt 3:4; Mk 1:6
1:9 [k]2Ki 6:14 [l]Ex 18:25; Isa 3:3
1:10 [m]1Ki 18:38; Lk 9:54; Rev 11:5; 13:13
1:13 [n]1Sa 26:21; Ps 72:14
1:15 [o]ver 3 [p]Isa 51:12; 57:11; Jer 1:17; Eze 2:6
1:16 [q]ver 2 [r]ver 4
1:17 [s]2Ki 8:15; Jer 20:6; 28:17 [t]2Ki 3:1; 8:16
2:1 [u]Ge 5:24; Heb 11:5 [v]ver 11; 1Ki 19:11; Isa 5:28; 66:15; Jer 4:13; Na 1:3

KEY PLACES IN 2 KINGS

The history of both Israel and Judah was much affected by the prophet Elisha's ministry. He served Israel for 50 years, fighting the idolatry of its kings and calling its people back to God.

Jericho Elijah's ministry had come to an end. He touched his cloak to the Jordan River, and he and Elisha crossed on dry ground. Elijah was taken by God in a whirlwind, and Elisha returned alone with the cloak. The prophets in Jericho realized that Elisha was Elijah's replacement (1:1–2:25).

Desert of Edom The king of Moab rebelled against Israel, so the nations of Israel, Judah, and Edom decided to attack from the Desert of Edom, but ran out of water. The kings consulted Elisha, who said God would send both water and victory (3:1-27).

Shunem Elisha cared for individuals and their needs. He helped a woman clear a debt by giving a supply of oil to sell. For another family in Shunem, he raised a son from the dead (4:1-37).

Gilgal Elisha cared for the young prophets in Gilgal—he removed poison from a stew, made a small amount of food feed everyone, and even caused an axhead to float so it could be retrieved. It was to Elisha that Naaman, a commander in the Aramean army, came to be healed of leprosy (4:38–6:7).

Dothan Although he cured an Aramean commander's leprosy, Elisha was loyal to Israel. He knew the Aramean army's battle plans and kept Israel's king informed. The Aramean king tracked Elisha down in Dothan and surrounded the city, hoping to kill him. But Elisha prayed that the Arameans would be blinded, then he led the blinded army into Samaria, Israel's capital city (6:8-23).

Samaria But the Arameans didn't learn their lesson. They later besieged Samaria. Ironically, Israel's king thought it was Elisha's fault, but Elisha said food would be available in abundance the next day. True to Elisha's word, the Lord caused panic in the Aramean camp, and the enemy ran, leaving their supplies to Samaria's starving people (6:24–7:20).

Damascus Despite Elisha's loyalty to Israel, he obeyed God and traveled to Damascus, the capital of Aram. King Ben-Hadad was sick, and he sent Hazael to ask Elisha if he would recover. Elisha knew the king would die, and told this to Hazael. But Hazael then murdered Ben-Hadad, making himself king. Later, Israel and Judah joined forces to fight this new Aramean threat (8:1-29).

Ramoth Gilead As Israel and Judah warred with Aram, Elisha sent a young prophet to Ramoth Gilead to anoint Jehu as Israel's next king. Jehu set out to destroy the wicked dynasties of Israel and Judah, killing kings Joram and Ahaziah, and wicked Queen Jezebel. He then destroyed King Ahab's family, and all the Baal worshipers in Israel (9:1–11:1).

Jerusalem Power-hungry Athaliah became queen of Judah when her son Ahaziah was killed. She had all her grandsons killed except Joash who was hidden by his aunt. Joash was crowned king at the age of seven and overthrew Athaliah. Meanwhile in Samaria, the Arameans continued to harass Israel. Israel's new king met with Elisha and was told that he would be victorious over Aram three times (11:2–13:19).

Following Elisha's death came a series of evil kings in Israel. Their idolatry and rejection of God caused their downfall. The Assyrian empire captured Samaria and took most of the Israelites into captivity (13:20–17:41). Judah had a short reprieve because of a few good kings who destroyed the idols and worshiped God. But many strayed from God. So Jerusalem fell to the next world power, Babylon (18:1–25:30).

Elijah and Elisha[a] were on their way
from Gilgal.[b] 2Elijah said to Elisha,
"Stay here;[c] the LORD has sent me to
Bethel."

But Elisha said, "As surely as the LORD
lives and as you live, I will not leave
you."[d] So they went down to Bethel.
3The company[e] of the prophets at
Bethel came out to Elisha and asked, "Do
you know that the LORD is going to take
your master from you today?"

"Yes, I know," Elisha replied, "but do
not speak of it."

4Then Elijah said to him, "Stay here,
Elisha; the LORD has sent me to Jericho.[f]"

And he replied, "As surely as the LORD
lives and as you live, I will not leave
you." So they went to Jericho.

5The company[g] of the prophets at Jericho went up to Elisha and asked him,
"Do you know that the LORD is going to
take your master from you today?"

"Yes, I know," he replied, "but do not
speak of it."

6Then Elijah said to him, "Stay here;[h]
the LORD has sent me to the Jordan."[i]

And he replied, "As surely as the LORD
lives and as you live, I will not leave
you."[j] So the two of them walked on.

7Fifty men of the company of the
prophets went and stood at a distance,
facing the place where Elijah and Elisha
had stopped at the Jordan. 8Elijah took
his cloak,[k] rolled it up and struck[l] the
water with it. The water divided[m] to
the right and to the left, and the two of
them crossed over on dry[n] ground.

A whirlwind takes Elijah to heaven.

9When they had crossed, Elijah said to
Elisha, "Tell me, what can I do for you
before I am taken from you?"

"Let me inherit a double[o] portion of
your spirit,"[p] Elisha replied.

10"You have asked a difficult thing,"
Elijah said, "yet if you see me when I
am taken from you, it will be yours—
otherwise not."

11As they were walking along and talking together, suddenly a chariot of fire[q]
and horses of fire appeared and separated
the two of them, and Elijah went up to
heaven[r] in a whirlwind.[s] 12Elisha saw
this and cried out, "My father! My father!
The chariots[t] and horsemen of Israel!"
And Elisha saw him no more. Then he
took hold of his own clothes and tore[u]
them apart.

Elisha succeeds Elijah.

13He picked up the cloak that had
fallen from Elijah and went back and
stood on the bank of the Jordan. 14Then
he took the cloak[v] that had fallen from
him and struck[w] the water with it.
"Where now is the LORD, the God of
Elijah?" he asked. When he struck the
water, it divided to the right and to the
left, and he crossed over.

15The company[x] of the prophets from
Jericho, who were watching, said, "The
spirit[y] of Elijah is resting on Elisha." And
they went to meet him and bowed to
the ground before him. 16"Look," they
said, "we your servants have fifty able
men. Let them go and look for your master. Perhaps the Spirit[z] of the LORD has
picked him up[a] and set him down on
some mountain or in some valley."

"No," Elisha replied, "do not send
them."

17But they persisted until he was too
ashamed[b] to refuse. So he said, "Send
them." And they sent fifty men, who
searched for three days but did not find
him. 18When they returned to Elisha,
who was staying in Jericho, he said to
them, "Didn't I tell you not to go?"

Elisha heals bad water.

19The men of the city said to Elisha,
"Look, our lord, this town is well situated, as you can see, but the water is bad
and the land is unproductive."

20"Bring me a new bowl," he said,
"and put salt in it." So they brought it
to him.

21Then he went out to the spring and
threw[c] the salt into it, saying, "This is
what the LORD says: 'I have healed this
water. Never again will it cause death
or make the land unproductive.'" 22And
the water has remained wholesome[d] to

2:1 [a]1Ki 19:16,21 [b]Dt 11:30; 2Ki 4:38
2:2 [c]ver 6 [d]Ru 1:16; 1Sa 1:26; 2Ki 4:30
2:3 [e]1Sa 10:5; 2Ki 4:1,38
2:4 [f]Jos 3:16; 6:26
2:5 [g]ver 3
2:6 [h]ver 2 [i]Jos 3:15 [j]Ru 1:16
2:8 [k]1Ki 19:19 [l]ver 14 [m]Ex 14:21 [n]Ex 14:22,29
2:9 [o]Dt 21:17 [p]Nu 11:17
2:11 [q]2Ki 6:17; Ps 68:17; 104:3,4; Isa 66:15; Hab 3:8; Zec 6:1 [r]Ge 5:24 [s]ver 1
2:12 [t]2Ki 6:17; 13:14 [u]Ge 37:29
2:14 [v]1Ki 19:19 [w]ver 8
2:15 [x]ver 7; 1Sa 10:5 [y]Nu 11:17
2:16 [z]1Ki 18:12 [a]Ac 8:39
2:17 [b]2Ki 8:11
2:21 [c]Ex 15:25; 2Ki 4:41; 6:6
2:22 [d]Ex 15:25

this day, according to the word Elisha
had spoken.

Bears maul jeering youths.

23From there Elisha went up to Bethel.
As he was walking along the road, some
youths came out of the town and jeered[a]
at him. "Go on up, you baldhead!" they
said. "Go on up, you baldhead!" 24He
turned around, looked at them and called
down a curse[b] on them in the name[c] of
the LORD. Then two bears came out of
the woods and mauled forty-two of the
youths. 25And he went on to Mount
Carmel[d] and from there returned to
Samaria.

Elisha predicts Israel's victory over Moab.

3 Joram[b][e] son of Ahab became king of
Israel in Samaria in the eighteenth
year of Jehoshaphat king of Judah, and
he reigned twelve years. 2He did evil[f]
in the eyes of the LORD, but not as his
father[g] and mother had done. He got
rid of the sacred stone[h] of Baal that his
father had made. 3Nevertheless he clung
to the sins[i] of Jeroboam son of Nebat,
which he had caused Israel to commit;
he did not turn away from them.
4Now Mesha king of Moab[j] raised
sheep, and he had to supply the king of
Israel with a hundred thousand lambs[k]
and with the wool of a hundred thousand
rams. 5But after Ahab died, the king of
Moab rebelled[l] against the king of Israel.
6So at that time King Joram set out from
Samaria and mobilized all Israel. 7He also
sent this message to Jehoshaphat king
of Judah: "The king of Moab has rebelled
against me. Will you go with me to
fight[m] against Moab?"
"I will go with you," he replied. "I am
as you are, my people as your people,
my horses as your horses."
8"By what route shall we attack?" he
asked.
"Through the Desert of Edom," he
answered.
9So the king of Israel set out with
the king of Judah and the king of Edom.[n]
After a roundabout march of seven days,
the army had no more water for themselves or for the animals with them.
10"What!" exclaimed the king of Israel.
"Has the LORD called us three kings together only to hand us over to Moab?"
11But Jehoshaphat asked, "Is there no
prophet of the LORD here, that we may
inquire[o] of the LORD through him?"
An officer of the king of Israel answered, "Elisha[p] son of Shaphat is here.
He used to pour water on the hands of
Elijah.[c][q]"
12Jehoshaphat said, "The word[r] of the
LORD is with him." So the king of Israel
and Jehoshaphat and the king of Edom
went down to him.
13Elisha said to the king of Israel,
"What do we have to do with each other? Go to the prophets of your father and
the prophets of your mother."
"No," the king of Israel answered,
"because it was the LORD who called us
three kings together to hand us over to
Moab."
14Elisha said, "As surely as the LORD
Almighty lives, whom I serve, if I did
not have respect for the presence of
Jehoshaphat king of Judah, I would not
look at you or even notice you. 15But
now bring me a harpist."[s]
While the harpist was playing, the
hand[t] of the LORD came upon Elisha
16and he said, "This is what the LORD
says: Make this valley full of ditches.
17For this is what the LORD says: You
will see neither wind nor rain, yet this
valley will be filled with water,[u] and you,
your cattle and your other animals will
drink. 18This is an easy[v] thing in the
eyes of the LORD; he will also hand Moab
over to you. 19You will overthrow every
fortified city and every major town. You
will cut down every good tree, stop up all
the springs, and ruin every good field
with stones."
20The next morning, about the
time[w] for offering the sacrifice, there it
was—water flowing from the direction

2:23 [a]Ex 22:28; 2Ch 36:16; Job 19:18; Ps 31:18
2:24 [b]Ge 4:11; Ne 13:25-27 [c]Dt 18:19
2:25 [d]1Ki 18:20; 2Ki 4:25
3:1 [e]2Ki 1:17
3:2 [f]1Ki 15:26 [g]1Ki 16:30-32 [h]Ex 23:24; 2Ki 10:18, 26-28
3:3 [i]1Ki 12:28-32; 14:9,16
3:4 [j]Ge 19:37; 2Ki 1:1 [k]Ezr 7:17; Isa 16:1
3:5 [l]2Ki 1:1
3:7 [m]1Ki 22:4
3:9 [n]1Ki 22:47
3:11 [o]Ge 25:22; 1Ki 22:7 [p]Ge 20:7 [q]1Ki 19:16
3:12 [r]Nu 11:17
3:15 [s]1Sa 16:23 [t]Jer 15:17; Eze 1:3
3:17 [u]Ps 107:35; Isa 32:2; 35:6; 41:18
3:18 [v]Ge 18:14; 2Ki 20:10; Isa 49:6; Jer 32:17,27; Mk 10:27
3:20 [w]Ex 29:39-40

b *1* Hebrew *Jehoram,* a variant of *Joram;* also in verse 6
c *11* That is, he was Elijah's personal servant.

of Edom! And the land was filled with
water.[a]
21Now all the Moabites had heard that
the kings had come to fight against
them; so every man, young and old, who
could bear arms was called up and stationed on the border. 22When they got
up early in the morning, the sun was
shining on the water. To the Moabites
across the way, the water looked red—
like blood. 23"That's blood!" they said.
"Those kings must have fought and
slaughtered each other. Now to the
plunder, Moab!"
24But when the Moabites came to the
camp of Israel, the Israelites rose up and
fought them until they fled. And the
Israelites invaded the land and slaughtered the Moabites. 25They destroyed
the towns, and each man threw a stone
on every good field until it was covered.
They stopped up all the springs and cut
down every good tree. Only Kir Hareseth[b] was left with its stones in place,
but men armed with slings surrounded
it and attacked it as well.
26When the king of Moab saw that
the battle had gone against him, he took
with him seven hundred swordsmen
to break through to the king of Edom,
but they failed. 27Then he took his firstborn[c] son, who was to succeed him as
king, and offered him as a sacrifice on
the city wall. The fury against Israel was
great; they withdrew and returned to
their own land.

Elisha and the widow's oil.

4 The wife of a man from the company[d] of the prophets cried out to
Elisha, "Your servant my husband is
dead, and you know that he revered
the LORD. But now his creditor[e] is coming to take my two boys as his slaves."
2Elisha replied to her, "How can I help
you? Tell me, what do you have in your
house?"
"Your servant has nothing there at all,"
she said, "except a little oil."[f]
3Elisha said, "Go around and ask all
your neighbors for empty jars. Don't
ask for just a few. 4Then go inside and
shut the door behind you and your sons.
Pour oil into all the jars, and as each is
filled, put it to one side."
5She left him and afterward shut the
door behind her and her sons. They
brought the jars to her and she kept
pouring. 6When all the jars were full,
she said to her son, "Bring me another
one."
But he replied, "There is not a jar left."
Then the oil stopped flowing.
7She went and told the man of God,[g]
and he said, "Go, sell the oil and pay
your debts. You and your sons can live
on what is left."

The Shunammite's son restored to life.

8One day Elisha went to Shunem.[h]
And a well-to-do woman was there,
who urged him to stay for a meal. So
whenever he came by, he stopped there
to eat. 9She said to her husband, "I know
that this man who often comes our way
is a holy man of God. 10Let's make a
small room on the roof and put in it a
bed and a table, a chair and a lamp for
him. Then he can stay[i] there whenever
he comes to us."
11One day when Elisha came, he went
up to his room and lay down there. 12He
said to his servant Gehazi, "Call the
Shunammite."[j] So he called her, and she
stood before him. 13Elisha said to him,
"Tell her, 'You have gone to all this trouble for us. Now what can be done for
you? Can we speak on your behalf to
the king or the commander of the army?'"
She replied, "I have a home among my
own people."
14"What can be done for her?" Elisha
asked.
Gehazi said, "Well, she has no son and
her husband is old."
15Then Elisha said, "Call her." So he
called her, and she stood in the doorway.
16"About this time[k] next year," Elisha
said, "you will hold a son in your arms."
"No, my lord," she objected. "Don't
mislead your servant, O man of God!"

3:20 [a]Ex 17:6
3:25 [b]ver 19; Isa 15:1; 16:7; Jer 48:31,36
3:27 [c]Dt 12:31; 2Ki 16:3; 21:6; 2Ch 28:3; Ps 106:38; Jer 19:4-5; Am 2:1; Mic 6:7
4:1 [d]1Sa 10:5; 2Ki 2:3 [e]Ex 22:26; Lev 25:39-43; Ne 5:3-5; Job 22:6; 24:9
4:2 [f]1Ki 17:12
4:7 [g]1Ki 12:22
4:8 [h]Jos 19:18
4:10 [i]Mt 10:41; Ro 12:13
4:12 [j]2Ki 8:1
4:16 [k]Ge 18:10

17But the woman became pregnant, and the next year about that same time she gave birth to a son, just as Elisha had told her.

18The child grew, and one day he went out to his father, who was with the reapers.[a] 19"My head! My head!" he said to his father.

His father told a servant, "Carry him to his mother." 20After the servant had lifted him up and carried him to his mother, the boy sat on her lap until noon, and then he died. 21She went up and laid him on the bed[b] of the man of God, then shut the door and went out.

22She called her husband and said, "Please send me one of the servants and a donkey so I can go to the man of God quickly and return."

23"Why go to him today?" he asked. "It's not the New Moon[c] or the Sabbath."

"It's all right," she said.

24She saddled the donkey and said to her servant, "Lead on; don't slow down for me unless I tell you." 25So she set out and came to the man of God at Mount Carmel.[d]

When he saw her in the distance, the man of God said to his servant Gehazi, "Look! There's the Shunammite! 26Run to meet her and ask her, 'Are you all right? Is your husband all right? Is your child all right?'"

"Everything is all right," she said.

27When she reached the man of God at the mountain, she took hold of his feet. Gehazi came over to push her away, but the man of God said, "Leave her alone! She is in bitter distress,[e] but the LORD has hidden it from me and has not told me why."

28"Did I ask you for a son, my lord?" she said. "Didn't I tell you, 'Don't raise my hopes'?"

29Elisha said to Gehazi, "Tuck your cloak into your belt,[f] take my staff[g] in your hand and run. If you meet anyone, do not greet him, and if anyone greets you, do not answer. Lay my staff on the boy's face."

30But the child's mother said, "As surely as the LORD lives and as you live, I will not leave you." So he got up and followed her.

31Gehazi went on ahead and laid the staff on the boy's face, but there was no sound or response. So Gehazi went back to meet Elisha and told him, "The boy has not awakened."

32When Elisha reached the house, there was the boy lying dead on his couch.[h] 33He went in, shut the door on the two of them and prayed[i] to the LORD. 34Then he got on the bed and lay upon the boy, mouth to mouth, eyes to eyes, hands to hands. As he stretched[j] himself out upon him, the boy's body grew warm. 35Elisha turned away and walked back and forth in the room and then got on the bed and stretched out upon him once more. The boy sneezed seven times[k] and opened his eyes.[l]

36Elisha summoned Gehazi and said, "Call the Shunammite." And he did. When she came, he said, "Take your son."[m] 37She came in, fell at his feet and bowed to the ground. Then she took her son and went out.

Poisonous stew made edible.

38Elisha returned to Gilgal[n] and there was a famine[o] in that region. While the company of the prophets was meeting with him, he said to his servant, "Put on the large pot and cook some stew for these men."

39One of them went out into the fields to gather herbs and found a wild vine. He gathered some of its gourds and filled the fold of his cloak. When he returned, he cut them up into the pot of stew, though no one knew what they were. 40The stew was poured out for the men, but as they began to eat it, they cried out, "O man of God, there is death in the pot!" And they could not eat it.

41Elisha said, "Get some flour." He put it into the pot and said, "Serve it to the people to eat." And there was nothing harmful in the pot.[p]

Provision of food for 100 men.

42A man came from Baal Shalishah,[q]

4:18 [a]Ru 2:3
4:21 [b]ver 32
4:23 [c]Nu 10:10; 1Ch 23:31; Ps 81:3
4:25 [d]1Ki 18:20; 2Ki 2:25
4:27 [e]1Sa 1:15
4:29 [f]1Ki 18:46; 2Ki 2:8, 14; 9:1 [g]Ex 4:2; 7:19; 14:16
4:32 [h]ver 21
4:33 [i]1Ki 17:20; Mt 6:6
4:34 [j]1Ki 17:21; Ac 20:10
4:35 [k]Jos 6:15 [l]2Ki 8:5
4:36 [m]Heb 11:35
4:38 [n]2Ki 2:1 [o]Lev 26:26; 2Ki 8:1
4:41 [p]Ex 15:25; 2Ki 2:21
4:42 [q]1Sa 9:4

bringing the man of God twenty loaves[a] of barley bread[b] baked from the first ripe grain, along with some heads of new grain. "Give it to the people to eat," Elisha said.

43"How can I set this before a hundred men?" his servant asked.

But Elisha answered, "Give it to the people to eat.[c] For this is what the LORD says: 'They will eat and have some left over.[d] '" 44Then he set it before them, and they ate and had some left over, according to the word of the LORD.

Naaman is healed of leprosy.

5 Now Naaman was commander of the army of the king of Aram.[e] He was a great man in the sight of his master and highly regarded, because through him the LORD had given victory to Aram. He was a valiant soldier, but he had leprosy.[d][f]

2Now bands[g] from Aram had gone out and had taken captive a young girl from Israel, and she served Naaman's wife. 3She said to her mistress, "If only my master would see the prophet[h] who is in Samaria! He would cure him of his leprosy."

4Naaman went to his master and told him what the girl from Israel had said. 5"By all means, go," the king of Aram replied. "I will send a letter to the king of Israel." So Naaman left, taking with him ten talents[e] of silver, six thousand shekels[f] of gold and ten sets of clothing.[i] 6The letter that he took to the king of Israel read: "With this letter I am sending my servant Naaman to you so that you may cure him of his leprosy."

7As soon as the king of Israel read the letter,[j] he tore his robes and said, "Am I God?[k] Can I kill and bring back to life?[l] Why does this fellow send someone to me to be cured of his leprosy? See how he is trying to pick a quarrel[m] with me!"

8When Elisha the man of God heard that the king of Israel had torn his robes, he sent him this message: "Why have you torn your robes? Have the man come to me and he will know that there is a

4:42 [a]Mt 14:17; 15:36 [b]1Sa 9:7
4:43 [c]Lk 9:13 [d]Mt 14:20; Jn 6:12
5:1 [e]Ge 10:22; 2Sa 10:19 [f]Ex 4:6; Nu 12:10; Lk 4:27
5:2 [g]2Ki 6:23; 13:20; 24:2
5:3 [h]Ge 20:7
5:5 [i]ver 22; Ge 24:53; Jdg 14:12; 1Sa 9:7
5:7 [j]2Ki 19:14 [k]Ge 30:2 [l]Dt 32:39; 1Sa 2:6 [m]1Ki 20:7
5:8 [n]1Ki 22:7
5:10 [o]Jn 9:7 [p]Ge 33:3; Lev 14:7
5:11 [q]Ex 7:19
5:12 [r]Isa 8:6 [s]Pr 14:17,29; 19:11; 29:11
5:13 [t]2Ki 6:21; 13:14
5:14 [u]Ge 33:3; Lev 14:7; Jos 6:15 [v]Ex 4:7 [w]Job 33:25; Lk 4:27
5:15 [x]Jos 2:11 [y]Jos 4:24; 1Sa 17:46; Da 2:47 [z]1Sa 9:7; 25:27
5:16 [a]ver 20,26; Ge 14:23; Da 5:17
5:17 [b]Ex 20:24
5:18 [c]2Ki 7:2

prophet[n] in Israel." 9So Naaman went with his horses and chariots and stopped at the door of Elisha's house. 10Elisha sent a messenger to say to him, "Go, wash[o] yourself seven times[p] in the Jordan, and your flesh will be restored and you will be cleansed."

11But Naaman went away angry and said, "I thought that he would surely come out to me and stand and call on the name of the LORD his God, wave his hand[q] over the spot and cure me of my leprosy. 12Are not Abana and Pharpar, the rivers of Damascus, better than any of the waters[r] of Israel? Couldn't I wash in them and be cleansed?" So he turned and went off in a rage.[s]

13Naaman's servants went to him and said, "My father,[t] if the prophet had told you to do some great thing, would you not have done it? How much more, then, when he tells you, 'Wash and be cleansed'!" 14So he went down and dipped himself in the Jordan seven times,[u] as the man of God had told him, and his flesh was restored[v] and became clean like that of a young boy.[w]

15Then Naaman and all his attendants went back to the man of God[x]. He stood before him and said, "Now I know[y] that there is no God in all the world except in Israel. Please accept now a gift[z] from your servant."

16The prophet answered, "As surely as the LORD lives, whom I serve, I will not accept a thing." And even though Naaman urged him, he refused.[a]

17"If you will not," said Naaman, "please let me, your servant, be given as much earth[b] as a pair of mules can carry, for your servant will never again make burnt offerings and sacrifices to any other god but the LORD. 18But may the LORD forgive your servant for this one thing: When my master enters the temple of Rimmon to bow down and he is leaning[c] on my arm and I bow there also—

[d]*1* The Hebrew word was used for various diseases affecting the skin—not necessarily leprosy; also in verses 3, 6, 7, 11 and 27. [e]*5* That is, about 750 pounds (about 340 kilograms) [f]*5* That is, about 150 pounds (about 70 kilograms)

when I bow down in the temple of
Rimmon, may the LORD forgive your
servant for this."
19"Go in peace,"[a] Elisha said.

Naaman's leprosy is put on Gehazi.

After Naaman had traveled some distance, 20Gehazi, the servant of Elisha
the man of God, said to himself, "My
master was too easy on Naaman, this Aramean, by not accepting from him what
he brought. As surely as the LORD[b] lives,
I will run after him and get something
from him."
21So Gehazi hurried after Naaman.
When Naaman saw him running toward
him, he got down from the chariot to
meet him. "Is everything all right?" he
asked.
22"Everything is all right," Gehazi
answered. "My master sent me to say,
'Two young men from the company of
the prophets have just come to me from
the hill country of Ephraim. Please give
them a talent[g] of silver and two sets of
clothing.'"[c]
23"By all means, take two talents," said
Naaman. He urged Gehazi to accept
them, and then tied up the two talents of
silver in two bags, with two sets of clothing. He gave them to two of his servants,
and they carried them ahead of Gehazi.
24When Gehazi came to the hill, he took
the things from the servants and put them
away in the house. He sent the men
away and they left. 25Then he went in
and stood before his master Elisha.
"Where have you been, Gehazi?"
Elisha asked.
"Your servant didn't go anywhere,"
Gehazi answered.
26But Elisha said to him, "Was not my
spirit with you when the man got down
from his chariot to meet you? Is this the
time[d] to take money, or to accept clothes,
olive groves, vineyards, flocks, herds, or
menservants and maidservants?[e] 27Naa-
man's leprosy[f] will cling to you and to
your descendants forever." Then Gehazi[g]
went from Elisha's presence and he was
leprous, as white as snow.[h]

5:19 [a]1Sa 1:17; Ac 15:33
5:20 [b]Ex 20:7
5:22 [c]ver 5; Ge 45:22
5:26 [d]ver 16 [e]Jer 45:5
5:27 [f]Nu 12:10; 2Ki 15:5 [g]Col 3:5 [h]Ex 4:6
6:1 [i]1Sa 10:5; 2Ki 4:38
6:6 [j]Ex 15:25; 2Ki 2:21
6:9 [k]ver 12
6:10 [l]Jer 11:18
6:12 [m]ver 9

An axhead floats.

6 The company[i] of the prophets said
to Elisha, "Look, the place where we
meet with you is too small for us. 2Let
us go to the Jordan, where each of us can
get a pole; and let us build a place there
for us to live."
And he said, "Go."
3Then one of them said, "Won't you
please come with your servants?"
"I will," Elisha replied. 4And he went
with them.
They went to the Jordan and began to
cut down trees. 5As one of them was
cutting down a tree, the iron axhead fell
into the water. "Oh, my lord," he cried
out, "it was borrowed!"
6The man of God asked, "Where did
it fall?" When he showed him the place,
Elisha cut a stick and threw[j] it there,
and made the iron float. 7"Lift it out," he
said. Then the man reached out his hand
and took it.

Elisha prays and the Arameans are blinded.

8Now the king of Aram was at war
with Israel. After conferring with his officers, he said, "I will set up my camp in
such and such a place."
9The man of God sent word to the
king[k] of Israel: "Beware of passing that
place, because the Arameans are going
down there." 10So the king of Israel
checked on the place indicated by the
man of God. Time and again Elisha
warned[l] the king, so that he was on his
guard in such places.
11This enraged the king of Aram. He
summoned his officers and demanded
of them, "Will you not tell me which of
us is on the side of the king of Israel?"
12"None of us, my lord the king,[m]"
said one of his officers, "but Elisha, the
prophet who is in Israel, tells the king
of Israel the very words you speak in
your bedroom."
13"Go, find out where he is," the
king ordered, "so I can send men and

g22 That is, about 75 pounds (about 34 kilograms)

capture him." The report came back:
"He is in Dothan."[a] 14Then he sent[b]
horses and chariots and a strong force
there. They went by night and surrounded the city.
15When the servant of the man of God
got up and went out early the next morning, an army with horses and chariots
had surrounded the city. "Oh, my lord,
what shall we do?" the servant asked.
16"Don't be afraid,"[c] the prophet answered. "Those who are with us are
more[d] than those who are with them."
17And Elisha prayed, "O LORD, open
his eyes so he may see." Then the LORD
opened the servant's eyes, and he looked
and saw the hills full of horses and chariots[e] of fire all around Elisha.
18As the enemy came down toward
him, Elisha prayed to the LORD, "Strike
these people with blindness."[f] So he
struck them with blindness, as Elisha had
asked.
19Elisha told them, "This is not the
road and this is not the city. Follow me,
and I will lead you to the man you are
looking for." And he led them to Samaria.
20After they entered the city, Elisha
said, "LORD, open the eyes of these men
so they can see." Then the LORD opened
their eyes and they looked, and there
they were, inside Samaria.
21When the king of Israel saw them,
he asked Elisha, "Shall I kill them, my
father?[g] Shall I kill them?"
22"Do not kill them," he answered.
"Would you kill men you have captured[h] with your own sword or bow?
Set food and water before them so that
they may eat and drink and then go back
to their master." 23So he prepared a
great feast for them, and after they had
finished eating and drinking, he sent
them away, and they returned to their
master. So the bands[i] from Aram stopped
raiding Israel's territory.

Famine strikes besieged Samaria.

24Some time later, Ben-Hadad[j] king of
Aram mobilized his entire army and
marched up and laid siege[k] to Samaria.
25There was a great famine[l] in the city;
the siege lasted so long that a donkey's
head sold for eighty shekels[h] of silver,
and a quarter of a cab[i] of seed pods[j][m]
for five shekels.[k]
26As the king of Israel was passing by
on the wall, a woman cried to him,
"Help me, my lord the king!"
27The king replied, "If the LORD does
not help you, where can I get help for
you? From the threshing floor? From
the winepress?" 28Then he asked her,
"What's the matter?"
She answered, "This woman said to
me, 'Give up your son so we may eat
him today, and tomorrow we'll eat my
son.' 29So we cooked my son and ate[n]
him. The next day I said to her, 'Give up
your son so we may eat him,' but she
had hidden him."

Elisha promises an end to the famine and siege.

30When the king heard the woman's
words, he tore[o] his robes. As he went
along the wall, the people looked, and
there, underneath, he had sackcloth[p]
on his body. 31He said, "May God deal
with me, be it ever so severely, if the
head of Elisha son of Shaphat remains
on his shoulders today!"
32Now Elisha was sitting in his house,
and the elders[q] were sitting with him.
The king sent a messenger ahead, but before he arrived, Elisha said to the elders,
"Don't you see how this murderer[r] is
sending someone to cut off my head?[s]
Look, when the messenger comes, shut
the door and hold it shut against him.
Is not the sound of his master's footsteps
behind him?"
33While he was still talking to them,
the messenger came down to him. And
⌊the king⌋ said, "This disaster is from
the LORD. Why should I wait[t] for the
LORD any longer?"

6:13 [a]Ge 37:17
6:14 [b]2Ki 1:9
6:16 [c]Ge 15:1 [d]2Ch 32:7; Ps 55:18; Ro 8:31; 1Jn 4:4
6:17 [e]2Ki 2:11,12; Ps 68:17; Zec 6:1-7
6:18 [f]Ge 19:11; Ac 13:11
6:21 [g]2Ki 5:13
6:22 [h]Dt 20:11; 2Ch 28:8-15; Ro 12:20
6:23 [i]2Ki 5:2
6:24 [j]1Ki 15:18; 20:1; 2Ki 8:7 [k]Dt 28:52
6:25 [l]Lev 26:26; Ru 1:1 [m]Isa 36:12
6:29 [n]Lev 26:29; Dt 28:53-55
6:30 [o]2Ki 18:37; Isa 22:15 [p]Ge 37:34; 1Ki 21:27
6:32 [q]Eze 8:1; 14:1; 20:1 [r]1Ki 18:4 [s]ver 31
6:33 [t]Lev 24:11; Job 2:9; 14:14; Isa 40:31

[h]*25* That is, about 2 pounds (about 1 kilogram)
[i]*25* That is, probably about 1/2 pint (about 0.3 liter)
[j]*25* Or *of dove's dung* [k]*25* That is, about 2 ounces (about 55 grams)

7 Elisha said, "Hear the word of the LORD. This is what the LORD says: About this time tomorrow, a seah[l] of flour will sell for a shekel[m] and two seahs[n] of barley for a shekel[a] at the gate of Samaria."

2The officer on whose arm the king was leaning[b] said to the man of God, "Look, even if the LORD should open the floodgates[c] of the heavens, could this happen?"

"You will see it with your own eyes," answered Elisha, "but you will not eat[d] any of it!"

3Now there were four men with leprosy[o][e] at the entrance of the city gate. They said to each other, "Why stay here until we die? 4If we say, 'We'll go into the city'—the famine is there, and we will die. And if we stay here, we will die. So let's go over to the camp of the Arameans and surrender. If they spare us, we live; if they kill us, then we die."

5At dusk they got up and went to the camp of the Arameans. When they reached the edge of the camp, not a man was there, 6for the Lord had caused the Arameans to hear the sound[f] of chariots and horses and a great army, so that they said to one another, "Look, the king of Israel has hired[g] the Hittite[h] and Egyptian kings to attack us!" 7So they got up and fled[i] in the dusk and abandoned their tents and their horses and donkeys. They left the camp as it was and ran for their lives.

8The men who had leprosy[j] reached the edge of the camp and entered one of the tents. They ate and drank, and carried away silver, gold and clothes, and went off and hid them. They returned and entered another tent and took some things from it and hid them also.

9Then they said to each other, "We're not doing right. This is a day of good news and we are keeping it to ourselves. If we wait until daylight, punishment will overtake us. Let's go at once and report this to the royal palace."

10So they went and called out to the city gatekeepers and told them, "We went into the Aramean camp and not a man was there—not a sound of anyone—only tethered horses and donkeys, and the tents left just as they were." 11The gatekeepers shouted the news, and it was reported within the palace.

12The king got up in the night and said to his officers, "I will tell you what the Arameans have done to us. They know we are starving; so they have left the camp to hide[k] in the countryside, thinking, 'They will surely come out, and then we will take them alive and get into the city.'"

13One of his officers answered, "Have some men take five of the horses that are left in the city. Their plight will be like that of all the Israelites left here—yes, they will only be like all these Israelites who are doomed. So let us send them to find out what happened."

14So they selected two chariots with their horses, and the king sent them after the Aramean army. He commanded the drivers, "Go and find out what has happened." 15They followed them as far as the Jordan, and they found the whole road strewn with the clothing and equipment the Arameans had thrown away in their headlong flight. So the messengers returned and reported to the king. 16Then the people went out and plundered[l] the camp of the Arameans. So a seah of flour sold for a shekel, and two seahs of barley sold for a shekel,[m] as the LORD had said.

17Now the king had put the officer on whose arm he leaned in charge of the gate, and the people trampled him in the gateway, and he died,[n] just as the man of God had foretold when the king came down to his house. 18It happened as the man of God had said to the king: "About this time tomorrow, a seah of flour will sell for a shekel and two seahs of barley for a shekel at the gate of Samaria."

7:1 [a]ver 16
7:2 [b]2Ki 5:18 [c]ver 19; Ge 7:11; Ps 78:23; Mal 3:10 [d]ver 17
7:3 [e]Lev 13:45-46; Nu 5:1-4
7:6 [f]Ex 14:24; 2Sa 5:24; Eze 1:24 [g]2Sa 10:6; Jer 46:21 [h]Nu 13:29
7:7 [i]Jdg 7:21; Ps 48:4-6; Pr 28:1; Isa 30:17
7:8 [j]Isa 33:23; 35:6
7:12 [k]Jos 8:4; 2Ki 6:25-29
7:16 [l]Isa 33:4,23 [m]ver 1
7:17 [n]ver 2; 2Ki 6:32

[l] *1* That is, probably about 7 quarts (about 7.3 liters); also in verses 16 and 18 [m] *1* That is, about 2/5 ounce (about 11 grams); also in verses 16 and 18 [n] *1* That is, probably about 13 quarts (about 15 liters); also in verses 16 and 18 [o] *3* The Hebrew word is used for various diseases affecting the skin—not necessarily leprosy; also in verse 8.

19The officer had said to the man of
God, "Look, even if the LORD should
open the floodgates[a] of the heavens,
could this happen?" The man of God had
replied, "You will see it with your own
eyes, but you will not eat any of it!"
20And that is exactly what happened
to him, for the people trampled him in
the gateway, and he died.

The Shunammite's possessions are restored.

8 Now Elisha had said to the woman[b] whose son he had restored to
life, "Go away with your family and stay
for a while wherever you can, because
the LORD has decreed a famine[c] in the
land that will last seven years."[d] 2The
woman proceeded to do as the man of
God said. She and her family went away
and stayed in the land of the Philistines seven years.
3At the end of the seven years she
came back from the land of the Philistines and went to the king to beg for
her house and land. 4The king was talking to Gehazi, the servant of the man
of God, and had said, "Tell me about all
the great things Elisha has done." 5Just
as Gehazi was telling the king how Elisha
had restored[e] the dead to life, the woman whose son Elisha had brought back
to life came to beg the king for her house
and land.
Gehazi said, "This is the woman, my
lord the king, and this is her son whom
Elisha restored to life." 6The king asked
the woman about it, and she told him.
Then he assigned an official to her case
and said to him, "Give back everything
that belonged to her, including all the
income from her land from the day she
left the country until now."

Ben-Hadad is murdered.

7Elisha went to Damascus,[f] and Ben-
Hadad[g] king of Aram was ill. When the
king was told, "The man of God has
come all the way up here," 8he said to
Hazael,[h] "Take a gift[i] with you and go to
meet the man of God. Consult[j] the LORD
through him; ask him, 'Will I recover
from this illness?'"
9Hazael went to meet Elisha, taking
with him as a gift forty camel-loads of all
the finest wares of Damascus. He went
in and stood before him, and said, "Your
son Ben-Hadad king of Aram has sent me
to ask, 'Will I recover from this illness?'"
10Elisha answered, "Go and say to
him, 'You will certainly recover';[k] but[p]
the LORD has revealed to me that he will
in fact die." 11He stared at him with a
fixed gaze until Hazael felt ashamed.[l]
Then the man of God began to weep.[m]
12"Why is my lord weeping?" asked
Hazael.
"Because I know the harm[n] you will
do to the Israelites," he answered. "You
will set fire to their fortified places, kill
their young men with the sword, dash[o]
their little children[p] to the ground, and
rip open[q] their pregnant women."
13Hazael said, "How could your servant, a mere dog,[r] accomplish such a
feat?"
"The LORD has shown me that you will
become king[s] of Aram," answered Elisha.
14Then Hazael left Elisha and returned
to his master. When Ben-Hadad asked,
"What did Elisha say to you?" Hazael
replied, "He told me that you would
certainly recover." 15But the next day
he took a thick cloth, soaked it in water
and spread it over the king's face, so that
he died.[t] Then Hazael succeeded him as
king.

Jehoram reigns in Judah.

8:16-24pp— 2Ch 21:5-10,20

16In the fifth year of Joram[u] son of
Ahab king of Israel, when Jehoshaphat
was king of Judah, Jehoram[v] son of Jehoshaphat began his reign as king of
Judah. 17He was thirty-two years old
when he became king, and he reigned
in Jerusalem eight years. 18He walked
in the ways of the kings of Israel, as
the house of Ahab had done, for he

7:19 [a]ver 2
8:1 [b]2Ki 4:8-37 [c]Lev 26:26; Dt 28:22; Ru 1:1 [d]Ge 12:10; Ps 105:16; Hag 1:11
8:5 [e]2Ki 4:35
8:7 [f]2Sa 8:5; 1Ki 11:24 [g]2Ki 6:24
8:8 [h]1Ki 19:15 [i]Ge 32:20; 1Sa 9:7; 2Ki 1:2 [j]Jdg 18:5
8:10 [k]Isa 38:1
8:11 [l]Jdg 3:25 [m]Lk 19:41
8:12 [n]1Ki 19:17; 2Ki 10:32; 12:17; 13:3,7 [o]Ps 137:9; Isa 13:16; Hos 13:16; Na 3:10; Lk 19:44 [p]Ge 34:29 [q]2Ki 15:16; Am 1:13
8:13 [r]1Sa 17:43; 2Sa 3:8 [s]1Ki 19:15
8:15 [t]2Ki 1:17
8:16 [u]2Ki 1:17; 3:1 [v]2Ch 21:1-4

p *10* The Hebrew may also be read *Go and say, 'You will certainly not recover,' for.*

married a daughter[a] of Ahab. He did
evil in the eyes of the LORD. 19Neverthe-
less, for the sake of his servant David,
the LORD was not willing to destroy[b]
Judah. He had promised to maintain a
lamp[c] for David and his descendants
forever.
20In the time of Jehoram, Edom rebelled against Judah and set up its own
king.[d] 21So Jehoram[q] went to Zair with
all his chariots. The Edomites surrounded him and his chariot commanders,
but he rose up and broke through by
night; his army, however, fled back
home. 22To this day Edom has been in
rebellion[e] against Judah. Libnah[f] revolted at the same time.
23As for the other events of Jehoram's
reign, and all he did, are they not written in the book of the annals of the kings
of Judah? 24Jehoram rested with his
fathers and was buried with them in
the City of David. And Ahaziah his son
succeeded him as king.

Ahaziah reigns in Judah.

8:25-29pp— 2Ch 22:1-6

25In the twelfth[g] year of Joram son of
Ahab king of Israel, Ahaziah son of Jehoram king of Judah began to reign. 26Aha-
ziah was twenty-two years old when he
became king, and he reigned in Jerusalem one year. His mother's name was
Athaliah,[h] a granddaughter of Omri[i]
king of Israel. 27He walked in the ways
of the house of Ahab[j] and did evil[k] in the
eyes of the LORD, as the house of Ahab
had done, for he was related by marriage
to Ahab's family.
28Ahaziah went with Joram son of
Ahab to war against Hazael king of
Aram at Ramoth Gilead.[l] The Arameans
wounded Joram; 29so King Joram returned to Jezreel[m] to recover from the
wounds the Arameans had inflicted on
him at Ramoth[r] in his battle with Hazael[n] king of Aram.
Then Ahaziah son of Jehoram king
of Judah went down to Jezreel to see
Joram son of Ahab, because he had
been wounded.

Jehu is anointed king of Israel.

9 The prophet Elisha summoned a
man from the company[o] of the
prophets and said to him, "Tuck your
cloak into your belt,[p] take this flask of
oil[q] with you and go to Ramoth Gilead.[r]
2When you get there, look for Jehu son
of Jehoshaphat, the son of Nimshi. Go
to him, get him away from his companions and take him into an inner
room. 3Then take the flask and pour
the oil[s] on his head and declare, 'This
is what the LORD says: I anoint you
king over Israel.' Then open the door
and run; don't delay!"
4So the young man, the prophet, went
to Ramoth Gilead. 5When he arrived,
he found the army officers sitting together. "I have a message for you, commander," he said.
"For which of us?" asked Jehu.
"For you, commander," he replied.
6Jehu got up and went into the house.
Then the prophet poured the oil[t] on
Jehu's head and declared, "This is what
the LORD, the God of Israel, says: 'I
anoint you king over the LORD's people
Israel. 7You are to destroy the house of
Ahab your master, and I will avenge[u]
the blood of my servants[v] the prophets
and the blood of all the LORD's servants
shed by Jezebel.[w] 8The whole house[x]
of Ahab will perish. I will cut off from
Ahab every last male[y] in Israel—slave
or free. 9I will make the house of Ahab
like the house of Jeroboam[z] son of
Nebat and like the house of Baasha[a]
son of Ahijah. 10As for Jezebel, dogs[b]
will devour her on the plot of ground
at Jezreel, and no one will bury her.'"
Then he opened the door and ran.
11When Jehu went out to his fellow
officers, one of them asked him, "Is
everything all right? Why did this madman[c] come to you?"
"You know the man and the sort of
things he says," Jehu replied.
12"That's not true!" they said. "Tell
us."

8:18 [a]ver 26; 2Ki 11:1
8:19 [b]Ge 6:13 [c]2Sa 21:17; 7:13; 1Ki 11:36; Rev 21:23
8:20 [d]1Ki 22:47
8:22 [e]Ge 27:40 [f]Nu 33:20; Jos 21:13; 2Ki 19:8
8:25 [g]2Ki 9:29
8:26 [h]ver 18 [i]1Ki 16:23
8:27 [j]1Ki 16:30 [k]1Ki 15:26
8:28 [l]Dt 4:43; 1Ki 22:3,29
8:29 [m]2Ki 9:15 [n]1Ki 19:15,17
9:1 [o]1Sa 10:5 [p]2Ki 4:29 [q]1Sa 10:1 [r]2Ki 8:28
9:3 [s]1Ki 19:16
9:6 [t]1Ki 19:16; 2Ch 22:7
9:7 [u]Ge 4:24; Rev 6:10 [v]Dt 32:43 [w]1Ki 18:4; 21:15
9:8 [x]2Ki 10:17 [y]Dt 32:36; 1Sa 25:22; 1Ki 21:21; 2Ki 14:26
9:9 [z]1Ki 14:10; 15:29; 16:3,11 [a]1Ki 16:3
9:10 [b]ver 35-36; 1Ki 21:23
9:11 [c]Jer 29:26; Jn 10:20; Ac 26:24

q21 Hebrew *Joram,* a variant of *Jehoram*; also in verses 23 and 24 r29 Hebrew *Ramah,* a variant of *Ramoth*

Jehu said, "Here is what he told me: 'This is what the LORD says: I anoint you king over Israel.'"

13 They hurried and took their cloaks and spread[a] them under him on the bare steps. Then they blew the trumpet[b] and shouted, "Jehu is king!"

Jehu slays Joram and Ahaziah.

9:21-29pp— 2Ch 22:7-9

14 So Jehu son of Jehoshaphat, the son of Nimshi, conspired against Joram. (Now Joram and all Israel had been defending Ramoth Gilead[c] against Hazael king of Aram, 15 but King Joram[s] had returned to Jezreel to recover[d] from the wounds the Arameans had inflicted on him in the battle with Hazael king of Aram.) Jehu said, "If this is the way you feel, don't let anyone slip out of the city to go and tell the news in Jezreel." 16 Then he got into his chariot and rode to Jezreel, because Joram was resting there and Ahaziah[e] king of Judah had gone down to see him.

17 When the lookout[f] standing on the tower in Jezreel saw Jehu's troops approaching, he called out, "I see some troops coming."

"Get a horseman," Joram ordered. "Send him to meet them and ask, 'Do you come in peace?[g]'"

18 The horseman rode off to meet Jehu and said, "This is what the king says: 'Do you come in peace?'"

"What do you have to do with peace?" Jehu replied. "Fall in behind me."

The lookout reported, "The messenger has reached them, but he isn't coming back."

19 So the king sent out a second horseman. When he came to them he said, "This is what the king says: 'Do you come in peace?'"

Jehu replied, "What do you have to do with peace? Fall in behind me."

20 The lookout reported, "He has reached them, but he isn't coming back either. The driving is like[h] that of Jehu son of Nimshi—he drives like a madman."

21 "Hitch up my chariot," Joram ordered. And when it was hitched up, Joram king of Israel and Ahaziah king of Judah rode out, each in his own chariot, to meet Jehu. They met him at the plot of ground that had belonged to Naboth[i] the Jezreelite. 22 When Joram saw Jehu he asked, "Have you come in peace, Jehu?"

"How can there be peace," Jehu replied, "as long as all the idolatry and witchcraft of your mother Jezebel[j] abound?"

23 Joram turned about and fled, calling out to Ahaziah, "Treachery,[k] Ahaziah!"

24 Then Jehu drew his bow[l] and shot Joram between the shoulders. The arrow pierced his heart and he slumped down in his chariot. 25 Jehu said to Bidkar, his chariot officer, "Pick him up and throw him on the field that belonged to Naboth the Jezreelite. Remember how you and I were riding together in chariots behind Ahab his father when the LORD made this prophecy[m] about him: 26 'Yesterday I saw the blood of Naboth[n] and the blood of his sons, declares the LORD, and I will surely make you pay for it on this plot of ground, declares the LORD.'[t] Now then, pick him up and throw him on that plot, in accordance with the word of the LORD."[o]

27 When Ahaziah king of Judah saw what had happened, he fled up the road to Beth Haggan.[u] Jehu chased him, shouting, "Kill him too!" They wounded him in his chariot on the way up to Gur near Ibleam,[p] but he escaped to Megiddo[q] and died there. 28 His servants took him by chariot[r] to Jerusalem and buried him with his fathers in his tomb in the City of David. 29 (In the eleventh[s] year of Joram son of Ahab, Ahaziah had become king of Judah.)

Jezebel's death.

30 Then Jehu went to Jezreel. When Jezebel heard about it, she painted[t] her eyes, arranged her hair and looked out

9:13 [a]Mt 21:8; Lk 19:36 [b]2Sa 15:10; 1Ki 1:34,39
9:14 [c]Dt 4:43; 2Ki 8:28
9:15 [d]2Ki 8:29
9:16 [e]2Ch 22:7
9:17 [f]Isa 21:6 [g]1Sa 16:4
9:20 [h]2Sa 18:27
9:21 [i]ver 26; 1Ki 21:1-7, 15-19
9:22 [j]1Ki 16:30-33; 18:19; 2Ch 21:13; Rev 2:20
9:23 [k]2Ki 11:14
9:24 [l]1Ki 22:34
9:25 [m]1Ki 21:19-22, 24-29
9:26 [n]1Ki 21:19 [o]1Ki 21:29
9:27 [p]Jdg 1:27 [q]2Ki 23:29
9:28 [r]2Ki 14:20; 23:30
9:29 [s]2Ki 8:25
9:30 [t]Jer 4:30; Eze 23:40

[s] *15* Hebrew *Jehoram,* a variant of *Joram*; also in verses 17 and 21-24 [t] *26* See 1 Kings 21:19. [u] *27* Or *fled by way of the garden house*

of a window. 31As Jehu entered the gate,
she asked, "Have you come in peace,
Zimri,[a] you murderer of your master?"[v]
32He looked up at the window and
called out, "Who is on my side? Who?"
Two or three eunuchs looked down at
him. 33"Throw her down!" Jehu said.
So they threw her down, and some of
her blood spattered the wall and the
horses as they trampled her underfoot.[b]
34Jehu went in and ate and drank.
"Take care of that cursed woman," he
said, "and bury her, for she was a king's
daughter."[c] 35But when they went out
to bury her, they found nothing except
her skull, her feet and her hands. 36They
went back and told Jehu, who said, "This
is the word of the LORD that he spoke
through his servant Elijah the Tishbite:
On the plot of ground at Jezreel dogs[d]
will devour Jezebel's flesh.[we] 37Jezebel's
body will be like refuse[f] on the ground
in the plot at Jezreel, so that no one will
be able to say, 'This is Jezebel.'"

Seventy of Ahab's sons are beheaded.

10 Now there were in Samaria[g] seventy sons[h] of the house of Ahab.
So Jehu wrote letters and sent them to
Samaria: to the officials of Jezreel,[xi] to
the elders and to the guardians[j] of Ahab's
children. He said, 2"As soon as this letter reaches you, since your master's sons
are with you and you have chariots and
horses, a fortified city and weapons,
3choose the best and most worthy of
your master's sons and set him on his
father's throne. Then fight for your master's house."
4But they were terrified and said, "If
two kings could not resist him, how
can we?"
5So the palace administrator, the city
governor, the elders and the guardians
sent this message to Jehu: "We are your
servants[k] and we will do anything you
say. We will not appoint anyone as king;
you do whatever you think best."
6Then Jehu wrote them a second letter, saying, "If you are on my side and
will obey me, take the heads of your
master's sons and come to me in Jezreel
by this time tomorrow."
Now the royal princes, seventy of
them, were with the leading men of the
city, who were rearing them. 7When the
letter arrived, these men took the
princes and slaughtered all seventy[l] of
them. They put their heads[m] in baskets and sent them to Jehu in Jezreel.
8When the messenger arrived, he told
Jehu, "They have brought the heads of
the princes."
Then Jehu ordered, "Put them in two
piles at the entrance of the city gate
until morning."
9The next morning Jehu went out. He
stood before all the people and said, "You
are innocent. It was I who conspired
against my master and killed him, but
who killed all these? 10Know then, that
not a word the LORD has spoken against
the house of Ahab will fail. The LORD
has done what he promised[n] through
his servant Elijah."[o] 11So Jehu[p] killed
everyone in Jezreel who remained of
the house of Ahab, as well as all his chief
men, his close friends and his priests,
leaving him no survivor.[q]

Jehu has forty-two of Ahaziah's relatives killed.

12Jehu then set out and went toward
Samaria. At Beth Eked of the Shepherds,
13he met some relatives of Ahaziah king
of Judah and asked, "Who are you?"
They said, "We are relatives of Ahaziah,[r] and we have come down to greet
the families of the king and of the queen
mother.[s]"
14"Take them alive!" he ordered. So
they took them alive and slaughtered
them by the well of Beth Eked—forty-
two men. He left no survivor.
15After he left there, he came upon
Jehonadab[t] son of Recab,[u] who was on
his way to meet him. Jehu greeted him

9:31 [a]1Ki 16:9-10
9:33 [b]Ps 7:5
9:34 [c]1Ki 16:31; 21:25
9:36 [d]Ps 68:23; Jer 15:3 [e]1Ki 21:23
9:37 [f]Ps 83:10; Isa 5:25; Jer 8:2; 9:22; 16:4; 25:33; Zep 1:17
10:1 [g]1Ki 13:32 [h]Jdg 8:30 [i]1Ki 21:1 [j]ver 5
10:5 [k]Jos 9:8; 1Ki 20:4,32
10:7 [l]1Ki 21:21 [m]2Sa 4:8
10:10 [n]2Ki 9:7-10 [o]1Ki 21:29
10:11 [p]Hos 1:4 [q]ver 14; Job 18:19
10:13 [r]2Ki 8:24,29; 2Ch 22:8 [s]1Ki 2:19
10:15 [t]Jer 35:6, 14-19 [u]1Ch 2:55; Jer 35:2

[v]*31* Or *"Did Zimri have peace, who murdered his master?"* [w]*36* See 1 Kings 21:23. [x]*1* Hebrew; some Septuagint manuscripts and Vulgate *of the city*

and said, "Are you in accord with me, as
I am with you?"
"I am," Jehonadab answered.
"If so," said Jehu, "give me your
hand."[a] So he did, and Jehu helped him
up into the chariot. 16Jehu said, "Come
with me and see my zeal[b] for the LORD."
Then he had him ride along in his chariot.
17When Jehu came to Samaria, he
killed all who were left there of Ahab's
family;[c] he destroyed them, according
to the word of the LORD spoken to Elijah.

Priests and ministers of Baal are killed.

18Then Jehu brought all the people together and said to them, "Ahab served[d]
Baal a little; Jehu will serve him much.
19Now summon[e] all the prophets of Baal,
all his ministers and all his priests. See
that no one is missing, because I am going to hold a great sacrifice for Baal. Anyone who fails to come will no longer live."
But Jehu was acting deceptively in order
to destroy the ministers of Baal.
20Jehu said, "Call an assembly[f] in hon-
or of Baal." So they proclaimed it.
21Then he sent word throughout Israel,
and all the ministers of Baal came; not
one stayed away. They crowded into
the temple of Baal until it was full from
one end to the other. 22And Jehu said
to the keeper of the wardrobe, "Bring
robes for all the ministers of Baal." So
he brought out robes for them.
23Then Jehu and Jehonadab son of
Recab went into the temple of Baal.
Jehu said to the ministers of Baal, "Look
around and see that no servants of the
LORD are here with you—only ministers
of Baal." 24So they went in to make
sacrifices and burnt offerings. Now Jehu
had posted eighty men outside with this
warning: "If one of you lets any of the
men I am placing in your hands escape,
it will be your life for his life."[g]
25As soon as Jehu had finished making
the burnt offering, he ordered the guards
and officers: "Go in and kill[h] them; let
no one escape."[i] So they cut them down

10:15 [a]Ezr 10:19; Eze 17:18
10:16 [b]Nu 25:13; 1Ki 19:10
10:17 [c]2Ki 9:8
10:18 [d]Jdg 2:11; 1Ki 16:31-32
10:19 [e]1Ki 18:19; 22:6
10:20 [f]Ex 32:5; Joel 1:14
10:24 [g]1Ki 20:39
10:25 [h]Ex 22:20; 2Ki 11:18 [i]1Ki 18:40
10:26 [j]1Ki 14:23
10:27 [k]1Ki 16:32
10:28 [l]1Ki 19:17
10:29 [m]1Ki 12:30 [n]1Ki 12:28-29 [o]1Ki 12:32
10:30 [p]ver 35; 2Ki 15:12
10:31 [q]Pr 4:23 [r]1Ki 12:30
10:32 [s]2Ki 13:25 [t]1Ki 19:17; 2Ki 8:12
10:33 [u]Nu 32:34; Dt 2:36; Jdg 11:26; Isa 17:2
10:34 [v]1Ki 15:31
11:1 [w]2Ki 8:18

with the sword. The guards and officers
threw the bodies out and then entered
the inner shrine of the temple of Baal.
26They brought the sacred stone[j] out of
the temple of Baal and burned it. 27They
demolished the sacred stone of Baal
and tore down the temple[k] of Baal, and
people have used it for a latrine to this
day.
28So Jehu[l] destroyed Baal worship in
Israel. 29However, he did not turn away
from the sins[m] of Jeroboam son of Nebat,
which he had caused Israel to commit—
the worship of the golden calves[n] at
Bethel[o] and Dan.
30The LORD said to Jehu, "Because you
have done well in accomplishing what
is right in my eyes and have done to the
house of Ahab all I had in mind to do,
your descendants will sit on the throne
of Israel to the fourth generation."[p] 31Yet
Jehu was not careful[q] to keep the law
of the LORD, the God of Israel, with all his
heart. He did not turn away from the
sins[r] of Jeroboam, which he had caused
Israel to commit.

Jehu's death.

32In those days the LORD began to
reduce[s] the size of Israel. Hazael[t] overpowered the Israelites throughout their
territory 33east of the Jordan in all the
land of Gilead (the region of Gad,
Reuben and Manasseh), from Aroer[u]
by the Arnon Gorge through Gilead to
Bashan.
34As for the other events of Jehu's
reign, all he did, and all his achievements, are they not written in the book
of the annals[v] of the kings of Israel?
35Jehu rested with his fathers and was
buried in Samaria. And Jehoahaz his son
succeeded him as king. 36The time that
Jehu reigned over Israel in Samaria was
twenty-eight years.

Joash becomes king of Judah.

11:1-21pp— 2Ch 22:10–23:21

11 When Athaliah[w] the mother of
Ahaziah saw that her son was
dead, she proceeded to destroy the

whole royal family. 2But Jehosheba, the daughter of King Jehoram[y] and sister of Ahaziah, took Joash[a] son of Ahaziah and stole him away from among the royal princes, who were about to be murdered. She put him and his nurse in a bedroom to hide him from Athaliah; so he was not killed.[b] 3He remained hidden with his nurse at the temple of the LORD for six years while Athaliah ruled the land.

4In the seventh year Jehoiada sent for the commanders of units of a hundred, the Carites[c] and the guards and had them brought to him at the temple of the LORD. He made a covenant with them and put them under oath at the temple of the LORD. Then he showed them the king's son. 5He commanded them, saying, "This is what you are to do: You who are in the three companies that are going on duty on the Sabbath[d]—a third of you guarding the royal palace,[e] 6a third at the Sur Gate, and a third at the gate behind the guard, who take turns guarding the temple— 7and you who are in the other two companies that normally go off Sabbath duty are all to guard the temple for the king. 8Station yourselves around the king, each man with his weapon in his hand. Anyone who approaches your ranks[z] must be put to death. Stay close to the king wherever he goes."

9The commanders of units of a hundred did just as Jehoiada the priest ordered. Each one took his men—those who were going on duty on the Sabbath and those who were going off duty—and came to Jehoiada the priest. 10Then he gave the commanders the spears and shields[f] that had belonged to King David and that were in the temple of the LORD. 11The guards, each with his weapon in his hand, stationed themselves around the king—near the altar and the temple, from the south side to the north side of the temple.

12Jehoiada brought out the king's son and put the crown on him; he presented him with a copy of the covenant[g] and proclaimed him king. They anointed[h] him, and the people clapped their hands[i] and shouted, "Long live the king!"[j]

11:2 [a]ver 21; 2Ki 12:1 [b]Jdg 9:5
11:4 [c]ver 19
11:5 [d]1Ch 9:25 [e]1Ki 14:27
11:10 [f]2Sa 8:7; 1Ch 18:7
11:12 [g]Ex 25:16; 2Ki 23:3 [h]1Sa 9:16; 1Ki 1:39 [i]Ps 47:1; 98:8; Isa 55:12 [j]1Sa 10:24
11:14 [k]1Ki 7:15; 2Ki 23:3; 2Ch 34:31 [l]1Ki 1:39 [m]Ge 37:29 [n]2Ki 9:23
11:15 [o]1Ki 2:30
11:16 [p]Ne 3:28; Jer 31:40 [q]Ge 4:14
11:17 [r]Ex 24:8; 2Sa 5:3; 2Ch 15:12; 23:3; 29:10; 34:31; Ezr 10:3 [s]2Ki 23:3; Jer 34:8
11:18 [t]1Ki 16:32 [u]Dt 12:3 [v]1Ki 18:40; 2Ki 10:25; 23:20
11:19 [w]ver 4
11:20 [x]Pr 11:10; 28:12; 29:2

Athaliah's death.

13When Athaliah heard the noise made by the guards and the people, she went to the people at the temple of the LORD. 14She looked and there was the king, standing by the pillar,[k] as the custom was. The officers and the trumpeters were beside the king, and all the people of the land were rejoicing and blowing trumpets.[l] Then Athaliah tore[m] her robes and called out, "Treason! Treason!"[n]

15Jehoiada the priest ordered the commanders of units of a hundred, who were in charge of the troops: "Bring her out between the ranks[a] and put to the sword anyone who follows her." For the priest had said, "She must not be put to death in the temple[o] of the LORD." 16So they seized her as she reached the place where the horses enter[p] the palace grounds, and there she was put to death.[q]

17Jehoiada then made a covenant[r] between the LORD and the king and people that they would be the LORD's people. He also made a covenant between the king and the people.[s] 18All the people of the land went to the temple[t] of Baal and tore it down. They smashed[u] the altars and idols to pieces and killed Mattan the priest[v] of Baal in front of the altars.

Then Jehoiada the priest posted guards at the temple of the LORD. 19He took with him the commanders of hundreds, the Carites,[w] the guards and all the people of the land, and together they brought the king down from the temple of the LORD and went into the palace, entering by way of the gate of the guards. The king then took his place on the royal throne, 20and all the people of the land rejoiced.[x] And the city was quiet, because Athaliah had been slain with the sword at the palace.

y*2* Hebrew *Joram,* a variant of *Jehoram* z*8* Or *approaches the precincts* a*15* Or *out from the precincts*

21 Joash[b] was seven years old when he began to reign.

Joash's instruction to repair the temple.

12:1-21pp— 2Ch 24:1-14; 24:23-27

12 In the seventh year of Jehu, Joash[c][a] became king, and he reigned in Jerusalem forty years. His mother's name was Zibiah; she was from Beersheba. 2 Joash did what was right in the eyes of the LORD all the years Jehoiada the priest instructed him. 3 The high places,[b] however, were not removed; the people continued to offer sacrifices and burn incense there.

4 Joash said to the priests, "Collect[c] all the money that is brought as sacred offerings[d] to the temple of the LORD—the money collected in the census,[e] the money received from personal vows and the money brought voluntarily[f] to the temple. 5 Let every priest receive the money from one of the treasurers, and let it be used to repair whatever damage is found in the temple."

6 But by the twenty-third year of King Joash the priests still had not repaired the temple. 7 Therefore King Joash summoned Jehoiada the priest and the other priests and asked them, "Why aren't you repairing the damage done to the temple? Take no more money from your treasurers, but hand it over for repairing the temple." 8 The priests agreed that they would not collect any more money from the people and that they would not repair the temple themselves.

9 Jehoiada the priest took a chest and bored a hole in its lid. He placed it beside the altar, on the right side as one enters the temple of the LORD. The priests who guarded the entrance[g] put into the chest all the money[h] that was brought to the temple of the LORD. 10 Whenever they saw that there was a large amount of money in the chest, the royal secretary[i] and the high priest came, counted the money that had been brought into the temple of the LORD and put it into bags. 11 When the amount had been determined, they gave the money to the men appointed to supervise the work on the temple. With it they paid those who worked on the temple of the LORD—the carpenters and builders, 12 the masons and stonecutters.[j] They purchased timber and dressed stone for the repair of the temple of the LORD, and met all the other expenses of restoring the temple.

13 The money brought into the temple was not spent for making silver basins, wick trimmers, sprinkling bowls, trumpets or any other articles of gold[k] or silver for the temple of the LORD; 14 it was paid to the workmen, who used it to repair the temple. 15 They did not require an accounting from those to whom they gave the money to pay the workers, because they acted with complete honesty.[l] 16 The money from the guilt offerings[m] and sin offerings[n] was not brought into the temple of the LORD; it belonged[o] to the priests.

17 About this time Hazael[p] king of Aram went up and attacked Gath and captured it. Then he turned to attack Jerusalem. 18 But Joash king of Judah took all the sacred objects dedicated by his fathers—Jehoshaphat, Jehoram and Ahaziah, the kings of Judah—and the gifts he himself had dedicated and all the gold found in the treasuries of the temple of the LORD and of the royal palace, and he sent[q] them to Hazael king of Aram, who then withdrew[r] from Jerusalem.

Joash's death.

19 As for the other events of the reign of Joash, and all he did, are they not written in the book of the annals of the kings of Judah? 20 His officials[s] conspired against him and assassinated[t] him at Beth Millo,[u] on the road down to Silla. 21 The officials who murdered him were Jozabad son of Shimeath and Jehozabad son of Shomer. He died and was buried with his fathers in the City of David. And Amaziah his son succeeded him as king.

12:1 [a]2Ki 11:2
12:3 [b]1Ki 3:3; 2Ki 14:4; 15:35; 18:4
12:4 [c]2Ki 22:4 [d]Ex 35:5 [e]Ex 30:12 [f]Ex 35:29; 1Ch 29:3-9
12:9 [g]Jer 35:4 [h]2Ch 24:8; Mk 12:41; Lk 21:1
12:10 [i]2Sa 8:17
12:12 [j]2Ki 22:5-6
12:13 [k]1Ki 7:48-51; 2Ch 24:14
12:15 [l]2Ki 22:7; 1Co 4:2
12:16 [m]Lev 5:14-19; Nu 18:9 [n]Lev 4:1-35 [o]Lev 7:7
12:17 [p]2Ki 8:12
12:18 [q]1Ki 15:18; 2Ch 21:16-17 [r]1Ki 15:21
12:20 [s]2Ki 14:5 [t]2Ch 24:25 [u]Jdg 9:6

b *21* Hebrew *Jehoash,* a variant of *Joash* c *1* Hebrew *Jehoash,* a variant of *Joash*; also in verses 2, 4, 6, 7 and 18

Jehoahaz reigns in Israel.

13 In the twenty-third year of Joash
son of Ahaziah king of Judah, Jehoahaz son of Jehu became king of Israel
in Samaria, and he reigned seventeen
years. 2He did evil[a] in the eyes of the
LORD by following the sins of Jeroboam
son of Nebat, which he had caused Israel
to commit, and he did not turn away
from them. 3So the LORD's anger[b] burned
against Israel, and for a long time he
kept them under the power[c] of Hazael
king of Aram and Ben-Hadad[d] his son.
4Then Jehoahaz sought[e] the LORD's
favor, and the LORD listened to him, for
he saw[f] how severely the king of Aram
was oppressing[g] Israel. 5The LORD provided a deliverer[h] for Israel, and they
escaped from the power of Aram. So
the Israelites lived in their own homes
as they had before. 6But they did not
turn away from the sins[i] of the house of
Jeroboam, which he had caused Israel to
commit; they continued in them. Also,
the Asherah pole[d][j] remained standing in
Samaria.
7Nothing had been left[k] of the army
of Jehoahaz except fifty horsemen, ten
chariots and ten thousand foot soldiers,
for the king of Aram had destroyed the
rest and made them like the dust[l] at
threshing time.
8As for the other events of the reign
of Jehoahaz, all he did and his achievements, are they not written in the book
of the annals of the kings of Israel? 9Je-
hoahaz rested with his fathers and was
buried in Samaria. And Jehoash[e] his son
succeeded him as king.

Jehoash reigns in Israel.

10In the thirty-seventh year of Joash
king of Judah, Jehoash son of Jehoahaz
became king of Israel in Samaria, and
he reigned sixteen years. 11He did evil
in the eyes of the LORD and did not turn
away from any of the sins of Jeroboam
son of Nebat, which he had caused Israel
to commit; he continued in them.
12As for the other events of the reign
of Jehoash, all he did and his achievements, including his war against Amaziah[m] king of Judah, are they not written
in the book of the annals[n] of the kings
of Israel? 13Jehoash rested with his fathers, and Jeroboam[o] succeeded him on
the throne. Jehoash was buried in Samaria with the kings of Israel.

Elisha's death.

14Now Elisha was suffering from the
illness from which he died. Jehoash king
of Israel went down to see him and
wept over him. "My father! My father!"
he cried. "The chariots[p] and horsemen
of Israel!"
15Elisha said, "Get a bow and some
arrows,"[q] and he did so. 16"Take the bow
in your hands," he said to the king of
Israel. When he had taken it, Elisha put
his hands on the king's hands.
17"Open the east window," he said,
and he opened it. "Shoot!"[r] Elisha said,
and he shot. "The LORD's arrow of victory, the arrow of victory over Aram!"
Elisha declared. "You will completely
destroy the Arameans at Aphek."[s]
18Then he said, "Take the arrows,"
and the king took them. Elisha told him,
"Strike the ground." He struck it three
times and stopped. 19The man of God
was angry with him and said, "You
should have struck the ground five or
six times; then you would have defeated Aram and completely destroyed it.
But now you will defeat it only three
times."[t]
20Elisha died and was buried.
Now Moabite raiders[u] used to enter
the country every spring. 21Once while
some Israelites were burying a man, suddenly they saw a band of raiders; so they
threw the man's body into Elisha's tomb.
When the body touched Elisha's bones,
the man came to life[v] and stood up on
his feet.
22Hazael king of Aram oppressed[w]
Israel throughout the reign of Jehoahaz.
23But the LORD was gracious to them

13:2 [a]1Ki 12:26-33
13:3 [b]Dt 31:17; Jdg 2:14 [c]1Ki 8:12; 12:17; 19:17 [d]ver 24
13:4 [e]Dt 4:29; Ps 78:34 [f]Ex 3:7; Dt 26:7 [g]2Ki 14:26
13:5 [h]ver 25; 2Ki 14:25,27
13:6 [i]1Ki 12:30 [j]1Ki 16:33
13:7 [k]2Ki 10:32-33 [l]2Sa 22:43
13:12 [m]2Ki 14:15 [n]1Ki 15:31
13:13 [o]2Ki 14:23; Hos 1:1
13:14 [p]2Ki 2:12
13:15 [q]1Sa 20:20
13:17 [r]Jos 8:18 [s]1Ki 20:26
13:19 [t]ver 25
13:20 [u]2Ki 3:7; 24:2
13:21 [v]Mt 27:52
13:22 [w]1Ki 19:17; 2Ki 8:12

[d]*6* That is, a symbol of the goddess Asherah; here and elsewhere in 2 Kings [e]*9* Hebrew *Joash,* a variant of *Jehoash*; also in verses 12-14 and 25

and had compassion and showed concern for them because of his covenant[a] with Abraham, Isaac and Jacob. To this day he has been unwilling to destroy[b] them or banish them from his presence.[c]

24 Hazael king of Aram died, and Ben-Hadad[d] his son succeeded him as king. 25 Then Jehoash son of Jehoahaz recaptured from Ben-Hadad son of Hazael the towns he had taken in battle from his father Jehoahaz. Three times[e] Jehoash defeated him, and so he recovered[f] the Israelite towns.

Amaziah reigns in Judah.

14:1-7pp— 2Ch 25:1-4,11-12
14:8-22pp— 2Ch 25:17–26:2

14 In the second year of Jehoash[f] son of Jehoahaz king of Israel, Amaziah son of Joash king of Judah began to reign. 2 He was twenty-five years old when he became king, and he reigned in Jerusalem twenty-nine years. His mother's name was Jehoaddin; she was from Jerusalem. 3 He did what was right in the eyes of the LORD, but not as his father David had done. In everything he followed the example of his father Joash. 4 The high places,[g] however, were not removed; the people continued to offer sacrifices and burn incense there.

5 After the kingdom was firmly in his grasp, he executed[h] the officials[i] who had murdered his father the king. 6 Yet he did not put the sons of the assassins to death, in accordance with what is written in the Book of the Law[j] of Moses where the LORD commanded: "Fathers shall not be put to death for their children, nor children put to death for their fathers; each is to die for his own sins."[g][k]

7 He was the one who defeated ten thousand Edomites in the Valley of Salt[l] and captured Sela[m] in battle, calling it Joktheel, the name it has to this day.

8 Then Amaziah sent messengers to Jehoash son of Jehoahaz, the son of Jehu, king of Israel, with the challenge: "Come, meet me face to face."

9 But Jehoash king of Israel replied to Amaziah king of Judah: "A thistle[n] in Lebanon sent a message to a cedar in Lebanon, 'Give your daughter to my son in marriage.' Then a wild beast in Lebanon came along and trampled the thistle underfoot. 10 You have indeed defeated Edom and now you are arrogant.[o] Glory in your victory, but stay at home! Why ask for trouble and cause your own downfall and that of Judah also?"

11 Amaziah, however, would not listen, so Jehoash king of Israel attacked. He and Amaziah king of Judah faced each other at Beth Shemesh[p] in Judah. 12 Judah was routed by Israel, and every man fled to his home.[q] 13 Jehoash king of Israel captured Amaziah king of Judah, the son of Joash, the son of Ahaziah, at Beth Shemesh. Then Jehoash went to Jerusalem and broke down the wall[r] of Jerusalem from the Ephraim Gate[s] to the Corner Gate[t]—a section about six hundred feet long.[h] 14 He took all the gold and silver and all the articles found in the temple of the LORD and in the treasuries of the royal palace. He also took hostages and returned to Samaria.

15 As for the other events of the reign of Jehoash, what he did and his achievements, including his war[u] against Amaziah king of Judah, are they not written in the book of the annals of the kings of Israel? 16 Jehoash rested with his fathers and was buried in Samaria with the kings of Israel. And Jeroboam his son succeeded him as king.

Amaziah is killed.

17 Amaziah son of Joash king of Judah lived for fifteen years after the death of Jehoash son of Jehoahaz king of Israel. 18 As for the other events of Amaziah's reign, are they not written in the book of the annals of the kings of Judah?

19 They conspired[v] against him in Jerusalem, and he fled to Lachish,[w] but they sent men after him to Lachish and killed him there. 20 He was brought back

13:23 [a]Ge 13:16-17; Ex 2:24 [b]Dt 29:20 [c]Ex 33:15; 2Ki 14:27; 17:18; 24:3,20
13:24 [d]ver 3
13:25 [e]ver 18,19 [f]2Ki 10:32
14:4 [g]2Ki 12:3; 16:4
14:5 [h]2Ki 21:24 [i]2Ki 12:20
14:6 [j]Dt 28:61 [k]Nu 26:11; Job 21:20; Jer 31:30; 44:3; Eze 18:4,20
14:7 [l]2Sa 8:13; 2Ch 25:11 [m]Jdg 1:36
14:9 [n]Jdg 9:8-15
14:10 [o]Dt 8:14; 2Ch 26:16; 32:25
14:11 [p]Jos 15:10
14:12 [q]2Sa 18:17
14:13 [r]1Ki 3:1; 2Ch 33:14; 36:19; Jer 39:2 [s]Ne 8:16; 12:39 [t]2Ch 25:23; Jer 31:38; Zec 14:10
14:15 [u]2Ki 13:12
14:19 [v]2Ki 12:20 [w]Jos 10:3; 2Ki 18:14,17

[f] *1* Hebrew *Joash,* a variant of *Jehoash*; also in verses 13, 23 and 27 [g] *6* Deut. 24:16 [h] *13* Hebrew *four hundred cubits* (about 180 meters)

by horse[a] and was buried in Jerusalem
with his fathers, in the City of David.

Azariah reigns in Judah.

21Then all the people of Judah took
Azariah,[i][b] who was sixteen years old,
and made him king in place of his father
Amaziah. 22He was the one who rebuilt
Elath[c] and restored it to Judah after
Amaziah rested with his fathers.

Jeroboam II reigns in Israel.

23In the fifteenth year of Amaziah son
of Joash king of Judah, Jeroboam[d] son
of Jehoash king of Israel became king in
Samaria, and he reigned forty-one years.
24He did evil in the eyes of the LORD and
did not turn away from any of the sins
of Jeroboam son of Nebat, which he had
caused Israel to commit.[e] 25He was the
one who restored the boundaries of
Israel from Lebo[j] Hamath[f] to the Sea of
the Arabah,[k][g] in accordance with the
word of the LORD, the God of Israel,
spoken through his servant Jonah[h] son
of Amittai, the prophet from Gath Hepher.
26The LORD had seen how bitterly everyone in Israel, whether slave or free,[i]
was suffering;[j] there was no one to help
them.[k] 27And since the LORD had not
said he would blot out[l] the name of Israel
from under heaven, he saved[m] them
by the hand of Jeroboam son of Jehoash.
28As for the other events of Jeroboam's
reign, all he did, and his military achievements, including how he recovered for
Israel both Damascus[n] and Hamath,[o]
which had belonged to Yaudi,[l] are they
not written in the book of the annals[p]
of the kings of Israel? 29Jeroboam rested with his fathers, the kings of Israel.
And Zechariah his son succeeded him
as king.

Azariah reigns in Judah.

15:1-7pp— 2Ch 26:3-4,21-23

15 In the twenty-seventh year of Jeroboam king of Israel, Azariah[q]
son of Amaziah king of Judah began to
reign. 2He was sixteen years old when
he became king, and he reigned in Jerusalem fifty-two years. His mother's
name was Jecoliah; she was from Jerusalem. 3He did what was right in the
eyes of the LORD, just as his father
Amaziah had done. 4The high places,
however, were not removed; the people
continued to offer sacrifices and burn
incense there.
5The LORD afflicted[r] the king with
leprosy[m] until the day he died, and he
lived in a separate house.[n][s] Jotham[t] the
king's son had charge of the palace[u]
and governed the people of the land.
6As for the other events of Azariah's
reign, and all he did, are they not written in the book of the annals of the kings
of Judah? 7Azariah rested[v] with his
fathers and was buried near them in the
City of David. And Jotham[w] his son succeeded him as king.

Zechariah reigns in Israel.

8In the thirty-eighth year of Azariah
king of Judah, Zechariah son of Jeroboam
became king of Israel in Samaria, and
he reigned six months. 9He did evil[x] in
the eyes of the LORD, as his fathers had
done. He did not turn away from the sins
of Jeroboam son of Nebat, which he had
caused Israel to commit.
10Shallum son of Jabesh conspired
against Zechariah. He attacked him in
front of the people,[o] assassinated[y] him
and succeeded him as king. 11The other
events of Zechariah's reign are written
in the book of the annals[z] of the kings
of Israel. 12So the word of the LORD spoken to Jehu was fulfilled:[a] "Your descendants will sit on the throne of Israel to
the fourth generation."[p]

Shallum reigns in Israel.

13Shallum son of Jabesh became king
in the thirty-ninth year of Uzziah king

14:20 [a]2Ki 9:28
14:21 [b]2Ki 15:1; 2Ch 26:23
14:22 [c]1Ki 9:26; 2Ki 16:6
14:23 [d]2Ki 13:13
14:24 [e]1Ki 15:30
14:25 [f]Nu 13:21; 1Ki 8:65 [g]Dt 3:17 [h]Jnh 1:1; Mt 12:39
14:26 [i]Dt 32:36 [j]2Ki 13:4 [k]Ps 18:41; 22:11; 72:12; 107:12; Isa 63:5; La 1:7
14:27 [l]2Ki 13:23 [m]Jdg 6:14
14:28 [n]2Sa 8:5; 1Ki 11:24 [o]2Ch 8:3 [p]1Ki 15:31
15:1 [q]ver 32; 2Ki 14:21
15:5 [r]Ge 12:17 [s]Lev 13:46 [t]2Ch 27:1 [u]Ge 41:40
15:7 [v]Isa 6:1; 14:28 [w]ver 5
15:9 [x]1Ki 15:26
15:10 [y]2Ki 12:20
15:11 [z]1Ki 15:31
15:12 [a]2Ki 10:30

[i]*21* Also called *Uzziah* [j]*25* Or *from the entrance to*
[k]*25* That is, the Dead Sea [l]*28* Or *Judah*
[m]*5* The Hebrew word was used for various diseases affecting the skin—not necessarily leprosy.
[n]*5* Or *in a house where he was relieved of responsibility* [o]*10* Hebrew; some Septuagint manuscripts *in Ibleam* [p]*12* 2 Kings 10:30

of Judah, and he reigned in Samaria[a] one month. 14 Then Menahem son of Gadi went from Tirzah[b] up to Samaria. He attacked Shallum son of Jabesh in Samaria, assassinated[c] him and succeeded him as king.

15 The other events of Shallum's reign, and the conspiracy he led, are written in the book of the annals[d] of the kings of Israel.

16 At that time Menahem, starting out from Tirzah, attacked Tiphsah[e] and everyone in the city and its vicinity, because they refused to open[f] their gates. He sacked Tiphsah and ripped open all the pregnant women.

Menahem reigns in Israel.

17 In the thirty-ninth year of Azariah king of Judah, Menahem son of Gadi became king of Israel, and he reigned in Samaria ten years. 18 He did evil in the eyes of the LORD. During his entire reign he did not turn away from the sins of Jeroboam son of Nebat, which he had caused Israel to commit.

19 Then Pul[q][g] king of Assyria invaded the land, and Menahem gave him a thousand talents[r] of silver to gain his support and strengthen his own hold on the kingdom. 20 Menahem exacted this money from Israel. Every wealthy man had to contribute fifty shekels[s] of silver to be given to the king of Assyria. So the king of Assyria withdrew[h] and stayed in the land no longer.

21 As for the other events of Menahem's reign, and all he did, are they not written in the book of the annals of the kings of Israel? 22 Menahem rested with his fathers. And Pekahiah his son succeeded him as king.

Pekahiah reigns in Israel.

23 In the fiftieth year of Azariah king of Judah, Pekahiah son of Menahem became king of Israel in Samaria, and he reigned two years. 24 Pekahiah did evil in the eyes of the LORD. He did not turn away from the sins of Jeroboam son of Nebat, which he had caused Israel to commit. 25 One of his chief officers, Pekah[i] son of Remaliah, conspired against him. Taking fifty men of Gilead with him, he assassinated[j] Pekahiah, along with Argob and Arieh, in the citadel of the royal palace at Samaria. So Pekah killed Pekahiah and succeeded him as king.

26 The other events of Pekahiah's reign, and all he did, are written in the book of the annals of the kings of Israel.

Pekah reigns in Israel.

27 In the fifty-second year of Azariah king of Judah, Pekah[k] son of Remaliah[l] became king of Israel in Samaria, and he reigned twenty years. 28 He did evil in the eyes of the LORD. He did not turn away from the sins of Jeroboam son of Nebat, which he had caused Israel to commit.

29 In the time of Pekah king of Israel, Tiglath-Pileser[m] king of Assyria came and took Ijon,[n] Abel Beth Maacah, Janoah, Kedesh and Hazor. He took Gilead and Galilee, including all the land of Naphtali,[o] and deported[p] the people to Assyria. 30 Then Hoshea[q] son of Elah conspired against Pekah son of Remaliah. He attacked and assassinated[r] him, and then succeeded him as king in the twentieth year of Jotham son of Uzziah.

31 As for the other events of Pekah's reign, and all he did, are they not written in the book of the annals of the kings of Israel?

Jotham reigns in Judah.

15:33-38pp— 2Ch 27:1-4,7-9

32 In the second year of Pekah son of Remaliah king of Israel, Jotham[s] son of Uzziah king of Judah began to reign. 33 He was twenty-five years old when he became king, and he reigned in Jerusalem sixteen years. His mother's name was Jerusha daughter of Zadok. 34 He did what was right[t] in the eyes of the LORD, just as his father Uzziah had done.

15:13 [a] ver 1,8
15:14 [b] 1Ki 14:17 [c] 2Ki 12:20
15:15 [d] 1Ki 15:31
15:16 [e] 1Ki 4:24 [f] 2Ki 8:12; Hos 13:16
15:19 [g] 1Ch 5:6,26
15:20 [h] 2Ki 12:18
15:25 [i] 2Ch 28:6; Isa 7:1 [j] 2Ki 12:20
15:27 [k] 2Ch 28:6; Isa 7:1 [l] Isa 7:4
15:29 [m] 2Ki 16:7; 17:6; 1Ch 5:26; 2Ch 28:20; Jer 50:17 [n] 1Ki 15:20 [o] 2Ki 16:9; 17:24; 2Ch 16:4; Isa 9:1 [p] 2Ki 24:14-16; 1Ch 5:22; Isa 14:6,17; 36:17; 45:13
15:30 [q] 2Ki 17:1 [r] 2Ki 12:20
15:32 [s] 1Ch 5:17
15:34 [t] ver 3; 1Ki 14:8; 2Ch 26:4-5

q *19* Also called *Tiglath-Pileser* r *19* That is, about 37 tons (about 34 metric tons) s *20* That is, about 1 1/4 pounds (about 0.6 kilogram)

35 The high places,[a] however, were not
removed; the people continued to offer
sacrifices and burn incense there. Jotham
rebuilt the Upper Gate[b] of the temple
of the LORD.
36 As for the other events of Jotham's
reign, and what he did, are they not written in the book of the annals of the kings
of Judah? 37 (In those days the LORD began
to send Rezin[c] king of Aram and Pekah
son of Remaliah against Judah.) 38 Jotham
rested with his fathers and was buried
with them in the City of David, the city
of his father. And Ahaz his son succeeded him as king.

Idolatry marks Ahaz's reign in Judah.

16:1-20pp— 2Ch 28:1-27

16 In the seventeenth year of Pekah
son of Remaliah, Ahaz[d] son of
Jotham king of Judah began to reign.
2 Ahaz was twenty years old when he
became king, and he reigned in Jerusalem sixteen years. Unlike David his
father, he did not do what was right[e] in
the eyes of the LORD his God. 3 He
walked in the ways of the kings of Israel and even sacrificed his son[f] in[t] the
fire, following the detestable[g] ways of the
nations the LORD had driven out before
the Israelites. 4 He offered sacrifices and
burned incense at the high places, on
the hilltops and under every spreading
tree.[h]
5 Then Rezin[i] king of Aram and Pekah
son of Remaliah king of Israel marched
up to fight against Jerusalem and besieged Ahaz, but they could not overpower him. 6 At that time, Rezin[j] king
of Aram recovered Elath[k] for Aram by
driving out the men of Judah. Edomites
then moved into Elath and have lived
there to this day.
7 Ahaz sent messengers to say to
Tiglath-Pileser[l] king of Assyria, "I am
your servant and vassal. Come up and
save[m] me out of the hand of the king of
Aram and of the king of Israel, who are
attacking me." 8 And Ahaz took the silver
and gold found in the temple of the LORD
and in the treasuries of the royal palace
and sent it as a gift[n] to the king of Assyria. 9 The king of Assyria complied by attacking Damascus[o] and capturing it. He
deported its inhabitants to Kir[p] and put
Rezin to death.
10 Then King Ahaz went to Damascus
to meet Tiglath-Pileser king of Assyria.
He saw an altar in Damascus and sent to
Uriah[q] the priest a sketch of the altar,
with detailed plans for its construction.
11 So Uriah the priest built an altar in
accordance with all the plans that King
Ahaz had sent from Damascus and finished it before King Ahaz returned.
12 When the king came back from Damascus and saw the altar, he approached
it and presented offerings[u] [r] on it. 13 He
offered up his burnt offering[s] and grain
offering, poured out his drink offering,
and sprinkled the blood of his fellowship
offerings[v] [t] on the altar. 14 The bronze
altar[u] that stood before the LORD he
brought from the front of the temple—
from between the new altar and the temple of the LORD—and put it on the north
side of the new altar.
15 King Ahaz then gave these orders
to Uriah the priest: "On the large new
altar, offer the morning[v] burnt offering
and the evening grain offering, the
king's burnt offering and his grain offering, and the burnt offering of all the people of the land, and their grain offering
and their drink offering. Sprinkle on the
altar all the blood of the burnt offerings
and sacrifices. But I will use the bronze
altar for seeking guidance."[w] 16 And Uriah the priest did just as King Ahaz had
ordered.
17 King Ahaz took away the side panels
and removed the basins from the movable stands. He removed the Sea from
the bronze bulls that supported it and
set it on a stone base.[x] 18 He took away
the Sabbath canopy[w] that had been built
at the temple and removed the royal

15:35 [a] 2Ki 12:3 [b] 2Ch 23:20
15:37 [c] 2Ki 16:5; Isa 7:1
16:1 [d] Isa 1:1; 14:28
16:2 [e] 1Ki 14:8
16:3 [f] Lev 18:21; 2Ki 21:6 [g] Lev 18:3; Dt 9:4; 12:31
16:4 [h] Dt 12:2; Eze 6:13
16:5 [i] 2Ki 15:37; Isa 7:1,4
16:6 [j] Isa 9:12 [k] 2Ki 14:22; 2Ch 26:2
16:7 [l] 2Ki 15:29 [m] Isa 2:6; Jer 2:18; Eze 16:28; Hos 10:6
16:8 [n] 2Ki 12:18
16:9 [o] 2Ki 15:29 [p] Isa 22:6; Am 1:5; 9:7
16:10 [q] Isa 8:2
16:12 [r] 2Ch 26:16
16:13 [s] Lev 6:8-13 [t] Lev 7:11-21
16:14 [u] 2Ch 4:1
16:15 [v] Ex 29:38-41 [w] 1Sa 9:9
16:17 [x] 1Ki 7:27

t3 Or *even made his son pass through* u12 Or *and went up* v13 Traditionally *peace offerings* w18 Or *the dais of his throne* (see Septuagint)

entryway outside the temple of the LORD,
in deference to the king of Assyria.[a]
19As for the other events of the reign
of Ahaz, and what he did, are they not
written in the book of the annals of
the kings of Judah? 20Ahaz rested with
his fathers and was buried with them
in the City of David. And Hezekiah his
son succeeded him as king.

Hoshea's reign in Israel.

17:3-7pp— 2Ki 18:9-12

17 In the twelfth year of Ahaz king
of Judah, Hoshea[b] son of Elah became king of Israel in Samaria, and he
reigned nine years. 2He did evil in the
eyes of the LORD, but not like the kings
of Israel who preceded him.
3Shalmaneser[c] king of Assyria came
up to attack Hoshea, who had been
Shalmaneser's vassal and had paid him
tribute. 4But the king of Assyria discovered that Hoshea was a traitor, for he
had sent envoys to So[x] king of Egypt,
and he no longer paid tribute to the king
of Assyria, as he had done year by year.
Therefore Shalmaneser seized him and
put him in prison. 5The king of Assyria
invaded the entire land, marched against
Samaria and laid siege[d] to it for three
years. 6In the ninth year of Hoshea, the
king of Assyria captured Samaria[e] and
deported[f] the Israelites to Assyria. He
settled them in Halah, in Gozan[g] on the
Habor River and in the towns of the
Medes.

Israel exiled because of sin.

7All this took place because the Israelites had sinned[h] against the LORD their
God, who had brought them up out of
Egypt[i] from under the power of Pharaoh
king of Egypt. They worshiped other
gods 8and followed the practices of the
nations[j] the LORD had driven out before
them, as well as the practices that the
kings of Israel had introduced. 9The Israelites secretly did things against the
LORD their God that were not right.
From watchtower to fortified city[k] they
built themselves high places in all their

16:18 [a]Eze 16:28
17:1 [b]2Ki 15:30
17:3 [c]2Ki 18:9-12; Hos 10:14
17:5 [d]Hos 13:16
17:6 [e]Hos 13:16 [f]Dt 28:36,64; 2Ki 18:10-11 [g]1Ch 5:26
17:7 [h]Jos 23:16; Jdg 6:10 [i]Ex 14:15-31
17:8 [j]Lev 18:3; Dt 18:9; 2Ki 16:3
17:9 [k]2Ki 18:8
17:10 [l]Ex 34:13; Mic 5:14 [m]1Ki 14:23
17:12 [n]Ex 20:4
17:13 [o]1Sa 9:9 [p]Jer 18:11; 25:5; 35:15
17:14 [q]Ex 32:9; Dt 31:27; Ac 7:51
17:15 [r]Dt 29:25 [s]Dt 32:21; Ro 1:21-23 [t]Dt 12:30-31

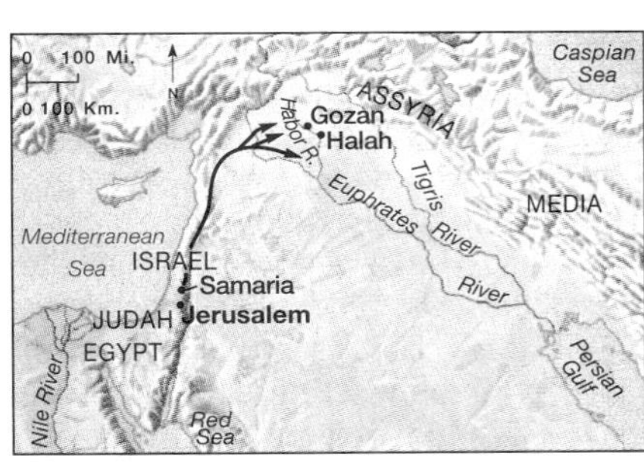

Israel Taken Captive

Finally the sins of Israel's people caught up with them. God allowed Assyria to defeat and disperse the people. They were led into captivity, swallowed up by the mighty, evil Assyrian empire. Sin always brings discipline, and the consequences of that sin are sometimes irreversible.

towns. 10They set up sacred stones and
Asherah poles[l] on every high hill and
under every spreading tree.[m] 11At every
high place they burned incense, as the
nations whom the LORD had driven out
before them had done. They did wicked
things that provoked the LORD to anger.
12They worshiped idols,[n] though the
LORD had said, "You shall not do this."[y]
13The LORD warned Israel and Judah
through all his prophets and seers:[o]
"Turn from your evil ways.[p] Observe
my commands and decrees, in accordance with the entire Law that I commanded your fathers to obey and that I
delivered to you through my servants the
prophets."
14But they would not listen and were
as stiff-necked[q] as their fathers, who did
not trust in the LORD their God. 15They
rejected his decrees and the covenant[r]
he had made with their fathers and the
warnings he had given them. They followed worthless idols[s] and themselves
became worthless. They imitated the nations[t] around them although the LORD
had ordered them, "Do not do as they
do," and they did the things the LORD
had forbidden them to do.
16They forsook all the commands of
the LORD their God and made for
themselves two idols cast in the shape

x4 Or *to Sais, to the*; *So* is possibly an abbreviation for *Osorkon.* y12 Exodus 20:4, 5

of calves,[a] and an Asherah[b] pole. They
bowed down to all the starry hosts,[c] and
they worshiped Baal.[d] 17 They sacrificed[e]
their sons and daughters in[z] the fire.
They practiced divination and sorcery[f]
and sold[g] themselves to do evil in the
eyes of the LORD, provoking him to anger.

18 So the LORD was very angry with
Israel and removed them from his presence. Only the tribe of Judah was left,
19 and even Judah did not keep the
commands of the LORD their God. They
followed the practices Israel had introduced.[h] 20 Therefore the LORD rejected all the people of Israel; he afflicted
them and gave them into the hands of
plunderers,[i] until he thrust them from
his presence.

21 When he tore[j] Israel away from the
house of David, they made Jeroboam son
of Nebat their king.[k] Jeroboam enticed
Israel away from following the LORD and
caused them to commit a great sin.
22 The Israelites persisted in all the sins
of Jeroboam and did not turn away from
them 23 until the LORD removed them
from his presence, as he had warned
through all his servants the prophets. So
the people of Israel were taken from
their homeland into exile in Assyria, and
they are still there.

Foreigners' resettlement of Samaria.

24 The king of Assyria[l] brought people
from Babylon, Cuthah, Avva, Hamath
and Sepharvaim[m] and settled them in the
towns of Samaria to replace the Israelites. They took over Samaria and lived
in its towns. 25 When they first lived
there, they did not worship the LORD;
so he sent lions[n] among them and they
killed some of the people. 26 It was reported to the king of Assyria: "The people you deported and resettled in the
towns of Samaria do not know what the
god of that country requires. He has sent
lions among them, which are killing
them off, because the people do not
know what he requires."

27 Then the king of Assyria gave this
order: "Have one of the priests you took
captive from Samaria go back to live there
and teach the people what the god of the
land requires." 28 So one of the priests
who had been exiled from Samaria came
to live in Bethel and taught them how to
worship the LORD.

29 Nevertheless, each national group
made its own gods in the several towns[o]
where they settled, and set them up in
the shrines[p] the people of Samaria had
made at the high places.[q] 30 The men
from Babylon made Succoth Benoth, the
men from Cuthah made Nergal, and
the men from Hamath made Ashima;
31 the Avvites made Nibhaz and Tartak,
and the Sepharvites burned their children in the fire as sacrifices to Adrammelech[r] and Anammelech, the gods of
Sepharvaim.[s] 32 They worshiped the
LORD, but they also appointed all sorts[t]
of their own people to officiate for them
as priests in the shrines at the high
places. 33 They worshiped the LORD, but
they also served their own gods in accordance with the customs of the nations from which they had been brought.

34 To this day they persist in their former practices. They neither worship the
LORD nor adhere to the decrees and
ordinances, the laws and commands that
the LORD gave the descendants of Jacob,
whom he named Israel.[u] 35 When the
LORD made a covenant with the Israelites, he commanded them: "Do not
worship[v] any other gods or bow down
to them, serve them or sacrifice to them.
36 But the LORD, who brought you up out
of Egypt with mighty power and outstretched arm,[w] is the one you must worship. To him you shall bow down and to
him offer sacrifices. 37 You must always
be careful[x] to keep the decrees and ordinances, the laws and commands he
wrote for you. Do not worship other
gods. 38 Do not forget[y] the covenant I
have made with you, and do not worship other gods. 39 Rather, worship the
LORD your God; it is he who will deliver
you from the hand of all your enemies."

17:16 [a] 1Ki 12:28 [b] 1Ki 14:15,23 [c] 2Ki 21:3 [d] 1Ki 16:31
17:17 [e] Dt 18:10-12; 2Ki 16:3 [f] Lev 19:26 [g] 1Ki 21:20
17:19 [h] 1Ki 14:22-23; 2Ki 16:3
17:20 [i] 2Ki 15:29
17:21 [j] 1Ki 11:11 [k] 1Ki 12:20
17:24 [l] Ezr 4:2,10 [m] 2Ki 18:34
17:25 [n] Ge 37:20
17:29 [o] Jer 2:28 [p] 1Ki 12:31 [q] Mic 4:5
17:31 [r] 2Ki 19:37 [s] ver 24
17:32 [t] 1Ki 12:31
17:34 [u] Ge 32:28; 35:10; 1Ki 18:31
17:35 [v] Ex 20:5; Jdg 6:10
17:36 [w] Ex 3:20; 6:6; Ps 136:12
17:37 [x] Dt 5:32
17:38 [y] Dt 4:23; 6:12

[z] 17 Or *They made their sons and daughters pass through*

40They would not listen, however, but
persisted in their former practices.
41Even while these people were worshiping the LORD,[a] they were serving their
idols. To this day their children and
grandchildren continue to do as their
fathers did.

Hezekiah destroys idol worship.

18:2-4pp— 2Ch 29:1-2; 31:1
18:5-7pp— 2Ch 31:20-21
18:9-12pp— 2Ki 17:3-7

18 In the third year of Hoshea son
of Elah king of Israel, Hezekiah[b]
son of Ahaz king of Judah began to reign.
2He was twenty-five years old when he
became king, and he reigned in Jerusalem twenty-nine years.[c] His mother's name was Abijah[a] daughter of
Zechariah. 3He did what was right in
the eyes of the LORD, just as his father
David[d] had done. 4He removed[e] the high
places, smashed the sacred stones[f] and
cut down the Asherah poles. He broke
into pieces the bronze snake[g] Moses had
made, for up to that time the Israelites
had been burning incense to it. (It was
called[b] Nehushtan.[c])
5Hezekiah trusted[h] in the LORD, the
God of Israel. There was no one like him
among all the kings of Judah, either
before him or after him. 6He held fast[i]
to the LORD and did not cease to follow
him; he kept the commands the LORD
had given Moses. 7And the LORD was
with him; he was successful[j] in whatever he undertook. He rebelled[k] against
the king of Assyria and did not serve
him. 8From watchtower to fortified city,[l]
he defeated the Philistines, as far as Gaza
and its territory.
9In King Hezekiah's fourth year,[m]
which was the seventh year of Hoshea
son of Elah king of Israel, Shalmaneser
king of Assyria marched against Samaria
and laid siege to it. 10At the end of three
years the Assyrians took it. So Samaria
was captured in Hezekiah's sixth year,
which was the ninth year of Hoshea king
of Israel. 11The king[n] of Assyria deported Israel to Assyria and settled them in
Halah, in Gozan on the Habor River
and in towns of the Medes. 12This happened because they had not obeyed the
LORD their God, but had violated his
covenant[o]—all that Moses the servant
of the LORD commanded.[p] They neither
listened to the commands[q] nor carried
them out.
13In the fourteenth year of King Hezekiah's reign, Sennacherib king of Assyria
attacked all the fortified cities of Judah[r]
and captured them. 14So Hezekiah king
of Judah sent this message to the king of
Assyria at Lachish: "I have done wrong.[s]
Withdraw from me, and I will pay whatever you demand of me." The king of
Assyria exacted from Hezekiah king of
Judah three hundred talents[d] of silver
and thirty talents[e] of gold. 15So Hezekiah
gave[t] him all the silver that was found
in the temple of the LORD and in the treasuries of the royal palace.
16At this time Hezekiah king of Judah
stripped off the gold with which he had
covered the doors and doorposts of the
temple of the LORD, and gave it to the
king of Assyria.

Sennacherib's confrontation with Judah.

18:13, 17-37pp— Isa 36:1-22
18:17-35pp— 2Ch 32:9-19

17The king of Assyria sent his supreme
commander,[u] his chief officer and his
field commander with a large army, from
Lachish to King Hezekiah at Jerusalem.
They came up to Jerusalem and stopped
at the aqueduct of the Upper Pool,[v] on
the road to the Washerman's Field.
18They called for the king; and Eliakim[w] son of Hilkiah the palace administrator, Shebna[x] the secretary, and Joah
son of Asaph the recorder went out to
them.
19The field commander said to them,
"Tell Hezekiah:

"'This is what the great king,
the king of Assyria, says: On what

17:41 [a]ver 32-33; 1Ki 18:21; Mt 6:24
18:1 [b]Isa 1:1; 2Ch 28:27
18:2 [c]Isa 38:5
18:3 [d]Isa 38:5
18:4 [e]2Ch 31:1 [f]Ex 23:24 [g]Nu 21:9
18:5 [h]2Ki 19:10; 23:25
18:6 [i]Dt 10:20; Jos 23:8
18:7 [j]Ge 39:3; 1Sa 18:14 [k]2Ki 16:7
18:8 [l]2Ki 17:9; Isa 14:29
18:9 [m]Isa 1:1
18:11 [n]Isa 37:12
18:12 [o]2Ki 17:15 [p]Da 9:6,10 [q]1Ki 9:6
18:13 [r]2Ch 32:1; Isa 1:7; Mic 1:9
18:14 [s]Isa 24:5
18:15 [t]1Ki 15:18; 2Ki 16:8
18:17 [u]Isa 20:1 [v]2Ki 20:20; 2Ch 32:4,30; Isa 7:3
18:18 [w]2Ki 19:2; Isa 22:20 [x]Isa 22:15

a *2* Hebrew *Abi,* a variant of *Abijah* b *4* Or *He called it* c *4* *Nehushtan* sounds like the Hebrew for *bronze* and *snake* and *unclean thing.* d *14* That is, about 11 tons (about 10 metric tons) e *14* That is, about 1 ton (about 1 metric ton)

are you basing this confidence of
yours? 20You say you have strategy
and military strength—but you
speak only empty words. On whom
are you depending, that you rebel
against me? 21Look now, you are
depending on Egypt,[a] that splintered
reed of a staff,[b] which pierces a
man's hand and wounds him if he
leans on it! Such is Pharaoh king
of Egypt to all who depend on him.
22And if you say to me, "We are
depending on the LORD our God"—
isn't he the one whose high places
and altars Hezekiah removed, saying to Judah and Jerusalem, "You
must worship before this altar in
Jerusalem"?

23"'Come now, make a bargain
with my master, the king of Assyria: I will give you two thousand
horses—if you can put riders on
them! 24How can you repulse one
officer[c] of the least of my master's
officials, even though you are depending on Egypt for chariots and
horsemen[†]? 25Furthermore, have I
come to attack and destroy this place
without word from the LORD?[d] The
LORD himself told me to march
against this country and destroy it.'"

26Then Eliakim son of Hilkiah, and
Shebna and Joah said to the field commander, "Please speak to your servants
in Aramaic,[e] since we understand it.
Don't speak to us in Hebrew in the hearing of the people on the wall."

27But the commander replied, "Was it
only to your master and you that my master sent me to say these things, and not
to the men sitting on the wall—who,
like you, will have to eat their own
filth and drink their own urine?"

28Then the commander stood and
called out in Hebrew: "Hear the word of
the great king, the king of Assyria! 29This
is what the king says: Do not let Hezekiah deceive[f] you. He cannot deliver you
from my hand. 30Do not let Hezekiah
persuade you to trust in the LORD when
he says, 'The LORD will surely deliver us;
this city will not be given into the hand
of the king of Assyria.'

31"Do not listen to Hezekiah. This is
what the king of Assyria says: Make
peace with me and come out to me.
Then every one of you will eat from his
own vine and fig tree[g] and drink water
from his own cistern,[h] 32until I come
and take you to a land like your own, a
land of grain and new wine, a land of
bread and vineyards, a land of olive trees
and honey. Choose life[i] and not death!

"Do not listen to Hezekiah, for he is
misleading you when he says, 'The LORD
will deliver us.' 33Has the god[j] of any
nation ever delivered his land from the
hand of the king of Assyria? 34Where are
the gods of Hamath[k] and Arpad?[l] Where
are the gods of Sepharvaim, Hena and
Ivvah? Have they rescued Samaria from
my hand? 35Who of all the gods of these
countries has been able to save his
land from me? How then can the LORD
deliver Jerusalem from my hand?"[m]

36But the people remained silent and
said nothing in reply, because the king
had commanded, "Do not answer him."

37Then Eliakim son of Hilkiah the
palace administrator, Shebna the secretary and Joah son of Asaph the recorder
went to Hezekiah, with their clothes
torn,[n] and told him what the field commander had said.

Hezekiah sends a message to Isaiah.

19:1-13pp— Isa 37:1-13

19 When King Hezekiah heard this,
he tore[o] his clothes and put on
sackcloth and went into the temple of
the LORD. 2He sent Eliakim the palace
administrator, Shebna the secretary and
the leading priests, all wearing sackcloth,
to the prophet Isaiah[p] son of Amoz.
3They told him, "This is what Hezekiah says: This day is a day of distress
and rebuke and disgrace, as when children come to the point of birth and
there is no strength to deliver them.
4It may be that the LORD your God will

18:21 [a]Isa 20:5; Eze 29:6 [b]Isa 30:5,7
18:24 [c]Isa 10:8
18:25 [d]2Ki 19:6,22
18:26 [e]Ezr 4:7
18:29 [f]2Ki 19:10
18:31 [g]Nu 13:23; 1Ki 4:25 [h]Jer 14:3; La 4:4
18:32 [i]Dt 8:7-9; 30:19
18:33 [j]2Ki 19:12; Isa 10:10-11
18:34 [k]2Ki 17:24; 19:13 [l]Isa 10:9
18:35 [m]Ps 2:1-2
18:37 [n]2Ki 6:30
19:1 [o]Ge 37:34; 1Ki 21:27; 2Ch 32:20-22
19:2 [p]Isa 1:1

†*24* Or *charioteers*

hear all the words of the field commander, whom his master, the king of Assyria, has sent to ridicule[a] the living God, and that he will rebuke[b] him for the words the LORD your God has heard. Therefore pray for the remnant that still survives."

5 When King Hezekiah's officials came to Isaiah, 6 Isaiah said to them, "Tell your master, 'This is what the LORD says: Do not be afraid of what you have heard—those words with which the underlings of the king of Assyria have blasphemed[c] me. 7 Listen! I am going to put such a spirit in him that when he hears a certain report, he will return to his own country, and there I will have him cut down with the sword.[d] '"

8 When the field commander heard that the king of Assyria had left Lachish,[e] he withdrew and found the king fighting against Libnah.

9 Now Sennacherib received a report that Tirhakah, the Cushite[g] king ⌊of Egypt⌋, was marching out to fight against him. So he again sent messengers to Hezekiah with this word: 10 "Say to Hezekiah king of Judah: Do not let the god you depend[f] on deceive[g] you when he says, 'Jerusalem will not be handed over to the king of Assyria.' 11 Surely you have heard what the kings of Assyria have done to all the countries, destroying them completely. And will you be delivered? 12 Did the gods of the nations that were destroyed by my forefathers deliver[h] them: the gods of Gozan,[i] Haran,[j] Rezeph and the people of Eden who were in Tel Assar? 13 Where is the king of Hamath, the king of Arpad, the king of the city of Sepharvaim, or of Hena or Ivvah?"[k]

Hezekiah prays.

19:14-19pp— Isa 37:14-20

14 Hezekiah received the letter from the messengers and read it. Then he went up to the temple of the LORD and spread it out before the LORD. 15 And Hezekiah prayed to the LORD: "O LORD, God of Israel, enthroned between the cherubim,[l] you alone are God over all the kingdoms of the earth. You have made heaven and earth. 16 Give ear,[m] O LORD, and hear;[n] open your eyes,[o] O LORD, and see; listen to the words Sennacherib has sent to insult the living God.

17 "It is true, O LORD, that the Assyrian kings have laid waste these nations and their lands. 18 They have thrown their gods into the fire and destroyed them, for they were not gods[p] but only wood and stone, fashioned by men's hands.[q] 19 Now, O LORD our God, deliver us from his hand, so that all kingdoms[r] on earth may know[s] that you alone, O LORD, are God."

Isaiah predicts Sennacherib's defeat.

19:20-37pp— Isa 37:21-38

20 Then Isaiah son of Amoz sent a message to Hezekiah: "This is what the LORD, the God of Israel, says: I have heard[t] your prayer concerning Sennacherib king of Assyria. 21 This is the word that the LORD has spoken against him:

"'The Virgin Daughter[u] of Zion
despises you and mocks[v] you.
The Daughter of Jerusalem
tosses her head[w] as you flee.
22 Who is it you have insulted and
blasphemed?
Against whom have you raised
your voice
and lifted your eyes in pride?
Against the Holy One[x] of Israel!
23 By your messengers
you have heaped insults on the Lord.
And you have said,[y]
"With my many chariots[z]
I have ascended the heights of the
mountains,
the utmost heights of Lebanon.
I have cut down its tallest cedars,
the choicest of its pines.
I have reached its remotest parts,
the finest of its forests.
24 I have dug wells in foreign lands

19:4 [a] 2Ki 18:35 [b] 2Sa 16:12
19:6 [c] 2Ki 18:25
19:7 [d] ver 37
19:8 [e] 2Ki 18:14
19:10 [f] 2Ki 18:5 [g] 2Ki 18:29
19:12 [h] 2Ki 18:33 [i] 2Ki 17:6 [j] Ge 11:31
19:13 [k] 2Ki 18:34
19:15 [l] Ex 25:22
19:16 [m] Ps 31:2 [n] 1Ki 8:29 [o] ver 4; 2Ch 6:40
19:18 [p] Isa 44:9-11; Jer 10:3-10 [q] Ps 115:4; Ac 17:29
19:19 [r] 1Ki 8:43 [s] Ps 83:18
19:20 [t] 2Ki 20:5
19:21 [u] Jer 14:17; La 2:13 [v] Ps 22:7-8 [w] Job 16:4; Ps 109:25
19:22 [x] Ps 71:22; Isa 5:24
19:23 [y] Isa 10:18 [z] Ps 20:7

g9 That is, from the upper Nile region

and drunk the water there.
With the soles of my feet
I have dried up all the streams of Egypt."

25"'Have you not heard?[a]
Long ago I ordained it.
In days of old I planned[b] it;
now I have brought it to pass,
that you have turned fortified cities
into piles of stone.[c]
26Their people, drained of power,
are dismayed[d] and put to shame.
They are like plants in the field,
like tender green shoots,[e]
like grass sprouting on the roof,
scorched[f] before it grows up.

27"'But I know[g] where you stay
and when you come and go
and how you rage against me.
28Because you rage against me
and your insolence has reached my ears,
I will put my hook[h] in your nose
and my bit[i] in your mouth,
and I will make you return[j]
by the way you came.'

29"This will be the sign[k] for you, O Hezekiah:

"This year you will eat what grows by itself,[l]
and the second year what springs from that.
But in the third year sow and reap,
plant vineyards[m] and eat their fruit.
30Once more a remnant of the house of Judah
will take root[n] below and bear fruit above.
31For out of Jerusalem will come a remnant,
and out of Mount Zion a band of survivors.

The zeal[o] of the LORD Almighty will accomplish this.

32"Therefore this is what the LORD says concerning the king of Assyria:

"He will not enter this city
or shoot an arrow here.

19:25 [a]Isa 40:21,28 [b]Isa 10:5; 45:7 [c]Mic 1:6
19:26 [d]Ps 6:10 [e]Isa 4:2 [f]Ps 129:6
19:27 [g]Ps 139:1-4
19:28 [h]Eze 19:9; 29:4 [i]Isa 30:28 [j]ver 33
19:29 [k]2Ki 20:8-9; Lk 2:12 [l]Lev 25:5 [m]Ps 107:37
19:30 [n]2Ch 32:22-23
19:31 [o]Isa 9:7
19:33 [p]ver 28
19:34 [q]2Ki 20:6 [r]1Ki 11:12-13
19:35 [s]Ex 12:23 [t]Job 24:24
19:36 [u]Ge 10:11; Jnh 1:2
19:37 [v]ver 7 [w]Ge 8:4 [x]Ezr 4:2
20:3 [y]Ne 13:22 [z]2Ki 18:3-6
20:5 [a]1Sa 9:16; 1Ki 9:3; 2Ki 19:20 [b]Ps 39:12; 56:8

He will not come before it with shield
or build a siege ramp against it.
33By the way that he came he will return;[p]
he will not enter this city,
declares the LORD.
34I will defend[q] this city and save it,
for my sake and for the sake of David[r] my servant."

Sennacherib and 185,000 Assyrians are killed.

19:35-37pp— 2Ch 32:20-21

35That night the angel of the LORD[s]
went out and put to death a hundred and
eighty-five thousand men in the Assyrian camp. When the people got up the
next morning—there were all the dead
bodies![t] 36So Sennacherib king of Assyria broke camp and withdrew. He returned to Nineveh[u] and stayed there.
37One day, while he was worshiping
in the temple of his god Nisroch, his
sons Adrammelech and Sharezer cut him
down with the sword,[v] and they escaped to the land of Ararat.[w] And Esarhaddon[x] his son succeeded him as king.

Hezekiah's life is extended.

20:1-11pp— 2Ch 32:24-26; Isa 38:1-8

20 In those days Hezekiah became
ill and was at the point of
death. The prophet Isaiah son of Amoz
went to him and said, "This is what
the LORD says: Put your house in order,
because you are going to die; you will
not recover."
2Hezekiah turned his face to the wall
and prayed to the LORD, 3"Remember,[y]
O LORD, how I have walked before you
faithfully[z] and with wholehearted devotion and have done what is good in your
eyes." And Hezekiah wept bitterly.
4Before Isaiah had left the middle
court, the word of the LORD came to him:
5"Go back and tell Hezekiah, the leader
of my people, 'This is what the LORD, the
God of your father David, says: I have
heard[a] your prayer and seen your tears;[b]
I will heal you. On the third day from
now you will go up to the temple of

the LORD. 6I will add fifteen years to your
life. And I will deliver you and this city
from the hand of the king of Assyria. I
will defend[a] this city for my sake and for
the sake of my servant David.'"
7Then Isaiah said, "Prepare a poultice
of figs." They did so and applied it to the
boil,[b] and he recovered.
8Hezekiah had asked Isaiah, "What
will be the sign that the LORD will heal
me and that I will go up to the temple
of the LORD on the third day from now?"
9Isaiah answered, "This is the LORD's
sign[c] to you that the LORD will do what
he has promised: Shall the shadow go
forward ten steps, or shall it go back
ten steps?"
10"It is a simple matter for the shadow
to go forward ten steps," said Hezekiah. "Rather, have it go back ten steps."
11Then the prophet Isaiah called upon
the LORD, and the LORD made the shadow go back[d] the ten steps it had gone
down on the stairway of Ahaz.

Isaiah predicts the Babylonian exile.

20:12-19pp— Isa 39:1-8

12At that time Merodach-Baladan son
of Baladan king of Babylon sent Hezekiah letters and a gift, because he had
heard of Hezekiah's illness. 13Hezekiah
received the messengers and showed
them all that was in his storehouses—
the silver, the gold, the spices and the
fine oil—his armory and everything
found among his treasures. There was
nothing in his palace or in all his kingdom that Hezekiah did not show them.
14Then Isaiah the prophet went to
King Hezekiah and asked, "What did
those men say, and where did they come
from?"
"From a distant land," Hezekiah replied. "They came from Babylon."
15The prophet asked, "What did they
see in your palace?"
"They saw everything in my palace,"
Hezekiah said. "There is nothing among
my treasures that I did not show them."
16Then Isaiah said to Hezekiah, "Hear
the word of the LORD: 17The time will
surely come when everything in your
palace, and all that your fathers have
stored up until this day, will be carried
off to Babylon.[e] Nothing will be left, says
the LORD. 18And some of your descendants,[f] your own flesh and blood, that
will be born to you, will be taken away,
and they will become eunuchs in the
palace of the king of Babylon."
19"The word of the LORD you have spoken is good," Hezekiah replied. For he
thought, "Will there not be peace and
security in my lifetime?"

Hezekiah's death.

20:20-21pp— 2Ch 32:32-33

20As for the other events of Hezekiah's
reign, all his achievements and how he
made the pool[g] and the tunnel by which
he brought water into the city, are they
not written in the book of the annals
of the kings of Judah? 21Hezekiah rested with his fathers. And Manasseh his
son succeeded him as king.

Manasseh's evil reign in Judah.

21:1-10pp— 2Ch 33:1-10
21:17-18pp— 2Ch 33:18-20

21 Manasseh was twelve years old
when he became king, and he
reigned in Jerusalem fifty-five years. His
mother's name was Hephzibah.[h] 2He
did evil[i] in the eyes of the LORD, following the detestable practices[j] of the nations the LORD had driven out before the
Israelites. 3He rebuilt the high places[k]
his father Hezekiah had destroyed; he
also erected altars to Baal[l] and made an
Asherah pole, as Ahab king of Israel had
done. He bowed down to all the starry
hosts[m] and worshiped them. 4He built
altars[n] in the temple of the LORD, of
which the LORD had said, "In Jerusalem
I will put my Name."[o] 5In both courts[p]
of the temple of the LORD, he built
altars to all the starry hosts. 6He sacrificed his own son[q] in[h] the fire, practiced sorcery and divination, and

20:6 [a]2Ki 19:34
20:7 [b]Isa 38:21
20:9 [c]Dt 13:2; Jer 44:29
20:11 [d]Jos 10:13
20:17 [e]2Ki 24:13; 25:13; 2Ch 36:10; Jer 27:22; 52:17-23
20:18 [f]2Ki 24:15; 2Ch 33:11; Da 1:3
20:20 [g]Ne 3:16
21:1 [h]Isa 62:4
21:2 [i]Jer 15:4 [j]2Ki 16:3
21:3 [k]2Ki 18:4 [l]Jdg 6:28; 1Ki 16:32 [m]Dt 17:3; 2Ki 17:16
21:4 [n]Jer 32:34 [o]2Sa 7:13; 1Ki 8:29
21:5 [p]1Ki 7:12; 2Ki 23:12
21:6 [q]Lev 18:21; Dt 18:10; 2Ki 16:3; 17:17

h6 Or *He made his own son pass through*

consulted mediums and spiritists.[a] He
did much evil in the eyes of the LORD,
provoking him to anger.
7He took the carved Asherah pole[b] he
had made and put it in the temple, of
which the LORD had said to David and to
his son Solomon, "In this temple and in
Jerusalem, which I have chosen out of
all the tribes of Israel, I will put my
Name[c] forever. 8I will not again[d] make
the feet of the Israelites wander from the
land I gave their forefathers, if only they
will be careful to do everything I commanded them and will keep the whole
Law that my servant Moses[e] gave them."
9But the people did not listen. Manasseh led them astray, so that they did
more evil[f] than the nations[g] the LORD
had destroyed before the Israelites.
10The LORD said through his servants
the prophets: 11"Manasseh king of Judah
has committed these detestable sins. He
has done more evil[h] than the Amorites[i]
who preceded him and has led Judah
into sin with his idols. 12Therefore this
is what the LORD, the God of Israel, says:
I am going to bring such disaster[j] on Jerusalem and Judah that the ears of everyone who hears of it will tingle.[k] 13I
will stretch out over Jerusalem the measuring line used against Samaria and the
plumb line[l] used against the house of
Ahab. I will wipe[m] out Jerusalem as one
wipes a dish, wiping it and turning it
upside down. 14I will forsake[n] the remnant[o] of my inheritance and hand them
over to their enemies. They will be looted and plundered by all their foes, 15be-
cause they have done evil[p] in my eyes
and have provoked[q] me to anger from
the day their forefathers came out of
Egypt until this day."
16Moreover, Manasseh also shed so
much innocent blood[r] that he filled Jerusalem from end to end—besides the
sin that he had caused Judah to commit,
so that they did evil in the eyes of the
LORD.
17As for the other events of Manasseh's reign, and all he did, including
the sin he committed, are they not written in the book of the annals of the

21:6 [a]Lev 19:31
21:7 [b]Dt 16:21; 2Ki 23:4 [c]2Sa 7:13; 1Ki 8:29; 9:3; 2Ki 23:27; Jer 32:34
21:8 [d]2Sa 7:10 [e]2Ki 18:12
21:9 [f]Pr 29:12 [g]Dt 9:4
21:11 [h]2Ki 24:3-4 [i]Ge 15:16; 1Ki 21:26
21:12 [j]2Ki 23:26; 24:3; Jer 15:4 [k]1Sa 3:11; Jer 19:3
21:13 [l]Isa 34:11; La 2:8; Am 7:7-9 [m]2Ki 23:27
21:14 [n]Ps 78:58-60 [o]2Ki 19:4; Mic 2:12
21:15 [p]Ex 32:22 [q]Jer 25:7
21:16 [r]2Ki 24:4
21:18 [s]ver 26
21:20 [t]ver 2-6
21:22 [u]1Ki 11:33
21:23 [v]2Ki 12:20; 2Ch 33:24-25
21:24 [w]2Ki 14:5
21:26 [x]ver 18
22:1 [y]Jos 15:39
22:2 [z]Dt 17:19 [a]Dt 5:32
22:3 [b]2Ch 34:20; Jer 39:14

kings of Judah? 18Manasseh rested with
his fathers and was buried in his palace
garden,[s] the garden of Uzza. And Amon
his son succeeded him as king.

Amon's reign in Judah.

21:19-24pp— 2Ch 33:21-25

19Amon was twenty-two years old
when he became king, and he reigned in
Jerusalem two years. His mother's name
was Meshullemeth daughter of Haruz;
she was from Jotbah. 20He did evil[t] in the
eyes of the LORD, as his father Manasseh
had done. 21He walked in all the ways
of his father; he worshiped the idols his
father had worshiped, and bowed down
to them. 22He forsook the LORD, the God
of his fathers, and did not walk[u] in the
way of the LORD.
23Amon's officials conspired against
him and assassinated[v] the king in his
palace. 24Then the people of the land
killed[w] all who had plotted against King
Amon, and they made Josiah his son king
in his place.
25As for the other events of Amon's
reign, and what he did, are they not written in the book of the annals of the kings
of Judah? 26He was buried in his grave
in the garden[x] of Uzza. And Josiah his
son succeeded him as king.

Hilkiah finds the Book of the Law.

22:1-20pp— 2Ch 34:1-2,8-28

22 Josiah was eight years old when
he became king, and he reigned
in Jerusalem thirty-one years. His mother's name was Jedidah daughter of Adaiah; she was from Bozkath.[y] 2He did
what was right[z] in the eyes of the LORD
and walked in all the ways of his father
David, not turning aside to the right[a] or
to the left.
3In the eighteenth year of his reign,
King Josiah sent the secretary, Shaphan[b]
son of Azaliah, the son of Meshullam,
to the temple of the LORD. He said:
4"Go up to Hilkiah the high priest and
have him get ready the money that has
been brought into the temple of the
LORD, which the doorkeepers have

collected[a] from the people. 5Have them
entrust it to the men appointed to supervise the work on the temple. And have
these men pay the workers who repair[b]
the temple of the LORD— 6the carpenters, the builders and the masons. Also
have them purchase timber and dressed
stone to repair the temple.[c] 7But they
need not account for the money entrusted to them, because they are acting faithfully."[d]

8Hilkiah the high priest said to
Shaphan the secretary, "I have found the
Book of the Law[e] in the temple of the
LORD." He gave it to Shaphan, who read
it. 9Then Shaphan the secretary went
to the king and reported to him: "Your
officials have paid out the money that
was in the temple of the LORD and have
entrusted it to the workers and supervisors at the temple." 10Then Shaphan
the secretary informed the king, "Hilkiah the priest has given me a book." And
Shaphan read from it in the presence
of the king.[f]

11When the king heard the words of
the Book of the Law, he tore his robes.
12He gave these orders to Hilkiah the
priest, Ahikam[g] son of Shaphan, Acbor
son of Micaiah, Shaphan the secretary
and Asaiah the king's attendant: 13"Go
and inquire of the LORD for me and for
the people and for all Judah about what
is written in this book that has been
found. Great is the LORD's anger[h] that
burns against us because our fathers have
not obeyed the words of this book; they
have not acted in accordance with all
that is written there concerning us."

Huldah predicts disaster on Jerusalem.

14Hilkiah the priest, Ahikam, Acbor,
Shaphan and Asaiah went to speak to the
prophetess Huldah, who was the wife of
Shallum son of Tikvah, the son of Harhas,
keeper of the wardrobe. She lived in Jerusalem, in the Second District.
15She said to them, "This is what the
LORD, the God of Israel, says: Tell the
man who sent you to me, 16'This is what
the LORD says: I am going to bring disaster[i] on this place and its people, according to everything written in the
book[j] the king of Judah has read.
17Because they have forsaken[k] me and
burned incense to other gods and
provoked me to anger by all the idols
their hands have made,[i] my anger will
burn against this place and will not be
quenched.' 18Tell the king of Judah,
who sent you to inquire[l] of the LORD,
'This is what the LORD, the God of Israel,
says concerning the words you heard:
19Because your heart was responsive and
you humbled[m] yourself before the LORD
when you heard what I have spoken
against this place and its people, that
they would become accursed[n] and laid
waste,[o] and because you tore your robes
and wept in my presence, I have heard
you, declares the LORD. 20Therefore I will
gather you to your fathers, and you will
be buried in peace.[p] Your eyes will not
see all the disaster I am going to bring
on this place.'"

So they took her answer back to the
king.

22:4 [a]2Ki 12:4-5
22:5 [b]2Ki 12:5, 11-14
22:6 [c]2Ki 12:11-12
22:7 [d]2Ki 12:15
22:8 [e]Dt 31:24
22:10 [f]Jer 36:21
22:12 [g]2Ki 25:22; Jer 26:24
22:13 [h]Dt 29:24-28; 31:17
22:16 [i]Dt 31:29; Jos 23:15 [j]Dt 29:27; Da 9:11
22:17 [k]Dt 29:25-27
22:18 [l]2Ch 34:26; Jer 21:2
22:19 [m]Ex 10:3; 1Ki 21:29; Ps 51:17; Isa 57:15; Mic 6:8 [n]Jer 26:6 [o]Lev 26:31
22:20 [p]Isa 57:1
23:2 [q]Dt 31:11; 2Ki 22:8
23:3 [r]2Ki 11:14,17 [s]Dt 13:4

Josiah directs the people to obey God.

23:1-3pp— 2Ch 34:29-32
23:4-20Ref— 2Ch 34:3-7,33
23:21-23pp— 2Ch 35:1,18-19
23:28-30pp— 2Ch 35:20–36:1

23 Then the king called together all
the elders of Judah and Jerusalem. 2He went up to the temple of the
LORD with the men of Judah, the people
of Jerusalem, the priests and the prophets—all the people from the least to the
greatest. He read[q] in their hearing all the
words of the Book of the Covenant,
which had been found in the temple of
the LORD. 3The king stood by the pillar
and renewed the covenant[r] in the presence of the LORD—to follow[s] the LORD
and keep his commands, regulations and
decrees with all his heart and all his
soul, thus confirming the words of the
covenant written in this book. Then all

[i] *17* Or *by everything they have done*

the people pledged themselves to the covenant.

4The king ordered Hilkiah the high priest, the priests next in rank and the doorkeepers[a] to remove[b] from the temple of the LORD all the articles made for Baal and Asherah and all the starry hosts. He burned them outside Jerusalem in the fields of the Kidron Valley and took the ashes to Bethel. 5He did away with the pagan priests appointed by the kings of Judah to burn incense on the high places of the towns of Judah and on those around Jerusalem—those who burned incense to Baal, to the sun and moon, to the constellations and to all the starry hosts.[c] 6He took the Asherah pole from the temple of the LORD to the Kidron Valley outside Jerusalem and burned it there. He ground it to powder and scattered the dust over the graves of the common people.[d] 7He also tore down the quarters of the male shrine prostitutes,[e] which were in the temple of the LORD and where women did weaving for Asherah.

8Josiah brought all the priests from the towns of Judah and desecrated the high places, from Geba[f] to Beersheba, where the priests had burned incense. He broke down the shrines[j] at the gates—at the entrance to the Gate of Joshua, the city governor, which is on the left of the city gate. 9Although the priests of the high places did not serve[g] at the altar of the LORD in Jerusalem, they ate unleavened bread with their fellow priests.

10He desecrated Topheth,[h] which was in the Valley of Ben Hinnom,[i] so no one could use it to sacrifice his son[j] or daughter in[k] the fire to Molech. 11He removed from the entrance to the temple of the LORD the horses that the kings of Judah had dedicated to the sun. They were in the court near the room of an official named Nathan-Melech. Josiah then burned the chariots dedicated to the sun.[k]

12He pulled down the altars the kings of Judah had erected on the roof[l] near the upper room of Ahaz, and the altars Manasseh had built in the two courts[m] of the temple of the LORD. He removed them from there, smashed them to pieces and threw the rubble into the Kidron Valley. 13The king also desecrated the high places that were east of Jerusalem on the south of the Hill of Corruption—the ones Solomon[n] king of Israel had built for Ashtoreth the vile goddess of the Sidonians, for Chemosh the vile god of Moab, and for Molech[l] the detestable god of the people of Ammon. 14Josiah smashed[o] the sacred stones and cut down the Asherah poles and covered the sites with human bones.

15Even the altar[p] at Bethel, the high place made by Jeroboam[q] son of Nebat, who had caused Israel to sin—even that altar and high place he demolished. He burned the high place and ground it to powder, and burned the Asherah pole also. 16Then Josiah[r] looked around, and when he saw the tombs that were there on the hillside, he had the bones removed from them and burned on the altar to defile it, in accordance with the word of the LORD proclaimed by the man of God who foretold these things.

17The king asked, "What is that tombstone I see?"

The men of the city said, "It marks the tomb of the man of God who came from Judah and pronounced against the altar of Bethel the very things you have done to it."

18"Leave it alone," he said. "Don't let anyone disturb his bones[s]." So they spared his bones and those of the prophet who had come from Samaria.

19Just as he had done at Bethel, Josiah removed and defiled all the shrines at the high places that the kings of Israel had built in the towns of Samaria that had provoked the LORD to anger. 20Josiah slaughtered[t] all the priests of those high places on the altars and burned human bones[u] on them. Then he went back to Jerusalem.

21The king gave this order to all the people: "Celebrate the Passover[v] to the

23:4 [a]2Ki 25:18 [b]2Ki 21:7
23:5 [c]2Ki 21:3; Jer 8:2
23:6 [d]Jer 26:23
23:7 [e]1Ki 14:24; 15:12; Eze 16:16
23:8 [f]1Ki 15:22
23:9 [g]Eze 44:10-14
23:10 [h]Isa 30:33; Jer 7:31,32; 19:6 [i]Jos 15:8 [j]Lev 18:21; Dt 18:10
23:11 [k]Dt 4:19
23:12 [l]Jer 19:13; Zep 1:5 [m]2Ki 21:5
23:13 [n]1Ki 11:7
23:14 [o]Ex 23:24; Dt 7:5,25
23:15 [p]1Ki 13:1-3 [q]1Ki 12:33
23:16 [r]1Ki 13:2
23:18 [s]1Ki 13:31
23:20 [t]Ex 22:20; 2Ki 10:25; 11:18 [u]1Ki 13:2
23:21 [v]Ex 12:11; Nu 9:2; Dt 16:1-8

j8 Or *high places* k10 Or *to make his son or daughter pass through* l13 Hebrew *Milcom*

LORD your God, as it is written in this
Book of the Covenant." 22Not since the
days of the judges who led Israel, nor
throughout the days of the kings of Israel and the kings of Judah, had any such
Passover been observed. 23But in the
eighteenth year of King Josiah, this
Passover was celebrated to the LORD in
Jerusalem.
24Furthermore, Josiah got rid of the
mediums and spiritists,[a] the household
gods,[b] the idols and all the other detestable things seen in Judah and Jerusalem. This he did to fulfill the requirements of the law written in the
book that Hilkiah the priest had discovered in the temple of the LORD.
25Neither before nor after Josiah was
there a king like him who turned[c] to
the LORD as he did—with all his heart
and with all his soul and with all his
strength, in accordance with all the Law
of Moses.
26Nevertheless, the LORD did not turn
away from the heat of his fierce anger,
which burned against Judah because of
all that Manasseh[d] had done to provoke
him to anger. 27So the LORD said, "I will
remove[e] Judah also from my presence[f]
as I removed Israel, and I will reject Jerusalem, the city I chose, and this temple, about which I said, 'There shall my
Name be.'[m]"
28As for the other events of Josiah's
reign, and all he did, are they not written in the book of the annals of the kings
of Judah?

Josiah is killed in battle.

29While Josiah was king, Pharaoh
Neco[g] king of Egypt went up to the Euphrates River to help the king of Assyria. King Josiah marched out to meet
him in battle, but Neco faced him and
killed him at Megiddo.[h] 30Josiah's servants brought his body in a chariot[i]
from Megiddo to Jerusalem and buried
him in his own tomb. And the people of
the land took Jehoahaz son of Josiah and
anointed him and made him king in
place of his father.

23:24 [a]Lev 19:31; Dt 18:11; 2Ki 21:6 [b]Ge 31:19
23:25 [c]2Ki 18:5
23:26 [d]2Ki 21:12; Jer 15:4
23:27 [e]2Ki 21:13 [f]2Ki 18:11
23:29 [g]Jer 46:2 [h]Zec 12:11
23:30 [i]2Ki 9:28
23:31 [j]1Ch 3:15; Jer 22:11 [k]2Ki 24:18
23:33 [l]2Ki 25:6 [m]1Ki 8:65
23:34 [n]1Ch 3:15; 2Ch 36:5-8 [o]Jer 22:12; Eze 19:3-4
23:35 [p]ver 33
23:36 [q]Jer 26:1
24:1 [r]Jer 25:1,9; Da 1:1
24:2 [s]Jer 35:11

Jehoahaz reigns in Judah.

23:31-34pp— 2Ch 36:2-4

31Jehoahaz[j] was twenty-three years old
when he became king, and he reigned
in Jerusalem three months. His mother's
name was Hamutal[k] daughter of Jeremiah; she was from Libnah. 32He did
evil in the eyes of the LORD, just as his
fathers had done. 33Pharaoh Neco put
him in chains at Riblah[l] in the land of
Hamath[n] [m] so that he might not reign
in Jerusalem, and he imposed on Judah
a levy of a hundred talents[o] of silver and
a talent[p] of gold. 34Pharaoh Neco made
Eliakim[n] son of Josiah king in place of
his father Josiah and changed Eliakim's
name to Jehoiakim. But he took Jehoahaz and carried him off to Egypt, and
there he died.[o] 35Jehoiakim paid Pharaoh
Neco the silver and gold he demanded.
In order to do so, he taxed the land
and exacted the silver and gold from
the people of the land according to their
assessments.[p]

Jehoiakim reigns in Judah.

23:36–24:6pp— 2Ch 36:5-8

36Jehoiakim[q] was twenty-five years old
when he became king, and he reigned
in Jerusalem eleven years. His mother's name was Zebidah daughter of
Pedaiah; she was from Rumah. 37And
he did evil in the eyes of the LORD, just
as his fathers had done.

Nebuchadnezzar invades Jerusalem.

24 During Jehoiakim's reign, Nebuchadnezzar[r] king of Babylon
invaded the land, and Jehoiakim became
his vassal for three years. But then he
changed his mind and rebelled against
Nebuchadnezzar. 2The LORD sent Babylonian,[q] Aramean,[s] Moabite and Ammonite raiders against him. He sent them to

[m]27 1 Kings 8:29 [n]33 Hebrew; Septuagint (see also 2 Chron. 36:3) *Neco at Riblah in Hamath removed him* [o]33 That is, about 3 3/4 tons (about 3.4 metric tons) [p]33 That is, about 75 pounds (about 34 kilograms) [q]2 Or *Chaldean*

destroy[a] Judah, in accordance with the word of the LORD proclaimed by his servants the prophets. 3Surely these things happened to Judah according to the LORD's command,[b] in order to remove them from his presence because of the sins of Manasseh[c] and all he had done, 4including the shedding of innocent blood.[d] For he had filled Jerusalem with innocent blood, and the LORD was not willing to forgive.

5As for the other events of Jehoiakim's reign, and all he did, are they not written in the book of the annals of the kings of Judah? 6Jehoiakim rested[e] with his fathers. And Jehoiachin his son succeeded him as king.

7The king of Egypt[f] did not march out from his own country again, because the king of Babylon[g] had taken all his territory, from the Wadi of Egypt to the Euphrates River.

Jehoiachin reigns in Judah.

24:8-17pp— 2Ch 36:9-10

8Jehoiachin[h] was eighteen years old when he became king, and he reigned in Jerusalem three months. His mother's name was Nehushta daughter of Elnathan; she was from Jerusalem. 9He did evil in the eyes of the LORD, just as his father had done.

10At that time the officers of Nebuchadnezzar[i] king of Babylon advanced on Jerusalem and laid siege to it, 11and Nebuchadnezzar himself came up to the city while his officers were besieging it. 12Jehoiachin king of Judah, his mother, his attendants, his nobles and his officials all surrendered[j] to him.

In the eighth year of the reign of the king of Babylon, he took Jehoiachin prisoner. 13As the LORD had declared,[k] Nebuchadnezzar removed all the treasures[l] from the temple of the LORD and from the royal palace, and took away all the gold articles[m] that Solomon[n] king of Israel had made for the temple of the LORD. 14He carried into exile[o] all Jerusalem: all the officers and fighting men, and all the craftsmen and artisans—a total of ten thousand. Only the poorest[p] people of the land were left.

15Nebuchadnezzar took Jehoiachin captive to Babylon. He also took from Jerusalem to Babylon the king's mother,[q] his wives, his officials and the leading men[r] of the land. 16The king of Babylon also deported to Babylon the entire force of seven thousand fighting men, strong and fit for war, and a thousand craftsmen and artisans.[s] 17He made Mattaniah, Jehoiachin's uncle, king in his place and changed his name to Zedekiah.[t]

Zedekiah reigns in Judah.

24:18-20pp— 2Ch 36:11-16; Jer 52:1-3

18Zedekiah[u] was twenty-one years old when he became king, and he reigned in Jerusalem eleven years. His mother's name was Hamutal[v] daughter of Jeremiah; she was from Libnah. 19He did evil in the eyes of the LORD, just as Jehoiakim had done. 20It was because of the LORD's anger that all this happened to Jerusalem and Judah, and in the end he thrust[w] them from his presence.

Jerusalem and the temple are destroyed.

25:1-12pp— Jer 39:1-10
25:1-21pp— 2Ch 36:17-20; Jer 52:4-27

Now Zedekiah rebelled against the king of Babylon.

25 So in the ninth year of Zedekiah's reign, on the tenth day of the tenth month, Nebuchadnezzar[x] king of Babylon marched against Jerusalem with his whole army. He encamped outside the city and built siege works[y] all around it. 2The city was kept under siege until the eleventh year of King Zedekiah. 3By the ninth day of the ⌞fourth⌟[r] month the famine[z] in the city had become so severe that there was no food for the people to eat. 4Then the city wall was broken through,[a] and the whole army fled at night through the gate between the two walls near the king's

24:2 [a]Jer 25:9
24:3 [b]2Ki 18:25 [c]2Ki 21:12; 23:26
24:4 [d]2Ki 21:16
24:6 [e]Jer 22:19
24:7 [f]Ge 15:18 [g]Jer 37:5-7; 46:2
24:8 [h]1Ch 3:16
24:10 [i]Da 1:1
24:12 [j]2Ki 25:27; Jer 22:24-30; 24:1; 25:1; 29:2; 52:28
24:13 [k]2Ki 20:17 [l]2Ki 25:15; Isa 39:6 [m]2Ki 25:14; Jer 20:5 [n]1Ki 7:51
24:14 [o]Jer 24:1; 52:28 [p]2Ki 25:12; Jer 40:7; 52:16
24:15 [q]Jer 22:24-28 [r]Est 2:6; Eze 17:12-14
24:16 [s]Jer 52:28
24:17 [t]1Ch 3:15; 2Ch 36:11; Jer 37:1
24:18 [u]Jer 52:1 [v]2Ki 23:31
24:20 [w]Dt 4:26; 29:27
25:1 [x]Jer 34:1-7 [y]Eze 24:2
25:3 [z]Jer 14:18; La 4:9
25:4 [a]Eze 33:21

r3 See Jer. 52:6.

garden, though the Babylonians[s] were surrounding[a] the city. They fled toward the Arabah,[t] 5 but the Babylonian[u] army pursued the king and overtook him in the plains of Jericho. All his soldiers were separated from him and scattered,[b] 6 and he was captured.[c] He was taken to the king of Babylon at Riblah,[d] where sentence was pronounced on him. 7 They killed the sons of Zedekiah before his eyes. Then they put out his eyes, bound him with bronze shackles and took him to Babylon.[e]

8 On the seventh day of the fifth month, in the nineteenth year of Nebuchadnezzar king of Babylon, Nebuzaradan commander of the imperial guard, an official of the king of Babylon, came to Jerusalem. 9 He set fire[f] to the temple of the LORD, the royal palace and all the houses of Jerusalem. Every important building he burned down.[g] 10 The whole Babylonian army, under the commander of the imperial guard, broke down the walls[h] around Jerusalem. 11 Nebuzaradan the commander of the guard carried into exile[i] the people who remained in the city, along with the rest of the populace and those who had gone over to the king of Babylon.[j] 12 But the commander left behind some of the poorest people[k] of the land to work the vineyards and fields.

13 The Babylonians broke up the bronze pillars, the movable stands and the bronze Sea that were at the temple of the LORD and they carried the bronze to Babylon. 14 They also took away the pots, shovels, wick trimmers, dishes and all the bronze articles[l] used in the temple service. 15 The commander of the imperial guard took away the censers and sprinkling bowls—all that were made of pure gold or silver.

16 The bronze from the two pillars, the Sea and the movable stands, which Solomon had made for the temple of the LORD, was more than could be weighed. 17 Each pillar[m] was twenty-seven feet[v] high. The bronze capital on top of one pillar was four and a half feet[w] high and was decorated with a network and pomegranates of bronze all around. The other pillar, with its network, was similar.

18 The commander of the guard took as prisoners Seraiah[n] the chief priest, Zephaniah[o] the priest next in rank and the three doorkeepers. 19 Of those still in the city, he took the officer in charge of the fighting men and five royal advisers. He also took the secretary who was chief officer in charge of conscripting the people of the land and sixty of his men who were found in the city. 20 Nebuzaradan the commander took them all and brought them to the king of Babylon at Riblah. 21 There at Riblah, in the land of Hamath, the king had them executed.

So Judah went into captivity, away from her land.[p]

Gedaliah is appointed governor of Judah.

25:22-26pp—Jer 40:7-9; 41:1-3, 16-18

22 Nebuchadnezzar king of Babylon appointed Gedaliah[q] son of Ahikam, the son of Shaphan, to be over the people he had left behind in Judah. 23 When all the army officers and their men heard that the king of Babylon had appointed Gedaliah as governor, they came to Gedaliah at Mizpah—Ishmael son of Nethaniah, Johanan son of Kareah, Seraiah son of Tanhumeth the Netophathite, Jaazaniah the son of the Maacathite, and their men. 24 Gedaliah took an oath to reassure them and their men. "Do not be afraid of the Babylonian officials," he said. "Settle down in the land and serve the king of Babylon, and it will go well with you."

25 In the seventh month, however, Ishmael son of Nethaniah, the son of Elishama, who was of royal blood, came with ten men and assassinated Gedaliah and also the men of Judah and the Babylonians who were with him at Mizpah. 26 At this, all the people from the least to the greatest, together with the army

25:4 [a]Jer 4:17
25:5 [b]Eze 12:14
25:6 [c]Jer 34:21-22 [d]2Ki 23:33
25:7 [e]Jer 21:7; 32:4-5; Eze 12:11
25:9 [f]Isa 60:7 [g]Ps 74:3-8; Jer 2:15; Am 2:5; Mic 3:12
25:10 [h]Ne 1:3
25:11 [i]2Ki 24:14 [j]2Ki 24:1
25:12 [k]2Ki 24:14
25:14 [l]Ex 27:3; 1Ki 7:47-50
25:17 [m]1Ki 7:15-22
25:18 [n]1Ch 6:14; Ezr 7:1; Ne 11:11 [o]Jer 21:1; 29:25
25:21 [p]Ge 12:7; Dt 28:64; Jos 23:13; 2Ki 23:27
25:22 [q]Jer 39:14; 40:5,7

[s]4 Or *Chaldeans*; also in verses 13, 25 and 26 [t]4 Or *the Jordan Valley* [u]5 Or *Chaldean*; also in verses 10 and 24 [v]17 Hebrew *eighteen cubits* (about 8.1 meters) [w]17 Hebrew *three cubits* (about 1.3 meters)

officers, fled to Egypt[a] for fear of the
Babylonians.

Jehoiachin is released from prison.

25:27-30pp— Jer 52:31-34

27In the thirty-seventh year of the exile
of Jehoiachin king of Judah, in the year
Evil-Merodach[x] became king of Babylon,
he released Jehoiachin[b] from prison on
the twenty-seventh day of the twelfth
month. **28**He spoke kindly to him and
gave him a seat of honor[c] higher than
those of the other kings who were
with him in Babylon. **29**So Jehoiachin
put aside his prison clothes and for the
rest of his life ate regularly at the
king's table.[d] **30**Day by day the king
gave Jehoiachin a regular allowance as
long as he lived.[e]

25:26 [a]Isa 30:2; Jer 43:7
25:27 [b]2Ki 24:12; Jer 52:31-34
25:28 [c]Ezr 5:5; Ne 2:1; Da 2:48
25:29 [d]2Sa 9:7
25:30 [e]Est 2:9; Jer 28:4

[x]*27* Also called *Amel-Marduk*

1 CHRONICLES

Author: Unknown (possibly Ezra).

Date Written: Between 450 and 400 B.C. (compiled from earlier sources).

Time Span: Chapters 1-9 cover approximately 3,500 years from the creation of Adam to the birth of David. Chapters 10-29 cover 33-40 years describing the reign of David.

Title: The books of 1 and 2 Chronicles are so named because they "chronicle" the entire history of God's people from Genesis through Kings. The title used in the Hebrew Bible means "the accounts of the days."

Background: The last book of the Hebrew Bible has been broken down into 1 and 2 Chronicles in modern translations. The Chronicles are different in perspective from the books of Samuel and Kings, even though they cover much of the same material. Instead of prophetic, moral and political views, the Chronicles are presented from a priest's point of view, evaluating the nation's religious history.

Where Written: Unknown (possibly Jerusalem).

To Whom: To the remnant of Judah returning from Babylon.

Content: There are 2 distinct sections of this book. First, the royal lineage from Adam to David is given. Then, the righteous reign of David is discussed. Chronicles evaluates David's achievements and his religious guidance of the nation as he seeks God's leadership. David's trials, sins and failures are de-emphasized in Chronicles since the covenant relationship between God and the people is the focus here. 1 Chronicles ends with the death of David and the succession of his son Solomon to the throne.

Key Words: "Royal"; "Chosen." Chronicles recounts the "royal" line of David (which eventually leads to the absolute royalty of Jesus Christ). David is "chosen" by God to rule over Israel; and his son Solomon is "chosen" to rule after him and to build a house for the Lord (chapter 28).

Themes: • God will never forsake his people, his promises or his covenant. • We must fulfill our covenant with God to be totally obedient to his Word. • In order to do a great work for God...we must first have a great heart for God. • God is always working in our lives...even when we don't understand his ways or see his hand. • Even though people and nations sometimes fail...God never fails. • We should appreciate our heritage and significance in God's eyes. • God blesses obedience...and punishes disobedience.

Outline:

1. Genealogies from Adam to David. 1:1-9:44
2. Anointing of David as king over Israel. 10:1-12:40
3. Bringing the ark of the covenant to Jerusalem. 13:1-17:27
4. Battle victories of David. 18:1-20:8
5. Census of Israel. 21:1-27:34
6. Plans for the temple. 28:1-29:9
7. Final words and deeds of David. 29:10-29:30

1 CHRONICLES

Family records from Adam to Noah's sons.

1 Adam,[a] Seth, Enosh, 2Kenan,[b] Mahalalel,[c] Jared,[d] 3Enoch,[e] Methuselah,[f] Lamech,[g] Noah.[h]

4The sons of Noah:[a][i]
Shem, Ham and Japheth.[j]

The Japhethites.

1:5-7pp— Ge 10:2-5

5The sons[b] of Japheth:
Gomer, Magog, Madai, Javan, Tubal, Meshech and Tiras.
6The sons of Gomer:
Ashkenaz, Riphath[c] and Togarmah.
7The sons of Javan:
Elishah, Tarshish, the Kittim and the Rodanim.

The Hamites.

1:8-16pp— Ge 10:6-20

8The sons of Ham:
Cush, Mizraim,[d] Put and Canaan.
9The sons of Cush:
Seba, Havilah, Sabta, Raamah and Sabteca.
The sons of Raamah:
Sheba and Dedan.
10Cush was the father[e] of
Nimrod, who grew to be a mighty warrior on earth.
11Mizraim was the father of
the Ludites, Anamites, Lehabites,
Naphtuhites, 12Pathrusites, Casluhites (from whom the Philistines came) and Caphtorites.
13Canaan was the father of
Sidon his firstborn,[f] and of the
Hittites, 14Jebusites, Amorites,
Girgashites, 15Hivites, Arkites, Sinites, 16Arvadites, Zemarites and Hamathites.

The Semites.

1:17-23pp— Ge 10:21-31; 11:10-27

17The sons of Shem:
Elam, Asshur, Arphaxad, Lud and Aram.
The sons of Aram[g]:
Uz, Hul, Gether and Meshech.
18Arphaxad was the father of Shelah,
and Shelah the father of Eber.
19Two sons were born to Eber:
One was named Peleg,[h] because in his time the earth was divided; his brother was named Joktan.
20Joktan was the father of
Almodad, Sheleph, Hazarmaveth,
Jerah, 21Hadoram, Uzal, Diklah,
22Obal,[i] Abimael, Sheba, 23Ophir,
Havilah and Jobab. All these were sons of Joktan.

24Shem,[k] Arphaxad,[j] Shelah,
25Eber, Peleg, Reu,
26Serug, Nahor, Terah
27and Abram (that is, Abraham).

Family records of Abraham.

28The sons of Abraham:
Isaac and Ishmael.

Descendants of Hagar.

1:29-31pp— Ge 25:12-16

29These were their descendants:
Nebaioth the firstborn of Ishmael, Kedar, Adbeel, Mibsam,
30Mishma, Dumah, Massa, Hadad, Tema, 31Jetur, Naphish and
Kedemah. These were the sons of Ishmael.

1:1 [a]Ge 5:1-32; Lk 3:36-38
1:2 [b]Ge 5:9 [c]Ge 5:12 [d]Ge 5:15
1:3 [e]Ge 5:18; Jude 14 [f]Ge 5:21 [g]Ge 5:25 [h]Ge 5:29
1:4 [i]Ge 6:10; 10:1 [j]Ge 5:32
1:24 [k]Ge 10:21-25; Lk 3:34-36

[a] *4* Septuagint; Hebrew does not have *The sons of Noah:* [b] *5* *Sons* may mean *descendants* or *successors* or *nations*; also in verses 6-10, 17 and 20. [c] *6* Many Hebrew manuscripts and Vulgate (see also Septuagint and Gen. 10:3); most Hebrew manuscripts *Diphath* [d] *8* That is, Egypt; also in verse 11
[e] *10* *Father* may mean *ancestor* or *predecessor* or *founder*; also in verses 11, 13, 18 and 20.
[f] *13* Or *of the Sidonians, the foremost*
[g] *17* One Hebrew manuscript and some Septuagint manuscripts (see also Gen. 10:23); most Hebrew manuscripts do not have this line. [h] *19* *Peleg* means *division.* [i] *22* Some Hebrew manuscripts and Syriac (see also Gen. 10:28); most Hebrew manuscripts *Ebal* [j] *24* Hebrew; some Septuagint manuscripts *Arphaxad, Cainan* (see also note at Gen. 11:10)

KEY PLACES IN 1 CHRONICLES

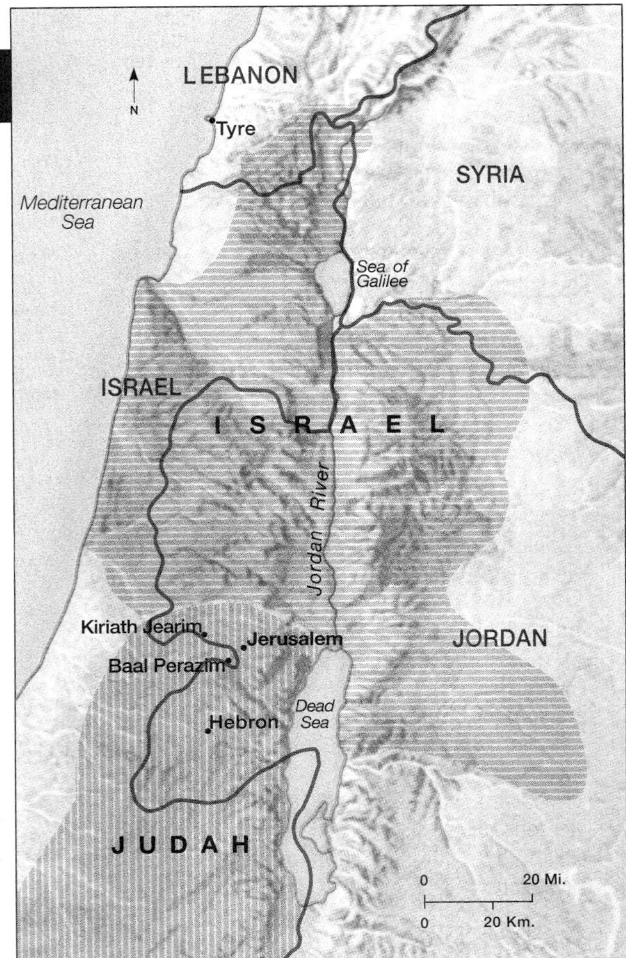

The genealogies of 1 Chronicles present an overview of Israel's history. The first nine chapters are filled with genealogies tracing the lineages of people from the creation to the exile in Babylon. Saul's death is recorded in chapter 10. Chapter 11 begins the history of David's reign over Israel.

Hebron Although David had been anointed king years earlier, his reign began when the leaders of Israel accepted him as king at Hebron (11:1-3).

Jerusalem David set out to complete the conquest of the land begun by Joshua. He attacked Jerusalem, captured it, and made it his capital (11:4–12:40).

Kiriath Jearim The ark of the covenant, which had been captured by the Philistines in battle and returned (1 Samuel 4–6), was in safekeeping in Kiriath Jearim. David summoned all Israel to this city to join in bringing the ark to Jerusalem. Unfortunately, it was not moved according to God's instructions, and as a result one man died. David left the ark in the home of Obed-Edom until he could discover how to transport it correctly (13:1-14).

Tyre David did much building in Jerusalem. King Hiram of Tyre sent workers and supplies to help build David's palace. Cedar, abundant in the mountains north of Israel, was a valuable and hardy wood for the beautiful buildings in Jerusalem (14:1–17:27).

Baal Perazim David was not very popular with the Philistines because he had slain Goliath, one of their greatest warriors (1 Samuel 17). When David began to rule over a united Israel, the Philistines set out to capture him. But David and his army attacked the Philistines at Baal Perazim as they approached Jerusalem. His army defeated the mighty Philistines twice, causing all the surrounding nations to fear David's power (14:11-17). After this battle, David moved the ark to Jerusalem (this time in accordance with God's instructions for the transportation of the ark). There was a great celebration as the ark was brought into Jerusalem (15:1–17:27). David spent the remainder of his life making preparations for the building of the temple, a central place for the worship of God (18:1–29:30).

Descendants of Keturah.

1:32-33pp— Ge 25:1-4

32The sons born to Keturah, Abraham's concubine:[a]
Zimran, Jokshan, Medan, Midian, Ishbak and Shuah.
The sons of Jokshan:
Sheba and Dedan.[b]
33The sons of Midian:
Ephah, Epher, Hanoch, Abida and Eldaah.
All these were descendants of Keturah.

Descendants of Sarah.

1:35-37pp— Ge 36:10-14

34Abraham[c] was the father of Isaac.[d]
The sons of Isaac:
Esau and Israel.[e]
35The sons of Esau:[f]
Eliphaz, Reuel,[g] Jeush, Jalam and Korah.
36The sons of Eliphaz:
Teman, Omar, Zepho,[k] Gatam and Kenaz;
by Timna: Amalek.[l][h]
37The sons of Reuel:[i]
Nahath, Zerah, Shammah and Mizzah.

The sons of Seir in Edom.

1:38-42pp— Ge 36:20-28

38The sons of Seir:
Lotan, Shobal, Zibeon, Anah, Dishon, Ezer and Dishan.
39The sons of Lotan:
Hori and Homam. Timna was Lotan's sister.
40The sons of Shobal:
Alvan,[m] Manahath, Ebal, Shepho and Onam.
The sons of Zibeon:
Aiah and Anah.[j]
41The son of Anah:
Dishon.
The sons of Dishon:
Hemdan,[n] Eshban, Ithran and Keran.

1:32 *a*Ge 22:24 *b*Ge 10:7
1:34 *c*Lk 3:34 *d*Ge 21:2-3; Mt 1:2; Ac 7:8 *e*Ge 17:5; 25:25-26
1:35 *f*Ge 36:19 *g*Ge 36:4
1:36 *h*Ex 17:14
1:37 *i*Ge 36:17
1:40 *j*Ge 36:2
1:45 *k*Ge 36:11

42The sons of Ezer:
Bilhan, Zaavan and Akan.[o]
The sons of Dishan[p]:
Uz and Aran.

The kings of Edom.

1:43-54pp— Ge 36:31-43

43These were the kings who reigned in Edom before any Israelite king reigned[q]:
Bela son of Beor, whose city was named Dinhabah.
44When Bela died, Jobab son of Zerah from Bozrah succeeded him as king.
45When Jobab died, Husham from the land of the Temanites[k] succeeded him as king.
46When Husham died, Hadad son of Bedad, who defeated Midian in the country of Moab, succeeded him as king. His city was named Avith.
47When Hadad died, Samlah from Masrekah succeeded him as king.
48When Samlah died, Shaul from Rehoboth on the river[r] succeeded him as king.
49When Shaul died, Baal-Hanan son of Acbor succeeded him as king.
50When Baal-Hanan died, Hadad succeeded him as king. His city was named Pau,[s] and his wife's name was Mehetabel daughter of Matred, the daughter of Me-Zahab.
51Hadad also died.

k*36* Many Hebrew manuscripts, some Septuagint manuscripts and Syriac (see also Gen. 36:11); most Hebrew manuscripts *Zephi* l*36* Some Septuagint manuscripts (see also Gen. 36:12); Hebrew *Gatam, Kenaz, Timna and Amalek* m*40* Many Hebrew manuscripts and some Septuagint manuscripts (see also Gen. 36:23); most Hebrew manuscripts *Alian* n*41* Many Hebrew manuscripts and some Septuagint manuscripts (see also Gen. 36:26); most Hebrew manuscripts *Hamran* o*42* Many Hebrew and Septuagint manuscripts (see also Gen. 36:27); most Hebrew manuscripts *Zaavan, Jaakan* p*42* Hebrew *Dishon,* a variant of *Dishan* q*43* Or *before an Israelite king reigned over them* r*48* Possibly the Euphrates s*50* Many Hebrew manuscripts, some Septuagint manuscripts, Vulgate and Syriac (see also Gen. 36:39); most Hebrew manuscripts *Pa*

The chiefs of Edom were:
Timna, Alvah, Jetheth, 52Oholiba-
mah, Elah, Pinon, 53Kenaz, Teman, Mibzar, 54Magdiel and Iram.
These were the chiefs of Edom.

Family records of Israel's sons.

2:1-2pp— Ge 35:23-26

2 These were the sons of Israel:
Reuben, Simeon, Levi, Judah, Is-
sachar, Zebulun, 2Dan, Joseph,
Benjamin, Naphtali, Gad and
Asher.

Judah.

2:5-15pp— Ru 4:18-22; Mt 1:3-6

3The sons of Judah:[a]
Er, Onan and Shelah.[b] These
three were born to him by a
Canaanite woman, the daughter
of Shua.[c] Er, Judah's firstborn,
was wicked in the LORD's sight;
so the LORD put him to death.[d]
4Tamar,[e] Judah's daughter-in-law,[f]
bore him Perez[g] and Zerah. Judah
had five sons in all.

5The sons of Perez:[h]
Hezron[i] and Hamul.
6The sons of Zerah:
Zimri, Ethan, Heman, Calcol and
Darda[t]—five in all.
7The son of Carmi:
Achar,[u][j] who brought trouble on
Israel by violating the ban on tak-
ing devoted things.[v][k]
8The son of Ethan:
Azariah.
9The sons born to Hezron[l] were:
Jerahmeel, Ram and Caleb.[w]

10Ram[m] was the father of
Amminadab[n], and Amminadab
the father of Nahshon,[o] the leader of the people of Judah. 11Nah-
shon was the father of Salmon,[x]
Salmon the father of Boaz,
12Boaz[p] the father of Obed and
Obed the father of Jesse.[q]
13Jesse[r] was the father of

2:3 [a]Ge 29:35; 38:2-10 [b]Ge 38:5 [c]Ge 38:2 [d]Nu 26:19
2:4 [e]Ge 38:11-30 [f]Ge 11:31 [g]Ge 38:29
2:5 [h]Ge 46:12 [i]Nu 26:21
2:7 [j]Jos 7:1 [k]Jos 6:18
2:9 [l]Nu 26:21
2:10 [m]Lk 3:32-33 [n]Ex 6:23 [o]Nu 1:7
2:12 [p]Ru 2:1 [q]Ru 4:17
2:13 [r]Ru 4:17 [s]1Sa 16:6
2:16 [t]1Sa 26:6 [u]2Sa 2:18 [v]2Sa 2:13
2:17 [w]2Sa 17:25
2:19 [x]ver 42,50
2:20 [y]Ex 31:2
2:21 [z]Nu 27:1
2:23 [a]Nu 32:41; Dt 3:14; Jos 13:30 [b]Nu 32:42
2:24 [c]1Ch 4:5

Eliab[s] his firstborn; the second
son was Abinadab, the third
Shimea, 14the fourth Nethanel,
the fifth Raddai, 15the sixth Ozem
and the seventh David. 16Their
sisters were Zeruiah[t] and Abigail.
Zeruiah's[u] three sons were Abishai, Joab[v] and Asahel. 17Abigail was
the mother of Amasa,[w] whose
father was Jether the Ishmaelite.

18Caleb son of Hezron had children
by his wife Azubah (and by Jeri-
oth). These were her sons: Jesh-
er, Shobab and Ardon. 19When
Azubah died, Caleb[x] married Ephrath, who bore him Hur. 20Hur
was the father of Uri, and Uri the
father of Bezalel.[y]
21Later, Hezron lay with the daughter
of Makir the father of Gilead[z]
(he had married her when he
was sixty years old), and she
bore him Segub. 22Segub was the
father of Jair, who controlled
twenty-three towns in Gilead.
23(But Geshur and Aram captured Havvoth Jair,[y][a] as well as
Kenath[b] with its surrounding settlements—sixty towns.) All these
were descendants of Makir the
father of Gilead.

24After Hezron died in Caleb Ephrathah, Abijah the wife of Hezron
bore him Ashhur[c] the father[z] of
Tekoa.

25The sons of Jerahmeel the firstborn
of Hezron:
Ram his firstborn, Bunah, Oren,
Ozem and[a] Ahijah. 26Jerahmeel
had another wife, whose name

t *6* Many Hebrew manuscripts, some Septuagint manuscripts and Syriac (see also 1 Kings 4:31); most Hebrew manuscripts *Dara* u *7* *Achar* means *trouble*; *Achar* is called *Achan* in Joshua. v *7* The Hebrew term refers to the irrevocable giving over of things or persons to the LORD, often by totally destroying them.
w *9* Hebrew *Kelubai,* a variant of *Caleb*
x *11* Septuagint (see also Ruth 4:21); Hebrew *Salma*
y *23* Or *captured the settlements of Jair* z *24* *Father* may mean *civic leader* or *military leader*; also in verses 42, 45, 49-52 and possibly elsewhere. a *25* Or *Oren and Ozem, by*

was Atarah; she was the mother of Onam.
27The sons of Ram the firstborn of Jerahmeel:
Maaz, Jamin and Eker.
28The sons of Onam:
Shammai and Jada.
The sons of Shammai:
Nadab and Abishur.
29Abishur's wife was named Abihail, who bore him Ahban and Molid.
30The sons of Nadab:
Seled and Appaim. Seled died without children.
31The son of Appaim:
Ishi, who was the father of Sheshan.
Sheshan was the father of Ahlai.
32The sons of Jada, Shammai's brother:
Jether and Jonathan. Jether died without children.
33The sons of Jonathan:
Peleth and Zaza.
These were the descendants of Jerahmeel.
34Sheshan had no sons—only daughters.
He had an Egyptian servant named Jarha.
35Sheshan gave his daughter in marriage to his servant Jarha, and she bore him Attai.
36Attai was the father of Nathan,
Nathan the father of Zabad,[a]
37Zabad the father of Ephlal,
Ephlal the father of Obed,
38Obed the father of Jehu,
Jehu the father of Azariah,
39Azariah the father of Helez,
Helez the father of Eleasah,
40Eleasah the father of Sismai,
Sismai the father of Shallum,
41Shallum the father of Jekamiah,
and Jekamiah the father of Elishama.

42The sons of Caleb[b] the brother of Jerahmeel:
Mesha his firstborn, who was the father of Ziph, and his son Mareshah,[b] who was the father of Hebron.

2:36
[a]1Ch 11:41
2:42
[b]ver 19
2:45
[c]Jos 15:55
[d]Jos 15:58
2:49
[e]Jos 15:31
[f]Jos 15:16
2:50
[g]1Ch 4:4
[h]ver 19
2:53
[i]2Sa 23:38
2:54
[j]Ezr 2:22; Ne 7:26; 12:28
2:55
[k]Ge 15:19; Jdg 1:16; Jdg 4:11
[l]Jos 19:35
[m]2Ki 10:15, 23; Jer 35:2-19

43The sons of Hebron:
Korah, Tappuah, Rekem and Shema.
44Shema was the father of Raham, and Raham the father of Jorkeam. Rekem was the father of Shammai.
45The son of Shammai was Maon[c], and Maon was the father of Beth Zur.[d]
46Caleb's concubine Ephah was the mother of Haran, Moza and Gazez. Haran was the father of Gazez.
47The sons of Jahdai:
Regem, Jotham, Geshan, Pelet, Ephah and Shaaph.
48Caleb's concubine Maacah was the mother of Sheber and Tirhanah.
49She also gave birth to Shaaph the father of Madmannah[e] and to Sheva the father of Macbenah and Gibea. Caleb's daughter was Acsah.[f]
50These were the descendants of Caleb.

The sons of Hur[g] the firstborn of Ephrathah:
Shobal the father of Kiriath Jearim,[h]
51Salma the father of Bethlehem, and Hareph the father of Beth Gader.
52The descendants of Shobal the father of Kiriath Jearim were:
Haroeh, half the Manahathites,
53and the clans of Kiriath Jearim: the Ithrites,[i] Puthites, Shumathites and Mishraites. From these descended the Zorathites and Eshtaolites.
54The descendants of Salma:
Bethlehem, the Netophathites,[j] Atroth Beth Joab, half the Manahathites, the Zorites,
55and the clans of scribes[c] who lived at Jabez: the Tirathites, Shimeathites and Sucathites. These are the Kenites[k] who came from Hammath,[l] the father of the house of Recab.[d][m]

[b]*42* The meaning of the Hebrew for this phrase is uncertain. [c]*55* Or *of the Sopherites* [d]*55* Or *father of Beth Recab*

Family records of David's sons.

3:1-4pp— 2Sa 3:2-5
3:5-8pp— 2Sa 5:14-16; 1Ch 14:4-7

3 These were the sons of David[a] born
to him in Hebron:
The firstborn was Amnon the
son of Ahinoam of Jezreel;[b]
the second, Daniel the son of Abigail[c] of Carmel;
2the third, Absalom the son of
Maacah daughter of Talmai king
of Geshur;
the fourth, Adonijah[d] the son of
Haggith;
3the fifth, Shephatiah the son of
Abital;
and the sixth, Ithream, by his
wife Eglah.
4These six were born to David in
Hebron,[e] where he reigned sev-
en years and six months.[f]
David reigned in Jerusalem thirty-three
years, 5and these were the children
born to him there:
Shammua,[e] Shobab, Nathan and
Solomon. These four were by
Bathsheba[f][g] daughter of Ammiel. 6There were also Ibhar,
Elishua,[g] Eliphelet, 7Nogah, Nepheg, Japhia, 8Elishama, Eliada
and Eliphelet—nine in all. 9All
these were the sons of David,
besides his sons by his concubines. And Tamar[h] was their
sister.[i]

10Solomon's son was Rehoboam,[j]
Abijah his son,
Asa his son,
Jehoshaphat[k] his son,
11Jehoram[h][l] his son,
Ahaziah[m] his son,
Joash[n] his son,
12Amaziah[o] his son,
Azariah his son,
Jotham[p] his son,
13Ahaz[q] his son,
Hezekiah[r] his son,
Manasseh[s] his son,
14Amon[t] his son,
Josiah[u] his son.

3:1 [a]1Ch 14:3; 28:5 [b]Jos 15:56 [c]1Sa 25:42
3:2 [d]1Ki 2:22
3:4 [e]2Sa 5:4; 1Ch 29:27 [f]2Sa 2:11; 5:5
3:5 [g]2Sa 11:3; 12:24
3:9 [h]2Sa 13:1 [i]1Ch 14:4
3:10 [j]1Ki 11:43; 14:21-31; 2Ch 12:16 [k]2Ch 17:1–21:3
3:11 [l]2Ki 8:16-24; 2Ch 21:1 [m]2Ch 22:1-10 [n]2Ki 11:1–12:21
3:12 [o]2Ki 14:1-22; 2Ch 25:1-28 [p]Isa 1:1; Hos 1:1; Mic 1:1
3:13 [q]2Ki 16:1-20; 2Ch 28:1; Isa 7:1 [r]2Ki 18:1–20:21; 2Ch 29:1; Jer 26:19 [s]2Ch 33:1
3:14 [t]2Ki 21:19-26; 2Ch 33:21; Zep 1:1 [u]2Ch 34:1; Jer 1:2; 3:6; 25:3
3:15 [v]2Ki 23:34 [w]Jer 37:1 [x]2Ki 23:31
3:16 [y]2Ki 24:6,8; Mt 1:11 [z]2Ki 24:18
3:17 [a]Ezr 3:2
3:18 [b]Ezr 1:8; 5:14 [c]Jer 22:30

15The sons of Josiah:
Johanan the firstborn,
Jehoiakim[v] the second son,
Zedekiah[w] the third,
Shallum[x] the fourth.
16The successors of Jehoiakim:
Jehoiachin[i][y] his son,
and Zedekiah.[z]

17The descendants of Jehoiachin the
captive:
Shealtiel[a] his son, 18Malkiram,
Pedaiah, Shenazzar,[b] Jekamiah,
Hoshama and Nedabiah.[c]
19The sons of Pedaiah:
Zerubbabel[d] and Shimei.
The sons of Zerubbabel:
Meshullam and Hananiah.
Shelomith was their sister.
20There were also five others:
Hashubah, Ohel, Berekiah, Hasa-
diah and Jushab-Hesed.
21The descendants of Hananiah:
Pelatiah and Jeshaiah, and the
sons of Rephaiah, of Arnan, of
Obadiah and of Shecaniah.
22The descendants of Shecaniah:
Shemaiah and his sons:
Hattush,[e] Igal, Bariah, Neariah
and Shaphat—six in all.
23The sons of Neariah:
Elioenai, Hizkiah and Azrikam—
three in all.
24The sons of Elioenai:
Hodaviah, Eliashib, Pelaiah, Akkub, Johanan, Delaiah and Ana-
ni—seven in all.

Other clans of Judah.

4 The descendants of Judah:[f]
Perez, Hezron,[g] Carmi, Hur and
Shobal.

3:19 [d]Ezr 2:2; 3:2; 5:2; Ne 7:7; 12:1; Hag 1:1; 2:2; Zec 4:6 **3:22** [e]Ezr 8:2-3 **4:1** [f]Ge 29:35; 46:12; 1Ch 2:3 [g]Nu 26:21

e*5* Hebrew *Shimea,* a variant of *Shammua* f*5* One Hebrew manuscript and Vulgate (see also Septuagint and 2 Samuel 11:3); most Hebrew manuscripts *Bathshua* g*6* Two Hebrew manuscripts (see also 2 Samuel 5:15 and 1 Chron. 14:5); most Hebrew manuscripts *Elishama* h*11* Hebrew *Joram,* a variant of *Jehoram* i*16* Hebrew *Jeconiah,* a variant of *Jehoiachin*; also in verse 17

2 Reaiah son of Shobal was the father of Jahath, and Jahath the father of Ahumai and Lahad. These
were the clans of the Zorathites.
3 These were the sons[j] of Etam:
Jezreel, Ishma and Idbash. Their
sister was named Hazzelelponi.
4 Penuel was the father of Gedor,
and Ezer the father of Hushah.
These were the descendants of
Hur,[a] the firstborn of Ephrathah
and father[k] of Bethlehem.[b]
5 Ashhur[c] the father of Tekoa had two
wives, Helah and Naarah.
6 Naarah bore him Ahuzzam, Hepher, Temeni and Haahashtari.
These were the descendants of
Naarah.
7 The sons of Helah:
Zereth, Zohar, Ethnan, 8 and Koz,
who was the father of Anub and
Hazzobebah and of the clans of
Aharhel son of Harum.

9 Jabez was more honorable than his
brothers. His mother had named him
Jabez,[l] saying, "I gave birth to him in
pain." 10 Jabez cried out to the God of
Israel, "Oh, that you would bless me
and enlarge my territory! Let your hand
be with me, and keep me from harm so
that I will be free from pain." And God
granted his request.

11 Kelub, Shuhah's brother, was the
father of Mehir, who was the
father of Eshton. 12 Eshton was
the father of Beth Rapha, Paseah
and Tehinnah the father of Ir
Nahash.[m] These were the men
of Recah.

13 The sons of Kenaz:
Othniel[d] and Seraiah.
The sons of Othniel:
Hathath and Meonothai.[n] 14 Meonothai was the father of Ophrah.
Seraiah was the father of Joab,
the father of Ge Harashim.[o] It
was called this because its people were craftsmen.
15 The sons of Caleb son of Jephunneh:
Iru, Elah and Naam.

4:4 [a] 1Ch 2:50 [b] Ru 1:19
4:5 [c] 1Ch 2:24
4:13 [d] Jos 15:17
4:17 [e] Ex 15:20
4:18 [f] Jos 15:34
4:19 [g] Jos 15:44 [h] Dt 3:14
4:21 [i] Ge 38:5
4:24 [j] Ge 29:33 [k] Nu 26:12

The son of Elah:
Kenaz.
16 The sons of Jehallelel:
Ziph, Ziphah, Tiria and Asarel.
17 The sons of Ezrah:
Jether, Mered, Epher and Jalon.
One of Mered's wives gave birth
to Miriam,[e] Shammai and Ishbah
the father of Eshtemoa. 18 (His
Judean wife gave birth to Jered
the father of Gedor, Heber the
father of Soco, and Jekuthiel the
father of Zanoah.[f]) These were
the children of Pharaoh's daughter Bithiah, whom Mered had
married.
19 The sons of Hodiah's wife, the sister of Naham:
the father of Keilah[g] the Garmite,
and Eshtemoa the Maacathite.[h]
20 The sons of Shimon:
Amnon, Rinnah, Ben-Hanan and
Tilon.
The descendants of Ishi:
Zoheth and Ben-Zoheth.
21 The sons of Shelah[i] son of Judah:
Er the father of Lecah, Laadah
the father of Mareshah and the
clans of the linen workers at Beth
Ashbea, 22 Jokim, the men of Co-
zeba, and Joash and Saraph, who
ruled in Moab and Jashubi Lehem. (These records are from
ancient times.) 23 They were the
potters who lived at Netaim and
Gederah; they stayed there and
worked for the king.

Simeon.

4:28-33pp—Jos 19:2-10

24 The descendants of Simeon:[j]
Nemuel, Jamin, Jarib,[k] Zerah and
Shaul;

j *3* Some Septuagint manuscripts (see also Vulgate); Hebrew *father* k *4* *Father* may mean *civic leader* or *military leader*; also in verses 12, 14, 17, 18 and possibly elsewhere. l *9* *Jabez* sounds like the Hebrew for *pain.* m *12* Or *of the city of Nahash*
n *13* Some Septuagint manuscripts and Vulgate; Hebrew does not have *and Meonothai.*
o *14* *Ge Harashim* means *valley of craftsmen.*

25Shallum was Shaul's son, Mibsam
his son and Mishma his son.
26The descendants of Mishma:
Hammuel his son, Zaccur his
son and Shimei his son.
27Shimei had sixteen sons and six
daughters, but his brothers did not have
many children; so their entire clan did
not become as numerous as the people
of Judah. 28They lived in Beersheba,[a]
Moladah,[b] Hazar Shual, 29Bilhah,
Ezem,[c] Tolad, 30Bethuel, Hormah,[d] Ziklag, 31Beth Marcaboth, Hazar Susim,
Beth Biri and Shaaraim.[e] These were
their towns until the reign of David.
32Their surrounding villages were Etam,
Ain,[f] Rimmon, Token and Ashan[g]—five
towns— 33and all the villages around
these towns as far as Baalath.[p] These
were their settlements. And they kept
a genealogical record.

34Meshobab, Jamlech, Joshah son of
Amaziah, 35Joel, Jehu son of Joshibi-
ah, the son of Seraiah, the son of
Asiel, 36also Elioenai, Jaakobah, Jesh-
ohaiah, Asaiah, Adiel, Jesimiel, Benaiah, 37and Ziza son of Shiphi, the
son of Allon, the son of Jedaiah,
the son of Shimri, the son of Shemaiah.

38The men listed above by name were
leaders of their clans. Their families
increased greatly, 39and they went to the
outskirts of Gedor[h] to the east of the
valley in search of pasture for their
flocks. 40They found rich, good pasture, and the land was spacious, peaceful and quiet.[i] Some Hamites had lived
there formerly.
41The men whose names were listed
came in the days of Hezekiah king of
Judah. They attacked the Hamites in
their dwellings and also the Meunites[j]
who were there and completely destroyed[q] them, as is evident to this day.
Then they settled in their place, because
there was pasture for their flocks. 42And
five hundred of these Simeonites, led by
Pelatiah, Neariah, Rephaiah and Uzziel,
the sons of Ishi, invaded the hill country
of Seir.[k] 43They killed the remaining
Amalekites[l] who had escaped, and they
have lived there to this day.

Reuben.

5 The sons of Reuben[m] the firstborn
of Israel (he was the firstborn, but
when he defiled his father's marriage
bed,[n] his rights as firstborn were given
to the sons of Joseph[o] son of Israel;[p] so
he could not be listed in the genealogical
record in accordance with his birthright,[q] 2and though Judah[r] was the
strongest of his brothers and a ruler[s]
came from him, the rights of the firstborn[t] belonged to Joseph)— 3the sons
of Reuben[u] the firstborn of Israel:
Hanoch, Pallu,[v] Hezron and Carmi.
4The descendants of Joel:
Shemaiah his son, Gog his son,
Shimei his son, 5Micah his son,
Reaiah his son, Baal his son,
6and Beerah his son, whom
Tiglath-Pileser[r][w] king of Assyria
took into exile. Beerah was a
leader of the Reubenites.
7Their relatives by clans,[x] listed
according to their genealogical
records:
Jeiel the chief, Zechariah, 8and
Bela son of Azaz, the son of Shema, the son of Joel. They settled
in the area from Aroer[y] to Nebo
and Baal Meon.[z] 9To the east
they occupied the land up to the
edge of the desert that extends
to the Euphrates River, because
their livestock had increased in
Gilead.[a]
10During Saul's reign they waged
war against the Hagrites[b], who
were defeated at their hands; they
occupied the dwellings of the Hagrites throughout the entire region
east of Gilead.

4:28 [a]Ge 21:14 [b]Jos 15:26
4:29 [c]Jos 15:29
4:30 [d]Nu 14:45
4:31 [e]Jos 15:36
4:32 [f]Nu 34:11 [g]Jos 15:42
4:39 [h]Jos 15:58
4:40 [i]Jdg 18:7-10
4:41 [j]2Ch 20:1; 26:7
4:42 [k]Ge 14:6
4:43 [l]1Sa 15:8; 30:17; 2Sa 8:12; Est 3:1; 9:16
5:1 [m]Ge 29:32 [n]Ge 35:22; 49:4 [o]Ge 48:16,22; 49:26 [p]Ge 48:5 [q]1Ch 26:10
5:2 [r]Ge 49:10,12 [s]1Sa 9:16; 12:12; 2Sa 6:21; 1Ch 11:2; 2Ch 7:18; Ps 60:7; Mic 5:2; Mt 2:6 [t]Ge 25:31
5:3 [u]Ge 29:32; 46:9; Ex 6:14; Nu 26:5-11 [v]Nu 26:5
5:6 [w]ver 26; 2Ki 15:19; 16:10; 2Ch 28:20
5:7 [x]ver 17
5:8 [y]Nu 32:34 [z]Jos 13:17
5:9 [a]Nu 32:26; Jos 22:9
5:10 [b]ver 18-21

p *33* Some Septuagint manuscripts (see also Joshua 19:8); Hebrew *Baal* q *41* The Hebrew term refers to the irrevocable giving over of things or persons to the LORD, often by totally destroying them. r *6* Hebrew *Tilgath-Pilneser,* a variant of *Tiglath-Pileser;* also in verse 26

Gad.

11The Gadites[a] lived next to them in
Bashan, as far as Salecah:[b]
12Joel was the chief, Shapham the
second, then Janai and Shaphat,
in Bashan.
13Their relatives, by families, were:
Michael, Meshullam, Sheba, Jorai,
Jacan, Zia and Eber—seven in all.
14These were the sons of Abihail
son of Huri, the son of Jaroah, the
son of Gilead, the son of Michael,
the son of Jeshishai, the son of
Jahdo, the son of Buz.
15Ahi son of Abdiel, the son of
Guni, was head of their family.
16The Gadites lived in Gilead, in Bashan and its outlying villages, and
on all the pasturelands of Sharon
as far as they extended.
17All these were entered in the
genealogical records during the reigns of
Jotham[c] king of Judah and Jeroboam[d]
king of Israel.

18The Reubenites, the Gadites and the
half-tribe of Manasseh had 44,760 men
ready for military service[e]—able-bodied men who could handle shield and
sword, who could use a bow, and who
were trained for battle. 19They waged
war against the Hagrites, Jetur,[f] Naphish
and Nodab. 20They were helped[g] in
fighting them, and God handed the
Hagrites and all their allies over to them,
because they cried[h] out to him during
the battle. He answered their prayers,
because they trusted[i] in him. 21They
seized the livestock of the Hagrites—
fifty thousand camels, two hundred fifty
thousand sheep and two thousand donkeys. They also took one hundred thousand people captive, 22and many others
fell slain, because the battle[j] was God's.
And they occupied the land until the
exile.[k]

The half-tribe of Manasseh.

23The people of the half-tribe of Manasseh were numerous; they settled in
the land from Bashan to Baal Hermon,
that is, to Senir (Mount Hermon).[l]
24These were the heads of their families: Epher, Ishi, Eliel, Azriel, Jeremiah,
Hodaviah and Jahdiel. They were brave
warriors, famous men, and heads of
their families. 25But they were unfaithful[m] to the God of their fathers and
prostituted[n] themselves to the gods of
the peoples of the land, whom God
had destroyed before them. 26So the
God of Israel stirred up the spirit of
Pul[o] king of Assyria (that is, Tiglath-
Pileser[p] king of Assyria), who took the
Reubenites, the Gadites and the half-
tribe of Manasseh into exile. He took
them to Halah,[q] Habor, Hara and the
river of Gozan, where they are to this
day.

Levi.

6 The sons of Levi:[r]
Gershon, Kohath and Merari.
2The sons of Kohath:
Amram, Izhar, Hebron and Uzziel.
3The children of Amram:
Aaron, Moses and Miriam.
The sons of Aaron:
Nadab, Abihu,[s] Eleazar and Ithamar.
4Eleazar was the father of Phinehas,
Phinehas the father of Abishua,
5Abishua the father of Bukki,
Bukki the father of Uzzi,
6Uzzi the father of Zerahiah,
Zerahiah the father of Meraioth,
7Meraioth the father of Amariah,
Amariah the father of Ahitub,
8Ahitub the father of Zadok,[t]
Zadok the father of Ahimaaz,
9Ahimaaz the father of Azariah,
Azariah the father of Johanan,
10Johanan the father of Azariah[u]
(it was he who served as priest
in the temple Solomon built in
Jerusalem),
11Azariah the father of Amariah,
Amariah the father of Ahitub,
12Ahitub the father of Zadok,

5:11 [a]Jos 13:24-28 [b]Dt 3:10; Jos 13:11
5:17 [c]2Ki 15:32 [d]2Ki 14:16, 28
5:18 [e]Nu 1:3
5:19 [f]ver 10; Ge 25:15; 1Ch 1:31
5:20 [g]Ps 37:40 [h]1Ki 8:44; 2Ch 13:14; 14:11; Ps 20:7-9; 22:5 [i]Ps 26:1; Da 6:23
5:22 [j]2Ch 32:8 [k]2Ki 15:29; 17:6
5:23 [l]Dt 3:8,9; SS4:8
5:25 [m]Dt 32:15-18; 2Ki 17:7; 1Ch 9:1; 2Ch 26:16 [n]Ex 34:15
5:26 [o]2Ki 15:19 [p]2Ki 15:29 [q]2Ki 17:6; 18:11
6:1 [r]Ge 46:11; Ex 6:16; Nu 26:57; 1Ch 23:6
6:3 [s]Lev 10:1
6:8 [t]2Sa 8:17; 15:27; Ezr 7:2
6:10 [u]1Ki 4:2; 6:1; 2Ch 3:1; 26:17-18

Zadok the father of Shallum,
[13]Shallum the father of Hilkiah,[a]
Hilkiah the father of Azariah,
[14]Azariah the father of Seraiah,[b]
and Seraiah the father of Jehozadak.

[15]Jehozadak[c] was deported when the LORD sent Judah and Jerusalem into exile by the hand of Nebuchadnezzar.

[16]The sons of Levi:[d]
Gershon,[s] Kohath and Merari.[e]
[17]These are the names of the sons of Gershon:
Libni and Shimei.
[18]The sons of Kohath:
Amram, Izhar, Hebron and Uzziel.
[19]The sons of Merari:[f]
Mahli and Mushi.
These are the clans of the Levites listed according to their fathers:
[20]Of Gershon:
Libni his son, Jehath his son,
Zimmah his son, [21]Joah his son,
Iddo his son, Zerah his son
and Jeatherai his son.
[22]The descendants of Kohath:
Amminadab his son, Korah[g] his son,
Assir his son, [23]Elkanah his son,
Ebiasaph his son, Assir his son,
[24]Tahath his son, Uriel[h] his son,
Uzziah his son and Shaul his son.
[25]The descendants of Elkanah:
Amasai, Ahimoth,
[26]Elkanah his son,[t] Zophai his son,
Nahath his son, [27]Eliab his son,
Jeroham his son, Elkanah[i] his son
and Samuel[j] his son.[u]
[28]The sons of Samuel:
Joel[v][k] the firstborn
and Abijah the second son.
[29]The descendants of Merari:
Mahli, Libni his son,
Shimei his son, Uzzah his son,
[30]Shimea his son, Haggiah his son
and Asaiah his son.

The temple musicians.

[31]These are the men[l] David put in
charge of the music[m] in the house of the
LORD after the ark came to rest there.
[32]They ministered with music before
the tabernacle, the Tent of Meeting,
until Solomon built the temple of the
LORD in Jerusalem. They performed their
duties according to the regulations laid
down for them.

[33]Here are the men who served,
together with their sons:
From the Kohathites:
Heman,[n] the musician,
the son of Joel,[o] the son of Samuel,
[34]the son of Elkanah,[p] the son of Jeroham,
the son of Eliel, the son of Toah,
[35]the son of Zuph, the son of Elkanah,
the son of Mahath, the son of Amasai,
[36]the son of Elkanah, the son of Joel,
the son of Azariah, the son of Zephaniah,
[37]the son of Tahath, the son of Assir,
the son of Ebiasaph, the son of Korah,[q]
[38]the son of Izhar,[r] the son of Kohath,
the son of Levi, the son of Israel;
[39]and Heman's associate Asaph,[s] who served at his right hand:
Asaph son of Berekiah, the son of Shimea,[t]
[40]the son of Michael, the son of Baaseiah,[w]
the son of Malkijah, [41]the son of Ethni,
the son of Zerah, the son of Adaiah,

6:13 [a]2Ki 22:1-20; 2Ch 34:9; 35:8
6:14 [b]2Ki 25:18; Ezr 2:2; Ne 11:11
6:15 [c]2Ki 25:18; Ne 12:1; Hag 1:1,14; 2:2,4; Zec 6:11
6:16 [d]Ge 29:34; Ex 6:16; Nu 3:17-20 [e]Nu 26:57
6:19 [f]Ge 46:11; 1Ch 23:21; 24:26
6:22 [g]Ex 6:24
6:24 [h]1Ch 15:5
6:27 [i]1Sa 1:1 [j]1Sa 1:20
6:28 [k]ver 33; 1Sa 8:2
6:31 [l]1Ch 25:1; 2Ch 29:25-26; Ne 12:45 [m]1Ch 9:33; 15:19; Ezr 3:10; Ps 68:25
6:33 [n]1Ki 4:31; 1Ch 15:17; 25:1 [o]ver 28
6:34 [p]1Sa 1:1
6:37 [q]Ex 6:24
6:38 [r]Ex 6:21
6:39 [s]1Ch 25:1,9; 2Ch 29:13; Ne 11:17 [t]1Ch 15:17

[s]*16* Hebrew *Gershom,* a variant of *Gershon*; also in verses 17, 20, 43, 62 and 71 [t]*26* Some Hebrew manuscripts, Septuagint and Syriac; most Hebrew manuscripts *Ahimoth* [26]*and Elkanah. The sons of Elkanah:* [u]*27* Some Septuagint manuscripts (see also 1 Samuel 1:19,20 and 1 Chron. 6:33,34); Hebrew does not have *and Samuel his son.* [v]*28* Some Septuagint manuscripts and Syriac (see also 1 Samuel 8:2 and 1 Chron. 6:33); Hebrew does not have *Joel.* [w]*40* Most Hebrew manuscripts; some Hebrew manuscripts, one Septuagint manuscript and Syriac *Maaseiah*

42 the son of Ethan, the son of
Zimmah,
the son of Shimei, 43 the son of
Jahath,
the son of Gershon, the son of
Levi;
44 and from their associates, the Merarites, at his left hand:
Ethan son of Kishi, the son of
Abdi,
the son of Malluch, 45 the son of
Hashabiah,
the son of Amaziah, the son of
Hilkiah,
46 the son of Amzi, the son of Bani,
the son of Shemer, 47 the son of
Mahli,
the son of Mushi, the son of
Merari,
the son of Levi.

Descendants of Aaron and their settlements.

6:54-80pp—Jos 21:4-39

48 Their fellow Levites[a] were assigned
to all the other duties of the tabernacle,
the house of God. 49 But Aaron and his
descendants were the ones who presented offerings on the altar[b] of burnt
offering and on the altar of incense[c] in
connection with all that was done in the
Most Holy Place, making atonement for
Israel, in accordance with all that Moses
the servant of God had commanded.

50 These were the descendants of
Aaron:
Eleazar his son, Phinehas his son,
Abishua his son, 51 Bukki his son,
Uzzi his son, Zerahiah his son,
52 Meraioth his son, Amariah his
son,
Ahitub his son, 53 Zadok[d] his son
and Ahimaaz his son.

54 These were the locations of their
settlements[e] allotted as their territory
(they were assigned to the descendants
of Aaron who were from the Kohathite
clan, because the first lot was for them):
55 They were given Hebron in
Judah with its surrounding pasturelands. 56 But the fields and villages
around the city were given to Caleb
son of Jephunneh.[f]
57 So the descendants of Aaron
were given Hebron (a city of refuge),
and Libnah,[x][g] Jattir,[h] Eshtemoa,
58 Hilen, Debir,[i] 59 Ashan,[j] Juttah[y]
and Beth Shemesh, together with
their pasturelands. 60 And from the
tribe of Benjamin they were given
Gibeon,[z] Geba, Alemeth and Anathoth,[k] together with their pasturelands.
These towns, which were distributed among the Kohathite clans,
were thirteen in all.
61 The rest of Kohath's descendants
were allotted ten towns from the clans
of half the tribe of Manasseh.
62 The descendants of Gershon, clan by
clan, were allotted thirteen towns from
the tribes of Issachar, Asher and Naphtali,
and from the part of the tribe of Manasseh that is in Bashan.
63 The descendants of Merari, clan by
clan, were allotted twelve towns from
the tribes of Reuben, Gad and Zebulun.
64 So the Israelites gave the Levites
these towns[l] and their pasturelands.
65 From the tribes of Judah, Simeon and
Benjamin they allotted the previously
named towns.
66 Some of the Kohathite clans were
given as their territory towns from the
tribe of Ephraim.
67 In the hill country of Ephraim
they were given Shechem (a city of
refuge), and Gezer,[a][m] 68 Jokmeam,[n]
Beth Horon,[o] 69 Aijalon[p] and Gath
Rimmon,[q] together with their pasturelands.
70 And from half the tribe of
Manasseh the Israelites gave Aner
and Bileam, together with their pasturelands, to the rest of the Kohathite clans.

6:48 [a] 1Ch 23:32
6:49 [b] Ex 27:1-8 [c] Ex 30:1-7,10; 2Ch 26:18
6:53 [d] 2Sa 8:17
6:54 [e] Nu 31:10
6:56 [f] Jos 14:13; 15:13
6:57 [g] Nu 33:20 [h] Jos 15:48
6:58 [i] Jos 10:3
6:59 [j] Jos 15:42
6:60 [k] Jer 1:1
6:64 [l] Nu 35:1-8; Jos 21:3, 41-42
6:67 [m] Jos 10:33
6:68 [n] 1Ki 4:12 [o] Jos 10:10
6:69 [p] Jos 10:12 [q] Jos 19:45

[x] *57* See Joshua 21:13; Hebrew *given the cities of refuge: Hebron, Libnah.* [y] *59* Syriac (see also Septuagint and Joshua 21:16); Hebrew does not have *Juttah.* [z] *60* See Joshua 21:17; Hebrew does not have *Gibeon.* [a] *67* See Joshua 21:21; Hebrew *given the cities of refuge: Shechem, Gezer.*

71The Gershonites[a] received the following:
From the clan of the half-tribe of
Manasseh
they received Golan in Bashan[b]
and also Ashtaroth, together with
their pasturelands;
72from the tribe of Issachar
they received Kedesh, Daberath,[c]
73Ramoth and Anem, together
with their pasturelands;
74from the tribe of Asher
they received Mashal, Abdon,[d]
75Hukok[e] and Rehob,[f] together
with their pasturelands;
76and from the tribe of Naphtali
they received Kedesh in Galilee,
Hammon[g] and Kiriathaim,[h] together with their pasturelands.

77The Merarites (the rest of the
Levites) received the following:
From the tribe of Zebulun
they received Jokneam, Kartah,[b]
Rimmono and Tabor, together
with their pasturelands;
78from the tribe of Reuben across the
Jordan east of Jericho
they received Bezer[i] in the
desert, Jahzah, 79Kedemoth[j] and
Mephaath, together with their
pasturelands;
80and from the tribe of Gad
they received Ramoth in Gilead,[k]
Mahanaim,[l] 81Heshbon and Jazer,[m] together with their pasturelands.[n]

Issachar.

7 The sons of Issachar:[o]
Tola, Puah,[p] Jashub and Shimron—four in all.
2The sons of Tola:
Uzzi, Rephaiah, Jeriel, Jahmai, Ib-
sam and Samuel—heads of their
families. During the reign of
David, the descendants of Tola
listed as fighting men in their genealogy numbered 22,600.
3The son of Uzzi:
Izrahiah.
The sons of Izrahiah:
Michael, Obadiah, Joel and Isshiah. All five of them were chiefs.
4According to their family genealogy, they had 36,000 men ready
for battle, for they had many
wives and children.
5The relatives who were fighting
men belonging to all the clans of
Issachar, as listed in their genealogy, were 87,000 in all.

Benjamin.

6Three sons of Benjamin:[q]
Bela, Beker and Jediael.
7The sons of Bela:
Ezbon, Uzzi, Uzziel, Jerimoth
and Iri, heads of families—five
in all. Their genealogical record
listed 22,034 fighting men.
8The sons of Beker:
Zemirah, Joash, Eliezer, Elioenai,
Omri, Jeremoth, Abijah, Anathoth
and Alemeth. All these were the
sons of Beker. 9Their genealogical record listed the heads of families and 20,200 fighting men.
10The son of Jediael:
Bilhan.
The sons of Bilhan:
Jeush, Benjamin, Ehud, Kenaanah, Zethan, Tarshish and
Ahishahar. 11All these sons of
Jediael were heads of families.
There were 17,200 fighting men
ready to go out to war.
12The Shuppites and Huppites were
the descendants of Ir, and the
Hushites the descendants of
Aher.

Naphtali.

13The sons of Naphtali:[r]
Jahziel, Guni, Jezer and Shillem[c]—the descendants of Bilhah.

6:71 [a]1Ch 23:7 [b]Jos 20:8
6:72 [c]Jos 19:12
6:74 [d]Jos 19:28
6:75 [e]Jos 19:34 [f]Nu 13:21
6:76 [g]Jos 19:28 [h]Nu 32:37
6:78 [i]Jos 20:8
6:79 [j]Dt 2:26
6:80 [k]Jos 20:8 [l]Ge 32:2
6:81 [m]Nu 21:32 [n]2Ch 11:14
7:1 [o]Ge 30:18; Nu 26:23 [p]Ge 46:13
7:6 [q]Ge 46:21; Nu 26:38; 1Ch 8:1-40
7:13 [r]Ge 30:8; 46:24

b *77* See Septuagint and Joshua 21:34; Hebrew does not have *Jokneam, Kartah.* c *13* Some Hebrew and Septuagint manuscripts (see also Gen. 46:24 and Num. 26:49); most Hebrew manuscripts *Shallum*

Manasseh.

14The descendants of Manasseh:[a]
Asriel was his descendant
through his Aramean concubine.
She gave birth to Makir the father
of Gilead.[b] 15Makir took a wife from
among the Huppites and Shuppites.
His sister's name was Maacah.
Another descendant was named
Zelophehad,[c] who had only daughters.
16Makir's wife Maacah gave birth
to a son and named him Peresh. His
brother was named Sheresh, and
his sons were Ulam and Rakem.
17The son of Ulam:
Bedan.
These were the sons of Gilead[d]
son of Makir, the son of Manasseh. 18His sister Hammoleketh
gave birth to Ishhod, Abiezer[e]
and Mahlah.
19The sons of Shemida were:
Ahian, Shechem, Likhi and Ani-
am.

Ephraim.

20The descendants of Ephraim:[f]
Shuthelah, Bered his son,
Tahath his son, Eleadah his son,
Tahath his son, 21Zabad his son
and Shuthelah his son.
Ezer and Elead were killed by
the native-born men of Gath, when
they went down to seize their
livestock. 22Their father Ephraim
mourned for them many days, and
his relatives came to comfort him.
23Then he lay with his wife again,
and she became pregnant and gave
birth to a son. He named him Beriah,[d] because there had been misfortune in his family. 24His daughter
was Sheerah, who built Lower and
Upper Beth Horon[g] as well as Uzzen
Sheerah.
25Rephah was his son, Resheph his
son,[e]
Telah his son, Tahan his son,
26Ladan his son, Ammihud his son,

7:14 [a]Ge 41:51; Jos 17:1; 1Ch 5:23 [b]Nu 26:30
7:15 [c]Nu 26:33; 36:1-12
7:17 [d]Nu 26:30; 1Sa 12:11
7:18 [e]Jos 17:2
7:20 [f]Ge 41:52; Nu 1:33; 26:35
7:24 [g]Jos 10:10; 16:3,5
7:28 [h]Jos 10:33; 16:7
7:29 [i]Jos 17:11 [j]Jos 11:2
7:30 [k]Ge 46:17; Nu 1:40; 26:44

Elishama his son, 27Nun his son
and Joshua his son.
28Their lands and settlements included Bethel and its surrounding villages,
Naaran to the east, Gezer[h] and its villages to the west, and Shechem and its
villages all the way to Ayyah and its villages. 29Along the borders of Manasseh
were Beth Shan,[i] Taanach, Megiddo and
Dor,[j] together with their villages. The
descendants of Joseph son of Israel lived
in these towns.

Asher.

30The sons of Asher:[k]
Imnah, Ishvah, Ishvi and Beriah.
Their sister was Serah.
31The sons of Beriah:
Heber and Malkiel, who was the
father of Birzaith.
32Heber was the father of Japhlet, Shomer and Hotham and of their sister Shua.
33The sons of Japhlet:
Pasach, Bimhal and Ashvath.
These were Japhlet's sons.
34The sons of Shomer:
Ahi, Rohgah,[f] Hubbah and Aram.
35The sons of his brother Helem:
Zophah, Imna, Shelesh and Amal.
36The sons of Zophah:
Suah, Harnepher, Shual, Beri, Im-
rah, 37Bezer, Hod, Shamma, Shil-
shah, Ithran[g] and Beera.
38The sons of Jether:
Jephunneh, Pispah and Ara.
39The sons of Ulla:
Arah, Hanniel and Rizia.
40All these were descendants of Asher—heads of families, choice men, brave
warriors and outstanding leaders. The
number of men ready for battle, as listed in their genealogy, was 26,000.

d *23* *Beriah* sounds like the Hebrew for *misfortune.* e *25* Some Septuagint manuscripts; Hebrew does not have *his son.* f *34* Or *of his brother Shomer: Rohgah* g *37* Possibly a variant of *Jether*

Family records of Benjamin.

8:28-38pp— 1Ch 9:34-44

8 Benjamin[a] was the father of Bela his
firstborn,
Ashbel the second son, Aharah
the third,
2Nohah the fourth and Rapha the
fifth.
3The sons of Bela were:
Addar,[b] Gera, Abihud,[h] 4Abishua,
Naaman, Ahoah,[c] 5Gera, She-
phuphan and Huram.
6These were the descendants of
Ehud,[d] who were heads of families of those living in Geba and
were deported to Manahath:
7Naaman, Ahijah, and Gera, who
deported them and who was the
father of Uzza and Ahihud.
8Sons were born to Shaharaim in
Moab after he had divorced his
wives Hushim and Baara. 9By his
wife Hodesh he had Jobab, Zibia,
Mesha, Malcam, 10Jeuz, Sakia
and Mirmah. These were his
sons, heads of families. 11By Hushim he had Abitub and Elpaal.
12The sons of Elpaal:
Eber, Misham, Shemed (who
built Ono[e] and Lod with its surrounding villages), 13and Beriah
and Shema, who were heads of
families of those living in Aijalon[f] and who drove out the
inhabitants of Gath.[g]
14Ahio, Shashak, Jeremoth, 15Zeba-
diah, Arad, Eder, 16Michael, Ish-
pah and Joha were the sons of
Beriah.
17Zebadiah, Meshullam, Hizki, Heber,
18Ishmerai, Izliah and Jobab were
the sons of Elpaal.
19Jakim, Zicri, Zabdi, 20Elienai, Zillethai, Eliel, 21Adaiah, Beraiah
and Shimrath were the sons of
Shimei.
22Ishpan, Eber, Eliel, 23Abdon, Zicri,
Hanan, 24Hananiah, Elam, An-
thothijah, 25Iphdeiah and Penuel
were the sons of Shashak.
26Shamsherai, Shehariah, Athaliah,
27Jaareshiah, Elijah and Zicri were
the sons of Jeroham.
28All these were heads of families,
chiefs as listed in their genealogy, and
they lived in Jerusalem.

29Jeiel[i] the father[j] of Gibeon lived in
Gibeon.[h]
His wife's name was Maacah,
30and his firstborn son was Abdon, followed by Zur, Kish, Baal,
Ner,[k] Nadab, 31Gedor, Ahio, Ze-
ker 32and Mikloth, who was the
father of Shimeah. They too lived
near their relatives in Jerusalem.
33Ner[i] was the father of Kish,[j] Kish
the father of Saul[k], and Saul the
father of Jonathan, Malki-Shua,
Abinadab and Esh-Baal.[l][l]
34The son of Jonathan:[m]
Merib-Baal,[m][n] who was the father
of Micah.
35The sons of Micah:
Pithon, Melech, Tarea and Ahaz.
36Ahaz was the father of Jehoaddah, Jehoaddah was the father
of Alemeth, Azmaveth and Zimri,
and Zimri was the father of Moza.
37Moza was the father of Binea;
Raphah was his son, Eleasah his
son and Azel his son.
38Azel had six sons, and these were
their names:
Azrikam, Bokeru, Ishmael, Shea-
riah, Obadiah and Hanan. All
these were the sons of Azel.
39The sons of his brother Eshek:
Ulam his firstborn, Jeush the second son and Eliphelet the third.
40The sons of Ulam were brave
warriors who could handle the
bow. They had many sons and
grandsons—150 in all.
All these were the descendants of
Benjamin.[o]

8:1 *a* Ge 46:21; 1Ch 7:6
8:3 *b* Ge 46:21
8:4 *c* 2Sa 23:9
8:6 *d* Jdg 3:12-30; 1Ch 2:52
8:12 *e* Ezr 2:33; Ne 6:2; 7:37; 11:35
8:13 *f* Jos 10:12 *g* Jos 11:22
8:29 *h* Jos 9:3
8:33 *i* 1Sa 28:19 *j* 1Sa 9:1 *k* 1Sa 14:49 *l* 2Sa 2:8
8:34 *m* 2Sa 9:12 *n* 2Sa 4:4
8:40 *o* Nu 26:38

h3 Or *Gera the father of Ehud* i29 Some Septuagint manuscripts (see also 1 Chron. 9:35); Hebrew does not have *Jeiel.* j29 *Father* may mean *civic leader* or *military leader.* k30 Some Septuagint manuscripts (see also 1 Chron. 9:36); Hebrew does not have *Ner.* l33 Also known as *Ish-Bosheth* m34 Also known as *Mephibosheth*

9 All Israel was listed in the genealogies recorded in the book of the
kings of Israel.

Those returning from Babylonian captivity.

9:1-17pp— Ne 11:3-19

The people of Judah were taken captive to Babylon because of their unfaithfulness.[a] 2Now the first to resettle on
their own property in their own towns[b]
were some Israelites, priests, Levites
and temple servants.[c]
3Those from Judah, from Benjamin,
and from Ephraim and Manasseh who
lived in Jerusalem were:
4Uthai son of Ammihud, the son of
Omri, the son of Imri, the son of
Bani, a descendant of Perez son
of Judah.[d]
5Of the Shilonites:
Asaiah the firstborn and his sons.
6Of the Zerahites:
Jeuel.
The people from Judah numbered 690.
7Of the Benjamites:
Sallu son of Meshullam, the son
of Hodaviah, the son of Hassenuah;
8Ibneiah son of Jeroham; Elah son
of Uzzi, the son of Micri; and Meshullam son of Shephatiah, the
son of Reuel, the son of Ibnijah.
9The people from Benjamin, as listed in their genealogy, numbered
956. All these men were heads of
their families.
10Of the priests:
Jedaiah; Jehoiarib; Jakin;
11Azariah son of Hilkiah, the son of
Meshullam, the son of Zadok, the
son of Meraioth, the son of Ahitub, the official in charge of the
house of God;
12Adaiah son of Jeroham, the son of
Pashhur,[e] the son of Malkijah; and
Maasai son of Adiel, the son of
Jahzerah, the son of Meshullam,
the son of Meshillemith, the son
of Immer.

9:1 [a]1Ch 5:25
9:2 [b]Jos 9:27; Ezr 2:70 [c]Ezr 2:43,58; 8:20; Ne 7:60
9:4 [d]Ge 38:29; 46:12
9:12 [e]Ezr 2:38; 10:22; Ne 10:3; Jer 21:1; 38:1
9:15 [f]2Ch 20:14; Ne 11:22
9:16 [g]Ne 12:28
9:17 [h]ver 22; 1Ch 26:1; 2Ch 8:14; 31:14; Ezr 2:42; Ne 7:45
9:18 [i]1Ch 26:14; Eze 43:1; 46:1
9:19 [j]Jer 35:4
9:20 [k]Nu 25:7-13
9:21 [l]1Ch 26:2,14
9:22 [m]ver 17; 1Ch 26:1-2; 2Ch 31:15,18 [n]1Sa 9:9

13The priests, who were heads of
families, numbered 1,760. They
were able men, responsible for
ministering in the house of God.
14Of the Levites:
Shemaiah son of Hasshub, the
son of Azrikam, the son of Hashabiah, a Merarite; 15Bakbakkar,
Heresh, Galal and Mattaniah[f] son
of Mica, the son of Zicri, the son
of Asaph; 16Obadiah son of Shemaiah, the son of Galal, the son
of Jeduthun; and Berekiah son
of Asa, the son of Elkanah, who
lived in the villages of the
Netophathites.[g]

Duties of the Levites.

17The gatekeepers:[h]
Shallum, Akkub, Talmon, Ahiman and their brothers, Shallum
their chief 18being stationed at
the King's Gate[i] on the east, up
to the present time. These were
the gatekeepers belonging to the
camp of the Levites. 19Shallum[j]
son of Kore, the son of Ebiasaph,
the son of Korah, and his fellow
gatekeepers from his family (the
Korahites) were responsible for
guarding the thresholds of the
Tent[n] just as their fathers had
been responsible for guarding the
entrance to the dwelling of the
LORD. 20In earlier times Phinehas[k] son of Eleazar was in charge
of the gatekeepers, and the LORD
was with him. 21Zechariah[l] son of
Meshelemiah was the gatekeeper at the entrance to the Tent of
Meeting.
22Altogether, those chosen to be gatekeepers[m] at the thresholds numbered
212. They were registered by genealogy
in their villages. The gatekeepers had
been assigned to their positions of trust
by David and Samuel the seer.[n] 23They
and their descendants were in charge of
guarding the gates of the house of the
LORD—the house called the Tent. 24The

[n] *19* That is, the temple; also in verses 21 and 23

gatekeepers were on the four sides:
east, west, north and south. 25Their
brothers in their villages had to come
from time to time and share their duties
for seven-day[a] periods. 26But the four
principal gatekeepers, who were Levites,
were entrusted with the responsibility
for the rooms and treasuries[b] in the
house of God. 27They would spend the
night stationed around the house of
God,[c] because they had to guard it; and
they had charge of the key[d] for opening
it each morning.
28Some of them were in charge of the
articles used in the temple service; they
counted them when they were brought
in and when they were taken out.
29Others were assigned to take care of
the furnishings and all the other articles
of the sanctuary,[e] as well as the flour and
wine, and the oil, incense and spices.
30But some[f] of the priests took care of
mixing the spices. 31A Levite named
Mattithiah, the firstborn son of Shallum
the Korahite, was entrusted with the
responsibility for baking the offering
bread. 32Some of their Kohathite brothers were in charge of preparing for every
Sabbath the bread set out on the table.[g]
33Those who were musicians,[h] heads
of Levite families, stayed in the rooms of
the temple and were exempt from other
duties because they were responsible
for the work day and night.[i]
34All these were heads of Levite families, chiefs as listed in their genealogy,
and they lived in Jerusalem.

Family records of Saul and Jonathan.

9:34-44pp— 1Ch 8:28-38

35Jeiel[j] the father[o] of Gibeon lived in
Gibeon.
His wife's name was Maacah,
36and his firstborn son was Abdon, followed by Zur, Kish, Baal,
Ner, Nadab, 37Gedor, Ahio, Zechariah and Mikloth. 38Mikloth was
the father of Shimeam. They too
lived near their relatives in
Jerusalem.

9:25 [a]2Ki 11:5; 2Ch 23:8
9:26 [b]1Ch 26:22
9:27 [c]Nu 3:38; 1Ch 23:30-32 [d]Isa 22:22
9:29 [e]Nu 3:28; 1Ch 23:29
9:30 [f]Ex 30:23-25
9:32 [g]Lev 24:5-8; 1Ch 23:29; 2Ch 13:11
9:33 [h]1Ch 6:31; 25:1-31 [i]Ps 134:1
9:35 [j]1Ch 8:29
9:39 [k]1Ch 8:33 [l]1Sa 9:1 [m]1Sa 13:22 [n]2Sa 2:8
9:40 [o]2Sa 4:4

39Ner[k] was the father of Kish,[l] Kish
the father of Saul, and Saul the
father of Jonathan,[m] Malki-Shua,
Abinadab and Esh-Baal.[p][n]
40The son of Jonathan:
Merib-Baal,[q][o] who was the father
of Micah.
41The sons of Micah:
Pithon, Melech, Tahrea and Ahaz.[r]
42Ahaz was the father of Jadah, Jadah[s] was the father of Alemeth,
Azmaveth and Zimri, and Zimri
was the father of Moza. 43Moza
was the father of Binea; Rephaiah
was his son, Eleasah his son and
Azel his son.
44Azel had six sons, and these were
their names:
Azrikam, Bokeru, Ishmael, Sheari-
ah, Obadiah and Hanan. These
were the sons of Azel.

Saul takes his life after his sons are killed.

10:1-12pp— 1Sa 31:1-13; 2Sa 1:4-12

10 Now the Philistines fought against
Israel; the Israelites fled before
them, and many fell slain on Mount
Gilboa. 2The Philistines pressed hard
after Saul and his sons, and they killed
his sons Jonathan, Abinadab and Malki-
Shua. 3The fighting grew fierce around
Saul, and when the archers overtook
him, they wounded him.
4Saul said to his armor-bearer, "Draw
your sword and run me through, or these
uncircumcised fellows will come and
abuse me."
But his armor-bearer was terrified and
would not do it; so Saul took his own
sword and fell on it. 5When the armor-
bearer saw that Saul was dead, he too
fell on his sword and died. 6So Saul and
his three sons died, and all his house
died together.

o35 *Father* may mean *civic leader* or *military leader.*
p39 Also known as *Ish-Bosheth*
q40 Also known as *Mephibosheth*
r41 Vulgate and Syriac (see also Septuagint and 1 Chron. 8:35); Hebrew does not have *and Ahaz.*
s42 Some Hebrew manuscripts and Septuagint (see also 1 Chron. 8:36); most Hebrew manuscripts *Jarah, Jarah*

7When all the Israelites in the valley
saw that the army had fled and that Saul
and his sons had died, they abandoned
their towns and fled. And the Philistines
came and occupied them.
8The next day, when the Philistines
came to strip the dead, they found Saul
and his sons fallen on Mount Gilboa.
9They stripped him and took his head
and his armor, and sent messengers
throughout the land of the Philistines
to proclaim the news among their idols
and their people. 10They put his armor
in the temple of their gods and hung up
his head in the temple of Dagon.[a]
11When all the inhabitants of Jabesh
Gilead[b] heard of everything the Philistines had done to Saul, 12all their valiant
men went and took the bodies of Saul
and his sons and brought them to Jabesh.
Then they buried their bones under the
great tree in Jabesh, and they fasted sev-
en days.
13Saul died[c] because he was unfaithful[d] to the LORD; he did not keep[e] the
word of the LORD and even consulted a
medium[f] for guidance, 14and did not
inquire of the LORD. So the LORD put him
to death and turned[g] the kingdom[h] over
to David son of Jesse.

David is anointed king over Israel.

11:1-3pp— 2Sa 5:1-3

11 All Israel[i] came together to David
at Hebron[j] and said, "We are your
own flesh and blood. 2In the past, even
while Saul was king, you were the one
who led Israel on their military campaigns.[k] And the LORD your God said to
you, 'You will shepherd[l] my people Israel,
and you will become their ruler.[m]'"
3When all the elders of Israel had
come to King David at Hebron, he made
a compact with them at Hebron before
the LORD, and they anointed[n] David king
over Israel, as the LORD had promised
through Samuel.

David conquers Jerusalem.

11:4-9pp— 2Sa 5:6-10

4David and all the Israelites marched
to Jerusalem (that is, Jebus). The Jebusites[o] who lived there 5said to David,
"You will not get in here." Nevertheless,
David captured the fortress of Zion, the
City of David.
6David had said, "Whoever leads the
attack on the Jebusites will become com-
mander-in-chief." Joab[p] son of Zeruiah
went up first, and so he received the
command.
7David then took up residence in the
fortress, and so it was called the City of
David. 8He built up the city around it,
from the supporting terraces[t][q] to the
surrounding wall, while Joab restored
the rest of the city. 9And David became
more and more powerful,[r] because the
LORD Almighty was with him.

David's mighty men.

11:10-41pp— 2Sa 23:8-39

10These were the chiefs of David's
mighty men—they, together with all
Israel,[s] gave his kingship strong support
to extend it over the whole land, as the
LORD had promised[t]— 11this is the list
of David's mighty men:[u]
Jashobeam,[u] a Hacmonite, was chief of
the officers[v]; he raised his spear against
three hundred men, whom he killed in
one encounter.
12Next to him was Eleazar son of
Dodai the Ahohite, one of the three
mighty men. 13He was with David at
Pas Dammim when the Philistines gathered there for battle. At a place where
there was a field full of barley, the troops
fled from the Philistines. 14But they took
their stand in the middle of the field.
They defended it and struck the Philistines down, and the LORD brought about
a great victory.[v]
15Three of the thirty chiefs came
down to David to the rock at the cave of
Adullam, while a band of Philistines was
encamped in the Valley[w] of Rephaim.
16At that time David was in the stronghold,[x] and the Philistine garrison was at

10:10 [a]Jdg 16:23
10:11 [b]Jdg 21:8
10:13 [c]2Sa 1:1 [d]1Sa 15:23; 1Ch 5:25 [e]1Sa 13:13 [f]Lev 19:31; 20:6; Dt 18:9-14; 1Sa 28:7
10:14 [g]1Ch 12:23 [h]1Sa 13:14; 15:28
11:1 [i]1Ch 9:1 [j]Ge 13:18; 23:19
11:2 [k]1Sa 18:5,16 [l]Ps 78:71; Mt 2:6 [m]1Ch 5:2
11:3 [n]1Sa 16:1-13
11:4 [o]Ge 10:16; 15:18-21; Jos 3:10; 15:8; Jdg 1:21; 19:10
11:6 [p]2Sa 2:13; 8:16
11:8 [q]2Sa 5:9; 2Ch 32:5
11:9 [r]2Sa 3:1; Est 9:4
11:10 [s]ver 1 [t]ver 3; 1Ch 12:23
11:11 [u]2Sa 17:10
11:14 [v]Ex 14:30; 1Sa 11:13
11:15 [w]1Ch 14:9; Isa 17:5
11:16 [x]2Sa 5:17

t *8* Or *the Millo* u *11* Possibly a variant of *Jashob-Baal* v *11* Or *Thirty*; some Septuagint manuscripts *Three* (see also 2 Samuel 23:8)

Bethlehem. 17David longed for water
and said, "Oh, that someone would get
me a drink of water from the well near
the gate of Bethlehem!" 18So the Three
broke through the Philistine lines, drew
water from the well near the gate of
Bethlehem and carried it back to David.
But he refused to drink it; instead, he
poured[a] it out before the LORD. 19"God
forbid that I should do this!" he said.
"Should I drink the blood of these men
who went at the risk of their lives?"
Because they risked their lives to bring
it back, David would not drink it.

Such were the exploits of the three
mighty men.

20Abishai[b] the brother of Joab was
chief of the Three. He raised his spear
against three hundred men, whom he
killed, and so he became as famous as
the Three. 21He was doubly honored
above the Three and became their commander, even though he was not included among them.

22Benaiah son of Jehoiada was a valiant fighter from Kabzeel,[c] who performed great exploits. He struck down
two of Moab's best men. He also went
down into a pit on a snowy day and
killed a lion.[d] 23And he struck down an
Egyptian who was seven and a half feet[w]
tall. Although the Egyptian had a spear
like a weaver's rod[e] in his hand, Benaiah
went against him with a club. He
snatched the spear from the Egyptian's
hand and killed him with his own spear.
24Such were the exploits of Benaiah son
of Jehoiada; he too was as famous as the
three mighty men. 25He was held in
greater honor than any of the Thirty, but
he was not included among the Three.
And David put him in charge of his
bodyguard.

26The mighty men were:
Asahel[f] the brother of Joab,
Elhanan son of Dodo from Bethlehem,
27Shammoth[g] the Harorite,
Helez the Pelonite,
28Ira son of Ikkesh from Tekoa,
Abiezer[h] from Anathoth,
29Sibbecai[i] the Hushathite,
Ilai the Ahohite,
30Maharai the Netophathite,
Heled son of Baanah the Netophathite,
31Ithai son of Ribai from Gibeah
in Benjamin,
Benaiah[j] the Pirathonite,[k]
32Hurai from the ravines of Gaash,
Abiel the Arbathite,
33Azmaveth the Baharumite,
Eliahba the Shaalbonite,
34the sons of Hashem the Gizonite,
Jonathan son of Shagee the Hararite,
35Ahiam son of Sacar the Hararite,
Eliphal son of Ur,
36Hepher the Mekerathite,
Ahijah the Pelonite,
37Hezro the Carmelite,
Naarai son of Ezbai,
38Joel the brother of Nathan,
Mibhar son of Hagri,
39Zelek the Ammonite,
Naharai the Berothite, the armor-
bearer of Joab son of Zeruiah,
40Ira the Ithrite,
Gareb the Ithrite,
41Uriah[l] the Hittite,
Zabad[m] son of Ahlai,
42Adina son of Shiza the Reubenite,
who was chief of the Reubenites, and the thirty with him,
43Hanan son of Maacah,
Joshaphat the Mithnite,
44Uzzia the Ashterathite,[n]
Shama and Jeiel the sons of
Hotham the Aroerite,
45Jediael son of Shimri,
his brother Joha the Tizite,
46Eliel the Mahavite,
Jeribai and Joshaviah the sons of
Elnaam,
Ithmah the Moabite,
47Eliel, Obed and Jaasiel the Mezo-
baite.

Warriors join David at Ziklag.

12 These were the men who came
to David at Ziklag,[o] while he was

11:18 [a]Dt 12:16
11:20 [b]1Sa 26:6
11:22 [c]Jos 15:21 [d]1Sa 17:36
11:23 [e]1Sa 17:7
11:26 [f]2Sa 2:18
11:27 [g]1Ch 27:8
11:28 [h]1Ch 27:12
11:29 [i]2Sa 21:18
11:31 [j]1Ch 27:14 [k]Jdg 12:13
11:41 [l]2Sa 11:6 [m]1Ch 2:36
11:44 [n]Dt 1:4
12:1 [o]Jos 15:31; 1Sa 27:2-6

w23 Hebrew *five cubits* (about 2.3 meters)

banished from the presence of Saul son
of Kish (they were among the warriors
who helped him in battle; 2they were
armed with bows and were able to
shoot arrows or to sling stones right-
handed or left-handed;[a] they were kinsmen of Saul[b] from the tribe of Benjamin):

3Ahiezer their chief and Joash the
sons of Shemaah the Gibeathite;
Jeziel and Pelet the sons of Azmaveth; Beracah, Jehu the Anathothite, 4and Ishmaiah the Gibeonite, a
mighty man among the Thirty, who
was a leader of the Thirty; Jeremiah, Jahaziel, Johanan, Jozabad the
Gederathite,[c] 5Eluzai, Jerimoth, Be-
aliah, Shemariah and Shephatiah
the Haruphite; 6Elkanah, Isshiah,
Azarel, Joezer and Jashobeam the
Korahites; 7and Joelah and Zebadiah
the sons of Jeroham from Gedor.[d]

8Some Gadites[e] defected to David at
his stronghold in the desert. They were
brave warriors, ready for battle and able
to handle the shield and spear. Their
faces were the faces of lions,[f] and they
were as swift as gazelles[g] in the mountains.

9Ezer was the chief,
Obadiah the second in command,
Eliab the third,
10Mishmannah the fourth, Jeremiah
the fifth,
11Attai the sixth, Eliel the seventh,
12Johanan the eighth, Elzabad the
ninth,
13Jeremiah the tenth and Macbannai
the eleventh.

14These Gadites were army commanders; the least was a match for a
hundred,[h] and the greatest for a thousand.[i] 15It was they who crossed the
Jordan in the first month when it was
overflowing all its banks,[j] and they put
to flight everyone living in the valleys,
to the east and to the west.

16Other Benjamites[k] and some men
from Judah also came to David in his
stronghold. 17David went out to meet
them and said to them, "If you have
come to me in peace, to help me, I am

12:2 [a]Jdg 3:15; 20:16 [b]2Sa 3:19
12:4 [c]Jos 15:36
12:7 [d]Jos 15:58
12:8 [e]Ge 30:11 [f]2Sa 17:10 [g]2Sa 2:18
12:14 [h]Lev 26:8 [i]Dt 32:30
12:15 [j]Jos 3:15
12:16 [k]2Sa 3:19
12:18 [l]Jdg 3:10; 6:34; 1Ch 28:12; 2Ch 15:1; 20:14; 24:20 [m]2Sa 17:25 [n]1Sa 25:5-6
12:19 [o]1Sa 29:2-11
12:20 [p]1Sa 27:6
12:23 [q]2Sa 2:3-4 [r]1Ch 10:14 [s]1Sa 16:1; 1Ch 11:10
12:28 [t]2Sa 8:17; 1Ch 6:8; 15:11; 16:39; 27:17
12:29 [u]2Sa 3:19 [v]2Sa 2:8-9

ready to have you unite with me. But if
you have come to betray me to my enemies when my hands are free from violence, may the God of our fathers see it
and judge you."

18Then the Spirit[l] came upon Amasai,[m] chief of the Thirty, and he said:

"We are yours, O David!
We are with you, O son of Jesse!
Success,[n] success to you,
and success to those who help you,
for your God will help you."

So David received them and made
them leaders of his raiding bands.

19Some of the men of Manasseh
defected to David when he went with
the Philistines to fight against Saul. (He
and his men did not help the Philistines
because, after consultation, their rulers
sent him away. They said, "It will cost
us our heads if he deserts to his master
Saul.")[o] 20When David went to Ziklag,[p]
these were the men of Manasseh who
defected to him: Adnah, Jozabad, Jediael,
Michael, Jozabad, Elihu and Zillethai,
leaders of units of a thousand in Manasseh. 21They helped David against raiding bands, for all of them were brave
warriors, and they were commanders
in his army. 22Day after day men came
to help David, until he had a great army,
like the army of God.[x]

Warriors join David at Hebron.

23These are the numbers of the men
armed for battle who came to David at
Hebron[q] to turn[r] Saul's kingdom over to
him, as the LORD had said:[s]

24men of Judah, carrying shield and
spear—6,800 armed for battle;
25men of Simeon, warriors ready for
battle—7,100;
26men of Levi—4,600, 27including
Jehoiada, leader of the family of
Aaron, with 3,700 men, 28and
Zadok,[t] a brave young warrior,
with 22 officers from his family;
29men of Benjamin,[u] Saul's kinsmen—
3,000, most[v] of whom had

[x]22 Or *a great and mighty army*

remained loyal to Saul's house
until then;
30 men of Ephraim, brave warriors,
famous in their own clans—
20,800;
31 men of half the tribe of Manasseh,
designated by name to come and
make David king—18,000;
32 men of Issachar, who understood
the times and knew what Israel
should do[a]—200 chiefs, with all
their relatives under their command;
33 men of Zebulun, experienced soldiers prepared for battle with
every type of weapon, to help
David with undivided loyalty—
50,000;
34 men of Naphtali—1,000 officers,
together with 37,000 men carrying shields and spears;
35 men of Dan, ready for battle—
28,600;
36 men of Asher, experienced soldiers
prepared for battle—40,000;
37 and from east of the Jordan, men of
Reuben, Gad and the half-tribe of
Manasseh, armed with every
type of weapon—120,000.

38 All these were fighting men who
volunteered to serve in the ranks. They
came to Hebron fully determined to
make David king over all Israel.[b] All the
rest of the Israelites were also of one
mind to make David king. 39 The men
spent three days there with David, eating and drinking,[c] for their families had
supplied provisions for them. 40 Also,
their neighbors from as far away as Issachar, Zebulun and Naphtali came bringing food on donkeys, camels, mules and
oxen. There were plentiful supplies[d] of
flour, fig cakes, raisin[e] cakes, wine, oil,
cattle and sheep, for there was joy[f] in
Israel.

Uzzah is struck down for touching the ark.

13:1-14pp— 2Sa 6:1-11

13 David conferred with each of
his officers, the commanders of
thousands and commanders of hundreds. 2 He then said to the whole
assembly of Israel, "If it seems good to
you and if it is the will of the LORD our
God, let us send word far and wide to
the rest of our brothers throughout the
territories of Israel, and also to the
priests and Levites who are with them
in their towns and pasturelands, to come
and join us. 3 Let us bring the ark of our
God back to us,[g] for we did not inquire[h]
of[y] it[z] during the reign of Saul." 4 The
whole assembly agreed to do this,
because it seemed right to all the people.

5 So David assembled all the Israelites,[i]
from the Shihor River[j] in Egypt to Lebo[a]
Hamath,[k] to bring the ark of God from
Kiriath Jearim.[l] 6 David and all the
Israelites with him went to Baalah[m] of
Judah (Kiriath Jearim) to bring up from
there the ark of God the LORD, who is
enthroned between the cherubim[n]—the
ark that is called by the Name.

7 They moved the ark of God from
Abinadab's[o] house on a new cart, with
Uzzah and Ahio guiding it. 8 David and
all the Israelites were celebrating with
all their might before God, with songs
and with harps, lyres, tambourines, cymbals and trumpets.[p]

9 When they came to the threshing
floor of Kidon, Uzzah reached out his
hand to steady the ark, because the oxen
stumbled. 10 The LORD's anger[q] burned
against Uzzah, and he struck him down[r]
because he had put his hand on the ark.
So he died there before God.

11 Then David was angry because the
LORD's wrath had broken out against
Uzzah, and to this day that place is
called Perez Uzzah.[b][s]

12 David was afraid of God that day
and asked, "How can I ever bring the
ark of God to me?" 13 He did not take
the ark to be with him in the City of
David. Instead, he took it aside to the
house of Obed-Edom[t] the Gittite. 14 The
ark of God remained with the family of
Obed-Edom in his house for three

12:32 [a]Est 1:13
12:38 [b]2Sa 5:1-3; 1Ch 9:1
12:39 [c]2Sa 3:20; Isa 25:6-8
12:40 [d]2Sa 16:1; 17:29 [e]1Sa 25:18 [f]1Ch 29:22
13:3 [g]1Sa 7:1-2 [h]2Ch 1:5
13:5 [i]1Ch 11:1; 15:3 [j]Jos 13:3 [k]Nu 13:21 [l]1Sa 6:21; 7:2
13:6 [m]Jos 15:9; 2Sa 6:2 [n]Ex 25:22; 2Ki 19:15
13:7 [o]Nu 4:15; 1Sa 7:1
13:8 [p]2Sa 6:5; 1Ch 15:16, 19,24; 2Ch 5:12; Ps 92:3
13:10 [q]1Ch 15:13, 15 [r]Lev 10:2
13:11 [s]1Ch 15:13; Ps 7:11
13:13 [t]1Ch 15:18, 24; 16:38; 26:4-5,15

[y]3 Or *we neglected* [z]3 Or *him* [a]5 Or *to the entrance to* [b]11 *Perez Uzzah* means *outbreak against Uzzah.*

months, and the LORD blessed his household[a] and everything he had.

David's family.

14:1-7pp— 2Sa 5:11-16; 1Ch 3:5-8

14 Now Hiram king of Tyre sent messengers to David, along with cedar logs,[b] stonemasons and carpenters to build a palace for him. 2And David knew that the LORD had established him as king over Israel and that his kingdom had been highly exalted[c] for the sake of his people Israel.

3In Jerusalem David took more wives and became the father of more sons[d] and daughters. 4These are the names of the children born to him there:[e] Shammua, Shobab, Nathan, Solomon, 5Ibhar, Elishua, Elpelet, 6Nogah, Nepheg, Japhia, 7Elishama, Beeliada[c] and Eliphelet.

David defeats the Philistines.

14:8-17pp— 2Sa 5:17-25

8When the Philistines heard that David had been anointed king over all Israel,[f] they went up in full force to search for him, but David heard about it and went out to meet them. 9Now the Philistines had come and raided the Valley[g] of Rephaim; 10so David inquired of God: "Shall I go and attack the Philistines? Will you hand them over to me?"

The LORD answered him, "Go, I will hand them over to you."

11So David and his men went up to Baal Perazim,[h] and there he defeated them. He said, "As waters break out, God has broken out against my enemies by my hand." So that place was called Baal Perazim.[d] 12The Philistines had abandoned their gods there, and David gave orders to burn[i] them in the fire.[j]

13Once more the Philistines raided the valley;[k] 14so David inquired of God again, and God answered him, "Do not go straight up, but circle around them and attack them in front of the balsam trees. 15As soon as you hear the sound of marching in the tops of the balsam trees, move out to battle, because that will mean God has gone out in front of you to strike the Philistine army." 16So David did as God commanded him, and they struck down the Philistine army, all the way from Gibeon[l] to Gezer.[m]

17So David's fame[n] spread throughout every land, and the LORD made all the nations fear[o] him.

David returns the ark to Jerusalem.

15:25–16:3pp— 2Sa 6:12-19

15 After David had constructed buildings for himself in the City of David, he prepared[p] a place for the ark of God and pitched[q] a tent for it. 2Then David said, "No one but the Levites[r] may carry[s] the ark of God, because the LORD chose them to carry the ark of the LORD and to minister[t] before him forever."

3David assembled all Israel[u] in Jerusalem to bring up the ark of the LORD to the place he had prepared for it. 4He called together the descendants of Aaron and the Levites:

5From the descendants of Kohath,
Uriel the leader and 120 relatives;
6from the descendants of Merari,
Asaiah the leader and 220 relatives;
7from the descendants of Gershon,[e]
Joel the leader and 130 relatives;
8from the descendants of Elizaphan,[v]
Shemaiah the leader and 200 relatives;
9from the descendants of Hebron,[w]
Eliel the leader and 80 relatives;
10from the descendants of Uzziel,
Amminadab the leader and 112 relatives.

11Then David summoned Zadok[x] and Abiathar[y] the priests, and Uriel, Asaiah, Joel, Shemaiah, Eliel and Amminadab the Levites. 12He said to them, "You are the heads of the Levitical families; you and your fellow Levites are to consecrate[z] yourselves and bring up the ark of the LORD, the God of Israel, to the place

13:14 [a]2Sa 6:11; 1Ch 26:4-5
14:1 [b]2Ch 2:3; Ezr 3:7
14:2 [c]Nu 24:7; Dt 26:19
14:3 [d]1Ch 3:1
14:4 [e]1Ch 3:9
14:8 [f]1Ch 11:1
14:9 [g]ver 13; Jos 15:8; 1Ch 11:15
14:11 [h]Isa 28:21
14:12 [i]Ex 32:20 [j]Jos 7:15
14:13 [k]ver 9
14:16 [l]Jos 9:3 [m]Jos 10:33
14:17 [n]Jos 6:27; 2Ch 26:8 [o]Ex 15:14-16; Dt 2:25
15:1 [p]Ps 132:1-18 [q]1Ch 16:1; 17:1
15:2 [r]Nu 4:15; Dt 10:8; 2Ch 5:5 [s]Dt 31:9 [t]1Ch 23:13
15:3 [u]1Ki 8:1; 1Ch 13:5
15:8 [v]Ex 6:22
15:9 [w]Ex 6:18
15:11 [x]1Ch 12:28 [y]1Sa 22:20
15:12 [z]Ex 19:14-15; Lev 11:44; 2Ch 35:6

c7 A variant of *Eliada* d11 *Baal Perazim* means *the lord who breaks out.* e7 Hebrew *Gershom,* a variant of *Gershon*

I have prepared for it. 13It was because you, the Levites,[a] did not bring it up the first time that the LORD our God broke out in anger against us.[b] We did not inquire of him about how to do it in the prescribed way." 14So the priests and Levites consecrated themselves in order to bring up the ark of the LORD, the God of Israel. 15And the Levites carried the ark of God with the poles on their shoulders, as Moses had commanded[c] in accordance with the word of the LORD.

16David told the leaders of the Levites to appoint their brothers as singers[d] to sing joyful songs, accompanied by musical instruments: lyres, harps and cymbals.[e]

17So the Levites appointed Heman[f] son of Joel; from his brothers, Asaph[g] son of Berekiah; and from their brothers the Merarites,[h] Ethan son of Kushaiah; 18and with them their brothers next in rank: Zechariah,[f] Jaaziel, Shemiramoth, Jehiel, Unni, Eliab, Benaiah, Maaseiah, Mattithiah, Eliphelehu, Mikneiah, Obed-Edom[i] and Jeiel,[g] the gatekeepers.

19The musicians Heman,[j] Asaph and Ethan were to sound the bronze cymbals; 20Zechariah, Aziel, Shemiramoth, Jehiel, Unni, Eliab, Maaseiah and Benaiah were to play the lyres according to *alamoth*,[h] 21and Mattithiah, Eliphelehu, Mikneiah, Obed-Edom, Jeiel and Azaziah were to play the harps, directing according to *sheminith*.[h] 22Kenaniah the head Levite was in charge of the singing; that was his responsibility because he was skillful at it.

23Berekiah and Elkanah were to be doorkeepers for the ark. 24Shebaniah, Joshaphat, Nethanel, Amasai, Zechariah, Benaiah and Eliezer the priests were to blow trumpets[k] before the ark of God. Obed-Edom and Jehiah were also to be doorkeepers for the ark.

25So David and the elders of Israel and the commanders of units of a thousand went to bring up the ark[l] of the covenant of the LORD from the house of Obed-Edom, with rejoicing. 26Because God had helped the Levites who were carrying the ark of the covenant of the LORD, seven bulls and seven rams[m] were sacrificed. 27Now David was clothed in a robe of fine linen, as were all the Levites who were carrying the ark, and as were the singers, and Kenaniah, who was in charge of the singing of the choirs. David also wore a linen ephod. 28So all Israel brought up the ark of the covenant of the LORD with shouts, with the sounding of rams' horns[n] and trumpets, and of cymbals, and the playing of lyres and harps.

29As the ark of the covenant of the LORD was entering the City of David, Michal daughter of Saul watched from a window. And when she saw King David dancing and celebrating, she despised him in her heart.

16 They brought the ark of God and set it inside the tent that David had pitched[o] for it, and they presented burnt offerings and fellowship offerings[i] before God. 2After David had finished sacrificing the burnt offerings and fellowship offerings, he blessed[p] the people in the name of the LORD. 3Then he gave a loaf of bread, a cake of dates and a cake of raisins to each Israelite man and woman.

4He appointed some of the Levites to minister[q] before the ark of the LORD, to make petition, to give thanks, and to praise the LORD, the God of Israel: 5Asaph was the chief, Zechariah second, then Jeiel, Shemiramoth, Jehiel, Mattithiah, Eliab, Benaiah, Obed-Edom and Jeiel. They were to play the lyres and harps, Asaph was to sound the cymbals, 6and Benaiah and Jahaziel the priests were to blow the trumpets regularly before the ark of the covenant of God.

David's psalm of thanks.

16:8-22pp— Ps 105:1-15
16:23-33pp— Ps 96:1-13
16:34-36pp— Ps 106:1,47-48

7That day David first committed to

15:13 [a]1Ki 8:4 [b]2Sa 6:3; 1Ch 13:7-10
15:15 [c]Ex 25:14; Nu 4:5,15
15:16 [d]Ps 68:25 [e]1Ch 13:8; 25:1; Ne 12:27,36
15:17 [f]1Ch 6:33 [g]1Ch 6:39 [h]1Ch 6:44
15:18 [i]1Ch 26:4-5
15:19 [j]1Ch 25:6
15:24 [k]ver 28; 1Ch 16:6; 2Ch 7:6
15:25 [l]1Ch 13:13; 2Ch 1:4
15:26 [m]Nu 23:1-4,29
15:28 [n]1Ch 13:8
16:1 [o]1Ch 15:1
16:2 [p]Ex 39:43
16:4 [q]1Ch 15:2

[f] *18* Three Hebrew manuscripts and most Septuagint manuscripts (see also verse 20 and 1 Chron. 16:5); most Hebrew manuscripts *Zechariah son and* or *Zechariah, Ben and* [g] *18* Hebrew; Septuagint (see also verse 21) *Jeiel and Azaziah* [h] *20,21* Probably a musical term [i] *1* Traditionally *peace offerings*; also in verse 2

Asaph and his associates this psalm[a] of thanks to the LORD:

8Give thanks[b] to the LORD, call on his name;
make known among the nations[c] what he has done.
9Sing to him, sing praise[d] to him;
tell of all his wonderful acts.
10Glory in his holy name;
let the hearts of those who seek the LORD rejoice.
11Look to the LORD and his strength;
seek[e] his face always.
12Remember[f] the wonders he has done,
his miracles,[g] and the judgments he pronounced,
13O descendants of Israel his servant,
O sons of Jacob, his chosen ones.

14He is the LORD our God;
his judgments[h] are in all the earth.
15He remembers[j] his covenant forever,
the word he commanded, for a thousand generations,
16the covenant[i] he made with Abraham,
the oath he swore to Isaac.
17He confirmed it to Jacob[j] as a decree,
to Israel as an everlasting covenant:
18"To you I will give the land of Canaan[k]
as the portion you will inherit."

19When they were but few in number,[l]
few indeed, and strangers in it,
20they[k] wandered from nation to nation,
from one kingdom to another.
21He allowed no man to oppress them;
for their sake he rebuked kings:[m]
22"Do not touch my anointed ones;
do my prophets[n] no harm."

23Sing to the LORD, all the earth;
proclaim his salvation day after day.
24Declare his glory among the nations,
his marvelous deeds among all peoples.
25For great is the LORD and most worthy of praise;[o]
he is to be feared[p] above all gods.[q]
26For all the gods of the nations are idols,
but the LORD made the heavens.[r]
27Splendor and majesty are before him;
strength and joy in his dwelling place.

16:7 [a]2Sa 23:1 **16:8** [b]ver 34; Ps 136:1 [c]2Ki 19:19 **16:9** [d]Ex 15:1 **16:11** [e]1Ch 28:9; 2Ch 7:14; Ps 24:6; 119:2,58 **16:12** [f]Ps 77:11 [g]Ps 78:43 **16:14** [h]Isa 26:9 **16:16** [i]Ge 12:7; 15:18; 17:2; 22:16-18; 26:3; 28:13; 35:11 **16:17** [j]Ge 35:9-12 **16:18** [k]Ge 13:14-17 **16:19** [l]Ge 34:30; Dt 7:7 **16:21** [m]Ge 12:17; 20:3; Ex 7:15-18 **16:22** [n]Ge 20:7 **16:25** [o]Ps 48:1 [p]Ps 76:7; 89:7 [q]Dt 32:39 **16:26** [r]Lev 19:4; Ps 102:25 **16:28** [s]Ps 29:1-2 **16:29** [t]Ps 29:1-2 **16:30** [u]Ps 114:7 **16:31** [v]Isa 44:23; 49:13 [w]Ps 93:1 **16:32** [x]Ps 98:7 **16:33** [y]Isa 55:12 [z]Ps 96:10; 98:9 **16:34** [a]ver 8 [b]Na 1:7 [c]2Ch 5:13; 7:3; Ezr 3:11; Ps 136:1-26; Jer 33:11

28Ascribe to the LORD, O families of nations,
ascribe to the LORD glory and strength,[s]
29 ascribe to the LORD the glory due his name.
Bring an offering and come before him;
worship the LORD in the splendor of his[l] holiness.[t]
30Tremble[u] before him, all the earth!
The world is firmly established; it cannot be moved.
31Let the heavens rejoice, let the earth be glad;[v]
let them say among the nations,
"The LORD reigns![w]"
32Let the sea resound, and all that is in it;[x]
let the fields be jubilant, and everything in them!
33Then the trees[y] of the forest will sing,
they will sing for joy before the LORD,
for he comes to judge[z] the earth.

34Give thanks[a] to the LORD, for he is good;[b]
his love endures forever.[c]
35Cry out, "Save us, O God our Savior;[d]
gather us and deliver us from the nations,
that we may give thanks to your holy name,
that we may glory in your praise."
36Praise be to the LORD, the God of Israel,[e]
from everlasting to everlasting.

Then all the people said "Amen" and "Praise the LORD."

Asaph ministers regularly before the ark.

37David left Asaph and his associates before the ark of the covenant of the

16:35 [d]Mic 7:7 **16:36** [e]Dt 27:15; 1Ki 8:15; Ps 72:18-19

j*15* Some Septuagint manuscripts (see also Psalm 105:8); Hebrew *Remember* k*18-20* One Hebrew manuscript, Septuagint and Vulgate (see also Psalm 105:12); most Hebrew manuscripts *inherit, / [19]though you are but few in number, / few indeed, and strangers in it." / [20]They* l*29* Or *LORD with the splendor of*

LORD to minister there regularly, according to each day's requirements.[a] 38He
also left Obed-Edom[b] and his sixty-eight
associates to minister with them. Obed-
Edom son of Jeduthun, and also Hosah,[c]
were gatekeepers.
39David left Zadok[d] the priest and his
fellow priests before the tabernacle of the
LORD at the high place in Gibeon[e] 40to
present burnt offerings to the LORD on
the altar of burnt offering regularly,
morning and evening, in accordance
with everything written in the Law[f] of
the LORD, which he had given Israel.
41With them were Heman[g] and Jeduthun and the rest of those chosen and
designated by name to give thanks to
the LORD, "for his love endures forever."
42Heman and Jeduthun were responsible for the sounding of the trumpets and
cymbals and for the playing of the other
instruments for sacred song.[h] The sons
of Jeduthun were stationed at the gate.
43Then all the people left, each for his
own home, and David returned home to
bless his family.

One of David's sons will build a house for God.

17:1-15pp— 2Sa 7:1-17

17 After David was settled in his
palace, he said to Nathan the
prophet, "Here I am, living in a palace
of cedar, while the ark of the covenant
of the LORD is under a tent.[i]"
2Nathan replied to David, "Whatever
you have in mind,[j] do it, for God is with
you."
3That night the word of God came to
Nathan, saying:

4"Go and tell my servant David,
'This is what the LORD says: You[k]
are not the one to build me a house
to dwell in. 5I have not dwelt in a
house from the day I brought Israel
up out of Egypt to this day. I have
moved from one tent site to another, from one dwelling place to another. 6Wherever I have moved with all
the Israelites, did I ever say to any of
their leaders[m] whom I commanded
to shepherd my people, "Why have
you not built me a house of cedar?"'
7"Now then, tell my servant
David, 'This is what the LORD
Almighty says: I took you from the
pasture and from following the
flock, to be ruler[l] over my people
Israel. 8I have been with you wherever you have gone, and I have cut
off all your enemies from before
you. Now I will make your name
like the names of the greatest men
of the earth. 9And I will provide a
place for my people Israel and will
plant them so that they can have a
home of their own and no longer be
disturbed. Wicked people will not
oppress them anymore, as they did
at the beginning 10and have done
ever since the time I appointed
leaders[m] over my people Israel. I
will also subdue all your enemies.
"'I declare to you that the LORD
will build a house for you: 11When
your days are over and you go to be
with your fathers, I will raise up
your offspring to succeed you, one
of your own sons, and I will establish his kingdom. 12He is the one
who will build[n] a house for me, and
I will establish his throne forever.[o]
13I will be his father,[p] and he will
be my son.[q] I will never take my
love away from him, as I took it
away from your predecessor. 14I will
set him over my house and my
kingdom forever; his throne[r] will be
established forever.[s]'"

15Nathan reported to David all the
words of this entire revelation.

David praises God in prayer.

17:16-27pp— 2Sa 7:18-29

16Then King David went in and sat
before the LORD, and he said:

"Who am I, O LORD God, and
what is my family, that you have

16:37 [a]2Ch 8:14
16:38 [b]1Ch 13:13 [c]1Ch 26:10
16:39 [d]2Sa 8:17; 1Ch 15:11 [e]1Ki 3:4; 2Ch 1:3
16:40 [f]Ex 29:38; Nu 28:1-8
16:41 [g]1Ch 6:33; 25:1-6; 2Ch 5:13
16:42 [h]2Ch 7:6
17:1 [i]1Ch 15:1
17:2 [j]2Ch 6:7
17:4 [k]1Ch 28:3
17:7 [l]2Sa 6:21
17:10 [m]Jdg 2:16
17:12 [n]1Ki 5:5 [o]2Ch 7:18
17:13 [p]2Co 6:18 [q]Lk 1:32; Heb 1:5*
17:14 [r]1Ki 2:12; 1Ch 28:5 [s]Ps 132:11; Jer 33:17

m6 Traditionally *judges*; also in verse 10

brought me this far? 17And as if this were not enough in your sight, O God, you have spoken about the future of the house of your servant. You have looked on me as though I were the most exalted of men, O LORD God.

18"What more can David say to you for honoring your servant? For you know your servant, 19O LORD. For the sake[a] of your servant and according to your will, you have done this great thing and made known all these great promises.[b]

20"There is no one like you, O LORD, and there is no God but you,[c] as we have heard with our own ears. 21And who is like your people Israel—the one nation on earth whose God went out to redeem[d] a people for himself, and to make a name for yourself, and to perform great and awesome wonders by driving out nations from before your people, whom you redeemed from Egypt? 22You made your people Israel your very own forever,[e] and you, O LORD, have become their God.

23"And now, LORD, let the promise[f] you have made concerning your servant and his house be established forever. Do as you promised, 24so that it will be established and that your name will be great forever. Then men will say, 'The LORD Almighty, the God over Israel, is Israel's God!' And the house of your servant David will be established before you.

25"You, my God, have revealed to your servant that you will build a house for him. So your servant has found courage to pray to you. 26O LORD, you are God! You have promised these good things to your servant. 27Now you have been pleased to bless the house of your servant, that it may continue forever in your sight;[g] for you, O LORD, have blessed it, and it will be blessed forever."

17:19 [a]2Sa 7:16-17; 2Ki 20:6; Isa 9:7; 37:35; 55:3 [b]2Sa 7:25
17:20 [c]Ex 8:10; 9:14; 15:11; Isa 44:6; 46:9
17:21 [d]Ex 6:6
17:22 [e]Ex 19:5-6
17:23 [f]1Ki 8:25
17:27 [g]Ps 16:11; 21:6
18:2 [h]Nu 21:29
18:3 [i]1Ch 19:6 [j]Ge 2:14
18:4 [k]Ge 49:6
18:5 [l]2Ki 16:9; 1Ch 19:6
18:8 [m]1Ki 7:23; 2Ch 4:12, 15-16
18:11 [n]Nu 24:18 [o]Nu 24:20

David's victories.

18:1-13pp— 2Sa 8:1-14

18 In the course of time, David defeated the Philistines and subdued them, and he took Gath and its surrounding villages from the control of the Philistines.

2David also defeated the Moabites,[h] and they became subject to him and brought tribute.

3Moreover, David fought Hadadezer king of Zobah,[i] as far as Hamath, when he went to establish his control along the Euphrates River.[j] 4David captured a thousand of his chariots, seven thousand charioteers and twenty thousand foot soldiers. He hamstrung[k] all but a hundred of the chariot horses.

5When the Arameans of Damascus[l] came to help Hadadezer king of Zobah, David struck down twenty-two thousand of them. 6He put garrisons in the Aramean kingdom of Damascus, and the Arameans became subject to him and brought tribute. The LORD gave David victory everywhere he went.

7David took the gold shields carried by the officers of Hadadezer and brought them to Jerusalem. 8From Tebah[n] and Cun, towns that belonged to Hadadezer, David took a great quantity of bronze, which Solomon used to make the bronze Sea,[m] the pillars and various bronze articles.

9When Tou king of Hamath heard that David had defeated the entire army of Hadadezer king of Zobah, 10he sent his son Hadoram to King David to greet him and congratulate him on his victory in battle over Hadadezer, who had been at war with Tou. Hadoram brought all kinds of articles of gold and silver and bronze.

11King David dedicated these articles to the LORD, as he had done with the silver and gold he had taken from all these nations: Edom[n] and Moab, the Ammonites and the Philistines, and Amalek.[o]

12Abishai son of Zeruiah struck down

[n]8 Hebrew *Tibhath,* a variant of *Tebah*

eighteen thousand Edomites[a] in the Valley of Salt. 13He put garrisons in Edom, and all the Edomites became subject to David. The LORD gave David victory everywhere he went.

David's officials.

18:14-17pp— 2Sa 8:15-18

14David reigned[b] over all Israel,[c] doing what was just and right for all his people. 15Joab[d] son of Zeruiah was over the army; Jehoshaphat son of Ahilud was recorder; 16Zadok[e] son of Ahitub and Ahimelech[o][f] son of Abiathar were priests; Shavsha was secretary; 17Benaiah son of Jehoiada was over the Kerethites and Pelethites;[g] and David's sons were chief officials at the king's side.

David's delegation is humiliated.

19:1-19pp— 2Sa 10:1-19

19 In the course of time, Nahash king of the Ammonites[h] died, and his son succeeded him as king. 2David thought, "I will show kindness to Hanun son of Nahash, because his father showed kindness to me." So David sent a delegation to express his sympathy to Hanun concerning his father.

When David's men came to Hanun in the land of the Ammonites to express sympathy to him, 3the Ammonite nobles said to Hanun, "Do you think David is honoring your father by sending men to you to express sympathy? Haven't his men come to you to explore and spy out[i] the country and overthrow it?" 4So Hanun seized David's men, shaved them, cut off their garments in the middle at the buttocks, and sent them away.

5When someone came and told David about the men, he sent messengers to meet them, for they were greatly humiliated. The king said, "Stay at Jericho till your beards have grown, and then come back."

David defeats the Ammonites and the Arameans.

6When the Ammonites realized that they had become a stench[j] in David's nostrils, Hanun and the Ammonites sent a thousand talents[p] of silver to hire chariots and charioteers from Aram Naharaim,[q] Aram Maacah and Zobah.[k] 7They hired thirty-two thousand chariots and charioteers, as well as the king of Maacah with his troops, who came and camped near Medeba,[l] while the Ammonites were mustered from their towns and moved out for battle.

8On hearing this, David sent Joab out with the entire army of fighting men. 9The Ammonites came out and drew up in battle formation at the entrance to their city, while the kings who had come were by themselves in the open country.

10Joab saw that there were battle lines in front of him and behind him; so he selected some of the best troops in Israel and deployed them against the Arameans. 11He put the rest of the men under the command of Abishai[m] his brother, and they were deployed against the Ammonites. 12Joab said, "If the Arameans are too strong for me, then you are to rescue me; but if the Ammonites are too strong for you, then I will rescue you. 13Be strong and let us fight bravely for our people and the cities of our God. The LORD will do what is good in his sight."

14Then Joab and the troops with him advanced to fight the Arameans, and they fled before him. 15When the Ammonites saw that the Arameans were fleeing, they too fled before his brother Abishai and went inside the city. So Joab went back to Jerusalem.

16After the Arameans saw that they had been routed by Israel, they sent messengers and had Arameans brought from beyond the River,[r] with Shophach the commander of Hadadezer's army leading them.

17When David was told of this, he

18:12 [a]1Ki 11:15
18:14 [b]1Ch 29:26 [c]1Ch 11:1
18:15 [d]2Sa 5:6-8; 1Ch 11:6
18:16 [e]2Sa 8:17; 1Ch 6:8 [f]1Ch 24:6
18:17 [g]1Sa 30:14; 2Sa 8:18; 15:18
19:1 [h]Ge 19:38; Jdg 10:17–11:33; 2Ch 20:1-2; Zep 2:8-11
19:3 [i]Nu 21:32
19:6 [j]Ge 34:30 [k]1Ch 18:3,5,9
19:7 [l]Nu 21:30; Jos 13:9,16
19:11 [m]1Sa 26:6

[o]*16* Some Hebrew manuscripts, Vulgate and Syriac (see also 2 Samuel 8:17); most Hebrew manuscripts *Abimelech* [p]*6* That is, about 37 tons (about 34 metric tons) [q]*6* That is, Northwest Mesopotamia [r]*16* That is, the Euphrates

gathered all Israel[a] and crossed the Jordan; he advanced against them and
formed his battle lines opposite them.
David formed his lines to meet the
Arameans in battle, and they fought
against him. 18But they fled before
Israel, and David killed seven thousand
of their charioteers and forty thousand
of their foot soldiers. He also killed
Shophach the commander of their army.
19When the vassals of Hadadezer saw
that they had been defeated by Israel,
they made peace with David and became
subject to him.
So the Arameans were not willing to
help the Ammonites anymore.

Capture of Rabbah.

20:1-3pp— 2Sa 11:1; 12:29-31

20 In the spring, at the time when
kings go off to war, Joab led
out the armed forces. He laid waste the
land of the Ammonites and went to Rabbah[b] and besieged it, but David remained
in Jerusalem. Joab attacked Rabbah and
left it in ruins.[c] 2David took the crown
from the head of their king[s]—its weight
was found to be a talent[t] of gold, and it
was set with precious stones—and it was
placed on David's head. He took a great
quantity of plunder from the city 3and
brought out the people who were there,
consigning them to labor with saws
and with iron picks and axes.[d] David did
this to all the Ammonite towns. Then
David and his entire army returned to
Jerusalem.

War with the Philistines.

20:4-8pp— 2Sa 21:15-22

4In the course of time, war broke out
with the Philistines, at Gezer.[e] At that
time Sibbecai the Hushathite killed Sip-
pai, one of the descendants of the
Rephaites,[f] and the Philistines were sub-
jugated.
5In another battle with the Philistines,
Elhanan son of Jair killed Lahmi the
brother of Goliath the Gittite, who had
a spear with a shaft like a weaver's rod.[g]

19:17 [a]1Ch 9:1
20:1 [b]Dt 3:11; 2Sa 12:26 [c]Am 1:13-15
20:3 [d]Dt 29:11
20:4 [e]Jos 10:33 [f]Ge 14:5
20:5 [g]1Sa 17:7
21:1 [h]2Ch 18:21; Ps 109:6 [i]2Ch 14:8; 25:5
21:2 [j]1Ch 27:23-24
21:3 [k]Dt 1:11
21:5 [l]1Ch 9:1
21:9 [m]1Sa 22:5 [n]1Sa 9:9

6In still another battle, which took
place at Gath, there was a huge man
with six fingers on each hand and six
toes on each foot—twenty-four in all.
He also was descended from Rapha.
7When he taunted Israel, Jonathan son
of Shimea, David's brother, killed him.
8These were descendants of Rapha in
Gath, and they fell at the hands of David
and his men.

David takes a census of the fighting men.

21:1-26pp— 2Sa 24:1-25

21 Satan[h] rose up against Israel and
incited David to take a census[i] of
Israel. 2So David said to Joab and the
commanders of the troops, "Go and
count[j] the Israelites from Beersheba to
Dan. Then report back to me so that I
may know how many there are."
3But Joab replied, "May the LORD multiply his troops a hundred times over.[k]
My lord the king, are they not all my
lord's subjects? Why does my lord want
to do this? Why should he bring guilt on
Israel?"
4The king's word, however, overruled
Joab; so Joab left and went throughout
Israel and then came back to Jerusalem.
5Joab reported the number of the fighting men to David: In all Israel[l] there
were one million one hundred thousand
men who could handle a sword, including four hundred and seventy thousand
in Judah.
6But Joab did not include Levi and
Benjamin in the numbering, because
the king's command was repulsive to
him. 7This command was also evil in
the sight of God; so he punished Israel.
8Then David said to God, "I have
sinned greatly by doing this. Now, I beg
you, take away the guilt of your servant.
I have done a very foolish thing."

David chooses a plague as his punishment.

9The LORD said to Gad,[m] David's seer,[n]

s *2* Or *of Milcom,* that is, Molech t *2* That is, about 75 pounds (about 34 kilograms)

10"Go and tell David, 'This is what the LORD says: I am giving you three options. Choose one of them for me to carry out against you.'"

11So Gad went to David and said to him, "This is what the LORD says: 'Take your choice: 12three years of famine,[a] three months of being swept away[u] before your enemies, with their swords overtaking you, or three days of the sword[b] of the LORD[c]—days of plague in the land, with the angel of the LORD ravaging every part of Israel.' Now then, decide how I should answer the one who sent me."

13David said to Gad, "I am in deep distress. Let me fall into the hands of the LORD, for his mercy[d] is very great; but do not let me fall into the hands of men."

14So the LORD sent a plague on Israel, and seventy thousand men of Israel fell dead.[e] 15And God sent an angel[f] to destroy Jerusalem.[g] But as the angel was doing so, the LORD saw it and was grieved[h] because of the calamity and said to the angel who was destroying[i] the people, "Enough! Withdraw your hand." The angel of the LORD was then standing at the threshing floor of Araunah[v] the Jebusite.

16David looked up and saw the angel of the LORD standing between heaven and earth, with a drawn sword in his hand extended over Jerusalem. Then David and the elders, clothed in sackcloth, fell facedown.[j]

17David said to God, "Was it not I who ordered the fighting men to be counted? I am the one who has sinned and done wrong. These are but sheep.[k] What have they done? O LORD my God, let your hand fall upon me and my family,[l] but do not let this plague remain on your people."

David builds an altar to the LORD.

18Then the angel of the LORD ordered Gad to tell David to go up and build an altar to the LORD on the threshing floor[m] of Araunah the Jebusite. 19So David went up in obedience to the word that Gad had spoken in the name of the LORD.

20While Araunah was threshing wheat,[n] he turned and saw the angel; his four sons who were with him hid themselves. 21Then David approached, and when Araunah looked and saw him, he left the threshing floor and bowed down before David with his face to the ground.

22David said to him, "Let me have the site of your threshing floor so I can build an altar to the LORD, that the plague on the people may be stopped. Sell it to me at the full price."

23Araunah said to David, "Take it! Let my lord the king do whatever pleases him. Look, I will give the oxen for the burnt offerings, the threshing sledges for the wood, and the wheat for the grain offering. I will give all this."

24But King David replied to Araunah, "No, I insist on paying the full price. I will not take for the LORD what is yours, or sacrifice a burnt offering that costs me nothing."

25So David paid Araunah six hundred shekels[w] of gold for the site. 26David built an altar to the LORD there and sacrificed burnt offerings and fellowship offerings.[x] He called on the LORD, and the LORD answered him with fire[o] from heaven on the altar of burnt offering.

27Then the LORD spoke to the angel, and he put his sword back into its sheath. 28At that time, when David saw that the LORD had answered him on the threshing floor of Araunah the Jebusite, he offered sacrifices there. 29The tabernacle of the LORD, which Moses had made in the desert, and the altar of burnt offering were at that time on the high place at Gibeon.[p] 30But David could not go before it to inquire of God, because he was afraid of the sword of the angel of the LORD.

21:12 [a]Dt 32:24 [b]Eze 30:25 [c]Ge 19:13
21:13 [d]Ps 6:4; 86:15; 130:4,7
21:14 [e]1Ch 27:24
21:15 [f]Ge 32:1 [g]Ps 125:2 [h]Ge 6:6; Ex 32:14 [i]Ge 19:13
21:16 [j]Nu 14:5; Jos 7:6
21:17 [k]2Sa 7:8; Ps 74:1 [l]Jnh 1:12
21:18 [m]2Ch 3:1
21:20 [n]Jdg 6:11
21:26 [o]Lev 9:24; Jdg 6:21
21:29 [p]1Ki 3:4; 1Ch 16:39

u *12* Hebrew; Septuagint and Vulgate (see also 2 Samuel 24:13) *of fleeing* v *15* Hebrew *Ornan,* a variant of *Araunah*; also in verses 18-28
w *25* That is, about 15 pounds (about 7 kilograms)
x *26* Traditionally *peace offerings*

22

Then David said, "The house of
the LORD God[a] is to be here, and
also the altar of burnt offering for Israel."

David makes preparations for building the temple.

2So David gave orders to assemble the
aliens[b] living in Israel, and from among
them he appointed stonecutters[c] to prepare dressed stone for building the
house of God. 3He provided a large
amount of iron to make nails for the
doors of the gateways and for the fit-
tings, and more bronze than could be
weighed.[d] 4He also provided more cedar
logs[e] than could be counted, for the
Sidonians and Tyrians had brought large
numbers of them to David.
5David said, "My son Solomon is
young[f] and inexperienced, and the
house to be built for the LORD should be
of great magnificence and fame and
splendor in the sight of all the nations.
Therefore I will make preparations for
it." So David made extensive preparations before his death.
6Then he called for his son Solomon
and charged him to build[g] a house for
the LORD, the God of Israel. 7David said
to Solomon: "My son, I had it in my
heart[h] to build[i] a house for the Name[j] of
the LORD my God. 8But this word of the
LORD came to me: 'You have shed much
blood and have fought many wars.[k] You
are not to build a house for my Name,[l]
because you have shed much blood on
the earth in my sight. 9But you will have
a son who will be a man of peace[m] and
rest, and I will give him rest from all his
enemies on every side. His name will be
Solomon,[y][n] and I will grant Israel peace
and quiet[o] during his reign. 10He is the
one who will build a house for my
Name.[p] He will be my son,[q] and I will
be his father. And I will establish the
throne of his kingdom over Israel forever.'[r]
11"Now, my son, the LORD be with[s]
you, and may you have success and
build the house of the LORD your God,
as he said you would. 12May the LORD
give you discretion and understanding[t]
when he puts you in command over
Israel, so that you may keep the law of
the LORD your God. 13Then you will
have success if you are careful to observe
the decrees and laws[u] that the LORD gave
Moses for Israel. Be strong and courageous.[v] Do not be afraid or discouraged.
14"I have taken great pains to provide
for the temple of the LORD a hundred
thousand talents[z] of gold, a million talents[a] of silver, quantities of bronze and
iron too great to be weighed, and wood
and stone. And you may add to them.[w]
15You have many workmen: stonecutters, masons and carpenters, as well as
men skilled in every kind of work 16in
gold and silver, bronze and iron—craftsmen[x] beyond number. Now begin the
work, and the LORD be with you."

David orders help for Solomon.

17Then David ordered[y] all the leaders
of Israel to help his son Solomon. 18He
said to them, "Is not the LORD your God
with you? And has he not granted you
rest[z] on every side?[a] For he has handed
the inhabitants of the land over to me,
and the land is subject to the LORD and
to his people. 19Now devote your heart
and soul to seeking the LORD your God.[b]
Begin to build the sanctuary of the LORD
God, so that you may bring the ark of the
covenant of the LORD and the sacred articles belonging to God into the temple
that will be built for the Name of the
LORD."

The Levites are counted, and duties are assigned.

23

When David was old and full of
years, he made his son Solomon[c] king over Israel.[d]
2He also gathered together all the
leaders of Israel, as well as the priests

22:1 [a]Ge 28:17; 1Ch 21:18-29; 2Ch 3:1
22:2 [b]1Ki 9:21; Isa 56:6 [c]1Ki 5:17-18
22:3 [d]ver 14; 1Ki 7:47; 1Ch 29:2-5
22:4 [e]1Ki 5:6
22:5 [f]1Ki 3:7; 1Ch 29:1
22:6 [g]Ac 7:47
22:7 [h]1Ch 17:2 [i]2Sa 7:2; 1Ki 8:17 [j]Dt 12:5,11
22:8 [k]1Ki 5:3 [l]1Ch 28:3
22:9 [m]1Ki 5:4 [n]2Sa 12:24 [o]1Ki 4:20
22:10 [p]1Ch 17:12 [q]2Sa 7:13 [r]2Sa 7:14; 2Ch 6:15
22:11 [s]ver 16
22:12 [t]1Ki 3:9-12; 2Ch 1:10
22:13 [u]1Ch 28:7 [v]Dt 31:6; Jos 1:6-9; 1Ch 28:20
22:14 [w]ver 3; 1Ch 29:2-5,19
22:16 [x]ver 11; 2Ch 2:7
22:17 [y]1Ch 28:1-6
22:18 [z]ver 9; 1Ch 23:25 [a]2Sa 7:1
22:19 [b]ver 7; 1Ki 8:6; 1Ch 28:9; 2Ch 5:7; 7:14

23:1 [c]1Ki 1:33-39; 1Ch 28:5 [d]1Ki 1:30; 1Ch 29:28

[y]9 *Solomon* sounds like and may be derived from the Hebrew for *peace.* [z]14 That is, about 3,750 tons (about 3,450 metric tons) [a]14 That is, about 37,500 tons (about 34,500 metric tons)

and Levites. 3The Levites thirty years old
or more[a] were counted, and the total
number of men was thirty-eight thousand.[b] 4David said, "Of these, twenty-
four thousand are to supervise[c] the work
of the temple of the LORD and six thousand are to be officials and judges.[d]
5Four thousand are to be gatekeepers
and four thousand are to praise the LORD
with the musical instruments[e] I have
provided for that purpose."[f]
6David divided[g] the Levites into
groups corresponding to the sons of
Levi: Gershon, Kohath and Merari.

7Belonging to the Gershonites:
Ladan and Shimei.
8The sons of Ladan:
Jehiel the first, Zetham and
Joel—three in all.
9The sons of Shimei:
Shelomoth, Haziel and Haran—
three in all.
These were the heads of the families of Ladan.
10And the sons of Shimei:
Jahath, Ziza,[b] Jeush and Beriah.
These were the sons of Shimei—
four in all.
11Jahath was the first and Ziza the
second, but Jeush and Beriah did
not have many sons; so they
were counted as one family with
one assignment.

12The sons of Kohath:[h]
Amram, Izhar, Hebron and
Uzziel—four in all.
13The sons of Amram:[i]
Aaron and Moses.
Aaron was set apart,[j] he and his
descendants forever, to consecrate the most holy things, to
offer sacrifices before the LORD,
to minister before him and to
pronounce blessings[k] in his name
forever. 14The sons of Moses the
man[l] of God were counted as
part of the tribe of Levi.
15The sons of Moses:
Gershom and Eliezer.[m]
16The descendants of Gershom:[n]
Shubael was the first.

23:3 [a]ver 24; Nu 8:24 [b]Nu 4:3-49
23:4 [c]Ezr 3:8 [d]1Ch 26:29; 2Ch 19:8
23:5 [e]1Ch 15:16 [f]Ne 12:45
23:6 [g]2Ch 8:14; 29:25
23:12 [h]Ex 6:18
23:13 [i]Ex 6:20; 28:1 [j]Ex 30:7-10; Dt 21:5 [k]Nu 6:23
23:14 [l]Dt 33:1
23:15 [m]Ex 18:4
23:16 [n]1Ch 26:24-28
23:19 [o]1Ch 24:23
23:21 [p]1Ch 24:26
23:24 [q]Nu 4:3; 10:17,21
23:25 [r]1Ch 22:9
23:26 [s]Nu 4:5,15; 7:9; Dt 10:8
23:28 [t]2Ch 29:15; Ne 13:9; Mal 3:3
23:29 [u]Ex 25:30 [v]Lev 2:4-7; 6:20-23

17The descendants of Eliezer:
Rehabiah was the first.
Eliezer had no other sons, but
the sons of Rehabiah were very
numerous.
18The sons of Izhar:
Shelomith was the first.
19The sons of Hebron:[o]
Jeriah the first, Amariah the second, Jahaziel the third and Jekameam the fourth.
20The sons of Uzziel:
Micah the first and Isshiah the
second.

21The sons of Merari:[p]
Mahli and Mushi.
The sons of Mahli:
Eleazar and Kish.
22Eleazar died without having sons:
he had only daughters. Their
cousins, the sons of Kish, married
them.
23The sons of Mushi:
Mahli, Eder and Jerimoth—
three in all.

24These were the descendants of Levi
by their families—the heads of families
as they were registered under their
names and counted individually, that is,
the workers twenty years old or more[q]
who served in the temple of the LORD.
25For David had said, "Since the LORD,
the God of Israel, has granted rest[r] to his
people and has come to dwell in Jerusalem forever, 26the Levites no longer
need to carry the tabernacle or any of
the articles used in its service."[s] 27Ac-
cording to the last instructions of David,
the Levites were counted from those
twenty years old or more.
28The duty of the Levites was to help
Aaron's descendants in the service of
the temple of the LORD: to be in charge
of the courtyards, the side rooms, the
purification[t] of all sacred things and the
performance of other duties at the house
of God. 29They were in charge of the
bread set out on the table,[u] the flour for
the grain offerings,[v] the unleavened

[b] *10* One Hebrew manuscript, Septuagint and Vulgate (see also verse 11); most Hebrew manuscripts *Zina*

wafers, the baking and the mixing, and
all measurements of quantity and size.[a]
30They were also to stand every morning to thank and praise the LORD. They
were to do the same in the evening[b]
31and whenever burnt offerings were
presented to the LORD on Sabbaths and
at New Moon[c] festivals and at appointed
feasts.[d] They were to serve before the
LORD regularly in the proper number
and in the way prescribed for them.
32And so the Levites[e] carried out their
responsibilities for the Tent of Meeting,[f] for the Holy Place and, under their
brothers the descendants of Aaron, for
the service of the temple of the LORD.[g]

Divisions of Aaron's sons.

24 These were the divisions[h] of
the sons of Aaron:[i]
The sons of Aaron were Nadab, Abihu, Eleazar and Ithamar.[j] 2But Nadab
and Abihu died before their father did,[k]
and they had no sons; so Eleazar and
Ithamar served as the priests. 3With the
help of Zadok[l] a descendant of Eleazar
and Ahimelech a descendant of Ithamar,
David separated them into divisions for
their appointed order of ministering. 4A
larger number of leaders were found
among Eleazar's descendants than among
Ithamar's, and they were divided accordingly: sixteen heads of families from
Eleazar's descendants and eight heads
of families from Ithamar's descendants.
5They divided them impartially by
drawing lots,[m] for there were officials of
the sanctuary and officials of God among
the descendants of both Eleazar and Ithamar.
6The scribe Shemaiah son of Nethanel, a Levite, recorded their names in the
presence of the king and of the officials:
Zadok the priest, Ahimelech[n] son of Abiathar and the heads of families of the
priests and of the Levites—one family
being taken from Eleazar and then one
from Ithamar.

7The first lot fell to Jehoiarib,
the second to Jedaiah,[o]
8the third to Harim,[p]

23:29 [a]Lev 19:35-36; 1Ch 9:29,32
23:30 [b]1Ch 9:33; Ps 134:1
23:31 [c]2Ki 4:23 [d]Lev 23:4; Nu 28:9–29:39; Isa 1:13-14; Col 2:16
23:32 [e]Nu 1:53; 1Ch 6:48 [f]Nu 3:6-8,38 [g]2Ch 23:18; 31:2; Eze 44:14
24:1 [h]1Ch 23:6; 28:13; 2Ch 5:11; 8:14; 23:8; 31:2; 35:4,5; Ezr 6:18 [i]Nu 3:2-4 [j]Ex 6:23
24:2 [k]Lev 10:1-2; Nu 3:4
24:3 [l]2Sa 8:17
24:5 [m]ver 31; 1Ch 25:8
24:6 [n]1Ch 18:16
24:7 [o]Ezr 2:36; Ne 12:6
24:8 [p]Ezr 2:39; Ne 10:5
24:10 [q]Ne 12:4,17; Lk 1:5
24:14 [r]Jer 20:1
24:15 [s]Ne 10:20
24:20 [t]1Ch 23:6
24:21 [u]1Ch 23:17
24:23 [v]1Ch 23:19

the fourth to Seorim,
9the fifth to Malkijah,
the sixth to Mijamin,
10the seventh to Hakkoz,
the eighth to Abijah,[q]
11the ninth to Jeshua,
the tenth to Shecaniah,
12the eleventh to Eliashib,
the twelfth to Jakim,
13the thirteenth to Huppah,
the fourteenth to Jeshebeab,
14the fifteenth to Bilgah,
the sixteenth to Immer,[r]
15the seventeenth to Hezir,[s]
the eighteenth to Happizzez,
16the nineteenth to Pethahiah,
the twentieth to Jehezkel,
17the twenty-first to Jakin,
the twenty-second to Gamul,
18the twenty-third to Delaiah
and the twenty-fourth to Maaziah.

19This was their appointed order of
ministering when they entered the temple of the LORD, according to the regulations prescribed for them by their
forefather Aaron, as the LORD, the God of
Israel, had commanded him.

Other descendants of Levi.

20As for the rest of the descendants of
Levi:[t]
from the sons of Amram: Shubael;
from the sons of Shubael: Jehdeiah.
21As for Rehabiah,[u] from his sons:
Isshiah was the first.
22From the Izharites: Shelomoth;
from the sons of Shelomoth:
Jahath.
23The sons of Hebron:[v] Jeriah the
first,[c] Amariah the second, Jahaziel the third and Jekameam the
fourth.
24The son of Uzziel: Micah;
from the sons of Micah: Shamir.
25The brother of Micah: Isshiah;
from the sons of Isshiah: Zechariah.

c *23* Two Hebrew manuscripts and some Septuagint manuscripts (see also 1 Chron. 23:19); most Hebrew manuscripts *The sons of Jeriah:*

26The sons of Merari:[a] Mahli and
Mushi.
The son of Jaaziah: Beno.
27The sons of Merari:
from Jaaziah: Beno, Shoham, Zaccur and Ibri.
28From Mahli: Eleazar, who had no
sons.
29From Kish: the son of Kish:
Jerahmeel.
30And the sons of Mushi: Mahli, Eder
and Jerimoth.

These were the Levites, according to
their families. 31They also cast lots,[b] just
as their brothers the descendants of
Aaron did, in the presence of King David
and of Zadok, Ahimelech, and the heads
of families of the priests and of the Levites. The families of the oldest brother
were treated the same as those of the
youngest.

Numbering and duties of the musicians.

25 David, together with the commanders of the army, set apart
some of the sons of Asaph,[c] Heman[d] and
Jeduthun[e] for the ministry of prophesying,[f] accompanied by harps, lyres and
cymbals.[g] Here is the list of the men[h]
who performed this service:[i]

2From the sons of Asaph:
Zaccur, Joseph, Nethaniah and
Asarelah. The sons of Asaph were
under the supervision of Asaph,
who prophesied under the king's
supervision.
3As for Jeduthun, from his sons:[j]
Gedaliah, Zeri, Jeshaiah, Shimei,[d]
Hashabiah and Mattithiah, six in all,
under the supervision of their father
Jeduthun, who prophesied, using
the harp[k] in thanking and praising
the LORD.
4As for Heman, from his sons:
Bukkiah, Mattaniah, Uzziel, Shubael
and Jerimoth; Hananiah, Hanani,
Eliathah, Giddalti and Romamti-Ezer; Joshbekashah, Mallothi, Hothir
and Mahazioth. 5All these were
sons of Heman the king's seer. They
were given him through the promises of God to exalt him.[e] God gave
Heman fourteen sons and three
daughters.

6All these men were under the supervision of their fathers[l] for the music of
the temple of the LORD, with cymbals,
lyres and harps, for the ministry at the
house of God. Asaph, Jeduthun and
Heman[m] were under the supervision of
the king.[n] 7Along with their relatives—
all of them trained and skilled in music
for the LORD—they numbered 288.
8Young and old alike, teacher as well as
student, cast lots[o] for their duties.

9The first lot, which was for
Asaph,[p] fell to Joseph,
his sons and relatives,[f] 12[g]
the second to Gedaliah,
he and his relatives
and sons, 12
10the third to Zaccur,
his sons and relatives, 12
11the fourth to Izri,[h]
his sons and relatives, 12
12the fifth to Nethaniah,
his sons and relatives, 12
13the sixth to Bukkiah,
his sons and relatives, 12
14the seventh to Jesarelah,[i]
his sons and relatives, 12
15the eighth to Jeshaiah,
his sons and relatives, 12
16the ninth to Mattaniah,
his sons and relatives, 12
17the tenth to Shimei,
his sons and relatives, 12
18the eleventh to Azarel,[j]
his sons and relatives, 12
19the twelfth to Hashabiah,
his sons and relatives, 12
20the thirteenth to Shubael,
his sons and relatives, 12

24:26 [a] 1Ch 6:19; 23:21
24:31 [b] ver 5
25:1 [c] 1Ch 6:39 [d] 1Ch 6:33 [e] 1Ch 16:41, 42; Ne 11:17 [f] 1Sa 10:5; 2Ki 3:15 [g] 1Ch 15:16 [h] 1Ch 6:31 [i] 2Ch 5:12; 8:14; 34:12; 35:15; Ezr 3:10
25:3 [j] 1Ch 16:41-42 [k] Ge 4:21; Ps 33:2
25:6 [l] 1Ch 15:16 [m] 1Ch 15:19 [n] 2Ch 23:18; 29:25
25:8 [o] 1Ch 26:13
25:9 [p] 1Ch 6:39

d *3* One Hebrew manuscript and some Septuagint manuscripts (see also verse 17); most Hebrew manuscripts do not have *Shimei.* e *5* Hebrew *exalt the horn* f *9* See Septuagint; Hebrew does not have *his sons and relatives.* g *9* See the total in verse 7; Hebrew does not have *twelve.* h *11* A variant of *Zeri* i *14* A variant of *Asarelah* j *18* A variant of *Uzziel*

21the fourteenth to Mattithiah,
his sons and relatives, 12
22the fifteenth to Jerimoth,
his sons and relatives, 12
23the sixteenth to Hananiah,
his sons and relatives, 12
24the seventeenth to Joshbekashah,
his sons and relatives, 12
25the eighteenth to Hanani,
his sons and relatives, 12
26the nineteenth to Mallothi,
his sons and relatives, 12
27the twentieth to Eliathah,
his sons and relatives, 12
28the twenty-first to Hothir,
his sons and relatives, 12
29the twenty-second to Giddalti,
his sons and relatives, 12
30the twenty-third to Mahazioth,
his sons and relatives, 12
31the twenty-fourth to Romamti-Ezer,
his sons and relatives, 12[a]

The temple gatekeepers.

26 The divisions of the gatekeepers:[b]

From the Korahites: Meshelemiah son of Kore, one of the sons of Asaph.
2Meshelemiah had sons:
Zechariah[c] the firstborn,
Jediael the second,
Zebadiah the third,
Jathniel the fourth,
3Elam the fifth,
Jehohanan the sixth
and Eliehoenai the seventh.
4Obed-Edom also had sons:
Shemaiah the firstborn,
Jehozabad the second,
Joah the third,
Sacar the fourth,
Nethanel the fifth,
5Ammiel the sixth,
Issachar the seventh
and Peullethai the eighth.
(For God had blessed Obed-Edom.[d])

6His son Shemaiah also had sons,
who were leaders in their father's
family because they were very
capable men. 7The sons of Shemaiah: Othni, Rephael, Obed and
Elzabad; his relatives Elihu and
Semakiah were also able men.
8All these were descendants of
Obed-Edom; they and their sons
and their relatives were capable
men with the strength to do the
work—descendants of Obed-Edom, 62 in all.
9Meshelemiah had sons and relatives, who were able men—18
in all.

10Hosah the Merarite had sons: Shimri the first (although he was not
the firstborn, his father had
appointed him the first),[e] 11Hilki-
ah the second, Tabaliah the third
and Zechariah the fourth. The
sons and relatives of Hosah were
13 in all.

12These divisions of the gatekeepers,
through their chief men, had duties for
ministering[f] in the temple of the LORD,
just as their relatives had. 13Lots[g] were
cast for each gate, according to their
families, young and old alike.
14The lot for the East Gate[h] fell to
Shelemiah.[k] Then lots were cast for his
son Zechariah,[i] a wise counselor, and
the lot for the North Gate fell to him.
15The lot for the South Gate fell to
Obed-Edom,[j] and the lot for the storehouse fell to his sons. 16The lots for the
West Gate and the Shalleketh Gate on
the upper road fell to Shuppim and
Hosah.
Guard was alongside of guard: 17There
were six Levites a day on the east, four a
day on the north, four a day on the south
and two at a time at the storehouse. 18As
for the court to the west, there were
four at the road and two at the court
itself.
19These were the divisions of the
gatekeepers who were descendants of
Korah and Merari.[k]

25:31 [a]1Ch 9:33
26:1 [b]1Ch 9:17
26:2 [c]1Ch 9:21
26:5 [d]2Sa 6:10; 1Ch 13:13; 16:38
26:10 [e]Dt 21:16; 1Ch 5:1
26:12 [f]1Ch 9:22
26:13 [g]1Ch 24:5,31; 25:8
26:14 [h]1Ch 9:18 [i]1Ch 9:21
26:15 [j]1Ch 13:13; 2Ch 25:24
26:19 [k]2Ch 35:15; Ne 7:1; Eze 44:11

k *14* A variant of *Meshelemiah*

The treasurers and other officials.

20Their fellow Levites[a] were[l] in charge
of the treasuries of the house of God and
the treasuries for the dedicated things.[b]
21The descendants of Ladan, who
were Gershonites through Ladan and
who were heads of families belonging
to Ladan the Gershonite,[c] were Jehieli,
22the sons of Jehieli, Zetham and his
brother Joel. They were in charge of the
treasuries[d] of the temple of the LORD.
23From the Amramites, the Izharites,
the Hebronites and the Uzzielites:[e]

24Shubael,[f] a descendant of Gershom
son of Moses, was the officer in
charge of the treasuries. 25His
relatives through Eliezer: Rehabiah his son, Jeshaiah his son,
Joram his son, Zicri his son and
Shelomith[g] his son. 26Shelomith
and his relatives were in charge
of all the treasuries for the
things dedicated[h] by King David,
by the heads of families who were
the commanders of thousands
and commanders of hundreds,
and by the other army commanders. 27Some of the plunder tak-
en in battle they dedicated for the
repair of the temple of the LORD.
28And everything dedicated by
Samuel the seer[i] and by Saul son
of Kish, Abner son of Ner and
Joab son of Zeruiah, and all the
other dedicated things were in
the care of Shelomith and his relatives.
29From the Izharites: Kenaniah and
his sons were assigned duties
away from the temple, as officials
and judges[j] over Israel.
30From the Hebronites: Hashabiah[k]
and his relatives—seventeen hundred able men—were responsible
in Israel west of the Jordan for all
the work of the LORD and for the
king's service. 31As for the Hebronites,[l] Jeriah was their chief
according to the genealogical
records of their families. In the
fortieth[m] year of David's reign a
search was made in the records,
and capable men among the
Hebronites were found at Jazer
in Gilead. 32Jeriah had twenty-
seven hundred relatives, who
were able men and heads of families, and King David put them in
charge of the Reubenites, the
Gadites and the half-tribe of Manasseh for every matter pertaining to God and for the affairs of
the king.

Commanders for the twelve months.

27 This is the list of the Israelites—
heads of families, commanders
of thousands and commanders of hundreds, and their officers, who served the
king in all that concerned the army divisions that were on duty month by month
throughout the year. Each division consisted of 24,000 men.

2In charge of the first division, for the
first month, was Jashobeam[n] son of
Zabdiel. There were 24,000 men
in his division. 3He was a descendant of Perez and chief of all the
army officers for the first month.
4In charge of the division for the second month was Dodai[o] the Ahohite;
Mikloth was the leader of his division. There were 24,000 men in
his division.
5The third army commander, for the
third month, was Benaiah[p] son of
Jehoiada the priest. He was chief
and there were 24,000 men in his
division. 6This was the Benaiah who
was a mighty man among the Thirty
and was over the Thirty. His son
Ammizabad was in charge of his
division.
7The fourth, for the fourth month, was
Asahel[q] the brother of Joab; his son
Zebadiah was his successor. There
were 24,000 men in his division.
8The fifth, for the fifth month, was

26:20 [a]2Ch 24:5 [b]1Ch 28:12
26:21 [c]1Ch 23:7; 29:8
26:22 [d]1Ch 9:26
26:23 [e]Nu 3:27
26:24 [f]1Ch 23:16
26:25 [g]1Ch 23:18
26:26 [h]2Sa 8:11
26:28 [i]1Sa 9:9
26:29 [j]Dt 17:8-13; 1Ch 23:4; Ne 11:16
26:30 [k]1Ch 27:17
26:31 [l]1Ch 23:19 [m]2Sa 5:4
27:2 [n]2Sa 23:8; 1Ch 11:11
27:4 [o]2Sa 23:9
27:5 [p]2Sa 23:20
27:7 [q]2Sa 2:18; 1Ch 11:26

[l]20 Septuagint; Hebrew *As for the Levites, Ahijah was*

the commander Shamhuth[a] the Izrahite. There were 24,000 men in his division.
9The sixth, for the sixth month, was Ira[b] the son of Ikkesh the Tekoite. There were 24,000 men in his division.
10The seventh, for the seventh month, was Helez[c] the Pelonite, an Ephraimite. There were 24,000 men in his division.
11The eighth, for the eighth month, was Sibbecai[d] the Hushathite, a Zerahite. There were 24,000 men in his division.
12The ninth, for the ninth month, was Abiezer[e] the Anathothite, a Benjamite. There were 24,000 men in his division.
13The tenth, for the tenth month, was Maharai[f] the Netophathite, a Zerahite. There were 24,000 men in his division.
14The eleventh, for the eleventh month, was Benaiah[g] the Pirathonite, an Ephraimite. There were 24,000 men in his division.
15The twelfth, for the twelfth month, was Heldai[h] the Netophathite, from the family of Othniel.[i] There were 24,000 men in his division.

Officers for the twelve tribes.

16The officers over the tribes of Israel:

over the Reubenites: Eliezer son of Zicri;
over the Simeonites: Shephatiah son of Maacah;
17over Levi: Hashabiah[j] son of Kemuel;
over Aaron: Zadok;[k]
18over Judah: Elihu, a brother of David;
over Issachar: Omri son of Michael;
19over Zebulun: Ishmaiah son of Obadiah;
over Naphtali: Jerimoth son of Azriel;
20over the Ephraimites: Hoshea son of Azaziah;
over half the tribe of Manasseh: Joel son of Pedaiah;
21over the half-tribe of Manasseh in Gilead: Iddo son of Zechariah;
over Benjamin: Jaasiel son of Abner;
22over Dan: Azarel son of Jeroham.

These were the officers over the tribes of Israel.

23David did not take the number of the men twenty years old or less,[l] because the LORD had promised to make Israel as numerous as the stars[m] in the sky. 24Joab son of Zeruiah began to count the men but did not finish. Wrath came on Israel on account of this numbering,[n] and the number was not entered in the book[m] of the annals of King David.

David's officials.

25Azmaveth son of Adiel was in charge of the royal storehouses.

Jonathan son of Uzziah was in charge of the storehouses in the outlying districts, in the towns, the villages and the watchtowers.

26Ezri son of Kelub was in charge of the field workers who farmed the land.

27Shimei the Ramathite was in charge of the vineyards.

Zabdi the Shiphmite was in charge of the produce of the vineyards for the wine vats.

28Baal-Hanan the Gederite was in charge of the olive and sycamore-fig[o] trees in the western foothills.

Joash was in charge of the supplies of olive oil.

29Shitrai the Sharonite was in charge of the herds grazing in Sharon.

Shaphat son of Adlai was in charge of the herds in the valleys.

30Obil the Ishmaelite was in charge of the camels.

Jehdeiah the Meronothite was in charge of the donkeys.

31Jaziz the Hagrite[p] was in charge of the flocks.

27:8 [a]1Ch 11:27
27:9 [b]2Sa 23:26; 1Ch 11:28
27:10 [c]2Sa 23:26; 1Ch 11:27
27:11 [d]2Sa 21:18
27:12 [e]2Sa 23:27; 1Ch 11:28
27:13 [f]2Sa 23:28; 1Ch 11:30
27:14 [g]1Ch 11:31
27:15 [h]2Sa 23:29 [i]Jos 15:17
27:17 [j]1Ch 26:30 [k]2Sa 8:17; 1Ch 12:28
27:23 [l]1Ch 21:2-5 [m]Ge 15:5
27:24 [n]2Sa 24:15; 1Ch 21:7
27:28 [o]1Ki 10:27; 2Ch 1:15
27:31 [p]1Ch 5:10

[m]24 Septuagint; Hebrew *number*

All these were the officials in charge
of King David's property.

32Jonathan, David's uncle, was a counselor, a man of insight and a scribe.
Jehiel son of Hacmoni took care of the
king's sons.
33Ahithophel[a] was the king's counselor.
Hushai[b] the Arkite was the king's
friend. 34Ahithophel was succeeded by
Jehoiada son of Benaiah and by Abiathar.[c]
Joab[d] was the commander of the royal army.

David exhorts Solomon to build the temple.

28 David summoned all the officials[e] of Israel to assemble at
Jerusalem: the officers over the tribes,
the commanders of the divisions in the
service of the king, the commanders of
thousands and commanders of hundreds, and the officials in charge of all
the property and livestock belonging to
the king and his sons, together with the
palace officials, the mighty men and all
the brave warriors.
2King David rose to his feet and said:
"Listen to me, my brothers and my
people. I had it in my heart[f] to build a
house as a place of rest for the ark of the
covenant of the LORD, for the footstool[g]
of our God, and I made plans to build it.
3But God said to me,[h] 'You are not to
build a house for my Name,[i] because
you are a warrior and have shed blood.'[j]
4"Yet the LORD, the God of Israel,
chose me[k] from my whole family[l] to be
king over Israel forever. He chose
Judah[m] as leader, and from the house of
Judah he chose my family, and from my
father's sons he was pleased to make me
king over all Israel. 5Of all my sons—and
the LORD has given me many[n]—he has
chosen my son Solomon[o] to sit on the
throne of the kingdom of the LORD over
Israel. 6He said to me: 'Solomon your
son is the one who will build my house
and my courts, for I have chosen him to
be my son,[p] and I will be his father. 7I

27:33 [a]2Sa 15:12 [b]2Sa 15:37
27:34 [c]1Ki 1:7 [d]1Ch 11:6
28:1 [e]1Ch 11:10; 27:1-31
28:2 [f]1Ch 17:2 [g]Ps 99:5; 132:7
28:3 [h]2Sa 7:5 [i]1Ch 22:8 [j]1Ki 5:3; 1Ch 17:4
28:4 [k]1Ch 17:23,27; 2Ch 6:6 [l]1Sa 16:1-13 [m]Ge 49:10; 1Ch 5:2
28:5 [n]1Ch 3:1 [o]1Ch 22:9; 23:1
28:6 [p]2Sa 7:13; 1Ch 22:9-10
28:7 [q]1Ch 22:13
28:8 [r]Dt 6:1 [s]Dt 4:1
28:9 [t]1Ch 29:19 [u]1Sa 16:7; Ps 7:9 [v]Ps 40:16; Jer 29:13 [w]Jos 24:20; 2Ch 15:2 [x]Ps 44:23
28:11 [y]Ex 25:9
28:12 [z]1Ch 12:18 [a]1Ch 26:20
28:13 [b]1Ch 24:1
28:15 [c]Ex 25:31
28:16 [d]Ex 25:23

will establish his kingdom forever if he
is unswerving in carrying out my commands and laws,[q] as is being done at
this time.'
8"So now I charge you in the sight of
all Israel and of the assembly of the
LORD, and in the hearing of our God: Be
careful to follow all the commands[r] of
the LORD your God, that you may possess this good land and pass it on as an
inheritance to your descendants forever.[s]
9"And you, my son Solomon, acknowledge the God of your father, and serve
him with wholehearted devotion[t] and
with a willing mind, for the LORD
searches every heart[u] and understands
every motive behind the thoughts. If
you seek him,[v] he will be found by you;
but if you forsake[w] him, he will reject[x]
you forever. 10Consider now, for the
LORD has chosen you to build a temple as
a sanctuary. Be strong and do the work."

David gives Solomon the plans for the temple.

11Then David gave his son Solomon
the plans[y] for the portico of the temple,
its buildings, its storerooms, its upper
parts, its inner rooms and the place of
atonement. 12He gave him the plans of
all that the Spirit[z] had put in his mind
for the courts of the temple of the LORD
and all the surrounding rooms, for the
treasuries of the temple of God and for
the treasuries for the dedicated things.[a]
13He gave him instructions for the divisions[b] of the priests and Levites, and for
all the work of serving in the temple of
the LORD, as well as for all the articles to
be used in its service. 14He designated
the weight of gold for all the gold articles
to be used in various kinds of service,
and the weight of silver for all the silver
articles to be used in various kinds of
service: 15the weight of gold for the gold
lampstands[c] and their lamps, with the
weight for each lampstand and its lamps;
and the weight of silver for each silver
lampstand and its lamps, according to
the use of each lampstand; 16the weight
of gold for each table[d] for consecrated

bread; the weight of silver for the silver
tables; 17 the weight of pure gold for the
forks, sprinkling bowls[a] and pitchers;
the weight of gold for each gold dish;
the weight of silver for each silver dish;
18 and the weight of the refined gold for
the altar of incense.[b] He also gave him
the plan for the chariot,[c] that is, the
cherubim of gold that spread their wings
and shelter[d] the ark of the covenant of
the LORD.

19 "All this," David said, "I have in
writing from the hand of the LORD upon
me, and he gave me understanding in
all the details[e] of the plan.[f]"

20 David also said to Solomon his son,
"Be strong and courageous,[g] and do the
work. Do not be afraid or discouraged,
for the LORD God, my God, is with you.
He will not fail you or forsake[h] you until
all the work for the service of the temple of the LORD is finished.[i] 21 The divisions of the priests and Levites are ready
for all the work on the temple of God,
and every willing man skilled[j] in any
craft will help you in all the work. The
officials and all the people will obey your
every command."

Abundant offerings for building the temple.

29 Then King David said to the
whole assembly: "My son
Solomon, the one whom God has chosen, is young and inexperienced.[k] The
task is great, because this palatial structure is not for man but for the LORD
God. 2 With all my resources I have provided for the temple of my God—gold[l]
for the gold work, silver for the silver,
bronze for the bronze, iron for the iron
and wood for the wood, as well as onyx
for the settings, turquoise,[n][m] stones of
various colors, and all kinds of fine stone
and marble—all of these in large quantities.[n] 3 Besides, in my devotion to the
temple of my God I now give my personal treasures of gold and silver for the
temple of my God, over and above
everything I have provided[o] for this holy
temple: 4 three thousand talents[o] of gold
(gold of Ophir)[p] and seven thousand
talents[p] of refined silver,[q] for the overlay-
ing of the walls of the buildings, 5 for the
gold work and the silver work, and for
all the work to be done by the craftsmen. Now, who is willing to consecrate
himself today to the LORD?"

6 Then the leaders of families, the
officers of the tribes of Israel, the commanders of thousands and commanders
of hundreds, and the officials[r] in charge
of the king's work gave willingly.[s] 7 They[t]
gave toward the work on the temple of
God five thousand talents[q] and ten thousand darics[r] of gold, ten thousand talents[s] of silver, eighteen thousand talents[t]
of bronze and a hundred thousand talents[u] of iron. 8 Any who had precious
stones[u] gave them to the treasury of the
temple of the LORD in the custody of
Jehiel the Gershonite.[v] 9 The people rejoiced at the willing response of their
leaders, for they had given freely and
wholeheartedly[w] to the LORD. David
the king also rejoiced greatly.

David's praise and thanks to God.

10 David praised the LORD in the presence of the whole assembly, saying,

"Praise be to you, O LORD,
  God of our father Israel,
  from everlasting to everlasting.
11 Yours, O LORD, is the greatness and
    the power[x]
  and the glory and the majesty and
    the splendor,
  for everything in heaven and earth
    is yours.[y]
Yours, O LORD, is the kingdom;
  you are exalted as head over all.[z]
12 Wealth and honor[a] come from you;
  you are the ruler[b] of all things.

28:17 [a]Ex 27:3
28:18 [b]Ex 30:1-10 [c]Ex 25:18-22 [d]Ex 25:20
28:19 [e]1Ki 6:38 [f]Ex 25:9
28:20 [g]Dt 31:6; 1Ch 22:13; 2Ch 19:11; Hag 2:4 [h]Dt 4:31; Jos 24:20 [i]1Ki 6:14; 2Ch 7:11
28:21 [j]Ex 35:25–36:5
29:1 [k]1Ki 3:7; 1Ch 22:5; 2Ch 13:7
29:2 [l]ver 7,14,16; Ezr 1:4; 6:5; Hag 2:8 [m]Isa 54:11 [n]1Ch 22:2-5
29:3 [o]2Ch 24:10; 31:3; 35:8
29:4 [p]Ge 10:29 [q]1Ch 22:14
29:6 [r]1Ch 27:1; 28:1 [s]ver 9; Ex 25:1-8; 35:20-29; 36:2; 2Ch 24:10; Ezr 7:15
29:7 [t]Ex 25:2; Ne 7:70-71
29:8 [u]Ex 35:27 [v]1Ch 26:21
29:9 [w]1Ki 8:61; 2Co 9:7
29:11 [x]Ps 24:8; 59:17; 62:11 [y]Ps 89:11 [z]Rev 5:12-13
29:12 [a]2Ch 1:12 [b]2Ch 20:6; Ro 11:36

[n]*2* The meaning of the Hebrew for this word is uncertain. [o]*4* That is, about 110 tons (about 100 metric tons) [p]*4* That is, about 260 tons (about 240 metric tons) [q]*7* That is, about 190 tons (about 170 metric tons) [r]*7* That is, about 185 pounds (about 84 kilograms) [s]*7* That is, about 375 tons (about 345 metric tons) [t]*7* That is, about 675 tons (about 610 metric tons) [u]*7* That is, about 3,750 tons (about 3,450 metric tons)

In your hands are strength and power
to exalt and give strength to all.
13Now, our God, we give you thanks,
and praise your glorious name.

14"But who am I, and who are my
people, that we should be able to give
as generously as this? Everything comes
from you, and we have given you only
what comes from your hand. 15We are
aliens and strangers[a] in your sight, as
were all our forefathers. Our days on
earth are like a shadow,[b] without hope.
16O LORD our God, as for all this abundance that we have provided for building you a temple for your Holy Name,
it comes from your hand, and all of it
belongs to you. 17I know, my God, that
you test the heart[c] and are pleased with
integrity. All these things have I given
willingly and with honest intent. And
now I have seen with joy how willingly
your people who are here have given to
you.[d] 18O LORD, God of our fathers Abraham, Isaac and Israel, keep this desire in
the hearts of your people forever, and
keep their hearts loyal to you. 19And
give my son Solomon the wholehearted
devotion[e] to keep your commands, requirements and decrees[f] and to do
everything to build the palatial structure
for which I have provided."[g]

20Then David said to the whole
assembly, "Praise the LORD your God."
So they all praised the LORD, the God of
their fathers; they bowed low and fell
prostrate before the LORD and the king.

Anointing of Solomon as king.

29:21-25pp—1Ki 1:28-53

21The next day they made sacrifices to
the LORD and presented burnt offerings
to him:[h] a thousand bulls, a thousand
rams and a thousand male lambs,
together with their drink offerings, and
other sacrifices in abundance for all
Israel. 22They ate and drank with great
joy[i] in the presence of the LORD that day.

Then they acknowledged Solomon
son of David as king a second time,
anointing him before the LORD to be
ruler and Zadok[j] to be priest. 23So Solomon sat on the throne[k] of the LORD as
king in place of his father David. He
prospered and all Israel obeyed him.
24All the officers and mighty men, as
well as all of King David's sons, pledged
their submission to King Solomon.

25The LORD highly exalted Solomon in
the sight of all Israel and bestowed on
him royal splendor[l] such as no king over
Israel ever had before.[m]

David's death.

29:26-28pp— 1Ki 2:10-12

26David son of Jesse was king[n] over all
Israel. 27He ruled over Israel forty
years—seven in Hebron and thirty-three
in Jerusalem.[o] 28He died[p] at a good old
age, having enjoyed long life, wealth
and honor. His son Solomon succeeded
him as king.[q]

29As for the events of King David's
reign, from beginning to end, they are
written in the records of Samuel the
seer,[r] the records of Nathan[s] the prophet
and the records of Gad[t] the seer,
30together with the details of his reign
and power, and the circumstances that
surrounded him and Israel and the kingdoms of all the other lands.

29:15 [a]Ps 39:12; Heb 11:13 [b]Job 14:2
29:17 [c]Ps 139:23; Pr 15:11; 17:3; Jer 11:20; 17:10 [d]1Ch 28:9; Ps 15:1-5
29:19 [e]1Ch 28:9 [f]Ps 72:1 [g]1Ch 22:14
29:21 [h]1Ki 8:62
29:22 [i]1Ch 23:1 [j]1Ki 1:33-39
29:23 [k]1Ki 2:12
29:25 [l]2Ch 1:1,12 [m]1Ki 3:13; Ecc 2:9
29:26 [n]1Ch 18:14
29:27 [o]2Sa 5:4-5; 1Ki 2:11; 1Ch 3:4
29:28 [p]Ge 15:15; Ac 13:36 [q]1Ch 23:1
29:29 [r]1Sa 9:9 [s]2Sa 7:2 [t]1Sa 22:5

2 CHRONICLES

Author: Unknown (possibly Ezra).

Date Written: Between 450 and 400 B.C. (compiled from earlier sources).

Time Span: 430-440 years (period of time from Solomon's reign through the Babylonian captivity).

Title: The books of 1 and 2 Chronicles are so named because they "chronicle" the entire history of God's people from Genesis through Kings. The title used in the Hebrew Bible means "the accounts of the days."

Background: The last book of the Hebrew Bible has been broken down into 1 and 2 Chronicles in modern translations. The Chronicles are different in perspective from the books of Samuel and Kings, even though they cover much of the same material. Instead of prophetic, moral and political views, they are presented from a priest's point of view, evaluating the nation's religious history. 2 Chronicles is a sequel to the book of 1 Chronicles.

Where Written: Unknown (possibly Judah).

To Whom: To the remnant of Judah returning from Babylon.

Content: 2 Chronicles records the history of the southern kingdom of Judah, from the reign of Solomon to the conclusion of the Babylonian exile. The decline of Judah is disappointing, but emphasis is given to the spiritual reformers who zealously seek to turn the people back to God. Little is said about the bad kings or of the failures of good kings; only goodness is stressed. Since Chronicles takes a priestly perspective, the northern kingdom of Israel is rarely mentioned because of her false worship and refusal to acknowledge the temple in Jerusalem. 2 Chronicles concludes with the final destruction of Jerusalem and the temple.

Key Words: "Temple"; "Revival." The "temple" of God is repeatedly emphasized: its construction; dedication (chapter 7); service; worship; destruction; and, finally, Cyrus's edict to rebuild it. Great "revivals" take place under the direction of Asa, Jehoshaphat, Joash, Hezekiah and Josiah.

Themes: • Obedience is victory...disobedience is defeat. • God desires to forgive and heal those who will humbly pray and repent. • A nation's leaders are a reflection of a nation's people. • No worthy project can be completed right without the help of Almighty God. • God hates sin and will not tolerate it. • Our personal efforts are worthless if done outside the will of God.

Outline:
1. The reign of Solomon. 1:1-1:17
2. Solomon's building of the temple. 2:1-7:22
3. Latter years of Solomon's reign. 8:1-9:31
4. The reigns of the kings of Judah. 10:1-36:14
5. The fall of Jerusalem. 36:15-36:23

2 CHRONICLES

Solomon asks for wisdom.

1:2-13pp— 1Ki 3:4-15

1 Solomon son of David established[a]
himself firmly over his kingdom, for
the LORD his God was with[b] him and
made him exceedingly great.[c]
2Then Solomon spoke to all
Israel[d]—to the commanders of thousands and commanders of hundreds, to
the judges and to all the leaders in
Israel, the heads of families— 3and
Solomon and the whole assembly went
to the high place at Gibeon, for God's
Tent of Meeting[e] was there, which
Moses[f] the LORD's servant had made in
the desert. 4Now David had brought
up the ark[g] of God from Kiriath Jearim
to the place he had prepared for it,
because he had pitched a tent[h] for it in
Jerusalem. 5But the bronze altar[i] that
Bezalel[j] son of Uri, the son of Hur, had
made was in Gibeon in front of the
tabernacle of the LORD; so Solomon and
the assembly inquired[k] of him there.
6Solomon went up to the bronze altar
before the LORD in the Tent of Meeting
and offered a thousand burnt offerings
on it.
7That night God appeared[l] to Solomon
and said to him, "Ask for whatever you
want me to give you."
8Solomon answered God, "You have
shown great kindness to David my father
and have made me[m] king in his place.
9Now, LORD God, let your promise[n] to
my father David be confirmed, for you
have made me king over a people who
are as numerous as the dust of the
earth.[o] 10Give me wisdom and knowledge, that I may lead[p] this people, for
who is able to govern this great people
of yours?"
11God said to Solomon, "Since this is
your heart's desire and you have not
asked for wealth,[q] riches or honor, nor
for the death of your enemies, and since
you have not asked for a long life but for
wisdom and knowledge to govern my
people over whom I have made you
king, 12therefore wisdom and knowledge
will be given you. And I will also give
you wealth, riches and honor,[r] such as
no king who was before you ever had
and none after you will have.[s]"
13Then Solomon went to Jerusalem
from the high place at Gibeon, from before the Tent of Meeting. And he reigned
over Israel.

Solomon's wealth.

1:14-17pp— 1Ki 10:26-29; 2Ch 9:25-28

14Solomon accumulated chariots[t] and
horses; he had fourteen hundred chariots and twelve thousand horses,[a] which
he kept in the chariot cities and also
with him in Jerusalem. 15The king made
silver and gold[u] as common in Jerusalem
as stones, and cedar as plentiful as sycamore-fig trees in the foothills. 16Solo-
mon's horses were imported from Egypt[b]
and from Kue[c]—the royal merchants
purchased them from Kue. 17They imported a chariot[v] from Egypt for six hundred shekels[d] of silver, and a horse for a
hundred and fifty.[e] They also exported
them to all the kings of the Hittites and
of the Arameans.

Hiram supplies timber for building the temple.

2:1-18pp— 1Ki 5:1-16

2 Solomon gave orders to build a
temple[w] for the Name of the LORD
and a royal palace for himself.[x] 2He conscripted seventy thousand men as carriers and eighty thousand as stonecutters
in the hills and thirty-six hundred as
foremen over them.[y]
3Solomon sent this message to
Hiram[f][z] king of Tyre:

"Send me cedar logs[a] as you did
for my father David when you sent

1:1 [a]1Ki 2:12,26; 2Ch 12:1 [b]Ge 21:22; 39:2; Nu 14:43 [c]1Ch 29:25
1:2 [d]1Ch 9:1; 28:1
1:3 [e]Ex 36:8 [f]Ex 40:18
1:4 [g]2Sa 6:2; 1Ch 15:25 [h]2Sa 6:17; 1Ch 15:1
1:5 [i]Ex 38:2 [j]Ex 31:2 [k]1Ch 13:3
1:7 [l]2Ch 7:12
1:8 [m]1Ch 23:1; 28:5
1:9 [n]2Sa 7:25; 1Ki 8:25 [o]Ge 12:2
1:10 [p]Nu 27:17; 2Sa 5:2; Pr 8:15-16
1:11 [q]Dt 17:17
1:12 [r]1Ch 29:12 [s]1Ch 29:25; 2Ch 9:22; Ne 13:26
1:14 [t]1Sa 8:11; 1Ki 4:26; 9:19
1:15 [u]1Ki 9:28; Isa 60:5
1:17 [v]SS 1:9
2:1 [w]Dt 12:5 [x]Ecc 2:4
2:2 [y]ver 18; 2Ch 10:4
2:3 [z]2Sa 5:11 [a]1Ch 14:1

a *14* Or *charioteers* b *16* Or possibly *Muzur,* a region in Cilicia; also in verse 17 c *16* Probably Cilicia d *17* That is, about 15 pounds (about 7 kilograms) e *17* That is, about 3 3/4 pounds (about 1.7 kilograms) f *3* Hebrew *Huram,* a variant of *Hiram*; also in verses 11 and 12

KEY PLACES IN 2 CHRONICLES

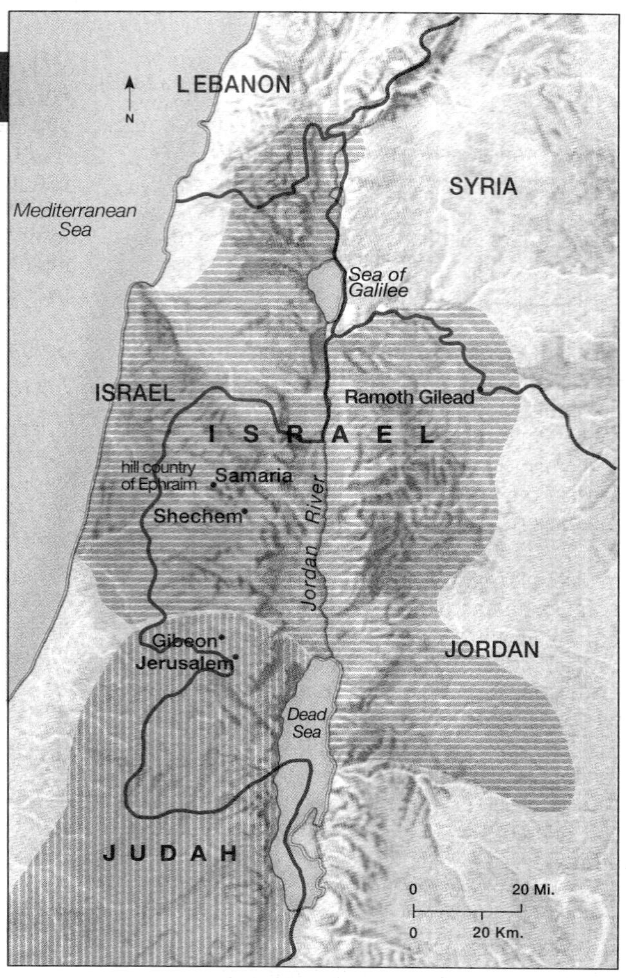

Gibeon David's son Solomon became king over Israel. He summoned the nation's leaders to a ceremony in Gibeon. Here God told Solomon to ask for whatever he desired. Solomon asked for wisdom and knowledge to rule Israel (1:1-12).

Jerusalem After the ceremony in Gibeon, Solomon returned to the capital city, Jerusalem. His reign began a golden age for Israel. Solomon implemented the plans for the temple which had been drawn up by his father, David. It was a magnificent construction. It symbolized Solomon's wealth and wisdom, which became known worldwide (1:13–9:31).

Shechem After Solomon's death, his son Rehoboam was ready to be crowned in Shechem. However, his promise of higher taxes and harder work for the people led to rebellion. Everyone but the tribes of Judah and Benjamin deserted Rehoboam and set up their own kingdom to the north called Israel. Rehoboam returned to Jerusalem as ruler over the southern kingdom called Judah (10:1–12:16). The remainder of 2 Chronicles records the history of Judah.

Hill Country of Ephraim Abijah became the next king of Judah, and soon war broke out between Israel and Judah. When the armies of the two nations arrived for battle in the hill country of Ephraim, Israel had twice as many troops as Judah. It looked like Judah's defeat was certain. But they cried out to God, and God gave them victory over Israel. In their history as separate nations, Judah had a few godly kings who instituted reforms and brought the people back to God. Israel, however, had a succession of only evil kings (13:1-22).

Aram Asa, a godly king, removed every trace of pagan worship from Judah and renewed the people's covenant with God in Jerusalem. But King Baasha of Israel built a fortress to control traffic into Judah. Instead of looking to God for guidance, Asa took silver and gold from the temple and sent it to the king of Aram requesting his help against King Baasha. As a result, God became angry with Judah (14:1–16:14).

Samaria Although Jehoshaphat was a godly king, he allied himself with Israel's most evil king, Ahab. Ahab's capital was in Samaria. Ahab wanted help fighting against Ramoth Gilead. Jehoshaphat wanted advice, but rather than listening to God's prophet who had promised defeat, he joined Ahab in battle (17:1–18:27).

Ramoth Gilead The alliance with Israel against Ramoth Gilead ended in defeat and Ahab's death. Although shaken by his defeat, Jehoshaphat returned to Jerusalem and to God. But his son Jehoram was a wicked king, as was his son Ahaziah, and history repeated itself. Ahaziah formed an alliance with Israel's King Joram to do battle with the Arameans at Ramoth Gilead. This led to the death of both kings (18:28–22:9).

Jerusalem The rest of Judah's history recorded in 2 Chronicles centers on Jerusalem. Some kings caused Judah to sin by bringing idol worship into their midst. Others cleaned up the idol worship, reopened and restored the temple and, in the case of Josiah, tried to follow God's laws as they were written by Moses. In spite of the few good influences, a series of evil kings sent Judah into a downward spiral that ended with the Babylonian empire overrunning the country. The temple was burned, the walls of the city were broken down, and the people were deported to Babylon.

him cedar to build a palace to live
in. 4Now I am about to build a temple[a] for the Name of the LORD my
God and to dedicate it to him for
burning fragrant incense[b] before
him, for setting out the consecrated
bread[c] regularly, and for making
burnt offerings[d] every morning and
evening and on Sabbaths[e] and New
Moons and at the appointed feasts
of the LORD our God. This is a lasting ordinance for Israel.

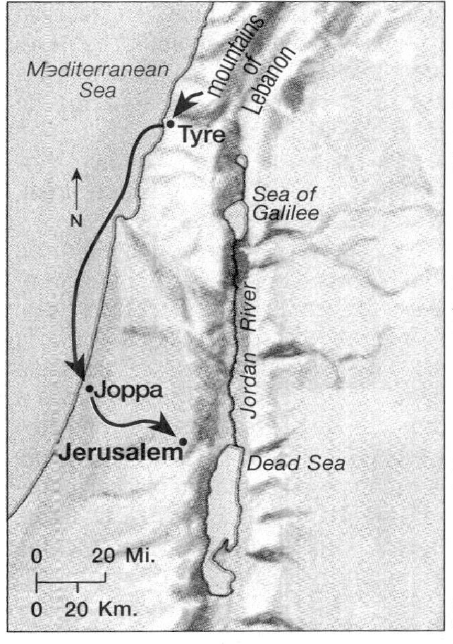

Shipping Resources for the Temple

Solomon asked King Hiram of Tyre to provide supplies and skilled workmen to help build God's temple in Jerusalem. The plan was to cut the cedar logs in the mountains of Lebanon, float them by sea to Joppa, then bring them inland to Jerusalem by the shortest and easiest route.

5"The temple I am going to build
will be great,[f] because our God is
greater than all other gods.[g] 6But
who is able to build a temple for
him, since the heavens, even the
highest heavens, cannot contain
him?[h] Who then am I[i] to build a
temple for him, except as a place to
burn sacrifices before him?
7"Send me, therefore, a man
skilled to work in gold and silver,
bronze and iron, and in purple,
crimson and blue yarn, and experienced in the art of engraving, to
work in Judah and Jerusalem with
my skilled craftsmen,[j] whom my
father David provided.
8"Send me also cedar, pine and
algum[g] logs from Lebanon, for I
know that your men are skilled in
cutting timber there. My men will
work with yours 9to provide me
with plenty of lumber, because the
temple I build must be large and
magnificent. 10I will give your servants, the woodsmen who cut the
timber, twenty thousand cors[h] of
ground wheat, twenty thousand cors
of barley, twenty thousand baths[i]
of wine and twenty thousand baths
of olive oil.[k]"

11Hiram king of Tyre replied by letter
to Solomon:

"Because the LORD loves[l] his people, he has made you their king."

12And Hiram added:

"Praise be to the LORD, the God
of Israel, who made heaven and
earth![m] He has given King David a
wise son, endowed with intelligence and discernment, who will
build a temple for the LORD and a
palace for himself.
13"I am sending you Huram-
Abi,[n] a man of great skill, 14whose
mother was from Dan[o] and whose
father was from Tyre. He is trained[p]
to work in gold and silver, bronze
and iron, stone and wood, and with
purple and blue[q] and crimson yarn
and fine linen. He is experienced in
all kinds of engraving and can execute any design given to him. He
will work with your craftsmen and
with those of my lord, David your
father.

2:4 [a]ver 1; Dt 12:5 [b]Ex 30:7 [c]Ex 25:30 [d]Ex 29:42; 2Ch 13:11 [e]Nu 28:9-10
2:5 [f]1Ch 22:5; Ps 135:5 [g]1Ch 16:25
2:6 [h]1Ki 8:27; 2Ch 6:18; Jer 23:24 [i]Ex 3:11
2:7 [j]ver 13-14; Ex 35:31; 1Ch 22:16
2:10 [k]Ezr 3:7
2:11 [l]1Ki 10:9; 2Ch 9:8
2:12 [m]Ne 9:6; Ps 8:3; 33:6; 102:25
2:13 [n]1Ki 7:13
2:14 [o]Ex 31:6 [p]Ex 35:31 [q]Ex 35:35

g *8* Probably a variant of *almug*; possibly juniper
h *10* That is, probably about 125,000 bushels (about 4,400 kiloliters)
i *10* That is, probably about 115,000 gallons (about 440 kiloliters)

15"Now let my lord send his servants the wheat and barley and the
olive oil[a] and wine he promised,
16and we will cut all the logs from
Lebanon that you need and will
float them in rafts by sea down to
Joppa.[b] You can then take them up
to Jerusalem."

17Solomon took a census of all the
aliens[c] who were in Israel, after the census[d] his father David had taken; and
they were found to be 153,600. 18He
assigned[e] 70,000 of them to be carriers and 80,000 to be stonecutters in the
hills, with 3,600 foremen over them to
keep the people working.

Details concerning the temple's construction.

3:1-14pp— 1Ki 6:1-29

3 Then Solomon began to build[f] the
temple of the LORD[g] in Jerusalem on
Mount Moriah, where the LORD had appeared to his father David. It was on the
threshing floor of Araunah[i][h] the Jebusite,
the place provided by David. 2He began
building on the second day of the second
month in the fourth year of his reign.[i]

3The foundation Solomon laid for
building the temple of God was sixty
cubits long and twenty cubits wide[k][j]
(using the cubit of the old standard).
4The portico at the front of the temple
was twenty cubits[l] long across the width
of the building and twenty cubits[m] high.

He overlaid the inside with pure gold.
5He paneled the main hall with pine
and covered it with fine gold and decorated it with palm tree[k] and chain designs. 6He adorned the temple with
precious stones. And the gold he used
was gold of Parvaim. 7He overlaid the
ceiling beams, doorframes, walls and
doors of the temple with gold, and he
carved cherubim[l] on the walls.

8He built the Most Holy Place,[m] its
length corresponding to the width of the
temple—twenty cubits long and twenty
cubits wide. He overlaid the inside with
six hundred talents[n] of fine gold. 9The
gold nails[n] weighed fifty shekels.[o] He
also overlaid the upper parts with gold.

10In the Most Holy Place he made a
pair[o] of sculptured cherubim and overlaid them with gold. 11The total wing-
span of the cherubim was twenty cubits.
One wing of the first cherub was five
cubits[p] long and touched the temple
wall, while its other wing, also five cubits long, touched the wing of the other
cherub. 12Similarly one wing of the second cherub was five cubits long and
touched the other temple wall, and its
other wing, also five cubits long, touched
the wing of the first cherub. 13The wings
of these cherubim[p] extended twenty cubits. They stood on their feet, facing the
main hall.[q]

14He made the curtain[q] of blue, purple and crimson yarn and fine linen,
with cherubim[r] worked into it.

15In the front of the temple he made
two pillars,[s] which ⌊together⌋ were
thirty-five cubits[r] long, each with a capital[t] on top measuring five cubits. 16He
made interwoven chains[s][u] and put them
on top of the pillars. He also made a
hundred pomegranates[v] and attached
them to the chains. 17He erected the pillars in the front of the temple, one to the
south and one to the north. The one to
the south he named Jakin[t] and the one
to the north Boaz.[u]

Details concerning the temple's furnishings.

4:2-6,10–5:1pp— 1Ki 7:23-26,38-51

4 He made a bronze altar[w] twenty cubits long, twenty cubits wide and

2:15 [a]ver 10; Ezr 3:7
2:16 [b]Jos 19:46; Jnh 1:3
2:17 [c]1Ch 22:2 [d]2Sa 24:2
2:18 [e]ver 2; 1Ch 22:2; 2Ch 8:8
3:1 [f]Ac 7:47 [g]Ge 28:17 [h]2Sa 24:18; 1Ch 21:18
3:2 [i]Ezr 5:11
3:3 [j]Eze 41:2
3:5 [k]Eze 40:16
3:7 [l]Ge 3:24; 1Ki 6:29-35; Eze 41:18
3:8 [m]Ex 26:33
3:9 [n]Ex 26:32
3:10 [o]Ex 25:18
3:13 [p]Ex 25:18
3:14 [q]Ex 26:31,33; Heb 9:3 [r]Ge 3:24
3:15 [s]1Ki 7:15; Rev 3:12 [t]1Ki 7:22
3:16 [u]1Ki 7:17 [v]1Ki 7:20
4:1 [w]Ex 20:24; 27:1-2; 40:6; 1Ki 8:64; 2Ki 16:14

[i]*1* Hebrew *Ornan,* a variant of *Araunah* [k]*3* That is, about 90 feet (about 27 meters) long and 30 feet (about 9 meters) wide [l]*4* That is, about 30 feet (about 9 meters); also in verses 8, 11 and 13 [m]*4* Some Septuagint and Syriac manuscripts; Hebrew *and a hundred and twenty* [n]*8* That is, about 23 tons (about 21 metric tons) [o]*9* That is, about 1 1/4 pounds (about 0.6 kilogram) [p]*11* That is, about 7 1/2 feet (about 2.3 meters); also in verse 15 [q]*13* Or *facing inward* [r]*15* That is, about 52 feet (about 16 meters) [s]*16* Or possibly *made chains in the inner sanctuary;* the meaning of the Hebrew for this phrase is uncertain. [t]*17* *Jakin* probably means *he establishes.* [u]*17* *Boaz* probably means *in him is strength.*

ten cubits high.[v] 2He made the Sea[a] of
cast metal, circular in shape, measuring
ten cubits from rim to rim and five cubits[w] high. It took a line of thirty cubits[x]
to measure around it. 3Below the rim,
figures of bulls encircled it—ten to a
cubit.[y] The bulls were cast in two rows
in one piece with the Sea.
4The Sea stood on twelve bulls, three
facing north, three facing west, three
facing south and three facing east.[b] The
Sea rested on top of them, and their
hindquarters were toward the center. 5It
was a handbreadth[z] in thickness, and
its rim was like the rim of a cup, like a
lily blossom. It held three thousand
baths.[a]
6He then made ten basins[c] for washing and placed five on the south side and
five on the north. In them the things to
be used for the burnt offerings[d] were
rinsed, but the Sea was to be used by
the priests for washing.
7He made ten gold lampstands[e] according to the specifications[f] for them
and placed them in the temple, five on
the south side and five on the north.
8He made ten tables[g] and placed them
in the temple, five on the south side and
five on the north. He also made a hundred gold sprinkling bowls.[h]
9He made the courtyard[i] of the priests,
and the large court and the doors for the
court, and overlaid the doors with
bronze. 10He placed the Sea on the
south side, at the southeast corner.
11He also made the pots and shovels
and sprinkling bowls.
So Huram finished[j] the work he had
undertaken for King Solomon in the
temple of God:

12the two pillars;
the two bowl-shaped capitals on top
of the pillars;
the two sets of network decorating
the two bowl-shaped capitals on
top of the pillars;
13the four hundred pomegranates
for the two sets of network (two
rows of pomegranates for each
network, decorating the bowl-
shaped capitals on top of the
pillars);
14the stands[k] with their basins;
15the Sea and the twelve bulls under
it;
16the pots, shovels, meat forks and all
related articles.

All the objects that Huram-Abi[l] made
for King Solomon for the temple of the
LORD were of polished bronze. 17The
king had them cast in clay molds in the
plain of the Jordan between Succoth[m]
and Zarethan.[b] 18All these things that
Solomon made amounted to so much
that the weight of the bronze[n] was not
determined.
19Solomon also made all the furnishings that were in God's temple:

the golden altar;
the tables[o] on which was the bread
of the Presence;
20the lampstands[p] of pure gold with
their lamps, to burn in front of
the inner sanctuary as prescribed;
21the gold floral work and lamps and
tongs (they were solid gold);
22the pure gold wick trimmers, sprinkling bowls, dishes[q] and censers;[r] and the gold doors of the
temple: the inner doors to the
Most Holy Place and the doors of
the main hall.

5 When all the work Solomon had
done for the temple of the LORD was
finished,[s] he brought in the things his
father David had dedicated[t]—the silver
and gold and all the furnishings—and he
placed them in the treasuries of God's
temple.

4:2 [a]Rev 4:6; 15:2
4:4 [b]Nu 2:3-25; Eze 48:30-34; Rev 21:13
4:6 [c]Ex 30:18 [d]Ne 13:5,9; Eze 40:38
4:7 [e]Ex 25:31 [f]Ex 25:40
4:8 [g]Ex 25:23 [h]Nu 4:14
4:9 [i]1Ki 6:36; 2Ki 21:5; 2Ch 33:5
4:11 [j]1Ki 7:14
4:14 [k]1Ki 7:27-30
4:16 [l]1Ki 7:13
4:17 [m]Ge 33:17
4:18 [n]1Ki 7:23
4:19 [o]Ex 25:23,30
4:20 [p]Ex 25:31
4:22 [q]Nu 7:14 [r]Lev 10:1
5:1 [s]1Ki 6:14 [t]2Sa 8:11

v *1* That is, about 30 feet (about 9 meters) long and wide, and about 15 feet (about 4.5 meters) high
w *2* That is, about 7 1/2 feet (about 2.3 meters)
x *2* That is, about 45 feet (about 13.5 meters)
y *3* That is, about 1 1/2 feet (about 0.5 meter)
z *5* That is, about 3 inches (about 8 centimeters)
a *5* That is, about 17,500 gallons (about 66 kiloliters)
b *17* Hebrew *Zeredatha,* a variant of *Zarethan*

The ark is brought into the Most Holy Place.

5:2–6:11pp— 1Ki 8:1-21

[2]Then Solomon summoned to Jerusalem the elders of Israel, all the heads of the tribes and the chiefs of the Israelite families, to bring up the ark[a] of the LORD's covenant from Zion, the City of David. [3]And all the men of Israel[b] came together to the king at the time of the festival in the seventh month.

[4]When all the elders of Israel had arrived, the Levites took up the ark, [5]and they brought up the ark and the Tent of Meeting and all the sacred furnishings in it. The priests, who were Levites,[c] carried them up; [6]and King Solomon and the entire assembly of Israel that had gathered about him were before the ark, sacrificing so many sheep and cattle that they could not be recorded or counted.

[7]The priests then brought the ark[d] of the LORD's covenant to its place in the inner sanctuary of the temple, the Most Holy Place, and put it beneath the wings of the cherubim. [8]The cherubim[e] spread their wings over the place of the ark and covered the ark and its carrying poles. [9]These poles were so long that their ends, extending from the ark, could be seen from in front of the inner sanctuary, but not from outside the Holy Place; and they are still there today. [10]There was nothing in the ark except[f] the two tablets[g] that Moses had placed in it at Horeb, where the LORD made a covenant with the Israelites after they came out of Egypt.

[11]The priests then withdrew from the Holy Place. All the priests who were there had consecrated themselves, regardless of their divisions.[h] [12]All the Levites who were musicians[i]—Asaph, Heman, Jeduthun and their sons and relatives—stood on the east side of the altar, dressed in fine linen and playing cymbals, harps and lyres. They were accompanied by 120 priests sounding trumpets.[j] [13]The trumpeters and singers joined in unison, as with one voice, to give praise and thanks to the LORD. Accompanied by trumpets, cymbals and other instruments, they raised their voices in praise to the LORD and sang:

> "He is good;
> his love endures forever."[k]

Then the temple of the LORD was filled with a cloud, [14]and the priests could not perform[l] their service because of the cloud,[m] for the glory[n] of the LORD filled the temple of God.

6 Then Solomon said, "The LORD has said that he would dwell in a dark cloud;[o] [2]I have built a magnificent temple for you, a place for you to dwell forever.[p]"

[3]While the whole assembly of Israel was standing there, the king turned around and blessed them. [4]Then he said:

> "Praise be to the LORD, the God of Israel, who with his hands has fulfilled what he promised with his mouth to my father David. For he said, [5]'Since the day I brought my people out of Egypt, I have not chosen a city in any tribe of Israel to have a temple built for my Name to be there, nor have I chosen anyone to be the leader over my people Israel. [6]But now I have chosen Jerusalem[q] for my Name[r] to be there, and I have chosen David[s] to rule my people Israel.'
>
> [7]"My father David had it in his heart[t] to build a temple for the Name of the LORD, the God of Israel. [8]But the LORD said to my father David, 'Because it was in your heart to build a temple for my Name, you did well to have this in your heart. [9]Nevertheless, you are not the one to build the temple, but your son, who is your own flesh and blood—he is the one who will build the temple for my Name.'
>
> [10]"The LORD has kept the promise he made. I have succeeded David my father and now I sit on the throne of Israel, just as the

5:2 [a]Nu 3:31; 2Sa 6:12; 1Ch 15:25
5:3 [b]1Ch 9:1; 2Ch 7:8-10
5:5 [c]Nu 3:31; 1Ch 15:2
5:7 [d]Rev 11:19
5:8 [e]Ge 3:24
5:10 [f]Heb 9:4 [g]Ex 16:34; Dt 10:2
5:11 [h]1Ch 24:1
5:12 [i]1Ki 10:12; 1Ch 25:1; Ps 68:25 [j]1Ch 13:8; 15:24
5:13 [k]1Ch 16:34, 41; 2Ch 7:3; 20:21; Ezr 3:11; Ps 100:5; 136:1; Jer 33:11
5:14 [l]Ex 40:35; Rev 15:8 [m]Ex 19:16 [n]Ex 29:43; 2Ch 7:2
6:1 [o]Ex 19:9; 1Ki 8:12-50
6:2 [p]Ezr 6:12; 7:15; Ps 135:21
6:6 [q]Dt 12:5; Isa 14:1 [r]Ex 20:24; 2Ch 12:13 [s]1Ch 28:4
6:7 [t]1Sa 10:7; 1Ch 17:2; 28:2; Ac 7:46

LORD promised, and I have built the
temple for the Name of the LORD,
the God of Israel. 11There I have
placed the ark, in which is the covenant[a] of the LORD that he made
with the people of Israel."

Solomon's prayer of dedication.

6:12-40pp— 1Ki 8:22-53
6:41-42pp— Ps 132:8-10

12Then Solomon stood before the altar
of the LORD in front of the whole assembly of Israel and spread out his hands.
13Now he had made a bronze plat-
form,[b] five cubits[c] long, five cubits wide
and three cubits[d] high, and had placed
it in the center of the outer court. He
stood on the platform and then knelt
down[c] before the whole assembly of
Israel and spread out his hands toward
heaven. 14He said:

"O LORD, God of Israel, there is
no God like you[d] in heaven or on
earth—you who keep your covenant of love[e] with your servants
who continue wholeheartedly in
your way. 15You have kept your
promise to your servant David my
father; with your mouth you have
promised[f] and with your hand you
have fulfilled it—as it is today.
16"Now LORD, God of Israel, keep
for your servant David my father
the promises you made to him
when you said, 'You shall never
fail[g] to have a man to sit before me
on the throne of Israel, if only your
sons are careful in all they do to
walk before me according to my
law,[h] as you have done.' 17And now,
O LORD, God of Israel, let your word
that you promised your servant
David come true.
18"But will God really dwell[i] on
earth with men? The heavens,[j]
even the highest heavens, cannot
contain you. How much less this
temple I have built! 19Yet give attention to your servant's prayer and his
plea for mercy, O LORD my God.
Hear the cry and the prayer that
your servant is praying in your presence. 20May your eyes[k] be open
toward this temple day and night,
this place of which you said you
would put your Name[l] there. May
you hear[m] the prayer your servant
prays toward this place. 21Hear the
supplications of your servant and of
your people Israel when they pray
toward this place. Hear from heav-
en, your dwelling place; and when
you hear, forgive.[n]
22"When a man wrongs his
neighbor and is required to take an
oath[o] and he comes and swears the
oath before your altar in this temple,
23then hear from heaven and act.
Judge between your servants, repaying[p] the guilty by bringing down on
his own head what he has done.
Declare the innocent not guilty and
so establish his innocence.
24"When your people Israel have
been defeated[q] by an enemy because they have sinned against you
and when they turn back and confess your name, praying and making
supplication before you in this temple, 25then hear from heaven and
forgive the sin of your people Israel
and bring them back to the land
you gave to them and their fathers.
26"When the heavens are shut up
and there is no rain[r] because your
people have sinned against you, and
when they pray toward this place
and confess your name and turn
from their sin because you have
afflicted them, 27then hear from
heaven and forgive[s] the sin of your
servants, your people Israel. Teach
them the right way to live, and send
rain on the land you gave your people for an inheritance.
28"When famine[t] or plague comes
to the land, or blight or mildew, locusts or grasshoppers, or when enemies besiege them in any of their

6:11 [a]Dt 10:2; 2Ch 5:10; Ps 25:10; 50:5
6:13 [b]Ne 8:4 [c]Ps 95:6
6:14 [d]Ex 8:10; 15:11 [e]Dt 7:9
6:15 [f]1Ch 22:10
6:16 [g]2Sa 7:13,15; 1Ki 2:4; 2Ch 7:18; 23:3 [h]Ps 132:12
6:18 [i]Rev 21:3 [j]2Ch 2:6; Ps 11:4; Isa 40:22; 66:1; Ac 7:49
6:20 [k]Ex 3:16; Ps 34:15 [l]Dt 12:11 [m]2Ch 7:14; 30:20
6:21 [n]Ps 51:1; Isa 33:24; 40:2; 43:25; 44:22; 55:7; Mic 7:18
6:22 [o]Ex 22:11
6:23 [p]Isa 3:11; 65:6; Mt 16:27
6:24 [q]Lev 26:17
6:26 [r]Lev 26:19; Dt 11:17; 28:24; 2Sa 1:21; 1Ki 17:1
6:27 [s]ver 30,39; 2Ch 7:14
6:28 [t]2Ch 20:9

c *13* That is, about 7 1/2 feet (about 2.3 meters)
d *13* That is, about 4 1/2 feet (about 1.3 meters)

cities, whatever disaster or disease may come, 29 and when a prayer or plea is made by any of your people Israel—each one aware of his afflictions and pains, and spreading out his hands toward this temple— 30 then hear from heaven, your dwelling place. Forgive,[a] and deal with each man according to all he does, since you know his heart (for you alone know the hearts of men),[b] 31 so that they will fear you[c] and walk in your ways all the time they live in the land you gave our fathers.

32 "As for the foreigner who does not belong to your people Israel but has come[d] from a distant land because of your great name and your mighty hand[e] and your outstretched arm—when he comes and prays toward this temple, 33 then hear from heaven, your dwelling place, and do whatever the foreigner[f] asks of you, so that all the peoples of the earth may know your name and fear you, as do your own people Israel, and may know that this house I have built bears your Name.

34 "When your people go to war against their enemies,[g] wherever you send them, and when they pray[h] to you toward this city you have chosen and the temple I have built for your Name, 35 then hear from heaven their prayer and their plea, and uphold their cause.

36 "When they sin against you—for there is no one who does not sin[i]—and you become angry with them and give them over to the enemy, who takes them captive[j] to a land far away or near; 37 and if they have a change of heart[k] in the land where they are held captive, and repent and plead with you in the land of their captivity and say, 'We have sinned, we have done wrong and acted wickedly'; 38 and if they turn back to you with all their heart and soul in the land of their captivity where they were taken, and pray toward the land you gave their fathers, toward the city you have chosen and toward the temple I have built for your Name; 39 then from heaven, your dwelling place, hear their prayer and their pleas, and uphold their cause. And forgive your people, who have sinned against you.

40 "Now, my God, may your eyes be open and your ears attentive[l] to the prayers offered in this place.

41 "Now arise,[m] O LORD God, and
come to your resting
place,[n]
you and the ark of your might.
May your priests,[o] O LORD God,
be clothed with salvation,
may your saints rejoice in your
goodness.[p]
42 O LORD God, do not reject your
anointed one.
Remember the great love[q]
promised to David your
servant."

The temple is dedicated to the LORD.

7:1-10pp— 1Ki 8:62-66

7 When Solomon finished praying, fire[r] came down from heaven and consumed the burnt offering and the sacrifices, and the glory of the LORD filled[s] the temple.[t] 2 The priests could not enter[u] the temple of the LORD because the glory[v] of the LORD filled it. 3 When all the Israelites saw the fire coming down and the glory of the LORD above the temple, they knelt on the pavement with their faces to the ground, and they worshiped and gave thanks to the LORD, saying,

"He is good;
his love endures forever."[w]

4 Then the king and all the people offered sacrifices before the LORD. 5 And King Solomon offered a sacrifice of twenty-two thousand head of cattle and a hundred and twenty thousand sheep and goats. So the king and all the people

6:30 [a]ver 27 [b]1Sa 16:7; 1Ch 28:9; Ps 7:9; 44:21; Pr 16:2; 17:3
6:31 [c]Ps 103:11, 13; Pr 8:13
6:32 [d]2Ch 9:6; Jn 12:20; Ac 8:27 [e]Ex 3:19,20
6:33 [f]2Ch 7:14
6:34 [g]Dt 28:7 [h]1Ch 5:20
6:36 [i]Job 15:14; Ps 143:2; Ecc 7:20; Jer 17:9; Jas 3:1; 1Jn 1:8-10 [j]Lev 26:44
6:37 [k]2Ch 7:14; 33:12,19,23; Jer 29:13
6:40 [l]2Ch 7:15; Ne 1:6,11; Ps 17:1,6
6:41 [m]Isa 33:10 [n]1Ch 28:2 [o]Ps 132:16 [p]Ps 116:12
6:42 [q]Ps 89:24,28; Isa 55:3
7:1 [r]Lev 9:24; 1Ki 18:38 [s]Ex 16:10 [t]Ps 26:8
7:2 [u]1Ki 8:11 [v]Ex 29:43; 40:35; 2Ch 5:14
7:3 [w]1Ch 16:34; 2Ch 5:13; 20:21

dedicated the temple of God. 6The
priests took their positions, as did the
Levites[a] with the LORD's musical instruments,[b] which King David had made for
praising the LORD and which were used
when he gave thanks, saying, "His love
endures forever." Opposite the Levites,
the priests blew their trumpets, and all
the Israelites were standing.
7Solomon consecrated the middle part
of the courtyard in front of the temple of
the LORD, and there he offered burnt
offerings and the fat of the fellowship
offerings,[e] because the bronze altar he
had made could not hold the burnt offerings, the grain offerings and the fat portions.
8So Solomon observed the festival[c] at
that time for seven days, and all Israel
with him—a vast assembly, people from
Lebo[f] Hamath to the Wadi of Egypt.[d]
9On the eighth day they held an assembly, for they had celebrated the dedication of the altar for seven days and the
festival[e] for seven days more. 10On the
twenty-third day of the seventh month
he sent the people to their homes, joyful
and glad in heart for the good things the
LORD had done for David and Solomon
and for his people Israel.

The LORD appears to Solomon.

7:11-22pp— 1Ki 9:1-9

11When Solomon had finished the
temple of the LORD and the royal palace,
and had succeeded in carrying out all he
had in mind to do in the temple of the
LORD and in his own palace, 12the LORD
appeared to him at night and said:

"I have heard your prayer and
have chosen this place for myself[f]
as a temple for sacrifices.
13"When I shut up the heavens
so that there is no rain,[g] or command locusts to devour the land or
send a plague among my people,
14if my people, who are called by
my name, will humble[h] themselves
and pray and seek my face[i] and
turn[j] from their wicked ways, then
will I hear from heaven and will
forgive[k] their sin and will heal[l]
their land. 15Now my eyes will be
open and my ears attentive to the
prayers offered in this place.[m] 16I
have chosen[n] and consecrated this
temple so that my Name may be
there forever. My eyes and my
heart will always be there.
17"As for you, if you walk before
me[o] as David your father did, and
do all I command, and observe my
decrees and laws, 18I will establish
your royal throne, as I covenanted
with David your father when I said,
'You shall never fail to have a man[p]
to rule over Israel.'[q]
19"But if you[g] turn away[r] and forsake[s] the decrees and commands I
have given you[g] and go off to serve
other gods and worship them,
20then I will uproot[t] Israel from my
land,[u] which I have given them,
and will reject this temple I have
consecrated for my Name. I will
make it a byword and an object of
ridicule[v] among all peoples. 21And
though this temple is now so imposing, all who pass by will be appalled and say,[w] 'Why has the LORD
done such a thing to this land and
to this temple?' 22People will answer, 'Because they have forsaken
the LORD, the God of their fathers,
who brought them out of Egypt,
and have embraced other gods,
worshiping and serving them—that
is why he brought all this disaster
on them.'"

Solomon's various accomplishments and activities.

8:1-18pp— 1Ki 9:10-28

8 At the end of twenty years, during
which Solomon built the temple of
the LORD and his own palace, 2Solomon
rebuilt the villages that Hiram[h] had giv-
en him, and settled Israelites in them.

7:6 [a]1Ch 15:16 [b]2Ch 5:12
7:8 [c]2Ch 30:26 [d]Ge 15:18
7:9 [e]Lev 23:36
7:12 [f]Dt 12:5
7:13 [g]2Ch 6:26-28; Am 4:7
7:14 [h]Lev 26:41; 2Ch 6:37; Jas 4:10 [i]1Ch 16:11 [j]Isa 55:7; Zec 1:4 [k]2Ch 6:27 [l]2Ch 30:20; Isa 30:26; 57:18
7:15 [m]2Ch 6:40
7:16 [n]ver 12; 2Ch 6:6
7:17 [o]1Ki 9:4
7:18 [p]2Ch 6:16 [q]2Sa 7:13; 2Ch 13:5
7:19 [r]Dt 28:15 [s]Lev 26:14,33
7:20 [t]Dt 29:28 [u]1Ki 14:15 [v]Dt 28:37
7:21 [w]Dt 29:24

[e]7 Traditionally *peace offerings* [f]8 Or *from the entrance to* [g]19 The Hebrew is plural. [h]2 Hebrew *Huram,* a variant of *Hiram*; also in verse 18

3Solomon then went to Hamath Zobah and captured it. 4He also built up Tadmor in the desert and all the store cities he had built in Hamath. 5He rebuilt Upper Beth Horon[a] and Lower Beth Horon as fortified cities, with walls and with gates and bars, 6as well as Baalath and all his store cities, and all the cities for his chariots and for his horses[i]—whatever he desired to build in Jerusalem, in Lebanon and throughout all the territory he ruled.

7All the people left from the Hittites, Amorites, Perizzites, Hivites and Jebusites[b] (these peoples were not Israelites), 8that is, their descendants remaining in the land, whom the Israelites had not destroyed—these Solomon conscripted[c] for his slave labor force, as it is to this day. 9But Solomon did not make slaves of the Israelites for his work; they were his fighting men, commanders of his captains, and commanders of his chariots and charioteers. 10They were also King Solomon's chief officials—two hundred and fifty officials supervising the men.

11Solomon brought Pharaoh's daughter[d] up from the City of David to the palace he had built for her, for he said, "My wife must not live in the palace of David king of Israel, because the places the ark of the LORD has entered are holy."

12On the altar[e] of the LORD that he had built in front of the portico, Solomon sacrificed burnt offerings to the LORD, 13according to the daily requirement[f] for offerings commanded by Moses for Sabbaths,[g] New Moons and the three[h] annual feasts—the Feast of Unleavened Bread, the Feast of Weeks[i] and the Feast of Tabernacles. 14In keeping with the ordinance of his father David, he appointed the divisions[j] of the priests for their duties, and the Levites[k] to lead the praise and to assist the priests according to each day's requirement. He also appointed the gatekeepers[l] by divisions for the various gates, because this was what David the man of God[m] had ordered.[n] 15They did not deviate from the king's commands to the priests or to the Levites in any matter, including that of the treasuries.

16All Solomon's work was carried out, from the day the foundation of the temple of the LORD was laid until its completion. So the temple of the LORD was finished.

17Then Solomon went to Ezion Geber and Elath on the coast of Edom. 18And Hiram sent him ships commanded by his own officers, men who knew the sea. These, with Solomon's men, sailed to Ophir and brought back four hundred and fifty talents[j] of gold,[o] which they delivered to King Solomon.

The queen of Sheba visits Solomon.

9:1-12pp— 1Ki 10:1-13

9 When the queen of Sheba[p] heard of Solomon's fame, she came to Jerusalem to test him with hard questions. Arriving with a very great caravan—with camels carrying spices, large quantities of gold, and precious stones—she came to Solomon and talked with him about all she had on her mind. 2Solomon answered all her questions; nothing was too hard for him to explain to her. 3When the queen of Sheba saw the wisdom of Solomon,[q] as well as the palace he had built, 4the food on his table, the seating of his officials, the attending servants in their robes, the cupbearers in their robes and the burnt offerings he made at[k] the temple of the LORD, she was overwhelmed.

5She said to the king, "The report I heard in my own country about your achievements and your wisdom is true. 6But I did not believe what they said until I came[r] and saw with my own eyes. Indeed, not even half the greatness of your wisdom was told me; you have far exceeded the report I heard. 7How happy your men must be! How happy your officials, who continually stand before you and hear your wisdom! 8Praise be to the LORD your God, who

i6 Or *charioteers* j18 That is, about 17 tons (about 16 metric tons) k4 Or *the ascent by which he went up to*

8:5 [a]1Ch 7:24; 2Ch 14:7
8:7 [b]Ge 10:16
8:8 [c]1Ki 4:6; 9:21
8:11 [d]1Ki 3:1; 7:8
8:12 [e]1Ki 8:64; 2Ch 4:1; 15:8
8:13 [f]Ex 29:38; Nu 28:3 [g]Nu 28:9 [h]Ex 23:14; Dt 16:16 [i]Ex 23:16
8:14 [j]1Ch 24:1 [k]1Ch 25:1 [l]1Ch 9:17; 26:1 [m]Ne 12:24, 36 [n]1Ch 23:6; Ne 12:45
8:18 [o]2Ch 9:9
9:1 [p]Ge 10:7; Eze 23:42; Mt 12:42; Lk 11:31
9:3 [q]1Ki 5:12
9:6 [r]2Ch 6:32

has delighted in you and placed you on
his throne[a] as king to rule for the LORD
your God. Because of the love of your
God for Israel and his desire to uphold
them forever, he has made you king[b]
over them, to maintain justice and righteousness."
9 Then she gave the king 120 talents[l]
of gold,[c] large quantities of spices, and
precious stones. There had never been
such spices as those the queen of Sheba
gave to King Solomon.
10 (The men of Hiram and the men of
Solomon brought gold from Ophir;[d] they
also brought algumwood[m] and precious
stones. 11 The king used the algumwood
to make steps for the temple of the LORD
and for the royal palace, and to make
harps and lyres for the musicians. Nothing like them had ever been seen in
Judah.)
12 King Solomon gave the queen of
Sheba all she desired and asked for; he
gave her more than she had brought to
him. Then she left and returned with
her retinue to her own country.

Solomon's wisdom and riches are described.

9:13-28pp— 1Ki 10:14-29; 2Ch 1:14-17

13 The weight of the gold that Solomon received yearly was 666 talents,[n]
14 not including the revenues brought in
by merchants and traders. Also all the
kings of Arabia[e] and the governors of
the land brought gold and silver to Solomon.
15 King Solomon made two hundred
large shields of hammered gold; six hundred bekas[o] of hammered gold went
into each shield. 16 He also made three
hundred small shields[f] of hammered
gold, with three hundred bekas[p] of gold
in each shield. The king put them in the
Palace of the Forest of Lebanon.[g]
17 Then the king made a great throne
inlaid with ivory[h] and overlaid with
pure gold. 18 The throne had six steps,
and a footstool of gold was attached to
it. On both sides of the seat were armrests, with a lion standing beside each
of them. 19 Twelve lions stood on the six
steps, one at either end of each step.
Nothing like it had ever been made for
any other kingdom. 20 All King Solomon's
goblets were gold, and all the household
articles in the Palace of the Forest of
Lebanon were pure gold. Nothing was
made of silver, because silver was considered of little value in Solomon's day.
21 The king had a fleet of trading ships[q]
manned by Hiram's[r] men. Once every
three years it returned, carrying gold,
silver and ivory, and apes and baboons.
22 King Solomon was greater in riches
and wisdom than all the other kings of
the earth.[i] 23 All the kings[j] of the earth
sought audience with Solomon to hear
the wisdom God had put in his heart.
24 Year after year, everyone who came
brought a gift[k]—articles of silver and
gold, and robes, weapons and spices,
and horses and mules.
25 Solomon had four thousand stalls
for horses and chariots,[l] and twelve
thousand horses,[s] which he kept in the
chariot cities and also with him in Jerusalem. 26 He ruled[m] over all the kings
from the River[t][n] to the land of the Philistines, as far as the border of Egypt.[o]
27 The king made silver as common in
Jerusalem as stones, and cedar as plentiful as sycamore-fig trees in the foothills.
28 Solomon's horses were imported from
Egypt[u] and from all other countries.

Solomon's death and burial.

9:29-31pp— 1Ki 11:41-43

29 As for the other events of Solomon's
reign, from beginning to end, are they
not written in the records of Nathan[p]
the prophet, in the prophecy of Ahijah[q]
the Shilonite and in the visions of Iddo
the seer concerning Jeroboam[r] son of
Nebat? 30 Solomon reigned in Jerusalem

9:8 [a] 1Ki 2:12; 1Ch 17:14; 28:5; 29:23; 2Ch 13:8 [b] 2Ch 2:11
9:9 [c] 2Ch 8:18
9:10 [d] 2Ch 8:18
9:14 [e] 2Ch 17:11; Isa 21:13; Jer 25:24; Eze 27:21; 30:5
9:16 [f] 2Ch 12:9 [g] 1Ki 7:2
9:17 [h] 1Ki 22:39
9:22 [i] 1Ki 3:13; 2Ch 1:12
9:23 [j] 1Ki 4:34
9:24 [k] 2Ch 32:23; Ps 45:12; 68:29; 72:10; Isa 18:7
9:25 [l] 1Sa 8:11; 1Ki 4:26
9:26 [m] 1Ki 4:21 [n] Ps 72:8-9 [o] Ge 15:18-21
9:29 [p] 2Sa 7:2; 1Ch 29:29 [q] 1Ki 11:29 [r] 2Ch 10:2

[l] *9* That is, about 4 1/2 tons (about 4 metric tons)
[m] *10* Probably a variant of *almugwood*
[n] *13* That is, about 25 tons (about 23 metric tons)
[o] *15* That is, about 7 1/2 pounds (about 3.5 kilograms)
[p] *16* That is, about 3 3/4 pounds (about 1.7 kilograms)
[q] *21* Hebrew *of ships that could go to Tarshish*
[r] *21* Hebrew *Huram,* a variant of *Hiram*
[s] *25* Or *charioteers*
[t] *26* That is, the Euphrates
[u] *28* Or possibly *Muzur,* a region in Cilicia

over all Israel forty years. 31 Then he
rested with his fathers and was buried
in the city of David[a] his father. And
Rehoboam his son succeeded him as
king.

Rehoboam rejects the advice of the elders.

10:1–11:4pp— 1Ki 12:1-24

10 Rehoboam went to Shechem, for
all the Israelites had gone there to
make him king. 2 When Jeroboam[b] son
of Nebat heard this (he was in Egypt,
where he had fled[c] from King Solomon),
he returned from Egypt. 3 So they sent
for Jeroboam, and he and all Israel[d]
went to Rehoboam and said to him:
4 "Your father put a heavy yoke on us,[e]
but now lighten the harsh labor and the
heavy yoke he put on us, and we will
serve you."

5 Rehoboam answered, "Come back to
me in three days." So the people went
away.

6 Then King Rehoboam consulted the
elders[f] who had served his father Solomon during his lifetime. "How would
you advise me to answer these people?"
he asked.

7 They replied, "If you will be kind to
these people and please them and give
them a favorable answer,[g] they will always be your servants."

8 But Rehoboam rejected[h] the advice
the elders[i] gave him and consulted the
young men who had grown up with him
and were serving him. 9 He asked them,
"What is your advice? How should we
answer these people who say to me,
'Lighten the yoke your father put on
us'?"

10 The young men who had grown up
with him replied, "Tell the people who
have said to you, 'Your father put a
heavy yoke on us, but make our yoke
lighter'—tell them, 'My little finger is
thicker than my father's waist. 11 My
father laid on you a heavy yoke; I will
make it even heavier. My father
scourged you with whips; I will scourge
you with scorpions.'"

12 Three days later Jeroboam and all
the people returned to Rehoboam, as
the king had said, "Come back to me in
three days." 13 The king answered them
harshly. Rejecting the advice of the
elders, 14 he followed the advice of the
young men and said, "My father made
your yoke heavy; I will make it even
heavier. My father scourged you with
whips; I will scourge you with scorpions." 15 So the king did not listen to the
people, for this turn of events was from
God,[j] to fulfill the word the LORD had
spoken to Jeroboam son of Nebat
through Ahijah the Shilonite.[k]

Ten tribes of Israel rebel.

16 When all Israel[l] saw that the king
refused to listen to them, they answered
the king:

"What share do we have in David,[m]
what part in Jesse's son?
To your tents, O Israel!
Look after your own house,
O David!"

So all the Israelites went home. 17 But as
for the Israelites who were living in the
towns of Judah, Rehoboam still ruled
over them.

18 King Rehoboam sent out Adoniram,[v][n] who was in charge of forced
labor, but the Israelites stoned him to
death. King Rehoboam, however, managed to get into his chariot and escape
to Jerusalem. 19 So Israel has been in
rebellion against the house of David to
this day.

The LORD instructs Rehoboam not to fight against his brothers.

11 When Rehoboam arrived in Jerusalem,[o] he mustered the house of
Judah and Benjamin—a hundred and
eighty thousand fighting men—to make
war against Israel and to regain the
kingdom for Rehoboam.

2 But this word of the LORD came to
Shemaiah[p] the man of God: 3 "Say to

9:31 [a] 1Ki 2:10
10:2 [b] 2Ch 9:29 [c] 1Ki 11:40
10:3 [d] 1Ch 9:1
10:4 [e] 2Ch 2:2
10:6 [f] Job 8:8-9; 12:12; 15:10; 32:7
10:7 [g] Pr 15:1
10:8 [h] 2Sa 17:14 [i] Pr 13:20
10:15 [j] 2Ch 11:4; 25:16-20 [k] 1Ki 11:29
10:16 [l] 1Ch 9:1 [m] ver 19; 2Sa 20:1
10:18 [n] 1Ki 5:14
11:1 [o] 1Ki 12:21
11:2 [p] 2Ch 12:5-7, 15

[v] *18* Hebrew *Hadoram,* a variant of *Adoniram*

Rehoboam son of Solomon king of Judah and to all the Israelites in Judah and Benjamin, 4'This is what the LORD says: Do not go up to fight against your brothers.[a] Go home, every one of you, for this is my doing.'" So they obeyed the words of the LORD and turned back from marching against Jeroboam.

5Rehoboam lived in Jerusalem and built up towns for defense in Judah: 6Bethlehem, Etam, Tekoa, 7Beth Zur, Soco, Adullam, 8Gath, Mareshah, Ziph, 9Adoraim, Lachish, Azekah, 10Zorah, Aijalon and Hebron. These were fortified cities in Judah and Benjamin. 11He strengthened their defenses and put commanders in them, with supplies of food, olive oil and wine. 12He put shields and spears in all the cities, and made them very strong. So Judah and Benjamin were his.

The priests and Levites move to Judah.

13The priests and Levites from all their districts throughout Israel sided with him. 14The Levites[b] even abandoned their pasturelands and property,[c] and came to Judah and Jerusalem because Jeroboam and his sons had rejected them as priests of the LORD. 15And he appointed[d] his own priests[e] for the high places and for the goat[f] and calf[g] idols he had made. 16Those from every tribe of Israel[h] who set their hearts on seeking the LORD, the God of Israel, followed the Levites to Jerusalem to offer sacrifices to the LORD, the God of their fathers. 17They strengthened[i] the kingdom of Judah and supported Rehoboam son of Solomon three years, walking in the ways of David and Solomon during this time.

Rehoboam's family.

18Rehoboam married Mahalath, who was the daughter of David's son Jerimoth and of Abihail, the daughter of Jesse's son Eliab. 19She bore him sons: Jeush, Shemariah and Zaham. 20Then he married Maacah[j] daughter of Absalom, who bore him Abijah,[k] Attai, Ziza and Shelomith. 21Rehoboam loved Maacah daughter of Absalom more than any of his other wives and concubines. In all, he had eighteen wives[l] and sixty concubines, twenty-eight sons and sixty daughters.

22Rehoboam appointed Abijah[m] son of Maacah to be the chief prince among his brothers, in order to make him king. 23He acted wisely, dispersing some of his sons throughout the districts of Judah and Benjamin, and to all the fortified cities. He gave them abundant provisions and took many wives for them.

Shishak attacks Jerusalem.

12:9-16pp— 1Ki 14:21, 25-31

12 After Rehoboam's position as king was established[n] and he had become strong,[o] he and all Israel[w] with him abandoned the law of the LORD. 2Because they had been unfaithful[p] to the LORD, Shishak[q] king of Egypt attacked Jerusalem in the fifth year of King Rehoboam. 3With twelve hundred chariots and sixty thousand horsemen and the innumerable troops of Libyans, Sukkites and Cushites[x][r] that came with him from Egypt, 4he captured the fortified cities[s] of Judah and came as far as Jerusalem.

5Then the prophet Shemaiah[t] came to Rehoboam and to the leaders of Judah who had assembled in Jerusalem for fear of Shishak, and he said to them, "This is what the LORD says, 'You have abandoned me; therefore, I now abandon[u] you to Shishak.'"

6The leaders of Israel and the king humbled themselves and said, "The LORD is just."[v]

7When the LORD saw that they humbled themselves, this word of the LORD came to Shemaiah: "Since they have humbled themselves, I will not destroy them but will soon give them deliverance.[w] My wrath will not be poured out on Jerusalem through Shishak. 8They

11:4 [a]2Ch 28:8-11
11:14 [b]Nu 35:2-5 [c]2Ch 13:9
11:15 [d]1Ki 13:33 [e]1Ki 12:31 [f]Lev 17:7 [g]1Ki 12:28; 2Ch 13:8
11:16 [h]2Ch 15:9
11:17 [i]2Ch 12:1
11:20 [j]1Ki 15:2 [k]2Ch 13:2
11:21 [l]Dt 17:17
11:22 [m]Dt 21:15-17
12:1 [n]ver 13 [o]2Ch 11:17
12:2 [p]1Ki 14:22-24 [q]1Ki 11:40
12:3 [r]2Ch 16:8; Na 3:9
12:4 [s]2Ch 11:10
12:5 [t]2Ch 11:2 [u]Dt 28:15; 2Ch 15:2
12:6 [v]Ex 9:27; Da 9:14
12:7 [w]1Ki 21:29; Ps 78:38

w *1* That is, Judah, as frequently in 2 Chronicles
x *3* That is, people from the upper Nile region

will, however, become subject[a] to him, so that they may learn the difference between serving me and serving the kings of other lands."

9When Shishak king of Egypt attacked Jerusalem, he carried off the treasures of the temple of the LORD and the treasures of the royal palace. He took everything, including the gold shields[b] Solomon had made. 10So King Rehoboam made bronze shields to replace them and assigned these to the commanders of the guard on duty at the entrance to the royal palace. 11Whenever the king went to the LORD's temple, the guards went with him, bearing the shields, and afterward they returned them to the guardroom.

12Because Rehoboam humbled himself, the LORD's anger turned from him, and he was not totally destroyed. Indeed, there was some good[c] in Judah.

Rehoboam's death.

13King Rehoboam established himself firmly in Jerusalem and continued as king. He was forty-one years old when he became king, and he reigned seventeen years in Jerusalem, the city the LORD had chosen out of all the tribes of Israel in which to put his Name.[d] His mother's name was Naamah; she was an Ammonite. 14He did evil because he had not set his heart on seeking the LORD.

15As for the events of Rehoboam's reign, from beginning to end, are they not written in the records of Shemaiah[e] the prophet and of Iddo the seer that deal with genealogies? There was continual warfare between Rehoboam and Jeroboam. 16Rehoboam rested with his fathers and was buried in the City of David. And Abijah[f] his son succeeded him as king.

Abijah reigns in Judah.

13:1-2,22–14:1pp— 1Ki 15:1-2,6-8

13 In the eighteenth year of the reign of Jeroboam, Abijah became king of Judah, 2and he reigned in Jerusalem three years. His mother's name was Maacah,[y] a daughter[z] of Uriel of Gibeah.

There was war between Abijah[g] and Jeroboam.[h] 3Abijah went into battle with a force of four hundred thousand able fighting men, and Jeroboam drew up a battle line against him with eight hundred thousand able troops.

4Abijah stood on Mount Zemaraim,[i] in the hill country of Ephraim, and said, "Jeroboam and all Israel,[j] listen to me! 5Don't you know that the LORD, the God of Israel, has given the kingship of Israel to David and his descendants forever[k] by a covenant of salt?[l] 6Yet Jeroboam son of Nebat, an official of Solomon son of David, rebelled[m] against his master. 7Some worthless scoundrels[n] gathered around him and opposed Rehoboam son of Solomon when he was young and indecisive and not strong enough to resist them.

8"And now you plan to resist the kingdom of the LORD, which is in the hands of David's descendants. You are indeed a vast army and have with you the golden calves[o] that Jeroboam made to be your gods. 9But didn't you drive out the priests of the LORD,[p] the sons of Aaron, and the Levites, and make priests of your own as the peoples of other lands do? Whoever comes to consecrate himself with a young bull[q] and seven rams may become a priest of what are not gods.[r]

10"As for us, the LORD is our God, and we have not forsaken him. The priests who serve the LORD are sons of Aaron, and the Levites assist them. 11Every morning and evening[s] they present burnt offerings and fragrant incense to the LORD. They set out the bread on the ceremonially clean table[t] and light the lamps on the gold lampstand every evening. We are observing the requirements of the LORD our God. But you have forsaken him. 12God is with us; he is our leader. His priests with their trumpets will sound the battle cry against you.[u]

12:8 [a]Dt 28:48
12:9 [b]2Ch 9:16
12:12 [c]1Ki 14:13; 2Ch 19:3
12:13 [d]Dt 12:5; 2Ch 6:6
12:15 [e]2Ch 9:29; 11:2
12:16 [f]2Ch 11:20
13:2 [g]2Ch 11:20 [h]1Ki 15:6
13:4 [i]Jos 18:22 [j]1Ch 11:1
13:5 [k]2Sa 7:13 [l]Lev 2:13; Nu 18:19
13:6 [m]1Ki 11:26
13:7 [n]Jdg 9:4
13:8 [o]1Ki 12:28; 2Ch 11:15
13:9 [p]2Ch 11:14-15 [q]Ex 29:35-36 [r]Jer 2:11
13:11 [s]Ex 29:39; 2Ch 2:4 [t]Lev 24:5-9
13:12 [u]Nu 10:8-9

y2 Most Septuagint manuscripts and Syriac (see also 2 Chron. 11:20 and 1 Kings 15:2); Hebrew *Micaiah*
z2 Or *granddaughter*

Men of Israel, do not fight against the LORD,[a] the God of your fathers, for you will not succeed."

Abijah defeats Jeroboam.

13Now Jeroboam had sent troops around to the rear, so that while he was in front of Judah the ambush[b] was behind them. 14Judah turned and saw that they were being attacked at both front and rear. Then they cried out[c] to the LORD. The priests blew their trumpets 15and the men of Judah raised the battle cry. At the sound of their battle cry, God routed Jeroboam and all Israel[d] before Abijah and Judah. 16The Israelites fled before Judah, and God delivered[e] them into their hands. 17Abijah and his men inflicted heavy losses on them, so that there were five hundred thousand casualties among Israel's able men. 18The men of Israel were subdued on that occasion, and the men of Judah were victorious because they relied[f] on the LORD, the God of their fathers.

19Abijah pursued Jeroboam and took from him the towns of Bethel, Jeshanah and Ephron, with their surrounding villages. 20Jeroboam did not regain power during the time of Abijah. And the LORD struck him down and he died.

21But Abijah grew in strength. He married fourteen wives and had twenty-two sons and sixteen daughters.

22The other events of Abijah's reign, what he did and what he said, are written in the annotations of the prophet Iddo.

14 And Abijah rested with his fathers and was buried in the City of David. Asa his son succeeded him as king, and in his days the country was at peace for ten years.

Asa's obedient reign in Judah.

14:2-3pp— 1Ki 15:11-12

2Asa did what was good and right in the eyes of the LORD his God. 3He removed the foreign altars and the high places, smashed the sacred stones and cut down the Asherah poles.[a][g] 4He commanded Judah to seek the LORD, the God of their fathers, and to obey his laws and commands. 5He removed the high places and incense altars[h] in every town in Judah, and the kingdom was at peace under him. 6He built up the fortified cities of Judah, since the land was at peace. No one was at war with him during those years, for the LORD gave him rest.[i]

7"Let us build up these towns," he said to Judah, "and put walls around them, with towers, gates and bars. The land is still ours, because we have sought the LORD our God; we sought him and he has given us rest on every side." So they built and prospered.

8Asa had an army of three hundred thousand men from Judah, equipped with large shields and with spears, and two hundred and eighty thousand from Benjamin, armed with small shields and with bows. All these were brave fighting men.

9Zerah the Cushite[j] marched out against them with a vast army[b] and three hundred chariots, and came as far as Mareshah.[k] 10Asa went out to meet him, and they took up battle positions in the Valley of Zephathah near Mareshah.

11Then Asa called[l] to the LORD his God and said, "LORD, there is no one like you to help the powerless against the mighty. Help us, O LORD our God, for we rely[m] on you, and in your name[n] we have come against this vast army. O LORD, you are our God; do not let man prevail[o] against you."

12The LORD struck down[p] the Cushites before Asa and Judah. The Cushites fled, 13and Asa and his army pursued them as far as Gerar.[q] Such a great number of Cushites fell that they could not recover; they were crushed before the LORD and his forces. The men of Judah carried off a large amount of plunder. 14They destroyed all the villages around

13:12 [a]Ac 5:39
13:13 [b]Jos 8:9
13:14 [c]2Ch 14:11
13:15 [d]2Ch 14:12
13:16 [e]2Ch 16:8
13:18 [f]1Ch 5:20; 2Ch 14:11; Ps 22:5
14:3 [g]Ex 34:13; Dt 7:5; 1Ki 15:12-14
14:5 [h]2Ch 34:4,7
14:6 [i]1Ch 22:9; 2Ch 15:15
14:9 [j]2Ch 12:3; 16:8 [k]2Ch 11:8
14:11 [l]2Ch 13:14 [m]2Ch 13:18 [n]1Sa 17:45 [o]1Sa 14:6; Ps 9:19
14:12 [p]2Ch 13:15
14:13 [q]Ge 10:19

a*3* That is, symbols of the goddess Asherah; here and elsewhere in 2 Chronicles b*9* Hebrew *with an army of a thousand thousands* or *with an army of thousands upon thousands*

Gerar, for the terror[a] of the LORD had
fallen upon them. They plundered all
these villages, since there was much
booty there. 15They also attacked the
camps of the herdsmen and carried off
droves of sheep and goats and camels.
Then they returned to Jerusalem.

Asa removes the idols from the land.

15:16-19pp— 1Ki 15:13-16

15 The Spirit of God came upon[b]
Azariah son of Oded. 2He went
out to meet Asa and said to him, "Listen
to me, Asa and all Judah and Benjamin.
The LORD is with you[c] when you are
with him.[d] If you seek[e] him, he will be
found by you, but if you forsake him, he
will forsake you.[f] 3For a long time Israel
was without the true God, without a
priest to teach[g] and without the law.[h]
4But in their distress they turned to the
LORD, the God of Israel, and sought
him,[i] and he was found by them. 5In
those days it was not safe to travel
about,[j] for all the inhabitants of the
lands were in great turmoil. 6One nation was being crushed by another and
one city by another,[k] because God was
troubling them with every kind of distress. 7But as for you, be strong[l] and do
not give up, for your work will be
rewarded."[m]
8When Asa heard these words and
the prophecy of Azariah son of[c] Oded
the prophet, he took courage. He removed the detestable idols from the
whole land of Judah and Benjamin and
from the towns he had captured[n] in the
hills of Ephraim. He repaired the altar[o]
of the LORD that was in front of the portico of the LORD's temple.
9Then he assembled all Judah and
Benjamin and the people from Ephraim,
Manasseh and Simeon who had settled
among them, for large numbers[p] had
come over to him from Israel when they
saw that the LORD his God was with
him.
10They assembled at Jerusalem in the
third month of the fifteenth year of Asa's
reign. 11At that time they sacrificed to
the LORD seven hundred head of cattle
and seven thousand sheep and goats
from the plunder[q] they had brought
back. 12They entered into a covenant[r] to
seek the LORD,[s] the God of their fathers,
with all their heart and soul. 13All who
would not seek the LORD, the God of
Israel, were to be put to death,[t] whether
small or great, man or woman. 14They
took an oath to the LORD with loud ac-
clamation, with shouting and with trumpets and horns. 15All Judah rejoiced
about the oath because they had sworn
it wholeheartedly. They sought God[u]
eagerly, and he was found by them. So
the LORD gave them rest[v] on every side.
16King Asa also deposed his grandmother Maacah from her position as
queen mother, because she had made a
repulsive Asherah pole.[w] Asa cut the
pole down, broke it up and burned it in
the Kidron Valley. 17Although he did not
remove the high places from Israel,
Asa's heart was fully committed ⌊to the
LORD⌋ all his life. 18He brought into the
temple of God the silver and gold and
the articles that he and his father had
dedicated.
19There was no more war until the
thirty-fifth year of Asa's reign.

Asa's treaty with Ben-Hadad.

16:1-6pp— 1Ki 15:17-22

16 In the thirty-sixth year of Asa's
reign Baasha[x] king of Israel went
up against Judah and fortified Ramah to
prevent anyone from leaving or entering the territory of Asa king of Judah.
2Asa then took the silver and gold out
of the treasuries of the LORD's temple
and of his own palace and sent it to
Ben-Hadad king of Aram, who was ruling in Damascus. 3"Let there be a treaty[y] between me and you," he said, "as
there was between my father and your
father. See, I am sending you silver and
gold. Now break your treaty with Baasha

14:14 [a]Ge 35:5; 2Ch 17:10
15:1 [b]Nu 11:25,26; 24:2; 2Ch 20:14; 24:20
15:2 [c]ver 4,15; 2Ch 20:17 [d]Jas 4:8 [e]Jer 29:13 [f]1Ch 28:9; 2Ch 24:20
15:3 [g]Lev 10:11 [h]2Ch 17:9; La 2:9
15:4 [i]Dt 4:29
15:5 [j]Jdg 5:6
15:6 [k]Mt 24:7
15:7 [l]Jos 1:7,9 [m]Ps 58:11
15:8 [n]2Ch 13:19 [o]2Ch 8:12
15:9 [p]2Ch 11:16-17
15:11 [q]2Ch 14:13
15:12 [r]2Ki 11:17; 2Ch 23:16; 34:31 [s]1Ch 16:11
15:13 [t]Ex 22:20; Dt 13:9-16
15:15 [u]Dt 4:29 [v]1Ch 22:9; 2Ch 14:7
15:16 [w]Ex 34:13; 2Ch 14:2-5
16:1 [x]Jer 41:9
16:3 [y]2Ch 20:35

c8 Vulgate and Syriac (see also Septuagint and verse 1); Hebrew does not have *Azariah son of*.

king of Israel so he will withdraw
from me."
4Ben-Hadad agreed with King Asa and
sent the commanders of his forces
against the towns of Israel. They conquered Ijon, Dan, Abel Maim[d] and all
the store cities of Naphtali. 5When Baasha heard this, he stopped building
Ramah and abandoned his work. 6Then
King Asa brought all the men of Judah,
and they carried away from Ramah the
stones and timber Baasha had been
using. With them he built up Geba and
Mizpah.

Hanani's imprisonment for rebuking Asa.

7At that time Hanani[a] the seer came
to Asa king of Judah and said to him:
"Because you relied on the king of Aram
and not on the LORD your God, the army
of the king of Aram has escaped from
your hand. 8Were not the Cushites[e][b]
and Libyans a mighty army with great
numbers of chariots and horsemen[f]? Yet
when you relied on the LORD, he delivered[c] them into your hand. 9For the
eyes[d] of the LORD range throughout the
earth to strengthen those whose hearts
are fully committed to him. You have
done a foolish[e] thing, and from now on
you will be at war."
10Asa was angry with the seer because
of this; he was so enraged that he put
him in prison. At the same time Asa
brutally oppressed some of the people.

Asa's death.

16:11–17:1pp— 1Ki 15:23-24

11The events of Asa's reign, from beginning to end, are written in the book
of the kings of Judah and Israel. 12In the
thirty-ninth year of his reign Asa was
afflicted with a disease in his feet.
Though his disease was severe, even in
his illness he did not seek help from the
LORD,[f] but only from the physicians.
13Then in the forty-first year of his reign
Asa died and rested with his fathers.
14They buried him in the tomb that he
had cut out for himself in the City of
David. They laid him on a bier covered
with spices and various blended perfumes,[g] and they made a huge fire[h] in
his honor.

Jehoshaphat's prosperous reign in Judah.

17 Jehoshaphat his son succeeded
him as king and strengthened
himself against Israel. 2He stationed
troops in all the fortified cities of Judah
and put garrisons in Judah and in the
towns of Ephraim that his father Asa
had captured.[i]
3The LORD was with Jehoshaphat because in his early years he walked in the
ways his father David[j] had followed. He
did not consult the Baals 4but sought[k]
the God of his father and followed his
commands rather than the practices of
Israel. 5The LORD established the kingdom under his control; and all Judah
brought gifts[l] to Jehoshaphat, so that he
had great wealth and honor.[m] 6His heart
was devoted[n] to the ways of the LORD;
furthermore, he removed the high
places[o] and the Asherah poles[p] from
Judah.[q]
7In the third year of his reign he sent
his officials Ben-Hail, Obadiah, Zechariah, Nethanel and Micaiah to teach[r] in
the towns of Judah. 8With them were
certain Levites[s]—Shemaiah, Nethaniah,
Zebadiah, Asahel, Shemiramoth, Jehonathan, Adonijah, Tobijah and Tob-Adoni-
jah—and the priests Elishama and
Jehoram. 9They taught throughout Judah, taking with them the Book of the
Law[t] of the LORD; they went around to
all the towns of Judah and taught the
people.
10The fear[u] of the LORD fell on all the
kingdoms of the lands surrounding Judah, so that they did not make war with
Jehoshaphat. 11Some Philistines brought
Jehoshaphat gifts and silver as tribute,
and the Arabs[v] brought him flocks:[w] sev-
en thousand seven hundred rams and
seven thousand seven hundred goats.

16:7 [a]1Ki 16:1
16:8 [b]2Ch 12:3; 14:9 [c]2Ch 13:16
16:9 [d]Pr 15:3; Jer 16:17; Zec 4:10 [e]1Sa 13:13
16:12 [f]Jer 17:5-6
16:14 [g]Ge 50:2; Jn 19:39-40 [h]2Ch 21:19; Jer 34:5
17:2 [i]2Ch 15:8
17:3 [j]1Ki 22:43
17:4 [k]1Ki 12:28; 2Ch 22:9
17:5 [l]1Sa 10:27 [m]2Ch 18:1
17:6 [n]1Ki 8:61; 2Ch 15:17 [o]1Ki 15:14; 2Ch 19:3; 20:33 [p]Ex 34:13 [q]2Ch 21:12
17:7 [r]Lev 10:11; Dt 6:4-9; 2Ch 15:3; 35:3
17:8 [s]2Ch 19:8; Ne 8:7-8
17:9 [t]Dt 6:4-9; 28:61
17:10 [u]Ge 35:5; Dt 2:25; 2Ch 14:14
17:11 [v]2Ch 9:14; 26:8 [w]2Ch 21:16

d*4* Also known as *Abel Beth Maacah* e*8* That is, people from the upper Nile region f*8* Or *charioteers*

12 Jehoshaphat became more and more powerful; he built forts and store cities in Judah 13 and had large supplies in the towns of Judah. He also kept experienced fighting men in Jerusalem. 14 Their enrollment[a] by families was as follows:

From Judah, commanders of units of 1,000:
Adnah the commander, with 300,000 fighting men;
15 next, Jehohanan the commander, with 280,000;
16 next, Amasiah son of Zicri, who volunteered[b] himself for the service of the LORD, with 200,000.
17 From Benjamin:[c]
Eliada, a valiant soldier, with 200,000 men armed with bows and shields;
18 next, Jehozabad, with 180,000 men armed for battle.

19 These were the men who served the king, besides those he stationed in the fortified cities[d] throughout Judah.[e]

Micaiah contradicts Ahab's false prophets.

18:1-27pp— 1Ki 22:1-28

18 Now Jehoshaphat had great wealth and honor,[f] and he allied[g] himself with Ahab[h] by marriage. 2 Some years later he went down to visit Ahab in Samaria. Ahab slaughtered many sheep and cattle for him and the people with him and urged him to attack Ramoth Gilead. 3 Ahab king of Israel asked Jehoshaphat king of Judah, "Will you go with me against Ramoth Gilead?"

Jehoshaphat replied, "I am as you are, and my people as your people; we will join you in the war." 4 But Jehoshaphat also said to the king of Israel, "First seek the counsel of the LORD."

5 So the king of Israel brought together the prophets—four hundred men—and asked them, "Shall we go to war against Ramoth Gilead, or shall I refrain?"

"Go," they answered, "for God will give it into the king's hand."

6 But Jehoshaphat asked, "Is there not a prophet of the LORD here whom we can inquire of?"

7 The king of Israel answered Jehoshaphat, "There is still one man through whom we can inquire of the LORD, but I hate him because he never prophesies anything good about me, but always bad. He is Micaiah son of Imlah."

"The king should not say that," Jehoshaphat replied.

8 So the king of Israel called one of his officials and said, "Bring Micaiah son of Imlah at once."

9 Dressed in their royal robes, the king of Israel and Jehoshaphat king of Judah were sitting on their thrones at the threshing floor by the entrance to the gate of Samaria, with all the prophets prophesying before them. 10 Now Zedekiah son of Kenaanah had made iron horns, and he declared, "This is what the LORD says: 'With these you will gore the Arameans until they are destroyed.'"

11 All the other prophets were prophesying the same thing. "Attack Ramoth Gilead[i] and be victorious," they said, "for the LORD will give it into the king's hand."

12 The messenger who had gone to summon Micaiah said to him, "Look, as one man the other prophets are predicting success for the king. Let your word agree with theirs, and speak favorably."

13 But Micaiah said, "As surely as the LORD lives, I can tell him only what my God says."[j]

14 When he arrived, the king asked him, "Micaiah, shall we go to war against Ramoth Gilead, or shall I refrain?"

"Attack and be victorious," he answered, "for they will be given into your hand."

15 The king said to him, "How many times must I make you swear to tell me nothing but the truth in the name of the LORD?"

16 Then Micaiah answered, "I saw all Israel[k] scattered on the hills like sheep without a shepherd,[l] and the LORD said, 'These people have no master. Let each one go home in peace.'"

17:14 [a] 2Sa 24:2
17:16 [b] Jdg 5:9; 1Ch 29:9
17:17 [c] Nu 1:36
17:19 [d] 2Ch 11:10 [e] 2Ch 25:5
18:1 [f] 2Ch 17:5 [g] 2Ch 19:1-3; 22:3 [h] 2Ch 21:6
18:11 [i] 2Ch 22:5
18:13 [j] Nu 22:18,20, 35
18:16 [k] 1Ch 9:1 [l] Nu 27:17; Eze 34:5-8

17The king of Israel said to Jehoshaphat, "Didn't I tell you that he never
prophesies anything good about me, but
only bad?"
18Micaiah continued, "Therefore hear
the word of the LORD: I saw the LORD
sitting on his throne[a] with all the host of
heaven standing on his right and on his
left. 19And the LORD said, 'Who will entice Ahab king of Israel into attacking
Ramoth Gilead and going to his death
there?'
"One suggested this, and another that.
20Finally, a spirit came forward, stood
before the LORD and said, 'I will entice
him.'
"'By what means?' the LORD asked.
21"'I will go and be a lying spirit[b] in
the mouths of all his prophets,' he said.
"'You will succeed in enticing him,'
said the LORD. 'Go and do it.'
22"So now the LORD has put a lying
spirit in the mouths of these prophets of
yours.[c] The LORD has decreed disaster
for you."
23Then Zedekiah son of Kenaanah
went up and slapped[d] Micaiah in the
face. "Which way did the spirit from[g]
the LORD go when he went from me to
speak to you?" he asked.
24Micaiah replied, "You will find out
on the day you go to hide in an inner
room."
25The king of Israel then ordered,
"Take Micaiah and send him back to
Amon the ruler of the city and to Joash
the king's son, 26and say, 'This is what
the king says: Put this fellow in prison[e]
and give him nothing but bread and
water until I return safely.'"
27Micaiah declared, "If you ever return safely, the LORD has not spoken
through me." Then he added, "Mark
my words, all you people!"

Ahab's death.

18:28-34pp— 1Ki 22:29-36

28So the king of Israel and Jehoshaphat king of Judah went up to Ramoth
Gilead. 29The king of Israel said to Jehoshaphat, "I will enter the battle in
disguise, but you wear your royal robes."
So the king of Israel disguised[f] himself
and went into battle.
30Now the king of Aram had ordered
his chariot commanders, "Do not fight
with anyone, small or great, except the
king of Israel." 31When the chariot commanders saw Jehoshaphat, they thought,
"This is the king of Israel." So they
turned to attack him, but Jehoshaphat
cried out,[g] and the LORD helped him.
God drew them away from him, 32for
when the chariot commanders saw that
he was not the king of Israel, they stopped pursuing him.
33But someone drew his bow at random and hit the king of Israel between
the sections of his armor. The king told
the chariot driver, "Wheel around and
get me out of the fighting. I've been
wounded." 34All day long the battle
raged, and the king of Israel propped
himself up in his chariot facing the
Arameans until evening. Then at sunset
he died.[h]

Jehoshaphat appoints judges.

19 When Jehoshaphat king of Judah
returned safely to his palace in
Jerusalem, 2Jehu[i] the seer, the son of
Hanani, went out to meet him and said
to the king, "Should you help the wicked[j] and love[h] those who hate the LORD?[k]
Because of this, the wrath[l] of the LORD
is upon you. 3There is, however, some
good[m] in you, for you have rid the land
of the Asherah poles[n] and have set your
heart on seeking God.[o]"
4Jehoshaphat lived in Jerusalem, and
he went out again among the people
from Beersheba to the hill country of
Ephraim and turned them back to the
LORD, the God of their fathers. 5He appointed judges[p] in the land, in each of
the fortified cities of Judah. 6He told
them, "Consider carefully what you do,[q]
because you are not judging for man[r]
but for the LORD, who is with you
whenever you give a verdict. 7Now let
the fear of the LORD be upon you. Judge

g23 Or *Spirit of*   h2 Or *and make alliances with*

18:18 [a]Da 7:9
18:21 [b]1Ch 21:1; Job 1:6; Zec 3:1; Jn 8:44
18:22 [c]Job 12:16; Isa 19:14; Eze 14:9
18:23 [d]Jer 20:2; Mk 14:65; Ac 23:2
18:26 [e]2Ch 16:10; Heb 11:36
18:29 [f]1Sa 28:8
18:31 [g]2Ch 13:14
18:34 [h]2Ch 22:5
19:2 [i]1Ki 16:1 [j]2Ch 16:2-9 [k]Ps 139:21-22 [l]2Ch 24:18; 32:25; Ps 7:11
19:3 [m]1Ki 14:13; 2Ch 12:12 [n]2Ch 17:6 [o]2Ch 18:1; 20:35; 25:7; Ezr 7:10
19:5 [p]Ge 47:6; Ex 18:26
19:6 [q]Lev 19:15 [r]Dt 1:17; 16:18-20; 17:8-13

carefully, for with the LORD our God
there is no injustice[a] or partiality[b] or
bribery."
8 In Jerusalem also, Jehoshaphat appointed some of the Levites, priests and
heads of Israelite families to administer[c]
the law of the LORD and to settle disputes. And they lived in Jerusalem. 9 He
gave them these orders: "You must serve
faithfully and wholeheartedly in the fear
of the LORD. 10 In every case that comes
before you from your fellow countrymen
who live in the cities—whether bloodshed or other concerns of the law, commands, decrees or ordinances—you are
to warn them not to sin against the
LORD;[d] otherwise his wrath will come
on you and your brothers. Do this, and
you will not sin.
11 "Amariah the chief priest will be
over you in any matter concerning the
LORD, and Zebadiah son of Ishmael, the
leader of the tribe of Judah, will be over
you in any matter concerning the king,
and the Levites will serve as officials
before you. Act with courage,[e] and may
the LORD be with those who do well."

Jehoshaphat proclaims a fast for all Judah.

20 After this, the Moabites and
Ammonites with some of the
Meunites[i][f] came to make war on Jehoshaphat.
2 Some men came and told Jehoshaphat, "A vast army is coming against
you from Edom,[j] from the other side of
the Sea.[k] It is already in Hazazon Tamar[g]" (that is, En Gedi). 3 Alarmed, Jehoshaphat resolved to inquire of the
LORD, and he proclaimed a fast[h] for all
Judah. 4 The people of Judah came together to seek help from the LORD;
indeed, they came from every town in
Judah to seek him.
5 Then Jehoshaphat stood up in the
assembly of Judah and Jerusalem at
the temple of the LORD in the front
of the new courtyard 6 and said:

"O LORD, God of our fathers,[i] are
you not the God who is in heaven?[j]
You rule over all the kingdoms[k] of
the nations. Power and might are in
your hand, and no one can withstand you. 7 O our God, did you not
drive out the inhabitants of this
land before your people Israel and
give it forever to the descendants of
Abraham your friend?[l] 8 They have
lived in it and have built in it a sanctuary[m] for your Name, saying, 9 'If
calamity comes upon us, whether
the sword of judgment, or plague
or famine,[n] we will stand in your
presence before this temple that
bears your Name and will cry out
to you in our distress, and you will
hear us and save us.'
10 "But now here are men from
Ammon, Moab and Mount Seir,
whose territory you would not
allow Israel to invade when they
came from Egypt;[o] so they turned
away from them and did not destroy
them. 11 See how they are repaying
us by coming to drive us out of the
possession[p] you gave us as an inheritance. 12 O our God, will you
not judge them?[q] For we have no
power to face this vast army that
is attacking us. We do not know
what to do, but our eyes are upon
you.[r]"

13 All the men of Judah, with their
wives and children and little ones, stood
there before the LORD.
14 Then the Spirit[s] of the LORD came
upon Jahaziel son of Zechariah, the son
of Benaiah, the son of Jeiel, the son of
Mattaniah, a Levite and descendant of
Asaph, as he stood in the assembly.
15 He said: "Listen, King Jehoshaphat
and all who live in Judah and Jerusalem! This is what the LORD says to
you: 'Do not be afraid or discouraged[t]
because of this vast army. For the battle[u]
is not yours, but God's. 16 Tomorrow
march down against them. They will

19:7 [a]Ge 18:25; Dt 32:4 [b]Dt 10:17; Job 34:19; Ro 2:11; Col 3:25
19:8 [c]2Ch 17:8-9
19:10 [d]Dt 17:8-13
19:11 [e]1Ch 28:20
20:1 [f]1Ch 4:41
20:2 [g]Ge 14:7
20:3 [h]1Sa 7:6; 2Ch 19:3; Ezr 8:21; Jer 36:9; Jnh 3:5,7
20:6 [i]Mt 6:9 [j]Dt 4:39 [k]1Ch 29:11-12
20:7 [l]Isa 41:8; Jas 2:23
20:8 [m]2Ch 6:20
20:9 [n]2Ch 6:28
20:10 [o]Nu 20:14-21; Dt 2:4-6,9, 18-19
20:11 [p]Ps 83:1-12
20:12 [q]Jdg 11:27 [r]Ps 25:15; 121:1-2
20:14 [s]2Ch 15:1
20:15 [t]2Ch 32:7 [u]Ex 14:13-14; 1Sa 17:47

[i]1 Some Septuagint manuscripts; Hebrew *Ammonites* [j]2 One Hebrew manuscript; most Hebrew manuscripts, Septuagint and Vulgate *Aram* [k]2 That is, the Dead Sea

be climbing up by the Pass of Ziz, and
you will find them at the end of the
gorge in the Desert of Jeruel. 17You will
not have to fight this battle. Take up
your positions; stand firm and see[a] the
deliverance the LORD will give you, O
Judah and Jerusalem. Do not be afraid;
do not be discouraged. Go out to face
them tomorrow, and the LORD will be
with you.' "

18Jehoshaphat bowed[b] with his face to
the ground, and all the people of Judah
and Jerusalem fell down in worship
before the LORD. 19Then some Levites
from the Kohathites and Korahites stood
up and praised the LORD, the God of
Israel, with very loud voice.

20Early in the morning they left for
the Desert of Tekoa. As they set out,
Jehoshaphat stood and said, "Listen to
me, Judah and people of Jerusalem!
Have faith[c] in the LORD your God and
you will be upheld; have faith in his
prophets and you will be successful.[d]"
21After consulting the people, Jehoshaphat appointed men to sing to the
LORD and to praise him for the splendor
of his[l] holiness[e] as they went out at the
head of the army, saying:

"Give thanks to the LORD,
for his love endures forever."[f]

22As they began to sing and praise,
the LORD set ambushes[g] against the men
of Ammon and Moab and Mount Seir
who were invading Judah, and they
were defeated. 23The men of Ammon[h]
and Moab rose up against the men from
Mount Seir[i] to destroy and annihilate
them. After they finished slaughtering
the men from Seir, they helped to destroy one another.[j]

24When the men of Judah came to
the place that overlooks the desert and
looked toward the vast army, they saw
only dead bodies lying on the ground;
no one had escaped. 25So Jehoshaphat
and his men went to carry off their plunder, and they found among them a great
amount of equipment and clothing[m] and
also articles of value—more than they
could take away. There was so much
plunder that it took three days to collect
it. 26On the fourth day they assembled
in the Valley of Beracah, where they
praised the LORD. This is why it is called
the Valley of Beracah[n] to this day.

27Then, led by Jehoshaphat, all the
men of Judah and Jerusalem returned
joyfully to Jerusalem, for the LORD had
given them cause to rejoice over their
enemies. 28They entered Jerusalem and
went to the temple of the LORD with
harps and lutes and trumpets.

29The fear[k] of God came upon all the
kingdoms of the countries when they
heard how the LORD had fought[l] against
the enemies of Israel. 30And the kingdom of Jehoshaphat was at peace, for his
God had given him rest[m] on every side.

Jehoshaphat reigns in Judah.

20:31–21:1pp— 1Ki 22:41-50

31So Jehoshaphat reigned over Judah.
He was thirty-five years old when he became king of Judah, and he reigned in
Jerusalem twenty-five years. His mother's name was Azubah daughter of Shilhi. 32He walked in the ways of his father
Asa and did not stray from them; he did
what was right in the eyes of the LORD.
33The high places,[n] however, were not
removed, and the people still had not
set their hearts on the God of their
fathers.

34The other events of Jehoshaphat's
reign, from beginning to end, are written in the annals of Jehu[o] son of Hanani,
which are recorded in the book of the
kings of Israel.

35Later, Jehoshaphat king of Judah
made an alliance[p] with Ahaziah king of
Israel, who was guilty of wickedness.[q]
36He agreed with him to construct a
fleet of trading ships.[o] After these were
built at Ezion Geber, 37Eliezer son of Do-
davahu of Mareshah prophesied against
Jehoshaphat, saying, "Because you have
made an alliance with Ahaziah, the LORD

20:17 [a]Ex 14:13; 2Ch 15:2
20:18 [b]Ex 4:31
20:20 [c]Isa 7:9 [d]Ge 39:3; Pr 16:3
20:21 [e]1Ch 16:29; Ps 29:2 [f]2Ch 5:13; Ps 136:1
20:22 [g]Jdg 7:22; 2Ch 13:13
20:23 [h]Ge 19:38 [i]2Ch 21:8 [j]Jdg 7:22; 1Sa 14:20; Eze 38:21
20:29 [k]Ge 35:5; Dt 2:25; 2Ch 14:14; 17:10 [l]Ex 14:14
20:30 [m]1Ch 22:9; 2Ch 14:6-7; 15:15
20:33 [n]2Ch 17:6; 19:3
20:34 [o]1Ki 16:1
20:35 [p]2Ch 16:3 [q]2Ch 19:1-3

[l]*21* Or *him with the splendor of* [m]*25* Some Hebrew manuscripts and Vulgate; most Hebrew manuscripts *corpses* [n]*26* *Beracah* means *praise.* [o]*36* Hebrew *of ships that could go to Tarshish*

will destroy what you have made." The
ships[a] were wrecked and were not able
to set sail to trade.[p]
21 Then Jehoshaphat rested with
his fathers and was buried with
them in the City of David. And Jehoram[b] his son succeeded him as king.
2Jehoram's brothers, the sons of Jehoshaphat, were Azariah, Jehiel, Zechariah,
Azariahu, Michael and Shephatiah. All
these were sons of Jehoshaphat king of
Israel.[q] 3Their father had given them
many gifts[c] of silver and gold and articles of value, as well as fortified cities[d]
in Judah, but he had given the kingdom
to Jehoram because he was his firstborn
son.

Jehoram's reign in Judah.

21:5-10,20pp— 2Ki 8:16-24

4When Jehoram established[e] himself
firmly over his father's kingdom, he put
all his brothers[f] to the sword along with
some of the princes of Israel. 5Jehoram
was thirty-two years old when he became king, and he reigned in Jerusalem
eight years. 6He walked in the ways of
the kings of Israel,[g] as the house of Ahab
had done, for he married a daughter of
Ahab.[h] He did evil in the eyes of the
LORD. 7Nevertheless, because of the
covenant the LORD had made with
David,[i] the LORD was not willing to destroy the house of David.[j] He had promised to maintain a lamp[k] for him and
his descendants forever.
8In the time of Jehoram, Edom[l] rebelled against Judah and set up its own
king. 9So Jehoram went there with his
officers and all his chariots. The Edomites surrounded him and his chariot
commanders, but he rose up and broke
through by night. 10To this day Edom
has been in rebellion against Judah.
Libnah[m] revolted at the same time,
because Jehoram had forsaken the LORD,
the God of his fathers. 11He had also
built high places on the hills of Judah
and had caused the people of Jerusalem to prostitute themselves and had
led Judah astray.

Elijah's prophecy against Jehoram.

12Jehoram received a letter from Elijah[n] the prophet, which said:

"This is what the LORD, the God of
your father[o] David, says: 'You have
not walked in the ways of your
father Jehoshaphat or of Asa[p] king
of Judah. 13But you have walked in
the ways of the kings of Israel, and
you have led Judah and the people
of Jerusalem to prostitute themselves, just as the house of Ahab
did.[q] You have also murdered your
own brothers, members of your
father's house, men who were better[r] than you. 14So now the LORD is
about to strike your people, your
sons, your wives and everything
that is yours, with a heavy blow.
15You yourself will be very ill with
a lingering disease[s] of the bowels,
until the disease causes your bowels
to come out.'"

16The LORD aroused against Jehoram
the hostility of the Philistines and of the
Arabs[t] who lived near the Cushites.
17They attacked Judah, invaded it and
carried off all the goods found in the
king's palace, together with his sons and
wives. Not a son was left to him except
Ahaziah,[r] the youngest.[u]

Jehoram's death and burial.

18After all this, the LORD afflicted Jehoram with an incurable disease of the
bowels. 19In the course of time, at the
end of the second year, his bowels came
out because of the disease, and he died
in great pain. His people made no fire in
his honor,[v] as they had for his fathers.
20Jehoram was thirty-two years old
when he became king, and he reigned in
Jerusalem eight years. He passed away,
to no one's regret, and was buried[w] in
the City of David, but not in the tombs
of the kings.

20:37 [a]1Ki 9:26; 2Ch 9:21
21:1 [b]1Ch 3:11
21:3 [c]2Ch 11:23 [d]2Ch 11:10
21:4 [e]1Ki 2:12 [f]Jdg 9:5
21:6 [g]1Ki 12:28-30 [h]2Ch 18:1; 22:3
21:7 [i]2Sa 7:13 [j]2Sa 7:15; 2Ch 23:3 [k]2Sa 21:17; 1Ki 11:36
21:8 [l]2Ch 20:22-23
21:10 [m]Nu 33:20
21:12 [n]2Ki 1:16-17 [o]2Ch 17:3-6 [p]2Ch 14:2
21:13 [q]ver 6,11; 1Ki 16:29-33 [r]ver 4; 1Ki 2:32
21:15 [s]ver 18-19; Nu 12:10
21:16 [t]2Ch 17:10-11; 22:1; 26:7
21:17 [u]2Ki 12:18; 2Ch 22:1; 25:23; Joel 3:5
21:19 [v]2Ch 16:14
21:20 [w]2Ch 24:25; 28:27; 33:20; Jer 22:18,28

p*37* Hebrew *sail for Tarshish* q*2* That is, Judah, as frequently in 2 Chronicles r*17* Hebrew *Jehoahaz,* a variant of *Ahaziah*

Ahaziah reigns in Judah.

22:1-6pp— 2Ki 8:25-29

22 The people[a] of Jerusalem[b] made Ahaziah, Jehoram's youngest son, king in his place, since the raiders,[c] who came with the Arabs into the camp, had killed all the older sons. So Ahaziah son of Jehoram king of Judah began to reign.

2 Ahaziah was twenty-two[s] years old when he became king, and he reigned in Jerusalem one year. His mother's name was Athaliah, a granddaughter of Omri.

3 He too walked[d] in the ways of the house of Ahab,[e] for his mother encouraged him in doing wrong. 4 He did evil in the eyes of the LORD, as the house of Ahab had done, for after his father's death they became his advisers, to his undoing. 5 He also followed their counsel when he went with Joram[t] son of Ahab king of Israel to war against Hazael king of Aram at Ramoth Gilead.[f] The Arameans wounded Joram; 6 so he returned to Jezreel to recover from the wounds they had inflicted on him at Ramoth[u] in his battle with Hazael[g] king of Aram.

Then Ahaziah[v] son of Jehoram king of Judah went down to Jezreel to see Joram son of Ahab because he had been wounded.

Jehu murders Ahaziah.

22:7-9pp— 2Ki 9:21-29

7 Through Ahaziah's[h] visit to Joram, God brought about Ahaziah's downfall. When Ahaziah arrived, he went out with Joram to meet Jehu son of Nimshi, whom the LORD had anointed to destroy the house of Ahab. 8 While Jehu was executing judgment on the house of Ahab,[i] he found the princes of Judah and the sons of Ahaziah's relatives, who had been attending Ahaziah, and he killed them. 9 He then went in search of Ahaziah, and his men captured him while he was hiding[j] in Samaria. He was brought to Jehu and put to death. They buried him, for they said, "He was a son of Jehoshaphat, who sought[k] the LORD with all his heart." So there was no one in the house of Ahaziah powerful enough to retain the kingdom.

Athaliah seeks to kill Joash.

22:10–23:21pp— 2Ki 11:1-21

10 When Athaliah the mother of Ahaziah saw that her son was dead, she proceeded to destroy the whole royal family of the house of Judah. 11 But Jehosheba,[w] the daughter of King Jehoram, took Joash son of Ahaziah and stole him away from among the royal princes who were about to be murdered and put him and his nurse in a bedroom. Because Jehosheba,[w] the daughter of King Jehoram and wife of the priest Jehoiada, was Ahaziah's sister, she hid the child from Athaliah so she could not kill him. 12 He remained hidden with them at the temple of God for six years while Athaliah ruled the land.

Jehoiada crowns Joash king.

23 In the seventh year Jehoiada showed his strength. He made a covenant with the commanders of units of a hundred: Azariah son of Jeroham, Ishmael son of Jehohanan, Azariah son of Obed, Maaseiah son of Adaiah, and Elishaphat son of Zicri. 2 They went throughout Judah and gathered the Levites[l] and the heads of Israelite families from all the towns. When they came to Jerusalem, 3 the whole assembly made a covenant[m] with the king at the temple of God.

Jehoiada said to them, "The king's son shall reign, as the LORD promised concerning the descendants of David.[n] 4 Now this is what you are to do: A third of you priests and Levites who are going on duty on the Sabbath are to keep watch at the doors, 5 a third of you at the

22:1 [a]2Ch 33:25; 36:1 [b]2Ch 23:20-21; 26:1 [c]2Ch 21:16-17
22:3 [d]2Ch 18:1 [e]2Ch 21:6
22:5 [f]2Ch 18:11, 34
22:6 [g]1Ki 19:15; 2Ki 8:13-15; 9:15
22:7 [h]2Ki 9:16; 2Ch 10:15
22:8 [i]2Ki 10:13
22:9 [j]Jdg 9:5 [k]2Ch 17:4
23:2 [l]Nu 35:2-5
23:3 [m]2Ki 11:17 [n]2Sa 7:12; 1Ki 2:4; 2Ch 6:16; 7:18; 21:7

[s]*2* Some Septuagint manuscripts and Syriac (see also 2 Kings 8:26); Hebrew *forty-two* [t]*5* Hebrew *Jehoram,* a variant of *Joram*; also in verses 6 and 7 [u]*6* Hebrew *Ramah,* a variant of *Ramoth* [v]*6* Some Hebrew manuscripts, Septuagint, Vulgate and Syriac (see also 2 Kings 8:29); most Hebrew manuscripts *Azariah* [w]*11* Hebrew *Jehoshabeath,* a variant of *Jehosheba*

royal palace and a third at the Foundation Gate, and all the other men are to
be in the courtyards of the temple of the
LORD. 6 No one is to enter the temple of
the LORD except the priests and Levites
on duty; they may enter because they
are consecrated, but all the other men
are to guard[a] what the LORD has assigned to them.[x] 7 The Levites are to station
themselves around the king, each man
with his weapons in his hand. Anyone
who enters the temple must be put to
death. Stay close to the king wherever
he goes."
8 The Levites and all the men of Judah
did just as Jehoiada the priest ordered.[b]
Each one took his men—those who
were going on duty on the Sabbath and
those who were going off duty—for
Jehoiada the priest had not released any
of the divisions.[c] 9 Then he gave the
commanders of units of a hundred the
spears and the large and small shields
that had belonged to King David and
that were in the temple of God. 10 He stationed all the men, each with his weapon in his hand, around the king— near
the altar and the temple, from the south
side to the north side of the temple.
11 Jehoiada and his sons brought out
the king's son and put the crown on
him; they presented him with a copy[d] of
the covenant and proclaimed him king.
They anointed him and shouted, "Long
live the king!"

Athaliah's death.

12 When Athaliah heard the noise of
the people running and cheering the
king, she went to them at the temple of
the LORD. 13 She looked, and there was
the king,[e] standing by his pillar[f] at the
entrance. The officers and the trumpeters were beside the king, and all the
people of the land were rejoicing and
blowing trumpets, and singers with
musical instruments were leading the
praises. Then Athaliah tore her robes
and shouted, "Treason! Treason!"
14 Jehoiada the priest sent out the
commanders of units of a hundred, who
were in charge of the troops, and said
to them: "Bring her out between the
ranks[y] and put to the sword anyone
who follows her." For the priest had
said, "Do not put her to death at the
temple of the LORD." 15 So they seized
her as she reached the entrance of the
Horse Gate[g] on the palace grounds, and
there they put her to death.
16 Jehoiada then made a covenant[h]
that he and the people and the king[z]
would be the LORD's people. 17 All the
people went to the temple of Baal and
tore it down. They smashed the altars
and idols and killed[i] Mattan the priest of
Baal in front of the altars.
18 Then Jehoiada placed the oversight
of the temple of the LORD in the hands
of the priests, who were Levites,[j] to
whom David had made assignments in
the temple,[k] to present the burnt offerings of the LORD as written in the Law
of Moses, with rejoicing and singing, as
David had ordered. 19 He also stationed
doorkeepers[l] at the gates of the LORD's
temple so that no one who was in any
way unclean might enter.
20 He took with him the commanders
of hundreds, the nobles, the rulers of
the people and all the people of the
land and brought the king down from
the temple of the LORD. They went into
the palace through the Upper Gate[m] and
seated the king on the royal throne,
21 and all the people of the land rejoiced.
And the city was quiet, because Athaliah had been slain with the sword.[n]

Joash's order to restore the temple.

24:1-14pp— 2Ki 12:1-16

24 Joash was seven years old when
he became king, and he reigned
in Jerusalem forty years. His mother's
name was Zibiah; she was from Beersheba. 2 Joash did what was right in the
eyes of the LORD[o] all the years of Jehoiada the priest. 3 Jehoiada chose two wives
for him, and he had sons and daughters.

23:6 [a] 1Ch 23:28-29; Zec 3:7
23:8 [b] 2Ki 11:9 [c] 1Ch 24:1
23:11 [d] Ex 25:16; Dt 17:18; 1Sa 10:24
23:13 [e] 1Ki 1:41 [f] 1Ki 7:15
23:15 [g] Ne 3:28; Jer 31:40
23:16 [h] 2Ch 29:10; 34:31; Ne 9:38
23:17 [i] Dt 13:6-9
23:18 [j] 1Ch 23:28-32; 2Ch 5:5 [k] 1Ch 23:6; 25:6
23:19 [l] 1Ch 9:22
23:20 [m] 2Ki 15:35
23:21 [n] 2Ch 22:1
24:2 [o] 2Ch 25:2; 26:5

[x] 6 Or *to observe the LORD's command* ⌊*not to enter*⌋
[y] 14 Or *out from the precincts* [z] 16 Or *covenant between* ⌊*the LORD*⌋ *and the people and the king that they* (see 2 Kings 11:17)

4 Some time later Joash decided to
restore the temple of the LORD. 5 He
called together the priests and Levites
and said to them, "Go to the towns of
Judah and collect the money[a] due annu-
ally from all Israel,[b] to repair the temple
of your God. Do it now." But the Levites[c] did not act at once.
6 Therefore the king summoned Jehoiada the chief priest and said to him,
"Why haven't you required the Levites
to bring in from Judah and Jerusalem
the tax imposed by Moses the servant of
the LORD and by the assembly of Israel
for the Tent of the Testimony?"[d]
7 Now the sons of that wicked woman
Athaliah had broken into the temple of
God and had used even its sacred objects for the Baals.
8 At the king's command, a chest was
made and placed outside, at the gate of
the temple of the LORD. 9 A proclamation
was then issued in Judah and Jerusalem
that they should bring to the LORD the
tax that Moses the servant of God had
required of Israel in the desert. 10 All the
officials and all the people brought their
contributions gladly,[e] dropping them into
the chest until it was full. 11 Whenever
the chest was brought in by the Levites
to the king's officials and they saw that
there was a large amount of money,
the royal secretary and the officer of the
chief priest would come and empty the
chest and carry it back to its place. They
did this regularly and collected a great
amount of money. 12 The king and Jehoiada gave it to the men who carried out
the work required for the temple of the
LORD. They hired[f] masons and carpenters to restore the LORD's temple, and
also workers in iron and bronze to repair
the temple.
13 The men in charge of the work were
diligent, and the repairs progressed
under them. They rebuilt the temple of
God according to its original design and
reinforced it. 14 When they had finished,
they brought the rest of the money to
the king and Jehoiada, and with it were
made articles for the LORD's temple:
articles for the service and for the burnt
offerings, and also dishes and other
objects of gold and silver. As long as
Jehoiada lived, burnt offerings were presented continually in the temple of the
LORD.
15 Now Jehoiada was old and full of
years, and he died at the age of a hundred and thirty. 16 He was buried with
the kings in the City of David, because
of the good he had done in Israel for
God and his temple.

Joash's apostasy.

17 After the death of Jehoiada, the officials of Judah came and paid homage
to the king, and he listened to them.
18 They abandoned[g] the temple of the
LORD, the God of their fathers, and worshiped Asherah poles and idols.[h] Because
of their guilt, God's anger[i] came upon
Judah and Jerusalem. 19 Although the
LORD sent prophets to the people to
bring them back to him, and though
they testified against them, they would
not listen.[j]
20 Then the Spirit[k] of God came upon
Zechariah[l] son of Jehoiada the priest.
He stood before the people and said,
"This is what God says: 'Why do you
disobey the LORD's commands? You will
not prosper.[m] Because you have forsaken
the LORD, he has forsaken[n] you.'"
21 But they plotted against him, and
by order of the king they stoned[o] him
to death[p] in the courtyard of the LORD's
temple.[q] 22 King Joash did not remember
the kindness Zechariah's father Jehoiada
had shown him but killed his son, who
said as he lay dying, "May the LORD see
this and call you to account."[r]

Joash's death and burial.

24:23-27pp— 2Ki 12:17-21

23 At the turn of the year,[a] the army of
Aram marched against Joash; it invaded
Judah and Jerusalem and killed all the
leaders of the people.[s] They sent all
the plunder to their king in Damascus.

24:5 [a]Ex 30:16; Ne 10:32-33; Mt 17:24 [b]1Ch 11:1 [c]1Ch 26:20
24:6 [d]Ex 30:12-16; Nu 1:50
24:10 [e]Ex 25:2; 1Ch 29:3,6,9
24:12 [f]2Ch 34:11
24:18 [g]ver 4; Jos 24:20; 2Ch 7:19 [h]Ex 34:13; 1Ki 14:23; 2Ch 33:3; Jer 17:2 [i]Jos 22:20; 2Ch 19:2
24:19 [j]Nu 11:29; Jer 7:25; Zec 1:4
24:20 [k]Jdg 3:10; 1Ch 12:18; 2Ch 20:14 [l]Mt 23:35; Lk 11:51 [m]Nu 14:41 [n]Dt 31:17; 2Ch 15:2
24:21 [o]Jos 7:25; Ac 7:58-59 [p]Ne 9:26; Jer 26:21 [q]Jer 20:2; Mt 23:35
24:22 [r]Ge 9:5
24:23 [s]2Ki 12:17-18

a23 Probably in the spring

24Although the Aramean army had come
with only a few men,[a] the LORD delivered into their hands a much larger
army.[b] Because Judah had forsaken the
LORD, the God of their fathers, judgment
was executed on Joash. 25When the Arameans withdrew, they left Joash severely
wounded. His officials conspired against
him for murdering the son of Jehoiada
the priest, and they killed him in his
bed. So he died and was buried[c] in the
City of David, but not in the tombs of
the kings.
26Those who conspired against him
were Zabad,[b] son of Shimeath an Ammonite woman, and Jehozabad, son of
Shimrith[c][d] a Moabite woman.[e] 27The
account of his sons, the many prophecies about him, and the record of the
restoration of the temple of God are
written in the annotations on the book
of the kings. And Amaziah his son succeeded him as king.

Amaziah reigns in Judah.

25:1-4pp— 2Ki 14:1-6
25:11-12pp— 2Ki 14:7
25:17-28pp— 2Ki 14:8-20

25 Amaziah was twenty-five years
old when he became king, and
he reigned in Jerusalem twenty-nine
years. His mother's name was Jehoaddin[d]; she was from Jerusalem. 2He did
what was right in the eyes of the LORD,
but not wholeheartedly.[f] 3After the kingdom was firmly in his control, he executed the officials who had murdered
his father the king. 4Yet he did not put
their sons to death, but acted in accordance with what is written in the Law,
in the Book of Moses,[g] where the LORD
commanded: "Fathers shall not be put
to death for their children, nor children
put to death for their fathers; each is to
die for his own sins."[e][h]
5Amaziah called the people of Judah
together and assigned them according to
their families to commanders of thousands and commanders of hundreds for
all Judah and Benjamin. He then mustered[i] those twenty years old[j] or more
and found that there were three hundred
thousand men ready for military service,[k] able to handle the spear and
shield. 6He also hired a hundred thousand fighting men from Israel for a hundred talents[f] of silver.
7But a man of God came to him and
said, "O king, these troops from Israel[l]
must not march with you, for the LORD
is not with Israel—not with any of the
people of Ephraim. 8Even if you go and
fight courageously in battle, God will
overthrow you before the enemy, for
God has the power to help or to overthrow."[m]
9Amaziah asked the man of God, "But
what about the hundred talents I paid
for these Israelite troops?"
The man of God replied, "The LORD
can give you much more than that."[n]
10So Amaziah dismissed the troops
who had come to him from Ephraim
and sent them home. They were furious
with Judah and left for home in a great
rage.[o]
11Amaziah then marshaled his strength
and led his army to the Valley of Salt,
where he killed ten thousand men of
Seir. 12The army of Judah also captured
ten thousand men alive, took them to
the top of a cliff and threw them down
so that all were dashed to pieces.[p]
13Meanwhile the troops that Amaziah
had sent back and had not allowed to
take part in the war raided Judean
towns from Samaria to Beth Horon.
They killed three thousand people and
carried off great quantities of plunder.
14When Amaziah returned from
slaughtering the Edomites, he brought
back the gods of the people of Seir. He
set them up as his own gods,[q] bowed
down to them and burned sacrifices to
them. 15The anger of the LORD burned
against Amaziah, and he sent a prophet
to him, who said, "Why do you consult
this people's gods, which could not
save[r] their own people from your hand?"
16While he was still speaking, the king

24:24 [a]2Ch 14:9; 16:8; 20:2,12 [b]Lev 26:23-25; Dt 28:25
24:25 [c]2Ch 21:20
24:26 [d]2Ki 12:21 [e]Ru 1:4
25:2 [f]ver 14; 1Ki 8:61; 2Ch 24:2
25:4 [g]Dt 28:61 [h]Nu 26:11; Dt 24:16
25:5 [i]2Sa 24:2 [j]Ex 30:14 [k]Nu 1:3; 1Ch 21:1; 2Ch 17:14-19
25:7 [l]2Ch 16:2-9; 19:1-3
25:8 [m]2Ch 14:11; 20:6
25:9 [n]Dt 8:18; Pr 10:22
25:10 [o]ver 13
25:12 [p]Ps 141:6; Ob 3
25:14 [q]Ex 20:3; 2Ch 28:23; Isa 44:15
25:15 [r]Ps 96:5; Isa 36:20

b*26* A variant of *Jozabad* c*26* A variant of *Shomer*
d*1* Hebrew *Jehoaddan,* a variant of *Jehoaddin*
e*4* Deut. 24:16 f*6* That is, about 3 3/4 tons (about 3.4 metric tons); also in verse 9

said to him, "Have we appointed you an adviser to the king? Stop! Why be struck down?"

So the prophet stopped but said, "I know that God has determined to destroy you, because you have done this and have not listened to my counsel."

[17]After Amaziah king of Judah consulted his advisers, he sent this challenge to Jehoash[g] son of Jehoahaz, the son of Jehu, king of Israel: "Come, meet me face to face."

[18]But Jehoash king of Israel replied to Amaziah king of Judah: "A thistle[a] in Lebanon sent a message to a cedar in Lebanon, 'Give your daughter to my son in marriage.' Then a wild beast in Lebanon came along and trampled the thistle underfoot. [19]You say to yourself that you have defeated Edom, and now you are arrogant and proud. But stay at home! Why ask for trouble and cause your own downfall and that of Judah also?"

[20]Amaziah, however, would not listen, for God so worked that he might hand them over to ⌊Jehoash⌋, because they sought the gods of Edom.[b] [21]So Jehoash king of Israel attacked. He and Amaziah king of Judah faced each other at Beth Shemesh in Judah. [22]Judah was routed by Israel, and every man fled to his home. [23]Jehoash king of Israel captured Amaziah king of Judah, the son of Joash, the son of Ahaziah,[h] at Beth Shemesh. Then Jehoash brought him to Jerusalem and broke down the wall of Jerusalem from the Ephraim Gate[c] to the Corner Gate[d]—a section about six hundred feet[i] long. [24]He took all the gold and silver and all the articles found in the temple of God that had been in the care of Obed-Edom,[e] together with the palace treasures and the hostages, and returned to Samaria.

Amaziah is assassinated.

[25]Amaziah son of Joash king of Judah lived for fifteen years after the death of Jehoash son of Jehoahaz king of Israel. [26]As for the other events of Amaziah's

25:18 [a]Jdg 9:8-15
25:20 [b]1Ki 12:15; 2Ch 10:15; 22:7
25:23 [c]2Ki 14:13; Ne 8:16; 12:39 [d]2Ch 26:9; Jer 31:38
25:24 [e]1Ch 26:15
25:27 [f]Jos 10:3
26:1 [g]2Ch 22:1
26:5 [h]2Ch 15:2; 24:2; Da 1:17 [i]2Ch 27:6
26:6 [j]Isa 2:6; 11:14; 14:29; Jer 25:20 [k]Am 1:8; 3:9
26:7 [l]2Ch 21:16 [m]2Ch 20:1
26:8 [n]Ge 19:38; 2Ch 17:11
26:9 [o]2Ki 14:13; 2Ch 25:23 [p]Ne 2:13; 3:13

reign, from beginning to end, are they not written in the book of the kings of Judah and Israel? [27]From the time that Amaziah turned away from following the LORD, they conspired against him in Jerusalem and he fled to Lachish[f], but they sent men after him to Lachish and killed him there. [28]He was brought back by horse and was buried with his fathers in the City of Judah.

Uzziah replaces Amaziah as king over Judah.

26:1-4pp— 2Ki 14:21-22; 15:1-3

26 Then all the people of Judah[g] took Uzziah,[j] who was sixteen years old, and made him king in place of his father Amaziah. [2]He was the one who rebuilt Elath and restored it to Judah after Amaziah rested with his fathers.

[3]Uzziah was sixteen years old when he became king, and he reigned in Jerusalem fifty-two years. His mother's name was Jecoliah; she was from Jerusalem. [4]He did what was right in the eyes of the LORD, just as his father Amaziah had done. [5]He sought God during the days of Zechariah, who instructed him in the fear[k] of God.[h] As long as he sought the LORD, God gave him success.[i]

[6]He went to war against the Philistines[j] and broke down the walls of Gath, Jabneh and Ashdod.[k] He then rebuilt towns near Ashdod and elsewhere among the Philistines. [7]God helped him against the Philistines and against the Arabs[l] who lived in Gur Baal and against the Meunites.[m] [8]The Ammonites[n] brought tribute to Uzziah, and his fame spread as far as the border of Egypt, because he had become very powerful.

[9]Uzziah built towers in Jerusalem at the Corner Gate,[o] at the Valley Gate[p] and at the angle of the wall, and he fortified

g *17* Hebrew *Joash,* a variant of *Jehoash*; also in verses 18, 21, 23 and 25 h *23* Hebrew *Jehoahaz,* a variant of *Ahaziah* i *23* Hebrew *four hundred cubits* (about 180 meters) j *1* Also called *Azariah* k *5* Many Hebrew manuscripts, Septuagint and Syriac; other Hebrew manuscripts *vision*

them. 10He also built towers in the desert
and dug many cisterns, because he had
much livestock in the foothills and in
the plain. He had people working his
fields and vineyards in the hills and in
the fertile lands, for he loved the soil.
11Uzziah had a well-trained army,
ready to go out by divisions according
to their numbers as mustered by Jeiel
the secretary and Maaseiah the officer
under the direction of Hananiah, one of
the royal officials. 12The total number of
family leaders over the fighting men
was 2,600. 13Under their command was
an army of 307,500 men trained for
war, a powerful force to support the
king against his enemies. 14Uzziah provided shields, spears, helmets, coats of
armor, bows and slingstones for the
entire army.[a] 15In Jerusalem he made
machines designed by skillful men for
use on the towers and on the corner
defenses to shoot arrows and hurl large
stones. His fame spread far and wide, for
he was greatly helped until he became
powerful.

The LORD *afflicts Uzziah with leprosy.*

26:21-23pp— 2Ki 15:5-7

16But after Uzziah became powerful,
his pride[b] led to his downfall.[c] He was
unfaithful[d] to the LORD his God, and
entered the temple of the LORD to burn
incense[e] on the altar of incense. 17Azari-
ah[f] the priest with eighty other courageous priests of the LORD followed him
in. 18They confronted him and said, "It
is not right for you, Uzziah, to burn
incense to the LORD. That is for the
priests,[g] the descendants[h] of Aaron,[i]
who have been consecrated to burn
incense.[j] Leave the sanctuary, for you
have been unfaithful; and you will not
be honored by the LORD God."
19Uzziah, who had a censer in his
hand ready to burn incense, became
angry. While he was raging at the priests
in their presence before the incense
altar in the LORD's temple, leprosy[l][k]
broke out on his forehead. 20When

26:14 [a]Jer 46:4
26:16 [b]2Ki 14:10 [c]Dt 32:15; 2Ch 25:19 [d]1Ch 5:25 [e]2Ki 16:12
26:17 [f]1Ki 4:2; 1Ch 6:10
26:18 [g]Nu 16:39 [h]Nu 18:1-7 [i]Ex 30:7 [j]1Ch 6:49
26:19 [k]Nu 12:10; 2Ki 5:25-27
26:21 [l]Ex 4:6; Lev 13:46; 14:8; Nu 5:2; 19:12
26:22 [m]2Ki 15:1; Isa 1:1; 6:1
26:23 [n]Isa 1:1; 6:1 [o]2Ki 14:21; 15:7; Am 1:1
27:1 [p]2Ki 15:5,32; 1Ch 3:12
27:3 [q]2Ch 33:14; Ne 3:26
27:5 [r]Ge 19:38

Azariah the chief priest and all the other
priests looked at him, they saw that he
had leprosy on his forehead, so they
hurried him out. Indeed, he himself was
eager to leave, because the LORD had afflicted him.
21King Uzziah had leprosy until the
day he died. He lived in a separate
house[m][l]—leprous, and excluded from
the temple of the LORD. Jotham his son
had charge of the palace and governed
the people of the land.
22The other events of Uzziah's reign,
from beginning to end, are recorded by
the prophet Isaiah[m] son of Amoz. 23Uzzi-
ah[n] rested with his fathers and was buried near them in a field for burial that
belonged to the kings, for people said,
"He had leprosy." And Jotham his son
succeeded him as king.[o]

Jotham reigns in Judah.

27:1-4,7-9pp— 2Ki 15:33-38

27 Jotham[p] was twenty-five years
old when he became king, and
he reigned in Jerusalem sixteen years.
His mother's name was Jerusha daughter
of Zadok. 2He did what was right in the
eyes of the LORD, just as his father Uzziah had done, but unlike him he did not
enter the temple of the LORD. The people, however, continued their corrupt
practices. 3Jotham rebuilt the Upper
Gate of the temple of the LORD and did
extensive work on the wall at the hill of
Ophel.[q] 4He built towns in the Judean
hills and forts and towers in the wooded
areas.
5Jotham made war on the king of the
Ammonites[r] and conquered them. That
year the Ammonites paid him a hundred
talents[n] of silver, ten thousand cors[o] of
wheat and ten thousand cors of barley.
The Ammonites brought him the same
amount also in the second and third
years.

[l] *19* The Hebrew word was used for various diseases affecting the skin—not necessarily leprosy; also in verses 20, 21 and 23. [m] *21* Or *in a house where he was relieved of responsibilities* [n] *5* That is, about 3 3/4 tons (about 3.4 metric tons) [o] *5* That is, probably about 62,000 bushels (about 2,200 kiloliters)

6Jotham grew powerful[a] because he
walked steadfastly before the LORD his
God.

Jotham's death.

7The other events in Jotham's reign,
including all his wars and the other
things he did, are written in the book of
the kings of Israel and Judah. 8He was
twenty-five years old when he became
king, and he reigned in Jerusalem sixteen years. 9Jotham rested with his
fathers and was buried in the City of
David. And Ahaz his son succeeded him
as king.

Ahaz's wicked reign in Judah.

28:1-27pp— 2Ki 16:1-20

28 Ahaz[b] was twenty years old
when he became king, and he
reigned in Jerusalem sixteen years.
Unlike David his father, he did not do
what was right in the eyes of the LORD.
2He walked in the ways of the kings of
Israel and also made cast idols[c] for
worshiping the Baals. 3He burned sacrifices in the Valley of Ben Hinnom[d] and
sacrificed his sons[e] in the fire, following
the detestable[f] ways of the nations the
LORD had driven out before the Israelites. 4He offered sacrifices and burned
incense at the high places, on the hilltops and under every spreading tree.
5Therefore the LORD his God handed
him over to the king of Aram.[g] The Arameans defeated him and took many of
his people as prisoners and brought
them to Damascus.
He was also given into the hands of
the king of Israel, who inflicted heavy
casualties on him. 6In one day Pekah[h]
son of Remaliah killed a hundred and
twenty thousand soldiers in Judah[i]—
because Judah had forsaken the LORD,
the God of their fathers. 7Zicri, an Ephraimite warrior, killed Maaseiah the king's
son, Azrikam the officer in charge of the
palace, and Elkanah, second to the king.
8The Israelites took captive from their
kinsmen[j] two hundred thousand wives,
sons and daughters. They also took a
great deal of plunder, which they carried
back to Samaria.[k]
9But a prophet of the LORD named
Oded was there, and he went out to
meet the army when it returned to
Samaria. He said to them, "Because the
LORD, the God of your fathers, was
angry[l] with Judah, he gave them into
your hand. But you have slaughtered
them in a rage that reaches to heaven.[m]
10And now you intend to make the men
and women of Judah and Jerusalem your
slaves.[n] But aren't you also guilty of sins
against the LORD your God? 11Now listen
to me! Send back your fellow countrymen you have taken as prisoners, for
the LORD's fierce anger rests on you.[o]"
12Then some of the leaders in Ephraim—Azariah son of Jehohanan, Berekiah
son of Meshillemoth, Jehizkiah son of
Shallum, and Amasa son of Hadlai—
confronted those who were arriving
from the war. 13"You must not bring
those prisoners here," they said, "or we
will be guilty before the LORD. Do you
intend to add to our sin and guilt? For
our guilt is already great, and his fierce
anger rests on Israel."
14So the soldiers gave up the prisoners and plunder in the presence of the
officials and all the assembly. 15The men
designated by name took the prisoners,
and from the plunder they clothed all
who were naked. They provided them
with clothes and sandals, food and
drink,[p] and healing balm. All those who
were weak they put on donkeys. So they
took them back to their fellow countrymen at Jericho, the City of Palms,[q] and
returned to Samaria.
16At that time King Ahaz sent to the
king[p] of Assyria[r] for help. 17The Edomites[s] had again come and attacked Judah
and carried away prisoners,[t] 18while the
Philistines[u] had raided towns in the
foothills and in the Negev of Judah.
They captured and occupied Beth Shemesh, Aijalon[v] and Gederoth, as well
as Soco, Timnah and Gimzo, with their

27:6 [a]2Ch 26:5

28:1 [b]1Ch 3:13; Isa 1:1

28:2 [c]Ex 34:17; 2Ch 22:3

28:3 [d]Jos 15:8; 2Ki 23:10 [e]Lev 18:21; 2Ki 3:27; 2Ch 33:6; Eze 20:26 [f]Dt 18:9; 2Ch 33:2

28:5 [g]Isa 7:1

28:6 [h]2Ki 15:25,27 [i]ver 8; Isa 9:21; 11:13

28:8 [j]Dt 28:25-41; 2Ch 11:4 [k]2Ch 29:9

28:9 [l]2Ch 25:15; Isa 10:6; 47:6; Zec 1:15 [m]Ezr 9:6; Rev 18:5

28:10 [n]Lev 25:39-46

28:11 [o]2Ch 11:4; Jas 2:13

28:15 [p]2Ki 6:22; Pr 25:21-22 [q]Dt 34:3; Jdg 1:16

28:16 [r]2Ki 16:7

28:17 [s]Ps 137:7; Isa 34:5 [t]2Ch 29:9

28:18 [u]Eze 16:27,57 [v]Jos 10:12

p *16* One Hebrew manuscript, Septuagint and Vulgate (see also 2 Kings 16:7); most Hebrew manuscripts *kings*

surrounding villages. 19The LORD had
humbled Judah because of Ahaz king of
Israel,[q] for he had promoted wickedness
in Judah and had been most unfaithful[a]
to the LORD. 20Tiglath-Pileser[r][b] king of
Assyria came to him, but he gave him
trouble instead of help.[c] 21Ahaz took
some of the things from the temple of
the LORD and from the royal palace and
from the princes and presented them to
the king of Assyria, but that did not help
him.

22In his time of trouble King Ahaz became even more unfaithful[d] to the LORD.
23He offered sacrifices to the gods[e] of
Damascus, who had defeated him; for
he thought, "Since the gods of the kings
of Aram have helped them, I will sacrifice to them so they will help me."[f] But
they were his downfall and the downfall
of all Israel.

24Ahaz gathered together the furnishings from the temple of God[g] and took
them away.[s] He shut the doors[h] of the
LORD's temple and set up altars[i] at every
street corner in Jerusalem. 25In every
town in Judah he built high places to
burn sacrifices to other gods and provoked the LORD, the God of his fathers,
to anger.

Ahaz's death.

26The other events of his reign and
all his ways, from beginning to end, are
written in the book of the kings of Judah
and Israel. 27Ahaz rested[j] with his fathers and was buried[k] in the city of
Jerusalem, but he was not placed in the
tombs of the kings of Israel. And Hezekiah his son succeeded him as king.

Hezekiah consecrates the temple.

29:1-2pp— 2Ki 18:2-3

29 Hezekiah[l] was twenty-five years
old when he became king, and
he reigned in Jerusalem twenty-nine
years. His mother's name was Abijah
daughter of Zechariah. 2He did what was
right in the eyes of the LORD, just as his
father David[m] had done.

3In the first month of the first year of
his reign, he opened the doors of the
temple of the LORD and repaired[n] them.
4He brought in the priests and the Levites, assembled them in the square on
the east side 5and said: "Listen to me,
Levites! Consecrate[o] yourselves now and
consecrate the temple of the LORD, the
God of your fathers. Remove all defile-
ment from the sanctuary. 6Our fathers[p]
were unfaithful;[q] they did evil in the
eyes of the LORD our God and forsook
him. They turned their faces away from
the LORD's dwelling place and turned
their backs on him. 7They also shut the
doors of the portico and put out the
lamps. They did not burn incense or
present any burnt offerings at the sanctuary to the God of Israel. 8Therefore,
the anger of the LORD has fallen on Judah
and Jerusalem; he has made them an
object of dread and horror[r] and scorn,[s]
as you can see with your own eyes.
9This is why our fathers have fallen by
the sword and why our sons and daughters and our wives are in captivity.[t]
10Now I intend to make a covenant[u]
with the LORD, the God of Israel, so that
his fierce anger will turn away from us.
11My sons, do not be negligent now, for
the LORD has chosen you to stand before
him and serve him,[v] to minister[w] before
him and to burn incense."

12Then these Levites[x] set to work:
from the Kohathites,
Mahath son of Amasai and Joel son of Azariah;
from the Merarites,
Kish son of Abdi and Azariah son of Jehallelel;
from the Gershonites,
Joah son of Zimmah and Eden[y] son of Joah;
13from the descendants of Elizaphan,
Shimri and Jeiel;
from the descendants of Asaph,[z]
Zechariah and Mattaniah;
14from the descendants of Heman,
Jehiel and Shimei;

28:19 [a]2Ch 21:2
28:20 [b]2Ki 15:29; 1Ch 5:6 [c]2Ki 16:7
28:22 [d]Jer 5:3
28:23 [e]2Ch 25:14 [f]Jer 44:17-18
28:24 [g]2Ki 16:18 [h]2Ch 29:7 [i]2Ch 30:14
28:27 [j]Isa 14:28-32 [k]2Ch 21:20; 24:25
29:1 [l]1Ch 3:13
29:2 [m]2Ch 28:1; 34:2
29:3 [n]2Ch 28:24
29:5 [o]2Ch 35:6
29:6 [p]Ps 106:6-47; Jer 2:27 [q]1Ch 5:25; Eze 8:16
29:8 [r]Dt 28:25; 2Ch 24:18 [s]Jer 18:16; 19:8; 25:9,18
29:9 [t]2Ch 28:5-8, 17
29:10 [u]2Ch 15:12; 23:16
29:11 [v]Nu 3:6; 8:6,14 [w]1Ch 15:2
29:12 [x]Nu 3:17-20 [y]2Ch 31:15
29:13 [z]1Ch 6:39

q *19* That is, Judah, as frequently in 2 Chronicles
r *20* Hebrew *Tilgath-Pilneser,* a variant of *Tiglath-Pileser*
s *24* Or *and cut them up*

from the descendants of Jeduthun,
Shemaiah and Uzziel.
15 When they had assembled their
brothers and consecrated themselves,
they went in to purify[a] the temple of the
LORD, as the king had ordered, following
the word of the LORD. 16 The priests went
into the sanctuary of the LORD to purify
it. They brought out to the courtyard of
the LORD's temple everything unclean
that they found in the temple of the
LORD. The Levites took it and carried it
out to the Kidron Valley.[b] 17 They began
the consecration on the first day of the
first month, and by the eighth day of the
month they reached the portico of the
LORD. For eight more days they consecrated the temple of the LORD itself, finishing on the sixteenth day of the first
month.
18 Then they went in to King Hezekiah
and reported: "We have purified the entire temple of the LORD, the altar of
burnt offering with all its utensils, and
the table for setting out the consecrated
bread, with all its articles. 19 We have
prepared and consecrated all the articles[c] that King Ahaz removed in his
unfaithfulness while he was king. They
are now in front of the LORD's altar."
20 Early the next morning King Hezekiah gathered the city officials together
and went up to the temple of the LORD.
21 They brought seven bulls, seven rams,
seven male lambs and seven male goats
as a sin offering[d] for the kingdom, for
the sanctuary and for Judah. The king
commanded the priests, the descendants
of Aaron, to offer these on the altar of
the LORD. 22 So they slaughtered the
bulls, and the priests took the blood and
sprinkled it on the altar; next they
slaughtered the rams and sprinkled their
blood on the altar; then they slaughtered
the lambs and sprinkled their blood[e] on
the altar. 23 The goats for the sin offering
were brought before the king and the
assembly, and they laid their hands[f] on
them. 24 The priests then slaughtered the
goats and presented their blood on the
altar for a sin offering to atone[g] for all
Israel, because the king had ordered the
burnt offering and the sin offering for
all Israel.
25 He stationed the Levites in the temple of the LORD with cymbals, harps and
lyres in the way prescribed by David[h]
and Gad[i] the king's seer and Nathan
the prophet; this was commanded by
the LORD through his prophets. 26 So the
Levites stood ready with David's instruments,[j] and the priests with their trumpets.[k]
27 Hezekiah gave the order to sacrifice
the burnt offering on the altar. As the
offering began, singing to the LORD
began also, accompanied by trumpets
and the instruments[l] of David king of
Israel. 28 The whole assembly bowed in
worship, while the singers sang and the
trumpeters played. All this continued
until the sacrifice of the burnt offering
was completed.
29 When the offerings were finished,
the king and everyone present with him
knelt down and worshiped.[m] 30 King
Hezekiah and his officials ordered the
Levites to praise the LORD with the
words of David and of Asaph the seer.
So they sang praises with gladness and
bowed their heads and worshiped.
31 Then Hezekiah said, "You have now
dedicated yourselves to the LORD. Come
and bring sacrifices[n] and thank offerings
to the temple of the LORD." So the assembly brought sacrifices and thank
offerings, and all whose hearts were
willing[o] brought burnt offerings.
32 The number of burnt offerings the
assembly brought was seventy bulls, a
hundred rams and two hundred male
lambs—all of them for burnt offerings
to the LORD. 33 The animals consecrated
as sacrifices amounted to six hundred
bulls and three thousand sheep and
goats. 34 The priests, however, were too
few to skin all the burnt offerings;[p] so
their kinsmen the Levites helped them
until the task was finished and until
other priests had been consecrated,[q] for
the Levites had been more conscientious
in consecrating themselves than the
priests had been. 35 There were burnt
offerings in abundance, together with

29:15 [a] ver 5; 1Ch 23:28; 2Ch 30:12
29:16 [b] 2Sa 15:23
29:19 [c] 2Ch 28:24
29:21 [d] Lev 4:13-14
29:22 [e] Lev 4:18
29:23 [f] Lev 4:15
29:24 [g] Ex 29:36; Lev 4:26
29:25 [h] 1Ch 25:6; 2Ch 8:14 [i] 1Sa 22:5; 2Sa 24:11
29:26 [j] 1Ch 15:16 [k] 1Ch 15:24; 23:5; 2Ch 5:12
29:27 [l] 2Ch 23:18
29:29 [m] 2Ch 20:18
29:31 [n] Heb 13:15-16 [o] Ex 25:2; 35:22
29:34 [p] 2Ch 35:11 [q] 2Ch 30:3,15

the fat[a] of the fellowship offerings[t][b] and the drink offerings[c] that accompanied the burnt offerings.

So the service of the temple of the LORD was reestablished. 36Hezekiah and all the people rejoiced at what God had brought about for his people, because it was done so quickly.

Hezekiah celebrates the Passover.

30 Hezekiah sent word to all Israel and Judah and also wrote letters to Ephraim and Manasseh,[d] inviting them to come to the temple of the LORD in Jerusalem and celebrate the Passover[e] to the LORD, the God of Israel. 2The king and his officials and the whole assembly in Jerusalem decided to celebrate[f] the Passover in the second month. 3They had not been able to celebrate it at the regular time because not enough priests had consecrated[g] themselves and the people had not assembled in Jerusalem. 4The plan seemed right both to the king and to the whole assembly. 5They decided to send a proclamation throughout Israel, from Beersheba to Dan,[h] calling the people to come to Jerusalem and celebrate the Passover to the LORD, the God of Israel. It had not been celebrated in large numbers according to what was written.

6At the king's command, couriers went throughout Israel and Judah with letters from the king and from his officials, which read:

"People of Israel, return to the LORD, the God of Abraham, Isaac and Israel, that he may return to you who are left, who have escaped from the hand of the kings of Assyria. 7Do not be like your fathers[i] and brothers, who were unfaithful to the LORD, the God of their fathers, so that he made them an object of horror,[j] as you see. 8Do not be stiff-necked,[k] as your fathers were; submit to the LORD. Come to the sanctuary, which he has consecrated forever. Serve the LORD your God, so that his fierce anger[l] will turn away from you. 9If you return[m] to the LORD, then your brothers and your children will be shown compassion[n] by their captors and will come back to this land, for the LORD your God is gracious and compassionate.[o] He will not turn his face from you if you return to him."

10The couriers went from town to town in Ephraim and Manasseh, as far as Zebulun, but the people scorned and ridiculed[p] them. 11Nevertheless, some men of Asher, Manasseh and Zebulun humbled themselves and went to Jerusalem.[q] 12Also in Judah the hand of God was on the people to give them unity[r] of mind to carry out what the king and his officials had ordered, following the word of the LORD.

13A very large crowd of people assembled in Jerusalem to celebrate the Feast of Unleavened Bread[s] in the second month. 14They removed the altars[t] in Jerusalem and cleared away the incense altars and threw them into the Kidron Valley.[u]

15They slaughtered the Passover lamb on the fourteenth day of the second month. The priests and the Levites were ashamed and consecrated[v] themselves and brought burnt offerings to the temple of the LORD. 16Then they took up their regular positions[w] as prescribed in the Law of Moses the man of God. The priests sprinkled the blood handed to them by the Levites. 17Since many in the crowd had not consecrated themselves, the Levites had to kill[x] the Passover lambs for all those who were not ceremonially clean and could not consecrate ⌊their lambs⌋ to the LORD. 18Although most of the many people who came from Ephraim, Manasseh, Issachar and Zebulun had not purified themselves,[y] yet they ate the Passover, contrary to what was written. But Hezekiah prayed for them, saying, "May the LORD, who is good, pardon everyone 19who sets his heart on seeking God—the

29:35 [a]Ex 29:13; Lev 3:16 [b]Lev 7:11-21 [c]Nu 15:5-10
30:1 [d]Ge 41:52 [e]Ex 12:11; Nu 28:16
30:2 [f]Nu 9:10
30:3 [g]2Ch 29:34
30:5 [h]Jdg 20:1
30:7 [i]Ps 78:8,57; 106:6; Eze 20:18 [j]2Ch 29:8
30:8 [k]Ex 32:9 [l]Nu 25:4; 2Ch 29:10
30:9 [m]Dt 30:2-5; Isa 1:16; 55:7 [n]1Ki 8:50; Ps 106:46 [o]Ex 34:6-7; Dt 4:31; Mic 7:18
30:10 [p]2Ch 36:16
30:11 [q]ver 25
30:12 [r]Jer 32:39; Eze 11:19; Php 2:13
30:13 [s]Nu 28:16
30:14 [t]2Ch 28:24 [u]2Sa 15:23
30:15 [v]2Ch 29:34
30:16 [w]2Ch 35:10
30:17 [x]2Ch 29:34
30:18 [y]Ex 12:43-49; Nu 9:6-10

t*35* Traditionally *peace offerings*

LORD, the God of his fathers—even if he is not clean according to the rules of the sanctuary." 20And the LORD heard[a] Hezekiah and healed[b] the people.[c]

21The Israelites who were present in Jerusalem celebrated the Feast of Unleavened Bread[d] for seven days with great rejoicing, while the Levites and priests sang to the LORD every day, accompanied by the LORD's instruments of praise.[u]

22Hezekiah spoke encouragingly to all the Levites, who showed good understanding of the service of the LORD. For the seven days they ate their assigned portion and offered fellowship offerings[v] and praised the LORD, the God of their fathers.

23The whole assembly then agreed to celebrate[e] the festival seven more days; so for another seven days they celebrated joyfully. 24Hezekiah king of Judah provided[f] a thousand bulls and seven thousand sheep and goats for the assembly, and the officials provided them with a thousand bulls and ten thousand sheep and goats. A great number of priests consecrated themselves. 25The entire assembly of Judah rejoiced, along with the priests and Levites and all who had assembled from Israel[g], including the aliens who had come from Israel and those who lived in Judah. 26There was great joy in Jerusalem, for since the days of Solomon[h] son of David king of Israel there had been nothing like this in Jerusalem. 27The priests and the Levites stood to bless[i] the people, and God heard them, for their prayer reached heaven, his holy dwelling place.

The people forsake their idolatry.

31 When all this had ended, the Israelites who were there went out to the towns of Judah, smashed the sacred stones and cut down[j] the Asherah poles. They destroyed the high places and the altars throughout Judah and Benjamin and in Ephraim and Manasseh. After they had destroyed all of them, the Israelites returned to their own towns and to their own property.

The people bring contributions.

31:20-21pp— 2Ki 18:5-7

2Hezekiah[k] assigned the priests and Levites to divisions[l]—each of them according to their duties as priests or Levites—to offer burnt offerings and fellowship offerings,[v] to minister,[m] to give thanks and to sing praises[n] at the gates of the LORD's dwelling.[o] 3The king contributed[p] from his own possessions for the morning and evening burnt offerings and for the burnt offerings on the Sabbaths, New Moons and appointed feasts as written in the Law of the LORD.[q] 4He ordered the people living in Jerusalem to give the portion[r] due the priests and Levites so they could devote themselves to the Law of the LORD. 5As soon as the order went out, the Israelites generously gave the firstfruits[s] of their grain, new wine,[t] oil and honey and all that the fields produced. They brought a great amount, a tithe of everything. 6The men of Israel and Judah who lived in the towns of Judah also brought a tithe[u] of their herds and flocks and a tithe of the holy things dedicated to the LORD their God, and they piled them in heaps.[v] 7They began doing this in the third month and finished in the seventh month.[w] 8When Hezekiah and his officials came and saw the heaps, they praised the LORD and blessed[x] his people Israel.

9Hezekiah asked the priests and Levites about the heaps; 10and Azariah the chief priest, from the family of Zadok,[y] answered, "Since the people began to bring their contributions to the temple of the LORD, we have had enough to eat and plenty to spare, because the LORD has blessed his people, and this great amount is left over."[z]

11Hezekiah gave orders to prepare storerooms in the temple of the LORD, and this was done. 12Then they faithfully brought in the contributions, tithes and dedicated gifts. Conaniah,[a] a Levite, was

30:20 [a]2Ch 6:20 [b]2Ch 7:14; Mal 4:2 [c]Jas 5:16
30:21 [d]Ex 12:15,17; 13:6
30:23 [e]1Ki 8:65; 2Ch 7:9
30:24 [f]1Ki 8:5; 2Ch 29:34; 35:7; Ezr 6:17; 8:35
30:25 [g]ver 11
30:26 [h]2Ch 7:8
30:27 [i]Ex 39:43; Nu 6:23; Dt 26:15; 2Ch 23:18; Ps 68:5
31:1 [j]2Ki 18:4; 2Ch 32:12; Isa 36:7
31:2 [k]2Ch 29:9 [l]1Ch 24:1 [m]1Ch 15:2 [n]Ps 7:17; 9:2; 47:6; 71:22 [o]1Ch 23:28-32
31:3 [p]1Ch 29:3; 2Ch 35:7; Eze 45:17 [q]Nu 28:1–29:40
31:4 [r]Nu 18:8; Dt 18:8; Ne 13:10; Mal 2:7
31:5 [s]Nu 18:12,24; Ne 13:12; Eze 44:30 [t]Dt 12:17
31:6 [u]Lev 27:30; Ne 13:10-12 [v]Dt 14:28; Ru 3:7
31:7 [w]Ex 23:16
31:8 [x]Ps 144:13-15
31:10 [y]2Sa 8:17 [z]Ex 36:5; Eze 44:30; Mal 3:10-12
31:12 [a]2Ch 35:9

u21 Or *priests praised the LORD every day with resounding instruments belonging to the LORD*
v22, 2 Traditionally *peace offerings*

in charge of these things, and his brother Shimei was next in rank. 13 Jehiel, Azaziah, Nahath, Asahel, Jerimoth, Jozabad,[a] Eliel, Ismakiah, Mahath and Benaiah were supervisors under Conaniah and Shimei his brother, by appointment of King Hezekiah and Azariah the official in charge of the temple of God.

14 Kore son of Imnah the Levite, keeper of the East Gate, was in charge of the freewill offerings given to God, distributing the contributions made to the LORD and also the consecrated gifts. 15 Eden,[b] Miniamin, Jeshua, Shemaiah, Amariah and Shecaniah assisted him faithfully in the towns[c] of the priests, distributing to their fellow priests according to their divisions, old and young alike.

16 In addition, they distributed to the males three years old or more whose names were in the genealogical records[d]—all who would enter the temple of the LORD to perform the daily duties of their various tasks, according to their responsibilities and their divisions. 17 And they distributed to the priests enrolled by their families in the genealogical records and likewise to the Levites twenty years old or more, according to their responsibilities and their divisions. 18 They included all the little ones, the wives, and the sons and daughters of the whole community listed in these genealogical records. For they were faithful in consecrating themselves.

19 As for the priests, the descendants of Aaron, who lived on the farm lands around their towns or in any other towns,[e] men were designated by name to distribute portions to every male among them and to all who were recorded in the genealogies of the Levites.

20 This is what Hezekiah did throughout Judah, doing what was good and right and faithful[f] before the LORD his God. 21 In everything that he undertook in the service of God's temple and in obedience to the law and the commands, he sought his God and worked wholeheartedly. And so he prospered.[g]

31:13 [a]2Ch 35:9
31:15 [b]2Ch 29:12 [c]Jos 21:9-19
31:16 [d]1Ch 23:3; Ezr 3:4
31:19 [e]ver 12-15; Lev 25:34; Nu 35:2-5
31:20 [f]2Ki 20:3; 22:2
31:21 [g]Dt 29:9
32:1 [h]2Ki 18:13-19; Isa 36:1; 37:9,17,37
32:2 [i]Isa 22:7; Jer 1:15
32:4 [j]2Ki 18:17; 20:20; Isa 22:9,11; Na 3:14
32:5 [k]2Ch 25:23; Isa 22:10 [l]1Ki 9:24; 1Ch 11:8 [m]Isa 22:8
32:7 [n]Dt 31:6; 1Ch 22:13 [o]2Ch 20:15 [p]Nu 14:9; 2Ki 6:16
32:8 [q]Job 40:9; Isa 52:10; Jer 17:5; 32:21 [r]Dt 3:22; 1Sa 17:45; 2Ch 13:12 [s]1Ch 5:22; 2Ch 20:17; Ps 20:7; Isa 28:6
32:9 [t]Jos 10:3,31
32:10 [u]Eze 29:16

Sennacherib's invasion of Judah.

32:9-19pp— 2Ki 18:17-35; Isa 36:2-20
32:20-21pp— 2Ki 19:35-37; Isa 37:36-38

32 After all that Hezekiah had so faithfully done, Sennacherib[h] king of Assyria came and invaded Judah. He laid siege to the fortified cities, thinking to conquer them for himself. 2 When Hezekiah saw that Sennacherib had come and that he intended to make war on Jerusalem,[i] 3 he consulted with his officials and military staff about blocking off the water from the springs outside the city, and they helped him. 4 A large force of men assembled, and they blocked all the springs[j] and the stream that flowed through the land. "Why should the kings[w] of Assyria come and find plenty of water?" they said. 5 Then he worked hard repairing all the broken sections of the wall[k] and building towers on it. He built another wall outside that one and reinforced the supporting terraces[x][l] of the City of David. He also made large numbers of weapons[m] and shields.

6 He appointed military officers over the people and assembled them before him in the square at the city gate and encouraged them with these words: 7 "Be strong and courageous.[n] Do not be afraid or discouraged[o] because of the king of Assyria and the vast army with him, for there is a greater power with us than with him.[p] 8 With him is only the arm of flesh,[q] but with us[r] is the LORD our God to help us and to fight our battles."[s] And the people gained confidence from what Hezekiah the king of Judah said.

9 Later, when Sennacherib king of Assyria and all his forces were laying siege to Lachish,[t] he sent his officers to Jerusalem with this message for Hezekiah king of Judah and for all the people of Judah who were there:

> 10 "This is what Sennacherib king of Assyria says: On what are you basing your confidence,[u] that you

[w]4 Hebrew; Septuagint and Syriac *king* [x]5 Or *the Millo*

remain in Jerusalem under siege? 11When Hezekiah says, 'The LORD our God will save us from the hand of the king of Assyria,' he is misleading[a] you, to let you die of hunger and thirst. 12Did not Hezekiah himself remove this god's high places and altars, saying to Judah and Jerusalem, 'You must worship before one altar[b] and burn sacrifices on it'?

13"Do you not know what I and my fathers have done to all the peoples of the other lands? Were the gods of those nations ever able to deliver their land from my hand?[c] 14Who of all the gods of these nations that my fathers destroyed has been able to save his people from me? How then can your god deliver you from my hand? 15Now do not let Hezekiah deceive[d] you and mislead you like this. Do not believe him, for no god of any nation or kingdom has been able to deliver[e] his people from my hand or the hand of my fathers.[f] How much less will your god deliver you from my hand!"

16Sennacherib's officers spoke further against the LORD God and against his servant Hezekiah. 17The king also wrote letters[g] insulting[h] the LORD, the God of Israel, and saying this against him: "Just as the gods[i] of the peoples of the other lands did not rescue their people from my hand, so the god of Hezekiah will not rescue his people from my hand." 18Then they called out in Hebrew to the people of Jerusalem who were on the wall to terrify them and make them afraid in order to capture the city. 19They spoke about the God of Jerusalem as they did about the gods of the other peoples of the world—the work of men's hands.[j]

20King Hezekiah and the prophet Isaiah son of Amoz cried out in prayer to heaven about this. 21And the LORD sent an angel,[k] who annihilated all the fighting men and the leaders and officers in the camp of the Assyrian king. So he withdrew to his own land in disgrace. And when he went into the temple of his god, some of his sons cut him down with the sword.[l]

22So the LORD saved Hezekiah and the people of Jerusalem from the hand of Sennacherib king of Assyria and from the hand of all others. He took care of them[y] on every side. 23Many brought offerings to Jerusalem for the LORD and valuable gifts[m] for Hezekiah king of Judah. From then on he was highly regarded by all the nations.

Hezekiah's repentance and death.

32:24-33pp— 2Ki 20:1-21; Isa 37:21-38; 38:1-8

24In those days Hezekiah became ill and was at the point of death. He prayed to the LORD, who answered him and gave him a miraculous sign. 25But Hezekiah's heart was proud[n] and he did not respond to the kindness shown him; therefore the LORD's wrath[o] was on him and on Judah and Jerusalem. 26Then Hezekiah repented[p] of the pride of his heart, as did the people of Jerusalem; therefore the LORD's wrath did not come upon them during the days of Hezekiah.[q]

27Hezekiah had very great riches and honor,[r] and he made treasuries for his silver and gold and for his precious stones, spices, shields and all kinds of valuables. 28He also made buildings to store the harvest of grain, new wine and oil; and he made stalls for various kinds of cattle, and pens for the flocks. 29He built villages and acquired great numbers of flocks and herds, for God had given him very great riches.[s]

30It was Hezekiah who blocked[t] the upper outlet of the Gihon[u] spring and channeled the water down to the west side of the City of David. He succeeded in everything he undertook. 31But when envoys were sent by the rulers of Babylon[v] to ask him about the miraculous sign[w] that had occurred in the land, God

32:11 [a]Isa 37:10
32:12 [b]2Ch 31:1
32:13 [c]ver 15
32:15 [d]Isa 37:10 [e]Da 3:15 [f]Ex 5:2
32:17 [g]Isa 37:14 [h]Ps 74:22; Isa 37:4,17 [i]2Ki 19:12
32:19 [j]2Ki 19:18; Ps 115:4,4-8; Isa 2:8; 17:8
32:21 [k]Ge 19:13 [l]2Ki 19:7
32:23 [m]2Ch 9:24; 17:5; Isa 45:14; Zec 14:16-17
32:25 [n]2Ki 14:10; 2Ch 26:16 [o]2Ch 19:2; 24:18
32:26 [p]Jer 26:18-19 [q]2Ch 34:27,28; Isa 39:8
32:27 [r]1Ch 29:12
32:29 [s]1Ch 29:12
32:30 [t]2Ki 18:17 [u]1Ki 1:33
32:31 [v]Isa 39:1 [w]ver 24; Isa 38:7

[y]22 Hebrew; Septuagint and Vulgate *He gave them rest*

left him to test[a] him and to know everything that was in his heart.
32The other events of Hezekiah's reign
and his acts of devotion are written in
the vision of the prophet Isaiah son of
Amoz in the book of the kings of Judah
and Israel. 33Hezekiah rested with his
fathers and was buried on the hill where
the tombs of David's descendants are.
All Judah and the people of Jerusalem
honored him when he died. And Manasseh his son succeeded him as king.

Manasseh's reign in Judah.

33:1-10pp— 2Ki 21:1-10

33 Manasseh[b] was twelve years old
when he became king, and he
reigned in Jerusalem fifty-five years. 2He
did evil in the eyes of the LORD,[c] following the detestable[d] practices of the nations the LORD had driven out before the
Israelites. 3He rebuilt the high places
his father Hezekiah had demolished; he
also erected altars to the Baals and made
Asherah poles.[e] He bowed down[f] to all
the starry hosts and worshiped them.
4He built altars in the temple of the
LORD, of which the LORD had said, "My
Name[g] will remain in Jerusalem forever." 5In both courts of the temple of the
LORD,[h] he built altars to all the starry
hosts. 6He sacrificed his sons[i] in[z] the fire
in the Valley of Ben Hinnom, practiced
sorcery, divination and witchcraft, and
consulted mediums[j] and spiritists.[k] He
did much evil in the eyes of the LORD,
provoking him to anger.
7He took the carved image he had
made and put it in God's temple,[l] of
which God had said to David and to his
son Solomon, "In this temple and in Jerusalem, which I have chosen out of all
the tribes of Israel, I will put my Name
forever. 8I will not again make the feet
of the Israelites leave the land[m] I assigned to your forefathers, if only they
will be careful to do everything I commanded them concerning all the laws,
decrees and ordinances given through
Moses." 9But Manasseh led Judah and
the people of Jerusalem astray, so that
they did more evil than the nations the
LORD had destroyed before the Israelites.[n]
10The LORD spoke to Manasseh and his
people, but they paid no attention. 11So
the LORD brought against them the army
commanders of the king of Assyria, who
took Manasseh prisoner,[o] put a hook in
his nose, bound him with bronze shackles[p] and took him to Babylon. 12In his
distress he sought the favor of the LORD
his God and humbled[q] himself greatly
before the God of his fathers. 13And
when he prayed to him, the LORD was
moved by his entreaty and listened to
his plea; so he brought him back to Jerusalem and to his kingdom. Then Manasseh knew that the LORD is God.
14Afterward he rebuilt the outer wall
of the City of David, west of the Gihon[r]
spring in the valley, as far as the entrance of the Fish Gate[s] and encircling
the hill of Ophel;[t] he also made it much
higher. He stationed military commanders in all the fortified cities in Judah.
15He got rid of the foreign gods and
removed[u] the image from the temple of
the LORD, as well as all the altars he had
built on the temple hill and in Jerusalem; and he threw them out of the
city. 16Then he restored the altar of the
LORD and sacrificed fellowship offerings[a]
and thank offerings[v] on it, and told Judah to serve the LORD, the God of Israel.
17The people, however, continued to
sacrifice at the high places, but only to
the LORD their God.

Manasseh's death.

33:18-20pp— 2Ki 21:17-18

18The other events of Manasseh's
reign, including his prayer to his God
and the words the seers spoke to him
in the name of the LORD, the God of
Israel, are written in the annals of the
kings of Israel.[b] 19His prayer and how
God was moved by his entreaty, as well
as all his sins and unfaithfulness, and

32:31 [a]Ge 22:1; Dt 8:16
33:1 [b]1Ch 3:13
33:2 [c]Jer 15:4 [d]Dt 18:9; 2Ch 28:3
33:3 [e]Dt 16:21-22 [f]Dt 17:3; 2Ch 31:1
33:4 [g]2Ch 7:16
33:5 [h]2Ch 4:9
33:6 [i]Lev 18:21; Dt 18:10; 2Ch 28:3 [j]Lev 19:31 [k]1Sa 28:13
33:7 [l]2Ch 7:16
33:8 [m]2Sa 7:10
33:9 [n]Jer 15:4
33:11 [o]Dt 28:36 [p]Ps 149:8
33:12 [q]2Ch 6:37; 32:26; 1Pe 5:6
33:14 [r]1Ki 1:33 [s]Ne 3:3; 12:39; Zep 1:10 [t]2Ch 27:3; Ne 3:26
33:15 [u]ver 3-7; 2Ki 23:12
33:16 [v]Lev 7:11-18

z *6* Or *He made his sons pass through*
a *16* Traditionally *peace offerings*
b *18* That is, Judah, as frequently in 2 Chronicles

the sites where he built high places and set up Asherah poles and idols before he humbled[a] himself—all are written in the records of the seers.[c][b] 20 Manasseh rested with his fathers and was buried[c] in his palace. And Amon his son succeeded him as king.

Amon's reign and death.

33:21-25pp— 2Ki 21:19-24

21 Amon[d] was twenty-two years old when he became king, and he reigned in Jerusalem two years. 22 He did evil in the eyes of the LORD, as his father Manasseh had done. Amon worshiped and offered sacrifices to all the idols Manasseh had made. 23 But unlike his father Manasseh, he did not humble[e] himself before the LORD; Amon increased his guilt.

24 Amon's officials conspired against him and assassinated him in his palace. 25 Then the people[f] of the land killed all who had plotted against King Amon, and they made Josiah his son king in his place.

Josiah purges the land of idolatry.

34:1-2pp— 2Ki 22:1-2
34:3-7Ref— 2Ki 23:4-20
34:8-13pp— 2Ki 22:3-7

34 Josiah[g] was eight years old when he became king,[h] and he reigned in Jerusalem thirty-one years. 2 He did what was right in the eyes of the LORD and walked in the ways of his father David,[i] not turning aside to the right or to the left.

3 In the eighth year of his reign, while he was still young, he began to seek the God[j] of his father David. In his twelfth year he began to purge Judah and Jerusalem of high places, Asherah poles, carved idols and cast images. 4 Under his direction the altars of the Baals were torn down; he cut to pieces the incense altars that were above them, and smashed the Asherah poles,[k] the idols and the images. These he broke to pieces and scattered over the graves of those who had sacrificed to them.[l] 5 He burned[m] the bones of the priests on their altars, and so he purged Judah and Jerusalem. 6 In the towns of Manasseh, Ephraim and Simeon, as far as Naphtali, and in the ruins around them, 7 he tore down the altars and the Asherah poles and crushed the idols to powder[n] and cut to pieces all the incense altars throughout Israel. Then he went back to Jerusalem.

8 In the eighteenth year of Josiah's reign, to purify the land and the temple, he sent Shaphan son of Azaliah and Maaseiah the ruler of the city, with Joah son of Joahaz, the recorder, to repair the temple of the LORD his God.

9 They went to Hilkiah[o] the high priest and gave him the money that had been brought into the temple of God, which the Levites who were the doorkeepers had collected from the people of Manasseh, Ephraim and the entire remnant of Israel and from all the people of Judah and Benjamin and the inhabitants of Jerusalem. 10 Then they entrusted it to the men appointed to supervise the work on the LORD's temple. These men paid the workers who repaired and restored the temple. 11 They also gave money[p] to the carpenters and builders to purchase dressed stone, and timber for joists and beams for the buildings that the kings of Judah had allowed to fall into ruin.[q]

12 The men did the work faithfully.[r] Over them to direct them were Jahath and Obadiah, Levites descended from Merari, and Zechariah and Meshullam, descended from Kohath. The Levites—all who were skilled in playing musical instruments—[s] 13 had charge of the laborers[t] and supervised all the workers from job to job. Some of the Levites were secretaries, scribes and doorkeepers.

Hilkiah finds the Book of the Law.

34:14-28pp— 2Ki 22:8-20

14 While they were bringing out the money that had been taken into the temple of the LORD, Hilkiah the priest

33:19 [a]2Ch 6:37 [b]2Ki 21:17
33:20 [c]2Ki 21:18; 2Ch 21:20
33:21 [d]1Ch 3:14
33:23 [e]ver 12; Ex 10:3; 2Ch 7:14; Ps 18:27; 147:6; Pr 3:34
33:25 [f]2Ch 22:1
34:1 [g]1Ch 3:14 [h]Zep 1:1
34:2 [i]2Ch 29:2
34:3 [j]1Ki 13:2; 1Ch 16:11; 2Ch 15:2; 33:17,22
34:4 [k]Ex 34:13 [l]Ex 32:20; Lev 26:30; 2Ki 23:11; Mic 1:5
34:5 [m]1Ki 13:2
34:7 [n]Ex 32:20; 2Ch 31:1
34:9 [o]1Ch 6:13; 2Ch 35:8
34:11 [p]2Ch 24:12 [q]2Ch 33:4-7
34:12 [r]2Ki 12:15 [s]1Ch 25:1
34:13 [t]1Ch 23:4

c *19* One Hebrew manuscript and Septuagint; most Hebrew manuscripts *of Hozai*

found the Book of the Law of the LORD
that had been given through Moses.
15Hilkiah said to Shaphan the secretary,
"I have found the Book of the Law[a] in
the temple of the LORD." He gave it to
Shaphan.
16Then Shaphan took the book to the
king and reported to him: "Your officials
are doing everything that has been
committed to them. 17They have paid
out the money that was in the temple
of the LORD and have entrusted it to the
supervisors and workers." 18Then Shaphan the secretary informed the king,
"Hilkiah the priest has given me a
book." And Shaphan read from it in the
presence of the king.
19When the king heard the words of
the Law,[b] he tore[c] his robes. 20He gave
these orders to Hilkiah, Ahikam son of
Shaphan[d], Abdon son of Micah,[d] Shaphan the secretary and Asaiah the king's
attendant: 21"Go and inquire of the LORD
for me and for the remnant in Israel and
Judah about what is written in this book
that has been found. Great is the LORD's
anger that is poured out[e] on us because
our fathers have not kept the word of
the LORD; they have not acted in accordance with all that is written in this
book."

Huldah predicts disaster on Jerusalem.

22Hilkiah and those the king had sent
with him[e] went to speak to the prophetess[f] Huldah, who was the wife of
Shallum son of Tokhath,[f] the son of Has-
rah,[g] keeper of the wardrobe. She lived
in Jerusalem, in the Second District.
23She said to them, "This is what the
LORD, the God of Israel, says: Tell the
man who sent you to me, 24'This is
what the LORD says: I am going to bring
disaster[g] on this place and its people[h]—
all the curses[i] written in the book that
has been read in the presence of the
king of Judah. 25Because they have forsaken me[j] and burned incense to other
gods and provoked me to anger by all
that their hands have made,[h] my anger
will be poured out on this place and will
not be quenched.' 26Tell the king of
Judah, who sent you to inquire of the
LORD, 'This is what the LORD, the God
of Israel, says concerning the words you
heard: 27Because your heart was responsive[k] and you humbled[l] yourself before
God when you heard what he spoke
against this place and its people, and
because you humbled yourself before me
and tore your robes and wept in my
presence, I have heard you, declares the
LORD. 28Now I will gather you to your
fathers,[m] and you will be buried in
peace. Your eyes will not see all the disaster I am going to bring on this place
and on those who live here.'"[n]
So they took her answer back to the
king.

Josiah covenants to obey God.

34:29-32pp— 2Ki 23:1-3

29Then the king called together all the
elders of Judah and Jerusalem. 30He
went up to the temple of the LORD[o]
with the men of Judah, the people of
Jerusalem, the priests and the Levites—
all the people from the least to the
greatest. He read in their hearing all the
words of the Book of the Covenant,
which had been found in the temple of
the LORD. 31The king stood by his pillar[p]
and renewed the covenant[q] in the presence of the LORD—to follow[r] the LORD
and keep his commands, regulations
and decrees with all his heart and all
his soul, and to obey the words of the
covenant written in this book.
32Then he had everyone in Jerusalem
and Benjamin pledge themselves to it;
the people of Jerusalem did this in accordance with the covenant of God, the
God of their fathers.
33Josiah removed all the detestable[s]
idols from all the territory belonging to
the Israelites, and he had all who were
present in Israel serve the LORD their

34:15 [a]2Ki 22:8; Ezr 7:6; Ne 8:1
34:19 [b]Dt 28:3-68 [c]Jos 7:6; Isa 36:22; 37:1
34:20 [d]2Ki 22:3
34:21 [e]2Ch 29:8; La 2:4; 4:11; Eze 36:18
34:22 [f]Ex 15:20; Ne 6:14
34:24 [g]Pr 16:4; Isa 3:9; Jer 40:2; 42:10; 44:2,11 [h]2Ch 36:14-20 [i]Dt 28:15-68
34:25 [j]2Ch 33:3-6; Jer 22:9
34:27 [k]2Ch 12:7; 32:26 [l]Ex 10:3; 2Ch 6:37
34:28 [m]2Ch 35:20-25 [n]2Ch 32:26
34:30 [o]2Ki 23:2; Ne 8:1-3
34:31 [p]1Ki 7:15; 2Ki 11:14 [q]2Ki 11:17; 2Ch 23:16; 29:10 [r]Dt 13:4
34:33 [s]ver 3-7; Dt 18:9

d *20* Also called *Acbor son of Micaiah* e *22* One Hebrew manuscript, Vulgate and Syriac; most Hebrew manuscripts do not have *had sent with him.*
f *22* Also called *Tikvah* g *22* Also called *Harhas*
h *25* Or *by everything they have done*

God. As long as he lived, they did not
fail to follow the LORD, the God of their
fathers.

Josiah celebrates the Passover.

35:1,18-19pp— 2Ki 23:21-23

35 Josiah celebrated the Passover[a]
to the LORD in Jerusalem, and the
Passover lamb was slaughtered on the
fourteenth day of the first month. 2He
appointed the priests to their duties and
encouraged them in the service of the
LORD's temple. 3He said to the Levites,
who instructed[b] all Israel and who had
been consecrated to the LORD: "Put the
sacred ark in the temple that Solomon
son of David king of Israel built. It is not
to be carried about on your shoulders.
Now serve the LORD your God and his
people Israel. 4Prepare yourselves by
families in your divisions,[c] according to
the directions written by David king of
Israel and by his son Solomon.
5"Stand in the holy place with a group
of Levites for each subdivision of the
families of your fellow countrymen, the
lay people. 6Slaughter the Passover
lambs, consecrate yourselves[d] and prepare ⌊the lambs⌋ for your fellow countrymen, doing what the LORD commanded
through Moses."
7Josiah provided for all the lay people
who were there a total of thirty thousand sheep and goats for the Passover
offerings,[e] and also three thousand cattle—all from the king's own possessions.[f]
8His officials also contributed[g] voluntarily to the people and the priests and
Levites. Hilkiah,[h] Zechariah and Jehiel,
the administrators of God's temple, gave
the priests twenty-six hundred Passover
offerings and three hundred cattle. 9Also
Conaniah[i] along with Shemaiah and
Nethanel, his brothers, and Hashabiah,
Jeiel and Jozabad,[j] the leaders of the
Levites, provided five thousand Passover
offerings and five hundred head of cattle
for the Levites.
10The service was arranged and the
priests stood in their places with the
Levites in their divisions[k] as the king
had ordered.[l] 11The Passover lambs were
slaughtered,[m] and the priests sprinkled
the blood handed to them, while the
Levites skinned the animals. 12They set
aside the burnt offerings to give them
to the subdivisions of the families of the
people to offer to the LORD, as is written
in the Book of Moses. They did the
same with the cattle. 13They roasted the
Passover animals over the fire as prescribed,[n] and boiled the holy offerings in
pots, caldrons and pans and served them
quickly to all the people. 14After this,
they made preparations for themselves
and for the priests, because the priests,
the descendants of Aaron, were sacrificing the burnt offerings and the fat portions[o] until nightfall. So the Levites
made preparations for themselves and
for the Aaronic priests.

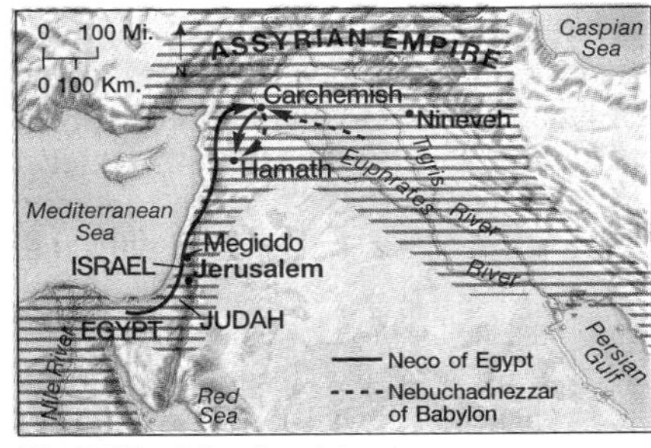

The Battle at Carchemish

A world war was brewing in 609 B.C. when Pharaoh Neco of Egypt set out for the city of Carchemish to join the Assyrians in an attempt to defeat the Babylonians, who were rising to great power. Neco marched his armies through Judah, where King Josiah tried to stop him at Megiddo, but was killed. The battle began at Carchemish in 605 B.C., and the Egyptians and Assyrians were soundly defeated, chased to Hamath, and defeated again. Babylon was now the new world power.

15The musicians,[p] the descendants of
Asaph, were in the places prescribed
by David, Asaph, Heman and Jeduthun
the king's seer. The gatekeepers at each
gate did not need to leave their posts,
because their fellow Levites made the
preparations for them.
16So at that time the entire service
of the LORD was carried out for the celebration of the Passover and the offering
of burnt offerings on the altar of the

35:1 [a]Ex 12:1-30; Nu 9:3; 28:16
35:3 [b]Dt 33:10; 1Ch 23:26; 2Ch 5:7; 17:7
35:4 [c]ver 10; 1Ch 9:10-13; 24:1; 2Ch 8:14; Ezr 6:18
35:6 [d]Lev 11:44; 2Ch 29:5,15
35:7 [e]2Ch 30:24 [f]2Ch 31:3
35:8 [g]1Ch 29:3; 2Ch 29:31-36 [h]1Ch 6:13
35:9 [i]2Ch 31:12 [j]2Ch 31:13
35:10 [k]ver 4; Ezr 6:18 [l]2Ch 30:16
35:11 [m]2Ch 29:22, 34; 30:17
35:13 [n]Ex 12:2-11; Lev 6:25; 1Sa 2:13-15
35:14 [o]Ex 29:13
35:15 [p]1Ch 25:1; 26:12-19; 2Ch 29:30; Ne 12:46; Ps 68:25

LORD, as King Josiah had ordered. 17The
Israelites who were present celebrated
the Passover at that time and observed
the Feast of Unleavened Bread for seven
days. 18The Passover had not been observed like this in Israel since the days
of the prophet Samuel; and none of the
kings of Israel had ever celebrated such
a Passover as did Josiah, with the priests,
the Levites and all Judah and Israel who
were there with the people of Jerusalem.
19This Passover was celebrated in the
eighteenth year of Josiah's reign.

Josiah's death.

35:20–36:1pp— 2Ki 23:28-30

20After all this, when Josiah had set
the temple in order, Neco king of Egypt
went up to fight at Carchemish[a] on the
Euphrates,[b] and Josiah marched out to
meet him in battle. 21But Neco sent
messengers to him, saying, "What quarrel is there between you and me, O king
of Judah? It is not you I am attacking at
this time, but the house with which I
am at war. God has told[c] me to hurry;
so stop opposing God, who is with me,
or he will destroy you."

22Josiah, however, would not turn
away from him, but disguised[d] himself
to engage him in battle. He would not
listen to what Neco had said at God's
command but went to fight him on the
plain of Megiddo.

23Archers[e] shot King Josiah, and he
told his officers, "Take me away; I am
badly wounded." 24So they took him
out of his chariot, put him in the other
chariot he had and brought him to Jerusalem, where he died. He was buried in
the tombs of his fathers, and all Judah
and Jerusalem mourned for him.

25Jeremiah composed laments for Josiah, and to this day all the men and
women singers commemorate Josiah in
the laments.[f] These became a tradition
in Israel and are written in the Laments.

26The other events of Josiah's reign
and his acts of devotion, according to
what is written in the Law of the LORD—
27all the events, from beginning to end,
are written in the book of the kings of
Israel and Judah.

36

1And the peo-
ple of the land took Jehoahaz son
of Josiah and made him king in Jerusalem in place of his father.

Jehoahaz reigns in Judah.

36:2-4pp— 2Ki 23:31-34

2Jehoahaz[i] was twenty-three years old
when he became king, and he reigned
in Jerusalem three months. 3The king of
Egypt dethroned him in Jerusalem and
imposed on Judah a levy of a hundred
talents[j] of silver and a talent[k] of gold.
4The king of Egypt made Eliakim, a
brother of Jehoahaz, king over Judah
and Jerusalem and changed Eliakim's
name to Jehoiakim. But Neco[g] took Eliakim's brother Jehoahaz and carried him
off to Egypt.

Jehoiakim reigns in Judah.

36:5-8pp— 2Ki 23:36–24:6

5Jehoiakim[h] was twenty-five years old
when he became king, and he reigned
in Jerusalem eleven years. He did evil
in the eyes of the LORD his God. 6Neb-
uchadnezzar[i] king of Babylon attacked
him and bound him with bronze shackles to take him to Babylon.[j] 7Nebuchad-
nezzar also took to Babylon articles from
the temple of the LORD and put them in
his temple[l] there.[k]

8The other events of Jehoiakim's reign,
the detestable things he did and all that
was found against him, are written in
the book of the kings of Israel and Judah.
And Jehoiachin his son succeeded him
as king.

Jehoiachin reigns in Judah.

36:9-10pp— 2Ki 24:8-17

9Jehoiachin[l] was eighteen[m] years old
when he became king, and he reigned

35:20 [a]Isa 10:9; Jer 46:2 [b]Ge 2:14
35:21 [c]1Ki 13:18; 2Ki 18:25
35:22 [d]Jdg 5:19; 1Sa 28:8; 2Ch 18:29
35:23 [e]1Ki 22:34
35:25 [f]Jer 22:10, 15-16
36:4 [g]Jer 22:10-12
36:5 [h]Jer 22:18; 26:1; 35:1
36:6 [i]Jer 25:9; 27:6; Eze 29:18 [j]2Ch 33:11; Eze 19:9; Da 1:1
36:7 [k]2Ki 24:13; Ezr 1:7; Da 1:2
36:9 [l]Jer 22:24-28; 52:31

[i]2 Hebrew *Joahaz,* a variant of *Jehoahaz*; also in verse 4 [j]3 That is, about 3 3/4 tons (about 3.4 metric tons) [k]3 That is, about 75 pounds (about 34 kilograms) [l]7 Or *palace* [m]9 One Hebrew manuscript, some Septuagint manuscripts and Syriac (see also 2 Kings 24:8); most Hebrew manuscripts *eight*

in Jerusalem three months and ten days.
He did evil in the eyes of the LORD. 10In
the spring, King Nebuchadnezzar sent
for him and brought him to Babylon,[a]
together with articles of value from the
temple of the LORD, and he made Jehoiachin's uncle,[n] Zedekiah, king over Judah
and Jerusalem.

Zedekiah reigns in Judah.

36:11-16pp— 2Ki 24:18-20; Jer 52:1-3

11Zedekiah[b] was twenty-one years old
when he became king, and he reigned
in Jerusalem eleven years. 12He did evil
in the eyes of the LORD[c] his God and did
not humble[d] himself before Jeremiah
the prophet, who spoke the word of the
LORD. 13He also rebelled against King
Nebuchadnezzar, who had made him
take an oath[e] in God's name. He became
stiff-necked[f] and hardened his heart and
would not turn to the LORD, the God of
Israel. 14Furthermore, all the leaders of
the priests and the people became more
and more unfaithful,[g] following all the
detestable practices of the nations and
defiling the temple of the LORD, which
he had consecrated in Jerusalem.

The fall of Jerusalem.

36:17-20pp— 2Ki 25:1-21; Jer 52:4-27

15The LORD, the God of their fathers,
sent word to them through his messengers[h] again and again,[i] because he had
pity on his people and on his dwelling
place. 16But they mocked God's messengers, despised his words and scoffed[j] at
his prophets until the wrath[k] of the
LORD was aroused against his people and
there was no remedy.[l] 17He brought up
against them the king of the Babylonians,[o] who killed their young men with
the sword in the sanctuary, and spared
neither young man[m] nor young woman,
old man or aged. God handed all of them
over to Nebuchadnezzar.[n] 18He carried
to Babylon all the articles[o] from the
temple of God, both large and small, and
the treasures of the LORD's temple and
the treasures of the king and his officials.
19They set fire[p] to God's temple[q] and
broke down the wall[r] of Jerusalem; they
burned all the palaces and destroyed[s]
everything of value there.[t]
20He carried into exile[u] to Babylon the
remnant, who escaped from the sword,
and they became servants[v] to him and
his sons until the kingdom of Persia
came to power. 21The land enjoyed its
sabbath rests;[w] all the time of its desolation it rested,[x] until the seventy years[y]
were completed in fulfillment of the
word of the LORD spoken by Jeremiah.

The proclamation of Cyrus.

36:22-23pp— Ezr 1:1-3

22In the first year of Cyrus[z] king of
Persia, in order to fulfill the word of the
LORD spoken by Jeremiah, the LORD
moved the heart of Cyrus king of Persia
to make a proclamation throughout his
realm and to put it in writing:

23"This is what Cyrus king of Persia
says:

"'The LORD, the God of heaven,
has given me all the kingdoms of
the earth and he has appointed[a] me
to build a temple for him at Jerusalem in Judah. Anyone of his people
among you—may the LORD his God
be with him, and let him go up.'"

36:10 [a]ver 18; 2Ki 20:17; Ezr 1:7; Jer 22:25; 24:1; 29:1; 37:1; Eze 17:12 **36:11** [b]2Ki 24:17; Jer 27:1; 28:1 **36:12** [c]Jer 37:1-39:18 [d]Dt 8:3; 2Ch 7:14; 2Ch 33:23; Jer 21:3-7 **36:13** [e]Eze 17:13 [f]2Ki 17:14; 2Ch 30:8 **36:14** [g]1Ch 5:25 **36:15** [h]Isa 5:4; 44:26; Jer 7:25; Hag 1:13; Zec 1:4; Mal 2:7; 3:1 [i]Jer 7:13,25; 25:3-4; 35:14,15; 44:4-6 **36:16** [j]2Ki 2:23; Pr 1:25; Jer 5:13 [k]Ezr 5:12; Pr 1:30-31 [l]2Ch 30:10; Pr 29:1; Zec 1:2 **36:17** [m]Jer 6:11 [n]Ezr 5:12; Jer 32:28 **36:18** [o]ver 7,10 **36:19** [p]Jer 11:16; 17:27; 21:10,14; 22:7; 32:29; 39:8; La 4:11; Eze 20:47; Am 2:5; Zec 11:1 [q]1Ki 9:8-9 [r]2Ki 14:13

36:19 [s]La 2:6 [t]Ps 79:1-3 **36:20** [u]Lev 26:44; 2Ki 24:14; Ezr 2:1; Ne 7:6 [v]Jer 27:7
36:21 [w]Lev 25:4; 26:34 [x]1Ch 22:9 [y]Jer 1:1; 25:11; 27:22; 29:10; 40:1; Da 9:2; Zec 1:12; 7:5
36:22 [z]Isa 44:28; 45:1,13; Jer 25:12; 29:10; Da 1:21; 6:28; 10:1 **36:23** [a]Jdg 4:10

[n] *10* Hebrew *brother,* that is, relative (see 2 Kings 24:17) [o] *17* Or *Chaldeans*

EZRA

Author: Probably Ezra.

Date Written: Between 457 and 444 B.C.

Time Span: About 81 years.

Title: From one of the book's chief characters: Ezra.

Background: Ezra continues from the exact place where 2 Chronicles ends: Cyrus, king of Persia, issues a decree which permits the Jews of his kingdom to return to Jerusalem after 70 years of captivity. The exodus of Israel from Egypt included some 3 million people, but fewer than 50,000 people take advantage of this "second exodus" of 900 miles from Babylon back to Jerusalem. At least parts of this period coincide in time with these historical figures: Gautama Buddha in India; Confucius in China; Socrates in Greece (followed by his pupil, Plato); and Pericles in Athens (erecting the Parthenon).

Where Written: Jerusalem.

To Whom: To the Israelites.

Content: After Cyrus's edict, Zerubbabel leads the first return of God's people to rebuild the ruins of Jerusalem and the temple that have been destroyed by Nebuchadnezzar. The work is repeatedly hampered by shortages of resources and external opposition. These discouragements bring all work to a halt until God sends the prophets Haggai and Zechariah to encourage the people, who then enthusiastically rebuild the altar and the temple of God. Some years later, Ezra leads a return of priests from captivity to Jerusalem. Ezra's effective ministry includes: teaching the Word of God, initiating reforms, restoring worship and leading spiritual revival in Jerusalem.

Key Words: "Return"; "Rededicate." From bondage, God's people are now ready to "return" to their land, their worship and their God. They have to "rededicate" themselves to rebuilding all they have lost: the altar, the temple, and their faith in God and his Word.

Themes: • God sovereignly looks over and protects his children. • God always keeps his promises. • When God's people receive punishment for sin, it shows that pure love includes correction. • In return for God's enduring love, we ought to obey his Word. • No problem is too big to stop a plan made in the will of God. • Our goals should be worthy in God's eyes as well as our own. • Our sorrows of yesterday can be our successes of today.

Outline:

1. The exiles return to Jerusalem. 1:1-2:70
2. The temple of God is rebuilt. 3:1-6:22
3. Ezra comes to Jerusalem and reforms the people. 7:1-10:44

EZRA

Cyrus's proclamation helps the exiles return to Jerusalem.

1:1-3pp— 2Ch 36:22-23

1 In the first year of Cyrus king of
Persia, in order to fulfill the word of
the LORD spoken by Jeremiah,[a] the LORD
moved the heart[b] of Cyrus king of Persia to make a proclamation throughout
his realm and to put it in writing:

2"This is what Cyrus king of Persia
says:
"'The LORD, the God of heaven,
has given me all the kingdoms of
the earth and he has appointed[c] me
to build[d] a temple for him at Jerusalem in Judah. 3Anyone of his people among you—may his God be
with him, and let him go up to Jerusalem in Judah and build the temple of the LORD, the God of Israel,
the God who is in Jerusalem. 4And
the people of any place where survivors[e] may now be living are to
provide him with silver and gold,
with goods and livestock, and with
freewill offerings[f] for the temple
of God in Jerusalem.'"[g]

5Then the family heads of Judah and
Benjamin,[h] and the priests and Levites—everyone whose heart God had
moved[i]—prepared to go up and build
the house[j] of the LORD in Jerusalem.
6All their neighbors assisted them with
articles of silver and gold, with goods
and livestock, and with valuable gifts,
in addition to all the freewill offerings.
7Moreover, King Cyrus brought out the
articles belonging to the temple of the
LORD, which Nebuchadnezzar had carried away from Jerusalem and had placed
in the temple of his god.[a][k] 8Cyrus king
of Persia had them brought by Mithredath the treasurer, who counted them
out to Sheshbazzar[l] the prince of Judah.
9This was the inventory:

gold dishes	30
silver dishes	1,000
silver pans[b]	29
10gold bowls	30
matching silver bowls	410
other articles	1,000

11In all, there were 5,400 articles of
gold and of silver. Sheshbazzar brought
all these along when the exiles came
up from Babylon to Jerusalem.

List of the exiles who returned to Jerusalem.

2:1-70pp— Ne 7:6-73

2 Now these are the people of the
province who came up from the
captivity of the exiles,[m] whom Nebuchadnezzar king of Babylon[n] had taken
captive to Babylon (they returned to
Jerusalem and Judah, each to his own
town,[o] 2in company with Zerubbabel,[p]
Jeshua,[q] Nehemiah, Seraiah,[r] Reelaiah,
Mordecai, Bilshan, Mispar, Bigvai, Rehum and Baanah):

The list of the men of the people of Israel:

3the descendants of Parosh[s]	2,172
4of Shephatiah	372
5of Arah	775
6of Pahath-Moab (through the line of Jeshua and Joab)	2,812
7of Elam	1,254
8of Zattu	945
9of Zaccai	760
10of Bani	642
11of Bebai	623
12of Azgad	1,222
13of Adonikam[t]	666
14of Bigvai	2,056
15of Adin	454
16of Ater (through Hezekiah)	98
17of Bezai	323
18of Jorah	112
19of Hashum	223
20of Gibbar	95
21the men of Bethlehem[u]	123
22of Netophah	56
23of Anathoth	128

1:1 [a]Jer 25:11-12; 29:10-14 [b]2Ch 36:22,23
1:2 [c]Isa 44:28; 45:13 [d]Ezr 5:13
1:4 [e]Isa 10:20-22 [f]Nu 15:3; Ps 50:14; 54:6; 116:17 [g]Ezr 4:3; 5:13; 6:3,14
1:5 [h]Ezr 4:1; Ne 11:4 [i]ver 1; Ex 35:20-22; 2Ch 36:22; Hag 1:14; Php 2:13 [j]Ps 127:1
1:7 [k]2Ki 24:13; 2Ch 36:7,10; Ezr 5:14; 6:5
1:8 [l]Ezr 5:14
2:1 [m]2Ch 36:20; Ne 7:6 [n]2Ki 24:16; 25:12 [o]Ne 7:73
2:2 [p]1Ch 3:19 [q]Ezr 3:2 [r]Ne 10:2
2:3 [s]Ezr 8:3
2:13 [t]Ezr 8:13
2:21 [u]Mic 5:2

a7 Or *gods* b9 The meaning of the Hebrew for this word is uncertain.

[24]of Azmaveth 42
[25]of Kiriath Jearim,[c] Kephirah and Beeroth 743
[26]of Ramah[a] and Geba 621
[27]of Micmash 122
[28]of Bethel and Ai[b] 223
[29]of Nebo 52
[30]of Magbish 156
[31]of the other Elam 1,254
[32]of Harim 320
[33]of Lod, Hadid and Ono 725
[34]of Jericho[c] 345
[35]of Senaah 3,630

[36]The priests:

the descendants of Jedaiah[d] (through the family of Jeshua) 973
[37]of Immer[e] 1,052
[38]of Pashhur[f] 1,247
[39]of Harim[g] 1,017

[40]The Levites:[h]

the descendants of Jeshua[i] and Kadmiel (through the line of Hodaviah) 74

[41]The singers:[j]

the descendants of Asaph 128

[42]The gatekeepers[k] of the temple:

the descendants of Shallum, Ater, Talmon, Akkub, Hatita and Shobai 139

[43]The temple servants:[l]

the descendants of
Ziha, Hasupha, Tabbaoth,
[44]Keros, Siaha, Padon,
[45]Lebanah, Hagabah, Akkub,
[46]Hagab, Shalmai, Hanan,
[47]Giddel, Gahar, Reaiah,
[48]Rezin, Nekoda, Gazzam,
[49]Uzza, Paseah, Besai,
[50]Asnah, Meunim, Nephussim,
[51]Bakbuk, Hakupha, Harhur,
[52]Bazluth, Mehida, Harsha,
[53]Barkos, Sisera, Temah,
[54]Neziah and Hatipha

[55]The descendants of the servants of Solomon:

the descendants of
Sotai, Hassophereth, Peruda,
[56]Jaala, Darkon, Giddel,
[57]Shephatiah, Hattil,
Pokereth-Hazzebaim and Ami

[58]The temple servants[m] and the descendants of the servants of Solomon 392

[59]The following came up from
the towns of Tel Melah, Tel Harsha,
Kerub, Addon and Immer, but they
could not show that their families
were descended[n] from Israel:

[60]The descendants of
Delaiah, Tobiah and Nekoda 652

[61]And from among the priests:

The descendants of
Hobaiah, Hakkoz and Barzillai (a man who had married a daughter of Barzillai the Gileadite[o] and was called by that name).

[62]These searched for their family records, but they could not find
them and so were excluded from
the priesthood[p] as unclean. [63]The
governor ordered them not to eat
any of the most sacred food[q] until
there was a priest ministering with
the Urim and Thummim.[r]

[64]The whole company numbered
42,360, [65]besides their 7,337 menservants and maidservants; and they
also had 200 men and women
singers.[s] [66]They had 736 horses,[t]
245 mules, [67]435 camels and 6,720
donkeys.

[68]When they arrived at the house of
the LORD in Jerusalem, some of the heads
of the families[u] gave freewill offerings
toward the rebuilding of the house of
God on its site. [69]According to their
ability they gave to the treasury for
this work 61,000 drachmas[d] of gold,

2:26 [a]Jos 18:25
2:28 [b]Ge 12:8
2:34 [c]1Ki 16:34; 2Ch 28:15
2:36 [d]1Ch 24:7
2:37 [e]1Ch 24:14
2:38 [f]1Ch 9:12
2:39 [g]1Ch 24:8
2:40 [h]Ge 29:34; Nu 3:9; Dt 18:6-7; 1Ch 16:4; Ezr 7:7; 8:15; Ne 12:24 [i]Ezr 3:9
2:41 [j]1Ch 15:16
2:42 [k]1Sa 3:15; 1Ch 9:17
2:43 [l]1Ch 9:2; Ne 11:21
2:58 [m]1Ki 9:21; 1Ch 9:2
2:59 [n]Nu 1:18
2:61 [o]2Sa 17:27
2:62 [p]Nu 3:10; 16:39-40
2:63 [q]Lev 2:3,10 [r]Ex 28:30; Nu 27:21
2:65 [s]2Sa 19:35
2:66 [t]Isa 66:20
2:68 [u]Ex 25:2

c25 See Septuagint (see also Neh. 7:29); Hebrew *Kiriath Arim.* d69 That is, about 1,100 pounds (about 500 kilograms)

5,000 minas[e] of silver and 100 priestly garments.

70The priests, the Levites, the singers, the gatekeepers and the temple servants settled in their own towns, along with some of the other people, and the rest of the Israelites settled in their towns.[a]

Rebuilding of the altar and the temple begins.

3 When the seventh month came and the Israelites had settled in their towns,[b] the people assembled[c] as one man in Jerusalem. 2Then Jeshua[d] son of Jozadak[e] and his fellow priests and Zerubbabel son of Shealtiel[f] and his associates began to build the altar of the God of Israel to sacrifice burnt offerings on it, in accordance with what is written in the Law of Moses[g] the man of God. 3Despite their fear[h] of the peoples around them, they built the altar on its foundation and sacrificed burnt offerings on it to the LORD, both the morning and evening sacrifices.[i] 4Then in accordance with what is written, they celebrated the Feast of Tabernacles[j] with the required number of burnt offerings prescribed for each day. 5After that, they presented the regular burnt offerings, the New Moon[k] sacrifices and the sacrifices for all the appointed sacred feasts of the LORD,[l] as well as those brought as freewill offerings to the LORD. 6On the first day of the seventh month they began to offer burnt offerings to the LORD, though the foundation of the LORD's temple had not yet been laid.

7Then they gave money to the masons and carpenters, and gave food and drink and oil to the people of Sidon and Tyre, so that they would bring cedar logs[m] by sea from Lebanon[n] to Joppa, as authorized by Cyrus[o] king of Persia.

8In the second month of the second year after their arrival at the house of God in Jerusalem, Zerubbabel[p] son of Shealtiel, Jeshua son of Jozadak and the rest of their brothers (the priests and the Levites and all who had returned from the captivity to Jerusalem) began the work, appointing Levites twenty[q] years of age and older to supervise the building of the house of the LORD. 9Jeshua[r] and his sons and brothers and Kadmiel and his sons (descendants of Hodaviah[f]) and the sons of Henadad and their sons and brothers—all Levites—joined together in supervising those working on the house of God.

10When the builders laid[s] the foundation of the temple of the LORD, the priests in their vestments and with trumpets,[t] and the Levites (the sons of Asaph) with cymbals, took their places to praise[u] the LORD, as prescribed by David[v] king of Israel.[w] 11With praise and thanksgiving they sang to the LORD:

"He is good;
his love to Israel endures
forever."[x]

And all the people gave a great shout[y] of praise to the LORD, because the foundation of the house of the LORD was laid. 12But many of the older priests and Levites and family heads, who had seen the former temple,[z] wept aloud when they saw the foundation of this temple being laid, while many others shouted for joy. 13No one could distinguish the sound of the shouts of joy[a] from the sound of weeping, because the people made so much noise. And the sound was heard far away.

Enemies oppose rebuilding the temple.

4 When the enemies of Judah and Benjamin heard that the exiles were building a temple for the LORD, the God of Israel, 2they came to Zerubbabel and to the heads of the families and said, "Let us help you build because, like you, we seek your God and have been sacrificing to him since the time of Esarhaddon[b] king of Assyria, who brought us here."[c]

3But Zerubbabel, Jeshua and the rest

2:70 [a]ver 1; 1Ch 9:2; Ne 11:3-4
3:1 [b]Ne 7:73; 8:1 [c]Lev 23:24
3:2 [d]Ezr 2:2; Ne 12:1,8; Hag 2:2 [e]Hag 1:1; Zec 6:11 [f]1Ch 3:17 [g]Ex 20:24; Dt 12:5-6
3:3 [h]Ezr 4:4; Da 9:25 [i]Ex 29:39; Nu 28:1-8
3:4 [j]Ex 23:16; Nu 29:12-38; Ne 8:14-18; Zec 14:16-19
3:5 [k]Nu 28:3,11, 14; Col 2:16 [l]Lev 23:1-44; Nu 29:39
3:7 [m]1Ch 14:1 [n]Isa 35:2 [o]Ezr 1:2-4; 6:3
3:8 [p]Zec 4:9 [q]1Ch 23:24
3:9 [r]Ezr 2:40
3:10 [s]Ezr 5:16 [t]Nu 10:2; 1Ch 16:6 [u]1Ch 25:1 [v]1Ch 6:31 [w]Zec 6:12
3:11 [x]1Ch 16:34,41; 2Ch 7:3; Ps 107:1; 118:1 [y]Ne 12:24
3:12 [z]Hag 2:3,9
3:13 [a]Job 8:21; Ps 27:6; Isa 16:9
4:2 [b]2Ki 17:24; 19:37 [c]2Ki 17:41

e *69* That is, about 3 tons (about 2.9 metric tons)
f *9* Hebrew *Yehudah,* probably a variant of *Hodaviah*

of the heads of the families of Israel answered, "You have no part with us in
building a temple to our God. We alone
will build it for the LORD, the God of
Israel, as King Cyrus, the king of Persia,
commanded us."[a]

4 Then the peoples around them set
out to discourage the people of Judah
and make them afraid to go on building.[g][b] 5 They hired counselors to work
against them and frustrate their plans
during the entire reign of Cyrus king of
Persia and down to the reign of Darius
king of Persia.

A letter is sent to Artaxerxes.

6 At the beginning of the reign of Xerxes,[h][c] they lodged an accusation against
the people of Judah and Jerusalem.[d]

7 And in the days of Artaxerxes[e] king
of Persia, Bishlam, Mithredath, Tabeel
and the rest of his associates wrote a
letter to Artaxerxes. The letter was written in Aramaic script and in the Aramaic[f] language.[i,j]

8 Rehum the commanding officer and
Shimshai the secretary wrote a letter
against Jerusalem to Artaxerxes the king
as follows:

9 Rehum the commanding officer
and Shimshai the secretary, together with the rest of their associates[g]—the judges and officials
over the men from Tripolis, Persia,[k]
Erech and Babylon, the Elamites of
Susa, 10 and the other people whom
the great and honorable Ashurbanipal[l] deported and settled in the
city of Samaria and elsewhere in
Trans-Euphrates.[h]

11 (This is a copy of the letter they
sent him.)

To King Artaxerxes,

From your servants, the men of
Trans-Euphrates:

12 The king should know that the
Jews who came up to us from you
have gone to Jerusalem and are rebuilding that rebellious and wicked
city. They are restoring the walls
and repairing the foundations.[i]

13 Furthermore, the king should
know that if this city is built and
its walls are restored, no more taxes, tribute or duty[j] will be paid,
and the royal revenues will suffer.
14 Now since we are under obligation to the palace and it is not proper for us to see the king dishonored,
we are sending this message to inform the king, 15 so that a search
may be made in the archives[k] of
your predecessors. In these records
you will find that this city is a rebellious city, troublesome to kings
and provinces, a place of rebellion
from ancient times. That is why
this city was destroyed.[l] 16 We inform the king that if this city is
built and its walls are restored,
you will be left with nothing in
Trans-Euphrates.

Artaxerxes orders the work to stop.

17 The king sent this reply:

To Rehum the commanding officer,
Shimshai the secretary and the rest
of their associates living in Samaria
and elsewhere in Trans-Euphrates:[m]

Greetings.

18 The letter you sent us has been
read and translated in my presence.
19 I issued an order and a search was
made, and it was found that this city
has a long history of revolt[n] against
kings and has been a place of rebellion and sedition. 20 Jerusalem has
had powerful kings ruling over the
whole of Trans-Euphrates,[o] and taxes, tribute and duty were paid to
them. 21 Now issue an order to these
men to stop work, so that this city
will not be rebuilt until I so order.

4:3 [a] Ezr 1:1-4; Ne 2:20
4:4 [b] Ezr 3:3
4:6 [c] Est 1:1; Da 9:1 [d] Est 3:13; 9:5
4:7 [e] Ezr 7:1; Ne 2:1 [f] 2Ki 18:26; Isa 36:11; Da 2:4
4:9 [g] Ezr 5:6; 6:6,13
4:10 [h] ver 17; Ne 4:2
4:12 [i] Ezr 5:3,9
4:13 [j] Ezr 7:24; Ne 5:4
4:15 [k] Ezr 5:17; 6:1 [l] Est 3:8
4:17 [m] ver 10
4:19 [n] 2Ki 18:7
4:20 [o] Ge 15:18-21; Ex 23:31; Jos 1:4; 1Ki 4:21; 1Ch 18:3; Ps 72:8-11

[g] *4* Or *and troubled them as they built* [h] *6* Hebrew *Ahasuerus,* a variant of Xerxes' Persian name [i] *7* Or *written in Aramaic and translated* [j] *7* The text of Ezra 4:8—6:18 is in Aramaic. [k] *9* Or *officials, magistrates and governors over the men from* [l] *10* Aramaic *Osnappar,* a variant of *Ashurbanipal*

22 Be careful not to neglect this matter. Why let this threat grow, to the detriment of the royal interests?[a]

23 As soon as the copy of the letter of King Artaxerxes was read to Rehum and Shimshai the secretary and their associates,[b] they went immediately to the Jews in Jerusalem and compelled them by force to stop.

24 Thus the work on the house of God in Jerusalem came to a standstill until the second year of the reign of Darius[c] king of Persia.

Zerubbabel and Jeshua resume work on the temple.

5 Now Haggai[d] the prophet and Zechariah[e] the prophet, a descendant of Iddo, prophesied[f] to the Jews in Judah and Jerusalem in the name of the God of Israel, who was over them. 2 Then Zerubbabel[g] son of Shealtiel and Jeshua[h] son of Jozadak set to work[i] to rebuild the house of God in Jerusalem. And the prophets of God were with them, helping them.

Tattenai sends a letter to Darius opposing the Jews.

3 At that time Tattenai,[j] governor of Trans-Euphrates, and Shethar-Bozenai[k] and their associates went to them and asked, "Who authorized you to rebuild this temple and restore this structure?"[l] 4 They also asked, "What are the names of the men constructing this building?"[m] 5 But the eye of their God[m] was watching over the elders of the Jews, and they were not stopped until a report could go to Darius and his written reply be received.

6 This is a copy of the letter that Tattenai, governor of Trans-Euphrates, and Shethar-Bozenai and their associates, the officials of Trans-Euphrates, sent to King Darius. 7 The report they sent him read as follows:

To King Darius:

Cordial greetings.

8 The king should know that we went to the district of Judah, to the temple of the great God. The people are building it with large stones and placing the timbers in the walls. The work[n] is being carried on with diligence and is making rapid progress under their direction.

9 We questioned the elders and asked them, "Who authorized you to rebuild this temple and restore this structure?"[o] 10 We also asked them their names, so that we could write down the names of their leaders for your information.

11 This is the answer they gave us:

"We are the servants of the God of heaven and earth, and we are rebuilding the temple[p] that was built many years ago, one that a great king of Israel built and finished. 12 But because our fathers angered[q] the God of heaven, he handed them over to Nebuchadnezzar the Chaldean, king of Babylon, who destroyed this temple and deported the people to Babylon.[r]

13 "However, in the first year of Cyrus king of Babylon, King Cyrus issued a decree[s] to rebuild this house of God. 14 He even removed from the temple[n] of Babylon the gold and silver articles of the house of God, which Nebuchadnezzar had taken from the temple in Jerusalem and brought to the temple[n] in Babylon.[t]

"Then King Cyrus gave them to a man named Sheshbazzar,[u] whom he had appointed governor, 15 and he told him, 'Take these articles and go and deposit them in the temple in Jerusalem. And rebuild the house of God on its site.' 16 So this Sheshbazzar came and laid the foundations of the house of God[v] in Jerusalem. From that day to the present it has been under construction but is not yet finished."

4:22 [a]Da 6:2
4:23 [b]ver 9
4:24 [c]Ne 2:1-8; Da 9:25; Hag 1:1,15; Zec 1:1
5:1 [d]Ezr 6:14; Hag 1:1,3,12; 2:1,10,20 [e]Zec 1:1; 7:1 [f]Hag 1:14–2:9; Zec 4:9-10; 8:9
5:2 [g]1Ch 3:19; Hag 1:14; 2:21; Zec 4:6-10 [h]Ezr 2:2; 3:2 [i]ver 8; Hag 2:2-5
5:3 [j]Ezr 6:6 [k]Ezr 6:6 [l]ver 9; Ezr 1:3; 4:12
5:5 [m]2Ki 25:28; Ezr 7:6,9,28; 8:18,22,31; Ne 2:8,18; Ps 33:18; Isa 66:14
5:8 [n]ver 2
5:9 [o]Ezr 4:12
5:11 [p]1Ki 6:1; 2Ch 3:1-2
5:12 [q]2Ch 36:16 [r]Dt 21:10; 28:36; 2Ki 24:1; 25:8,9,11; Jer 1:3
5:13 [s]Ezr 1:1
5:14 [t]Ezr 1:7; 6:5; Da 5:2 [u]1Ch 3:18
5:16 [v]Ezr 3:10; 6:15

m4 See Septuagint; Aramaic *4We told them the names of the men constructing this building.*
n14 Or *palace*

17Now if it pleases the king, let a search be made in the royal archives[a] of Babylon to see if King Cyrus did in fact issue a decree to rebuild this house of God in Jerusalem. Then let the king send us his decision in this matter.

Darius issues a new decree.

6 King Darius then issued an order, and they searched in the archives[b] stored in the treasury at Babylon. 2A scroll was found in the citadel of Ecbatana in the province of Media, and this was written on it:

Memorandum:

3In the first year of King Cyrus, the king issued a decree concerning the temple of God in Jerusalem:

Let the temple be rebuilt as a place to present sacrifices, and let its foundations be laid.[c] It is to be ninety feet[o] high and ninety feet wide, 4with three courses[d] of large stones and one of timbers. The costs are to be paid by the royal treasury.[e] 5Also, the gold[f] and silver articles of the house of God, which Nebuchadnezzar took from the temple in Jerusalem and brought to Babylon, are to be returned to their places in the temple in Jerusalem; they are to be deposited in the house of God.[g]

6Now then, Tattenai,[h] governor of Trans-Euphrates, and Shethar-Bozenai[i] and you, their fellow officials of that province, stay away from there. 7Do not interfere with the work on this temple of God. Let the governor of the Jews and the Jewish elders rebuild this house of God on its site.

8Moreover, I hereby decree what you are to do for these elders of the Jews in the construction of this house of God:

The expenses of these men are to be fully paid out of the royal treasury,[j] from the revenues[k] of Trans-Euphrates, so that the work will not stop. 9Whatever is needed—young bulls, rams, male lambs for burnt offerings[l] to the God of heaven, and wheat, salt, wine and oil, as requested by the priests in Jerusalem—must be given them daily without fail, 10so that they may offer sacrifices pleasing to the God of heaven and pray for the well-being of the king and his sons.[m]

11Furthermore, I decree that if anyone changes this edict, a beam is to be pulled from his house and he is to be lifted up and impaled[n] on it. And for this crime his house is to be made a pile of rubble.[o] 12May God, who has caused his Name to dwell there,[p] overthrow any king or people who lifts a hand to change this decree or to destroy this temple in Jerusalem.

I Darius[q] have decreed it. Let it be carried out with diligence.

The temple is completed and dedicated.

13Then, because of the decree King Darius had sent, Tattenai, governor of Trans-Euphrates, and Shethar-Bozenai and their associates[r] carried it out with diligence. 14So the elders of the Jews continued to build and prosper under the preaching[s] of Haggai the prophet and Zechariah, a descendant of Iddo. They finished building the temple according to the command of the God of Israel and the decrees of Cyrus,[t] Darius[u] and Artaxerxes,[v] kings of Persia. 15The temple was completed on the third day of the month Adar, in the sixth year of the reign of King Darius.[w]

16Then the people of Israel—the priests, the Levites and the rest of the exiles—celebrated the dedication[x] of the house of God with joy. 17For the dedication of this house of God they offered[y] a hundred bulls, two hundred rams, four hundred male lambs and, as a sin offering for all Israel, twelve male goats,

5:17 [a]Ezr 4:15; 6:1,2
6:1 [b]Ezr 4:15; 5:17
6:3 [c]Ezr 3:10; Hag 2:3
6:4 [d]1Ki 6:36 [e]ver 8; Ezr 7:20
6:5 [f]1Ch 29:2 [g]Ezr 1:7; 5:14
6:6 [h]Ezr 5:3 [i]Ezr 5:3
6:8 [j]ver 4 [k]1Sa 9:20
6:9 [l]Lev 1:3,10
6:10 [m]Ezr 7:23; 1Ti 2:1-2
6:11 [n]Dt 21:22-23; Est 2:23; 5:14; 9:14 [o]Ezr 7:26; Da 2:5; 3:29
6:12 [p]Ex 20:24; Dt 12:5; 1Ki 9:3; 2Ch 6:2 [q]ver 14
6:13 [r]Ezr 4:9
6:14 [s]Ezr 5:1 [t]Ezr 1:1-4 [u]ver 12 [v]Ezr 7:1; Ne 2:1
6:15 [w]Zec 1:1; 4:9
6:16 [x]1Ki 8:63; 2Ch 7:5
6:17 [y]2Sa 6:13; 2Ch 29:21; 30:24; Ezr 8:35

[o]3 Aramaic *sixty cubits* (about 27 meters)

one for each of the tribes of Israel. 18 And
they installed the priests in their divisions[a] and the Levites in their groups[b]
for the service of God at Jerusalem, according to what is written in the Book
of Moses.[c]
19 On the fourteenth day of the first
month, the exiles celebrated the Passover.[d] 20 The priests and Levites had
purified themselves and were all ceremonially clean. The Levites slaughtered[e]
the Passover lamb for all the exiles, for
their brothers the priests and for themselves. 21 So the Israelites who had returned from the exile ate it, together
with all who had separated themselves[f]
from the unclean practices[g] of their
Gentile neighbors in order to seek the
LORD,[h] the God of Israel. 22 For seven
days they celebrated with joy the Feast
of Unleavened Bread,[i] because the LORD
had filled them with joy by changing
the attitude[j] of the king of Assyria, so
that he assisted them in the work on
the house of God, the God of Israel.

Ezra comes to Jerusalem.

7 After these things, during the reign
of Artaxerxes[k] king of Persia, Ezra
son of Seraiah, the son of Azariah, the
son of Hilkiah,[l] 2 the son of Shallum,
the son of Zadok,[m] the son of Ahitub,[n]
3 the son of Amariah, the son of Azariah, the son of Meraioth, 4 the son of Zerahiah, the son of Uzzi, the son of Bukki,
5 the son of Abishua, the son of Phinehas,
the son of Eleazar, the son of Aaron the
chief priest— 6 this Ezra[o] came up from
Babylon. He was a teacher well versed
in the Law of Moses, which the LORD,
the God of Israel, had given. The king
had granted him everything he asked,
for the hand of the LORD his God was
on him.[p] 7 Some of the Israelites, including priests, Levites, singers, gatekeepers and temple servants, also came up
to Jerusalem in the seventh year of
King Artaxerxes.[q]
8 Ezra arrived in Jerusalem in the
fifth month of the seventh year of the
king. 9 He had begun his journey from

6:18 [a] 1Ch 23:6; 2Ch 35:4; Lk 1:5 [b] 1Ch 24:1 [c] Nu 3:6-9; 8:9-11; 18:1-32
6:19 [d] Ex 12:11; Nu 28:16
6:20 [e] 2Ch 30:15, 17; 35:11
6:21 [f] Ezr 9:1; Ne 9:2 [g] Dt 18:9; Ezr 9:11; Eze 36:25 [h] 1Ch 22:19; Ps 14:2
6:22 [i] Ex 12:17 [j] Ezr 1:1
7:1 [k] Ezr 4:7; 6:14; Ne 2:1 [l] 2Ki 22:4
7:2 [m] 1Ki 1:8; 1Ch 6:8 [n] Ne 11:11
7:6 [o] Ne 12:36 [p] Ezr 5:5; Isa 41:20
7:7 [q] Ezr 8:1
7:9 [r] ver 6
7:10 [s] ver 25; Dt 33:10; Ne 8:1-8
7:12 [t] Eze 26:7; Da 2:37
7:14 [u] Est 1:14
7:15 [v] 1Ch 29:6 [w] 1Ch 29:6,9; 2Ch 6:2
7:16 [x] Ezr 8:25 [y] Zec 6:10
7:17 [z] 2Ki 3:4 [a] Nu 15:5-12 [b] Dt 12:5-11
7:19 [c] Ezr 5:14; Jer 27:22

Babylon on the first day of the first
month, and he arrived in Jerusalem on
the first day of the fifth month, for the
gracious hand of his God was on him.[r]
10 For Ezra had devoted himself to the
study and observance of the Law of the
LORD, and to teaching[s] its decrees and
laws in Israel.

Artaxerxes' letter supports Ezra.

11 This is a copy of the letter King
Artaxerxes had given to Ezra the priest
and teacher, a man learned in matters
concerning the commands and decrees
of the LORD for Israel:

12 [p]Artaxerxes, king of kings,[t]

To Ezra the priest, a teacher of the
Law of the God of heaven:

Greetings.

13 Now I decree that any of the
Israelites in my kingdom, including priests and Levites, who wish
to go to Jerusalem with you, may
go. 14 You are sent by the king and
his seven advisers[u] to inquire about
Judah and Jerusalem with regard
to the Law of your God, which is
in your hand. 15 Moreover, you are
to take with you the silver and gold
that the king and his advisers have
freely given[v] to the God of Israel,
whose dwelling[w] is in Jerusalem,
16 together with all the silver and
gold[x] you may obtain from the
province of Babylon, as well as the
freewill offerings of the people and
priests for the temple of their God
in Jerusalem.[y] 17 With this money
be sure to buy bulls, rams and male
lambs,[z] together with their grain
offerings and drink offerings,[a] and
sacrifice[b] them on the altar of the
temple of your God in Jerusalem.
18 You and your brother Jews
may then do whatever seems best
with the rest of the silver and
gold, in accordance with the will
of your God. 19 Deliver[c] to the God

p *12* The text of Ezra 7:12-26 is in Aramaic.

of Jerusalem all the articles entrusted to you for worship in the temple
of your God. 20And anything else
needed for the temple of your God
that you may have occasion to supply, you may provide from the royal
treasury.[a]
21Now I, King Artaxerxes, order
all the treasurers of Trans-Euphrates to provide with diligence whatever Ezra the priest, a teacher of
the Law of the God of heaven, may
ask of you— 22up to a hundred talents[q] of silver, a hundred cors[r] of
wheat, a hundred baths[s] of wine,
a hundred baths[s] of olive oil, and
salt without limit. 23Whatever the
God of heaven has prescribed, let
it be done with diligence for the
temple of the God of heaven. Why
should there be wrath against the
realm of the king and of his sons?[b]
24You are also to know that you
have no authority to impose taxes,
tribute or duty[c] on any of the priests,
Levites, singers, gatekeepers, temple servants or other workers at
this house of God.[d]
25And you, Ezra, in accordance
with the wisdom of your God, which
you possess, appoint[e] magistrates and
judges to administer justice to all
the people of Trans-Euphrates—all
who know the laws of your God.
And you are to teach[f] any who do
not know them. 26Whoever does not
obey the law of your God and the law
of the king must surely be punished
by death, banishment, confiscation
of property, or imprisonment.[g]
27Praise be to the LORD, the God of
our fathers, who has put it into the
king's heart[h] to bring honor[i] to the
house of the LORD in Jerusalem in this
way 28and who has extended his good
favor[j] to me before the king and his
advisers and all the king's powerful
officials. Because the hand of the LORD
my God was on me,[k] I took courage and
gathered leading men from Israel to go
up with me.

7:20 [a]Ezr 6:4
7:23 [b]Ezr 6:10
7:24 [c]Ezr 4:13 [d]Ezr 8:36
7:25 [e]Ex 18:21,26; Dt 16:18 [f]ver 10; Lev 10:11
7:26 [g]Ezr 6:11
7:27 [h]Ezr 1:1; 6:22 [i]1Ch 29:12
7:28 [j]2Ki 25:28 [k]Ezr 5:5; 9:9
8:1 [l]Ezr 7:7
8:3 [m]1Ch 3:22 [n]Ezr 2:3
8:4 [o]Ezr 2:6
8:6 [p]Ezr 2:15; Ne 7:20; 10:16

List of family heads who came up from Babylon.

8 These are the family heads and
those registered with them who
came up with me from Babylon during the reign of King Artaxerxes:[l]

2of the descendants of Phinehas,
Gershom;
of the descendants of Ithamar,
Daniel;
of the descendants of David, Hattush 3of the descendants of
Shecaniah;[m]

of the descendants of Parosh,[n] Zechariah, and with him were registered 150 men;
4of the descendants of Pahath-Moab,[o] Eliehoenai son of Zerahiah,
and with him 200 men;
5of the descendants of Zattu,[t] Shecaniah son of Jahaziel, and with
him 300 men;
6of the descendants of Adin,[p] Ebed
son of Jonathan, and with him
50 men;
7of the descendants of Elam, Jeshaiah son of Athaliah, and with
him 70 men;
8of the descendants of Shephatiah,
Zebadiah son of Michael, and with
him 80 men;
9of the descendants of Joab, Obadiah son of Jehiel, and with him
218 men;
10of the descendants of Bani,[u] Shelomith son of Josiphiah, and with
him 160 men;
11of the descendants of Bebai, Zechariah son of Bebai, and with him
28 men;
12of the descendants of Azgad, Johanan son of Hakkatan, and with
him 110 men;

q*22* That is, about 3 3/4 tons (about 3.4 metric tons) r*22* That is, probably about 600 bushels (about 22 kiloliters) s*22* That is, probably about 600 gallons (about 2.2 kiloliters) t*5* Some Septuagint manuscripts (also 1 Esdras 8:32); Hebrew does not have *Zattu.* u*10* Some Septuagint manuscripts (also 1 Esdras 8:36); Hebrew does not have *Bani.*

13 of the descendants of Adonikam,[a]
the last ones, whose names were
Eliphelet, Jeuel and Shemaiah,
and with them 60 men;
14 of the descendants of Bigvai, Uthai
and Zaccur, and with them 70
men.

Attendants for the temple.

15 I assembled them at the canal that
flows toward Ahava,[b] and we camped
there three days. When I checked among
the people and the priests, I found no
Levites[c] there. 16 So I summoned Eliezer,
Ariel, Shemaiah, Elnathan, Jarib, Elnathan, Nathan, Zechariah and Meshullam, who were leaders, and Joiarib and
Elnathan, who were men of learning,
17 and I sent them to Iddo, the leader in
Casiphia. I told them what to say to Iddo
and his kinsmen, the temple servants[d]
in Casiphia, so that they might bring attendants to us for the house of our God.
18 Because the gracious hand of our God
was on us,[e] they brought us Sherebiah,
a capable man, from the descendants of
Mahli son of Levi, the son of Israel, and
Sherebiah's sons and brothers, 18 men;
19 and Hashabiah, together with Jeshaiah from the descendants of Merari, and
his brothers and nephews, 20 men.
20 They also brought 220 of the temple
servants[f]—a body that David and the
officials had established to assist the
Levites. All were registered by name.

Prayer for safe journey to Jerusalem.

21 There, by the Ahava Canal,[g] I proclaimed a fast, so that we might humble ourselves before our God and ask
him for a safe journey[h] for us and our
children, with all our possessions. 22 I
was ashamed to ask the king for soldiers[i] and horsemen to protect us from
enemies on the road, because we had
told the king, "The gracious hand of our
God is on everyone[j] who looks to him,
but his great anger is against all who
forsake him.[k]" 23 So we fasted[l] and petitioned our God about this, and he answered our prayer.

8:13 [a]Ezr 2:13
8:15 [b]ver 21,31 [c]Ezr 2:40; 7:7
8:17 [d]Ezr 2:43
8:18 [e]Ezr 5:5
8:20 [f]1Ch 9:2; Ezr 2:43
8:21 [g]ver 15; 2Ch 20:3 [h]Ps 5:8; 107:7
8:22 [i]Ne 2:9; Ezr 7:6,9,28 [j]Ezr 5:5 [k]Dt 31:17; 2Ch 15:2
8:23 [l]2Ch 20:3; 33:13
8:24 [m]ver 18
8:25 [n]ver 33; Ezr 7:15,16
8:28 [o]Lev 21:6; 22:2-3
8:31 [p]ver 15
8:32 [q]Ge 40:13; Ne 2:11
8:33 [r]Ne 3:4,21 [s]Ne 3:24

24 Then I set apart twelve of the leading priests, together with Sherebiah,[m]
Hashabiah and ten of their brothers,
25 and I weighed out[n] to them the offering of silver and gold and the articles
that the king, his advisers, his officials
and all Israel present there had donated
for the house of our God. 26 I weighed
out to them 650 talents[v] of silver, silver
articles weighing 100 talents,[w] 100 talents[w] of gold, 27 20 bowls of gold valued
at 1,000 darics,[x] and two fine articles of
polished bronze, as precious as gold.
28 I said to them, "You as well as these
articles are consecrated to the LORD.[o]
The silver and gold are a freewill offering to the LORD, the God of your fathers. 29 Guard them carefully until you
weigh them out in the chambers of the
house of the LORD in Jerusalem before
the leading priests and the Levites and
the family heads of Israel." 30 Then the
priests and Levites received the silver
and gold and sacred articles that had
been weighed out to be taken to the
house of our God in Jerusalem.
31 On the twelfth day of the first month
we set out from the Ahava Canal[p] to
go to Jerusalem. The hand of our God
was on us, and he protected us from
enemies and bandits along the way.
32 So we arrived in Jerusalem, where
we rested three days.[q]
33 On the fourth day, in the house of
our God, we weighed out the silver and
gold and the sacred articles into the
hands of Meremoth[r] son of Uriah, the
priest. Eleazar son of Phinehas was
with him, and so were the Levites Jozabad son of Jeshua and Noadiah son of
Binnui.[s] 34 Everything was accounted
for by number and weight, and the entire
weight was recorded at that time.
35 Then the exiles who had returned
from captivity sacrificed burnt offerings
to the God of Israel: twelve bulls for all
Israel, ninety-six rams, seventy-seven
male lambs and, as a sin offering, twelve

[v] *26* That is, about 25 tons (about 22 metric tons)
[w] *26* That is, about 3 3/4 tons (about 3.4 metric tons)
[x] *27* That is, about 19 pounds (about 8.5 kilograms)

male goats.[a] All this was a burnt offering to the LORD. 36They also delivered the king's orders[b] to the royal satraps and to the governors of Trans-Euphrates, who then gave assistance to the people and to the house of God.[c]

Ezra prays about Israel's intermarriages.

9 After these things had been done, the leaders came to me and said, "The people of Israel, including the priests and the Levites, have not kept themselves separate[d] from the neighboring peoples with their detestable practices, like those of the Canaanites, Hittites, Perizzites, Jebusites, Ammonites,[e] Moabites, Egyptians and Amorites.[f] 2They have taken some of their daughters[g] as wives for themselves and their sons, and have mingled the holy race[h] with the peoples around them. And the leaders and officials have led the way in this unfaithfulness."[i]

3When I heard this, I tore my tunic and cloak, pulled hair from my head and beard and sat down appalled. 4Then everyone who trembled[j] at the words of the God of Israel gathered around me because of this unfaithfulness of the exiles. And I sat there appalled until the evening sacrifice.

5Then, at the evening sacrifice,[k] I rose from my self-abasement, with my tunic and cloak torn, and fell on my knees with my hands spread out to the LORD my God 6and prayed:

"O my God, I am too ashamed and disgraced to lift up my face to you, my God, because our sins are higher than our heads and our guilt has reached to the heavens.[l] 7From the days of our forefathers[m] until now, our guilt has been great. Because of our sins, we and our kings and our priests have been subjected to the sword[n] and captivity,[o] to pillage and humiliation[p] at the hand of foreign kings, as it is today.

8"But now, for a brief moment, the LORD our God has been gracious[q] in leaving us a remnant[r] and giving us a firm place[s] in his sanctuary, and so our God gives light to our eyes[t] and a little relief in our bondage. 9Though we are slaves,[u] our God has not deserted us in our bondage. He has shown us kindness[v] in the sight of the kings of Persia: He has granted us new life to rebuild the house of our God and repair its ruins,[w] and he has given us a wall of protection in Judah and Jerusalem.

10"But now, O our God, what can we say after this? For we have disregarded the commands[x] 11you gave through your servants the prophets when you said: 'The land you are entering to possess is a land polluted[y] by the corruption of its peoples. By their detestable practices[z] they have filled it with their impurity from one end to the other. 12Therefore, do not give your daughters in marriage to their sons or take their daughters for your sons. Do not seek a treaty of friendship with them[a] at any time, that you may be strong and eat the good things of the land and leave it to your children as an everlasting inheritance.'

13"What has happened to us is a result of our evil deeds and our great guilt, and yet, our God, you have punished us less than our sins have deserved[b] and have given us a remnant like this. 14Shall we again break your commands and intermarry[c] with the peoples who commit such detestable practices? Would you not be angry enough with us to destroy us,[d] leaving us no remnant[e] or survivor? 15O LORD, God of Israel, you are righteous![f] We are left this day as a remnant. Here we are before you in our guilt, though because of it not one of us can stand[g] in your presence.[h]"

8:35 [a]2Ch 29:21; Ezr 6:17
8:36 [b]Ezr 7:21-24 [c]Est 9:3
9:1 [d]Ezr 6:21; Ne 9:2 [e]Ge 19:38 [f]Ex 13:5
9:2 [g]Ex 34:16 [h]Ex 22:31 [i]Ezr 10:2
9:4 [j]Ezr 10:3
9:5 [k]Ex 29:41
9:6 [l]2Ch 28:9; Job 42:6; Ps 38:4; Rev 18:5
9:7 [m]2Ch 29:6 [n]Eze 21:1-32 [o]Dt 28:64 [p]Dt 28:37
9:8 [q]Ps 25:16; Isa 33:2 [r]Ge 45:7 [s]Ecc 12:11; Isa 22:23 [t]Ps 13:3
9:9 [u]Ex 1:14; Ne 9:36 [v]Ezr 7:28 [w]Ps 69:35; Isa 43:1; Jer 32:44
9:10 [x]Dt 11:8; Isa 1:19-20
9:11 [y]Lev 18:25-28 [z]Dt 9:4
9:12 [a]Ex 34:15; Dt 7:3; 23:6
9:13 [b]Job 11:6; Ps 103:10
9:14 [c]Ne 13:27 [d]Dt 9:8 [e]Dt 9:14
9:15 [f]Ge 18:25; Ps 51:4; Jer 12:1; Da 9:7 [g]Ne 9:33; Ps 130:3; Mal 3:2 [h]1Ki 8:47

The people confess their sins.

10 While Ezra was praying and confessing,[a] weeping and throwing
himself down before the house of God,
a large crowd of Israelites—men, wom-
en and children—gathered around him.
They too wept bitterly. [2]Then Shecaniah son of Jehiel, one of the descendants
of Elam, said to Ezra, "We have been
unfaithful[b] to our God by marrying foreign women from the peoples around
us. But in spite of this, there is still hope
for Israel.[c] [3]Now let us make a covenant[d] before our God to send away[e] all
these women and their children, in accordance with the counsel of my lord
and of those who fear the commands
of our God. Let it be done according to
the Law. [4]Rise up; this matter is in your
hands. We will support you, so take courage and do it."
[5]So Ezra rose up and put the leading
priests and Levites and all Israel under
oath[f] to do what had been suggested.
And they took the oath. [6]Then Ezra withdrew from before the house of God and
went to the room of Jehohanan son of
Eliashib. While he was there, he ate no
food and drank no water,[g] because he
continued to mourn over the unfaithfulness of the exiles.
[7]A proclamation was then issued
throughout Judah and Jerusalem for all
the exiles to assemble in Jerusalem.
[8]Anyone who failed to appear within

10:1 [a]2Ch 20:9; Da 9:20
10:2 [b]Ezr 9:2; Ne 13:27 [c]Dt 30:8-10
10:3 [d]2Ch 34:31 [e]Ex 34:16; Dt 7:2-3; Ezr 9:4
10:5 [f]Ne 5:12; 13:25
10:6 [g]Ex 34:28; Dt 9:18

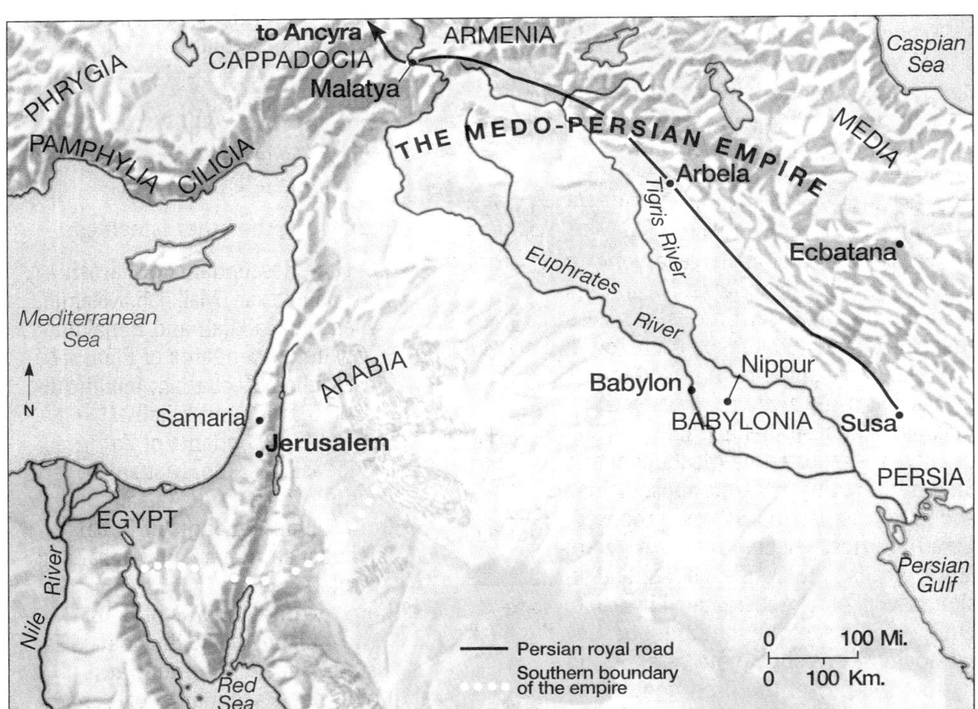

The Medo-Persian Empire

The events in the books of Ezra, Nehemiah, and Esther took place during the rule of the Medes and Persians. These two kingdoms came from the northeast of Mesopotamia (present-day Iran) and joined forces to defeat the Babylonians (Daniel 5:30,31). The Persians ruled until the rise of the Greek empire under Alexander the Great. The Persians had a relaxed policy toward their captives, allowing them to own land and homes. King Cyrus of Persia went a step further, allowing many groups of exiles, including the Jews, to return to their homelands. In the books of Ezra and Nehemiah, groups of Jewish exiles were allowed to return to Palestine to rebuild their capital city and temple. The first group of returnees led by Zerubbabel arrived in 538 B.C. The second group returned with Ezra in 458 B.C. Nehemiah came in 455 B.C. to encourage the rebuilding of Jerusalem's wall. Esther became queen of the kingdom in 479 B.C. between the first and second returns.

three days would forfeit all his property, in accordance with the decision of the officials and elders, and would himself be expelled from the assembly of the exiles.

9Within the three days, all the men of Judah and Benjamin[a] had gathered in Jerusalem. And on the twentieth day of the ninth month, all the people were sitting in the square before the house of God, greatly distressed by the occasion and because of the rain. 10Then Ezra the priest stood up and said to them, "You have been unfaithful; you have married foreign women, adding to Israel's guilt. 11Now make confession to the LORD, the God of your fathers, and do his will. Separate yourselves from the peoples around you and from your foreign wives."[b]

12The whole assembly responded with a loud voice:[c] "You are right! We must do as you say. 13But there are many people here and it is the rainy season; so we cannot stand outside. Besides, this matter cannot be taken care of in a day or two, because we have sinned greatly in this thing. 14Let our officials act for the whole assembly. Then let everyone in our towns who has married a foreign woman come at a set time, along with the elders and judges[d] of each town, until the fierce anger[e] of our God in this matter is turned away from us." 15Only Jonathan son of Asahel and Jahzeiah son of Tikvah, supported by Meshullam and Shabbethai[f] the Levite, opposed this.

16So the exiles did as was proposed. Ezra the priest selected men who were family heads, one from each family division, and all of them designated by name. On the first day of the tenth month they sat down to investigate the cases, 17and by the first day of the first month they finished dealing with all the men who had married foreign women.

Names of those with foreign wives are listed.

18Among the descendants of the priests, the following had married foreign women:[g]

From the descendants of Jeshua[h] son of Jozadak, and his brothers: Maaseiah, Eliezer, Jarib and Gedaliah. 19(They all gave their hands[i] in pledge to put away their wives, and for their guilt they each presented a ram from the flock as a guilt offering.)[j]

20From the descendants of Immer:[k] Hanani and Zebadiah.

21From the descendants of Harim:[l] Maaseiah, Elijah, Shemaiah, Jehiel and Uzziah.

22From the descendants of Pashhur:[m] Elioenai, Maaseiah, Ishmael, Nethanel, Jozabad and Elasah.

23Among the Levites:[n]

Jozabad, Shimei, Kelaiah (that is, Kelita), Pethahiah, Judah and Eliezer.

24From the singers: Eliashib.[o]

From the gatekeepers: Shallum, Telem and Uri.

25And among the other Israelites:

From the descendants of Parosh:[p] Ramiah, Izziah, Malkijah, Mijamin, Eleazar, Malkijah and Benaiah.

26From the descendants of Elam:[q] Mattaniah, Zechariah, Jehiel, Abdi, Jeremoth and Elijah.

27From the descendants of Zattu: Elioenai, Eliashib, Mattaniah, Jeremoth, Zabad and Aziza.

28From the descendants of Bebai: Jehohanan, Hananiah, Zabbai and Athlai.

29From the descendants of Bani: Meshullam, Malluch, Adaiah, Jashub, Sheal and Jeremoth.

30From the descendants of Pahath-Moab: Adna, Kelal, Benaiah, Maaseiah, Mattaniah, Bezalel, Binnui and Manasseh.

31From the descendants of Harim: Eliezer, Ishijah, Malkijah, Shemaiah, Shimeon, 32Benjamin, Malluch and Shemariah.

33From the descendants of Hashum:

10:9 [a]Ezr 1:5
10:11 [b]ver 3; Dt 24:1; Ne 9:2; Mal 2:10-16
10:12 [c]Jos 6:5
10:14 [d]Dt 16:18 [e]Nu 25:4; 2Ch 29:10; 30:8
10:15 [f]Ne 11:16
10:18 [g]Jdg 3:6 [h]Ezr 2:2
10:19 [i]2Ki 10:15 [j]Lev 5:15; 6:6
10:20 [k]1Ch 24:14
10:21 [l]1Ch 24:8
10:22 [m]1Ch 9:12
10:23 [n]Ne 8:7; 9:4
10:24 [o]Ne 3:1; 12:10; 13:7,28
10:25 [p]Ezr 2:3
10:26 [q]ver 2

Mattenai, Mattattah, Zabad, Eliph-
elet, Jeremai, Manasseh and
Shimei.
34From the descendants of Bani:
Maadai, Amram, Uel, 35Benaiah,
Bedeiah, Keluhi, 36Vaniah, Mer-
emoth, Eliashib, 37Mattaniah, Mat-
tenai and Jaasu.
38From the descendants of Binnui:[y]
Shimei, 39Shelemiah, Nathan,
Adaiah, 40Macnadebai, Shashai,
Sharai, 41Azarel, Shelemiah,
Shemariah, 42Shallum, Amariah
and Joseph.
43From the descendants of Nebo:
Jeiel, Mattithiah, Zabad, Zebina,
Jaddai, Joel and Benaiah.

44All these had married foreign women, and some of them had children by these wives.[z]

y *37,38* See Septuagint (also 1 Esdras 9:34); Hebrew *Jaasu 38and Bani and Binnui,* z *44* Or *and they sent them away with their children*

NEHEMIAH

Author: Probably Nehemiah. (However, some scholars suggest that Ezra may have written parts of the book while using Nehemiah's memoirs to record the rest.)

Date Written: Between 445 and 420 B.C.

Time Span: 19-25 years.

Title: From the book's chief character: Nehemiah.

Background: Some 12 years after the book of Ezra ends with Ezra's reforms in Jerusalem, the book of Nehemiah begins with Nehemiah receiving word that Jerusalem is again in shambles both physically and spiritually. This breaks Nehemiah's heart, and he weeps for many days. Nehemiah is the cupbearer for Artaxerxes, the king of Persia, and is granted permission to return to Jerusalem on a mission of restoration.

Where Written: Probably Jerusalem.

To Whom: To the Israelites.

Content: Nehemiah is given permission by the king of Persia to return to Jerusalem, where he rebuilds the walls of the city and is made governor. The people, inspired by Nehemiah, give tithes of much money, supplies and manpower to complete the wall in a remarkable 52 days—despite much opposition. This united effort is short-lived, however, because Jerusalem falls back into apostasy when Nehemiah leaves for a while. But he then returns to reestablish true worship through prayer and by encouraging the people to revival by reading and adhering to the Word of God.

Key Words: "Goal"; "Rebuild." We all need goals—goals that reflect vision, goals that really matter, goals that include God. Nehemiah's "goal" is to "rebuild" the walls of Jerusalem. Nothing less than total completion will be satisfactory.

Themes: • Each of us ought to have genuine compassion for others who have spiritual or physical hurts. • To feel compassion, yet do nothing to help, is unfounded Biblically. • At times we may have to give up our own comfort in order to minister properly to others. • We must totally believe in a cause before we will give our time or money to it with a right heart. • When we allow God to minister through us, even unbelievers will know it is God's work.

Outline:

1. Nehemiah rebuilds Jerusalem's walls. 1:1-6:19
2. Ezra ministers the law to the people. 7:1-10:39
3. Laws and reforms are obeyed. 11:1-13:31

NEHEMIAH

Nehemiah learns
of Jerusalem's desolation.

1 The words of Nehemiah son of
Hacaliah:

In the month of Kislev[a] in the twentieth year, while I was in the citadel of
Susa, 2Hanani,[b] one of my brothers,
came from Judah with some other men,
and I questioned them about the Jewish
remnant[c] that survived the exile, and
also about Jerusalem.
3They said to me, "Those who survived the exile and are back in the province are in great trouble and disgrace.
The wall of Jerusalem is broken down,
and its gates have been burned with
fire.[d]"

Nehemiah weeps, fasts and prays.

4When I heard these things, I sat down
and wept.[e] For some days I mourned and
fasted[f] and prayed before the God of
heaven. 5Then I said:

"O LORD, God of heaven, the great
and awesome God,[g] who keeps his
covenant of love[h] with those who
love him and obey his commands,
6let your ear be attentive and your
eyes open to hear[i] the prayer[j] your
servant is praying before you day
and night for your servants, the people of Israel. I confess the sins we Israelites, including myself and my
father's house, have committed
against you. 7We have acted very
wickedly[k] toward you. We have not
obeyed the commands, decrees and
laws you gave your servant Moses.
8"Remember[l] the instruction you
gave your servant Moses, saying, 'If
you are unfaithful, I will scatter[m]
you among the nations, 9but if you
return to me and obey my commands, then even if your exiled people are at the farthest horizon, I will
gather[n] them from there and bring
them to the place I have chosen as
a dwelling for my Name.'[o]

10"They are your servants and
your people, whom you redeemed
by your great strength and your
mighty hand.[p] 11O Lord, let your ear
be attentive[q] to the prayer of this
your servant and to the prayer of your
servants who delight in revering
your name. Give your servant success today by granting him favor in
the presence of this man."

I was cupbearer[r] to the king.

Artaxerxes sends Nehemiah
to Jerusalem.

2 In the month of Nisan in the twentieth year of King Artaxerxes,[s] when
wine was brought for him, I took the
wine and gave it to the king. I had not
been sad in his presence before; 2so the
king asked me, "Why does your face look
so sad when you are not ill? This can be
nothing but sadness of heart."
I was very much afraid, 3but I said to
the king, "May the king live forever![t]
Why should my face not look sad when
the city[u] where my fathers are buried
lies in ruins, and its gates have been destroyed by fire?[v]"
4The king said to me, "What is it you
want?"
Then I prayed to the God of heaven,
5and I answered the king, "If it pleases
the king and if your servant has found
favor in his sight, let him send me to the
city in Judah where my fathers are
buried so that I can rebuild it."
6Then the king[w], with the queen sitting beside him, asked me, "How long
will your journey take, and when will
you get back?" It pleased the king to
send me; so I set a time.
7I also said to him, "If it pleases the
king, may I have letters to the governors
of Trans-Euphrates,[x] so that they will provide me safe-conduct until I arrive in
Judah? 8And may I have a letter to
Asaph, keeper of the king's forest, so he
will give me timber to make beams for
the gates of the citadel[y] by the temple

1:1 [a]Ne 10:1; Zec 7:1
1:2 [b]Ne 7:2 [c]Jer 52:28
1:3 [d]2Ki 25:10; Ne 2:3,13,17
1:4 [e]Ps 137:1 [f]Ezr 9:4
1:5 [g]Dt 7:21; Ne 4:14 [h]Ex 20:6; Da 9:4
1:6 [i]1Ki 8:29 [j]Da 9:17
1:7 [k]Dt 28:14-15; Ps 106:6
1:8 [l]2Ki 20:3 [m]Lev 26:33
1:9 [n]Dt 30:4 [o]1Ki 8:48; Jer 29:14
1:10 [p]Ex 32:11; Dt 9:29
1:11 [q]ver 6 [r]Ge 40:1
2:1 [s]Ezr 7:1
2:3 [t]1Ki 1:31; Da 2:4; 5:10; 6:6,21 [u]Ps 137:6 [v]Ne 1:3
2:6 [w]Ne 5:14; 13:6
2:7 [x]Ezr 8:36
2:8 [y]Ne 7:2

and for the city wall and for the residence I will occupy?" And because the
gracious hand of my God was upon me,[a]
the king granted my requests. 9So I
went to the governors of Trans-Euphrates
and gave them the king's letters. The
king had also sent army officers and cavalry[b] with me.

10When Sanballat[c] the Horonite and
Tobiah[d] the Ammonite official heard
about this, they were very much disturbed that someone had come to promote the welfare of the Israelites.[e]

Nehemiah inspects the broken walls.

11I went to Jerusalem, and after staying there three days[f] 12I set out during
the night with a few men. I had not told
anyone what my God had put in my
heart to do for Jerusalem. There were
no mounts with me except the one I was
riding on.

13By night I went out through the Valley Gate[g] toward the Jackal[a] Well and the
Dung Gate,[h] examining the walls[i] of Jerusalem, which had been broken down,
and its gates, which had been destroyed
by fire. 14Then I moved on toward the
Fountain Gate[j] and the King's Pool,[k] but
there was not enough room for my
mount to get through; 15so I went up the
valley by night, examining the wall.
Finally, I turned back and reentered
through the Valley Gate. 16The officials
did not know where I had gone or what
I was doing, because as yet I had said
nothing to the Jews or the priests or
nobles or officials or any others who
would be doing the work.

17Then I said to them, "You see the
trouble we are in: Jerusalem lies in ruins,
and its gates have been burned with
fire.[l] Come, let us rebuild the wall[m] of
Jerusalem, and we will no longer be in
disgrace.[n]" 18I also told them about the
gracious hand of my God upon me[o] and
what the king had said to me.

They replied, "Let us start rebuilding."
So they began this good work.

19But when Sanballat the Horonite,
Tobiah the Ammonite official and
Geshem[p] the Arab heard about it, they
mocked and ridiculed us.[q] "What is this
you are doing?" they asked. "Are you rebelling against the king?"

20I answered them by saying, "The
God of heaven will give us success. We
his servants will start rebuilding, but as
for you, you have no share[r] in Jerusalem
or any claim or historic right to it."

Names and duties of those building the wall.

3 Eliashib[s] the high priest and his fellow priests went to work and rebuilt[t] the Sheep Gate.[u] They dedicated
it and set its doors in place, building as
far as the Tower of the Hundred, which
they dedicated, and as far as the Tower
of Hananel.[v] 2The men of Jericho[w] built
the adjoining section, and Zaccur son of
Imri built next to them.

3The Fish Gate[x] was rebuilt by the
sons of Hassenaah. They laid its beams
and put its doors and bolts and bars in
place. 4Meremoth son of Uriah, the son
of Hakkoz, repaired the next section.
Next to him Meshullam son of Berekiah, the son of Meshezabel, made repairs,
and next to him Zadok son of Baana also
made repairs. 5The next section was repaired by the men of Tekoa,[y] but their
nobles would not put their shoulders to
the work under their supervisors.[b]

6The Jeshanah[c] Gate[z] was repaired
by Joiada son of Paseah and Meshullam son of Besodeiah. They laid its
beams and put its doors and bolts and
bars in place. 7Next to them, repairs
were made by men from Gibeon[a] and
Mizpah—Melatiah of Gibeon and Jadon
of Meronoth—places under the authority of the governor of Trans-Euphrates.
8Uzziel son of Harhaiah, one of the
goldsmiths, repaired the next section;
and Hananiah, one of the perfume-mak-
ers, made repairs next to that. They restored[d] Jerusalem as far as the Broad

2:8 [a]ver 18; Ezr 5:5; 7:6
2:9 [b]Ezr 8:22
2:10 [c]ver 19; Ne 4:1,7 [d]Ne 4:3; 13:4-7 [e]Est 10:3
2:11 [f]Ge 40:13
2:13 [g]2Ch 26:9 [h]Ne 3:13 [i]Ne 1:3
2:14 [j]Ne 3:15 [k]2Ki 18:17
2:17 [l]Ne 1:3 [m]Ps 102:16; Isa 30:13; 58:12 [n]Eze 5:14
2:18 [o]2Sa 2:7
2:19 [p]Ne 6:1,2,6 [q]Ps 44:13-16
2:20 [r]Ezr 4:3
3:1 [s]Ezr 10:24 [t]Isa 58:12 [u]ver 32; Ne 12:39 [v]Ne 12:39; Jer 31:38; Zec 14:10
3:2 [w]Ne 7:36
3:3 [x]2Ch 33:14; Ne 12:39
3:5 [y]2Sa 14:2
3:6 [z]Ne 12:39
3:7 [a]Jos 9:3; Ne 2:7

a *13* Or *Serpent* or *Fig* b *5* Or *their Lord* or *the governor* c *6* Or *Old* d *8* Or *They left out part of*

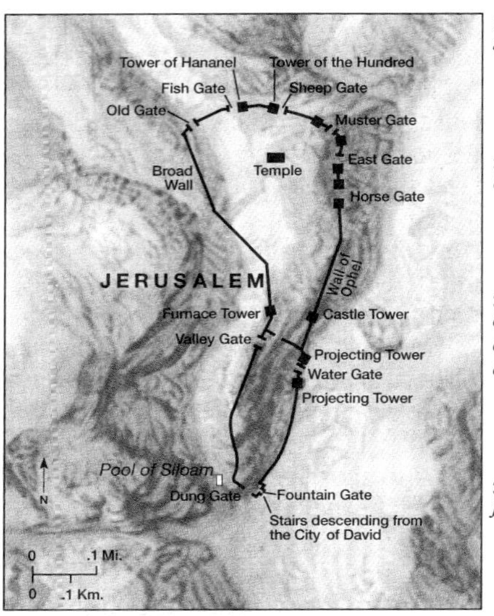

The Restoration of the City Walls

Nehemiah takes us on a counter-clockwise tour around Jerusalem (beginning with the Sheep Gate). He describes for us each section, gate, and tower on the wall and who worked to rebuild it.

Wall.[a] 9 Rephaiah son of Hur, ruler of a
half-district of Jerusalem, repaired the
next section. 10 Adjoining this, Jedaiah
son of Harumaph made repairs opposite
his house, and Hattush son of Hashab-
neiah made repairs next to him. 11 Malkijah son of Harim and Hasshub son of
Pahath-Moab repaired another section
and the Tower of the Ovens.[b] 12 Shallum
son of Hallohesh, ruler of a half-district
of Jerusalem, repaired the next section
with the help of his daughters.

13 The Valley Gate[c] was repaired by
Hanun and the residents of Zanoah.[d]
They rebuilt it and put its doors and bolts
and bars in place. They also repaired
five hundred yards[e] of the wall as far as
the Dung Gate.[e]

14 The Dung Gate was repaired by Malkijah son of Recab, ruler of the district
of Beth Hakkerem.[f] He rebuilt it and put
its doors and bolts and bars in place.

15 The Fountain Gate was repaired by
Shallun son of Col-Hozeh, ruler of the
district of Mizpah. He rebuilt it, roofing
it over and putting its doors and bolts
and bars in place. He also repaired the
wall of the Pool of Siloam,[f][g] by the King's
Garden, as far as the steps going down
from the City of David. 16 Beyond him,
Nehemiah son of Azbuk, ruler of a half-
district of Beth Zur,[h] made repairs up
to a point opposite the tombs[g][i] of David,
as far as the artificial pool and the House
of the Heroes.

17 Next to him, the repairs were made
by the Levites under Rehum son of Bani.
Beside him, Hashabiah, ruler of half the
district of Keilah,[j] carried out repairs for
his district. 18 Next to him, the repairs
were made by their countrymen under
Binnui[h] son of Henadad, ruler of the other half-district of Keilah. 19 Next to him,
Ezer son of Jeshua, ruler of Mizpah,
repaired another section, from a point
facing the ascent to the armory as far
as the angle. 20 Next to him, Baruch son
of Zabbai zealously repaired another section, from the angle to the entrance of
the house of Eliashib the high priest.
21 Next to him, Meremoth[k] son of Uriah,
the son of Hakkoz, repaired another
section, from the entrance of Eliashib's
house to the end of it.

22 The repairs next to him were made
by the priests from the surrounding
region. 23 Beyond them, Benjamin and
Hasshub made repairs in front of their
house; and next to them, Azariah son
of Maaseiah, the son of Ananiah, made
repairs beside his house. 24 Next to him,
Binnui[l] son of Henadad repaired another section, from Azariah's house to the
angle and the corner, 25 and Palal son of
Uzai worked opposite the angle and the
tower projecting from the upper palace
near the court of the guard.[m] Next to
him, Pedaiah son of Parosh[n] 26 and the
temple servants[o] living on the hill of
Ophel[p] made repairs up to a point opposite the Water Gate[q] toward the east and
the projecting tower. 27 Next to them, the

3:8 [a]Ne 12:38
3:11 [b]Ne 12:38
3:13 [c]2Ch 26:9 [d]Jos 15:34 [e]Ne 2:13
3:14 [f]Jer 6:1
3:15 [g]Isa 8:6; Jn 9:7
3:16 [h]Jos 15:58 [i]Ac 2:29
3:17 [j]Jos 15:44
3:21 [k]Ezr 8:33
3:24 [l]Ezr 8:33
3:25 [m]Jer 32:2; 37:21; 39:14 [n]Ezr 2:3
3:26 [o]Ne 7:46; 11:21 [p]2Ch 33:14 [q]Ne 8:1,3,16; 12:37

[e] *13* Hebrew *a thousand cubits* (about 450 meters) [f] *15* Hebrew *Shelah,* a variant of *Shiloah,* that is, Siloam [g] *16* Hebrew; Septuagint, some Vulgate manuscripts and Syriac *tomb* [h] *18* Two Hebrew manuscripts and Syriac (see also Septuagint and verse 24); most Hebrew manuscripts *Bavvai*

men of Tekoa[a] repaired another section, from the great projecting tower[b] to the wall of Ophel.

28Above the Horse Gate,[c] the priests made repairs, each in front of his own house. 29Next to them, Zadok son of Immer made repairs opposite his house. Next to him, Shemaiah son of Shecaniah, the guard at the East Gate, made repairs. 30Next to him, Hananiah son of Shelemiah, and Hanun, the sixth son of Zalaph, repaired another section. Next to them, Meshullam son of Berekiah made repairs opposite his living quarters. 31Next to him, Malkijah, one of the goldsmiths, made repairs as far as the house of the temple servants and the merchants, opposite the Inspection Gate, and as far as the room above the corner; 32and between the room above the corner and the Sheep Gate[d] the goldsmiths and merchants made repairs.

Rebuilding continues despite opposition.

4 When Sanballat[e] heard that we were rebuilding the wall, he became angry and was greatly incensed. He ridiculed the Jews, 2and in the presence of his associates[f] and the army of Samaria, he said, "What are those feeble Jews doing? Will they restore their wall? Will they offer sacrifices? Will they finish in a day? Can they bring the stones back to life from those heaps of rubble[g]—burned as they are?"

3Tobiah[h] the Ammonite, who was at his side, said, "What they are building—if even a fox climbed up on it, he would break down their wall of stones!"[i]

4Hear us, O our God, for we are despised.[j] Turn their insults back on their own heads. Give them over as plunder in a land of captivity. 5Do not cover up their guilt[k] or blot out their sins from your sight,[l] for they have thrown insults in the face of[i] the builders.

6So we rebuilt the wall till all of it reached half its height, for the people worked with all their heart.

7But when Sanballat, Tobiah,[m] the Arabs, the Ammonites and the men of Ashdod heard that the repairs to Jerusalem's walls had gone ahead and that the gaps were being closed, they were very angry. 8They all plotted together[n] to come and fight against Jerusalem and stir up trouble against it. 9But we prayed to our God and posted a guard day and night to meet this threat.

10Meanwhile, the people in Judah said, "The strength of the laborers[o] is giving out, and there is so much rubble that we cannot rebuild the wall."

11Also our enemies said, "Before they know it or see us, we will be right there among them and will kill them and put an end to the work."

12Then the Jews who lived near them came and told us ten times over, "Wherever you turn, they will attack us."

13Therefore I stationed some of the people behind the lowest points of the wall at the exposed places, posting them by families, with their swords, spears and bows. 14After I looked things over, I stood up and said to the nobles, the officials and the rest of the people, "Don't be afraid[p] of them. Remember[q] the Lord, who is great and awesome,[r] and fight[s] for your brothers, your sons and your daughters, your wives and your homes."

15When our enemies heard that we were aware of their plot and that God had frustrated it,[t] we all returned to the wall, each to his own work.

16From that day on, half of my men did the work, while the other half were equipped with spears, shields, bows and armor. The officers posted themselves behind all the people of Judah 17who were building the wall. Those who carried materials did their work with one hand and held a weapon[u] in the other, 18and each of the builders wore his sword at his side as he worked. But the man who sounded the trumpet[v] stayed with me.

19Then I said to the nobles, the officials and the rest of the people, "The work is extensive and spread out, and we are

3:27 [a]ver 5 [b]Ps 48:12
3:28 [c]2Ki 11:16; 2Ch 23:15; Jer 31:40
3:32 [d]ver 1; Jn 5:2
4:1 [e]Ne 2:10
4:2 [f]Ezr 4:9-10 [g]Ps 79:1; Jer 26:18
4:3 [h]Ne 2:10 [i]Job 13:12; 15:3
4:4 [j]Ps 44:13; 79:12; 123:3-4; Jer 33:24
4:5 [k]Isa 2:9; La 1:22 [l]2Ki 14:27; Ps 51:1; 69:27-28; 109:14; Jer 18:23
4:7 [m]Ne 2:10
4:8 [n]Ps 2:2; 83:1-18
4:10 [o]1Ch 23:4
4:14 [p]Ge 28:15; Nu 14:9; Dt 1:29 [q]Ne 1:8 [r]Ne 1:5 [s]2Sa 10:12
4:15 [t]2Sa 17:14; Job 5:12
4:17 [u]Ps 149:6
4:18 [v]Nu 10:2

[i]5 Or *have provoked you to anger before*

widely separated from each other along
the wall. 20Wherever you hear the sound
of the trumpet,[a] join us there. Our God
will fight[b] for us!"
21So we continued the work with half
the men holding spears, from the first
light of dawn till the stars came out.
22At that time I also said to the people,
"Have every man and his helper stay inside Jerusalem at night, so they can serve
us as guards by night and workmen by
day." 23Neither I nor my brothers nor
my men nor the guards with me took off
our clothes; each had his weapon, even
when he went for water.[j]

Oppressive usurers
are to make restoration.

5 Now the men and their wives raised
a great outcry against their Jewish
brothers. 2Some were saying, "We and
our sons and daughters are numerous; in
order for us to eat and stay alive, we
must get grain."
3Others were saying, "We are mortgag-
ing our fields,[c] our vineyards and our
homes to get grain during the famine."[d]
4Still others were saying, "We have
had to borrow money to pay the king's
tax[e] on our fields and vineyards. 5Al-
though we are of the same flesh and
blood[f] as our countrymen and though
our sons are as good as theirs, yet we
have to subject our sons and daughters
to slavery.[g] Some of our daughters have
already been enslaved, but we are powerless, because our fields and our vineyards belong to others."[h]
6When I heard their outcry and these
charges, I was very angry. 7I pondered
them in my mind and then accused the
nobles and officials. I told them, "You
are exacting usury[i] from your own countrymen!" So I called together a large
meeting to deal with them 8and said:
"As far as possible, we have bought[j] back
our Jewish brothers who were sold to
the Gentiles. Now you are selling your
brothers, only for them to be sold back
to us!" They kept quiet, because they
could find nothing to say.[k]

4:20 [a]Eze 33:3 [b]Ex 14:14; Dt 1:30; 20:4; Jos 10:14
5:3 [c]Ps 109:11 [d]Ge 47:23
5:4 [e]Ezr 4:13
5:5 [f]Ge 29:14 [g]Lev 25:39-43, 47; 2Ki 4:1; Isa 50:1 [h]Dt 15:7-11; 2Ki 4:1
5:7 [i]Ex 22:25-27; Lev 25:35-37; Dt 23:19-20; 24:10-13
5:8 [j]Lev 25:47 [k]Jer 34:8
5:9 [l]Isa 52:5
5:10 [m]Ex 22:25
5:11 [n]Isa 58:6
5:12 [o]Ezr 10:5
5:13 [p]Mt 10:14; Ac 18:6 [q]Dt 27:15-26
5:14 [r]Ne 2:6; 13:6 [s]Ge 42:6; Ezr 6:7; Jer 40:7; Hag 1:1
5:15 [t]Ge 20:11
5:16 [u]2Th 3:7-10
5:18 [v]1Ki 4:23

9So I continued, "What you are doing
is not right. Shouldn't you walk in the
fear of our God to avoid the reproach[l] of
our Gentile enemies? 10I and my brothers
and my men are also lending the people
money and grain. But let the exacting of
usury stop![m] 11Give back to them immediately their fields, vineyards, olive groves
and houses, and also the usury[n] you are
charging them—the hundredth part of
the money, grain, new wine and oil."
12"We will give it back," they said.
"And we will not demand anything more
from them. We will do as you say."
Then I summoned the priests and
made the nobles and officials take an
oath[o] to do what they had promised. 13I
also shook[p] out the folds of my robe and
said, "In this way may God shake out of
his house and possessions every man
who does not keep this promise. So may
such a man be shaken out and emptied!"
At this the whole assembly said,
"Amen,"[q] and praised the LORD. And the
people did as they had promised.
14Moreover, from the twentieth year
of King Artaxerxes,[r] when I was appointed to be their governor[s] in the land
of Judah, until his thirty-second year—
twelve years—neither I nor my brothers ate the food allotted to the governor. 15But the earlier governors—those
preceding me—placed a heavy burden
on the people and took forty shekels[k]
of silver from them in addition to food
and wine. Their assistants also lorded it
over the people. But out of reverence
for God[t] I did not act like that. 16Instead,[u]
I devoted myself to the work on this wall.
All my men were assembled there for the
work; we[l] did not acquire any land.
17Furthermore, a hundred and fifty
Jews and officials ate at my table, as well
as those who came to us from the surrounding nations. 18Each day one ox, six
choice sheep and some poultry[v] were
prepared for me, and every ten days an
abundant supply of wine of all kinds.

[j] *23* The meaning of the Hebrew for this clause is uncertain. [k] *15* That is, about 1 pound (about 0.5 kilogram) [l] *16* Most Hebrew manuscripts; some Hebrew manuscripts, Septuagint, Vulgate and Syriac *I*

In spite of all this, I never demanded the
food allotted to the governor, because the
demands were heavy on these people.
19Remember[a] me with favor, O my
God, for all I have done for these people.

Sanballat conspires
to oppose the rebuilding.

6 When word came to Sanballat, Tobiah,[b] Geshem[c] the Arab and the rest
of our enemies that I had rebuilt the wall
and not a gap was left in it—though up
to that time I had not set the doors in the
gates— 2Sanballat and Geshem sent me
this message: "Come, let us meet together in one of the villages[m] on the plain of
Ono.[d]"
But they were scheming to harm me;
3so I sent messengers to them with this
reply: "I am carrying on a great project
and cannot go down. Why should the
work stop while I leave it and go down
to you?" 4Four times they sent me the
same message, and each time I gave
them the same answer.
5Then, the fifth time, Sanballat[e] sent
his aide to me with the same message,
and in his hand was an unsealed letter
6in which was written:

> "It is reported among the nations—and Geshem[n][f] says it is true—that you and the Jews are plotting to revolt, and therefore you are building the wall. Moreover, according to these reports you are about to become their king
> 7and have even appointed prophets to make this proclamation about you in Jerusalem: 'There is a king in Judah!' Now this report will get back to the king; so come, let us confer together."

8I sent him this reply: "Nothing like
what you are saying is happening; you
are just making it up out of your head."
9They were all trying to frighten us,
thinking, "Their hands will get too weak
for the work, and it will not be completed."
⌞But I prayed,⌟ "Now strengthen my
hands."

5:19 [a]Ge 8:1; 2Ki 20:3; Ne 1:8; 13:14,22,31
6:1 [b]Ne 2:10 [c]Ne 2:19
6:2 [d]1Ch 8:12
6:5 [e]Ne 2:10
6:6 [f]Ne 2:19
6:10 [g]Nu 18:7
6:12 [h]Eze 13:22-23 [i]Ne 2:10
6:13 [j]Jer 20:10
6:14 [k]Ne 1:8 [l]Ne 2:10 [m]Ex 15:20; Eze 13:17-23; Ac 21:9; Rev 2:20 [n]Ne 13:29; Jer 23:9-40; Zec 13:2-3
7:1 [o]1Ch 9:27; 26:12-19; Ne 6:1,15 [p]Ps 68:25 [q]Ne 8:9
7:2 [r]Ne 1:2

10One day I went to the house of Shemaiah son of Delaiah, the son of Mehetabel, who was shut in at his home.
He said, "Let us meet in the house of
God, inside the temple[g], and let us close
the temple doors, because men are coming to kill you—by night they are coming
to kill you."
11But I said, "Should a man like me
run away? Or should one like me go into
the temple to save his life? I will not go!"
12I realized that God had not sent him,
but that he had prophesied against me[h]
because Tobiah and Sanballat[i] had hired
him. 13He had been hired to intimidate
me so that I would commit a sin by doing
this, and then they would give me a bad
name to discredit me.[j]
14Remember[k] Tobiah and Sanballat,[l]
O my God, because of what they have
done; remember also the prophetess[m]
Noadiah and the rest of the prophets[n]
who have been trying to intimidate me.

The wall is completed.

15So the wall was completed on the
twenty-fifth of Elul, in fifty-two days.
16When all our enemies heard about this,
all the surrounding nations were afraid
and lost their self-confidence, because
they realized that this work had been
done with the help of our God.
17Also, in those days the nobles of
Judah were sending many letters to Tobiah, and replies from Tobiah kept coming to them. 18For many in Judah were
under oath to him, since he was son-
in-law to Shecaniah son of Arah, and his
son Jehohanan had married the daughter of Meshullam son of Berekiah.
19Moreover, they kept reporting to me
his good deeds and then telling him
what I said. And Tobiah sent letters to
intimidate me.

7 After the wall had been rebuilt and
I had set the doors in place, the
gatekeepers[o] and the singers[p] and the
Levites[q] were appointed. 2I put in charge
of Jerusalem my brother Hanani,[r] along

[m]2 Or *in Kephirim* [n]6 Hebrew *Gashmu,* a variant of *Geshem*

with[o] Hananiah[a] the commander of the
citadel,[b] because he was a man of integrity and feared[c] God more than most
men do. 3 I said to them, "The gates of
Jerusalem are not to be opened until the
sun is hot. While the gatekeepers are
still on duty, have them shut the doors
and bar them. Also appoint residents
of Jerusalem as guards, some at their
posts and some near their own houses."

List of the exiles who returned to Judah.

7:6-73pp— Ezr 2:1-70

4 Now the city was large and spacious,
but there were few people in it,[d] and
the houses had not yet been rebuilt. 5 So
my God put it into my heart to assemble the nobles, the officials and the common people for registration by families.
I found the genealogical record of those
who had been the first to return. This
is what I found written there:

6 These are the people of the province who came up from the captivity of the exiles[e] whom Nebuchadnezzar king of Babylon had taken
captive (they returned to Jerusalem
and Judah, each to his own town,
7 in company with Zerubbabel,[f]
Jeshua, Nehemiah, Azariah, Raami-
ah, Nahamani, Mordecai, Bilshan,
Mispereth, Bigvai, Nehum and
Baanah):

The list of the men of Israel:

8 the descendants of Parosh 2,172
9 of Shephatiah 372
10 of Arah 652
11 of Pahath-Moab (through the line of Jeshua and Joab) 2,818
12 of Elam 1,254
13 of Zattu 845
14 of Zaccai 760
15 of Binnui 648
16 of Bebai 628
17 of Azgad 2,322
18 of Adonikam 667
19 of Bigvai 2,067
20 of Adin[g] 655
21 of Ater (through Hezekiah) 98
22 of Hashum 328
23 of Bezai 324
24 of Hariph 112
25 of Gibeon 95

26 the men of Bethlehem and Netophah[h] 188
27 of Anathoth[i] 128
28 of Beth Azmaveth 42
29 of Kiriath Jearim, Kephirah[j] and Beeroth[k] 743
30 of Ramah and Geba 621
31 of Micmash 122
32 of Bethel and Ai[l] 123
33 of the other Nebo 52
34 of the other Elam 1,254
35 of Harim 320
36 of Jericho[m] 345
37 of Lod, Hadid and Ono[n] 721
38 of Senaah 3,930

39 The priests:

the descendants of Jedaiah (through the family of Jeshua) 973
40 of Immer 1,052
41 of Pashhur 1,247
42 of Harim 1,017

43 The Levites:

the descendants of Jeshua (through Kadmiel through the line of Hodaviah) 74

44 The singers:[o]

the descendants of Asaph 148

45 The gatekeepers:[p]

the descendants of Shallum, Ater, Talmon, Akkub, Hatita and Shobai 138

46 The temple servants:[q]

the descendants of
Ziha, Hasupha, Tabbaoth,
47 Keros, Sia, Padon,
48 Lebana, Hagaba, Shalmai,
49 Hanan, Giddel, Gahar,
50 Reaiah, Rezin, Nekoda,
51 Gazzam, Uzza, Paseah,

7:2 [a]Ne 10:23 [b]Ne 2:8 [c]1Ki 18:3
7:4 [d]Ne 11:1
7:6 [e]2Ch 36:20; Ezr 2:1-70; Ne 1:2
7:7 [f]1Ch 3:19; Ezr 2:2
7:20 [g]Ezr 8:6
7:26 [h]2Sa 23:28; 1Ch 2:54
7:27 [i]Jos 21:18
7:29 [j]Jos 18:26 [k]Jos 18:25
7:32 [l]Ge 12:8
7:36 [m]Ne 3:2
7:37 [n]1Ch 8:12
7:44 [o]Ne 11:23
7:45 [p]1Ch 9:17
7:46 [q]Ne 3:26

[o]2 Or *Hanani, that is,*

[52]Besai, Meunim, Nephussim,
[53]Bakbuk, Hakupha, Harhur,
[54]Bazluth, Mehida, Harsha,
[55]Barkos, Sisera, Temah,
[56]Neziah and Hatipha

[57]The descendants of the servants of Solomon:

the descendants of
Sotai, Sophereth, Perida,
[58]Jaala, Darkon, Giddel,
[59]Shephatiah, Hattil,
Pokereth-Hazzebaim and Amon

[60]The temple servants and the descendants of the servants of Solomon[a] 392

[61]The following came up from the
towns of Tel Melah, Tel Harsha,
Kerub, Addon and Immer, but they
could not show that their families
were descended from Israel:

[62]the descendants of
Delaiah, Tobiah and Nekoda 642

[63]And from among the priests:

the descendants of
Hobaiah, Hakkoz and Barzillai
(a man who had married a
daughter of Barzillai the
Gileadite and was called by
that name).

[64]These searched for their family
records, but they could not find
them and so were excluded from the
priesthood as unclean. [65]The governor, therefore, ordered them not to
eat any of the most sacred food until
there should be a priest ministering with the Urim and Thummim.[b]

[66]The whole company numbered
42,360, [67]besides their 7,337 menservants and maidservants; and they
also had 245 men and women singers. [68]There were 736 horses, 245
mules,[p] [69]435 camels and 6,720
donkeys.

[70]Some of the heads of the families contributed to the work. The
governor gave to the treasury 1,000
drachmas[q] of gold, 50 bowls and
530 garments for priests. [71]Some of
the heads of the families[c] gave to
the treasury for the work 20,000
drachmas[r] of gold and 2,200 minas[s]
of silver. [72]The total given by the
rest of the people was 20,000 drachmas of gold, 2,000 minas[t] of silver
and 67 garments for priests.[d]

[73]The priests, the Levites, the
gatekeepers, the singers and the
temple servants,[e] along with certain
of the people and the rest of the Israelites, settled in their own towns.[f]

Ezra publicly reads the Book of the Law.

When the seventh month came and the
Israelites had settled in their towns,[g] [1]all
8 the people assembled as one man
in the square before the Water
Gate.[h] They told Ezra the scribe to bring
out the Book of the Law of Moses,[i]
which the LORD had commanded for
Israel.

[2]So on the first day of the seventh
month[j] Ezra the priest brought the
Law[k] before the assembly, which was
made up of men and women and all
who were able to understand. [3]He read
it aloud from daybreak till noon as he
faced the square before the Water Gate[l]
in the presence of the men, women and
others who could understand. And all
the people listened attentively to the
Book of the Law.

[4]Ezra the scribe stood on a high wood-
en platform[m] built for the occasion. Beside him on his right stood Mattithiah,
Shema, Anaiah, Uriah, Hilkiah and Maaseiah; and on his left were Pedaiah,
Mishael, Malkijah, Hashum, Hashbad-
danah, Zechariah and Meshullam.

[5]Ezra opened the book. All the people
could see him because he was standing[n]

7:60 [a]1Ch 9:2
7:65 [b]Ex 28:30; Ne 8:9
7:71 [c]1Ch 29:7
7:72 [d]Ex 25:2
7:73 [e]Ne 1:10; Ps 34:22; 103:21; 113:1; 135:1 [f]Ezr 3:1; Ne 11:1 [g]Ezr 3:1
8:1 [h]Ne 3:26 [i]Dt 28:61; 2Ch 34:15; Ezr 7:6
8:2 [j]Lev 23:23-25; Nu 29:1-6 [k]Dt 31:11
8:3 [l]Ne 3:26
8:4 [m]2Ch 6:13
8:5 [n]Jdg 3:20

[p]*68* Some Hebrew manuscripts (see also Ezra 2:66); most Hebrew manuscripts do not have this verse.
[q]*70* That is, about 19 pounds (about 8.5 kilograms)
[r]*71* That is, about 375 pounds (about 170 kilograms); also in verse 72
[s]*71* That is, about 1 1/3 tons (about 1.2 metric tons)
[t]*72* That is, about 1 1/4 tons (about 1.1 metric tons)

above them; and as he opened it, the
people all stood up. 6Ezra praised the
LORD, the great God; and all the people
lifted their hands[a] and responded,
"Amen! Amen!" Then they bowed down
and worshiped the LORD with their faces
to the ground.
7The Levites[b]—Jeshua, Bani, Sherebiah, Jamin, Akkub, Shabbethai, Hodiah,
Maaseiah, Kelita, Azariah, Jozabad,
Hanan and Pelaiah—instructed[c] the people in the Law while the people were
standing there. 8They read from the
Book of the Law of God, making it clear[u]
and giving the meaning so that the people could understand what was being
read.
9Then Nehemiah the governor, Ezra
the priest and scribe, and the Levites[d]
who were instructing the people said to
them all, "This day is sacred to the LORD
your God. Do not mourn or weep."[e]
For all the people had been weeping as
they listened to the words of the Law.
10Nehemiah said, "Go and enjoy choice
food and sweet drinks, and send some
to those who have nothing[f] prepared.
This day is sacred to our Lord. Do not
grieve, for the joy[g] of the LORD is your
strength."
11The Levites calmed all the people,
saying, "Be still, for this is a sacred day.
Do not grieve."
12Then all the people went away to eat
and drink, to send portions of food and
to celebrate with great joy,[h] because they
now understood the words that had been
made known to them.
13On the second day of the month, the
heads of all the families, along with the
priests and the Levites, gathered around
Ezra the scribe to give attention to the
words of the Law. 14They found written in the Law, which the LORD had
commanded through Moses, that the
Israelites were to live in booths during
the feast of the seventh month 15and
that they should proclaim this word and
spread it throughout their towns and in
Jerusalem: "Go out into the hill country and bring back branches from olive
and wild olive trees, and from myrtles,
palms and shade trees, to make booths"—
as it is written.[v]
16So the people went out and brought
back branches and built themselves
booths on their own roofs, in their courtyards, in the courts of the house of God
and in the square by the Water Gate and
the one by the Gate of Ephraim.[i] 17The
whole company that had returned from
exile built booths and lived in them.
From the days of Joshua son of Nun until
that day, the Israelites had not celebrated[j] it like this. And their joy was very
great.
18Day after day, from the first day to
the last, Ezra read[k] from the Book of the
Law of God. They celebrated the feast for
seven days, and on the eighth day, in
accordance with the regulation,[l] there
was an assembly.

The people fast and confess their sins.

9 On the twenty-fourth day of the
same month, the Israelites gathered
together, fasting and wearing sackcloth
and having dust on their heads.[m] 2Those
of Israelite descent had separated themselves from all foreigners.[n] They stood
in their places and confessed their sins
and the wickedness of their fathers.[o]
3They stood where they were and read
from the Book of the Law of the LORD
their God for a quarter of the day, and
spent another quarter in confession and
in worshiping the LORD their God.
4Standing on the stairs were the
Levites[p]—Jeshua, Bani, Kadmiel, Shebaniah, Bunni, Sherebiah, Bani and
Kenani—who called with loud voices
to the LORD their God. 5And the
Levites—Jeshua, Kadmiel, Bani, Hashab-
neiah, Sherebiah, Hodiah, Shebaniah
and Pethahiah—said: "Stand up and
praise the LORD your God,[q] who is from
everlasting to everlasting.[w]"

"Blessed be your glorious name,
and may it be exalted above all blessing and praise. 6You alone are the

8:6 [a]Ex 4:31; Ezr 9:5; 1Ti 2:8
8:7 [b]Ezr 10:23 [c]Lev 10:11; 2Ch 17:7
8:9 [d]Ne 7:1,65,70 [e]Dt 12:7,12; 16:14-15
8:10 [f]1Sa 25:8; Lk 14:12-14 [g]Lev 23:40; Dt 12:18; 16:11,14-15
8:12 [h]Est 9:22
8:16 [i]2Ki 14:13; Ne 12:39
8:17 [j]2Ch 7:8; 8:13; 30:21
8:18 [k]Dt 31:11 [l]Lev 23:36,40; Nu 29:35
9:1 [m]Jos 7:6; 1Sa 4:12
9:2 [n]Ne 13:3,30 [o]Ezr 10:11; Ps 106:6
9:4 [p]Ezr 10:23
9:5 [q]Ps 78:4

[u]*8* Or *God, translating it* [v]*15* See Lev. 23:37-40.
[w]*5* Or *God for ever and ever*

LORD.[a] You made the heavens,[b] even
the highest heavens, and all their
starry host, the earth[c] and all that
is on it, the seas[d] and all that is in
them.[e] You give life to everything,
and the multitudes of heaven worship you.
7“You are the LORD God, who
chose Abram and brought him out
of Ur of the Chaldeans[f] and named
him Abraham.[g] 8You found his heart
faithful to you, and you made a covenant with him to give to his descendants the land of the Canaanites, Hittites, Amorites, Perizzites,
Jebusites and Girgashites.[h] You have
kept your promise[i] because you are
righteous.[j]
9“You saw the suffering of our
forefathers in Egypt;[k] you heard their
cry at the Red Sea.[x][l] 10You sent miraculous signs[m] and wonders against
Pharaoh, against all his officials and
all the people of his land, for you
knew how arrogantly the Egyptians
treated them. You made a name[n]
for yourself, which remains to this
day. 11You divided the sea before
them,[o] so that they passed through
it on dry ground, but you hurled
their pursuers into the depths, like
a stone into mighty waters.[p] 12By
day you led[q] them with a pillar of
cloud,[r] and by night with a pillar
of fire to give them light on the way
they were to take.
13“You came down on Mount
Sinai;[s] you spoke[t] to them from heav-
en. You gave them regulations and
laws that are just[u] and right, and decrees and commands that are good.[v]
14You made known to them your
holy Sabbath[w] and gave them commands, decrees and laws through
your servant Moses. 15In their hunger you gave them bread from heav-
en[x] and in their thirst you brought
them water from the rock;[y] you told
them to go in and take possession of
the land you had sworn with uplifted hand to give them.[z]
16“But they, our forefathers, be-

9:6
[a]Dt 6:4
[b]2Ki 19:15
[c]Ge 1:1;
Isa 37:16
[d]Ps 95:5
[e]Dt 10:14
9:7
[f]Ge 11:31
[g]Ge 17:5
9:8
[h]Ge 15:18-21
[i]Jos 21:45
[j]Ge 15:6;
Ezr 9:15
9:9
[k]Ex 3:7
[l]Ex 14:10-30
9:10
[m]Ex 10:1
[n]Jer 32:20;
Da 9:15
9:11
[o]Ex 14:21;
Ps 78:13
[p]Ex 15:4-5,10;
Heb 11:29
9:12
[q]Ex 15:13
[r]Ex 13:21
9:13
[s]Ex 19:11
[t]Ex 19:19
[u]Ps 119:137
[v]Ex 20:1
9:14
[w]Ge 2:3;
Ex 20:8-11
9:15
[x]Ex 16:4;
Jn 6:31
[y]Ex 17:6;
Nu 20:7-13
[z]Dt 1:8,21
9:16
[a]Dt 1:26-33;
31:29
9:17
[b]Ps 78:42
[c]Nu 14:1-4
[d]Ex 34:6
[e]Nu 14:17-19
[f]Ps 78:11
9:18
[g]Ex 32:4
9:20
[h]Nu 11:17;
Isa 63:11,14
[i]Ex 16:15
[j]Ex 17:6
9:21
[k]Dt 2:7
[l]Dt 8:4
9:22
[m]Nu 21:21
[n]Nu 21:33
9:24
[o]Jos 11:23

came arrogant and stiff-necked, and
did not obey your commands.[a]
17They refused to listen and failed
to remember[b] the miracles you
performed among them. They
became stiff-necked and in their
rebellion appointed a leader in
order to return to their slavery.[c]
But you are a forgiving God, gracious and compassionate, slow to
anger[d] and abounding in love.[e]
Therefore you did not desert
them,[f] 18even when they cast for
themselves an image of a calf[g] and
said, ‘This is your god, who brought
you up out of Egypt,’ or when they
committed awful blasphemies.
19“Because of your great compassion you did not abandon them in
the desert. By day the pillar of cloud
did not cease to guide them on their
path, nor the pillar of fire by night
to shine on the way they were to
take. 20You gave your good Spirit[h]
to instruct them. You did not
withhold your manna[i] from their
mouths, and you gave them water[j]
for their thirst. 21For forty years you
sustained them in the desert; they
lacked nothing,[k] their clothes did
not wear out nor did their feet become swollen.[l]
22“You gave them kingdoms and
nations, allotting to them even the
remotest frontiers. They took over
the country of Sihon[y][m] king of Heshbon and the country of Og king of
Bashan.[n] 23You made their sons as
numerous as the stars in the sky,
and you brought them into the land
that you told their fathers to enter
and possess. 24Their sons went in
and took possession of the land.[o] You
subdued before them the Canaanites, who lived in the land; you
handed the Canaanites over to them,
along with their kings and the peoples of the land, to deal with them
as they pleased. 25They captured

[x]*9* Hebrew *Yam Suph*; that is, Sea of Reeds
[y]*22* One Hebrew manuscript and Septuagint; most Hebrew manuscripts *Sihon, that is, the country of the*

fortified cities and fertile land; they
took possession of houses filled with
all kinds of good things, wells already
dug, vineyards, olive groves and fruit
trees in abundance. They ate to the
full and were well-nourished;[a] they
reveled in your great goodness.[b]
26“But they were disobedient and
rebelled against you; they put your
law behind their backs.[c] They killed
your prophets,[d] who had admonished them in order to turn them
back to you; they committed awful
blasphemies.[e] 27So you handed them
over to their enemies,[f] who oppressed them. But when they were
oppressed they cried out to you.
From heaven you heard them, and
in your great compassion[g] you gave
them deliverers, who rescued them
from the hand of their enemies.
28“But as soon as they were at
rest, they again did what was evil in
your sight. Then you abandoned
them to the hand of their enemies
so that they ruled over them. And
when they cried out to you again,
you heard from heaven, and in your
compassion you delivered them[h]
time after time.
29“You warned them to return to
your law, but they became arrogant[i]
and disobeyed your commands. They
sinned against your ordinances, by
which a man will live if he obeys
them.[j] Stubbornly they turned their
backs on you, became stiff-necked
and refused to listen.[k] 30For many
years you were patient with them.
By your Spirit you admonished them
through your prophets.[l] Yet they
paid no attention, so you handed
them over to the neighboring peoples. 31But in your great mercy you
did not put an end[m] to them or abandon them, for you are a gracious and
merciful God.
32“Now therefore, O our God, the
great, mighty[n] and awesome God,
who keeps his covenant of love,[o] do
not let all this hardship seem trifling
in your eyes—the hardship that has
come upon us, upon our kings and
leaders, upon our priests and prophets, upon our fathers and all your
people, from the days of the kings
of Assyria until today. 33In all that
has happened to us, you have been
just;[p] you have acted faithfully, while
we did wrong.[q] 34Our kings,[r] our
leaders, our priests and our fathers[s]
did not follow your law; they did
not pay attention to your commands
or the warnings you gave them.
35Even while they were in their
kingdom, enjoying your great goodness[t] to them in the spacious and
fertile land you gave them, they did
not serve you[u] or turn from their
evil ways.
36“But see, we are slaves[v] today,
slaves in the land you gave our forefathers so they could eat its fruit and
the other good things it produces.
37Because of our sins, its abundant
harvest goes to the kings you have
placed over us. They rule over our
bodies and our cattle as they please.
We are in great distress.[w]

Names of leaders who sealed the agreement.

38“In view of all this, we are making a
binding agreement,[x] putting it in writing,[y] and our leaders, our Levites and our
priests are affixing their seals to it.”

10

Those who sealed it were:

Nehemiah the governor, the son
of Hacaliah.

Zedekiah, 2Seraiah,[z] Azariah, Jeremiah,
3Pashhur,[a] Amariah, Malkijah,
4Hattush, Shebaniah, Malluch,
5Harim,[b] Meremoth, Obadiah,
6Daniel, Ginnethon, Baruch,
7Meshullam, Abijah, Mijamin,
8Maaziah, Bilgai and Shemaiah.
These were the priests.

9The Levites:[c]

Jeshua son of Azaniah, Binnui of
the sons of Henadad, Kadmiel,

9:25 [a]Dt 6:10-12 [b]Nu 13:27; Dt 32:12-15
9:26 [c]1Ki 14:9 [d]Mt 21:35-36 [e]Jdg 2:12-13
9:27 [f]Jdg 2:14 [g]Ps 106:45
9:28 [h]Ps 106:43
9:29 [i]Ps 5:5; Isa 2:11; Jer 43:2 [j]Dt 30:16 [k]Zec 7:11-12
9:30 [l]2Ki 17:13-18; 2Ch 36:16
9:31 [m]Isa 48:9; Jer 4:27
9:32 [n]Ps 24:8 [o]Dt 7:9
9:33 [p]Ge 18:25 [q]Jer 44:3; Da 9:7-8,14
9:34 [r]2Ki 23:11 [s]Jer 44:17
9:35 [t]Isa 63:7 [u]Dt 28:45-48
9:36 [v]Dt 28:48; Ezr 9:9
9:37 [w]Dt 28:33; La 5:5
9:38 [x]2Ch 23:16 [y]Isa 44:5
10:2 [z]Ezr 2:2
10:3 [a]1Ch 9:12
10:5 [b]1Ch 24:8
10:9 [c]Ne 12:1

10and their associates: Shebaniah,
Hodiah, Kelita, Pelaiah, Hanan,
11Mica, Rehob, Hashabiah,
12Zaccur, Sherebiah, Shebaniah,
13Hodiah, Bani and Beninu.

14The leaders of the people:

Parosh, Pahath-Moab, Elam, Zattu,
Bani,
15Bunni, Azgad, Bebai,
16Adonijah, Bigvai, Adin,[a]
17Ater, Hezekiah, Azzur,
18Hodiah, Hashum, Bezai,
19Hariph, Anathoth, Nebai,
20Magpiash, Meshullam, Hezir,[b]
21Meshezabel, Zadok, Jaddua,
22Pelatiah, Hanan, Anaiah,
23Hoshea, Hananiah,[c] Hasshub,
24Hallohesh, Pilha, Shobek,
25Rehum, Hashabnah, Maaseiah,
26Ahiah, Hanan, Anan,
27Malluch, Harim and Baanah.

Provisions of the agreement.

28"The rest of the people—priests,
Levites, gatekeepers, singers, temple servants[d] and all who separated themselves from the neighboring
peoples[e] for the sake of the Law of
God, together with their wives and
all their sons and daughters who
are able to understand— 29all these
now join their brothers the nobles,
and bind themselves with a curse
and an oath[f] to follow the Law of
God given through Moses the servant of God and to obey carefully
all the commands, regulations and
decrees of the LORD our Lord.
30"We promise not to give our
daughters in marriage to the peoples
around us or take their daughters
for our sons.[g]
31"When the neighboring peoples
bring merchandise or grain to sell on
the Sabbath,[h] we will not buy from
them on the Sabbath or on any holy
day. Every seventh year we will for-
go working the land[i] and will cancel all debts.[j]
32"We assume the responsibility
for carrying out the commands to
give a third of a shekel[z] each year
for the service of the house of our
God: 33for the bread set out on the
table;[k] for the regular grain offerings
and burnt offerings; for the offerings on the Sabbaths, New Moon[l]
festivals and appointed feasts; for the
holy offerings; for sin offerings to
make atonement for Israel; and for
all the duties of the house of our
God.[m]
34"We—the priests, the Levites
and the people—have cast lots[n] to
determine when each of our families is to bring to the house of our
God at set times each year a contribution of wood[o] to burn on the altar
of the LORD our God, as it is written in the Law.
35"We also assume responsibility
for bringing to the house of the LORD
each year the firstfruits[p] of our crops
and of every fruit tree.[q]
36"As it is also written in the Law,
we will bring the firstborn[r] of our
sons and of our cattle, of our herds
and of our flocks to the house of our
God, to the priests ministering
there.[s]
37"Moreover, we will bring to the
storerooms of the house of our God,
to the priests, the first of our ground
meal, of our ⌊grain⌋ offerings, of the
fruit of all our trees and of our new
wine and oil.[t] And we will bring a
tithe[u] of our crops to the Levites,[v]
for it is the Levites who collect the
tithes in all the towns where we
work.[w] 38A priest descended from
Aaron is to accompany the Levites
when they receive the tithes, and
the Levites are to bring a tenth of the
tithes[x] up to the house of our God,
to the storerooms of the treasury.
39The people of Israel, including the
Levites, are to bring their contributions of grain, new wine and oil
to the storerooms where the articles
for the sanctuary are kept and where

z32 That is, about 1/8 ounce (about 4 grams)

10:16 [a]Ezr 8:6
10:20 [b]1Ch 24:15
10:23 [c]Ne 7:2
10:28 [d]Ps 135:1 [e]2Ch 6:26; Ne 9:2
10:29 [f]Nu 5:21; Ps 119:106
10:30 [g]Ex 34:16; Dt 7:3; Ne 13:23
10:31 [h]Ne 13:16,18; Jer 17:27; Eze 23:38; Am 8:5 [i]Ex 23:11; Lev 25:1-7 [j]Dt 15:1
10:33 [k]Lev 24:6 [l]Nu 10:10; Ps 81:3; Isa 1:14 [m]2Ch 24:5
10:34 [n]Lev 16:8 [o]Ne 13:31
10:35 [p]Ex 22:29; 23:19; Nu 18:12 [q]Dt 26:1-11
10:36 [r]Ex 13:2; Nu 18:14-16 [s]Ne 13:31
10:37 [t]Lev 23:17; Nu 18:12 [u]Lev 27:30; Nu 18:21 [v]Dt 14:22-29 [w]Eze 44:30
10:38 [x]Nu 18:26

the ministering priests, the gatekeepers and the singers stay.
"We will not neglect the house of
our God."[a]

The new residents of Jerusalem.

11:3-19pp— 1Ch 9:1-17

11 Now the leaders of the people
settled in Jerusalem, and the rest
of the people cast lots to bring one out
of every ten to live in Jerusalem,[b] the
holy city,[c] while the remaining nine
were to stay in their own towns.[d] 2The
people commended all the men who
volunteered to live in Jerusalem.
3These are the provincial leaders who
settled in Jerusalem (now some Israelites, priests, Levites, temple servants
and descendants of Solomon's servants
lived in the towns of Judah, each on his
own property in the various towns,[e]
4while other people from both Judah
and Benjamin[f] lived in Jerusalem):[g]

From the descendants of Judah:

Athaiah son of Uzziah, the son of
Zechariah, the son of Amariah, the
son of Shephatiah, the son of Mahalalel, a descendant of Perez; 5and
Maaseiah son of Baruch, the son of
Col-Hozeh, the son of Hazaiah, the
son of Adaiah, the son of Joiarib,
the son of Zechariah, a descendant
of Shelah. 6The descendants of Perez
who lived in Jerusalem totaled 468
able men.

7From the descendants of Benjamin:

Sallu son of Meshullam, the son of
Joed, the son of Pedaiah, the son of
Kolaiah, the son of Maaseiah, the
son of Ithiel, the son of Jeshaiah,
8and his followers, Gabbai and Sal-
lai—928 men. 9Joel son of Zicri was
their chief officer, and Judah son
of Hassenuah was over the Second
District of the city.

10From the priests:

Jedaiah; the son of Joiarib; Jakin;
11Seraiah[h] son of Hilkiah, the son of
Meshullam, the son of Zadok, the
son of Meraioth, the son of Ahitub,[i]
supervisor in the house of God,
12and their associates, who carried
on work for the temple—822 men;
Adaiah son of Jeroham, the son of
Pelaliah, the son of Amzi, the son of
Zechariah, the son of Pashhur, the
son of Malkijah, 13and his associates, who were heads of families—
242 men; Amashsai son of Azarel,
the son of Ahzai, the son of Meshillemoth, the son of Immer, 14and
his[a] associates, who were able
men—128. Their chief officer was
Zabdiel son of Haggedolim.

15From the Levites:

Shemaiah son of Hasshub, the son
of Azrikam, the son of Hashabiah,
the son of Bunni; 16Shabbethai[j] and
Jozabad,[k] two of the heads of the
Levites, who had charge of the
outside work of the house of God;
17Mattaniah[l] son of Mica, the son of
Zabdi, the son of Asaph,[m] the director who led in thanksgiving and
prayer; Bakbukiah, second among
his associates; and Abda son of
Shammua, the son of Galal, the son
of Jeduthun.[n] 18The Levites in the
holy city[o] totaled 284.

19The gatekeepers:

Akkub, Talmon and their associates,
who kept watch at the gates—172
men.

20The rest of the Israelites, with the
priests and Levites, were in all the towns
of Judah, each on his ancestral property.
21The temple servants[p] lived on the
hill of Ophel, and Ziha and Gishpa were
in charge of them.
22The chief officer of the Levites in Jerusalem was Uzzi son of Bani, the son of
Hashabiah, the son of Mattaniah,[q] the
son of Mica. Uzzi was one of Asaph's descendants, who were the singers responsible for the service of the house of
God. 23The singers[r] were under the

10:39 [a]Dt 12:6; Ne 13:11,12
11:1 [b]Ne 7:4 [c]ver 18; Isa 48:2; 52:1; 64:10; Zec 14:20-21 [d]Ne 7:73
11:3 [e]1Ch 9:2-3; Ezr 2:1
11:4 [f]Ezr 1:5 [g]Ezr 2:70
11:11 [h]2Ki 25:18; Ezr 2:2 [i]Ezr 7:2
11:16 [j]Ezr 10:15 [k]Ezr 8:33
11:17 [l]1Ch 9:15; Ne 12:8 [m]2Ch 5:12 [n]1Ch 25:1
11:18 [o]Rev 21:2
11:21 [p]Ezr 2:43; Ne 3:26
11:22 [q]1Ch 9:15
11:23 [r]Ne 7:44

a *14* Most Septuagint manuscripts; Hebrew *their*

king's orders, which regulated their daily activity.
24 Pethahiah son of Meshezabel, one of
the descendants of Zerah[a] son of Judah,
was the king's agent in all affairs relating to the people.
25 As for the villages with their fields,
some of the people of Judah lived in
Kiriath Arba[b] and its surrounding settlements, in Dibon[c] and its settlements, in
Jekabzeel and its villages, 26 in Jeshua,
in Moladah, in Beth Pelet,[d] 27 in Hazar
Shual, in Beersheba[e] and its settlements,
28 in Ziklag,[f] in Meconah and its settlements, 29 in En Rimmon, in Zorah,[g] in
Jarmuth,[h] 30 Zanoah, Adullam[i] and their
villages, in Lachish[j] and its fields, and
in Azekah[k] and its settlements. So they
were living all the way from Beersheba[l]
to the Valley of Hinnom.
31 The descendants of the Benjamites
from Geba[m] lived in Micmash,[n] Aija,
Bethel and its settlements, 32 in Anathoth,[o] Nob[p] and Ananiah, 33 in Hazor,[q]
Ramah and Gittaim,[r] 34 in Hadid, Zeboim[s] and Neballat, 35 in Lod and Ono,[t]
and in the Valley of the Craftsmen.
36 Some of the divisions of the Levites
of Judah settled in Benjamin.

Names of the priests and Levites who returned.

12 These were the priests[u] and
Levites who returned with Zerubbabel[v] son of Shealtiel and with
Jeshua:[w]
Seraiah,[x] Jeremiah, Ezra,
2 Amariah, Malluch, Hattush,
3 Shecaniah, Rehum, Meremoth,
4 Iddo,[y] Ginnethon,[b] Abijah,[z]
5 Mijamin,[c] Moadiah, Bilgah,
6 Shemaiah, Joiarib, Jedaiah,[a]
7 Sallu, Amok, Hilkiah and Jedaiah.
These were the leaders of the priests and
their associates in the days of Jeshua.
8 The Levites were Jeshua, Binnui, Kadmiel, Sherebiah, Judah, and also Mattaniah,[b] who, together with his associates,
was in charge of the songs of thanksgiving. 9 Bakbukiah and Unni, their associates, stood opposite them in the services.

11:24 [a]Ge 38:30
11:25 [b]Ge 35:27; Jos 14:15 [c]Nu 21:30
11:26 [d]Jos 15:27
11:27 [e]Ge 21:14
11:28 [f]1Sa 27:6
11:29 [g]Jos 15:33 [h]Jos 10:3
11:30 [i]Jos 15:35 [j]Jos 10:3 [k]Jos 10:10 [l]Jos 15:28
11:31 [m]Jos 21:17; Isa 10:29 [n]1Sa 13:2
11:32 [o]Jos 21:18; Isa 10:30 [p]1Sa 21:1
11:33 [q]Jos 11:1 [r]2Sa 4:3
11:34 [s]1Sa 13:18
11:35 [t]1Ch 8:12
12:1 [u]Ne 10:1-8 [v]1Ch 3:19 [w]Ezr 2:2 [x]Ezr 2:2
12:4 [y]Zec 1:1 [z]Lk 1:5
12:6 [a]1Ch 24:7
12:8 [b]Ne 11:17
12:10 [c]Ezr 10:24
12:16 [d]ver 4
12:24 [e]Ezr 2:40

10 Jeshua was the father of Joiakim,
Joiakim the father of Eliashib,[c] Eliashib
the father of Joiada, 11 Joiada the father of
Jonathan, and Jonathan the father of Jaddua.
12 In the days of Joiakim, these were
the heads of the priestly families:
of Seraiah's family, Meraiah;
of Jeremiah's, Hananiah;
13 of Ezra's, Meshullam;
of Amariah's, Jehohanan;
14 of Malluch's, Jonathan;
of Shecaniah's,[d] Joseph;
15 of Harim's, Adna;
of Meremoth's,[e] Helkai;
16 of Iddo's,[d] Zechariah;
of Ginnethon's, Meshullam;
17 of Abijah's, Zicri;
of Miniamin's and of Moadiah's,
Piltai;
18 of Bilgah's, Shammua;
of Shemaiah's, Jehonathan;
19 of Joiarib's, Mattenai;
of Jedaiah's, Uzzi;
20 of Sallu's, Kallai;
of Amok's, Eber;
21 of Hilkiah's, Hashabiah;
of Jedaiah's, Nethanel.
22 The family heads of the Levites in
the days of Eliashib, Joiada, Johanan and
Jaddua, as well as those of the priests,
were recorded in the reign of Darius the
Persian. 23 The family heads among the
descendants of Levi up to the time of
Johanan son of Eliashib were recorded in
the book of the annals. 24 And the leaders
of the Levites[e] were Hashabiah, Sherebiah, Jeshua son of Kadmiel, and their
associates, who stood opposite them to
give praise and thanksgiving, one section
responding to the other, as prescribed by
David the man of God.
25 Mattaniah, Bakbukiah, Obadiah,
Meshullam, Talmon and Akkub were
gatekeepers who guarded the storerooms
at the gates. 26 They served in the days of

[b]*4* Many Hebrew manuscripts and Vulgate (see also Neh. 12:16); most Hebrew manuscripts *Ginnethoi* [c]*5* A variant of *Miniamin* [d]*14* Very many Hebrew manuscripts, some Septuagint manuscripts and Syriac (see also Neh. 12:3); most Hebrew manuscripts *Shebaniah's* [e]*15* Some Septuagint manuscripts (see also Neh. 12:3); Hebrew *Meraioth's*

Joiakim son of Jeshua, the son of Jozadak, and in the days of Nehemiah the governor and of Ezra the priest and scribe.

Dedication of the wall.

27At the dedication[a] of the wall of Jerusalem, the Levites were sought out from where they lived and were brought to Jerusalem to celebrate joyfully the dedication with songs of thanksgiving and with the music of cymbals,[b] harps and lyres.[c] 28The singers also were brought together from the region around Jerusalem—from the villages of the Netophathites,[d] 29from Beth Gilgal, and from the area of Geba and Azmaveth, for the singers had built villages for themselves around Jerusalem. 30When the priests and Levites had purified themselves ceremonially, they purified the people,[e] the gates and the wall.

31I had the leaders of Judah go up on top[f] of the wall. I also assigned two large choirs to give thanks. One was to proceed on top[g] of the wall to the right, toward the Dung Gate.[f] 32Hoshaiah and half the leaders of Judah followed them, 33along with Azariah, Ezra, Meshullam, 34Judah, Benjamin,[g] Shemaiah, Jeremiah, 35as well as some priests with trumpets,[h] and also Zechariah son of Jonathan, the son of Shemaiah, the son of Mattaniah, the son of Micaiah, the son of Zaccur, the son of Asaph, 36and his associates—Shemaiah, Azarel, Milalai, Gilalai, Maai, Nethanel, Judah and Hanani—with musical instruments[i] ⌊prescribed by⌋ David the man of God.[j] Ezra[k] the scribe led the procession. 37At the Fountain Gate[l] they continued directly up the steps of the City of David on the ascent to the wall and passed above the house of David to the Water Gate[m] on the east.

38The second choir proceeded in the opposite direction. I followed them on top[h] of the wall, together with half the people—past the Tower of the Ovens[n] to the Broad Wall,[o] 39over the Gate of Ephraim,[p] the Jeshanah[i] Gate,[q] the Fish Gate,[r] the Tower of Hananel[s] and the Tower of the Hundred,[t] as far as the Sheep Gate.[u] At the Gate of the Guard they stopped.

40The two choirs that gave thanks then took their places in the house of God; so did I, together with half the officials, 41as well as the priests—Eliakim, Maaseiah, Miniamin, Micaiah, Elioenai, Zechariah and Hananiah with their trumpets— 42and also Maaseiah, Shemaiah, Eleazar, Uzzi, Jehohanan, Malkijah, Elam and Ezer. The choirs sang under the direction of Jezrahiah. 43And on that day they offered great sacrifices, rejoicing because God had given them great joy. The women and children also rejoiced. The sound of rejoicing in Jerusalem could be heard far away.

Appointment of temple duties.

44At that time men were appointed to be in charge of the storerooms[v] for the contributions, firstfruits and tithes.[w] From the fields around the towns they were to bring into the storerooms the portions required by the Law for the priests and the Levites, for Judah was pleased with the ministering priests and Levites.[x] 45They performed the service of their God and the service of purification, as did also the singers and gatekeepers, according to the commands of David[y] and his son Solomon.[z] 46For long ago, in the days of David and Asaph,[a] there had been directors for the singers and for the songs of praise[b] and thanksgiving to God. 47So in the days of Zerubbabel and of Nehemiah, all Israel contributed the daily portions for the singers and gatekeepers. They also set aside the portion for the other Levites, and the Levites set aside the portion for the descendants of Aaron.[c]

Nehemiah's various reforms.

13 On that day the Book of Moses was read aloud in the hearing of the people and there it was found written that no Ammonite or Moabite should

12:27 [a]Dt 20:5 [b]2Sa 6:5 [c]1Ch 15:16,28; 25:6; Ps 92:3
12:28 [d]1Ch 2:54; 9:16
12:30 [e]Ex 19:10; Job 1:5
12:31 [f]Ne 2:13
12:34 [g]Ezr 1:5
12:35 [h]Ezr 3:10
12:36 [i]1Ch 15:16 [j]2Ch 8:14 [k]Ezr 7:6
12:37 [l]Ne 2:14; 3:15 [m]Ne 3:26
12:38 [n]Ne 3:11 [o]Ne 3:8
12:39 [p]2Ki 14:13; Ne 8:16 [q]Ne 3:6 [r]2Ch 33:14; Ne 3:3 [s]Ne 3:1 [t]Ne 3:1 [u]Ne 3:1
12:44 [v]Ne 13:4,13 [w]Lev 27:30 [x]Dt 18:8
12:45 [y]1Ch 25:1; 2Ch 8:14 [z]1Ch 6:31; 23:5
12:46 [a]2Ch 35:15 [b]2Ch 29:27; Ps 137:4
12:47 [c]Nu 18:21; Dt 18:8

[f]31 Or *go alongside* [g]31 Or *proceed alongside*
[h]38 Or *them alongside* [i]39 Or *Old*

ever be admitted into the assembly of
God,[a] 2because they had not met the Israelites with food and water but had
hired Balaam[b] to call a curse down on
them.[c] (Our God, however, turned the
curse into a blessing.)[d] 3When the people heard this law, they excluded from
Israel all who were of foreign descent.[e]

4Before this, Eliashib the priest had
been put in charge of the storerooms[f] of
the house of our God. He was closely
associated with Tobiah,[g] 5and he had provided him with a large room formerly
used to store the grain offerings and
incense and temple articles, and also the
tithes[h] of grain, new wine and oil prescribed for the Levites, singers and gatekeepers, as well as the contributions for
the priests.

6But while all this was going on, I was
not in Jerusalem, for in the thirty-second
year of Artaxerxes[i] king of Babylon I had
returned to the king. Some time later I
asked his permission 7and came back to
Jerusalem. Here I learned about the evil
thing Eliashib[j] had done in providing
Tobiah a room in the courts of the house
of God. 8I was greatly displeased and
threw all Tobiah's household goods out
of the room.[k] 9I gave orders to purify the
rooms,[l] and then I put back into them
the equipment of the house of God, with
the grain offerings and the incense.

10I also learned that the portions assigned to the Levites had not been giv-
en to them,[m] and that all the Levites and
singers responsible for the service had
gone back to their own fields. 11So I
rebuked the officials and asked them,
"Why is the house of God neglected?"[n]
Then I called them together and stationed
them at their posts.

12All Judah brought the tithes[o] of grain,
new wine and oil into the storerooms.[p]
13I put Shelemiah the priest, Zadok the
scribe, and a Levite named Pedaiah in
charge of the storerooms and made
Hanan son of Zaccur, the son of Mattaniah, their assistant, because these men
were considered trustworthy. They were
made responsible for distributing the
supplies to their brothers.[q]

13:1 [a]ver 23; Dt 23:3
13:2 [b]Nu 22:3-11 [c]Nu 23:7; Dt 23:3 [d]Nu 23:11; Dt 23:4-5
13:3 [e]ver 23; Ne 9:2
13:4 [f]Ne 12:44 [g]Ne 2:10
13:5 [h]Lev 27:30; Nu 18:21
13:6 [i]Ne 2:6; 5:14
13:7 [j]Ezr 10:24
13:8 [k]Mt 21:12-13; Jn 2:13-16
13:9 [l]1Ch 23:28; 2Ch 29:5
13:10 [m]Dt 12:19
13:11 [n]Ne 10:37-39; Hag 1:1-9
13:12 [o]2Ch 31:6 [p]1Ki 7:51; Ne 10:37-39; Mal 3:10
13:13 [q]Ne 12:44; Ac 6:1-5
13:14 [r]Ge 8:1
13:15 [s]Ex 20:8-11; 34:21; Dt 5:12-15; Ne 10:31
13:16 [t]Ne 10:31
13:18 [u]Ne 10:31; Jer 17:21-23
13:19 [v]Lev 23:32
13:22 [w]Ge 8:1; Ne 12:30
13:23 [x]Ezr 9:1-2; Mal 2:11 [y]ver 1; Ne 10:30

14Remember[r] me for this, O my God,
and do not blot out what I have so faithfully done for the house of my God and
its services.

15In those days I saw men in Judah
treading winepresses on the Sabbath and
bringing in grain and loading it on donkeys, together with wine, grapes, figs
and all other kinds of loads. And they
were bringing all this into Jerusalem on
the Sabbath.[s] Therefore I warned them
against selling food on that day. 16Men
from Tyre who lived in Jerusalem were
bringing in fish and all kinds of merchandise and selling them in Jerusalem
on the Sabbath[t] to the people of Judah.
17I rebuked the nobles of Judah and said
to them, "What is this wicked thing you
are doing—desecrating the Sabbath day?
18Didn't your forefathers do the same
things, so that our God brought all this
calamity upon us and upon this city?
Now you are stirring up more wrath
against Israel by desecrating the Sabbath."[u]

19When evening shadows fell on the
gates of Jerusalem before the Sabbath,[v]
I ordered the doors to be shut and not
opened until the Sabbath was over. I stationed some of my own men at the gates
so that no load could be brought in on
the Sabbath day. 20Once or twice the
merchants and sellers of all kinds of
goods spent the night outside Jerusalem.
21But I warned them and said, "Why do
you spend the night by the wall? If you
do this again, I will lay hands on you."
From that time on they no longer came
on the Sabbath. 22Then I commanded
the Levites to purify themselves and go
and guard the gates in order to keep
the Sabbath day holy.

Remember[w] me for this also, O my
God, and show mercy to me according to
your great love.

23Moreover, in those days I saw men
of Judah who had married[x] women from
Ashdod, Ammon and Moab.[y] 24Half of
their children spoke the language of Ashdod or the language of one of the other

peoples, and did not know how to speak
the language of Judah. 25I rebuked them
and called curses down on them. I beat
some of the men and pulled out their
hair. I made them take an oath[a] in God's
name and said: "You are not to give your
daughters in marriage to their sons, nor
are you to take their daughters in marriage for your sons or for yourselves.
26Was it not because of marriages like
these that Solomon king of Israel sinned?
Among the many nations there was no
king like him.[b] He was loved by his
God,[c] and God made him king over all
Israel, but even he was led into sin by
foreign women.[d] 27Must we hear now
that you too are doing all this terrible
wickedness and are being unfaithful to
our God by marrying[e] foreign women?"
28One of the sons of Joiada son of
Eliashib[f] the high priest was son-in-law
to Sanballat[g] the Horonite. And I drove
him away from me.

29Remember[h] them, O my God, because they defiled the priestly office and
the covenant of the priesthood and of the
Levites.

30So I purified the priests and the
Levites of everything foreign,[i] and assigned them duties, each to his own task.
31I also made provision for contributions
of wood[j] at designated times, and for the
firstfruits.

Remember[k] me with favor, O my God.

13:25 [a]Ezr 10:5
13:26 [b]1Ki 3:13; 2Ch 1:12 [c]2Sa 12:25 [d]1Ki 11:3
13:27 [e]Ezr 9:14; 10:2
13:28 [f]Ezr 10:24 [g]Ne 2:10
13:29 [h]Ne 6:14
13:30 [i]Ne 10:30
13:31 [j]Ne 10:34 [k]ver 14,22; Ge 8:1

ESTHER

Author: Unknown.

Date Written: Between 485 and 435 B.C.

Time Span: About 10 years.

Title: From the book's chief character: Esther.

Background: The story of Esther takes place during that period of time between the separate returns to Jerusalem led by Zerubbabel and Ezra (between chapters 6 and 7 of the book of Ezra). After 70 years of captivity, about 50,000 Israelites return to their homeland of Jerusalem, but the vast majority determine to remain in Media-Persia. Esther's story takes place against this background while in the king's palace in Susa, the Persian capital. Ruth and Esther are the only books of the Bible named after women. Esther is a Jewish woman who marries a Gentile; Ruth, a Gentile woman who marries a Jew.

Where Written: Unknown (probably Media-Persia).

To Whom: To the Jews who remain in Media-Persia instead of returning to Jerusalem.

Content: Esther, whose Jewish heritage has been kept secret, is chosen queen to King Xerxes after Vashti is demoted from the same position. Haman, an evil adviser to the king, plans to exterminate the Jewish people (chapter 3). But Esther has the faith and courage to carry out the plan of her wise cousin, Mordecai, and risks her very life, which results in the deliverance of the Jewish people. The Feast of Purim is instituted to remind the people of God's deliverance (chapter 9). Even to this day there is public reading of the book of Esther during this celebration.

Key Words: "Beauty"; "Providence." God has blessed Esther with much outward physical "beauty," but it is the "beauty" of her heart that sets her apart for the "providence" of God to be shown. It is not by chance that this Jewish girl rises from total obscurity to become the queen of the most powerful empire of the world. The name of God does not appear once in the book of Esther, but God's providential care and leading are not to be denied.

Themes: • God may have bigger plans for our lives than we have for ourselves. • God may put us into positions of leadership or influence so we can more thoroughly accomplish his purposes. • God answers prayer and fasting by enabling us to overcome our human obstacles. • God providentially provides for his own. • God uses ordinary people to accomplish extraordinary things for him. • God at times may have to discipline us...but he will never abandon us.

Outline:
1. Esther becomes queen. 1:1-2:18
2. Haman plots to destroy the Jews. 2:19-5:14
3. Mordecai is honored at Haman's expense. 6:1-8:2
4. The Jews triumph. 8:3-10:3

ESTHER

Xerxes deposes Queen Vashti.

1 This is what happened during the
time of Xerxes,[a][a] the Xerxes who
ruled over 127 provinces[b] stretching
from India to Cush[b]:[c] 2At that time King
Xerxes reigned from his royal throne in
the citadel of Susa,[d] 3and in the third year
of his reign he gave a banquet[e] for all
his nobles and officials. The military leaders of Persia and Media, the princes, and
the nobles of the provinces were present.
4For a full 180 days he displayed the
vast wealth of his kingdom and the splendor and glory of his majesty. 5When these
days were over, the king gave a banquet,
lasting seven days,[f] in the enclosed
garden[g] of the king's palace, for all the
people from the least to the greatest, who
were in the citadel of Susa. 6The garden
had hangings of white and blue linen,
fastened with cords of white linen and
purple material to silver rings on marble
pillars. There were couches[h] of gold and
silver on a mosaic pavement of porphyry,
marble, mother-of-pearl and other costly
stones. 7Wine was served in goblets of
gold, each one different from the other,
and the royal wine was abundant, in
keeping with the king's liberality.[i] 8By
the king's command each guest was allowed to drink in his own way, for the
king instructed all the wine stewards to
serve each man what he wished.
9Queen Vashti also gave a banquet[j]
for the women in the royal palace of King
Xerxes.

1:1 [a]Ezr 4:6; Da 9:1 [b]Est 9:30; Da 3:2; 6:1 [c]Est 8:9
1:2 [d]Ezr 4:9; Ne 1:1; Est 2:8
1:3 [e]1Ki 3:15; Est 2:18
1:5 [f]Jdg 14:17 [g]2Ki 21:18; Est 7:7-8
1:6 [h]Est 7:8; Eze 23:41; Am 3:12; 6:4
1:7 [i]Est 2:18; Da 5:2
1:9 [j]1Ki 3:15

a *1* Hebrew *Ahasuerus,* a variant of Xerxes' Persian name; here and throughout Esther b *1* That is, the upper Nile region

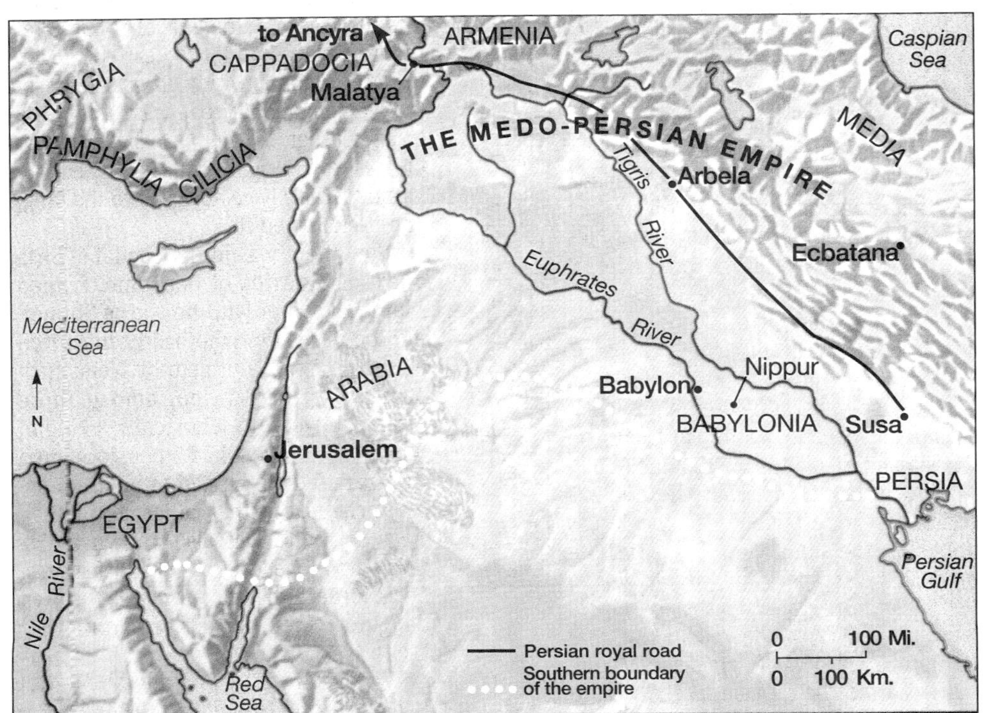

The World of Esther's Day

Esther lived in the capital of the vast Medo-Persian empire, which incorporated the provinces of Media and Persia, as well as the previous empires of Assyria and Babylon. Esther, a Jewess, was chosen by King Xerxes to be his queen. The story of how she saved her people takes place in the palace of Susa.

10On the seventh day, when King
Xerxes was in high spirits[a] from wine,[b]
he commanded the seven eunuchs who
served him—Mehuman, Biztha, Harbona,[c] Bigtha, Abagtha, Zethar and Car-
cas— 11to bring[d] before him Queen
Vashti, wearing her royal crown, in order
to display her beauty[e] to the people and
nobles, for she was lovely to look at.
12But when the attendants delivered
the king's command, Queen Vashti refused to come. Then the king became
furious and burned with anger.[f]
13Since it was customary for the king
to consult experts in matters of law and
justice, he spoke with the wise men who
understood the times[g] 14and were closest
to the king—Carshena, Shethar, Adma-
tha, Tarshish, Meres, Marsena and Memucan, the seven nobles[h] of Persia and
Media who had special access to the king
and were highest in the kingdom.
15"According to law, what must be
done to Queen Vashti?" he asked. "She
has not obeyed the command of King
Xerxes that the eunuchs have taken to
her."
16Then Memucan replied in the presence of the king and the nobles, "Queen
Vashti has done wrong, not only against
the king but also against all the nobles
and the peoples of all the provinces of
King Xerxes. 17For the queen's conduct
will become known to all the women,
and so they will despise their husbands
and say, 'King Xerxes commanded Queen
Vashti to be brought before him, but she
would not come.' 18This very day the
Persian and Median women of the nobility who have heard about the queen's
conduct will respond to all the king's
nobles in the same way. There will be
no end of disrespect and discord.[i]
19"Therefore, if it pleases the king,[j]
let him issue a royal decree and let it be
written in the laws of Persia and Media,
which cannot be repealed,[k] that Vashti
is never again to enter the presence of
King Xerxes. Also let the king give her
royal position to someone else who is
better than she. 20Then when the king's
edict is proclaimed throughout all his
vast realm, all the women will respect
their husbands, from the least to the
greatest."
21The king and his nobles were pleased
with this advice, so the king did as Memucan proposed. 22He sent dispatches to
all parts of the kingdom, to each province in its own script and to each people
in its own language,[l] proclaiming in each
people's tongue that every man should
be ruler over his own household.

Xerxes chooses Esther as queen.

2 Later when the anger of King Xerxes had subsided,[m] he remembered
Vashti and what she had done and what
he had decreed about her. 2Then the
king's personal attendants proposed, "Let
a search be made for beautiful young
virgins for the king. 3Let the king appoint
commissioners in every province of his
realm to bring all these beautiful girls
into the harem at the citadel of Susa. Let
them be placed under the care of Hegai,
the king's eunuch, who is in charge of
the women; and let beauty treatments be
given to them. 4Then let the girl who
pleases the king be queen instead of
Vashti." This advice appealed to the king,
and he followed it.
5Now there was in the citadel of Susa
a Jew of the tribe of Benjamin, named
Mordecai son of Jair, the son of Shimei,
the son of Kish,[n] 6who had been carried
into exile from Jerusalem by Nebuchadnezzar king of Babylon, among those
taken captive with Jehoiachin[c][o] king of
Judah.[p] 7Mordecai had a cousin named
Hadassah, whom he had brought up because she had neither father nor mother.
This girl, who was also known as Esther,[q] was lovely[r] in form and features,
and Mordecai had taken her as his own
daughter when her father and mother
died.
8When the king's order and edict
had been proclaimed, many girls were
brought to the citadel of Susa[s] and put
under the care of Hegai. Esther also was
taken to the king's palace and entrusted

1:10 [a]Jdg 16:25; Ru 3:7 [b]Ge 14:18; Est 3:15; 5:6; 7:2; Pr 31:4-7; Da 5:1-4 [c]Est 7:9
1:11 [d]SS 2:4 [e]Ps 45:11; Eze 16:14
1:12 [f]Ge 39:19; Est 2:21; 7:7; Pr 19:12
1:13 [g]1Ch 12:32; Jer 10:7; Da 2:12
1:14 [h]2Ki 25:19; Ezr 7:14
1:18 [i]Pr 19:13; 27:15
1:19 [j]Ecc 8:4 [k]Est 8:8; Da 6:8,12
1:22 [l]Ne 13:24; Est 8:9; Eph 5:22-24; 1Ti 2:12
2:1 [m]Est 1:19-20; 7:10
2:5 [n]1Sa 9:1; Est 3:2
2:6 [o]2Ki 24:6,15; 2Ch 36:10,20 [p]Da 1:1-5; 5:13
2:7 [q]Ge 41:45 [r]Ge 39:6
2:8 [s]ver 3,15; Ne 1:1; Est 1:2; Da 8:2

c6 Hebrew *Jeconiah,* a variant of *Jehoiachin*

to Hegai, who had charge of the harem.
[9]The girl pleased him and won his favor.[a] Immediately he provided her with
her beauty treatments and special food.[b]
He assigned to her seven maids selected from the king's palace and moved
her and her maids into the best place
in the harem.
[10]Esther had not revealed her nationality and family background, because
Mordecai had forbidden her to do so.[c]
[11]Every day he walked back and forth
near the courtyard of the harem to find
out how Esther was and what was happening to her.
[12]Before a girl's turn came to go in to
King Xerxes, she had to complete twelve
months of beauty treatments prescribed
for the women, six months with oil of
myrrh and six with perfumes[d] and cos-
metics. [13]And this is how she would go
to the king: Anything she wanted was
given her to take with her from the harem to the king's palace. [14]In the evening
she would go there and in the morning
return to another part of the harem to the
care of Shaashgaz, the king's eunuch who
was in charge of the concubines.[e] She
would not return to the king unless he
was pleased with her and summoned
her by name.[f]
[15]When the turn came for Esther
(the girl Mordecai had adopted, the
daughter of his uncle Abihail[g]) to go
to the king,[h] she asked for nothing other than what Hegai, the king's eunuch
who was in charge of the harem, suggested. And Esther won the favor[i] of
everyone who saw her. [16]She was tak-
en to King Xerxes in the royal residence in the tenth month, the month
of Tebeth, in the seventh year of his
reign.
[17]Now the king was attracted to
Esther more than to any of the other
women, and she won his favor and approval more than any of the other virgins. So he set a royal crown on her
head and made her queen[j] instead of
Vashti. [18]And the king gave a great
banquet,[k] Esther's banquet, for all his
nobles and officials.[l] He proclaimed a
holiday throughout the provinces and
distributed gifts with royal liberality.[m]

Mordecai uncovers a conspiracy.

[19]When the virgins were assembled a
second time, Mordecai was sitting at the
king's gate.[n] [20]But Esther had kept secret
her family background and nationality
just as Mordecai had told her to do, for
she continued to follow Mordecai's instructions as she had done when he
was bringing her up.[o]
[21]During the time Mordecai was sitting
at the king's gate, Bigthana[d] and Teresh,
two of the king's officers[p] who guarded
the doorway, became angry[q] and conspired to assassinate King Xerxes. [22]But
Mordecai found out about the plot and
told Queen Esther, who in turn reported
it to the king, giving credit to Mordecai.
[23]And when the report was investigated
and found to be true, the two officials
were hanged[r] on a gallows.[e] All this was
recorded in the book of the annals[s] in the
presence of the king.

Haman plots to have all Jews killed.

3 After these events, King Xerxes
honored Haman son of Hamme-
datha, the Agagite,[t] elevating him and
giving him a seat of honor higher than
that of all the other nobles. [2]All the royal
officials at the king's gate knelt down
and paid honor to Haman, for the king
had commanded this concerning him.
But Mordecai would not kneel down or
pay him honor.
[3]Then the royal officials at the king's
gate asked Mordecai, "Why do you disobey the king's command?"[u] [4]Day after
day they spoke to him but he refused
to comply.[v] Therefore they told Haman
about it to see whether Mordecai's
behavior would be tolerated, for he
had told them he was a Jew.
[5]When Haman saw that Mordecai
would not kneel down or pay him honor,

2:9 [a]Ge 39:21 [b]ver 3,12; Ge 37:3; 1Sa 9:22-24; 2Ki 25:30; Eze 16:9-13; Da 1:5
2:10 [c]ver 20
2:12 [d]Pr 27:9; SS 1:3; Isa 3:24
2:14 [e]1Ki 11:3; SS 6:8; Da 5:2 [f]Est 4:11
2:15 [g]Est 9:29 [h]Ps 45:14 [i]Ge 18:3; 30:27; Est 5:8
2:17 [j]Est 1:11; Eze 16:9-13
2:18 [k]1Ki 3:15; Est 1:3 [l]Ge 40:20 [m]Est 1:7
2:19 [n]ver 21; Est 3:2; 4:2; 5:13
2:20 [o]ver 10
2:21 [p]Ge 40:2; Est 6:2 [q]Est 1:12; 3:5; 5:9; 7:7
2:23 [r]Ge 40:19; Ps 7:14-16; Pr 26:27 [s]Est 6:1; 10:2
3:1 [t]ver 10; Ex 17:8-16; Nu 24:7; Dt 25:17-19; 1Sa 14:48; Est 5:11
3:3 [u]Est 5:9; Da 3:12
3:4 [v]Ge 39:10

d21 Hebrew *Bigthan,* a variant of *Bigthana* e23 Or *were hung* (or *impaled*) *on poles*; similarly elsewhere in Esther

he was enraged.[a] 6 Yet having learned who Mordecai's people were, he scorned the idea of killing only Mordecai. Instead Haman looked for a way[b] to destroy[c] all Mordecai's people, the Jews,[d] throughout the whole kingdom of Xerxes.

7 In the twelfth year of King Xerxes, in the first month, the month of Nisan, they cast the *pur*[e] (that is, the lot[f]) in the presence of Haman to select a day and month. And the lot fell on[f] the twelfth month, the month of Adar.[g]

8 Then Haman said to King Xerxes, "There is a certain people dispersed and scattered among the peoples in all the provinces of your kingdom whose customs[h] are different from those of all other people and who do not obey[i] the king's laws; it is not in the king's best interest to tolerate them.[j] 9 If it pleases the king, let a decree be issued to destroy them, and I will put ten thousand talents[g] of silver into the royal treasury for the men who carry out this business."[k]

10 So the king took his signet ring[l] from his finger and gave it to Haman son of Hammedatha, the Agagite, the enemy of the Jews. 11 "Keep the money," the king said to Haman, "and do with the people as you please."

12 Then on the thirteenth day of the first month the royal secretaries were summoned. They wrote out in the script of each province and in the language[m] of each people all Haman's orders to the king's satraps, the governors of the various provinces and the nobles of the various peoples. These were written in the name of King Xerxes himself and sealed[n] with his own ring. 13 Dispatches were sent by couriers to all the king's provinces with the order to destroy, kill and annihilate all the Jews[o]—young and old, women and little children—on a single day, the thirteenth day of the twelfth month, the month of Adar,[p] and to plunder[q] their goods. 14 A copy of the text of the edict was to be issued as law in every province and made known to the people of every nationality so they would be ready for that day.[r]

15 Spurred on by the king's command, the couriers went out, and the edict was issued in the citadel of Susa.[s] The king and Haman sat down to drink,[t] but the city of Susa was bewildered.[u]

Mordecai persuades Esther to help the Jews.

4 When Mordecai learned of all that had been done, he tore his clothes,[v] put on sackcloth and ashes,[w] and went out into the city, wailing[x] loudly and bitterly. 2 But he went only as far as the king's gate,[y] because no one clothed in sackcloth was allowed to enter it. 3 In every province to which the edict and order of the king came, there was great mourning among the Jews, with fasting, weeping and wailing. Many lay in sackcloth and ashes.

4 When Esther's maids and eunuchs came and told her about Mordecai, she was in great distress. She sent clothes for him to put on instead of his sackcloth, but he would not accept them. 5 Then Esther summoned Hathach, one of the king's eunuchs assigned to attend her, and ordered him to find out what was troubling Mordecai and why.

6 So Hathach went out to Mordecai in the open square of the city in front of the king's gate. 7 Mordecai told him everything that had happened to him, including the exact amount of money Haman had promised to pay into the royal treasury for the destruction of the Jews.[z] 8 He also gave him a copy of the text of the edict for their annihilation, which had been published in Susa, to show to Esther and explain it to her, and he told him to urge her to go into the king's presence to beg for mercy and plead with him for her people.

9 Hathach went back and reported to Esther what Mordecai had said. 10 Then she instructed him to say to Mordecai, 11 "All the king's officials and the people of the royal provinces know that for any man or woman who approaches the king

3:5 [a]Est 2:21; 5:9
3:6 [b]Pr 16:25 [c]Ps 74:8; 83:4 [d]Est 9:24
3:7 [e]Est 9:24,26 [f]Lev 16:8; 1Sa 10:21 [g]ver 13; Ezr 6:15; Est 9:19
3:8 [h]Ac 16:20-21 [i]Jer 29:7; Da 6:13 [j]Ezr 4:15
3:9 [k]Est 7:4
3:10 [l]Ge 41:42; Est 7:6; 8:2
3:12 [m]Ne 13:24 [n]Ge 38:18; 1Ki 21:8; Est 8:8-10
3:13 [o]1Sa 15:3; Ezr 4:6; Est 8:10-14 [p]ver 7 [q]Est 8:11; 9:10
3:14 [r]Est 8:8; 9:1
3:15 [s]Est 8:14 [t]Est 1:10 [u]Est 8:15
4:1 [v]Nu 14:6 [w]2Sa 13:19; Eze 27:30-31; Jnh 3:5-6 [x]Ex 11:6; Ps 30:11
4:2 [y]Est 2:19
4:7 [z]Est 3:9; 7:4

[f]7 Septuagint; Hebrew does not have *And the lot fell on.* [g]9 That is, about 375 tons (about 345 metric tons)

in the inner court without being summoned[a] the king has but one law:[b] that
he be put to death. The only exception
to this is for the king to extend the gold
scepter[c] to him and spare his life. But
thirty days have passed since I was called
to go to the king."
12When Esther's words were reported
to Mordecai, 13he sent back this answer:
"Do not think that because you are in
the king's house you alone of all the Jews
will escape. 14For if you remain silent[d] at
this time, relief[e] and deliverance[f] for the
Jews will arise from another place, but
you and your father's family will perish.
And who knows but that you have come
to royal position for such a time as this?"[g]
15Then Esther sent this reply to Mordecai: 16"Go, gather together all the Jews
who are in Susa, and fast[h] for me. Do
not eat or drink for three days, night
or day. I and my maids will fast as you
do. When this is done, I will go to the
king, even though it is against the law.
And if I perish, I perish."[i]
17So Mordecai went away and carried
out all of Esther's instructions.

The king and Haman come to Esther's banquet.

5 On the third day Esther put on her
royal robes[j] and stood in the inner
court of the palace, in front of the king's[k]
hall. The king was sitting on his royal
throne in the hall, facing the entrance.
2When he saw Queen Esther standing in
the court, he was pleased with her and
held out to her the gold scepter that
was in his hand. So Esther approached
and touched the tip of the scepter.[l]
3Then the king asked, "What is it,
Queen Esther? What is your request?
Even up to half the kingdom,[m] it will be
given you."
4"If it pleases the king," replied Esther, "let the king, together with Haman, come today to a banquet I have
prepared for him."
5"Bring Haman at once," the king said,
"so that we may do what Esther asks."
So the king and Haman went to the
banquet Esther had prepared. 6As they
were drinking wine,[n] the king again
asked Esther, "Now what is your petition? It will be given you. And what is
your request? Even up to half the kingdom,[o] it will be granted."[p]
7Esther replied, "My petition and my
request is this: 8If the king regards me
with favor[q] and if it pleases the king to
grant my petition and fulfill my request,
let the king and Haman come tomorrow
to the banquet[r] I will prepare for them.
Then I will answer the king's question."

Gallows are built to hang Mordecai.

9Haman went out that day happy and
in high spirits. But when he saw Mordecai at the king's gate and observed that
he neither rose nor showed fear in his
presence, he was filled with rage[s] against
Mordecai.[t] 10Nevertheless, Haman restrained himself and went home.
Calling together his friends and Zeresh,[u] his wife, 11Haman boasted[v] to
them about his vast wealth, his many
sons,[w] and all the ways the king had
honored him and how he had elevated
him above the other nobles and officials.
12"And that's not all," Haman added.
"I'm the only person[x] Queen Esther
invited to accompany the king to the
banquet she gave. And she has invited
me along with the king tomorrow.
13But all this gives me no satisfaction
as long as I see that Jew Mordecai sitting
at the king's gate.[y]"
14His wife Zeresh and all his friends
said to him, "Have a gallows built, seventy-five feet[h] high,[z] and ask the king
in the morning to have Mordecai
hanged[a] on it. Then go with the king
to the dinner and be happy." This sug-
gestion delighted Haman, and he had
the gallows built.

Haman unintentionally honors Mordecai.

6 That night the king could not
sleep;[b] so he ordered the book of the

4:11 [a]Est 2:14 [b]Da 2:9 [c]Est 5:1,2; 8:4
4:14 [d]Ecc 3:7; Isa 62:1; Am 5:13 [e]Est 9:16,22 [f]Ge 45:7; Dt 28:29 [g]Ge 50:20
4:16 [h]2Ch 20:3; Est 9:31 [i]Ge 43:14
5:1 [j]Est 4:16; Eze 16:13 [k]Est 6:4; Pr 21:1
5:2 [l]Est 4:11; 8:4; Pr 21:1
5:3 [m]Est 7:2; Da 5:16; Mk 6:23
5:6 [n]Est 1:10 [o]Mk 6:23 [p]Est 7:2; 9:12
5:8 [q]Est 2:15; 7:3; 8:5 [r]1Ki 3:15; Est 6:14
5:9 [s]Est 2:21; Pr 14:17 [t]Est 3:3,5
5:10 [u]Est 6:13
5:11 [v]Pr 13:16 [w]Est 9:7-10,13
5:12 [x]Job 22:29; Pr 16:18; 29:23
5:13 [y]Est 2:19
5:14 [z]Est 7:9 [a]Ezr 6:11; Est 6:4
6:1 [b]Da 2:1; 6:18

h *14* Hebrew *fifty cubits* (about 23 meters)

chronicles,[a] the record of his reign, to be
brought in and read to him. 2It was found
recorded there that Mordecai had exposed Bigthana and Teresh, two of the
king's officers who guarded the doorway,
who had conspired to assassinate King
Xerxes.
3"What honor and recognition has
Mordecai received for this?" the king
asked.

"Nothing has been done for him,"[b]
his attendants answered.

4The king said, "Who is in the court?"
Now Haman had just entered the outer
court of the palace to speak to the king
about hanging Mordecai on the gallows
he had erected for him.

5His attendants answered, "Haman
is standing in the court."

"Bring him in," the king ordered.

6When Haman entered, the king asked
him, "What should be done for the man
the king delights to honor?"

Now Haman thought to himself, "Who
is there that the king would rather honor
than me?" 7So he answered the king,
"For the man the king delights to hon-
or, 8have them bring a royal robe[c] the
king has worn and a horse[d] the king
has ridden, one with a royal crest placed
on its head. 9Then let the robe and horse
be entrusted to one of the king's most
noble princes. Let them robe the man
the king delights to honor, and lead him
on the horse through the city streets,
proclaiming before him, 'This is what
is done for the man the king delights
to honor![e]'"

10"Go at once," the king commanded Haman. "Get the robe and the horse
and do just as you have suggested for
Mordecai the Jew, who sits at the king's
gate. Do not neglect anything you have
recommended."

11So Haman got[f] the robe and the
horse. He robed Mordecai, and led him
on horseback through the city streets,
proclaiming before him, "This is what
is done for the man the king delights
to honor!"

12Afterward Mordecai returned to
the king's gate. But Haman rushed home,
with his head covered[g] in grief, 13and
told Zeresh[h] his wife and all his friends
everything that had happened to him.

His advisers and his wife Zeresh said
to him, "Since Mordecai, before whom
your downfall[i] has started, is of Jewish
origin, you cannot stand against him—
you will surely come to ruin!" 14While
they were still talking with him, the
king's eunuchs arrived and hurried Haman away to the banquet[j] Esther had
prepared.

Haman is hanged instead of Mordecai.

7 So the king and Haman went to
dine[k] with Queen Esther, 2and as
they were drinking wine[l] on that second
day, the king again asked, "Queen Esther,
what is your petition? It will be given
you. What is your request? Even up to
half the kingdom,[m] it will be granted.[n]"
3Then Queen Esther answered, "If I
have found favor[o] with you, O king,
and if it pleases your majesty, grant me
my life—this is my petition. And spare
my people—this is my request. 4For I
and my people have been sold for destruction and slaughter and annihilation.[p] If we had merely been sold as
male and female slaves, I would have
kept quiet, because no such distress
would justify disturbing the king.[i]"

5King Xerxes asked Queen Esther,
"Who is he? Where is the man who has
dared to do such a thing?"

6Esther said, "The adversary and enemy is this vile Haman."

Then Haman was terrified before the
king and queen. 7The king got up in a
rage,[q] left his wine and went out into
the palace garden.[r] But Haman, realizing
that the king had already decided his
fate,[s] stayed behind to beg Queen Esther
for his life.

8Just as the king returned from the
palace garden to the banquet hall, Haman
was falling on the couch[t] where Esther
was reclining.[u]

6:1 [a]Est 2:23; 10:2
6:3 [b]Ecc 9:13-16
6:8 [c]Ge 41:42; Isa 52:1 [d]1Ki 1:33
6:9 [e]Ge 41:43
6:11 [f]Ge 41:42
6:12 [g]2Sa 15:30; Jer 14:3,4; Mic 3:7
6:13 [h]Est 5:10 [i]Ps 57:6; Pr 26:27; 28:18
6:14 [j]1Ki 3:15; Est 5:8
7:1 [k]Ge 40:20-22; Mt 22:1-14
7:2 [l]Est 1:10 [m]Est 5:3 [n]Est 9:12
7:3 [o]Est 2:15
7:4 [p]Est 3:9
7:7 [q]Ge 34:7; Est 1:12; Pr 19:12; 20:1-2 [r]2Ki 21:18 [s]Est 6:13
7:8 [t]Est 1:6 [u]Ge 39:14

i4 Or *quiet, but the compensation our adversary offers cannot be compared with the loss the king would suffer*

The king exclaimed, "Will he even molest the queen while she is with me in
the house?"[a]
As soon as the word left the king's
mouth, they covered Haman's face.[b]
9Then Harbona,[c] one of the eunuchs attending the king, said, "A gallows seventy-five feet[j] high[d] stands by Haman's
house. He had it made for Mordecai, who
spoke up to help the king."
The king said, "Hang him on it!"[e] 10So
they hanged Haman[f] on the gallows[g]
he had prepared for Mordecai.[h] Then the
king's fury subsided.[i]

The Jews' right to protect themselves.

8 That same day King Xerxes gave
Queen Esther the estate of Haman,[j]
the enemy of the Jews. And Mordecai
came into the presence of the king, for
Esther had told how he was related to
her. 2The king took off his signet ring,[k]
which he had reclaimed from Haman,
and presented it to Mordecai. And Esther
appointed him over Haman's estate.[l]
3Esther again pleaded with the king,
falling at his feet and weeping. She
begged him to put an end to the evil
plan of Haman the Agagite, which he had
devised against the Jews. 4Then the king
extended the gold scepter[m] to Esther and
she arose and stood before him.
5"If it pleases the king," she said, "and
if he regards me with favor and thinks it
the right thing to do, and if he is pleased
with me, let an order be written over-
ruling the dispatches that Haman son
of Hammedatha, the Agagite, devised
and wrote to destroy the Jews in all the
king's provinces. 6For how can I bear
to see disaster fall on my people? How
can I bear to see the destruction of my
family?"[n]
7King Xerxes replied to Queen Esther
and to Mordecai the Jew, "Because Haman attacked the Jews, I have given his
estate to Esther, and they have hanged
him on the gallows. 8Now write another decree[o] in the king's name in behalf
of the Jews as seems best to you, and seal
it with the king's signet ring[p]—for no
document written in the king's name and
sealed with his ring can be revoked."[q]
9At once the royal secretaries were
summoned—on the twenty-third day of
the third month, the month of Sivan.
They wrote out all Mordecai's orders to
the Jews, and to the satraps, governors
and nobles of the 127 provinces stretching from India to Cush.[k][r] These orders
were written in the script of each province and the language of each people
and also to the Jews in their own script
and language.[s] 10Mordecai wrote in the
name of King Xerxes, sealed the dispatches with the king's signet ring, and sent
them by mounted couriers, who rode
fast horses especially bred for the king.
11The king's edict granted the Jews
in every city the right to assemble and
protect themselves; to destroy, kill and
annihilate any armed force of any nationality or province that might attack them
and their women and children; and to
plunder[t] the property of their enemies.
12The day appointed for the Jews to do
this in all the provinces of King Xerxes
was the thirteenth day of the twelfth
month, the month of Adar.[u] 13A copy
of the text of the edict was to be issued
as law in every province and made
known to the people of every nationality so that the Jews would be ready on
that day[v] to avenge themselves on their
enemies.
14The couriers, riding the royal horses,
raced out, spurred on by the king's command. And the edict was also issued in
the citadel of Susa.
15Mordecai[w] left the king's presence
wearing royal garments of blue and
white, a large crown of gold and a purple robe of fine linen.[x] And the city of
Susa held a joyous celebration.[y] 16For
the Jews it was a time of happiness
and joy,[z] gladness and honor.[a] 17In
every province and in every city, wherever the edict of the king went, there
was joy[b] and gladness among the Jews,
with feasting and celebrating. And many
people of other nationalities became

7:8 [a]Ge 34:7 [b]Est 6:12
7:9 [c]Est 1:10 [d]Est 5:14 [e]Ps 7:14-16; 9:16; Pr 11:5-6; 26:27; Mt 7:2
7:10 [f]Pr 10:28 [g]Est 9:25 [h]Da 6:24 [i]Est 2:1
8:1 [j]Est 2:7; 7:6; Pr 22:22-23
8:2 [k]Ge 41:42; Est 3:10 [l]Pr 13:22; Da 2:48
8:4 [m]Est 4:11; 5:2
8:6 [n]Est 7:4; 9:1
8:8 [o]Est 3:12-14 [p]Ge 41:42 [q]Est 1:19; Da 6:15
8:9 [r]Est 1:1 [s]Est 1:22
8:11 [t]Est 9:10, 15,16
8:12 [u]Est 3:13; 9:1
8:13 [v]Est 3:14
8:15 [w]Est 9:4 [x]Ge 41:42 [y]Est 3:15
8:16 [z]Ps 97:10-12 [a]Ps 112:4
8:17 [b]Est 9:19,27; Ps 35:27; Pr 11:10

j9 Hebrew *fifty cubits* (about 23 meters) k9 That is, the upper Nile region

Jews because fear[a] of the Jews had seized
them.[b]

Triumph of Jews over their enemies.

9 On the thirteenth day of the twelfth
month, the month of Adar,[c] the edict
commanded by the king was to be carried out. On this day the enemies of the
Jews had hoped to overpower them,
but now the tables were turned and the
Jews got the upper hand[d] over those who
hated them.[e] 2The Jews assembled in
their cities[f] in all the provinces of King
Xerxes to attack those seeking their destruction. No one could stand against
them,[g] because the people of all the other
nationalities were afraid of them. 3And
all the nobles of the provinces, the satraps, the governors and the king's administrators helped the Jews,[h] because
fear of Mordecai had seized them. 4Mor-
decai was prominent[i] in the palace; his
reputation spread throughout the provinces, and he became more and more
powerful.[j]
5The Jews struck down all their enemies with the sword, killing and destroying them,[k] and they did what they
pleased to those who hated them. 6In
the citadel of Susa, the Jews killed and
destroyed five hundred men. 7They also
killed Parshandatha, Dalphon, Aspatha,
8Poratha, Adalia, Aridatha, 9Parmashta,
Arisai, Aridai and Vaizatha, 10the ten
sons[l] of Haman son of Hammedatha,
the enemy of the Jews. But they did not
lay their hands on the plunder.[m]
11The number of those slain in the
citadel of Susa was reported to the
king that same day. 12The king said to
Queen Esther, "The Jews have killed
and destroyed five hundred men and
the ten sons of Haman in the citadel of
Susa. What have they done in the rest
of the king's provinces? Now what is
your petition? It will be given you.
What is your request? It will also be
granted."[n]
13"If it pleases the king," Esther answered, "give the Jews in Susa permission to carry out this day's edict
tomorrow also, and let Haman's ten
sons[o] be hanged[p] on gallows."
14So the king commanded that this be
done. An edict was issued in Susa, and
they hanged[q] the ten sons of Haman.
15The Jews in Susa came together on the
fourteenth day of the month of Adar,
and they put to death in Susa three hundred men, but they did not lay their
hands on the plunder.[r]
16Meanwhile, the remainder of the
Jews who were in the king's provinces
also assembled to protect themselves
and get relief[s] from their enemies.[t] They
killed seventy-five thousand of them[u]
but did not lay their hands on the plunder. 17This happened on the thirteenth
day of the month of Adar, and on the
fourteenth they rested and made it a
day of feasting[v] and joy.

Feast of Purim.

18The Jews in Susa, however, had assembled on the thirteenth and fourteenth, and then on the fifteenth they
rested and made it a day of feasting and
joy.
19That is why rural Jews—those living in villages—observe the fourteenth
of the month of Adar[w] as a day of joy
and feasting, a day for giving presents
to each other.[x]
20Mordecai recorded these events, and
he sent letters to all the Jews throughout the provinces of King Xerxes, near
and far, 21to have them celebrate annu-
ally the fourteenth and fifteenth days
of the month of Adar 22as the time when
the Jews got relief[y] from their enemies,
and as the month when their sorrow was
turned into joy and their mourning into
a day of celebration.[z] He wrote them to
observe the days as days of feasting and
joy and giving presents of food[a] to one
another and gifts to the poor.
23So the Jews agreed to continue the
celebration they had begun, doing what
Mordecai had written to them. 24For
Haman son of Hammedatha, the Agagite,[b] the enemy of all the Jews, had plotted against the Jews to destroy them

8:17 [a]Ex 15:14,16; Dt 11:25 [b]Est 9:3
9:1 [c]Est 8:12 [d]Jer 29:4-7 [e]Est 3:12-14; Pr 22:22-23
9:2 [f]ver 15-18 [g]Est 8:11,17; Ps 71:13,24
9:3 [h]Ezr 8:36
9:4 [i]Ex 11:3 [j]2Sa 3:1; 1Ch 11:9
9:5 [k]Ezr 4:6
9:10 [l]Est 5:11 [m]Ge 14:23; 1Sa 14:32; Est 3:13; 8:11
9:12 [n]Est 5:6; 7:2
9:13 [o]Est 5:11 [p]Dt 21:22-23
9:14 [q]Ezr 6:11
9:15 [r]Ge 14:23; Est 8:11
9:16 [s]Est 4:14 [t]Dt 25:19 [u]1Ch 4:43
9:17 [v]1Ki 3:15
9:19 [w]Est 3:7 [x]ver 22; Dt 16:11,14; Ne 8:10,12; Est 2:9; Rev 11:10
9:22 [y]Est 4:14 [z]Ne 8:12; Ps 30:11-12 [a]2Ki 25:30
9:24 [b]Ex 17:8-16

and had cast the *pur*[a] (that is, the lot[b])
for their ruin and destruction. 25But when
the plot came to the king's attention,[l]
he issued written orders that the evil
scheme Haman had devised against the
Jews should come back onto his own
head,[c] and that he and his sons should be
hanged[d] on the gallows.[e] 26(Therefore
these days were called Purim, from the
word *pur*.[f]) Because of everything written in this letter and because of what
they had seen and what had happened
to them, 27the Jews took it upon themselves to establish the custom that they
and their descendants and all who join
them should without fail observe these
two days every year, in the way prescribed and at the time appointed.
28These days should be remembered
and observed in every generation by
every family, and in every province and
in every city. And these days of Purim
should never cease to be celebrated by
the Jews, nor should the memory of
them die out among their descendants.
29So Queen Esther, daughter of Abihail,[g] along with Mordecai the Jew,
wrote with full authority to confirm this
second letter concerning Purim. 30And
Mordecai sent letters to all the Jews in
the 127 provinces[h] of the kingdom of
Xerxes—words of goodwill and assurance— 31to establish these days of Purim
at their designated times, as Mordecai
the Jew and Queen Esther had decreed
for them, and as they had established
for themselves and their descendants
in regard to their times of fasting[i] and
lamentation.[j] 32Esther's decree confirmed these regulations about Purim,
and it was written down in the records.

The greatness of Xerxes and Mordecai.

10 King Xerxes imposed tribute
throughout the empire, to its distant shores.[k] 2And all his acts of power
and might, together with a full account
of the greatness of Mordecai[l] to which
the king had raised him,[m] are they not
written in the book of the annals[n] of
the kings of Media and Persia? 3Mordecai
the Jew was second[o] in rank[p] to King
Xerxes,[q] preeminent among the Jews,
and held in high esteem by his many
fellow Jews, because he worked for the
good of his people and spoke up for the
welfare of all the Jews.[r]

9:24 [a]Est 3:7 [b]Lev 16:8
9:25 [c]Ps 7:16 [d]Dt 21:22-23 [e]Est 7:10
9:26 [f]ver 20; Est 3:7
9:29 [g]Est 2:15
9:30 [h]Est 1:1
9:31 [i]Est 4:16 [j]Est 4:1-3
10:1 [k]Ps 72:10; 97:1; Isa 24:15
10:2 [l]Est 8:15; 9:4 [m]Ge 41:44 [n]Est 2:23
10:3 [o]Da 5:7 [p]Ge 41:43 [q]Ge 41:40 [r]Ne 2:10; Jer 29:4-7; Da 6:3

[l]*25* Or *when Esther came before the king*

JOB

Author: Unknown. (However, suggestions include Job, Elihu, Moses and Solomon.)

Date Written: Scholars place the date of the authorship of Job anywhere from the time of Abraham to the time the Jews return from their Babylonian exile.

Time Span: Not specified.

Title: From the book's chief character: Job.

Background: As the book of Job begins, Job is one of the wealthiest and most prosperous men on the face of the earth. He fears God and lives an upright life during the ancient patriarchal period in the land of Uz (region of northern Arabia).

Where Written: Unknown (possibly the Palestinian area).

To Whom: To no specific people.

Content: Why do the righteous suffer? This is the question raised after Job loses his family, his wealth and his health. Job's 3 friends—Eliphaz, Bildad and Zophar—come to comfort him and to discuss his crushing series of tragedies. They insist his suffering is punishment for sin in his life. Job, though, remains devoted to God through all of this and contends that his life has not been one of sin. A fourth man, Elihu, tells Job he needs to humble himself and submit to God's use of trials to purify his life. Finally, Job questions God himself and learns valuable lessons about the sovereignty of God and his need to totally trust in the Lord. Job is then restored to health, happiness and prosperity...even beyond his earlier state.

Key Words: "Trouble"; "Suffering"; "Comfort." To live a life of faith requires perseverance. Despite torment and "trouble," Job was steadfast in his belief in God, for as he told his wife, "Shall we accept good from God, and not trouble?" (2:10). Christians today are not exempt from broken hearts or "suffering," but through it all we, like Job, can rest in the fact that God is fair, omnipotent, omniscient and sovereign. He will "comfort" us if we will turn to him.

Themes: • Satan cannot bring financial and physical destruction upon us unless it is God's permissive will, and God will set the limits. • It is beyond our human ability to understand the "why's" behind all the suffering in the world. • Rest assured...the wicked will receive their just dues. • We cannot blame all suffering on the sin in a sufferer's life. • Suffering may sometimes be allowed in our lives to purify, to test, to teach or to strengthen the soul by showing us that when we have lost all, and only God remains...God remains enough. • God deserves and requests our love and praise regardless of our lot in life. • God will deliver all suffering believers either in this life or in that which is to come.

Outline:

1. Job's background and assaults from Satan. 1:1-2:13
2. Job's debates with his 3 friends. 3:1-31:40
3. Elihu's speaking out for God's fairness. 32:1-37:24
4. God's intervention. 38:1-41:34
5. Job's restoration. 42:1-42:17

JOB

The LORD allows Satan to test Job.

1 In the land of Uz[a] there lived a man whose name was Job.[b] This man was blameless[c] and upright; he feared God[d] and shunned evil. 2He had seven sons and three daughters,[e] 3and he owned seven thousand sheep, three thousand camels, five hundred yoke of oxen and five hundred donkeys, and had a large number of servants. He was the greatest man[f] among all the people of the East.

4His sons used to take turns holding feasts in their homes, and they would invite their three sisters to eat and drink with them. 5When a period of feasting had run its course, Job would send and have them purified. Early in the morning he would sacrifice a burnt offering[g] for each of them, thinking, "Perhaps my children have sinned[h] and cursed God[i] in their hearts." This was Job's regular custom.

6One day the angels[a][j] came to present themselves before the LORD, and Satan[b] also came with them.[k] 7The LORD said to Satan, "Where have you come from?"

Satan answered the LORD, "From roaming through the earth and going back and forth in it."[l]

8Then the LORD said to Satan, "Have you considered my servant Job?[m] There is no one on earth like him; he is blameless and upright, a man who fears God and shuns evil."[n]

9"Does Job fear God for nothing?"[o] Satan replied. 10"Have you not put a hedge around him and his household and everything he has?[p] You have blessed the work of his hands, so that his flocks and herds are spread throughout the land.[q] 11But stretch out your hand and strike everything he has,[r] and he will surely curse you to your face."[s]

12The LORD said to Satan, "Very well, then, everything he has is in your hands, but on the man himself do not lay a finger."

Then Satan went out from the presence of the LORD.

13One day when Job's sons and daughters were feasting and drinking wine at the oldest brother's house, 14a messenger came to Job and said, "The oxen were plowing and the donkeys were grazing nearby, 15and the Sabeans[t] attacked and carried them off. They put the servants to the sword, and I am the only one who has escaped to tell you!"

16While he was still speaking, another messenger came and said, "The fire of God fell from the sky[u] and burned up the sheep and the servants,[v] and I am the only one who has escaped to tell you!"

17While he was still speaking, another messenger came and said, "The Chaldeans[w] formed three raiding parties and swept down on your camels and carried them off. They put the servants to the sword, and I am the only one who has escaped to tell you!"

18While he was still speaking, yet another messenger came and said, "Your sons and daughters were feasting and drinking wine at the oldest brother's house, 19when suddenly a mighty wind[x] swept in from the desert and struck the four corners of the house. It collapsed on them and they are dead, and I am the only one who has escaped to tell you!"

20At this, Job got up and tore his robe[y] and shaved his head. Then he fell to the ground in worship[z] 21and said:

"Naked I came from my mother's
womb,
and naked I will depart.[c][a]
The LORD gave and the LORD has
taken away;[b]
may the name of the LORD be
praised."[c]

22In all this, Job did not sin by charging God with wrongdoing.[d]

Satan afflicts Job with painful sores.

2 On another day the angels[a] came to present themselves before the LORD,

1:1 [a]Jer 25:20 [b]Eze 14:14,20; Jas 5:11 [c]Ge 6:9; 17:1 [d]Ge 22:12; Ex 18:21
1:2 [e]Job 42:13
1:3 [f]Job 29:25
1:5 [g]Ge 8:20; Job 42:8 [h]Job 8:4 [i]1Ki 21:10,13
1:6 [j]Job 38:7 [k]Job 2:1
1:7 [l]1Pe 5:8
1:8 [m]Jos 1:7; Job 42:7-8 [n]ver 1
1:9 [o]1Ti 6:5
1:10 [p]Ps 34:7 [q]ver 3; Job 29:6; 31:25; Ps 128:1-2
1:11 [r]Job 19:21 [s]Job 2:5
1:15 [t]Ge 10:7; Job 6:19
1:16 [u]Ge 19:24 [v]Lev 10:2; Nu 11:1-3
1:17 [w]Ge 11:28,31
1:19 [x]Jer 4:11; 13:24
1:20 [y]Ge 37:29 [z]1Pe 5:6
1:21 [a]Ecc 5:15; 1Ti 6:7 [b]1Sa 2:7 [c]Job 2:10; Eph 5:20; 1Th 5:18
1:22 [d]Job 2:10

[a]*6,1* Hebrew *the sons of God* [b]*6* *Satan* means *accuser.* [c]*21* Or *will return there*

and Satan also came with them[a] to present himself before him. 2And the LORD
said to Satan, "Where have you come
from?"

Satan answered the LORD, "From roaming through the earth and going back and
forth in it."

3Then the LORD said to Satan, "Have
you considered my servant Job? There is
no one on earth like him; he is blameless
and upright, a man who fears God and
shuns evil.[b] And he still maintains his
integrity,[c] though you incited me against
him to ruin him without any reason."[d]

4"Skin for skin!" Satan replied. "A man
will give all he has for his own life. 5But
stretch out your hand and strike his flesh
and bones,[e] and he will surely curse you
to your face."[f]

6The LORD said to Satan, "Very well,
then, he is in your hands; but you must
spare his life."[g]

7So Satan went out from the presence
of the LORD and afflicted Job with painful
sores from the soles of his feet to the top
of his head.[h] 8Then Job took a piece of
broken pottery and scraped himself with
it as he sat among the ashes.[i]

9His wife said to him, "Are you still
holding on to your integrity? Curse God
and die!"

10He replied, "You are talking like a
foolish[d] woman. Shall we accept good
from God, and not trouble?"[j]

In all this, Job did not sin in what he
said.[k]

Job's three friends come to comfort him.

11When Job's three friends, Eliphaz the
Temanite,[l] Bildad the Shuhite[m] and Zophar the Naamathite, heard about all the
troubles that had come upon him, they
set out from their homes and met together by agreement to go and sympathize with him and comfort him.[n]
12When they saw him from a distance,
they could hardly recognize him; they began to weep aloud, and they tore their
robes and sprinkled dust on their heads.[o]
13Then they sat on the ground with him
for seven days and seven nights.[p] No one
said a word to him, because they saw
how great his suffering was.

Job: The day of his birth is cursed.

3 After this, Job opened his mouth and
cursed the day of his birth. 2He said:

3"May the day of my birth perish,
and the night it was said, 'A boy is
born!'[q]
4That day—may it turn to darkness;
may God above not care about it;
may no light shine upon it.
5May darkness and deep shadow[e][r]
claim it once more;
may a cloud settle over it;
may blackness overwhelm its light.
6That night—may thick darkness[s]
seize it;
may it not be included among the
days of the year
nor be entered in any of the
months.
7May that night be barren;
may no shout of joy be heard in it.
8May those who curse days[f] curse
that day,
those who are ready to rouse
Leviathan.[t]
9May its morning stars become dark;
may it wait for daylight in vain
and not see the first rays of dawn,[u]
10for it did not shut the doors of the
womb on me
to hide trouble from my eyes.

11"Why did I not perish at birth,
and die as I came from the womb?[v]
12Why were there knees to receive
me[w]
and breasts that I might be nursed?
13For now I would be lying down[x] in
peace;
I would be asleep and at rest[y]
14with kings and counselors of the
earth,[z]
who built for themselves places
now lying in ruins,[a]

2:1 [a]Job 1:6 **2:3** [b]Job 1:1,8 [c]Job 27:6 [d]Job 9:17 **2:5** [e]Job 19:20 [f]Job 1:11 **2:6** [g]Job 1:12 **2:7** [h]Dt 28:35; Job 7:5 **2:8** [i]Job 42:6; Jer 6:26; Eze 27:30; Mt 11:21 **2:10** [j]Job 1:21 [k]Job 1:22; Ps 39:1; Jas 1:12; 5:11 **2:11** [l]Ge 36:11; Jer 49:7 [m]Ge 25:2 [n]Job 42:11; Ro 12:15 **2:12** [o]Jos 7:6; Ne 9:1; La 2:10; Eze 27:30 **2:13** [p]Ge 50:10; Eze 3:15 **3:3** [q]Job 10:18-19; Jer 20:14-18 **3:5** [r]Job 10:21,22; Ps 23:4; Jer 2:6; 13:16 **3:6** [s]Job 23:17 **3:8** [t]Job 41:1,8, 10,25 **3:9** [u]Job 41:18 **3:11** [v]Job 10:18 **3:12** [w]Ge 30:3; Isa 66:12 **3:13** [x]Job 17:13 [y]Job 7:8-10, 21; 10:22; 14:10-12; 19:27; 21:13,23 **3:14** [z]Job 12:17 [a]Job 15:28

[d] *10* The Hebrew word rendered *foolish* denotes moral deficiency. [e] *5* Or *and the shadow of death*
[f] *8* Or *the sea*

15with rulers[a] who had gold,
who filled their houses with silver.[b]
16Or why was I not hidden in the ground like a stillborn child,[c]
like an infant who never saw the light of day?
17There the wicked cease from turmoil,
and there the weary are at rest.[d]
18Captives also enjoy their ease;
they no longer hear the slave driver's shout.[e]
19The small and the great are there,
and the slave is freed from his master.

20"Why is light given to those in misery,
and life to the bitter of soul,[f]
21to those who long for death that does not come,[g]
who search for it more than for hidden treasure,[h]
22who are filled with gladness
and rejoice when they reach the grave?
23Why is life given to a man
whose way is hidden,
whom God has hedged in?[i]
24For sighing comes to me instead of food;[j]
my groans pour out like water.[k]
25What I feared has come upon me;
what I dreaded[l] has happened to me.
26I have no peace, no quietness;
I have no rest,[m] but only turmoil."

Eliphaz: God does not punish the innocent.

4 Then Eliphaz the Temanite replied:

2"If someone ventures a word with you, will you be impatient?
But who can keep from speaking?[n]
3Think how you have instructed many,
how you have strengthened feeble hands.[o]
4Your words have supported those who stumbled;
you have strengthened faltering knees.[p]
5But now trouble comes to you, and you are discouraged;
it strikes[q] you, and you are dismayed.[r]
6Should not your piety be your confidence[s]
and your blameless[t] ways your hope?

7"Consider now: Who, being innocent, has ever perished?[u]
Where were the upright ever destroyed?[v]
8As I have observed, those who plow evil[w]
and those who sow trouble reap it.[x]
9At the breath of God[y] they are destroyed;
at the blast of his anger they perish.[z]
10The lions may roar and growl,
yet the teeth of the great lions are broken.[a]
11The lion perishes for lack of prey,[b]
and the cubs of the lioness are scattered.

12"A word was secretly brought to me,
my ears caught a whisper[c] of it.[d]
13Amid disquieting dreams in the night,
when deep sleep falls on men,[e]
14fear and trembling seized me
and made all my bones shake.[f]
15A spirit glided past my face,
and the hair on my body stood on end.
16It stopped,
but I could not tell what it was.
A form stood before my eyes,
and I heard a hushed voice:
17'Can a mortal be more righteous than God?[g]
Can a man be more pure than his Maker?[h]
18If God places no trust in his servants,
if he charges his angels with error,[i]

3:15 [a]Job 12:21 [b]Job 27:17
3:16 [c]Ps 58:8; Ecc 6:3
3:17 [d]Job 17:16
3:18 [e]Job 39:7
3:20 [f]1Sa 1:10; Jer 20:18; Eze 27:30-31
3:21 [g]Rev 9:6 [h]Pr 2:4
3:23 [i]Job 19:6,8, 12; Ps 88:8; La 3:7
3:24 [j]Job 6:7; 33:20 [k]Ps 42:3,4
3:25 [l]Job 30:15
3:26 [m]Job 7:4,14
4:2 [n]Job 32:20
4:3 [o]Isa 35:3; Heb 12:12
4:4 [p]Isa 35:3; Heb 12:12
4:5 [q]Job 19:21 [r]Job 6:14
4:6 [s]Pr 3:26 [t]Job 1:1
4:7 [u]Job 36:7 [v]Job 8:20; Ps 37:25
4:8 [w]Job 15:35 [x]Pr 22:8; Hos 10:13; Gal 6:7-8
4:9 [y]Job 15:30; Isa 30:33; 2Th 2:8 [z]Job 40:13
4:10 [a]Job 5:15; Ps 58:6
4:11 [b]Job 27:14; Ps 34:10
4:12 [c]Job 26:14 [d]Job 33:14
4:13 [e]Job 33:15

4:14 [f]Jer 23:9; Hab 3:16 **4:17** [g]Job 9:2 [h]Job 35:10
4:18 [i]Job 15:15

[19]how much more those who live in
houses of clay,[a]
whose foundations[b] are in the
dust,[c]
who are crushed more readily than a
moth!
[20]Between dawn and dusk they are
broken to pieces;
unnoticed, they perish forever.[d]
[21]Are not the cords of their tent pulled
up,[e]
so that they die without wisdom?'[g][f]

Eliphaz: Job should appeal to God.

5 "Call if you will, but who will
answer you?
To which of the holy ones[g] will
you turn?
[2]Resentment kills a fool,
and envy slays the simple.[h]
[3]I myself have seen a fool taking
root,[i]
but suddenly his house was cursed.[j]
[4]His children are far from safety,[k]
crushed in court[l] without a
defender.
[5]The hungry consume his harvest,[m]
taking it even from among thorns,
and the thirsty pant after his
wealth.
[6]For hardship does not spring from
the soil,
nor does trouble sprout from the
ground.
[7]Yet man is born to trouble[n]
as surely as sparks fly upward.

[8]"But if it were I, I would appeal to
God;
I would lay my cause before him.[o]
[9]He performs wonders that cannot be
fathomed,[p]
miracles that cannot be counted.
[10]He bestows rain on the earth;
he sends water upon the
countryside.[q]
[11]The lowly he sets on high,[r]
and those who mourn are lifted to
safety.
[12]He thwarts the plans[s] of the crafty,
so that their hands achieve no
success.
[13]He catches the wise in their
craftiness,[t]
and the schemes of the wily are
swept away.
[14]Darkness[u] comes upon them in the
daytime;
at noon they grope as in the
night.[v]
[15]He saves the needy[w] from the sword
in their mouth;
he saves them from the clutches of
the powerful.[x]
[16]So the poor have hope,
and injustice shuts its mouth.[y]

[17]"Blessed is the man whom God
corrects;[z]
so do not despise the discipline[a] of
the Almighty.[h][b]
[18]For he wounds, but he also binds
up;[c]
he injures, but his hands also
heal.[d]
[19]From six calamities he will rescue
you;
in seven no harm will befall you.[e]
[20]In famine[f] he will ransom you from
death,
and in battle from the stroke of the
sword.[g]
[21]You will be protected from the lash
of the tongue,[h]
and need not fear[i] when
destruction comes.
[22]You will laugh at destruction and
famine,
and need not fear the beasts of the
earth.[j]
[23]For you will have a covenant with
the stones[k] of the field,
and the wild animals will be at
peace with you.[l]
[24]You will know that your tent is
secure;
you will take stock of your property
and find nothing missing.[m]

4:19 [a]Job 10:9 [b]Job 22:16 [c]Ge 2:7 **4:20** [d]Job 14:2,20; 20:7; Ps 90:5-6 **4:21** [e]Job 8:22 [f]Job 18:21; 36:12 **5:1** [g]Job 15:15 **5:2** [h]Pr 12:16 **5:3** [i]Ps 37:35; Jer 12:2 [j]Job 24:18 **5:4** [k]Job 4:11 [l]Am 5:12 **5:5** [m]Job 18:8-10 **5:7** [n]Job 14:1 **5:8** [o]Ps 35:23; 50:15 **5:9** [p]Job 42:3; Ps 40:5 **5:10** [q]Job 36:28 **5:11** [r]Ps 113:7-8 **5:12** [s]Ne 4:15; Ps 33:10 **5:13** [t]1Co 3:19* **5:14** [u]Job 12:25 [v]Dt 28:29 **5:15** [w]Ps 35:10 [x]Job 4:10 **5:16** [y]Ps 107:42 **5:17** [z]Jas 1:12 [a]Ps 94:12; Pr 3:11 [b]Heb 12:5-11 **5:18** [c]Isa 30:26 [d]1Sa 2:6 **5:19** [e]Ps 34:19; 91:10 **5:20** [f]Ps 33:19 [g]Ps 144:10 **5:21** [h]Ps 31:20 [i]Ps 91:5 **5:22** [j]Ps 91:13; Eze 34:25 **5:23** [k]Ps 91:12 [l]Isa 11:6-9 **5:24** [m]Job 8:6

g *21* Some interpreters end the quotation after verse 17. h *17* Hebrew *Shaddai*; here and throughout Job

[25]You will know that your children
will be many,[a]
and your descendants like the grass
of the earth.[b]
[26]You will come to the grave in full
vigor,[c]
like sheaves gathered in season.

[27]"We have examined this, and it is true.
So hear it and apply it to yourself."

Job: Defense of his integrity.

6 Then Job replied:

[2]"If only my anguish could be
weighed
and all my misery be placed on the
scales![d]
[3]It would surely outweigh the sand[e]
of the seas—
no wonder my words have been
impetuous.[f]
[4]The arrows[g] of the Almighty are in
me,[h]
my spirit drinks[i] in their poison;
God's terrors[j] are marshaled
against me.[k]
[5]Does a wild donkey bray when it has
grass,
or an ox bellow when it has
fodder?
[6]Is tasteless food eaten without salt,
or is there flavor in the white of an
egg[i]?
[7]I refuse to touch it;
such food makes me ill.[l]

[8]"Oh, that I might have my request,
that God would grant what I hope
for,[m]
[9]that God would be willing to crush
me,
to let loose his hand and cut me off![n]
[10]Then I would still have this
consolation—
my joy in unrelenting pain—
that I had not denied the words[o] of
the Holy One.[p]

[11]"What strength do I have, that I
should still hope?
What prospects, that I should be
patient?[q]
[12]Do I have the strength of stone?
Is my flesh bronze?
[13]Do I have any power to help
myself,[r]
now that success has been driven
from me?

[14]"A despairing man[s] should have the
devotion[t] of his friends,
even though he forsakes the fear of
the Almighty.
[15]But my brothers are as undependable
as intermittent streams,[u]
as the streams that overflow
[16]when darkened by thawing ice
and swollen with melting snow,
[17]but that cease to flow in the dry
season,
and in the heat[v] vanish from their
channels.
[18]Caravans turn aside from their
routes;
they go up into the wasteland and
perish.
[19]The caravans of Tema[w] look for
water,
the traveling merchants of Sheba
look in hope.
[20]They are distressed, because they
had been confident;
they arrive there, only to be
disappointed.[x]
[21]Now you too have proved to be of no
help;
you see something dreadful and are
afraid.[y]
[22]Have I ever said, 'Give something on
my behalf,
pay a ransom for me from your
wealth,
[23]deliver me from the hand of the
enemy,
ransom me from the clutches of
the ruthless'?

[24]"Teach me, and I will be quiet;[z]
show me where I have been
wrong.

5:25 [a]Ps 112:2 [b]Ps 72:16; Isa 44:3-4
5:26 [c]Ge 15:15
6:2 [d]Job 31:6
6:3 [e]Pr 27:3 [f]Job 23:2
6:4 [g]Ps 38:2 [h]Job 16:12,13 [i]Job 21:20 [j]Job 30:15 [k]Ps 88:15-18
6:7 [l]Job 3:24
6:8 [m]Job 14:13
6:9 [n]Nu 11:15; 1Ki 19:4
6:10 [o]Job 22:22; 23:12 [p]Lev 19:2; Isa 57:15
6:11 [q]Job 21:4
6:13 [r]Job 26:2
6:14 [s]Job 4:5 [t]Job 15:4
6:15 [u]Ps 38:11; Jer 15:18
6:17 [v]Job 24:19
6:19 [w]Ge 25:15; Isa 21:14
6:20 [x]Jer 14:3
6:21 [y]Ps 38:11
6:24 [z]Ps 39:1

[i]6 The meaning of the Hebrew for this phrase is uncertain.

25 How painful are honest words![a]
But what do your arguments prove?
26 Do you mean to correct what I say,
and treat the words of a despairing
man as wind?[b]
27 You would even cast lots[c] for the
fatherless
and barter away your friend.

28 "But now be so kind as to look at me.
Would I lie to your face?[d]
29 Relent, do not be unjust;
reconsider, for my integrity is at
stake.[j][e]
30 Is there any wickedness on my lips?[f]
Can my mouth not discern[g]
malice?

Job: Desire to die.

7 "Does not man have hard service[h]
on earth?[i]
Are not his days like those of a
hired man?[j]
2 Like a slave longing for the evening
shadows,
or a hired man waiting eagerly for
his wages,[k]
3 so I have been allotted months of
futility,
and nights of misery have been
assigned to me.[l]
4 When I lie down I think, 'How long
before I get up?'[m]
The night drags on, and I toss till
dawn.
5 My body is clothed with worms[n] and
scabs,
my skin is broken and festering.

6 "My days are swifter than a weaver's
shuttle,[o]
and they come to an end without
hope.[p]
7 Remember, O God, that my life is
but a breath;[q]
my eyes will never see happiness
again.[r]
8 The eye that now sees me will see
me no longer;
you will look for me, but I will be
no more.[s]
9 As a cloud vanishes and is gone,
so he who goes down to the grave[k][t]
does not return.[u]
10 He will never come to his house again;
his place[v] will know him no more.[w]

11 "Therefore I will not keep silent;[x]
I will speak out in the anguish of
my spirit,
I will complain in the bitterness of
my soul.[y]
12 Am I the sea, or the monster of the
deep,[z]
that you put me under guard?
13 When I think my bed will comfort me
and my couch will ease my
complaint,[a]
14 even then you frighten me with
dreams
and terrify[b] me with visions,
15 so that I prefer strangling and
death,[c]
rather than this body of mine.
16 I despise my life;[d] I would not live
forever.
Let me alone; my days have no
meaning.

17 "What is man that you make so
much of him,
that you give him so much
attention,[e]
18 that you examine him every morning
and test him every moment?[f]
19 Will you never look away from me,
or let me alone even for an instant?[g]
20 If I have sinned, what have I done to
you,[h]
O watcher of men?
Why have you made me your
target?[i]
Have I become a burden to you?[l]
21 Why do you not pardon my offenses
and forgive my sins?[j]
For I will soon lie down in the dust;[k]
you will search for me, but I will
be no more."

6:25 [a]Ecc 12:11
6:26 [b]Job 8:2; 15:3
6:27 [c]Joel 3:3; Na 3:10; 2Pe 2:3
6:28 [d]Job 27:4; 33:1,3; 36:3,4
6:29 [e]Job 23:7,10; 34:5,36; 42:6
6:30 [f]Job 27:4 [g]Job 12:11
7:1 [h]Job 14:14; Isa 40:2 [i]Job 5:7 [j]Job 14:6
7:2 [k]Lev 19:13
7:3 [l]Job 16:7; Ps 6:6
7:4 [m]Dt 28:67
7:5 [n]Job 17:14; Isa 14:11
7:6 [o]Job 9:25 [p]Job 13:15; 17:11,15
7:7 [q]Ps 78:39; Jas 4:14 [r]Job 9:25
7:8 [s]Job 20:7,9,21
7:9 [t]Job 11:8 [u]2Sa 12:23; Job 30:15
7:10 [v]Job 27:21,23 [w]Job 8:18
7:11 [x]Ps 40:9 [y]1Sa 1:10
7:12 [z]Eze 32:2-3
7:13 [a]Job 9:27
7:14 [b]Job 9:34
7:15 [c]1Ki 19:4
7:16 [d]Job 9:21; 10:1
7:17 [e]Ps 8:4; 144:3; Heb 2:6
7:18 [f]Job 14:3 **7:19** [g]Job 9:18 **7:20** [h]Job 35:6 [i]Job 16:12 **7:21** [j]Job 10:14 [k]Job 10:9; Ps 104:29

j29 Or *my righteousness still stands* k9 Hebrew *Sheol* l20 A few manuscripts of the Masoretic Text, an ancient Hebrew scribal tradition and Septuagint; most manuscripts of the Masoretic Text *I have become a burden to myself.*

Bildad: God is totally just.

8 Then Bildad the Shuhite replied:

2“How long will you say such
things?
Your words are a blustering wind.[a]
3Does God pervert justice?[b]
Does the Almighty pervert what is
right?[c]
4When your children sinned against
him,
he gave them over to the penalty
of their sin.[d]
5But if you will look to God
and plead[e] with the Almighty,
6if you are pure and upright,
even now he will rouse himself on
your behalf[f]
and restore you to your rightful
place.[g]
7Your beginnings will seem humble,
so prosperous[h] will your future be.

8“Ask the former generations[i]
and find out what their fathers
learned,
9for we were born only yesterday and
know nothing,[j]
and our days on earth are but a
shadow.[k]
10Will they not instruct you and tell you?
Will they not bring forth words
from their understanding?
11Can papyrus grow tall where there is
no marsh?
Can reeds thrive without water?
12While still growing and uncut,
they wither more quickly than
grass.[l]
13Such is the destiny of all who forget
God;[m]
so perishes the hope of the godless.[n]
14What he trusts in is fragile[m];
what he relies on is a spider's
web.[o]
15He leans on his web,[p] but it gives way;
he clings to it, but it does not
hold.[q]
16He is like a well-watered plant in the
sunshine,
spreading its shoots[r] over the
garden;[s]
17it entwines its roots around a pile of
rocks
and looks for a place among the
stones.
18But when it is torn from its spot,
that place disowns it and says, ‘I
never saw you.’[t]
19Surely its life withers[u] away,
and[n] from the soil other plants
grow.[v]

20“Surely God does not reject a
blameless[w] man
or strengthen the hands of
evildoers.[x]
21He will yet fill your mouth with
laughter[y]
and your lips with shouts of joy.[z]
22Your enemies will be clothed in
shame,[a]
and the tents of the wicked will be
no more.”[b]

Job: God destroys the blameless and the wicked.

9 Then Job replied:

2“Indeed, I know that this is true.
But how can a mortal be righteous
before God?[c]
3Though one wished to dispute with
him,
he could not answer him one time
out of a thousand.[d]
4His wisdom[e] is profound, his power
is vast.[f]
Who has resisted him and come
out unscathed?[g]
5He moves mountains without their
knowing it
and overturns them in his anger.[h]
6He shakes the earth[i] from its place
and makes its pillars tremble.[j]
7He speaks to the sun and it does not
shine;
he seals off the light of the stars.[k]

8:2 [a]Job 6:26 **8:3** [b]Dt 32:4; 2Ch 19:7; Ro 3:5 [c]Ge 18:25 **8:4** [d]Job 1:19 **8:5** [e]Job 11:13 **8:6** [f]Ps 7:6 [g]Job 5:24 **8:7** [h]Job 42:12 **8:8** [i]Dt 4:32; 32:7; Job 15:18 **8:9** [j]Ge 47:9 [k]1Ch 29:15; Job 7:6 **8:12** [l]Ps 129:6; Jer 17:6 **8:13** [m]Ps 9:17 [n]Job 11:20; 13:16; 15:34; Pr 10:28 **8:14** [o]Isa 59:5 **8:15** [p]Job 27:18 [q]Ps 49:11 **8:16** [r]Ps 80:11 [s]Ps 37:35; Jer 11:16 **8:18** [t]Job 7:8; Ps 37:36 **8:19** [u]Job 20:5 [v]Ecc 1:4 **8:20** [w]Job 1:1 [x]Job 21:30 **8:21** [y]Job 5:22 [z]Ps 126:2; 132:16 **8:22** [a]Ps 35:26; 109:29; 132:18 [b]Job 18:6, 14,21 **9:2** [c]Job 4:17; Ps 143:2; Ro 3:20 **9:3** [d]Job 10:2; 40:2 **9:4** [e]Job 11:6 [f]Job 36:5 [g]2Ch 13:12 **9:5** [h]Mic 1:4 **9:6** [i]Isa 2:21; Hag 2:6; Heb 12:26 [j]Job 26:11 **9:7** [k]Isa 13:10; Eze 32:8

m *14* The meaning of the Hebrew for this word is uncertain. n *19* Or *Surely all the joy it has / is that*

8He alone stretches out the heavens[a]
and treads on the waves of the
sea.[b]
9He is the Maker of the Bear and
Orion,
the Pleiades and the constellations
of the south.[c]
10He performs wonders[d] that cannot
be fathomed,
miracles that cannot be counted.[e]
11When he passes me, I cannot see him;
when he goes by, I cannot perceive
him.[f]
12If he snatches away, who can stop
him?[g]
Who can say to him, 'What are you
doing?'[h]
13God does not restrain his anger;
even the cohorts of Rahab[i]
cowered at his feet.

14"How then can I dispute with him?
How can I find words to argue with
him?
15Though I were innocent, I could not
answer him;[j]
I could only plead[k] with my Judge
for mercy.
16Even if I summoned him and he
responded,
I do not believe he would give me
a hearing.
17He would crush me[l] with a storm[m]
and multiply[n] my wounds for no
reason.[o]
18He would not let me regain my breath
but would overwhelm me with
misery.[p]
19If it is a matter of strength, he is
mighty!
And if it is a matter of justice, who
will summon him[o]?
20Even if I were innocent, my mouth
would condemn me;
if I were blameless, it would
pronounce me guilty.

21"Although I am blameless,[q]
I have no concern for myself;
I despise my own life.[r]
22It is all the same; that is why I say,
'He destroys both the blameless
and the wicked.'[s]
23When a scourge[t] brings sudden death,
he mocks the despair of the
innocent.[u]
24When a land falls into the hands of
the wicked,[v]
he blindfolds its judges.[w]
If it is not he, then who is it?

25"My days are swifter than a runner;[x]
they fly away without a glimpse of
joy.
26They skim past like boats of
papyrus,[y]
like eagles swooping down on their
prey.[z]
27If I say, 'I will forget my complaint,[a]
I will change my expression, and
smile,'
28I still dread[b] all my sufferings,
for I know you will not hold me
innocent.[c]
29Since I am already found guilty,
why should I struggle in vain?[d]
30Even if I washed myself with soap[p]
and my hands[e] with washing soda,[f]
31you would plunge me into a slime pit
so that even my clothes would
detest me.

32"He is not a man like me that I
might answer him,[g]
that we might confront each other
in court.[h]
33If only there were someone to
arbitrate between us,[i]
to lay his hand upon us both,
34someone to remove God's rod from
me,[j]
so that his terror would frighten
me no more.
35Then I would speak up without fear
of him,
but as it now stands with me, I
cannot.[k]

Job: More grievances.

10 "I loathe my very life;[l]
therefore I will give free rein to
my complaint

9:8 [a]Ge 1:6; Ps 104:2-3 [b]Job 38:16; Ps 77:19 **9:9** [c]Ge 1:16; Job 38:31; Am 5:8 **9:10** [d]Ps 71:15 [e]Job 5:9 **9:11** [f]Job 23:8-9; 35:14 **9:12** [g]Job 11:10 [h]Isa 45:9; Ro 9:20 **9:13** [i]Job 26:12; Ps 89:10; Isa 30:7; 51:9 **9:15** [j]Job 10:15 [k]Job 8:5 **9:17** [l]Job 16:12 [m]Job 30:22 [n]Job 16:14 [o]Job 2:3 **9:18** [p]Job 7:19; 27:2 **9:21** [q]Job 1:1 [r]Job 7:16 **9:22** [s]Job 10:8; Ecc 9:2,3; Eze 21:3 **9:23** [t]Heb 11:36 [u]Job 24:1,12 **9:24** [v]Job 10:3; 16:11 [w]Job 12:6 **9:25** [x]Job 7:6 **9:26** [y]Isa 18:2 [z]Hab 1:8 **9:27** [a]Job 7:11 **9:28** [b]Job 3:25; Ps 119:120 [c]Job 7:21 **9:29** [d]Ps 37:33 **9:30** [e]Job 31:7 [f]Jer 2:22 **9:32** [g]Ro 9:20 [h]Ps 143:2; Ecc 6:10

9:33 [i]1Sa 2:25 **9:34** [j]Job 13:21; Ps 39:10
9:35 [k]Job 13:21 **10:1** [l]1Ki 19:4

o *19* See Septuagint; Hebrew *me.* p *30* Or *snow*

and speak out in the bitterness of
my soul.[a]
2I will say to God: Do not condemn me,
but tell me what charges[b] you have
against me.
3Does it please you to oppress me,[c]
to spurn the work of your hands,[d]
while you smile on the schemes of
the wicked?[e]
4Do you have eyes of flesh?
Do you see as a mortal sees?[f]
5Are your days like those of a mortal
or your years like those of a man,[g]
6that you must search out my faults
and probe after my sin[h]—
7though you know that I am not guilty
and that no one can rescue me
from your hand?

8"Your hands shaped[i] me and made me.
Will you now turn and destroy me?
9Remember that you molded me like
clay.[j]
Will you now turn me to dust
again?[k]
10Did you not pour me out like milk
and curdle me like cheese,
11clothe me with skin and flesh
and knit me together[l] with bones
and sinews?
12You gave me life[m] and showed me
kindness,
and in your providence watched
over my spirit.

13"But this is what you concealed in
your heart,
and I know that this was in your
mind:[n]
14If I sinned, you would be watching me
and would not let my offense go
unpunished.[o]
15If I am guilty—woe to me![p]
Even if I am innocent, I cannot lift
my head,[q]
for I am full of shame
and drowned in[q] my affliction.
16If I hold my head high, you stalk me
like a lion[r]
and again display your awesome
power against me.[s]
17You bring new witnesses against me[t]
and increase your anger toward me;[u]
your forces come against me wave
upon wave.

18"Why then did you bring me out of
the womb?[v]
I wish I had died before any eye
saw me.
19If only I had never come into being,
or had been carried straight from
the womb to the grave!
20Are not my few days[w] almost over?[x]
Turn away from me[y] so I can have
a moment's joy
21before I go to the place of no
return,[z]
to the land of gloom and deep
shadow,[r][a]
22to the land of deepest night,
of deep shadow and disorder,
where even the light is like
darkness."

Zophar: God is justified in his dealings.

11 Then Zophar the Naamathite replied:

2"Are all these words to go
unanswered?[b]
Is this talker to be vindicated?
3Will your idle talk reduce men to
silence?
Will no one rebuke you when you
mock?[c]
4You say to God, 'My beliefs are
flawless[d]
and I am pure[e] in your sight.'
5Oh, how I wish that God would
speak,
that he would open his lips against
you
6and disclose to you the secrets of
wisdom,[f]
for true wisdom has two sides.
Know this: God has even forgotten
some of your sin.[g]

7"Can you fathom[h] the mysteries of
God?
Can you probe the limits of the
Almighty?

10:1 [a]Job 7:11 **10:2** [b]Job 9:29 **10:3** [c]Job 9:22 [d]Job 14:15; Ps 138:8; Isa 64:8 [e]Job 21:16; 22:18 **10:4** [f]1Sa 16:7 **10:5** [g]Ps 90:2,4; 2Pe 3:8 **10:6** [h]Job 14:16 **10:8** [i]Ps 119:73 **10:9** [j]Isa 64:8 [k]Ge 2:7 **10:11** [l]Ps 139:13,15 **10:12** [m]Job 33:4 **10:13** [n]Job 23:13 **10:14** [o]Job 7:21 **10:15** [p]Job 9:13; Isa 3:11 [q]Job 9:15 **10:16** [r]Isa 38:13; La 3:10 [s]Job 5:9 **10:17** [t]Job 16:8 [u]Ru 1:21 **10:18** [v]Job 3:11 **10:20** [w]Job 14:1 [x]Job 7:19 [y]Job 7:16 **10:21** [z]2Sa 12:23; Job 3:13; 16:22 [a]Ps 23:4; 88:12 **11:2** [b]Job 8:2 **11:3** [c]Job 17:2; 21:3 **11:4** [d]Job 6:10 [e]Job 10:7 **11:6** [f]Job 9:4 [g]Ezr 9:13; Job 15:5 **11:7** [h]Ecc 3:11; Ro 11:33

q *15* Or *and aware of* r *21* Or *and the shadow of death*; also in verse 22

8They are higher than the heavens[a]—what can you do?
They are deeper than the depths of the grave[s]—what can you know?
9Their measure is longer than the earth
and wider than the sea.

10"If he comes along and confines you in prison
and convenes a court, who can oppose him?[b]
11Surely he recognizes deceitful men;
and when he sees evil, does he not take note?[c]
12But a witless man can no more become wise
than a wild donkey's colt can be born a man.[t]

13"Yet if you devote your heart[d] to him
and stretch out your hands to him,[e]
14if you put away the sin that is in your hand
and allow no evil[f] to dwell in your tent,[g]
15then you will lift up your face[h] without shame;
you will stand firm and without fear.
16You will surely forget your trouble,[i]
recalling it only as waters gone by.[j]
17Life will be brighter than noonday,[k]
and darkness will become like morning.
18You will be secure, because there is hope;
you will look about you and take your rest[l] in safety.[m]
19You will lie down, with no one to make you afraid,[n]
and many will court your favor.[o]
20But the eyes of the wicked will fail,[p]
and escape will elude them;[q]
their hope will become a dying gasp."[r]

Job: Wisdom and power are God's.

12 Then Job replied:

2"Doubtless you are the people,
and wisdom will die with you![s]
3But I have a mind as well as you;
I am not inferior to you.
Who does not know all these things?[t]

4"I have become a laughingstock[u] to my friends,
though I called upon God and he answered[v]—
a mere laughingstock, though righteous and blameless![w]
5Men at ease have contempt for misfortune
as the fate of those whose feet are slipping.
6The tents of marauders are undisturbed,[x]
and those who provoke God are secure[y]—
those who carry their god in their hands.[u]

7"But ask the animals, and they will teach you,
or the birds of the air, and they will tell you;
8or speak to the earth, and it will teach you,
or let the fish of the sea inform you.
9Which of all these does not know
that the hand of the LORD has done this?[z]
10In his hand is the life of every creature
and the breath of all mankind.[a]
11Does not the ear test words
as the tongue tastes food?[b]
12Is not wisdom found among the aged?[c]
Does not long life bring understanding?[d]

13"To God belong wisdom[e] and power;[f]
counsel and understanding are his.[g]
14What he tears down[h] cannot be rebuilt;[i]
the man he imprisons cannot be released.

11:8 [a]Job 22:12 **11:10** [b]Job 9:12; Rev 3:7 **11:11** [c]Job 34:21-25; Ps 10:14 **11:13** [d]1Sa 7:3; Ps 78:8 [e]Ps 88:9 **11:14** [f]Ps 101:4 [g]Job 22:23 **11:15** [h]Job 22:26; 1Jn 3:21 **11:16** [i]Isa 65:16 [j]Job 22:11 **11:17** [k]Job 22:28; Ps 37:6; Isa 58:8,10 **11:18** [l]Ps 3:5 [m]Lev 26:6; Pr 3:24 **11:19** [n]Lev 26:6 [o]Isa 45:14 **11:20** [p]Dt 28:65; Job 17:5 [q]Job 27:22; 34:22 [r]Job 8:13 **12:2** [s]Job 17:10 **12:3** [t]Job 13:2 **12:4** [u]Job 21:3 [v]Ps 91:15 [w]Job 6:29 **12:6** [x]Job 22:18 [y]Job 9:24; 21:9 **12:9** [z]Isa 41:20 **12:10** [a]Job 27:3; 33:4; Ac 17:28 **12:11** [b]Job 34:3 **12:12** [c]Job 15:10 [d]Job 32:7,9 **12:13** [e]Job 11:6 [f]Job 9:4 [g]Job 32:8; 38:36 **12:14** [h]Job 19:10 [i]Job 37:7; Isa 25:2

s8 Hebrew *than Sheol* t12 Or *wild donkey can be born tame* u6 Or *secure / in what God's hand brings them*

15 If he holds back the waters,[a] there is drought;[b]
if he lets them loose, they devastate the land.[c]
16 To him belong strength and victory;
both deceived and deceiver are his.[d]
17 He leads counselors away stripped[e]
and makes fools of judges.[f]
18 He takes off the shackles[g] put on by kings
and ties a loincloth[v] around their waist.
19 He leads priests away stripped
and overthrows men long established.[h]
20 He silences the lips of trusted advisers
and takes away the discernment of elders.[i]
21 He pours contempt on nobles
and disarms the mighty.
22 He reveals the deep things of darkness[j]
and brings deep shadows[k] into the light.[l]
23 He makes nations great, and destroys them;[m]
he enlarges nations,[n] and disperses them.
24 He deprives the leaders of the earth of their reason;
he sends them wandering through a trackless waste.[o]
25 They grope in darkness with no light;[p]
he makes them stagger like drunkards.[q]

Job: Request that God show him his sins.

13 "My eyes have seen all this,
my ears have heard and understood it.
2 What you know, I also know;
I am not inferior to you.[r]
3 But I desire to speak to the Almighty
and to argue my case with God.[s]
4 You, however, smear me with lies;[t]
you are worthless physicians, all of you!
5 If only you would be altogether silent!
For you, that would be wisdom.[u]
6 Hear now my argument;
listen to the plea of my lips.
7 Will you speak wickedly on God's behalf?
Will you speak deceitfully for him?[v]
8 Will you show him partiality?[w]
Will you argue the case for God?
9 Would it turn out well if he examined you?
Could you deceive him as you might deceive men?[x]
10 He would surely rebuke you
if you secretly showed partiality.
11 Would not his splendor[y] terrify you?
Would not the dread of him fall on you?
12 Your maxims are proverbs of ashes;
your defenses are defenses of clay.

13 "Keep silent and let me speak;
then let come to me what may.
14 Why do I put myself in jeopardy
and take my life in my hands?
15 Though he slay me, yet will I hope[z] in him;[a]
I will surely[w] defend my ways to his face.[b]
16 Indeed, this will turn out for my deliverance,[c]
for no godless man would dare come before him!
17 Listen carefully to my words;[d]
let your ears take in what I say.
18 Now that I have prepared my case,[e]
I know I will be vindicated.
19 Can anyone bring charges against me?[f]
If so, I will be silent and die.[g]

20 "Only grant me these two things, O God,
and then I will not hide from you:
21 Withdraw your hand[h] far from me,
and stop frightening me with your terrors.

12:15 [a]1Ki 8:35 [b]1Ki 17:1 [c]Ge 7:11
12:16 [d]Job 13:7,9
12:17 [e]Job 19:9 [f]Job 3:14
12:18 [g]Ps 116:16
12:19 [h]Job 24:12,22; 34:20,28; 35:9
12:20 [i]Job 32:9
12:22 [j]1Co 4:5 [k]Job 3:5 [l]Da 2:22
12:23 [m]Jer 25:9 [n]Ps 107:38; Isa 9:3; 26:15
12:24 [o]Ps 107:40
12:25 [p]Job 5:14 [q]Ps 107:27; Isa 24:20
13:2 [r]Job 12:3
13:3 [s]Job 23:3-4
13:4 [t]Ps 119:69; Jer 23:32
13:5 [u]Pr 17:28
13:7 [v]Job 36:4
13:8 [w]Lev 19:15
13:9 [x]Job 12:16; Gal 6:7
13:11 [y]Job 31:23
13:15 [z]Job 7:6 [a]Ps 23:4; Pr 14:32 [b]Job 27:5
13:16 [c]Isa 12:1
13:17 [d]Job 21:2
13:18 [e]Job 23:4
13:19 [f]Job 40:4; Isa 50:8 [g]Job 10:8
13:21 [h]Ps 39:10

v *18* Or *shackles of kings / and ties a belt* w *15* Or *He will surely slay me; I have no hope— / yet I will*

22Then summon me and I will
answer,[a]
or let me speak, and you reply.[b]
23How many wrongs and sins have I
committed?[c]
Show me my offense and my sin.
24Why do you hide your face[d]
and consider me your enemy?[e]
25Will you torment a windblown leaf?[f]
Will you chase after dry chaff?[g]
26For you write down bitter things
against me
and make me inherit the sins of
my youth.[h]
27You fasten my feet in shackles;[i]
you keep close watch on all my
paths
by putting marks on the soles of
my feet.

28"So man wastes away like something
rotten,
like a garment eaten by moths.[j]

Job: Remember the shortness of life.

14 "Man born of woman
is of few days and full of
trouble.[k]
2He springs up like a flower[l] and
withers away;[m]
like a fleeting shadow,[n] he does not
endure.
3Do you fix your eye on such a one?[o]
Will you bring him[x] before you for
judgment?[p]
4Who can bring what is pure[q] from
the impure?[r]
No one![s]
5Man's days are determined;
you have decreed the number of
his months[t]
and have set limits he cannot
exceed.
6So look away from him and let him
alone,[u]
till he has put in his time like a
hired man.[v]

7"At least there is hope for a tree:
If it is cut down, it will sprout again,
and its new shoots will not fail.
8Its roots may grow old in the ground
and its stump die in the soil,
9yet at the scent of water it will bud
and put forth shoots like a plant.
10But man dies and is laid low;
he breathes his last and is no
more.[w]
11As water disappears from the sea
or a riverbed becomes parched and
dry,[x]
12so man lies down and does not rise;
till the heavens are no more,[y] men
will not awake
or be roused from their sleep.[z]

13"If only you would hide me in the
grave[y]
and conceal me till your anger has
passed![a]
If only you would set me a time
and then remember me!
14If a man dies, will he live again?
All the days of my hard service
I will wait for my renewal[z] to
come.
15You will call and I will answer you;[b]
you will long for the creature your
hands have made.
16Surely then you will count my steps[c]
but not keep track of my sin.[d]
17My offenses will be sealed up in a
bag;[e]
you will cover over my sin.[f]

18"But as a mountain erodes and
crumbles
and as a rock is moved from its
place,
19as water wears away stones
and torrents wash away the soil,
so you destroy man's hope.[g]
20You overpower him once for all, and
he is gone;
you change his countenance and
send him away.
21If his sons are honored, he does not
know it;
if they are brought low, he does
not see it.[h]

13:22 [a]Job 14:15 [b]Job 9:16 **13:23** [c]1Sa 26:18 **13:24** [d]Dt 32:20; Ps 13:1; Isa 8:17 [e]Job 19:11; La 2:5 **13:25** [f]Lev 26:36 [g]Job 21:18; Isa 42:3 **13:26** [h]Ps 25:7 **13:27** [i]Job 33:11 **13:28** [j]Isa 50:9; Jas 5:2 **14:1** [k]Job 5:7; Ecc 2:23 **14:2** [l]Jas 1:10 [m]Ps 90:5-6 [n]Job 8:9 **14:3** [o]Ps 8:4; 144:3 [p]Ps 143:2 **14:4** [q]Ps 51:10 [r]Eph 2:1-3 [s]Jn 3:6; Ro 5:12 **14:5** [t]Job 21:21 **14:6** [u]Job 7:19 [v]Job 7:1,2; Ps 39:13 **14:10** [w]Job 13:19 **14:11** [x]Isa 19:5 **14:12** [y]Rev 20:11; 21:1 [z]Ac 3:21 **14:13** [a]Isa 26:20 **14:15** [b]Job 13:22 **14:16** [c]Ps 139:1-3; Pr 5:21; Jer 32:19 [d]Job 10:6 **14:17** [e]Dt 32:34 [f]Hos 13:12 **14:19** [g]Job 7:6 **14:21** [h]Ecc 9:5; Isa 63:16

x3 Septuagint, Vulgate and Syriac; Hebrew *me*
y13 Hebrew *Sheol* z14 Or *release*

22He feels but the pain of his own body
and mourns only for himself."

Eliphaz: Job's remarks are self-condemning.

15 Then Eliphaz the Temanite replied:

2"Would a wise man answer with empty notions
or fill his belly with the hot east wind?[a]
3Would he argue with useless words,
with speeches that have no value?
4But you even undermine piety
and hinder devotion to God.
5Your sin prompts your mouth;
you adopt the tongue of the crafty.[b]
6Your own mouth condemns you, not mine;
your own lips testify against you.[c]

7"Are you the first man ever born?[d]
Were you brought forth before the hills?[e]
8Do you listen in on God's council?[f]
Do you limit wisdom to yourself?
9What do you know that we do not know?
What insights do you have that we do not have?[g]
10The gray-haired and the aged[h] are on our side,
men even older than your father.
11Are God's consolations[i] not enough for you,
words[j] spoken gently to you?[k]
12Why has your heart[l] carried you away,
and why do your eyes flash,
13so that you vent your rage against God
and pour out such words from your mouth?

14"What is man, that he could be pure,
or one born of woman,[m] that he could be righteous?[n]
15If God places no trust in his holy ones,
if even the heavens are not pure in his eyes,[o]
16how much less man, who is vile and corrupt,[p]
who drinks up evil like water![q]

17"Listen to me and I will explain to you;
let me tell you what I have seen,
18what wise men have declared,
hiding nothing received from their fathers[r]
19(to whom alone the land was given
when no alien passed among them):
20All his days the wicked man suffers torment,
the ruthless through all the years stored up for him.[s]
21Terrifying sounds fill his ears;[t]
when all seems well, marauders attack him.[u]
22He despairs of escaping the darkness;
he is marked for the sword.[v]
23He wanders about[w]—food for vultures[a];
he knows the day of darkness is at hand.[x]
24Distress and anguish fill him with terror;
they overwhelm him, like a king poised to attack,
25because he shakes his fist at God
and vaunts himself against the Almighty,[y]
26defiantly charging against him
with a thick, strong shield.

27"Though his face is covered with fat
and his waist bulges with flesh,[z]
28he will inhabit ruined towns
and houses where no one lives,[a]
houses crumbling to rubble.[b]
29He will no longer be rich and his wealth will not endure,[c]
nor will his possessions spread over the land.
30He will not escape the darkness;[d]
a flame[e] will wither his shoots,
and the breath of God's mouth[f] will carry him away.

15:2 [a]Job 6:26 **15:5** [b]Job 5:13 **15:6** [c]Lk 19:22 **15:7** [d]Job 38:21 [e]Ps 90:2; Pr 8:25 **15:8** [f]Ro 11:34; 1Co 2:11 **15:9** [g]Job 13:2 **15:10** [h]Job 32:6-7 **15:11** [i]2Co 1:3-4 [j]Zec 1:13 [k]Job 36:16 **15:12** [l]Job 11:13 **15:14** [m]Job 14:4; 25:4 [n]Pr 20:9; Ecc 7:20 **15:15** [o]Job 4:18; 25:5 **15:16** [p]Ps 14:1 [q]Job 34:7; Pr 19:28 **15:18** [r]Job 8:8 **15:20** [s]Job 24:1; 27:13-23 **15:21** [t]Job 18:11; 20:25 [u]Job 27:20; 1Th 5:3 **15:22** [v]Job 19:29; 27:14 **15:23** [w]Ps 59:15; 109:10 [x]Job 18:12 **15:25** [y]Job 36:9 **15:27** [z]Ps 17:10 **15:28** [a]Isa 5:9 [b]Job 3:14 **15:29** [c]Job 27:16-17 **15:30** [d]Job 5:14 [e]Job 22:20 [f]Job 4:9

a23 Or *about, looking for food*

31Let him not deceive himself by
trusting what is worthless,[a]
for he will get nothing in return.
32Before his time[b] he will be paid in
full,[c]
and his branches will not flourish.[d]
33He will be like a vine stripped of its
unripe grapes,[e]
like an olive tree shedding its
blossoms.
34For the company of the godless will
be barren,
and fire will consume the tents of
those who love bribes.[f]
35They conceive trouble and give birth
to evil;[g]
their womb fashions deceit."

Job: Friends should comfort.

16

Then Job replied:

2"I have heard many things like
these;
miserable comforters are you all![h]
3Will your long-winded speeches
never end?
What ails you that you keep on
arguing?[i]
4I also could speak like you,
if you were in my place;
I could make fine speeches against you
and shake my head[j] at you.
5But my mouth would encourage you;
comfort from my lips would bring
you relief.

6"Yet if I speak, my pain is not
relieved;
and if I refrain, it does not go away.
7Surely, O God, you have worn me
out;[k]
you have devastated my entire
household.
8You have bound me—and it has
become a witness;
my gauntness[l] rises up and testifies
against me.[m]
9God assails me and tears[n] me in his
anger
and gnashes his teeth at me;[o]
my opponent fastens on me his
piercing eyes.[p]
10Men open their mouths[q] to jeer at
me;
they strike my cheek[r] in scorn
and unite together against me.[s]
11God has turned me over to evil men
and thrown me into the clutches of
the wicked.[t]
12All was well with me, but he
shattered me;
he seized me by the neck and
crushed me.[u]
He has made me his target;[v]
13 his archers surround me.
Without pity, he pierces[w] my kidneys
and spills my gall on the ground.
14Again and again[x] he bursts upon me;
he rushes at me like a warrior.[y]

15"I have sewed sackcloth[z] over my skin
and buried my brow in the dust.
16My face is red with weeping,
deep shadows ring my eyes;
17yet my hands have been free of
violence[a]
and my prayer is pure.

18"O earth, do not cover my blood;[b]
may my cry never be laid to rest![c]
19Even now my witness[d] is in heaven;
my advocate is on high.
20My intercessor is my friend[b]
as my eyes pour out[e] tears to God;
21on behalf of a man he pleads[f] with God
as a man pleads for his friend.

Job: Broken spirit.

22"Only a few years will pass
before I go on the journey of no
return.[g]

17

1My spirit is broken,
my days are cut short,
the grave awaits me.[h]
2Surely mockers[i] surround me;
my eyes must dwell on their hostility.

3"Give me, O God, the pledge you
demand.[j]
Who else will put up security[k] for
me?[l]

15:31 [a]Isa 59:4 **15:32** [b]Ecc 7:17 [c]Job 22:16; Ps 55:23 [d]Job 18:16 **15:33** [e]Hab 3:17 **15:34** [f]Job 8:22 **15:35** [g]Ps 7:14; Isa 59:4; Hos 10:13 **16:2** [h]Job 13:4 **16:3** [i]Job 6:26 **16:4** [j]Ps 22:7; 109:25; La 2:15; Zep 2:15; Mt 27:39 **16:7** [k]Job 7:3 **16:8** [l]Job 19:20 [m]Job 10:17 **16:9** [n]Hos 6:1 [o]Ps 35:16; La 2:16; Ac 7:54 [p]Job 13:24 **16:10** [q]Ps 22:13 [r]Isa 50:6; La 3:30; Mic 5:1; Ac 23:2 [s]Ps 35:15 **16:11** [t]Job 1:15,17 **16:12** [u]Job 9:17 [v]La 3:12 **16:13** [w]Job 20:24 **16:14** [x]Job 9:17 [y]Joel 2:7 **16:15** [z]Ge 37:34 **16:17** [a]Isa 59:6; Jnh 3:8 **16:18** [b]Isa 26:21 [c]Ps 66:18-19 **16:19** [d]Ge 31:50; Ro 1:9; 1Th 2:5 **16:20** [e]La 2:19 **16:21** [f]Ps 9:4

16:22 [g]Ecc 12:5 **17:1** [h]Ps 88:3-4 **17:2** [i]1Sa 1:6-7 **17:3** [j]Ps 119:122 [k]Pr 6:1 [l]Isa 38:14

b*20* Or *My friends treat me with scorn*

4You have closed their minds to
understanding;
therefore you will not let them
triumph.
5If a man denounces his friends for
reward,
the eyes of his children will fail.[a]

6"God has made me a byword[b] to
everyone,
a man in whose face people spit.
7My eyes have grown dim with grief;[c]
my whole frame is but a shadow.
8Upright men are appalled at this;
the innocent are aroused[d] against
the ungodly.
9Nevertheless, the righteous[e] will
hold to their ways,
and those with clean hands[f] will
grow stronger.

10"But come on, all of you, try again!
I will not find a wise man among
you.[g]
11My days have passed, my plans are
shattered,
and so are the desires of my heart.[h]
12These men turn night into day;
in the face of darkness they say,
'Light is near.'
13If the only home I hope for is the
grave,[c][i]
if I spread out my bed in darkness,
14if I say to corruption,[j] 'You are my
father,'
and to the worm,[k] 'My mother' or
'My sister,'
15where then is my hope?[l]
Who can see any hope for me?
16Will it go down to the gates of
death[c]?[m]
Will we descend together into the
dust?"

Bildad: The wicked are punished.

18 Then Bildad the Shuhite replied:

2"When will you end these speeches?
Be sensible, and then we can talk.
3Why are we regarded as cattle
and considered stupid in your
sight?[n]
4You who tear yourself[o] to pieces in
your anger,
is the earth to be abandoned for
your sake?
Or must the rocks be moved from
their place?

5"The lamp of the wicked is snuffed
out;[p]
the flame of his fire stops burning.
6The light in his tent becomes dark;
the lamp beside him goes out.
7The vigor of his step is weakened;[q]
his own schemes[r] throw him down.[s]
8His feet thrust him into a net[t]
and he wanders into its mesh.
9A trap seizes him by the heel;
a snare holds him fast.
10A noose is hidden for him on the
ground;
a trap lies in his path.
11Terrors startle him on every side[u]
and dog[v] his every step.
12Calamity is hungry[w] for him;
disaster is ready for him when he
falls.
13It eats away parts of his skin;
death's firstborn devours his limbs.[x]
14He is torn from the security of his
tent[y]
and marched off to the king of
terrors.
15Fire resides[d] in his tent;
burning sulfur[z] is scattered over
his dwelling.
16His roots dry up below[a]
and his branches wither above.[b]
17The memory of him perishes from
the earth;
he has no name in the land.[c]
18He is driven from light into darkness[d]
and is banished from the world.
19He has no offspring[e] or descendants[f]
among his people,
no survivor where once he lived.[g]
20Men of the west are appalled at his
fate;[h]
men of the east are seized with
horror.

17:5 [a]Job 11:20
17:6 [b]Job 30:9
17:7 [c]Job 16:8
17:8 [d]Job 22:19
17:9 [e]Pr 4:18 [f]Job 22:30
17:10 [g]Job 12:2
17:11 [h]Job 7:6
17:13 [i]Job 3:13
17:14 [j]Job 13:28; 30:28,30; Ps 16:10 [k]Job 21:26
17:15 [l]Job 7:6
17:16 [m]Job 3:17-19; Jnh 2:6
18:3 [n]Ps 73:22
18:4 [o]Job 13:14
18:5 [p]Job 21:17; Pr 13:9; 20:20; 24:20
18:7 [q]Pr 4:12 [r]Job 5:13 [s]Job 15:6
18:8 [t]Job 22:10; Ps 9:15; 35:7
18:11 [u]Job 15:21; Jer 6:25; 20:3 [v]Job 20:8
18:12 [w]Isa 8:21
18:13 [x]Zec 14:12
18:14 [y]Job 8:22
18:15 [z]Ps 11:6
18:16 [a]Isa 5:24; Hos 9:1-16; Am 2:9 [b]Job 15:30; Mal 4:1
18:17 [c]Ps 34:16; Pr 2:22; 10:7
18:18 [d]Job 5:14
18:19 [e]Jer 22:30 [f]Isa 14:22 [g]Job 27:14-15
18:20 [h]Ps 37:13; Jer 50:27,31

c *13,16* Hebrew *Sheol* d *15* Or *Nothing he had remains*

21Surely such is the dwelling[a] of an evil man;
such is the place of one who knows not God."[b]

Job: His Redeemer lives.

19 Then Job replied:

2"How long will you torment me
and crush me with words?
3Ten times now you have reproached me;
shamelessly you attack me.
4If it is true that I have gone astray,
my error[c] remains my concern alone.
5If indeed you would exalt yourselves above me[d]
and use my humiliation against me,
6then know that God has wronged me[e]
and drawn his net[f] around me.

7"Though I cry, 'I've been wronged!' I get no response;[g]
though I call for help, there is no justice.[h]
8He has blocked my way so I cannot pass;[i]
he has shrouded my paths in darkness.[j]
9He has stripped[k] me of my honor
and removed the crown from my head.[l]
10He tears me down[m] on every side till I am gone;
he uproots my hope[n] like a tree.[o]
11His anger[p] burns against me;
he counts me among his enemies.[q]
12His troops advance in force;[r]
they build a siege ramp[s] against me
and encamp around my tent.

13"He has alienated my brothers[t] from me;
my acquaintances are completely estranged from me.[u]
14My kinsmen have gone away;
my friends have forgotten me.
15My guests and my maidservants count me a stranger;
they look upon me as an alien.
16I summon my servant, but he does not answer,
though I beg him with my own mouth.
17My breath is offensive to my wife;
I am loathsome to my own brothers.
18Even the little boys[v] scorn me;
when I appear, they ridicule me.
19All my intimate friends[w] detest me;[x]
those I love have turned against me.
20I am nothing but skin and bones;[y]
I have escaped with only the skin of my teeth.[e]

21"Have pity on me, my friends, have pity,
for the hand of God has struck me.
22Why do you pursue[z] me as God does?
Will you never get enough of my flesh?[a]

23"Oh, that my words were recorded,
that they were written on a scroll,[b]
24that they were inscribed with an iron tool on[f] lead,
or engraved in rock forever!
25I know that my Redeemer[g][c] lives,[d]
and that in the end he will stand upon the earth.[h]
26And after my skin has been destroyed,
yet[i] in[j] my flesh I will see God;[e]
27I myself will see him
with my own eyes—I, and not another.
How my heart yearns[f] within me!

28"If you say, 'How we will hound him,
since the root of the trouble lies in him,[k]'
29you should fear the sword yourselves;
for wrath will bring punishment by the sword,[g]
and then you will know that there is judgment.[l]"[h]

18:21 [a]Job 21:28 [b]Jer 9:3; 1Th 4:5 **19:4** [c]Job 6:24 **19:5** [d]Ps 35:26; 38:16; 55:12 **19:6** [e]Job 27:2 [f]Job 18:8 **19:7** [g]Job 30:20 [h]Job 9:24; Hab 1:2-4 **19:8** [i]Job 3:23; La 3:7 [j]Job 30:26 **19:9** [k]Job 12:17 [l]Ps 89:39,44; La 5:16 **19:10** [m]Job 12:14 [n]Job 7:6 [o]Job 24:20 **19:11** [p]Job 16:9 [q]Job 13:24 **19:12** [r]Job 16:13 [s]Job 30:12 **19:13** [t]Ps 69:8 [u]Job 16:7; Ps 88:8 **19:18** [v]2Ki 2:23 **19:19** [w]Ps 55:12-13 [x]Ps 38:11 **19:20** [y]Job 33:21; Ps 102:5 **19:22** [z]Job 13:25; 16:11 [a]Ps 69:26 **19:23** [b]Isa 30:8 **19:25** [c]Ps 78:35; Pr 23:11; Isa 43:14; Jer 50:34 [d]Job 16:19 **19:26** [e]Ps 17:15; Mt 5:8; 1Co 13:12; 1Jn 3:2 **19:27** [f]Ps 73:26 **19:29** [g]Job 15:22 [h]Job 22:4; Ps 1:5; 9:7

e20 Or *only my gums* f24 Or *and* g25 Or *defender* h25 Or *upon my grave* i26 Or *And after I awake, / though this ⌊body⌋ has been destroyed, / then* j26 Or */ apart from* k28 Many Hebrew manuscripts, Septuagint and Vulgate; most Hebrew manuscripts *me* l29 Or */ that you may come to know the Almighty*

Zophar: Joy of the godless is brief.

20 Then Zophar the Naamathite replied:

2 "My troubled thoughts prompt me to answer
because I am greatly disturbed.
3 I hear a rebuke[a] that dishonors me,
and my understanding inspires me to reply.

4 "Surely you know how it has been from of old,
ever since man[m] was placed on the earth,
5 that the mirth of the wicked is brief,
the joy of the godless lasts but a moment.[b]
6 Though his pride reaches to the heavens
and his head touches the clouds,[c]
7 he will perish forever,[d] like his own dung;
those who have seen him will say, 'Where is he?'[e]
8 Like a dream[f] he flies away,[g] no more to be found,
banished[h] like a vision of the night.[i]
9 The eye that saw him will not see him again;
his place will look on him no more.[j]
10 His children[k] must make amends to the poor;
his own hands must give back his wealth.[l]
11 The youthful vigor[m] that fills his bones
will lie with him in the dust.[n]

12 "Though evil is sweet in his mouth
and he hides it under his tongue,
13 though he cannot bear to let it go
and keeps it in his mouth,[o]
14 yet his food will turn sour in his stomach;
it will become the venom of serpents within him.
15 He will spit out the riches he swallowed;
God will make his stomach vomit them up.
16 He will suck the poison[p] of serpents;
the fangs of an adder will kill him.[q]
17 He will not enjoy the streams,
the rivers flowing with honey[r] and cream.[s]
18 What he toiled for he must give back uneaten;
he will not enjoy the profit from his trading.
19 For he has oppressed the poor and left them destitute;[t]
he has seized houses he did not build.

20 "Surely he will have no respite from his craving;[u]
he cannot save himself by his treasure.
21 Nothing is left for him to devour;
his prosperity will not endure.[v]
22 In the midst of his plenty, distress will overtake him;
the full force of misery will come upon him.
23 When he has filled his belly,
God will vent his burning anger against him
and rain down his blows upon him.[w]
24 Though he flees[x] from an iron weapon,
a bronze-tipped arrow pierces him.
25 He pulls it out of his back,
the gleaming point out of his liver.
Terrors[y] will come over him;[z]
26 total darkness[a] lies in wait for his treasures.
A fire unfanned will consume him[b]
and devour what is left in his tent.
27 The heavens will expose his guilt;
the earth will rise up against him.[c]
28 A flood will carry off his house,[d]
rushing waters[n] on the day of God's wrath.[e]
29 Such is the fate God allots the wicked,
the heritage appointed for them by God."[f]

20:3 [a]Job 19:3
20:5 [b]Job 8:12; Ps 37:35-36; 73:19
20:6 [c]Isa 14:13-14; Ob 3-4
20:7 [d]Job 4:20 [e]Job 7:10; 8:18
20:8 [f]Ps 73:20 [g]Job 27:21-23 [h]Job 18:18 [i]Ps 90:5
20:9 [j]Job 7:8
20:10 [k]Job 5:4 [l]Job 27:16-17
20:11 [m]Job 13:26 [n]Job 21:26
20:13 [o]Nu 11:18-20
20:16 [p]Dt 32:32 [q]Dt 32:24
20:17 [r]Dt 32:13 [s]Job 29:6
20:19 [t]Job 24:4,14; 35:9
20:20 [u]Ecc 5:12-14
20:21 [v]Job 15:29
20:23 [w]Ps 78:30-31
20:24 [x]Isa 24:18; Am 5:19
20:25 [y]Job 18:11 [z]Job 16:13
20:26 [a]Job 18:18 [b]Ps 21:9
20:27 [c]Dt 31:28
20:28 [d]Dt 28:31 [e]Job 21:17, 20,30
20:29 [f]Job 27:13

m4 Or *Adam* n28 Or *The possessions in his house will be carried off, / washed away*

Job: Wicked people sometimes prosper.

21

Then Job replied:

2 “Listen carefully to my words;
let this be the consolation you give me.
3 Bear with me while I speak,
and after I have spoken, mock on.[a]

4 “Is my complaint directed to man?
Why should I not be impatient?[b]
5 Look at me and be astonished;
clap your hand over your mouth.[c]
6 When I think about this, I am terrified;
trembling seizes my body.
7 Why do the wicked live on,
growing old and increasing in power?[d]
8 They see their children established around them,
their offspring before their eyes.[e]
9 Their homes are safe and free from fear;[f]
the rod of God is not upon them.
10 Their bulls never fail to breed;
their cows calve and do not miscarry.[g]
11 They send forth their children as a flock;
their little ones dance about.
12 They sing to the music of tambourine and harp;
they make merry to the sound of the flute.[h]
13 They spend their years in prosperity[i]
and go down to the grave[o] in peace.[p]
14 Yet they say to God, ‘Leave us alone![j]
We have no desire to know your ways.[k]
15 Who is the Almighty, that we should serve him?
What would we gain by praying to him?’[l]
16 But their prosperity is not in their own hands,
so I stand aloof from the counsel of the wicked.

17 “Yet how often is the lamp of the wicked snuffed out?[m]
How often does calamity come upon them,
the fate God allots in his anger?
18 How often are they like straw before the wind,
like chaff[n] swept away by a gale?
19 ⌊It is said,⌋ ‘God stores up a man’s punishment for his sons.’[o]
Let him repay the man himself, so that he will know it!
20 Let his own eyes see his destruction;
let him drink[p] of the wrath of the Almighty.[q][q]
21 For what does he care about the family he leaves behind
when his allotted months[r] come to an end?

22 “Can anyone teach knowledge to God,[s]
since he judges even the highest?[t]
23 One man dies in full vigor,
completely secure and at ease,
24 his body[r] well nourished,
his bones rich with marrow.[u]
25 Another man dies in bitterness of soul,
never having enjoyed anything good.
26 Side by side they lie in the dust,
and worms cover them both.[v]

27 “I know full well what you are thinking,
the schemes by which you would wrong me.
28 You say, ‘Where now is the great man’s[w] house,
the tents where wicked men lived?’[x]
29 Have you never questioned those who travel?
Have you paid no regard to their accounts—
30 that the evil man is spared from the day of calamity,[y]
that he is delivered from[s] the day of wrath?[z]

21:3 [a]Job 16:10
21:4 [b]Job 6:11
21:5 [c]Jdg 18:19; Job 29:9; 40:4
21:7 [d]Job 12:6; Ps 73:3; Jer 12:1; Hab 1:13
21:8 [e]Ps 17:14
21:9 [f]Ps 73:5
21:10 [g]Ex 23:26
21:12 [h]Ps 81:2
21:13 [i]Job 36:11
21:14 [j]Job 22:17 [k]Pr 1:29
21:15 [l]Ex 5:2; Job 34:9; Mal 3:14
21:17 [m]Job 18:5
21:18 [n]Job 13:25; Ps 1:4
21:19 [o]Ex 20:5; Jer 31:29; Eze 18:2
21:20 [p]Ps 75:8; Isa 51:17 [q]Jer 25:15; Rev 14:10
21:21 [r]Job 14:5
21:22 [s]Job 35:11; 36:22; Isa 40:13-14; Ro 11:34 [t]Ps 82:1
21:24 [u]Pr 3:8
21:26 [v]Job 24:20; Ecc 9:2-3; Isa 14:11
21:28 [w]Job 1:3; 12:21; 31:37 [x]Job 8:22
21:30 [y]Pr 16:4 [z]Job 20:22,28; 2Pe 2:9

[o] *13* Hebrew *Sheol* [p] *13* Or *in an instant* [q] *17-20* Verses 17 and 18 may be taken as exclamations and 19 and 20 as declarations. [r] *24* The meaning of the Hebrew for this word is uncertain. [s] *30* Or *man is reserved for the day of calamity, / that he is brought forth to*

31Who denounces his conduct to his
face?
Who repays him for what he has
done?
32He is carried to the grave,
and watch is kept over his tomb.
33The soil in the valley is sweet to
him;[a]
all men follow after him,
and a countless throng goes[t] before
him.[b]

34"So how can you console me[c] with
your nonsense?
Nothing is left of your answers but
falsehood!"

Eliphaz: Job needs to repent of many sins.

22 Then Eliphaz the Temanite replied:

2"Can a man be of benefit to God?[d]
Can even a wise man benefit him?
3What pleasure would it give the
Almighty if you were
righteous?
What would he gain if your ways
were blameless?

4"Is it for your piety that he rebukes
you
and brings charges against you?[e]
5Is not your wickedness great?
Are not your sins[f] endless?
6You demanded security[g] from your
brothers for no reason;
you stripped men of their clothing,
leaving them naked.
7You gave no water to the weary
and you withheld food from the
hungry,[h]
8though you were a powerful man,
owning land—
an honored man,[i] living on it.
9And you sent widows away empty-
handed[j]
and broke the strength of the
fatherless.
10That is why snares are all around you,
why sudden peril terrifies you,
11why it is so dark[k] you cannot see,
and why a flood of water covers you.[l]

12"Is not God in the heights of
heaven?[m]
And see how lofty are the highest
stars!
13Yet you say, 'What does God know?[n]
Does he judge through such
darkness?[o]
14Thick clouds[p] veil him, so he does
not see us
as he goes about in the vaulted
heavens.'
15Will you keep to the old path
that evil men have trod?
16They were carried off before their
time,[q]
their foundations washed away by
a flood.[r]
17They said to God, 'Leave us alone!
What can the Almighty do to us?'[s]
18Yet it was he who filled their houses
with good things,[t]
so I stand aloof from the counsel of
the wicked.[u]

19"The righteous see their ruin and
rejoice;[v]
the innocent mock[w] them, saying,
20'Surely our foes are destroyed,
and fire[x] devours their wealth.'

21"Submit to God and be at peace with
him;
in this way prosperity will come to
you.[y]
22Accept instruction from his mouth
and lay up his words in your heart.
23If you return[z] to the Almighty, you
will be restored:[a]
If you remove wickedness far from
your tent[b]
24and assign your nuggets to the dust,
your gold of Ophir to the rocks in
the ravines,[c]
25then the Almighty will be your gold,
the choicest silver for you.[d]
26Surely then you will find delight in
the Almighty[e]
and will lift up your face to God.

21:33 [a]Job 3:22; 17:16; 24:24 [b]Job 3:19
21:34 [c]Job 16:2
22:2 [d]Lk 17:10
22:4 [e]Job 14:3; 19:29; Ps 143:2
22:5 [f]Job 11:6; 15:5
22:6 [g]Ex 22:26; Dt 24:6,17; Eze 18:12,16
22:7 [h]Job 31:17, 21,31
22:8 [i]Isa 3:3; 9:15
22:9 [j]Job 24:3,21
22:11 [k]Job 5:14 [l]Ps 69:1-2; 124:4-5; La 3:54
22:12 [m]Job 11:8
22:13 [n]Ps 10:11; Isa 29:15 [o]Eze 8:12
22:14 [p]Job 26:9
22:16 [q]Job 15:32 [r]Job 14:19; Mt 7:26-27
22:17 [s]Job 21:15
22:18 [t]Job 12:6 [u]Job 21:16
22:19 [v]Ps 58:10; 107:42 [w]Ps 52:6
22:20 [x]Job 15:30
22:21 [y]Ps 34:8-10
22:23 [z]Job 8:5; Isa 31:6; Zec 1:3 [a]Isa 19:22; Ac 20:32 [b]Job 11:14
22:24 [c]Job 31:25
22:25 [d]Isa 33:6
22:26 [e]Job 27:10; Isa 58:14

t33 Or / *as a countless throng went*

27You will pray to him,[a] and he will
hear you,
and you will fulfill your vows.
28What you decide on will be done,
and light will shine on your ways.
29When men are brought low and you
say, 'Lift them up!'
then he will save the downcast.[b]
30He will deliver even one who is not
innocent,
who will be delivered through the
cleanness of your hands."[c]

Job: When tested, he will come forth as gold.

23 Then Job replied:

2"Even today my complaint[d] is
bitter;[e]
his hand[u] is heavy in spite of[v]
my groaning.
3If only I knew where to find him;
if only I could go to his dwelling!
4I would state my case[f] before him
and fill my mouth with arguments.
5I would find out what he would
answer me,
and consider what he would say.
6Would he oppose me with great
power?[g]
No, he would not press charges
against me.
7There an upright man could present
his case before him,[h]
and I would be delivered forever
from my judge.

8"But if I go to the east, he is not
there;
if I go to the west, I do not find
him.
9When he is at work in the north, I
do not see him;
when he turns to the south, I catch
no glimpse of him.[i]
10But he knows the way that I take;
when he has tested me,[j] I will
come forth as gold.[k]
11My feet have closely followed his
steps;[l]
I have kept to his way without
turning aside.[m]
12I have not departed from the
commands of his lips;[n]
I have treasured the words of his
mouth more than my daily
bread.[o]

13"But he stands alone, and who can
oppose him?
He does whatever he pleases.[p]
14He carries out his decree against me,
and many such plans he still has in
store.[q]
15That is why I am terrified before
him;
when I think of all this, I fear him.
16God has made my heart faint;[r]
the Almighty[s] has terrified me.
17Yet I am not silenced by the
darkness,[t]
by the thick darkness that covers
my face.

Job: Wicked people sometimes seem to go unpunished.

24 "Why does the Almighty not
set times for judgment?[u]
Why must those who know him
look in vain for such days?[v]
2Men move boundary stones;[w]
they pasture flocks they have
stolen.
3They drive away the orphan's
donkey
and take the widow's ox in
pledge.[x]
4They thrust the needy from the path
and force all the poor[y] of the land
into hiding.[z]
5Like wild donkeys in the desert,
the poor go about their labor[a] of
foraging food;
the wasteland provides food for
their children.
6They gather fodder in the fields
and glean in the vineyards of the
wicked.
7Lacking clothes, they spend the
night naked;
they have nothing to cover
themselves in the cold.[b]

22:27 [a]Job 33:26; 34:28; Isa 58:9
22:29 [b]Mt 23:12; 1Pe 5:5
22:30 [c]Job 42:7-8
23:2 [d]Job 7:11 [e]Job 6:3
23:4 [f]Job 13:18
23:6 [g]Job 9:4
23:7 [h]Job 13:3
23:9 [i]Job 9:11
23:10 [j]Ps 66:10; 139:1-3 [k]1Pe 1:7
23:11 [l]Ps 17:5 [m]Ps 44:18
23:12 [n]Job 6:10 [o]Jn 4:32,34
23:13 [p]Ps 115:3
23:14 [q]1Th 3:3
23:16 [r]Dt 20:3; Ps 22:14; Jer 51:46 [s]Job 27:2
23:17 [t]Job 19:8
24:1 [u]Jer 46:10 [v]Ac 1:7
24:2 [w]Dt 19:14; 27:17; Pr 23:10
24:3 [x]Dt 24:6,10, 12,17; Job 22:6
24:4 [y]Job 29:12; 30:25; Ps 41:1 [z]Pr 28:28
24:5 [a]Ps 104:23
24:7 [b]Ex 22:27; Job 22:6

u2 Septuagint and Syriac; Hebrew / *the hand on me*
v2 Or *heavy on me in*

8They are drenched by mountain rains
and hug[a] the rocks for lack of
shelter.
9The fatherless[b] child is snatched
from the breast;
the infant of the poor is seized for
a debt.
10Lacking clothes, they go about
naked;
they carry the sheaves, but still go
hungry.
11They crush olives among the
terraces[w];
they tread the winepresses, yet
suffer thirst.
12The groans of the dying rise from the
city,
and the souls of the wounded cry
out for help.[c]
But God charges no one with
wrongdoing.[d]

13"There are those who rebel against
the light,[e]
who do not know its ways
or stay in its paths.[f]
14When daylight is gone, the murderer
rises up
and kills the poor and needy;
in the night he steals forth like a
thief.[g]
15The eye of the adulterer watches for
dusk;[h]
he thinks, 'No eye will see me,'[i]
and he keeps his face concealed.
16In the dark, men break into houses,[j]
but by day they shut themselves in;
they want nothing to do with the
light.[k]
17For all of them, deep darkness is
their morning[x];
they make friends with the terrors
of darkness.[y]

18"Yet they are foam[l] on the surface of
the water;[m]
their portion of the land is cursed,
so that no one goes to the
vineyards.
19As heat and drought snatch away the
melted snow,[n]
so the grave[z][o] snatches away those
who have sinned.
20The womb forgets them,
the worm feasts on them;
evil men are no longer
remembered[p]
but are broken like a tree.[q]
21They prey on the barren and
childless woman,
and to the widow show no
kindness.[r]
22But God drags away the mighty by
his power;
though they become established,
they have no assurance of
life.[s]
23He may let them rest in a feeling of
security,[t]
but his eyes are on their ways.[u]
24For a little while they are exalted,
and then they are gone;[v]
they are brought low and gathered
up like all others;
they are cut off like heads of
grain.[w]

25"If this is not so, who can prove me
false
and reduce my words to nothing?"[x]

Bildad: Man cannot be righteous before God.

25 Then Bildad the Shuhite replied:

2"Dominion and awe belong to God;[y]
he establishes order in the heights
of heaven.
3Can his forces be numbered?
Upon whom does his light not rise?[z]
4How then can a man be righteous
before God?
How can one born of woman be
pure?[a]
5If even the moon[b] is not bright
and the stars are not pure in his
eyes,[c]
6how much less man, who is but a
maggot—
a son of man,[d] who is only a
worm!"[e]

24:8 [a]La 4:5
24:9 [b]Dt 24:17
24:12 [c]Eze 26:15 [d]Job 9:23
24:13 [e]Jn 3:19-20 [f]Isa 5:20
24:14 [g]Ps 10:9
24:15 [h]Pr 7:8-9 [i]Ps 10:11
24:16 [j]Ex 22:2; Mt 6:19 [k]Jn 3:20
24:18 [l]Job 9:26 [m]Job 22:16
24:19 [n]Job 6:17 [o]Job 21:13
24:20 [p]Job 18:17; Pr 10:7 [q]Ps 31:12; Da 4:14
24:21 [r]Job 22:9
24:22 [s]Dt 28:66
24:23 [t]Job 12:6 [u]Job 11:11
24:24 [v]Job 14:21; Ps 37:10 [w]Isa 17:5
24:25 [x]Job 6:28; 27:4
25:2 [y]Job 9:4; Rev 1:6
25:3 [z]Jas 1:17
25:4 [a]Job 4:17; 14:4
25:5 [b]Job 31:26 [c]Job 15:15
25:6 [d]Job 7:17 [e]Ps 22:6

w 11 Or *olives between the millstones*; the meaning of the Hebrew for this word is uncertain. x 17 Or *them, their morning is like the shadow of death* y 17 Or *of the shadow of death* z 19 Hebrew *Sheol*

Job: Who can understand God's power?

26 Then Job replied:

2"How you have helped the
powerless![a]
How you have saved the arm that
is feeble![b]
3What advice you have offered to one
without wisdom!
And what great insight you have
displayed!
4Who has helped you utter these words?
And whose spirit spoke from your
mouth?

5"The dead are in deep anguish,[c]
those beneath the waters and all
that live in them.
6Death[a][d] is naked before God;
Destruction[b] lies uncovered.[e]
7He spreads out the northern ⌊skies⌋[f]
over empty space;
he suspends the earth over nothing.
8He wraps up the waters[g] in his
clouds,[h]
yet the clouds do not burst under
their weight.
9He covers the face of the full moon,
spreading his clouds[i] over it.
10He marks out the horizon on the
face of the waters[j]
for a boundary between light and
darkness.[k]
11The pillars of the heavens quake,
aghast at his rebuke.
12By his power he churned up the sea;[l]
by his wisdom[m] he cut Rahab to
pieces.
13By his breath the skies became fair;
his hand pierced the gliding
serpent.[n]
14And these are but the outer fringe of
his works;
how faint the whisper we hear of
him!
Who then can understand the
thunder of his power?"[o]

Job: Integrity will not be denied.

27 And Job continued his discourse:[p]

2"As surely as God lives, who has
denied me justice,[q]
the Almighty, who has made me
taste bitterness of soul,[r]
3as long as I have life within me,
the breath of God[s] in my nostrils,
4my lips will not speak wickedness,
and my tongue will utter no
deceit.[t]
5I will never admit you are in the
right;
till I die, I will not deny my
integrity.[u]
6I will maintain my righteousness and
never let go of it;
my conscience will not reproach
me as long as I live.[v]

7"May my enemies be like the
wicked,
my adversaries like the unjust!
8For what hope has the godless[w]
when he is cut off,
when God takes away his life?[x]
9Does God listen to his cry
when distress comes upon him?[y]
10Will he find delight in the
Almighty?[z]
Will he call upon God at all times?

11"I will teach you about the power of
God;
the ways of the Almighty I will not
conceal.
12You have all seen this yourselves.
Why then this meaningless talk?

13"Here is the fate God allots to the
wicked,
the heritage a ruthless man
receives from the Almighty:[a]
14However many his children, their
fate is the sword;[b]
his offspring will never have
enough to eat.[c]
15The plague will bury those who
survive him,
and their widows will not weep for
them.[d]
16Though he heaps up silver like dust
and clothes like piles of clay,[e]

26:2 [a]Job 6:12 [b]Ps 71:9 **26:5** [c]Ps 88:10 **26:6** [d]Ps 139:8 [e]Job 41:11; Pr 15:11; Heb 4:13 **26:7** [f]Job 9:8 **26:8** [g]Pr 30:4 [h]Job 37:11 **26:9** [i]Job 22:14; Ps 97:2 **26:10** [j]Pr 8:27,29 [k]Job 38:8-11 **26:12** [l]Ex 14:21; Isa 51:15; Jer 31:35 [m]Job 12:13 **26:13** [n]Isa 27:1 **26:14** [o]Job 36:29 **27:1** [p]Job 29:1 **27:2** [q]Job 34:5 [r]Job 9:18 **27:3** [s]Job 32:8; 33:4 **27:4** [t]Job 6:28 **27:5** [u]Job 2:9; 13:15 **27:6** [v]Job 2:3 **27:8** [w]Job 8:13 [x]Job 11:20; Lk 12:20 **27:9** [y]Job 35:12; Pr 1:28; Isa 1:15; Jer 14:12; Mic 3:4 **27:10** [z]Job 22:26 **27:13** [a]Job 15:20; 20:29 **27:14** [b]Dt 28:41; Job 15:22; Hos 9:13 [c]Job 20:10 **27:15** [d]Ps 78:64 **27:16** [e]Zec 9:3

a*6* Hebrew *Sheol* b*6* Hebrew *Abaddon*

17what he lays up the righteous will wear,[a]
and the innocent will divide his silver.
18The house he builds is like a moth's cocoon,[b]
like a hut[c] made by a watchman.
19He lies down wealthy, but will do so no more;[d]
when he opens his eyes, all is gone.
20Terrors overtake him like a flood;[e]
a tempest snatches him away in the night.[f]
21The east wind carries him off, and he is gone;
it sweeps him out of his place.[g]
22It hurls itself against him without mercy[h]
as he flees headlong from its power.[i]
23It claps its hands in derision
and hisses him out of his place.[j]

Job: The fear of the Lord is wisdom.

28 "There is a mine for silver
and a place where gold is refined.
2Iron is taken from the earth,
and copper is smelted from ore.[k]
3Man puts an end to the darkness;[l]
he searches the farthest recesses
for ore in the blackest darkness.
4Far from where people dwell he cuts a shaft,
in places forgotten by the foot of man;
far from men he dangles and sways.
5The earth, from which food comes,[m]
is transformed below as by fire;
6sapphires[c] come from its rocks,
and its dust contains nuggets of gold.
7No bird of prey knows that hidden path,
no falcon's eye has seen it.
8Proud beasts do not set foot on it,
and no lion prowls there.
9Man's hand assaults the flinty rock
and lays bare the roots of the mountains.
10He tunnels through the rock;
his eyes see all its treasures.
11He searches[d] the sources of the rivers
and brings hidden things to light.

12"But where can wisdom be found?[n]
Where does understanding dwell?
13Man does not comprehend its worth;[o]
it cannot be found in the land of the living.
14The deep says, 'It is not in me';
the sea says, 'It is not with me.'
15It cannot be bought with the finest gold,
nor can its price be weighed in silver.[p]
16It cannot be bought with the gold of Ophir,
with precious onyx or sapphires.
17Neither gold nor crystal can compare with it,
nor can it be had for jewels of gold.[q]
18Coral and jasper are not worthy of mention;
the price of wisdom is beyond rubies.[r]
19The topaz of Cush cannot compare with it;
it cannot be bought with pure gold.[s]

20"Where then does wisdom come from?
Where does understanding dwell?[t]
21It is hidden from the eyes of every living thing,
concealed even from the birds of the air.
22Destruction[e][u] and Death say,
'Only a rumor of it has reached our ears.'
23God understands the way to it
and he alone knows where it dwells,[v]
24for he views the ends of the earth[w]
and sees everything under the heavens.[x]

27:17 [a]Pr 28:8; Ecc 2:26
27:18 [b]Job 8:14 [c]Isa 1:8
27:19 [d]Job 7:8
27:20 [e]Job 15:21 [f]Job 20:8
27:21 [g]Job 7:10; 21:18
27:22 [h]Jer 13:14; Eze 5:11; 24:14 [i]Job 11:20
27:23 [j]Job 18:18
28:2 [k]Dt 8:9
28:3 [l]Ecc 1:13
28:5 [m]Ps 104:14
28:12 [n]Ecc 7:24
28:13 [o]Pr 3:15; Mt 13:44-46
28:15 [p]Pr 3:13-14; 8:10-11; 16:16
28:17 [q]Pr 16:16
28:18 [r]Pr 3:15
28:19 [s]Pr 8:19
28:20 [t]ver 23,28
28:22 [u]Job 26:6
28:23 [v]Pr 8:22-31
28:24 [w]Ps 33:13-14 [x]Pr 15:3

c*6* Or *lapis lazuli*; also in verse 16 d*11* Septuagint, Aquila and Vulgate; Hebrew *He dams up*
e*22* Hebrew *Abaddon*

[25]When he established the force of the wind
and measured out the waters,[a]
[26]when he made a decree for the rain
and a path for the thunderstorm,[b]
[27]then he looked at wisdom and appraised it;
he confirmed it and tested it.
[28]And he said to man,
'The fear of the Lord—that is wisdom,
and to shun evil is understanding.[c]'"

Job: Longing for blessed days gone by.

29 Job continued his discourse:[d]
[2]"How I long for the months gone by,
for the days when God watched over me,[e]
[3]when his lamp shone upon my head
and by his light I walked through darkness![f]
[4]Oh, for the days when I was in my prime,
when God's intimate friendship blessed my house,[g]
[5]when the Almighty was still with me
and my children were around me,
[6]when my path was drenched with cream[h]
and the rock[i] poured out for me streams of olive oil.[j]

[7]"When I went to the gate[k] of the city
and took my seat in the public square,
[8]the young men saw me and stepped aside
and the old men rose to their feet;
[9]the chief men refrained from speaking
and covered their mouths with their hands;[l]
[10]the voices of the nobles were hushed,
and their tongues stuck to the roof of their mouths.[m]
[11]Whoever heard me spoke well of me,
and those who saw me commended me,
[12]because I rescued the poor[n] who cried for help,
and the fatherless[o] who had none to assist him.[p]
[13]The man who was dying blessed me;[q]
I made the widow's[r] heart sing.
[14]I put on righteousness[s] as my clothing;
justice was my robe and my turban.
[15]I was eyes[t] to the blind
and feet to the lame.
[16]I was a father to the needy;[u]
I took up the case of the stranger.
[17]I broke the fangs of the wicked
and snatched the victims from their teeth.[v]

[18]"I thought, 'I will die in my own house,
my days as numerous as the grains of sand.[w]
[19]My roots will reach to the water,[x]
and the dew will lie all night on my branches.
[20]My glory will remain fresh in me,
the bow[y] ever new in my hand.'[z]

[21]"Men listened to me expectantly,
waiting in silence for my counsel.
[22]After I had spoken, they spoke no more;
my words fell gently on their ears.[a]
[23]They waited for me as for showers
and drank in my words as the spring rain.
[24]When I smiled at them, they scarcely believed it;
the light of my face was precious to them.[f]
[25]I chose the way for them and sat as their chief;
I dwelt as a king[b] among his troops;
I was like one who comforts mourners.[c]

Job: Reasons for mourning.

30 "But now they mock me,[d]
men younger than I,
whose fathers I would have disdained
to put with my sheep dogs.

28:25 [a]Job 12:15; Ps 135:7
28:26 [b]Job 37:3, 8,11; 38:25,27
28:28 [c]Dt 4:6; Ps 111:10; Pr 1:7; 9:10
29:1 [d]Job 13:12; 27:1
29:2 [e]Jer 31:28
29:3 [f]Job 11:17
29:4 [g]Ps 25:14; Pr 3:32
29:6 [h]Job 20:17 [i]Ps 81:16 [j]Dt 32:13
29:7 [k]Job 31:21
29:9 [l]Job 21:5
29:10 [m]Ps 137:6
29:12 [n]Job 24:4 [o]Job 31:17,21 [p]Ps 72:12; Pr 21:13
29:13 [q]Job 31:20 [r]Job 22:9
29:14 [s]Job 27:6; Ps 132:9; Isa 59:17; 61:10; Eph 6:14
29:15 [t]Nu 10:31
29:16 [u]Job 24:4; Pr 29:7
29:17 [v]Ps 3:7
29:18 [w]Ps 30:6
29:19 [x]Job 18:16; Jer 17:8
29:20 [y]Ps 18:34 [z]Ge 49:24
29:22 [a]Dt 32:2
29:25 [b]Job 1:3; 31:37 [c]Job 4:4
30:1 [d]Job 12:4

f24 The meaning of the Hebrew for this clause is uncertain.

[2]Of what use was the strength of
their hands to me,
since their vigor had gone from
them?
[3]Haggard from want and hunger,
they roamed[g] the parched land
in desolate wastelands at night.
[4]In the brush they gathered salt herbs,
and their food[h] was the root of the
broom tree.
[5]They were banished from their
fellow men,
shouted at as if they were thieves.
[6]They were forced to live in the dry
stream beds,
among the rocks and in holes in
the ground.
[7]They brayed among the bushes
and huddled in the undergrowth.
[8]A base and nameless brood,
they were driven out of the land.

[9]"And now their sons mock me[a] in
song;[b]
I have become a byword[c] among
them.
[10]They detest me and keep their
distance;
they do not hesitate to spit in my
face.[d]
[11]Now that God has unstrung my bow
and afflicted me,[e]
they throw off restraint[f] in my
presence.
[12]On my right the tribe[i] attacks;
they lay snares for my feet,[g]
they build their siege ramps
against me.[h]
[13]They break up my road;[i]
they succeed in destroying me—
without anyone's helping them.[j]
[14]They advance as through a gaping
breach;
amid the ruins they come rolling in.
[15]Terrors overwhelm me;[j]
my dignity is driven away as by the
wind,
my safety vanishes like a cloud.[k]

[16]"And now my life ebbs away;[l]
days of suffering grip me.
[17]Night pierces my bones;
my gnawing pains never rest.

30:9 [a]Ps 69:11 [b]Job 12:4; La 3:14,63 [c]Job 17:6
30:10 [d]Nu 12:14; Dt 25:9; Isa 50:6; Mt 26:67
30:11 [e]Ru 1:21 [f]Ps 32:9
30:12 [g]Ps 140:4-5 [h]Job 19:12
30:13 [i]Isa 3:12
30:15 [j]Job 31:23; Ps 55:4-5 [k]Job 3:25; Hos 13:3
30:16 [l]Job 3:24; Ps 22:14; 42:4
30:19 [m]Ps 69:2,14
30:20 [n]Job 19:7
30:21 [o]Job 19:6,22 [p]Job 16:9,14 [q]Job 10:3
30:22 [r]Job 27:21 [s]Job 9:17
30:23 [t]Job 9:22; 10:8 [u]Job 3:19
30:24 [v]Job 19:7
30:25 [w]Job 24:4; Ps 35:13-14; Ro 12:15
30:26 [x]Job 3:25-26; 19:8; Jer 8:15
30:27 [y]La 2:11
30:28 [z]Ps 38:6; 42:9; 43:2 [a]Job 19:7
30:29 [b]Ps 44:19 [c]Ps 102:6; Mic 1:8
30:30 [d]La 4:8 [e]Ps 102:3
30:31 [f]Isa 24:8

[18]In his great power ⌊God⌋ becomes
like clothing to me[k];
he binds me like the neck of my
garment.
[19]He throws me into the mud,[m]
and I am reduced to dust and
ashes.

[20]"I cry out to you, O God, but you do
not answer;[n]
I stand up, but you merely look at
me.
[21]You turn on me ruthlessly;[o]
with the might of your hand[p] you
attack me.[q]
[22]You snatch me up and drive me
before the wind;[r]
you toss me about in the storm.[s]
[23]I know you will bring me down to
death,[t]
to the place appointed for all the
living.[u]

[24]"Surely no one lays a hand on a
broken man
when he cries for help in his
distress.[v]
[25]Have I not wept for those in trouble?
Has not my soul grieved for the
poor?[w]
[26]Yet when I hoped for good, evil
came;
when I looked for light, then came
darkness.[x]
[27]The churning inside me never
stops;[y]
days of suffering confront me.
[28]I go about blackened,[z] but not by the
sun;
I stand up in the assembly and cry
for help.[a]
[29]I have become a brother of jackals,[b]
a companion of owls.[c]
[30]My skin grows black and peels;[d]
my body burns with fever.[e]
[31]My harp is tuned to mourning,[f]
and my flute to the sound of
wailing.

[g]3 Or *gnawed* [h]4 Or *fuel* [i]12 The meaning of the Hebrew for this word is uncertain. [j]13 Or *me. / 'No one can help him,' ⌊they say⌋.* [k]18 Hebrew; Septuagint *⌊God⌋ grasps my clothing*

Job: Concluding words.

31 "I made a covenant with my eyes
not to look lustfully at a girl.[a]
[2]For what is man's lot from God above,
his heritage from the Almighty on high?[b]
[3]Is it not ruin[c] for the wicked,
disaster for those who do wrong?[d]
[4]Does he not see my ways[e]
and count my every step?[f]

[5]"If I have walked in falsehood
or my foot has hurried after deceit[g]—
[6]let God weigh me in honest scales[h]
and he will know that I am blameless—
[7]if my steps have turned from the path,[i]
if my heart has been led by my eyes,
or if my hands[j] have been defiled,
[8]then may others eat what I have sown,[k]
and may my crops be uprooted.[l]

[9]"If my heart has been enticed[m] by a woman,
or if I have lurked at my neighbor's door,
[10]then may my wife grind another man's grain,
and may other men sleep with her.[n]
[11]For that would have been shameful,
a sin to be judged.[o]
[12]It is a fire[p] that burns to Destruction[1];[q]
it would have uprooted my harvest.[r]

[13]"If I have denied justice to my menservants and maidservants
when they had a grievance against me,[s]
[14]what will I do when God confronts me?
What will I answer when called to account?
[15]Did not he who made me in the womb make them?
Did not the same one form us both within our mothers?[t]

[16]"If I have denied the desires of the poor[u]
or let the eyes of the widow[v] grow weary,
[17]if I have kept my bread to myself,
not sharing it with the fatherless[w]—
[18]but from my youth I reared him as would a father,
and from my birth I guided the widow—
[19]if I have seen anyone perishing for lack of clothing,[x]
or a needy[y] man without a garment,
[20]and his heart did not bless me
for warming him with the fleece from my sheep,
[21]if I have raised my hand against the fatherless,[z]
knowing that I had influence in court,
[22]then let my arm fall from the shoulder,
let it be broken off at the joint.[a]
[23]For I dreaded destruction from God,
and for fear of his splendor[b] I could not do such things.

[24]"If I have put my trust in gold[c]
or said to pure gold, 'You are my security,'[d]
[25]if I have rejoiced over my great wealth,[e]
the fortune my hands had gained,
[26]if I have regarded the sun[f] in its radiance
or the moon moving in splendor,
[27]so that my heart was secretly enticed
and my hand offered them a kiss of homage,
[28]then these also would be sins to be judged,[g]
for I would have been unfaithful to God on high.

[29]"If I have rejoiced at my enemy's misfortune[h]
or gloated over the trouble that came to him[i]—

[1]12 Hebrew *Abaddon*

31:1 [a]Mt 5:28 **31:2** [b]Job 20:29 **31:3** [c]Job 21:30 [d]Job 34:22 **31:4** [e]2Ch 16:9 [f]Pr 5:21 **31:5** [g]Mic 2:11 **31:6** [h]Job 6:2; 27:5-6 **31:7** [i]Job 23:11 [j]Job 9:30 **31:8** [k]Lev 26:16; Job 20:18 [l]Mic 6:15 **31:9** [m]Job 24:15 **31:10** [n]Dt 28:30; Jer 8:10 **31:11** [o]Ge 38:24; Lev 20:10; Dt 22:22-24 **31:12** [p]Job 15:30 [q]Job 26:6 [r]Job 20:28 **31:13** [s]Dt 24:14-15 **31:15** [t]Job 10:3 **31:16** [u]Job 5:16; 20:19 [v]Job 22:9 **31:17** [w]Job 22:7; 29:12 **31:19** [x]Job 22:6 [y]Job 24:4 **31:21** [z]Job 22:9 **31:22** [a]Job 38:15 **31:23** [b]Job 13:11 **31:24** [c]Job 22:25 [d]Mt 6:24; Mk 10:24 **31:25** [e]Ps 62:10 **31:26** [f]Eze 8:16 **31:28** [g]Dt 17:2-7 **31:29** [h]Ob 12 [i]Pr 17:5; 24:17-18

30I have not allowed my mouth to sin
by invoking a curse against his
life—
31if the men of my household have
never said,
'Who has not had his fill of Job's
meat?'[a]—
32but no stranger had to spend the
night in the street,
for my door was always open to
the traveler[b]—
33if I have concealed[c] my sin as men
do,[m]
by hiding[d] my guilt in my heart
34because I so feared the crowd[e]
and so dreaded the contempt of
the clans
that I kept silent and would not go
outside
35("Oh, that I had someone to hear
me![f]
I sign now my defense—let the
Almighty answer me;
let my accuser[g] put his indictment
in writing.
36Surely I would wear it on my
shoulder,
I would put it on like a crown.
37I would give him an account of my
every step;
like a prince[h] I would approach
him.)—

38"if my land cries out against me[i]
and all its furrows are wet with
tears,
39if I have devoured its yield without
payment[j]
or broken the spirit of its tenants,[k]
40then let briers[l] come up instead of
wheat
and weeds instead of barley."

The words of Job are ended.

Elihu: Words have failed Job and his three friends.

32 So these three men stopped
answering Job, because he was
righteous in his own eyes.[m] 2But Elihu
son of Barakel the Buzite,[n] of the family
of Ram, became very angry with Job for
justifying himself rather than God.[o] 3He
was also angry with the three friends, because they had found no way to refute
Job, and yet had condemned him.[n] 4Now
Elihu had waited before speaking to Job
because they were older than he. 5But
when he saw that the three men had
nothing more to say, his anger was
aroused.
6So Elihu son of Barakel the Buzite
said:

"I am young in years,
and you are old;[p]
that is why I was fearful,
not daring to tell you what I know.
7I thought, 'Age should speak;
advanced years should teach
wisdom.'
8But it is the spirit[o] in a man,
the breath of the Almighty,[q] that
gives him understanding.[r]
9It is not only the old[p] who are wise,[s]
not only the aged who understand
what is right.

10"Therefore I say: Listen to me;
I too will tell you what I know.
11I waited while you spoke,
I listened to your reasoning;
while you were searching for words,
12 I gave you my full attention.
But not one of you has proved Job
wrong;
none of you has answered his
arguments.
13Do not say, 'We have found wisdom;[t]
let God refute him, not man.'
14But Job has not marshaled his words
against me,
and I will not answer him with
your arguments.

15"They are dismayed and have no
more to say;
words have failed them.
16Must I wait, now that they are silent,
now that they stand there with no
reply?

31:31 [a]Job 22:7
31:32 [b]Ge 19:2-3; Ro 12:13
31:33 [c]Pr 28:13 [d]Ge 3:8
31:34 [e]Ex 23:2
31:35 [f]Job 19:7; 30:28 [g]Job 27:7; 35:14
31:37 [h]Job 1:3; 29:25
31:38 [i]Ge 4:10
31:39 [j]1Ki 21:19 [k]Lev 19:13; Jas 5:4
31:40 [l]Ge 3:18
32:1 [m]Job 10:7; 33:9
32:2 [n]Ge 22:21 [o]Job 27:5; 30:21
32:6 [p]Job 15:10
32:8 [q]Job 27:3; 33:4 [r]Pr 2:6
32:9 [s]1Co 1:26
32:13 [t]Jer 9:23

m33 Or *as Adam did* n3 Masoretic Text; an ancient Hebrew scribal tradition *Job, and so had condemned God* o8 Or *Spirit*; also in verse 18 p9 Or *many*; or *great*

17I too will have my say;
I too will tell what I know.
18For I am full of words,
and the spirit within me compels me;
19inside I am like bottled-up wine,
like new wineskins ready to burst.
20I must speak and find relief;
I must open my lips and reply.
21I will show partiality[a] to no one,[b]
nor will I flatter any man;
22for if I were skilled in flattery,
my Maker would soon take me
away.

Elihu: God sometimes uses afflictions.

33 "But now, Job, listen to my
words;
pay attention to everything I say.[c]
2I am about to open my mouth;
my words are on the tip of my
tongue.
3My words come from an upright heart;
my lips sincerely speak what I
know.[d]
4The Spirit of God has made me;[e]
the breath of the Almighty[f] gives
me life.
5Answer me[g] then, if you can;
prepare[h] yourself and confront me.
6I am just like you before God;
I too have been taken from clay.[i]
7No fear of me should alarm you,
nor should my hand be heavy upon
you.[j]

8"But you have said in my hearing—
I heard the very words—
9'I am pure[k] and without sin;[l]
I am clean and free from guilt.
10Yet God has found fault with me;
he considers me his enemy.[m]
11He fastens my feet in shackles;[n]
he keeps close watch on all my
paths.'[o]

12"But I tell you, in this you are not
right,
for God is greater than man.[p]
13Why do you complain to him[q]
that he answers none of man's
words[q]?
14For God does speak[r]—now one way,
now another—
though man may not perceive it.
15In a dream,[s] in a vision of the night,
when deep sleep falls on men
as they slumber in their beds,
16he may speak[t] in their ears
and terrify them with warnings,
17to turn man from wrongdoing
and keep him from pride,
18to preserve his soul from the pit,[r][u]
his life from perishing by the
sword.[s][v]
19Or a man may be chastened on a bed
of pain
with constant distress in his
bones,[w]
20so that his very being finds food[x]
repulsive
and his soul loathes the choicest
meal.[y]
21His flesh wastes away to nothing,
and his bones, once hidden, now
stick out.[z]
22His soul draws near to the pit,[t]
and his life to the messengers of
death.[u][a]

23"Yet if there is an angel on his side
as a mediator, one out of a
thousand,
to tell a man what is right for
him,[b]
24to be gracious to him and say,
'Spare him from going down to the
pit[v];[c]
I have found a ransom for him'—
25then his flesh is renewed like a
child's;
it is restored as in the days of his
youth.[d]
26He prays to God and finds favor with
him,[e]
he sees God's face and shouts for
joy;[f]
he is restored by God to his
righteous state.[g]

32:21 [a]Lev 19:15; Job 13:10 [b]Mt 22:16
33:1 [c]Job 13:6
33:3 [d]Job 6:28; 27:4; 36:4
33:4 [e]Ge 2:7; Job 10:3 [f]Job 27:3
33:5 [g]ver 32 [h]Job 13:18
33:6 [i]Job 4:19
33:7 [j]Job 9:34; 13:21; 2Co 2:4
33:9 [k]Job 10:7 [l]Job 13:23; 16:17
33:10 [m]Job 13:24
33:11 [n]Job 13:27 [o]Job 14:16
33:12 [p]Ecc 7:20
33:13 [q]Job 40:2; Isa 45:9
33:14 [r]Ps 62:11
33:15 [s]Job 4:13
33:16 [t]Job 36:10,15
33:18 [u]ver 22,24, 28,30 [v]Job 15:22
33:19 [w]Job 30:17
33:20 [x]Ps 107:18 [y]Job 3:24; 6:6
33:21 [z]Job 16:8; 19:20
33:22 [a]Ps 88:3
33:23 [b]Mic 6:8
33:24 [c]Isa 38:17
33:25 [d]2Ki 5:14
33:26 [e]Job 34:28 [f]Job 22:26 [g]Ps 50:15; 51:12

[q]*13* Or *that he does not answer for any of his actions* [r]*18* Or *preserve him from the grave* [s]*18* Or *from crossing the River* [t]*22* Or *He draws near to the grave* [u]*22* Or *to the dead* [v]*24* Or *grave*

27Then he comes to men and says,
'I sinned,[a] and perverted what was right,[b]
but I did not get what I deserved.[c]
28He redeemed my soul from going down to the pit,[w]
and I will live to enjoy the light.'[d]

29"God does all these things to a man[e]—
twice, even three times—
30to turn back his soul from the pit,[x]
that the light of life[f] may shine on him.

31"Pay attention, Job, and listen to me;
be silent, and I will speak.
32If you have anything to say, answer me;
speak up, for I want you to be cleared.
33But if not, then listen to me;
be silent, and I will teach you wisdom.[g]"

Elihu: It is unthinkable that God would do wrong.

34 Then Elihu said:

2"Hear my words, you wise men;
listen to me, you men of learning.
3For the ear tests words
as the tongue tastes food.[h]
4Let us discern for ourselves what is right;
let us learn together what is good.[i]

5"Job says, 'I am innocent,[j]
but God denies me justice.[k]
6Although I am right,
I am considered a liar;
although I am guiltless,
his arrow inflicts an incurable wound.'[l]
7What man is like Job,
who drinks scorn like water?[m]
8He keeps company with evildoers;
he associates with wicked men.[n]
9For he says, 'It profits a man nothing
when he tries to please God.'[o]

10"So listen to me, you men of understanding.
Far be it from God to do evil,[p]
from the Almighty to do wrong.[q]
11He repays a man for what he has done;[r]
he brings upon him what his conduct deserves.[s]
12It is unthinkable that God would do wrong,
that the Almighty would pervert justice.[t]
13Who appointed him over the earth?
Who put him in charge of the whole world?[u]
14If it were his intention
and he withdrew his spirit[y] and breath,[v]
15all mankind would perish together
and man would return to the dust.[w]

16"If you have understanding, hear this;
listen to what I say.
17Can he who hates justice govern?[x]
Will you condemn the just and mighty One?[y]
18Is he not the One who says to kings,
'You are worthless,'
and to nobles, 'You are wicked,'[z]
19who shows no partiality[a] to princes
and does not favor the rich over the poor,[b]
for they are all the work of his hands?[c]
20They die in an instant, in the middle of the night;[d]
the people are shaken and they pass away;
the mighty are removed without human hand.[e]

21"His eyes are on the ways of men;
he sees their every step.[f]
22There is no dark place,[g] no deep shadow,[h]
where evildoers can hide.
23God has no need to examine men further,
that they should come before him for judgment.[i]

33:27 [a]2Sa 12:13 [b]Lk 15:21 [c]Ro 6:21 **33:28** [d]Job 22:28 **33:29** [e]1Co 12:6; Eph 1:11; Php 2:13 **33:30** [f]Ps 56:13 **33:33** [g]Ps 34:11 **34:3** [h]Job 12:11 **34:4** [i]1Th 5:21 **34:5** [j]Job 33:9 [k]Job 27:2 **34:6** [l]Job 6:4 **34:7** [m]Job 15:16 **34:8** [n]Job 22:15; Ps 50:18 **34:9** [o]Job 21:15; 35:3 **34:10** [p]Ge 18:25 [q]Dt 32:4; Job 8:3; Ro 9:14 **34:11** [r]Ps 62:12; Mt 16:27; Ro 2:6; 2Co 5:10 [s]Jer 32:19; Eze 33:20 **34:12** [t]Job 8:3 **34:13** [u]Job 38:4,6 **34:14** [v]Ps 104:29 **34:15** [w]Ge 3:19; Job 9:22 **34:17** [x]2Sa 23:3-4 [y]Job 40:8 **34:18** [z]Ex 22:28 **34:19** [a]Dt 10:17; Ac 10:34 [b]Lev 19:15 [c]Job 10:3 **34:20** [d]Ex 12:29 [e]Job 12:19 **34:21** [f]Job 31:4; Pr 15:3

34:22 [g]Ps 139:12 [h]Am 9:2-3 **34:23** [i]Job 11:11

[w] *28* Or *redeemed me from going down to the grave*
[x] *30* Or *turn him back from the grave*
[y] *14* Or *Spirit*

24Without inquiry he shatters the
mighty[a]
and sets up others in their place.[b]
25Because he takes note of their deeds,
he overthrows them in the night
and they are crushed.
26He punishes them for their
wickedness
where everyone can see them,
27because they turned from following
him[c]
and had no regard for any of his
ways.[d]
28They caused the cry of the poor to
come before him,
so that he heard the cry of the
needy.[e]
29But if he remains silent, who can
condemn him?
If he hides his face, who can see him?
Yet he is over man and nation alike,
30 to keep a godless man from ruling,
from laying snares for the people.[f]

31"Suppose a man says to God,
'I am guilty but will offend no more.
32Teach me what I cannot see;[g]
if I have done wrong, I will not do
so again.'[h]
33Should God then reward you on your
terms,
when you refuse to repent?[i]
You must decide, not I;
so tell me what you know.

34"Men of understanding declare,
wise men who hear me say to me,
35'Job speaks without knowledge;[j]
his words lack insight.'
36Oh, that Job might be tested to the
utmost
for answering like a wicked man![k]
37To his sin he adds rebellion;
scornfully he claps his hands[l]
among us
and multiplies his words against
God."[m]

Elihu: Job has been self-righteous.

35 Then Elihu said:

2"Do you think this is just?
You say, 'I will be cleared by God.[z]'
3Yet you ask him, 'What profit is it to
me,[a]
and what do I gain by not
sinning?'[n]

4"I would like to reply to you
and to your friends with you.
5Look up at the heavens[o] and see;
gaze at the clouds so high
above you.[p]
6If you sin, how does that affect him?
If your sins are many, what does
that do to him?[q]
7If you are righteous, what do you
give to him,[r]
or what does he receive[s] from your
hand?[t]
8Your wickedness affects only a man
like yourself,
and your righteousness only the
sons of men.

9"Men cry out[u] under a load of
oppression;
they plead for relief from the arm
of the powerful.[v]
10But no one says, 'Where is God my
Maker,[w]
who gives songs in the night,[x]
11who teaches[y] more to us than to[b]
the beasts of the earth
and makes us wiser than[c] the birds
of the air?'
12He does not answer[z] when men cry
out
because of the arrogance of the
wicked.
13Indeed, God does not listen to their
empty plea;
the Almighty pays no attention to it.[a]
14How much less, then, will he listen
when you say that you do not see
him,[b]
that your case[c] is before him
and you must wait for him,
15and further, that his anger never
punishes
and he does not take the least
notice of wickedness.[d]

34:24 [a]Job 12:19 [b]Da 2:21
34:27 [c]Ps 28:5; Isa 5:12 [d]1Sa 15:11
34:28 [e]Ex 22:23; Job 35:9; Jas 5:4
34:30 [f]Pr 29:2-12
34:32 [g]Job 35:11; Ps 25:4 [h]Job 33:27
34:33 [i]Job 41:11
34:35 [j]Job 35:16; 38:2
34:36 [k]Job 22:15
34:37 [l]Job 27:23 [m]Job 23:2
35:3 [n]Job 9:29-31; 34:9
35:5 [o]Ge 15:5 [p]Job 22:12
35:6 [q]Pr 8:36
35:7 [r]Ro 11:35 [s]Pr 9:12 [t]Job 22:2-3; Lk 17:10
35:9 [u]Ex 2:23 [v]Job 12:19
35:10 [w]Job 27:10; Isa 51:13 [x]Ps 42:8; 149:5; Ac 16:25
35:11 [y]Ps 94:12
35:12 [z]Pr 1:28
35:13 [a]Job 27:9; Pr 15:29; Isa 1:15; Jer 11:11
35:14 [b]Job 9:11 [c]Ps 37:6

z*2* Or *My righteousness is more than God's* a*3* Or *you* b*11* Or *teaches us by* c*11* Or *us wise by* d*15* Symmachus, Theodotion and Vulgate; the meaning of the Hebrew for this word is uncertain.

16So Job opens his mouth with empty talk;
without knowledge he multiplies words."[a]

Elihu: God is great beyond understanding.

36 Elihu continued:
2"Bear with me a little longer and I will show you
that there is more to be said in God's behalf.
3I get my knowledge from afar;
I will ascribe justice to my Maker.[b]
4Be assured that my words are not false;[c]
one perfect in knowledge[d] is with you.

5"God is mighty, but does not despise men;[e]
he is mighty, and firm in his purpose.[f]
6He does not keep the wicked alive[g]
but gives the afflicted their rights.[h]
7He does not take his eyes off the righteous;[i]
he enthrones them with kings[j]
and exalts them forever.
8But if men are bound in chains,[k]
held fast by cords of affliction,
9he tells them what they have done—
that they have sinned arrogantly.[l]
10He makes them listen[m] to correction
and commands them to repent of their evil.[n]
11If they obey and serve him,[o]
they will spend the rest of their days in prosperity
and their years in contentment.
12But if they do not listen,
they will perish by the sword[e][p]
and die without knowledge.[q]

13"The godless in heart[r] harbor resentment;
even when he fetters them, they do not cry for help.
14They die in their youth,
among male prostitutes of the shrines.[s]
15But those who suffer he delivers in their suffering;
he speaks to them in their affliction.

16"He is wooing[t] you from the jaws of distress
to a spacious place free from restriction,
to the comfort of your table[u] laden with choice food.
17But now you are laden with the judgment due the wicked;
judgment and justice have taken hold of you.[v]
18Be careful that no one entices you by riches;
do not let a large bribe turn you aside.[w]
19Would your wealth
or even all your mighty efforts
sustain you so you would not be in distress?
20Do not long for the night,[x]
to drag people away from their homes.[f]
21Beware of turning to evil,[y]
which you seem to prefer to affliction.[z]

22"God is exalted in his power.
Who is a teacher like him?[a]
23Who has prescribed his ways for him,[b]
or said to him, 'You have done wrong'?[c]
24Remember to extol his work,[d]
which men have praised in song.[e]
25All mankind has seen it;
men gaze on it from afar.
26How great is God—beyond our understanding![f]
The number of his years is past finding out.[g]

27"He draws up the drops of water,
which distill as rain to the streams[g];[h]
28the clouds pour down their moisture
and abundant showers fall on mankind.[i]

35:16 [a]Job 34:35,37
36:3 [b]Job 8:3; 37:23
36:4 [c]Job 33:3 [d]Job 37:5, 16,23
36:5 [e]Ps 22:24 [f]Job 12:13
36:6 [g]Job 8:22 [h]Job 5:15
36:7 [i]Ps 33:18 [j]Ps 113:8
36:8 [k]Ps 107:10,14
36:9 [l]Job 15:25
36:10 [m]Job 33:16 [n]2Ki 17:13
36:11 [o]Isa 1:19
36:12 [p]Job 15:22 [q]Job 4:21
36:13 [r]Ro 2:5
36:14 [s]Dt 23:17
36:16 [t]Hos 2:14 [u]Ps 23:5
36:17 [v]Job 22:11
36:18 [w]Job 34:33
36:20 [x]Job 34:20,25
36:21 [y]Ps 66:18 [z]Heb 11:25
36:22 [a]Isa 40:13; 1Co 2:16
36:23 [b]Job 34:13 [c]Job 8:3
36:24 [d]Ps 92:5; 138:5 [e]Ps 59:16; Rev 15:3
36:26 [f]1Co 13:12 [g]Job 10:5; Ps 90:2; 102:24; Heb 1:12
36:27 [h]Job 38:28; Ps 147:8
36:28 [i]Job 5:10

e *12* Or *will cross the River* f *20* The meaning of the Hebrew for verses 18-20 is uncertain. g *27* Or *distill from the mist as rain*

29Who can understand how he spreads out the clouds,
how he thunders from his pavilion?[a]
30See how he scatters his lightning about him,
bathing the depths of the sea.
31This is the way he governs[h] the nations[b]
and provides food in abundance.[c]
32He fills his hands with lightning
and commands it to strike its mark.[d]
33His thunder announces the coming storm;
even the cattle make known its approach.[i]

Elihu: God's works are wondrous.

37 "At this my heart pounds
and leaps from its place.
2Listen! Listen to the roar of his voice,
to the rumbling that comes from his mouth.[e]
3He unleashes his lightning beneath the whole heaven
and sends it to the ends of the earth.
4After that comes the sound of his roar;
he thunders with his majestic voice.
When his voice resounds,
he holds nothing back.
5God's voice thunders in marvelous ways;
he does great things beyond our understanding.[f]
6He says to the snow,[g] 'Fall on the earth,'
and to the rain shower, 'Be a mighty downpour.'[h]
7So that all men he has made may know his work,
he stops every man from his labor.[j][i]
8The animals take cover;
they remain in their dens.[j]
9The tempest comes out from its chamber,
the cold from the driving winds.
10The breath of God produces ice,
and the broad waters become frozen.[k]

36:29 [a]Job 26:14; 37:16
36:31 [b]Job 37:13 [c]Ps 136:25; Ac 14:17
36:32 [d]Job 37:12,15
37:2 [e]Ps 29:3-9
37:5 [f]Job 5:9
37:6 [g]Job 38:22 [h]Job 36:27
37:7 [i]Job 12:14
37:8 [j]Job 38:40; Ps 104:22
37:10 [k]Job 38:29-30; Ps 147:17
37:11 [l]Job 36:27,29
37:12 [m]Ps 148:8
37:13 [n]1Sa 12:17 [o]Ex 9:18; 1Ki 18:45; Job 38:27
37:16 [p]Job 36:4
37:18 [q]Job 9:8; Ps 104:2; Isa 44:24
37:23 [r]Job 9:4; 36:4; 1Ti 6:16 [s]Job 8:3 [t]Isa 63:9; Eze 18:23,32
37:24 [u]Mt 10:28 [v]Mt 11:25

11He loads the clouds with moisture;
he scatters his lightning through them.[l]
12At his direction they swirl around
over the face of the whole earth
to do whatever he commands them.[m]
13He brings the clouds to punish men,[n]
or to water his earth[k] and show his love.[o]

14"Listen to this, Job;
stop and consider God's wonders.
15Do you know how God controls the clouds
and makes his lightning flash?
16Do you know how the clouds hang poised,
those wonders of him who is perfect in knowledge?[p]
17You who swelter in your clothes
when the land lies hushed under the south wind,
18can you join him in spreading out the skies,[q]
hard as a mirror of cast bronze?

19"Tell us what we should say to him;
we cannot draw up our case because of our darkness.
20Should he be told that I want to speak?
Would any man ask to be swallowed up?
21Now no one can look at the sun,
bright as it is in the skies
after the wind has swept them clean.
22Out of the north he comes in golden splendor;
God comes in awesome majesty.
23The Almighty is beyond our reach
and exalted in power;[r]
in his justice[s] and great righteousness, he does not oppress.[t]
24Therefore, men revere him,[u]
for does he not have regard for all the wise[v] in heart?[l]"

h*31* Or *nourishes* i*33* Or *announces his coming— / the One zealous against evil*
j*7* Or */ he fills all men with fear by his power*
k*13* Or *to favor them* l*24* Or *for he does not have regard for any who think they are wise.*

The LORD *answers Job out of a storm.*

38 Then the LORD answered Job out of the storm.[a] He said:

2"Who is this that darkens my counsel
with words without knowledge?[b]
3Brace yourself like a man;
I will question you,
and you shall answer me.[c]

4"Where were you when I laid the earth's foundation?[d]
Tell me, if you understand.
5Who marked off its dimensions?[e]
Surely you know!
Who stretched a measuring line across it?
6On what were its footings set,
or who laid its cornerstone[f]—
7while the morning stars sang together
and all the angels[m] shouted for joy?

8"Who shut up the sea behind doors[g]
when it burst forth from the womb,[h]
9when I made the clouds its garment
and wrapped it in thick darkness,
10when I fixed limits for it[i]
and set its doors and bars in place,[j]
11when I said, 'This far you may come and no farther;
here is where your proud waves halt'?[k]

12"Have you ever given orders to the morning,
or shown the dawn its place,
13that it might take the earth by the edges
and shake the wicked[l] out of it?
14The earth takes shape like clay under a seal;
its features stand out like those of a garment.
15The wicked are denied their light,[m]
and their upraised arm is broken.[n]

16"Have you journeyed to the springs of the sea
or walked in the recesses of the deep?[o]
17Have the gates of death[p] been shown to you?
Have you seen the gates of the shadow of death[n]?
18Have you comprehended the vast expanses of the earth?[q]
Tell me, if you know all this.

19"What is the way to the abode of light?
And where does darkness reside?
20Can you take them to their places?
Do you know the paths[r] to their dwellings?
21Surely you know, for you were already born![s]
You have lived so many years!

22"Have you entered the storehouses of the snow[t]
or seen the storehouses of the hail,
23which I reserve for times of trouble,[u]
for days of war and battle?[v]
24What is the way to the place where the lightning is dispersed,
or the place where the east winds are scattered over the earth?
25Who cuts a channel for the torrents of rain,
and a path for the thunderstorm,[w]
26to water[x] a land where no man lives,
a desert with no one in it,
27to satisfy a desolate wasteland
and make it sprout with grass?[y]
28Does the rain have a father?[z]
Who fathers the drops of dew?
29From whose womb comes the ice?
Who gives birth to the frost from the heavens[a]
30when the waters become hard as stone,
when the surface of the deep is frozen?[b]

31"Can you bind the beautiful[o] Pleiades?
Can you loose the cords of Orion?[c]
32Can you bring forth the constellations in their seasons[p]
or lead out the Bear[q] with its cubs?

38:1 [a]Job 40:6
38:2 [b]Job 35:16; 42:3; 1Ti 1:7
38:3 [c]Job 40:7
38:4 [d]Ps 104:5; Pr 8:29
38:5 [e]Pr 8:29; Isa 40:12
38:6 [f]Job 26:7
38:8 [g]Jer 5:22 [h]Ge 1:9-10
38:10 [i]Ps 33:7; 104:9 [j]Job 26:10
38:11 [k]Ps 89:9
38:13 [l]Ps 104:35
38:15 [m]Job 18:5 [n]Ps 10:15
38:16 [o]Ps 77:19
38:17 [p]Ps 9:13
38:18 [q]Job 28:24
38:20 [r]Job 26:10
38:21 [s]Job 15:7
38:22 [t]Job 37:6
38:23 [u]Isa 30:30; Eze 13:11 [v]Ex 9:18; Jos 10:11; Rev 16:21
38:25 [w]Job 28:26
38:26 [x]Job 36:27
38:27 [y]Ps 104:14; 107:35
38:28 [z]Ps 147:8; Jer 14:22
38:29 [a]Ps 147:16-17
38:30 [b]Job 37:10
38:31 [c]Job 9:9; Am 5:8

m*7* Hebrew *the sons of God* n*17* Or *gates of deep shadows* o*31* Or *the twinkling*; or *the chains of the* p*32* Or *the morning star in its season* q*32* Or *out Leo*

33Do you know the laws[a] of the
heavens?
Can you set up ⌊God's[r]⌋ dominion
over the earth?

34"Can you raise your voice to the
clouds
and cover yourself with a flood of
water?[b]
35Do you send the lightning bolts on
their way?[c]
Do they report to you, 'Here we
are'?
36Who endowed the heart[s] with
wisdom[d]
or gave understanding[e] to the mind[s]?
37Who has the wisdom to count the
clouds?
Who can tip over the water jars of
the heavens
38when the dust becomes hard
and the clods of earth stick
together?

The LORD uses animals to illustrate his majesty.

39"Do you hunt the prey for the
lioness
and satisfy the hunger of the lions[f]
40when they crouch in their dens[g]
or lie in wait in a thicket?
41Who provides food for the raven[h]
when its young cry out to God
and wander about for lack of
food?[i]

39

"Do you know when the
mountain goats[j] give birth?
Do you watch when the doe bears
her fawn?
2Do you count the months till they
bear?
Do you know the time they give
birth?
3They crouch down and bring forth
their young;
their labor pains are ended.
4Their young thrive and grow strong
in the wilds;
they leave and do not return.

5"Who let the wild donkey[k] go free?
Who untied his ropes?
6I gave him the wasteland[l] as his
home,
the salt flats as his habitat.[m]
7He laughs at the commotion in the
town;
he does not hear a driver's shout.[n]
8He ranges the hills for his pasture
and searches for any green thing.

9"Will the wild ox[o] consent to serve
you?
Will he stay by your manger at
night?
10Can you hold him to the furrow with
a harness?
Will he till the valleys behind you?
11Will you rely on him for his great
strength?
Will you leave your heavy work to
him?
12Can you trust him to bring in your
grain
and gather it to your threshing
floor?

13"The wings of the ostrich flap
joyfully,
but they cannot compare with the
pinions and feathers of the
stork.
14She lays her eggs on the ground
and lets them warm in the sand,
15unmindful that a foot may crush
them,
that some wild animal may trample
them.
16She treats her young harshly,[p] as if
they were not hers;
she cares not that her labor was in
vain,
17for God did not endow her with
wisdom
or give her a share of good sense.[q]
18Yet when she spreads her feathers to
run,
she laughs at horse and rider.

19"Do you give the horse his strength
or clothe his neck with a flowing
mane?

38:33 [a]Ps 148:6; Jer 31:36
38:34 [b]Job 22:11; 36:27-28
38:35 [c]Job 36:32; 37:3
38:36 [d]Job 9:4 [e]Job 32:8; Ps 51:6; Ecc 2:26
38:39 [f]Ps 104:21
38:40 [g]Job 37:8
38:41 [h]Lk 12:24 [i]Ps 147:9; Mt 6:26
39:1 [j]Dt 14:5
39:5 [k]Job 6:5; 11:12; 24:5
39:6 [l]Job 24:5; Ps 107:34; Jer 2:24 [m]Hos 8:9
39:7 [n]Job 3:18
39:9 [o]Nu 23:22; Dt 33:17
39:16 [p]La 4:3
39:17 [q]Job 35:11

[r]33 Or *his*; or *their* [s]36 The meaning of the Hebrew for this word is uncertain.

20 Do you make him leap like a locust,[a]
striking terror with his proud
snorting?[b]
21 He paws fiercely, rejoicing in his
strength,
and charges into the fray.[c]
22 He laughs at fear, afraid of nothing;
he does not shy away from the
sword.
23 The quiver rattles against his side,
along with the flashing spear and
lance.
24 In frenzied excitement he eats up
the ground;
he cannot stand still when the
trumpet sounds.[d]
25 At the blast of the trumpet[e] he
snorts, 'Aha!'
He catches the scent of battle from
afar,
the shout of commanders and the
battle cry.[f]

26 "Does the hawk take flight by your
wisdom
and spread his wings toward the
south?
27 Does the eagle soar at your command
and build his nest on high?[g]
28 He dwells on a cliff and stays there
at night;
a rocky crag is his stronghold.
29 From there he seeks out his food;[h]
his eyes detect it from afar.
30 His young ones feast on blood,
and where the slain are, there is
he."[i]

The LORD *seeks an answer from Job.*

40

The LORD said to Job:[j]

2 "Will the one who contends
with the Almighty correct him?
Let him who accuses God answer
him!"

Job has no answer.

3 Then Job answered the LORD:

4 "I am unworthy[k]—how can I reply
to you?
I put my hand over my mouth.[l]
5 I spoke once, but I have no
answer[m]—
twice, but I will say no more."[n]

The LORD *tells Job to save himself if he is able.*

6 Then the LORD spoke to Job out of
the storm:[o]

7 "Brace yourself like a man;
I will question you,
and you shall answer me.[p]

8 "Would you discredit my justice?[q]
Would you condemn me to justify
yourself?
9 Do you have an arm like God's,[r]
and can your voice thunder like
his?[s]
10 Then adorn yourself with glory and
splendor,
and clothe yourself in honor and
majesty.[t]
11 Unleash the fury of your wrath,[u]
look at every proud man and bring
him low,[v]
12 look at every proud man and humble
him,[w]
crush[x] the wicked where they
stand.
13 Bury them all in the dust together;
shroud their faces in the grave.
14 Then I myself will admit to you
that your own right hand can save
you.[y]

15 "Look at the behemoth,[t]
which I made along with you
and which feeds on grass like an ox.
16 What strength he has in his loins,
what power in the muscles of his
belly!
17 His tail[u] sways like a cedar;
the sinews of his thighs are close-
knit.
18 His bones are tubes of bronze,
his limbs like rods of iron.
19 He ranks first among the works of
God,[z]
yet his Maker can approach him
with his sword.

39:20 [a] Joel 2:4-5 [b] Jer 8:16
39:21 [c] Jer 8:6
39:24 [d] Jer 4:5,19; Eze 7:14; Am 3:6
39:25 [e] Jos 6:5 [f] Am 1:14; 2:2
39:27 [g] Jer 49:16; Ob 4
39:29 [h] Job 9:26
39:30 [i] Mt 24:28; Lk 17:37
40:1 [j] Job 10:2; 13:3; 23:4; 31:35; 33:13
40:4 [k] Job 42:6 [l] Job 29:9
40:5 [m] Job 9:3 [n] Job 9:15
40:6 [o] Job 38:1
40:7 [p] Job 38:3; 42:4
40:8 [q] Job 27:2; Ro 3:3
40:9 [r] 2Ch 32:8 [s] Job 37:5; Ps 29:3-4
40:10 [t] Ps 93:1; 104:1
40:11 [u] Isa 42:25; Na 1:6 [v] Isa 2:11,12,17; Da 4:37
40:12 [w] 1Sa 2:7 [x] Isa 13:11; 63:2-3,6
40:14 [y] Ps 20:6; 60:5; 108:6
40:19 [z] Job 41:33

t *15* Possibly the hippopotamus or the elephant
u *17* Possibly trunk

20The hills bring him their produce,[a]
and all the wild animals play[b]
nearby.
21Under the lotus plants he lies,
hidden among the reeds in the
marsh.
22The lotuses conceal him in their
shadow;
the poplars by the stream[c]
surround him.
23When the river rages, he is not
alarmed;
he is secure, though the Jordan
should surge against his
mouth.
24Can anyone capture him by the
eyes,[v]
or trap him and pierce his nose?[d]

The LORD further illustrates his power and majesty.

41 "Can you pull in the leviathan[w][e]
with a fishhook
or tie down his tongue with a
rope?
2Can you put a cord through his nose
or pierce his jaw with a hook?[f]
3Will he keep begging you for mercy?
Will he speak to you with gentle
words?
4Will he make an agreement with you
for you to take him as your slave
for life?[g]
5Can you make a pet of him like a bird
or put him on a leash for your
girls?
6Will traders barter for him?
Will they divide him up among the
merchants?
7Can you fill his hide with harpoons
or his head with fishing spears?
8If you lay a hand on him,
you will remember the struggle
and never do it again!
9Any hope of subduing him is false;
the mere sight of him is
overpowering.
10No one is fierce enough to rouse
him.[h]
Who then is able to stand against
me?[i]
11Who has a claim against me that I
must pay?[j]
Everything under heaven belongs
to me.[k]
12"I will not fail to speak of his limbs,
his strength and his graceful form.
13Who can strip off his outer coat?
Who would approach him with a
bridle?
14Who dares open the doors of his
mouth,
ringed about with his fearsome
teeth?
15His back has[x] rows of shields
tightly sealed together;
16each is so close to the next
that no air can pass between.
17They are joined fast to one another;
they cling together and cannot be
parted.
18His snorting throws out flashes of light;
his eyes are like the rays of dawn.[l]
19Firebrands stream from his mouth;
sparks of fire shoot out.
20Smoke pours from his nostrils
as from a boiling pot over a fire of
reeds.
21His breath[m] sets coals ablaze,
and flames dart from his mouth.[n]
22Strength resides in his neck;
dismay goes before him.
23The folds of his flesh are tightly joined;
they are firm and immovable.
24His chest is hard as rock,
hard as a lower millstone.
25When he rises up, the mighty are
terrified;
they retreat before his thrashing.
26The sword that reaches him has no
effect,
nor does the spear or the dart or
the javelin.
27Iron he treats like straw
and bronze like rotten wood.
28Arrows do not make him flee;
slingstones are like chaff to him.
29A club seems to him but a piece of
straw;
he laughs at the rattling of the lance.

40:20 [a]Ps 104:14 [b]Ps 104:26
40:22 [c]Isa 44:4
40:24 [d]Job 41:2,7,26
41:1 [e]Job 3:8; Ps 104:26; Isa 27:1
41:2 [f]Isa 37:29
41:4 [g]Ex 21:6
41:10 [h]Job 3:8 [i]Jer 50:44
41:11 [j]Ro 11:35 [k]Ex 19:5; Dt 10:14; Ps 24:1; 50:12; 1Co 10:26
41:18 [l]Job 3:9
41:21 [m]Isa 40:7 [n]Ps 18:8

v24 Or *by a water hole* w1 Possibly the crocodile
x15 Or *His pride is his*

[30]His undersides are jagged potsherds,
leaving a trail in the mud like a threshing sledge.[a]
[31]He makes the depths churn like a boiling caldron
and stirs up the sea like a pot of ointment.
[32]Behind him he leaves a glistening wake;
one would think the deep had white hair.
[33]Nothing on earth is his equal[b]—
a creature without fear.
[34]He looks down on all that are haughty;
he is king over all that are proud.[c]"

Job repents in dust and ashes.

42 Then Job replied to the LORD:

[2]"I know that you can do all things;[d]
no plan of yours can be thwarted.[e]
[3]⌊You asked,⌋ 'Who is this that obscures my counsel without knowledge?'[f]
Surely I spoke of things I did not understand,
things too wonderful for me to know.[g]

[4]⌊"You said,⌋ 'Listen now, and I will speak;
I will question you,
and you shall answer me.'[h]
[5]My ears had heard of you[i]
but now my eyes have seen you.[j]
[6]Therefore I despise myself[k]
and repent in dust and ashes."[l]

Job prays for his friends.

[7]After the LORD had said these things
to Job, he said to Eliphaz the Temanite, "I am angry with you and your two
friends,[m] because you have not spoken
of me what is right, as my servant Job
has. [8]So now take seven bulls and seven
rams[n] and go to my servant Job and sacrifice a burnt offering[o] for yourselves. My
servant Job will pray for you, and I will
accept his prayer[p] and not deal with you
according to your folly.[q] You have not
spoken of me what is right, as my servant Job has." [9]So Eliphaz the Temanite, Bildad the Shuhite and Zophar the
Naamathite did what the LORD told them;
and the LORD accepted Job's prayer.

The LORD restores and doubles Job's possessions.

[10]After Job had prayed for his friends,
the LORD made him prosperous again[r]
and gave him twice as much as he had
before.[s] [11]All his brothers and sisters and
everyone who had known him before[t]
came and ate with him in his house.
They comforted and consoled him over
all the trouble the LORD had brought upon
him, and each one gave him a piece of
silver[y] and a gold ring.
[12]The LORD blessed the latter part of
Job's life more than the first. He had fourteen thousand sheep, six thousand camels, a thousand yoke of oxen and a
thousand donkeys. [13]And he also had sev-
en sons and three daughters. [14]The first
daughter he named Jemimah, the second
Keziah and the third Keren-Happuch.
[15]Nowhere in all the land were there
found women as beautiful as Job's daughters, and their father granted them an inheritance along with their brothers.

Job's death.

[16]After this, Job lived a hundred and
forty years; he saw his children and their
children to the fourth generation. [17]And
so he died, old and full of years.[u]

41:30 [a]Isa 41:15
41:33 [b]Job 40:19
41:34 [c]Job 28:8
42:2 [d]Ge 18:14; Mt 19:26 [e]2Ch 20:6
42:3 [f]Job 38:2 [g]Ps 40:5; 131:1; 139:6
42:4 [h]Job 38:3; 40:7
42:5 [i]Job 26:14; Ro 10:17 [j]Jdg 13:22; Isa 6:5; Eph 1:17-18
42:6 [k]Job 40:4 [l]Ezr 9:6
42:7 [m]Job 32:3
42:8 [n]Nu 23:1,29 [o]Job 1:5 [p]Ge 20:17; Jas 5:15-16; 1Jn 5:16 [q]Job 22:30
42:10 [r]Dt 30:3; Ps 14:7 [s]Job 1:3; Ps 85:1-3; 126:5-6
42:11 [t]Job 19:13
42:17 [u]Ge 15:15; 25:8

y *11* Hebrew *him a kesitah*; a kesitah was a unit of money of unknown weight and value.

PSALMS

Author: Primarily David, but also at least 7 other writers: Moses, Solomon, Asaph, Ethan, Heman and the sons of Korah. Some of the psalms are anonymous.

Date Written: Between 1450 and 430 B.C. (Due to the numerous authors, the time span is great. However, the majority were written about 1000 B.C.)

Time Span: About 1,000 years (the period from the time of Moses to the return of the Israelites from Babylonian exile).

Title: The word "psalms" means "praises," a term that reflects much of the book's content. "Psalm" comes from a Greek word which means "a song sung to the accompaniment of a plucked instrument." The Hebrew title of this book means "Praise Songs."

Background: Psalms is the longest book in the Bible and includes the longest chapter in the Bible (119). The book of Psalms is made up of 150 poems composed to be set to music.

Where Written: Numerous areas due to the numerous authors.

To Whom: To the Israelites.

Content: The book of Psalms is used as the temple hymnbook during the kingdom period for both public and private worship. The 5 divisions or books of Psalms correspond in order and in thought to the 5 books of Moses. By virtue of several authors contributing to this collection over an extended period of time, the psalms cover almost every area of human experience and emotion: fear vs. confidence; anger vs. compassion; sorrow vs. joy; and prayer and praises for the psalmist's majestic God. David writes the majority of his psalms while fleeing from Saul and his army. Several psalms refer to the Messiah of God, Jesus Christ: his coming, his death and his resurrection.

Key Words: "Praise"; "Trust." These 150 psalms abound in "praise" to God for all that he is, all that he has done and all that he will do. God's people are continually commended to "trust" God for his protection, love and deliverance.

Themes: • Sin is always rebellion against God. • Sin will always be punished. • A life of consecrated righteousness hates sin. • God loves each of us and is concerned for every area of our lives. • We can approach God just as we are, with all our concerns. • A life of praise is a life of victory. • God can be trusted during our times of sorrow as well as our times of joy.

Outline:

1. Book One: Psalms. 1-41
2. Book Two: Psalms. 42-72
3. Book Three: Psalms. 73-89
4. Book Four: Psalms. 90-106
5. Book Five: Psalms. 107-150

PSALMS

BOOK I

Psalms 1–41

Psalm 1

Righteous and wicked people are contrasted.

1 Blessed is the man
who does not walk[a] in the counsel of the wicked
or stand in the way of sinners
or sit[b] in the seat of mockers.
2 But his delight[c] is in the law of the LORD,[d]
and on his law he meditates[e] day and night.
3 He is like a tree[f] planted by streams of water,[g]
which yields its fruit[h] in season
and whose leaf does not wither.
Whatever he does prospers.[i]

4 Not so the wicked!
They are like chaff[j]
that the wind blows away.
5 Therefore the wicked will not stand[k] in the judgment,[l]
nor sinners in the assembly of the righteous.

6 For the LORD watches over[m] the way of the righteous,
but the way of the wicked will perish.[n]

Psalm 2

The King is installed on Zion.

1 Why do the nations conspire[a]
and the peoples plot[o] in vain?
2 The kings[p] of the earth take their stand
and the rulers gather together
against the LORD
and against his Anointed[q] One.[b] [r]
3 "Let us break their chains," they say,
"and throw off their fetters."[s]

4 The One enthroned in heaven laughs;[t]
the Lord scoffs at them.
5 Then he rebukes them in his anger
and terrifies them in his wrath,[u]
saying,
6 "I have installed my King[c]
on Zion, my holy hill."

7 I will proclaim the decree of the LORD:

He said to me, "You are my Son[d];
today I have become your Father.[e] [v]
8 Ask of me,
and I will make the nations your inheritance,
the ends of the earth[w] your possession.
9 You will rule them with an iron scepter[f];[x]
you will dash them to pieces[y] like pottery.[z]"

10 Therefore, you kings, be wise;
be warned, you rulers of the earth.
11 Serve the LORD with fear
and rejoice[a] with trembling.[b]
12 Kiss the Son,[c] lest he be angry
and you be destroyed in your way,
for his wrath[d] can flare up in a moment.
Blessed are all who take refuge[e] in him.

Psalm 3

A psalm of David. When he fled from his son Absalom.[f]

God is a shield.

1 O LORD, how many are my foes!
How many rise up against me!
2 Many are saying of me,
"God will not deliver him.[g]"
Selah[g]

3 But you are a shield[h] around me,
O LORD;

1:1 [a]Pr 4:14 [b]Ps 26:4; Jer 15:17
1:2 [c]Ps 119:16, 35 [d]Ps 119:1 [e]Jos 1:8
1:3 [f]Ps 128:3 [g]Jer 17:8 [h]Eze 47:12 [i]Ge 39:3
1:4 [j]Job 21:18; Isa 17:13
1:5 [k]Ps 5:5 [l]Ps 9:7-8,16
1:6 [m]Ps 37:18; 2Ti 2:19 [n]Ps 9:6
2:1 [o]Ps 21:11
2:2 [p]Ps 48:4 [q]Jn 1:41 [r]Ps 74:18,23; Ac 4:25-26*
2:3 [s]Jer 5:5
2:4 [t]Ps 37:13; 59:8; Pr 1:26
2:5 [u]Ps 21:9; 78:49-50
2:7 [v]Ac 13:33*; Heb 1:5*
2:8 [w]Ps 22:27
2:9 [x]Rev 12:5 [y]Ps 89:23 [z]Rev 2:27*
2:11 [a]Heb 12:28 [b]Ps 119:119-120
2:12 [c]Jn 5:23 [d]Rev 6:16 [e]Ps 34:8; Ro 9:33
3:1 [f]2Sa 15:14
3:2 [g]Ps 71:11
3:3 [h]Ge 15:1; Ps 28:7

a *1* Hebrew; Septuagint *rage* b *2* Or *anointed one* c *6* Or *king* d *7* Or *son*; also in verse 12 e *7* Or *have begotten you* f *9* Or *will break them with a rod of iron* g *2* A word of uncertain meaning, occurring frequently in the Psalms; possibly a musical term

you bestow glory on me and lift[h]
up my head.[a]
4To the LORD I cry aloud,
and he answers me from his holy
hill.[b] *Selah*

5I lie down and sleep;[c]
I wake again, because the LORD
sustains me.
6I will not fear[d] the tens of thousands
drawn up against me on every side.

7Arise,[e] O LORD!
Deliver me,[f] O my God!
Strike[g] all my enemies on the jaw;
break the teeth[h] of the wicked.

8From the LORD comes deliverance.[i]
May your blessing be on your
people. *Selah*

Psalm 4

For the director of music. With stringed instruments. A psalm of David.

Trust in the LORD.

1Answer me when I call to you,
O my righteous God.
Give me relief from my distress;
be merciful[j] to me and hear my
prayer.[k]

2How long, O men, will you turn my
glory into shame[i]?
How long will you love delusions
and seek false gods[j]?[l] *Selah*
3Know that the LORD has set apart the
godly[m] for himself;
the LORD will hear[n] when I call to
him.

4In your anger do not sin;[o]
when you are on your beds,[p]
search your hearts and be silent.
Selah
5Offer right sacrifices
and trust in the LORD.[q]

6Many are asking, "Who can show us
any good?"
Let the light of your face shine
upon us,[r] O LORD.

3:3 [a]Ps 27:6
3:4 [b]Ps 2:6
3:5 [c]Lev 26:6; Pr 3:24
3:6 [d]Ps 27:3
3:7 [e]Ps 7:6 [f]Ps 6:4 [g]Job 16:10 [h]Ps 58:6
3:8 [i]Isa 43:3,11
4:1 [j]Ps 25:16 [k]Ps 17:6
4:2 [l]Ps 31:6
4:3 [m]Ps 31:23 [n]Ps 6:8
4:4 [o]Eph 4:26* [p]Ps 77:6
4:5 [q]Dt 33:19; Ps 37:3
4:6 [r]Nu 6:25
4:7 [s]Ac 14:17 [t]Isa 9:3
4:8 [u]Ps 3:5 [v]Lev 25:18
5:2 [w]Ps 3:4 [x]Ps 84:3
5:3 [y]Ps 88:13
5:4 [z]Ps 11:5; 92:15
5:5 [a]Ps 73:3 [b]Ps 1:5 [c]Ps 11:5
5:6 [d]Ps 55:23; Rev 21:8
5:7 [e]Ps 138:2
5:8 [f]Ps 31:1 [g]Ps 27:11
5:9 [h]Lk 11:44 [i]Ro 3:13*

7You have filled my heart[s] with
greater joy[t]
than when their grain and new
wine abound.
8I will lie down and sleep[u] in peace,
for you alone, O LORD,
make me dwell in safety.[v]

Psalm 5

For the director of music. For flutes. A psalm of David.

Prayer for deliverance from enemies.

1Give ear to my words, O LORD,
consider my sighing.
2Listen to my cry for help,[w]
my King and my God,[x]
for to you I pray.
3In the morning,[y] O LORD, you hear
my voice;
in the morning I lay my requests
before you
and wait in expectation.

4You are not a God who takes
pleasure in evil;
with you the wicked[z] cannot dwell.
5The arrogant[a] cannot stand[b] in your
presence;
you hate[c] all who do wrong.
6You destroy those who tell lies;[d]
bloodthirsty and deceitful men
the LORD abhors.

7But I, by your great mercy,
will come into your house;
in reverence will I bow down[e]
toward your holy temple.
8Lead me, O LORD, in your
righteousness[f]
because of my enemies—
make straight your way[g] before me.

9Not a word from their mouth can be
trusted;
their heart is filled with destruction.
Their throat is an open grave;[h]
with their tongue they speak deceit.[i]
10Declare them guilty, O God!

h3 Or *LORD, / my Glorious One, who lifts* i2 Or *you dishonor my Glorious One* j2 Or *seek lies*

Let their intrigues be their downfall.
Banish them for their many sins,[a]
for they have rebelled[b] against you.

11 But let all who take refuge in you be glad;
let them ever sing for joy.[c]
Spread your protection over them,
that those who love your name[d]
may rejoice in you.[e]
12 For surely, O LORD, you bless the righteous;
you surround them[f] with your favor as with a shield.

Psalm 6

For the director of music. With stringed instruments. According to *sheminith*.[k] A psalm of David.

Prayer for the LORD's mercy.

1 O LORD, do not rebuke me in your anger[g]
or discipline me in your wrath.
2 Be merciful to me, LORD, for I am faint;
O LORD, heal me,[h] for my bones are in agony.[i]
3 My soul is in anguish.[j]
How long,[k] O LORD, how long?

4 Turn, O LORD, and deliver me;
save me because of your unfailing love.[l]
5 No one remembers you when he is dead.
Who praises you from the grave[l]?[m]

6 I am worn out[n] from groaning;
all night long I flood my bed with weeping
and drench my couch with tears.[o]
7 My eyes grow weak[p] with sorrow;
they fail because of all my foes.

8 Away from me,[q] all you who do evil,[r]
for the LORD has heard my weeping.
9 The LORD has heard my cry for mercy;[s]
the LORD accepts my prayer.
10 All my enemies will be ashamed and dismayed;
they will turn back in sudden disgrace.[t]

5:10 [a]Ps 9:16 [b]Ps 107:11
5:11 [c]Ps 2:12 [d]Ps 69:36 [e]Isa 65:13
5:12 [f]Ps 32:7
6:1 [g]Ps 38:1
6:2 [h]Hos 6:1 [i]Ps 22:14; 31:10
6:3 [j]Jn 12:27 [k]Ps 90:13
6:4 [l]Ps 17:13
6:5 [m]Ps 30:9; 88:10-12; Ecc 9:10; Isa 38:18
6:6 [n]Ps 69:3 [o]Ps 42:3
6:7 [p]Ps 31:9
6:8 [q]Ps 119:115 [r]Mt 7:23; Lk 13:27
6:9 [s]Ps 116:1
6:10 [t]Ps 71:24; 73:19
7:1 [u]Ps 31:15
7:2 [v]Isa 38:13 [w]Ps 50:22
7:3 [x]1Sa 24:11; Isa 59:3
7:6 [y]Ps 94:2 [z]Ps 138:7 [a]Ps 44:23
7:8 [b]Ps 18:20; 96:13
7:9 [c]Jer 11:20 [d]1Ch 28:9; Ps 26:2; Rev 2:23 [e]Ps 37:23
7:10 [f]Ps 125:4
7:11 [g]Ps 50:6

Psalm 7

A *shiggaion*[m] of David, which he sang to the LORD concerning Cush, a Benjamite.

Prayer for deliverance from the wicked.

1 O LORD my God, I take refuge in you;
save and deliver me from all who pursue me,[u]
2 or they will tear me like a lion[v]
and rip me to pieces with no one to rescue[w] me.

3 O LORD my God, if I have done this
and there is guilt on my hands[x]—
4 if I have done evil to him who is at peace with me
or without cause have robbed my foe—
5 then let my enemy pursue and overtake me;
let him trample my life to the ground
and make me sleep in the dust.
Selah

6 Arise,[y] O LORD, in your anger;
rise up against the rage of my enemies.[z]
Awake,[a] my God; decree justice.
7 Let the assembled peoples gather around you.
Rule over them from on high;
8 let the LORD judge the peoples.
Judge me, O LORD, according to my righteousness,[b]
according to my integrity, O Most High.
9 O righteous God,[c]
who searches minds and hearts,[d]
bring to an end the violence of the wicked
and make the righteous secure.[e]

10 My shield[n] is God Most High,
who saves the upright in heart.[f]
11 God is a righteous judge,[g]
a God who expresses his wrath every day.

[k] Title: Probably a musical term [l] *5* Hebrew *Sheol*
[m] Title: Probably a literary or musical term
[n] *10* Or *sovereign*

[12]If he does not relent,
he[o] will sharpen his sword;[a]
he will bend and string his bow.
[13]He has prepared his deadly weapons;
he makes ready his flaming arrows.

[14]He who is pregnant with evil
and conceives trouble gives birth[b]
to disillusionment.
[15]He who digs a hole and scoops it out
falls into the pit he has made.[c]
[16]The trouble he causes recoils on
himself;
his violence comes down on his
own head.

[17]I will give thanks to the LORD
because of his righteousness[d]
and will sing praise[e] to the name of
the LORD Most High.

Psalm 8

For the director of music.
According to *gittith.*[p] A psalm
of David.

The dominion God has given man.

[1]O LORD, our Lord,
how majestic is your name in all
the earth!

You have set your glory
above the heavens.[f]
[2]From the lips of children and infants
you have ordained praise[q] [g]
because of your enemies,
to silence the foe[h] and the avenger.
[3]When I consider your heavens,[i]
the work of your fingers,
the moon and the stars,[j]
which you have set in place,
[4]what is man that you are mindful of
him,
the son of man that you care for
him?[k]
[5]You made him a little lower than the
heavenly beings[r]
and crowned him with glory and
honor.[l]
[6]You made him ruler[m] over the works
of your hands;
you put everything under his
feet:[n] [o]
[7]all flocks and herds,
and the beasts of the field,
[8]the birds of the air,
and the fish of the sea,
all that swim the paths of the seas.

[9]O LORD, our Lord,
how majestic is your name in all
the earth![p]

Psalm 9[s]

For the director of music. To
⌊the tune of⌋ "The Death of the
Son." A psalm of David.

*Praises for the protection
and justice of God.*

[1]I will praise you, O LORD, with all my
heart;[q]
I will tell of all your wonders.[r]
[2]I will be glad and rejoice[s] in you;
I will sing praise to your name,[t]
O Most High.

[3]My enemies turn back;
they stumble and perish before you.
[4]For you have upheld my right and
my cause;[u]
you have sat on your throne,
judging righteously.[v]
[5]You have rebuked the nations and
destroyed the wicked;
you have blotted out their name[w]
for ever and ever.
[6]Endless ruin has overtaken the enemy,
you have uprooted their cities;
even the memory of them[x] has
perished.

[7]The LORD reigns forever;
he has established his throne[y] for
judgment.

7:12 [a]Dt 32:41
7:14 [b]Job 15:35; Isa 59:4; Jas 1:15
7:15 [c]Job 4:8
7:17 [d]Ps 71:15-16 [e]Ps 9:2
8:1 [f]Ps 57:5; 113:4; 148:13
8:2 [g]Mt 21:16* [h]Ps 44:16; 1Co 1:27
8:3 [i]Ps 89:11 [j]Ps 136:9
8:4 [k]Job 7:17; Ps 144:3; Heb 2:6
8:5 [l]Ps 21:5; 103:4
8:6 [m]Ge 1:28 [n]Heb 2:6-8* [o]1Co 15:25, 27*; Eph 1:22
8:9 [p]ver 1
9:1 [q]Ps 86:12 [r]Ps 26:7
9:2 [s]Ps 5:11 [t]Ps 92:1; 83:18
9:4 [u]Ps 140:12 [v]1Pe 2:23
9:5 [w]Pr 10:7
9:6 [x]Ps 34:16
9:7 [y]Ps 89:14

[o]*12* Or *If a man does not repent, / God* [p]Title: Probably a musical term [q]*2* Or *strength* [r]*5* Or *than God* [s]Psalms 9 and 10 may have been originally a single acrostic poem, the stanzas of which begin with the successive letters of the Hebrew alphabet. In the Septuagint they constitute one psalm.

8He will judge the world in
righteousness;[a]
he will govern the peoples with
justice.
9The LORD is a refuge for the oppressed,
a stronghold in times of trouble.[b]
10Those who know your name[c] will
trust in you,
for you, LORD, have never
forsaken[d] those who seek you.

11Sing praises to the LORD, enthroned
in Zion;[e]
proclaim among the nations[f] what
he has done.[g]
12For he who avenges blood[h]
remembers;
he does not ignore the cry of the
afflicted.

13O LORD, see how my enemies[i]
persecute me!
Have mercy and lift me up from
the gates of death,
14that I may declare your praises[j]
in the gates of the Daughter of Zion
and there rejoice in your salvation.[k]
15The nations have fallen into the pit
they have dug;[l]
their feet are caught in the net
they have hidden.[m]
16The LORD is known by his justice;
the wicked are ensnared by the
work of their hands.
Higgaion.[t] *Selah*
17The wicked return to the grave,[u] [n]
all the nations that forget God.[o]
18But the needy will not always be
forgotten,
nor the hope[p] of the afflicted[q] ever
perish.

19Arise, O LORD, let not man triumph;
let the nations be judged in your
presence.
20Strike them with terror, O LORD;
let the nations know they are but
men.[r] *Selah*

Psalm 10[v]

Prayer for God to protect the weak.

1Why, O LORD, do you stand far off?[s]
Why do you hide yourself[t] in times
of trouble?

2In his arrogance the wicked man
hunts down the weak,
who are caught in the schemes he
devises.
3He boasts[u] of the cravings of his heart;
he blesses the greedy and reviles
the LORD.
4In his pride the wicked does not
seek him;
in all his thoughts there is no room
for God.[v]
5His ways are always prosperous;
he is haughty and your laws are far
from him;
he sneers at all his enemies.
6He says to himself, "Nothing will
shake me;
I'll always be happy[w] and never
have trouble."
7His mouth is full of curses[x] and lies
and threats;[y]
trouble and evil are under his
tongue.[z]
8He lies in wait near the villages;
from ambush he murders the
innocent,[a]
watching in secret for his victims.
9He lies in wait like a lion in cover;
he lies in wait to catch the helpless;[b]
he catches the helpless and drags
them off in his net.
10His victims are crushed, they collapse;
they fall under his strength.
11He says to himself, "God has
forgotten;[c]
he covers his face and never sees."

12Arise, LORD! Lift up your hand,[d]
O God.
Do not forget the helpless.[e]
13Why does the wicked man revile God?
Why does he say to himself,
"He won't call me to account"?
14But you, O God, do see trouble[f] and
grief;

9:8 [a]Ps 96:13
9:9 [b]Ps 32:7
9:10 [c]Ps 91:14 [d]Ps 37:28
9:11 [e]Ps 76:2 [f]Ps 107:22 [g]Ps 105:1
9:12 [h]Ge 9:5
9:13 [i]Ps 38:19
9:14 [j]Ps 106:2 [k]Ps 13:5; 51:12
9:15 [l]Ps 7:15-16 [m]Ps 35:8; 57:6
9:17 [n]Ps 49:14 [o]Job 8:13; Ps 50:22
9:18 [p]Ps 71:5; Pr 23:18 [q]Ps 12:5
9:20 [r]Ps 62:9; Isa 31:3
10:1 [s]Ps 22:1,11 [t]Ps 13:1
10:3 [u]Ps 94:4
10:4 [v]Ps 14:1; 36:1
10:6 [w]Rev 18:7
10:7 [x]Ro 3:14* [y]Ps 73:8 [z]Ps 140:3
10:8 [a]Ps 94:6
10:9 [b]Ps 17:12; 59:3; 140:5
10:11 [c]Job 22:13
10:12 [d]Ps 17:7; Mic 5:9 [e]Ps 9:12
10:14 [f]Ps 22:11

t *16* Or *Meditation*; possibly a musical notation
u *17* Hebrew *Sheol* v Psalms 9 and 10 may have been originally a single acrostic poem, the stanzas of which begin with the successive letters of the Hebrew alphabet. In the Septuagint they constitute one psalm.

you consider it to take it in hand.
The victim commits himself to you;[a]
you are the helper[b] of the fatherless.
15Break the arm of the wicked and evil
man;[c]
call him to account for his
wickedness
that would not be found out.

16The LORD is King for ever and ever;[d]
the nations[e] will perish from his land.
17You hear, O LORD, the desire of the
afflicted;[f]
you encourage them, and you
listen to their cry,
18defending the fatherless[g] and the
oppressed,[h]
in order that man, who is of the
earth, may terrify no more.

Psalm 11

For the director of music.
Of David.

The LORD is righteous and just.

1In the LORD I take refuge.[i]
How then can you say to me:
"Flee like a bird to your mountain.
2For look, the wicked bend their bows;
they set their arrows[j] against the
strings
to shoot from the shadows
at the upright in heart.[k]
3When the foundations[l] are being
destroyed,
what can the righteous do[w]?"

4The LORD is in his holy temple;[m]
the LORD is on his heavenly throne.[n]
He observes the sons of men;[o]
his eyes examine[p] them.
5The LORD examines the righteous,[q]
but the wicked[x] and those who
love violence
his soul hates.[r]
6On the wicked he will rain
fiery coals and burning sulfur;[s]
a scorching wind[t] will be their lot.

7For the LORD is righteous,[u]
he loves justice;[v]
upright men will see his face.[w]

10:14 [a]Ps 37:5 [b]Ps 68:5
10:15 [c]Ps 37:17
10:16 [d]Ps 29:10 [e]Dt 8:20
10:17 [f]1Ch 29:18; Ps 34:15
10:18 [g]Ps 82:3 [h]Ps 9:9
11:1 [i]Ps 56:11
11:2 [j]Ps 7:13 [k]Ps 64:3-4
11:3 [l]Ps 82:5
11:4 [m]Ps 18:6 [n]Ps 103:19 [o]Ps 33:13 [p]Ps 34:15-16
11:5 [q]Ge 22:1; Jas 1:12 [r]Ps 5:5
11:6 [s]Eze 38:22 [t]Jer 4:11-12
11:7 [u]Ps 7:9,11; 45:7 [v]Ps 33:5 [w]Ps 17:15
12:1 [x]Isa 57:1
12:2 [y]Ps 10:7; 41:6; 55:21; Ro 16:18
12:3 [z]Da 7:8; Rev 13:5
12:5 [a]Ps 10:18; 34:6
12:6 [b]2Sa 22:31; Ps 18:30; Pr 30:5
12:7 [c]Ps 37:28
12:8 [d]Ps 55:10-11
13:1 [e]Job 13:24; Ps 44:24

Psalm 12

For the director of music.
According to *sheminith.*[y]
A psalm of David.

The LORD will protect the oppressed.

1Help, LORD, for the godly are no more;[x]
the faithful have vanished from
among men.
2Everyone lies to his neighbor;
their flattering lips speak with
deception.[y]

3May the LORD cut off all flattering lips
and every boastful tongue[z]
4that says, "We will triumph with our
tongues;
we own our lips[z]—who is our
master?"

5"Because of the oppression of the weak
and the groaning of the needy,
I will now arise," says the LORD.
"I will protect them[a] from those
who malign them."
6And the words of the LORD are
flawless,[b]
like silver refined in a furnace of clay,
purified seven times.

7O LORD, you will keep us safe
and protect us from such people
forever.[c]
8The wicked freely strut[d] about
when what is vile is honored
among men.

Psalm 13

For the director of music.
A psalm of David.

Trust in God's unfailing love.

1How long, O LORD? Will you forget
me forever?
How long will you hide your face[e]
from me?

w*3* Or *what is the Righteous One doing*
x*5* Or *The LORD, the Righteous One, examines the wicked, /* y Title: Probably a musical term
z*4* Or */ our lips are our plowshares*

2How long must I wrestle with my
thoughts[a]
and every day have sorrow in my
heart?
How long will my enemy triumph
over me?[b]

3Look on me and answer,[c] O LORD my
God.
Give light to my eyes,[d] or I will
sleep in death;[e]
4my enemy will say, "I have
overcome him,[f]"
and my foes will rejoice when I fall.

5But I trust in your unfailing love;[g]
my heart rejoices in your salvation.[h]
6I will sing[i] to the LORD,
for he has been good to me.

Psalm 14

14:1-7pp— Ps53:1-6

For the director of music.
Of David.

Vile deeds of the corrupt.

1The fool[a] says in his heart,
"There is no God."[j]
They are corrupt, their deeds are vile;
there is no one who does good.

2The LORD looks down from heaven[k]
on the sons of men
to see if there are any who understand,[l]
any who seek God.
3All have turned aside,
they have together become corrupt;[m]
there is no one who does good,[n]
not even one.[o]

4Will evildoers never learn—[p]
those who devour my people[q] as
men eat bread
and who do not call on the LORD?[r]
5There they are, overwhelmed with
dread,
for God is present in the company
of the righteous.
6You evildoers frustrate the plans of
the poor,
but the LORD is their refuge.[s]

13:2 [a]Ps 42:4 [b]Ps 42:9
13:3 [c]Ps 5:1 [d]Ezr 9:8 [e]Jer 51:39
13:4 [f]Ps 25:2
13:5 [g]Ps 52:8 [h]Ps 9:14
13:6 [i]Ps 116:7
14:1 [j]Ps 10:4
14:2 [k]Ps 33:13 [l]Ps 92:6
14:3 [m]Ps 58:3 [n]Ps 143:2 [o]Ro 3:10-12*
14:4 [p]Ps 82:5 [q]Ps 27:2 [r]Ps 79:6; Isa 64:7
14:6 [s]Ps 9:9; 40:17
14:7 [t]Ps 53:6
15:1 [u]Ps 27:5-6 [v]Ps 24:3-5
15:2 [w]Ps 24:4; Zec 8:3,16; Eph 4:25
15:3 [x]Ex 23:1
15:4 [y]Ac 28:10 [z]Jdg 11:35
15:5 [a]Ex 22:25 [b]Ex 23:8; Dt 16:19 [c]2Pe 1:10
16:1 [d]Ps 17:8 [e]Ps 7:1
16:2 [f]Ps 73:25
16:3 [g]Ps 101:6

7Oh, that salvation for Israel would
come out of Zion!
When the LORD restores the
fortunes[t] of his people,
let Jacob rejoice and Israel be glad!

Psalm 15

A psalm of David.

*Those who may dwell
in the LORD's sanctuary.*

1LORD, who may dwell in your
sanctuary?[u]
Who may live on your holy hill?[v]

2He whose walk is blameless
and who does what is righteous,
who speaks the truth[w] from his heart
3 and has no slander[x] on his tongue,
who does his neighbor no wrong
and casts no slur on his fellowman,
4who despises a vile man
but honors[y] those who fear the LORD,
who keeps his oath[z]
even when it hurts,
5who lends his money without usury[a]
and does not accept a bribe[b]
against the innocent.

He who does these things
will never be shaken.[c]

Psalm 16

A *miktam*[b] of David.

The LORD reveals the path of life.

1Keep me safe,[d] O God,
for in you I take refuge.[e]

2I said to the LORD, "You are my Lord;
apart from you I have no good
thing."[f]
3As for the saints who are in the land,[g]
they are the glorious ones in whom
is all my delight.[c]

a *1* The Hebrew words rendered *fool* in Psalms denote one who is morally deficient. b Title: Probably a literary or musical term c *3* Or *As for the pagan priests who are in the land / and the nobles in whom all delight, I said:*

4The sorrows[a] of those will increase
who run after other gods.[b]
I will not pour out their libations of blood
or take up their names[c] on my lips.

5LORD, you have assigned me my portion[d] and my cup;[e]
you have made my lot secure.
6The boundary lines have fallen for me in pleasant places;
surely I have a delightful inheritance.[f]

7I will praise the LORD, who counsels me;[g]
even at night[h] my heart instructs me.
8I have set the LORD always before me.
Because he is at my right hand,[i]
I will not be shaken.

9Therefore my heart is glad[j] and my tongue rejoices;
my body also will rest secure,[k]
10because you will not abandon me to the grave,[d]
nor will you let your Holy One[e] see decay.[l]
11You have made[f] known to me the path of life;[m]
you will fill me with joy in your presence,[n]
with eternal pleasures[o] at your right hand.

Psalm 17

A prayer of David.

Prayer to hide in the shadow of God's wings.

1Hear, O LORD, my righteous plea;
listen to my cry.[p]
Give ear to my prayer—
it does not rise from deceitful lips.[q]
2May my vindication come from you;
may your eyes see what is right.

3Though you probe my heart and examine me at night,
though you test me,[r] you will find nothing;[s]
I have resolved that my mouth will not sin.[t]
4As for the deeds of men—
by the word of your lips
I have kept myself
from the ways of the violent.
5My steps have held to your paths;[u]
my feet have not slipped.[v]

6I call on you, O God, for you will answer me;[w]
give ear to me[x] and hear my prayer.[y]
7Show the wonder of your great love,[z]
you who save by your right hand[a]
those who take refuge in you from their foes.
8Keep me as the apple of your eye;[b]
hide me in the shadow of your wings
9from the wicked who assail me,
from my mortal enemies who surround me.[c]

10They close up their callous hearts,[d]
and their mouths speak with arrogance.[e]
11They have tracked me down, they now surround me,[f]
with eyes alert, to throw me to the ground.
12They are like a lion[g] hungry for prey,
like a great lion crouching in cover.

13Rise up, O LORD, confront them, bring them down;[h]
rescue me from the wicked by your sword.
14O LORD, by your hand save me from such men,
from men of this world[i] whose reward is in this life.

You still the hunger of those you cherish;
their sons have plenty,
and they store up wealth[j] for their children.
15And I—in righteousness I will see your face;
when I awake, I will be satisfied with seeing your likeness.[k]

16:4 [a]Ps 32:10 [b]Ps 106:37-38 [c]Ex 23:13 **16:5** [d]Ps 73:26 [e]Ps 23:5 **16:6** [f]Ps 78:55; Jer 3:19 **16:7** [g]Ps 73:24 [h]Ps 77:6 **16:8** [i]Ps 73:23 **16:9** [j]Ps 4:7; 30:11 [k]Ps 4:8 **16:10** [l]Ac 13:35* **16:11** [m]Mt 7:14 [n]Ac 2:25-28* [o]Ps 36:7-8 **17:1** [p]Ps 61:1 [q]Isa 29:13 **17:3** [r]Ps 26:2; 66:10 [s]Job 23:10; Jer 50:20 [t]Ps 39:1 **17:5** [u]Ps 44:18; 119:133 [v]Ps 18:36 **17:6** [w]Ps 86:7 [x]Ps 116:2 [y]Ps 88:2 **17:7** [z]Ps 31:21 [a]Ps 20:6 **17:8** [b]Dt 32:10 **17:9** [c]Ps 31:20; 109:3 **17:10** [d]Ps 73:7 [e]1Sa 2:3 **17:11** [f]Ps 37:14; 88:17 **17:12** [g]Ps 7:2; 10:9 **17:13** [h]Ps 7:12; 22:20; 73:18 **17:14** [i]Lk 16:8 [j]Ps 73:3-7 **17:15** [k]Nu 12:8; Ps 4:6-7; 16:11; 1Jn 3:2

d *10* Hebrew *Sheol* e *10* Or *your faithful one* f *11* Or *You will make*

Psalm 18

18:Title–50pp— 2Sa22:1-51

For the director of music. Of David the servant of the LORD. He sang to the LORD the words of this song when the LORD delivered him from the hand of all his enemies and from the hand of Saul. He said:

The LORD is a rock, fortress and deliverer.

1 I love you, O LORD, my strength.

2 The LORD is my rock,[a] my fortress
and my deliverer;
my God is my rock, in whom I take
refuge.
He is my shield[b] and the horn[g] of
my salvation,[c] my stronghold.
3 I call to the LORD, who is worthy of
praise,[d]
and I am saved from my enemies.

4 The cords of death[e] entangled me;
the torrents[f] of destruction
overwhelmed me.
5 The cords of the grave[h] coiled
around me;
the snares of death[g] confronted me.
6 In my distress I called to the LORD;
I cried to my God for help.
From his temple he heard my voice;[h]
my cry came before him, into
his ears.

7 The earth trembled and quaked,[i]
and the foundations of the
mountains shook;
they trembled because he was
angry.[j]
8 Smoke rose from his nostrils;
consuming fire[k] came from his
mouth,
burning coals blazed out of it.
9 He parted the heavens and came
down;[l]
dark clouds were under his feet.
10 He mounted the cherubim[m] and flew;
he soared on the wings of the
wind.[n]

18:2 [a]Ps 19:14 [b]Ps 59:11 [c]Ps 75:10
18:3 [d]Ps 48:1
18:4 [e]Ps 116:3 [f]Ps 124:4
18:5 [g]Ps 116:3
18:6 [h]Ps 34:15
18:7 [i]Jdg 5:4 [j]Ps 68:7-8
18:8 [k]Ps 50:3
18:9 [l]Ps 144:5
18:10 [m]Ps 80:1 [n]Ps 104:3
18:11 [o]Dt 4:11; Ps 97:2
18:12 [p]Ps 104:2 [q]Ps 97:3
18:13 [r]Ps 29:3; 104:7
18:14 [s]Ps 144:6
18:15 [t]Ps 76:6; 106:9
18:16 [u]Ps 144:7
18:17 [v]Ps 35:10
18:18 [w]Ps 59:16
18:19 [x]Ps 31:8 [y]Ps 118:5
18:20 [z]Ps 24:4
18:21 [a]2Ch 34:33 [b]Ps 119:102
18:22 [c]Ps 119:30

11 He made darkness his covering,[o] his
canopy around him—
the dark rain clouds of the sky.
12 Out of the brightness of his presence[p]
clouds advanced,
with hailstones and bolts of
lightning.[q]
13 The LORD thundered[r] from heaven;
the voice of the Most High
resounded.[i]
14 He shot his arrows and scattered ⌊the
enemies⌋,
great bolts of lightning and routed
them.[s]
15 The valleys of the sea were exposed
and the foundations of the earth
laid bare
at your rebuke,[t] O LORD,
at the blast of breath from your
nostrils.

16 He reached down from on high and
took hold of me;
he drew me out of deep waters.[u]
17 He rescued me from my powerful
enemy,
from my foes, who were too
strong for me.[v]
18 They confronted me in the day of my
disaster,
but the LORD was my support.[w]
19 He brought me out into a spacious
place;[x]
he rescued me because he
delighted in me.[y]

20 The LORD has dealt with me
according to my righteousness;
according to the cleanness of my
hands[z] he has rewarded me.
21 For I have kept the ways of the
LORD;[a]
I have not done evil by turning[b]
from my God.
22 All his laws are before me;[c]
I have not turned away from his
decrees.
23 I have been blameless before him
and have kept myself from sin.

g2 *Horn* here symbolizes strength. h5 Hebrew *Sheol* i13 Some Hebrew manuscripts and Septuagint (see also 2 Samuel 22:14); most Hebrew manuscripts *resounded, / amid hailstones and bolts of lightning*

[24]The LORD has rewarded me according
to my righteousness,[a]
according to the cleanness of my
hands in his sight.

[25]To the faithful[b] you show yourself
faithful,
to the blameless you show yourself
blameless,
[26]to the pure you show yourself pure,
but to the crooked you show
yourself shrewd.[c]
[27]You save the humble
but bring low those whose eyes are
haughty.[d]
[28]You, O LORD, keep my lamp burning;
my God turns my darkness into
light.[e]
[29]With your help[f] I can advance
against a troop[j];
with my God I can scale a wall.

[30]As for God, his way is perfect;[g]
the word of the LORD is flawless.[h]
He is a shield
for all who take refuge[i] in him.
[31]For who is God besides the LORD?[j]
And who is the Rock[k] except our
God?
[32]It is God who arms me with strength[l]
and makes my way perfect.
[33]He makes my feet like the feet of a
deer;[m]
he enables me to stand on the
heights.[n]
[34]He trains my hands for battle;[o]
my arms can bend a bow of bronze.
[35]You give me your shield of victory,
and your right hand sustains[p] me;
you stoop down to make me great.
[36]You broaden the path beneath me,
so that my ankles do not turn.

[37]I pursued my enemies[q] and overtook
them;
I did not turn back till they were
destroyed.
[38]I crushed them so that they could
not rise;[r]
they fell beneath my feet.[s]
[39]You armed me with strength for battle;
you made my adversaries bow at
my feet.

18:24 [a]1Sa 26:23 **18:25** [b]1Ki 8:32; Ps 62:12; Mt 5:7 **18:26** [c]Pr 3:34 **18:27** [d]Pr 6:17 **18:28** [e]Job 18:6; 29:3 **18:29** [f]Heb 11:34 **18:30** [g]Dt 32:4; Rev 15:3 [h]Ps 12:6 [i]Ps 17:7 **18:31** [j]Dt 32:39; 86:8; Isa 45:5,6,14, 18,21 [k]Dt 32:31; 1Sa 2:2 **18:32** [l]Isa 45:5 **18:33** [m]Hab 3:19 [n]Dt 32:13 **18:34** [o]Ps 144:1 **18:35** [p]Ps 119:116 **18:37** [q]Ps 37:20; 44:5 **18:38** [r]Ps 36:12 [s]Ps 47:3 **18:40** [t]Ps 21:12 [u]Ps 94:23 **18:41** [v]Ps 50:22 [w]Job 27:9; Pr 1:28 **18:43** [x]2Sa 8:1-14 [y]Isa 52:15; 55:5 **18:44** [z]Ps 66:3 **18:45** [a]Mic 7:17 **18:46** [b]Ps 51:14 **18:47** [c]Ps 47:3 **18:48** [d]Ps 59:1 **18:49** [e]Ps 108:1 [f]Ro 15:9* **18:50** [g]Ps 144:10 [h]Ps 89:4

[40]You made my enemies turn their
backs[t] in flight,
and I destroyed[u] my foes.
[41]They cried for help, but there was no
one to save them[v]—
to the LORD, but he did not answer.[w]
[42]I beat them as fine as dust borne on
the wind;
I poured them out like mud in the
streets.

[43]You have delivered me from the
attacks of the people;
you have made me the head of
nations;[x]
people I did not know[y] are subject
to me.
[44]As soon as they hear me, they obey
me;
foreigners[z] cringe before me.
[45]They all lose heart;
they come trembling from their
strongholds.[a]

[46]The LORD lives! Praise be to my Rock!
Exalted be God my Savior![b]
[47]He is the God who avenges me,
who subdues nations[c] under me,
[48] who saves[d] me from my enemies.
You exalted me above my foes;
from violent men you rescued me.
[49]Therefore I will praise you among
the nations, O LORD;
I will sing[e] praises to your name.[f]
[50]He gives his king great victories;
he shows unfailing kindness to his
anointed,
to David[g] and his descendants
forever.[h]

Psalm 19

For the director of music.
A psalm of David.

God's creation and his law.

[1]The heavens[i] declare[j] the glory of God;
the skies proclaim the work of his
hands.

19:1 [i]Isa 40:22 [j]Ps 50:6; Ro 1:19

j29 Or *can run through a barricade*

2Day after day they pour forth speech;
night after night they display
knowledge.[a]
3There is no speech or language
where their voice is not heard.[k]
4Their voice[l] goes out into all the earth,
their words to the ends of the
world.[b]

In the heavens he has pitched a
tent[c] for the sun,
5 which is like a bridegroom coming
forth from his pavilion,
like a champion rejoicing to run
his course.
6It rises at one end of the heavens
and makes its circuit to the other;[d]
nothing is hidden from its heat.

7The law of the LORD is perfect,
reviving the soul.[e]
The statutes of the LORD are
trustworthy,[f]
making wise the simple.[g]
8The precepts of the LORD are right,[h]
giving joy to the heart.
The commands of the LORD are radiant,
giving light to the eyes.
9The fear of the LORD is pure,
enduring forever.
The ordinances of the LORD are sure
and altogether righteous.[i]
10They are more precious than gold,[j]
than much pure gold;
they are sweeter than honey,
than honey from the comb.
11By them is your servant warned;
in keeping them there is great
reward.

12Who can discern his errors?
Forgive my hidden faults.[k]
13Keep your servant also from willful
sins;
may they not rule over me.
Then will I be blameless,
innocent of great transgression.

14May the words of my mouth and the
meditation of my heart
be pleasing[l] in your sight,
O LORD, my Rock[m] and my
Redeemer.[n]

19:2 [a]Ps 74:16
19:4 [b]Ro 10:18* [c]Ps 104:2
19:6 [d]Ps 113:3; Ecc 1:5
19:7 [e]Ps 23:3 [f]Ps 93:5; 111:7 [g]Ps 119:98-100
19:8 [h]Ps 12:6; 119:128
19:9 [i]Ps 119:138, 142
19:10 [j]Pr 8:10
19:12 [k]Ps 51:2; 90:8; 139:6
19:14 [l]Ps 104:34 [m]Ps 18:2 [n]Isa 47:4
20:1 [o]Ps 46:7,11 [p]Ps 91:14
20:2 [q]Ps 3:4
20:3 [r]Ac 10:4 [s]Ps 51:19
20:4 [t]Ps 21:2; 145:16,19
20:5 [u]Ps 9:14; 60:4 [v]1Sa 1:17
20:6 [w]Ps 28:8; 41:11; Isa 58:9
20:7 [x]Ps 33:17; Isa 31:1 [y]2Ch 32:8
20:8 [z]Mic 7:8 [a]Ps 37:23
20:9 [b]Ps 3:7; 17:6

Psalm 20

For the director of music.
A psalm of David.

The LORD saves his anointed.

1May the LORD answer you when you
are in distress;
may the name of the God of
Jacob[o] protect you.[p]
2May he send you help from the
sanctuary[q]
and grant you support from Zion.
3May he remember[r] all your sacrifices
and accept your burnt offerings.[s]
Selah
4May he give you the desire of your
heart[t]
and make all your plans succeed.
5We will shout for joy when you are
victorious
and will lift up our banners[u] in the
name of our God.
May the LORD grant all your requests.[v]

6Now I know that the LORD saves his
anointed;[w]
he answers him from his holy heaven
with the saving power of his right
hand.
7Some trust in chariots and some in
horses,[x]
but we trust in the name of the
LORD our God.[y]
8They are brought to their knees and fall,
but we rise up[z] and stand firm.[a]

9O LORD, save the king!
Answer[m] us[b] when we call!

Psalm 21

For the director of music.
A psalm of David.

Rejoicing in the LORD's blessings.

1O LORD, the king rejoices in your
strength.

k3 Or *They have no speech, there are no words; / no sound is heard from them* l4 Septuagint, Jerome and Syriac; Hebrew *line* m9 Or *save! / O King, answer*

How great is his joy in the victories
you give![a]
2You have granted him the desire of
his heart[b]
and have not withheld the request
of his lips. *Selah*
3You welcomed him with rich
blessings
and placed a crown of pure gold[c]
on his head.
4He asked you for life, and you gave it
to him—
length of days, for ever and
ever.[d]
5Through the victories[e] you gave, his
glory is great;
you have bestowed on him
splendor and majesty.
6Surely you have granted him eternal
blessings
and made him glad with the joy[f] of
your presence.[g]
7For the king trusts in the LORD;
through the unfailing love of the
Most High
he will not be shaken.

8Your hand will lay hold[h] on all your
enemies;
your right hand will seize your
foes.
9At the time of your appearing
you will make them like a fiery
furnace.
In his wrath the LORD will swallow
them up,
and his fire will consume them.[i]
10You will destroy their descendants
from the earth,
their posterity from mankind.[j]
11Though they plot evil[k] against
you
and devise wicked schemes,[l] they
cannot succeed;
12for you will make them turn their
backs[m]
when you aim at them with drawn
bow.

13Be exalted, O LORD, in your
strength;
we will sing and praise your
might.

21:1 [a]Ps 59:16-17
21:2 [b]Ps 37:4
21:3 [c]2Sa 12:30
21:4 [d]Ps 61:5-6; 91:16; 133:3
21:5 [e]Ps 18:50
21:6 [f]Ps 43:4 [g]1Ch 17:27
21:8 [h]Isa 10:10
21:9 [i]Ps 50:3; La 2:2; Mal 4:1
21:10 [j]Dt 28:18; Ps 37:28
21:11 [k]Ps 2:1 [l]Ps 10:2
21:12 [m]Ps 7:12-13; 18:40
22:1 [n]Mt 27:46*; Mk 15:34* [o]Ps 10:1
22:2 [p]Ps 42:3
22:3 [q]Ps 99:9 [r]Dt 10:21
22:5 [s]Isa 49:23
22:6 [t]Job 25:6; Isa 41:14 [u]Ps 31:11 [v]Isa 49:7; 53:3
22:7 [w]Mt 27:39,44 [x]Mk 15:29
22:8 [y]Ps 91:14 [z]Mt 27:43
22:9 [a]Ps 71:6
22:10 [b]Isa 46:3
22:11 [c]Ps 72:12
22:12 [d]Ps 68:30 [e]Dt 32:14
22:13 [f]Ps 17:12 [g]Ps 35:21
22:14 [h]Ps 31:10

Psalm 22

For the director of music. To ⌊the tune of⌋ "The Doe of the Morning." A psalm of David.

Prayer of despair and praises.

1My God, my God, why have you
forsaken me?[n]
Why are you so far[o] from saving me,
so far from the words of my
groaning?
2O my God, I cry out by day, but you
do not answer,
by night,[p] and am not silent.

3Yet you are enthroned as the Holy
One;[q]
you are the praise[r] of Israel.[n]
4In you our fathers put their trust;
they trusted and you delivered them.
5They cried to you and were saved;
in you they trusted and were not
disappointed.[s]

6But I am a worm[t] and not a man,
scorned by men[u] and despised[v] by
the people.
7All who see me mock me;
they hurl insults,[w] shaking their
heads:[x]
8"He trusts in the LORD;
let the LORD rescue him.[y]
Let him deliver him,
since he delights[z] in him."

9Yet you brought me out of the womb;[a]
you made me trust in you
even at my mother's breast.
10From birth[b] I was cast upon you;
from my mother's womb you have
been my God.
11Do not be far from me,
for trouble is near
and there is no one to help.[c]

12Many bulls[d] surround me;
strong bulls of Bashan[e] encircle me.
13Roaring lions[f] tearing their prey
open their mouths wide[g] against me.
14I am poured out like water,
and all my bones are out of joint.[h]

n3 Or *Yet you are holy, / enthroned on the praises of Israel*

My heart has turned to wax;
it has melted away[a] within me.
15My strength is dried up like a potsherd,
and my tongue sticks to the roof of my mouth;[b]
you lay me[o] in the dust[c] of death.
16Dogs[d] have surrounded me;
a band of evil men has encircled me,
they have pierced[p][e] my hands and my feet.
17I can count all my bones;
people stare[f] and gloat over me.[g]
18They divide my garments among them
and cast lots[h] for my clothing.

19But you, O LORD, be not far off;
O my Strength, come quickly[i] to help me.
20Deliver my life from the sword,
my precious life[j] from the power of the dogs.
21Rescue me from the mouth of the lions;
save[q] me from the horns of the wild oxen.

22I will declare your name to my brothers;
in the congregation I will praise you.[k]
23You who fear the LORD, praise him![l]
All you descendants of Jacob, honor him!
Revere him,[m] all you descendants of Israel!
24For he has not despised or disdained
the suffering of the afflicted one;
he has not hidden his face[n] from him
but has listened to his cry for help.[o]

25From you comes the theme of my praise in the great assembly;[p]
before those who fear you[r] will I fulfill my vows.[q]
26The poor will eat[r] and be satisfied;
they who seek the LORD will praise him—[s]
may your hearts live forever!
27All the ends of the earth[t]
will remember and turn to the LORD,
and all the families of the nations
will bow down before him,[u]
28for dominion belongs to the LORD[v]
and he rules over the nations.
29All the rich[w] of the earth will feast and worship;
all who go down to the dust[x] will kneel before him—
those who cannot keep themselves alive.
30Posterity[y] will serve him;
future generations will be told about the Lord.
31They will proclaim his righteousness
to a people yet unborn[z]—
for he has done it.

22:14 [a]Job 30:16; Da 5:6
22:15 [b]Ps 38:10; Jn 19:28 [c]Ps 104:29
22:16 [d]Ps 59:6 [e]Isa 53:5; Zec 12:10; Jn 19:34
22:17 [f]Lk 23:35 [g]Lk 23:27
22:18 [h]Mt 27:35*; Lk 23:34; Jn 19:24*
22:19 [i]Ps 70:5
22:20 [j]Ps 35:17
22:22 [k]Heb 2:12*
22:23 [l]Ps 86:12; 135:19 [m]Ps 33:8
22:24 [n]Ps 69:17 [o]Heb 5:7
22:25 [p]Ps 35:18 [q]Ecc 5:4
22:26 [r]Ps 107:9 [s]Ps 40:16
22:27 [t]Ps 2:8 [u]Ps 86:9
22:28 [v]Ps 47:7-8
22:29 [w]Ps 45:12 [x]Isa 26:19
22:30 [y]Ps 102:28
22:31 [z]Ps 78:6
23:1 [a]Isa 40:11; Jn 10:11; 1Pe 2:25 [b]Php 4:19
23:2 [c]Eze 34:14; Rev 7:17
23:3 [d]Ps 19:7 [e]Ps 5:8; 85:13
23:4 [f]Job 10:21-22 [g]Ps 3:6; 27:1 [h]Isa 43:2

Psalm 23

A psalm of David.

The Shepherd's Psalm.

1The LORD is my shepherd,[a] I shall not be in want.[b]
2 He makes me lie down in green pastures,
he leads me beside quiet waters,[c]
3 he restores my soul.[d]
He guides me in paths of righteousness[e]
for his name's sake.
4Even though I walk
through the valley of the shadow of death,[s][f]
I will fear no evil,[g]
for you are with me;[h]
your rod and your staff,
they comfort me.

5You prepare a table before me
in the presence of my enemies.
You anoint my head with oil;[i]
my cup[j] overflows.
6Surely goodness and love will follow me
all the days of my life,
and I will dwell in the house of the LORD
forever.

23:5 [i]Ps 92:10 [j]Ps 16:5

[o]*15* Or */ I am laid* [p]*16* Some Hebrew manuscripts, Septuagint and Syriac; most Hebrew manuscripts */ like the lion,* [q]*21* Or */ you have heard* [r]*25* Hebrew *him* [s]*4* Or *through the darkest valley*

Psalm 24

Of David. A psalm.

The King of glory.

1The earth is the LORD's,[a] and everything in it,
the world, and all who live in it;[b]
2for he founded it upon the seas
and established it upon the waters.

3Who may ascend the hill[c] of the LORD?
Who may stand in his holy place?[d]
4He who has clean hands[e] and a pure heart,[f]
who does not lift up his soul to an idol
or swear by what is false.[t]
5He will receive blessing from the LORD
and vindication from God his Savior.
6Such is the generation of those who seek him,
who seek your face,[g] O God of Jacob.[u] *Selah*

7Lift up your heads, O you gates;[h]
be lifted up, you ancient doors,
that the King of glory[i] may come in.
8Who is this King of glory?
The LORD strong and mighty,
the LORD mighty in battle.[j]
9Lift up your heads, O you gates;
lift them up, you ancient doors,
that the King of glory may come in.
10Who is he, this King of glory?
The LORD Almighty—
he is the King of glory. *Selah*

Psalm 25[v]

Of David.

Prayer seeking forgiveness.

1To you, O LORD, I lift up my soul;[k]
2 in you I trust,[l] O my God.
Do not let me be put to shame,
nor let my enemies triumph over me.
3No one whose hope is in you
will ever be put to shame,[m]
but they will be put to shame
who are treacherous without excuse.

24:1 [a]Ex 9:29; Job 41:11; Ps 89:11 [b]1Co 10:26* **24:3** [c]Ps 2:6 [d]Ps 15:1; 65:4 **24:4** [e]Job 17:9 [f]Mt 5:8 **24:6** [g]Ps 27:8 **24:7** [h]Isa 26:2 [i]Ps 97:6; 1Co 2:8 **24:8** [j]Ps 76:3-6 **25:1** [k]Ps 86:4 **25:2** [l]Ps 41:11 **25:3** [m]Isa 49:23 **25:4** [n]Ex 33:13 **25:6** [o]Ps 103:17; Isa 63:7,15 **25:7** [p]Job 13:26; Jer 3:25 [q]Ps 51:1 **25:8** [r]Ps 92:15 [s]Ps 32:8 **25:9** [t]Ps 23:3 [u]Ps 27:11 **25:10** [v]Ps 40:11 [w]Ps 103:18 **25:11** [x]Ps 31:3; 79:9 **25:12** [y]Ps 37:23 **25:13** [z]Pr 19:23 [a]Ps 37:11 **25:14** [b]Pr 3:32 [c]Jn 7:17 **25:15** [d]Ps 141:8 **25:16** [e]Ps 69:16 **25:17** [f]Ps 107:6 **25:18** [g]2Sa 16:12

4Show me your ways, O LORD,
teach me your paths;[n]
5guide me in your truth and teach me,
for you are God my Savior,
and my hope is in you all day long.
6Remember, O LORD, your great mercy and love,[o]
for they are from of old.
7Remember not the sins of my youth[p]
and my rebellious ways;
according to your love[q] remember me,
for you are good, O LORD.

8Good and upright[r] is the LORD;
therefore he instructs[s] sinners in his ways.
9He guides[t] the humble in what is right
and teaches them[u] his way.
10All the ways of the LORD are loving and faithful[v]
for those who keep the demands of his covenant.[w]
11For the sake of your name,[x] O LORD,
forgive my iniquity, though it is great.
12Who, then, is the man that fears the LORD?
He will instruct him in the way[y] chosen for him.
13He will spend his days in prosperity,[z]
and his descendants will inherit the land.[a]
14The LORD confides[b] in those who fear him;
he makes his covenant known[c] to them.
15My eyes are ever on the LORD,[d]
for only he will release my feet from the snare.

16Turn to me[e] and be gracious to me,
for I am lonely and afflicted.
17The troubles of my heart have multiplied;
free me from my anguish.[f]
18Look upon my affliction and my distress[g]
and take away all my sins.

t4 Or *swear falsely* u6 Two Hebrew manuscripts and Syriac (see also Septuagint); most Hebrew manuscripts *face, Jacob* v This psalm is an acrostic poem, the verses of which begin with the successive letters of the Hebrew alphabet.

[19]See how my enemies[a] have
increased
and how fiercely they hate me!
[20]Guard my life[b] and rescue me;
let me not be put to shame,
for I take refuge in you.
[21]May integrity[c] and uprightness
protect me,
because my hope is in you.

[22]Redeem Israel,[d] O God,
from all their troubles!

Psalm 26

Of David.

Prayer proclaiming a blameless life.

[1]Vindicate me, O LORD,
for I have led a blameless life;[e]
I have trusted[f] in the LORD
without wavering.[g]
[2]Test me,[h] O LORD, and try me,
examine my heart and my mind;[i]
[3]for your love is ever before me,
and I walk continually[j] in your
truth.
[4]I do not sit[k] with deceitful men,
nor do I consort with hypocrites;
[5]I abhor[l] the assembly of evildoers
and refuse to sit with the wicked.
[6]I wash my hands in innocence,[m]
and go about your altar, O LORD,
[7]proclaiming aloud your praise
and telling of all your wonderful
deeds.[n]
[8]I love[o] the house where you live,
O LORD,
the place where your glory dwells.

[9]Do not take away my soul along with
sinners,
my life with bloodthirsty men,[p]
[10]in whose hands are wicked schemes,
whose right hands are full of
bribes.[q]
[11]But I lead a blameless life;
redeem me[r] and be merciful to me.

[12]My feet stand on level ground;[s]
in the great assembly[t] I will praise
the LORD.

25:19 [a]Ps 3:1
25:20 [b]Ps 86:2
25:21 [c]Ps 41:12
25:22 [d]Ps 130:8
26:1 [e]Ps 7:8; Pr 20:7 [f]Ps 28:7 [g]2Ki 20:3; Heb 10:23
26:2 [h]Ps 17:3 [i]Ps 7:9
26:3 [j]2Ki 20:3
26:4 [k]Ps 1:1
26:5 [l]Ps 31:6; 139:21
26:6 [m]Ps 73:13
26:7 [n]Ps 9:1
26:8 [o]Ps 27:4
26:9 [p]Ps 28:3
26:10 [q]1Sa 8:3
26:11 [r]Ps 69:18
26:12 [s]Ps 27:11; 40:2 [t]Ps 22:22
27:1 [u]Isa 60:19 [v]Ex 15:2 [w]Ps 118:6
27:2 [x]Ps 9:3; 14:4
27:3 [y]Ps 3:6 [z]Job 4:6
27:4 [a]Ps 90:17 [b]Ps 23:6; 26:8
27:5 [c]Ps 17:8; 31:20 [d]Ps 40:2
27:6 [e]Ps 3:3 [f]Ps 107:22
27:7 [g]Ps 13:3
27:9 [h]Ps 69:17

Psalm 27

Of David.

Strength from the LORD.

[1]The LORD is my light[u] and my
salvation[v]—
whom shall I fear?
The LORD is the stronghold of my life—
of whom shall I be afraid?[w]
[2]When evil men advance against me
to devour my flesh,[w]
when my enemies and my foes
attack me,
they will stumble and fall.[x]
[3]Though an army besiege me,
my heart will not fear;[y]
though war break out against me,
even then will I be confident.[z]

[4]One thing[a] I ask of the LORD,
this is what I seek:
that I may dwell in the house of the
LORD
all the days of my life,[b]
to gaze upon the beauty of the LORD
and to seek him in his temple.
[5]For in the day of trouble
he will keep me safe in his dwelling;
he will hide me[c] in the shelter of his
tabernacle
and set me high upon a rock.[d]
[6]Then my head will be exalted[e]
above the enemies who surround
me;
at his tabernacle will I sacrifice[f] with
shouts of joy;
I will sing and make music to the
LORD.

[7]Hear my voice when I call, O LORD;
be merciful to me and answer me.[g]
[8]My heart says of you, "Seek his[x] face!"
Your face, LORD, I will seek.
[9]Do not hide your face[h] from me,
do not turn your servant away in
anger;
you have been my helper.
Do not reject me or forsake me,
O God my Savior.

[w]2 Or *to slander me* [x]8 Or *To you, O my heart, he has said, "Seek my*

10Though my father and mother
forsake me,
the LORD will receive me.
11Teach me your way, O LORD;
lead me in a straight path[a]
because of my oppressors.
12Do not turn me over to the desire of
my foes,
for false witnesses[b] rise up against
me,
breathing out violence.

13I am still confident of this:
I will see the goodness of the LORD[c]
in the land of the living.[d]
14Wait[e] for the LORD;
be strong and take heart
and wait for the LORD.

Psalm 28

Of David.

A cry for mercy.

1To you I call, O LORD my Rock;
do not turn a deaf ear to me.
For if you remain silent,[f]
I will be like those who have gone
down to the pit.[g]
2Hear my cry for mercy[h]
as I call to you for help,
as I lift up my hands
toward your Most Holy Place.[i]

3Do not drag me away with the wicked,
with those who do evil,
who speak cordially with their
neighbors
but harbor malice in their hearts.[j]
4Repay them for their deeds
and for their evil work;
repay them for what their hands
have done[k]
and bring back upon them what
they deserve.[l]
5Since they show no regard for the
works of the LORD
and what his hands have done,[m]
he will tear them down
and never build them up again.

6Praise be to the LORD,
for he has heard my cry for mercy.

27:11 [a]Ps 5:8; 25:4; 86:11
27:12 [b]Mt 26:60; Ac 9:1
27:13 [c]Ps 31:19 [d]Jer 11:19; Eze 26:20
27:14 [e]Ps 40:1
28:1 [f]Ps 83:1 [g]Ps 88:4
28:2 [h]Ps 138:2; 140:6 [i]Ps 5:7
28:3 [j]Ps 12:2; Ps 26:9; Jer 9:8
28:4 [k]2Ti 4:14; Rev 22:12 [l]Rev 18:6
28:5 [m]Isa 5:12
28:7 [n]Ps 18:1 [o]Ps 13:5 [p]Ps 40:3; 69:30
28:8 [q]Ps 20:6
28:9 [r]Dt 9:29; Ezr 1:4 [s]Isa 40:11 [t]Dt 1:31; 32:11
29:1 [u]1Ch 16:28 [v]Ps 96:7-9
29:2 [w]2Ch 20:21
29:3 [x]Job 37:5 [y]Ps 18:13
29:4 [z]Ps 68:33
29:5 [a]Jdg 9:15
29:6 [b]Ps 114:4 [c]Dt 3:9
29:8 [d]Nu 13:26

7The LORD is my strength[n] and my
shield;
my heart trusts[o] in him, and I am
helped.
My heart leaps for joy
and I will give thanks to him in
song.[p]

8The LORD is the strength of his people,
a fortress of salvation for his
anointed one.[q]
9Save your people and bless your
inheritance;[r]
be their shepherd[s] and carry
them[t] forever.

Psalm 29

A psalm of David.

The majesty of the LORD's voice.

1Ascribe to the LORD,[u] O mighty ones,
ascribe to the LORD glory[v] and
strength.
2Ascribe to the LORD the glory due his
name;
worship the LORD in the splendor
of his[y] holiness.[w]

3The voice[x] of the LORD is over the
waters;
the God of glory thunders,[y]
the LORD thunders over the mighty
waters.
4The voice of the LORD is powerful;[z]
the voice of the LORD is majestic.
5The voice of the LORD breaks the
cedars;
the LORD breaks in pieces the
cedars of Lebanon.[a]
6He makes Lebanon skip[b] like a calf,
Sirion[z] [c] like a young wild ox.
7The voice of the LORD strikes
with flashes of lightning.
8The voice of the LORD shakes the
desert;
the LORD shakes the Desert of
Kadesh.[d]
9The voice of the LORD twists the oaks[a]
and strips the forests bare.

y2 Or *LORD with the splendor of* z6 That is, Mount Hermon a9 Or *LORD makes the deer give birth*

And in his temple all cry, "Glory!"[a]

10The LORD sits[b] enthroned over the flood;[b]
the LORD is enthroned as King forever.[c]

11The LORD gives strength to his people;[d]
the LORD blesses his people with peace.[e]

Psalm 30

A psalm. A song. For the dedication of the temple.[c] Of David.

Praise for God's mercy and favor.

1I will exalt you, O LORD,
for you lifted me out of the depths
and did not let my enemies gloat over me.[f]
2O LORD my God, I called to you for help[g]
and you healed me.[h]
3O LORD, you brought me up from the grave[d];
you spared me from going down into the pit.[i]

4Sing to the LORD, you saints[j] of his;
praise his holy name.[k]
5For his anger[l] lasts only a moment,
but his favor lasts a lifetime;
weeping may remain for a night,
but rejoicing comes in the morning.[m]

6When I felt secure, I said,
"I will never be shaken."
7O LORD, when you favored me,
you made my mountain[e] stand firm;
but when you hid your face,[n]
I was dismayed.

8To you, O LORD, I called;
to the Lord I cried for mercy:
9"What gain is there in my destruction,[f]
in my going down into the pit?
Will the dust praise you?
Will it proclaim your faithfulness?[o]
10Hear, O LORD, and be merciful to me;
O LORD, be my help."

11You turned my wailing into dancing;
you removed my sackcloth and clothed me with joy,[p]
12that my heart may sing to you and not be silent.
O LORD my God, I will give you thanks[q] forever.[r]

Psalm 31

31:1-4pp— Ps71:1-3

For the director of music. A psalm of David.

Cry for the LORD's mercy during time of trouble.

1In you, O LORD, I have taken refuge;
let me never be put to shame;
deliver me in your righteousness.
2Turn your ear to me,
come quickly to my rescue;
be my rock of refuge,[s]
a strong fortress to save me.
3Since you are my rock and my fortress,[t]
for the sake of your name[u] lead and guide me.
4Free me from the trap that is set for me,
for you are my refuge.[v]
5Into your hands I commit my spirit;[w]
redeem me, O LORD, the God of truth.

6I hate those who cling to worthless idols;
I trust in the LORD.[x]
7I will be glad and rejoice in your love,
for you saw my affliction[y]
and knew the anguish[z] of my soul.
8You have not handed me over[a] to the enemy
but have set my feet in a spacious place.

9Be merciful to me, O LORD, for I am in distress;
my eyes grow weak with sorrow,[b]
my soul and my body with grief.
10My life is consumed by anguish
and my years by groaning;[c]

29:9 [a]Ps 26:8
29:10 [b]Ge 6:17 [c]Ps 10:16
29:11 [d]Ps 28:8 [e]Ps 37:11
30:1 [f]Ps 25:2; 28:9
30:2 [g]Ps 88:13 [h]Ps 6:2
30:3 [i]Ps 28:1; 86:13
30:4 [j]Ps 149:1 [k]Ps 97:12
30:5 [l]Ps 103:9 [m]2Co 4:17
30:7 [n]Dt 31:17; Ps 104:29
30:9 [o]Ps 6:5
30:11 [p]Ps 4:7; Jer 31:4,13
30:12 [q]Ps 16:9 [r]Ps 44:8
31:2 [s]Ps 18:2
31:3 [t]Ps 18:2 [u]Ps 23:3
31:4 [v]Ps 25:15
31:5 [w]Lk 23:46; Ac 7:59
31:6 [x]Jnh 2:8
31:7 [y]Ps 90:14 [z]Ps 10:14; Jn 10:27
31:8 [a]Dt 32:30
31:9 [b]Ps 6:7
31:10 [c]Ps 13:2

[b] *10* Or *sat* [c] Title: Or *palace* [d] *3* Hebrew *Sheol* [e] *7* Or *hill country* [f] *9* Or *there if I am silenced*

my strength fails because of my
affliction,[g]
and my bones grow weak.[a]
11Because of all my enemies,
I am the utter contempt of my
neighbors;[b]
I am a dread to my friends—
those who see me on the street
flee from me.
12I am forgotten by them as though I
were dead;[c]
I have become like broken pottery.
13For I hear the slander of many;
there is terror on every side;[d]
they conspire against me
and plot to take my life.[e]
14But I trust[f] in you, O LORD;
I say, "You are my God."
15My times[g] are in your hands;
deliver me from my enemies
and from those who pursue me.
16Let your face shine[h] on your servant;
save me in your unfailing love.
17Let me not be put to shame,[i] O LORD,
for I have cried out to you;
but let the wicked be put to shame
and lie silent[j] in the grave.[h]
18Let their lying lips[k] be silenced,
for with pride and contempt
they speak arrogantly[l] against the
righteous.

19How great is your goodness,[m]
which you have stored up for those
who fear you,
which you bestow in the sight of
men[n]
on those who take refuge in you.
20In the shelter of your presence you
hide[o] them
from the intrigues of men;[p]
in your dwelling you keep them safe
from accusing tongues.

21Praise be to the LORD,
for he showed his wonderful love[q]
to me
when I was in a besieged city.[r]
22In my alarm[s] I said,
"I am cut off from your sight!"
Yet you heard my cry[t] for mercy
when I called to you for help.

23Love the LORD, all his saints![u]
The LORD preserves the faithful,[v]
but the proud he pays back[w] in full.
24Be strong and take heart,[x]
all you who hope in the LORD.

31:10 [a]Ps 38:3; 39:11
31:11 [b]Job 19:13; Ps 38:11; 64:8; Isa 53:4
31:12 [c]Ps 88:4
31:13 [d]Jer 20:3,10; La 2:22 [e]Mt 27:1
31:14 [f]Ps 140:6
31:15 [g]Job 24:1; Ps 143:9
31:16 [h]Nu 6:25; Ps 4:6
31:17 [i]Ps 25:2-3 [j]Ps 115:17
31:18 [k]Ps 120:2 [l]Ps 94:4
31:19 [m]Ro 11:22 [n]Isa 64:4
31:20 [o]Ps 27:5 [p]Job 5:21
31:21 [q]Ps 17:7 [r]1Sa 23:7
31:22 [s]Ps 116:11 [t]La 3:54
31:23 [u]Ps 34:9 [v]Ps 145:20 [w]Ps 94:2
31:24 [x]Ps 27:14
32:1 [y]Ps 85:2
32:2 [z]Ro 4:7-8*; 2Co 5:19 [a]Jn 1:47
32:3 [b]Ps 31:10
32:4 [c]Job 33:7
32:5 [d]Pr 28:13 [e]Ps 103:12 [f]Lev 26:40
32:6 [g]Ps 69:13; Isa 55:6 [h]Isa 43:2
32:7 [i]Ps 9:9 [j]Ex 15:1
32:8 [k]Ps 25:8 [l]Ps 33:18

Psalm 32

Of David. A *maskil.*[i]

Blessed is one whose sins are forgiven.

1Blessed is he
whose transgressions are forgiven,
whose sins are covered.[y]
2Blessed is the man
whose sin the LORD does not count
against him[z]
and in whose spirit is no deceit.[a]

3When I kept silent,
my bones wasted away[b]
through my groaning all day long.
4For day and night
your hand was heavy[c] upon me;
my strength was sapped
as in the heat of summer. *Selah*
5Then I acknowledged my sin to you
and did not cover up my iniquity.
I said, "I will confess[d]
my transgressions[e] to the LORD"—
and you forgave
the guilt of my sin.[f] *Selah*
6Therefore let everyone who is godly
pray to you
while you may be found;[g]
surely when the mighty waters rise,
they will not reach him.[h]
7You are my hiding place;
you will protect me from trouble[i]
and surround me with songs of
deliverance.[j] *Selah*

8I will instruct[k] you and teach you in
the way you should go;
I will counsel you and watch over[l]
you.
9Do not be like the horse or the mule,
which have no understanding

[g]*10* Or *guilt* [h]*17* Hebrew *Sheol* [i]Title: Probably a literary or musical term

but must be controlled by bit and
bridle[a]
or they will not come to you.
[10]Many are the woes of the wicked,[b]
but the LORD's unfailing love
surrounds the man who trusts[c] in
him.

[11]Rejoice in the LORD[d] and be glad,
you righteous;
sing, all you who are upright in
heart!

Psalm 33

God's creation and providence.

[1]Sing joyfully to the LORD, you
righteous;
it is fitting[e] for the upright[f] to
praise him.
[2]Praise the LORD with the harp;
make music to him on the ten-
stringed lyre.[g]
[3]Sing to him a new song;[h]
play skillfully, and shout for joy.

[4]For the word of the LORD is right[i]
and true;
he is faithful in all he does.
[5]The LORD loves righteousness and
justice;[j]
the earth is full of his unfailing love.[k]

[6]By the word[l] of the LORD were the
heavens made,
their starry host by the breath of
his mouth.
[7]He gathers the waters of the sea into
jars[j];
he puts the deep into storehouses.
[8]Let all the earth fear the LORD;
let all the people of the world
revere him.[m]
[9]For he spoke, and it came to be;
he commanded,[n] and it stood firm.
[10]The LORD foils the plans of the
nations;[o]
he thwarts the purposes of the
peoples.
[11]But the plans of the LORD stand firm
forever,
the purposes[p] of his heart through
all generations.

[12]Blessed is the nation whose God is
the LORD,[q]
the people he chose[r] for his
inheritance.
[13]From heaven the LORD looks down
and sees all mankind;[s]
[14]from his dwelling place[t] he watches
all who live on earth—
[15]he who forms[u] the hearts of all,
who considers everything they
do.[v]
[16]No king is saved by the size of his
army;[w]
no warrior escapes by his great
strength.
[17]A horse[x] is a vain hope for
deliverance;
despite all its great strength it
cannot save.
[18]But the eyes[y] of the LORD are on
those who fear him,
on those whose hope is in his
unfailing love,[z]
[19]to deliver them from death
and keep them alive in famine.[a]

[20]We wait[b] in hope for the LORD;
he is our help and our shield.
[21]In him our hearts rejoice,[c]
for we trust in his holy name.
[22]May your unfailing love rest upon us,
O LORD,
even as we put our hope in you.

Psalm 34[k]

Of David. When he pretended to
be insane before Abimelech, who
drove him away, and he left.

Praise and fear the LORD.

[1]I will extol the LORD at all times;[d]
his praise will always be on my
lips.
[2]My soul will boast[e] in the LORD;
let the afflicted hear and rejoice.[f]
[3]Glorify the LORD with me;
let us exalt[g] his name together.

32:9 [a]Pr 26:3
32:10 [b]Ro 2:9 [c]Pr 16:20
32:11 [d]Ps 64:10
33:1 [e]Ps 147:1 [f]Ps 32:11
33:2 [g]Ps 92:3
33:3 [h]Ps 96:1
33:4 [i]Ps 19:8
33:5 [j]Ps 11:7 [k]Ps 119:64
33:6 [l]Heb 11:3
33:8 [m]Ps 67:7; 96:9
33:9 [n]Ge 1:3; Ps 148:5
33:10 [o]Isa 8:10
33:11 [p]Job 23:13
33:12 [q]Ps 144:15 [r]Ex 19:5; Dt 7:6
33:13 [s]Job 28:24; Ps 11:4
33:14 [t]1Ki 8:39
33:15 [u]Job 10:8 [v]Jer 32:19
33:16 [w]Ps 44:6
33:17 [x]Ps 20:7; Pr 21:31
33:18 [y]Job 36:7; Ps 34:15 [z]Ps 147:11
33:19 [a]Job 5:20
33:20 [b]Ps 130:6
33:21 [c]Zec 10:7; Jn 16:22
34:1 [d]Ps 71:6; Eph 5:20
34:2 [e]Jer 9:24; 1Co 1:31 [f]Ps 119:74
34:3 [g]Lk 1:46

[j]7 Or *sea as into a heap* [k]This psalm is an acrostic poem, the verses of which begin with the successive letters of the Hebrew alphabet.

4 I sought the LORD,[a] and he answered me;
he delivered me from all my fears.
5 Those who look to him are radiant;[b]
their faces are never covered with shame.[c]
6 This poor man called, and the LORD heard him;
he saved him out of all his troubles.
7 The angel of the LORD[d] encamps around those who fear him,
and he delivers them.

8 Taste and see that the LORD is good;[e]
blessed is the man who takes refuge[f] in him.
9 Fear the LORD, you his saints,
for those who fear him lack nothing.[g]
10 The lions may grow weak and hungry,
but those who seek the LORD lack no good thing.[h]

11 Come, my children, listen to me;
I will teach you[i] the fear of the LORD.
12 Whoever of you loves life[j]
and desires to see many good days,
13 keep your tongue from evil
and your lips from speaking lies.[k]
14 Turn from evil and do good;[l]
seek peace[m] and pursue it.

15 The eyes of the LORD[n] are on the righteous[o]
and his ears are attentive to their cry;
16 the face of the LORD is against[p] those who do evil,[q]
to cut off the memory[r] of them from the earth.

17 The righteous cry out, and the LORD hears[s] them;
he delivers them from all their troubles.
18 The LORD is close[t] to the brokenhearted[u]
and saves those who are crushed in spirit.

19 A righteous man may have many troubles,[v]
but the LORD delivers him from them all;[w]
20 he protects all his bones,
not one of them will be broken.[x]

21 Evil will slay the wicked;[y]
the foes of the righteous will be condemned.
22 The LORD redeems[z] his servants;
no one will be condemned who takes refuge in him.

Psalm 35

Of David.

Prayer to be rescued from the enemy.

1 Contend, O LORD, with those who contend with me;
fight[a] against those who fight against me.
2 Take up shield and buckler;
arise[b] and come to my aid.
3 Brandish spear and javelin[1]
against those who pursue me.
Say to my soul,
"I am your salvation."

4 May those who seek my life
be disgraced[c] and put to shame;
may those who plot my ruin
be turned back in dismay.
5 May they be like chaff[d] before the wind,
with the angel of the LORD driving them away;
6 may their path be dark and slippery,
with the angel of the LORD pursuing them.
7 Since they hid their net for me without cause
and without cause dug a pit for me,
8 may ruin overtake them by surprise—[e]
may the net they hid entangle them,
may they fall into the pit,[f] to their ruin.
9 Then my soul will rejoice[g] in the LORD
and delight in his salvation.[h]
10 My whole being will exclaim,
"Who is like you,[i] O LORD?

34:4 [a] Mt 7:7
34:5 [b] Ps 36:9 [c] Ps 25:3
34:7 [d] 2Ki 6:17; Da 6:22
34:8 [e] 1Pe 2:3 [f] Ps 2:12
34:9 [g] Ps 23:1
34:10 [h] Ps 84:11
34:11 [i] Ps 32:8
34:12 [j] 1Pe 3:10
34:13 [k] 1Pe 2:22
34:14 [l] Ps 37:27 [m] Heb 12:14
34:15 [n] Ps 33:18 [o] Job 36:7
34:16 [p] Lev 17:10; Jer 44:11 [q] 1Pe 3:10-12* [r] Pr 10:7
34:17 [s] Ps 145:19
34:18 [t] Ps 145:18 [u] Isa 57:15
34:19 [v] ver 17 [w] ver 4,6; Pr 24:16
34:20 [x] Jn 19:36*
34:21 [y] Ps 94:23
34:22 [z] 1Ki 1:29; Ps 71:23
35:1 [a] Ps 43:1
35:2 [b] Ps 62:2
35:4 [c] Ps 70:2
35:5 [d] Job 21:18; Ps 1:4; Isa 29:5
35:8 [e] 1Th 5:3 [f] Ps 9:15
35:9 [g] Lk 1:47 [h] Isa 61:10
35:10 [i] Ex 15:11

[1] 3 Or *and block the way*

You rescue the poor from those too strong[a] for them,
the poor and needy[b] from those who rob them."

[11]Ruthless witnesses[c] come forward;
they question me on things I know nothing about.
[12]They repay me evil for good[d]
and leave my soul forlorn.
[13]Yet when they were ill, I put on sackcloth
and humbled myself with fasting.[e]
When my prayers returned to me unanswered,
[14] I went about mourning
as though for my friend or brother.
I bowed my head in grief
as though weeping for my mother.
[15]But when I stumbled, they gathered in glee;
attackers gathered against me when I was unaware.
They slandered[f] me without ceasing.
[16]Like the ungodly they maliciously mocked[m];
they gnashed their teeth[g] at me.
[17]O Lord, how long[h] will you look on?
Rescue my life from their ravages,
my precious life[i] from these lions.
[18]I will give you thanks in the great assembly;[j]
among throngs of people I will praise you.[k]

[19]Let not those gloat over me
who are my enemies without cause;
let not those who hate me without reason[l]
maliciously wink the eye.[m]
[20]They do not speak peaceably,
but devise false accusations
against those who live quietly in the land.
[21]They gape[n] at me and say, "Aha! Aha![o]
With our own eyes we have seen it."
[22]O LORD, you have seen[p] this; be not silent.
Do not be far[q] from me, O Lord.
[23]Awake,[r] and rise to my defense!
Contend for me, my God and Lord.
[24]Vindicate me in your righteousness,
O LORD my God;
do not let them gloat over me.
[25]Do not let them think, "Aha, just what we wanted!"
or say, "We have swallowed him up."[s]

[26]May all who gloat over my distress
be put to shame[t] and confusion;
may all who exalt themselves over me[u]
be clothed with shame and disgrace.
[27]May those who delight in my vindication[v]
shout for joy[w] and gladness;
may they always say, "The LORD be exalted,
who delights[x] in the well-being of his servant."
[28]My tongue will speak of your righteousness[y]
and of your praises all day long.

Psalm 36

For the director of music. Of David the servant of the LORD.

The wickedness of man and the love of God.

[1]An oracle is within my heart
concerning the sinfulness of the wicked:[n]
There is no fear of God
before his eyes.[z]
[2]For in his own eyes he flatters himself
too much to detect or hate his sin.
[3]The words of his mouth[a] are wicked and deceitful;
he has ceased to be wise[b] and to do good.[c]
[4]Even on his bed he plots evil;[d]
he commits himself to a sinful course[e]
and does not reject what is wrong.[f]
[5]Your love, O LORD, reaches to the heavens,
your faithfulness to the skies.

35:10 [a]Ps 18:17 [b]Ps 37:14
35:11 [c]Ps 27:12
35:12 [d]Jn 10:32
35:13 [e]Job 30:25; Ps 69:10
35:15 [f]Job 30:1,8
35:16 [g]Job 16:9; La 2:16
35:17 [h]Hab 1:13 [i]Ps 22:20
35:18 [j]Ps 22:25 [k]Ps 22:22
35:19 [l]Ps 38:19; 69:4; Jn 15:25* [m]Ps 13:4; Pr 6:13
35:21 [n]Ps 22:13 [o]Ps 40:15
35:22 [p]Ex 3:7 [q]Ps 10:1; 28:1
35:23 [r]Ps 44:23
35:25 [s]La 2:16
35:26 [t]Ps 40:14; 109:29 [u]Ps 38:16
35:27 [v]Ps 9:4 [w]Ps 32:11 [x]Ps 40:16; 147:11
35:28 [y]Ps 51:14
36:1 [z]Ro 3:18*
36:3 [a]Ps 10:7 [b]Ps 94:8 [c]Jer 4:22
36:4 [d]Pr 4:16; Mic 2:1 [e]Isa 65:2 [f]Ps 52:3; Ro 12:9

[m] *16* Septuagint; Hebrew may mean *ungodly circle of mockers.* [n] *1* Or *heart: / Sin proceeds from the wicked.*

6Your righteousness is like the mighty
mountains,
your justice like the great deep.[a]
O LORD, you preserve both man and
beast.
7 How priceless is your unfailing love!
Both high and low among men
find[o] refuge in the shadow of your
wings.[b]
8They feast on the abundance of your
house;[c]
you give them drink from your
river[d] of delights.
9For with you is the fountain of life;[e]
in your light[f] we see light.

10Continue your love to those who
know you,
your righteousness to the upright
in heart.
11May the foot of the proud not come
against me,
nor the hand of the wicked drive
me away.
12See how the evildoers lie fallen—
thrown down, not able to rise![g]

Psalm 37[p]

Of David.

The LORD laughs at the wicked.

1Do not fret because of evil men
or be envious[h] of those who do
wrong;[i]
2for like the grass they will soon wither,
like green plants they will soon die
away.[j]

3Trust in the LORD and do good;
dwell in the land[k] and enjoy safe
pasture.[l]
4Delight[m] yourself in the LORD
and he will give you the desires of
your heart.

5Commit your way to the LORD;
trust in him[n] and he will do this:
6He will make your righteousness[o]
shine like the dawn,[p]
the justice of your cause like the
noonday sun.

7Be still[q] before the LORD and wait
patiently[r] for him;
do not fret when men succeed in
their ways,
when they carry out their wicked
schemes.

8Refrain from anger[s] and turn from
wrath;
do not fret—it leads only to evil.
9For evil men will be cut off,
but those who hope in the LORD
will inherit the land.[t]

10A little while, and the wicked will be
no more;[u]
though you look for them, they will
not be found.
11But the meek will inherit the land[v]
and enjoy great peace.

12The wicked plot against the
righteous
and gnash their teeth[w] at them;
13but the Lord laughs at the wicked,
for he knows their day is coming.[x]

14The wicked draw the sword
and bend the bow[y]
to bring down the poor and needy,[z]
to slay those whose ways are
upright.
15But their swords will pierce their
own hearts,[a]
and their bows will be broken.

16Better the little that the righteous
have
than the wealth[b] of many wicked;
17for the power of the wicked will be
broken,[c]
but the LORD upholds the righteous.

18The days of the blameless are known
to the LORD,[d]
and their inheritance will endure
forever.
19In times of disaster they will not
wither;
in days of famine they will enjoy
plenty.

o7 Or *love, O God! / Men find*; or *love! / Both heavenly beings and men / find* p This psalm is an acrostic poem, the stanzas of which begin with the successive letters of the Hebrew alphabet.

36:6 [a]Job 11:8; Ps 77:19; Ro 11:33
36:7 [b]Ru 2:12; Ps 17:8
36:8 [c]Ps 65:4 [d]Job 20:17; Rev 22:1
36:9 [e]Jer 2:13 [f]1Pe 2:9
36:12 [g]Ps 140:10
37:1 [h]Pr 23:17-18 [i]Ps 73:3
37:2 [j]Ps 90:6
37:3 [k]Dt 30:20 [l]Isa 40:11; Jn 10:9
37:4 [m]Isa 58:14
37:5 [n]Ps 4:5; Ps 55:22; Pr 16:3; 1Pe 5:7
37:6 [o]Mic 7:9 [p]Job 11:17
37:7 [q]Ps 62:5; La 3:26 [r]Ps 40:1
37:8 [s]Eph 4:31; Col 3:8
37:9 [t]Isa 57:13; 60:21
37:10 [u]Job 7:10; 24:24
37:11 [v]Mt 5:5
37:12 [w]Ps 35:16
37:13 [x]1Sa 26:10; Ps 2:4
37:14 [y]Ps 11:2 [z]Ps 35:10
37:15 [a]Ps 9:16
37:16 [b]Pr 15:16
37:17 [c]Job 38:15; Ps 10:15
37:18 [d]Ps 1:6

20 But the wicked will perish:
The LORD's enemies will be like the beauty of the fields,
they will vanish—vanish like smoke.[a]
21 The wicked borrow and do not repay,
but the righteous give generously;[b]
22 those the LORD blesses will inherit the land,
but those he curses[c] will be cut off.
23 If the LORD delights[d] in a man's way,
he makes his steps firm;[e]
24 though he stumble, he will not fall,[f]
for the LORD upholds[g] him with his hand.
25 I was young and now I am old,
yet I have never seen the righteous forsaken[h]
or their children begging bread.
26 They are always generous and lend freely;
their children will be blessed.[i]

27 Turn from evil and do good;[j]
then you will dwell in the land forever.
28 For the LORD loves the just
and will not forsake his faithful ones.

They will be protected forever,
but the offspring of the wicked will be cut off;[k]
29 the righteous will inherit the land[l]
and dwell in it forever.

30 The mouth of the righteous man utters wisdom,
and his tongue speaks what is just.
31 The law of his God is in his heart;[m]
his feet do not slip.[n]

32 The wicked lie in wait[o] for the righteous,
seeking their very lives;
33 but the LORD will not leave them in their power
or let them be condemned when brought to trial.[p]

34 Wait for the LORD[q]
and keep his way.
He will exalt you to inherit the land;
when the wicked are cut off, you will see[r] it.

35 I have seen a wicked and ruthless man
flourishing[s] like a green tree in its native soil,
36 but he soon passed away and was no more;
though I looked for him, he could not be found.[t]

37 Consider the blameless, observe the upright;
there is a future[q] for the man of peace.[u]
38 But all sinners will be destroyed;
the future[r] of the wicked will be cut off.[v]
39 The salvation[w] of the righteous comes from the LORD;
he is their stronghold in time of trouble.[x]
40 The LORD helps[y] them and delivers[z] them;
he delivers them from the wicked and saves them,
because they take refuge in him.

Psalm 38

A psalm of David. A petition.

Sorrow for sin.

1 O LORD, do not rebuke me in your anger
or discipline me in your wrath.[a]
2 For your arrows[b] have pierced me,
and your hand has come down upon me.
3 Because of your wrath there is no health in my body;
my bones[c] have no soundness because of my sin.
4 My guilt has overwhelmed me
like a burden too heavy to bear.[d]

5 My wounds fester and are loathsome
because of my sinful folly.[e]
6 I am bowed down and brought very low;
all day long I go about mourning.[f]
7 My back is filled with searing pain;[g]
there is no health in my body.

37:20 [a]Ps 102:3 **37:21** [b]Ps 112:5 **37:22** [c]Job 5:3; Pr 3:33 **37:23** [d]Ps 147:11 [e]1Sa 2:9 **37:24** [f]Pr 24:16 [g]Ps 145:14; 147:6 **37:25** [h]Heb 13:5 **37:26** [i]Ps 147:13 **37:27** [j]Ps 34:14 **37:28** [k]Ps 21:10; Isa 14:20 **37:29** [l]ver 9; Pr 2:21 **37:31** [m]Dt 6:6; Ps 40:8; Isa 51:7 [n]ver 23 **37:32** [o]Ps 10:8 **37:33** [p]Ps 109:31; 2Pe 2:9 **37:34** [q]Ps 27:14 [r]Ps 52:6 **37:35** [s]Job 5:3 **37:36** [t]Job 20:5 **37:37** [u]Isa 57:1-2 **37:38** [v]Ps 1:4 **37:39** [w]Ps 3:8 [x]Ps 9:9 **37:40** [y]1Ch 5:20 [z]Isa 31:5 **38:1** [a]Ps 6:1 **38:2** [b]Job 6:4; Ps 32:4 **38:3** [c]Ps 6:2; Isa 1:6 **38:4** [d]Ezr 9:6 **38:5** [e]Ps 69:5 **38:6** [f]Job 30:28; Ps 35:14; 42:9 **38:7** [g]Ps 102:3

[q]37 Or *there will be posterity* [r]38 Or *posterity*

8 I am feeble and utterly crushed;
I groan[a] in anguish of heart.

9 All my longings lie open before you,
O Lord;
my sighing[b] is not hidden from you.
10 My heart pounds, my strength fails[c]
me;
even the light has gone from my
eyes.[d]
11 My friends and companions avoid
me because of my wounds;[e]
my neighbors stay far away.
12 Those who seek my life set their traps,[f]
those who would harm me talk of
my ruin;[g]
all day long they plot deception.[h]
13 I am like a deaf man, who cannot hear,
like a mute, who cannot open his
mouth;
14 I have become like a man who does
not hear,
whose mouth can offer no reply.
15 I wait[i] for you, O LORD;
you will answer,[j] O Lord my God.
16 For I said, "Do not let them gloat[k]
or exalt themselves over me when
my foot slips."[l]

17 For I am about to fall,
and my pain is ever with me.
18 I confess my iniquity;[m]
I am troubled by my sin.
19 Many are those who are my vigorous
enemies;[n]
those who hate me without
reason[o] are numerous.
20 Those who repay my good with evil[p]
slander me when I pursue what is
good.
21 O LORD, do not forsake me;
be not far[q] from me, O my God.
22 Come quickly to help me,[r]
O Lord my Savior.[s]

Psalm 39

For the director of music. For
Jeduthun. A psalm of David.

The brevity of life.

1 I said, "I will watch my ways[t]
and keep my tongue from sin;[u]
I will put a muzzle on my mouth
as long as the wicked are in my
presence."
2 But when I was silent[v] and still,
not even saying anything good,
my anguish increased.
3 My heart grew hot within me,
and as I meditated, the fire burned;
then I spoke with my tongue:

4 "Show me, O LORD, my life's end
and the number of my days;[w]
let me know how fleeting is my
life.[x]
5 You have made my days[y] a mere
handbreadth;
the span of my years is as nothing
before you.
Each man's life is but a breath.[z]
Selah
6 Man is a mere phantom[a] as he goes
to and fro:
He bustles about, but only in
vain;[b]
he heaps up wealth, not knowing
who will get it.[c]

7 "But now, Lord, what do I look for?
My hope is in you.[d]
8 Save me[e] from all my transgressions;[f]
do not make me the scorn of fools.
9 I was silent; I would not open my
mouth,[g]
for you are the one who has done
this.
10 Remove your scourge from me;
I am overcome by the blow of your
hand.[h]
11 You rebuke[i] and discipline men for
their sin;
you consume their wealth like a
moth[j]—
each man is but a breath. *Selah*
12 "Hear my prayer, O LORD,
listen to my cry for help;
be not deaf to my weeping.
For I dwell with you as an alien,[k]
a stranger,[l] as all my fathers were.
13 Look away from me, that I may
rejoice again
before I depart and am no more."[m]

38:8 [a]Ps 22:1
38:9 [b]Job 3:24; Ps 6:6; 10:17
38:10 [c]Ps 31:10 [d]Ps 6:7
38:11 [e]Ps 31:11
38:12 [f]Ps 140:5 [g]Ps 35:4; 54:3 [h]Ps 35:20
38:15 [i]Ps 39:7 [j]Ps 17:6
38:16 [k]Ps 35:26 [l]Ps 13:4
38:18 [m]Ps 32:5
38:19 [n]Ps 18:17 [o]Ps 35:19
38:20 [p]Ps 35:12; 1Jn 3:12
38:21 [q]Ps 35:22
38:22 [r]Ps 40:13 [s]Ps 27:1
39:1 [t]1Ki 2:4 [u]Job 2:10; Jas 3:2
39:2 [v]Ps 38:13
39:4 [w]Ps 90:12 [x]Ps 103:14
39:5 [y]Ps 89:45 [z]Ps 62:9
39:6 [a]1Pe 1:24 [b]Ps 127:2 [c]Lk 12:20
39:7 [d]Ps 38:15
39:8 [e]Ps 51:9 [f]Ps 44:13
39:9 [g]Job 2:10
39:10 [h]Job 9:34; Ps 32:4
39:11 [i]2Pe 2:16 [j]Job 13:28
39:12 [k]1Pe 2:11 [l]Heb 11:13
39:13 [m]Job 10:21; 14:10

Psalm 40

40:13-17pp— Ps70:1-5

For the director of music.
Of David. A psalm.

Desire to do the will of God.

1I waited patiently[a] for the LORD;
he turned to me and heard my cry.[b]
2He lifted me out of the slimy pit,
out of the mud and mire;[c]
he set my feet on a rock[d]
and gave me a firm place to stand.
3He put a new song[e] in my mouth,
a hymn of praise to our God.
Many will see and fear
and put their trust in the LORD.

4Blessed is the man[f]
who makes the LORD his trust,[g]
who does not look to the proud,
to those who turn aside to false
gods.[s]
5Many, O LORD my God,
are the wonders[h] you have done.
The things you planned for us
no one can recount[i] to you;
were I to speak and tell of them,
they would be too many to declare.

6Sacrifice and offering you did not
desire,[j]
but my ears you have pierced[t,u];
burnt offerings[k] and sin offerings
you did not require.
7Then I said, "Here I am, I have
come—
it is written about me in the scroll.[v]
8I desire to do your will,[l] O my God;
your law is within my heart."[m]

9I proclaim righteousness in the great
assembly;[n]
I do not seal my lips,
as you know,[o] O LORD.
10I do not hide your righteousness in
my heart;
I speak of your faithfulness[p] and
salvation.
I do not conceal your love and your
truth
from the great assembly.[q]

40:1 [a]Ps 27:14 [b]Ps 34:15
40:2 [c]Ps 69:14 [d]Ps 27:5
40:3 [e]Ps 33:3
40:4 [f]Ps 34:8 [g]Ps 84:12
40:5 [h]Ps 136:4 [i]Ps 139:18; Isa 55:8
40:6 [j]1Sa 15:22; Am 5:22 [k]Isa 1:11
40:8 [l]Jn 4:34 [m]Ps 37:31
40:9 [n]Ps 22:25 [o]Jos 22:22; Ps 119:13
40:10 [p]Ps 89:1 [q]Ac 20:20
40:11 [r]Pr 20:28 [s]Ps 43:3
40:12 [t]Ps 116:3 [u]Ps 38:4 [v]Ps 69:4 [w]Ps 73:26
40:13 [x]Ps 70:1
40:14 [y]Ps 35:4
40:16 [z]Ps 35:27
40:17 [a]Ps 70:5
41:1 [b]Ps 82:3-4; Pr 14:21
41:2 [c]Ps 37:22 [d]Ps 27:12

11Do not withhold your mercy from
me, O LORD;
may your love[r] and your truth[s]
always protect me.
12For troubles[t] without number
surround me;
my sins have overtaken me, and I
cannot see.[u]
They are more than the hairs of my
head,[v]
and my heart fails[w] within me.

13Be pleased, O LORD, to save me;
O LORD, come quickly to help me.[x]
14May all who seek to take my life
be put to shame and confusion;
may all who desire my ruin[y]
be turned back in disgrace.
15May those who say to me, "Aha! Aha!"
be appalled at their own shame.
16But may all who seek you
rejoice and be glad in you;
may those who love your salvation
always say,
"The LORD be exalted!"[z]
17Yet I am poor and needy;
may the Lord think of me.
You are my help and my deliverer;
O my God, do not delay.[a]

Psalm 41

For the director of music.
A psalm of David.

Have regard for the weak.

1Blessed is he who has regard for the
weak;[b]
the LORD delivers him in times of
trouble.
2The LORD will protect him and
preserve his life;
he will bless him in the land[c]
and not surrender him to the
desire of his foes.[d]
3The LORD will sustain him on his
sickbed

[s]4 Or *to falsehood* [t]6 Hebrew; Septuagint *but a body you have prepared for me* (see also Symmachus and Theodotion) [u]6 Or *opened* [v]7 Or *come / with the scroll written for me*

and restore him from his bed of
illness.

4I said, "O LORD, have mercy[a] on me;
heal me, for I have sinned[b] against
you."

5My enemies say of me in malice,
"When will he die and his name
perish?[c]"

6Whenever one comes to see me,
he speaks falsely,[d] while his heart
gathers slander;[e]
then he goes out and spreads it
abroad.

7All my enemies whisper together[f]
against me;
they imagine the worst for me,
saying,

8"A vile disease has beset him;
he will never get up from the place
where he lies."

9Even my close friend,[g] whom I trusted,
he who shared my bread,
has lifted up his heel against me.[h]

10But you, O LORD, have mercy on me;
raise me up,[i] that I may repay them.

11I know that you are pleased with me,[j]
for my enemy does not triumph
over me.[k]

12In my integrity you uphold me[l]
and set me in your
presence forever.[m]

13Praise be to the LORD, the God of
Israel,[n]
from everlasting to everlasting.
Amen and Amen.[o]

BOOK II

Psalms 42–72

Psalm 42[w]

For the director of music. A
maskil[x] of the Sons of Korah.

The downcast have hope in God.

1As the deer pants for streams of water,
so my soul pants[p] for you, O God.

2My soul thirsts[q] for God, for the
living God.[r]
When can I go[s] and meet with God?

3My tears[t] have been my food
day and night,
while men say to me all day long,
"Where is your God?"[u]

4These things I remember
as I pour out my soul:
how I used to go with the multitude,
leading the procession to the house
of God,[v]
with shouts of joy and thanksgiving[w]
among the festive throng.

5Why are you downcast,[x] O my soul?
Why so disturbed within me?
Put your hope in God,[y]
for I will yet praise him,
my Savior[z] and 6my God.

My[y] soul is downcast within me;
therefore I will remember you
from the land of the Jordan,
the heights of Hermon—from
Mount Mizar.

7Deep calls to deep
in the roar of your waterfalls;
all your waves and breakers
have swept over me.[a]

8By day the LORD directs his love,[b]
at night[c] his song[d] is with me—
a prayer to the God of my life.

9I say to God my Rock,
"Why have you forgotten me?
Why must I go about mourning,[e]
oppressed by the enemy?"

10My bones suffer mortal agony
as my foes taunt me,
saying to me all day long,
"Where is your God?"

11Why are you downcast, O my soul?
Why so disturbed within me?
Put your hope in God,
for I will yet praise him,
my Savior and my God.[f]

41:4 [a]Ps 6:2 [b]Ps 51:4
41:5 [c]Ps 38:12
41:6 [d]Ps 12:2 [e]Pr 26:24
41:7 [f]Ps 56:5; 71:10-11
41:9 [g]2Sa 15:12; Ps 55:12 [h]Job 19:19; Ps 55:20; Mt 26:23; Jn 13:18*
41:10 [i]Ps 3:3
41:11 [j]Ps 147:11 [k]Ps 25:2
41:12 [l]Ps 37:17 [m]Job 36:7
41:13 [n]Ps 72:18 [o]Ps 89:52; 106:48
42:1 [p]Ps 119:131
42:2 [q]Ps 63:1 [r]Jer 10:10 [s]Ps 43:4
42:3 [t]Ps 80:5 [u]Ps 79:10
42:4 [v]Isa 30:29 [w]Ps 100:4
42:5 [x]Ps 38:6; 77:3 [y]La 3:24 [z]Ps 44:3
42:7 [a]Ps 88:7; Jnh 2:3
42:8 [b]Ps 57:3 [c]Job 35:10 [d]Ps 63:6; 149:5
42:9 [e]Ps 38:6
42:11 [f]Ps 43:5

[w]In many Hebrew manuscripts Psalms 42 and 43 constitute one psalm. [x]Title: Probably a literary or musical term [y]*5,6* A few Hebrew manuscripts, Septuagint and Syriac; most Hebrew manuscripts *praise him for his saving help. / 6O my God, my*

Psalm 43 [z]

Hope in God despite oppression.

1 Vindicate me, O God,
and plead my cause[a] against an ungodly nation;
rescue me from deceitful and wicked men.[b]
2 You are God my stronghold.
Why have you rejected[c] me?
Why must I go about mourning,
oppressed by the enemy?[d]
3 Send forth your light[e] and your truth,
let them guide me;
let them bring me to your holy mountain,[f]
to the place where you dwell.[g]
4 Then will I go to the altar[h] of God,
to God, my joy and my delight.
I will praise you with the harp,[i]
O God, my God.

5 Why are you downcast, O my soul?
Why so disturbed within me?
Put your hope in God,
for I will yet praise him,
my Savior and my God.[j]

Psalm 44

For the director of music. Of the Sons of Korah. A *maskil.* [a]

Past victories and present defeats.

1 We have heard with our ears, O God;
our fathers have told us[k]
what you did in their days,
in days long ago.
2 With your hand you drove out[l] the nations
and planted[m] our fathers;
you crushed the peoples
and made our fathers flourish.[n]
3 It was not by their sword[o] that they won the land,
nor did their arm bring them victory;
it was your right hand, your arm,[p]
and the light of your face, for you loved[q] them.

4 You are my King[r] and my God,
who decrees[b] victories for Jacob.
5 Through you we push back our enemies;
through your name we trample[s] our foes.
6 I do not trust in my bow,[t]
my sword does not bring me victory;
7 but you give us victory[u] over our enemies,
you put our adversaries to shame.[v]
8 In God we make our boast[w] all day long,
and we will praise your name forever.[x] *Selah*

9 But now you have rejected[y] and humbled us;
you no longer go out with our armies.[z]
10 You made us retreat[a] before the enemy,
and our adversaries have plundered us.
11 You gave us up to be devoured like sheep[b]
and have scattered us among the nations.[c]
12 You sold your people for a pittance,[d]
gaining nothing from their sale.

13 You have made us a reproach to our neighbors,[e]
the scorn[f] and derision of those around us.
14 You have made us a byword among the nations;
the peoples shake their heads[g] at us.
15 My disgrace is before me all day long,
and my face is covered with shame
16 at the taunts of those who reproach and revile[h] me,
because of the enemy, who is bent on revenge.

17 All this happened to us,
though we had not forgotten[i] you
or been false to your covenant.
18 Our hearts had not turned[j] back;
our feet had not strayed from your path.

43:1 [a] 1Sa 24:15; Ps 26:1; 35:1 [b] Ps 5:6
43:2 [c] Ps 44:9 [d] Ps 42:9
43:3 [e] Ps 36:9 [f] Ps 42:4 [g] Ps 84:1
43:4 [h] Ps 26:6 [i] Ps 33:2
43:5 [j] Ps 42:6
44:1 [k] Ex 12:26; Ps 78:3
44:2 [l] Ps 78:55 [m] Ex 15:17 [n] Ps 80:9
44:3 [o] Dt 8:17; Jos 24:12 [p] Ps 77:15 [q] Dt 4:37; 7:7-8
44:4 [r] Ps 74:12
44:5 [s] Ps 108:13
44:6 [t] Ps 33:16
44:7 [u] Ps 136:24 [v] Ps 53:5
44:8 [w] Ps 34:2 [x] Ps 30:12
44:9 [y] Ps 74:1 [z] Ps 60:1,10
44:10 [a] Lev 26:17; Jos 7:8; Ps 89:41
44:11 [b] Ro 8:36 [c] Dt 4:27; 28:64; Ps 106:27
44:12 [d] Isa 52:3; Jer 15:13; 52:3; Jer 15:13
44:13 [e] Ps 79:4; 80:6 [f] Dt 28:37
44:14 [g] Ps 109:25; Jer 24:9
44:16 [h] Ps 74:10
44:17 [i] Ps 78:7,57; Da 9:13
44:18 [j] Job 23:11

[z] In many Hebrew manuscripts Psalms 42 and 43 constitute one psalm. [a] Title: Probably a literary or musical term [b] 4 Septuagint, Aquila and Syriac; Hebrew *King, O God; / command*

19But you crushed[a] us and made us a
haunt for jackals
and covered us over with deep
darkness.[b]

20If we had forgotten[c] the name of our
God
or spread out our hands to a
foreign god,[d]
21would not God have discovered it,
since he knows the secrets of the
heart?[e]
22Yet for your sake we face death all
day long;
we are considered as sheep to be
slaughtered.[f]

23Awake,[g] O Lord! Why do you sleep?[h]
Rouse yourself! Do not reject us
forever.[i]
24Why do you hide your face[j]
and forget our misery and
oppression?[k]

25We are brought down to the dust;[l]
our bodies cling to the ground.
26Rise up[m] and help us;
redeem[n] us because of your
unfailing love.

Psalm 45

For the director of music. To ⌊the tune of⌋ "Lilies." Of the Sons of Korah. A *maskil.*[c] A wedding song.

A song for the king.

1My heart is stirred by a noble theme
as I recite my verses for the king;
my tongue is the pen of a skillful
writer.

2You are the most excellent of men
and your lips have been anointed
with grace,[o]
since God has blessed you forever.
3Gird your sword[p] upon your side,
O mighty one;[q]
clothe yourself with splendor and
majesty.
4In your majesty ride forth
victoriously[r]
in behalf of truth, humility and
righteousness;
let your right hand display
awesome deeds.
5Let your sharp arrows pierce the
hearts of the king's enemies;
let the nations fall beneath your feet.
6Your throne, O God, will last for ever
and ever;[s]
a scepter of justice will be the
scepter of your kingdom.
7You love righteousness[t] and hate
wickedness;
therefore God, your God, has set
you above your companions
by anointing[u] you with the oil of
joy.[v]
8All your robes are fragrant[w] with
myrrh and aloes and cassia;
from palaces adorned with ivory
the music of the strings makes you
glad.
9Daughters of kings[x] are among your
honored women;
at your right hand[y] is the royal
bride in gold of Ophir.

10Listen, O daughter, consider and give
ear:
Forget your people[z] and your
father's house.
11The king is enthralled by your beauty;
honor[a] him, for he is your lord.[b]
12The Daughter of Tyre will come with
a gift,[d] [c]
men of wealth will seek your favor.

13All glorious[d] is the princess within
⌊her chamber⌋;
her gown is interwoven with gold.
14In embroidered garments she is led
to the king;[e]
her virgin companions follow her
and are brought to you.
15They are led in with joy and gladness;
they enter the palace of the king.

16Your sons will take the place of your
fathers;
you will make them princes
throughout the land.

44:19 [a]Ps 51:8 [b]Job 3:5
44:20 [c]Ps 78:11 [d]Dt 6:14; Ps 81:9
44:21 [e]Ps 139:1-2; Jer 17:10
44:22 [f]Isa 53:7; Ro 8:36*
44:23 [g]Ps 7:6 [h]Ps 78:65 [i]Ps 77:7
44:24 [j]Job 13:24 [k]Ps 42:9
44:25 [l]Ps 119:25
44:26 [m]Ps 35:2 [n]Ps 25:22
45:2 [o]Lk 4:22
45:3 [p]Heb 4:12; Rev 1:16 [q]Isa 9:6
45:4 [r]Rev 6:2
45:6 [s]Ps 93:2; 98:9
45:7 [t]Ps 33:5 [u]Isa 61:1 [v]Ps 21:6; Heb 1:8-9*
45:8 [w]SS 1:3
45:9 [x]SS 6:8 [y]1Ki 2:19
45:10 [z]Dt 21:13
45:11 [a]Ps 95:6 [b]Isa 54:5
45:12 [c]Ps 22:29; Isa 49:23
45:13 [d]Isa 61:10
45:14 [e]SS 1:4

c Title: Probably a literary or musical term
d *12* Or *A Tyrian robe is among the gifts*

[17]I will perpetuate your memory
through all generations;[a]
therefore the nations will praise
you[b] for ever and ever.

Psalm 46

For the director of music. Of the
Sons of Korah. According to
alamoth.[e] A song.

Confidence in God our refuge.

[1]God is our refuge[c] and strength,
an ever-present[d] help in trouble.
[2]Therefore we will not fear,[e] though
the earth give way[f]
and the mountains fall[g] into the
heart of the sea,
[3]though its waters roar[h] and foam
and the mountains quake with
their surging. *Selah*

[4]There is a river whose streams make
glad the city of God,[i]
the holy place where the Most
High dwells.
[5]God is within her,[j] she will not fall;
God will help[k] her at break of day.
[6]Nations[l] are in uproar, kingdoms[m]
fall;
he lifts his voice, the earth melts.[n]

[7]The LORD Almighty is with us;[o]
the God of Jacob is our fortress.[p]
Selah

[8]Come and see the works of the
LORD,[q]
the desolations[r] he has brought on
the earth.
[9]He makes wars[s] cease to the ends of
the earth;
he breaks the bow[t] and shatters
the spear,
he burns the shields[f] with fire.[u]
[10]"Be still, and know that I am God;[v]
I will be exalted[w] among the
nations,
I will be exalted in the earth."

[11]The LORD Almighty is with us;
the God of Jacob is our fortress.
Selah

Psalm 47

For the director of music. Of the
Sons of Korah. A psalm.

*Nations exhorted
to sing praises to God.*

[1]Clap your hands,[x] all you nations;
shout to God with cries of joy.[y]
[2]How awesome[z] is the LORD Most
High,
the great King[a] over all the earth!
[3]He subdued[b] nations under us,
peoples under our feet.
[4]He chose our inheritance[c] for us,
the pride of Jacob, whom he loved.
Selah

[5]God has ascended amid shouts of joy,
the LORD amid the sounding of
trumpets.[d]
[6]Sing praises[e] to God, sing praises;
sing praises to our King, sing
praises.

[7]For God is the King of all the earth;[f]
sing to him a psalm[g][g] of praise.
[8]God reigns[h] over the nations;
God is seated on his holy throne.
[9]The nobles of the nations assemble
as the people of the God of Abraham,
for the kings[h] of the earth belong to
God;[i]
he is greatly exalted.[j]

Psalm 48

A song. A psalm of the Sons
of Korah.

Mount Zion, the city of God.

[1]Great is the LORD,[k] and most worthy
of praise,
in the city of our God,[l] his holy
mountain.[m]
[2]It is beautiful[n] in its loftiness,
the joy of the whole earth.

45:17 [a]Mal 1:11 [b]Ps 138:4
46:1 [c]Ps 9:9; 14:6 [d]Dt 4:7
46:2 [e]Ps 23:4 [f]Ps 82:5 [g]Ps 18:7
46:3 [h]Ps 93:3
46:4 [i]Ps 48:1,8; Isa 60:14
46:5 [j]Isa 12:6; Eze 43:7 [k]Ps 37:40
46:6 [l]Ps 2:1 [m]Ps 68:32 [n]Mic 1:4
46:7 [o]2Ch 13:12 [p]Ps 9:9
46:8 [q]Ps 66:5 [r]Isa 61:4
46:9 [s]Isa 2:4 [t]Ps 76:3 [u]Eze 39:9
46:10 [v]Ps 100:3 [w]Isa 2:11
47:1 [x]Ps 98:8; Isa 55:12 [y]Ps 106:47
47:2 [z]Dt 7:21 [a]Mal 1:14
47:3 [b]Ps 18:39,47
47:4 [c]1Pe 1:4
47:5 [d]Ps 68:33; 98:6
47:6 [e]Ps 68:4; 89:18
47:7 [f]Zec 14:9 [g]Col 3:16
47:8 [h]1Ch 16:31
47:9 [i]Ps 72:11; 89:18 [j]Ps 97:9
48:1 [k]Ps 96:4 [l]Ps 46:4 [m]Isa 2:2-3; Mic 4:1; Zec 8:3
48:2 [n]Ps 50:2; La 2:15

[e]Title: Probably a musical term [f]*9* Or *chariots*
[g]*7* Or *a maskil* (probably a literary or musical term)
[h]*9* Or *shields*

Like the utmost heights of Zaphon[i]
is Mount Zion,
the[j] city of the Great King.[a]
3God is in her citadels;
he has shown himself to be her
fortress.[b]

4When the kings joined forces,
when they advanced together,[c]
5they saw ⌊her⌋ and were astounded;
they fled in terror.[d]
6Trembling seized them there,
pain like that of a woman in labor.
7You destroyed them like ships of
Tarshish
shattered by an east wind.[e]

8As we have heard,
so have we seen
in the city of the LORD Almighty,
in the city of our God:
God makes her secure forever.[f]
Selah

9Within your temple, O God,
we meditate on your unfailing love.[g]
10Like your name,[h] O God,
your praise reaches to the ends of
the earth;[i]
your right hand is filled with
righteousness.
11Mount Zion rejoices,
the villages of Judah are glad
because of your judgments.[j]

12Walk about Zion, go around her,
count her towers,
13consider well her ramparts,
view her citadels,[k]
that you may tell of them to the
next generation.[l]
14For this God is our God for ever and
ever;
he will be our guide[m] even to the
end.

Psalm 49

For the director of music. Of the Sons of Korah. A psalm.

Foolishness of trusting in wealth.

1Hear this, all you peoples;[n]
listen, all who live in this world,[o]
2both low and high,
rich and poor alike:
3My mouth will speak words of
wisdom;[p]
the utterance from my heart will
give understanding.[q]
4I will turn my ear to a proverb;[r]
with the harp I will expound my
riddle:[s]

5Why should I fear[t] when evil days
come,
when wicked deceivers surround
me—
6those who trust in their wealth[u]
and boast of their great riches?
7No man can redeem the life of another
or give to God a ransom for him—
8the ransom for a life is costly,
no payment is ever enough—[v]
9that he should live on[w] forever
and not see decay.

10For all can see that wise men die;[x]
the foolish and the senseless alike
perish
and leave their wealth to others.[y]
11Their tombs will remain their
houses[k] forever,
their dwellings for endless
generations,
though they had[l] named[z] lands
after themselves.

12But man, despite his riches, does not
endure;
he is[m] like the beasts that perish.

13This is the fate of those who trust in
themselves,[a]
and of their followers, who approve
their sayings. *Selah*
14Like sheep they are destined for the
grave,[n] [b]
and death will feed on them.
The upright will rule[c] over them in
the morning;
their forms will decay in the grave,[n]

48:2 [a]Mt 5:35
48:3 [b]Ps 46:7
48:4 [c]2Sa 10:1-19
48:5 [d]Ex 15:16
48:7 [e]Jer 18:17; Eze 27:26
48:8 [f]Ps 87:5
48:9 [g]Ps 26:3
48:10 [h]Dt 28:58; Jos 7:9 [i]Isa 41:10
48:11 [j]Ps 97:8
48:13 [k]ver 3; Ps 122:7 [l]Ps 78:6
48:14 [m]Ps 23:4
49:1 [n]Ps 78:1 [o]Ps 33:8
49:3 [p]Ps 37:30 [q]Ps 119:130
49:4 [r]Ps 78:2 [s]Nu 12:8
49:5 [t]Ps 23:4
49:6 [u]Job 31:24
49:8 [v]Mt 16:26
49:9 [w]Ps 22:29; 89:48
49:10 [x]Ecc 2:16 [y]Ecc 2:18,21
49:11 [z]Ge 4:17; Dt 3:14
49:13 [a]Lk 12:20
49:14 [b]Job 24:19; Ps 9:17 [c]Da 7:18; Mal 4:3; 1Co 6:2; Rev 2:26

[i]2 *Zaphon* can refer to a sacred mountain or the direction north. [j]2 Or *earth, / Mount Zion, on the northern side / of the* [k]11 Septuagint and Syriac; Hebrew *In their thoughts their houses will remain* [l]11 Or */ for they have* [m]12 Hebrew; Septuagint and Syriac read verse 12 the same as verse 20. [n]14 Hebrew *Sheol*; also in verse 15

far from their princely mansions.
15But God will redeem my life[o] from the grave;[a]
he will surely take me to himself.[b] *Selah*

16Do not be overawed when a man grows rich,
when the splendor of his house increases;
17for he will take nothing with him when he dies,
his splendor will not descend with him.[c]
18Though while he lived he counted himself blessed—[d]
and men praise you when you prosper—
19he will join the generation of his fathers,[e]
who will never see the light[f] ⌊of life⌋.

20A man who has riches without understanding
is like the beasts that perish.[g]

Psalm 50

A psalm of Asaph.

God desires commitment more than sacrifices.

1The Mighty One, God, the LORD,[h]
speaks and summons the earth
from the rising of the sun to the place where it sets.[i]
2From Zion, perfect in beauty,[j]
God shines forth.[k]
3Our God comes[l] and will not be silent;
a fire devours before him,[m]
and around him a tempest rages.
4He summons the heavens above,
and the earth,[n] that he may judge his people:
5"Gather to me my consecrated ones,[o]
who made a covenant[p] with me by sacrifice."
6And the heavens proclaim[q] his righteousness,
for God himself is judge.[r] *Selah*
7"Hear, O my people, and I will speak,
O Israel, and I will testify[s] against you:
I am God, your God.[t]
8I do not rebuke you for your sacrifices
or your burnt offerings,[u] which are ever before me.
9I have no need of a bull[v] from your stall
or of goats from your pens,
10for every animal of the forest is mine,
and the cattle on a thousand hills.[w]
11I know every bird in the mountains,
and the creatures of the field are mine.
12If I were hungry I would not tell you,
for the world[x] is mine, and all that is in it.
13Do I eat the flesh of bulls
or drink the blood of goats?
14Sacrifice thank offerings[y] to God,
fulfill your vows[z] to the Most High,
15and call[a] upon me in the day of trouble;
I will deliver you, and you will honor[b] me."

16But to the wicked, God says:

"What right have you to recite my laws
or take my covenant on your lips?[c]
17You hate my instruction
and cast my words behind[d] you.
18When you see a thief, you join[e] with him;
you throw in your lot with adulterers.
19You use your mouth for evil
and harness your tongue to deceit.[f]
20You speak continually against your brother[g]
and slander your own mother's son.
21These things you have done and I kept silent;[h]
you thought I was altogether[p] like you.
But I will rebuke you
and accuse[i] you to your face.

22"Consider this, you who forget God,[j]
or I will tear you to pieces, with none to rescue:[k]

49:15 [a]Ps 56:13; Hos 13:14 [b]Ps 73:24 **49:17** [c]Ps 17:14; 1Ti 6:7 **49:18** [d]Dt 29:19; Lk 12:19 **49:19** [e]Ge 15:15 [f]Job 33:30 **49:20** [g]Ecc 3:19 **50:1** [h]Jos 22:22 [i]Ps 113:3 **50:2** [j]Ps 48:2 [k]Dt 33:2; Ps 80:1 **50:3** [l]Ps 96:13 [m]Ps 97:3; Da 7:10 **50:4** [n]Dt 4:26; Isa 1:2 **50:5** [o]Ps 30:4 [p]Ex 24:7 **50:6** [q]Ps 89:5 [r]Ps 75:7 **50:7** [s]Ps 81:8 [t]Ex 20:2 **50:8** [u]Ps 40:6; Hos 6:6 **50:9** [v]Ps 69:31 **50:10** [w]Ps 104:24 **50:12** [x]Ex 19:5 **50:14** [y]Heb 13:15 [z]Dt 23:21 **50:15** [a]Ps 81:7 [b]Ps 22:23 **50:16** [c]Isa 29:13 **50:17** [d]Ne 9:26; Ro 2:21-22 **50:18** [e]Ro 1:32; 1Ti 5:22 **50:19** [f]Ps 10:7; 52:2 **50:20** [g]Mt 10:21 **50:21** [h]Ecc 8:11; Isa 42:14 [i]Ps 90:8 **50:22** [j]Job 8:13; Ps 9:17 [k]Ps 7:2

o *15* Or *soul* p *21* Or *thought the 'I AM' was*

[23]He who sacrifices thank offerings
honors me,
and he prepares the way[a]
so that I may show him[q] the
salvation of God.[b]"

Psalm 51

For the director of music. A psalm of David. When the prophet Nathan came to him after David had committed adultery with Bathsheba.

Confession and prayer for God's pardon.

[1]Have mercy on me, O God,
according to your unfailing love;
according to your great compassion
blot out[c] my transgressions.[d]
[2]Wash away[e] all my iniquity
and cleanse[f] me from my sin.

[3]For I know my transgressions,
and my sin is always before me.[g]
[4]Against you, you only, have I sinned
and done what is evil in your
sight,[h]
so that you are proved right when
you speak
and justified when you judge.[i]
[5]Surely I was sinful[j] at birth,
sinful from the time my mother
conceived me.
[6]Surely you desire truth in the inner
parts[r];
you teach[s] me wisdom[k] in the
inmost place.[l]

[7]Cleanse me with hyssop,[m] and I will
be clean;
wash me, and I will be whiter than
snow.[n]
[8]Let me hear joy and gladness;[o]
let the bones you have crushed
rejoice.
[9]Hide your face from my sins[p]
and blot out all my iniquity.

[10]Create in me a pure heart,[q] O God,
and renew a steadfast spirit within
me.[r]

50:23 [a]Ps 85:13 [b]Ps 91:16
51:1 [c]Ac 3:19 [d]Isa 43:25; Col 2:14
51:2 [e]1Jn 1:9 [f]Heb 9:14
51:3 [g]Isa 59:12
51:4 [h]Ge 20:6; Lk 15:21 [i]Ro 3:4*
51:5 [j]Job 14:4
51:6 [k]Pr 2:6 [l]Ps 15:2
51:7 [m]Lev 14:4; Heb 9:19 [n]Isa 1:18
51:8 [o]Isa 35:10
51:9 [p]Jer 16:17
51:10 [q]Ps 78:37; Ac 15:9 [r]Eze 18:31
51:11 [s]Eph 4:30
51:12 [t]Ps 13:5
51:13 [u]Ac 9:21-22 [v]Ps 22:27
51:14 [w]2Sa 12:9 [x]Ps 25:5 [y]Ps 35:28
51:15 [z]Ps 9:14
51:16 [a]1Sa 15:22; Ps 40:6
51:17 [b]Ps 34:18
51:18 [c]Ps 102:16; Isa 51:3
51:19 [d]Ps 4:5 [e]Ps 66:13 [f]Ps 66:15
52:1 [g]1Sa 22:9 [h]Ps 94:4

[11]Do not cast me from your presence
or take your Holy Spirit[s] from me.
[12]Restore to me the joy of your
salvation[t]
and grant me a willing spirit, to
sustain me.

[13]Then I will teach transgressors your
ways,[u]
and sinners will turn back to you.[v]
[14]Save me from bloodguilt,[w] O God,
the God who saves me,[x]
and my tongue will sing of your
righteousness.[y]
[15]O Lord, open my lips,[z]
and my mouth will declare your
praise.
[16]You do not delight in sacrifice,[a] or I
would bring it;
you do not take pleasure in burnt
offerings.
[17]The sacrifices of God are[t] a broken
spirit;
a broken and contrite heart,[b]
O God, you will not despise.

[18]In your good pleasure make Zion[c]
prosper;
build up the walls of Jerusalem.
[19]Then there will be righteous
sacrifices,[d]
whole burnt offerings[e] to delight you;
then bulls[f] will be offered on your
altar.

Psalm 52

For the director of music. A *maskil*[u] of David. When Doeg the Edomite[g] had gone to Saul and told him: "David has gone to the house of Ahimelech."

God will bring down the evil man.

[1]Why do you boast of evil, you mighty
man?
Why do you boast[h] all day long,

[q]23 Or *and to him who considers his way / I will show* [r]6 The meaning of the Hebrew for this phrase is uncertain. [s]6 Or *you desired . . . ; / you taught* [t]17 Or *My sacrifice, O God, is* [u]Title: Probably a literary or musical term

you who are a disgrace in the eyes
of God?
2Your tongue plots destruction;
it is like a sharpened razor,[a]
you who practice deceit.[b]
3You love evil rather than good,
falsehood[c] rather than speaking
the truth. *Selah*
4You love every harmful word,
O you deceitful tongue![d]

5Surely God will bring you down to
everlasting ruin:
He will snatch you up and tear[e]
you from your tent;
he will uproot[f] you from the land
of the living.[g] *Selah*
6The righteous will see and fear;
they will laugh[h] at him, saying,
7"Here now is the man
who did not make God his
stronghold
but trusted in his great wealth[i]
and grew strong by destroying
others!"

8But I am like an olive tree[j]
flourishing in the house of God;
I trust[k] in God's unfailing love
for ever and ever.
9I will praise you forever[l] for what
you have done;
in your name I will hope, for your
name is good.[m]
I will praise you in the presence of
your saints.

Psalm 53

53:1-6pp— Ps 14:1-7

For the director of music.
According to *mahalath*.[v]
A *maskil*[w] of David.

Description of a fool.

1The fool[n] says in his heart,
"There is no God."[o]
They are corrupt, and their ways are
vile;
there is no one who does good.

2God looks down from heaven[p]
on the sons of men
to see if there are any who understand,
any who seek God.[q]
3Everyone has turned away,
they have together become corrupt;
there is no one who does good,
not even one.[r]

4Will the evildoers never learn—
those who devour my people as
men eat bread
and who do not call on God?
5There they were, overwhelmed with
dread,
where there was nothing to dread.[s]
God scattered the bones[t] of those
who attacked you;
you put them to shame, for God
despised them.

6Oh, that salvation for Israel would
come out of Zion!
When God restores the fortunes of
his people,
let Jacob rejoice and Israel be glad!

Psalm 54

For the director of music. With
stringed instruments. A *maskil*[w]
of David. When the Ziphites had
gone to Saul and said, "Is not
David hiding among us?"

Prayer to triumph over ruthless men.

1Save me, O God, by your name;[u]
vindicate me by your might.[v]
2Hear my prayer, O God;[w]
listen to the words of my mouth.

3Strangers are attacking me;[x]
ruthless men seek my life[y]—
men without regard for God.[z]
Selah

4Surely God is my help;[a]
the Lord is the one who sustains
me.[b]

5Let evil recoil[c] on those who slander
me;
in your faithfulness[d] destroy them.

52:2 [a]Ps 57:4 [b]Ps 50:19
52:3 [c]Jer 9:5
52:4 [d]Ps 120:2,3
52:5 [e]Isa 22:19 [f]Pr 2:22 [g]Ps 27:13
52:6 [h]Job 22:19; Ps 37:34; 40:3
52:7 [i]Ps 49:6
52:8 [j]Jer 11:16 [k]Ps 13:5
52:9 [l]Ps 30:12 [m]Ps 54:6
53:1 [n]Ps 14:1-7; Ro 3:10 [o]Ps 10:4
53:2 [p]Ps 33:13 [q]2Ch 15:2
53:3 [r]Ro 3:10-12*
53:5 [s]Lev 26:17 [t]Eze 6:5
54:1 [u]Ps 20:1 [v]2Ch 20:6
54:2 [w]Ps 5:1; 55:1
54:3 [x]Ps 86:14 [y]Ps 40:14 [z]Ps 36:1
54:4 [a]Ps 118:7 [b]Ps 41:12
54:5 [c]Ps 94:23 [d]Ps 89:49; 143:12

[v]Title: Probably a musical term [w]Title: Probably a literary or musical term

6I will sacrifice a freewill offering[a] to you;
I will praise your name, O LORD, for it is good.[b]
7For he has delivered me[c] from all my troubles,
and my eyes have looked in triumph on my foes.[d]

Psalm 55

For the director of music.
With stringed instruments. A *maskil*[x] of David.

Prayer for friends who betray.

1Listen to my prayer, O God,
do not ignore my plea;[e]
2 hear me and answer me.[f]
My thoughts trouble me and I am distraught[g]
3 at the voice of the enemy,
at the stares of the wicked;
for they bring down suffering upon me[h]
and revile me in their anger.[i]
4My heart is in anguish within me;
the terrors[j] of death assail me.
5Fear and trembling[k] have beset me;
horror has overwhelmed me.
6I said, "Oh, that I had the wings of a dove!
I would fly away and be at rest—
7I would flee far away
and stay in the desert; *Selah*
8I would hurry to my place of shelter,
far from the tempest and storm.[l]"

9Confuse the wicked, O Lord, confound their speech,
for I see violence and strife[m] in the city.
10Day and night they prowl about on its walls;
malice and abuse are within it.
11Destructive forces[n] are at work in the city;
threats and lies[o] never leave its streets.

12If an enemy were insulting me,
I could endure it;
if a foe were raising himself against me,
I could hide from him.
13But it is you, a man like myself,
my companion, my close friend,[p]
14with whom I once enjoyed sweet fellowship
as we walked with the throng at the house of God.[q]

15Let death take my enemies by surprise;[r]
let them go down alive to the grave,[y][s]
for evil finds lodging among them.

16But I call to God,
and the LORD saves me.
17Evening,[t] morning[u] and noon
I cry out in distress,
and he hears my voice.
18He ransoms me unharmed
from the battle waged against me,
even though many oppose me.
19God, who is enthroned forever,[v]
will hear[w] them and afflict them— *Selah*
men who never change their ways
and have no fear of God.

20My companion attacks his friends;[x]
he violates his covenant.[y]
21His speech is smooth as butter,
yet war is in his heart;
his words are more soothing than oil,[z]
yet they are drawn swords.[a]

22Cast your cares on the LORD
and he will sustain you;[b]
he will never let the righteous fall.[c]
23But you, O God, will bring down the wicked
into the pit[d] of corruption;
bloodthirsty and deceitful men[e]
will not live out half their days.[f]

But as for me, I trust in you.[g]

54:6 [a]Ps 50:14 [b]Ps 52:9
54:7 [c]Ps 34:6 [d]Ps 59:10
55:1 [e]Ps 27:9; 61:1
55:2 [f]Ps 66:19 [g]Ps 77:3; Isa 38:14
55:3 [h]2Sa 16:6-8; Ps 17:9 [i]Ps 71:11
55:4 [j]Ps 116:3
55:5 [k]Job 21:6; Ps 119:120
55:8 [l]Isa 4:6
55:9 [m]Jer 6:7
55:11 [n]Ps 5:9 [o]Ps 10:7
55:13 [p]2Sa 15:12; Ps 41:9
55:14 [q]Ps 42:4
55:15 [r]Ps 64:7 [s]Nu 16:30,33
55:17 [t]Ps 141:2; Ac 3:1 [u]Ps 5:3
55:19 [v]Dt 33:27 [w]Ps 78:59
55:20 [x]Ps 7:4 [y]Ps 89:34
55:21 [z]Pr 5:3 [a]Ps 28:3; Ps 57:4; 59:7
55:22 [b]Ps 37:5; Mt 6:25-34; 1Pe 5:7 [c]Ps 37:24
55:23 [d]Ps 73:18 [e]Ps 5:6 [f]Job 15:32; Pr 10:27 [g]Ps 25:2

[x]Title: Probably a literary or musical term
[y]*15* Hebrew *Sheol*

Psalm 56

For the director of music. To ⌊the tune of⌋ "A Dove on Distant Oaks." Of David. A *miktam.*[z] When the Philistines had seized him in Gath.

Trust God in times of fear.

[1]Be merciful to me, O God, for men
hotly pursue me;[a]
all day long they press their attack.
[2]My slanderers pursue me all day long;[b]
many are attacking me in their
pride.[c]

[3]When I am afraid,[d]
I will trust in you.
[4]In God, whose word I praise,
in God I trust; I will not be afraid.
What can mortal man do to me?[e]

[5]All day long they twist my words;[f]
they are always plotting to harm me.
[6]They conspire,[g] they lurk,
they watch my steps,
eager to take my life.[h]

[7]On no account let them escape;
in your anger, O God, bring down
the nations.[i]
[8]Record my lament;
list my tears on your scroll[a]—
are they not in your record?[j]

[9]Then my enemies will turn back[k]
when I call for help.[l]
By this I will know that God is for
me.[m]
[10]In God, whose word I praise,
in the LORD, whose word I
praise—
[11]in God I trust; I will not be afraid.
What can man do to me?

[12]I am under vows[n] to you, O God;
I will present my thank offerings to
you.
[13]For you have delivered me[b] from
death[o]
and my feet from stumbling,
that I may walk before God
in the light of life.[c][p]

56:1 [a]Ps 57:1-3
56:2 [b]Ps 57:3 [c]Ps 35:1
56:3 [d]Ps 55:4-5
56:4 [e]Ps 118:6; Heb 13:6
56:5 [f]Ps 41:7
56:6 [g]Ps 59:3 [h]Ps 71:10
56:7 [i]Ps 36:12; 55:23
56:8 [j]Mal 3:16
56:9 [k]Ps 9:3 [l]Ps 102:2 [m]Ro 8:31
56:12 [n]Ps 50:14
56:13 [o]Ps 116:8 [p]Job 33:30
57:1 [q]Ps 2:12 [r]Ps 17:8 [s]Isa 26:20
57:2 [t]Ps 138:8
57:3 [u]Ps 18:9,16 [v]Ps 56:1 [w]Ps 40:11
57:4 [x]Ps 35:17 [y]Ps 55:21; Pr 30:14
57:5 [z]Ps 108:5
57:6 [a]Ps 145:14 [b]Ps 35:7 [c]Ps 7:15; Pr 28:10
57:7 [d]Ps 108:1
57:8 [e]Ps 16:9; 30:12; 150:3

Psalm 57

57:7-11pp— Ps108:1-5

For the director of music. ⌊To the tune of⌋ "Do Not Destroy." Of David. A *miktam.*[z] When he had fled from Saul into the cave.

The love and faithfulness of God.

[1]Have mercy on me, O God, have
mercy on me,
for in you my soul takes refuge.[q]
I will take refuge in the shadow of
your wings[r]
until the disaster has passed.[s]

[2]I cry out to God Most High,
to God, who fulfills ⌊his purpose⌋
for me.[t]
[3]He sends from heaven and saves me,[u]
rebuking those who hotly pursue
me;[v] *Selah*
God sends his love and his
faithfulness.[w]

[4]I am in the midst of lions;[x]
I lie among ravenous beasts—
men whose teeth are spears and
arrows,
whose tongues are sharp swords.[y]

[5]Be exalted, O God, above the heavens;
let your glory be over all the earth.[z]

[6]They spread a net for my feet—
I was bowed down[a] in distress.
They dug a pit[b] in my path—
but they have fallen into it
themselves.[c] *Selah*

[7]My heart is steadfast, O God,
my heart is steadfast;[d]
I will sing and make music.
[8]Awake, my soul!
Awake, harp and lyre![e]
I will awaken the dawn.

[9]I will praise you, O Lord, among the
nations;
I will sing of you among the peoples.

z Title: Probably a literary or musical term
a *8* Or */ put my tears in your wineskin* b *13* Or *my soul* c *13* Or *the land of the living*

10For great is your love, reaching to
the heavens;
your faithfulness reaches to the
skies.[a]
11Be exalted, O God, above the heavens;
let your glory be over all the earth.[b]

Psalm 58

For the director of music. ⌊To the tune of⌋ "Do Not Destroy." Of David. A *miktam.* [d]

The righteous are avenged.

1Do you rulers indeed speak justly?[c]
Do you judge uprightly among men?
2No, in your heart you devise
injustice,
and your hands mete out violence
on the earth.[d]
3Even from birth the wicked go astray;
from the womb they are wayward
and speak lies.
4Their venom is like the venom of a
snake,[e]
like that of a cobra that has
stopped its ears,
5that will not heed the tune of the
charmer,
however skillful the enchanter may
be.

6Break the teeth in their mouths,
O God;[f]
tear out, O LORD, the fangs of the
lions![g]
7Let them vanish like water that flows
away;[h]
when they draw the bow, let their
arrows be blunted.[i]
8Like a slug melting away as it moves
along,
like a stillborn child,[j] may they not
see the sun.

9Before your pots can feel ⌊the heat
of⌋ the thorns[k]—
whether they be green or dry—the
wicked will be swept away.[e] [l]
10The righteous will be glad when
they are avenged,[m]
when they bathe their feet in the
blood of the wicked.[n]
11Then men will say,
"Surely the righteous still are
rewarded;
surely there is a God who judges
the earth."[o]

57:10 [a]Ps 36:5; 103:11
57:11 [b]ver 5
58:1 [c]Ps 82:2
58:2 [d]Ps 94:20; Mal 3:15
58:4 [e]Ps 140:3; Ecc 10:11
58:6 [f]Ps 3:7 [g]Job 4:10
58:7 [h]Jos 7:5; Ps 112:10 [i]Ps 64:3
58:8 [j]Job 3:16
58:9 [k]Ps 118:12 [l]Pr 10:25
58:10 [m]Ps 64:10; 91:8 [n]Ps 68:23
58:11 [o]Ps 9:8; 18:20
59:1 [p]Ps 143:9
59:2 [q]Ps 139:19
59:3 [r]Ps 56:6
59:4 [s]Ps 35:19,23
59:5 [t]Jer 18:23
59:6 [u]ver 14
59:7 [v]Ps 57:4 [w]Ps 10:11
59:8 [x]Ps 37:13; Pr 1:26 [y]Ps 2:4

Psalm 59

For the director of music. ⌊To the tune of⌋ "Do Not Destroy." Of David. A *miktam.* [d] When Saul had sent men to watch David's house in order to kill him.

Prayer for God's protection.

1Deliver me from my enemies,
O God;[p]
protect me from those who rise up
against me.
2Deliver me from evildoers
and save me from bloodthirsty
men.[q]

3See how they lie in wait for me!
Fierce men conspire[r] against me
for no offense or sin of mine,
O LORD.
4I have done no wrong, yet they are
ready to attack me.[s]
Arise to help me; look on my
plight!
5O LORD God Almighty, the God of
Israel,
rouse yourself to punish all the
nations;
show no mercy to wicked
traitors.[t] *Selah*
6They return at evening,
snarling like dogs,[u]
and prowl about the city.
7See what they spew from their
mouths—
they spew out swords[v] from their
lips,
and they say, "Who can hear us?"[w]
8But you, O LORD, laugh at them;[x]
you scoff at all those nations.[y]

[d]Title: Probably a literary or musical term [e]9 The meaning of the Hebrew for this verse is uncertain.

[9]O my Strength, I watch for you;
you, O God, are my fortress,[a] [10]my
loving God.

God will go before me
and will let me gloat over those
who slander me.
[11]But do not kill them, O Lord our
shield,[f] [b]
or my people will forget.[c]
In your might make them wander
about,
and bring them down.[d]
[12]For the sins of their mouths,[e]
for the words of their lips,[f]
let them be caught in their pride.[g]
For the curses and lies they utter,
[13] consume them in wrath,
consume them till they are no more.[h]
Then it will be known to the ends of
the earth
that God rules over Jacob.[i]
Selah

[14]They return at evening,
snarling like dogs,
and prowl about the city.
[15]They wander about for food[j]
and howl if not satisfied.
[16]But I will sing of your strength,[k]
in the morning[l] I will sing of your
love;[m]
for you are my fortress,
my refuge in times of trouble.[n]

[17]O my Strength, I sing praise to you;
you, O God, are my fortress, my
loving God.

Psalm 60

60:5-12pp— Ps 108:6-13

For the director of music. To ⌊the tune of⌋ "The Lily of the Covenant." A *miktam*[g] of David. For teaching. When he fought Aram Naharaim[h] and Aram Zobah,[i] and when Joab returned and struck down twelve thousand Edomites in the Valley of Salt.

Petition for God's help.

[1]You have rejected us,[o] O God, and

59:9 [a]Ps 9:9; 62:2
59:11 [b]Ps 84:9 [c]Dt 4:9 [d]Ps 106:27
59:12 [e]Ps 10:7 [f]Pr 12:13 [g]Zep 3:11
59:13 [h]Ps 104:35 [i]Ps 83:18
59:15 [j]Job 15:23
59:16 [k]Ps 21:13 [l]Ps 88:13 [m]Ps 101:1 [n]Ps 46:1
60:1 [o]2Sa 5:20; Ps 44:9 [p]Ps 79:5 [q]Ps 80:3
60:2 [r]Ps 18:7 [s]2Ch 7:14
60:3 [t]Ps 71:20 [u]Isa 51:17; Jer 25:16
60:5 [v]Ps 17:7; 108:6 [w]Ps 127:2
60:6 [x]Ge 12:6
60:7 [y]Jos 13:31 [z]Dt 33:17 [a]Ge 49:10
60:8 [b]2Sa 8:1
60:10 [c]Jos 7:12; Ps 44:9; 108:11
60:11 [d]Ps 146:3
60:12 [e]Nu 24:18; Ps 44:5

burst forth upon us;
you have been angry[p]—now
restore us![q]
[2]You have shaken the land[r] and torn
it open;
mend its fractures,[s] for it is
quaking.
[3]You have shown your people
desperate times;[t]
you have given us wine that makes
us stagger.[u]

[4]But for those who fear you, you have
raised a banner
to be unfurled against the bow.
Selah

[5]Save us and help us with your right
hand,[v]
that those you love[w] may be
delivered.
[6]God has spoken from his sanctuary:
"In triumph I will parcel out
Shechem[x]
and measure off the Valley of
Succoth.
[7]Gilead[y] is mine, and Manasseh is
mine;
Ephraim is my helmet,
Judah[z] my scepter.[a]
[8]Moab is my washbasin,
upon Edom I toss my sandal;
over Philistia I shout in triumph.[b]"

[9]Who will bring me to the fortified
city?
Who will lead me to Edom?
[10]Is it not you, O God, you who have
rejected us
and no longer go out with our
armies?[c]
[11]Give us aid against the enemy,
for the help of man is worthless.[d]
[12]With God we will gain the victory,
and he will trample down our
enemies.[e]

[f]*11* Or *sovereign* [g]Title: Probably a literary or musical term [h]Title: That is, Arameans of Northwest Mesopotamia [i]Title: That is, Arameans of central Syria

Psalm 61

For the director of music. With stringed instruments. Of David.

Desire to dwell in God's tent forever.

[1]Hear my cry, O God;[a]
listen to my prayer.[b]

[2]From the ends of the earth I call to you,
I call as my heart grows faint;[c]
lead me to the rock[d] that is higher than I.
[3]For you have been my refuge,[e]
a strong tower against the foe.[f]

[4]I long to dwell[g] in your tent forever
and take refuge in the shelter of your wings.[h] *Selah*
[5]For you have heard my vows,[i] O God;
you have given me the heritage of those who fear your name.[j]

[6]Increase the days of the king's life,
his years for many generations.[k]
[7]May he be enthroned in God's presence forever;[l]
appoint your love and faithfulness to protect him.[m]

[8]Then will I ever sing praise to your name[n]
and fulfill my vows day after day.

Psalm 62

For the director of music. For Jeduthun. A psalm of David.

Trust in God at all times.

[1]My soul finds rest[o] in God alone;
my salvation comes from him.
[2]He alone is my rock[p] and my salvation;
he is my fortress, I will never be shaken.

[3]How long will you assault a man?
Would all of you throw him down—
this leaning wall,[q] this tottering fence?

61:1 [a]Ps 64:1 [b]Ps 86:6
61:2 [c]Ps 77:3 [d]Ps 18:2
61:3 [e]Ps 62:7 [f]Pr 18:10
61:4 [g]Ps 23:6 [h]Ps 91:4
61:5 [i]Ps 56:12 [j]Ps 86:11
61:6 [k]Ps 21:4
61:7 [l]Ps 41:12 [m]Ps 40:11
61:8 [n]Ps 65:1; 71:22
62:1 [o]Ps 33:20
62:2 [p]Ps 89:26
62:3 [q]Isa 30:13
62:4 [r]Ps 28:3
62:7 [s]Ps 46:1; 85:9; Jer 3:23
62:8 [t]1Sa 1:15; Ps 42:4; La 2:19
62:9 [u]Ps 39:5,11 [v]Isa 40:15
62:10 [w]Isa 61:8 [x]Job 31:25; 1Ti 6:6-10
62:12 [y]Job 34:11; Mt 16:27
63:1 [z]Ps 42:2; 84:2

[4]They fully intend to topple him
from his lofty place;
they take delight in lies.
With their mouths they bless,
but in their hearts they curse.[r] *Selah*

[5]Find rest, O my soul, in God alone;
my hope comes from him.
[6]He alone is my rock and my salvation;
he is my fortress, I will not be shaken.
[7]My salvation and my honor depend on God[j];
he is my mighty rock, my refuge.[s]
[8]Trust in him at all times, O people;
pour out your hearts to him,[t]
for God is our refuge. *Selah*

[9]Lowborn men are but a breath,[u]
the highborn are but a lie;
if weighed on a balance,[v] they are nothing;
together they are only a breath.
[10]Do not trust in extortion
or take pride in stolen goods;[w]
though your riches increase,
do not set your heart on them.[x]

[11]One thing God has spoken,
two things have I heard:
that you, O God, are strong,
[12] and that you, O Lord, are loving.
Surely you will reward each person
according to what he has done.[y]

Psalm 63

A psalm of David. When he was in the Desert of Judah.

Thirsting for God.

[1]O God, you are my God,
earnestly I seek you;
my soul thirsts for you,[z]
my body longs for you,
in a dry and weary land
where there is no water.

j7 Or / *God Most High is my salvation and my honor*

[2]I have seen you in the sanctuary[a]
and beheld your power and your
glory.
[3]Because your love is better than life,[b]
my lips will glorify you.
[4]I will praise you as long as I live,[c]
and in your name I will lift up my
hands.[d]
[5]My soul will be satisfied as with the
richest of foods;[e]
with singing lips my mouth will
praise you.

[6]On my bed I remember you;
I think of you through the watches
of the night.[f]
[7]Because you are my help,[g]
I sing in the shadow of your wings.
[8]My soul clings to you;
your right hand upholds me.[h]

[9]They who seek my life will be
destroyed;[i]
they will go down to the depths of
the earth.[j]
[10]They will be given over to the sword
and become food for jackals.

[11]But the king will rejoice in God;
all who swear by God's name will
praise him,[k]
while the mouths of liars will be
silenced.

Psalm 64

For the director of music.
A psalm of David.

A refuge from the conspiracy of the wicked.

[1]Hear me, O God, as I voice my
complaint;[l]
protect my life from the threat of
the enemy.[m]
[2]Hide me from the conspiracy of the
wicked,[n]
from that noisy crowd of evildoers.

[3]They sharpen their tongues like
swords
and aim their words like deadly
arrows.[o]

63:2 [a]Ps 27:4
63:3 [b]Ps 69:16
63:4 [c]Ps 104:33 [d]Ps 28:2
63:5 [e]Ps 36:8
63:6 [f]Ps 42:8
63:7 [g]Ps 27:9
63:8 [h]Ps 18:35
63:9 [i]Ps 40:14 [j]Ps 55:15
63:11 [k]Dt 6:13; Ps 21:1; Isa 45:23
64:1 [l]Ps 55:2 [m]Ps 140:1
64:2 [n]Ps 56:6; 59:2
64:3 [o]Ps 58:7
64:4 [p]Ps 11:2 [q]Ps 55:19
64:5 [r]Ps 10:11
64:8 [s]Ps 9:3; Pr 18:7 [t]Ps 22:7
64:9 [u]Jer 51:10
64:10 [v]Ps 25:20 [w]Ps 32:11
65:1 [x]Ps 116:18
65:2 [y]Isa 66:23
65:3 [z]Ps 38:4 [a]Heb 9:14
65:4 [b]Ps 4:3; 33:12 [c]Ps 36:8

[4]They shoot from ambush at the
innocent man;[p]
they shoot at him suddenly,
without fear.[q]

[5]They encourage each other in evil
plans,
they talk about hiding their snares;
they say, "Who will see them[k]?"[r]
[6]They plot injustice and say,
"We have devised a perfect plan!"
Surely the mind and heart of man
are cunning.

[7]But God will shoot them with arrows;
suddenly they will be struck down.
[8]He will turn their own tongues
against them[s]
and bring them to ruin;
all who see them will shake their
heads[t] in scorn.

[9]All mankind will fear;
they will proclaim the works of God
and ponder what he has done.[u]
[10]Let the righteous rejoice in the LORD
and take refuge in him;[v]
let all the upright in heart praise
him![w]

Psalm 65

For the director of music. A
psalm of David. A song.

God's forgiveness and provisionary care.

[1]Praise awaits[l] you, O God, in Zion;
to you our vows will be fulfilled.[x]
[2]O you who hear prayer,
to you all men will come.[y]
[3]When we were overwhelmed by
sins,[z]
you forgave[m] our transgressions.[a]
[4]Blessed are those you choose[b]
and bring near to live in your courts!
We are filled with the good things of
your house,[c]
of your holy temple.

[k]5 Or *us* [l]1 Or *befits*; the meaning of the Hebrew for this word is uncertain. [m]3 Or *made atonement for*

[5]You answer us with awesome deeds
of righteousness,
O God our Savior,[a]
the hope of all the ends of the earth
and of the farthest seas,[b]
[6]who formed the mountains by your
power,
having armed yourself with
strength,[c]
[7]who stilled the roaring of the seas,[d]
the roaring of their waves,
and the turmoil of the nations.[e]
[8]Those living far away fear your
wonders;
where morning dawns and evening
fades
you call forth songs of joy.

[9]You care for the land and water it;[f]
you enrich it abundantly.
The streams of God are filled with
water
to provide the people with grain,[g]
for so you have ordained it.[n]
[10]You drench its furrows
and level its ridges;
you soften it with showers
and bless its crops.
[11]You crown the year with your bounty,
and your carts overflow with
abundance.
[12]The grasslands of the desert overflow;[h]
the hills are clothed with gladness.
[13]The meadows are covered with flocks[i]
and the valleys are mantled with
grain;[j]
they shout for joy and sing.[k]

Psalm 66

For the director of music.
A song. A psalm.

God's awesome power and deeds.

[1]Shout with joy to God, all the earth![l]
[2] Sing the glory of his name;[m]
make his praise glorious!
[3]Say to God, "How awesome are your
deeds![n]
So great is your power
that your enemies cringe[o] before
you.
[4]All the earth bows down[p] to you;
they sing praise[q] to you,
they sing praise to your name."
Selah

[5]Come and see what God has done,
how awesome his works[r] in man's
behalf!
[6]He turned the sea into dry land,[s]
they passed through the waters on
foot—
come, let us rejoice in him.
[7]He rules forever[t] by his power,
his eyes watch[u] the nations—
let not the rebellious[v] rise up
against him. *Selah*

[8]Praise[w] our God, O peoples,
let the sound of his praise be heard;
[9]he has preserved our lives
and kept our feet from slipping.[x]
[10]For you, O God, tested us;
you refined us like silver.[y]
[11]You brought us into prison
and laid burdens[z] on our backs.
[12]You let men ride over our heads;[a]
we went through fire and water,
but you brought us to a place of
abundance.[b]

[13]I will come to your temple with
burnt offerings
and fulfill my vows[c] to you—
[14]vows my lips promised and my
mouth spoke
when I was in trouble.
[15]I will sacrifice fat animals to you
and an offering of rams;
I will offer bulls and goats.[d]
Selah

[16]Come and listen,[e] all you who fear
God;
let me tell[f] you what he has done
for me.
[17]I cried out to him with my mouth;
his praise was on my tongue.
[18]If I had cherished sin in my heart,
the Lord would not have listened;[g]
[19]but God has surely listened
and heard my voice[h] in prayer.

65:5 [a]Ps 85:4 [b]Ps 107:23
65:6 [c]Ps 93:1
65:7 [d]Mt 8:26 [e]Isa 17:12-13
65:9 [f]Ps 68:9-10 [g]Ps 46:4; 104:14
65:12 [h]Job 28:26
65:13 [i]Ps 144:13 [j]Ps 72:16 [k]Ps 98:8; Isa 55:12
66:1 [l]Ps 100:1
66:2 [m]Ps 79:9
66:3 [n]Ps 65:5 [o]Ps 18:44
66:4 [p]Ps 22:27 [q]Ps 67:3
66:5 [r]Ps 106:22
66:6 [s]Ex 14:22
66:7 [t]Ps 145:13 [u]Ps 11:4 [v]Ps 140:8
66:8 [w]Ps 98:4
66:9 [x]Ps 121:3
66:10 [y]Ps 17:3; Isa 48:10; Zec 13:9; 1Pe 1:6-7
66:11 [z]La 1:13
66:12 [a]Isa 51:23 [b]Isa 43:2
66:13 [c]Ecc 5:4
66:15 [d]Nu 6:14; Ps 51:19
66:16 [e]Ps 34:11 [f]Ps 71:15,24
66:18 [g]Job 36:21; Isa 1:15; Jas 4:3
66:19 [h]Ps 116:1-2

n9 Or *for that is how you prepare the land*

20 Praise be to God,
who has not rejected[a] my prayer
or withheld his love from me!

Psalm 67

For the director of music. With stringed instruments. A psalm. A song.

Let the nations praise God.

1 May God be gracious to us and bless us
and make his face shine upon us,[b] *Selah*
2 that your ways may be known on earth,
your salvation[c] among all nations.[d]
3 May the peoples praise you, O God;
may all the peoples praise you.
4 May the nations be glad and sing for joy,
for you rule the peoples justly[e]
and guide the nations of the earth. *Selah*
5 May the peoples praise you, O God;
may all the peoples praise you.
6 Then the land will yield its harvest,[f]
and God, our God, will bless us.
7 God will bless us,
and all the ends of the earth will fear him.[g]

Psalm 68

For the director of music. Of David. A psalm. A song.

Let the righteous rejoice.

1 May God arise, may his enemies be scattered;
may his foes flee[h] before him.
2 As smoke[i] is blown away by the wind,
may you blow them away;
as wax melts[j] before the fire,
may the wicked perish before God.
3 But may the righteous be glad
and rejoice[k] before God;
may they be happy and joyful.
4 Sing to God, sing praise to his name,[l]
extol him who rides on the clouds[o] [m]—
his name is the LORD[n]—
and rejoice before him.
5 A father to the fatherless,[o] a defender of widows,[p]
is God in his holy dwelling.[q]
6 God sets the lonely in families,[p] [r]
he leads forth the prisoners[s] with singing;
but the rebellious live in a sun-scorched land.[t]

7 When you went out[u] before your people, O God,
when you marched through the wasteland, *Selah*
8 the earth shook,
the heavens poured down rain,[v]
before God, the One of Sinai,[w]
before God, the God of Israel.
9 You gave abundant showers,[x] O God;
you refreshed your weary inheritance.
10 Your people settled in it,
and from your bounty, O God, you provided[y] for the poor.

11 The Lord announced the word,
and great was the company of those who proclaimed it:
12 "Kings and armies flee[z] in haste;
in the camps men divide the plunder.
13 Even while you sleep among the campfires,[q] [a]
the wings of ⌊my⌋ dove are sheathed with silver,
its feathers with shining gold."
14 When the Almighty[r] scattered[b] the kings in the land,
it was like snow fallen on Zalmon.

15 The mountains of Bashan are majestic mountains;
rugged are the mountains of Bashan.
16 Why gaze in envy, O rugged mountains,
at the mountain where God chooses[c] to reign,

66:20 [a]Ps 22:24; 68:35
67:1 [b]Nu 6:24-26; Ps 4:6
67:2 [c]Isa 52:10 [d]Tit 2:11
67:4 [e]Ps 96:10-13
67:6 [f]Lev 26:4; Ps 85:12; Eze 34:27
67:7 [g]Ps 33:8
68:1 [h]Nu 10:35; Isa 33:3
68:2 [i]Hos 13:3 [j]Isa 9:18; Mic 1:4
68:3 [k]Ps 32:11
68:4 [l]Ps 66:2 [m]Dt 33:26 [n]Ex 6:3; Ps 83:18
68:5 [o]Ps 10:14 [p]Dt 10:18 [q]Dt 26:15
68:6 [r]Ps 113:9 [s]Ac 12:6 [t]Ps 107:34
68:7 [u]Ex 13:21; Jdg 4:14
68:8 [v]Jdg 5:4 [w]Ex 19:16,18
68:9 [x]Dt 11:11
68:10 [y]Ps 74:19
68:12 [z]Jos 10:16
68:13 [a]Ge 49:14
68:14 [b]Jos 10:10
68:16 [c]Dt 12:5

o4 Or / *prepare the way for him who rides through the deserts* p6 Or *the desolate in a homeland* q13 Or *saddlebags* r14 Hebrew *Shaddai*

where the LORD himself will dwell
forever?
17The chariots of God are tens of
thousands
and thousands of thousands;[a]
the Lord ⌊has come⌋ from Sinai into
his sanctuary.
18When you ascended on high,
you led captives[b] in your train;
you received gifts from men,[c]
even from[s] the rebellious—
that you,[t] O LORD God, might
dwell there.

19Praise be to the Lord, to God our
Savior,[d]
who daily bears our burdens.[e]
Selah
20Our God is a God who saves;
from the Sovereign LORD comes
escape from death.[f]

21Surely God will crush the heads[g] of
his enemies,
the hairy crowns of those who go
on in their sins.
22The Lord says, "I will bring them
from Bashan;
I will bring them from the depths
of the sea,[h]
23that you may plunge your feet in the
blood of your foes,[i]
while the tongues of your dogs[j]
have their share."

24Your procession has come into view,
O God,
the procession of my God and King
into the sanctuary.[k]
25In front are the singers, after them
the musicians;
with them are the maidens playing
tambourines.[l]
26Praise God in the great congregation;
praise the LORD in the assembly of
Israel.[m]
27There is the little tribe[n] of Benjamin,
leading them,
there the great throng of Judah's
princes,
and there the princes of Zebulun
and of Naphtali.

68:17 [a]Dt 33:2; Da 7:10
68:18 [b]Jdg 5:12 [c]Eph 4:8*
68:19 [d]Ps 65:5 [e]Ps 55:22
68:20 [f]Ps 56:13
68:21 [g]Ps 110:5; Hab 3:13
68:22 [h]Nu 21:33
68:23 [i]Ps 58:10 [j]1Ki 21:19
68:24 [k]Ps 63:2
68:25 [l]Jdg 11:34; 1Ch 13:8
68:26 [m]Ps 26:12; Isa 48:1
68:27 [n]1Sa 9:21
68:29 [o]Ps 72:10
68:30 [p]Ps 22:12 [q]Ps 89:10
68:31 [r]Isa 19:19; 45:14
68:33 [s]Ps 18:10 [t]Ps 29:4
68:34 [u]Ps 29:1
68:35 [v]Ps 29:11 [w]Ps 66:20
69:1 [x]Jnh 2:5
69:2 [y]Ps 40:2
69:3 [z]Ps 6:6 [a]Ps 119:82; Isa 38:14
69:4 [b]Jn 15:25*

28Summon your power, O God[u];
show us your strength, O God, as
you have done before.
29Because of your temple at Jerusalem
kings will bring you gifts.[o]
30Rebuke the beast among the reeds,
the herd of bulls[p] among the calves
of the nations.
Humbled, may it bring bars of silver.
Scatter the nations[q] who delight in
war.
31Envoys will come from Egypt;[r]
Cush[v] will submit herself to God.

32Sing to God, O kingdoms of the earth,
sing praise to the Lord, *Selah*
33to him who rides[s] the ancient skies
above,
who thunders with mighty voice.[t]
34Proclaim the power[u] of God,
whose majesty is over Israel,
whose power is in the skies.
35You are awesome, O God, in your
sanctuary;
the God of Israel gives power and
strength to his people.[v]

Praise be to God![w]

Psalm 69

For the director of music. To ⌊the
tune of⌋ "Lilies." Of David.

Comfort for the brokenhearted.

1Save me, O God,
for the waters have come up to my
neck.[x]
2I sink in the miry depths,[y]
where there is no foothold.
I have come into the deep waters;
the floods engulf me.
3I am worn out calling for help;[z]
my throat is parched.
My eyes fail,[a]
looking for my God.
4Those who hate me without reason[b]
outnumber the hairs of my head;

[s]*18* Or *gifts for men, / even* [t]*18* Or *they*
[u]*28* Many Hebrew manuscripts, Septuagint and Syriac; most Hebrew manuscripts *Your God has summoned power for you* [v]*31* That is, the upper Nile region

many are my enemies without cause,[a]
those who seek to destroy me.
I am forced to restore
what I did not steal.

5You know my folly,[b] O God;
my guilt is not hidden from you.[c]

6May those who hope in you
not be disgraced because of me,
O Lord, the LORD Almighty;
may those who seek you
not be put to shame because of me,
O God of Israel.
7For I endure scorn for your sake,[d]
and shame covers my face.[e]
8I am a stranger to my brothers,
an alien to my own mother's sons;[f]
9for zeal for your house consumes me,[g]
and the insults of those who insult
you fall on me.[h]
10When I weep and fast,[i]
I must endure scorn;
11when I put on sackcloth,[j]
people make sport of me.
12Those who sit at the gate mock me,
and I am the song of the drunkards.[k]

13But I pray to you, O LORD,
in the time of your favor;[l]
in your great love,[m] O God,
answer me with your sure salvation.
14Rescue me from the mire,
do not let me sink;
deliver me from those who hate me,
from the deep waters.[n]
15Do not let the floodwaters[o] engulf me
or the depths swallow me up[p]
or the pit close its mouth over me.
16Answer me, O LORD, out of the
goodness of your love;[q]
in your great mercy turn to me.
17Do not hide your face[r] from your
servant;
answer me quickly, for I am in
trouble.[s]
18Come near and rescue me;
redeem[t] me because of my foes.

19You know how I am scorned,[u]
disgraced and shamed;
all my enemies are before you.
20Scorn has broken my heart
and has left me helpless;
I looked for sympathy, but there was
none,
for comforters,[v] but I found none.[w]
21They put gall in my food
and gave me vinegar for my thirst.[x]

22May the table set before them
become a snare;
may it become retribution and[w] a
trap.
23May their eyes be darkened so they
cannot see,
and their backs be bent forever.[y]
24Pour out your wrath[z] on them;
let your fierce anger overtake them.
25May their place be deserted;[a]
let there be no one to dwell in
their tents.[b]
26For they persecute those you wound
and talk about the pain of those
you hurt.[c]
27Charge them with crime upon crime;[d]
do not let them share in your
salvation.[e]
28May they be blotted out of the book
of life[f]
and not be listed with the
righteous.[g]

29I am in pain and distress;
may your salvation, O God, protect
me.[h]

30I will praise God's name in song[i]
and glorify him[j] with thanksgiving.
31This will please the LORD more than
an ox,
more than a bull with its horns and
hoofs.[k]
32The poor will see and be glad[l]—
you who seek God, may your
hearts live![m]
33The LORD hears the needy[n]
and does not despise his captive
people.

34Let heaven and earth praise him,
the seas and all that move in them,[o]

69:4 [a]Ps 35:19; 38:19 **69:5** [b]Ps 38:5 [c]Ps 44:21 **69:7** [d]Jer 15:15 [e]Ps 44:15 **69:8** [f]Ps 31:11; Isa 53:3 **69:9** [g]Jn 2:17* [h]Ps 89:50-51; Ro 15:3* **69:10** [i]Ps 35:13 **69:11** [j]Ps 35:13 **69:12** [k]Job 30:9 **69:13** [l]Isa 49:8; 2Co 6:2 [m]Ps 51:1 **69:14** [n]ver 2; Ps 144:7 **69:15** [o]Ps 124:4-5 [p]Nu 16:33 **69:16** [q]Ps 63:3 **69:17** [r]Ps 27:9 [s]Ps 66:14 **69:18** [t]Ps 49:15 **69:19** [u]Ps 22:6 **69:20** [v]Job 16:2 [w]Isa 63:5 **69:21** [x]Mt 27:34; Mk 15:23; Jn 19:28-30 **69:23** [y]Isa 6:9-10; Ro 11:9-10* **69:24** [z]Ps 79:6 **69:25** [a]Mt 23:38 [b]Ac 1:20* **69:26** [c]Isa 53:4; Zec 1:15 **69:27** [d]Ne 4:5 [e]Ps 109:14; Isa 26:10 **69:28** [f]Ex 32:32-33; Lk 10:20; Php 4:3 [g]Eze 13:9

69:29 [h]Ps 59:1; 70:5 **69:30** [i]Ps 28:7 [j]Ps 34:3 **69:31** [k]Ps 50:9-13 **69:32** [l]Ps 34:2 [m]Ps 22:26 **69:33** [n]Ps 12:5; 68:6 **69:34** [o]Ps 96:11; 148:1; Isa 44:23; 49:13; 55:12

w22 Or *snare / and their fellowship become*

35 for God will save Zion[a]
and rebuild the cities of Judah.[b]
Then people will settle there and
possess it;
36 the children of his servants will
inherit it,
and those who love his name will
dwell there.[c]

Psalm 70

70:1-5pp— Ps40:13-17

For the director of music. Of
David. A petition.

Help for the poor and needy.

1 Hasten, O God, to save me;
O LORD, come quickly to help me.[d]
2 May those who seek my life[e]
be put to shame and confusion;
may all who desire my ruin
be turned back in disgrace.[f]
3 May those who say to me, "Aha! Aha!"
turn back because of their shame.
4 But may all who seek you
rejoice and be glad in you;
may those who love your salvation
always say,
"Let God be exalted!"

5 Yet I am poor and needy;[g]
come quickly to me,[h] O God.
You are my help and my deliverer;
O LORD, do not delay.

Psalm 71

71:1-3pp— Ps31:1-4

God's protection during old age.

1 In you, O LORD, I have taken refuge;
let me never be put to shame.[i]
2 Rescue me and deliver me in your
righteousness;
turn your ear[j] to me and save me.
3 Be my rock of refuge,
to which I can always go;
give the command to save me,
for you are my rock and my fortress.[k]
4 Deliver me, O my God, from the
hand of the wicked,[l]
from the grasp of evil and cruel men.

5 For you have been my hope,
O Sovereign LORD,
my confidence[m] since my youth.
6 From birth[n] I have relied on you;
you brought me forth from my
mother's womb.[o]
I will ever praise[p] you.
7 I have become like a portent[q] to many,
but you are my strong refuge.[r]
8 My mouth[s] is filled with your praise,
declaring your splendor[t] all day
long.

9 Do not cast[u] me away when I am old;[v]
do not forsake me when my
strength is gone.
10 For my enemies speak against me;
those who wait to kill[w] me
conspire[x] together.
11 They say, "God has forsaken him;
pursue him and seize him,
for no one will rescue[y] him."
12 Be not far[z] from me, O God;
come quickly, O my God, to help[a]
me.
13 May my accusers perish in shame;
may those who want to harm me
be covered with scorn and
disgrace.[b]

14 But as for me, I will always have
hope;[c]
I will praise you more and more.
15 My mouth will tell[d] of your
righteousness,
of your salvation all day long,
though I know not its measure.
16 I will come and proclaim your
mighty acts,[e] O Sovereign LORD;
I will proclaim your righteousness,
yours alone.
17 Since my youth, O God, you have
taught[f] me,
and to this day I declare your
marvelous deeds.[g]
18 Even when I am old and gray,[h]
do not forsake me, O God,
till I declare your power to the next
generation,
your might to all who are to come.[i]

69:35 [a]Ob 1:17 [b]Ps 51:18; Isa 44:26
69:36 [c]Ps 37:29; 102:28
70:1 [d]Ps 40:13
70:2 [e]Ps 35:4 [f]Ps 35:26
70:5 [g]Ps 40:17 [h]Ps 141:1
71:1 [i]Ps 25:2-3; 31:1
71:2 [j]Ps 17:6
71:3 [k]Ps 18:2; 31:2-3; 44:4
71:4 [l]Ps 140:4
71:5 [m]Job 4:6; Jer 17:7
71:6 [n]Ps 22:10 [o]Ps 22:9; Isa 46:3 [p]Ps 9:1; 34:1; 52:9; 119:164; 145:2
71:7 [q]Isa 8:18; 1Co 4:9 [r]2Sa 22:3; Ps 61:3
71:8 [s]Ps 51:15; 63:5 [t]Ps 35:28; 96:6; 104:1
71:9 [u]Ps 51:11 [v]ver 18; Ps 92:14; Isa 46:4
71:10 [w]Ps 10:8; 59:3; Pr 1:18 [x]Ps 31:13; 56:6; Mt 12:14
71:11 [y]Ps 7:2
71:12 [z]Ps 35:22; 38:21 [a]Ps 38:22; 70:1
71:13 [b]ver 24
71:14 [c]Ps 130:7
71:15 [d]Ps 35:28; 40:5
71:16 [e]Ps 106:2

71:17 [f]Dt 4:5 [g]Ps 26:7 **71:18** [h]ver 9 [i]Ps 22:30,31; 78:4

19Your righteousness reaches to the skies,[a] O God,
you who have done great things.[b]
Who, O God, is like you?[c]
20Though you have made me see troubles,[d] many and bitter,
you will restore[e] my life again;
from the depths of the earth
you will again bring me up.
21You will increase my honor[f]
and comfort[g] me once again.

22I will praise you with the harp[h]
for your faithfulness, O my God;
I will sing praise to you with the lyre,[i]
O Holy One of Israel.[j]
23My lips will shout for joy
when I sing praise to you—
I, whom you have redeemed.[k]
24My tongue will tell of your righteous acts
all day long,[l]
for those who wanted to harm me[m]
have been put to shame and confusion.

Psalm 72

Of Solomon.

Praise to the king.

1Endow the king with your justice, O God,
the royal son with your righteousness.
2He will[x] judge your people in righteousness,[n]
your afflicted ones with justice.
3The mountains will bring prosperity to the people,
the hills the fruit of righteousness.
4He will defend the afflicted among the people
and save the children of the needy;[o]
he will crush the oppressor.

5He will endure[y] as long as the sun,
as long as the moon, through all generations.
6He will be like rain[p] falling on a mown field,
like showers watering the earth.
7In his days the righteous will flourish;[q]
prosperity will abound till the moon is no more.

8He will rule from sea to sea
and from the River[z][r] to the ends of the earth.[a][s]
9The desert tribes will bow before him
and his enemies will lick the dust.
10The kings of Tarshish and of distant shores
will bring tribute to him;
the kings of Sheba[t] and Seba
will present him gifts.[u]
11All kings will bow down to him
and all nations will serve him.

12For he will deliver the needy who cry out,
the afflicted who have no one to help.
13He will take pity on the weak and the needy
and save the needy from death.
14He will rescue[v] them from oppression and violence,
for precious[w] is their blood in his sight.

15Long may he live!
May gold from Sheba[x] be given him.
May people ever pray for him
and bless him all day long.
16Let grain abound throughout the land;
on the tops of the hills may it sway.
Let its fruit flourish like Lebanon;[y]
let it thrive like the grass of the field.
17May his name endure forever;[z]
may it continue as long as the sun.[a]

All nations will be blessed through him,
and they will call him blessed.[b]

18Praise be to the LORD God, the God of Israel,[c]
who alone does marvelous deeds.[d]
19Praise be to his glorious name forever;
may the whole earth be filled with his glory.[e]
Amen and Amen.[f]

20This concludes the prayers of David son of Jesse.

71:19 [a]Ps 36:5; 57:10 [b]Ps 126:2; Lk 1:49 [c]Ps 35:10
71:20 [d]Ps 60:3 [e]Hos 6:2
71:21 [f]Ps 18:35 [g]Ps 23:4; 86:17; Isa 12:1; 49:13
71:22 [h]Ps 33:2 [i]Ps 92:3; 144:9 [j]2Ki 19:22
71:23 [k]Ps 103:4
71:24 [l]Ps 35:28 [m]ver 13
72:2 [n]Isa 9:7; 11:4-5; 32:1
72:4 [o]Isa 11:4
72:6 [p]Dt 32:2; Hos 6:3
72:7 [q]Ps 92:12; Isa 2:4
72:8 [r]Ex 23:31 [s]Zec 9:10
72:10 [t]Ge 10:7 [u]2Ch 9:24
72:14 [v]Ps 69:18 [w]1Sa 26:21; Ps 116:15
72:15 [x]Isa 60:6
72:16 [y]Ps 104:16
72:17 [z]Ex 3:15 [a]Ps 89:36 [b]Ge 12:3; Lk 1:48
72:18 [c]1Ch 29:10; Ps 41:13; 106:48 [d]Job 5:9
72:19 [e]Nu 14:21; Ne 9:5 [f]Ps 41:13

[x]*2* Or *May he*; similarly in verses 3-11 and 17
[y]*5* Septuagint; Hebrew *You will be feared* [z]*8* That is, the Euphrates [a]*8* Or *the end of the land*

BOOK III

Psalms 73–89

Psalm 73

A psalm of Asaph.

Destruction of the wicked.

[1]Surely God is good to Israel,
to those who are pure in heart.[a]

[2]But as for me, my feet had almost slipped;
I had nearly lost my foothold.
[3]For I envied[b] the arrogant
when I saw the prosperity of the wicked.[c]

[4]They have no struggles;
their bodies are healthy and strong.[b]
[5]They are free[d] from the burdens common to man;
they are not plagued by human ills.
[6]Therefore pride is their necklace;[e]
they clothe themselves with violence.[f]
[7]From their callous hearts[g] comes iniquity[c];
the evil conceits of their minds know no limits.
[8]They scoff, and speak with malice;
in their arrogance[h] they threaten oppression.
[9]Their mouths lay claim to heaven,
and their tongues take possession of the earth.
[10]Therefore their people turn to them
and drink up waters in abundance.[d]
[11]They say, "How can God know?
Does the Most High have knowledge?"

[12]This is what the wicked are like—
always carefree, they increase in wealth.[i]

[13]Surely in vain[j] have I kept my heart pure;
in vain have I washed my hands in innocence.[k]
[14]All day long I have been plagued;
I have been punished every morning.

[15]If I had said, "I will speak thus,"
I would have betrayed your children.
[16]When I tried to understand[l] all this,
it was oppressive to me
[17]till I entered the sanctuary[m] of God;
then I understood their final destiny.[n]

[18]Surely you place them on slippery ground;[o]
you cast them down to ruin.
[19]How suddenly[p] are they destroyed,
completely swept away by terrors!
[20]As a dream[q] when one awakes,[r]
so when you arise, O Lord,
you will despise them as fantasies.

[21]When my heart was grieved
and my spirit embittered,
[22]I was senseless[s] and ignorant;
I was a brute beast[t] before you.

[23]Yet I am always with you;
you hold me by my right hand.
[24]You guide[u] me with your counsel,[v]
and afterward you will take me into glory.
[25]Whom have I in heaven but you?
And earth has nothing I desire besides you.[w]
[26]My flesh and my heart[x] may fail,[y]
but God is the strength of my heart
and my portion forever.

[27]Those who are far from you will perish;[z]
you destroy all who are unfaithful to you.
[28]But as for me, it is good to be near God.[a]
I have made the Sovereign LORD my refuge;
I will tell of all your deeds.[b]

73:1 [a]Mt 5:8
73:3 [b]Ps 37:1; Pr 23:17 [c]Job 21:7; Jer 12:1
73:5 [d]Job 21:9
73:6 [e]Ge 41:42 [f]Ps 109:18
73:7 [g]Ps 17:10
73:8 [h]Ps 17:10; Jude 16
73:12 [i]Ps 49:6
73:13 [j]Job 21:15; 34:9 [k]Ps 26:6
73:16 [l]Ecc 8:17
73:17 [m]Ps 77:13 [n]Ps 37:38
73:18 [o]Ps 35:6
73:19 [p]Isa 47:11
73:20 [q]Job 20:8 [r]Ps 78:65
73:22 [s]Ps 49:10; 92:6 [t]Ecc 3:18
73:24 [u]Ps 48:14 [v]Ps 32:8
73:25 [w]Php 3:8
73:26 [x]Ps 84:2 [y]Ps 40:12
73:27 [z]Ps 119:155
73:28 [a]Heb 10:22; Jas 4:8 [b]Ps 40:5

b*4* With a different word division of the Hebrew; Masoretic Text *struggles at their death; / their bodies are healthy* c*7* Syriac (see also Septuagint); Hebrew *Their eyes bulge with fat* d*10* The meaning of the Hebrew for this verse is uncertain.

Psalm 74

A *maskil* [e] of Asaph.

Prayer for Mount Zion.

1Why have you rejected us forever,[a]
O God?
Why does your anger smolder against
the sheep of your pasture?[b]
2Remember the people you purchased[c]
of old,[d]
the tribe of your inheritance,
whom you redeemed[e]—
Mount Zion, where you dwelt.[f]
3Turn your steps toward these
everlasting ruins,
all this destruction the enemy has
brought on the sanctuary.

4Your foes roared[g] in the place where
you met with us;
they set up their standards[h] as signs.
5They behaved like men wielding axes
to cut through a thicket of trees.[i]
6They smashed all the carved[j] paneling
with their axes and hatchets.
7They burned your sanctuary to the
ground;
they defiled the dwelling place of
your Name.
8They said in their hearts, "We will
crush[k] them completely!"
They burned every place where God
was worshiped in the land.
9We are given no miraculous signs;
no prophets[l] are left,
and none of us knows how long
this will be.

10How long will the enemy mock you,
O God?
Will the foe revile[m] your name
forever?
11Why do you hold back your hand,
your right hand?[n]
Take it from the folds of your
garment and destroy them!

12But you, O God, are my king[o] from
of old;
you bring salvation upon the earth.
13It was you who split open the sea[p]
by your power;
you broke the heads of the
monster[q] in the waters.
14It was you who crushed the heads of
Leviathan
and gave him as food to the
creatures of the desert.
15It was you who opened up springs[r]
and streams;
you dried up[s] the ever flowing rivers.
16The day is yours, and yours also the
night;
you established the sun and moon.[t]
17It was you who set all the
boundaries[u] of the earth;
you made both summer and winter.[v]

18Remember how the enemy has
mocked you, O LORD,
how foolish people[w] have reviled
your name.
19Do not hand over the life of your
dove to wild beasts;
do not forget the lives of your
afflicted[x] people forever.
20Have regard for your covenant,[y]
because haunts of violence fill the
dark places of the land.
21Do not let the oppressed[z] retreat in
disgrace;
may the poor and needy[a] praise
your name.

22Rise up, O God, and defend your cause;
remember how fools[b] mock you all
day long.
23Do not ignore the clamor of your
adversaries,[c]
the uproar of your enemies, which
rises continually.

Psalm 75

For the director of music. ⌊To the tune of⌋ "Do Not Destroy." A psalm of Asaph. A song.

It is God who judges.

1We give thanks to you, O God,
we give thanks, for your Name is
near;[d]
men tell of your wonderful deeds.[e]

74:1 [a]Dt 29:20; Ps 44:23 [b]Ps 79:13; 95:7; 100:3
74:2 [c]Ex 15:16 [d]Dt 32:7 [e]Ex 15:13 [f]Ps 68:16
74:4 [g]La 2:7 [h]Nu 2:2
74:5 [i]Jer 46:22
74:6 [j]1Ki 6:18
74:8 [k]Ps 83:4
74:9 [l]1Sa 3:1
74:10 [m]Ps 44:16
74:11 [n]La 2:3
74:12 [o]Ps 44:4
74:13 [p]Ex 14:21 [q]Isa 51:9; Eze 29:3
74:15 [r]Ex 17:6; Nu 20:11 [s]Jos 2:10; 3:13
74:16 [t]Ge 1:16; Ps 136:7-9
74:17 [u]Dt 32:8; Ac 17:26 [v]Ge 8:22
74:18 [w]Dt 32:6; Ps 39:8
74:19 [x]Ps 9:18
74:20 [y]Ge 17:7; Ps 106:45
74:21 [z]Ps 103:6 [a]Ps 35:10
74:22 [b]Ps 53:1
74:23 [c]Ps 65:7
75:1 [d]Ps 145:18 [e]Ps 44:1; 71:16

e Title: Probably a literary or musical term

2You say, "I choose the appointed time;
it is I who judge uprightly.
3When the earth and all its people quake,[a]
it is I who hold its pillars[b] firm.
Selah
4To the arrogant I say, 'Boast no more,'
and to the wicked, 'Do not lift up your horns.[c]
5Do not lift your horns against heaven;
do not speak with outstretched neck.' "

6No one from the east or the west
or from the desert can exalt a man.
7But it is God who judges:[d]
He brings one down, he exalts another.[e]
8In the hand of the LORD is a cup
full of foaming wine mixed[f] with spices;
he pours it out, and all the wicked of the earth
drink it down to its very dregs.[g]

9As for me, I will declare[h] this forever;
I will sing praise to the God of Jacob.
10I will cut off the horns of all the wicked,
but the horns of the righteous will be lifted up.[i]

Psalm 76

For the director of music. With stringed instruments. A psalm of Asaph. A song.

The majesty and judgment of God.

1In Judah God is known;
his name is great in Israel.
2His tent is in Salem,[j]
his dwelling place in Zion.
3There he broke the flashing arrows,
the shields and the swords, the weapons of war.[k] *Selah*

4You are resplendent with light,
more majestic than mountains rich with game.
5Valiant men lie plundered,
they sleep their last sleep;[l]

75:3 [a]Isa 24:19 [b]1Sa 2:8
75:4 [c]Zec 1:21
75:7 [d]Ps 50:6 [e]1Sa 2:7; Ps 147:6; Da 2:21
75:8 [f]Pr 23:30 [g]Job 21:20; Jer 25:15
75:9 [h]Ps 40:10
75:10 [i]Ps 89:17; 92:10; 148:14
76:2 [j]Ge 14:18
76:3 [k]Ps 46:9
76:5 [l]Ps 13:3
76:6 [m]Ex 15:1
76:7 [n]1Ch 16:25 [o]Ezr 9:15; Rev 6:17 [p]Ps 2:5; Na 1:6
76:8 [q]1Ch 16:30; 2Ch 20:29-30
76:9 [r]Ps 9:8
76:10 [s]Ex 9:16; Ro 9:17
76:11 [t]Ps 50:14; Ecc 5:4-5 [u]2Ch 32:23; Ps 68:29
77:1 [v]Ps 3:4
77:2 [w]Ps 50:15; Isa 26:9,16 [x]Job 11:13 [y]Ge 37:35
77:3 [z]Ps 143:4
77:5 [a]Dt 32:7; Ps 44:1; 143:5; Isa 51:9

not one of the warriors
can lift his hands.
6At your rebuke, O God of Jacob,
both horse and chariot[m] lie still.
7You alone are to be feared.[n]
Who can stand[o] before you when you are angry?[p]
8From heaven you pronounced judgment,
and the land feared[q] and was quiet—
9when you, O God, rose up to judge,[r]
to save all the afflicted of the land.
Selah
10Surely your wrath against men brings you praise,[s]
and the survivors of your wrath are restrained.[f]

11Make vows to the LORD your God
and fulfill them;[t]
let all the neighboring lands
bring gifts[u] to the One to be feared.
12He breaks the spirit of rulers;
he is feared by the kings of the earth.

Psalm 77

For the director of music. For Jeduthun. Of Asaph. A psalm.

Remember the deeds of the LORD.

1I cried out to God[v] for help;
I cried out to God to hear me.
2When I was in distress,[w] I sought the Lord;
at night I stretched out untiring hands[x]
and my soul refused to be comforted.[y]

3I remembered you, O God, and I groaned;
I mused, and my spirit grew faint.[z]
Selah
4You kept my eyes from closing;
I was too troubled to speak.
5I thought about the former days,[a]
the years of long ago;
6I remembered my songs in the night.
My heart mused and my spirit inquired:

[f]*10* Or *Surely the wrath of men brings you praise, / and with the remainder of wrath you arm yourself*

[7]"Will the Lord reject forever?
Will he never show his favor[a] again?
[8]Has his unfailing love vanished
forever?
Has his promise[b] failed for all time?
[9]Has God forgotten to be merciful?[c]
Has he in anger withheld his
compassion?[d]" *Selah*

[10]Then I thought, "To this I will appeal:
the years of the right hand[e] of the
Most High."
[11]I will remember the deeds of the LORD;
yes, I will remember your
miracles[f] of long ago.
[12]I will meditate on all your works
and consider all your mighty deeds.

[13]Your ways, O God, are holy.
What god is so great as our God?[g]
[14]You are the God who performs
miracles;
you display your power among the
peoples.
[15]With your mighty arm you redeemed
your people,[h]
the descendants of Jacob and
Joseph. *Selah*

[16]The waters[i] saw you, O God,
the waters saw you and writhed;[j]
the very depths were convulsed.
[17]The clouds poured down water,[k]
the skies resounded with thunder;
your arrows flashed back and forth.
[18]Your thunder was heard in the
whirlwind,
your lightning lit up the world;
the earth trembled and quaked.[l]
[19]Your path led through the sea,[m]
your way through the mighty waters,
though your footprints were not seen.

[20]You led your people[n] like a flock[o]
by the hand of Moses and Aaron.

Psalm 78

A *maskil* [g] of Asaph.

Teach the children the deeds of the LORD.

[1]O my people, hear my teaching;[p]
listen to the words of my mouth.
[2]I will open my mouth in parables,[q]
I will utter hidden things, things
from of old—
[3]what we have heard and known,
what our fathers have told us.[r]
[4]We will not hide them from their
children;[s]
we will tell the next generation
the praiseworthy deeds[t] of the LORD,
his power, and the wonders he has
done.
[5]He decreed statutes[u] for Jacob[v]
and established the law in Israel,
which he commanded our forefathers
to teach their children,
[6]so the next generation would know
them,
even the children yet to be born,[w]
and they in turn would tell their
children.
[7]Then they would put their trust in God
and would not forget[x] his deeds
but would keep his commands.[y]
[8]They would not be like their
forefathers[z]—
a stubborn[a] and rebellious[b]
generation,
whose hearts were not loyal to God,
whose spirits were not faithful to
him.

[9]The men of Ephraim, though armed
with bows,[c]
turned back on the day of battle;[d]
[10]they did not keep God's covenant[e]
and refused to live by his law.
[11]They forgot what he had done,[f]
the wonders he had shown them.
[12]He did miracles[g] in the sight of their
fathers
in the land of Egypt,[h] in the region
of Zoan.[i]
[13]He divided the sea[j] and led them
through;
he made the water stand firm like
a wall.[k]
[14]He guided them with the cloud by day
and with light from the fire all night.[l]

77:7 [a]Ps 85:1
77:8 [b]2Pe 3:9
77:9 [c]Ps 25:6; 40:11; 51:1 [d]Isa 49:15
77:10 [e]Ps 31:22
77:11 [f]Ps 143:5
77:13 [g]Ex 15:11; Ps 71:19; 86:8
77:15 [h]Ex 6:6; Dt 9:29
77:16 [i]Ex 14:21,28; Hab 3:8 [j]Ps 114:4; Hab 3:10
77:17 [k]Jdg 5:4
77:18 [l]Jdg 5:4
77:19 [m]Hab 3:15
77:20 [n]Ex 13:21 [o]Ps 78:52; Isa 63:11
78:1 [p]Isa 51:4; 55:3
78:2 [q]Ps 49:4; Mt 13:35*
78:3 [r]Ps 44:1
78:4 [s]Dt 11:19 [t]Ps 26:7; 71:17
78:5 [u]Ps 19:7; 81:5 [v]Ps 147:19
78:6 [w]Ps 22:31; 102:18
78:7 [x]Dt 6:12 [y]Dt 5:29
78:8 [z]2Ch 30:7 [a]Ex 32:9 [b]ver 37; Isa 30:9
78:9 [c]ver 57; 1Ch 12:2 [d]Jdg 20:39
78:10 [e]2Ki 17:15
78:11 [f]Ps 106:13
78:12 [g]Ps 106:22 [h]Ex 7-12 [i]Nu 13:22
78:13 [j]Ex 14:21; Ps 136:13 [k]Ex 15:8
78:14 [l]Ex 13:21; Ps 105:39

[g]Title: Probably a literary or musical term

15He split the rocks[a] in the desert
and gave them water as abundant as the seas;
16he brought streams out of a rocky crag
and made water flow down like rivers.

17But they continued to sin[b] against him,
rebelling in the desert against the Most High.
18They willfully put God to the test[c]
by demanding the food they craved.[d]
19They spoke against God,[e] saying,
"Can God spread a table in the desert?
20When he struck the rock, water gushed out,[f]
and streams flowed abundantly.
But can he also give us food?
Can he supply meat[g] for his people?"
21When the LORD heard them, he was very angry;
his fire broke out[h] against Jacob,
and his wrath rose against Israel,
22for they did not believe in God
or trust[i] in his deliverance.
23Yet he gave a command to the skies above
and opened the doors of the heavens;[j]
24he rained down manna[k] for the people to eat,
he gave them the grain of heaven.
25Men ate the bread of angels;
he sent them all the food they could eat.
26He let loose the east wind[l] from the heavens
and led forth the south wind by his power.
27He rained meat down on them like dust,
flying birds like sand on the seashore.
28He made them come down inside their camp,
all around their tents.
29They ate till they had more than enough,[m]
for he had given them what they craved.

30But before they turned from the food they craved,
even while it was still in their mouths,[n]
31God's anger rose against them;
he put to death the sturdiest[o] among them,
cutting down the young men of Israel.

32In spite of all this, they kept on sinning;
in spite of his wonders,[p] they did not believe.[q]
33So he ended their days in futility[r]
and their years in terror.
34Whenever God slew them, they would seek[s] him;
they eagerly turned to him again.
35They remembered that God was their Rock,[t]
that God Most High was their Redeemer.[u]
36But then they would flatter him with their mouths,[v]
lying to him with their tongues;
37their hearts were not loyal[w] to him,
they were not faithful to his covenant.
38Yet he was merciful;[x]
he forgave[y] their iniquities[z]
and did not destroy them.
Time after time he restrained his anger
and did not stir up his full wrath.
39He remembered that they were but flesh,[a]
a passing breeze[b] that does not return.

40How often they rebelled[c] against him in the desert[d]
and grieved him[e] in the wasteland!
41Again and again they put God to the test;[f]
they vexed the Holy One of Israel.[g]
42They did not remember his power—
the day he redeemed them from the oppressor,
43the day he displayed his miraculous signs in Egypt,
his wonders in the region of Zoan.

78:15 [a]Nu 20:11; 1Co 10:4
78:17 [b]Dt 9:22; Isa 63:10; Heb 3:16
78:18 [c]1Co 10:9 [d]Ex 16:2; Nu 11:4
78:19 [e]Nu 21:5
78:20 [f]Nu 20:11 [g]Nu 11:18
78:21 [h]Nu 11:1
78:22 [i]Dt 1:32; Heb 3:19
78:23 [j]Ge 7:11; Mal 3:10
78:24 [k]Ex 16:4; Jn 6:31*
78:26 [l]Nu 11:31
78:29 [m]Nu 11:20
78:30 [n]Nu 11:33
78:31 [o]Isa 10:16
78:32 [p]ver 11 [q]ver 22
78:33 [r]Nu 14:29,35
78:34 [s]Hos 5:15
78:35 [t]Dt 32:4 [u]Dt 9:26
78:36 [v]Eze 33:31
78:37 [w]ver 8; Ac 8:21
78:38 [x]Ex 34:6 [y]Isa 48:10 [z]Nu 14:18,20
78:39 [a]Ge 6:3; Ps 103:14 [b]Job 7:7; Jas 4:14
78:40 [c]Heb 3:16 [d]Ps 95:8; 106:14 [e]Eph 4:30
78:41 [f]Nu 14:22 [g]2Ki 19:22; Ps 89:18

44He turned their rivers to blood;[a]
they could not drink from their streams.
45He sent swarms of flies[b] that devoured them,
and frogs[c] that devastated them.
46He gave their crops to the grasshopper,
their produce to the locust.[d]
47He destroyed their vines with hail[e]
and their sycamore-figs with sleet.
48He gave over their cattle to the hail,
their livestock[f] to bolts of lightning.
49He unleashed against them his hot anger,[g]
his wrath, indignation and hostility—
a band of destroying angels.
50He prepared a path for his anger;
he did not spare them from death
but gave them over to the plague.
51He struck down all the firstborn of Egypt,[h]
the firstfruits of manhood in the tents of Ham.[i]
52But he brought his people out like a flock;[j]
he led them like sheep through the desert.
53He guided them safely, so they were unafraid;
but the sea engulfed[k] their enemies.[l]
54Thus he brought them to the border of his holy land,
to the hill country his right hand[m] had taken.
55He drove out nations[n] before them
and allotted their lands to them as an inheritance;[o]
he settled the tribes of Israel in their homes.

56But they put God to the test
and rebelled against the Most High;
they did not keep his statutes.
57Like their fathers[p] they were disloyal and faithless,
as unreliable as a faulty bow.[q]
58They angered him[r] with their high places;[s]
they aroused his jealousy with their idols.[t]
59When God heard them, he was very angry;
he rejected Israel[u] completely.
60He abandoned the tabernacle of Shiloh,[v]
the tent he had set up among men.
61He sent ⌊the ark of⌋ his might[w] into captivity,[x]
his splendor into the hands of the enemy.
62He gave his people over to the sword;
he was very angry with his inheritance.
63Fire consumed[y] their young men,
and their maidens had no wedding songs;[z]
64their priests were put to the sword,[a]
and their widows could not weep.

65Then the Lord awoke as from sleep,[b]
as a man wakes from the stupor of wine.
66He beat back his enemies;
he put them to everlasting shame.[c]
67Then he rejected the tents of Joseph,
he did not choose the tribe of Ephraim;
68but he chose the tribe of Judah,
Mount Zion,[d] which he loved.
69He built his sanctuary like the heights,
like the earth that he established forever.
70He chose David[e] his servant
and took him from the sheep pens;
71from tending the sheep he brought him
to be the shepherd[f] of his people Jacob,
of Israel his inheritance.
72And David shepherded them with integrity of heart;[g]
with skillful hands he led them.

Psalm 79

A psalm of Asaph.

Prayer for the desolate Jerusalem.

1O God, the nations have invaded your inheritance;[h]
they have defiled your holy temple,
they have reduced Jerusalem to rubble.[i]

78:44 [a]Ex 7:20-21; Ps 105:29
78:45 [b]Ex 8:24; Ps 105:31 [c]Ex 8:2,6
78:46 [d]Ex 10:13
78:47 [e]Ex 9:23; Ps 105:32
78:48 [f]Ex 9:25
78:49 [g]Ex 15:7
78:51 [h]Ex 12:29; Ps 135:8 [i]Ps 105:23; 106:22
78:52 [j]Ps 77:20
78:53 [k]Ex 14:28 [l]Ps 106:10
78:54 [m]Ex 15:17; Ps 44:3
78:55 [n]Ps 44:2 [o]Jos 13:7
78:57 [p]Eze 20:27 [q]Hos 7:16
78:58 [r]Jdg 2:12 [s]Lev 26:30 [t]Ex 20:4; Dt 32:21
78:59 [u]Dt 32:19
78:60 [v]Jos 18:1
78:61 [w]Ps 132:8 [x]1Sa 4:17
78:63 [y]Nu 11:1 [z]Jer 7:34; 16:9
78:64 [a]1Sa 4:17; 22:18
78:65 [b]Ps 44:23
78:66 [c]1Sa 5:6
78:68 [d]Ps 87:2
78:70 [e]1Sa 16:1
78:71 [f]2Sa 5:2; Ps 28:9
78:72 [g]1Ki 9:4
79:1 [h]Ps 74:2 [i]2Ki 25:9

2They have given the dead bodies of
your servants
as food to the birds of the air,
the flesh of your saints to the
beasts of the earth.[a]
3They have poured out blood like water
all around Jerusalem,
and there is no one to bury the
dead.[b]
4We are objects of reproach to our
neighbors,
of scorn and derision to those
around us.[c]

5How long,[d] O LORD? Will you be
angry[e] forever?
How long will your jealousy burn
like fire?[f]
6Pour out your wrath[g] on the nations
that do not acknowledge[h] you,
on the kingdoms
that do not call on your name;[i]
7for they have devoured Jacob
and destroyed his homeland.
8Do not hold against us the sins of the
fathers;[j]
may your mercy come quickly to
meet us,
for we are in desperate need.[k]

9Help us,[l] O God our Savior,
for the glory of your name;
deliver us and forgive our sins
for your name's sake.[m]
10Why should the nations say,
"Where is their God?"[n]
Before our eyes, make known among
the nations
that you avenge[o] the outpoured
blood of your servants.
11May the groans of the prisoners
come before you;
by the strength of your arm
preserve those condemned to die.

12Pay back into the laps[p] of our
neighbors seven times[q]
the reproach they have hurled at
you, O Lord.
13Then we your people, the sheep of
your pasture,[r]
will praise you forever;[s]
from generation to generation
we will recount your praise.

79:2 [a]Dt 28:26; Jer 7:33
79:3 [b]Jer 16:4
79:4 [c]Ps 44:13; 80:6
79:5 [d]Ps 74:10 [e]Ps 74:1; 85:5 [f]Dt 29:20; Ps 89:46; Zep 3:8
79:6 [g]Ps 69:24; Rev 16:1 [h]Jer 10:25; 2Th 1:8 [i]Ps 14:4
79:8 [j]Isa 64:9 [k]Ps 116:6; 142:6
79:9 [l]2Ch 14:11 [m]Ps 25:11; 31:3; Jer 14:7
79:10 [n]Ps 42:10 [o]Ps 94:1
79:12 [p]Isa 65:6; Jer 32:18 [q]Ge 4:15
79:13 [r]Ps 74:1; 95:7 [s]Ps 44:8
80:1 [t]Ps 77:20 [u]Ex 25:22
80:2 [v]Nu 2:18-24 [w]Ps 35:23
80:3 [x]Ps 85:4; La 5:21 [y]Nu 6:25
80:5 [z]Ps 42:3; Isa 30:20
80:6 [a]Ps 79:4
80:8 [b]Isa 5:1-2; Jer 2:21 [c]Jos 13:6; Ac 7:45
80:11 [d]Ps 72:8
80:12 [e]Ps 89:40; Isa 5:5
80:13 [f]Jer 5:6

Psalm 80

For the director of music. To ⌊the tune of⌋ "The Lilies of the Covenant." Of Asaph. A psalm.

Petition for God to restore Israel.

1Hear us, O Shepherd of Israel,
you who lead Joseph like a flock;[t]
you who sit enthroned between the
cherubim,[u] shine forth
2 before Ephraim, Benjamin and
Manasseh.[v]
Awaken[w] your might;
come and save us.

3Restore[x] us,[y] O God;
make your face shine upon us,
that we may be saved.

4O LORD God Almighty,
how long will your anger smolder
against the prayers of your people?
5You have fed them with the bread of
tears;
you have made them drink tears by
the bowlful.[z]
6You have made us a source of
contention to our neighbors,
and our enemies mock us.[a]

7Restore us, O God Almighty;
make your face shine upon us,
that we may be saved.

8You brought a vine[b] out of Egypt;
you drove out[c] the nations and
planted it.
9You cleared the ground for it,
and it took root and filled the land.
10The mountains were covered with
its shade,
the mighty cedars with its branches.
11It sent out its boughs to the Sea,[h]
its shoots as far as the River.[i] [d]

12Why have you broken down its walls[e]
so that all who pass by pick its
grapes?
13Boars from the forest ravage[f] it
and the creatures of the field feed
on it.

[h]*11* Probably the Mediterranean [i]*11* That is, the Euphrates

14 Return to us, O God Almighty!
Look down from heaven and see![a]
Watch over this vine,
15 the root your right hand has planted,
the son[j] you have raised up for
yourself.

16 Your vine is cut down, it is burned
with fire;
at your rebuke[b] your people perish.
17 Let your hand rest on the man at
your right hand,
the son of man you have raised up
for yourself.
18 Then we will not turn away from you;
revive us, and we will call on your
name.

19 Restore us, O LORD God Almighty;
make your face shine upon us,
that we may be saved.

Psalm 81

For the director of music.
According to *gittith*.[k] Of Asaph.

Sing for joy to God.

1 Sing for joy to God our strength;
shout aloud to the God of Jacob![c]
2 Begin the music, strike the
tambourine,[d]
play the melodious harp[e] and lyre.

3 Sound the ram's horn at the New
Moon,
and when the moon is full, on the
day of our Feast;
4 this is a decree for Israel,
an ordinance of the God of Jacob.
5 He established it as a statute for Joseph
when he went out against Egypt,[f]
where we heard a language we did
not understand.[l][g]

6 He says, "I removed the burden from
their shoulders;[h]
their hands were set free from the
basket.
7 In your distress you called[i] and I
rescued you,
I answered[j] you out of a
thundercloud;
I tested you at the waters of
Meribah.[k] *Selah*

8 "Hear, O my people,[l] and I will warn
you—
if you would but listen to me,
O Israel!
9 You shall have no foreign god[m]
among you;
you shall not bow down to an alien
god.
10 I am the LORD your God,
who brought you up out of Egypt.[n]
Open wide your mouth and I will
fill[o] it.

11 "But my people would not listen to me;
Israel would not submit to me.[p]
12 So I gave them over[q] to their
stubborn hearts
to follow their own devices.

13 "If my people would but listen to me,[r]
if Israel would follow my ways,
14 how quickly would I subdue[s] their
enemies
and turn my hand against[t] their
foes!
15 Those who hate the LORD would
cringe before him,
and their punishment would last
forever.
16 But you would be fed with the finest
of wheat;[u]
with honey from the rock I would
satisfy you."

Psalm 82

A psalm of Asaph.

Petition for God to rescue the weak.

1 God presides in the great assembly;
he gives judgment[v] among the
"gods":

2 "How long will you[m] defend the unjust
and show partiality[w] to the
wicked?[x] *Selah*

80:14 [a]Isa 63:15
80:16 [b]Ps 39:11; 76:6
81:1 [c]Ps 66:1
81:2 [d]Ex 15:20 [e]Ps 92:3
81:5 [f]Ex 11:4 [g]Ps 114:1
81:6 [h]Isa 9:4
81:7 [i]Ex 2:23; Ps 50:15 [j]Ex 19:19 [k]Ex 17:7
81:8 [l]Ps 50:7
81:9 [m]Ex 20:3; Dt 32:12; Isa 43:12
81:10 [n]Ex 20:2 [o]Ps 107:9
81:11 [p]Ex 32:1-6
81:12 [q]Ac 7:42; Ro 1:24
81:13 [r]Dt 5:29; Isa 48:18
81:14 [s]Ps 47:3 [t]Am 1:8
81:16 [u]Dt 32:14
82:1 [v]Ps 58:11; Isa 3:13
82:2 [w]Dt 1:17 [x]Ps 58:1-2; Pr 18:5

j *15* Or *branch* k Title: Probably a musical term
l *5* Or / *and we heard a voice we had not known*
m *2* The Hebrew is plural.

3 Defend the cause of the weak and
fatherless;[a]
maintain the rights of the poor[b]
and oppressed.
4 Rescue the weak and needy;
deliver them from the hand of the
wicked.

5 "They know nothing, they
understand nothing.[c]
They walk about in darkness;[d]
all the foundations[e] of the earth
are shaken.

6 "I said, 'You are "gods";[f]
you are all sons of the Most High.'
7 But you will die[g] like mere men;
you will fall like every other ruler."

8 Rise up,[h] O God, judge the earth,
for all the nations are your
inheritance.[i]

Psalm 83

A song. A psalm of Asaph.

Petition to cover Israel's enemies with shame.

1 O God, do not keep silent;[j]
be not quiet, O God, be not still.
2 See how your enemies are astir,[k]
how your foes rear their heads.[l]
3 With cunning they conspire[m] against
your people;
they plot against those you cherish.
4 "Come," they say, "let us destroy[n]
them as a nation,
that the name of Israel be
remembered[o] no more."

5 With one mind they plot together;[p]
they form an alliance against
you—
6 the tents of Edom[q] and
the Ishmaelites,
of Moab[r] and the Hagrites,[s]
7 Gebal,[n][t] Ammon and Amalek,
Philistia, with the people of Tyre.[u]
8 Even Assyria has joined them
to lend strength to the descendants
of Lot.[v] *Selah*

9 Do to them as you did to Midian,[w]
as you did to Sisera and Jabin at
the river Kishon,[x]
10 who perished at Endor
and became like refuse[y] on the
ground.
11 Make their nobles like Oreb and
Zeeb,[z]
all their princes like Zebah and
Zalmunna,[a]
12 who said, "Let us take possession[b]
of the pasturelands of God."

13 Make them like tumbleweed, O my
God,
like chaff[c] before the wind.
14 As fire consumes the forest
or a flame sets the mountains
ablaze,[d]
15 so pursue them with your tempest
and terrify them with your storm.[e]
16 Cover their faces with shame[f]
so that men will seek your name,
O LORD.

17 May they ever be ashamed and
dismayed;
may they perish in disgrace.[g]
18 Let them know that you, whose
name is the LORD—
that you alone are the Most High
over all the earth.[h]

Psalm 84

For the director of music.
According to *gittith.*[o] Of the
Sons of Korah. A psalm.

Yearning to dwell in God's house.

1 How lovely is your dwelling place,[i]
O LORD Almighty!
2 My soul yearns,[j] even faints,
for the courts of the LORD;
my heart and my flesh cry out
for the living God.

3 Even the sparrow has found a home,
and the swallow a nest for herself,
where she may have her young—

82:3 [a]Dt 24:17 [b]Jer 22:16
82:5 [c]Ps 14:4; Mic 3:1 [d]Isa 59:9 [e]Ps 11:3
82:6 [f]Jn 10:34*
82:7 [g]Ps 49:12; Eze 31:14
82:8 [h]Ps 12:5 [i]Ps 2:8; Rev 11:15
83:1 [j]Ps 28:1; 35:22
83:2 [k]Ps 2:1; Isa 17:12 [l]Jdg 8:28; Ps 81:15
83:3 [m]Ps 31:13
83:4 [n]Est 3:6 [o]Jer 11:19
83:5 [p]Ps 2:2
83:6 [q]Ps 137:7 [r]2Ch 20:1 [s]Ge 25:16
83:7 [t]Jos 13:5 [u]Eze 27:3
83:8 [v]Dt 2:9
83:9 [w]Jdg 7:1-23 [x]Jdg 4:23-24
83:10 [y]Zep 1:17
83:11 [z]Jdg 7:25 [a]Jdg 8:12,21
83:12 [b]2Ch 20:11
83:13 [c]Ps 35:5; Isa 17:13
83:14 [d]Dt 32:22; Isa 9:18
83:15 [e]Job 9:17
83:16 [f]Ps 109:29; 132:18
83:17 [g]Ps 35:4
83:18 [h]Ps 59:13
84:1 [i]Ps 27:4; 43:3; 132:5
84:2 [j]Ps 42:1-2

[n]7 That is, Byblos [o]Title: Probably a musical term

a place near your altar,[a]
O LORD Almighty, my King and my God.[b]
4Blessed are those who dwell in your house;
they are ever praising you. *Selah*
5Blessed are those whose strength[c] is in you,
who have set their hearts on pilgrimage.[d]
6As they pass through the Valley of Baca,
they make it a place of springs;
the autumn[e] rains also cover it with pools.[p]
7They go from strength to strength,[f]
till each appears[g] before God in Zion.
8Hear my prayer, O LORD God Almighty;
listen to me, O God of Jacob. *Selah*
9Look upon our shield,[q][h] O God;
look with favor on your anointed one.[i]
10Better is one day in your courts
than a thousand elsewhere;
I would rather be a doorkeeper[j] in the house of my God
than dwell in the tents of the wicked.
11For the LORD God is a sun[k] and shield;[l]
the LORD bestows favor and honor;
no good thing does he withhold[m]
from those whose walk is blameless.
12O LORD Almighty,
blessed[n] is the man who trusts in you.

Psalm 85

For the director of music. Of the Sons of Korah. A psalm.

Prayer for God's unfailing love.

1You showed favor to your land, O LORD;
you restored the fortunes[o] of Jacob.
2You forgave[p] the iniquity[q] of your people
and covered all their sins. *Selah*
3You set aside all your wrath[r]
and turned from your fierce anger.[s]
4Restore[t] us again, O God our Savior,
and put away your displeasure toward us.
5Will you be angry with us forever?[u]
Will you prolong your anger through all generations?
6Will you not revive[v] us again,
that your people may rejoice in you?
7Show us your unfailing love, O LORD,
and grant us your salvation.
8I will listen to what God the LORD will say;
he promises peace[w] to his people, his saints—
but let them not return to folly.
9Surely his salvation[x] is near those who fear him,
that his glory[y] may dwell in our land.
10Love and faithfulness[z] meet together;
righteousness[a] and peace kiss each other.
11Faithfulness springs forth from the earth,
and righteousness[b] looks down from heaven.
12The LORD will indeed give what is good,[c]
and our land will yield[d] its harvest.
13Righteousness goes before him
and prepares the way for his steps.

Psalm 86

A prayer of David.

Desire to walk in God's truth.

1Hear, O LORD, and answer[e] me,
for I am poor and needy.
2Guard my life, for I am devoted to you.
You are my God; save your servant
who trusts in you.[f]
3Have mercy[g] on me, O Lord,
for I call[h] to you all day long.
4Bring joy to your servant,
for to you, O Lord,
I lift[i] up my soul.

84:3 [a]Ps 43:4 [b]Ps 5:2 **84:5** [c]Ps 81:1 [d]Jer 31:6 **84:6** [e]Joel 2:23 **84:7** [f]Pr 4:18 [g]Dt 16:16 **84:9** [h]Ps 59:11 [i]1Sa 16:6; Ps 2:2; 132:17 **84:10** [j]1Ch 23:5 **84:11** [k]Isa 60:19; Rev 21:23 [l]Ge 15:1 [m]Ps 34:10 **84:12** [n]Ps 2:12 **85:1** [o]Ps 14:7; Jer 30:18; Eze 39:25 **85:2** [p]Nu 14:19 [q]Ps 78:38 **85:3** [r]Ps 106:23 [s]Ex 32:12; Dt 13:17; Ps 78:38; Jnh 3:9 **85:4** [t]Ps 80:3,7 **85:5** [u]Ps 79:5 **85:6** [v]Ps 80:18; Hab 3:2 **85:8** [w]Zec 9:10 **85:9** [x]Isa 46:13 [y]Zec 2:5 **85:10** [z]Ps 89:14; Pr 3:3 [a]Ps 72:2-3; Isa 32:17 **85:11** [b]Isa 45:8 **85:12** [c]Ps 84:11; Jas 1:17 [d]Lev 26:4; Ps 67:6; Zec 8:12 **86:1** [e]Ps 17:6 **86:2** [f]Ps 25:2; 31:14 **86:3** [g]Ps 4:1; 57:1 [h]Ps 88:9 **86:4** [i]Ps 25:1; 143:8

[p]6 Or *blessings* [q]9 Or *sovereign*

5You are forgiving and good,
O Lord,
abounding in love[a] to all who call
to you.
6Hear my prayer, O LORD;
listen to my cry for mercy.
7In the day of my trouble[b] I will call
to you,
for you will answer me.

8Among the gods there is none like
you,[c] O Lord;
no deeds can compare with
yours.
9All the nations you have made
will come and worship[d] before
you, O Lord;
they will bring glory[e] to your
name.
10For you are great and do marvelous
deeds;[f]
you alone[g] are God.

11Teach me your way,[h] O LORD,
and I will walk in your truth;
give me an undivided[i] heart,
that I may fear your name.
12I will praise you, O Lord my God,
with all my heart;
I will glorify your name forever.
13For great is your love toward me;
you have delivered me from the
depths of the grave.[r]

14The arrogant are attacking me,
O God;
a band of ruthless men seeks my
life—
men without regard for you.[j]
15But you, O Lord, are a compassionate
and gracious[k] God,
slow to anger, abounding in love
and faithfulness.[l]
16Turn to me and have mercy on me;
grant your strength to your servant
and save the son of your
maidservant.[s] [m]
17Give me a sign of your goodness,
that my enemies may see it and be
put to shame,
for you, O LORD, have helped me
and comforted me.

86:5 [a]Ex 34:6; Ne 9:17; Ps 103:8; 145:8; Joel 2:13; Jnh 4:2
86:7 [b]Ps 50:15
86:8 [c]Ex 15:11; Dt 3:24; Ps 89:6
86:9 [d]Ps 66:4; Rev 15:4 [e]Isa 43:7
86:10 [f]Ps 72:18 [g]Dt 6:4; Mk 12:29; 1Co 8:4
86:11 [h]Ps 25:5 [i]Jer 32:39
86:14 [j]Ps 54:3
86:15 [k]Ps 103:8 [l]Ex 34:6; Ne 9:17; Joel 2:13
86:16 [m]Ps 116:16
87:2 [n]Ps 78:68
87:3 [o]Ps 46:4; Isa 60:1
87:4 [p]Job 9:13 [q]Ps 45:12 [r]Isa 19:25
87:6 [s]Ps 69:28; Isa 4:3; Eze 13:9
87:7 [t]Ps 149:3 [u]Ps 36:9
88:1 [v]Ps 51:14 [w]Ps 22:2; 27:9; Lk 18:7

Psalm 87

Of the Sons of Korah. A psalm.
A song.

The glorious city of God.

1He has set his foundation on the
holy mountain;
2 the LORD loves the gates of Zion[n]
more than all the dwellings of Jacob.
3Glorious things are said of you,
O city of God:[o] *Selah*
4"I will record Rahab[t] [p] and Babylon
among those who acknowledge me—
Philistia too, and Tyre[q], along with
Cush[u]—
and will say, 'This[v] one was born
in Zion.[r] ' "

5Indeed, of Zion it will be said,
"This one and that one were born
in her,
and the Most High himself will
establish her."
6The LORD will write in the register[s]
of the peoples:
"This one was born in Zion."
Selah
7As they make music[t] they will sing,
"All my fountains[u] are in you."

Psalm 88

A song. A psalm of the Sons of
Korah. For the director of music.
According to *mahalath
leannoth.*[w] A *maskil*[x] of Heman
the Ezrahite.

Prayer for God to rescue from death.

1O LORD, the God who saves me,[v]
day and night I cry out[w] before you.
2May my prayer come before you;
turn your ear to my cry.

[r]*13* Hebrew *Sheol* [s]*16* Or *save your faithful son*
[t]*4* A poetic name for Egypt [u]*4* That is, the upper Nile region [v]*4* Or *"O Rahab and Babylon, / Philistia, Tyre and Cush, / I will record concerning those who acknowledge me: / 'This*
[w]Title: Possibly a tune, "The Suffering of Affliction"
[x]Title: Probably a literary or musical term

3For my soul is full of trouble
and my life draws near the grave.[y][a]
4I am counted among those who go
down to the pit;[b]
I am like a man without strength.
5I am set apart with the dead,
like the slain who lie in the grave,
whom you remember no more,
who are cut off[c] from your care.

6You have put me in the lowest pit,
in the darkest depths.[d]
7Your wrath lies heavily upon me;
you have overwhelmed me with all
your waves.[e] *Selah*
8You have taken from me my closest
friends[f]
and have made me repulsive to
them.
I am confined[g] and cannot escape;
9 my eyes[h] are dim with grief.

I call[i] to you, O LORD, every day;
I spread out my hands[j] to you.
10Do you show your wonders to the
dead?
Do those who are dead rise up and
praise you?[k] *Selah*
11Is your love declared in the grave,
your faithfulness[l] in Destruction[z]?
12Are your wonders known in the
place of darkness,
or your righteous deeds in the land
of oblivion?

13But I cry to you for help,[m] O LORD;
in the morning[n] my prayer comes
before you.[o]
14Why, O LORD, do you reject[p] me
and hide your face[q] from me?

15From my youth I have been afflicted
and close to death;
I have suffered your terrors[r] and
am in despair.
16Your wrath has swept over me;
your terrors have destroyed me.
17All day long they surround me like a
flood;[s]
they have completely engulfed me.
18You have taken my companions[t] and
loved ones from me;
the darkness is my closest friend.

88:3 [a]Ps 107:18,26
88:4 [b]Ps 28:1
88:5 [c]Ps 31:22; Isa 53:8
88:6 [d]Ps 69:15; La 3:55
88:7 [e]Ps 42:7
88:8 [f]Job 19:13; Ps 31:11 [g]Jer 32:2
88:9 [h]Ps 38:10 [i]Ps 86:3 [j]Job 11:13; Ps 143:6
88:10 [k]Ps 6:5
88:11 [l]Ps 30:9
88:13 [m]Ps 30:2 [n]Ps 5:3 [o]Ps 119:147
88:14 [p]Ps 43:2 [q]Job 13:24; Ps 13:1
88:15 [r]Job 6:4
88:17 [s]Ps 22:16; 124:4
88:18 [t]ver 8; Job 19:13; Ps 38:11
89:1 [u]Ps 59:16; Ps 101:1 [v]Ps 36:5; 40:10
89:2 [w]Ps 36:5
89:4 [x]2Sa 7:12-16; 1Ki 8:16; Ps 132:11-12; Isa 9:7; Lk 1:33
89:5 [y]Ps 19:1
89:6 [z]Ps 113:5
89:7 [a]Ps 47:2
89:8 [b]Ps 71:19
89:9 [c]Ps 65:7
89:10 [d]Ps 87:4 [e]Ps 68:1
89:11 [f]1Ch 29:11; Ps 24:1

Psalm 89

A *maskil*[a] of Ethan the Ezrahite.

The LORD's covenant with David.

1I will sing[u] of the LORD's great love
forever;
with my mouth I will make your
faithfulness known[v] through
all generations.
2I will declare that your love stands
firm forever,
that you established your
faithfulness in heaven itself.[w]

3You said, "I have made a covenant
with my chosen one,
I have sworn to David my servant,
4'I will establish your line forever
and make your throne firm through
all generations.'"[x] *Selah*

5The heavens[y] praise your wonders,
O LORD,
your faithfulness too, in the
assembly of the holy ones.
6For who in the skies above can
compare with the LORD?
Who is like the LORD among the
heavenly beings?[z]
7In the council of the holy ones God
is greatly feared;
he is more awesome than all who
surround him.[a]
8O LORD God Almighty, who is like
you?[b]
You are mighty, O LORD, and your
faithfulness surrounds you.

9You rule over the surging sea;
when its waves mount up, you still
them.[c]
10You crushed Rahab[d] like one of the
slain;
with your strong arm you
scattered[e] your enemies.
11The heavens are yours, and yours
also the earth;[f]

y3 Hebrew *Sheol* z11 Hebrew *Abaddon*
aTitle: Probably a literary or musical term

you founded the world and all that
is in it.[a]
12You created the north and the south;
Tabor[b] and Hermon[c] sing for joy[d]
at your name.
13Your arm is endued with power;
your hand is strong, your right
hand exalted.

14Righteousness and justice are the
foundation of your throne;[e]
love and faithfulness go before you.
15Blessed are those who have learned
to acclaim you,
who walk in the light[f] of your
presence, O LORD.
16They rejoice in your name[g] all day
long;
they exult in your righteousness.
17For you are their glory and strength,
and by your favor you exalt our
horn.[b][h]
18Indeed, our shield[c] belongs to the
LORD,
our king[i] to the Holy One of Israel.

19Once you spoke in a vision,
to your faithful people you said:
"I have bestowed strength on a
warrior;
I have exalted a young man from
among the people.
20I have found David[j] my servant;[k]
with my sacred oil I have
anointed[l] him.
21My hand will sustain him;
surely my arm will strengthen him.[m]
22No enemy will subject him to
tribute;
no wicked man will oppress[n] him.
23I will crush his foes before him[o]
and strike down his adversaries.[p]
24My faithful love will be with him,[q]
and through my name his horn[d]
will be exalted.
25I will set his hand over the sea,
his right hand over the rivers.[r]
26He will call out to me, 'You are my
Father,[s]
my God, the Rock my Savior.'[t]
27I will also appoint him my firstborn,[u]
the most exalted[v] of the kings[w] of
the earth.

89:11 [a]Ge 1:1
89:12 [b]Jos 19:22 [c]Dt 3:8; Jos 12:1 [d]Ps 98:8
89:14 [e]Ps 97:2
89:15 [f]Ps 44:3
89:16 [g]Ps 105:3
89:17 [h]Ps 75:10; 92:10; 148:14
89:18 [i]Ps 47:9
89:20 [j]Ac 13:22 [k]Ps 78:70 [l]1Sa 16:1,12
89:21 [m]Ps 18:35
89:22 [n]2Sa 7:10
89:23 [o]Ps 18:40 [p]2Sa 7:9
89:24 [q]2Sa 7:15
89:25 [r]Ps 72:8
89:26 [s]2Sa 7:14 [t]2Sa 22:47
89:27 [u]Col 1:18 [v]Nu 24:7 [w]Rev 1:5; 19:16
89:28 [x]ver 33-34; Isa 55:3
89:29 [y]ver 4,36; Dt 11:21; Jer 33:17
89:32 [z]2Sa 7:14
89:33 [a]2Sa 7:15
89:34 [b]Nu 23:19
89:38 [c]Dt 32:19; 1Ch 28:9; Ps 44:9
89:39 [d]La 5:16
89:40 [e]Ps 80:12 [f]La 2:2
89:41 [g]Ps 44:13
89:42 [h]Ps 13:2; 80:6
89:43 [i]Ps 44:10

28I will maintain my love to him forever,
and my covenant with him will
never fail.[x]
29I will establish his line forever,
his throne as long as the heavens
endure.[y]

30"If his sons forsake my law
and do not follow my statutes,
31if they violate my decrees
and fail to keep my commands,
32I will punish their sin with the rod,
their iniquity with flogging;[z]
33but I will not take my love from him,[a]
nor will I ever betray my faithfulness.
34I will not violate my covenant
or alter what my lips have uttered.[b]
35Once for all, I have sworn by my
holiness—
and I will not lie to David—
36that his line will continue forever
and his throne endure before me
like the sun;
37it will be established forever like the
moon,
the faithful witness in the sky."
Selah

38But you have rejected,[c] you have
spurned,
you have been very angry with
your anointed one.
39You have renounced the covenant
with your servant
and have defiled his crown in the
dust.[d]
40You have broken through all his
walls[e]
and reduced his strongholds[f] to ruins.
41All who pass by have plundered him;
he has become the scorn of his
neighbors.[g]
42You have exalted the right hand of
his foes;
you have made all his
enemies rejoice.[h]
43You have turned back the edge of his
sword
and have not supported him in
battle.[i]

b *17 Horn* here symbolizes strong one. c *18* Or *sovereign* d *24 Horn* here symbolizes strength.

[44]You have put an end to his splendor
and cast his throne to the ground.
[45]You have cut short the days of his
youth;
you have covered him with a
mantle of shame.[a] *Selah*

[46]How long, O LORD? Will you hide
yourself forever?
How long will your wrath burn like
fire?[b]
[47]Remember how fleeting is my life.[c]
For what futility you have created
all men!
[48]What man can live and not see
death,
or save himself from the power of
the grave[e]?[d] *Selah*
[49]O Lord, where is your former great
love,
which in your faithfulness you
swore to David?
[50]Remember, Lord, how your servant
has[f] been mocked,[e]
how I bear in my heart the taunts
of all the nations,
[51]the taunts with which your enemies
have mocked, O LORD,
with which they have mocked every
step of your anointed one.[f]

[52]Praise be to the LORD forever!
Amen and Amen.[g]

BOOK IV

Psalms 90–106

Psalm 90

A prayer of Moses the man of God.

*God is from everlasting
to everlasting.*

[1]Lord, you have been our dwelling
place[h]
throughout all generations.
[2]Before the mountains were born[i]
or you brought forth the earth and
the world,
from everlasting to everlasting you
are God.[j]

89:45 [a]Ps 44:15; 109:29
89:46 [b]Ps 79:5
89:47 [c]Job 7:7; Ps 39:5
89:48 [d]Ps 22:29; 49:9
89:50 [e]Ps 69:19
89:51 [f]Ps 74:10
89:52 [g]Ps 41:13; 72:19
90:1 [h]Dt 33:27; Eze 11:16
90:2 [i]Job 15:7; Pr 8:25 [j]Ps 102:24-27
90:3 [k]Ge 3:19; Job 34:15
90:4 [l]2Pe 3:8
90:5 [m]Ps 73:20; Isa 40:6
90:6 [n]Mt 6:30; Jas 1:10
90:8 [o]Ps 19:12
90:9 [p]Ps 78:33
90:10 [q]Job 20:8
90:11 [r]Ps 76:7
90:12 [s]Ps 39:4 [t]Dt 32:29
90:13 [u]Ps 6:3 [v]Dt 32:36; Ps 135:14
90:14 [w]Ps 103:5 [x]Ps 85:6 [y]Ps 31:7
90:16 [z]Ps 44:1; Hab 3:2

[3]You turn men back to dust,
saying, "Return to dust, O sons of
men."[k]
[4]For a thousand years in your sight
are like a day that has just gone by,
or like a watch in the night.[l]
[5]You sweep men away[m] in the sleep
of death;
they are like the new grass of the
morning—
[6]though in the morning it springs up
new,
by evening it is dry and withered.[n]

[7]We are consumed by your anger
and terrified by your indignation.
[8]You have set our iniquities before you,
our secret sins[o] in the light of your
presence.
[9]All our days pass away under your
wrath;
we finish our years with a moan.[p]
[10]The length of our days is
seventy years—
or eighty, if we have the strength;
yet their span[g] is but trouble and
sorrow,
for they quickly pass, and we fly
away.[q]

[11]Who knows the power of your anger?
For your wrath is as great as the
fear that is due you.[r]
[12]Teach us to number our days[s] aright,
that we may gain a heart of
wisdom.[t]

[13]Relent, O LORD! How long[u] will it be?
Have compassion on your
servants.[v]
[14]Satisfy[w] us in the morning with your
unfailing love,
that we may sing for joy[x] and be
glad all our days.[y]
[15]Make us glad for as many days as you
have afflicted us,
for as many years as we have seen
trouble.
[16]May your deeds be shown to your
servants,
your splendor to their children.[z]

[e]*48* Hebrew *Sheol* [f]*50* Or *your servants have*
[g]*10* Or *yet the best of them*

[17]May the favor[h] of the Lord our God
rest upon us;
establish the work of our hands for
us—
yes, establish the work of our
hands.[a]

Psalm 91

In the shadow of the Almighty.

[1]He who dwells in the shelter[b] of the
Most High
will rest in the shadow[c] of the
Almighty.[i]
[2]I will say[j] of the LORD, "He is my
refuge[d] and my fortress,
my God, in whom I trust."

[3]Surely he will save you from the
fowler's snare[e]
and from the deadly pestilence.[f]
[4]He will cover you with his feathers,
and under his wings you will find
refuge;[g]
his faithfulness will be your
shield[h] and rampart.
[5]You will not fear[i] the terror of night,
nor the arrow that flies by day,
[6]nor the pestilence that stalks in the
darkness,
nor the plague that destroys at
midday.
[7]A thousand may fall at your side,
ten thousand at your right hand,
but it will not come near you.
[8]You will only observe with your eyes
and see the punishment of the
wicked.[j]

[9]If you make the Most High your
dwelling—
even the LORD, who is my refuge—
[10]then no harm[k] will befall you,
no disaster will come near your tent.
[11]For he will command his angels[l]
concerning you
to guard you in all your ways;[m]
[12]they will lift you up in their hands,
so that you will not strike your foot
against a stone.[n]
[13]You will tread upon the lion and the
cobra;
you will trample the great lion and
the serpent.[o]

[14]"Because he loves me," says the
LORD, "I will rescue him;
I will protect him, for he
acknowledges my name.
[15]He will call upon me, and I will
answer him;
I will be with him in trouble,
I will deliver him and honor him.[p]
[16]With long life[q] will I satisfy him
and show him my salvation.[r]"

Psalm 92

A psalm. A song. For the
Sabbath day.

The righteous will flourish.

[1]It is good to praise the LORD
and make music to your name,[s]
O Most High,[t]
[2]to proclaim your love in the morning[u]
and your faithfulness at night,
[3]to the music of the ten-stringed lyre
and the melody of the harp.[v]

[4]For you make me glad by your deeds,
O LORD;
I sing for joy at the works of your
hands.[w]
[5]How great are your works,[x] O LORD,
how profound your thoughts![y]
[6]The senseless man[z] does not know,
fools do not understand,
[7]that though the wicked spring up
like grass
and all evildoers flourish,
they will be forever destroyed.

[8]But you, O LORD, are exalted forever.

[9]For surely your enemies, O LORD,
surely your enemies will perish;
all evildoers will be scattered.[a]
[10]You have exalted my horn[k] [b] like that
of a wild ox;
fine oils[c] have been poured upon me.

90:17 [a]Isa 26:12
91:1 [b]Ps 31:20 [c]Ps 17:8
91:2 [d]Ps 142:5
91:3 [e]Ps 124:7; Pr 6:5 [f]1Ki 8:37
91:4 [g]Ps 17:8 [h]Ps 35:2
91:5 [i]Job 5:21
91:8 [j]Ps 37:34; 58:10; Mal 1:5
91:10 [k]Pr 12:21
91:11 [l]Heb 1:14 [m]Ps 34:7
91:12 [n]Mt 4:6*; Lk 4:10-11*
91:13 [o]Da 6:22; Lk 10:19
91:15 [p]1Sa 2:30; Ps 50:15; Jn 12:26
91:16 [q]Dt 6:2; Ps 21:4 [r]Ps 50:23
92:1 [s]Ps 147:1 [t]Ps 135:3
92:2 [u]Ps 89:1
92:3 [v]1Sa 10:5; Ne 12:27; Ps 33:2
92:4 [w]Ps 8:6; 143:5
92:5 [x]Rev 15:3 [y]Ps 40:5; 139:17; Isa 28:29; Ro 11:33
92:6 [z]Ps 73:22
92:9 [a]Ps 68:1; 89:10
92:10 [b]Ps 89:17 [c]Ps 23:5

h *17* Or *beauty* i *1* Hebrew *Shaddai*
j *2* Or *He says* k *10* *Horn* here symbolizes strength.

[11]My eyes have seen the defeat of my
adversaries;
my ears have heard the rout of my
wicked foes.[a]

[12]The righteous will flourish like a
palm tree,
they will grow like a cedar of
Lebanon;[b]
[13]planted in the house of the LORD,
they will flourish in the courts of
our God.[c]
[14]They will still bear fruit[d] in old age,
they will stay fresh and green,
[15]proclaiming, "The LORD is upright;
he is my Rock, and there is no
wickedness in him.[e]"

Psalm 93

The LORD is robed in majesty.

[1]The LORD reigns,[f] he is robed in
majesty;[g]
the LORD is robed in majesty
and is armed with strength.[h]
The world is firmly established;
it cannot be moved.[i]
[2]Your throne was established long ago;
you are from all eternity.[j]

[3]The seas[k] have lifted up, O LORD,
the seas have lifted up their voice;
the seas have lifted up their
pounding waves.
[4]Mightier than the thunder[l] of the
great waters,
mightier than the breakers of the
sea—
the LORD on high is mighty.

[5]Your statutes stand firm;
holiness[m] adorns your house
for endless days, O LORD.

Psalm 94

God avenges.

[1]O LORD, the God who avenges,[n]
O God who avenges, shine forth.[o]
[2]Rise up, O Judge[p] of the earth;
pay back[q] to the proud what they
deserve.
[3]How long will the wicked, O LORD,
how long will the wicked be jubilant?

[4]They pour out arrogant[r] words;
all the evildoers are full of
boasting.[s]
[5]They crush your people,[t] O LORD;
they oppress your inheritance.
[6]They slay the widow and the alien;
they murder the fatherless.
[7]They say, "The LORD does not see;[u]
the God of Jacob pays no heed."

[8]Take heed, you senseless ones[v]
among the people;
you fools, when will you become
wise?

[9]Does he who implanted the ear not
hear?
Does he who formed the eye not
see?[w]
[10]Does he who disciplines nations not
punish?
Does he who teaches[x] man lack
knowledge?
[11]The LORD knows the thoughts of man;
he knows that they are futile.[y]

[12]Blessed is the man you discipline,[z]
O LORD,
the man you teach[a] from your law;
[13]you grant him relief from days of
trouble,
till a pit[b] is dug for the wicked.
[14]For the LORD will not reject his
people;[c]
he will never forsake his
inheritance.
[15]Judgment will again be founded on
righteousness,[d]
and all the upright in heart will
follow it.

[16]Who will rise up[e] for me against the
wicked?
Who will take a stand for me
against evildoers?[f]
[17]Unless the LORD had given me help,[g]
I would soon have dwelt in the
silence of death.
[18]When I said, "My foot is slipping,[h]"
your love, O LORD, supported me.
[19]When anxiety was great within me,
your consolation brought joy to my
soul.

92:11 [a]Ps 54:7; 91:8 **92:12** [b]Ps 1:3; 52:8; Jer 17:8; Hos 14:6 **92:13** [c]Ps 100:4 **92:14** [d]Jn 15:2 **92:15** [e]Job 34:10 **93:1** [f]Ps 97:1 [g]Ps 104:1 [h]Ps 65:6 [i]Ps 96:10 **93:2** [j]Ps 45:6 **93:3** [k]Ps 96:11 **93:4** [l]Ps 65:7 **93:5** [m]Ps 29:2 **94:1** [n]Na 1:2; Ro 12:19 [o]Ps 80:1 **94:2** [p]Ge 18:25 [q]Ps 31:23 **94:4** [r]Ps 31:18 [s]Ps 52:1 **94:5** [t]Isa 3:15 **94:7** [u]Job 22:14; Ps 10:11 **94:8** [v]Ps 92:6 **94:9** [w]Ex 4:11; Pr 20:12 **94:10** [x]Job 35:11; Isa 28:26 **94:11** [y]1Co 3:20* **94:12** [z]Job 5:17; Heb 12:5 [a]Dt 8:3 **94:13** [b]Ps 55:23 **94:14** [c]1Sa 12:22; Ps 37:28; Ro 11:2 **94:15** [d]Ps 97:2 **94:16** [e]Nu 10:35; Ps 17:13 [f]Ps 59:2 **94:17** [g]Ps 124:2 **94:18** [h]Ps 38:16

[20]Can a corrupt throne be allied with
you—
one that brings on misery by its
decrees?[a]
[21]They band together[b] against the
righteous
and condemn the innocent[c] to death.
[22]But the LORD has become my fortress,
and my God the rock in whom I
take refuge.[d]
[23]He will repay[e] them for their sins
and destroy them for their
wickedness;
the LORD our God will destroy them.

Psalm 95

The great King above all gods.

[1]Come, let us sing for joy to the LORD;
let us shout aloud[f] to the Rock[g] of
our salvation.
[2]Let us come before him[h] with
thanksgiving
and extol him with music[i] and song.

[3]For the LORD is the great God,[j]
the great King above all gods.[k]
[4]In his hand are the depths of the earth,
and the mountain peaks belong to
him.
[5]The sea is his, for he made it,
and his hands formed the dry land.[l]

[6]Come, let us bow down[m] in worship,
let us kneel[n] before the LORD our
Maker;[o]
[7]for he is our God
and we are the people of his
pasture,[p]
the flock under his care.

Today, if you hear his voice,
[8] do not harden your hearts as you
did at Meribah,[l][q]
as you did that day at Massah[m] in
the desert,
[9]where your fathers tested[r] and tried
me,
though they had seen what I did.
[10]For forty years[s] I was angry with that
generation;
I said, "They are a people whose
hearts go astray,
and they have not known my ways."
[11]So I declared on oath[t] in my anger,
"They shall never enter my rest."[u]

Psalm 96

96:1-13pp— 1Ch16:23-33

Worship the LORD in his holiness.

[1]Sing to the LORD[v] a new song;
sing to the LORD, all the earth.
[2]Sing to the LORD, praise his name;
proclaim his salvation[w] day after day.
[3]Declare his glory among the nations,
his marvelous deeds among all
peoples.

[4]For great is the LORD and most
worthy of praise;[x]
he is to be feared[y] above all gods.[z]
[5]For all the gods of the nations are idols,
but the LORD made the heavens.[a]
[6]Splendor and majesty are before him;
strength and glory[b] are in his
sanctuary.

[7]Ascribe to the LORD,[c] O families of
nations,[d]
ascribe to the LORD glory and
strength.
[8]Ascribe to the LORD the glory due his
name;
bring an offering[e] and come into
his courts.
[9]Worship the LORD in the splendor of
his[n] holiness;[f]
tremble[g] before him, all the earth.[h]

[10]Say among the nations, "The LORD
reigns.[i]"
The world is firmly established, it
cannot be moved;[j]
he will judge the peoples with
equity.[k]
[11]Let the heavens rejoice, let the earth
be glad;[l]
let the sea resound, and all that is
in it;

94:20 [a]Ps 58:2 **94:21** [b]Ps 56:6 [c]Ps 106:38; Pr 17:15,26 **94:22** [d]Ps 18:2; 59:9 **94:23** [e]Ps 7:16 **95:1** [f]Ps 81:1 [g]2Sa 22:47 **95:2** [h]Mic 6:6 [i]Ps 81:2; Eph 5:19 **95:3** [j]Ps 48:1; 145:3 [k]Ps 96:4; 97:9 **95:5** [l]Ge 1:9; Ps 146:6 **95:6** [m]Php 2:10 [n]2Ch 6:13 [o]Ps 100:3; 149:2; Isa 17:7; Da 6:10-11; Hos 8:14 **95:7** [p]Ps 74:1; 79:13 **95:8** [q]Ex 17:7 **95:9** [r]Nu 14:22; Ps 78:18; 1Co 10:9 **95:10** [s]Ac 7:36; Heb 3:17 **95:11** [t]Nu 14:23 [u]Dt 1:35; Heb 4:3* **96:1** [v]1Ch 16:23 **96:2** [w]Ps 71:15 **96:4** [x]Ps 18:3; 145:3 [y]Ps 89:7 [z]Ps 95:3 **96:5** [a]Ps 115:15 **96:6** [b]Ps 29:1 **96:7** [c]Ps 29:1 [d]Ps 22:27 **96:8** [e]Ps 45:12; 72:10 **96:9** [f]Ps 29:2 [g]Ps 114:7 [h]Ps 33:8

96:10 [i]Ps 97:1 [j]Ps 93:1 [k]Ps 67:4 **96:11** [l]Ps 97:1; 98:7; Isa 49:13

[l]*8 Meribah* means *quarreling.* [m]*8 Massah* means *testing.* [n]*9* Or *LORD with the splendor of*

12 let the fields be jubilant, and
everything in them.
Then all the trees of the forest[a] will
sing for joy;[b]
13 they will sing before the LORD, for
he comes,
he comes to judge[c] the earth.
He will judge the world in
righteousness
and the peoples in his truth.

Psalm 97

The heavens proclaim
the LORD's righteousness.

1The LORD reigns,[d] let the earth be
glad;[e]
let the distant shores rejoice.

2Clouds and thick darkness[f] surround
him;
righteousness and justice are the
foundation of his throne.[g]
3Fire[h] goes before[i] him
and consumes[j] his foes on every
side.
4His lightning lights up the world;
the earth sees and trembles.[k]
5The mountains melt[l] like wax before
the LORD,
before the Lord of all the earth.[m]
6The heavens proclaim his
righteousness,[n]
and all the peoples see his glory.[o]

7All who worship images[p] are put to
shame,[q]
those who boast in idols—
worship him,[r] all you gods!

8Zion hears and rejoices
and the villages of Judah are glad
because of your judgments,[s] O LORD.
9For you, O LORD, are the Most High
over all the earth;[t]
you are exalted[u] far above all gods.

10Let those who love the LORD hate
evil,[v]
for he guards the lives of his
faithful ones[w]
and delivers[x] them from the hand
of the wicked.[y]

96:12 [a]Isa 44:23 [b]Ps 65:13
96:13 [c]Rev 19:11
97:1 [d]Ps 96:10 [e]Ps 96:11
97:2 [f]Ex 19:9; Ps 18:11 [g]Ps 89:14
97:3 [h]Da 7:10 [i]Hab 3:5 [j]Ps 18:8
97:4 [k]Ps 104:32
97:5 [l]Ps 46:2,6; Mic 1:4 [m]Jos 3:11
97:6 [n]Ps 50:6 [o]Ps 19:1
97:7 [p]Lev 26:1 [q]Jer 10:14 [r]Heb 1:6
97:8 [s]Ps 48:11
97:9 [t]Ps 83:18; 95:3 [u]Ex 18:11
97:10 [v]Ps 34:14; Am 5:15; Ro 12:9 [w]Pr 2:8 [x]Da 3:28 [y]Ps 37:40; Jer 15:21
97:11 [z]Job 22:28
97:12 [a]Ps 30:4
98:1 [b]Ps 96:1 [c]Ps 96:3 [d]Ex 15:6 [e]Isa 52:10
98:2 [f]Isa 52:10
98:3 [g]Lk 1:54
98:4 [h]Isa 44:23
98:5 [i]Ps 92:3 [j]Isa 51:3
98:6 [k]Nu 10:10 [l]Ps 47:7
98:7 [m]Ps 24:1
98:8 [n]Isa 55:12

11Light is shed[z] upon the righteous
and joy on the upright in heart.
12Rejoice in the LORD, you who are
righteous,
and praise his holy name.[a]

Psalm 98

A psalm.

Sing praises to the LORD.

1Sing to the LORD a new song,[b]
for he has done marvelous things;[c]
his right hand[d] and his holy arm[e]
have worked salvation for him.
2The LORD has made his salvation
known[f]
and revealed his righteousness to
the nations.
3He has remembered[g] his love
and his faithfulness to the house of
Israel;
all the ends of the earth have seen
the salvation of our God.

4Shout for joy[h] to the LORD, all the
earth,
burst into jubilant song with
music;
5make music to the LORD with the
harp,[i]
with the harp and the sound of
singing,[j]
6with trumpets[k] and the blast of the
ram's horn—
shout for joy before the LORD, the
King.[l]

7Let the sea resound, and everything
in it,
the world, and all who live in it.[m]
8Let the rivers clap their hands,
let the mountains[n] sing together
for joy;
9let them sing before the LORD,
for he comes to judge the earth.
He will judge the world in
righteousness
and the peoples with equity.[o]

98:9 [o]Ps 96:10

Psalm 99

The holy God of Zion.

[1]The LORD reigns,[a]
let the nations tremble;
he sits enthroned between the cherubim,[b]
let the earth shake.
[2]Great is the LORD[c] in Zion;
he is exalted[d] over all the nations.
[3]Let them praise your great and awesome name[e]—
he is holy.

[4]The King is mighty, he loves justice[f]—
you have established equity;[g]
in Jacob you have done
what is just and right.
[5]Exalt[h] the LORD our God
and worship at his footstool;
he is holy.

[6]Moses[i] and Aaron were among his priests,
Samuel[j] was among those who called on his name;
they called on the LORD
and he answered[k] them.
[7]He spoke to them from the pillar of cloud;[l]
they kept his statutes and the decrees he gave them.

[8]O LORD our God,
you answered them;
you were to Israel[o] a forgiving God,[m]
though you punished their misdeeds.[p]
[9]Exalt the LORD our God
and worship at his holy mountain,
for the LORD our God is holy.

Psalm 100

A psalm. For giving thanks.

Worship the LORD with gladness.

[1]Shout for joy[n] to the LORD, all the earth.
[2] Worship the LORD with gladness;
come before him[o] with joyful songs.
[3]Know that the LORD is God.[p]
It is he who made us,[q] and we are his[q];
we are his people, the sheep of his pasture.[r]

[4]Enter his gates with thanksgiving
and his courts with praise;
give thanks to him and praise his name.[s]
[5]For the LORD is good[t] and his love endures forever;[u]
his faithfulness[v] continues through all generations.

Psalm 101

Of David. A psalm.

A blameless life, heart and walk.

[1]I will sing of your love[w] and justice;
to you, O LORD, I will sing praise.
[2]I will be careful to lead a blameless life—
when will you come to me?

I will walk in my house
with blameless heart.
[3]I will set before my eyes
no vile thing.[x]

The deeds of faithless men I hate;[y]
they will not cling to me.
[4]Men of perverse heart[z] shall be far from me;
I will have nothing to do with evil.

[5]Whoever slanders his neighbor[a] in secret,
him will I put to silence;
whoever has haughty eyes[b] and a proud heart,
him will I not endure.

[6]My eyes will be on the faithful in the land,
that they may dwell with me;
he whose walk is blameless[c]
will minister to me.

99:1 [a]Ps 97:1 [b]Ex 25:22
99:2 [c]Ps 48:1 [d]Ps 97:9; 113:4
99:3 [e]Ps 76:1
99:4 [f]Ps 11:7 [g]Ps 98:9
99:5 [h]Ps 132:7
99:6 [i]Ex 24:6 [j]Jer 15:1 [k]1Sa 7:9
99:7 [l]Ex 33:9
99:8 [m]Nu 14:20
100:1 [n]Ps 98:4
100:2 [o]Ps 95:2
100:3 [p]Ps 46:10 [q]Job 10:3 [r]Ps 74:1; Eze 34:31
100:4 [s]Ps 116:17
100:5 [t]1Ch 16:34; Ps 25:8 [u]Ezr 3:11; Ps 106:1 [v]Ps 119:90
101:1 [w]Ps 51:14; 89:1; 145:7
101:3 [x]Dt 15:9 [y]Ps 40:4
101:4 [z]Pr 11:20
101:5 [a]Ps 50:20 [b]Ps 10:5; Pr 6:17
101:6 [c]Ps 119:1

[o]8 Hebrew *them* [p]8 Or / *an avenger of the wrongs done to them* [q]3 Or *and not we ourselves*

7No one who practices deceit
will dwell in my house;
no one who speaks falsely
will stand in my presence.

8Every morning[a] I will put to silence
all the wicked[b] in the land;
I will cut off every evildoer[c]
from the city of the LORD.[d]

Psalm 102

A prayer of an afflicted man.
When he is faint and pours out
his lament before the LORD.

Prayer of the distressed and destitute.

1Hear my prayer, O LORD;
let my cry for help[e] come to you.
2Do not hide your face[f] from me
when I am in distress.
Turn your ear to me;
when I call, answer me quickly.

3For my days vanish like smoke;[g]
my bones burn like glowing
embers.
4My heart is blighted and withered
like grass;[h]
I forget to eat my food.
5Because of my loud groaning
I am reduced to skin and bones.
6I am like a desert owl,[i]
like an owl among the ruins.
7I lie awake;[j] I have become
like a bird alone[k] on a roof.
8All day long my enemies taunt me;
those who rail against me use my
name as a curse.
9For I eat ashes as my food
and mingle my drink with tears[l]
10because of your great wrath,[m]
for you have taken me up and
thrown me aside.
11My days are like the evening shadow;[n]
I wither away like grass.

12But you, O LORD, sit enthroned
forever;[o]
your renown endures[p] through all
generations.
13You will arise and have compassion[q]
on Zion,
for it is time to show favor to her;
the appointed time has come.
14For her stones are dear to your
servants;
her very dust moves them to pity.
15The nations will fear[r] the name of
the LORD,
all the kings[s] of the earth will
revere your glory.
16For the LORD will rebuild Zion
and appear in his glory.[t]
17He will respond to the prayer[u] of the
destitute;
he will not despise their plea.

18Let this be written[v] for a future
generation,
that a people not yet created[w] may
praise the LORD:
19"The LORD looked down[x] from his
sanctuary on high,
from heaven he viewed the earth,
20to hear the groans of the prisoners[y]
and release those condemned to
death."
21So the name of the LORD will be
declared[z] in Zion
and his praise in Jerusalem
22when the peoples and the kingdoms
assemble to worship the LORD.

23In the course of my life[r] he broke my
strength;
he cut short my days.
24So I said:
"Do not take me away, O my God,
in the midst of my days;
your years go on[a] through all
generations.
25In the beginning[b] you laid the
foundations of the earth,
and the heavens are the work of
your hands.
26They will perish,[c] but you remain;
they will all wear out like a garment.
Like clothing you will change them
and they will be discarded.
27But you remain the same,[d]
and your years will never end.

101:8 [a]Jer 21:12 [b]Ps 75:10 [c]Ps 118:10-12 [d]Ps 46:4
102:1 [e]Ex 2:23
102:2 [f]Ps 69:17
102:3 [g]Jas 4:14
102:4 [h]Ps 37:2
102:6 [i]Job 30:29; Isa 34:11
102:7 [j]Ps 77:4 [k]Ps 38:11
102:9 [l]Ps 42:3
102:10 [m]Ps 38:3
102:11 [n]Job 14:2
102:12 [o]Ps 9:7 [p]Ps 135:13
102:13 [q]Isa 60:10
102:15 [r]1Ki 8:43 [s]Ps 138:4
102:16 [t]Isa 60:1-2
102:17 [u]Ne 1:6
102:18 [v]Ro 15:4 [w]Ps 22:31
102:19 [x]Dt 26:15
102:20 [y]Ps 79:11
102:21 [z]Ps 22:22
102:24 [a]Ps 90:2; Isa 38:10
102:25 [b]Ge 1:1; Heb 1:10-12*
102:26 [c]Isa 34:4; Mt 24:35; 2Pe 3:7-10; Rev 20:11
102:27 [d]Mal 3:6; Heb 13:8; Jas 1:17

[r]23 Or *By his power*

[28]The children of your servants[a] will
live in your presence;
their descendants[b] will be
established before you."

Psalm 103

Of David.

The LORD is compassionate.

[1]Praise the LORD, O my soul;[c]
all my inmost being, praise his holy
name.
[2]Praise the LORD, O my soul,
and forget not all his benefits—
[3]who forgives all your sins[d]
and heals[e] all your diseases,
[4]who redeems your life from the pit
and crowns you with love and
compassion,
[5]who satisfies your desires with good
things
so that your youth is renewed like
the eagle's.[f]

[6]The LORD works righteousness
and justice for all the oppressed.

[7]He made known[g] his ways[h] to Moses,
his deeds[i] to the people of Israel:
[8]The LORD is compassionate and
gracious,[j]
slow to anger, abounding in love.
[9]He will not always accuse,
nor will he harbor his anger
forever;[k]
[10]he does not treat us as our sins
deserve[l]
or repay us according to our
iniquities.
[11]For as high as the heavens are above
the earth,
so great is his love[m] for those who
fear him;
[12]as far as the east is from the west,
so far has he removed our
transgressions[n] from us.
[13]As a father has compassion[o] on his
children,
so the LORD has compassion on
those who fear him;
[14]for he knows how we are formed,[p]
he remembers that we are dust.
[15]As for man, his days are like grass,[q]
he flourishes like a flower[r] of the
field;
[16]the wind blows[s] over it and it is gone,
and its place[t] remembers it no more.
[17]But from everlasting to everlasting
the LORD's love is with those who
fear him,
and his righteousness with their
children's children—
[18]with those who keep his covenant
and remember to obey his
precepts.[u]

[19]The LORD has established his throne
in heaven,
and his kingdom rules[v] over all.

[20]Praise the LORD, you his angels,[w]
you mighty ones[x] who do his
bidding,
who obey his word.
[21]Praise the LORD, all his heavenly
hosts,[y]
you his servants who do his will.
[22]Praise the LORD, all his works[z]
everywhere in his dominion.

Praise the LORD, O my soul.

Psalm 104

God's creation and providence.

[1]Praise the LORD, O my soul.[a]

O LORD my God, you are very great;
you are clothed with splendor and
majesty.
[2]He wraps[b] himself in light as with a
garment;
he stretches out the heavens[c] like
a tent
[3] and lays the beams[d] of his upper
chambers on their waters.
He makes the clouds[e] his chariot
and rides on the wings of the wind.[f]
[4]He makes winds his messengers,[s][g]
flames of fire[h] his servants.

[5]He set the earth[i] on its foundations;
it can never be moved.

102:28 [a]Ps 69:36 [b]Ps 89:4
103:1 [c]Ps 104:1
103:3 [d]Ps 130:8 [e]Ex 15:26
103:5 [f]Isa 40:31
103:7 [g]Ps 99:7; 147:19 [h]Ex 33:13 [i]Ps 106:22
103:8 [j]Ex 34:6; Ps 86:15; Jas 5:11
103:9 [k]Ps 30:5; Isa 57:16; Jer 3:5,12; Mic 7:18
103:10 [l]Ezr 9:13
103:11 [m]Ps 57:10
103:12 [n]2Sa 12:13
103:13 [o]Mal 3:17
103:14 [p]Isa 29:16
103:15 [q]Ps 90:5 [r]Job 14:2; Jas 1:10; 1Pe 1:24
103:16 [s]Isa 40:7 [t]Job 7:10
103:18 [u]Dt 7:9
103:19 [v]Ps 47:2
103:20 [w]Ps 148:2; Heb 1:14 [x]Ps 29:1
103:21 [y]1Ki 22:19
103:22 [z]Ps 145:10
104:1 [a]Ps 103:22
104:2 [b]Da 7:9 [c]Isa 40:22
104:3 [d]Am 9:6 [e]Isa 19:1 [f]Ps 18:10
104:4 [g]Ps 148:8; Heb 1:7* [h]2Ki 2:11
104:5 [i]Job 26:7; Ps 24:1-2

s4 Or *angels*

[6]You covered it[a] with the deep[b] as
with a garment;
the waters stood above the
mountains.
[7]But at your rebuke[c] the waters fled,
at the sound of your thunder they
took to flight;
[8]they flowed over the mountains,
they went down into the valleys,
to the place you assigned[d] for them.
[9]You set a boundary they cannot cross;
never again will they cover the earth.

[10]He makes springs[e] pour water into
the ravines;
it flows between the mountains.
[11]They give water to all the beasts of
the field;
the wild donkeys quench their thirst.
[12]The birds of the air[f] nest by the waters;
they sing among the branches.
[13]He waters the mountains[g] from his
upper chambers;
the earth is satisfied by the fruit of
his work.
[14]He makes grass grow[h] for the cattle,
and plants for man to cultivate—
bringing forth food[i] from the earth:
[15]wine[j] that gladdens the heart of man,
oil[k] to make his face shine,
and bread that sustains his heart.
[16]The trees of the LORD are well watered,
the cedars of Lebanon that he
planted.
[17]There the birds[l] make their nests;
the stork has its home in the pine
trees.
[18]The high mountains belong to the
wild goats;
the crags are a refuge for the
coneys.[t] [m]

[19]The moon marks off the seasons,[n]
and the sun[o] knows when to go
down.
[20]You bring darkness,[p] it becomes
night,[q]
and all the beasts of the forest[r] prowl.
[21]The lions roar for their prey
and seek their food from God.[s]
[22]The sun rises, and they steal away;
they return and lie down in their
dens.[t]

104:6 [a]Ge 7:19 [b]Ge 1:2 **104:7** [c]Ps 18:15 **104:8** [d]Ps 33:7 **104:10** [e]Ps 107:33; Isa 41:18 **104:12** [f]Mt 8:20 **104:13** [g]Ps 147:8; Jer 10:13 **104:14** [h]Job 38:27; Ps 147:8 [i]Ge 1:30; Job 28:5 **104:15** [j]Jdg 9:13 [k]Ps 23:5; 92:10; Lk 7:46 **104:17** [l]ver 12 **104:18** [m]Pr 30:26 **104:19** [n]Ge 1:14 [o]Ps 19:6 **104:20** [p]Isa 45:7 [q]Ps 74:16 [r]Ps 50:10 **104:21** [s]Job 38:39; Ps 145:15; Joel 1:20 **104:22** [t]Job 37:8 **104:23** [u]Ge 3:19 **104:24** [v]Ps 40:5 [w]Pr 3:19 **104:25** [x]Ps 69:34 **104:26** [y]Ps 107:23; Eze 27:9 [z]Job 41:1 **104:27** [a]Job 36:31; Ps 136:25; 145:15; 147:9 **104:28** [b]Ps 145:16 **104:29** [c]Dt 31:17 [d]Job 34:14; Ecc 12:7 **104:31** [e]Ge 1:31 **104:32** [f]Ps 97:4 [g]Ex 19:18 [h]Ps 144:5

[23]Then man goes out to his work,[u]
to his labor until evening.

[24]How many are your works,[v] O LORD!
In wisdom you made[w] them all;
the earth is full of your creatures.
[25]There is the sea,[x] vast and spacious,
teeming with creatures beyond
number—
living things both large and small.
[26]There the ships[y] go to and fro,
and the leviathan,[z] which you
formed to frolic there.

[27]These all look to you
to give them their food[a] at the
proper time.
[28]When you give it to them,
they gather it up;
when you open your hand,
they are satisfied[b] with good things.
[29]When you hide your face,[c]
they are terrified;
when you take away their breath,
they die and return to the dust.[d]
[30]When you send your Spirit,
they are created,
and you renew the face of the earth.

[31]May the glory of the LORD endure
forever;
may the LORD rejoice in his works[e]—
[32]he who looks at the earth, and it
trembles,[f]
who touches the mountains,[g] and
they smoke.[h]

[33]I will sing[i] to the LORD all my life;
I will sing praise to my God as long
as I live.
[34]May my meditation be pleasing to him,
as I rejoice[j] in the LORD.
[35]But may sinners vanish[k] from the
earth
and the wicked be no more.

Praise the LORD, O my soul.

Praise the LORD.[u] [l]

104:33 [i]Ps 63:4 **104:34** [j]Ps 9:2 **104:35** [k]Ps 37:38 [l]Ps 105:45; 106:48

[t]*18* That is, the hyrax or rock badger [u]*35* Hebrew *Hallelu Yah*; in the Septuagint this line stands at the beginning of Psalm 105.

Psalm 105

105:1-15pp— 1Ch16:8-22

Recalling the LORD's provisions for his people.

1Give thanks to the LORD,[a] call on his
name;[b]
make known among the nations
what he has done.
2Sing to him,[c] sing praise to him;
tell of all his wonderful acts.
3Glory in his holy name;
let the hearts of those who seek
the LORD rejoice.
4Look to the LORD and his strength;
seek his face[d] always.

5Remember the wonders[e] he has
done,
his miracles, and the judgments he
pronounced,[f]
6O descendants of Abraham his
servant,[g]
O sons of Jacob, his chosen[h] ones.
7He is the LORD our God;
his judgments are in all the earth.

8He remembers his covenant[i] forever,
the word he commanded, for a
thousand generations,
9the covenant he made with Abraham,[j]
the oath he swore to Isaac.
10He confirmed it[k] to Jacob as a decree,
to Israel as an everlasting covenant:
11"To you I will give the land of Canaan[l]
as the portion you will inherit."

12When they were but few in number,[m]
few indeed, and strangers in it,[n]
13they wandered from nation to nation,
from one kingdom to another.
14He allowed no one to oppress[o] them;
for their sake he rebuked kings:[p]
15"Do not touch[q] my anointed ones;
do my prophets no harm."

16He called down famine[r] on the land
and destroyed all their supplies of
food;
17and he sent a man before them—
Joseph, sold as a slave.[s]
18They bruised his feet with shackles,[t]
his neck was put in irons,
19till what he foretold[u] came to pass,
till the word of the LORD proved
him true.
20The king sent and released him,
the ruler of peoples set him free.[v]
21He made him master of his household,
ruler over all he possessed,
22to instruct his princes[w] as he pleased
and teach his elders wisdom.

23Then Israel entered Egypt;[x]
Jacob lived as an alien in the land
of Ham.
24The LORD made his people very fruitful;
he made them too numerous[y] for
their foes,
25whose hearts he turned[z] to hate his
people,
to conspire[a] against his servants.
26He sent Moses[b] his servant,
and Aaron, whom he had chosen.[c]
27They performed[d] his miraculous
signs among them,
his wonders in the land of Ham.
28He sent darkness[e] and made the land
dark—
for had they not rebelled against
his words?
29He turned their waters into blood,[f]
causing their fish to die.[g]
30Their land teemed with frogs,[h]
which went up into the bedrooms
of their rulers.
31He spoke, and there came swarms of
flies,[i]
and gnats[j] throughout their country.
32He turned their rain into hail,[k]
with lightning throughout their
land;
33he struck down their vines[l] and fig
trees
and shattered the trees of their
country.
34He spoke, and the locusts came,[m]
grasshoppers without number;
35they ate up every green thing in
their land,
ate up the produce of their soil.

105:1 [a]1Ch 16:34 [b]Ps 99:6
105:2 [c]Ps 96:1
105:4 [d]Ps 27:8
105:5 [e]Ps 40:5 [f]Ps 77:11
105:6 [g]ver 42 [h]Ps 106:5
105:8 [i]Ps 106:45; Lk 1:72
105:9 [j]Ge 12:7; 17:2; 22:16-18; Gal 3:15-18
105:10 [k]Ge 28:13-15
105:11 [l]Ge 13:15; 15:18
105:12 [m]Ge 34:30; Dt 7:7 [n]Ge 23:4; Heb 11:9
105:14 [o]Ge 35:5 [p]Ge 12:17-20
105:15 [q]Ge 26:11
105:16 [r]Ge 41:54; Lev 26:26; Isa 3:1; Eze 4:16
105:17 [s]Ge 37:28; 45:5; Ac 7:9
105:18 [t]Ge 40:15
105:19 [u]Ge 40:20-22
105:20 [v]Ge 41:14
105:22 [w]Ge 41:43-44
105:23 [x]Ge 46:6; Ac 13:17
105:24 [y]Ex 1:7,9
105:25 [z]Ex 4:21 [a]Ex 1:6-10; Ac 7:19
105:26 [b]Ex 3:10 [c]Nu 16:5; 17:5-8
105:27 [d]Ex 7:8–12:51
105:28 [e]Ex 10:22
105:29 [f]Ps 78:44 [g]Ex 7:21 **105:30** [h]Ex 8:2,6
105:31 [i]Ex 8:21-24 [j]Ex 8:16-18 **105:32** [k]Ex 9:22-25
105:33 [l]Ps 78:47 **105:34** [m]Ex 10:4,12-15

[36]Then he struck down all the
firstborn[a] in their land,
the firstfruits of all their manhood.
[37]He brought out Israel, laden with
silver and gold,[b]
and from among their tribes no
one faltered.
[38]Egypt was glad when they left,
because dread of Israel[c] had fallen
on them.
[39]He spread out a cloud[d] as a covering,
and a fire to give light at night.[e]
[40]They asked,[f] and he brought them
quail[g]
and satisfied them with the bread
of heaven.[h]
[41]He opened the rock,[i] and water
gushed out;
like a river it flowed in the desert.

[42]For he remembered his holy promise[j]
given to his servant Abraham.
[43]He brought out his people with
rejoicing,[k]
his chosen ones with shouts of joy;
[44]he gave them the lands of the nations,[l]
and they fell heir to what others
had toiled for—
[45]that they might keep his precepts
and observe his laws.[m]

Praise the LORD.[v]

Psalm 106

106:1,47-48pp— 1Ch16:34-36

Recalling the sins of God's people.

[1]Praise the LORD.[w]

Give thanks to the LORD, for he is
good;[n]
his love endures forever.
[2]Who can proclaim the mighty acts[o]
of the LORD
or fully declare his praise?
[3]Blessed are they who maintain justice,
who constantly do what is right.[p]
[4]Remember me,[q] O LORD, when you
show favor to your people,
come to my aid when you save them,
[5]that I may enjoy the prosperity[r] of
your chosen ones,
that I may share in the joy[s] of your
nation
and join your inheritance in giving
praise.

[6]We have sinned,[t] even as our fathers
did;
we have done wrong and acted
wickedly.
[7]When our fathers were in Egypt,
they gave no thought to your
miracles;
they did not remember[u] your many
kindnesses,
and they rebelled by the sea,[v] the
Red Sea.[x]
[8]Yet he saved them for his name's
sake,[w]
to make his mighty power known.
[9]He rebuked[x] the Red Sea, and it
dried up;[y]
he led them through[z] the depths
as through a desert.
[10]He saved them[a] from the hand of
the foe;
from the hand of the enemy he
redeemed them.[b]
[11]The waters covered[c] their
adversaries;
not one of them survived.
[12]Then they believed his promises
and sang his praise.[d]

[13]But they soon forgot[e] what he had
done
and did not wait for his counsel.
[14]In the desert they gave in to their
craving;
in the wasteland they put God to
the test.[f]
[15]So he gave them[g] what they asked for,
but sent a wasting disease[h] upon
them.

[16]In the camp they grew envious[i] of
Moses
and of Aaron, who was
consecrated to the LORD.

105:36 [a]Ex 12:29 **105:37** [b]Ex 12:35 **105:38** [c]Ex 12:33; 15:16 **105:39** [d]Ex 13:21 [e]Ne 9:12; Ps 78:14 **105:40** [f]Ps 78:18,24 [g]Ex 16:13 [h]Jn 6:31 **105:41** [i]Ex 17:6; Nu 20:11; Ps 78:15-16; 1Co 10:4 **105:42** [j]Ge 15:13-16 **105:43** [k]Ex 15:1-18; Ps 106:12 **105:44** [l]Jos 13:6-7 **105:45** [m]Dt 4:40; 6:21-24 **106:1** [n]Ps 100:5; 105:1 **106:2** [o]Ps 145:4,12 **106:3** [p]Ps 15:2 **106:4** [q]Ps 119:132 **106:5** [r]Ps 1:3 [s]Ps 118:15 **106:6** [t]Da 9:5 **106:7** [u]Ps 78:11,42 [v]Ex 14:11-12 **106:8** [w]Ex 9:16 **106:9** [x]Ps 18:15 [y]Ex 14:21; Na 1:4 [z]Isa 63:11-14 **106:10** [a]Ex 14:30 [b]Ps 107:2 **106:11** [c]Ex 14:28; 15:5 **106:12** [d]Ex 15:1-21 **106:13** [e]Ex 15:24 **106:14** [f]1Co 10:9 **106:15** [g]Nu 11:31 [h]Isa 10:16 **106:16** [i]Nu 16:1-3

[v]*45* Hebrew *Hallelu Yah* [w]*1* Hebrew *Hallelu Yah*; also in verse 48 [x]*7* Hebrew *Yam Suph*; that is, Sea of Reeds; also in verses 9 and 22

17The earth opened[a] up and
swallowed Dathan;
it buried the company of Abiram.
18Fire blazed[b] among their followers;
a flame consumed the wicked.

19At Horeb they made a calf[c]
and worshiped an idol cast from
metal.
20They exchanged their Glory[d]
for an image of a bull, which eats
grass.
21They forgot the God[e] who saved them,
who had done great things[f] in
Egypt,
22miracles in the land of Ham[g]
and awesome deeds by the Red Sea.
23So he said he would destroy[h] them—
had not Moses, his chosen one,
stood in the breach[i] before him
to keep his wrath from destroying
them.

24Then they despised the pleasant
land;[j]
they did not believe[k] his promise.
25They grumbled[l] in their tents
and did not obey the LORD.
26So he swore[m] to them with uplifted
hand
that he would make them fall in
the desert,[n]
27make their descendants fall among
the nations
and scatter[o] them throughout the
lands.

28They yoked themselves to the Baal of
Peor[p]
and ate sacrifices offered to lifeless
gods;
29they provoked the LORD to anger by
their wicked deeds,
and a plague broke out among them.
30But Phinehas stood up and intervened,
and the plague was checked.[q]
31This was credited to him[r] as
righteousness
for endless generations to come.

32By the waters of Meribah[s] they
angered the LORD,
and trouble came to Moses
because of them;
33for they rebelled against the Spirit of
God,
and rash words came from Moses'
lips.[y][t]

34They did not destroy[u] the peoples
as the LORD had commanded[v] them,
35but they mingled[w] with the nations
and adopted their customs.
36They worshiped their idols,[x]
which became a snare to them.
37They sacrificed their sons[y]
and their daughters to demons.
38They shed innocent blood,
the blood of their sons[z] and
daughters,
whom they sacrificed to the idols of
Canaan,
and the land was desecrated by
their blood.
39They defiled themselves[a] by what
they did;
by their deeds they prostituted[b]
themselves.

40Therefore the LORD was angry[c] with
his people
and abhorred his inheritance.[d]
41He handed them over[e] to the nations,
and their foes ruled over them.
42Their enemies oppressed them
and subjected them to their power.
43Many times he delivered them,
but they were bent on rebellion[f]
and they wasted away in their sin.

44But he took note of their distress
when he heard their cry;[g]
45for their sake he remembered his
covenant[h]
and out of his great love[i] he relented.
46He caused them to be pitied[j]
by all who held them captive.

47Save us, O LORD our God,
and gather us[k] from the nations,
that we may give thanks to your holy
name
and glory in your praise.

106:17 [a]Dt 11:6
106:18 [b]Nu 16:35
106:19 [c]Ex 32:4
106:20 [d]Jer 2:11; Ro 1:23
106:21 [e]Ps 78:11 [f]Dt 10:21
106:22 [g]Ps 105:27
106:23 [h]Ex 32:10 [i]Ex 32:11-14
106:24 [j]Dt 8:7; Eze 20:6 [k]Heb 3:18-19
106:25 [l]Nu 14:2
106:26 [m]Eze 20:15; Heb 3:11 [n]Nu 14:28-35
106:27 [o]Lev 26:33; Ps 44:11
106:28 [p]Nu 25:2-3; Hos 9:10
106:30 [q]Nu 25:8
106:31 [r]Nu 25:11-13
106:32 [s]Nu 20:2-13; Ps 81:7
106:33 [t]Nu 20:8-12
106:34 [u]Jdg 1:21 [v]Dt 7:16
106:35 [w]Jdg 3:5-6
106:36 [x]Jdg 2:12
106:37 [y]2Ki 16:3; 17:17
106:38 [z]Nu 35:33
106:39 [a]Eze 20:18 [b]Lev 17:7; Nu 15:39
106:40 [c]Jdg 2:14; Ps 78:59 [d]Dt 9:29
106:41 [e]Jdg 2:14; Ne 9:27
106:43 [f]Jdg 2:16-19
106:44 [g]Jdg 3:9; 10:10 **106:45** [h]Lev 26:42; Ps 105:8 [i]Jdg 2:18 **106:46** [j]Ezr 9:9; Jer 42:12
106:47 [k]Ps 147:2

y33 Or *against his spirit, / and rash words came from his lips*

[48]Praise be to the LORD, the God of Israel,
from everlasting to everlasting.
Let all the people say, "Amen!"[a]

Praise the LORD.

BOOK V

Psalms 107–150

Psalm 107

Thanks to the LORD for his unfailing love.

[1]Give thanks to the LORD,[b] for he is good;
his love endures forever.
[2]Let the redeemed[c] of the LORD say this—
those he redeemed from the hand of the foe,
[3]those he gathered[d] from the lands,
from east and west, from north and south.[z]

[4]Some wandered in desert[e] wastelands,
finding no way to a city where they could settle.
[5]They were hungry and thirsty,
and their lives ebbed away.
[6]Then they cried out[f] to the LORD in their trouble,
and he delivered them from their distress.
[7]He led them by a straight way[g]
to a city where they could settle.
[8]Let them give thanks to the LORD for his unfailing love
and his wonderful deeds for men,
[9]for he satisfies[h] the thirsty
and fills the hungry with good things.[i]

[10]Some sat in darkness[j] and the deepest gloom,
prisoners suffering in iron chains,[k]
[11]for they had rebelled[l] against the words of God
and despised the counsel[m] of the Most High.
[12]So he subjected them to bitter labor;
they stumbled, and there was no one to help.[n]
[13]Then they cried to the LORD in their trouble,
and he saved them from their distress.
[14]He brought them out of darkness and the deepest gloom
and broke away their chains.[o]
[15]Let them give thanks to the LORD for his unfailing love
and his wonderful deeds for men,
[16]for he breaks down gates of bronze
and cuts through bars of iron.

[17]Some became fools through their rebellious ways
and suffered affliction[p] because of their iniquities.
[18]They loathed all food[q]
and drew near the gates of death.[r]
[19]Then they cried to the LORD in their trouble,
and he saved them from their distress.
[20]He sent forth his word[s] and healed them;[t]
he rescued[u] them from the grave.[v]
[21]Let them give thanks to the LORD for his unfailing love
and his wonderful deeds for men.
[22]Let them sacrifice thank offerings[w]
and tell of his works[x] with songs of joy.

[23]Others went out on the sea in ships;
they were merchants on the mighty waters.
[24]They saw the works of the LORD,
his wonderful deeds in the deep.
[25]For he spoke[y] and stirred up a tempest[z]
that lifted high the waves.[a]
[26]They mounted up to the heavens
and went down to the depths;
in their peril their courage melted[b] away.
[27]They reeled and staggered like drunken men;
they were at their wits' end.

106:48 [a]Ps 41:13
107:1 [b]Ps 106:1
107:2 [c]Ps 106:10
107:3 [d]Ps 106:47; Isa 43:5-6
107:4 [e]Nu 14:33; 32:13
107:6 [f]Ps 50:15
107:7 [g]Ezr 8:21
107:9 [h]Ps 22:26; Lk 1:53 [i]Ps 34:10
107:10 [j]Lk 1:79 [k]Job 36:8
107:11 [l]Ps 106:7; La 3:42 [m]2Ch 36:16
107:12 [n]Ps 22:11
107:14 [o]Ps 116:16; Lk 13:16; Ac 12:7
107:17 [p]Isa 65:6-7; La 3:39
107:18 [q]Job 33:20 [r]Job 33:22; Ps 9:13; 88:3
107:20 [s]Mt 8:8 [t]Ps 103:3 [u]Job 33:28 [v]Ps 30:3; 49:15
107:22 [w]Lev 7:12; Ps 50:14; 116:17 [x]Ps 9:11; 73:28; 118:17
107:25 [y]Ps 105:31 [z]Jnh 1:4 [a]Ps 93:3
107:26 [b]Ps 22:14

z3 Hebrew *north and the sea*

28Then they cried out to the LORD in
their trouble,
and he brought them out of their
distress.
29He stilled the storm[a] to a whisper;
the waves[b] of the sea were hushed.
30They were glad when it grew
calm,
and he guided them to their
desired haven.
31Let them give thanks to the LORD for
his unfailing love
and his wonderful deeds for men.
32Let them exalt him in the assembly[c]
of the people
and praise him in the council of
the elders.

33He turned rivers into a desert,[d]
flowing springs into thirsty ground,
34and fruitful land into a salt waste,[e]
because of the wickedness of those
who lived there.
35He turned the desert into pools of
water[f]
and the parched ground into
flowing springs;
36there he brought the hungry to
live,
and they founded a city where they
could settle.
37They sowed fields and planted
vineyards[g]
that yielded a fruitful harvest;
38he blessed them, and their numbers
greatly increased,[h]
and he did not let their herds
diminish.

39Then their numbers decreased,[i] and
they were humbled
by oppression, calamity and
sorrow;
40he who pours contempt on nobles[j]
made them wander in a trackless
waste.[k]
41But he lifted the needy[l] out of their
affliction
and increased their families like
flocks.
42The upright see and rejoice,[m]
but all the wicked shut their
mouths.[n]

43Whoever is wise,[o] let him heed
these things
and consider the great love[p] of the
LORD.

Psalm 108

108:1-5pp— Ps57:7-11
108:6-13pp— Ps60:5-12

A song. A psalm of David.

Petition for God's help.

1My heart is steadfast, O God;
I will sing and make music with all
my soul.
2Awake, harp and lyre!
I will awaken the dawn.
3I will praise you, O LORD, among the
nations;
I will sing of you among the peoples.
4For great is your love, higher than
the heavens;
your faithfulness reaches to the skies.
5Be exalted, O God, above the heavens,
and let your glory be over all the
earth.[q]

6Save us and help us with your right
hand,
that those you love may be delivered.
7God has spoken from his sanctuary:
"In triumph I will parcel out
Shechem
and measure off the Valley of Succoth.
8Gilead is mine, Manasseh is mine;
Ephraim is my helmet,
Judah[r] my scepter.
9Moab is my washbasin,
upon Edom I toss my sandal;
over Philistia I shout in triumph."
10Who will bring me to the fortified city?
Who will lead me to Edom?
11Is it not you, O God, you who have
rejected us
and no longer go out with our
armies?[s]
12Give us aid against the enemy,
for the help of man is worthless.
13With God we will gain the victory,
and he will trample down our
enemies.

107:29 [a]Mt 8:26 [b]Ps 89:9
107:32 [c]Ps 22:22,25; 35:18
107:33 [d]1Ki 17:1; Ps 74:15
107:34 [e]Ge 13:10; 14:3; 19:25
107:35 [f]Ps 114:8; Isa 41:18
107:37 [g]Isa 65:21
107:38 [h]Ge 12:2; 17:16,20; Ex 1:7
107:39 [i]2Ki 10:32; Eze 5:12
107:40 [j]Job 12:21 [k]Job 12:24
107:41 [l]1Sa 2:8; Ps 113:7-9
107:42 [m]Job 22:19 [n]Job 5:16; Ps 63:11; Ro 3:19
107:43 [o]Jer 9:12; Hos 14:9 [p]Ps 64:9
108:5 [q]Ps 57:5
108:8 [r]Ge 49:10
108:11 [s]Ps 44:9

Psalm 109

For the director of music.
Of David. A psalm.

Judgment against those with lying tongues.

1O God, whom I praise,
do not remain silent,[a]
2for wicked and deceitful men
have opened their mouths against me;
they have spoken against me with lying tongues.[b]
3With words of hatred[c] they surround me;
they attack me without cause.[d]
4In return for my friendship they accuse me,
but I am a man of prayer.[e]
5They repay me evil for good,[f]
and hatred for my friendship.

6Appoint[a] an evil man[b] to oppose him;
let an accuser[c][g] stand at his right hand.
7When he is tried, let him be found guilty,
and may his prayers condemn[h] him.
8May his days be few;
may another take his place[i] of leadership.
9May his children be fatherless
and his wife a widow.[j]
10May his children be wandering beggars;
may they be driven[d] from their ruined homes.
11May a creditor seize all he has;
may strangers plunder the fruits of his labor.[k]
12May no one extend kindness to him
or take pity[l] on his fatherless children.
13May his descendants be cut off,[m]
their names blotted out[n] from the next generation.
14May the iniquity of his fathers[o] be remembered before the LORD;
may the sin of his mother never be blotted out.
15May their sins always remain before the LORD,
that he may cut off the memory[p] of them from the earth.

16For he never thought of doing a kindness,
but hounded to death the poor
and the needy[q] and the brokenhearted.[r]
17He loved to pronounce a curse—
may it[e] come on him;[s]
he found no pleasure in blessing—
may it be[f] far from him.
18He wore cursing[t] as his garment;
it entered into his body like water,[u]
into his bones like oil.
19May it be like a cloak wrapped about him,
like a belt tied forever around him.
20May this be the LORD's payment[v] to my accusers,
to those who speak evil[w] of me.

21But you, O Sovereign LORD,
deal well with me for your name's sake;[x]
out of the goodness of your love,[y]
deliver me.
22For I am poor and needy,
and my heart is wounded within me.
23I fade away like an evening shadow;[z]
I am shaken off like a locust.
24My knees give[a] way from fasting;
my body is thin and gaunt.
25I am an object of scorn[b] to my accusers;
when they see me, they shake their heads.[c]

26Help me,[d] O LORD my God;
save me in accordance with your love.
27Let them know[e] that it is your hand,
that you, O LORD, have done it.
28They may curse,[f] but you will bless;
when they attack they will be put to shame,
but your servant will rejoice.[g]

109:1 [a]Ps 83:1 **109:2** [b]Ps 52:4; 120:2 **109:3** [c]Ps 69:4 [d]Ps 35:7; Jn 15:25 **109:4** [e]Ps 69:13 **109:5** [f]Ps 35:12; 38:20 **109:6** [g]Zec 3:1 **109:7** [h]Pr 28:9 **109:8** [i]Ac 1:20* **109:9** [j]Ex 22:24 **109:11** [k]Job 5:5 **109:12** [l]Isa 9:17 **109:13** [m]Job 18:19; Ps 37:28 [n]Pr 10:7 **109:14** [o]Ex 20:5; Ne 4:5; Jer 18:23 **109:15** [p]Job 18:17; Ps 34:16 **109:16** [q]Ps 37:14,32 [r]Ps 34:18 **109:17** [s]Pr 14:14; Eze 35:6 **109:18** [t]Ps 73:6 [u]Nu 5:22 **109:20** [v]Ps 94:23; 2Ti 4:14 [w]Ps 71:10 **109:21** [x]Ps 79:9 [y]Ps 69:16 **109:23** [z]Ps 102:11 **109:24** [a]Heb 12:12 **109:25** [b]Ps 22:6 [c]Mt 27:39; Mk 15:29 **109:26** [d]Ps 119:86 **109:27** [e]Job 37:7 **109:28** [f]2Sa 16:12 [g]Isa 65:14

[a]*6* Or *⌊They say:⌋ "Appoint* (with quotation marks at the end of verse 19) [b]*6* Or *the Evil One*
[c]*6* Or *let Satan* [d]*10* Septuagint; Hebrew *sought*
[e]*17* Or *curse, / and it has* [f]*17* Or *blessing, / and it is*

29My accusers will be clothed with
disgrace
and wrapped in shame[a] as in a
cloak.

30With my mouth I will greatly extol
the LORD;
in the great throng[b] I will praise him.
31For he stands at the right hand[c] of
the needy one,
to save his life from those who
condemn him.

Psalm 110

Of David. A psalm.

A priest in the order of Melchizedek.

1The LORD says[d] to my Lord:
"Sit at my right hand
until I make your enemies
a footstool for your feet."[e]

2The LORD will extend your mighty
scepter[f] from Zion;
you will rule in the midst of your
enemies.
3Your troops will be willing
on your day of battle.
Arrayed in holy majesty,[g]
from the womb of the dawn
you will receive the dew of your
youth.[g]

4The LORD has sworn
and will not change his mind:[h]
"You are a priest forever,[i]
in the order of Melchizedek.[j]"

5The Lord is at your right hand;[k]
he will crush kings[l] on the day of
his wrath.[m]
6He will judge the nations,[n] heaping
up the dead[o]
and crushing the rulers[p] of the
whole earth.
7He will drink from a brook beside
the way[h];
therefore he will lift up his head.[q]

Psalm 111[i]

The LORD's glorious works.

1Praise the LORD.[j]

I will extol the LORD with all my heart
in the council of the upright and in
the assembly.

2Great are the works[r] of the LORD;
they are pondered by all who
delight in them.
3Glorious and majestic are his deeds,
and his righteousness endures
forever.
4He has caused his wonders to be
remembered;
the LORD is gracious and
compassionate.[s]
5He provides food[t] for those who fear
him;
he remembers his covenant
forever.
6He has shown his people the power
of his works,
giving them the lands of other
nations.
7The works of his hands are faithful
and just;
all his precepts are trustworthy.[u]
8They are steadfast for ever[v] and ever,
done in faithfulness and
uprightness.
9He provided redemption[w] for his
people;
he ordained his covenant forever—
holy and awesome[x] is his name.

10The fear of the LORD is the beginning
of wisdom;[y]
all who follow his precepts have
good understanding.[z]
To him belongs eternal praise.[a]

Psalm 112[i]

Fear the LORD.

1Praise the LORD.[j]

Blessed is the man who fears the
LORD,[b]
who finds great delight[c] in his
commands.

109:29 [a]Ps 35:26; 132:18
109:30 [b]Ps 35:18; 111:1
109:31 [c]Ps 16:8; 73:23; 121:5
110:1 [d]Mt 22:44*; Mk 12:36*; Lk 20:42*; Ac 2:34* [e]1Co 15:25
110:2 [f]Ps 45:6
110:3 [g]Jdg 5:2; Ps 96:9
110:4 [h]Nu 23:19 [i]Heb 5:6*; 7:21* [j]Heb 7:15-17*
110:5 [k]Ps 16:8 [l]Ps 2:12 [m]Ps 2:5; Ro 2:5
110:6 [n]Isa 2:4 [o]Isa 66:24 [p]Ps 68:21
110:7 [q]Ps 27:6
111:2 [r]Ps 92:5; 143:5
111:4 [s]Ps 103:8
111:5 [t]Mt 6:26,31-33
111:7 [u]Ps 19:7; Rev 15:3
111:8 [v]Isa 40:8; Mt 5:18
111:9 [w]Lk 1:68 [x]Ps 99:3; Lk 1:49
111:10 [y]Pr 9:10 [z]Ecc 12:13 [a]Ps 145:2
112:1 [b]Ps 128:1 [c]Ps 119:14, 16,47,92

g3 Or / *your young men will come to you like the dew* h7 Or / *The One who grants succession will set him in authority* i This psalm is an acrostic poem, the lines of which begin with the successive letters of the Hebrew alphabet. j1 Hebrew *Hallelu Yah*

2His children will be mighty in the land;
the generation of the upright will
be blessed.
3Wealth and riches are in his house,
and his righteousness endures
forever.
4Even in darkness light dawns[a] for
the upright,
for the gracious and compassionate
and righteous[b] man.[k]
5Good will come to him who is
generous and lends freely,[c]
who conducts his affairs with justice.
6Surely he will never be shaken;
a righteous man will be
remembered[d] forever.
7He will have no fear of bad news;
his heart is steadfast,[e] trusting in
the LORD.
8His heart is secure, he will have no
fear;
in the end he will look in triumph
on his foes.[f]
9He has scattered abroad his gifts to
the poor,[g]
his righteousness endures forever;
his horn[l] will be lifted[h] high in
honor.

10The wicked man will see[i] and be
vexed,
he will gnash his teeth[j] and waste
away;[k]
the longings of the wicked will
come to nothing.[l]

Psalm 113

Praise the name of the LORD.

1Praise the LORD.[m]

Praise, O servants of the LORD,[m]
praise the name of the LORD.
2Let the name of the LORD be praised,
both now and forevermore.[n]
3From the rising of the sun[o] to the
place where it sets,
the name of the LORD is to be
praised.

4The LORD is exalted[p] over all the
nations,
his glory above the heavens.[q]
5Who is like the LORD our God,[r]
the One who sits enthroned[s] on
high,
6who stoops down to look[t]
on the heavens and the earth?

7He raises the poor[u] from the dust
and lifts the needy[v] from the ash
heap;
8he seats them[w] with princes,
with the princes of their people.
9He settles the barren[x] woman in her
home
as a happy mother of children.

Praise the LORD.

Psalm 114

God's power delivers.

1When Israel came out of Egypt,[y]
the house of Jacob from a people of
foreign tongue,
2Judah became God's sanctuary,
Israel his dominion.

3The sea looked and fled,[z]
the Jordan turned back;[a]
4the mountains skipped like rams,
the hills like lambs.

5Why was it, O sea, that you fled,
O Jordan, that you turned back,
6you mountains, that you skipped like
rams,
you hills, like lambs?

7Tremble, O earth,[b] at the presence of
the Lord,
at the presence of the God of Jacob,
8who turned the rock into a pool,
the hard rock into springs of water.[c]

Psalm 115

115:4-11pp— Ps135:15-20

Idols are useless.

1Not to us, O LORD, not to us
but to your name be the glory,[d]
because of your love and faithfulness.

112:4 [a]Job 11:17 [b]Ps 97:11
112:5 [c]Ps 37:21,26
112:6 [d]Pr 10:7
112:7 [e]Ps 57:7; Pr 1:33
112:8 [f]Ps 59:10
112:9 [g]2Co 9:9* [h]Ps 75:10
112:10 [i]Ps 86:17 [j]Ps 37:12 [k]Ps 58:7-8 [l]Pr 11:7
113:1 [m]Ps 135:1
113:2 [n]Da 2:20
113:3 [o]Isa 59:19; Mal 1:11
113:4 [p]Ps 99:2 [q]Ps 8:1; 97:9
113:5 [r]Ps 89:6 [s]Ps 103:19
113:6 [t]Ps 11:4; 138:6; Isa 57:15
113:7 [u]1Sa 2:8 [v]Ps 107:41
113:8 [w]Job 36:7
113:9 [x]1Sa 2:5; Ps 68:6; Isa 54:1
114:1 [y]Ex 13:3
114:3 [z]Ex 14:21; Ps 77:16 [a]Jos 3:16
114:7 [b]Ps 96:9
114:8 [c]Ex 17:6; Nu 20:11; Ps 107:35
115:1 [d]Ps 96:8; Isa 48:11; Eze 36:32

[k]4 Or */ for ⌊the LORD⌋ is gracious and compassionate and righteous* [l]9 *Horn* here symbolizes dignity.
[m]1 Hebrew *Hallelu Yah*; also in verse 9

2Why do the nations say,
"Where is their God?"[a]
3Our God is in heaven;[b]
he does whatever pleases him.[c]
4But their idols are silver and gold,
made by the hands of men.[d]
5They have mouths, but cannot speak,[e]
eyes, but they cannot see;
6they have ears, but cannot hear,
noses, but they cannot smell;
7they have hands, but cannot feel,
feet, but they cannot walk;
nor can they utter a sound with
their throats.
8Those who make them will be like
them,
and so will all who trust in them.

9O house of Israel, trust in the LORD—
he is their help and shield.
10O house of Aaron,[f] trust in the LORD—
he is their help and shield.
11You who fear him, trust in the LORD—
he is their help and shield.

12The LORD remembers us and will
bless us:
He will bless the house of Israel,
he will bless the house of Aaron,
13he will bless those who fear[g] the
LORD—
small and great alike.

14May the LORD make you increase,[h]
both you and your children.
15May you be blessed by the LORD,
the Maker of heaven[i] and earth.

16The highest heavens belong to the
LORD,[j]
but the earth he has given[k] to man.
17It is not the dead[l] who praise the LORD,
those who go down to silence;
18it is we who extol the LORD,
both now and forevermore.[m]

Praise the LORD.[n]

Psalm 116

Love for the LORD proclaimed.

1I love the LORD,[n] for he heard my
voice;
he heard my cry[o] for mercy.
2Because he turned his ear[p] to me,
I will call on him as long as I live.

3The cords of death[q] entangled me,
the anguish of the grave[o] came
upon me;
I was overcome by trouble and
sorrow.
4Then I called on the name[r] of the
LORD:
"O LORD, save me![s]"

5The LORD is gracious and righteous;[t]
our God is full of compassion.
6The LORD protects the simplehearted;
when I was in great need,[u] he
saved me.

7Be at rest[v] once more, O my soul,
for the LORD has been good[w] to you.

8For you, O LORD, have delivered my
soul[x] from death,
my eyes from tears,
my feet from stumbling,
9that I may walk before the LORD
in the land of the living.[y]
10I believed;[z] therefore[p] I said,
"I am greatly afflicted."
11And in my dismay I said,
"All men are liars."[a]

12How can I repay the LORD
for all his goodness to me?
13I will lift up the cup of salvation
and call on the name[b] of the LORD.
14I will fulfill my vows[c] to the LORD
in the presence of all his people.

15Precious in the sight[d] of the LORD
is the death of his saints.
16O LORD, truly I am your servant;[e]
I am your servant, the son of your
maidservant[q];[f]
you have freed me from my chains.

17I will sacrifice a thank offering[g] to you
and call on the name of the LORD.
18I will fulfill my vows to the LORD
in the presence of all his people,

115:2 [a]Ps 42:3; 79:10
115:3 [b]Ps 103:19 [c]Ps 135:6; Da 4:35
115:4 [d]Dt 4:28; Jer 10:3-5
115:5 [e]Jer 10:5
115:10 [f]Ps 118:3
115:13 [g]Ps 128:1,4
115:14 [h]Dt 1:11
115:15 [i]Ge 1:1; 14:19; Ps 96:5
115:16 [j]Ps 89:11 [k]Ps 8:6-8
115:17 [l]Ps 6:5; 88:10-12; Isa 38:18
115:18 [m]Ps 113:2; Da 2:20
116:1 [n]Ps 18:1 [o]Ps 66:19
116:2 [p]Ps 40:1
116:3 [q]Ps 18:4-5
116:4 [r]Ps 118:5 [s]Ps 22:20
116:5 [t]Ezr 9:15; Ne 9:8; Ps 103:8; 145:17
116:6 [u]Ps 19:7; 79:8
116:7 [v]Jer 6:16; Mt 11:29 [w]Ps 13:6
116:8 [x]Ps 56:13
116:9 [y]Ps 27:13
116:10 [z]2Co 4:13*
116:11 [a]Ro 3:4
116:13 [b]Ps 16:5; 80:18
116:14 [c]Ps 22:25; Jnh 2:9
116:15 [d]Ps 72:14
116:16 [e]Ps 119:125; 143:12 [f]Ps 86:16
116:17 [g]Lev 7:12; Ps 50:14

[n]*18* Hebrew *Hallelu Yah* [o]*3* Hebrew *Sheol*
[p]*10* Or *believed even when* [q]*16* Or *servant, your faithful son*

19in the courts[a] of the house of the
LORD—
in your midst, O Jerusalem.

Praise the LORD.[r]

Psalm 117

Praise the LORD, all nations.

1Praise the LORD, all you nations;[b]
extol him, all you peoples.
2For great is his love toward us,
and the faithfulness of the LORD[c]
endures forever.

Praise the LORD.[r]

Psalm 118

The LORD's love endures forever.

1Give thanks to the LORD,[d] for he is
good;
his love endures forever.[e]

2Let Israel say:[f]
"His love endures forever."
3Let the house of Aaron say:
"His love endures forever."
4Let those who fear the LORD say:
"His love endures forever."

5In my anguish[g] I cried to the LORD,
and he answered[h] by setting me free.
6The LORD is with me;[i] I will not be
afraid.
What can man do to me?[j]
7The LORD is with me; he is my helper.[k]
I will look in triumph on my
enemies.[l]

8It is better to take refuge in the LORD[m]
than to trust in man.[n]
9It is better to take refuge in the LORD
than to trust in princes.[o]

10All the nations surrounded me,
but in the name of the LORD I cut
them off.[p]
11They surrounded me[q] on every side,[r]
but in the name of the LORD I cut
them off.
12They swarmed around me like bees,[s]
but they died out as quickly as
burning thorns;[t]

116:19 [a]Ps 96:8; 135:2
117:1 [b]Ro 15:11*
117:2 [c]Ps 100:5
118:1 [d]1Ch 16:8 [e]Ps 106:1; 136:1
118:2 [f]Ps 115:9
118:5 [g]Ps 120:1 [h]Ps 18:19
118:6 [i]Heb 13:6* [j]Ps 27:1; 56:4
118:7 [k]Ps 54:4 [l]Ps 59:10
118:8 [m]Ps 40:4 [n]Jer 17:5
118:9 [o]Ps 146:3
118:10 [p]Ps 18:40
118:11 [q]Ps 88:17 [r]Ps 3:6
118:12 [s]Dt 1:44 [t]Ps 58:9
118:13 [u]Ps 86:17; 140:4
118:14 [v]Ex 15:2 [w]Isa 12:2
118:15 [x]Ps 68:3 [y]Ps 89:13
118:17 [z]Ps 6:5; Hab 1:12 [a]Ex 15:6; Ps 73:28
118:18 [b]2Co 6:9
118:19 [c]Isa 26:2
118:20 [d]Ps 24:7; Isa 35:8; Rev 22:14
118:21 [e]Ps 116:1
118:22 [f]Mt 21:42; Mk 12:10; Lk 20:17*; Ac 4:11*; 1Pe 2:7*

in the name of the LORD I cut them
off.

13I was pushed back and about to fall,
but the LORD helped me.[u]
14The LORD is my strength[v] and my song;
he has become my salvation.[w]

15Shouts of joy[x] and victory
resound in the tents of the righteous:
"The LORD's right hand[y] has done
mighty things!
16 The LORD's right hand is lifted high;
the LORD's right hand has done
mighty things!"

17I will not die[z] but live,
and will proclaim[a] what the LORD
has done.
18The LORD has chastened me severely,
but he has not given me over to
death.[b]

19Open for me the gates[c] of
righteousness;
I will enter and give thanks to the
LORD.
20This is the gate of the LORD
through which the righteous may
enter.[d]
21I will give you thanks, for you
answered me;[e]
you have become my salvation.

22The stone the builders rejected
has become the capstone;[f]
23the LORD has done this,
and it is marvelous in our eyes.
24This is the day the LORD has made;
let us rejoice and be glad in it.

25O LORD, save us;
O LORD, grant us success.
26Blessed is he who comes[g] in the
name of the LORD.
From the house of the LORD we
bless you.[s]
27The LORD is God,
and he has made his light shine[h]
upon us.

118:26 [g]Mt 21:9*; Mk 11:9*; Lk 13:35*; 19:38*; Jn 12:13* **118:27** [h]1Pe 2:9

[r] *19,2* Hebrew *Hallelu Yah* [s] *26* The Hebrew is plural.

With boughs in hand, join in the
festal procession
up[t] to the horns of the altar.

28You are my God, and I will give you
thanks;
you are my God,[a] and I will exalt[b]
you.

29Give thanks to the LORD, for he is good;
his love endures forever.

Psalm 119[u]

The excellency of God's Word.

א Aleph

1Blessed are they whose ways are
blameless,
who walk[c] according to the law of
the LORD.
2Blessed are they who keep his statutes
and seek him with all their heart.[d]
3They do nothing wrong;[e]
they walk in his ways.
4You have laid down precepts
that are to be fully obeyed.
5Oh, that my ways were steadfast
in obeying your decrees!
6Then I would not be put to shame
when I consider all your commands.
7I will praise you with an upright heart
as I learn your righteous laws.
8I will obey your decrees;
do not utterly forsake me.

ב Beth

9How can a young man keep his way
pure?
By living according to your word.[f]
10I seek you with all my heart;[g]
do not let me stray from your
commands.[h]
11I have hidden your word in my
heart[i]
that I might not sin against you.
12Praise be to you, O LORD;
teach me your decrees.[j]
13With my lips I recount
all the laws that come from your
mouth.[k]

118:28 [a]Isa 25:1 [b]Ex 15:2
119:1 [c]Ps 128:1
119:2 [d]Dt 6:5
119:3 [e]1Jn 3:9; 5:18
119:9 [f]2Ch 6:16
119:10 [g]2Ch 15:15 [h]ver 21,118
119:11 [i]Ps 37:31; Lk 2:19,51
119:12 [j]ver 26
119:13 [k]Ps 40:9
119:15 [l]Ps 1:2
119:16 [m]Ps 1:2
119:17 [n]Ps 13:6; 116:7
119:19 [o]1Ch 29:15; Ps 39:12; 2Co 5:6; Heb 11:13
119:20 [p]Ps 42:2; 84:2 [q]Ps 63:1
119:21 [r]ver 10
119:22 [s]Ps 39:8
119:25 [t]Ps 44:25 [u]Ps 143:11
119:26 [v]Ps 25:4; 27:11; 86:11
119:27 [w]Ps 145:5
119:28 [x]Ps 107:26 [y]Ps 20:2; 1Pe 5:10

14I rejoice in following your statutes
as one rejoices in great riches.
15I meditate on your precepts[l]
and consider your ways.
16I delight[m] in your decrees;
I will not neglect your word.

ג Gimel

17Do good to your servant,[n] and I will
live;
I will obey your word.
18Open my eyes that I may see
wonderful things in your law.
19I am a stranger on earth;[o]
do not hide your commands from
me.
20My soul is consumed[p] with longing
for your laws[q] at all times.
21You rebuke the arrogant, who are
cursed
and who stray[r] from your commands.
22Remove from me scorn[s] and
contempt,
for I keep your statutes.
23Though rulers sit together and
slander me,
your servant will meditate on your
decrees.
24Your statutes are my delight;
they are my counselors.

ד Daleth

25I am laid low in the dust;[t]
preserve my life[u] according to your
word.
26I recounted my ways and you
answered me;
teach me your decrees.[v]
27Let me understand the teaching of
your precepts;
then I will meditate on your
wonders.[w]
28My soul is weary with sorrow;[x]
strengthen me[y] according to your
word.
29Keep me from deceitful ways;
be gracious to me through your law.
30I have chosen the way of truth;
I have set my heart on your laws.

t*27* Or *Bind the festal sacrifice with ropes / and take it*
uThis psalm is an acrostic poem; the verses of each stanza begin with the same letter of the Hebrew alphabet.

[31]I hold fast[a] to your statutes, O LORD;
do not let me be put to shame.
[32]I run in the path of your commands,
for you have set my heart free.

ה He

[33]Teach me,[b] O LORD, to follow your
decrees;
then I will keep them to the end.
[34]Give me understanding, and I will
keep your law
and obey it with all my heart.
[35]Direct me in the path of your
commands,
for there I find delight.
[36]Turn my heart[c] toward your statutes
and not toward selfish gain.[d]
[37]Turn my eyes away from worthless
things;
preserve my life[e] according to your
word.[v]
[38]Fulfill your promise[f] to your servant,
so that you may be feared.
[39]Take away the disgrace I dread,
for your laws are good.
[40]How I long[g] for your precepts!
Preserve my life in your
righteousness.

ו Waw

[41]May your unfailing love come to me,
O LORD,
your salvation according to your
promise;
[42]then I will answer[h] the one who
taunts me,
for I trust in your word.
[43]Do not snatch the word of truth from
my mouth,
for I have put my hope in your
laws.
[44]I will always obey your law,
for ever and ever.
[45]I will walk about in freedom,
for I have sought out your precepts.
[46]I will speak of your statutes before
kings[i]
and will not be put to shame,
[47]for I delight in your commands
because I love them.

119:31 [a]Dt 11:22
119:33 [b]ver 12
119:36 [c]1Ki 8:58 [d]Eze 33:31; Mk 7:21-22; Lk 12:15; Heb 13:5
119:37 [e]Ps 71:20; Isa 33:15
119:38 [f]2Sa 7:25
119:40 [g]ver 20
119:42 [h]Pr 27:11
119:46 [i]Mt 10:18; Ac 26:1-2
119:50 [j]Ro 15:4
119:51 [k]Jer 20:7 [l]ver 157; Job 23:11; Ps 44:18
119:52 [m]Ps 103:18
119:53 [n]Ezr 9:3 [o]Ps 89:30
119:55 [p]Ps 63:6
119:57 [q]Ps 16:5; La 3:24
119:58 [r]1Ki 13:6 [s]ver 41
119:59 [t]Lk 15:17-18
119:61 [u]Ps 140:5
119:62 [v]Ac 16:25
119:63 [w]Ps 101:6-7
119:64 [x]Ps 33:5

[48]I lift up my hands to[w] your
commands, which I love,
and I meditate on your decrees.

ז Zayin

[49]Remember your word to your servant,
for you have given me hope.
[50]My comfort in my suffering is this:
Your promise preserves my life.[j]
[51]The arrogant mock me[k] without
restraint,
but I do not turn[l] from your law.
[52]I remember[m] your ancient laws,
O LORD,
and I find comfort in them.
[53]Indignation grips me[n] because of the
wicked,
who have forsaken your law.[o]
[54]Your decrees are the theme of my song
wherever I lodge.
[55]In the night I remember[p] your
name, O LORD,
and I will keep your law.
[56]This has been my practice:
I obey your precepts.

ח Heth

[57]You are my portion,[q] O LORD;
I have promised to obey your words.
[58]I have sought your face with all my
heart;
be gracious to me[r] according to
your promise.[s]
[59]I have considered my ways[t]
and have turned my steps to your
statutes.
[60]I will hasten and not delay
to obey your commands.
[61]Though the wicked bind me with
ropes,
I will not forget[u] your law.
[62]At midnight[v] I rise to give you thanks
for your righteous laws.
[63]I am a friend to all who fear you,[w]
to all who follow your precepts.
[64]The earth is filled with your love,[x]
O LORD;
teach me your decrees.

[v]*37* Two manuscripts of the Masoretic Text and Dead Sea Scrolls; most manuscripts of the Masoretic Text *life in your way* [w]*48* Or *for*

ט Teth

[65]Do good to your servant
according to your word, O LORD.
[66]Teach me knowledge and good
judgment,
for I believe in your commands.
[67]Before I was afflicted I went astray,[a]
but now I obey your word.
[68]You are good,[b] and what you do is
good;
teach me your decrees.[c]
[69]Though the arrogant have smeared
me with lies,[d]
I keep your precepts with all my
heart.
[70]Their hearts are callous[e] and unfeeling,
but I delight in your law.
[71]It was good for me to be afflicted
so that I might learn your decrees.
[72]The law from your mouth is more
precious to me
than thousands of pieces of silver
and gold.[f]

י Yodh

[73]Your hands made me[g] and formed me;
give me understanding to learn
your commands.
[74]May those who fear you rejoice[h]
when they see me,
for I have put my hope in your word.
[75]I know, O LORD, that your laws are
righteous,
and in faithfulness[i] you have
afflicted me.
[76]May your unfailing love be my
comfort,
according to your promise to your
servant.
[77]Let your compassion[j] come to me
that I may live,
for your law is my delight.
[78]May the arrogant[k] be put to shame
for wronging me without cause;[l]
but I will meditate on your
precepts.
[79]May those who fear you turn to me,
those who understand your statutes.
[80]May my heart be blameless toward
your decrees,
that I may not be put to shame.

119:67 [a]Jer 31:18-19; Heb 12:11
119:68 [b]Ps 106:1; 107:1; Mt 19:17 [c]ver 12
119:69 [d]Job 13:4; Ps 109:2
119:70 [e]Ps 17:10; Isa 6:10; Ac 28:27
119:72 [f]Ps 19:10; Pr 8:10-11,19
119:73 [g]Job 10:8; Ps 100:3; 138:8; 139:13-16
119:74 [h]Ps 34:2
119:75 [i]Heb 12:5-11
119:77 [j]ver 41
119:78 [k]Jer 50:32 [l]ver 86,161
119:81 [m]Ps 84:2
119:82 [n]Ps 69:3; La 2:11
119:84 [o]Ps 39:4; Rev 6:10
119:85 [p]Ps 35:7; Jer 18:20,22
119:86 [q]Ps 35:19 [r]Ps 109:26 [s]ver 78
119:87 [t]Isa 58:2
119:89 [u]Mt 24:34-35; 1Pe 1:25
119:90 [v]Ps 36:5 [w]Ps 148:6; Ecc 1:4
119:91 [x]Jer 33:25
119:97 [y]Ps 1:2

כ Kaph

[81]My soul faints[m] with longing for
your salvation,
but I have put my hope in your word.
[82]My eyes fail,[n] looking for your promise;
I say, "When will you comfort me?"
[83]Though I am like a wineskin in the
smoke,
I do not forget your decrees.
[84]How long[o] must your servant wait?
When will you punish my
persecutors?
[85]The arrogant dig pitfalls[p] for me,
contrary to your law.
[86]All your commands are trustworthy;[q]
help me,[r] for men persecute me
without cause.[s]
[87]They almost wiped me from the earth,
but I have not forsaken[t] your
precepts.
[88]Preserve my life according to your
love,
and I will obey the statutes of your
mouth.

ל Lamedh

[89]Your word, O LORD, is eternal;[u]
it stands firm in the heavens.
[90]Your faithfulness[v] continues through
all generations;
you established the earth, and it
endures.[w]
[91]Your laws endure[x] to this day,
for all things serve you.
[92]If your law had not been my delight,
I would have perished in my
affliction.
[93]I will never forget your precepts,
for by them you have preserved my
life.
[94]Save me, for I am yours;
I have sought out your precepts.
[95]The wicked are waiting to destroy me,
but I will ponder your statutes.
[96]To all perfection I see a limit;
but your commands are boundless.

מ Mem

[97]Oh, how I love your law!
I meditate[y] on it all day long.

[98]Your commands make me wiser[a]
than my enemies,
for they are ever with me.
[99]I have more insight than all my
teachers,
for I meditate on your statutes.
[100]I have more understanding than the
elders,
for I obey your precepts.[b]
[101]I have kept my feet[c] from every evil
path
so that I might obey your word.
[102]I have not departed from your laws,
for you yourself have taught me.
[103]How sweet are your words to my
taste,
sweeter than honey[d] to my mouth![e]
[104]I gain understanding from your
precepts;
therefore I hate every wrong path.[f]

נ Nun

[105]Your word is a lamp to my feet
and a light[g] for my path.
[106]I have taken an oath[h] and
confirmed it,
that I will follow your righteous laws.
[107]I have suffered much;
preserve my life, O LORD,
according to your word.
[108]Accept, O LORD, the willing praise
of my mouth,[i]
and teach me your laws.
[109]Though I constantly take my life in
my hands,[j]
I will not forget your law.
[110]The wicked have set a snare[k] for me,
but I have not strayed[l] from your
precepts.
[111]Your statutes are my heritage forever;
they are the joy of my heart.
[112]My heart is set on keeping your
decrees
to the very end.[m]

ס Samekh

[113]I hate double-minded men,[n]
but I love your law.
[114]You are my refuge and my shield;[o]
I have put my hope[p] in your word.
[115]Away from me,[q] you evildoers,
that I may keep the commands of
my God!
[116]Sustain me[r] according to your
promise, and I will live;
do not let my hopes be dashed.[s]
[117]Uphold me, and I will be delivered;
I will always have regard for your
decrees.
[118]You reject all who stray from your
decrees,
for their deceitfulness is in vain.
[119]All the wicked of the earth you
discard like dross;[t]
therefore I love your statutes.
[120]My flesh trembles[u] in fear of you;
I stand in awe of your laws.

ע Ayin

[121]I have done what is righteous and
just;
do not leave me to my oppressors.
[122]Ensure your servant's well-being;[v]
let not the arrogant oppress me.
[123]My eyes fail, looking for your
salvation,
looking for your righteous promise.[w]
[124]Deal with your servant according to
your love
and teach me your decrees.[x]
[125]I am your servant;[y] give me
discernment
that I may understand your statutes.
[126]It is time for you to act, O LORD;
your law is being broken.
[127]Because I love your commands
more than gold,[z] more than pure
gold,
[128]and because I consider all your
precepts right,
I hate every wrong path.[a]

פ Pe

[129]Your statutes are wonderful;
therefore I obey them.
[130]The unfolding of your words gives
light;[b]
it gives understanding to the
simple.[c]
[131]I open my mouth and pant,[d]
longing for your commands.[e]
[132]Turn to me and have mercy[f] on me,

119:98 [a]Dt 4:6
119:100 [b]Job 32:7-9
119:101 [c]Pr 1:15
119:103 [d]Ps 19:10; Pr 8:11 [e]Pr 24:13-14
119:104 [f]ver 128
119:105 [g]Pr 6:23
119:106 [h]Ne 10:29
119:108 [i]Hos 14:2; Heb 13:15
119:109 [j]Jdg 12:3; Job 13:14
119:110 [k]Ps 140:5; 141:9 [l]ver 10
119:112 [m]ver 33
119:113 [n]Jas 1:8
119:114 [o]Ps 32:7; 91:1 [p]ver 74
119:115 [q]Ps 6:8; 139:19; Mt 7:23
119:116 [r]Ps 54:4 [s]Ps 25:2; Ro 5:5; 9:33
119:119 [t]Eze 22:18,19
119:120 [u]Hab 3:16
119:122 [v]Job 17:3
119:123 [w]ver 82
119:124 [x]ver 12
119:125 [y]Ps 116:16
119:127 [z]Ps 19:10
119:128 [a]ver 104,163
119:130 [b]Pr 6:23 [c]Ps 19:7
119:131 [d]Ps 42:1 [e]ver 20
119:132 [f]Ps 25:16; 106:4

as you always do to those who love
your name.
133Direct my footsteps according to
your word;[a]
let no sin rule[b] over me.
134Redeem me from the oppression of
men,[c]
that I may obey your precepts.
135Make your face shine[d] upon your
servant
and teach me your decrees.
136Streams of tears[e] flow from my eyes,
for your law is not obeyed.[f]

צ Tsadhe

137Righteous are you,[g] O LORD,
and your laws are right.[h]
138The statutes you have laid down are
righteous;[i]
they are fully trustworthy.
139My zeal wears me out,[j]
for my enemies ignore your words.
140Your promises have been
thoroughly tested,[k]
and your servant loves them.
141Though I am lowly and despised,[l]
I do not forget your precepts.
142Your righteousness is everlasting
and your law is true.[m]
143Trouble and distress have come
upon me,
but your commands are my delight.
144Your statutes are forever right;
give me understanding[n] that I may
live.

ק Qoph

145I call with all my heart; answer me,
O LORD,
and I will obey your decrees.
146I call out to you; save me
and I will keep your statutes.
147I rise before dawn[o] and cry for help;
I have put my hope in your word.
148My eyes stay open through the
watches of the night,[p]
that I may meditate on your promises.
149Hear my voice in accordance with
your love;
preserve my life, O LORD,
according to your laws.
150Those who devise wicked schemes
are near,
but they are far from your law.
151Yet you are near,[q] O LORD,
and all your commands are true.[r]
152Long ago I learned from your statutes
that you established them to last
forever.[s]

ר Resh

153Look upon my suffering[t] and
deliver me,
for I have not forgotten[u] your law.
154Defend my cause[v] and redeem me;[w]
preserve my life according to your
promise.
155Salvation is far from the wicked,
for they do not seek out[x] your
decrees.
156Your compassion is great, O LORD;
preserve my life[y] according to your
laws.
157Many are the foes who
persecute me,[z]
but I have not turned from your
statutes.
158I look on the faithless with loathing,[a]
for they do not obey your word.
159See how I love your precepts;
preserve my life, O LORD,
according to your love.
160All your words are true;
all your righteous laws are eternal.

ש Sin and Shin

161Rulers persecute me[b] without cause,
but my heart trembles at your word.
162I rejoice in your promise
like one who finds great spoil.[c]
163I hate and abhor falsehood
but I love your law.
164Seven times a day I praise you
for your righteous laws.
165Great peace[d] have they who love
your law,
and nothing can make them
stumble.
166I wait for your salvation,[e] O LORD,
and I follow your commands.
167I obey your statutes,
for I love them greatly.

119:133 [a]Ps 17:5 [b]Ps 19:13; Ro 6:12
119:134 [c]Ps 142:6; Lk 1:74
119:135 [d]Nu 6:25; Ps 4:6
119:136 [e]Jer 9:1,18 [f]Eze 9:4
119:137 [g]Ezr 9:15; Jer 12:1 [h]Ne 9:13
119:138 [i]Ps 19:7
119:139 [j]Ps 69:9; Jn 2:17
119:140 [k]Ps 12:6
119:141 [l]Ps 22:6
119:142 [m]Ps 19:7
119:144 [n]Ps 19:9
119:147 [o]Ps 5:3; 57:8; 108:2
119:148 [p]Ps 63:6
119:151 [q]Ps 34:18; 145:18 [r]ver 142
119:152 [s]Lk 21:33
119:153 [t]La 5:1 [u]Pr 3:1
119:154 [v]Mic 7:9 [w]1Sa 24:15
119:155 [x]Job 5:4
119:156 [y]2Sa 24:14
119:157 [z]Ps 7:1
119:158 [a]Ps 139:21
119:161 [b]1Sa 24:11
119:162 [c]1Sa 30:16
119:165 [d]Pr 3:2; Isa 26:3,12; 32:17
119:166 [e]Ge 49:18

[168]I obey your precepts and your statutes,
for all my ways are known[a] to you.

ת Taw

[169]May my cry come[b] before you,
O LORD;
give me understanding according
to your word.
[170]May my supplication come[c] before
you;
deliver me[d] according to your
promise.
[171]May my lips overflow with praise,[e]
for you teach me[f] your decrees.
[172]May my tongue sing of your word,
for all your commands are righteous.
[173]May your hand be ready to help[g] me,
for I have chosen[h] your precepts.
[174]I long for your salvation,[i] O LORD,
and your law is my delight.
[175]Let me live[j] that I may praise you,
and may your laws sustain me.
[176]I have strayed like a lost sheep.[k]
Seek your servant,
for I have not forgotten your
commands.

Psalm 120

A song of ascents.

Prayer for the LORD
to save from lying lips.

[1]I call on the LORD in my distress,[l]
and he answers me.
[2]Save me, O LORD, from lying lips[m]
and from deceitful tongues.[n]

[3]What will he do to you,
and what more besides, O deceitful
tongue?
[4]He will punish you with a warrior's
sharp arrows,[o]
with burning coals of the broom tree.

[5]Woe to me that I dwell in Meshech,
that I live among the tents of Kedar![p]
[6]Too long have I lived
among those who hate peace.
[7]I am a man of peace;
but when I speak, they are for war.

119:168 [a]Pr 5:21
119:169 [b]Ps 18:6
119:170 [c]Ps 28:2 [d]Ps 31:2
119:171 [e]Ps 51:15 [f]Ps 94:12
119:173 [g]Ps 37:24 [h]Jos 24:22
119:174 [i]ver 166
119:175 [j]Isa 55:3
119:176 [k]Isa 53:6
120:1 [l]Ps 102:2; Jnh 2:2
120:2 [m]Pr 12:22 [n]Ps 52:4
120:4 [o]Ps 45:5
120:5 [p]Ge 25:13; Jer 49:28
121:2 [q]Ps 115:15; 124:8
121:5 [r]Isa 25:4
121:6 [s]Ps 91:5; Isa 49:10; Rev 7:16
121:7 [t]Ps 41:2; 91:10-12
121:8 [u]Dt 28:6
122:6 [v]Ps 51:18

Psalm 121

A song of ascents.

The LORD will keep you
from all harm.

[1]I lift up my eyes to the hills—
where does my help come from?
[2]My help comes from the LORD,
the Maker of heaven and earth.[q]

[3]He will not let your foot slip—
he who watches over you will not
slumber;
[4]indeed, he who watches over Israel
will neither slumber nor sleep.

[5]The LORD watches over[r] you—
the LORD is your shade at your
right hand;
[6]the sun[s] will not harm you by day,
nor the moon by night.

[7]The LORD will keep you from all
harm[t]—
he will watch over your life;
[8]the LORD will watch over your
coming and going
both now and forevermore.[u]

Psalm 122

A song of ascents. Of David.

Peace for Jerusalem.

[1]I rejoiced with those who said to me,
"Let us go to the house of the LORD."
[2]Our feet are standing
in your gates, O Jerusalem.

[3]Jerusalem is built like a city
that is closely compacted together.
[4]That is where the tribes go up,
the tribes of the LORD,
to praise the name of the LORD
according to the statute given to
Israel.
[5]There the thrones for judgment stand,
the thrones of the house of David.

[6]Pray for the peace of Jerusalem:
"May those who love[v] you be secure.

[7]May there be peace within your walls
and security within your citadels."
[8]For the sake of my brothers and friends,
I will say, "Peace be within you."
[9]For the sake of the house of the LORD our God,
I will seek your prosperity.[a]

Psalm 123

A song of ascents.

Prayer for mercy.

[1]I lift up my eyes to you,
to you whose throne[b] is in heaven.
[2]As the eyes of slaves look to the hand of their master,
as the eyes of a maid look to the hand of her mistress,
so our eyes look to the LORD[c] our God,
till he shows us his mercy.

[3]Have mercy on us, O LORD, have mercy on us,
for we have endured much contempt.
[4]We have endured much ridicule from the proud,
much contempt from the arrogant.

Psalm 124

A song of ascents. Of David.

Praise for God's deliverance of Israel.

[1]If the LORD had not been on our side—
let Israel say[d]—
[2]if the LORD had not been on our side
when men attacked us,
[3]when their anger flared against us,
they would have swallowed us alive;
[4]the flood would have engulfed us,
the torrent would have swept over us,
[5]the raging waters
would have swept us away.

[6]Praise be to the LORD,
who has not let us be torn by their teeth.

122:9
[a]Ne 2:10

123:1
[b]Ps 11:4; 121:1; 141:8

123:2
[c]Ps 25:15

124:1
[d]Ps 129:1

124:7
[e]Ps 91:3; Pr 6:5

124:8
[f]Ge 1:1; Ps 121:2; 134:3

125:1
[g]Ps 46:5

125:2
[h]Ps 121:8; Zec 2:4-5

125:3
[i]Ps 89:22; Pr 22:8; Isa 14:5
[j]1Sa 24:10; Ps 55:20

125:4
[k]Ps 119:68
[l]Ps 7:10; 36:10; 94:15

125:5
[m]Job 23:11
[n]Pr 2:15; Isa 59:8
[o]Ps 128:6

126:1
[p]Ps 85:1; Hos 6:11

126:2
[q]Job 8:21; Ps 51:14

[7]We have escaped like a bird
out of the fowler's snare;[e]
the snare has been broken,
and we have escaped.
[8]Our help is in the name of the LORD,
the Maker of heaven[f] and earth.

Psalm 125

A song of ascents.

Those who trust will endure forever.

[1]Those who trust in the LORD are like Mount Zion,
which cannot be shaken[g] but endures forever.
[2]As the mountains surround Jerusalem,
so the LORD surrounds[h] his people
both now and forevermore.

[3]The scepter of the wicked will not remain[i]
over the land allotted to the righteous,
for then the righteous might use
their hands to do evil.[j]

[4]Do good, O LORD,[k] to those who are good,
to those who are upright in heart.[l]
[5]But those who turn[m] to crooked ways[n]
the LORD will banish with the evildoers.

Peace be upon Israel.[o]

Psalm 126

A song of ascents.

Joy for returning captives.

[1]When the LORD brought back[p] the captives to[x] Zion,
we were like men who dreamed.[y]
[2]Our mouths were filled with laughter,
our tongues with songs of joy.[q]

[x] 1 Or *LORD restored the fortunes of* [y] 1 Or *men restored to health*

Then it was said among the nations,
"The LORD has done great things[a]
for them."
3 The LORD has done great things for us,
and we are filled with joy.[b]

4 Restore our fortunes,[z] O LORD,
like streams in the Negev.[c]
5 Those who sow in tears
will reap with songs of joy.[d]
6 He who goes out weeping,
carrying seed to sow,
will return with songs of joy,
carrying sheaves with him.

Psalm 127

A song of ascents. Of Solomon.

Children are a reward from the LORD.

1 Unless the LORD builds[e] the house,
its builders labor in vain.
Unless the LORD watches[f] over the
city,
the watchmen stand guard in vain.
2 In vain you rise early
and stay up late,
toiling for food[g] to eat—
for he grants sleep[h] to[a] those he
loves.

3 Sons are a heritage from the LORD,
children a reward[i] from him.
4 Like arrows in the hands of a warrior
are sons born in one's youth.
5 Blessed is the man
whose quiver is full of them.
They will not be put to shame
when they contend with their
enemies[j] in the gate.

Psalm 128

A song of ascents.

Blessings for those who fear the LORD.

1 Blessed are all who fear the LORD,[k]
who walk in his ways.[l]
2 You will eat the fruit of your labor;[m]

126:2 [a]Ps 71:19
126:3 [b]Isa 25:9
126:4 [c]Isa 35:6; 43:19
126:5 [d]Isa 35:10
127:1 [e]Ps 78:69 [f]Ps 121:4
127:2 [g]Ge 3:17 [h]Job 11:18
127:3 [i]Ge 33:5
127:5 [j]Pr 27:11
128:1 [k]Ps 112:1 [l]Ps 119:1-3
128:2 [m]Isa 3:10 [n]Ecc 8:12
128:3 [o]Eze 19:10 [p]Ps 52:8; 144:12
128:5 [q]Ps 20:2; 134:3
128:6 [r]Ge 50:23; Job 42:16 [s]Ps 125:5
129:1 [t]Ps 88:15; Hos 2:15 [u]Ps 124:1
129:2 [v]Mt 16:18
129:4 [w]Ps 119:137
129:5 [x]Mic 4:11 [y]Ps 71:13
129:6 [z]Ps 37:2
129:8 [a]Ru 2:4; Ps 118:26

blessings and prosperity[n] will be
yours.
3 Your wife will be like a fruitful vine[o]
within your house;
your sons will be like olive shoots[p]
around your table.
4 Thus is the man blessed
who fears the LORD.

5 May the LORD bless you from Zion[q]
all the days of your life;
may you see the prosperity of
Jerusalem,
6 and may you live to see your
children's children.[r]

Peace be upon Israel.[s]

Psalm 129

A song of ascents.

Shame on all who hate Zion.

1 They have greatly oppressed me
from my youth[t]—
let Israel say[u]—
2 they have greatly oppressed me from
my youth,
but they have not gained the
victory[v] over me.
3 Plowmen have plowed my back
and made their furrows long.
4 But the LORD is righteous;[w]
he has cut me free from the cords
of the wicked.

5 May all who hate Zion[x]
be turned back in shame.[y]
6 May they be like grass on the roof,
which withers[z] before it can grow;
7 with it the reaper cannot fill his
hands,
nor the one who gathers fill his
arms.
8 May those who pass by not say,
"The blessing of the LORD be upon
you;
we bless you[a] in the name of the
LORD."

z4 Or *Bring back our captives*   a2 Or *eat— / for while they sleep he provides for*

Psalm 130

A song of ascents.

Wait for the LORD.

[1]Out of the depths[a] I cry to you, O LORD;
[2] O Lord, hear my voice.[b]
Let your ears be attentive[c]
to my cry for mercy.

[3]If you, O LORD, kept a record of sins,
O Lord, who could stand?[d]
[4]But with you there is forgiveness;[e]
therefore you are feared.[f]

[5]I wait for the LORD,[g] my soul waits,
and in his word[h] I put my hope.
[6]My soul waits for the Lord
more than watchmen[i] wait for the
morning,
more than watchmen wait for the
morning.[j]

[7]O Israel, put your hope[k] in the LORD,
for with the LORD is unfailing love
and with him is full redemption.
[8]He himself will redeem[l] Israel
from all their sins.

Psalm 131

A song of ascents. Of David.

Childlike hope in the LORD.

[1]My heart is not proud,[m] O LORD,
my eyes are not haughty;
I do not concern myself with great
matters
or things too wonderful for me.
[2]But I have stilled and quieted my soul;
like a weaned child with its mother,
like a weaned child is my soul[n]
within me.

[3]O Israel, put your hope[o] in the LORD
both now and forevermore.

Psalm 132

132:8-10pp— 2Ch6:41-42

A song of ascents.

The LORD has chosen Zion.

[1]O LORD, remember David
and all the hardships he endured.
[2]He swore an oath to the LORD
and made a vow to the Mighty One
of Jacob:[p]
[3]"I will not enter my house
or go to my bed—
[4]I will allow no sleep to my eyes,
no slumber to my eyelids,
[5]till I find a place[q] for the LORD,
a dwelling for the Mighty One of
Jacob."

[6]We heard it in Ephrathah,[r]
we came upon it in the fields of
Jaar[b]:[c][s]
[7]"Let us go to his dwelling place;[t]
let us worship at his footstool[u]—
[8]arise, O LORD,[v] and come to your
resting place,
you and the ark of your might.
[9]May your priests be clothed with
righteousness;[w]
may your saints sing for joy."

[10]For the sake of David your servant,
do not reject your anointed one.

[11]The LORD swore an oath to David,[x]
a sure oath that he will not revoke:
"One of your own descendants[y]
I will place on your throne—
[12]if your sons keep my covenant
and the statutes I teach them,
then their sons will sit
on your throne[z] for ever and ever."

[13]For the LORD has chosen Zion,[a]
he has desired it for his dwelling:
[14]"This is my resting place for ever
and ever;[b]
here I will sit enthroned, for I have
desired it—
[15]I will bless her with abundant
provisions;
her poor will I satisfy with food.[c]
[16]I will clothe her priests[d] with salvation,
and her saints will ever sing for joy.

[17]"Here I will make a horn[d] grow[e] for
David
and set up a lamp[f] for my anointed
one.

130:1 [a]Ps 42:7; 69:2; La 3:55
130:2 [b]Ps 28:2 [c]2Ch 6:40; Ps 64:1
130:3 [d]Ps 76:7; 143:2
130:4 [e]Ex 34:7; Isa 55:7; Jer 33:8 [f]1Ki 8:40
130:5 [g]Ps 27:14; 33:20; Isa 8:17 [h]Ps 119:81
130:6 [i]Ps 63:6 [j]Ps 119:147
130:7 [k]Ps 131:3
130:8 [l]Lk 1:68
131:1 [m]Ps 101:5; Ro 12:16
131:2 [n]Mt 18:3; 1Co 14:20
131:3 [o]Ps 130:7
132:2 [p]Ge 49:24
132:5 [q]Ac 7:46
132:6 [r]1Sa 17:12 [s]1Sa 7:2
132:7 [t]Ps 5:7 [u]Ps 99:5
132:8 [v]Nu 10:35; Ps 78:61
132:9 [w]Job 29:14; Isa 61:3,10
132:11 [x]Ps 89:3-4,35 [y]2Sa 7:12
132:12 [z]Lk 1:32; Ac 2:30
132:13 [a]Ps 48:1-2
132:14 [b]Ps 68:16
132:15 [c]Ps 107:9; 147:14
132:16 [d]2Ch 6:41
132:17 [e]Eze 29:21; Lk 1:69 [f]1Ki 11:36; 2Ch 21:7

b*6* That is, Kiriath Jearim c*6* Or *heard of it in Ephrathah, / we found it in the fields of Jaar.* (And no quotes around verses 7-9) d*17 Horn* here symbolizes strong one, that is, king.

[18]I will clothe his enemies with shame,[a]
but the crown on his head will be resplendent."

Psalm 133

A song of ascents. Of David.

Psalm for brothers to live in unity.

[1]How good and pleasant it is
when brothers live together[b] in unity!
[2]It is like precious oil poured on the head,[c]
running down on the beard,
running down on Aaron's beard,
down upon the collar of his robes.
[3]It is as if the dew of Hermon[d]
were falling on Mount Zion.
For there the LORD bestows his blessing,[e]
even life forevermore.[f]

Psalm 134

A song of ascents.

Exhortation to praise the LORD.

[1]Praise the LORD, all you servants[g] of the LORD
who minister by night[h] in the house of the LORD.
[2]Lift up your hands[i] in the sanctuary
and praise the LORD.
[3]May the LORD, the Maker of heaven[j] and earth,
bless you from Zion.[k]

Psalm 135

135:15-20pp— Ps 115:4-11

The LORD is greater than all other gods.

[1]Praise the LORD.[e]

Praise the name of the LORD;
praise him, you servants[l] of the LORD,
[2]you who minister in the house[m] of the LORD,
in the courts[n] of the house of our God.

[3]Praise the LORD, for the LORD is good;[o]
sing praise to his name, for that is pleasant.[p]
[4]For the LORD has chosen Jacob[q] to be his own,
Israel to be his treasured possession.[r]

[5]I know that the LORD is great,[s]
that our Lord is greater than all gods.[t]
[6]The LORD does whatever pleases him,[u]
in the heavens and on the earth,
in the seas and all their depths.
[7]He makes clouds rise from the ends of the earth;
he sends lightning with the rain[v]
and brings out the wind[w] from his storehouses.[x]

[8]He struck down the firstborn[y] of Egypt,
the firstborn of men and animals.
[9]He sent his signs[z] and wonders into your midst, O Egypt,
against Pharaoh and all his servants.[a]
[10]He struck down many[b] nations
and killed mighty kings—
[11]Sihon[c] king of the Amorites,
Og king of Bashan
and all the kings of Canaan[d]—
[12]and he gave their land as an inheritance,[e]
an inheritance to his people Israel.

[13]Your name, O LORD, endures forever,[f]
your renown,[g] O LORD, through all generations.
[14]For the LORD will vindicate his people
and have compassion on his servants.[h]

[15]The idols of the nations are silver and gold,
made by the hands of men.
[16]They have mouths, but cannot speak,
eyes, but they cannot see;
[17]they have ears, but cannot hear,
nor is there breath in their mouths.

132:18 [a]Ps 35:26; 109:29
133:1 [b]Ge 13:8; Heb 13:1
133:2 [c]Ex 30:25
133:3 [d]Dt 4:48 [e]Lev 25:21; Dt 28:8 [f]Ps 42:8
134:1 [g]Ps 135:1-2 [h]1Ch 9:33
134:2 [i]Ps 28:2; 1Ti 2:8
134:3 [j]Ps 124:8 [k]Ps 128:5
135:1 [l]Ps 113:1; 134:1
135:2 [m]Lk 2:37 [n]Ps 116:19
135:3 [o]Ps 119:68 [p]Ps 147:1
135:4 [q]Dt 10:15; 1Pe 2:9 [r]Ex 19:5; Dt 7:6
135:5 [s]Ps 48:1 [t]Ps 97:9
135:6 [u]Ps 115:3
135:7 [v]Jer 10:13; Zec 10:1 [w]Job 28:25 [x]Job 38:22
135:8 [y]Ex 12:12; Ps 78:51
135:9 [z]Dt 6:22 [a]Ps 136:10-15
135:10 [b]Nu 21:21-25; Ps 136:17-21
135:11 [c]Nu 21:21 [d]Jos 12:7-24
135:12 [e]Ps 78:55
135:13 [f]Ex 3:15 [g]Ps 102:12
135:14 [h]Dt 32:36

e *1* Hebrew *Hallelu Yah*; also in verses 3 and 21

18Those who make them will be like
them,
and so will all who trust in them.

19O house of Israel, praise the LORD;
O house of Aaron, praise the LORD;
20O house of Levi, praise the LORD;
you who fear him, praise the LORD.
21Praise be to the LORD from Zion,[a]
to him who dwells in Jerusalem.

Praise the LORD.

Psalm 136

God's love endures forever.

1Give thanks to the LORD, for he is
good.[b]
His love endures forever.[c]
2Give thanks to the God of gods.[d]
His love endures forever.
3Give thanks to the Lord of lords:
His love endures forever.

4to him who alone does great
wonders,[e]
His love endures forever.
5who by his understanding[f] made the
heavens,[g]
His love endures forever.
6who spread out the earth[h] upon the
waters,[i]
His love endures forever.
7who made the great lights[j]—
His love endures forever.
8the sun to govern[k] the day,
His love endures forever.
9the moon and stars to govern the
night;
His love endures forever.

10to him who struck down the
firstborn[l] of Egypt
His love endures forever.
11and brought Israel out[m] from among
them
His love endures forever.
12with a mighty hand and outstretched
arm;[n]
His love endures forever.

13to him who divided the Red Sea[f][o]
asunder
His love endures forever.
14and brought Israel through[p] the
midst of it,
His love endures forever.
15but swept Pharaoh and his army into
the Red Sea;[q]
His love endures forever.

16to him who led his people through
the desert,[r]
His love endures forever.
17who struck down great kings,[s]
His love endures forever.
18and killed mighty kings[t]—
His love endures forever.
19Sihon king of the Amorites[u]
His love endures forever.
20and Og king of Bashan—
His love endures forever.
21and gave their land[v] as an
inheritance,
His love endures forever.
22an inheritance to his servant Israel;
His love endures forever.

23to the One who remembered us[w] in
our low estate
His love endures forever.
24and freed us from our enemies,[x]
His love endures forever.
25and who gives food[y] to every
creature.
His love endures forever.

26Give thanks to the God of heaven.
His love endures forever.

Psalm 137

Captives in Babylon.

1By the rivers of Babylon[z] we sat and
wept[a]
when we remembered Zion.
2There on the poplars
we hung our harps,
3for there our captors asked us for
songs,
our tormentors demanded[b] songs
of joy;
they said, "Sing us one of the songs
of Zion!"

135:21 [a]Ps 134:3
136:1 [b]Ps 106:1 [c]1Ch 16:34; 2Ch 20:21
136:2 [d]Dt 10:17
136:4 [e]Ps 72:18
136:5 [f]Pr 3:19; Jer 51:15 [g]Ge 1:1
136:6 [h]Ge 1:9; Jer 10:12 [i]Ps 24:2
136:7 [j]Ge 1:14,16
136:8 [k]Ge 1:16
136:10 [l]Ex 12:29; Ps 135:8
136:11 [m]Ex 6:6; 12:51
136:12 [n]Dt 4:34; Ps 44:3
136:13 [o]Ex 14:21; Ps 78:13
136:14 [p]Ex 14:22
136:15 [q]Ex 14:27; Ps 135:9
136:16 [r]Ex 13:18
136:17 [s]Ps 135:9-12
136:18 [t]Dt 29:7
136:19 [u]Nu 21:21-25
136:21 [v]Jos 12:1
136:23 [w]Ps 113:7
136:24 [x]Ps 107:2
136:25 [y]Ps 104:27; 145:15
137:1 [z]Eze 1:1,3 [a]Ne 1:4
137:3 [b]Ps 80:6

f *13* Hebrew *Yam Suph*; that is, Sea of Reeds; also in verse 15

4How can we sing the songs of the LORD
while in a foreign land?
5If I forget you, O Jerusalem,
may my right hand forget ⌊its skill⌋.
6May my tongue cling to the roof[a] of
my mouth
if I do not remember you,
if I do not consider Jerusalem
my highest joy.

7Remember, O LORD, what the
Edomites[b] did
on the day Jerusalem fell.[c]
"Tear it down," they cried,
"tear it down to its foundations!"

8O Daughter of Babylon, doomed to
destruction,[d]
happy is he who repays you
for what you have done to us—
9he who seizes your infants
and dashes them[e] against the
rocks.

Psalm 138

Of David.

The LORD's love and faithfulness.

1I will praise you, O LORD, with all my
heart;
before the "gods"[f] I will sing your
praise.
2I will bow down toward your holy
temple[g]
and will praise your name
for your love and your faithfulness,
for you have exalted above all things
your name and your word.[h]
3When I called, you answered me;
you made me bold and
stouthearted.[i]

4May all the kings of the earth[j] praise
you, O LORD,
when they hear the words of your
mouth.
5May they sing of the ways of the LORD,
for the glory of the LORD is great.

6Though the LORD is on high, he looks
upon the lowly,[k]
but the proud[l] he knows from afar.
7Though I walk[m] in the midst of
trouble,
you preserve my life;
you stretch out your hand against
the anger of my foes,[n]
with your right hand[o] you save me.[p]
8The LORD will fulfill ⌊his purpose⌋[q]
for me;
your love, O LORD, endures forever—
do not abandon the works of your
hands.[r]

Psalm 139

For the director of music.
Of David. A psalm.

God knows all things.

1O LORD, you have searched me[s]
and you know[t] me.
2You know when I sit and when I
rise;[u]
you perceive my thoughts[v] from afar.
3You discern my going out and my
lying down;
you are familiar with all my ways.[w]
4Before a word is on my tongue
you know it completely,[x] O LORD.

5You hem me in[y]—behind and before;
you have laid your hand upon me.
6Such knowledge is too wonderful for
me,
too lofty[z] for me to attain.

7Where can I go from your Spirit?
Where can I flee[a] from your
presence?
8If I go up to the heavens,[b] you are
there;
if I make my bed[c] in the depths,[g]
you are there.
9If I rise on the wings of the dawn,
if I settle on the far side of the sea,
10even there your hand will guide me,[d]
your right hand will hold me fast.

11If I say, "Surely the darkness will
hide me
and the light become night around
me,"

137:6 [a]Eze 3:26
137:7 [b]Jer 49:7; La 4:21-22; Eze 25:12 [c]Ob 1:11
137:8 [d]Isa 13:1,19; Jer 25:12,26; Jer 50:15; Rev 18:6
137:9 [e]2Ki 8:12; Isa 13:16
138:1 [f]Ps 95:3; 96:4
138:2 [g]1Ki 8:29; Ps 5:7; 28:2 [h]Isa 42:21
138:3 [i]Ps 28:7
138:4 [j]Ps 102:15
138:6 [k]Ps 113:6; Isa 57:15 [l]Pr 3:34; Jas 4:6
138:7 [m]Ps 23:4 [n]Jer 51:25 [o]Ps 20:6 [p]Ps 71:20
138:8 [q]Ps 57:2; Php 1:6 [r]Job 10:3,8; 14:15
139:1 [s]Ps 17:3 [t]Jer 12:3
139:2 [u]2Ki 19:27 [v]Mt 9:4; Jn 2:24
139:3 [w]Job 31:4
139:4 [x]Heb 4:13
139:5 [y]Ps 34:7
139:6 [z]Job 42:3; Ro 11:33
139:7 [a]Jer 23:24; Jnh 1:3
139:8 [b]Am 9:2-3 [c]Pr 15:11
139:10 [d]Ps 23:3

g8 Hebrew *Sheol*

[12]even the darkness will not be dark[a]
to you;
the night will shine like the day,
for darkness is as light to you.

[13]For you created my inmost being;[b]
you knit me together[c] in my
mother's womb.
[14]I praise you because I am fearfully
and wonderfully made;
your works are wonderful,[d]
I know that full well.
[15]My frame was not hidden from you
when I was made in the secret
place.
When I was woven together[e] in the
depths of the earth,[f]
[16] your eyes saw my unformed body.
All the days ordained for me
were written in your book
before one of them came to be.

[17]How precious to[h] me are your
thoughts, O God![g]
How vast is the sum of them!
[18]Were I to count them,
they would outnumber the grains
of sand.
When I awake,
I am still with you.

[19]If only you would slay the wicked,[h]
O God!
Away from me,[i] you bloodthirsty
men!
[20]They speak of you with evil intent;
your adversaries misuse your
name.[j]
[21]Do I not hate those[k] who hate you,
O LORD,
and abhor those who rise up
against you?
[22]I have nothing but hatred for them;
I count them my enemies.

[23]Search me,[l] O God, and know my
heart;[m]
test me and know my anxious
thoughts.
[24]See if there is any offensive way in
me,
and lead me[n] in the way
everlasting.

139:12 [a]Job 34:22; Da 2:22
139:13 [b]Ps 119:73 [c]Job 10:11
139:14 [d]Ps 40:5
139:15 [e]Job 10:11 [f]Ps 63:9
139:17 [g]Ps 40:5
139:19 [h]Isa 11:4 [i]Ps 119:115
139:20 [j]Jude 15
139:21 [k]2Ch 19:2; Ps 31:6; 119:113; Ps 119:158
139:23 [l]Job 31:6; Ps 26:2 [m]Jer 11:20
139:24 [n]Ps 5:8; 143:10; Pr 15:9
140:1 [o]Ps 17:13 [p]Ps 18:48
140:2 [q]Ps 36:4; 56:6
140:3 [r]Ps 57:4 [s]Ps 58:4; Jas 3:8
140:4 [t]Ps 141:9 [u]Ps 71:4
140:5 [v]Ps 31:4; 35:7
140:6 [w]Ps 16:2 [x]Ps 116:1; 143:1
140:7 [y]Ps 28:8
140:8 [z]Ps 10:2-3
140:9 [a]Ps 7:16
140:10 [b]Ps 11:6; 21:9
140:11 [c]Ps 34:21

Psalm 140

For the director of music.
A psalm of David.

Prayer for protection from evil men.

[1]Rescue me,[o] O LORD, from evil men;
protect me from men of violence,[p]
[2]who devise evil plans[q] in their
hearts
and stir up war every day.
[3]They make their tongues as sharp
as[r] a serpent's;
the poison of vipers[s] is on their
lips. *Selah*

[4]Keep me,[t] O LORD, from the hands of
the wicked;[u]
protect me from men of violence
who plan to trip my feet.
[5]Proud men have hidden a snare for
me;
they have spread out the cords of
their net
and have set traps[v] for me along
my path. *Selah*

[6]O LORD, I say to you, "You are my
God."[w]
Hear, O LORD, my cry for mercy.[x]
[7]O Sovereign LORD,[y] my strong
deliverer,
who shields my head in the day of
battle—
[8]do not grant the wicked[z] their
desires, O LORD;
do not let their plans succeed,
or they will become proud.
Selah

[9]Let the heads of those who surround
me
be covered with the trouble their
lips have caused.[a]
[10]Let burning coals fall upon them;
may they be thrown into the fire,[b]
into miry pits, never to rise.
[11]Let slanderers not be established in
the land;
may disaster hunt down men of
violence.[c]

h *17* Or *concerning*

[12]I know that the LORD secures justice
for the poor
and upholds the cause[a] of the
needy.[b]
[13]Surely the righteous will praise your
name[c]
and the upright will live[d] before you.

Psalm 141

A psalm of David.

Let not hearts be drawn to evil.

[1]O LORD, I call to you; come quickly[e]
to me.
Hear my voice[f] when I call to you.
[2]May my prayer be set before you like
incense;[g]
may the lifting up of my hands[h] be
like the evening sacrifice.[i]

[3]Set a guard over my mouth, O LORD;
keep watch over the door of my lips.
[4]Let not my heart be drawn to what is
evil,
to take part in wicked deeds
with men who are evildoers;
let me not eat of their delicacies.[j]

[5]Let a righteous man[i] strike me—it is
a kindness;
let him rebuke me[k]—it is oil on
my head.[l]
My head will not refuse it.

Yet my prayer is ever against the
deeds of evildoers;
[6] their rulers will be thrown down
from the cliffs,
and the wicked will learn that my
words were well spoken.
[7]⌊They will say,⌋ "As one plows and
breaks up the earth,
so our bones have been scattered
at the mouth[m] of the grave.[j]"

[8]But my eyes are fixed[n] on you,
O Sovereign LORD;
in you I take refuge[o]—do not give
me over to death.
[9]Keep me[p] from the snares they have
laid for me,
from the traps set[q] by evildoers.

140:12
[a]Ps 9:4
[b]Ps 35:10

140:13
[c]Ps 97:12
[d]Ps 11:7

141:1
[e]Ps 22:19; 70:5
[f]Ps 143:1

141:2
[g]Rev 5:8; 8:3
[h]1Ti 2:8
[i]Ex 29:39,41

141:4
[j]Pr 23:6

141:5
[k]Pr 9:8
[l]Ps 23:5

141:7
[m]Ps 53:5

141:8
[n]Ps 25:15
[o]Ps 2:12

141:9
[p]Ps 140:4
[q]Ps 38:12

141:10
[r]Ps 35:8

142:1
[s]Ps 30:8

142:2
[t]Isa 26:16

142:3
[u]Ps 140:5; 143:4,7

142:4
[v]Ps 31:11; Jer 30:17

142:5
[w]Ps 46:1
[x]Ps 16:5
[y]Ps 27:13

142:6
[z]Ps 17:1
[a]Ps 79:8; 116:6

142:7
[b]Ps 146:7
[c]Ps 13:6

143:1
[d]Ps 140:6
[e]Ps 89:1-2
[f]Ps 71:2

[10]Let the wicked fall[r] into their own
nets,
while I pass by in safety.

Psalm 142

A *maskil*[k] of David. When he
was in the cave. A prayer.

The comfort of prayer.

[1]I cry aloud to the LORD;
I lift up my voice to the LORD for
mercy.[s]
[2]I pour out my complaint[t] before him;
before him I tell my trouble.

[3]When my spirit grows faint[u] within
me,
it is you who know my way.
In the path where I walk
men have hidden a snare for me.
[4]Look to my right and see;
no one is concerned for me.
I have no refuge;
no one cares[v] for my life.

[5]I cry to you, O LORD;
I say, "You are my refuge,[w]
my portion[x] in the land of the
living."[y]
[6]Listen to my cry,[z]
for I am in desperate need;[a]
rescue me from those who pursue me,
for they are too strong for me.
[7]Set me free from my prison,[b]
that I may praise your name.

Then the righteous will gather about
me
because of your goodness to me.[c]

Psalm 143

A psalm of David.

Prayer for rescue.

[1]O LORD, hear my prayer,
listen to my cry for mercy;[d]
in your faithfulness[e] and
righteousness[f]
come to my relief.

[i]5 Or *Let the Righteous One* [j]7 Hebrew *Sheol*
[k]Title: Probably a literary or musical term

2Do not bring your servant into
judgment,
for no one living is righteous[a]
before you.
3The enemy pursues me,
he crushes me to the ground;
he makes me dwell in darkness
like those long dead.
4So my spirit grows faint within me;
my heart within me is dismayed.[b]
5I remember[c] the days of long ago;
I meditate on all your works
and consider what your hands have
done.
6I spread out my hands[d] to you;
my soul thirsts for you like a
parched land. *Selah*
7Answer me quickly,[e] O LORD;
my spirit fails.
Do not hide your face[f] from me
or I will be like those who go
down to the pit.
8Let the morning bring me word of
your unfailing love,[g]
for I have put my trust in you.
Show me the way[h] I should go,
for to you I lift up my soul.[i]
9Rescue me from my enemies,[j] O LORD,
for I hide myself in you.
10Teach me to do your will,
for you are my God;
may your good Spirit
lead[k] me on level ground.
11For your name's sake, O LORD,
preserve my life;[l]
in your righteousness,[m] bring me
out of trouble.
12In your unfailing love, silence my
enemies;
destroy all my foes,[n]
for I am your servant.[o]

Psalm 144

Of David.

Petition for God's deliverance.

1Praise be to the LORD my Rock,[p]
who trains my hands for war,
my fingers for battle.
2He is my loving God and my fortress,[q]
my stronghold and my deliverer,
my shield,[r] in whom I take refuge,
who subdues peoples[l] under me.
3O LORD, what is man[s] that you care
for him,
the son of man that you think of him?
4Man is like a breath;
his days are like a fleeting
shadow.[t]
5Part your heavens,[u] O LORD, and
come down;
touch the mountains, so that they
smoke.[v]
6Send forth lightning and scatter ⌊the
enemies⌋;
shoot your arrows[w] and rout them.
7Reach down your hand from on high;
deliver me and rescue me
from the mighty waters,[x]
from the hands of foreigners[y]
8whose mouths are full of lies,[z]
whose right hands are deceitful.
9I will sing a new song to you, O God;
on the ten-stringed lyre[a] I will
make music to you,
10to the One who gives victory to kings,
who delivers his servant David[b]
from the deadly sword.
11Deliver me and rescue me
from the hands of foreigners
whose mouths are full of lies,
whose right hands are deceitful.[c]
12Then our sons in their youth
will be like well-nurtured plants,[d]
and our daughters will be like pillars
carved to adorn a palace.
13Our barns will be filled
with every kind of provision.
Our sheep will increase by thousands,
by tens of thousands in our fields;
14 our oxen will draw heavy loads.[m]
There will be no breaching of walls,
no going into captivity,
no cry of distress in our streets.

143:2 [a]Ps 14:3; Ecc 7:20; Ro 3:20
143:4 [b]Ps 142:3
143:5 [c]Ps 77:6
143:6 [d]Ps 63:1; 88:9
143:7 [e]Ps 69:17 [f]Ps 27:9; 28:1
143:8 [g]Ps 46:5; 90:14 [h]Ps 27:11 [i]Ps 25:1-2
143:9 [j]Ps 31:15
143:10 [k]Ne 9:20; Ps 23:3; 25:4-5
143:11 [l]Ps 119:25 [m]Ps 31:1
143:12 [n]Ps 52:5; 54:5 [o]Ps 116:16
144:1 [p]Ps 18:2,34
144:2 [q]Ps 59:9; 91:2 [r]Ps 84:9
144:3 [s]Ps 8:4; Heb 2:6
144:4 [t]Ps 39:11; 102:11
144:5 [u]Ps 18:9; Isa 64:1 [v]Ps 104:32
144:6 [w]Ps 7:12-13; 18:14
144:7 [x]Ps 69:2 [y]Ps 18:44
144:8 [z]Ps 12:2
144:9 [a]Ps 33:2-3
144:10 [b]Ps 18:50
144:11 [c]Ps 12:2; Isa 44:20
144:12 [d]Ps 128:3

l *2* Many manuscripts of the Masoretic Text, Dead Sea Scrolls, Aquila, Jerome and Syriac; most manuscripts of the Masoretic Text *subdues my people* m *14* Or *our chieftains will be firmly established*

15 Blessed are the people[a] of whom this is true;
blessed are the people whose God is the LORD.

Psalm 145[n]

A psalm of praise. Of David.

Praise to God for his many virtues.

1 I will exalt you,[b] my God the King;[c]
I will praise your name for ever and ever.
2 Every day I will praise[d] you
and extol your name for ever and ever.

3 Great is the LORD and most worthy of praise;
his greatness no one can fathom.[e]
4 One generation[f] will commend your works to another;
they will tell of your mighty acts.
5 They will speak of the glorious splendor of your majesty,
and I will meditate on your wonderful works.[o] [g]
6 They will tell of the power of your awesome works,[h]
and I will proclaim[i] your great deeds.
7 They will celebrate your abundant goodness[j]
and joyfully sing of your righteousness.[k]

8 The LORD is gracious and compassionate,[l]
slow to anger and rich in love.[m]
9 The LORD is good[n] to all;
he has compassion on all he has made.
10 All you have made will praise you,[o] O LORD;
your saints will extol you.[p]
11 They will tell of the glory of your kingdom
and speak of your might,
12 so that all men may know of your mighty acts[q]
and the glorious splendor of your kingdom.
13 Your kingdom is an everlasting kingdom,[r]
and your dominion endures through all generations.

The LORD is faithful to all his promises
and loving toward all he has made.[p]
14 The LORD upholds[s] all those who fall
and lifts up all[t] who are bowed down.
15 The eyes of all look to you,
and you give them their food[u] at the proper time.
16 You open your hand
and satisfy the desires[v] of every living thing.

17 The LORD is righteous in all his ways
and loving toward all he has made.
18 The LORD is near[w] to all who call on him,[x]
to all who call on him in truth.
19 He fulfills the desires[y] of those who fear him;
he hears their cry[z] and saves them.
20 The LORD watches over all who love him,[a]
but all the wicked he will destroy.[b]

21 My mouth will speak[c] in praise of the LORD.
Let every creature[d] praise his holy name
for ever and ever.

Psalm 146

Blessed is the one whose help is God.

1 Praise the LORD.[q]

Praise the LORD,[e] O my soul.
2 I will praise the LORD all my life;[f]
I will sing praise to my God as long as I live.

144:15 [a]Ps 33:12
145:1 [b]Ps 30:1; 34:1 [c]Ps 5:2
145:2 [d]Ps 71:6
145:3 [e]Job 5:9; Ps 147:5; Ro 11:33
145:4 [f]Isa 38:19
145:5 [g]Ps 119:27
145:6 [h]Ps 66:3 [i]Dt 32:3
145:7 [j]Isa 63:7 [k]Ps 51:14
145:8 [l]Ps 86:15 [m]Ex 34:6; Nu 14:18
145:9 [n]Ps 100:5
145:10 [o]Ps 19:1 [p]Ps 68:26
145:12 [q]Ps 105:1
145:13 [r]1Ti 1:17; 2Pe 1:11
145:14 [s]Ps 37:24 [t]Ps 146:8
145:15 [u]Ps 104:27; 136:25
145:16 [v]Ps 104:28
145:18 [w]Dt 4:7 [x]Jn 4:24
145:19 [y]Ps 37:4 [z]Pr 15:29
145:20 [a]Ps 31:23; 97:10 [b]Ps 9:5
145:21 [c]Ps 71:8 [d]Ps 65:2
146:1 [e]Ps 103:1
146:2 [f]Ps 104:33

[n] This psalm is an acrostic poem, the verses of which (including verse 13b) begin with the successive letters of the Hebrew alphabet. [o] *5* Dead Sea Scrolls and Syriac (see also Septuagint); Masoretic Text *On the glorious splendor of your majesty / and on your wonderful works I will meditate* [p] *13* One manuscript of the Masoretic Text, Dead Sea Scrolls and Syriac (see also Septuagint); most manuscripts of the Masoretic Text do not have the last two lines of verse 13. [q] *1* Hebrew *Hallelu Yah*; also in verse 10

3Do not put your trust in princes,[a]
in mortal men,[b] who cannot save.
4When their spirit departs, they
return to the ground;[c]
on that very day their plans come
to nothing.[d]

5Blessed is he[e] whose help[f] is the
God of Jacob,
whose hope is in the LORD his God,
6the Maker of heaven[g] and earth,
the sea, and everything in them—
the LORD, who remains faithful[h]
forever.
7He upholds the cause of the
oppressed[i]
and gives food to the hungry.[j]
The LORD sets prisoners free,[k]
8 the LORD gives sight to the blind,[l]
the LORD lifts up those who are
bowed down,
the LORD loves the righteous.
9The LORD watches over the alien
and sustains the fatherless and the
widow,[m]
but he frustrates the ways of the
wicked.

10The LORD reigns[n] forever,
your God, O Zion, for all generations.

Praise the LORD.

Psalm 147

The LORD is worthy of praise.

1Praise the LORD.[r]

How good it is to sing praises to our
God,
how pleasant[o] and fitting to praise
him![p]

2The LORD builds up Jerusalem;[q]
he gathers the exiles[r] of Israel.
3He heals the brokenhearted
and binds up their wounds.

4He determines the number of the
stars[s]
and calls them each by name.
5Great is our Lord[t] and mighty in
power;
his understanding has no limit.[u]
6The LORD sustains the humble[v]
but casts the wicked to the ground.

7Sing to the LORD[w] with thanksgiving;
make music to our God on the harp.
8He covers the sky with clouds;
he supplies the earth with rain[x]
and makes grass grow[y] on the hills.
9He provides food[z] for the cattle
and for the young ravens[a] when
they call.

10His pleasure is not in the strength[b]
of the horse,[c]
nor his delight in the legs of a man;
11the LORD delights in those who fear
him,
who put their hope in his unfailing
love.

12Extol the LORD, O Jerusalem;
praise your God, O Zion,
13for he strengthens the bars of your
gates
and blesses your people within you.
14He grants peace[d] to your borders
and satisfies you[e] with the finest of
wheat.

15He sends his command[f] to the earth;
his word runs swiftly.
16He spreads the snow[g] like wool
and scatters the frost[h] like ashes.
17He hurls down his hail like pebbles.
Who can withstand his icy blast?
18He sends his word[i] and melts them;
he stirs up his breezes, and the
waters flow.

19He has revealed his word to Jacob,
his laws and decrees[j] to Israel.
20He has done this for no other nation;[k]
they do not know his laws.

Praise the LORD.

Psalm 148

All creation is to praise the LORD.

1Praise the LORD.[s]

Praise the LORD from the heavens,

146:3 [a]Ps 118:9 [b]Isa 2:22
146:4 [c]Ps 104:29; Ecc 12:7 [d]Ps 33:10; 1Co 2:6
146:5 [e]Ps 144:15; Jer 17:7 [f]Ps 71:5
146:6 [g]Ps 115:15; Ac 14:15; Rev 14:7 [h]Ps 117:2
146:7 [i]Ps 103:6 [j]Ps 107:9 [k]Ps 68:6
146:8 [l]Mt 9:30
146:9 [m]Ex 22:22; Dt 10:18; Ps 68:5
146:10 [n]Ex 15:18; Ps 10:16
147:1 [o]Ps 135:3 [p]Ps 33:1
147:2 [q]Ps 102:16 [r]Dt 30:3
147:4 [s]Isa 40:26
147:5 [t]Ps 48:1 [u]Isa 40:28
147:6 [v]Ps 146:8-9
147:7 [w]Ps 33:3
147:8 [x]Job 38:26 [y]Ps 104:14
147:9 [z]Ps 104:27-28; Mt 6:26 [a]Job 38:41
147:10 [b]1Sa 16:7 [c]Ps 33:16-17
147:14 [d]Isa 60:17-18 [e]Ps 132:15
147:15 [f]Job 37:12
147:16 [g]Job 37:6 [h]Job 38:29
147:18 [i]Ps 33:9
147:19 [j]Dt 33:4; Mal 4:4
147:20 [k]Dt 4:7-8,32-34

r *1* Hebrew *Hallelu Yah*; also in verse 20 s *1* Hebrew *Hallelu Yah*; also in verse 14

praise him in the heights above.
[2]Praise him, all his angels,[a]
praise him, all his heavenly hosts.
[3]Praise him, sun and moon,
praise him, all you shining stars.
[4]Praise him, you highest heavens
and you waters above the skies.[b]
[5]Let them praise the name of the LORD,
for he commanded[c] and they were
created.
[6]He set them in place for ever and ever;
he gave a decree[d] that will never
pass away.

[7]Praise the LORD from the earth,
you great sea creatures[e] and all
ocean depths,
[8]lightning and hail, snow and clouds,
stormy winds that do his bidding,[f]
[9]you mountains and all hills,[g]
fruit trees and all cedars,
[10]wild animals and all cattle,
small creatures and flying birds,
[11]kings of the earth and all nations,
you princes and all rulers on earth,
[12]young men and maidens,
old men and children.

[13]Let them praise the name of the LORD,[h]
for his name alone is exalted;
his splendor is above the earth and
the heavens.[i]
[14]He has raised up for his people a
horn,[t][j]
the praise of all his saints,
of Israel, the people close to his heart.

Praise the LORD.

Psalm 149

Praise the LORD in dance and song.

[1]Praise the LORD.[u][k]

Sing to the LORD a new song,
his praise in the assembly[l] of the
saints.

[2]Let Israel rejoice in their Maker;[m]
let the people of Zion be glad in
their King.[n]

148:2 [a]Ps 103:20 **148:4** [b]Ge 1:7; 1Ki 8:27 **148:5** [c]Ge 1:1,6; Ps 33:6,9 **148:6** [d]Job 38:33; Ps 89:37; Jer 33:25 **148:7** [e]Ps 74:13-14 **148:8** [f]Ps 147:15-18 **148:9** [g]Isa 44:23; 49:13; 55:12 **148:13** [h]Isa 12:4 [i]Ps 8:1; 113:4 **148:14** [j]Ps 75:10 **149:1** [k]Ps 33:2 [l]Ps 35:18 **149:2** [m]Ps 95:6 [n]Ps 47:6; Zec 9:9 **149:3** [o]Ps 81:2; 150:4 **149:4** [p]Ps 35:27 [q]Ps 132:16 **149:5** [r]Ps 132:16 [s]Job 35:10 **149:6** [t]Ps 66:17 [u]Heb 4:12; Rev 1:16 **149:9** [v]Dt 7:1; Eze 28:26 [w]Ps 148:14 **150:1** [x]Ps 102:19 [y]Ps 19:1 **150:2** [z]Dt 3:24 [a]Ps 145:5-6 **150:3** [b]Ps 149:3 **150:4** [c]Ex 15:20 [d]Isa 38:20 **150:5** [e]1Ch 13:8; 15:16 **150:6** [f]Ps 145:21

[3]Let them praise his name with dancing
and make music to him with
tambourine and harp.[o]
[4]For the LORD takes delight[p] in his
people;
he crowns the humble with
salvation.[q]
[5]Let the saints rejoice[r] in this honor
and sing for joy on their beds.[s]

[6]May the praise of God be in their
mouths[t]
and a double-edged[u] sword in their
hands,
[7]to inflict vengeance on the nations
and punishment on the peoples,
[8]to bind their kings with fetters,
their nobles with shackles of iron,
[9]to carry out the sentence written
against them.[v]
This is the glory of all his saints.[w]

Praise the LORD.

Psalm 150

Praise God with musical instruments.

[1]Praise the LORD.[v]

Praise God in his sanctuary;[x]
praise him in his mighty heavens.[y]
[2]Praise him for his acts of power;[z]
praise him for his surpassing
greatness.[a]
[3]Praise him with the sounding of the
trumpet,
praise him with the harp and lyre,[b]
[4]praise him with tambourine and
dancing,[c]
praise him with the strings[d] and flute,
[5]praise him with the clash of cymbals,[e]
praise him with resounding cymbals.

[6]Let everything[f] that has breath
praise the LORD.

Praise the LORD.

t*14* *Horn* here symbolizes strong one, that is, king.
u*1* Hebrew *Hallelu Yah*; also in verse 9 v*1* Hebrew *Hallelu Yah*; also in verse 6

PROVERBS

Author: Principally King Solomon, but Agur, King Lemuel and others made contributions.

Date Written: Between 1000 and 700 B.C. However, the majority of the proverbs were written by Solomon by 931 B.C. (The book was not edited into its present-day form until some years later.)

Time Span: Unknown, but primarily during the years of Solomon's life.

Title: The Hebrew title of this book means "Proverbs of Solomon."

Background: Solomon succeeds his father David to rule as king of Israel. After asking God for wisdom, Solomon is so blessed that people come from far away to learn from him. This collection of wise sayings is a part of these teachings. The book of Proverbs is a collection of roughly one-fourth of the 3,000 proverbs and 1,005 songs attributed to Solomon.

Where Written: Probably Judah.

To Whom: Primarily to young people.

Content: Proverbs is an assortment of wise sayings relating spiritual truths and common sense. These proverbs give instruction concerning every conceivable area of human life, often contrasting the ungodly view of the fool versus the godly perspective of the wise. These truths give counsel which helps both to prevent and to correct ungodly lifestyles. Proverbs are practical, timeless and ideal for memorizing. The book ends with a close look at the qualities of a godly woman in relation to her husband, her children and her neighbors (chapter 31).

Key Words: "Wisdom"; "Folly." The ability to live with practical righteousness is scrutinized. This "wisdom" helps us to discern between good and evil, truth and error, and divine and human perspectives. "The fear of the LORD is the beginning of wisdom" (9:10), but "Folly is loud...undisciplined and without knowledge" (9:13).

Themes: • True wisdom cannot be gained apart from God. • God is concerned that we submit even seemingly insignificant areas of our lives to his lordship. • We should not rely on our own understanding, but on the truths that God teaches us. • God will direct our paths. • Godly success in life comes from obedience to the Word and ways of God. • God desires for us to be happy. • God has made happiness available to us if we will only fear, trust and obey him.

Outline:

1. Purpose and theme of Proverbs. 1:1-1:6
2. Wisdom and folly contrasted. 1:7-9:18
3. Proverbs of Solomon. 10:1-24:34
4. Proverbs of Solomon collected by King Hezekiah's men. 25:1-29:27
5. Sayings of Agur. 30:1-30:33
6. Sayings of King Lemuel. 31:1-31:31

PROVERBS

Proverbs of Solomon: Attaining wisdom.

1 The proverbs of Solomon[a] son of David, king of Israel:[b]

[2]for attaining wisdom and discipline;
for understanding words of insight;
[3]for acquiring a disciplined and prudent life,
doing what is right and just and fair;
[4]for giving prudence to the simple,[c]
knowledge and discretion[d] to the young—
[5]let the wise listen and add to their learning,[e]
and let the discerning get guidance—
[6]for understanding proverbs and parables,[f]
the sayings and riddles[g] of the wise.

[7]The fear of the LORD[h] is the beginning of knowledge,
but fools[a] despise wisdom and discipline.

Warning against enticement of sinners.

[8]Listen, my son,[i] to your father's instruction
and do not forsake your mother's teaching.[j]
[9]They will be a garland to grace your head
and a chain to adorn your neck.[k]

[10]My son, if sinners entice[l] you,
do not give in[m] to them.[n]
[11]If they say, "Come along with us;
let's lie in wait[o] for someone's blood,
let's waylay some harmless soul;
[12]let's swallow them alive, like the grave,[b]
and whole, like those who go down to the pit;[p]
[13]we will get all sorts of valuable things
and fill our houses with plunder;
[14]throw in your lot with us,
and we will share a common purse"—
[15]my son, do not go along with them,
do not set foot[q] on their paths;[r]
[16]for their feet rush into sin,
they are swift to shed blood.[s]
[17]How useless to spread a net
in full view of all the birds!
[18]These men lie in wait for their own blood;
they waylay only themselves!
[19]Such is the end of all who go after ill-gotten gain;
it takes away the lives of those who get it.[t]

Warning against rejecting wisdom.

[20]Wisdom calls aloud[u] in the street,
she raises her voice in the public squares;
[21]at the head of the noisy streets[c] she cries out,
in the gateways of the city she makes her speech:

[22]"How long will you simple ones[d][v] love your simple ways?
How long will mockers delight in mockery
and fools hate knowledge?
[23]If you had responded to my rebuke,
I would have poured out my heart to you
and made my thoughts known to you.
[24]But since you rejected me when I called[w]
and no one gave heed when I stretched out my hand,
[25]since you ignored all my advice
and would not accept my rebuke,
[26]I in turn will laugh[x] at your disaster;
I will mock when calamity overtakes you[y]—

1:1 [a]1Ki 4:29-34 [b]Pr 10:1;25:1; Ecc 1:1
1:4 [c]Pr 8:5 [d]Pr 2:10-11; 8:12
1:5 [e]Pr 9:9
1:6 [f]Ps 49:4; 78:2 [g]Nu 12:8
1:7 [h]Job 28:28; Ps 111:10; Pr 9:10; 15:33; Ecc 12:13
1:8 [i]Pr 4:1 [j]Pr 6:20
1:9 [k]Pr 4:1-9
1:10 [l]Ge 39:7 [m]Dt 13:8 [n]Pr 16:29; Eph 5:11
1:11 [o]Ps 10:8
1:12 [p]Ps 28:1
1:15 [q]Ps 119:101 [r]Ps 1:1; Pr 4:14
1:16 [s]Pr 6:18; Isa 59:7
1:19 [t]Pr 15:27
1:20 [u]Pr 8:1; 9:1-3,13-15
1:22 [v]Pr 8:5; 9:4,16
1:24 [w]Isa 65:12; 66:4; Jer 7:13; Zec 7:11
1:26 [x]Ps 2:4 [y]Pr 6:15; 10:24

a *7* The Hebrew words rendered *fool* in Proverbs, and often elsewhere in the Old Testament, denote one who is morally deficient. b *12* Hebrew *Sheol*
c *21* Hebrew; Septuagint / *on the tops of the walls*
d *22* The Hebrew word rendered *simple* in Proverbs generally denotes one without moral direction and inclined to evil.

27when calamity overtakes you like a
storm,
when disaster sweeps over you like
a whirlwind,
when distress and trouble
overwhelm you.

28"Then they will call to me but I will
not answer;[a]
they will look for me but will not
find me.[b]
29Since they hated knowledge
and did not choose to fear the
LORD,[c]
30since they would not accept my
advice
and spurned my rebuke,[d]
31they will eat the fruit of their ways
and be filled with the fruit of their
schemes.[e]
32For the waywardness of the simple
will kill them,
and the complacency of fools will
destroy them;[f]
33but whoever listens to me will live
in safety[g]
and be at ease, without fear of
harm."[h]

Wisdom for the upright.

2 My son, if you accept my words
and store up my commands
within you,
2turning your ear to wisdom
and applying your heart to
understanding,[i]
3and if you call out for insight
and cry aloud for understanding,
4and if you look for it as for silver
and search for it as for hidden
treasure,[j]
5then you will understand the fear of
the LORD
and find the knowledge of God.[k]
6For the LORD gives wisdom,[l]
and from his mouth come
knowledge and understanding.
7He holds victory in store for the
upright,
he is a shield[m] to those whose
walk is blameless,[n]
8for he guards the course of the just
and protects the way of his faithful
ones.[o]

9Then you will understand what is
right and just
and fair—every good path.
10For wisdom will enter your heart,[p]
and knowledge will be pleasant to
your soul.
11Discretion will protect you,
and understanding will guard
you.[q]

12Wisdom will save you from the ways
of wicked men,
from men whose words are
perverse,
13who leave the straight paths
to walk in dark ways,[r]
14who delight in doing wrong
and rejoice in the perverseness of
evil,[s]
15whose paths are crooked[t]
and who are devious in their
ways.[u]

16It will save you also from the
adulteress,[v]
from the wayward wife with her
seductive words,
17who has left the partner of her youth
and ignored the covenant she
made before God.[e] [w]
18For her house leads down to death
and her paths to the spirits of the
dead.[x]
19None who go to her return
or attain the paths of life.[y]

20Thus you will walk in the ways of
good men
and keep to the paths of the
righteous.
21For the upright will live in the
land,[z]
and the blameless will remain in it;
22but the wicked will be cut off from
the land,[a]
and the unfaithful will be torn
from it.[b]

1:28 [a]1Sa 8:18; Isa 1:15; Jer 11:11; Mic 3:4 [b]Job 27:9; Pr 8:17; Eze 8:18; Zec 7:13
1:29 [c]Job 21:14
1:30 [d]ver 25; Ps 81:11
1:31 [e]Job 4:8; Pr 14:14; Isa 3:11; Jer 6:19
1:32 [f]Jer 2:19
1:33 [g]Ps 25:12; Pr 3:23 [h]Ps 112:8
2:2 [i]Pr 22:17
2:4 [j]Job 3:21; Pr 3:14; Mt 13:44
2:5 [k]Pr 1:7
2:6 [l]1Ki 3:9,12; Jas 1:5
2:7 [m]Pr 30:5-6 [n]Ps 84:11
2:8 [o]1Sa 2:9; Ps 66:9
2:10 [p]Pr 14:33
2:11 [q]Pr 4:6; 6:22
2:13 [r]Pr 4:19; Jn 3:19
2:14 [s]Pr 10:23; Jer 11:15
2:15 [t]Ps 125:5 [u]Pr 21:8
2:16 [v]Pr 5:1-6; 6:20-29;7:5-27
2:17 [w]Mal 2:14
2:18 [x]Pr 7:27
2:19 [y]Ecc 7:26
2:21 [z]Ps 37:29
2:22 [a]Job 18:17; Ps 37:38 [b]Dt 28:63; Pr 10:30

e *17* Or *covenant of her God*

Wisdom brings blessings.

3 My son, do not forget my teaching,[a]
but keep my commands in your heart,
[2]for they will prolong your life many years[b]
and bring you prosperity.

[3]Let love and faithfulness never leave you;
bind them around your neck,
write them on the tablet of your heart.[c]
[4]Then you will win favor and a good name
in the sight of God and man.[d]
[5]Trust in the LORD[e] with all your heart
and lean not on your own understanding;
[6]in all your ways acknowledge him,
and he will make your paths[f] straight.[f][g]

[7]Do not be wise in your own eyes;[h]
fear the LORD and shun evil.[i]
[8]This will bring health to your body[j]
and nourishment to your bones.[k]
[9]Honor the LORD with your wealth,
with the firstfruits[l] of all your crops;
[10]then your barns will be filled[m] to overflowing,
and your vats will brim over with new wine.[n]
[11]My son, do not despise the LORD's discipline[o]
and do not resent his rebuke,
[12]because the LORD disciplines those he loves,[p]
as a father[g] the son he delights in.[q]

[13]Blessed is the man who finds wisdom,
the man who gains understanding,
[14]for she is more profitable than silver
and yields better returns than gold.[r]
[15]She is more precious than rubies;[s]
nothing you desire can compare with her.[t]

3:1 [a]Pr 4:5
3:2 [b]Pr 4:10
3:3 [c]Ex 13:9; Pr 6:21; 7:3; 2Co 3:3
3:4 [d]1Sa 2:26; Lk 2:52
3:5 [e]Ps 37:3,5
3:6 [f]1Ch 28:9 [g]Pr 16:3; Isa 45:13
3:7 [h]Ro 12:16 [i]Job 1:1; Pr 16:6
3:8 [j]Pr 4:22 [k]Job 21:24
3:9 [l]Ex 22:29; 23:19; Dt 26:1-15
3:10 [m]Dt 28:8 [n]Joel 2:24
3:11 [o]Job 5:17
3:12 [p]Pr 13:24; Rev 3:19 [q]Dt 8:5; Heb 12:5-6*
3:14 [r]Job 28:15; Pr 8:19; 16:16
3:15 [s]Job 28:18 [t]Pr 8:11
3:16 [u]Pr 8:18
3:17 [v]Pr 16:7; Mt 11:28-30
3:18 [w]Ge 2:9; Pr 11:30; Rev 2:7
3:19 [x]Ps 104:24 [y]Pr 8:27-29
3:21 [z]Pr 4:20-22
3:22 [a]Pr 1:8-9
3:23 [b]Ps 37:24; Pr 4:12
3:24 [c]Lev 26:6; Ps 3:5 [d]Job 11:18

[16]Long life is in her right hand;
in her left hand are riches and honor.[u]
[17]Her ways are pleasant ways,
and all her paths are peace.[v]
[18]She is a tree of life[w] to those who embrace her;
those who lay hold of her will be blessed.

[19]By wisdom the LORD laid the earth's foundations,[x]
by understanding he set the heavens[y] in place;
[20]by his knowledge the deeps were divided,
and the clouds let drop the dew.

[21]My son, preserve sound judgment and discernment,
do not let them out of your sight;[z]
[22]they will be life for you,
an ornament to grace your neck.[a]
[23]Then you will go on your way in safety,
and your foot will not stumble;[b]
[24]when you lie down,[c] you will not be afraid;
when you lie down, your sleep[d] will be sweet.
[25]Have no fear of sudden disaster
or of the ruin that overtakes the wicked,
[26]for the LORD will be your confidence
and will keep your foot[e] from being snared.

[27]Do not withhold good from those who deserve it,
when it is in your power to act.
[28]Do not say to your neighbor,
"Come back later; I'll give it tomorrow"—
when you now have it with you.[f]

[29]Do not plot harm against your neighbor,
who lives trustfully near you.
[30]Do not accuse a man for no reason—
when he has done you no harm.

3:26 [e]1Sa 2:9 **3:28** [f]Lev 19:13; Dt 24:15

[f]6 Or *will direct your paths* [g]12 Hebrew; Septuagint / *and he punishes*

31Do not envy[a] a violent man
or choose any of his ways,
32for the LORD detests a perverse man[b]
but takes the upright into his confidence.[c]

33The LORD's curse[d] is on the house of the wicked,[e]
but he blesses the home of the righteous.[f]
34He mocks proud mockers
but gives grace to the humble.[g]
35The wise inherit honor,
but fools he holds up to shame.

Fatherly advice on the importance of wisdom.

4 Listen, my sons,[h] to a father's instruction;
pay attention and gain understanding.
2I give you sound learning,
so do not forsake my teaching.
3When I was a boy in my father's house,
still tender, and an only child of my mother,
4he taught me and said,
"Lay hold of my words with all your heart;
keep my commands and you will live.[i]
5Get wisdom,[j] get understanding;
do not forget my words or swerve from them.
6Do not forsake wisdom, and she will protect you;[k]
love her, and she will watch over you.
7Wisdom is supreme; therefore get wisdom.
Though it cost all[l] you have,[h] get understanding.[m]
8Esteem her, and she will exalt you;
embrace her, and she will honor you.[n]
9She will set a garland of grace on your head
and present you with a crown of splendor.[o]"
10Listen, my son, accept what I say,
and the years of your life will be many.[p]
11I guide[q] you in the way of wisdom
and lead you along straight paths.
12When you walk, your steps will not be hampered;
when you run, you will not stumble.[r]
13Hold on to instruction, do not let it go;
guard it well, for it is your life.[s]
14Do not set foot on the path of the wicked
or walk in the way of evil men.[t]
15Avoid it, do not travel on it;
turn from it and go on your way.
16For they cannot sleep till they do evil;[u]
they are robbed of slumber till they make someone fall.
17They eat the bread of wickedness
and drink the wine of violence.

18The path of the righteous[v] is like the first gleam of dawn,
shining ever brighter till the full light of day.[w]
19But the way of the wicked is like deep darkness;[x]
they do not know what makes them stumble.

20My son, pay attention to what I say;
listen closely to my words.[y]
21Do not let them out of your sight,[z]
keep them within your heart;
22for they are life to those who find them
and health to a man's whole body.[a]
23Above all else, guard your heart,
for it is the wellspring of life.[b]
24Put away perversity from your mouth;
keep corrupt talk far from your lips.
25Let your eyes look straight ahead,
fix your gaze directly before you.
26Make level[i] paths for your feet[c]
and take only ways that are firm.
27Do not swerve to the right or the left;[d]
keep your foot from evil.

3:31 [a]Ps 37:1; Pr 24:1-2 **3:32** [b]Pr 11:20 [c]Job 29:4; Ps 25:14 **3:33** [d]Dt 11:28; Mal 2:2 [e]Zec 5:4 [f]Ps 1:3 **3:34** [g]Jas 4:6*; 1Pe 5:5* **4:1** [h]Pr 1:8 **4:4** [i]Pr 7:2 **4:5** [j]Pr 16:16 **4:6** [k]2Th 2:10 **4:7** [l]Mt 13:44-46 [m]Pr 23:23 **4:8** [n]1Sa 2:30; Pr 3:18 **4:9** [o]Pr 1:8-9 **4:10** [p]Pr 3:2 **4:11** [q]1Sa 12:23 **4:12** [r]Job 18:7; Pr 3:23 **4:13** [s]Pr 3:22 **4:14** [t]Ps 1:1; Pr 1:15 **4:16** [u]Ps 36:4; Mic 2:1 **4:18** [v]Isa 26:7 [w]2Sa 23:4; Da 12:3; Mt 5:14; Php 2:15 **4:19** [x]Job 18:5; Pr 2:13; Isa 59:9-10; Jn 12:35 **4:20** [y]Pr 5:1 **4:21** [z]Pr 3:21;7:1-2 **4:22** [a]Pr 3:8; 12:18 **4:23** [b]Mt 12:34; Lk 6:45 **4:26** [c]Heb 12:13* **4:27** [d]Dt 5:32; 28:14

[h]7 Or *Whatever else you get* [i]26 Or *Consider the*

Warning against adultery.

5 My son, pay attention to my
wisdom,
listen well to my words[a] of insight,
2that you may maintain discretion
and your lips may preserve
knowledge.
3For the lips of an adulteress drip
honey,
and her speech is smoother than
oil;[b]
4but in the end she is bitter as gall,[c]
sharp as a double-edged sword.
5Her feet go down to death;
her steps lead straight to the
grave.[j][d]
6She gives no thought to the way of
life;
her paths are crooked, but she
knows it not.[e]

7Now then, my sons, listen[f] to me;
do not turn aside from what I say.
8Keep to a path far from her,[g]
do not go near the door of her
house,
9lest you give your best strength to
others
and your years to one who is cruel,
10lest strangers feast on your wealth
and your toil enrich another man's
house.
11At the end of your life you will groan,
when your flesh and body are
spent.
12You will say, "How I hated discipline!
How my heart spurned
correction![h]
13I would not obey my teachers
or listen to my instructors.
14I have come to the brink of utter ruin
in the midst of the whole
assembly."

15Drink water from your own cistern,
running water from your own well.
16Should your springs overflow in the
streets,
your streams of water in the public
squares?
17Let them be yours alone,
never to be shared with strangers.
18May your fountain[i] be blessed,
and may you rejoice in the wife of
your youth.[j]
19A loving doe, a graceful deer[k]—
may her breasts satisfy you always,
may you ever be captivated by her
love.
20Why be captivated, my son, by an
adulteress?
Why embrace the bosom of
another man's wife?

21For a man's ways are in full view[l] of
the LORD,
and he examines all his paths.[m]
22The evil deeds of a wicked man
ensnare him;[n]
the cords of his sin hold him fast.[o]
23He will die for lack of discipline,[p]
led astray by his own great folly.

Warning against laziness.

6 My son, if you have put up
security for your neighbor,[q]
if you have struck hands in pledge[r]
for another,
2if you have been trapped by what
you said,
ensnared by the words of your
mouth,
3then do this, my son, to free
yourself,
since you have fallen into your
neighbor's hands:
Go and humble yourself;
press your plea with your
neighbor!
4Allow no sleep to your eyes,
no slumber to your eyelids.[s]
5Free yourself, like a gazelle from the
hand of the hunter,
like a bird from the snare of the
fowler.[t]

6Go to the ant, you sluggard;[u]
consider its ways and be wise!
7It has no commander,
no overseer or ruler,
8yet it stores its provisions in
summer
and gathers its food at harvest.[v]

5:1 [a]Pr 4:20; 22:17
5:3 [b]Ps 55:21; Pr 2:16; 7:5
5:4 [c]Ecc 7:26
5:5 [d]Pr 7:26-27
5:6 [e]Pr 30:20
5:7 [f]Pr 7:24
5:8 [g]Pr 7:1-27
5:12 [h]Pr 1:29; 12:1
5:18 [i]SS 4:12-15 [j]Ecc 9:9; Mal 2:14
5:19 [k]SS 2:9; 4:5
5:21 [l]Ps 119:168; Hos 7:2 [m]Job 14:16; Job 31:4; 34:21; Pr 15:3; Jer 16:17; 32:19; Heb 4:13
5:22 [n]Ps 9:16 [o]Nu 32:23; Ps 7:15-16; Pr 1:31-32
5:23 [p]Job 4:21; 36:12
6:1 [q]Pr 17:18 [r]Pr 11:15; 22:26-27
6:4 [s]Ps 132:4
6:5 [t]Ps 91:3
6:6 [u]Pr 20:4
6:8 [v]Pr 10:4

j5 Hebrew *Sheol*

[9]How long will you lie there, you
sluggard?[a]
When will you get up from your
sleep?
[10]A little sleep, a little slumber,
a little folding of the hands to
rest[b]—
[11]and poverty[c] will come on you like a
bandit
and scarcity like an armed man.[k]

[12]A scoundrel and villain,
who goes about with a corrupt
mouth,
[13] who winks with his eye,[d]
signals with his feet
and motions with his fingers,
[14] who plots evil[e] with deceit in his
heart—
he always stirs up dissension.[f]
[15]Therefore disaster will overtake him
in an instant;
he will suddenly be
destroyed—without remedy.[g]

Seven things hated by the LORD.

[16]There are six things the LORD hates,
seven that are detestable to him:
[17] haughty eyes,
a lying tongue,[h]
hands that shed innocent blood,[i]
[18] a heart that devises wicked
schemes,
feet that are quick to rush into
evil,[j]
[19] a false witness[k] who pours out
lies
and a man who stirs up
dissension among brothers.[l]

Further warning against adultery.

[20]My son, keep your father's
commands
and do not forsake your mother's
teaching.[m]
[21]Bind them upon your heart forever;
fasten them around your neck.[n]
[22]When you walk, they will guide you;
when you sleep, they will watch
over you;
when you awake, they will speak
to you.

6:9 [a]Pr 24:30-34
6:10 [b]Pr 24:33
6:11 [c]Pr 24:30-34
6:13 [d]Ps 35:19
6:14 [e]Mic 2:1 [f]ver 16-19
6:15 [g]2Ch 36:16
6:17 [h]Ps 120:2; Pr 12:22 [i]Dt 19:10; Isa 1:15; 59:7
6:18 [j]Ge 6:5
6:19 [k]Ps 27:12 [l]ver 12-15
6:20 [m]Pr 1:8
6:21 [n]Pr 3:3; 7:1-3
6:23 [o]Ps 19:8; 119:105
6:24 [p]Pr 2:16; 7:5
6:26 [q]Pr 7:22-23; 29:3
6:29 [r]Ex 20:14 [s]Pr 2:16-19; 5:8
6:31 [t]Ex 22:1-14
6:32 [u]Ex 20:14 [v]Pr 7:7; 9:4,16
6:33 [w]Pr 5:9-14
6:34 [x]Nu 5:14 [y]Ge 34:7
6:35 [z]Job 31:9-11; SS 8:7
7:1 [a]Pr 1:8; 2:1

[23]For these commands are a lamp,
this teaching is a light,[o]
and the corrections of discipline
are the way to life,
[24]keeping you from the immoral
woman,
from the smooth tongue of the
wayward wife.[p]
[25]Do not lust in your heart after her
beauty
or let her captivate you with her
eyes,
[26]for the prostitute reduces you to a
loaf of bread,
and the adulteress preys upon your
very life.[q]
[27]Can a man scoop fire into his lap
without his clothes being burned?
[28]Can a man walk on hot coals
without his feet being scorched?
[29]So is he who sleeps[r] with another
man's wife;[s]
no one who touches her will go
unpunished.

[30]Men do not despise a thief if he steals
to satisfy his hunger when he is
starving.
[31]Yet if he is caught, he must pay
sevenfold,[t]
though it costs him all the wealth
of his house.
[32]But a man who commits adultery[u]
lacks judgment;[v]
whoever does so destroys himself.
[33]Blows and disgrace are his lot,
and his shame will never[w] be
wiped away;
[34]for jealousy[x] arouses a husband's
fury,[y]
and he will show no mercy when
he takes revenge.
[35]He will not accept any compensation;
he will refuse the bribe, however
great it is.[z]

Warning against the adulteress.

7 My son,[a] keep my words
and store up my commands
within you.

[k]11 Or *like a vagrant / and scarcity like a beggar*

2 Keep my commands and you will live;[a]
guard my teachings as the apple of your eye.
3 Bind them on your fingers;
write them on the tablet of your heart.[b]
4 Say to wisdom, "You are my sister,"
and call understanding your kinsman;
5 they will keep you from the adulteress,
from the wayward wife with her seductive words.[c]

6 At the window of my house
I looked out through the lattice.
7 I saw among the simple,
I noticed among the young men,
a youth who lacked judgment.[d]
8 He was going down the street near her corner,
walking along in the direction of her house
9 at twilight,[e] as the day was fading,
as the dark of night set in.

10 Then out came a woman to meet him,
dressed like a prostitute and with crafty intent.
11 (She is loud[f] and defiant,
her feet never stay at home;
12 now in the street, now in the squares,
at every corner she lurks.)[g]
13 She took hold of him[h] and kissed him
and with a brazen face she said:[i]

14 "I have fellowship offerings[l][j] at home;
today I fulfilled my vows.
15 So I came out to meet you;
I looked for you and have found you!
16 I have covered my bed
with colored linens from Egypt.
17 I have perfumed my bed[k]
with myrrh,[l] aloes and cinnamon.
18 Come, let's drink deep of love till morning;
let's enjoy ourselves with love![m]
19 My husband is not at home;
he has gone on a long journey.
20 He took his purse filled with money
and will not be home till full moon."

21 With persuasive words she led him astray;
she seduced him with her smooth talk.[n]
22 All at once he followed her
like an ox going to the slaughter,
like a deer[m] stepping into a noose[n][o]
23 till an arrow pierces[p] his liver,
like a bird darting into a snare,
little knowing it will cost him his life.[q]

24 Now then, my sons, listen[r] to me;
pay attention to what I say.
25 Do not let your heart turn to her ways
or stray into her paths.[s]
26 Many are the victims she has brought down;
her slain are a mighty throng.
27 Her house is a highway to the grave,[o]
leading down to the chambers of death.[t]

The excellency of wisdom.

8 Does not wisdom call out?[u]
Does not understanding raise her voice?
2 On the heights along the way,
where the paths meet, she takes her stand;
3 beside the gates leading into the city,
at the entrances, she cries aloud:[v]
4 "To you, O men, I call out;
I raise my voice to all mankind.
5 You who are simple,[w] gain prudence;[x]
you who are foolish, gain understanding.
6 Listen, for I have worthy things to say;
I open my lips to speak what is right.
7 My mouth speaks what is true,[y]
for my lips detest wickedness.
8 All the words of my mouth are just;

7:2 [a]Pr 4:4
7:3 [b]Dt 6:8; Pr 3:3
7:5 [c]ver 21; Job 31:9; Pr 2:16; 6:24
7:7 [d]Pr 1:22; 6:32
7:9 [e]Job 24:15
7:11 [f]Pr 9:13; 1Ti 5:13
7:12 [g]Pr 8:1-36; 23:26-28
7:13 [h]Ge 39:12 [i]Pr 1:20
7:14 [j]Lev 7:11-18
7:17 [k]Est 1:6; Isa 57:7; Eze 23:41; Am 6:4 [l]Ge 37:25
7:18 [m]Ge 39:7
7:21 [n]Pr 5:3
7:22 [o]Job 18:10
7:23 [p]Job 15:22; 16:13 [q]Pr 6:26; Ecc 7:26; 9:12
7:24 [r]Pr 1:8-9; 5:7; 8:32
7:25 [s]Pr 5:7-8
7:27 [t]Pr 2:18; 5:5; 9:18; Rev 22:15
8:1 [u]Pr 1:20; 9:3
8:3 [v]Job 29:7
8:5 [w]Pr 1:22 [x]Pr 1:4
8:7 [y]Ps 37:30; Jn 8:14

l 14 Traditionally *peace offerings* m 22 Syriac (see also Septuagint); Hebrew *fool* n 22 The meaning of the Hebrew for this line is uncertain. o 27 Hebrew *Sheol*

none of them is crooked or
perverse.
9To the discerning all of them are right;
they are faultless to those who
have knowledge.
10Choose my instruction instead of
silver,
knowledge rather than choice
gold,[a]
11for wisdom is more precious[b] than
rubies,
and nothing you desire can
compare with her.[c]

12"I, wisdom, dwell together with
prudence;
I possess knowledge and
discretion.[d]
13To fear the LORD is to hate evil;[e]
I hate[f] pride and arrogance,
evil behavior and perverse speech.
14Counsel and sound judgment are
mine;
I have understanding and power.[g]
15By me kings reign
and rulers[h] make laws that are just;
16by me princes govern,
and all nobles who rule on earth.[p]
17I love those who love me,[i]
and those who seek me find me.[j]
18With me are riches and honor,[k]
enduring wealth and prosperity.[l]
19My fruit is better than fine gold;
what I yield surpasses choice
silver.[m]
20I walk in the way of righteousness,
along the paths of justice,
21bestowing wealth on those who love
me
and making their treasuries full.[n]

22"The LORD brought me forth as the
first of his works,[q,r]
before his deeds of old;
23I was appointed[s] from eternity,
from the beginning, before the
world began.
24When there were no oceans, I was
given birth,
when there were no springs
abounding with water;[o]
25before the mountains were settled in
place,
before the hills, I was given birth,[p]
26before he made the earth or its fields
or any of the dust of the world.[q]
27I was there when he set the heavens
in place,[r]
when he marked out the horizon
on the face of the deep,
28when he established the clouds
above
and fixed securely the fountains of
the deep,
29when he gave the sea its boundary[s]
so the waters would not overstep
his command,[t]
and when he marked out the
foundations of the earth.[u]
30 Then I was the craftsman at his
side.[v]
I was filled with delight day after day,
rejoicing always in his presence,
31rejoicing in his whole world
and delighting in mankind.[w]

32"Now then, my sons, listen to me;
blessed are[x] those who keep my
ways.[y]
33Listen to my instruction and be wise;
do not ignore it.
34Blessed is the man who listens[z] to
me,
watching daily at my doors,
waiting at my doorway.
35For whoever finds me[a] finds life
and receives favor from the LORD.[b]
36But whoever fails to find me harms
himself;[c]
all who hate me love death."

Wisdom's call.

9 Wisdom has built[d] her house;
she has hewn out its seven pillars.
2She has prepared her meat and
mixed her wine;
she has also set her table.[e]
3She has sent out her maids, and she
calls[f]
from the highest point of the city.[g]

8:10 [a]Pr 3:14-15
8:11 [b]Job 28:17-19 [c]Pr 3:13-15
8:12 [d]Pr 1:4
8:13 [e]Pr 16:6 [f]Jer 44:4
8:14 [g]Pr 21:22; Ecc 7:19
8:15 [h]Da 2:21; Ro 13:1
8:17 [i]1Sa 2:30; Ps 91:14; Jn 14:21-24 [j]Pr 1:28; Jas 1:5
8:18 [k]Pr 3:16 [l]Dt 8:18; Mt 6:33
8:19 [m]Pr 3:13-14; 10:20
8:21 [n]Pr24:4
8:24 [o]Ge 7:11
8:25 [p]Job 15:7
8:26 [q]Ps 90:2
8:27 [r]Pr 3:19
8:29 [s]Ge 1:9; Job 38:10; Ps 16:6 [t]Ps 104:9 [u]Job 38:5
8:30 [v]Jn 1:1-3
8:31 [w]Ps 16:3; 104:1-30
8:32 [x]Lk 11:28 [y]Ps 119:1-2
8:34 [z]Pr 3:13,18
8:35 [a]Pr 3:13-18 [b]Pr 12:2
8:36 [c]Pr 15:32
9:1 [d]Eph 2:20-22; 1Pe 2:5
9:2 [e]Lk 14:16-23
9:3 [f]Pr 8:1-3 [g]ver 14

p *16* Many Hebrew manuscripts and Septuagint; most Hebrew manuscripts *and nobles—all righteous rulers*
q *22* Or *way*; or *dominion* r *22* Or *The LORD possessed me at the beginning of his work*; or *The LORD brought me forth at the beginning of his work*
s *23* Or *fashioned*

4"Let all who are simple come in here!"
she says to those who lack
judgment.[a]
5"Come, eat my food
and drink the wine I have mixed.[b]
6Leave your simple ways and you will
live;[c]
walk in the way of understanding.

7"Whoever corrects a mocker invites
insult;
whoever rebukes a wicked man
incurs abuse.[d]
8Do not rebuke a mocker[e] or he will
hate you;
rebuke a wise man and he will
love you.[f]
9Instruct a wise man and he will be
wiser still;
teach a righteous man and he will
add to his learning.[g]

10"The fear of the LORD[h] is the
beginning of wisdom,
and knowledge of the Holy One is
understanding.
11For through me your days will be
many,
and years will be added to your
life.[i]
12If you are wise, your wisdom will
reward you;
if you are a mocker, you alone will
suffer."

Folly's call.

13The woman Folly is loud;[j]
she is undisciplined and without
knowledge.[k]
14She sits at the door of her house,
on a seat at the highest point of the
city,[l]
15calling out to those who pass by,
who go straight on their way.
16"Let all who are simple come in
here!"
she says to those who lack
judgment.
17"Stolen water is sweet;
food eaten in secret is delicious![m]"
18But little do they know that the dead
are there,
that her guests are in the depths of
the grave.[t][n]

Proverbs of Solomon: Miscellaneous.

10 The proverbs of Solomon:[o]

A wise son brings joy to his
father,[p]
but a foolish son grief to his mother.

2Ill-gotten treasures are of no value,[q]
but righteousness delivers from
death.[r]

3The LORD does not let the righteous
go hungry[s]
but he thwarts the craving of the
wicked.

4Lazy hands make a man poor,[t]
but diligent hands bring wealth.[u]

5He who gathers crops in summer is a
wise son,
but he who sleeps during harvest is
a disgraceful son.

6Blessings crown the head of the
righteous,
but violence overwhelms the
mouth of the wicked.[u][v]

7The memory of the righteous[w] will
be a blessing,
but the name of the wicked[x] will
rot.[y]

8The wise in heart accept commands,
but a chattering fool comes to
ruin.[z]

9The man of integrity[a] walks
securely,[b]
but he who takes crooked paths
will be found out.[c]

10He who winks maliciously[d] causes
grief,
and a chattering fool comes to
ruin.

11The mouth of the righteous is a
fountain of life,[e]
but violence overwhelms the
mouth of the wicked.[f]

9:4 [a]Pr 6:32
9:5 [b]Isa 55:1
9:6 [c]Pr 8:35
9:7 [d]Pr 23:9
9:8 [e]Pr 15:12 [f]Ps 141:5
9:9 [g]Pr 1:5,7
9:10 [h]Job 28:28; Pr 1:7
9:11 [i]Pr 3:16; 10:27
9:13 [j]Pr 7:11 [k]Pr 5:6
9:14 [l]ver 3
9:17 [m]Pr 20:17
9:18 [n]Pr 2:18; 7:26-27
10:1 [o]Pr 1:1 [p]Pr 15:20; 29:3
10:2 [q]Pr 21:6 [r]Pr 11:4,19
10:3 [s]Mt 6:25-34
10:4 [t]Pr 19:15 [u]Pr 12:24; 13:4; 21:5
10:6 [v]ver 8,11,14
10:7 [w]Ps 112:6 [x]Ps 109:13 [y]Ps 9:6
10:8 [z]Mt 7:24-27
10:9 [a]Isa 33:15 [b]Ps 23:4 [c]Pr 28:18
10:10 [d]Ps 35:19
10:11 [e]Ps 37:30; Pr 13:12,14,19 [f]ver 6

t *18* Hebrew *Sheol*   u *6* Or *but the mouth of the wicked conceals violence*; also in verse 11

[12]Hatred stirs up dissension,
but love covers over all wrongs.[a]

[13]Wisdom is found on the lips of the discerning,[b]
but a rod is for the back of him who lacks judgment.[c]

[14]Wise men store up knowledge,
but the mouth of a fool invites ruin.[d]

[15]The wealth of the rich is their fortified city,[e]
but poverty is the ruin of the poor.[f]

[16]The wages of the righteous bring them life,
but the income of the wicked brings them punishment.[g]

[17]He who heeds discipline shows the way to life,[h]
but whoever ignores correction leads others astray.

[18]He who conceals his hatred has lying lips,
and whoever spreads slander is a fool.

[19]When words are many, sin is not absent,
but he who holds his tongue is wise.[i]

[20]The tongue of the righteous is choice silver,
but the heart of the wicked is of little value.

[21]The lips of the righteous nourish many,
but fools die for lack of judgment.[j]

[22]The blessing of the LORD brings wealth,[k]
and he adds no trouble to it.

[23]A fool finds pleasure in evil conduct,[l]
but a man of understanding delights in wisdom.

[24]What the wicked dreads[m] will overtake him;
what the righteous desire will be granted.[n]

[25]When the storm has swept by, the wicked are gone,
but the righteous stand firm[o] forever.[p]

[26]As vinegar to the teeth and smoke to the eyes,
so is a sluggard to those who send him.[q]

[27]The fear of the LORD adds length to life,[r]
but the years of the wicked are cut short.[s]

[28]The prospect of the righteous is joy,
but the hopes of the wicked come to nothing.[t]

[29]The way of the LORD is a refuge for the righteous,
but it is the ruin of those who do evil.[u]

[30]The righteous will never be uprooted,
but the wicked will not remain in the land.[v]

[31]The mouth of the righteous brings forth wisdom,[w]
but a perverse tongue will be cut out.

[32]The lips of the righteous know what is fitting,[x]
but the mouth of the wicked only what is perverse.

11

The LORD abhors dishonest scales,[y]
but accurate weights are his delight.[z]

[2]When pride comes, then comes disgrace,[a]
but with humility comes wisdom.[b]

[3]The integrity of the upright guides them,
but the unfaithful are destroyed by their duplicity.[c]

[4]Wealth is worthless in the day of wrath,[d]
but righteousness delivers from death.[e]

10:12 [a]Pr 17:9; 1Co 13:4-7; 1Pe 4:8 **10:13** [b]ver 31 [c]Pr 26:3 **10:14** [d]Pr 18:6,7 **10:15** [e]Pr 18:11 [f]Pr 19:7 **10:16** [g]Pr 11:18-19 **10:17** [h]Pr 6:23 **10:19** [i]Pr 17:28; Ecc 5:3; Jas 1:19; 3:2-12 **10:21** [j]Pr 5:22-23; Hos 4:1,6,14 **10:22** [k]Ge 24:35; Ps 37:22 **10:23** [l]Pr 2:14; 15:21 **10:24** [m]Isa 66:4 [n]Ps 145:17-19; Mt 5:6; 1Jn 5:14-15 **10:25** [o]Ps 15:5 [p]Pr 12:3,7; Mt 7:24-27 **10:26** [q]Pr 26:6 **10:27** [r]Pr 9:10-11 [s]Job 15:32 **10:28** [t]Job 8:13; Pr 11:7 **10:29** [u]Pr 21:15 **10:30** [v]Ps 37:9,28-29; Pr 2:20-22 **10:31** [w]Ps 37:30 **10:32** [x]Ecc 10:12 **11:1** [y]Lev 19:36; Dt 25:13-16; Pr 20:10,23 [z]Pr 16:11 **11:2** [a]Pr 16:18 [b]Pr 18:12; 29:23 **11:3** [c]Pr 13:6

11:4 [d]Eze 7:19; Zep 1:18 [e]Ge 7:1; Pr 10:2

5The righteousness of the blameless
makes a straight way for them,
but the wicked are brought down
by their own wickedness.[a]

6The righteousness of the upright
delivers them,
but the unfaithful are trapped by
evil desires.

7When a wicked man dies, his hope
perishes;
all he expected from his power
comes to nothing.[b]

8The righteous man is rescued from
trouble,
and it comes on the wicked
instead.[c]

9With his mouth the godless destroys
his neighbor,
but through knowledge the
righteous escape.

10When the righteous prosper, the city
rejoices;[d]
when the wicked perish, there are
shouts of joy.

11Through the blessing of the upright a
city is exalted,
but by the mouth of the wicked it
is destroyed.[e]

12A man who lacks judgment derides
his neighbor,[f]
but a man of understanding holds
his tongue.

13A gossip betrays a confidence,[g]
but a trustworthy man keeps a
secret.

14For lack of guidance a nation falls,[h]
but many advisers make victory
sure.[i]

15He who puts up security[j] for another
will surely suffer,
but whoever refuses to strike
hands in pledge is safe.

16A kindhearted woman gains
respect,[k]
but ruthless men gain only wealth.

17A kind man benefits himself,
but a cruel man brings trouble on
himself.

18The wicked man earns deceptive
wages,
but he who sows righteousness
reaps a sure reward.[l]

19The truly righteous man attains life,
but he who pursues evil goes to his
death.

20The LORD detests men of perverse
heart
but he delights in those whose
ways are blameless.[m]

21Be sure of this: The wicked will not
go unpunished,
but those who are righteous will go
free.[n]

22Like a gold ring in a pig's snout
is a beautiful woman who shows
no discretion.

23The desire of the righteous ends only
in good,
but the hope of the wicked only in
wrath.

24One man gives freely, yet gains even
more;
another withholds unduly, but
comes to poverty.

25A generous man will prosper;
he who refreshes others will
himself be refreshed.[o]

26People curse the man who hoards
grain,
but blessing crowns him who is
willing to sell.

27He who seeks good finds goodwill,
but evil comes to him who
searches for it.[p]

28Whoever trusts in his riches will
fall,[q]
but the righteous will thrive like a
green leaf.[r]

29He who brings trouble on his family
will inherit only wind,
and the fool will be servant to the
wise.[s]

11:5 [a]Pr 5:21-23
11:7 [b]Pr 10:28
11:8 [c]Pr 21:18
11:10 [d]Pr 28:12
11:11 [e]Pr 29:8
11:12 [f]Pr 14:21
11:13 [g]Lev 19:16; Pr 20:19; 1Ti 5:13
11:14 [h]Pr 20:18 [i]Pr 15:22; 24:6
11:15 [j]Pr 6:1
11:16 [k]Pr 31:31
11:18 [l]Hos 10:12-13
11:20 [m]1Ch 29:17; Ps 119:1; Pr 12:2,22
11:21 [n]Pr 16:5
11:25 [o]Mt 5:7; 2Co 9:6-9
11:27 [p]Est 7:10; Ps 7:15-16
11:28 [q]Job 31:24-28; Ps 49:6; 52:7; Mk 10:25; 1Ti 6:17 [r]Ps 1:3; 92:12-14; Jer 17:8
11:29 [s]Pr 14:19

30The fruit of the righteous is a tree of life,[a]
and he who wins souls is wise.

31If the righteous receive their due[b] on earth,
how much more the ungodly and the sinner!

12

Whoever loves discipline loves knowledge,
but he who hates correction is stupid.[c]

2A good man obtains favor from the LORD,
but the LORD condemns a crafty man.

3A man cannot be established through wickedness,
but the righteous cannot be uprooted.[d]

4A wife of noble character is her husband's crown,
but a disgraceful wife is like decay in his bones.[e]

5The plans of the righteous are just,
but the advice of the wicked is deceitful.

6The words of the wicked lie in wait for blood,
but the speech of the upright rescues them.[f]

7Wicked men are overthrown and are no more,[g]
but the house of the righteous stands firm.[h]

8A man is praised according to his wisdom,
but men with warped minds are despised.

9Better to be a nobody and yet have a servant
than pretend to be somebody and have no food.

10A righteous man cares for the needs of his animal,
but the kindest acts of the wicked are cruel.

11He who works his land will have abundant food,
but he who chases fantasies lacks judgment.[i]

12The wicked desire the plunder of evil men,
but the root of the righteous flourishes.

13An evil man is trapped by his sinful talk,[j]
but a righteous man escapes trouble.[k]

14From the fruit of his lips a man is filled with good things[l]
as surely as the work of his hands rewards him.[m]

15The way of a fool seems right to him,[n]
but a wise man listens to advice.

16A fool shows his annoyance at once,
but a prudent man overlooks an insult.[o]

17A truthful witness gives honest testimony,
but a false witness tells lies.[p]

18Reckless words pierce like a sword,[q]
but the tongue of the wise brings healing.[r]

19Truthful lips endure forever,
but a lying tongue lasts only a moment.

20There is deceit in the hearts of those who plot evil,
but joy for those who promote peace.

21No harm befalls the righteous,[s]
but the wicked have their fill of trouble.

22The LORD detests lying lips,[t]
but he delights in men who are truthful.[u]

23A prudent man keeps his knowledge to himself,[v]
but the heart of fools blurts out folly.

11:30 [a]Jas 5:20
11:31 [b]Pr 13:21; Jer 25:29; 1Pe 4:18
12:1 [c]Pr 9:7-9; 15:5,10,12,32
12:3 [d]Pr 10:25
12:4 [e]Pr 14:30
12:6 [f]Pr 14:3
12:7 [g]Ps 37:36 [h]Pr 10:25
12:11 [i]Pr 28:19
12:13 [j]Pr 18:7 [k]Pr 21:23; 2Pe 2:9
12:14 [l]Pr 13:2; 15:23; 18:20 [m]Isa 3:10-11
12:15 [n]Pr 14:12; 16:2,25; Lk 18:11
12:16 [o]Pr 29:11
12:17 [p]Pr 14:5,25
12:18 [q]Ps 57:4 [r]Pr 15:4
12:21 [s]Ps 91:10
12:22 [t]Pr 6:17; Rev 22:15 [u]Pr 11:20
12:23 [v]Pr 10:14; 13:16

[24]Diligent hands will rule,
but laziness ends in slave labor.[a]

[25]An anxious heart weighs a man down,[b]
but a kind word cheers him up.

[26]A righteous man is cautious in friendship,[v]
but the way of the wicked leads them astray.

[27]The lazy man does not roast[w] his game,
but the diligent man prizes his possessions.

[28]In the way of righteousness there is life;[c]
along that path is immortality.

13 A wise son heeds his father's instruction,
but a mocker does not listen to rebuke.[d]

[2]From the fruit of his lips a man enjoys good things,[e]
but the unfaithful have a craving for violence.

[3]He who guards his lips[f] guards his life,[g]
but he who speaks rashly will come to ruin.[h]

[4]The sluggard craves and gets nothing,
but the desires of the diligent are fully satisfied.

[5]The righteous hate what is false,
but the wicked bring shame and disgrace.

[6]Righteousness guards the man of integrity,
but wickedness overthrows the sinner.[i]

[7]One man pretends to be rich, yet has nothing;
another pretends to be poor, yet has great wealth.[j]

[8]A man's riches may ransom his life,
but a poor man hears no threat.

[9]The light of the righteous shines brightly,
but the lamp of the wicked is snuffed out.[k]

[10]Pride only breeds quarrels,
but wisdom is found in those who take advice.

[11]Dishonest money dwindles away,[l]
but he who gathers money little by little makes it grow.

[12]Hope deferred makes the heart sick,
but a longing fulfilled is a tree of life.

[13]He who scorns instruction will pay for it,[m]
but he who respects a command is rewarded.

[14]The teaching of the wise is a fountain of life,[n]
turning a man from the snares of death.[o]

[15]Good understanding wins favor,
but the way of the unfaithful is hard.[x]

[16]Every prudent man acts out of knowledge,
but a fool exposes his folly.[p]

[17]A wicked messenger falls into trouble,
but a trustworthy envoy brings healing.[q]

[18]He who ignores discipline comes to poverty and shame,
but whoever heeds correction is honored.[r]

[19]A longing fulfilled is sweet to the soul,
but fools detest turning from evil.

[20]He who walks with the wise grows wise,
but a companion of fools suffers harm.[s]

[21]Misfortune pursues the sinner,
but prosperity is the reward of the righteous.[t]

12:24 [a]Pr 10:4
12:25 [b]Pr 15:13; Isa 50:4
12:28 [c]Dt 30:15
13:1 [d]Pr 10:1
13:2 [e]Pr 12:14
13:3 [f]Jas 3:2 [g]Pr 21:23 [h]Pr 18:7,20-21
13:6 [i]Pr 11:3,5
13:7 [j]2Co 6:10
13:9 [k]Job 18:5; Pr 4:18-19; 24:20
13:11 [l]Pr 10:2
13:13 [m]Nu 15:31; 2Ch 36:16
13:14 [n]Pr 10:11 [o]Pr 14:27
13:16 [p]Pr 12:23
13:17 [q]Pr 25:13
13:18 [r]Pr 15:5,31-32
13:20 [s]Pr 15:31
13:21 [t]Ps 32:10

[v]*26* Or *man is a guide to his neighbor* [w]*27* The meaning of the Hebrew for this word is uncertain. [x]*15* Or *unfaithful does not endure*

[22]A good man leaves an inheritance for
his children's children,
but a sinner's wealth is stored up
for the righteous.[a]

[23]A poor man's field may produce
abundant food,
but injustice sweeps it away.

[24]He who spares the rod hates his son,
but he who loves him is careful to
discipline him.[b]

[25]The righteous eat to their hearts'
content,
but the stomach of the wicked goes
hungry.[c]

14

The wise woman builds her
house,[d]
but with her own hands the foolish
one tears hers down.

[2]He whose walk is upright fears the
LORD,
but he whose ways are devious
despises him.

[3]A fool's talk brings a rod to his back,
but the lips of the wise protect
them.[e]

[4]Where there are no oxen, the
manger is empty,
but from the strength of an ox
comes an abundant harvest.

[5]A truthful witness does not deceive,
but a false witness pours out lies.[f]

[6]The mocker seeks wisdom and finds
none,
but knowledge comes easily to the
discerning.

[7]Stay away from a foolish man,
for you will not find knowledge on
his lips.

[8]The wisdom of the prudent is to give
thought to their ways,
but the folly of fools is deception.[g]

[9]Fools mock at making amends for sin,
but goodwill is found among the
upright.

[10]Each heart knows its own bitterness,
and no one else can share its joy.

13:22 [a]Job 27:17; Ecc 2:26
13:24 [b]Pr 19:18; 22:15; 23:13-14; 29:15,17; Heb 12:7
13:25 [c]Ps 34:10; Pr 10:3
14:1 [d]Pr 24:3
14:3 [e]Pr 12:6
14:5 [f]Pr 6:19; 12:17
14:8 [g]ver 24
14:11 [h]Pr 3:33; 12:7
14:12 [i]Pr 12:15 [j]Pr 16:25
14:13 [k]Ecc 2:2
14:14 [l]Pr 1:31 [m]Pr 12:14
14:16 [n]Pr 22:3
14:17 [o]ver 29
14:19 [p]Pr 11:29
14:20 [q]Pr 19:4,7
14:21 [r]Pr 11:12 [s]Ps 41:1; Pr 19:17

[11]The house of the wicked will be
destroyed,
but the tent of the upright will
flourish.[h]

[12]There is a way that seems right to a
man,[i]
but in the end it leads to death.[j]

[13]Even in laughter[k] the heart may ache,
and joy may end in grief.

[14]The faithless will be fully repaid for
their ways,[l]
and the good man rewarded for his.[m]

[15]A simple man believes anything,
but a prudent man gives thought to
his steps.

[16]A wise man fears the LORD and
shuns evil,[n]
but a fool is hotheaded and
reckless.

[17]A quick-tempered man does foolish
things,[o]
and a crafty man is hated.

[18]The simple inherit folly,
but the prudent are crowned with
knowledge.

[19]Evil men will bow down in the
presence of the good,
and the wicked at the gates of the
righteous.[p]

[20]The poor are shunned even by their
neighbors,
but the rich have many friends.[q]

[21]He who despises his neighbor sins,[r]
but blessed is he who is kind to
the needy.[s]

[22]Do not those who plot evil go astray?
But those who plan what is good
find[y] love and faithfulness.

[23]All hard work brings a profit,
but mere talk leads only to poverty.

[24]The wealth of the wise is their crown,
but the folly of fools yields folly.

[y]22 Or *show*

25A truthful witness saves lives,
but a false witness is deceitful.[a]

26He who fears the LORD has a secure fortress,[b]
and for his children it will be a refuge.

27The fear of the LORD is a fountain of life,
turning a man from the snares of death.[c]

28A large population is a king's glory,
but without subjects a prince is ruined.

29A patient man has great understanding,
but a quick-tempered man displays folly.[d]

30A heart at peace gives life to the body,
but envy rots the bones.[e]

31He who oppresses the poor shows contempt for their Maker,[f]
but whoever is kind to the needy honors God.

32When calamity comes, the wicked are brought down,[g]
but even in death the righteous have a refuge.[h]

33Wisdom reposes in the heart of the discerning[i]
and even among fools she lets herself be known.[z]

34Righteousness exalts a nation,[j]
but sin is a disgrace to any people.

35A king delights in a wise servant,
but a shameful servant incurs his wrath.[k]

15 A gentle answer turns away wrath,[l]
but a harsh word stirs up anger.

2The tongue of the wise commends knowledge,
but the mouth of the fool gushes folly.[m]

3The eyes[n] of the LORD are everywhere,[o]
keeping watch on the wicked and the good.[p]

4The tongue that brings healing is a tree of life,
but a deceitful tongue crushes the spirit.

5A fool spurns his father's discipline,
but whoever heeds correction shows prudence.[q]

6The house of the righteous contains great treasure,[r]
but the income of the wicked brings them trouble.

7The lips of the wise spread knowledge;
not so the hearts of fools.

8The LORD detests the sacrifice of the wicked,[s]
but the prayer of the upright pleases him.[t]

9The LORD detests the way of the wicked
but he loves those who pursue righteousness.[u]

10Stern discipline awaits him who leaves the path;
he who hates correction will die.[v]

11Death and Destruction[a] lie open before the LORD[w]—
how much more the hearts of men![x]

12A mocker resents correction;[y]
he will not consult the wise.

13A happy heart makes the face cheerful,
but heartache crushes the spirit.[z]

14The discerning heart seeks knowledge,[a]
but the mouth of a fool feeds on folly.

15All the days of the oppressed are wretched,
but the cheerful heart has a continual feast.[b]

14:25 [a]ver 5
14:26 [b]Pr 18:10; 19:23; Isa 33:6
14:27 [c]Pr 13:14
14:29 [d]Ecc 7:8-9; Jas 1:19
14:30 [e]Pr 12:4
14:31 [f]Pr 17:5
14:32 [g]Pr 6:15 [h]Job 13:15; 2Ti 4:18
14:33 [i]Pr 2:6-10
14:34 [j]Pr 11:11
14:35 [k]Mt 24:45-51; 25:14-30
15:1 [l]Pr 25:15
15:2 [m]Pr 12:23
15:3 [n]2Ch 16:9 [o]Job 31:4; Heb 4:13 [p]Job 34:21; Jer 16:17
15:5 [q]Pr 13:1
15:6 [r]Pr 8:21
15:8 [s]Pr 21:27; Isa 1:11; Jer 6:20 [t]ver 29
15:9 [u]Pr 21:21; 1Ti 6:11
15:10 [v]Pr 1:31-32; 5:12
15:11 [w]Job 26:6; Ps 139:8 [x]2Ch 6:30; Ps 44:21
15:12 [y]Am 5:10
15:13 [z]Pr 12:25; 17:22; 18:14
15:14 [a]Pr 18:15
15:15 [b]ver 13

z*33* Hebrew; Septuagint and Syriac / *but in the heart of fools she is not known* a*11* Hebrew *Sheol and Abaddon*

16Better a little with the fear of the LORD
than great wealth with turmoil.[a]

17Better a meal of vegetables where there is love
than a fattened calf with hatred.[b]

18A hot-tempered man stirs up dissension,[c]
but a patient man calms a quarrel.[d]

19The way of the sluggard is blocked with thorns,[e]
but the path of the upright is a highway.

20A wise son brings joy to his father,[f]
but a foolish man despises his mother.

21Folly delights a man who lacks judgment,[g]
but a man of understanding keeps a straight course.

22Plans fail for lack of counsel,
but with many advisers they succeed.[h]

23A man finds joy in giving an apt reply[i]—
and how good is a timely word![j]

24The path of life leads upward for the wise
to keep him from going down to the grave.[b]

25The LORD tears down the proud man's house[k]
but he keeps the widow's boundaries intact.[l]

26The LORD detests the thoughts of the wicked,[m]
but those of the pure are pleasing to him.

27A greedy man brings trouble to his family,
but he who hates bribes will live.[n]

28The heart of the righteous weighs its answers,[o]
but the mouth of the wicked gushes evil.

15:16 [a]Ps 37:16-17; Pr 16:8; 1Ti 6:6
15:17 [b]Pr 17:1
15:18 [c]Pr 26:21 [d]Ge 13:8
15:19 [e]Pr 22:5
15:20 [f]Pr 10:1
15:21 [g]Pr 10:23
15:22 [h]Pr 11:14
15:23 [i]Pr 12:14 [j]Pr 25:11
15:25 [k]Pr 12:7 [l]Dt 19:14; Ps 68:5-6; Pr 23:10-11
15:26 [m]Pr 6:16
15:27 [n]Ex 23:8; Isa 33:15
15:28 [o]1Pe 3:15
15:29 [p]Ps 145:18-19
15:31 [q]ver 5
15:32 [r]Pr 1:7
15:33 [s]Pr 1:7 [t]Pr 18:12
16:1 [u]Pr 19:21
16:2 [v]Pr 21:2
16:3 [w]Ps 37:5-6; Pr 3:5-6
16:4 [x]Isa 43:7 [y]Ro 9:22
16:5 [z]Pr 6:16 [a]Pr 11:20-21
16:6 [b]Pr 14:16

29The LORD is far from the wicked
but he hears the prayer of the righteous.[p]

30A cheerful look brings joy to the heart,
and good news gives health to the bones.

31He who listens to a life-giving rebuke
will be at home among the wise.[q]

32He who ignores discipline despises himself,[r]
but whoever heeds correction gains understanding.

33The fear of the LORD[s] teaches a man wisdom,[c]
and humility comes before honor.[t]

16

To man belong the plans of the heart,
but from the LORD comes the reply of the tongue.[u]

2All a man's ways seem innocent to him,
but motives are weighed by the LORD.[v]

3Commit to the LORD whatever you do,
and your plans will succeed.[w]

4The LORD works out everything for his own ends[x]—
even the wicked for a day of disaster.[y]

5The LORD detests all the proud of heart.[z]
Be sure of this: They will not go unpunished.[a]

6Through love and faithfulness sin is atoned for;
through the fear of the LORD a man avoids evil.[b]

7When a man's ways are pleasing to the LORD,
he makes even his enemies live at peace with him.

8Better a little with righteousness

b24 Hebrew *Sheol* c33 Or *Wisdom teaches the fear of the LORD*

than much gain[a] with injustice.

9In his heart a man plans his course,
but the LORD determines his steps.[b]

10The lips of a king speak as an oracle,
and his mouth should not betray
justice.

11Honest scales and balances are from
the LORD;
all the weights in the bag are of his
making.[c]

12Kings detest wrongdoing,
for a throne is established through
righteousness.[d]

13Kings take pleasure in honest lips;
they value a man who speaks the
truth.[e]

14A king's wrath is a messenger of
death,[f]
but a wise man will appease it.

15When a king's face brightens, it
means life;[g]
his favor is like a rain cloud in
spring.

16How much better to get wisdom
than gold,
to choose understanding rather
than silver![h]

17The highway of the upright avoids
evil;
he who guards his way guards his
life.

18Pride goes before destruction,
a haughty spirit before a fall.[i]

19Better to be lowly in spirit and
among the oppressed
than to share plunder with the
proud.

20Whoever gives heed to instruction
prospers,
and blessed is he who trusts in the
LORD.[j]

21The wise in heart are called
discerning,
and pleasant words promote
instruction.[d] [k]

16:8 [a]Ps 37:16
16:9 [b]Jer 10:23
16:11 [c]Pr 11:1
16:12 [d]Pr 25:5
16:13 [e]Pr 14:35
16:14 [f]Pr 19:12
16:15 [g]Job 29:24
16:16 [h]Pr 8:10,19
16:18 [i]Pr 11:2; 18:12
16:20 [j]Ps 2:12; 34:8; Pr 19:8; Jer 17:7
16:21 [k]ver 23
16:22 [l]Pr 13:14
16:24 [m]Pr 24:13-14
16:25 [n]Pr 12:15 [o]Pr 14:12
16:27 [p]Jas 3:6
16:28 [q]Pr 15:18 [r]Pr 17:9
16:29 [s]Pr 1:10; 12:26
16:31 [t]Pr 20:29
16:33 [u]Pr 18:18; 29:26
17:1 [v]Pr 15:16,17

22Understanding is a fountain of life to
those who have it,[l]
but folly brings punishment to
fools.

23A wise man's heart guides his
mouth,
and his lips promote instruction.[e]

24Pleasant words are a honeycomb,
sweet to the soul and healing to
the bones.[m]

25There is a way that seems right to a
man,[n]
but in the end it leads to death.[o]

26The laborer's appetite works for him;
his hunger drives him on.

27A scoundrel plots evil,
and his speech is like a scorching
fire.[p]

28A perverse man stirs up dissension,[q]
and a gossip separates close
friends.[r]

29A violent man entices his neighbor
and leads him down a path that is
not good.[s]

30He who winks with his eye is
plotting perversity;
he who purses his lips is bent on
evil.

31Gray hair is a crown of splendor;[t]
it is attained by a righteous life.

32Better a patient man than a warrior,
a man who controls his temper
than one who takes a city.

33The lot is cast into the lap,
but its every decision is from the
LORD.[u]

17 Better a dry crust with peace
and quiet
than a house full of feasting,[f] with
strife.[v]

2A wise servant will rule over a
disgraceful son,

d*21* Or *words make a man persuasive*
e*23* Or *mouth / and makes his lips persuasive*
f*1* Hebrew *sacrifices*

and will share the inheritance as
one of the brothers.

3The crucible for silver and the
furnace for gold,[a]
but the LORD tests the heart.[b]

4A wicked man listens to evil lips;
a liar pays attention to a malicious
tongue.

5He who mocks the poor shows
contempt for their Maker;[c]
whoever gloats over disaster[d] will
not go unpunished.[e]

6Children's children[f] are a crown to
the aged,
and parents are the pride of their
children.

7Arrogant[g] lips are unsuited to a
fool—
how much worse lying lips to a
ruler!

8A bribe is a charm to the one who
gives it;
wherever he turns, he succeeds.

9He who covers over an offense
promotes love,[g]
but whoever repeats the matter
separates close friends.[h]

10A rebuke impresses a man of
discernment
more than a hundred lashes a fool.

11An evil man is bent only on
rebellion;
a merciless official will be sent
against him.

12Better to meet a bear robbed of her
cubs
than a fool in his folly.

13If a man pays back evil[i] for good,
evil will never leave his house.

14Starting a quarrel is like breaching a
dam;
so drop the matter before a dispute
breaks out.[j]

15Acquitting the guilty and
condemning the innocent[k]—
the LORD detests them both.[l]

16Of what use is money in the hand of
a fool,
since he has no desire to get
wisdom?[m]

17A friend loves at all times,
and a brother is born for adversity.

18A man lacking in judgment strikes
hands in pledge
and puts up security for his
neighbor.[n]

19He who loves a quarrel loves sin;
he who builds a high gate invites
destruction.

20A man of perverse heart does not
prosper;
he whose tongue is deceitful falls
into trouble.

21To have a fool for a son brings grief;
there is no joy for the father of a
fool.[o]

22A cheerful heart is good medicine,
but a crushed spirit dries up the
bones.[p]

23A wicked man accepts a bribe[q] in
secret
to pervert the course of justice.

24A discerning man keeps wisdom in
view,
but a fool's eyes[r] wander to the
ends of the earth.

25A foolish son brings grief to his
father
and bitterness to the one who bore
him.[s]

26It is not good to punish an innocent
man,[t]
or to flog officials for their
integrity.

27A man of knowledge uses words
with restraint,
and a man of understanding is
even-tempered.[u]

17:3 [a]Pr 27:21 [b]1Ch 29:17; Ps 26:2; Jer 17:10
17:5 [c]Pr 14:31 [d]Job 31:29 [e]Ob 1:12
17:6 [f]Pr 13:22
17:9 [g]Pr 10:12 [h]Pr 16:28
17:13 [i]Ps 109:4-5; Jer 18:20
17:14 [j]Pr 20:3
17:15 [k]Pr 18:5 [l]Ex 23:6-7; Isa 5:23
17:16 [m]Pr 23:23
17:18 [n]Pr 6:1-5; 11:15; 22:26-27
17:21 [o]Pr 10:1
17:22 [p]Ps 22:15; Pr 15:13
17:23 [q]Ex 23:8
17:24 [r]Ecc 2:14
17:25 [s]Pr 10:1
17:26 [t]Pr 18:5
17:27 [u]Pr 14:29; Jas 1:19

[g]7 Or *Eloquent*

[28]Even a fool is thought wise if he
keeps silent,
and discerning if he holds his
tongue.[a]

18 An unfriendly man pursues
selfish ends;
he defies all sound judgment.

[2]A fool finds no pleasure in
understanding
but delights in airing his own
opinions.[b]

[3]When wickedness comes, so does
contempt,
and with shame comes disgrace.

[4]The words of a man's mouth are
deep waters,
but the fountain of wisdom is a
bubbling brook.

[5]It is not good to be partial to the
wicked[c]
or to deprive the innocent of
justice.[d]

[6]A fool's lips bring him strife,
and his mouth invites a beating.

[7]A fool's mouth is his undoing,
and his lips are a snare[e] to his soul.[f]

[8]The words of a gossip are like choice
morsels;
they go down to a man's inmost
parts.[g]

[9]One who is slack in his work
is brother to one who destroys.[h]

[10]The name of the LORD is a strong
tower;[i]
the righteous run to it and are safe.

[11]The wealth of the rich is their
fortified city;[j]
they imagine it an unscalable wall.

[12]Before his downfall a man's heart is
proud,
but humility comes before honor.[k]

[13]He who answers before listening—
that is his folly and his shame.[l]

[14]A man's spirit sustains him in
sickness,
but a crushed spirit who can
bear?[m]

[15]The heart of the discerning acquires
knowledge;[n]
the ears of the wise seek it out.

[16]A gift[o] opens the way for the giver
and ushers him into the presence
of the great.

[17]The first to present his case seems
right,
till another comes forward and
questions him.

[18]Casting the lot settles disputes[p]
and keeps strong opponents apart.

[19]An offended brother is more
unyielding than a fortified city,
and disputes are like the barred
gates of a citadel.

[20]From the fruit of his mouth a man's
stomach is filled;
with the harvest from his lips he is
satisfied.[q]

[21]The tongue has the power of life and
death,
and those who love it will eat its
fruit.[r]

[22]He who finds a wife finds what is
good[s]
and receives favor from the LORD.[t]

[23]A poor man pleads for mercy,
but a rich man answers harshly.

[24]A man of many companions may
come to ruin,
but there is a friend who sticks
closer than a brother.[u]

19 Better a poor man whose walk
is blameless
than a fool whose lips are
perverse.[v]

[2]It is not good to have zeal without
knowledge,
nor to be hasty and miss the way.[w]

[3]A man's own folly ruins his life,
yet his heart rages against the
LORD.

17:28 [a]Job 13:5
18:2 [b]Pr 12:23
18:5 [c]Lev 19:15; Pr 24:23-25; 28:21 [d]Ps 82:2; Pr 17:15
18:7 [e]Ps 140:9 [f]Ps 64:8; Pr 10:14; 12:13; 13:3; Ecc 10:12
18:8 [g]Pr 26:22
18:9 [h]Pr 28:24
18:10 [i]2Sa 22:3; Ps 61:3
18:11 [j]Pr 10:15
18:12 [k]Pr 11:2; 15:33; 16:18
18:13 [l]Pr 20:25; Jn 7:51
18:14 [m]Pr 15:13; 17:22
18:15 [n]Pr 15:14
18:16 [o]Ge 32:20
18:18 [p]Pr 16:33
18:20 [q]Pr 12:14
18:21 [r]Pr 13:2-3; Mt 12:37
18:22 [s]Pr 12:4 [t]Pr 19:14; 31:10
18:24 [u]Pr 17:17; Jn 15:13-15
19:1 [v]Pr 28:6
19:2 [w]Pr 29:20

4Wealth brings many friends,
but a poor man's friend deserts him.[a]

5A false witness[b] will not go unpunished,
and he who pours out lies will not go free.[c]

6Many curry favor with a ruler,[d]
and everyone is the friend of a man who gives gifts.[e]

7A poor man is shunned by all his relatives—
how much more do his friends avoid him!
Though he pursues them with pleading,
they are nowhere to be found.[h][f]

8He who gets wisdom loves his own soul;
he who cherishes understanding prospers.[g]

9A false witness will not go unpunished,
and he who pours out lies will perish.[h]

10It is not fitting for a fool[i] to live in luxury—
how much worse for a slave to rule over princes![j]

11A man's wisdom gives him patience;[k]
it is to his glory to overlook an offense.

12A king's rage is like the roar of a lion,
but his favor is like dew[l] on the grass.[m]

13A foolish son is his father's ruin,[n]
and a quarrelsome wife is like a constant dripping.[o]

14Houses and wealth are inherited from parents,[p]
but a prudent wife is from the LORD.[q]

15Laziness brings on deep sleep,
and the shiftless man goes hungry.[r]

19:4 [a]Pr 14:20
19:5 [b]Ex 23:1 [c]Dt 19:19; Pr 21:28
19:6 [d]Pr 29:26 [e]Pr 17:8; 18:16
19:7 [f]ver 4; Ps 38:11
19:8 [g]Pr 16:20
19:9 [h]ver 5
19:10 [i]Pr 26:1 [j]Pr 30:21-23; Ecc 10:5-7
19:11 [k]Pr 16:32
19:12 [l]Ps 133:3 [m]Pr 16:14-15
19:13 [n]Pr 10:1 [o]Pr 21:9
19:14 [p]2Co 12:14 [q]Pr 18:22
19:15 [r]Pr 6:9; 10:4
19:16 [s]Pr 16:17; Lk 10:28
19:17 [t]Mt 10:42; 2Co 9:6-8
19:18 [u]Pr 13:24; 23:13-14
19:20 [v]Pr 4:1 [w]Pr 12:15
19:21 [x]Ps 33:11; Pr 16:9; Isa 14:24,27
19:23 [y]Ps 25:13; Pr 12:21; 1Ti 4:8
19:24 [z]Pr 26:15
19:25 [a]Pr 9:9; 21:11
19:26 [b]Pr 28:24

16He who obeys instructions guards his life,
but he who is contemptuous of his ways will die.[s]

17He who is kind to the poor lends to the LORD,
and he will reward him for what he has done.[t]

18Discipline your son, for in that there is hope;
do not be a willing party to his death.[u]

19A hot-tempered man must pay the penalty;
if you rescue him, you will have to do it again.

20Listen to advice and accept instruction,[v]
and in the end you will be wise.[w]

21Many are the plans in a man's heart,
but it is the LORD's purpose that prevails.[x]

22What a man desires is unfailing love[i];
better to be poor than a liar.

23The fear of the LORD leads to life:
Then one rests content, untouched by trouble.[y]

24The sluggard buries his hand in the dish;
he will not even bring it back to his mouth![z]

25Flog a mocker, and the simple will learn prudence;
rebuke a discerning man, and he will gain knowledge.[a]

26He who robs his father and drives out his mother[b]
is a son who brings shame and disgrace.

27Stop listening to instruction, my son,
and you will stray from the words of knowledge.

28A corrupt witness mocks at justice,

h *7* The meaning of the Hebrew for this sentence is uncertain. i *22* Or *A man's greed is his shame*

and the mouth of the wicked gulps
down evil.[a]

29Penalties are prepared for mockers,
and beatings for the backs of
fools.[b]

20 Wine is a mocker and beer a
brawler;
whoever is led astray by them is
not wise.[c]

2A king's wrath is like the roar of a
lion;[d]
he who angers him forfeits his
life.[e]

3It is to a man's honor to avoid strife,
but every fool is quick to quarrel.[f]

4A sluggard does not plow in season;
so at harvest time he looks but
finds nothing.

5The purposes of a man's heart are
deep waters,
but a man of understanding draws
them out.

6Many a man claims to have unfailing
love,
but a faithful man who can find?[g]

7The righteous man leads a blameless
life;
blessed are his children after him.[h]

8When a king sits on his throne to
judge,
he winnows out all evil with his
eyes.[i]

9Who can say, "I have kept my heart
pure;
I am clean and without sin"?[j]

10Differing weights and differing
measures—
the LORD detests them both.[k]

11Even a child is known by his actions,
by whether his conduct is pure[l]
and right.

12Ears that hear and eyes that see—
the LORD has made them both.[m]

13Do not love sleep or you will grow
poor;[n]
stay awake and you will have food
to spare.

14"It's no good, it's no good!" says the
buyer;
then off he goes and boasts about
his purchase.

15Gold there is, and rubies in
abundance,
but lips that speak knowledge are a
rare jewel.

16Take the garment of one who puts
up security for a stranger;
hold it in pledge[o] if he does it for a
wayward woman.[p]

17Food gained by fraud tastes sweet to
a man,[q]
but he ends up with a mouth full of
gravel.

18Make plans by seeking advice;
if you wage war, obtain guidance.[r]

19A gossip betrays a confidence;[s]
so avoid a man who talks too much.

20If a man curses his father or mother,[t]
his lamp will be snuffed out in
pitch darkness.[u]

21An inheritance quickly gained at the
beginning
will not be blessed at the end.

22Do not say, "I'll pay you back for this
wrong!"[v]
Wait for the LORD, and he will
deliver you.[w]

23The LORD detests differing weights,
and dishonest scales do not please
him.[x]

24A man's steps are directed by the
LORD.
How then can anyone understand
his own way?[y]

25It is a trap for a man to dedicate
something rashly
and only later to consider his
vows.[z]

26A wise king winnows out the
wicked;

19:28 [a]Job 15:16
19:29 [b]Pr 26:3
20:1 [c]Pr 31:4
20:2 [d]Pr 19:12 [e]Pr 8:36
20:3 [f]Pr 17:14
20:6 [g]Ps 12:1
20:7 [h]Ps 37:25-26; 112:2
20:8 [i]ver 26; Pr 25:4-5
20:9 [j]1Ki 8:46; Ecc 7:20; 1Jn 1:8
20:10 [k]ver 23; Pr 11:1
20:11 [l]Mt 7:16
20:12 [m]Ps 94:9
20:13 [n]Pr 6:11; 19:15
20:16 [o]Ex 22:26 [p]Pr 27:13
20:17 [q]Pr 9:17
20:18 [r]Pr 11:14; 24:6
20:19 [s]Pr 11:13
20:20 [t]Pr 30:11 [u]Ex 21:17; Job 18:5
20:22 [v]Pr 24:29 [w]Ro 12:19
20:23 [x]ver 10
20:24 [y]Jer 10:23
20:25 [z]Ecc 5:2,4-5

he drives the threshing wheel over
them.[a]

27 The lamp of the LORD searches the
spirit of a man[j];
it searches out his inmost being.

28 Love and faithfulness keep a king
safe;
through love his throne is made
secure.[b]

29 The glory of young men is their
strength,
gray hair the splendor of the old.[c]

30 Blows and wounds cleanse[d] away
evil,
and beatings purge the inmost
being.

21

1 The king's heart is in the hand
of the LORD;
he directs it like a watercourse
wherever he pleases.

2 All a man's ways seem right to him,
but the LORD weighs the heart.[e]

3 To do what is right and just
is more acceptable to the LORD
than sacrifice.[f]

4 Haughty eyes[g] and a proud heart,
the lamp of the wicked, are sin!

5 The plans of the diligent lead to
profit[h]
as surely as haste leads to poverty.

6 A fortune made by a lying tongue
is a fleeting vapor and a deadly
snare.[k][i]

7 The violence of the wicked will drag
them away,
for they refuse to do what is right.

8 The way of the guilty is devious,[j]
but the conduct of the innocent is
upright.

9 Better to live on a corner of the roof
than share a house with a
quarrelsome wife.[k]

10 The wicked man craves evil;
his neighbor gets no mercy from
him.

11 When a mocker is punished, the
simple gain wisdom;
when a wise man is instructed, he
gets knowledge.[l]

12 The Righteous One[l] takes note of the
house of the wicked
and brings the wicked to ruin.[m]

13 If a man shuts his ears to the cry of
the poor,
he too will cry out and not be
answered.[n]

14 A gift given in secret soothes anger,
and a bribe concealed in the cloak
pacifies great wrath.[o]

15 When justice is done, it brings joy to
the righteous
but terror to evildoers.[p]

16 A man who strays from the path of
understanding
comes to rest in the company of
the dead.[q]

17 He who loves pleasure will become
poor;
whoever loves wine and oil will
never be rich.[r]

18 The wicked become a ransom[s] for
the righteous,
and the unfaithful for the upright.

19 Better to live in a desert
than with a quarrelsome and ill-
tempered wife.[t]

20 In the house of the wise are stores of
choice food and oil,
but a foolish man devours all he
has.

21 He who pursues righteousness and
love
finds life, prosperity[m] and honor.[u]

22 A wise man attacks the city of the
mighty[v]
and pulls down the stronghold in
which they trust.

20:26 [a]ver 8
20:28 [b]Pr 29:14
20:29 [c]Pr 16:31
20:30 [d]Pr 22:15
21:2 [e]Pr 16:2; 24:12; Lk 16:15
21:3 [f]1Sa 15:22; Pr 15:8; Isa 1:11; Hos 6:6; Mic 6:6-8
21:4 [g]Pr 6:17
21:5 [h]Pr 10:4; 28:22
21:6 [i]2Pe 2:3
21:8 [j]Pr 2:15
21:9 [k]Pr 25:24
21:11 [l]Pr 19:25
21:12 [m]Pr 14:11
21:13 [n]Mt 18:30-34; Jas 2:13
21:14 [o]Pr 18:16; 19:6
21:15 [p]Pr 10:29
21:16 [q]Ps 49:14
21:17 [r]Pr 23:20-21, 29-35
21:18 [s]Pr 11:8; Isa 43:3
21:19 [t]ver 9
21:21 [u]Mt 5:6
21:22 [v]Ecc 9:15-16

j *27* Or *The spirit of man is the LORD's lamp*
k *6* Some Hebrew manuscripts, Septuagint and Vulgate; most Hebrew manuscripts *vapor for those who seek death*
l *12* Or *The righteous man*
m *21* Or *righteousness*

23 He who guards his mouth[a] and his
tongue
keeps himself from calamity.[b]

24 The proud and arrogant[c]
man—"Mocker" is his name;
he behaves with overweening pride.

25 The sluggard's craving will be the
death of him,[d]
because his hands refuse to work.
26 All day long he craves for more,
but the righteous give without
sparing.[e]

27 The sacrifice of the wicked is
detestable[f]—
how much more so when brought
with evil intent![g]

28 A false witness will perish,[h]
and whoever listens to him will be
destroyed forever.[n]

29 A wicked man puts up a bold front,
but an upright man gives thought
to his ways.

30 There is no wisdom,[i] no insight, no
plan
that can succeed against the LORD.[j]

31 The horse is made ready for the day
of battle,
but victory rests with the LORD.[k]

22

A good name is more desirable
than great riches;
to be esteemed is better than silver
or gold.[l]

2 Rich and poor have this in common:
The LORD is the Maker of them all.[m]

3 A prudent man sees danger and
takes refuge,[n]
but the simple keep going and
suffer for it.[o]

4 Humility and the fear of the LORD
bring wealth and honor and life.

5 In the paths of the wicked lie thorns
and snares,[p]
but he who guards his soul stays
far from them.

6 Train[o] a child in the way he should go,[q]
and when he is old he will not turn
from it.

7 The rich rule over the poor,
and the borrower is servant to the
lender.

8 He who sows wickedness reaps
trouble,[r]
and the rod of his fury will be
destroyed.[s]

9 A generous man will himself be
blessed,[t]
for he shares his food with the
poor.[u]

10 Drive out the mocker, and out goes
strife;
quarrels and insults are ended.[v]

11 He who loves a pure heart and
whose speech is gracious
will have the king for his friend.[w]

12 The eyes of the LORD keep watch
over knowledge,
but he frustrates the words of the
unfaithful.

13 The sluggard says, "There is a lion
outside!"[x]
or, "I will be murdered in the
streets!"

14 The mouth of an adulteress is a deep
pit;[y]
he who is under the LORD's wrath
will fall into it.[z]

15 Folly is bound up in the heart of a
child,
but the rod of discipline will drive
it far from him.[a]

16 He who oppresses the poor to
increase his wealth
and he who gives gifts to the
rich—both come to poverty.

Sayings of the wise.

17 Pay attention and listen to the
sayings of the wise;[b]
apply your heart to what I teach,

21:23 [a]Jas 3:2 [b]Pr 12:13; 13:3
21:24 [c]Ps 1:1; Pr 1:22; Isa 16:6; Jer 48:29
21:25 [d]Pr 13:4
21:26 [e]Ps 37:26; Mt 5:42; Eph 4:28
21:27 [f]Isa 66:3; Jer 6:20; Am 5:22 [g]Pr 15:8
21:28 [h]Pr 19:5
21:30 [i]Jer 9:23 [j]Isa 8:10; Ac 5:39
21:31 [k]Ps 3:8; 33:12-19; Isa 31:1
22:1 [l]Ecc 7:1
22:2 [m]Job 31:15
22:3 [n]Pr 14:16 [o]Pr 27:12
22:5 [p]Pr 15:19
22:6 [q]Eph 6:4
22:8 [r]Job 4:8 [s]Ps 125:3
22:9 [t]2Co 9:6 [u]Pr 19:17
22:10 [v]Pr 18:6; 26:20
22:11 [w]Pr 16:13; Mt 5:8
22:13 [x]Pr 26:13
22:14 [y]Pr 2:16; 5:3-5; 7:5; 23:27 [z]Ecc 7:26
22:15 [a]Pr 13:24; 23:14
22:17 [b]Pr 5:1

[n]*28* Or */ but the words of an obedient man will live on*
[o]*6* Or *Start*

18 for it is pleasing when you keep
them in your heart
and have all of them ready on your
lips.
19 So that your trust may be in the LORD,
I teach you today, even you.
20 Have I not written thirty[p] sayings for
you,
sayings of counsel and knowledge,
21 teaching you true and reliable
words,[a]
so that you can give sound answers
to him who sent you?

22 Do not exploit the poor[b] because
they are poor
and do not crush the needy in
court,[c]
23 for the LORD will take up their case[d]
and will plunder those who
plunder them.[e]

24 Do not make friends with a hot-
tempered man,
do not associate with one easily
angered,
25 or you may learn his ways
and get yourself ensnared.[f]

26 Do not be a man who strikes hands
in pledge[g]
or puts up security for debts;
27 if you lack the means to pay,
your very bed will be snatched
from under you.[h]

28 Do not move an ancient boundary
stone[i]
set up by your forefathers.

29 Do you see a man skilled in his
work?
He will serve[j] before kings;
he will not serve before obscure
men.

23 When you sit to dine with a
ruler,
note well what[q] is before you,
2 and put a knife to your throat
if you are given to gluttony.
3 Do not crave his delicacies,[k]
for that food is deceptive.

4 Do not wear yourself out to get rich;
have the wisdom to show restraint.
5 Cast but a glance at riches, and they
are gone,
for they will surely sprout wings
and fly off to the sky like an eagle.[l]

6 Do not eat the food of a stingy man,
do not crave his delicacies;[m]
7 for he is the kind of man
who is always thinking about the
cost.[r]
"Eat and drink," he says to you,
but his heart is not with you.
8 You will vomit up the little you have
eaten
and will have wasted your
compliments.

9 Do not speak to a fool,
for he will scorn the wisdom of
your words.[n]

10 Do not move an ancient boundary
stone[o]
or encroach on the fields of the
fatherless,
11 for their Defender[p] is strong;
he will take up their case against
you.[q]

12 Apply your heart to instruction
and your ears to words of
knowledge.

13 Do not withhold discipline from a
child;
if you punish him with the rod, he
will not die.
14 Punish him with the rod
and save his soul from death.[s]

15 My son, if your heart is wise,
then my heart will be glad;
16 my inmost being will rejoice
when your lips speak what is
right.[r]

17 Do not let your heart envy[s] sinners,
but always be zealous for the fear
of the LORD.
18 There is surely a future hope for you,

22:21 [a]Lk 1:3-4; 1Pe 3:15
22:22 [b]Zec 7:10 [c]Ex 23:6; Mal 3:5
22:23 [d]Ps 12:5 [e]1Sa 25:39; Pr 23:10-11
22:25 [f]1Co 15:33
22:26 [g]Pr 11:15
22:27 [h]Pr 17:18
22:28 [i]Dt 19:14; Pr 23:10
22:29 [j]Ge 41:46
23:3 [k]ver 6-8
23:5 [l]Pr 27:24
23:6 [m]Ps 141:4
23:9 [n]Pr 1:7; 9:7; Mt 7:6
23:10 [o]Dt 19:14; Pr 22:28
23:11 [p]Job 19:25 [q]Pr 22:22-23
23:16 [r]ver 24; Pr 27:11
23:17 [s]Ps 37:1; Pr 28:14

p *20* Or *not formerly written*; or *not written excellent*
q *1* Or *who* r *7* Or *for as he thinks within himself, / so he is*; or *for as he puts on a feast, / so he is*
s *14* Hebrew *Sheol*

and your hope will not be cut off.[a]

19Listen, my son, and be wise,
and keep your heart on the right path.

20Do not join those who drink too much wine[b]
or gorge themselves on meat,
21for drunkards and gluttons become poor,[c]
and drowsiness clothes them in rags.

22Listen to your father, who gave you life,
and do not despise your mother when she is old.[d]

23Buy the truth and do not sell it;
get wisdom, discipline and understanding.[e]

24The father of a righteous man has great joy;
he who has a wise son delights in him.[f]
25May your father and mother be glad;
may she who gave you birth rejoice!

26My son,[g] give me your heart
and let your eyes keep to my ways,[h]
27for a prostitute is a deep pit[i]
and a wayward wife is a narrow well.
28Like a bandit she lies in wait,[j]
and multiplies the unfaithful among men.

29Who has woe? Who has sorrow?
Who has strife? Who has complaints?
Who has needless bruises? Who has bloodshot eyes?
30Those who linger over wine,[k]
who go to sample bowls of mixed wine.
31Do not gaze at wine when it is red,
when it sparkles in the cup,
when it goes down smoothly!
32In the end it bites like a snake
and poisons like a viper.
33Your eyes will see strange sights
and your mind imagine confusing things.
34You will be like one sleeping on the high seas,
lying on top of the rigging.
35"They hit me," you will say, "but I'm not hurt!
They beat me, but I don't feel it!
When will I wake up
so I can find another drink?"

24 Do not envy[l] wicked men,
do not desire their company;
2for their hearts plot violence,
and their lips talk about making trouble.[m]

3By wisdom a house is built,[n]
and through understanding it is established;
4through knowledge its rooms are filled
with rare and beautiful treasures.[o]

5A wise man has great power,
and a man of knowledge increases strength;
6for waging war you need guidance,
and for victory many advisers.[p]

7Wisdom is too high for a fool;
in the assembly at the gate he has nothing to say.

8He who plots evil
will be known as a schemer.
9The schemes of folly are sin,
and men detest a mocker.

10If you falter in times of trouble,
how small is your strength![q]

11Rescue those being led away to death;
hold back those staggering toward slaughter.[r]
12If you say, "But we knew nothing about this,"
does not he who weighs[s] the heart perceive it?
Does not he who guards your life know it?
Will he not repay each person according to what he has done?[t]

13Eat honey, my son, for it is good;
honey from the comb is sweet to your taste.

23:18 [a]Ps 9:18; Pr 24:14,19-20
23:20 [b]Isa 5:11,22; Ro 13:13; Eph 5:18
23:21 [c]Pr 21:17
23:22 [d]Lev 19:32; Pr 1:8; 30:17; Eph 6:1-2
23:23 [e]Pr 4:7
23:24 [f]ver 15-16; Pr 10:1; 15:20
23:26 [g]Pr 3:1; 5:1-6 [h]Ps 18:21; Pr 4:4
23:27 [i]Pr 22:14
23:28 [j]Pr 7:11-12; Ecc 7:26
23:30 [k]Ps 75:8; Isa 5:11; Eph 5:18
24:1 [l]Ps 37:1; 73:3; Pr 3:31-32; 23:17-18
24:2 [m]Ps 10:7
24:3 [n]Pr 14:1
24:4 [o]Pr 8:21
24:6 [p]Pr 11:14; 20:18; Lk 14:31
24:10 [q]Job 4:5; Jer 51:46; Heb 12:3
24:11 [r]Ps 82:4; Isa 58:6-7
24:12 [s]Pr 21:2 [t]Job 34:11; Ps 62:12; Ro 2:6*

[14]Know also that wisdom is sweet to
your soul;
if you find it, there is a future hope
for you,
and your hope will not be cut off.[a] [b]

[15]Do not lie in wait like an outlaw
against a righteous man's house,
do not raid his dwelling place;
[16]for though a righteous man falls
seven times, he rises again,
but the wicked are brought down
by calamity. [c]

[17]Do not gloat[d] when your enemy
falls;
when he stumbles, do not let your
heart rejoice,[e]
[18]or the LORD will see and disapprove
and turn his wrath away from him.

[19]Do not fret[f] because of evil men
or be envious of the wicked,
[20]for the evil man has no future hope,
and the lamp of the wicked will be
snuffed out.[g]

[21]Fear the LORD and the king,[h] my son,
and do not join with the
rebellious,
[22]for those two will send sudden
destruction upon them,
and who knows what calamities
they can bring?

More sayings of the wise.

[23]These also are sayings of the wise:[i]

To show partiality[j] in judging is not
good:[k]
[24]Whoever says to the guilty, "You are
innocent"[l]—
peoples will curse him and nations
denounce him.
[25]But it will go well with those who
convict the guilty,
and rich blessing will come upon
them.

[26]An honest answer
is like a kiss on the lips.

[27]Finish your outdoor work
and get your fields ready;
after that, build your house.

24:14 [a]Ps 119:103; Pr 16:24 [b]Pr 23:18
24:16 [c]Job 5:19; Ps 34:19; Mic 7:8
24:17 [d]Ob 1:12 [e]Job 31:29
24:19 [f]Ps 37:1
24:20 [g]Job 18:5; Pr 13:9; 23:17-18
24:21 [h]Ro 13:1-5; 1Pe 2:17
24:23 [i]Pr 1:6 [j]Lev 19:15 [k]Pr 28:21
24:24 [l]Pr 17:15
24:28 [m]Ps 7:4; Pr 25:18; Eph 4:25
24:29 [n]Pr 20:22; Mt 5:38-41; Ro 12:17
24:30 [o]Pr 6:6-11; 26:13-16
24:33 [p]Pr 6:10
24:34 [q]Pr 10:4; Ecc 10:18
25:1 [r]1Ki 4:32 [s]Pr 1:1
25:2 [t]Pr 16:10-15
25:5 [u]Pr 20:8 [v]2Sa 7:13 [w]Pr 16:12; 29:14

[28]Do not testify against your neighbor
without cause,[m]
or use your lips to deceive.
[29]Do not say, "I'll do to him as he has
done to me;
I'll pay that man back for what he
did."[n]

[30]I went past the field of the
sluggard,[o]
past the vineyard of the man who
lacks judgment;
[31]thorns had come up everywhere,
the ground was covered with weeds,
and the stone wall was in ruins.
[32]I applied my heart to what I
observed
and learned a lesson from what I
saw:
[33]A little sleep, a little slumber,
a little folding of the hands to
rest[p]—
[34]and poverty will come on you like a
bandit
and scarcity like an armed man.[t] [q]

Proverbs of Solomon: Kings.

25 These are more proverbs[r] of Solomon, copied by the men of Hezekiah king of Judah:[s]

[2]It is the glory of God to conceal a
matter;
to search out a matter is the glory
of kings.[t]

[3]As the heavens are high and the
earth is deep,
so the hearts of kings are
unsearchable.

[4]Remove the dross from the silver,
and out comes material for[u] the
silversmith;
[5]remove the wicked from the king's
presence,[u]
and his throne will be established[v]
through righteousness.[w]

[6]Do not exalt yourself in the king's
presence,

t34 Or *like a vagrant / and scarcity like a beggar*
u4 Or *comes a vessel from*

and do not claim a place among
great men;
[7]it is better for him to say to you,
"Come up here,"[a]
than for him to humiliate you
before a nobleman.

Neighbors.

What you have seen with your eyes
[8] do not bring[v] hastily to court,
for what will you do in the end
if your neighbor puts you to shame?[b]

[9]If you argue your case with a neighbor,
do not betray another man's
confidence,
[10]or he who hears it may shame you
and you will never lose your bad
reputation.

[11]A word aptly spoken
is like apples of gold in settings of
silver.[c]

[12]Like an earring of gold or an
ornament of fine gold
is a wise man's rebuke to a
listening ear.[d]

[13]Like the coolness of snow at harvest
time
is a trustworthy messenger to
those who send him;
he refreshes the spirit of his
masters.[e]

[14]Like clouds and wind without rain
is a man who boasts of gifts he
does not give.

[15]Through patience a ruler can be
persuaded,[f]
and a gentle tongue can break a
bone.[g]

[16]If you find honey, eat just enough—
too much of it, and you will vomit.[h]
[17]Seldom set foot in your neighbor's
house—
too much of you, and he will hate you.

[18]Like a club or a sword or a sharp arrow
is the man who gives false
testimony against his
neighbor.[i]

25:7
[a]Lk 14:7-10

25:8
[b]Mt 5:25-26

25:11
[c]ver 12;
Pr 15:23

25:12
[d]ver 11;
Ps 141:5;
Pr 13:18;
15:31

25:13
[e]Pr 10:26;
13:17

25:15
[f]Ecc 10:4
[g]Pr 15:1

25:16
[h]ver 27

25:18
[i]Ps 57:4;
Pr 12:18

25:22
[j]Ps 18:8
[k]2Sa 16:12;
2Ch 28:15;
Mt 5:44;
Ro 12:20*

25:24
[l]Pr 21:9

25:25
[m]Pr 15:30

25:27
[n]ver 16
[o]Pr 27:2;
Mt 23:12

26:1
[p]1Sa 12:17
[q]ver 8;
Pr 19:10

26:2
[r]Nu 23:8;
Dt 23:5

[19]Like a bad tooth or a lame foot
is reliance on the unfaithful in
times of trouble.

[20]Like one who takes away a garment
on a cold day,
or like vinegar poured on soda,
is one who sings songs to a heavy
heart.

Enemies.

[21]If your enemy is hungry, give him
food to eat;
if he is thirsty, give him water to
drink.
[22]In doing this, you will heap burning
coals[j] on his head,
and the LORD will reward you.[k]

[23]As a north wind brings rain,
so a sly tongue brings angry looks.

[24]Better to live on a corner of the roof
than share a house with a
quarrelsome wife.[l]

[25]Like cold water to a weary soul
is good news from a distant land.[m]

[26]Like a muddied spring or a polluted
well
is a righteous man who gives way
to the wicked.

[27]It is not good to eat too much honey,[n]
nor is it honorable to seek one's
own honor.[o]

[28]Like a city whose walls are broken
down
is a man who lacks self-control.

Fools.

26 Like snow in summer or rain[p]
in harvest,
honor is not fitting for a fool.[q]

[2]Like a fluttering sparrow or a darting
swallow,
an undeserved curse does not
come to rest.[r]

[v]*7,8* Or *nobleman / on whom you had set your eyes. /* [8]*Do not go*

3 A whip for the horse, a halter for the donkey,[a]
and a rod for the backs of fools![b]

4 Do not answer a fool according to his folly,
or you will be like him yourself.[c]

5 Answer a fool according to his folly,
or he will be wise in his own eyes.[d]

6 Like cutting off one's feet or drinking violence
is the sending of a message by the hand of a fool.[e]

7 Like a lame man's legs that hang limp
is a proverb in the mouth of a fool.[f]

8 Like tying a stone in a sling
is the giving of honor to a fool.[g]

9 Like a thornbush in a drunkard's hand
is a proverb in the mouth of a fool.[h]

10 Like an archer who wounds at random
is he who hires a fool or any passer-by.

11 As a dog returns to its vomit,[i]
so a fool repeats his folly.[j]

12 Do you see a man wise in his own eyes?[k]
There is more hope for a fool than for him.[l]

The sluggard.

13 The sluggard says,[m] "There is a lion in the road,
a fierce lion roaming the streets!"[n]

14 As a door turns on its hinges,
so a sluggard turns on his bed.[o]

15 The sluggard buries his hand in the dish;
he is too lazy to bring it back to his mouth.[p]

16 The sluggard is wiser in his own eyes
than seven men who answer discreetly.

Speech.

17 Like one who seizes a dog by the ears
is a passer-by who meddles in a quarrel not his own.

18 Like a madman shooting firebrands or deadly arrows
19 is a man who deceives his neighbor
and says, "I was only joking!"

20 Without wood a fire goes out;
without gossip a quarrel dies down.[q]

21 As charcoal to embers and as wood to fire,
so is a quarrelsome man for kindling strife.[r]

22 The words of a gossip are like choice morsels;
they go down to a man's inmost parts.[s]

23 Like a coating of glaze[w] over earthenware
are fervent lips with an evil heart.

24 A malicious man disguises himself with his lips,[t]
but in his heart he harbors deceit.[u]
25 Though his speech is charming,[v] do not believe him,
for seven abominations fill his heart.[w]
26 His malice may be concealed by deception,
but his wickedness will be exposed in the assembly.

27 If a man digs a pit,[x] he will fall into it;[y]
if a man rolls a stone, it will roll back on him.[z]

28 A lying tongue hates those it hurts,
and a flattering mouth[a] works ruin.

Miscellaneous proverbs.

27 Do not boast[b] about tomorrow,
for you do not know what a day may bring forth.[c]

26:3 [a]Ps 32:9 [b]Pr 10:13
26:4 [c]ver 5; Isa 36:21
26:5 [d]ver 4; Pr 3:7
26:6 [e]Pr 10:26
26:7 [f]ver 9
26:8 [g]ver 1
26:9 [h]ver 7
26:11 [i]2Pe 2:22* [j]Ex 8:15; Ps 85:8
26:12 [k]Pr 3:7 [l]Pr 29:20
26:13 [m]Pr 6:6-11; 24:30-34 [n]Pr 22:13
26:14 [o]Pr 6:9
26:15 [p]Pr 19:24
26:20 [q]Pr 22:10
26:21 [r]Pr 14:17; 15:18
26:22 [s]Pr 18:8
26:24 [t]Ps 31:18 [u]Ps 41:6; Pr 10:18; 12:20
26:25 [v]Ps 28:3 [w]Jer 9:4-8
26:27 [x]Ps 7:15 [y]Est 6:13 [z]Est 2:23; 7:9; Ps 35:8; 141:10; Pr 28:10; 29:6; Isa 50:11
26:28 [a]Ps 12:3; Pr 29:5
27:1 [b]1Ki 20:11 [c]Mt 6:34; Lk 12:19-20; Jas 4:13-16

w *23* With a different word division of the Hebrew; Masoretic Text *of silver dross*

2Let another praise you, and not your
own mouth;
someone else, and not your own
lips.[a]

3Stone is heavy and sand[b] a burden,
but provocation by a fool is heavier
than both.

4Anger is cruel and fury
overwhelming,
but who can stand before jealousy?[c]

5Better is open rebuke
than hidden love.

6Wounds from a friend can be trusted,
but an enemy multiplies kisses.[d]

7He who is full loathes honey,
but to the hungry even what is
bitter tastes sweet.

8Like a bird that strays from its nest[e]
is a man who strays from his
home.

9Perfume[f] and incense bring joy to
the heart,
and the pleasantness of one's
friend springs from his earnest
counsel.

10Do not forsake your friend and the
friend of your father,
and do not go to your brother's
house when disaster[g] strikes
you—
better a neighbor nearby than a
brother far away.

11Be wise, my son, and bring joy to my
heart;[h]
then I can answer anyone who
treats me with contempt.[i]

12The prudent see danger and take
refuge,
but the simple keep going and
suffer for it.[j]

13Take the garment of one who puts
up security for a stranger;
hold it in pledge if he does it for a
wayward woman.[k]

14If a man loudly blesses his neighbor
early in the morning,
it will be taken as a curse.

15A quarrelsome wife is like
a constant dripping[l] on a rainy day;
16restraining her is like restraining the
wind
or grasping oil with the hand.

17As iron sharpens iron,
so one man sharpens another.

18He who tends a fig tree will eat its
fruit,[m]
and he who looks after his master
will be honored.[n]

19As water reflects a face,
so a man's heart reflects the man.

20Death and Destruction[x] are never
satisfied,[o]
and neither are the eyes of man.[p]

21The crucible for silver and the
furnace for gold,[q]
but man is tested by the praise he
receives.

22Though you grind a fool in a mortar,
grinding him like grain with a
pestle,
you will not remove his folly from
him.

23Be sure you know the condition of
your flocks,[r]
give careful attention to your
herds;
24for riches do not endure forever,[s]
and a crown is not secure for all
generations.
25When the hay is removed and new
growth appears
and the grass from the hills is
gathered in,
26the lambs will provide you with
clothing,
and the goats with the price of a
field.
27You will have plenty of goats' milk
to feed you and your family
and to nourish your servant girls.

27:2 [a]Pr 25:27
27:3 [b]Job 6:3
27:4 [c]Nu 5:14
27:6 [d]Ps 141:5; Pr 28:23
27:8 [e]Isa 16:2
27:9 [f]Est 2:12; Ps 45:8
27:10 [g]Pr 17:17; 18:24
27:11 [h]Pr 10:1; 23:15-16 [i]Ge 24:60
27:12 [j]Pr 22:3
27:13 [k]Pr 20:16
27:15 [l]Est 1:18; Pr 19:13
27:18 [m]1Co 9:7 [n]Lk 19:12-27
27:20 [o]Pr 30:15-16; Hab 2:5 [p]Ecc 1:8; 6:7
27:21 [q]Pr 17:3
27:23 [r]Pr 12:10
27:24 [s]Pr 23:5

[x]20 Hebrew *Sheol and Abaddon*

28 The wicked man flees[a] though no one pursues,[b]
but the righteous are as bold as a lion.[c]

2When a country is rebellious, it has many rulers,
but a man of understanding and knowledge maintains order.

3A ruler[y] who oppresses the poor
is like a driving rain that leaves no crops.

4Those who forsake the law praise the wicked,
but those who keep the law resist them.

5Evil men do not understand justice,
but those who seek the LORD understand it fully.

6Better a poor man whose walk is blameless
than a rich man whose ways are perverse.[d]

7He who keeps the law is a discerning son,
but a companion of gluttons disgraces his father.[e]

8He who increases his wealth by exorbitant interest[f]
amasses it for another,[g] who will be kind to the poor.[h]

9If anyone turns a deaf ear to the law,
even his prayers are detestable.[i]

10He who leads the upright along an evil path
will fall into his own trap,[j]
but the blameless will receive a good inheritance.

11A rich man may be wise in his own eyes,
but a poor man who has discernment sees through him.

12When the righteous triumph, there is great elation;[k]
but when the wicked rise to power, men go into hiding.[l]

13He who conceals his sins[m] does not prosper,
but whoever confesses and renounces them finds mercy.[n]

14Blessed is the man who always fears the LORD,
but he who hardens his heart falls into trouble.

15Like a roaring lion or a charging bear
is a wicked man ruling over a helpless people.

16A tyrannical ruler lacks judgment,
but he who hates ill-gotten gain will enjoy a long life.

17A man tormented by the guilt of murder
will be a fugitive[o] till death;
let no one support him.

18He whose walk is blameless is kept safe,
but he whose ways are perverse will suddenly fall.[p]

19He who works his land will have abundant food,
but the one who chases fantasies will have his fill of poverty.[q]

20A faithful man will be richly blessed,
but one eager to get rich will not go unpunished.[r]

21To show partiality is not good[s] —
yet a man will do wrong for a piece of bread.[t]

22A stingy man is eager to get rich
and is unaware that poverty awaits him.[u]

23He who rebukes a man will in the end gain more favor
than he who has a flattering tongue.[v]

24He who robs his father or mother[w]
and says, "It's not wrong"—
he is partner to him who destroys.[x]

25A greedy man stirs up dissension,
but he who trusts in the LORD[y] will prosper.

28:1 [a]2Ki 7:7 [b]Lev 26:17; Ps 53:5 [c]Ps 138:3
28:6 [d]Pr 19:1
28:7 [e]Pr 23:19-21
28:8 [f]Ex 18:21 [g]Job 27:17; Pr 13:22 [h]Ps 112:9; Pr 14:31; Lk 14:12-14
28:9 [i]Ps 66:18; 109:7; Pr 15:8; Isa 1:13
28:10 [j]Pr 26:27
28:12 [k]2Ki 11:20 [l]Pr 11:10; 29:2
28:13 [m]Job 31:33 [n]Ps 32:1-5; 1Jn 1:9
28:17 [o]Ge 9:6
28:18 [p]Pr 10:9
28:19 [q]Pr 12:11
28:20 [r]ver 22; Pr 10:6; 1Ti 6:9
28:21 [s]Pr 18:5 [t]Eze 13:19
28:22 [u]ver 20; Pr 23:6
28:23 [v]Pr 27:5-6
28:24 [w]Pr 19:26 [x]Pr 18:9
28:25 [y]Pr 29:25

y3 Or *A poor man*

26 He who trusts in himself is a fool,[a]
but he who walks in wisdom is
kept safe.

27 He who gives to the poor will lack
nothing,[b]
but he who closes his eyes to them
receives many curses.

28 When the wicked rise to power,
people go into hiding;[c]
but when the wicked perish, the
righteous thrive.

Rulers and authority.

29 A man who remains stiff-
necked after many rebukes
will suddenly be
destroyed—without remedy.[d]

2 When the righteous thrive, the
people rejoice;[e]
when the wicked rule, the people
groan.[f]

3 A man who loves wisdom brings joy
to his father,[g]
but a companion of prostitutes
squanders his wealth.[h]

4 By justice a king gives a country
stability,[i]
but one who is greedy for bribes
tears it down.

5 Whoever flatters his neighbor
is spreading a net for his feet.

6 An evil man is snared by his own
sin,[j]
but a righteous one can sing and
be glad.

7 The righteous care about justice for
the poor,[k]
but the wicked have no such
concern.

8 Mockers stir up a city,
but wise men turn away anger.[l]

9 If a wise man goes to court with a fool,
the fool rages and scoffs, and there
is no peace.

10 Bloodthirsty men hate a man of
integrity
and seek to kill the upright.[m]

11 A fool gives full vent to his anger,
but a wise man keeps himself
under control.[n]

12 If a ruler listens to lies,
all his officials become wicked.

13 The poor man and the oppressor
have this in common:
The LORD gives sight to the eyes of
both.[o]

14 If a king judges the poor with
fairness,
his throne will always be secure.[p]

15 The rod of correction imparts wisdom,
but a child left to himself disgraces
his mother.[q]

16 When the wicked thrive, so does sin,
but the righteous will see their
downfall.[r]

17 Discipline your son, and he will give
you peace;
he will bring delight to your soul.[s]

18 Where there is no revelation, the
people cast off restraint;
but blessed is he who keeps the
law.[t]

19 A servant cannot be corrected by
mere words;
though he understands, he will not
respond.

20 Do you see a man who speaks in
haste?
There is more hope for a fool than
for him.[u]

21 If a man pampers his servant from
youth,
he will bring grief[z] in the end.

22 An angry man stirs up dissension,
and a hot-tempered one commits
many sins.[v]

23 A man's pride brings him low,
but a man of lowly spirit gains
honor.[w]

28:26 [a]Ps 4:5; Pr 3:5
28:27 [b]Dt 15:7; 24:19; Pr 19:17; 22:9
28:28 [c]ver 12
29:1 [d]2Ch 36:16; Pr 6:15
29:2 [e]Est 8:15 [f]Pr 28:12
29:3 [g]Pr 10:1 [h]Pr 5:8-10; Lk 15:11-32
29:4 [i]Pr 8:15-16
29:6 [j]Ecc 9:12
29:7 [k]Job 29:16; Ps 41:1; Pr 31:8-9
29:8 [l]Pr 11:11; 16:14
29:10 [m]1Jn 3:12
29:11 [n]Pr 12:16; 19:11
29:13 [o]Pr 22:2; Mt 5:45
29:14 [p]Ps 72:1-5; Pr 16:12
29:15 [q]Pr 10:1; 13:24; 17:21,25
29:16 [r]Ps 37:35-36; 58:10; 91:8; 92:11
29:17 [s]ver 15; Pr 10:1
29:18 [t]Ps 1:1-2; 119:1-2; Jn 13:17
29:20 [u]Pr 26:12; Jas 1:19
29:22 [v]Pr 14:17; 15:18; 26:21
29:23 [w]Pr 11:2; 15:33; 16:18; Isa 66:2; Mt 23:12

[z]*21* The meaning of the Hebrew for this word is uncertain.

[24]The accomplice of a thief is his own enemy;
he is put under oath and dare not testify.[a]

[25]Fear of man will prove to be a snare,
but whoever trusts in the LORD[b] is kept safe.

[26]Many seek an audience with a ruler,[c]
but it is from the LORD that man gets justice.

[27]The righteous detest the dishonest;
the wicked detest the upright.[d]

Sayings of Agur

30 The sayings of Agur son of Jakeh—an oracle [a]:

This man declared to Ithiel,
to Ithiel and to Ucal:[b]

[2]"I am the most ignorant of men;
I do not have a man's understanding.
[3]I have not learned wisdom,
nor have I knowledge of the Holy One.[e]
[4]Who has gone up[f] to heaven and come down?
Who has gathered up the wind in the hollow[g] of his hands?
Who has wrapped up the waters[h] in his cloak?[i]
Who has established all the ends of the earth?
What is his name,[j] and the name of his son?
Tell me if you know!

[5]"Every word of God is flawless;[k]
he is a shield[l] to those who take refuge in him.
[6]Do not add[m] to his words,
or he will rebuke you and prove you a liar.

[7]"Two things I ask of you, O LORD;
do not refuse me before I die:
[8]Keep falsehood and lies far from me;
give me neither poverty nor riches,
but give me only my daily bread.[n]
[9]Otherwise, I may have too much and disown[o] you
and say, 'Who is the LORD?'[p]
Or I may become poor and steal,
and so dishonor the name of my God.[q]

[10]"Do not slander a servant to his master,
or he will curse you, and you will pay for it.

[11]"There are those who curse their fathers
and do not bless their mothers;[r]
[12]those who are pure in their own eyes[s]
and yet are not cleansed of their filth;[t]
[13]those whose eyes are ever so haughty,[u]
whose glances are so disdainful;
[14]those whose teeth[v] are swords
and whose jaws are set with knives[w]
to devour[x] the poor[y] from the earth,
the needy from among mankind.[z]

[15]"The leech has two daughters.
'Give! Give!' they cry.

"There are three things that are never satisfied,[a]
four that never say, 'Enough!':
[16]the grave,[c] [b] the barren womb,
land, which is never satisfied with water,
and fire, which never says, 'Enough!'

[17]"The eye that mocks[c] a father,
that scorns obedience to a mother,
will be pecked out by the ravens of the valley,
will be eaten by the vultures.[d]

[18]"There are three things that are too amazing for me,
four that I do not understand:

29:24 [a]Lev 5:1 **29:25** [b]Pr 28:25 **29:26** [c]Pr 19:6 **29:27** [d]ver 10 **30:3** [e]Pr 9:10 **30:4** [f]Ps 24:1-2; Jn 3:13; Eph 4:7-10 [g]Ps 104:3; Isa 40:12 [h]Job 26:8; 38:8-9 [i]Ge 1:2 [j]Rev 19:12 **30:5** [k]Ps 12:6; 18:30 [l]Ge 15:1; Ps 84:11 **30:6** [m]Dt 4:2; 12:32; Rev 22:18 **30:8** [n]Mt 6:11 **30:9** [o]Jos 24:27; Isa 1:4; 59:13 [p]Dt 6:12; 8:10-14; Hos 13:6 [q]Dt 8:12 **30:11** [r]Pr 20:20 **30:12** [s]Pr 16:2; Lk 18:11 [t]Jer 2:23,35 **30:13** [u]2Sa 22:28; Job 41:34; Ps 131:1; Pr 6:17 **30:14** [v]Job 4:11; 29:17; Ps 3:7 [w]Ps 57:4 [x]Job 24:9; Ps 14:4 [y]Am 8:4; Mic 2:2 [z]Job 19:22 **30:15** [a]Pr 27:20 **30:16** [b]Pr 27:20; Isa 5:14; 14:9,11; Hab 2:5

30:17 [c]Dt 21:18-21; Pr 23:22 [d]Job 15:23

a *1* Or *Jakeh of Massa* b *1* Masoretic Text; with a different word division of the Hebrew *declared, "I am weary, O God; / I am weary, O God, and faint.*
c *16* Hebrew *Sheol*

19the way of an eagle in the sky,
the way of a snake on a rock,
the way of a ship on the high seas,
and the way of a man with a maiden.

20"This is the way of an adulteress:
She eats and wipes her mouth
and says, 'I've done nothing wrong.'[a]

21"Under three things the earth trembles,
under four it cannot bear up:
22a servant who becomes king,[b]
a fool who is full of food,
23an unloved woman who is married,
and a maidservant who displaces her mistress.

24"Four things on earth are small,
yet they are extremely wise:
25Ants are creatures of little strength,
yet they store up their food in the summer;[c]
26coneys[d] [d] are creatures of little power,
yet they make their home in the crags;
27locusts[e] have no king,
yet they advance together in ranks;
28a lizard can be caught with the hand,
yet it is found in kings' palaces.

29"There are three things that are stately in their stride,
four that move with stately bearing:
30a lion, mighty among beasts,
who retreats before nothing;
31a strutting rooster, a he-goat,
and a king with his army around him.[e]

32"If you have played the fool and exalted yourself,
or if you have planned evil,
clap your hand over your mouth![f]
33For as churning the milk produces butter,
and as twisting the nose produces blood,
so stirring up anger produces strife."

30:20 [a]Pr 5:6
30:22 [b]Pr 19:10; 29:2
30:25 [c]Pr 6:6-8
30:26 [d]Ps 104:18
30:27 [e]Ex 10:4
30:32 [f]Job 21:5; 29:9
31:1 [g]Pr 22:17
31:2 [h]Jdg 11:30; Isa 49:15
31:3 [i]Dt 17:17; 1Ki 11:3; Ne 13:26; Pr 5:1-14
31:4 [j]Pr 20:1; Ecc 10:16-17; Isa 5:22
31:5 [k]1Ki 16:9 [l]Pr 16:12; Hos 4:11
31:6 [m]Ge 14:18
31:7 [n]Est 1:10
31:8 [o]1Sa 19:4; Job 29:12-17
31:9 [p]Lev 19:15; Dt 1:16; Pr 24:23; 29:7; Isa 1:17; Jer 22:16
31:10 [q]Ru 3:11; Pr 12:4; 18:22 [r]Pr 8:35; 19:14
31:11 [s]Ge 2:18 [t]Pr 12:4
31:13 [u]1Ti 2:9-10

Sayings of King Lemuel.

31 The sayings[g] of King Lemuel—an oracle[f] his mother taught him:

2"O my son, O son of my womb,
O son of my vows,[g] [h]
3do not spend your strength on women,
your vigor on those who ruin kings.[i]

4"It is not for kings, O Lemuel—
not for kings to drink wine,[j]
not for rulers to crave beer,
5lest they drink[k] and forget what the law decrees,[l]
and deprive all the oppressed of their rights.
6Give beer to those who are perishing,
wine[m] to those who are in anguish;
7let them drink[n] and forget their poverty
and remember their misery no more.

8"Speak[o] up for those who cannot speak for themselves,
for the rights of all who are destitute.
9Speak up and judge fairly;
defend the rights of the poor and needy."[p]

Description of a wife of noble character.

10[h]A wife of noble character[q] who can find?[r]
She is worth far more than rubies.
11Her husband[s] has full confidence in her
and lacks nothing of value.[t]
12She brings him good, not harm,
all the days of her life.
13She selects wool and flax
and works with eager hands.[u]
14She is like the merchant ships,
bringing her food from afar.

[d]*26* That is, the hyrax or rock badger [e]*31* Or *king secure against revolt* [f]*1* Or *of Lemuel king of Massa, which* [g]*2* Or */ the answer to my prayers* [h]*10* Verses 10-31 are an acrostic, each verse beginning with a successive letter of the Hebrew alphabet.

15She gets up while it is still dark;
she provides food for her family
and portions for her servant girls.
16She considers a field and buys it;
out of her earnings she plants a vineyard.
17She sets about her work vigorously;
her arms are strong for her tasks.
18She sees that her trading is profitable,
and her lamp does not go out at night.
19In her hand she holds the distaff
and grasps the spindle with her fingers.
20She opens her arms to the poor
and extends her hands to the needy.[a]
21When it snows, she has no fear for her household;
for all of them are clothed in scarlet.
22She makes coverings for her bed;
she is clothed in fine linen and purple.
23Her husband is respected at the city gate,
where he takes his seat among the elders[b] of the land.

31:20
[a]Dt 15:11; Eph 4:28; Heb 13:16

31:23
[b]Ex 3:16; Ru 4:1,11; Pr 12:4

31:26
[c]Pr 10:31

31:31
[d]Pr 11:16

24She makes linen garments and sells them,
and supplies the merchants with sashes.
25She is clothed with strength and dignity;
she can laugh at the days to come.
26She speaks with wisdom,
and faithful instruction is on her tongue.[c]
27She watches over the affairs of her household
and does not eat the bread of idleness.
28Her children arise and call her blessed;
her husband also, and he praises her:
29"Many women do noble things,
but you surpass them all."
30Charm is deceptive, and beauty is fleeting;
but a woman who fears the LORD is to be praised.
31Give her the reward she has earned,
and let her works bring her praise[d] at the city gate.

ECCLESIASTES

Author: Probably Solomon.

Date Written: Between 940 and 935 B.C.

Time Span: Unknown (probably during the latter years of Solomon's reign).

Title: This title from the Greek means "Teacher."

Background: Though the author has a life full of pleasures, wealth, power and prestige...he still seeks happiness. The majority of Ecclesiastes is probably written as Solomon analyzes past failures and apostasy in his life.

Where Written: Jerusalem.

To Whom: Primarily to young people.

Content: The book of Ecclesiastes begins with the author sharing his reasons for viewing life as meaningless and futile. His thoughts contend that despite man's labor, attainments, popularity or possessions...death awaits all. He realizes that there is a time and a season for all things (chapter 3), but does not know how man can fully understand when these times are relevant. This confession of pessimism eventually gives way to the truth that there is no joy for man apart from his Creator. The author realizes and enthusiastically proclaims the answer: satisfaction, meaning and happiness do not come from the attainments of life...but from the Lord of life.

Key Words: "Meaningless"; "Labor." Without God, there is no sense to be made out of our lives. All is empty, hopeless and "meaningless." Our earthly "labor" will continually frustrate and disappoint us if we seek it as an end to itself.

Themes: • Earthly goals apart from God will not bring us happiness. • Money will not bring us happiness. • Fame will not bring us happiness. • Power will not bring us happiness. • Accomplishments will not bring us happiness. • Human wisdom will not bring us happiness. • A life that is totally submissive and devoted to God will bring happiness. • A youthful life obedient to God will bring joy to our latter years...a youthful life disobedient to God will bring sorrow to our latter years. • We ought to enjoy life even though at times we will have troubles. • The closer we walk with God, the more aware we become of his blessings in our lives. • Today could be our last on this earth...we should view it as a precious gift from God.

Outline:

1. Everything is meaningless. 1:1-2:26
2. A time for everything. 3:1-3:22
3. Disappointments and inequalities of life. 4:1-8:17
4. A common destiny for all. 9:1-12:8
5. Conclusion: Fear God and keep his commandments. 12:9-12:14

ECCLESIASTES

The Teacher declares that everything is meaningless.

1 The words of the Teacher,[a][a] son of David, king in Jerusalem:[b]

2"Meaningless! Meaningless!"
says the Teacher.
"Utterly meaningless!
Everything is meaningless."[c]
3What does man gain from all his labor
at which he toils under the sun?[d]
4Generations come and generations go,
but the earth remains forever.[e]
5The sun rises and the sun sets,
and hurries back to where it rises.[f]
6The wind blows to the south
and turns to the north;
round and round it goes,
ever returning on its course.
7All streams flow into the sea,
yet the sea is never full.
To the place the streams come from,
there they return again.[g]
8All things are wearisome,
more than one can say.
The eye never has enough of seeing,[h]
nor the ear its fill of hearing.
9What has been will be again,
what has been done will be done
again;[i]
there is nothing new under the sun.
10Is there anything of which one can say,
"Look! This is something new"?
It was here already, long ago;
it was here before our time.
11There is no remembrance of men of old,
and even those who are yet to come
will not be remembered
by those who follow.[j]

Wisdom is meaningless.

12I, the Teacher,[k] was king over Israel
in Jerusalem. 13I devoted myself to study
and to explore by wisdom all that is done
under heaven. What a heavy burden God
has laid on men![l] 14I have seen all the
things that are done under the sun; all of
them are meaningless, a chasing after
the wind.[m]

15What is twisted cannot be
straightened;[n]
what is lacking cannot be counted.

16I thought to myself, "Look, I have
grown and increased in wisdom more
than anyone who has ruled over Jerusalem before me;[o] I have experienced much
of wisdom and knowledge." 17Then I
applied myself to the understanding of
wisdom,[p] and also of madness and folly,[q] but I learned that this, too, is a chasing after the wind.

18For with much wisdom comes much
sorrow;
the more knowledge, the more
grief.[r]

Pleasure is meaningless.

2 I thought in my heart, "Come now, I
will test you with pleasure[s] to find
out what is good." But that also proved
to be meaningless. 2"Laughter,"[t] I said, "is
foolish. And what does pleasure accomplish?" 3I tried cheering myself with
wine,[u] and embracing folly[v]—my mind
still guiding me with wisdom. I wanted
to see what was worthwhile for men to
do under heaven during the few days
of their lives.

4I undertook great projects: I built
houses for myself[w] and planted vineyards.[x] 5I made gardens and parks and
planted all kinds of fruit trees in them.
6I made reservoirs to water groves of
flourishing trees. 7I bought male and
female slaves and had other slaves who
were born in my house. I also owned
more herds and flocks than anyone in Jerusalem before me. 8I amassed silver and
gold[y] for myself, and the treasure of
kings and provinces. I acquired men
and women singers,[z] and a harem[b] as
well—the delights of the heart of man.
9I became greater by far than anyone
in Jerusalem before me.[a] In all this my
wisdom stayed with me.

1:1 [a] ver 12; Ecc 7:27; 12:10 [b] Pr 1:1
1:2 [c] Ps 39:5-6; 62:9; 144:4; Ecc 12:8; Ro 8:20-21
1:3 [d] Ecc 2:11,22; 3:9; 5:15-16
1:4 [e] Ps 104:5; 119:90
1:5 [f] Ps 19:5-6
1:7 [g] Job 36:28
1:8 [h] Pr 27:20
1:9 [i] Ecc 2:12; 3:15
1:11 [j] Ecc 2:16
1:12 [k] ver 1
1:13 [l] Ge 3:17; Ecc 3:10
1:14 [m] Ecc 2:11,17
1:15 [n] Ecc 7:13
1:16 [o] 1Ki 3:12; 4:30; Ecc 2:9
1:17 [p] Ecc 7:23 [q] Ecc 2:3,12; 7:25
1:18 [r] Ecc 2:23; 12:12
2:1 [s] Ecc 7:4; 8:15; Lk 12:19
2:2 [t] Pr 14:13; Ecc 7:6
2:3 [u] ver 24-25; Ecc 3:12-13 [v] Ecc 1:17
2:4 [w] 1Ki 7:1-12 [x] SS 8:11
2:8 [y] 1Ki 9:28; 10:10,14,21 [z] 2Sa 19:35
2:9 [a] 1Ch 29:25; Ecc 1:16

a *1* Or *leader of the assembly*; also in verses 2 and 12
b *8* The meaning of the Hebrew for this phrase is uncertain.

[10]I denied myself nothing my eyes
desired;
I refused my heart no pleasure.
My heart took delight in all my work,
and this was the reward for all my
labor.
[11]Yet when I surveyed all that my
hands had done
and what I had toiled to achieve,
everything was meaningless, a chasing
after the wind;[a]
nothing was gained under the sun.[b]

Wisdom and folly are meaningless.

[12]Then I turned my thoughts to
consider wisdom,
and also madness and folly.[c]
What more can the king's successor do
than what has already been done?[d]
[13]I saw that wisdom[e] is better than
folly,[f]
just as light is better than darkness.
[14]The wise man has eyes in his head,
while the fool walks in the darkness;
but I came to realize
that the same fate overtakes them
both.[g]

[15]Then I thought in my heart,

"The fate of the fool will overtake
me also.
What then do I gain by being
wise?"[h]
I said in my heart,
"This too is meaningless."
[16]For the wise man, like the fool, will
not be long remembered;
in days to come both will be
forgotten.[i]
Like the fool, the wise man too must
die!

Work is meaningless.

[17]So I hated life, because the work that
is done under the sun was grievous to
me. All of it is meaningless, a chasing
after the wind.[j] [18]I hated all the things
I had toiled for under the sun, because I
must leave them to the one who comes
after me.[k] [19]And who knows whether he
will be a wise man or a fool? Yet he will
have control over all the work into
which I have poured my effort and skill
under the sun. This too is meaningless.
[20]So my heart began to despair over all
my toilsome labor under the sun. [21]For
a man may do his work with wisdom,
knowledge and skill, and then he must
leave all he owns to someone who has
not worked for it. This too is meaningless and a great misfortune. [22]What does
a man get for all the toil and anxious
striving with which he labors under the
sun?[l] [23]All his days his work is pain and
grief;[m] even at night his mind does not
rest. This too is meaningless.
[24]A man can do nothing better than to
eat and drink[n] and find satisfaction in his
work.[o] This too, I see, is from the hand
of God,[p] [25]for without him, who can eat
or find enjoyment? [26]To the man who
pleases him, God gives wisdom, knowledge and happiness, but to the sinner he
gives the task of gathering and storing
up wealth[q] to hand it over to the one
who pleases God.[r] This too is meaningless, a chasing after the wind.

A time for everything.

3 There is a time[s] for everything,
and a season for every activity
under heaven:

2 a time to be born and a time to die,
a time to plant and a time to uproot,
3 a time to kill and a time to heal,
a time to tear down and a time to
build,
4 a time to weep and a time to laugh,
a time to mourn and a time to
dance,
5 a time to scatter stones and a time
to gather them,
a time to embrace and a time to
refrain,
6 a time to search and a time to give
up,
a time to keep and a time to throw
away,
7 a time to tear and a time to mend,
a time to be silent[t] and a time to
speak,

2:11 [a]Ecc 1:14 [b]Ecc 1:3
2:12 [c]Ecc 1:17 [d]Ecc 1:9; 7:25
2:13 [e]Ecc 7:19; 9:18 [f]Ecc 7:11-12
2:14 [g]Ps 49:10; Pr 17:24; Ecc 3:19; 6:6; 7:2; 9:3,11-12
2:15 [h]Ecc 6:8
2:16 [i]Ecc 1:11; 9:5
2:17 [j]Ecc 4:2
2:18 [k]Ps 39:6; 49:10
2:22 [l]Ecc 1:3; 3:9
2:23 [m]Job 5:7; 14:1; Ecc 1:18
2:24 [n]Ecc 8:15; 1Co 15:32 [o]Ecc 3:22 [p]Ecc 3:12-13; 5:17-19; 9:7-10
2:26 [q]Job 27:17 [r]Pr 13:22
3:1 [s]ver 11,17; Ecc 8:6
3:7 [t]Am 5:13

8 a time to love and a time to hate,
a time for war and a time for
peace.

9 What does the worker gain from his
toil?[a] 10 I have seen the burden God has
laid on men.[b] 11 He has made everything
beautiful in its time.[c] He has also set eternity in the hearts of men; yet they cannot fathom[d] what God has done from
beginning to end.[e] 12 I know that there
is nothing better for men than to be happy and do good while they live. 13 That
everyone may eat and drink,[f] and find
satisfaction[g] in all his toil—this is the gift
of God.[h] 14 I know that everything God
does will endure forever; nothing can be
added to it and nothing taken from it.
God does it so that men will revere him.[i]

15 Whatever is has already been,[j]
and what will be has been before;[k]
and God will call the past to
account.[c]

16 And I saw something else under
the sun:

In the place of judgment—wickedness
was there,
in the place of justice—wickedness
was there.

17 I thought in my heart,

"God will bring to judgment[l]
both the righteous and the wicked,
for there will be a time for every
activity,
a time for every deed."[m]

18 I also thought, "As for men, God tests
them so that they may see that they are
like the animals.[n] 19 Man's fate[o] is like
that of the animals; the same fate awaits
them both: As one dies, so dies the other. All have the same breath[d]; man has
no advantage over the animal. Everything is meaningless. 20 All go to the same
place; all come from dust, and to dust
all return.[p] 21 Who knows if the spirit of
man rises upward[q] and if the spirit of the
animal[e] goes down into the earth?"

22 So I saw that there is nothing better
for a man than to enjoy his work,[r] because that is his lot.[s] For who can bring
him to see what will happen after him?

Oppression without comforters.

4 Again I looked and saw all the oppression[t] that was taking place
under the sun:

I saw the tears of the oppressed—
and they have no comforter;
power was on the side of their
oppressors—
and they have no comforter.[u]
2 And I declared that the dead,[v]
who had already died,
are happier than the living,
who are still alive.[w]
3 But better than both
is he who has not yet been,[x]
who has not seen the evil
that is done under the sun.[y]

4 And I saw that all labor and all
achievement spring from man's envy of
his neighbor. This too is meaningless, a
chasing after the wind.[z]

5 The fool folds his hands[a]
and ruins himself.
6 Better one handful with tranquillity
than two handfuls with toil[b]
and chasing after the wind.

7 Again I saw something meaningless
under the sun:

8 There was a man all alone;
he had neither son nor brother.
There was no end to his toil,
yet his eyes were not content[c]
with his wealth.
"For whom am I toiling," he asked,
"and why am I depriving myself of
enjoyment?"
This too is meaningless—
a miserable business!

Comfort in companionship.

9 Two are better than one,
because they have a good return
for their work:

3:9 [a]Ecc 1:3
3:10 [b]Ecc 1:13
3:11 [c]ver 1 [d]Job 11:7; Ecc 8:17 [e]Job 28:23; Ro 11:33
3:13 [f]Ecc 2:3 [g]Ps 34:12 [h]Dt 12:7,18; Ecc 2:24; 5:19
3:14 [i]Job 23:15; Ecc 5:7; 7:18; 8:12-13; Jas 1:17
3:15 [j]Ecc 6:10 [k]Ecc 1:9
3:17 [l]Job 19:29; Ecc 11:9; Mt 16:27; Ro 2:6-8; 2Th 1:6-7 [m]ver 1
3:18 [n]Ps 73:22
3:19 [o]Ecc 2:14
3:20 [p]Ge 2:7; 3:19; Job 34:15
3:21 [q]Ecc 12:7
3:22 [r]Ecc 2:24; 5:18 [s]Job 31:2
4:1 [t]Ps 12:5; Ecc 3:16 [u]La 1:16
4:2 [v]Jer 20:17-18; 22:10 [w]Job 3:17; 10:18
4:3 [x]Job 3:16; Ecc 6:3 [y]Job 3:22
4:4 [z]Ecc 1:14
4:5 [a]Pr 6:10
4:6 [b]Pr 15:16-17; 16:8
4:8 [c]Pr 27:20

c *15* Or *God calls back the past* d *19* Or *spirit*
e *21* Or *Who knows the spirit of man, which rises upward, or the spirit of the animal, which*

10If one falls down,
his friend can help him up.
But pity the man who falls
and has no one to help him up!
11Also, if two lie down together, they
will keep warm.
But how can one keep warm alone?
12Though one may be overpowered,
two can defend themselves.
A cord of three strands is not quickly
broken.

Advancement is meaningless.

13Better a poor but wise youth than
an old but foolish king who no longer
knows how to take warning. 14The youth
may have come from prison to the kingship, or he may have been born in poverty within his kingdom. 15I saw that all
who lived and walked under the sun followed the youth, the king's successor.
16There was no end to all the people
who were before them. But those who
came later were not pleased with the
successor. This too is meaningless, a
chasing after the wind.

Quick mouth of a fool.

5 Guard your steps when you go to the house of God. Go near to listen rather than to offer the sacrifice of fools, who do not know that they do wrong.

2Do not be quick with your mouth,
do not be hasty in your heart
to utter anything before God.[a]
God is in heaven
and you are on earth,
so let your words be few.[b]
3As a dream[c] comes when there are
many cares,
so the speech of a fool when there
are many words.[d]

4When you make a vow to God, do not
delay in fulfilling it.[e] He has no pleasure
in fools; fulfill your vow.[f] 5It is better not
to vow than to make a vow and not fulfill it.[g] 6Do not let your mouth lead you
into sin. And do not protest to the ⌊tem-
ple⌋ messenger, "My vow was a mistake."
Why should God be angry at what you
say and destroy the work of your hands?
7Much dreaming and many words are
meaningless. Therefore stand in awe of
God.[h]

Wealth is meaningless.

8If you see the poor oppressed[i] in a
district, and justice and rights denied, do
not be surprised at such things; for one
official is eyed by a higher one, and over
them both are others higher still. 9The
increase from the land is taken by all; the
king himself profits from the fields.

10Whoever loves money never has
money enough;
whoever loves wealth is never
satisfied with his income.
This too is meaningless.

11As goods increase,
so do those who consume them.
And what benefit are they to the
owner
except to feast his eyes on them?

12The sleep of a laborer is sweet,
whether he eats little or much,
but the abundance of a rich man
permits him no sleep.[j]

13I have seen a grievous evil under
the sun:[k]

wealth hoarded to the harm of its
owner,
14 or wealth lost through some
misfortune,
so that when he has a son
there is nothing left for him.
15Naked a man comes from his
mother's womb,
and as he comes, so he departs.[l]
He takes nothing from his labor[m]
that he can carry in his hand.[n]

16This too is a grievous evil:

As a man comes, so he departs,
and what does he gain,
since he toils for the wind?[o]
17All his days he eats in darkness,
with great frustration, affliction
and anger.

5:2 [a]Jdg 11:35 [b]Job 6:24; Pr 10:19; 20:25
5:3 [c]Job 20:8 [d]Ecc 10:14
5:4 [e]Dt 23:21; Jdg 11:35; Ps 119:60 [f]Nu 30:2; Ps 66:13-14; 76:11
5:5 [g]Nu 30:2-4; Pr 20:25; Jnh 2:9; Ac 5:4
5:7 [h]Ecc 3:14; 12:13
5:8 [i]Ps 12:5; Ecc 4:1
5:12 [j]Job 20:20
5:13 [k]Ecc 6:1-2
5:15 [l]Job 1:21 [m]Ps 49:17; 1Ti 6:7 [n]Ecc 1:3
5:16 [o]Pr 11:29; Ecc 1:3

18Then I realized that it is good and
proper for a man to eat and drink,[a] and to
find satisfaction in his toilsome labor[b]
under the sun during the few days of life
God has given him—for this is his lot.
19Moreover, when God gives any man
wealth and possessions,[c] and enables
him to enjoy them,[d] to accept his lot[e]
and be happy in his work—this is a gift
of God.[f] 20He seldom reflects on the days
of his life, because God keeps him occupied with gladness of heart.[g]

6 I have seen another evil under the
sun, and it weighs heavily on men:
2God gives a man wealth, possessions and
honor, so that he lacks nothing his heart
desires, but God does not enable him to
enjoy them,[h] and a stranger enjoys them
instead. This is meaningless, a grievous
evil.[i]

3A man may have a hundred children
and live many years; yet no matter how
long he lives, if he cannot enjoy his prosperity and does not receive proper burial, I say that a stillborn[j] child is better off
than he.[k] 4It comes without meaning, it
departs in darkness, and in darkness its
name is shrouded. 5Though it never saw
the sun or knew anything, it has more
rest than does that man— 6even if he
lives a thousand years twice over but fails
to enjoy his prosperity. Do not all go to
the same place?

7All man's efforts are for his mouth,
yet his appetite is never satisfied.[l]
8What advantage has a wise man
over a fool?[m]
What does a poor man gain
by knowing how to conduct himself
before others?
9Better what the eye sees
than the roving of the appetite.
This too is meaningless,
a chasing after the wind.[n]

10Whatever exists has already been named,
and what man is has been known;
no man can contend
with one who is stronger than he.
11The more the words,
the less the meaning,
and how does that profit anyone?

5:18 [a]Ecc 2:3 [b]Ecc 2:10,24
5:19 [c]1Ch 29:12; 2Ch 1:12 [d]Ecc 6:2 [e]Job 31:2 [f]Ecc 2:24; 3:13
5:20 [g]Dt 12:7,18
6:2 [h]Ps 17:14; Ecc 5:19 [i]Ecc 5:13
6:3 [j]Job 3:16; Ecc 4:3 [k]Job 3:3
6:7 [l]Pr 16:26; 27:20
6:8 [m]Ecc 2:15
6:9 [n]Ecc 1:14
6:12 [o]Job 10:20 [p]Job 14:2; Ps 39:6; Jas 4:14
7:1 [q]Pr 22:1; SS 1:3
7:2 [r]Pr 11:19 [s]Ps 90:12
7:3 [t]Pr 14:13
7:4 [u]Ecc 2:1; Jer 16:8
7:5 [v]Ps 141:5; Pr 13:18; 15:31-32
7:6 [w]Ps 58:9; 118:12 [x]Ecc 2:2
7:7 [y]Ex 18:21; 23:8; Dt 16:19
7:8 [z]Pr 14:29; Gal 5:22; Eph 4:2
7:9 [a]Mt 5:22; Pr 14:17; Jas 1:19
7:11 [b]Pr 8:10-11; Ecc 2:13 [c]Ecc 11:7

12For who knows what is good for a
man in life, during the few and meaningless days[o] he passes through like a shadow?[p] Who can tell him what will happen
under the sun after he is gone?

The Teacher searches out wisdom.

7 A good name is better than fine
perfume,[q]
and the day of death better than
the day of birth.
2It is better to go to a house of mourning
than to go to a house of feasting,
for death[r] is the destiny[s] of every man;
the living should take this to heart.
3Sorrow is better than laughter,[t]
because a sad face is good for the
heart.
4The heart of the wise is in the house
of mourning,
but the heart of fools is in the
house of pleasure.[u]
5It is better to heed a wise man's
rebuke[v]
than to listen to the song of fools.
6Like the crackling of thorns[w] under
the pot,
so is the laughter[x] of fools.
This too is meaningless.

7Extortion turns a wise man into a fool,
and a bribe[y] corrupts the heart.

8The end of a matter is better than its
beginning,
and patience[z] is better than pride.
9Do not be quickly provoked[a] in
your spirit,
for anger resides in the lap of fools.

10Do not say, "Why were the old days
better than these?"
For it is not wise to ask such
questions.

11Wisdom, like an inheritance, is a
good thing[b]
and benefits those who see the sun.[c]
12Wisdom is a shelter
as money is a shelter,
but the advantage of knowledge is this:
that wisdom preserves the life of
its possessor.

13Consider what God has done:[a]

Who can straighten
what he has made crooked?[b]
14When times are good, be happy;
but when times are bad, consider:
God has made the one
as well as the other.
Therefore, a man cannot discover
anything about his future.

15In this meaningless life[c] of mine I
have seen both of these:

a righteous man perishing in his
righteousness,
and a wicked man living long in
his wickedness.[d]
16Do not be overrighteous,
neither be overwise—
why destroy yourself?
17Do not be overwicked,
and do not be a fool—
why die before your time?[e]
18It is good to grasp the one
and not let go of the other.
The man who fears God[f] will avoid
all ⌊extremes⌋.[f]

19Wisdom[g] makes one wise man more
powerful[h]
than ten rulers in a city.

20There is not a righteous man[i] on earth
who does what is right and never
sins.[j]

21Do not pay attention to every word
people say,
or you[k] may hear your servant
cursing you—
22for you know in your heart
that many times you yourself have
cursed others.

23All this I tested by wisdom and I said,

"I am determined to be wise"[l]—
but this was beyond me.
24Whatever wisdom may be,
it is far off and most profound—
who can discover it?[m]
25So I turned my mind to understand,
to investigate and to search out
wisdom and the scheme of
things[n]
and to understand the stupidity of
wickedness
and the madness of folly.[o]

26I find more bitter than death
the woman who is a snare,[p]
whose heart is a trap
and whose hands are chains.
The man who pleases God will
escape her,
but the sinner she will ensnare.[q]

27"Look," says the Teacher,[g] [r] "this is
what I have discovered:

"Adding one thing to another to
discover the scheme of things—
28 while I was still searching
but not finding—
I found one ⌊upright⌋ man among a
thousand,
but not one ⌊upright⌋ woman[s]
among them all.
29This only have I found:
God made mankind upright,
but men have gone in search of
many schemes."

8

Who is like the wise man?
Who knows the explanation of
things?
Wisdom brightens a man's face
and changes its hard appearance.

Wisdom of obeying the king.

2Obey the king's command, I say, because you took an oath before God. 3Do
not be in a hurry to leave the king's presence.[t] Do not stand up for a bad cause,
for he will do whatever he pleases. 4Since
a king's word is supreme, who can say
to him, "What are you doing?[u]"

5Whoever obeys his command will
come to no harm,
and the wise heart will know the
proper time and procedure.
6For there is a proper time and
procedure for every matter,[v]
though a man's misery weighs
heavily upon him.

7:13 [a]Ecc 2:24 [b]Ecc 1:15
7:15 [c]Job 7:7 [d]Ecc 8:12-14; Jer 12:1
7:17 [e]Job 15:32; Ps 55:23
7:18 [f]Ecc 3:14
7:19 [g]Ecc 2:13 [h]Ecc 9:13-18
7:20 [i]Ps 14:3 [j]1Ki 8:46; 2Ch 6:36; Pr 20:9; Ro 3:23
7:21 [k]Pr 30:10
7:23 [l]Ecc 1:17; Ro 1:22
7:24 [m]Job 28:12
7:25 [n]Job 28:3 [o]Ecc 1:17
7:26 [p]Ex 10:7; Jdg 14:15 [q]Pr 2:16-19; 5:3-5; 7:23; 22:14
7:27 [r]Ecc 1:1
7:28 [s]1Ki 11:3
8:3 [t]Ecc 10:4
8:4 [u]Job 9:12; Est 1:19; Da 4:35
8:6 [v]Ecc 3:1

[f]18 Or *will follow them both*
[g]27 Or *leader of the assembly*

7Since no man knows the future,
who can tell him what is to come?
8No man has power over the wind to
contain it[h];
so no one has power over the day
of his death.
As no one is discharged in time of war,
so wickedness will not release
those who practice it.

Death for the wicked.

9All this I saw, as I applied my mind to
everything done under the sun. There
is a time when a man lords it over others
to his own[i] hurt. 10Then too, I saw the
wicked buried[a]—those who used to
come and go from the holy place and receive praise[j] in the city where they did
this. This too is meaningless.
11When the sentence for a crime is not
quickly carried out, the hearts of the people are filled with schemes to do wrong.
12Although a wicked man commits a
hundred crimes and still lives a long
time, I know that it will go better[b] with
God-fearing men,[c] who are reverent before God.[d] 13Yet because the wicked do
not fear God,[e] it will not go well with
them, and their days[f] will not lengthen
like a shadow.
14There is something else meaningless
that occurs on earth: righteous men who
get what the wicked deserve, and wicked
men who get what the righteous deserve.[g] This too, I say, is meaningless.[h]
15So I commend the enjoyment of life[i],
because nothing is better for a man under
the sun than to eat and drink[j] and be
glad.[k] Then joy will accompany him in
his work all the days of the life God has
given him under the sun.
16When I applied my mind to know
wisdom[l] and to observe man's labor on
earth[m]—his eyes not seeing sleep day or
night— 17then I saw all that God has
done.[n] No one can comprehend what
goes on under the sun. Despite all his
efforts to search it out, man cannot discover its meaning. Even if a wise man
claims he knows, he cannot really comprehend it.[o]

A common destiny for all.

9 So I reflected on all this and concluded that the righteous and the
wise and what they do are in God's
hands, but no man knows whether love
or hate awaits him.[p] 2All share a common destiny—the righteous and the
wicked, the good and the bad,[k] the clean
and the unclean, those who offer sacrifices and those who do not.

As it is with the good man,
so with the sinner;
as it is with those who take oaths,
so with those who are afraid to
take them.[q]

3This is the evil in everything that happens under the sun: The same destiny
overtakes all.[r] The hearts of men, moreover, are full of evil and there is madness
in their hearts while they live,[s] and afterward they join the dead.[t] 4Anyone who
is among the living has hope[l]—even a
live dog is better off than a dead lion!

5For the living know that they will die,
but the dead know nothing;[u]
they have no further reward,
and even the memory of them[v] is
forgotten.[w]
6Their love, their hate
and their jealousy have long since
vanished;
never again will they have a part
in anything that happens under
the sun.[x]

7Go, eat your food with gladness, and
drink your wine[y] with a joyful heart,[z]
for it is now that God favors what you
do. 8Always be clothed in white,[a] and
always anoint your head with oil. 9Enjoy
life with your wife,[b] whom you love, all
the days of this meaningless life that God
has given you under the sun— all your
meaningless days. For this is your lot[c]
in life and in your toilsome labor under

8:10 [a]Ecc 1:11
8:12 [b]Dt 12:28; Ps 37:11,18-19; Pr 1:32-33; Isa 3:10-11 [c]Ex 1:20 [d]Ecc 3:14
8:13 [e]Ecc 3:14; Isa 3:11 [f]Dt 4:40; Job 5:26; Ps 34:12; Isa 65:20
8:14 [g]Job 21:7; Ps 73:14; Mal 3:15 [h]Ecc 7:15
8:15 [i]Ps 42:8 [j]Ex 32:6; Ecc 2:3 [k]Ecc 2:24; 3:12-13; 5:18; 9:7
8:16 [l]Ecc 1:17 [m]Ecc 1:13
8:17 [n]Job 28:3 [o]Job 5:9; 28:23; Ecc 3:11; Ro 11:33
9:1 [p]Dt 33:3; Job 12:10; Ecc 10:14
9:2 [q]Job 9:22; Ecc 2:14; 6:6; 7:2
9:3 [r]Job 9:22; Ecc 2:14 [s]Jer 11:8; 13:10; 16:12; 17:9 [t]Job 21:26
9:5 [u]Job 14:21 [v]Ps 9:6 [w]Ecc 1:11; 2:16; Isa 26:14
9:6 [x]Job 21:21
9:7 [y]Nu 6:20 [z]Ecc 2:24; 8:15
9:8 [a]Ps 23:5; Rev 3:4
9:9 [b]Pr 5:18 [c]Job 31:2

h*8* Or *over his spirit to retain it* i*9* Or *to their*
j*10* Some Hebrew manuscripts and Septuagint (Aquila); most Hebrew manuscripts *and are forgotten*
k*2* Septuagint (Aquila), Vulgate and Syriac; Hebrew does not have *and the bad.* l*4* Or *What then is to be chosen? With all who live, there is hope*

the sun. [10]Whatever[a] your hand finds to
do, do it with all your might,[b] for in the
grave,[m c] where you are going, there is
neither working nor planning nor knowledge nor wisdom.[d]

[11]I have seen something else under
the sun:

The race is not to the swift
  or the battle to the strong,[e]
nor does food come to the wise[f]
  or wealth to the brilliant
  or favor to the learned;
but time and chance[g] happen to
    them all.[h]

[12]Moreover, no man knows when his
hour will come:

As fish are caught in a cruel net,
  or birds are taken in a snare,
so men are trapped by evil times[i]
  that fall unexpectedly upon them.[j]

Contrast of wisdom and folly.

[13]I also saw under the sun this example of wisdom[k] that greatly impressed
me: [14]There was once a small city with
only a few people in it. And a powerful
king came against it, surrounded it and
built huge siegeworks against it. [15]Now
there lived in that city a man poor but
wise, and he saved the city by his wisdom. But nobody remembered that poor
man.[l] [16]So I said, "Wisdom is better than
strength." But the poor man's wisdom
is despised, and his words are no longer
heeded.[m]

[17]The quiet words of the wise are more
    to be heeded
  than the shouts of a ruler of fools.
[18]Wisdom[n] is better than weapons of
    war,
  but one sinner destroys much good.

10 As dead flies give perfume a bad
    smell,
  so a little folly[o] outweighs wisdom
    and honor.
[2]The heart of the wise inclines to the
    right,
  but the heart of the fool to the left.
[3]Even as he walks along the road,
  the fool lacks sense
  and shows everyone[p] how stupid
    he is.
[4]If a ruler's anger rises against you,
  do not leave your post;[q]
  calmness can lay great errors to rest.[r]

[5]There is an evil I have seen under
    the sun,
  the sort of error that arises from a
    ruler:
[6]Fools are put in many high positions,[s]
  while the rich occupy the low ones.
[7]I have seen slaves on horseback,
  while princes go on foot like slaves.[t]

[8]Whoever digs a pit may fall into it;[u]
  whoever breaks through a wall may
    be bitten by a snake.[v]
[9]Whoever quarries stones may be
    injured by them;
  whoever splits logs may be
    endangered by them.[w]

[10]If the ax is dull
  and its edge unsharpened,
more strength is needed
  but skill will bring success.

[11]If a snake bites before it is charmed,
  there is no profit for the charmer.[x]

[12]Words from a wise man's mouth are
    gracious,[y]
  but a fool is consumed by his own
    lips.[z]
[13]At the beginning his words are folly;
  at the end they are wicked
    madness—
[14] and the fool multiplies words.[a]

No one knows what is coming—
  who can tell him what will happen
    after him?[b]

[15]A fool's work wearies him;
  he does not know the way to town.

[16]Woe to you, O land whose king was
    a servant[n c]
  and whose princes feast in the
    morning.

9:10 [a]1Sa 10:7 [b]Ecc 11:6; Ro 12:11; Col 3:23 [c]Nu 16:33 [d]Ecc 2:24
9:11 [e]Am 2:14-15 [f]Job 32:13; Isa 47:10; Jer 9:23 [g]Ecc 2:14 [h]Dt 8:18
9:12 [i]Pr 29:6 [j]Ps 73:22; Ecc 2:14; 8:7
9:13 [k]2Sa 20:22
9:15 [l]Ge 40:14; Ecc 1:11; 2:16; 4:13
9:16 [m]Pr 21:22; Ecc 7:19
9:18 [n]ver 16
10:1 [o]Pr 13:16; 18:2
10:3 [p]Pr 13:16; 18:2
10:4 [q]Ecc 8:3 [r]Pr 16:14; 25:15
10:6 [s]Pr 29:2
10:7 [t]Pr 19:10
10:8 [u]Ps 7:15; 57:6; Pr 26:27 [v]Est 2:23; Ps 9:16; Am 5:19
10:9 [w]Pr 26:27
10:11 [x]Ps 58:5; Isa 3:3
10:12 [y]Pr 10:32 [z]Pr 10:14; 14:3; 15:2; 18:7
10:14 [a]Pr 15:2; Ecc 5:3; 6:12; 8:7 [b]Ecc 9:1
10:16 [c]Isa 3:4-5,12

[m]*10* Hebrew *Sheol* [n]*16* Or *king is a child*

17Blessed are you, O land whose king
is of noble birth
and whose princes eat at a proper
time—
for strength and not for
drunkenness.[a]

18If a man is lazy, the rafters sag;
if his hands are idle, the house leaks.[b]

19A feast is made for laughter,
and wine[c] makes life merry,
but money is the answer for
everything.

20Do not revile the king[d] even in your
thoughts,
or curse the rich in your bedroom,
because a bird of the air may carry
your words,
and a bird on the wing may report
what you say.

The unknown.

11 Cast[e] your bread upon the
waters,
for after many days you will find it
again.[f]
2Give portions to seven, yes to eight,
for you do not know what disaster
may come upon the land.

3If clouds are full of water,
they pour rain upon the earth.
Whether a tree falls to the south or
to the north,
in the place where it falls, there
will it lie.
4Whoever watches the wind will not
plant;
whoever looks at the clouds will
not reap.

5As you do not know the path of the
wind,[g]
or how the body is formed[o] in a
mother's womb,[h]
so you cannot understand the work
of God,
the Maker of all things.

6Sow your seed in the morning,
and at evening let not your hands
be idle,[i]
for you do not know which will
succeed,
whether this or that,
or whether both will do equally well.

Be happy while young.

7Light is sweet,
and it pleases the eyes to see the
sun.[j]
8However many years a man may live,
let him enjoy them all.
But let him remember[k] the days of
darkness,
for they will be many.
Everything to come is meaningless.

9Be happy, young man, while you are
young,
and let your heart give you joy in
the days of your youth.
Follow the ways of your heart
and whatever your eyes see,
but know that for all these things
God will bring you to judgment.[l]
10So then, banish anxiety[m] from your
heart
and cast off the troubles of your body,
for youth and vigor are
meaningless.[n]

Remember your Creator while young.

12 Remember[o] your Creator
in the days of your youth,
before the days of trouble[p] come
and the years approach when you
will say,
"I find no pleasure in them"—
2before the sun and the light
and the moon and the stars grow
dark,
and the clouds return after the rain;
3when the keepers of the house
tremble,
and the strong men stoop,
when the grinders cease because
they are few,
and those looking through the
windows grow dim;

[o]5 Or *know how life* (or *the spirit*) / *enters the body being formed*

10:17 [a]Dt 14:26; 1Sa 25:36; Pr 31:4
10:18 [b]Pr 20:4; 24:30-34
10:19 [c]Ge 14:18; Jdg 9:13
10:20 [d]Ex 22:28
11:1 [e]ver 6; Isa 32:20; Hos 10:12 [f]Dt 24:19; Pr 19:17; Mt 10:42
11:5 [g]Jn 3:8-10 [h]Ps 139:14-16
11:6 [i]Ecc 9:10
11:7 [j]Ecc 7:11
11:8 [k]Ecc 12:1
11:9 [l]Job 19:29; Ecc 2:24; 3:17; 12:14; Ro 14:10
11:10 [m]Ps 94:19 [n]Ecc 2:24
12:1 [o]Ecc 11:8 [p]2Sa 19:35

4when the doors to the street are closed
and the sound of grinding fades;
when men rise up at the sound of birds,
but all their songs grow faint;[a]
5when men are afraid of heights
and of dangers in the streets;
when the almond tree blossoms
and the grasshopper drags himself along
and desire no longer is stirred.
Then man goes to his eternal home[b]
and mourners[c] go about the streets.

6Remember him—before the silver cord is severed,
or the golden bowl is broken;
before the pitcher is shattered at the spring,
or the wheel broken at the well,
7and the dust returns[d] to the ground it came from,
and the spirit returns to God[e] who gave it.[f]

8"Meaningless! Meaningless!" says the Teacher.[p]
"Everything is meaningless![g]"

12:4 [a]Jer 25:10
12:5 [b]Job 17:13; 10:21 [c]Jer 9:17; Am 5:16
12:7 [d]Ge 3:19; Job 34:15; Ps 146:4 [e]Ecc 3:21 [f]Job 20:8; Zec 12:1
12:8 [g]Ecc 1:2
12:9 [h]1Ki 4:32
12:10 [i]Pr 22:20-21
12:11 [j]Ezr 9:8
12:12 [k]Ecc 1:18
12:13 [l]Dt 4:2; 10:12 [m]Mic 6:8
12:14 [n]Ecc 3:17 [o]Mt 10:26; 1Co 4:5

Conclusion: Fear God and keep his commandments.

9Not only was the Teacher wise, but
also he imparted knowledge to the people. He pondered and searched out and
set in order many proverbs.[h] 10The Teacher searched to find just the right words,
and what he wrote was upright and true.[i]
11The words of the wise are like goads,
their collected sayings like firmly embed-
ded nails[j]—given by one Shepherd. 12Be
warned, my son, of anything in addition
to them.

Of making many books there is no end, and much study wearies the body.[k]

13Now all has been heard;
here is the conclusion of the matter:
Fear God and keep his commandments,[l]
for this is the whole ⌊duty⌋ of man.[m]
14For God will bring every deed into judgment,[n]
including every hidden thing,[o]
whether it is good or evil.

[p]8 Or *the leader of the assembly*; also in verses 9 and 10

SONG OF SONGS

Author: Probably Solomon.

Date Written: Between 965 and 960 B.C.

Time Span: About 1 year.

Title: This book's title, "Song of Songs," means "the supreme song." This book is also called the "Song of Solomon" because it is a love song about Solomon and his bride.

Background: The setting of the book is probably early in Solomon's reign. Most of the story takes place in the palace at Jerusalem or in the surrounding country leading to the bride's home. The Song of Songs more explicitly deals with the topics of sex and marriage than any other book in the Bible. While there are many interpretations of this story, many view it as allegorically portraying God's love for Israel and/or Christ's love for his church.

Where Written: Jerusalem.

To Whom: To the bride.

Content: The Song of Songs is a celebration of love between a man (Solomon) and a woman (the Shulammite shepherd girl). This collection of poems, in the form of songs, portrays the deep and pure love of two who are now looking back over memories of their relationship. The poor Shulammite girl had worked in the country in a vineyard owned by King Solomon. Upon visiting the vineyard, Solomon and the Shulammite fell in love, and he took her to his palace in Jerusalem to be his wife. The lyrics following cover almost every area of their mutual feelings: admiration for each other's physical attributes, their marriage, sexuality, desires and joys. The problems of separation and jealousy arise but are quickly resolved by emphasizing their original true love.

Key Words: "Love"; "Marriage." The Song of Songs beautifully portrays the qualities of a pure "love" and ingredients for a successful "marriage." To develop this kind of a relationship requires total honesty, unselfishness and unconditional support.

Themes: • Sex and marriage are ordained by God and are good in his sight when combined. • God's love for Israel (and Christ's love for the church, his bride) is much greater than any human love. • Although a person may be poverty-stricken financially, he can be rich spiritually by loving God and knowing that God unconditionally loves him. • An ideal marriage will be tender and affectionate, yet strong during times of trial.

Outline:

1. Solomon and the Shulamite girl fall in love. 1:1-3:5
2. The two are united in marriage. 3:6-5:1
3. The bride and groom face painful struggles. 5:2-7:9a
4. The bride and groom reunite and grow in their love. 7:9b-8:14

SONG OF SONGS

1 Solomon's Song of Songs.[a]

Words of love.

Beloved[a]

2Let him kiss me with the kisses of
his mouth—
for your love[b] is more delightful
than wine.
3Pleasing is the fragrance of your
perfumes;[c]
your name[d] is like perfume poured
out.
No wonder the maidens[e] love you!
4Take me away with you—let us
hurry!
Let the king bring me into his
chambers.[f]

Friends

We rejoice and delight in you[b];
we will praise your love more than
wine.

Beloved

How right they are to adore you!

5Dark am I, yet lovely,[g]
O daughters of Jerusalem,[h]
dark like the tents of Kedar,
like the tent curtains of Solomon.[c]
6Do not stare at me because I am dark,
because I am darkened by the sun.
My mother's sons were angry with me
and made me take care of the
vineyards;[i]
my own vineyard I have neglected.
7Tell me, you whom I love, where
you graze your flock
and where you rest your sheep[j] at
midday.
Why should I be like a veiled woman
beside the flocks of your friends?

Friends

8If you do not know, most beautiful of
women,[k]
follow the tracks of the sheep
and graze your young goats
by the tents of the shepherds.

Lover

9I liken you, my darling, to a mare
harnessed to one of the chariots[l] of
Pharaoh.
10Your cheeks[m] are beautiful with
earrings,
your neck with strings of jewels.[n]
11We will make you earrings of gold,
studded with silver.

Beloved

12While the king was at his table,
my perfume spread its fragrance.[o]
13My lover is to me a sachet of myrrh
resting between my breasts.
14My lover is to me a cluster of
henna[p] blossoms
from the vineyards of En Gedi.[q]

Lover

15How beautiful[r] you are, my darling!
Oh, how beautiful!
Your eyes are doves.[s]

Beloved

16How handsome you are, my lover!
Oh, how charming!
And our bed is verdant.

Lover

17The beams of our house are cedars;[t]
our rafters are firs.

The bride and her lover delight in each other.

Beloved[d]

2 I am a rose[e][u] of Sharon,[v]
a lily[w] of the valleys.

Lover

2Like a lily among thorns

1:1 [a]1Ki 4:32
1:2 [b]SS 4:10
1:3 [c]SS 4:10 [d]Ecc 7:1 [e]Ps 45:14
1:4 [f]Ps 45:15
1:5 [g]SS 2:14; 4:3 [h]SS 2:7; 5:8; 5:16
1:6 [i]Ps 69:8; SS 8:12
1:7 [j]SS 3:1-4; Isa 13:20
1:8 [k]SS 5:9; 6:1
1:9 [l]2Ch 1:17
1:10 [m]SS 5:13 [n]Isa 61:10
1:12 [o]SS 4:11-14
1:14 [p]SS 4:13 [q]1Sa 23:29
1:15 [r]SS 4:7 [s]SS 2:14; 4:1; 5:2,12; 6:9
1:17 [t]1Ki 6:9
2:1 [u]Isa 35:1 [v]1Ch 27:29 [w]SS 5:13; Hos 14:5

a Primarily on the basis of the gender of the Hebrew pronouns used, male and female speakers are indicated in the margins by the captions *Lover* and *Beloved* respectively. The words of others are marked *Friends.* In some instances the divisions and their captions are debatable. b *4* The Hebrew is masculine singular. c *5* Or *Salma* d *1* Or *Lover* e *1* Possibly a member of the crocus family

is my darling among the maidens.

Beloved

[3]Like an apple tree among the trees of the forest
is my lover[a] among the young men.
I delight[b] to sit in his shade,
and his fruit is sweet to my taste.[c]
[4]He has taken me to the banquet hall,[d]
and his banner[e] over me is love.
[5]Strengthen me with raisins,
refresh me with apples,[f]
for I am faint with love.[g]
[6]His left arm is under my head,
and his right arm embraces me.[h]
[7]Daughters of Jerusalem, I charge you[i]
by the gazelles and by the does of the field:
Do not arouse or awaken love
until it so desires.[j]

[8]Listen! My lover!
Look! Here he comes,
leaping across the mountains,
bounding over the hills.[k]
[9]My lover is like a gazelle[l] or a young stag.[m]
Look! There he stands behind our wall,
gazing through the windows,
peering through the lattice.
[10]My lover spoke and said to me,
"Arise, my darling,
my beautiful one, and come with me.
[11]See! The winter is past;
the rains are over and gone.
[12]Flowers appear on the earth;
the season of singing has come,
the cooing of doves
is heard in our land.
[13]The fig tree forms its early fruit;[n]
the blossoming[o] vines spread their fragrance.
Arise, come, my darling;
my beautiful one, come with me."

Lover

[14]My dove[p] in the clefts of the rock,
in the hiding places on the mountainside,
show me your face,
let me hear your voice;
for your voice is sweet,
and your face is lovely.[q]
[15]Catch for us the foxes,[r]
the little foxes
that ruin the vineyards,[s]
our vineyards that are in bloom.[t]

Beloved

[16]My lover is mine and I am his;[u]
he browses among the lilies.[v]
[17]Until the day breaks
and the shadows flee,[w]
turn, my lover,[x]
and be like a gazelle
or like a young stag[y]
on the rugged hills.[f][z]

The bride looks for her lover.

3 All night long on my bed
I looked[a] for the one my heart loves;
I looked for him but did not find him.
[2]I will get up now and go about the city,
through its streets and squares;
I will search for the one my heart loves.
So I looked for him but did not find him.
[3]The watchmen found me
as they made their rounds in the city.[b]
"Have you seen the one my heart loves?"
[4]Scarcely had I passed them
when I found the one my heart loves.
I held him and would not let him go
till I had brought him to my mother's house,[c]
to the room of the one who conceived me.[d]
[5]Daughters of Jerusalem, I charge you[e]
by the gazelles and by the does of the field:
Do not arouse or awaken love
until it so desires.[f]

[f]17 Or *the hills of Bether*

2:3 [a]SS 1:14 [b]SS 1:4 [c]SS 4:16
2:4 [d]Est 1:11 [e]Nu 1:52
2:5 [f]SS 7:8 [g]SS 5:8
2:6 [h]SS 8:3
2:7 [i]SS 5:8 [j]SS 3:5; 8:4
2:8 [k]ver 17; SS 8:14
2:9 [l]2Sa 2:18 [m]ver 17; SS 8:14
2:13 [n]Isa 28:4; Jer 24:2; Hos 9:10; Mic 7:1; Na 3:12 [o]SS 7:12
2:14 [p]Ge 8:8; SS 1:15 [q]SS 1:5; 8:13
2:15 [r]Jdg 15:4 [s]SS 1:6 [t]SS 7:12
2:16 [u]SS 7:10 [v]SS 4:5; 6:3
2:17 [w]SS 4:6 [x]SS 1:14 [y]ver 9 [z]ver 8
3:1 [a]SS 5:6; Isa 26:9
3:3 [b]SS 5:7
3:4 [c]SS 8:2 [d]SS 6:9
3:5 [e]SS 2:7 [f]SS 8:4

Solomon approaches.

[6]Who is this coming up from the
desert[a]
like a column of smoke,
perfumed with myrrh[b] and incense
made from all the spices[c] of the
merchant?
[7]Look! It is Solomon's carriage,
escorted by sixty warriors,[d]
the noblest of Israel,
[8]all of them wearing the sword,
all experienced in battle,
each with his sword at his side,
prepared for the terrors of the
night.[e]
[9]King Solomon made for himself the
carriage;
he made it of wood from Lebanon.
[10]Its posts he made of silver,
its base of gold.
Its seat was upholstered with purple,
its interior lovingly inlaid
by[g] the daughters of Jerusalem.
[11]Come out, you daughters of Zion,[f]
and look at King Solomon wearing
the crown,
the crown with which his mother
crowned him
on the day of his wedding,
the day his heart rejoiced.[g]

The lover commends the bride's beauty.

Lover

4 How beautiful you are, my darling!
Oh, how beautiful!
Your eyes behind your veil are
doves.[h]
Your hair is like a flock of goats
descending from Mount Gilead.[i]
[2]Your teeth are like a flock of sheep
just shorn,
coming up from the washing.
Each has its twin;
not one of them is alone.[j]
[3]Your lips are like a scarlet ribbon;
your mouth[k] is lovely.
Your temples behind your veil
are like the halves of a
pomegranate.[l]
[4]Your neck is like the tower[m] of
David,
built with elegance[h];
on it hang a thousand shields,[n]
all of them shields of warriors.
[5]Your two breasts[o] are like two fawns,
like twin fawns of a gazelle[p]
that browse among the lilies.[q]
[6]Until the day breaks
and the shadows flee,[r]
I will go to the mountain of myrrh[s]
and to the hill of incense.
[7]All beautiful[t] you are, my darling;
there is no flaw in you.

[8]Come with me from Lebanon, my
bride,[u]
come with me from Lebanon.
Descend from the crest of Amana,
from the top of Senir,[v] the summit
of Hermon,[w]
from the lions' dens
and the mountain haunts of the
leopards.
[9]You have stolen my heart, my sister,
my bride;
you have stolen my heart
with one glance of your eyes,
with one jewel of your necklace.[x]
[10]How delightful[y] is your love[z], my
sister, my bride!
How much more pleasing is your
love than wine,
and the fragrance of your perfume
than any spice!
[11]Your lips drop sweetness as the
honeycomb, my bride;
milk and honey are under your
tongue.[a]
The fragrance of your garments is
like that of Lebanon.[b]
[12]You are a garden locked up, my
sister, my bride;
you are a spring enclosed, a sealed
fountain.[c]
[13]Your plants are an orchard of
pomegranates[d]
with choice fruits,
with henna[e] and nard,
[14] nard and saffron,

3:6 [a]SS 8:5 [b]SS 1:13; 4:6,14 [c]Ex 30:34
3:7 [d]1Sa 8:11
3:8 [e]Job 15:22; Ps 91:5
3:11 [f]Isa 4:4 [g]Isa 62:5
4:1 [h]SS 1:15; 5:12 [i]SS 6:5; Mic 7:14
4:2 [j]SS 6:6
4:3 [k]SS 5:16 [l]SS 6:7
4:4 [m]SS 7:4 [n]Eze 27:10
4:5 [o]SS 7:3 [p]Pr 5:19 [q]SS 2:16; 6:2-3
4:6 [r]SS 2:17 [s]ver 14
4:7 [t]SS 1:15
4:8 [u]SS 5:1 [v]Dt 3:9 [w]1Ch 5:23
4:9 [x]Ge 41:42
4:10 [y]SS 7:6 [z]SS 1:2
4:11 [a]Ps 19:10; SS 5:1 [b]Hos 14:6
4:12 [c]Pr 5:15-18
4:13 [d]SS 6:11; 7:12 [e]SS 1:14

g *10* Or *its inlaid interior a gift of love / from* h *4* The meaning of the Hebrew for this word is uncertain.

calamus and cinnamon,[a]
with every kind of incense tree,
with myrrh[b] and aloes
and all the finest spices.[c]
15You are[i] a garden fountain,
a well of flowing water
streaming down from Lebanon.

Beloved

16Awake, north wind,
and come, south wind!
Blow on my garden,
that its fragrance may spread
abroad.
Let my lover come into his garden
and taste its choice fruits.[d]

Lover

5 I have come into my garden, my
sister, my bride;[e]
I have gathered my myrrh with my
spice.
I have eaten my honeycomb and my
honey;
I have drunk my wine and my
milk.[f]

Friends

Eat, O friends, and drink;
drink your fill, O lovers.

The bride again cannot find her lover.

Beloved

2I slept but my heart was awake.
Listen! My lover is knocking:
"Open to me, my sister, my darling,
my dove, my flawless[g] one.[h]
My head is drenched with dew,
my hair with the dampness of the
night."
3I have taken off my robe—
must I put it on again?
I have washed my feet—
must I soil them again?
4My lover thrust his hand through the
latch-opening;
my heart began to pound for him.
5I arose to open for my lover,
and my hands dripped with myrrh,[i]

4:14 [a]Ex 30:23 [b]SS 3:6 [c]SS 1:12
4:16 [d]SS 2:3; 5:1
5:1 [e]SS 4:8 [f]SS 4:11; Isa 55:1
5:2 [g]SS 4:7 [h]SS 6:9
5:5 [i]ver 13
5:6 [j]SS 6:1 [k]SS 6:2 [l]SS 3:1
5:7 [m]SS 3:3
5:8 [n]SS 2:7; 3:5 [o]SS 2:5
5:9 [p]SS 1:8; 6:1
5:10 [q]Ps 45:2
5:12 [r]SS 1:15; 4:1 [s]Ge 49:12
5:13 [t]SS 1:10 [u]SS 6:2 [v]SS 2:1
5:14 [w]Job 28:6

my fingers with flowing myrrh,
on the handles of the lock.
6I opened for my lover,[j]
but my lover had left; he was gone.[k]
My heart sank at his departure.[j]
I looked[l] for him but did not find him.
I called him but he did not answer.
7The watchmen found me
as they made their rounds in the
city.[m]
They beat me, they bruised me;
they took away my cloak,
those watchmen of the walls!
8O daughters of Jerusalem, I charge
you[n]—
if you find my lover,
what will you tell him?
Tell him I am faint with love.[o]

The lover's handsomeness is commended.

Friends

9How is your beloved better than
others,
most beautiful of women?[p]
How is your beloved better than
others,
that you charge us so?

Beloved

10My lover is radiant and ruddy,
outstanding among ten thousand.[q]
11His head is purest gold;
his hair is wavy
and black as a raven.
12His eyes are like doves[r]
by the water streams,
washed in milk,[s]
mounted like jewels.
13His cheeks[t] are like beds of spice[u]
yielding perfume.
His lips are like lilies[v]
dripping with myrrh.
14His arms are rods of gold
set with chrysolite.
His body is like polished ivory
decorated with sapphires.[k][w]

[i]*15* Or *I am* (spoken by the *Beloved*) [j]*6* Or *heart had gone out to him when he spoke* [k]*14* Or *lapis lazuli*

15His legs are pillars of marble
set on bases of pure gold.
His appearance is like Lebanon,[a]
choice as its cedars.
16His mouth[b] is sweetness itself;
he is altogether lovely.
This is my lover,[c] this my friend,
O daughters of Jerusalem.[d]

Friends

6 Where has your lover[e] gone,
most beautiful of women?[f]
Which way did your lover turn,
that we may look for him with you?

Beloved

2My lover has gone[g] down to his
garden,[h]
to the beds of spices,[i]
to browse in the gardens
and to gather lilies.
3I am my lover's and my lover is mine;[j]
he browses among the lilies.[k]

The bride's virtues are commended.

Lover

4You are beautiful, my darling, as
Tirzah,[l]
lovely as Jerusalem,[m]
majestic as troops with banners.[n]
5Turn your eyes from me;
they overwhelm me.
Your hair is like a flock of goats
descending from Gilead.[o]
6Your teeth are like a flock of sheep
coming up from the washing.
Each has its twin,
not one of them is alone.[p]
7Your temples behind your veil[q]
are like the halves of a pomegranate.[r]
8Sixty queens[s] there may be,
and eighty concubines,[t]
and virgins beyond number;
9but my dove,[u] my perfect one,[v] is
unique,
the only daughter of her mother,
the favorite of the one who bore
her.[w]
The maidens saw her and called her
blessed;
the queens and concubines praised
her.

Friends

10Who is this that appears like the
dawn,
fair as the moon, bright as the sun,
majestic as the stars in procession?

Lover

11I went down to the grove of nut
trees
to look at the new growth in the
valley,
to see if the vines had budded
or the pomegranates were in
bloom.[x]
12Before I realized it,
my desire set me among the royal
chariots of my people.[l]

Friends

13Come back, come back,
O Shulammite;
come back, come back, that we
may gaze on you!

Lover

Why would you gaze on the
Shulammite
as on the dance[y] of Mahanaim?

7 How beautiful your sandaled
feet,
O prince's[z] daughter!
Your graceful legs are like jewels,
the work of a craftsman's hands.
2Your navel is a rounded goblet
that never lacks blended wine.
Your waist is a mound of wheat
encircled by lilies.
3Your breasts[a] are like two fawns,
twins of a gazelle.
4Your neck is like an ivory tower.[b]
Your eyes are the pools of Heshbon[c]
by the gate of Bath Rabbim.
Your nose is like the tower of
Lebanon[d]
looking toward Damascus.

5:15 [a]1Ki 4:33; SS 7:4
5:16 [b]SS 4:3 [c]SS 7:9 [d]SS 1:5
6:1 [e]SS 5:6 [f]SS 1:8
6:2 [g]SS 5:6 [h]SS 4:12 [i]SS 5:13
6:3 [j]SS 7:10 [k]SS 2:16
6:4 [l]Jos 12:24 [m]Ps 48:2; 50:2 [n]ver 10
6:5 [o]SS 4:1
6:6 [p]SS 4:2
6:7 [q]Ge 24:65 [r]SS 4:3
6:8 [s]Ps 45:9 [t]Ge 22:24
6:9 [u]SS 1:15 [v]SS 5:2 [w]SS 3:4
6:11 [x]SS 7:12
6:13 [y]Ex 15:20
7:1 [z]Ps 45:13
7:3 [a]SS 4:5
7:4 [b]Ps 144:12; SS 4:4 [c]Nu 21:26 [d]SS 5:15

l12 Or *among the chariots of Amminadab*; or *among the chariots of the people of the prince*

[5]Your head crowns you like Mount
Carmel.[a]
Your hair is like royal tapestry;
the king is held captive by its
tresses.
[6]How beautiful[b] you are and how
pleasing,
O love, with your delights![c]
[7]Your stature is like that of the palm,
and your breasts[d] like clusters of
fruit.
[8]I said, "I will climb the palm tree;
I will take hold of its fruit."
May your breasts be like the clusters
of the vine,
the fragrance of your breath like
apples,[e]
[9] and your mouth like the best wine.

The bride's promise of her love.

Beloved

May the wine go straight to my
lover,[f]
flowing gently over lips and teeth.[m]
[10]I belong to my lover,
and his desire[g] is for me.[h]
[11]Come, my lover, let us go to the
countryside,
let us spend the night in the
villages.[n]
[12]Let us go early to the vineyards[i]
to see if the vines have budded,[j]
if their blossoms[k] have opened,
and if the pomegranates[l] are in
bloom[m]—
there I will give you my love.
[13]The mandrakes[n] send out their
fragrance,
and at our door is every delicacy,
both new and old,
that I have stored up for you, my
lover.[o]

8 If only you were to me like a
brother,
who was nursed at my mother's
breasts!
Then, if I found you outside,
I would kiss you,
and no one would despise me.
[2]I would lead you
and bring you to my mother's
house[p]—
she who has taught me.
I would give you spiced wine to
drink,
the nectar of my pomegranates.
[3]His left arm is under my head
and his right arm embraces me.[q]
[4]Daughters of Jerusalem, I charge
you:
Do not arouse or awaken love
until it so desires.[r]

Friends

[5]Who is this coming up from the
desert[s]
leaning on her lover?

Beloved

Under the apple tree I roused you;
there your mother conceived[t] you,
there she who was in labor gave
you birth.
[6]Place me like a seal over your heart,
like a seal on your arm;
for love[u] is as strong as death,
its jealousy[o][v] unyielding as the
grave.[p]
It burns like blazing fire,
like a mighty flame.[q]
[7]Many waters cannot quench love;
rivers cannot wash it away.
If one were to give
all the wealth of his house for love,
it[r] would be utterly scorned.[w]

Friends

[8]We have a young sister,
and her breasts are not yet grown.
What shall we do for our sister
for the day she is spoken for?
[9]If she is a wall,
we will build towers of silver on
her.
If she is a door,
we will enclose her with panels of
cedar.

7:5 [a]Isa 35:2
7:6 [b]SS 1:15 [c]SS 4:10
7:7 [d]SS 4:5
7:8 [e]SS 2:5
7:9 [f]SS 5:16
7:10 [g]Ps 45:11 [h]SS 2:16; 6:3
7:12 [i]SS 1:6 [j]SS 2:15 [k]SS 2:13 [l]SS 4:13 [m]SS 6:11
7:13 [n]Ge 30:14 [o]SS 4:16
8:2 [p]SS 3:4
8:3 [q]SS 2:6
8:4 [r]SS 2:7; 3:5
8:5 [s]SS 3:6 [t]SS 3:4
8:6 [u]SS 1:2 [v]Nu 5:14
8:7 [w]Pr 6:35

[m] *9* Septuagint, Aquila, Vulgate and Syriac; Hebrew *lips of sleepers* [n] *11* Or *henna bushes* [o] *6* Or *ardor* [p] *6* Hebrew *Sheol* [q] *6* Or */ like the very flame of the LORD* [r] *7* Or *he*

Beloved

10 I am a wall,
and my breasts are like towers.
Thus I have become in his eyes
like one bringing contentment.
11 Solomon had a vineyard[a] in Baal
Hamon;
he let out his vineyard to tenants.
Each was to bring for its fruit
a thousand shekels[s][b] of silver.
12 But my own vineyard[c] is mine to give;
the thousand shekels are for you,
O Solomon,
and two hundred[t] are for those
who tend its fruit.

8:11
[a]Ecc 2:4
[b]Isa 7:23

8:12
[c]SS 1:6

8:14
[d]Pr 5:19
[e]SS 2:9
[f]SS 2:8,17

Lover

13 You who dwell in the gardens
with friends in attendance,
let me hear your voice!

Beloved

14 Come away, my lover,
and be like a gazelle[d]
or like a young stag[e]
on the spice-laden mountains.[f]

s *11* That is, about 25 pounds (about 11.5 kilograms); also in verse 12 t *12* That is, about 5 pounds (about 2.3 kilograms)

ISAIAH

Author: Isaiah.

Date Written: Between 745 and 680 B.C.

Time Span: Isaiah's prophetic ministry lasts about 60 years during the reigns of 4 kings of Judah: Uzziah, Jotham, Ahaz and Hezekiah.

Title: This book is named after its author: the prophet Isaiah.

Background: The well-educated, politically astute Isaiah lives in Jerusalem, the capital of Judah. Isaiah has messages for all of Israel, but his ministry is primarily directed to Judah. Hosea and Micah are prophesying God's word at this same time. Tradition has it that Isaiah is sawn into pieces during the reign of evil Manasseh. The book of Isaiah begins the prophetical section of the Old Testament.

Where Written: Probably Jerusalem.

To Whom: Primarily to the nation of Judah, but also to all the surrounding nations.

Content: While Judah is spiritually destitute, Israel is even more corrupt. After Isaiah prophesies the destruction of Israel by Assyria, which indeed takes place shortly thereafter, he turns his attention to Judah. His message to Judah and the surrounding nations is that the judgment of God will come upon them also. If they do not turn from their evil ways, they will be led into captivity by the Babylonians. All is not gloom, however, as Isaiah assures the people: those in captivity will be allowed to return to Jerusalem under Cyrus's edict; a "suffering Servant" will be born as the virgin child of God to be the Messiah and bring salvation to the world; and the restoration of Jerusalem will take place and bring abundant blessings to the new Zion. Isaiah's prophecies concerning Jesus Christ are crystal clear, thorough and probably more detailed than in any other Old Testament book.

Key Words: "Judgment"; "Salvation." Isaiah's 66 chapters can be likened to a miniature Bible. The first 39 chapters correspond to the 39 books of the Old Testament by emphasizing God's "judgment" upon those who refuse to repent and turn to him in faith. The final 27 chapters parallel the 27 books of the New Testament by focusing on the Messiah, who is our "salvation."

Themes: • God is our eternal Comforter, Redeemer and Savior. • God will pardon us of our sins if we will forsake our past and turn to him. • The fleeting pleasure of sin in our lives will never be worth the extreme price we must pay for it (judgment from God). • God is holy and will not tarry while unholiness persists in his covenant people. • Deliverance is of God, not of man. • The greatest success in the world is being obedient to the will of God.

Outline:

1. Isaiah's commission to proclaim judgment. 1:1-6:13
2. Destruction of Israel by Assyria. 7:1-10:4
3. Destruction of Assyria by God. 10:5-12:6
4. Prophecies concerning other pagan nations. 13:1-23:18
5. Israel's judgment and deliverance. 24:1-27:13
6. Zion's restoration. 28:1-35:10
7. Delay of judgment for Jerusalem through Hezekiah's prayers. 36:1-39:8
8. Prophecy of Israel's deliverance and Deliverer. 40:1-57:21
9. The final kingdom and its glory. 58:1-66:24

ISAIAH

1 The vision[a] concerning Judah and
Jerusalem[b] that Isaiah son of Amoz
saw[c] during the reigns of Uzziah,[d] Jotham, Ahaz[e] and Hezekiah, kings of
Judah.

Isaiah mourns the judgment of Judah.

2Hear, O heavens! Listen, O earth!
For the LORD has spoken:[f]
"I reared children and brought
them up,
but they have rebelled[g] against me.
3The ox knows his master,
the donkey his owner's manger,
but Israel does not know,[h]
my people do not understand."

4Ah, sinful nation,
a people loaded with guilt,
a brood of evildoers,[i]
children given to corruption!
They have forsaken the LORD;
they have spurned the Holy One[j]
of Israel
and turned their backs on him.

5Why should you be beaten anymore?
Why do you persist in rebellion?[k]
Your whole head is injured,
your whole heart afflicted.[l]
6From the sole of your foot to the
top of your head
there is no soundness[m]—
only wounds and welts
and open sores,
not cleansed or bandaged[n]
or soothed with oil.[o]

7Your country is desolate,[p]
your cities burned with fire;
your fields are being stripped by
foreigners
right before you,
laid waste as when overthrown
by strangers.
8The Daughter of Zion is left
like a shelter in a vineyard,
like a hut[q] in a field of melons,
like a city under siege.
9Unless the LORD Almighty
had left us some survivors,[r]
we would have become like Sodom,
we would have been like Gomorrah.[s]

10Hear the word of the LORD,[t]
you rulers of Sodom;[u]
listen to the law[v] of our God,
you people of Gomorrah!
11"The multitude of your sacrifices—
what are they to me?" says the LORD.
"I have more than enough of burnt
offerings,
of rams and the fat of fattened
animals;[w]
I have no pleasure
in the blood of bulls[x] and lambs
and goats.[y]
12When you come to appear before me,
who has asked this of you,[z]
this trampling of my courts?
13Stop bringing meaningless offerings![a]
Your incense[b] is detestable to me.
New Moons, Sabbaths and
convocations[c]—
I cannot bear your evil assemblies.
14Your New Moon festivals and your
appointed feasts[d]
my soul hates.
They have become a burden to me;
I am weary[e] of bearing them.
15When you spread out your hands in
prayer,
I will hide[f] my eyes from you;
even if you offer many prayers,
I will not listen.
Your hands are full of blood;[g]
16 wash and make yourselves clean.
Take your evil deeds
out of my sight![h]
Stop doing wrong,[i]
17 learn to do right!
Seek justice,[j]
encourage the oppressed.[a]
Defend the cause of the fatherless,[k]
plead the case of the widow.

1:1 [a]Nu 12:6 [b]Isa 40:9 [c]Isa 2:1 [d]2Ch 26:22 [e]2Ki 16:1
1:2 [f]Mic 1:2 [g]Isa 30:1,9; 65:2
1:3 [h]Jer 8:7; 9:3,6
1:4 [i]Isa 14:20 [j]Isa 5:19,24
1:5 [k]Isa 31:6 [l]Isa 33:6,24
1:6 [m]Ps 38:3 [n]Isa 30:26; Jer 8:22 [o]Lk 10:34
1:7 [p]Lev 26:34
1:8 [q]Job 27:18
1:9 [r]Isa 10:20-22; 37:4,31-32 [s]Ge 19:24; Ro 9:29*
1:10 [t]Isa 28:14 [u]Isa 3:9; Eze 16:49; Ro 9:29; Rev 11:8 [v]Isa 8:20
1:11 [w]Ps 50:8 [x]Jer 6:20 [y]1Sa 15:22; Mal 1:10
1:12 [z]Ex 23:17
1:13 [a]Isa 66:3 [b]Jer 7:9 [c]1Ch 23:31
1:14 [d]Lev 23:1-44; Nu 28:11–29:39; Isa 29:1 [e]Isa 7:13; 43:22,24
1:15 [f]Isa 8:17; 59:2; Mic 3:4 [g]Isa 59:3
1:16 [h]Isa 52:11 [i]Isa 55:7; Jer 25:5
1:17 [j]Zep 2:3 [k]Ps 82:3

a *17* Or */ rebuke the oppressor*

[18]"Come now, let us reason together,"[a]
says the LORD.
"Though your sins are like scarlet,
they shall be as white as snow;[b]
though they are red as crimson,
they shall be like wool.
[19]If you are willing and obedient,
you will eat the best from the land;[c]
[20]but if you resist and rebel,
you will be devoured by the sword."[d]
For the mouth of the LORD
has spoken.[e]

[21]See how the faithful city
has become a harlot![f]
She once was full of justice;
righteousness used to dwell in her—
but now murderers!
[22]Your silver has become dross,
your choice wine is diluted with
water.
[23]Your rulers are rebels,
companions of thieves;
they all love bribes[g]
and chase after gifts.
They do not defend the cause of the
fatherless;
the widow's case does not come
before them.[h]
[24]Therefore the Lord, the LORD
Almighty,
the Mighty One of Israel, declares:
"Ah, I will get relief from my foes
and avenge[i] myself on my enemies.
[25]I will turn my hand against you;
I will thoroughly purge away your
dross
and remove all your impurities.[j]
[26]I will restore your judges as in days
of old,[k]
your counselors as at the
beginning.
Afterward you will be called
the City of Righteousness,[l]
the Faithful City.[m]"
[27]Zion will be redeemed with justice,
her penitent ones with
righteousness.[n]
[28]But rebels and sinners will both be
broken,
and those who forsake the LORD
will perish.[o]

1:18 [a]Isa 41:1; 43:9,26 [b]Ps 51:7; Rev 7:14
1:19 [c]Dt 30:15-16; Isa 55:2
1:20 [d]Isa 3:25; 65:12 [e]Isa 34:16; 40:5; 58:14; Mic 4:4
1:21 [f]Isa 57:3-9; Jer 2:20
1:23 [g]Ex 23:8 [h]Isa 10:2; Jer 5:28; Eze 22:6-7; Zec 7:10
1:24 [i]Isa 35:4; 59:17; 61:2; 63:4
1:25 [j]Eze 22:22; Mal 3:3
1:26 [k]Jer 33:7,11 [l]Isa 33:5; 62:1; Zec 8:3 [m]Isa 60:14; 62:2
1:27 [n]Isa 35:10; 62:12; 63:4
1:28 [o]Ps 9:5; Isa 24:20; 66:24; 2Th 1:8-9
1:29 [p]Isa 57:5 [q]Isa 65:3; 66:17
1:31 [r]Isa 5:24; 9:18-19; 26:11; 33:14; 66:15-16,24
2:1 [s]Isa 1:1
2:2 [t]Isa 27:13; 56:7; 66:20; Mic 4:7
2:3 [u]Isa 51:4,7 [v]Lk 24:47

[29]"You will be ashamed because of the
sacred oaks[p]
in which you have delighted;
you will be disgraced because of the
gardens[q]
that you have chosen.
[30]You will be like an oak with fading
leaves,
like a garden without water.
[31]The mighty man will become tinder
and his work a spark;
both will burn together,
with no one to quench the fire.[r]"

The mountain of the LORD.

2:1-4pp— Mic 4:1-3

2 This is what Isaiah son of Amoz saw concerning Judah and Jerusalem:[s]

[2]In the last days

the mountain[t] of the LORD's temple
will be established
as chief among the mountains;
it will be raised above the hills,
and all nations will stream to it.
[3]Many peoples will come and say,

"Come, let us go up to the mountain
of the LORD,
to the house of the God of Jacob.
He will teach us his ways,
so that we may walk in his paths."
The law[u] will go out from Zion,
the word of the LORD from
Jerusalem.[v]
[4]He will judge between the nations
and will settle disputes for many
peoples.
They will beat their swords into
plowshares
and their spears into pruning
hooks.[w]
Nation will not take up sword
against nation,[x]
nor will they train for war anymore.
[5]Come, O house of Jacob,[y]
let us walk in the light[z] of the LORD.

2:4 [w]Joel 3:10 [x]Ps 46:9; Isa 9:5; 11:6-9; 32:18; Hos 2:18; Zec 9:10
2:5 [y]Isa 58:1 [z]Isa 60:1,19-20; 1Jn 1:5,7

The day of the LORD.

6You have abandoned[a] your people,
the house of Jacob.
They are full of superstitions from
the East;
they practice divination like the
Philistines[b]
and clasp hands[c] with pagans.[d]
7Their land is full of silver and gold;
there is no end to their treasures.
Their land is full of horses;[e]
there is no end to their chariots.[f]
8Their land is full of idols;[g]
they bow down to the work of
their hands,
to what their fingers[h] have made.
9So man will be brought low[i]
and mankind humbled[j]—
do not forgive them.[b][k]

10Go into the rocks,
hide in the ground
from dread of the LORD
and the splendor of his majesty![l]
11The eyes of the arrogant man will be
humbled
and the pride[m] of men brought low;
the LORD alone will be exalted in
that day.

12The LORD Almighty has a day in store
for all the proud and lofty,
for all that is exalted[n]
(and they will be humbled),[o]
13for all the cedars of Lebanon, tall and
lofty,
and all the oaks of Bashan,[p]
14for all the towering mountains
and all the high hills,[q]
15for every lofty tower
and every fortified wall,[r]
16for every trading ship[c][s]
and every stately vessel.
17The arrogance of man will be
brought low
and the pride of men humbled;
the LORD alone will be exalted in
that day,[t]
18 and the idols will totally
disappear.[u]

19Men will flee to caves in the rocks
and to holes in the ground
from dread of the LORD
and the splendor of his majesty,
when he rises to shake the earth.[v]
20In that day men will throw away
to the rodents and bats[w]
their idols of silver and idols of gold,
which they made to worship.
21They will flee to caverns in the rocks
and to the overhanging crags
from dread of the LORD
and the splendor of his majesty,
when he rises to shake the earth.[x]

22Stop trusting in man,[y]
who has but a breath in his nostrils.
Of what account is he?[z]

Judgment against Jerusalem and Judah.

3 See now, the Lord,
the LORD Almighty,
is about to take from Jerusalem and
Judah
both supply and support:
all supplies of food[a] and all supplies
of water,[b]
2 the hero and warrior,[c]
the judge and prophet,
the soothsayer and elder,[d]
3the captain of fifty and man of rank,
the counselor, skilled craftsman and
clever enchanter.

4I will make boys their officials;
mere children will govern them.[e]
5People will oppress each other—
man against man, neighbor against
neighbor.[f]
The young will rise up against the old,
the base against the honorable.

6A man will seize one of his brothers
at his father's home, and say,
"You have a cloak, you be our leader;
take charge of this heap of ruins!"
7But in that day he will cry out,
"I have no remedy.[g]
I have no food or clothing in my house;
do not make me the leader of the
people."

2:6 [a]Dt 31:17 [b]2Ki 1:2 [c]Pr 6:1 [d]2Ki 16:7
2:7 [e]Dt 17:16 [f]Isa 31:1; Mic 5:10
2:8 [g]Isa 10:9-11 [h]Isa 17:8
2:9 [i]Ps 62:9 [j]Isa 5:15 [k]Ne 4:5
2:10 [l]2Th 1:9; Rev 6:15-16
2:11 [m]Isa 5:15; 37:23
2:12 [n]Isa 24:4,21; Mal 4:1 [o]Job 40:11
2:13 [p]Zec 11:2
2:14 [q]Isa 30:25; 40:4
2:15 [r]Isa 25:2,12
2:16 [s]1Ki 10:22
2:17 [t]ver 11
2:18 [u]Isa 21:9
2:19 [v]Heb 12:26
2:20 [w]Lev 11:19
2:21 [x]ver 19
2:22 [y]Ps 146:3; Jer 17:5 [z]Ps 8:4; 144:3; Isa 40:15; Jas 4:14
3:1 [a]Lev 26:26 [b]Isa 5:13; Eze 4:16
3:2 [c]Eze 17:13 [d]2Ki 24:14; Isa 9:14-15
3:4 [e]Ecc 10:16*fn*
3:5 [f]Isa 9:19; Jer 9:8; Mic 7:2,6
3:7 [g]Eze 34:4; Hos 5:13

b9 Or *not raise them up* c16 Hebrew *every ship of Tarshish*

8Jerusalem staggers,
Judah is falling;[a]
their words[b] and deeds are against
the LORD,
defying[c] his glorious presence.
9The look on their faces testifies
against them;
they parade their sin like Sodom;[d]
they do not hide it.
Woe to them!
They have brought disaster[e] upon
themselves.

10Tell the righteous it will be well[f]
with them,
for they will enjoy the fruit of their
deeds.[g]
11Woe to the wicked! Disaster[h] is
upon them!
They will be paid back for what their
hands have done.

Oppressive rulers.

12Youths[i] oppress my people,
women rule over them.
O my people, your guides lead you
astray;[j]
they turn you from the path.
13The LORD takes his place in court;
he rises to judge[k] the people.
14The LORD enters into judgment[l]
against the elders and leaders of
his people:
"It is you who have ruined my
vineyard;
the plunder[m] from the poor is in
your houses.
15What do you mean by crushing my
people[n]
and grinding the faces of the poor?"
declares the Lord,
the LORD Almighty.

Judgments on haughty women.

16The LORD says,
"The women of Zion[o] are haughty,
walking along with outstretched necks,
flirting with their eyes,
tripping along with mincing steps,
with ornaments jingling on their
ankles.
17Therefore the Lord will bring sores on
the heads of the women of Zion;
the LORD will make their scalps bald."

18In that day the Lord will snatch away
their finery: the bangles and headbands
and crescent necklaces,[p] 19the earrings
and bracelets and veils, 20the head-
dresses[q] and ankle chains and sashes,
the perfume bottles and charms, 21the
signet rings and nose rings, 22the fine
robes and the capes and cloaks, the
purses 23and mirrors, and the linen garments and tiaras and shawls.

24Instead of fragrance[r] there will be
a stench;
instead of a sash,[s] a rope;
instead of well-dressed hair, baldness;[t]
instead of fine clothing, sackcloth;[u]
instead of beauty,[v] branding.
25Your men will fall by the sword,[w]
your warriors in battle.
26The gates of Zion will lament and
mourn;[x]
destitute, she will sit on the ground.[y]

4 In that day seven women
will take hold of one man[z]
and say, "We will eat our own food[a]
and provide our own clothes;
only let us be called by your name.
Take away our disgrace!"[b]

The glorious Branch of the LORD.

2In that day the Branch of the LORD[c]
will be beautiful and glorious, and the
fruit[d] of the land will be the pride and
glory of the survivors in Israel. 3Those
who are left in Zion, who remain[e] in Jerusalem, will be called holy,[f] all who are
recorded[g] among the living in Jerusalem. 4The Lord will wash away the filth[h]
of the women of Zion; he will cleanse
the bloodstains[i] from Jerusalem by a
spirit[d] of judgment[j] and a spirit[d] of fire.[k]
5Then the LORD will create over all of
Mount Zion and over those who assemble there a cloud of smoke by day and a
glow of flaming fire by night;[l] over all
the glory[m] will be a canopy. 6It will be a
shelter[n] and shade from the heat of the

3:8 [a]Isa 1:7 [b]Isa 9:15,17 [c]Ps 73:9,11
3:9 [d]Ge 13:13 [e]Pr 8:36; Ro 6:23
3:10 [f]Dt 28:1-14 [g]Ps 128:2
3:11 [h]Dt 28:15-68
3:12 [i]ver 4 [j]Isa 9:16
3:13 [k]Mic 6:2
3:14 [l]Job 22:4 [m]Job 24:9; Jas 2:6
3:15 [n]Ps 94:5
3:16 [o]SS 3:11
3:18 [p]Jdg 8:21
3:20 [q]Ex 39:28
3:24 [r]Est 2:12 [s]Pr 31:24 [t]Isa 22:12 [u]La 2:10; Eze 27:30-31 [v]1Pe 3:3
3:25 [w]Isa 1:20
3:26 [x]Jer 14:2 [y]La 2:10
4:1 [z]Isa 13:12 [a]2Th 3:12 [b]Ge 30:23
4:2 [c]Isa 11:1-5; 53:2; Jer 23:5-6; Zec 3:8; 6:12 [d]Ps 72:16
4:3 [e]Ro 11:5 [f]Isa 52:1; 60:21 [g]Lk 10:20
4:4 [h]Isa 3:24 [i]Isa 1:15 [j]Isa 28:6 [k]Isa 1:31; Mt 3:11
4:5 [l]Ex 13:21 [m]Isa 60:1
4:6 [n]Ps 27:5

d*4* Or *the Spirit*

day, and a refuge[a] and hiding place from the storm and rain.

Song of the vineyard.

5 I will sing for the one I love
a song about his vineyard:[b]
My loved one had a vineyard
on a fertile hillside.
2He dug it up and cleared it of stones
and planted it with the choicest vines.[c]
He built a watchtower in it
and cut out a winepress as well.
Then he looked for a crop of good grapes,
but it yielded only bad fruit.[d]

3"Now you dwellers in Jerusalem and men of Judah,
judge between me and my vineyard.[e]
4What more could have been done for my vineyard
than I have done for it?[f]
When I looked for good grapes,
why did it yield only bad?
5Now I will tell you
what I am going to do to my vineyard:
I will take away its hedge,
and it will be destroyed;
I will break down its wall,[g]
and it will be trampled.[h]
6I will make it a wasteland,
neither pruned nor cultivated,
and briers and thorns[i] will grow there.
I will command the clouds
not to rain on it."

7The vineyard[j] of the LORD Almighty
is the house of Israel,
and the men of Judah
are the garden of his delight.
And he looked for justice,[k] but saw bloodshed;
for righteousness, but heard cries of distress.

Woes to the people.

8Woe[l] to you who add house to house
and join field to field[m]
till no space is left
and you live alone in the land.

9The LORD Almighty has declared in my hearing:[n]

"Surely the great houses will become desolate,[o]
the fine mansions left without occupants.
10A ten-acre[e] vineyard will produce only a bath[f] of wine,
a homer[g] of seed only an ephah[h] of grain."[p]

11Woe to those who rise early in the morning
to run after their drinks,
who stay up late at night
till they are inflamed with wine.[q]
12They have harps and lyres at their banquets,
tambourines and flutes and wine,
but they have no regard[r] for the deeds of the LORD,
no respect for the work of his hands.[s]
13Therefore my people will go into exile[t]
for lack of understanding;[u]
their men of rank will die of hunger
and their masses will be parched with thirst.
14Therefore the grave[i] [v] enlarges its appetite
and opens its mouth[w] without limit;
into it will descend their nobles and masses
with all their brawlers and revelers.
15So man will be brought low[x]
and mankind humbled,[y]
the eyes of the arrogant[z] humbled.
16But the LORD Almighty will be exalted by his justice,[a]
and the holy God will show himself holy[b] by his righteousness.
17Then sheep will graze as in their own pasture;[c]
lambs will feed[j] among the ruins of the rich.

4:6 [a]Isa 25:4
5:1 [b]Ps 80:8-9
5:2 [c]Jer 2:21 [d]Mt 21:19; Mk 11:13; Lk 13:6
5:3 [e]Mt 21:40
5:4 [f]2Ch 36:15; Jer 2:5-7; Mic 6:3-4; Mt 23:37
5:5 [g]Ps 80:12 [h]Isa 28:3,18; La 1:15; Lk 21:24
5:6 [i]Isa 7:23,24; Heb 6:8
5:7 [j]Ps 80:8 [k]Isa 59:15
5:8 [l]Jer 22:13 [m]Mic 2:2; Hab 2:9-12
5:9 [n]Isa 22:14 [o]Isa 6:11-12; Mt 23:38
5:10 [p]Lev 26:26
5:11 [q]Pr 23:29-30
5:12 [r]Job 34:27 [s]Ps 28:5; Am 6:5-6
5:13 [t]Hos 4:6 [u]Isa 1:3; Hos 4:6
5:14 [v]Pr 30:16 [w]Nu 16:30
5:15 [x]Isa 10:33 [y]Isa 2:9 [z]Isa 2:11
5:16 [a]Isa 28:17; 30:18; 33:5; 61:8 [b]Isa 29:23
5:17 [c]Isa 7:25; Zep 2:6,14

e *10* Hebrew *ten-yoke,* that is, the land plowed by 10 yoke of oxen in one day f *10* That is, probably about 6 gallons (about 22 liters) g *10* That is, probably about 6 bushels (about 220 liters) h *10* That is, probably about 3/5 bushel (about 22 liters) i *14* Hebrew *Sheol* j *17* Septuagint; Hebrew */ strangers will eat*

18Woe to those who draw sin along
with cords of deceit,
and wickedness[a] as with cart ropes,
19to those who say, "Let God hurry,
let him hasten his work
so we may see it.
Let it approach,
let the plan of the Holy One of
Israel come,
so we may know it."[b]

20Woe to those who call evil good
and good evil,
who put darkness for light
and light for darkness,[c]
who put bitter for sweet
and sweet for bitter.[d]

21Woe to those who are wise in their
own eyes[e]
and clever in their own sight.

22Woe to those who are heroes at
drinking wine[f]
and champions at mixing drinks,
23who acquit the guilty for a bribe,[g]
but deny justice[h] to the innocent.[i]
24Therefore, as tongues of fire lick up
straw
and as dry grass sinks down in the
flames,
so their roots will decay[j]
and their flowers blow away
like dust;
for they have rejected the law of the
LORD Almighty
and spurned the word[k] of the Holy
One of Israel.
25Therefore the LORD's anger[l] burns
against his people;
his hand is raised and he strikes
them down.
The mountains shake,
and the dead bodies are like
refuse[m] in the streets.

Yet for all this, his anger is not
turned away,[n]
his hand is still upraised.[o]

26He lifts up a banner for the distant
nations,
he whistles[p] for those at the ends
of the earth.[q]
Here they come,
swiftly and speedily!
27Not one of them grows tired or
stumbles,
not one slumbers or sleeps;
not a belt is loosened at the waist,[r]
not a sandal thong is broken.[s]
28Their arrows are sharp,[t]
all their bows[u] are strung;
their horses' hoofs seem like flint,
their chariot wheels like a
whirlwind.
29Their roar is like that of the lion,[v]
they roar like young lions;
they growl as they seize[w] their prey
and carry it off with no one to
rescue.[x]
30In that day they will roar over it
like the roaring of the sea.[y]
And if one looks at the land,
he will see darkness and distress;[z]
even the light will be darkened[a]
by the clouds.

The Lord commissions Isaiah.

6 In the year that King Uzziah[b] died,[c]
I saw the Lord[d] seated on a throne,[e]
high and exalted, and the train of his
robe filled the temple. 2Above him were
seraphs,[f] each with six wings: With two
wings they covered their faces, with
two they covered their feet,[g] and with
two they were flying. 3And they were
calling to one another:

"Holy, holy, holy is the LORD Almighty;
the whole earth is full of his glory."[h]

4At the sound of their voices the doorposts and thresholds shook and the temple was filled with smoke.
5"Woe to me!" I cried. "I am ruined!
For I am a man of unclean lips, and I
live among a people of unclean lips,[i] and
my eyes have seen the King,[j] the LORD
Almighty."
6Then one of the seraphs flew to me
with a live coal in his hand, which he had
taken with tongs from the altar. 7With it
he touched my mouth and said, "See,

5:18 [a]Isa 59:4-8; Jer 23:14
5:19 [b]Jer 17:15; Eze 12:22; 2Pe 3:4
5:20 [c]Mt 6:22-23; Lk 11:34-35 [d]Am 5:7
5:21 [e]Pr 3:7; Ro 12:16; 1Co 3:18-20
5:22 [f]Pr 23:20
5:23 [g]Ex 23:8 [h]Isa 10:2 [i]Ps 94:21; Jas 5:6
5:24 [j]Job 18:16 [k]Isa 8:6; 30:9,12
5:25 [l]2Ki 22:13 [m]2Ki 9:37 [n]Jer 4:8; Da 9:16 [o]Isa 9:12,17, 21; 10:4
5:26 [p]Isa 7:18; Zec 10:8 [q]Dt 28:49; Isa 13:5; 18:3
5:27 [r]Job 12:18 [s]Joel 2:7-8
5:28 [t]Ps 45:5 [u]Ps 7:12
5:29 [v]Jer 51:38; Zep 3:3; Zec 11:3 [w]Isa 10:6; 49:24-25 [x]Isa 42:22; Mic 5:8
5:30 [y]Lk 21:25 [z]Isa 8:22; Jer 4:23-28 [a]Joel 2:10
6:1 [b]2Ch 26:22,23 [c]2Ki 15:7 [d]Jn 12:41 [e]Rev 4:2
6:2 [f]Rev 4:8 [g]Eze 1:11
6:3 [h]Ps 72:19; Rev 4:8

6:5 [i]Jer 9:3-8 [j]Jer 51:57

this has touched your lips;[a] your guilt is
taken away and your sin atoned for.[b]"
8Then I heard the voice[c] of the Lord
saying, "Whom shall I send? And who
will go for us?"
And I said, "Here am I. Send me!"
9He said, "Go[d] and tell this people:

"'Be ever hearing, but never
understanding;
be ever seeing, but never
perceiving.'[e]
10Make the heart of this people
calloused;[f]
make their ears dull
and close their eyes.[k]
Otherwise they might see with their
eyes,
hear with their ears,[g]
understand with their hearts,
and turn and be healed."[h]

11Then I said, "For how long, O Lord?"[i]
And he answered:

"Until the cities lie ruined[j]
and without inhabitant,
until the houses are left deserted
and the fields ruined and ravaged,
12until the LORD has sent everyone far
away[k]
and the land is utterly forsaken.[l]
13And though a tenth remains[m] in the
land,
it will again be laid waste.
But as the terebinth and oak
leave stumps when they are cut
down,
so the holy seed will be the stump
in the land."[n]

Ahaz should not be afraid.

7 When Ahaz son of Jotham, the son
of Uzziah, was king of Judah, King
Rezin[o] of Aram[p] and Pekah[q] son of Remaliah king of Israel marched up to fight
against Jerusalem, but they could not
overpower it.
2Now the house of David[r] was told,
"Aram has allied itself with[l] Ephraim[s]";
so the hearts of Ahaz and his people
were shaken, as the trees of the forest
are shaken by the wind.

3Then the LORD said to Isaiah, "Go out,
you and your son Shear-Jashub,[m] to meet
Ahaz at the end of the aqueduct of the
Upper Pool, on the road to the Washerman's Field.[t] 4Say to him, 'Be careful,
keep calm[u] and don't be afraid.[v] Do not
lose heart[w] because of these two smoldering stubs[x] of firewood—because of
the fierce anger[y] of Rezin and Aram and
of the son of Remaliah. 5Aram, Ephraim and Remaliah's son have plotted your
ruin, saying, 6"Let us invade Judah; let us
tear it apart and divide it among ourselves, and make the son of Tabeel king
over it." 7Yet this is what the Sovereign
LORD says:

"'It will not take place,
it will not happen,[z]
8for the head of Aram is Damascus,[a]
and the head of Damascus is only
Rezin.
Within sixty-five years
Ephraim will be too shattered[b] to
be a people.
9The head of Ephraim is Samaria,
and the head of Samaria is only
Remaliah's son.
If you do not stand firm in your faith,[c]
you will not stand at all.'"[d]

A virgin will be with child.

10Again the LORD spoke to Ahaz, 11"Ask
the LORD your God for a sign, whether
in the deepest depths or in the highest
heights."
12But Ahaz said, "I will not ask; I will
not put the LORD to the test."
13Then Isaiah said, "Hear now, you
house of David! Is it not enough to try
the patience of men? Will you try the
patience of my God[e] also? 14Therefore
the Lord himself will give you[n] a sign:
The virgin will be with child and will
give birth to a son,[f] and[o] will call him

6:7 [a]Jer 1:9 [b]1Jn 1:7
6:8 [c]Ac 9:4
6:9 [d]Eze 3:11 [e]Mt 13:15*; Lk 8:10*
6:10 [f]Dt 32:15; Ps 119:70 [g]Jer 5:21 [h]Mt 13:13-15; Mk 4:12*; Ac 28:26-27*
6:11 [i]Ps 79:5 [j]Lev 26:31
6:12 [k]Dt 28:64 [l]Jer 4:29
6:13 [m]Isa 1:9 [n]Job 14:7
7:1 [o]2Ki 15:37 [p]2Ch 28:5 [q]2Ki 15:25
7:2 [r]ver 13; Isa 22:22 [s]Isa 9:9
7:3 [t]2Ki 18:17; Isa 36:2
7:4 [u]Isa 30:15 [v]Isa 35:4 [w]Dt 20:3 [x]Zec 3:2 [y]Isa 10:24
7:7 [z]Isa 8:10; Ac 4:25
7:8 [a]Ge 14:15 [b]Isa 17:1-3
7:9 [c]2Ch 20:20 [d]Isa 8:6-8; 30:12-14
7:13 [e]Isa 25:1
7:14 [f]Lk 1:31

[k] *9,10* Hebrew; Septuagint *'You will be ever hearing, but never understanding; / you will be ever seeing, but never perceiving.' / 10This people's heart has become calloused; / they hardly hear with their ears, / and they have closed their eyes* [l] *2* Or *has set up camp in* [m] *3* *Shear-Jashub* means *a remnant will return.* [n] *14* The Hebrew is plural. [o] *14* Masoretic Text; Dead Sea Scrolls *and he* or *and they*

Immanuel.[p][a] 15He will eat curds and
honey[b] when he knows enough to reject
the wrong and choose the right. 16But
before the boy knows[c] enough to reject
the wrong and choose the right, the
land of the two kings you dread will be
laid waste.[d] 17The LORD will bring on you
and on your people and on the house
of your father a time unlike any since
Ephraim broke away[e] from Judah—he
will bring the king of Assyria.[f]"

18In that day the LORD will whistle[g]
for flies from the distant streams of Egypt
and for bees from the land of Assyria.[h]
19They will all come and settle in the
steep ravines and in the crevices[i] in the
rocks, on all the thornbushes and at all
the water holes. 20In that day the Lord
will use[j] a razor hired from beyond the
River[q]—the king of Assyria[k]—to shave
your head and the hair of your legs, and
to take off your beards also. 21In that day,
a man will keep alive a young cow and
two goats. 22And because of the abundance of the milk they give, he will have
curds to eat. All who remain in the land
will eat curds and honey. 23In that day,
in every place where there were a thousand vines worth a thousand silver
shekels,[r] there will be only briers and
thorns.[l] 24Men will go there with bow
and arrow, for the land will be covered
with briers and thorns. 25As for all the
hills once cultivated by the hoe, you
will no longer go there for fear of the
briers and thorns; they will become
places where cattle are turned loose and
where sheep run.[m]

Assyria will subdue the land.

8 The LORD said to me, "Take a large
scroll[n] and write on it with an ordinary pen: Maher-Shalal-Hash-Baz.[s][o] 2And
I will call in Uriah[p] the priest and Zechariah son of Jeberekiah as reliable witnesses for me."

3Then I went to the prophetess, and
she conceived and gave birth to a son.
And the LORD said to me, "Name him
Maher-Shalal-Hash-Baz. 4Before the boy
knows[q] how to say 'My father' or 'My
mother,' the wealth of Damascus and the
plunder of Samaria will be carried off by
the king of Assyria.[r]"

5The LORD spoke to me again:

6"Because this people has rejected[s]
the gently flowing waters of Shiloah[t]
and rejoices over Rezin
and the son of Remaliah,[u]
7therefore the Lord is about to bring
against them
the mighty floodwaters[v] of the
River[q]—
the king of Assyria[w] with all his
pomp.
It will overflow all its channels,
run over all its banks
8and sweep on into Judah, swirling
over it,
passing through it and reaching up
to the neck.
Its outspread wings will cover the
breadth of your land,
O Immanuel[t]!"[x]

9Raise the war cry,[u][y] you nations, and
be shattered!
Listen, all you distant lands.
Prepare[z] for battle, and be shattered!
Prepare for battle, and be shattered!
10Devise your strategy, but it will be
thwarted;[a]
propose your plan, but it will not
stand,[b]
for God is with us.[v][c]

11The LORD spoke to me with his strong
hand upon me,[d] warning me not to follow[e] the way of this people. He said:

12"Do not call conspiracy[f]
everything that these people call
conspiracy[w];
do not fear what they fear,
and do not dread it.[g]
13The LORD Almighty is the one you
are to regard as holy,[h]

7:14 [a]Isa 8:8,10; Mt 1:23* **7:15** [b]ver 22 **7:16** [c]Isa 8:4 [d]Isa 17:3; Hos 5:9,13; Am 1:3-5 **7:17** [e]1Ki 12:16 [f]2Ch 28:20 **7:18** [g]Isa 5:26 [h]Isa 13:5 **7:19** [i]Isa 2:19 **7:20** [j]Isa 10:15 [k]Isa 8:7; 10:5 **7:23** [l]Isa 5:6 **7:25** [m]Isa 5:17 **8:1** [n]Isa 30:8; Hab 2:2 [o]ver 3; Hab 2:2 **8:2** [p]2Ki 16:10 **8:4** [q]Isa 7:16 [r]Isa 7:8 **8:6** [s]Isa 5:24 [t]Jn 9:7 [u]Isa 7:1 **8:7** [v]Isa 17:12-13 [w]Isa 7:20 **8:8** [x]Isa 7:14 **8:9** [y]Isa 17:12-13 [z]Joel 3:9 **8:10** [a]Job 5:12 [b]Isa 7:7 [c]Isa 7:14; Ro 8:31 **8:11** [d]Eze 3:14 [e]Eze 2:8 **8:12** [f]Isa 7:2; 30:1 [g]1Pe 3:14* **8:13** [h]Nu 20:12

p *14 Immanuel* means *God with us.* q *20, 7* That is, the Euphrates r *23* That is, about 25 pounds (about 11.5 kilograms) s *1 Maher-Shalal-Hash-Baz* means *quick to the plunder, swift to the spoil*; also in verse 3. t *8 Immanuel* means *God with us.* u *9* Or *Do your worst* v *10* Hebrew *Immanuel* w *12* Or *Do not call for a treaty / every time these people call for a treaty*

he is the one you are to fear,
he is the one you are to dread,[a]
14and he will be a sanctuary;[b]
but for both houses of Israel he will be
a stone that causes men to stumble
and a rock that makes them fall.[c]
And for the people of Jerusalem he will be
a trap and a snare.[d]
15Many of them will stumble;[e]
they will fall and be broken,
they will be snared and captured."

16Bind up the testimony
and seal[f] up the law among my disciples.
17I will wait[g] for the LORD,
who is hiding[h] his face from the house of Jacob.
I will put my trust in him.

18Here am I, and the children the LORD
has given me.[i] We are signs[j] and symbols
in Israel from the LORD Almighty, who
dwells on Mount Zion.[k]
19When men tell you to consult[l] mediums and spiritists, who whisper and mutter,[m] should not a people inquire of their
God? Why consult the dead on behalf of
the living? 20To the law[n] and to the testimony! If they do not speak according to
this word, they have no light[o] of dawn.
21Distressed and hungry, they will roam
through the land; when they are famished, they will become enraged and,
looking upward, will curse[p] their king
and their God. 22Then they will look toward the earth and see only distress and
darkness and fearful gloom, and they will
be thrust into utter darkness.[q]

The Prince of Peace is born.

9 Nevertheless, there will be no more gloom for those who were in distress. In the past he humbled the land of Zebulun and the land of Naphtali,[r] but in the future he will honor Galilee of the Gentiles, by the way of the sea, along the Jordan—

2The people walking in darkness
have seen a great light;[s]
on those living in the land of the shadow of death[x] [t]
a light has dawned.[u]
3You have enlarged the nation
and increased their joy;
they rejoice before you
as people rejoice at the harvest,
as men rejoice
when dividing the plunder.
4For as in the day of Midian's defeat,[v]
you have shattered
the yoke[w] that burdens them,
the bar across their shoulders,[x]
the rod of their oppressor.[y]
5Every warrior's boot used in battle
and every garment rolled in blood
will be destined for burning,[z]
will be fuel for the fire.
6For to us a child is born,[a]
to us a son is given,[b]
and the government[c] will be on his shoulders.
And he will be called
Wonderful Counselor,[y] [d] Mighty God,[e]
Everlasting Father, Prince of Peace.[f]
7Of the increase of his government and peace
there will be no end.[g]
He will reign on David's throne
and over his kingdom,
establishing and upholding it
with justice[h] and righteousness
from that time on and forever.
The zeal[i] of the LORD Almighty
will accomplish this.

Judgment against Israel.

8The Lord has sent a message against Jacob;
it will fall on Israel.
9All the people will know it—
Ephraim and the inhabitants of Samaria[j]—
who say with pride
and arrogance[k] of heart,
10"The bricks have fallen down,
but we will rebuild with dressed stone;

8:13 [a]Isa 29:23 **8:14** [b]Isa 4:6; Eze 11:16 [c]Lk 2:34; Ro 9:33*; 1Pe 2:8* [d]Isa 24:17-18 **8:15** [e]Isa 28:13; 59:10; Lk 20:18; Ro 9:32 **8:16** [f]Isa 29:11-12 **8:17** [g]Hab 2:3 [h]Dt 31:17; Isa 54:8 **8:18** [i]Heb 2:13* [j]Lk 2:34 [k]Ps 9:11 **8:19** [l]1Sa 28:8 [m]Isa 29:4 **8:20** [n]Isa 1:10; Lk 16:29 [o]Mic 3:6 **8:21** [p]Rev 16:11 **8:22** [q]ver 20; Isa 5:30 **9:1** [r]2Ki 15:29 **9:2** [s]Eph 5:8 [t]Lk 1:79 [u]Mt 4:15-16* **9:4** [v]Jdg 7:25 [w]Isa 14:25 [x]Isa 10:27 [y]Isa 14:4; 49:26; 51:13; 54:14 **9:5** [z]Isa 2:4 **9:6** [a]Isa 53:2; Lk 2:11 [b]Jn 3:16 [c]Mt 28:18 [d]Isa 28:29 [e]Isa 10:21; 11:2 [f]Isa 26:3,12; 66:12 **9:7** [g]Da 2:44; Lk 1:33 [h]Isa 11:4; 16:5; 32:1,16 [i]Isa 37:32; 59:17 **9:9** [j]Isa 7:9 [k]Isa 46:12

x2 Or *land of darkness* y6 Or *Wonderful, Counselor*

the fig trees have been felled,
but we will replace them with cedars."
11 But the LORD has strengthened Rezin's[a] foes against them
and has spurred their enemies on.
12 Arameans[b] from the east and Philistines[c] from the west
have devoured[d] Israel with open mouth.

Yet for all this, his anger is not turned away,
his hand is still upraised.[e]

13 But the people have not returned to him who struck[f] them,
nor have they sought[g] the LORD Almighty.
14 So the LORD will cut off from Israel both head and tail,
both palm branch and reed[h] in a single day;[i]
15 the elders[j] and prominent men are the head,
the prophets who teach lies are the tail.
16 Those who guide[k] this people mislead them,
and those who are guided are led astray.[l]
17 Therefore the Lord will take no pleasure in the young men,[m]
nor will he pity[n] the fatherless and widows,
for everyone is ungodly[o] and wicked,[p]
every mouth speaks vileness.[q]

Yet for all this, his anger is not turned away,
his hand is still upraised.[r]

18 Surely wickedness burns like a fire;[s]
it consumes briers and thorns,
it sets the forest thickets ablaze,[t]
so that it rolls upward in a column of smoke.
19 By the wrath[u] of the LORD Almighty
the land will be scorched
and the people will be fuel for the fire;[v]
no one will spare his brother.[w]
20 On the right they will devour,
but still be hungry;[x]
on the left they will eat,[y]
but not be satisfied.
Each will feed on the flesh of his own offspring[z]:
21 Manasseh will feed on Ephraim,
and Ephraim on Manasseh;
together they will turn against Judah.[z]

Yet for all this, his anger is not turned away,
his hand is still upraised.[a]

10 Woe to those who make unjust laws,
to those who issue oppressive decrees,[b]
2 to deprive[c] the poor of their rights
and withhold justice from the oppressed of my people,[d]
making widows their prey
and robbing the fatherless.
3 What will you do on the day of reckoning,[e]
when disaster[f] comes from afar?
To whom will you run for help?[g]
Where will you leave your riches?
4 Nothing will remain but to cringe among the captives[h]
or fall among the slain.[i]

Yet for all this, his anger is not turned away,[j]
his hand is still upraised.

Judgment against Assyria.

5 "Woe to the Assyrian,[k] the rod of my anger,
in whose hand is the club[l] of my wrath![m]
6 I send him against a godless[n] nation,
I dispatch him against a people who anger me,[o]
to seize loot and snatch plunder,[p]
and to trample them down like mud in the streets.
7 But this is not what he intends,[q]
this is not what he has in mind;
his purpose is to destroy,

9:11 [a]Isa 7:8 **9:12** [b]2Ki 16:6 [c]2Ch 28:18 [d]Ps 79:7 [e]Isa 5:25 **9:13** [f]Jer 5:3 [g]Isa 31:1; Hos 7:7,10 **9:14** [h]Isa 19:15 [i]Rev 18:8 **9:15** [j]Isa 3:2-3 **9:16** [k]Mt 15:14; 23:16,24 [l]Isa 3:12 **9:17** [m]Jer 18:21 [n]Isa 27:11 [o]Isa 10:6 [p]Isa 1:4 [q]Mt 12:34 [r]Isa 5:25 **9:18** [s]Mal 4:1 [t]Ps 83:14 **9:19** [u]Isa 13:9,13 [v]Isa 1:31 [w]Mic 7:2,6 **9:20** [x]Lev 26:26 [y]Isa 49:26 **9:21** [z]2Ch 28:6 [a]Isa 5:25 **10:1** [b]Ps 58:2 **10:2** [c]Isa 3:14 [d]Isa 5:23 **10:3** [e]Job 31:14; Hos 9:7 [f]Lk 19:44 [g]Isa 20:6 **10:4** [h]Isa 24:22 [i]Isa 22:2; 34:3; 66:16 [j]Isa 5:25 **10:5** [k]Isa 14:25; Zep 2:13 [l]Jer 51:20 [m]Isa 13:3,5, 13; 30:30; 66:14 **10:6** [n]Isa 9:17 [o]Isa 9:19 [p]Isa 5:29 **10:7** [q]Ge 50:20; Ac 4:23-28

z20 Or *arm*

to put an end to many nations.
8'Are not my commanders[a] all kings?'
he says.
9 'Has not Calno[b] fared like
Carchemish?[c]
Is not Hamath like Arpad,
and Samaria[d] like Damascus?[e]
10As my hand seized the kingdoms of
the idols,[f]
kingdoms whose images excelled
those of Jerusalem and
Samaria—
11shall I not deal with Jerusalem and
her images
as I dealt with Samaria and her
idols?'"

12When the Lord has finished all his
work[g] against Mount Zion[h] and Jerusalem, he will say, "I will punish the king
of Assyria[i] for the willful pride of his
heart and the haughty look in his eyes.
13For he says:

"'By the strength of my hand I have
done this,[j]
and by my wisdom, because I have
understanding.
I removed the boundaries of nations,
I plundered their treasures;[k]
like a mighty one I subdued[a] their
kings.
14As one reaches into a nest,[l]
so my hand reached for the wealth[m]
of the nations;
as men gather abandoned eggs,
so I gathered all the countries;
not one flapped a wing,
or opened its mouth to chirp.'"

15Does the ax raise itself above him
who swings it,
or the saw boast against him who
uses it?[n]
As if a rod were to wield him who
lifts it up,
or a club[o] brandish him who is
not wood!
16Therefore, the Lord, the LORD Almighty,
will send a wasting disease[p] upon
his sturdy warriors;
under his pomp[q] a fire will be kindled
like a blazing flame.

10:8 [a]2Ki 18:24
10:9 [b]Ge 10:10 [c]2Ch 35:20 [d]2Ki 17:6 [e]2Ki 16:9
10:10 [f]2Ki 19:18
10:12 [g]Isa 28:21-22; 65:7 [h]2Ki 19:31 [i]Jer 50:18
10:13 [j]Isa 37:24; Da 4:30 [k]Eze 28:4
10:14 [l]Jer 49:16; Ob 4 [m]Job 31:25
10:15 [n]Isa 45:9; Ro 9:20-21 [o]ver 5
10:16 [p]ver 18; Isa 17:4 [q]Isa 8:7
10:17 [r]Isa 31:9 [s]Isa 37:23 [t]Nu 11:1-3 [u]Isa 9:18
10:18 [v]2Ki 19:23
10:19 [w]Isa 21:17
10:20 [x]Isa 11:10,11 [y]2Ki 16:7 [z]2Ch 28:20 [a]Isa 17:7
10:21 [b]Isa 6:13 [c]Isa 9:6
10:22 [d]Ro 9:27-28 [e]Isa 28:22; Da 9:27
10:23 [f]Isa 28:22; Ro 9:27-28*
10:24 [g]Ps 87:5-6 [h]Ex 5:14
10:25 [i]Isa 17:14 [j]ver 5; Da 11:36
10:26 [k]Isa 37:36-38 [l]Isa 9:4

17The Light of Israel will become a fire,[r]
their Holy One[s] a flame;
in a single day it will burn and
consume
his thorns[t] and his briers.[u]
18The splendor of his forests[v] and
fertile fields
it will completely destroy,
as when a sick man wastes away.
19And the remaining trees of his
forests will be so few[w]
that a child could write them down.

A remnant of Israel will return.

20In that day[x] the remnant of Israel,
the survivors of the house of Jacob,
will no longer rely[y] on him
who struck them down[z]
but will truly rely[a] on the LORD,
the Holy One of Israel.
21A remnant[b] will return,[b] a remnant
of Jacob
will return to the Mighty God.[c]
22Though your people, O Israel, be like
the sand by the sea,
only a remnant will return.[d]
Destruction has been decreed,[e]
overwhelming and righteous.
23The Lord, the LORD Almighty, will
carry out
the destruction decreed upon the
whole land.[f]

24Therefore, this is what the Lord, the
LORD Almighty, says:

"O my people who live in Zion,[g]
do not be afraid of the Assyrians,
who beat[h] you with a rod
and lift up a club against you, as
Egypt did.
25Very soon[i] my anger against you
will end
and my wrath[j] will be directed to
their destruction."

26The LORD Almighty will lash[k] them
with a whip,
as when he struck down Midian[l]
at the rock of Oreb;

a *13* Or / *I subdued the mighty,*
b *21* Hebrew *shear-jashub*; also in verse 22

and he will raise his staff over the
waters,[a]
as he did in Egypt.
27In that day their burden will be lifted
from your shoulders,
their yoke[b] from your neck;[c]
the yoke will be broken
because you have grown so fat.[c]

28They enter Aiath;
they pass through Migron;[d]
they store supplies at Micmash.[e]
29They go over the pass, and say,
"We will camp overnight at Geba."
Ramah[f] trembles;
Gibeah of Saul flees.
30Cry out, O Daughter of Gallim![g]
Listen, O Laishah!
Poor Anathoth![h]
31Madmenah is in flight;
the people of Gebim take cover.
32This day they will halt at Nob;[i]
they will shake their fist
at the mount of the Daughter of Zion,[j]
at the hill of Jerusalem.

33See, the Lord, the LORD Almighty,
will lop off the boughs with great
power.
The lofty trees will be felled,
the tall[k] ones will be brought low.
34He will cut down the forest thickets
with an ax;
Lebanon will fall before the Mighty
One.

Branch from the roots of Jesse.

11 A shoot will come up from the
stump of Jesse;[l]
from his roots a Branch[m] will
bear fruit.
2The Spirit[n] of the LORD will rest
on him—
the Spirit of wisdom[o] and of
understanding,
the Spirit of counsel and of power,[p]
the Spirit of knowledge and of the
fear of the LORD—
3and he will delight in the fear of the
LORD.

He will not judge by what he sees
with his eyes,[q]
or decide by what he hears with
his ears;[r]
4but with righteousness[s] he will
judge the needy,
with justice[t] he will give decisions
for the poor[u] of the earth.
He will strike[v] the earth with the
rod of his mouth;
with the breath[w] of his lips he will
slay the wicked.
5Righteousness will be his belt
and faithfulness[x] the sash around
his waist.[y]

6The wolf will live with the lamb,[z]
the leopard will lie down with
the goat,
the calf and the lion and the
yearling[d] together;
and a little child will lead them.
7The cow will feed with the bear,
their young will lie down together,
and the lion will eat straw like the ox.
8The infant will play near the hole of
the cobra,
and the young child put his hand
into the viper's nest.
9They will neither harm nor destroy[a]
on all my holy mountain,
for the earth[b] will be full of the
knowledge[c] of the LORD
as the waters cover the sea.

Gathering of the remnant.

10In that day the Root of Jesse will
stand as a banner[d] for the peoples; the
nations[e] will rally to him,[f] and his place
of rest[g] will be glorious. 11In that day[h]
the Lord will reach out his hand a second time to reclaim the remnant that is
left of his people from Assyria,[i] from Lower Egypt, from Upper Egypt,[e] from Cush,[f]
from Elam,[j] from Babylonia,[g] from Hamath and from the islands[k] of the sea.

12He will raise a banner for the nations
and gather the exiles of Israel;
he will assemble the scattered
people[l] of Judah

10:26 [a]Ex 14:16
10:27 [b]Isa 9:4 [c]Isa 14:25
10:28 [d]1Sa 14:2 [e]1Sa 13:2
10:29 [f]Jos 18:25
10:30 [g]1Sa 25:44 [h]Ne 11:32
10:32 [i]1Sa 21:1 [j]Jer 6:23
10:33 [k]Am 2:9
11:1 [l]ver 10; Isa 9:7; Rev 5:5 [m]Isa 4:2
11:2 [n]Isa 42:1; 48:16; 61:1; Mt 3:16; Jn 1:32-33 [o]Eph 1:17 [p]2Ti 1:7
11:3 [q]Jn 7:24 [r]Jn 2:25
11:4 [s]Ps 72:2 [t]Isa 9:7 [u]Isa 3:14 [v]Mal 4:6 [w]Job 4:9; 2Th 2:8
11:5 [x]Isa 25:1 [y]Eph 6:14
11:6 [z]Isa 65:25
11:9 [a]Job 5:23 [b]Ps 98:2-3; Isa 52:10 [c]Isa 45:6,14; Hab 2:14
11:10 [d]Jn 12:32 [e]Isa 49:23; Lk 2:32 [f]Ro 15:12* [g]Isa 14:3; 28:12; 32:17-18
11:11 [h]Isa 10:20 [i]Isa 19:24; Hos 11:11; Mic 7:12; Zec 10:10 [j]Ge 10:22 [k]Isa 42:4,10,12; 66:19
11:12 [l]Zep 3:10

c*27* Hebrew; Septuagint *broken / from your shoulders* d*6* Hebrew; Septuagint *lion will feed* e*11* Hebrew *from Pathros* f*11* That is, the upper Nile region g*11* Hebrew *Shinar*

from the four quarters of the earth.
13 Ephraim's jealousy will vanish,
and Judah's enemies[h] will be cut off;
Ephraim will not be jealous of Judah,
nor Judah hostile toward Ephraim.[a]
14 They will swoop down on the slopes
of Philistia to the west;
together they will plunder the
people to the east.
They will lay hands on Edom[b] and
Moab,[c]
and the Ammonites will be subject
to them.
15 The LORD will dry up
the gulf of the Egyptian sea;
with a scorching wind he will sweep
his hand[d]
over the Euphrates River.[i][e]
He will break it up into seven streams
so that men can cross over in
sandals.
16 There will be a highway[f] for the
remnant of his people
that is left from Assyria,
as there was for Israel
when they came up from Egypt.[g]

Songs of praise to the LORD.

12 In that day you will say:

"I will praise[h] you, O LORD.
Although you were angry with me,
your anger has turned away
and you have comforted me.
2 Surely God is my salvation;
I will trust[i] and not be afraid.
The LORD, the LORD, is my strength
and my song;
he has become my salvation.[j]"
3 With joy you will draw water[k]
from the wells of salvation.

4 In that day you will say:

"Give thanks to the LORD, call on
his name;[l]
make known among the nations
what he has done,
and proclaim that his name is
exalted.
5 Sing[m] to the LORD, for he has done
glorious things;[n]
let this be known to all the world.
6 Shout aloud and sing for joy, people
of Zion,
for great is the Holy One of Israel[o]
among you.[p]"

Isaiah's prophecy against Babylon.

13 An oracle concerning Babylon that Isaiah son of Amoz saw:

2 Raise a banner[q] on a bare hilltop,
shout to them;
beckon to them
to enter the gates of the nobles.
3 I have commanded my holy ones;
I have summoned my warriors[r] to
carry out my wrath—
those who rejoice[s] in my triumph.

4 Listen, a noise on the mountains,
like that of a great multitude![t]
Listen, an uproar among the
kingdoms,
like nations massing together!
The LORD Almighty is mustering
an army for war.
5 They come from faraway lands,
from the ends of the heavens[u]—
the LORD and the weapons of his
wrath—
to destroy[v] the whole country.

6 Wail,[w] for the day[x] of the LORD is near;
it will come like destruction from
the Almighty.[j]
7 Because of this, all hands will go limp,
every man's heart will melt.[y]
8 Terror[z] will seize them,
pain and anguish will grip them;
they will writhe like a woman
in labor.
They will look aghast at each other,
their faces aflame.[a]

9 See, the day of the LORD is coming
—a cruel day, with wrath and
fierce anger—
to make the land desolate
and destroy the sinners within it.
10 The stars of heaven and their
constellations
will not show their light.

11:13 [a]Jer 3:18; Eze 37:16-17, 22; Hos 1:11
11:14 [b]Da 11:41; Joel 3:19 [c]Isa 16:14; 25:10
11:15 [d]Isa 19:16 [e]Isa 7:20
11:16 [f]Isa 19:23; 62:10 [g]Ex 14:26-31
12:1 [h]Isa 25:1
12:2 [i]Isa 26:3 [j]Ex 15:2; Ps 118:14
12:3 [k]Jn 4:10,14
12:4 [l]Ps 105:1; Isa 24:15
12:5 [m]Ex 15:1 [n]Ps 98:1
12:6 [o]Isa 49:26 [p]Zep 3:14-17
13:2 [q]Jer 50:2; 51:27
13:3 [r]Joel 3:11 [s]Ps 149:2
13:4 [t]Joel 3:14
13:5 [u]Isa 5:26 [v]Isa 24:1
13:6 [w]Eze 30:2 [x]Isa 2:12; Joel 1:15
13:7 [y]Eze 21:7
13:8 [z]Isa 21:4 [a]Na 2:10

h 13 Or *hostility* i 15 Hebrew *the River*
j 6 Hebrew *Shaddai*

The rising sun[a] will be darkened[b]
and the moon will not give its light.[c]
11I will punish[d] the world for its evil,
the wicked for their sins.
I will put an end to the arrogance of the haughty
and will humble the pride of the ruthless.
12I will make man[e] scarcer than pure gold,
more rare than the gold of Ophir.
13Therefore I will make the heavens tremble;[f]
and the earth will shake from its place
at the wrath of the LORD Almighty,
in the day of his burning anger.

14Like a hunted gazelle,
like sheep without a shepherd,[g]
each will return to his own people,
each will flee to his native land.[h]
15Whoever is captured will be thrust through;
all who are caught will fall[i] by the sword.[j]
16Their infants[k] will be dashed to pieces before their eyes;
their houses will be looted and their wives ravished.

17See, I will stir up[l] against them the Medes,
who do not care for silver
and have no delight in gold.[m]
18Their bows will strike down the young men;
they will have no mercy on infants
nor will they look with compassion on children.
19Babylon, the jewel of kingdoms,
the glory[n] of the Babylonians'[k] pride,
will be overthrown[o] by God
like Sodom and Gomorrah.[p]
20She will never be inhabited[q]
or lived in through all generations;
no Arab[r] will pitch his tent there,
no shepherd will rest his flocks there.
21But desert creatures[s] will lie there,
jackals will fill her houses;
there the owls will dwell,
and there the wild goats will leap about.
22Hyenas will howl in her strongholds,[t]
jackals[u] in her luxurious palaces.
Her time is at hand,[v]
and her days will not be prolonged.

Restoration of Israel.

14 The LORD will have compassion[w] on Jacob;
once again he will choose[x] Israel
and will settle them in their own land.
Aliens[y] will join them
and unite with the house of Jacob.
2Nations will take them
and bring[z] them to their own place.
And the house of Israel will possess the nations[a]
as menservants and maidservants in the LORD's land.
They will make captives of their captors
and rule over their oppressors.[b]

3On the day the LORD gives you relief[c]
from suffering and turmoil and cruel
bondage, 4you will take up this taunt[d]
against the king of Babylon:

How the oppressor[e] has come to an end!
How his fury[l] has ended!
5The LORD has broken the rod of the wicked,[f]
the scepter of the rulers,
6which in anger struck down peoples[g]
with unceasing blows,
and in fury subdued nations
with relentless aggression.[h]
7All the lands are at rest and at peace;
they break into singing.[i]
8Even the pine trees[j] and the cedars of Lebanon
exult over you and say,
"Now that you have been laid low,
no woodsman comes to cut us down."

9The grave[m] [k] below is all astir
to meet you at your coming;

13:10 [a]Isa 24:23 [b]Isa 5:30; Rev 8:12 [c]Eze 32:7; Mt 24:29*; Mk 13:24* **13:11** [d]Isa 3:11; 11:4; 26:21 **13:12** [e]Isa 4:1 **13:13** [f]Isa 34:4; 51:6; Hag 2:6 **13:14** [g]1Ki 22:17 [h]Jer 50:16 **13:15** [i]Jer 51:4 [j]Isa 14:19; Jer 50:25 **13:16** [k]Ps 137:9 **13:17** [l]Jer 51:1 [m]Pr 6:34-35 **13:19** [n]Da 4:30 [o]Rev 14:8 [p]Ge 19:24 **13:20** [q]Isa 14:23; 34:10-15 [r]2Ch 17:11 **13:21** [s]Rev 18:2 **13:22** [t]Isa 25:2 [u]Isa 34:13 [v]Jer 51:33 **14:1** [w]Ps 102:13; Isa 49:10,13; 54:7-8,10 [x]Isa 41:8; 44:1; 49:7; Zec 1:17; 2:12 [y]Eph 2:12-19 **14:2** [z]Isa 60:9 [a]Isa 49:7,23 [b]Isa 60:14; 61:5 **14:3** [c]Isa 11:10 **14:4** [d]Hab 2:6 [e]Isa 9:4 **14:5** [f]Ps 125:3 **14:6** [g]Isa 10:14 [h]Isa 47:6 **14:7** [i]Ps 98:1; 126:1-3 **14:8** [j]Eze 31:16 **14:9** [k]Eze 32:21

[k]19 Or *Chaldeans'* [l]4 Dead Sea Scrolls, Septuagint and Syriac; the meaning of the word in the Masoretic Text is uncertain. [m]9 Hebrew *Sheol*; also in verses 11 and 15

it rouses the spirits of the departed
to greet you—
all those who were leaders in
the world;
it makes them rise from their
thrones—
all those who were kings over the
nations.
10They will all respond,
they will say to you,
"You also have become weak, as we are;
you have become like us."[a]
11All your pomp has been brought down
to the grave,
along with the noise of your harps;
maggots are spread out beneath you
and worms[b] cover you.

Fall from heaven.

12How you have fallen[c] from heaven,
O morning star,[d] son of the dawn!
You have been cast down to the earth,
you who once laid low the nations!
13You said in your heart,
"I will ascend[e] to heaven;
I will raise my throne[f]
above the stars of God;
I will sit enthroned on the mount of
assembly,
on the utmost heights of the sacred
mountain.[n]
14I will ascend above the tops of
the clouds;
I will make myself like the Most
High."[g]
15But you are brought down to the grave,
to the depths[h] of the pit.

16Those who see you stare at you,
they ponder your fate:[i]
"Is this the man who shook the earth
and made kingdoms tremble,
17the man who made the world
a desert,[j]
who overthrew its cities
and would not let his captives
go home?"

18All the kings of the nations lie in state,
each in his own tomb.
19But you are cast out[k] of your tomb
like a rejected branch;

14:10 [a]Eze 32:21
14:11 [b]Isa 51:8
14:12 [c]Isa 34:4; Lk 10:18 [d]2Pe 1:19; Rev 2:28; 8:10; 9:1
14:13 [e]Da 5:23; 8:10; Mt 11:23 [f]Eze 28:2; 2Th 2:4
14:14 [g]Isa 47:8; 2Th 2:4
14:15 [h]Mt 11:23; Lk 10:15
14:16 [i]Jer 50:23
14:17 [j]Joel 2:3
14:19 [k]Isa 22:16-18 [l]Jer 41:7-9
14:20 [m]Job 18:19 [n]Isa 1:4 [o]Ps 21:10
14:21 [p]Ex 20:5; Lev 26:39
14:22 [q]1Ki 14:10; Job 18:19
14:23 [r]Isa 34:11-15; Zep 2:14
14:24 [s]Isa 45:23 [t]Ac 4:28
14:25 [u]Isa 10:5,12 [v]Isa 9:4 [w]Isa 10:27
14:26 [x]Isa 23:9 [y]Ex 15:12
14:27 [z]2Ch 20:6; Isa 43:13; Da 4:35

you are covered with the slain,
with those pierced by the sword,
those who descend to the stones of
the pit.[l]
Like a corpse trampled underfoot,
20 you will not join them in burial,
for you have destroyed your land
and killed your people.

The offspring[m] of the wicked[n]
will never be mentioned[o] again.
21Prepare a place to slaughter his sons
for the sins of their forefathers;[p]
they are not to rise to inherit the land
and cover the earth with their cities.

Judgment against Babylon.

22"I will rise up against them,"
declares the LORD Almighty.
"I will cut off from Babylon her
name and survivors,
her offspring and descendants,[q]"
declares the LORD.
23"I will turn her into a place for owls[r]
and into swampland;
I will sweep her with the broom of
destruction,"
declares the LORD Almighty.

Judgment against Assyria.

24The LORD Almighty has sworn,[s]

"Surely, as I have planned, so it will be,
and as I have purposed, so it will
stand.[t]
25I will crush the Assyrian[u] in my land;
on my mountains I will trample
him down.
His yoke[v] will be taken from my
people,
and his burden removed from their
shoulders.[w]"

26This is the plan[x] determined for the
whole world;
this is the hand[y] stretched out
over all nations.
27For the LORD Almighty has purposed,
and who can thwart him?
His hand is stretched out, and who
can turn it back?[z]

[n]*13* Or *the north*; Hebrew *Zaphon*

Judgment against Philistia.

28This oracle[a] came in the year King
Ahaz[b] died:

29Do not rejoice, all you Philistines,[c]
that the rod that struck you is broken;
from the root of that snake will
spring up a viper,[d]
its fruit will be a darting,
venomous serpent.
30The poorest of the poor will find
pasture,
and the needy[e] will lie down
in safety.[f]
But your root I will destroy by
famine;[g]
it will slay[h] your survivors.

31Wail, O gate![i] Howl, O city!
Melt away, all you Philistines!
A cloud of smoke comes from the
north,[j]
and there is not a straggler in its
ranks.
32What answer shall be given
to the envoys[k] of that nation?
"The LORD has established Zion,[l]
and in her his afflicted people will
find refuge.[m]"

Judgment against Moab.

15 An oracle concerning Moab:[n]

Ar in Moab is ruined,[o]
destroyed in a night!
Kir in Moab is ruined,
destroyed in a night!
2Dibon goes up to its temple,
to its high places[p] to weep;
Moab wails over Nebo and Medeba.
Every head is shaved[q]
and every beard cut off.
3In the streets they wear sackcloth;
on the roofs and in the public
squares[r]
they all wail,
prostrate with weeping.[s]
4Heshbon and Elealeh[t] cry out,
their voices are heard all the way
to Jahaz.
Therefore the armed men of Moab
cry out,
and their hearts are faint.

5My heart cries out over Moab;[u]
her fugitives flee as far as Zoar,
as far as Eglath Shelishiyah.
They go up the way to Luhith,
weeping as they go;
on the road to Horonaim[v]
they lament their destruction.[w]
6The waters of Nimrim are dried up[x]
and the grass is withered;[y]
the vegetation is gone
and nothing green is left.
7So the wealth they have acquired[z]
and stored up
they carry away over the Ravine of
the Poplars.
8Their outcry echoes along the border
of Moab;
their wailing reaches as far as
Eglaim,
their lamentation as far as Beer Elim.
9Dimon's[o] waters are full of blood,
but I will bring still more upon
Dimon[o]—
a lion[a] upon the fugitives of Moab
and upon those who remain in
the land.

16 Send lambs[b] as tribute
to the ruler of the land,
from Sela,[c] across the desert,
to the mount of the Daughter of
Zion.[d]
2Like fluttering birds
pushed from the nest,[e]
so are the women of Moab
at the fords of the Arnon.[f]

3"Give us counsel,
render a decision.
Make your shadow like night—
at high noon.
Hide the fugitives,[g]
do not betray the refugees.
4Let the Moabite fugitives stay with you;
be their shelter from the destroyer."

The oppressor[h] will come to an end,
and destruction will cease;
the aggressor will vanish from
the land.

o9 Masoretic Text; Dead Sea Scrolls, some Septuagint manuscripts and Vulgate *Dibon*

14:28 [a]Isa 13:1 [b]2Ki 16:20
14:29 [c]2Ch 26:6 [d]Isa 11:8
14:30 [e]Isa 3:15 [f]Isa 7:21-22 [g]Isa 8:21; 9:20; 51:19 [h]Jer 25:16
14:31 [i]Isa 3:26 [j]Jer 1:14
14:32 [k]Isa 37:9 [l]Ps 87:2,5; Isa 44:28; 54:11 [m]Isa 4:6; Jas 2:5
15:1 [n]Isa 11:14 [o]Jer 48:24,41
15:2 [p]Jer 48:35 [q]Lev 21:5
15:3 [r]Jer 48:38 [s]Isa 22:4
15:4 [t]Nu 32:3
15:5 [u]Jer 48:31 [v]Jer 48:3,34 [w]Jer 4:20; 48:5
15:6 [x]Isa 19:5-7; Jer 48:34 [y]Joel 1:12
15:7 [z]Isa 30:6; Jer 48:36
15:9 [a]2Ki 17:25
16:1 [b]2Ki 3:4 [c]2Ki 14:7 [d]Isa 10:32
16:2 [e]Pr 27:8 [f]Nu 21:13-14; Jer 48:20
16:3 [g]1Ki 18:4
16:4 [h]Isa 9:4

5In love a throne[a] will be established;
in faithfulness a man will sit on it—
one from the house[p] of David[b]—
one who in judging seeks justice[c]
and speeds the cause of
righteousness.

Moab's pride.

16:6-12pp—Jer 48:29-36

6We have heard of Moab's[d] pride[e]—
her overweening pride and conceit,
her pride and her insolence—
but her boasts are empty.
7Therefore the Moabites wail,[f]
they wail together for Moab.
Lament and grieve
for the men[q][g] of Kir Hareseth.[h]
8The fields of Heshbon wither,
the vines of Sibmah also.
The rulers of the nations
have trampled down the
choicest vines,
which once reached Jazer
and spread toward the desert.
Their shoots spread out
and went as far as the sea.
9So I weep,[i] as Jazer weeps,
for the vines of Sibmah.
O Heshbon, O Elealeh,
I drench you with tears!
The shouts of joy over your ripened
fruit
and over your harvests[j] have been
stilled.
10Joy and gladness are taken away
from the orchards;[k]
no one sings or shouts in the
vineyards;
no one treads[l] out wine at the
presses,[m]
for I have put an end to the shouting.
11My heart laments for Moab[n] like
a harp,
my inmost being[o] for Kir Hareseth.
12When Moab appears at her high place,
she only wears herself out;
when she goes to her shrine[p] to pray,
it is to no avail.[q]

13This is the word the LORD has already spoken concerning Moab. 14But
now the LORD says: "Within three years,
as a servant bound by contract would
count them, Moab's splendor and all her
many people will be despised,[r] and her
survivors will be very few and feeble."[s]

Prophecy against Damascus.

17 An oracle concerning Damascus:[t]

"See, Damascus will no longer be a city
but will become a heap of ruins.[u]
2The cities of Aroer will be deserted
and left to flocks,[v] which will lie
down,
with no one to make them afraid.[w]
3The fortified city will disappear from
Ephraim,
and royal power from Damascus;
the remnant of Aram will be
like the glory[x] of the Israelites,"[y]
declares the LORD Almighty.

4"In that day the glory of Jacob will fade;
the fat of his body will waste[z] away.
5It will be as when a reaper gathers
the standing grain
and harvests[a] the grain with
his arm—
as when a man gleans heads of grain
in the Valley of Rephaim.
6Yet some gleanings will remain,[b]
as when an olive tree is beaten,[c]
leaving two or three olives on the
topmost branches,
four or five on the fruitful boughs,"
declares the LORD, the
God of Israel.

7In that day men will look[d] to their
Maker
and turn their eyes to the Holy
One[e] of Israel.
8They will not look to the altars,
the work of their hands,[f]
and they will have no regard for the
Asherah poles[r]
and the incense altars their fingers
have made.

16:5 [a]Da 7:14; Mic 4:7 [b]Lk 1:32 [c]Isa 9:7
16:6 [d]Am 2:1; Zep 2:8 [e]Ob 3; Zep 2:10
16:7 [f]Jer 48:20 [g]1Ch 16:3 [h]2Ki 3:25
16:9 [i]Isa 15:3 [j]Jer 40:12
16:10 [k]Isa 24:7-8 [l]Jdg 9:27 [m]Job 24:11
16:11 [n]Isa 15:5 [o]Isa 63:15; Hos 11:8; Php 2:1
16:12 [p]Isa 15:2 [q]1Ki 18:29
16:14 [r]Isa 25:10; Jer 48:42 [s]Isa 21:17
17:1 [t]Ge 14:15; Jer 49:23; Ac 9:2 [u]Isa 25:2; Am 1:3; Zec 9:1
17:2 [v]Isa 7:21; Eze 25:5 [w]Jer 7:33; Mic 4:4
17:3 [x]ver 4; Hos 9:11 [y]Isa 7:8,16; 8:4
17:4 [z]Isa 10:16
17:5 [a]ver 11; Jer 51:33; Joel 3:13; Mt 13:30
17:6 [b]Dt 4:27; Isa 24:13 [c]Isa 27:12
17:7 [d]Isa 10:20 [e]Mic 7:7
17:8 [f]Isa 2:18,20; 30:22

p5 Hebrew *tent* q7 Or "*raisin cakes*," a wordplay
r8 That is, symbols of the goddess Asherah

[9]In that day their strong cities, which they left because of the Israelites, will be like places abandoned to thickets and undergrowth. And all will be desolation.

[10]You have forgotten[a] God your Savior;[b]
you have not remembered the
Rock, your fortress.
Therefore, though you set out the
finest plants
and plant imported vines,
[11]though on the day you set them out,
you make them grow,
and on the morning[c] when you plant
them, you bring them to bud,
yet the harvest will be as nothing[d]
in the day of disease and
incurable pain.[e]

[12]Oh, the raging of many nations—
they rage like the raging sea![f]
Oh, the uproar of the peoples—
they roar like the roaring of great
waters!
[13]Although the peoples roar like the
roar of surging waters,
when he rebukes[g] them they flee[h]
far away,
driven before the wind like chaff[i]
on the hills,
like tumbleweed before a gale.[j]
[14]In the evening, sudden terror!
Before the morning, they are gone![k]
This is the portion of those who
loot us,
the lot of those who plunder us.

Prophecy against Cush.

18 Woe to the land of whirring
wings[s]
along the rivers of Cush,[t][l]
[2]which sends envoys by sea
in papyrus[m] boats over the water.

Go, swift messengers,
to a people tall and smooth-skinned,
to a people feared far and wide,
an aggressive[n] nation of strange
speech,
whose land is divided by rivers.[o]

[3]All you people of the world,
you who live on the earth,
when a banner[p] is raised on the
mountains,
you will see it,
and when a trumpet sounds,
you will hear it.
[4]This is what the LORD says to me:
"I will remain quiet and will look
on from my dwelling place,[q]
like shimmering heat in the sunshine,
like a cloud of dew[r] in the heat
of harvest."
[5]For, before the harvest, when the
blossom is gone
and the flower becomes a ripening
grape,
he will cut off the shoots with
pruning knives,
and cut down and take away the
spreading branches.[s]
[6]They will all be left to the mountain
birds of prey
and to the wild animals;[t]
the birds will feed on them all summer,
the wild animals all winter.

[7]At that time gifts will be brought to
the LORD Almighty

from a people tall and smooth-skinned,
from a people feared far and wide,
an aggressive nation of strange speech,
whose land is divided by rivers—

the gifts will be brought to Mount Zion,
the place of the Name of the LORD Almighty.[u]

Prophecy against Egypt.

19 An oracle[v] concerning Egypt:[w][x]

See, the LORD rides on a swift
cloud[y]
and is coming to Egypt.
The idols of Egypt tremble before him,
and the hearts of the Egyptians
melt[z] within them.

[2]"I will stir up Egyptian against
Egyptian—
brother will fight against brother,[a]
neighbor against neighbor,
city against city,
kingdom against kingdom.[b]

17:10 [a]Isa 51:13 [b]Ps 68:19; Isa 12:2
17:11 [c]Ps 90:6 [d]Hos 8:7 [e]Job 4:8
17:12 [f]Ps 18:4; Jer 6:23; Lk 21:25
17:13 [g]Ps 9:5 [h]Isa 13:14 [i]Isa 41:2, 15-16 [j]Job 21:18
17:14 [k]2Ki 19:35
18:1 [l]Isa 20:3-5; Eze 30:4-5,9; Zep 2:12; 3:10
18:2 [m]Ex 2:3 [n]Ge 10:8-9; 2Ch 12:3 [o]ver 7
18:3 [p]Isa 5:26
18:4 [q]Isa 26:21; Hos 5:15 [r]Isa 26:19; Hos 14:5
18:5 [s]Isa 17:10-11; Eze 17:6
18:6 [t]Isa 56:9; Jer 7:33; Eze 32:4; 39:17
18:7 [u]Ps 68:31
19:1 [v]Isa 13:1; Jer 43:12 [w]Joel 3:19 [x]Ex 12:12 [y]Ps 18:10; 104:3; Rev 1:7 [z]Jos 2:11
19:2 [a]Jdg 7:22; Mt 10:21,36 [b]2Ch 20:23

[s]1 Or *of locusts* [t]1 That is, the upper Nile region

3The Egyptians will lose heart,
and I will bring their plans to nothing;
they will consult the idols and the spirits of the dead,
the mediums and the spiritists.[a]
4I will hand the Egyptians over
to the power of a cruel master,
and a fierce king[b] will rule over them,"
declares the Lord, the LORD Almighty.

5The waters of the river will dry up,[c]
and the riverbed will be parched and dry.
6The canals will stink;[d]
the streams of Egypt will dwindle and dry up.[e]
The reeds and rushes will wither,[f]
7 also the plants along the Nile,
at the mouth of the river.
Every sown field[g] along the Nile
will become parched, will blow away and be no more.
8The fishermen[h] will groan and lament,
all who cast hooks[i] into the Nile;
those who throw nets on the water
will pine away.
9Those who work with combed flax
will despair,
the weavers of fine linen[j] will lose hope.
10The workers in cloth will be dejected,
and all the wage earners will be sick at heart.

11The officials of Zoan[k] are nothing but fools;
the wise counselors of Pharaoh
give senseless advice.
How can you say to Pharaoh,
"I am one of the wise men,[l]
a disciple of the ancient kings"?

12Where are your wise men[m] now?
Let them show you and make known
what the LORD Almighty
has planned[n] against Egypt.
13The officials of Zoan have become fools,
the leaders of Memphis[u][o] are deceived;
the cornerstones of her peoples
have led Egypt astray.
14The LORD has poured into them
a spirit of dizziness;[p]
they make Egypt stagger in all that she does,
as a drunkard staggers around in his vomit.
15There is nothing Egypt can do—
head or tail, palm branch or reed.[q]

16In that day the Egyptians will be like
women.[r] They will shudder with fear[s]
at the uplifted hand[t] that the LORD
Almighty raises against them. 17And the
land of Judah will bring terror to the
Egyptians; everyone to whom Judah is
mentioned will be terrified, because of
what the LORD Almighty is planning[u]
against them.
18In that day five cities in Egypt will
speak the language of Canaan and swear
allegiance[v] to the LORD Almighty. One
of them will be called the City of Destruction.[v]
19In that day there will be an altar[w]
to the LORD in the heart of Egypt, and
a monument[x] to the LORD at its border.
20It will be a sign and witness to the
LORD Almighty in the land of Egypt.
When they cry out to the LORD because
of their oppressors, he will send them a
savior and defender, and he will rescue[y]
them. 21So the LORD will make himself
known to the Egyptians, and in that day
they will acknowledge[z] the LORD. They
will worship[a] with sacrifices and grain
offerings; they will make vows to the
LORD and keep them. 22The LORD will
strike[b] Egypt with a plague; he will strike
them and heal them. They will turn[c] to
the LORD, and he will respond to their
pleas and heal[d] them.
23In that day there will be a highway[e]
from Egypt to Assyria. The Assyrians will
go to Egypt and the Egyptians to Assyria.
The Egyptians and Assyrians will worship[f] together. 24In that day Israel will be
the third, along with Egypt and Assyria,
a blessing on the earth. 25The LORD Almighty will bless them, saying, "Blessed

19:3 [a]Isa 8:19; 47:13; Da 2:2,10
19:4 [b]Isa 20:4; Jer 46:26; Eze 29:19
19:5 [c]Jer 51:36
19:6 [d]Ex 7:18 [e]Isa 37:25; Eze 30:12 [f]Isa 15:6
19:7 [g]Isa 23:3
19:8 [h]Eze 47:10 [i]Hab 1:15
19:9 [j]Pr 7:16; Eze 27:7
19:11 [k]Nu 13:22 [l]1Ki 4:30; Ac 7:22
19:12 [m]1Co 1:20 [n]Isa 14:24; Ro 9:17
19:13 [o]Jer 2:16; Eze 30:13,16
19:14 [p]Mt 17:17
19:15 [q]Isa 9:14
19:16 [r]Jer 51:30; Na 3:13 [s]Heb 10:31 [t]Isa 11:15
19:17 [u]Isa 14:24
19:18 [v]Zep 3:9
19:19 [w]Jos 22:10 [x]Ge 28:18
19:20 [y]Isa 49:24-26
19:21 [z]Isa 11:9 [a]Isa 56:7; Mal 1:11
19:22 [b]Heb 12:11 [c]Isa 45:14; Hos 14:1 [d]Dt 32:39
19:23 [e]Isa 11:16 [f]Isa 27:13

u *13* Hebrew *Noph* v *18* Most manuscripts of the Masoretic Text; some manuscripts of the Masoretic Text, Dead Sea Scrolls and Vulgate *City of the Sun* (that is, Heliopolis)

be Egypt my people,[a] Assyria my hand-
iwork,[b] and Israel my inheritance.[c]"

Isaiah goes stripped and barefoot.

20 In the year that the supreme
commander,[d] sent by Sargon king
of Assyria, came to Ashdod and attacked
and captured it— ²at that time the LORD
spoke through Isaiah son of Amoz.[e] He
said to him, "Take off the sackcloth[f] from
your body and the sandals[g] from your
feet." And he did so, going around
stripped[h] and barefoot.[i]
³Then the LORD said, "Just as my servant Isaiah has gone stripped and barefoot for three years, as a sign[j] and
portent against Egypt and Cush,[w][k] ⁴so
the king[l] of Assyria will lead away
stripped and barefoot the Egyptian captives and Cushite exiles, young and old,
with buttocks bared—to Egypt's shame.[m]
⁵Those who trusted in Cush and boasted in Egypt[n] will be afraid and put to
shame. ⁶In that day the people who live
on this coast will say, 'See what has happened to those we relied on, those we
fled to for help[o] and deliverance from
the king of Assyria! How then can we
escape?[p] '"

Prophecy against Babylon.

21 An oracle concerning the Desert[q] by the Sea:

Like whirlwinds sweeping through
the southland,[r]
an invader comes from the desert,
from a land of terror.

²A dire[s] vision has been shown to me:
The traitor betrays,[t] the looter
takes loot.
Elam,[u] attack! Media, lay siege!
I will bring to an end all the
groaning she caused.

³At this my body is racked with pain,
pangs seize me, like those of a
woman in labor;[v]
I am staggered by what I hear,
I am bewildered by what I see.
⁴My heart falters,
fear makes me tremble;

19:25 [a]Ps 100:3 [b]Isa 29:23; 45:11; 60:21; 64:8; Eph 2:10 [c]Hos 2:23
20:1 [d]2Ki 18:17
20:2 [e]Isa 13:1 [f]Zec 13:4; Mt 3:4 [g]Eze 24:17,23 [h]1Sa 19:24 [i]Mic 1:8
20:3 [j]Isa 8:18 [k]Isa 37:9; 43:3
20:4 [l]Isa 19:4 [m]Isa 47:3; Jer 13:22,26
20:5 [n]2Ki 18:21; Isa 30:5
20:6 [o]Isa 10:3 [p]Jer 30:15-17; Mt 23:33; 1Th 5:3; Heb 2:3
21:1 [q]Isa 13:21; Jer 51:43 [r]Zec 9:14
21:2 [s]Ps 60:3 [t]Isa 33:1 [u]Isa 22:6; Jer 49:34
21:3 [v]Ps 48:6; Isa 26:17
21:5 [w]Jer 51:39,57; Da 5:2
21:7 [x]ver 9
21:8 [y]Hab 2:1
21:9 [z]Rev 14:8 [a]Jer 51:8; Rev 18:2 [b]Isa 46:1; Jer 50:2; 51:44
21:10 [c]Jer 51:33
21:11 [d]Ge 25:14 [e]Ge 32:3

the twilight I longed for
has become a horror to me.

⁵They set the tables,
they spread the rugs,
they eat, they drink![w]
Get up, you officers,
oil the shields!

⁶This is what the Lord says to me:

"Go, post a lookout
and have him report what he sees.
⁷When he sees chariots[x]
with teams of horses,
riders on donkeys
or riders on camels,
let him be alert,
fully alert."

⁸And the lookout[x][y] shouted,

"Day after day, my lord, I stand on
the watchtower;
every night I stay at my post.
⁹Look, here comes a man in a chariot
with a team of horses.
And he gives back the answer:
'Babylon[z] has fallen,[a] has fallen!
All the images of its gods[b]
lie shattered on the ground!'"

¹⁰O my people, crushed on the
threshing floor,[c]
I tell you what I have heard
from the LORD Almighty,
from the God of Israel.

Prophecy against Edom.

¹¹An oracle concerning Dumah[y]:[d]

Someone calls to me from Seir,[e]
"Watchman, what is left of the night?
Watchman, what is left of the
night?"
¹²The watchman replies,
"Morning is coming, but also
the night.
If you would ask, then ask;
and come back yet again."

w *3* That is, the upper Nile region; also in verse 5
x *8* Dead Sea Scrolls and Syriac; Masoretic Text *A lion*
y *11* *Dumah* means *silence* or *stillness*, a wordplay on *Edom*.

Prophecy against Arabia.

13 An oracle[a] concerning Arabia:

You caravans of Dedanites,
who camp in the thickets of Arabia,
14 bring water for the thirsty;
you who live in Tema,[b]
bring food for the fugitives.
15 They flee[c] from the sword,
from the drawn sword,
from the bent bow
and from the heat of battle.

16 This is what the Lord says to me:
"Within one year, as a servant bound by
contract[d] would count it, all the pomp[e]
of Kedar[f] will come to an end. 17 The
survivors of the bowmen, the warriors
of Kedar, will be few.[g]" The LORD, the
God of Israel, has spoken.

Prophecy against Jerusalem.

22 An oracle[h] concerning the Valley[i] of Vision:

What troubles you now,
that you have all gone up on
the roofs,
2 O town full of commotion,
O city of tumult and revelry?[j]
Your slain were not killed by the
sword,
nor did they die in battle.
3 All your leaders have fled together;
they have been captured without
using the bow.
All you who were caught were taken
prisoner together,
having fled while the enemy was
still far away.
4 Therefore I said, "Turn away from me;
let me weep[k] bitterly.
Do not try to console me
over the destruction of my people."[l]

5 The Lord, the LORD Almighty, has a day
of tumult and trampling and terror[m]
in the Valley of Vision,
a day of battering down walls
and of crying out to the mountains.
6 Elam[n] takes up the quiver,[o]
with her charioteers and horses;
Kir[p] uncovers the shield.
7 Your choicest valleys are full of chariots,
and horsemen are posted at the
city gates;[q]
8 the defenses of Judah are
stripped away.

And you looked in that day
to the weapons[r] in the Palace of
the Forest;[s]
9 you saw that the City of David
had many breaches in its defenses;
you stored up water
in the Lower Pool.[t]
10 You counted the buildings in Jerusalem
and tore down houses to
strengthen the wall.
11 You built a reservoir between the
two walls[u]
for the water of the Old Pool,[v]
but you did not look to the One who
made it,
or have regard for the One who
planned it long ago.

12 The Lord, the LORD Almighty,
called you on that day
to weep[w] and to wail,
to tear out your hair[x] and put
on sackcloth.[y]
13 But see, there is joy and revelry,
slaughtering of cattle and killing
of sheep,
eating of meat and drinking of
wine![z]
"Let us eat and drink," you say,
"for tomorrow we die!"[a]

14 The LORD Almighty has revealed this
in my hearing:[b] "Till your dying day this
sin will not be atoned[c] for," says the
Lord, the LORD Almighty.

Eliakim replaces Shebna.

15 This is what the Lord, the LORD Almighty, says:

"Go, say to this steward,
to Shebna,[d] who is in charge of the
palace:
16 What are you doing here and who
gave you permission
to cut out a grave[e] for yourself
here,

21:13 [a]Isa 13:1
21:14 [b]Ge 25:15
21:15 [c]Isa 13:14
21:16 [d]Isa 16:14 [e]Isa 17:3 [f]Ps 120:5; Isa 60:7
21:17 [g]Isa 10:19
22:1 [h]Isa 13:1 [i]Ps 125:2; Jer 21:13; Joel 3:2,12,14
22:2 [j]Isa 32:13
22:4 [k]Isa 15:3; Lk 19:41 [l]Jer 9:1
22:5 [m]La 1:5
22:6 [n]Isa 21:2 [o]Jer 49:35 [p]2Ki 16:9
22:7 [q]2Ch 32:1-2
22:8 [r]2Ch 32:5 [s]1Ki 7:2
22:9 [t]2Ch 32:4
22:11 [u]2Ki 25:4; Jer 39:4 [v]2Ch 32:4
22:12 [w]Joel 2:17 [x]Mic 1:16 [y]Joel 1:13
22:13 [z]Isa 5:22; 28:7-8; 56:12; Lk 17:26-29 [a]1Co 15:32*
22:14 [b]Isa 5:9 [c]Isa 13:11; 26:21; 30:13-14; Eze 24:13
22:15 [d]2Ki 18:18; Isa 36:3
22:16 [e]Mt 27:60

hewing your grave on the height
and chiseling your resting place in the rock?

17“Beware, the LORD is about to take firm hold of you
and hurl you away, O you mighty man.
18He will roll you up tightly like a ball
and throw[a] you into a large country.
There you will die
and there your splendid chariots will remain—
you disgrace to your master’s house!
19I will depose you from your office,
and you will be ousted from your position.

20“In that day I will summon my servant, Eliakim[b] son of Hilkiah. 21I will
clothe him with your robe and fasten
your sash around him and hand your authority over to him. He will be a father
to those who live in Jerusalem and to
the house of Judah. 22I will place on his
shoulder the key[c] to the house of David;[d]
what he opens no one can shut, and what
he shuts no one can open.[e] 23I will drive
him like a peg[f] into a firm place;[g] he will
be a seat[z] of honor[h] for the house of his
father. 24All the glory of his family will
hang on him: its offspring and offshoots—
all its lesser vessels, from the bowls to all
the jars.

25“In that day,” declares the LORD Almighty, “the peg[i] driven into the firm
place will give way; it will be sheared off
and will fall, and the load hanging on it
will be cut down.” The LORD has spoken.[j]

Prophecy against Tyre.

23

An oracle concerning Tyre:[k]

Wail, O ships[l] of Tarshish![m]
For Tyre is destroyed
and left without house or harbor.
From the land of Cyprus[a]
word has come to them.

2Be silent, you people of the island
and you merchants of Sidon,
whom the seafarers have enriched.
3On the great waters
came the grain of the Shihor;
the harvest of the Nile[b][n] was the revenue of Tyre,[o]
and she became the marketplace of the nations.

4Be ashamed, O Sidon,[p] and you, O fortress of the sea,
for the sea has spoken:
“I have neither been in labor nor given birth;
I have neither reared sons nor brought up daughters.”
5When word comes to Egypt,
they will be in anguish at the report from Tyre.

6Cross over to Tarshish;
wail, you people of the island.
7Is this your city of revelry,[q]
the old, old city,
whose feet have taken her
to settle in far-off lands?
8Who planned this against Tyre,
the bestower of crowns,
whose merchants are princes,
whose traders are renowned in the earth?
9The LORD Almighty planned it,
to bring low[r] the pride of all glory
and to humble[s] all who are renowned[t] on the earth.

10Till[c] your land as along the Nile,
O Daughter of Tarshish,
for you no longer have a harbor.
11The LORD has stretched out his hand[u] over the sea
and made its kingdoms tremble.
He has given an order concerning Phoenicia[d]
that her fortresses be destroyed.[v]
12He said, “No more of your reveling,[w]
O Virgin Daughter[x] of Sidon, now crushed!

22:18 [a]Isa 17:13
22:20 [b]2Ki 18:18; Isa 36:3
22:22 [c]Rev 3:7 [d]Isa 7:2 [e]Job 12:14
22:23 [f]Zec 10:4 [g]Ezr 9:8 [h]1Sa 2:7-8; Job 36:7
22:25 [i]ver 23 [j]Isa 46:11; Mic 4:4
23:1 [k]Jos 19:29; 1Ki 5:1; Jer 47:4; Eze 26,27,28; Joel 3:4-8; Am 1:9-10; Zec 9:2-4 [l]1Ki 10:22 [m]Ge 10:4; Isa 2:16*fn*
23:3 [n]Isa 19:7 [o]Eze 27:3
23:4 [p]Ge 10:15,19
23:7 [q]Isa 22:2; 32:13
23:9 [r]Job 40:11 [s]Isa 13:11 [t]Isa 5:13; 9:15
23:11 [u]Ex 14:21 [v]Isa 25:2; Zec 9:3-4
23:12 [w]Rev 18:22 [x]Isa 47:1

[z]*23* Or *throne* [a]*1* Hebrew *Kittim*
[b]*2,3* Masoretic Text; one Dead Sea Scroll *Sidon, / who cross over the sea; / your envoys ³are on the great waters. / The grain of the Shihor, / the harvest of the Nile,* [c]*10* Dead Sea Scrolls and some Septuagint manuscripts; Masoretic Text *Go through*
[d]*11* Hebrew *Canaan*

"Up, cross over to Cyprus[e];
even there you will find no rest."
13 Look at the land of the Babylonians,[f]
this people that is now of no account!
The Assyrians[a] have made it
a place for desert creatures;
they raised up their siege towers,
they stripped its fortresses bare
and turned it into a ruin.[b]

14 Wail, you ships of Tarshish;[c]
your fortress is destroyed!

15 At that time Tyre[d] will be forgotten
for seventy years, the span of a king's life.
But at the end of these seventy years,
it will happen to Tyre as in the song of
the prostitute:

16 "Take up a harp, walk through the city,
O prostitute forgotten;
play the harp well, sing many a song,
so that you will be remembered."

17 At the end of seventy years, the LORD
will deal with Tyre. She will return to
her hire as a prostitute[e] and will ply her
trade with all the kingdoms on the face
of the earth. 18 Yet her profit and her
earnings will be set apart for the LORD;[f]
they will not be stored up or hoarded.
Her profits will go to those who live before the LORD,[g] for abundant food and
fine clothes.

The earth will be completely laid waste.

24 See, the LORD is going to lay
waste the earth[h]
and devastate it;
he will ruin its face
and scatter its inhabitants—
2 it will be the same
for priest as for people,[i]
for master as for servant,
for mistress as for maid,
for seller as for buyer,[j]
for borrower as for lender,
for debtor as for creditor.[k]
3 The earth will be completely laid waste
and totally plundered.[l]
The LORD has spoken
this word.

4 The earth dries up and withers,
the world languishes and withers,
the exalted[m] of the earth languish.
5 The earth is defiled[n] by its people;
they have disobeyed[o] the laws,
violated the statutes
and broken the everlasting covenant.
6 Therefore a curse consumes the earth;
its people must bear their guilt.
Therefore earth's inhabitants are
burned up,[p]
and very few are left.
7 The new wine dries up and the vine
withers;[q]
all the merrymakers groan.[r]
8 The gaiety of the tambourines[s] is
stilled,
the noise[t] of the revelers has
stopped,
the joyful harp[u] is silent.[v]
9 No longer do they drink wine[w] with
a song;
the beer is bitter[x] to its drinkers.
10 The ruined city lies desolate;
the entrance to every house is barred.
11 In the streets they cry out for wine;
all joy turns to gloom,[y]
all gaiety is banished from the earth.
12 The city is left in ruins,
its gate is battered to pieces.
13 So will it be on the earth
and among the nations,
as when an olive tree is beaten,[z]
or as when gleanings are left after
the grape harvest.

14 They raise their voices, they shout
for joy;[a]
from the west they acclaim the
LORD's majesty.
15 Therefore in the east give glory[b] to
the LORD;
exalt[c] the name of the LORD,
the God of Israel,
in the islands of the sea.
16 From the ends of the earth we
hear singing:
"Glory[d] to the Righteous One."

But I said, "I waste away, I waste away!
Woe to me!

23:13 [a]Isa 10:5 [b]Isa 10:7
23:14 [c]Isa 2:16 *fn*
23:15 [d]Jer 25:22
23:17 [e]Eze 16:26; Na 3:4; Rev 17:1
23:18 [f]Ex 28:36; Ps 72:10 [g]Isa 60:5-9; Mic 4:13
24:1 [h]ver 20; Isa 2:19-21; 33:9
24:2 [i]Hos 4:9 [j]Eze 7:12 [k]Lev 25:35-37; Dt 23:19-20
24:3 [l]Isa 6:11-12
24:4 [m]Isa 2:12
24:5 [n]Ge 3:17; Nu 35:33 [o]Isa 10:6; 59:12
24:6 [p]Isa 1:31
24:7 [q]Joel 1:10-12 [r]Isa 16:8-10
24:8 [s]Isa 5:12 [t]Jer 7:34; 16:9; 25:10; Hos 2:11 [u]Rev 18:22 [v]Eze 26:13
24:9 [w]Isa 5:11,22 [x]Isa 5:20
24:11 [y]Isa 16:10; 32:13; Jer 14:3
24:13 [z]Isa 17:6
24:14 [a]Isa 12:6
24:15 [b]Isa 66:19 [c]Isa 25:3; Mal 1:11
24:16 [d]Isa 28:5

[e] *12* Hebrew *Kittim* [f] *13* Or *Chaldeans*

The treacherous betray!
With treachery the treacherous betray![a]"
17Terror and pit and snare[b] await you,
O people of the earth.
18Whoever flees at the sound of terror
will fall into a pit;
whoever climbs out of the pit
will be caught in a snare.

The floodgates of the heavens[c] are opened,
the foundations of the earth shake.[d]
19The earth is broken up,
the earth is split asunder,[e]
the earth is thoroughly shaken.
20The earth reels like a drunkard,[f]
it sways like a hut in the wind;
so heavy upon it is the guilt of its rebellion[g]
that it falls—never to rise again.

21In that day the LORD will punish[h]
the powers in the heavens above
and the kings on the earth below.
22They will be herded together
like prisoners[i] bound in a dungeon;[j]
they will be shut up in prison
and be punished[g] after many days.[k]
23The moon will be abashed, the sun[l] ashamed;
for the LORD Almighty will reign[m]
on Mount Zion[n] and in Jerusalem,
and before its elders, gloriously.[o]

Praises to God for his faithfulness.

25 O LORD, you are my God;
I will exalt you and praise your name,
for in perfect faithfulness
you have done marvelous things,[p]
things planned[q] long ago.
2You have made the city a heap of rubble,[r]
the fortified[s] town a ruin,
the foreigners' stronghold[t] a city no more;
it will never be rebuilt.
3Therefore strong peoples will honor you;
cities of ruthless[u] nations will revere you.
4You have been a refuge[v] for the poor,
a refuge for the needy in his distress,
a shelter from the storm
and a shade from the heat.
For the breath of the ruthless[w]
is like a storm driving against a wall
5 and like the heat of the desert.
You silence[x] the uproar of foreigners;
as heat is reduced by the shadow of a cloud,
so the song of the ruthless is stilled.

6On this mountain[y] the LORD Almighty will prepare
a feast[z] of rich food for all peoples,
a banquet of aged wine—
the best of meats and the finest of wines.[a]
7On this mountain he will destroy
the shroud[b] that enfolds all peoples,
the sheet that covers all nations;
8 he will swallow up death[c] forever.
The Sovereign LORD will wipe away the tears[d]
from all faces;
he will remove the disgrace[e] of his people
from all the earth.
The LORD has spoken.

9In that day they will say,

"Surely this is our God;[f]
we trusted in him, and he saved[g] us.
This is the LORD, we trusted in him;
let us rejoice[h] and be glad in his salvation."

10The hand of the LORD will rest on this mountain;
but Moab[i] will be trampled under him
as straw is trampled down in the manure.
11They will spread out their hands in it,
as a swimmer spreads out his hands to swim.
God will bring down[j] their pride[k]
despite the cleverness[h] of their hands.

24:16 [a]Isa 21:2; Jer 5:11 **24:17** [b]Jer 48:43 **24:18** [c]Ge 7:11 [d]Ps 18:7 **24:19** [e]Dt 11:6 **24:20** [f]Isa 19:14 [g]Isa 1:2,28; 43:27 **24:21** [h]Isa 10:12 **24:22** [i]Isa 10:4 [j]Isa 42:7,22 [k]Eze 38:8 **24:23** [l]Isa 13:10 [m]Rev 22:5 [n]Heb 12:22 [o]Isa 60:19 **25:1** [p]Ps 98:1 [q]Nu 23:19 **25:2** [r]Isa 17:1 [s]Isa 17:3 [t]Isa 13:22 **25:3** [u]Isa 13:11 **25:4** [v]Isa 4:6; 17:10; 27:5; 33:16 [w]Isa 29:5; 49:25 **25:5** [x]Jer 51:55 **25:6** [y]Isa 2:2 [z]Isa 1:19; Mt 8:11; 22:4 [a]Pr 9:2 **25:7** [b]2Co 3:15-16; Eph 4:18 **25:8** [c]Hos 13:14; 1Co 15:54-55* [d]Isa 30:19; 35:10; 51:11; 65:19; Rev 7:17; 21:4 [e]Mt 5:11; 1Pe 4:14 **25:9** [f]Isa 40:9 [g]Ps 20:5; Isa 33:22; 35:4; 49:25-26,26; 60:16 [h]Isa 35:2,10 **25:10** [i]Am 2:1-3 **25:11** [j]Isa 5:25; 14:26; 16:14 [k]Job 40:12

g22 Or *released* h11 The meaning of the Hebrew for this word is uncertain.

[12]He will bring down your high
fortified walls
and lay them low;[a]
he will bring them down to the
ground,
to the very dust.

Praises in the land of Judah.

26 In that day this song will be
sung in the land of Judah:

We have a strong city;[b]
God makes salvation
its walls[c] and ramparts.
[2]Open the gates
that the righteous[d] nation may enter,
the nation that keeps faith.
[3]You will keep in perfect peace
him whose mind is steadfast,
because he trusts in you.
[4]Trust[e] in the LORD forever,
for the LORD, the LORD, is the Rock
eternal.
[5]He humbles those who dwell on high,
he lays the lofty city low;
he levels it to the ground[f]
and casts it down to the dust.
[6]Feet trample it down—
the feet of the oppressed,
the footsteps of the poor.[g]

[7]The path of the righteous is level;
O upright One, you make the way of
the righteous smooth.[h]
[8]Yes, LORD, walking in the way of
your laws,[i][i]
we wait for you;
your name[j] and renown
are the desire of our hearts.
[9]My soul yearns for you in the night;
in the morning my spirit longs[k]
for you.
When your judgments come upon
the earth,
the people of the world learn
righteousness.[l]
[10]Though grace is shown to the wicked,
they do not learn righteousness;
even in a land of uprightness they go
on doing evil[m]
and regard[n] not the majesty of
the LORD.
[11]O LORD, your hand is lifted high,
but they do not see[o] it.
Let them see your zeal for your
people and be put to shame;
let the fire[p] reserved for your
enemies consume them.

[12]LORD, you establish peace for us;
all that we have accomplished you
have done for us.
[13]O LORD, our God, other lords[q] besides
you have ruled over us,
but your name alone do we honor.[r]
[14]They are now dead,[s] they live no more;
those departed spirits do not rise.
You punished them and brought
them to ruin;[t]
you wiped out all memory of them.
[15]You have enlarged the nation, O LORD;
you have enlarged the nation.
You have gained glory for yourself;
you have extended all the
borders[u] of the land.

[16]LORD, they came to you in their
distress;[v]
when you disciplined them,
they could barely whisper a prayer.[j]
[17]As a woman with child and about to
give birth[w]
writhes and cries out in her pain,
so were we in your presence,
O LORD.
[18]We were with child, we writhed in
pain,
but we gave birth[x] to wind.
We have not brought salvation[y] to
the earth;
we have not given birth to people
of the world.

[19]But your dead[z] will live;
their bodies will rise.
You who dwell in the dust,
wake up and shout for joy.
Your dew is like the dew of the
morning;
the earth will give birth to her
dead.[a]

[20]Go, my people, enter your rooms
and shut the doors[b] behind you;

25:12 [a]Isa 15:1
26:1 [b]Isa 14:32 [c]Isa 60:18
26:2 [d]Isa 54:14; 58:8; 62:2
26:4 [e]Isa 12:2; 50:10
26:5 [f]Isa 25:12
26:6 [g]Isa 3:15
26:7 [h]Isa 42:16
26:8 [i]Isa 56:1 [j]Isa 12:4
26:9 [k]Ps 63:1; 78:34; Isa 55:6 [l]Mt 6:33
26:10 [m]Isa 32:6 [n]Isa 22:12-13; Hos 11:7; Jn 5:37-38; Ro 2:4
26:11 [o]Isa 44:9,18 [p]Heb 10:27
26:13 [q]Isa 2:8; 10:5,11 [r]Isa 63:7
26:14 [s]Dt 4:28 [t]Isa 10:3
26:15 [u]Isa 33:17
26:16 [v]Hos 5:15
26:17 [w]Jn 16:21
26:18 [x]Isa 33:11; 59:4 [y]Ps 17:14
26:19 [z]Isa 25:8; Eph 5:14 [a]Eze 37:1-14; Da 12:2
26:20 [b]Ex 12:23

i *8* Or *judgments* j *16* The meaning of the Hebrew for this clause is uncertain.

hide[a] yourselves for a little while
until his wrath has passed by.[b]
21See, the LORD is coming[c] out of his
dwelling[d]
to punish[e] the people of the earth
for their sins.
The earth will disclose the blood[f] shed
upon her;
she will conceal her slain no longer.

Israel will bud and blossom.

27 In that day,
the LORD will punish with his
sword,[g]
his fierce, great and powerful sword,
Leviathan[h] the gliding serpent,
Leviathan the coiling serpent;
he will slay the monster[i] of the sea.

2In that day—

"Sing about a fruitful vineyard:[j]
3 I, the LORD, watch over it;
I water[k] it continually.
I guard it day and night
so that no one may harm it.
4 I am not angry.
If only there were briers and thorns
confronting me!
I would march against them in battle;
I would set them all on fire.[l]
5Or else let them come to me for
refuge;[m]
let them make peace[n] with me,
yes, let them make peace with me."

6In days to come Jacob will take root,
Israel will bud and blossom[o]
and fill all the world with fruit.[p]

7Has ⌊the LORD⌋ struck her
as he struck[q] down those who
struck her?
Has she been killed
as those were killed who killed her?
8By warfare[k] and exile[r] you contend
with her—
with his fierce blast he drives her out,
as on a day the east wind blows.
9By this, then, will Jacob's guilt be
atoned for,
and this will be the full fruitage of
the removal of his sin:[s]

When he makes all the altar stones
to be like chalk stones crushed to
pieces,
no Asherah poles[l] [t] or incense altars
will be left standing.
10The fortified city stands desolate,[u]
an abandoned settlement, forsaken
like the desert;
there the calves graze,
there they lie down;[v]
they strip its branches bare.
11When its twigs are dry, they are
broken off
and women come and make fires
with them.
For this is a people without
understanding;[w]
so their Maker has no compassion
on them,
and their Creator[x] shows them
no favor.[y]

The exiled will be gathered at Jerusalem.

12In that day the LORD will thresh from
the flowing Euphrates[m] to the Wadi of
Egypt,[z] and you, O Israelites, will be
gathered[a] up one by one. 13And in that
day a great trumpet[b] will sound. Those
who were perishing in Assyria and those
who were exiled in Egypt[c] will come and
worship the LORD on the holy mountain
in Jerusalem.

Woe to Ephraim.

28 Woe to that wreath, the pride of
Ephraim's[d] drunkards,
to the fading flower, his glorious
beauty,
set on the head of a fertile valley[e]—
to that city, the pride of those laid
low by wine![f]
2See, the Lord has one who is
powerful[g] and strong.
Like a hailstorm[h] and a destructive
wind,[i]

26:20 [a]Ps 91:1,4 [b]Ps 30:5; Isa 54:7-8 **26:21** [c]Jude 14 [d]Mic 1:3 [e]Isa 13:9,11; 30:12-14 [f]Job 16:18; Lk 11:50-51 **27:1** [g]Isa 34:6; 66:16 [h]Job 3:8 [i]Ps 74:13 **27:2** [j]Jer 2:21 **27:3** [k]Isa 58:11 **27:4** [l]Isa 10:17; Mt 3:12; Heb 6:8 **27:5** [m]Isa 25:4 [n]Job 22:21; Ro 5:1; 2Co 5:20 **27:6** [o]Hos 14:5-6 [p]Isa 37:31 **27:7** [q]Isa 37:36-38 **27:8** [r]Isa 50:1; 54:7 **27:9** [s]Ro 11:27* [t]Ex 34:13 **27:10** [u]Isa 32:14; Jer 26:6 [v]Isa 17:2 **27:11** [w]Dt 32:28; Isa 1:3; Jer 8:7 [x]Dt 32:18; Isa 43:1,7,15; 44:1-2,21,24 [y]Isa 9:17 **27:12** [z]Ge 15:18 [a]Dt 30:4; Isa 11:12; 17:6 **27:13** [b]Lev 25:9; Mt 24:31 [c]Isa 19:21,25 **28:1** [d]ver 3; Isa 9:9 [e]ver 4 [f]Hos 7:5

28:2 [g]Isa 40:10 [h]Isa 30:30; Eze 13:11 [i]Isa 29:6

[k]8 See Septuagint; the meaning of the Hebrew for this word is uncertain. [l]9 That is, symbols of the goddess Asherah [m]12 Hebrew *River*

like a driving rain and a flooding[a]
downpour,
he will throw it forcefully to the
ground.
3That wreath, the pride of Ephraim's[b]
drunkards,
will be trampled underfoot.
4That fading flower, his glorious beauty,
set on the head of a fertile valley,[c]
will be like a fig[d] ripe before harvest—
as soon as someone sees it and
takes it in his hand,
he swallows it.

5In that day the LORD Almighty
will be a glorious crown,[e]
a beautiful wreath
for the remnant of his people.
6He will be a spirit of justice[f]
to him who sits in judgment,[g]
a source of strength
to those who turn back the battle[h]
at the gate.

7And these also stagger from wine[i]
and reel[j] from beer:
Priests[k] and prophets[l] stagger
from beer
and are befuddled with wine;
they reel from beer,
they stagger when seeing visions,[m]
they stumble when rendering
decisions.
8All the tables are covered with vomit[n]
and there is not a spot without filth.

9"Who is it he is trying to teach?[o]
To whom is he explaining his
message?
To children weaned[p] from their milk,[q]
to those just taken from the breast?
10For it is:
Do and do, do and do,
rule on rule, rule on rule[n];
a little here, a little there."

11Very well then, with foreign lips and
strange tongues[r]
God will speak to this people,[s]
12to whom he said,
"This is the resting place, let the
weary rest";[t]
and, "This is the place of repose"—
but they would not listen.

28:2 [a]Isa 8:7
28:3 [b]ver 1
28:4 [c]ver 1 [d]Hos 9:10; Na 3:12
28:5 [e]Isa 62:3
28:6 [f]Isa 11:2-4; 32:1,16 [g]Jn 5:30 [h]2Ch 32:8
28:7 [i]Isa 22:13 [j]Isa 56:10-12 [k]Isa 24:2 [l]Isa 9:15 [m]Isa 29:11; Hos 4:11
28:8 [n]Jer 48:26
28:9 [o]ver 26; Isa 30:20; 48:17; 50:4; 54:13 [p]Ps 131:2 [q]Heb 5:12-13
28:11 [r]Isa 33:19 [s]1Co 14:21*
28:12 [t]Isa 11:10; Mt 11:28-29
28:13 [u]Mt 21:44 [v]Isa 8:15
28:14 [w]Isa 1:10
28:15 [x]ver 2,18; Isa 8:7-8; 30:28; Da 11:22 [y]Isa 9:15 [z]Isa 29:15
28:16 [a]Ps 118:22; Isa 8:14-15; Mt 21:42; Ac 4:11; Eph 2:20 [b]Ro 9:33*; 10:11*; 1Pe 2:6*
28:17 [c]Isa 5:16 [d]2Ki 21:13
28:18 [e]Isa 7:7 [f]ver 15 [g]Da 8:13
28:19 [h]2Ki 24:2

13So then, the word of the LORD to
them will become:
Do and do, do and do,
rule on rule, rule on rule;
a little here, a little there—
so that they will go and fall backward,
be injured[u] and snared and
captured.[v]

14Therefore hear the word of the
LORD,[w] you scoffers
who rule this people in Jerusalem.
15You boast, "We have entered into a
covenant with death,
with the grave[o] we have made an
agreement.
When an overwhelming scourge
sweeps by,[x]
it cannot touch us,
for we have made a lie[y] our refuge
and falsehood[p] our hiding place.[z] "

Zion's precious cornerstone.

16So this is what the Sovereign LORD
says:

"See, I lay a stone in Zion,
a tested stone,[a]
a precious cornerstone for a sure
foundation;
the one who trusts will never be
dismayed.[b]
17I will make justice[c] the measuring line
and righteousness the plumb line;[d]
hail will sweep away your refuge,
the lie,
and water will overflow your
hiding place.
18Your covenant with death will be
annulled;
your agreement with the grave will
not stand.[e]
When the overwhelming scourge
sweeps by,[f]
you will be beaten down[g] by it.
19As often as it comes it will carry
you away;[h]

[n] *10* Hebrew / *sav lasav sav lasav / kav lakav kav lakav* (possibly meaningless sounds; perhaps a mimicking of the prophet's words); also in verse 13
[o] *15* Hebrew *Sheol*; also in verse 18
[p] *15* Or *false gods*

morning after morning, by day and
by night,
it will sweep through."

The understanding of this message
will bring sheer terror.[a]
20The bed is too short to stretch out on,
the blanket too narrow to wrap
around you.[b]
21The LORD will rise up as he did at
Mount Perazim,[c]
he will rouse himself as in the
Valley of Gibeon[d]—
to do his work,[e] his strange work,
and perform his task, his alien task.
22Now stop your mocking,
or your chains will become
heavier;
the Lord, the LORD Almighty, has
told me
of the destruction decreed[f] against
the whole land.[g]

23Listen and hear my voice;
pay attention and hear what I say.
24When a farmer plows for planting,
does he plow continually?
Does he keep on breaking up and
harrowing the soil?
25When he has leveled the surface,
does he not sow caraway and
scatter cummin?[h]
Does he not plant wheat in its place,[q]
barley in its plot,[q]
and spelt[i] in its field?
26His God instructs him
and teaches him the right way.

27Caraway is not threshed with a sledge,
nor is a cartwheel rolled over
cummin;
caraway is beaten out with a rod,
and cummin with a stick.
28Grain must be ground to make bread;
so one does not go on threshing it
forever.
Though he drives the wheels of his
threshing cart over it,
his horses do not grind it.
29All this also comes from the LORD
Almighty,
wonderful in counsel[j] and
magnificent in wisdom.[k]

28:19 [a]Job 18:11
28:20 [b]Isa 59:6
28:21 [c]1Ch 14:11 [d]Jos 10:10,12; 1Ch 14:16 [e]Isa 10:12; Lk 19:41-44
28:22 [f]Isa 10:22 [g]Isa 10:23
28:25 [h]Mt 23:23 [i]Ex 9:32
28:29 [j]Isa 9:6 [k]Ro 11:33
29:1 [l]Isa 22:12-13 [m]2Sa 5:9 [n]Isa 1:14
29:2 [o]Isa 3:26; La 2:5
29:3 [p]Lk 19:43-44
29:4 [q]Isa 8:19
29:5 [r]Isa 17:13 [s]Isa 17:14; 1Th 5:3
29:6 [t]Mt 24:7; Mk 13:8; Lk 21:11; Rev 11:19
29:7 [u]Mic 4:11-12; Zec 12:9 [v]Job 20:8
29:8 [w]Ps 73:20

Woe to the city of David.

29 Woe[l] to you, Ariel, Ariel,[m]
the city where David settled!
Add year to year
and let your cycle of festivals[n] go on.
2Yet I will besiege Ariel;
she will mourn and lament,[o]
she will be to me like an altar
hearth.[r]
3I will encamp against you all around;
I will encircle[p] you with towers
and set up my siege works against
you.
4Brought low, you will speak from the
ground;
your speech will mumble[q] out of
the dust.
Your voice will come ghostlike from
the earth;
out of the dust your speech will
whisper.

5But your many enemies will become
like fine dust,
the ruthless hordes like blown
chaff.[r]
Suddenly,[s] in an instant,
6 the LORD Almighty will come
with thunder and earthquake[t] and
great noise,
with windstorm and tempest and
flames of a devouring fire.
7Then the hordes of all the nations[u]
that fight against Ariel,
that attack her and her fortress and
besiege her,
will be as it is with a dream,[v]
with a vision in the night—
8as when a hungry man dreams that
he is eating,
but he awakens,[w] and his hunger
remains;
as when a thirsty man dreams that
he is drinking,
but he awakens faint, with his
thirst unquenched.
So will it be with the hordes of all
the nations
that fight against Mount Zion.

q25 The meaning of the Hebrew for this word is uncertain. r2 The Hebrew for *altar hearth* sounds like the Hebrew for *Ariel.*

[9]Be stunned and amazed,
blind yourselves and be sightless;
be drunk,[a] but not from wine,[b]
stagger, but not from beer.
[10]The LORD has brought over you a deep sleep:
He has sealed your eyes[c] (the prophets);[d]
he has covered your heads (the seers).[e]

[11]For you this whole vision is nothing
but words sealed[f] in a scroll. And if you
give the scroll to someone who can read,
and say to him, "Read this, please," he
will answer, "I can't; it is sealed." [12]Or if
you give the scroll to someone who cannot read, and say, "Read this, please," he
will answer, "I don't know how to read."

[13]The Lord says:

"These people come near to me with their mouth
and honor me with their lips,
but their hearts are far from me.[g]
Their worship of me
is made up only of rules taught by men.[s] [h]
[14]Therefore once more I will astound these people
with wonder upon wonder;[i]
the wisdom of the wise[j] will perish,
the intelligence of the intelligent will vanish.[k]"
[15]Woe to those who go to great depths
to hide their plans from the LORD,
who do their work in darkness and think,
"Who sees us?[l] Who will know?"[m]
[16]You turn things upside down,
as if the potter were thought to be like the clay!
Shall what is formed say to him who formed it,
"He did not make me"?
Can the pot say of the potter,[n]
"He knows nothing"?

Restoration promised.

[17]In a very short time, will not Lebanon
be turned into a fertile field[o]
and the fertile field seem like a forest?[p]
[18]In that day the deaf[q] will hear the words of the scroll,
and out of gloom and darkness
the eyes of the blind will see.[r]
[19]Once more the humble[s] will rejoice in the LORD;
the needy[t] will rejoice in the Holy One of Israel.
[20]The ruthless will vanish,
the mockers[u] will disappear,
and all who have an eye for evil[v] will be cut down—
[21]those who with a word make a man out to be guilty,
who ensnare the defender in court[w]
and with false testimony deprive the innocent of justice.[x]

[22]Therefore this is what the LORD, who
redeemed Abraham,[y] says to the house
of Jacob:

"No longer will Jacob be ashamed;[z]
no longer will their faces grow pale.
[23]When they see among them their children,[a]
the work of my hands,[b]
they will keep my name holy;
they will acknowledge the holiness of the Holy One of Jacob,
and will stand in awe of the God of Israel.
[24]Those who are wayward[c] in spirit will gain understanding;[d]
those who complain will accept instruction."[e]

Egyptian alliance is rebuked.

30 "Woe[f] to the obstinate children,"[g]
declares the LORD,
"to those who carry out plans that are not mine,
forming an alliance,[h] but not by my Spirit,
heaping sin upon sin;
[2]who go down to Egypt[i]
without consulting[j] me;

29:9 [a]Isa 51:17 [b]Isa 51:21-22 **29:10** [c]Ps 69:23; Isa 6:9-10; Ro 11:8* [d]Mic 3:6 [e]1Sa 9:9 **29:11** [f]Isa 8:16; Mt 13:11; Rev 5:1-2 **29:13** [g]Eze 33:31 [h]Mt 15:8-9*; Mk 7:6-7*; Col 2:22 **29:14** [i]Hab 1:5 [j]Jer 8:9; 49:7 [k]Isa 6:9-10; 1Co 1:19* **29:15** [l]Ps 10:11-13; 94:7; Isa 57:12 [m]Job 22:13 **29:16** [n]Isa 45:9; 64:8; Ro 9:20-21* **29:17** [o]Ps 84:6 [p]Isa 32:15 **29:18** [q]Mk 7:37 [r]Isa 32:3; 35:5; Mt 11:5 **29:19** [s]Isa 61:1; Mt 5:5; 11:29 [t]Isa 14:30; Mt 11:5; Jas 1:9; 2:5 **29:20** [u]Isa 28:22 [v]Isa 59:4; Mic 2:1 **29:21** [w]Am 5:10,15 [x]Isa 32:7 **29:22** [y]Isa 41:8; 63:16 [z]Isa 49:23 **29:23** [a]Isa 49:20-26 [b]Isa 19:25 **29:24** [c]Isa 28:7; Heb 5:2 [d]Isa 41:20; 60:16 [e]Isa 30:21 **30:1** [f]Isa 29:15 [g]Isa 1:2 [h]Isa 8:12

30:2 [i]Isa 31:1 [j]Nu 27:21

[s] *13* Hebrew; Septuagint *They worship me in vain; / their teachings are but rules taught by men*

who look for help to Pharaoh's
protection,[a]
to Egypt's shade for refuge.
3But Pharaoh's protection will be to
your shame,
Egypt's shade will bring you
disgrace.[b]
4Though they have officials in Zoan[c]
and their envoys have arrived
in Hanes,
5everyone will be put to shame
because of a people[d] useless to them,
who bring neither help nor advantage,
but only shame and disgrace."

6An oracle concerning the animals of the Negev:

Through a land of hardship and
distress,[e]
of lions and lionesses,
of adders and darting snakes,[f]
the envoys carry their riches on
donkeys' backs,
their treasures[g] on the humps
of camels,
to that unprofitable nation,
7 to Egypt, whose help is utterly
useless.
Therefore I call her
Rahab the Do-Nothing.

8Go now, write it on a tablet for them,
inscribe it on a scroll,[h]
that for the days to come
it may be an everlasting witness.
9These are rebellious people,
deceitful[i] children,
children unwilling to listen to the
LORD's instruction.[j]
10They say to the seers,
"See no more visions[k]!"
and to the prophets,
"Give us no more visions of what
is right!
Tell us pleasant things,[l]
prophesy illusions.[m]
11Leave this way,
get off this path,
and stop confronting[n] us
with the Holy One of Israel!"

12Therefore, this is what the Holy One of Israel says:

"Because you have rejected this
message,[o]
relied on oppression[p]
and depended on deceit,
13this sin will become for you
like a high wall,[q] cracked and
bulging,
that collapses[r] suddenly,[s] in an
instant.
14It will break in pieces like pottery,[t]
shattered so mercilessly
that among its pieces not a fragment
will be found
for taking coals from a hearth
or scooping water out of a cistern."

15This is what the Sovereign LORD, the Holy One of Israel, says:

"In repentance and rest is your
salvation,
in quietness and trust[u] is your
strength,
but you would have none of it.
16You said, 'No, we will flee on horses.'[v]
Therefore you will flee!
You said, 'We will ride off on swift
horses.'
Therefore your pursuers will
be swift!
17A thousand will flee
at the threat of one;
at the threat of five[w]
you will all flee[x] away,
till you are left
like a flagstaff on a mountaintop,
like a banner on a hill."

The LORD shows compassion.

18Yet the LORD longs[y] to be gracious
to you;
he rises to show you compassion.
For the LORD is a God of justice.[z]
Blessed are all who wait for him![a]

19O people of Zion, who live in Jerusalem, you will weep no more.[b] How gracious he will be when you cry for help!
As soon as he hears, he will answer[c]
you. 20Although the Lord gives you the
bread[d] of adversity and the water of
affliction, your teachers will be hidden[e]
no more; with your own eyes you will

30:2 [a]Isa 36:9
30:3 [b]Isa 20:4-5; 36:6
30:4 [c]Isa 19:11
30:5 [d]ver 7
30:6 [e]Ex 5:10,21; Isa 8:22; Jer 11:4 [f]Dt 8:15 [g]Isa 15:7
30:8 [h]Isa 8:1; Hab 2:2
30:9 [i]Isa 28:15; 59:3-4 [j]Isa 1:10
30:10 [k]Jer 11:21; Am 7:13 [l]1Ki 22:8 [m]Eze 13:7; Ro 16:18
30:11 [n]Job 21:14
30:12 [o]Isa 5:24 [p]Isa 5:7
30:13 [q]Ps 62:3 [r]1Ki 20:30 [s]Isa 29:5
30:14 [t]Ps 2:9; Jer 19:10-11
30:15 [u]Isa 32:17
30:16 [v]Isa 31:1,3
30:17 [w]Lev 26:8; Jos 23:10 [x]Lev 26:36; Dt 28:25
30:18 [y]Isa 42:14; 2Pe 3:9,15 [z]Isa 5:16 [a]Isa 25:9
30:19 [b]Isa 60:20; 61:3 [c]Ps 50:15; Isa 58:9; 65:24; Mt 7:7-11
30:20 [d]1Ki 22:27 [e]Ps 74:9; Am 8:11

see them. 21Whether you turn to the
right or to the left, your ears will hear
a voice[a] behind you, saying, "This is the
way; walk in it." 22Then you will defile
your idols[b] overlaid with silver and your
images covered with gold; you will throw
them away like a menstrual cloth and
say to them, "Away with you!"

23He will also send you rain[c] for the
seed you sow in the ground, and the food
that comes from the land will be rich and
plentiful. In that day your cattle will
graze in broad meadows.[d] 24The oxen
and donkeys that work the soil will eat
fodder and mash, spread out with fork[e]
and shovel. 25In the day of great slaughter, when the towers[f] fall, streams of
water will flow[g] on every high mountain and every lofty hill. 26The moon will
shine like the sun,[h] and the sunlight will
be seven times brighter, like the light of
seven full days, when the LORD binds
up the bruises of his people and heals[i]
the wounds he inflicted.

The LORD will shatter Assyria.

27See, the Name[j] of the LORD comes
from afar,
with burning anger[k] and dense
clouds of smoke;
his lips are full of wrath,[l]
and his tongue is a consuming fire.
28His breath[m] is like a rushing torrent,
rising up to the neck.[n]
He shakes the nations in the sieve[o]
of destruction;
he places in the jaws of the peoples
a bit[p] that leads them astray.
29And you will sing
as on the night you celebrate a
holy festival;
your hearts will rejoice
as when people go up with flutes
to the mountain[q] of the LORD,
to the Rock of Israel.
30The LORD will cause men to hear his
majestic voice
and will make them see his arm
coming down
with raging anger and
consuming fire,
with cloudburst, thunderstorm and
hail.
31The voice of the LORD will shatter
Assyria;[r]
with his scepter he will strike[s]
them down.
32Every stroke the LORD lays on them
with his punishing rod
will be to the music of tambourines
and harps,
as he fights them in battle with the
blows of his arm.[t]
33Topheth[u] has long been prepared;
it has been made ready for the king.
Its fire pit has been made deep and
wide,
with an abundance of fire and wood;
the breath of the LORD,
like a stream of burning sulfur,[v]
sets it ablaze.

Woe to those who seek Egypt's help.

31 Woe to those who go down to
Egypt[w] for help,
who rely on horses,
who trust in the multitude of their
chariots[x]
and in the great strength of their
horsemen,
but do not look to the Holy One of
Israel,
or seek help from the LORD.[y]
2Yet he too is wise[z] and can bring
disaster;[a]
he does not take back his words.[b]
He will rise up against the house of
the wicked,[c]
against those who help evildoers.
3But the Egyptians[d] are men and
not God;[e]
their horses are flesh and not spirit.
When the LORD stretches out his
hand,[f]
he who helps will stumble,
he who is helped[g] will fall;
both will perish together.

4This is what the LORD says to me:

"As a lion[h] growls,
a great lion over his prey—

30:21 [a]Isa 29:24
30:22 [b]Ex 32:4
30:23 [c]Isa 65:21-22 [d]Ps 65:13
30:24 [e]Mt 3:12; Lk 3:17
30:25 [f]Isa 2:15 [g]Isa 41:18
30:26 [h]Isa 24:23; 60:19-20; Rev 21:23; 22:5 [i]Dt 32:39; Isa 1:5
30:27 [j]Isa 59:19 [k]Isa 66:14 [l]Isa 10:5
30:28 [m]Isa 11:4 [n]Isa 8:8 [o]Am 9:9 [p]2Ki 19:28; Isa 37:29
30:29 [q]Ps 42:4
30:31 [r]Isa 10:5,12 [s]Isa 11:4
30:32 [t]Isa 11:15; Eze 32:10
30:33 [u]2Ki 23:10 [v]Ge 19:24
31:1 [w]Dt 17:16; Isa 30:2,5 [x]Isa 2:7 [y]Ps 20:7; Da 9:13
31:2 [z]Ro 16:27 [a]Isa 45:7 [b]Nu 23:19 [c]Isa 32:6
31:3 [d]Isa 36:9 [e]Eze 28:9; 2Th 2:4 [f]Isa 9:17,21 [g]Isa 30:5-7
31:4 [h]Nu 24:9; Hos 11:10; Am 3:8

and though a whole band of shepherds
is called together against him,
he is not frightened by their shouts
or disturbed by their clamor—
so the LORD Almighty will
come down[a]
to do battle on Mount Zion and on
its heights.
5Like birds hovering overhead,
the LORD Almighty will shield[b]
Jerusalem;
he will shield it and deliver[c] it,
he will 'pass over' it and will
rescue it."

6Return to him you have so greatly revolted against, O Israelites. 7For in that
day every one of you will reject the idols
of silver and gold[d] your sinful hands have
made.

8"Assyria[e] will fall by a sword that is
not of man;
a sword, not of mortals, will
devour[f] them.
They will flee before the sword
and their young men will be put to
forced labor.[g]
9Their stronghold[h] will fall because
of terror;
at sight of the battle standard their
commanders will panic,"
declares the LORD,
whose fire[i] is in Zion,
whose furnace is in Jerusalem.

A righteous king.

32 See, a king[j] will reign in
righteousness
and rulers will rule with justice.[k]
2Each man will be like a shelter[l] from
the wind
and a refuge from the storm,
like streams of water in the desert
and the shadow of a great rock in a
thirsty land.

3Then the eyes of those who see will
no longer be closed,[m]
and the ears of those who hear
will listen.
4The mind of the rash will know and
understand,[n]
and the stammering tongue will be
fluent and clear.
5No longer will the fool[o] be called noble
nor the scoundrel be highly
respected.
6For the fool speaks folly,[p]
his mind is busy with evil:
He practices ungodliness[q]
and spreads error[r] concerning
the LORD;
the hungry he leaves empty[s]
and from the thirsty he
withholds water.
7The scoundrel's methods are wicked,[t]
he makes up evil schemes[u]
to destroy the poor with lies,
even when the plea of the needy[v]
is just.
8But the noble man makes noble plans,
and by noble deeds[w] he stands.

Judgments on complacent women.

9You women who are so complacent,
rise up and listen[x] to me;
you daughters who feel secure,[y]
hear what I have to say!
10In little more than a year
you who feel secure will tremble;
the grape harvest will fail,[z]
and the harvest of fruit will not come.
11Tremble, you complacent women;
shudder, you daughters who feel
secure!
Strip off your clothes,[a]
put sackcloth around your waists.
12Beat your breasts[b] for the pleasant
fields,
for the fruitful vines
13and for the land of my people,
a land overgrown with thorns
and briers[c]—
yes, mourn for all houses of merriment
and for this city of revelry.[d]
14The fortress[e] will be abandoned,
the noisy city deserted;[f]
citadel and watchtower[g] will become
a wasteland forever,
the delight of donkeys,[h] a pasture
for flocks,
15till the Spirit[i] is poured upon us
from on high,

31:4 [a]Isa 42:13
31:5 [b]Ps 91:4 [c]Isa 37:35; 38:6
31:7 [d]Isa 2:20; 30:22
31:8 [e]Isa 10:12 [f]Isa 14:25; 37:7 [g]Ge 49:15
31:9 [h]Dt 32:31,37 [i]Isa 10:17
32:1 [j]Eze 37:24 [k]Ps 72:1-4; Isa 9:7
32:2 [l]Isa 4:6
32:3 [m]Isa 29:18
32:4 [n]Isa 29:24
32:5 [o]1Sa 25:25
32:6 [p]Pr 19:3 [q]Isa 9:17 [r]Isa 9:16 [s]Isa 3:15
32:7 [t]Jer 5:26-28 [u]Mic 7:3 [v]Isa 61:1
32:8 [w]Pr 11:25
32:9 [x]Isa 28:23 [y]Isa 47:8; Am 6:1; Zep 2:15
32:10 [z]Isa 5:5-6; 24:7
32:11 [a]Isa 47:2
32:12 [b]Na 2:7
32:13 [c]Isa 5:6 [d]Isa 22:2
32:14 [e]Isa 13:22 [f]Isa 6:11; 27:10 [g]Isa 34:13 [h]Ps 104:11
32:15 [i]Isa 11:2; Joel 2:28

and the desert becomes a fertile
field,[a]
and the fertile field seems like
a forest.[b]

Quietness and confidence forever.

16Justice will dwell in the desert
and righteousness live in the
fertile field.
17The fruit of righteousness will be
peace;[c]
the effect of righteousness will be
quietness and confidence[d]
forever.
18My people will live in peaceful
dwelling places,
in secure homes,
in undisturbed places of rest.[e]
19Though hail[f] flattens the forest[g]
and the city is leveled[h] completely,
20how blessed you will be,
sowing[i] your seed by every stream,
and letting your cattle and donkeys
range free.[j]

Judgments on the enemies of God's people.

33 Woe to you, O destroyer,
you who have not been
destroyed!
Woe to you, O traitor,
you who have not been betrayed!
When you stop destroying,
you will be destroyed;[k]
when you stop betraying,
you will be betrayed.[l]

2O LORD, be gracious to us;
we long for you.
Be our strength[m] every morning,
our salvation[n] in time of distress.
3At the thunder of your voice, the
peoples flee;
when you rise up,[o] the nations
scatter.
4Your plunder, O nations, is harvested
as by young locusts;
like a swarm of locusts men
pounce on it.
5The LORD is exalted,[p] for he dwells
on high;
he will fill Zion with justice[q] and
righteousness.[r]
6He will be the sure foundation for
your times,
a rich store of salvation[s] and
wisdom and knowledge;
the fear[t] of the LORD is the key to
this treasure.[t]

7Look, their brave men cry aloud in
the streets;
the envoys[u] of peace weep bitterly.
8The highways are deserted,
no travelers are on the roads.[v]
The treaty is broken,
its witnesses[u] are despised,
no one is respected.
9The land mourns[v] [w] and wastes away,
Lebanon[x] is ashamed and withers;[y]
Sharon is like the Arabah,
and Bashan and Carmel drop
their leaves.

10"Now will I arise,[z]" says the LORD.
"Now will I be exalted;
now will I be lifted up.
11You conceive[a] chaff,
you give birth[b] to straw;
your breath is a fire[c] that
consumes you.
12The peoples will be burned as if
to lime;
like cut thornbushes they will be
set ablaze.[d]"

The LORD is judge, lawgiver and king.

13You who are far away,[e] hear[f] what
I have done;
you who are near, acknowledge
my power!
14The sinners in Zion are terrified;
trembling[g] grips the godless:
"Who of us can dwell with the
consuming fire?[h]
Who of us can dwell with
everlasting burning?"
15He who walks righteously[i]
and speaks what is right,[j]

32:15 [a]Ps 107:35; Isa 35:1-2 [b]Isa 29:17
32:17 [c]Ps 119:165; Ro 14:17; Jas 3:18 [d]Isa 30:15
32:18 [e]Hos 2:18-23
32:19 [f]Isa 28:17; 30:30 [g]Isa 10:19; Zec 11:2 [h]Isa 24:10; 27:10
32:20 [i]Ecc 11:1 [j]Isa 30:24
33:1 [k]Hab 2:8; Mt 7:2 [l]Isa 21:2
33:2 [m]Isa 40:10; 51:9; 59:16 [n]Isa 25:9
33:3 [o]Isa 59:16-18
33:5 [p]Ps 97:9 [q]Isa 28:6 [r]Isa 1:26
33:6 [s]Isa 51:6 [t]Isa 11:2-3; Mt 6:33
33:7 [u]2Ki 18:37
33:8 [v]Jdg 5:6; Isa 35:8
33:9 [w]Isa 3:26 [x]Isa 2:13; 35:2 [y]Isa 24:4
33:10 [z]Ps 12:5; Isa 2:21
33:11 [a]Ps 7:14; Isa 59:4; Jas 1:15 [b]Isa 26:18 [c]Isa 1:31
33:12 [d]Isa 10:17
33:13 [e]Ps 48:10; 49:1 [f]Isa 49:1
33:14 [g]Isa 32:11 [h]Isa 30:30; Heb 12:29
33:15 [i]Isa 58:8 [j]Ps 15:2; 24:4

t6 Or *is a treasure from him* u8 Dead Sea Scrolls; Masoretic Text / *the cities* v9 Or *dries up*

who rejects gain from extortion
and keeps his hand from accepting bribes,
who stops his ears against plots of murder
and shuts his eyes[a] against contemplating evil—
16this is the man who will dwell on the heights,
whose refuge[b] will be the mountain fortress.[c]
His bread will be supplied,
and water will not fail[d] him.

17Your eyes will see the king[e] in his beauty
and view a land that stretches afar.[f]
18In your thoughts you will ponder the former terror:[g]
"Where is that chief officer?
Where is the one who took the revenue?
Where is the officer in charge of the towers?"
19You will see those arrogant people no more,
those people of an obscure speech,
with their strange, incomprehensible tongue.[h]

20Look upon Zion, the city of our festivals;
your eyes will see Jerusalem,
a peaceful abode,[i] a tent that will not be moved;[j]
its stakes will never be pulled up,
nor any of its ropes broken.
21There the LORD will be our Mighty One.
It will be like a place of broad rivers and streams.[k]
No galley with oars will ride them,
no mighty ship will sail them.
22For the LORD is our judge,[l]
the LORD is our lawgiver,[m]
the LORD is our king;[n]
it is he who will save[o] us.

23Your rigging hangs loose:
The mast is not held secure,
the sail is not spread.
Then an abundance of spoils will be divided
and even the lame[p] will carry off plunder.[q]
24No one living in Zion will say,
"I am ill";[r]
and the sins of those who dwell there will be forgiven.[s]

Judgment against the nations.

34 Come near, you nations, and listen;
pay attention, you peoples![t]
Let the earth[u] hear, and all that is in it,
the world, and all that comes out of it![v]
2The LORD is angry with all nations;
his wrath is upon all their armies.
He will totally destroy[w w] them,
he will give them over to slaughter.[x]
3Their slain will be thrown out,
their dead bodies will send up a stench;[y]
the mountains will be soaked with their blood.[z]
4All the stars of the heavens will be dissolved[a]
and the sky rolled up[b] like a scroll;
all the starry host will fall[c]
like withered leaves from the vine,
like shriveled figs from the fig tree.

5My sword[d] has drunk its fill in the heavens;
see, it descends in judgment on Edom,[e]
the people I have totally destroyed.[f]
6The sword of the LORD is bathed in blood,
it is covered with fat—
the blood of lambs and goats,
fat from the kidneys of rams.
For the LORD has a sacrifice in Bozrah
and a great slaughter in Edom.
7And the wild oxen will fall with them,
the bull calves and the great bulls.[g]
Their land will be drenched with blood,
and the dust will be soaked with fat.

33:15 [a]Ps 119:37
33:16 [b]Isa 25:4 [c]Isa 26:1 [d]Isa 49:10
33:17 [e]Isa 6:5 [f]Isa 26:15
33:18 [g]Isa 17:14
33:19 [h]Isa 28:11; Jer 5:15
33:20 [i]Isa 32:18 [j]Ps 46:5; 125:1-2
33:21 [k]Isa 41:18; 48:18; 66:12
33:22 [l]Isa 11:4 [m]Isa 2:3; Jas 4:12 [n]Ps 89:18 [o]Isa 25:9
33:23 [p]2Ki 7:8 [q]2Ki 7:16
33:24 [r]Isa 30:26 [s]Jer 50:20; 1Jn 1:7-9
34:1 [t]Isa 41:1; 43:9 [u]Ps 49:1 [v]Dt 32:1
34:2 [w]Isa 13:5 [x]Isa 30:25
34:3 [y]Joel 2:20; Am 4:10 [z]ver 7; Eze 14:19; 35:6; 38:22
34:4 [a]Isa 13:13; 2Pe 3:10 [b]Eze 32:7-8 [c]Joel 2:31; Mt 24:29*; Rev 6:13
34:5 [d]Dt 32:41-42; Jer 46:10; Eze 21:5 [e]Am 1:11-12 [f]Isa 24:6; Mal 1:4
34:7 [g]Ps 68:30

w2 The Hebrew term refers to the irrevocable giving over of things or persons to the LORD, often by totally destroying them; also in verse 5.

8For the LORD has a day of vengeance,[a]
a year of retribution, to uphold
Zion's cause.
9Edom's streams will be turned
into pitch,
her dust into burning sulfur;
her land will become blazing pitch!
10It will not be quenched night
and day;
its smoke will rise forever.[b]
From generation to generation it will
lie desolate;[c]
no one will ever pass through
it again.
11The desert owl[x] [d] and screech owl[x]
will possess it;
the great owl[x] and the raven will
nest there.
God will stretch out over Edom
the measuring line of chaos
and the plumb line[e] of desolation.
12Her nobles will have nothing there
to be called a kingdom,
all her princes[f] will vanish[g] away.
13Thorns will overrun her citadels,
nettles and brambles her
strongholds.[h]
She will become a haunt for jackals,[i]
a home for owls.
14Desert creatures will meet with
hyenas,[j]
and wild goats will bleat to
each other;
there the night creatures will
also repose
and find for themselves places
of rest.
15The owl will nest there and lay eggs,
she will hatch them, and care for
her young under the shadow
of her wings;
there also the falcons[k] will gather,
each with its mate.

16Look in the scroll[l] of the LORD and
read:

None of these will be missing,
not one will lack her mate.
For it is his mouth[m] that has given
the order,
and his Spirit will gather them
together.
17He allots their portions;[n]
his hand distributes them by measure.
They will possess it forever
and dwell there from generation to
generation.[o]

Joyful return to Zion.

35 The desert[p] and the parched
land will be glad;
the wilderness will rejoice and
blossom.[q]
Like the crocus,2it will burst into
bloom;
it will rejoice greatly and shout
for joy.[r]
The glory of Lebanon[s] will be
given to it,
the splendor of Carmel[t] and Sharon;
they will see the glory of the LORD,
the splendor of our God.[u]

3Strengthen the feeble hands,
steady the knees[v] that give way;
4say to those with fearful hearts,
"Be strong, do not fear;
your God will come,
he will come with vengeance;[w]
with divine retribution
he will come to save you."

5Then will the eyes of the blind
be opened[x]
and the ears of the deaf[y] unstopped.
6Then will the lame[z] leap like a deer,
and the mute tongue[a] shout for joy.
Water will gush forth in the wilderness
and streams[b] in the desert.
7The burning sand will become a pool,
the thirsty ground bubbling springs.[c]
In the haunts where jackals[d] once lay,
grass and reeds and papyrus
will grow.

8And a highway[e] will be there;
it will be called the Way of Holiness.[f]
The unclean[g] will not journey on it;
it will be for those who walk in
that Way;
wicked fools will not go about on it.[y]

34:8 [a]Isa 63:4
34:10 [b]Rev 14:10-11; 19:3 [c]Isa 13:20; 24:1; Eze 29:12; Mal 1:3
34:11 [d]Zep 2:14; Rev 18:2 [e]2Ki 21:13; La 2:8
34:12 [f]Jer 27:20; 39:6 [g]Isa 41:11-12
34:13 [h]Isa 13:22; 32:13 [i]Ps 44:19; Jer 9:11; 10:22
34:14 [j]Isa 13:22
34:15 [k]Dt 14:13
34:16 [l]Isa 30:8 [m]Isa 1:20; 58:14
34:17 [n]Isa 17:14; Jer 13:25 [o]ver 10
35:1 [p]Isa 27:10; 41:18-19 [q]Isa 51:3
35:2 [r]Isa 25:9; 55 :12 [s]Isa 32:15 [t]SS7:5 [u]Isa 25:9
35:3 [v]Job 4:4; Heb 12:12
35:4 [w]Isa 1:24; 34:8
35:5 [x]Mt 11:5; Jn 9:6-7 [y]Isa 29:18; 50:4
35:6 [z]Mt 15:30; Jn 5:8-9; Ac 3:8 [a]Isa 32:4; Mt 9:32-33; 12:22; Lk 11:14 [b]Isa 41:18; Jn 7:38
35:7 [c]Isa 49:10 [d]Isa 13:22 **35:8** [e]Isa 11:16; 33:8; Mt 7:13-14 [f]Isa 4:3; 1Pe 1:15 [g]Isa 52:1

x *11* The precise identification of these birds is uncertain. y *8* Or / *the simple will not stray from it*

9No lion[a] will be there,
nor will any ferocious beast[b] get up on it;
they will not be found there.
But only the redeemed[c] will walk there,
10 and the ransomed of the LORD will return.
They will enter Zion with singing;
everlasting joy[d] will crown their heads.
Gladness and joy will overtake them,
and sorrow and sighing will flee away.[e]

Sennacherib leads Assyria against Judah.

36:1-22pp— 2Ki 18:13,17-37; 2Ch 32:9-19

36 In the fourteenth year of King
Hezekiah's reign, Sennacherib[f]
king of Assyria attacked all the fortified
cities of Judah and captured them. 2Then
the king of Assyria sent his field commander with a large army from Lachish
to King Hezekiah at Jerusalem. When the
commander stopped at the aqueduct of
the Upper Pool, on the road to the
Washerman's Field,[g] 3Eliakim[h] son of
Hilkiah the palace administrator, Shebna[i]
the secretary, and Joah son of Asaph the
recorder went out to him.

4The field commander said to them,
"Tell Hezekiah,

"'This is what the great king, the
king of Assyria, says: On what are
you basing this confidence of yours?
5You say you have strategy and military strength—but you speak only
empty words. On whom are you depending, that you rebel[j] against me?
6Look now, you are depending on
Egypt,[k] that splintered reed[l] of a
staff, which pierces a man's hand
and wounds him if he leans on it!

35:9 [a]Isa 30:6 [b]Isa 34:14 [c]Isa 51:11; 62:12; 63:4
35:10 [d]Isa 25:9 [e]Isa 30:19; 51:11; Rev 7:17; 21:4
36:1 [f]2Ch 32:1
36:2 [g]Isa 7:3
36:3 [h]Isa 22:20-21 [i]2Ki 18:18
36:5 [j]2Ki 18:7
36:6 [k]Isa 30:2,5 [l]Eze 29:6-7

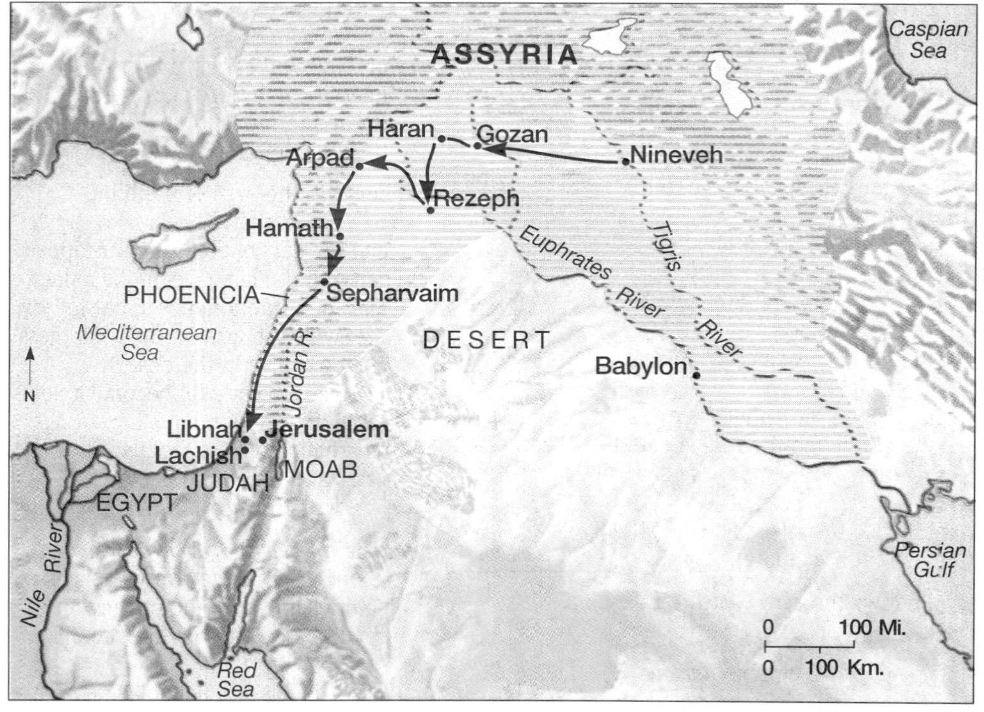

Assyria Advances

As Sennacherib beautified his capital city, Nineveh, Hezekiah withheld tribute and prepared for battle. The Assyrians advanced toward their rebellious western border, attacking swiftly down the Mediterranean coast. From Lachish, Sennacherib threatened to take Jerusalem, but Isaiah knew his threats would die with him on his return to Nineveh.

Such is Pharaoh king of Egypt to all who depend on him. 7And if you say to me, "We are depending on the LORD our God"—isn't he the one whose high places and altars Hezekiah removed,[a] saying to Judah and Jerusalem, "You must worship before this altar"?[b]

8" 'Come now, make a bargain with my master, the king of Assyria: I will give you two thousand horses—if you can put riders on them! 9How then can you repulse one officer of the least of my master's officials, even though you are depending on Egypt[c] for chariots and horsemen?[d] 10Furthermore, have I come to attack and destroy this land without the LORD? The LORD himself told[e] me to march against this country and destroy it.' "

11Then Eliakim, Shebna and Joah said to the field commander, "Please speak to your servants in Aramaic,[f] since we understand it. Don't speak to us in Hebrew in the hearing of the people on the wall."

12But the commander replied, "Was it only to your master and you that my master sent me to say these things, and not to the men sitting on the wall—who, like you, will have to eat their own filth and drink their own urine?"

13Then the commander stood and called out in Hebrew,[g] "Hear the words of the great king, the king of Assyria! 14This is what the king says: Do not let Hezekiah deceive you. He cannot deliver you! 15Do not let Hezekiah persuade you to trust in the LORD when he says, 'The LORD will surely deliver us; this city will not be given into the hand of the king of Assyria.'[h]

16"Do not listen to Hezekiah. This is what the king of Assyria says: Make peace with me and come out to me. Then every one of you will eat from his own vine and fig tree[i] and drink water from his own cistern,[j] 17until I come and take you to a land like your own—a land of grain and new wine, a land of bread and vineyards.

18"Do not let Hezekiah mislead you when he says, 'The LORD will deliver us.' Has the god of any nation ever delivered his land from the hand of the king of Assyria? 19Where are the gods of Hamath and Arpad? Where are the gods of Sepharvaim? Have they rescued Samaria from my hand? 20Who of all the gods[k] of these countries has been able to save his land from me? How then can the LORD deliver Jerusalem from my hand?"

21But the people remained silent and said nothing in reply, because the king had commanded, "Do not answer him."[l]

22Then Eliakim son of Hilkiah the palace administrator, Shebna the secretary, and Joah son of Asaph the recorder went to Hezekiah, with their clothes torn, and told him what the field commander had said.

Isaiah encourages Hezekiah.

37:1-13pp— 2Ki 19:1-13

37 When King Hezekiah heard this, he tore his clothes and put on sackcloth and went into the temple of the LORD. 2He sent Eliakim the palace administrator, Shebna the secretary, and the leading priests, all wearing sackcloth, to the prophet Isaiah son of Amoz.[m] 3They told him, "This is what Hezekiah says: This day is a day of distress and rebuke and disgrace, as when children come to the point of birth[n] and there is no strength to deliver them. 4It may be that the LORD your God will hear the words of the field commander, whom his master, the king of Assyria, has sent to ridicule the living God, and that he will rebuke him for the words the LORD your God has heard.[o] Therefore pray for the remnant[p] that still survives."

5When King Hezekiah's officials came to Isaiah, 6Isaiah said to them, "Tell your master, 'This is what the LORD says: Do not be afraid[q] of what you have heard—those words with which the underlings of the king of Assyria have blasphemed me. 7Listen! I am going to put a spirit in him so that when he hears a certain

36:7 [a]2Ki 18:4 [b]Dt 12:2-5
36:9 [c]Isa 31:3 [d]Isa 30:2-5
36:10 [e]1Ki 13:18
36:11 [f]Ezr 4:7
36:13 [g]2Ch 32:18
36:15 [h]Isa 37:10
36:16 [i]1Ki 4:25; Zec 3:10 [j]Pr 5:15
36:20 [k]1Ki 20:23
36:21 [l]Pr 9:7-8; 26:4
37:2 [m]Isa 1:1
37:3 [n]Isa 26:18; 66:9; Hos 13:13
37:4 [o]Isa 36:13,18-20 [p]Isa 1:9
37:6 [q]Isa 7:4

report,[a] he will return to his own country, and there I will have him cut down
with the sword.' "
8When the field commander heard
that the king of Assyria had left Lachish,
he withdrew and found the king fighting against Libnah.[b]
9Now Sennacherib received a report[c]
that Tirhakah, the Cushite[z] king ⌊of
Egypt⌋, was marching out to fight against
him. When he heard it, he sent messengers to Hezekiah with this word: 10"Say
to Hezekiah king of Judah: Do not let the
god you depend on deceive you when he
says, 'Jerusalem will not be handed over
to the king of Assyria.'[d] 11Surely you have
heard what the kings of Assyria have
done to all the countries, destroying
them completely. And will you be delivered?[e] 12Did the gods of the nations that
were destroyed by my forefathers[f] deliver them—the gods of Gozan, Haran,[g]
Rezeph and the people of Eden who
were in Tel Assar? 13Where is the king of
Hamath, the king of Arpad, the king
of the city of Sepharvaim, or of Hena
or Ivvah?"

Hezekiah prays for help.

37:14-20pp— 2Ki 19:14-19

14Hezekiah received the letter from
the messengers and read it. Then he
went up to the temple of the LORD and
spread it out before the LORD. 15And
Hezekiah prayed to the LORD: 16"O LORD
Almighty, God of Israel, enthroned between the cherubim, you alone are God[h]
over all the kingdoms of the earth. You
have made heaven and earth. 17Give ear,
O LORD, and hear;[i] open your eyes, O
LORD, and see;[j] listen to all the words
Sennacherib has sent to insult the living God.
18"It is true, O LORD, that the Assyrian
kings have laid waste all these peoples
and their lands.[k] 19They have thrown
their gods into the fire and destroyed
them,[l] for they were not gods[m] but only
wood and stone, fashioned by human
hands. 20Now, O LORD our God, deliver
us from his hand, so that all kingdoms
on earth may know that you alone, O
LORD, are God.[a] [n]"

Isaiah prophesies Sennacherib's defeat.

37:21-38pp— 2Ki 19:20-37; 2Ch 32:20-21

21Then Isaiah son of Amoz[o] sent a
message to Hezekiah: "This is what the
LORD, the God of Israel, says: Because
you have prayed to me concerning Sennacherib king of Assyria, 22this is the
word the LORD has spoken against him:

"The Virgin Daughter of Zion
despises and mocks you.
The Daughter of Jerusalem
tosses her head[p] as you flee.
23Who is it you have insulted and
blasphemed?[q]
Against whom have you raised
your voice
and lifted your eyes in pride?[r]
Against the Holy One of Israel!
24By your messengers
you have heaped insults on the Lord.
And you have said,
'With my many chariots
I have ascended the heights of the
mountains,
the utmost heights of Lebanon.[s]
I have cut down its tallest cedars,
the choicest of its pines.
I have reached its remotest heights,
the finest of its forests.
25I have dug wells in foreign lands[b]
and drunk the water there.
With the soles of my feet
I have dried up all the streams
of Egypt.[t]'

26"Have you not heard?
Long ago I ordained[u] it.
In days of old I planned[v] it;
now I have brought it to pass,
that you have turned fortified cities
into piles of stone.[w]
27Their people, drained of power,
are dismayed and put to shame.

37:7 [a]ver 9
37:8 [b]Nu 33:20
37:9 [c]ver 7
37:10 [d]Isa 36:15
37:11 [e]Isa 36:18-20
37:12 [f]2Ki 18:11 [g]Ge 11:31; 12:1-4; Ac 7:2
37:16 [h]Dt 10:17; Ps 86:10; 136:2-3
37:17 [i]2Ch 6:40 [j]Da 9:18
37:18 [k]2Ki 15:29; Na 2:11-12
37:19 [l]Isa 26:14 [m]Isa 41:24,29
37:20 [n]Ps 46:10
37:21 [o]ver 2
37:22 [p]Job 16:4
37:23 [q]ver 4 [r]Isa 2:11
37:24 [s]Isa 14:8
37:25 [t]Dt 11:10
37:26 [u]Ac 2:23; 4:27-28; 1Pe 2:8 [v]Isa 10:6; 25:1 [w]Isa 25:2

z*9* That is, from the upper Nile region
a*20* Dead Sea Scrolls (see also 2 Kings 19:19); Masoretic Text *alone are the LORD* b*25* Dead Sea Scrolls (see also 2 Kings 19:24); Masoretic Text does not have *in foreign lands.*

They are like plants in the field,
like tender green shoots,
like grass sprouting on the roof,[a]
scorched[c] before it grows up.

28"But I know where you stay
and when you come and go[b]
and how you rage[c] against me.
29Because you rage against me
and because your insolence[d] has
reached my ears,
I will put my hook in your nose[e]
and my bit in your mouth,
and I will make you return
by the way you came.[f]

30"This will be the sign for you,
O Hezekiah:

"This year you will eat what grows
by itself,
and the second year what springs
from that.
But in the third year sow and reap,
plant vineyards and eat their fruit.
31Once more a remnant of the house
of Judah
will take root below and bear
fruit[g] above.
32For out of Jerusalem will come a
remnant,
and out of Mount Zion a band of
survivors.
The zeal[h] of the LORD Almighty
will accomplish this.

33"Therefore this is what the LORD
says concerning the king of Assyria:

"He will not enter this city
or shoot an arrow here.
He will not come before it with shield
or build a siege ramp against it.
34By the way that he came he
will return;[i]
he will not enter this city,"
declares the LORD.
35"I will defend[j] this city and save it,
for my sake[k] and for the sake of
David[l] my servant!"

Sennacherib and the 185,000 Assyrians are slain.

36Then the angel of the LORD went

37:27
[a]Ps 129:6
37:28
[b]Ps 139:1-3
[c]Ps 2:1
37:29
[d]Isa 10:12
[e]Isa 30:28; Eze 38:4
[f]ver 34
37:31
[g]Isa 27:6
37:32
[h]Isa 9:7
37:34
[i]ver 29
37:35
[j]Isa 31:5; 38:6
[k]Isa 43:25; 48:9,11
[l]2Ki 20:6
37:36
[m]Isa 10:12
37:37
[n]Ge 10:11
37:38
[o]Ge 8:4; Jer 51:27
38:1
[p]Isa 37:2
[q]2Sa 17:23
38:3
[r]Ne 13:14; Ps 26:3
[s]1Ch 29:19
[t]Dt 6:18
[u]Ps 6:8
38:5
[v]2Ki 18:2
38:6
[w]Isa 31:5; 37:35
38:7
[x]Isa 7:11,14
38:8
[y]Jos 10:13
38:10
[z]Ps 102:24

out and put to death a hundred and
eighty-five thousand men in the Assyrian[m] camp. When the people got up the
next morning—there were all the dead
bodies! 37So Sennacherib king of Assyria
broke camp and withdrew. He returned
to Nineveh[n] and stayed there.
38One day, while he was worshiping in
the temple of his god Nisroch, his sons
Adrammelech and Sharezer cut him
down with the sword, and they escaped
to the land of Ararat.[o] And Esarhaddon
his son succeeded him as king.

Fifteen extra years of life.

38:1-8pp— 2Ki 20:1-11; 2Ch 32:24-26

38 In those days Hezekiah became
ill and was at the point of death.
The prophet Isaiah son of Amoz[p] went
to him and said, "This is what the LORD
says: Put your house in order,[q] because
you are going to die; you will not recover."
2Hezekiah turned his face to the wall
and prayed to the LORD, 3"Remember,
O LORD, how I have walked[r] before you
faithfully and with wholehearted devotion[s] and have done what is good in your
eyes.[t]" And Hezekiah wept[u] bitterly.
4Then the word of the LORD came to
Isaiah: 5"Go and tell Hezekiah, 'This is
what the LORD, the God of your father
David, says: I have heard your prayer and
seen your tears; I will add fifteen years[v]
to your life. 6And I will deliver you and
this city from the hand of the king of
Assyria. I will defend[w] this city.
7" 'This is the LORD's sign[x] to you that
the LORD will do what he has promised:
8I will make the shadow cast by the sun
go back the ten steps it has gone down
on the stairway of Ahaz.' " So the sunlight went back the ten steps it had
gone down.[y]
9A writing of Hezekiah king of Judah
after his illness and recovery:

10I said, "In the prime of my life[z]

c*27* Some manuscripts of the Masoretic Text, Dead Sea Scrolls and some Septuagint manuscripts (see also 2 Kings 19:26); most manuscripts of the Masoretic Text *roof / and terraced fields*

must I go through the gates of
death[d][a]
and be robbed of the rest of my
years?[b]"
11I said, "I will not again see the LORD,
the LORD, in the land of the living;[c]
no longer will I look on mankind,
or be with those who now dwell in
this world.[e]
12Like a shepherd's tent[d] my house
has been pulled down[e] and taken
from me.
Like a weaver I have rolled[f] up my life,
and he has cut me off from the
loom;[g]
day and night[h] you made an end
of me.
13I waited patiently till dawn,
but like a lion he broke[i] all my
bones;[j]
day and night you made an end of me.
14I cried like a swift or thrush,
I moaned like a mourning dove.[k]
My eyes grew weak as I looked to
the heavens.
I am troubled; O Lord, come to
my aid!"[l]

15But what can I say?
He has spoken to me, and he
himself has done this.[m]
I will walk humbly[n] all my years
because of this anguish of my soul.[o]
16Lord, by such things men live;
and my spirit finds life in them too.
You restored me to health
and let me live.[p]
17Surely it was for my benefit
that I suffered such anguish.
In your love you kept me
from the pit[q] of destruction;
you have put all my sins[r]
behind your back.[s]
18For the grave[d][t] cannot praise you,
death cannot sing your praise;[u]
those who go down to the pit[v]
cannot hope for your faithfulness.
19The living, the living—they
praise[w] you,
as I am doing today;
fathers tell their children[x]
about your faithfulness.

38:10 [a]Ps 107:18; 2Co 1:9 [b]Job 17:11
38:11 [c]Ps 27:13; 116:9
38:12 [d]2Co 5:1,4; 2Pe 1:13-14 [e]Job 4:21 [f]Heb 1:12 [g]Job 7:6 [h]Ps 73:14
38:13 [i]Ps 51:8 [j]Job 10:16; Da 6:24
38:14 [k]Isa 59:11 [l]Job 17:3
38:15 [m]Ps 39:9 [n]1Ki 21:27 [o]Job 7:11
38:16 [p]Ps 119:25
38:17 [q]Ps 30:3 [r]Jer 31:34 [s]Isa 43:25; Mic 7:19
38:18 [t]Ecc 9:10 [u]Ps 6:5; 88:10-11; 115:17 [v]Ps 30:9
38:19 [w]Dt 6:7; Ps 118:17; 119:175 [x]Dt 11:19
38:20 [y]Ps 68:25 [z]Ps 33:2 [a]Ps 116:2 [b]Ps 116:17-19
39:1 [c]2Ch 32:31
39:2 [d]2Ch 32:31 [e]2Ki 18:15
39:3 [f]Dt 28:49
39:6 [g]2Ki 24:13; Jer 20:5
39:7 [h]2Ki 24:15; Da 1:1-7

20The LORD will save me,
and we will sing[y] with stringed
instruments[z]
all the days of our lives[a]
in the temple[b] of the LORD.

21Isaiah had said, "Prepare a poultice
of figs and apply it to the boil, and he
will recover."
22Hezekiah had asked, "What will be
the sign that I will go up to the temple
of the LORD?"

Isaiah prophesies the Babylonian exile.

39:1-8pp— 2Ki 20:12-19

39 At that time Merodach-Baladan
son of Baladan king of Babylon[c]
sent Hezekiah letters and a gift, because
he had heard of his illness and recovery.
2Hezekiah received the envoys[d] gladly
and showed them what was in his storehouses—the silver, the gold,[e] the spices,
the fine oil, his entire armory and everything found among his treasures. There
was nothing in his palace or in all his
kingdom that Hezekiah did not show
them.
3Then Isaiah the prophet went to King
Hezekiah and asked, "What did those men
say, and where did they come from?"
"From a distant land,[f]" Hezekiah replied. "They came to me from Babylon."
4The prophet asked, "What did they
see in your palace?"
"They saw everything in my palace,"
Hezekiah said. "There is nothing among
my treasures that I did not show them."
5Then Isaiah said to Hezekiah, "Hear
the word of the LORD Almighty: 6The
time will surely come when everything
in your palace, and all that your fathers
have stored up until this day, will be carried off to Babylon.[g] Nothing will be left,
says the LORD. 7And some of your descendants, your own flesh and blood who will
be born to you, will be taken away, and
they will become eunuchs in the palace
of the king of Babylon.[h]"

[d] *10, 18* Hebrew *Sheol* [e] *11* A few Hebrew manuscripts; most Hebrew manuscripts *in the place of cessation*

8"The word of the LORD you have spoken is good," Hezekiah replied. For he
thought, "There will be peace and security in my lifetime.[a]"

Prepare the way for the LORD.

40 Comfort, comfort[b] my people,
says your God.
2Speak tenderly[c] to Jerusalem,
and proclaim to her
that her hard service has been
completed,[d]
that her sin has been paid for,
that she has received from the
LORD's hand
double[e] for all her sins.

3A voice of one calling:
"In the desert prepare
the way[f] for the LORD[f];
make straight in the wilderness
a highway for our God.[g] [g]
4Every valley shall be raised up,
every mountain and hill made low;
the rough ground shall become level,[h]
the rugged places a plain.
5And the glory of the LORD will be
revealed,
and all mankind together will see it.[i]
For the mouth of the
LORD has spoken."[j]

6A voice says, "Cry out."
And I said, "What shall I cry?"

"All men are like grass,[k]
and all their glory is like the
flowers of the field.
7The grass withers and the flowers fall,
because the breath[l] of the LORD
blows on them.
Surely the people are grass.
8The grass withers and the flowers fall,
but the word[m] of our God stands
forever."[n]

9You who bring good tidings[o] to Zion,
go up on a high mountain.
You who bring good tidings to
Jerusalem,[h]
lift up your voice with a shout,
lift it up, do not be afraid;
say to the towns of Judah,
"Here is your God!"[p]
10See, the Sovereign LORD comes[q]
with power,
and his arm[r] rules[s] for him.
See, his reward[t] is with him,
and his recompense accompanies
him.
11He tends his flock like a shepherd:[u]
He gathers the lambs in his arms
and carries them close to his heart;
he gently leads those that
have young.

12Who has measured the waters[v] in
the hollow of his hand,[w]
or with the breadth of his hand
marked off the heavens?[x]
Who has held the dust of the earth
in a basket,
or weighed the mountains on
the scales
and the hills in a balance?
13Who has understood the mind[i]
of the LORD,
or instructed him as his
counselor?[y]
14Whom did the LORD consult to
enlighten him,
and who taught him the
right way?
Who was it that taught him
knowledge[z]
or showed him the path of
understanding?

15Surely the nations are like a drop
in a bucket;
they are regarded as dust on
the scales;
he weighs the islands as though
they were fine dust.
16Lebanon is not sufficient for
altar fires,
nor its animals[a] enough for
burnt offerings.

39:8 [a]2Ch 32:26
40:1 [b]Isa 12:1; 49:13; 51:3,12; 52:9; 61:2; 66:13; Jer 31:13; Zep 3:14-17; 2Co 1:3
40:2 [c]Isa 35:4 [d]Isa 41:11-13; 49:25 [e]Isa 61:7; Jer 16:18; Zec 9:12; Rev 18:6
40:3 [f]Mal 3:1 [g]Mt 3:3*; Mk 1:3*; Jn 1:23*
40:4 [h]Isa 45:2,13
40:5 [i]Isa 52:10; Lk 3:4-6* [j]Isa 1:20; 58:14
40:6 [k]Job 14:2
40:7 [l]Job 41:21
40:8 [m]Isa 55:11; 59:21 [n]Mt 5:18; 1Pe 1:24-25*
40:9 [o]Isa 52:7-10; 61:1; Ro 10:15 [p]Isa 25:9
40:10 [q]Rev 22:7 [r]Isa 59:16 [s]Isa 9:6-7 [t]Isa 62:11; Rev 22:12
40:11 [u]Eze 34:23; Mic 5:4; Jn 10:11
40:12 [v]Job 38:10 [w]Pr 30:4 [x]Heb 1:10-12
40:13 [y]Ro 11:34*; 1Co 2:16*
40:14 [z]Job 21:22; Col 2:3
40:16 [a]Ps 50:9-11; Mic 6:7; Heb 10:5-9

f3 Or *A voice of one calling in the desert: / "Prepare the way for the LORD* g3 Hebrew; Septuagint *make straight the paths of our God* h9 Or *O Zion, bringer of good tidings, / go up on a high mountain. / O Jerusalem, bringer of good tidings* i13 Or *Spirit*; or *spirit*

17Before him all the nations[a] are
as nothing;[b]
they are regarded by him as
worthless
and less than nothing.[c]

18To whom, then, will you compare
God?[d]
What image[e] will you compare
him to?
19As for an idol,[f] a craftsman casts it,
and a goldsmith[g] overlays it
with gold[h]
and fashions silver chains for it.
20A man too poor to present such
an offering
selects wood that will not rot.
He looks for a skilled craftsman
to set up an idol that will
not topple.[i]

21Do you not know?
Have you not heard?
Has it not been told[j] you from the
beginning?
Have you not understood[k] since
the earth was founded?[l]
22He sits enthroned above the circle
of the earth,
and its people are like
grasshoppers.[m]
He stretches out the heavens like
a canopy,[n]
and spreads them out like a tent[o]
to live in.
23He brings princes[p] to naught
and reduces the rulers of this
world to nothing.[q]
24No sooner are they planted,
no sooner are they sown,
no sooner do they take root in
the ground,
than he blows[r] on them and
they wither,
and a whirlwind sweeps them
away like chaff.

25"To whom will you compare me?[s]
Or who is my equal?" says the
Holy One.
26Lift your eyes and look to the
heavens:[t]
Who created[u] all these?
He who brings out the starry host[v]
one by one,
and calls them each by name.
Because of his great power and
mighty strength,
not one of them is missing.[w]

27Why do you say, O Jacob,
and complain, O Israel,
"My way is hidden from the LORD;
my cause is disregarded by my
God"?[x]
28Do you not know?
Have you not heard?[y]
The LORD is the everlasting[z] God,
the Creator of the ends of the earth.
He will not grow tired or weary,
and his understanding no one
can fathom.[a]
29He gives strength to the weary[b]
and increases the power of the weak.
30Even youths grow tired and weary,
and young men[c] stumble and fall;
31but those who hope[d] in the LORD
will renew their strength.[e]
They will soar on wings like eagles;[f]
they will run and not grow weary,
they will walk and not be faint.[g]

The LORD strengthens Israel.

41 "Be silent[h] before me, you
islands![i]
Let the nations renew their strength!
Let them come forward[j] and speak;
let us meet together[k] at the place
of judgment.

2"Who has stirred[l] up one from
the east,[m]
calling him in righteousness to
his service[j]?
He hands nations over to him
and subdues kings before him.
He turns them to dust[n] with his sword,
to windblown chaff[o] with his bow.
3He pursues them and moves on
unscathed,
by a path his feet have not traveled
before.

40:17 [a]Isa 30:28 [b]Isa 29:7 [c]Da 4:35 **40:18** [d]Ex 8:10; 1Sa 2:2; Isa 46:5 [e]Ac 17:29 **40:19** [f]Ps 115:4 [g]Isa 41:7; Jer 10:3 [h]Isa 2:20 **40:20** [i]1Sa 5:3 **40:21** [j]Ps 19:1; 50:6; Ac 14:17 [k]Ro 1:19 [l]Isa 48:13; 51:13 **40:22** [m]Nu 13:33; Ps 104:2; Isa 42:5 [n]Job 22:14 [o]Job 36:29 **40:23** [p]Isa 34:12 [q]Job 12:21; Ps 107:40 **40:24** [r]Isa 41:16 **40:25** [s]ver 18 **40:26** [t]Isa 51:6 [u]Ps 89:11-13; Isa 42:5 [v]Ps 147:4 [w]Isa 34:16 **40:27** [x]Job 27:2; Lk 18:7-8 **40:28** [y]ver 21 [z]Ps 90:2 [a]Ps 147:5; Ro 11:33 **40:29** [b]Isa 50:4; Jer 31:25 **40:30** [c]Isa 9:17; Jer 6:11; 9:21 **40:31** [d]Lk 18:1 [e]2Co 4:16 [f]Ex 19:4; Ps 103:5 [g]2Co 4:1; Heb 12:1-3 **41:1** [h]Hab 2:20; Zec 2:13 [i]Isa 11:11 [j]Isa 48:16

41:1 [k]Isa 1:18; 34:1; 50:8 **41:2** [l]Ezr 1:2 [m]ver 25; Isa 45:1,13 [n]2Sa 22:43 [o]Isa 40:24

j2 Or / *whom victory meets at every step*

4Who has done this and carried
it through,
calling forth the generations from
the beginning?[a]
I, the LORD—with the first of them
and with the last[b]—I am he."

5The islands[c] have seen it and fear;
the ends of the earth tremble.
They approach and come forward;
6 each helps the other
and says to his brother, "Be strong!"
7The craftsman encourages the
goldsmith,[d]
and he who smooths with
the hammer
spurs on him who strikes the anvil.
He says of the welding, "It is good."
He nails down the idol so it will
not topple.

8"But you, O Israel, my servant,
Jacob, whom I have chosen,
you descendants of Abraham[e] my
friend,[f]
9I took you from the ends of
the earth,[g]
from its farthest corners I called you.
I said, 'You are my servant';
I have chosen[h] you and have not
rejected you.
10So do not fear, for I am with you;[i]
do not be dismayed, for I am
your God.
I will strengthen you and help[j] you;
I will uphold you with my
righteous right hand.

11"All who rage[k] against you
will surely be ashamed and
disgraced;[l]
those who oppose[m] you
will be as nothing and perish.[n]
12Though you search for your enemies,
you will not find them.[o]
Those who wage war against you
will be as nothing[p] at all.
13For I am the LORD, your God,
who takes hold of your right hand[q]
and says to you, Do not fear;
I will help[r] you.
14Do not be afraid, O worm Jacob,
O little Israel,
for I myself will help you," declares
the LORD,
your Redeemer, the Holy One of
Israel.
15"See, I will make you into a
threshing sledge,[s]
new and sharp, with many teeth.
You will thresh the mountains and
crush them,
and reduce the hills to chaff.
16You will winnow[t] them, the wind
will pick them up,
and a gale will blow them away.
But you will rejoice in the LORD
and glory[u] in the Holy One of Israel.

17"The poor and needy search for water,[v]
but there is none;
their tongues are parched with thirst.
But I the LORD will answer[w] them;
I, the God of Israel, will not
forsake them.
18I will make rivers flow[x] on barren
heights,
and springs within the valleys.
I will turn the desert[y] into pools
of water,
and the parched ground into
springs.[z]
19I will put in the desert
the cedar and the acacia, the
myrtle and the olive.
I will set pines in the wasteland,
the fir and the cypress together,[a]
20so that people may see and know,
may consider and understand,
that the hand of the LORD has
done this,
that the Holy One of Israel has
created[b] it.

21"Present your case," says the LORD.
"Set forth your arguments," says
Jacob's King.[c]
22"Bring in ⌊your idols⌋ to tell us
what is going to happen.[d]
Tell us what the former things were,
so that we may consider them
and know their final outcome.
Or declare to us the things to come,[e]
23 tell us what the future holds,
so we may know[f] that you are gods.
Do something, whether good or bad,[g]

41:4 [a]ver 26; Isa 46:10 [b]Isa 44:6; 48:12; Rev 1:8,17; 22:13
41:5 [c]Eze 26:17-18
41:7 [d]Isa 40:19
41:8 [e]Isa 29:22; 51:2; 63:16 [f]2Ch 20:7; Jas 2:23
41:9 [g]Isa 11:12 [h]Dt 7:6
41:10 [i]Jos 1:9; Isa 43:2,5; Ro 8:31 [j]ver 13-14; Isa 44:2; 49:8
41:11 [k]Isa 17:12 [l]Isa 45:24 [m]Ex 23:22 [n]Isa 29:8
41:12 [o]Ps 37:35-36 [p]Isa 17:14
41:13 [q]Isa 42:6; 45:1 [r]ver 10
41:15 [s]Mic 4:13
41:16 [t]Jer 51:2 [u]Isa 45:25
41:17 [v]Isa 43:20 [w]Isa 30:19
41:18 [x]Isa 30:25 [y]Isa 43:19 [z]Isa 35:7
41:19 [a]Isa 60:13
41:20 [b]Job 12:9
41:21 [c]Isa 43:15
41:22 [d]Isa 43:9; 45:21 [e]Isa 46:10
41:23 [f]Isa 42:9; 44:7-8; 45:3 [g]Jer 10:5

so that we will be dismayed and
filled with fear.
24But you are less than nothing[a]
and your works are utterly worthless;
he who chooses you is detestable.[b]

25"I have stirred up one from the
north,[c] and he comes—
one from the rising sun who calls
on my name.
He treads[d] on rulers as if they were
mortar,
as if he were a potter treading
the clay.
26Who told of this from the beginning,
so we could know,
or beforehand, so we could say,
'He was right'?
No one told of this,
no one foretold it,
no one heard any words[e] from you.
27I was the first to tell[f] Zion, 'Look,
here they are!'
I gave to Jerusalem a messenger
of good tidings.[g]
28I look but there is no one[h]—
no one among them to give counsel,[i]
no one to give answer when
I ask them.
29See, they are all false!
Their deeds amount to nothing;[j]
their images are but wind[k]
and confusion.

Chosen servant of the LORD.

42 "Here is my servant, whom I
uphold,
my chosen one[l] in whom I delight;
I will put my Spirit[m] on him
and he will bring justice to
the nations.
2He will not shout or cry out,
or raise his voice in the streets.
3A bruised reed he will not break,
and a smoldering wick he will
not snuff out.
In faithfulness he will bring forth
justice;[n]
4 he will not falter or be discouraged
till he establishes justice on earth.
In his law the islands will put
their hope."[o]

41:24
[a]Isa 37:19; 44:9; 1Co 8:4
[b]Ps 115:8
41:25
[c]ver 2
[d]2Sa 22:43
41:26
[e]Hab 2:18-19
41:27
[f]Isa 48:3,16
[g]Isa 40:9
41:28
[h]Isa 50:2; 59:16; 63:5
[i]Isa 40:13-14
41:29
[j]ver 24
[k]Jer 5:13
42:1
[l]Isa 43:10; Lk 9:35; 1Pe 2:4,6
[m]Isa 11:2; Mt 3:16-17; Jn 3:34
42:3
[n]Ps 72:2
42:4
[o]Ge 49:10; Mt 12:18-21*
42:5
[p]Ps 24:2
[q]Ac 17:25
42:6
[r]Isa 43:1
[s]Jer 23:6
[t]Isa 26:3
[u]Isa 49:8
[v]Lk 2:32; Ac 13:47
42:7
[w]Isa 35:5
[x]Isa 49:9; 61:1
[y]Lk 4:19; 2Ti 2:26; Heb 2:14-15
42:8
[z]Ex 3:15
[a]Isa 48:11
42:10
[b]Ps 33:3; 40:3; 98:1
[c]Isa 49:6
[d]1Ch 16:32; Ps 96:11
42:11
[e]Isa 32:16
[f]Isa 60:7
[g]Isa 52:7; Na 1:15
42:12
[h]Isa 24:15
42:13
[i]Isa 9:6
[j]Isa 26:11
[k]Hos 11:10
[l]Isa 66:14

5This is what God the LORD says—
he who created the heavens and
stretched them out,
who spread out the earth and all
that comes out of it,[p]
who gives breath[q] to its people,
and life to those who walk on it:
6"I, the LORD, have called[r] you
in righteousness;[s]
I will take hold of your hand.
I will keep[t] you and will make you
to be a covenant[u] for the people
and a light for the Gentiles,[v]
7to open eyes that are blind,[w]
to free[x] captives from prison[y]
and to release from the dungeon
those who sit in darkness.

8"I am the LORD; that is my name![z]
I will not give my glory to another[a]
or my praise to idols.
9See, the former things have
taken place,
and new things I declare;
before they spring into being
I announce them to you."

Song of praise to the LORD.

10Sing to the LORD a new song,[b]
his praise from the ends of the
earth,[c]
you who go down to the sea, and all
that is in it,[d]
you islands, and all who live in them.
11Let the desert[e] and its towns raise
their voices;
let the settlements where Kedar[f]
lives rejoice.
Let the people of Sela sing for joy;
let them shout from the
mountaintops.[g]
12Let them give glory[h] to the LORD
and proclaim his praise in the islands.
13The LORD will march out like a
mighty[i] man,
like a warrior he will stir up
his zeal;[j]
with a shout[k] he will raise the
battle cry
and will triumph over his
enemies.[l]

14 "For a long time I have kept silent,
I have been quiet and held
myself back.
But now, like a woman in childbirth,
I cry out, I gasp and pant.
15 I will lay waste[a] the mountains
and hills
and dry up all their vegetation;
I will turn rivers into islands
and dry up[b] the pools.
16 I will lead[c] the blind[d] by ways they
have not known,
along unfamiliar paths I will
guide them;
I will turn the darkness into light
before them
and make the rough places smooth.[e]
These are the things I will do;
I will not forsake[f] them.
17 But those who trust in idols,
who say to images, 'You are
our gods,'
will be turned back in utter shame.[g]

Rebuke for Israel's disobedience.

18 "Hear, you deaf;[h]
look, you blind, and see!
19 Who is blind[i] but my servant,[j]
and deaf like the messenger[k] I send?
Who is blind like the one
committed[l] to me,
blind like the servant of the LORD?
20 You have seen many things, but have
paid no attention;
your ears are open, but you hear
nothing."[m]
21 It pleased the LORD
for the sake of his righteousness
to make his law[n] great and glorious.
22 But this is a people plundered and
looted,
all of them trapped in pits[o]
or hidden away in prisons.[p]
They have become plunder,
with no one to rescue them;
they have been made loot,
with no one to say, "Send
them back."

23 Which of you will listen to this
or pay close attention[q] in time
to come?
24 Who handed Jacob over to
become loot,
and Israel to the plunderers?
Was it not the LORD,
against whom we have sinned?
For they would not follow[r] his ways;
they did not obey his law.
25 So he poured out on them his
burning anger,
the violence of war.
It enveloped them in flames,[s] yet they
did not understand;
it consumed them, but they did not
take it to heart.[t]

God proclaims Israel's redemption.

43 But now, this is what the LORD
says—
he who created you, O Jacob,
he who formed[u] you, O Israel:[v]
"Fear not, for I have redeemed[w] you;
I have summoned you by name;[x]
you are mine.
2 When you pass through the waters,[y]
I will be with you;[z]
and when you pass through the rivers,
they will not sweep over you.
When you walk through the fire,[a]
you will not be burned;
the flames will not set you ablaze.[b]
3 For I am the LORD, your God,[c]
the Holy One of Israel, your Savior;
I give Egypt for your ransom,
Cush[k][d] and Seba in your stead.[e]
4 Since you are precious and honored
in my sight,
and because I love[f] you,
I will give men in exchange for you,
and people in exchange for your life.
5 Do not be afraid,[g] for I am with you;[h]
I will bring your children[i] from
the east
and gather you from the west.
6 I will say to the north, 'Give them up!'
and to the south,[j] 'Do not hold
them back.'
Bring my sons from afar
and my daughters[k] from the ends
of the earth—

42:15 [a]Eze 38:20 [b]Isa 50:2; Na 1:4-6
42:16 [c]Lk 1:78-79 [d]Isa 32:3 [e]Lk 3:5 [f]Heb 13:5
42:17 [g]Ps 97:7; Isa 1:29; 44:11; 45:16
42:18 [h]Isa 35:5
42:19 [i]Isa 43:8; Eze 12:2 [j]Isa 41:8-9 [k]Isa 44:26 [l]Isa 26:3
42:20 [m]Jer 6:10
42:21 [n]ver 4
42:22 [o]Isa 24:18 [p]Isa 24:22
42:23 [q]Isa 48:18
42:24 [r]Isa 30:15
42:25 [s]2Ki 25:9 [t]Isa 29:13; 47:7; 57:1,11; Hos 7:9
43:1 [u]ver 7 [v]Ge 32:28; Isa 44:21 [w]Isa 44:2,6 [x]Isa 42:6; 45:3-4
43:2 [y]Isa 8:7 [z]Dt 31:6,8 [a]Isa 29:6; 30:27 [b]Ps 66:12; Da 3:25-27
43:3 [c]Ex 20:2 [d]Isa 20:3 [e]Pr 21:18
43:4 [f]Isa 63:9
43:5 [g]Isa 44:2 [h]Jer 30:10-11 [i]Isa 41:8
43:6 [j]Ps 107:3 [k]2Co 6:18

k3 That is, the upper Nile region

[7]everyone who is called by my name,[a]
whom I created for my glory,
whom I formed and made.[b]"

[8]Lead out those who have eyes but
are blind,[c]
who have ears but are deaf.[d]
[9]All the nations gather together[e]
and the peoples assemble.
Which of them foretold[f] this
and proclaimed to us the
former things?
Let them bring in their witnesses to
prove they were right,
so that others may hear and say,
"It is true."
[10]"You are my witnesses," declares
the LORD,
"and my servant[g] whom I have
chosen,
so that you may know and believe me
and understand that I am he.
Before me no god[h] was formed,
nor will there be one after me.
[11]I, even I, am the LORD,
and apart from me there is no savior.[i]
[12]I have revealed and saved and
proclaimed—
I, and not some foreign god[j]
among you.
You are my witnesses,[k]" declares
the LORD, "that I am God.
[13] Yes, and from ancient days[l] I am he.
No one can deliver out of my hand.
When I act, who can reverse it?"[m]

Israel wearies the LORD.

[14]This is what the LORD says—
your Redeemer, the Holy One of
Israel:
"For your sake I will send to Babylon
and bring down as fugitives[n] all
the Babylonians,[1][o]
in the ships in which they took pride.
[15]I am the LORD, your Holy One,
Israel's Creator, your King."

[16]This is what the LORD says—
he who made a way through
the sea,
a path through the mighty
waters,[p]
[17]who drew out[q] the chariots and horses,
the army and reinforcements
together,[r]
and they lay there, never to rise again,
extinguished, snuffed out like a wick:
[18]"Forget the former things;
do not dwell on the past.
[19]See, I am doing a new thing![s]
Now it springs up; do you not
perceive it?
I am making a way in the desert[t]
and streams in the wasteland.
[20]The wild animals honor me,
the jackals[u] and the owls,
because I provide water[v] in
the desert
and streams in the wasteland,
to give drink to my people, my chosen,
[21] the people I formed for myself
that they may proclaim my praise.[w]

[22]"Yet you have not called upon me,
O Jacob,
you have not wearied yourselves
for me, O Israel.[x]
[23]You have not brought me sheep for
burnt offerings,
nor honored[y] me with your
sacrifices.[z]
I have not burdened you with
grain offerings
nor wearied you with demands[a]
for incense.[b]
[24]You have not bought any fragrant
calamus[c] for me,
or lavished on me the fat of
your sacrifices.
But you have burdened me with
your sins
and wearied[d] me with your
offenses.[e]

[25]"I, even I, am he who blots out
your transgressions,[f] for my
own sake,[g]
and remembers your sins no more.[h]
[26]Review the past for me,
let us argue the matter together;[i]
state the case[j] for your innocence.

43:7 [a]Isa 56:5; 63:19; Jas 2:7 [b]ver 1,21; Ps 100:3; Eph 2:10
43:8 [c]Isa 6:9-10 [d]Isa 42:20; Eze 12:2
43:9 [e]Isa 41:1 [f]Isa 41:26
43:10 [g]Isa 41:8-9 [h]Isa 44:6,8
43:11 [i]Isa 45:21
43:12 [j]Dt 32:12; Ps 81:9 [k]Isa 44:8
43:13 [l]Ps 90:2 [m]Job 9:12; Isa 14:27
43:14 [n]Isa 13:14-15 [o]Isa 23:13
43:16 [p]Ps 77:19; Isa 11:15; 51:10
43:17 [q]Ps 118:12; Isa 1:31 [r]Ex 14:9
43:19 [s]2Co 5:17; Rev 21:5 [t]Ex 17:6; Nu 20:11
43:20 [u]Isa 13:22 [v]Isa 48:21
43:21 [w]Ps 102:18; 1Pe 2:9
43:22 [x]Isa 30:11
43:23 [y]Zec 7:5-6; Mal 1:6-8 [z]Am 5:25 [a]Jer 7:22 [b]Ex 30:35; Lev 2:1
43:24 [c]Ex 30:23 [d]Isa 1:14; 7:13 [e]Mal 2:17
43:25 [f]Ac 3:19 [g]Isa 37:35; Eze 36:22 [h]Isa 38:17; Jer 31:34 **43:26** [i]Isa 1:18 [j]Isa 41:1; 50:8

[1]*14* Or *Chaldeans*

27Your first father sinned;
your spokesmen[a] rebelled against me.
28So I will disgrace the dignitaries of your temple,
and I will consign Jacob to destruction[m]
and Israel to scorn.[b]

The LORD promises blessings.

44 "But now listen, O Jacob, my servant,[c]
Israel, whom I have chosen.
2This is what the LORD says—
he who made you, who formed you in the womb,
and who will help[d] you:
Do not be afraid, O Jacob, my servant,
Jeshurun,[e] whom I have chosen.
3For I will pour water[f] on the thirsty land,
and streams on the dry ground;
I will pour out my Spirit[g] on your offspring,
and my blessing on your descendants.[h]
4They will spring up like grass in a meadow,
like poplar trees[i] by flowing streams.[j]
5One will say, 'I belong to the LORD';
another will call himself by the name of Jacob;
still another will write on his hand,[k] 'The LORD's,'[l]
and will take the name Israel.

The LORD is the first and the last.

6"This is what the LORD says—
Israel's King[m] and Redeemer,[n] the LORD Almighty:
I am the first and I am the last;[o]
apart from me there is no God.
7Who then is like me? Let him proclaim it.
Let him declare and lay out before me
what has happened since I established my ancient people,
and what is yet to come—
yes, let him foretell[p] what will come.

43:27 [a]Isa 9:15; 28:7; Jer 5:31
43:28 [b]Jer 24:9; Eze 5:15
44:1 [c]ver 21; Jer 30:10; 46:27-28
44:2 [d]Isa 41:10 [e]Dt 32:15
44:3 [f]Joel 3:18 [g]Joel 2:28; Ac 2:17 [h]Isa 61:9; 65:23
44:4 [i]Lev 23:40 [j]Job 40:22
44:5 [k]Ex 13:9 [l]Zec 8:20-22
44:6 [m]Isa 41:21 [n]Isa 43:1 [o]Isa 41:4; Rev 1:8,17; 22:13
44:7 [p]Isa 41:22,26
44:8 [q]Isa 43:10 [r]Dt 4:35; 1Sa 2:2
44:9 [s]Isa 41:24
44:10 [t]Isa 41:29; Jer 10:5; Ac 19:26
44:11 [u]Isa 1:29 [v]Isa 42:17
44:12 [w]Isa 40:19; 41:6-7 [x]Jer 10:3-5; Ac 17:29
44:13 [y]Isa 41:7 [z]Ps 115:4-7 [a]Jdg 17:4-5
44:15 [b]ver 19

8Do not tremble, do not be afraid.
Did I not proclaim this and foretell it long ago?
You are my witnesses. Is there any God[q] besides me?
No, there is no other Rock;[r] I know not one."

Idols are worthless.

9All who make idols are nothing,
and the things they treasure are worthless.[s]
Those who would speak up for them are blind;
they are ignorant, to their own shame.
10Who shapes a god and casts an idol,
which can profit him nothing?[t]
11He and his kind will be put to shame;[u]
craftsmen are nothing but men.
Let them all come together and take their stand;
they will be brought down to terror and infamy.[v]

12The blacksmith[w] takes a tool
and works with it in the coals;
he shapes an idol with hammers,
he forges it with the might of his arm.[x]
He gets hungry and loses his strength;
he drinks no water and grows faint.
13The carpenter[y] measures with a line
and makes an outline with a marker;
he roughs it out with chisels
and marks it with compasses.
He shapes it in the form of man,[z]
of man in all his glory,
that it may dwell in a shrine.[a]
14He cut down cedars,
or perhaps took a cypress or oak.
He let it grow among the trees of the forest,
or planted a pine, and the rain made it grow.
15It is man's fuel[b] for burning;
some of it he takes and warms himself,
he kindles a fire and bakes bread.

[m]28 The Hebrew term refers to the irrevocable giving over of things or persons to the LORD, often by totally destroying them.

But he also fashions a god and
worships it;
he makes an idol and bows[a] down
to it.
16 Half of the wood he burns in the fire;
over it he prepares his meal,
he roasts his meat and eats his fill.
He also warms himself and says,
"Ah! I am warm; I see the fire."
17 From the rest he makes a god, his idol;
he bows down to it and worships.
He prays[b] to it and says,
"Save[c] me; you are my god."
18 They know nothing, they
understand[d] nothing;
their eyes[e] are plastered over so
they cannot see,
and their minds closed so they
cannot understand.
19 No one stops to think,
no one has the knowledge or
understanding[f] to say,
"Half of it I used for fuel;
I even baked bread over its coals,
I roasted meat and I ate.
Shall I make a detestable[g] thing from
what is left?
Shall I bow down to a block of
wood?"
20 He feeds on ashes,[h] a deluded[i] heart
misleads him;
he cannot save himself, or say,
"Is not this thing in my right hand
a lie?[j]"

The LORD has promised redemption.

21 "Remember[k] these things, O Jacob,
for you are my servant, O Israel.
I have made you, you are my servant;[l]
O Israel, I will not forget you.[m]
22 I have swept away[n] your offenses
like a cloud,
your sins like the morning mist.
Return[o] to me,
for I have redeemed[p] you."

23 Sing for joy,[q] O heavens, for the
LORD has done this;
shout aloud, O earth[r] beneath.
Burst into song, you mountains,[s]
you forests and all your trees,
for the LORD has redeemed Jacob,
he displays his glory[t] in Israel.

24 "This is what the LORD says—
your Redeemer,[u] who formed you
in the womb:

I am the LORD,
who has made all things,
who alone stretched out the heavens,[v]
who spread out the earth by myself,

25 who foils[w] the signs of false prophets
and makes fools of diviners,[x]
who overthrows the learning of
the wise[y]
and turns it into nonsense,[z]
26 who carries out the words[a] of
his servants
and fulfills[b] the predictions of
his messengers,

who says of Jerusalem, 'It shall
be inhabited,'
of the towns of Judah, 'They shall
be built,'
and of their ruins, 'I will restore
them,'[c]
27 who says to the watery deep, 'Be dry,
and I will dry up your streams,'
28 who says of Cyrus,[d] 'He is my
shepherd
and will accomplish all that I please;
he will say of Jerusalem,[e] "Let
it be rebuilt,"
and of the temple,[f] "Let its
foundations be laid."'

Cyrus will subdue nations.

45

"This is what the LORD says to
his anointed,
to Cyrus, whose right hand I take
hold[g] of
to subdue nations[h] before him
and to strip kings of their armor,
to open doors before him
so that gates will not be shut:
2 I will go before you
and will level[i] the mountains[n];
I will break down gates of bronze
and cut through bars of iron.[j]

44:15 [a]2Ch 25:14
44:17 [b]1Ki 18:26 [c]Isa 45:20
44:18 [d]Isa 1:3 [e]Isa 6:9-10
44:19 [f]Isa 5:13; 27:11; 45:20 [g]Dt 27:15
44:20 [h]Ps 102:9 [i]Job 15:31; Ro 1:21-23,28; 2Th 2:11; 2Ti 3:13 [j]Isa 59:3,4,13; Ro 1:25
44:21 [k]Isa 46:8; Zec 10:9 [l]ver 1-2 [m]Isa 49:15
44:22 [n]Isa 43:25; Ac 3:19 [o]Isa 55:7 [p]1Co 6:20
44:23 [q]Isa 42:10 [r]Ps 148:7 [s]Ps 98:8 [t]Isa 61:3
44:24 [u]Isa 43:14 [v]Isa 42:5
44:25 [w]Ps 33:10 [x]Isa 47:13 [y]1Co 1:27 [z]2Sa 15:31; 1Co 1:19-20
44:26 [a]Zec 1:6 [b]Isa 55:11; Mt 5:18 [c]Isa 49:8-21
44:28 [d]2Ch 36:22 [e]Isa 14:32 [f]Ezr 1:2-4
45:1 [g]Ps 73:23; Isa 41:13; 42:6 [h]Jer 50:35
45:2 [i]Isa 40:4 [j]Ps 107:16; Jer 51:30

n2 Dead Sea Scrolls and Septuagint; the meaning of the word in the Masoretic Text is uncertain.

3 I will give you the treasures[a] of darkness,
riches stored in secret places,[b]
so that you may know[c] that I am the LORD,
the God of Israel, who summons you by name.[d]
4 For the sake of Jacob my servant,[e]
of Israel my chosen,
I summon you by name
and bestow on you a title of honor,
though you do not acknowledge[f] me.
5 I am the LORD, and there is no other;[g]
apart from me there is no God.[h]
I will strengthen you,[i]
though you have not acknowledged me,
6 so that from the rising of the sun
to the place of its setting[j]
men may know there is none besides me.[k]
I am the LORD, and there is no other.
7 I form the light and create darkness,
I bring prosperity and create disaster;[l]
I, the LORD, do all these things.

8 "You heavens above, rain[m] down righteousness;[n]
let the clouds shower it down.
Let the earth open wide,
let salvation[o] spring up,
let righteousness grow with it;
I, the LORD, have created it.

9 "Woe to him who quarrels[p] with his Maker,
to him who is but a potsherd among the potsherds on the ground.
Does the clay say to the potter,[q]
'What are you making?'
Does your work say,
'He has no hands'?
10 Woe to him who says to his father,
'What have you begotten?'
or to his mother,
'What have you brought to birth?'

11 "This is what the LORD says—
the Holy One of Israel, and its Maker:
Concerning things to come,
do you question me about my children,
or give me orders about the work of my hands?[r]
12 It is I who made the earth
and created mankind upon it.
My own hands stretched out the heavens;[s]
I marshaled their starry hosts.[t]
13 I will raise up Cyrus[o] [u] in my righteousness:
I will make all his ways straight.
He will rebuild my city
and set my exiles free,
but not for a price or reward,[v]
says the LORD Almighty."

14 This is what the LORD says:

"The products of Egypt and the merchandise of Cush,[p]
and those tall Sabeans—
they will come over to you
and will be yours;
they will trudge behind you,
coming over to you in chains.[w]
They will bow down before you
and plead[x] with you, saying,
'Surely God is with you,[y] and there is no other;
there is no other god.'"

15 Truly you are a God who hides[z] himself,
O God and Savior of Israel.
16 All the makers of idols will be put to shame and disgraced;[a]
they will go off into disgrace together.
17 But Israel will be saved[b] by the LORD
with an everlasting salvation;[c]
you will never be put to shame or disgraced,
to ages everlasting.

18 For this is what the LORD says—
he who created the heavens,
he is God;
he who fashioned and made the earth,
he founded it;
he did not create it to be empty,[d]
but formed it to be inhabited[e]—
he says:

45:3 [a]Jer 50:37 [b]Jer 41:8 [c]Isa 41:23 [d]Ex 33:12; Isa 43:1
45:4 [e]Isa 41:8-9 [f]Ac 17:23
45:5 [g]Isa 44:8 [h]Ps 18:31 [i]Ps 18:39
45:6 [j]Isa 43:5; Mal 1:11 [k]ver 5,18
45:7 [l]Isa 31:2; Am 3:6
45:8 [m]Ps 72:6; Joel 3:18 [n]Ps 85:11; Isa 60:21; 61:10,11; Hos 10:12 [o]Isa 12:3
45:9 [p]Job 15:25 [q]Isa 29:16; Ro 9:20-21*
45:11 [r]Isa 19:25
45:12 [s]Ge 2:1; Isa 42:5 [t]Ne 9:6
45:13 [u]2Ch 36:22; Isa 41:2 [v]Isa 52:3
45:14 [w]Isa 14:1-2 [x]Jer 16:19; Zec 8:20-23 [y]1Co 14:25
45:15 [z]Ps 44:24
45:16 [a]Isa 44:9,11
45:17 [b]Ro 11:26 [c]Isa 26:4
45:18 [d]Ge 1:2 [e]Ge 1:26; Isa 42:5

[o] 13 Hebrew *him* [p] 14 That is, the upper Nile region

"I am the LORD,
and there is no other.[a]
19I have not spoken in secret,[b]
from somewhere in a land
of darkness;
I have not said to Jacob's descendants,[c]
'Seek me in vain.'
I, the LORD, speak the truth;
I declare what is right.[d]

20"Gather together[e] and come;
assemble, you fugitives from
the nations.
Ignorant[f] are those who carry[g]
about idols of wood,
who pray to gods that cannot save.[h]
21Declare what is to be, present it—
let them take counsel together.
Who foretold[i] this long ago,
who declared it from the
distant past?
Was it not I, the LORD?
And there is no God apart
from me,[j]
a righteous God and a Savior;
there is none but me.

22"Turn[k] to me and be saved,[l]
all you ends of the earth;[m]
for I am God, and there is no other.
23By myself I have sworn,[n]
my mouth has uttered in
all integrity[o]
a word that will not be revoked:[p]
Before me every knee will bow;
by me every tongue will swear.[q]
24They will say of me, 'In the LORD alone
are righteousness[r] and strength.'"
All who have raged against him
will come to him and be put
to shame.[s]
25But in the LORD all the descendants
of Israel
will be found righteous and
will exult.[t]

Babylon's idols are unable to rescue.

46 Bel[u] bows down, Nebo
stoops low;
their idols are borne by beasts
of burden.[q]
The images that are carried[v] about
are burdensome,
a burden for the weary.
2They stoop and bow down together;
unable to rescue the burden,
they themselves go off into
captivity.[w]

3"Listen[x] to me, O house of Jacob,
all you who remain of the house
of Israel,
you whom I have upheld since you
were conceived,
and have carried since your birth.
4Even to your old age and gray hairs[y]
I am he,[z] I am he who will
sustain you.
I have made you and I will carry you;
I will sustain you and I will
rescue you.

5"To whom will you compare me or
count me equal?
To whom will you liken me that
we may be compared?[a]
6Some pour out gold from their bags
and weigh out silver on the scales;
they hire a goldsmith[b] to make it
into a god,
and they bow down and worship it.[c]
7They lift it to their shoulders and
carry[d] it;
they set it up in its place, and
there it stands.
From that spot it cannot move.
Though one cries out to it, it does
not answer;
it cannot save[e] him from his troubles.

8"Remember[f] this, fix it in mind,
take it to heart, you rebels.
9Remember the former things, those
of long ago;[g]
I am God, and there is no other;
I am God, and there is none
like me.[h]
10I make known the end from the
beginning,
from ancient times,[i] what is still
to come.
I say: My purpose will stand,[j]
and I will do all that I please.

q1 Or *are but beasts and cattle*

45:18 [a]ver 5
45:19 [b]Isa 48:16 [c]Isa 41:8 [d]Dt 30:11
45:20 [e]Isa 43:9 [f]Isa 44:19 [g]Isa 46:1; Jer 10:5 [h]Isa 44:17; 46:6-7
45:21 [i]Isa 41:22 [j]ver 5
45:22 [k]Zec 12:10 [l]Nu 21:8-9; 2Ch 20:12 [m]Isa 49:6,12
45:23 [n]Ge 22:16 [o]Heb 6:13 [p]Isa 55:11 [q]Ps 63:11; Isa 19:18; Ro 14:11*; Php 2:10-11
45:24 [r]Jer 33:16 [s]Isa 41:11
45:25 [t]Isa 41:16
46:1 [u]Isa 21:9; Jer 50:2; 51:44 [v]Isa 45:20
46:2 [w]Jdg 18:17-18; 2Sa 5:21
46:3 [x]ver 12
46:4 [y]Ps 71:18 [z]Isa 43:13
46:5 [a]Isa 40:18,25
46:6 [b]Isa 40:19 [c]Isa 44:17
46:7 [d]ver 1 [e]Isa 44:17; Isa 45:20
46:8 [f]Isa 44:21
46:9 [g]Dt 32:7 [h]Isa 45:5,21
46:10 [i]Isa 45:21 [j]Pr 19:21; Ac 5:39

[11]From the east I summon a bird of prey;
from a far-off land, a man to fulfill
my purpose.
What I have said, that will I
bring about;
what I have planned, that will I do.
[12]Listen[a] to me, you stubborn-hearted,
you who are far from
righteousness.[b]
[13]I am bringing my righteousness near,
it is not far away;
and my salvation will not be delayed.
I will grant salvation to Zion,
my splendor[c] to Israel.

The fall of Babylon.

47 "Go down, sit in the dust,
Virgin Daughter[d] of Babylon;
sit on the ground without a throne,
Daughter of the Babylonians.[r][e]
No more will you be called
tender or delicate.[f]
[2]Take millstones[g] and grind[h] flour;
take off your veil.[i]
Lift up your skirts,[j] bare your legs,
and wade through the streams.
[3]Your nakedness[k] will be exposed
and your shame[l] uncovered.
I will take vengeance;[m]
I will spare no one."

[4]Our Redeemer—the LORD Almighty
is his name[n]—
is the Holy One of Israel.

[5]"Sit in silence, go into darkness,[o]
Daughter of the Babylonians;
no more will you be called
queen of kingdoms.[p]
[6]I was angry[q] with my people
and desecrated my inheritance;
I gave them into your hand,[r]
and you showed them no mercy.
Even on the aged
you laid a very heavy yoke.
[7]You said, 'I will continue forever—
the eternal queen!'[s]
But you did not consider these things
or reflect[t] on what might happen.[u]

[8]"Now then, listen, you wanton
creature,
lounging in your security[v]
and saying to yourself,
'I am, and there is none
besides me.[w]
I will never be a widow[x]
or suffer the loss of children.'
[9]Both of these will overtake you
in a moment,[y] on a single day:
loss of children[z] and widowhood.
They will come upon you in
full measure,
in spite of your many sorceries[a]
and all your potent spells.[b]
[10]You have trusted[c] in your
wickedness
and have said, 'No one sees me.'[d]
Your wisdom[e] and knowledge
mislead[f] you
when you say to yourself,
'I am, and there is none besides me.'
[11]Disaster will come upon you,
and you will not know how to
conjure it away.
A calamity will fall upon you
that you cannot ward off with
a ransom;
a catastrophe you cannot foresee
will suddenly[g] come upon you.

[12]"Keep on, then, with your
magic spells
and with your many sorceries,[h]
which you have labored at since
childhood.
Perhaps you will succeed,
perhaps you will cause terror.
[13]All the counsel you have received
has only worn you out![i]
Let your astrologers[j] come forward,
those stargazers who make
predictions month by month,
let them save[k] you from what is
coming upon you.
[14]Surely they are like stubble;[l]
the fire will burn them up.
They cannot even save themselves
from the power of the flame.[m]
Here are no coals to warm anyone;
here is no fire to sit by.

46:12 [a]ver 3 [b]Ps 119:150; Isa 48:1; Jer 2:5
46:13 [c]Isa 44:23
47:1 [d]Isa 23:12 [e]Ps 137:8; Jer 50:42; 51:33; Zec 2:7 [f]Dt 28:56
47:2 [g]Ex 11:5; Mt 24:41 [h]Jdg 16:21 [i]Ge 24:65 [j]Isa 32:11
47:3 [k]Eze 16:37; Na 3:5 [l]Isa 20:4 [m]Isa 34:8
47:4 [n]Jer 50:34
47:5 [o]Isa 13:10 [p]Isa 13:19
47:6 [q]2Ch 28:9 [r]Isa 10:13
47:7 [s]ver 5; Rev 18:7 [t]Isa 42:23,25 [u]Dt 32:29
47:8 [v]Isa 32:9 [w]Isa 45:6; Zep 2:15 [x]Rev 18:7
47:9 [y]Ps 73:19; 1Th 5:3; Rev 18:8-10 [z]Isa 13:18 [a]Na 3:4 [b]Rev 18:23
47:10 [c]Ps 52:7; 62:10 [d]Isa 29:15 [e]Isa 5:21 [f]Isa 44:20
47:11 [g]1Th 5:3
47:12 [h]ver 9
47:13 [i]Isa 57:10; Jer 51:58 [j]Isa 44:25 [k]ver 15
47:14 [l]Isa 5:24; Na 1:10 [m]Isa 10:17; Jer 51:30,32,58

[r]*1* Or *Chaldeans*; also in verse 5

[15]That is all they can do for you—
these you have labored with
and trafficked[a] with since childhood.
Each of them goes on in his error;
there is not one that can save you.

Stubborn Israel is rebuked.

48 "Listen to this, O house of Jacob,
you who are called by the name of Israel
and come from the line of Judah,
you who take oaths in the name of the LORD
and invoke[b] the God of Israel—
but not in truth[c] or righteousness—
[2]you who call yourselves citizens of the holy city[d]
and rely[e] on the God of Israel—
the LORD Almighty is his name:
[3]I foretold the former things[f] long ago,
my mouth announced[g] them and I made them known;
then suddenly I acted, and they came to pass.
[4]For I knew how stubborn[h] you were;
the sinews of your neck[i] were iron,
your forehead[j] was bronze.
[5]Therefore I told you these things long ago;
before they happened I announced them to you
so that you could not say,
'My idols did them;[k]
my wooden image and metal god ordained them.'
[6]You have heard these things; look at them all.
Will you not admit them?

"From now on I will tell you of new things,
of hidden things unknown to you.
[7]They are created now, and not long ago;
you have not heard of them before today.
So you cannot say,
'Yes, I knew of them.'
[8]You have neither heard nor understood;
from of old your ear has not been open.
Well do I know how treacherous you are;
you were called a rebel[l] from birth.

God saves Israel for his own sake.

[9]For my own name's sake I delay my wrath;[m]
for the sake of my praise I hold it back from you,
so as not to cut you off.[n]
[10]See, I have refined you, though not as silver;
I have tested you in the furnace[o] of affliction.
[11]For my own sake,[p] for my own sake, I do this.
How can I let myself be defamed?[q]
I will not yield my glory to another.[r]

[12]"Listen[s] to me, O Jacob,
Israel, whom I have called:
I am he;
I am the first and I am the last.[t]
[13]My own hand laid the foundations of the earth,[u]
and my right hand spread out the heavens;[v]
when I summon them,
they all stand up together.[w]

[14]"Come together,[x] all of you, and listen:
Which of ⌞the idols⌟ has foretold these things?
The LORD's chosen ally
will carry out his purpose[y] against Babylon;
his arm will be against the Babylonians.[s]
[15]I, even I, have spoken;
yes, I have called[z] him.
I will bring him,
and he will succeed in his mission.

[16]"Come near[a] me and listen to this:

"From the first announcement I have not spoken in secret;[b]
at the time it happens, I am there."

And now the Sovereign LORD has sent[c] me,
with his Spirit.

47:15 [a]Rev 18:11
48:1 [b]Isa 58:2 [c]Jer 4:2
48:2 [d]Isa 52:1 [e]Isa 10:20; Mic 3:11; Ro 2:17
48:3 [f]Isa 41:22 [g]Isa 45:21
48:4 [h]Dt 31:27 [i]Ex 32:9; Ac 7:51 [j]Eze 3:9
48:5 [k]Jer 44:15-18
48:8 [l]Dt 9:7,24; Ps 58:3
48:9 [m]Ps 78:38; Isa 30:18 [n]Ne 9:31
48:10 [o]1Ki 8:51
48:11 [p]1Sa 12:22; Isa 37:35 [q]Dt 32:27; Jer 14:7,21; Eze 20:9,14, 22,44 [r]Isa 42:8
48:12 [s]Isa 46:3 [t]Isa 41:4; Rev 1:17; 22:13
48:13 [u]Heb 1:10-12 [v]Ex 20:11 [w]Isa 40:26
48:14 [x]Isa 43:9 [y]Isa 46:10-11
48:15 [z]Isa 45:1
48:16 [a]Isa 41:1 [b]Isa 45:19 [c]Zec 2:9,11

s *14* Or *Chaldeans*; also in verse 20

17 This is what the LORD says—
your Redeemer,[a] the Holy One[b]
of Israel:
"I am the LORD your God,
who teaches you what is best for you,
who directs[c] you in the way[d]
you should go.
18 If only you had paid attention[e] to
my commands,
your peace[f] would have been like
a river,
your righteousness[g] like the waves
of the sea.
19 Your descendants would have been
like the sand,
your children like its numberless
grains;[h]
their name would never be cut off[i]
nor destroyed from before me."

20 Leave Babylon,
flee[j] from the Babylonians!
Announce this with shouts of joy[k]
and proclaim it.
Send it out to the ends of the earth;
say, "The LORD has redeemed[l]
his servant Jacob."
21 They did not thirst[m] when he led
them through the deserts;
he made water flow[n] for them
from the rock;
he split the rock
and water gushed out.[o]

22 "There is no peace," says the LORD,
"for the wicked."[p]

A light for the Gentiles.

49 Listen to me, you islands;
hear this, you distant nations:
Before I was born[q] the LORD
called[r] me;
from my birth he has made
mention of my name.
2 He made my mouth like a
sharpened sword,[s]
in the shadow of his hand he hid me;
he made me into a polished arrow
and concealed me in his quiver.
3 He said to me, "You are my servant,[t]
Israel, in whom I will display my
splendor."[u]

4 But I said, "I have labored to
no purpose;
I have spent my strength in vain[v]
and for nothing.
Yet what is due me is in the
LORD's hand,
and my reward[w] is with my God."

5 And now the LORD says—
he who formed me in the womb
to be his servant
to bring Jacob back to him
and gather Israel[x] to himself,
for I am honored[y] in the eyes
of the LORD
and my God has been my
strength—
6 he says:
"It is too small a thing for you to be
my servant
to restore the tribes of Jacob
and bring back those of Israel I
have kept.
I will also make you a light for
the Gentiles,[z]
that you may bring my salvation to
the ends of the earth."[a]

7 This is what the LORD says—
the Redeemer and Holy One of
Israel[b]—
to him who was despised[c] and
abhorred by the nation,
to the servant of rulers:
"Kings[d] will see you and rise up,
princes will see and bow down,
because of the LORD, who is faithful,
the Holy One of Israel, who has
chosen you."

8 This is what the LORD says:

"In the time of my favor[e] I will
answer you,
and in the day of salvation I will
help you;[f]
I will keep[g] you and will make you
to be a covenant for the people,[h]
to restore the land[i]
and to reassign its desolate
inheritances,
9 to say to the captives,[j] 'Come out,'
and to those in darkness, 'Be free!'

48:17 [a]Isa 49:7 [b]Isa 43:14 [c]Isa 49:10 [d]Ps 32:8
48:18 [e]Dt 32:29 [f]Ps 119:165; Isa 66:12 [g]Isa 45:8
48:19 [h]Ge 22:17 [i]Isa 56:5; 66:22
48:20 [j]Jer 50:8; 51:6,45; Zec 2:6-7; Rev 18:4 [k]Isa 49:13 [l]Isa 52:9; 63:9
48:21 [m]Isa 41:17 [n]Isa 30:25 [o]Ex 17:6; Nu 20:11; Ps 105:41; Isa 35:6
48:22 [p]Isa 57:21
49:1 [q]Isa 44:24; 46:3; Mt 1:20 [r]Isa 7:14; 9:6; 44:2; Jer 1:5; Gal 1:15
49:2 [s]Isa 11:4; Rev 1:16
49:3 [t]Zec 3:8 [u]Isa 44:23
49:4 [v]Isa 65:23 [w]Isa 35:4
49:5 [x]Isa 11:12 [y]Isa 43:4
49:6 [z]Lk 2:32 [a]Ac 13:47*
49:7 [b]Isa 48:17 [c]Ps 22:6; 69:7-9 [d]Isa 52:15
49:8 [e]Ps 69:13 [f]2Co 6:2* [g]Isa 26:3 [h]Isa 42:6 [i]Isa 44:26
49:9 [j]Isa 42:7; 61:1; Lk 4:19

"They will feed beside the roads
and find pasture on every
barren hill.[a]
10 They will neither hunger nor thirst,[b]
nor will the desert heat or the sun
beat upon them.[c]
He who has compassion[d] on them
will guide them
and lead them beside springs[e]
of water.
11 I will turn all my mountains into roads,
and my highways[f] will be raised up.[g]
12 See, they will come from afar[h]—
some from the north, some from
the west,
some from the region of Aswan.[t]"

13 Shout for joy, O heavens;
rejoice, O earth;
burst into song, O mountains![i]
For the LORD comforts[j] his people
and will have compassion on his
afflicted ones.

14 But Zion said, "The LORD has
forsaken me,
the Lord has forgotten me."

15 "Can a mother forget the baby
at her breast
and have no compassion on the
child she has borne?
Though she may forget,
I will not forget you![k]
16 See, I have engraved[l] you on the
palms of my hands;
your walls[m] are ever before me.
17 Your sons hasten back,
and those who laid you waste[n]
depart from you.
18 Lift up your eyes and look around;
all your sons gather[o] and come
to you.
As surely as I live,[p]" declares the LORD,
"you will wear[q] them all as
ornaments;
you will put them on, like a bride.

19 "Though you were ruined and
made desolate[r]
and your land laid waste,[s]
now you will be too small for
your people,[t]
and those who devoured you will
be far away.
20 The children born during your
bereavement
will yet say in your hearing,
'This place is too small for us;
give us more space to live in.'[u]
21 Then you will say in your heart,
'Who bore me these?
I was bereaved and barren;
I was exiled and rejected.[v]
Who brought these up?
I was left[w] all alone,
but these—where have they
come from?'"

22 This is what the Sovereign LORD
says:

"See, I will beckon to the Gentiles,
I will lift up my banner[x] to the
peoples;
they will bring your sons in their arms
and carry your daughters on their
shoulders.[y]
23 Kings[z] will be your foster fathers,
and their queens your nursing
mothers.[a]
They will bow down before you with
their faces to the ground;
they will lick the dust[b] at your feet.
Then you will know that I am
the LORD;[c]
those who hope in me will not
be disappointed."

24 Can plunder be taken from warriors,[d]
or captives rescued from the
fierce[u]?

25 But this is what the LORD says:

"Yes, captives[e] will be taken from
warriors,[f]
and plunder retrieved from
the fierce;
I will contend with those who
contend with you,
and your children I will save.[g]
26 I will make your oppressors[h] eat[i]
their own flesh;

49:9 [a]Isa 41:18
49:10 [b]Isa 33:16 [c]Ps 121:6; Rev 7:16 [d]Isa 14:1 [e]Isa 35:7
49:11 [f]Isa 11:16 [g]Isa 40:4
49:12 [h]Isa 43:5-6
49:13 [i]Isa 44:23 [j]Isa 40:1
49:15 [k]Isa 44:21
49:16 [l]SS 8:6 [m]Ps 48:12-13; Isa 62:6
49:17 [n]Isa 10:6
49:18 [o]Isa 43:5; 54:7; Isa 60:4 [p]Isa 45:23 [q]Isa 52:1
49:19 [r]Isa 54:1,3 [s]Isa 5:6 [t]Zec 10:10
49:20 [u]Isa 54:1-3
49:21 [v]Isa 5:13 [w]Isa 1:8
49:22 [x]Isa 11:10 [y]Isa 60:4
49:23 [z]Isa 60:3,10-11 [a]Isa 60:16 [b]Ps 72:9 [c]Mic 7:17
49:24 [d]Mt 12:29; Lk 11:21
49:25 [e]Isa 14:2 [f]Jer 50:33-34 [g]Isa 25:9; 35:4
49:26 [h]Isa 9:4 [i]Isa 9:20

[t]*12* Dead Sea Scrolls; Masoretic Text *Sinim*
[u]*24* Dead Sea Scrolls, Vulgate and Syriac (see also Septuagint and verse 25); Masoretic Text *righteous*

they will be drunk on their own
blood,[a] as with wine.
Then all mankind will know[b]
that I, the LORD, am your Savior,
your Redeemer, the Mighty One
of Jacob."

The LORD's servant is obedient.

50 This is what the LORD says:
"Where is your mother's
certificate of divorce[c]
with which I sent her away?
Or to which of my creditors
did I sell[d] you?
Because of your sins you were sold;[e]
because of your transgressions your
mother was sent away.
2When I came, why was there no one?
When I called, why was there no
one to answer?[f]
Was my arm too short[g] to ransom you?
Do I lack the strength[h] to rescue you?
By a mere rebuke I dry up the sea,[i]
I turn rivers into a desert;
their fish rot for lack of water
and die of thirst.
3I clothe the sky with darkness
and make sackcloth[j] its covering."

4The Sovereign LORD has given me an
instructed tongue,[k]
to know the word that sustains
the weary.[l]
He wakens me morning by morning,[m]
wakens my ear to listen like one
being taught.
5The Sovereign LORD has opened
my ears,[n]
and I have not been rebellious;[o]
I have not drawn back.
6I offered my back to those who
beat[p] me,
my cheeks to those who pulled out
my beard;
I did not hide my face
from mocking and spitting.[q]
7Because the Sovereign LORD helps[r] me,
I will not be disgraced.
Therefore have I set my face like flint,[s]
and I know I will not be put
to shame.
8He who vindicates me is near.
Who then will bring charges
against me?[t]
Let us face each other![u]
Who is my accuser?
Let him confront me!
9It is the Sovereign LORD who
helps[v] me.
Who is he that will condemn me?
They will all wear out like a garment;
the moths[w] will eat them up.

10Who among you fears the LORD
and obeys the word of his servant?[x]
Let him who walks in the dark,
who has no light,
trust[y] in the name of the LORD
and rely on his God.
11But now, all you who light fires
and provide yourselves with
flaming torches,[z]
go, walk in the light of your fires[a]
and of the torches you have
set ablaze.
This is what you shall receive from
my hand:
You will lie down in torment.[b]

The LORD will comfort Zion.

51 "Listen[c] to me, you who pursue
righteousness[d]
and who seek the LORD:
Look to the rock from which you
were cut
and to the quarry from which you
were hewn;
2look to Abraham,[e] your father,
and to Sarah, who gave you birth.
When I called him he was but one,
and I blessed him and made
him many.[f]
3The LORD will surely comfort[g] Zion
and will look with compassion on
all her ruins;[h]
he will make her deserts like Eden,[i]
her wastelands like the garden of
the LORD.
Joy and gladness[j] will be found in her,
thanksgiving and the sound of
singing.

49:26 [a]Rev 16:6 [b]Eze 39:7
50:1 [c]Dt 24:1; Jer 3:8; Hos 2:2 [d]Ne 5:5; Mt 18:25 [e]Dt 32:30; Isa 52:3
50:2 [f]Isa 41:28 [g]Nu 11:23; Isa 59:1 [h]Ge 18:14 [i]Ex 14:22; Jos 3:16
50:3 [j]Rev 6:12
50:4 [k]Ex 4:12 [l]Mt 11:28 [m]Ps 5:3; 119:147; 143:8
50:5 [n]Isa 35:5 [o]Mt 26:39; Jn 8:29; 14:31; 15:10; Ac 26:19; Heb 5:8
50:6 [p]Isa 53:5; Mt 27:30; Mk 14:65; 15:19; Lk 22:63 [q]La 3:30; Mt 26:67
50:7 [r]Isa 42:1 [s]Eze 3:8-9
50:8 [t]Isa 43:26; Ro 8:32-34 [u]Isa 41:1
50:9 [v]Isa 41:10 [w]Job 13:28; Isa 51:8
50:10 [x]Isa 49:3 [y]Isa 26:4
50:11 [z]Pr 26:18 [a]Jas 3:6 [b]Isa 65:13-15
51:1 [c]Isa 46:3 [d]ver 7; Ps 94:15; Ro 9:30-31
51:2 [e]Isa 29:22; Ro 4:16; Heb 11:11 [f]Ge 12:2
51:3 [g]Isa 40:1 [h]Isa 52:9 [i]Ge 2:8 [j]Isa 25:9; 66:10

4“Listen to me, my people;[a]
hear me, my nation:
The law will go out from me;
my justice[b] will become a light to
the nations.[c]
5My righteousness draws near speedily,
my salvation is on the way,[d]
and my arm[e] will bring justice
to the nations.
The islands will look to me
and wait in hope for my arm.
6Lift up your eyes to the heavens,
look at the earth beneath;
the heavens will vanish like smoke,[f]
the earth will wear out like
a garment[g]
and its inhabitants die like flies.
But my salvation will last forever,
my righteousness will never fail.

7“Hear me, you who know what
is right,[h]
you people who have my law in
your hearts:[i]
Do not fear the reproach of men
or be terrified by their insults.[j]
8For the moth will eat them up like
a garment;[k]
the worm will devour them
like wool.
But my righteousness will last forever,[l]
my salvation through all
generations.”

9Awake, awake! Clothe yourself
with strength,[m]
O arm of the LORD;
awake, as in days gone by,
as in generations of old.[n]
Was it not you who cut Rahab
to pieces,
who pierced that monster[o]
through?
10Was it not you who dried up the sea,[p]
the waters of the great deep,
who made a road in the depths of
the sea
so that the redeemed might
cross over?
11The ransomed[q] of the LORD will return.
They will enter Zion with singing;
everlasting joy will crown
their heads.

51:4 [a]Ps 50:7 [b]Isa 2:4 [c]Isa 42:4,6
51:5 [d]Isa 46:13 [e]Isa 40:10; 63:1,5
51:6 [f]Mt 24:35; 2Pe 3:10 [g]Ps 102:25-26
51:7 [h]ver 1 [i]Ps 37:31 [j]Mt 5:11; Ac 5:41
51:8 [k]Isa 50:9 [l]ver 6
51:9 [m]Isa 52:1 [n]Dt 4:34 [o]Ps 74:13
51:10 [p]Ex 14:22
51:11 [q]Isa 35:9 [r]Jer 33:11 [s]Rev 7:17
51:12 [t]2Co 1:4 [u]Ps 118:6; Isa 2:22 [v]Isa 40:6-7; 1Pe 1:24
51:13 [w]Isa 17:10 [x]Isa 45:11 [y]Ps 104:2; Isa 48:13 [z]Isa 7:4
51:14 [a]Isa 49:10
51:15 [b]Jer 31:35
51:16 [c]Dt 18:18; Isa 59:21 [d]Ex 33:22
51:17 [e]Isa 52:1 [f]Job 21:20; Rev 14:10; 16:19 [g]Ps 60:3
51:18 [h]Ps 88:18 [i]Isa 49:21
51:19 [j]Isa 47:9

Gladness and joy[r] will overtake them,
and sorrow and sighing will
flee away.[s]

12“I, even I, am he who comforts[t] you.
Who are you that you fear
mortal men,[u]
the sons of men, who are
but grass,[v]
13that you forget[w] the LORD your Maker,[x]
who stretched out the heavens[y]
and laid the foundations of the earth,
that you live in constant terror[z]
every day
because of the wrath of
the oppressor,
who is bent on destruction?
For where is the wrath of
the oppressor?
14 The cowering prisoners will soon
be set free;
they will not die in their dungeon,
nor will they lack bread.[a]
15For I am the LORD your God,
who churns up the sea[b] so that
its waves roar—
the LORD Almighty is his name.
16I have put my words in your mouth[c]
and covered you with the shadow
of my hand[d]—
I who set the heavens in place,
who laid the foundations of
the earth,
and who say to Zion, ‘You are
my people.’”

The LORD's wrath against Jerusalem.

17Awake, awake![e]
Rise up, O Jerusalem,
you who have drunk from the hand
of the LORD
the cup of his wrath,[f]
you who have drained to its dregs
the goblet that makes men stagger.[g]
18Of all the sons[h] she bore
there was none to guide her;[i]
of all the sons she reared
there was none to take her by
the hand.
19These double calamities[j] have come
upon you—
who can comfort you?—

ruin and destruction, famine[a] and
sword—
who can[v] console you?
20Your sons have fainted;
they lie at the head of every street,[b]
like antelope caught in a net.
They are filled with the wrath of
the LORD
and the rebuke of your God.

21Therefore hear this, you afflicted one,
made drunk,[c] but not with wine.
22This is what your Sovereign LORD says,
your God, who defends[d]
his people:
"See, I have taken out of your hand
the cup[e] that made you stagger;
from that cup, the goblet of
my wrath,
you will never drink again.
23I will put it into the hands of
your tormentors,[f]
who said to you,
'Fall prostrate[g] that we may walk[h]
over you.'
And you made your back like
the ground,
like a street to be walked over."

The end of Jerusalem's captivity.

52 Awake, awake,[i] O Zion,
clothe yourself with strength.[j]
Put on your garments of splendor,[k]
O Jerusalem, the holy city.[l]
The uncircumcised and defiled
will not enter you again.[m]
2Shake off your dust;[n]
rise up, sit enthroned, O Jerusalem.
Free yourself from the chains on
your neck,
O captive Daughter of Zion.

3For this is what the LORD says:

"You were sold for nothing,[o]
and without money[p] you will
be redeemed."

4For this is what the Sovereign LORD
says:

"At first my people went down to
Egypt[q] to live;
lately, Assyria has oppressed them.

5"And now what do I have here?"
declares the LORD.

"For my people have been taken
away for nothing,
and those who rule them mock,[w]"
declares the LORD.
"And all day long
my name is constantly
blasphemed.[r]
6Therefore my people will know[s]
my name;
therefore in that day they
will know
that it is I who foretold it.
Yes, it is I."

7How beautiful on the mountains
are the feet of those who bring
good news,[t]
who proclaim peace,[u]
who bring good tidings,
who proclaim salvation,
who say to Zion,
"Your God reigns!"[v]
8Listen! Your watchmen[w] lift up
their voices;
together they shout for joy.
When the LORD returns to Zion,
they will see it with their own eyes.
9Burst into songs of joy[x] together,
you ruins[y] of Jerusalem,
for the LORD has comforted
his people,
he has redeemed Jerusalem.[z]
10The LORD will lay bare his holy arm
in the sight of all the nations,[a]
and all the ends of the earth will see
the salvation[b] of our God.

11Depart,[c] depart, go out from there!
Touch no unclean thing![d]
Come out from it and be pure,[e]
you who carry the vessels of
the LORD.
12But you will not leave in haste[f]
or go in flight;
for the LORD will go before you,[g]
the God of Israel will be your
rear guard.[h]

51:19 [a]Isa 14:30
51:20 [b]Isa 5:25; Jer 14:16
51:21 [c]ver 17; Isa 29:9
51:22 [d]Isa 49:25 [e]ver 17
51:23 [f]Isa 49:26; Jer 25:15-17, 26,28; 49:12 [g]Zec 12:2 [h]Jos 10:24
52:1 [i]Isa 51:17 [j]Isa 51:9 [k]Ex 28:2,40; Ps 110:3; Zec 3:4 [l]Ne 11:1; Mt 4:5; Rev 21:2 [m]Na 1:15; Rev 21:27
52:2 [n]Isa 29:4
52:3 [o]Ps 44:12 [p]Isa 45:13
52:4 [q]Ge 46:6
52:5 [r]Eze 36:20; Ro 2:24*
52:6 [s]Isa 49:23
52:7 [t]Isa 40:9; Ro 10:15* [u]Na 1:15; Eph 6:15 [v]Ps 93:1
52:8 [w]Isa 62:6
52:9 [x]Ps 98:4 [y]Isa 51:3 [z]Isa 48:20
52:10 [a]Isa 66:18 [b]Ps 98:2-3; Lk 3:6
52:11 [c]Isa 48:20 [d]Isa 1:16; 2Co 6:17* [e]2Ti 2:19
52:12 [f]Ex 12:11 [g]Mic 2:13 [h]Ex 14:19

v *19* Dead Sea Scrolls, Septuagint, Vulgate and Syriac; Masoretic Text / *how can I* w *5* Dead Sea Scrolls and Vulgate; Masoretic Text *wail*

The suffering of God's servant.

[13]See, my servant[a] will act wisely[x];
he will be raised and lifted up and
highly exalted.[b]
[14]Just as there were many who were
appalled at him[y]—
his appearance was so disfigured
beyond that of any man
and his form marred beyond
human likeness—
[15]so will he sprinkle many nations,[z]
and kings will shut their mouths
because of him.
For what they were not told, they
will see,
and what they have not heard,
they will understand.[c]

53 Who has believed our
message[d]
and to whom has the arm of the
LORD been revealed?[e]
[2]He grew up before him like a
tender shoot,
and like a root out of dry ground.
He had no beauty or majesty to
attract us to him,
nothing in his appearance[f] that we
should desire him.
[3]He was despised and rejected by men,
a man of sorrows, and familiar
with suffering.[g]
Like one from whom men hide
their faces
he was despised,[h] and we
esteemed him not.
[4]Surely he took up our infirmities
and carried our sorrows,[i]
yet we considered him stricken
by God,[j]
smitten by him, and afflicted.
[5]But he was pierced for our
transgressions,[k]
he was crushed for our iniquities;
the punishment that brought us
peace was upon him,
and by his wounds we are healed.[l]
[6]We all, like sheep, have gone astray,
each of us has turned to his own way;
and the LORD has laid on him
the iniquity of us all.

52:13 [a]Isa 42:1 [b]Isa 57:15; Php 2:9
52:15 [c]Ro 15:21*; Eph 3:4-5
53:1 [d]Ro 10:16* [e]Jn 12:38*
53:2 [f]Isa 52:14
53:3 [g]ver 4,10; Lk 18:31-33 [h]Ps 22:6; Jn 1:10-11
53:4 [i]Mt 8:17* [j]Jn 19:7
53:5 [k]Ro 4:25; 1Co 15:3; Heb 9:28 [l]1Pe 2:24-25
53:7 [m]Mk 14:61
53:8 [n]Da 9:26; Ac 8:32-33* [o]ver 12
53:9 [p]Mt 27:57-60 [q]Isa 42:1-3 [r]1Pe 2:22*
53:10 [s]Isa 46:10 [t]ver 5 [u]ver 3 [v]Ps 22:30
53:11 [w]Jn 10:14-18 [x]Ro 5:18-19
53:12 [y]Php 2:9 [z]Mt 26:28, 38,39,42 [a]Mk 15:27*; Lk 22:37*; 23:32

[7]He was oppressed and afflicted,
yet he did not open his mouth;[m]
he was led like a lamb to the slaughter,
and as a sheep before her shearers
is silent,
so he did not open his mouth.
[8]By oppression[a] and judgment he was
taken away.
And who can speak of his
descendants?
For he was cut off from the land
of the living;[n]
for the transgression[o] of my people
he was stricken.[b]
[9]He was assigned a grave with
the wicked,
and with the rich[p] in his death,
though he had done no violence,[q]
nor was any deceit in his mouth.[r]
[10]Yet it was the LORD's will[s] to crush[t]
him and cause him to suffer,[u]
and though the LORD makes[c] his
life a guilt offering,
he will see his offspring[v] and
prolong his days,
and the will of the LORD will
prosper in his hand.
[11]After the suffering[w] of his soul,
he will see the light ⌊of life⌋[d] and
be satisfied[e];
by his knowledge[f] my righteous
servant will justify[x] many,
and he will bear their iniquities.
[12]Therefore I will give him a portion
among the great,[g][y]
and he will divide the spoils with
the strong,[h]
because he poured out his life
unto death,[z]
and was numbered with the
transgressors.[a]

[x]*13* Or *will prosper* [y]*14* Hebrew *you*
[z]*15* Hebrew; Septuagint *so will many nations marvel at him* [a]*8* Or *From arrest* [b]*8* Or *away. / Yet who of his generation considered / that he was cut off from the land of the living / for the transgression of my people, / to whom the blow was due?*
[c]*10* Hebrew *though you make* [d]*11* Dead Sea Scrolls (see also Septuagint); Masoretic Text does not have *the light ⌊of life⌋.* [e]*11* Or (with Masoretic Text) *[11]He will see the result of the suffering of his soul / and be satisfied* [f]*11* Or *by knowledge of him*
[g]*12* Or *many* [h]*12* Or *numerous*

For he bore the sin of many,
and made intercession for the
transgressors.

The heritage of the servants of the LORD.

54 "Sing, O barren woman,
you who never bore a child;
burst into song, shout for joy,
you who were never in labor;
because more are the children[a] of
the desolate woman
than of her who has a husband,[b]"
says the LORD.
2 "Enlarge the place of your tent,[c]
stretch your tent curtains wide,
do not hold back;
lengthen your cords,
strengthen your stakes.[d]
3 For you will spread out to the right
and to the left;
your descendants will dispossess
nations
and settle in their desolate[e] cities.

4 'Do not be afraid; you will not
suffer shame.
Do not fear disgrace; you will not
be humiliated.
You will forget the shame of your youth
and remember no more the
reproach[f] of your widowhood.
5 For your Maker is your husband[g]—
the LORD Almighty is his name—
the Holy One of Israel is your
Redeemer;[h]
he is called the God of all the earth.[i]
6 The LORD will call you back[j]
as if you were a wife deserted[k]
and distressed in spirit—
a wife who married young,
only to be rejected," says
your God.
7 "For a brief moment[l] I abandoned
you,
but with deep compassion I will
bring you back.[m]
8 In a surge of anger[n]
I hid my face from you for a moment,
but with everlasting kindness[o]
I will have compassion on you,"
says the LORD your Redeemer.

54:1 [a] Isa 49:20 [b] 1Sa 2:5; Gal 4:27*
54:2 [c] Isa 49:19-20 [d] Ex 35:18; 39:40
54:3 [e] Isa 49:19
54:4 [f] Isa 51:7
54:5 [g] Jer 3:14 [h] Isa 48:17 [i] Isa 6:3
54:6 [j] Isa 49:14-21 [k] Isa 50:1-2; 62:4,12
54:7 [l] Isa 26:20 [m] Isa 49:18
54:8 [n] Isa 60:10 [o] ver 10
54:9 [p] Ge 8:21 [q] Isa 12:1
54:10 [r] Ps 46:2 [s] Isa 51:6 [t] Ps 89:34 [u] ver 8
54:11 [v] Isa 14:32 [w] Isa 28:2; 29:6 [x] Isa 51:19 [y] 1Ch 29:2; Rev 21:18 [z] Isa 28:16; Rev 21:19-20
54:13 [a] Jn 6:45* [b] Isa 48:18
54:14 [c] Isa 9:4
54:15 [d] Isa 41:11-16
54:17 [e] Isa 29:8 [f] Isa 45:24-25

9 "To me this is like the days of Noah,
when I swore that the waters of
Noah would never again cover
the earth.[p]
So now I have sworn not to be
angry[q] with you,
never to rebuke you again.
10 Though the mountains be shaken[r]
and the hills be removed,
yet my unfailing love for you will
not be shaken[s]
nor my covenant[t] of peace
be removed,"
says the LORD, who has
compassion[u] on you.

11 "O afflicted[v] city, lashed by storms[w]
and not comforted,[x]
I will build you with stones of
turquoise,[i] [y]
your foundations[z] with sapphires.[j]
12 I will make your battlements of rubies,
your gates of sparkling jewels,
and all your walls of
precious stones.
13 All your sons will be taught by
the LORD,[a]
and great will be your children's
peace.[b]
14 In righteousness you will be
established:
Tyranny[c] will be far from you;
you will have nothing to fear.
Terror will be far removed;
it will not come near you.
15 If anyone does attack you, it will
not be my doing;
whoever attacks you will
surrender[d] to you.

16 "See, it is I who created the blacksmith
who fans the coals into flame
and forges a weapon fit for
its work.
And it is I who have created the
destroyer to work havoc;
17 no weapon forged against you
will prevail,[e]
and you will refute[f] every tongue
that accuses you.

[i] *11* The meaning of the Hebrew for this word is uncertain. [j] *11* Or *lapis lazuli*

This is the heritage of the servants
of the LORD,
and this is their vindication
from me,"
declares the LORD.

Seek the LORD while he may be found.

55 "Come, all you who are
thirsty,[a]
come to the waters;
and you who have no money,
come, buy[b] and eat!
Come, buy wine and milk[c]
without money and without cost.[d]
2Why spend money on what is
not bread,
and your labor on what does
not satisfy?[e]
Listen, listen to me, and eat what
is good,[f]
and your soul will delight in the
richest of fare.
3Give ear and come to me;
hear me, that your soul may live.[g]
I will make an everlasting
covenant[h] with you,
my faithful love[i] promised to
David.[j]
4See, I have made him a witness to
the peoples,
a leader and commander[k] of
the peoples.
5Surely you will summon nations[l]
you know not,
and nations that do not know you
will hasten to you,
because of the LORD your God,
the Holy One of Israel,
for he has endowed you with
splendor."[m]

6Seek the LORD while he may
be found;[n]
call[o] on him while he is near.
7Let the wicked forsake his way
and the evil man his thoughts.[p]
Let him turn[q] to the LORD, and he
will have mercy[r] on him,
and to our God, for he will
freely pardon.[s]

55:1 [a]Jn 4:14; 7:37 [b]La 5:4; Mt 13:44; Rev 3:18 [c]SS 5:1 [d]Hos 14:4; Mt 10:8; Rev 21:6
55:2 [e]Ps 22:26; Ecc 6:2; Hos 8:7 [f]Isa 1:19
55:3 [g]Lev 18:5; Ro 10:5 [h]Isa 61:8 [i]Isa 54:8 [j]Ac 13:34*
55:4 [k]Jer 30:9; Eze 34:23-24
55:5 [l]Isa 49:6 [m]Isa 60:9
55:6 [n]Ps 32:6; Isa 49:8; 2Co 6:1-2 [o]Isa 65:24
55:7 [p]Isa 32:7; 59:7 [q]Isa 44:22 [r]Isa 54:10 [s]Isa 1:18; 40:2
55:8 [t]Isa 53:6
55:9 [u]Ps 103:11
55:10 [v]Isa 30:23 [w]2Co 9:10
55:11 [x]Isa 45:23 [y]Isa 44:26
55:12 [z]Isa 54:10,13 [a]1Ch 16:33 [b]Ps 98:8
55:13 [c]Isa 5:6 [d]Isa 41:19 [e]Isa 63:12
56:1 [f]Isa 1:17 [g]Ps 85:9
56:2 [h]Ps 119:2 [i]Ex 20:8,10; Isa 58:13

God's word will not return empty.

8"For my thoughts are not
your thoughts,
neither are your ways my ways,"[t]
declares the LORD.
9"As the heavens are higher than
the earth,[u]
so are my ways higher than
your ways
and my thoughts than your thoughts.
10As the rain[v] and the snow
come down from heaven,
and do not return to it
without watering the earth
and making it bud and flourish,
so that it yields seed for the sower
and bread for the eater,[w]
11so is my word that goes out from
my mouth:
It will not return to me empty,[x]
but will accomplish what I desire
and achieve the purpose[y] for
which I sent it.
12You will go out in joy
and be led forth in peace;[z]
the mountains and hills
will burst into song before you,
and all the trees[a] of the field
will clap their hands.[b]
13Instead of the thornbush will grow
the pine tree,
and instead of briers[c] the myrtle[d]
will grow.
This will be for the LORD's renown,[e]
for an everlasting sign,
which will not be destroyed."

Salvation available to all.

56 This is what the LORD says:
"Maintain justice[f]
and do what is right,
for my salvation[g] is close at hand
and my righteousness will soon
be revealed.
2Blessed[h] is the man who does this,
the man who holds it fast,
who keeps the Sabbath[i] without
desecrating it,
and keeps his hand from doing
any evil."

3Let no foreigner who has bound
himself to the LORD say,
"The LORD will surely exclude me
from his people."
And let not any eunuch[a] complain,
"I am only a dry tree."

4For this is what the LORD says:

"To the eunuchs who keep my
Sabbaths,
who choose what pleases me
and hold fast to my covenant—
5to them I will give within my temple
and its walls[b]
a memorial and a name
better than sons and daughters;
I will give them an everlasting name
that will not be cut off.[c]
6And foreigners who bind themselves
to the LORD
to serve[d] him,
to love the name of the LORD,
and to worship him,
all who keep the Sabbath[e] without
desecrating it
and who hold fast to my covenant—
7these I will bring to my holy
mountain[f]
and give them joy in my house
of prayer.
Their burnt offerings and sacrifices[g]
will be accepted on my altar;
for my house will be called
a house of prayer for all nations.[h]"[i]
8The Sovereign LORD declares—
he who gathers the exiles of Israel:
"I will gather[j] still others to them
besides those already gathered."

Israel's evil watchmen.

9Come, all you beasts of the field,[k]
come and devour, all you beasts of
the forest!
10Israel's watchmen[l] are blind,
they all lack knowledge;
they are all mute dogs,
they cannot bark;
they lie around and dream,
they love to sleep.[m]
11They are dogs with mighty appetites;
they never have enough.
They are shepherds[n] who lack
understanding;[o]
they all turn to their own way,
each seeks his own gain.[p]
12"Come," each one cries, "let me
get wine!
Let us drink our fill of beer!
And tomorrow will be like today,
or even far better."[q]

Peace for the righteous at death.

57 The righteous perish,[r]
and no one ponders it in his
heart;[s]
devout men are taken away,
and no one understands
that the righteous are taken away
to be spared from evil.[t]
2Those who walk uprightly[u]
enter into peace;
they find rest as they lie in death.

Israel's gross idolatry.

3"But you—come here, you sons
of a sorceress,
you offspring of adulterers[v] and
prostitutes![w]
4Whom are you mocking?
At whom do you sneer
and stick out your tongue?
Are you not a brood of rebels,
the offspring of liars?
5You burn with lust among the oaks
and under every spreading tree;[x]
you sacrifice your children[y] in
the ravines
and under the overhanging crags.
6⌊The idols⌋[z] among the smooth
stones of the ravines are
your portion;
they, they are your lot.
Yes, to them you have poured out
drink offerings[a]
and offered grain offerings.
In the light of these things, should
I relent?[b]
7You have made your bed on a high
and lofty hill;[c]
there you went up to offer
your sacrifices.

56:3 [a]Jer 38:7*fn*; Ac 8:27
56:5 [b]Isa 26:1; 60:18 [c]Isa 48:19; 55:13
56:6 [d]Isa 60:7,10; 61:5 [e]ver 2,4
56:7 [f]Isa 2:2 [g]Ro 12:1; Heb 13:15 [h]Mt 21:13*; Lk 19:46* [i]Mk 11:17*
56:8 [j]Isa 11:12; 60:3-11; Jn 10:16
56:9 [k]Isa 18:6; Jer 12:9
56:10 [l]Eze 3:17 [m]Na 3:18
56:11 [n]Eze 34:2 [o]Isa 1:3 [p]Isa 57:17; Eze 13:19; Mic 3:11
56:12 [q]Ps 10:6; Lk 12:18-19
57:1 [r]Ps 12:1 [s]Isa 42:25 [t]2Ki 22:20
57:2 [u]Isa 26:7
57:3 [v]Mt 16:4 [w]Isa 1:21
57:5 [x]2Ki 16:4 [y]Lev 18:21; Ps 106:37-38; Eze 16:20
57:6 [z]Jer 3:9 [a]Jer 7:18 [b]Jer 5:9,29; 9:9
57:7 [c]Jer 3:6; Eze 16:16

8Behind your doors and your doorposts
you have put your pagan symbols.
Forsaking me, you uncovered
your bed,
you climbed into it and opened
it wide;
you made a pact with those whose
beds you love,[a]
and you looked on their nakedness.[b]
9You went to Molech[k] with olive oil
and increased your perfumes.
You sent your ambassadors[l] [c] far away;
you descended to the grave[m] itself!
10You were wearied by all your ways,
but you would not say, 'It is
hopeless.'[d]
You found renewal of your strength,
and so you did not faint.

11"Whom have you so dreaded
and feared[e]
that you have been false to me,
and have neither remembered[f] me
nor pondered this in your hearts?
Is it not because I have long
been silent[g]
that you do not fear me?
12I will expose your righteousness and
your works,[h]
and they will not benefit you.
13When you cry out[i] for help,
let your collection ⌊of idols⌋ save you!
The wind will carry all of them off,
a mere breath will blow them away.
But the man who makes me his refuge
will inherit the land[j]
and possess my holy mountain."[k]

Comfort for the contrite.

14And it will be said:

"Build up, build up, prepare
the road!
Remove the obstacles out of the
way of my people."[l]
15For this is what the high and lofty[m]
One says—
he who lives forever,[n] whose
name is holy:
"I live in a high and holy place,
but also with him who is contrite[o]
and lowly in spirit,[p]
to revive the spirit of the lowly
and to revive the heart of
the contrite.[q]
16I will not accuse forever,
nor will I always be angry,[r]
for then the spirit of man would
grow faint before me—
the breath of man that I have
created.
17I was enraged by his sinful greed;[s]
I punished him, and hid my face
in anger,
yet he kept on in his willful ways.[t]
18I have seen his ways, but I will
heal[u] him;
I will guide him and restore
comfort[v] to him,
19 creating praise on the lips[w] of the
mourners in Israel.
Peace, peace,[x] to those far and near,"[y]
says the LORD. "And I will heal them."
20But the wicked[z] are like the tossing sea,
which cannot rest,
whose waves cast up mire and mud.
21"There is no peace," [a] says my God,
"for the wicked."[b]

Proper fasting.

58 "Shout it aloud,[c] do not
hold back.
Raise your voice like a trumpet.
Declare to my people their rebellion[d]
and to the house of Jacob their sins.
2For day after day they seek[e] me out;
they seem eager to know my ways,
as if they were a nation that does
what is right
and has not forsaken the
commands of its God.
They ask me for just decisions
and seem eager for God to come
near[f] them.
3'Why have we fasted,'[g] they say,
'and you have not seen it?
Why have we humbled ourselves,
and you have not noticed?'[h]

"Yet on the day of your fasting, you
do as you please[i]
and exploit all your workers.

57:8 [a]Eze 16:26; 23:7 [b]Eze 23:18
57:9 [c]Eze 23:16,40
57:10 [d]Jer 2:25; 18:12
57:11 [e]Pr 29:25 [f]Jer 2:32; 3:21 [g]Ps 50:21
57:12 [h]Isa 29:15; Mic 3:2-4,8
57:13 [i]Jer 22:20; 30:15 [j]Ps 37:9 [k]Isa 65:9-11
57:14 [l]Isa 62:10; Jer 18:15
57:15 [m]Isa 52:13 [n]Dt 33:27 [o]Ps 147:3 [p]Ps 34:18; 51:17; Isa 66:2 [q]Isa 61:1
57:16 [r]Ps 85:5; 103:9; Mic 7:18
57:17 [s]Isa 56:11 [t]Isa 1:4
57:18 [u]Isa 30:26 [v]Isa 61:1-3
57:19 [w]Isa 6:7; Heb 13:15 [x]Eph 2:17 [y]Ac 2:39
57:20 [z]Job 18:5-21
57:21 [a]Isa 59:8 [b]Isa 48:22
58:1 [c]Isa 40:6 [d]Isa 48:8
58:2 [e]Isa 48:1; Tit 1:16; Jas 4:8 [f]Isa 29:13
58:3 [g]Lev 16:29 [h]Mal 3:14 [i]Isa 22:13; Zec 7:5-6

[k]9 Or *to the king* [l]9 Or *idols*
[m]9 Hebrew *Sheol*

4Your fasting ends in quarreling
and strife,[a]
and in striking each other with
wicked fists.
You cannot fast as you do today
and expect your voice to be heard[b]
on high.
5Is this the kind of fast[c] I
have chosen,
only a day for a man to humble[d]
himself?
Is it only for bowing one's head
like a reed
and for lying on sackcloth and
ashes?[e]
Is that what you call a fast,
a day acceptable to the LORD?
6"Is not this the kind of fasting I
have chosen:
to loose the chains of injustice[f]
and untie the cords of the yoke,
to set the oppressed[g] free
and break every yoke?
7Is it not to share your food with
the hungry[h]
and to provide the poor wanderer
with shelter[i]—
when you see the naked, to
clothe[j] him,
and not to turn away from your
own flesh and blood?[k]
8Then your light will break forth like
the dawn,[l]
and your healing[m] will quickly
appear;
then your righteousness[n] will go
before you,
and the glory of the LORD will be
your rear guard.[n]
9Then you will call,[o] and the LORD
will answer;
you will cry for help, and he will
say: Here am I.

"If you do away with the yoke
of oppression,
with the pointing finger[p] and
malicious talk,[q]
10and if you spend yourselves in
behalf of the hungry
and satisfy the needs of the
oppressed,[r]
then your light[s] will rise in the
darkness,
and your night will become like
the noonday.[t]
11The LORD will guide you always;
he will satisfy your needs[u] in a
sun-scorched land
and will strengthen your frame.
You will be like a well-watered
garden,[v]
like a spring[w] whose waters
never fail.
12Your people will rebuild the
ancient ruins[x]
and will raise up the age-old
foundations;[y]
you will be called Repairer of
Broken Walls,
Restorer of Streets with Dwellings.
13"If you keep your feet from breaking
the Sabbath[z]
and from doing as you please on
my holy day,
if you call the Sabbath a delight[a]
and the LORD's holy day honorable,
and if you honor it by not going
your own way
and not doing as you please or
speaking idle words,
14then you will find your joy[b] in
the LORD,
and I will cause you to ride on the
heights[c] of the land
and to feast on the inheritance of
your father Jacob."
The mouth of the LORD
has spoken.[d]

Sin separates Israel from God.

59 Surely the arm of the LORD is
not too short[e] to save,
nor his ear too dull to hear.[f]
2But your iniquities have separated
you from your God;
your sins have hidden his face
from you,
so that he will not hear.[g]
3For your hands are stained
with blood,[h]
your fingers with guilt.

58:4 [a]1Ki 21:9-13; Isa 59:6 [b]Isa 59:2
58:5 [c]Zec 7:5 [d]1Ki 21:27 [e]Job 2:8
58:6 [f]Ne 5:10-11 [g]Jer 34:9
58:7 [h]Eze 18:16; Lk 3:11 [i]Isa 16:4; Heb 13:2 [j]Job 31:19-20; Mt 25:36 [k]Ge 29:14; Lk 10:31-32
58:8 [l]Job 11:17 [m]Isa 30:26 [n]Ex 14:19
58:9 [o]Ps 50:15 [p]Pr 6:13 [q]Ps 12:2; Isa 59:13
58:10 [r]Dt 15:7-8 [s]Isa 42:16 [t]Job 11:17
58:11 [u]Ps 107:9 [v]SS 4:15 [w]Jn 4:14
58:12 [x]Isa 49:8 [y]Isa 44:28
58:13 [z]Isa 56:2 [a]Ps 84:2,10
58:14 [b]Job 22:26 [c]Dt 32:13 [d]Isa 1:20
59:1 [e]Nu 11:23; Isa 50:2 [f]Isa 58:9; 65:24
59:2 [g]Isa 1:15; 58:4
59:3 [h]Isa 1:15

n8 Or *your righteous One*

Your lips have spoken lies,
and your tongue mutters
wicked things.
4No one calls for justice;
no one pleads his case with integrity.
They rely on empty arguments and
speak lies;
they conceive trouble and give
birth to evil.[a]
5They hatch the eggs of vipers
and spin a spider's web.[b]
Whoever eats their eggs will die,
and when one is broken, an adder
is hatched.
6Their cobwebs are useless for clothing;
they cannot cover themselves with
what they make.[c]
Their deeds are evil deeds,
and acts of violence[d] are in
their hands.
7Their feet rush into sin;
they are swift to shed innocent
blood.[e]
Their thoughts are evil thoughts;[f]
ruin and destruction mark
their ways.[g]
8The way of peace they do not know;
there is no justice in their paths.
They have turned them into
crooked roads;
no one who walks in them will
know peace.[h]

Israel's confession.

9So justice is far from us,
and righteousness does not reach us.
We look for light, but all is darkness;[i]
for brightness, but we walk in
deep shadows.
10Like the blind[j] we grope along
the wall,
feeling our way like men
without eyes.
At midday we stumble[k] as if it were
twilight;
among the strong, we are like
the dead.[l]
11We all growl like bears;
we moan mournfully like doves.[m]
We look for justice, but find none;
for deliverance, but it is far away.
12For our offenses[n] are many in
your sight,
and our sins testify[o] against us.
Our offenses are ever with us,
and we acknowledge our iniquities:
13rebellion and treachery against
the LORD,
turning our backs[p] on our God,
fomenting oppression[q] and revolt,
uttering lies[r] our hearts have
conceived.
14So justice is driven back,
and righteousness[s] stands at
a distance;
truth[t] has stumbled in the streets,
honesty cannot enter.
15Truth is nowhere to be found,
and whoever shuns evil becomes
a prey.

Zion's Redeemer.

The LORD looked and was displeased
that there was no justice.
16He saw that there was no one,[u]
he was appalled that there was no
one to intervene;
so his own arm worked salvation[v]
for him,
and his own righteousness
sustained him.
17He put on righteousness as his
breastplate,[w]
and the helmet[x] of salvation on
his head;
he put on the garments[y] of vengeance
and wrapped himself in zeal[z] as
in a cloak.
18According to what they have done,
so will he repay
wrath to his enemies
and retribution to his foes;
he will repay the islands their due.
19From the west,[a] men will fear the
name of the LORD,
and from the rising of the sun,[b]
they will revere his glory.
For he will come like a pent-up flood
that the breath of the LORD
drives along.[o]

59:4 [a]Job 15:35; Ps 7:14
59:5 [b]Job 8:14
59:6 [c]Isa 28:20 [d]Isa 58:4
59:7 [e]Pr 6:17 [f]Mk 7:21-22 [g]Ro 3:15-17*
59:8 [h]Isa 57:21; Lk 1:79
59:9 [i]Isa 5:30; 8:20
59:10 [j]Dt 28:29 [k]Isa 8:15 [l]La 3:6
59:11 [m]Isa 38:14; Eze 7:16
59:12 [n]Ezr 9:6 [o]Isa 3:9
59:13 [p]Pr 30:9; Mt 10:33; Tit 1:16 [q]Isa 5:7 [r]Mk 7:21-22
59:14 [s]Isa 1:21 [t]Isa 48:1
59:16 [u]Isa 41:28 [v]Ps 98:1; Isa 63:5
59:17 [w]Eph 6:14 [x]Eph 6:17; 1Th 5:8 [y]Isa 63:3 [z]Isa 9:7
59:19 [a]Isa 49:12 [b]Ps 113:3

o *19* Or *When the enemy comes in like a flood, / the Spirit of the LORD will put him to flight*

20 "The Redeemer will come to Zion,
to those in Jacob who repent of
their sins,"[a]
declares the LORD.

21 "As for me, this is my covenant with them," says the LORD. "My Spirit,[b] who is on you, and my words that I have put in your mouth will not depart from your mouth, or from the mouths of your children, or from the mouths of their descendants from this time on and forever," says the LORD.

The glory of the LORD shines from Zion.

60 "Arise,[c] shine, for your light[d]
has come,
and the glory of the LORD rises
upon you.
2 See, darkness covers the earth
and thick darkness[e] is over the
peoples,
but the LORD rises upon you
and his glory appears over you.
3 Nations[f] will come to your light,
and kings[g] to the brightness of
your dawn.

4 'Lift up your eyes and look about you:
All assemble[h] and come to you;
your sons come from afar,
and your daughters[i] are carried on
the arm.[j]
5 Then you will look and be radiant,
your heart will throb and swell
with joy;
the wealth on the seas will be
brought to you,
to you the riches of the nations
will come.
6 Herds of camels will cover your land,
young camels of Midian[k]
and Ephah.[l]
And all from Sheba[m] will come,
bearing gold and incense[n]
and proclaiming the praise[o]
of the LORD.
7 All Kedar's[p] flocks will be gathered
to you,
the rams of Nebaioth will
serve you;
they will be accepted as offerings on
my altar,
and I will adorn my glorious
temple.[q]

8 "Who are these[r] that fly along
like clouds,
like doves to their nests?
9 Surely the islands[s] look to me;
in the lead are the ships of
Tarshish,[p][t]
bringing[u] your sons from afar,
with their silver and gold,
to the honor of the LORD your God,
the Holy One of Israel,
for he has endowed you with
splendor.[v]

10 "Foreigners[w] will rebuild your walls,
and their kings[x] will serve you.
Though in anger I struck you,
in favor I will show you
compassion.[y]
11 Your gates[z] will always stand open,
they will never be shut, day or night,
so that men may bring you the
wealth of the nations[a]—
their kings[b] led in triumphal
procession.
12 For the nation or kingdom that will
not serve[c] you will perish;
it will be utterly ruined.

13 "The glory of Lebanon[d] will come
to you,
the pine, the fir and the cypress
together,[e]
to adorn the place of my sanctuary;
and I will glorify the place of
my feet.[f]
14 The sons of your oppressors[g] will
come bowing before you;
all who despise you will bow
down[h] at your feet
and will call you the City of the LORD,
Zion[i] of the Holy One of Israel.

15 "Although you have been forsaken[j]
and hated,
with no one traveling[k] through,
I will make you the everlasting pride[l]
and the joy[m] of all generations.

59:20 [a]Ac 2:38-39; Ro 11:26-27*
59:21 [b]Isa 11:2; 44:3
60:1 [c]Isa 52:2 [d]Eph 5:14
60:2 [e]Jer 13:16; Col 1:13
60:3 [f]Isa 45:14; Rev 21:24 [g]Isa 49:23
60:4 [h]Isa 11:12 [i]Isa 43:6 [j]Isa 49:20-22
60:6 [k]Ge 25:2 [l]Ge 25:4 [m]Ps 72:10 [n]Isa 43:23; Mt 2:11 [o]Isa 42:10
60:7 [p]Ge 25:13 [q]ver 13; Hag 2:3,7,9
60:8 [r]Isa 49:21
60:9 [s]Isa 11:11 [t]Isa 2:16*fn* [u]Isa 14:2; 43:6 [v]Isa 55:5
60:10 [w]Isa 14:1-2 [x]Isa 49:23; Rev 21:24 [y]Isa 54:8
60:11 [z]ver 18; Isa 62:10; Rev 21:25 [a]ver 5; Rev 21:26 [b]Ps 149:8
60:12 [c]Isa 14:2
60:13 [d]Isa 35:2 [e]Isa 41:19 [f]1Ch 28:2; Ps 132:7
60:14 [g]Isa 14:2 [h]Isa 49:23; Rev 3:9 [i]Heb 12:22
60:15 [j]Isa 1:7-9; 6:12 [k]Isa 33:8 [l]Isa 4:2 [m]Isa 65:18

[p]9 Or *the trading ships*

16You will drink the milk of nations
and be nursed[a] at royal breasts.
Then you will know that I, the LORD,
am your Savior,
your Redeemer,[b] the Mighty One
of Jacob.
17Instead of bronze I will bring you gold,
and silver in place of iron.
Instead of wood I will bring you
bronze,
and iron in place of stones.
I will make peace your governor
and righteousness your ruler.
18No longer will violence be heard in
your land,
nor ruin or destruction within
your borders,
but you will call your walls Salvation[c]
and your gates Praise.
19The sun will no more be your light
by day,
nor will the brightness of the moon
shine on you,
for the LORD will be your
everlasting light,[d]
and your God will be your glory.[e]
20Your sun[f] will never set again,
and your moon will wane no more;
the LORD will be your everlasting light,
and your days of sorrow[g] will end.
21Then will all your people be righteous[h]
and they will possess[i] the land
forever.
They are the shoot I have planted,[j]
the work of my hands,[k]
for the display of my splendor.[l]
22The least of you will become
a thousand,
the smallest a mighty nation.
I am the LORD;
in its time I will do this swiftly."

The year of the LORD's favor.

61 The Spirit[m] of the Sovereign
LORD is on me,
because the LORD has anointed[n] me
to preach good news to the poor.[o]
He has sent me to bind up[p] the
brokenhearted,
to proclaim freedom for the
captives[q]
and release from darkness for
the prisoners,[q]
2to proclaim the year of the LORD's
favor[r]
and the day of vengeance[s] of
our God,
to comfort[t] all who mourn,
3 and provide for those who grieve
in Zion—
to bestow on them a crown
of beauty
instead of ashes,
the oil of gladness
instead of mourning,
and a garment of praise
instead of a spirit of despair.
They will be called oaks of
righteousness,
a planting of the LORD
for the display of his splendor.[u]

4They will rebuild the ancient ruins[v]
and restore the places long
devastated;
they will renew the ruined cities
that have been devastated for
generations.
5Aliens[w] will shepherd your flocks;
foreigners will work your fields
and vineyards.
6And you will be called priests[x] of
the LORD,
you will be named ministers of
our God.
You will feed on the wealth[y]
of nations,
and in their riches you will boast.

7Instead of their shame
my people will receive a
double[z] portion,
and instead of disgrace
they will rejoice in their inheritance;
and so they will inherit a double
portion in their land,
and everlasting joy will be theirs.

8"For I, the LORD, love justice;[a]
I hate robbery and iniquity.
In my faithfulness I will reward them
and make an everlasting covenant[b]
with them.

60:16 [a]Isa 49:23; 66:11,12 [b]Isa 59:20
60:18 [c]Isa 26:1
60:19 [d]Rev 22:5 [e]Zec 2:5; Rev 21:23
60:20 [f]Isa 30:26 [g]Isa 35:10
60:21 [h]Rev 21:27 [i]Ps 37:11,22; Isa 57:13; 61:7 [j]Mt 15:13 [k]Isa 19:25; 29:23; Eph 2:10 [l]Isa 52:1
61:1 [m]Isa 11:2 [n]Ps 45:7 [o]Mt 11:5; Lk 7:22 [p]Isa 57:15 [q]Isa 42:7; 49:9
61:2 [r]Isa 49:8; Lk 4:18-19* [s]Isa 34:8 [t]Isa 57:18; Mt 5:4
61:3 [u]Isa 60:20-21
61:4 [v]Isa 49:8; Eze 36:33; Am 9:14
61:5 [w]Isa 14:1-2
61:6 [x]Ex 19:6; 1Pe 2:5 [y]Isa 60:11
61:7 [z]Isa 40:2; Zec 9:12
61:8 [a]Ps 11:7; Isa 5:16 [b]Isa 55:3

q *1* Hebrew; Septuagint *the blind*

9Their descendants will be known
among the nations
and their offspring among the
peoples.
All who see them will acknowledge
that they are a people the LORD
has blessed."

10I delight greatly in the LORD;
my soul rejoices[a] in my God.
For he has clothed me with
garments of salvation
and arrayed me in a robe of
righteousness,[b]
as a bridegroom adorns his head
like a priest,
and as a bride[c] adorns herself
with her jewels.
11For as the soil makes the sprout
come up
and a garden causes seeds to grow,
so the Sovereign LORD will make
righteousness[d] and praise
spring up before all nations.

A new name for Zion.

62 For Zion's sake I will not
keep silent,
for Jerusalem's sake I will not
remain quiet,
till her righteousness[e] shines out
like the dawn,
her salvation like a blazing torch.
2The nations[f] will see your
righteousness,
and all kings your glory;
you will be called by a new name[g]
that the mouth of the LORD
will bestow.
3You will be a crown[h] of splendor in
the LORD's hand,
a royal diadem in the hand of
your God.
4No longer will they call you
Deserted,[i]
or name your land Desolate.
But you will be called Hephzibah,[r]
and your land Beulah[s];
for the LORD will take delight[j] in you,
and your land will be married.[k]
5As a young man marries a maiden,
so will your sons[t] marry you;
as a bridegroom rejoices over his bride,
so will your God rejoice[l] over you.

6I have posted watchmen[m] on your
walls, O Jerusalem;
they will never be silent day or night.
You who call on the LORD,
give yourselves no rest,
7and give him no rest[n] till he
establishes Jerusalem
and makes her the praise of
the earth.

8The LORD has sworn by his right hand
and by his mighty arm:
"Never again will I give your grain[o]
as food for your enemies,
and never again will foreigners drink
the new wine
for which you have toiled;
9but those who harvest it will eat it
and praise the LORD,
and those who gather the grapes
will drink it
in the courts of my sanctuary."

10Pass through, pass through the gates![p]
Prepare the way for the people.
Build up, build up the highway![q r]
Remove the stones.
Raise a banner[s] for the nations.

11The LORD has made proclamation
to the ends of the earth:
"Say to the Daughter of Zion,[t]
'See, your Savior comes![u]
See, his reward is with him,
and his recompense accompanies
him.'"[v]
12They will be called[w] the Holy People,[x]
the Redeemed[y] of the LORD;
and you will be called Sought After,
the City No Longer Deserted.[z]

The day of God's vengeance.

63 Who is this coming from Edom,
from Bozrah,[a] with his garments
stained crimson?
Who is this, robed in splendor,
striding forward in the greatness of
his strength?

61:10 [a]Isa 25:9; Hab 3:18 [b]Ps 132:9; Isa 52:1 [c]Isa 49:18; Rev 21:2
61:11 [d]Ps 85:11
62:1 [e]Isa 1:26
62:2 [f]Isa 52:10; 60:3 [g]ver 4,12
62:3 [h]Isa 28:5; Zec 9:16; 1Th 2:19
62:4 [i]Isa 54:6 [j]Jer 32:41; Zep 3:17 [k]Jer 3:14; Hos 2:19
62:5 [l]Isa 65:19
62:6 [m]Isa 52:8; Eze 3:17
62:7 [n]Mt 15:21-28; Lk 18:1-8
62:8 [o]Dt 28:30-33; Isa 1:7; Jer 5:17
62:10 [p]Isa 60:11 [q]Isa 57:14 [r]Isa 11:16 [s]Isa 11:10
62:11 [t]Zec 9:9; Mt 21:5 [u]Rev 22:12 [v]Isa 40:10
62:12 [w]ver 4 [x]1Pe 2:9 [y]Isa 35:9 [z]Isa 42:16
63:1 [a]Am 1:12

r4 *Hephzibah* means *my delight is in her.*
s4 *Beulah* means *married.* t5 Or *Builder*

"It is I, speaking in righteousness,
mighty to save."[a]

2Why are your garments red,
like those of one treading the
winepress?

3"I have trodden the winepress[b] alone;
from the nations no one was with me.
I trampled them in my anger
and trod them down in my wrath;[c]
their blood spattered my garments,[d]
and I stained all my clothing.
4For the day of vengeance was in
my heart,
and the year of my redemption
has come.
5I looked, but there was no one[e]
to help,
I was appalled that no one
gave support;
so my own arm[f] worked salvation
for me,
and my own wrath sustained me.[g]
6I trampled the nations in my anger;
in my wrath I made them drunk[h]
and poured their blood[i] on
the ground."

Praise and prayer for the LORD's kindnesses.

7I will tell of the kindnesses[j] of
the LORD,
the deeds for which he is to
be praised,
according to all the LORD has
done for us—
yes, the many good things he has done
for the house of Israel,
according to his compassion[k] and
many kindnesses.
8He said, "Surely they are my people,[l]
sons who will not be false to me";
and so he became their Savior.
9In all their distress he too was
distressed,
and the angel of his presence[m]
saved them.
In his love and mercy he
redeemed[n] them;
he lifted them up and carried[o] them
all the days of old.

10Yet they rebelled[p]
and grieved his Holy Spirit.[q]
So he turned and became their enemy[r]
and he himself fought against them.

11Then his people recalled[u] the days
of old,
the days of Moses and his people—
where is he who brought them
through the sea,[s]
with the shepherd of his flock?
Where is he who set
his Holy Spirit[t] among them,
12who sent his glorious arm of power
to be at Moses' right hand,
who divided the waters[u] before them,
to gain for himself everlasting
renown,
13who led[v] them through the depths?
Like a horse in open country,
they did not stumble;[w]
14like cattle that go down to the plain,
they were given rest by the Spirit
of the LORD.
This is how you guided your people
to make for yourself a glorious name.

15Look down from heaven[x] and see
from your lofty throne,[y] holy
and glorious.
Where are your zeal[z] and your might?
Your tenderness and compassion[a]
are withheld from us.
16But you are our Father,
though Abraham does not know us
or Israel acknowledge[b] us;
you, O LORD, are our Father,
our Redeemer[c] from of old is
your name.
17Why, O LORD, do you make us
wander from your ways
and harden our hearts so we do
not revere[d] you?
Return[e] for the sake of your
servants,
the tribes that are your inheritance.
18For a little while your people
possessed your holy place,
but now our enemies have
trampled down your
sanctuary.[f]

u *11* Or *But may he recall*

63:1 [a]Zep 3:17
63:3 [b]Rev 14:20; 19:15 [c]Isa 22:5 [d]Rev 19:13
63:5 [e]Isa 41:28 [f]Ps 44:3; 98:1 [g]Isa 59:16
63:6 [h]Isa 29:9 [i]Isa 34:3
63:7 [j]Isa 54:8 [k]Ps 51:1; Eph 2:4
63:8 [l]Isa 51:4
63:9 [m]Ex 33:14 [n]Dt 7:7-8 [o]Dt 1:31
63:10 [p]Ps 78:40 [q]Ps 51:11; Ac 7:51; Eph 4:30 [r]Ps 106:40
63:11 [s]Ex 14:22,30 [t]Nu 11:17
63:12 [u]Ex 14:21-22; Isa 11:15
63:13 [v]Dt 32:12 [w]Jer 31:9
63:15 [x]Dt 26:15; Ps 80:14 [y]Ps 123:1 [z]Isa 9:7; 26:11 [a]Jer 31:20; Hos 11:8
63:16 [b]Job 14:21 [c]Isa 41:14; 44:6
63:17 [d]Isa 29:13 [e]Nu 10:36
63:18 [f]Ps 74:3-8

19 We are yours from of old;
but you have not ruled over them,
they have not been called by your
name.[v]

64 Oh, that you would rend the
heavens[a] and come down,[b]
that the mountains[c] would tremble
before you!
2 As when fire sets twigs ablaze
and causes water to boil,
come down to make your name
known to your enemies
and cause the nations to quake[d]
before you!
3 For when you did awesome[e] things
that we did not expect,
you came down, and the mountains
trembled before you.
4 Since ancient times no one has heard,
no ear has perceived,
no eye has seen any God besides you,
who acts on behalf of those who
wait for him.[f]
5 You come to the help of those who
gladly do right,[g]
who remember your ways.
But when we continued to sin
against them,
you were angry.
How then can we be saved?
6 All of us have become like one who
is unclean,
and all our righteous[h] acts are like
filthy rags;
we all shrivel up like a leaf,[i]
and like the wind our sins sweep
us away.
7 No one[j] calls on your name
or strives to lay hold of you;
for you have hidden[k] your face from us
and made us waste away[l] because
of our sins.

The potter and the clay.

8 Yet, O LORD, you are our Father.[m]
We are the clay, you are the potter;[n]
we are all the work of your hand.
9 Do not be angry[o] beyond measure,
O LORD;
do not remember our sins[p] forever.

64:1 [a]Ps 18:9; 144:5 [b]Mic 1:3 [c]Ex 19:18
64:2 [d]Ps 99:1; Jer 5:22; 33:9
64:3 [e]Ps 65:5
64:4 [f]Isa 30:18; 1Co 2:9*
64:5 [g]Isa 26:8
64:6 [h]Isa 46:12; 48:1 [i]Ps 90:5-6
64:7 [j]Isa 59:4 [k]Dt 31:18; Isa 1:15; 54:8 [l]Isa 9:18
64:8 [m]Isa 63:16 [n]Isa 29:16
64:9 [o]Isa 57:17; 60:10 [p]Isa 43:25
64:11 [q]Ps 74:3-7 [r]La 1:7,10
64:12 [s]Ps 74:10-11; Isa 42:14 [t]Ps 83:1
65:1 [u]Hos 1:10; Ro 9:24-26; 10:20* [v]Eph 2:12
65:2 [w]Isa 1:2,23; Ro 10:21* [x]Ps 81:11-12; Isa 66:18
65:3 [y]Job 1:11 [z]Isa 1:29
65:4 [a]Lev 11:7
65:5 [b]Mt 9:11; Lk 7:39; 18:9-12
65:6 [c]Ps 50:3 [d]Jer 16:18 [e]Ps 79:12

Oh, look upon us, we pray,
for we are all your people.
10 Your sacred cities have become
a desert;
even Zion is a desert, Jerusalem
a desolation.
11 Our holy and glorious temple,[q]
where our fathers praised you,
has been burned with fire,
and all that we treasured[r] lies
in ruins.
12 After all this, O LORD, will you hold
yourself back?[s]
Will you keep silent[t] and punish
us beyond measure?

Judgment and salvation.

65 "I revealed myself to those who
did not ask for me;
I was found by those who did not
seek me.[u]
To a nation[v] that did not call on
my name,
I said, 'Here am I, here am I.'
2 All day long I have held out my hands
to an obstinate people,[w]
who walk in ways not good,
pursuing their own imaginations[x]—
3 a people who continually provoke me
to my very face,[y]
offering sacrifices in gardens[z]
and burning incense on altars
of brick;
4 who sit among the graves
and spend their nights keeping
secret vigil;
who eat the flesh of pigs,[a]
and whose pots hold broth of
unclean meat;
5 who say, 'Keep away; don't come
near me,
for I am too sacred[b] for you!'
Such people are smoke in my nostrils,
a fire that keeps burning all day.
6 "See, it stands written before me:
I will not keep silent[c] but will pay
back[d] in full;
I will pay it back into their laps[e]—

v 19 Or *We are like those you have never ruled, / like those never called by your name*

7both your sins[a] and the sins of
your fathers,"[b]
says the LORD.
"Because they burned sacrifices on
the mountains
and defied me on the hills,[c]
I will measure into their laps
the full payment for their
former deeds."

8This is what the LORD says:

"As when juice is still found in a
cluster of grapes
and men say, 'Don't destroy it,
there is yet some good in it,'
so will I do in behalf of my servants;
I will not destroy them all.
9I will bring forth descendants[d]
from Jacob,
and from Judah those who will
possess[e] my mountains;
my chosen people will inherit them,
and there will my servants live.[f]
10Sharon[g] will become a pasture
for flocks,
and the Valley of Achor[h] a resting
place for herds,
for my people who seek[i] me.

11"But as for you who forsake[j] the LORD
and forget my holy mountain,
who spread a table for Fortune
and fill bowls of mixed wine for
Destiny,
12I will destine you for the sword,[k]
and you will all bend down for
the slaughter;
for I called but you did not answer,[l]
I spoke but you did not listen.[m]
You did evil in my sight
and chose what displeases me."

13Therefore this is what the Sovereign LORD says:

"My servants will eat,[n]
but you will go hungry;
my servants will drink,
but you will go thirsty;[o]
my servants will rejoice,
but you will be put to shame.[p]
14My servants will sing
out of the joy of their hearts,
but you will cry out[q]
from anguish of heart
and wail in brokenness of spirit.
15You will leave your name
to my chosen ones as a curse;[r]
the Sovereign LORD will put you
to death,
but to his servants he will give
another name.
16Whoever invokes a blessing in the land
will do so by the God of truth;[s]
he who takes an oath in the land
will swear[t] by the God of truth.
For the past troubles will be forgotten
and hidden from my eyes.

New heavens and a new earth.

17"Behold, I will create
new heavens and a new earth.[u]
The former things will not be
remembered,[v]
nor will they come to mind.
18But be glad and rejoice[w] forever
in what I will create,
for I will create Jerusalem to be
a delight
and its people a joy.
19I will rejoice[x] over Jerusalem
and take delight in my people;
the sound of weeping and of crying[y]
will be heard in it no more.

20"Never again will there be in it
an infant who lives but a few days,
or an old man who does not live
out his years;[z]
he who dies at a hundred
will be thought a mere youth;
he who fails to reach[w] a hundred
will be considered accursed.
21They will build houses[a] and dwell
in them;
they will plant vineyards and eat
their fruit.[b]
22No longer will they build houses and
others live in them,
or plant and others eat.
For as the days of a tree,[c]
so will be the days[d] of my people;
my chosen ones will long enjoy
the works of their hands.

65:7 [a]Isa 22:14 [b]Ex 20:5 [c]Isa 57:7
65:9 [d]Isa 45:19 [e]Am 9:11-15 [f]Isa 32:18
65:10 [g]Isa 35:2 [h]Jos 7:26 [i]Isa 51:1
65:11 [j]Dt 29:24-25; Isa 1:28
65:12 [k]Isa 27:1 [l]Pr 1:24-25; Isa 41:28; 66:4 [m]2Ch 36:15-16; Jer 7:13
65:13 [n]Isa 1:19 [o]Isa 41:17 [p]Isa 44:9
65:14 [q]Mt 8:12; Lk 13:28
65:15 [r]Zec 8:13
65:16 [s]Ps 31:5 [t]Isa 19:18
65:17 [u]Isa 66:22; 2Pe 3:13 [v]Isa 43:18; Jer 3:16
65:18 [w]Ps 98:1-9; Isa 25:9
65:19 [x]Isa 35:10; 62:5 [y]Isa 25:8; Rev 7:17
65:20 [z]Ecc 8:13
65:21 [a]Isa 32:18 [b]Isa 37:30; Am 9:14
65:22 [c]Ps 92:12-14 [d]Ps 21:4; 91:16

w20 Or / *the sinner who reaches*

[23]They will not toil in vain
or bear children doomed to misfortune;
for they will be a people blessed[a] by the LORD,
they and their descendants[b] with them.
[24]Before they call[c] I will answer;
while they are still speaking[d] I will hear.
[25]The wolf and the lamb[e] will feed together,
and the lion will eat straw like the ox,
but dust will be the serpent's[f] food.
They will neither harm nor destroy
on all my holy mountain,"
says the LORD.

The people choose evil.

66 This is what the LORD says:

"Heaven is my throne,[g]
and the earth is my footstool.[h]
Where is the house[i] you will build for me?
Where will my resting place be?
[2]Has not my hand made all these things,[j]
and so they came into being?"
declares the LORD.

"This is the one I esteem:
he who is humble and contrite in spirit,[k]
and trembles at my word.[l]
[3]But whoever sacrifices a bull[m]
is like one who kills a man,
and whoever offers a lamb,
like one who breaks a dog's neck;
whoever makes a grain offering
is like one who presents pig's blood,
and whoever burns memorial incense,[n]
like one who worships an idol.
They have chosen their own ways,[o]
and their souls delight in their abominations;
[4]so I also will choose harsh treatment for them
and will bring upon them what they dread.[p]
For when I called, no one answered,[q]
when I spoke, no one listened.
They did evil[r] in my sight
and chose what displeases me."[s]

Jerusalem is comforted.

[5]Hear the word of the LORD,
you who tremble at his word:
"Your brothers who hate[t] you,
and exclude you because of my name, have said,
'Let the LORD be glorified,
that we may see your joy!'
Yet they will be put to shame.[u]
[6]Hear that uproar from the city,
hear that noise from the temple!
It is the sound of the LORD
repaying[v] his enemies all they deserve.

[7]"Before she goes into labor,[w]
she gives birth;
before the pains come upon her,
she delivers a son.[x]
[8]Who has ever heard of such a thing?
Who has ever seen[y] such things?
Can a country be born in a day
or a nation be brought forth in a moment?
Yet no sooner is Zion in labor
than she gives birth to her children.
[9]Do I bring to the moment of birth[z]
and not give delivery?" says the LORD.
"Do I close up the womb
when I bring to delivery?" says your God.
[10]"Rejoice[a] with Jerusalem and be glad for her,
all you who love[b] her;
rejoice greatly with her,
all you who mourn over her.
[11]For you will nurse[c] and be satisfied
at her comforting breasts;
you will drink deeply
and delight in her overflowing abundance."

[12]For this is what the LORD says:

"I will extend peace to her like a river,[d]
and the wealth[e] of nations like a flooding stream;

65:23 [a]Dt 28:3-12; Isa 61:9 [b]Ac 2:39
65:24 [c]Isa 55:6 [d]Da 9:20-23; 10:12
65:25 [e]Isa 11:6 [f]Ge 3:14; Mic 7:17
66:1 [g]Mt 23:22 [h]1Ki 8:27; Mt 5:34-35 [i]2Sa 7:7; Jn 4:20-21; Ac 7:49*; 17:24
66:2 [j]Isa 40:26; Ac 7:50* [k]Isa 57:15; Mt 5:3-4; Lk 18:13-14 [l]Ezr 9:4
66:3 [m]Isa 1:11 [n]Lev 2:2 [o]Isa 57:17
66:4 [p]Pr 10:24 [q]Pr 1:24; Jer 7:13 [r]2Ki 21:2,4,6 [s]Isa 65:12
66:5 [t]Ps 38:20; Isa 60:15 [u]Lk 13:17
66:6 [v]Isa 65:6; Joel 3:7
66:7 [w]Isa 54:1 [x]Rev 12:5
66:8 [y]Isa 64:4
66:9 [z]Isa 37:3
66:10 [a]Dt 32:43; Ro 15:10 [b]Ps 26:8
66:11 [c]Isa 60:16
66:12 [d]Isa 48:18 [e]Ps 72:3; Isa 60:5; 61:6

you will nurse and be carried[a] on
her arm
and dandled on her knees.
13 As a mother comforts her child,
so will I comfort[b] you;
and you will be comforted over
Jerusalem."

The rebellious will meet their end.

14 When you see this, your heart
will rejoice
and you will flourish like grass;
the hand of the LORD will be made
known to his servants,
but his fury[c] will be shown to
his foes.
15 See, the LORD is coming with fire,
and his chariots[d] are like
a whirlwind;
he will bring down his anger with fury,
and his rebuke[e] with flames of fire.
16 For with fire[f] and with his sword[g]
the LORD will execute judgment
upon all men,
and many will be those slain by
the LORD.

17 "Those who consecrate and purify
themselves to go into the gardens,[h] following the one in the midst of[x] those
who eat the flesh of pigs[i] and rats and
other abominable things—they will meet
their end[j] together," declares the LORD.
18 "And I, because of their actions and
their imaginations, am about to come[y]
and gather all nations and tongues, and
they will come and see my glory.

19 "I will set a sign[k] among them, and
I will send some of those who survive
to the nations—to Tarshish,[l] to the Libyans[z] and Lydians[m] (famous as archers),
to Tubal[n] and Greece, and to the distant
islands[o] that have not heard of my fame
or seen my glory.[p] They will proclaim
my glory among the nations.
20 And they
will bring all your brothers, from all the
nations, to my holy mountain in Jerusalem as an offering to the LORD—on
horses, in chariots and wagons, and on
mules and camels," says the LORD. "They
will bring them, as the Israelites bring
their grain offerings, to the temple of
the LORD in ceremonially clean vessels.[q]
21 And I will select some of them also to
be priests[r] and Levites," says the LORD.

22 "As the new heavens and the new
earth[s] that I make will endure before
me," declares the LORD, "so will your
name and descendants endure.[t]
23 From
one New Moon to another and from
one Sabbath[u] to another, all mankind will
come and bow down[v] before me," says
the LORD.
24 "And they will go out and
look upon the dead bodies of those who
rebelled against me; their worm[w] will
not die, nor will their fire be quenched,[x] and they will be loathsome to all
mankind."

66:12 [a]Isa 60:4
66:13 [b]Isa 40:1; 2Co 1:4
66:14 [c]Isa 10:5
66:15 [d]Ps 68:17 [e]Ps 9:5
66:16 [f]Isa 30:30 [g]Isa 27:1
66:17 [h]Isa 1:29 [i]Lev 11:7 [j]Ps 37:20; Isa 1:28
66:19 [k]Isa 11:10; 49:22 [l]Isa 2:16 [m]Eze 27:10 [n]Ge 10:2 [o]Isa 11:11 [p]1Ch 16:24; Isa 24:15
66:20 [q]Isa 52:11
66:21 [r]Ex 19:6; Isa 61:6; 1Pe 2:5,9
66:22 [s]Isa 65:17; Heb 12:26-27; 2Pe 3:13; Rev 21:1 [t]Jn 10:27-29; 1Pe 1:4-5
66:23 [u]Eze 46:1-3 [v]Isa 19:21
66:24 [w]Isa 14:11 [x]Isa 1:31; Mk 9:48*

x 17 Or *gardens behind one of your temples, and*
y 18 The meaning of the Hebrew for this clause is uncertain. z 19 Some Septuagint manuscripts *Put* (Libyans); Hebrew *Pul*

JEREMIAH

Author: Jeremiah, as dictated to his secretary, Baruch.

Date Written: Between 627 and 580 B.C.

Time Span: 40-47 years. (Jeremiah's ministry begins under Judah's last good king, Josiah, and continues under the remaining 4 evil kings: Jehoahaz, Jehoiakim, Jehoiachin and Zedekiah.)

Title: This book is named after its author: the prophet Jeremiah.

Background: Although 70 years earlier Assyria was powerful enough to destroy the northern kingdom of Israel, her power has since declined, and Babylon eventually defeats both Assyria and Egypt to attain world supremacy. Jeremiah's life covers the 40 years that lead to the destruction of Jerusalem, also at the hands of Babylon. Other prophets of the time include Zephaniah, Habakkuk, Daniel and Ezekiel. Jeremiah, "the weeping prophet," begins his ministry from Jerusalem when he is about 20 years old. Apostasy, idolatry and perverted worship are the rule of the day in Judah.

Where Written: Probably Jerusalem. (However, some scholars suggest Egypt.)

To Whom: Primarily to the nation of Judah, but also to all the surrounding nations.

Content: Jeremiah boldly undertakes the unenviable task of proclaiming God's judgment upon an unrepentant nation. He even remains celibate as a sign that judgment will come during his lifetime (chapter 16), which it surely does. Persecution becomes his lot when false prophets of the land, such as Hananiah, tell the people what they desire to hear rather than the truth of God. Jeremiah's unpopular message brings him sorrows of opposition, imprisonment, excommunication from the temple and beatings (chapters 20 and 38). Nothing can stop Jeremiah. Yet even as he prophesies destruction, Jeremiah promises a coming time of blessing, restoration and a new covenant. After Judah's exile to Babylon, he remains with the remnant in Jerusalem. But when Gedaliah, the governor placed over Jerusalem, is murdered, Jeremiah is taken as a hostage to Egypt, where he continues his prophetic ministry.

Key Words: "Sin"; "Weeping." It is the responsibility of Jeremiah to proclaim Judah's coming judgment for her continuance in "sin," for the people's wickedness is too great. Jeremiah is "weeping," not only for his own persecutions, but also for his nation's bitter affliction.

Themes: • God is patient and loving. • God's love for us may require divine discipline for our own good. • It grieves the heart of God to have to discipline his children. • Nations which reject God will pay the price for their disobedience. • The time to repent and turn to God is now. • God may have to rebuke sin in our lives, but he will never abandon or forsake us.

Outline:

1. The call of Jeremiah. 1:1-1:19
2. Prophecies against Judah. 2:1-29:32
3. The future restoration of Israel. 30:1-33:26
4. The fall of Jerusalem and her flight to Egypt. 34:1-45:5
5. Prophecies against the foreign nations. 46:1-51:64
6. The capture and destruction of Jerusalem. 52:1-52:34

JEREMIAH

1 The words of Jeremiah son of Hilkiah, one of the priests at Anathoth[a] in the territory of Benjamin. 2 The word of the LORD came to him in the thirteenth year of the reign of Josiah son of Amon king of Judah, 3 and through the reign of Jehoiakim[b] son of Josiah king of Judah, down to the fifth month of the eleventh year of Zedekiah[c] son of Josiah king of Judah, when the people of Jerusalem went into exile.[d]

God's call of Jeremiah.

4 The word of the LORD came to me, saying,

5 "Before I formed you in the womb I
knew[a][e] you,
before you were born[f] I set you
apart;
I appointed you as a prophet to the
nations.[g]"

6 "Ah, Sovereign LORD," I said, "I do not know how to speak;[h] I am only a child."[i]

7 But the LORD said to me, "Do not say, 'I am only a child.' You must go to everyone I send you to and say whatever I command you. 8 Do not be afraid[j] of them, for I am with you[k] and will rescue you," declares the LORD.

9 Then the LORD reached out his hand and touched[l] my mouth and said to me, "Now, I have put my words in your mouth.[m] 10 See, today I appoint you over nations and kingdoms to uproot and tear down, to destroy and overthrow, to build and to plant."[n]

The branch of an almond tree and a boiling pot.

11 The word of the LORD came to me: "What do you see, Jeremiah?"[o]

"I see the branch of an almond tree," I replied.

12 The LORD said to me, "You have seen correctly, for I am watching[b] to see that my word is fulfilled."

13 The word of the LORD came to me again: "What do you see?"[p]

"I see a boiling pot, tilting away from the north," I answered.

14 The LORD said to me, "From the north disaster will be poured out on all who live in the land. 15 I am about to summon all the peoples of the northern kingdoms," declares the LORD.

"Their kings will come and set up
their thrones
in the entrance of the gates of
Jerusalem;
they will come against all her
surrounding walls
and against all the towns of
Judah.[q]
16 I will pronounce my judgments on
my people
because of their wickedness[r] in
forsaking me,[s]
in burning incense to other gods[t]
and in worshiping what their
hands have made.

17 "Get yourself ready! Stand up and say to them whatever I command you. Do not be terrified[u] by them, or I will terrify you before them. 18 Today I have made you[v] a fortified city, an iron pillar and a bronze wall to stand against the whole land—against the kings of Judah, its officials, its priests and the people of the land. 19 They will fight against you but will not overcome you, for I am with you[w] and will rescue[x] you," declares the LORD.

Israel forsakes the LORD.

2 The word of the LORD came to me: 2 "Go and proclaim in the hearing of Jerusalem:

"'I remember the devotion of your
youth,[y]
how as a bride you loved me
and followed me through the desert,[z]
through a land not sown.

1:1 [a]Jos 21:18; 1Ch 6:60; Jer 32:7-9
1:3 [b]2Ki 23:34 [c]2Ki 24:17; Jer 39:2 [d]Jer 52:15
1:5 [e]Ps 139:16 [f]Isa 49:1 [g]ver 10; Jer 25:15-26
1:6 [h]Ex 4:10; 6:12 [i]1Ki 3:7
1:8 [j]Eze 2:6 [k]Jos 1:5; Jer 15:20
1:9 [l]Isa 6:7 [m]Ex 4:12
1:10 [n]Jer 18:7-10; 24:6; 31:4,28
1:11 [o]Jer 24:3; Am 7:8
1:13 [p]Zec 4:2
1:15 [q]Jer 4:16; 9:11
1:16 [r]Dt 28:20 [s]Jer 17:13 [t]Jer 7:9; 19:4
1:17 [u]Eze 2:6
1:18 [v]Isa 50:7
1:19 [w]Jer 20:11 [x]ver 8
2:2 [y]Eze 16:8-14, 60; Hos 2:15 [z]Dt 2:7

a5 Or *chose* b12 The Hebrew for *watching* sounds like the Hebrew for *almond tree.*

[3]Israel was holy[a] to the LORD,[b]
the firstfruits[c] of his harvest;
all who devoured[d] her were held
guilty,[e]
and disaster overtook them,' "
declares the LORD.

[4]Hear the word of the LORD, O house of
Jacob,
all you clans of the house of Israel.

[5]This is what the LORD says:

"What fault did your fathers find in
me,
that they strayed so far from me?
They followed worthless idols
and became worthless[f] themselves.
[6]They did not ask, 'Where is the LORD,
who brought us up out of Egypt[g]
and led us through the barren
wilderness,
through a land of deserts[h] and rifts,[i]
a land of drought and darkness,[c]
a land where no one travels and no
one lives?'
[7]I brought you into a fertile land
to eat its fruit and rich produce.[j]
But you came and defiled my land
and made my inheritance
detestable.[k]
[8]The priests did not ask,
'Where is the LORD?'
Those who deal with the law did not
know me;[l]
the leaders rebelled against me.
The prophets prophesied by Baal,[m]
following worthless idols.[n]

[9]"Therefore I bring charges[o] against
you again,"
declares the LORD.
"And I will bring charges against
your children's children.
[10]Cross over to the coasts of Kittim[d]
and look,
send to Kedar[e] and observe closely;
see if there has ever been anything
like this:
[11]Has a nation ever changed its gods?
(Yet they are not gods[p] at all.)
But my people have exchanged their[f]
Glory[q]
for worthless idols.

2:3 [a]Dt 7:6 [b]Ex 19:6 [c]Jas 1:18; Rev 14:4 [d]Isa 41:11; Jer 30:16 [e]Jer 50:7
2:5 [f]2Ki 17:15
2:6 [g]Hos 13:4 [h]Dt 8:15 [i]Dt 32:10
2:7 [j]Nu 13:27; Dt 8:7-9; 11:10-12 [k]Ps 106:34-39; Jer 16:18
2:8 [l]Jer 4:22 [m]Jer 23:13 [n]Jer 16:19
2:9 [o]Eze 20:35-36; Mic 6:2
2:11 [p]Isa 37:19; Jer 16:20 [q]Ps 106:20; Ro 1:23
2:13 [r]Ps 36:9; Jn 4:14
2:14 [s]Ex 4:22
2:15 [t]Jer 4:7; 50:17 [u]Isa 1:7
2:16 [v]Isa 19:13 [w]Jer 43:7-9
2:17 [x]Jer 4:18
2:18 [y]Isa 30:2 [z]Jos 13:3
2:19 [a]Jer 3:11,22 [b]Isa 3:9; Hos 5:5 [c]Job 20:14; Am 8:10 [d]Ps 36:1
2:20 [e]Lev 26:13 [f]Isa 57:7; Jer 17:2 [g]Dt 12:2
2:21 [h]Ex 15:17 [i]Ps 80:8 [j]Isa 5:4

[12]Be appalled at this, O heavens,
and shudder with great horror,"
declares the LORD.
[13]"My people have committed two sins:
They have forsaken me,
the spring of living water,[r]
and have dug their own cisterns,
broken cisterns that cannot hold
water.
[14]Is Israel a servant, a slave[s] by birth?
Why then has he become plunder?
[15]Lions[t] have roared;
they have growled at him.
They have laid waste[u] his land;
his towns are burned and deserted.
[16]Also, the men of Memphis[g][v] and
Tahpanhes[w]
have shaved the crown of your
head.[h]
[17]Have you not brought this on
yourselves[x]
by forsaking the LORD your God
when he led you in the way?
[18]Now why go to Egypt[y]
to drink water from the Shihor[i]?[z]
And why go to Assyria
to drink water from the River[j]?
[19]Your wickedness will punish you;
your backsliding[a] will rebuke[b] you.
Consider then and realize
how evil and bitter[c] it is for you
when you forsake the LORD your God
and have no awe[d] of me,"
declares the Lord,
the LORD Almighty.

[20]"Long ago you broke off your yoke[e]
and tore off your bonds;
you said, 'I will not serve you!'
Indeed, on every high hill[f]
and under every spreading tree[g]
you lay down as a prostitute.
[21]I had planted[h] you like a choice vine[i]
of sound and reliable stock.
How then did you turn against me
into a corrupt,[j] wild vine?

c*6* Or *and the shadow of death* d*10* That is, Cyprus and western coastlands e*10* The home of Bedouin tribes in the Syro-Arabian desert f*11* Masoretic Text; an ancient Hebrew scribal tradition *my* g*16* Hebrew *Noph* h*16* Or *have cracked your skull* i*18* That is, a branch of the Nile j*18* That is, the Euphrates

22 Although you wash yourself with soda
and use an abundance of soap,
the stain of your guilt is still before me,"
declares the Sovereign LORD.
23 "How can you say, 'I am not defiled;[a]
I have not run after the Baals'?[b]
See how you behaved in the valley;[c]
consider what you have done.
You are a swift she-camel
running[d] here and there,
24 a wild donkey[e] accustomed to the desert,
sniffing the wind in her craving—
in her heat who can restrain her?
Any males that pursue her need not tire themselves;
at mating time they will find her.
25 Do not run until your feet are bare
and your throat is dry.
But you said, 'It's no use!
I love foreign gods,[f]
and I must go after them.'

26 "As a thief is disgraced[g] when he is caught,
so the house of Israel is disgraced—
they, their kings and their officials,
their priests and their prophets.
27 They say to wood, 'You are my father,'
and to stone,[h] 'You gave me birth.'
They have turned their backs to me
and not their faces;[i]
yet when they are in trouble,[j] they say,
'Come and save us!'
28 Where then are the gods[k] you made for yourselves?
Let them come if they can save you
when you are in trouble![l]
For you have as many gods
as you have towns,[m] O Judah.

29 "Why do you bring charges against me?
You have all[n] rebelled against me,"
declares the LORD.
30 "In vain I punished your people;
they did not respond to correction.
Your sword has devoured your prophets[o]
like a ravening lion.

2:23 [a]Pr 30:12 [b]Jer 9:14 [c]Jer 7:31 [d]ver 33; Jer 31:22
2:24 [e]Jer 14:6
2:25 [f]Dt 32:16; Jer 3:13; 14:10
2:26 [g]Jer 48:27
2:27 [h]Jer 3:9 [i]Jer 18:17; 32:33 [j]Jdg 10:10; Isa 26:16
2:28 [k]Isa 45:20 [l]Dt 32:37 [m]2Ki 17:29; Jer 11:13
2:29 [n]Jer 5:1; 6:13; Da 9:11
2:30 [o]Ne 9:26; Ac 7:52; 1Th 2:15
2:31 [p]Isa 45:19
2:34 [q]2Ki 21:16 [r]Ex 22:2
2:35 [s]Jer 25:31 [t]1Jn 1:8,10
2:36 [u]Jer 31:22 [v]Isa 30:2,3,7
2:37 [w]2Sa 13:19 [x]Jer 37:7
3:1 [y]Dt 24:1-4 [z]Jer 2:20,25; Eze 16:26,29
3:2 [a]Ge 38:14; Eze 16:25

31 "You of this generation, consider the word of the LORD:

"Have I been a desert to Israel
or a land of great darkness?[p]
Why do my people say, 'We are free to roam;
we will come to you no more'?
32 Does a maiden forget her jewelry,
a bride her wedding ornaments?
Yet my people have forgotten me,
days without number.
33 How skilled you are at pursuing love!
Even the worst of women can learn from your ways.
34 On your clothes men find
the lifeblood[q] of the innocent poor,
though you did not catch them breaking in.[r]
Yet in spite of all this
35 you say, 'I am innocent;
he is not angry with me.'
But I will pass judgment[s] on you
because you say, 'I have not sinned.'[t]
36 Why do you go about so much,
changing[u] your ways?
You will be disappointed by Egypt[v]
as you were by Assyria.
37 You will also leave that place
with your hands on your head,[w]
for the LORD has rejected those you trust;
you will not be helped[x] by them.

Adulterous Israel and Judah.

3 "If a man divorces[y] his wife
and she leaves him and marries another man,
should he return to her again?
Would not the land be completely defiled?
But you have lived as a prostitute with many lovers[z]—
would you now return to me?"
declares the LORD.
2 "Look up to the barren heights and see.
Is there any place where you have not been ravished?
By the roadside[a] you sat waiting for lovers,

sat like a nomad[k] in the desert.
You have defiled the land[a]
with your prostitution and
wickedness.
3Therefore the showers have been
withheld,[b]
and no spring rains[c] have fallen.
Yet you have the brazen look of a
prostitute;
you refuse to blush with shame.[d]
4Have you not just called to me:
'My Father,[e] my friend from my
youth,[f]
5will you always be angry?[g]
Will your wrath continue forever?'
This is how you talk,
but you do all the evil you can."

6During the reign of King Josiah, the
LORD said to me, "Have you seen what
faithless Israel has done? She has gone
up on every high hill and under every
spreading tree[h] and has committed adultery[i] there. 7I thought that after she had
done all this she would return to me but
she did not, and her unfaithful sister[j]
Judah saw it. 8I gave faithless Israel her
certificate of divorce and sent her away
because of all her adulteries. Yet I saw
that her unfaithful sister Judah had no
fear;[k] she also went out and committed
adultery. 9Because Israel's immorality
mattered so little to her, she defiled the
land[l] and committed adultery with
stone[m] and wood.[n] 10In spite of all this,
her unfaithful sister Judah did not return
to me with all her heart, but only in pretense,[o]" declares the LORD.

Exhortation for the faithless to return to the LORD.

11The LORD said to me, "Faithless Israel is more righteous[p] than unfaithful[q]
Judah. 12Go, proclaim this message toward the north:[r]

"'Return,[s] faithless Israel,' declares
the LORD,
'I will frown on you no longer,
for I am merciful,' declares the LORD,
'I will not be angry[t] forever.
13Only acknowledge[u] your guilt—
you have rebelled against the LORD
your God,
you have scattered your favors to
foreign gods[v]
under every spreading tree,[w]
and have not obeyed[x] me,'"
declares the LORD.

14"Return,[y] faithless people," declares
the LORD, "for I am your husband. I will
choose you—one from a town and two
from a clan—and bring you to Zion.
15Then I will give you shepherds[z] after
my own heart, who will lead you with
knowledge and understanding. 16In those
days, when your numbers have increased
greatly in the land," declares the LORD,
"men will no longer say, 'The ark of the
covenant of the LORD.' It will never enter
their minds or be remembered;[a] it will
not be missed, nor will another one be
made. 17At that time they will call Jerusalem The Throne[b] of the LORD, and all
nations will gather in Jerusalem to hon-
or[c] the name of the LORD. No longer will
they follow the stubbornness of their
evil hearts.[d] 18In those days the house of
Judah will join the house of Israel,[e] and
together[f] they will come from a northern[g] land to the land[h] I gave your forefathers as an inheritance.

19"I myself said,

"'How gladly would I treat you like
sons
and give you a desirable land,
the most beautiful inheritance of any
nation.'
I thought you would call me
'Father'[i]
and not turn away from following
me.
20But like a woman unfaithful to her
husband,
so you have been unfaithful to me,
O house of Israel,"
declares the LORD.
21A cry is heard on the barren
heights,[j]
the weeping and pleading of the
people of Israel,

3:2 [a]Jer 2:7
3:3 [b]Lev 26:19 [c]Jer 14:4 [d]Jer 6:15; 8:12; Zep 3:5
3:4 [e]ver 19 [f]Jer 2:2
3:5 [g]Ps 103:9; Isa 57:16
3:6 [h]Jer 17:2 [i]Jer 2:20
3:7 [j]Eze 16:46
3:8 [k]Eze 16:47; 23:11
3:9 [l]ver 2 [m]Isa 57:6 [n]Jer 2:27
3:10 [o]Jer 12:2
3:11 [p]Eze 16:52; 23:11 [q]ver 7
3:12 [r]2Ki 17:3-6 [s]ver 14; Jer 31:21,22; Eze 33:11 [t]Ps 86:15
3:13 [u]Dt 30:1-3; Jer 14:20; 1Jn 1:9 [v]Jer 2:25 [w]Dt 12:2 [x]ver 25
3:14 [y]Hos 2:19
3:15 [z]Ac 20:28
3:16 [a]Isa 65:17
3:17 [b]Jer 17:12; Eze 43:7 [c]Isa 60:9 [d]Jer 11:8
3:18 [e]Hos 1:11 [f]Isa 11:13; Jer 50:4 [g]Jer 16:15; 31:8 [h]Am 9:15
3:19 [i]ver 4; Isa 63:16
3:21 [j]ver 2

[k]2 Or *an Arab*

because they have perverted their
ways
and have forgotten the LORD their
God.

22"Return,[a] faithless people;
I will cure[b] you of backsliding."

"Yes, we will come to you,
for you are the LORD our God.
23Surely the ⌊idolatrous⌋ commotion on
the hills
and mountains is a deception;
surely in the LORD our God
is the salvation[c] of Israel.
24From our youth shameful[d] gods have
consumed
the fruits of our fathers' labor—
their flocks and herds,
their sons and daughters.
25Let us lie down in our shame,[e]
and let our disgrace cover us.
We have sinned against the LORD our
God,
both we and our fathers;
from our youth[f] till this day
we have not obeyed the LORD our
God."

4 "If you will return[g], O Israel,
return to me,"
declares the LORD.
"If you put your detestable idols[h] out
of my sight
and no longer go astray,
2and if in a truthful, just and
righteous way
you swear,[i] 'As surely as the LORD
lives,'[j]
then the nations will be blessed[k] by
him
and in him they will glory."

3This is what the LORD says to the
men of Judah and to Jerusalem:

"Break up your unplowed ground[l]
and do not sow among thorns.[m]
4Circumcise yourselves to the LORD,
circumcise your hearts,[n]
you men of Judah and people of
Jerusalem,
or my wrath[o] will break out and
burn like fire
because of the evil you have done—
burn with no one to quench[p] it.

Disaster from the north.

5"Announce in Judah and proclaim in
Jerusalem and say:
'Sound the trumpet throughout the
land!'
Cry aloud and say:
'Gather together!
Let us flee to the fortified cities!'[q]
6Raise the signal to go to Zion!
Flee for safety without delay!
For I am bringing disaster from the
north,[r]
even terrible destruction."

7A lion[s] has come out of his lair;
a destroyer of nations has set out.
He has left his place
to lay waste[t] your land.
Your towns will lie in ruins[u]
without inhabitant.
8So put on sackcloth,[v]
lament and wail,
for the fierce anger[w] of the LORD
has not turned away from us.

9"In that day," declares the LORD,
"the king and the officials will lose
heart,
the priests will be horrified,
and the prophets will be appalled."[x]

10Then I said, "Ah, Sovereign LORD,
how completely you have deceived[y] this
people and Jerusalem by saying, 'You
will have peace,'[z] when the sword is at
our throats."
11At that time this people and Jerusalem will be told, "A scorching wind[a]
from the barren heights in the desert
blows toward my people, but not to winnow or cleanse; 12a wind too strong for
that comes from me.[1] Now I pronounce
my judgments[b] against them."

13Look! He advances like the clouds,[c]
his chariots[d] come like a
whirlwind,[e]
his horses are swifter than eagles.[f]
Woe to us! We are ruined!

3:22 [a]Hos 14:4 [b]Jer 33:6; Hos 6:1
3:23 [c]Ps 3:8; Jer 17:14
3:24 [d]Hos 9:10
3:25 [e]Ezr 9:6 [f]Jer 22:21
4:1 [g]Jer 3:1,22; Joel 2:12 [h]Jer 35:15
4:2 [i]Dt 10:20; Isa 65:16 [j]Jer 12:16 [k]Ge 22:18; Gal 3:8
4:3 [l]Hos 10:12 [m]Mk 4:18
4:4 [n]Dt 10:16; Jer 9:26; Ro 2:28-29 [o]Zep 2:2 [p]Am 5:6
4:5 [q]Jos 10:20; Jer 8:14
4:6 [r]Jer 1:13-15; 50:3
4:7 [s]2Ki 24:1; Jer 2:15 [t]Isa 1:7 [u]Jer 25:9
4:8 [v]Isa 22:12; Jer 6:26 [w]Jer 30:24
4:9 [x]Isa 29:9
4:10 [y]2Th 2:11 [z]Jer 14:13
4:11 [a]Eze 17:10; Hos 13:15
4:12 [b]Jer 1:16
4:13 [c]Isa 19:1 [d]Isa 66:15 [e]Isa 5:28 [f]Dt 28:49; Hab 1:8

[1]12 Or *comes at my command*

14O Jerusalem, wash[a] the evil from your heart and be saved.
How long will you harbor wicked thoughts?
15A voice is announcing from Dan,[b]
proclaiming disaster from the hills of Ephraim.
16"Tell this to the nations,
proclaim it to Jerusalem:
'A besieging army is coming from a distant land,
raising a war cry[c] against the cities of Judah.
17They surround[d] her like men guarding a field,
because she has rebelled[e] against me,'"
declares the LORD.
18"Your own conduct and actions[f]
have brought this upon you.[g]
This is your punishment.
How bitter[h] it is!
How it pierces to the heart!"

19Oh, my anguish, my anguish![i]
I writhe in pain.
Oh, the agony of my heart!
My heart pounds within me,
I cannot keep silent.[j]
For I have heard the sound of the trumpet;
I have heard the battle cry.[k]
20Disaster follows disaster;[l]
the whole land lies in ruins.
In an instant my tents[m] are destroyed,
my shelter in a moment.
21How long must I see the battle standard
and hear the sound of the trumpet?

22"My people are fools;[n]
they do not know me.[o]
They are senseless children;
they have no understanding.
They are skilled in doing evil;[p]
they know not how to do good."[q]

23I looked at the earth,
and it was formless and empty;[r]
and at the heavens,
and their light was gone.
24I looked at the mountains,
and they were quaking;[s]
all the hills were swaying.
25I looked, and there were no people;
every bird in the sky had flown away.[t]
26I looked, and the fruitful land was a desert;
all its towns lay in ruins
before the LORD, before his fierce anger.

27This is what the LORD says:

"The whole land will be ruined,
though I will not destroy[u] it completely.
28Therefore the earth will mourn[v]
and the heavens above grow dark,[w]
because I have spoken and will not relent,[x]
I have decided and will not turn back.[y]"

29At the sound of horsemen and archers[z]
every town takes to flight.[a]
Some go into the thickets;
some climb up among the rocks.
All the towns are deserted;[b]
no one lives in them.

30What are you doing,[c] O devastated one?
Why dress yourself in scarlet
and put on jewels[d] of gold?
Why shade your eyes with paint?[e]
You adorn yourself in vain.
Your lovers[f] despise you;
they seek your life.

31I hear a cry as of a woman in labor,[g]
a groan as of one bearing her first child—
the cry of the Daughter of Zion
gasping for breath,[h]
stretching out her hands[i] and saying,
"Alas! I am fainting;
my life is given over to murderers."

Judgments against Israel and Judah.

5 "Go up and down[j] the streets of Jerusalem,
look around and consider,
search through her squares.

4:14 [a]Jas 4:8
4:15 [b]Jer 8:16
4:16 [c]Eze 21:22
4:17 [d]2Ki 25:1,4 [e]Jer 5:23
4:18 [f]Ps 107:17; Isa 50:1 [g]Jer 2:17 [h]Jer 2:19
4:19 [i]Isa 16:11; 22:4; Jer 9:10 [j]Jer 20:9 [k]Nu 10:9
4:20 [l]Ps 42:7; Eze 7:26 [m]Jer 10:20
4:22 [n]Jer 10:8 [o]Jer 2:8 [p]Jer 13:23; 1Co 14:20 [q]Ro 16:19
4:23 [r]Ge 1:2
4:24 [s]Isa 5:25; Eze 38:20
4:25 [t]Jer 9:10; 12:4; Zep 1:3
4:27 [u]Jer 5:10,18; 12:12; 30:11; 46:28
4:28 [v]Jer 12:4,11; 14:2; Hos 4:3 [w]Isa 5:30; 50:3 [x]Nu 23:19 [y]Jer 23:20; 30:24
4:29 [z]Jer 6:23 [a]2Ki 25:4 [b]ver 7
4:30 [c]Isa 10:3-4 [d]Eze 23:40 [e]2Ki 9:30 [f]La 1:2; Eze 23:9,22
4:31 [g]Jer 13:21 [h]Isa 42:14 [i]Isa 1:15; La 1:17
5:1 [j]2Ch 16:9; Eze 22:30

If you can find but one person[a]
who deals honestly and seeks the truth,
I will forgive[b] this city.
2Although they say, 'As surely as the LORD lives,'[c]
still they are swearing falsely."

3O LORD, do not your eyes[d] look for truth?
You struck[e] them, but they felt no pain;
you crushed them, but they refused correction.[f]
They made their faces harder than stone[g]
and refused to repent.
4I thought, "These are only the poor;
they are foolish,
for they do not know[h] the way of the LORD,
the requirements of their God.
5So I will go to the leaders[i]
and speak to them;
surely they know the way of the LORD,
the requirements of their God."
But with one accord they too had broken off the yoke
and torn off the bonds.[j]
6Therefore a lion from the forest will attack them,
a wolf from the desert will ravage them,
a leopard[k] will lie in wait near their towns
to tear to pieces any who venture out,
for their rebellion is great
and their backslidings many.[l]

7"Why should I forgive you?
Your children have forsaken me
and sworn[m] by gods that are not gods.[n]
I supplied all their needs,
yet they committed adultery[o]
and thronged to the houses of prostitutes.
8They are well-fed, lusty stallions,
each neighing for another man's wife.[p]
9Should I not punish them for this?"[q]
declares the LORD.
"Should I not avenge myself
on such a nation as this?

10"Go through her vineyards and ravage them,
but do not destroy them completely.[r]
Strip off her branches,
for these people do not belong to the LORD.
11The house of Israel and the house of Judah
have been utterly unfaithful[s] to me,"
declares the LORD.

12They have lied about the LORD;
they said, "He will do nothing!
No harm will come to us;[t]
we will never see sword or famine.[u]
13The prophets[v] are but wind
and the word is not in them;
so let what they say be done to them."

14Therefore this is what the LORD God Almighty says:

"Because the people have spoken these words,
I will make my words in your mouth[w] a fire[x]
and these people the wood it consumes.
15O house of Israel," declares the LORD,
"I am bringing a distant nation[y] against you—
an ancient and enduring nation,
a people whose language[z] you do not know,
whose speech you do not understand.
16Their quivers are like an open grave;
all of them are mighty warriors.
17They will devour[a] [b] your harvests and food,
devour[c] [d] your sons and daughters;
they will devour[e] your flocks and herds,
devour your vines and fig trees.
With the sword they will destroy
the fortified cities in which you trust.[f]

5:1 [a]Ge 18:32 [b]Ge 18:24
5:2 [c]Jer 4:2
5:3 [d]2Ch 16:9 [e]Isa 9:13 [f]Jer 2:30; Zep 3:2 [g]Jer 7:26; 19:15; Eze 3:8-9
5:4 [h]Jer 8:7
5:5 [i]Mic 3:1,9 [j]Ps 2:3; Jer 2:20
5:6 [k]Hos 13:7 [l]Jer 30:14
5:7 [m]Jos 23:7; Zep 1:5 [n]Dt 32:21; Jer 2:11; Gal 4:8 [o]Nu 25:1
5:8 [p]Jer 29:23; Eze 22:11
5:9 [q]ver 29; Jer 9:9
5:10 [r]Jer 4:27
5:11 [s]Jer 3:20
5:12 [t]Jer 23:17 [u]2Ch 36:16; Jer 14:13
5:13 [v]Jer 14:15
5:14 [w]Jer 1:9; Hos 6:5 [x]Jer 23:29
5:15 [y]Dt 28:49; Isa 5:26; Jer 4:16 [z]Isa 28:11
5:17 [a]Jer 8:16 [b]Lev 26:16 [c]Jer 50:7,17 [d]Dt 28:32 [e]Dt 28:31 [f]Dt 28:33

18"Yet even in those days," declares
the LORD, "I will not destroy[a] you completely. 19And when the people ask,[b]
'Why has the LORD our God done all this
to us?' you will tell them, 'As you have
forsaken me and served foreign gods[c] in
your own land, so now you will serve
foreigners[d] in a land not your own.'

20"Announce this to the house of Jacob
and proclaim it in Judah:
21Hear this, you foolish and senseless
people,
who have eyes[e] but do not see,
who have ears but do not hear:[f]
22Should you not fear[g] me?" declares
the LORD.
"Should you not tremble in my
presence?
I made the sand a boundary for the sea,
an everlasting barrier it cannot
cross.
The waves may roll, but they cannot
prevail;
they may roar, but they cannot
cross it.
23But these people have stubborn and
rebellious[h] hearts;
they have turned aside and gone
away.
24They do not say to themselves,
'Let us fear the LORD our God,
who gives autumn and spring rains[i] in
season,
who assures us of the regular weeks
of harvest.'[j]
25Your wrongdoings have kept these
away;
your sins have deprived you of good.

26"Among my people are wicked men
who lie in wait[k] like men who snare
birds
and like those who set traps to catch
men.
27Like cages full of birds,
their houses are full of deceit;[l]
they have become rich[m] and
powerful
28 and have grown fat[n] and sleek.
Their evil deeds have no limit;
they do not plead the case of the
fatherless[o] to win it,
they do not defend the rights of the
poor.[p]
29Should I not punish them for this?"
declares the LORD.
"Should I not avenge myself
on such a nation as this?

30"A horrible[q] and shocking thing
has happened in the land:
31The prophets prophesy lies,[r]
the priests rule by their own
authority,
and my people love it this way.
But what will you do in the end?

Jerusalem's coming destruction.

6 "Flee for safety, people of
Benjamin!
Flee from Jerusalem!
Sound the trumpet in Tekoa![s]
Raise the signal over Beth
Hakkerem![t]
For disaster looms out of the north,[u]
even terrible destruction.
2I will destroy the Daughter of Zion,
so beautiful and delicate.
3Shepherds[v] with their flocks will
come against her;
they will pitch their tents around[w]
her,
each tending his own portion."

4"Prepare for battle against her!
Arise, let us attack at noon![x]
But, alas, the daylight is fading,
and the shadows of evening grow
long.
5So arise, let us attack at night
and destroy her fortresses!"

6This is what the LORD Almighty says:

"Cut down the trees[y]
and build siege ramps[z] against
Jerusalem.
This city must be punished;
it is filled with oppression.
7As a well pours out its water,
so she pours out her wickedness.
Violence[a] and destruction[b] resound
in her;
her sickness and wounds are ever
before me.

5:18 [a]Jer 4:27
5:19 [b]Dt 29:24-26; 1Ki 9:9 [c]Jer 16:13 [d]Dt 28:48
5:21 [e]Isa 6:10; Eze 12:2 [f]Mt 13:15; Mk 8:18
5:22 [g]Dt 28:58
5:23 [h]Dt 21:18
5:24 [i]Ps 147:8; Joel 2:23 [j]Ge 8:22; Ac 14:17
5:26 [k]Ps 10:8; Pr 1:11
5:27 [l]Jer 9:6 [m]Jer 12:1
5:28 [n]Dt 32:15 [o]Zec 7:10 [p]Isa 1:23; Jer 7:6
5:30 [q]Jer 23:14; Hos 6:10
5:31 [r]Eze 13:6; Mic 2:11
6:1 [s]2Ch 11:6 [t]Ne 3:14 [u]Jer 4:6
6:3 [v]Jer 12:10 [w]2Ki 25:4; Lk 19:43
6:4 [x]Jer 15:8
6:6 [y]Dt 20:19-20 [z]Jer 32:24
6:7 [a]Ps 55:9; Eze 7:11,23 [b]Jer 20:8

[8]Take warning, O Jerusalem,
or I will turn away[a] from you
and make your land desolate
so no one can live in it."

[9]This is what the LORD Almighty says:

"Let them glean the remnant of Israel
as thoroughly as a vine;
pass your hand over the branches
again,
like one gathering grapes."

[10]To whom can I speak and give
warning?
Who will listen to me?
Their ears are closed[m][b]
so they cannot hear.
The word[c] of the LORD is offensive to
them;
they find no pleasure in it.
[11]But I am full of the wrath[d] of the
LORD,
and I cannot hold it in.[e]

"Pour it out on the children in the
street
and on the young men[f] gathered
together;
both husband and wife will be caught
in it,
and the old, those weighed down
with years.
[12]Their houses will be turned over to
others,[g]
together with their fields and their
wives,[h]
when I stretch out my hand[i]
against those who live in the land,"
declares the LORD.
[13]"From the least to the greatest,
all are greedy for gain;[j]
prophets and priests alike,
all practice deceit.[k]
[14]They dress the wound of my people
as though it were not serious.
'Peace, peace,' they say,
when there is no peace.[l]
[15]Are they ashamed of their loathsome
conduct?
No, they have no shame at all;
they do not even know how to
blush.[m]
So they will fall among the fallen;
they will be brought down when I
punish them,"
says the LORD.

[16]This is what the LORD says:

"Stand at the crossroads and look;
ask for the ancient paths,[n]
ask where the good way[o] is, and
walk in it,
and you will find rest[p] for your
souls.
But you said, 'We will not walk in it.'
[17]I appointed watchmen[q] over you and
said,
'Listen to the sound of the
trumpet!'
But you said, 'We will not listen.'[r]
[18]Therefore hear, O nations;
observe, O witnesses,
what will happen to them.
[19]Hear, O earth:[s]
I am bringing disaster on this people,
the fruit of their schemes,[t]
because they have not listened to my
words
and have rejected my law.[u]
[20]What do I care about incense from
Sheba
or sweet calamus[v] from a distant
land?
Your burnt offerings are not
acceptable;[w]
your sacrifices[x] do not please
me."[y]

[21]Therefore this is what the LORD
says:

"I will put obstacles before this
people.
Fathers and sons alike will
stumble[z] over them;
neighbors and friends will perish."

[22]This is what the LORD says:

"Look, an army is coming
from the land of the north;[a]
a great nation is being stirred up
from the ends of the earth.

6:8 [a]Eze 23:18; Hos 9:12
6:10 [b]Ac 7:51 [c]Jer 20:8
6:11 [d]Jer 7:20 [e]Job 32:20; Jer 20:9 [f]Jer 9:21
6:12 [g]Dt 28:30 [h]Jer 8:10; 38:22 [i]Isa 5:25
6:13 [j]Isa 56:11 [k]Jer 8:10
6:14 [l]Jer 4:10; 8:11; Eze 13:10
6:15 [m]Jer 3:3; 8:10-12
6:16 [n]Jer 18:15 [o]Ps 119:3 [p]Mt 11:29
6:17 [q]Eze 3:17 [r]Jer 11:7-8; 25:4
6:19 [s]Isa 1:2; Jer 22:29 [t]Pr 1:31 [u]Jer 8:9
6:20 [v]Ex 30:23 [w]Am 5:22 [x]Ps 50:8-10; Jer 7:21; Mic 6:7-8 [y]Isa 1:11
6:21 [z]Isa 8:14
6:22 [a]Jer 1:15; 10:22

[m]10 Hebrew *uncircumcised*

23 They are armed with bow and spear;
they are cruel and show no mercy.[a]
They sound like the roaring sea
as they ride on their horses;[b]
they come like men in battle
formation
to attack you, O Daughter of Zion."

24 We have heard reports about them,
and our hands hang limp.
Anguish[c] has gripped us,
pain like that of a woman in labor.[d]
25 Do not go out to the fields
or walk on the roads,
for the enemy has a sword,
and there is terror on every side.[e]
26 O my people, put on sackcloth[f]
and roll in ashes;[g]
mourn with bitter wailing
as for an only son,[h]
for suddenly the destroyer
will come upon us.

27 "I have made you a tester[i] of metals
and my people the ore,
that you may observe
and test their ways.
28 They are all hardened rebels,[j]
going about to slander.[k]
They are bronze and iron;[l]
they all act corruptly.
29 The bellows blow fiercely
to burn away the lead with fire,
but the refining goes on in vain;
the wicked are not purged out.
30 They are called rejected silver,
because the LORD has rejected
them."[m]

False religion worthless.

7 This is the word that came to
Jeremiah from the LORD: 2 "Stand[n]
at the gate of the LORD's house and there
proclaim this message:
"'Hear the word of the LORD, all you
people of Judah who come through
these gates to worship the LORD. 3 This is
what the LORD Almighty, the God of
Israel, says: Reform your ways[o] and your
actions, and I will let you live in this
place. 4 Do not trust in deceptive[p] words
and say, "This is the temple of the LORD,
the temple of the LORD, the temple of the
LORD!" 5 If you really change your ways
and your actions and deal with each other justly,[q] 6 if you do not oppress the
alien, the fatherless or the widow and do
not shed innocent blood[r] in this place,
and if you do not follow other gods[s] to
your own harm, 7 then I will let you live
in this place, in the land[t] I gave your
forefathers for ever and ever. 8 But look,
you are trusting in deceptive words that
are worthless.
9 "'Will you steal and murder, commit
adultery and perjury,[n] burn incense to
Baal[u] and follow other gods[v] you have
not known, 10 and then come and stand
before me in this house,[w] which bears
my Name, and say, "We are safe"—safe
to do all these detestable things? 11 Has
this house,[x] which bears my Name,
become a den of robbers[y] to you? But I
have been watching![z] declares the LORD.
12 "'Go now to the place in Shiloh[a]
where I first made a dwelling for my
Name, and see what I did[b] to it because
of the wickedness of my people Israel.
13 While you were doing all these things,
declares the LORD, I spoke to you again
and again,[c] but you did not listen;[d] I
called you, but you did not answer.[e]
14 Therefore, what I did to Shiloh I will
now do to the house that bears my
Name,[f] the temple you trust in, the
place I gave to you and your fathers. 15 I
will thrust you from my presence, just
as I did all your brothers, the people of
Ephraim.'[g]
16 "So do not pray for this people nor
offer any plea[h] or petition for them; do
not plead with me, for I will not listen
to you. 17 Do you not see what they are
doing in the towns of Judah and in the
streets of Jerusalem? 18 The children
gather wood, the fathers light the fire,
and the women knead the dough and
make cakes of bread for the Queen of
Heaven.[i] They pour out drink offerings[j]
to other gods to provoke[k] me to anger.
19 But am I the one they are provoking?

6:23 [a]Isa 13:18 [b]Jer 4:29
6:24 [c]Jer 4:19 [d]Jer 4:31; 50:41-43
6:25 [e]Jer 49:29
6:26 [f]Jer 4:8 [g]Jer 25:34; Mic 1:10 [h]Zec 12:10
6:27 [i]Jer 9:7
6:28 [j]Jer 5:23 [k]Jer 9:4 [l]Eze 22:18
6:30 [m]Ps 119:119; Jer 7:29; Hos 9:17
7:2 [n]Jer 17:19
7:3 [o]Jer 18:11; 26:13
7:4 [p]Mic 3:11
7:5 [q]Jer 22:3
7:6 [r]Jer 2:34; 19:4 [s]Dt 8:19
7:7 [t]Dt 4:40
7:9 [u]Jer 11:13,17 [v]Ex 20:3
7:10 [w]Jer 32:34; Eze 23:38-39
7:11 [x]Isa 56:7 [y]Mt 21:13*; Mk 11:17*; Lk 19:46* [z]Jer 29:23
7:12 [a]Jos 18:1 [b]1Sa 4:10-11, 22; Ps 78:60-64
7:13 [c]2Ch 36:15 [d]Isa 65:12 [e]Jer 35:17
7:14 [f]1Ki 9:7
7:15 [g]Ps 78:67
7:16 [h]Ex 32:10; Dt 9:14; Jer 15:1

7:18 [i]Jer 44:17-19 [j]Jer 19:13 [k]1Ki 14:9

n9 Or *and swear by false gods*

declares the LORD. Are they not rather
harming themselves, to their own
shame?[a]
20“ ‘Therefore this is what the Sovereign LORD says: My anger[b] and my
wrath will be poured out on this place,
on man and beast, on the trees of the
field and on the fruit of the ground, and
it will burn and not be quenched.
21“ ‘This is what the LORD Almighty,
the God of Israel, says: Go ahead, add
your burnt offerings to your other sacrifices[c] and eat[d] the meat yourselves!
22For when I brought your forefathers
out of Egypt and spoke to them, I did
not just give them commands about
burnt offerings and sacrifices,[e] 23but I
gave them this command: Obey[f] me,
and I will be your God and you will be
my people.[g] Walk in all the ways I command you, that it may go well[h] with you.
24But they did not listen or pay attention;[i] instead, they followed the stubborn inclinations of their evil hearts.
They went backward and not forward.
25From the time your forefathers left
Egypt until now, day after day, again and
again I sent you my servants the prophets.[j] 26But they did not listen to me or
pay attention. They were stiff-necked and
did more evil than their forefathers.’[k]
27“When you tell[l] them all this, they
will not listen[m] to you; when you call
to them, they will not answer. 28There-
fore say to them, ‘This is the nation that
has not obeyed the LORD its God or
responded to correction. Truth has perished; it has vanished from their lips.
29Cut off[n] your hair and throw it away;
take up a lament on the barren heights,
for the LORD has rejected and abandoned[o] this generation that is under his
wrath.

The Valley of Slaughter.

30“ ‘The people of Judah have done
evil in my eyes, declares the LORD. They
have set up their detestable idols[p] in the
house that bears my Name and have
defiled[q] it. 31They have built the high
places of Topheth[r] in the Valley of Ben
Hinnom to burn their sons and daughters[s] in the fire—something I did not
command, nor did it enter my mind.[t]
32So beware, the days are coming,
declares the LORD, when people will no
longer call it Topheth or the Valley of Ben
Hinnom, but the Valley of Slaughter,[u]
for they will bury[v] the dead in Topheth
until there is no more room. 33Then the
carcasses of this people will become
food[w] for the birds of the air and the
beasts of the earth, and there will be no
one to frighten them away. 34I will bring
an end to the sounds[x] of joy and gladness and to the voices of bride and bridegroom[y] in the towns of Judah and the
streets of Jerusalem, for the land will
become desolate.[z]

8 “ ‘At that time, declares the LORD,
the bones of the kings and officials
of Judah, the bones of the priests and
prophets, and the bones of the people of
Jerusalem will be removed from their
graves. 2They will be exposed to the sun
and the moon and all the stars of the
heavens, which they have loved and
served[a] and which they have followed
and consulted and worshiped. They will
not be gathered up or buried, but will be
like refuse lying on the ground. 3Wher-
ever I banish them, all the survivors of
this evil nation will prefer death to life,[b]
declares the LORD Almighty.’

4“Say to them, ‘This is what the LORD
says:

“ ‘When men fall down, do they not
get up?[c]
When a man turns away, does he
not return?
5Why then have these people turned
away?
Why does Jerusalem always turn
away?
They cling to deceit;[d]
they refuse to return.[e]
6I have listened attentively,
but they do not say what is right.
No one repents[f] of his wickedness,
saying, “What have I done?”
Each pursues his own course[g]
like a horse charging into battle.

7:19 [a]Jer 9:19
7:20 [b]Jer 42:18; La 2:3-5
7:21 [c]Isa 1:11; Am 5:21-22 [d]Hos 8:13
7:22 [e]1Sa 15:22; Ps 51:16; Hos 6:6
7:23 [f]Ex 19:5 [g]Lev 26:12 [h]Ex 15:26
7:24 [i]Ps 81:11-12; Jer 11:8
7:25 [j]Jer 25:4
7:26 [k]Jer 16:12
7:27 [l]Eze 2:7 [m]Eze 3:7
7:29 [n]Job 1:20; Isa 15:2; Mic 1:16 [o]Jer 6:30
7:30 [p]Eze 7:20-22 [q]Jer 32:34
7:31 [r]2Ki 23:10 [s]Ps 106:38 [t]Jer 19:5
7:32 [u]Jer 19:6 [v]Jer 19:11
7:33 [w]Dt 28:26
7:34 [x]Isa 24:8; Eze 26:13 [y]Rev 18:23 [z]Lev 26:34
8:2 [a]2Ki 23:5; Ac 7:42
8:3 [b]Job 3:22; Rev 9:6
8:4 [c]Pr 24:16
8:5 [d]Jer 5:27 [e]Jer 7:24; 9:6
8:6 [f]Rev 9:20 [g]Ps 14:1-3

7Even the stork in the sky
knows her appointed seasons,
and the dove, the swift and the thrush
observe the time of their migration.
But my people do not know[a]
the requirements of the LORD.

8" 'How can you say, "We are wise,
for we have the law[b] of the LORD,"
when actually the lying pen of the scribes
has handled it falsely?
9The wise[c] will be put to shame;
they will be dismayed and trapped.
Since they have rejected the word[d] of the LORD,
what kind of wisdom do they have?
10Therefore I will give their wives to other men
and their fields to new owners.[e]
From the least to the greatest,
all are greedy for gain;[f]
prophets and priests alike,
all practice deceit.
11They dress the wound of my people
as though it were not serious.
"Peace, peace," they say,
when there is no peace.[g]
12Are they ashamed of their loathsome conduct?
No, they have no shame[h] at all;
they do not even know how to blush.
So they will fall among the fallen;
they will be brought down when they are punished,[i]
says the LORD.[j]

13" 'I will take away their harvest,
declares the Lord.
There will be no grapes on the vine.[k]
There will be no figs[l] on the tree,
and their leaves will wither.[m]
What I have given them
will be taken[n] from them.[o] ' "

14"Why are we sitting here?
Gather together!
Let us flee to the fortified cities[o]
and perish there!
For the LORD our God has doomed us
to perish
and given us poisoned water[p] to drink,
because we have sinned[q] against him.
15We hoped for peace[r]
but no good has come,
for a time of healing
but there was only terror.[s]
16The snorting of the enemy's horses
is heard from Dan;[t]
at the neighing of their stallions
the whole land trembles.
They have come to devour
the land and everything in it,
the city and all who live there."

17"See, I will send venomous snakes[u]
among you,
vipers that cannot be charmed,[v]
and they will bite you,"
declares the LORD.

Jeremiah mourns for his people.

18O my Comforter[p] in sorrow,
my heart is faint[w] within me.
19Listen to the cry of my people
from a land far away:[x]
"Is the LORD not in Zion?
Is her King no longer there?"

"Why have they provoked me to
anger with their images,
with their worthless foreign idols?"[y]

20"The harvest is past,
the summer has ended,
and we are not saved."

21Since my people are crushed, I am crushed;
I mourn,[z] and horror grips me.
22Is there no balm in Gilead?[a]
Is there no physician there?
Why then is there no healing[b]
for the wound of my people?

9

1Oh, that my head were a spring of water
and my eyes a fountain of tears!
I would weep[c] day and night
for the slain of my people.[d]

8:7 [a]Isa 1:3; Jer 5:4-5
8:8 [b]Ro 2:17
8:9 [c]Jer 6:15 [d]Jer 6:19
8:10 [e]Jer 6:12 [f]Isa 56:11
8:11 [g]Jer 6:14
8:12 [h]Jer 3:3 [i]Ps 52:5-7; Isa 3:9 [j]Jer 6:15
8:13 [k]Joel 1:7 [l]Lk 13:6 [m]Mt 21:19 [n]Jer 5:17
8:14 [o]Jer 4:5; Jer 35:11 [p]Dt 29:18; Jer 9:15; 23:15 [q]Jer 14:7,20
8:15 [r]ver 11 [s]Jer 14:19
8:16 [t]Jer 4:15
8:17 [u]Nu 21:6; Dt 32:24 [v]Ps 58:5
8:18 [w]La 5:17
8:19 [x]Jer 9:16 [y]Dt 32:21
8:21 [z]Jer 14:17
8:22 [a]Ge 37:25 [b]Jer 30:12
9:1 [c]Jer 13:17; La 2:11,18 [d]Isa 22:4

o *13* The meaning of the Hebrew for this sentence is uncertain. p *18* The meaning of the Hebrew for this word is uncertain.

[2]Oh, that I had in the desert
a lodging place for travelers,
so that I might leave my people
and go away from them;
for they are all adulterers,[a]
a crowd of unfaithful people.

[3]"They make ready their tongue
like a bow, to shoot lies;[b]
it is not by truth
that they triumph[q] in the land.
They go from one sin to another;
they do not acknowledge me,"
declares the LORD.
[4]"Beware of your friends;
do not trust your brothers.[c]
For every brother is a deceiver,[r][d]
and every friend a slanderer.
[5]Friend deceives friend,
and no one speaks the truth.
They have taught their tongues to lie;
they weary themselves with sinning.
[6]You[s] live in the midst of deception;[e]
in their deceit they refuse to
acknowledge me,"
declares the LORD.

[7]Therefore this is what the LORD
Almighty says:

"See, I will refine[f] and test[g] them,
for what else can I do
because of the sin of my people?
[8]Their tongue[h] is a deadly arrow;
it speaks with deceit.
With his mouth each speaks cordially
to his neighbor,
but in his heart he sets a trap[i] for
him.
[9]Should I not punish them for this?"
declares the LORD.
"Should I not avenge[j] myself
on such a nation as this?"

[10]I will weep and wail for the mountains
and take up a lament concerning
the desert pastures.
They are desolate and untraveled,
and the lowing of cattle is not heard.
The birds of the air[k] have fled
and the animals are gone.

[11]"I will make Jerusalem a heap of ruins,
a haunt of jackals;[l]
and I will lay waste the towns of
Judah
so no one can live there."[m]

[12]What man is wise[n] enough to understand this? Who has been instructed by
the LORD and can explain it? Why has
the land been ruined and laid waste like
a desert that no one can cross?
[13]The LORD said, "It is because they
have forsaken my law, which I set
before them; they have not obeyed me
or followed my law.[o] [14]Instead, they have
followed[p] the stubbornness of their
hearts;[q] they have followed the Baals, as
their fathers taught them." [15]Therefore,
this is what the LORD Almighty, the God
of Israel, says: "See, I will make this people eat bitter food[r] and drink poisoned
water.[s] [16]I will scatter them among nations[t] that neither they nor their fathers
have known,[u] and I will pursue them
with the sword[v] until I have destroyed
them."[w]

[17]This is what the LORD Almighty
says:

"Consider now! Call for the wailing
women[x] to come;
send for the most skillful of them.
[18]Let them come quickly
and wail over us
till our eyes overflow with tears
and water streams from our
eyelids.[y]
[19]The sound of wailing is heard from
Zion:
'How ruined[z] we are!
How great is our shame!
We must leave our land
because our houses are in ruins.'"

[20]Now, O women, hear the word of the
LORD;
open your ears to the words of his
mouth.
Teach your daughters how to wail;
teach one another a lament.[a]
[21]Death has climbed in through our
windows

9:2 [a]Jer 5:7-8; 23:10; Hos 4:2
9:3 [b]Ps 64:3
9:4 [c]Mic 7:5-6 [d]Ge 27:35
9:6 [e]Jer 5:27
9:7 [f]Isa 1:25 [g]Jer 6:27
9:8 [h]ver 3 [i]Jer 5:26
9:9 [j]Jer 5:9,29
9:10 [k]Jer 4:25; 12:4; Hos 4:3
9:11 [l]Isa 34:13 [m]Isa 25:2; Jer 26:9
9:12 [n]Ps 107:43; Hos 14:9
9:13 [o]2Ch 7:19; Ps 89:30-32
9:14 [p]Jer 2:8,23 [q]Jer 7:24
9:15 [r]La 3:15 [s]Jer 8:14
9:16 [t]Lev 26:33 [u]Dt 28:64 [v]Eze 5:2 [w]Jer 44:27; Eze 5:12
9:17 [x]2Ch 35:25; Ecc 12:5; Am 5:16
9:18 [y]Jer 14:17
9:19 [z]Jer 4:13
9:20 [a]Isa 32:9-13

q3 Or *lies; / they are not valiant for truth* r4 Or *a deceiving Jacob* s6 That is, Jeremiah (the Hebrew is singular)

and has entered our fortresses;
it has cut off the children from the streets
and the young men[a] from the public squares.

22Say, "This is what the LORD declares:

" 'The dead bodies of men will lie
like refuse[b] on the open field,
like cut grain behind the reaper,
with no one to gather them.' "

23This is what the LORD says:

"Let not the wise man boast of his wisdom[c]
or the strong man boast of his strength[d]
or the rich man boast of his riches,[e]
24but let him who boasts boast[f] about this:
that he understands and knows me,
that I am the LORD,[g] who exercises kindness,[h]
justice and righteousness[i] on earth,
for in these I delight,"
declares the LORD.

25"The days are coming," declares the
LORD, "when I will punish all who are
circumcised only in the flesh[j]— 26Egypt,
Judah, Edom, Ammon, Moab and all
who live in the desert in distant places.[t][k]
For all these nations are really uncir-
cumcised, and even the whole house of
Israel is uncircumcised in heart.[l]"

Idols are worthless.

10:12-16pp—Jer 51:15-19

10 Hear what the LORD says to you,
O house of Israel. 2This is what
the LORD says:

"Do not learn the ways of the nations[m]
or be terrified by signs in the sky,
though the nations are terrified by them.
3For the customs of the peoples are worthless;
they cut a tree out of the forest,
and a craftsman[n] shapes it with his chisel.
4They adorn it with silver and gold;
they fasten it with hammer and nails
so it will not totter.[o]
5Like a scarecrow in a melon patch,
their idols cannot speak;[p]
they must be carried
because they cannot walk.[q]
Do not fear them;
they can do no harm
nor can they do any good."[r]

6No one is like you, O LORD;
you are great,[s]
and your name is mighty in power.
7Who should not revere you,
O King of the nations?[t]
This is your due.
Among all the wise men of the nations
and in all their kingdoms,
there is no one like you.
8They are all senseless and foolish;[u]
they are taught by worthless wooden idols.
9Hammered silver is brought from Tarshish
and gold from Uphaz.
What the craftsman and goldsmith have made[v]
is then dressed in blue and purple—
all made by skilled workers.
10But the LORD is the true God;
he is the living God, the eternal King.
When he is angry, the earth trembles;
the nations cannot endure his wrath.[w]

11"Tell them this: 'These gods, who
did not make the heavens and the earth,
will perish[x] from the earth and from
under the heavens.' "[u]

12But God made the earth by his power;
he founded the world by his wisdom
and stretched out the heavens[y] by his understanding.
13When he thunders,[z] the waters in the heavens roar;

9:21 [a]2Ch 36:17
9:22 [b]Jer 8:2
9:23 [c]Ecc 9:11 [d]1Ki 20:11 [e]Eze 28:4-5
9:24 [f]1Co 1:31*; Gal 6:14 [g]2Co 10:17* [h]Ps 51:1; Mic 7:18 [i]Ps 36:6
9:25 [j]Ro 2:8-9
9:26 [k]Jer 25:23 [l]Lev 26:41; Ac 7:51; Ro 2:28
10:2 [m]Lev 20:23
10:3 [n]Isa 40:19
10:4 [o]Isa 41:7
10:5 [p]1Co 12:2 [q]Ps 115:5,7 [r]Isa 41:24; 46:7
10:6 [s]Ps 48:1
10:7 [t]Ps 22:28; Rev 15:4
10:8 [u]Isa 40:19; Jer 4:22
10:9 [v]Ps 115:4; Isa 40:19
10:10 [w]Ps 76:7
10:11 [x]Ps 96:5; Isa 2:18
10:12 [y]Ge 1:1,8; Job 9:8; Isa 40:22
10:13 [z]Job 36:29

[t]26 Or *desert and who clip the hair by their foreheads* [u]11 The text of this verse is in Aramaic.

he makes clouds rise from the ends
of the earth.
He sends lightning with the rain[a]
and brings out the wind from his
storehouses.

14Everyone is senseless and without
knowledge;
every goldsmith is shamed by his
idols.
His images are a fraud;
they have no breath in them.
15They are worthless,[b] the objects of
mockery;
when their judgment comes, they
will perish.
16He who is the Portion[c] of Jacob is not
like these,
for he is the Maker of all things,[d]
including Israel, the tribe of his
inheritance[e]—
the LORD Almighty is his name.[f]

God will judge Judah.

17Gather up your belongings[g] to leave
the land,
you who live under siege.
18For this is what the LORD says:
"At this time I will hurl[h] out
those who live in this land;
I will bring distress on them
so that they may be captured."

19Woe to me because of my injury!
My wound[i] is incurable!
Yet I said to myself,
"This is my sickness, and I must
endure[j] it."
20My tent[k] is destroyed;
all its ropes are snapped.
My sons are gone from me and are no
more;[l]
no one is left now to pitch my tent
or to set up my shelter.
21The shepherds are senseless
and do not inquire of the LORD;
so they do not prosper
and all their flock is scattered.[m]
22Listen! The report is coming—
a great commotion from the land of
the north!
It will make the towns of Judah
desolate,
a haunt of jackals.[n]

Jeremiah prays.

23I know, O LORD, that a man's life is not
his own;
it is not for man to direct his steps.[o]
24Correct me, LORD, but only with
justice—
not in your anger,[p]
lest you reduce me to nothing.[q]
25Pour out your wrath on the nations[r]
that do not acknowledge you,
on the peoples who do not call on
your name.[s]
For they have devoured[t] Jacob;
they have devoured him
completely
and destroyed his homeland.[u]

Judah breaks covenant with God.

11 This is the word that came to Jeremiah from the LORD: 2"Listen to
the terms of this covenant and tell them
to the people of Judah and to those who
live in Jerusalem. 3Tell them that this is
what the LORD, the God of Israel, says:
'Cursed[v] is the man who does not obey
the terms of this covenant— 4the terms
I commanded your forefathers when I
brought them out of Egypt, out of the
iron-smelting furnace.[w]' I said, 'Obey[x]
me and do everything I command you,
and you will be my people,[y] and I will
be your God. 5Then I will fulfill the oath
I swore[z] to your forefathers, to give
them a land flowing with milk and honey'—the land you possess today."
I answered, "Amen, LORD."
6The LORD said to me, "Proclaim all
these words in the towns of Judah and
in the streets of Jerusalem: 'Listen to the
terms of this covenant and follow[a] them.
7From the time I brought your forefathers up from Egypt until today, I warned
them again and again,[b] saying, "Obey
me." 8But they did not listen or pay
attention;[c] instead, they followed the
stubbornness of their evil hearts. So I
brought on them all the curses[d] of the

10:13 [a]Ps 135:7
10:15 [b]Isa 41:24; Jer 14:22
10:16 [c]Dt 32:9; Ps 119:57 [d]ver 12 [e]Ps 74:2 [f]Jer 31:35; 32:18
10:17 [g]Eze 12:3-12
10:18 [h]1Sa 25:29
10:19 [i]Jer 14:17 [j]Mic 7:9
10:20 [k]Jer 4:20 [l]Jer 31:15; La 1:5
10:21 [m]Jer 23:2
10:22 [n]Jer 9:11
10:23 [o]Pr 20:24
10:24 [p]Ps 6:1; 38:1 [q]Jer 30:11
10:25 [r]Zep 3:8 [s]Job 18:21; Ps 14:4 [t]Ps 79:7; Jer 8:16 [u]Ps 79:6-7
11:3 [v]Dt 27:26; Gal 3:10
11:4 [w]Dt 4:20; 1Ki 8:51 [x]Ex 24:8 [y]Jer 7:23; 31:33
11:5 [z]Ex 13:5; Dt 7:12; Ps 105:8-11
11:6 [a]Dt 15:5; Ro 2:13; Jas 1:22
11:7 [b]2Ch 36:15
11:8 [c]Jer 7:26 [d]Lev 26:14-43

covenant I had commanded them to follow but that they did not keep.'"
9Then the LORD said to me, "There is
a conspiracy[a] among the people of Judah
and those who live in Jerusalem. 10They
have returned to the sins of their forefathers,[b] who refused to listen to my
words. They have followed other gods[c]
to serve them. Both the house of Israel
and the house of Judah have broken the
covenant I made with their forefathers.
11Therefore this is what the LORD says:
'I will bring on them a disaster[d] they
cannot escape. Although they cry[e] out
to me, I will not listen[f] to them. 12The
towns of Judah and the people of Jerusalem will go and cry out to the gods to
whom they burn incense,[g] but they will
not help them at all when disaster[h]
strikes. 13You have as many gods as you
have towns, O Judah; and the altars you
have set up to burn incense[i] to that
shameful[j] god Baal are as many as the
streets of Jerusalem.'
14"Do not pray[k] for this people nor
offer any plea or petition for them, because I will not listen[l] when they call to
me in the time of their distress.

15"What is my beloved doing in my
 temple
 as she works out her evil schemes
 with many?
 Can consecrated meat avert ⌊your
 punishment⌋?
When you engage in your
 wickedness,
 then you rejoice.[v]"

16The LORD called you a thriving olive
 tree
 with fruit beautiful in form.
But with the roar of a mighty
 storm
 he will set it on fire,[m]
 and its branches will be broken.[n]

17The LORD Almighty, who planted[o] you,
has decreed disaster for you, because the
house of Israel and the house of Judah
have done evil and provoked me to
anger by burning incense to Baal.[p]

11:9 [a]Eze 22:25
11:10 [b]Dt 9:7 [c]Jdg 2:12-13
11:11 [d]2Ki 22:16 [e]Jer 14:12; Eze 8:18 [f]ver 14; Pr 1:28; Isa 1:15; Zec 7:13
11:12 [g]Jer 44:17 [h]Dt 32:37
11:13 [i]Jer 7:9 [j]Jer 3:24
11:14 [k]Ex 32:10 [l]ver 11
11:16 [m]Jer 21:14 [n]Isa 27:11; Ro 11:17-24
11:17 [o]Isa 5:2; Jer 12:2 [p]Jer 7:9
11:19 [q]Jer 18:18; 20:10 [r]Job 28:13; Isa 53:8 [s]Ps 83:4
11:20 [t]Ps 7:9
11:21 [u]Jer 12:6 [v]Jer 26:8,11; 38:4
11:22 [w]Jer 18:21
11:23 [x]Jer 6:9 [y]Jer 23:12
12:1 [z]Ezr 9:15 [a]Jer 5:27-28
12:2 [b]Jer 11:17

Men of Anathoth plot against Jeremiah.

18Because the LORD revealed their plot
to me, I knew it, for at that time he
showed me what they were doing. 19I
had been like a gentle lamb led to the
slaughter; I did not realize that they had
plotted[q] against me, saying,

"Let us destroy the tree and its fruit;
 let us cut him off from the land of
 the living,[r]
 that his name be remembered[s] no
 more."
20But, O LORD Almighty, you who
 judge righteously
 and test the heart and mind,[t]
let me see your vengeance upon
 them,
 for to you I have committed my
 cause.

21"Therefore this is what the LORD
says about the men of Anathoth who are
seeking your life[u] and saying, 'Do not
prophesy in the name of the LORD or
you will die[v] by our hands'— 22therefore
this is what the LORD Almighty says: 'I
will punish them. Their young men[w] will
die by the sword, their sons and daughters by famine. 23Not even a remnant[x]
will be left to them, because I will bring
disaster on the men of Anathoth in the
year of their punishment.[y]'"

Jeremiah questions God.

12 You are always righteous,[z]
 O LORD,
 when I bring a case before you.
Yet I would speak with you about your
 justice:
 Why does the way of the wicked
 prosper?[a]
 Why do all the faithless live at
 ease?
2You have planted[b] them, and they
 have taken root;
 they grow and bear fruit.

v 15 Or *Could consecrated meat avert your punishment? / Then you would rejoice*

You are always on their lips
but far from their hearts.[a]
3 Yet you know me, O LORD;
you see me and test[b] my thoughts
about you.
Drag them off like sheep to be
butchered!
Set them apart for the day of
slaughter![c]
4 How long will the land lie parched[w][d]
and the grass in every field be
withered?[e]
Because those who live in it are
wicked,
the animals and birds have
perished.[f]
Moreover, the people are saying,
"He will not see what happens to
us."

God answers Jeremiah.

5 "If you have raced with men on foot
and they have worn you out,
how can you compete with horses?
If you stumble in safe country,[x]
how will you manage in the
thickets[g] by[y] the Jordan?
6 Your brothers, your own family—
even they have betrayed you;
they have raised a loud cry against
you.[h]
Do not trust them,
though they speak well of you.[i]

7 "I will forsake my house,
abandon[j] my inheritance;
I will give the one I love
into the hands of her enemies.
8 My inheritance has become to me
like a lion in the forest.
She roars at me;
therefore I hate her.[k]
9 Has not my inheritance become to
me
like a speckled bird of prey
that other birds of prey surround
and attack?
Go and gather all the wild beasts;
bring them to devour.[l]
10 Many shepherds[m] will ruin my
vineyard
and trample down my field;
they will turn my pleasant field
into a desolate wasteland.[n]
11 It will be made a wasteland,
parched and desolate before me;[o]
the whole land will be laid waste
because there is no one who cares.
12 Over all the barren heights in the
desert
destroyers will swarm,
for the sword of the LORD[p] will devour
from one end of the land to the
other;[q]
no one will be safe.
13 They will sow wheat but reap thorns;
they will wear themselves out but
gain nothing.[r]
So bear the shame of your harvest
because of the LORD's fierce anger."[s]

14 This is what the LORD says: "As for
all my wicked neighbors who seize the
inheritance I gave my people Israel, I
will uproot[t] them from their lands and
I will uproot the house of Judah from
among them. 15 But after I uproot them,
I will again have compassion and will
bring[u] each of them back to his own
inheritance and his own country. 16 And
if they learn well the ways of my people
and swear by my name, saying, 'As surely as the LORD lives'[v]—even as they once
taught my people to swear by Baal[w]—
then they will be established among my
people.[x] 17 But if any nation does not listen, I will completely uproot and destroy[y] it," declares the LORD.

A linen belt.

13 This is what the LORD said to me:
"Go and buy a linen belt and put
it around your waist, but do not let it
touch water." 2 So I bought a belt, as the
LORD directed, and put it around my
waist.

3 Then the word of the LORD came to
me a second time: 4 "Take the belt you
bought and are wearing around your
waist, and go now to Perath[z] and hide it
there in a crevice in the rocks." 5 So I

12:2 [a] Isa 29:13; Jer 3:10; Mt 15:8; Tit 1:16
12:3 [b] Ps 7:9; 11:5; 139:1-4; Jer 11:20 [c] Jer 17:18
12:4 [d] Jer 4:28 [e] Joel 1:10-12 [f] Jer 4:25; 9:10
12:5 [g] Jer 49:19; 50:44
12:6 [h] Pr 26:24-25; Jer 9:4 [i] Ps 12:2
12:7 [j] Jer 7:29
12:8 [k] Hos 9:15; Am 6:8
12:9 [l] Isa 56:9; Jer 15:3; Eze 23:25
12:10 [m] Jer 23:1 [n] Isa 5:1-7
12:11 [o] ver 4; Isa 42:25; Jer 23:10
12:12 [p] Jer 47:6 [q] Jer 3:2
12:13 [r] Lev 26:20; Dt 28:38; Mic 6:15; Hag 1:6 [s] Jer 4:26
12:14 [t] Zec 2:7-9
12:15 [u] Am 9:14-15
12:16 [v] Jer 4:2 [w] Jos 23:7 [x] Isa 49:6; Jer 3:17
12:17 [y] Isa 60:12

w4 Or *land mourn* x5 Or *If you put your trust in a land of safety* y5 Or *the flooding of* z4 Or possibly *the Euphrates*; also in verses 5-7

went and hid it at Perath, as the LORD
told me.[a]
6Many days later the LORD said to me,
"Go now to Perath and get the belt I
told you to hide there." 7So I went to
Perath and dug up the belt and took it
from the place where I had hidden it,
but now it was ruined and completely
useless.
8Then the word of the LORD came to
me: 9"This is what the LORD says: 'In
the same way I will ruin the pride of
Judah and the great pride[b] of Jerusalem.
10These wicked people, who refuse to
listen to my words, who follow the stubbornness of their hearts[c] and go after
other gods[d] to serve and worship them,
will be like this belt—completely useless! 11For as a belt is bound around a
man's waist, so I bound the whole house
of Israel and the whole house of Judah
to me,' declares the LORD, 'to be my
people for my renown[e] and praise and
honor.[f] But they have not listened.'[g]

Wineskins filled with wine.

12"Say to them: 'This is what the
LORD, the God of Israel, says: Every
wineskin should be filled with wine.'
And if they say to you, 'Don't we know
that every wineskin should be filled with
wine?' 13then tell them, 'This is what
the LORD says: I am going to fill with
drunkenness[h] all who live in this land,
including the kings who sit on David's
throne, the priests, the prophets and
all those living in Jerusalem. 14I will
smash them one against the other,
fathers and sons alike, declares the LORD.
I will allow no pity or mercy or compassion[i] to keep me from destroying[j]
them.'"

The cause of the coming captivity.

15Hear and pay attention,
do not be arrogant,
for the LORD has spoken.
16Give glory[k] to the LORD your God
before he brings the darkness,
before your feet stumble[l]
on the darkening hills.
You hope for light,
but he will turn it to thick darkness
and change it to deep gloom.[m]
17But if you do not listen,[n]
I will weep in secret
because of your pride;
my eyes will weep bitterly,
overflowing with tears,[o]
because the LORD's flock[p] will be
taken captive.[q]

18Say to the king and to the queen
mother,
"Come down from your thrones,
for your glorious crowns
will fall from your heads."
19The cities in the Negev will be shut
up,
and there will be no one to open
them.
All Judah[r] will be carried into exile,
carried completely away.

20Lift up your eyes and see
those who are coming from the
north.[s]
Where is the flock[t] that was
entrusted to you,
the sheep of which you boasted?
21What will you say when ⌊the LORD⌋
sets over you
those you cultivated as your special
allies?[u]
Will not pain grip you
like that of a woman in labor?[v]
22And if you ask yourself,
"Why has this happened to me?"—
it is because of your many sins[w]
that your skirts have been torn off
and your body mistreated.[x]
23Can the Ethiopian[a] change his skin
or the leopard its spots?
Neither can you do good
who are accustomed to doing evil.

24"I will scatter you like chaff[y]
driven by the desert wind.[z]
25This is your lot,
the portion[a] I have decreed for you,"
declares the LORD,

13:5 [a]Ex 40:16
13:9 [b]Lev 26:19
13:10 [c]Jer 11:8; 16:12 [d]Jer 9:14
13:11 [e]Jer 32:20; 33:9 [f]Ex 19:5-6 [g]Jer 7:26
13:13 [h]Ps 60:3; 75:8; Isa 51:17; 63:6; Jer 51:57
13:14 [i]Jer 16:5 [j]Dt 29:20; Eze 5:10
13:16 [k]Jos 7:19 [l]Jer 23:12 [m]Isa 59:9
13:17 [n]Mal 2:2 [o]Jer 9:1 [p]Ps 80:1; Jer 23:1 [q]Jer 14:18
13:19 [r]Jer 20:4; 52:30
13:20 [s]Jer 6:22; Hab 1:6 [t]Jer 23:2
13:21 [u]Jer 38:22 [v]Jer 4:31
13:22 [w]Jer 9:2-6; 16:10-12 [x]Eze 16:37; Na 3:5-6
13:24 [y]Ps 1:4 [z]Lev 26:33
13:25 [a]Job 20:29; Mt 24:51

a23 Hebrew *Cushite* (probably a person from the upper Nile region)

"because you have forgotten me
and trusted in false gods.
26 I will pull up your skirts over your face
that your shame may be seen[a]—
27 your adulteries and lustful neighings,
your shameless prostitution![b]
I have seen your detestable acts
on the hills and in the fields.[c]
Woe to you, O Jerusalem!
How long will you be unclean?"[d]

Drought in Judah.

14 This is the word of the LORD to Jeremiah concerning the drought:

2 "Judah mourns,[e]
her cities languish;
they wail for the land,
and a cry goes up from Jerusalem.
3 The nobles send their servants for
water;
they go to the cisterns
but find no water.[f]
They return with their jars unfilled;
dismayed and despairing,
they cover their heads.[g]
4 The ground is cracked
because there is no rain in the
land;[h]
the farmers are dismayed
and cover their heads.
5 Even the doe in the field
deserts her newborn fawn
because there is no grass.[i]
6 Wild donkeys stand on the barren
heights[j]
and pant like jackals;
their eyesight fails
for lack of pasture."

Jeremiah's prayer.

7 Although our sins testify[k] against us,
O LORD, do something for the sake
of your name.
For our backsliding[l] is great;
we have sinned[m] against you.
8 O Hope[n] of Israel,
its Savior in times of distress,
why are you like a stranger in the
land,
like a traveler who stays only a
night?
9 Why are you like a man taken by
surprise,
like a warrior powerless to save?[o]
You are among[p] us, O LORD,
and we bear your name;[q]
do not forsake us!

10 This is what the LORD says about
this people:

"They greatly love to wander;
they do not restrain their feet.[r]
So the LORD does not accept[s] them;
he will now remember[t] their
wickedness
and punish them for their sins."[u]

11 Then the LORD said to me, "Do not
pray[v] for the well-being of this people.
12 Although they fast, I will not listen to
their cry;[w] though they offer burnt offerings[x] and grain offerings, I will not accept[y] them. Instead, I will destroy them
with the sword, famine and plague."
13 But I said, "Ah, Sovereign LORD, the
prophets keep telling them, 'You will
not see the sword or suffer famine.[z] Indeed, I will give you lasting peace in this
place.'"
14 Then the LORD said to me, "The
prophets are prophesying lies[a] in my
name. I have not sent[b] them or appointed them or spoken to them. They are
prophesying to you false visions,[c] divinations,[d] idolatries[b] and the delusions
of their own minds. 15 Therefore, this is
what the LORD says about the prophets
who are prophesying in my name: I
did not send them, yet they are saying,
'No sword or famine will touch this
land.' Those same prophets will perish[e]
by sword and famine.[f] 16 And the people
they are prophesying to will be thrown
out into the streets of Jerusalem because
of the famine and sword. There will be
no one to bury[g] them or their wives,
their sons or their daughters.[h] I will pour
out on them the calamity they deserve.[i]
17 "Speak this word to them:

"'Let my eyes overflow with tears[j]
night and day without ceasing;

13:26 [a]La 1:8; Eze 16:37; Hos 2:10
13:27 [b]Jer 2:20 [c]Eze 6:13 [d]Hos 8:5
14:2 [e]Isa 3:26; Jer 8:21
14:3 [f]2Ki 18:31; Job 6:19-20 [g]2Sa 15:30
14:4 [h]Jer 3:3
14:5 [i]Isa 15:6
14:6 [j]Job 39:5-6; Jer 2:24
14:7 [k]Hos 5:5 [l]Jer 5:6 [m]Jer 8:14
14:8 [n]Jer 17:13
14:9 [o]Isa 50:2 [p]Jer 8:19 [q]Isa 63:19; Jer 15:16
14:10 [r]Ps 119:101; Jer 2:25 [s]Jer 6:20; Am 5:22 [t]Hos 9:9 [u]Jer 44:21-23; Hos 8:13
14:11 [v]Ex 32:10
14:12 [w]Isa 1:15; Jer 11:11 [x]Jer 7:21 [y]Jer 6:20
14:13 [z]Jer 5:12
14:14 [a]Jer 27:14 [b]Jer 23:21,32 [c]Jer 23:16 [d]Eze 12:24
14:15 [e]Eze 14:9 [f]Jer 5:12-13
14:16 [g]Ps 79:3 [h]Jer 7:33 [i]Pr 1:31
14:17 [j]Jer 9:1

b 14 Or *visions, worthless divinations*

for my virgin daughter—my people—
has suffered a grievous wound,
a crushing blow.[a]
18If I go into the country,
I see those slain by the sword;
if I go into the city,
I see the ravages of famine.[b]
Both prophet and priest
have gone to a land they know
not.' "
19Have you rejected Judah
completely?[c]
Do you despise Zion?
Why have you afflicted us
so that we cannot be healed?[d]
We hoped for peace
but no good has come,
for a time of healing
but there is only terror.[e]
20O LORD, we acknowledge our
wickedness
and the guilt of our fathers;
we have indeed sinned[f] against you.
21For the sake of your name[g] do not
despise us;
do not dishonor your glorious
throne.[h]
Remember your covenant with us
and do not break it.
22Do any of the worthless idols of the
nations bring rain?[i]
Do the skies themselves send
down showers?
No, it is you, O LORD our God.
Therefore our hope is in you,
for you are the one who does all
this.

Four kinds of destroyers.

15 Then the LORD said to me: "Even
if Moses[j] and Samuel[k] were to
stand before me, my heart would not go
out to this people.[l] Send them away
from my presence![m] Let them go! 2And
if they ask you, 'Where shall we go?' tell
them, 'This is what the LORD says:

" 'Those destined for death, to death;
those for the sword, to the sword;[n]
those for starvation, to starvation;[o]
those for captivity, to captivity.'[p]

3"I will send four kinds of destroyers[q]
against them," declares the LORD, "the
sword to kill and the dogs to drag away
and the birds[r] of the air and the beasts
of the earth to devour and destroy.[s] 4I
will make them abhorrent[t] to all the
kingdoms of the earth[u] because of what
Manasseh[v] son of Hezekiah king of Judah
did in Jerusalem.

5"Who will have pity[w] on you,
O Jerusalem?
Who will mourn for you?
Who will stop to ask how you are?
6You have rejected[x] me," declares the
LORD.
"You keep on backsliding.
So I will lay hands[y] on you and
destroy you;
I can no longer show compassion.
7I will winnow them with a
winnowing fork
at the city gates of the land.
I will bring bereavement and
destruction on my people,[z]
for they have not changed their
ways.
8I will make their widows more
numerous
than the sand of the sea.
At midday I will bring a destroyer[a]
against the mothers of their young
men;
suddenly I will bring down on them
anguish and terror.
9The mother of seven will grow faint[b]
and breathe her last.
Her sun will set while it is still day;
she will be disgraced and
humiliated.
I will put the survivors to the sword[c]
before their enemies,"
declares the LORD.

Jeremiah's prayer and God's answer.

10Alas, my mother, that you gave me
birth,[d]
a man with whom the whole land
strives and contends![e]
I have neither lent[f] nor borrowed,
yet everyone curses me.

14:17 [a]Jer 8:21
14:18 [b]Eze 7:15
14:19 [c]Jer 7:29 [d]Jer 30:12-13 [e]Jer 8:15
14:20 [f]Da 9:7-8
14:21 [g]ver 7 [h]Jer 3:17
14:22 [i]Ps 135:7
15:1 [j]Ex 32:11; Nu 14:13-20 [k]1Sa 7:9 [l]Jer 7:16; Eze 14:14,20 [m]2Ki 17:20
15:2 [n]Jer 43:11 [o]Jer 14:12 [p]Rev 13:10
15:3 [q]Lev 26:16 [r]Dt 28:26 [s]Lev 26:22; Eze 14:21
15:4 [t]Jer 24:9; 29:18 [u]Dt 28:25 [v]2Ki 21:2; 23:26-27
15:5 [w]Isa 51:19; Jer 13:14; 21:7; Na 3:7
15:6 [x]Jer 6:19; 7:24 [y]Zep 1:4
15:7 [z]Jer 18:21
15:8 [a]Jer 6:4
15:9 [b]1Sa 2:5 [c]Jer 21:7
15:10 [d]Job 3:1 [e]Jer 1:19 [f]Lev 25:36

[11]The LORD said,

"Surely I will deliver you[a] for a good
purpose;
surely I will make your enemies
plead[b] with you
in times of disaster and times of
distress.

[12]"Can a man break iron—
iron from the north[c]—or bronze?
[13]Your wealth and your treasures
I will give as plunder, without
charge,[d]
because of all your sins
throughout your country.[e]
[14]I will enslave you to your enemies
in[c] a land you do not know,[f]
for my anger will kindle a fire[g]
that will burn against you."

[15]You understand, O LORD;
remember me and care for me.
Avenge me on my persecutors.[h]
You are long-suffering—do not take
me away;
think of how I suffer reproach for
your sake.[i]
[16]When your words came, I ate[j] them;
they were my joy and my heart's
delight,[k]
for I bear your name,[l]
O LORD God Almighty.
[17]I never sat[m] in the company of
revelers,
never made merry with them;
I sat alone because your hand was
on me
and you had filled me with
indignation.
[18]Why is my pain unending
and my wound grievous and
incurable?[n]
Will you be to me like a deceptive
brook,
like a spring that fails?[o]

[19]Therefore this is what the LORD says:

"If you repent, I will restore you
that you may serve[p] me;
if you utter worthy, not worthless,
words,
you will be my spokesman.

15:11 [a]Jer 40:4 [b]Jer 21:1-2; 37:3; 42:1-3
15:12 [c]Jer 28:14
15:13 [d]Ps 44:12 [e]Jer 17:3
15:14 [f]Dt 28:36; Jer 16:13 [g]Dt 32:22; Ps 21:9
15:15 [h]Jer 12:3 [i]Ps 69:7-9
15:16 [j]Eze 3:3; Rev 10:10 [k]Ps 119:72,103 [l]Jer 14:9
15:17 [m]Ps 1:1; 26:4-5; Jer 16:8
15:18 [n]Jer 30:15; Mic 1:9 [o]Job 6:15
15:19 [p]Zec 3:7
15:20 [q]Jer 20:11; Eze 3:8
15:21 [r]Jer 50:34 [s]Ge 48:16
16:2 [t]1Co 7:26-27
16:3 [u]Jer 6:21
16:4 [v]Jer 25:33 [w]Ps 83:10; Jer 9:22 [x]Ps 79:1-3; Jer 15:3; 34:20
16:6 [y]Eze 9:5-6 [z]Lev 19:28 [a]Jer 41:5; 47:5
16:7 [b]Eze 24:17; Hos 9:4
16:8 [c]Ecc 7:2-4; Jer 15:17

Let this people turn to you,
but you must not turn to them.
[20]I will make you a wall to this people,
a fortified wall of bronze;
they will fight against you
but will not overcome you,
for I am with you
to rescue and save you,"[q]
declares the LORD.
[21]"I will save you from the hands of
the wicked
and redeem[r] you from the grasp of
the cruel."[s]

Jeremiah is commanded not to marry.

16 Then the word of the LORD came
to me: [2]"You must not marry[t] and
have sons or daughters in this place."
[3]For this is what the LORD says about the
sons and daughters born in this land and
about the women who are their mothers and the men who are their fathers:[u]
[4]"They will die of deadly diseases. They
will not be mourned or buried[v] but will
be like refuse lying on the ground.[w]
They will perish by sword and famine,
and their dead bodies will become food
for the birds of the air and the beasts of
the earth."[x]
[5]For this is what the LORD says: "Do
not enter a house where there is a funeral meal; do not go to mourn or show
sympathy, because I have withdrawn
my blessing, my love and my pity from
this people," declares the LORD. [6]"Both
high and low will die in this land.[y] They
will not be buried or mourned, and no
one will cut[z] himself or shave[a] his head
for them. [7]No one will offer food to comfort those who mourn[b] for the dead—
not even for a father or a mother—nor
will anyone give them a drink to console
them.
[8]"And do not enter a house where
there is feasting and sit down to eat and
drink.[c] [9]For this is what the LORD Almighty, the God of Israel, says: Before
your eyes and in your days I will bring

c *14* Some Hebrew manuscripts, Septuagint and Syriac (see also Jer. 17:4); most Hebrew manuscripts *I will cause your enemies to bring you / into*

an end to the sounds[a] of joy and gladness and to the voices of bride and
bridegroom in this place.[b]
10"When you tell these people all this
and they ask you, 'Why has the LORD
decreed such a great disaster against us?
What wrong have we done? What sin
have we committed against the LORD
our God?'[c] 11then say to them, 'It is because your fathers forsook me,' declares
the LORD, 'and followed other gods and
served and worshiped them. They forsook me and did not keep my law.[d]
12But you have behaved more wickedly
than your fathers.[e] See how each of you
is following the stubbornness of his evil
heart[f] instead of obeying me. 13So I will
throw you out of this land into a land
neither you nor your fathers have
known,[g] and there you will serve other
gods[h] day and night, for I will show you
no favor.'[i]

God promises to restore Israel.

14"However, the days are coming,"
declares the LORD, "when men will no
longer say, 'As surely as the LORD lives,
who brought the Israelites up out of
Egypt,'[j] 15but they will say, 'As surely as
the LORD lives, who brought the Israelites up out of the land of the north
and out of all the countries where he
had banished them.'[k] For I will restore[l]
them to the land I gave their forefathers.
16"But now I will send for many fishermen," declares the LORD, "and they
will catch them.[m] After that I will send
for many hunters, and they will hunt[n]
them down on every mountain and hill
and from the crevices of the rocks.[o]
17My eyes are on all their ways; they are
not hidden[p] from me, nor is their sin
concealed from my eyes.[q] 18I will repay
them double[r] for their wickedness and
their sin, because they have defiled my
land[s] with the lifeless forms of their vile
images and have filled my inheritance
with their detestable idols."

19O LORD, my strength and my
fortress,
my refuge in time of distress,
to you the nations will come[t]
from the ends of the earth and say,
"Our fathers possessed nothing but
false gods,[u]
worthless idols that did them no
good.
20Do men make their own gods?
Yes, but they are not gods!"[v]

21"Therefore I will teach them—
this time I will teach them
my power and might.
Then they will know
that my name is the LORD.

The LORD searches the heart.

17 "Judah's sin is engraved with an
iron tool,[w]
inscribed with a flint point,
on the tablets of their hearts[x]
and on the horns of their altars.
2Even their children remember
their altars and Asherah poles[d][y]
beside the spreading trees
and on the high hills.[z]
3My mountain in the land
and your[e] wealth and all your
treasures
I will give away as plunder,[a]
together with your high places,[b]
because of sin throughout your
country.[c]
4Through your own fault you will lose
the inheritance[d] I gave you.
I will enslave you to your enemies[e]
in a land[f] you do not know,
for you have kindled my anger,
and it will burn[g] forever."

5This is what the LORD says:

"Cursed is the one who trusts in
man,[h]
who depends on flesh for his
strength
and whose heart turns away from
the LORD.
6He will be like a bush in the
wastelands;

16:9 [a]Isa 24:8; Eze 26:13; Hos 2:11 [b]Rev 18:23
16:10 [c]Dt 29:24; Jer 5:19
16:11 [d]Dt 29:25-26; 1Ki 9:9; Ps 106:35-43; Jer 22:9
16:12 [e]Jer 7:26 [f]Ecc 9:3; Jer 13:10
16:13 [g]Dt 28:36; Jer 5:19 [h]Dt 4:28 [i]Jer 15:5
16:14 [j]Dt 15:15; Jer 23:7-8
16:15 [k]Isa 11:11; Jer 23:8 [l]Jer 24:6
16:16 [m]Am 4:2; Hab 1:14-15 [n]Am 9:3; Mic 7:2 [o]1Sa 26:20
16:17 [p]1Co 4:5; Heb 4:13 [q]Pr 15:3
16:18 [r]Isa 40:2; Rev 18:6 [s]Nu 35:34; Jer 2:7
16:19 [t]Isa 2:2; Jer 3:17 [u]Ps 4:2
16:20 [v]Ps 115:4-7; Isa 37:19; Jer 2:11
17:1 [w]Job 19:24 [x]Pr 3:3; 2Co 3:3
17:2 [y]2Ch 24:18 [z]Jer 2:20
17:3 [a]2Ki 24:13 [b]Jer 26:18; Mic 3:12 [c]Jer 15:13
17:4 [d]La 5:2 [e]Dt 28:48; Jer 12:7 [f]Jer 16:13 [g]Jer 7:20; 15:14 **17:5** [h]Isa 2:22; 30:1-3

d*2* That is, symbols of the goddess Asherah e*2,3* Or *hills / 3and the mountains of the land. / Your*

he will not see prosperity when it
comes.
He will dwell in the parched places of
the desert,
in a salt[a] land where no one lives.

7"But blessed is the man who trusts[b]
in the LORD,
whose confidence is in him.
8He will be like a tree planted by the
water
that sends out its roots by the
stream.
It does not fear when heat comes;
its leaves are always green.
It has no worries in a year of drought[c]
and never fails to bear fruit."[d]

9The heart[e] is deceitful above all things
and beyond cure.
Who can understand it?

10"I the LORD search the heart[f]
and examine the mind,[g]
to reward[h] a man according to his
conduct,
according to what his deeds
deserve."[i]

11Like a partridge that hatches eggs it
did not lay
is the man who gains riches by
unjust means.
When his life is half gone, they will
desert him,
and in the end he will prove to be
a fool.[j]

12A glorious throne,[k] exalted from the
beginning,
is the place of our sanctuary.
13O LORD, the hope[l] of Israel,
all who forsake[m] you will be put to
shame.
Those who turn away from you will
be written in the dust
because they have forsaken the
LORD,
the spring of living water.

14Heal me, O LORD, and I will be healed;
save me and I will be saved,
for you are the one I praise.[n]
15They keep saying to me,
"Where is the word of the LORD?
Let it now be fulfilled!"[o]
16I have not run away from being your
shepherd;
you know I have not desired the
day of despair.
What passes my lips is open before
you.
17Do not be a terror[p] to me;
you are my refuge[q] in the day of
disaster.
18Let my persecutors be put to shame,
but keep me from shame;
let them be terrified,
but keep me from terror.
Bring on them the day of disaster;
destroy them with double
destruction.[r]

Keep the Sabbath day holy.

19This is what the LORD said to me:
"Go and stand at the gate of the people,
through which the kings of Judah go in
and out; stand also at all the other gates
of Jerusalem.[s] 20Say to them, 'Hear the
word of the LORD, O kings of Judah and
all people of Judah and everyone living
in Jerusalem[t] who come through these
gates.[u] 21This is what the LORD says: Be
careful not to carry a load on the Sabbath[v] day or bring it through the gates of
Jerusalem. 22Do not bring a load out of
your houses or do any work on the Sabbath, but keep the Sabbath day holy, as I
commanded your forefathers.[w] 23Yet
they did not listen or pay attention;[x] they
were stiff-necked[y] and would not listen
or respond to discipline.[z] 24But if you are
careful to obey me, declares the LORD,
and bring no load through the gates of
this city on the Sabbath, but keep the
Sabbath day holy by not doing any work
on it, 25then kings who sit on David's
throne[a] will come through the gates of
this city with their officials. They and
their officials will come riding in chariots and on horses, accompanied by the
men of Judah and those living in Jerusalem, and this city will be inhabited forever. 26People will come from the towns of
Judah and the villages around Jerusalem,

17:6 [a]Dt 29:23; Job 39:6
17:7 [b]Ps 34:8; 40:4; Pr 16:20
17:8 [c]Jer 14:1-6 [d]Ps 1:3; 92:12-14
17:9 [e]Ecc 9:3; Mt 13:15; Mk 7:21-22
17:10 [f]1Sa 16:7; Rev 2:23 [g]Ps 17:3; 139:23; Jer 11:20; 20:12; Ro 8:27 [h]Ps 62:12; Jer 32:19 [i]Ro 2:6
17:11 [j]Lk 12:20
17:12 [k]Jer 3:17
17:13 [l]Jer 14:8 [m]Isa 1:28; Jer 2:17
17:14 [n]Ps 109:1
17:15 [o]Isa 5:19; 2Pe 3:4
17:17 [p]Ps 88:15-16 [q]Jer 16:19; Na 1:7
17:18 [r]Ps 35:1-8
17:19 [s]Jer 7:2; 26:2
17:20 [t]Jer 19:3 [u]Jer 22:2
17:21 [v]Nu 15:32-36; Ne 13:15-21; Jn 5:10
17:22 [w]Ex 20:8; 31:13; Isa 56:2-6; Eze 20:12
17:23 [x]Jer 7:26 [y]Jer 19:15 [z]Jer 7:28
17:25 [a]2Sa 7:13; Isa 9:7; Jer 22:2,4; Lk 1:32

from the territory of Benjamin and the
western foothills, from the hill country
and the Negev,[a] bringing burnt offerings
and sacrifices, grain offerings, incense
and thank offerings to the house of the
LORD. 27But if you do not obey[b] me to
keep the Sabbath day holy by not carrying any load as you come through the
gates of Jerusalem on the Sabbath day,
then I will kindle an unquenchable fire[c]
in the gates of Jerusalem that will
consume her fortresses.' "[d]

Clay in the potter's hand.

18 This is the word that came to Jeremiah from the LORD: 2"Go down
to the potter's house, and there I will
give you my message." 3So I went down
to the potter's house, and I saw him
working at the wheel. 4But the pot he
was shaping from the clay was marred
in his hands; so the potter formed it into
another pot, shaping it as seemed best
to him.
5Then the word of the LORD came to
me: 6"O house of Israel, can I not do
with you as this potter does?" declares
the LORD. "Like clay[e] in the hand of the
potter, so are you in my hand, O house
of Israel. 7If at any time I announce that
a nation or kingdom is to be uprooted,[f]
torn down and destroyed, 8and if that
nation I warned repents of its evil, then
I will relent[g] and not inflict on it the disaster[h] I had planned. 9And if at another
time I announce that a nation or kingdom is to be built[i] up and planted, 10and
if it does evil[j] in my sight and does not
obey me, then I will reconsider[k] the
good I had intended to do for it.
11"Now therefore say to the people of
Judah and those living in Jerusalem,
'This is what the LORD says: Look! I am
preparing a disaster[l] for you and devis-
ing a plan against you. So turn[m] from
your evil ways,[n] each one of you, and
reform your ways and your actions.'
12But they will reply, 'It's no use.[o] We
will continue with our own plans; each
of us will follow the stubbornness of his
evil heart.' "

13Therefore this is what the LORD
says:

"Inquire among the nations:
Who has ever heard anything like
this?[p]
A most horrible[q] thing has been done
by Virgin Israel.
14Does the snow of Lebanon
ever vanish from its rocky slopes?
Do its cool waters from distant sources
ever cease to flow?[†]
15Yet my people have forgotten me;
they burn incense to worthless
idols,[r]
which made them stumble in their
ways
and in the ancient paths.[s]
They made them walk in bypaths
and on roads not built up.[t]
16Their land will be laid waste,[u]
an object of lasting scorn;[v]
all who pass by will be appalled
and will shake their heads.[w]
17Like a wind[x] from the east,
I will scatter them before their
enemies;
I will show them my back and not
my face[y]
in the day of their disaster."

18They said, "Come, let's make plans[z]
against Jeremiah; for the teaching of the
law by the priest[a] will not be lost, nor
will counsel from the wise, nor the word
from the prophets.[b] So come, let's attack
him with our tongues[c] and pay no attention to anything he says."

19Listen to me, O LORD;
hear what my accusers are saying!
20Should good be repaid with evil?
Yet they have dug a pit[d] for me.
Remember that I stood before you
and spoke in their behalf[e]
to turn your wrath away from them.
21So give their children over to famine;[f]
hand them over to the power of
the sword.
Let their wives be made childless
and widows;[g]

† *14* The meaning of the Hebrew for this sentence is uncertain.

17:26 [a]Jer 32:44; 33:13; Zec 7:7
17:27 [b]Jer 22:5 [c]Jer 7:20 [d]2Ki 25:9; Am 2:5
18:6 [e]Isa 45:9; Ro 9:20-21
18:7 [f]Jer 1:10
18:8 [g]Jer 26:13; Jnh 3:8-10 [h]Eze 18:21; Hos 11:8-9
18:9 [i]Jer 1:10; 31:28
18:10 [j]Eze 33:18 [k]1Sa 2:29-30
18:11 [l]Jer 4:6 [m]2Ki 17:13; Isa 1:16-19 [n]Jer 7:3
18:12 [o]Isa 57:10; Jer 2:25
18:13 [p]Isa 66:8; Jer 2:10 [q]Jer 5:30
18:15 [r]Jer 10:15 [s]Jer 6:16 [t]Isa 57:14; 62:10
18:16 [u]Jer 25:9 [v]Jer 19:8 [w]Ps 22:7
18:17 [x]Jer 13:24 [y]Jer 2:27
18:18 [z]Jer 11:19 [a]Mal 2:7 [b]Jer 5:13 [c]Ps 52:2
18:20 [d]Ps 35:7; 57:6 [e]Ps 106:23
18:21 [f]Jer 11:22 [g]Ps 109:9

let their men be put to death,
their young men slain by the
sword in battle.
22Let a cry[a] be heard from their houses
when you suddenly bring invaders
against them,
for they have dug a pit to capture me
and have hidden snares[b] for my feet.
23But you know, O LORD,
all their plots to kill[c] me.
Do not forgive[d] their crimes
or blot out their sins from your
sight.
Let them be overthrown before you;
deal with them in the time of your
anger.

The potter's jar is smashed.

19 This is what the LORD says: "Go and buy a clay jar from a potter.[e] Take along some of the elders[f] of the people and of the priests 2and go out to the Valley of Ben Hinnom,[g] near the entrance of the Potsherd Gate. There proclaim the words I tell you, 3and say, 'Hear the word of the LORD, O kings[h] of Judah and people of Jerusalem. This is what the LORD Almighty, the God of Israel, says: Listen! I am going to bring a disaster[i] on this place that will make the ears of everyone who hears of it tingle.[j] 4For they have forsaken[k] me and made this a place of foreign gods; they have burned sacrifices[l] in it to gods that neither they nor their fathers nor the kings of Judah ever knew, and they have filled this place with the blood of the innocent.[m] 5They have built the high places of Baal to burn their sons[n] in the fire as offerings to Baal—something I did not command or mention, nor did it enter my mind.[o] 6So beware, the days are coming, declares the LORD, when people will no longer call this place Topheth or the Valley of Ben Hinnom,[p] but the Valley of Slaughter.[q]

7" 'In this place I will ruin[g] the plans of Judah and Jerusalem. I will make them fall by the sword before their enemies,[r] at the hands of those who seek their lives, and I will give their carcasses[s] as food[t] to the birds of the air and the beasts of the earth. 8I will devastate this city and make it an object of scorn;[u] all who pass by will be appalled and will scoff because of all its wounds. 9I will make them eat[v] the flesh of their sons and daughters, and they will eat one another's flesh during the stress of the siege imposed on them by the enemies[w] who seek their lives.'

10"Then break the jar[x] while those who go with you are watching, 11and say to them, 'This is what the LORD Almighty says: I will smash[y] this nation and this city just as this potter's jar is smashed and cannot be repaired. They will bury[z] the dead in Topheth until there is no more room. 12This is what I will do to this place and to those who live here, declares the LORD. I will make this city like Topheth. 13The houses[a] in Jerusalem and those of the kings of Judah will be defiled like this place, Topheth—all the houses where they burned incense on the roofs to all the starry hosts[b] and poured out drink offerings[c] to other gods.' "

14Jeremiah then returned from Topheth, where the LORD had sent him to prophesy, and stood in the court[d] of the LORD's temple and said to all the people, 15"This is what the LORD Almighty, the God of Israel, says: 'Listen! I am going to bring on this city and the villages around it every disaster I pronounced against them, because they were stiff-necked[e] and would not listen to my words.' "

Pashhur has Jeremiah put in stocks.

20 When the priest Pashhur son of Immer,[f] the chief officer[g] in the temple of the LORD, heard Jeremiah prophesying these things, 2he had Jeremiah the prophet beaten[h] and put in the stocks[i] at the Upper Gate of Benjamin[j] at the LORD's temple. 3The next day, when Pashhur released him from the stocks, Jeremiah said to him, "The

18:22 [a]Jer 6:26 [b]Ps 140:5
18:23 [c]Jer 11:21 [d]Ps 109:14
19:1 [e]Jer 18:2 [f]Nu 11:17
19:2 [g]Jos 15:8
19:3 [h]Jer 17:20 [i]Jer 6:19 [j]1Sa 3:11
19:4 [k]Dt 28:20; Isa 65:11 [l]Lev 18:21 [m]2Ki 21:16; Jer 2:34
19:5 [n]Lev 18:21; Ps 106:37-38 [o]Jer 7:31; 32:35
19:6 [p]Jos 15:8 [q]Jer 7:32
19:7 [r]Lev 26:17; Dt 28:25 [s]Jer 16:4; 34:20 [t]Ps 79:2
19:8 [u]Jer 18:16
19:9 [v]Lev 26:29; Dt 28:49-57; La 4:10 [w]Isa 9:20
19:10 [x]ver 1
19:11 [y]Ps 2:9; Isa 30:14 [z]Jer 7:32
19:13 [a]Jer 32:29; 52:13 [b]Dt 4:19; Ac 7:42 [c]Jer 7:18; Eze 20:28
19:14 [d]2Ch 20:5; Jer 26:2
19:15 [e]Ne 9:16; Jer 7:26; 17:23
20:1 [f]1Ch 24:14 [g]2Ki 25:18
20:2 [h]Jer 1:19 [i]Job 13:27 [j]Jer 37:13; 38:7; Zec 14:10

g7 The Hebrew for *ruin* sounds like the Hebrew for *jar* (see verses 1 and 10).

LORD's name for you is not Pashhur, but
Magor-Missabib.[h][a] 4For this is what the
LORD says: 'I will make you a terror to
yourself and to all your friends; with
your own eyes[b] you will see them fall by
the sword of their enemies. I will hand[c]
all Judah over to the king of Babylon,
who will carry[d] them away to Babylon or
put them to the sword. 5I will hand over
to their enemies all the wealth[e] of this
city—all its products, all its valuables and
all the treasures of the kings of Judah.
They will take it away[f] as plunder and
carry it off to Babylon. 6And you, Pashhur, and all who live in your house will
go into exile to Babylon. There you will
die and be buried, you and all your
friends to whom you have prophesied[g]
lies.'"

Jeremiah cries out to the LORD.

7O LORD, you deceived[i] me, and I was
deceived[i];
you overpowered me and
prevailed.
I am ridiculed all day long;
everyone mocks me.
8Whenever I speak, I cry out
proclaiming violence and
destruction.[h]
So the word of the LORD has brought
me
insult and reproach[i] all day long.
9But if I say, "I will not mention him
or speak any more in his name,"
his word is in my heart like a fire,[j]
a fire shut up in my bones.
I am weary of holding it in;[k]
indeed, I cannot.
10I hear many whispering,
"Terror[l] on every side!
Report[m] him! Let's report him!"
All my friends[n]
are waiting for me to slip,[o] saying,
"Perhaps he will be deceived;
then we will prevail[p] over him
and take our revenge on him."
11But the LORD[q] is with me like a
mighty warrior;
so my persecutors[r] will stumble
and not prevail.[s]
They will fail and be thoroughly
disgraced;[t]
their dishonor will never be
forgotten.
12O LORD Almighty, you who examine
the righteous
and probe the heart and mind,[u]
let me see your vengeance[v] upon
them,
for to you I have committed[w] my
cause.

13Sing to the LORD!
Give praise to the LORD!
He rescues[x] the life of the needy
from the hands of the wicked.

14Cursed be the day I was born![y]
May the day my mother bore me
not be blessed!
15Cursed be the man who brought my
father the news,
who made him very glad, saying,
"A child is born to you—a son!"
16May that man be like the towns[z]
the LORD overthrew without pity.
May he hear wailing in the morning,
a battle cry at noon.
17For he did not kill me in the womb,[a]
with my mother as my grave,
her womb enlarged forever.
18Why did I ever come out of the womb
to see trouble and sorrow
and to end my days in shame?[b]

God rejects Zedekiah's request.

21 The word came to Jeremiah from
the LORD when King Zedekiah[c]
sent to him Pashhur[d] son of Malkijah and
the priest Zephaniah[e] son of Maaseiah.
They said: 2"Inquire[f] now of the LORD
for us because Nebuchadnezzar[j][g] king
of Babylon is attacking us. Perhaps the
LORD will perform wonders[h] for us as in
times past so that he will withdraw
from us."
3But Jeremiah answered them, "Tell
Zedekiah, 4'This is what the LORD, the
God of Israel, says: I am about to turn[i]

20:3 [a]ver 10
20:4 [b]Jer 29:21 [c]Jer 21:10 [d]Jer 52:27
20:5 [e]Jer 17:3 [f]2Ki 20:17
20:6 [g]Jer 14:15; La 2:14
20:8 [h]Jer 6:7 [i]2Ch 36:16; Jer 6:10
20:9 [j]Ps 39:3 [k]Job 32:18-20; Ac 4:20
20:10 [l]Ps 31:13; Jer 6:25 [m]Isa 29:21 [n]Ps 41:9 [o]Lk 11:53-54 [p]1Ki 19:2
20:11 [q]Jer 1:8; Ro 8:31 [r]Jer 17:18 [s]Jer 15:20 [t]Jer 23:40
20:12 [u]Jer 17:10 [v]Ps 54:7; 59:10 [w]Ps 62:8; Jer 11:20
20:13 [x]Ps 35:10
20:14 [y]Job 3:3; Jer 15:10
20:16 [z]Ge 19:25
20:17 [a]Job 10:18-19
20:18 [b]Ps 90:9
21:1 [c]2Ki 24:18; Jer 52:1 [d]Jer 38:1 [e]2Ki 25:18; Jer 29:25; 37:3
21:2 [f]Jer 37:3,7 [g]2Ki 25:1 [h]Ps 44:1-4; Jer 32:17
21:4 [i]Jer 32:5

h*3* *Magor-Missabib* means *terror on every side.*
i*7* Or *persuaded* j*2* Hebrew *Nebuchadrezzar,* of which *Nebuchadnezzar* is a variant; here and often in Jeremiah and Ezekiel

against you the weapons of war that are
in your hands, which you are using to
fight the king of Babylon and the Babylonians[k] who are outside the wall besieging[a] you. And I will gather them inside
this city. 5I myself will fight against you
with an outstretched hand[b] and a mighty
arm in anger and fury and great wrath.
6I will strike down those who live in
this city—both men and animals—and
they will die of a terrible plague.[c] 7After
that, declares the LORD, I will hand over
Zedekiah[d] king of Judah, his officials and
the people in this city who survive the
plague, sword and famine, to Nebuchadnezzar king of Babylon[e] and to their enemies who seek their lives. He will put
them to the sword; he will show them
no mercy or pity or compassion.'[f]
8"Furthermore, tell the people, 'This
is what the LORD says: See, I am setting
before you the way of life and the way of
death. 9Whoever stays in this city will
die by the sword, famine or plague.[g] But
whoever goes out and surrenders to the
Babylonians who are besieging you will
live; he will escape with his life.[h] 10I
have determined to do this city harm[i]
and not good, declares the LORD. It will
be given into the hands[j] of the king of
Babylon, and he will destroy it with
fire.'[k]
11"Moreover, say to the royal house[l]
of Judah, 'Hear the word of the LORD;
12O house of David, this is what the
LORD says:

"'Administer justice[m] every morning;
rescue from the hand of his oppressor
the one who has been robbed,
or my wrath will break out and burn like fire
because of the evil you have done—
burn with no one to quench[n] it.
13I am against[o] you, ⌊Jerusalem,⌋
you who live above this valley[p]
on the rocky plateau,
declares the LORD—
you who say, "Who can come against us?
Who can enter our refuge?"[q]
14I will punish you as your deeds[r] deserve,
declares the LORD.
I will kindle a fire[s] in your forests[t]
that will consume everything around you.'"

Judgment against Shallum.

22 This is what the LORD says: "Go
down to the palace of the king
of Judah and proclaim this message
there: 2'Hear the word of the LORD, O
king of Judah, you who sit on David's
throne[u]—you, your officials and your
people who come through these gates.[v]
3This is what the LORD says: Do what is
just[w] and right. Rescue from the hand of
his oppressor[x] the one who has been
robbed. Do no wrong or violence to the
alien, the fatherless or the widow,[y] and
do not shed innocent blood in this place.
4For if you are careful to carry out these
commands, then kings[z] who sit on
David's throne will come through the
gates of this palace, riding in chariots
and on horses, accompanied by their officials and their people. 5But if you do not
obey[a] these commands, declares the
LORD, I swear[b] by myself that this palace
will become a ruin.'"
6For this is what the LORD says about
the palace of the king of Judah:

"Though you are like Gilead to me,
like the summit of Lebanon,
I will surely make you like a desert,[c]
like towns not inhabited.
7I will send destroyers[d] against you,
each man with his weapons,
and they will cut[e] up your fine cedar beams
and throw them into the fire.

8"People from many nations will pass
by this city and will ask one another,
'Why has the LORD done such a thing to
this great city?'[f] 9And the answer will
be: 'Because they have forsaken the covenant of the LORD their God and have
worshiped and served other gods.[g]'"

21:4 [a]Jer 37:8-10
21:5 [b]Jer 6:12
21:6 [c]Jer 14:12
21:7 [d]2Ki 25:7; Jer 52:9 [e]Jer 37:17; 39:5 [f]2Ch 36:17; Eze 7:9; Hab 1:6
21:9 [g]Jer 14:12 [h]Jer 38:2,17; 39:18; 45:5
21:10 [i]Jer 44:11,27; Am 9:4 [j]Jer 32:28; 38:2-3 [k]Jer 52:13
21:11 [l]Jer 13:18
21:12 [m]Jer 22:3 [n]Isa 1:31
21:13 [o]Eze 13:8 [p]Ps 125:2 [q]Jer 49:4; Ob 3-4
21:14 [r]Isa 3:10-11 [s]2Ch 36:19; Jer 52:13 [t]Eze 20:47
22:2 [u]Jer 17:25; Lk 1:32 [v]Jer 17:20
22:3 [w]Mic 6:8; Zec 7:9 [x]Ps 72:4; Jer 21:12 [y]Ex 22:22
22:4 [z]Jer 17:25
22:5 [a]Jer 17:27 [b]Heb 6:13
22:6 [c]Mic 3:12
22:7 [d]Jer 4:7 [e]Isa 10:34
22:8 [f]Dt 29:25-26; 1Ki 9:8-9; Jer 16:10-11
22:9 [g]2Ki 22:17; 2Ch 34:25

[k]4 Or *Chaldeans*; also in verse 9

10Do not weep for the dead[a] ⌊king⌋ or
mourn[b] his loss;
rather, weep bitterly for him who
is exiled,
because he will never return
nor see his native land again.

11For this is what the LORD says about
Shallum[l][c] son of Josiah, who succeeded
his father as king of Judah but has gone
from this place: "He will never return.
12He will die[d] in the place where they
have led him captive; he will not see this
land again."

Judgment against Jehoiakim.

13"Woe to him who builds[e] his palace
by unrighteousness,
his upper rooms by injustice,
making his countrymen work for
nothing,
not paying[f] them for their labor.
14He says, 'I will build myself a great
palace[g]
with spacious upper rooms.'
So he makes large windows in it,
panels it with cedar[h]
and decorates it in red.

15"Does it make you a king
to have more and more cedar?
Did not your father have food and
drink?
He did what was right and just,[i]
so all went well[j] with him.
16He defended the cause of the poor
and needy,[k]
and so all went well.
Is that not what it means to know
me?"
declares the LORD.
17"But your eyes and your heart
are set only on dishonest gain,
on shedding innocent blood[l]
and on oppression and extortion."

18Therefore this is what the LORD says
about Jehoiakim son of Josiah king of
Judah:

"They will not mourn for him:
'Alas, my brother! Alas, my sister!'
They will not mourn for him:
'Alas, my master! Alas, his
splendor!'
19He will have the burial of a donkey—
dragged away and thrown[m]
outside the gates of Jerusalem."

20"Go up to Lebanon and cry out,
let your voice be heard in Bashan,
cry out from Abarim,[n]
for all your allies are crushed.
21I warned you when you felt secure,
but you said, 'I will not listen!'
This has been your way from your
youth;[o]
you have not obeyed[p] me.
22The wind will drive all your
shepherds away,
and your allies will go into exile.
Then you will be ashamed and
disgraced
because of all your wickedness.
23You who live in 'Lebanon,[m]'
who are nestled in cedar buildings,
how you will groan when pangs
come upon you,
pain[q] like that of a woman in labor!

Judgment against Jehoiachin.

24"As surely as I live," declares the
LORD, "even if you, Jehoiachin[n][r] son of
Jehoiakim king of Judah, were a signet
ring on my right hand, I would still pull
you off. 25I will hand you over[s] to those
who seek your life, those you fear—to
Nebuchadnezzar king of Babylon and
to the Babylonians.[o] 26I will hurl[t] you
and the mother who gave you birth into
another country, where neither of you
was born, and there you both will die.
27You will never come back to the land
you long to return to."

28Is this man Jehoiachin a despised,
broken pot,[u]
an object no one wants?
Why will he and his children be
hurled[v] out,
cast into a land[w] they do not know?

22:10 [a]Ecc 4:2 [b]ver 18
22:11 [c]2Ki 23:31
22:12 [d]2Ki 23:34
22:13 [e]Mic 3:10; Hab 2:9 [f]Lev 19:13; Jas 5:4
22:14 [g]Isa 5:8-9 [h]2Sa 7:2
22:15 [i]2Ki 23:25 [j]Ps 128:2; Isa 3:10
22:16 [k]Ps 72:1-4, 12-13
22:17 [l]2Ki 24:4
22:19 [m]Jer 36:30
22:20 [n]Nu 27:12
22:21 [o]Jer 3:25; 32:30 [p]Jer 7:23-28
22:23 [q]Jer 4:31
22:24 [r]2Ki 24:6,8; Jer 37:1
22:25 [s]2Ki 24:16; Jer 34:20
22:26 [t]2Ki 24:8; 2Ch 36:10
22:28 [u]Ps 31:12; Jer 48:38; Hos 8:8 [v]Jer 15:1 [w]Jer 17:4

[l]*11* Also called *Jehoahaz* [m]*23* That is, the palace in Jerusalem (see 1 Kings 7:2) [n]*24* Hebrew *Coniah,* a variant of *Jehoiachin*; also in verse 28 [o]*25* Or *Chaldeans*

29O land,[a] land, land,
hear the word of the LORD!
30This is what the LORD says:
"Record this man as if childless,[b]
a man who will not prosper[c] in his lifetime,
for none of his offspring will prosper,
none will sit on the throne[d] of David
or rule anymore in Judah."

The righteous Branch.

23 "Woe to the shepherds[e] who
are destroying and scattering[f]
the sheep of my pasture!"[g] declares the
LORD. 2Therefore this is what the LORD,
the God of Israel, says to the shepherds
who tend my people: "Because you have
scattered my flock and driven them away
and have not bestowed care on them, I
will bestow punishment on you for the
evil[h] you have done," declares the LORD.
3"I myself will gather the remnant[i] of my
flock out of all the countries where I
have driven them and will bring them
back to their pasture, where they will be
fruitful and increase in number. 4I will
place shepherds[j] over them who will
tend them, and they will no longer be
afraid[k] or terrified, nor will any be missing,[l]" declares the LORD.

5"The days are coming," declares the LORD,
"when I will raise up to David[p] a righteous Branch,[m]
a King who will reign[n] wisely
and do what is just and right[o] in the land.
6In his days Judah will be saved
and Israel will live in safety.
This is the name[p] by which he will be called:
The LORD Our Righteousness.[q]

7"So then, the days are coming," declares the LORD, "when people will no
longer say, 'As surely as the LORD lives,
who brought the Israelites up out of
Egypt,'[r] 8but they will say, 'As surely as
the LORD lives, who brought the descendants of Israel up out of the land of the
north and out of all the countries where
he had banished them.' Then they will
live in their own land."[s]

Wickedness of the false prophets.

9Concerning the prophets:

My heart is broken within me;
all my bones tremble.
I am like a drunken man,
like a man overcome by wine,
because of the LORD
and his holy words.[t]
10The land is full of adulterers;[u]
because of the curse[q] the land lies parched[r]
and the pastures[v] in the desert are withered.[w]
The ⌊prophets⌋ follow an evil course
and use their power unjustly.

11"Both prophet and priest are godless;[x]
even in my temple[y] I find their wickedness,"
declares the LORD.
12"Therefore their path will become slippery;[z]
they will be banished to darkness
and there they will fall.
I will bring disaster on them
in the year they are punished,[a]"
declares the LORD.

13"Among the prophets of Samaria
I saw this repulsive thing:
They prophesied by Baal[b]
and led my people Israel astray.
14And among the prophets of Jerusalem
I have seen something horrible:[c]
They commit adultery and live a lie.[d]
They strengthen the hands of evildoers,[e]
so that no one turns from his wickedness.
They are all like Sodom[f] to me;
the people of Jerusalem are like Gomorrah."[g]

15Therefore, this is what the LORD
Almighty says concerning the prophets:

22:29 [a]Jer 6:19; Mic 1:2
22:30 [b]1Ch 3:18; Mt 1:12 [c]Jer 10:21 [d]Ps 94:20
23:1 [e]Jer 10:21; Eze 34:1-10; Zec 11:15-17 [f]Isa 56:11 [g]Eze 34:31
23:2 [h]Jer 21:12
23:3 [i]Isa 11:10-12; Jer 32:37; Eze 34:11-16
23:4 [j]Jer 3:15; 31:10; Eze 34:23 [k]Jer 30:10; 46:27-28 [l]Jn 6:39
23:5 [m]Isa 4:2 [n]Isa 9:7 [o]Isa 11:1; Zec 6:12
23:6 [p]Jer 33:16; Mt 1:21-23 [q]Ro 3:21-22; 1Co 1:30
23:7 [r]Jer 16:14
23:8 [s]Isa 43:5-6; Am 9:14-15
23:9 [t]Jer 20:8-9
23:10 [u]Jer 9:2 [v]Ps 107:34; Jer 9:10 [w]Hos 4:2-3
23:11 [x]Jer 6:13; 8:10; Zep 3:4 [y]Jer 7:10
23:12 [z]Ps 35:6; Jer 13:16 [a]Jer 11:23
23:13 [b]Jer 2:8
23:14 [c]Jer 5:30 [d]Jer 29:23 [e]Eze 13:22 [f]Ge 18:20 [g]Isa 1:9-10; Jer 20:16

p5 Or *up from David's line* q10 Or *because of these things* r10 Or *land mourns*

"I will make them eat bitter food
and drink poisoned water,[a]
because from the prophets of Jerusalem
ungodliness has spread throughout the land."

16This is what the LORD Almighty says:

"Do not listen[b] to what the prophets are prophesying to you;
they fill you with false hopes.
They speak visions[c] from their own minds,
not from the mouth[d] of the LORD.
17They keep saying to those who despise me,
'The LORD says: You will have peace.'[e]
And to all who follow the stubbornness[f] of their hearts
they say, 'No harm[g] will come to you.'
18But which of them has stood in the council of the LORD
to see or to hear his word?
Who has listened and heard his word?
19See, the storm[h] of the LORD
will burst out in wrath,
a whirlwind swirling down
on the heads of the wicked.
20The anger[i] of the LORD will not turn back[j]
until he fully accomplishes
the purposes of his heart.
In days to come
you will understand it clearly.
21I did not send[k] these prophets,
yet they have run with their message;
I did not speak to them,
yet they have prophesied.
22But if they had stood in my council,
they would have proclaimed my words to my people
and would have turned[l] them from their evil ways
and from their evil deeds.

23"Am I only a God nearby,[m]"
declares the LORD,
"and not a God far away?
24Can anyone hide[n] in secret places
so that I cannot see him?"
declares the LORD.
"Do not I fill heaven and earth?"[o]
declares the LORD.

25"I have heard what the prophets say
who prophesy lies[p] in my name. They
say, 'I had a dream![q] I had a dream!'
26How long will this continue in the
hearts of these lying prophets, who
prophesy the delusions[r] of their own
minds? 27They think the dreams they
tell one another will make my people
forget[s] my name, just as their fathers forgot[t] my name through Baal worship.
28Let the prophet who has a dream tell
his dream, but let the one who has my
word speak it faithfully. For what has
straw to do with grain?" declares the
LORD. 29"Is not my word like fire," [u] declares the LORD, "and like a hammer
that breaks a rock in pieces?
30"Therefore," declares the LORD, "I
am against[v] the prophets[w] who steal from
one another words supposedly from me.
31Yes," declares the LORD, "I am against
the prophets who wag their own tongues
and yet declare, 'The LORD declares.'[x]
32Indeed, I am against those who prophesy false dreams,[y]" declares the LORD.
"They tell them and lead my people
astray with their reckless lies, yet I did
not send or appoint them. They do not
benefit[z] these people in the least," declares the LORD.
33"When these people, or a prophet or
a priest, ask you, 'What is the oracle[s][a]
of the LORD?' say to them, 'What oracle?[t]
I will forsake[b] you, declares the LORD.'
34If a prophet or a priest or anyone else
claims, 'This is the oracle[c] of the LORD,'
I will punish[d] that man and his household. 35This is what each of you keeps
on saying to his friend or relative: 'What
is the LORD's answer?'[e] or 'What has the
LORD spoken?' 36But you must not mention 'the oracle of the LORD' again,
because every man's own word becomes

23:15 [a]Jer 8:14; 9:15
23:16 [b]Jer 27:9-10, 14; Mt 7:15 [c]Jer 14:14 [d]Jer 9:20
23:17 [e]Jer 8:11 [f]Jer 13:10 [g]Jer 5:12; Am 9:10; Mic 3:11
23:19 [h]Jer 25:32; 30:23
23:20 [i]2Ki 23:26 [j]Jer 30:24
23:21 [k]Jer 14:14; 27:15
23:22 [l]Jer 25:5; Zec 1:4
23:23 [m]Ps 139:1-10
23:24 [n]Job 22:12-14 [o]1Ki 8:27
23:25 [p]Jer 14:14 [q]ver 28,32; Jer 29:8
23:26 [r]1Ti 4:1-2
23:27 [s]Dt 13:1-3; Jer 29:8 [t]Jdg 3:7; 8:33-34
23:29 [u]Jer 5:14
23:30 [v]Ps 34:16 [w]Dt 18:20; Jer 14:15
23:31 [x]ver 17
23:32 [y]ver 25 [z]Jer 7:8; La 2:14
23:33 [a]Mal 1:1 [b]ver 39
23:34 [c]La 2:14 [d]Zec 13:3
23:35 [e]Jer 33:3; 42:4

s*33* Or *burden* (see Septuagint and Vulgate)
t*33* Hebrew; Septuagint and Vulgate *'You are the burden.* (The Hebrew for *oracle* and *burden* is the same.)

his oracle and so you distort[a] the words of the living God, the LORD Almighty, our God. 37This is what you keep saying to a prophet: 'What is the LORD's answer to you?' or 'What has the LORD spoken?' 38Although you claim, 'This is the oracle of the LORD,' this is what the LORD says: You used the words, 'This is the oracle of the LORD,' even though I told you that you must not claim, 'This is the oracle of the LORD.' 39Therefore, I will surely forget you and cast[b] you out of my presence along with the city I gave to you and your fathers. 40I will bring upon you everlasting disgrace[c]—everlasting shame that will not be forgotten."

Two baskets of figs.

24 After Jehoiachin[u][d] son of Jehoiakim king of Judah and the officials, the craftsmen and the artisans of Judah were carried into exile from Jerusalem to Babylon by Nebuchadnezzar king of Babylon, the LORD showed me two baskets of figs[e] placed in front of the temple of the LORD. 2One basket had very good figs, like those that ripen early; the other basket had very poor[f] figs, so bad they could not be eaten.

3Then the LORD asked me, "What do you see,[g] Jeremiah?"

"Figs," I answered. "The good ones are very good, but the poor ones are so bad they cannot be eaten."

4Then the word of the LORD came to me: 5"This is what the LORD, the God of Israel, says: 'Like these good figs, I regard as good the exiles from Judah, whom I sent away from this place to the land of the Babylonians.[v] 6My eyes will watch over them for their good, and I will bring them back[h] to this land. I will build[i] them up and not tear them down; I will plant them and not uproot them. 7I will give them a heart to know me, that I am the LORD. They will be my people,[j] and I will be their God, for they will return[k] to me with all their heart.[l]

8"'But like the poor[m] figs, which are so bad they cannot be eaten,' says the LORD, 'so will I deal with Zedekiah king of Judah, his officials[n] and the survivors[o] from Jerusalem, whether they remain in this land or live in Egypt.[p] 9I will make them abhorrent[q] and an offense to all the kingdoms of the earth, a reproach and a byword,[r] an object of ridicule and cursing,[s] wherever I banish[t] them. 10I will send the sword,[u] famine and plague[v] against them until they are destroyed from the land I gave to them and their fathers.'"

Seventy years of captivity.

25 The word came to Jeremiah concerning all the people of Judah in the fourth year of Jehoiakim[w] son of Josiah king of Judah, which was the first year of Nebuchadnezzar[x] king of Babylon. 2So Jeremiah the prophet said to all the people of Judah[y] and to all those living in Jerusalem: 3For twenty-three years—from the thirteenth year of Josiah[z] son of Amon king of Judah until this very day—the word of the LORD has come to me and I have spoken to you again and again,[a] but you have not listened.[b]

4And though the LORD has sent all his servants the prophets[c] to you again and again, you have not listened or paid any attention. 5They said, "Turn now, each of you, from your evil ways and your evil practices, and you can stay in the land the LORD gave to you and your fathers for ever and ever. 6Do not follow other gods[d] to serve and worship them; do not provoke me to anger with what your hands have made. Then I will not harm you."

7"But you did not listen to me," declares the LORD, "and you have provoked me with what your hands have made,[e] and you have brought harm[f] to yourselves."

8Therefore the LORD Almighty says this: "Because you have not listened to my words, 9I will summon[g] all the peoples of the north[h] and my servant[i] Nebuchadnezzar king of Babylon," declares

23:36 [a]Gal 1:7-8; 2Pe 3:16
23:39 [b]Jer 7:15
23:40 [c]Jer 20:11; Eze 5:14-15
24:1 [d]2Ki 24:16; 2Ch 36:9; Jer 29:2 [e]Am 8:1-2
24:2 [f]Isa 5:4
24:3 [g]Jer 1:11; Am 8:2
24:6 [h]Jer 29:10; Eze 11:17 [i]Jer 33:7; 42:10
24:7 [j]Isa 51:16; Jer 31:33; Heb 8:10 [k]Jer 32:40 [l]Eze 11:19
24:8 [m]Jer 29:17 [n]Jer 39:6 [o]Jer 39:9 [p]Jer 44:1,26
24:9 [q]Jer 15:4; 34:17 [r]Dt 28:25; 1Ki 9:7 [s]Jer 29:18 [t]Dt 28:37
24:10 [u]Isa 51:19 [v]Jer 27:8
25:1 [w]2Ki 24:2; Jer 36:1 [x]2Ki 24:1
25:2 [y]Jer 18:11
25:3 [z]Jer 1:2 [a]Jer 11:7; 26:5 [b]Jer 7:26
25:4 [c]Jer 7:25
25:6 [d]Dt 8:19
25:7 [e]Dt 32:21 [f]2Ki 21:15
25:9 [g]Isa 13:3-5 [h]Jer 1:15 [i]Jer 27:6

u *1* Hebrew *Jeconiah,* a variant of *Jehoiachin*
v *5* Or *Chaldeans*

the LORD, "and I will bring them against
this land and its inhabitants and against
all the surrounding nations. I will completely destroy[w] them and make them
an object of horror and scorn,[a] and an
everlasting ruin. 10I will banish from
them the sounds[b] of joy and gladness,
the voices of bride and bridegroom,[c] the
sound of millstones[d] and the light of the
lamp.[e] 11This whole country will become
a desolate wasteland,[f] and these nations
will serve the king of Babylon seventy
years.[g]

12"But when the seventy years[h] are
fulfilled, I will punish the king of Babylon and his nation, the land of the Babylonians,[x] for their guilt," declares the
LORD, "and will make it desolate[i] forever. 13I will bring upon that land all the
things I have spoken against it, all that
are written in this book and prophesied
by Jeremiah against all the nations.
14They themselves will be enslaved[j] by
many nations[k] and great kings; I will
repay[l] them according to their deeds
and the work of their hands."

God's wrath against the nations.

15This is what the LORD, the God of
Israel, said to me: "Take from my hand
this cup[m] filled with the wine of my
wrath and make all the nations to whom
I send you drink it. 16When they drink
it, they will stagger[n] and go mad[o] because of the sword I will send among
them."

17So I took the cup from the LORD's
hand and made all the nations to whom
he sent[p] me drink it: 18Jerusalem and
the towns of Judah, its kings and officials, to make them a ruin and an object
of horror and scorn and cursing,[q] as they
are today;[r] 19Pharaoh king of Egypt, his
attendants, his officials and all his people, 20and all the foreign people there;
all the kings of Uz;[s] all the kings of the
Philistines (those of Ashkelon,[t] Gaza,
Ekron, and the people left at Ashdod);
21Edom, Moab and Ammon;[u] 22all the
kings of Tyre and Sidon;[v] the kings of the
coastlands[w] across the sea; 23Dedan,
Tema, Buz and all who are in distant
places[y];[x] 24all the kings of Arabia[y] and
all the kings of the foreign people who
live in the desert; 25all the kings of Zimri, Elam[z] and Media; 26and all the kings
of the north,[a] near and far, one after the
other—all the kingdoms on the face of
the earth. And after all of them, the king
of Sheshach[z][b] will drink it too.

27"Then tell them, 'This is what the
LORD Almighty, the God of Israel, says:
Drink, get drunk[c] and vomit, and fall to
rise no more because of the sword[d] I will
send among you.' 28But if they refuse
to take the cup from your hand and
drink, tell them, 'This is what the LORD
Almighty says: You must drink it! 29See,
I am beginning to bring disaster[e] on the
city that bears my Name,[f] and will you
indeed go unpunished?[g] You will not go
unpunished, for I am calling down a
sword upon all[h] who live on the earth,
declares the LORD Almighty.'

30"Now prophesy all these words
against them and say to them:

"'The LORD will roar[i] from on high;
he will thunder[j] from his holy
dwelling
and roar mightily against his land.
He will shout like those who tread
the grapes,
shout against all who live on the
earth.
31The tumult will resound to the ends
of the earth,
for the LORD will bring charges[k]
against the nations;
he will bring judgment on all mankind
and put the wicked to the sword,'"
declares the LORD.

32This is what the LORD Almighty
says:

"Look! Disaster is spreading
from nation to nation;[l]

25:9 [a]Jer 18:16 **25:10** [b]Isa 24:8; Eze 26:13 [c]Jer 7:34 [d]Ecc 12:3-4 [e]Rev 18:22-23 **25:11** [f]Jer 4:26-27; 12:11-12 [g]2Ch 36:21 **25:12** [h]Jer 29:10 [i]Isa 13:19-22; 14:22-23 **25:14** [j]Jer 27:7 [k]Jer 50:9; 51:27-28 [l]Jer 51:6 **25:15** [m]Isa 51:17; Ps 75:8; Rev 14:10 **25:16** [n]Na 3:11 [o]Jer 51:7 **25:17** [p]Jer 1:10 **25:18** [q]Jer 24:9 [r]Jer 44:22 **25:20** [s]Job 1:1 [t]Jer 47:5 **25:21** [u]Jer 49:1 **25:22** [v]Jer 47:4 [w]Jer 31:10 **25:23** [x]Jer 9:26; 49:32 **25:24** [y]2Ch 9:14 **25:25** [z]Ge 10:22 **25:26** [a]Jer 50:3,9 [b]Jer 51:41 **25:27** [c]ver 16,28; Hab 2:16 [d]Eze 21:4 **25:29** [e]Jer 13:12-14 [f]1Pe 4:17 [g]Pr 11:31 [h]ver 30-31 **25:30** [i]Isa 16:10; 42:13 [j]Joel 3:16; Am 1:2 **25:31** [k]Hos 4:1; Joel 3:2; Mic 6:2

25:32 [l]Isa 34:2

w9 The Hebrew term refers to the irrevocable giving over of things or persons to the LORD, often by totally destroying them. x12 Or *Chaldeans*
y23 Or *who clip the hair by their foreheads*
z26 *Sheshach* is a cryptogram for Babylon.

a mighty storm[a] is rising
from the ends of the earth."

33At that time those slain[b] by the LORD
will be everywhere—from one end of
the earth to the other. They will not be
mourned or gathered[c] up or buried,[d] but
will be like refuse lying on the ground.

34Weep and wail, you shepherds;
roll[e] in the dust, you leaders of the
flock.
For your time to be slaughtered[f] has
come;
you will fall and be shattered like
fine pottery.
35The shepherds will have nowhere to
flee,
the leaders of the flock no place to
escape.[g]
36Hear the cry of the shepherds,
the wailing of the leaders of the
flock,
for the LORD is destroying their
pasture.
37The peaceful meadows will be laid
waste
because of the fierce anger of the
LORD.
38Like a lion[h] he will leave his lair,
and their land will become desolate
because of the sword[a] of the oppressor
and because of the LORD's fierce
anger.

Jeremiah escapes a death sentence.

26 Early in the reign of Jehoiakim[i]
son of Josiah king of Judah, this
word came from the LORD: 2"This is
what the LORD says: Stand in the courtyard[j] of the LORD's house and speak to
all the people of the towns of Judah who
come to worship in the house of the
LORD. Tell[k] them everything I command
you; do not omit[l] a word. 3Perhaps they
will listen and each will turn[m] from his
evil way. Then I will relent[n] and not
bring on them the disaster I was planning because of the evil they have done.
4Say to them, 'This is what the LORD
says: If you do not listen[o] to me and follow my law,[p] which I have set before
you, 5and if you do not listen to the
words of my servants the prophets,
whom I have sent to you again and again
(though you have not listened[q]), 6then
I will make this house like Shiloh[r] and
this city an object of cursing[s] among all
the nations of the earth.'"
7The priests, the prophets and all the
people heard Jeremiah speak these
words in the house of the LORD. 8But
as soon as Jeremiah finished telling all
the people everything the LORD had
commanded him to say, the priests,
the prophets and all the people seized
him and said, "You must die! 9Why do
you prophesy in the LORD's name that
this house will be like Shiloh and this
city will be desolate and deserted?"[t] And
all the people crowded around Jeremiah
in the house of the LORD.
10When the officials of Judah heard
about these things, they went up from
the royal palace to the house of the LORD
and took their places at the entrance of
the New Gate of the LORD's house.
11Then the priests and the prophets said
to the officials and all the people, "This
man should be sentenced to death[u] because he has prophesied against this city.
You have heard it with your own ears!"
12Then Jeremiah said to all the officials[v] and all the people: "The LORD sent
me to prophesy[w] against this house and
this city all the things you have heard.[x]
13Now reform[y] your ways and your
actions and obey the LORD your God.
Then the LORD will relent and not bring
the disaster he has pronounced against
you. 14As for me, I am in your hands;[z]
do with me whatever you think is good
and right. 15Be assured, however, that if
you put me to death, you will bring the
guilt of innocent blood on yourselves
and on this city and on those who live in
it, for in truth the LORD has sent me to
you to speak all these words in your
hearing."
16Then the officials[a] and all the people
said to the priests and the prophets,

25:32 [a]Jer 23:19
25:33 [b]Isa 66:16; Eze 39:17-20 [c]Jer 16:4 [d]Ps 79:3
25:34 [e]Jer 6:26 [f]Isa 34:6; Jer 50:27
25:35 [g]Job 11:20
25:38 [h]Jer 4:7
26:1 [i]2Ki 23:36
26:2 [j]Jer 19:14 [k]Jer 1:17; Mt 28:20; Ac 20:27 [l]Dt 4:2
26:3 [m]Jer 36:7 [n]Jer 18:8
26:4 [o]Lev 26:14 [p]1Ki 9:6
26:5 [q]Jer 25:4
26:6 [r]Jos 18:1 [s]2Ki 22:19
26:9 [t]Jer 9:11
26:11 [u]Dt 18:20; Jer 18:23; 38:4; Mt 26:66; Ac 6:11
26:12 [v]Jer 1:18 [w]Am 7:15; Ac 4:18-20; 5:29 [x]ver 2,15
26:13 [y]Jer 7:5; Joel 2:12-14
26:14 [z]Jer 38:5
26:16 [a]Ac 23:9

a *38* Some Hebrew manuscripts and Septuagint (see also Jer. 46:16 and 50:16); most Hebrew manuscripts *anger*

"This man should not be sentenced to
death![a] He has spoken to us in the name
of the LORD our God."
17Some of the elders of the land
stepped forward and said to the entire
assembly of people, 18"Micah[b] of Moresheth prophesied in the days of Hezekiah
king of Judah. He told all the people of
Judah, 'This is what the LORD Almighty
says:

"'Zion[c] will be plowed like a field,
Jerusalem will become a heap of
rubble,[d]
the temple hill[e] a mound overgrown
with thickets.'[b][f]

19"Did Hezekiah king of Judah or anyone else in Judah put him to death? Did
not Hezekiah[g] fear the LORD and seek
his favor? And did not the LORD relent,[h]
so that he did not bring the disaster[i] he
pronounced against them? We are about
to bring a terrible disaster[j] on ourselves!"
20(Now Uriah son of Shemaiah from
Kiriath Jearim[k] was another man who
prophesied in the name of the LORD; he
prophesied the same things against this
city and this land as Jeremiah did.
21When King Jehoiakim[l] and all his officers and officials heard his words, the
king sought to put him to death. But Uriah heard of it and fled[m] in fear to Egypt.
22King Jehoiakim, however, sent Elnathan[n] son of Acbor to Egypt, along with
some other men. 23They brought Uriah
out of Egypt and took him to King Jehoiakim, who had him struck down with a
sword and his body thrown into the
burial place of the common people.)
24Furthermore, Ahikam[o] son of Shaphan supported Jeremiah, and so he was
not handed over to the people to be put
to death.

A yoke for Jeremiah's neck.

27 Early in the reign of Zedekiah[c][p]
son of Josiah king of Judah, this
word came to Jeremiah from the LORD:
2This is what the LORD said to me:
"Make a yoke[q] out of straps and crossbars and put it on your neck. 3Then send
word to the kings of Edom, Moab,
Ammon,[r] Tyre and Sidon through the
envoys who have come to Jerusalem to
Zedekiah king of Judah. 4Give them a
message for their masters and say, 'This
is what the LORD Almighty, the God of
Israel, says: "Tell this to your masters:
5With my great power and outstretched
arm[s] I made the earth and its people and
the animals that are on it, and I give[t] it
to anyone I please. 6Now I will hand all
your countries over to my servant[u] Nebuchadnezzar[v] king of Babylon; I will
make even the wild animals subject to
him.[w] 7All nations will serve[x] him and
his son and his grandson until the time[y]
for his land comes; then many nations
and great kings will subjugate[z] him.
8"'"If, however, any nation or kingdom will not serve Nebuchadnezzar king
of Babylon or bow its neck under his
yoke, I will punish that nation with the
sword, famine and plague, declares the
LORD, until I destroy it by his hand. 9So
do not listen to your prophets, your
diviners, your interpreters of dreams,
your mediums[a] or your sorcerers who
tell you, 'You will not serve the king of
Babylon.' 10They prophesy lies[b] to you
that will only serve to remove you far
from your lands; I will banish you and
you will perish. 11But if any nation will
bow its neck under the yoke[c] of the king
of Babylon and serve him, I will let that
nation remain in its own land to till it
and to live there, declares the LORD."'"
12I gave the same message to Zedekiah king of Judah. I said, "Bow your neck
under the yoke of the king of Babylon;
serve him and his people, and you will
live. 13Why will you and your people
die[d] by the sword, famine and plague
with which the LORD has threatened any
nation that will not serve the king of
Babylon? 14Do not listen to the words of
the prophets who say to you, 'You will
not serve the king of Babylon,' for they
are prophesying lies[e] to you. 15'I have

26:16 [a]Ac 5:34-39; 23:29
26:18 [b]Mic 1:1 [c]Isa 2:3 [d]Ne 4:2; Jer 9:11 [e]Mic 4:1; Zec 8:3 [f]Jer 17:3
26:19 [g]2Ch 32:24-26; Isa 37:14-20 [h]Ex 32:14; 2Sa 24:16 [i]Jer 44:7 [j]Hab 2:10
26:20 [k]Jos 9:17
26:21 [l]1Ki 19:2 [m]Mt 10:23
26:22 [n]Jer 36:12,25
26:24 [o]2Ki 22:12
27:1 [p]2Ch 36:11
27:2 [q]Jer 28:10,13
27:3 [r]Jer 25:21
27:5 [s]Dt 9:29 [t]Ps 115:16
27:6 [u]Jer 25:9 [v]Jer 21:7; Eze 29:18-20 [w]Jer 28:14; Da 2:37-38
27:7 [x]2Ch 36:20 [y]Jer 25:12 [z]Jer 25:14; Da 5:28
27:9 [a]Dt 18:11
27:10 [b]Jer 23:25
27:11 [c]Jer 21:9
27:13 [d]Eze 18:31
27:14 [e]Jer 14:14

b *18* Micah 3:12 c *1* A few Hebrew manuscripts and Syriac (see also Jer. 27:3, 12 and 28:1); most Hebrew manuscripts *Jehoiakim* (Most Septuagint manuscripts do not have this verse.)

not sent[a] them,' declares the LORD. 'They
are prophesying lies in my name.[b] Therefore, I will banish you and you will perish,[c] both you and the prophets who
prophesy to you.'"
16Then I said to the priests and all
these people, "This is what the LORD
says: Do not listen to the prophets who
say, 'Very soon now the articles[d] from
the LORD's house will be brought back
from Babylon.' They are prophesying lies
to you. 17Do not listen to them. Serve
the king of Babylon, and you will live.
Why should this city become a ruin? 18If
they are prophets and have the word of
the LORD, let them plead[e] with the LORD
Almighty that the furnishings remaining in the house of the LORD and in the
palace of the king of Judah and in Jerusalem not be taken to Babylon. 19For this
is what the LORD Almighty says about
the pillars, the Sea,[f] the movable stands
and the other furnishings[g] that are left
in this city, 20which Nebuchadnezzar
king of Babylon did not take away when
he carried[h] Jehoiachin[d][i] son of Jehoiakim
king of Judah into exile from Jerusalem
to Babylon, along with all the nobles of
Judah and Jerusalem— 21yes, this is
what the LORD Almighty, the God of
Israel, says about the things that are left
in the house of the LORD and in the
palace of the king of Judah and in Jerusalem: 22'They will be taken[j] to Babylon
and there they will remain until the
day[k] I come for them,' declares the
LORD. 'Then I will bring[l] them back and
restore them to this place.'"

Hananiah falsely prophesies Judah's return.

28 In the fifth month of that same
year, the fourth year, early in the
reign of Zedekiah[m] king of Judah, the
prophet Hananiah son of Azzur, who
was from Gibeon,[n] said to me in the
house of the LORD in the presence of the
priests and all the people: 2"This is what
the LORD Almighty, the God of Israel,
says: 'I will break the yoke[o] of the king
of Babylon. 3Within two years I will
bring back to this place all the articles[p]
of the LORD's house that Nebuchadnezzar king of Babylon removed from here
and took to Babylon. 4I will also bring
back to this place Jehoiachin[d][q] son of
Jehoiakim king of Judah and all the other
exiles from Judah who went to Babylon,'
declares the LORD, 'for I will break the
yoke of the king of Babylon.'"
5Then the prophet Jeremiah replied to
the prophet Hananiah before the priests
and all the people who were standing in
the house of the LORD. 6He said, "Amen!
May the LORD do so! May the LORD fulfill
the words you have prophesied by bringing the articles of the LORD's house and
all the exiles back to this place from
Babylon. 7Nevertheless, listen to what I
have to say in your hearing and in the
hearing of all the people: 8From early
times the prophets who preceded you
and me have prophesied war, disaster
and plague[r] against many countries and
great kingdoms. 9But the prophet who
prophesies peace will be recognized as
one truly sent by the LORD only if his
prediction comes true.[s]"
10Then the prophet Hananiah took the
yoke[t] off the neck of the prophet Jeremiah and broke it, 11and he said[u] before all
the people, "This is what the LORD says:
'In the same way will I break the yoke
of Nebuchadnezzar king of Babylon off
the neck of all the nations within two
years.'" At this, the prophet Jeremiah
went on his way.
12Shortly after the prophet Hananiah
had broken the yoke off the neck of the
prophet Jeremiah, the word of the LORD
came to Jeremiah: 13"Go and tell Hananiah, 'This is what the LORD says: You
have broken a wooden yoke, but in its
place you will get a yoke of iron. 14This
is what the LORD Almighty, the God of
Israel, says: I will put an iron yoke[v] on
the necks of all these nations to make
them serve[w] Nebuchadnezzar king of
Babylon, and they will serve him. I will
even give him control over the wild
animals.[x]'"

27:15 [a]Jer 23:21 [b]Jer 29:9 [c]Jer 6:15
27:16 [d]2Ki 24:13; 2Ch 36:7,10; Jer 28:3; Da 1:2
27:18 [e]1Sa 7:8
27:19 [f]2Ki 25:13 [g]Jer 52:17-23
27:20 [h]2Ch 36:10; Jer 24:1 [i]Jer 22:24
27:22 [j]2Ki 25:13 [k]2Ch 36:21 [l]Ezr 1:7; 7:19
28:1 [m]Jer 27:1,3 [n]Jos 9:3
28:2 [o]Jer 27:12
28:3 [p]2Ki 24:13
28:4 [q]Jer 22:24-27
28:8 [r]Lev 26:14-17; Isa 5:5-7
28:9 [s]Dt 18:22
28:10 [t]Jer 27:2
28:11 [u]Jer 14:14; 27:10
28:14 [v]Dt 28:48 [w]Jer 25:11 [x]Jer 27:6

d *20,4* Hebrew *Jeconiah,* a variant of *Jehoiachin*

15Then the prophet Jeremiah said to
Hananiah the prophet, "Listen, Hananiah! The LORD has not sent[a] you, yet you
have persuaded this nation to trust in
lies.[b] 16Therefore, this is what the LORD
says: 'I am about to remove you from
the face of the earth.[c] This very year you
are going to die, because you have
preached rebellion[d] against the LORD.'"
17In the seventh month of that same
year, Hananiah the prophet died.

Jeremiah sends a letter to the exiles.

29 This is the text of the letter that
the prophet Jeremiah sent from
Jerusalem to the surviving elders among
the exiles and to the priests, the proph-
ets and all the other people Nebuchad-
nezzar had carried into exile from
Jerusalem to Babylon.[e] 2(This was after
King Jehoiachin[e][f] and the queen mother,
the court officials and the leaders of
Judah and Jerusalem, the craftsmen and
the artisans had gone into exile from
Jerusalem.) 3He entrusted the letter to
Elasah son of Shaphan and to Gemariah
son of Hilkiah, whom Zedekiah king of
Judah sent to King Nebuchadnezzar in
Babylon. It said:

4This is what the LORD Almighty,
the God of Israel, says to all those
I carried[g] into exile from Jerusalem
to Babylon: 5"Build[h] houses and settle down; plant gardens and eat
what they produce. 6Marry and
have sons and daughters; find wives
for your sons and give your daughters in marriage, so that they too
may have sons and daughters.
Increase in number there; do not decrease. 7Also, seek the peace and
prosperity of the city to which I have
carried you into exile. Pray[i] to the
LORD for it, because if it prospers,
you too will prosper." 8Yes, this is
what the LORD Almighty, the God of
Israel, says: "Do not let the prophets
and diviners among you deceive[j]
you. Do not listen to the dreams you
encourage them to have.[k] 9They
are prophesying lies[l] to you in my
name. I have not sent them," declares the LORD.

10This is what the LORD says:
"When seventy years[m] are completed for Babylon, I will come to you
and fulfill my gracious promise to
bring you back[n] to this place. 11For I
know the plans[o] I have for you,"
declares the LORD, "plans to prosper
you and not to harm you, plans to
give you hope and a future. 12Then
you will call upon me and come and
pray to me, and I will listen[p] to you.
13You will seek[q] me and find me
when you seek me with all your
heart.[r] 14I will be found by you,"
declares the LORD, "and will bring
you back[s] from captivity.[f] I will gather you from all the nations and
places where I have banished you,"
declares the LORD, "and will bring
you back to the place from which I
carried you into exile."[t]

15You may say, "The LORD has
raised up prophets for us in Babylon," 16but this is what the LORD
says about the king who sits on
David's throne and all the people
who remain in this city, your countrymen who did not go with you
into exile— 17yes, this is what the
LORD Almighty says: "I will send the
sword, famine and plague[u] against
them and I will make them like
poor figs[v] that are so bad they cannot be eaten. 18I will pursue them
with the sword, famine and plague
and will make them abhorrent[w] to
all the kingdoms of the earth and an
object of cursing and horror,[x] of
scorn and reproach, among all the
nations where I drive them. 19For
they have not listened to my
words,"[y] declares the LORD, "words
that I sent to them again and again
by my servants the prophets.[z] And
you exiles have not listened either,"
declares the LORD.

20Therefore, hear the word of

28:15 [a]Jer 29:31 [b]Jer 20:6; 29:21; La 2:14; Eze 13:6
28:16 [c]Ge 7:4 [d]Dt 13:5; Jer 29:32
29:1 [e]2Ch 36:10
29:2 [f]2Ki 24:12; Jer 22:24-28
29:4 [g]Jer 24:5
29:5 [h]ver 28
29:7 [i]Ezr 6:10; 1Ti 2:1-2
29:8 [j]Jer 37:9 [k]Jer 23:27
29:9 [l]Jer 14:14; 27:15
29:10 [m]2Ch 36:21; Jer 25:12; Da 9:2 [n]Jer 21:22
29:11 [o]Ps 40:5
29:12 [p]Ps 145:19
29:13 [q]Mt 7:7 [r]Dt 4:29; Jer 24:7
29:14 [s]Dt 30:3; Jer 30:3 [t]Jer 23:3-4
29:17 [u]Jer 27:8 [v]Jer 24:8-10
29:18 [w]Jer 15:4 [x]Dt 28:25; Jer 42:18
29:19 [y]Jer 6:19 [z]Jer 25:4

e*2* Hebrew *Jeconiah,* a variant of *Jehoiachin*
f*14* Or *will restore your fortunes*

the LORD, all you exiles whom I
have sent[a] away from Jerusalem to
Babylon. 21This is what the LORD
Almighty, the God of Israel, says
about Ahab son of Kolaiah and Zedekiah son of Maaseiah, who are
prophesying lies[b] to you in my name:
"I will hand them over to Nebuchadnezzar king of Babylon, and he will
put them to death before your very
eyes. 22Because of them, all the
exiles from Judah who are in Babylon will use this curse: 'The LORD
treat you like Zedekiah and Ahab,
whom the king of Babylon burned[c]
in the fire.' 23For they have done
outrageous things in Israel; they
have committed adultery[d] with their
neighbors' wives and in my name
have spoken lies, which I did not
tell them to do. I know[e] it and am
a witness to it," declares the LORD.

Shemaiah preaches rebellion.

24Tell Shemaiah the Nehelamite,
25"This is what the LORD Almighty, the
God of Israel, says: You sent letters in
your own name to all the people in Jerusalem, to Zephaniah[f] son of Maaseiah
the priest, and to all the other priests.
You said to Zephaniah, 26'The LORD has
appointed you priest in place of Jehoiada
to be in charge of the house of the LORD;
you should put any madman[g] who acts
like a prophet into the stocks[h] and neck-
irons. 27So why have you not repri-
manded Jeremiah from Anathoth, who
poses as a prophet among you? 28He has
sent this message[i] to us in Babylon: It
will be a long time.[j] Therefore build[k]
houses and settle down; plant gardens
and eat what they produce.'"
29Zephaniah the priest, however, read
the letter to Jeremiah the prophet.
30Then the word of the LORD came to
Jeremiah: 31"Send this message to all
the exiles: 'This is what the LORD says
about Shemaiah[l] the Nehelamite: Because Shemaiah has prophesied to you,
even though I did not send[m] him, and
has led you to believe a lie, 32this is what
the LORD says: I will surely punish Shemaiah the Nehelamite and his descendants.[n] He will have no one left among
this people, nor will he see the good[o]
things I will do for my people, declares
the LORD, because he has preached
rebellion[p] against me.'"

Restoration of Israel and Judah to their land.

30 This is the word that came to
Jeremiah from the LORD: 2"This
is what the LORD, the God of Israel, says:
'Write[q] in a book all the words I have
spoken to you. 3The days are coming,'
declares the LORD, 'when I will bring[r]
my people Israel and Judah back from
captivity[g] and restore[s] them to the land
I gave their forefathers to possess,' says
the LORD."
4These are the words the LORD spoke
concerning Israel and Judah: 5"This is
what the LORD says:

"'Cries of fear[t] are heard—
terror, not peace.
6Ask and see:
Can a man bear children?
Then why do I see every strong man
with his hands on his stomach like
a woman in labor,[u]
every face turned deathly pale?
7How awful that day[v] will be!
None will be like it.
It will be a time of trouble[w] for Jacob,
but he will be saved[x] out of it.

8"'In that day,' declares the LORD
Almighty,
'I will break the yoke[y] off their necks
and will tear off their bonds;
no longer will foreigners enslave
them.[z]
9Instead, they will serve the LORD
their God
and David[a] their king,[b]
whom I will raise up for them.

10"'So do not fear,[c] O Jacob my servant;[d]
do not be dismayed, O Israel,'
declares the LORD.

29:20 [a]Jer 24:5
29:21 [b]ver 9; Jer 14:14
29:22 [c]Da 3:6
29:23 [d]Jer 23:14 [e]Heb 4:13
29:25 [f]2Ki 25:18; Jer 21:1
29:26 [g]2Ki 9:11; Hos 9:7; Jn 10:20 [h]Jer 20:2
29:28 [i]ver 1 [j]ver 10 [k]ver 5
29:31 [l]ver 24 [m]Jer 14:14; 28:15
29:32 [n]1Sa 2:30-33 [o]ver 10 [p]Jer 28:16
30:2 [q]Isa 30:8
30:3 [r]Jer 29:14 [s]Jer 16:15
30:5 [t]Jer 6:25
30:6 [u]Jer 4:31
30:7 [v]Isa 2:12; Joel 2:11 [w]Zep 1:15 [x]ver 10
30:8 [y]Isa 9:4 [z]Eze 34:27
30:9 [a]Isa 55:3-4; Lk 1:69; Ac 2:30; 13:23 [b]Eze 34:23-24; 37:24; Hos 3:5
30:10 [c]Isa 43:5; Jer 46:27-28 [d]Isa 44:2

g3 Or *will restore the fortunes of my people Israel and Judah*

'I will surely save[a] you out of a distant place,
your descendants from the land of their exile.
Jacob will again have peace and security,[b]
and no one will make him afraid.
11I am with you and will save you,'
declares the LORD.
'Though I completely destroy all the nations
among which I scatter you,
I will not completely destroy[c] you.
I will discipline[d] you but only with justice;
I will not let you go entirely unpunished.'[e]

12"This is what the LORD says:

"'Your wound is incurable,
your injury beyond healing.[f]
13There is no one to plead your cause,
no remedy for your sore,
no healing[g] for you.
14All your allies[h] have forgotten you;
they care nothing for you.
I have struck you as an enemy[i] would
and punished you as would the cruel,[j]
because your guilt is so great
and your sins[k] so many.
15Why do you cry out over your wound,
your pain that has no cure?
Because of your great guilt and many sins
I have done these things to you.

16"'But all who devour[l] you will be devoured;
all your enemies will go into exile.[m]
Those who plunder[n] you will be plundered;
all who make spoil of you I will despoil.
17But I will restore you to health
and heal your wounds,'
declares the LORD,
'because you are called an outcast,[o]
Zion for whom no one cares.'

18"This is what the LORD says:

"'I will restore the fortunes[p] of Jacob's tents
and have compassion[q] on his dwellings;
the city will be rebuilt[r] on her ruins,
and the palace will stand in its proper place.
19From them will come songs[s] of thanksgiving[t]
and the sound of rejoicing.[u]
I will add to their numbers,[v]
and they will not be decreased;
I will bring them honor,[w]
and they will not be disdained.
20Their children[x] will be as in days of old,
and their community will be established[y] before me;
I will punish all who oppress them.
21Their leader[z] will be one of their own;
their ruler will arise from among them.
I will bring him near[a] and he will come close to me,
for who is he who will devote himself
to be close to me?'
declares the LORD.
22"'So you will be my people,
and I will be your God.'"

23See, the storm[b] of the LORD
will burst out in wrath,
a driving wind swirling down
on the heads of the wicked.
24The fierce anger[c] of the LORD will not turn back[d]
until he fully accomplishes
the purposes of his heart.
In days to come
you will understand[e] this.

31 "At that time," declares the LORD, "I will be the God[f] of all the clans of Israel, and they will be my people."
2This is what the LORD says:

"The people who survive the sword
will find favor[g] in the desert;
I will come to give rest[h] to Israel."

30:10 [a]Jer 29:14 [b]Isa 35:9
30:11 [c]Jer 4:27; 46:28 [d]Jer 10:24 [e]Am 9:8
30:12 [f]Jer 15:18
30:13 [g]Jer 8:22; 14:19; 46:11
30:14 [h]Jer 22:20; La 1:2 [i]Job 13:24 [j]Job 30:21 [k]Jer 5:6
30:16 [l]Isa 33:1; Jer 2:3; 10:25 [m]Isa 14:2; Joel 3:4-8 [n]Jer 50:10
30:17 [o]Jer 33:24
30:18 [p]ver 3; Jer 31:23 [q]Ps 102:13 [r]Jer 31:4,24, 38
30:19 [s]Isa 35:10; 51:11 [t]Isa 51:3 [u]Ps 126:1-2; Jer 31:4 [v]Jer 33:22 [w]Isa 60:9
30:20 [x]Isa 54:13; Jer 31:17 [y]Isa 54:14
30:21 [z]ver 9 [a]Nu 16:5
30:23 [b]Jer 23:19
30:24 [c]Jer 4:8 [d]Jer 4:28 [e]Jer 23:19-20
31:1 [f]Jer 30:22
31:2 [g]Nu 14:20 [h]Ex 33:14

[3]The LORD appeared to us in the past,[h] saying:

"I have loved[a] you with an
everlasting love;
I have drawn[b] you with loving-
kindness.
[4]I will build you up again
and you will be rebuilt, O Virgin
Israel.
Again you will take up your
tambourines
and go out to dance with the joyful.[c]
[5]Again you will plant vineyards
on the hills of Samaria;[d]
the farmers will plant them
and enjoy their fruit.[e]
[6]There will be a day when watchmen
cry out
on the hills of Ephraim,
'Come, let us go up to Zion,
to the LORD our God.'"[f]

[7]This is what the LORD says:

"Sing with joy for Jacob;
shout for the foremost[g] of the
nations.
Make your praises heard, and say,
'O LORD, save[h] your people,
the remnant[i] of Israel.'
[8]See, I will bring them from the land
of the north[j]
and gather[k] them from the ends of
the earth.
Among them will be the blind[l] and
the lame,[m]
expectant mothers and women in
labor;
a great throng will return.
[9]They will come with weeping;[n]
they will pray as I bring them back.
I will lead[o] them beside streams of
water
on a level[p] path where they will not
stumble,
because I am Israel's father,[q]
and Ephraim is my firstborn son.

[10]"Hear the word of the LORD,
O nations;
proclaim it in distant coastlands:[r]
'He who scattered Israel will gather[s]
them
and will watch over his flock like a
shepherd.'[t]
[11]For the LORD will ransom Jacob
and redeem[u] them from the hand
of those stronger[v] than they.
[12]They will come and shout for joy on
the heights[w] of Zion;
they will rejoice in the bounty[x] of
the LORD—
the grain, the new wine and the oil,[y]
the young of the flocks and herds.
They will be like a well-watered
garden,[z]
and they will sorrow[a] no more.
[13]Then maidens will dance and be glad,
young men and old as well.
I will turn their mourning[b] into
gladness;
I will give them comfort and joy[c]
instead of sorrow.
[14]I will satisfy[d] the priests with
abundance,
and my people will be filled with
my bounty,"
declares the LORD.

[15]This is what the LORD says:

"A voice is heard in Ramah,[e]
mourning and great weeping,
Rachel weeping for her children
and refusing to be comforted,[f]
because her children are no more."[g]

[16]This is what the LORD says:

"Restrain your voice from weeping
and your eyes from tears,[h]
for your work will be rewarded,[i]"
declares the LORD.
"They will return[j] from the land of
the enemy.
[17]So there is hope for your future,"
declares the LORD.
"Your children will return to their
own land.

[18]"I have surely heard Ephraim's
moaning:
'You disciplined[k] me like an unruly
calf,[l]
and I have been disciplined.

31:3 [a]Dt 4:37 [b]Hos 11:4
31:4 [c]Jer 30:19
31:5 [d]Jer 50:19 [e]Isa 65:21; Am 9:14
31:6 [f]Isa 2:3; Jer 50:4-5; Mic 4:2
31:7 [g]Dt 28:13; Isa 61:9 [h]Ps 14:7; 28:9 [i]Isa 37:31
31:8 [j]Jer 3:18; 23:8 [k]Dt 30:4; Eze 34:12-14 [l]Isa 42:16 [m]Eze 34:16; Mic 4:6
31:9 [n]Ps 126:5 [o]Isa 63:13 [p]Isa 49:11 [q]Ex 4:22; Jer 3:4
31:10 [r]Isa 66:19; Jer 25:22 [s]Jer 50:19 [t]Isa 40:11; Eze 34:12
31:11 [u]Isa 44:23; 48:20 [v]Ps 142:6
31:12 [w]Eze 17:23; Mic 4:1 [x]Joel 3:18 [y]Hos 2:21-22 [z]Isa 58:11 [a]Isa 65:19; Jn 16:22; Rev 7:17
31:13 [b]Isa 61:3 [c]Ps 30:11; Isa 51:11
31:14 [d]ver 25
31:15 [e]Jos 18:25 [f]Ge 37:35 [g]Jer 10:20; Mt 2:17-18*
31:16 [h]Isa 25:8; 30:19 [i]Ru 2:12 [j]Jer 30:3; Eze 11:17
31:18 [k]Job 5:17 [l]Hos 4:16

[h]3 Or *LORD has appeared to us from afar*

Restore[a] me, and I will return,
because you are the LORD my
God.
19After I strayed,[b]
I repented;
after I came to understand,
I beat[c] my breast.
I was ashamed and humiliated
because I bore the disgrace of my
youth.'
20Is not Ephraim my dear son,
the child in whom I delight?
Though I often speak against him,
I still remember[d] him.
Therefore my heart yearns for him;
I have great compassion[e] for him,"
declares the LORD.

21"Set up road signs;
put up guideposts.
Take note of the highway,[f]
the road that you take.
Return,[g] O Virgin[h] Israel,
return to your towns.
22How long will you wander,[i]
O unfaithful[j] daughter?
The LORD will create a new thing
on earth—
a woman will surround[i] a man."

23This is what the LORD Almighty, the
God of Israel, says: "When I bring them
back from captivity,[jk] the people in the
land of Judah and in its towns will once
again use these words: 'The LORD bless
you, O righteous dwelling,[l] O sacred
mountain.'[m] 24People will live[n] together
in Judah and all its towns—farmers and
those who move about with their flocks.
25I will refresh the weary and satisfy
the faint."[o]

26At this I awoke[p] and looked around.
My sleep had been pleasant to me.
27"The days are coming," declares the
LORD, "when I will plant[q] the house of
Israel and the house of Judah with the
offspring of men and of animals. 28Just
as I watched over them to uproot and
tear down, and to overthrow, destroy
and bring disaster,[r] so I will watch over
them to build and to plant,"[s] declares
the LORD. 29"In those days people will
no longer say,

'The fathers[t] have eaten sour grapes,
and the children's teeth are set on
edge.'[u]

30Instead, everyone will die for his own
sin;[v] whoever eats sour grapes—his
own teeth will be set on edge.

A new covenant with Israel and Judah.

31"The time is coming," declares the
LORD,
"when I will make a new
covenant[w]
with the house of Israel
and with the house of Judah.
32It will not be like the covenant[x]
I made with their forefathers[y]
when I took them by the hand
to lead them out of Egypt,
because they broke my covenant,
though I was a husband to[k] them,[l]"
declares the LORD.
33"This is the covenant I will make
with the house of Israel
after that time," declares the LORD.
"I will put my law in their minds
and write it on their hearts.[z]
I will be their God,
and they will be my people.[a]
34No longer will a man teach[b] his
neighbor,
or a man his brother, saying,
'Know the LORD,'
because they will all know[c] me,
from the least of them to the
greatest,"
declares the LORD.
"For I will forgive[d] their wickedness
and will remember their sins[e] no
more."

35This is what the LORD says,

he who appoints[f] the sun
to shine by day,
who decrees the moon and stars
to shine by night,[g]

31:18 [a]Ps 80:3
31:19 [b]Eze 36:31 [c]Eze 21:12; Lk 18:13
31:20 [d]Hos 4:4; 11:8 [e]Isa 55:7; 63:15; Mic 7:18
31:21 [f]Jer 50:5 [g]Isa 52:11 [h]ver 4
31:22 [i]Jer 2:23 [j]Jer 3:6
31:23 [k]Jer 30:18 [l]Isa 1:26 [m]Ps 48:1; Zec 8:3
31:24 [n]Zec 8:4-8
31:25 [o]Jn 4:14
31:26 [p]Zec 4:1
31:27 [q]Eze 36:9-11; Hos 2:23
31:28 [r]Jer 18:8; 44:27 [s]Jer 1:10
31:29 [t]La 5:7 [u]Eze 18:2
31:30 [v]Isa 3:11; Gal 6:7
31:31 [w]Jer 32:40; Eze 37:26; Lk 22:20; Heb 8:8-12*; 10:16-17
31:32 [x]Ex 24:8 [y]Dt 5:3
31:33 [z]2Co 3:3 [a]Jer 24:7; Heb 10:16
31:34 [b]1Jn 2:27 [c]Jn 6:45 [d]Isa 54:13; Jer 33:8; 50:20 [e]Ro 11:27; Mic 7:19; Heb 10:17*
31:35 [f]Ps 136:7-9 [g]Ge 1:16

[i]22 Or *will go about* ⌊*seeking*⌋; or *will protect*
[j]23 Or *I restore their fortunes* [k]32 Hebrew; Septuagint and Syriac / *and I turned away from*
[l]32 Or *was their master*

who stirs up the sea
so that its waves roar—
the LORD Almighty is his name:[a]
36"Only if these decrees[b] vanish from my sight,"
declares the LORD,
"will the descendants[c] of Israel ever cease
to be a nation before me."

37This is what the LORD says:

"Only if the heavens above can be measured[d]
and the foundations of the earth below be searched out
will I reject[e] all the descendants of Israel
because of all they have done,"
declares the LORD.

38"The days are coming," declares the LORD, "when this city will be rebuilt[f] for me from the Tower of Hananel[g] to the Corner Gate.[h] 39The measuring line will stretch from there straight to the hill of Gareb and then turn to Goah. 40The whole valley[i] where dead bodies[j] and ashes are thrown, and all the terraces out to the Kidron Valley[k] on the east as far as the corner of the Horse Gate,[l] will be holy[m] to the LORD. The city will never again be uprooted or demolished."

Jeremiah's purchase of a field.

32 This is the word that came to Jeremiah from the LORD in the tenth[n] year of Zedekiah king of Judah, which was the eighteenth[o] year of Nebuchadnezzar. 2The army of the king of Babylon was then besieging Jerusalem, and Jeremiah the prophet was confined in the courtyard of the guard[p] in the royal palace of Judah.

3Now Zedekiah king of Judah had imprisoned him there, saying, "Why do you prophesy[q] as you do? You say, 'This is what the LORD says: I am about to hand this city over to the king of Babylon, and he will capture[r] it. 4Zedekiah king of Judah will not escape[s] out of the hands of the Babylonians[m] but will certainly be handed over to the king of Babylon, and will speak with him face to face and see him with his own eyes. 5He will take[t] Zedekiah to Babylon, where he will remain until I deal with him, declares the LORD. If you fight against the Babylonians, you will not succeed.'"[u]

6Jeremiah said, "The word of the LORD came to me: 7Hanamel son of Shallum your uncle is going to come to you and say, 'Buy my field at Anathoth, because as nearest relative it is your right and duty[v] to buy it.'

8"Then, just as the LORD had said, my cousin Hanamel came to me in the courtyard of the guard and said, 'Buy my field at Anathoth in the territory of Benjamin. Since it is your right to redeem it and possess it, buy it for yourself.'

"I knew that this was the word of the LORD; 9so I bought the field at Anathoth from my cousin Hanamel and weighed out for him seventeen shekels[n] of silver.[w] 10I signed and sealed the deed, had it witnessed,[x] and weighed out the silver on the scales. 11I took the deed of purchase—the sealed copy containing the terms and conditions, as well as the unsealed copy— 12and I gave this deed to Baruch[y] son of Neriah,[z] the son of Mahseiah, in the presence of my cousin Hanamel and of the witnesses who had signed the deed and of all the Jews sitting in the courtyard of the guard.

13"In their presence I gave Baruch these instructions: 14'This is what the LORD Almighty, the God of Israel, says: Take these documents, both the sealed and unsealed copies of the deed of purchase, and put them in a clay jar so they will last a long time. 15For this is what the LORD Almighty, the God of Israel, says: Houses, fields and vineyards will again be bought in this land.'[a]

Jeremiah's prayer.

16"After I had given the deed of purchase to Baruch son of Neriah, I prayed to the LORD:

31:35 [a]Jer 10:16
31:36 [b]Isa 54:9-10; Jer 33:20-26 [c]Ps 89:36-37
31:37 [d]Jer 33:22 [e]Jer 33:24-26; Ro 11:1-5
31:38 [f]Jer 30:18 [g]Ne 3:1 [h]2Ki 14:13; Zec 14:10
31:40 [i]Jer 7:31-32 [j]Jer 8:2 [k]2Sa 15:23; Jn 18:1 [l]2Ki 11:16 [m]Joel 3:17; Zec 14:21
32:1 [n]2Ki 25:1 [o]Jer 25:1; 39:1
32:2 [p]Ne 3:25; Jer 37:21
32:3 [q]Jer 26:8-9 [r]ver 28; Jer 34:2-3
32:4 [s]Jer 38:18,23; 39:5-7; 52:9
32:5 [t]Jer 39:7; Eze 12:13 [u]Jer 21:4
32:7 [v]Lev 25:24-25; Ru 4:3-4; Mt 27:10*
32:9 [w]Ge 23:16
32:10 [x]Ru 4:9
32:12 [y]ver 16; Jer 36:4; 43:3,6; 45:1 [z]Jer 51:59
32:15 [a]ver 43-44; Jer 30:18; Am 9:14-15

[m]*4* Or *Chaldeans*; also in verses 5, 24, 25, 28, 29 and 43 [n]*9* That is, about 7 ounces (about 200 grams)

17“Ah, Sovereign LORD,[a] you have made the heavens and the earth by your great power and outstretched arm.[b] Nothing is too hard[c] for you. 18You show love[d] to thousands but bring the punishment for the fathers' sins into the laps of their children[e] after them. O great and powerful God, whose name is the LORD Almighty,[f] 19great are your purposes and mighty are your deeds.[g] Your eyes are open to all the ways of men;[h] you reward everyone according to his conduct and as his deeds deserve.[i] 20You performed miraculous signs and wonders in Egypt[j] and have continued them to this day, both in Israel and among all mankind, and have gained the renown that is still yours. 21You brought your people Israel out of Egypt with signs and wonders, by a mighty hand[k] and an outstretched arm and with great terror.[l] 22You gave them this land you had sworn to give their forefathers, a land flowing with milk and honey.[m] 23They came in and took possession[n] of it, but they did not obey you or follow your law;[o] they did not do what you commanded them to do. So you brought all this disaster[p] upon them.

24“See how the siege ramps are built up to take the city. Because of the sword, famine and plague,[q] the city will be handed over to the Babylonians who are attacking it. What you said[r] has happened, as you now see. 25And though the city will be handed over to the Babylonians, you, O Sovereign LORD, say to me, ‘Buy the field with silver and have the transaction witnessed.’ ”

26Then the word of the LORD came to Jeremiah: 27“I am the LORD, the God of all mankind.[s] Is anything too hard for me? 28Therefore, this is what the LORD says: I am about to hand this city over to the Babylonians and to Nebuchadnezzar[t] king of Babylon, who will capture it.[u] 29The Babylonians who are attacking this city will come in and set it on fire; they will burn it down,[v] along with the houses[w] where the people provoked me to anger by burning incense on the roofs to Baal and by pouring out drink offerings[x] to other gods.

30“The people of Israel and Judah have done nothing but evil in my sight from their youth;[y] indeed, the people of Israel have done nothing but provoke[z] me with what their hands have made,[a] declares the LORD. 31From the day it was built until now, this city has so aroused my anger and wrath that I must remove[b] it from my sight. 32The people of Israel and Judah have provoked me by all the evil[c] they have done—they, their kings and officials, their priests and prophets, the men of Judah and the people of Jerusalem. 33They turned their backs[d] to me and not their faces; though I taught[e] them again and again, they would not listen or respond to discipline. 34They set up their abominable idols in the house that bears my Name and defiled[f] it. 35They built high places for Baal in the Valley of Ben Hinnom to sacrifice their sons and daughters° to Molech,[g] though I never commanded, nor did it enter my mind,[h] that they should do such a detestable thing and so make Judah sin.

36“You are saying about this city, ‘By the sword, famine and plague[i] it will be handed over to the king of Babylon’; but this is what the LORD, the God of Israel, says: 37I will surely gather[j] them from all the lands where I banish them in my furious anger and great wrath; I will bring them back to this place and let them live in safety.[k] 38They will be my people,[l] and I will be their God. 39I will give them singleness[m] of heart and action, so that they will always fear me for their own good and the good of their children after them. 40I will make an everlasting covenant[n] with them: I will

32:17 [a]Jer 1:6 [b]2Ki 19:15; Ps 102:25 [c]Mt 19:26
32:18 [d]Dt 5:10 [e]Ex 20:5 [f]Jer 10:16
32:19 [g]Isa 28:29 [h]Pr 5:21; Jer 16:17 [i]Jer 17:10; Mt 16:27
32:20 [j]Ex 9:16
32:21 [k]Ex 6:6; 1Ch 17:21; Da 9:15 [l]Dt 26:8
32:22 [m]Ex 3:8; Jer 11:5
32:23 [n]Ps 44:2; 78:54-55 [o]Ne 9:26; Jer 11:8 [p]Da 9:14
32:24 [q]Jer 14:12 [r]Dt 4:25-26; Jos 23:15-16
32:27 [s]Nu 16:22
32:28 [t]2Ch 36:17 [u]ver 3
32:29 [v]2Ch 36:19; Jer 21:10; 37:8,10; 52:13 [w]Jer 19:13 [x]Jer 44:18
32:30 [y]Jer 22:21 [z]Jer 8:19 [a]Jer 25:7
32:31 [b]2Ki 23:27; 24:3
32:32 [c]Isa 1:4-6; Da 9:8
32:33 [d]Jer 2:27; Eze 8:16 [e]Jer 7:13
32:34 [f]Jer 7:30
32:35 [g]Lev 18:21 [h]Jer 7:31; 19:5
32:36 [i]ver 24
32:37 [j]Jer 23:3,6 [k]Dt 30:3; Eze 34:28
32:38 [l]Jer 24:7; 2Co 6:16* **32:39** [m]Eze 11:19
32:40 [n]Isa 55:3

°35 Or *to make their sons and daughters pass through* ⌊*the fire*⌋

never stop doing good to them, and I will inspire them to fear me, so that they will never turn away from me.[a] 41 I will rejoice in doing them good[b] and will assuredly plant[c] them in this land with all my heart and soul.

42 "This is what the LORD says: As I have brought all this great calamity on this people, so I will give them all the prosperity I have promised[d] them. 43 Once more fields will be bought[e] in this land of which you say, 'It is a desolate waste, without men or animals, for it has been handed over to the Babylonians.' 44 Fields will be bought for silver, and deeds[f] will be signed, sealed and witnessed in the territory of Benjamin, in the villages around Jerusalem, in the towns of Judah and in the towns of the hill country, of the western foothills and of the Negev,[g] because I will restore[h] their fortunes,[p] declares the LORD."

The nation's restoration and prosperity.

33 While Jeremiah was still confined in the courtyard[i] of the guard, the word of the LORD came to him a second time: 2 "This is what the LORD says, he who made the earth,[j] the LORD who formed it and established it—the LORD is his name:[k] 3 'Call[l] to me and I will answer you and tell you great and unsearchable things you do not know.' 4 For this is what the LORD, the God of Israel, says about the houses in this city and the royal palaces of Judah that have been torn down to be used against the siege[m] ramps[n] and the sword 5 in the fight with the Babylonians[q]: 'They will be filled with the dead bodies of the men I will slay in my anger and wrath.[o] I will hide my face[p] from this city because of all its wickedness.

6 " 'Nevertheless, I will bring health and healing to it; I will heal my people and will let them enjoy abundant peace and security. 7 I will bring Judah[q] and Israel back from captivity[r] and will rebuild them as they were before.[s] 8 I will cleanse[t] them from all the sin they have committed against me and will forgive[u] all their sins of rebellion against me. 9 Then this city will bring me renown, joy, praise[v] and honor[w] before all nations on earth that hear of all the good things I do for it; and they will be in awe and will tremble at the abundant prosperity and peace I provide for it.'

10 "This is what the LORD says: 'You say about this place, "It is a desolate waste, without men or animals."[x] Yet in the towns of Judah and the streets of Jerusalem that are deserted, inhabited by neither men nor animals, there will be heard once more 11 the sounds of joy and gladness,[y] the voices of bride and bridegroom, and the voices of those who bring thank offerings[z] to the house of the LORD, saying,

"Give thanks to the LORD Almighty,
for the LORD is good;[a]
his love endures forever."[b]

For I will restore the fortunes of the land as they were before,' says the LORD.

12 "This is what the LORD Almighty says: 'In this place, desolate[c] and without men or animals—in all its towns there will again be pastures for shepherds to rest their flocks.[d] 13 In the towns of the hill country, of the western foothills and of the Negev,[e] in the territory of Benjamin, in the villages around Jerusalem and in the towns of Judah, flocks will again pass under the hand[f] of the one who counts them,' says the LORD.

14 " 'The days are coming,' declares the LORD, 'when I will fulfill the gracious promise[g] I made to the house of Israel and to the house of Judah.

15 " 'In those days and at that time
I will make a righteous[h] Branch[i]
sprout from David's line;
he will do what is just and right in
the land.

32:40 [a]Jer 24:7 **32:41** [b]Dt 30:9 [c]Jer 24:6; 31:28; Am 9:15 **32:42** [d]Jer 31:28 **32:43** [e]ver 15 **32:44** [f]ver 10 [g]Jer 17:26 [h]Jer 33:7,11, 26 **33:1** [i]Jer 32:2-3; 37:21; 38:28 **33:2** [j]Jer 10:16 [k]Ex 3:15; 15:3 **33:3** [l]Isa 55:6; Jer 29:12 **33:4** [m]Eze 4:2 [n]Jer 32:24; Hab 1:10 **33:5** [o]Jer 21:4-7 [p]Isa 8:17 **33:7** [q]Jer 32:44 [r]Jer 30:3; Am 9:14 [s]Isa 1:26 **33:8** [t]Heb 9:13-14 [u]Jer 31:34; Mic 7:18; Zec 13:1 **33:9** [v]Jer 13:11 [w]Isa 62:7; Jer 3:17 **33:10** [x]Jer 32:43 **33:11** [y]Isa 51:3 [z]Lev 7:12 [a]1Ch 16:8; Ps 136:1 [b]1Ch 16:34; 2Ch 5:13; Ps 100:4-5 **33:12** [c]Jer 32:43 [d]Isa 65:10; Eze 34:11-15 **33:13** [e]Jer 17:26 [f]Lev 27:32 **33:14** [g]Jer 29:10

33:15 [h]Ps 72:2 [i]Isa 4:2; 11:1; Jer 23:5

p44 Or *will bring them back from captivity*
q5 Or *Chaldeans* r7 Or *will restore the fortunes of Judah and Israel*

16In those days Judah will be saved[a]
and Jerusalem will live in safety.
This is the name by which it[s] will be
called:
The LORD Our Righteousness.'[b]

17For this is what the LORD says: 'David
will never fail[c] to have a man to sit on
the throne of the house of Israel, 18nor
will the priests, who are Levites,[d] ever
fail to have a man to stand before me
continually to offer burnt offerings, to
burn grain offerings and to present sacrifices.[e]' "
19The word of the LORD came to Jeremiah: 20"This is what the LORD says: 'If
you can break my covenant with the
day[f] and my covenant with the night, so
that day and night no longer come at
their appointed time, 21then my covenant[g] with David my servant—and my
covenant with the Levites who are
priests ministering before me—can be
broken and David will no longer have a
descendant to reign on his throne.[h] 22I
will make the descendants of David my
servant and the Levites who minister
before me as countless[i] as the stars of
the sky and as measureless as the sand
on the seashore.' "
23The word of the LORD came to Jeremiah: 24"Have you not noticed that
these people are saying, 'The LORD has
rejected the two kingdoms[t][j] he chose'?
So they despise[k] my people and no
longer regard them as a nation.[l] 25This is
what the LORD says: 'If I have not established my covenant with day and night[m]
and the fixed laws of heaven and earth,[n]
26then I will reject[o] the descendants of
Jacob[p] and David my servant and will
not choose one of his sons to rule over
the descendants of Abraham, Isaac and
Jacob. For I will restore their fortunes[u][q]
and have compassion on them.' "

The capture of Zedekiah.

34 While Nebuchadnezzar king of
Babylon and all his army and all
the kingdoms and peoples[r] in the empire
he ruled were fighting against Jerusalem[s] and all its surrounding towns, this

33:16 [a]Isa 45:17 [b]1Co 1:30
33:17 [c]2Sa 7:13; 1Ki 2:4; Ps 89:29-37; Lk 1:33
33:18 [d]Dt 18:1 [e]Heb 13:15
33:20 [f]Ps 89:36
33:21 [g]Ps 89:34 [h]2Ch 7:18
33:22 [i]Ge 15:5
33:24 [j]Eze 37:22 [k]Ne 4:4 [l]Jer 30:17
33:25 [m]Jer 31:35-36 [n]Ps 74:16-17
33:26 [o]Jer 31:37 [p]Isa 14:1 [q]ver 7
34:1 [r]Jer 27:7 [s]2Ki 25:1; Jer 39:1
34:2 [t]2Ch 36:11 [u]ver 22; Jer 32:29; 37:8
34:3 [v]2Ki 25:7; Jer 21:7; 32:4
34:5 [w]2Ch 16:14; 21:19 [x]Jer 22:18

word came to Jeremiah from the LORD:
2"This is what the LORD, the God of Israel, says: Go to Zedekiah[t] king of Judah
and tell him, 'This is what the LORD
says: I am about to hand this city over to
the king of Babylon, and he will burn it
down.[u] 3You will not escape from his
grasp but will surely be captured and
handed over[v] to him. You will see the
king of Babylon with your own eyes, and
he will speak with you face to face. And
you will go to Babylon.

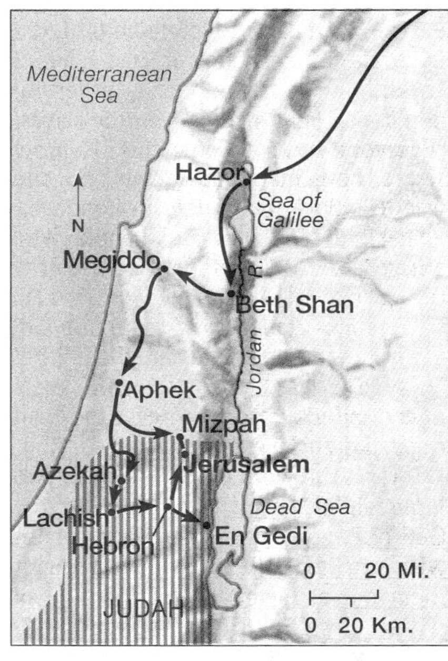

Babylon Attacks Judah

Zedekiah incurred Babylon's wrath in allying with Egypt (37:5) and not surrendering as God told him through Jeremiah (38:17). Nebuchadnezzar attacked Judah for the third and final time, moving systematically until all its cities fell. Jerusalem withstood siege for several months but was burned as Jeremiah predicted (chapter 39).

4" 'Yet hear the promise of the LORD,
O Zedekiah king of Judah. This is what
the LORD says concerning you: You will
not die by the sword; 5you will die peacefully. As people made a funeral fire[w] in
honor of your fathers, the former kings
who preceded you, so they will make a
fire in your honor and lament, "Alas,[x]

[s]16 Or *he* [t]24 Or *families* [u]26 Or *will bring them back from captivity*

O master!" I myself make this promise,
declares the LORD.'"
6Then Jeremiah the prophet told all
this to Zedekiah king of Judah, in Jerusalem, 7while the army of the king of
Babylon was fighting against Jerusalem
and the other cities of Judah that were
still holding out—Lachish[a] and Azekah.[b]
These were the only fortified cities left
in Judah.

Freedom for Hebrew slaves.

8The word came to Jeremiah from the
LORD after King Zedekiah had made a
covenant with all the people[c] in Jerusalem to proclaim freedom[d] for the slaves.
9Everyone was to free his Hebrew
slaves, both male and female; no one
was to hold a fellow Jew in bondage.[e]
10So all the officials and people who
entered into this covenant agreed that
they would free their male and female
slaves and no longer hold them in bondage. They agreed, and set them free.
11But afterward they changed their
minds and took back the slaves they had
freed and enslaved them again.
12Then the word of the LORD came to
Jeremiah: 13"This is what the LORD, the
God of Israel, says: I made a covenant
with your forefathers[f] when I brought
them out of Egypt, out of the land of
slavery. I said, 14'Every seventh year
each of you must free any fellow Hebrew
who has sold himself to you. After he
has served you six years, you must let
him go free.'[v][g] Your fathers, however,
did not listen to me or pay attention[h] to
me. 15Recently you repented and did
what is right in my sight: Each of you
proclaimed freedom to his countrymen.[i]
You even made a covenant before me in
the house that bears my Name.[j] 16But
now you have turned around[k] and profaned[l] my name; each of you has taken
back the male and female slaves you had
set free to go where they wished. You
have forced them to become your slaves
again.
17"Therefore, this is what the LORD
says: You have not obeyed me; you have
not proclaimed freedom for your fellow
countrymen. So I now proclaim 'freedom' for you,[m] declares the LORD—'freedom' to fall by the sword, plague and
famine. I will make you abhorrent to all
the kingdoms of the earth.[n] 18The men
who have violated my covenant and
have not fulfilled the terms of the covenant they made before me, I will treat
like the calf they cut in two and then
walked between its pieces.[o] 19The leaders of Judah and Jerusalem, the court
officials,[p] the priests and all the people
of the land who walked between the
pieces of the calf, 20I will hand over[q] to
their enemies who seek their lives.[r]
Their dead bodies will become food for
the birds of the air and the beasts of the
earth.[s]
21"I will hand Zedekiah[t] king of Judah
and his officials[u] over to their enemies
who seek their lives, to the army of the
king of Babylon, which has withdrawn[v]
from you. 22I am going to give the order,
declares the LORD, and I will bring them
back to this city. They will fight against
it, take[w] it and burn[x] it down. And I will
lay waste the towns of Judah so no one
can live there."

Obedient Recabites are blessed.

35 This is the word that came to
Jeremiah from the LORD during
the reign of Jehoiakim[y] son of Josiah
king of Judah: 2"Go to the Recabite[z]
family and invite them to come to one
of the side rooms[a] of the house of the
LORD and give them wine to drink."
3So I went to get Jaazaniah son of
Jeremiah, the son of Habazziniah, and
his brothers and all his sons—the whole
family of the Recabites. 4I brought them
into the house of the LORD, into the
room of the sons of Hanan son of Igdali-
ah the man of God.[b] It was next to the
room of the officials, which was over
that of Maaseiah son of Shallum[c] the
doorkeeper.[d] 5Then I set bowls full of
wine and some cups before the men of

34:7 [a]Jos 10:3 [b]Jos 10:10; 2Ch 11:9
34:8 [c]2Ki 11:17 [d]Ex 21:2; Lev 25:10, 39-41; Ne 5:5-8
34:9 [e]Lev 25:39-46
34:13 [f]Ex 24:8
34:14 [g]Ex 21:2 [h]Dt 15:12; 2Ki 17:14
34:15 [i]ver 8 [j]Jer 7:10-11; 32:34
34:16 [k]Eze 3:20; 18:24 [l]Ex 20:7; Lev 19:12
34:17 [m]Mt 7:2; Gal 6:7 [n]Dt 28:25,64; Jer 29:18
34:18 [o]Ge 15:10
34:19 [p]Zep 3:3-4
34:20 [q]Jer 21:7 [r]Jer 11:21 [s]Dt 28:26; Jer 7:33; 19:7
34:21 [t]Jer 32:4 [u]Jer 39:6; 52:24-27 [v]Jer 37:5
34:22 [w]Jer 39:1-2 [x]Jer 39:8
35:1 [y]2Ch 36:5
35:2 [z]2Ki 10:15; 1Ch 2:55 [a]1Ki 6:5
35:4 [b]Dt 33:1 [c]1Ch 9:19 [d]2Ki 12:9

v *14* Deut. 15:12

the Recabite family and said to them,
"Drink some wine."
6But they replied, "We do not drink
wine, because our forefather Jonadab[a]
son of Recab gave us this command:
'Neither you nor your descendants must
ever drink wine.[b] 7Also you must never
build houses, sow seed or plant vineyards; you must never have any of these
things, but must always live in tents.[c]
Then you will live a long time in the
land[d] where you are nomads.' 8We have
obeyed everything our forefather[e] Jonadab son of Recab commanded us. Neither we nor our wives nor our sons and
daughters have ever drunk wine 9or
built houses to live in or had vineyards,
fields or crops.[f] 10We have lived in tents
and have fully obeyed everything our
forefather Jonadab commanded us. 11But
when Nebuchadnezzar king of Babylon
invaded[g] this land, we said, 'Come, we
must go to Jerusalem[h] to escape the
Babylonian[w] and Aramean armies.' So
we have remained in Jerusalem."
12Then the word of the LORD came to
Jeremiah, saying: 13"This is what the
LORD Almighty, the God of Israel, says:
Go and tell the men of Judah and the
people of Jerusalem, 'Will you not learn
a lesson[i] and obey my words?' declares
the LORD. 14'Jonadab son of Recab
ordered his sons not to drink wine and
this command has been kept. To this
day they do not drink wine, because
they obey their forefather's command.
But I have spoken to you again and
again,[j] yet you have not obeyed[k] me.
15Again and again I sent all my servants
the prophets[l] to you. They said, "Each
of you must turn[m] from your wicked
ways and reform[n] your actions; do not
follow other gods to serve them. Then
you will live in the land[o] I have given to
you and your fathers." But you have
not paid attention or listened[p] to me.
16The descendants of Jonadab son of
Recab have carried out the command
their forefather[q] gave them, but these
people have not obeyed me.'
17"Therefore, this is what the LORD
God Almighty, the God of Israel, says:
'Listen! I am going to bring on Judah
and on everyone living in Jerusalem
every disaster[r] I pronounced against
them. I spoke to them, but they did not
listen;[s] I called to them, but they did not
answer.'"[t]
18Then Jeremiah said to the family of
the Recabites, "This is what the LORD
Almighty, the God of Israel, says: 'You
have obeyed the command of your
forefather Jonadab and have followed all
his instructions and have done everything he ordered.' 19Therefore, this is
what the LORD Almighty, the God of
Israel, says: 'Jonadab son of Recab will
never fail[u] to have a man to serve[v] me.'"

Baruch reads Jeremiah's scroll.

36 In the fourth year of Jehoiakim[w]
son of Josiah king of Judah, this
word came to Jeremiah from the LORD:
2"Take a scroll[x] and write on it all the
words I have spoken to you concerning
Israel, Judah and all the other nations
from the time I began speaking to you in
the reign of Josiah[y] till now. 3Perhaps[z]
when the people of Judah hear[a] about
every disaster I plan to inflict on them,
each of them will turn[b] from his wicked
way; then I will forgive[c] their wickedness and their sin."
4So Jeremiah called Baruch[d] son of
Neriah, and while Jeremiah dictated[e] all
the words the LORD had spoken to him,
Baruch wrote them on the scroll.[f] 5Then
Jeremiah told Baruch, "I am restricted;
I cannot go to the LORD's temple. 6So
you go to the house of the LORD on a day
of fasting[g] and read to the people from
the scroll the words of the LORD that you
wrote as I dictated. Read them to all the
people of Judah who come in from their
towns. 7Perhaps they will bring their
petition before the LORD, and each will
turn[h] from his wicked ways, for the
anger[i] and wrath pronounced against
this people by the LORD are great."
8Baruch son of Neriah did everything
Jeremiah the prophet told him to do; at
the LORD's temple he read the words of

[w]*11* Or *Chaldean*

35:6 [a]2Ki 10:15 [b]Lev 10:9; Nu 6:2-4; Lk 1:15
35:7 [c]Heb 11:9 [d]Ex 20:12; Eph 6:2-3
35:8 [e]Pr 1:8; Col 3:20
35:9 [f]1Ti 6:6
35:11 [g]2Ki 24:1 [h]Jer 8:14
35:13 [i]Jer 6:10; 32:33
35:14 [j]Jer 7:13; 25:3 [k]Isa 30:9
35:15 [l]Jer 7:25 [m]Jer 26:3 [n]Isa 1:16-17; Jer 4:1; 18:11; Eze 18:30 [o]Jer 25:5 [p]Jer 7:26
35:16 [q]Mal 1:6
35:17 [r]Jos 23:15; Jer 21:4-7 [s]Pr 1:24; Ro 10:21 [t]Isa 65:12; 66:4; Jer 7:13
35:19 [u]Jer 33:17 [v]Jer 15:19
36:1 [w]2Ch 36:5
36:2 [x]Ex 17:14; Jer 30:2; Hab 2:2 [y]Jer 1:2; 25:3
36:3 [z]ver 7; Eze 12:3 [a]Mk 4:12 [b]Jer 26:3; Jnh 3:8; Ac 3:19 [c]Jer 18:8
36:4 [d]Jer 32:12 [e]ver 18 [f]Eze 2:9
36:6 [g]ver 9
36:7 [h]Jer 26:3 [i]Dt 31:17

the LORD from the scroll. 9In the ninth month[a] of the fifth year of Jehoiakim son of Josiah king of Judah, a time of fasting[b] before the LORD was proclaimed for all the people in Jerusalem and those who had come from the towns of Judah. 10From the room of Gemariah son of Shaphan the secretary,[c] which was in the upper courtyard at the entrance of the New Gate[d] of the temple, Baruch read to all the people at the LORD's temple the words of Jeremiah from the scroll.

11When Micaiah son of Gemariah, the son of Shaphan, heard all the words of the LORD from the scroll, 12he went down to the secretary's room in the royal palace, where all the officials were sitting: Elishama the secretary, Delaiah son of Shemaiah, Elnathan[e] son of Acbor, Gemariah son of Shaphan, Zedekiah son of Hananiah, and all the other officials. 13After Micaiah told them everything he had heard Baruch read to the people from the scroll, 14all the officials sent Jehudi[f] son of Nethaniah, the son of Shelemiah, the son of Cushi, to say to Baruch, "Bring the scroll from which you have read to the people and come." So Baruch son of Neriah went to them with the scroll in his hand. 15They said to him, "Sit down, please, and read it to us."

So Baruch read it to them. 16When they heard all these words, they looked at each other in fear and said to Baruch, "We must report all these words to the king." 17Then they asked Baruch, "Tell us, how did you come to write all this? Did Jeremiah dictate it?"

18"Yes," Baruch replied, "he dictated[g] all these words to me, and I wrote them in ink on the scroll."

19Then the officials said to Baruch, "You and Jeremiah, go and hide.[h] Don't let anyone know where you are."

Jehoiakim burns Jeremiah's scroll.

20After they put the scroll in the room of Elishama the secretary, they went to the king in the courtyard and reported everything to him. 21The king sent Jehudi[i] to get the scroll, and Jehudi brought it from the room of Elishama the secretary and read it to the king[j] and all the officials standing beside him. 22It was the ninth month and the king was sitting in the winter apartment,[k] with a fire burning in the firepot in front of him. 23Whenever Jehudi had read three or four columns of the scroll, the king cut them off with a scribe's knife and threw them into the firepot, until the entire scroll was burned in the fire.[l] 24The king and all his attendants who heard all these words showed no fear,[m] nor did they tear their clothes.[n] 25Even though Elnathan, Delaiah and Gemariah urged the king not to burn the scroll, he would not listen to them. 26Instead, the king commanded Jerahmeel, a son of the king, Seraiah son of Azriel and Shelemiah son of Abdeel to arrest[o] Baruch the scribe and Jeremiah the prophet. But the LORD had hidden[p] them.

Baruch rewrites Jeremiah's scroll.

27After the king burned the scroll containing the words that Baruch had written at Jeremiah's dictation,[q] the word of the LORD came to Jeremiah: 28"Take another scroll and write on it all the words that were on the first scroll, which Jehoiakim king of Judah burned up. 29Also tell Jehoiakim king of Judah, 'This is what the LORD says: You burned that scroll and said, "Why did you write on it that the king of Babylon would certainly come and destroy this land and cut off both men and animals from it?"[r] 30Therefore, this is what the LORD says about Jehoiakim king of Judah: He will have no one to sit on the throne of David; his body will be thrown out[s] and exposed to the heat by day and the frost by night. 31I will punish him and his children and his attendants for their wickedness; I will bring on them and those living in Jerusalem and the people of Judah every disaster[t] I pronounced against them, because they have not listened.'"

32So Jeremiah took another scroll and

36:9 [a]ver 22 [b]2Ch 20:3
36:10 [c]Jer 52:25 [d]Jer 26:10
36:12 [e]Jer 26:22
36:14 [f]ver 21
36:18 [g]ver 4
36:19 [h]1Ki 17:3
36:21 [i]ver 14 [j]2Ki 22:10
36:22 [k]Am 3:15
36:23 [l]1Ki 22:8
36:24 [m]Ps 36:1 [n]Ge 37:29; 2Ki 22:11; Isa 37:1
36:26 [o]Mt 23:34 [p]Jer 15:21
36:27 [q]ver 4
36:29 [r]Isa 30:10
36:30 [s]Jer 22:19
36:31 [t]Pr 29:1

gave it to the scribe Baruch son of Neriah, and as Jeremiah dictated,[a] Baruch
wrote[b] on it all the words of the scroll
that Jehoiakim king of Judah had
burned[c] in the fire. And many similar
words were added to them.

Jeremiah is imprisoned in a dungeon.

37 Zedekiah[d] son of Josiah was
made king[e] of Judah by Nebuchadnezzar king of Babylon; he reigned
in place of Jehoiachin[x][f] son of Jehoiakim.
2Neither he nor his attendants nor the
people of the land paid any attention[g]
to the words the LORD had spoken
through Jeremiah the prophet.
3King Zedekiah, however, sent Jehucal son of Shelemiah with the priest
Zephaniah[h] son of Maaseiah to Jeremiah
the prophet with this message: "Please
pray[i] to the LORD our God for us."
4Now Jeremiah was free to come and
go among the people, for he had not yet
been put in prison.[j] 5Pharaoh's army
had marched out of Egypt,[k] and when
the Babylonians[y] who were besieging
Jerusalem heard the report about them,
they withdrew[l] from Jerusalem.[m]
6Then the word of the LORD came to
Jeremiah the prophet: 7"This is what
the LORD, the God of Israel, says: Tell
the king of Judah, who sent you to
inquire[n] of me, 'Pharaoh's army, which
has marched out to support you, will go
back to its own land, to Egypt.[o] 8Then
the Babylonians will return and attack
this city; they will capture it and burn[p]
it down.'
9"This is what the LORD says: Do not
deceive[q] yourselves, thinking, 'The Babylonians will surely leave us.' They will
not! 10Even if you were to defeat the
entire Babylonian[z] army that is attacking
you and only wounded men were left in
their tents, they would come out and
burn this city down."
11After the Babylonian army had withdrawn[r] from Jerusalem because of Pharaoh's army, 12Jeremiah started to leave
the city to go to the territory of Benjamin
to get his share of the property[s] among
the people there. 13But when he reached
the Benjamin Gate, the captain of the
guard, whose name was Irijah son of
Shelemiah, the son of Hananiah, arrested him and said, "You are deserting to
the Babylonians!"
14"That's not true!" Jeremiah said. "I
am not deserting to the Babylonians."
But Irijah would not listen to him; instead, he arrested[t] Jeremiah and brought
him to the officials. 15They were angry
with Jeremiah and had him beaten[u] and
imprisoned in the house[v] of Jonathan
the secretary, which they had made into
a prison.
16Jeremiah was put into a vaulted cell
in a dungeon, where he remained a long
time. 17Then King Zedekiah sent for him
and had him brought to the palace,
where he asked[w] him privately,[x] "Is
there any word from the LORD?"
"Yes," Jeremiah replied, "you will be
handed over[y] to the king of Babylon."
18Then Jeremiah said to King Zedekiah, "What crime[z] have I committed
against you or your officials or this people, that you have put me in prison?
19Where are your prophets who prophesied to you, 'The king of Babylon will
not attack you or this land'? 20But now,
my lord the king, please listen. Let me
bring my petition before you: Do not
send me back to the house of Jonathan
the secretary, or I will die there."
21King Zedekiah then gave orders for
Jeremiah to be placed in the courtyard
of the guard and given bread from the
street of the bakers each day until all the
bread[a] in the city was gone.[b] So Jeremiah
remained in the courtyard of the guard.[c]

Jeremiah is thrown into a cistern.

38 Shephatiah son of Mattan, Gedaliah son of Pashhur, Jehucal[a][d]
son of Shelemiah, and Pashhur son of
Malkijah heard what Jeremiah was
telling all the people when he said,

36:32 [a]ver 4 [b]Ex 34:1 [c]ver 23
37:1 [d]2Ki 24:17 [e]Eze 17:13 [f]2Ki 24:8,12; 2Ch 36:10; Jer 22:24
37:2 [g]2Ki 24:19; 2Ch 36:12,14
37:3 [h]Jer 29:25; 52:24 [i]1Ki 13:6; Jer 21:1-2; 42:2
37:4 [j]ver 15; Jer 32:2
37:5 [k]Eze 17:15 [l]Jer 34:21 [m]2Ki 24:7
37:7 [n]2Ki 22:18 [o]Jer 2:36; La 4:17
37:8 [p]Jer 34:22; 39:8
37:9 [q]Jer 29:8
37:11 [r]ver 5
37:12 [s]Jer 32:9
37:14 [t]Jer 40:4
37:15 [u]Jer 20:2 [v]Jer 38:26
37:17 [w]Jer 15:11 [x]Jer 38:16 [y]Jer 21:7
37:18 [z]1Sa 26:18; Jn 10:32; Ac 25:8
37:21 [a]Isa 33:16; Jer 38:9 [b]2Ki 25:3; Jer 52:6 [c]Jer 32:2; 38:6,13,28
38:1 [d]Jer 37:3

x *1* Hebrew *Coniah,* a variant of *Jehoiachin*
y *5* Or *Chaldeans;* also in verses 8, 9, 13 and 14
z *10* Or *Chaldean;* also in verse 11
a *1* Hebrew *Jucal,* a variant of *Jehucal*

2"This is what the LORD says: 'Whoever
stays in this city will die by the sword,
famine or plague,[a] but whoever goes
over to the Babylonians[b] will live. He
will escape with his life; he will live.'[b]
3And this is what the LORD says: 'This
city will certainly be handed over to the
army of the king of Babylon, who will
capture it.'"[c]
4Then the officials[d] said to the king,
"This man should be put to death.[e] He
is discouraging the soldiers who are left
in this city, as well as all the people, by
the things he is saying to them. This
man is not seeking the good of these
people but their ruin."
5"He is in your hands," King Zedekiah answered. "The king can do nothing
to oppose you."
6So they took Jeremiah and put him
into the cistern of Malkijah, the king's
son, which was in the courtyard of the
guard.[f] They lowered Jeremiah by ropes
into the cistern; it had no water in it,
only mud, and Jeremiah sank down into
the mud.
7But Ebed-Melech,[g] a Cushite,[c] an
official[d][h] in the royal palace, heard that
they had put Jeremiah into the cistern.
While the king was sitting in the Benjamin Gate,[i] 8Ebed-Melech went out of
the palace and said to him, 9"My lord
the king, these men have acted wickedly in all they have done to Jeremiah the
prophet. They have thrown him into a
cistern, where he will starve to death
when there is no longer any bread[j] in
the city."
10Then the king commanded Ebed-
Melech the Cushite, "Take thirty men
from here with you and lift Jeremiah the
prophet out of the cistern before he
dies."
11So Ebed-Melech took the men with
him and went to a room under the treasury in the palace. He took some old rags
and worn-out clothes from there and let
them down with ropes to Jeremiah in
the cistern. 12Ebed-Melech the Cushite
said to Jeremiah, "Put these old rags and
worn-out clothes under your arms to
pad the ropes." Jeremiah did so, 13and
they pulled him up with the ropes and
lifted him out of the cistern. And Jeremiah remained in the courtyard of the
guard.[k]

Zedekiah seeks Jeremiah's counsel.

14Then King Zedekiah sent for Jeremiah the prophet and had him brought to
the third entrance to the temple of the
LORD. "I am going to ask you something," the king said to Jeremiah. "Do
not hide[l] anything from me."
15Jeremiah said to Zedekiah, "If I give
you an answer, will you not kill me?
Even if I did give you counsel, you would
not listen to me."
16But King Zedekiah swore this oath
secretly[m] to Jeremiah: "As surely as the
LORD lives, who has given us breath,[n] I
will neither kill you nor hand you over
to those who are seeking your life."[o]
17Then Jeremiah said to Zedekiah,
"This is what the LORD God Almighty,
the God of Israel, says: 'If you surrender
to the officers of the king of Babylon,
your life will be spared and this city will
not be burned down; you and your family will live.[p] 18But if you will not surrender to the officers of the king of
Babylon, this city will be handed over[q]
to the Babylonians and they will burn[r] it
down; you yourself will not escape[s] from
their hands.'"
19King Zedekiah said to Jeremiah, "I
am afraid[t] of the Jews who have gone
over[u] to the Babylonians, for the Babylonians may hand me over to them and
they will mistreat me."
20"They will not hand you over,"
Jeremiah replied. "Obey[v] the LORD by
doing what I tell you. Then it will go well
with you, and your life[w] will be spared.
21But if you refuse to surrender, this is
what the LORD has revealed to me: 22All
the women[x] left in the palace of the king
of Judah will be brought out to the officials of the king of Babylon. Those wom-
en will say to you:

38:2 [a]Jer 34:17 [b]Jer 21:9; 39:18; 45:5
38:3 [c]Jer 21:4,10; 32:3
38:4 [d]Jer 36:12 [e]Jer 26:11
38:6 [f]Jer 37:21
38:7 [g]Jer 39:16 [h]Ac 8:27 [i]Job 29:7
38:9 [j]Jer 37:21
38:13 [k]Jer 37:21
38:14 [l]1Sa 3:17
38:16 [m]Jer 37:17 [n]Isa 42:5; 57:16 [o]ver 4
38:17 [p]2Ki 24:12; Jer 21:9
38:18 [q]ver 3; Jer 34:3 [r]Jer 37:8 [s]Jer 24:8; 32:4
38:19 [t]Isa 51:12; Jn 12:42 [u]Jer 39:9
38:20 [v]Jer 11:4 [w]Isa 55:3
38:22 [x]Jer 6:12

[b]*2* Or *Chaldeans*; also in verses 18, 19 and 23
[c]*7* Probably from the upper Nile region [d]*7* Or *a eunuch*

"They misled you and overcame
you—
those trusted friends of yours.
Your feet are sunk in the mud;
your friends have deserted you.'

23"All your wives and children[a] will be
brought out to the Babylonians. You yourself will not escape from their hands but
will be captured[b] by the king of Babylon;
and this city will[e] be burned down."
24Then Zedekiah said to Jeremiah,
"Do not let anyone know about this
conversation, or you may die. 25If the
officials hear that I talked with you, and
they come to you and say, 'Tell us what
you said to the king and what the king
said to you; do not hide it from us or we
will kill you,' 26then tell them, 'I was
pleading with the king not to send me
back to Jonathan's house[c] to die there.'"
27All the officials did come to Jeremiah and question him, and he told them
everything the king had ordered him to
say. So they said no more to him, for no
one had heard his conversation with the
king.
28And Jeremiah remained in the courtyard of the guard[d] until the day Jerusalem was captured.

Jerusalem falls to Nebuchadnezzar.

39:1-10pp— 2Ki 25:1-12; Jer 52:4-16

39 This is how Jerusalem was taken:
1In the ninth year of Zedekiah
king of Judah, in the tenth month, Nebuchadnezzar king of Babylon marched
against Jerusalem with his whole army
and laid siege[e] to it. 2And on the ninth
day of the fourth month of Zedekiah's
eleventh year, the city wall was broken
through. 3Then all the officials[f] of the
king of Babylon came and took seats in
the Middle Gate: Nergal-Sharezer of Sam-
gar, Nebo-Sarsekim[f] a chief officer, Nergal-Sharezer a high official and all the
other officials of the king of Babylon.
4When Zedekiah king of Judah and all
the soldiers saw them, they fled; they left
the city at night by way of the king's garden, through the gate between the two
walls, and headed toward the Arabah.[g]

38:23 [a]2Ki 25:6 [b]Jer 41:10
38:26 [c]Jer 37:15
38:28 [d]Jer 37:21; 39:14
39:1 [e]2Ki 25:1; Jer 52:4; Eze 24:2
39:3 [f]Jer 21:4
39:5 [g]Jer 32:4 [h]2Ki 23:33
39:7 [i]Eze 12:13 [j]Jer 32:5
39:8 [k]Jer 38:18 [l]Ne 1:3
39:9 [m]Jer 40:1
39:12 [n]Pr 16:7; 1Pe 3:13
39:14 [o]Jer 38:28 [p]2Ki 22:12 [q]Jer 40:5
39:16 [r]Jer 38:7

Zedekiah's eyes are put out.

5But the Babylonian[h] army pursued
them and overtook Zedekiah[g] in the
plains of Jericho. They captured him and
took him to Nebuchadnezzar king of
Babylon at Riblah[h] in the land of Hamath, where he pronounced sentence on
him. 6There at Riblah the king of Babylon slaughtered the sons of Zedekiah
before his eyes and also killed all the
nobles of Judah. 7Then he put out Zedekiah's eyes[i] and bound him with bronze
shackles to take him to Babylon.[j]
8The Babylonians[i] set fire[k] to the royal
palace and the houses of the people
and broke down the walls[l] of Jerusalem.
9Nebuzaradan commander of the imperial guard carried into exile to Babylon
the people who remained in the city,
along with those who had gone over to
him, and the rest of the people.[m] 10But
Nebuzaradan the commander of the
guard left behind in the land of Judah
some of the poor people, who owned
nothing; and at that time he gave them
vineyards and fields.

Jeremiah is freed.

11Now Nebuchadnezzar king of Babylon had given these orders about Jeremiah through Nebuzaradan commander
of the imperial guard: 12"Take him and
look after him; don't harm[n] him but do
for him whatever he asks." 13So Nebuzaradan the commander of the guard,
Nebushazban a chief officer, Nergal-
Sharezer a high official and all the other
officers of the king of Babylon 14sent and
had Jeremiah taken out of the courtyard
of the guard.[o] They turned him over to
Gedaliah son of Ahikam,[p] the son of Shaphan, to take him back to his home. So
he remained among his own people.[q]
15While Jeremiah had been confined
in the courtyard of the guard, the word
of the LORD came to him: 16"Go and tell
Ebed-Melech[r] the Cushite, 'This is what
the LORD Almighty, the God of Israel,

e23 Or *and you will cause this city to* f3 Or *Nergal-Sharezer, Samgar-Nebo, Sarsekim* g4 Or *the Jordan Valley* h5 Or *Chaldean* i8 Or *Chaldeans*

says: I am about to fulfill my words against this city through disaster,[a] not prosperity. At that time they will be fulfilled before your eyes. 17But I will rescue[b] you on that day, declares the LORD; you will not be handed over to those you fear. 18I will save you; you will not fall by the sword[c] but will escape with your life,[d] because you trust[e] in me, declares the LORD.'"

Jeremiah lives with Gedaliah.

40 The word came to Jeremiah from the LORD after Nebuzaradan commander of the imperial guard had released him at Ramah. He had found Jeremiah bound in chains among all the captives from Jerusalem and Judah who were being carried into exile to Babylon. 2When the commander of the guard found Jeremiah, he said to him, "The LORD your God decreed this disaster for this place.[f] 3And now the LORD has brought it about; he has done just as he said he would. All this happened because you people sinned[g] against the LORD and did not obey[h] him. 4But today I am freeing you from the chains on your wrists. Come with me to Babylon, if you like, and I will look after you; but if you do not want to, then don't come. Look, the whole country lies before you; go wherever you please."[i] 5However, before Jeremiah turned to go,[j] Nebuzaradan added, "Go back to Gedaliah[j] son of Ahikam, the son of Shaphan, whom the king of Babylon has appointed over the towns of Judah, and live with him among the people, or go anywhere else you please."[k]

Then the commander gave him provisions and a present and let him go. 6So Jeremiah went to Gedaliah son of Ahikam at Mizpah[l] and stayed with him among the people who were left behind in the land.

Ishmael assassinates Gedaliah.

40:7-9; 41:1-3pp— 2Ki 25:22-26

7When all the army officers and their men who were still in the open country heard that the king of Babylon had appointed Gedaliah son of Ahikam as governor over the land and had put him in charge of the men, women and children who were the poorest[m] in the land and who had not been carried into exile to Babylon, 8they came to Gedaliah at Mizpah[n]—Ishmael[o] son of Nethaniah, Johanan and Jonathan the sons of Kareah, Seraiah son of Tanhumeth, the sons of Ephai the Netophathite,[p] and Jaazaniah[k] the son of the Maacathite,[q] and their men. 9Gedaliah son of Ahikam, the son of Shaphan, took an oath to reassure them and their men. "Do not be afraid to serve[r] the Babylonians,[l]" he said. "Settle down in the land and serve the king of Babylon, and it will go well with you.[s] 10I myself will stay at Mizpah[t] to represent you before the Babylonians who come to us, but you are to harvest the wine, summer fruit and oil, and put them in your storage jars, and live in the towns you have taken over."[u]

11When all the Jews in Moab,[v] Ammon, Edom and all the other countries heard that the king of Babylon had left a remnant in Judah and had appointed Gedaliah son of Ahikam, the son of Shaphan, as governor over them, 12they all came back to the land of Judah, to Gedaliah at Mizpah, from all the countries where they had been scattered.[w] And they harvested an abundance of wine and summer fruit.

13Johanan son of Kareah and all the army officers still in the open country came to Gedaliah at Mizpah[x] 14and said to him, "Don't you know that Baalis king of the Ammonites[y] has sent Ishmael son of Nethaniah to take your life?" But Gedaliah son of Ahikam did not believe them.

15Then Johanan son of Kareah said privately to Gedaliah in Mizpah, "Let me go and kill Ishmael son of Nethaniah, and no one will know it. Why should he take your life and cause all the Jews who

39:16 [a]Jer 21:10; Da 9:12
39:17 [b]Ps 41:1-2
39:18 [c]Jer 45:5 [d]Jer 21:9; 38:2 [e]Jer 17:7
40:2 [f]Jer 50:7
40:3 [g]Da 9:11 [h]Dt 29:24-28; Ro 2:5-9
40:4 [i]Ge 13:9; Jer 39:11-12
40:5 [j]2Ki 25:22 [k]Jer 39:14
40:6 [l]Jdg 20:1; 1Sa 7:5-17
40:7 [m]Jer 39:10
40:8 [n]ver 13 [o]ver 14; Jer 41:1,2 [p]2Sa 23:28 [q]Dt 3:14
40:9 [r]Jer 27:11 [s]Jer 38:20
40:10 [t]ver 6 [u]Dt 1:39
40:11 [v]Nu 25:1
40:12 [w]Jer 43:5
40:13 [x]ver 8
40:14 [y]2Sa 10:1-19; Jer 25:21; 41:10

j5 Or *Jeremiah answered* k8 Hebrew *Jezaniah,* a variant of *Jaazaniah* l9 Or *Chaldeans*; also in verse 10

are gathered around you to be scattered and the remnant of Judah to perish?”

16 But Gedaliah son of Ahikam said to Johanan son of Kareah, “Don’t do such a thing! What you are saying about Ishmael is not true.”

41 In the seventh month Ishmael[a] son of Nethaniah, the son of Elishama, who was of royal blood and had been one of the king’s officers, came with ten men to Gedaliah son of Ahikam at Mizpah. While they were eating together there, 2 Ishmael[b] son of Nethaniah and the ten men who were with him got up and struck down Gedaliah son of Ahikam, the son of Shaphan, with the sword, killing the one whom the king of Babylon had appointed[c] as governor over the land.[d] 3 Ishmael also killed all the Jews who were with Gedaliah at Mizpah, as well as the Babylonian[m] soldiers who were there.

4 The day after Gedaliah’s assassination, before anyone knew about it, 5 eighty men who had shaved off their beards,[e] torn their clothes and cut themselves came from Shechem,[f] Shiloh[g] and Samaria,[h] bringing grain offerings and incense with them to the house of the LORD.[i] 6 Ishmael son of Nethaniah went out from Mizpah to meet them, weeping[j] as he went. When he met them, he said, “Come to Gedaliah son of Ahikam.” 7 When they went into the city, Ishmael son of Nethaniah and the men who were with him slaughtered them and threw them into a cistern. 8 But ten of them said to Ishmael, “Don’t kill us! We have wheat and barley, oil and honey, hidden in a field.”[k] So he let them alone and did not kill them with the others. 9 Now the cistern where he threw all the bodies of the men he had killed along with Gedaliah was the one King Asa[l] had made as part of his defense[m] against Baasha[n] king of Israel. Ishmael son of Nethaniah filled it with the dead.

10 Ishmael made captives of all the rest of the people[o] who were in Mizpah—the king’s daughters along with all the others who were left there, over whom Nebuzaradan commander of the imperial guard had appointed Gedaliah son of Ahikam. Ishmael son of Nethaniah took them captive and set out to cross over to the Ammonites.[p]

11 When Johanan[q] son of Kareah and all the army officers who were with him heard about all the crimes Ishmael son of Nethaniah had committed, 12 they took all their men and went to fight Ishmael son of Nethaniah. They caught up with him near the great pool[r] in Gibeon. 13 When all the people[s] Ishmael had with him saw Johanan son of Kareah and the army officers who were with him, they were glad. 14 All the people Ishmael had taken captive at Mizpah turned and went over to Johanan son of Kareah. 15 But Ishmael son of Nethaniah and eight of his men escaped[t] from Johanan and fled to the Ammonites.

Jeremiah warns against entering Egypt.

16 Then Johanan son of Kareah and all the army officers who were with him led away all the survivors[u] from Mizpah whom he had recovered from Ishmael son of Nethaniah after he had assassinated Gedaliah son of Ahikam: the soldiers, women, children and court officials he had brought from Gibeon. 17 And they went on, stopping at Geruth Kimham[v] near Bethlehem on their way to Egypt[w] 18 to escape the Babylonians.[n] They were afraid[x] of them because Ishmael son of Nethaniah had killed Gedaliah[y] son of Ahikam, whom the king of Babylon had appointed as governor over the land.

42 Then all the army officers, including Johanan[z] son of Kareah and Jezaniah[o] son of Hoshaiah, and all the people from the least to the greatest[a] approached 2 Jeremiah the prophet and said to him, “Please hear our petition and pray[b] to the LORD your God for this entire remnant.[c] For as you now see, though we were once many, now only a few[d] are left. 3 Pray that the LORD your God will tell us where we should go and what we should do.”[e]

41:1 [a] Jer 40:8
41:2 [b] Ps 41:9; 109:5 [c] Jer 40:5 [d] 2Sa 3:27; 20:9-10
41:5 [e] Lev 19:27 [f] Ge 33:18; Jdg 9:1-57; 1Ki 12:1 [g] Jos 18:1 [h] 1Ki 16:24 [i] 2Ki 25:9
41:6 [j] 2Sa 3:16
41:8 [k] Isa 45:3
41:9 [l] 1Ki 15:22; 2Ch 16:6 [m] Jdg 6:2 [n] 2Ch 16:1
41:10 [o] Jer 40:7,12 [p] Jer 40:14
41:11 [q] Jer 40:8
41:12 [r] 2Sa 2:13
41:13 [s] ver 10
41:15 [t] Job 21:30; Pr 28:17
41:16 [u] Jer 43:4
41:17 [v] 2Sa 19:37 [w] Jer 42:14
41:18 [x] Isa 51:12; Jer 42:16; Lk 12:4-5 [y] Jer 40:5
42:1 [z] Jer 40:13; 41:11 [a] Jer 6:13; 44:12
42:2 [b] Jer 36:7; Ac 8:24; Jas 5:16 [c] Isa 1:9 [d] Lev 26:22; La 1:1
42:3 [e] Ps 86:11; Pr 3:6

m *3* Or *Chaldean* n *18* Or *Chaldeans* o *1* Hebrew; Septuagint (see also 43:2) *Azariah*

4“I have heard you,” replied Jeremiah the prophet. “I will certainly pray[a] to the LORD your God as you have requested; I will tell you everything the LORD says and will keep nothing back from you.”[b]

5Then they said to Jeremiah, “May the LORD be a true and faithful witness[c] against us if we do not act in accordance with everything the LORD your God sends you to tell us. 6Whether it is favorable or unfavorable, we will obey the LORD our God, to whom we are sending you, so that it will go well[d] with us, for we will obey[e] the LORD our God.”

7Ten days later the word of the LORD came to Jeremiah. 8So he called together Johanan son of Kareah and all the army officers[f] who were with him and all the people from the least to the greatest. 9He said to them, “This is what the LORD, the God of Israel, to whom you sent me to present your petition, says:[g] 10‘If you stay in this land, I will build[h] you up and not tear you down; I will plant[i] you and not uproot you,[j] for I am grieved over the disaster I have inflicted on you.[k] 11Do not be afraid of the king of Babylon,[l] whom you now fear.[m] Do not be afraid of him, declares the LORD, for I am with you and will save[n] you and deliver you from his hands.[o] 12I will show you compassion so that he will have compassion on you and restore you to your land.’[p]

13“However, if you say, ‘We will not stay in this land,’ and so disobey[q] the LORD your God, 14and if you say, ‘No, we will go and live in Egypt,[r] where we will not see war or hear the trumpet or be hungry for bread,’ 15then hear the word of the LORD, O remnant of Judah. This is what the LORD Almighty, the God of Israel, says: ‘If you are determined to go to Egypt and you do go to settle there, 16then the sword[s] you fear will overtake you there, and the famine you dread will follow you into Egypt, and there you will die. 17Indeed, all who are determined to go to Egypt to settle there will die by the sword, famine and plague;[t] not one of them will survive or escape the disaster I will bring on them.’ 18This is what the LORD Almighty, the God of Israel, says: ‘As my anger and wrath[u] have been poured out on those who lived in Jerusalem,[v] so will my wrath be poured out on you when you go to Egypt. You will be an object of cursing and horror,[w] of condemnation and reproach; you will never see this place again.’[x]

19“O remnant of Judah, the LORD has told you, ‘Do not go to Egypt.’[y] Be sure of this: I warn you today 20that you made a fatal mistake[p] when you sent me to the LORD your God and said, ‘Pray to the LORD our God for us; tell us everything he says and we will do it.’[z] 21I have told you today, but you still have not obeyed the LORD your God in all he sent me to tell you.[a] 22So now, be sure of this: You will die by the sword, famine and plague[b] in the place where you want to go to settle.”[c]

Johanan leads the remnant into Egypt.

43 When Jeremiah finished telling the people all the words of the LORD their God—everything the LORD had sent him to tell them[d]— 2Azariah son of Hoshaiah and Johanan[e] son of Kareah and all the arrogant men said to Jeremiah, “You are lying! The LORD our God has not sent you to say, ‘You must not go to Egypt to settle there.’ 3But Baruch son of Neriah is inciting you against us to hand us over to the Babylonians,[q] so they may kill us or carry us into exile to Babylon.”[f]

4So Johanan son of Kareah and all the army officers and all the people disobeyed the LORD’s command[g] to stay in the land of Judah.[h] 5Instead, Johanan son of Kareah and all the army officers led away all the remnant of Judah who had come back to live in the land of Judah from all the nations where they had been scattered.[i] 6They also led away all the men, women and children and the king’s daughters whom Nebuzaradan commander of the imperial guard had left with Gedaliah son of Ahikam, the

42:4 [a]Ex 8:29; 1Sa 12:23 [b]1Ki 22:14; 1Sa 3:17
42:5 [c]Ge 31:50
42:6 [d]Dt 5:29; 6:3; Jer 7:23 [e]Ex 24:7; Jos 24:24
42:8 [f]ver 1
42:9 [g]2Ki 22:15
42:10 [h]Jer 24:6 [i]Jer 31:28 [j]Eze 36:36 [k]Jer 18:8
42:11 [l]Jer 27:11 [m]Nu 14:9 [n]Isa 43:5 [o]Jer 1:8; Ro 8:31
42:12 [p]Ps 106:44-46
42:13 [q]Jer 44:16
42:14 [r]Nu 11:4-5
42:16 [s]Eze 11:8
42:17 [t]ver 22; Jer 44:13
42:18 [u]Dt 29:18-20; Jer 7:20 [v]2Ch 36:19; Jer 39:1-9 [w]Jer 29:18 [x]Jer 22:10
42:19 [y]Dt 17:16; Isa 30:7
42:20 [z]ver 2
42:21 [a]Eze 2:7; Zec 7:11-12
42:22 [b]ver 17; Eze 6:11 [c]Hos 9:6
43:1 [d]Jer 26:8; 42:9-22
43:2 [e]Jer 42:1
43:3 [f]Jer 38:4
43:4 [g]Jer 42:5-6 [h]Jer 42:10
43:5 [i]Jer 40:12

p20 Or *you erred in your hearts* q3 Or *Chaldeans*

son of Shaphan, and Jeremiah the prophet and Baruch son of Neriah. 7So they
entered Egypt in disobedience to the
LORD and went as far as Tahpanhes.[a]
8In Tahpanhes[b] the word of the LORD
came to Jeremiah: 9"While the Jews are
watching, take some large stones with
you and bury them in clay in the brick
pavement at the entrance to Pharaoh's
palace in Tahpanhes. 10Then say to
them, 'This is what the LORD Almighty,
the God of Israel, says: I will send for
my servant[c] Nebuchadnezzar king of
Babylon, and I will set his throne over
these stones I have buried here; he will
spread his royal canopy above them.
11He will come and attack Egypt,[d]
bringing death to those destined for
death, captivity to those destined for captivity, and the sword to those destined
for the sword.[e] 12He[r] will set fire to the
temples of the gods[f] of Egypt; he will
burn their temples and take their gods
captive. As a shepherd wraps[g] his garment around him, so will he wrap Egypt
around himself and depart from there
unscathed. 13There in the temple of the
sun[s] in Egypt he will demolish the sacred
pillars and will burn down the temples
of the gods of Egypt.'"

The Jews are punished for their idolatry.

44 This word came to Jeremiah
concerning all the Jews living
in Lower Egypt—in Migdol,[h] Tahpanhes[i]
and Memphis[t][j]—and in Upper Egypt[u]:[k]
2"This is what the LORD Almighty, the
God of Israel, says: You saw the great
disaster I brought on Jerusalem and on
all the towns of Judah. Today they lie
deserted and in ruins[l] 3because of the
evil they have done. They provoked me
to anger by burning incense and by worshiping other gods[m] that neither they
nor you nor your fathers[n] ever knew.
4Again and again[o] I sent my servants the
prophets,[p] who said, 'Do not do this
detestable thing that I hate!' 5But they
did not listen or pay attention; they did
not turn from their wickedness or stop
burning incense to other gods.[q] 6There-
fore, my fierce anger was poured out;
it raged against the towns of Judah and
the streets of Jerusalem and made them
the desolate ruins they are today.
7"Now this is what the LORD God
Almighty, the God of Israel, says: Why
bring such great disaster[r] on yourselves
by cutting off from Judah the men and
women,[s] the children and infants, and
so leave yourselves without a remnant?
8Why provoke me to anger with what
your hands have made,[t] burning incense
to other gods in Egypt, where you have
come to live?[u] You will destroy yourselves and make yourselves an object
of cursing and reproach[v] among all the
nations on earth. 9Have you forgotten
the wickedness committed by your
fathers and by the kings and queens of
Judah and the wickedness committed by
you and your wives in the land of Judah
and the streets of Jerusalem?[w] 10To this
day they have not humbled themselves
or shown reverence, nor have they followed my law[x] and the decrees I set
before you and your fathers.[y]
11"Therefore, this is what the LORD
Almighty, the God of Israel, says: I am
determined to bring disaster[z] on you
and to destroy all Judah. 12I will take
away the remnant[a] of Judah who were
determined to go to Egypt to settle
there. They will all perish in Egypt; they
will fall by the sword or die from famine. From the least to the greatest,
they will die by sword or famine.[b] They
will become an object of cursing and
horror, of condemnation and reproach.[c]
13I will punish those who live in Egypt
with the sword, famine and plague,[d] as I
punished Jerusalem. 14None of the remnant of Judah who have gone to live in
Egypt will escape or survive to return to
the land of Judah, to which they long to
return and live; none will return except
a few fugitives."[e]
15Then all the men who knew that
their wives were burning incense to

43:7 [a]Jer 2:16; 44:1
43:8 [b]Jer 2:16
43:10 [c]Isa 44:28; Jer 25:9; 27:6
43:11 [d]Jer 46:13-26; Eze 29:19-20 [e]Jer 15:2; 44:13; Zec 11:9
43:12 [f]Jer 46:25; Eze 30:13 [g]Ps 104:2; 109:18-19
44:1 [h]Ex 14:2 [i]Jer 43:7,8 [j]Isa 19:13 [k]Isa 11:11; Jer 46:14
44:2 [l]Isa 6:11; Jer 9:11; 34:22
44:3 [m]ver 8; Dt 13:6-11; 29:26 [n]Dt 32:17; Jer 19:4
44:4 [o]Jer 7:13 [p]Jer 7:25; 25:4; 26:5
44:5 [q]Jer 11:8-10
44:7 [r]Jer 26:19 [s]Jer 51:22
44:8 [t]Jer 25:6-7 [u]1Co 10:22 [v]Jer 42:18
44:9 [w]ver 17,21
44:10 [x]Jos 1:7 [y]1Ki 9:6-9
44:11 [z]Jer 21:10; Am 9:4
44:12 [a]ver 7 [b]Isa 1:28 [c]Jer 29:18; 42:15-18
44:13 [d]Jer 42:17
44:14 [e]ver 28; Jer 22:24-27; Ro 9:27

r *12* Or *I* s *13* Or *in Heliopolis* t *1* Hebrew *Noph*
u *1* Hebrew *in Pathros*

other gods, along with all the women who were present—a large assembly—and all the people living in Lower and Upper Egypt,[v] said to Jeremiah, 16“We will not listen[a] to the message you have spoken to us in the name of the LORD! 17We will certainly do everything we said we would:[b] We will burn incense to the Queen of Heaven[c] and will pour out drink offerings to her just as we and our fathers, our kings and our officials did in the towns of Judah and in the streets of Jerusalem. At that time we had plenty of food and were well off and suffered no harm.[d] 18But ever since we stopped burning incense to the Queen of Heaven and pouring out drink offerings to her, we have had nothing and have been perishing by sword and famine.[e]”

19The women added, “When we burned incense to the Queen of Heaven[f] and poured out drink offerings to her, did not our husbands know that we were making cakes like her image and pouring out drink offerings to her?”

20Then Jeremiah said to all the people, both men and women, who were answering him, 21“Did not the LORD remember[g] and think about the incense[h] burned in the towns of Judah and the streets of Jerusalem[i] by you and your fathers,[j] your kings and your officials and the people of the land? 22When the LORD could no longer endure your wicked actions and the detestable things you did, your land became an object of cursing[k] and a desolate waste without inhabitants, as it is today.[l] 23Because you have burned incense and have sinned against the LORD and have not obeyed him or followed his law or his decrees or his stipulations, this disaster[m] has come upon you, as you now see.”[n]

24Then Jeremiah said to all the people, including the women,[o] “Hear the word of the LORD, all you people of Judah in Egypt.[p] 25This is what the LORD Almighty, the God of Israel, says: You and your wives have shown by your actions what you promised when you said, ‘We will certainly carry out the vows we made to burn incense and pour out drink offerings to the Queen of Heaven.’[q]

“Go ahead then, do what you promised! Keep your vows![r] 26But hear the word of the LORD, all Jews living in Egypt: ‘I swear[s] by my great name,’ says the LORD, ‘that no one from Judah living anywhere in Egypt will ever again invoke my name or swear, “As surely as the Sovereign LORD lives.”[t] 27For I am watching over them for harm,[u] not for good; the Jews in Egypt will perish by sword and famine until they are all destroyed. 28Those who escape the sword and return to the land of Judah from Egypt will be very few.[v] Then the whole remnant of Judah who came to live in Egypt will know whose word will stand—mine or theirs.[w]

29“ ‘This will be the sign to you that I will punish you in this place,’ declares the LORD, ‘so that you will know that my threats of harm against you will surely stand.’[x] 30This is what the LORD says: ‘I am going to hand Pharaoh[y] Hophra king of Egypt over to his enemies who seek his life, just as I handed Zedekiah[z] king of Judah over to Nebuchadnezzar king of Babylon, the enemy who was seeking his life.’ ”[a]

Baruch receives God’s message.

45 This is what Jeremiah the prophet told Baruch[b] son of Neriah in the fourth year of Jehoiakim[c] son of Josiah king of Judah, after Baruch had written on a scroll the words Jeremiah was then dictating: 2“This is what the LORD, the God of Israel, says to you, Baruch: 3You said, ‘Woe to me! The LORD has added sorrow to my pain; I am worn out with groaning[d] and find no rest.’ ”

4⌊The LORD said,⌋ “Say this to him: ‘This is what the LORD says: I will overthrow what I have built and uproot what I have planted,[e] throughout the land.[f] 5Should you then seek great things for yourself? Seek them not.[g] For I will bring disaster on all people, declares the LORD,

44:16 [a]Jer 11:8-10
44:17 [b]Dt 23:23 [c]ver 25; Jer 7:18 [d]Hos 2:5-13
44:18 [e]Mal 3:13-15
44:19 [f]Jer 7:18
44:21 [g]Isa 64:9; Jer 14:10 [h]Jer 11:13 [i]ver 9 [j]Ps 79:8
44:22 [k]Jer 25:18 [l]Ge 19:13; Ps 107:33-34
44:23 [m]Jer 40:2 [n]1Ki 9:9; Jer 7:13-15; Da 9:11-12
44:24 [o]ver 15 [p]Jer 43:7
44:25 [q]ver 17 [r]Eze 20:39
44:26 [s]Ge 22:16; Isa 48:1; Heb 6:13-17 [t]Dt 32:40; Ps 50:16
44:27 [u]Jer 31:28
44:28 [v]ver 13-14; Isa 10:19 [w]ver 17,25-26
44:29 [x]Pr 19:21
44:30 [y]Jer 46:26; Eze 30:21 [z]2Ki 25:1-7 [a]Jer 39:5
45:1 [b]Jer 32:12; 36:4,18,32 [c]2Ch 36:5
45:3 [d]Ps 69:3
45:4 [e]Jer 11:17 [f]Isa 5:5-7; Jer 18:7-10
45:5 [g]Mt 6:25-27, 33

[v] *15* Hebrew *in Egypt and Pathros*

but wherever you go I will let you escape with your life.' "[a]

Message against Egypt.

46 This is the word of the LORD that came to Jeremiah the prophet concerning the nations:[b]

[2]Concerning Egypt:

This is the message against the army of Pharaoh Neco[c] king of Egypt, which was defeated at Carchemish[d] on the Euphrates River by Nebuchadnezzar king of Babylon in the fourth year of Jehoiakim[e] son of Josiah king of Judah:

[3]"Prepare your shields,[f] both large
and small,
and march out for battle!
[4]Harness the horses,
mount the steeds!
Take your positions
with helmets on!
Polish[g] your spears,
put on your armor![h]
[5]What do I see?
They are terrified,
they are retreating,
their warriors are defeated.
They flee[i] in haste
without looking back,
and there is terror[j] on every side,"
declares the LORD.
[6]"The swift cannot flee[k]
nor the strong escape.
In the north by the River Euphrates
they stumble and fall.[l]

[7]"Who is this that rises like the Nile,
like rivers of surging waters?[m]
[8]Egypt rises like the Nile,
like rivers of surging waters.
She says, 'I will rise and cover the
earth;
I will destroy cities and their
people.'
[9]Charge, O horses!
Drive furiously, O charioteers![n]
March on, O warriors—
men of Cush[w] and Put who carry
shields,
men of Lydia[o] who draw the bow.

45:5 [a]Jer 21:9; 38:2; 39:18
46:1 [b]Jer 1:10; 25:15-38
46:2 [c]2Ki 23:29 [d]2Ch 35:20 [e]Jer 45:1
46:3 [f]Isa 21:5; Jer 51:11-12
46:4 [g]Eze 21:9-11 [h]1Sa 17:5,38; 2Ch 26:14; Ne 4:16
46:5 [i]ver 21 [j]Jer 49:29
46:6 [k]Isa 30:16 [l]ver 12,16; Da 11:19
46:7 [m]Jer 47:2
46:9 [n]Jer 47:3 [o]Isa 66:19
46:10 [p]Joel 1:15 [q]Dt 32:42 [r]Zep 1:7
46:11 [s]Jer 8:22 [t]Isa 47:1 [u]Jer 30:13; Mic 1:9
46:12 [v]Isa 19:4; Na 3:8-10
46:13 [w]Isa 19:1
46:14 [x]Jer 43:8
46:15 [y]Isa 66:15-16
46:16 [z]Lev 26:37 [a]ver 6
46:17 [b]Isa 19:11-16
46:18 [c]Jer 48:15

[10]But that day[p] belongs to the Lord,
the LORD Almighty—
a day of vengeance, for vengeance
on his foes.
The sword will devour[q] till it is
satisfied,
till it has quenched its thirst with
blood.
For the Lord, the LORD Almighty, will
offer sacrifice[r]
in the land of the north by the
River Euphrates.

[11]"Go up to Gilead and get balm,[s]
O Virgin[t] Daughter of Egypt.
But you multiply remedies in vain;
there is no healing[u] for you.
[12]The nations will hear of your shame;
your cries will fill the earth.
One warrior will stumble over
another;
both will fall[v] down together."

[13]This is the message the LORD spoke
to Jeremiah the prophet about the coming of Nebuchadnezzar king of Babylon
to attack Egypt:[w]

[14]"Announce this in Egypt, and
proclaim it in Migdol;
proclaim it also in Memphis[x] and
Tahpanhes:[x]
'Take your positions and get ready,
for the sword devours those
around you.'
[15]Why will your warriors be laid low?
They cannot stand, for the LORD
will push them down.[y]
[16]They will stumble[z] repeatedly;
they will fall[a] over each other.
They will say, 'Get up, let us go back
to our own people and our native
lands,
away from the sword of the
oppressor.'
[17]There they will exclaim,
'Pharaoh king of Egypt is only a
loud noise;
he has missed his opportunity.[b]'
[18]"As surely as I live," declares the
King,[c]

[w]*9* That is, the upper Nile region [x]*14* Hebrew *Noph*; also in verse 19

whose name is the LORD Almighty,
"one will come who is like Tabor[a]
among the mountains,
like Carmel[b] by the sea.
19 Pack your belongings for exile,[c]
you who live in Egypt,
for Memphis will be laid waste
and lie in ruins without inhabitant.

20 "Egypt is a beautiful heifer,
but a gadfly is coming
against her from the north.[d]
21 The mercenaries[e] in her ranks
are like fattened calves.
They too will turn and flee[f] together,
they will not stand their ground,
for the day[g] of disaster is coming
upon them,
the time for them to be punished.
22 Egypt will hiss like a fleeing serpent
as the enemy advances in force;
they will come against her with axes,
like men who cut down trees.
23 They will chop down her forest,"
declares the LORD,
"dense though it be.
They are more numerous than
locusts,[h]
they cannot be counted.
24 The Daughter of Egypt will be put to
shame,
handed over to the people of the
north.[i]"

25 The LORD Almighty, the God of
Israel, says: "I am about to bring punishment on Amon god of Thebes,[y][j] on
Pharaoh, on Egypt and her gods[k] and
her kings, and on those who rely[l] on
Pharaoh. 26 I will hand them over[m] to
those who seek their lives, to Nebuchadnezzar king[n] of Babylon and his officers.
Later, however, Egypt will be inhabited[o]
as in times past," declares the LORD.

Israel will be preserved.

27 "Do not fear,[p] O Jacob my servant;
do not be dismayed, O Israel.
I will surely save you out of a distant
place,
your descendants from the land of
their exile.[q]
Jacob will again have peace and
security,
and no one will make him afraid.
28 Do not fear, O Jacob my servant,
for I am with you,"[r] declares the
LORD.
"Though I completely destroy[s] all the
nations
among which I scatter you,
I will not completely destroy you.
I will discipline you but only with
justice;
I will not let you go entirely
unpunished."

Message against Philistia.

47 This is the word of the LORD that came to Jeremiah the prophet concerning the Philistines before Pharaoh attacked Gaza:[t]

2 This is what the LORD says:

"See how the waters are rising in
the north;[u]
they will become an overflowing
torrent.
They will overflow the land and
everything in it,
the towns and those who live in
them.
The people will cry out;
all who dwell in the land will wail
3 at the sound of the hoofs of galloping
steeds,
at the noise of enemy chariots
and the rumble of their wheels.
Fathers will not turn to help their
children;
their hands will hang limp.
4 For the day has come
to destroy all the Philistines
and to cut off all survivors
who could help Tyre[v] and Sidon.[w]
The LORD is about to destroy the
Philistines,[x]
the remnant from the coasts of
Caphtor.[z][y]
5 Gaza will shave[z] her head in
mourning;
Ashkelon[a] will be silenced.

46:18 [a]Jos 19:22 [b]1Ki 18:42
46:19 [c]Isa 20:4
46:20 [d]ver 24; Jer 47:2
46:21 [e]2Ki 7:6 [f]ver 5 [g]Ps 37:13
46:23 [h]Jdg 7:12
46:24 [i]Jer 1:15
46:25 [j]Eze 30:14; Na 3:8 [k]Jer 43:12 [l]Isa 20:6
46:26 [m]Jer 44:30 [n]Eze 32:11 [o]Eze 29:11-16
46:27 [p]Isa 41:13; 43:5 [q]Isa 11:11; Jer 50:19
46:28 [r]Isa 8:9-10 [s]Jer 4:27
47:1 [t]Ge 10:19; Am 1:6; Zec 9:5-7
47:2 [u]Isa 8:7; 14:31
47:4 [v]Am 1:9-10; Zec 9:2-4 [w]Jer 25:22 [x]Ge 10:14; Joel 3:4 [y]Dt 2:23
47:5 [z]Jer 41:5; Mic 1:16 [a]Jer 25:20

y25 Hebrew *No* z4 That is, Crete

O remnant on the plain,
how long will you cut yourselves?

6"'Ah, sword[a] of the LORD,' ⌊you cry,⌋
'how long till you rest?
Return to your scabbard;
cease and be still.'
7But how can it rest
when the LORD has commanded it,
when he has ordered it
to attack Ashkelon and the coast?"

Message against Moab.

48:29-36pp— Isa 16:6-12

48 Concerning Moab:

This is what the LORD Almighty, the God of Israel, says:

"Woe to Nebo,[b] for it will be ruined.
Kiriathaim[c] will be disgraced and captured;
the stronghold[a] will be disgraced and shattered.
2Moab will be praised[d] no more;
in Heshbon[b][e] men will plot her downfall:
'Come, let us put an end to that nation.'
You too, O Madmen,[c] will be silenced;
the sword will pursue you.
3Listen to the cries from Horonaim,[f]
cries of great havoc and destruction.
4Moab will be broken;
her little ones will cry out.[d]
5They go up the way to Luhith,[g]
weeping bitterly as they go;
on the road down to Horonaim
anguished cries over the destruction are heard.
6Flee! Run for your lives;
become like a bush[e] in the desert.[h]
7Since you trust in your deeds and riches,
you too will be taken captive,
and Chemosh[i] will go into exile,[j]
together with his priests and officials.
8The destroyer will come against every town,
and not a town will escape.
The valley will be ruined
and the plateau destroyed,
because the LORD has spoken.
9Put salt on Moab,
for she will be laid waste[f];
her towns will become desolate,
with no one to live in them.

10"A curse on him who is lax in doing the LORD's work!
A curse on him who keeps his sword[k] from bloodshed![l]

11"Moab has been at rest[m] from youth,
like wine left on its dregs,[n]
not poured from one jar to another—
she has not gone into exile.
So she tastes as she did,
and her aroma is unchanged.
12But days are coming,"
declares the LORD,
"when I will send men who pour from jars,
and they will pour her out;
they will empty her jars
and smash her jugs.
13Then Moab will be ashamed[o] of Chemosh,
as the house of Israel was ashamed
when they trusted in Bethel.

14"How can you say, 'We are warriors,[p]
men valiant in battle'?
15Moab will be destroyed and her towns invaded;
her finest young men will go down in the slaughter,[q]"
declares the King,[r] whose name is the LORD Almighty.[s]
16"The fall of Moab is at hand;[t]
her calamity will come quickly.
17Mourn for her, all who live around her,
all who know her fame;
say, 'How broken is the mighty scepter,
how broken the glorious staff!'

47:6 [a]Jer 12:12
48:1 [b]Nu 32:38 [c]Nu 32:37
48:2 [d]Isa 16:14 [e]Nu 21:25
48:3 [f]Isa 15:5
48:5 [g]Isa 15:5
48:6 [h]Jer 17:6
48:7 [i]Nu 21:29 [j]Isa 46:1-2; Jer 49:3
48:10 [k]Jer 47:6 [l]1Ki 20:42; 2Ki 13:15-19
48:11 [m]Zec 1:15 [n]Zep 1:12
48:13 [o]Hos 10:6
48:14 [p]Ps 33:16
48:15 [q]Jer 50:27 [r]Jer 46:18 [s]Jer 51:57
48:16 [t]Isa 13:22

a*1* Or */ Misgab* b*2* The Hebrew for *Heshbon* sounds like the Hebrew for *plot.* c*2* The name of the Moabite town Madmen sounds like the Hebrew for *be silenced.* d*4* Hebrew; Septuagint */ proclaim it to Zoar* e*6* Or *like Aroer* f*9* Or *Give wings to Moab, / for she will fly away*

18“Come down from your glory
and sit on the parched ground,[a]
O inhabitants of the Daughter of Dibon,[b]
for he who destroys Moab
will come up against you
and ruin your fortified cities.[c]
19Stand by the road and watch,
you who live in Aroer.[d]
Ask the man fleeing and the woman escaping,
ask them, ‘What has happened?’
20Moab is disgraced, for she is shattered.
Wail[e] and cry out!
Announce by the Arnon[f]
that Moab is destroyed.
21Judgment has come to the plateau—
to Holon, Jahzah[g] and Mephaath,[h]
22 to Dibon,[i] Nebo and Beth Diblathaim,
23 to Kiriathaim, Beth Gamul and Beth Meon,[j]
24 to Kerioth[k] and Bozrah—
to all the towns of Moab, far and near.
25Moab’s horn[g][l] is cut off;
her arm[m] is broken,”
declares the LORD.

26“Make her drunk,[n]
for she has defied the LORD.
Let Moab wallow in her vomit;
let her be an object of ridicule.
27Was not Israel the object of your ridicule?[o]
Was she caught among thieves,
that you shake your head[p] in scorn[q]
whenever you speak of her?
28Abandon your towns and dwell among the rocks,
you who live in Moab.
Be like a dove[r] that makes its nest
at the mouth of a cave.[s]

29“We have heard of Moab’s pride[t]—
her overweening pride and conceit,
her pride and arrogance
and the haughtiness of her heart.
30I know her insolence but it is futile,”
declares the LORD,
“and her boasts accomplish nothing.

48:18 [a]Isa 47:1 [b]Nu 21:30; Jos 13:9 [c]ver 8
48:19 [d]Dt 2:36
48:20 [e]Isa 16:7 [f]Nu 21:13
48:21 [g]Nu 21:23; Isa 15:4 [h]Jos 13:18
48:22 [i]Jos 13:9,17
48:23 [j]Jos 13:17
48:24 [k]Am 2:2
48:25 [l]Ps 75:10 [m]Ps 10:15; Eze 30:21
48:26 [n]Jer 25:16,27
48:27 [o]Jer 2:26 [p]Job 16:4; Jer 18:16 [q]Mic 7:8-10
48:28 [r]Ps 55:6-7 [s]Jdg 6:2
48:29 [t]Job 40:12; Isa 16:6
48:31 [u]Isa 15:5-8 [v]2Ki 3:25
48:32 [w]Isa 16:8-9
48:33 [x]Isa 16:10 [y]Joel 1:12
48:34 [z]Nu 32:3 [a]Isa 15:4 [b]Ge 13:10 [c]Isa 15:5 [d]Isa 15:6
48:35 [e]Isa 15:2; 16:12 [f]Jer 11:13
48:36 [g]Isa 16:11 [h]Isa 15:7
48:37 [i]Isa 15:2; Jer 41:5 [j]Ge 37:34
48:38 [k]Jer 22:28

31Therefore I wail[u] over Moab,
for all Moab I cry out,
I moan for the men of Kir Hareseth.[v]
32I weep for you, as Jazer weeps,
O vines of Sibmah.[w]
Your branches spread as far as the sea;
they reached as far as the sea of Jazer.
The destroyer has fallen
on your ripened fruit and grapes.
33Joy and gladness are gone
from the orchards and fields of Moab.
I have stopped the flow of wine[x]
from the presses;
no one treads them with shouts of joy.[y]
Although there are shouts,
they are not shouts of joy.

34“The sound of their cry rises
from Heshbon to Elealeh[z] and Jahaz,[a]
from Zoar[b] as far as Horonaim[c] and Eglath Shelishiyah,
for even the waters of Nimrim are dried up.[d]
35In Moab I will put an end
to those who make offerings on the high places[e]
and burn incense[f] to their gods,”
declares the LORD.
36“So my heart laments[g] for Moab like a flute;
it laments like a flute for the men of Kir Hareseth.
The wealth they acquired[h] is gone.
37Every head is shaved[i]
and every beard cut off;
every hand is slashed
and every waist is covered with sackcloth.[j]
38On all the roofs in Moab
and in the public squares
there is nothing but mourning,
for I have broken Moab
like a jar[k] that no one wants,”
declares the LORD.
39“How shattered she is! How they wail!

g25 *Horn* here symbolizes strength.

How Moab turns her back in shame!
Moab has become an object of ridicule,
an object of horror to all those around her."

40This is what the LORD says:

"Look! An eagle is swooping[a] down,
spreading its wings[b] over Moab.
41Kerioth[h] will be captured
and the strongholds taken.
In that day the hearts of Moab's warriors
will be like the heart of a woman in labor.[c]
42Moab will be destroyed[d] as a nation[e]
because she defied[f] the LORD.
43Terror and pit and snare[g] await you,
O people of Moab,"
declares the LORD.
44"Whoever flees[h] from the terror
will fall into a pit,
whoever climbs out of the pit
will be caught in a snare;
for I will bring upon Moab
the year[i] of her punishment,"
declares the LORD.

45"In the shadow of Heshbon
the fugitives stand helpless,
for a fire has gone out from Heshbon,
a blaze from the midst of Sihon;[j]
it burns the foreheads of Moab,
the skulls[k] of the noisy boasters.
46Woe to you, O Moab![l]
The people of Chemosh are destroyed;
your sons are taken into exile
and your daughters into captivity.

47"Yet I will restore[m] the fortunes of Moab
in days to come,"
declares the LORD.

Here ends the judgment on Moab.

Message against Ammon.

49 Concerning the Ammonites:[n]
This is what the LORD says:

"Has Israel no sons?
Has she no heirs?
Why then has Molech[i] taken possession of Gad?
Why do his people live in its towns?
2But the days are coming,"
declares the LORD,
"when I will sound the battle cry[o]
against Rabbah[p] of the Ammonites;
it will become a mound of ruins,
and its surrounding villages will be set on fire.
Then Israel will drive out
those who drove her out,[q]"
says the LORD.
3"Wail, O Heshbon, for Ai[r] is destroyed!
Cry out, O inhabitants of Rabbah!
Put on sackcloth and mourn;
rush here and there inside the walls,
for Molech will go into exile,[s]
together with his priests and officials.
4Why do you boast of your valleys,
boast of your valleys so fruitful?
O unfaithful daughter,
you trust in your riches[t] and say,
'Who will attack me?'[u]
5I will bring terror on you
from all those around you,"
declares the Lord,
the LORD Almighty.
"Every one of you will be driven away,
and no one will gather the fugitives.

6"Yet afterward, I will restore[v] the fortunes of the Ammonites,"
declares the LORD.

Message against Edom.

49:9-10pp— Ob 5-6
49:14-16pp— Ob 1-4

7Concerning Edom:[w]

This is what the LORD Almighty says:

"Is there no longer wisdom in Teman?[x]
Has counsel perished from the prudent?
Has their wisdom decayed?
8Turn and flee, hide in deep caves,
you who live in Dedan,[y]

48:40 [a]Dt 28:49; Hab 1:8 [b]Isa 8:8
48:41 [c]Isa 21:3
48:42 [d]Ps 83:4; Isa 16:14 [e]ver 2 [f]ver 26
48:43 [g]Isa 24:17
48:44 [h]1Ki 19:17; Isa 24:18 [i]Jer 11:23
48:45 [j]Nu 21:21, 26-28 [k]Nu 24:17
48:46 [l]Nu 21:29
48:47 [m]Jer 12:15; 49:6,39
49:1 [n]Am 1:13; Zep 2:8-9
49:2 [o]Jer 4:19 [p]Dt 3:11 [q]Isa 14:2; Eze 21:28-32; 25:2-11
49:3 [r]Jos 8:28 [s]Jer 48:7
49:4 [t]Jer 9:23; 1Ti 6:17 [u]Jer 21:13
49:6 [v]ver 39; Jer 48:47
49:7 [w]Ge 25:30; Eze 25:12 [x]Ge 36:11,15, 34
49:8 [y]Jer 25:23

h*41* Or *The cities* i*1* Or *their king*; Hebrew *malcam*; also in verse 3

for I will bring disaster on Esau
at the time I punish him.
9If grape pickers came to you,
would they not leave a few grapes?
If thieves came during the night,
would they not steal only as much
as they wanted?
10But I will strip Esau bare;
I will uncover his hiding places,
so that he cannot conceal himself.
His children, relatives and neighbors
will perish,
and he will be no more.[a]
11Leave your orphans;[b] I will protect
their lives.
Your widows too can trust in me."

12This is what the LORD says: "If those
who do not deserve to drink the cup[c]
must drink it, why should you go unpunished?[d] You will not go unpunished, but
must drink it. 13I swear[e] by myself,"
declares the LORD, "that Bozrah[f] will
become a ruin and an object of horror,
of reproach and of cursing; and all its
towns will be in ruins forever."

14I have heard a message from the
LORD:
An envoy was sent to the nations
to say,
"Assemble yourselves to attack it!
Rise up for battle!"

15"Now I will make you small among
the nations,
despised among men.
16The terror you inspire
and the pride of your heart have
deceived you,
you who live in the clefts of the
rocks,
who occupy the heights of the
hill.
Though you build your nest[g] as
high as the eagle's,
from there I will bring you down,"
declares the LORD.
17"Edom will become an object of
horror;[h]
all who pass by will be appalled and
will scoff
because of all its wounds.[i]

49:10 [a]Mal 1:2-5
49:11 [b]Hos 14:3
49:12 [c]Jer 25:15 [d]Jer 25:28-29
49:13 [e]Ge 22:16 [f]Ge 36:33; Isa 34:6
49:16 [g]Job 39:27; Am 9:2
49:17 [h]ver 13 [i]Jer 50:13; Eze 35:7
49:18 [j]Ge 19:24; Dt 29:23 [k]ver 33
49:19 [l]Jer 12:5 [m]Jer 50:44
49:20 [n]Isa 14:27 [o]Jer 50:45 [p]Mal 1:3-4
49:21 [q]Eze 26:15 [r]Jer 50:46; Eze 26:18
49:22 [s]Hos 8:1 [t]Isa 13:8; Jer 48:40-41
49:23 [u]Ge 14:15; 2Ch 16:2; Ac 9:2 [v]Isa 10:9; Am 6:2; Zec 9:2 [w]2Ki 18:34 [x]Ge 49:4; Isa 57:20

18As Sodom and Gomorrah[j] were
overthrown,
along with their neighboring
towns,"
says the LORD,
"so no one will live there;
no man will dwell[k] in it.

19"Like a lion coming up from Jordan's
thickets[l]
to a rich pastureland,
I will chase Edom from its land in an
instant.
Who is the chosen one I will
appoint for this?
Who is like me and who can
challenge me?[m]
And what shepherd can stand
against me?"
20Therefore, hear what the LORD has
planned against Edom,
what he has purposed[n] against
those who live in Teman:
The young of the flock[o] will be
dragged away;
he will completely destroy[p] their
pasture because of them.
21At the sound of their fall the earth
will tremble;[q]
their cry[r] will resound to the Red
Sea.[j]
22Look! An eagle will soar and swoop[s]
down,
spreading its wings over Bozrah.
In that day the hearts of Edom's
warriors
will be like the heart of a woman
in labor.[t]

Message against Damascus.

23Concerning Damascus:[u]

"Hamath[v] and Arpad[w] are dismayed,
for they have heard bad news.
They are disheartened,
troubled like[k] the restless sea.[x]
24Damascus has become feeble,
she has turned to flee
and panic has gripped her;
anguish and pain have seized her,
pain like that of a woman in labor.

j *21* Hebrew *Yam Suph*; that is, Sea of Reeds
k *23* Hebrew *on* or *by*

25Why has the city of renown not been abandoned,
the town in which I delight?
26Surely, her young men will fall in the streets;
all her soldiers will be silenced[a] in that day,"
declares the LORD Almighty.
27"I will set fire[b] to the walls of Damascus;
it will consume the fortresses of Ben-Hadad.[c]"

Message against Kedar and Hazor.

28Concerning Kedar[d] and the kingdoms of Hazor, which Nebuchadnezzar king of Babylon attacked:

This is what the LORD says:

"Arise, and attack Kedar
and destroy the people of the East.[e]
29Their tents and their flocks will be taken;
their shelters will be carried off
with all their goods and camels.
Men will shout to them,
'Terror[f] on every side!'

30"Flee quickly away!
Stay in deep caves, you who live in Hazor,"
declares the LORD.
"Nebuchadnezzar king of Babylon has plotted against you;
he has devised a plan against you.

31"Arise and attack a nation at ease,
which lives in confidence,"
declares the LORD,
"a nation that has neither gates nor bars;[g]
its people live alone.
32Their camels will become plunder,
and their large herds will be booty.
I will scatter to the winds those who are in distant places[l][h]
and will bring disaster on them from every side,"
declares the LORD.
33"Hazor will become a haunt of jackals,
a desolate[i] place forever.
No one will live there;
no man will dwell[j] in it."

Message against Elam.

34This is the word of the LORD that
came to Jeremiah the prophet concerning Elam,[k] early in the reign of Zedekiah[l] king of Judah:

35This is what the LORD Almighty says:

"See, I will break the bow[m] of Elam,
the mainstay of their might.
36I will bring against Elam the four winds[n]
from the four quarters of the heavens;
I will scatter them to the four winds,
and there will not be a nation
where Elam's exiles do not go.
37I will shatter Elam before their foes,
before those who seek their lives;
I will bring disaster upon them,
even my fierce anger,"[o]
declares the LORD.
"I will pursue them with the sword[p]
until I have made an end of them.
38I will set my throne in Elam
and destroy her king and officials,"
declares the LORD.

39"Yet I will restore[q] the fortunes of Elam
in days to come,"
declares the LORD.

Destruction of Babylon and restoration of Israel.

51:15-19pp—Jer 10:12-16

50 This is the word the LORD spoke
through Jeremiah the prophet
concerning Babylon[r] and the land of
the Babylonians[m]:

2"Announce and proclaim[s] among the nations,
lift up a banner and proclaim it;
keep nothing back, but say,
'Babylon will be captured;[t]
Bel[u] will be put to shame,
Marduk[v] filled with terror.

49:26 [a]Jer 50:30
49:27 [b]Jer 43:12; Am 1:4 [c]1Ki 15:18
49:28 [d]Ge 25:13 [e]Jdg 6:3
49:29 [f]Jer 6:25; 46:5
49:31 [g]Eze 38:11
49:32 [h]Jer 9:26
49:33 [i]Jer 10:22 [j]ver 18; Jer 51:37
49:34 [k]Ge 10:22 [l]2Ki 24:18
49:35 [m]Isa 22:6
49:36 [n]ver 32
49:37 [o]Jer 30:24 [p]Jer 9:16
49:39 [q]Jer 48:47
50:1 [r]Ge 10:10; Isa 13:1
50:2 [s]Jer 4:16 [t]Jer 51:31 [u]Isa 46:1 [v]Jer 51:47

l32 Or *who clip the hair by their foreheads* m1 Or *Chaldeans*; also in verses 8, 25, 35 and 45

Her images will be put to shame
and her idols filled with terror.'
3A nation from the north will attack her
and lay waste her land.
No one will live[a] in it;
both men and animals[b] will flee away.

4"In those days, at that time,"
declares the LORD,
"the people of Israel and the people of Judah together[c]
will go in tears[d] to seek[e] the LORD their God.
5They will ask the way to Zion
and turn their faces toward it.
They will come[f] and bind themselves to the LORD
in an everlasting covenant[g]
that will not be forgotten.

6"My people have been lost sheep;[h]
their shepherds have led them astray
and caused them to roam on the mountains.
They wandered over mountain and hill[i]
and forgot their own resting place.[j]
7Whoever found them devoured them;
their enemies said, 'We are not guilty,[k]
for they sinned against the LORD,
their true pasture,
the LORD, the hope[l] of their fathers.'

8"Flee[m] out of Babylon;
leave the land of the Babylonians,
and be like the goats that lead the flock.
9For I will stir up and bring against Babylon
an alliance of great nations from the land of the north.
They will take up their positions against her,
and from the north she will be captured.
Their arrows will be like skilled warriors
who do not return empty-handed.

50:3 [a]ver 13; Isa 14:22-23 [b]Zep 1:3
50:4 [c]Jer 3:18; Hos 1:11 [d]Ezr 3:12; Jer 31:9 [e]Hos 3:5
50:5 [f]Jer 33:7 [g]Isa 55:3; Jer 32:40; Heb 8:6-10
50:6 [h]Isa 53:6; Mt 9:36; 10:6 [i]Jer 3:6; Eze 34:6 [j]ver 19
50:7 [k]Jer 2:3 [l]Jer 14:8
50:8 [m]Isa 48:20; Jer 51:6; Rev 18:4
50:11 [n]Isa 47:6
50:13 [o]Jer 18:16 [p]Jer 49:17
50:14 [q]ver 29,42
50:15 [r]Jer 51:14 [s]Jer 51:44,58 [t]Jer 51:6 [u]Ps 137:8; Rev 18:6
50:16 [v]Jer 25:38 [w]Isa 13:14 [x]Jer 51:9
50:17 [y]Jer 2:15 [z]2Ki 17:6 [a]2Ki 24:10,14 [b]2Ki 25:7

10So Babylonia[n] will be plundered;
all who plunder her will have their fill,"
declares the LORD.

11"Because you rejoice and are glad,
you who pillage my inheritance,[n]
because you frolic like a heifer threshing grain
and neigh like stallions,
12your mother will be greatly ashamed;
she who gave you birth will be disgraced.
She will be the least of the nations—
a wilderness, a dry land, a desert.
13Because of the LORD's anger she will not be inhabited
but will be completely desolate.
All who pass Babylon will be horrified and scoff[o]
because of all her wounds.[p]

14"Take up your positions around Babylon,
all you who draw the bow.[q]
Shoot at her! Spare no arrows,
for she has sinned against the LORD.
15Shout[r] against her on every side!
She surrenders, her towers fall,
her walls[s] are torn down.
Since this is the vengeance[t] of the LORD,
take vengeance on her;
do to her[u] as she has done to others.
16Cut off from Babylon the sower,
and the reaper with his sickle at harvest.
Because of the sword[v] of the oppressor
let everyone return to his own people,[w]
let everyone flee to his own land.[x]

17"Israel is a scattered flock
that lions[y] have chased away.
The first to devour him
was the king[z] of Assyria;
the last to crush his bones
was Nebuchadnezzar[a] king[b] of Babylon."

18Therefore this is what the LORD Almighty, the God of Israel, says:

[n]10 Or *Chaldea*

"I will punish the king of Babylon
and his land
as I punished the king[a] of Assyria.[b]
19But I will bring[c] Israel back to his
own pasture
and he will graze on Carmel and
Bashan;
his appetite will be satisfied
on the hills[d] of Ephraim and Gilead.
20In those days, at that time,"
declares the LORD,
"search will be made for Israel's guilt,
but there will be none,
and for the sins[e] of Judah,
but none will be found,
for I will forgive[f] the remnant[g] I
spare.

21"Attack the land of Merathaim
and those who live in Pekod.[h]
Pursue, kill and completely destroy[o]
them,"
declares the LORD.
"Do everything I have commanded
you.
22The noise[i] of battle is in the land,
the noise of great destruction!
23How broken and shattered
is the hammer of the whole earth!
How desolate[j] is Babylon
among the nations!
24I set a trap[k] for you, O Babylon,
and you were caught before you
knew it;
you were found and captured[l]
because you opposed[m] the LORD.
25The LORD has opened his arsenal
and brought out the weapons[n] of
his wrath,
for the Sovereign LORD Almighty has
work to do
in the land of the Babylonians.[o]
26Come against her from afar.
Break open her granaries;
pile her up like heaps of grain.
Completely destroy[p] her
and leave her no remnant.
27Kill all her young bulls;
let them go down to the slaughter!
Woe to them! For their day has
come,
the time for them to be punished.
28Listen to the fugitives and refugees
from Babylon
declaring in Zion[q]
how the LORD our God has taken
vengeance,[r]
vengeance for his temple.

29"Summon archers against Babylon,
all those who draw the bow.[s]
Encamp all around her;
let no one escape.
Repay[t] her for her deeds;[u]
do to her as she has done.
For she has defied[v] the LORD,
the Holy One of Israel.
30Therefore, her young men[w] will fall
in the streets;
all her soldiers will be silenced in
that day,"
declares the LORD.
31"See, I am against[x] you, O arrogant
one,"
declares the Lord, the LORD
Almighty,
"for your day has come,
the time for you to be punished.
32The arrogant one will stumble and fall
and no one will help her up;
I will kindle a fire[y] in her towns
that will consume all who are
around her."

33This is what the LORD Almighty says:

"The people of Israel are oppressed,[z]
and the people of Judah as well.
All their captors hold them fast,
refusing to let them go.[a]
34Yet their Redeemer is strong;
the LORD Almighty[b] is his name.
He will vigorously defend their cause[c]
so that he may bring rest[d] to their
land,
but unrest to those who live in
Babylon.

35"A sword[e] against the Babylonians!"
declares the LORD—
"against those who live in Babylon
and against her officials and wise[f]
men!

50:18 [a]Isa 10:12 [b]Eze 31:3
50:19 [c]Jer 31:10; Eze 34:13 [d]Jer 31:5; 33:12
50:20 [e]Mic 7:18,19 [f]Jer 31:34 [g]Isa 1:9
50:21 [h]Eze 23:23
50:22 [i]Jer 4:19-21; 51:54
50:23 [j]Isa 14:16
50:24 [k]Da 5:30-31 [l]Jer 51:31 [m]Job 9:4
50:25 [n]Isa 13:5 [o]Jer 51:25,55
50:26 [p]Isa 14:22-23
50:28 [q]Isa 48:20; Jer 51:10 [r]ver 15
50:29 [s]ver 14 [t]Rev 18:6 [u]Jer 51:56 [v]Isa 47:10
50:30 [w]Isa 13:18; Jer 49:26
50:31 [x]Jer 21:13
50:32 [y]Jer 21:14; 49:27
50:33 [z]Isa 58:6 [a]Isa 14:17
50:34 [b]Jer 51:19 [c]Jer 15:21; 51:36 [d]Isa 14:7
50:35 [e]Jer 47:6 [f]Da 5:7

[o]*21* The Hebrew term refers to the irrevocable giving over of things or persons to the LORD, often by totally destroying them; also in verse 26.

36A sword against her false prophets!
They will become fools.
A sword against her warriors![a]
They will be filled with terror.
37A sword against her horses and chariots[b]
and all the foreigners in her ranks!
They will become women.[c]
A sword against her treasures!
They will be plundered.
38A drought on[p] her waters!
They will dry[d] up.
For it is a land of idols,[e]
idols that will go mad with terror.

39"So desert creatures and hyenas will live there,
and there the owl will dwell.
It will never again be inhabited
or lived in from generation to generation.[f]
40As God overthrew Sodom and Gomorrah[g]
along with their neighboring towns,"
declares the LORD,
"so no one will live there;
no man will dwell in it.

41"Look! An army is coming from the north;[h]
a great nation and many kings
are being stirred up from the ends of the earth.[i]
42They are armed with bows[j] and spears;
they are cruel and without mercy.[k]
They sound like the roaring sea[l]
as they ride on their horses;
they come like men in battle formation
to attack you, O Daughter of Babylon.[m]
43The king of Babylon has heard reports about them,
and his hands hang limp.
Anguish has gripped him,
pain like that of a woman in labor.
44Like a lion coming up from Jordan's thickets
to a rich pastureland,
I will chase Babylon from its land in an instant.

50:36 [a]Jer 49:22
50:37 [b]Jer 51:21 [c]Jer 51:30; Na 3:13
50:38 [d]Jer 51:36 [e]ver 2
50:39 [f]Isa 13:19-22; 34:13-15; Jer 51:37; Rev 18:2
50:40 [g]Ge 19:24
50:41 [h]Jer 6:22 [i]Isa 13:4; Jer 51:22-28
50:42 [j]ver 14 [k]Isa 13:18 [l]Isa 5:30 [m]Jer 6:23
50:44 [n]Nu 16:5 [o]Job 41:10; Isa 46:9; Jer 49:19
50:45 [p]Ps 33:11; Isa 14:24; Jer 51:11
50:46 [q]Rev 18:9-10
51:2 [r]Isa 41:16; Jer 15:7; Mt 3:12
51:3 [s]Jer 50:29 [t]Jer 46:4
51:4 [u]Isa 13:15 [v]Jer 49:26; 50:30
51:5 [w]Isa 54:6-8 [x]Hos 4:1
51:6 [y]Jer 50:8 [z]Nu 16:26; Rev 18:4

Who is the chosen[n] one I will appoint for this?
Who is like me and who can challenge me?[o]
And what shepherd can stand against me?"
45Therefore, hear what the LORD has planned against Babylon,
what he has purposed[p] against the land of the Babylonians:
The young of the flock will be dragged away;
he will completely destroy their pasture because of them.
46At the sound of Babylon's capture
the earth will tremble;
its cry[q] will resound among the nations.

51

This is what the LORD says:
"See, I will stir up the spirit of a destroyer
against Babylon and the people of Leb Kamai.[q]
2I will send foreigners to Babylon
to winnow[r] her and to devastate her land;
they will oppose her on every side
in the day of her disaster.
3Let not the archer string his bow,[s]
nor let him put on his armor.[t]
Do not spare her young men;
completely destroy[r] her army.
4They will fall[u] down slain in Babylon,[s]
fatally wounded in her streets.[v]
5For Israel and Judah have not been forsaken[w]
by their God, the LORD Almighty,
though their land[t] is full of guilt[x]
before the Holy One of Israel.

6"Flee[y] from Babylon!
Run for your lives!
Do not be destroyed because of her sins.[z]

p38 Or *A sword against* q1 *Leb Kamai* is a cryptogram for Chaldea, that is, Babylonia.
r3 The Hebrew term refers to the irrevocable giving over of things or persons to the LORD, often by totally destroying them. s4 Or *Chaldea* t5 Or */ and the land ⌊of the Babylonians⌋*

It is time for the LORD's vengeance;[a]
he will pay[b] her what she deserves.
7Babylon was a gold cup[c] in the LORD's hand;
she made the whole earth drunk.
The nations drank her wine;
therefore they have now gone mad.
8Babylon will suddenly fall[d] and be broken.
Wail over her!
Get balm[e] for her pain;
perhaps she can be healed.

9" 'We would have healed Babylon,
but she cannot be healed;
let us leave[f] her and each go to his own land,
for her judgment[g] reaches to the skies,
it rises as high as the clouds.'

10" 'The LORD has vindicated[h] us;
come, let us tell in Zion
what the LORD our God has done.'[i]

11"Sharpen the arrows,[j]
take up the shields![k]
The LORD has stirred up the kings of the Medes,[l]
because his purpose[m] is to destroy Babylon.
The LORD will take vengeance,
vengeance for his temple.[n]
12Lift up a banner against the walls of Babylon!
Reinforce the guard,
station the watchmen,
prepare an ambush!
The LORD will carry out his purpose,
his decree against the people of Babylon.
13You who live by many waters[o]
and are rich in treasures,[p]
your end has come,
the time for you to be cut off.
14The LORD Almighty has sworn by himself:[q]
I will surely fill you with men, as with a swarm of locusts,[r]
and they will shout[s] in triumph over you.

15"He made the earth by his power;
he founded the world by his wisdom
and stretched[t] out the heavens by his understanding.
16When he thunders,[u] the waters in the heavens roar;
he makes clouds rise from the ends of the earth.
He sends lightning with the rain
and brings out the wind from his storehouses.[v]

17"Every man is senseless and without knowledge;
every goldsmith is shamed by his idols.
His images are a fraud;[w]
they have no breath in them.
18They are worthless,[x] the objects of mockery;
when their judgment comes, they will perish.
19He who is the Portion of Jacob is not like these,
for he is the Maker of all things,
including the tribe of his inheritance—
the LORD Almighty is his name.

20"You are my war club,[y]
my weapon for battle—
with you I shatter[z] nations,
with you I destroy kingdoms,
21with you I shatter horse and rider,[a]
with you I shatter chariot and driver,
22with you I shatter man and woman,
with you I shatter old man and youth,
with you I shatter young man and maiden,[b]
23with you I shatter shepherd and flock,
with you I shatter farmer and oxen,
with you I shatter governors and officials.[c]

24"Before your eyes I will repay[d] Babylon and all who live in Babylonia[u] for all the wrong they have done in Zion," declares the LORD.

25"I am against you, O destroying mountain,
you who destroy the whole earth,"
declares the LORD.

51:6 [a]Jer 50:15 [b]Jer 25:14
51:7 [c]Jer 25:15-16; Rev 14:8-10; 17:4
51:8 [d]Isa 21:9; Rev 14:8 [e]Jer 46:11
51:9 [f]Isa 13:14; Jer 50:16 [g]Rev 18:4-5
51:10 [h]Mic 7:9 [i]Jer 50:28
51:11 [j]Jer 50:9 [k]Jer 46:4 [l]ver 28 [m]Jer 50:45 [n]Jer 50:28
51:13 [o]Rev 17:1,15 [p]Isa 45:3; Hab 2:9
51:14 [q]Am 6:8 [r]ver 27; Na 3:15 [s]Jer 50:15
51:15 [t]Ge 1:1; Job 9:8; Ps 104:2
51:16 [u]Ps 18:11-13 [v]Ps 135:7; Jnh 1:4
51:17 [w]Isa 44:20; Hab 2:18-19
51:18 [x]Jer 18:15
51:20 [y]Isa 10:5 [z]Mic 4:13
51:21 [a]Ex 15:1
51:22 [b]2Ch 36:17; Isa 13:17-18
51:23 [c]ver 57
51:24 [d]Jer 50:15

[u] *24* Or *Chaldea*; also in verse 35

"I will stretch out my hand against
you,
roll you off the cliffs,
and make you a burned-out
mountain.[a]
26No rock will be taken from you for a
cornerstone,
nor any stone for a foundation,
for you will be desolate[b] forever,"
declares the LORD.

27"Lift up a banner[c] in the land!
Blow the trumpet among the
nations!
Prepare the nations for battle against
her;
summon against her these
kingdoms:[d]
Ararat,[e] Minni and Ashkenaz.[f]
Appoint a commander against her;
send up horses like a swarm of
locusts.
28Prepare the nations for battle against
her—
the kings of the Medes,[g]
their governors and all their officials,
and all the countries they rule.
29The land trembles and writhes,
for the LORD's purposes against
Babylon stand—
to lay waste the land of Babylon
so that no one will live there.[h]
30Babylon's warriors[i] have stopped
fighting;
they remain in their strongholds.
Their strength is exhausted;
they have become like women.[j]
Her dwellings are set on fire;
the bars[k] of her gates are broken.
31One courier[l] follows another
and messenger follows messenger
to announce to the king of Babylon
that his entire city is captured,
32the river crossings seized,
the marshes set on fire,
and the soldiers terrified.[m]"

33This is what the LORD Almighty, the
God of Israel, says:

"The Daughter of Babylon is like a
threshing floor[n]
at the time it is trampled;
the time to harvest[o] her will soon
come."

34"Nebuchadnezzar[p] king of Babylon
has devoured us,
he has thrown us into confusion,
he has made us an empty jar.
Like a serpent he has swallowed us
and filled his stomach with our
delicacies,
and then has spewed us out.
35May the violence done to our flesh[v]
be upon Babylon,"
say the inhabitants of Zion.
"May our blood be on those who live
in Babylonia,"
says Jerusalem.[q]

36Therefore, this is what the LORD
says:

"See, I will defend your cause[r]
and avenge[s] you;
I will dry up[t] her sea
and make her springs dry.
37Babylon will be a heap of ruins,
a haunt[u] of jackals,
an object of horror and scorn,
a place where no one lives.[v]
38Her people all roar like young lions,
they growl like lion cubs.
39But while they are aroused,
I will set out a feast for them
and make them drunk,
so that they shout with laughter—
then sleep forever and not awake,"
declares the LORD.[w]
40"I will bring them down
like lambs to the slaughter,
like rams and goats.

41"How Sheshach[w][x] will be captured,[y]
the boast of the whole earth seized!
What a horror Babylon will be
among the nations!
42The sea will rise over Babylon;
its roaring waves[z] will cover her.
43Her towns will be desolate,
a dry and desert land,
a land where no one lives,
through which no man travels.[a]

51:25 [a]Zec 4:7
51:26 [b]ver 29; Isa 13:19-22; Jer 50:12
51:27 [c]Isa 13:2; Jer 50:2 [d]Jer 25:14 [e]Ge 8:4 [f]Ge 10:3
51:28 [g]ver 11
51:29 [h]ver 43; Isa 13:20
51:30 [i]Jer 50:36 [j]Isa 19:16 [k]Isa 45:2; La 2:9; Na 3:13
51:31 [l]2Sa 18:19-31
51:32 [m]Jer 50:36
51:33 [n]Isa 21:10 [o]Isa 17:5; Hos 6:11
51:34 [p]Jer 50:17
51:35 [q]ver 24; Ps 137:8
51:36 [r]Ps 140:12; Jer 50:34; La 3:58 [s]ver 6; Ro 12:19 [t]Jer 50:38
51:37 [u]Isa 13:22; Rev 18:2 [v]Jer 50:13,39
51:39 [w]ver 57
51:41 [x]Jer 25:26 [y]Isa 13:19
51:42 [z]Isa 8:7
51:43 [a]ver 29,62; Isa 13:20; Jer 2:6

v35 Or *done to us and to our children*
w41 *Sheshach* is a cryptogram for Babylon.

44I will punish Bel[a] in Babylon
and make him spew out[b] what he has swallowed.
The nations will no longer stream to him.
And the wall[c] of Babylon will fall.

45"Come out[d] of her, my people!
Run[e] for your lives!
Run from the fierce anger of the LORD.
46Do not lose heart or be afraid[f]
when rumors[g] are heard in the land;
one rumor comes this year, another the next,
rumors of violence in the land
and of ruler against ruler.
47For the time will surely come
when I will punish the idols[h] of Babylon;
her whole land will be disgraced[i]
and her slain will all lie fallen within her.
48Then heaven and earth and all that is in them
will shout[j] for joy over Babylon,
for out of the north[k]
destroyers will attack her,"
declares the LORD.

49"Babylon must fall because of Israel's slain,
just as the slain in all the earth
have fallen because of Babylon.[l]
50You who have escaped the sword,
leave[m] and do not linger!
Remember[n] the LORD in a distant land,
and think on Jerusalem."

51"We are disgraced,[o]
for we have been insulted
and shame covers our faces,
because foreigners have entered
the holy places of the LORD's house."[p]

52"But days are coming," declares the LORD,
"when I will punish her idols,[q]
and throughout her land
the wounded will groan.
53Even if Babylon reaches the sky[r]
and fortifies her lofty stronghold,
I will send destroyers[s] against her,"
declares the LORD.

51:44 [a]Isa 46:1 [b]ver 34 [c]ver 58; Jer 50:15
51:45 [d]Rev 18:4 [e]ver 6; Isa 48:20; Jer 50:8
51:46 [f]Jer 46:27 [g]2Ki 19:7
51:47 [h]ver 52; Isa 46:1-2; Jer 50:2 [i]Jer 50:12
51:48 [j]Isa 44:23; Rev 18:20 [k]ver 11
51:49 [l]Ps 137:8; Jer 50:29
51:50 [m]ver 45 [n]Ps 137:6
51:51 [o]Ps 44:13-16; 79:4 [p]La 1:10
51:52 [q]ver 47
51:53 [r]Ge 11:4; Isa 14:13-14 [s]Jer 49:16
51:54 [t]Jer 50:22
51:55 [u]Ps 18:4
51:56 [v]ver 48 [w]Ps 46:9 [x]ver 6; Ps 94:1-2; Hab 2:8
51:57 [y]Ps 76:5; Jer 25:27 [z]Jer 46:18; 48:15
51:58 [a]ver 44 [b]ver 64 [c]Hab 2:13
51:59 [d]Jer 36:4 [e]Jer 52:1 [f]Jer 28:1
51:60 [g]Jer 30:2; 36:2
51:62 [h]Isa 13:20; Jer 50:13,39

54"The sound of a cry comes from Babylon,
the sound of great destruction[t]
from the land of the Babylonians.[x]
55The LORD will destroy Babylon;
he will silence her noisy din.
Waves[u] ⌊of enemies⌋ will rage like great waters;
the roar of their voices will resound.
56A destroyer[v] will come against Babylon;
her warriors will be captured,
and their bows will be broken.[w]
For the LORD is a God of retribution;
he will repay[x] in full.
57I will make her officials and wise men drunk,
her governors, officers and warriors as well;
they will sleep[y] forever and not awake,"
declares the King,[z] whose name is the LORD Almighty.

58This is what the LORD Almighty says:

"Babylon's thick wall[a] will be leveled
and her high gates set on fire;
the peoples[b] exhaust themselves for nothing,
the nations' labor is only fuel for the flames."[c]

Scroll thrown into the Euphrates.

59This is the message Jeremiah gave
to the staff officer Seraiah son of Neriah,[d] the son of Mahseiah, when he
went to Babylon with Zedekiah[e] king of
Judah in the fourth[f] year of his reign.
60Jeremiah had written on a scroll[g]
about all the disasters that would come
upon Babylon—all that had been recorded concerning Babylon. 61He said to
Seraiah, "When you get to Babylon, see
that you read all these words aloud.
62Then say, 'O LORD, you have said you
will destroy this place, so that neither
man nor animal will live in it; it will be
desolate[h] forever.' 63When you finish
reading this scroll, tie a stone to it and

[x]54 Or *Chaldeans*

throw it into the Euphrates. 64 Then say, 'So will Babylon sink to rise no more because of the disaster I will bring upon her. And her people[a] will fall.'"

The words of Jeremiah end[b] here.

The fall of Jerusalem.

52:1-3pp— 2Ki 24:18-20; 2Ch 36:11-16
52:4-16pp— Jer 39:1-10
52:4-21pp— 2Ki 25:1-21; 2Ch 36:17-20

52 Zedekiah[c] was twenty-one years old when he became king, and he reigned in Jerusalem eleven years. His mother's name was Hamutal daughter of Jeremiah; she was from Libnah.[d] 2 He did evil in the eyes of the LORD, just as Jehoiakim[e] had done. 3 It was because of the LORD's anger that all this happened to Jerusalem and Judah,[f] and in the end he thrust them from his presence.

Now Zedekiah rebelled[g] against the king of Babylon.

4 So in the ninth year of Zedekiah's reign, on the tenth[h] day of the tenth month, Nebuchadnezzar king of Babylon marched against Jerusalem[i] with his whole army. They camped outside the city and built siege works all around it.[j] 5 The city was kept under siege until the eleventh year of King Zedekiah.

6 By the ninth day of the fourth month the famine in the city had become so severe that there was no food for the people to eat.[k] 7 Then the city wall was broken through, and the whole army fled. They left the city at night through the gate between the two walls near the king's garden, though the Babylonians[y] were surrounding the city. They fled toward the Arabah,[z] 8 but the Babylonian[a] army pursued King Zedekiah and overtook him in the plains of Jericho. All his soldiers were separated from him and scattered, 9 and he was captured.[l]

He was taken to the king of Babylon at Riblah[m] in the land of Hamath,[n] where he pronounced sentence on him. 10 There at Riblah the king of Babylon slaughtered the sons[o] of Zedekiah before his eyes; he also killed all the officials of Judah. 11 Then he put out Zedekiah's eyes, bound him with bronze shackles and took him to Babylon, where he put him in prison till the day of his death.[p]

12 On the tenth day of the fifth[q] month, in the nineteenth year of Nebuchadnezzar king of Babylon, Nebuzaradan[r] commander of the imperial guard, who served the king of Babylon, came to Jerusalem. 13 He set fire[s] to the temple[t] of the LORD, the royal palace and all the houses of Jerusalem. Every important building he burned down. 14 The whole Babylonian army under the commander of the imperial guard broke down all the walls[u] around Jerusalem. 15 Nebuzaradan the commander of the guard carried into exile some of the poorest people and those who remained in the city, along with the rest of the craftsmen[b] and those who had gone over to the king of Babylon. 16 But Nebuzaradan left behind[v] the rest of the poorest people of the land to work the vineyards and fields.

17 The Babylonians broke up the bronze pillars,[w] the movable stands[x] and the bronze Sea[y] that were at the temple of the LORD and they carried all the bronze to Babylon.[z] 18 They also took away the pots, shovels, wick trimmers, sprinkling bowls, dishes and all the bronze articles used in the temple service.[a] 19 The commander of the imperial guard took away the basins, censers,[b] sprinkling bowls, pots, lampstands, dishes and bowls used for drink offerings—all that were made of pure gold or silver.

20 The bronze from the two pillars, the Sea and the twelve bronze bulls under it, and the movable stands, which King Solomon had made for the temple of the LORD, was more than could be weighed.[c] 21 Each of the pillars was eighteen cubits high and twelve cubits in circumference[c]; each was four fingers thick, and hollow.[d] 22 The bronze capital[e] on top of the one pillar was five cubits[d] high and

51:64 [a]ver 58 [b]Job 31:40
52:1 [c]2Ki 24:17 [d]Jos 10:29; 2Ki 8:22
52:2 [e]Jer 36:30
52:3 [f]Isa 3:1 [g]Eze 17:12-16
52:4 [h]Zec 8:19 [i]2Ki 25:1-7; Jer 39:1 [j]Eze 24:1-2
52:6 [k]Isa 3:1
52:9 [l]Jer 32:4 [m]Nu 34:11 [n]Nu 13:21
52:10 [o]Jer 22:30
52:11 [p]Eze 12:13
52:12 [q]Zec 7:5; 8:19 [r]Jer 39:9
52:13 [s]2Ch 36:19; Ps 74:8; La 2:6 [t]Ps 79:1; Mic 3:12
52:14 [u]Ne 1:3
52:16 [v]Jer 40:6
52:17 [w]1Ki 7:15 [x]1Ki 7:27-37 [y]1Ki 7:23 [z]Jer 27:19-22
52:18 [a]Ex 27:3; 1Ki 7:45
52:19 [b]1Ki 7:50
52:20 [c]1Ki 7:47
52:21 [d]1Ki 7:15
52:22 [e]1Ki 7:16

y *7* Or *Chaldeans*; also in verse 17 z *7* Or *the Jordan Valley* a *8* Or *Chaldean*; also in verse 14 b *15* Or *populace* c *21* That is, about 27 feet (about 8.1 meters) high and 18 feet (about 5.4 meters) in circumference d *22* That is, about 7 1/2 feet (about 2.3 meters)

was decorated with a network and pomegranates of bronze all around. The other
pillar, with its pomegranates, was similar.
23There were ninety-six pomegranates
on the sides; the total number of pomegranates[a] above the surrounding network was a hundred.

Judah's exile to Babylon.

24The commander of the guard took
as prisoners Seraiah[b] the chief priest,
Zephaniah[c] the priest next in rank and
the three doorkeepers. 25Of those still in
the city, he took the officer in charge of
the fighting men, and seven royal advisers. He also took the secretary who was
chief officer in charge of conscripting the
people of the land and sixty of his men
who were found in the city. 26Nebuzar-
adan[d] the commander took them all and
brought them to the king of Babylon at
Riblah. 27There at Riblah, in the land of
Hamath, the king had them executed.
So Judah went into captivity, away[e]
from her land. 28This is the number of
the people Nebuchadnezzar carried into
exile:[f]

in the seventh year, 3,023 Jews;
29in Nebuchadnezzar's eighteenth
year,
832 people from Jerusalem;
30in his twenty-third year,
745 Jews taken into exile by Nebuzaradan the commander of the
imperial guard.
There were 4,600 people in all.

Jehoiachin's release from prison.

52:31-34pp— 2Ki 25:27-30

31In the thirty-seventh year of the
exile of Jehoiachin king of Judah, in the
year Evil-Merodach[e] became king of
Babylon, he released Jehoiachin king of
Judah and freed him from prison on the
twenty-fifth day of the twelfth month.
32He spoke kindly to him and gave him
a seat of honor higher than those of the
other kings who were with him in Babylon. 33So Jehoiachin put aside his prison
clothes and for the rest of his life ate
regularly at the king's table.[g] 34Day by
day the king of Babylon gave Jehoiachin
a regular allowance[h] as long as he lived,
till the day of his death.

52:23 [a]1Ki 7:20
52:24 [b]2Ki 25:18 [c]Jer 21:1; 37:3
52:26 [d]ver 12
52:27 [e]Jer 20:4
52:28 [f]2Ki 24:14-16; 2Ch 36:20
52:33 [g]2Sa 9:7
52:34 [h]2Sa 9:10

e*31* Also called *Amel-Marduk*

LAMENTATIONS

Author: Probably Jeremiah.

Date Written: Between 586 and 585 B.C.

Time Span: An uncertain period of time soon after the destruction of Jerusalem, at the beginning of the exile.

Title: The book takes its name from its content: poetic laments about the destruction of Jerusalem. It is also called the "Lamentations of Jeremiah."

Background: Lamentations (a look at the past) is a sequel to the book of Jeremiah (a look toward the future). Both books center around the destruction of Jerusalem and her subsequent captivity. Lamentations is one of 5 books which make up the Megilloth. These books of the Megilloth are read publicly at the following Jewish festivals: Ninth of Aba (Lamentations); Purim (Esther); Pentecost (Ruth); Tabernacles (Ecclesiastes); and Passover (Song of Songs). The first 4 poems of Lamentations, a 5-poem song, are in "acrostic" or alphabetical fashion. The 22 letters of the Hebrew alphabet correspond successively to the first letter of each verse in chapters 1, 2 and 4. However, in chapter 3 each letter is allotted 3 verses.

Where Written: Jerusalem or Egypt.

To Whom: To the fallen city of Jerusalem.

Content: Nebuchadnezzar brings to pass that which Jeremiah has been prophesying for 40 years. Jerusalem is destroyed, as is the temple, and the people are exiled to Babylon. Now Jeremiah sits among the ashes and weeps. His anguish is not only for himself, but for the exiles and those left behind destitute. "My eyes fail from weeping, I am in torment within, my heart is poured out on the ground because my people are destroyed" (2:11). These 5 poems make up a funeral song for the death of Jerusalem. But even during this barren hour, in Jeremiah's contrite heart he has a glimmer of hope. He begins again to pray for mercy on his people. Jeremiah praises God for his power, his fairness and his faithfulness. He looks to God for the future restoration of Jerusalem.

Key Words: "Wrath"; "Lament." The "wrath" of God has crushed Jerusalem and vindicated his righteousness and justice. All Jeremiah can do now is "lament" over what was once his proud and glorious city.

Themes: • The suffering we experience may at times be a direct result of the sin in our lives. • Suffering may be allowed in our lives as a means of helping us to repent. • A forgiven sin may still have consequences with which we must deal. • During our darkest hours God will strengthen and comfort us if we will only let him. • If we have ever experienced sorrow, we are great candidates to console another who is hurting now. • Even as Jeremiah mourned, our Father mourns (when we refuse to take the message of his Son to heart). • The judgment of God is certain...the time it will arrive is not.

Outline:

1. Destruction and desolation of Jerusalem. 1:1-1:22
2. God's anger with Jerusalem. 2:1-2:22
3. Prayer for God's mercy on Jerusalem. 3:1-3:66
4. Repentance of Jerusalem. 4:1-4:22
5. Prayer for God's restoration of Jerusalem. 5:1-5:22

LAMENTATIONS

Jerusalem is desolate.

1 [a] How deserted lies the city,
once so full of people!
How like a widow[a] is she,
who once was great[b] among the nations!
She who was queen among the provinces
has now become a slave.[c]

2 Bitterly she weeps[d] at night,
tears are upon her cheeks.
Among all her lovers[e]
there is none to comfort her.
All her friends have betrayed[f] her;
they have become her enemies.[g]

3 After affliction and harsh labor,
Judah has gone into exile.[h]
She dwells among the nations;
she finds no resting place.[i]
All who pursue her have overtaken her
in the midst of her distress.

4 The roads to Zion mourn,
for no one comes to her appointed feasts.
All her gateways are desolate,[j]
her priests groan,
her maidens grieve,
and she is in bitter anguish.[k]

5 Her foes have become her masters;
her enemies are at ease.
The LORD has brought her grief[l]
because of her many sins.
Her children have gone into exile,[m]
captive before the foe.

6 All the splendor has departed
from the Daughter of Zion.[n]
Her princes are like deer
that find no pasture;
in weakness they have fled
before the pursuer.

7 In the days of her affliction and wandering
Jerusalem remembers all the treasures
that were hers in days of old.
When her people fell into enemy hands,
there was no one to help her.[o]
Her enemies looked at her
and laughed at her destruction.

8 Jerusalem has sinned[p] greatly
and so has become unclean.
All who honored her despise her,
for they have seen her nakedness;[q]
she herself groans[r]
and turns away.

9 Her filthiness clung to her skirts;
she did not consider her future.[s]
Her fall[t] was astounding;
there was none to comfort[u] her.
"Look, O LORD, on my affliction,[v]
for the enemy has triumphed."

10 The enemy laid hands
on all her treasures;[w]
she saw pagan nations
enter her sanctuary[x]—
those you had forbidden[y]
to enter your assembly.

11 All her people groan[z]
as they search for bread;[a]
they barter their treasures for food
to keep themselves alive.
"Look, O LORD, and consider,
for I am despised."

12 "Is it nothing to you, all you who pass by?[b]
Look around and see.
Is any suffering like my suffering[c]
that was inflicted on me,
that the LORD brought on me
in the day of his fierce anger?[d]

13 "From on high he sent fire,
sent it down into my bones.[e]
He spread a net for my feet
and turned me back.
He made me desolate,[f]
faint[g] all the day long.

1:1 [a]Isa 47:8 [b]1Ki 4:21 [c]Isa 3:26; Jer 40:9
1:2 [d]Ps 6:6 [e]Jer 3:1 [f]Jer 4:30; Mic 7:5 [g]ver 16
1:3 [h]Jer 13:19 [i]Dt 28:65
1:4 [j]Jer 9:11 [k]Joel 1:8-13
1:5 [l]Jer 30:15 [m]Jer 39:9; 52:28-30
1:6 [n]Jer 13:18
1:7 [o]Jer 37:7; La 4:17
1:8 [p]ver 20; Isa 59:2-13 [q]Jer 13:22,26 [r]ver 21,22
1:9 [s]Dt 32:28-29; Isa 47:7; Eze 24:13 [t]Jer 13:18 [u]Ecc 4:1; Jer 16:7 [v]Ps 25:18
1:10 [w]Isa 64:11 [x]Ps 74:7-8; Jer 51:51 [y]Dt 23:3
1:11 [z]Ps 38:8 [a]Jer 52:6
1:12 [b]Jer 18:16 [c]ver 18 [d]Isa 13:13; Jer 30:24
1:13 [e]Job 30:30 [f]Jer 44:6 [g]Hab 3:16

a This chapter is an acrostic poem, the verses of which begin with the successive letters of the Hebrew alphabet.

14“My sins have been bound into a
yoke[b];[a]
by his hands they were woven
together.
They have come upon my neck
and the Lord has sapped my strength.
He has handed me over[b]
to those I cannot withstand.

15“The Lord has rejected
all the warriors in my midst;[c]
he has summoned an army[d] against
me
to[c] crush my young men.[e]
In his winepress the Lord has
trampled
the Virgin Daughter of Judah.

Jeremiah mourns for Jerusalem.

16“This is why I weep
and my eyes overflow with tears.[f]
No one is near to comfort[g] me,
no one to restore my spirit.
My children are destitute
because the enemy has prevailed.”[h]

17Zion stretches out her hands,[i]
but there is no one to comfort her.
The LORD has decreed for Jacob
that his neighbors become his foes;
Jerusalem has become
an unclean thing among them.

18“The LORD is righteous,
yet I rebelled[j] against his
command.
Listen, all you peoples;
look upon my suffering.[k]
My young men and maidens
have gone into exile.[l]

19“I called to my allies
but they betrayed me.
My priests and my elders
perished[m] in the city
while they searched for food
to keep themselves alive.

20“See, O LORD, how distressed[n] I am!
I am in torment[o] within,
and in my heart I am disturbed,
for I have been most rebellious.
Outside, the sword bereaves;
inside, there is only death.[p]

21“People have heard my groaning,[q]
but there is no one to comfort me.[r]
All my enemies have heard of my
distress;
they rejoice[s] at what you have done.
May you bring the day[t] you have
announced
so they may become like me.

22“Let all their wickedness come
before you;
deal with them
as you have dealt with me
because of all my sins.[u]
My groans are many
and my heart is faint.”

2[d] How the Lord has covered the
Daughter of Zion
with the cloud of his anger[e]![v]
He has hurled down the splendor of
Israel
from heaven to earth;
he has not remembered his footstool[w]
in the day of his anger.

2Without pity[x] the Lord has
swallowed[y] up
all the dwellings of Jacob;
in his wrath he has torn down
the strongholds[z] of the Daughter of
Judah.
He has brought her kingdom and its
princes
down to the ground[a] in dishonor.

3In fierce anger he has cut off
every horn[f][b] of Israel.
He has withdrawn his right hand[c]
at the approach of the enemy.
He has burned in Jacob like a
flaming fire
that consumes everything around it.[d]

4Like an enemy he has strung his
bow;[e]
his right hand is ready.

1:14 [a]Dt 28:48; Isa 47:6 [b]Jer 32:5
1:15 [c]Jer 37:10 [d]Isa 41:2 [e]Isa 28:18; Jer 18:21
1:16 [f]La 2:11,18; 3:48-49 [g]Ps 69:20; Ecc 4:1 [h]ver 2; Jer 13:17; 14:17
1:17 [i]Jer 4:31
1:18 [j]1Sa 12:14 [k]ver 12 [l]Dt 28:32,41
1:19 [m]Jer 14:15; La 2:20
1:20 [n]Jer 4:19 [o]La 2:11 [p]Dt 32:25; Eze 7:15
1:21 [q]ver 8 [r]ver 4 [s]La 2:15 [t]Isa 47:11; Jer 30:16
1:22 [u]Ne 4:5
2:1 [v]La 3:44 [w]Ps 99:5; 132:7
2:2 [x]La 3:43 [y]Ps 21:9 [z]Ps 89:39-40; Mic 5:11 [a]Isa 25:12
2:3 [b]Ps 75:5,10 [c]Ps 74:11 [d]Isa 42:25; Jer 21:4-5,14
2:4 [e]Job 16:13; La 3:12-13

[b] *14* Most Hebrew manuscripts; Septuagint *He kept watch over my sins* [c] *15* Or *has set a time for me / when he will* [d] This chapter is an acrostic poem, the verses of which begin with the successive letters of the Hebrew alphabet. [e] *1* Or *How the Lord in his anger / has treated the Daughter of Zion with contempt* [f] *3* Or */ all the strength*; or *every king*; *horn* here symbolizes strength.

Like a foe he has slain
all who were pleasing to the eye;[a]
he has poured out his wrath like fire[b]
on the tent of the Daughter of Zion.

5The Lord is like an enemy;[c]
he has swallowed up Israel.
He has swallowed up all her palaces
and destroyed her strongholds.[d]
He has multiplied mourning and lamentation
for the Daughter of Judah.[e]

6He has laid waste his dwelling like a garden;
he has destroyed his place of meeting.[f]
The LORD has made Zion forget
her appointed feasts and her Sabbaths;[g]
in his fierce anger he has spurned
both king and priest.[h]

7The Lord has rejected his altar
and abandoned his sanctuary.
He has handed over to the enemy
the walls of her palaces;[i]
they have raised a shout in the house of the LORD
as on the day of an appointed feast.

8The LORD determined to tear down
the wall around the Daughter of Zion.
He stretched out a measuring line[j]
and did not withhold his hand from destroying.
He made ramparts and walls lament;
together they wasted away.[k]

9Her gates[l] have sunk into the ground;
their bars he has broken and destroyed.
Her king and her princes are exiled[m] among the nations,
the law[n] is no more,
and her prophets no longer find
visions[o] from the LORD.

10The elders of the Daughter of Zion
sit on the ground in silence;
they have sprinkled dust on their heads[p]
and put on sackcloth.[q]
The young women of Jerusalem
have bowed their heads to the ground.[r]

11My eyes fail from weeping,[s]
I am in torment within,[t]
my heart is poured out[u] on the ground
because my people are destroyed,
because children and infants faint[v]
in the streets of the city.

12They say to their mothers,
"Where is bread and wine?"
as they faint like wounded men
in the streets of the city,
as their lives ebb away
in their mothers' arms.[w]

13What can I say for you?
With what can I compare you,
O Daughter of Jerusalem?
To what can I liken you,
that I may comfort you,
O Virgin Daughter of Zion?[x]
Your wound is as deep as the sea.[y]
Who can heal you?

14The visions of your prophets
were false and worthless;
they did not expose your sin
to ward off your captivity.[z]
The oracles they gave you
were false and misleading.[a]

15All who pass your way
clap their hands at you;[b]
they scoff[c] and shake their heads
at the Daughter of Jerusalem:
"Is this the city that was called
the perfection of beauty,[d]
the joy of the whole earth?"[e]

16All your enemies open their mouths
wide against you;[f]
they scoff and gnash their teeth[g]
and say, "We have swallowed her up.[h]
This is the day we have waited for;
we have lived to see it."

17The LORD has done what he planned;
he has fulfilled his word,
which he decreed long ago.[i]

2:4 [a]Eze 24:16,25 [b]Isa 42:25; Jer 7:20
2:5 [c]Jer 30:14 [d]ver 2 [e]Jer 9:17-20
2:6 [f]Jer 52:13 [g]La 1:4; Zep 3:18 [h]La 4:16
2:7 [i]Ps 74:7-8; Isa 64:11; Jer 33:4-5
2:8 [j]2Ki 21:13; Isa 34:11 [k]Isa 3:26
2:9 [l]Ne 1:3 [m]Dt 28:36; 2Ki 24:15 [n]2Ch 15:3 [o]Jer 14:14
2:10 [p]Job 2:12 [q]Isa 15:3 [r]Job 2:13; Isa 3:26
2:11 [s]La 1:16; 3:48-51 [t]La 1:20 [u]ver 19; Ps 22:14 [v]La 4:4
2:12 [w]La 4:4
2:13 [x]Isa 37:22 [y]Jer 14:17; La 1:12
2:14 [z]Isa 58:1 [a]Jer 2:8; 23:25-32, 33-40; 29:9; Eze 13:3; 22:28
2:15 [b]Eze 25:6 [c]Jer 19:8 [d]Ps 50:2 [e]Ps 48:2
2:16 [f]Ps 56:2; La 3:46 [g]Job 16:9 [h]Ps 35:25
2:17 [i]Dt 28:15-45

He has overthrown you without pity,[a]
he has let the enemy gloat over you,
he has exalted the horn[g] of your
foes.[b]

18 The hearts of the people
cry out to the Lord.[c]
O wall of the Daughter of Zion,
let your tears[d] flow like a river
day and night;[e]
give yourself no relief,
your eyes no rest.[f]

19 Arise, cry out in the night,
as the watches of the night begin;
pour out your heart[g] like water
in the presence of the Lord.[h]
Lift up your hands to him
for the lives of your children,
who faint[i] from hunger
at the head of every street.

20 "Look, O LORD, and consider:
Whom have you ever treated like
this?
Should women eat their offspring,[j]
the children they have cared for?[k]
Should priest and prophet be killed[l]
in the sanctuary of the Lord?

21 "Young and old lie together
in the dust of the streets;
my young men and maidens
have fallen by the sword.[m]
You have slain them in the day of
your anger;
you have slaughtered them without
pity.[n]

22 "As you summon to a feast day,
so you summoned against me
terrors[o] on every side.
In the day of the LORD's anger
no one escaped or survived;
those I cared for and reared,[p]
my enemy has destroyed."

Jeremiah cries to the LORD.

3 [h] I am the man who has seen
affliction
by the rod of his wrath.[q]
2 He has driven me away and made
me walk
in darkness[r] rather than light;
3 indeed, he has turned his hand
against me[s]
again and again, all day long.

4 He has made my skin and my flesh
grow old
and has broken my bones.[t]
5 He has besieged me and surrounded
me
with bitterness[u] and hardship.[v]
6 He has made me dwell in darkness
like those long dead.[w]

7 He has walled me in so I cannot
escape;[x]
he has weighed me down with
chains.[y]
8 Even when I call out or cry for help,
he shuts out my prayer.[z]
9 He has barred my way with blocks of
stone;
he has made my paths crooked.[a]

10 Like a bear lying in wait,
like a lion in hiding,
11 he dragged me from the path and
mangled[b] me
and left me without help.
12 He drew his bow[c]
and made me the target[d] for his
arrows.[e]

13 He pierced my heart
with arrows from his quiver.[f]
14 I became the laughingstock[g] of all
my people;
they mock me in song[h] all day
long.
15 He has filled me with bitter herbs
and sated me with gall.[i]

16 He has broken my teeth with gravel;[j]
he has trampled me in the dust.
17 I have been deprived of peace;
I have forgotten what prosperity is.
18 So I say, "My splendor is gone
and all that I had hoped from the
LORD."[k]

2:17 [a]ver 2; Eze 5:11 [b]Ps 89:42
2:18 [c]Ps 119:145 [d]La 1:16 [e]Jer 9:1 [f]La 3:49
2:19 [g]1Sa 1:15; Ps 62:8 [h]Isa 26:9 [i]Isa 51:20
2:20 [j]Dt 28:53; Jer 19:9 [k]La 4:10 [l]Ps 78:64; Jer 14:15
2:21 [m]2Ch 36:17; Ps 78:62-63; Jer 6:11 [n]Jer 13:14; La 3:43; Zec 11:6
2:22 [o]Ps 31:13; Jer 6:25 [p]Hos 9:13
3:1 [q]Job 19:21; Ps 88:7
3:2 [r]Jer 4:23
3:3 [s]Isa 5:25
3:4 [t]Ps 51:8; Isa 38:13; Jer 50:17
3:5 [u]ver 19 [v]Jer 23:15
3:6 [w]Ps 88:5-6
3:7 [x]Job 3:23 [y]Jer 40:4
3:8 [z]Job 30:20; Ps 22:2
3:9 [a]Isa 63:17; Hos 2:6
3:11 [b]Hos 6:1
3:12 [c]La 2:4 [d]Job 7:20 [e]Ps 7:12-13; 38:2
3:13 [f]Job 6:4
3:14 [g]Jer 20:7 [h]Job 30:9
3:15 [i]Jer 9:15 **3:16** [j]Pr 20:17 **3:18** [k]Job 17:15

[g] *17 Horn* here symbolizes strength. [h] This chapter is an acrostic poem; the verses of each stanza begin with the successive letters of the Hebrew alphabet, and the verses within each stanza begin with the same letter.

19I remember my affliction and my wandering,
the bitterness and the gall.
20I well remember them,
and my soul is downcast[a] within me.[b]
21Yet this I call to mind
and therefore I have hope:

22Because of the LORD's great love we are not consumed,
for his compassions never fail.[c]
23They are new every morning;
great is your faithfulness.[d]
24I say to myself, "The LORD is my portion;[e]
therefore I will wait for him."

25The LORD is good to those whose hope is in him,
to the one who seeks him;[f]
26it is good to wait quietly
for the salvation of the LORD.[g]
27It is good for a man to bear the yoke
while he is young.

28Let him sit alone in silence,[h]
for the LORD has laid it on him.
29Let him bury his face in the dust—
there may yet be hope.[i]
30Let him offer his cheek to one who would strike him,[j]
and let him be filled with disgrace.

31For men are not cast off
by the Lord forever.[k]
32Though he brings grief, he will show compassion,
so great is his unfailing love.[l]
33For he does not willingly bring affliction
or grief to the children of men.[m]

34To crush underfoot
all prisoners in the land,
35to deny a man his rights
before the Most High,
36to deprive a man of justice—
would not the Lord see such things?[n]

37Who can speak and have it happen
if the Lord has not decreed it?[o]
38Is it not from the mouth of the Most High
that both calamities and good things come?[p]
39Why should any living man complain
when punished for his sins?[q]

40Let us examine our ways and test them,[r]
and let us return to the LORD.[s]
41Let us lift up our hearts and our hands
to God in heaven,[t] and say:
42"We have sinned and rebelled[u]
and you have not forgiven.[v]

43"You have covered yourself with anger and pursued us;
you have slain without pity.[w]
44You have covered yourself with a cloud[x]
so that no prayer[y] can get through.
45You have made us scum[z] and refuse
among the nations.

46"All our enemies have opened their mouths
wide against us.[a]
47We have suffered terror and pitfalls,[b]
ruin and destruction.[c]"
48Streams of tears flow from my eyes[d]
because my people are destroyed.[e]

49My eyes will flow unceasingly,
without relief,[f]
50until the LORD looks down
from heaven and sees.[g]
51What I see brings grief to my soul
because of all the women of my city.

52Those who were my enemies without cause
hunted me like a bird.[h]
53They tried to end my life in a pit[i]
and threw stones at me;
54the waters closed over my head,[j]
and I thought I was about to be cut off.

55I called on your name, O LORD,
from the depths of the pit.[k]
56You heard my plea:[l] "Do not close your ears
to my cry for relief."

3:20 [a]Ps 42:5 [b]Ps 42:11 **3:22** [c]Ps 78:38; Mal 3:6 **3:23** [d]Zep 3:5 **3:24** [e]Ps 16:5 **3:25** [f]Isa 25:9; 30:18 **3:26** [g]Ps 37:7; 40:1 **3:28** [h]Jer 15:17 **3:29** [i]Jer 31:17 **3:30** [j]Job 16:10; Isa 50:6 **3:31** [k]Ps 94:14; Isa 54:7 **3:32** [l]Ps 78:38; Hos 11:8 **3:33** [m]Eze 33:11 **3:36** [n]Jer 22:3; Hab 1:13 **3:37** [o]Ps 33:9-11 **3:38** [p]Job 2:10; Isa 45:7; Jer 32:42 **3:39** [q]Jer 30:15; Mic 7:9 **3:40** [r]2Co 13:5 [s]Ps 119:59; 139:23-24 **3:41** [t]Ps 25:1; 28:2 **3:42** [u]Da 9:5 [v]Jer 5:7-9 **3:43** [w]La 2:2,17,21 **3:44** [x]Ps 97:2 [y]ver 8 **3:45** [z]1Co 4:13 **3:46** [a]La 2:16 **3:47** [b]Jer 48:43 [c]Isa 24:17-18; 51:19

3:48 [d]La 1:16, [e]La 2:11 **3:49** [f]Jer 14:17 **3:50** [g]Isa 63:15 **3:52** [h]Ps 35:7 **3:53** [i]Jer 37:16 **3:54** [j]Ps 69:2; Jnh 2:3-5 **3:55** [k]Ps 130:1; Jnh 2:2 **3:56** [l]Ps 55:1

57You came near when I called you,
and you said, "Do not fear." [a]

58O Lord, you took up my case; [b]
you redeemed my life. [c]
59You have seen, O LORD, the wrong
done to me. [d]
Uphold my cause!
60You have seen the depth of their
vengeance,
all their plots against me. [e]

61O LORD, you have heard their insults,
all their plots against me—
62what my enemies whisper and mutter
against me all day long. [f]
63Look at them! Sitting or standing,
they mock me in their songs.

64Pay them back what they deserve,
O LORD,
for what their hands have done. [g]
65Put a veil over their hearts, [h]
and may your curse be on them!
66Pursue them in anger and destroy
them
from under the heavens of the LORD.

Jerusalem is punished for her sins.

4 [i] How the gold has lost its luster,
the fine gold become dull!
The sacred gems are scattered
at the head of every street. [i]

2How the precious sons of Zion,
once worth their weight in gold,
are now considered as pots of clay,
the work of a potter's hands!

3Even jackals offer their breasts
to nurse their young,
but my people have become heartless
like ostriches in the desert. [j]

4Because of thirst the infant's tongue
sticks to the roof of its mouth; [k]
the children beg for bread,
but no one gives it to them. [l]

5Those who once ate delicacies
are destitute in the streets.
Those nurtured in purple [m]
now lie on ash heaps. [n]

6The punishment of my people
is greater than that of Sodom, [o]
which was overthrown in a moment
without a hand turned to help her.

7Their princes were brighter than snow
and whiter than milk,
their bodies more ruddy than rubies,
their appearance like sapphires. [j]

8But now they are blacker [p] than soot;
they are not recognized in the
streets.
Their skin has shriveled on their
bones; [q]
it has become as dry as a stick.

9Those killed by the sword are better off
than those who die of famine;
racked with hunger, they waste away
for lack of food from the field. [r]

10With their own hands compassionate
women
have cooked their own children, [s]
who became their food
when my people were destroyed.

11The LORD has given full vent to his
wrath;
he has poured out his fierce anger.
He kindled a fire [t] in Zion
that consumed her foundations. [u]

12The kings of the earth did not believe,
nor did any of the world's people,
that enemies and foes could enter
the gates of Jerusalem. [v]

13But it happened because of the sins
of her prophets
and the iniquities of her priests, [w]
who shed within her
the blood of the righteous.

14Now they grope through the streets
like men who are blind. [x]
They are so defiled with blood [y]
that no one dares to touch their
garments.

15"Go away! You are unclean!" men
cry to them.
"Away! Away! Don't touch us!"

3:57 [a]Isa 41:10
3:58 [b]Jer 51:36 [c]Ps 34:22; Jer 50:34
3:59 [d]Jer 18:19-20
3:60 [e]Jer 11:20; 18:18
3:62 [f]Eze 36:3
3:64 [g]Ps 28:4
3:65 [h]Isa 6:10
4:1 [i]Eze 7:19
4:3 [j]Job 39:16
4:4 [k]Ps 22:15 [l]La 2:11,12
4:5 [m]Jer 6:2 [n]Am 6:3-7
4:6 [o]Ge 19:25
4:8 [p]Job 30:28 [q]Ps 102:3-5
4:9 [r]Jer 15:2; 16:4
4:10 [s]Lev 26:29; Dt 28:53-57; Jer 19:9; La 2:20; Eze 5:10
4:11 [t]Jer 17:27 [u]Dt 32:22; Jer 7:20; Eze 22:31
4:12 [v]1Ki 9:9; Jer 21:13
4:13 [w]Jer 5:31; 6:13; Eze 22:28; Mic 3:11
4:14 [x]Isa 59:10 [y]Jer 2:34; 19:4

[i] This chapter is an acrostic poem, the verses of which begin with the successive letters of the Hebrew alphabet. [j]7 Or *lapis lazuli*

When they flee and wander about,
people among the nations say,
"They can stay here no longer." [a]

16The LORD himself has scattered them;
he no longer watches over them. [b]
The priests are shown no honor,
the elders [c] no favor.

17Moreover, our eyes failed,
looking in vain [d] for help; [e]
from our towers we watched
for a nation [f] that could not save us.

18Men stalked us at every step,
so we could not walk in our streets.
Our end was near, our days were numbered,
for our end had come. [g]

19Our pursuers were swifter
than eagles [h] in the sky;
they chased us [i] over the mountains
and lay in wait for us in the desert.

20The LORD's anointed, [j] our very life breath,
was caught in their traps. [k]
We thought that under his shadow
we would live among the nations.

21Rejoice and be glad, O Daughter of Edom,
you who live in the land of Uz.
But to you also the cup [l] will be passed;
you will be drunk and stripped naked. [m]

22O Daughter of Zion, your punishment will end; [n]
he will not prolong your exile.
But, O Daughter of Edom, he will punish your sin
and expose your wickedness. [o]

Jeremiah prays for restoration.

5

Remember, O LORD, what has happened to us;
look, and see our disgrace. [p]
2Our inheritance [q] has been turned over to aliens,
our homes [r] to foreigners.
3We have become orphans and fatherless,
our mothers like widows. [s]
4We must buy the water we drink;
our wood can be had only at a price. [t]
5Those who pursue us are at our heels;
we are weary [u] and find no rest.
6We submitted to Egypt and Assyria [v]
to get enough bread.
7Our fathers sinned and are no more,
and we bear their punishment. [w]
8Slaves [x] rule over us,
and there is none to free us from their hands. [y]
9We get our bread at the risk of our lives
because of the sword in the desert.
10Our skin is hot as an oven,
feverish from hunger. [z]
11Women have been ravished [a] in Zion,
and virgins in the towns of Judah.
12Princes have been hung up by their hands;
elders are shown no respect. [b]
13Young men toil at the millstones;
boys stagger under loads of wood.
14The elders are gone from the city gate;
the young men have stopped their music. [c]
15Joy is gone from our hearts;
our dancing has turned to mourning. [d]
16The crown [e] has fallen from our head.
Woe to us, for we have sinned! [f]
17Because of this our hearts [g] are faint,
because of these things our eyes [h] grow dim
18for Mount Zion, which lies desolate, [i]
with jackals prowling over it.

19You, O LORD, reign forever;
your throne endures [j] from generation to generation.
20Why do you always forget us? [k]
Why do you forsake us so long?
21Restore [l] us to yourself, O LORD, that we may return;
renew our days as of old
22unless you have utterly rejected us
and are angry with us beyond measure. [m]

4:15 [a]Lev 13:46 **4:16** [b]Isa 9:14-16 [c]La 5:12 **4:17** [d]Isa 20:5; Eze 29:16 [e]La 1:7 [f]Jer 37:7 **4:18** [g]Eze 7:2-12; Am 8:2 **4:19** [h]Dt 28:49 [i]Isa 5:26-28 **4:20** [j]2Sa 19:21 [k]Jer 39:5; Eze 12:12-13; 19:4,8 **4:21** [l]Jer 25:15 [m]Isa 34:6-10; Am 1:11-12; Ob 16 **4:22** [n]Isa 40:2; Jer 33:8 [o]Ps 137:7; Mal 1:4 **5:1** [p]Ps 44:13-16; 89:50 **5:2** [q]Ps 79:1 [r]Zep 1:13 **5:3** [s]Jer 15:8; 18:21 **5:4** [t]Isa 3:1 **5:5** [u]Ne 9:37 **5:6** [v]Hos 9:3 **5:7** [w]Jer 14:20; 16:12 **5:8** [x]Ne 5:15 [y]Zec 11:6 **5:10** [z]La 4:8-9 **5:11** [a]Zec 14:2 **5:12** [b]La 4:16 **5:14** [c]Isa 24:8; Jer 7:34 **5:15** [d]Jer 25:10 **5:16** [e]Ps 89:39 [f]Isa 3:11

5:17 [g]Isa 1:5, [h]Ps 6:7 **5:18** [i]Mic 3:12 **5:19** [j]Ps 45:6; 102:12,24-27 **5:20** [k]Ps 13:1; 44:24 **5:21** [l]Ps 80:3 **5:22** [m]Isa 64:9

EZEKIEL

Author: Ezekiel.

Date Written: Between 593 and 565 B.C.

Time Span: About 22 years.

Title: This book is named after its author: the prophet Ezekiel. The name Ezekiel means "God strengthens."

Background: Ezekiel, who grew up in Jerusalem and served as a priest in the temple, is among the second group of captives taken to Babylon along with King Jehoiachin. While in Babylon he becomes a prophet of God. Jeremiah has already prophesied in Jerusalem for about 35 years, and Daniel, having been exiled to Babylon 9 years earlier, is also a well-established prophet, as shown by his being mentioned 3 times in Ezekiel's messages. Both Ezekiel and Daniel are several years younger than the prophet Jeremiah.

Where Written: Babylon.

To Whom: Principally to the Babylonian exiles.

Content: Ezekiel's ministry begins in Babylon with condemnation and judgment of the nation Judah. But after the destruction of Jerusalem takes place, Ezekiel's perspective changes. The past is gone, but there is a glimmer of hope shining through for the future. Ezekiel, who wants to help the people learn from their failures, announces impending judgment upon the nations that surround Judah and reestablishes hope for the restoration of Israel. His vision of the valley of dry bones pictures new life being breathed into the nation (chapter 37). Ezekiel concludes with his return to Jerusalem in a vision to receive details on the new temple, the new Jerusalem and the new land. Israel and Judah will once again be restored to unity from the ends of the earth, as God's glory also returns.

Key Words: "Visions"; "Watchman." Ezekiel receives a variety of beautiful and unusual "visions" concerning the immediate and long-term plans of God. These help to establish Ezekiel as God's "watchman" to warn and encourage the people. "Son of man, I have made you a watchman for the house of Israel; so hear the word I speak and give them warning from me" (3:17; 33:7).

Themes: • God always has and always will hate sin. • The ways of God contrast with the ways of the world. • We are each responsible for our own sins. • We are together accountable for the sins of our nation. • As will any loving father, God will discipline us for our disobedience. • God's promises of restoration for his people will undeniably be fulfilled.

Outline:

1. Call and commission of Ezekiel. 1:1-3:27
2. Judgment on sinful Judah. 4:1-24:27
3. Judgment on the Gentiles. 25:1-32:32
4. Promised restoration of Israel. 33:1-39:29
5. The new temple. 40:1-48:35

EZEKIEL

1 In the[a] thirtieth year, in the fourth month on the fifth day, while I was among the exiles[a] by the Kebar River, the heavens were opened[b] and I saw visions[c] of God.

2On the fifth of the month—it was the fifth year of the exile of King Jehoiachin[d]— **3**the word of the LORD came to Ezekiel the priest, the son of Buzi,[b] by the Kebar River in the land of the Babylonians.[c] There the hand of the LORD was upon him.[e]

Ezekiel's vision of four living creatures.

4I looked, and I saw a windstorm coming out of the north[f]—an immense cloud with flashing lightning and surrounded by brilliant light. The center of the fire looked like glowing metal,[g] **5**and in the fire was what looked like four living creatures.[h] In appearance their form was that of a man,[i] **6**but each of them had four faces[j] and four wings. **7**Their legs were straight; their feet were like those of a calf and gleamed like burnished bronze.[k] **8**Under their wings on their four sides they had the hands of a man.[l] All four of them had faces and wings, **9**and their wings touched one another. Each one went straight ahead; they did not turn as they moved.[m]

10Their faces looked like this: Each of the four had the face of a man, and on the right side each had the face of a lion, and on the left the face of an ox; each also had the face of an eagle.[n] **11**Such were their faces. Their wings[o] were spread out upward; each had two wings, one touching the wing of another creature on either side, and two wings covering its body. **12**Each one went straight ahead. Wherever the spirit would go, they would go, without turning as they went. **13**The appearance of the living creatures was like burning coals of fire or like torches. Fire moved back and forth among the creatures; it was bright, and lightning[p] flashed out of it. **14**The creatures sped back and forth like flashes of lightning.[q]

Four wheels.

15As I looked at the living creatures, I saw a wheel on the ground beside each creature with its four faces. **16**This was the appearance and structure of the wheels: They sparkled like chrysolite,[r] and all four looked alike. Each appeared to be made like a wheel intersecting a wheel. **17**As they moved, they would go in any one of the four directions the creatures faced; the wheels did not turn[s] about[d] as the creatures went. **18**Their rims were high and awesome, and all four rims were full of eyes[t] all around.

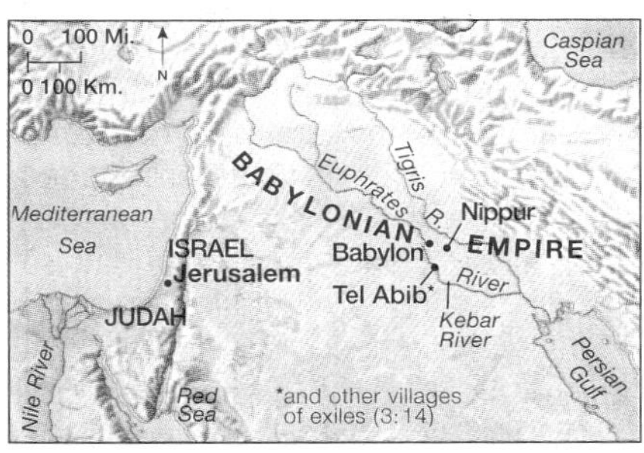

Exile in Babylon

Ezekiel worked for God right where he was—among the exiles in various colonies near the Kebar River in Babylonia. Jerusalem and its temple lay over 500 miles away, but Ezekiel helped the people understand that although they were far from home, they did not need to be far from God.

19When the living creatures moved, the wheels beside them moved; and when the living creatures rose from the ground, the wheels also rose. **20**Wherever the spirit would go, they would go,[u] and the wheels would rise along with them, because the spirit of the living creatures was in the wheels. **21**When the creatures moved, they also moved; when the creatures stood still, they also stood still; and when the creatures rose from the ground, the wheels rose along

1:1 [a]Eze 11:24-25 [b]Mt 3:16; Ac 7:56 [c]Ex 24:10
1:2 [d]2Ki 24:15
1:3 [e]2Ki 3:15; Eze 3:14,22
1:4 [f]Jer 1:14 [g]Eze 8:2
1:5 [h]Rev 4:6 [i]ver 26
1:6 [j]Eze 10:14
1:7 [k]Da 10:6; Rev 1:15
1:8 [l]Eze 10:8
1:9 [m]Eze 10:22
1:10 [n]Eze 10:14; Rev 4:7
1:11 [o]Isa 6:2
1:13 [p]Rev 4:5
1:14 [q]Ps 29:7
1:16 [r]Eze 10:9-11; Da 10:6
1:17 [s]ver 9
1:18 [t]Eze 10:12; Rev 4:6
1:20 [u]ver 12

a *1* Or ⌊*my*⌋ b *3* Or *Ezekiel son of Buzi the priest*
c *3* Or *Chaldeans* d *17* Or *aside*

with them, because the spirit of the living creatures was in the wheels.[a]

22 Spread out above the heads of the living creatures was what looked like an expanse,[b] sparkling like ice, and awesome. 23 Under the expanse their wings were stretched out one toward the other, and each had two wings covering its body. 24 When the creatures moved, I heard the sound of their wings, like the roar of rushing waters, like the voice[c] of the Almighty,[e] like the tumult of an army.[d] When they stood still, they lowered their wings.

25 Then there came a voice from above the expanse over their heads as they stood with lowered wings. 26 Above the expanse over their heads was what looked like a throne of sapphire,[f][e] and high above on the throne was a figure like that of a man.[f] 27 I saw that from what appeared to be his waist up he looked like glowing metal, as if full of fire, and that from there down he looked like fire; and brilliant light surrounded him.[g] 28 Like the appearance of a rainbow[h] in the clouds on a rainy day, so was the radiance around him.[i]

This was the appearance of the likeness of the glory[j] of the LORD. When I saw it, I fell facedown,[k] and I heard the voice of one speaking.

The LORD sends Ezekiel to Israel.

2 He said to me, "Son of man, stand[l] up on your feet and I will speak to you." 2 As he spoke, the Spirit came into me and raised me[m] to my feet, and I heard him speaking to me.

3 He said: "Son of man, I am sending you to the Israelites, to a rebellious nation that has rebelled against me; they and their fathers have been in revolt against me to this very day.[n] 4 The people to whom I am sending you are obstinate and stubborn.[o] Say to them, 'This is what the Sovereign LORD says.' 5 And whether they listen or fail to listen[p]—for they are a rebellious house[q]—they will know that a prophet has been among them.[r] 6 And you, son of man, do not be afraid[s] of them or their words. Do not be afraid, though briers and thorns[t] are all around you and you live among scorpions. Do not be afraid of what they say or terrified by them, though they are a rebellious house.[u] 7 You must speak my words to them, whether they listen or fail to listen, for they are rebellious.[v] 8 But you, son of man, listen to what I say to you. Do not rebel like that rebellious house;[w] open your mouth and eat[x] what I give you."

Ezekiel eats a scroll.

9 Then I looked, and I saw a hand[y] stretched out to me. In it was a scroll, 10 which he unrolled before me. On both sides of it were written words of lament and mourning and woe.[z]

3 And he said to me, "Son of man, eat what is before you, eat this scroll; then go and speak to the house of Israel." 2 So I opened my mouth, and he gave me the scroll to eat.

3 Then he said to me, "Son of man, eat this scroll I am giving you and fill your stomach with it." So I ate[a] it, and it tasted as sweet as honey[b] in my mouth.

4 He then said to me: "Son of man, go now to the house of Israel and speak my words to them. 5 You are not being sent to a people of obscure speech and difficult language,[c] but to the house of Israel— 6 not to many peoples of obscure speech and difficult language, whose words you cannot understand. Surely if I had sent you to them, they would have listened to you.[d] 7 But the house of Israel is not willing to listen to you because they are not willing to listen to me, for the whole house of Israel is hardened and obstinate.[e] 8 But I will make you as unyielding and hardened as they are.[f] 9 I will make your forehead like the hardest stone, harder than flint. Do not be afraid of them or terrified by them, though they are a rebellious house.[g]"

10 And he said to me, "Son of man,

1:21 [a]Eze 10:17
1:22 [b]Eze 10:1
1:24 [c]Eze 10:5; 43:2; Da 10:6; Rev 1:15; 19:6 [d]2Ki 7:6
1:26 [e]Ex 24:10; Eze 10:1 [f]Rev 1:13
1:27 [g]Eze 8:2
1:28 [h]Ge 9:13; Rev 10:1 [i]Rev 4:2 [j]Eze 8:4 [k]Eze 3:23; Da 8:17; Rev 1:17
2:1 [l]Da 10:11
2:2 [m]Eze 3:24; Da 8:18
2:3 [n]Jer 3:25; Eze 20:8-24
2:4 [o]Eze 3:7
2:5 [p]Eze 3:11 [q]Eze 3:27 [r]Eze 33:33
2:6 [s]Jer 1:8,17 [t]Isa 9:18; Mic 7:4 [u]Eze 3:9
2:7 [v]Jer 1:7; Eze 3:10-11
2:8 [w]Isa 50:5 [x]Jer 15:16; Rev 10:9
2:9 [y]Eze 8:3
2:10 [z]Rev 8:13
3:3 [a]Jer 15:16 [b]Ps 19:10; Ps 119:103; Rev 10:9-10
3:5 [c]Isa 28:11; Jnh 1:2
3:6 [d]Mt 11:21-23
3:7 [e]Eze 2:4; Jn 15:20-23
3:8 [f]Jer 1:18 **3:9** [g]Isa 50:7; Eze 2:6; Mic 3:8

e24 Hebrew *Shaddai* f26 Or *lapis lazuli*

listen carefully and take to heart all the
words I speak to you. 11Go now to your
countrymen in exile and speak to them.
Say to them, 'This is what the Sovereign
LORD says,' whether they listen or fail to
listen.[a]"
12Then the Spirit lifted me up,[b] and
I heard behind me a loud rumbling
sound—May the glory of the LORD be
praised in his dwelling place!— 13the
sound of the wings of the living creatures brushing against each other and
the sound of the wheels beside them, a
loud rumbling sound.[c] 14The Spirit then
lifted me up and took me away, and I
went in bitterness and in the anger of
my spirit, with the strong hand of the
LORD upon me. 15I came to the exiles
who lived at Tel Abib near the Kebar
River.[d] And there, where they were living, I sat among them for seven days[e]—
overwhelmed.

Ezekiel is made a watchman for Israel.

16At the end of seven days the word of
the LORD came to me:[f] 17"Son of man, I
have made you a watchman[g] for the
house of Israel; so hear the word I speak
and give them warning from me. 18When
I say to a wicked man, 'You will surely
die,' and you do not warn him or speak
out to dissuade him from his evil ways in
order to save his life, that wicked man
will die for[g] his sin, and I will hold you
accountable for his blood.[h] 19But if you
do warn the wicked man and he does
not turn from his wickedness or from
his evil ways, he will die for his sin; but
you will have saved yourself.[i]
20"Again, when a righteous man turns
from his righteousness and does evil, and
I put a stumbling block before him, he
will die. Since you did not warn him, he
will die for his sin. The righteous things
he did will not be remembered, and I
will hold you accountable for his blood.[j]
21But if you do warn the righteous man
not to sin and he does not sin, he will
surely live because he took warning,
and you will have saved yourself.[k]"

3:11 [a]Eze 2:4-5,7
3:12 [b]Eze 8:3; Ac 8:39
3:13 [c]Eze 1:24; 10:5,16-17
3:15 [d]Ps 137:1 [e]Job 2:13
3:16 [f]Jer 42:7
3:17 [g]Isa 52:8; Jer 6:17; Eze 33:7-9
3:18 [h]ver 20; Eze 33:6
3:19 [i]2Ki 17:13; Eze 14:14,20; Ac 18:6; 20:26; 1Ti 4:14-16
3:20 [j]Ps 125:5; Eze 18:24; 33:12,18
3:21 [k]Ac 20:31
3:22 [l]Eze 1:3 [m]Ac 9:6 [n]Eze 8:4
3:23 [o]Eze 1:1 [p]Eze 1:28
3:24 [q]Eze 2:2
3:25 [r]Eze 4:8
3:26 [s]Eze 2:5; 24:27; 33:22
3:27 [t]ver 11 [u]Eze 12:3; 24:27; 33:22
4:2 [v]Jer 6:6 [w]Eze 21:22
4:3 [x]Isa 8:18; 20:3; Eze 12:3-6; 24:24,27 [y]Jer 39:1

22The hand of the LORD[l] was upon me
there, and he said to me, "Get up and
go[m] out to the plain,[n] and there I will
speak to you." 23So I got up and went
out to the plain. And the glory of the
LORD was standing there, like the glory
I had seen by the Kebar River,[o] and I
fell facedown.[p]
24Then the Spirit came into me and
raised me[q] to my feet. He spoke to me
and said: "Go, shut yourself inside your
house. 25And you, son of man, they will
tie with ropes; you will be bound so that
you cannot go out among the people.[r]
26I will make your tongue stick to the
roof of your mouth so that you will be silent and unable to rebuke them, though
they are a rebellious house.[s] 27But when
I speak to you, I will open your mouth
and you shall say to them, 'This is what
the Sovereign LORD says.'[t] Whoever will
listen let him listen, and whoever will
refuse let him refuse; for they are a
rebellious house.[u]

A clay tablet and an iron pan.

4 "Now, son of man, take a clay tablet, put it in front of you and draw
the city of Jerusalem on it. 2Then lay
siege to it: Erect siege works against it,
build a ramp[v] up to it, set up camps
against it and put battering rams around
it.[w] 3Then take an iron pan, place it as
an iron wall between you and the city
and turn your face toward it. It will be
under siege, and you shall besiege it.
This will be a sign[x] to the house of
Israel.[y]

Ezekiel lies on his side.

4"Then lie on your left side and put
the sin of the house of Israel upon yourself.[h] You are to bear their sin for the
number of days you lie on your side. 5I
have assigned you the same number of
days as the years of their sin. So for 390
days you will bear the sin of the house
of Israel.

g *18* Or *in*; also in verses 19 and 20 h *4* Or *your side*

6 "After you have finished this, lie down again, this time on your right side, and bear the sin of the house of Judah. I have assigned you 40 days, a day for each year.[a] 7 Turn your face toward the siege of Jerusalem and with bared arm prophesy against her. 8 I will tie you up with ropes so that you cannot turn from one side to the other until you have finished the days of your siege.[b]

Defiled food.

9 "Take wheat and barley, beans and lentils, millet and spelt;[c] put them in a storage jar and use them to make bread for yourself. You are to eat it during the 390 days you lie on your side. 10 Weigh out twenty shekels[i] of food to eat each day and eat it at set times. 11 Also measure out a sixth of a hin[j] of water and drink it at set times. 12 Eat the food as you would a barley cake; bake it in the sight of the people, using human excrement[d] for fuel." 13 The LORD said, "In this way the people of Israel will eat defiled food among the nations where I will drive them."[e]

14 Then I said, "Not so, Sovereign LORD![f] I have never defiled myself. From my youth until now I have never eaten anything found dead[g] or torn by wild animals. No unclean meat has ever entered my mouth.[h]"

15 "Very well," he said, "I will let you bake your bread over cow manure instead of human excrement."

16 He then said to me: "Son of man, I will cut off[i] the supply of food in Jerusalem. The people will eat rationed food in anxiety and drink rationed water in despair,[j] 17 for food and water will be scarce. They will be appalled at the sight of each other and will waste away because of[k] their sin.[k]

Ezekiel must shave, burn and scatter his hair.

5 "Now, son of man, take a sharp sword and use it as a barber's razor[l] to shave[m] your head and your beard.[n] Then take a set of scales and divide up the hair. 2 When the days of your siege come to an end, burn a third of the hair with fire inside the city. Take a third and strike it with the sword all around the city. And scatter a third to the wind. For I will pursue them with drawn sword.[o] 3 But take a few strands of hair and tuck them away in the folds of your garment.[p] 4 Again, take a few of these and throw them into the fire and burn them up. A fire will spread from there to the whole house of Israel.

5 "This is what the Sovereign LORD says: This is Jerusalem, which I have set in the center of the nations, with countries all around her. 6 Yet in her wickedness she has rebelled against my laws and decrees more than the nations and countries around her. She has rejected my laws and has not followed my decrees.[q]

7 "Therefore this is what the Sovereign LORD says: You have been more unruly than the nations around you and have not followed my decrees or kept my laws. You have not even[l] conformed to the standards of the nations around you.[r]

8 "Therefore this is what the Sovereign LORD says: I myself am against you, Jerusalem, and I will inflict punishment on you in the sight of the nations.[s] 9 Because of all your detestable idols, I will do to you what I have never done before and will never do again.[t] 10 Therefore in your midst fathers will eat their children, and children will eat their fathers.[u] I will inflict punishment on you and will scatter all your survivors to the winds.[v] 11 Therefore as surely as I live, declares the Sovereign LORD, because you have defiled my sanctuary with all your vile images[w] and detestable practices,[x] I myself will withdraw my favor; I will not look on you with pity or spare you.[y] 12 A third of your people will die of the plague or perish by famine inside you; a third will fall by the sword outside your walls; and

4:6 [a] Nu 14:34; Da 9:24-26; 12:11-12
4:8 [b] Eze 3:25
4:9 [c] Isa 28:25
4:12 [d] Isa 36:12
4:13 [e] Hos 9:3
4:14 [f] Jer 1:6; Eze 9:8; 20:49 [g] Lev 11:39 [h] Ex 22:31; Dt 14:3; Ac 10:14
4:16 [i] Ps 105:16; Eze 5:16 [j] ver 10-11; Lev 26:26; Isa 3:1; Eze 12:19
4:17 [k] Lev 26:39; Eze 24:23; 33:10
5:1 [l] Isa 7:20 [m] Eze 44:20 [n] Lev 21:5
5:2 [o] ver 12; Lev 26:33
5:3 [p] Jer 39:10
5:6 [q] Jer 11:10; Eze 16:47-51; Zec 7:11
5:7 [r] 2Ch 33:9; Jer 2:10-11; Eze 16:47
5:8 [s] Eze 15:7
5:9 [t] Da 9:12; Mt 24:21
5:10 [u] Lev 26:29; La 2:20 [v] Lev 26:33; Ps 44:11; Eze 12:14; Zec 2:6
5:11 [w] Eze 7:20 [x] 2Ch 36:14; Eze 8:6 [y] Eze 7:4,9

i *10* That is, about 8 ounces (about 0.2 kilogram)
j *11* That is, about 2/3 quart (about 0.6 liter)
k *17* Or *away in*
l *7* Most Hebrew manuscripts; some Hebrew manuscripts and Syriac *You have*

a third I will scatter to the winds and
pursue with drawn sword.[a]
13“Then my anger will cease and my
wrath[b] against them will subside, and I
will be avenged.[c] And when I have spent
my wrath upon them, they will know
that I the LORD have spoken in my zeal.
14“I will make you a ruin and a reproach among the nations around you,
in the sight of all who pass by.[d] 15You
will be a reproach and a taunt, a warning
and an object of horror to the nations
around you when I inflict punishment
on you in anger and in wrath and with
stinging rebuke.[e] I the LORD have spoken.[f] 16When I shoot at you with my
deadly and destructive arrows of famine,
I will shoot to destroy you. I will bring
more and more famine upon you and cut
off your supply of food.[g] 17I will send
famine and wild beasts against you, and
they will leave you childless. Plague and
bloodshed[h] will sweep through you, and
I will bring the sword against you. I the
LORD have spoken.[i]”

Prophecy against idolatrous Israel.

6 The word of the LORD came to me:
2“Son of man, set your face against
the mountains[j] of Israel; prophesy against
them 3and say: ‘O mountains of Israel,
hear the word of the Sovereign LORD.
This is what the Sovereign LORD says to
the mountains and hills, to the ravines
and valleys:[k] I am about to bring a sword
against you, and I will destroy your
high places.[l] 4Your altars will be demolished and your incense altars[m] will be
smashed; and I will slay your people in
front of your idols. 5I will lay the dead
bodies of the Israelites in front of their
idols, and I will scatter your bones[n]
around your altars. 6Wherever you live,
the towns will be laid waste and the
high places demolished, so that your
altars will be laid waste and devastated,
your idols[o] smashed and ruined, your incense altars[p] broken down, and what
you have made wiped out.[q] 7Your people will fall slain among you, and you
will know that I am the LORD.

5:12 [a]ver 2,17; Jer 15:2; 21:9; Eze 6:11-12; 12:14
5:13 [b]Eze 21:17; 36:6 [c]Isa 1:24
5:14 [d]Lev 26:32; Ne 2:17; Ps 74:3-10; 79:1-4
5:15 [e]1Ki 9:7; Jer 22:8-9; 24:9 [f]Eze 25:17
5:16 [g]Dt 32:24
5:17 [h]Eze 38:22 [i]Eze 14:21
6:2 [j]Eze 36:1
6:3 [k]Eze 36:4 [l]Lev 26:30
6:4 [m]2Ch 14:5
6:5 [n]Jer 8:1-2
6:6 [o]Mic 1:7; Zec 13:2 [p]Lev 26:30 [q]Isa 6:11; Eze 5:14
6:8 [r]Jer 44:28 [s]Isa 6:13; Jer 44:14; Eze 12:16; 14:22
6:9 [t]Ps 78:40; Isa 7:13 [u]Eze 20:7,24 [v]Eze 20:43; 36:31
6:11 [w]Eze 5:12; 21:14,17; 25:6
6:12 [x]Eze 5:12
6:13 [y]Isa 57:5 [z]1Ki 14:23; Jer 2:20; Eze 20:28; Hos 4:13
6:14 [a]Isa 5:25 [b]Eze 14:13

A remnant to escape.

8“ ‘But I will spare some, for some of
you will escape[r] the sword when you are
scattered among the lands and nations.[s]
9Then in the nations where they have
been carried captive, those who escape
will remember me—how I have been
grieved[t] by their adulterous hearts,
which have turned away from me, and
by their eyes, which have lusted after
their idols.[u] They will loathe themselves
for the evil they have done and for all
their detestable practices.[v] 10And they
will know that I am the LORD; I did not
threaten in vain to bring this calamity
on them.
11“ ‘This is what the Sovereign LORD
says: Strike your hands together and
stamp your feet and cry out “Alas!” because of all the wicked and detestable
practices of the house of Israel, for they
will fall by the sword, famine and
plague.[w] 12He that is far away will die of
the plague, and he that is near will fall
by the sword, and he that survives and
is spared will die of famine. So will I
spend my wrath upon them.[x] 13And they
will know that I am the LORD, when
their people lie slain among their idols
around their altars, on every high hill
and on all the mountaintops, under
every spreading tree and every leafy
oak[y]—places where they offered fragrant incense to all their idols.[z] 14And I
will stretch out my hand[a] against them
and make the land a desolate waste from
the desert to Diblah[m]—wherever they
live. Then they will know that I am the
LORD.[b]’ ”

The end has come.

7 The word of the LORD came to me:
2“Son of man, this is what the Sovereign LORD says to the land of Israel:
The end![c] The end has come upon the
four corners[d] of the land. 3The end is
now upon you and I will unleash my

7:2 [c]Am 8:2,10 [d]Rev 7:1; 20:8

[m] *14* Most Hebrew manuscripts; a few Hebrew manuscripts *Riblah*

anger against you. I will judge you according to your conduct and repay you for all your detestable practices. **4**I will not look on you with pity[a] or spare you; I will surely repay you for your conduct and the detestable practices among you. Then you will know that I am the LORD.

5"This is what the Sovereign LORD says: Disaster![b] An unheard-of[n] disaster is coming. **6**The end has come! The end has come! It has roused itself against you. It has come! **7**Doom has come upon you—you who dwell in the land. The time has come, the day is near;[c] there is panic, not joy, upon the mountains. **8**I am about to pour out my wrath[d] on you and spend my anger against you; I will judge you according to your conduct and repay you for all your detestable practices.[e] **9**I will not look on you with pity or spare you; I will repay you in accordance with your conduct and the detestable practices among you. Then you will know that it is I the LORD who strikes the blow.

10"The day is here! It has come! Doom has burst forth, the rod[f] has budded, arrogance has blossomed! **11**Violence has grown into[o] a rod to punish wickedness; none of the people will be left, none of that crowd—no wealth, nothing of value.[g] **12**The time has come, the day has arrived. Let not the buyer rejoice nor the seller grieve, for wrath is upon the whole crowd.[h] **13**The seller will not recover the land he has sold as long as both of them live, for the vision concerning the whole crowd will not be reversed. Because of their sins, not one of them will preserve his life.[i] **14**Though they blow the trumpet and get everything ready, no one will go into battle, for my wrath is upon the whole crowd.

15"Outside is the sword, inside are plague and famine; those in the country will die by the sword, and those in the city will be devoured by famine and plague.[j] **16**All who survive and escape will be in the mountains, moaning like doves[k] of the valleys, each because of his sins.[l] **17**Every hand will go limp,[m] and every knee will become as weak as water. **18**They will put on sackcloth and be clothed with terror.[n] Their faces will be covered with shame and their heads will be shaved.[o] **19**They will throw their silver into the streets, and their gold will be an unclean thing. Their silver and gold will not be able to save them in the day of the LORD's wrath.[p] They will not satisfy their hunger or fill their stomachs with it, for it has made them stumble[q] into sin.[r] **20**They were proud of their beautiful jewelry and used it to make their detestable idols and vile images.[s] Therefore I will turn these into an unclean thing for them. **21**I will hand it all over as plunder to foreigners and as loot to the wicked of the earth, and they will defile it.[t] **22**I will turn my face[u] away from them, and they will desecrate my treasured place; robbers will enter it and desecrate it.

23"Prepare chains, because the land is full of bloodshed[v] and the city is full of violence. **24**I will bring the most wicked of the nations to take possession of their houses; I will put an end to the pride of the mighty, and their sanctuaries[w] will be desecrated.[x] **25**When terror comes, they will seek peace, but there will be none.[y] **26**Calamity upon calamity[z] will come, and rumor upon rumor. They will try to get a vision from the prophet; the teaching of the law by the priest will be lost, as will the counsel of the elders.[a] **27**The king will mourn, the prince will be clothed with despair,[b] and the hands of the people of the land will tremble. I will deal with them according to their conduct,[c] and by their own standards I will judge them. Then they will know that I am the LORD.[d]"

Israel does detestable things.

8 In the sixth year, in the sixth month on the fifth day, while I was sitting in my house and the elders[e] of Judah

7:4 [a]Eze 5:11
7:5 [b]2Ki 21:12
7:7 [c]Eze 12:23; Zep 1:14
7:8 [d]Isa 42:25; Eze 9:8; 14:19; Na 1:6 [e]Eze 20:8,21; 36:19
7:10 [f]Ps 89:32; Isa 10:5
7:11 [g]Jer 16:6; Zep 1:18
7:12 [h]ver 7; Isa 5:13-14; Eze 30:3
7:13 [i]Lev 25:24-28
7:15 [j]Dt 32:25; Jer 14:18; La 1:20; Eze 5:12
7:16 [k]Isa 59:11 [l]Ezr 9:15; Eze 6:8
7:17 [m]Isa 13:7; Eze 21:7; 22:14
7:18 [n]Ps 55:5 [o]Isa 15:2-3; Eze 27:31; Am 8:10
7:19 [p]Eze 13:5; Zep 1:7,18 [q]Eze 14:3 [r]Pr 11:4
7:20 [s]Jer 7:30
7:21 [t]2Ki 24:13
7:22 [u]Eze 39:23-24
7:23 [v]2Ki 21:16
7:24 [w]Eze 24:21 [x]2Ch 7:20; Eze 28:7
7:25 [y]Eze 13:10,16
7:26 [z]Jer 4:20 [a]Isa 47:11; Eze 20:1-3; Mic 3:6
7:27 [b]Ps 109:19; Eze 26:16 [c]Eze 18:20 [d]ver 4
8:1 [e]Eze 14:1

[n]*5* Most Hebrew manuscripts; some Hebrew manuscripts and Syriac *Disaster after* [o]*11* Or *The violent one has become*

were sitting before[a] me, the hand of the Sovereign LORD came upon me there.[b] 2I looked, and I saw a figure like that of a man.[p] From what appeared to be his waist down he was like fire, and from there up his appearance was as bright as glowing metal.[c] 3He stretched out what looked like a hand and took me by the hair of my head. The Spirit lifted me up[d] between earth and heaven and in visions of God he took me to Jerusalem, to the entrance to the north gate of the inner court, where the idol that provokes to jealousy[e] stood. 4And there before me was the glory[f] of the God of Israel, as in the vision I had seen in the plain.[g]

5Then he said to me, "Son of man, look toward the north." So I looked, and in the entrance north of the gate of the altar I saw this idol[h] of jealousy.

6And he said to me, "Son of man, do you see what they are doing—the utterly detestable[i] things the house of Israel is doing here, things that will drive me far from my sanctuary? But you will see things that are even more detestable."

7Then he brought me to the entrance to the court. I looked, and I saw a hole in the wall. 8He said to me, "Son of man, now dig into the wall." So I dug into the wall and saw a doorway there.

9And he said to me, "Go in and see the wicked and detestable things they are doing here." 10So I went in and looked, and I saw portrayed all over the walls all kinds of crawling things and detestable animals and all the idols of the house of Israel.[j] 11In front of them stood seventy elders of the house of Israel, and Jaazaniah son of Shaphan was standing among them. Each had a censer[k] in his hand, and a fragrant cloud of incense[l] was rising.

12He said to me, "Son of man, have you seen what the elders of the house of Israel are doing in the darkness, each at the shrine of his own idol? They say, 'The LORD does not see[m] us; the LORD has forsaken the land.'" 13Again, he said, "You will see them doing things that are even more detestable."

14Then he brought me to the entrance to the north gate of the house of the LORD, and I saw women sitting there, mourning for Tammuz. 15He said to me, "Do you see this, son of man? You will see things that are even more detestable than this."

16He then brought me into the inner court of the house of the LORD, and there at the entrance to the temple, between the portico and the altar,[n] were about twenty-five men. With their backs toward the temple of the LORD and their faces toward the east, they were bowing down to the sun in the east.[o]

17He said to me, "Have you seen this, son of man? Is it a trivial matter for the house of Judah to do the detestable things they are doing here? Must they also fill the land with violence[p] and continually provoke me to anger?[q] Look at them putting the branch to their nose! 18Therefore I will deal with them in anger; I will not look on them with pity[r] or spare them. Although they shout in my ears, I will not listen[s] to them."

Idolaters are killed.

9 Then I heard him call out in a loud voice, "Bring the guards of the city here, each with a weapon in his hand." 2And I saw six men coming from the direction of the upper gate, which faces north, each with a deadly weapon in his hand. With them was a man clothed in linen[t] who had a writing kit at his side. They came in and stood beside the bronze altar.

3Now the glory[u] of the God of Israel went up from above the cherubim,[v] where it had been, and moved to the threshold of the temple. Then the LORD called to the man clothed in linen who had the writing kit at his side 4and said to him, "Go throughout the city of Jerusalem and put a mark[w] on the foreheads of those who grieve and lament[x] over all the detestable things that are done in it.[y]"

5As I listened, he said to the others, "Follow him through the city and kill,

8:1 [a]Eze 33:31 [b]Eze 1:1-3
8:2 [c]Eze 1:4,26-27
8:3 [d]Eze 3:12; 11:1 [e]Ex 20:5; Dt 32:16
8:4 [f]Eze 1:28 [g]Eze 3:22
8:5 [h]Ps 78:58; Jer 32:34
8:6 [i]Eze 5:11
8:10 [j]Ex 20:4
8:11 [k]Nu 16:17 [l]Nu 16:35
8:12 [m]Ps 10:11; Isa 29:15; Eze 9:9
8:16 [n]Joel 2:17 [o]Dt 4:19; 17:3; Job 31:28; Jer 2:27; Eze 11:1,12
8:17 [p]Eze 9:9 [q]Eze 16:26
8:18 [r]Eze 9:10; 24:14 [s]Isa 1:15; Jer 11:11; Mic 3:4; Zec 7:13
9:2 [t]Lev 16:4; Eze 10:2; Rev 15:6
9:3 [u]Eze 10:4 [v]Eze 11:22
9:4 [w]Ex 12:7; 2Co 1:22; Rev 7:3; 9:4 [x]Ps 119:136; Jer 13:17; Eze 21:6 [y]Ps 119:53

p2 Or *saw a fiery figure*

without showing pity[a] or compassion. 6 Slaughter old men, young men and maidens, women and children, but do not touch anyone who has the mark. Begin at my sanctuary." So they began with the elders[b] who were in front of the temple.[c]

7 Then he said to them, "Defile the temple and fill the courts with the slain. Go!" So they went out and began killing throughout the city. 8 While they were killing and I was left alone, I fell facedown,[d] crying out, "Ah, Sovereign LORD! Are you going to destroy the entire remnant of Israel in this outpouring of your wrath on Jerusalem?[e]"

9 He answered me, "The sin of the house of Israel and Judah is exceedingly great; the land is full of bloodshed and the city is full of injustice.[f] They say, 'The LORD has forsaken the land; the LORD does not see.'[g] 10 So I will not look on them with pity[h] or spare them, but I will bring down on their own heads what they have done.[i]"

11 Then the man in linen with the writing kit at his side brought back word, saying, "I have done as you commanded."

Cherubim and wheels.

10 I looked, and I saw the likeness of a throne[j] of sapphire[q][k] above the expanse[l] that was over the heads of the cherubim. 2 The LORD said to the man clothed in linen,[m] "Go in among the wheels[n] beneath the cherubim. Fill[o] your hands with burning coals from among the cherubim and scatter them over the city." And as I watched, he went in.

3 Now the cherubim were standing on the south side of the temple when the man went in, and a cloud filled the inner court. 4 Then the glory of the LORD[p] rose from above the cherubim and moved to the threshold of the temple. The cloud filled the temple, and the court was full of the radiance of the glory of the LORD. 5 The sound of the wings of the cherubim could be heard as far away as the outer court, like the voice[q] of God Almighty[r] when he speaks.

6 When the LORD commanded the man in linen, "Take fire from among the wheels, from among the cherubim," the man went in and stood beside a wheel. 7 Then one of the cherubim reached out his hand to the fire that was among them. He took up some of it and put it into the hands of the man in linen, who took it and went out. 8 (Under the wings of the cherubim could be seen what looked like the hands of a man.)[r]

9 I looked, and I saw beside the cherubim four wheels, one beside each of the cherubim; the wheels sparkled like chrysolite.[s] 10 As for their appearance, the four of them looked alike; each was like a wheel intersecting a wheel. 11 As they moved, they would go in any one of the four directions the cherubim faced; the wheels did not turn about[s] as the cherubim went. The cherubim went in whatever direction the head faced, without turning as they went. 12 Their entire bodies, including their backs, their hands and their wings, were completely full of eyes,[t] as were their four wheels.[u] 13 I heard the wheels being called "the whirling wheels." 14 Each of the cherubim[v] had four faces:[w] One face was that of a cherub, the second the face of a man, the third the face of a lion, and the fourth the face of an eagle.[x]

15 Then the cherubim rose upward. These were the living creatures[y] I had seen by the Kebar River. 16 When the cherubim moved, the wheels beside them moved; and when the cherubim spread their wings to rise from the ground, the wheels did not leave their side. 17 When the cherubim stood still, they also stood still; and when the cherubim rose, they rose with them, because the spirit of the living creatures was in them.[z]

18 Then the glory of the LORD departed from over the threshold of the temple and stopped above the cherubim.[a]

9:5 [a]Eze 5:11
9:6 [b]Eze 8:11-13, 16 [c]2Ch 36:17; Jer 25:29; 1Pe 4:17
9:8 [d]Jos 7:6 [e]Eze 11:13; Am 7:1-6
9:9 [f]Eze 22:29 [g]Job 22:13; Eze 8:12
9:10 [h]Eze 7:4; 8:18 [i]Isa 65:6; Eze 11:21
10:1 [j]Rev 4:2 [k]Ex 24:10 [l]Eze 1:22
10:2 [m]Eze 9:2 [n]Eze 1:15 [o]Rev 8:5
10:4 [p]Eze 1:28; 9:3
10:5 [q]Job 40:9; Eze 1:24
10:8 [r]Eze 1:8
10:9 [s]Eze 1:15-16; Rev 21:20
10:12 [t]Rev 4:6-8 [u]Eze 1:15-21
10:14 [v]1Ki 7:36 [w]Eze 1:6 [x]Eze 1:10; Rev 4:7
10:15 [y]Eze 1:3,5
10:17 [z]Eze 1:20-21
10:18 [a]Ps 18:10

[q] *1* Or *lapis lazuli* [r] *5* Hebrew *El-Shaddai* [s] *11* Or *aside*

19While I watched, the cherubim spread
their wings and rose from the ground,
and as they went, the wheels went with
them.[a] They stopped at the entrance to
the east gate of the LORD's house, and
the glory of the God of Israel was above
them.
20These were the living creatures I
had seen beneath the God of Israel by
the Kebar River,[b] and I realized that they
were cherubim. 21Each had four faces[c]
and four wings,[d] and under their wings
was what looked like the hands of a
man. 22Their faces had the same appearance as those I had seen by the Kebar
River. Each one went straight ahead.

Ezekiel prophesies against twenty-five men.

11 Then the Spirit lifted me up and
brought me to the gate of the
house of the LORD that faces east. There
at the entrance to the gate were twenty-
five men, and I saw among them Jaazaniah son of Azzur and Pelatiah son of
Benaiah, leaders of the people.[e] 2The
LORD said to me, "Son of man, these are
the men who are plotting evil and giving wicked advice in this city. 3They say,
'Will it not soon be time to build houses?[t] This city is a cooking pot,[f] and we
are the meat.'[g] 4Therefore prophesy[h]
against them; prophesy, son of man."
5Then the Spirit of the LORD came
upon me, and he told me to say: "This
is what the LORD says: That is what you
are saying, O house of Israel, but I know
what is going through your mind.[i] 6You
have killed many people in this city
and filled its streets with the dead.[j]
7"Therefore this is what the Sovereign LORD says: The bodies you have
thrown there are the meat and this city
is the pot, but I will drive you out of it.[k]
8You fear the sword, and the sword is
what I will bring against you, declares
the Sovereign LORD.[l] 9I will drive you
out of the city and hand you over[m] to
foreigners and inflict punishment on
you.[n] 10You will fall by the sword, and I
will execute judgment on you at the
borders of Israel.[o] Then you will know
that I am the LORD. 11This city will not
be a pot[p] for you, nor will you be the
meat in it; I will execute judgment on
you at the borders of Israel. 12And you
will know that I am the LORD, for you
have not followed my decrees[q] or kept
my laws but have conformed to the
standards of the nations around you.[r]"
13Now as I was prophesying, Pelatiah[s] son of Benaiah died. Then I fell
facedown and cried out in a loud voice,
"Ah, Sovereign LORD! Will you completely destroy the remnant of Israel?[t]"
14The word of the LORD came to me:
15"Son of man, your brothers—your
brothers who are your blood relatives[u]
and the whole house of Israel—are
those of whom the people of Jerusalem
have said, 'They are[v] far away from the
LORD; this land was given to us as our
possession.'[u]

God promises restoration of Israel.

16"Therefore say: 'This is what the
Sovereign LORD says: Although I sent
them far away among the nations and
scattered them among the countries,
yet for a little while I have been a sanctuary[v] for them in the countries where
they have gone.'
17"Therefore say: 'This is what the
Sovereign LORD says: I will gather you
from the nations and bring you back
from the countries where you have been
scattered, and I will give you back the
land of Israel again.'[w]
18"They will return to it and remove
all its vile images[x] and detestable idols.[y]
19I will give them an undivided heart[z]
and put a new spirit in them; I will remove from them their heart of stone[a]
and give them a heart of flesh.[b] 20Then
they will follow my decrees and be careful to keep my laws.[c] They will be my
people, and I will be their God.[d] 21But
as for those whose hearts are devoted
to their vile images and detestable idols,

10:19 [a]Eze 11:1,22
10:20 [b]Eze 1:1
10:21 [c]Eze 41:18 [d]Eze 1:6
11:1 [e]Eze 8:16; 10:19; 43:4-5
11:3 [f]Jer 1:13; Eze 24:3 [g]ver 7,11
11:4 [h]Eze 3:4,17
11:5 [i]Jer 17:10
11:6 [j]Eze 7:23; 22:6
11:7 [k]Eze 24:3-13; Mic 3:2-3
11:8 [l]Pr 10:24
11:9 [m]Ps 106:41 [n]Dt 28:36; Eze 5:8
11:10 [o]2Ki 14:25
11:11 [p]ver 3
11:12 [q]Lev 18:4; Eze 18:9 [r]Eze 8:10
11:13 [s]ver 1 [t]Eze 9:8
11:15 [u]Eze 33:24
11:16 [v]Ps 90:1; 91:9; Isa 8:14
11:17 [w]Jer 3:18; 24:5-6; Eze 28:25; 34:13
11:18 [x]Eze 5:11 [y]Eze 37:23
11:19 [z]Jer 32:39 [a]Zec 7:12 [b]Eze 18:31; 36:26; 2Co 3:3
11:20 [c]Ps 105:45 [d]Eze 14:11; 36:26-28

t3 Or *This is not the time to build houses.* u15 Or *are in exile with you* (see Septuagint and Syriac) v15 Or *those to whom the people of Jerusalem have said, 'Stay*

I will bring down on their own heads
what they have done, declares the Sovereign LORD.[a]"
22Then the cherubim, with the wheels
beside them, spread their wings, and
the glory of the God of Israel was above
them.[b] 23The glory[c] of the LORD went up
from within the city and stopped above
the mountain[d] east of it. 24The Spirit[e]
lifted me up and brought me to the exiles in Babylonia[w] in the vision[f] given by
the Spirit of God.

Then the vision I had seen went up
from me, 25and I told the exiles everything the LORD had shown me.[g]

Ezekiel packs belongings for exile.

12 The word of the LORD came to
me: 2"Son of man, you are living
among a rebellious people. They have
eyes to see but do not see and ears to
hear but do not hear, for they are a
rebellious people.[h]

3"Therefore, son of man, pack your
belongings for exile and in the daytime,
as they watch, set out and go from
where you are to another place. Perhaps[i] they will understand,[j] though they
are a rebellious house.[k] 4During the daytime, while they watch, bring out your
belongings packed for exile. Then in the
evening, while they are watching, go
out like those who go into exile.[l] 5While
they watch, dig through the wall and
take your belongings out through it.
6Put them on your shoulder as they are
watching and carry them out at dusk.
Cover your face so that you cannot see
the land, for I have made you a sign[m] to
the house of Israel."

7So I did as I was commanded.[n] During the day I brought out my things
packed for exile. Then in the evening I
dug through the wall with my hands. I
took my belongings out at dusk, carrying them on my shoulders while they
watched.

8In the morning the word of the LORD
came to me: 9"Son of man, did not that
rebellious house of Israel ask you, 'What
are you doing?'[o]

10"Say to them, 'This is what the Sovereign LORD says: This oracle concerns
the prince in Jerusalem and the whole
house of Israel who are there.' 11Say to
them, 'I am a sign to you.'

"As I have done, so it will be done
to them. They will go into exile as captives.[p]

12"The prince among them will put
his things on his shoulder at dusk[q] and
leave, and a hole will be dug in the wall
for him to go through. He will cover his
face so that he cannot see the land.[r] 13I
will spread my net[s] for him, and he will
be caught in my snare;[t] I will bring him
to Babylonia, the land of the Chaldeans,
but he will not see[u] it, and there he will
die.[v] 14I will scatter to the winds all
those around him—his staff and all his
troops—and I will pursue them with
drawn sword.[w]

15"They will know that I am the LORD,
when I disperse them among the nations
and scatter them through the countries.
16But I will spare a few of them from
the sword, famine and plague, so that
in the nations where they go they may
acknowledge all their detestable practices. Then they will know that I am
the LORD.[x]"

Ezekiel trembles and shudders.

17The word of the LORD came to me:
18"Son of man, tremble as you eat your
food,[y] and shudder in fear as you drink
your water. 19Say to the people of the
land: 'This is what the Sovereign LORD
says about those living in Jerusalem and
in the land of Israel: They will eat their
food in anxiety and drink their water in
despair, for their land will be stripped of
everything[z] in it because of the violence
of all who live there.[a] 20The inhabited
towns will be laid waste and the land
will be desolate. Then you will know
that I am the LORD.[b]'"

21The word of the LORD came to me:
22"Son of man, what is this proverb you

11:21 [a]Eze 9:10; 16:43
11:22 [b]Eze 10:19
11:23 [c]Eze 8:4; 10:4 [d]Zec 14:4
11:24 [e]Eze 8:3 [f]2Co 12:2-4
11:25 [g]Eze 3:4,11
12:2 [h]Isa 6:10; Eze 2:6-8; Mt 13:15
12:3 [i]Jer 36:3 [j]Jer 26:3 [k]2Ti 2:25-26
12:4 [l]ver 12; Jer 39:4
12:6 [m]ver 12; Isa 8:18; 20:3; Eze 4:3; 24:24
12:7 [n]Eze 24:18; 37:10
12:9 [o]Eze 17:12; 20:49; 24:19
12:11 [p]2Ki 25:7; Jer 15:2; 52:15
12:12 [q]Jer 39:4 [r]Jer 52:7
12:13 [s]Eze 17:20; 19:8; Hos 7:12 [t]Isa 24:17-18 [u]Jer 39:7 [v]Jer 52:11; Eze 17:16
12:14 [w]2Ki 25:5; Eze 5:10,12
12:16 [x]Jer 22:8-9; Eze 6:8-10; 14:22
12:18 [y]La 5:9; Eze 4:16
12:19 [z]Eze 6:6-14; Mic 7:13; Zec 7:14 [a]Eze 4:16; 23:33
12:20 [b]Isa 7:23-24; Jer 4:7

w*24* Or *Chaldea*

have in the land of Israel: 'The days go by and every vision comes to nothing'?[a] 23Say to them, 'This is what the Sovereign LORD says: I am going to put an end to this proverb, and they will no longer quote it in Israel.' Say to them, 'The days are near when every vision will be fulfilled.[b] 24For there will be no more false visions or flattering divinations[c] among the people of Israel. 25But I the LORD will speak what I will, and it shall be fulfilled without delay. For in your days, you rebellious house, I will fulfill whatever I say, declares the Sovereign LORD.[d]' "

26The word of the LORD came to me: 27"Son of man, the house of Israel is saying, 'The vision he sees is for many years from now, and he prophesies about the distant future.'[e]

28"Therefore say to them, 'This is what the Sovereign LORD says: None of my words will be delayed any longer; whatever I say will be fulfilled, declares the Sovereign LORD.' "

Judgment against false prophets.

13 The word of the LORD came to me: 2"Son of man, prophesy against the prophets of Israel who are now prophesying. Say to those who prophesy out of their own imagination: 'Hear the word of the LORD![f] 3This is what the Sovereign LORD says: Woe to the foolish[x] prophets[g] who follow their own spirit and have seen nothing![h] 4Your prophets, O Israel, are like jackals among ruins. 5You have not gone up to the breaks in the wall to repair[i] it for the house of Israel so that it will stand firm in the battle on the day of the LORD.[j] 6Their visions are false and their divinations a lie. They say, "The LORD declares," when the LORD has not sent them; yet they expect their words to be fulfilled.[k] 7Have you not seen false visions and uttered lying divinations when you say, "The LORD declares," though I have not spoken?

8" 'Therefore this is what the Sovereign LORD says: Because of your false words and lying visions, I am against you, declares the Sovereign LORD. 9My hand will be against the prophets who see false visions and utter lying divinations. They will not belong to the council of my people or be listed in the records[l] of the house of Israel, nor will they enter the land of Israel. Then you will know that I am the Sovereign LORD.[m]

10" 'Because they lead my people astray,[n] saying, "Peace," when there is no peace, and because, when a flimsy wall is built, they cover it with whitewash,[o] 11therefore tell those who cover it with whitewash that it is going to fall. Rain will come in torrents, and I will send hailstones hurtling down, and violent winds will burst forth.[p] 12When the wall collapses, will people not ask you, "Where is the whitewash you covered it with?"

13" 'Therefore this is what the Sovereign LORD says: In my wrath I will unleash a violent wind, and in my anger hailstones[q] and torrents of rain will fall with destructive fury.[r] 14I will tear down the wall you have covered with whitewash and will level it to the ground so that its foundation[s] will be laid bare. When it[y] falls,[t] you will be destroyed in it; and you will know that I am the LORD. 15So I will spend my wrath against the wall and against those who covered it with whitewash. I will say to you, "The wall is gone and so are those who whitewashed it, 16those prophets of Israel who prophesied to Jerusalem and saw visions of peace for her when there was no peace, declares the Sovereign LORD.[u]" '

17"Now, son of man, set your face against the daughters[v] of your people who prophesy out of their own imagination. Prophesy against them[w] 18and say, 'This is what the Sovereign LORD says: Woe to the women who sew magic charms on all their wrists and make veils of various lengths for their heads in order to ensnare people. Will you ensnare the lives of my people but preserve

12:22 [a]Eze 11:3; Am 6:3; 2Pe 3:4
12:23 [b]Ps 37:13; Joel 2:1; Zep 1:14
12:24 [c]Jer 14:14; Eze 13:23; Zec 13:2-4
12:25 [d]Isa 14:24; Hab 1:5
12:27 [e]Da 10:14
13:2 [f]ver 17; Jer 23:16; 37:19
13:3 [g]La 2:14 [h]Jer 23:25-32
13:5 [i]Isa 58:12; Eze 22:30 [j]Eze 7:19
13:6 [k]Jer 28:15; Eze 22:28
13:9 [l]Jer 17:13 [m]Eze 20:38
13:10 [n]Jer 50:6 [o]Eze 7:25; 22:28
13:11 [p]Eze 38:22
13:13 [q]Rev 11:19; 16:21 [r]Ex 9:25; Isa 30:30
13:14 [s]Mic 1:6 [t]Jer 6:15
13:16 [u]Isa 57:21; Jer 6:14
13:17 [v]Rev 2:20 [w]ver 2

[x]3 Or *wicked* [y]14 Or *the city*

your own? 19You have profaned[a] me
among my people for a few handfuls of
barley and scraps of bread. By lying to
my people, who listen to lies, you have
killed those who should not have died
and have spared those who should not
live.[b]
20"'Therefore this is what the Sovereign LORD says: I am against your magic
charms with which you ensnare people
like birds and I will tear them from your
arms; I will set free the people that you
ensnare like birds. 21I will tear off your
veils and save my people from your
hands, and they will no longer fall prey
to your power. Then you will know that
I am the LORD.[c] 22Because you disheartened the righteous with your lies, when
I had brought them no grief, and because you encouraged the wicked not to
turn from their evil ways and so save
their lives,[d] 23therefore you will no
longer see false visions or practice divination.[e] I will save my people from your
hands. And then you will know that I
am the LORD.[f]'"

Idolatrous elders rebuked.

14 Some of the elders of Israel came
to me and sat down in front of
me.[g] 2Then the word of the LORD came
to me: 3"Son of man, these men have set
up idols in their hearts and put wicked
stumbling blocks[h] before their faces.
Should I let them inquire of me at all?[i]
4Therefore speak to them and tell them,
'This is what the Sovereign LORD says:
When any Israelite sets up idols in his
heart and puts a wicked stumbling block
before his face and then goes to a
prophet, I the LORD will answer him myself in keeping with his great idolatry.
5I will do this to recapture the hearts of
the people of Israel, who have all deserted[j] me for their idols.'[k]
6"Therefore say to the house of Israel,
'This is what the Sovereign LORD says:
Repent! Turn from your idols and renounce all your detestable practices![l]
7"'When any Israelite or any alien[m]
living in Israel separates himself from
me and sets up idols in his heart and
puts a wicked stumbling block before
his face and then goes to a prophet to
inquire of me, I the LORD will answer
him myself. 8I will set my face against[n]
that man and make him an example and
a byword.[o] I will cut him off from my
people. Then you will know that I am
the LORD.
9"'And if the prophet[p] is enticed[q] to
utter a prophecy, I the LORD have enticed that prophet, and I will stretch out
my hand against him and destroy him
from among my people Israel.[r] 10They
will bear their guilt—the prophet will
be as guilty as the one who consults
him. 11Then the people of Israel will
no longer stray[s] from me, nor will they
defile themselves anymore with all their
sins. They will be my people, and I will
be their God, declares the Sovereign
LORD.[t]'"

Four dreadful judgments.

12The word of the LORD came to me:
13"Son of man, if a country sins against
me by being unfaithful and I stretch out
my hand against it to cut off its food
supply[u] and send famine upon it and
kill its men and their animals,[v] 14even if
these three men—Noah,[w] Daniel[z][x] and
Job[y]—were in it, they could save only
themselves by their righteousness,[z] declares the Sovereign LORD.
15"Or if I send wild beasts[a] through
that country and they leave it childless
and it becomes desolate so that no one
can pass through it because of the
beasts,[b] 16as surely as I live, declares
the Sovereign LORD, even if these three
men were in it, they could not save
their own sons or daughters. They alone
would be saved, but the land would be
desolate.[c]
17"Or if I bring a sword[d] against that
country and say, 'Let the sword pass
throughout the land,' and I kill its men
and their animals,[e] 18as surely as I live,
declares the Sovereign LORD, even if

13:19 [a]Eze 20:39; 22:26 [b]Pr 28:21
13:21 [c]Ps 91:3
13:22 [d]Jer 23:14; Eze 33:14-16
13:23 [e]ver 6; Eze 12:24 [f]Mic 3:6
14:1 [g]Eze 8:1; 20:1
14:3 [h]ver 7; Eze 7:19 [i]Isa 1:15; Eze 20:31
14:5 [j]Zec 11:8 [k]Jer 2:11
14:6 [l]Isa 2:20; 30:22
14:7 [m]Ex 12:48; 20:10
14:8 [n]Eze 15:7 [o]Eze 5:15
14:9 [p]Jer 14:15 [q]Jer 4:10 [r]1Ki 22:23
14:11 [s]Eze 48:11 [t]Eze 11:19-20; 37:23
14:13 [u]Lev 26:26 [v]Eze 5:16; 6:14; 15:8
14:14 [w]Ge 6:8 [x]ver 20; Eze 28:3; Da 1:6; 6:13 [y]Job 1:1 [z]Job 42:9; Jer 15:1; Eze 18:20
14:15 [a]Eze 5:17 [b]Lev 26:22
14:16 [c]Eze 18:20
14:17 [d]Lev 26:25; Eze 5:12; 21:3-4 [e]Eze 25:13; Zep 1:3

[z]14 Or *Danel*; the Hebrew spelling may suggest a person other than the prophet Daniel; also in verse 20.

these three men were in it, they could
not save their own sons or daughters.
They alone would be saved.
19 "Or if I send a plague into that land
and pour out my wrath[a] upon it through
bloodshed, killing its men and their
animals,[b] 20 as surely as I live, declares
the Sovereign LORD, even if Noah, Daniel
and Job were in it, they could save neither son nor daughter. They would save
only themselves by their righteousness.[c]
21 "For this is what the Sovereign LORD
says: How much worse will it be when
I send against Jerusalem my four dreadful judgments—sword and famine and
wild beasts and plague—to kill its men
and their animals![d] 22 Yet there will be
some survivors—sons and daughters
who will be brought out of it.[e] They will
come to you, and when you see their
conduct[f] and their actions, you will be
consoled regarding the disaster I have
brought upon Jerusalem—every disaster
I have brought upon it. 23 You will be
consoled when you see their conduct
and their actions, for you will know that
I have done nothing in it without cause,
declares the Sovereign LORD.[g]"

A useless vine.

15 The word of the LORD came to
me: 2 "Son of man, how is the
wood of a vine[h] better than that of a
branch on any of the trees in the forest?
3 Is wood ever taken from it to make
anything useful? Do they make pegs
from it to hang things on? 4 And after it
is thrown on the fire as fuel and the fire
burns both ends and chars the middle,
is it then useful for anything?[i] 5 If it was
not useful for anything when it was
whole, how much less can it be made
into something useful when the fire has
burned it and it is charred?
6 "Therefore this is what the Sovereign
LORD says: As I have given the wood of
the vine among the trees of the forest as
fuel for the fire, so will I treat the people
living in Jerusalem. 7 I will set my face
against[j] them. Although they have
come out of the fire, the fire will yet
consume them. And when I set my face
against them, you will know that I am
the LORD.[k] 8 I will make the land desolate[l] because they have been unfaithful,[m] declares the Sovereign LORD."

Woe to adulterous Jerusalem.

16 The word of the LORD came to
me: 2 "Son of man, confront Jerusalem with her detestable practices[n]
3 and say, 'This is what the Sovereign
LORD says to Jerusalem: Your ancestry[o]
and birth were in the land of the Canaanites; your father was an Amorite
and your mother a Hittite.[p] 4 On the
day you were born[q] your cord was not
cut, nor were you washed with water to
make you clean, nor were you rubbed
with salt or wrapped in cloths. 5 No one
looked on you with pity or had compassion enough to do any of these things for
you. Rather, you were thrown out into
the open field, for on the day you were
born you were despised.
6 " 'Then I passed by and saw you
kicking about in your blood, and as you
lay there in your blood I said to you,
"Live!"[a][r] 7 I made you grow[s] like a plant
of the field. You grew up and developed
and became the most beautiful of jewels.[b] Your breasts were formed and your
hair grew, you who were naked and
bare.[t]
8 " 'Later I passed by, and when I
looked at you and saw that you were old
enough for love, I spread the corner of
my garment[u] over you and covered your
nakedness. I gave you my solemn oath
and entered into a covenant with you,
declares the Sovereign LORD, and you
became mine.[v]
9 " 'I bathed[c] you with water and
washed[w] the blood from you and put
ointments on you. 10 I clothed you with
an embroidered[x] dress and put leather
sandals on you. I dressed you in fine
linen[y] and covered you with costly garments.[z] 11 I adorned you with jewelry:[a]

14:19 [a]Eze 7:8 [b]Eze 38:22
14:20 [c]ver 14
14:21 [d]Jer 15:3; Eze 5:17; 33:27; Am 4:6-10; Rev 6:8
14:22 [e]Eze 12:16 [f]Eze 20:43
14:23 [g]Jer 22:8-9
15:2 [h]Isa 5:1-7; Jer 2:21; Hos 10:1
15:4 [i]Eze 19:14; Jn 15:6
15:7 [j]Ps 34:16; Eze 14:8 [k]Isa 24:18; Am 9:1-4
15:8 [l]Eze 14:13 [m]Eze 17:20
16:2 [n]Eze 20:4; 22:2
16:3 [o]Eze 21:30 [p]ver 45
16:4 [q]Hos 2:3
16:6 [r]Ex 19:4
16:7 [s]Dt 1:10 [t]Ex 1:7
16:8 [u]Ru 3:9 [v]Jer 2:2; Hos 2:7,19-20
16:9 [w]Ru 3:3
16:10 [x]Ex 26:36 [y]Eze 27:16 [z]ver 18
16:11 [a]Eze 23:40

a *6* A few Hebrew manuscripts, Septuagint and Syriac; most Hebrew manuscripts *"Live!" And as you lay there in your blood I said to you, "Live!"* b *7* Or *became mature* c *9* Or *I had bathed*

I put bracelets[a] on your arms and a
necklace[b] around your neck, 12and I put
a ring on your nose,[c] earrings on your
ears and a beautiful crown[d] on your
head. 13So you were adorned with gold
and silver; your clothes were of fine
linen and costly fabric and embroidered
cloth. Your food was fine flour, honey
and olive oil.[e] You became very beautiful and rose to be a queen.[f] 14And your
fame[g] spread among the nations on account of your beauty,[h] because the
splendor I had given you made your
beauty perfect, declares the Sovereign
LORD.

15" 'But you trusted in your beauty
and used your fame to become a prostitute. You lavished your favors on anyone
who passed by[i] and your beauty became
his.[d] [j] 16You took some of your garments
to make gaudy high places, where you
carried on your prostitution.[k] Such
things should not happen, nor should
they ever occur. 17You also took the fine
jewelry I gave you, the jewelry made
of my gold and silver, and you made for
yourself male idols and engaged in prostitution with them.[l] 18And you took your
embroidered clothes to put on them,
and you offered my oil and incense before them. 19Also the food I provided for
you—the fine flour, olive oil and honey
I gave you to eat—you offered as fragrant
incense before them. That is what happened, declares the Sovereign LORD.[m]

20" 'And you took your sons and
daughters[n] whom you bore to me[o] and
sacrificed them as food to the idols. Was
your prostitution not enough?[p] 21You
slaughtered my children and sacrificed
them[e] to the idols.[q] 22In all your detestable practices and your prostitution you
did not remember the days of your
youth,[r] when you were naked and bare,
kicking about in your blood.[s]

23" 'Woe! Woe to you, declares the
Sovereign LORD. In addition to all your
other wickedness, 24you built a mound
for yourself and made a lofty shrine[t] in
every public square.[u] 25At the head of
every street you built your lofty shrines
and degraded your beauty, offering your
body with increasing promiscuity to
anyone who passed by.[v] 26You engaged
in prostitution with the Egyptians, your
lustful neighbors, and provoked[w] me to
anger with your increasing promiscuity.[x]
27So I stretched out my hand[y] against
you and reduced your territory; I gave
you over to the greed of your enemies,
the daughters of the Philistines,[z] who
were shocked by your lewd conduct.
28You engaged in prostitution with the
Assyrians[a] too, because you were insa-
tiable; and even after that, you still were
not satisfied. 29Then you increased your
promiscuity to include Babylonia,[f] [b] a
land of merchants, but even with this
you were not satisfied.

30" 'How weak-willed you are, declares the Sovereign LORD, when you do
all these things, acting like a brazen
prostitute![c] 31When you built your
mounds at the head of every street and
made your lofty shrines[d] in every public
square, you were unlike a prostitute, because you scorned payment.

32" 'You adulterous wife! You prefer
strangers to your own husband! 33Every
prostitute receives a fee, but you give
gifts[e] to all your lovers, bribing them to
come to you from everywhere for your
illicit favors.[f] 34So in your prostitution
you are the opposite of others; no one
runs after you for your favors. You are
the very opposite, for you give payment
and none is given to you.

35" 'Therefore, you prostitute, hear the
word of the LORD! 36This is what the
Sovereign LORD says: Because you
poured out your wealth[g] and exposed
your nakedness in your promiscuity
with your lovers, and because of all your
detestable idols, and because you gave
them your children's blood,[g] 37therefore
I am going to gather all your lovers, with
whom you found pleasure, those you
loved as well as those you hated. I will

16:11 [a]Isa 3:19; Eze 23:42 [b]Ge 41:42
16:12 [c]Isa 3:21 [d]Isa 28:5; Jer 13:18
16:13 [e]1Sa 10:1 [f]Dt 32:13-14; 1Ki 4:21
16:14 [g]1Ki 10:24 [h]La 2:15
16:15 [i]ver 25 [j]Isa 57:8; Jer 2:20; Eze 23:3; 27:3
16:16 [k]2Ki 23:7
16:17 [l]Eze 7:20
16:19 [m]Hos 2:8
16:20 [n]Jer 7:31 [o]Ex 13:2 [p]Ps 106:37-38; Isa 57:5; Eze 23:37
16:21 [q]2Ki 17:17; Jer 19:5
16:22 [r]Jer 2:2; Hos 11:1 [s]ver 6
16:24 [t]ver 31; Isa 57:7 [u]Ps 78:58; Jer 2:20; 3:2; Eze 20:28
16:25 [v]ver 15; Pr 9:14
16:26 [w]Eze 8:17 [x]Eze 20:8; 23:19-21
16:27 [y]Eze 20:33 [z]2Ch 28:18
16:28 [a]2Ki 16:7
16:29 [b]Eze 23:14-17
16:30 [c]Jer 3:3
16:31 [d]ver 24
16:33 [e]Isa 30:6; 57:9 [f]Hos 8:9-10
16:36 [g]Jer 19:5; Eze 23:10

[d] *15* Most Hebrew manuscripts; one Hebrew manuscript (see some Septuagint manuscripts) *by. Such a thing should not happen*
[e] *21* Or *and made them pass through* ⌊*the fire*⌋
[f] *29* Or *Chaldea*
[g] *36* Or *lust*

gather them against you from all around
and will strip you in front of them, and
they will see all your nakedness.[a] **38**I
will sentence you to the punishment of
women who commit adultery and who
shed blood;[b] I will bring upon you the
blood vengeance of my wrath and jealous anger.[c] **39**Then I will hand you over
to your lovers, and they will tear down
your mounds and destroy your lofty
shrines. They will strip you of your
clothes and take your fine jewelry and
leave you naked and bare.[d] **40**They will
bring a mob against you, who will
stone[e] you and hack you to pieces with
their swords. **41**They will burn down[f]
your houses and inflict punishment on
you in the sight of many women.[g] I will
put a stop[h] to your prostitution, and you
will no longer pay your lovers. **42**Then
my wrath against you will subside and
my jealous anger will turn away from
you; I will be calm and no longer angry.[i]

43"'Because you did not remember[j]
the days of your youth but enraged me
with all these things, I will surely bring
down[k] on your head what you have
done, declares the Sovereign LORD. Did
you not add lewdness to all your other
detestable practices?[l]

44"'Everyone who quotes proverbs
will quote this proverb about you: "Like
mother, like daughter." **45**You are a true
daughter of your mother, who despised
her husband and her children; and you
are a true sister of your sisters, who despised their husbands and their children.
Your mother was a Hittite and your father an Amorite.[m] **46**Your older sister was
Samaria, who lived to the north of you
with her daughters; and your younger
sister, who lived to the south of you with
her daughters, was Sodom.[n] **47**You not
only walked in their ways and copied
their detestable practices, but in all your
ways you soon became more depraved
than they.[o] **48**As surely as I live, declares
the Sovereign LORD, your sister Sodom
and her daughters never did what you
and your daughters have done.[p]

49"'Now this was the sin of your sister Sodom:[q] She and her daughters were
arrogant,[r] overfed and unconcerned; they
did not help the poor and needy.[s] **50**They
were haughty and did detestable things
before me. Therefore I did away with
them as you have seen.[t] **51**Samaria did
not commit half the sins you did. You
have done more detestable things than
they, and have made your sisters seem
righteous by all these things you have
done.[u] **52**Bear your disgrace, for you have
furnished some justification for your sisters. Because your sins were more vile
than theirs, they appear more righteous
than you. So then, be ashamed and bear
your disgrace, for you have made your
sisters appear righteous.

53"'However, I will restore[v] the fortunes of Sodom and her daughters and
of Samaria and her daughters, and your
fortunes along with them, **54**so that you
may bear your disgrace[w] and be ashamed
of all you have done in giving them
comfort. **55**And your sisters, Sodom with
her daughters and Samaria with her
daughters, will return to what they
were before; and you and your daughters will return to what you were before.[x] **56**You would not even mention
your sister Sodom in the day of your
pride, **57**before your wickedness was uncovered. Even so, you are now scorned
by the daughters of Edom[h][y] and all her
neighbors and the daughters of the
Philistines—all those around you who
despise you. **58**You will bear the consequences of your lewdness and your detestable practices, declares the LORD.[z]

The LORD will remember his covenant.

59"'This is what the Sovereign LORD
says: I will deal with you as you deserve,
because you have despised my oath by
breaking the covenant.[a] **60**Yet I will remember the covenant I made with you
in the days of your youth, and I will
establish an everlasting covenant[b] with
you. **61**Then you will remember your
ways and be ashamed[c] when you receive

16:37 [a]Jer 13:22
16:38 [b]Eze 23:45 [c]Lev 20:10; Eze 23:25
16:39 [d]Eze 23:26; Hos 2:3
16:40 [e]Jn 8:5,7
16:41 [f]Dt 13:16 [g]Eze 23:10 [h]Eze 23:27,48
16:42 [i]Isa 54:9; Eze 5:13; 39:29
16:43 [j]Ps 78:42 [k]Eze 22:31 [l]ver 22; Eze 11:21
16:45 [m]Eze 23:2
16:46 [n]Ge 13:10-13; Eze 23:4
16:47 [o]2Ki 21:9; Eze 5:7
16:48 [p]Mt 10:15; 11:23-24
16:49 [q]Ge 13:13 [r]Ps 138:6 [s]Eze 18:7,12, 16; Lk 12:16-20
16:50 [t]Ge 18:20-21; 19:5
16:51 [u]Jer 3:8-11
16:53 [v]Isa 19:24-25
16:54 [w]Jer 2:26; Eze 14:22
16:55 [x]Mal 3:4
16:57 [y]2Ki 16:6
16:58 [z]Eze 23:49
16:59 [a]Eze 17:19
16:60 [b]Jer 32:40; Eze 37:26
16:61 [c]Eze 20:43

[h]*57* Many Hebrew manuscripts and Syriac; most Hebrew manuscripts, Septuagint and Vulgate *Aram*

your sisters, both those who are older
than you and those who are younger. I
will give them to you as daughters, but
not on the basis of my covenant with
you. 62So I will establish my covenant
with you, and you will know that I am
the LORD.[a] 63Then, when I make atonement[b] for you for all you have done,
you will remember and be ashamed and
never again open your mouth[c] because
of your humiliation, declares the Sovereign LORD.[d] ' "

Two eagles and a vine.

17 The word of the LORD came to
me: 2"Son of man, set forth an
allegory and tell the house of Israel a
parable.[e] 3Say to them, 'This is what the
Sovereign LORD says: A great eagle[f]
with powerful wings, long feathers and
full plumage of varied colors came to
Lebanon.[g] Taking hold of the top of a
cedar, 4he broke off its topmost shoot
and carried it away to a land of merchants, where he planted it in a city of
traders.

5" 'He took some of the seed of your
land and put it in fertile soil. He planted
it like a willow by abundant water,[h] 6and
it sprouted and became a low, spreading
vine. Its branches turned toward him,
but its roots remained under it. So it
became a vine and produced branches
and put out leafy boughs.

7" 'But there was another great eagle
with powerful wings and full plumage.
The vine now sent out its roots toward
him from the plot where it was planted
and stretched out its branches to him
for water.[i] 8It had been planted in good
soil by abundant water so that it would
produce branches, bear fruit and become
a splendid vine.'

9"Say to them, 'This is what the Sovereign LORD says: Will it thrive? Will it
not be uprooted and stripped of its fruit
so that it withers? All its new growth
will wither. It will not take a strong arm
or many people to pull it up by the
roots. 10Even if it[j] is transplanted, will
it thrive? Will it not wither completely
when the east wind strikes it—wither
away in the plot where it grew?' "

11Then the word of the LORD came to
me: 12"Say to this rebellious house,
'Do you not know what these things
mean?[k] ' Say to them: 'The king of Babylon went to Jerusalem and carried off
her king and her nobles,[l] bringing them
back with him to Babylon.[m] 13Then he
took a member of the royal family and
made a treaty with him, putting him
under oath.[n] He also carried away the
leading men of the land, 14so that the
kingdom would be brought low,[o] unable
to rise again, surviving only by keeping
his treaty. 15But the king rebelled[p]
against him by sending his envoys to
Egypt to get horses and a large
army.[q] Will he succeed? Will he who
does such things escape? Will he break
the treaty and yet escape?[r]

16" 'As surely as I live, declares the
Sovereign LORD, he shall die[s] in Babylon, in the land of the king who put him
on the throne, whose oath he despised
and whose treaty he broke.[t] 17Pharaoh[u]
with his mighty army and great horde
will be of no help to him in war, when
ramps[v] are built and siege works erected
to destroy many lives.[w] 18He despised
the oath by breaking the covenant. Because he had given his hand in pledge[x]
and yet did all these things, he shall not
escape.

19" 'Therefore this is what the Sovereign LORD says: As surely as I live, I will
bring down on his head my oath that
he despised and my covenant that he
broke.[y] 20I will spread my net[z] for him,
and he will be caught in my snare. I will
bring him to Babylon and execute judgment[a] upon him there because he was
unfaithful to me. 21All his fleeing troops
will fall by the sword,[b] and the survivors[c] will be scattered to the winds.[d]
Then you will know that I the LORD
have spoken.

22" 'This is what the Sovereign LORD
says: I myself will take a shoot from the
very top of a cedar and plant it; I will
break off a tender sprig from its topmost
shoots and plant it on a high and lofty

16:62 [a]Jer 24:7; Eze 20:37, 43-44; Hos 2:19-20
16:63 [b]Ps 65:3; 79:9 [c]Ro 3:19 [d]Ps 39:9; Da 9:7-8
17:2 [e]Eze 20:49
17:3 [f]Hos 8:1 [g]Jer 22:23
17:5 [h]Dt 8:7-9; Isa 44:4
17:7 [i]Eze 31:4
17:10 [j]Hos 13:15
17:12 [k]Eze 12:9 [l]2Ki 24:15 [m]Eze 24:19
17:13 [n]2Ch 36:13
17:14 [o]Eze 29:14
17:15 [p]Jer 52:3 [q]Dt 17:16 [r]Jer 34:3; 38:18
17:16 [s]Jer 52:11; Eze 12:13 [t]2Ki 24:17
17:17 [u]Jer 37:7 [v]Eze 4:2 [w]Isa 36:6; Jer 37:5; Eze 29:6-7
17:18 [x]1Ch 29:24
17:19 [y]Eze 16:59
17:20 [z]Eze 12:13; 32:3 [a]Jer 2:35; Eze 20:36
17:21 [b]Eze 12:14 [c]2Ki 25:11 [d]2Ki 25:5

mountain.[a] 23On the mountain heights
of Israel I will plant it; it will produce
branches and bear fruit and become a
splendid cedar. Birds of every kind will
nest in it; they will find shelter in the
shade of its branches.[b] 24All the trees of
the field[c] will know that I the LORD bring
down the tall tree and make the low tree
grow tall. I dry up the green tree and
make the dry tree flourish.

"'I the LORD have spoken, and I will
do it.[d]'"

The soul who sins will die.

18 The word of the LORD came to
me: 2"What do you people mean
by quoting this proverb about the land
of Israel:

"'The fathers eat sour grapes,
and the children's teeth are set on
edge'?[e]

3"As surely as I live, declares the Sovereign LORD, you will no longer quote
this proverb in Israel. 4For every living
soul belongs to me, the father as well as
the son—both alike belong to me. The
soul who sins is the one who will die.[f]

5"Suppose there is a righteous man
who does what is just and right.
6He does not eat at the mountain[g]
shrines
or look to the idols[h] of the house of
Israel.
He does not defile his neighbor's
wife
or lie with a woman during her
period.
7He does not oppress[i] anyone,
but returns what he took in
pledge[j] for a loan.
He does not commit robbery
but gives his food to the hungry
and provides clothing for the
naked.[k]
8He does not lend at usury
or take excessive interest.[i][l]
He withholds his hand from doing
wrong
and judges fairly[m] between man
and man.
9He follows my decrees
and faithfully keeps my laws.
That man is righteous;[n]
he will surely live,[o]
declares the Sovereign
LORD.

10"Suppose he has a violent son, who
sheds blood[p] or does any of these other
things[j] 11(though the father has done
none of them):

"He eats at the mountain shrines.
He defiles his neighbor's wife.
12He oppresses the poor[q] and needy.
He commits robbery.
He does not return what he took in
pledge.
He looks to the idols.
He does detestable things.[r]
13He lends at usury and takes
excessive interest.[s]

Will such a man live? He will not! Because he has done all these detestable
things, he will surely be put to death
and his blood will be on his own head.[t]

14"But suppose this son has a son who
sees all the sins his father commits, and
though he sees them, he does not do
such things:[u]

15"He does not eat at the mountain
shrines
or look to the idols of the house of
Israel.
He does not defile his neighbor's wife.
16He does not oppress anyone
or require a pledge for a loan.
He does not commit robbery
but gives his food to the hungry
and provides clothing for the
naked.[v]
17He withholds his hand from sin[k]
and takes no usury or excessive
interest.
He keeps my laws and follows my
decrees.

He will not die for his father's sin; he
will surely live. 18But his father will die

17:22 [a]Jer 23:5; Eze 20:40; 36:1,36; 37:22
17:23 [b]Ps 92:12; Isa 2:2; Eze 31:6; Da 4:12; Hos 14:5-7; Mt 13:32
17:24 [c]Ps 96:12 [d]Eze 19:12; 21:26; 22:14; Am 9:11
18:2 [e]Isa 3:15; Jer 31:29; La 5:7
18:4 [f]ver 20; Isa 42:5; Ro 6:23
18:6 [g]Eze 22:9 [h]Dt 4:19; Eze 6:13; 20:24
18:7 [i]Ex 22:21 [j]Ex 22:26; Dt 24:12 [k]Dt 15:11; Mt 25:36
18:8 [l]Ex 22:25; Lev 25:35-37; Dt 23:19-20 [m]Zec 8:16
18:9 [n]Hab 2:4 [o]Lev 18:5; Eze 20:11; Am 5:4
18:10 [p]Ex 21:12
18:12 [q]Am 4:1 [r]2Ki 21:11; Isa 59:6-7; Jer 22:17; Eze 8:6,17
18:13 [s]Ex 22:25 [t]Eze 33:4-5
18:14 [u]2Ch 34:21; Pr 23:24
18:16 [v]Ps 41:1; Isa 58:10

[i]8 Or *take interest*; similarly in verses 13 and 17
[j]10 Or *things to a brother*
[k]17 Septuagint (see also verse 8); Hebrew *from the poor*

for his own sin, because he practiced extortion, robbed his brother and did what
was wrong among his people.
19"Yet you ask, 'Why does the son not
share the guilt of his father?' Since the
son has done what is just and right and
has been careful to keep all my decrees,
he will surely live.[a] 20The soul who sins
is the one who will die. The son will not
share the guilt of the father, nor will the
father share the guilt of the son. The
righteousness of the righteous man will
be credited to him, and the wickedness
of the wicked will be charged against
him.[b]
21"But if a wicked man turns away
from all the sins he has committed and
keeps all my decrees and does what is
just and right, he will surely live; he will
not die.[c] 22None of the offenses he has
committed will be remembered against
him. Because of the righteous things he
has done, he will live.[d] 23Do I take any
pleasure in the death of the wicked? declares the Sovereign LORD. Rather, am I
not pleased[e] when they turn from their
ways and live?[f]
24"But if a righteous man turns from
his righteousness and commits sin and
does the same detestable things the
wicked man does, will he live? None of
the righteous things he has done will be
remembered. Because of the unfaithfulness he is guilty of and because of the
sins he has committed, he will die.[g]
25"Yet you say, 'The way of the Lord
is not just.' Hear, O house of Israel: Is
my way unjust?[h] Is it not your ways that
are unjust? 26If a righteous man turns
from his righteousness and commits sin,
he will die for it; because of the sin he
has committed he will die. 27But if a
wicked man turns away from the wickedness he has committed and does what
is just and right, he will save his life.[i]
28Because he considers all the offenses
he has committed and turns away from
them, he will surely live; he will not
die. 29Yet the house of Israel says, 'The
way of the Lord is not just.' Are my ways
unjust, O house of Israel? Is it not your
ways that are unjust?

18:19 [a]Ex 20:5; Dt 5:9; Jer 15:4; Zec 1:3-6
18:20 [b]Dt 24:16; 1Ki 8:32; 2Ki 14:6; Isa 3:11; Mt 16:27; Ro 2:9
18:21 [c]Eze 33:12,19
18:22 [d]Ps 18:20-24; Isa 43:25; Mic 7:19
18:23 [e]Ps 147:11 [f]Eze 33:11; 1Ti 2:4
18:24 [g]1Sa 15:11; 2Ch 24:17-20; Eze 3:20; 20:27; 2Pe 2:20-22
18:25 [h]Ge 18:25; Jer 12:1; Eze 33:17; Zep 3:5; Mal 2:17; 3:13-15
18:27 [i]Isa 1:18
18:30 [j]Mt 3:2 [k]Eze 7:3; 33:20; Hos 12:6
18:31 [l]Ps 51:10 [m]Isa 1:16-17; Eze 11:19; 36:26
18:32 [n]Eze 33:11
19:1 [o]Eze 26:17; 27:2,32 [p]2Ki 24:6
19:4 [q]2Ki 23:33-34; 2Ch 36:4
19:5 [r]2Ki 23:34
19:6 [s]2Ki 24:9; 2Ch 36:9
19:7 [t]Eze 30:12
19:8 [u]2Ki 24:2 [v]2Ki 24:11
19:9 [w]2Ch 36:6 [x]2Ki 24:15

30"Therefore, O house of Israel, I will
judge you, each one according to his
ways, declares the Sovereign LORD. Repent![j] Turn away from all your offenses;
then sin will not be your downfall.[k]
31Rid yourselves of all the offenses you
have committed, and get a new heart[l]
and a new spirit. Why will you die, O
house of Israel?[m] 32For I take no pleasure in the death of anyone, declares
the Sovereign LORD. Repent and live![n]

Lament for Israel's princes.

19 "Take up a lament[o] concerning
the princes[p] of Israel 2and say:

"'What a lioness was your mother
among the lions!
She lay down among the young lions
and reared her cubs.
3She brought up one of her cubs,
and he became a strong lion.
He learned to tear the prey
and he devoured men.
4The nations heard about him,
and he was trapped in their pit.
They led him with hooks
to the land of Egypt.[q]

5"'When she saw her hope unfulfilled,
her expectation gone,
she took another of her cubs
and made him a strong lion.[r]
6He prowled among the lions,
for he was now a strong lion.
He learned to tear the prey
and he devoured men.[s]
7He broke down[1] their strongholds
and devastated[t] their towns.
The land and all who were in it
were terrified by his roaring.
8Then the nations[u] came against him,
those from regions round about.
They spread their net for him,
and he was trapped in their pit.[v]
9With hooks they pulled him into a cage
and brought him to the king of
Babylon.[w]
They put him in prison,
so his roar was heard no longer
on the mountains of Israel.[x]

[1]7 Targum (see Septuagint); Hebrew *He knew*

The shriveled vine.

10"'Your mother was like a vine in
your vineyard[m]
planted by the water;
it was fruitful and full of branches
because of abundant water.[a]
11Its branches were strong,
fit for a ruler's scepter.
It towered high
above the thick foliage,
conspicuous for its height
and for its many branches.[b]
12But it was uprooted[c] in fury
and thrown to the ground.
The east wind made it shrivel,
it was stripped of its fruit;
its strong branches withered
and fire consumed them.[d]
13Now it is planted in the desert,[e]
in a dry and thirsty land.[f]
14Fire spread from one of its main[n]
branches
and consumed[g] its fruit.
No strong branch is left on it
fit for a ruler's scepter.'[h]

This is a lament and is to be used as a
lament."

Rebellious Israel.

20 In the seventh year, in the fifth
month on the tenth day, some
of the elders of Israel came to inquire of
the LORD, and they sat down in front
of me.[i]
2Then the word of the LORD came to
me: 3"Son of man, speak to the elders of
Israel and say to them, 'This is what the
Sovereign LORD says: Have you come
to inquire[j] of me? As surely as I live, I
will not let you inquire of me, declares
the Sovereign LORD.[k]'
4"Will you judge them? Will you judge
them, son of man? Then confront them
with the detestable practices of their
fathers[l] 5and say to them: 'This is what
the Sovereign LORD says: On the day I
chose[m] Israel, I swore with uplifted hand
to the descendants of the house of Jacob
and revealed myself to them in Egypt.
With uplifted hand I said to them, "I am
the LORD your God.[n]" 6On that day I
swore to them that I would bring them
out of Egypt into a land I had searched
out for them, a land flowing with milk
and honey,[o] the most beautiful of all
lands.[p] 7And I said to them, "Each of
you, get rid of the vile images[q] you have
set your eyes on, and do not defile yourselves with the idols of Egypt. I am the
LORD your God.[r]"
8"'But they rebelled against me and
would not listen to me; they did not get
rid of the vile images they had set their
eyes on, nor did they forsake the idols
of Egypt.[s] So I said I would pour out my
wrath on them and spend my anger
against them in Egypt.[t] 9But for the sake
of my name I did what would keep it
from being profaned in the eyes of the
nations they lived among and in whose
sight I had revealed myself to the Israelites by bringing them out of Egypt.[u]
10Therefore I led them out of Egypt
and brought them into the desert.[v] 11I
gave them my decrees and made known
to them my laws, for the man who
obeys them will live by them.[w] 12Also I
gave them my Sabbaths as a sign[x] between us, so they would know that I
the LORD made them holy.
13"'Yet the people of Israel rebelled[y]
against me in the desert. They did not
follow my decrees but rejected my
laws—although the man who obeys
them will live by them—and they utterly desecrated my Sabbaths. So I said
I would pour out my wrath[z] on them
and destroy them in the desert.[a] 14But
for the sake of my name I did what
would keep it from being profaned in
the eyes of the nations in whose sight I
had brought them out.[b] 15Also with uplifted hand I swore to them in the desert
that I would not bring them into the
land I had given them—a land flowing
with milk and honey, most beautiful of
all lands[c]— 16because they rejected my
laws and did not follow my decrees
and desecrated my Sabbaths. For their

19:10 [a]Ps 80:8-11
19:11 [b]Eze 31:3; Da 4:11
19:12 [c]Eze 17:10 [d]Isa 27:11; Eze 28:17; Hos 13:15
19:13 [e]Eze 20:35 [f]Hos 2:3
19:14 [g]Eze 20:47 [h]Eze 15:4
20:1 [i]Eze 8:1
20:3 [j]Eze 14:3 [k]Mic 3:7
20:4 [l]Eze 16:2; 22:2; Mt 23:32
20:5 [m]Dt 7:6 [n]Ex 6:7
20:6 [o]Ex 3:8; Jer 32:22 [p]Dt 8:7; Ps 48:2; Da 8:9
20:7 [q]Ex 20:4 [r]Ex 20:2; Lev 18:3; Dt 29:18
20:8 [s]Eze 7:8 [t]Isa 63:10
20:9 [u]Eze 36:22; 39:7
20:10 [v]Ex 13:18
20:11 [w]Lev 18:5; Dt 4:7-8; Ro 10:5
20:12 [x]Ex 31:13
20:13 [y]Ps 78:40 [z]Dt 9:8 [a]Nu 14:29; Ps 95:8-10; Isa 56:6
20:14 [b]Eze 36:23
20:15 [c]Ps 95:11; 106:26

[m] *10* Two Hebrew manuscripts; most Hebrew manuscripts *your blood* [n] *14* Or *from under its*

hearts[a] were devoted to their idols.[b]
17 Yet I looked on them with pity and did
not destroy them or put an end to them
in the desert. 18 I said to their children
in the desert, "Do not follow the statutes
of your fathers[c] or keep their laws or
defile yourselves with their idols. 19 I am
the LORD your God;[d] follow my decrees
and be careful to keep my laws.[e] 20 Keep
my Sabbaths holy, that they may be a
sign between us. Then you will know
that I am the LORD your God.[f]"
21 "'But the children rebelled against
me: They did not follow my decrees,
they were not careful to keep my laws—
although the man who obeys them will
live by them—and they desecrated my
Sabbaths. So I said I would pour out my
wrath on them and spend my anger
against them in the desert. 22 But I
withheld[g] my hand, and for the sake of
my name I did what would keep it from
being profaned in the eyes of the nations in whose sight I had brought them
out. 23 Also with uplifted hand I swore
to them in the desert that I would disperse them among the nations and
scatter[h] them through the countries,
24 because they had not obeyed my laws
but had rejected my decrees and desecrated my Sabbaths,[i] and their eyes
⌊lusted⌋ after[j] their fathers' idols.[k] 25 I also
gave them over[l] to statutes that were not
good and laws they could not live by;[m]
26 I let them become defiled through their
gifts—the sacrifice of every firstborn[o]—
that I might fill them with horror so they
would know that I am the LORD.[n]'
27 "Therefore, son of man, speak to the
people of Israel and say to them, 'This is
what the Sovereign LORD says: In this
also your fathers blasphemed[o] me by
forsaking me:[p] 28 When I brought them
into the land[q] I had sworn to give them
and they saw any high hill or any leafy
tree, there they offered their sacrifices,
made offerings that provoked me to
anger, presented their fragrant incense
and poured out their drink offerings.[r]
29 Then I said to them: What is this high
place you go to?'" (It is called Bamah[p] to
this day.)

Israel's judgment and restoration.

30 "Therefore say to the house of Israel:
'This is what the Sovereign LORD says:
Will you defile yourselves[s] the way your
fathers did and lust after their vile images?[t] 31 When you offer your gifts—the
sacrifice of your sons[u] in[q] the fire—you
continue to defile yourselves with all
your idols to this day. Am I to let you
inquire of me, O house of Israel? As
surely as I live, declares the Sovereign
LORD, I will not let you inquire of me.[v]
32 "'You say, "We want to be like the
nations, like the peoples of the world,
who serve wood and stone." But what
you have in mind will never happen.
33 As surely as I live, declares the Sovereign LORD, I will rule over you with a
mighty hand and an outstretched arm
and with outpoured wrath.[w] 34 I will
bring you from the nations[x] and gather
you from the countries where you have
been scattered—with a mighty hand
and an outstretched arm and with outpoured wrath.[y] 35 I will bring you into
the desert of the nations and there, face
to face, I will execute judgment[z] upon
you. 36 As I judged your fathers in the
desert of the land of Egypt, so I will
judge you, declares the Sovereign LORD.[a]
37 I will take note of you as you pass
under my rod,[b] and I will bring you
into the bond of the covenant.[c] 38 I will
purge[d] you of those who revolt and
rebel against me. Although I will bring
them out of the land where they are
living, yet they will not enter the land
of Israel. Then you will know that I am
the LORD.[e]
39 "'As for you, O house of Israel, this
is what the Sovereign LORD says: Go and
serve your idols,[f] every one of you! But
afterward you will surely listen to me
and no longer profane my holy name
with your gifts and idols.[g] 40 For on my
holy mountain, the high mountain of Israel, declares the Sovereign LORD, there
in the land the entire house of Israel will

20:16 [a]Nu 15:39 [b]Am 5:26
20:18 [c]Zec 1:4
20:19 [d]Ex 20:2 [e]Dt 5:32-33; 6:1-2; 8:1; 11:1; 12:1
20:20 [f]Jer 17:22
20:22 [g]Ps 78:38
20:23 [h]Lev 26:33; Dt 28:64
20:24 [i]ver 13 [j]Eze 6:9 [k]ver 16
20:25 [l]Ps 81:12 [m]2Th 2:11
20:26 [n]2Ki 17:17
20:27 [o]Ro 2:24 [p]Eze 18:24
20:28 [q]Ps 78:55,58 [r]Eze 6:13
20:30 [s]ver 43 [t]Jer 16:12
20:31 [u]Eze 16:20 [v]Ps 106:37-39; Jer 7:31
20:33 [w]Jer 21:5
20:34 [x]2Co 6:17*
[y]Isa 27:12-13; Jer 44:6; La 2:4
20:35 [z]Jer 2:35
20:36 [a]Nu 11:1-35; 1Co 10:5-10
20:37 [b]Lev 27:32; Jer 33:13 [c]Eze 16:62
20:38 [d]Eze 34:17-22; Am 9:9-10 [e]Ps 95:11; Jer 44:14; Eze 13:9; Mal 3:3; Heb 4:3
20:39 [f]Jer 44:25 [g]Isa 1:13; Eze 43:7; Am 4:4

[o]26 Or *—making every firstborn pass through ⌊the fire⌋* [p]29 *Bamah* means *high place.* [q]31 Or *—making your sons pass through*

serve me, and there I will accept them. There I will require your offerings[a] and your choice gifts,[r] along with all your holy sacrifices.[b] [41]I will accept you as fragrant incense when I bring you out from the nations and gather you from the countries where you have been scattered, and I will show myself holy[c] among you in the sight of the nations.[d] [42]Then you will know that I am the LORD,[e] when I bring you into the land of Israel,[f] the land I had sworn with uplifted hand to give to your fathers. [43]There you will remember your conduct and all the actions by which you have defiled yourselves, and you will loathe yourselves for all the evil you have done.[g] [44]You will know that I am the LORD, when I deal with you for my name's sake[h] and not according to your evil ways and your corrupt practices, O house of Israel, declares the Sovereign LORD.[i]'"

The unquenchable forest fire.

[45]The word of the LORD came to me: [46]"Son of man, set your face toward the south; preach against the south and prophesy against[j] the forest of the southland.[k] [47]Say to the southern forest: 'Hear the word of the LORD. This is what the Sovereign LORD says: I am about to set fire to you, and it will consume all your trees, both green and dry. The blazing flame will not be quenched, and every face from south to north will be scorched by it.[l] [48]Everyone will see that I the LORD have kindled it; it will not be quenched.[m]'"

[49]Then I said, "Ah, Sovereign LORD! They are saying of me, 'Isn't he just telling parables?[n]'"

Babylon, the sword of the LORD's judgment.

21 The word of the LORD came to me: [2]"Son of man, set your face against Jerusalem and preach against the sanctuary. Prophesy against[o] the land of Israel [3]and say to her: 'This is what the LORD says: I am against you.[p] I will draw my sword from its scabbard and cut off from you both the righteous and the wicked.[q] [4]Because I am going to cut off the righteous and the wicked, my sword will be unsheathed against everyone from south to north.[r] [5]Then all people will know that I the LORD have drawn my sword from its scabbard; it will not return[s] again.'[t]

[6]"Therefore groan, son of man! Groan before them with broken heart and bitter grief.[u] [7]And when they ask you, 'Why are you groaning?' you shall say, 'Because of the news that is coming. Every heart will melt and every hand go limp;[v] every spirit will become faint and every knee become as weak as water.' It is coming! It will surely take place, declares the Sovereign LORD."

[8]The word of the LORD came to me: [9]"Son of man, prophesy and say, 'This is what the Lord says:

"'A sword, a sword,
sharpened and polished—
[10]sharpened for the slaughter,[w]
polished to flash like lightning!

"'Shall we rejoice in the scepter of my son ⌊Judah⌋? The sword despises every such stick.

[11]"'The sword is appointed to be polished,[x]
to be grasped with the hand;
it is sharpened and polished,
made ready for the hand of the slayer.
[12]Cry out and wail, son of man,
for it is against my people;
it is against all the princes of Israel.
They are thrown to the sword
along with my people.
Therefore beat your breast.[y]

[13]"'Testing will surely come. And what if the scepter ⌊of Judah⌋, which the sword despises, does not continue? declares the Sovereign LORD.'

[14]"So then, son of man, prophesy
and strike your hands[z] together.

20:40 [a]Isa 60:7 [b]Isa 56:7; Mal 3:4
20:41 [c]Eze 28:25; 36:23 [d]Eze 11:17
20:42 [e]Eze 38:23 [f]Eze 34:13; 36:24
20:43 [g]Eze 6:9; 16:61; Hos 5:15
20:44 [h]Eze 36:22 [i]Eze 24:24
20:46 [j]Eze 21:2; Am 7:16 [k]Isa 30:6; Jer 13:19
20:47 [l]Isa 9:18-19; 13:8; Jer 21:14
20:48 [m]Jer 7:20
20:49 [n]Mt 13:13; Jn 16:25
21:2 [o]Eze 20:46
21:3 [p]Jer 21:13 [q]ver 9-11; Job 9:22
21:4 [r]Eze 20:47
21:5 [s]ver 30 [t]Na 1:9
21:6 [u]Isa 22:4
21:7 [v]Eze 22:14; 7:17
21:10 [w]Ps 110:5-6; Isa 34:5-6
21:11 [x]Jer 46:4
21:12 [y]Jer 31:19
21:14 [z]Nu 24:10

[r]40 Or *and the gifts of your firstfruits*

Let the sword strike twice,
even three times.
It is a sword for slaughter—
a sword for great slaughter,
closing in on them from every
side.[a]
15So that hearts may melt[b]
and the fallen be many,
I have stationed the sword for
slaughter[s]
at all their gates.
Oh! It is made to flash like lightning,
it is grasped for slaughter.[c]
16O sword, slash to the right,
then to the left,
wherever your blade is turned.
17I too will strike my hands[d] together,
and my wrath[e] will subside.
I the LORD have spoken."

18The word of the LORD came to me:
19"Son of man, mark out two roads for
the sword of the king of Babylon to take,
both starting from the same country.
Make a signpost where the road branches off to the city. 20Mark out one road
for the sword to come against Rabbah of
the Ammonites[f] and another against
Judah and fortified Jerusalem. 21For the
king of Babylon will stop at the fork in
the road, at the junction of the two
roads, to seek an omen: He will cast
lots[g] with arrows, he will consult his
idols, he will examine the liver.[h] 22Into
his right hand will come the lot for Jerusalem, where he is to set up battering
rams, to give the command to slaughter,
to sound the battle cry, to set battering
rams against the gates, to build a ramp
and to erect siege works.[i] 23It will seem
like a false omen to those who have
sworn allegiance to him, but he will remind[j] them of their guilt and take them
captive.

24"Therefore this is what the Sovereign LORD says: 'Because you people
have brought to mind your guilt by your
open rebellion, revealing your sins in
all that you do—because you have done
this, you will be taken captive.

25" 'O profane and wicked prince of
Israel, whose day has come, whose time
of punishment has reached its climax,[k]
26this is what the Sovereign LORD says:
Take off the turban, remove the crown.[l]
It will not be as it was: The lowly will be
exalted and the exalted will be brought
low.[m] 27A ruin! A ruin! I will make it a
ruin! It will not be restored until he
comes to whom it rightfully belongs; to
him I will give it.'[n]

21:14 [a]Eze 6:11; 30:24
21:15 [b]2Sa 17:10 [c]Ps 22:14
21:17 [d]ver 14; Eze 22:13 [e]Eze 5:13
21:20 [f]Dt 3:11; Jer 49:2; Am 1:14
21:21 [g]Pr 16:33 [h]Nu 22:7; 23:23
21:22 [i]Eze 4:2; 26:9
21:23 [j]Nu 5:15
21:25 [k]Eze 35:5
21:26 [l]Jer 13:18 [m]Ps 75:7; Eze 17:24
21:27 [n]Ps 2:6; Jer 23:5-6; Eze 37:24; Hag 2:21-22
21:28 [o]Zep 2:8 [p]Jer 12:12
21:29 [q]ver 25; Eze 22:28; 35:5
21:30 [r]Jer 47:6 [s]Eze 16:3
21:31 [t]Eze 22:20-21 [u]Jer 51:20-23
21:32 [v]Mal 4:1 [w]Eze 25:10
22:2 [x]Eze 24:6,9; Na 3:1 [y]Eze 16:2

Judgment against the Ammonites.

28"And you, son of man, prophesy and
say, 'This is what the Sovereign LORD
says about the Ammonites[o] and their
insults:

" 'A sword,[p] a sword,
drawn for the slaughter,
polished to consume
and to flash like lightning!
29Despite false visions concerning you
and lying divinations about you,
it will be laid on the necks
of the wicked who are to be slain,
whose day has come,
whose time of punishment has
reached its climax.[q]
30Return the sword to its scabbard.[r]
In the place where you were
created,
in the land of your ancestry,[s]
I will judge you.
31I will pour out my wrath upon you
and breathe out my fiery anger[t]
against you;
I will hand you over to brutal men,
men skilled in destruction.[u]
32You will be fuel for the fire,[v]
your blood will be shed in your
land,
you will be remembered[w] no more;
for I the LORD have spoken.' "

Jerusalem's guilt.

22 The word of the LORD came to
me: 2"Son of man, will you
judge her? Will you judge this city of
bloodshed?[x] Then confront her with all
her detestable practices[y] 3and say: 'This

s *15* Septuagint; the meaning of the Hebrew for this word is uncertain.

is what the Sovereign LORD says: O city that brings on herself doom by shedding blood[a] in her midst and defiles herself by making idols, 4 you have become guilty because of the blood you have shed[b] and have become defiled by the idols you have made. You have brought your days to a close, and the end of your years has come.[c] Therefore I will make you an object of scorn to the nations and a laughingstock to all the countries.[d] 5 Those who are near and those who are far away will mock you, O infamous city, full of turmoil.

6 "'See how each of the princes of Israel who are in you uses his power to shed blood.[e] 7 In you they have treated father and mother with contempt;[f] in you they have oppressed the alien and mistreated the fatherless and the widow.[g] 8 You have despised my holy things and desecrated my Sabbaths.[h] 9 In you are slanderous men[i] bent on shedding blood; in you are those who eat at the mountain shrines[j] and commit lewd acts.[k] 10 In you are those who dishonor their fathers' bed; in you are those who violate women during their period, when they are ceremonially unclean.[l] 11 In you one man commits a detestable offense with his neighbor's wife, another shamefully defiles his daughter-in-law,[m] and another violates his sister,[n] his own father's daughter. 12 In you men accept bribes[o] to shed blood; you take usury and excessive interest[t] and make unjust gain from your neighbors[p] by extortion. And you have forgotten me, declares the Sovereign LORD.

13 "'I will surely strike my hands[q] together at the unjust gain[r] you have made and at the blood[s] you have shed in your midst. 14 Will your courage endure or your hands be strong in the day I deal with you? I the LORD have spoken,[t] and I will do it.[u] 15 I will disperse you among the nations and scatter[v] you through the countries; and I will put an end to your uncleanness.[w] 16 When you have been defiled[u] in the eyes of the nations, you will know that I am the LORD.'"

17 Then the word of the LORD came to me: 18 "Son of man, the house of Israel has become dross[x] to me; all of them are the copper, tin, iron and lead left inside a furnace. They are but the dross of silver.[y] 19 Therefore this is what the Sovereign LORD says: 'Because you have all become dross, I will gather you into Jerusalem. 20 As men gather silver, copper, iron, lead and tin into a furnace to melt it with a fiery blast, so will I gather you in my anger and my wrath and put you inside the city and melt you.[z] 21 I will gather you and I will blow on you with my fiery wrath, and you will be melted inside her. 22 As silver is melted[a] in a furnace, so you will be melted inside her, and you will know that I the LORD have poured out my wrath upon you.'"[b]

23 Again the word of the LORD came to me: 24 "Son of man, say to the land, 'You are a land that has had no rain or showers[v] in the day of wrath.'[c] 25 There is a conspiracy[d] of her princes[w] within her like a roaring lion tearing its prey; they devour people,[e] take treasures and precious things and make many widows[f] within her. 26 Her priests do violence to my law[g] and profane my holy things; they do not distinguish between the holy and the common;[h] they teach that there is no difference between the unclean and the clean;[i] and they shut their eyes to the keeping of my Sabbaths, so that I am profaned among them.[j] 27 Her officials within her are like wolves tearing their prey; they shed blood and kill people to make unjust gain.[k] 28 Her prophets whitewash[l] these deeds for them by false visions and lying divinations. They say, 'This is what the Sovereign LORD says'—when the LORD has not spoken.[m] 29 The people of the land practice extortion and commit robbery; they oppress the poor and needy and mistreat the alien,[n] denying them justice.[o]

30 "I looked for a man among them

22:3 [a]ver 6,13,27; Eze 23:37,45
22:4 [b]2Ki 21:16 [c]Eze 21:25 [d]Eze 5:14
22:6 [e]Isa 1:23
22:7 [f]Dt 5:16; 27:16 [g]Ex 22:21-22
22:8 [h]Eze 23:38-39
22:9 [i]Lev 19:16 [j]Eze 18:11 [k]Hos 4:10,14
22:10 [l]Lev 18:8,19
22:11 [m]Lev 18:15 [n]Lev 18:9; 2Sa 13:14
22:12 [o]Dt 27:25; Mic 7:3 [p]Lev 19:13
22:13 [q]Eze 21:17 [r]Isa 33:15 [s]ver 3
22:14 [t]Eze 24:14 [u]Eze 17:24; 21:7
22:15 [v]Dt 4:27; Zec 7:14 [w]Eze 23:27
22:18 [x]Ps 119:119; Isa 1:22 [y]Jer 6:28-30
22:20 [z]Mal 3:2
22:22 [a]Isa 1:25 [b]Eze 20:8,33
22:24 [c]Eze 24:13
22:25 [d]Jer 11:9 [e]Hos 6:9 [f]Jer 15:8
22:26 [g]Mal 2:7-8 [h]Eze 44:23 [i]Lev 10:10 [j]1Sa 2:12-17; Jer 2:8,26; Hag 2:11-14
22:27 [k]Isa 1:23
22:28 [l]Eze 13:10 [m]Eze 13:2,6-7 **22:29** [n]Ex 22:21; 23:9 [o]Isa 5:7

[t]*12* Or *usury and interest* [u]*16* Or *When I have allotted you your inheritance* [v]*24* Septuagint; Hebrew *has not been cleansed or rained on* [w]*25* Septuagint; Hebrew *prophets*

who would build up the wall[a] and stand before me in the gap on behalf of the land so I would not have to destroy it, but I found none.[b] 31 So I will pour out my wrath on them and consume them with my fiery anger, bringing down[c] on their own heads all they have done, declares the Sovereign LORD.[d]"

Two adulterous sisters.

23 The word of the LORD came to me: 2 "Son of man, there were two women, daughters of the same mother.[e] 3 They became prostitutes in Egypt,[f] engaging in prostitution[g] from their youth. In that land their breasts were fondled and their virgin bosoms caressed. 4 The older was named Oholah, and her sister was Oholibah. They were mine and gave birth to sons and daughters. Oholah is Samaria, and Oholibah is Jerusalem.

5 "Oholah engaged in prostitution while she was still mine; and she lusted after her lovers, the Assyrians[h]—warriors[i] 6 clothed in blue, governors and commanders, all of them handsome young men, and mounted horsemen. 7 She gave herself as a prostitute to all the elite of the Assyrians and defiled herself with all the idols of everyone she lusted after.[j] 8 She did not give up the prostitution she began in Egypt,[k] when during her youth men slept with her, caressed her virgin bosom and poured out their lust upon her.[l]

9 "Therefore I handed her over[m] to her lovers, the Assyrians, for whom she lusted.[n] 10 They stripped[o] her naked, took away her sons and daughters and killed her with the sword. She became a byword among women,[p] and punishment was inflicted on her.[q]

11 "Her sister Oholibah saw this, yet in her lust and prostitution she was more depraved than her sister.[r] 12 She too lusted after the Assyrians—governors and commanders, warriors in full dress, mounted horsemen, all handsome young men.[s] 13 I saw that she too defiled herself; both of them went the same way.

14 "But she carried her prostitution still further. She saw men portrayed on a wall,[t] figures of Chaldeans[x] portrayed in red,[u] 15 with belts around their waists and flowing turbans on their heads; all of them looked like Babylonian chariot officers, natives of Chaldea.[y] 16 As soon as she saw them, she lusted after them and sent messengers to them in Chaldea. 17 Then the Babylonians came to her, to the bed of love, and in their lust they defiled her. After she had been defiled by them, she turned away from them in disgust. 18 When she carried on her prostitution openly and exposed her nakedness, I turned away[v] from her in disgust, just as I had turned away from her sister.[w] 19 Yet she became more and more promiscuous as she recalled the days of her youth, when she was a prostitute in Egypt. 20 There she lusted after her lovers, whose genitals were like those of donkeys and whose emission was like that of horses. 21 So you longed for the lewdness of your youth, when in Egypt your bosom was caressed and your young breasts fondled.[z][x]

22 "Therefore, Oholibah, this is what the Sovereign LORD says: I will stir up your lovers against you, those you turned away from in disgust, and I will bring them against you from every side[y]— 23 the Babylonians[z] and all the Chaldeans, the men of Pekod[a] and Shoa and Koa, and all the Assyrians with them, handsome young men, all of them governors and commanders, chariot officers and men of high rank, all mounted on horses.[b] 24 They will come against you with weapons,[a] chariots and wagons[c] and with a throng of people; they will take up positions against you on every side with large and small shields and with helmets. I will turn you over to them for punishment,[d] and they will punish you according to their standards. 25 I will direct my jealous anger against you, and they will deal with you in fury.

22:30 [a]Eze 13:5 [b]Ps 106:23; Jer 5:1
22:31 [c]Eze 16:43 [d]Eze 7:8-9; 9:10; Ro 2:8
23:2 [e]Jer 3:7; Eze 16:45
23:3 [f]Jos 24:14 [g]Lev 17:7
23:5 [h]2Ki 16:7; Hos 5:13 [i]Hos 8:9
23:7 [j]Hos 5:3; 6:10
23:8 [k]Ex 32:4 [l]Eze 16:15
23:9 [m]2Ki 18:11 [n]Hos 11:5
23:10 [o]Hos 2:10 [p]Eze 16:41 [q]Eze 16:36
23:11 [r]Jer 3:8-11; Eze 16:51
23:12 [s]2Ki 16:7-15; 2Ch 28:16
23:14 [t]Eze 8:10 [u]Jer 22:14
23:18 [v]Ps 78:59; 106:40; Jer 6:8 [w]Jer 12:8; Am 5:21
23:21 [x]Eze 16:26
23:22 [y]Eze 16:37
23:23 [z]2Ki 20:14-18 [a]Jer 50:21 [b]2Ki 24:2
23:24 [c]Jer 47:3; Eze 26:7,10; Na 2:4 [d]Jer 39:5-6

[x]*14* Or *Babylonians* [y]*15* Or *Babylonia*; also in verse 16 [z]*21* Syriac (see also verse 3); Hebrew *caressed because of your young breasts* [a]*24* The meaning of the Hebrew for this word is uncertain.

They will cut off your noses and your
ears, and those of you who are left will
fall by the sword. They will take away
your sons and daughters,[a] and those of
you who are left will be consumed by
fire.[b] 26 They will also strip[c] you of your
clothes and take your fine jewelry.[d] 27 So
I will put a stop[e] to the lewdness and
prostitution you began in Egypt. You will
not look on these things with longing or
remember Egypt anymore.

28 "For this is what the Sovereign LORD
says: I am about to hand you over[f] to
those you hate, to those you turned
away from in disgust. 29 They will deal
with you in hatred and take away everything you have worked for. They will
leave you naked and bare, and the
shame of your prostitution will be exposed. Your lewdness and promiscuity[g]
30 have brought this upon you, because
you lusted after the nations and defiled
yourself with their idols.[h] 31 You have
gone the way of your sister; so I will put
her cup[i] into your hand.[j]

32 "This is what the Sovereign LORD
says:

"You will drink your sister's cup,
a cup large and deep;
it will bring scorn and derision,
for it holds so much.[k]
33 You will be filled with drunkenness
and sorrow,
the cup of ruin and desolation,
the cup of your sister Samaria.[l]
34 You will drink it[m] and drain it dry;
you will dash it to pieces
and tear your breasts.

I have spoken, declares the Sovereign
LORD.

35 "Therefore this is what the Sovereign LORD says: Since you have forgotten[n] me and thrust me behind your
back,[o] you must bear the consequences
of your lewdness and prostitution."

36 The LORD said to me: "Son of man,
will you judge Oholah and Oholibah?
Then confront[p] them with their detestable practices,[q] 37 for they have committed adultery and blood is on their hands.
They committed adultery with their
idols; they even sacrificed their children,
whom they bore to me,[b] as food for
them.[r] 38 They have also done this to
me: At that same time they defiled my
sanctuary and desecrated my Sabbaths.
39 On the very day they sacrificed their
children to their idols, they entered my
sanctuary and desecrated[s] it. That is
what they did in my house.[t]

40 "They even sent messengers for men
who came from far away,[u] and when they
arrived you bathed yourself for them,
painted your eyes[v] and put on your jewelry.[w] 41 You sat on an elegant couch,[x]
with a table[y] spread before it on which
you had placed the incense and oil that
belonged to me.

42 "The noise of a carefree crowd was
around her; Sabeans[c] were brought from
the desert along with men from the rabble, and they put bracelets[z] on the arms
of the woman and her sister and beautiful crowns on their heads.[a] 43 Then I said
about the one worn out by adultery,
'Now let them use her as a prostitute,[b]
for that is all she is.' 44 And they slept
with her. As men sleep with a prostitute,
so they slept with those lewd women,
Oholah and Oholibah. 45 But righteous
men will sentence them to the punishment of women who commit adultery
and shed blood, because they are adulterous and blood is on their hands.[c]

46 "This is what the Sovereign LORD
says: Bring a mob[d] against them and give
them over to terror and plunder. 47 The
mob will stone them and cut them down
with their swords; they will kill their
sons and daughters and burn[e] down
their houses.[f]

48 "So I will put an end to lewdness in
the land, that all women may take warning and not imitate you.[g] 49 You will suffer the penalty for your lewdness and
bear the consequences of your sins of
idolatry. Then you will know that I am
the Sovereign LORD.[h]"

23:25 [a]ver 47 [b]Eze 20:47-48
23:26 [c]Jer 13:22 [d]Isa 3:18-23; Eze 16:39
23:27 [e]Eze 16:41
23:28 [f]Jer 34:20
23:29 [g]Dt 28:48
23:30 [h]Eze 6:9
23:31 [i]Jer 25:15 [j]2Ki 21:13
23:32 [k]Ps 60:3; Isa 51:17; Jer 25:15
23:33 [l]Jer 25:15-16
23:34 [m]Ps 75:8; Isa 51:17
23:35 [n]Isa 17:10; Jer 3:21 [o]1Ki 14:9
23:36 [p]Eze 16:2 [q]Isa 58:1; Eze 22:2; Mic 3:8
23:37 [r]Eze 16:36
23:39 [s]2Ki 21:4 [t]Jer 7:10
23:40 [u]Isa 57:9 [v]2Ki 9:30 [w]Jer 4:30; Eze 16:13-19
23:41 [x]Est 1:6; Pr 7:17; Am 6:4 [y]Isa 65:11; Eze 44:16
23:42 [z]Ge 24:30 [a]Eze 16:11-12
23:43 [b]ver 3
23:45 [c]Lev 20:10; Eze 16:38; Hos 6:5
23:46 [d]Eze 16:40
23:47 [e]2Ch 36:19 [f]2Ch 36:17; Eze 16:40-41
23:48 [g]2Pe 2:6 **23:49** [h]Eze 7:4; 9:10; 20:38

b 37 Or *even made the children they bore to me pass through* ⌊*the fire*⌋ c 42 Or *drunkards*

The cooking pot.

24 In the ninth year, in the tenth
month on the tenth day, the
word of the LORD came to me:[a] 2"Son of
man, record this date, this very date, because the king of Babylon has laid siege
to Jerusalem this very day.[b] 3Tell this
rebellious house[c] a parable[d] and say to
them: 'This is what the Sovereign LORD
says:

"'Put on the cooking pot;[e] put it on
and pour water into it.
4Put into it the pieces of meat,
all the choice pieces—the leg and
the shoulder.
Fill it with the best of these bones;
5 take the pick of the flock.[f]
Pile wood beneath it for the bones;
bring it to a boil
and cook the bones in it.[g]

6"'For this is what the Sovereign LORD
says:

"'Woe to the city of bloodshed,[h]
to the pot now encrusted,
whose deposit will not go away!
Empty it piece by piece
without casting lots[i] for them.

7"'For the blood she shed is in her
midst:
She poured it on the bare rock;
she did not pour it on the ground,
where the dust would cover it.[j]
8To stir up wrath and take revenge
I put her blood on the bare rock,
so that it would not be covered.

9"'Therefore this is what the Sovereign
LORD says:

"'Woe to the city of bloodshed!
I, too, will pile the wood high.
10So heap on the wood
and kindle the fire.
Cook the meat well,
mixing in the spices;
and let the bones be charred.
11Then set the empty pot on the coals
till it becomes hot and its copper
glows

24:1 [a]Eze 8:1
24:2 [b]2Ki 25:1; Jer 39:1; 52:4
24:3 [c]Isa 1:2; Eze 2:3,6 [d]Eze 17:2; 20:49 [e]Jer 1:13; Eze 11:3
24:5 [f]Jer 52:10 [g]Jer 52:24-27
24:6 [h]Eze 22:2 [i]Ob 11; Na 3:10
24:7 [j]Lev 17:13
24:11 [k]Jer 21:10; Eze 22:15
24:13 [l]Jer 6:28-30; Eze 16:42; 22:24
24:14 [m]Eze 36:19 [n]Eze 18:30
24:16 [o]Jer 13:17; 16:5; 22:10
24:17 [p]Jer 16:7
24:19 [q]Eze 12:9; 37:18
24:21 [r]Ps 27:4 [s]Eze 23:25 [t]Jer 7:14,15; Eze 23:47
24:22 [u]Jer 16:7

so its impurities may be melted
and its deposit burned away.[k]
12It has frustrated all efforts;
its heavy deposit has not been
removed,
not even by fire.

13"'Now your impurity is lewdness.
Because I tried to cleanse you but you
would not be cleansed from your impurity, you will not be clean again until
my wrath against you has subsided.[l]

14"'I the LORD have spoken. The time
has come for me to act. I will not hold
back; I will not have pity, nor will I
relent. You will be judged according to
your conduct and your actions,[m] declares
the Sovereign LORD.[n]'"

No weeping at the death of Ezekiel's wife.

15The word of the LORD came to me:
16"Son of man, with one blow I am
about to take away from you the delight
of your eyes. Yet do not lament or weep
or shed any tears.[o] 17Groan quietly; do
not mourn for the dead. Keep your turban fastened and your sandals on your
feet; do not cover the lower part of
your face or eat the customary food ⌊of
mourners⌋.[p]"
18So I spoke to the people in the morning, and in the evening my wife died.
The next morning I did as I had been
commanded.
19Then the people asked me, "Won't
you tell us what these things have to do
with us?[q]"
20So I said to them, "The word of the
LORD came to me: 21Say to the house of
Israel, 'This is what the Sovereign LORD
says: I am about to desecrate my sanctuary—the stronghold in which you
take pride, the delight of your eyes,[r]
the object of your affection. The sons
and daughters[s] you left behind will fall
by the sword.[t] 22And you will do as I
have done. You will not cover the lower
part of your face or eat the customary
food ⌊of mourners⌋.[u] 23You will keep your
turbans on your heads and your sandals

on your feet. You will not mourn[a] or
weep but will waste away because of[d]
your sins and groan among yourselves.[b]
24Ezekiel will be a sign[c] to you; you will
do just as he has done. When this happens, you will know that I am the Sovereign LORD.'
25"And you, son of man, on the day I
take away their stronghold, their joy and
glory, the delight of their eyes, their
heart's desire, and their sons and daughters[d] as well— 26on that day a fugitive
will come to tell you[e] the news. 27At that
time your mouth will be opened; you
will speak with him and will no longer
be silent. So you will be a sign to them,
and they will know that I am the LORD.[f]"

Judgment against Ammon.

25 The word of the LORD came to
me: 2"Son of man, set your face
against the Ammonites[g] and prophesy
against them.[h] 3Say to them, 'Hear the
word of the Sovereign LORD. This is
what the Sovereign LORD says: Because
you said "Aha![i]" over my sanctuary
when it was desecrated and over the
land of Israel when it was laid waste
and over the people of Judah when they
went into exile,[j] 4therefore I am going
to give you to the people of the East[k]
as a possession. They will set up their
camps and pitch their tents among you;
they will eat your fruit and drink your
milk.[l] 5I will turn Rabbah[m] into a pasture
for camels and Ammon into a resting
place for sheep.[n] Then you will know
that I am the LORD. 6For this is what
the Sovereign LORD says: Because you
have clapped your hands and stamped
your feet, rejoicing with all the malice of
your heart against the land of Israel,[o]
7therefore I will stretch out my hand[p]
against you and give you as plunder to
the nations. I will cut you off from the
nations and exterminate you from the
countries. I will destroy[q] you, and you
will know that I am the LORD.[r]'"

Judgment against Moab.

8"This is what the Sovereign LORD
says: 'Because Moab[s] and Seir said,
"Look, the house of Judah has become
like all the other nations," 9therefore I
will expose the flank of Moab, beginning at its frontier towns—Beth Jeshimoth[t], Baal Meon[u] and Kiriathaim[v]—
the glory of that land. 10I will give Moab
along with the Ammonites to the people
of the East as a possession, so that the
Ammonites will not be remembered[w]
among the nations; 11and I will inflict
punishment on Moab. Then they will
know that I am the LORD.'"

Judgment against Edom.

12"This is what the Sovereign LORD
says: 'Because Edom[x] took revenge on
the house of Judah and became very
guilty by doing so, 13therefore this is
what the Sovereign LORD says: I will
stretch out my hand against Edom and
kill its men and their animals.[y] I will lay
it waste, and from Teman to Dedan[z]
they will fall by the sword. 14I will take
vengeance on Edom by the hand of my
people Israel, and they will deal with
Edom in accordance with my anger[a]
and my wrath; they will know my vengeance, declares the Sovereign LORD.'"

Judgment against Philistia.

15"This is what the Sovereign LORD
says: 'Because the Philistines[b] acted in
vengeance and took revenge with malice
in their hearts, and with ancient hostility sought to destroy Judah, 16therefore
this is what the Sovereign LORD says: I
am about to stretch out my hand against
the Philistines,[c] and I will cut off the
Kerethites[d] and destroy those remaining
along the coast. 17I will carry out great
vengeance on them and punish them in
my wrath. Then they will know that I
am the LORD, when I take vengeance on
them.'"

Judgment against Tyre.

26 In the eleventh year, on the first
day of the month, the word of

24:23 [a]Job 27:15 [b]Ps 78:64
24:24 [c]Isa 20:3; Eze 4:3; 12:11
24:25 [d]Jer 11:22
24:26 [e]1Sa 4:12; Job 1:15-19
24:27 [f]Eze 3:26; 33:22
25:2 [g]Eze 21:28; Zep 2:8-9 [h]Jer 49:1-6
25:3 [i]Eze 26:2; 36:2 [j]Pr 17:5
25:4 [k]Jdg 6:3 [l]Dt 28:33,51; Jdg 6:33
25:5 [m]Dt 3:11; Eze 21:20 [n]Isa 17:2
25:6 [o]Ob 12; Zep 2:8
25:7 [p]Zep 1:4 [q]Eze 21:31 [r]Am 1:14-15
25:8 [s]Jer 48:1; Am 2:1
25:9 [t]Nu 33:49 [u]Nu 32:3; Jos 13:17 [v]Nu 32:37; Jos 13:19
25:10 [w]Eze 21:32
25:12 [x]2Ch 28:17
25:13 [y]Eze 29:8 [z]Jer 25:23
25:14 [a]Eze 35:11
25:15 [b]2Ch 28:18
25:16 [c]Jer 47:1-7 [d]1Sa 30:14; Zep 2:4-5

d23 Or *away in*

the LORD came to me: 2“Son of man, because Tyre[a] has said of Jerusalem, ‘Aha![b]
The gate to the nations is broken, and
its doors have swung open to me; now
that she lies in ruins I will prosper,’
3therefore this is what the Sovereign
LORD says: I am against you, O Tyre, and
I will bring many nations against you,
like the sea[c] casting up its waves. 4They
will destroy[d] the walls of Tyre[e] and pull
down her towers; I will scrape away her
rubble and make her a bare rock. 5Out
in the sea[f] she will become a place to
spread fishnets, for I have spoken, declares the Sovereign LORD. She will become plunder[g] for the nations, 6and her
settlements on the mainland will be
ravaged by the sword. Then they will
know that I am the LORD.

7“For this is what the Sovereign LORD
says: From the north I am going to bring
against Tyre Nebuchadnezzar[e][h] king of
Babylon, king of kings,[i] with horses and
chariots,[j] with horsemen and a great
army. 8He will ravage your settlements
on the mainland with the sword; he will
set up siege works[k] against you, build
a ramp[l] up to your walls and raise his
shields against you. 9He will direct the
blows of his battering rams against your
walls and demolish your towers with his
weapons. 10His horses will be so many
that they will cover you with dust. Your
walls will tremble at the noise of the war
horses, wagons and chariots[m] when he
enters your gates as men enter a city
whose walls have been broken through.
11The hoofs[n] of his horses will trample
all your streets; he will kill your people
with the sword, and your strong pillars[o]
will fall to the ground.[p] 12They will
plunder your wealth and loot your merchandise; they will break down your
walls and demolish your fine houses and
throw your stones, timber and rubble
into the sea.[q] 13I will put an end[r] to your
noisy songs, and the music of your
harps[s] will be heard no more.[t] 14I will
make you a bare rock, and you will become a place to spread fishnets. You will
never be rebuilt,[u] for I the LORD have
spoken, declares the Sovereign LORD.

15“This is what the Sovereign LORD
says to Tyre: Will not the coastlands[v]
tremble[w] at the sound of your fall,
when the wounded groan and the
slaughter takes place in you? 16Then all
the princes of the coast will step down
from their thrones and lay aside their
robes and take off their embroidered
garments. Clothed[x] with terror, they will
sit on the ground, trembling[y] every moment, appalled[z] at you. 17Then they will
take up a lament[a] concerning you and
say to you:

“ ‘How you are destroyed, O city of
renown,
peopled by men of the sea!
You were a power on the seas,
you and your citizens;
you put your terror
on all who lived there.[b]
18Now the coastlands tremble
on the day of your fall;
the islands in the sea
are terrified at your collapse.’[c]

19“This is what the Sovereign LORD
says: When I make you a desolate city,
like cities no longer inhabited, and when
I bring the ocean depths over you and
its vast waters cover you,[d] 20then I will
bring you down with those who go
down to the pit,[e] to the people of long
ago. I will make you dwell in the earth
below, as in ancient ruins, with those
who go down to the pit, and you will
not return or take your place[f] in the
land of the living.[f] 21I will bring you to
a horrible end and you will be no more.
You will be sought, but you will never
again be found, declares the Sovereign
LORD.”[g]

Ezekiel’s lament for Tyre.

27 The word of the LORD came to
me: 2“Son of man, take up a
lament concerning Tyre. 3Say to Tyre,

26:2 [a]2Sa 5:11; Isa 23 [b]Eze 25:3
26:3 [c]Isa 5:30; Jer 50:42; 51:42
26:4 [d]Isa 23:1,11 [e]Am 1:10
26:5 [f]Eze 27:32 [g]Eze 29:19
26:7 [h]Jer 27:6 [i]Ezr 7:12; Da 2:37 [j]Eze 23:24; Na 2:3-4
26:8 [k]Jer 6:6 [l]Eze 21:22
26:10 [m]Jer 4:13
26:11 [n]Isa 5:28 [o]Jer 43:13 [p]Isa 26:5
26:12 [q]Isa 23:8; Eze 27:3-27; 28:8
26:13 [r]Jer 7:34 [s]Isa 14:11 [t]Jer 25:10; Rev 18:22
26:14 [u]Job 12:14; Mal 1:4
26:15 [v]Eze 27:35 [w]Jer 49:21
26:16 [x]Job 8:22 [y]Hos 11:10 [z]Eze 32:10
26:17 [a]Eze 19:1; 27:32 [b]Isa 14:12
26:18 [c]Isa 23:5; 41:5; Eze 27:35
26:19 [d]Isa 8:7-8
26:20 [e]Eze 32:18; Am 9:2; Jnh 2:2,6 [f]Eze 32:24,30
26:21 [g]Eze 27:36; 28:19; Rev 18:21

e *7* Hebrew *Nebuchadrezzar,* of which *Nebuchadnezzar* is a variant; here and often in Ezekiel and Jeremiah f *20* Septuagint; Hebrew *return, and I will give glory*

situated at the gateway to the sea,[a] merchant of peoples on many coasts, 'This is
what the Sovereign LORD says:

"'You say, O Tyre,
"I am perfect in beauty.[b]"
4 Your domain was on the high seas;
your builders brought your beauty
to perfection.
5 They made all your timbers
of pine trees from Senir[g];[c]
they took a cedar from Lebanon
to make a mast for you.
6 Of oaks[d] from Bashan
they made your oars;
of cypress wood[h] from the coasts of
Cyprus[i][e]
they made your deck, inlaid with
ivory.
7 Fine embroidered linen from Egypt
was your sail
and served as your banner;
your awnings were of blue and
purple[f]
from the coasts of Elishah.
8 Men of Sidon and Arvad[g] were your
oarsmen;
your skilled men, O Tyre, were
aboard as your seamen.[h]
9 Veteran craftsmen of Gebal[j][i] were
on board
as shipwrights to caulk your seams.
All the ships of the sea and their
sailors
came alongside to trade for your
wares.

10 "'Men of Persia,[j] Lydia and Put[k]
served as soldiers in your army.
They hung their shields and helmets
on your walls,
bringing you splendor.
11 Men of Arvad and Helech
manned your walls on every side;
men of Gammad
were in your towers.
They hung their shields around your
walls;
they brought your beauty to
perfection.

12 "'Tarshish[l] did business with you
because of your great wealth of goods;[m]
they exchanged silver, iron, tin and lead
for your merchandise.
13 "'Greece, Tubal and Meshech[n] traded with you; they exchanged slaves[o]
and articles of bronze for your wares.
14 "'Men of Beth Togarmah[p] exchanged
work horses, war horses and mules for
your merchandise.
15 "'The men of Rhodes[k][q] traded with
you, and many coastlands[r] were your
customers; they paid you with ivory[s]
tusks and ebony.
16 "'Aram[l][t] did business with you
because of your many products; they exchanged turquoise,[u] purple fabric, embroidered work, fine linen, coral and
rubies for your merchandise.
17 "'Judah and Israel traded with you;
they exchanged wheat from Minnith[v]
and confections,[m] honey, oil and balm
for your wares.
18 "'Damascus,[w] because of your many
products and great wealth of goods, did
business with you in wine from Helbon
and wool from Zahar.
19 "'Danites and Greeks from Uzal
bought your merchandise; they exchanged wrought iron, cassia and calamus for your wares.
20 "'Dedan traded in saddle blankets
with you.
21 "'Arabia and all the princes of
Kedar[x] were your customers; they did
business with you in lambs, rams and
goats.
22 "'The merchants of Sheba[y] and Raamah traded with you; for your merchandise they exchanged the finest of all kinds
of spices[z] and precious stones, and gold.
23 "'Haran,[a] Canneh and Eden[b] and
merchants of Sheba, Asshur and Kilmad
traded with you. 24 In your marketplace
they traded with you beautiful garments, blue fabric, embroidered work
and multicolored rugs with cords twisted
and tightly knotted.

27:3 [a]ver 33 [b]Eze 28:2
27:5 [c]Dt 3:9
27:6 [d]Nu 21:33; Jer 22:20; Zec 11:2 [e]Ge 10:4; Isa 23:12
27:7 [f]Ex 25:4; Jer 10:9
27:8 [g]Ge 10:18 [h]1Ki 9:27
27:9 [i]Jos 13:5; 1Ki 5:18
27:10 [j]Eze 38:5 [k]Eze 30:5
27:12 [l]Ge 10:4 [m]ver 18,33
27:13 [n]Ge 10:2; Isa 66:19; Eze 38:2 [o]Rev 18:13
27:14 [p]Ge 10:3; Eze 38:6
27:15 [q]Ge 10:7 [r]Jer 25:22 [s]1Ki 10:22; Rev 18:12
27:16 [t]Jdg 10:6; Isa 7:1-8 [u]Eze 28:13
27:17 [v]Jdg 11:33
27:18 [w]Ge 14:15; Eze 47:16-18
27:21 [x]Ge 25:13; Isa 60:7
27:22 [y]Ge 10:7,28; 1Ki 10:1-2; Isa 60:6 [z]Ge 43:11
27:23 [a]2Ki 19:12 [b]Isa 37:12

[g] *5* That is, Hermon [h] *6* Targum; the Masoretic Text has a different division of the consonants. [i] *6* Hebrew *Kittim* [j] *9* That is, Byblos [k] *15* Septuagint; Hebrew *Dedan* [l] *16* Most Hebrew manuscripts; some Hebrew manuscripts and Syriac *Edom* [m] *17* The meaning of the Hebrew for this word is uncertain.

25“ ‘The ships of Tarshish[a] serve
as carriers for your wares.
You are filled with heavy cargo
in the heart of the sea.
26Your oarsmen take you
out to the high seas.
But the east wind[b] will break you to
pieces
in the heart of the sea.
27Your wealth,[c] merchandise and
wares,
your mariners, seamen and
shipwrights,
your merchants and all your soldiers,
and everyone else on board
will sink into the heart of the sea
on the day of your shipwreck.
28The shorelands will quake[d]
when your seamen cry out.
29All who handle the oars
will abandon their ships;
the mariners and all the seamen
will stand on the shore.
30They will raise their voice
and cry bitterly over you;
they will sprinkle dust[e] on their
heads
and roll[f] in ashes.[g]
31They will shave their heads because
of you
and will put on sackcloth.
They will weep[h] over you with
anguish of soul
and with bitter mourning.[i]
32As they wail and mourn over you,
they will take up a lament[j]
concerning you:
“Who was ever silenced like Tyre,
surrounded by the sea?”
33When your merchandise went out
on the seas,
you satisfied many nations;
with your great wealth[k] and your
wares
you enriched the kings of the
earth.
34Now you are shattered by the sea
in the depths of the waters;
your wares and all your company
have gone down with you.[l]
35All who live in the coastlands[m]
are appalled at you;
their kings shudder with horror
and their faces are distorted with
fear.
36The merchants among the nations
hiss at you;[n]
you have come to a horrible end
and will be no more.[o]’ ”

27:25 [a]Isa 2:16*fn*
27:26 [b]Ps 48:7; Jer 18:17
27:27 [c]Pr 11:4
27:28 [d]Eze 26:15
27:30 [e]2Sa 1:2 [f]Jer 6:26 [g]Rev 18:18-19
27:31 [h]Isa 16:9 [i]Isa 22:12; Eze 7:18
27:32 [j]Eze 26:17
27:33 [k]ver 12; Eze 28:4-5
27:34 [l]Zec 9:4
27:35 [m]Eze 26:15
27:36 [n]Jer 18:16; 19:8; 49:17; 50:13; Zep 2:15 [o]Ps 37:10,36; Eze 26:21
28:2 [p]Isa 14:13 [q]Ps 9:20; 82:6-7; Isa 31:3; 2Th 2:4
28:3 [r]Da 1:20; 5:11-12
28:4 [s]Zec 9:3
28:5 [t]Job 31:25; Ps 52:7; 62:10; Hos 12:8; 13:6
28:7 [u]Eze 30:11; 31:12; 32:12; Hab 1:6
28:8 [v]Eze 32:30 [w]Eze 27:27

Judgment against the king of Tyre.

28 The word of the LORD came to
me: 2“Son of man, say to the
ruler of Tyre, ‘This is what the Sovereign
LORD says:

“ ‘In the pride of your heart
you say, “I am a god;
I sit on the throne[p] of a god
in the heart of the seas.”
But you are a man and not a god,
though you think you are as wise
as a god.[q]
3Are you wiser than Daniel[n]?[r]
Is no secret hidden from you?
4By your wisdom and understanding
you have gained wealth for
yourself
and amassed gold and silver
in your treasuries.[s]
5By your great skill in trading
you have increased your wealth,
and because of your wealth
your heart has grown proud.[t]

6“ ‘Therefore this is what the Sovereign
LORD says:

“ ‘Because you think you are wise,
as wise as a god,
7I am going to bring foreigners against
you,
the most ruthless of nations;[u]
they will draw their swords against
your beauty and wisdom
and pierce your shining splendor.
8They will bring you down to the
pit,[v]
and you will die a violent death
in the heart of the seas.[w]
9Will you then say, “I am a god,”
in the presence of those who kill
you?

[n]3 Or *Danel*; the Hebrew spelling may suggest a person other than the prophet Daniel.

You will be but a man, not a god,
in the hands of those who slay you.[a]
10 You will die the death of the uncircumcised[a]
at the hands of foreigners.

I have spoken, declares the Sovereign LORD.'"

11 The word of the LORD came to me:
12 "Son of man, take up a lament[b] concerning the king of Tyre and say to him:
'This is what the Sovereign LORD says:

"'You were the model of perfection,
full of wisdom and perfect in beauty.[c]
13 You were in Eden,[d]
the garden of God;[e]
every precious stone adorned you:
ruby, topaz and emerald,
chrysolite, onyx and jasper,
sapphire,[o] turquoise[f] and beryl.[p]
Your settings and mountings[q] were made of gold;
on the day you were created they were prepared.
14 You were anointed[g] as a guardian cherub,[h]
for so I ordained you.
You were on the holy mount of God;
you walked among the fiery stones.
15 You were blameless in your ways
from the day you were created
till wickedness was found in you.
16 Through your widespread trade
you were filled with violence,[i]
and you sinned.
So I drove you in disgrace from the mount of God,
and I expelled you, O guardian cherub,[j]
from among the fiery stones.
17 Your heart became proud[k]
on account of your beauty,
and you corrupted your wisdom
because of your splendor.
So I threw you to the earth;
I made a spectacle of you before kings.
18 By your many sins and dishonest trade
you have desecrated your sanctuaries.
So I made a fire come out from you,
and it consumed you,
and I reduced you to ashes[l] on the ground
in the sight of all who were watching.
19 All the nations who knew you
are appalled at you;
you have come to a horrible end
and will be no more.[m]'"

Judgment against Sidon.

20 The word of the LORD came to me:
21 "Son of man, set your face against[n]
Sidon;[o] prophesy against her 22 and say:
'This is what the Sovereign LORD says:

"'I am against you, O Sidon,
and I will gain glory[p] within you.
They will know that I am the LORD,
when I inflict punishment[q] on her
and show myself holy within her.
23 I will send a plague upon her
and make blood flow in her streets.
The slain will fall within her,
with the sword against her on every side.
Then they will know that I am the LORD.[r]

The LORD will gather and restore Israel.

24 "'No longer will the people of Israel
have malicious neighbors who are painful briers and sharp thorns.[s] Then they
will know that I am the Sovereign LORD.
25 "'This is what the Sovereign LORD
says: When I gather[t] the people of Israel
from the nations where they have been
scattered,[u] I will show myself holy[v]
among them in the sight of the nations.
Then they will live in their own land,
which I gave to my servant Jacob.[w]
26 They will live there in safety[x] and will
build houses and plant vineyards; they
will live in safety when I inflict punishment on all their neighbors who maligned them. Then they will know that
I am the LORD their God.[y]'"

28:10 [a]Eze 31:18; 32:19,24
28:12 [b]Eze 19:1 [c]Eze 27:2-4
28:13 [d]Ge 2:8 [e]Eze 31:8-9 [f]Eze 27:16
28:14 [g]Ex 30:26; 40:9 [h]Ex 25:17-20
28:16 [i]Hab 2:17 [j]Ge 3:24
28:17 [k]Eze 31:10
28:18 [l]Mal 4:3
28:19 [m]Jer 51:64; Eze 26:21; 27:36
28:21 [n]Eze 6:2 [o]Ge 10:15; Jer 25:22
28:22 [p]Eze 39:13 [q]Eze 30:19
28:23 [r]Eze 38:22
28:24 [s]Nu 33:55; Jos 23:13; Eze 2:6
28:25 [t]Ps 106:47; Jer 32:37 [u]Isa 11:12 [v]Eze 20:41 [w]Jer 23:8; Eze 11:17; 34:27; 37:25
28:26 [x]Jer 23:6 [y]Isa 65:21; Jer 32:15; Eze 38:8; Am 9:14-15

[o] 13 Or *lapis lazuli* [p] 13 The precise identification of some of these precious stones is uncertain.
[q] 13 The meaning of the Hebrew for this phrase is uncertain.

Judgment against Egypt.

29 In the tenth year, in the tenth
month on the twelfth day, the
word of the LORD came to me:[a] 2“Son of
man, set your face against Pharaoh king
of Egypt[b] and prophesy against him and
against all Egypt.[c] 3Speak to him and say:
‘This is what the Sovereign LORD says:

“‘I am against you, Pharaoh[d] king of
Egypt,
you great monster[e] lying among
your streams.
You say, “The Nile is mine;
I made it for myself.”
4But I will put hooks[f] in your jaws
and make the fish of your streams
stick to your scales.
I will pull you out from among your
streams,
with all the fish sticking to your
scales.[g]
5I will leave you in the desert,
you and all the fish of your
streams.
You will fall on the open field
and not be gathered or picked up.
I will give you as food
to the beasts of the earth and the
birds of the air.[h]

6Then all who live in Egypt will know
that I am the LORD.

“‘You have been a staff of reed[i] for the
house of Israel. 7When they grasped you
with their hands, you splintered[j] and
you tore open their shoulders; when
they leaned on you, you broke and their
backs were wrenched.[r][k]
8“‘Therefore this is what the Sovereign LORD says: I will bring a sword
against you and kill your men and their
animals.[l] 9Egypt will become a desolate
wasteland. Then they will know that I
am the LORD.
“‘Because you said, “The Nile is mine;
I made it,[m]” 10therefore I am against you
and against your streams, and I will
make the land of Egypt a ruin and a desolate waste from Migdol to Aswan,[n] as
far as the border of Cush.[s] 11No foot of
man or animal will pass through it; no
one will live there for forty years.[o] 12I
will make the land of Egypt desolate
among devastated lands, and her cities
will lie desolate forty years among ruined
cities. And I will disperse the Egyptians
among the nations and scatter them
through the countries.[p]
13“‘Yet this is what the Sovereign
LORD says: At the end of forty years I
will gather the Egyptians from the nations where they were scattered. 14I will
bring them back from captivity and return them to Upper Egypt,[t][q] the land of
their ancestry. There they will be a lowly[r] kingdom. 15It will be the lowliest of
kingdoms and will never again exalt
itself above the other nations.[s] I will
make it so weak that it will never again
rule over the nations. 16Egypt will no
longer be a source of confidence[t] for the
people of Israel but will be a reminder
of their sin in turning to her for help.
Then they will know that I am the Sovereign LORD.[u]’”

Egypt will be given to Babylon.

17In the twenty-seventh year, in the
first month on the first day, the word of
the LORD came to me:[v] 18“Son of man,
Nebuchadnezzar[w] king of Babylon drove
his army in a hard campaign against
Tyre; every head was rubbed bare[x] and
every shoulder made raw. Yet he and his
army got no reward from the campaign
he led against Tyre. 19Therefore this is
what the Sovereign LORD says: I am
going to give Egypt to Nebuchadnezzar
king of Babylon, and he will carry off its
wealth. He will loot and plunder the
land as pay for his army.[y] 20I have given
him Egypt as a reward for his efforts because he and his army did it for me,
declares the Sovereign LORD.[z]
21“On that day I will make a horn[u][a]
grow for the house of Israel, and I will
open your mouth[b] among them. Then
they will know that I am the LORD.[c]”

29:1 [a]ver 17; Eze 26:1 **29:2** [b]Jer 25:19 [c]Isa 19:1-17; Jer 46:2; Eze 30:1-26; 31:1-18; 32:1-32 **29:3** [d]Jer 44:30 [e]Ps 74:13; Isa 27:1; Eze 32:2 **29:4** [f]2Ki 19:28 [g]Eze 38:4 **29:5** [h]Jer 7:33; 34:20; Eze 32:4-6; 39:4 **29:6** [i]2Ki 18:21; Isa 36:6 **29:7** [j]Isa 36:6 [k]Eze 17:15-17 **29:8** [l]Eze 14:17; 32:11-13 **29:9** [m]Eze 30:7-8, 13-19 **29:10** [n]Eze 30:6 **29:11** [o]Eze 32:13 **29:12** [p]Jer 46:19; Eze 30:7, 23,26 **29:14** [q]Eze 30:14 [r]Eze 17:14 **29:15** [s]Zec 10:11 **29:16** [t]Isa 36:4,6 [u]Isa 30:2; Hos 8:13 **29:17** [v]Eze 24:1 **29:18** [w]Jer 27:6; Eze 26:7-8 [x]Jer 48:37 **29:19** [y]Jer 43:10-13; Eze 30:4, 10,24-25 **29:20** [z]Isa 10:6-7; 45:1; Jer 25:9 **29:21** [a]Ps 132:17 [b]Eze 33:22 [c]Eze 24:27

r *7* Syriac (see also Septuagint and Vulgate); Hebrew *and you caused their backs to stand* s *10* That is, the upper Nile region t *14* Hebrew *to Pathros* u *21* *Horn* here symbolizes strength.

Anguish of Egypt and her allies.

30 The word of the LORD came to
me: 2"Son of man, prophesy and
say: 'This is what the Sovereign LORD
says:

"'Wail[a] and say,
'Alas for that day!"
3For the day is near,[b]
the day of the LORD[c] is near—
a day of clouds,
a time of doom for the nations.
4A sword will come against Egypt,
and anguish will come upon Cush.[v]
When the slain fall in Egypt,
her wealth will be carried away
and her foundations torn down.[d]

5Cush and Put,[e] Lydia and all Arabia,
Libya[w] and the people[f] of the covenant
land will fall by the sword along with
Egypt.
6"'This is what the LORD says:

"'The allies of Egypt will fall
and her proud strength will fail.
From Migdol to Aswan[g]
they will fall by the sword within
her,
declares the Sovereign
LORD.
7"'They will be desolate
among desolate lands,
and their cities will lie
among ruined cities.[h]
8Then they will know that I am the
LORD,
when I set fire to Egypt
and all her helpers are crushed.

9"'On that day messengers will go out
from me in ships to frighten Cush[i] out
of her complacency. Anguish[j] will take
hold of them on the day of Egypt's doom,
for it is sure to come.[k]

10"'This is what the Sovereign LORD
says:

"'I will put an end to the hordes of
Egypt
by the hand of Nebuchadnezzar
king of Babylon.[l]
11He and his army—the most ruthless
of nations[m]—
will be brought in to destroy the land.
They will draw their swords against
Egypt
and fill the land with the slain.
12I will dry up[n] the streams of the Nile[o]
and sell the land to evil men;
by the hand of foreigners
I will lay waste the land and
everything in it.

I the LORD have spoken.

13"'This is what the Sovereign LORD
says:

"'I will destroy the idols[p]
and put an end to the images in
Memphis.[x][q]
No longer will there be a prince in
Egypt,[r]
and I will spread fear throughout
the land.
14I will lay[s] waste Upper Egypt,[y]
set fire to Zoan[t]
and inflict punishment on Thebes.[z][u]
15I will pour out my wrath on
Pelusium,[a]
the stronghold of Egypt,
and cut off the hordes of Thebes.
16I will set fire to Egypt;
Pelusium will writhe in agony.
Thebes will be taken by storm;
Memphis will be in constant
distress.
17The young men of Heliopolis[b][v] and
Bubastis[c]
will fall by the sword,
and the cities themselves will go
into captivity.
18Dark will be the day at Tahpanhes
when I break the yoke of Egypt;[w]
there her proud strength will come
to an end.
She will be covered with clouds,
and her villages will go into
captivity.[x]

30:2 [a]Isa 13:6
30:3 [b]Eze 7:7; Joel 2:1,11; Ob 1:15 [c]ver 18; Eze 7:12,19
30:4 [d]Eze 29:19
30:5 [e]Eze 27:10 [f]Jer 25:20
30:6 [g]Eze 29:10
30:7 [h]Eze 29:12
30:9 [i]Isa 18:1-2 [j]Isa 23:5 [k]Eze 32:9-10
30:10 [l]Eze 29:19
30:11 [m]Eze 28:7
30:12 [n]Isa 19:6 [o]Eze 29:9
30:13 [p]Jer 43:12 [q]Isa 19:13 [r]Zec 10:11
30:14 [s]Eze 29:14 [t]Ps 78:12,43 [u]Jer 46:25
30:17 [v]Ge 41:45
30:18 [w]Lev 26:13 [x]ver 3

v*4* That is, the upper Nile region; also in verses 5 and 9 w*5* Hebrew *Cub* x*13* Hebrew *Noph*; also in verse 16 y*14* Hebrew *waste Pathros* z*14* Hebrew *No*; also in verses 15 and 16 a*15* Hebrew *Sin*; also in verse 16 b*17* Hebrew *Awen* (or *On*) c*17* Hebrew *Pi Beseth*

19 So I will inflict punishment on
Egypt,
and they will know that I am the
LORD.'"

20 In the eleventh year, in the first
month on the seventh day, the word of
the LORD came to me:[a] 21 "Son of man, I
have broken the arm[b] of Pharaoh king
of Egypt. It has not been bound up for
healing[c] or put in a splint so as to become strong enough to hold a sword.
22 Therefore this is what the Sovereign
LORD says: I am against Pharaoh king of
Egypt.[d] I will break both his arms, the
good arm as well as the broken one, and
make the sword fall from his hand.[e] 23 I
will disperse the Egyptians among the
nations and scatter them through the
countries.[f] 24 I will strengthen[g] the arms
of the king of Babylon and put my
sword[h] in his hand, but I will break the
arms of Pharaoh, and he will groan before him like a mortally wounded man.
25 I will strengthen the arms of the king
of Babylon, but the arms of Pharaoh will
fall limp. Then they will know that I am
the LORD, when I put my sword into
the hand of the king of Babylon and he
brandishes it against Egypt. 26 I will disperse the Egyptians among the nations
and scatter them through the countries.
Then they will know that I am the
LORD.[i]"

A cedar in Lebanon.

31 In the eleventh year,[j] in the third
month on the first day, the word
of the LORD came to me:[k] 2 "Son of man,
say to Pharaoh king of Egypt and to his
hordes:

"'Who can be compared with you in
majesty?
3 Consider Assyria, once a cedar in
Lebanon,
with beautiful branches
overshadowing the forest;
it towered on high,
its top above the thick foliage.[l]
4 The waters nourished it,
deep springs made it grow tall;
their streams flowed
all around its base
and sent their channels
to all the trees of the field.
5 So it towered higher
than all the trees of the field;
its boughs increased
and its branches grew long,
spreading because of abundant
waters.[m]
6 All the birds of the air
nested in its boughs,
all the beasts of the field
gave birth under its branches;
all the great nations
lived in its shade.[n]
7 It was majestic in beauty,
with its spreading boughs,
for its roots went down
to abundant waters.
8 The cedars[o] in the garden of God
could not rival it,
nor could the pine trees
equal its boughs,
nor could the plane trees
compare with its branches—
no tree in the garden of God
could match its beauty.[p]
9 I made it beautiful
with abundant branches,
the envy of all the trees of Eden[q]
in the garden of God.[r]

10 "'Therefore this is what the Sovereign LORD says: Because it towered on
high, lifting its top above the thick foliage, and because it was proud[s] of its
height, 11 I handed it over to the ruler of
the nations, for him to deal with according to its wickedness. I cast it aside,[t]
12 and the most ruthless of foreign nations[u] cut it down and left it. Its boughs
fell on the mountains and in all the valleys;[v] its branches lay broken in all the
ravines of the land. All the nations of the
earth came out from under its shade and
left it.[w] 13 All the birds of the air settled
on the fallen tree, and all the beasts of
the field were among its branches.[x]
14 Therefore no other trees by the waters
are ever to tower proudly on high, lifting
their tops above the thick foliage. No

30:20 [a]Eze 26:1; 29:17; 31:1
30:21 [b]Jer 48:25 [c]Jer 30:13; 46:11
30:22 [d]Jer 46:25 [e]Ps 37:17
30:23 [f]Eze 29:12
30:24 [g]Zec 10:6,12 [h]Eze 21:14; Zep 2:12
30:26 [i]Eze 29:12
31:1 [j]Jer 52:5 [k]Eze 30:20
31:3 [l]Isa 10:34
31:5 [m]Eze 17:5
31:6 [n]Eze 17:23; Mt 13:32
31:8 [o]Ps 80:10 [p]Ge 2:8-9
31:9 [q]Ge 2:8 [r]Ge 13:10; Eze 28:13
31:10 [s]Isa 14:13-14; Eze 28:17
31:11 [t]Da 5:20
31:12 [u]Eze 28:7 [v]Eze 32:5; 35:8 [w]Eze 32:11-12; Da 4:14
31:13 [x]Isa 18:6; Eze 29:5; 32:4

other trees so well-watered are ever to
reach such a height; they are all destined
for death,[a] for the earth below, among
mortal men, with those who go down to
the pit.[b]
15"'This is what the Sovereign LORD
says: On the day it was brought down to
the grave[d] I covered the deep springs
with mourning for it; I held back its
streams, and its abundant waters were
restrained. Because of it I clothed Lebanon with gloom, and all the trees of the
field withered away. 16I made the nations tremble[c] at the sound of its fall
when I brought it down to the grave
with those who go down to the pit.
Then all the trees[d] of Eden, the choicest
and best of Lebanon, all the trees that
were well-watered, were consoled[e] in
the earth below.[f] 17Those who lived in
its shade, its allies among the nations,
had also gone down to the grave with it,
joining those killed by the sword.[g]
18"'Which of the trees of Eden can be
compared with you in splendor and majesty? Yet you, too, will be brought down
with the trees of Eden to the earth below; you will lie among the uncircumcised,[h] with those killed by the sword.
"'This is Pharaoh and all his hordes,
declares the Sovereign LORD.'"

Ezekiel's lament for Pharaoh.

32 In the twelfth year, in the
twelfth month on the first day,
the word of the LORD came to me:[i] 2"Son
of man, take up a lament[j] concerning
Pharaoh king of Egypt and say to him:

"'You are like a lion[k] among the
nations;
you are like a monster in the seas
thrashing about in your streams,
churning the water with your feet
and muddying the streams.[l]

3"'This is what the Sovereign LORD
says:

"'With a great throng of people
I will cast my net over you,
and they will haul you up in my
net.[m]

31:14 [a]Ps 82:7 [b]Ps 63:9; Eze 26:20; 32:24
31:16 [c]Eze 26:15 [d]Isa 14:8 [e]Eze 14:22; 32:31 [f]Isa 14:15; Eze 32:18
31:17 [g]Ps 9:17
31:18 [h]Jer 9:26; Eze 32:19,21
32:1 [i]Eze 31:1; 33:21
32:2 [j]Eze 19:1; 27:2 [k]Eze 19:3,6; Na 2:11-13 [l]Eze 29:3; 34:18
32:3 [m]Eze 12:13
32:4 [n]Isa 18:6; Eze 31:12-13
32:5 [o]Eze 31:12
32:6 [p]Isa 34:3
32:7 [q]Isa 13:10; 34:4; Eze 30:3; Joel 2:2,31; 3:15; Mt 24:29; Rev 8:12
32:10 [r]Jer 46:10 [s]Eze 26:16; 27:35
32:11 [t]Jer 46:26
32:12 [u]Eze 28:7

4I will throw you on the land
and hurl you on the open field.
I will let all the birds of the air settle
on you
and all the beasts of the earth
gorge themselves on you.[n]
5I will spread your flesh on the
mountains
and fill the valleys[o] with your
remains.
6I will drench the land with your
flowing blood[p]
all the way to the mountains,
and the ravines will be filled with
your flesh.
7When I snuff you out, I will cover the
heavens
and darken their stars;
I will cover the sun with a cloud,
and the moon will not give its
light.[q]
8All the shining lights in the heavens
I will darken over you;
I will bring darkness over your
land,
declares the Sovereign
LORD.
9I will trouble the hearts of many
peoples
when I bring about your
destruction among the nations,
among[e] lands you have not known.
10I will cause many peoples to be
appalled at you,
and their kings will shudder with
horror because of you
when I brandish my sword before
them.
On the day[r] of your downfall
each of them will tremble
every moment for his life.[s]

11"'For this is what the Sovereign
LORD says:

"'The sword of the king of Babylon[t]
will come against you.
12I will cause your hordes to fall
by the swords of mighty men—
the most ruthless of all nations.[u]

d *15* Hebrew *Sheol*; also in verses 16 and 17
e *9* Hebrew; Septuagint *bring you into captivity among the nations, / to*

They will shatter the pride of Egypt,
and all her hordes will be
overthrown.[a]
13 I will destroy all her cattle
from beside abundant waters
no longer to be stirred by the foot of
man
or muddied by the hoofs of cattle.[b]
14 Then I will let her waters settle
and make her streams flow like oil,
declares the Sovereign
LORD.
15 When I make Egypt desolate
and strip the land of everything in it,
when I strike down all who live
there,
then they will know that I am the
LORD.[c]'

16 "This is the lament[d] they will chant
for her. The daughters of the nations will
chant it; for Egypt and all her hordes
they will chant it, declares the Sovereign
LORD."

Egypt is consigned to the pit.

17 In the twelfth year, on the fifteenth
day of the month, the word of the LORD
came to me:[e] 18 "Son of man, wail for
the hordes of Egypt and consign[f] to the
earth below both her and the daughters
of mighty nations, with those who go
down to the pit.[g] 19 Say to them, 'Are
you more favored than others? Go down
and be laid among the uncircumcised.'[h]
20 They will fall among those killed by
the sword. The sword is drawn; let her
be dragged[i] off with all her hordes.
21 From within the grave[f][j] the mighty
leaders will say of Egypt and her allies,
'They have come down and they lie with
the uncircumcised, with those killed by
the sword.'
22 "Assyria is there with her whole
army; she is surrounded by the graves of
all her slain, all who have fallen by the
sword. 23 Their graves are in the depths
of the pit[k] and her army lies around her
grave. All who had spread terror in the
land of the living are slain, fallen by the
sword.
24 "Elam[l] is there, with all her hordes
around her grave. All of them are slain,
fallen by the sword.[m] All who had spread
terror in the land of the living[n] went
down uncircumcised to the earth below.
They bear their shame with those who
go down to the pit.[o] 25 A bed is made for
her among the slain, with all her hordes
around her grave. All of them are uncircumcised, killed by the sword. Because their terror had spread in the land
of the living, they bear their shame with
those who go down to the pit; they are
laid among the slain.
26 "Meshech and Tubal[p] are there,
with all their hordes around their graves.
All of them are uncircumcised, killed by
the sword because they spread their terror in the land of the living. 27 Do they
not lie with the other uncircumcised
warriors who have fallen, who went
down to the grave with their weapons
of war, whose swords were placed under
their heads? The punishment for their
sins rested on their bones, though the
terror of these warriors had stalked
through the land of the living.
28 "You too, O Pharaoh, will be broken
and will lie among the uncircumcised,
with those killed by the sword.
29 "Edom[q] is there, her kings and all
her princes; despite their power, they
are laid with those killed by the sword.
They lie with the uncircumcised, with
those who go down to the pit.[r]
30 "All the princes of the north[s] and
all the Sidonians[t] are there; they went
down with the slain in disgrace despite
the terror caused by their power. They
lie uncircumcised with those killed by
the sword and bear their shame with
those who go down to the pit.
31 "Pharaoh—he and all his army—
will see them and he will be consoled[u]
for all his hordes that were killed by the
sword, declares the Sovereign LORD.
32 Although I had him spread terror in
the land of the living, Pharaoh and all
his hordes will be laid among the uncircumcised, with those killed by the
sword, declares the Sovereign LORD."

32:12 [a] Eze 31:11-12
32:13 [b] Eze 29:8,11
32:15 [c] Ex 7:5; 14:4,18; Ps 107:33-34; Eze 6:7
32:16 [d] 2Sa 1:17; 2Ch 35:25; Eze 26:17
32:17 [e] ver 1
32:18 [f] Jer 1:10 [g] Eze 31:14,16; Mic 1:8
32:19 [h] ver 29-30; Eze 28:10; 31:18
32:20 [i] Ps 28:3
32:21 [j] Isa 14:9
32:23 [k] Isa 14:15
32:24 [l] Ge 10:22 [m] Jer 49:37 [n] Job 28:13 [o] Eze 26:20
32:26 [p] Ge 10:2; Eze 27:13
32:29 [q] Isa 34:5-15; Jer 49:7; Eze 35:15; Ob 1 [r] Eze 25:12-14
32:30 [s] Jer 25:26; Eze 38:6; 39:2 [t] Jer 25:22; Eze 28:21
32:31 [u] Eze 14:22; 31:16

[f] *21* Hebrew *Sheol*; also in verse 27

Ezekiel's duty as a watchman.

33 The word of the LORD came to me: 2"Son of man, speak to your countrymen and say to them: 'When I bring the sword[a] against a land, and the people of the land choose one of their men and make him their watchman,[b] 3and he sees the sword coming against the land and blows the trumpet[c] to warn the people, 4then if anyone hears the trumpet but does not take warning[d] and the sword comes and takes his life, his blood will be on his own head.[e] 5Since he heard the sound of the trumpet but did not take warning, his blood will be on his own head. If he had taken warning, he would have saved himself. 6But if the watchman sees the sword coming and does not blow the trumpet to warn the people and the sword comes and takes the life of one of them, that man will be taken away because of his sin, but I will hold the watchman accountable for his blood.'[f]

7"Son of man, I have made you a watchman for the house of Israel; so hear the word I speak and give them warning from me.[g] 8When I say to the wicked, 'O wicked man, you will surely die,[h]' and you do not speak out to dissuade him from his ways, that wicked man will die for[g] his sin, and I will hold you accountable for his blood.[i] 9But if you do warn the wicked man to turn from his ways and he does not do so, he will die for his sin, but you will have saved yourself.[j]

10"Son of man, say to the house of Israel, 'This is what you are saying: "Our offenses and sins weigh us down, and we are wasting away[k] because of[h] them. How then can we live?[l]"' 11Say to them, 'As surely as I live, declares the Sovereign LORD, I take no pleasure in the death of the wicked, but rather that they turn from their ways and live.[m] Turn! Turn from your evil ways! Why will you die, O house of Israel?'[n]

12"Therefore, son of man, say to your countrymen, 'The righteousness of the righteous man will not save him when he disobeys, and the wickedness of the wicked man will not cause him to fall when he turns from it. The righteous man, if he sins, will not be allowed to live because of his former righteousness.'[o] 13If I tell the righteous man that he will surely live, but then he trusts in his righteousness and does evil, none of the righteous things he has done will be remembered; he will die for the evil he has done.[p] 14And if I say to the wicked man, 'You will surely die,' but he then turns away from his sin and does what is just[q] and right— 15if he gives back what he took in pledge for a loan, returns what he has stolen,[r] follows the decrees that give life, and does no evil, he will surely live; he will not die.[s] 16None of the sins he has committed will be remembered against him. He has done what is just and right; he will surely live.[t]

17"Yet your countrymen say, 'The way of the Lord is not just.' But it is their way that is not just. 18If a righteous man turns from his righteousness and does evil, he will die for it.[u] 19And if a wicked man turns away from his wickedness and does what is just and right, he will live by doing so. 20Yet, O house of Israel, you say, 'The way of the Lord is not just.' But I will judge each of you according to his own ways."

Desolation of Jerusalem.

21In the twelfth year of our exile, in the tenth month on the fifth day, a man who had escaped[v] from Jerusalem came to me and said, "The city has fallen![w]" 22Now the evening before the man arrived, the hand of the LORD was upon me,[x] and he opened my mouth[y] before the man came to me in the morning. So my mouth was opened and I was no longer silent.[z]

23Then the word of the LORD came to me: 24"Son of man, the people living in those ruins[a] in the land of Israel are saying, 'Abraham was only one man, yet he possessed the land. But we are many;

33:2 [a]Jer 12:12 [b]Eze 3:11
33:3 [c]Hos 8:1
33:4 [d]2Ch 25:16 [e]Jer 6:17; Eze 18:13; Zec 1:4; Ac 18:6
33:6 [f]Eze 3:18
33:7 [g]Jer 26:2; Eze 3:17
33:8 [h]ver 14 [i]Eze 18:4
33:9 [j]Eze 3:17-19
33:10 [k]Eze 24:23 [l]Lev 26:39; Eze 4:17
33:11 [m]Eze 18:32; 2Pe 3:9 [n]Eze 18:23
33:12 [o]2Ch 7:14; Eze 3:20
33:13 [p]Eze 18:24; Heb 10:38; 2Pe 2:20-21
33:14 [q]Eze 18:27
33:15 [r]Ex 22:1-4; Lev 6:2-5 [s]Eze 20:11; Lk 19:8
33:16 [t]Isa 43:25; Eze 18:22
33:18 [u]Eze 3:20; Eze 18:26
33:21 [v]Eze 24:26 [w]2Ki 25:4,10; Jer 39:1-2; Eze 32:1
33:22 [x]Eze 1:3 [y]Lk 1:64 [z]Eze 3:26-27; 24:27
33:24 [a]Eze 36:4

g*8* Or *in*; also in verse 9 h*10* Or *away in*

surely the land has been given to us as
our possession.'[a] 25Therefore say to
them, 'This is what the Sovereign LORD
says: Since you eat meat with the blood[b]
still in it and look to your idols and shed
blood, should you then possess the
land?[c] 26You rely on your sword, you do
detestable things, and each of you defiles
his neighbor's wife.[d] Should you then
possess the land?'

27"Say this to them: 'This is what the
Sovereign LORD says: As surely as I live,
those who are left in the ruins will fall
by the sword, those out in the country
I will give to the wild animals to be
devoured, and those in strongholds and
caves will die of a plague.[e] 28I will make
the land a desolate waste, and her proud
strength will come to an end, and the
mountains of Israel will become desolate so that no one will cross them.
29Then they will know that I am the
LORD, when I have made the land a desolate waste because of all the detestable
things they have done.'

30"As for you, son of man, your countrymen are talking together about you
by the walls and at the doors of the
houses, saying to each other, 'Come and
hear the message that has come from
the LORD.' 31My people come to you, as
they usually do, and sit before[f] you to
listen to your words, but they do not put
them into practice. With their mouths
they express devotion, but their hearts
are greedy for unjust gain.[g] 32Indeed, to
them you are nothing more than one
who sings love songs with a beautiful
voice and plays an instrument well, for
they hear your words but do not put
them into practice.[h]

33"When all this comes true—and it
surely will—then they will know that a
prophet has been among them.[i]"

Woe to Israel's unfaithful shepherds.

34 The word of the LORD came to
me: 2"Son of man, prophesy
against the shepherds of Israel; prophesy
and say to them: 'This is what the Sovereign LORD says: Woe to the shepherds

33:24 [a]Isa 51:2; Jer 40:7; Eze 11:15; Ac 7:5
33:25 [b]Ge 9:4; Dt 12:16 [c]Jer 7:9-10; Eze 22:6,27
33:26 [d]Eze 22:11
33:27 [e]1Sa 13:6; Isa 2:19; Jer 42:22; Eze 39:4
33:31 [f]Eze 8:1 [g]Ps 78:36-37; Isa 29:13; Eze 22:27; Mt 13:22; 1Jn 3:18
33:32 [h]Mk 6:20
33:33 [i]1Sa 3:20; Jer 28:9; Eze 2:5
34:2 [j]Ps 78:70-72; Isa 40:11; Jer 3:15; 23:1; Mic 3:11; Jn 10:11; 21:15-17
34:3 [k]Isa 56:11; Eze 22:27; Zec 11:16
34:4 [l]Zec 11:15-17
34:5 [m]Nu 27:17 [n]ver 28; Isa 56:9
34:6 [o]Ps 142:4; 1Pe 2:25
34:10 [p]Jer 21:13 [q]Ps 72:14 [r]1Sa 2:29-30; Zec 10:3
34:12 [s]Isa 40:11; Jer 31:10; Lk 19:10 [t]Eze 30:3
34:13 [u]Jer 23:3

of Israel who only take care of themselves! Should not shepherds take care
of the flock?[j] 3You eat the curds, clothe
yourselves with the wool and slaughter the choice animals, but you do not
take care of the flock.[k] 4You have not
strengthened the weak or healed the
sick or bound up the injured. You have
not brought back the strays or searched
for the lost. You have ruled them harshly and brutally.[l] 5So they were scattered
because there was no shepherd,[m] and
when they were scattered they became
food for all the wild animals.[n] 6My sheep
wandered over all the mountains and
on every high hill. They were scattered
over the whole earth, and no one
searched or looked for them.[o]

7"'Therefore, you shepherds, hear the
word of the LORD: 8As surely as I live,
declares the Sovereign LORD, because my
flock lacks a shepherd and so has been
plundered and has become food for all
the wild animals, and because my shepherds did not search for my flock but
cared for themselves rather than for my
flock, 9therefore, O shepherds, hear the
word of the LORD: 10This is what the
Sovereign LORD says: I am against[p] the
shepherds and will hold them accountable for my flock. I will remove them
from tending the flock so that the shepherds can no longer feed themselves. I
will rescue[q] my flock from their mouths,
and it will no longer be food for them.[r]

The LORD will care for his flock.

11"'For this is what the Sovereign
LORD says: I myself will search for my
sheep and look after them. 12As a shepherd[s] looks after his scattered flock
when he is with them, so will I look
after my sheep. I will rescue them from
all the places where they were scattered
on a day of clouds and darkness.[t] 13I will
bring them out from the nations and
gather them from the countries, and I
will bring them into their own land. I
will pasture them on the mountains of
Israel, in the ravines and in all the settlements in the land.[u] 14I will tend them

in a good pasture, and the mountain
heights of Israel[a] will be their grazing
land. There they will lie down in good
grazing land, and there they will feed
in a rich pasture[b] on the mountains of
Israel.[c] 15 I myself will tend my sheep
and have them lie down, declares the
Sovereign LORD.[d] 16 I will search for the
lost and bring back the strays. I will
bind up the injured and strengthen the
weak,[e] but the sleek and the strong I
will destroy. I will shepherd the flock
with justice.[f]
17 "'As for you, my flock, this is what
the Sovereign LORD says: I will judge between one sheep and another, and
between rams and goats.[g] 18 Is it not
enough for you to feed on the good pasture? Must you also trample the rest of
your pasture with your feet? Is it not
enough for you to drink clear water?
Must you also muddy the rest with your
feet? 19 Must my flock feed on what you
have trampled and drink what you have
muddied with your feet?
20 "'Therefore this is what the Sovereign LORD says to them: See, I myself
will judge between the fat sheep and
the lean sheep. 21 Because you shove
with flank and shoulder, butting all the
weak sheep with your horns[h] until you
have driven them away, 22 I will save my
flock, and they will no longer be plundered. I will judge between one sheep
and another.[i] 23 I will place over them
one shepherd, my servant David, and he
will tend[j] them; he will tend them and
be their shepherd. 24 I the LORD will be
their God,[k] and my servant David will
be prince among them. I the LORD have
spoken.[l]
25 "'I will make a covenant of peace
with them and rid the land of wild
beasts[m] so that they may live in the
desert and sleep in the forests in safety.[n]
26 I will bless[o] them and the places surrounding my hill.[i] I will send down
showers in season;[p] there will be showers of blessing.[q] 27 The trees of the field
will yield their fruit and the ground will
yield its crops; the people will be secure
in their land. They will know that I am

34:14 [a]Eze 20:40 [b]Ps 23:2 [c]Eze 36:29-30
34:15 [d]Ps 23:1-2
34:16 [e]Mic 4:6 [f]Isa 10:16; Lk 5:32
34:17 [g]Mt 25:32-33
34:21 [h]Dt 33:17
34:22 [i]Ps 72:12-14; Jer 23:2-3
34:23 [j]Isa 40:11
34:24 [k]Eze 36:28 [l]Jer 30:9
34:25 [m]Lev 26:6 [n]Isa 11:6-9; Hos 2:18
34:26 [o]Ge 12:2 [p]Ps 68:9 [q]Dt 11:13-15; Isa 44:3
34:27 [r]Lev 26:13 [s]Jer 30:8
34:28 [t]Jer 30:10; Eze 39:26
34:29 [u]Isa 4:2 [v]Eze 36:29 [w]Eze 36:6 [x]Eze 36:15
34:30 [y]Eze 14:11; 37:27
34:31 [z]Ps 100:3; Jer 23:1
35:3 [a]Jer 6:12 [b]Eze 25:12-14
35:4 [c]ver 9
35:5 [d]Ps 137:7; Eze 21:29
35:6 [e]Isa 63:2-6
35:8 [f]Eze 31:12
35:9 [g]Jer 49:13

the LORD, when I break the bars of their
yoke[r] and rescue them from the hands
of those who enslaved them.[s] 28 They
will no longer be plundered by the nations, nor will wild animals devour
them. They will live in safety, and no
one will make them afraid.[t] 29 I will provide for them a land renowned[u] for its
crops, and they will no longer be victims of famine[v] in the land or bear the
scorn[w] of the nations.[x] 30 Then they will
know that I, the LORD their God, am
with them and that they, the house of
Israel, are my people, declares the Sovereign LORD.[y] 31 You my sheep, the sheep
of my pasture,[z] are people, and I am your
God, declares the Sovereign LORD.'"

Judgment against Mount Seir

35 The word of the LORD came to
me: 2 "Son of man, set your face
against Mount Seir; prophesy against it
3 and say: 'This is what the Sovereign
LORD says: I am against you, Mount Seir,
and I will stretch out my hand[a] against
you and make you a desolate waste.[b] 4 I
will turn your towns into ruins and you
will be desolate. Then you will know
that I am the LORD.[c]
5 "'Because you harbored an ancient
hostility and delivered the Israelites over
to the sword at the time of their calamity, the time their punishment reached
its climax,[d] 6 therefore as surely as I live,
declares the Sovereign LORD, I will give
you over to bloodshed and it will pursue
you.[e] Since you did not hate bloodshed,
bloodshed will pursue you. 7 I will
make Mount Seir a desolate waste and
cut off from it all who come and go. 8 I
will fill your mountains with the slain;
those killed by the sword will fall on
your hills and in your valleys and in all
your ravines.[f] 9 I will make you desolate
forever; your towns will not be inhabited. Then you will know that I am the
LORD.[g]
10 "'Because you have said, "These
two nations and countries will be ours

[i]26 Or *I will make them and the places surrounding my hill a blessing*

and we will take possession[a] of them," even though I the LORD was there, 11therefore as surely as I live, declares the Sovereign LORD, I will treat you in accordance with the anger[b] and jealousy you showed in your hatred of them and I will make myself known among them when I judge you.[c] 12Then you will know that I the LORD have heard all the contemptible things you have said against the mountains of Israel. You said, "They have been laid waste and have been given over to us to devour.[d]" 13You boasted against me and spoke against me without restraint, and I heard it.[e] 14This is what the Sovereign LORD says: While the whole earth rejoices, I will make you desolate.[f] 15Because you rejoiced[g] when the inheritance of the house of Israel became desolate, that is how I will treat you. You will be desolate, O Mount Seir,[h] you and all of Edom.[i] Then they will know that I am the LORD.'"

Blessings and restoration promised.

36

"Son of man, prophesy to the mountains of Israel and say, 'O mountains of Israel, hear the word of the LORD. 2This is what the Sovereign LORD says: The enemy said of you, "Aha![j] The ancient heights[k] have become our possession.[l]"' 3Therefore prophesy and say, 'This is what the Sovereign LORD says: Because they ravaged and hounded you from every side so that you became the possession of the rest of the nations and the object of people's malicious talk and slander,[m] 4therefore, O mountains of Israel, hear the word of the Sovereign LORD: This is what the Sovereign LORD says to the mountains and hills, to the ravines and valleys,[n] to the desolate ruins and the deserted towns that have been plundered and ridiculed by the rest of the nations around you[o]— 5this is what the Sovereign LORD says: In my burning zeal I have spoken against the rest of the nations, and against all Edom, for with glee and with malice in their hearts they made my land their own possession so that they might plunder its pastureland.'[p] 6Therefore prophesy concerning the land of Israel and say to the mountains and hills, to the ravines and valleys: 'This is what the Sovereign LORD says: I speak in my jealous wrath because you have suffered the scorn of the nations.[q] 7Therefore this is what the Sovereign LORD says: I swear with uplifted hand that the nations around you will also suffer scorn.

8"'But you, O mountains of Israel, will produce branches and fruit[r] for my people Israel, for they will soon come home. 9I am concerned for you and will look on you with favor; you will be plowed and sown, 10and I will multiply the number of people upon you, even the whole house of Israel. The towns will be inhabited and the ruins rebuilt.[s] 11I will increase the number of men and animals upon you, and they will be fruitful and become numerous. I will settle people on you as in the past[t] and will make you prosper more than before.[u] Then you will know that I am the LORD. 12I will cause people, my people Israel, to walk upon you. They will possess you, and you will be their inheritance;[v] you will never again deprive them of their children.

13"'This is what the Sovereign LORD says: Because people say to you, "You devour men[w] and deprive your nation of its children," 14therefore you will no longer devour men or make your nation childless, declares the Sovereign LORD. 15No longer will I make you hear the taunts of the nations, and no longer will you suffer the scorn of the peoples or cause your nation to fall, declares the Sovereign LORD.[x]'"

16Again the word of the LORD came to me: 17"Son of man, when the people of Israel were living in their own land, they defiled it by their conduct and their actions. Their conduct was like a woman's monthly uncleanness in my sight.[y] 18So I poured out[z] my wrath on them because they had shed blood in the land and because they had defiled it with their idols. 19I dispersed them among the nations, and they were scat-

35:10 [a]Ps 83:12; Eze 36:2,5
35:11 [b]Eze 25:14 [c]Ps 9:16; Mt 7:2
35:12 [d]Jer 50:7
35:13 [e]Da 11:36
35:14 [f]Jer 51:48
35:15 [g]Ob 12 [h]ver 3 [i]Isa 34:5-6,11; Jer 50:11-13; La 4:21
36:2 [j]Eze 25:3 [k]Dt 32:13 [l]Eze 35:10
36:3 [m]Ps 44:13-14
36:4 [n]Eze 6:3 [o]Dt 11:11; Ps 79:4; Eze 34:28
36:5 [p]Jer 50:11; Eze 25:12-14; 35:10,15
36:6 [q]Ps 123:3-4; Eze 34:29
36:8 [r]Isa 27:6
36:10 [s]ver 33; Isa 49:17-23
36:11 [t]Mic 7:14 [u]Jer 31:28; Eze 16:55
36:12 [v]Eze 47:14,22
36:13 [w]Nu 13:32
36:15 [x]Ps 89:50-51; Eze 34:29
36:17 [y]Jer 2:7
36:18 [z]2Ch 34:21

tered[a] through the countries; I judged them according to their conduct and their actions.[b] 20And wherever they went among the nations they profaned[c] my holy name, for it was said of them, 'These are the LORD's people, and yet they had to leave his land.'[d] 21I had concern for my holy name, which the house of Israel profaned among the nations where they had gone.[e]

22"Therefore say to the house of Israel, 'This is what the Sovereign LORD says: It is not for your sake, O house of Israel, that I am going to do these things, but for the sake of my holy name, which you have profaned[f] among the nations where you have gone.[g] 23I will show the holiness of my great name, which has been profaned among the nations, the name you have profaned among them. Then the nations will know that I am the LORD, declares the Sovereign LORD, when I show myself holy[h] through you before their eyes.[i]

24"'For I will take you out of the nations; I will gather you from all the countries and bring you back into your own land.[j] 25I will sprinkle[k] clean water on you, and you will be clean; I will cleanse[l] you from all your impurities and from all your idols.[m] 26I will give you a new heart[n] and put a new spirit in you; I will remove from you your heart of stone and give you a heart of flesh.[o] 27And I will put my Spirit[p] in you and move you to follow my decrees and be careful to keep my laws. 28You will live in the land I gave your forefathers; you will be my people,[q] and I will be your God.[r] 29I will save you from all your uncleanness. I will call for the grain and make it plentiful and will not bring famine[s] upon you. 30I will increase the fruit of the trees and the crops of the field, so that you will no longer suffer disgrace among the nations because of famine.[t] 31Then you will remember your evil ways and wicked deeds, and you will loathe yourselves for your sins and detestable practices.[u] 32I want you to know that I am not doing this for your sake, declares the Sovereign LORD. Be ashamed and disgraced for your conduct, O house of Israel![v]

33"'This is what the Sovereign LORD says: On the day I cleanse you from all your sins, I will resettle your towns, and the ruins will be rebuilt. 34The desolate land will be cultivated instead of lying desolate in the sight of all who pass through it. 35They will say, "This land that was laid waste has become like the garden of Eden;[w] the cities that were lying in ruins, desolate and destroyed, are now fortified and inhabited.[x]" 36Then the nations around you that remain will know that I the LORD have rebuilt what was destroyed and have replanted what was desolate. I the LORD have spoken, and I will do it.'[y]

37"This is what the Sovereign LORD says: Once again I will yield to the plea of the house of Israel and do this for them: I will make their people as numerous as sheep, 38as numerous as the flocks for offerings[z] at Jerusalem during her appointed feasts. So will the ruined cities be filled with flocks of people. Then they will know that I am the LORD."

Valley of dry bones.

37 The hand of the LORD was upon me,[a] and he brought me out by the Spirit[b] of the LORD and set me in the middle of a valley;[c] it was full of bones.[d] 2He led me back and forth among them, and I saw a great many bones on the floor of the valley, bones that were very dry. 3He asked me, "Son of man, can these bones live?"

I said, "O Sovereign LORD, you alone know.[e]"

4Then he said to me, "Prophesy to these bones and say to them, 'Dry bones, hear the word of the LORD![f] 5This is what the Sovereign LORD says to these bones: I will make breath[j] enter you, and you will come to life.[g] 6I will attach tendons to you and make flesh come

36:19 [a]Dt 28:64 [b]Eze 39:24
36:20 [c]Ro 2:24 [d]Isa 52:5; Jer 33:24; Eze 12:16
36:21 [e]Ps 74:18; Isa 48:9
36:22 [f]Ro 2:24* [g]Ps 106:8
36:23 [h]Eze 20:41 [i]Ps 126:2; Isa 5:16
36:24 [j]Eze 34:13; 37:21
36:25 [k]Heb 9:13; 10:22 [l]Ps 51:2,7 [m]Zec 13:2
36:26 [n]Jer 24:7 [o]Ps 51:10; Eze 11:19
36:27 [p]Eze 37:14
36:28 [q]Jer 30:22 [r]Eze 14:11; 37:14,27
36:29 [s]Eze 34:29
36:30 [t]Lev 26:4-5; Eze 34:27; Hos 2:21-22
36:31 [u]Eze 6:9; 20:43
36:32 [v]Dt 9:5
36:35 [w]Joel 2:3 [x]Isa 51:3
36:36 [y]Eze 17:22; 22:14; 37:14; 39:27-28
36:38 [z]1Ki 8:63; 2Ch 35:7-9
37:1 [a]Eze 1:3; 8:3 [b]Eze 11:24; Lk 4:1; Ac 8:39 [c]Jer 7:32 [d]Jer 8:2; Eze 40:1
37:3 [e]Dt 32:39; 1Sa 2:6; Isa 26:19

37:4 [f]Jer 22:29 **37:5** [g]Ge 2:7; Ps 104:29-30

j5 The Hebrew for this word can also mean *wind* or *spirit* (see verses 6-14).

upon you and cover you with skin; I will
put breath in you, and you will come to
life. Then you will know that I am the
LORD.[a]'"
[7]So I prophesied as I was commanded.
And as I was prophesying, there was a
noise, a rattling sound, and the bones
came together, bone to bone. [8]I looked,
and tendons and flesh appeared on them
and skin covered them, but there was
no breath in them.
[9]Then he said to me, "Prophesy to the
breath;[b] prophesy, son of man, and say
to it, 'This is what the Sovereign LORD
says: Come from the four winds, O
breath, and breathe into these slain, that
they may live.'" [10]So I prophesied as he
commanded me, and breath entered
them; they came to life and stood up on
their feet—a vast army.[c]
[11]Then he said to me: "Son of man,
these bones are the whole house of Israel. They say, 'Our bones are dried up
and our hope is gone; we are cut off.'[d]
[12]Therefore prophesy and say to them:
'This is what the Sovereign LORD says:
O my people, I am going to open your
graves and bring you up from them; I
will bring you back to the land of Israel.[e]
[13]Then you, my people, will know that
I am the LORD, when I open your graves
and bring you up from them. [14]I will put
my Spirit[f] in you and you will live, and
I will settle you in your own land. Then
you will know that I the LORD have
spoken, and I have done it, declares the
LORD.[g]'"

Two sticks of wood.

[15]The word of the LORD came to me:
[16]"Son of man, take a stick of wood and
write on it, 'Belonging to Judah and
the Israelites[h] associated with him.[i]'
Then take another stick of wood, and
write on it, 'Ephraim's stick, belonging
to Joseph and all the house of Israel
associated with him.' [17]Join them together into one stick so that they will
become one in your hand.[j]
[18]"When your countrymen ask you,
'Won't you tell us what you mean by

37:6 [a]Eze 38:23; Joel 2:27; 3:17
37:9 [b]Ps 104:30
37:10 [c]Rev 11:11
37:11 [d]La 3:54
37:12 [e]Dt 32:39; 1Sa 2:6; Isa 26:19; Hos 13:14; Am 9:14-15
37:14 [f]Joel 2:28-29 [g]Eze 36:27-28, 36
37:16 [h]1Ki 12:20; 2Ch 10:17-19 [i]Nu 17:2-3; 2Ch 15:9
37:17 [j]ver 24; Isa 11:13; Jer 50:4; Hos 1:11
37:18 [k]Eze 24:19
37:19 [l]Zec 10:6
37:21 [m]Isa 43:5-6; Eze 36:24; 39:27
37:22 [n]Isa 11:13; Jer 3:18; Hos 1:11
37:23 [o]Eze 36:25; 43:7 [p]Eze 11:18; 36:28
37:24 [q]Hos 3:5 [r]Isa 40:11; Eze 34:23 [s]Ps 78:70-71
37:25 [t]Eze 28:25 [u]Am 9:15 [v]Isa 11:1
37:26 [w]Isa 55:3 [x]Jer 30:19 [y]Eze 16:62
37:27 [z]Lev 26:11; Jn 1:14 [a]2Co 6:16*
37:28 [b]Ex 31:13; Eze 20:12
38:2 [c]Ge 10:2

this?'[k] [19]say to them, 'This is what the
Sovereign LORD says: I am going to take
the stick of Joseph—which is in Ephraim's hand—and of the Israelite tribes
associated with him, and join it to Judah's stick, making them a single stick
of wood, and they will become one in
my hand.'[l] [20]Hold before their eyes the
sticks you have written on [21]and say to
them, 'This is what the Sovereign LORD
says: I will take the Israelites out of the
nations where they have gone. I will
gather them from all around and bring
them back into their own land.[m] [22]I will
make them one nation in the land, on
the mountains of Israel. There will be
one king over all of them and they will
never again be two nations or be divided into two kingdoms.[n] [23]They will no
longer defile[o] themselves with their idols
and vile images or with any of their offenses, for I will save them from all their
sinful backsliding,[k] and I will cleanse
them. They will be my people, and I
will be their God.[p]
[24]"'My servant David[q] will be king
over them, and they will all have one
shepherd.[r] They will follow my laws and
be careful to keep my decrees.[s] [25]They
will live in the land I gave to my servant
Jacob, the land where your fathers
lived.[t] They and their children and their
children's children will live there forever,[u] and David my servant will be their
prince forever.[v] [26]I will make a covenant
of peace[w] with them; it will be an everlasting covenant. I will establish them
and increase their numbers,[x] and I will
put my sanctuary among them forever.[y]
[27]My dwelling place[z] will be with them;
I will be their God, and they will be my
people.[a] [28]Then the nations will know
that I the LORD make Israel holy,[b] when
my sanctuary is among them forever.'"

Judgment against Gog.

38 The word of the LORD came to
me: [2]"Son of man, set your face
against Gog, of the land of Magog,[c] the

k*23* Many Hebrew manuscripts (see also Septuagint); most Hebrew manuscripts *all their dwelling places where they sinned*

chief prince of[l] Meshech and Tubal;[a]
prophesy against him 3and say: 'This is
what the Sovereign LORD says: I am
against you, O Gog, chief prince of[m]
Meshech and Tubal.[b] 4I will turn you
around, put hooks[c] in your jaws and
bring you out with your whole army—
your horses, your horsemen fully armed,
and a great horde with large and small
shields, all of them brandishing their
swords.[d] 5Persia, Cush[n][e] and Put[f] will
be with them, all with shields and helmets, 6also Gomer[g] with all its troops,
and Beth Togarmah[h] from the far north
with all its troops—the many nations
with you.
7" 'Get ready; be prepared,[i] you and
all the hordes gathered about you, and
take command of them. 8After many
days[j] you will be called to arms. In future years you will invade a land that
has recovered from war, whose people
were gathered from many nations[k] to the
mountains of Israel, which had long
been desolate. They had been brought
out from the nations, and now all of
them live in safety.[l] 9You and all your
troops and the many nations with you
will go up, advancing like a storm;[m] you
will be like a cloud[n] covering the land.
10" 'This is what the Sovereign LORD
says: On that day thoughts will come
into your mind and you will devise an
evil scheme.[o] 11You will say, "I will invade a land of unwalled villages; I will
attack a peaceful and unsuspecting people—all of them living without walls and
without gates and bars.[p] 12I will plunder
and loot and turn my hand against the
resettled ruins and the people gathered
from the nations, rich in livestock and
goods, living at the center of the land."
13Sheba[q] and Dedan and the merchants
of Tarshish and all her villages[o] will say
to you, "Have you come to plunder?
Have you gathered your hordes to loot,
to carry off silver and gold, to take away
livestock and goods and to seize much
plunder?[r]" '
14"Therefore, son of man, prophesy
and say to Gog: 'This is what the Sovereign LORD says: In that day, when my
people Israel are living in safety,[s] will
you not take notice of it? 15You will
come from your place in the far north,
you and many nations with you, all of
them riding on horses, a great horde, a
mighty army.[t] 16You will advance against
my people Israel like a cloud[u] that covers the land. In days to come, O Gog, I
will bring you against my land, so that
the nations may know me when I show
myself holy through you before their
eyes.[v]
17" 'This is what the Sovereign LORD
says: Are you not the one I spoke of in
former days by my servants the prophets
of Israel? At that time they prophesied
for years that I would bring you against
them. 18This is what will happen in that
day: When Gog attacks the land of Israel,
my hot anger will be aroused, declares
the Sovereign LORD. 19In my zeal and
fiery wrath I declare that at that time
there shall be a great earthquake in the
land of Israel.[w] 20The fish of the sea, the
birds of the air, the beasts of the field,
every creature that moves along the
ground, and all the people on the face of
the earth will tremble at my presence.
The mountains will be overturned, the
cliffs will crumble and every wall will
fall to the ground.[x] 21I will summon a
sword[y] against Gog on all my mountains,
declares the Sovereign LORD. Every
man's sword will be against his brother.[z] 22I will execute judgment[a] upon him
with plague and bloodshed; I will pour
down torrents of rain, hailstones[b] and
burning sulfur on him and on his troops
and on the many nations with him.
23And so I will show my greatness and
my holiness, and I will make myself
known in the sight of many nations.
Then they will know that I am the
LORD.[c]'

Seven months to bury Gog's dead.

39 "Son of man, prophesy against
Gog and say: 'This is what the
Sovereign LORD says: I am against you,

38:2 [a]Rev 20:8
38:3 [b]Eze 39:1
38:4 [c]2Ki 19:28 [d]Eze 29:4; Da 11:40
38:5 [e]Ge 10:6 [f]Eze 27:10
38:6 [g]Ge 10:2 [h]Eze 27:14
38:7 [i]Isa 8:9
38:8 [j]Isa 24:22 [k]Isa 11:11 [l]Jer 23:6
38:9 [m]Isa 28:2 [n]Jer 4:13; Joel 2:2
38:10 [o]Ps 36:4; Mic 2:1
38:11 [p]Jer 49:31; Zec 2:4
38:13 [q]Eze 27:22 [r]Isa 10:6; Jer 15:13
38:14 [s]ver 8; Zec 2:5
38:15 [t]Eze 39:2
38:16 [u]ver 9 [v]Isa 29:23; Eze 39:21
38:19 [w]Ps 18:7; Eze 5:13; Hag 2:6,21
38:20 [x]Hos 4:3; Na 1:5
38:21 [y]Eze 14:17 [z]1Sa 14:20; 2Ch 20:23; Hag 2:22
38:22 [a]Isa 66:16; Jer 25:31 [b]Ps 18:12; Rev 16:21
38:23 [c]Eze 36:23

[l]2 Or *the prince of Rosh,* [m]3 Or *Gog, prince of Rosh,* [n]5 That is, the upper Nile region [o]13 Or *her strong lions*

O Gog, chief prince of[p] Meshech and Tubal.[a] [2]I will turn you around and drag you along. I will bring you from the far north and send you against the mountains of Israel. [3]Then I will strike your bow[b] from your left hand and make your arrows[c] drop from your right hand. [4]On the mountains of Israel you will fall, you and all your troops and the nations with you. I will give you as food to all kinds of carrion birds and to the wild animals.[d] [5]You will fall in the open field, for I have spoken, declares the Sovereign LORD. [6]I will send fire[e] on Magog and on those who live in safety in the coastlands,[f] and they will know that I am the LORD.

[7]" 'I will make known my holy name among my people Israel. I will no longer let my holy name be profaned,[g] and the nations will know that I the LORD am the Holy One in Israel.[h] [8]It is coming! It will surely take place, declares the Sovereign LORD. This is the day I have spoken of.

[9]" 'Then those who live in the towns of Israel will go out and use the weapons for fuel and burn them up—the small and large shields, the bows and arrows, the war clubs and spears. For seven years they will use them for fuel.[i] [10]They will not need to gather wood from the fields or cut it from the forests, because they will use the weapons for fuel. And they will plunder those who plundered them and loot those who looted them, declares the Sovereign LORD.[j]

[11]" 'On that day I will give Gog a burial place in Israel, in the valley of those who travel east toward[q] the Sea.[r] It will block the way of travelers, because Gog and all his hordes will be buried there. So it will be called the Valley of Hamon Gog.[s][k]

[12]" 'For seven months the house of Israel will be burying them in order to cleanse the land.[l] [13]All the people of the land will bury them, and the day I am glorified[m] will be a memorable day for them, declares the Sovereign LORD.

[14]" 'Men will be regularly employed to cleanse the land. Some will go throughout the land and, in addition to them, others will bury those that remain on the ground. At the end of the seven months they will begin their search. [15]As they go through the land and one of them sees a human bone, he will set up a marker beside it until the gravediggers have buried it in the Valley of Hamon Gog. [16](Also a town called Hamonah[t] will be there.) And so they will cleanse the land.'

A sacrifice for the birds and animals.

[17]"Son of man, this is what the Sovereign LORD says: Call out to every kind of bird[n] and all the wild animals: 'Assemble and come together from all around to the sacrifice I am preparing for you, the great sacrifice on the mountains of Israel. There you will eat flesh and drink blood. [18]You will eat the flesh of mighty men and drink the blood of the princes of the earth as if they were rams and lambs, goats and bulls—all of them fattened animals from Bashan.[o] [19]At the sacrifice I am preparing for you, you will eat fat till you are glutted and drink blood till you are drunk. [20]At my table you will eat your fill of horses and riders, mighty men and soldiers of every kind,' declares the Sovereign LORD.[p]

[21]"I will display my glory among the nations, and all the nations will see the punishment I inflict and the hand I lay upon them.[q] [22]From that day forward the house of Israel will know that I am the LORD their God. [23]And the nations will know that the people of Israel went into exile for their sin, because they were unfaithful to me. So I hid my face from them and handed them over to their enemies, and they all fell by the sword.[r] [24]I dealt with them according to their uncleanness and their offenses, and I hid my face from them.[s]

[25]"Therefore this is what the Sovereign LORD says: I will now bring Jacob back from captivity[u][t] and will have compassion[u] on all the people of Israel, and

39:1 [a]Eze 38:2,3
39:3 [b]Hos 1:5 [c]Ps 76:3
39:4 [d]ver 17-20; Eze 29:5; 33:27
39:6 [e]Eze 30:8; Am 1:4 [f]Jer 25:22
39:7 [g]Ex 20:7 [h]Isa 12:6; Eze 36:16,23
39:9 [i]Ps 46:9
39:10 [j]Isa 14:2; 33:1; Hab 2:8
39:11 [k]Eze 38:2
39:12 [l]Dt 21:23
39:13 [m]Eze 28:22
39:17 [n]Rev 19:17
39:18 [o]Ps 22:12; Jer 51:40
39:20 [p]Rev 19:17-18
39:21 [q]Ex 9:16; Isa 37:20; Eze 38:16
39:23 [r]Isa 1:15; 59:2; Jer 22:8-9; 44:23
39:24 [s]Jer 2:17,19; 4:18; Eze 36:19
39:25 [t]Jer 33:7; Eze 34:13 [u]Jer 30:18

[p] *1* Or *Gog, prince of Rosh,* [q] *11* Or *of* [r] *11* That is, the Dead Sea [s] *11* *Hamon Gog* means *hordes of Gog.* [t] *16* *Hamonah* means *horde.* [u] *25* Or *now restore the fortunes of Jacob*

I will be zealous for my holy name.[a] 26 They will forget their shame and all the unfaithfulness they showed toward me when they lived in safety[b] in their land with no one to make them afraid.[c] 27 When I have brought them back from the nations and have gathered them from the countries of their enemies, I will show myself holy through them in the sight of many nations.[d] 28 Then they will know that I am the LORD their God, for though I sent them into exile among the nations, I will gather them to their own land, not leaving any behind. 29 I will no longer hide my face from them, for I will pour out my Spirit[e] on the house of Israel, declares the Sovereign LORD."

Visions of the temple and its measurements.

40 In the twenty-fifth year of our exile, at the beginning of the year, on the tenth of the month, in the fourteenth year after the fall of the city[f]—on that very day the hand of the LORD was upon me[g] and he took me there. 2 In visions[h] of God he took me to the land of Israel and set me on a very high mountain,[i] on whose south side were some buildings that looked like a city. 3 He took me there, and I saw a man whose appearance was like bronze;[j] he was standing in the gateway with a linen cord and a measuring rod[k] in his hand. 4 The man said to me, "Son of man, look with your eyes and hear with your ears and pay attention to everything I am going to show you, for that is why you have been brought here. Tell[l] the house of Israel everything you see.[m]"

5 I saw a wall completely surrounding the temple area. The length of the measuring rod in the man's hand was six long cubits, each of which was a cubit[v] and a handbreadth.[w] He measured[n] the wall; it was one measuring rod thick and one rod high.

6 Then he went to the gate facing east.[o] He climbed its steps and measured the threshold of the gate; it was one rod deep.[x] 7 The alcoves[p] for the guards were one rod long and one rod wide, and the projecting walls between the alcoves were five cubits thick. And the threshold of the gate next to the portico facing the temple was one rod deep.

8 Then he measured the portico of the gateway; 9 it[y] was eight cubits deep and its jambs were two cubits thick. The portico of the gateway faced the temple.

10 Inside the east gate were three alcoves on each side; the three had the same measurements, and the faces of the projecting walls on each side had the same measurements. 11 Then he measured the width of the entrance to the gateway; it was ten cubits and its length was thirteen cubits. 12 In front of each alcove was a wall one cubit high, and the alcoves were six cubits square. 13 Then he measured the gateway from the top of the rear wall of one alcove to the top of the opposite one; the distance was twenty-five cubits from one parapet opening to the opposite one. 14 He measured along the faces of the projecting walls all around the inside of the gateway—sixty cubits. The measurement was up to the portico[z] facing the courtyard.[a][q] 15 The distance from the entrance of the gateway to the far end of its portico was fifty cubits. 16 The alcoves and the projecting walls inside the gateway were surmounted by narrow parapet openings all around, as was the portico; the openings all around faced inward. The faces of the projecting walls were decorated with palm trees.[r]

17 Then he brought me into the outer court.[s] There I saw some rooms and a pavement that had been constructed all around the court; there were thirty rooms[t] along the pavement.[u] 18 It abutted

39:25 [a]Isa 27:12-13
39:26 [b]1Ki 4:25 [c]Isa 17:2; Eze 34:28; Mic 4:4
39:27 [d]Eze 36:23-24; 37:21; 38:16
39:29 [e]Joel 2:28; Ac 2:17
40:1 [f]2Ki 25:7; Jer 39:1-10; 52:4-11; Eze 33:21 [g]Eze 1:3
40:2 [h]Da 7:1,7 [i]Eze 17:22; Rev 21:10
40:3 [j]Eze 1:7; Da 10:6; Rev 1:15 [k]Eze 47:3; Zec 2:1-2; Rev 11:1; 21:15
40:4 [l]Jer 26:2 [m]Eze 44:5
40:5 [n]Eze 42:20
40:6 [o]Eze 8:16
40:7 [p]ver 36
40:14 [q]Ex 27:9
40:16 [r]ver 21-22; 2Ch 3:5; Eze 41:26
40:17 [s]Rev 11:2 [t]Eze 41:6 [u]Eze 42:1

v *5* The common cubit was about 1 1/2 feet (about 0.5 meter). w *5* That is, about 3 inches (about 8 centimeters) x *6* Septuagint; Hebrew *deep, the first threshold, one rod deep* y *8,9* Many Hebrew manuscripts, Septuagint, Vulgate and Syriac; most Hebrew manuscripts *gateway facing the temple; it was one rod deep. 9Then he measured the portico of the gateway; it* z *14* Septuagint; Hebrew *projecting wall* a *14* The meaning of the Hebrew for this verse is uncertain.

the sides of the gateways and was as
wide as they were long; this was the
lower pavement. 19Then he measured
the distance from the inside of the lower gateway to the outside of the inner
court;[a] it was a hundred cubits[b] on the
east side as well as on the north.
20Then he measured the length and
width of the gate facing north, leading
into the outer court. 21Its alcoves[c]—
three on each side—its projecting walls
and its portico had the same measurements as those of the first gateway. It
was fifty cubits long and twenty-five
cubits wide. 22Its openings, its portico[d]
and its palm tree decorations had the
same measurements as those of the gate
facing east. Seven steps led up to it, with
its portico opposite them. 23There was a
gate to the inner court facing the north
gate, just as there was on the east. He
measured from one gate to the opposite
one; it was a hundred cubits.[e]
24Then he led me to the south side
and I saw a gate facing south. He measured its jambs and its portico, and they
had the same measurements as the others. 25The gateway and its portico had
narrow openings all around, like the
openings of the others. It was fifty cubits
long and twenty-five cubits wide.[f] 26Sev-
en steps led up to it, with its portico
opposite them; it had palm tree decorations on the faces of the projecting walls
on each side.[g] 27The inner court[h] also
had a gate facing south, and he measured from this gate to the outer gate on
the south side; it was a hundred cubits.
28Then he brought me into the inner
court through the south gate, and he
measured the south gate; it had the
same measurements[i] as the others. 29Its
alcoves, its projecting walls and its portico had the same measurements as the
others. The gateway and its portico had
openings all around. It was fifty cubits
long and twenty-five cubits wide. 30(The
porticoes[j] of the gateways around the
inner court were twenty-five cubits wide
and five cubits deep.) 31Its portico[k] faced
the outer court; palm trees decorated its
jambs, and eight steps led up to it.

40:19 [a]Eze 46:1 [b]ver 23,27
40:21 [c]ver 7
40:22 [d]ver 49
40:23 [e]ver 19
40:25 [f]ver 33
40:26 [g]ver 22
40:27 [h]ver 32
40:28 [i]ver 35
40:30 [j]ver 21
40:31 [k]ver 22
40:34 [l]ver 22
40:35 [m]Eze 44:4; 47:2
40:36 [n]ver 7
40:38 [o]2Ch 4:6; Eze 42:13
40:39 [p]Eze 46:2 [q]Lev 4:3,28 [r]Lev 7:1
40:42 [s]Ex 20:25 [t]ver 39

32Then he brought me to the inner
court on the east side, and he measured
the gateway; it had the same measurements as the others. 33Its alcoves, its
projecting walls and its portico had the
same measurements as the others. The
gateway and its portico had openings
all around. It was fifty cubits long and
twenty-five cubits wide. 34Its portico[l]
faced the outer court; palm trees decorated the jambs on either side, and eight
steps led up to it.
35Then he brought me to the north
gate[m] and measured it. It had the same
measurements as the others, 36as did
its alcoves,[n] its projecting walls and its
portico, and it had openings all around.
It was fifty cubits long and twenty-five
cubits wide. 37Its portico[b] faced the outer court; palm trees decorated the jambs
on either side, and eight steps led up
to it.
38A room with a doorway was by the
portico in each of the inner gateways,
where the burnt offerings[o] were washed.
39In the portico of the gateway were
two tables on each side, on which the
burnt offerings,[p] sin offerings[q] and guilt
offerings[r] were slaughtered. 40By the
outside wall of the portico of the gateway, near the steps at the entrance to
the north gateway were two tables, and
on the other side of the steps were two
tables. 41So there were four tables on
one side of the gateway and four on the
other—eight tables in all—on which the
sacrifices were slaughtered. 42There
were also four tables of dressed stone[s]
for the burnt offerings, each a cubit and
a half long, a cubit and a half wide and
a cubit high. On them were placed the
utensils for slaughtering the burnt offerings and the other sacrifices.[t] 43And
double-pronged hooks, each a handbreadth long, were attached to the wall
all around. The tables were for the flesh
of the offerings.
44Outside the inner gate, within the
inner court, were two rooms, one[c] at the

[b]*37* Septuagint (see also verses 31 and 34); Hebrew *jambs* [c]*44* Septuagint; Hebrew *were rooms for singers, which were*

side of the north gate and facing south,
and another at the side of the south[d]
gate and facing north. 45He said to me,
"The room facing south is for the priests
who have charge of the temple,[a] 46and
the room facing north[b] is for the priests
who have charge of the altar.[c] These are
the sons of Zadok,[d] who are the only
Levites who may draw near to the LORD
to minister before him.[e]"
47Then he measured the court: It was
square—a hundred cubits long and a
hundred cubits wide. And the altar was
in front of the temple.
48He brought me to the portico of the
temple[f] and measured the jambs of the
portico; they were five cubits wide on
either side. The width of the entrance
was fourteen cubits and its projecting
walls were[e] three cubits wide on either
side. 49The portico[g] was twenty cubits
wide, and twelve[f] cubits from front to
back. It was reached by a flight of stairs,[g]
and there were pillars[h] on each side of
the jambs.

41 Then the man brought me to the
outer sanctuary[i] and measured
the jambs; the width of the jambs was
six cubits[h] on each side.[i] 2The entrance
was ten cubits wide, and the projecting
walls on each side of it were five cubits
wide. He also measured the outer sanctuary; it was forty cubits long and twenty
cubits wide.[j]
3Then he went into the inner sanctuary and measured the jambs of the entrance; each was two cubits wide. The
entrance was six cubits wide, and the
projecting walls on each side of it were
seven cubits wide. 4And he measured
the length of the inner sanctuary; it was
twenty cubits, and its width was twenty
cubits across the end of the outer sanctuary.[k] He said to me, "This is the Most
Holy Place.[l]"
5Then he measured the wall of the
temple; it was six cubits thick, and each
side room around the temple was four
cubits wide. 6The side rooms were on
three levels, one above another, thirty
on each level. There were ledges all
around the wall of the temple to serve
as supports for the side rooms, so that
the supports were not inserted into the
wall of the temple.[n] 7The side rooms all
around the temple were wider at each
successive level. The structure surrounding the temple was built in ascending
stages, so that the rooms widened as
one went upward. A stairway[o] went up
from the lowest floor to the top floor
through the middle floor.
8I saw that the temple had a raised
base all around it, forming the foundation of the side rooms. It was the length
of the rod, six long cubits. 9The outer
wall of the side rooms was five cubits
thick. The open area between the side
rooms of the temple 10and the ⌊priests'⌋
rooms was twenty cubits wide all around
the temple. 11There were entrances to
the side rooms from the open area, one
on the north and another on the south;
and the base adjoining the open area
was five cubits wide all around.
12The building facing the temple
courtyard on the west side was seventy
cubits wide. The wall of the building
was five cubits thick all around, and its
length was ninety cubits.
13Then he measured the temple; it
was a hundred cubits long, and the temple courtyard and the building with its
walls were also a hundred cubits long.
14The width of the temple courtyard on
the east, including the front of the temple, was a hundred cubits.[p]
15Then he measured the length of the
building facing the courtyard at the rear
of the temple, including its galleries[q] on
each side; it was a hundred cubits.
The outer sanctuary, the inner sanctuary and the portico facing the court,
16as well as the thresholds and the narrow windows[r] and galleries around the
three of them—everything beyond and
including the threshold was covered
with wood. The floor, the wall up to the

40:45 [a] 1Ch 9:23
40:46 [b] Eze 42:13 [c] Nu 18:5 [d] 1Ki 2:35 [e] Nu 16:5; Eze 43:19; 44:15; 45:4; 48:11
40:48 [f] 1Ki 6:2
40:49 [g] ver 22; 1Ki 6:3 [h] 1Ki 7:15
41:1 [i] ver 23
41:2 [j] 2Ch 3:3
41:4 [k] 1Ki 6:20 [l] Ex 26:33; Heb 9:3-8
41:6 [m] Eze 40:17 [n] 1Ki 6:5
41:7 [o] 1Ki 6:8
41:14 [p] Eze 40:47
41:15 [q] Eze 42:3
41:16 [r] 1Ki 6:4

d *44* Septuagint; Hebrew *east* e *48* Septuagint; Hebrew *entrance was* f *49* Septuagint; Hebrew *eleven* g *49* Hebrew; Septuagint *Ten steps led up to it* h *1* The common cubit was about 1 1/2 feet (about 0.5 meter). i *1* One Hebrew manuscript and Septuagint; most Hebrew manuscripts *side, the width of the tent*

windows, and the windows were covered.[a] 17In the space above the outside
of the entrance to the inner sanctuary
and on the walls at regular intervals all
around the inner and outer sanctuary
18were carved[b] cherubim[c] and palm
trees.[d] Palm trees alternated with cherubim. Each cherub had two faces:[e] 19the
face of a man toward the palm tree on
one side and the face of a lion toward
the palm tree on the other. They were
carved all around the whole temple.[f]
20From the floor to the area above the
entrance, cherubim and palm trees were
carved on the wall of the outer sanctuary.

21The outer sanctuary[g] had a rectangular doorframe, and the one at the
front of the Most Holy Place was similar.
22There was a wooden altar[h] three cubits
high and two cubits square[j]; its corners,
its base[k] and its sides were of wood.
The man said to me, "This is the table[i]
that is before the LORD." 23Both the outer sanctuary[j] and the Most Holy Place
had double doors.[k] 24Each door had two
leaves—two hinged leaves[l] for each
door. 25And on the doors of the outer
sanctuary were carved cherubim and
palm trees like those carved on the
walls, and there was a wooden over-
hang on the front of the portico. 26On
the sidewalls of the portico were narrow windows with palm trees carved on
each side. The side rooms of the temple
also had overhangs.[m]

42 Then the man led me northward into the outer court and
brought me to the rooms[n] opposite the
temple courtyard[o] and opposite the outer wall on the north side.[p] 2The building
whose door faced north was a hundred
cubits[l] long and fifty cubits wide. 3Both
in the section twenty cubits from the
inner court and in the section opposite
the pavement of the outer court, gallery[q] faced gallery at the three levels.[r]
4In front of the rooms was an inner
passageway ten cubits wide and a hundred cubits[m] long. Their doors were on
the north.[s] 5Now the upper rooms were
narrower, for the galleries took more
space from them than from the rooms on
the lower and middle floors of the building. 6The rooms on the third floor had
no pillars, as the courts had; so they
were smaller in floor space than those
on the lower and middle floors. 7There
was an outer wall parallel to the rooms
and the outer court; it extended in front
of the rooms for fifty cubits. 8While the
row of rooms on the side next to the
outer court was fifty cubits long, the row
on the side nearest the sanctuary was a
hundred cubits long. 9The lower rooms
had an entrance[t] on the east side as one
enters them from the outer court.

10On the south side[n] along the length
of the wall of the outer court, adjoining
the temple courtyard and opposite the
outer wall, were rooms[u] 11with a passageway in front of them. These were
like the rooms on the north; they had
the same length and width, with similar
exits and dimensions. Similar to the
doorways on the north 12were the doorways of the rooms on the south. There
was a doorway at the beginning of the
passageway that was parallel to the corresponding wall extending eastward, by
which one enters the rooms.

13Then he said to me, "The north[v]
and south rooms facing the temple
courtyard are the priests' rooms, where
the priests who approach the LORD will
eat the most holy offerings. There they
will put the most holy offerings—the
grain offerings, the sin offerings[w] and the
guilt offerings[x]—for the place is holy.[y]
14Once the priests enter the holy precincts, they are not to go into the outer
court until they leave behind the garments[z] in which they minister, for these
are holy. They are to put on other clothes
before they go near the places that are
for the people.[a]"

15When he had finished measuring
what was inside the temple area, he led
me out by the east gate[b] and measured

41:16 [a]ver 25-26; 1Ki 6:15; Eze 42:3
41:18 [b]1Ki 6:18 [c]Ex 37:7; 2Ch 3:7 [d]1Ki 6:29; 7:36 [e]Eze 10:21
41:19 [f]Eze 10:14
41:21 [g]ver 1
41:22 [h]Ex 30:1 [i]Ex 25:23; Eze 23:41; 44:16; Mal 1:7,12
41:23 [j]ver 1 [k]1Ki 6:32
41:24 [l]1Ki 6:34
41:26 [m]ver 15-16; Eze 40:16
42:1 [n]ver 13 [o]Eze 41:12-14 [p]Eze 40:17
42:3 [q]Eze 41:15 [r]Eze 41:16
42:4 [s]Eze 46:19
42:9 [t]Eze 44:5; 46:19
42:10 [u]ver 1
42:13 [v]Eze 40:46 [w]Lev 10:17; 6:25 [x]Lev 14:13 [y]Ex 29:31; Lev 6:29; 7:6; 10:12-13; Nu 18:9-10
42:14 [z]Eze 44:19 [a]Ex 29:9; Lev 8:7-9
42:15 [b]Eze 43:1

j*22* Septuagint; Hebrew *long* k*22* Septuagint; Hebrew *length* l*2* The common cubit was about 1 1/2 feet (about 0.5 meter). m*4* Septuagint and Syriac; Hebrew *and one cubit* n*10* Septuagint; Hebrew *Eastward*

the area all around: 16He measured the east side with the measuring rod; it was five hundred cubits.[o] 17He measured the north side; it was five hundred cubits[p] by the measuring rod. 18He measured the south side; it was five hundred cubits by the measuring rod. 19Then he turned to the west side and measured; it was five hundred cubits by the measuring rod. 20So he measured[a] the area on all four sides. It had a wall around it,[b] five hundred cubits long and five hundred cubits wide,[c] to separate the holy from the common.[d]

The glory of the LORD fills the temple.

43 Then the man brought me to the gate facing east,[e] 2and I saw the glory of the God of Israel coming from the east. His voice was like the roar of rushing waters,[f] and the land was radiant with his glory.[g] 3The vision I saw was like the vision I had seen when he[q] came to destroy the city and like the visions I had seen by the Kebar River, and I fell facedown. 4The glory[h] of the LORD entered the temple through the gate facing east.[i] 5Then the Spirit[j] lifted me up[k] and brought me into the inner court, and the glory of the LORD filled the temple.

6While the man was standing beside me, I heard someone speaking to me from inside the temple. 7He said: "Son of man, this is the place of my throne and the place for the soles of my feet. This is where I will live among the Israelites forever. The house of Israel will never again defile my holy name—neither they nor their kings—by their prostitution[r] and the lifeless idols[s] of their kings at their high places.[l] 8When they placed their threshold next to my threshold and their doorposts beside my doorposts, with only a wall between me and them, they defiled my holy name by their detestable practices. So I destroyed them in my anger. 9Now let them put away from me their prostitution and the lifeless idols of their kings, and I will live among them forever.[m]

10"Son of man, describe the temple to the people of Israel, that they may be ashamed[n] of their sins. Let them consider the plan, 11and if they are ashamed of all they have done, make known to them the design of the temple—its arrangement, its exits and entrances—its whole design and all its regulations[t] and laws. Write these down before them so that they may be faithful to its design and follow all its regulations.[o]

12"This is the law of the temple: All the surrounding area[p] on top of the mountain will be most holy. Such is the law of the temple.

Measurements of the altar.

13"These are the measurements of the altar[q] in long cubits, that cubit being a cubit[u] and a handbreadth[v]: Its gutter is a cubit deep and a cubit wide, with a rim of one span[w] around the edge. And this is the height of the altar: 14From the gutter on the ground up to the lower ledge it is two cubits high and a cubit wide, and from the smaller ledge up to the larger ledge it is four cubits high and a cubit wide. 15The altar hearth is four cubits high, and four horns[r] project upward from the hearth. 16The altar hearth is square, twelve cubits long and twelve cubits wide. 17The upper ledge also is square, fourteen cubits long and fourteen cubits wide, with a rim of half a cubit and a gutter of a cubit all around. The steps[s] of the altar face east."

Regulations: Offerings.

18Then he said to me, "Son of man, this is what the Sovereign LORD says: These will be the regulations for sacrificing burnt offerings[t] and sprinkling blood[u]

42:20 [a]Eze 40:5 [b]Zec 2:5 [c]Eze 45:2; Rev 21:16 [d]Eze 22:26
43:1 [e]Eze 10:19; 42:15; 44:1; 46:1
43:2 [f]Rev 1:15 [g]Isa 6:3; Eze 11:23; Rev 18:1
43:4 [h]Eze 1:28 [i]Eze 10:19
43:5 [j]Eze 11:24 [k]Eze 3:12; 8:3
43:7 [l]Lev 26:30
43:9 [m]Eze 37:26-28
43:10 [n]Eze 16:61
43:11 [o]Eze 44:5
43:12 [p]Eze 40:2
43:13 [q]2Ch 4:1
43:15 [r]Ex 27:2
43:17 [s]Ex 20:26
43:18 [t]Ex 40:29 [u]Lev 1:5,11; Heb 9:21-22

[o]*16* See Septuagint of verse 17; Hebrew *rods*; also in verses 18 and 19. [p]*17* Septuagint; Hebrew *rods* [q]*3* Some Hebrew manuscripts and Vulgate; most Hebrew manuscripts *I* [r]*7* Or *their spiritual adultery*; also in verse 9 [s]*7* Or *the corpses*; also in verse 9 [t]*11* Some Hebrew manuscripts and Septuagint; most Hebrew manuscripts *regulations and its whole design* [u]*13* The common cubit was about 1 1/2 feet (about 0.5 meter). [v]*13* That is, about 3 inches (about 8 centimeters) [w]*13* That is, about 9 inches (about 22 centimeters)

upon the altar when it is built: 19 You are to give a young bull[a] as a sin offering to the priests, who are Levites, of the family of Zadok,[b] who come near[c] to minister before me, declares the Sovereign LORD. 20 You are to take some of its blood and put it on the four horns of the altar and on the four corners of the upper ledge[d] and all around the rim, and so purify the altar[e] and make atonement for it. 21 You are to take the bull for the sin offering and burn it in the designated part of the temple area outside the sanctuary.[f]

22 "On the second day you are to offer a male goat without defect for a sin offering, and the altar is to be purified as it was purified with the bull. 23 When you have finished purifying it, you are to offer a young bull and a ram from the flock, both without defect.[g] 24 You are to offer them before the LORD, and the priests are to sprinkle salt[h] on them and sacrifice them as a burnt offering to the LORD.

25 "For seven days[i] you are to provide a male goat daily for a sin offering; you are also to provide a young bull and a ram from the flock, both without defect.[j] 26 For seven days they are to make atonement for the altar and cleanse it; thus they will dedicate it. 27 At the end of these days, from the eighth day[k] on, the priests are to present your burnt offerings and fellowship offerings[x][l] on the altar. Then I will accept you, declares the Sovereign LORD."

Regulations: Ministry and service.

44 Then the man brought me back to the outer gate of the sanctuary, the one facing east,[m] and it was shut. 2 The LORD said to me, "This gate is to remain shut. It must not be opened; no one may enter through it.[n] It is to remain shut because the LORD, the God of Israel, has entered through it. 3 The prince himself is the only one who may sit inside the gateway to eat in the presence[o] of the LORD. He is to enter by way of the portico of the gateway and go out the same way.[p]"

43:19 [a]Lev 4:3; Eze 45:18-19 [b]Eze 44:15 [c]Nu 16:40; Eze 40:46
43:20 [d]ver 17 [e]Lev 16:19
43:21 [f]Ex 29:14; Heb 13:11
43:23 [g]Ex 29:1
43:24 [h]Lev 2:13; Mk 9:49-50
43:25 [i]Lev 8:33 [j]Ex 29:37
43:27 [k]Lev 9:1 [l]Lev 17:5
44:1 [m]Eze 43:1
44:2 [n]Eze 43:4-5
44:3 [o]Ex 24:9-11 [p]Eze 46:2,8
44:4 [q]Isa 6:4; Rev 15:8 [r]Eze 1:28; 3:23
44:5 [s]Eze 40:4; 43:10-11
44:6 [t]Eze 3:9
44:7 [u]Lev 26:41 [v]Ge 17:14; Ex 12:48; Lev 22:25
44:8 [w]Lev 22:2; Nu 18:7
44:9 [x]Joel 3:17; Zec 14:21
44:10 [y]2Ki 23:8 [z]Nu 18:23
44:11 [a]2Ch 29:34 [b]Nu 3:5-37; 16:9; 1Ch 26:12-19
44:12 [c]Ps 106:26 [d]2Ki 16:10-16
44:13 [e]Eze 16:61 [f]Nu 18:3
44:14 [g]Nu 18:4; 1Ch 23:28-32

4 Then the man brought me by way of the north gate to the front of the temple. I looked and saw the glory of the LORD filling the temple[q] of the LORD, and I fell facedown.[r]

5 The LORD said to me, "Son of man, look carefully, listen closely and give attention to everything I tell you concerning all the regulations regarding the temple of the LORD. Give attention to the entrance of the temple and all the exits of the sanctuary.[s] 6 Say to the rebellious house[t] of Israel, 'This is what the Sovereign LORD says: Enough of your detestable practices, O house of Israel! 7 In addition to all your other detestable practices, you brought foreigners uncircumcised in heart[u] and flesh into my sanctuary, desecrating my temple while you offered me food, fat and blood, and you broke my covenant.[v] 8 Instead of carrying out your duty in regard to my holy things, you put others in charge of my sanctuary.[w] 9 This is what the Sovereign LORD says: No foreigner uncircumcised in heart and flesh is to enter my sanctuary, not even the foreigners who live among the Israelites.[x]

10 " 'The Levites who went far from me when Israel went astray[y] and who wandered from me after their idols must bear the consequences of their sin.[z] 11 They may serve in my sanctuary, having charge of the gates of the temple and serving in it; they may slaughter the burnt offerings[a] and sacrifices for the people and stand before the people and serve them.[b] 12 But because they served them in the presence of their idols and made the house of Israel fall into sin, therefore I have sworn with uplifted hand[c] that they must bear the consequences of their sin, declares the Sovereign LORD.[d] 13 They are not to come near to serve me as priests or come near any of my holy things or my most holy offerings; they must bear the shame[e] of their detestable practices.[f] 14 Yet I will put them in charge of the duties of the temple and all the work that is to be done in it.[g]

[x]27 Traditionally *peace offerings*

15"'But the priests, who are Levites
and descendants of Zadok and who faithfully carried out the duties of my sanctuary when the Israelites went astray from
me, are to come near to minister before
me; they are to stand before me to offer
sacrifices of fat and blood, declares the
Sovereign LORD.[a] 16They alone are to
enter my sanctuary; they alone are to
come near my table[b] to minister before
me and perform my service.[c]
17"'When they enter the gates of the
inner court, they are to wear linen
clothes;[d] they must not wear any woolen
garment while ministering at the gates
of the inner court or inside the temple.
18They are to wear linen turbans[e] on
their heads and linen undergarments[f]
around their waists. They must not wear
anything that makes them perspire.[g]
19When they go out into the outer court
where the people are, they are to take
off the clothes they have been ministering in and are to leave them in the
sacred rooms, and put on other clothes,
so that they do not consecrate[h] the people by means of their garments.[i]
20"'They must not shave their heads
or let their hair grow long, but they are
to keep the hair of their heads trimmed.[j]
21No priest is to drink wine when he
enters the inner court.[k] 22They must not
marry widows or divorced women; they
may marry only virgins of Israelite descent or widows of priests.[l] 23They are to
teach my people the difference between
the holy and the common[m] and show
them how to distinguish between the
unclean and the clean.[n]
24"'In any dispute, the priests are to
serve as judges[o] and decide it according
to my ordinances. They are to keep my
laws and my decrees for all my appointed feasts, and they are to keep my Sabbaths holy.[p]
25"'A priest must not defile himself
by going near a dead person; however, if
the dead person was his father or mother, son or daughter, brother or unmarried sister, then he may defile himself.[q]
26After he is cleansed, he must wait
seven days.[r] 27On the day he goes into
the inner court of the sanctuary to minister in the sanctuary, he is to offer a sin
offering for himself, declares the Sovereign LORD.
28"'I am to be the only inheritance[s]
the priests have. You are to give them
no possession in Israel; I will be their
possession. 29They will eat the grain offerings, the sin offerings and the guilt
offerings; and everything in Israel devoted[y] to the LORD[t] will belong to them.[u]
30The best of all the firstfruits[v] and of
all your special gifts will belong to the
priests. You are to give them the first
portion of your ground meal[w] so that a
blessing[x] may rest on your household.[y]
31The priests must not eat anything, bird
or animal, found dead or torn by wild
animals.[z]

Sacred portion of the land for the priests.

45 "'When you allot the land as an
inheritance,[a] you are to present
to the LORD a portion of the land as a
sacred district, 25,000 cubits long and
20,000[z] cubits wide; the entire area will
be holy.[b] 2Of this, a section 500 cubits
square[c] is to be for the sanctuary, with
50 cubits around it for open land. 3In
the sacred district, measure off a section
25,000 cubits[a] long and 10,000 cubits[b]
wide. In it will be the sanctuary, the
Most Holy Place. 4It will be the sacred
portion of the land for the priests,[d] who
minister in the sanctuary and who draw
near to minister before the LORD. It will
be a place for their houses as well as a
holy place for the sanctuary.[e] 5An area
25,000 cubits long and 10,000 cubits
wide will belong to the Levites, who
serve in the temple, as their possession for towns to live in.[c][f]
6"'You are to give the city as its property an area 5,000 cubits wide and

44:15 [a]Jer 33:18; Eze 40:46; Zec 3:7
44:16 [b]Eze 41:22 [c]Nu 18:5
44:17 [d]Ex 39:27-28; Rev 19:8
44:18 [e]Ex 28:39; Isa 3:20 [f]Ex 28:42 [g]Lev 16:4
44:19 [h]Lev 6:27; Eze 46:20 [i]Lev 6:10-11; Eze 42:14
44:20 [j]Lev 21:5; Nu 6:5
44:21 [k]Lev 10:9
44:22 [l]Lev 21:7
44:23 [m]Eze 22:26 [n]Mal 2:7
44:24 [o]Dt 17:8-9; 1Ch 23:4 [p]2Ch 19:8
44:25 [q]Lev 21:1-4
44:26 [r]Nu 19:14
44:28 [s]Nu 18:20; Dt 10:9; 18:1-2; Jos 13:33
44:29 [t]Lev 27:21 [u]Nu 18:9,14
44:30 [v]Nu 18:12-13 [w]Nu 15:18-21 [x]Mal 3:10 [y]Ne 10:35-37
44:31 [z]Ex 22:31; Lev 22:8
45:1 [a]Eze 47:21-22 [b]Eze 48:8-9,29
45:2 [c]Eze 42:20
45:4 [d]Eze 40:46 [e]Eze 48:10-11
45:5 [f]Eze 48:13

y*29* The Hebrew term refers to the irrevocable giving over of things or persons to the LORD. z*1* Septuagint (see also verses 3 and 5 and 48:9); Hebrew *10,000*
a*3* That is, about 7 miles (about 12 kilometers)
b*3* That is, about 3 miles (about 5 kilometers)
c*5* Septuagint; Hebrew *temple; they will have as their possession 20 rooms*

25,000 cubits long, adjoining the sacred
portion; it will belong to the whole
house of Israel.[a]
7"'The prince will have the land bordering each side of the area formed by
the sacred district and the property of the
city. It will extend westward from the
west side and eastward from the east
side, running lengthwise from the western to the eastern border parallel to one
of the tribal portions.[b] 8This land will be
his possession in Israel. And my princes
will no longer oppress my people but
will allow the house of Israel to possess
the land according to their tribes.[c]

Regulations: Duties of the prince.

9"'This is what the Sovereign LORD
says: You have gone far enough, O
princes of Israel! Give up your violence
and oppression and do what is just and
right.[d] Stop dispossessing my people,
declares the Sovereign LORD. 10You are to
use accurate scales,[e] an accurate ephah[d][f]
and an accurate bath.[e] 11The ephah[g]
and the bath are to be the same size, the
bath containing a tenth of a homer[f] and
the ephah a tenth of a homer; the homer
is to be the standard measure for both.
12The shekel[g] is to consist of twenty gerahs.[h] Twenty shekels plus twenty-five
shekels plus fifteen shekels equal one
mina.[h]
13"'This is the special gift you are to
offer: a sixth of an ephah from each
homer of wheat and a sixth of an ephah
from each homer of barley. 14The prescribed portion of oil, measured by the
bath, is a tenth of a bath from each cor
(which consists of ten baths or one
homer, for ten baths are equivalent to a
homer). 15Also one sheep is to be taken
from every flock of two hundred from
the well-watered pastures of Israel.
These will be used for the grain offerings, burnt offerings[i] and fellowship
offerings[i] to make atonement[j] for the
people, declares the Sovereign LORD.
16All the people of the land will participate in this special gift for the use of the
prince in Israel. 17It will be the duty of
the prince to provide the burnt offerings,
grain offerings and drink offerings at the
festivals, the New Moons and the Sabbaths[k]—at all the appointed feasts of the
house of Israel. He will provide the sin
offerings, grain offerings, burnt offerings and fellowship offerings to make
atonement for the house of Israel.[l]
18"'This is what the Sovereign LORD
says: In the first month[m] on the first
day you are to take a young bull without
defect[n] and purify the sanctuary.[o] 19The
priest is to take some of the blood of
the sin offering and put it on the doorposts of the temple, on the four corners
of the upper ledge[p] of the altar[q] and on
the gateposts of the inner court. 20You
are to do the same on the seventh day of
the month for anyone who sins unintentionally[r] or through ignorance; so you
are to make atonement for the temple.
21"'In the first month on the fourteenth day you are to observe the Passover,[s] a feast lasting seven days, during
which you shall eat bread made without yeast. 22On that day the prince is to
provide a bull as a sin offering for himself and for all the people of the land.[t]
23Every day during the seven days of the
Feast he is to provide seven bulls and
seven rams[u] without defect as a burnt
offering to the LORD, and a male goat for
a sin offering.[v] 24He is to provide as a
grain offering[w] an ephah for each bull
and an ephah for each ram, along with
a hin[j] of oil for each ephah.[x]
25"'During the seven days of the
Feast,[y] which begins in the seventh
month on the fifteenth day, he is to
make the same provision for sin offerings, burnt offerings, grain offerings and
oil.[z]

46

"'This is what the Sovereign
LORD says: The gate of the inner
court[a] facing east[b] is to be shut on the
six working days, but on the Sabbath

45:6 [a]Eze 48:15-18
45:7 [b]Eze 48:21
45:8 [c]Nu 26:53; Eze 46:18
45:9 [d]Jer 22:3; Zec 7:9-10; 8:16
45:10 [e]Dt 25:15; Pr 11:1; Am 8:4-6; Mic 6:10-11 [f]Lev 19:36
45:11 [g]Isa 5:10
45:12 [h]Ex 30:13; Lev 27:25; Nu 3:47
45:15 [i]Lev 1:4 [j]Lev 6:30
45:17 [k]Lev 23:38; Isa 66:23 [l]1Ki 8:62; 2Ch 31:3; Eze 46:4-12
45:18 [m]Ex 12:2 [n]Lev 22:20; Heb 9:14 [o]Lev 16:16,33
45:19 [p]Eze 43:17 [q]Lev 16:18-19; Eze 43:20
45:20 [r]Lev 4:27
45:21 [s]Ex 12:11; Lev 23:5-6
45:22 [t]Lev 4:14
45:23 [u]Job 42:8 [v]Nu 28:16-25
45:24 [w]Nu 28:12-13 [x]Eze 46:5-7
45:25 [y]Dt 16:13 [z]Lev 23:34-43; Nu 29:12-38
46:1 [a]Eze 40:19 [b]1Ch 9:18

d *10* An ephah was a dry measure. e *10* A bath was a liquid measure. f *11* A homer was a dry measure. g *12* A shekel weighed about 2/5 ounce (about 11.5 grams). h *12* That is, 60 shekels; the common mina was 50 shekels. i *15* Traditionally *peace offerings*; also in verse 17 j *24* That is, probably about 4 quarts (about 4 liters)

day and on the day of the New Moon[a] it
is to be opened. 2 The prince is to enter
from the outside through the portico[b] of
the gateway and stand by the gatepost.
The priests are to sacrifice his burnt
offering and his fellowship offerings.[k] He
is to worship at the threshold of the
gateway and then go out, but the gate
will not be shut until evening.[c] 3 On the
Sabbaths and New Moons the people of
the land are to worship in the presence
of the LORD at the entrance to that gateway.[d] 4 The burnt offering the prince
brings to the LORD on the Sabbath day
is to be six male lambs and a ram, all
without defect. 5 The grain offering giv-
en with the ram is to be an ephah,[l] and
the grain offering with the lambs is to
be as much as he pleases, along with a
hin[m] of oil for each ephah.[e] 6 On the day
of the New Moon[f] he is to offer a young
bull, six lambs and a ram, all without
defect. 7 He is to provide as a grain offering one ephah with the bull, one ephah
with the ram, and with the lambs as
much as he wants to give, along with a
hin of oil with each ephah.[g] 8 When the
prince enters, he is to go in through the
portico[h] of the gateway, and he is to
come out the same way.[i]
9 "'When the people of the land come
before the LORD at the appointed feasts,[j]
whoever enters by the north gate to
worship is to go out the south gate; and
whoever enters by the south gate is to
go out the north gate. No one is to return through the gate by which he
entered, but each is to go out the opposite gate. 10 The prince is to be among
them, going in when they go in and
going out when they go out.[k]
11 "'At the festivals and the appointed
feasts, the grain offering is to be an
ephah with a bull, an ephah with a ram,
and with the lambs as much as one
pleases, along with a hin of oil for each
ephah.[l] 12 When the prince provides[m] a
freewill offering[n] to the LORD—whether
a burnt offering or fellowship offerings—
the gate facing east is to be opened for
him. He shall offer his burnt offering or
his fellowship offerings as he does on
the Sabbath day. Then he shall go out,
and after he has gone out, the gate will
be shut.[o]
13 "'Every day you are to provide a
year-old lamb without defect for a burnt
offering to the LORD; morning by morning you shall provide it.[p] 14 You are also
to provide with it morning by morning
a grain offering, consisting of a sixth of
an ephah with a third of a hin of oil to
moisten the flour. The presenting of this
grain offering to the LORD is a lasting
ordinance.[q] 15 So the lamb and the grain
offering and the oil shall be provided
morning by morning for a regular[r] burnt
offering.[s]
16 "'This is what the Sovereign LORD
says: If the prince makes a gift from his
inheritance to one of his sons, it will
also belong to his descendants; it is to
be their property by inheritance.[t] 17 If,
however, he makes a gift from his inheritance to one of his servants, the servant
may keep it until the year of freedom;[u]
then it will revert to the prince. His inheritance belongs to his sons only; it is
theirs. 18 The prince must not take any
of the inheritance[v] of the people, driving
them off their property. He is to give his
sons their inheritance out of his own
property, so that none of my people
will be separated from his property.'"
19 Then the man brought me through
the entrance[w] at the side of the gate to
the sacred rooms facing north, which
belonged to the priests, and showed me
a place at the western end. 20 He said to
me, "This is the place where the priests
will cook the guilt offering and the sin
offering and bake the grain offering, to
avoid bringing them into the outer court
and consecrating[x] the people."[y]
21 He then brought me to the outer
court and led me around to its four corners, and I saw in each corner another
court. 22 In the four corners of the outer
court were enclosed[n] courts, forty cubits

46:1 [a] ver 6; Isa 66:23
46:2 [b] ver 8 [c] ver 12; Eze 44:3
46:3 [d] Lk 1:10
46:5 [e] ver 11; Eze 45:24
46:6 [f] ver 1; Nu 10:10
46:7 [g] Eze 45:24
46:8 [h] ver 2 [i] Eze 44:3
46:9 [j] Ex 23:14; 34:20
46:10 [k] 2Sa 6:14-15; Ps 42:4
46:11 [l] ver 5
46:12 [m] Eze 45:17 [n] Lev 7:16 [o] ver 2
46:13 [p] Ex 29:38; Nu 28:3
46:14 [q] Da 8:11
46:15 [r] Ex 29:42 [s] Ex 29:38; Nu 28:5-6
46:16 [t] 2Ch 21:3
46:17 [u] Lev 25:10
46:18 [v] Lev 25:23; Eze 45:8; Mic 2:1-2
46:19 [w] Eze 42:9
46:20 [x] Lev 6:27 [y] Zec 14:20

k *2* Traditionally *peace offerings*; also in verse 12
l *5* That is, probably about 3/5 bushel (about 22 liters)
m *5* That is, probably about 4 quarts (about 4 liters)
n *22* The meaning of the Hebrew for this word is uncertain.

long and thirty cubits wide; each of the
courts in the four corners was the same
size. [23]Around the inside of each of the
four courts was a ledge of stone, with
places for fire built all around under the
ledge. [24]He said to me, "These are the
kitchens where those who minister at
the temple will cook the sacrifices of the
people."

River from the temple.

47 The man brought me back to the
entrance of the temple, and I
saw water[a] coming out from under the
threshold of the temple toward the east
(for the temple faced east). The water
was coming down from under the south
side of the temple, south of the altar.[b]
[2]He then brought me out through the
north gate and led me around the outside to the outer gate facing east, and the
water was flowing from the south side.
[3]As the man went eastward with a
measuring line[c] in his hand, he measured off a thousand cubits[o] and then
led me through water that was ankle-
deep. [4]He measured off another thousand cubits and led me through water
that was knee-deep. He measured off
another thousand and led me through
water that was up to the waist. [5]He
measured off another thousand, but now
it was a river that I could not cross, because the water had risen and was deep
enough to swim in—a river that no one
could cross.[d] [6]He asked me, "Son of man,
do you see this?"
Then he led me back to the bank of
the river. [7]When I arrived there, I saw a
great number of trees on each side of the
river.[e] [8]He said to me, "This water flows
toward the eastern region and goes
down into the Arabah,[p][f] where it enters the Sea.[q] When it empties into the
Sea,[q] the water there becomes fresh.[g]
[9]Swarms of living creatures will live
wherever the river flows. There will be
large numbers of fish, because this water
flows there and makes the salt water
fresh; so where the river flows everything will live.[h] [10]Fishermen[i] will stand
along the shore; from En Gedi[j] to En
Eglaim there will be places for spreading
nets.[k] The fish will be of many kinds[l]—
like the fish of the Great Sea.[r][m] [11]But the
swamps and marshes will not become
fresh; they will be left for salt.[n] [12]Fruit
trees of all kinds will grow on both
banks of the river.[o] Their leaves will not
wither, nor will their fruit[p] fail. Every
month they will bear, because the water
from the sanctuary flows to them. Their
fruit will serve for food and their leaves
for healing.[q]"

Boundaries and inheritance of the land.

[13]This is what the Sovereign LORD
says: "These are the boundaries[r] by
which you are to divide the land for an
inheritance among the twelve tribes of
Israel, with two portions for Joseph.[s]
[14]You are to divide it equally among
them. Because I swore with uplifted
hand to give it to your forefathers, this
land will become your inheritance.[t]

[15]"This is to be the boundary of the
land:

"On the north side it will run from
the Great Sea by the Hethlon road[u]
past Lebo[s] Hamath to Zedad, [16]Bero-
thah[t][v] and Sibraim (which lies on
the border between Damascus and
Hamath),[w] as far as Hazer Hatticon,
which is on the border of Hauran.
[17]The boundary will extend from
the sea to Hazar Enan,[u] along the
northern border of Damascus, with
the border of Hamath to the north.
This will be the north boundary.[x]
[18]"On the east side the boundary will
run between Hauran and Damascus,
along the Jordan between Gilead
and the land of Israel, to the eastern

47:1 [a]Isa 55:1 [b]Ps 46:4; Joel 3:18; Rev 22:1
47:3 [c]Eze 40:3
47:5 [d]Isa 11:9; Hab 2:14
47:7 [e]ver 12; Rev 22:2
47:8 [f]Dt 3:17; Jos 3:16 [g]Isa 41:18
47:9 [h]Isa 12:3; 55:1; Jn 4:14; 7:37-38
47:10 [i]Mt 4:19 [j]Jos 15:62 [k]Eze 26:5 [l]Ps 104:25; Mt 13:47 [m]Nu 34:6
47:11 [n]Dt 29:23
47:12 [o]ver 7; Rev 22:2 [p]Ps 1:3 [q]Ge 2:9; Jer 17:8
47:13 [r]Nu 34:2-12 [s]Ge 48:5
47:14 [t]Ge 12:7; Dt 1:8; Eze 20:5-6
47:15 [u]Eze 48:1
47:16 [v]2Sa 8:8 [w]Nu 13:21; Eze 48:1
47:17 [x]Eze 48:1

o*3* That is, about 1,500 feet (about 450 meters)
p*8* Or *the Jordan Valley* q*8* That is, the Dead Sea
r*10* That is, the Mediterranean; also in verses 15, 19 and 20 s*15* Or *past the entrance to* t*15,16* See Septuagint and Ezekiel 48:1; Hebrew *road to go into Zedad, [16]Hamath, Berothah* u*17* Hebrew *Enon,* a variant of *Enan*

sea and as far as Tamar.[v] This will
be the east boundary.
19"On the south side it will run from
Tamar as far as the waters of Meribah Kadesh,[a] then along the Wadi
⌊of Egypt⌋[b] to the Great Sea.[c] This
will be the south boundary.
20"On the west side, the Great Sea will
be the boundary to a point opposite
Lebo[w] Hamath.[d] This will be the
west boundary.[e]

21"You are to distribute this land
among yourselves according to the
tribes of Israel. 22You are to allot it as an
inheritance for yourselves and for the
aliens[f] who have settled among you and
who have children. You are to consider
them as native-born Israelites; along
with you they are to be allotted an inheritance among the tribes of Israel.[g] 23In
whatever tribe the alien settles, there
you are to give him his inheritance," declares the Sovereign LORD.

Portions of land for the tribes.

48 "These are the tribes, listed by
name: At the northern frontier,
Dan[h] will have one portion; it will follow the Hethlon road[i] to Lebo[x] Hamath;[j]
Hazar Enan and the northern border of
Damascus next to Hamath will be part
of its border from the east side to the
west side.
2"Asher[k] will have one portion; it will
border the territory of Dan from east to
west.
3"Naphtali[l] will have one portion; it
will border the territory of Asher from
east to west.
4"Manasseh[m] will have one portion;
it will border the territory of Naphtali
from east to west.
5"Ephraim[n] will have one portion; it
will border the territory of Manasseh[o]
from east to west.[p]
6"Reuben[q] will have one portion; it
will border the territory of Ephraim from
east to west.
7"Judah[r] will have one portion; it will
border the territory of Reuben from east
to west.

8"Bordering the territory of Judah
from east to west will be the portion
you are to present as a special gift. It
will be 25,000 cubits[y] wide, and its
length from east to west will equal one
of the tribal portions; the sanctuary will
be in the center of it.[s]
9"The special portion you are to offer
to the LORD will be 25,000 cubits long
and 10,000 cubits[z] wide.[t] 10This will be
the sacred portion for the priests. It will
be 25,000 cubits long on the north side,
10,000 cubits wide on the west side,
10,000 cubits wide on the east side and
25,000 cubits long on the south side.
In the center of it will be the sanctuary
of the LORD.[u] 11This will be for the consecrated priests, the Zadokites,[v] who
were faithful in serving me[w] and did not
go astray as the Levites did when the
Israelites went astray.[x] 12It will be a
special gift to them from the sacred portion of the land, a most holy portion,
bordering the territory of the Levites.
13"Alongside the territory of the
priests, the Levites will have an allotment 25,000 cubits long and 10,000
cubits wide. Its total length will be
25,000 cubits and its width 10,000 cubits.[y] 14They must not sell or exchange
any of it. This is the best of the land and
must not pass into other hands, because
it is holy to the LORD.[z]
15"The remaining area, 5,000 cubits
wide and 25,000 cubits long, will be for
the common use of the city, for houses
and for pastureland. The city will be in
the center of it 16and will have these
measurements: the north side 4,500
cubits, the south side 4,500 cubits, the
east side 4,500 cubits, and the west side
4,500 cubits.[a] 17The pastureland for the
city will be 250 cubits on the north,
250 cubits on the south, 250 cubits on
the east, and 250 cubits on the west.
18What remains of the area, bordering
on the sacred portion and running the

47:19 [a]Dt 32:51 [b]Isa 27:12 [c]Eze 48:28
47:20 [d]Eze 48:1 [e]Nu 34:6
47:22 [f]Isa 14:1 [g]Nu 26:55-56; Isa 56:6-7; Ro 10:12; Eph 2:12-16; 3:6; Col 3:11
48:1 [h]Ge 30:6 [i]Eze 47:15-17 [j]Eze 47:20
48:2 [k]Jos 19:24-31
48:3 [l]Jos 19:32-39
48:4 [m]Jos 17:1-11
48:5 [n]Jos 16:5-9 [o]Jos 17:7-10 [p]Jos 17:17
48:6 [q]Jos 13:15-21
48:7 [r]Jos 15:1-63
48:8 [s]ver 21
48:9 [t]Eze 45:1
48:10 [u]ver 21; Eze 45:3-4
48:11 [v]2Sa 8:17 [w]Lev 8:35 [x]Eze 14:11; 44:15
48:13 [y]Eze 45:5
48:14 [z]Lev 25:34; 27:10,28
48:16 [a]Rev 21:16

v *18* Septuagint and Syriac; Hebrew *Israel. You will measure to the eastern sea* w *20* Or *opposite the entrance to* x *1* Or *to the entrance to* y *8* That is, about 7 miles (about 12 kilometers) z *9* That is, about 3 miles (about 5 kilometers)

length of it, will be 10,000 cubits on the east side and 10,000 cubits on the west side. Its produce will supply food for the workers of the city.[a] 19The workers from the city who farm it will come from all the tribes of Israel. 20The entire portion will be a square, 25,000 cubits on each side. As a special gift you will set aside the sacred portion, along with the property of the city.

21"What remains on both sides of the area formed by the sacred portion and the city property will belong to the prince. It will extend eastward from the 25,000 cubits of the sacred portion to the eastern border, and westward from the 25,000 cubits to the western border. Both these areas running the length of the tribal portions will belong to the prince, and the sacred portion with the temple sanctuary will be in the center of them.[b] 22So the property of the Levites and the property of the city will lie in the center of the area that belongs to the prince. The area belonging to the prince will lie between the border of Judah and the border of Benjamin.

23"As for the rest of the tribes: Benjamin[c] will have one portion; it will extend from the east side to the west side.

24"Simeon[d] will have one portion; it will border the territory of Benjamin from east to west.

25"Issachar[e] will have one portion; it will border the territory of Simeon from east to west.

26"Zebulun[f] will have one portion; it will border the territory of Issachar from east to west.

27"Gad[g] will have one portion; it will border the territory of Zebulun from east to west.

28"The southern boundary of Gad will run south from Tamar[h] to the waters of Meribah Kadesh, then along the Wadi ⌊of Egypt⌋ to the Great Sea.[a] [i]

29"This is the land you are to allot as an inheritance to the tribes of Israel, and these will be their portions," declares the Sovereign LORD.

Gates of the city.

30"These will be the exits of the city: Beginning on the north side, which is 4,500 cubits long, 31the gates of the city will be named after the tribes of Israel. The three gates on the north side will be the gate of Reuben, the gate of Judah and the gate of Levi.

32"On the east side, which is 4,500 cubits long, will be three gates: the gate of Joseph, the gate of Benjamin and the gate of Dan.

33"On the south side, which measures 4,500 cubits, will be three gates: the gate of Simeon, the gate of Issachar and the gate of Zebulun.

34"On the west side, which is 4,500 cubits long, will be three gates: the gate of Gad, the gate of Asher and the gate of Naphtali.

35"The distance all around will be 18,000 cubits.

"And the name of the city from that time on will be:

THE LORD IS THERE.[j]"

48:18 [a]Eze 45:6
48:21 [b]ver 8,10; Eze 45:7
48:23 [c]Jos 18:11-28
48:24 [d]Ge 29:33; Jos 19:1-9
48:25 [e]Jos 19:17-23
48:26 [f]Jos 19:10-16
48:27 [g]Jos 13:24-28
48:28 [h]Ge 14:7 [i]Eze 47:19
48:35 [j]Isa 12:6; 24:23; Jer 3:17; 14:9; Jer 33:16; Joel 3:21; Zec 2:10; Rev 21:3

a*28* That is, the Mediterranean

DANIEL

Author: Daniel.

Date Written: Between 605 and 530 B.C.

Time Span: 60-70 years. (During the early period of Babylonian captivity, Daniel prophesies under the reigns of Nebuchadnezzar, his captor; Belshazzar; Darius the Mede; and Cyrus.)

Title: From the book's author and chief character: Daniel. This book is sometimes referred to as the "Apocalypse of the Old Testament." The name Daniel means "God is my judge."

Background: As part of the first group deported to Babylon, Daniel is educated and groomed for service in the Gentile government. This devout Jewish teenager grows up in the courts of Nebuchadnezzar, where he continues to encourage both Jew and Gentile to trust in God. In contrast to the lives of most Biblical characters, Daniel is distinguished by never having anything negative written about him. A large segment of Daniel is composed in the Aramaic tongue, unlike other Old Testament books which are written in Hebrew.

Where Written: Babylon.

To Whom: Primarily to the Jews exiled in Babylon, but also to the Gentiles of Babylon and Persia.

Content: Daniel and his 3 friends—Shadrach, Meshach and Abednego—are ordered to compromise their faith by eating the king's food instead of what God has ordained. They are blessed for not compromising. But later, after Daniel has risen in prominence by identifying and interpreting Nebuchadnezzar's dream, more persecution arises. Eventually Daniel's friends are thrown into a fiery furnace for not bowing down to false gods, but God protects them. Daniel's power rises when he is able to interpret the handwriting which Belshazzar sees on the wall (chapter 5), but shortly thereafter Daniel is thrown into a lions' den for the offense of praying to his God (chapter 6). Once again God protects as Daniel walks away unharmed. Daniel's ministry continues with these visions: the 4 beasts—correlating to the kingdoms of Babylon, Persia, Greece and Rome (chapter 7); the ram and the goat (chapter 8); the 70 "sevens" (chapter 9); and, finally, the emergence of the righteous and eternal kingdom of God.

Key Words: "Courage"; "Preservation." The book of Daniel has several memorable stories illustrating the "courage" and commitment of men who place their faith in God. The "preservation" of God's people is assured for all who rely on him.

Themes: • God works through the lives of people to accomplish his desires. • Earthly kingdoms may rise and fall, but God and his Word will last forever. • If we will commit ourselves to God, good will triumph over evil in our lives. • God is concerned about every area of our lives...even our diets and eating habits. • Only God knows all, sees all and hears all...and thus only he is worthy of lordship of our lives.

Outline:

1. Daniel's training in Babylon. 1:1-1:21
2. Daniel and his friends during Nebuchadnezzar's reign. 2:1-4:37
3. The writing on the wall. 5:1-5:31
4. Daniel's faith tested in the lions' den. 6:1-6:28
5. Daniel's dream, visions and prayer. 7:1-9:27
6. Daniel's revelation of Israel's future. 10:1-12:13

DANIEL

God gives wisdom to Daniel.

1 In the third year of the reign of Jehoiakim king of Judah, Nebuchadnezzar[a]
king of Babylon came to Jerusalem and
besieged it.[b] 2And the Lord delivered
Jehoiakim king of Judah into his hand,
along with some of the articles from the
temple of God. These he carried off to
the temple of his god in Babylonia[a] and
put in the treasure house of his god.[c]
3Then the king ordered Ashpenaz,
chief of his court officials, to bring in
some of the Israelites from the royal
family and the nobility[d]— 4young men
without any physical defect, handsome,
showing aptitude for every kind of learning, well informed, quick to understand,
and qualified to serve in the king's palace.
He was to teach them the language and
literature of the Babylonians.[b] 5The king
assigned them a daily amount of food
and wine[e] from the king's table. They
were to be trained for three years, and
after that they were to enter the king's
service.[f]
6Among these were some from Judah:
Daniel,[g] Hananiah, Mishael and Azariah.
7The chief official gave them new names:
to Daniel, the name Belteshazzar;[h] to
Hananiah, Shadrach; to Mishael, Meshach; and to Azariah, Abednego.[i]
8But Daniel resolved not to defile[j]
himself with the royal food and wine,
and he asked the chief official for permission not to defile himself this way.
9Now God had caused the official to
show favor[k] and sympathy[l] to Daniel,
10but the official told Daniel, "I am afraid
of my lord the king, who has assigned
your[c] food and drink. Why should he
see you looking worse than the other
young men your age? The king would
then have my head because of you."
11Daniel then said to the guard whom
the chief official had appointed over
Daniel, Hananiah, Mishael and Azariah,
12"Please test your servants for ten days:
Give us nothing but vegetables to eat
and water to drink. 13Then compare our
appearance with that of the young men
who eat the royal food, and treat your
servants in accordance with what you
see." 14So he agreed to this and tested
them for ten days.
15At the end of the ten days they looked
healthier and better nourished than
any of the young men who ate the royal
food.[m] 16So the guard took away their
choice food and the wine they were to
drink and gave them vegetables instead.[n]

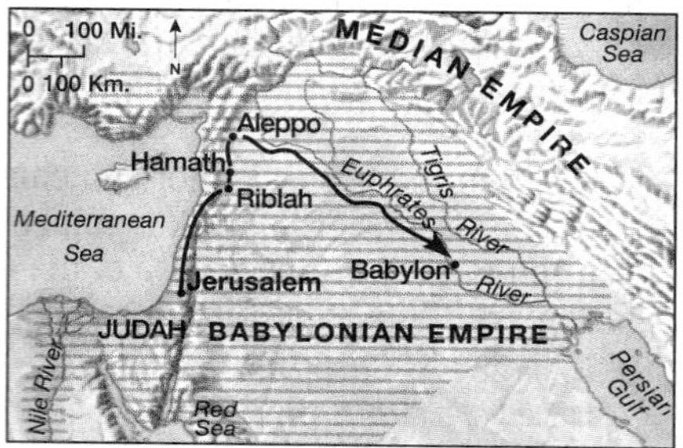

Taken to Babylon

Daniel, as a captive of Babylonian soldiers, faced a long and difficult march to a new land. The 500-mile trek, under harsh conditions, certainly tested his faith in God.

17To these four young men God gave
knowledge and understanding[o] of all
kinds of literature and learning.[p] And
Daniel could understand visions and
dreams of all kinds.[q]
18At the end of the time[r] set by the
king to bring them in, the chief official
presented them to Nebuchadnezzar.
19The king talked with them, and he
found none equal to Daniel, Hananiah,
Mishael and Azariah; so they entered
the king's service.[s] 20In every matter of
wisdom and understanding about which
the king questioned them, he found
them ten times better than all the magicians and enchanters in his whole
kingdom.[t]
21And Daniel remained there until
the first year of King Cyrus.[u]

1:1 [a]2Ki 24:1 [b]2Ch 36:6
1:2 [c]2Ch 36:7; Jer 27:19-20; Zec 5:5-11
1:3 [d]2Ki 20:18; 24:15; Isa 39:7
1:5 [e]ver 8,10 [f]ver 19
1:6 [g]Eze 14:14
1:7 [h]Da 4:8; 5:12 [i]Da 2:49; 3:12
1:8 [j]Eze 4:13-14
1:9 [k]Ge 39:21; Pr 16:7 [l]1Ki 8:50; Ps 106:46
1:15 [m]Ex 23:25
1:16 [n]ver 12-13
1:17 [o]1Ki 3:12 [p]Da 2:23; Jas 1:5 [q]Da 2:19,30; 7:1; 8:1
1:18 [r]ver 5
1:19 [s]Ge 41:46
1:20 [t]1Ki 4:30; Da 2:13,28
1:21 [u]Da 6:28; 10:1

a2 Hebrew *Shinar* b4 Or *Chaldeans* c10 The Hebrew for *your* and *you* in this verse is plural.

Nebuchadnezzar has a dream.

2 In the second year of his reign, Nebuchadnezzar had dreams;[a] his mind was troubled[b] and he could not sleep.[c] 2So the king summoned the magicians,[d] enchanters, sorcerers[e] and astrologers[d][f] to tell him what he had dreamed.[g] When they came in and stood before the king, 3he said to them, "I have had a dream that troubles[h] me and I want to know what it means.[e]"

4Then the astrologers answered the king in Aramaic,[f][i] "O king, live forever![j] Tell your servants the dream, and we will interpret it."

5The king replied to the astrologers, "This is what I have firmly decided: If you do not tell me what my dream was and interpret it, I will have you cut into pieces[k] and your houses turned into piles of rubble.[l] 6But if you tell me the dream and explain it, you will receive from me gifts and rewards and great honor.[m] So tell me the dream and interpret it for me."

7Once more they replied, "Let the king tell his servants the dream, and we will interpret it."

8Then the king answered, "I am certain that you are trying to gain time, because you realize that this is what I have firmly decided: 9If you do not tell me the dream, there is just one penalty[n] for you. You have conspired to tell me misleading and wicked things, hoping the situation will change. So then, tell me the dream, and I will know that you can interpret it for me."[o]

10The astrologers answered the king, "There is not a man on earth who can do what the king asks! No king, however great and mighty, has ever asked such a thing of any magician or enchanter or astrologer.[p] 11What the king asks is too difficult. No one can reveal it to the king except the gods,[q] and they do not live among men."

12This made the king so angry and furious[r] that he ordered the execution[s] of all the wise men of Babylon. 13So the decree was issued to put the wise men to death, and men were sent to look for Daniel and his friends to put them to death.[t]

14When Arioch, the commander of the king's guard, had gone out to put to death the wise men of Babylon, Daniel spoke to him with wisdom and tact. 15He asked the king's officer, "Why did the king issue such a harsh decree?" Arioch then explained the matter to Daniel. 16At this, Daniel went in to the king and asked for time, so that he might interpret the dream for him.

17Then Daniel returned to his house and explained the matter to his friends Hananiah, Mishael and Azariah.[u] 18He urged them to plead for mercy[v] from the God of heaven concerning this mystery,[w] so that he and his friends might not be executed with the rest of the wise men of Babylon. 19During the night the mystery[x] was revealed to Daniel in a vision.[y] Then Daniel praised the God of heaven 20and said:

"Praise be to the name of God for
ever and ever;[z]
wisdom and power[a] are his.
21He changes times and seasons;[b]
he sets up kings and deposes[c] them.
He gives wisdom[d] to the wise
and knowledge to the discerning.
22He reveals deep and hidden things;[e]
he knows what lies in darkness,[f]
and light[g] dwells with him.
23I thank and praise you, O God of my
fathers:[h]
You have given me wisdom[i] and
power,
you have made known to me what
we asked of you,
you have made known to us the
dream of the king."

Daniel interprets the dream.

24Then Daniel went to Arioch,[j] whom the king had appointed to execute the wise men of Babylon, and said to him, "Do not execute the wise men of Babylon.

2:1 [a]Job 33:15,18; Da 4:5 [b]Ge 41:8 [c]Est 6:1; Da 6:18
2:2 [d]Ge 41:8 [e]Ex 7:11 [f]ver 10; Da 5:7 [g]Da 4:6
2:3 [h]Da 4:5
2:4 [i]Ezr 4:7 [j]Da 3:9; 5:10
2:5 [k]ver 12 [l]Ezr 6:11; Da 3:29
2:6 [m]ver 48; Da 5:7,16
2:9 [n]Est 4:11 [o]Isa 41:22-24
2:10 [p]ver 27
2:11 [q]Da 5:11
2:12 [r]Da 3:13,19 [s]ver 5
2:13 [t]Da 1:20
2:17 [u]Da 1:6
2:18 [v]Isa 37:4 [w]Jer 33:3
2:19 [x]ver 28 [y]Job 33:15; Da 1:17
2:20 [z]Ps 113:2; 145:1-2 [a]Jer 32:19
2:21 [b]Da 7:25 [c]Job 12:19; Ps 75:6-7 [d]Jas 1:5
2:22 [e]Job 12:22; Ps 25:14; Da 5:11 [f]Ps 139:11-12; Jer 23:24; Heb 4:13 [g]Isa 45:7; Jas 1:17
2:23 [h]Ex 3:15 [i]Da 1:17
2:24 [j]ver 14

[d]2 Or *Chaldeans*; also in verses 4, 5 and 10 [e]3 Or *was* [f]4 The text from here through chapter 7 is in Aramaic.

Take me to the king, and I will interpret
his dream for him."
25 Arioch took Daniel to the king at once
and said, "I have found a man among
the exiles from Judah[a] who can tell the
king what his dream means."
26 The king asked Daniel (also called
Belteshazzar),[b] "Are you able to tell me
what I saw in my dream and interpret it?"
27 Daniel replied, "No wise man, enchanter, magician or diviner can explain
to the king the mystery he has asked
about,[c] 28 but there is a God in heaven
who reveals mysteries.[d] He has shown
King Nebuchadnezzar what will happen
in days to come.[e] Your dream and the
visions that passed through your mind[f]
as you lay on your bed are these:
29 "As you were lying there, O king,
your mind turned to things to come, and
the revealer of mysteries showed you
what is going to happen. 30 As for me,
this mystery has been revealed[g] to me,
not because I have greater wisdom than
other living men, but so that you, O
king, may know the interpretation and
that you may understand what went
through your mind.
31 "You looked, O king, and there before you stood a large statue—an enormous, dazzling statue,[h] awesome in
appearance. 32 The head of the statue
was made of pure gold, its chest and arms
of silver, its belly and thighs of bronze,
33 its legs of iron, its feet partly of iron
and partly of baked clay. 34 While you
were watching, a rock was cut out, but
not by human hands.[i] It struck the statue
on its feet of iron and clay and smashed
them.[j] 35 Then the iron, the clay, the
bronze, the silver and the gold were
broken to pieces at the same time and
became like chaff on a threshing floor
in the summer. The wind swept them
away[k] without leaving a trace. But the
rock that struck the statue became a huge
mountain[l] and filled the whole earth.
36 "This was the dream, and now we
will interpret it to the king. 37 You, O
king, are the king of kings.[m] The God
of heaven has given you dominion[n]
and power and might and glory; 38 in your
hands he has placed mankind and the
beasts of the field and the birds of the air.
Wherever they live, he has made you
ruler over them all.[o] You are that head
of gold.
39 "After you, another kingdom will rise,
inferior to yours. Next, a third kingdom,
one of bronze, will rule over the whole
earth. 40 Finally, there will be a fourth
kingdom, strong as iron—for iron breaks
and smashes everything—and as iron
breaks things to pieces, so it will crush
and break all the others.[p] 41 Just as you
saw that the feet and toes were partly
of baked clay and partly of iron, so this
will be a divided kingdom; yet it will
have some of the strength of iron in it,
even as you saw iron mixed with clay.
42 As the toes were partly iron and partly clay, so this kingdom will be partly
strong and partly brittle. 43 And just as
you saw the iron mixed with baked clay,
so the people will be a mixture and will
not remain united, any more than iron
mixes with clay.
44 "In the time of those kings, the God
of heaven will set up a kingdom that will
never be destroyed, nor will it be left to
another people. It will crush[q] all those
kingdoms[r] and bring them to an end,
but it will itself endure forever.[s] 45 This is
the meaning of the vision of the rock[t]
cut out of a mountain, but not by human
hands[u]—a rock that broke the iron, the
bronze, the clay, the silver and the gold
to pieces.
"The great God has shown the king
what will take place in the future. The
dream is true and the interpretation is
trustworthy."
46 Then King Nebuchadnezzar fell prostrate[v] before Daniel and paid him hon-
or and ordered that an offering[w] and
incense be presented to him. 47 The king
said to Daniel, "Surely your God is the
God of gods[x] and the Lord of kings[y] and
a revealer of mysteries,[z] for you were
able to reveal this mystery."
48 Then the king placed Daniel in a
high position and lavished many gifts on
him. He made him ruler over the entire

2:25 [a]Da 1:6; 5:13; 6:13
2:26 [b]Da 1:7
2:27 [c]ver 10
2:28 [d]Ge 40:8; Am 4:13 [e]Ge 49:1; Da 10:14 [f]Da 4:5
2:30 [g]Isa 45:3; Da 1:17; Am 4:13
2:31 [h]Hab 1:7
2:34 [i]Zec 4:6 [j]ver 44-45; Ps 2:9; Isa 60:12; Da 8:25
2:35 [k]Ps 1:4; 37:10; Isa 17:13 [l]Isa 2:3; Mic 4:1
2:37 [m]Eze 26:7 [n]Jer 27:7
2:38 [o]Jer 27:6; Da 4:21-22
2:40 [p]Da 7:7,23
2:44 [q]Ps 2:9; 1Co 15:24 [r]Isa 60:12 [s]Ps 145:13; Isa 9:7; Da 4:34; 6:26; 7:14,27; Mic 4:7,13; Lk 1:33
2:45 [t]Isa 28:16 [u]Da 8:25
2:46 [v]Da 8:17; Ac 10:25 [w]Ac 14:13
2:47 [x]Da 11:36 [y]Da 4:25 [z]ver 22,28

province of Babylon and placed him in charge of all its wise men.[a] 49Moreover, at Daniel's request the king appointed Shadrach, Meshach and Abednego administrators over the province of Babylon,[b] while Daniel himself remained at the royal court.

Three friends are rescued from the blazing furnace.

3 King Nebuchadnezzar made an image[c] of gold, ninety feet high and nine feet[g] wide, and set it up on the plain of Dura in the province of Babylon. 2He then summoned the satraps, prefects, governors, advisers, treasurers, judges, magistrates and all the other provincial officials[d] to come to the dedication of the image he had set up. 3So the satraps, prefects, governors, advisers, treasurers, judges, magistrates and all the other provincial officials assembled for the dedication of the image that King Nebuchadnezzar had set up, and they stood before it.

4Then the herald loudly proclaimed, "This is what you are commanded to do, O peoples, nations and men of every language:[e] 5As soon as you hear the sound of the horn, flute, zither, lyre, harp, pipes and all kinds of music, you must fall down and worship the image of gold that King Nebuchadnezzar has set up.[f] 6Whoever does not fall down and worship will immediately be thrown into a blazing furnace."[g]

7Therefore, as soon as they heard the sound of the horn, flute, zither, lyre, harp and all kinds of music, all the peoples, nations and men of every language fell down and worshiped the image of gold that King Nebuchadnezzar had set up.[h]

8At this time some astrologers[h][i] came forward and denounced the Jews. 9They said to King Nebuchadnezzar, "O king, live forever![j] 10You have issued a decree,[k] O king, that everyone who hears the sound of the horn, flute, zither, lyre, harp, pipes and all kinds of music must fall down and worship the image of gold,[l] 11and that whoever does not fall down and worship will be thrown into a blazing furnace. 12But there are some Jews whom you have set over the affairs of the province of Babylon—Shadrach, Meshach and Abednego[m]—who pay no attention[n] to you, O king. They neither serve your gods nor worship the image of gold you have set up."[o]

13Furious[p] with rage, Nebuchadnezzar summoned Shadrach, Meshach and Abednego. So these men were brought before the king, 14and Nebuchadnezzar said to them, "Is it true, Shadrach, Meshach and Abednego, that you do not serve my gods[q] or worship the image[r] of gold I have set up? 15Now when you hear the sound of the horn, flute, zither, lyre, harp, pipes and all kinds of music, if you are ready to fall down and worship the image I made, very good. But if you do not worship it, you will be thrown immediately into a blazing furnace. Then what god[s] will be able to rescue[t] you from my hand?"

16Shadrach, Meshach and Abednego[u] replied to the king, "O Nebuchadnezzar, we do not need to defend ourselves before you in this matter. 17If we are thrown into the blazing furnace, the God we serve is able to save[v] us from it, and he will rescue[w] us from your hand, O king. 18But even if he does not, we want you to know, O king, that we will not serve your gods or worship the image of gold you have set up.[x]"

19Then Nebuchadnezzar was furious with Shadrach, Meshach and Abednego, and his attitude toward them changed. He ordered the furnace heated seven[y] times hotter than usual 20and commanded some of the strongest soldiers in his army to tie up Shadrach, Meshach and Abednego and throw them into the blazing furnace. 21So these men, wearing their robes, trousers, turbans and other clothes, were bound and thrown into the blazing furnace. 22The king's command was so urgent and the furnace so hot that the flames of the fire killed the

2:48 [a]ver 6; Da 4:9; 5:11
2:49 [b]Da 1:7
3:1 [c]Isa 46:6; Jer 16:20; Hab 2:19
3:2 [d]ver 27; Da 6:7
3:4 [e]Da 4:1; 6:25
3:5 [f]ver 10,15
3:6 [g]ver 11,15,21; Jer 29:22; Da 6:7; Mt 13:42,50; Rev 13:15
3:7 [h]ver 5
3:8 [i]Da 2:10
3:9 [j]Ne 2:3; Da 5:10; 6:6
3:10 [k]Da 6:12 [l]ver 4-6
3:12 [m]Da 2:49 [n]Da 6:13 [o]Est 3:3
3:13 [p]Da 2:12
3:14 [q]Isa 46:1; Jer 50:2 [r]ver 1
3:15 [s]Isa 36:18-20 [t]Ex 5:2; 2Ch 32:15
3:16 [u]Da 1:7
3:17 [v]Ps 27:1-2 [w]Job 5:19; Jer 1:8
3:18 [x]ver 28; Jos 24:15
3:19 [y]Lev 26:18-28

g *1* Aramaic *sixty cubits high and six cubits wide* (about 27 meters high and 2.7 meters wide) h *8* Or *Chaldeans*

soldiers who took up Shadrach, Meshach and Abednego,[a] 23and these three men, firmly tied, fell into the blazing furnace.

24Then King Nebuchadnezzar leaped to his feet in amazement and asked his advisers, "Weren't there three men that we tied up and threw into the fire?"

They replied, "Certainly, O king."

25He said, "Look! I see four men walking around in the fire, unbound and unharmed, and the fourth looks like a son of the gods."

26Nebuchadnezzar then approached the opening of the blazing furnace and shouted, "Shadrach, Meshach and Abednego, servants of the Most High God,[b] come out! Come here!"

So Shadrach, Meshach and Abednego came out of the fire, 27and the satraps, prefects, governors and royal advisers[c] crowded around them.[d] They saw that the fire[e] had not harmed their bodies, nor was a hair of their heads singed; their robes were not scorched, and there was no smell of fire on them.

28Then Nebuchadnezzar said, "Praise be to the God of Shadrach, Meshach and Abednego, who has sent his angel[f] and rescued his servants! They trusted[g] in him and defied the king's command and were willing to give up their lives rather than serve or worship any god except their own God.[h] 29Therefore I decree[i] that the people of any nation or language who say anything against the God of Shadrach, Meshach and Abednego be cut into pieces and their houses be turned into piles of rubble,[j] for no other god can save[k] in this way."

30Then the king promoted Shadrach, Meshach and Abednego in the province of Babylon.[l]

Nebuchadnezzar dreams about a tree.

4 King Nebuchadnezzar,

To the peoples, nations and men of every language,[m] who live in all the world:

May you prosper greatly![n]

2It is my pleasure to tell you about the miraculous signs[o] and wonders that the Most High God[p] has performed for me.

3How great are his signs,
how mighty his wonders![q]
His kingdom is an eternal kingdom;
his dominion endures[r] from generation to generation.

4I, Nebuchadnezzar, was at home in my palace, contented[s] and prosperous. 5I had a dream[t] that made me afraid. As I was lying in my bed, the images and visions that passed through my mind[u] terrified me. 6So I commanded that all the wise men of Babylon be brought before me to interpret[v] the dream for me. 7When the magicians,[w] enchanters, astrologers[i] and diviners[x] came, I told them the dream, but they could not interpret it for me.[y] 8Finally, Daniel came into my presence and I told him the dream. (He is called Belteshazzar,[z] after the name of my god, and the spirit of the holy gods[a] is in him.)

9I said, "Belteshazzar, chief[b] of the magicians, I know that the spirit of the holy gods[c] is in you, and no mystery is too difficult for you. Here is my dream; interpret it for me. 10These are the visions I saw while lying in my bed:[d] I looked, and there before me stood a tree in the middle of the land. Its height was enormous.[e] 11The tree grew large and strong and its top touched the sky; it was visible to the ends of the earth. 12Its leaves were beautiful, its fruit abundant, and on it was food for all. Under it the beasts of the field found shelter, and the birds of the air lived in its branches;[f] from it every creature was fed.

13"In the visions I saw while lying in my bed,[g] I looked, and there

3:22 [a]Da 1:7
3:26 [b]Da 4:2,34
3:27 [c]ver 2 [d]Isa 43:2; Heb 11:32-34 [e]Da 6:23
3:28 [f]Ps 34:7; Da 6:22; Ac 5:19 [g]Job 13:15; Ps 26:1; 84:12; Jer 17:7 [h]ver 18
3:29 [i]Da 6:26 [j]Ezr 6:11 [k]Da 6:27
3:30 [l]Da 2:49
4:1 [m]Da 3:4 [n]Da 6:25
4:2 [o]Ps 74:9 [p]Da 3:26
4:3 [q]Ps 105:27; Da 6:27 [r]Da 2:44
4:4 [s]Ps 30:6
4:5 [t]Da 2:1 [u]Da 2:28
4:6 [v]Da 2:2
4:7 [w]Ge 41:8 [x]Isa 44:25; Da 2:2 [y]Da 2:10
4:8 [z]Da 1:7 [a]Da 5:11,14
4:9 [b]Da 2:48 [c]Da 5:11-12
4:10 [d]ver 5 [e]Eze 31:3-4
4:12 [f]Eze 17:23; Mt 13:32
4:13 [g]Da 7:1

i7 Or *Chaldeans*

before me was a messenger,[j] a holy
one,[a] coming down from heaven.
14He called in a loud voice: 'Cut
down the tree and trim off its
branches; strip off its leaves and
scatter its fruit. Let the animals flee
from under it and the birds from
its branches.[b] 15But let the stump
and its roots, bound with iron and
bronze, remain in the ground, in the
grass of the field.

"'Let him be drenched with the
dew of heaven, and let him live with
the animals among the plants of the
earth. 16Let his mind be changed
from that of a man and let him be
given the mind of an animal, till sev-
en times[k] pass by for him.[c]

17"'The decision is announced by
messengers, the holy ones declare
the verdict, so that the living may
know that the Most High[d] is sovereign[e] over the kingdoms of men and
gives them to anyone he wishes and
sets over them the lowliest[f] of men.'

18"This is the dream that I, King
Nebuchadnezzar, had. Now, Belteshazzar, tell me what it means, for
none of the wise men in my kingdom can interpret it for me.[g] But
you can,[h] because the spirit of the
holy gods is in you."[i]

Daniel interprets the dream.

19Then Daniel (also called Belteshazzar) was greatly perplexed for
a time, and his thoughts terrified[j]
him. So the king said, "Belteshazzar,
do not let the dream or its meaning
alarm you."

Belteshazzar answered, "My lord,
if only the dream applied to your enemies and its meaning to your adversaries! 20The tree you saw, which
grew large and strong, with its top
touching the sky, visible to the whole
earth, 21with beautiful leaves and
abundant fruit, providing food for
all, giving shelter to the beasts of
the field, and having nesting places
in its branches for the birds of the
air— 22you, O king, are that tree![k]
You have become great and strong;
your greatness has grown until it
reaches the sky, and your dominion
extends to distant parts of the earth.[l]

23"You, O king, saw a messenger, a
holy one,[m] coming down from heav-
en and saying, 'Cut down the tree
and destroy it, but leave the stump,
bound with iron and bronze, in the
grass of the field, while its roots remain in the ground. Let him be
drenched with the dew of heaven;
let him live like the wild animals,
until seven times pass by for him.'[n]

24"This is the interpretation, O
king, and this is the decree[o] the
Most High has issued against my
lord the king: 25You will be driven
away from people and will live with
the wild animals; you will eat grass
like cattle and be drenched with
the dew of heaven. Seven times will
pass by for you until you acknowledge that the Most High[p] is sovereign over the kingdoms of men and
gives them to anyone he wishes.[q]
26The command to leave the stump
of the tree with its roots[r] means
that your kingdom will be restored
to you when you acknowledge that
Heaven rules.[s] 27Therefore, O king,
be pleased to accept my advice: Renounce your sins by doing what is
right, and your wickedness by being
kind to the oppressed.[t] It may be that
then your prosperity will continue.[u]"

Nebuchadnezzar's dream is fulfilled.

28All this happened[v] to King Nebuchadnezzar. 29Twelve months later,
as the king was walking on the roof
of the royal palace of Babylon, 30he
said, "Is not this the great Babylon
I have built as the royal residence,
by my mighty power and for the
glory of my majesty?"[w]

31The words were still on his lips

4:13 [a]ver 23; Dt 33:2; Da 8:13
4:14 [b]Eze 31:12; Mt 3:10
4:16 [c]ver 23,32
4:17 [d]ver 2,25; Ps 83:18 [e]Jer 27:5-7; Da 2:21; 5:18-21 [f]Da 11:21
4:18 [g]Ge 41:8; Da 5:8,15 [h]Ge 41:15 [i]ver 7-9
4:19 [j]Da 7:15,28; 8:27; 10:16-17
4:22 [k]2Sa 12:7 [l]Jer 27:7; Da 2:37-38; 5:18-19
4:23 [m]ver 13 [n]Da 5:21
4:24 [o]Job 40:12; Ps 107:40
4:25 [p]ver 17; Ps 83:18 [q]Jer 27:5; Da 5:21
4:26 [r]ver 15 [s]Da 2:37
4:27 [t]Isa 55:6-7 [u]1Ki 21:29; Ps 41:3; Eze 18:22
4:28 [v]Nu 23:19
4:30 [w]Isa 37:24-25; Da 5:20; Hab 2:4

j*13* Or *watchman*; also in verses 17 and 23 k*16* Or *years*; also in verses 23, 25 and 32

when a voice came from heaven,
"This is what is decreed for you,
King Nebuchadnezzar: Your royal
authority has been taken from you.
32You will be driven away from people and will live with the wild animals; you will eat grass like cattle.
Seven times will pass by for you until you acknowledge that the Most
High is sovereign over the kingdoms
of men and gives them to anyone he
wishes."
33Immediately what had been said
about Nebuchadnezzar was fulfilled.
He was driven away from people and
ate grass like cattle. His body was
drenched with the dew of heaven
until his hair grew like the feathers
of an eagle and his nails like the
claws of a bird.[a]

34At the end of that time, I, Nebuchadnezzar, raised my eyes toward
heaven, and my sanity was restored.
Then I praised the Most High; I
honored and glorified him who lives
forever.[b]

His dominion is an eternal dominion;
his kingdom endures from
generation to generation.[c]
35All the peoples of the earth
are regarded as nothing.[d]
He does as he pleases[e]
with the powers of heaven
and the peoples of the earth.
No one can hold back his hand
or say to him: "What have you
done?"[f]

36At the same time that my sanity
was restored, my honor and splendor
were returned to me for the glory of
my kingdom.[g] My advisers and nobles sought me out, and I was restored to my throne and became even
greater than before. 37Now I, Nebuchadnezzar, praise and exalt and
glorify the King of heaven, because
everything he does is right and all
his ways are just.[h] And those who
walk in pride he is able to humble.[i]

4:33 [a]Da 5:20-21
4:34 [b]Da 12:7; Rev 4:10 [c]Ps 145:13; Da 2:44; 5:21; 6:26; Lk 1:33
4:35 [d]Isa 40:17 [e]Ps 115:3; 135:6 [f]Isa 45:9; Ro 9:20
4:36 [g]Pr 22:4
4:37 [h]Dt 32:4; Ps 33:4-5 [i]Ex 18:11; Job 40:11-12; Da 5:20,23
5:1 [j]Est 1:3
5:2 [k]2Ki 24:13; Jer 52:19 [l]Est 1:7; Da 1:2
5:4 [m]Ps 135:15-18; Hab 2:19; Rev 9:20
5:6 [n]Da 4:5 [o]Eze 7:17
5:7 [p]Isa 44:25 [q]Da 4:6-7 [r]Ge 41:42 [s]Da 2:5-6,48; 6:2-3
5:8 [t]Da 2:10,27
5:9 [u]Isa 21:4
5:10 [v]Da 3:9
5:11 [w]Da 4:8-9,19

The handwriting on the wall.

5 King Belshazzar gave a great banquet[j] for a thousand of his nobles
and drank wine with them. 2While Belshazzar was drinking his wine, he gave
orders to bring in the gold and silver
goblets[k] that Nebuchadnezzar his father[l]
had taken from the temple in Jerusalem,
so that the king and his nobles, his wives
and his concubines might drink from
them.[l] 3So they brought in the gold goblets that had been taken from the temple
of God in Jerusalem, and the king and his
nobles, his wives and his concubines
drank from them. 4As they drank the
wine, they praised the gods of gold and
silver, of bronze, iron, wood and stone.[m]
5Suddenly the fingers of a human hand
appeared and wrote on the plaster of the
wall, near the lampstand in the royal
palace. The king watched the hand as it
wrote. 6His face turned pale and he was
so frightened[n] that his knees knocked
together and his legs gave way.[o]
7The king called out for the enchanters,
astrologers[m] and diviners[p] to be brought
and said to these wise[q] men of Babylon,
"Whoever reads this writing and tells me
what it means will be clothed in purple
and have a gold chain placed around his
neck,[r] and he will be made the third
highest ruler in the kingdom."[s]
8Then all the king's wise men came in,
but they could not read the writing or
tell the king what it meant.[t] 9So King
Belshazzar became even more terrified[u]
and his face grew more pale. His nobles
were baffled.

Daniel's interpretation of the writing.

10The queen,[n] hearing the voices of
the king and his nobles, came into the
banquet hall. "O king, live forever!"[v] she
said. "Don't be alarmed! Don't look so
pale! 11There is a man in your kingdom
who has the spirit of the holy gods[w] in
him. In the time of your father he was

l *2* Or *ancestor*; or *predecessor*; also in verses 11, 13 and 18 m *7* Or *Chaldeans*; also in verse 11
n *10* Or *queen mother*

found to have insight and intelligence and
wisdom[a] like that of the gods. King Nebuchadnezzar your father—your father the
king, I say—appointed him chief of the
magicians, enchanters, astrologers and
diviners.[b] 12This man Daniel, whom the
king called Belteshazzar,[c] was found to
have a keen mind and knowledge and
understanding, and also the ability to interpret dreams, explain riddles and solve
difficult problems.[d] Call for Daniel, and
he will tell you what the writing means."
13So Daniel was brought before the
king, and the king said to him, "Are you
Daniel, one of the exiles my father the
king brought from Judah?[e] 14I have heard
that the spirit of the gods is in you and
that you have insight, intelligence and
outstanding wisdom. 15The wise men and
enchanters were brought before me to
read this writing and tell me what it
means, but they could not explain it.
16Now I have heard that you are able to
give interpretations and to solve difficult problems. If you can read this writing and tell me what it means, you will
be clothed in purple and have a gold
chain placed around your neck, and you
will be made the third highest ruler in
the kingdom."
17Then Daniel answered the king, "You
may keep your gifts for yourself and give
your rewards to someone else.[f] Nevertheless, I will read the writing for the king
and tell him what it means.
18"O king, the Most High God gave
your father Nebuchadnezzar sovereignty
and greatness and glory and splendor.[g]
19Because of the high position he gave
him, all the peoples and nations and men
of every language dreaded and feared
him. Those the king wanted to put to
death, he put to death;[h] those he wanted
to spare, he spared; those he wanted to
promote, he promoted; and those he
wanted to humble, he humbled. 20But
when his heart became arrogant and
hardened with pride,[i] he was deposed
from his royal throne and stripped[j] of
his glory.[k] 21He was driven away from
people and given the mind of an animal;
he lived with the wild donkeys and
ate grass like cattle; and his body was
drenched with the dew of heaven, until
he acknowledged that the Most High God
is sovereign[l] over the kingdoms of men
and sets over them anyone he wishes.[m]
22"But you his son,[o] O Belshazzar, have
not humbled[n] yourself, though you knew
all this. 23Instead, you have set yourself
up against[o] the Lord of heaven. You had
the goblets from his temple brought to
you, and you and your nobles, your wives
and your concubines drank wine from
them. You praised the gods of silver and
gold, of bronze, iron, wood and stone,
which cannot see or hear or understand.[p] But you did not honor the God
who holds in his hand your life[q] and all
your ways.[r] 24Therefore he sent the hand
that wrote the inscription.
25"This is the inscription that was
written:

MENE, MENE, TEKEL, PARSIN[p]

26"This is what these words mean:

Mene[q]: God has numbered
the days[s] of your reign and
brought it to an end.[t]
27*Tekel*[r]: You have been weighed
on the scales and found
wanting.[u]
28*Peres*[s]: Your kingdom is divided and given to the Medes[v]
and Persians."[w]

29Then at Belshazzar's command, Daniel was clothed in purple, a gold chain
was placed around his neck, and he
was proclaimed the third highest ruler
in the kingdom.
30That very night Belshazzar,[x] king of
the Babylonians,[t] was slain,[y] 31and Darius[z] the Mede took over the kingdom,
at the age of sixty-two.

Daniel is thrown into the lions' den.

6 It pleased Darius[a] to appoint 120
satraps[b] to rule throughout the

5:11 [a]ver 14; Da 1:17 [b]Da 2:47-48
5:12 [c]Da 1:7 [d]ver 14-16; Da 6:3
5:13 [e]Da 6:13
5:17 [f]2Ki 5:16
5:18 [g]Jer 27:7; Da 2:37-38
5:19 [h]Da 2:12-13; 3:6
5:20 [i]Da 4:30 [j]Jer 13:18 [k]Job 40:12; Isa 14:13-15
5:21 [l]Eze 17:24 [m]Da 4:16-17, 35
5:22 [n]Ex 10:3; 2Ch 33:23
5:23 [o]Jer 50:29 [p]Ps 115:4-8; Hab 2:19 [q]Job 12:10 [r]Job 31:4; Jer 10:23
5:26 [s]Jer 27:7 [t]Isa 13:6
5:27 [u]Ps 62:9
5:28 [v]Isa 13:17 [w]Da 6:28
5:30 [x]ver 1 [y]Isa 21:9; Jer 51:31
5:31 [z]Da 6:1; 9:1
6:1 [a]Da 5:31 [b]Est 1:1

o*22* Or *descendant*; or *successor* p*25* Aramaic *UPARSIN* (that is, *AND PARSIN*) q*26* *Mene* can mean *numbered* or *mina* (a unit of money). r*27* *Tekel* can mean *weighed* or *shekel.* s*28* *Peres* (the singular of *Parsin*) can mean *divided* or *Persia* or *a half mina* or *a half shekel.* t*30* Or *Chaldeans*

kingdom, 2with three administrators over them, one of whom was Daniel.[a] The satraps were made accountable[b] to them so that the king might not suffer loss. 3Now Daniel so distinguished himself among the administrators and the satraps by his exceptional qualities that the king planned to set him over the whole kingdom.[c] 4At this, the administrators and the satraps tried to find grounds for charges against Daniel in his conduct of government affairs, but they were unable to do so. They could find no corruption in him, because he was trustworthy and neither corrupt nor negligent. 5Finally these men said, "We will never find any basis for charges against this man Daniel unless it has something to do with the law of his God."[d]

6So the administrators and the satraps went as a group to the king and said: "O King Darius, live forever![e] 7The royal administrators, prefects, satraps, advisers and governors[f] have all agreed that the king should issue an edict and enforce the decree that anyone who prays to any god or man during the next thirty days, except to you, O king, shall be thrown into the lions' den.[g] 8Now, O king, issue the decree and put it in writing so that it cannot be altered—in accordance with the laws of the Medes and Persians, which cannot be repealed."[h] 9So King Darius put the decree in writing.

10Now when Daniel learned that the decree had been published, he went home to his upstairs room where the windows opened toward[i] Jerusalem. Three times a day he got down on his knees[j] and prayed, giving thanks to his God, just as he had done before.[k] 11Then these men went as a group and found Daniel praying and asking God for help. 12So they went to the king and spoke to him about his royal decree: "Did you not publish a decree that during the next thirty days anyone who prays to any god or man except to you, O king, would be thrown into the lions' den?"

The king answered, "The decree stands—in accordance with the laws of the Medes and Persians, which cannot be repealed."[l]

13Then they said to the king, "Daniel, who is one of the exiles from Judah,[m] pays no attention[n] to you, O king, or to the decree you put in writing. He still prays three times a day." 14When the king heard this, he was greatly distressed;[o] he was determined to rescue Daniel and made every effort until sundown to save him.

15Then the men went as a group to the king and said to him, "Remember, O king, that according to the law of the Medes and Persians no decree or edict that the king issues can be changed."[p]

16So the king gave the order, and they brought Daniel and threw him into the lions' den.[q] The king said to Daniel, "May your God, whom you serve continually, rescue[r] you!"

17A stone was brought and placed over the mouth of the den, and the king sealed[s] it with his own signet ring and with the rings of his nobles, so that Daniel's situation might not be changed. 18Then the king returned to his palace and spent the night without eating[t] and without any entertainment being brought to him. And he could not sleep.[u]

19At the first light of dawn, the king got up and hurried to the lions' den. 20When he came near the den, he called to Daniel in an anguished voice, "Daniel, servant of the living God, has your God, whom you serve continually, been able to rescue you from the lions?"[v]

21Daniel answered, "O king, live forever![w] 22My God sent his angel,[x] and he shut the mouths of the lions.[y] They have not hurt me, because I was found innocent in his sight.[z] Nor have I ever done any wrong before you, O king."

23The king was overjoyed and gave orders to lift Daniel out of the den. And when Daniel was lifted from the den, no wound[a] was found on him, because he had trusted[b] in his God.

24At the king's command, the men who had falsely accused Daniel were brought in and thrown into the lions' den,[c] along with their wives and children.[d] And

6:2 [a]Da 2:48-49 [b]Ezr 4:22
6:3 [c]Ge 41:41; Est 10:3; Da 5:12-14
6:5 [d]Ac 24:13-16
6:6 [e]Ne 2:3; Da 2:4
6:7 [f]Da 3:2 [g]Ps 59:3; 64:2-6; Da 3:6
6:8 [h]Est 1:19
6:10 [i]1Ki 8:48-49 [j]Ps 95:6 [k]Ac 5:29
6:12 [l]Est 1:19; Da 3:8-12
6:13 [m]Da 2:25; 5:13 [n]Est 3:8; Da 3:12
6:14 [o]Mk 6:26
6:15 [p]Est 8:8
6:16 [q]ver 7 [r]Job 5:19; Ps 37:39-40
6:17 [s]Mt 27:66
6:18 [t]2Sa 12:17 [u]Est 6:1; Da 2:1
6:20 [v]Da 3:17
6:21 [w]Da 2:4
6:22 [x]Da 3:28 [y]Ps 91:11-13; Heb 11:33 [z]Ac 12:11; 2Ti 4:17
6:23 [a]Da 3:27 [b]1Ch 5:20
6:24 [c]Dt 19:18-19; Est 7:9-10; Ps 54:5 [d]Dt 24:16; 2Ki 14:6

before they reached the floor of the den,
the lions overpowered them and crushed
all their bones.[a]

King Darius issues a decree.

25Then King Darius wrote to all the
peoples, nations and men of every language throughout the land:

'May you prosper greatly![b]

26"I issue a decree that in every
part of my kingdom people must fear
and reverence the God of Daniel.[c]

"For he is the living God
and he endures forever;
his kingdom will not be destroyed,
his dominion will never end.[d]
27He rescues and he saves;
he performs signs and wonders[e]
in the heavens and on the earth.
He has rescued Daniel
from the power of the lions."[f]

28So Daniel prospered during the reign
of Darius and the reign of Cyrus[u][g] the
Persian.

Daniel dreams about four beasts.

7 In the first year of Belshazzar[h] king
of Babylon, Daniel had a dream,
and visions passed through his mind[i] as
he was lying on his bed. He wrote[j] down
the substance of his dream.
2Daniel said: "In my vision at night I
looked, and there before me were the
four winds of heaven[k] churning up the
great sea. 3Four great beasts,[l] each different from the others, came up out of
the sea.
4"The first was like a lion,[m] and it had
the wings of an eagle.[n] I watched until
its wings were torn off and it was lifted
from the ground so that it stood on two
feet like a man, and the heart of a man
was given to it.
5"And there before me was a second
beast, which looked like a bear. It was
raised up on one of its sides, and it had
three ribs in its mouth between its teeth.
It was told, 'Get up and eat your fill of
flesh!'[o]
6"After that, I looked, and there before
me was another beast, one that looked
like a leopard.[p] And on its back it had
four wings like those of a bird. This beast
had four heads, and it was given authority to rule.
7"After that, in my vision at night I
looked, and there before me was a fourth
beast—terrifying and frightening and
very powerful. It had large iron[q] teeth;
it crushed and devoured its victims and
trampled underfoot whatever was left. It
was different from all the former beasts,
and it had ten horns.[r]
8"While I was thinking about the
horns, there before me was another horn,
a little[s] one, which came up among them;
and three of the first horns were uprooted before it. This horn had eyes like the
eyes of a man[t] and a mouth that spoke
boastfully.[u]
9"As I looked,

"thrones were set in place,
and the Ancient of Days took his
seat.
His clothing was as white as snow;
the hair of his head was white like
wool.[v]
His throne was flaming with fire,
and its wheels[w] were all ablaze.
10A river of fire[x] was flowing,
coming out from before him.[y]
Thousands upon thousands attended
him;
ten thousand times ten thousand
stood before him.
The court was seated,
and the books[z] were opened.

11"Then I continued to watch because
of the boastful words the horn was speaking. I kept looking until the beast was
slain and its body destroyed and thrown
into the blazing fire.[a] 12(The other beasts
had been stripped of their authority, but
were allowed to live for a period of time.)
13"In my vision at night I looked, and
there before me was one like a son of
man,[b] coming with the clouds of heav-
en.[c] He approached the Ancient of Days

6:24 [a]Isa 38:13
6:25 [b]Da 4:1
6:26 [c]Ps 99:1-3; Da 3:29 [d]Da 2:44; 4:34
6:27 [e]Da 4:3 [f]ver 22
6:28 [g]2Ch 36:22; Da 1:21
7:1 [h]Da 5:1 [i]Da 1:17 [j]Jer 36:4
7:2 [k]Rev 7:1
7:3 [l]Rev 13:1
7:4 [m]Jer 4:7 [n]Eze 17:3
7:5 [o]Da 2:39
7:6 [p]Rev 13:2
7:7 [q]Da 2:40 [r]Rev 12:3
7:8 [s]Da 8:9 [t]Rev 9:7 [u]Ps 12:3; Rev 13:5-6
7:9 [v]Rev 1:14 [w]Eze 1:15; 10:6
7:10 [x]Ps 50:3; 97:3; Isa 30:27 [y]Dt 33:2; Ps 68:17; Rev 5:11 [z]Rev 20:11-15
7:11 [a]Rev 19:20
7:13 [b]Mt 8:20*; Rev 1:13* [c]Mt 24:30; Rev 1:7

u*28* Or *Darius, that is, the reign of Cyrus*

and was led into his presence. 14He was given authority,[a] glory and sovereign power; all peoples, nations and men of every language worshiped him.[b] His dominion is an everlasting dominion that will not pass away, and his kingdom is one that will never be destroyed.[c]

Daniel's dream is interpreted.

15"I, Daniel, was troubled in spirit, and the visions that passed through my mind disturbed me.[d] 16I approached one of those standing there and asked him the true meaning of all this.

"So he told me and gave me the interpretation[e] of these things: 17'The four great beasts are four kingdoms that will rise from the earth. 18But the saints of the Most High will receive the kingdom and will possess it forever—yes, for ever and ever.'[f]

19"Then I wanted to know the true meaning of the fourth beast, which was different from all the others and most terrifying, with its iron teeth and bronze claws—the beast that crushed and devoured its victims and trampled underfoot whatever was left. 20I also wanted to know about the ten horns on its head and about the other horn that came up, before which three of them fell—the horn that looked more imposing than the others and that had eyes and a mouth that spoke boastfully. 21As I watched, this horn was waging war against the saints and defeating them,[g] 22until the Ancient of Days came and pronounced judgment in favor of the saints of the Most High, and the time came when they possessed the kingdom.

23"He gave me this explanation: 'The fourth beast is a fourth kingdom that will appear on earth. It will be different from all the other kingdoms and will devour the whole earth, trampling it down and crushing it.[h] 24The ten horns[i] are ten kings who will come from this kingdom. After them another king will arise, different from the earlier ones; he will subdue three kings. 25He will speak against the Most High[j] and oppress his saints and try to change the set times[k] and the laws. The saints will be handed over to him for a time, times and half a time.[v][l]

26"'But the court will sit, and his power will be taken away and completely destroyed forever. 27Then the sovereignty, power and greatness of the kingdoms under the whole heaven will be handed over to the saints, the people of the Most High. His kingdom will be an everlasting[m] kingdom, and all rulers will worship[n] and obey him.'

28"This is the end of the matter. I, Daniel, was deeply troubled[o] by my thoughts, and my face turned pale, but I kept the matter to myself."

Daniel's vision of a ram and a goat.

8 In the third year of King Belshazzar's reign, I, Daniel, had a vision, after the one that had already appeared to me. 2In my vision I saw myself in the citadel of Susa[p] in the province of Elam;[q] in the vision I was beside the Ulai Canal. 3I looked up,[r] and there before me was a ram with two horns, standing beside the canal, and the horns were long. One of the horns was longer than the other but grew up later. 4I watched the ram as he charged toward the west and the north and the south. No animal could stand against him, and none could rescue from his power. He did as he pleased[s] and became great.

5As I was thinking about this, suddenly a goat with a prominent horn between his eyes came from the west, crossing the whole earth without touching the ground. 6He came toward the two-horned ram I had seen standing beside the canal and charged at him in great rage. 7I saw him attack the ram furiously, striking the ram and shattering his two horns. The ram was powerless to stand against him; the goat knocked him to the ground and trampled on him,[t] and none could rescue the ram from his power. 8The goat became very great, but at the height of his power his large horn was broken

7:14 [a]Mt 28:18 [b]Ps 72:11; 102:22; 1Co 15:27; Eph 1:22 [c]Da 2:44; Heb 12:28; Rev 11:15
7:15 [d]Da 4:19
7:16 [e]Da 8:16; 9:22; Zec 1:9
7:18 [f]Isa 60:12-14; Rev 2:26; 20:4
7:21 [g]Rev 13:7
7:23 [h]Da 2:40
7:24 [i]Rev 17:12
7:25 [j]Isa 37:23; Da 11:36 [k]Da 2:21 [l]Da 8:24; 12:7; Rev 12:14
7:27 [m]Da 2:44; 4:34; Lk 1:33; Rev 11:15; 22:5 [n]Ps 22:27; 72:11; 86:9
7:28 [o]Da 4:19
8:2 [p]Est 1:2 [q]Ge 10:22
8:3 [r]Da 10:5
8:4 [s]Da 11:3,16
8:7 [t]Da 7:7

[v]25 Or *for a year, two years and half a year*

off,[a] and in its place four prominent
horns grew up toward the four winds of
heaven.[b]
9Out of one of them came another
horn, which started small but grew in
power to the south and to the east and
toward the Beautiful Land.[c] **10**It grew
until it reached[d] the host of the heavens,
and it threw some of the starry host
down to the earth[e] and trampled[f] on
them. **11**It set itself up to be as great as
the Prince of the host;[g] it took away the
daily sacrifice[h] from him, and the place
of his sanctuary was brought low.[i] **12**Because of rebellion, the host ⌊of the saints⌋[w]
and the daily sacrifice were given over
to it. It prospered in everything it did,
and truth was thrown to the ground.
13Then I heard a holy one[j] speaking,
and another holy one said to him, "How
long will it take for the vision to be fulfilled[k]—the vision concerning the daily
sacrifice, the rebellion that causes desolation, and the surrender of the sanctuary
and of the host that will be trampled[l]
underfoot?"
14He said to me, "It will take 2,300
evenings and mornings; then the sanctuary will be reconsecrated."[m]

Gabriel's interpretation of the vision.

15While I, Daniel, was watching the
vision[n] and trying to understand it,
there before me stood one who looked
like a man.[o] **16**And I heard a man's voice
from the Ulai calling, "Gabriel,[p] tell this
man the meaning of the vision."
17As he came near the place where I
was standing, I was terrified and fell prostrate.[q] "Son of man," he said to me, "understand that the vision concerns the
time of the end."[r]
18While he was speaking to me, I was
in a deep sleep, with my face to the
ground.[s] Then he touched me and raised
me to my feet.[t]
19He said: "I am going to tell you what
will happen later in the time of wrath,
because the vision concerns the appointed time of the end.[x][u] **20**The two-horned
ram that you saw represents the kings
of Media and Persia. **21**The shaggy goat
is the king of Greece,[v] and the large horn
between his eyes is the first king.[w] **22**The
four horns that replaced the one that
was broken off represent four kingdoms
that will emerge from his nation but will
not have the same power.
23"In the latter part of their reign, when
rebels have become completely wicked,
a stern-faced king, a master of intrigue,
will arise. **24**He will become very strong,
but not by his own power. He will cause
astounding devastation and will succeed
in whatever he does. He will destroy the
mighty men and the holy people.[x] **25**He
will cause deceit to prosper, and he will
consider himself superior. When they
feel secure, he will destroy many and
take his stand against the Prince of
princes.[y] Yet he will be destroyed, but
not by human power.[z]
26"The vision of the evenings and
mornings that has been given you is
true,[a] but seal[b] up the vision, for it concerns the distant future."[c]
27I, Daniel, was exhausted and lay ill
for several days. Then I got up and went
about the king's business.[d] I was appalled[e] by the vision; it was beyond understanding.

Daniel prays and fasts.

9 In the first year of Darius[f] son of
Xerxes[y] (a Mede by descent), who
was made ruler over the Babylonian[z]
kingdom— **2**in the first year of his reign,
I, Daniel, understood from the Scriptures,
according to the word of the LORD given
to Jeremiah the prophet, that the desolation of Jerusalem would last seventy[g]
years. **3**So I turned to the Lord God and
pleaded with him in prayer and petition,
in fasting, and in sackcloth and ashes.[h]
4I prayed to the LORD my God and
confessed:

"O Lord, the great and awesome
God,[i] who keeps his covenant of

8:8 [a]2Ch 26:16-21; Da 5:20 [b]Da 7:2; Rev 7:1
8:9 [c]Da 11:16
8:10 [d]Isa 14:13 [e]Rev 12:4 [f]Da 7:7
8:11 [g]Da 11:36-37 [h]Eze 46:13-14 [i]Da 11:31; 12:11
8:13 [j]Da 4:23 [k]Da 12:6 [l]Lk 21:24; Rev 11:2
8:14 [m]Da 12:11-12
8:15 [n]ver 1 [o]Da 10:16-18
8:16 [p]Da 9:21; Lk 1:19
8:17 [q]Eze 1:28; Da 2:46; Rev 1:17 [r]Hab 2:3
8:18 [s]Da 10:9 [t]Eze 2:2; Da 10:16-18
8:19 [u]Hab 2:3
8:21 [v]Da 10:20 [w]Da 11:3
8:24 [x]Da 7:25; 11:36
8:25 [y]Da 11:36 [z]Da 2:34; 11:21
8:26 [a]Da 10:1 [b]Rev 22:10 [c]Da 10:14
8:27 [d]Da 2:48 [e]Da 7:28
9:1 [f]Da 5:31
9:2 [g]2Ch 36:21; Jer 29:10; Zec 7:5
9:3 [h]Ne 1:4; Jer 29:12
9:4 [i]Dt 7:21

w *12* Or *rebellion, the armies* x *19* Or *because the end will be at the appointed time* y *1* Hebrew *Ahasuerus* z *1* Or *Chaldean*

love[a] with all who love him and obey his commands, 5 we have sinned and done wrong.[b] We have been wicked and have rebelled; we have turned away[c] from your commands and laws.[d] 6 We have not listened to your servants the prophets,[e] who spoke in your name to our kings, our princes and our fathers, and to all the people of the land.

7 "Lord, you are righteous, but this day we are covered with shame[f]—the men of Judah and people of Jerusalem and all Israel, both near and far, in all the countries where you have scattered[g] us because of our unfaithfulness to you.[h] 8 O LORD, we and our kings, our princes and our fathers are covered with shame because we have sinned against you. 9 The Lord our God is merciful and forgiving,[i] even though we have rebelled against him;[j] 10 we have not obeyed the LORD our God or kept the laws he gave us through his servants the prophets.[k] 11 All Israel has transgressed your law and turned away, refusing to obey you.

"Therefore the curses and sworn judgments written in the Law of Moses, the servant of God, have been poured out on us, because we have sinned[l] against you. 12 You have fulfilled[m] the words spoken against us and against our rulers by bringing upon us great disaster. Under the whole heaven nothing has ever been done like what has been done to Jerusalem.[n] 13 Just as it is written in the Law of Moses, all this disaster has come upon us, yet we have not sought the favor of the LORD our God by turning from our sins and giving attention to your truth.[o] 14 The LORD did not hesitate to bring the disaster[p] upon us, for the LORD our God is righteous in everything he does; yet we have not obeyed him.[q]

15 "Now, O Lord our God, who brought your people out of Egypt with a mighty hand[r] and who made for yourself a name[s] that endures to this day, we have sinned, we have done wrong. 16 O Lord, in keeping with all your righteous acts,[t] turn away your anger and your wrath from Jerusalem,[u] your city, your holy hill.[v] Our sins and the iniquities of our fathers have made Jerusalem and your people an object of scorn[w] to all those around us.

17 "Now, our God, hear the prayers and petitions of your servant. For your sake, O Lord, look with favor[x] on your desolate sanctuary. 18 Give ear, O God, and hear; open your eyes and see[y] the desolation of the city that bears your Name.[z] We do not make requests of you because we are righteous, but because of your great mercy. 19 O Lord, listen! O Lord, forgive![a] O Lord, hear and act! For your sake, O my God, do not delay, because your city and your people bear your Name."

Seventy "sevens" are decreed.

20 While I was speaking and praying, confessing my sin and the sin of my people Israel and making my request to the LORD my God for his holy hill[b]—21 while I was still in prayer, Gabriel,[c] the man I had seen in the earlier vision, came to me in swift flight about the time of the evening sacrifice.[d] 22 He instructed me and said to me, "Daniel, I have now come to give you insight and understanding. 23 As soon as you began to pray, an answer was given, which I have come to tell you, for you are highly esteemed.[e] Therefore, consider the message and understand the vision:[f]

24 "Seventy 'sevens'[a] are decreed for your people and your holy city to finish[b] transgression, to put an end to sin, to atone[g] for wickedness, to bring in everlasting righteousness,[h] to seal up vision and prophecy and to anoint the most holy.[c]

25 "Know and understand this: From

9:4 [a]Dt 7:9
9:5 [b]Ps 106:6 [c]Isa 53:6 [d]ver 11; La 1:20
9:6 [e]2Ch 36:16; Jer 44:5
9:7 [f]Ps 44:15 [g]Dt 4:27; Am 9:9 [h]Jer 3:25
9:9 [i]Ps 130:4 [j]Ne 9:17; Jer 14:7
9:10 [k]2Ki 17:13-15; 18:12
9:11 [l]Isa 1:4-6; Jer 8:5-10
9:12 [m]Isa 44:26; Zec 1:6 [n]Jer 44:2-6; Eze 5:9
9:13 [o]Isa 9:13; Jer 2:30
9:14 [p]Jer 44:27 [q]Ne 9:33
9:15 [r]Jer 32:21 [s]Ne 9:10
9:16 [t]Ps 31:1 [u]Jer 32:32 [v]Zec 8:3 [w]Eze 5:14
9:17 [x]Nu 6:24-26; Ps 80:19
9:18 [y]Ps 80:14 [z]Isa 37:17; Jer 7:10-12; 25:29
9:19 [a]Ps 44:23
9:20 [b]ver 3; Ps 145:18; Isa 58:9
9:21 [c]Da 8:16; Lk 1:19 [d]Ex 29:39
9:23 [e]Da 10:19; Lk 1:28 [f]Da 10:11-12; Mt 24:15
9:24 [g]Isa 53:10, [h]Isa 56:1

a24 Or *'weeks'*; also in verses 25 and 26 b24 Or *restrain* c24 Or *Most Holy Place*; or *most holy One*

the issuing of the decree[d] to restore and rebuild[a] Jerusalem until the Anointed One,[e][b] the ruler, comes, there will be seven 'sevens,' and sixty-two 'sevens.' It will be rebuilt with streets and a trench, but in times of trouble. 26 After the sixty-two 'sevens,' the Anointed One will be cut off[c] and will have nothing.[f] The people of the ruler who will come will destroy the city and the sanctuary. The end will come like a flood:[d] War will continue until the end, and desolations have been decreed. 27 He will confirm a covenant with many for one 'seven.'[g] In the middle of the 'seven'[g] he will put an end to sacrifice and offering. And on a wing ⌊of the temple⌋ he will set up an abomination that causes desolation, until the end that is decreed[e] is poured out on him.[h]"[i]

Daniel has a glorious vision.

10 In the third year of Cyrus[f] king of Persia, a revelation was given to Daniel (who was called Belteshazzar).[g] Its message was true[h] and it concerned a great war.[j] The understanding of the message came to him in a vision.

2 At that time I, Daniel, mourned[i] for three weeks. 3 I ate no choice food; no meat or wine touched my lips; and I used no lotions at all until the three weeks were over.

4 On the twenty-fourth day of the first month, as I was standing on the bank of the great river, the Tigris,[j] 5 I looked up and there before me was a man dressed in linen,[k] with a belt of the finest gold[l] around his waist. 6 His body was like chrysolite, his face like lightning,[m] his eyes like flaming torches,[n] his arms and legs like the gleam of burnished bronze,[o] and his voice like the sound of a multitude.

7 I, Daniel, was the only one who saw the vision; the men with me did not see it,[p] but such terror overwhelmed them that they fled and hid themselves. 8 So I was left alone,[q] gazing at this great vision; I had no strength left,[r] my face turned deathly pale and I was helpless.[s] 9 Then I heard him speaking, and as I listened to him, I fell into a deep sleep, my face to the ground.[t]

10 A hand touched me[u] and set me trembling on my hands and knees.[v] 11 He said, "Daniel, you who are highly esteemed,[w] consider carefully the words I am about to speak to you, and stand up,[x] for I have now been sent to you." And when he said this to me, I stood up trembling.

12 Then he continued, "Do not be afraid, Daniel. Since the first day that you set your mind to gain understanding and to humble[y] yourself before your God, your words were heard, and I have come in response to them.[z] 13 But the prince of the Persian kingdom resisted me twenty-one days. Then Michael,[a] one of the chief princes, came to help me, because I was detained there with the king of Persia. 14 Now I have come to explain[b] to you what will happen to your people in the future, for the vision concerns a time yet to come.[c]"

15 While he was saying this to me, I bowed with my face toward the ground and was speechless.[d] 16 Then one who looked like a man[k] touched my lips, and I opened my mouth and began to speak.[e] I said to the one standing before me, "I am overcome with anguish[f] because of the vision, my lord, and I am helpless. 17 How can I, your servant, talk with you, my lord? My strength is gone and I can hardly breathe."[g]

18 Again the one who looked like a man touched[h] me and gave me strength. 19 "Do not be afraid, O man highly esteemed," he said. "Peace![i] Be strong now; be strong."[j]

When he spoke to me, I was strengthened and said, "Speak, my lord, since you have given me strength."[k]

20 So he said, "Do you know why I have come to you? Soon I will return to fight

9:25 [a]Ezr 4:24 [b]Jn 4:25
9:26 [c]Isa 53:8 [d]Na 1:8
9:27 [e]Isa 10:22
10:1 [f]Da 1:21 [g]Da 1:7 [h]Da 8:26
10:2 [i]Ezr 9:4
10:4 [j]Ge 2:14
10:5 [k]Eze 9:2; Rev 15:6 [l]Jer 10:9
10:6 [m]Mt 17:2 [n]Rev 19:12 [o]Rev 1:15
10:7 [p]2Ki 6:17-20; Ac 9:7
10:8 [q]Ge 32:24 [r]Da 8:27 [s]Hab 3:16
10:9 [t]Da 8:18
10:10 [u]Jer 1:9 [v]Rev 1:17
10:11 [w]Da 9:23 [x]Eze 2:1
10:12 [y]Da 9:3 [z]Da 9:20
10:13 [a]ver 21; Da 12:1; Jude 9
10:14 [b]Da 9:22 [c]Da 2:28; 8:26; Hab 2:3
10:15 [d]Eze 24:27; Lk 1:20
10:16 [e]Isa 6:7; Jer 1:9; Da 8:15-18 [f]Isa 21:3
10:17 [g]Da 4:19
10:18 [h]ver 16
10:19 [i]Jdg 6:23; Isa 35:4 [j]Jos 1:9 [k]Isa 6:1-8

[d]*25* Or *word* [e]*25* Or *an anointed one*; also in verse 26 [f]*26* Or *off and will have no one*; or *off, but not for himself* [g]*27* Or *'week'* [h]*27* Or *it* [i]*27* Or *And one who causes desolation will come upon the pinnacle of the abominable ⌊temple⌋, until the end that is decreed is poured out on the desolated ⌊city⌋* [j]*1* Or *true and burdensome* [k]*16* Most manuscripts of the Masoretic Text; one manuscript of the Masoretic Text, Dead Sea Scrolls and Septuagint *Then something that looked like a man's hand*

against the prince of Persia, and when
I go, the prince of Greece[a] will come;
21 but first I will tell you what is written
in the Book of Truth.[b] (No one supports
me against them except Michael,[c] your
11 prince. 1 And in the first year of
Darius[d] the Mede, I took my stand
to support and protect him.)

Conflicts between kings of the South and the North.

2 "Now then, I tell you the truth:[e]
Three more kings will appear in Persia,
and then a fourth, who will be far richer
than all the others. When he has gained
power by his wealth, he will stir up everyone against the kingdom of Greece.[f]
3 Then a mighty king will appear, who
will rule with great power and do as he
pleases.[g] 4 After he has appeared, his
empire will be broken up and parceled
out toward the four winds of heaven.[h]
It will not go to his descendants, nor will
it have the power he exercised, because
his empire will be uprooted and given
to others.
5 "The king of the South will become
strong, but one of his commanders will
become even stronger than he and will
rule his own kingdom with great power.
6 After some years, they will become allies. The daughter of the king of the
South will go to the king of the North to
make an alliance, but she will not retain
her power, and he and his power[l] will
not last. In those days she will be handed
over, together with her royal escort and
her father[m] and the one who supported
her.
7 "One from her family line will arise to
take her place. He will attack the forces
of the king of the North[i] and enter his
fortress; he will fight against them and
be victorious. 8 He will also seize their
gods,[j] their metal images and their valuable articles of silver and gold and carry
them off to Egypt.[k] For some years he will
leave the king of the North alone. 9 Then
the king of the North will invade the
realm of the king of the South but will
retreat to his own country. 10 His sons will
prepare for war and assemble a great
army, which will sweep on like an irre-
sistible flood[l] and carry the battle as far
as his fortress.
11 "Then the king of the South will
march out in a rage and fight against the
king of the North, who will raise a large
army, but it will be defeated.[m] 12 When
the army is carried off, the king of the
South will be filled with pride and will
slaughter many thousands, yet he will
not remain triumphant. 13 For the king of
the North will muster another army,
larger than the first; and after several
years, he will advance with a huge army
fully equipped.
14 "In those times many will rise against
the king of the South. The violent men
among your own people will rebel in fulfillment of the vision, but without success. 15 Then the king of the North will
come and build up siege ramps[n] and
will capture a fortified city. The forces
of the South will be powerless to resist; even their best troops will not have
the strength to stand. 16 The invader will
do as he pleases;[o] no one will be able
to stand against him.[p] He will establish himself in the Beautiful Land and
will have the power to destroy it.[q] 17 He
will determine to come with the might
of his entire kingdom and will make an
alliance with the king of the South.
And he will give him a daughter in marriage in order to overthrow the kingdom, but his plans[n] will not succeed[r]
or help him. 18 Then he will turn his attention to the coastlands[s] and will take
many of them, but a commander will
put an end to his insolence and will
turn his insolence back upon him.[t]
19 After this, he will turn back toward
the fortresses of his own country but
will stumble and fall,[u] to be seen no
more.[v]
20 "His successor will send out a tax collector to maintain the royal splendor.[w]
In a few years, however, he will be destroyed, yet not in anger or in battle.

10:20 [a]Da 8:21; 11:2
10:21 [b]Da 11:2 [c]ver 13; Jude 9
11:1 [d]Da 5:31
11:2 [e]Da 10:21 [f]Da 10:20
11:3 [g]Da 8:4,21
11:4 [h]Da 7:2; 8:22
11:7 [i]ver 6
11:8 [j]Isa 37:19; 46:1-2 [k]Jer 43:12
11:10 [l]Isa 8:8; Jer 46:8; Da 9:26
11:11 [m]Da 8:7-8
11:15 [n]Eze 4:2
11:16 [o]Da 8:4 [p]Jos 1:5; Da 8:7 [q]Da 8:9
11:17 [r]Ps 20:4
11:18 [s]Isa 66:19; Jer 25:22 [t]Hos 12:14
11:19 [u]Ps 27:2 [v]Ps 37:36; Eze 26:21
11:20 [w]Isa 60:17

[l]*6* Or *offspring* [m]*6* Or *child* (see Vulgate and Syriac)
[n]*17* Or *but she*

Prophecy concerning a contemptible king.

21“He will be succeeded by a contemptible[a] person who has not been given the honor of royalty.[b] He will invade the kingdom when its people feel secure, and he will seize it through intrigue. 22Then an overwhelming army will be swept away before him; both it and a prince of the covenant will be destroyed.[c] 23After coming to an agreement with him, he will act deceitfully,[d] and with only a few people he will rise to power. 24When the richest provinces feel secure, he will invade them and will achieve what neither his fathers nor his forefathers did. He will distribute plunder, loot and wealth among his followers.[e] He will plot the overthrow of fortresses—but only for a time.

25“With a large army he will stir up his strength and courage against the king of the South. The king of the South will wage war with a large and very powerful army, but he will not be able to stand because of the plots devised against him. 26Those who eat from the king’s provisions will try to destroy him; his army will be swept away, and many will fall in battle. 27The two kings, with their hearts bent on evil,[f] will sit at the same table and lie[g] to each other, but to no avail, because an end will still come at the appointed time.[h] 28The king of the North will return to his own country with great wealth, but his heart will be set against the holy covenant. He will take action against it and then return to his own country.

29“At the appointed time he will invade the South again, but this time the outcome will be different from what it was before. 30Ships of the western coastlands[o][i] will oppose him, and he will lose heart. Then he will turn back and vent his fury against the holy covenant. He will return and show favor to those who forsake the holy covenant.

31“His armed forces will rise up to desecrate the temple fortress and will abolish the daily sacrifice. Then they will set up the abomination that causes desolation.[j] 32With flattery he will corrupt those who have violated the covenant, but the people who know their God will firmly resist[k] him.

33“Those who are wise will instruct[l] many, though for a time they will fall by the sword or be burned or captured or plundered.[m] 34When they fall, they will receive a little help, and many who are not sincere[n] will join them. 35Some of the wise will stumble, so that they may be refined,[o] purified and made spotless until the time of the end, for it will still come at the appointed time.

36“The king will do as he pleases. He will exalt and magnify himself above every god and will say unheard-of things[p] against the God of gods.[q] He will be successful until the time of wrath[r] is completed, for what has been determined must take place. 37He will show no regard for the gods of his fathers or for the one desired by women, nor will he regard any god, but will exalt himself above them all. 38Instead of them, he will honor a god of fortresses; a god unknown to his fathers he will honor with gold and silver, with precious stones and costly gifts. 39He will attack the mightiest fortresses with the help of a foreign god and will greatly honor those who acknowledge him. He will make them rulers over many people and will distribute the land at a price.[p]

40“At the time of the end the king of the South[s] will engage him in battle, and the king of the North will storm[t] out against him with chariots and cavalry and a great fleet of ships. He will invade many countries and sweep through them like a flood.[u] 41He will also invade the Beautiful Land. Many countries will fall, but Edom,[v] Moab[w] and the leaders of Ammon will be delivered from his hand. 42He will extend his power over many countries; Egypt will not escape. 43He will gain control of the treasures of gold and silver and all the riches of Egypt,[x] with the Libyans[y] and Nubians in submission. 44But

11:21 [a]Da 4:17 [b]Da 8:25
11:22 [c]Da 8:10-11
11:23 [d]Da 8:25
11:24 [e]Ne 9:25
11:27 [f]Ps 64:6 [g]Ps 12:2; Jer 9:5 [h]Hab 2:3
11:30 [i]Ge 10:4
11:31 [j]Da 8:11-13; 9:27; Mt 24:15*; Mk 13:14*
11:32 [k]Mic 5:7-9
11:33 [l]Mal 2:7 [m]Mt 24:9; Jn 16:2; Heb 11:32-38
11:34 [n]Mt 7:15; Ro 16:18
11:35 [o]Ps 78:38; Da 12:10; Zec 13:9; Jn 15:2
11:36 [p]Rev 13:5-6 [q]Dt 10:17; Isa 14:13-14; Da 7:25; 8:11-12,25; 2Th 2:4 [r]Isa 10:25; 26:20
11:40 [s]Isa 21:1 [t]Isa 5:28 [u]Eze 38:4
11:41 [v]Isa 11:14 [w]Jer 48:47
11:43 [x]Eze 30:4 [y]2Ch 12:3; Na 3:9

o30 Hebrew *of Kittim* p39 Or *land for a reward*

reports from the east and the north will
alarm him, and he will set out in a great
rage to destroy and annihilate many.
45He will pitch his royal tents between
the seas at[q] the beautiful holy mountain.
Yet he will come to his end, and no one
will help him.

A time of distress and deliverance.

12 "At that time Michael,[a] the great
prince who protects your people,
will arise. There will be a time of distress[b] such as has not happened from the
beginning of nations until then. But at
that time your people—everyone whose
name is found written in the book[c]—will
be delivered.[d] 2Multitudes who sleep in
the dust of the earth will awake: some
to everlasting life, others to shame and
everlasting contempt.[e] 3Those who are
wise[r][f] will shine[g] like the brightness of
the heavens, and those who lead many
to righteousness, like the stars for ever
and ever.[h] 4But you, Daniel, close up and
seal[i] the words of the scroll until the time
of the end.[j] Many will go here and there
to increase knowledge."

5Then I, Daniel, looked, and there before me stood two others, one on this
bank of the river and one on the opposite bank.[k] 6One of them said to the man
clothed in linen,[l] who was above the
waters of the river, "How long will it
be before these astonishing things are
fulfilled?"[m]

7The man clothed in linen, who was
above the waters of the river, lifted his
right hand and his left hand toward heav-
en, and I heard him swear by him who
lives forever,[n] saying, "It will be for a
time, times and half a time.[s][o] When
the power of the holy people[p] has been
finally broken, all these things will be
completed.[q]"

8I heard, but I did not understand. So
I asked, "My lord, what will the outcome
of all this be?"

9He replied, "Go your way, Daniel, because the words are closed up and sealed
until the time of the end.[r] 10Many will be
purified, made spotless and refined,[s] but
the wicked will continue to be wicked.[t]
None of the wicked will understand, but
those who are wise will understand.[u]

11"From the time that the daily sacrifice is abolished and the abomination that
causes desolation[v] is set up, there will
be 1,290 days. 12Blessed is the one who
waits[w] for and reaches the end of the
1,335 days.[x]

13"As for you, go your way till the end.
You will rest,[y] and then at the end of the
days you will rise to receive your allotted
inheritance.[z]"

12:1 [a]Da 10:13 [b]Da 9:12; Mt 24:21; Mk 13:19; Rev 16:18 [c]Ex 32:32; Ps 56:8 [d]Jer 30:7 **12:2** [e]Isa 26:19; Mt 25:46; Jn 5:28-29 **12:3** [f]Da 11:33 [g]Mt 13:43; Jn 5:35 [h]1Co 15:42 **12:4** [i]Isa 8:16 [j]ver 9,13; Rev 22:10 **12:5** [k]Da 10:4 **12:6** [l]Eze 9:2 [m]Da 8:13 **12:7** [n]Rev 10:5-6 [o]Da 7:25 [p]Da 8:24 [q]Lk 21:24; Rev 10:7 **12:9** [r]ver 4 **12:10** [s]Da 11:35 [t]Isa 32:7; Rev 22:11 [u]Hos 14:9 **12:11** [v]Da 8:11; 9:27; Mt 24:15*; Mk 13:14* **12:12** [w]Isa 30:18 [x]Da 8:14 **12:13** [y]Isa 57:2 [z]Ps 16:5; Rev 14:13

q45 Or *the sea and* r3 Or *who impart wisdom*
s7 Or *a year, two years and half a year*

HOSEA

Author: Hosea.

Date Written: Between 790 and 710 B.C.

Time Span: About 45 years. (Hosea's ministry overlaps those of the prophets Isaiah, Amos and Micah.)

Title: From the book's author and one of the chief characters: Hosea. Hosea has been called "the prophet with the broken heart."

Background: Hosea's ministry to the northern kingdom begins while Jeroboam II is reigning in Israel, and successively covers the reigns of Uzziah, Jotham, Ahaz and Hezekiah in Judah. The setting for this first book of the minor prophets is just before Israel is exiled to Assyria. While the nation is thriving in prosperity, its spiritual condition is deplorable with pagan and immoral worship of Baal and Ashtoreth, as well as the worship of the golden calves that Jeroboam I had set up at Bethel and Dan.

Where Written: Israel (northern kingdom).

To Whom: To the people of the northern kingdom.

Content: Hosea's personal life graphically illustrates his prophetic message. At the command of God, the prophet Hosea marries Gomer the prostitute. But instead of being faithful to her forgiving and loving husband, Gomer returns to her previous lovers. Hosea, though, is diligent as he compassionately seeks her out and is able to bring her back. Hosea's message is also revealed through the meaning of the names he gives his 3 children: Jezreel, Lo-Ruhamah and Lo-Ammi (chapter 1). Like Gomer wanton Israel is running after other "loves" instead of being faithful in her "marriage" to God. However, Israel's rebellion, apostasy and fornication eventually give way to God's love. Finally, Hosea outlines Israel's restoration and new marriage covenant.

Key Words: "Marriage"; "Forgiveness." Just as Hosea marries Gomer, so God's covenant relationship with Israel represents their "marriage." And just as Hosea reaches out in "forgiveness" to buy back his adulterous wife from a slave market (chapter 3), so God in "forgiveness" continues to seek his own.

Themes: • The love of God is unconditional, eternal and transforming. • God loves us enough to chasten us for our sins. • God hates physical and spiritual adultery. • There is absolutely nothing we can do which will separate us from God's compassion and love. • God's concern for our entire being includes the success of our marriage. • Unrequited love in our personal lives may help us to understand better the heartache God experiences when mankind rejects his love.

Outline:

1. Hosea is married to Gomer. 1:1-3:5
2. Israel commits spiritual adultery. 4:1-6:3
3. Israel is judged for refusing to repent. 6:4-10:15
4. God's love for Israel promises restoration. 11:1-14:9

HOSEA

1 The word of the LORD that came to
Hosea son of Beeri during the reigns
of Uzziah, Jotham, Ahaz and Hezekiah,
kings of Judah,[a] and during the reign of
Jeroboam[b] son of Jehoash[a] king of Israel:[c]

Hosea's wife and children.

2When the LORD began to speak
through Hosea, the LORD said to him,
"Go, take to yourself an adulterous[d] wife
and children of unfaithfulness, because
the land is guilty of the vilest adultery[e]
in departing from the LORD." 3So he married Gomer daughter of Diblaim, and she
conceived and bore him a son.
4Then the LORD said to Hosea, "Call
him Jezreel,[f] because I will soon punish the house of Jehu for the massacre at
Jezreel, and I will put an end to the kingdom of Israel. 5In that day I will break
Israel's bow in the Valley of Jezreel.[g]"
6Gomer[h] conceived again and gave
birth to a daughter. Then the LORD said
to Hosea, "Call her Lo-Ruhamah,[b] for I
will no longer show love to the house
of Israel,[i] that I should at all forgive
them. 7Yet I will show love to the house
of Judah; and I will save them—not by
bow,[j] sword or battle, or by horses
and horsemen, but by the LORD their
God.[k]"
8After she had weaned Lo-Ruhamah,
Gomer had another son. 9Then the LORD
said, "Call him Lo-Ammi,[c] for you are
not my people, and I am not your God.

Reuniting of Judah and Israel.

10"Yet the Israelites will be like the
sand on the seashore, which cannot be
measured or counted.[l] In the place where
it was said to them, 'You are not my people,' they will be called 'sons of the living
God.'[m] 11The people of Judah and the
people of Israel will be reunited,[n] and
they will appoint one leader[o] and will
come up out of the land,[p] for great will
be the day of Jezreel.

2 "Say of your brothers, 'My people,'
and of your sisters, 'My loved one.'[q]

Adulterous Israel.

2"Rebuke your mother,[r] rebuke her,
for she is not my wife,
and I am not her husband.
Let her remove the adulterous[s] look
from her face
and the unfaithfulness from
between her breasts.
3Otherwise I will strip her naked
and make her as bare as on the day
she was born;[t]
I will make her like a desert,[u]
turn her into a parched land,
and slay her with thirst.
4I will not show my love to her
children,[v]
because they are the children of
adultery.
5Their mother has been unfaithful
and has conceived them in disgrace.
She said, 'I will go after my lovers,[w]
who give me my food and my water,
my wool and my linen, my oil and
my drink.'[x]

The LORD's judgment on Israel.

6Therefore I will block her path with
thornbushes;
I will wall her in so that she cannot
find her way.[y]
7She will chase after her lovers but
not catch them;
she will look for them but not
find them.[z]
Then she will say,
'I will go back to my husband as
at first,[a]
for then I was better off[b] than now.'
8She has not acknowledged[c] that I
was the one
who gave her the grain, the new
wine and oil,
who lavished on her the silver and
gold—
which they used for Baal.[d]

1:1 [a]Isa 1:1; Mic 1:1 [b]2Ki 13:13 [c]Am 1:1
1:2 [d]Jer 3:1; Hos 2:2,5; 3:1 [e]Dt 31:16; Jer 3:14; Eze 23:3-21; Hos 5:3
1:4 [f]2Ki 10:1-14; Hos 2:22
1:5 [g]2Ki 15:29
1:6 [h]ver 3 [i]Hos 2:4
1:7 [j]Ps 44:6 [k]Zec 4:6
1:10 [l]Ge 22:17; Jer 33:22 [m]ver 9; Ro 9:26*
1:11 [n]Isa 11:12,13 [o]Jer 23:5-8 [p]Eze 37:15-28
2:1 [q]ver 23
2:2 [r]ver 5; Isa 50:1; Hos 1:2 [s]Eze 23:45
2:3 [t]Eze 16:4,22 [u]Isa 32:13-14
2:4 [v]Eze 8:18
2:5 [w]Jer 3:6 [x]Jer 44:17-18
2:6 [y]Job 3:23; 19:8; La 3:9
2:7 [z]Hos 5:13 [a]Jer 2:2; 3:1 [b]Eze 16:8
2:8 [c]Isa 1:3 [d]Eze 16:15-19; Hos 8:4

a *1* Hebrew *Joash,* a variant of *Jehoash*
b *6* *Lo-Ruhamah* means *not loved.*
c *9* *Lo-Ammi* means *not my people.*

9"Therefore I will take away my grain[a]
when it ripens,
and my new wine[b] when it is ready.
I will take back my wool and my linen,
intended to cover her nakedness.
10So now I will expose her lewdness
before the eyes of her lovers;
no one will take her out of my
hands.[c]
11I will stop[d] all her celebrations:
her yearly festivals, her New Moons,
her Sabbath days—all her
appointed feasts.[e]
12I will ruin her vines[f] and her fig trees,
which she said were her pay from
her lovers;
I will make them a thicket,[g]
and wild animals will devour them.[h]
13I will punish her for the days
she burned incense to the Baals;[i]
she decked herself with rings and
jewelry,[j]
and went after her lovers,[k]
but me she forgot,[l]"
declares the LORD.

Restoration of Israel.

14"Therefore I am now going to allure
her;
I will lead her into the desert
and speak tenderly to her.
15There I will give her back her
vineyards,
and will make the Valley of Achor[d] [m]
a door of hope.
There she will sing[e] [n] as in the days
of her youth,[o]
as in the day she came up out of
Egypt.[p]
16"In that day," declares the LORD,
"you will call me 'my husband';
you will no longer call me 'my
master.[f]'
17I will remove the names of the Baals
from her lips;[q]
no longer will their names be
invoked.[r]
18In that day I will make a covenant
for them
with the beasts of the field and the
birds of the air
and the creatures that move along
the ground.[s]
Bow and sword and battle
I will abolish[t] from the land,
so that all may lie down in safety.[u]
19I will betroth[v] you to me forever;
I will betroth you in[g] righteousness
and justice,[w]
in[h] love and compassion.
20I will betroth you in faithfulness,
and you will acknowledge[x] the LORD.
21"In that day I will respond,"
declares the LORD—
"I will respond[y] to the skies,
and they will respond to the earth;
22and the earth will respond to the grain,
the new wine and oil,[z]
and they will respond to Jezreel.[i]
23I will plant[a] her for myself in the land;
I will show my love to the one I
called 'Not my loved one.[j] [b]'
I will say to those called 'Not my
people,[k]' 'You are my people';[c]
and they will say, 'You are my
God.[d]'"

Reconciliation of Hosea and Gomer.

3 The LORD said to me, "Go, show
your love to your wife again, though
she is loved by another and is an adulteress.[e] Love her as the LORD loves the Israelites, though they turn to other gods and
love the sacred raisin cakes.[f]"
2So I bought her for fifteen shekels[l]
of silver and about a homer and a
lethek[m] of barley. 3Then I told her, "You
are to live with[n] me many days; you
must not be a prostitute or be intimate
with any man, and I will live with[n]
you."
4For the Israelites will live many days
without king or prince,[g] without sacrifice[h] or sacred stones, without ephod or
idol.[i] 5Afterward the Israelites will return

2:9 [a]Hos 8:7 [b]Hos 9:2
2:10 [c]Eze 16:37
2:11 [d]Jer 7:34 [e]Isa 1:14; Jer 16:9; Hos 3:4; Am 8:10
2:12 [f]Isa 7:23; Jer 8:13 [g]Isa 5:6 [h]Hos 13:8
2:13 [i]Hos 11:2 [j]Eze 16:17 [k]Hos 4:13 [l]Hos 4:6; 8:14; 13:6
2:15 [m]Jos 7:24,26 [n]Ex 15:1-18 [o]Jer 2:2 [p]Hos 12:9
2:17 [q]Ex 23:13; Ps 16:4 [r]Jos 23:7
2:18 [s]Job 5:22 [t]Isa 2:4 [u]Jer 23:6; Eze 34:25
2:19 [v]Isa 62:4 [w]Isa 1:27
2:20 [x]Jer 31:34; Hos 6:6; 13:4
2:21 [y]Isa 55:10; Zec 8:12
2:22 [z]Jer 31:12; Joel 2:19
2:23 [a]Jer 31:27 [b]Hos 1:6 [c]Hos 1:10 [d]Ro 9:25*; 1Pe 2:10
3:1 [e]Hos 1:2 [f]2Sa 6:19
3:4 [g]Hos 13:11 [h]Da 11:31; Hos 2:11 [i]Jdg 17:5-6; Zec 10:2

d *15* *Achor* means *trouble.* e *15* Or *respond*
f *16* Hebrew *baal* g *19* Or *with*; also in verse 20
h *19* Or *with* i *22* *Jezreel* means *God plants.*
j *23* Hebrew *Lo-Ruhamah* k *23* Hebrew *Lo-Ammi*
l *2* That is, about 6 ounces (about 170 grams)
m *2* That is, probably about 10 bushels (about 330 liters) n *3* Or *wait for*

and seek the LORD their God and David their king.[a] They will come trembling to the LORD and to his blessings in the last days.[b]

No faithfulness, love or acknowledgment of God.

4 Hear the word of the LORD, you Israelites,
because the LORD has a charge to bring
against you who live in the land:
"There is no faithfulness, no love,
no acknowledgment[c] of God in the land.
2 There is only cursing,[o] lying[d] and murder,[e]
stealing[f] and adultery;
they break all bounds,
and bloodshed follows bloodshed.
3 Because of this the land mourns,[p][g]
and all who live in it waste away;[h]
the beasts of the field and the birds of the air
and the fish of the sea are dying.[i]

4 "But let no man bring a charge,
let no man accuse another,
for your people are like those
who bring charges against a priest.[j]
5 You stumble[k] day and night,
and the prophets stumble with you.
So I will destroy your mother[l]—
6 my people are destroyed from lack of knowledge.[m]

"Because you have rejected knowledge,
I also reject you as my priests;
because you have ignored the law[n] of your God,
I also will ignore your children.
7 The more the priests increased,
the more they sinned against me;
they exchanged[q] their[r] Glory[o] for something disgraceful.[p]
8 They feed on the sins of my people
and relish their wickedness.[q]
9 And it will be: Like people, like priests.[r]
I will punish both of them for their ways
and repay them for their deeds.[s]

10 "They will eat but not have enough;[t]
they will engage in prostitution but not increase,
because they have deserted[u] the LORD
to give themselves 11 to prostitution,[v]
to old wine and new,
which take away the understanding[w] 12 of my people.
They consult a wooden idol[x]
and are answered by a stick of wood.[y]
A spirit of prostitution leads them astray;[z]
they are unfaithful to their God.
13 They sacrifice on the mountaintops
and burn offerings on the hills,
under oak,[a] poplar and terebinth,
where the shade is pleasant.[b]
Therefore your daughters turn to prostitution[c]
and your daughters-in-law to adultery.[d]

14 "I will not punish your daughters
when they turn to prostitution,
nor your daughters-in-law
when they commit adultery,
because the men themselves consort with harlots[e]
and sacrifice with shrine prostitutes—
a people without understanding will come to ruin!

15 "Though you commit adultery, O Israel,
let not Judah become guilty.

"Do not go to Gilgal;[f]
do not go up to Beth Aven.[s]
And do not swear, 'As surely as the LORD lives!'
16 The Israelites are stubborn,
like a stubborn heifer.
How then can the LORD pasture them
like lambs[g] in a meadow?
17 Ephraim is joined to idols;
leave him alone!

3:5 [a] Eze 34:23-24 [b] Jer 50:4-5
4:1 [c] Jer 7:28
4:2 [d] Hos 7:3; 10:4 [e] Hos 6:9 [f] Hos 7:1
4:3 [g] Jer 4:28 [h] Isa 33:9 [i] Jer 4:25; Zep 1:3
4:4 [j] Dt 17:12; Eze 3:26
4:5 [k] Eze 14:7 [l] Hos 2:2
4:6 [m] Hos 2:13; Mal 2:7-8 [n] Hos 8:1,12
4:7 [o] Hab 2:16 [p] Hos 10:1,6; 13:6
4:8 [q] Isa 56:11; Mic 3:11
4:9 [r] Isa 24:2 [s] Jer 5:31; Hos 8:13; 9:9,15
4:10 [t] Lev 26:26; Mic 6:14 [u] Hos 7:14; 9:17
4:11 [v] Hos 5:4 [w] Pr 20:1
4:12 [x] Jer 2:27 [y] Hab 2:19 [z] Isa 44:20
4:13 [a] Isa 1:29 [b] Jer 3:6; Hos 11:2 [c] Jer 2:20; Am 7:17 [d] Hos 2:13
4:14 [e] ver 11
4:15 [f] Hos 9:15; 12:11; Am 4:4
4:16 [g] Isa 5:17; 7:25

[o] *2* That is, to pronounce a curse upon [p] *3* Or *dries up* [q] *7* Syriac and an ancient Hebrew scribal tradition; Masoretic Text *I will exchange* [r] *7* Masoretic Text; an ancient Hebrew scribal tradition *my* [s] *15* *Beth Aven* means *house of wickedness* (a name for Bethel, which means *house of God*).

[18]Even when their drinks are gone,
they continue their prostitution;
their rulers dearly love shameful
ways.
[19]A whirlwind[a] will sweep them away,
and their sacrifices will bring them
shame.[b]

Judgments against Judah and Israel.

5 "Hear this, you priests!
Pay attention, you Israelites!
Listen, O royal house!
This judgment is against you:
You have been a snare[c] at Mizpah,
a net spread out on Tabor.
[2]The rebels are deep in slaughter.[d]
I will discipline all of them.[e]
[3]I know all about Ephraim;
Israel is not hidden from me.
Ephraim, you have now turned to
prostitution;
Israel is corrupt.[f]

[4]"Their deeds do not permit them
to return to their God.
A spirit of prostitution[g] is in their
heart;
they do not acknowledge[h] the LORD.
[5]Israel's arrogance testifies[i] against
them;
the Israelites, even Ephraim, stumble
in their sin;
Judah also stumbles with them.
[6]When they go with their flocks and
herds
to seek the LORD,[j]
they will not find him;
he has withdrawn[k] himself from
them.
[7]They are unfaithful[l] to the LORD;
they give birth to illegitimate[m]
children.
Now their New Moon festivals
will devour[n] them and their fields.

[8]"Sound the trumpet in Gibeah,[o]
the horn in Ramah.[p]
Raise the battle cry in Beth Aven[t];[q]
lead on, O Benjamin.
[9]Ephraim will be laid waste
on the day of reckoning.[r]

4:19 [a]Hos 12:1; 13:15 [b]Isa 1:29
5:1 [c]Hos 6:9; 9:8
5:2 [d]Hos 4:2 [e]Hos 9:15
5:3 [f]Hos 6:10
5:4 [g]Hos 4:11 [h]Hos 4:6
5:5 [i]Hos 7:10
5:6 [j]Mic 6:6-7 [k]Pr 1:28; Isa 1:15; Eze 8:6
5:7 [l]Hos 6:7 [m]Hos 2:4 [n]Hos 2:11-12
5:8 [o]Hos 9:9; 10:9 [p]Isa 10:29 [q]Hos 4:15
5:9 [r]Isa 37:3; Hos 9:11-17 [s]Isa 46:10; Zec 1:6
5:10 [t]Dt 19:14 [u]Eze 7:8
5:11 [v]Hos 9:16; Mic 6:16
5:12 [w]Isa 51:8
5:13 [x]Hos 7:11; 8:9 [y]Hos 10:6 [z]Hos 14:3 [a]Jer 30:12
5:14 [b]Am 3:4 [c]Mic 5:8
5:15 [d]Hos 3:5 [e]Jer 2:27 [f]Isa 64:9
6:1 [g]Hos 5:14 [h]Dt 32:39; Jer 30:17; Hos 14:4
6:2 [i]Ps 30:5
6:3 [j]Joel 2:23 [k]Ps 72:6
6:4 [l]Hos 11:8

Among the tribes of Israel
I proclaim what is certain.[s]
[10]Judah's leaders are like those
who move boundary stones.[t]
I will pour out my wrath[u] on them
like a flood of water.
[11]Ephraim is oppressed,
trampled in judgment,
intent on pursuing idols.[u][v]
[12]I am like a moth[w] to Ephraim,
like rot to the people of Judah.

[13]"When Ephraim saw his sickness,
and Judah his sores,
then Ephraim turned to Assyria,[x]
and sent to the great king for help.[y]
But he is not able to cure[z] you,
not able to heal your sores.[a]
[14]For I will be like a lion[b] to Ephraim,
like a great lion to Judah.
I will tear them to pieces and go away;
I will carry them off, with no one
to rescue them.[c]
[15]Then I will go back to my place
until they admit their guilt.
And they will seek my face;[d]
in their misery[e] they will earnestly
seek me.[f]"

Exhortation to repent.

6 "Come, let us return to the LORD.
He has torn us to pieces[g]
but he will heal us;
he has injured us
but he will bind up our wounds.[h]
[2]After two days he will revive us;[i]
on the third day he will restore us,
that we may live in his presence.
[3]Let us acknowledge the LORD;
let us press on to acknowledge him.
As surely as the sun rises,
he will appear;
he will come to us like the winter
rains,[j]
like the spring rains that water the
earth.[k]"

[4]"What can I do with you, Ephraim?[l]
What can I do with you, Judah?

[t]8 *Beth Aven* means *house of wickedness* (a name for Bethel, which means *house of God*). [u]11 The meaning of the Hebrew for this word is uncertain.

Your love is like the morning mist,
like the early dew that disappears.[a]
5Therefore I cut you in pieces with
my prophets,
I killed you with the words of my
mouth;[b]
my judgments flashed like
lightning upon you.[c]
6For I desire mercy, not sacrifice,[d]
and acknowledgment[e] of God
rather than burnt offerings.

Indictment of the wicked.

7Like Adam,[v] they have broken the
covenant[f]—
they were unfaithful[g] to me there.
8Gilead is a city of wicked men,
stained with footprints of blood.
9As marauders lie in ambush for a man,
so do bands of priests;
they murder on the road to Shechem,
committing shameful crimes.[h]
10I have seen a horrible[i] thing
in the house of Israel.
There Ephraim is given to
prostitution
and Israel is defiled.[j]

11"Also for you, Judah,
a harvest[k] is appointed.

"Whenever I would restore the
fortunes of my people,
7 1whenever I would heal Israel,
the sins of Ephraim are exposed
and the crimes of Samaria revealed.[l]
They practice deceit,[m]
thieves break into houses,[n]
bandits rob in the streets;
2but they do not realize
that I remember[o] all their evil deeds.
Their sins engulf them;[p]
they are always before me.

3"They delight the king with their
wickedness,
the princes with their lies.[q]
4They are all adulterers,[r]
burning like an oven
whose fire the baker need not stir
from the kneading of the dough till
it rises.
5On the day of the festival of our king
the princes become inflamed with
wine,[s]
and he joins hands with the
mockers.
6Their hearts are like an oven;[t]
they approach him with intrigue.
Their passion smolders all night;
in the morning it blazes like a
flaming fire.
7All of them are hot as an oven;
they devour their rulers.
All their kings fall,
and none of them calls[u] on me.

8"Ephraim mixes[v] with the nations;
Ephraim is a flat cake not
turned over.
9Foreigners sap his strength,[w]
but he does not realize it.
His hair is sprinkled with gray,
but he does not notice.
10Israel's arrogance testifies against
him,[x]
but despite all this
he does not return to the LORD his God
or search[y] for him.

11"Ephraim is like a dove,[z]
easily deceived and senseless—
now calling to Egypt,
now turning to Assyria.[a]
12When they go, I will throw my net[b]
over them;
I will pull them down like birds of
the air.
When I hear them flocking together,
I will catch them.
13Woe[c] to them,
because they have strayed[d] from me!
Destruction to them,
because they have rebelled
against me!
I long to redeem them
but they speak lies against me.[e]
14They do not cry out to me from their
hearts[f]
but wail upon their beds.
They gather together[w] for grain and
new wine[g]
but turn away from me.[h]

6:4 [a]Hos 7:1; 13:3 **6:5** [b]Jer 1:9-10; 23:29 [c]Heb 4:12 **6:6** [d]Isa 1:11; Mt 9:13*; 12:7* [e]Hos 2:20 **6:7** [f]Hos 8:1 [g]Hos 5:7 **6:9** [h]Jer 7:9-10; Eze 22:9; Hos 7:1 **6:10** [i]Jer 5:30 [j]Hos 5:3 **6:11** [k]Jer 51:33; Joel 3:13 **7:1** [l]Hos 6:4 [m]ver 13 [n]Hos 4:2 **7:2** [o]Jer 14:10; Hos 8:13 [p]Jer 2:19 **7:3** [q]Hos 4:2; Mic 7:3 **7:4** [r]Jer 9:2 **7:5** [s]Isa 28:1,7 **7:6** [t]Ps 21:9 **7:7** [u]ver 16 **7:8** [v]ver 11; Ps 106:35; Hos 5:13 **7:9** [w]Isa 1:7; Hos 8:7 **7:10** [x]Hos 5:5 [y]Isa 9:13 **7:11** [z]Hos 11:11 [a]Hos 5:13; 12:1 **7:12** [b]Eze 12:13 **7:13** [c]Hos 9:12 [d]Jer 14:10; Eze 34:4-6; Hos 9:17 [e]ver 1; Mt 23:37 **7:14** [f]Jer 3:10 [g]Am 2:8 [h]Hos 13:16

v *7* Or *As at Adam*; or *Like men*   w *14* Most Hebrew manuscripts; some Hebrew manuscripts and Septuagint *They slash themselves*

[15]I trained them and strengthened them,
but they plot evil[a] against me.
[16]They do not turn to the Most High;
they are like a faulty bow.[b]
Their leaders will fall by the sword
because of their insolent words.
For this they will be ridiculed[c]
in the land of Egypt.[d]

Israel will reap the whirlwind.

8 "Put the trumpet to your lips!
An eagle[e] is over the house of
the LORD
because the people have broken my
covenant
and rebelled against my law.[f]
[2]Israel cries out to me,
'O our God, we acknowledge you!'
[3]But Israel has rejected what is good;
an enemy will pursue him.
[4]They set up kings without my consent;
they choose princes without
my approval.[g]
With their silver and gold
they make idols[h] for themselves
to their own destruction.
[5]Throw out your calf-idol, O Samaria![i]
My anger burns against them.
How long will they be incapable of
purity?[j]
[6] They are from Israel!
This calf—a craftsman has made it;
it is not God.
It will be broken in pieces,
that calf of Samaria.

[7]"They sow the wind
and reap the whirlwind.[k]
The stalk has no head;
it will produce no flour.
Were it to yield grain,
foreigners would swallow it up.[l]
[8]Israel is swallowed up;[m]
now she is among the nations
like a worthless[n] thing.
[9]For they have gone up to Assyria
like a wild donkey wandering alone.
Ephraim has sold herself to lovers.
[10]Although they have sold themselves
among the nations,
I will now gather them together.[o]
They will begin to waste away[p]
under the oppression of the mighty
king.

[11]"Though Ephraim built many altars
for sin offerings,
these have become altars for
sinning.[q]
[12]I wrote for them the many things
of my law,
but they regarded them as
something alien.
[13]They offer sacrifices given to me
and they eat[r] the meat,
but the LORD is not pleased with
them.
Now he will remember[s] their
wickedness
and punish their sins:[t]
They will return to Egypt.[u]
[14]Israel has forgotten[v] his Maker
and built palaces;
Judah has fortified many towns.
But I will send fire upon their cities
that will consume their fortresses."[w]

Israel's days of reckoning.

9 Do not rejoice, O Israel;
do not be jubilant[x] like the other
nations.
For you have been unfaithful[y] to
your God;
you love the wages of a prostitute
at every threshing floor.
[2]Threshing floors and winepresses
will not feed the people;
the new wine[z] will fail them.
[3]They will not remain[a] in the LORD's
land;
Ephraim will return to Egypt[b]
and eat unclean[x] food in Assyria.[c]
[4]They will not pour out wine
offerings to the LORD,
nor will their sacrifices
please[d] him.
Such sacrifices will be to them like
the bread of mourners;
all who eat them will be unclean.[e]
This food will be for themselves;
it will not come into the temple of
the LORD.

x3 That is, ceremonially unclean

7:15 [a]Na 1:9,11
7:16 [b]Ps 78:9,57 [c]Eze 23:32 [d]Hos 9:3
8:1 [e]Dt 28:49; Jer 4:13 [f]Hos 4:6; 6:7
8:4 [g]Hos 13:10 [h]Hos 2:8
8:5 [i]Hos 10:5 [j]Jer 13:27
8:7 [k]Pr 22:8; Isa 66:15; Hos 10:12-13; Na 1:3 [l]Hos 2:9
8:8 [m]Jer 51:34 [n]Jer 22:28
8:10 [o]Eze 16:37; 22:20 [p]Jer 42:2
8:11 [q]Hos 10:1; 12:11
8:13 [r]Jer 7:21 [s]Hos 7:2 [t]Hos 4:9 [u]Hos 9:3,6
8:14 [v]Dt 32:18; Hos 2:13 [w]Jer 17:27
9:1 [x]Isa 22:12-13 [y]Hos 10:5
9:2 [z]Hos 2:9
9:3 [a]Lev 25:23 [b]Hos 8:13 [c]Eze 4:13; Hos 7:11
9:4 [d]Jer 6:20; Hos 8:13 [e]Hag 2:13-14

5What will you do[a] on the day of your
appointed feasts,[b]
on the festival days of the LORD?
6Even if they escape from destruction,
Egypt will gather them,
and Memphis[c] will bury them.
Their treasures of silver will be
taken over by briers,
and thorns[d] will overrun their tents.
7The days of punishment[e] are coming,
the days of reckoning are at hand.
Let Israel know this.
Because your sins[f] are so many
and your hostility so great,
the prophet is considered a fool,[g]
the inspired man a maniac.
8The prophet, along with my God,
is the watchman over Ephraim,[y]
yet snares[h] await him on all his paths,
and hostility in the house of his God.
9They have sunk deep into corruption,
as in the days of Gibeah.[i]
God will remember[j] their wickedness
and punish them for their sins.

10"When I found Israel,
it was like finding grapes in the
desert;
when I saw your fathers,
it was like seeing the early fruit on
the fig tree.
But when they came to Baal Peor,[k]
they consecrated themselves to
that shameful idol[l]
and became as vile as the thing
they loved.
11Ephraim's glory will fly away like a
bird[m]—
no birth, no pregnancy, no
conception.[n]
12Even if they rear children,
I will bereave them of every one.
Woe[o] to them
when I turn away from them![p]
13I have seen Ephraim, like Tyre,
planted in a pleasant place.[q]
But Ephraim will bring out
their children to the slayer."

14Give them, O LORD—
what will you give them?
Give them wombs that miscarry
and breasts that are dry.[r]

15"Because of all their wickedness in
Gilgal,[s]
I hated them there.
Because of their sinful deeds,[t]
I will drive them out of my house.
I will no longer love them;
all their leaders are rebellious.[u]
16Ephraim[v] is blighted,
their root is withered,
they yield no fruit.[w]
Even if they bear children,
I will slay[x] their cherished offspring."

17My God will reject them
because they have not obeyed[y] him;
they will be wanderers among the
nations.[z]

10 Israel was a spreading vine;[a]
he brought forth fruit for
himself.
As his fruit increased,
he built more altars;[b]
as his land prospered,
he adorned his sacred stones.[c]
2Their heart is deceitful,[d]
and now they must bear their guilt.[e]
The LORD will demolish their altars[f]
and destroy their sacred stones.[g]

3Then they will say, "We have no king
because we did not revere the LORD.
But even if we had a king,
what could he do for us?"
4They make many promises,
take false oaths[h]
and make agreements;[i]
therefore lawsuits spring up
like poisonous weeds in a plowed
field.
5The people who live in Samaria fear
for the calf-idol of Beth Aven.[z] [j]
Its people will mourn over it,
and so will its idolatrous priests,[k]
those who had rejoiced over its
splendor,
because it is taken from them into
exile.[l]

9:5 [a]Isa 10:3; Jer 5:31 [b]Hos 2:11
9:6 [c]Isa 19:13 [d]Isa 5:6; Hos 10:8
9:7 [e]Isa 34:8; Jer 10:15; Mic 7:4 [f]Jer 16:18 [g]Isa 44:25; La 2:14; Eze 14:9-10
9:8 [h]Hos 5:1
9:9 [i]Jdg 19:16-30; Hos 5:8; 10:9 [j]Hos 8:13
9:10 [k]Nu 25:1-5; Ps 106:28-29 [l]Jer 11:13; Hos 4:14
9:11 [m]Hos 4:7; 10:5 [n]ver 14
9:12 [o]Hos 7:13 [p]Dt 31:17
9:13 [q]Eze 27:3
9:14 [r]ver 11; Lk 23:29
9:15 [s]Hos 4:15 [t]Hos 7:2 [u]Isa 1:23; Hos 4:9; 5:2
9:16 [v]Hos 5:11 [w]Hos 8:7 [x]ver 12
9:17 [y]Hos 4:10 [z]Dt 28:65; Hos 7:13
10:1 [a]Eze 15:2 [b]1Ki 14:23 [c]Hos 8:11; 12:11
10:2 [d]1Ki 18:21 [e]Hos 13:16 [f]ver 8 [g]Mic 5:13
10:4 [h]Hos 4:2 [i]Eze 17:19; Am 5:7
10:5 [j]Hos 5:8 [k]2Ki 23:5 [l]Hos 8:5; 9:1,3,11

y8 Or *The prophet is the watchman over Ephraim, / the people of my God* z5 *Beth Aven* means *house of wickedness* (a name for Bethel, which means *house of God*).

6It will be carried to Assyria[a]
as tribute for the great king.[b]
Ephraim will be disgraced;[c]
Israel will be ashamed of its
wooden idols.[a]
7Samaria and its king will float away[d]
like a twig on the surface of the
waters.
8The high places of wickedness[b][e] will
be destroyed—
it is the sin of Israel.
Thorns[f] and thistles will grow up
and cover their altars.[g]
Then they will say to the mountains,
"Cover us!"
and to the hills, "Fall on us!"[h]

9"Since the days of Gibeah,[i] you have
sinned, O Israel,
and there you have remained.[c]
Did not war overtake
the evildoers in Gibeah?
10When I please, I will punish[j] them;
nations will be gathered against them
to put them in bonds for their
double sin.
11Ephraim is a trained heifer
that loves to thresh;
so I will put a yoke
on her fair neck.
I will drive Ephraim,
Judah must plow,
and Jacob must break up the ground.
12Sow for yourselves righteousness,[k]
reap the fruit of unfailing love,
and break up your unplowed ground;[l]
for it is time to seek[m] the LORD,
until he comes
and showers righteousness[n] on you.
13But you have planted wickedness,
you have reaped evil,[o]
you have eaten the fruit of
deception.
Because you have depended on your
own strength
and on your many warriors,[p]
14the roar of battle will rise against
your people,
so that all your fortresses will be
devastated[q]—
as Shalman devastated Beth Arbel on
the day of battle,
when mothers were dashed to the
ground with their children.[r]
15Thus will it happen to you, O Bethel,
because your wickedness is great.
When that day dawns,
the king of Israel will be
completely destroyed.[s]

God still loves rebellious Israel.

11 "When Israel was a child, I loved
him,
and out of Egypt I called my son.[t]
2But the more I[d] called Israel,
the further they went from me.[e]
They sacrificed to the Baals[u]
and they burned incense to images.[v]
3It was I who taught Ephraim to walk,
taking them by the arms;[w]
but they did not realize
it was I who healed[x] them.
4I led them with cords of human
kindness,
with ties of love;[y]
I lifted the yoke[z] from their neck
and bent down to feed[a] them.

5"Will they not return to Egypt[b]
and will not Assyria[c] rule over them
because they refuse to repent?
6Swords[d] will flash in their cities,
will destroy the bars of their gates
and put an end to their plans.
7My people are determined to turn
from me.[e]
Even if they call to the Most High,
he will by no means exalt them.

8"How can I give you up, Ephraim?[f]
How can I hand you over, Israel?
How can I treat you like Admah?
How can I make you like Zeboiim?[g]
My heart is changed within me;
all my compassion is aroused.
9I will not carry out my fierce anger,[h]
nor will I turn and devastate[i]
Ephraim.
For I am God, and not man[j]—
the Holy One among you.

10:6 [a]Hos 11:5 [b]Hos 5:13 [c]Isa 30:3; Hos 4:7
10:7 [d]Hos 13:11
10:8 [e]1Ki 12:28-30; Hos 4:13 [f]Hos 9:6 [g]ver 2; Isa 32:13 [h]Lk 23:30*; Rev 6:16
10:9 [i]Hos 5:8
10:10 [j]Eze 5:13; Hos 4:9
10:12 [k]Pr 11:18 [l]Jer 4:3 [m]Hos 12:6 [n]Isa 45:8
10:13 [o]Job 4:8; Hos 7:3; 11:12; Gal 6:7-8 [p]Ps 33:16
10:14 [q]Isa 17:3 [r]Hos 13:16
10:15 [s]ver 7
11:1 [t]Ex 4:22; Hos 12:9,13; 13:4; Mt 2:15*
11:2 [u]Hos 2:13 [v]2Ki 17:15; Isa 65:7; Jer 18:15
11:3 [w]Dt 1:31; Hos 7:15 [x]Jer 30:17
11:4 [y]Jer 31:2-3 [z]Lev 26:13 [a]Ex 16:32; Ps 78:25
11:5 [b]Hos 7:16 [c]Hos 10:6
11:6 [d]Hos 13:16
11:7 [e]Jer 3:6-7; 8:5
11:8 [f]Hos 6:4 [g]Ge 14:8
11:9 [h]Dt 13:17; Jer 30:11 [i]Mal 3:6 [j]Nu 23:19

a6 Or *its counsel* b8 Hebrew *aven,* a reference to Beth Aven (a derogatory name for Bethel) c9 Or *there a stand was taken* d2 Some Septuagint manuscripts; Hebrew *they* e2 Septuagint; Hebrew *them*

I will not come in wrath.[f]
10They will follow the LORD;
he will roar like a lion.
When he roars,
his children will come trembling
from the west.[a]
11They will come trembling
like birds from Egypt,
like doves from Assyria.[b]
I will settle them in their homes,"[c]
declares the LORD.

Israel is exhorted to repent.

12Ephraim has surrounded me with lies,[d]
the house of Israel with deceit.
And Judah is unruly against God,
even against the faithful Holy One.

12 1Ephraim feeds on the wind;[e]
he pursues the east wind all day
and multiplies lies and violence.
He makes a treaty with Assyria
and sends olive oil to Egypt.[f]
2The LORD has a charge[g] to bring
against Judah;
he will punish Jacob[g] according to
his ways
and repay him according to his
deeds.[h]
3In the womb he grasped his
brother's heel;[i]
as a man he struggled[j] with God.
4He struggled with the angel and
overcame him;
he wept and begged for his favor.
He found him at Bethel[k]
and talked with him there—
5the LORD God Almighty,
the LORD is his name[l] of renown!
6But you must return to your God;
maintain love and justice,[m]
and wait for your God always.[n]

7The merchant uses dishonest scales;[o]
he loves to defraud.
8Ephraim boasts,
"I am very rich; I have become
wealthy.[p]
With all my wealth they will not find
in me
any iniquity or sin."
9"I am the LORD your God,
who brought you out of[h] Egypt;[q]
I will make you live in tents[r] again,
as in the days of your appointed
feasts.
10I spoke to the prophets,
gave them many visions
and told parables[s] through them."[t]

11Is Gilead wicked?[u]
Its people are worthless!
Do they sacrifice bulls in Gilgal?[v]
Their altars will be like piles of stones
on a plowed field.[w]
12Jacob fled to the country of Aram[i];[x]
Israel served to get a wife,
and to pay for her he tended sheep.[y]
13The LORD used a prophet to bring
Israel up from Egypt,
by a prophet he cared for him.[z]
14But Ephraim has bitterly provoked
him to anger;
his Lord will leave upon him the
guilt of his bloodshed[a]
and will repay him for his contempt.[b]

The LORD's anger against idolatrous Israel.

13 When Ephraim spoke, men
trembled;[c]
he was exalted[d] in Israel.
But he became guilty of Baal
worship[e] and died.
2Now they sin more and more;
they make idols for themselves
from their silver,[f]
cleverly fashioned images,
all of them the work of craftsmen.
It is said of these people,
"They offer human sacrifice
and kiss[j] the calf-idols.[g]"
3Therefore they will be like the
morning mist,
like the early dew that disappears,[h]
like chaff[i] swirling from a
threshing floor,[j]
like smoke[k] escaping through a
window.

11:10 [a]Hos 6:1-3
11:11 [b]Isa 11:11 [c]Eze 28:26
11:12 [d]Hos 4:2
12:1 [e]Eze 17:10 [f]2Ki 17:4
12:2 [g]Mic 6:2 [h]Hos 4:9
12:3 [i]Ge 25:26 [j]Ge 32:24-29
12:4 [k]Ge 28:12-15; 35:15
12:5 [l]Ex 3:15
12:6 [m]Mic 6:8 [n]Hos 6:1-3; 10:12; Mic 7:7
12:7 [o]Am 8:5
12:8 [p]Ps 62:10; Rev 3:17
12:9 [q]Lev 23:43; Hos 11:1 [r]Ne 8:17
12:10 [s]Eze 20:49 [t]2Ki 17:13; Jer 7:25
12:11 [u]Hos 6:8 [v]Hos 4:15 [w]Hos 8:11
12:12 [x]Ge 28:5 [y]Ge 29:18
12:13 [z]Ex 13:3; Isa 63:11-14
12:14 [a]Eze 18:13 [b]Da 11:18
13:1 [c]Jdg 12:1 [d]Jdg 8:1 [e]Hos 11:2
13:2 [f]Isa 46:6; Jer 10:4 [g]Isa 44:17-20
13:3 [h]Hos 6:4 [i]Isa 17:13 [j]Da 2:35 [k]Ps 68:2

[f]9 Or *come against any city* [g]2 *Jacob* means *he grasps the heel* (figuratively, *he deceives*). [h]9 Or *God / ever since you were in* [i]12 That is, Northwest Mesopotamia [j]2 Or *"Men who sacrifice / kiss*

4"But I am the LORD your God,
⌊who brought you⌋ out of[k] Egypt.[a]
You shall acknowledge no God but me,[b]
no Savior[c] except me.
5I cared for you in the desert,
in the land of burning heat.
6When I fed them, they were satisfied;
when they were satisfied, they
became proud;
then they forgot me.[d]
7So I will come upon them like a lion,
like a leopard I will lurk by the path.
8Like a bear robbed of her cubs,[e]
I will attack them and rip them open.
Like a lion I will devour them;
a wild animal will tear them apart.[f]

9"You are destroyed, O Israel,
because you are against me,[g]
against your helper.[h]
10Where is your king,[i] that he may
save you?
Where are your rulers in all your
towns,
of whom you said,
'Give me a king and princes'?[j]
11So in my anger I gave you a king,
and in my wrath I took him away.[k]
12The guilt of Ephraim is stored up,
his sins are kept on record.[l]
13Pains as of a woman in childbirth[m]
come to him,
but he is a child without wisdom;
when the time arrives,
he does not come to the opening of
the womb.[n]

14"I will ransom them from the power
of the grave[l];[o]
I will redeem them from death.
Where, O death, are your plagues?
Where, O grave,[l] is your
destruction?[p]

"I will have no compassion,
15 even though he thrives[q] among his
brothers.
An east wind[r] from the LORD will come,
blowing in from the desert;
his spring will fail
and his well dry up.[s]
His storehouse will be plundered[t]
of all its treasures.

13:4 [a]Hos 12:9 [b]Ex 20:3 [c]Isa 43:11; 45:21-22
13:6 [d]Dt 32:12-15; Hos 2:13
13:8 [e]2Sa 17:8 [f]Ps 50:22
13:9 [g]Jer 2:17-19 [h]Dt 33:29
13:10 [i]2Ki 17:4 [j]1Sa 8:6; Hos 8:4
13:11 [k]1Ki 14:10; Hos 10:7
13:12 [l]Dt 32:34
13:13 [m]Isa 13:8; Mic 4:9-10 [n]Isa 66:9
13:14 [o]Ps 49:15; Eze 37:12-13 [p]1Co 15:55*
13:15 [q]Hos 10:1 [r]Eze 19:12 [s]Jer 51:36 [t]Jer 20:5
13:16 [u]Hos 10:2 [v]Hos 7:14 [w]Hos 11:6 [x]2Ki 8:12; Hos 10:14 [y]2Ki 15:16; Isa 13:16
14:1 [z]Hos 5:5
14:2 [a]Mic 7:18-19 [b]Heb 13:15
14:3 [c]Ps 33:17; Isa 31:1 [d]Hos 8:6 [e]Ps 10:14; 68:5
14:4 [f]Hos 6:1 [g]Zep 3:17
14:5 [h]SS 2:1 [i]Isa 35:2 [j]Job 29:19
14:6 [k]Ps 52:8; Jer 11:16 [l]SS 4:11

16The people of Samaria must bear
their guilt,[u]
because they have rebelled[v]
against their God.
They will fall by the sword;[w]
their little ones will be dashed[x] to
the ground,
their pregnant women[y] ripped
open."

Blessings promised for repentance.

14 Return, O Israel, to the LORD
your God.
Your sins have been your
downfall![z]
2Take words with you
and return to the LORD.
Say to him:
"Forgive all our sins
and receive us graciously,[a]
that we may offer the fruit of
our lips.[m][b]
3Assyria cannot save us;
we will not mount war-horses.[c]
We will never again say 'Our gods'[d]
to what our own hands have made,
for in you the fatherless[e] find
compassion."

4"I will heal[f] their waywardness
and love them freely,[g]
for my anger has turned away
from them.
5I will be like the dew to Israel;
he will blossom like a lily.[h]
Like a cedar of Lebanon[i]
he will send down his roots;[j]
6 his young shoots will grow.
His splendor will be like an olive tree,[k]
his fragrance like a cedar of
Lebanon.[l]
7Men will dwell again in his shade.[m]
He will flourish like the grain.
He will blossom like a vine,
and his fame will be like the
wine[n] from Lebanon.[o]

14:7 [m]Ps 91:1-4 [n]Hos 2:22 [o]Eze 17:23

[k]4 Or *God / ever since you were in* [l]14 Hebrew *Sheol* [m]2 Or *offer our lips as sacrifices of bulls*

8 O Ephraim, what more have I[n] to do
with idols?[a]
I will answer him and care for him.
I am like a green pine tree;
your fruitfulness comes from me."
9 Who is wise?[b] He will realize these
things.
Who is discerning? He will
understand them.[c]
The ways of the LORD are right;[d]
the righteous walk[e] in them,
but the rebellious stumble in them.

14:8 [a]ver 3
14:9 [b]Ps 107:43 [c]Pr 10:29; Isa 1:28 [d]Ps 111:7-8; Zep 3:5; Ac 13:10 [e]Isa 26:7

[n]*8* Or *What more has Ephraim*

JOEL

Author: Joel.

Date Written: Between 835 and 800 B.C.

Time Span: While the exact length of Joel's ministry is not known, his prophecies span the time until the future restoration of Jerusalem is complete.

Title: The book is named after its author: the prophet Joel. Joel has been called the "prophet of Pentecost." The name Joel means "Yahweh is God."

Background: Judah, the setting for the book of Joel, is devastated by a vast horde of locusts. This invasion of locusts destroys everything: the fields of grain, the vineyards, the gardens and the trees. Joel symbolically describes the locusts as a marching human army and views all of this as divine judgment coming against the nation for her sins.

Where Written: Probably Jerusalem.

To Whom: Primarily to the southern kingdom of Judah, but also to all Jews and Gentiles.

Content: A terrible locust plague is followed by a severe famine throughout the land. Joel uses these happenings as the catalyst to send words of warning to Judah that unless the people repent quickly and completely, enemy armies will devour the land as did the natural elements. Joel appeals to all the people and the priests of the land to fast and humble themselves as they seek God's forgiveness. If they will but respond, there will be renewed material and spiritual blessings for the nation. But the day of the Lord is coming. At this time the dreaded locusts will seem as gnats in comparison, as all nations receive their judgment. Finally, Joel gives an account of Jerusalem's ultimate restoration and prosperity.

Key Words: "Locusts"; "Spirit." The book of Joel is highlighted by 2 major events. One is the invasion of "locusts," which devastates the lands of rebellious Judah. The other is God pouring out his "Spirit" on all people, which will result in sons and daughters prophesying, old men dreaming dreams and young men seeing visions (2:28). The initial fulfillment of this is quoted by Peter in Acts as having taken place at Pentecost.

Themes: • Without repentance, judgment will be harsh, thorough and certain. • Our trust should not be in our possessions—which can be taken from us—but in the Lord our God. • God at times may use nature, sorrow or other common occurrences to draw us closer to him. • God's covenant with his people will endure forever.

Outline:

1. Invasion of locusts. 1:1-2:11
2. God's mercy on the repentant. 2:12-2:27
3. Final judgment and triumph of God. 2:28-3:21

JOEL

1 The word of the LORD that came[a] to Joel[b] son of Pethuel.

Joel's prophecy of a locust invasion.

[2]Hear this,[c] you elders;
listen, all who live in the land.[d]
Has anything like this ever happened in your days
or in the days of your forefathers?[e]
[3]Tell it to your children,[f]
and let your children tell it to their children,
and their children to the next generation.
[4]What the locust swarm has left
the great locusts have eaten;
what the great locusts have left
the young locusts have eaten;
what the young locusts have left
other locusts[a] have eaten.[g]

[5]Wake up, you drunkards, and weep!
Wail, all you drinkers of wine;[h]
wail because of the new wine,
for it has been snatched from your lips.
[6]A nation has invaded my land,
powerful and without number;[i]
it has the teeth[j] of a lion,
the fangs of a lioness.
[7]It has laid waste[k] my vines
and ruined my fig trees.[l]
It has stripped off their bark
and thrown it away,
leaving their branches white.

[8]Mourn like a virgin[b] in sackcloth[m]
grieving for the husband[c] of her youth.
[9]Grain offerings and drink offerings[n]
are cut off from the house of the LORD.
The priests are in mourning,
those who minister before the LORD.
[10]The fields are ruined,
the ground is dried up[d];[o]
the grain is destroyed,
the new wine[p] is dried up,
the oil fails.
[11]Despair, you farmers,[q]
wail, you vine growers;
grieve for the wheat and the barley,
because the harvest of the field is destroyed.[r]
[12]The vine is dried up
and the fig tree is withered;
the pomegranate, the palm and the apple tree—
all the trees of the field—are dried up.[s]
Surely the joy of mankind
is withered away.

A call to repentance.

[13]Put on sackcloth,[t] O priests, and mourn;
wail, you who minister[u] before the altar.
Come, spend the night in sackcloth,
you who minister before my God;
for the grain offerings and drink offerings[v]
are withheld from the house of your God.
[14]Declare a holy fast;[w]
call a sacred assembly.
Summon the elders
and all who live in the land
to the house of the LORD your God,
and cry out[x] to the LORD.

[15]Alas for that[y] day!
For the day of the LORD[z] is near;
it will come like destruction from the Almighty.[e]

[16]Has not the food been cut off[a]
before our very eyes—
joy and gladness
from the house of our God?[b]
[17]The seeds are shriveled
beneath the clods.[f][c]
The storehouses are in ruins,
the granaries have been broken down,
for the grain has dried up.
[18]How the cattle moan!

1:1 [a]Jer 1:2 [b]Ac 2:16
1:2 [c]Hos 5:1 [d]Hos 4:1 [e]Joel 2:2
1:3 [f]Ex 10:2; Ps 78:4
1:4 [g]Dt 28:39; Na 3:15
1:5 [h]Joel 3:3
1:6 [i]Joel 2:2,11,25 [j]Rev 9:8
1:7 [k]Isa 5:6 [l]Am 4:9
1:8 [m]ver 13; Isa 22:12; Am 8:10
1:9 [n]Hos 9:4; Joel 2:14,17
1:10 [o]Isa 24:4 [p]Hos 9:2
1:11 [q]Jer 14:3-4; Am 5:16 [r]Isa 17:11
1:12 [s]Hag 2:19
1:13 [t]Jer 4:8 [u]Joel 2:17 [v]ver 9
1:14 [w]2Ch 20:3 [x]Jnh 3:8
1:15 [y]Jer 30:7 [z]Isa 13:6,9; Joel 2:1,11,31
1:16 [a]Isa 3:7 [b]Dt 12:7
1:17 [c]Isa 17:10-11

a *4* The precise meaning of the four Hebrew words used here for locusts is uncertain. b *8* Or *young woman* c *8* Or *betrothed* d *10* Or *ground mourns* e *15* Hebrew *Shaddai* f *17* The meaning of the Hebrew for this word is uncertain.

The herds mill about
because they have no pasture;
even the flocks of sheep are
suffering.

19To you, O LORD, I call,[a]
for fire[b] has devoured the open
pastures[c]
and flames have burned up all the
trees of the field.
20Even the wild animals pant for you;[d]
the streams of water have dried up[e]
and fire has devoured the open
pastures.

An army of locusts.

2 Blow the trumpet[f] in Zion;[g]
sound the alarm on my holy hill.
Let all who live in the land tremble,
for the day of the LORD[h] is coming.
It is close at hand[i]—
2 a day of darkness[j] and gloom,[k]
a day of clouds and blackness.
Like dawn spreading across the
mountains
a large and mighty army[l] comes,
such as never was of old[m]
nor ever will be in ages to come.

3Before them fire devours,
behind them a flame blazes.
Before them the land is like the
garden of Eden,[n]
behind them, a desert waste[o]—
nothing escapes them.
4They have the appearance of horses;[p]
they gallop along like cavalry.
5With a noise like that of chariots[q]
they leap over the mountaintops,
like a crackling fire[r] consuming
stubble,
like a mighty army drawn up for
battle.

6At the sight of them, nations are in
anguish;[s]
every face turns pale.[t]
7They charge like warriors;
they scale walls like soldiers.
They all march in line,
not swerving[u] from their course.
8They do not jostle each other;
each marches straight ahead.
They plunge through defenses
without breaking ranks.
9They rush upon the city;
they run along the wall.
They climb into the houses;
like thieves they enter through the
windows.[v]

10Before them the earth shakes,[w]
the sky trembles,
the sun and moon are darkened,[x]
and the stars no longer shine.[y]
11The LORD[z] thunders
at the head of his army;
his forces are beyond number,
and mighty are those who obey his
command.
The day of the LORD is great;[a]
it is dreadful.
Who can endure it?[b]

A command to return to the LORD.

12"Even now," declares the LORD,
"return[c] to me with all your heart,
with fasting and weeping and
mourning."

13Rend your heart[d]
and not your garments.[e]
Return to the LORD your God,
for he is gracious and
compassionate,
slow to anger and abounding in love,[f]
and he relents from sending
calamity.[g]
14Who knows? He may turn[h] and have
pity
and leave behind a blessing[i]—
grain offerings and drink offerings[j]
for the LORD your God.

15Blow the trumpet[k] in Zion,
declare a holy fast,[l]
call a sacred assembly.[m]
16Gather the people,
consecrate[n] the assembly;
bring together the elders,
gather the children,
those nursing at the breast.
Let the bridegroom[o] leave his room
and the bride her chamber.
17Let the priests, who minister before
the LORD,

1:19
[a]Ps 50:15
[b]Am 7:4
[c]Jer 9:10
1:20
[d]Ps 104:21
[e]1Ki 17:7
2:1
[f]Jer 4:5
[g]ver 15
[h]Joel 1:15;
Zep 1:14-16
[i]Ob 1:15
2:2
[j]Am 5:18
[k]Da 9:12
[l]Joel 1:6
[m]Joel 1:2
2:3
[n]Ge 2:8
[o]Ps 105:34-35
2:4
[p]Rev 9:7
2:5
[q]Rev 9:9
[r]Isa 5:24;
30:30
2:6
[s]Isa 13:8
[t]Na 2:10
2:7
[u]Isa 5:27
2:9
[v]Jer 9:21
2:10
[w]Ps 18:7
[x]Mt 24:29
[y]Isa 13:10;
Eze 32:8
2:11
[z]Joel 1:15
[a]Zep 1:14;
Rev 18:8
[b]Eze 22:14
2:12
[c]Jer 4:1;
Hos 12:6
2:13
[d]Ps 34:18;
Isa 57:15
[e]Job 1:20
[f]Ex 34:6
[g]Jer 18:8
2:14
[h]Jer 26:3
[i]Hag 2:19
[j]Joel 1:13
2:15
[k]Nu 10:2
[l]Jer 36:9
[m]Joel 1:14
2:16
[n]Ex 19:10,22
[o]Ps 19:5

weep between the temple porch
and the altar.[a]
Let them say, "Spare your people,
O LORD.
Do not make your inheritance an
object of scorn,[b]
a byword among the nations.
Why should they say among the
peoples,
'Where is their God?[c]'"

18 Then the LORD will be jealous[d] for
his land
and take pity on his people.

19 The LORD will reply[g] to them:

"I am sending you grain, new wine
and oil,[e]
enough to satisfy you fully;
never again will I make you
an object of scorn[f] to the nations.

20 "I will drive the northern army[g] far
from you,
pushing it into a parched and
barren land,
with its front columns going into the
eastern[h] sea[h]
and those in the rear into the
western sea.[i]
And its stench[i] will go up;
its smell will rise."

Surely he has done great things.[j]
21 Be not afraid,[j] O land;
be glad and rejoice.
Surely the LORD has done great things.[k]
22 Be not afraid, O wild animals,
for the open pastures are becoming
green.[l]
The trees are bearing their fruit;
the fig tree and the vine yield their
riches.[m]
23 Be glad, O people of Zion,
rejoice[n] in the LORD your God,
for he has given you
the autumn rains in
righteousness.[k]
He sends you abundant showers,
both autumn and spring rains,[o] as
before.
24 The threshing floors will be filled
with grain;
the vats will overflow[p] with new
wine[q] and oil.

25 "I will repay you for the years the
locusts have eaten—
the great locust and the young
locust,
the other locusts and the locust
swarm[l]—
my great army that I sent among
you.
26 You will have plenty to eat, until you
are full,[r]
and you will praise[s] the name of
the LORD your God,
who has worked wonders[t] for you;
never again will my people be
shamed.
27 Then you will know that I am in
Israel,
that I am the LORD[u] your God,
and that there is no other;
never again will my people be
shamed.

A pouring out of God's Spirit.

28 "And afterward,
I will pour out my Spirit[v] on all
people.
Your sons and daughters will
prophesy,
your old men will dream dreams,
your young men will see visions.
29 Even on my servants,[w] both men and
women,
I will pour out my Spirit in those
days.
30 I will show wonders in the heavens[x]
and on the earth,[y]
blood and fire and billows of
smoke.
31 The sun will be turned to darkness[z]
and the moon to blood
before the coming of the great and
dreadful day of the LORD.[a]

2:17 [a]Eze 8:16; Mt 23:35 [b]Dt 9:26-29; Ps 44:13 [c]Ps 42:3
2:18 [d]Zec 1:14
2:19 [e]Jer 31:12 [f]Eze 34:29
2:20 [g]Jer 1:14-15 [h]Zec 14:8 [i]Isa 34:3
2:21 [j]Isa 54:4; Zep 3:16-17 [k]Ps 126:3
2:22 [l]Ps 65:12 [m]Joel 1:18-20
2:23 [n]Ps 149:2; Isa 12:6; 41:16; Hab 3:18; Zec 10:7 [o]Lev 26:4
2:24 [p]Lev 26:10; Mal 3:10 [q]Am 9:13
2:26 [r]Lev 26:5 [s]Isa 62:9 [t]Ps 126:3; Isa 25:1
2:27 [u]Joel 3:17
2:28 [v]Eze 39:29
2:29 [w]1Co 12:13; Gal 3:28
2:30 [x]Lk 21:11 [y]Mk 13:24-25
2:31 [z]Mt 24:29 [a]Isa 13:9-10; Mal 4:1,5

[g] *18,19* Or *LORD was jealous . . . / and took pity . . . / 19The LORD replied* [h] *20* That is, the Dead Sea [i] *20* That is, the Mediterranean [j] *20* Or *rise. / Surely it has done great things."* [k] *23* Or / *the teacher for righteousness:* [l] *25* The precise meaning of the four Hebrew words used here for locusts is uncertain.

32 And everyone who calls
on the name of the LORD will be
saved;[a]
for on Mount Zion[b] and in Jerusalem
there will be deliverance,[c]
as the LORD has said,
among the survivors[d]
whom the LORD calls.

Judgment against the nations.

3 "In those days and at that time,
when I restore the fortunes[e] of
Judah and Jerusalem,
2 I will gather all nations
and bring them down to the Valley
of Jehoshaphat.[m]
There I will enter into judgment[f]
against them
concerning my inheritance, my
people Israel,
for they scattered my people among
the nations
and divided up my land.
3 They cast lots for my people
and traded boys for prostitutes;
they sold girls for wine[g]
that they might drink.

4 "Now what have you against me, O
Tyre and Sidon[h] and all you regions of
Philistia? Are you repaying me for something I have done? If you are paying
me back, I will swiftly and speedily return on your own heads what you have
done.[i] 5 For you took my silver and my
gold and carried off my finest treasures
to your temples.[j] 6 You sold the people
of Judah and Jerusalem to the Greeks,
that you might send them far from their
homeland.
7 "See, I am going to rouse them out
of the places to which you sold them,[k]
and I will return on your own heads
what you have done. 8 I will sell your
sons[l] and daughters to the people of Judah,[m] and they will sell them to the Sabeans, a nation far away." The LORD has
spoken.

9 Proclaim this among the nations:
Prepare for war![n]
Rouse the warriors![o]
Let all the fighting men draw near
and attack.
10 Beat your plowshares into swords
and your pruning hooks[p] into
spears.
Let the weakling[q] say,
"I am strong!"
11 Come quickly, all you nations from
every side,
and assemble[r] there.

Bring down your warriors,[s] O LORD!

12 "Let the nations be roused;
let them advance into the Valley of
Jehoshaphat,
for there I will sit
to judge[t] all the nations on every
side.
13 Swing the sickle,
for the harvest[u] is ripe.
Come, trample the grapes,
for the winepress[v] is full
and the vats overflow—
so great is their wickedness!"

14 Multitudes, multitudes
in the valley of decision!
For the day of the LORD[w] is near
in the valley of decision.
15 The sun and moon will be darkened,
and the stars no longer shine.
16 The LORD will roar from Zion
and thunder from Jerusalem;[x]
the earth and the sky will
tremble.[y]
But the LORD will be a refuge for his
people,
a stronghold[z] for the people of
Israel.

Blessings for God's people.

17 "Then you will know that I, the LORD
your God,[a]
dwell in Zion,[b] my holy hill.
Jerusalem will be holy;
never again will foreigners invade
her.

18 "In that day the mountains will drip
new wine,

2:32 [a] Ac 2:17-21*; Ro 10:13* [b] Isa 46:13 [c] Ob 1:17 [d] Isa 11:11; Mic 4:7; Ro 9:27
3:1 [e] Jer 16:15
3:2 [f] Eze 36:5
3:3 [g] Am 2:6
3:4 [h] Mt 11:21 [i] Isa 34:8
3:5 [j] 2Ch 21:16-17
3:7 [k] Isa 43:5-6; Jer 23:8
3:8 [l] Isa 60:14 [m] Isa 14:2
3:9 [n] Isa 8:9 [o] Jer 46:4
3:10 [p] Isa 2:4; Mic 4:3 [q] Zec 12:8
3:11 [r] Eze 38:15-16; Zep 3:8 [s] Isa 13:3
3:12 [t] Isa 2:4
3:13 [u] Hos 6:11; Mt 13:39; Rev 14:15-19 [v] Rev 14:20
3:14 [w] Isa 34:2-8; Joel 1:15
3:16 [x] Am 1:2 [y] Eze 38:19 [z] Jer 16:19
3:17 [a] Joel 2:27 [b] Isa 4:3

[m] 2 *Jehoshaphat* means *the LORD judges*; also in verse 12.

and the hills will flow with milk;[a]
all the ravines of Judah will run
with water.[b]
A fountain will flow out of the LORD's
house[c]
and will water the valley of
acacias.[n][d]
19But Egypt will be desolate,
Edom a desert waste,
because of violence[e] done to the
people of Judah,
in whose land they shed innocent
blood.
20Judah will be inhabited forever[f]
and Jerusalem through all
generations.
21Their bloodguilt, which I have not
pardoned,
I will pardon.[g]"

The LORD dwells in Zion!

3:18 [a]Ex 3:8 [b]Isa 30:25; 35:6 [c]Rev 22:1-2 [d]Eze 47:1; Am 9:13
3:19 [e]Ob 1:10
3:20 [f]Am 9:15
3:21 [g]Eze 36:25

[n] *18* Or *Valley of Shittim*

AMOS

Author: Amos.

Date Written: Between 760 and 753 B.C.

Time Span: 7-10 years.

Title: The book is named after its author: Amos. Amos is often referred to as the "sycamore-fig grower from the south" or the "shepherd of Tekoa."

Background: Amos is a shepherd and a fruit picker from the Judean village of Tekoa (due south of Bethlehem) when God calls him—even though he lacks an education or a priestly background. Amos's mission is directed to his neighbor to the north, Israel. His messages of impending doom and captivity for the nation because of her sins are largely unpopular and unheeded, however, because not since the days of Solomon have times been so good in Israel. Amos's ministry takes place while Jeroboam II reigns over Israel, and Uzziah reigns over Judah (about 40 years prior to Israel's exile to Assyria). Contemporary prophets are Isaiah, Hosea and Micah.

Where Written: Near Jerusalem.

To Whom: Primarily to Israel, but also to Judah and the surrounding nations.

Content: Amos can see that beneath Israel's external prosperity and power, internally the nation is corrupt to the core. The sins for which Amos chastens the people are extensive: neglect of God's Word, idolatry, pagan worship, greed, corrupted leadership and oppression of the poor. Amos begins by pronouncing a judgment upon all the surrounding nations, then upon his own nation of Judah, and finally the harshest judgment is given to Israel. His visions from God reveal the same emphatic message: judgment is near. The book ends with God's promise to Amos of future restoration of the remnant.

Key Words: "Plumb line"; "Hope." God's vision to Amos reveals the "plumb line" (standard) by which the people will be tested and judged (chapter 7). God's nature shines through by the "hope" he offers in his restoration of the land and of the people.

Themes: • Because God is eternally righteous, he demands that we be satisfied with nothing less than his righteousness in our lives. • God hates sin. • The cost for having sin in our lives is expensive. • God often selects individuals to do his work whom the world would reject. • God holds those, to whom more has been given, accountable for more. • God's judgment is certain. • God-fearing people receive blessings from God both now and for all eternity.

Outline:

1. God judges Israel's neighbors. 1:1-2:5
2. God judges Israel. 2:6-6:14
3. Amos has 5 visions. 7:1-9:10
4. Israel is promised restoration.9:11-9:15

AMOS

1 The words of Amos, one of the shepherds of Tekoa[a]—what he saw concerning Israel two years before the earthquake,[b] when Uzziah[c] was king of Judah and Jeroboam[d] son of Jehoash[a] was king of Israel.[e]

2He said:

"The LORD roars[f] from Zion
and thunders from Jerusalem;[g]
the pastures of the shepherds dry up,[b]
and the top of Carmel[h] withers."[i]

Judgments against Damascus, Gaza, Tyre, Edom and Ammon.

3This is what the LORD says:

"For three sins of Damascus,[j]
even for four, I will not turn back ⌊my wrath⌋.[k]
Because she threshed Gilead
with sledges having iron teeth,
4I will send fire[l] upon the house of Hazael
that will consume the fortresses[m] of Ben-Hadad.[n]
5I will break down the gate[o] of Damascus;
I will destroy the king who is in[c] the Valley of Aven[d]
and the one who holds the scepter in Beth Eden.
The people of Aram will go into exile to Kir,[p]"
says the LORD.

6This is what the LORD says:

"For three sins of Gaza,[q]
even for four, I will not turn back ⌊my wrath⌋.
Because she took captive whole communities
and sold them to Edom,[r]
7I will send fire upon the walls of Gaza
that will consume her fortresses.
8I will destroy the king[e] of Ashdod[s]
and the one who holds the scepter in Ashkelon.
I will turn my hand[t] against Ekron,
till the last of the Philistines[u] is dead,"
says the Sovereign LORD.[v]

9This is what the LORD says:

"For three sins of Tyre,[w]
even for four, I will not turn back ⌊my wrath⌋.
Because she sold whole communities of captives to Edom,
disregarding a treaty of brotherhood,
10I will send fire upon the walls of Tyre
that will consume her fortresses.[x]"

11This is what the LORD says:

"For three sins of Edom,[y]
even for four, I will not turn back ⌊my wrath⌋.
Because he pursued his brother with a sword,
stifling all compassion,[f]
because his anger raged continually
and his fury flamed unchecked,[z]
12I will send fire upon Teman[a]
that will consume the fortresses of Bozrah."

13This is what the LORD says:

"For three sins of Ammon,[b]
even for four, I will not turn back ⌊my wrath⌋.
Because he ripped open the pregnant women[c] of Gilead
in order to extend his borders,
14I will set fire to the walls of Rabbah[d]
that will consume her fortresses
amid war cries[e] on the day of battle,
amid violent winds on a stormy day.
15Her king[g] will go into exile,
he and his officials together,"
says the LORD.

1:1 [a]2Sa 14:2 [b]Zec 14:5 [c]2Ch 26:23 [d]2Ki 14:23 [e]Hos 1:1
1:2 [f]Isa 42:13 [g]Joel 3:16 [h]Am 9:3 [i]Jer 12:4
1:3 [j]Isa 8:4; 17:1-3 [k]Am 2:6
1:4 [l]Jer 49:27 [m]Jer 17:27 [n]1Ki 20:1; 2Ki 6:24
1:5 [o]Jer 51:30 [p]2Ki 16:9
1:6 [q]1Sa 6:17; Zep 2:4 [r]Ob 11
1:8 [s]2Ch 26:6 [t]Ps 81:14 [u]Eze 25:16 [v]Isa 14:28-32; Zep 2:4-7
1:9 [w]1Ki 5:1; 9:11-14; Isa 23:1-18; Jer 25:22; Joel 3:4; Mt 11:21
1:10 [x]Zec 9:1-4
1:11 [y]Nu 20:14-21; 2Ch 28:17; Jer 49:7-22 [z]Eze 25:12-14
1:12 [a]Ob 9-10
1:13 [b]Jer 49:1-6; Eze 21:28; 25:2-7 [c]Hos 13:16
1:14 [d]Dt 3:11 [e]Am 2:2

a *1* Hebrew *Joash,* a variant of *Jehoash*
b *2* Or *shepherds mourn* c *5* Or *the inhabitants of*
d *5* *Aven* means *wickedness.* e *8* Or *inhabitants*
f *11* Or *sword / and destroyed his allies*
g *15* Or / *Molech*; Hebrew *malcam*

Judgments against Moab, Judah and Israel.

2 This is what the LORD says:
"For three sins of Moab,
even for four, I will not turn back ⌊my wrath⌋.
Because he burned, as if to lime,
the bones of Edom's king,
2I will send fire upon Moab
that will consume the fortresses of Kerioth.[h]
Moab will go down in great tumult
amid war cries and the blast of the trumpet.
3I will destroy her ruler[a]
and kill all her officials with him,"[b]
says the LORD.

4This is what the LORD says:

"For three sins of Judah,[c]
even for four, I will not turn back ⌊my wrath⌋.
Because they have rejected the law[d] of the LORD
and have not kept his decrees,[e]
because they have been led astray[f] by false gods,[i][g]
the gods[j] their ancestors followed,[h]
5I will send fire upon Judah
that will consume the fortresses of Jerusalem.[i]"

6This is what the LORD says:

"For three sins of Israel,
even for four, I will not turn back ⌊my wrath⌋.
They sell the righteous for silver,
and the needy for a pair of sandals.[j]
7They trample on the heads of the poor
as upon the dust of the ground
and deny justice to the oppressed.
Father and son use the same girl
and so profane my holy name.[k]
8They lie down beside every altar
on garments taken in pledge.[l]
In the house of their god
they drink wine[m] taken as fines.

9"I destroyed the Amorite[n] before them,
though he was tall as the cedars
and strong as the oaks.
I destroyed his fruit above
and his roots[o] below.

10"I brought you up out of Egypt,[p]
and I led you forty years in the desert[q]
to give you the land of the Amorites.[r]
11I also raised up prophets[s] from among your sons
and Nazirites[t] from among your young men.
Is this not true, people of Israel?"
declares the LORD.
12"But you made the Nazirites drink wine
and commanded the prophets not to prophesy.[u]

13"Now then, I will crush you
as a cart crushes when loaded with grain.
14The swift will not escape,
the strong[v] will not muster their strength,
and the warrior will not save his life.[w]
15The archer[x] will not stand his ground,
the fleet-footed soldier will not get away,
and the horseman will not save his life.
16Even the bravest warriors[y]
will flee naked on that day,"
declares the LORD.

Punishment of Israel for her sins.

3 Hear this word the LORD has spoken against you, O people of Israel—against the whole family I brought up out of Egypt:[z]

2"You only have I chosen[a]
of all the families of the earth;
therefore I will punish you
for all your sins.[b]"

3Do two walk together
unless they have agreed to do so?

2:3 [a]Ps 2:10 [b]Isa 40:23
2:4 [c]2Ki 17:19; Hos 12:2 [d]Jer 6:19 [e]Eze 20:24 [f]Isa 9:16 [g]Isa 28:15 [h]2Ki 22:13; Jer 16:12
2:5 [i]Jer 17:27; Hos 8:14
2:6 [j]Joel 3:3; Am 8:6
2:7 [k]Am 5:11-12; 8:4
2:8 [l]Ex 22:26 [m]Am 4:1; 6:6
2:9 [n]Nu 21:23-26; Jos 10:12 [o]Eze 17:9; Mal 4:1
2:10 [p]Ex 20:2; Am 3:1 [q]Dt 2:7 [r]Ex 3:8; Am 9:7
2:11 [s]Dt 18:18; Jer 7:25 [t]Nu 6:2-3; Jdg 13:5
2:12 [u]Isa 30:10; Jer 11:21; Am 7:12-13; Mic 2:6
2:14 [v]Jer 9:23 [w]Ps 33:16; Isa 30:16-17
2:15 [x]Eze 39:3
2:16 [y]Jer 48:41
3:1 [z]Am 2:10
3:2 [a]Dt 7:6; Lk 12:47 [b]Jer 14:10

h2 Or *of her cities* i4 Or *by lies* j4 Or *lies*

4Does a lion roar in the thicket
when he has no prey?[a]
Does he growl in his den
when he has caught nothing?
5Does a bird fall into a trap on the
ground
where no snare has been set?
Does a trap spring up from the earth
when there is nothing to catch?
6When a trumpet sounds in a city,
do not the people tremble?
When disaster comes to a city,
has not the LORD caused it?[b]

7Surely the Sovereign LORD does
nothing
without revealing his plan[c]
to his servants the prophets.[d]

8The lion has roared—
who will not fear?
The Sovereign LORD has spoken—
who can but prophesy?[e]

9Proclaim to the fortresses of Ashdod
and to the fortresses of Egypt:
"Assemble yourselves on the
mountains of Samaria;[f]
see the great unrest within her
and the oppression among her
people."

10"They do not know how to do right,[g]"
declares the LORD,
"who hoard plunder[h] and loot in
their fortresses."[i]

11Therefore this is what the Sovereign
LORD says:

"An enemy will overrun the land;
he will pull down your strongholds
and plunder your fortresses.[j]"

12This is what the LORD says:

"As a shepherd saves from the
lion's[k] mouth
only two leg bones or a piece of an
ear,
so will the Israelites be saved,
those who sit in Samaria
on the edge of their beds
and in Damascus on their
couches.[k l]"

13"Hear this and testify[m] against the
house of Jacob," declares the Lord, the
LORD God Almighty.

14"On the day I punish Israel for her
sins,
I will destroy the altars of Bethel;[n]
the horns of the altar will be cut off
and fall to the ground.
15I will tear down the winter house[o]
along with the summer house;[p]
the houses adorned with ivory[q] will
be destroyed
and the mansions will be
demolished,"
declares the LORD.

Israel's refusal to return to God.

4 Hear this word, you cows of
Bashan[r] on Mount Samaria,[s]
you women who oppress the poor
and crush the needy
and say to your husbands, "Bring us
some drinks![t]"
2The Sovereign LORD has sworn by his
holiness:
"The time will surely come
when you will be taken away[u] with
hooks,
the last of you with fishhooks.
3You will each go straight out
through breaks in the wall,[v]
and you will be cast out toward
Harmon,[l]"
declares the LORD.
4"Go to Bethel and sin;
go to Gilgal[w] and sin yet more.
Bring your sacrifices every morning,[x]
your tithes[y] every three years.[m z]
5Burn leavened bread[a] as a thank
offering
and brag about your freewill
offerings[b]—
boast about them, you Israelites,
for this is what you love to do,"
declares the Sovereign
LORD.

3:4 [a]Ps 104:21; Hos 5:14
3:6 [b]Isa 14:24-27; 45:7
3:7 [c]Ge 18:17; Da 9:22; Jn 15:15; Rev 10:7 [d]Jer 23:22
3:8 [e]Jer 20:9; Jnh 1:1-3; 3:1-3; Ac 4:20
3:9 [f]Am 4:1; 6:1
3:10 [g]Jer 4:22; Am 5:7; 6:12 [h]Hab 2:8 [i]Zep 1:9
3:11 [j]Am 2:5; 6:14
3:12 [k]1Sa 17:34 [l]Am 6:4
3:13 [m]Eze 2:7
3:14 [n]Am 5:5-6
3:15 [o]Jer 36:22 [p]Jdg 3:20 [q]1Ki 22:39
4:1 [r]Ps 22:12; Eze 39:18 [s]Am 3:9 [t]Am 2:8; 5:11; 8:6
4:2 [u]Am 6:8
4:3 [v]Eze 12:5
4:4 [w]Hos 4:15 [x]Nu 28:3 [y]Dt 14:28 [z]Eze 20:39; Am 5:21-22
4:5 [a]Lev 7:13 [b]Lev 22:18-21

[k] *12* The meaning of the Hebrew for this line is uncertain. [l] *3* Masoretic Text; with a different word division of the Hebrew (see Septuagint) *out, O mountain of oppression* [m] *4* Or *tithes on the third day*

6"I gave you empty stomachs[n] in
every city
and lack of bread in every town,
yet you have not returned to me,"
declares the LORD.[a]

7"I also withheld rain from you
when the harvest was still three
months away.
I sent rain on one town,
but withheld it from another.[b]
One field had rain;
another had none and dried up.
8People staggered from town to town
for water[c]
but did not get enough to drink,
yet you have not returned[d] to me,"
declares the LORD.[e]

9"Many times I struck your gardens
and vineyards,
I struck them with blight and
mildew.[f]
Locusts devoured your fig and olive
trees,[g]
yet you have not returned[h] to me,"
declares the LORD.

10"I sent plagues[i] among you
as I did to Egypt.
I killed your young men with the
sword,
along with your captured horses.
I filled your nostrils with the stench
of your camps,
yet you have not returned to me,"
declares the LORD.[j]

11"I overthrew some of you
as I[o] overthrew Sodom and
Gomorrah.[k]
You were like a burning stick
snatched from the fire,
yet you have not returned to me,"
declares the LORD.

12"Therefore this is what I will do to
you, Israel,
and because I will do this to you,
prepare to meet your God,
O Israel."

13He who forms the mountains,[l]
creates the wind,
and reveals his thoughts[m] to man,
he who turns dawn to darkness,
and treads the high places of the
earth[n]—
the LORD God Almighty is his name.[o]

A lament concerning Israel.

5 Hear this word, O house of Israel,
this lament[p] I take up concerning
you:

2"Fallen is Virgin[q] Israel,
never to rise again,
deserted in her own land,
with no one to lift her up.[r]"

3This is what the Sovereign LORD says:

"The city that marches out a
thousand strong for Israel
will have only a hundred left;
the town that marches out a
hundred strong
will have only ten left.[s]"

4This is what the LORD says to the
house of Israel:

"Seek me and live;[t]
5 do not seek Bethel,
do not go to Gilgal,[u]
do not journey to Beersheba.[v]
For Gilgal will surely go into exile,
and Bethel will be reduced to
nothing.[p] [w]"
6Seek[x] the LORD and live,[y]
or he will sweep through the house
of Joseph like a fire;[z]
it will devour,
and Bethel[a] will have no one to
quench it.

7You who turn justice into bitterness[b]
and cast righteousness to the ground
8(he who made the Pleiades and
Orion,[c]
who turns blackness into dawn[d]
and darkens day into night,[e]
who calls for the waters of the sea
and pours them out over the face of
the land—
the LORD is his name[f]—

4:6 [a]Isa 3:1; Jer 5:3; Hag 2:17
4:7 [b]Ex 9:4,26; Dt 11:17; 2Ch 7:13
4:8 [c]Eze 4:16-17 [d]Jer 3:7 [e]Jer 14:4
4:9 [f]Dt 28:22 [g]Joel 1:7 [h]Jer 3:10; Hag 2:17
4:10 [i]Ex 9:3; Dt 28:27 [j]Isa 9:13
4:11 [k]Ge 19:24; Jer 23:14
4:13 [l]Ps 65:6 [m]Da 2:28 [n]Mic 1:3 [o]Isa 47:4; Am 5:8,27; 9:6
5:1 [p]Eze 19:1
5:2 [q]Jer 14:17 [r]Jer 50:32; Am 8:14
5:3 [s]Isa 6:13; Am 6:9
5:4 [t]Isa 55:3; Jer 29:13
5:5 [u]1Sa 11:14; Am 4:4 [v]Am 8:14 [w]1Sa 7:16
5:6 [x]Isa 55:6 [y]ver 14 [z]Dt 4:24 [a]Am 3:14
5:7 [b]Am 6:12
5:8 [c]Job 9:9 [d]Isa 42:16 [e]Ps 104:20; Am 8:9 [f]Ps 104:6-9; Am 4:13

n6 Hebrew *you cleanness of teeth* o11 Hebrew *God* p5 Or *grief*; or *wickedness*; Hebrew *aven,* a reference to Beth Aven (a derogatory name for Bethel)

[9]he flashes destruction on the
 stronghold
 and brings the fortified city to ruin),[a]
[10]you hate the one who reproves in
 court[b]
 and despise him who tells the truth.[c]

[11]You trample on the poor[d]
 and force him to give you grain.
Therefore, though you have built
 stone mansions,[e]
 you will not live in them;
though you have planted lush
 vineyards,
 you will not drink their wine.[f]
[12]For I know how many are your
 offenses
 and how great your sins.

You oppress the righteous and take
 bribes
 and you deprive the poor of justice
 in the courts.[g]
[13]Therefore the prudent man keeps
 quiet in such times,
 for the times are evil.

[14]Seek good, not evil,
 that you may live.
Then the LORD God Almighty will be
 with you,
 just as you say he is.
[15]Hate evil,[h] love good;
 maintain justice in the courts.
Perhaps the LORD God Almighty will
 have mercy[i]
 on the remnant[j] of Joseph.

[16]Therefore this is what the Lord, the
LORD God Almighty, says:

"There will be wailing[k] in all the
 streets
 and cries of anguish in every public
 square.
The farmers[l] will be summoned to
 weep
 and the mourners to wail.
[17]There will be wailing in all the
 vineyards,
 for I will pass through[m] your
 midst,"
 says the LORD.[n]

5:9 [a]Mic 5:11
5:10 [b]Isa 29:21 [c]1Ki 22:8
5:11 [d]Am 8:6 [e]Am 3:15 [f]Mic 6:15
5:12 [g]Isa 5:23; Am 2:6-7
5:15 [h]Ps 97:10; Ro 12:9 [i]Joel 2:14 [j]Mic 5:7,8
5:16 [k]Jer 9:17 [l]Joel 1:11
5:17 [m]Ex 12:12 [n]Isa 16:10; Jer 48:33
5:18 [o]Joel 1:15 [p]Joel 2:2 [q]Isa 5:19,30; Jer 30:7
5:19 [r]Job 20:24; Isa 24:17-18; Jer 15:2-3; 48:44
5:20 [s]Isa 13:10; Zep 1:15
5:21 [t]Lev 26:31 [u]Isa 1:11-16
5:22 [v]Am 4:4; Mic 6:6-7 [w]Isa 66:3
5:23 [x]Am 6:5
5:24 [y]Jer 22:3 [z]Mic 6:8
5:25 [a]Isa 43:23 [b]Dt 32:17
5:27 [c]Am 4:13; Ac 7:42-43*

The day of the LORD.

[18]Woe to you who long
 for the day of the LORD![o]
Why do you long for the day of the
 LORD?
 That day will be darkness,[p] not
 light.[q]
[19]It will be as though a man fled from
 a lion
 only to meet a bear,
as though he entered his house
 and rested his hand on the wall
 only to have a snake bite him.[r]
[20]Will not the day of the LORD be
 darkness, not light—
 pitch-dark, without a ray of
 brightness?[s]

[21]"I hate, I despise your religious
 feasts;[t]
 I cannot stand your assemblies.[u]
[22]Even though you bring me burnt
 offerings and grain offerings,
 I will not accept them.
Though you bring choice fellowship
 offerings,[q]
 I will have no regard for them.[v] [w]
[23]Away with the noise of your songs!
 I will not listen to the music of
 your harps.[x]
[24]But let justice[y] roll on like a river,
 righteousness like a never-failing
 stream![z]

[25]"Did you bring me sacrifices[a] and
 offerings
 forty years[b] in the desert, O house
 of Israel?
[26]You have lifted up the shrine of
 your king,
 the pedestal of your idols,
 the star of your god[r]—
 which you made for yourselves.
[27]Therefore I will send you into exile
 beyond Damascus,"
 says the LORD, whose name is God
 Almighty.[c]

[q]22 Traditionally *peace offerings* [r]26 Or *lifted up Sakkuth your king / and Kaiwan your idols, / your star-gods*; Septuagint *lifted up the shrine of Molech / and the star of your god Rephan, / their idols*

Woe to the complacent.

6 Woe to you[a] who are complacent
in Zion,
and to you who feel secure on
Mount Samaria,
you notable men of the foremost
nation,
to whom the people of Israel
come![b]
2Go to Calneh[c] and look at it;
go from there to great Hamath,[d]
and then go down to Gath[e] in
Philistia.
Are they better off than[f] your two
kingdoms?
Is their land larger than yours?
3You put off the evil day
and bring near a reign of terror.[g]
4You lie on beds inlaid with ivory
and lounge on your couches.
You dine on choice lambs
and fattened calves.[h]
5You strum away on your harps[i] like
David
and improvise on musical
instruments.[j]
6You drink wine[k] by the bowlful
and use the finest lotions,
but you do not grieve[l] over the ruin
of Joseph.
7Therefore you will be among the first
to go into exile;
your feasting and lounging will end.

Pride of Israel abhorred.

8The Sovereign LORD has sworn by
himself[m]—the LORD God Almighty
declares:

"I abhor[n] the pride of Jacob[o]
and detest his fortresses;
I will deliver up[p] the city
and everything in it.[q]"

9If ten[r] men are left in one house,
they too will die. 10And if a relative
who is to burn the bodies[s] comes to
carry them out of the house and asks
anyone still hiding there, "Is anyone
with you?" and he says, "No," then he
will say, "Hush![t] We must not mention
the name of the LORD."

6:1 [a]Lk 6:24 [b]Isa 32:9-11
6:2 [c]Ge 10:10 [d]2Ki 18:34 [e]2Ch 26:6 [f]Na 3:8
6:3 [g]Isa 56:12; Am 9:10
6:4 [h]Eze 34:2-3; Am 3:12
6:5 [i]Isa 5:12; Am 5:23 [j]1Ch 15:16
6:6 [k]Am 2:8 [l]Eze 9:4
6:8 [m]Ge 22:16; Heb 6:13 [n]Lev 26:30 [o]Ps 47:4 [p]Am 4:2 [q]Dt 32:19
6:9 [r]Am 5:3
6:10 [s]1Sa 31:12 [t]Am 8:3
6:11 [u]Am 3:15 [v]Isa 55:11
6:12 [w]Hos 10:4 [x]Am 5:7
6:13 [y]Job 8:15; Isa 28:14-15
6:14 [z]Jer 5:15 [a]1Ki 8:65 [b]Am 3:11
7:1 [c]Am 8:1 [d]Joel 1:4
7:2 [e]Ex 10:15 [f]Isa 37:4 [g]Eze 11:13
7:3 [h]Dt 32:36; Jer 26:19; Jnh 3:10 [i]Hos 11:8
7:4 [j]Isa 66:16 [k]Dt 32:22
7:5 [l]ver 1-2; Joel 2:17
7:6 [m]Jnh 3:10

11For the LORD has given the command,
and he will smash the great house[u]
into pieces
and the small house into bits.[v]

12Do horses run on the rocky crags?
Does one plow there with oxen?
But you have turned justice into
poison[w]
and the fruit of righteousness into
bitterness[x]—
13you who rejoice in the conquest of
Lo Debar[s]
and say, "Did we not take Karnaim[t]
by our own strength?[y]"

14For the LORD God Almighty declares,
"I will stir up a nation[z] against you,
O house of Israel,
that will oppress you all the way
from Lebo[u] Hamath[a] to the valley
of the Arabah.[b]"

Locusts, fire and a plumb line.

7 This is what the Sovereign LORD
showed me:[c] He was preparing
swarms of locusts[d] after the king's share
had been harvested and just as the second crop was coming up. 2When they
had stripped the land clean,[e] I cried out,
"Sovereign LORD, forgive! How can Jacob
survive?[f] He is so small![g]"
3So the LORD relented.[h]
"This will not happen," the LORD said.[i]
4This is what the Sovereign LORD
showed me: The Sovereign LORD was
calling for judgment by fire;[j] it dried up
the great deep and devoured[k] the land.
5Then I cried out, "Sovereign LORD, I beg
you, stop! How can Jacob survive? He is
so small![l]"
6So the LORD relented.[m]
"This will not happen either," the
Sovereign LORD said.

7This is what he showed me: The Lord
was standing by a wall that had been
built true to plumb, with a plumb line in

[s]13 *Lo Debar* means *nothing.* [t]13 *Karnaim* means *horns; horn* here symbolizes strength. [u]14 Or *from the entrance to*

his hand. [8]And the LORD asked me, "What do you see,[a] Amos?[b]"

"A plumb line,[c]" I replied.

Then the Lord said, "Look, I am setting a plumb line among my people Israel; I will spare them no longer.[d]

[9]"The high places of Isaac will be
destroyed
and the sanctuaries[e] of Israel will
be ruined;
with my sword I will rise against
the house of Jeroboam.[f]"

Amaziah's opposition to Amos.

[10]Then Amaziah the priest of Bethel[g] sent a message to Jeroboam[h] king of Israel: "Amos is raising a conspiracy[i] against you in the very heart of Israel. The land cannot bear all his words.[j] [11]For this is what Amos is saying:

"'Jeroboam will die by the sword,
and Israel will surely go into exile,
away from their native land.'"

[12]Then Amaziah said to Amos, "Get out, you seer! Go back to the land of Judah. Earn your bread there and do your prophesying there.[k] [13]Don't prophesy anymore at Bethel, because this is the king's sanctuary and the temple of the kingdom.[l]"

[14]Amos answered Amaziah, "I was neither a prophet[m] nor a prophet's son, but I was a shepherd, and I also took care of sycamore-fig trees. [15]But the LORD took me from tending the flock[n] and said to me, 'Go, prophesy to my people Israel.'[o] [16]Now then, hear the word of the LORD. You say,

"'Do not prophesy against[p] Israel,
and stop preaching against the
house of Isaac.'

[17]"Therefore this is what the LORD says:

"'Your wife will become a prostitute[q]
in the city,
and your sons and daughters will
fall by the sword.
Your land will be measured and
divided up,
and you yourself will die in a
pagan[v] country.
And Israel will certainly go into exile,
away from their native land.[r]'"

7:8 [a]Jer 1:11,13 [b]Isa 28:17; La 2:8; Am 8:2 [c]2Ki 21:13 [d]Jer 15:6; Eze 7:2-9
7:9 [e]Lev 26:31 [f]2Ki 15:9; Isa 63:18; Hos 10:8
7:10 [g]1Ki 12:32 [h]2Ki 14:23 [i]Jer 38:4 [j]Jer 26:8-11
7:12 [k]Mt 8:34
7:13 [l]Am 2:12; Ac 4:18
7:14 [m]2Ki 2:5; 4:38
7:15 [n]2Sa 7:8 [o]Jer 7:1-2; Eze 2:3-4
7:16 [p]Eze 20:46; Mic 2:6
7:17 [q]Hos 4:13 [r]2Ki 17:6; Eze 4:13; Hos 9:3
8:2 [s]Jer 24:3 [t]Am 7:8 [u]Eze 7:2-9
8:3 [v]Am 5:16 [w]Am 5:23; 6:10
8:4 [x]Pr 30:14 [y]Ps 14:4; Am 2:7
8:5 [z]2Ki 4:23; Ne 13:15-16; Hos 12:7; Mic 6:10-11
8:6 [a]Am 2:6
8:7 [b]Am 6:8 [c]Hos 8:13
8:8 [d]Hos 4:3 [e]Ps 18:7; Jer 46:8; Am 9:5

A basket of ripe fruit.

8 This is what the Sovereign LORD showed me: a basket of ripe fruit. [2]"What do you see,[s] Amos?[t]" he asked.

"A basket of ripe fruit," I answered.

Then the LORD said to me, "The time is ripe for my people Israel; I will spare them no longer.[u]

[3]"In that day," declares the Sovereign LORD, "the songs in the temple will turn to wailing.[w] [v] Many, many bodies—flung everywhere! Silence![w]"

[4]Hear this, you who trample the needy
and do away with the poor[x] of the
land,[y]

[5]saying,

"When will the New Moon be over
that we may sell grain,
and the Sabbath be ended
that we may market wheat?"—
skimping the measure,
boosting the price
and cheating with dishonest scales,[z]
[6]buying the poor with silver
and the needy for a pair of sandals,
selling even the sweepings with
the wheat.[a]

[7]The LORD has sworn by the Pride of Jacob:[b] "I will never forget[c] anything they have done.

[8]"Will not the land tremble[d] for this,
and all who live in it mourn?
The whole land will rise like the Nile;
it will be stirred up and then sink
like the river of Egypt.[e]

[9]"In that day," declares the Sovereign LORD,

v17 Hebrew *an unclean* w3 Or *"the temple singers will wail*

'I will make the sun go down at noon
and darken the earth in broad daylight.[a]
10 I will turn your religious feasts into mourning
and all your singing into weeping.
I will make all of you wear sackcloth[b]
and shave your heads.
I will make that time like mourning for an only son[c]
and the end of it like a bitter day.[d]

A famine of hearing the words of the LORD.

11 "The days are coming," declares the Sovereign LORD,
"when I will send a famine through the land—
not a famine of food or a thirst for water,
but a famine of hearing the words of the LORD.[e]
12 Men will stagger from sea to sea
and wander from north to east,
searching for the word of the LORD,
but they will not find it.[f]

13 "In that day

"the lovely young women and strong young men
will faint because of thirst.[g]
14 They who swear by the shame[x] of Samaria,
or say, 'As surely as your god lives, O Dan,'[h]
or, 'As surely as the god[y] of Beersheba[i] lives'—
they will fall,
never to rise again.[j]"

Destruction of Israel.

9 I saw the Lord standing by the altar, and he said:

"Strike the tops of the pillars
so that the thresholds shake.
Bring them down on the heads[k] of all the people;
those who are left I will kill with the sword.
Not one will get away,
none will escape.

8:9 [a]Job 5:14; Isa 59:9-10; Jer 15:9; Am 5:8; Mic 3:6
8:10 [b]Jer 48:37 [c]Jer 6:26; Zec 12:10 [d]Eze 7:18
8:11 [e]1Sa 3:1; 2Ch 15:3; Eze 7:26
8:12 [f]Eze 20:3,31
8:13 [g]Isa 41:17; Hos 2:3
8:14 [h]1Ki 12:29 [i]Am 5:5 [j]Am 5:2
9:1 [k]Ps 68:21
9:2 [l]Ps 139:8 [m]Jer 51:53 [n]Ob 4
9:3 [o]Am 1:2 [p]Ps 139:8-10 [q]Jer 16:16-17
9:4 [r]Lev 26:33; Eze 5:12 [s]Jer 21:10 [t]Jer 39:16 [u]Jer 44:11
9:5 [v]Ps 46:2; Mic 1:4 [w]Am 8:8
9:6 [x]Ps 104:1-3, 5-6,13; Am 5:8
9:7 [y]Isa 20:4; 43:3 [z]Dt 2:23; Jer 47:4 [a]2Ki 16:9; Isa 22:6; Am 1:5; 2:10

2 Though they dig down to the depths of the grave,[z][l]
from there my hand will take them.
Though they climb up to the heavens,[m]
from there I will bring them down.[n]
3 Though they hide themselves on the top of Carmel,[o]
there I will hunt them down and seize them.[p]
Though they hide from me at the bottom of the sea,
there I will command the serpent to bite them.[q]
4 Though they are driven into exile by their enemies,
there I will command the sword[r] to slay them.
I will fix my eyes upon them
for evil[s] and not for good.[t]"[u]

5 The Lord, the LORD Almighty,
he who touches the earth and it melts,[v]
and all who live in it mourn—
the whole land rises like the Nile,
then sinks like the river of Egypt[w]—
6 he who builds his lofty palace[a] in the heavens
and sets its foundation[b] on the earth,
who calls for the waters of the sea
and pours them out over the face of the land—
the LORD is his name.[x]

7 "Are not you Israelites
the same to me as the Cushites[c]?"[y]
declares the LORD.
"Did I not bring Israel up from Egypt,
the Philistines from Caphtor[d][z]
and the Arameans from Kir?[a]

8 "Surely the eyes of the Sovereign LORD
are on the sinful kingdom.
I will destroy it
from the face of the earth—

x 14 Or *by Ashima*; or *by the idol* y 14 Or *power*
z 2 Hebrew *to Sheol* a 6 The meaning of the Hebrew for this phrase is uncertain. b 6 The meaning of the Hebrew for this word is uncertain.
c 7 That is, people from the upper Nile region
d 7 That is, Crete

yet I will not totally destroy
the house of Jacob,"
declares the LORD.[a]
9"For I will give the command,
and I will shake the house of Israel
among all the nations
as grain[b] is shaken in a sieve,[c]
and not a pebble will reach the
ground.
10All the sinners among my people
will die by the sword,
all those who say,
'Disaster will not overtake or
meet us.'[d]

Restoration of Israel.

11"In that day I will restore
David's fallen tent.
I will repair its broken places,
restore its ruins,
and build it as it used to be,[e]
12so that they may possess the
remnant of Edom[f]
and all the nations that bear my
name,[e] [g]"
declares the LORD, who will
do these things.[h]

13"The days are coming," declares
the LORD,

"when the reaper will be overtaken
by the plowman[i]
and the planter by the one treading
grapes.
New wine will drip from the
mountains
and flow from all the hills.[j]
14I will bring back my exiled[f] people
Israel;
they will rebuild the ruined cities[k]
and live in them.
They will plant vineyards and drink
their wine;
they will make gardens and eat
their fruit.[l]
15I will plant[m] Israel in their own land,
never again to be uprooted
from the land I have given them,"
says the LORD your God.[n]

9:8 [a]Jer 44:27
9:9 [b]Lk 22:31 [c]Isa 30:28
9:10 [d]Am 6:3
9:11 [e]Ps 80:12
9:12 [f]Nu 24:18 [g]Isa 43:7 [h]Ac 15:16-17*
9:13 [i]Lev 26:5 [j]Joel 3:18
9:14 [k]Isa 61:4 [l]Jer 30:18; 31:28; Eze 28:25-26
9:15 [m]Isa 60:21 [n]Jer 24:6; Eze 34:25-28; 37:12,25

e *12* Hebrew; Septuagint *so that the remnant of men / and all the nations that bear my name may seek* ⌊*the Lord*⌋ f *14* Or *will restore the fortunes of my*

OBADIAH

Author: Obadiah.

Date Written: Obadiah was written during one of the invasions of Jerusalem. If written when the city was destroyed by the Philistines and Arabians, the date can be set between 848 and 840 B.C. If written during the invasion of Jerusalem by Babylon under Nebuchadnezzar, the suggested date is about 586 B.C.

Time Span: While the length of Obadiah's ministry is not certain, his prophecies cover thousands of years.

Title: The book is named after its author: Obadiah. The name Obadiah means "servant of the LORD."

Background: Obadiah, the shortest book in the Old Testament, is only 21 verses long. Obadiah is a prophet of God who uses this opportunity to condemn Edom for sins against both God and Israel. The Edomites are descendants of Esau, and the Israelites are descendants of his twin brother, Jacob. A quarrel between the brothers has affected their descendants for over 1,000 years. This division caused the Edomites to forbid Israel to cross their land during the Israelites' exodus from Egypt. Edom's sins of pride now require a strong word of judgment from the Lord.

Where Written: Judah.

To Whom: To the Edomites.

Content: Obadiah's message is final and it's sure: the kingdom of Edom will be destroyed completely. Edom has been arrogant—gloating over Israel's misfortunes—and when enemy armies attack Israel and the Israelites ask for help, the Edomites refuse... and choose to fight against them, not for them (verses 10-14). These sins of pride can be overlooked no longer. The book ends with the promise of the fulfillment and deliverance of Zion in the last days when the land will be restored to God's people as he rules over them.

Key Words: "Pride"; "Brother." The Edomites' security (living in a fortified city in Mount Seir) causes an evil "pride" to develop. Their "brother" descendants are thus treated with treachery and abandonment. The only kind of "pride" which is good, and will cause man to treat his "brother" with compassion and love, is that which is placed in the Lord.

Themes: • God will overcome in our behalf if we will stay true to him. • Unlike Edom, we must be willing to help others in times of need. • Like a loving father, God may at times need to punish his children. • Pride is sin. (We have nothing to be proud of except Jesus Christ and what he has done for us.) • Loving all mankind can be easy, but we may need God's help to love the man next door.

Outline:
1. Prophecy of Edom's judgment. 1-9
2. The sins of Edom. 10-14
3. God's vengeance on Edom. 15-18
4. The possession of Edom by Israel. 19-21

OBADIAH

[1]The vision of Obadiah.

Edom's destruction.

1-4pp—Jer 49:14-16
5-6pp—Jer 49:9-10

This is what the Sovereign LORD says about Edom[a]—

We have heard a message from the LORD:
An envoy[b] was sent to the nations to say,
"Rise, and let us go against her for battle"[c]—

[2]"See, I will make you small among the nations;
you will be utterly despised.
[3]The pride[d] of your heart has deceived you,
you who live in the clefts of the rocks[a]
and make your home on the heights,
you who say to yourself,
'Who can bring me down to the ground?'[e]
[4]Though you soar like the eagle
and make your nest[f] among the stars,
from there I will bring you down,"[g]
declares the LORD.[h]
[5]"If thieves came to you,
if robbers in the night—
Oh, what a disaster awaits you—
would they not steal only as much as they wanted?
If grape pickers came to you,
would they not leave a few grapes?[i]
[6]But how Esau will be ransacked,
his hidden treasures pillaged!
[7]All your allies[j] will force you to the border;
your friends will deceive and overpower you;
those who eat your bread[k] will set a trap for you,[b]
but you will not detect it.

[8]"In that day," declares the LORD,
"will I not destroy[l] the wise men of Edom,
men of understanding in the mountains of Esau?
[9]Your warriors, O Teman,[m] will be terrified,
and everyone in Esau's mountains
will be cut down in the slaughter.
[10]Because of the violence[n] against your brother Jacob,[o]
you will be covered with shame;
you will be destroyed forever.[p]
[11]On the day you stood aloof
while strangers carried off his wealth
and foreigners entered his gates
and cast lots[q] for Jerusalem,
you were like one of them.
[12]You should not look down on your brother
in the day of his misfortune,
nor rejoice[r] over the people of Judah
in the day of their destruction,[s]
nor boast so much
in the day of their trouble.[t]
[13]You should not march through the gates of my people
in the day of their disaster,
nor look down on them in their calamity[u]
in the day of their disaster,
nor seize their wealth
in the day of their disaster.
[14]You should not wait at the crossroads
to cut down their fugitives,
nor hand over their survivors
in the day of their trouble.

[15]"The day of the LORD is near[v]
for all nations.
As you have done, it will be done to you;
your deeds[w] will return upon your own head.
[16]Just as you drank on my holy hill,
so all the nations will drink[x] continually;
they will drink and drink
and be as if they had never been.

1:1 [a]Isa 63:1-6; Jer 49:7-22; Eze 25:12-14; Am 1:11-12 [b]Isa 18:2 [c]Jer 6:4-5
1:3 [d]Isa 16:6 [e]Isa 14:13-15; Rev 18:7
1:4 [f]Hab 2:9 [g]Isa 14:13 [h]Job 20:6
1:5 [i]Dt 24:21
1:7 [j]Jer 30:14 [k]Ps 41:9
1:8 [l]Job 5:12; Isa 29:14
1:9 [m]Ge 36:11,34
1:10 [n]Joel 3:19 [o]Ps 137:7; Am 1:11-12 [p]Eze 35:9
1:11 [q]Na 3:10
1:12 [r]Eze 35:15 [s]Pr 17:5 [t]Mic 4:11
1:13 [u]Eze 35:5
1:15 [v]Eze 30:3 [w]Jer 50:29; Hab 2:8
1:16 [x]Jer 25:15; 49:12

a *3* Or *of Sela* b *7* The meaning of the Hebrew for this clause is uncertain.

Deliverance on holy Mount Zion.

[17]But on Mount Zion will be
deliverance;[a]
it will be holy,[b]
and the house of Jacob
will possess its inheritance.
[18]The house of Jacob will be a fire
and the house of Joseph a flame;
the house of Esau will be stubble,
and they will set it on fire and
consume[c] it.
There will be no survivors
from the house of Esau."
The LORD has spoken.

[19]People from the Negev will occupy
the mountains of Esau,
and people from the foothills
will possess
the land of the Philistines.[d]
They will occupy the fields of
Ephraim and Samaria,[e]
and Benjamin will possess Gilead.
[20]This company of Israelite exiles who
are in Canaan
will possess ⌞the land⌟ as far as
Zarephath;[f]
the exiles from Jerusalem who are in
Sepharad
will possess the towns of the
Negev.[g]
[21]Deliverers will go up on[c]
Mount Zion
to govern the mountains of Esau.
And the kingdom will be
the LORD's.[h]

1:17 [a]Am 9:11-15 [b]Isa 4:3
1:18 [c]Zec 12:6
1:19 [d]Isa 11:14 [e]Jer 31:5
1:20 [f]1Ki 17:9-10 [g]Jer 33:13
1:21 [h]Ps 22:28; Zec 14:9,16; Rev 11:15

c*21* Or *from*

JONAH

Author: Jonah.

Date Written: Between 793 and 753 B.C.

Time Span: Uncertain.

Title: From the book's author and chief character: Jonah.

Background: Jonah—the only Old Testament prophet from Galilee—was born in Israel and grew up in a city called Gath Hepher, about 3 miles from Nazareth. Jonah is commissioned by God to preach repentance to the Gentile nation of Assyria and its capital of Nineveh. This is an especially hard assignment since the Assyrians have a brutal and oppressive reputation, in addition to being long-standing enemies of Israel. King Jeroboam II reigns over Israel at this time.

Where Written: Near Jerusalem.

To Whom: Primarily to Israel.

Content: Jonah's fear and pride cause him to run from God. He does not wish to go to Nineveh to preach repentance to the people—as God has commanded—because he feels they are his enemy, and he is convinced that God will not carry out his threat to destroy the city. Instead he boards a ship for Tarshish, which is in the opposite direction. Soon a raging storm causes the crew to cast lots to determine that Jonah is the problem. They throw him overboard, and he is swallowed by a great fish. In its belly for 3 days and 3 nights (1:17), Jonah repents of his sin to God, and the fish vomits him on to dry land. Jonah then makes the 500-mile trip to Nineveh and leads the city in a great revival (chapter 3). But the prophet is displeased instead of thankful when Nineveh repents. Jonah learns his lesson, however, when God uses a vine, a worm and a wind to teach him that God is merciful.

Key Words: "Fish"; "Revival." Jonah is not merely swallowed by a great "fish"; this event represents God extending his helping hand to save the prophet. It gives Jonah a unique opportunity...to seek a unique deliverance...as he repents during this equally unique retreat. Many classify the "revival" which Jonah brings to Nineveh as one of the greatest evangelistic efforts of all time.

Themes: • We can never successfully hide from God...he sees our every move. • God many times does his greatest works through the least likely candidates. • What we may consider as impossible, God may consider as a great opportunity given to us. • Regardless of our patriotism...we must never put our country ahead of our God. • Regardless of our reputation, nationality or race...God loves us. • Rejoicing in the salvation of others is an experience God wants us to share with him. • God at times may use nature, animals, the weather or any other part of his creation to bring us to a closer union with him.

Outline:

1. Jonah runs away from the Lord. 1:1-1:17
2. Jonah is delivered from the fish. 2:1-2:10
3. Jonah obeys God and goes to Nineveh. 3:1-3:10
4. Jonah is angered at God's mercy. 4:1-4:11

JONAH

Jonah flees from the LORD.

1 The word of the LORD came to Jonah[a]
son of Amittai:[b] 2"Go to the great
city of Nineveh[c] and preach against it,
because its wickedness has come up before me."
3But Jonah ran[d] away from the LORD
and headed for Tarshish. He went down
to Joppa,[e] where he found a ship bound
for that port. After paying the fare, he
went aboard and sailed for Tarshish to
flee from the LORD.
4Then the LORD sent a great wind on
the sea, and such a violent storm arose
that the ship threatened to break up.[f]
5All the sailors were afraid and each
cried out to his own god. And they threw
the cargo into the sea to lighten the
ship.[g]

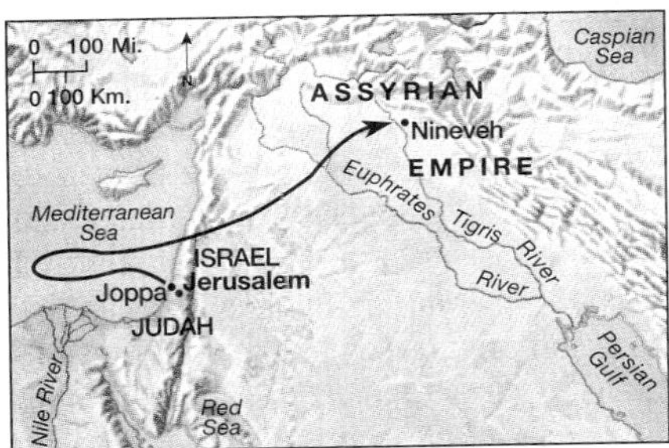

Jonah's Roundabout Journey

God told Jonah to go to Nineveh, the capital of the Assyrian empire. Many of Jonah's countrymen had experienced the atrocities of these fierce people. The last place Jonah wanted to go on a missionary trip was to Nineveh! So he went in the opposite direction. He boarded a ship in Joppa that was headed for Tarshish. But Jonah could not run from God.

But Jonah had gone below deck, where
he lay down and fell into a deep sleep.
6The captain went to him and said,
"How can you sleep? Get up and call[h] on
your god! Maybe he will take notice of us,
and we will not perish."[i]
7Then the sailors said to each other,
"Come, let us cast lots to find out who
is responsible for this calamity."[j] They
cast lots and the lot fell on Jonah.
8So they asked him, "Tell us, who is
responsible for making all this trouble for
us? What do you do? Where do you come
from? What is your country? From what
people are you?"
9He answered, "I am a Hebrew and I
worship the LORD, the God of heaven,[k]
who made the sea and the land.[l]"
10This terrified them and they asked,
"What have you done?" (They knew he
was running away from the LORD, because he had already told them so.)
11The sea was getting rougher and
rougher. So they asked him, "What
should we do to you to make the sea calm
down for us?"
12"Pick me up and throw me into the
sea," he replied, "and it will become
calm. I know that it is my fault that this
great storm has come upon you."[m]
13Instead, the men did their best to
row back to land. But they could not, for
the sea grew even wilder than before.[n]
14Then they cried to the LORD, "O LORD,
please do not let us die for taking this
man's life. Do not hold us accountable
for killing an innocent man,[o] for you,
O LORD, have done as you pleased."[p]
15Then they took Jonah and threw him
overboard, and the raging sea grew
calm.[q] 16At this the men greatly feared[r]
the LORD, and they offered a sacrifice to
the LORD and made vows to him.

A great fish swallows Jonah.

17But the LORD provided a great fish to
swallow Jonah,[s] and Jonah was inside
the fish three days and three nights.

Jonah prays from inside the fish.

2 From inside the fish Jonah prayed to
the LORD his God. 2He said:

"In my distress I called to the LORD,[t]
and he answered me.
From the depths of the grave[a] I
called for help,
and you listened to my cry.
3You hurled me into the deep,[u]
into the very heart of the seas,
and the currents swirled about me;

1:1 [a]Mt 12:39-41 [b]2Ki 14:25
1:2 [c]Ge 10:11
1:3 [d]Ps 139:7 [e]Jos 19:46; Ac 9:36,43
1:4 [f]Ps 107:23-26
1:5 [g]Ac 27:18-19
1:6 [h]Jnh 3:8 [i]Ps 107:28
1:7 [j]Jos 7:10-18; 1Sa 14:42
1:9 [k]Ac 17:24 [l]Ps 146:6
1:12 [m]2Sa 24:17; 1Ch 21:17
1:13 [n]Pr 21:30
1:14 [o]Dt 21:8 [p]Ps 115:3
1:15 [q]Ps 107:29; Lk 8:24
1:16 [r]Mk 4:41
1:17 [s]Mt 12:40; 16:4; Lk 11:30
2:2 [t]Ps 18:6; 120:1
2:3 [u]Ps 88:6

a2 Hebrew *Sheol*

all your waves and breakers
swept over me.[a]
4I said, 'I have been banished
from your sight;[b]
yet I will look again
toward your holy temple.'
5The engulfing waters threatened me,[b]
the deep surrounded me;
seaweed was wrapped around my
head.[c]
6To the roots of the mountains I sank
down;
the earth beneath barred me in
forever.
But you brought my life up from the
pit,
O LORD my God.

7"When my life was ebbing away,
I remembered[d] you, LORD,
and my prayer[e] rose to you,
to your holy temple.[f]

8"Those who cling to worthless idols[g]
forfeit the grace that could be theirs.
9But I, with a song of thanksgiving,
will sacrifice[h] to you.
What I have vowed[i] I will make good.
Salvation[j] comes from the LORD."

10And the LORD commanded the fish,
and it vomited Jonah onto dry land.

Jonah preaches at Nineveh and the people believe.

3 Then the word of the LORD came to
Jonah[k] a second time: 2"Go to the
great city of Nineveh and proclaim to it
the message I give you."
3Jonah obeyed the word of the LORD
and went to Nineveh. Now Nineveh was
a very important city—a visit required
three days. 4On the first day, Jonah started into the city. He proclaimed: "Forty
more days and Nineveh will be overturned." 5The Ninevites believed God.
They declared a fast, and all of them,
from the greatest to the least, put on
sackcloth.[l]
6When the news reached the king of
Nineveh, he rose from his throne, took
off his royal robes, covered himself with
sackcloth and sat down in the dust.[m]
7Then he issued a proclamation in
Nineveh:

"By the decree of the king and his
nobles:

Do not let any man or beast, herd
or flock, taste anything; do not let
them eat or drink.[n] 8But let man and
beast be covered with sackcloth. Let
everyone call[o] urgently on God. Let
them give up their evil ways and
their violence. 9Who knows?[p] God
may yet relent and with compassion turn[q] from his fierce anger so
that we will not perish."

10When God saw what they did and
how they turned from their evil ways, he
had compassion[r] and did not bring upon
them the destruction[s] he had threatened.[t]

The LORD's compassion angers Jonah.

4 But Jonah was greatly displeased
and became angry.[u] 2He prayed to
the LORD, "O LORD, is this not what I said
when I was still at home? That is why I
was so quick to flee to Tarshish. I knew[v]
that you are a gracious and compassionate God, slow to anger and abounding in
love,[w] a God who relents from sending
calamity.[x] 3Now, O LORD, take away my
life,[y] for it is better for me to die[z] than
to live."
4But the LORD replied, "Have you any
right to be angry?"[a]

God has a lesson for Jonah.

5Jonah went out and sat down at a
place east of the city. There he made
himself a shelter, sat in its shade and
waited to see what would happen to the
city. 6Then the LORD God provided a vine
and made it grow up over Jonah to give
shade for his head to ease his discom-
fort, and Jonah was very happy about the
vine. 7But at dawn the next day God provided a worm, which chewed the vine so

2:3 [a]Ps 42:7
2:4 [b]Ps 31:22
2:5 [c]Ps 69:1-2
2:7 [d]Ps 77:11-12 [e]2Ch 30:27 [f]Ps 11:4; 18:6
2:8 [g]2Ki 17:15; Jer 10:8
2:9 [h]Ps 50:14,23; Hos 14:2 [i]Ecc 5:4-5 [j]Ps 3:8
3:1 [k]Jnh 1:1
3:5 [l]Da 9:3; Lk 11:32
3:6 [m]Job 2:8,13; Eze 27:30-31
3:7 [n]2Ch 20:3
3:8 [o]Ps 130:1; Jnh 1:6
3:9 [p]2Sa 12:22 [q]Joel 2:14
3:10 [r]Am 7:6 [s]Jer 18:8 [t]Ex 32:14
4:1 [u]ver 4; Lk 15:28
4:2 [v]Jer 20:7-8 [w]Ex 34:6; Ps 86:5,15 [x]Joel 2:13
4:3 [y]1Ki 19:4 [z]Job 7:15
4:4 [a]Mt 20:11-15

b*5* Or *waters were at my throat*

that it withered.[a] 8When the sun rose,
God provided a scorching east wind, and
the sun blazed on Jonah's head so that
he grew faint. He wanted to die, and said,
"It would be better for me to die than to
live."
9But God said to Jonah, "Do you have
a right to be angry about the vine?"
"I do," he said. "I am angry enough
to die."

10But the LORD said, "You have been
concerned about this vine, though you
did not tend it or make it grow. It
sprang up overnight and died overnight.
11But Nineveh[b] has more than a hundred and twenty thousand people who
cannot tell their right hand from their
left, and many cattle as well. Should I
not be concerned[c] about that great
city?"

4:7
[a]Joel 1:12

4:11
[b]Jnh 1:2; 3:2
[c]Jnh 3:10

MICAH

Author: Micah.

Date Written: Between 735 and 698 B.C.

Time Span: About 25 years.

Title: From the book's author: Micah. This name means "who is like Yahweh."

Background: Micah is a prophet of the common people (rugged, direct and convincing) from the prominent Judean city of Moresheth, about 25 miles southwest of Jerusalem. Micah's ministry spans the reigns of Jotham, Ahaz and Hezekiah. These are turbulent times of great oppression, corruption and exploitation. Israel and Judah are deep in sin, despite their wealth, and Micah's message of imminent judgment upon them is neither pleasant nor popular.

Where Written: Judah.

To Whom: To both Israel and Judah.

Content: Micah's message is directed against the sins of the people in Jerusalem and Samaria, the capitals of Judah and Israel. The corrupt rulers, false prophets, ungodly priests and cheating merchants are the main reasons for God's judgment coming against the nations. But in the midst of their destruction, Micah prophesies the birth of the Messiah in Bethlehem (5:2)—700 years before Jesus Christ is born. This once insignificant village now gains eternal prominence. God also reveals through Micah these promises: a remnant will remain; he will gather his own from all the ends of the earth; and Zion will be restored.

Key Words: "Justice"; "Mercy"; "Humility." Micah's repeated and emphatic cry is for the people of God to show "justice" in all their dealings, to love "mercy" by showing the same to others, and to walk in "humility" with their God (6:8).

Themes: • God gives warnings so we will not have to suffer his wrath. • Judgment is certain if God's warnings are not heeded. • God disciplines us because he loves us. • God knows that sin destroys, and he wants us to be whole. • God's promise of restoration awaits those who remain true to him.

Outline:

1. Micah's vision of judgment against Samaria and Jerusalem. 1:1-1:16
2. Judgment of leaders and prophets. 2:1-3:12
3. The coming King and his restoration. 4:1-5:9
4. God's punishment and subsequent blessings for Israel. 5:10-7:20

MICAH

1 The word of the LORD that came to Micah of Moresheth[a] during the reigns of Jotham,[b] Ahaz[c] and Hezekiah, kings of Judah[d]—the vision[e] he saw concerning Samaria and Jerusalem.

Micah's prophecy against Samaria and Jerusalem.

2Hear, O peoples, all of you,[f]
listen, O earth[g] and all who are in it,
that the Sovereign LORD may witness[h] against you,
the Lord from his holy temple.[i]
3Look! The LORD is coming from his dwelling[j] place;
he comes down and treads the high places of the earth.[k]
4The mountains melt[l] beneath him
and the valleys split apart,[m]
like wax before the fire,
like water rushing down a slope.
5All this is because of Jacob's transgression,
because of the sins of the house of Israel.
What is Jacob's transgression?
Is it not Samaria?[n]
What is Judah's high place?
Is it not Jerusalem?

6"Therefore I will make Samaria a heap of rubble,
a place for planting vineyards.
I will pour her stones[o] into the valley
and lay bare her foundations.[p]
7All her idols[q] will be broken to pieces;
all her temple gifts will be burned with fire;
I will destroy all her images.[r]
Since she gathered her gifts from the wages of prostitutes,[s]
as the wages of prostitutes they will again be used."

Weeping and mourning.

8Because of this I will weep[t] and wail;
I will go about barefoot and naked.
I will howl like a jackal
and moan like an owl.
9For her wound[u] is incurable;
it has come to Judah.[v]
It[a] has reached the very gate[w] of my people,
even to Jerusalem itself.
10Tell it not in Gath[b];
weep not at all.[c]
In Beth Ophrah[d]
roll in the dust.
11Pass on in nakedness[x] and shame,
you who live in Shaphir.[e]
Those who live in Zaanan[f]
will not come out.
Beth Ezel is in mourning;
its protection is taken from you.
12Those who live in Maroth[g] writhe in pain,
waiting for relief,[y]
because disaster has come from the LORD,
even to the gate of Jerusalem.
13You who live in Lachish,[h] [z]
harness the team to the chariot.
You were the beginning of sin
to the Daughter of Zion,
for the transgressions of Israel
were found in you.
14Therefore you will give parting gifts[a]
to Moresheth Gath.
The town of Aczib[i] [b] will prove deceptive[c]
to the kings of Israel.
15I will bring a conqueror against you
who live in Mareshah.[j] [d]
He who is the glory of Israel
will come to Adullam.[e]
16Shave[f] your heads in mourning
for the children in whom you delight;
make yourselves as bald as the vulture,
for they will go from you into exile.

1:1 [a]Jer 26:18 [b]1Ch 3:12 [c]1Ch 3:13 [d]Hos 1:1 [e]Isa 1:1
1:2 [f]Ps 50:7 [g]Jer 6:19 [h]Ge 31:50; Dt 4:26; Isa 1:2 [i]Ps 11:4
1:3 [j]Isa 18:4 [k]Am 4:13
1:4 [l]Ps 46:2,6 [m]Nu 16:31; Na 1:5
1:5 [n]Am 8:14
1:6 [o]Am 5:11 [p]Eze 13:14
1:7 [q]Eze 6:6 [r]Dt 9:21 [s]Dt 23:17-18
1:8 [t]Isa 15:3
1:9 [u]Jer 46:11 [v]2Ki 18:13 [w]Isa 3:26
1:11 [x]Eze 23:29
1:12 [y]Jer 14:19
1:13 [z]Jos 10:3
1:14 [a]2Ki 16:8 [b]Jos 15:44 [c]Jer 15:18
1:15 [d]Jos 15:44 [e]Jos 12:15
1:16 [f]Job 1:20

[a] *9* Or *He* [b] *10* *Gath* sounds like the Hebrew for *tell.* [c] *10* Hebrew; Septuagint may suggest *not in Acco.* The Hebrew for *in Acco* sounds like the Hebrew for *weep.* [d] *10* *Beth Ophrah* means *house of dust.* [e] *11* *Shaphir* means *pleasant.* [f] *11* *Zaanan* sounds like the Hebrew for *come out.* [g] *12* *Maroth* sounds like the Hebrew for *bitter.* [h] *13* *Lachish* sounds like the Hebrew for *team.* [i] *14* *Aczib* means *deception.* [j] *15* *Mareshah* sounds like the Hebrew for *conqueror.*

Woe to those who plot evil.

2 Woe to those who plan iniquity,
to those who plot evil on their
beds![a]
At morning's light they carry it out
because it is in their power to do it.
2They covet fields[b] and seize them,
and houses, and take them.
They defraud[c] a man of his home,
a fellowman of his inheritance.

3Therefore, the LORD says:

"I am planning disaster[d] against this
people,
from which you cannot save
yourselves.
You will no longer walk proudly,[e]
for it will be a time of calamity.
4In that day men will ridicule you;
they will taunt you with this
mournful song:
'We are utterly ruined;[f]
my people's possession is divided up.
He takes it from me!
He assigns our fields to traitors.'"

5Therefore you will have no one in
the assembly of the LORD
to divide the land[g] by lot.

6"Do not prophesy," their prophets say.
"Do not prophesy about these things;
disgrace[h] will not overtake us.[i]"
7Should it be said, O house of Jacob:
"Is the Spirit of the LORD angry?
Does he do such things?"

"Do not my words do good[j]
to him whose ways are upright?[k]
8Lately my people have risen up
like an enemy.
You strip off the rich robe
from those who pass by without
a care,
like men returning from battle.
9You drive the women of my people
from their pleasant homes.[l]
You take away my blessing
from their children forever.
10Get up, go away!
For this is not your resting place,[m]
because it is defiled,[n]
it is ruined, beyond all remedy.

2:1 [a]Ps 36:4
2:2 [b]Isa 5:8 [c]Jer 22:17
2:3 [d]Jer 18:11; Am 3:1-2 [e]Isa 2:12
2:4 [f]Jer 4:13
2:5 [g]Jos 18:4
2:6 [h]Mic 6:16 [i]Am 2:12
2:7 [j]Ps 119:65 [k]Ps 15:2; 84:11
2:9 [l]Jer 10:20
2:10 [m]Dt 12:9 [n]Lev 18:25-29; Ps 106:38-39
2:11 [o]Jer 5:31 [p]Isa 30:10
2:12 [q]Mic 4:7; 5:7; 7:18
2:13 [r]Isa 52:12
3:1 [s]Jer 5:5
3:2 [t]Ps 53:4; Eze 22:27
3:3 [u]Ps 14:4 [v]Zep 3:3 [w]Eze 11:7
3:4 [x]Ps 18:41; Isa 1:15 [y]Dt 31:17
3:5 [z]Isa 3:12; 9:16

11If a liar and deceiver[o] comes and says,
'I will prophesy for you plenty of
wine and beer,'
he would be just the prophet for
this people![p]

Promise of Israel's restoration.

12"I will surely gather all of you,
O Jacob;
I will surely bring together the
remnant[q] of Israel.
I will bring them together like sheep
in a pen,
like a flock in its pasture;
the place will throng with people.
13One who breaks open the way will
go up before[r] them;
they will break through the gate
and go out.
Their king will pass through before
them,
the LORD at their head."

Rebuke of the leaders and prophets.

3 Then I said,

"Listen, you leaders[s] of Jacob,
you rulers of the house of Israel.
Should you not know justice,
2 you who hate good and love evil;
who tear the skin from my people
and the flesh from their bones;[t]
3who eat my people's flesh,[u]
strip off their skin
and break their bones in pieces;[v]
who chop them up like meat for the
pan,
like flesh for the pot?[w]"
4Then they will cry out to the LORD,
but he will not answer them.[x]
At that time he will hide his face[y]
from them
because of the evil they have done.

5This is what the LORD says:

"As for the prophets
who lead my people astray,[z]
if one feeds them,
they proclaim 'peace';
if he does not,
they prepare to wage war against him.

6Therefore night will come over you,
without visions,
and darkness, without divination.[a]
The sun will set for the prophets,[b]
and the day will go dark for them.
7The seers will be ashamed[c]
and the diviners disgraced.[d]
They will all cover their faces
because there is no answer from
God."
8But as for me, I am filled with power,
with the Spirit of the LORD,
and with justice and might,
to declare to Jacob his transgression,
to Israel his sin.[e]
9Hear this, you leaders of the house
of Jacob,
you rulers of the house of Israel,
who despise justice
and distort all that is right;[f]
10who build[g] Zion with bloodshed,[h]
and Jerusalem with wickedness.[i]
11Her leaders judge for a bribe,
her priests teach for a price,
and her prophets tell fortunes for
money.[j]
Yet they lean upon the LORD and say,
"Is not the LORD among us?
No disaster will come upon us."[k]
12Therefore because of you,
Zion will be plowed like a field,
Jerusalem will become a heap of
rubble,[l]
the temple hill a mound overgrown
with thickets.

The mountain of the LORD.

4:1-3pp— Isa 2:1-4

4 In the last days
the mountain[m] of the LORD's
temple will be established
as chief among the mountains;
it will be raised above the hills,[n]
and peoples will stream to it.[o]

2Many nations will come and say,

"Come, let us go up to the mountain
of the LORD,[p]
to the house of the God of Jacob.[q]
He will teach us his ways,[r]
so that we may walk in his paths."
The law will go out from Zion,
the word of the LORD from Jerusalem.
3He will judge between many peoples
and will settle disputes for strong
nations far and wide.[s]
They will beat their swords into
plowshares
and their spears into pruning hooks.[t]
Nation will not take up sword
against nation,
nor will they train for war anymore.[u]
4Every man will sit under his own vine
and under his own fig tree,[v]
and no one will make them afraid,[w]
for the LORD Almighty has spoken.[x]
5All the nations may walk
in the name of their gods;[y]
we will walk in the name of the LORD
our God for ever and ever.[z]

6"In that day," declares the LORD,

"I will gather the lame;
I will assemble the exiles[a]
and those I have brought to grief.[b]
7I will make the lame a remnant,[c]
those driven away a strong nation.
The LORD will rule over them in
Mount Zion
from that day and forever.[d]
8As for you, O watchtower of the flock,
O stronghold[k] of the Daughter of
Zion,
the former dominion will be
restored[e] to you;
kingship will come to the Daughter
of Jerusalem."

9Why do you now cry aloud—
have you no king?[f]
Has your counselor perished,
that pain seizes you like that of a
woman in labor?[g]
10Writhe in agony, O Daughter of Zion,
like a woman in labor,
for now you must leave the city
to camp in the open field.
You will go to Babylon;[h]
there you will be rescued.
There the LORD will redeem[i] you
out of the hand of your enemies.

3:6 [a]Isa 8:19-22 [b]Isa 29:10
3:7 [c]Mic 7:16 [d]Isa 44:25
3:8 [e]Isa 58:1
3:9 [f]Ps 58:1-2; Isa 1:23
3:10 [g]Jer 22:13 [h]Hab 2:12 [i]Eze 22:27
3:11 [j]Isa 1:23; Jer 6:13; Hos 4:8,18 [k]Jer 7:4
3:12 [l]Jer 26:18
4:1 [m]Zec 8:3 [n]Eze 17:22 [o]Ps 22:27; 86:9; Jer 3:17
4:2 [p]Jer 31:6 [q]Zec 2:11; 14:16 [r]Ps 25:8-9; Isa 54:13
4:3 [s]Isa 11:4 [t]Joel 3:10 [u]Isa 2:4
4:4 [v]1Ki 4:25 [w]Lev 26:6 [x]Isa 1:20; Zec 3:10
4:5 [y]2Ki 17:29 [z]Jos 24:14-15; Isa 26:8; Zec 10:12
4:6 [a]Ps 147:2 [b]Eze 34:13,16; 37:21; Zep 3:19
4:7 [c]Mic 2:12 [d]Da 7:14; Lk 1:33; Rev 11:15
4:8 [e]Isa 1:26
4:9 [f]Jer 8:19 [g]Jer 30:6
4:10 [h]2Ki 20:18; Isa 43:14 [i]Isa 48:20

[k]8 Or *hill*

[11]But now many nations
are gathered against you.
They say, "Let her be defiled,
let our eyes gloat[a] over Zion!"
[12]But they do not know
the thoughts of the LORD;
they do not understand his plan,[b]
he who gathers them like sheaves
to the threshing floor.

[13]"Rise and thresh, O Daughter of Zion,
for I will give you horns of iron;
I will give you hoofs of bronze
and you will break to pieces many
nations."[c]
You will devote their ill-gotten gains
to the LORD,
their wealth to the Lord of all the
earth.

Promise of a ruler from Bethlehem.

5 Marshal your troops, O city of
troops,[l]
for a siege is laid against us.
They will strike Israel's ruler
on the cheek[d] with a rod.

[2]"But you, Bethlehem[e] Ephrathah,[f]
though you are small among the
clans[m] of Judah,
out of you will come for me
one who will be ruler over Israel,
whose origins[n] are from of old,[g]
from ancient times.[o]"[h]

[3]Therefore Israel will be abandoned
until the time when she who is in
labor gives birth
and the rest of his brothers return
to join the Israelites.

[4]He will stand and shepherd his
flock[i]
in the strength of the LORD,
in the majesty of the name of the
LORD his God.
And they will live securely, for then
his greatness[j]
will reach to the ends of the earth.
[5] And he will be their peace.[k]

When the Assyrian invades[l] our land
and marches through our fortresses,
we will raise against him seven
shepherds,
even eight leaders of men.[m]
[6]They will rule[p] the land of Assyria
with the sword,
the land of Nimrod[n] with drawn
sword.[q] [o]
He will deliver us from the Assyrian
when he invades our land
and marches into our borders.[p]

[7]The remnant[q] of Jacob will be
in the midst of many peoples
like dew from the LORD,
like showers on the grass,[r]
which do not wait for man
or linger for mankind.
[8]The remnant of Jacob will be among
the nations,
in the midst of many peoples,
like a lion among the beasts of the
forest,[s]
like a young lion among flocks of
sheep,
which mauls and mangles[t] as it goes,
and no one can rescue.[u]
[9]Your hand will be lifted up[v] in
triumph over your enemies,
and all your foes will be destroyed.

[10]"In that day," declares the LORD,

"I will destroy your horses from
among you
and demolish your chariots.[w]
[11]I will destroy the cities[x] of your land
and tear down all your strongholds.[y]
[12]I will destroy your witchcraft
and you will no longer cast spells.[z]
[13]I will destroy your carved images
and your sacred stones from
among you;
you will no longer bow down
to the work of your hands.[a]
[14]I will uproot from among you your
Asherah poles[r] [b]
and demolish your cities.
[15]I will take vengeance[c] in anger
and wrath

4:11 [a]La 2:16; Ob 1:12
4:12 [b]Isa 55:8; Ro 11:33-34
4:13 [c]Da 2:44
5:1 [d]La 3:30
5:2 [e]Jn 7:42 [f]Ge 48:7 [g]Ps 102:25 [h]Mt 2:6*
5:4 [i]Isa 40:11; 49:9; Eze 34:11-15, 23; Mic 7:14 [j]Isa 52:13; Lk 1:32
5:5 [k]Isa 9:6; Lk 2:14; Col 1:19-20 [l]Isa 8:7 [m]Isa 10:24-27
5:6 [n]Ge 10:8 [o]Zep 2:13 [p]Na 2:11-13
5:7 [q]Mic 2:12 [r]Isa 44:4
5:8 [s]Ge 49:9 [t]Mic 4:13; Zec 10:5 [u]Ps 50:22; Hos 5:14
5:9 [v]Ps 10:12
5:10 [w]Hos 14:3; Zec 9:10
5:11 [x]Isa 6:11 [y]Hos 10:14; Am 5:9
5:12 [z]Dt 18:10-12; Isa 2:6; 8:19
5:13 [a]Eze 6:9; Zec 13:2
5:14 [b]Ex 34:13
5:15 [c]Isa 65:12

[l]1 Or *Strengthen your walls, O walled city* [m]2 Or *rulers* [n]2 Hebrew *goings out* [o]2 Or *from days of eternity* [p]6 Or *crush* [q]6 Or *Nimrod in its gates* [r]14 That is, symbols of the goddess Asherah

upon the nations that have not
obeyed me."

The LORD's case against Israel.

6 Listen to what the LORD says:
"Stand up, plead your case
before the mountains;[a]
let the hills hear what you have
to say.
2Hear,[b] O mountains, the LORD's
accusation;[c]
listen, you everlasting foundations
of the earth.
For the LORD has a case against his
people;
he is lodging a charge[d] against Israel.

3"My people, what have I done to you?
How have I burdened[e] you?
Answer me.
4I brought you up out of Egypt
and redeemed you from the land
of slavery.[f]
I sent Moses[g] to lead you,
also Aaron[h] and Miriam.[i]
5My people, remember
what Balak[j] king of Moab counseled
and what Balaam son of Beor
answered.
Remember ⌊your journey⌋ from
Shittim[k] to Gilgal,[l]
that you may know the righteous
acts[m] of the LORD."

6With what shall I come before the LORD
and bow down before the exalted
God?
Shall I come before him with burnt
offerings,
with calves a year old?[n]
7Will the LORD be pleased with
thousands of rams,[o]
with ten thousand rivers of oil?[p]
Shall I offer my firstborn[q] for my
transgression,
the fruit of my body for the sin of
my soul?[r]
8He has showed you, O man, what
is good.
And what does the LORD require
of you?
To act justly[s] and to love mercy
and to walk humbly[t] with your
God.[u]

9Listen! The LORD is calling to the city—
and to fear your name is wisdom—
"Heed the rod and the One who
appointed it.[s]
10Am I still to forget, O wicked house,
your ill-gotten treasures
and the short ephah,[t] which is
accursed?[v]
11Shall I acquit a man with dishonest
scales,[w]
with a bag of false weights?
12Her rich men are violent;[x]
her people are liars[y]
and their tongues speak deceitfully.[z]
13Therefore, I have begun to destroy[a]
you,
to ruin you because of your sins.
14You will eat but not be satisfied;[b]
your stomach will still be empty.[u]
You will store up but save nothing,[c]
because what you save I will give to
the sword.
15You will plant but not harvest;[d]
you will press olives but not use
the oil on yourselves,
you will crush grapes but not drink
the wine.[e]
16You have observed the statutes
of Omri[f]
and all the practices of Ahab's[g]
house,
and you have followed their
traditions.[h]
Therefore I will give you over to ruin[i]
and your people to derision;
you will bear the scorn[j] of the
nations.[v]"

Misery over the sins of Israel.

7 What misery is mine!
I am like one who gathers
summer fruit

6:1 [a]Ps 50:1; Eze 6:2
6:2 [b]Dt 32:1 [c]Hos 12:2 [d]Ps 50:7
6:3 [e]Jer 2:5
6:4 [f]Dt 7:8 [g]Ex 4:16 [h]Ps 77:20 [i]Ex 15:20
6:5 [j]Nu 22:5-6 [k]Nu 25:1 [l]Jos 5:9-10 [m]Jdg 5:11; 1Sa 12:7
6:6 [n]Ps 40:6-8; 51:16-17
6:7 [o]Isa 40:16 [p]Ps 50:8-10 [q]Lev 18:21 [r]2Ki 16:3
6:8 [s]Isa 1:17; Jer 22:3 [t]Isa 57:15 [u]Dt 10:12-13; 1Sa 15:22; Hos 6:6
6:10 [v]Eze 45:9-10; Am 3:10; 8:4-6
6:11 [w]Lev 19:36; Hos 12:7
6:12 [x]Isa 1:23 [y]Isa 3:8 [z]Jer 9:3
6:13 [a]Isa 1:7; 6:11
6:14 [b]Isa 9:20 [c]Isa 30:6
6:15 [d]Dt 28:38; Jer 12:13 [e]Am 5:11; Zep 1:13
6:16 [f]1Ki 16:25 [g]1Ki 16:29-33 [h]Jer 7:24 [i]Jer 25:9 [j]Jer 51:51

s *9* The meaning of the Hebrew for this line is uncertain. t *10* An ephah was a dry measure. u *14* The meaning of the Hebrew for this word is uncertain. v *16* Septuagint; Hebrew *scorn due my people*

at the gleaning of the vineyard;
there is no cluster of grapes to eat,
none of the early figs that I crave.
2The godly have been swept from the land;[a]
not one upright man remains.
All men lie in wait to shed blood;[b]
each hunts his brother with a net.[c]
3Both hands are skilled in doing evil;[d]
the ruler demands gifts,
the judge accepts bribes,
the powerful dictate what they desire—
they all conspire together.
4The best of them is like a brier,[e]
the most upright worse than a thorn hedge.
The day of your watchmen has come,
the day God visits you.
Now is the time of their confusion.[f]
5Do not trust a neighbor;
put no confidence in a friend.[g]
Even with her who lies in your embrace
be careful of your words.
6For a son dishonors his father,
a daughter rises up against her mother,[h]
a daughter-in-law against her mother-in-law—
a man's enemies are the members of his own household.[i]

7But as for me, I watch in hope[j] for the LORD,
I wait for God my Savior;
my God will hear[k] me.

8Do not gloat over me,[l] my enemy!
Though I have fallen, I will rise.[m]
Though I sit in darkness,
the LORD will be my light.[n]
9Because I have sinned against him,
I will bear the LORD's wrath,[o]
until he pleads my case
and establishes my right.
He will bring me out into the light;
I will see his righteousness.[p]
10Then my enemy will see it
and will be covered with shame,[q]
she who said to me,
"Where is the LORD your God?"

7:2 [a]Ps 12:1 [b]Mic 3:10 [c]Jer 5:26
7:3 [d]Pr 4:16
7:4 [e]Eze 2:6 [f]Isa 22:5; Hos 9:7
7:5 [g]Jer 9:4
7:6 [h]Eze 22:7 [i]Mt 10:35-36*
7:7 [j]Ps 130:5; Isa 25:9 [k]Ps 4:3
7:8 [l]Pr 24:17 [m]Ps 37:24; Am 9:11 [n]Isa 9:2
7:9 [o]La 3:39-40 [p]Isa 46:13
7:10 [q]Ps 35:26 [r]Isa 51:23 [s]Zec 10:5
7:11 [t]Isa 54:11
7:12 [u]Isa 19:23-25
7:13 [v]Isa 3:10-11
7:14 [w]Mic 5:4 [x]Ps 23:4 [y]Jer 50:19
7:15 [z]Ex 3:20; Ps 78:12
7:16 [a]Isa 26:11
7:17 [b]Isa 25:3; 49:23; 59:19
7:18 [c]Isa 43:25; Jer 50:20 [d]Ps 103:8-13 [e]Mic 2:12 [f]Ex 34:9 [g]Ps 103:9 [h]Jer 32:41

My eyes will see her downfall;[r]
even now she will be trampled[s] underfoot
like mire in the streets.

11The day for building your walls[t] will come,
the day for extending your boundaries.
12In that day people will come to you
from Assyria and the cities of Egypt,
even from Egypt to the Euphrates
and from sea to sea
and from mountain to mountain.[u]
13The earth will become desolate
because of its inhabitants,
as the result of their deeds.[v]

Prayer and praise.

14Shepherd[w] your people with your staff,[x]
the flock of your inheritance,
which lives by itself in a forest,
in fertile pasturelands.[w]
Let them feed in Bashan and Gilead[y]
as in days long ago.

15"As in the days when you came out of Egypt,
I will show them my wonders.[z]"

16Nations will see and be ashamed,[a]
deprived of all their power.
They will lay their hands on their mouths
and their ears will become deaf.
17They will lick dust like a snake,
like creatures that crawl on the ground.
They will come trembling out of their dens;
they will turn in fear[b] to the LORD our God
and will be afraid of you.
18Who is a God like you,
who pardons sin[c] and forgives[d] the transgression
of the remnant[e] of his inheritance?[f]
You do not stay angry[g] forever
but delight to show mercy.[h]

w14 Or *in the middle of Carmel*

19 You will again have compassion
on us;
you will tread our sins underfoot
and hurl all our iniquities[a] into the
depths of the sea.[b]

20 You will be true to Jacob,
and show mercy to Abraham,
as you pledged on oath to our
fathers[c]
in days long ago.

7:19 [a]Isa 43:25 [b]Jer 31:34
7:20 [c]Dt 7:8; Lk 1:72

NAHUM

Author: Nahum.

Date Written: Between 663 and 612 B.C.

Time Span: Not specified.

Title: From the book's author: Nahum. This name means "comfort."

Background: The book of Nahum is a sequel to the book of Jonah, wherein Jonah led the city of Nineveh (Assyria's capital) in a tremendous revival, which delayed God's judgment against them. But that happened about 150 years before, and now after years of falling away Nineveh has become even more wicked. Assyria is at the peak of her reign, exuding pride, wealth and power. Nahum, a prophet from the Judean town of Elkosh, has this mission: to preach God's coming judgment against Nineveh and God's comfort to the Israelites.

Where Written: Judah.

To Whom: To Assyria and her capital city, Nineveh, but as comfort to God's people in Judah as well.

Content: Assyria has progressively conquered nation after nation. The Assyrians are a brutal people—cruel, defiant and immoral—and their sins against God's people bring the judgment of God upon themselves. Nahum predicts the desolation of Nineveh, which takes place some years later when a flood of the Tigris River destroys part of her previously invincible city wall. Forces from Babylon then enter the city to fulfill Nahum's words. Nineveh's destruction will be final; whereas, Judah at her destruction will leave behind a remnant.

Key Words: "Wrath"; "Comfort." By all human standards Nineveh has might and power. The city is surrounded by a great wall 100 feet high—that reportedly could hold 6 chariots riding abreast—as well as a great moat 60 feet in depth. 200 towers ascend another 100 feet above the wall. But despite this formidable opposition, Nineveh will not escape God's "wrath." Nahum has constant words of "comfort" for his people: "the LORD will not leave the guilty unpunished" (1:3).

Themes: • God is patient and slow to anger. • The praise from our lips and the works of our hands together enable us to worship God. • One plus God is a majority. • God's promises are sure...whether for blessing or for punishment. • We should lean not on our own might...but on our Mighty One. • Vengeance is a right reserved for God alone.

Outline:

1. Nahum's vision of God's power and the deliverance of Judah. 1:1-1:14
2. Destruction of Nineveh. 1:15-2:13
3. Reasons for the fall of Nineveh. 3:1-3:19

NAHUM

1 An oracle[a] concerning Nineveh.[b] The book of the vision of Nahum the Elkoshite.

The LORD's wrath against Nineveh.

[2]The LORD is a jealous[c] and avenging God;
the LORD takes vengeance[d] and is filled with wrath.
The LORD takes vengeance on his foes
and maintains his wrath against his enemies.
[3]The LORD is slow to anger[e] and great in power;
the LORD will not leave the guilty unpunished.[f]
His way is in the whirlwind and the storm,
and clouds[g] are the dust of his feet.
[4]He rebukes the sea and dries it up;
he makes all the rivers run dry.
Bashan and Carmel[h] wither
and the blossoms of Lebanon fade.
[5]The mountains quake[i] before him
and the hills melt away.[j]
The earth trembles at his presence,
the world and all who live in it.
[6]Who can withstand his indignation?
Who can endure[k] his fierce anger?
His wrath is poured out like fire;[l]
the rocks are shattered[m] before him.

[7]The LORD is good,[n]
a refuge in times of trouble.
He cares for[o] those who trust in him,
[8] but with an overwhelming flood
he will make an end of ⌊Nineveh⌋;
he will pursue his foes into darkness.

[9]Whatever they plot against the LORD
he[a] will bring to an end;
trouble will not come a second time.
[10]They will be entangled among thorns[p]
and drunk from their wine;
they will be consumed like dry stubble.[b] [q]
[11]From you, ⌊O Nineveh,⌋ has one come forth
who plots evil against the LORD
and counsels wickedness.

1:1 [a]Isa 13:1; 19:1; Jer 23:33-34 [b]Jnh 1:2; Na 2:8; Zep 2:13
1:2 [c]Ex 20:5 [d]Dt 32:41; Ps 94:1
1:3 [e]Ne 9:17 [f]Ex 34:7 [g]Ps 104:3
1:4 [h]Isa 33:9
1:5 [i]Ex 19:18 [j]Mic 1:4
1:6 [k]Mal 3:2 [l]Jer 10:10 [m]1Ki 19:11
1:7 [n]Jer 33:11 [o]Ps 1:6
1:10 [p]2Sa 23:6 [q]Isa 5:24; Mal 4:1
1:12 [r]Isa 10:34 [s]Isa 54:6-8; La 3:31-32
1:13 [t]Isa 9:4
1:14 [u]Isa 14:22 [v]Mic 5:13 [w]Eze 32:22-23
1:15 [x]Isa 40:9; Ro 10:15 [y]Isa 52:7 [z]Lev 23:2-4 [a]Isa 52:1
2:1 [b]Jer 51:20
2:2 [c]Eze 37:23 [d]Isa 60:15
2:3 [e]Eze 23:14-15

[12]This is what the LORD says:

"Although they have allies and are numerous,
they will be cut off[r] and pass away.
Although I have afflicted you, ⌊O Judah,⌋
I will afflict you no more.[s]
[13]Now I will break their yoke[t] from your neck
and tear your shackles away."

[14]The LORD has given a command concerning you, ⌊Nineveh⌋:
"You will have no descendants to bear your name.[u]
I will destroy the carved images[v] and cast idols
that are in the temple of your gods.
I will prepare your grave,[w]
for you are vile."

[15]Look, there on the mountains,
the feet of one who brings good news,[x]
who proclaims peace![y]
Celebrate your festivals,[z] O Judah,
and fulfill your vows.
No more will the wicked invade you;[a]
they will be completely destroyed.

The destruction of Nineveh.

2 An attacker[b] advances against you, ⌊Nineveh⌋.
Guard the fortress,
watch the road,
brace yourselves,
marshal all your strength!

[2]The LORD will restore[c] the splendor[d] of Jacob
like the splendor of Israel,
though destroyers have laid them waste
and have ruined their vines.

[3]The shields of his soldiers are red;
the warriors are clad in scarlet.[e]
The metal on the chariots flashes

a *9* Or *What do you foes plot against the LORD? / He*
b *10* The meaning of the Hebrew for this verse is uncertain.

on the day they are made ready;
the spears of pine are brandished.[c]
4The chariots[a] storm through the streets,
rushing back and forth through the squares.
They look like flaming torches;
they dart about like lightning.

5He summons his picked troops,
yet they stumble[b] on their way.
They dash to the city wall;
the protective shield is put in place.
6The river gates[c] are thrown open
and the palace collapses.
7It is decreed[d] that ⌊the city⌋
be exiled and carried away.
Its slave girls moan[d] like doves
and beat upon their breasts.[e]
8Nineveh is like a pool,
and its water is draining away.
"Stop! Stop!" they cry,
but no one turns back.
9Plunder the silver!
Plunder the gold!
The supply is endless,
the wealth from all its treasures!
10She is pillaged, plundered, stripped!
Hearts melt, knees give way,
bodies tremble, every face grows pale.[f]

11Where now is the lions' den,[g]
the place where they fed their young,
where the lion and lioness went,
and the cubs, with nothing to fear?
12The lion killed[h] enough for his cubs
and strangled the prey for his mate,
filling his lairs with the kill
and his dens with the prey.

13"I am against[i] you,"
declares the LORD Almighty.
"I will burn up your chariots in smoke,[j]
and the sword will devour your young lions.
I will leave you no prey on the earth.
The voices of your messengers
will no longer be heard."

2:4 [a]Jer 4:13
2:5 [b]Jer 46:12
2:6 [c]Na 3:13
2:7 [d]Isa 59:11 [e]Isa 32:12
2:10 [f]Isa 29:22
2:11 [g]Isa 5:29
2:12 [h]Jer 51:34
2:13 [i]Jer 21:13; Na 3:5 [j]Ps 46:9
3:1 [k]Eze 22:2; Mic 3:10
3:3 [l]2Ki 19:35; Isa 34:3
3:4 [m]Isa 47:9 [n]Isa 23:17; Eze 16:25-29
3:5 [o]Na 2:13 [p]Jer 13:22 [q]Isa 47:3
3:6 [r]Job 9:31 [s]1Sa 2:30; Jer 51:37 [t]Isa 14:16
3:7 [u]Na 1:1 [v]Jer 15:5 [w]Isa 51:19
3:8 [x]Am 6:2 [y]Jer 46:25 [z]Isa 19:6-9
3:9 [a]2Ch 12:3 [b]Eze 27:10 [c]Eze 30:5

Woe to Nineveh.

3 Woe to the city of blood,[k]
full of lies,
full of plunder,
never without victims!
2The crack of whips,
the clatter of wheels,
galloping horses
and jolting chariots!
3Charging cavalry,
flashing swords
and glittering spears!
Many casualties,
piles of dead,
bodies without number,
people stumbling over the corpses[l]—
4all because of the wanton lust of a harlot,
alluring, the mistress of sorceries,[m]
who enslaved nations by her prostitution[n]
and peoples by her witchcraft.

5"I am against[o] you," declares the LORD Almighty.
"I will lift your skirts[p] over your face.
I will show the nations your nakedness[q]
and the kingdoms your shame.
6I will pelt you with filth,[r]
I will treat you with contempt[s]
and make you a spectacle.[t]
7All who see you will flee from you
and say,
'Nineveh[u] is in ruins—who will mourn for her?'[v]
Where can I find anyone to comfort[w] you?"

8Are you better than[x] Thebes,[e][y]
situated on the Nile,[z]
with water around her?
The river was her defense,
the waters her wall.
9Cush[f][a] and Egypt were her boundless strength;
Put[b] and Libya[c] were among her allies.

c3 Hebrew; Septuagint and Syriac / *the horsemen rush to and fro* d7 The meaning of the Hebrew for this word is uncertain. e8 Hebrew *No Amon* f9 That is, the upper Nile region

[10]Yet she was taken captive[a]
and went into exile.
Her infants were dashed[b] to pieces
at the head of every street.
Lots were cast for her nobles,
and all her great men were put in chains.
[11]You too will become drunk;[c]
you will go into hiding[d]
and seek refuge from the enemy.

[12]All your fortresses are like fig trees
with their first ripe fruit;
when they are shaken,
the figs[e] fall into the mouth of the eater.
[13]Look at your troops—
they are all women![f]
The gates[g] of your land
are wide open to your enemies;
fire has consumed their bars.[h]

[14]Draw water for the siege,[i]
strengthen your defenses![j]
Work the clay,
tread the mortar,
repair the brickwork!
[15]There the fire will devour you;
the sword will cut you down
and, like grasshoppers, consume you.
Multiply like grasshoppers,
multiply like locusts![k]
[16]You have increased the number of your merchants
till they are more than the stars of the sky,
but like locusts they strip the land
and then fly away.
[17]Your guards are like locusts,[l]
your officials like swarms of locusts
that settle in the walls on a cold day—
but when the sun appears they fly away,
and no one knows where.

[18]O king of Assyria, your shepherds[g] slumber;[m]
your nobles lie down to rest.[n]
Your people are scattered[o] on the mountains
with no one to gather them.
[19]Nothing can heal your wound;[p]
your injury is fatal.
Everyone who hears the news about you
claps his hands[q] at your fall,
for who has not felt
your endless cruelty?

3:10 [a]Isa 20:4 [b]Isa 13:16; Hos 13:16
3:11 [c]Isa 49:26 [d]Isa 2:10
3:12 [e]Isa 28:4
3:13 [f]Isa 19:16; Jer 50:37 [g]Na 2:6 [h]Isa 45:2
3:14 [i]2Ch 32:4 [j]Na 2:1
3:15 [k]Joel 1:4
3:17 [l]Jer 51:27
3:18 [m]Ps 76:5-6 [n]Isa 56:10 [o]1Ki 22:17
3:19 [p]Jer 30:13; Mic 1:9 [q]Job 27:23; La 2:15; Zep 2:15

[g]*18* Or *rulers*

HABAKKUK

Author: Habakkuk.

Date Written: Between 609 and 589 B.C.

Time Span: Not specified.

Title: From the book's author: Habakkuk. This name may mean"one who embraces."

Background: The prophet Habakkuk is called by God to warn the people of Judah of their coming judgment. These latter days before Judah's fall are a violent time of extensive sin throughout the land. Habakkuk, from Judah, is a contemporary of Jeremiah.

Where Written: Judah.

To Whom: To Judah.

Content: Habakkuk, witnessing Judah's apostasy, bribery and oppression, enters into a dialogue with God. He wants to know why God is allowing these people to prosper and escape judgment. God's reply is that he is sending the Babylonians as his chastening rod upon the nation of Judah. But this bothers Habakkuk even more: why would a just God bring judgment upon a wicked Judah with an even more wicked Babylon? God then gives Habakkuk a new understanding and insight into the very nature of God. God is good, fair and wise, and man's responsibility is to confidently place faith in him. God lets Habakkuk know that future judgment of Babylon will bring sure and thorough destruction. Habakkuk has learned his lesson: to trust God and praise him always.

Key Words: "Faith"; "Woe." A predominant lesson to be learned from this book is our need to have total "faith" in God, for "the righteous will live by his faith" (2:4). We may not always understand why God does everything he does, but we can be assured that God loves us and that his ultimate plans consistently include his judgment of the wicked. "Woe" to those who build their realm by unjust gain (2:9) and bloodshed (2:12). "Woe" to those who put their trust in idols (2:18,19).

Themes: • It is a timeless truth that God hates sin and is unwilling to compromise with it. • No matter what our circumstances may be, we can still trust the Lord and praise his holy name. • A life lived by faith will also be a life full of God's joy. • We can talk to God about anything...even our doubts and fears. • If we will get to know our Creator better, we will better understand his plans for his creation.

Outline:

1. Habakkuk complains against injustice. 1:1-1:4
2. The Lord answers 1:5-1:11
3. Habakkuk complains that the wicked prevail. 1:12-2:1
4. The Lord answers again. 2:2-2:20
5. Habakkuk praises God in prayer. 3:1-3:19

HABAKKUK

1 The oracle[a] that Habakkuk the prophet received.

Habakkuk complains to the LORD.

2How long, O LORD, must I call for help,
but you do not listen?[b]
Or cry out to you, "Violence!"
but you do not save?[c]
3Why do you make me look at injustice?
Why do you tolerate[d] wrong?
Destruction and violence[e] are before me;
there is strife,[f] and conflict abounds.
4Therefore the law[g] is paralyzed,
and justice never prevails.
The wicked hem in the righteous,
so that justice is perverted.[h]

The LORD answers.

5"Look at the nations and watch—
and be utterly amazed.[i]
For I am going to do something in your days
that you would not believe,
even if you were told.[j]
6I am raising up the Babylonians,[a][k]
that ruthless and impetuous people,
who sweep across the whole earth
to seize dwelling places not their own.[l]
7They are a feared and dreaded people;[m]
they are a law to themselves
and promote their own honor.
8Their horses are swifter[n] than leopards,
fiercer than wolves at dusk.
Their cavalry gallops headlong;
their horsemen come from afar.
They fly like a vulture swooping to devour;
9 they all come bent on violence.
Their hordes[b] advance like a desert wind
and gather prisoners[o] like sand.
10They deride kings
and scoff at rulers.[p]
They laugh at all fortified cities;
they build earthen ramps and capture them.
11Then they sweep past like the wind[q]
and go on—
guilty men, whose own strength is their god."[r]

Habakkuk complains again.

12O LORD, are you not from everlasting?
My God, my Holy One,[s] we will not die.
O LORD, you have appointed[t] them to execute judgment;
O Rock, you have ordained them to punish.
13Your eyes are too pure to look on evil;
you cannot tolerate wrong.[u]
Why then do you tolerate the treacherous?
Why are you silent while the wicked
swallow up those more righteous than themselves?
14You have made men like fish in the sea,
like sea creatures that have no ruler.
15The wicked foe pulls all of them up with hooks,[v]
he catches them in his net,[w]
he gathers them up in his dragnet;
and so he rejoices and is glad.
16Therefore he sacrifices to his net
and burns incense[x] to his dragnet,
for by his net he lives in luxury
and enjoys the choicest food.
17Is he to keep on emptying his net,
destroying nations without mercy?[y]

2 I will stand at my watch[z]
and station myself on the ramparts;[a]
I will look to see what he will say[b] to me,
and what answer I am to give to this complaint.[c][c]

The LORD answers that the righteous live by faith.

2Then the LORD replied:

"Write[d] down the revelation
and make it plain on tablets

a6 Or *Chaldeans* b9 The meaning of the Hebrew for this word is uncertain. c1 Or *and what to answer when I am rebuked*

1:1 [a]Na 1:1
1:2 [b]Ps 13:1-2; 22:1-2 [c]Jer 14:9
1:3 [d]ver 13 [e]Jer 20:8 [f]Ps 55:9
1:4 [g]Ps 119:126 [h]Job 19:7; Isa 1:23; 5:20; Eze 9:9
1:5 [i]Isa 29:9 [j]Ac 13:41*
1:6 [k]2Ki 24:2 [l]Jer 13:20
1:7 [m]Isa 18:7; Jer 39:5-9
1:8 [n]Jer 4:13
1:9 [o]Hab 2:5
1:10 [p]2Ch 36:6
1:11 [q]Jer 4:11-12 [r]Da 4:30
1:12 [s]Isa 31:1 [t]Isa 10:6
1:13 [u]La 3:34-36
1:15 [v]Isa 19:8 [w]Jer 16:16
1:16 [x]Jer 44:8
1:17 [y]Isa 14:6; 19:8
2:1 [z]Isa 21:8 [a]Ps 48:13 [b]Ps 85:8 [c]Ps 5:3
2:2 [d]Rev 1:19

so that a herald[d] may run with it.
[3]For the revelation awaits an
appointed time;
it speaks of the end[a]
and will not prove false.
Though it linger, wait[b] for it;
it[e] will certainly come and will not
delay.[c]

[4]"See, he is puffed up;
his desires are not upright—
but the righteous will live by his
faith[f][d]—
[5]indeed, wine[e] betrays him;
he is arrogant and never at rest.
Because he is as greedy as the grave[g]
and like death is never satisfied,[f]
he gathers to himself all the nations
and takes captive all the peoples.

[6]"Will not all of them taunt[g] him with
ridicule and scorn, saying,

"'Woe to him who piles up stolen
goods
and makes himself wealthy by
extortion![h]
How long must this go on?'
[7]Will not your debtors[h] suddenly arise?
Will they not wake up and make
you tremble?
Then you will become their victim.[i]
[8]Because you have plundered many
nations,
the peoples who are left will
plunder you.[j]
For you have shed man's blood;[k]
you have destroyed lands and cities
and everyone in them.

[9]"Woe to him who builds[l] his realm by
unjust gain
to set his nest on high,
to escape the clutches of ruin!
[10]You have plotted the ruin[m] of many
peoples,
shaming[n] your own house and
forfeiting your life.
[11]The stones[o] of the wall will cry out,
and the beams of the woodwork
will echo it.

[12]"Woe to him who builds a city with
bloodshed[p]

2:3 [a]Da 8:17; 10:14 [b]Ps 27:14 [c]Eze 12:25; Heb 10:37-38
2:4 [d]Ro 1:17*; Gal 3:11*; Heb 10:37-38*
2:5 [e]Pr 20:1 [f]Pr 27:20; 30:15-16
2:6 [g]Isa 14:4 [h]Am 2:8
2:7 [i]Pr 29:1
2:8 [j]Isa 33:1; Zec 2:8-9 [k]ver 17
2:9 [l]Jer 22:13
2:10 [m]Jer 26:19 [n]ver 16
2:11 [o]Jos 24:27; Lk 19:40
2:12 [p]Mic 3:10
2:13 [q]Isa 50:11 [r]Isa 47:13
2:14 [s]Nu 14:21 [t]Isa 11:9
2:16 [u]ver 10 [v]La 4:21 [w]Isa 51:22
2:17 [x]Jer 51:35 [y]Jer 50:15 [z]ver 8
2:18 [a]Jer 5:21 [b]Ps 115:4-5; Jer 10:14
2:19 [c]1Ki 18:27 [d]Jer 10:4
2:20 [e]Ps 11:4 [f]Isa 41:1

and establishes a town by crime!
[13]Has not the LORD Almighty determined
that the people's labor is only fuel
for the fire,[q]
that the nations exhaust
themselves for nothing?[r]
[14]For the earth will be filled with the
knowledge of the glory[s] of the
LORD,
as the waters cover the sea.[t]

[15]"Woe to him who gives drink to his
neighbors,
pouring it from the wineskin till
they are drunk,
so that he can gaze on their naked
bodies.
[16]You will be filled with shame[u]
instead of glory.
Now it is your turn! Drink and be
exposed[i]![v]
The cup[w] from the LORD's right hand
is coming around to you,
and disgrace will cover your glory.
[17]The violence[x] you have done to
Lebanon will overwhelm you,
and your destruction of animals
will terrify you.[y]
For you have shed man's blood;[z]
you have destroyed lands and cities
and everyone in them.

[18]"Of what value is an idol,[a] since a
man has carved it?
Or an image that teaches lies?
For he who makes it trusts in his
own creation;
he makes idols that cannot speak.[b]
[19]Woe to him who says to wood,
'Come to life!'
Or to lifeless stone, 'Wake up!'[c]
Can it give guidance?
It is covered with gold and silver;[d]
there is no breath in it.
[20]But the LORD is in his holy temple;[e]
let all the earth be silent[f] before
him."

d2 Or *so that whoever reads it* e3 Or *Though he linger, wait for him; / he* f4 Or *faithfulness* g5 Hebrew *Sheol* h7 Or *creditors* i16 Masoretic Text; Dead Sea Scrolls, Aquila, Vulgate and Syriac (see also Septuagint) *and stagger*

Habakkuk prays for mercy.

3 A prayer of Habakkuk the prophet. On *shigionoth.*[j]

[2]LORD, I have heard[a] of your fame;
I stand in awe[b] of your deeds,
O LORD.
Renew[c] them in our day,
in our time make them known;
in wrath remember mercy.[d]

[3]God came from Teman,
the Holy One from Mount Paran.
Selah[k]
His glory covered the heavens
and his praise filled the earth.[e]
[4]His splendor was like the sunrise;
rays flashed from his hand,
where his power was hidden.
[5]Plague went before him;
pestilence followed his steps.
[6]He stood, and shook the earth;
he looked, and made the nations
tremble.
The ancient mountains crumbled
and the age-old hills collapsed.[f]
His ways are eternal.
[7]I saw the tents of Cushan in distress,
the dwellings of Midian[g] in anguish.[h]

[8]Were you angry with the rivers,[i]
O LORD?
Was your wrath against the
streams?
Did you rage against the sea
when you rode with your horses
and your victorious chariots?[j]
[9]You uncovered your bow,
you called for many arrows.[k]
Selah
You split the earth with rivers;
[10] the mountains saw you and writhed.
Torrents of water swept by;
the deep roared[l]
and lifted its waves[m] on high.

[11]Sun and moon stood still[n] in the
heavens
at the glint of your flying arrows,[o]
at the lightning of your flashing
spear.
[12]In wrath you strode through the earth
and in anger you threshed[p] the
nations.
[13]You came out to deliver[q] your people,
to save your anointed one.
You crushed[r] the leader of the land
of wickedness,
you stripped him from head to foot.
Selah
[14]With his own spear you pierced his
head
when his warriors stormed out to
scatter us,[s]
gloating as though about to devour
the wretched[t] who were in hiding.
[15]You trampled the sea with your horses,
churning the great waters.[u]

Habakkuk determines to rejoice in the LORD.

[16]I heard and my heart pounded,
my lips quivered at the sound;
decay crept into my bones,
and my legs trembled.
Yet I will wait patiently for the day of
calamity
to come on the nation invading us.
[17]Though the fig tree does not bud
and there are no grapes on the vines,
though the olive crop fails
and the fields produce no food,[v]
though there are no sheep in the pen
and no cattle in the stalls,[w]
[18]yet I will rejoice in the LORD,[x]
I will be joyful in God my Savior.

[19]The Sovereign LORD is my strength;[y]
he makes my feet like the feet of a
deer,
he enables me to go on the heights.[z]

For the director of music. On my
stringed instruments.

3:2 [a]Ps 44:1 [b]Ps 119:120 [c]Ps 85:6 [d]Isa 54:8
3:3 [e]Ps 48:10
3:6 [f]Ps 114:1-6
3:7 [g]Jdg 7:24-25 [h]Ex 15:14
3:8 [i]Ex 7:20 [j]Ps 68:17
3:9 [k]Ps 7:12-13
3:10 [l]Ps 98:7 [m]Ps 93:3
3:11 [n]Jos 10:13 [o]Ps 18:14
3:12 [p]Isa 41:15
3:13 [q]Ps 20:6; 28:8 [r]Ps 68:21; 110:6
3:14 [s]Jdg 7:22 [t]Ps 64:2-5
3:15 [u]Ex 15:8; Ps 77:19
3:17 [v]Joel 1:10-12, 18 [w]Jer 5:17
3:18 [x]Isa 61:10; Php 4:4
3:19 [y]Dt 33:29; Ps 46:1-5 [z]Dt 32:13; 2Sa 22:34; Ps 18:33

j*1* Probably a literary or musical term k*3* A word of uncertain meaning; possibly a musical term; also in verses 9 and 13

ZEPHANIAH

Author: Zephaniah.

Date Written: Between 640 and 612 B.C.

Time Span: Not specified.

Title: From the book's author: Zephaniah. This name means "Yahweh protects."

Background: Zephaniah ministers to Judah—during the years before total destruction comes—when the young Josiah is king. Josiah begins as a very good king and institutes sweeping reforms, probably influenced by the prophet Zephaniah. But even these efforts are not enough, for Judah falls deeper and deeper into apostasy and sin. Zephaniah, a contemporary of Jeremiah, resides in Jerusalem. His prophecy concerns both Judah's immediate and long-range judgments by God. Zephaniah is probably the great-grandson of a former king of Judah, Hezekiah.

Where Written: Judah.

To Whom: Primarily to Judah.

Content: The book of Zephaniah is a message of judgment. The prophet graphically uses the 53 verses of this book to describe the wrath which will come upon Judah, Philistia, Moab, Ammon, Cush and Assyria. The sins and subsequent destruction of Jerusalem are given special attention. Future blessings, though, are available to all God's people, Jew and Gentile alike, if they will obediently turn to him. The promised remnant of Israel will be restored, and there will be worldwide rejoicing (chapter 3).

Key Words: "Great Day of the LORD"; "Remnant." Zephaniah emphatically announces that God's vengeance and holiness will lead him to judge all nations for their sins in the coming "great day of the LORD" (chapter 1). But God has promised to exalt a "remnant," which will be regathered from the ends of the earth to live in the comfort and joy of the Lord.

Themes: • God is not prejudiced...he hates sin and loves obedience universally. • God wants us to have pure hearts, not hypocritical, outward shows of piety. • The coming day of the Lord will bring judgment far greater than anything the world has ever known. • Renewed fellowship with God is available to all who have genuinely repentant hearts.

Outline:

1. God's judgment of Judah. 1:1-2:3
2. God's judgment of Judah's neighbors. 2:4-3:8
3. God's restoration of Judah. 3:9-3:20

ZEPHANIAH

1 The word of the LORD that came to
Zephaniah son of Cushi, the son of
Gedaliah, the son of Amariah, the son of
Hezekiah, during the reign of Josiah[a] son
of Amon king of Judah:

Judah's coming destruction.

2"I will sweep away everything
from the face of the earth,"[b]
declares the LORD.
3"I will sweep away both men and
animals;
I will sweep away the birds of the
air[c]
and the fish of the sea.
The wicked will have only heaps of
rubble[a]
when I cut off man from the face of
the earth,"[d]
declares the LORD.

4"I will stretch out my hand[e] against
Judah
and against all who live in Jerusalem.
I will cut off from this place every
remnant of Baal,[f]
the names of the pagan and the
idolatrous priests[g]—
5those who bow down on the roofs
to worship the starry host,
those who bow down and swear by
the LORD
and who also swear by Molech,[b][h]
6those who turn back from following[i]
the LORD
and neither seek[j] the LORD nor
inquire[k] of him.
7Be silent[l] before the Sovereign LORD,
for the day of the LORD[m] is near.
The LORD has prepared a sacrifice;[n]
he has consecrated those he has
invited.
8On the day of the LORD's sacrifice
I will punish[o] the princes
and the king's sons[p]
and all those clad
in foreign clothes.
9On that day I will punish
all who avoid stepping on the
threshold,[c]
who fill the temple of their gods
with violence and deceit.[q]

10"On that day," declares the LORD,
"a cry will go up from the Fish
Gate,[r]
wailing from the New Quarter,
and a loud crash from the hills.
11Wail,[s] you who live in the market
district[d];
all your merchants will be wiped out,
all who trade with[e] silver will be
ruined.[t]
12At that time I will search Jerusalem
with lamps
and punish those who are
complacent,[u]
who are like wine left on its dregs,[v]
who think, 'The LORD will do
nothing,[w]
either good or bad.'
13Their wealth will be plundered,[x]
their houses demolished.
They will build houses
but not live in them;
they will plant vineyards
but not drink the wine.[y]

The great day of the LORD.

14"The great day of the LORD[z] is near[a]—
near and coming quickly.
Listen! The cry on the day of the
LORD will be bitter,
the shouting of the warrior there.
15That day will be a day of wrath,
a day of distress and anguish,
a day of trouble and ruin,
a day of darkness and gloom,
a day of clouds and blackness,[b]
16a day of trumpet and battle cry[c]
against the fortified cities
and against the corner towers.[d]
17I will bring distress on the people
and they will walk like blind[e] men,
because they have sinned against
the LORD.

1:1 [a]2Ki 22:1; 2Ch 34:1–35:25
1:2 [b]Ge 6:7
1:3 [c]Jer 4:25 [d]Hos 4:3
1:4 [e]Jer 6:12 [f]Mic 5:13 [g]Hos 10:5
1:5 [h]Jer 5:7
1:6 [i]Isa 1:4; Jer 2:13 [j]Isa 9:13 [k]Hos 7:7
1:7 [l]Hab 2:20; Zec 2:13 [m]ver 14; Isa 13:6 [n]Isa 34:6; Jer 46:10
1:8 [o]Isa 24:21 [p]Jer 39:6
1:9 [q]Am 3:10
1:10 [r]2Ch 33:14
1:11 [s]Jas 5:1 [t]Hos 9:6
1:12 [u]Am 6:1 [v]Jer 48:11 [w]Eze 8:12
1:13 [x]Jer 15:13 [y]Dt 28:30,39; Am 5:11; Mic 6:15
1:14 [z]ver 7; Joel 1:15 [a]Eze 7:7
1:15 [b]Isa 22:5; Joel 2:2
1:16 [c]Jer 4:19 [d]Isa 2:15
1:17 [e]Isa 59:10

a*3* The meaning of the Hebrew for this line is uncertain. b*5* Hebrew *Malcam,* that is, Milcom
c*9* See 1 Samuel 5:5. d*11* Or *the Mortar*
e*11* Or *in*

Their blood will be poured out[a] like
dust
and their entrails like filth.[b]
18Neither their silver nor their gold
will be able to save them
on the day of the LORD's wrath.[c]
In the fire of his jealousy
the whole world will be consumed,[d]
for he will make a sudden end
of all who live in the earth.[e]"

Repentance urged.

2 Gather together,[f] gather together,
O shameful[g] nation,
2before the appointed time arrives
and that day sweeps on like chaff,[h]
before the fierce anger[i] of the LORD
comes upon you,
before the day of the LORD's wrath
comes upon you.
3Seek[j] the LORD, all you humble of the
land,
you who do what he commands.
Seek righteousness, seek humility;[k]
perhaps you will be sheltered[l]
on the day of the LORD's anger.

Judgment against Philistia.

4Gaza[m] will be abandoned
and Ashkelon left in ruins.
At midday Ashdod will be emptied
and Ekron uprooted.
5Woe to you who live by the sea,
O Kerethite[n] people;
the word of the LORD is against you,[o]
O Canaan, land of the Philistines.

"I will destroy you,
and none will be left."[p]

6The land by the sea, where the
Kerethites[f] dwell,
will be a place for shepherds and
sheep pens.[q]
7It will belong to the remnant of the
house of Judah;
there they will find pasture.
In the evening they will lie down
in the houses of Ashkelon.
The LORD their God will care for
them;
he will restore their fortunes.[g][r]

1:17 [a]Ps 79:3 [b]Jer 9:22
1:18 [c]Eze 7:19 [d]ver 2-3; Zep 3:8 [e]Ge 6:7
2:1 [f]2Ch 20:4; Joel 1:14 [g]Jer 3:3; 6:15
2:2 [h]Isa 17:13; Hos 13:3 [i]La 4:11
2:3 [j]Am 5:6 [k]Ps 45:4; Am 5:14-15 [l]Ps 57:1
2:4 [m]Am 1:6,7-8; Zec 9:5-7
2:5 [n]Eze 25:16 [o]Am 3:1 [p]Isa 14:30
2:6 [q]Isa 5:17
2:7 [r]Ps 126:4; Jer 32:44
2:8 [s]Jer 48:27 [t]Eze 25:3
2:9 [u]Isa 15:1-16:14; Jer 48:1-47 [v]Dt 29:23 [w]Jer 49:1-6; Eze 25:1-7 [x]Isa 11:14 [y]Am 2:1-3
2:10 [z]Isa 16:6 [a]Jer 48:27
2:11 [b]Joel 2:11 [c]Zep 1:4 [d]Zep 3:9
2:12 [e]Isa 18:1; 20:4 [f]Jer 46:10
2:13 [g]Na 1:1 [h]Mic 5:6
2:14 [i]Isa 14:23

Judgment against Moab and Ammon.

8"I have heard the insults[s] of Moab
and the taunts of the Ammonites,
who insulted[t] my people
and made threats against their land.
9Therefore, as surely as I live,"
declares the LORD Almighty, the
God of Israel,
"surely Moab[u] will become like
Sodom,[v]
the Ammonites[w] like Gomorrah—
a place of weeds and salt pits,
a wasteland forever.
The remnant of my people will
plunder[x] them;
the survivors of my nation will
inherit their land.[y]"

10This is what they will get in return
for their pride,[z]
for insulting[a] and mocking the
people of the LORD Almighty.
11The LORD will be awesome[b] to them
when he destroys all the gods[c] of
the land.
The nations on every shore will
worship him,[d]
every one in its own land.

Judgment against Cush.

12"You too, O Cushites,[h][e]
will be slain by my sword.[f]"

Judgment against Assyria.

13He will stretch out his hand against
the north
and destroy Assyria,
leaving Nineveh[g] utterly desolate
and dry as the desert.[h]
14Flocks and herds will lie down there,
creatures of every kind.
The desert owl[i] and the screech owl
will roost on her columns.
Their calls will echo through the
windows,
rubble will be in the doorways,
the beams of cedar will be exposed.

f6 The meaning of the Hebrew for this word is uncertain. g7 Or *will bring back their captives* h12 That is, people from the upper Nile region

15This is the carefree[a] city
that lived in safety.[b]
She said to herself,
"I am, and there is none besides
me."[c]
What a ruin she has become,
a lair for wild beasts!
All who pass by her scoff[d]
and shake their fists.

Woe to rebellious Jerusalem.

3 Woe to the city of oppressors,[e]
rebellious and defiled![f]
2She obeys[g] no one,
she accepts no correction.[h]
She does not trust in the LORD,
she does not draw near[i] to her
God.
3Her officials are roaring lions,
her rulers are evening wolves,[j]
who leave nothing for the
morning.
4Her prophets are arrogant;
they are treacherous[k] men.
Her priests profane the sanctuary
and do violence to the law.[l]
5The LORD within her is righteous;
he does no wrong.[m]
Morning by morning he dispenses
his justice,
and every new day he does not fail,
yet the unrighteous know no shame.

6"I have cut off nations;
their strongholds are demolished.
I have left their streets deserted,
with no one passing through.
Their cities are destroyed;[n]
no one will be left—no one at all.
7I said to the city,
'Surely you will fear me
and accept correction!'
Then her dwelling would not be cut
off,
nor all my punishments come upon
her.
But they were still eager
to act corruptly[o] in all they did.
8Therefore wait[p] for me," declares the
LORD,
"for the day I will stand up to
testify.[i]

2:15
[a]Isa 32:9
[b]Isa 47:8
[c]Eze 28:2
[d]Na 3:19

3:1
[e]Jer 6:6
[f]Eze 23:30

3:2
[g]Jer 22:21
[h]Jer 7:28
[i]Ps 73:28; Jer 5:3

3:3
[j]Eze 22:27

3:4
[k]Jer 9:4
[l]Eze 22:26

3:5
[m]Dt 32:4

3:6
[n]Lev 26:31

3:7
[o]Hos 9:9

3:8
[p]Ps 27:14
[q]Joel 3:2
[r]Zep 1:18

3:9
[s]Zep 2:11
[t]Isa 19:18

3:10
[u]Ps 68:31
[v]Isa 60:7

3:11
[w]Joel 2:26-27

3:12
[x]Isa 14:32
[y]Na 1:7

3:13
[z]Isa 10:21; Mic 4:7
[a]Ps 119:3
[b]Rev 14:5
[c]Eze 34:15; Zep 2:7
[d]Eze 34:25-28

3:14
[e]Zec 2:10
[f]Isa 12:6

3:15
[g]Eze 37:26-28
[h]Isa 54:14

I have decided to assemble the
nations,[q]
to gather the kingdoms
and to pour out my wrath on them—
all my fierce anger.
The whole world will be consumed[r]
by the fire of my jealous anger.

9"Then will I purify the lips of the
peoples,
that all of them may call[s] on the
name of the LORD
and serve[t] him shoulder to shoulder.
10From beyond the rivers of Cush[j] [u]
my worshipers, my scattered
people,
will bring me offerings.[v]
11On that day you will not be put to
shame[w]
for all the wrongs you have done to
me,
because I will remove from this city
those who rejoice in their pride.
Never again will you be haughty
on my holy hill.
12But I will leave within you
the meek[x] and humble,
who trust[y] in the name of the LORD.
13The remnant[z] of Israel will do no
wrong;[a]
they will speak no lies,[b]
nor will deceit be found in their
mouths.
They will eat and lie down[c]
and no one will make them afraid.[d]"

Call for rejoicing.

14Sing, O Daughter of Zion;[e]
shout aloud,[f] O Israel!
Be glad and rejoice with all your
heart,
O Daughter of Jerusalem!
15The LORD has taken away your
punishment,
he has turned back your enemy.
The LORD, the King of Israel, is with
you;[g]
never again will you fear[h] any
harm.

i8 Septuagint and Syriac; Hebrew *will rise up to plunder*   j10 That is, the upper Nile region

[16]On that day they will say to Jerusalem,
"Do not fear, O Zion;
do not let your hands hang limp.[a]
[17]The LORD your God is with you,
he is mighty to save.[b]
He will take great delight[c] in you,
he will quiet you with his love,
he will rejoice over you with
singing."

[18]"The sorrows for the appointed feasts
I will remove from you;
they are a burden and a reproach
to you.[k]
[19]At that time I will deal
with all who oppressed you;
I will rescue the lame
and gather those who have been
scattered.[d]
I will give them praise[e] and honor
in every land where they were put
to shame.
[20]At that time I will gather you;
at that time I will bring[f] you home.
I will give you honor[g] and praise
among all the peoples of the earth
when I restore your fortunes[l][h]
before your very eyes,"
says the LORD.

3:16 [a]Job 4:3; Isa 35:3-4; Heb 12:12
3:17 [b]Isa 63:1 [c]Isa 62:4
3:19 [d]Eze 34:16; Mic 4:6 [e]Isa 60:18
3:20 [f]Jer 29:14; Eze 37:12 [g]Isa 56:5; 66:22 [h]Joel 3:1

[k]*18* Or *"I will gather you who mourn for the appointed feasts; / your reproach is a burden to you*
[l]*20* Or *I bring back your captives*

HAGGAI

Author: Haggai.

Date Written: About 520 B.C.

Time Span: Slightly less than 4 months.

Title: From the book's author: Haggai.

Background: It has been several years since Zerubbabel (the governor) and Joshua (the high priest) led the first return of exiles to Jerusalem to rebuild the temple of God. Haggai, already an old man, came with them. Now, this small group with great aspirations has come upon hard times. They have allowed the negative influences of opposition and scanty resources to discourage them to the point of quitting, after having completed only the temple's foundation. The Jews' neglect of the temple is made worse by their preoccupation with constructing elaborate homes for themselves. The Spirit of the Lord comes upon the prophet Haggai and prompts him to stir the people to resume building the temple.

Where Written: Jerusalem.

To Whom: To Zerubbabel and Joshua in particular, but also to all Jews who returned from exile to Jerusalem.

Content: The elderly Haggai exhorts the people to get excited and committed to the work of rebuilding the temple, which has ceased. The best way possible for Haggai to do this is to give them a glimpse of what they have lost—that blessings come to those who put God first in their lives, and the vision of God's glory filling the new temple when it is completed. But even his message of hope is not lacking a rebuke and judgment of the people for their sins. Zerubbabel and Joshua are commissioned to let the Lord's presence guide their leadership of the people. Finally, the establishment of God's eternal kingdom is foretold, where Zerubbabel will be honored for his part in helping complete the temple.

Key Words: "Careful thought"; "Glory." Before the reconstruction of the temple can be completed, first the hearts of the people need to be renewed as the Lord tells them, "Give careful thought to your ways" (1:7). Haggai encourages the people to seek proper priorities, which will result in God's "glory" filling the new temple (2:7).

Themes: • In order for a project to be completed...it first must be started. • A job half done is a job not done. • If we commit our ways to God, he will guide and bless our walk. • We should avoid compromising situations. • Sometimes we settle for good... when we could have the best. • Prosperity and other standards of success hold no lasting contentment when we place our concerns ahead of God's.

Outline:

1. Haggai's proclamation of God's message to rebuild his temple. 1:1-1:15
2. The glory of the new temple. 2:1-2:9
3. The promise of blessings. 2:10-2:19
4. God's triumph and Zerubbabel's recognition. 2:20-2:23

HAGGAI

1 In the second year of King Darius,[a]
on the first day of the sixth month,
the word of the LORD came through the
prophet Haggai[b] to Zerubbabel[c] son of
Shealtiel, governor[d] of Judah, and to
Joshua[a][e] son of Jehozadak,[f] the high
priest:

Haggai's call to build the LORD's house.

[2]This is what the LORD Almighty says:
"These people say, 'The time has not
yet come for the LORD's house to be
built.'"
[3]Then the word of the LORD came
through the prophet Haggai:[g] [4]"Is it a
time for you yourselves to be living in
your paneled houses,[h] while this house
remains a ruin?[i]"
[5]Now this is what the LORD Almighty
says: "Give careful thought[j] to your ways.
[6]You have planted much, but have harvested little.[k] You eat, but never have
enough. You drink, but never have your
fill. You put on clothes, but are not warm.
You earn wages,[l] only to put them in a
purse with holes in it."
[7]This is what the LORD Almighty says:
"Give careful thought to your ways. [8]Go
up into the mountains and bring down
timber and build the house, so that I may
take pleasure[m] in it and be honored,"
says the LORD. [9]"You expected much,
but see, it turned out to be little. What
you brought home, I blew away. Why?"
declares the LORD Almighty. "Because of
my house, which remains a ruin,[n] while
each of you is busy with his own house.
[10]Therefore, because of you the heavens
have withheld their dew and the earth its
crops.[o] [11]I called for a drought[p] on the
fields and the mountains, on the grain,
the new wine, the oil and whatever the
ground produces, on men and cattle, and
on the labor of your hands.[q]"

The people do the work obediently.

[12]Then Zerubbabel[r] son of Shealtiel,
Joshua son of Jehozadak, the high priest,
and the whole remnant[s] of the people
obeyed[t] the voice of the LORD their God
and the message of the prophet Haggai,
because the LORD their God had sent
him. And the people feared[u] the LORD.
[13]Then Haggai, the LORD's messenger,
gave this message of the LORD to the people: "I am with[v] you," declares the LORD.
[14]So the LORD stirred up the spirit of Zerubbabel[w] son of Shealtiel, governor of
Judah, and the spirit of Joshua son of
Jehozadak, the high priest, and the spirit
of the whole remnant[x] of the people.
They came and began to work on the
house of the LORD Almighty, their God,
[15]on the twenty-fourth day of the sixth
month[y] in the second year of King
Darius.

Greater glory is promised.

2 On the twenty-first day of the seventh month, the word of the LORD
came through the prophet Haggai:
[2]"Speak to Zerubbabel son of Shealtiel,
governor of Judah, to Joshua son of Jehozadak, the high priest, and to the remnant
of the people. Ask them, [3]'Who of you is
left who saw this house[z] in its former
glory? How does it look to you now? Does
it not seem to you like nothing?[a] [4]But
now be strong, O Zerubbabel,' declares
the LORD. 'Be strong,[b] O Joshua son of
Jehozadak, the high priest. Be strong, all
you people of the land,' declares the
LORD, 'and work. For I am with[c] you,' declares the LORD Almighty. [5]'This is what
I covenanted with you when you came
out of Egypt.[d] And my Spirit[e] remains
among you. Do not fear.'
[6]"This is what the LORD Almighty
says: 'In a little while[f] I will once more
shake the heavens and the earth,[g] the
sea and the dry land. [7]I will shake all
nations, and the desired of all nations
will come, and I will fill this house[h] with
glory,' says the LORD Almighty. [8]'The silver is mine and the gold is mine,'
declares the LORD Almighty. [9]'The glory[i]

1:1 [a]Ezr 4:24 [b]Ezr 5:1 [c]Mt 1:12-13 [d]Ezr 5:3 [e]Ezr 2:2 [f]1Ch 6:15; Ezr 3:2
1:3 [g]Ezr 5:1
1:4 [h]2Sa 7:2 [i]ver 9; Jer 33:12
1:5 [j]La 3:40
1:6 [k]Dt 28:38 [l]Hag 2:16; Zec 8:10
1:8 [m]Ps 132:13-14
1:9 [n]ver 4
1:10 [o]Lev 26:19; Dt 28:23
1:11 [p]Dt 28:22; 1Ki 17:1 [q]Hag 2:17
1:12 [r]ver 1 [s]ver 14; Isa 1:9; Hag 2:2 [t]Isa 50:10 [u]Dt 31:12
1:13 [v]Mt 28:20; Ro 8:31
1:14 [w]Ezr 5:2 [x]ver 12
1:15 [y]ver 1
2:3 [z]Ezr 3:12 [a]Zec 4:10
2:4 [b]1Ch 28:20; Zec 8:9; Eph 6:10 [c]2Sa 5:10; Ac 7:9
2:5 [d]Ex 29:46 [e]Ne 9:20; Isa 63:11
2:6 [f]Isa 10:25 [g]Heb 12:26*
2:7 [h]Isa 60:7
2:9 [i]Ps 85:9

a *1* A variant of *Jeshua*; here and elsewhere in Haggai

of this present house will be greater
than the glory of the former house,'
says the LORD Almighty. 'And in this
place I will grant peace,' declares the
LORD Almighty."

The people's service is defiled.

10On the twenty-fourth day of the
ninth month,[a] in the second year of Darius, the word of the LORD came to the
prophet Haggai: 11"This is what the LORD
Almighty says: 'Ask the priests[b] what the
law says: 12If a person carries consecrated
meat in the fold of his garment, and that
fold touches some bread or stew, some
wine, oil or other food, does it become
consecrated?[c]'"
The priests answered, "No."
13Then Haggai said, "If a person defiled
by contact with a dead body touches one
of these things, does it become defiled?"
"Yes," the priests replied, "it becomes
defiled.[d]"
14Then Haggai said, "'So it is with this
people and this nation in my sight,'
declares the LORD. 'Whatever they do and
whatever they offer[e] there is defiled.
15"'Now give careful thought[f] to this
from this day on[b]—consider how things
were before one stone was laid[g] on another in the LORD's temple.[h] 16When anyone came to a heap of twenty measures,
there were only ten. When anyone went
to a wine vat to draw fifty measures,
there were only twenty.[i] 17I struck all the
work of your hands[j] with blight,[k] mildew
and hail, yet you did not turn to me,'
declares the LORD.[l] 18'From this day on,
from this twenty-fourth day of the ninth
month, give careful thought to the day
when the foundation[m] of the LORD's temple was laid. Give careful thought: 19Is
there yet any seed left in the barn? Until
now, the vine and the fig tree, the pomegranate and the olive tree have not borne
fruit.
"'From this day on I will bless you.'"

The LORD chooses Zerubbabel.

20The word of the LORD came to Haggai a second time on the twenty-fourth
day of the month: 21"Tell Zerubbabel[n]
governor of Judah that I will shake the
heavens and the earth. 22I will overturn
royal thrones and shatter the power of
the foreign kingdoms.[o] I will overthrow
chariots[p] and their drivers; horses and
their riders will fall, each by the sword
of his brother.[q]
23"'On that day,' declares the LORD Almighty, 'I will take you, my servant[r]
Zerubbabel son of Shealtiel,' declares the
LORD, 'and I will make you like my signet
ring, for I have chosen you,' declares the
LORD Almighty."

2:10 [a]ver 1
2:11 [b]Lev 10:10-11; Dt 17:8-11; Mal 2:7
2:12 [c]Lev 6:27; Mt 23:19
2:13 [d]Lev 22:4-6
2:14 [e]Isa 1:13
2:15 [f]Hag 1:5 [g]Ezr 3:10 [h]Ezr 4:24
2:16 [i]Hag 1:6
2:17 [j]Hag 1:11 [k]Dt 28:22; 1Ki 8:37; Am 4:9 [l]Am 4:6
2:18 [m]Zec 8:9
2:21 [n]Ezr 5:2
2:22 [o]Da 2:44 [p]Mic 5:10 [q]Jdg 7:22
2:23 [r]Isa 43:10

b *15* Or *to the days past*

ZECHARIAH

Author: Zechariah.

Date Written: Between 520 and 518 B.C., chapters 1-8; chapters 9-14 authored some years later, possibly between 480 and 470 B.C.

Time Span: Chapters 1-8 cover about 2 years during the rebuilding of the temple. Chapters 9-14 cover about 10 years after the temple is completed.

Title: From the book's author: Zechariah. This name means "God remembers."

Background: About 2 months after Haggai's first message to Jerusalem, Zechariah begins a similar ministry. Zechariah is the son of Berekiah and the grandson of Iddo, who were among the exiles that returned to Jerusalem under Zerubbabel. Zechariah's message for those rebuilding the temple of God is one of encouragement, comfort and judgment.

Where Written: Jerusalem.

To Whom: To a restored Israel.

Content: Zechariah's message begins with a series of night visions, which offer both comfort to the people of God in rebuilding the temple and judgment of the disobedient people and nations. Zechariah joins the older Haggai in exhorting the people to finish construction of the temple (which they accomplish in about 4 years time) and encouraging a closer walk in obedience to God. The people's devotion to the task increases when they are finally made to realize that the glory of God cannot return to the temple...if the temple does not exist. Zechariah's prophecies concerning the Messiah include: the righteous Branch (chapter 6); the Triumphal Entry on the colt of a donkey (chapter 9); and the betrayal for 30 pieces of silver (chapter 11). The book closes with the day of the Lord and the restoration of Israel.

Key Words: "Obedience"; "Messiah." Zechariah lets the nation know that future blessings are contingent upon the people's "obedience" to God and his Word. The coming of the "Messiah" is central to the book: his power, betrayal and kingdom.

Themes: • God's ways are not just best for God...they are also best for us. • We need to fear no obstacle when we are on the side of God. • God desires pure actions, but even more he desires pure motives for our actions. • A person in love with the Lord will also have love and compassion for others. • God's plan of redemption (through Jesus Christ) was established from the time sin first entered the world.

Outline:

1. Zechariah gives God's call to repentance. 1:1-1:6
2. Zechariah has 8 visions from the Lord. 1:7-6:8
3. Joshua is crowned. 6:9-6:15
4. God seeks obedience, not hypocrisy. 7:1-7:14
5. The Lord promises blessings for Israel. 8:1-8:23
6. Israel's enemies are judged. 9:1-9:8
7. The coming of the Messiah and his reign. 9:9-14:21

ZECHARIAH

1 In the eighth month of the second
year of Darius,[a] the word of the LORD
came to the prophet Zechariah[b] son of
Berekiah,[c] the son of Iddo:[d]

Zechariah's call for repentance.

2"The LORD was very angry[e] with your
forefathers. 3Therefore tell the people:
This is what the LORD Almighty says:
'Return to me,' declares the LORD Almighty, 'and I will return to you,'[f] says
the LORD Almighty. 4Do not be like your
forefathers,[g] to whom the earlier prophets proclaimed: This is what the LORD
Almighty says: 'Turn from your evil
ways[h] and your evil practices.' But they
would not listen or pay attention to me,[i]
declares the LORD. 5Where are your forefathers now? And the prophets, do they
live forever? 6But did not my words
and my decrees, which I commanded my
servants the prophets, overtake your
forefathers?

"Then they repented and said, 'The
LORD Almighty has done to us what our
ways and practices deserve,[j] just as he
determined to do.'"

*Man and horses
among myrtle trees.*

7On the twenty-fourth day of the eleventh month, the month of Shebat, in
the second year of Darius, the word of
the LORD came to the prophet Zechariah son of Berekiah, the son of Iddo.
8During the night I had a vision—
and there before me was a man riding a
red[k] horse! He was standing among the
myrtle trees in a ravine. Behind him
were red, brown and white horses.[l]
9I asked, "What are these, my lord?"
The angel[m] who was talking with me
answered, "I will show you what they
are."
10Then the man standing among the
myrtle trees explained, "They are the
ones the LORD has sent to go throughout the earth."[n]

11And they reported to the angel of
the LORD, who was standing among the
myrtle trees, "We have gone throughout
the earth and found the whole world at
rest and in peace."[o]
12Then the angel of the LORD said,
"LORD Almighty, how long will you withhold mercy from Jerusalem and from the
towns of Judah, which you have been
angry with these seventy[p] years?" 13So
the LORD spoke kind and comforting
words to the angel who talked with me.[q]
14Then the angel who was speaking to
me said, "Proclaim this word: This is
what the LORD Almighty says: 'I am very
jealous[r] for Jerusalem and Zion, 15but I
am very angry with the nations that feel
secure.[s] I was only a little angry, but
they added to the calamity.'[t]
16"Therefore, this is what the LORD
says: 'I will return[u] to Jerusalem with
mercy, and there my house will be rebuilt. And the measuring line[v] will be
stretched out over Jerusalem,' declares
the LORD Almighty.
17"Proclaim further: This is what the
LORD Almighty says: 'My towns will
again overflow with prosperity, and the
LORD will again comfort[w] Zion and
choose[x] Jerusalem.'"[y]

Four horns and four craftsmen.

18Then I looked up—and there before me were four horns! 19I asked the
angel who was speaking to me, "What
are these?"

He answered me, "These are the
horns[z] that scattered Judah, Israel and
Jerusalem."
20Then the LORD showed me four
craftsmen. 21I asked, "What are these
coming to do?"

He answered, "These are the horns
that scattered Judah so that no one could
raise his head, but the craftsmen have
come to terrify them and throw down
these horns of the nations who lifted
up their horns[a] against the land of Judah
to scatter its people."[b]

1:1 [a]Ezr 4:24; 6:15 [b]Ezr 5:1 [c]Mt 23:35; Lk 11:51 [d]ver 7; Ne 12:4
1:2 [e]2Ch 36:16
1:3 [f]Mal 3:7; Jas 4:8
1:4 [g]2Ch 36:15 [h]Ps 106:6 [i]2Ch 24:19; Ps 78:8; Jer 6:17
1:6 [j]Jer 12:14-17; La 2:17
1:8 [k]Rev 6:4 [l]Zec 6:2-7
1:9 [m]Zec 4:1,4-5
1:10 [n]Zec 6:5-8
1:11 [o]Isa 14:7
1:12 [p]Da 9:2
1:13 [q]Zec 4:1
1:14 [r]Joel 2:18; Zec 8:2
1:15 [s]Jer 48:11 [t]Ps 123:3-4; Am 1:11
1:16 [u]Zec 8:3 [v]Zec 2:1-2
1:17 [w]Isa 51:3 [x]Isa 14:1 [y]Zec 2:12
1:19 [z]Am 6:13
1:21 [a]Ps 75:4 [b]Ps 75:10

A man with a measuring line.

2 Then I looked up—and there before
me was a man with a measuring
line in his hand! 2 I asked, "Where are
you going?"
He answered me, "To measure Jerusalem, to find out how wide and how long
it is."[a]
3 Then the angel who was speaking to
me left, and another angel came to meet
him 4 and said to him: "Run, tell that
young man, 'Jerusalem will be a city
without walls[b] because of the great number[c] of men and livestock in it. 5 And I
myself will be a wall[d] of fire around it,'
declares the LORD, 'and I will be its glory[e] within.'

Shout and be glad.

6 "Come! Come! Flee from the land
of the north," declares the LORD, "for I
have scattered you to the four winds of
heaven,"[f] declares the LORD.
7 "Come, O Zion! Escape, you who live
in the Daughter of Babylon!"[g] 8 For this
is what the LORD Almighty says: "After
he has honored me and has sent me
against the nations that have plundered
you—for whoever touches you touches the apple of his eye[h]— 9 I will surely
raise my hand against them so that their
slaves will plunder them.[a][i] Then you will
know that the LORD Almighty has sent
me.[j]
10 "Shout and be glad, O Daughter of
Zion.[k] For I am coming,[l] and I will live
among you,"[m] declares the LORD. 11 "Many
nations will be joined with the LORD in
that day and will become my people. I
will live among you and you will know
that the LORD Almighty has sent me to
you. 12 The LORD will inherit[n] Judah as
his portion in the holy land and will
again choose[o] Jerusalem. 13 Be still[p]
before the LORD, all mankind, because
he has roused himself from his holy
dwelling."

Joshua receives clean garments.

3 Then he showed me Joshua[b][q] the
high priest standing before the angel
of the LORD, and Satan[c][r] standing at his
right side to accuse him. 2 The LORD said
to Satan, "The LORD rebuke you,[s] Satan!
The LORD, who has chosen[t] Jerusalem,
rebuke you! Is not this man a burning
stick snatched from the fire?"[u]
3 Now Joshua was dressed in filthy
clothes as he stood before the angel.
4 The angel said to those who were
standing before him, "Take off his filthy
clothes."
Then he said to Joshua, "See, I have
taken away your sin,[v] and I will put rich
garments[w] on you."
5 Then I said, "Put a clean turban[x] on
his head." So they put a clean turban on
his head and clothed him, while the
angel of the LORD stood by.
6 The angel of the LORD gave this
charge to Joshua: 7 "This is what the LORD
Almighty says: 'If you will walk in my
ways and keep my requirements, then
you will govern my house[y] and have
charge of my courts, and I will give you
a place among these standing here.
8 " 'Listen, O high priest Joshua and
your associates seated before you, who
are men symbolic[z] of things to come: I
am going to bring my servant, the
Branch.[a] 9 See, the stone I have set in
front of Joshua! There are seven eyes[d]
on that one stone,[b] and I will engrave an
inscription on it,' says the LORD Almighty, 'and I will remove the sin[c] of
this land in a single day.
10 " 'In that day each of you will invite
his neighbor to sit under his vine and
fig tree,[d]' declares the LORD Almighty."

A gold lampstand and two olive trees.

4 Then the angel who talked with me
returned and wakened[e] me, as a
man is wakened from his sleep.[f] 2 He
asked me, "What do you see?"[g]
I answered, "I see a solid gold lampstand[h] with a bowl at the top and seven
lights[i] on it, with seven channels to the

2:2 [a]Eze 40:3; Rev 21:15
2:4 [b]Eze 38:11 [c]Isa 49:20; Jer 30:19; 33:22
2:5 [d]Isa 26:1 [e]Rev 21:23
2:6 [f]Eze 17:21
2:7 [g]Isa 48:20
2:8 [h]Dt 32:10
2:9 [i]Isa 14:2 [j]Zec 4:9
2:10 [k]Zep 3:14 [l]Zec 9:9 [m]Lev 26:12; Zec 8:3
2:12 [n]Dt 32:9; Ps 33:12; Jer 10:16 [o]Zec 1:17
2:13 [p]Hab 2:20
3:1 [q]Hag 1:1; Zec 6:11 [r]Ps 109:6
3:2 [s]Jude 9 [t]Isa 14:1 [u]Am 4:11; Jude 23
3:4 [v]Eze 36:25; Mic 7:18 [w]Isa 52:1; Rev 19:8
3:5 [x]Ex 29:6
3:7 [y]Dt 17:8-11; Eze 44:15-16
3:8 [z]Eze 12:11 [a]Isa 4:2
3:9 [b]Isa 28:16 [c]Jer 50:20
3:10 [d]1Ki 4:25; Mic 4:4
4:1 [e]Da 8:18 [f]Jer 31:26
4:2 [g]Jer 1:13 [h]Ex 25:31; Rev 1:12 [i]Rev 4:5

a *8,9* Or *says after . . . eye:* 9 "*I . . . plunder them.*"
b *1* A variant of *Jeshua*; here and elsewhere in Zechariah
c *1* *Satan* means *accuser.*
d *9* Or *facets*

lights. 3 Also there are two olive trees[a] by it, one on the right of the bowl and the other on its left."

4 I asked the angel who talked with me, "What are these, my lord?"

5 He answered, "Do you not know what these are?"

"No, my lord," I replied.[b]

6 So he said to me, "This is the word of the LORD to Zerubbabel:[c] 'Not by might nor by power, but by my Spirit,'[d] says the LORD Almighty.

7 "What[e] are you, O mighty mountain? Before Zerubbabel you will become level ground.[e] Then he will bring out the capstone[f] to shouts of 'God bless it! God bless it!' "

8 Then the word of the LORD came to me: 9 "The hands of Zerubbabel have laid the foundation[g] of this temple; his hands will also complete it.[h] Then you will know that the LORD Almighty has sent me[i] to you.

10 "Who despises the day of small things?[j] Men will rejoice when they see the plumb line in the hand of Zerubbabel.

"(These seven are the eyes[k] of the LORD, which range throughout the earth.)"

11 Then I asked the angel, "What are these two olive trees[l] on the right and the left of the lampstand?"

12 Again I asked him, "What are these two olive branches beside the two gold pipes that pour out golden oil?"

13 He replied, "Do you not know what these are?"

"No, my lord," I said.

14 So he said, "These are the two who are anointed[m] to[f] serve the Lord of all the earth."

A flying scroll.

5 I looked again—and there before me was a flying scroll![n]

2 He asked me, "What do you see?"

I answered, "I see a flying scroll, thirty feet long and fifteen feet wide.[g]"

3 And he said to me, "This is the curse[o] that is going out over the whole land; for according to what it says on one side, every thief[p] will be banished, and according to what it says on the other, everyone who swears falsely[q] will be banished. 4 The LORD Almighty declares, 'I will send it out, and it will enter the house of the thief and the house of him who swears falsely by my name. It will remain in his house and destroy it, both its timbers and its stones.[r]' "

A woman sitting in a basket.

5 Then the angel who was speaking to me came forward and said to me, "Look up and see what this is that is appearing."

6 I asked, "What is it?"

He replied, "It is a measuring basket.[h]" And he added, "This is the iniquity[i] of the people throughout the land."

7 Then the cover of lead was raised, and there in the basket sat a woman! 8 He said, "This is wickedness," and he pushed her back into the basket and pushed the lead cover down over its mouth.[s]

9 Then I looked up—and there before me were two women, with the wind in their wings! They had wings like those of a stork,[t] and they lifted up the basket between heaven and earth.

10 "Where are they taking the basket?" I asked the angel who was speaking to me.

11 He replied, "To the country of Babylonia[j][u] to build a house[v] for it. When it is ready, the basket will be set there in its place."[w]

Four chariots.

6 I looked up again—and there before me were four chariots[x] coming out from between two mountains—mountains of bronze! 2 The first chariot had red horses, the second black,[y] 3 the third white,[z] and the fourth dappled—all of them powerful. 4 I asked the angel who

4:3 [a] ver 11; Rev 11:4
4:5 [b] Zec 1:9
4:6 [c] Ezr 5:2 [d] Isa 11:2-4; Hos 1:7
4:7 [e] Jer 51:25 [f] Ps 118:22
4:9 [g] Ezr 3:11 [h] Ezr 3:8; 6:15; Zec 6:12 [i] Zec 2:9
4:10 [j] Hag 2:3 [k] Zec 3:9; Rev 5:6
4:11 [l] ver 3; Rev 11:4
4:14 [m] Ex 29:7; 40:15; Da 9:24-26; Zec 3:1-7
5:1 [n] Eze 2:9; Rev 5:1
5:3 [o] Isa 24:6; 43:28; Mal 3:9; 4:6 [p] Ex 20:15; Mal 3:8 [q] Isa 48:1
5:4 [r] Lev 14:34-45; Hab 2:9-11; Mal 3:5
5:8 [s] Mic 6:11
5:9 [t] Lev 11:19
5:11 [u] Ge 10:10 [v] Jer 29:5,28 [w] Da 1:2
6:1 [x] ver 5
6:2 [y] Rev 6:5
6:3 [z] Rev 6:2

e *7* Or *Who* f *14* Or *two who bring oil and*
g *2* Hebrew *twenty cubits long and ten cubits wide* (about 9 meters long and 4.5 meters wide)
h *6* Hebrew *an ephah*; also in verses 7-11
i *6* Or *appearance* j *11* Hebrew *Shinar*

was speaking to me, "What are these, my lord?"

5The angel answered me, "These are the four spirits[k][a] of heaven, going out from standing in the presence of the Lord of the whole world. 6The one with the black horses is going toward the north country, the one with the white horses toward the west,[l] and the one with the dappled horses toward the south."

7When the powerful horses went out, they were straining to go throughout the earth.[b] And he said, "Go throughout the earth!" So they went throughout the earth.

8Then he called to me, "Look, those going toward the north country have given my Spirit[m] rest[c] in the land of the north."

A crown for Joshua.

9The word of the LORD came to me: 10"Take ⌊silver and gold⌋ from the exiles Heldai, Tobijah and Jedaiah, who have arrived from Babylon.[d] Go the same day to the house of Josiah son of Zephaniah. 11Take the silver and gold and make a crown,[e] and set it on the head of the high priest, Joshua[f] son of Jehozadak.[g] 12Tell him this is what the LORD Almighty says: 'Here is the man whose name is the Branch,[h] and he will branch out from his place and build the temple of the LORD.[i] 13It is he who will build the temple of the LORD, and he will be clothed with majesty and will sit and rule on his throne. And he will be a priest[j] on his throne. And there will be harmony between the two.' 14The crown will be given to Heldai,[n] Tobijah, Jedaiah and Hen[o] son of Zephaniah as a memorial in the temple of the LORD. 15Those who are far away will come and help to build the temple of the LORD,[k] and you will know that the LORD Almighty has sent me to you.[l] This will happen if you diligently obey[m] the LORD your God."

Selfish fasting.

7 In the fourth year of King Darius, the word of the LORD came to Zechariah on the fourth day of the ninth month, the month of Kislev.[n] 2The people of Bethel had sent Sharezer and Regem-Melech, together with their men, to entreat[o] the LORD 3by asking the priests of the house of the LORD Almighty and the prophets, "Should I mourn[p] and fast in the fifth[q] month, as I have done for so many years?"

4Then the word of the LORD Almighty came to me: 5"Ask all the people of the land and the priests, 'When you fasted[r] and mourned in the fifth and seventh months for the past seventy years, was it really for me that you fasted? 6And when you were eating and drinking, were you not just feasting for yourselves? 7Are these not the words the LORD proclaimed through the earlier prophets[s] when Jerusalem and its surrounding towns were at rest[t] and prosperous, and the Negev and the western foothills[u] were settled?'"

8And the word of the LORD came again to Zechariah: 9"This is what the LORD Almighty says: 'Administer true justice;[v] show mercy and compassion to one another. 10Do not oppress the widow or the fatherless, the alien[w] or the poor. In your hearts do not think evil of each other.'[x]

11"But they refused to pay attention; stubbornly they turned their backs and stopped up their ears.[y] 12They made their hearts as hard as flint[z] and would not listen to the law or to the words that the LORD Almighty had sent by his Spirit through the earlier prophets.[a] So the LORD Almighty was very angry.[b]

13"'When I called, they did not listen;[c] so when they called, I would not listen,'[d] says the LORD Almighty.[e] 14'I scattered[f] them with a whirlwind[g] among all the nations, where they were strangers. The land was left so desolate behind them that no one could come or go. This is how they made the pleasant land desolate.[h]'"

6:5 [a]Eze 37:9; Mt 24:31; Rev 7:1 **6:7** [b]Zec 1:10 **6:8** [c]Eze 5:13; 24:13 **6:10** [d]Ezr 7:14-16; Jer 28:6 **6:11** [e]Ps 21:3 [f]Zec 3:1 [g]Ezr 3:2 **6:12** [h]Isa 4:2; Zec 3:8 [i]Ezr 3:8-10; Zec 4:6-9 **6:13** [j]Ps 110:4 **6:15** [k]Isa 60:10 [l]Zec 2:9-11 [m]Isa 58:12; Jer 7:23; Zec 3:7 **7:1** [n]Ne 1:1 **7:2** [o]Jer 26:19; Zec 8:21 **7:3** [p]Zec 12:12-14 [q]Jer 52:12-14; Zec 8:19 **7:5** [r]Isa 58:5 **7:7** [s]Zec 1:4 [t]Jer 22:21 [u]Jer 17:26 **7:9** [v]Zec 8:16 **7:10** [w]Ex 22:21 [x]Ex 22:22; Isa 1:17 **7:11** [y]Jer 8:5; 11:10; 17:23 **7:12** [z]Jer 17:1; Eze 11:19 [a]Ne 9:29 [b]Da 9:12 **7:13** [c]Pr 1:24 [d]Isa 1:15; Jer 11:11; 14:12; Mic 3:4 [e]Pr 1:28 **7:14** [f]Dt 4:27; 28:64-67 [g]Jer 23:19 [h]Jer 44:6

[k]*5* Or *winds* [l]*6* Or *horses after them* [m]*8* Or *spirit* [n]*14* Syriac; Hebrew *Helem* [o]*14* Or *and the gracious one, the*

The LORD's promise to bless and restore his people.

8 Again the word of the LORD Almighty came to me. 2This is what the LORD Almighty says: "I am very jealous for Zion; I am burning with jealousy for her."

3This is what the LORD says: "I will return[a] to Zion and dwell in Jerusalem.[b] Then Jerusalem will be called the City of Truth, and the mountain of the LORD Almighty will be called the Holy Mountain."

4This is what the LORD Almighty says: "Once again men and women of ripe old age will sit in the streets of Jerusalem,[c] each with cane in hand because of his age. 5The city streets will be filled with boys and girls playing there.[d]"

6This is what the LORD Almighty says: "It may seem marvelous to the remnant of this people at that time,[e] but will it seem marvelous to me?[f]" declares the LORD Almighty.

7This is what the LORD Almighty says: "I will save my people from the countries of the east and the west.[g] 8I will bring them back[h] to live in Jerusalem; they will be my people,[i] and I will be faithful and righteous to them as their God."

9This is what the LORD Almighty says: "You who now hear these words spoken by the prophets[j] who were there when the foundation was laid for the house of the LORD Almighty, let your hands be strong[k] so that the temple may be built. 10Before that time there were no wages[l] for man or beast. No one could go about his business safely because of his enemy, for I had turned every man against his neighbor. 11But now I will not deal with the remnant of this people as I did in the past,"[m] declares the LORD Almighty.

12"The seed will grow well, the vine will yield its fruit,[n] the ground will produce its crops,[o] and the heavens will drop their dew.[p] I will give all these things as an inheritance[q] to the remnant of this people. 13As you have been an object of cursing[r] among the nations, O Judah and Israel, so will I save you, and you will be a blessing.[s] Do not be afraid, but let your hands be strong."

14This is what the LORD Almighty says: "Just as I had determined to bring disaster[t] upon you and showed no pity when your fathers angered me," says the LORD Almighty, 15"so now I have determined to do good[u] again to Jerusalem and Judah. Do not be afraid. 16These are the things you are to do: Speak the truth[v] to each other, and render true and sound judgment in your courts;[w] 17do not plot evil[x] against your neighbor, and do not love to swear falsely.[y] I hate all this," declares the LORD.

18Again the word of the LORD Almighty came to me. 19This is what the LORD Almighty says: "The fasts of the fourth,[z] fifth,[a] seventh[b] and tenth[c] months will become joyful[d] and glad occasions and happy festivals for Judah. Therefore love truth[e] and peace."

20This is what the LORD Almighty says: "Many peoples and the inhabitants of many cities will yet come, 21and the inhabitants of one city will go to another and say, 'Let us go at once to entreat[f] the LORD and seek the LORD Almighty. I myself am going.' 22And many peoples and powerful nations will come to Jerusalem to seek the LORD Almighty and to entreat him."[g]

23This is what the LORD Almighty says: "In those days ten men from all languages and nations will take firm hold of one Jew by the hem of his robe and say, 'Let us go with you, because we have heard that God is with you.'"[h]

Judgment on Israel's enemies.

An Oracle

9 The word of the LORD is against
the land of Hadrach
and will rest upon Damascus[i]—
for the eyes of men and all the tribes
of Israel
are on the LORD—[p]

8:3 [a]Zec 1:16 [b]Zec 2:10
8:4 [c]Isa 65:20
8:5 [d]Jer 30:20; 31:13
8:6 [e]Ps 118:23; 126:1-3 [f]Jer 32:17,27
8:7 [g]Ps 107:3; Isa 11:11; 43:5
8:8 [h]Zec 10:10 [i]Eze 11:19-20; 36:28; Zec 2:11
8:9 [j]Ezr 5:1 [k]Hag 2:4
8:10 [l]Hag 1:6
8:11 [m]Isa 12:1
8:12 [n]Joel 2:22 [o]Ps 67:6 [p]Ge 27:28 [q]Ob 1:17
8:13 [r]Jer 42:18 [s]Ge 12:2
8:14 [t]Jer 31:28; Eze 24:14
8:15 [u]ver 13; Jer 29:11; Mic 7:18-20
8:16 [v]Ps 15:2; Eph 4:25 [w]Zec 7:9
8:17 [x]Pr 3:29 [y]Pr 6:16-19
8:19 [z]Jer 39:2 [a]Jer 52:12 [b]2Ki 25:25 [c]Jer 52:4 [d]Ps 30:11 [e]ver 16
8:21 [f]Zec 7:2
8:22 [g]Ps 117:1; Isa 60:3; Zec 2:11
8:23 [h]Isa 45:14; 1Co 14:25
9:1 [i]Isa 17:1

p *1* Or *Damascus. / For the eye of the* LORD *is on all mankind, / as well as on the tribes of Israel,*

2 and upon Hamath[a] too, which borders
on it,
and upon Tyre[b] and Sidon, though
they are very skillful.
3 Tyre has built herself a stronghold;
she has heaped up silver like dust,
and gold like the dirt of the streets.[c]
4 But the Lord will take away her
possessions
and destroy her power on the sea,
and she will be consumed by fire.[d]
5 Ashkelon will see it and fear;
Gaza will writhe in agony,
and Ekron too, for her hope will
wither.
Gaza will lose her king
and Ashkelon will be deserted.
6 Foreigners will occupy Ashdod,
and I will cut off the pride of the
Philistines.
7 I will take the blood from their
mouths,
the forbidden food from between
their teeth.
Those who are left will belong to our
God
and become leaders in Judah,
and Ekron will be like the Jebusites.
8 But I will defend my house
against marauding forces.
Never again will an oppressor
overrun my people,
for now I am keeping watch.[e]

Rejoicing for Zion's coming king.

9 Rejoice greatly, O Daughter of Zion!
Shout, Daughter of Jerusalem!
See, your king[q] comes to you,
righteous and having salvation,[f]
gentle and riding on a donkey,
on a colt, the foal of a donkey.[g]
10 I will take away the chariots from
Ephraim
and the war-horses from Jerusalem,
and the battle bow will be broken.[h]
He will proclaim peace to the nations.
His rule will extend from sea to sea
and from the River[r] to the ends of
the earth.[s] [i]
11 As for you, because of the blood of my
covenant[j] with you,
I will free your prisoners[k] from the
waterless pit.
12 Return to your fortress,[l] O prisoners
of hope;
even now I announce that I will
restore twice as much to you.
13 I will bend Judah as I bend my bow
and fill it with Ephraim.[m]
I will rouse your sons, O Zion,
against your sons, O Greece,[n]
and make you like a warrior's
sword.[o]

14 Then the LORD will appear over
them;[p]
his arrow will flash like lightning.[q]
The Sovereign LORD will sound the
trumpet;
he will march in the storms[r] of the
south,
15 and the LORD Almighty will shield[s]
them.
They will destroy
and overcome with slingstones.
They will drink and roar as with wine;
they will be full like a bowl
used for sprinkling[t] the corners[t] of
the altar.
16 The LORD their God will save them on
that day
as the flock of his people.
They will sparkle in his land
like jewels in a crown.[u]
17 How attractive and beautiful they
will be!
Grain will make the young men
thrive,
and new wine the young women.

The LORD will strengthen his people.

10 Ask the LORD for rain in the
springtime;
it is the LORD who makes the storm
clouds.
He gives showers of rain to men,
and plants of the field to everyone.
2 The idols[v] speak deceit,
diviners see visions that lie;

9:2 [a]Jer 49:23 [b]Eze 28:1-19
9:3 [c]Job 27:16; Eze 28:4
9:4 [d]Isa 23:1; Eze 26:3-5; 28:18
9:8 [e]Isa 52:1; 54:14
9:9 [f]Isa 9:6-7; 43:3-11; Jer 23:5-6; Zep 3:14-15; Zec 2:10 [g]Mt 21:5*; Jn 12:15*
9:10 [h]Hos 1:7; 2:18; Mic 4:3; 5:10; Zec 10:4 [i]Ps 72:8
9:11 [j]Ex 24:8 [k]Isa 42:7
9:12 [l]Joel 3:16
9:13 [m]Isa 49:2 [n]Joel 3:6 [o]Jer 51:20
9:14 [p]Isa 31:5 [q]Ps 18:14; Hab 3:11 [r]Isa 21:1; 66:15
9:15 [s]Isa 37:35; Zec 12:8 [t]Ex 27:2
9:16 [u]Isa 62:3; Jer 31:11
10:2 [v]Eze 21:21

q *9* Or *King* r *10* That is, the Euphrates
s *10* Or *the end of the land* t *15* Or *bowl, / like*

they tell dreams that are false,
they give comfort in vain.
Therefore the people wander like sheep
oppressed for lack of a shepherd.[a]

3"My anger burns against the shepherds,
and I will punish the leaders;[b]
for the LORD Almighty will care
for his flock, the house of Judah,
and make them like a proud horse in battle.
4From Judah will come the cornerstone,
from him the tent peg,[c]
from him the battle bow,[d]
from him every ruler.
5Together they[u] will be like mighty men
trampling the muddy streets in battle.[e]
Because the LORD is with them,
they will fight and overthrow the horsemen.[f]

6"I will strengthen the house of Judah
and save the house of Joseph.
I will restore them
because I have compassion on them.[g]
They will be as though
I had not rejected them,
for I am the LORD their God
and I will answer[h] them.
7The Ephraimites will become like mighty men,
and their hearts will be glad as with wine.[i]
Their children will see it and be joyful;
their hearts will rejoice in the LORD.
8I will signal[j] for them
and gather them in.
Surely I will redeem them;
they will be as numerous[k] as before.
9Though I scatter them among the peoples,
yet in distant lands they will remember me.[l]
They and their children will survive,
and they will return.
10I will bring them back from Egypt
and gather them from Assyria.[m]
I will bring them to Gilead[n] and Lebanon,
and there will not be room[o] enough for them.
11They will pass through the sea of trouble;
the surging sea will be subdued
and all the depths of the Nile will dry up.[p]
Assyria's pride[q] will be brought down
and Egypt's scepter[r] will pass away.
12I will strengthen them in the LORD
and in his name they will walk,[s]"
declares the LORD.

11 Open your doors, O Lebanon,[t]
so that fire may devour your cedars!
2Wail, O pine tree, for the cedar has fallen;
the stately trees are ruined!
Wail, oaks of Bashan;
the dense forest[u] has been cut down!
3Listen to the wail of the shepherds;
their rich pastures are destroyed!
Listen to the roar of the lions;
the lush thicket of the Jordan is ruined![v]

Two staffs called Favor and Union.

4This is what the LORD my God says:
"Pasture the flock marked for slaughter.
5Their buyers slaughter them and go
unpunished. Those who sell them say,
'Praise the LORD, I am rich!' Their own
shepherds do not spare them.[w] 6For I
will no longer have pity on the people
of the land," declares the LORD. "I will
hand everyone over to his neighbor[x]
and his king. They will oppress the land,
and I will not rescue them from their
hands."[y]
7So I pastured the flock marked for
slaughter, particularly the oppressed of
the flock. Then I took two staffs and
called one Favor and the other Union,
and I pastured the flock. 8In one month
I got rid of the three shepherds.
The flock detested me, and I grew
weary of them 9and said, "I will not be
your shepherd. Let the dying die, and

10:2 [a]Eze 34:5; Hos 3:4; Mt 9:36
10:3 [b]Jer 25:34
10:4 [c]Isa 22:23 [d]Zec 9:10
10:5 [e]2Sa 22:43 [f]Am 2:15; Hag 2:22
10:6 [g]Zec 8:7-8 [h]Zec 13:9
10:7 [i]Zec 9:15
10:8 [j]Isa 5:26 [k]Jer 33:22; Eze 36:11
10:9 [l]Eze 6:9
10:10 [m]Isa 11:11 [n]Jer 50:19 [o]Isa 49:19
10:11 [p]Isa 19:5-7; 51:10 [q]Zep 2:13 [r]Eze 30:13
10:12 [s]Mic 4:5
11:1 [t]Eze 31:3
11:2 [u]Isa 32:19
11:3 [v]Jer 2:15; 50:44
11:5 [w]Jer 50:7; Eze 34:2-3
11:6 [x]Zec 14:13 [y]Isa 9:19-21; Jer 13:14; Mic 5:8; 7:2-6

u4,5 Or *ruler, all of them together.* / 5*They*

the perishing perish.[a] Let those who are
left eat one another's flesh."
10Then I took my staff called Favor[b]
and broke it, revoking[c] the covenant I
had made with all the nations. 11It was
revoked on that day, and so the afflicted
of the flock who were watching me
knew it was the word of the LORD.
12I told them, "If you think it best, give
me my pay; but if not, keep it." So they
paid me thirty pieces of silver.[d]
13And the LORD said to me, "Throw it
to the potter"—the handsome price at
which they priced me! So I took the
thirty pieces of silver and threw them
into the house of the LORD to the potter.[e]
14Then I broke my second staff called
Union, breaking the brotherhood between Judah and Israel.
15Then the LORD said to me, "Take
again the equipment of a foolish shepherd. 16For I am going to raise up a
shepherd over the land who will not care
for the lost, or seek the young, or heal
the injured, or feed the healthy, but will
eat the meat of the choice sheep, tearing off their hoofs.

17"Woe to the worthless shepherd,[f]
who deserts the flock!
May the sword strike his arm[g] and his
right eye!
May his arm be completely withered,
his right eye totally blinded!"[h]

Destruction of Jerusalem's enemies.

An Oracle

12 This is the word of the LORD concerning Israel. The LORD, who
stretches out the heavens,[i] who lays the
foundation of the earth,[j] and who forms
the spirit of man[k] within him, declares:
2"I am going to make Jerusalem a cup[l]
that sends all the surrounding peoples
reeling.[m] Judah[n] will be besieged as well
as Jerusalem. 3On that day, when all the
nations[o] of the earth are gathered against
her, I will make Jerusalem an immovable
rock[p] for all the nations. All who try to
move it will injure[q] themselves. 4On that
day I will strike every horse with panic
and its rider with madness," declares the
LORD. "I will keep a watchful eye over
the house of Judah, but I will blind all
the horses of the nations.[r] 5Then the
leaders of Judah will say in their hearts,
'The people of Jerusalem are strong, because the LORD Almighty is their God.'
6"On that day I will make the leaders
of Judah like a firepot[s] in a woodpile, like
a flaming torch among sheaves. They
will consume[t] right and left all the surrounding peoples, but Jerusalem will remain intact in her place.
7"The LORD will save the dwellings of
Judah first, so that the honor of the
house of David and of Jerusalem's inhabitants may not be greater than that of
Judah.[u] 8On that day the LORD will
shield[v] those who live in Jerusalem, so
that the feeblest among them will be like
David, and the house of David will be
like God,[w] like the Angel of the LORD
going before[x] them. 9On that day I will
set out to destroy all the nations that
attack Jerusalem.[y]

Mourning for the One they pierced.

10"And I will pour out on the house
of David and the inhabitants of Jerusalem a spirit[v] of grace and supplication.[z]
They will look on[w] me, the one they have
pierced,[a] and they will mourn for him as
one mourns for an only child, and grieve
bitterly for him as one grieves for a firstborn son. 11On that day the weeping in
Jerusalem will be great, like the weeping of Hadad Rimmon in the plain of
Megiddo.[b] 12The land will mourn,[c] each
clan by itself, with their wives by themselves: the clan of the house of David and
their wives, the clan of the house of
Nathan and their wives, 13the clan of the
house of Levi and their wives, the clan
of Shimei and their wives, 14and all the
rest of the clans and their wives.

A fountain to cleanse from sin.

13 "On that day a fountain[d] will be
opened to the house of David and

11:9 [a]Jer 15:2; 43:11
11:10 [b]ver 7 [c]Ps 89:39; Jer 14:21
11:12 [d]Ex 21:32; Mt 26:15
11:13 [e]Mt 27:9-10*; Ac 1:18-19
11:17 [f]Jer 23:1 [g]Eze 30:21-22 [h]Jer 23:1
12:1 [i]Isa 42:5; Jer 51:15 [j]Ps 102:25; Heb 1:10 [k]Isa 57:16
12:2 [l]Ps 75:8 [m]Isa 51:23 [n]Zec 14:14
12:3 [o]Zec 14:2 [p]Da 2:34-35 [q]Mt 21:44
12:4 [r]Ps 76:6
12:6 [s]Isa 10:17-18; Zec 11:1 [t]Ob 1:18
12:7 [u]Jer 30:18; Am 9:11
12:8 [v]Joel 3:16; Zec 9:15 [w]Ps 82:6 [x]Mic 7:8
12:9 [y]Zec 14:2-3
12:10 [z]Isa 44:3; Eze 39:29; Joel 2:28-29 [a]Jn 19:34,37*; Rev 1:7
12:11 [b]2Ki 23:29
12:12 [c]Mt 24:30; Rev 1:7
13:1 [d]Jer 17:13

[v] 10 Or *the Spirit* [w] 10 Or *to*

the inhabitants of Jerusalem, to cleanse[a]
them from sin and impurity.
2“On that day, I will banish the names
of the idols[b] from the land, and they will
be remembered no more,” declares the
LORD Almighty. “I will remove both the
prophets[c] and the spirit of impurity from
the land. 3And if anyone still prophesies,
his father and mother, to whom he was
born, will say to him, ‘You must die, because you have told lies in the LORD’s
name.’ When he prophesies, his own
parents will stab him.[d]
4“On that day every prophet will be
ashamed[e] of his prophetic vision. He will
not put on a prophet’s garment[f] of hair[g]
in order to deceive. 5He will say, ‘I am
not a prophet. I am a farmer; the land has
been my livelihood since my youth.[x]’[h]
6If someone asks him, ‘What are these
wounds on your body[y]?’ he will answer,
‘The wounds I was given at the house
of my friends.’

The shepherd struck,
the sheep scattered.

7“Awake, O sword,[i] against my
shepherd,[j]
against the man who is close to me!”
declares the LORD Almighty.
“Strike the shepherd,
and the sheep will be scattered,[k]
and I will turn my hand against the
little ones.
8In the whole land,” declares the LORD,
“two-thirds will be struck down
and perish;
yet one-third will be left in it.[l]
9This third I will bring into the fire;[m]
I will refine them like silver[n]
and test them like gold.
They will call[o] on my name
and I will answer[p] them;
I will say, ‘They are my people,’[q]
and they will say, ‘The LORD is our
God.[r]’”

The LORD will be king
over the whole earth.

14 A day of the LORD[s] is coming
when your plunder will be divided among you.
2I will gather all the nations to Jerusalem to fight against it; the city will be
captured, the houses ransacked, and the
women raped. Half of the city will go
into exile, but the rest of the people
will not be taken from the city.[t]
3Then the LORD will go out and fight[u]
against those nations, as he fights in the
day of battle. 4On that day his feet will
stand on the Mount of Olives,[v] east of
Jerusalem, and the Mount of Olives
will be split in two from east to west,
forming a great valley, with half of the
mountain moving north and half moving south. 5You will flee by my mountain valley, for it will extend to Azel.
You will flee as you fled from the earthquake[z][w] in the days of Uzziah king of
Judah. Then the LORD my God will
come,[x] and all the holy ones with him.[y]
6On that day there will be no light,[z]
no cold or frost. 7It will be a unique[a]
day, without daytime or nighttime[b]—a
day known to the LORD. When evening
comes, there will be light.[c]
8On that day living water[d] will flow
out from Jerusalem, half to the eastern[e]
sea[a] and half to the western sea,[b] in summer and in winter.
9The LORD will be king over the whole
earth.[f] On that day there will be one
LORD, and his name the only name.[g]
10The whole land, from Geba[h] to Rimmon, south of Jerusalem, will become
like the Arabah. But Jerusalem will be
raised up[i] and remain in its place,[j] from
the Benjamin Gate to the site of the First
Gate, to the Corner Gate, and from the
Tower of Hananel to the royal winepresses. 11It will be inhabited; never
again will it be destroyed. Jerusalem
will be secure.[k]
12This is the plague with which the
LORD will strike all the nations that

13:1 [a]Ps 51:2; Heb 9:14
13:2 [b]Ex 23:13; Eze 36:25; Hos 2:17 [c]1Ki 22:22; Jer 23:14-15
13:3 [d]Dt 13:6-11; 18:20; Jer 23:34; Eze 14:9
13:4 [e]Jer 6:15; Mic 3:6-7 [f]Mt 3:4 [g]2Ki 1:8; Isa 20:2
13:5 [h]Am 7:14
13:7 [i]Jer 47:6 [j]Isa 40:11; 53:4; Eze 37:24 [k]Mt 26:31*; Mk 14:27*
13:8 [l]Eze 5:2-4,12
13:9 [m]Mal 3:2 [n]Isa 48:10; 1Pe 1:6-7 [o]Ps 50:15 [p]Zec 10:6 [q]Jer 30:22 [r]Jer 29:12
14:1 [s]Isa 13:9; Mal 4:1
14:2 [t]Isa 13:6; Zec 13:8
14:3 [u]Zec 9:14-15
14:4 [v]Eze 11:23
14:5 [w]Am 1:1 [x]Isa 29:6; 66:15-16 [y]Mt 16:27; 25:31
14:6 [z]Isa 13:10; Jer 4:23
14:7 [a]Jer 30:7 [b]Rev 21:23-25; 22:5 [c]Isa 30:26
14:8 [d]Eze 47:1-12; Jn 7:38; Rev 22:1-2 [e]Joel 2:20
14:9 [f]Dt 6:4; Isa 45:24; Rev 11:15 [g]Eph 4:5-6
14:10 [h]1Ki 15:22 [i]Jer 30:18; Am 9:11 [j]Zec 12:6
14:11 [k]Eze 34:25-28

[x]5 Or *farmer; a man sold me in my youth*
[y]6 Or *wounds between your hands* [z]5 Or [5]*My mountain valley will be blocked and will extend to Azel. It will be blocked as it was blocked because of the earthquake* [a]8 That is, the Dead Sea
[b]8 That is, the Mediterranean

fought against Jerusalem: Their flesh will
rot while they are still standing on their
feet, their eyes will rot in their sockets,
and their tongues will rot in their
mouths.[a] 13On that day men will be
stricken by the LORD with great panic.
Each man will seize the hand of another, and they will attack each other.[b]
14Judah[c] too will fight at Jerusalem. The
wealth of all the surrounding nations
will be collected[d]—great quantities of
gold and silver and clothing. 15A similar
plague[e] will strike the horses and mules,
the camels and donkeys, and all the
animals in those camps.

16Then the survivors from all the
nations that have attacked Jerusalem will
go up year after year to worship the
King, the LORD Almighty, and to celebrate the Feast of Tabernacles.[f] 17If any
of the peoples of the earth do not go up
to Jerusalem to worship the King, the
LORD Almighty, they will have no rain.[g]
18If the Egyptian people do not go up and
take part, they will have no rain. The
LORD[c] will bring on them the plague he
inflicts on the nations that do not go
up to celebrate the Feast of Tabernacles.[h]
19This will be the punishment of Egypt
and the punishment of all the nations
that do not go up to celebrate the Feast
of Tabernacles.

20On that day HOLY TO THE LORD will be
inscribed on the bells of the horses, and
the cooking pots[i] in the LORD's house will
be like the sacred bowls[j] in front of the
altar. 21Every pot in Jerusalem and Judah
will be holy[k] to the LORD Almighty, and
all who come to sacrifice will take some
of the pots and cook in them. And on
that day[l] there will no longer be a
Canaanite[d][m] in the house of the LORD
Almighty.[n]

14:12 [a]Lev 26:16; Dt 28:22
14:13 [b]Zec 11:6
14:14 [c]Zec 12:2 [d]Isa 23:18
14:15 [e]ver 12
14:16 [f]Isa 60:6-9
14:17 [g]Jer 14:4; Am 4:7
14:18 [h]ver 12
14:20 [i]Eze 46:20 [j]Zec 9:15
14:21 [k]Ro 14:6-7; 1Co 10:31 [l]Ne 8:10 [m]Zec 9:8 [n]Eze 44:9

c *18* Or *part, then the LORD* d *21* Or *merchant*

MALACHI

Author: Malachi.

Date Written: Between 450 and 400 B.C.

Time Span: About 7 years.

Title: From the book's author: Malachi. This name means "my messenger."

Background: The temple of God is now complete. The ministries of Haggai and Zechariah are over, but prophecy continues through Malachi and his contemporary, Nehemiah. Once again the nation has fallen into a wide variety of sins: divorce; intermarriage to pagan spouses; neglect of the temple and its tithes; ungodly leadership; and indifference. It has been about 100 years since the Jews' return to Jerusalem, and now God's people are discouraged due to the trying times of drought and famine.

Where Written: Jerusalem.

To Whom: To all Israelites, but especially to the remnant that returned from captivity in Babylon.

Content: The prophet Malachi brings a message of judgment upon the people because they have not learned from their past sins. In a dialogue with God, the sins and apathy of the people are rebuked. Malachi is distinguished as being the only prophetic book which ends not in deliverance...but judgment. Mankind has made very little progress spiritually through the years, and, thus, the Old Testament ends with the word "curse." However, this word is contained in a promise that Elijah will come to restore the hearts of the fathers. This is fulfilled with the coming of John the Baptist who prepares the way for Jesus Christ, 400 years after Malachi's message.

Key Words: "Tithe"; "Prepare." When the people do not "tithe," they are actually robbing from God what is rightfully his (3:8,9). But the people owe to God more than just their money, they owe their time, talents and praises as well. Part of Malachi's ministry is to "prepare" the hearts of God's people and the way for John the Baptist, who will then "prepare" the way for the Messiah, Jesus Christ our Lord.

Themes: • Remembering God's past victories will help during our times of need today. • Giving to God and his work is a privilege, not a punishment. • Try as we may...we can never outgive the Lord. • There is no overlooking the issue of sin. • God has a plan that includes all of history.

Outline:
1. God's love for Israel. 1:1-1:5
2. Israel's defiled sacrifices. 1:6-1:14
3. God's admonition for the priests. 2:1-2:9
4. Israel's sins shown offensive to God. 2:10-3:15
5. Promises and rewards for those who fear God. 3:16-4:6

MALACHI

1 An oracle:[a] The word[b] of the LORD
to Israel through Malachi.[a]

Malachi's reminder of the LORD's love.

2"I have loved[c] you," says the LORD.
"But you ask, 'How have you
loved us?'
"Was not Esau Jacob's brother?" the
LORD says. "Yet I have loved Jacob,[d] 3but
Esau I have hated, and I have turned his
mountains into a wasteland[e] and left his
inheritance to the desert jackals.[f]"
4Edom may say, "Though we have
been crushed, we will rebuild[g] the
ruins."
But this is what the LORD Almighty
says: "They may build, but I will demolish. They will be called the Wicked Land,
a people always under the wrath of the
LORD.[h] 5You will see it with your own
eyes and say, 'Great[i] is the LORD—even
beyond the borders of Israel!'[j]

Blemished sacrifices.

6"A son honors his father, and a servant his master. If I am a father, where
is the honor due me? If I am a master,
where is the respect[k] due me?" says
the LORD Almighty.[l] "It is you, O priests,
who show contempt for my name.
"But you ask, 'How have we shown
contempt for your name?'
7"You place defiled food[m] on my altar.
"But you ask, 'How have we defiled
you?'
"By saying that the LORD's table is
contemptible. 8When you bring blind
animals for sacrifice, is that not wrong?
When you sacrifice crippled or diseased
animals,[n] is that not wrong? Try offering
them to your governor! Would he be
pleased with you? Would he accept you?"
says the LORD Almighty.[o]
9"Now implore God to be gracious to
us. With such offerings[p] from your
hands, will he accept you?"—says the
LORD Almighty.
10"Oh, that one of you would shut the
temple doors, so that you would not
light useless fires on my altar! I am not
pleased[q] with you," says the LORD Almighty, "and I will accept no offering[r]
from your hands. 11My name will be
great among the nations, from the rising
to the setting of the sun. In every place
incense[s] and pure offerings will be
brought to my name, because my name
will be great among the nations," says
the LORD Almighty.
12"But you profane it by saying of the
Lord's table, 'It is defiled,' and of its
food,[t] 'It is contemptible.' 13And you say,
'What a burden!'[u] and you sniff at it con-
temptuously," says the LORD Almighty.
"When you bring injured, crippled or
diseased animals and offer them as sacrifices, should I accept them from your
hands?" says the LORD. 14"Cursed is the
cheat who has an acceptable male in his
flock and vows to give it, but then sacrifices a blemished animal[v] to the Lord. For
I am a great king,[w]" says the LORD Almighty, "and my name is to be feared
among the nations.

Warning for the priests.

2 "And now this admonition is for
you, O priests.[x] 2If you do not listen,
and if you do not set your heart to honor
my name," says the LORD Almighty, "I
will send a curse[y] upon you, and I will
curse your blessings. Yes, I have already
cursed them, because you have not set
your heart to honor me.
3"Because of you I will rebuke[b] your
descendants[c]; I will spread on your
faces the offal[z] from your festival sacrifices, and you will be carried off with
it.[a] 4And you will know that I have sent
you this admonition so that my covenant
with Levi[b] may continue," says the LORD
Almighty. 5"My covenant was with him,
a covenant[c] of life and peace,[d] and I
gave them to him; this called for reverence and he revered me and stood in

1:1 [a]Na 1:1 [b]1Pe 4:11
1:2 [c]Dt 4:37 [d]Ro 9:13*
1:3 [e]Isa 34:10 [f]Eze 35:3-9
1:4 [g]Isa 9:10 [h]Eze 25:12-14
1:5 [i]Ps 35:27; Mic 5:4 [j]Am 1:11-12
1:6 [k]Isa 1:2 [l]Job 5:17
1:7 [m]ver 12; Lev 21:6
1:8 [n]Lev 22:22; Dt 15:21 [o]Isa 43:23
1:9 [p]Lev 23:33-44
1:10 [q]Hos 5:6 [r]Isa 1:11-14; Jer 14:12
1:11 [s]Isa 60:6-7; Rev 8:3
1:12 [t]ver 7
1:13 [u]Isa 43:22-24
1:14 [v]Lev 22:18-21 [w]1Ti 6:15
2:1 [x]ver 7
2:2 [y]Dt 28:20
2:3 [z]Ex 29:14 [a]1Ki 14:10
2:4 [b]Nu 3:12
2:5 [c]Dt 33:9 [d]Nu 25:12

a *1 Malachi* means *my messenger.* b *3* Or *cut off* (see Septuagint) c *3* Or *will blight your grain*

awe of my name. 6True instruction[a] was in his mouth and nothing false was found on his lips. He walked with me in peace and uprightness, and turned many from sin.[b]

7"For the lips of a priest[c] ought to preserve knowledge, and from his mouth men should seek instruction[d]—because he is the messenger[e] of the LORD Almighty. 8But you have turned from the way and by your teaching have caused many to stumble;[f] you have violated the covenant with Levi," says the LORD Almighty. 9"So I have caused you to be despised[g] and humiliated before all the people, because you have not followed my ways but have shown partiality in matters of the law."

10Have we not all one Father[d]?[h] Did not one God create us? Why do we profane the covenant[i] of our fathers by breaking faith with one another?

11Judah has broken faith. A detestable thing has been committed in Israel and in Jerusalem: Judah has desecrated the sanctuary the LORD loves, by marrying[j] the daughter of a foreign god.[k] 12As for the man who does this, whoever he may be, may the LORD cut him off[l] from the tents of Jacob[e]—even though he brings offerings[m] to the LORD Almighty.

13Another thing you do: You flood the LORD's altar with tears. You weep and wail because he no longer pays attention[n] to your offerings or accepts them with pleasure from your hands. 14You ask, "Why?" It is because the LORD is acting as the witness between you and the wife of your youth,[o] because you have broken faith with her, though she is your partner, the wife of your marriage covenant.

15Has not ⌊the LORD⌋ made them one?[p] In flesh and spirit they are his. And why one? Because he was seeking godly offspring.[f][q] So guard yourself in your spirit, and do not break faith with the wife of your youth.

16"I hate divorce,[r]" says the LORD God of Israel, "and I hate a man's covering himself[g] with violence as well as with his garment," says the LORD Almighty.

2:6 [a]Dt 33:10 [b]Jer 23:22; Jas 5:19-20
2:7 [c]Jer 18:18 [d]Lev 10:11 [e]Nu 27:21
2:8 [f]Jer 18:15
2:9 [g]1Sa 2:30
2:10 [h]1Co 8:6 [i]Ex 19:5
2:11 [j]Ne 13:23 [k]Ezr 9:1; Jer 3:7-9
2:12 [l]Eze 24:21 [m]Mal 1:10
2:13 [n]Jer 14:12
2:14 [o]Pr 5:18
2:15 [p]Ge 2:24; Mt 19:4-6 [q]1Co 7:14
2:16 [r]Dt 24:1; Mt 5:31-32; 19:4-9
2:17 [s]Isa 43:24
3:1 [t]Isa 40:3; Mt 11:10*; Mk 1:2*; Lk 7:27*
3:2 [u]Eze 22:14; Rev 6:17 [v]Zec 13:9; Mt 3:10-12
3:3 [w]Da 12:10 [x]Isa 1:25
3:4 [y]2Ch 7:12; Ps 51:19; Mal 1:11 [z]2Ch 7:3
3:5 [a]Jer 7:9 [b]Lev 19:13; Jas 5:4 [c]Ex 22:22
3:6 [d]Nu 23:19; Jas 1:17
3:7 [e]Jer 7:26; Ac 7:51 [f]Zec 1:3

So guard yourself in your spirit, and do not break faith.

17You have wearied[s] the LORD with your words.

"How have we wearied him?" you ask.

By saying, "All who do evil are good in the eyes of the LORD, and he is pleased with them" or "Where is the God of justice?"

3 "See, I will send my messenger, who will prepare the way before me.[t] Then suddenly the Lord you are seeking will come to his temple; the messenger of the covenant, whom you desire, will come," says the LORD Almighty.

2But who can endure[u] the day of his coming? Who can stand when he appears? For he will be like a refiner's fire[v] or a launderer's soap. 3He will sit as a refiner and purifier of silver;[w] he will purify[x] the Levites and refine them like gold and silver. Then the LORD will have men who will bring offerings in righteousness, 4and the offerings[y] of Judah and Jerusalem will be acceptable to the LORD, as in days gone by, as in former years.[z]

5"So I will come near to you for judgment. I will be quick to testify against sorcerers, adulterers and perjurers,[a] against those who defraud laborers of their wages,[b] who oppress the widows[c] and the fatherless, and deprive aliens of justice, but do not fear me," says the LORD Almighty.

The people rob God.

6"I the LORD do not change.[d] So you, O descendants of Jacob, are not destroyed. 7Ever since the time of your forefathers you have turned away[e] from my decrees and have not kept them. Return to me, and I will return to you,"[f] says the LORD Almighty.

"But you ask, 'How are we to return?'

[d]*10* Or *father* [e]*12* Or *12May the LORD cut off from the tents of Jacob anyone who gives testimony in behalf of the man who does this* [f]*15* Or *15But the one ⌊who is our father⌋ did not do this, not as long as life remained in him. And what was he seeking? An offspring from God* [g]*16* Or *his wife*

8"Will a man rob God? Yet you rob me.
"But you ask, 'How do we rob you?'
"In tithes[a] and offerings. 9You are
under a curse—the whole nation of
you—because you are robbing me.
10Bring the whole tithe into the storehouse,[b] that there may be food in my
house. Test me in this," says the LORD
Almighty, "and see if I will not throw
open the floodgates[c] of heaven and pour
out so much blessing that you will not
have room enough for it. 11I will prevent
pests from devouring your crops, and
the vines in your fields will not cast their
fruit," says the LORD Almighty. 12"Then
all the nations will call you blessed,[d]
for yours will be a delightful land,"[e] says
the LORD Almighty.
13"You have said harsh things[f] against
me," says the LORD.
"Yet you ask, 'What have we said
against you?'
14"You have said, 'It is futile[g] to serve
God. What did we gain by carrying out
his requirements and going about like
mourners[h] before the LORD Almighty?
15But now we call the arrogant blessed.
Certainly the evildoers[i] prosper, and even
those who challenge God escape.'"

A scroll of remembrance.

16Then those who feared the LORD
talked with each other, and the LORD
listened and heard.[j] A scroll[k] of remembrance was written in his presence concerning those who feared the LORD and
honored his name.

17"They will be mine," says the LORD
Almighty, "in the day when I make up
my treasured possession.[h] [l] I will spare[m]
them, just as in compassion a man spares
his son who serves him. 18And you will
again see the distinction between the
righteous[n] and the wicked, between
those who serve God and those who do
not.

The day of the LORD.

4 "Surely the day is coming;[o] it will
burn like a furnace. All the arrogant
and every evildoer will be stubble,[p] and
that day that is coming will set them on
fire," says the LORD Almighty. "Not a root
or a branch will be left to them. 2But for
you who revere my name, the sun of
righteousness[q] will rise with healing[r] in
its wings. And you will go out and leap[s]
like calves released from the stall. 3Then
you will trample[t] down the wicked; they
will be ashes[u] under the soles of your feet
on the day when I do these things," says
the LORD Almighty.
4"Remember the law[v] of my servant
Moses, the decrees and laws I gave him
at Horeb for all Israel.
5"See, I will send you the prophet Elijah[w] before that great and dreadful day of
the LORD comes.[x] 6He will turn the hearts
of the fathers to their children,[y] and the
hearts of the children to their fathers; or
else I will come and strike[z] the land with
a curse."[a]

h *17* Or *Almighty, "my treasured possession, in the day when I act*

3:8
[a]Ne 13:10-12
3:10
[b]Ne 13:12
[c]2Ki 7:2
3:12
[d]Isa 61:9
[e]Isa 62:4
3:13
[f]Mal 2:17
3:14
[g]Ps 73:13
[h]Isa 58:3
3:15
[i]Jer 7:10
3:16
[j]Ps 34:15
[k]Ps 56:8
3:17
[l]Dt 7:6
[m]Ps 103:13; Isa 26:20
3:18
[n]Ge 18:25
4:1
[o]Joel 2:31
[p]Isa 5:24; Ob 18
4:2
[q]Lk 1:78; Eph 5:14
[r]Isa 30:26
[s]Isa 35:6
4:3
[t]Job 40:12
[u]Eze 28:18
4:4
[v]Ps 147:19
4:5
[w]Mt 11:14; Lk 1:17
[x]Joel 2:31
4:6
[y]Lk 1:17
[z]Isa 11:4; Rev 19:15
[a]Zec 5:3

THE NEW TESTAMENT

New International Version

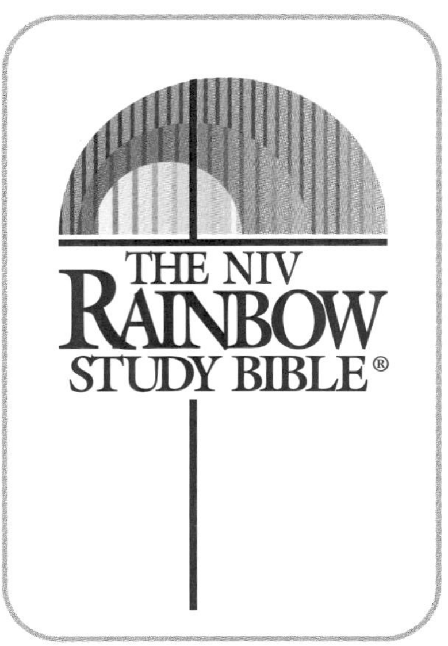

Every Verse Color-Coded

Bold Line® Edition

MATTHEW

Author: Matthew.

Date Written: Between A.D. 50 and 70.

Time Span: About 37 years (4 B.C.-A.D. 33).

Title: From the book's author: Matthew.

Background: The Old Testament ended with the prophets of God predicting the coming of the Anointed One, who would enter history to bring redemption and deliverance to his people. Some 400 years later, the New Testament begins with the book of Matthew revealing the fulfillment of these prophecies in Jesus Christ, the long-awaited Messiah. Matthew, a Jewish tax collector for the Roman government, is called by Jesus to become one of the twelve apostles. Thus, his Gospel often gives an eye-witness account.

Where Written: Possibly at Antioch.

To Whom: Primarily to Jews, but also to Gentiles who have become Christians.

Content: Matthew's Gospel provides the vital link between the Old and New Testaments. Matthew begins by tracing the genealogy of Jesus through Joseph; the birth of Jesus to the virgin Mary; the baptism of Jesus by John the Baptist; and Satan's temptation of Jesus while in the desert. Jesus speaks more in Matthew than in the other Gospels, and his teaching discourses include: the Sermon on the Mount (chapters 5-7); sending out the Twelve (chapter 10); parables of the kingdom (chapter 13); fellowship of the kingdom (chapter 18); and the Olivet Discourse concerning the future (chapters 24,25). During Jesus' final week his betrayal, trial, crucifixion, burial and resurrection take place. Matthew concludes with the call of the Great Commission to all believers.

Key Words: "Fulfillment"; "Kingdom of Heaven." Matthew quotes from many books of the Old Testament to solidify further the claim that indeed Jesus is the "fulfillment" of the promised Messiah, the Savior of the world. The term "kingdom of heaven" is used repeatedly by Matthew to introduce the Good News that God is present in Jesus Christ and lives to reign in men's lives. This term appears nowhere else in the New Testament.

Themes: • Jesus came to save both the Jews and the Gentiles. • There is one true God, but with the essence of 3, the Trinity: God the Father; God the Son; and God the Holy Spirit. • The standards of God are high, but the example he gave us is perfect...Jesus. • Christ is sufficient for whatever need we might have. • The ways of God are infinitely higher than the ways of the world. • Jesus willingly laid down his life to redeem a sinful world with his perfect and acceptable sacrifice.

Outline:

1. Jesus' birth and infancy. 1:1-2:23
2. The preparation and beginnings of Jesus' ministry. 3:1-4:25
3. The Sermon on the Mount. 5:1-7:29
4. Jesus' ministry of miracles. 8:1-9:34
5. Jesus' sending out the Twelve. 9:35-11:1
6. The continuation of Jesus' ministry with claims and parables. 11:2-25:46
7. Jesus' betrayal and crucifixion. 26:1-27:56
8. Jesus' burial, resurrection and ascension. 27:57-28:20

MATTHEW

Jesus' genealogy.

1:1-17pp— Lk 3:23-38
1:3-6pp— Ru 4:18-22
1:7-11pp— 1Ch 3:10-17

1 A record of the genealogy of Jesus Christ the son of David,[a] the son of Abraham:[b]

2Abraham was the father of Isaac,[c]
Isaac the father of Jacob,[d]
Jacob the father of Judah and his brothers,[e]
3Judah the father of Perez and Zerah, whose mother was Tamar,[f]
Perez the father of Hezron,
Hezron the father of Ram,
4Ram the father of Amminadab,
Amminadab the father of Nahshon,
Nahshon the father of Salmon,
5Salmon the father of Boaz, whose mother was Rahab,
Boaz the father of Obed, whose mother was Ruth,
Obed the father of Jesse,
6and Jesse the father of King David.[g]

David was the father of Solomon, whose mother had been Uriah's wife,[h]

1:1 [a]2Sa 7:12-16; Isa 9:6,7; 11:1; Jer 23:5,6; Mt 9:27; Lk 1:32,69; Ro 1:3; Rev 22:16 [b]Ge 22:18; Gal 3:16
1:2 [c]Ge 21:3,12 [d]Ge 25:26 [e]Ge 29:35
1:3 [f]Ge 38:27-30
1:6 [g]1Sa 16:1; 17:12 [h]2Sa 12:24

KEY PLACES IN MATTHEW

Jesus' earthly story begins in the town of Bethlehem in the Roman province of Judea (2:1). A threat to kill the infant king led Joseph to take his family to Egypt (2:14). When they returned, God led them to settle in Nazareth in Galilee (2:22,23). At about age 30, Jesus was baptized in the Jordan River and was tempted by Satan in the Judean desert (3:13;4:1). Jesus set up his base of operations in Capernaum (4:12,13) and from there ministered throughout Israel, telling parables, teaching about the kingdom, and healing the sick. He traveled to the region of the Gadarenes and healed two demon-possessed men (8:28ff); fed over 5,000 people with five loaves and two fish on the shores of Galilee near Bethsaida (14:15ff); healed the sick in Gennesaret (14:34ff); ministered to the Gentiles in Tyre and Sidon (15:21ff); visited Caesarea Philippi, where Peter declared him as the Messiah (16:13ff); and taught in Perea, across the Jordan (19:1). As he set out on his last visit to Jerusalem, he told the disciples what would happen to him there (20:17ff). He spent some time in Jericho (20:29) and then stayed in Bethany at night as he went back and forth into Jerusalem during his last week (21:17ff). In Jerusalem he would be crucified, but he would rise again.

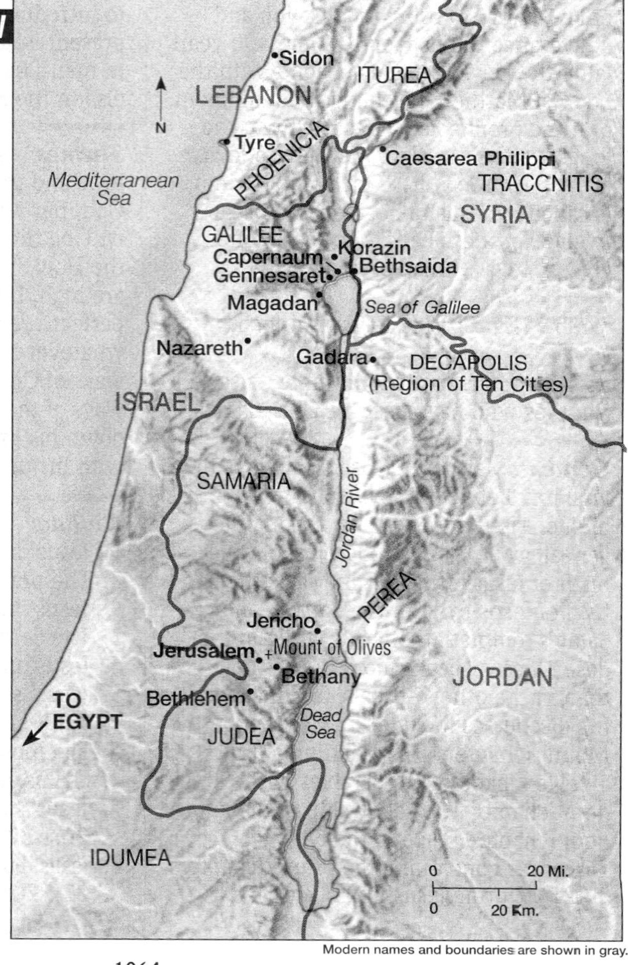

Modern names and boundaries are shown in gray.

7 Solomon the father of Rehoboam,
Rehoboam the father of Abijah,
Abijah the father of Asa,
8 Asa the father of Jehoshaphat,
Jehoshaphat the father of Jehoram,
Jehoram the father of Uzziah,
9 Uzziah the father of Jotham,
Jotham the father of Ahaz,
Ahaz the father of Hezekiah,
10 Hezekiah the father of Manasseh,[a]
Manasseh the father of Amon,
Amon the father of Josiah,
11 and Josiah the father of Jeconiah[a]
and his brothers at the time of
the exile to Babylon.[b]

12 After the exile to Babylon:
Jeconiah was the father of Shealtiel,[c]
Shealtiel the father of Zerubbabel,[d]
13 Zerubbabel the father of Abiud,
Abiud the father of Eliakim,
Eliakim the father of Azor,
14 Azor the father of Zadok,
Zadok the father of Akim,
Akim the father of Eliud,
15 Eliud the father of Eleazar,
Eleazar the father of Matthan,
Matthan the father of Jacob,
16 and Jacob the father of Joseph,
the husband of Mary,[e] of whom
was born Jesus, who is called
Christ.[f]

17 Thus there were fourteen generations in all from Abraham to David, fourteen from David to the exile to Babylon, and fourteen from the exile to the Christ.[b]

Jesus' birth to Mary.

18 This is how the birth of Jesus Christ
came about: His mother Mary was
pledged to be married to Joseph, but
before they came together, she was
found to be with child through the Holy
Spirit.[g] 19 Because Joseph her husband
was a righteous man and did not want
to expose her to public disgrace, he had
in mind to divorce[h] her quietly.

20 But after he had considered this,
an angel of the Lord appeared to him
in a dream and said, "Joseph son of
David, do not be afraid to take Mary
home as your wife, because what is conceived in her is from the Holy Spirit.
21 She will give birth to a son, and you
are to give him the name Jesus,[c][i] because
he will save his people from their sins."[j]
22 All this took place to fulfill what
the Lord had said through the prophet:
23 "The virgin will be with child and
will give birth to a son, and they will
call him Immanuel"[d][k]—which means,
"God with us."
24 When Joseph woke up, he did
what the angel of the Lord had commanded him and took Mary home as his
wife. 25 But he had no union with her
until she gave birth to a son. And he
gave him the name Jesus.[l]

Magi seek Jesus.

2 After Jesus was born in Bethlehem in Judea,[m] during the time of
King Herod,[n] Magi[e] from the east came
to Jerusalem 2 and asked, "Where is the
one who has been born king of the
Jews?[o] We saw his star[p] in the east[f] and
have come to worship him."
3 When King Herod heard this he was
disturbed, and all Jerusalem with him.
4 When he had called together all the
people's chief priests and teachers of the
law, he asked them where the Christ[g]
was to be born. 5 "In Bethlehem[q] in
Judea," they replied, "for this is what the
prophet has written:

6 " 'But you, Bethlehem, in the land of
Judah,
are by no means least among the
rulers of Judah;
for out of you will come a ruler
who will be the shepherd of my
people Israel.'[h]"[r]

1:10 [a]2Ki 20:21
1:11 [b]2Ki 24:14-16; Jer 27:20; Da 1:1,2
1:12 [c]1Ch 3:17 [d]1Ch 3:19; Ezr 3:2
1:16 [e]Lk 1:27 [f]Mt 27:17
1:18 [g]Lk 1:35
1:19 [h]Dt 24:1
1:21 [i]Lk 1:31 [j]Lk 2:11; Ac 5:31; 13:23,28
1:23 [k]Isa 7:14; 8:8,10
1:25 [l]ver 21
2:1 [m]Lk 2:4-7 [n]Lk 1:5
2:2 [o]Jer 23:5; Mt 27:11; Mk 15:2; Jn 1:49; 18:33-37 [p]Nu 24:17
2:5 [q]Jn 7:42
2:6 [r]Mic 5:2; 2Sa 5:2

[a] *11* That is, Jehoiachin; also in verse 12 [b] *17* Or *Messiah.* "The Christ" (Greek) and "the Messiah" (Hebrew) both mean "the Anointed One." [c] *21* *Jesus* is the Greek form of *Joshua,* which means *the LORD saves.* [d] *23* Isaiah 7:14 [e] *1* Traditionally *Wise Men* [f] *2* Or *star when it rose* [g] *4* Or *Messiah* [h] *6* Micah 5:2

[7]Then Herod called the Magi secretly and found out from them the exact
time the star had appeared. [8]He sent
them to Bethlehem and said, "Go and
make a careful search for the child. As
soon as you find him, report to me, so
that I too may go and worship him."
[9]After they had heard the king, they
went on their way, and the star they had
seen in the east[i] went ahead of them
until it stopped over the place where
the child was. [10]When they saw the star,
they were overjoyed. [11]On coming to the
house, they saw the child with his mother Mary, and they bowed down and
worshiped him.[a] Then they opened their
treasures and presented him with gifts[b]
of gold and of incense and of myrrh.
[12]And having been warned[c] in a dream[d]
not to go back to Herod, they returned
to their country by another route.

Mary and Joseph flee with Jesus to Egypt.

[13]When they had gone, an angel[e] of
the Lord appeared to Joseph in a dream.[f]
"Get up," he said, "take the child and
his mother and escape to Egypt. Stay
there until I tell you, for Herod is going
to search for the child to kill him."
[14]So he got up, took the child and
his mother during the night and left for
Egypt, [15]where he stayed until the death
of Herod. And so was fulfilled what the
Lord had said through the prophet: "Out
of Egypt I called my son."[j][g]
[16]When Herod realized that he had
been outwitted by the Magi, he was
furious, and he gave orders to kill all
the boys in Bethlehem and its vicinity
who were two years old and under, in
accordance with the time he had learned
from the Magi. [17]Then what was said
through the prophet Jeremiah was fulfilled:

[18]"A voice is heard in Ramah,
weeping and great mourning,
Rachel weeping for her children
and refusing to be comforted,
because they are no more."[k][h]

2:11 [a]Isa 60:3 [b]Ps 72:10
2:12 [c]Heb 11:7 [d]ver 13,19,22; Mt 27:19
2:13 [e]Ac 5:19 [f]ver 12,19,22
2:15 [g]Hos 11:1; Ex 4:22,23
2:18 [h]Jer 31:15
2:19 [i]ver 12,13,22
2:22 [j]ver 12,13,19; Mt 27:19 [k]Lk 2:39
2:23 [l]Lk 1:26; Jn 1:45,46 [m]Mt 1:22 [n]Mk 1:24

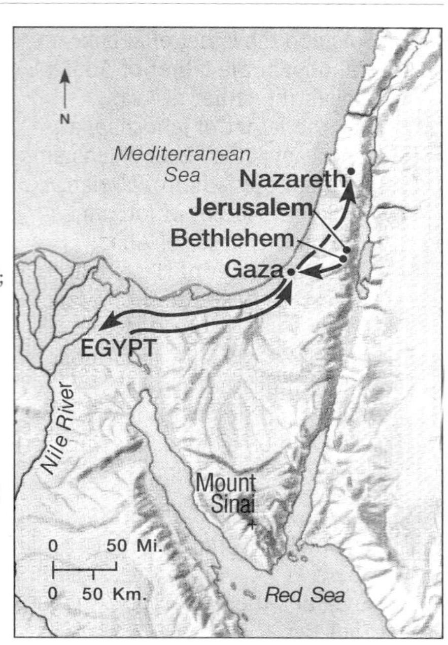

The Flight to Egypt

Herod planned to kill the baby Jesus, whom he perceived to be a future threat to his position. Warned of this treachery in a dream, Joseph took his family to Egypt until Herod's death, which occurred a year or two later. They then planned to return to Judea, but God led them instead to Nazareth in Galilee.

Jesus and his parents return to Nazareth.

[19]After Herod died, an angel of the
Lord appeared in a dream[i] to Joseph in
Egypt [20]and said, "Get up, take the child
and his mother and go to the land of
Israel, for those who were trying to take
the child's life are dead."
[21]So he got up, took the child and
his mother and went to the land of
Israel. [22]But when he heard that Arche-
laus was reigning in Judea in place of
his father Herod, he was afraid to go
there. Having been warned in a dream,[j]
he withdrew to the district of Galilee,[k]
[23]and he went and lived in a town called
Nazareth.[l] So was fulfilled[m] what was
said through the prophets: "He will be
called a Nazarene."[n]

i *9* Or *seen when it rose* j *15* Hosea 11:1 k *18* Jer. 31:15

John the Baptist begins his ministry.

3:1-12pp— Mk 1:3-8; Lk 3:2-17

3 In those days John the Baptist[a] came, preaching in the Desert of Judea 2and saying, "Repent, for the kingdom of heaven[b] is near." 3This is he who was spoken of through the prophet Isaiah:

"A voice of one calling in the desert,
'Prepare the way for the Lord,
make straight paths for him.'"[l][c]

4John's clothes were made of camel's hair, and he had a leather belt around his waist.[d] His food was locusts[e] and wild honey. 5People went out to him from Jerusalem and all Judea and the whole region of the Jordan. 6Confessing their sins, they were baptized by him in the Jordan River.

7But when he saw many of the Pharisees and Sadducees coming to where he was baptizing, he said to them: "You brood of vipers![f] Who warned you to flee from the coming wrath?[g] 8Produce fruit in keeping with repentance.[h] 9And do not think you can say to yourselves, 'We have Abraham as our father.' I tell you that out of these stones God can raise up children for Abraham. 10The ax is already at the root of the trees, and every tree that does not produce good fruit will be cut down and thrown into the fire.[i]

11"I baptize you with[m] water for repentance. But after me will come one who is more powerful than I, whose sandals I am not fit to carry. He will baptize you with the Holy Spirit[j] and with fire.[k] 12His winnowing fork is in his hand, and he will clear his threshing floor, gathering his wheat into the barn and burning up the chaff with unquenchable fire."[l]

Jesus is baptized by John the Baptist in the Jordan.

3:13-17pp— Mk 1:9-11; Lk 3:21,22; Jn 1:31-34

13Then Jesus came from Galilee to the Jordan to be baptized by John.[m] 14But John tried to deter him, saying, "I need to be baptized by you, and do you come to me?"

15Jesus replied, "Let it be so now; it is proper for us to do this to fulfill all righteousness." Then John consented.

16As soon as Jesus was baptized, he went up out of the water. At that moment heaven was opened, and he saw the Spirit of God[n] descending like a dove and lighting on him. 17And a voice from heaven[o] said, "This is my Son,[p] whom I love; with him I am well pleased."[q]

The devil tempts Jesus in the desert.

4:1-11pp— Mk 1:12,13; Lk 4:1-13

4 Then Jesus was led by the Spirit into the desert to be tempted by the devil. 2After fasting forty days and forty nights,[r] he was hungry. 3The tempter[s] came to him and said, "If you are the Son of God,[t] tell these stones to become bread."

4Jesus answered, "It is written: 'Man does not live on bread alone, but on every word that comes from the mouth of God.'[n]"[u]

5Then the devil took him to the holy city[v] and had him stand on the highest point of the temple. 6"If you are the Son of God," he said, "throw yourself down. For it is written:

"'He will command his angels
concerning you,
and they will lift you up in their
hands,
so that you will not strike your foot
against a stone.'[o]"[w]

7Jesus answered him, "It is also written: 'Do not put the Lord your God to the test.'[p]"[x]

8Again, the devil took him to a very high mountain and showed him all the kingdoms of the world and their splendor. 9"All this I will give you," he said, "if you will bow down and worship me."

10Jesus said to him, "Away from me,

3:1 [a]Lk 1:13, 57-66; 3:2-19
3:2 [b]Da 2:44; Mt 4:17; 6:10; Lk 11:20; 21:31; Jn 3:3,5; Ac 1:3,6
3:3 [c]Isa 40:3; Mal 3:1; Lk 1:76; Jn 1:23
3:4 [d]2Ki 1:8 [e]Lev 11:22
3:7 [f]Mt 12:34; 23:33 [g]Ro 1:18; 1Th 1:10
3:8 [h]Ac 26:20
3:10 [i]Mt 7:19; Lk 13:6-9; Jn 15:2,6
3:11 [j]Mk 1:8 [k]Isa 4:4; Ac 2:3,4
3:12 [l]Mt 13:30
3:13 [m]Mk 1:4
3:16 [n]Isa 11:2; 42:1
3:17 [o]Mt 17:5; Jn 12:28 [p]Ps 2:7; 2Pe 1:17,18 [q]Isa 42:1; Mt 12:18; 17:5; Mk 1:11; 9:7; Lk 9:35
4:2 [r]Ex 34:28; 1Ki 19:8
4:3 [s]1Th 3:5 [t]Mt 3:17; Jn 5:25; Ac 9:20
4:4 [u]Dt 8:3
4:5 [v]Ne 11:1; Da 9:24; Mt 27:53
4:6 [w]Ps 91:11,12
4:7 [x]Dt 6:16

[l]*3* Isaiah 40:3 [m]*11* Or *in* [n]*4* Deut. 8:3
[o]*6* Psalm 91:11,12 [p]*7* Deut. 6:16

Satan![a] For it is written: 'Worship the
Lord your God, and serve him only.'[q]"[b]
11 Then the devil left him, and angels
came and attended him.[c]

Jesus begins his Galilean ministry.

12 When Jesus heard that John had
been put in prison,[d] he returned to Galilee.[e] 13 Leaving Nazareth, he went and
lived in Capernaum,[f] which was by the
lake in the area of Zebulun and Naphtali— 14 to fulfill what was said through
the prophet Isaiah:

15 "Land of Zebulun and land of
Naphtali,
the way to the sea, along the Jordan,
Galilee of the Gentiles—
16 the people living in darkness
have seen a great light;
on those living in the land of the
shadow of death
a light has dawned."[r][g]

17 From that time on Jesus began to
preach, "Repent, for the kingdom of
heaven[h] is near."

Jesus calls four fishermen to follow him.

4:18-22pp— Mk 1:16-20; Lk 5:2-11; Jn 1:35-42

18 As Jesus was walking beside the
Sea of Galilee,[i] he saw two brothers,
Simon called Peter[j] and his brother Andrew. They were casting a net into the
lake, for they were fishermen. 19 "Come,
follow me,"[k] Jesus said, "and I will
make you fishers of men." 20 At once
they left their nets and followed him.
21 Going on from there, he saw two
other brothers, James son of Zebedee
and his brother John.[l] They were in a
boat with their father Zebedee, preparing their nets. Jesus called them, 22 and
immediately they left the boat and their
father and followed him.
23 Jesus went throughout Galilee,[m]
teaching in their synagogues,[n] preaching the good news[o] of the kingdom,[p]
and healing every disease and sickness
among the people.[q] 24 News about him
spread all over Syria,[r] and people brought
to him all who were ill with various
diseases, those suffering severe pain,
the demon-possessed,[s] those having
seizures,[t] and the paralyzed,[u] and he
healed them. 25 Large crowds from
Galilee, the Decapolis,[s] Jerusalem, Judea
and the region across the Jordan followed him.[v]

The Sermon on the Mount begins.

5 Now when he saw the crowds, he
went up on a mountainside and sat
down. His disciples came to him, 2 and
he began to teach them, saying:

The Beatitudes.

5:3-12pp— Lk 6:20-23

3 "Blessed are the poor in spirit,
for theirs is the kingdom of
heaven.[w]
4 Blessed are those who mourn,
for they will be comforted.[x]
5 Blessed are the meek,
for they will inherit the earth.[y]
6 Blessed are those who hunger and
thirst for righteousness,
for they will be filled.[z]
7 Blessed are the merciful,
for they will be shown mercy.
8 Blessed are the pure in heart,[a]
for they will see God.[b]
9 Blessed are the peacemakers,
for they will be called sons of God.[c]
10 Blessed are those who are
persecuted because of
righteousness,[d]
for theirs is the kingdom of
heaven.

11 "Blessed are you when people insult
you,[e] persecute you and falsely say all
kinds of evil against you because of
me. 12 Rejoice and be glad,[f] because great
is your reward in heaven, for in the
same way they persecuted the prophets
who were before you.[g]

4:10 [a]1Ch 21:1 [b]Dt 6:13
4:11 [c]Mt 26:53; Lk 22:43; Heb 1:14
4:12 [d]Mt 14:3 [e]Mk 1:14
4:13 [f]Mk 1:21; Lk 4:23,31; Jn 2:12; 4:46,47
4:16 [g]Isa 9:1,2; Lk 2:32
4:17 [h]Mt 3:2
4:18 [i]Mt 15:29; Mk 7:31; Jn 6:1 [j]Mt 16:17,18
4:19 [k]Mk 10:21, 28,52
4:21 [l]Mt 20:20
4:23 [m]Mk 1:39; Lk 4:15,44 [n]Mt 9:35; 13:54; Mk 1:21; Lk 4:15; Jn 6:59 [o]Mk 1:14 [p]Mt 3:2; Ac 20:25 [q]Mt 8:16; 15:30; Ac 10:38
4:24 [r]Lk 2:2 [s]Mt 8:16,28; 9:32; 15:22; Mk 1:32; 5:15,16,18 [t]Mt 17:15 [u]Mt 8:6; 9:2; Mk 2:3
4:25 [v]Mk 3:7,8; Lk 6:17
5:3 [w]ver 10,19; Mt 25:34
5:4 [x]Isa 61:2,3; Rev 7:17
5:5 [y]Ps 37:11; Ro 4:13
5:6 [z]Isa 55:1,2
5:8 [a]Ps 24:3,4 [b]Heb 12:14; Rev 22:4 **5:9** [c]ver 44,45; Ro 8:14 **5:10** [d]1Pe 3:14 **5:11** [e]1Pe 4:14 **5:12** [f]Ac 5:41; 1Pe 4:13,16 [g]Mt 23:31,37; Ac 7:52; 1Th 2:15

[q] *10* Deut. 6:13 [r] *16* Isaiah 9:1,2 [s] *25* That is, the Ten Cities

13"You are the salt of the earth. But if the salt loses its saltiness, how can it be made salty again? It is no longer good for anything, except to be thrown out and trampled by men.[a]

14"You are the light of the world.[b] A city on a hill cannot be hidden. 15Neither do people light a lamp and put it under a bowl. Instead they put it on its stand, and it gives light to everyone in the house.[c] 16In the same way, let your light shine before men, that they may see your good deeds and praise[d] your Father in heaven.

17"Do not think that I have come to abolish the Law or the Prophets; I have not come to abolish them but to fulfill them.[e] 18I tell you the truth, until heaven and earth disappear, not the smallest letter, not the least stroke of a pen, will by any means disappear from the Law until everything is accomplished.[f] 19Anyone who breaks one of the least of these commandments[g] and teaches others to do the same will be called least in the kingdom of heaven, but whoever practices and teaches these commands will be called great in the kingdom of heaven. 20For I tell you that unless your righteousness surpasses that of the Pharisees and the teachers of the law, you will certainly not enter the kingdom of heaven.

Judgment on anger and murder.

5:25,26pp — Lk 12:58,59

21"You have heard that it was said to the people long ago, 'Do not murder,[t][h] and anyone who murders will be subject to judgment.' 22But I tell you that anyone who is angry with his brother[u] will be subject to judgment.[i] Again, anyone who says to his brother, 'Raca,[v]' is answerable to the Sanhedrin.[j] But anyone who says, 'You fool!' will be in danger of the fire of hell.[k]

23"Therefore, if you are offering your gift at the altar and there remember that your brother has something against you, 24leave your gift there in front of the altar. First go and be reconciled to your brother; then come and offer your gift.

25"Settle matters quickly with your adversary who is taking you to court. Do it while you are still with him on the way, or he may hand you over to the judge, and the judge may hand you over to the officer, and you may be thrown into prison. 26I tell you the truth, you will not get out until you have paid the last penny.[w]

27"You have heard that it was said, 'Do not commit adultery.'[x][l] 28But I tell you that anyone who looks at a woman lustfully has already committed adultery with her in his heart.[m] 29If your right eye causes you to sin,[n] gouge it out and throw it away. It is better for you to lose one part of your body than for your whole body to be thrown into hell. 30And if your right hand causes you to sin, cut it off and throw it away. It is better for you to lose one part of your body than for your whole body to go into hell.

31"It has been said, 'Anyone who divorces his wife must give her a certificate of divorce.'[y][o] 32But I tell you that anyone who divorces his wife, except for marital unfaithfulness, causes her to become an adulteress, and anyone who marries the divorced woman commits adultery.[p]

33"Again, you have heard that it was said to the people long ago, 'Do not break your oath,[q] but keep the oaths you have made to the Lord.'[r] 34But I tell you, Do not swear at all:[s] either by heaven, for it is God's throne;[t] 35or by the earth, for it is his footstool; or by Jerusalem, for it is the city of the Great King.[u] 36And do not swear by your head, for you cannot make even one hair white or black. 37Simply let your 'Yes' be 'Yes,' and your 'No,' 'No';[v] anything beyond this comes from the evil one.[w]

38"You have heard that it was said, 'Eye for eye, and tooth for tooth.'[z][x] 39But I tell you, Do not resist an evil person.

5:13 [a]Mk 9:50; Lk 14:34,35
5:14 [b]Jn 8:12
5:15 [c]Mk 4:21; Lk 8:16
5:16 [d]Mt 9:8
5:17 [e]Ro 3:31
5:18 [f]Lk 16:17
5:19 [g]Jas 2:10
5:21 [h]Ex 20:13; Dt 5:17
5:22 [i]1Jn 3:15 [j]Mt 26:59 [k]Jas 3:6
5:27 [l]Ex 20:14; Dt 5:18
5:28 [m]Pr 6:25
5:29 [n]Mt 18:6,8,9; Mk 9:42-47
5:31 [o]Dt 24:1-4
5:32 [p]Lk 16:18
5:33 [q]Lev 19:12 [r]Nu 30:2; Dt 23:21; Mt 23:16-22
5:34 [s]Jas 5:12 [t]Isa 66:1; Mt 23:22
5:35 [u]Ps 48:2
5:37 [v]Jas 5:12 [w]Mt 6:13; 13:19,38; Jn 17:15; 2Th 3:3; 1Jn 2:13,14; 3:12; 5:18,19
5:38 [x]Ex 21:24; Lev 24:20; Dt 19:21

[t]*21* Exodus 20:13 [u]*22* Some manuscripts *brother without cause* [v]*22* An Aramaic term of contempt [w]*26* Greek *kodrantes* [x]*27* Exodus 20:14 [y]*31* Deut. 24:1 [z]*38* Exodus 21:24; Lev. 24:20; Deut. 19:21

If someone strikes you on the right
cheek, turn to him the other also.[a] **40**And
if someone wants to sue you and take
your tunic, let him have your cloak as
well. **41**If someone forces you to go one
mile, go with him two miles. **42**Give to
the one who asks you, and do not turn
away from the one who wants to borrow from you.[b]

43"You have heard that it was said,
'Love your neighbor[a][c] and hate your
enemy.'[d] **44**But I tell you: Love your enemies[b] and pray for those who persecute you,[e] **45**that you may be sons[f] of
your Father in heaven. He causes his
sun to rise on the evil and the good,
and sends rain on the righteous and
the unrighteous.[g] **46**If you love those who
love you, what reward will you get?[h]
Are not even the tax collectors doing
that? **47**And if you greet only your brothers, what are you doing more than others? Do not even pagans do that? **48**Be
perfect, therefore, as your heavenly
Father is perfect.[i]

The Sermon on the Mount continues.

6 "Be careful not to do your 'acts of
righteousness' before men, to be
seen by them.[j] If you do, you will have
no reward from your Father in heaven.

2"So when you give to the needy, do
not announce it with trumpets, as the
hypocrites do in the synagogues and
on the streets, to be honored by men.
I tell you the truth, they have received
their reward in full. **3**But when you give
to the needy, do not let your left hand
know what your right hand is doing,
4so that your giving may be in secret.
Then your Father, who sees what is
done in secret, will reward you.[k]

The model prayer.

6:9-13pp— Lk 11:2-4

5"And when you pray, do not be like
the hypocrites, for they love to pray
standing[l] in the synagogues and on the
street corners to be seen by men. I tell
you the truth, they have received their
reward in full. **6**But when you pray, go
into your room, close the door and
pray to your Father,[m] who is unseen.
Then your Father, who sees what is
done in secret, will reward you. **7**And
when you pray, do not keep on bab-
bling[n] like pagans, for they think they
will be heard because of their many
words.[o] **8**Do not be like them, for your
Father knows what you need[p] before
you ask him.

9"This, then, is how you should
pray:

"'Our Father in heaven,
hallowed be your name,
10your kingdom[q] come,
your will be done[r]
on earth as it is in heaven.
11Give us today our daily bread.[s]
12Forgive us our debts,
as we also have forgiven our
debtors.[t]
13And lead us not into temptation,[u]
but deliver us from the evil one.[c]'[v]

14For if you forgive men when they sin
against you, your heavenly Father will
also forgive you.[w] **15**But if you do not
forgive men their sins, your Father
will not forgive your sins.[x]

16"When you fast, do not look
somber[y] as the hypocrites do, for they
disfigure their faces to show men they
are fasting. I tell you the truth, they
have received their reward in full. **17**But
when you fast, put oil on your head
and wash your face, **18**so that it will not
be obvious to men that you are fasting,
but only to your Father, who is unseen;
and your Father, who sees what is
done in secret, will reward you.[z]

Treasures in heaven.

6:22,23pp— Lk 11:34-36

19"Do not store up for yourselves
treasures on earth,[a] where moth and
rust destroy,[b] and where thieves break

5:39 [a]Lk 6:29; Ro 12:17,19; 1Co 6:7; 1Pe 3:9
5:42 [b]Dt 15:8; Lk 6:30
5:43 [c]Lev 19:18 [d]Dt 23:6
5:44 [e]Lk 6:27,28; 23:34; Ac 7:60; Ro 12:14; 1Co 4:12; 1Pe 2:23
5:45 [f]ver 9 [g]Job 25:3
5:46 [h]Lk 6:32
5:48 [i]Lev 19:2; 1Pe 1:16
6:1 [j]Mt 23:5
6:4 [k]ver 6,18; Col 3:23,24
6:5 [l]Mk 11:25; Lk 18:10-14
6:6 [m]2Ki 4:33
6:7 [n]Ecc 5:2 [o]1Ki 18:26-29
6:8 [p]ver 32
6:10 [q]Mt 3:2 [r]Mt 26:39
6:11 [s]Pr 30:8
6:12 [t]Mt 18:21-35
6:13 [u]Jas 1:13 [v]Mt 5:37
6:14 [w]Mt 18:21-35; Mk 11:25,26; Eph 4:32; Col 3:13
6:15 [x]Mt 18:35
6:16 [y]Isa 58:5
6:18 [z]ver 4,6
6:19 [a]Pr 23:4; Heb 13:5 [b]Jas 5:2,3

[a]*43* Lev. 19:18 [b]*44* Some late manuscripts *enemies, bless those who curse you, do good to those who hate you* [c]*13* Or *from evil*; some late manuscripts *one, / for yours is the kingdom and the power and the glory forever. Amen.*

in and steal. **20**But store up for yourselves treasures in heaven,[a] where moth
and rust do not destroy, and where
thieves do not break in and steal.[b] **21**For
where your treasure is, there your heart
will be also.[c]
22"The eye is the lamp of the body.
If your eyes are good, your whole body
will be full of light. **23**But if your eyes
are bad, your whole body will be full
of darkness. If then the light within you
is darkness, how great is that darkness!
24"No one can serve two masters.
Either he will hate the one and love the
other, or he will be devoted to the one
and despise the other. You cannot serve
both God and Money.[d]

Freedom from worry.

6:25-33pp— Lk 12:22-31

25"Therefore I tell you, do not worry[e]
about your life, what you will eat or
drink; or about your body, what you
will wear. Is not life more important
than food, and the body more important than clothes? **26**Look at the birds
of the air; they do not sow or reap or
store away in barns, and yet your heavenly Father feeds them.[f] Are you not
much more valuable than they?[g] **27**Who
of you by worrying can add a single hour
to his life[d]?[h]
28"And why do you worry about
clothes? See how the lilies of the field
grow. They do not labor or spin. **29**Yet I
tell you that not even Solomon in all
his splendor[i] was dressed like one of
these. **30**If that is how God clothes the
grass of the field, which is here today
and tomorrow is thrown into the fire,
will he not much more clothe you, O
you of little faith?[j] **31**So do not worry,
saying, 'What shall we eat?' or 'What
shall we drink?' or 'What shall we wear?'
32For the pagans run after all these
things, and your heavenly Father knows
that you need them.[k] **33**But seek first
his kingdom and his righteousness, and
all these things will be given to you as
well.[l] **34**Therefore do not worry about
tomorrow, for tomorrow will worry
about itself. Each day has enough trouble of its own.

Judging and being judged.

7:3-5pp— Lk 6:41,42

7 "Do not judge, or you too will be
judged.[m] **2**For in the same way
you judge others, you will be judged,
and with the measure you use, it will
be measured to you.[n]
3"Why do you look at the speck of
sawdust in your brother's eye and pay
no attention to the plank in your own
eye? **4**How can you say to your brother, 'Let me take the speck out of your
eye,' when all the time there is a plank
in your own eye? **5**You hypocrite, first
take the plank out of your own eye, and
then you will see clearly to remove the
speck from your brother's eye.
6"Do not give dogs what is sacred;
do not throw your pearls to pigs. If you
do, they may trample them under their
feet, and then turn and tear you to
pieces.

Ask, seek and knock.

7:7-11pp— Lk 11:9-13

7"Ask and it will be given to you;[o]
seek and you will find; knock and the
door will be opened to you. **8**For everyone who asks receives; he who seeks
finds;[p] and to him who knocks, the door
will be opened.
9"Which of you, if his son asks for
bread, will give him a stone? **10**Or if he
asks for a fish, will give him a snake?
11If you, then, though you are evil,
know how to give good gifts to your
children, how much more will your
Father in heaven give good gifts to
those who ask him! **12**So in everything,
do to others what you would have them
do to you,[q] for this sums up the Law
and the Prophets.[r]

Enter the narrow gate.

13"Enter through the narrow gate.[s]
For wide is the gate and broad is the

6:20 [a]Mt 19:21; Lk 12:33; 18:22; 1Ti 6:19 [b]Lk 12:33
6:21 [c]Lk 12:34
6:24 [d]Lk 16:13
6:25 [e]ver 27,28,31, 34; Lk 10:41; 12:11,22; Php 4:6; 1Pe 5:7
6:26 [f]Job 38:41; Ps 147:9 [g]Mt 10:29-31
6:27 [h]Ps 39:5
6:29 [i]1Ki 10:4-7
6:30 [j]Mt 8:26; 14:31; 16:8
6:32 [k]ver 8
6:33 [l]Mt 19:29; Mk 10:29-30
7:1 [m]Lk 6:37; Ro 14:4,10, 13; 1Co 4:5; Jas 4:11,12
7:2 [n]Mk 4:24; Lk 6:38
7:7 [o]Mt 21:22; Mk 11:24; Jn 14:13,14; 15:7,16; 16:23,24; Jas 1:5-8; 4:2,3; 1Jn 3:22; 5:14,15
7:8 [p]Pr 8:17; Jer 29:12,13
7:12 [q]Lk 6:31 [r]Ro 13:8-10; Gal 5:14
7:13 [s]Lk 13:24

d27 Or *single cubit to his height*

road that leads to destruction, and many
enter through it. [14]But small is the gate
and narrow the road that leads to life,
and only a few find it.

[15]"Watch out for false prophets.[a] They
come to you in sheep's clothing, but
inwardly they are ferocious wolves.[b]
[16]By their fruit you will recognize them.[c]
Do people pick grapes from thornbushes, or figs from thistles?[d] [17]Like-
wise every good tree bears good fruit,
but a bad tree bears bad fruit. [18]A good
tree cannot bear bad fruit, and a bad
tree cannot bear good fruit. [19]Every
tree that does not bear good fruit is cut
down and thrown into the fire.[e] [20]Thus,
by their fruit you will recognize them.

[21]"Not everyone who says to me,
'Lord, Lord,'[f] will enter the kingdom of
heaven, but only he who does the will
of my Father who is in heaven.[g] [22]Many
will say to me on that day,[h] 'Lord, Lord,
did we not prophesy in your name,
and in your name drive out demons
and perform many miracles?'[i] [23]Then I
will tell them plainly, 'I never knew you.
Away from me, you evildoers!'[j]

The wise man builds on a rock. (The Sermon on the Mount concludes.)

7:24-27pp— Lk 6:47-49

[24]"Therefore everyone who hears
these words of mine and puts them
into practice[k] is like a wise man who
built his house on the rock. [25]The rain
came down, the streams rose, and the
winds blew and beat against that house;
yet it did not fall, because it had its
foundation on the rock. [26]But everyone who hears these words of mine
and does not put them into practice is
like a foolish man who built his house
on sand. [27]The rain came down, the
streams rose, and the winds blew and
beat against that house, and it fell with
a great crash."

[28]When Jesus had finished saying
these things,[l] the crowds were amazed
at his teaching,[m] [29]because he taught as
one who had authority, and not as their
teachers of the law.

7:15 [a]Jer 23:16; Mt 24:24; Mk 13:22; Lk 6:26; 2Pe 2:1; 1Jn 4:1; Rev 16:13 [b]Ac 20:29
7:16 [c]Mt 12:33; Lk 6:44 [d]Jas 3:12
7:19 [e]Mt 3:10
7:21 [f]Hos 8:2; Mt 25:11 [g]Ro 2:13; Jas 1:22
7:22 [h]Mt 10:15 [i]1Co 13:1-3
7:23 [j]Ps 6:8; Mt 25:12,41; Lk 13:25-27
7:24 [k]Jas 1:22-25
7:28 [l]Mt 11:1; 13:53; 19:1; 26:1 [m]Mt 13:54; Mk 1:22; 6:2; Lk 4:32; Jn 7:46
8:2 [n]Lk 5:12 [o]Mt 9:18; 15:25; 18:26; 20:20
8:4 [p]Mt 9:30; Mk 5:43; 7:36; 8:30 [q]Lev 14:2-32
8:8 [r]Ps 107:20
8:10 [s]Mt 15:28
8:11 [t]Ps 107:3; Isa 49:12; 59:19; Mal 1:11 [u]Lk 13:29
8:12 [v]Mt 13:38

Jesus heals man with leprosy.

8:2-4pp— Mk 1:40-44; Lk 5:12-14

8 When he came down from the
mountainside, large crowds followed
him. [2]A man with leprosy[e][n] came and
knelt before him[o] and said, "Lord, if you
are willing, you can make me clean."

[3]Jesus reached out his hand and
touched the man. "I am willing," he
said. "Be clean!" Immediately he was
cured[f] of his leprosy. [4]Then Jesus said
to him, "See that you don't tell anyone.[p]
But go, show yourself to the priest and
offer the gift Moses commanded,[q] as a
testimony to them."

Jesus heals centurion's servant.

8:5-13pp— Lk 7:1-10

[5]When Jesus had entered Capernaum,
a centurion came to him, asking for
help. [6]"Lord," he said, "my servant lies
at home paralyzed and in terrible suffering."

[7]Jesus said to him, "I will go and
heal him."

[8]The centurion replied, "Lord, I do
not deserve to have you come under
my roof. But just say the word, and my
servant will be healed.[r] [9]For I myself
am a man under authority, with soldiers under me. I tell this one, 'Go,'
and he goes; and that one, 'Come,'
and he comes. I say to my servant, 'Do
this,' and he does it."

[10]When Jesus heard this, he was
astonished and said to those following
him, "I tell you the truth, I have not
found anyone in Israel with such great
faith.[s] [11]I say to you that many will
come from the east and the west,[t] and
will take their places at the feast with
Abraham, Isaac and Jacob in the kingdom of heaven.[u] [12]But the subjects of
the kingdom[v] will be thrown outside,
into the darkness, where there will be

e2 The Greek word was used for various diseases affecting the skin—not necessarily leprosy. f3 Greek *made clean*

weeping and gnashing of teeth."[a]

13Then Jesus said to the centurion, "Go! It will be done just as you believed it would."[b] And his servant was healed at that very hour.

Jesus heals Peter's mother-in-law.

8:14-16pp— Mk 1:29-34; Lk 4:38-41

14When Jesus came into Peter's house, he saw Peter's mother-in-law lying in bed with a fever. 15He touched her hand and the fever left her, and she got up and began to wait on him.

16When evening came, many who were demon-possessed were brought to him, and he drove out the spirits with a word and healed all the sick.[c] 17This was to fulfill[d] what was spoken through the prophet Isaiah:

> "He took up our infirmities
> and carried our diseases."[g][e]

Jesus lacks place to lay his head.

8:19-22pp— Lk 9:57-60

18When Jesus saw the crowd around him, he gave orders to cross to the other side of the lake.[f] 19Then a teacher of the law came to him and said, "Teacher, I will follow you wherever you go."

20Jesus replied, "Foxes have holes and birds of the air have nests, but the Son of Man[g] has no place to lay his head."

21Another disciple said to him, "Lord, first let me go and bury my father."

22But Jesus told him, "Follow me,[h] and let the dead bury their own dead."

Jesus calms storm on lake.

8:23-27pp— Mk 4:36-41; Lk 8:22-25
8:23-27Ref— Mt 14:22-33

23Then he got into the boat and his disciples followed him. 24Without warning, a furious storm came up on the lake, so that the waves swept over the boat. But Jesus was sleeping. 25The disciples went and woke him, saying, "Lord, save us! We're going to drown!"

26He replied, "You of little faith,[i] why are you so afraid?" Then he got up and rebuked the winds and the waves, and it was completely calm.[j]

27The men were amazed and asked, "What kind of man is this? Even the winds and the waves obey him!"

Jesus sends demons into herd of pigs.

8:28-34pp— Mk 5:1-17; Lk 8:26-37

28When he arrived at the other side in the region of the Gadarenes,[h] two demon-possessed[k] men coming from the tombs met him. They were so violent that no one could pass that way. 29"What do you want with us,[l] Son of God?" they shouted. "Have you come here to torture us before the appointed time?"[m]

30Some distance from them a large herd of pigs was feeding. 31The demons begged Jesus, "If you drive us out, send us into the herd of pigs."

32He said to them, "Go!" So they came out and went into the pigs, and the whole herd rushed down the steep bank into the lake and died in the water. 33Those tending the pigs ran off, went into the town and reported all this, including what had happened to the demon-possessed men. 34Then the whole town went out to meet Jesus. And when they saw him, they pleaded with him to leave their region.[n]

A paralytic is healed.

9:2-8pp— Mk 2:3-12; Lk 5:18-26

9 Jesus stepped into a boat, crossed over and came to his own town.[o] 2Some men brought to him a paralytic,[p] lying on a mat. When Jesus saw their faith,[q] he said to the paralytic, "Take heart,[r] son; your sins are forgiven."[s]

3At this, some of the teachers of the law said to themselves, "This fellow is blaspheming!"[t]

4Knowing their thoughts,[u] Jesus said, "Why do you entertain evil thoughts in your hearts? 5Which is easier: to say, 'Your sins are forgiven,' or to say, 'Get

8:12 [a]Mt 13:42, 50; 22:13; 24:51; 25:30; Lk 13:28
8:13 [b]Mt 9:22
8:16 [c]Mt 4:23,24
8:17 [d]Mt 1:22 [e]Isa 53:4
8:18 [f]Mk 4:35
8:20 [g]Da 7:13; Mt 12:8,32, 40;16:13,27, 28;17:9;19:28; Mk 2:10; 8:31
8:22 [h]Mt 4:19
8:26 [i]Mt 6:30 [j]Ps 65:7; 89:9; 107:29
8:28 [k]Mt 4:24
8:29 [l]Jdg 11:12; 2Sa 16:10; 1Ki 17:18; Mk 1:24; Lk 4:34; Jn 2:4 [m]2Pe 2:4
8:34 [n]Lk 5:8; Ac 16:39
9:1 [o]Mt 4:13
9:2 [p]Mt 4:24 [q]ver 22 [r]Jn 16:33 [s]Lk 7:48
9:3 [t]Mt 26:65; Jn 10:33
9:4 [u]Ps 94:11; Mt 12:25; Lk 6:8; 9:47; 11:17

g *17* Isaiah 53:4 h *28* Some manuscripts *Gergesenes*; others *Gerasenes*

up and walk'? 6But so that you may know that the Son of Man[a] has authority on earth to forgive sins. . . ." Then he said to the paralytic, "Get up, take your mat and go home." 7And the man got up and went home. 8When the crowd saw this, they were filled with awe; and they praised God,[b] who had given such authority to men.

Jesus calls Matthew and eats with tax collectors.

9:9-13pp— Mk 2:14-17; Lk 5:27-32

9As Jesus went on from there, he saw a man named Matthew sitting at the tax collector's booth. "Follow me," he told him, and Matthew got up and followed him.

10While Jesus was having dinner at Matthew's house, many tax collectors and "sinners" came and ate with him and his disciples. 11When the Pharisees saw this, they asked his disciples, "Why does your teacher eat with tax collectors and 'sinners'?"[c]

12On hearing this, Jesus said, "It is not the healthy who need a doctor, but the sick. 13But go and learn what this means: 'I desire mercy, not sacrifice.'[i][d] For I have not come to call the righteous, but sinners."[e]

Jesus is questioned about fasting.

9:14-17pp— Mk 2:18-22; Lk 5:33-39

14Then John's disciples came and asked him, "How is it that we and the Pharisees fast,[f] but your disciples do not fast?"

15Jesus answered, "How can the guests of the bridegroom mourn while he is with them?[g] The time will come when the bridegroom will be taken from them; then they will fast.[h]

16"No one sews a patch of unshrunk cloth on an old garment, for the patch will pull away from the garment, making the tear worse. 17Neither do men pour new wine into old wineskins. If they do, the skins will burst, the wine will run out and the wineskins will be ruined. No, they pour new wine into new wineskins, and both are preserved."

A ruler's daughter is brought back to life, and other healings are performed.

9:18-26pp— Mk 5:22-43; Lk 8:41-56

18While he was saying this, a ruler came and knelt before him[i] and said, "My daughter has just died. But come and put your hand on her,[j] and she will live." 19Jesus got up and went with him, and so did his disciples.

20Just then a woman who had been subject to bleeding for twelve years came up behind him and touched the edge of his cloak.[k] 21She said to herself, "If I only touch his cloak, I will be healed."

22Jesus turned and saw her. "Take heart, daughter," he said, "your faith has healed you."[l] And the woman was healed from that moment.[m]

23When Jesus entered the ruler's house and saw the flute players and the noisy crowd,[n] 24he said, "Go away. The girl is not dead[o] but asleep."[p] But they laughed at him. 25After the crowd had been put outside, he went in and took the girl by the hand, and she got up. 26News of this spread through all that region.[q]

27As Jesus went on from there, two blind men followed him, calling out, "Have mercy on us, Son of David!"[r]

28When he had gone indoors, the blind men came to him, and he asked them, "Do you believe that I am able to do this?"

"Yes, Lord," they replied.

29Then he touched their eyes and said, "According to your faith will it be done to you";[s] 30and their sight was restored. Jesus warned them sternly, "See that no one knows about this."[t] 31But they went out and spread the news about him all over that region.[u]

32While they were going out, a man who was demon-possessed[v] and could not talk[w] was brought to Jesus. 33And when the demon was driven out, the

9:6 [a]Mt 8:20
9:8 [b]Mt 5:16; 15:31; Lk 7:16; 13:13; 17:15; 23:47; Jn 15:8; Ac 4:21; 11:18; 21:20
9:11 [c]Mt 11:19; Lk 5:30; 15:2; Gal 2:15
9:13 [d]Hos 6:6; Mic 6:6-8; Mt 12:7 [e]1Ti 1:15
9:14 [f]Lk 18:12
9:15 [g]Jn 3:29 [h]Ac 13:2,3; 14:23
9:18 [i]Mt 8:2 [j]Mk 5:23
9:20 [k]Mt 14:36; Mk 3:10
9:22 [l]Mk 10:52; Lk 7:50; 17:19; 18:42 [m]Mt 15:28
9:23 [n]2Ch 35:25; Jer 9:17,18
9:24 [o]Ac 20:10 [p]Jn 11:11-14
9:26 [q]Mt 4:24
9:27 [r]Mt 15:22; Mk 10:47; Lk 18:38-39
9:29 [s]ver 22
9:30 [t]Mt 8:4
9:31 [u]ver 26; Mk 7:36
9:32 [v]Mt 4:24 [w]Mt 12:22-24

[i]13 Hosea 6:6

man who had been mute spoke. The
crowd was amazed and said, "Nothing
like this has ever been seen in Israel."[a]
34But the Pharisees said, "It is by the
prince of demons that he drives out
demons."[b]
35Jesus went through all the towns
and villages, teaching in their synagogues, preaching the good news of the
kingdom and healing every disease and
sickness.[c] 36When he saw the crowds,
he had compassion on them,[d] because
they were harassed and helpless, like
sheep without a shepherd.[e] 37Then he
said to his disciples, "The harvest[f] is
plentiful but the workers are few.[g]
38Ask the Lord of the harvest, therefore, to send out workers into his harvest field."

Jesus commissions and instructs the twelve apostles in the ministry.

10:2-4pp— Mk 3:16-19; Lk 6:14-16; Ac 1:13
10:9-15pp— Mk 6:8-11; Lk 9:3-5; 10:4-12
10:19-22pp— Mk 13:11-13; Lk 21:12-17
10:26-33pp— Lk 12:2-9
10:34,35pp— Lk 12:51-53

10 He called his twelve disciples to
him and gave them authority to
drive out evil[j] spirits[h] and to heal every
disease and sickness.
2These are the names of the twelve
apostles: first, Simon (who is called
Peter) and his brother Andrew; James
son of Zebedee, and his brother John;
3Philip and Bartholomew; Thomas and
Matthew the tax collector; James son of
Alphaeus, and Thaddaeus; 4Simon the
Zealot and Judas Iscariot, who betrayed
him.[i]
5These twelve Jesus sent out with
the following instructions: "Do not go
among the Gentiles or enter any town
of the Samaritans.[j] 6Go rather to the
lost sheep of Israel.[k] 7As you go, preach
this message: 'The kingdom of heaven[l]
is near.' 8Heal the sick, raise the dead,
cleanse those who have leprosy,[k] drive
out demons. Freely you have received,
freely give. 9Do not take along any
gold or silver or copper in your belts;[m]
10take no bag for the journey, or extra
tunic, or sandals or a staff; for the worker is worth his keep.[n]
11"Whatever town or village you
enter, search for some worthy person
there and stay at his house until you
leave. 12As you enter the home, give it
your greeting.[o] 13If the home is deserving, let your peace rest on it; if it is
not, let your peace return to you. 14If
anyone will not welcome you or listen
to your words, shake the dust off your
feet[p] when you leave that home or
town. 15I tell you the truth, it will be
more bearable for Sodom and Gomorrah[q] on the day of judgment[r] than for
that town.[s] 16I am sending you out like
sheep among wolves.[t] Therefore be as
shrewd as snakes and as innocent as
doves.[u]
17"Be on your guard against men;
they will hand you over to the local
councils[v] and flog you in their synagogues.[w] 18On my account you will be
brought before governors and kings[x] as
witnesses to them and to the Gentiles.
19But when they arrest you, do not
worry about what to say or how to say
it.[y] At that time you will be given what
to say, 20for it will not be you speaking, but the Spirit of your Father[z]
speaking through you.
21"Brother will betray brother to
death, and a father his child; children
will rebel against their parents[a] and
have them put to death. 22All men will
hate you because of me, but he who
stands firm to the end will be saved.[b]
23When you are persecuted in one
place, flee to another. I tell you the
truth, you will not finish going through
the cities of Israel before the Son of
Man comes.
24"A student is not above his teacher, nor a servant above his master.[c] 25It
is enough for the student to be like his
teacher, and the servant like his master. If the head of the house has been

9:33 [a]Mk 2:12
9:34 [b]Mt 12:24; Lk 11:15
9:35 [c]Mt 4:23
9:36 [d]Mt 14:14 [e]Nu 27:17; Eze 34:5,6; Zec 10:2; Mk 6:34
9:37 [f]Jn 4:35 [g]Lk 10:2
10:1 [h]Mk 3:13-15; Lk 9:1
10:4 [i]Mt 26:14-16, 25,47; Jn 13:2,26,27
10:5 [j]2Ki 17:24; Lk 9:52; Jn 4:4-26, 39,40; Ac 8:5,25
10:6 [k]Jer 50:6; Mt 15:24
10:7 [l]Mt 3:2
10:9 [m]Lk 22:35
10:10 [n]1Ti 5:18
10:12 [o]1Sa 25:6
10:14 [p]Ne 5:13; Lk 10:11; Ac 13:51
10:15 [q]2Pe 2:6 [r]Mt 12:36; 2Pe 2:9; 1Jn 4:17 [s]Mt 11:22,24
10:16 [t]Lk 10:3 [u]Ro 16:19
10:17 [v]Mt 5:22 [w]Mt 23:34; Mk 13:9; Ac 5:40; 26:11
10:18 [x]Ac 25:24-26
10:19 [y]Ex 4:12
10:20 [z]Ac 4:8
10:21 [a]ver 35,36; Mic 7:6
10:22 [b]Mt 24:13; Mk 13:13 **10:24** [c]Lk 6:40; Jn 13:16; 15:20

j1 Greek *unclean* k8 The Greek word was used for various diseases affecting the skin—not necessarily leprosy.

called Beelzebub,[l][a] how much more
the members of his household!
26"So do not be afraid of them. There
is nothing concealed that will not be
disclosed, or hidden that will not be
made known.[b] 27What I tell you in the
dark, speak in the daylight; what is whispered in your ear, proclaim from the
roofs. 28Do not be afraid of those who
kill the body but cannot kill the soul.
Rather, be afraid of the One[c] who can
destroy both soul and body in hell. 29Are
not two sparrows sold for a penny[m]?
Yet not one of them will fall to the
ground apart from the will of your
Father. 30And even the very hairs of
your head are all numbered.[d] 31So don't
be afraid; you are worth more than many
sparrows.[e]
32"Whoever acknowledges me before
men,[f] I will also acknowledge him
before my Father in heaven. 33But whoever disowns me before men, I will disown him before my Father in heaven.[g]
34"Do not suppose that I have come
to bring peace to the earth. I did not
come to bring peace, but a sword. 35For
I have come to turn

"'a man against his father,
a daughter against her mother,
a daughter-in-law against her
mother-in-law[h]—
36 a man's enemies will be the
members of his own
household.'[n][i]

37"Anyone who loves his father or
mother more than me is not worthy of
me; anyone who loves his son or daughter more than me is not worthy of me;[j]
38and anyone who does not take his
cross and follow me is not worthy of
me.[k] 39Whoever finds his life will lose
it, and whoever loses his life for my sake
will find it.[l]
40"He who receives you receives me,[m]
and he who receives me receives the
one who sent me.[n] 41Anyone who
receives a prophet because he is a
prophet will receive a prophet's reward,
and anyone who receives a righteous
man because he is a righteous man will

10:25 [a]Mk 3:22
10:26 [b]Mk 4:22; Lk 8:17
10:28 [c]Isa 8:12,13; Heb 10:31
10:30 [d]1Sa 14:45; 2Sa 14:11; Lk 21:18; Ac 27:34
10:31 [e]Mt 12:12
10:32 [f]Ro 10:9
10:33 [g]Mk 8:38; 2Ti 2:12
10:35 [h]ver 21
10:36 [i]Mic 7:6
10:37 [j]Lk 14:26
10:38 [k]Mt 16:24; Lk 14:27
10:39 [l]Lk 17:33; Jn 12:25
10:40 [m]Mt 18:5; Gal 4:14 [n]Lk 9:48; Jn 12:44; 13:20
10:42 [o]Mt 25:40; Mk 9:41; Heb 6:10
11:1 [p]Mt 7:28
11:2 [q]Mt 14:3
11:3 [r]Ps 118:26; Jn 11:27; Heb 10:37
11:5 [s]Isa 35:4-6; 61:1; Lk 4:18,19
11:6 [t]Mt 13:21
11:7 [u]Mt 3:1
11:9 [v]Mt 21:26; Lk 1:76
11:10 [w]Mal 3:1; Mk 1:2

receive a righteous man's reward. 42And
if anyone gives even a cup of cold
water to one of these little ones because
he is my disciple, I tell you the truth,
he will certainly not lose his reward."[o]

Jesus testifies to the validity of John the Baptist's ministry.

11:2-19pp— Lk 7:18-35

11 After Jesus had finished instructing his twelve disciples,[p] he went
on from there to teach and preach in
the towns of Galilee.[o]
2When John heard in prison[q] what
Christ was doing, he sent his disciples
3to ask him, "Are you the one who was
to come,[r] or should we expect someone else?"
4Jesus replied, "Go back and report
to John what you hear and see: 5The
blind receive sight, the lame walk, those
who have leprosy[p] are cured, the deaf
hear, the dead are raised, and the good
news is preached to the poor.[s] 6Blessed
is the man who does not fall away on
account of me."[t]
7As John's[u] disciples were leaving,
Jesus began to speak to the crowd
about John: "What did you go out into
the desert to see? A reed swayed by the
wind? 8If not, what did you go out to
see? A man dressed in fine clothes? No,
those who wear fine clothes are in
kings' palaces. 9Then what did you go
out to see? A prophet?[v] Yes, I tell you,
and more than a prophet. 10This is the
one about whom it is written:

"'I will send my messenger ahead of
you,
who will prepare your way before
you.'[q][w]

11I tell you the truth: Among those born
of women there has not risen anyone
greater than John the Baptist; yet he
who is least in the kingdom of heaven
is greater than he. 12From the days of

[l]*25* Greek *Beezeboul* or *Beelzeboul* [m]*29* Greek *an assarion* [n]*36* Micah 7:6 [o]*1* Greek *in their towns* [p]*5* The Greek word was used for various diseases affecting the skin—not necessarily leprosy. [q]*10* Mal. 3:1

John the Baptist until now, the kingdom of heaven has been forcefully advancing, and forceful men lay hold of it. 13For all the Prophets and the Law prophesied until John. 14And if you are willing to accept it, he is the Elijah who was to come.[a] 15He who has ears, let him hear.[b]

16"To what can I compare this generation? They are like children sitting in the marketplaces and calling out to others:

17" 'We played the flute for you,
  and you did not dance;
we sang a dirge,
  and you did not mourn.'

18For John came neither eating[c] nor drinking,[d] and they say, 'He has a demon.' 19The Son of Man came eating and drinking, and they say, 'Here is a glutton and a drunkard, a friend of tax collectors and "sinners." '[e] But wisdom is proved right by her actions."

Jesus denounces unrepentant cities.

11:21-23pp— Lk 10:13-15

20Then Jesus began to denounce the cities in which most of his miracles had been performed, because they did not repent. 21"Woe to you, Korazin! Woe to you, Bethsaida![f] If the miracles that were performed in you had been performed in Tyre and Sidon,[g] they would have repented long ago in sackcloth and ashes.[h] 22But I tell you, it will be more bearable for Tyre and Sidon on the day of judgment than for you.[i] 23And you, Capernaum,[j] will you be lifted up to the skies? No, you will go down to the depths.[r][k] If the miracles that were performed in Sodom, it would have remained to this day. 24But I tell you that it will be more bearable for Sodom on the day of judgment than for you."[l]

Jesus gives rest to the weary.

11:25-27pp— Lk 10:21,22

25At that time Jesus said, "I praise you, Father,[m] Lord of heaven and earth, because you have hidden these things from the wise and learned, and revealed them to little children.[n] 26Yes, Father, for this was your good pleasure.

27"All things have been committed to me[o] by my Father.[p] No one knows the Son except the Father, and no one knows the Father except the Son and those to whom the Son chooses to reveal him.[q]

28"Come to me,[r] all you who are weary and burdened, and I will give you rest. 29Take my yoke upon you and learn from me,[s] for I am gentle and humble in heart, and you will find rest for your souls.[t] 30For my yoke is easy and my burden is light."[u]

Disciples pick grain and illustrate Jesus' lordship of the Sabbath.

12:1-8pp— Mk 2:23-28; Lk 6:1-5
12:9-14pp— Mk 3:1-6; Lk 6:6-11

12 At that time Jesus went through the grainfields on the Sabbath. His disciples were hungry and began to pick some heads of grain[v] and eat them. 2When the Pharisees saw this, they said to him, "Look! Your disciples are doing what is unlawful on the Sabbath."[w]

3He answered, "Haven't you read what David did when he and his companions were hungry?[x] 4He entered the house of God, and he and his companions ate the consecrated bread—which was not lawful for them to do, but only for the priests.[y] 5Or haven't you read in the Law that on the Sabbath the priests in the temple desecrate the day[z] and yet are innocent? 6I tell you that one[s] greater than the temple is here.[a] 7If you had known what these words mean, 'I desire mercy, not sacrifice,'[t][b] you would not have condemned the innocent. 8For the Son of Man[c] is Lord of the Sabbath."

9Going on from that place, he went into their synagogue, 10and a man with

11:14 [a]Mal 4:5; Mt 17:10-13; Mk 9:11-13; Lk 1:17; Jn 1:21
11:15 [b]Mt 13:9,43; Mk 4:23; Lk 14:35; Rev 2:7
11:18 [c]Mt 3:4 [d]Lk 1:15
11:19 [e]Mt 9:11
11:21 [f]Mk 6:45; Lk 9:10; Jn 12:21 [g]Mt 15:21; Lk 6:17; Ac 12:20 [h]Jnh 3:5-9
11:22 [i]ver 24; Mt 10:15
11:23 [j]Mt 4:13 [k]Isa 14:13-15
11:24 [l]Mt 10:15
11:25 [m]Lk 22:42; Jn 11:41 [n]1Co 1:26-29
11:27 [o]Mt 28:18 [p]Jn 3:35; 13:3; 17:2 [q]Jn 10:15
11:28 [r]Jn 7:37
11:29 [s]Jn 13:15; Php 2:5; 1Pe 2:21; 1Jn 2:6 [t]Jer 6:16
11:30 [u]1Jn 5:3
12:1 [v]Dt 23:25
12:2 [w]ver 10; Lk 13:14; 14:3; Jn 5:10; 7:23; 9:16
12:3 [x]1Sa 21:6
12:4 [y]Lev 24:5,9
12:5 [z]Nu 28:9,10; Jn 7:22,23
12:6 [a]ver 41,42
12:7 [b]Hos 6:6; Mic 6:6-8; Mt 9:13 **12:8** [c]Mt 8:20

r*23* Greek *Hades* s*6* Or *something*; also in verses 41 and 42 t*7* Hosea 6:6

a shriveled hand was there. Looking for
a reason to accuse Jesus, they asked him,
"Is it lawful to heal on the Sabbath?"[a]
11He said to them, "If any of you has
a sheep and it falls into a pit on the
Sabbath, will you not take hold of it
and lift it out?[b] 12How much more valuable is a man than a sheep![c] Therefore
it is lawful to do good on the Sabbath."
13Then he said to the man, "Stretch
out your hand." So he stretched it out
and it was completely restored, just as
sound as the other. 14But the Pharisees
went out and plotted how they might
kill Jesus.[d]
15Aware of this, Jesus withdrew from
that place. Many followed him, and he
healed all their sick,[e] 16warning them
not to tell who he was.[f] 17This was to
fulfill what was spoken through the
prophet Isaiah:

18"Here is my servant whom I have
chosen,
the one I love, in whom I delight;[g]
I will put my Spirit on him,
and he will proclaim justice to the
nations.
19He will not quarrel or cry out;
no one will hear his voice in the
streets.
20A bruised reed he will not break,
and a smoldering wick he will not
snuff out,
till he leads justice to victory.
21 In his name the nations will put
their hope."[u][h]

Pharisees accuse Jesus of healing by the power of Beelzebub.

12:25-29pp— Mk 3:23-27; Lk 11:17-22

22Then they brought him a demon-
possessed man who was blind and mute,
and Jesus healed him, so that he could
both talk and see.[i] 23All the people
were astonished and said, "Could this
be the Son of David?"[j]
24But when the Pharisees heard this,
they said, "It is only by Beelzebub,[v][k] the
prince of demons, that this fellow drives
out demons."[l]
25Jesus knew their thoughts[m] and
said to them, "Every kingdom divided
against itself will be ruined, and every
city or household divided against itself
will not stand. 26If Satan[n] drives out
Satan, he is divided against himself. How
then can his kingdom stand? 27And if I
drive out demons by Beelzebub, by
whom do your people[o] drive them out?
So then, they will be your judges. 28But
if I drive out demons by the Spirit of
God, then the kingdom of God has come
upon you.
29"Or again, how can anyone enter a
strong man's house and carry off his
possessions unless he first ties up the
strong man? Then he can rob his house.
30"He who is not with me is against
me, and he who does not gather with
me scatters.[p] 31And so I tell you, every
sin and blasphemy will be forgiven
men, but the blasphemy against the
Spirit will not be forgiven.[q] 32Anyone
who speaks a word against the Son of
Man will be forgiven, but anyone who
speaks against the Holy Spirit will not
be forgiven, either in this age[r] or in
the age to come.[s]
33"Make a tree good and its fruit will
be good, or make a tree bad and its
fruit will be bad, for a tree is recognized
by its fruit.[t] 34You brood of vipers,[u]
how can you who are evil say anything
good? For out of the overflow of the
heart the mouth speaks.[v] 35The good
man brings good things out of the good
stored up in him, and the evil man
brings evil things out of the evil stored
up in him. 36But I tell you that men will
have to give account on the day of
judgment for every careless word they
have spoken. 37For by your words you
will be acquitted, and by your words
you will be condemned."

Pharisees ask Jesus for a miraculous sign.

12:39-42pp— Lk 11:29-32
12:43-45pp— Lk 11:24-26

38Then some of the Pharisees and

12:10 [a]ver 2; Lk 13:14; 14:3; Jn 9:16
12:11 [b]Lk 14:5
12:12 [c]Mt 10:31
12:14 [d]Mt 26:4; 27:1; Mk 3:6; Lk 6:11; Jn 5:18; 11:53
12:15 [e]Mt 4:23
12:16 [f]Mt 8:4
12:18 [g]Mt 3:17
12:21 [h]Isa 42:1-4
12:22 [i]Mt 4:24; 9:32-33
12:23 [j]Mt 9:27
12:24 [k]Mk 3:22 [l]Mt 9:34
12:25 [m]Mt 9:4
12:26 [n]Mt 4:10
12:27 [o]Ac 19:13
12:30 [p]Mk 9:40; Lk 11:23
12:31 [q]Mk 3:28,29; Lk 12:10
12:32 [r]Tit 2:12 [s]Mk 10:30; Lk 20:34,35; Eph 1:21; Heb 6:5
12:33 [t]Mt 7:16,17; Lk 6:43,44
12:34 [u]Mt 3:7; 23:33 [v]Mt 15:18; Lk 6:45

u *21* Isaiah 42:1-4 v *24* Greek *Beezeboul* or *Beelzeboul*; also in verse 27

teachers of the law said to him, "Teacher, we want to see a miraculous sign
from you."[a]
39He answered, "A wicked and adulterous generation asks for a miraculous sign! But none will be given it
except the sign of the prophet Jonah.[b]
40For as Jonah was three days and
three nights in the belly of a huge
fish,[c] so the Son of Man[d] will be three
days and three nights in the heart of
the earth.[e] 41The men of Nineveh[f]
will stand up at the judgment with
this generation and condemn it; for they
repented at the preaching of Jonah,[g]
and now one[w] greater than Jonah is
here. 42The Queen of the South will
rise at the judgment with this generation and condemn it; for she came[h]
from the ends of the earth to listen to
Solomon's wisdom, and now one greater
than Solomon is here.
43"When an evil[x] spirit comes out of
a man, it goes through arid places seeking rest and does not find it. 44Then it
says, 'I will return to the house I left.'
When it arrives, it finds the house unoccupied, swept clean and put in order.
45Then it goes and takes with it seven
other spirits more wicked than itself,
and they go in and live there. And the
final condition of that man is worse than
the first.[i] That is how it will be with
this wicked generation."

Jesus identifies his mother and brothers.

12:46-50pp— Mk 3:31-35; Lk 8:19-21

46While Jesus was still talking to the
crowd, his mother[j] and brothers[k] stood
outside, wanting to speak to him. 47Some-
one told him, "Your mother and brothers are standing outside, wanting to speak
to you."[y]
48He replied to him, "Who is my mother, and who are my brothers?" 49Point-
ing to his disciples, he said, "Here are
my mother and my brothers. 50For
whoever does the will of my Father in
heaven[l] is my brother and sister and
mother."

Jesus teaches in a parable: The sower.

13:1-15pp— Mk 4:1-12; Lk8:4-10
13:16,17pp— Lk 10:23,24
13:18-23pp— Mk 4:13-20; Lk8:11-15

13 That same day Jesus went out of
the house[m] and sat by the lake.
2Such large crowds gathered around
him that he got into a boat[n] and sat in
it, while all the people stood on the
shore. 3Then he told them many things
in parables, saying: "A farmer went
out to sow his seed. 4As he was scattering the seed, some fell along the
path, and the birds came and ate it up.
5Some fell on rocky places, where it
did not have much soil. It sprang up
quickly, because the soil was shallow.
6But when the sun came up, the plants
were scorched, and they withered because they had no root. 7Other seed
fell among thorns, which grew up and
choked the plants. 8Still other seed fell
on good soil, where it produced a
crop—a hundred,[o] sixty or thirty times
what was sown. 9He who has ears, let
him hear."[p]
10The disciples came to him and
asked, "Why do you speak to the people in parables?"
11He replied, "The knowledge of the
secrets of the kingdom of heaven has
been given to you,[q] but not to them.
12Whoever has will be given more, and
he will have an abundance. Whoever
does not have, even what he has will be
taken from him.[r] 13This is why I speak
to them in parables:

"Though seeing, they do not see;
though hearing, they do not hear
or understand.[s]

14In them is fulfilled the prophecy of
Isaiah:

"'You will be ever hearing but never
understanding;
you will be ever seeing but never
perceiving.

12:38 [a]Mt 16:1; Mk 8:11,12; Lk 11:16; Jn 2:18; 6:30; 1Co 1:22
12:39 [b]Mt 16:4; Lk 11:29
12:40 [c]Jnh 1:17 [d]Mt 8:20 [e]Mt 16:21
12:41 [f]Jnh 1:2 [g]Jnh 3:5
12:42 [h]1Ki 10:1; 2Ch 9:1
12:45 [i]2Pe 2:20
12:46 [j]Mt 1:18; 2:11,13,14,20; Lk 1:43; 2:33,34,48,51; Jn 2:1,5; 19:25,26 [k]Mt 13:55; Jn 2:12; 7:3,5; Ac 1:14; 1Co 9:5; Gal 1:19
12:50 [l]Jn 15:14
13:1 [m]ver 36; Mt 9:28
13:2 [n]Lk 5:3
13:8 [o]Ge 26:12
13:9 [p]Mt 11:15
13:11 [q]Mt 11:25; 16:17; 19:11; Jn 6:65; 1Co 2:10,14; Col 1:27; 1Jn 2:20,27
13:12 [r]Mt 25:29; Lk 19:26
13:13 [s]Dt 29:4; Jer 5:21; Eze 12:2

w*41* Or *something*; also in verse 42 x*43* Greek *unclean* y*47* Some manuscripts do not have verse 47.

[15]For this people's heart has become
calloused;
they hardly hear with their ears,
and they have closed their eyes.
Otherwise they might see with their
eyes,
hear with their ears,
understand with their hearts
and turn, and I would heal them.'[z][a]

[16]But blessed are your eyes because
they see, and your ears because they
hear.[b] [17]For I tell you the truth, many
prophets and righteous men longed to
see what you see[c] but did not see it,
and to hear what you hear but did not
hear it.
[18]"Listen then to what the parable of
the sower means: [19]When anyone hears
the message about the kingdom[d] and
does not understand it, the evil one[e]
comes and snatches away what was
sown in his heart. This is the seed sown
along the path. [20]The one who received
the seed that fell on rocky places is the
man who hears the word and at once
receives it with joy. [21]But since he has
no root, he lasts only a short time. When
trouble or persecution comes because
of the word, he quickly falls away.[f]
[22]The one who received the seed that
fell among the thorns is the man who
hears the word, but the worries of this
life and the deceitfulness of wealth[g]
choke it, making it unfruitful. [23]But the
one who received the seed that fell on
good soil is the man who hears the word
and understands it. He produces a crop,
yielding a hundred, sixty or thirty times
what was sown."[h]

A parable: Wheat and weeds.

[24]Jesus told them another parable:
"The kingdom of heaven is like[i] a man
who sowed good seed in his field. [25]But
while everyone was sleeping, his enemy came and sowed weeds among the
wheat, and went away. [26]When the
wheat sprouted and formed heads, then
the weeds also appeared.
[27]"The owner's servants came to him
and said, 'Sir, didn't you sow good seed
in your field? Where then did the weeds
come from?'
[28]" 'An enemy did this,' he replied.
"The servants asked him, 'Do you
want us to go and pull them up?'
[29]" 'No,' he answered, 'because while
you are pulling the weeds, you may
root up the wheat with them. [30]Let both
grow together until the harvest. At
that time I will tell the harvesters: First
collect the weeds and tie them in bundles to be burned; then gather the
wheat and bring it into my barn.' "[j]

Parables: The mustard seed, and the yeast.

13:31,32pp— Mk 4:30-32
13:31-33pp— Lk 13:18-21

[31]He told them another parable: "The
kingdom of heaven is like[k] a mustard
seed,[l] which a man took and planted
in his field. [32]Though it is the smallest
of all your seeds, yet when it grows, it
is the largest of garden plants and becomes a tree, so that the birds of the
air come and perch in its branches."[m]
[33]He told them still another parable:
"The kingdom of heaven is like[n] yeast
that a woman took and mixed into a
large amount[a] of flour[o] until it worked
all through the dough."[p]
[34]Jesus spoke all these things to the
crowd in parables; he did not say anything to them without using a parable.[q]
[35]So was fulfilled what was spoken
through the prophet:

"I will open my mouth in parables,
I will utter things hidden since the
creation of the world."[b][r]

[36]Then he left the crowd and went
into the house. His disciples came to
him and said, "Explain to us the parable[s] of the weeds in the field."
[37]He answered, "The one who sowed
the good seed is the Son of Man.[t]
[38]The field is the world, and the good
seed stands for the sons of the kingdom. The weeds are the sons of the
evil one,[u] [39]and the enemy who sows

13:15 [a]Isa 6:9,10; Jn 12:40; Ac 28:26,27; Ro 11:8
13:16 [b]Mt 16:17
13:17 [c]Jn 8:56; Heb 11:13; 1Pe 1:10-12
13:19 [d]Mt 4:23 [e]Mt 5:37
13:21 [f]Mt 11:6
13:22 [g]Mt 19:23; 1Ti 6:9,10,17
13:23 [h]ver 8
13:24 [i]ver 31,33,45, 47; Mt 18:23; 20:1; 22:2; 25:1; Mk 4:26,30
13:30 [j]Mt 3:12
13:31 [k]ver 24 [l]Mt 17:20; Lk 17:6
13:32 [m]Ps 104:12; Eze 17:23; 31:6; Da 4:12
13:33 [n]ver 24 [o]Ge 18:6 [p]Gal 5:9
13:34 [q]Mk 4:33; Jn 16:25
13:35 [r]Ps 78:2; Ro 16:25,26; 1Co 2:7; Eph 3:9; Col 1:26
13:36 [s]Mt 15:15
13:37 [t]Mt 8:20
13:38 [u]Jn 8:44,45; 1Jn 3:10

z *15* Isaiah 6:9,10 a *33* Greek *three satas* (probably about 1/2 bushel or 22 liters) b *35* Psalm 78:2

them is the devil. The harvest[a] is the
end of the age,[b] and the harvesters are
angels.[c]
40"As the weeds are pulled up and
burned in the fire, so it will be at the
end of the age. 41The Son of Man[d] will
send out his angels,[e] and they will weed
out of his kingdom everything that
causes sin and all who do evil. 42They
will throw them into the fiery furnace,
where there will be weeping and gnashing of teeth.[f] 43Then the righteous will
shine like the sun[g] in the kingdom of
their Father. He who has ears, let him
hear.[h]

Parables: The hidden treasure, and the pearl.

44"The kingdom of heaven is like[i] treasure hidden in a field. When a man
found it, he hid it again, and then in
his joy went and sold all he had and
bought that field.[j]
45"Again, the kingdom of heaven is
like[k] a merchant looking for fine pearls.
46When he found one of great value,
he went away and sold everything he
had and bought it.

A parable: The net.

47"Once again, the kingdom of heav-
en is like[l] a net that was let down into
the lake and caught all kinds[m] of fish.
48When it was full, the fishermen pulled
it up on the shore. Then they sat down
and collected the good fish in baskets,
but threw the bad away. 49This is how
it will be at the end of the age. The
angels will come and separate the
wicked from the righteous[n] 50and throw
them into the fiery furnace, where there
will be weeping and gnashing of teeth.[o]
51"Have you understood all these
things?" Jesus asked.
"Yes," they replied.
52He said to them, "Therefore every
teacher of the law who has been instructed about the kingdom of heaven is like
the owner of a house who brings out
of his storeroom new treasures as well
as old."

13:39 [a]Joel 3:13 [b]Mt 24:3; 28:20 [c]Rev 14:15
13:41 [d]Mt 8:20 [e]Mt 24:31
13:42 [f]ver 50; Mt 8:12
13:43 [g]Da 12:3 [h]Mt 11:15
13:44 [i]ver 24 [j]Isa 55:1; Php 3:7,8
13:45 [k]ver 24
13:47 [l]ver 24 [m]Mt 22:10
13:49 [n]Mt 25:32
13:50 [o]Mt 8:12
13:53 [p]Mt 7:28
13:54 [q]Mt 4:23 [r]Mt 7:28
13:55 [s]Lk 3:23; Jn 6:42 [t]Mt 12:46
13:57 [u]Jn 6:61 [v]Lk 4:24; Jn 4:44
14:1 [w]Mk 8:15; Lk 3:1,19; 13:31; 23:7,8; Ac 4:27; 12:1 [x]Lk 9:7-9
14:2 [y]Mt 3:1
14:3 [z]Mt 4:12; 11:2 [a]Lk 3:19,20
14:4 [b]Lev 18:16; 20:21
14:5 [c]Mt 11:9

A prophet is without honor in his hometown.

13:54-58pp— Mk 6:1-6

53When Jesus had finished these parables,[p] he moved on from there. 54Com-
ing to his hometown, he began teaching
the people in their synagogue,[q] and
they were amazed.[r] "Where did this
man get this wisdom and these miraculous powers?" they asked. 55"Isn't this
the carpenter's son?[s] Isn't his mother's[t]
name Mary, and aren't his brothers
James, Joseph, Simon and Judas? 56Aren't
all his sisters with us? Where then did
this man get all these things?" 57And
they took offense[u] at him.
But Jesus said to them, "Only in his
hometown and in his own house is a
prophet without honor."[v]
58And he did not do many miracles
there because of their lack of faith.

King Herod has John the Baptist beheaded.

14:1-12pp— Mk 6:14-29

14 At that time Herod[w] the tetrarch
heard the reports about Jesus,[x]
2and he said to his attendants, "This is
John the Baptist;[y] he has risen from
the dead! That is why miraculous powers are at work in him."
3Now Herod had arrested John and
bound him and put him in prison[z]
because of Herodias, his brother
Philip's wife,[a] 4for John had been saying to him: "It is not lawful for you to
have her."[b] 5Herod wanted to kill John,
but he was afraid of the people,
because they considered him a prophet.[c]
6On Herod's birthday the daughter
of Herodias danced for them and
pleased Herod so much 7that he
promised with an oath to give her
whatever she asked. 8Prompted by her
mother, she said, "Give me here on a
platter the head of John the Baptist."
9The king was distressed, but because
of his oaths and his dinner guests, he
ordered that her request be granted

10 and had John beheaded[a] in the
prison. 11 His head was brought in on a
platter and given to the girl, who carried it to her mother. 12 John's disciples
came and took his body and buried
it.[b] Then they went and told Jesus.

Jesus feeds 5,000 with five loaves and two fish.

14:13-21pp— Mk 6:32-44; Lk 9:10-17; Jn 6:1-13
14:13-21Ref— Mt 15:32-38

13 When Jesus heard what had happened, he withdrew by boat privately
to a solitary place. Hearing of this, the
crowds followed him on foot from the
towns. 14 When Jesus landed and saw a
large crowd, he had compassion on
them[c] and healed their sick.[d]
15 As evening approached, the disciples came to him and said, "This is a
remote place, and it's already getting
late. Send the crowds away, so they
can go to the villages and buy themselves some food."
16 Jesus replied, "They do not need
to go away. You give them something
to eat."
17 "We have here only five loaves[e] of
bread and two fish," they answered.
18 "Bring them here to me," he said.
19 And he directed the people to sit
down on the grass. Taking the five
loaves and the two fish and looking up
to heaven, he gave thanks and broke
the loaves.[f] Then he gave them to the
disciples, and the disciples gave them
to the people. 20 They all ate and were
satisfied, and the disciples picked up
twelve basketfuls of broken pieces that
were left over. 21 The number of those
who ate was about five thousand men,
besides women and children.

Jesus walks on water.

14:22-33pp— Mk 6:45-51; Jn 6:15-21
14:34-36pp— Mk 6:53-56

22 Immediately Jesus made the disciples get into the boat and go on ahead
of him to the other side, while he
dismissed the crowd. 23 After he had
dismissed them, he went up on a
mountainside by himself to pray.[g]
When evening came, he was there
alone, 24 but the boat was already a
considerable distance[c] from land, buf-
feted by the waves because the wind
was against it.
25 During the fourth watch of the
night Jesus went out to them, walking
on the lake. 26 When the disciples saw
him walking on the lake, they were
terrified. "It's a ghost,"[h] they said, and
cried out in fear.
27 But Jesus immediately said to
them: "Take courage![i] It is I. Don't be
afraid."[j]
28 "Lord, if it's you," Peter replied,
"tell me to come to you on the water."
29 "Come," he said.
Then Peter got down out of the boat,
walked on the water and came toward
Jesus. 30 But when he saw the wind, he
was afraid and, beginning to sink,
cried out, "Lord, save me!"
31 Immediately Jesus reached out his
hand and caught him. "You of little
faith,"[k] he said, "why did you doubt?"
32 And when they climbed into the
boat, the wind died down. 33 Then
those who were in the boat worshiped
him, saying, "Truly you are the Son of
God."[l]
34 When they had crossed over, they
landed at Gennesaret. 35 And when the
men of that place recognized Jesus,
they sent word to all the surrounding
country. People brought all their sick
to him 36 and begged him to let the
sick just touch the edge of his cloak,[m]
and all who touched him were healed.

Tradition without obedience is condemned.

15:1-20pp— Mk 7:1-23

15 Then some Pharisees and teachers of the law came to Jesus from
Jerusalem and asked, 2 "Why do your
disciples break the tradition of the
elders? They don't wash their hands
before they eat!"[n]
3 Jesus replied, "And why do you

14:10 [a] Mt 17:12
14:12 [b] Ac 8:2
14:14 [c] Mt 9:36 [d] Mt 4:23
14:17 [e] Mt 16:9
14:19 [f] 1Sa 9:13; Mt 26:26; Mk 8:6; Lk 24:30; Ac 2:42; 27:35; 1Ti 4:4
14:23 [g] Lk 3:21
14:26 [h] Lk 24:37
14:27 [i] Mt 9:2; Ac 23:11 [j] Da 10:12; Mt 17:7; 28:10; Lk 1:13,30; 2:10; Ac 18:9; 23:11; Rev 1:17
14:31 [k] Mt 6:30
14:33 [l] Ps 2:7; Mt 4:3
14:36 [m] Mt 9:20
15:2 [n] Lk 11:38

c *24* Greek *many stadia*

break the command of God for the
sake of your tradition? 4For God said,
'Honor your father and mother'[d][a] and
'Anyone who curses his father or
mother must be put to death.'[e][b] 5But
you say that if a man says to his father
or mother, 'Whatever help you might
otherwise have received from me is a
gift devoted to God,' 6he is not to
'honor his father[f]' with it. Thus you
nullify the word of God for the sake of
your tradition. 7You hypocrites! Isaiah
was right when he prophesied about
you:

8" 'These people honor me with their
lips,
but their hearts are far from me.
9They worship me in vain;
their teachings are but rules taught
by men.'[c][g][d]"

10Jesus called the crowd to him and
said, "Listen and understand. 11What
goes into a man's mouth does not
make him 'unclean,'[e] but what comes
out of his mouth, that is what makes
him 'unclean.'"[f]
12Then the disciples came to him
and asked, "Do you know that the
Pharisees were offended when they
heard this?"
13He replied, "Every plant that my
heavenly Father has not planted[g] will
be pulled up by the roots. 14Leave
them; they are blind guides.[h][h] If a
blind man leads a blind man, both will
fall into a pit."[i]
15Peter said, "Explain the parable
to us."[j]
16"Are you still so dull?"[k] Jesus
asked them. 17"Don't you see that
whatever enters the mouth goes into
the stomach and then out of the body?
18But the things that come out of the
mouth come from the heart,[l] and these
make a man 'unclean.' 19For out of the
heart come evil thoughts, murder,
adultery, sexual immorality, theft, false
testimony, slander.[m] 20These are what
make a man 'unclean';[n] but eating with
unwashed hands does not make him
'unclean.'"

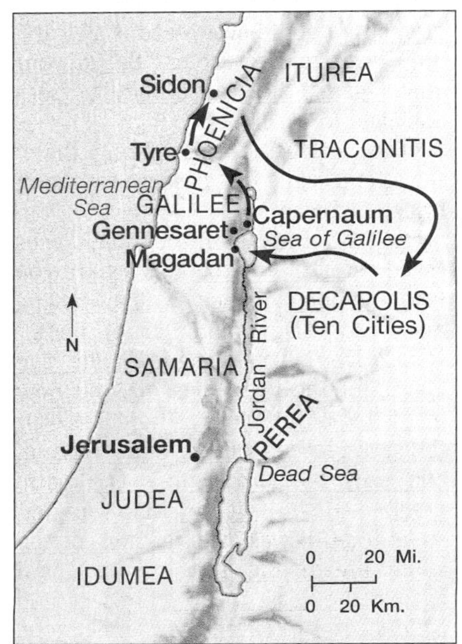

Ministry in Phoenicia

After preaching again in Capernaum, Jesus left Galilee for Phoenicia, where he preached in Tyre and Sidon. On his return, he traveled through the region of the Decapolis (Ten Cities), fed the 4,000 beside the sea, then crossed to Magadan.

Daughter of Canaanite woman is healed.

15:21-28pp— Mk 7:24-30

21Leaving that place, Jesus withdrew
to the region of Tyre and Sidon.[o] 22A
Canaanite woman from that vicinity
came to him, crying out, "Lord, Son of
David,[p] have mercy on me! My daughter is suffering terribly from demon-
possession."[q]
23Jesus did not answer a word. So his
disciples came to him and urged him,
"Send her away, for she keeps crying
out after us."
24He answered, "I was sent only to
the lost sheep of Israel."[r]
25The woman came and knelt before
him.[s] "Lord, help me!" she said.
26He replied, "It is not right to take

15:4 [a]Ex 20:12; Dt 5:16; Eph 6:2 [b]Ex 21:17; Lev 20:9
15:9 [c]Col 2:20-22 [d]Isa 29:13; Mal 2:2
15:11 [e]Ac 10:14,15 [f]ver 18
15:13 [g]Isa 60:21; 61:3; Jn 15:2
15:14 [h]Mt 23:16,24; Ro 2:19 [i]Lk 6:39
15:15 [j]Mt 13:36
15:16 [k]Mt 16:9
15:18 [l]Mt 12:34; Lk 6:45; Jas 3:6
15:19 [m]Gal 5:19-21
15:20 [n]Ro 14:14
15:21 [o]Mt 11:21
15:22 [p]Mt 9:27 [q]Mt 4:24
15:24 [r]Mt 10:6,23; Ro 15:8
15:25 [s]Mt 8:2

d*4* Exodus 20:12; Deut. 5:16 e*4* Exodus 21:17; Lev. 20:9 f*6* Some manuscripts *father or his mother* g*9* Isaiah 29:13 h*14* Some manuscripts *guides of the blind*

the children's bread and toss it to their
dogs."
27"Yes, Lord," she said, "but even the
dogs eat the crumbs that fall from their
masters' table."
28Then Jesus answered, "Woman, you
have great faith![a] Your request is granted." And her daughter was healed from
that very hour.

Jesus feeds 4,000.

15:29-31pp— Mk 7:31-37
15:32-39pp— Mk 8:1-10
15:32-39Ref— Mt 14:13-21

29Jesus left there and went along the
Sea of Galilee. Then he went up on a
mountainside and sat down. 30Great
crowds came to him, bringing the
lame, the blind, the crippled, the mute
and many others, and laid them at his
feet; and he healed them.[b] 31The people
were amazed when they saw the mute
speaking, the crippled made well, the
lame walking and the blind seeing.
And they praised the God of Israel.[c]
32Jesus called his disciples to him
and said, "I have compassion for these
people;[d] they have already been with
me three days and have nothing to eat.
I do not want to send them away hungry, or they may collapse on the way."
33His disciples answered, "Where
could we get enough bread in this
remote place to feed such a crowd?"
34"How many loaves do you have?"
Jesus asked.
"Seven," they replied, "and a few
small fish."
35He told the crowd to sit down on
the ground. 36Then he took the seven
loaves and the fish, and when he had
given thanks, he broke them[e] and gave
them to the disciples, and they in turn
to the people. 37They all ate and were
satisfied. Afterward the disciples picked
up seven basketfuls of broken pieces
that were left over.[f] 38The number of
those who ate was four thousand,
besides women and children. 39After
Jesus had sent the crowd away, he got
into the boat and went to the vicinity
of Magadan.

15:28 [a]Mt 9:22
15:30 [b]Mt 4:23
15:31 [c]Mt 9:8
15:32 [d]Mt 9:36
15:36 [e]Mt 14:19
15:37 [f]Mt 16:10
16:1 [g]Ac 4:1 [h]Mt 12:38
16:3 [i]Lk 12:54-56
16:4 [j]Mt 12:39
16:6 [k]Lk 12:1
16:8 [l]Mt 6:30
16:9 [m]Mt 14:17-21
16:10 [n]Mt 15:34-38
16:12 [o]Ac 4:1

Jesus is asked for a sign from heaven.

16:1-12pp— Mk 8:11-21

16 The Pharisees and Sadducees[g]
came to Jesus and tested him by
asking him to show them a sign from
heaven.[h]
2He replied,[i] "When evening comes,
you say, 'It will be fair weather, for the
sky is red,' 3and in the morning, 'Today
it will be stormy, for the sky is red and
overcast.' You know how to interpret
the appearance of the sky, but you cannot interpret the signs of the times.[i] 4A
wicked and adulterous generation looks
for a miraculous sign, but none will be
given it except the sign of Jonah."[j]
Jesus then left them and went away.

Jesus cautions against the teachings of the Pharisees and Sadducees.

5When they went across the lake, the
disciples forgot to take bread. 6"Be careful," Jesus said to them. "Be on your
guard against the yeast of the Pharisees
and Sadducees."[k]
7They discussed this among themselves and said, "It is because we didn't
bring any bread."
8Aware of their discussion, Jesus
asked, "You of little faith,[l] why are you
talking among yourselves about having
no bread? 9Do you still not understand? Don't you remember the five
loaves for the five thousand, and how
many basketfuls you gathered?[m] 10Or
the seven loaves for the four thousand,
and how many basketfuls you gathered?[n] 11How is it you don't understand that I was not talking to you
about bread? But be on your guard
against the yeast of the Pharisees and
Sadducees." 12Then they understood
that he was not telling them to guard
against the yeast used in bread, but
against the teaching of the Pharisees
and Sadducees.[o]

[i]*2* Some early manuscripts do not have the rest of verse 2 and all of verse 3.

Peter proclaims Jesus to be the Christ.

16:13-16pp— Mk 8:27-29; Lk 9:18-20

13When Jesus came to the region of
Caesarea Philippi, he asked his disciples, "Who do people say the Son of
Man is?"
14They replied, "Some say John the
Baptist;[a] others say Elijah; and still others, Jeremiah or one of the prophets."[b]
15"But what about you?" he asked.
"Who do you say I am?"
16Simon Peter answered, "You are the
Christ,[j] the Son of the living God."[c]
17Jesus replied, "Blessed are you,
Simon son of Jonah, for this was not
revealed to you by man,[d] but by my
Father in heaven. 18And I tell you that
you are Peter,[k][e] and on this rock I will
build my church,[f] and the gates of Hades[l]
will not overcome it.[m] 19I will give you
the keys[g] of the kingdom of heaven;
whatever you bind on earth will be[n]
bound in heaven, and whatever you
loose on earth will be[n] loosed in heav-
en."[h] 20Then he warned his disciples
not to tell anyone[i] that he was the Christ.

Jesus reveals his coming death and resurrection.

16:21-28pp— Mk 8:31–9:1; Lk 9:22-27

21From that time on Jesus began to
explain to his disciples that he must go
to Jerusalem and suffer many things[j] at
the hands of the elders, chief priests
and teachers of the law, and that he
must be killed and on the third day[k] be
raised to life.[l]
22Peter took him aside and began to
rebuke him. "Never, Lord!" he said.
"This shall never happen to you!"
23Jesus turned and said to Peter,
"Get behind me, Satan![m] You are a
stumbling block to me; you do not have
in mind the things of God, but the
things of men."
24Then Jesus said to his disciples, "If
anyone would come after me, he must
deny himself and take up his cross and
follow me.[n] 25For whoever wants to

16:14 [a]Mt 3:1; 14:2 [b]Mk 6:15; Jn 1:21
16:16 [c]Mt 4:3; Ps 42:2; Jn 11:27; Ac 14:15; 2Co 6:16; 1Th 1:9; 1Ti 3:15; Heb 10:31; 12:22
16:17 [d]1Co 15:50; Gal 1:16; Eph 6:12; Heb 2:14
16:18 [e]Jn 1:42 [f]Eph 2:20
16:19 [g]Isa 22:22; Rev 3:7 [h]Mt 18:18; Jn 20:23
16:20 [i]Mk 8:30
16:21 [j]Mk 10:34; Lk 17:25 [k]Jn 2:19 [l]Mt 17:22,23; Mk 9:31; Lk 9:22; 18:31-33; 24:6,7
16:23 [m]Mt 4:10
16:24 [n]Mt 10:38; Lk 14:27
16:25 [o]Jn 12:25
16:27 [p]Mt 8:20 [q]Ac 1:11 [r]Job 34:11; Ps 62:12; Jer 17:10; Ro 2:6; 2Co 5:10; Rev 22:12
17:5 [s]Mt 3:17; 2Pe 1:17 [t]Ac 3:22,23
17:7 [u]Mt 14:27
17:9 [v]Mk 8:30 [w]Mt 8:20 [x]Mt 16:21

save his life[o] will lose it, but whoever
loses his life for me will find it.[o]
26What good will it be for a man if he
gains the whole world, yet forfeits his
soul? Or what can a man give in
exchange for his soul? 27For the Son of
Man[p] is going to come[q] in his Father's
glory with his angels, and then he will
reward each person according to what
he has done.[r] 28I tell you the truth,
some who are standing here will not
taste death before they see the Son of
Man coming in his kingdom."

The transfiguration of Jesus Christ.

17:1-8pp— Lk 9:28-36
17:1-13pp— Mk 9:2-13

17 After six days Jesus took with
him Peter, James and John the
brother of James, and led them up a
high mountain by themselves. 2There
he was transfigured before them. His
face shone like the sun, and his clothes
became as white as the light. 3Just then
there appeared before them Moses and
Elijah, talking with Jesus.
4Peter said to Jesus, "Lord, it is good
for us to be here. If you wish, I will put
up three shelters—one for you, one for
Moses and one for Elijah."
5While he was still speaking, a bright
cloud enveloped them, and a voice from
the cloud said, "This is my Son, whom
I love; with him I am well pleased.[s]
Listen to him!"[t]
6When the disciples heard this, they
fell facedown to the ground, terrified.
7But Jesus came and touched them.
"Get up," he said. "Don't be afraid."[u]
8When they looked up, they saw no one
except Jesus.
9As they were coming down the
mountain, Jesus instructed them, "Don't
tell anyone[v] what you have seen, until
the Son of Man[w] has been raised from
the dead."[x]
10The disciples asked him, "Why

j16 Or *Messiah*; also in verse 20 k18 *Peter* means *rock.* l18 Or *hell* m18 Or *not prove stronger than it* n19 Or *have been* o25 The Greek word means either *life* or *soul*; also in verse 26.

then do the teachers of the law say that Elijah must come first?"

11 Jesus replied, "To be sure, Elijah comes and will restore all things.[a] 12 But I tell you, Elijah has already come,[b] and they did not recognize him, but have done to him everything they wished.[c] In the same way the Son of Man is going to suffer[d] at their hands." 13 Then the disciples understood that he was talking to them about John the Baptist.

The failure of the disciples.

17:14-19pp— Mk 9:14-28; Lk 9:37-42

14 When they came to the crowd, a man approached Jesus and knelt before him. 15 "Lord, have mercy on my son," he said. "He has seizures[e] and is suffering greatly. He often falls into the fire or into the water. 16 I brought him to your disciples, but they could not heal him."

17 "O unbelieving and perverse generation," Jesus replied, "how long shall I stay with you? How long shall I put up with you? Bring the boy here to me." 18 Jesus rebuked the demon, and it came out of the boy, and he was healed from that moment.

19 Then the disciples came to Jesus in private and asked, "Why couldn't we drive it out?"

20 He replied, "Because you have so little faith. I tell you the truth, if you have faith[f] as small as a mustard seed,[g] you can say to this mountain, 'Move from here to there' and it will move.[h] Nothing will be impossible for you.[p]"

22 When they came together in Galilee, he said to them, "The Son of Man[i] is going to be betrayed into the hands of men. 23 They will kill him,[j] and on the third day[k] he will be raised to life."[l] And the disciples were filled with grief.

Coin from a fish's mouth.

24 After Jesus and his disciples arrived in Capernaum, the collectors of the two-drachma tax[m] came to Peter and asked, "Doesn't your teacher pay the temple tax[q]?"

25 "Yes, he does," he replied.

When Peter came into the house, Jesus was the first to speak. "What do you think, Simon?" he asked. "From whom do the kings of the earth collect duty and taxes[n]—from their own sons or from others?"

26 "From others," Peter answered.

"Then the sons are exempt," Jesus said to him. 27 "But so that we may not offend[o] them, go to the lake and throw out your line. Take the first fish you catch; open its mouth and you will find a four-drachma coin. Take it and give it to them for my tax and yours."

How to be the greatest.

18:1-5pp— Mk 9:33-37; Lk 9:46-48

18 At that time the disciples came to Jesus and asked, "Who is the greatest in the kingdom of heaven?"

2 He called a little child and had him stand among them. 3 And he said: "I tell you the truth, unless you change and become like little children,[p] you will never enter the kingdom of heaven.[q] 4 Therefore, whoever humbles himself like this child is the greatest in the kingdom of heaven.[r]

5 "And whoever welcomes a little child like this in my name welcomes me.[s] 6 But if anyone causes one of these little ones who believe in me to sin,[t] it would be better for him to have a large millstone hung around his neck and to be drowned in the depths of the sea.[u]

7 "Woe to the world because of the things that cause people to sin! Such things must come, but woe to the man through whom they come![v] 8 If your hand or your foot causes you to sin,[w] cut it off and throw it away. It is better for you to enter life maimed or crippled than to have two hands or two feet and be thrown into eternal fire. 9 And if your eye causes you to sin,[x]

17:11 [a]Mal 4:6; Lk 1:16,17
17:12 [b]Mt 11:14 [c]Mt 14:3,10 [d]Mt 16:21
17:15 [e]Mt 4:24
17:20 [f]Mt 21:21 [g]Mt 13:31; Mk 11:23; Lk 17:6 [h]1Co 13:2
17:22 [i]Mt 8:20
17:23 [j]Ac 2:23; 3:13 [k]Mt 16:21 [l]Mt 16:21
17:24 [m]Ex 30:13
17:25 [n]Mt 22:17-21; Ro 13:7
17:27 [o]Jn 6:61
18:3 [p]Mt 19:14; 1Pe 2:2 [q]Mt 3:2
18:4 [r]Mk 9:35
18:5 [s]Mt 10:40
18:6 [t]Mt 5:29 [u]Mk 9:42; Lk 17:2
18:7 [v]Lk 17:1
18:8 [w]Mt 5:29; Mk 9:43,45
18:9 [x]Mt 5:29

p20 Some manuscripts *you.* 21 *But this kind does not go out except by prayer and fasting.* q24 Greek *the two drachmas*

gouge it out and throw it away. It is
better for you to enter life with one eye
than to have two eyes and be thrown
into the fire of hell.[a]

A parable: The lost sheep.

18:12-14pp— Lk 15:4-7

10"See that you do not look down on
one of these little ones. For I tell you
that their angels[b] in heaven always see
the face of my Father in heaven.[r]
12"What do you think? If a man owns
a hundred sheep, and one of them
wanders away, will he not leave the
ninety-nine on the hills and go to look
for the one that wandered off? 13And if
he finds it, I tell you the truth, he is
happier about that one sheep than
about the ninety-nine that did not wander off. 14In the same way your Father
in heaven is not willing that any of
these little ones should be lost.

How to discipline a sinner.

15"If your brother sins against you,[s]
go and show him his fault,[c] just between the two of you. If he listens to
you, you have won your brother over.
16But if he will not listen, take one or
two others along, so that 'every matter
may be established by the testimony of
two or three witnesses.'[t][d] 17If he refuses to listen to them, tell it to the
church;[e] and if he refuses to listen
even to the church, treat him as you
would a pagan or a tax collector.[f]
18"I tell you the truth, whatever you
bind on earth will be[u] bound in heav-
en, and whatever you loose on earth
will be[u] loosed in heaven.[g]
19"Again, I tell you that if two of you
on earth agree about anything you ask
for, it will be done for you[h] by my
Father in heaven. 20For where two or
three come together in my name, there
am I with them."

A parable: The unmerciful servant.

21Then Peter came to Jesus and
asked, "Lord, how many times shall I
forgive my brother when he sins
against me?[i] Up to seven times?"[j]
22Jesus answered, "I tell you, not sev-
en times, but seventy-seven times.[v][k]
23"Therefore, the kingdom of heav-
en is like[l] a king who wanted to settle
accounts[m] with his servants. 24As he
began the settlement, a man who owed
him ten thousand talents[w] was brought
to him. 25Since he was not able to pay,[n]
the master ordered that he and his
wife and his children and all that he
had be sold[o] to repay the debt.
26"The servant fell on his knees
before him.[p] 'Be patient with me,' he
begged, 'and I will pay back everything.' 27The servant's master took
pity on him, canceled the debt and
let him go.
28"But when that servant went out,
he found one of his fellow servants
who owed him a hundred denarii.[x] He
grabbed him and began to choke him.
'Pay back what you owe me!' he
demanded.
29"His fellow servant fell to his knees
and begged him, 'Be patient with me,
and I will pay you back.'
30"But he refused. Instead, he went
off and had the man thrown into prison
until he could pay the debt. 31When
the other servants saw what had happened, they were greatly distressed
and went and told their master everything that had happened.
32"Then the master called the servant
in. 'You wicked servant,' he said, 'I
canceled all that debt of yours because
you begged me to. 33Shouldn't you have
had mercy on your fellow servant just
as I had on you?' 34In anger his master
turned him over to the jailers to be
tortured, until he should pay back all
he owed.
35"This is how my heavenly Father
will treat each of you unless you forgive your brother from your heart."[q]

18:9 [a]Mt 5:22
18:10 [b]Ge 48:16; Ps 34:7; Ac 12:11,15; Heb 1:14
18:15 [c]Lev 19:17; Lk 17:3; Gal 6:1; Jas 5:19,20
18:16 [d]Nu 35:30; Dt 17:6; 19:15; Jn 8:17; 2Co 13:1; 1Ti 5:19; Heb 10:28
18:17 [e]1Co 6:1-6 [f]Ro 16:17; 2Th 3:6,14
18:18 [g]Mt 16:19; Jn 20:23
18:19 [h]Mt 7:7
18:21 [i]Mt 6:14 [j]Lk 17:4
18:22 [k]Ge 4:24
18:23 [l]Mt 13:24 [m]Mt 25:19
18:25 [n]Lk 7:42 [o]Lev 25:39; 2Ki 4:1; Ne 5:5,8
18:26 [p]Mt 8:2
18:35 [q]Mt 6:14; Jas 2:13

r *10* Some manuscripts *heaven.* [11] *The Son of Man came to save what was lost.* s *15* Some manuscripts do not have *against you.* t *16* Deut. 19:15 u *18* Or *have been* v *22* Or *seventy times seven* w *24* That is, millions of dollars x *28* That is, a few dollars

Jesus' instruction concerning marriage and divorce.

19:1-9pp— Mk 10:1-12

19 When Jesus had finished saying these things,[a] he left Galilee and went into the region of Judea to the other side of the Jordan. 2 Large crowds followed him, and he healed them[b] there.

3 Some Pharisees came to him to test him. They asked, "Is it lawful for a man to divorce his wife[c] for any and every reason?"

4 "Haven't you read," he replied, "that at the beginning the Creator 'made them male and female,'[y][d] 5 and said, 'For this reason a man will leave his father and mother and be united to his wife, and the two will become one flesh'[z]?[e] 6 So they are no longer two, but one. Therefore what God has joined together, let man not separate."

7 "Why then," they asked, "did Moses command that a man give his wife a certificate of divorce and send her away?"[f]

8 Jesus replied, "Moses permitted you to divorce your wives because your hearts were hard. But it was not this way from the beginning. 9 I tell you that anyone who divorces his wife, except for marital unfaithfulness, and marries another woman commits adultery."[g]

10 The disciples said to him, "If this is the situation between a husband and wife, it is better not to marry."

11 Jesus replied, "Not everyone can accept this word, but only those to whom it has been given.[h] 12 For some are eunuchs because they were born that way; others were made that way by men; and others have renounced marriage[a] because of the kingdom of heaven. The one who can accept this should accept it."

Jesus and the little children.

19:13-15pp— Mk 10:13-16; Lk 18:15-17

13 Then little children were brought to Jesus for him to place his hands on them[i] and pray for them. But the disciples rebuked those who brought them.

14 Jesus said, "Let the little children come to me, and do not hinder them, for the kingdom of heaven belongs[j] to such as these."[k] 15 When he had placed his hands on them, he went on from there.

The rich young man.

19:16-29pp— Mk 10:17-30; Lk 18:18-30

16 Now a man came up to Jesus and asked, "Teacher, what good thing must I do to get eternal life[l]?"[m]

17 "Why do you ask me about what is good?" Jesus replied. "There is only One who is good. If you want to enter life, obey the commandments."[n]

18 "Which ones?" the man inquired.

Jesus replied, "'Do not murder, do not commit adultery,[o] do not steal, do not give false testimony, 19 honor your father and mother,'[b][p] and 'love your neighbor as yourself.'[c]"[q]

20 "All these I have kept," the young man said. "What do I still lack?"

21 Jesus answered, "If you want to be perfect,[r] go, sell your possessions and give to the poor,[s] and you will have treasure in heaven.[t] Then come, follow me."

22 When the young man heard this, he went away sad, because he had great wealth.

23 Then Jesus said to his disciples, "I tell you the truth, it is hard for a rich man[u] to enter the kingdom of heaven. 24 Again I tell you, it is easier for a camel to go through the eye of a needle than for a rich man to enter the kingdom of God."

25 When the disciples heard this, they were greatly astonished and asked, "Who then can be saved?"

26 Jesus looked at them and said, "With man this is impossible, but with God all things are possible."[v]

27 Peter answered him, "We have left

19:1 [a]Mt 7:28
19:2 [b]Mt 4:23
19:3 [c]Mt 5:31
19:4 [d]Ge 1:27; 5:2
19:5 [e]Ge 2:24; 1Co 6:16; Eph 5:31
19:7 [f]Dt 24:1-4; Mt 5:31
19:9 [g]Mt 5:32; Lk 16:18
19:11 [h]Mt 13:11; 1Co 7:7-9,17
19:13 [i]Mk 5:23
19:14 [j]Mt 25:34 [k]Mt 18:3; 1Pe 2:2
19:16 [l]Mt 25:46 [m]Lk 10:25
19:17 [n]Lev 18:5
19:18 [o]Jas 2:11
19:19 [p]Ex 20:12-16; Dt 5:16-20 [q]Lev 19:18; Mt 5:43
19:21 [r]Mt 5:48 [s]Lk 12:33; Ac 2:45; 4:34-35 [t]Mt 6:20
19:23 [u]Mt 13:22; 1Ti 6:9,10
19:26 [v]Ge 18:14; Job 42:2; Jer 32:17; Zec 8:6; Lk 1:37; 18:27; Ro 4:21

y *4* Gen. 1:27 z *5* Gen. 2:24 a *12* Or *have made themselves eunuchs* b *19* Exodus 20:12-16; Deut. 5:16-20 c *19* Lev. 19:18

everything to follow you![a] What then will there be for us?"

28Jesus said to them, "I tell you the truth, at the renewal of all things, when the Son of Man sits on his glorious throne,[b] you who have followed me will also sit on twelve thrones, judging the twelve tribes of Israel.[c] 29And everyone who has left houses or brothers or sisters or father or mother[d] or children or fields for my sake will receive a hundred times as much and will inherit eternal life.[d] 30But many who are first will be last, and many who are last will be first.[e]

A parable: A landowner hiring workers.

20 "For the kingdom of heaven is like[f] a landowner who went out early in the morning to hire men to work in his vineyard.[g] 2He agreed to pay them a denarius for the day and sent them into his vineyard.

3"About the third hour he went out and saw others standing in the marketplace doing nothing. 4He told them, 'You also go and work in my vineyard, and I will pay you whatever is right.' 5So they went.

"He went out again about the sixth hour and the ninth hour and did the same thing. 6About the eleventh hour he went out and found still others standing around. He asked them, 'Why have you been standing here all day long doing nothing?'

7"'Because no one has hired us,' they answered.

"He said to them, 'You also go and work in my vineyard.'

8"When evening came,[h] the owner of the vineyard said to his foreman, 'Call the workers and pay them their wages beginning with the last ones hired and going on to the first.'

9"The workers who were hired about the eleventh hour came and each received a denarius. 10So when those came who were hired first, they expected to receive more. But each one of them also received a denarius. 11When they received it, they began to grumble[i] against the landowner. 12'These men who were hired last worked only one hour,' they said, 'and you have made them equal to us who have borne the burden of the work and the heat[j] of the day.'

13"But he answered one of them, 'Friend,[k] I am not being unfair to you. Didn't you agree to work for a denarius? 14Take your pay and go. I want to give the man who was hired last the same as I gave you. 15Don't I have the right to do what I want with my own money? Or are you envious because I am generous?'[l]

16"So the last will be first, and the first will be last."[m]

Prediction of Jesus' death.

20:17-19pp— Mk 10:32-34; Lk 18:31-33

17Now as Jesus was going up to Jerusalem, he took the twelve disciples aside and said to them, 18"We are going up to Jerusalem,[n] and the Son of Man[o] will be betrayed to the chief priests and the teachers of the law.[p] They will condemn him to death 19and will turn him over to the Gentiles to be mocked and flogged[q] and crucified.[r] On the third day[s] he will be raised to life!"[t]

Request by the mother of Zebedee's sons.

20:20-28pp— Mk 10:35-45

20Then the mother of Zebedee's sons[u] came to Jesus with her sons and, kneeling down,[v] asked a favor of him.

21"What is it you want?" he asked.

She said, "Grant that one of these two sons of mine may sit at your right and the other at your left in your kingdom."[w]

22"You don't know what you are asking," Jesus said to them. "Can you drink the cup[x] I am going to drink?"

"We can," they answered.

23Jesus said to them, "You will indeed drink from my cup,[y] but to sit

19:27 [a]Mt 4:19
19:28 [b]Mt 20:21; 25:31 [c]Lk 22:28-30; Rev 3:21; 4:4; 20:4
19:29 [d]Mt 6:33; 25:46
19:30 [e]Mt 20:16; Mk 10:31; Lk 13:30
20:1 [f]Mt 13:24 [g]Mt 21:28,33
20:8 [h]Lev 19:13; Dt 24:15
20:11 [i]Jnh 4:1
20:12 [j]Jnh 4:8; Lk 12:55; Jas 1:11
20:13 [k]Mt 22:12; 26:50
20:15 [l]Dt 15:9; Mk 7:22
20:16 [m]Mt 19:30
20:18 [n]Lk 9:51 [o]Mt 8:20 [p]Mt 16:21; 27:1,2
20:19 [q]Mt 16:21 [r]Ac 2:23 [s]Mt 16:21 [t]Mt 16:21
20:20 [u]Mt 4:21 [v]Mt 8:2
20:21 [w]Mt 19:28
20:22 [x]Isa 51:17,22; Jer 49:12; Mt 26:39,42; Mk 14:36; Lk 22:42; Jn 18:11
20:23 [y]Ac 12:2; Rev 1:9

d29 Some manuscripts *mother or wife*

at my right or left is not for me to grant.
These places belong to those for whom
they have been prepared by my Father."
24 When the ten heard about this, they
were indignant[a] with the two brothers.
25 Jesus called them together and said,
"You know that the rulers of the Gentiles lord it over them, and their high
officials exercise authority over them.
26 Not so with you. Instead, whoever
wants to become great among you must
be your servant,[b] 27 and whoever wants
to be first must be your slave— 28 just
as the Son of Man[c] did not come to be
served, but to serve,[d] and to give his life
as a ransom[e] for many."

Healing of two blind men by Jesus.

20:29-34pp— Mk 10:46-52; Lk 18:35-43

29 As Jesus and his disciples were
leaving Jericho, a large crowd followed
him. 30 Two blind men were sitting by
the roadside, and when they heard
that Jesus was going by, they shouted,
"Lord, Son of David,[f] have mercy on us!"
31 The crowd rebuked them and told
them to be quiet, but they shouted all
the louder, "Lord, Son of David, have
mercy on us!"
32 Jesus stopped and called them.
"What do you want me to do for you?"
he asked.
33 "Lord," they answered, "we want
our sight."
34 Jesus had compassion on them and
touched their eyes. Immediately they
received their sight and followed him.

The Triumphal Entry.

21:1-9pp— Mk 11:1-10; Lk 19:29-38
21:4-9pp— Jn 12:12-15

21 As they approached Jerusalem
and came to Bethphage on the
Mount of Olives,[g] Jesus sent two disciples, 2 saying to them, "Go to the village ahead of you, and at once you will
find a donkey tied there, with her colt
by her. Untie them and bring them to
me. 3 If anyone says anything to you,
tell him that the Lord needs them, and
he will send them right away."

20:24 [a]Lk 22:24,25
20:26 [b]Mt 23:11; Mk 9:35
20:28 [c]Mt 8:20 [d]Lk 22:27; Jn 13:13-16; 2Co 8:9; Php 2:7 [e]Isa 53:10; Mt 26:28; 1Ti 2:6; Tit 2:14; Heb 9:28; 1Pe 1:18,19
20:30 [f]Mt 9:27
21:1 [g]Mt 24:3; 26:30; Mk 14:26; Lk 19:37; 21:37; 22:39; Jn 8:1; Ac 1:12
21:5 [h]Zec 9:9; Isa 62:11
21:8 [i]2Ki 9:13
21:9 [j]ver 15; Mt 9:27 [k]Ps 118:26; Mt 23:39 [l]Lk 2:14

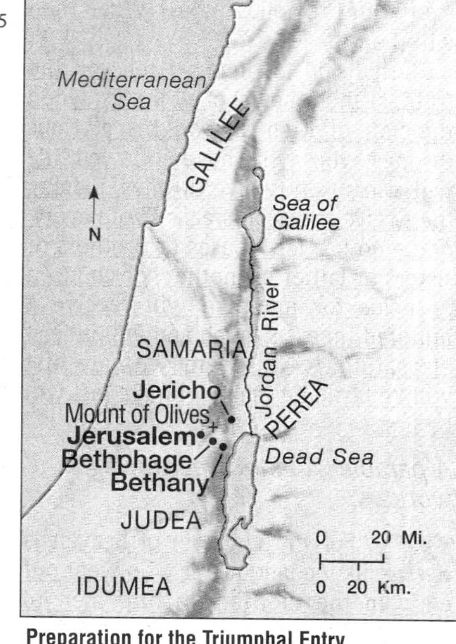

Preparation for the Triumphal Entry

On their way from Jericho, Jesus and the disciples neared Bethphage, on the slope of the Mount of Olives just outside Jerusalem. Two disciples went into the village, as Jesus told them, to bring back a donkey and its colt. Jesus rode into Jerusalem on the donkey, an unmistakable sign of his kingship.

4 This took place to fulfill what was
spoken through the prophet:
5 "Say to the Daughter of Zion,
'See, your king comes to you,
gentle and riding on a donkey,
on a colt, the foal of a donkey.' "[e][h]
6 The disciples went and did as Jesus
had instructed them. 7 They brought the
donkey and the colt, placed their cloaks
on them, and Jesus sat on them. 8 A
very large crowd spread their cloaks[i]
on the road, while others cut branches
from the trees and spread them on the
road. 9 The crowds that went ahead of
him and those that followed shouted,
"Hosanna[f] to the Son of David!"[j]
"Blessed is he who comes in the
name of the Lord!"[g][k]

[e]5 Zech. 9:9 [f]9 A Hebrew expression meaning "Save!" which became an exclamation of praise; also in verse 15 [g]9 Psalm 118:26

"Hosanna[f] in the highest!"[l]
[10]When Jesus entered Jerusalem, the
whole city was stirred and asked, "Who
is this?"
[11]The crowds answered, "This is Jesus,
the prophet[a] from Nazareth in Galilee."

Jesus' clearing of the temple.

21:12-16pp— Mk 11:15-18; Lk 19:45-47

[12]Jesus entered the temple area and
drove out all who were buying[b] and selling there. He overturned the tables of
the money changers[c] and the benches
of those selling doves.[d] [13]"It is written,"
he said to them, "'My house will be
called a house of prayer,'[h][e] but you are
making it a 'den of robbers.'[i]"[f]
[14]The blind and the lame came to him
at the temple, and he healed them.[g]
[15]But when the chief priests and the
teachers of the law saw the wonderful
things he did and the children shouting
in the temple area, "Hosanna to the Son
of David,"[h] they were indignant.[i]
[16]"Do you hear what these children
are saying?" they asked him.
"Yes," replied Jesus, "have you never
read,

"'From the lips of children and
infants
you have ordained praise'[j]?"[j]

[17]And he left them and went out of
the city to Bethany,[k] where he spent
the night.

The withered fig tree.

21:18-22pp— Mk 11:12-14,20-24

[18]Early in the morning, as he was on
his way back to the city, he was hungry.
[19]Seeing a fig tree by the road, he went
up to it but found nothing on it except
leaves. Then he said to it, "May you
never bear fruit again!" Immediately the
tree withered.[l]
[20]When the disciples saw this, they
were amazed. "How did the fig tree wither so quickly?" they asked.
[21]Jesus replied, "I tell you the truth, if
you have faith and do not doubt,[m] not

21:11 [a]Lk 7:16,39; 24:19; Jn 1:21,25; 6:14; 7:40
21:12 [b]Dt 14:26 [c]Ex 30:13 [d]Lev 1:14
21:13 [e]Isa 56:7 [f]Jer 7:11
21:14 [g]Mt 4:23
21:15 [h]ver 9; Mt 9:27 [i]Lk 19:39
21:16 [j]Ps 8:2
21:17 [k]Mt 26:6; Mk 11:1; Lk 24:50; Jn 11:1,18; 12:1
21:19 [l]Isa 34:4; Jer 8:13
21:21 [m]Mt 17:20; Lk 17:6; 1Co 13:2; Jas 1:6
21:22 [n]Mt 7:7
21:23 [o]Ac 4:7; 7:27
21:26 [p]Mt 11:9; Mk 6:20
21:28 [q]ver 33; Mt 20:1
21:31 [r]Lk 7:29 [s]Lk 7:50
21:32 [t]Mt 3:1-12 [u]Lk 3:12,13; 7:29 [v]Lk 7:36-50

only can you do what was done to the
fig tree, but also you can say to this
mountain, 'Go, throw yourself into the
sea,' and it will be done. [22]If you believe,
you will receive whatever you ask for[n]
in prayer."

Questioning of Jesus' authority.

21:23-27pp— Mk 11:27-33; Lk 20:1-8

[23]Jesus entered the temple courts,
and, while he was teaching, the chief
priests and the elders of the people
came to him. "By what authority[o] are
you doing these things?" they asked.
"And who gave you this authority?"
[24]Jesus replied, "I will also ask you
one question. If you answer me, I will
tell you by what authority I am doing
these things. [25]John's baptism—where
did it come from? Was it from heaven,
or from men?"
They discussed it among themselves
and said, "If we say, 'From heaven,' he
will ask, 'Then why didn't you believe
him?' [26]But if we say, 'From men'—
we are afraid of the people, for they all
hold that John was a prophet."[p]
[27]So they answered Jesus, "We don't
know."
Then he said, "Neither will I tell you
by what authority I am doing these
things.
[28]"What do you think? There was a
man who had two sons. He went to the
first and said, 'Son, go and work today
in the vineyard.'[q]
[29]"'I will not,' he answered, but later
he changed his mind and went.
[30]"Then the father went to the other
son and said the same thing. He answered, 'I will, sir,' but he did not go.
[31]"Which of the two did what his
father wanted?"
"The first," they answered.
Jesus said to them, "I tell you the
truth, the tax collectors[r] and the prostitutes[s] are entering the kingdom of
God ahead of you. [32]For John came to
you to show you the way of righteousness,[t] and you did not believe him, but

h *13* Isaiah 56:7 i *13* Jer. 7:11 j *16* Psalm 8:2

the tax collectors[u] and the prostitutes[v]
did. And even after you saw this, you
did not repent[a] and believe him.

A parable: The wretched tenants.

21:33-46pp— Mk 12:1-12; Lk 20:9-19

33“Listen to another parable: There
was a landowner who planted[b] a vineyard. He put a wall around it, dug a
winepress in it and built a watchtower.[c]
Then he rented the vineyard to some
farmers and went away on a journey.[d]
34When the harvest time approached,
he sent his servants[e] to the tenants to
collect his fruit.
35“The tenants seized his servants;
they beat one, killed another, and stoned
a third.[f] 36Then he sent other servants[g]
to them, more than the first time, and
the tenants treated them the same way.
37Last of all, he sent his son to them.
‘They will respect my son,’ he said.
38“But when the tenants saw the son,
they said to each other, ‘This is the
heir.[h] Come, let's kill him[i] and take his
inheritance.’[j] 39So they took him and
threw him out of the vineyard and killed
him.
40“Therefore, when the owner of the
vineyard comes, what will he do to
those tenants?”
41“He will bring those wretches to a
wretched end,”[k] they replied, “and he
will rent the vineyard to other tenants,[l]
who will give him his share of the crop
at harvest time.”
42Jesus said to them, “Have you never read in the Scriptures:

“ ‘The stone the builders rejected
has become the capstone[k];
the Lord has done this,
and it is marvelous in our eyes’[l]?[m]

43“Therefore I tell you that the kingdom of God will be taken away from
you[n] and given to a people who will
produce its fruit. 44He who falls on this
stone will be broken to pieces, but he
on whom it falls will be crushed.”[m][o]
45When the chief priests and the Pharisees heard Jesus' parables, they knew he
was talking about them. 46They looked
for a way to arrest him, but they were
afraid of the crowd because the people
held that he was a prophet.[p]

21:32 [a]Lk 7:30
21:33 [b]Ps 80:8 [c]Isa 5:1-7 [d]Mt 25:14,15
21:34 [e]Mt 22:3
21:35 [f]2Ch 24:21; Mt 23:34,37; Heb 11:36,37
21:36 [g]Mt 22:4
21:38 [h]Heb 1:2 [i]Mt 12:14 [j]Ps 2:8
21:41 [k]Mt 8:11,12 [l]Ac 13:46; 18:6; 28:28
21:42 [m]Ps 118:22, 23; Ac 4:11; 1Pe 2:7
21:43 [n]Mt 8:12
21:44 [o]Lk 2:34
21:46 [p]ver 11,26
22:2 [q]Mt 13:24
22:3 [r]Mt 21:34
22:4 [s]Mt 21:36
22:7 [t]Lk 19:27
22:9 [u]Eze 21:21
22:10 [v]Mt 13:47,48
22:12 [w]Mt 20:13; 26:50
22:13 [x]Mt 8:12
22:14 [y]Rev 17:14

A parable: The wedding banquet.

22:2-14Ref— Lk 14:16-24

22 Jesus spoke to them again in
parables, saying: 2“The kingdom
of heaven is like[q] a king who prepared
a wedding banquet for his son. 3He sent
his servants[r] to those who had been
invited to the banquet to tell them to
come, but they refused to come.
4“Then he sent some more servants[s]
and said, ‘Tell those who have been
invited that I have prepared my dinner:
My oxen and fattened cattle have been
butchered, and everything is ready. Come
to the wedding banquet.’
5“But they paid no attention and went
off—one to his field, another to his business. 6The rest seized his servants, mistreated them and killed them. 7The king
was enraged. He sent his army and
destroyed those murderers[t] and burned
their city.
8“Then he said to his servants, ‘The
wedding banquet is ready, but those I
invited did not deserve to come. 9Go to
the street corners[u] and invite to the banquet anyone you find.’ 10So the servants
went out into the streets and gathered
all the people they could find, both
good and bad,[v] and the wedding hall
was filled with guests.
11“But when the king came in to see
the guests, he noticed a man there who
was not wearing wedding clothes.
12‘Friend,’[w] he asked, ‘how did you get
in here without wedding clothes?’ The
man was speechless.
13“Then the king told the attendants,
‘Tie him hand and foot, and throw him
outside, into the darkness, where there
will be weeping and gnashing of teeth.’[x]
14“For many are invited, but few are
chosen.”[y]

[k]42 Or *cornerstone* [l]42 Psalm 118:22,23
[m]44 Some manuscripts do not have verse 44.

Taxes due Caesar.

22:15-22pp— Mk 12:13-17; Lk 20:20-26

15Then the Pharisees went out and laid
plans to trap him in his words. 16They
sent their disciples to him along with
the Herodians.[a] "Teacher," they said,
"we know you are a man of integrity
and that you teach the way of God in
accordance with the truth. You aren't
swayed by men, because you pay no
attention to who they are. 17Tell us
then, what is your opinion? Is it right
to pay taxes[b] to Caesar or not?"
18But Jesus, knowing their evil intent,
said, "You hypocrites, why are you trying to trap me? 19Show me the coin used
for paying the tax." They brought him a
denarius, 20and he asked them, "Whose
portrait is this? And whose inscription?"
21"Caesar's," they replied.
Then he said to them, "Give to Caesar what is Caesar's,[c] and to God what
is God's."
22When they heard this, they were
amazed. So they left him and went
away.[d]

Resurrection and marriage.

22:23-33pp— Mk 12:18-27; Lk 20:27-40

23That same day the Sadducees,[e]
who say there is no resurrection,[f] came
to him with a question. 24"Teacher,"
they said, "Moses told us that if a man
dies without having children, his brother must marry the widow and have
children for him.[g] 25Now there were
seven brothers among us. The first one
married and died, and since he had no
children, he left his wife to his brother. 26The same thing happened to the
second and third brother, right on
down to the seventh. 27Finally, the
woman died. 28Now then, at the resurrection, whose wife will she be of the
seven, since all of them were married
to her?"
29Jesus replied, "You are in error
because you do not know the Scriptures[h] or the power of God. 30At the
resurrection people will neither marry
nor be given in marriage;[i] they will be
like the angels in heaven. 31But about
the resurrection of the dead—have
you not read what God said to you, 32'I
am the God of Abraham, the God of
Isaac, and the God of Jacob'[n]?[j] He is
not the God of the dead but of the living."
33When the crowds heard this, they
were astonished at his teaching.[k]

The two greatest commandments.

22:34-40pp— Mk 12:28-31

34Hearing that Jesus had silenced the
Sadducees,[l] the Pharisees got together. 35One of them, an expert in the
law,[m] tested him with this question:
36"Teacher, which is the greatest commandment in the Law?"
37Jesus replied: "'Love the Lord your
God with all your heart and with all
your soul and with all your mind.'[o][n]
38This is the first and greatest commandment. 39And the second is like it:
'Love your neighbor as yourself.'[p][o]
40All the Law and the Prophets hang
on these two commandments."[p]

Questioning about Jesus' sonship.

22:41-46pp— Mk 12:35-37; Lk 20:41-44

41While the Pharisees were gathered
together, Jesus asked them, 42"What
do you think about the Christ[q]? Whose
son is he?"
"The son of David,"[q] they replied.
43He said to them, "How is it then
that David, speaking by the Spirit, calls
him 'Lord'? For he says,

44"'The Lord said to my Lord:
"Sit at my right hand
until I put your enemies
under your feet."'[r][r]

45If then David calls him 'Lord,' how
can he be his son?" 46No one could say
a word in reply, and from that day on
no one dared to ask him any more
questions.[s]

22:16 [a]Mk 3:6
22:17 [b]Mt 17:25
22:21 [c]Ro 13:7
22:22 [d]Mk 12:12
22:23 [e]Ac 4:1 [f]Ac 23:8; 1Co 15:12
22:24 [g]Dt 25:5,6
22:29 [h]Jn 20:9
22:30 [i]Mt 24:38
22:32 [j]Ex 3:6; Ac 7:32
22:33 [k]Mt 7:28
22:34 [l]Ac 4:1
22:35 [m]Lk 7:30; 10:25; 11:45; 14:3
22:37 [n]Dt 6:5
22:39 [o]Lev 19:18; Mt 5:43; 19:19; Gal 5:14
22:40 [p]Mt 7:12
22:42 [q]Mt 9:27
22:44 [r]Ps 110:1; Ac 2:34,35; 1Co 15:25; Heb 1:13; 10:13
22:46 [s]Mk 12:34; Lk 20:40

n *32* Exodus 3:6 o *37* Deut. 6:5 p *39* Lev. 19:18
q *42* Or *Messiah* r *44* Psalm 110:1

Jesus pronounces woes upon the religious leaders.

23:1-7pp— Mk 12:38,39; Lk 20:45,46
23:37-39pp— Lk 13:34,35

23 Then Jesus said to the crowds and to his disciples: 2“The teachers of the law[a] and the Pharisees sit in Moses' seat. 3So you must obey them and do everything they tell you. But do not do what they do, for they do not practice what they preach. 4They tie up heavy loads and put them on men's shoulders, but they themselves are not willing to lift a finger to move them.[b]

5“Everything they do is done for men to see:[c] They make their phylacteries[s][d] wide and the tassels on their garments[e] long; 6they love the place of honor at banquets and the most important seats in the synagogues;[f] 7they love to be greeted in the marketplaces and to have men call them ‘Rabbi.’[g]

8“But you are not to be called ‘Rabbi,’ for you have only one Master and you are all brothers. 9And do not call anyone on earth ‘father,’ for you have one Father,[h] and he is in heaven. 10Nor are you to be called ‘teacher,’ for you have one Teacher, the Christ.[t] 11The greatest among you will be your servant.[i] 12For whoever exalts himself will be humbled, and whoever humbles himself will be exalted.[j]

13“Woe to you, teachers of the law and Pharisees, you hypocrites![k] You shut the kingdom of heaven in men's faces. You yourselves do not enter, nor will you let those enter who are trying to.[u][l]

15“Woe to you, teachers of the law and Pharisees, you hypocrites! You travel over land and sea to win a single convert,[m] and when he becomes one, you make him twice as much a son of hell[n] as you are.

16“Woe to you, blind guides![o] You say, ‘If anyone swears by the temple, it means nothing; but if anyone swears by the gold of the temple, he is bound by his oath.’[p] 17You blind fools! Which is greater: the gold, or the temple that makes the gold sacred?[q] 18You also say, ‘If anyone swears by the altar, it means nothing; but if anyone swears by the gift on it, he is bound by his oath.’ 19You blind men! Which is greater: the gift, or the altar that makes the gift sacred?[r] 20Therefore, he who swears by the altar swears by it and by everything on it. 21And he who swears by the temple swears by it and by the one who dwells[s] in it. 22And he who swears by heaven swears by God's throne and by the one who sits on it.[t]

23“Woe to you, teachers of the law and Pharisees, you hypocrites! You give a tenth[u] of your spices—mint, dill and cummin. But you have neglected the more important matters of the law—justice, mercy and faithfulness.[v] You should have practiced the latter, without neglecting the former. 24You blind guides![w] You strain out a gnat but swallow a camel.

25“Woe to you, teachers of the law and Pharisees, you hypocrites! You clean the outside of the cup and dish,[x] but inside they are full of greed and self-indulgence.[y] 26Blind Pharisee! First clean the inside of the cup and dish, and then the outside also will be clean.

27“Woe to you, teachers of the law and Pharisees, you hypocrites! You are like whitewashed tombs,[z] which look beautiful on the outside but on the inside are full of dead men's bones and everything unclean. 28In the same way, on the outside you appear to people as righteous but on the inside you are full of hypocrisy and wickedness.

29“Woe to you, teachers of the law and Pharisees, you hypocrites! You build tombs for the prophets[a] and decorate the graves of the righteous. 30And you say, ‘If we had lived in the days of our forefathers, we would not have taken part with them in shedding the blood of the prophets.’ 31So you testify against

23:2 [a]Ezr 7:6,25; Ne 8:4
23:4 [b]Lk 11:46; Ac 15:10; Gal 6:13
23:5 [c]Mt 6:1,2, 5,16 [d]Ex 13:9; Dt 6:8 [e]Nu 15:38; Dt 22:12
23:6 [f]Lk 11:43; 14:7; 20:46
23:7 [g]ver 8; Mk 9:5; 10:51; Jn 1:38,49
23:9 [h]Mal 1:6; Mt 7:11
23:11 [i]Mt 20:26; Mk 9:35
23:12 [j]Lk 14:11
23:13 [k]ver 15,23, 25,27,29 [l]Lk 11:52
23:15 [m]Ac 2:11; 6:5; 13:43 [n]Mt 5:22
23:16 [o]ver 24; Mt 15:14 [p]Mt 5:33-35
23:17 [q]Ex 30:29
23:19 [r]Ex 29:37
23:21 [s]1Ki 8:13; Ps 26:8
23:22 [t]Ps 11:4; Mt 5:34
23:23 [u]Lev 27:30 [v]Mic 6:8; Lk 11:42
23:24 [w]ver 16
23:25 [x]Mk 7:4 [y]Lk 11:39
23:27 [z]Lk 11:44; Ac 23:3
23:29 [a]Lk 11:47,48

s *5* That is, boxes containing Scripture verses, worn on forehead and arm t *10* Or *Messiah* u *13* Some manuscripts *to.* *14Woe to you, teachers of the law and Pharisees, you hypocrites! You devour widows' houses and for a show make lengthy prayers. Therefore you will be punished more severely.*

yourselves that you are the descendants of those who murdered the prophets.[a] 32 Fill up, then, the measure[b] of the sin of your forefathers!

33 "You snakes! You brood of vipers![c] How will you escape being condemned to hell?[d] 34 Therefore I am sending you prophets and wise men and teachers. Some of them you will kill and crucify;[e] others you will flog in your synagogues[f] and pursue from town to town.[g] 35 And so upon you will come all the righteous blood that has been shed on earth, from the blood of righteous Abel[h] to the blood of Zechariah son of Berekiah,[i] whom you murdered between the temple and the altar.[j] 36 I tell you the truth, all this will come upon this generation.[k]

37 "O Jerusalem, Jerusalem, you who kill the prophets and stone those sent to you,[l] how often I have longed to gather your children together, as a hen gathers her chicks under her wings, but you were not willing. 38 Look, your house is left to you desolate.[m] 39 For I tell you, you will not see me again until you say, 'Blessed is he who comes in the name of the Lord.'[v]"[n]

Jesus' Olivet Discourse: The destruction of the temple, and the last days.

24:1-51pp— Mk 13:1-37; Lk 21:5-36

24 Jesus left the temple and was walking away when his disciples came up to him to call his attention to its buildings. 2 "Do you see all these things?" he asked. "I tell you the truth, not one stone here will be left on another;[o] every one will be thrown down."

3 As Jesus was sitting on the Mount of Olives,[p] the disciples came to him privately. "Tell us," they said, "when will this happen, and what will be the sign of your coming and of the end of the age?"

4 Jesus answered: "Watch out that no one deceives you. 5 For many will come in my name, claiming, 'I am the Christ,'[w] and will deceive many.[q] 6 You will hear of wars and rumors of wars, but see to it that you are not alarmed. Such things must happen, but the end is still to come. 7 Nation will rise against nation, and kingdom against kingdom.[r] There will be famines[s] and earthquakes in various places. 8 All these are the beginning of birth pains.

9 "Then you will be handed over to be persecuted[t] and put to death,[u] and you will be hated by all nations because of me. 10 At that time many will turn away from the faith and will betray and hate each other, 11 and many false prophets[v] will appear and deceive many people. 12 Because of the increase of wickedness, the love of most will grow cold, 13 but he who stands firm to the end will be saved.[w] 14 And this gospel of the kingdom[x] will be preached in the whole world[y] as a testimony to all nations, and then the end will come.

15 "So when you see standing in the holy place[z] 'the abomination that causes desolation,'[x][a] spoken of through the prophet Daniel—let the reader understand— 16 then let those who are in Judea flee to the mountains. 17 Let no one on the roof of his house[b] go down to take anything out of the house. 18 Let no one in the field go back to get his cloak. 19 How dreadful it will be in those days for pregnant women and nursing mothers![c] 20 Pray that your flight will not take place in winter or on the Sabbath. 21 For then there will be great distress, unequaled from the beginning of the world until now—and never to be equaled again.[d] 22 If those days had not been cut short, no one would survive, but for the sake of the elect[e] those days will be shortened. 23 At that time if anyone says to you, 'Look, here is the Christ!' or, 'There he is!' do not believe it.[f] 24 For false Christs and false prophets will appear and perform great

23:31 [a]Ac 7:51-52
23:32 [b]1Th 2:16
23:33 [c]Mt 3:7; 12:34 [d]Mt 5:22
23:34 [e]2Ch 36:15, 16; Lk 11:49 [f]Mt 10:17 [g]Mt 10:23
23:35 [h]Ge 4:8; Heb 11:4 [i]Zec 1:1 [j]2Ch 24:21
23:36 [k]Mt 10:23; 24:34
23:37 [l]2Ch 24:21; Mt 5:12
23:38 [m]1Ki 9:7,8; Jer 22:5
23:39 [n]Ps 118:26; Mt 21:9
24:2 [o]Lk 19:44
24:3 [p]Mt 21:1
24:5 [q]ver 11,23, 24; 1Jn 2:18
24:7 [r]Isa 19:2 [s]Ac 11:28
24:9 [t]Mt 10:17 [u]Jn 16:2
24:11 [v]Mt 7:15
24:13 [w]Mt 10:22
24:14 [x]Mt 4:23 [y]Ro 10:18; Col 1:6,23; Lk 2:1; 4:5; Ac 11:28; 17:6; Rev 3:10; 16:14
24:15 [z]Ac 6:13 [a]Da 9:27; 11:31; 12:11
24:17 [b]1Sa 9:25; Mt 10:27; Lk 12:3; Ac 10:9
24:19 [c]Lk 23:29 **24:21** [d]Da 12:1; Joel 2:2
24:22 [e]ver 24,31 **24:23** [f]Lk 17:23; 21:8

v *39* Psalm 118:26 w *5* Or *Messiah*; also in verse 23
x *15* Daniel 9:27; 11:31; 12:11

signs and miracles[a] to deceive even the
elect—if that were possible. 25See, I
have told you ahead of time.
26"So if anyone tells you, 'There he
is, out in the desert,' do not go out; or,
'Here he is, in the inner rooms,' do not
believe it. 27For as lightning[b] that comes
from the east is visible even in the
west, so will be the coming of the Son
of Man.[c] 28Wherever there is a carcass,
there the vultures will gather.[d]
29"Immediately after the distress of
those days

"'the sun will be darkened,
and the moon will not give its
light;
the stars will fall from the sky,
and the heavenly bodies will be
shaken.'[y][e]

30"At that time the sign of the Son of
Man will appear in the sky, and all the
nations of the earth will mourn. They
will see the Son of Man coming on the
clouds of the sky,[f] with power and
great glory. 31And he will send his
angels[g] with a loud trumpet call,[h] and
they will gather his elect from the four
winds, from one end of the heavens to
the other.
32"Now learn this lesson from the fig
tree: As soon as its twigs get tender
and its leaves come out, you know that
summer is near. 33Even so, when you
see all these things, you know that it[z]
is near, right at the door.[i] 34I tell you
the truth, this generation[a] will certainly not pass away until all these things
have happened.[j] 35Heaven and earth
will pass away, but my words will never pass away.[k]

The unknown day and hour.

24:37-39pp— Lk 17:26,27
24:45-51pp— Lk 12:42-46

36"No one knows about that day or
hour, not even the angels in heaven,
nor the Son,[b] but only the Father.[l] 37As
it was in the days of Noah,[m] so it will
be at the coming of the Son of Man.
38For in the days before the flood, people were eating and drinking, marrying and giving in marriage,[n] up to the
day Noah entered the ark; 39and they
knew nothing about what would happen until the flood came and took them
all away. That is how it will be at the
coming of the Son of Man. 40Two men
will be in the field; one will be taken
and the other left.[o] 41Two women will
be grinding with a hand mill; one will
be taken and the other left.[p]
42"Therefore keep watch, because
you do not know on what day your Lord
will come.[q] 43But understand this: If
the owner of the house had known at
what time of night the thief was coming,[r] he would have kept watch and
would not have let his house be broken into. 44So you also must be ready,[s]
because the Son of Man will come at
an hour when you do not expect him.
45"Who then is the faithful and wise
servant,[t] whom the master has put in
charge of the servants in his household to give them their food at the
proper time? 46It will be good for that
servant whose master finds him doing
so when he returns.[u] 47I tell you the
truth, he will put him in charge of all
his possessions.[v] 48But suppose that
servant is wicked and says to himself,
'My master is staying away a long
time,' 49and he then begins to beat his
fellow servants and to eat and drink
with drunkards.[w] 50The master of that
servant will come on a day when he
does not expect him and at an hour he
is not aware of. 51He will cut him to
pieces and assign him a place with the
hypocrites, where there will be weeping and gnashing of teeth.[x]

A parable: The ten virgins.

25 "At that time the kingdom of
heaven will be like[y] ten virgins
who took their lamps[z] and went out to
meet the bridegroom.[a] 2Five of them

24:24 [a]2Th 2:9-11; Rev 13:13
24:27 [b]Lk 17:24 [c]Mt 8:20
24:28 [d]Lk 17:37
24:29 [e]Isa 13:10; 34:4; Eze 32:7; Joel 2:10,31; Zep 1:15; Rev 6:12,13; 8:12
24:30 [f]Da 7:13; Rev 1:7
24:31 [g]Mt 13:41 [h]Isa 27:13; Zec 9:14; 1Co 15:52; 1Th 4:16; Rev 8:2; 10:7; 11:15
24:33 [i]Jas 5:9
24:34 [j]Mt 16:28; 23:36
24:35 [k]Mt 5:18
24:36 [l]Ac 1:7
24:37 [m]Ge 6:5; 7:6-23
24:38 [n]Mt 22:30
24:40 [o]Lk 17:34
24:41 [p]Lk 17:35
24:42 [q]Mt 25:13; Lk 12:40
24:43 [r]Lk 12:39
24:44 [s]1Th 5:6
24:45 [t]Mt 25:21,23
24:46 [u]Rev 16:15
24:47 [v]Mt 25:21,23
24:49 [w]Lk 21:34
24:51 [x]Mt 8:12

25:1 [y]Mt 13:24 [z]Lk 12:35-38; Ac 20:8; Rev 4:5 [a]Rev 19:7; 21:2

[y]*29* Isaiah 13:10; 34:4 [z]*33* Or *he* [a]*34* Or *race*
[b]*36* Some manuscripts do not have *nor the Son.*

were foolish and five were wise.[a] 3The
foolish ones took their lamps but did
not take any oil with them. 4The wise,
however, took oil in jars along with their
lamps. 5The bridegroom was a long time
in coming, and they all became drowsy
and fell asleep.[b]
6"At midnight the cry rang out: 'Here's
the bridegroom! Come out to meet him!'
7"Then all the virgins woke up and
trimmed their lamps. 8The foolish ones
said to the wise, 'Give us some of your
oil; our lamps are going out.'[c]
9"'No,' they replied, 'there may not be
enough for both us and you. Instead, go
to those who sell oil and buy some for
yourselves.'
10"But while they were on their way
to buy the oil, the bridegroom arrived.
The virgins who were ready went in
with him to the wedding banquet.[d]
And the door was shut.
11"Later the others also came. 'Sir!
Sir!' they said. 'Open the door for us!'
12"But he replied, 'I tell you the truth,
I don't know you.'
13"Therefore keep watch, because you
do not know the day or the hour.[e]

A parable: The talents.

25:14-30Ref— Lk 19:12-27

14"Again, it will be like a man going
on a journey,[f] who called his servants
and entrusted his property to them.
15To one he gave five talents[c] of money,
to another two talents, and to another
one talent, each according to his ability.[g] Then he went on his journey. 16The
man who had received the five talents
went at once and put his money to
work and gained five more. 17So also,
the one with the two talents gained two
more. 18But the man who had received
the one talent went off, dug a hole in
the ground and hid his master's money.
19"After a long time the master of those
servants returned and settled accounts
with them.[h] 20The man who had received
the five talents brought the other five.
'Master,' he said, 'you entrusted me with
five talents. See, I have gained five more.'

25:2 [a]Mt 24:45
25:5 [b]1Th 5:6
25:8 [c]Lk 12:35
25:10 [d]Rev 19:9
25:13 [e]Mt 24:42, 44; Mk 13:35; Lk 12:40
25:14 [f]Mt 21:33; Lk 19:12
25:15 [g]Mt 18:24,25
25:19 [h]Mt 18:23
25:21 [i]ver 23; Mt 24:45,47; Lk 16:10
25:23 [j]ver 21
25:29 [k]Mt 13:12; Mk 4:25; Lk 8:18; 19:26
25:30 [l]Mt 8:12
25:31 [m]Mt 16:27; Lk 17:30 [n]Mt 19:28
25:32 [o]Mal 3:18

21"His master replied, 'Well done,
good and faithful servant! You have
been faithful with a few things; I will
put you in charge of many things.[i] Come
and share your master's happiness!'
22"The man with the two talents also
came. 'Master,' he said, 'you entrusted
me with two talents; see, I have gained
two more.'
23"His master replied, 'Well done,
good and faithful servant! You have
been faithful with a few things; I will
put you in charge of many things.[j] Come
and share your master's happiness!'
24"Then the man who had received
the one talent came. 'Master,' he said,
'I knew that you are a hard man, harvesting where you have not sown and
gathering where you have not scattered seed. 25So I was afraid and went
out and hid your talent in the ground.
See, here is what belongs to you.'
26"His master replied, 'You wicked,
lazy servant! So you knew that I harvest where I have not sown and gather
where I have not scattered seed?
27Well then, you should have put my
money on deposit with the bankers, so
that when I returned I would have
received it back with interest.
28"'Take the talent from him and give
it to the one who has the ten talents.
29For everyone who has will be given
more, and he will have an abundance.
Whoever does not have, even what he
has will be taken from him.[k] 30And
throw that worthless servant outside,
into the darkness, where there will be
weeping and gnashing of teeth.'[l]

Separation of the sheep from the goats.

31"When the Son of Man comes[m] in
his glory, and all the angels with him,
he will sit on his throne[n] in heavenly
glory. 32All the nations will be gathered before him, and he will separate[o] the people one from another as a
shepherd separates the sheep from the

c*15* A talent was worth more than a thousand dollars.

goats.[a] 33He will put the sheep on his
right and the goats on his left.
34"Then the King will say to those
on his right, 'Come, you who are blessed
by my Father; take your inheritance,
the kingdom[b] prepared for you since
the creation of the world.[c] 35For I was
hungry and you gave me something to
eat, I was thirsty and you gave me
something to drink, I was a stranger and
you invited me in,[d] 36I needed clothes
and you clothed me,[e] I was sick and you
looked after me,[f] I was in prison and
you came to visit me.'[g]
37"Then the righteous will answer
him, 'Lord, when did we see you hungry and feed you, or thirsty and give
you something to drink? 38When did
we see you a stranger and invite you
in, or needing clothes and clothe you?
39When did we see you sick or in prison and go to visit you?'
40"The King will reply, 'I tell you the
truth, whatever you did for one of the
least of these brothers of mine, you did
for me.'[h]
41"Then he will say to those on his
left, 'Depart from me,[i] you who are
cursed, into the eternal fire[j] prepared
for the devil and his angels.[k] 42For I
was hungry and you gave me nothing
to eat, I was thirsty and you gave me
nothing to drink, 43I was a stranger
and you did not invite me in, I needed
clothes and you did not clothe me, I
was sick and in prison and you did not
look after me.'
44"They also will answer, 'Lord, when
did we see you hungry or thirsty or a
stranger or needing clothes or sick or
in prison, and did not help you?'
45"He will reply, 'I tell you the truth,
whatever you did not do for one of the
least of these, you did not do for me.'[l]
46"Then they will go away to eternal
punishment, but the righteous to eternal life."[m][n]

Plotting of Jesus' death.

26:2-5pp— Mk 14:1,2; Lk 22:1,2

26 When Jesus had finished saying all these things,[o] he said to
his disciples, 2"As you know, the Passover[p] is two days away—and the Son of
Man will be handed over to be crucified."
3Then the chief priests and the elders
of the people assembled[q] in the palace
of the high priest, whose name was
Caiaphas,[r] 4and they plotted to arrest
Jesus in some sly way and kill him.[s]
5"But not during the Feast," they said,
"or there may be a riot[t] among the
people."

Anointing of Jesus with perfume.

26:6-13pp— Mk 14:3-9
26:6-13Ref— Lk 7:37,38; Jn 12:1-8

6While Jesus was in Bethany[u] in the
home of a man known as Simon the
Leper, 7a woman came to him with an
alabaster jar of very expensive perfume,
which she poured on his head as he was
reclining at the table.
8When the disciples saw this, they
were indignant. "Why this waste?" they
asked. 9"This perfume could have been
sold at a high price and the money giv-
en to the poor."
10Aware of this, Jesus said to them,
"Why are you bothering this woman?
She has done a beautiful thing to me.
11The poor you will always have with
you,[v] but you will not always have me.
12When she poured this perfume on
my body, she did it to prepare me for
burial.[w] 13I tell you the truth, wherever this gospel is preached throughout
the world, what she has done will also
be told, in memory of her."

Judas's agreement of money for betrayal.

26:14-16pp— Mk 14:10,11; Lk 22:3-6

14Then one of the Twelve—the one
called Judas Iscariot[x]—went to the
chief priests 15and asked, "What are
you willing to give me if I hand him
over to you?" So they counted out for
him thirty silver coins.[y] 16From then

25:32 [a]Eze 34:17,20
25:34 [b]Mt 3:2; 5:3,10,19; 19:14; Ac 20:32; 1Co 15:50; Gal 5:21; Jas 2:5 [c]Heb 4:3; 9:26; Rev 13:8; 17:8
25:35 [d]Job 31:32; Isa 58:7; Eze 18:7; Heb 13:2
25:36 [e]Isa 58:7; Eze 18:7; Jas 2:15,16 [f]Jas 1:27 [g]2Ti 1:16
25:40 [h]Pr 19:17; Mt 10:40,42; Heb 6:10; 13:2
25:41 [i]Mt 7:23 [j]Isa 66:24; Mt 3:12; 5:22; Mk 9:43,48; Lk 3:17; Jude 7 [k]2Pe 2:4
25:45 [l]Pr 14:31; 17:5
25:46 [m]Mt 19:29; Jn 3:15,16,36; 17:2,3; Ro 2:7; Gal 6:8; 5:11,13,20 [n]Da 12:2; Jn 5:29; Ac 24:15; Ro 2:7,8; Gal 6:8
26:1 [o]Mt 7:28
26:2 [p]Jn 11:55; 13:1
26:3 [q]Ps 2:2 [r]ver 57; Jn 11:47-53; 18:13,14, 24,28
26:4 [s]Mt 12:14 **26:5** [t]Mt 27:24 **26:6** [u]Mt 21:17 **26:11** [v]Dt 15:11 **26:12** [w]Jn 19:40 **26:14** [x]ver 25, 47; Mt 10:4 **26:15** [y]Ex 21:32; Zec 11:12

on Judas watched for an opportunity to
hand him over.

The Last Supper.

26:17-19pp— Mk 14:12-16; Lk 22:7-13
26:20-24pp— Mk 14:17-21
26:26-29pp— Mk 14:22-25; Lk 22:17-20; 1Co 11:23-25

17On the first day of the Feast of
Unleavened Bread,[a] the disciples came
to Jesus and asked, "Where do you want
us to make preparations for you to eat
the Passover?"
18He replied, "Go into the city to a
certain man and tell him, 'The Teacher
says: My appointed time[b] is near. I am
going to celebrate the Passover with
my disciples at your house.'" 19So the
disciples did as Jesus had directed them
and prepared the Passover.
20When evening came, Jesus was
reclining at the table with the Twelve.
21And while they were eating, he said,
"I tell you the truth, one of you will
betray me."[c]

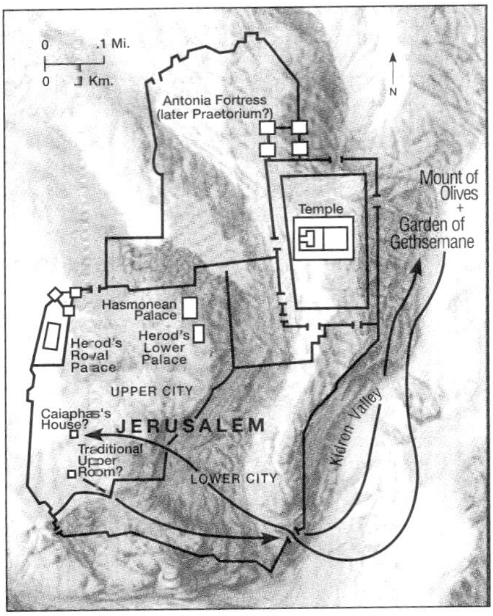

The Passover Meal and Gethsemane

Jesus, who would soon be the final Passover Lamb, ate the traditional Passover meal with his disciples in the upper room of a house in Jerusalem. During the meal they partook of the wine and bread, which would be the elements of future communion celebrations, and then went out to the Garden of Gethsemane on the Mount of Olives.

22They were very sad and began to
say to him one after the other, "Surely
not I, Lord?"
23Jesus replied, "The one who has
dipped his hand into the bowl with me
will betray me.[d] 24The Son of Man will
go just as it is written about him.[e] But
woe to that man who betrays the Son
of Man! It would be better for him if
he had not been born."
25Then Judas, the one who would
betray him, said, "Surely not I, Rabbi?"[f]
Jesus answered, "Yes, it is you."[d]
26While they were eating, Jesus took
bread, gave thanks and broke it,[g] and
gave it to his disciples, saying, "Take and
eat; this is my body."
27Then he took the cup, gave thanks
and offered it to them, saying, "Drink
from it, all of you. 28This is my blood
of the[e] covenant,[h] which is poured out
for many for the forgiveness of sins.[i]
29I tell you, I will not drink of this fruit
of the vine from now on until that day
when I drink it anew with you[j] in my
Father's kingdom."
30When they had sung a hymn, they
went out to the Mount of Olives.[k]

Prediction of Peter's denial.

26:31-35pp— Mk 14:27-31; Lk 22:31-34

31Then Jesus told them, "This very
night you will all fall away on account
of me,[l] for it is written:

"'I will strike the shepherd,
and the sheep of the flock will be
scattered.'[f][m]

32But after I have risen, I will go ahead
of you into Galilee."[n]
33Peter replied, "Even if all fall away
on account of you, I never will."
34"I tell you the truth," Jesus answered,
"this very night, before the
rooster crows, you will disown me three
times."[o]
35But Peter declared, "Even if I have to
die with you,[p] I will never disown you."
And all the other disciples said the same.

26:17 [a]Ex 12:18-20
26:18 [b]Jn 7:6,8,30; 12:23; 13:1; 17:1
26:21 [c]Lk 22:21-23; Jn 13:21
26:23 [d]Ps 41:9; Jn 13:18
26:24 [e]Isa 53; Da 9:26; Mk 9:12; Lk 24:25-27,46; Ac 17:2,3; 26:22,23
26:25 [f]Mt 23:7
26:26 [g]Mt 14:19; 1Co 10:16
26:28 [h]Ex 24:6-8; Heb 9:20 [i]Mt 20:28; Mk 1:4
26:29 [j]Ac 10:41
26:30 [k]Mt 21:1; Mk 14:26
26:31 [l]Mt 11:6 [m]Zec 13:7; Jn 16:32
26:32 [n]Mt 28:7,10,16
26:34 [o]ver 75; Jn 13:38
26:35 [p]Jn 13:37

d25 Or *"You yourself have said it"* e28 Some manuscripts *the new* f31 Zech. 13:7

The Garden of Gethsemane.

26:36-46pp— Mk 14:32-42; Lk 22:40-46

36Then Jesus went with his disciples to a place called Gethsemane, and he said to them, "Sit here while I go over there and pray." **37**He took Peter and the two sons of Zebedee[a] along with him, and he began to be sorrowful and troubled. **38**Then he said to them, "My soul is overwhelmed with sorrow[b] to the point of death. Stay here and keep watch with me."[c]

39Going a little farther, he fell with his face to the ground and prayed, "My Father, if it is possible, may this cup[d] be taken from me. Yet not as I will, but as you will."[e]

40Then he returned to his disciples and found them sleeping. "Could you men not keep watch with me[f] for one hour?" he asked Peter. **41**"Watch and pray so that you will not fall into temptation.[g] The spirit is willing, but the body is weak."

42He went away a second time and prayed, "My Father, if it is not possible for this cup to be taken away unless I drink it, may your will be done."

43When he came back, he again found them sleeping, because their eyes were heavy. **44**So he left them and went away once more and prayed the third time, saying the same thing.

45Then he returned to the disciples and said to them, "Are you still sleeping and resting? Look, the hour[h] is near, and the Son of Man is betrayed into the hands of sinners. **46**Rise, let us go! Here comes my betrayer!"

Jesus' betrayal and arrest.

26:47-56pp— Mk 14:43-50; Lk 22:47-53

47While he was still speaking, Judas, one of the Twelve, arrived. With him was a large crowd armed with swords and clubs, sent from the chief priests and the elders of the people. **48**Now the betrayer had arranged a signal with them: "The one I kiss is the man; arrest him." **49**Going at once to Jesus, Judas said, "Greetings, Rabbi!"[i] and kissed him.

50Jesus replied, "Friend,[j] do what you came for."[g]

Then the men stepped forward, seized Jesus and arrested him. **51**With that, one of Jesus' companions reached for his sword,[k] drew it out and struck the servant of the high priest, cutting off his ear.[l]

52"Put your sword back in its place," Jesus said to him, "for all who draw the sword will die by the sword.[m] **53**Do you think I cannot call on my Father, and he will at once put at my disposal more than twelve legions of angels?[n] **54**But how then would the Scriptures be fulfilled[o] that say it must happen in this way?"

55At that time Jesus said to the crowd, "Am I leading a rebellion, that you have come out with swords and clubs to capture me? Every day I sat in the temple courts teaching,[p] and you did not arrest me. **56**But this has all taken place that the writings of the prophets might be fulfilled."[q] Then all the disciples deserted him and fled.

Jesus' arraignment before the Sanhedrin.

26:57-68pp— Mk 14:53-65; Jn 18:12,13,19-24

57Those who had arrested Jesus took him to Caiaphas,[r] the high priest, where the teachers of the law and the elders had assembled. **58**But Peter followed him at a distance, right up to the courtyard of the high priest.[s] He entered and sat down with the guards[t] to see the outcome.

59The chief priests and the whole Sanhedrin[u] were looking for false evidence against Jesus so that they could put him to death. **60**But they did not find any, though many false witnesses[v] came forward.

Finally two[w] came forward **61**and declared, "This fellow said, 'I am able to destroy the temple of God and rebuild it in three days.'"[x]

26:37 [a]Mt 4:21
26:38 [b]Jn 12:27 [c]ver 40,41
26:39 [d]Mt 20:22 [e]ver 42; Ps 40:6-8; Isa 50:5; Jn 5:30; 6:38
26:40 [f]ver 38
26:41 [g]Mt 6:13
26:45 [h]ver 18
26:49 [i]ver 25
26:50 [j]Mt 20:13; 22:12
26:51 [k]Lk 22:36,38 [l]Jn 18:10
26:52 [m]Ge 9:6; Rev 13:10
26:53 [n]2Ki 6:17; Da 7:10; Mt 4:11
26:54 [o]ver 24
26:55 [p]Mk 12:35; Lk 21:37; Jn 7:14,28; 18:20
26:56 [q]ver 24
26:57 [r]ver 3
26:58 [s]Jn 18:15 [t]Jn 7:32, 45,46
26:59 [u]Mt 5:22
26:60 [v]Ps 27:12; 35:11; Ac 6:13 [w]Dt 19:15
26:61 [x]Jn 2:19

g50 Or *"Friend, why have you come?"*

62Then the high priest stood up and said to Jesus, "Are you not going to answer? What is this testimony that these men are bringing against you?" 63But Jesus remained silent.[a]

The high priest said to him, "I charge you under oath[b] by the living God:[c] Tell us if you are the Christ,[h] the Son of God."

64"Yes, it is as you say," Jesus replied. "But I say to all of you: In the future you will see the Son of Man sitting at the right hand of the Mighty One[d] and coming on the clouds of heaven."[e]

65Then the high priest tore his clothes[f] and said, "He has spoken blasphemy! Why do we need any more witnesses? Look, now you have heard the blasphemy. 66What do you think?"

"He is worthy of death,"[g] they answered.

67Then they spit in his face and struck him with their fists.[h] Others slapped him 68and said, "Prophesy to us, Christ. Who hit you?"[i]

Peter's denial.

26:69-75pp— Mk 14:66-72; Lk 22:55-62; Jn 18:16-18,25-27

69Now Peter was sitting out in the courtyard, and a servant girl came to him. "You also were with Jesus of Galilee," she said.

70But he denied it before them all. "I don't know what you're talking about," he said.

71Then he went out to the gateway, where another girl saw him and said to the people there, "This fellow was with Jesus of Nazareth."

72He denied it again, with an oath: "I don't know the man!"

73After a little while, those standing there went up to Peter and said, "Surely you are one of them, for your accent gives you away."

74Then he began to call down curses on himself and he swore to them, "I don't know the man!"

Immediately a rooster crowed. 75Then Peter remembered the word Jesus had spoken: "Before the rooster crows, you will disown me three times."[j] And he went outside and wept bitterly.

Judas hangs himself.

27 Early in the morning, all the chief priests and the elders of the people came to the decision to put Jesus to death.[k] 2They bound him, led him away and handed him over[l] to Pilate, the governor.[m]

3When Judas, who had betrayed him,[n] saw that Jesus was condemned, he was seized with remorse and returned the thirty silver coins[o] to the chief priests and the elders. 4"I have sinned," he said, "for I have betrayed innocent blood."

"What is that to us?" they replied. "That's your responsibility."[p]

5So Judas threw the money into the temple[q] and left. Then he went away and hanged himself.[r]

6The chief priests picked up the coins and said, "It is against the law to put this into the treasury, since it is blood money." 7So they decided to use the money to buy the potter's field as a burial place for foreigners. 8That is why it has been called the Field of Blood[s] to this day. 9Then what was spoken by Jeremiah the prophet was fulfilled:[t] "They took the thirty silver coins, the price set on him by the people of Israel, 10and they used them to buy the potter's field, as the Lord commanded me."[i][u]

Jesus appears before Pilate, the Roman governor.

27:11-26pp— Mk 15:2-15; Lk 23:2,3, 18-25; Jn 18:29-19:16

11Meanwhile Jesus stood before the governor, and the governor asked him, "Are you the king of the Jews?"[v]

"Yes, it is as you say," Jesus replied.

12When he was accused by the chief priests and the elders, he gave no answer.[w] 13Then Pilate asked him, "Don't you hear the testimony they are bring-

26:63 [a]Mt 27:12,14 [b]Lev 5:1 [c]Mt 16:16
26:64 [d]Ps 110:1 [e]Da 7:13; Rev 1:7
26:65 [f]Mk 14:63
26:66 [g]Lev 24:16; Jn 19:7
26:67 [h]Mt 16:21; 27:30
26:68 [i]Lk 22:63-65
26:75 [j]ver 34; Jn 13:38
27:1 [k]Mt 12:14; Mk 15:1; Lk 22:66
27:2 [l]Mt 20:19 [m]Mk 15:1; Lk 13:1; Ac 3:13; 1Ti 6:13
27:3 [n]Mt 10:4 [o]Mt 26:14,15
27:4 [p]ver 24
27:5 [q]Lk 1:9,21 [r]Ac 1:18
27:8 [s]Ac 1:19
27:9 [t]Mt 1:22
27:10 [u]Zec 11:12,13; Jer 32:6-9
27:11 [v]Mt 2:2
27:12 [w]Mt 26:63; Mk 14:61; Jn 19:9

h*63* Or *Messiah*; also in verse 68 i*10* See Zech. 11:12, 13; Jer. 19:1-13; 32:6-9.

ing against you?"[a] **14**But Jesus made no
reply,[b] not even to a single charge—to
the great amazement of the governor.
15Now it was the governor's custom
at the Feast to release a prisoner[c] chosen by the crowd. **16**At that time they
had a notorious prisoner, called Barabbas. **17**So when the crowd had gathered,
Pilate asked them, "Which one do you
want me to release to you: Barabbas,
or Jesus who is called Christ?"[d] **18**For
he knew it was out of envy that they
had handed Jesus over to him.
19While Pilate was sitting on the
judge's seat,[e] his wife sent him this
message: "Don't have anything to do
with that innocent[f] man, for I have suffered a great deal today in a dream[g]
because of him."
20But the chief priests and the elders
persuaded the crowd to ask for Barabbas and to have Jesus executed.[h]
21"Which of the two do you want me
to release to you?" asked the governor.
"Barabbas," they answered.
22"What shall I do, then, with Jesus
who is called Christ?"[i] Pilate asked.
They all answered, "Crucify him!"
23"Why? What crime has he committed?" asked Pilate.
But they shouted all the louder, "Crucify him!"
24When Pilate saw that he was getting nowhere, but that instead an uproar[j] was starting, he took water and
washed his hands[k] in front of the crowd.
"I am innocent of this man's blood,"[l]
he said. "It is your responsibility!"[m]
25All the people answered, "Let his
blood be on us and on our children!"[n]
26Then he released Barabbas to them.
But he had Jesus flogged,[o] and handed
him over to be crucified.

The soldiers mock Jesus.

27:27-31pp— Mk 15:16-20

27Then the governor's soldiers took
Jesus into the Praetorium[p] and gathered
the whole company of soldiers around
him. **28**They stripped him and put a
scarlet robe on him,[q] **29**and then twisted

27:13 [a]Mt 26:62
27:14 [b]Mk 14:61
27:15 [c]Jn 18:39
27:17 [d]ver 22; Mt 1:16
27:19 [e]Jn 19:13 [f]ver 24 [g]Ge 20:6; Nu 12:6; 1Ki 3:5; Job 33:14-16; Mt 1:20; 2:12,13,19,22
27:20 [h]Ac 3:14
27:22 [i]Mt 1:16
27:24 [j]Mt 26:5 [k]Ps 26:6 [l]Dt 21:6-8 [m]ver 4
27:25 [n]Jos 2:19; Ac 5:28
27:26 [o]Isa 53:5; Jn 19:1
27:27 [p]Jn 18:28,33; 19:9
27:28 [q]Jn 19:2
27:29 [r]Isa 53:3; Jn 19:2,3
27:30 [s]Mt 16:21; 26:67
27:31 [t]Isa 53:7
27:32 [u]Heb 13:12 [v]Ac 2:10; 6:9; 11:20; 13:1 [w]Mk 15:21; Lk 23:26
27:33 [x]Jn 19:17
27:34 [y]ver 48; Ps 69:21
27:35 [z]Ps 22:18
27:36 [a]ver 54
27:38 [b]Isa 53:12

together a crown of thorns and set it on
his head. They put a staff in his right
hand and knelt in front of him and
mocked him. "Hail, king of the Jews!"
they said.[r] **30**They spit on him, and took
the staff and struck him on the head
again and again.[s] **31**After they had mocked
him, they took off the robe and put his
own clothes on him. Then they led him
away to crucify him.[t]

Jesus' crucifixion.

27:33-44pp— Mk 15:22-32; Lk 23:33-43; Jn 19:17-24

32As they were going out,[u] they met
a man from Cyrene,[v] named Simon, and
they forced him to carry the cross.[w]
33They came to a place called Golgotha
(which means The Place of the Skull).[x]
34There they offered Jesus wine to
drink, mixed with gall;[y] but after tasting it, he refused to drink it. **35**When
they had crucified him, they divided
up his clothes by casting lots.[j][z] **36**And
sitting down, they kept watch[a] over him
there. **37**Above his head they placed
the written charge against him: THIS IS
JESUS, THE KING OF THE JEWS. **38**Two robbers were crucified with him,[b] one on
his right and one on his left. **39**Those
who passed by hurled insults at him,
shaking their heads[c] **40**and saying, "You
who are going to destroy the temple
and build it in three days,[d] save yourself![e] Come down from the cross, if
you are the Son of God!"[f]
41In the same way the chief priests,
the teachers of the law and the elders
mocked him. **42**"He saved others," they
said, "but he can't save himself! He's
the King of Israel![g] Let him come down
now from the cross, and we will believe[h] in him. **43**He trusts in God. Let
God rescue him[i] now if he wants him,
for he said, 'I am the Son of God.' " **44**In
the same way the robbers who were

27:39 [c]Ps 22:7; 109:25; La 2:15 **27:40** [d]Mt 26:61; Jn 2:19 [e]ver 42 [f]Mt 4:3,6 **27:42** [g]Jn 1:49; 12:13 [h]Jn 3:15 **27:43** [i]Ps 22:8

j35 A few late manuscripts *lots that the word spoken by the prophet might be fulfilled: "They divided my garments among themselves and cast lots for my clothing"* (Psalm 22:18)

crucified with him also heaped insults
on him.

Jesus' death.

27:45-56pp— Mk 15:33-41; Lk 23:44-49

45 From the sixth hour until the ninth
hour darkness[a] came over all the land.
46 About the ninth hour Jesus cried out
in a loud voice, "*Eloi, Eloi,*[k] *lama sa-*
bachthani?"—which means, "My God,
my God, why have you forsaken me?"[l][b]
47 When some of those standing there
heard this, they said, "He's calling Elijah."
48 Immediately one of them ran and
got a sponge. He filled it with wine vinegar,[c] put it on a stick, and offered it to
Jesus to drink. 49 The rest said, "Now
leave him alone. Let's see if Elijah comes
to save him."
50 And when Jesus had cried out again
in a loud voice, he gave up his spirit.[d]
51 At that moment the curtain of the
temple[e] was torn in two from top to
bottom. The earth shook and the rocks
split.[f] 52 The tombs broke open and the
bodies of many holy people who had
died were raised to life. 53 They came
out of the tombs, and after Jesus' resurrection they went into the holy city[g]
and appeared to many people.
54 When the centurion and those with
him who were guarding[h] Jesus saw the
earthquake and all that had happened,
they were terrified, and exclaimed,
"Surely he was the Son[m] of God!"[i]
55 Many women were there, watching from a distance. They had followed
Jesus from Galilee to care for his needs.[j]
56 Among them were Mary Magdalene,
Mary the mother of James and Joses,
and the mother of Zebedee's sons.[k]

Jesus' burial.

27:57-61pp— Mk 15:42-47; Lk 23:50-56; Jn 19:38-42

57 As evening approached, there came
a rich man from Arimathea, named
Joseph, who had himself become a disciple of Jesus. 58 Going to Pilate, he
asked for Jesus' body, and Pilate ordered
that it be given to him. 59 Joseph took
the body, wrapped it in a clean linen
cloth, 60 and placed it in his own new
tomb[l] that he had cut out of the rock.
He rolled a big stone in front of the
entrance to the tomb and went away.
61 Mary Magdalene and the other Mary
were sitting there opposite the tomb.
62 The next day, the one after Preparation Day, the chief priests and the
Pharisees went to Pilate. 63 "Sir," they
said, "we remember that while he was
still alive that deceiver said, 'After
three days I will rise again.'[m] 64 So give
the order for the tomb to be made
secure until the third day. Otherwise,
his disciples may come and steal the
body and tell the people that he has
been raised from the dead. This last
deception will be worse than the first."
65 "Take a guard,"[n] Pilate answered.
"Go, make the tomb as secure as you
know how." 66 So they went and made
the tomb secure by putting a seal[o] on
the stone[p] and posting the guard.[q]

Up from the grave he arose!

28:1-8pp— Mk 16:1-8; Lk 24:1-10

28 After the Sabbath, at dawn on
the first day of the week, Mary
Magdalene and the other Mary[r] went
to look at the tomb.
2 There was a violent earthquake,[s]
for an angel[t] of the Lord came down
from heaven and, going to the tomb,
rolled back the stone and sat on it.
3 His appearance was like lightning,
and his clothes were white as snow.[u]
4 The guards were so afraid of him that
they shook and became like dead men.
5 The angel said to the women, "Do
not be afraid,[v] for I know that you are
looking for Jesus, who was crucified.
6 He is not here; he has risen, just as he
said.[w] Come and see the place where
he lay. 7 Then go quickly and tell his
disciples: 'He has risen from the dead
and is going ahead of you into Galilee.[x] There you will see him.' Now I
have told you."

27:45 [a] Am 8:9
27:46 [b] Ps 22:1
27:48 [c] ver 34; Ps 69:21
27:50 [d] Jn 19:30
27:51 [e] Ex 26:31-33; Heb 9:3,8 [f] ver 54
27:53 [g] Mt 4:5
27:54 [h] ver 36 [i] Mt 4:3; 17:5
27:55 [j] Lk 8:2,3
27:56 [k] Mk 15:47; Lk 24:10; Jn 19:25
27:60 [l] Mt 27:66; 28:2; Mk 16:4
27:63 [m] Mt 16:21
27:65 [n] ver 66; Mt 28:11
27:66 [o] Da 6:17 [p] ver 60; Mt 28:2 [q] Mt 28:11
28:1 [r] Mt 27:56
28:2 [s] Mt 27:51 [t] Jn 20:12
28:3 [u] Da 10:6; Mk 9:3; Jn 20:12
28:5 [v] ver 10; Mt 14:27
28:6 [w] Mt 16:21
28:7 [x] ver 10,16; Mt 26:32

[k] *46* Some manuscripts *Eli, Eli* [l] *46* Psalm 22:1
[m] *54* Or *a son*

8 So the women hurried away from
the tomb, afraid yet filled with joy, and
ran to tell his disciples. 9 Suddenly Jesus
met them.[a] "Greetings," he said. They
came to him, clasped his feet and worshiped him. 10 Then Jesus said to them,
"Do not be afraid. Go and tell my
brothers[b] to go to Galilee; there they will
see me."

11 While the women were on their
way, some of the guards[c] went into the
city and reported to the chief priests
everything that had happened. 12 When
the chief priests had met with the elders
and devised a plan, they gave the soldiers a large sum of money, 13 telling
them, "You are to say, 'His disciples
came during the night and stole him
away while we were asleep.' 14 If this
report gets to the governor,[d] we will satisfy him and keep you out of trouble."
15 So the soldiers took the money and
did as they were instructed. And this
story has been widely circulated among
the Jews to this very day.

The Great Commission.

16 Then the eleven disciples went to
Galilee, to the mountain where Jesus
had told them to go.[e] 17 When they saw
him, they worshiped him; but some
doubted. 18 Then Jesus came to them
and said, "All authority in heaven and
on earth has been given to me.[f]
19 Therefore go and make disciples of
all nations,[g] baptizing them in[n] the
name of the Father and of the Son and
of the Holy Spirit,[h] 20 and teaching[i]
them to obey everything I have commanded you. And surely I am with you[j]
always, to the very end of the age."[k]

28:9 [a]Jn 20:14-18
28:10 [b]Jn 20:17; Ro 8:29; Heb 2:11-13,17
28:11 [c]Mt 27:65,66
28:14 [d]Mt 27:2
28:16 [e]ver 7,10; Mt 26:32
28:18 [f]Da 7:13,14; Lk 10:22; Jn 3:35; 17:2; 1Co 15:27; Eph 1:20-22; Php 2:9,10
28:19 [g]Mk 16:15, 16; Lk 24:47; Ac 1:8; 14:21 [h]Ac 2:38; 8:16; Ro 6:3,4
28:20 [i]Ac 2:42 [j]Mt 18:20; Ac 18:10 [k]Mt 13:39

[n] *19* Or *into*; see Acts 8:16; 19:5; Romans 6:3; 1 Cor. 1:13; 10:2 and Gal. 3:27.

MARK

Author: Mark.

Date Written: Between A.D. 50 and 70.

Time Span: About 3 1/2 years (A.D. 29-33).

Title: From the book's author: Mark.

Background: A book of action focusing more on Jesus' deeds than on his words, Mark is the shortest of the 4 Gospels. It is generally accepted that the preaching of Peter, a companion of Mark, is the source of most of this Gospel's material. Mark also spends time with Paul and Barnabas when he returns with them from Jerusalem to Antioch on their first missionary journey. Mark leaves early, however, and returns to Jerusalem. After this, Barnabas wants to bring Mark, his cousin, on the second missionary journey. But Paul disagrees and leaves instead with Silas. Paul and Barnabas reconcile at a later date, and Mark becomes a close friend and helper of Paul.

Where Written: Rome (possibly while Peter and Mark are in prison).

To Whom: Generally to all Gentiles, but primarily to the Romans.

Content: The Gospel according to Mark vividly portrays Jesus teaching, healing and ministering to the needs of others. Jesus is the perfect example and the perfect sacrifice for people of all time. His public ministry includes exhibits of his divine power over disease, nature, demons and even death. These miracles also reveal Jesus' compassion for a hurting world. However, opposition and hostility grow against Jesus from the chief priests, Pharisees and Sadducees. Finally, Jesus willingly allows his arrest and crucifixion to take place. But his resurrection seals the ultimate victory for all who trust him to save them.

Key Words: "Servant"; "Immediately." The ministry of Jesus Christ centers around his being a "servant" to all, giving his life as a ransom for many. Mark's Gospel uses the term "immediately" to emphasize the importance and urgency of believing in God's Son...now!

Themes: • Jesus is concerned about every aspect of our lives. • Jesus' actions paralleled his words, and so must ours if we hope to be a positive witness for him. • Jesus' death on the cross paid the price for each of our sins if we will but turn to him with a repentant heart and trust him as Savior. • There is none so down and out that he can ever be beyond the extending arms of God's love. • Even as Jesus came to serve us, so must we also serve others.

Outline:

1. The beginning of Jesus Christ's ministry. 1:1-1:13
2. Jesus' ministry of healing and teaching. 1:14-8:26
3. Jesus' instruction of his disciples. 8:27-13:37
4. Jesus' betrayal, trial and crucifixion. 14:1-15:41
5. Jesus' burial and resurrection. 15:42-16:20

MARK

John the Baptist prepares the way.

1:2-8pp— Mt 3:1-11; Lk 3:2-16

1 The beginning of the gospel about Jesus Christ, the Son of God.[a][a]

[2]It is written in Isaiah the prophet:

"I will send my messenger ahead of
you,
who will prepare your way"[b][b]—
[3]"a voice of one calling in the desert,
'Prepare the way for the Lord,
make straight paths for him.'"[c][c]

[4]And so John[d] came, baptizing in the
desert region and preaching a baptism
of repentance[e] for the forgiveness of
sins.[f] [5]The whole Judean countryside
and all the people of Jerusalem went
out to him. Confessing their sins, they
were baptized by him in the Jordan
River. [6]John wore clothing made of
camel's hair, with a leather belt around
his waist, and he ate locusts[g] and wild
honey. [7]And this was his message: "After
me will come one more powerful than
I, the thongs of whose sandals I am not
worthy to stoop down and untie.[h] [8]I

1:1 [a]Mt 4:3
1:2 [b]Mal 3:1; Mt 11:10; Lk 7:27
1:3 [c]Isa 40:3; Jn 1:23
1:4 [d]Mt 3:1 [e]Ac 13:24 [f]Lk 1:77
1:6 [g]Lev 11:22
1:7 [h]Ac 13:25

a *1* Some manuscripts do not have *the Son of God.*
b*2* Mal. 3:1 c*3* Isaiah 40:3

KEY PLACES IN MARK

Of the four Gospels, Mark's narrative is the most chronological—that is, most of the stories are positioned in the order they actually occurred. Though the shortest of the four, the Gospel of Mark contains the most events; it is action-packed. Most of this action centers in Galilee, where Jesus began his ministry. Capernaum served as his base of operation (1:21; 2:1; 9:33), from which he would go out to cities like Bethsaida—where he healed a blind man (8:22ff); Gennesaret—where he performed many healings (6:53ff); Tyre and Sidon (to the far north)—where he healed many, drove out demons, and met the Syrophoenician woman (3:8; 7:24ff); and Caesarea Philippi—where Peter declared him to be the Messiah (8:27ff). After his ministry in Galilee and the surrounding regions, Jesus headed for Jerusalem (10:1). Before going there, Jesus told his disciples three times that he would be crucified there and then come back to life (8:31; 9:31; 10:33, 34).

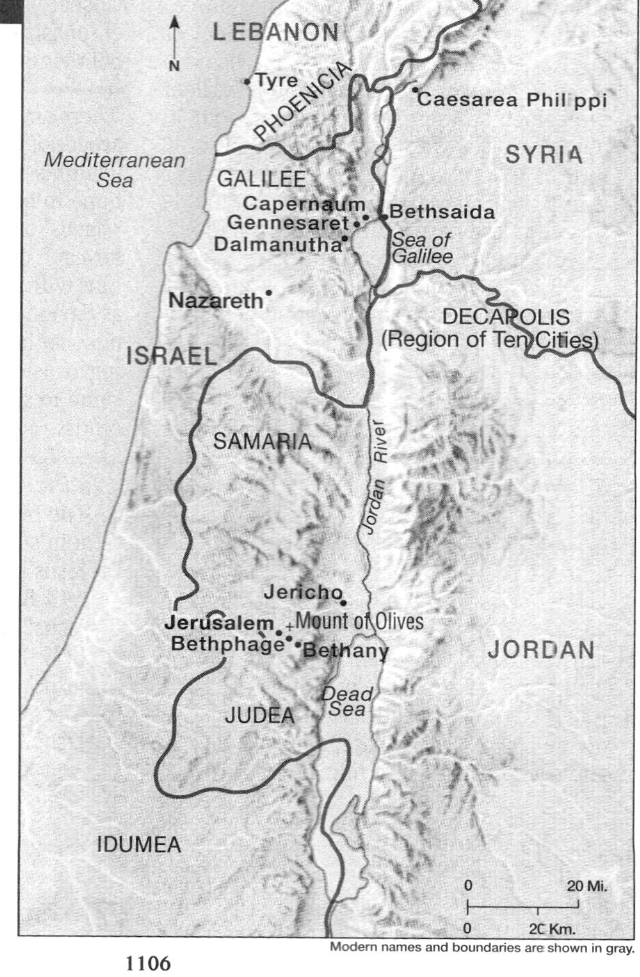

Modern names and boundaries are shown in gray.

baptize you with[d] water, but he will baptize you with the Holy Spirit."[a]

John baptizes Jesus.

1:9-11pp— Mt 3:13-17; Lk 3:21,22

9 At that time Jesus came from Nazareth[b] in Galilee and was baptized by
John in the Jordan. 10 As Jesus was coming up out of the water, he saw heaven
being torn open and the Spirit descending on him like a dove.[c] 11 And a voice
came from heaven: "You are my Son,[d]
whom I love; with you I am well
pleased."

Satan tempts Jesus in the desert.

1:12,13pp— Mt 4:1-11; Lk 4:1-13

12 At once the Spirit sent him out into
the desert, 13 and he was in the desert
forty days, being tempted by Satan.[e] He
was with the wild animals, and angels
attended him.

Jesus Begins His Ministry

When Jesus came from his home in Nazareth to begin his ministry, he first took two steps in preparation—baptism by John in the Jordan River, and temptation by Satan in the rough Judean desert. After the temptations, Jesus returned to Galilee and later set up his home base in Capernaum.

Jesus begins his ministry.

1:16-20pp— Mt 4:18-22; Lk 5:2-11; Jn 1:35-42

14 After John was put in prison, Jesus
went into Galilee,[f] proclaiming the good
news of God.[g] 15 "The time has come,"[h]
he said. "The kingdom of God is near.
Repent and believe the good news!"[i]
16 As Jesus walked beside the Sea of
Galilee, he saw Simon and his brother
Andrew casting a net into the lake, for
they were fishermen. 17 "Come, follow
me," Jesus said, "and I will make you
fishers of men." 18 At once they left their
nets and followed him.
19 When he had gone a little farther,
he saw James son of Zebedee and his
brother John in a boat, preparing their
nets. 20 Without delay he called them,
and they left their father Zebedee in the
boat with the hired men and followed
him.

Jesus orders evil spirit to leave a man.

1:21-28pp— Lk 4:31-37

21 They went to Capernaum, and when
the Sabbath came, Jesus went into the
synagogue and began to teach.[j] 22 The
people were amazed at his teaching,
because he taught them as one who had
authority, not as the teachers of the
law.[k] 23 Just then a man in their synagogue who was possessed by an evil[e]
spirit cried out, 24 "What do you want
with us,[l] Jesus of Nazareth?[m] Have you
come to destroy us? I know who you
are—the Holy One of God!"[n]
25 "Be quiet!" said Jesus sternly. "Come
out of him!"[o] 26 The evil spirit shook
the man violently and came out of him
with a shriek.[p]
27 The people were all so amazed[q] that
they asked each other, "What is this? A
new teaching—and with authority! He
even gives orders to evil spirits and they

1:8 [a]Isa 44:3; Joel 2:28; Ac 1:5; 2:4; 11:16; 19:4-6
1:9 [b]Mt 2:23
1:10 [c]Jn 1:32
1:11 [d]Mt 3:17
1:13 [e]Mt 4:10
1:14 [f]Mt 4:12 [g]Mt 4:23
1:15 [h]Gal 4:4; Eph 1:10 [i]Ac 20:21
1:21 [j]Mt 4:23; Mk 10:1
1:22 [k]Mt 7:28,29
1:24 [l]Mt 8:29 [m]Mt 2:23; Lk 24:19; Ac 24:5 [n]Lk 1:35; Jn 6:69; Ac 3:14
1:25 [o]ver 34
1:26 [p]Mk 9:20
1:27 [q]Mk 10:24,32

d *8* Or *in* e *23* Greek *unclean*; also in verses 26 and 27

obey him." **28**News about him spread quickly over the whole region[a] of Galilee.

Jesus heals Peter's mother-in-law.

1:29-31pp— Mt 8:14,15; Lk 4:38,39
1:32-34pp— Mt 8:16,17; Lk 4:40,41

29As soon as they left the synagogue,[b] they went with James and John to the home of Simon and Andrew. **30**Simon's mother-in-law was in bed with a fever, and they told Jesus about her. **31**So he went to her, took her hand and helped her up.[c] The fever left her and she began to wait on them.

32That evening after sunset the people brought to Jesus all the sick and demon-possessed.[d] **33**The whole town gathered at the door, **34**and Jesus healed many who had various diseases.[e] He also drove out many demons, but he would not let the demons speak because they knew who he was.[f]

Jesus prays early in the morning.

1:35-38pp— Lk 4:42,43

35Very early in the morning, while it was still dark, Jesus got up, left the house and went off to a solitary place, where he prayed.[g] **36**Simon and his companions went to look for him, **37**and when they found him, they exclaimed: "Everyone is looking for you!"

38Jesus replied, "Let us go somewhere else—to the nearby villages—so I can preach there also. That is why I have come."[h] **39**So he traveled throughout Galilee, preaching in their synagogues[i] and driving out demons.[j]

Jesus heals a man with leprosy.

1:40-44pp— Mt 8:2-4; Lk 5:12-14

40A man with leprosy[f] came to him and begged him on his knees,[k] "If you are willing, you can make me clean."

41Filled with compassion, Jesus reached out his hand and touched the man. "I am willing," he said. "Be clean!" **42**Immediately the leprosy left him and he was cured.

43Jesus sent him away at once with a strong warning: **44**"See that you don't tell this to anyone.[l] But go, show yourself to the priest[m] and offer the sacrifices that Moses commanded for your cleansing,[n] as a testimony to them." **45**Instead he went out and began to talk freely, spreading the news. As a result, Jesus could no longer enter a town openly but stayed outside in lonely places.[o] Yet the people still came to him from everywhere.[p]

Jesus heals a paralytic.

2:3-12pp— Mt 9:2-8; Lk 5:18-26

2 A few days later, when Jesus again entered Capernaum, the people heard that he had come home. **2**So many[q] gathered that there was no room left, not even outside the door, and he preached the word to them. **3**Some men came, bringing to him a paralytic,[r] carried by four of them. **4**Since they could not get him to Jesus because of the crowd, they made an opening in the roof above Jesus and, after digging through it, lowered the mat the paralyzed man was lying on. **5**When Jesus saw their faith, he said to the paralytic, "Son, your sins are forgiven."[s]

6Now some teachers of the law were sitting there, thinking to themselves, **7**"Why does this fellow talk like that? He's blaspheming! Who can forgive sins but God alone?"[t]

8Immediately Jesus knew in his spirit that this was what they were thinking in their hearts, and he said to them, "Why are you thinking these things? **9**Which is easier: to say to the paralytic, 'Your sins are forgiven,' or to say, 'Get up, take your mat and walk'? **10**But that you may know that the Son of Man[u] has authority on earth to forgive sins. . . ." He said to the paralytic, **11**"I tell you, get up, take your mat and go home." **12**He got up, took his mat and walked out in full view of them all. This amazed everyone and they praised God,[v] saying, "We have never seen anything like this!"[w]

1:28 [a]Mt 9:26
1:29 [b]ver 21,23
1:31 [c]Lk 7:14
1:32 [d]Mt 4:24
1:34 [e]Mt 4:23 [f]Mk 3:12; Ac 16:17,18
1:35 [g]Lk 3:21
1:38 [h]Isa 61:1
1:39 [i]Mt 4:23 [j]Mt 4:24
1:40 [k]Mk 10:17
1:44 [l]Mt 8:4 [m]Lev 13:49 [n]Lev 14:1-32
1:45 [o]Lk 5:15,16 [p]Mk 2:13; Lk 5:17; Jn 6:2
2:2 [q]ver 13; Mk 1:45
2:3 [r]Mt 4:24
2:5 [s]Lk 7:48
2:7 [t]Isa 43:25
2:10 [u]Mt 8:20
2:12 [v]Mt 9:8 [w]Mt 9:33

[f]*40* The Greek word was used for various diseases affecting the skin—not necessarily leprosy.

Levi (Matthew) follows Jesus.

2:14-17pp— Mt 9:9-13; Lk 5:27-32

13Once again Jesus went out beside
the lake. A large crowd came to him,[a]
and he began to teach them. 14As he
walked along, he saw Levi son of Alphaeus sitting at the tax collector's
booth. "Follow me,"[b] Jesus told him,
and Levi got up and followed him.
15While Jesus was having dinner at
Levi's house, many tax collectors and
"sinners" were eating with him and his
disciples, for there were many who followed him. 16When the teachers of the
law who were Pharisees[c] saw him eating with the "sinners" and tax collectors,
they asked his disciples: "Why does he
eat with tax collectors and 'sinners'?"[d]
17On hearing this, Jesus said to them,
"It is not the healthy who need a doctor, but the sick. I have not come to call
the righteous, but sinners."[e]

A parable: The cloth and wineskins.

2:18-22pp— Mt 9:14-17; Lk 5:33-38

18Now John's disciples and the Pharisees were fasting.[f] Some people came
and asked Jesus, "How is it that John's
disciples and the disciples of the Pharisees are fasting, but yours are not?"
19Jesus answered, "How can the guests
of the bridegroom fast while he is with
them? They cannot, so long as they have
him with them. 20But the time will come
when the bridegroom will be taken from
them,[g] and on that day they will fast.
21"No one sews a patch of unshrunk
cloth on an old garment. If he does, the
new piece will pull away from the old,
making the tear worse. 22And no one
pours new wine into old wineskins. If
he does, the wine will burst the skins,
and both the wine and the wineskins
will be ruined. No, he pours new wine
into new wineskins."

Disciples pick grain and illustrate Jesus' lordship of the Sabbath.

2:23-23pp— Mt 12:1-8; Lk 6:1-5

23One Sabbath Jesus was going
through the grainfields, and as his disciples walked along, they began to pick
some heads of grain.[h] 24The Pharisees
said to him, "Look, why are they doing
what is unlawful on the Sabbath?"[i]
25He answered, "Have you never read
what David did when he and his companions were hungry and in need? 26In
the days of Abiathar the high priest,[j]
he entered the house of God and ate
the consecrated bread, which is lawful
only for priests to eat.[k] And he also gave
some to his companions."[l]
27Then he said to them, "The Sabbath
was made for man,[m] not man for the
Sabbath.[n] 28So the Son of Man[o] is Lord
even of the Sabbath."

Jesus heals on the Sabbath.

3:1-6pp— Mt 12:9-14; Lk 6:6-11

3 Another time he went into the synagogue,[p] and a man with a shriveled hand was there. 2Some of them
were looking for a reason to accuse
Jesus, so they watched him closely[q] to
see if he would heal him on the Sabbath.[r] 3Jesus said to the man with the
shriveled hand, "Stand up in front of
everyone."
4Then Jesus asked them, "Which is
lawful on the Sabbath: to do good or to
do evil, to save life or to kill?" But they
remained silent.
5He looked around at them in anger
and, deeply distressed at their stubborn
hearts, said to the man, "Stretch out
your hand." He stretched it out, and his
hand was completely restored. 6Then
the Pharisees went out and began to plot
with the Herodians[s] how they might kill
Jesus.[t]

Crowds follow Jesus.

3:7-12pp— Mt 12:15,16; Lk 6:17-19

7Jesus withdrew with his disciples to
the lake, and a large crowd from Galilee followed.[u] 8When they heard all he
was doing, many people came to him
from Judea, Jerusalem, Idumea, and the
regions across the Jordan and around
Tyre and Sidon.[v] 9Because of the crowd
he told his disciples to have a small

2:13 [a]Mk 1:45; Lk 5:15; Jn 6:2
2:14 [b]Mt 4:19
2:16 [c]Ac 23:9 [d]Mt 9:11
2:17 [e]Lk 19:10; 1Ti 1:15
2:18 [f]Mt 6:16-18; Ac 13:2
2:20 [g]Lk 17:22
2:23 [h]Dt 23:25
2:24 [i]Mt 12:2
2:26 [j]1Ch 24:6; 2Sa 8:17 [k]Lev 24:5-9 [l]1Sa 21:1-6
2:27 [m]Ex 23:12; Dt 5:14 [n]Col 2:16
2:28 [o]Mt 8:20
3:1 [p]Mt 4:23; Mk 1:21
3:2 [q]Mt 12:10 [r]Lk 14:1
3:6 [s]Mt 22:16; Mk 12:13 [t]Mt 12:14
3:7 [u]Mt 4:25
3:8 [v]Mt 11:21

boat ready for him, to keep the people from crowding him. **10**For he had healed many,[a] so that those with diseases were pushing forward to touch him.[b] **11**Whenever the evil[g] spirits saw him, they fell down before him and cried out, "You are the Son of God."[c] **12**But he gave them strict orders not to tell who he was.[d]

The twelve apostles are appointed.

3:16-19pp— Mt 10:2-4; Lk 6:14-16; Ac 1:13

13Jesus went up on a mountainside and called to him those he wanted, and they came to him.[e] **14**He appointed twelve—designating them apostles[h][f]—that they might be with him and that he might send them out to preach **15**and to have authority to drive out demons.[g] **16**These are the twelve he appointed: Simon (to whom he gave the name Peter);[h] **17**James son of Zebedee and his brother John (to them he gave the name Boanerges, which means Sons of Thunder); **18**Andrew, Philip, Bartholomew, Matthew, Thomas, James son of Alphaeus, Thaddaeus, Simon the Zealot **19**and Judas Iscariot, who betrayed him.

Teachers claim Jesus to be possessed by Beelzebub.

3:23-27pp— Mt 12:25-29; Lk 11:17-22

20Then Jesus entered a house, and again a crowd gathered,[i] so that he and his disciples were not even able to eat.[j] **21**When his family heard about this, they went to take charge of him, for they said, "He is out of his mind."[k]

22And the teachers of the law who came down from Jerusalem[l] said, "He is possessed by Beelzebub[i]![m] By the prince of demons he is driving out demons."[n]

23So Jesus called them and spoke to them in parables:[o] "How can Satan[p] drive out Satan? **24**If a kingdom is divided against itself, that kingdom cannot stand. **25**If a house is divided against itself, that house cannot stand. **26**And if Satan opposes himself and is divided, he cannot stand; his end has come. **27**In fact, no one can enter a strong man's house and carry off his possessions unless he first ties up the strong man. Then he can rob his house.[q] **28**I tell you the truth, all the sins and blasphemies of men will be forgiven them. **29**But whoever blasphemes against the Holy Spirit will never be forgiven; he is guilty of an eternal sin."[r]

30He said this because they were saying, "He has an evil spirit."

Jesus identifies his mother and brothers.

3:31-35pp— Mt 12:46-50; Lk 8:19-21

31Then Jesus' mother and brothers arrived.[s] Standing outside, they sent someone in to call him. **32**A crowd was sitting around him, and they told him, "Your mother and brothers are outside looking for you."

33"Who are my mother and my brothers?" he asked.

34Then he looked at those seated in a circle around him and said, "Here are my mother and my brothers! **35**Whoever does God's will is my brother and sister and mother."

Parables: The sower, a lamp, and the growing seed.

4:1-12pp— Mt 13:1-15; Lk 8:4-10
4:13-20pp— Mt 13:18-23; Lk 8:11-15

4 Again Jesus began to teach by the lake.[t] The crowd that gathered around him was so large that he got into a boat and sat in it out on the lake, while all the people were along the shore at the water's edge. **2**He taught them many things by parables,[u] and in his teaching said: **3**"Listen! A farmer went out to sow his seed.[v] **4**As he was scattering the seed, some fell along the path, and the birds came and ate it up. **5**Some fell on rocky places, where it did not have much soil. It sprang up quickly, because the soil was shallow. **6**But when the sun came up, the plants were

3:10 [a]Mt 4:23 [b]Mt 9:20
3:11 [c]Mt 4:3; Mk 1:23,24
3:12 [d]Mt 8:4; Mk 1:24, 25,34; Ac 16:17,18
3:13 [e]Mt 5:1
3:14 [f]Mk 6:30
3:15 [g]Mt 10:1
3:16 [h]Jn 1:42
3:20 [i]ver 7 [j]Mk 6:31
3:21 [k]Jn 10:20; Ac 26:24
3:22 [l]Mt 15:1 [m]Mt 10:25; 11:18; 12:24; Jn 7:20; 8:48,52; 10:20 [n]Mt 9:34
3:23 [o]Mk 4:2 [p]Mt 4:10
3:27 [q]Isa 49:24,25
3:29 [r]Mt 12:31, 32; Lk 12:10
3:31 [s]ver 21
4:1 [t]Mk 2:13; 3:7
4:2 [u]ver 11; Mk 3:23
4:3 [v]ver 26

[g]11 Greek *unclean*; also in verse 30 [h]14 Some manuscripts do not have *designating them apostles.* [i]22 Greek *Beezeboul* or *Beelzeboul*

scorched, and they withered because they had no root. 7Other seed fell among thorns, which grew up and choked the plants, so that they did not bear grain. 8Still other seed fell on good soil. It came up, grew and produced a crop, multiplying thirty, sixty, or even a hundred times."[a]

9Then Jesus said, "He who has ears to hear, let him hear."[b]

10When he was alone, the Twelve and the others around him asked him about the parables. 11He told them, "The secret of the kingdom of God[c] has been given to you. But to those on the outside[d] everything is said in parables 12so that,

"'they may be ever seeing but never
perceiving,
and ever hearing but never
understanding;
otherwise they might turn and be
forgiven!'[j]"[e]

13Then Jesus said to them, "Don't you understand this parable? How then will you understand any parable? 14The farmer sows the word.[f] 15Some people are like seed along the path, where the word is sown. As soon as they hear it, Satan[g] comes and takes away the word that was sown in them. 16Others, like seed sown on rocky places, hear the word and at once receive it with joy. 17But since they have no root, they last only a short time. When trouble or persecution comes because of the word, they quickly fall away. 18Still others, like seed sown among thorns, hear the word; 19but the worries of this life, the deceitfulness of wealth[h] and the desires for other things come in and choke the word, making it unfruitful. 20Others, like seed sown on good soil, hear the word, accept it, and produce a crop—thirty, sixty or even a hundred times what was sown."

21He said to them, "Do you bring in a lamp to put it under a bowl or a bed? Instead, don't you put it on its stand?[i] 22For whatever is hidden is meant to be disclosed, and whatever is concealed is meant to be brought out into the open.[j] 23If anyone has ears to hear, let him hear."[k]

24"Consider carefully what you hear," he continued. "With the measure you use, it will be measured to you—and even more.[l] 25Whoever has will be given more; whoever does not have, even what he has will be taken from him."[m]

26He also said, "This is what the kingdom of God is like.[n] A man scatters seed on the ground. 27Night and day, whether he sleeps or gets up, the seed sprouts and grows, though he does not know how. 28All by itself the soil produces grain—first the stalk, then the head, then the full kernel in the head. 29As soon as the grain is ripe, he puts the sickle to it, because the harvest has come."[o]

A parable: The mustard seed.

4:30-32pp— Mt 13:31,32; Lk 13:18,19

30Again he said, "What shall we say the kingdom of God is like,[p] or what parable shall we use to describe it? 31It is like a mustard seed, which is the smallest seed you plant in the ground. 32Yet when planted, it grows and becomes the largest of all garden plants, with such big branches that the birds of the air can perch in its shade."

33With many similar parables Jesus spoke the word to them, as much as they could understand.[q] 34He did not say anything to them without using a parable.[r] But when he was alone with his own disciples, he explained everything.

Jesus calms a storm.

4:35-41pp— Mt 8:18,23-27; Lk 8:22-25

35That day when evening came, he said to his disciples, "Let us go over to the other side." 36Leaving the crowd behind, they took him along, just as he was, in the boat.[s] There were also other boats with him. 37A furious squall came up, and the waves broke over the

4:8 [a]Jn 15:5; Col 1:6
4:9 [b]ver 23; Mt 11:15
4:11 [c]Mt 3:2 [d]1Co 5:12, 13; Col 4:5; 1Th 4:12; 1Ti 3:7
4:12 [e]Isa 6:9,10; Mt 13:13-15
4:14 [f]Mk 16:20; Lk 1:2; Ac 4:31; 8:4; 16:6; 17:11; Php 1:14
4:15 [g]Mt 4:10
4:19 [h]Mt 19:23; 1Ti 6:9,10,17; 1Jn 2:15-17
4:21 [i]Mt 5:15
4:22 [j]Jer 16:17; Mt 10:26; Lk 8:17; 12:2
4:23 [k]ver 9; Mt 11:15
4:24 [l]Mt 7:2; Lk 6:38
4:25 [m]Mt 13:12; 25:29
4:26 [n]Mt 13:24
4:29 [o]Rev 14:15
4:30 [p]Mt 13:24
4:33 [q]Jn 16:12
4:34 [r]Jn 16:25
4:36 [s]ver 1; Mk 3:9; 5:2,21; 6:32,45

j *12* Isaiah 6:9,10

boat, so that it was nearly swamped.
38Jesus was in the stern, sleeping on a
cushion. The disciples woke him and
said to him, "Teacher, don't you care if
we drown?"
39He got up, rebuked the wind and
said to the waves, "Quiet! Be still!" Then
the wind died down and it was completely calm.
40He said to his disciples, "Why are
you so afraid? Do you still have no
faith?"[a]
41They were terrified and asked each
other, "Who is this? Even the wind and
the waves obey him!"

4:40 [a]Mt 14:31; Mk 16:14

Demons sent into herd of pigs.

5:1-17pp— Mt 8:28-34; Lk 8:26-37
5:18-20pp— Lk 8:38,39

5 They went across the lake to the
region of the Gerasenes.[k] 2When
Jesus got out of the boat,[b] a man with
an evil[l] spirit[c] came from the tombs to
meet him. 3This man lived in the tombs,
and no one could bind him any more,
not even with a chain. 4For he had often been chained hand and foot, but
he tore the chains apart and broke the
irons on his feet. No one was strong
enough to subdue him. 5Night and day
among the tombs and in the hills he
would cry out and cut himself with
stones.
6When he saw Jesus from a distance,
he ran and fell on his knees in front of
him. 7He shouted at the top of his voice,
"What do you want with me,[d] Jesus,
Son of the Most High God?[e] Swear to
God that you won't torture me!" 8For
Jesus had said to him, "Come out of this
man, you evil spirit!"
9Then Jesus asked him, "What is
your name?"
"My name is Legion,"[f] he replied,
"for we are many." 10And he begged
Jesus again and again not to send them
out of the area.
11A large herd of pigs was feeding
on the nearby hillside. 12The demons
begged Jesus, "Send us among the pigs;
allow us to go into them." 13He gave

5:2 [b]Mk 4:1 [c]Mk 1:23
5:7 [d]Mt 8:29 [e]Mt 4:3; Lk 1:32; 6:35; Ac 16:17; Heb 7:1
5:9 [f]ver 15
5:15 [g]ver 9 [h]ver 16,18; Mt 4:24

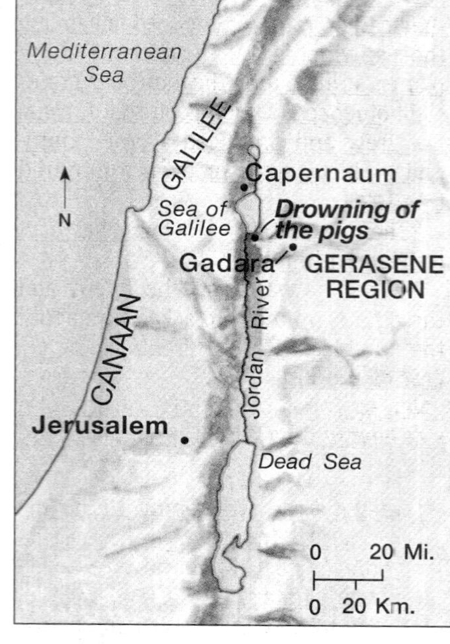

Healing a Demon-Possessed Man

From Capernaum, Jesus and his disciples crossed the Sea of Galilee. A storm blew up unexpectedly, but Jesus calmed it. Landing in the region of the Gerasenes, Jesus sent demons out of a man and into a herd of pigs that plunged over the steep bank into the lake.

them permission, and the evil spirits
came out and went into the pigs. The
herd, about two thousand in number,
rushed down the steep bank into the
lake and were drowned.
14Those tending the pigs ran off and
reported this in the town and countryside, and the people went out to see
what had happened. 15When they came
to Jesus, they saw the man who had
been possessed by the legion[g] of demons,[h] sitting there, dressed and in his
right mind; and they were afraid. 16Those
who had seen it told the people what
had happened to the demon-possessed
man—and told about the pigs as well.
17Then the people began to plead with
Jesus to leave their region.
18As Jesus was getting into the boat,
the man who had been demon-possessed

[k]*1* Some manuscripts *Gadarenes*; other manuscripts *Gergesenes* [l]*2* Greek *unclean*; also in verses 8 and 13

begged to go with him. 19 Jesus did not
let him, but said, "Go home to your
family and tell them[a] how much the
Lord has done for you, and how he has
had mercy on you." 20 So the man
went away and began to tell in the Decapolis[m][b] how much Jesus had done for
him. And all the people were amazed.

Jairus's daughter brought back to life, and woman healed.

5:22-43pp— Mt 9:18-26; Lk 8:41-56

21 When Jesus had again crossed over
by boat to the other side of the lake,[c] a
large crowd gathered around him while
he was by the lake.[d] 22 Then one of the
synagogue rulers,[e] named Jairus, came
there. Seeing Jesus, he fell at his feet
23 and pleaded earnestly with him, "My
little daughter is dying. Please come and
put your hands on[f] her so that she will
be healed and live." 24 So Jesus went
with him.
A large crowd followed and pressed
around him. 25 And a woman was there
who had been subject to bleeding[g] for
twelve years. 26 She had suffered a great
deal under the care of many doctors
and had spent all she had, yet instead of
getting better she grew worse. 27 When
she heard about Jesus, she came up behind him in the crowd and touched his
cloak, 28 because she thought, "If I just
touch his clothes,[h] I will be healed."
29 Immediately her bleeding stopped
and she felt in her body that she was
freed from her suffering.[i]
30 At once Jesus realized that power[j]
had gone out from him. He turned
around in the crowd and asked, "Who
touched my clothes?"
31 "You see the people crowding against
you," his disciples answered, "and yet
you can ask, 'Who touched me?' "
32 But Jesus kept looking around to
see who had done it. 33 Then the woman, knowing what had happened to
her, came and fell at his feet and, trembling with fear, told him the whole truth.
34 He said to her, "Daughter, your faith
has healed you.[k] Go in peace[l] and be
freed from your suffering."
35 While Jesus was still speaking, some
men came from the house of Jairus, the
synagogue ruler.[m] "Your daughter is
dead," they said. "Why bother the teacher any more?"
36 Ignoring what they said, Jesus told
the synagogue ruler, "Don't be afraid;
just believe."
37 He did not let anyone follow him
except Peter, James and John the brother of James.[n] 38 When they came to the
home of the synagogue ruler,[o] Jesus saw
a commotion, with people crying and
wailing loudly. 39 He went in and said
to them, "Why all this commotion and
wailing? The child is not dead but
asleep."[p] 40 But they laughed at him.
After he put them all out, he took the
child's father and mother and the disciples who were with him, and went in
where the child was. 41 He took her by
the hand[q] and said to her, *"Talitha
koum!"* (which means, "Little girl, I
say to you, get up!").[r] 42 Immediately the
girl stood up and walked around (she
was twelve years old). At this they were
completely astonished. 43 He gave strict
orders not to let anyone know about
this,[s] and told them to give her something to eat.

Jesus' hometown of Nazareth rejects him.

6:1-6pp— Mt 13:54-58

6 Jesus left there and went to his
hometown,[t] accompanied by his
disciples. 2 When the Sabbath came,[u] he
began to teach in the synagogue,[v] and
many who heard him were amazed.[w]
"Where did this man get these
things?" they asked. "What's this wisdom that has been given him, that he
even does miracles! 3 Isn't this the carpenter? Isn't this Mary's son and the
brother of James, Joseph,[n] Judas and
Simon?[x] Aren't his sisters here with
us?" And they took offense at him.[y]

[m]*20* That is, the Ten Cities [n]*3* Greek *Joses*, a variant of *Joseph*

5:19 [a]Mt 8:4
5:20 [b]Mt 4:25; Mk 7:31
5:21 [c]Mt 9:1 [d]Mk 4:1
5:22 [e]ver 35,36, 38; Lk 13:14; Ac 13:15; 18:8,17
5:23 [f]Mt 19:13; Mk 6:5; 7:32; 8:23; 16:18; Lk 4:40; 13:13; Ac 6:6
5:25 [g]Lev 15:25-30
5:28 [h]Mt 9:20
5:29 [i]ver 34
5:30 [j]Lk 5:17; 6:19
5:34 [k]Mt 9:22 [l]Ac 15:33
5:35 [m]ver 22
5:37 [n]Mt 4:21
5:38 [o]ver 22
5:39 [p]Mt 9:24
5:41 [q]Mk 1:31 [r]Lk 7:14; Ac 9:40
5:43 [s]Mt 8:4
6:1 [t]Mt 2:23
6:2 [u]Mk 1:21 [v]Mt 4:23 [w]Mt 7:28
6:3 [x]Mt 12:46 [y]Mt 11:6; Jn 6:61

4 Jesus said to them, "Only in his
hometown, among his relatives and in
his own house is a prophet without
honor."[a] 5 He could not do any miracles
there, except lay his hands on[b] a few
sick people and heal them. 6 And he
was amazed at their lack of faith.

The Twelve are sent to preach.

6:7-11pp— Mt 10:1,9-14; Lk 9:1,3-5

Then Jesus went around teaching
from village to village.[c] 7 Calling the
Twelve to him,[d] he sent them out two
by two[e] and gave them authority over
evil[o] spirits.[f]
8 These were his instructions: "Take
nothing for the journey except a
staff—no bread, no bag, no money in
your belts. 9 Wear sandals but not an
extra tunic. 10 Whenever you enter a
house, stay there until you leave that
town. 11 And if any place will not welcome you or listen to you, shake the
dust off your feet[g] when you leave, as a
testimony against them."
12 They went out and preached that
people should repent.[h] 13 They drove out
many demons and anointed many sick
people with oil[i] and healed them.

John the Baptist is beheaded.

6:14-29pp— Mt 14:1-12
6:14-16pp— Lk 9:7-9

14 King Herod heard about this, for
Jesus' name had become well known.
Some were saying,[p] "John the Baptist[j]
has been raised from the dead, and that
is why miraculous powers are at work
in him."
15 Others said, "He is Elijah."[k]
And still others claimed, "He is a
prophet,[l] like one of the prophets of
long ago."[m]
16 But when Herod heard this, he said,
"John, the man I beheaded, has been
raised from the dead!"
17 For Herod himself had given orders
to have John arrested, and he had him
bound and put in prison.[n] He did this
because of Herodias, his brother Philip's
wife, whom he had married. 18 For John
had been saying to Herod, "It is not
lawful for you to have your brother's
wife."[o] 19 So Herodias nursed a grudge
against John and wanted to kill him.
But she was not able to, 20 because Herod
feared John and protected him, knowing him to be a righteous and holy
man.[p] When Herod heard John, he was
greatly puzzled[q]; yet he liked to listen
to him.
21 Finally the opportune time came.
On his birthday Herod gave a banquet[q]
for his high officials and military commanders and the leading men of Galilee.[r] 22 When the daughter of Herodias
came in and danced, she pleased Herod
and his dinner guests.
The king said to the girl, "Ask me
for anything you want, and I'll give it
to you." 23 And he promised her with an
oath, "Whatever you ask I will give you,
up to half my kingdom."[s]
24 She went out and said to her mother, "What shall I ask for?"
"The head of John the Baptist," she
answered.
25 At once the girl hurried in to the
king with the request: "I want you to
give me right now the head of John
the Baptist on a platter."
26 The king was greatly distressed,
but because of his oaths and his dinner
guests, he did not want to refuse her.
27 So he immediately sent an execu-
tioner with orders to bring John's head.
The man went, beheaded John in the
prison, 28 and brought back his head on
a platter. He presented it to the girl,
and she gave it to her mother. 29 On
hearing of this, John's disciples came
and took his body and laid it in a tomb.

Jesus feeds 5,000.

6:32-44pp— Mt 14:13-21; Lk 9:10-17; Jn 6:5-13
6:32-44Ref— Mk 8:2-9

30 The apostles[t] gathered around Jesus
and reported to him all they had done
and taught.[u] 31 Then, because so many

6:4 [a] Lk 4:24; Jn 4:44
6:5 [b] Mk 5:23
6:6 [c] Mt 9:35; Mk 1:39; Lk 13:22
6:7 [d] Mk 3:13 [e] Dt 17:6; Lk 10:1 [f] Mt 10:1
6:11 [g] Mt 10:14
6:12 [h] Lk 9:6
6:13 [i] Jas 5:14
6:14 [j] Mt 3:1
6:15 [k] Mal 4:5 [l] Mt 21:11 [m] Mt 16:14; Mk 8:28
6:17 [n] Mt 4:12; 11:2; Lk 3:19,20
6:18 [o] Lev 18:16; 20:21
6:20 [p] Mt 11:9; 21:26
6:21 [q] Est 1:3; 2:18 [r] Lk 3:1
6:23 [s] Est 5:3,6; 7:2
6:30 [t] Mt 10:2; Lk 9:10; 17:5; 22:14; 24:10; Ac 1:2,26 [u] Lk 9:10

o *7* Greek *unclean* p *14* Some early manuscripts *He was saying* q *20* Some early manuscripts *he did many things*

people were coming and going that they did not even have a chance to eat,[a] he said to them, "Come with me by yourselves to a quiet place and get some rest."

32 So they went away by themselves in a boat[b] to a solitary place. 33 But many who saw them leaving recognized them and ran on foot from all the towns and got there ahead of them. 34 When Jesus landed and saw a large crowd, he had compassion on them, because they were like sheep without a shepherd.[c] So he began teaching them many things.

35 By this time it was late in the day, so his disciples came to him. "This is a remote place," they said, "and it's already very late. 36 Send the people away so they can go to the surrounding countryside and villages and buy themselves something to eat."

37 But he answered, "You give them something to eat."[d]

They said to him, "That would take eight months of a man's wages[r]! Are we to go and spend that much on bread and give it to them to eat?"

38 "How many loaves do you have?" he asked. "Go and see."

When they found out, they said, "Five—and two fish."[e]

39 Then Jesus directed them to have all the people sit down in groups on the green grass. 40 So they sat down in groups of hundreds and fifties. 41 Taking the five loaves and the two fish and looking up to heaven, he gave thanks and broke the loaves.[f] Then he gave them to his disciples to set before the people. He also divided the two fish among them all. 42 They all ate and were satisfied, 43 and the disciples picked up twelve basketfuls of broken pieces of bread and fish. 44 The number of the men who had eaten was five thousand.

Jesus walks on water.

6:45-51pp— Mt 14:22-32; Jn 6:15-21
6:53-56pp— Mt 14:34-36

45 Immediately Jesus made his disciples get into the boat[g] and go on ahead of him to Bethsaida,[h] while he dismissed the crowd. 46 After leaving them, he went up on a mountainside to pray.[i]

47 When evening came, the boat was in the middle of the lake, and he was alone on land. 48 He saw the disciples straining at the oars, because the wind was against them. About the fourth watch of the night he went out to them, walking on the lake. He was about to pass by them, 49 but when they saw him walking on the lake, they thought he was a ghost.[j] They cried out, 50 because they all saw him and were terrified.

Immediately he spoke to them and said, "Take courage! It is I. Don't be afraid."[k] 51 Then he climbed into the boat[l] with them, and the wind died down.[m] They were completely amazed, 52 for they had not understood about the loaves; their hearts were hardened.[n]

53 When they had crossed over, they landed at Gennesaret and anchored there.[o] 54 As soon as they got out of the boat, people recognized Jesus. 55 They ran throughout that whole region and carried the sick on mats to wherever they heard he was. 56 And wherever he went—into villages, towns or countryside—they placed the sick in the marketplaces. They begged him to let them touch even the edge of his cloak,[p] and all who touched him were healed.

Jesus condemns hypocrisy of tradition without obedience.

7:1-23pp— Mt 15:1-20

7 The Pharisees and some of the teachers of the law who had come from Jerusalem gathered around Jesus and 2 saw some of his disciples eating food with hands that were "unclean,"[q] that is, unwashed. 3 (The Pharisees and all the Jews do not eat unless they give their hands a ceremonial washing, holding to the tradition of the elders.[r] 4 When they come from the marketplace they do not eat unless they wash. And they observe many other traditions,

6:31 [a]Mk 3:20
6:32 [b]ver 45; Mk 4:36
6:34 [c]Mt 9:36
6:37 [d]2Ki 4:42-44
6:38 [e]Mt 15:34; Mk 8:5
6:41 [f]Mt 14:19
6:45 [g]ver 32 [h]Mt 11:21
6:46 [i]Lk 3:21
6:49 [j]Lk 24:37
6:50 [k]Mt 14:27
6:51 [l]ver 32 [m]Mk 4:39
6:52 [n]Mk 8:17-21
6:53 [o]Jn 6:24,25
6:56 [p]Mt 9:20
7:2 [q]Ac 10:14,28; 11:8; Ro 14:14
7:3 [r]ver 5,8,9,13; Lk 11:38

[r]37 Greek *take two hundred denarii*

such as the washing of cups, pitchers
and kettles.[s])[a]
5So the Pharisees and teachers of the
law asked Jesus, "Why don't your disciples live according to the tradition of
the elders[b] instead of eating their food
with 'unclean' hands?"
6He replied, "Isaiah was right when
he prophesied about you hypocrites; as
it is written:

"'These people honor me with their lips,
but their hearts are far from me.
7They worship me in vain;
their teachings are but rules taught by men.'[t][c]

8You have let go of the commands of
God and are holding on to the traditions of men."[d]
9And he said to them: "You have a
fine way of setting aside the commands
of God in order to observe[u] your own
traditions![e] 10For Moses said, 'Honor
your father and your mother,'[v][f] and,
'Anyone who curses his father or mother must be put to death.'[w][g] 11But you
say[h] that if a man says to his father or
mother: 'Whatever help you might otherwise have received from me is Cor-
ban' (that is, a gift devoted to God),
12then you no longer let him do anything for his father or mother. 13Thus
you nullify the word of God[i] by your
tradition[j] that you have handed down.
And you do many things like that."
14Again Jesus called the crowd to him
and said, "Listen to me, everyone, and
understand this. 15Nothing outside a
man can make him 'unclean' by going
into him. Rather, it is what comes out
of a man that makes him 'unclean.'[x]"
17After he had left the crowd and entered the house, his disciples asked him[k]
about this parable. 18"Are you so dull?"
he asked. "Don't you see that nothing
that enters a man from the outside can
make him 'unclean'? 19For it doesn't go
into his heart but into his stomach, and
then out of his body." (In saying this,
Jesus declared all foods[l] "clean.")[m]
20He went on: "What comes out of a

7:4 [a]Mt 23:25; Lk 11:39
7:5 [b]ver 3; Gal 1:14; Col 2:8
7:7 [c]Isa 29:13
7:8 [d]ver 3
7:9 [e]ver 3
7:10 [f]Ex 20:12; Dt 5:16 [g]Ex 21:17; Lev 20:9
7:11 [h]Mt 23:16,18
7:13 [i]Heb 4:12 [j]ver 3
7:17 [k]Mk 9:28
7:19 [l]Ro 14:1-12; Col 2:16; 1Ti 4:3-5 [m]Ac 10:15
7:22 [n]Mt 20:15
7:24 [o]Mt 11:21
7:25 [p]Mt 4:24
7:31 [q]ver 24; Mt 11:21 [r]Mt 4:18 [s]Mt 4:25; Mk 5:20
7:32 [t]Mt 9:32; Lk 11:14 [u]Mk 5:23

man is what makes him 'unclean.' 21For
from within, out of men's hearts, come
evil thoughts, sexual immorality, theft,
murder, adultery, 22greed,[n] malice,
deceit, lewdness, envy, slander, arrogance and folly. 23All these evils come
from inside and make a man 'unclean.'"

Demon driven from daughter of Syrophoenician woman.

7:24-30pp— Mt 15:21-28

24Jesus left that place and went to the
vicinity of Tyre.[y][o] He entered a house
and did not want anyone to know it;
yet he could not keep his presence secret. 25In fact, as soon as she heard
about him, a woman whose little daughter was possessed by an evil[z] spirit[p]
came and fell at his feet. 26The woman
was a Greek, born in Syrian Phoenicia.
She begged Jesus to drive the demon
out of her daughter.
27"First let the children eat all they
want," he told her, "for it is not right
to take the children's bread and toss it
to their dogs."
28"Yes, Lord," she replied, "but even
the dogs under the table eat the children's crumbs."
29Then he told her, "For such a reply,
you may go; the demon has left your
daughter."
30She went home and found her child
lying on the bed, and the demon gone.

Jesus heals a deaf and mute man.

7:31-37pp— Mt 15:29-31

31Then Jesus left the vicinity of Tyre[q]
and went through Sidon, down to the
Sea of Galilee[r] and into the region of
the Decapolis.[a][s] 32There some people
brought to him a man who was deaf
and could hardly talk,[t] and they begged
him to place his hand on[u] the man.

s *4* Some early manuscripts *pitchers, kettles and dining couches* t *6,7* Isaiah 29:13 u *9* Some manuscripts *set up* v *10* Exodus 20:12; Deut. 5:16 w *10* Exodus 21:17; Lev. 20:9 x *15* Some early manuscripts *'unclean.'* [16]*If anyone has ears to hear, let him hear.* y *24* Many early manuscripts *Tyre and Sidon* z *25* Greek *unclean* a *31* That is, the Ten Cities

33After he took him aside, away from the crowd, Jesus put his fingers into the man's ears. Then he spit[a] and touched the man's tongue. 34He looked up to heaven[b] and with a deep sigh[c] said to him, *"Ephphatha!"* (which means, "Be opened!"). 35At this, the man's ears were opened, his tongue was loosened and he began to speak plainly.[d]

36Jesus commanded them not to tell anyone.[e] But the more he did so, the more they kept talking about it. 37People were overwhelmed with amazement. "He has done everything well," they said. "He even makes the deaf hear and the mute speak."

Jesus feeds 4,000.

8:1-9pp— Mt 15:32-39
8:1-9Ref— Mk 6:32-44
8:11-21pp— Mt 16:1-12

8 During those days another large crowd gathered. Since they had nothing to eat, Jesus called his disciples to him and said, 2"I have compassion for these people;[f] they have already been with me three days and have nothing to eat. 3If I send them home hungry, they will collapse on the way, because some of them have come a long distance."

4His disciples answered, "But where in this remote place can anyone get enough bread to feed them?"

5"How many loaves do you have?" Jesus asked.

"Seven," they replied.

6He told the crowd to sit down on the ground. When he had taken the seven loaves and given thanks, he broke them and gave them to his disciples to set before the people, and they did so. 7They had a few small fish as well; he gave thanks for them also and told the disciples to distribute them.[g] 8The people ate and were satisfied. Afterward the disciples picked up seven basketfuls of broken pieces that were left over.[h] 9About four thousand men were present. And having sent them away, 10he got into the boat with his disciples and went to the region of Dalmanutha.

11The Pharisees came and began to question Jesus. To test him, they asked him for a sign from heaven.[i] 12He sighed deeply[j] and said, "Why does this generation ask for a miraculous sign? I tell you the truth, no sign will be given to it." 13Then he left them, got back into the boat and crossed to the other side.

14The disciples had forgotten to bring bread, except for one loaf they had with them in the boat. 15"Be careful," Jesus warned them. "Watch out for the yeast[k] of the Pharisees[l] and that of Herod."[m]

16They discussed this with one another and said, "It is because we have no bread."

17Aware of their discussion, Jesus asked them: "Why are you talking about having no bread? Do you still not see or understand? Are your hearts hardened?[n] 18Do you have eyes but fail to see, and ears but fail to hear? And don't you remember? 19When I broke the five loaves for the five thousand, how many basketfuls of pieces did you pick up?"

"Twelve,"[o] they replied.

20"And when I broke the seven loaves for the four thousand, how many basketfuls of pieces did you pick up?"

They answered, "Seven."[p]

21He said to them, "Do you still not understand?"[q]

Jesus heals a blind man.

22They came to Bethsaida,[r] and some people brought a blind man[s] and begged Jesus to touch him. 23He took the blind man by the hand and led him outside the village. When he had spit[t] on the man's eyes and put his hands on[u] him, Jesus asked, "Do you see anything?"

24He looked up and said, "I see people; they look like trees walking around."

25Once more Jesus put his hands on the man's eyes. Then his eyes were opened, his sight was restored, and he saw everything clearly. 26Jesus sent him home, saying, "Don't go into the village.[b]"

7:33 [a]Mk 8:23
7:34 [b]Mk 6:41; Jn 11:41 [c]Mk 8:12
7:35 [d]Isa 35:5,6
7:36 [e]Mt 8:4
8:2 [f]Mt 9:36
8:7 [g]Mt 14:19
8:8 [h]ver 20
8:11 [i]Mt 12:38
8:12 [j]Mk 7:34
8:15 [k]1Co 5:6-8 [l]Lk 12:1 [m]Mt 14:1; Mk 12:13
8:17 [n]Isa 6:9,10; Mk 6:52
8:19 [o]Mt 14:20; Mk 6:41-44; Lk 9:17; Jn 6:13
8:20 [p]ver 6-9; Mt 15:37
8:21 [q]Mk 6:52
8:22 [r]Mt 11:21 [s]Mk 10:46; Jn 9:1
8:23 [t]Mk 7:33 [u]Mk 5:23

[b]*26* Some manuscripts *Don't go and tell anyone in the village*

Peter confesses Jesus to be the Christ.

8:27-29pp— Mt 16:13-16; Lk 9:18-20

27Jesus and his disciples went on to
the villages around Caesarea Philippi.
On the way he asked them, "Who do
people say I am?"
28They replied, "Some say John the
Baptist;[a] others say Elijah;[b] and still others, one of the prophets."
29"But what about you?" he asked.
"Who do you say I am?"
Peter answered, "You are the Christ.[c]"[c]
30Jesus warned them not to tell anyone about him.[d]

Jesus predicts his death.

8:31— 9:1pp— Mt 16:21-28; Lk 9:22-27

31He then began to teach them that
the Son of Man[e] must suffer many
things[f] and be rejected by the elders,
chief priests and teachers of the law,[g]
and that he must be killed[h] and after
three days[i] rise again.[j] 32He spoke
plainly[k] about this, and Peter took him
aside and began to rebuke him.
33But when Jesus turned and looked
at his disciples, he rebuked Peter. "Get
behind me, Satan!"[l] he said. "You do
not have in mind the things of God,
but the things of men."
34Then he called the crowd to him
along with his disciples and said: "If
anyone would come after me, he must
deny himself and take up his cross and
follow me.[m] 35For whoever wants to
save his life[d] will lose it, but whoever
loses his life for me and for the gospel
will save it.[n] 36What good is it for a
man to gain the whole world, yet forfeit his soul? 37Or what can a man give
in exchange for his soul? 38If anyone is
ashamed of me and my words in this
adulterous and sinful generation, the
Son of Man[o] will be ashamed of him[p]
when he comes[q] in his Father's glory
with the holy angels."

9 And he said to them, "I tell you the
truth, some who are standing here
will not taste death before they see the
kingdom of God come[r] with power."[s]

8:28 [a]Mt 3:1 [b]Mal 4:5
8:29 [c]Jn 6:69; 11:27
8:30 [d]Mt 8:4; 16:20; 17:9; Mk 9:9; Lk 9:21
8:31 [e]Mt 8:20 [f]Mt 16:21 [g]Mt 27:1,2 [h]Ac 2:23; 3:13 [i]Mt 16:21 [j]Mt 16:21
8:32 [k]Jn 18:20
8:33 [l]Mt 4:10
8:34 [m]Mt 10:38; Lk 14:27
8:35 [n]Jn 12:25
8:38 [o]Mt 8:20 [p]Mt 10:33; Lk 12:9 [q]1Th 2:19
9:1 [r]Mk 13:30; Lk 22:18 [s]Mt 24:30; 25:31
9:2 [t]Mt 4:21
9:3 [u]Mt 28:3
9:5 [v]Mt 23:7
9:7 [w]Ex 24:16 [x]Mt 3:17
9:9 [y]Mk 8:30 [z]Mt 8:20
9:12 [a]Mt 8:20 [b]Mt 16:21 [c]Lk 23:11
9:13 [d]Mt 11:14

The transfiguration of Jesus Christ.

9:2-8pp— Lk 9:28-36
9:2-13pp— Mt 17:1-13

2After six days Jesus took Peter, James
and John[t] with him and led them up a
high mountain, where they were all
alone. There he was transfigured before
them. 3His clothes became dazzling
white,[u] whiter than anyone in the world
could bleach them. 4And there appeared before them Elijah and Moses,
who were talking with Jesus.
5Peter said to Jesus, "Rabbi,[v] it is good
for us to be here. Let us put up three
shelters—one for you, one for Moses
and one for Elijah." 6(He did not know
what to say, they were so frightened.)
7Then a cloud appeared and enveloped them, and a voice came from the
cloud:[w] "This is my Son, whom I love.
Listen to him!"[x]
8Suddenly, when they looked around,
they no longer saw anyone with them
except Jesus.
9As they were coming down the
mountain, Jesus gave them orders not
to tell anyone[y] what they had seen until
the Son of Man[z] had risen from the
dead. 10They kept the matter to themselves, discussing what "rising from the
dead" meant.
11And they asked him, "Why do the
teachers of the law say that Elijah must
come first?"
12Jesus replied, "To be sure, Elijah
does come first, and restores all things.
Why then is it written that the Son of
Man[a] must suffer much[b] and be rejected?[c] 13But I tell you, Elijah has come,[d]
and they have done to him everything
they wished, just as it is written about
him."

The healing of a possessed boy.

9:14-28; 30-32pp— Mt 17:14-19; 22,23; Lk 9:37-45

14When they came to the other

c29 Or *Messiah.* "The Christ" (Greek) and "the Messiah" (Hebrew) both mean "the Anointed One."
d35 The Greek word means either *life* or *soul*; also in verse 36.

disciples, they saw a large crowd around
them and the teachers of the law arguing with them. 15As soon as all the people saw Jesus, they were overwhelmed
with wonder and ran to greet him.
16"What are you arguing with them
about?" he asked.
17A man in the crowd answered,
"Teacher, I brought you my son, who
is possessed by a spirit that has robbed
him of speech. 18Whenever it seizes
him, it throws him to the ground. He
foams at the mouth, gnashes his teeth
and becomes rigid. I asked your disciples to drive out the spirit, but they
could not."
19"O unbelieving generation," Jesus
replied, "how long shall I stay with you?
How long shall I put up with you? Bring
the boy to me."
20So they brought him. When the
spirit saw Jesus, it immediately threw
the boy into a convulsion. He fell to the
ground and rolled around, foaming at
the mouth.[a]
21Jesus asked the boy's father, "How
long has he been like this?"
"From childhood," he answered. 22"It
has often thrown him into fire or water
to kill him. But if you can do anything,
take pity on us and help us."
23"'If you can'?" said Jesus. "Everything is possible for him who believes."[b]
24Immediately the boy's father exclaimed, "I do believe; help me overcome my unbelief!"
25When Jesus saw that a crowd was
running to the scene,[c] he rebuked the
evil[e] spirit. "You deaf and mute spirit,"
he said, "I command you, come out of
him and never enter him again."
26The spirit shrieked, convulsed him
violently and came out. The boy looked
so much like a corpse that many said,
"He's dead." 27But Jesus took him by
the hand and lifted him to his feet, and
he stood up.
28After Jesus had gone indoors, his
disciples asked him privately,[d] "Why
couldn't we drive it out?"
29He replied, "This kind can come out
only by prayer.[f]"

9:20 [a]Mk 1:26
9:23 [b]Mt 21:21; Mk 11:23; Jn 11:40
9:25 [c]ver 15
9:28 [d]Mk 7:17
9:31 [e]Mt 8:20 [f]ver 12; Ac 2:23; 3:13 [g]Mt 16:21 [h]Mt 16:21
9:32 [i]Lk 2:50; 9:45; 18:34; Jn 12:16
9:33 [j]Mt 4:13 [k]Mk 1:29
9:34 [l]Lk 22:24
9:35 [m]Mt 18:4; 20:26; Mk 10:43; Lk 22:26
9:36 [n]Mk 10:16
9:37 [o]Mt 10:40
9:38 [p]Nu 11:27-29
9:40 [q]Mt 12:30; Lk 11:23
9:41 [r]Mt 10:42

The coming death and resurrection of Jesus.

30They left that place and passed
through Galilee. Jesus did not want anyone to know where they were, 31be-
cause he was teaching his disciples. He
said to them, "The Son of Man[e] is going
to be betrayed into the hands of men.
They will kill him,[f] and after three days[g]
he will rise."[h] 32But they did not understand what he meant[i] and were afraid
to ask him about it.

Who is the greatest?

9:33-37pp— Mt 18:1-5; Lk 9:46-48

33They came to Capernaum.[j] When
he was in the house,[k] he asked them,
"What were you arguing about on the
road?" 34But they kept quiet because
on the way they had argued about who
was the greatest.[l]
35Sitting down, Jesus called the Twelve
and said, "If anyone wants to be first,
he must be the very last, and the servant of all."[m]
36He took a little child and had him
stand among them. Taking him in his
arms,[n] he said to them, 37"Whoever welcomes one of these little children in
my name welcomes me; and whoever
welcomes me does not welcome me
but the one who sent me."[o]

If not against us, then for us.

9:38-40pp— Lk 9:49,50

38"Teacher," said John, "we saw a
man driving out demons in your name
and we told him to stop, because he
was not one of us."[p]
39"Do not stop him," Jesus said. "No
one who does a miracle in my name can
in the next moment say anything bad
about me, 40for whoever is not against
us is for us.[q] 41I tell you the truth, anyone who gives you a cup of water in
my name because you belong to Christ
will certainly not lose his reward.[r]
42"And if anyone causes one of these

e *25* Greek *unclean* f *29* Some manuscripts *prayer and fasting*

little ones who believe in me to sin,[a] it
would be better for him to be thrown
into the sea with a large millstone tied
around his neck.[b] 43 If your hand causes you to sin,[c] cut it off. It is better for
you to enter life maimed than with two
hands to go into hell,[d] where the fire
never goes out.[g][e] 45 And if your foot
causes you to sin,[f] cut it off. It is better
for you to enter life crippled than to have
two feet and be thrown into hell.[h][g]
47 And if your eye causes you to sin,[h]
pluck it out. It is better for you to enter
the kingdom of God with one eye than
to have two eyes and be thrown into
hell,[i] 48 where

"'their worm does not die,
and the fire is not quenched.'[i][j]

49 Everyone will be salted[k] with fire.
50 "Salt is good, but if it loses its saltiness, how can you make it salty again?[l]
Have salt in yourselves,[m] and be at peace
with each other."[n]

Jesus' teaching on marriage and divorce.

10:1-12pp— Mt 19:1-9

10 Jesus then left that place and
went into the region of Judea and
across the Jordan.[o] Again crowds of people came to him, and as was his custom,
he taught them.[p]
2 Some Pharisees[q] came and tested him
by asking, "Is it lawful for a man to divorce his wife?"
3 "What did Moses command you?"
he replied.
4 They said, "Moses permitted a man
to write a certificate of divorce and send
her away."[r]
5 "It was because your hearts were
hard[s] that Moses wrote you this law,"
Jesus replied. 6 "But at the beginning of
creation God 'made them male and female.'[j][t] 7 'For this reason a man will leave
his father and mother and be united to
his wife,[k] 8 and the two will become one
flesh.'[l][u] So they are no longer two, but
one. 9 Therefore what God has joined
together, let man not separate."
10 When they were in the house again,
the disciples asked Jesus about this. 11 He
answered, "Anyone who divorces his
wife and marries another woman commits adultery against her.[v] 12 And if she
divorces her husband and marries
another man, she commits adultery."[w]

Jesus and the little children.

10:13-16pp— Mt 19:13-15; Lk 18:15-17

13 People were bringing little children
to Jesus to have him touch them, but
the disciples rebuked them. 14 When
Jesus saw this, he was indignant. He said
to them, "Let the little children come to
me, and do not hinder them, for the
kingdom of God belongs to such as
these.[x] 15 I tell you the truth, anyone who
will not receive the kingdom of God
like a little child will never enter it."[y]
16 And he took the children in his arms,[z]
put his hands on them and blessed them.

The rich young man.

10:17-31pp— Mt 19:16-30; Lk 18:18-30

17 As Jesus started on his way, a man
ran up to him and fell on his knees[a] before him. "Good teacher," he asked,
"what must I do to inherit eternal life?"[b]
18 "Why do you call me good?" Jesus
answered. "No one is good—except God
alone. 19 You know the commandments:
'Do not murder, do not commit adultery, do not steal, do not give false testimony, do not defraud, honor your
father and mother.'[m]"[c]
20 "Teacher," he declared, "all these I
have kept since I was a boy."
21 Jesus looked at him and loved him.
"One thing you lack," he said. "Go, sell
everything you have and give to the
poor,[d] and you will have treasure in
heaven.[e] Then come, follow me."[f]

9:42 [a]Mt 5:29 [b]Mt 18:6; Lk 17:2
9:43 [c]Mt 5:29 [d]Mt 5:30; 18:8 [e]Mt 25:41
9:45 [f]Mt 5:29 [g]Mt 18:8
9:47 [h]Mt 5:29 [i]Mt 5:29; 18:9
9:48 [j]Isa 66:24; Mt 25:41
9:49 [k]Lev 2:13
9:50 [l]Mt 5:13; Lk 14:34,35 [m]Col 4:6 [n]Ro 12:18; 2Co 13:11; 1Th 5:13
10:1 [o]Mk 1:5; Jn 10:40; 11:7 [p]Mt 4:23; Mk 2:13; 4:2; 6:6,34
10:2 [q]Mk 2:16
10:4 [r]Dt 24:1-4; Mt 5:31
10:5 [s]Ps 95:8; Heb 3:15
10:6 [t]Ge 1:27; 5:2
10:8 [u]Ge 2:24; 1Co 6:16
10:11 [v]Mt 5:32; Lk 16:18
10:12 [w]Ro 7:3; 1Co 7:10,11
10:14 [x]Mt 25:34
10:15 [y]Mt 18:3
10:16 [z]Mk 9:36
10:17 [a]Mk 1:40 [b]Lk 10:25; Ac 20:32
10:19 [c]Ex 20:12-16; Dt 5:16-20
10:21 [d]Ac 2:45 [e]Mt 6:20; Lk 12:33 [f]Mt 4:19

[g] *43* Some manuscripts *out,* [44] *where / "'their worm does not die, / and the fire is not quenched.'*
[h] *45* Some manuscripts *hell,* [46] *where / "'their worm does not die, / and the fire is not quenched.'*
[i] *48* Isaiah 66:24 [j] *6* Gen. 1:27 [k] *7* Some early manuscripts do not have *and be united to his wife.*
[l] *8* Gen. 2:24 [m] *19* Exodus 20:12-16; Deut. 5:16-20

22At this the man's face fell. He went
away sad, because he had great wealth.
23Jesus looked around and said to his
disciples, "How hard it is for the rich[a]
to enter the kingdom of God!"
24The disciples were amazed at his
words. But Jesus said again, "Children,
how hard it is[n] to enter the kingdom of
God![b] **25**It is easier for a camel to go
through the eye of a needle than for a
rich man to enter the kingdom of
God."[c]
26The disciples were even more
amazed, and said to each other, "Who
then can be saved?"
27Jesus looked at them and said, "With
man this is impossible, but not with
God; all things are possible with God."[d]
28Peter said to him, "We have left
everything to follow you!"[e]
29"I tell you the truth," Jesus replied,
"no one who has left home or brothers
or sisters or mother or father or children
or fields for me and the gospel **30**will
fail to receive a hundred times as much[f]
in this present age (homes, brothers,
sisters, mothers, children and fields—and
with them, persecutions) and in the age
to come,[g] eternal life.[h] **31**But many who
are first will be last, and the last first."[i]

Jesus' prediction of his death.

10:32-34pp— Mt 20:17-19; Lk 18:31-33

32They were on their way up to Jerusalem, with Jesus leading the way,
and the disciples were astonished, while
those who followed were afraid. Again
he took the Twelve[j] aside and told
them what was going to happen to
him. **33**"We are going up to Jerusalem,"[k] he said, "and the Son of Man[l]
will be betrayed to the chief priests and
teachers of the law.[m] They will condemn him to death and will hand him
over to the Gentiles, **34**who will mock
him and spit on him, flog him[n] and kill
him.[o] Three days later[p] he will rise."[q]

Request by James and John.

10:35-45pp— Mt 20:20-28

35Then James and John, the sons of
Zebedee, came to him. "Teacher," they
said, "we want you to do for us whatever we ask."
36"What do you want me to do for
you?" he asked.
37They replied, "Let one of us sit at
your right and the other at your left in
your glory."[r]
38"You don't know what you are asking,"[s] Jesus said. "Can you drink the
cup[t] I drink or be baptized with the
baptism I am baptized with?"[u]
39"We can," they answered.
Jesus said to them, "You will drink
the cup I drink and be baptized with the
baptism I am baptized with,[v] **40**but to
sit at my right or left is not for me to
grant. These places belong to those for
whom they have been prepared."
41When the ten heard about this, they
became indignant with James and John.
42Jesus called them together and said,
"You know that those who are regarded as rulers of the Gentiles lord it over
them, and their high officials exercise
authority over them. **43**Not so with
you. Instead, whoever wants to become
great among you must be your servant,[w] **44**and whoever wants to be first
must be slave of all. **45**For even the
Son of Man did not come to be served,
but to serve,[x] and to give his life as a
ransom for many."[y]

Restoration of Bartimaeus's sight.

10:46-52pp— Mt 20:29-34; Lk 18:35-43

46Then they came to Jericho. As Jesus
and his disciples, together with a large
crowd, were leaving the city, a blind
man, Bartimaeus (that is, the Son of
Timaeus), was sitting by the roadside
begging. **47**When he heard that it was
Jesus of Nazareth,[z] he began to shout,
"Jesus, Son of David,[a] have mercy
on me!"
48Many rebuked him and told him to
be quiet, but he shouted all the more,
"Son of David, have mercy on me!"
49Jesus stopped and said, "Call him."
So they called to the blind man,

10:23 [a]Ps 52:7; 62:10; 1Ti 6:9,10,17
10:24 [b]Mt 7:13,14
10:25 [c]Lk 12:16-20
10:27 [d]Mt 19:26
10:28 [e]Mt 4:19
10:30 [f]Mt 6:33 [g]Mt 12:32 [h]Mt 25:46
10:31 [i]Mt 19:30
10:32 [j]Mk 3:16-19
10:33 [k]Lk 9:51 [l]Mt 8:20 [m]Mt 27:1,2
10:34 [n]Mt 16:21 [o]Ac 2:23; 3:13 [p]Mt 16:21 [q]Mt 16:21
10:37 [r]Mt 19:28
10:38 [s]Job 38:2 [t]Mt 20:22 [u]Lk 12:50
10:39 [v]Ac 12:2; Rev 1:9
10:43 [w]Mk 9:35
10:45 [x]Mt 20:28 [y]Mt 20:28
10:47 [z]Mk 1:24 [a]Mt 9:27

[n]*24* Some manuscripts *is for those who trust in riches*

"Cheer up! On your feet! He's calling
you." 50 Throwing his cloak aside, he
jumped to his feet and came to Jesus.
51 "What do you want me to do for
you?" Jesus asked him.
The blind man said, "Rabbi,[a] I want
to see."
52 "Go," said Jesus, "your faith has
healed you."[b] Immediately he received
his sight and followed[c] Jesus along the
road.

Jesus' Triumphal Entry.

11:1-10pp— Mt 21:1-9; Lk 19:29-38
11:7-10pp— Jn 12:12-15

11 As they approached Jerusalem and
came to Bethphage and Bethany[d]
at the Mount of Olives,[e] Jesus sent two
of his disciples, 2 saying to them, "Go
to the village ahead of you, and just as
you enter it, you will find a colt tied
there, which no one has ever ridden.[f]
Untie it and bring it here. 3 If anyone
asks you, 'Why are you doing this?' tell
him, 'The Lord needs it and will send
it back here shortly.' "
4 They went and found a colt outside
in the street, tied at a doorway.[g] As they
untied it, 5 some people standing there
asked, "What are you doing, untying that
colt?" 6 They answered as Jesus had told
them to, and the people let them go.
7 When they brought the colt to Jesus and
threw their cloaks over it, he sat on it.
8 Many people spread their cloaks on the
road, while others spread branches they
had cut in the fields. 9 Those who went
ahead and those who followed shouted,

"Hosanna![o]"

"Blessed is he who comes in the
name of the Lord!"[p][h]

10 "Blessed is the coming kingdom of
our father David!"

"Hosanna in the highest!"[i]

11 Jesus entered Jerusalem and went
to the temple. He looked around at
everything, but since it was already
late, he went out to Bethany with the
Twelve.[j]

10:51 [a]Mt 23:7
10:52 [b]Mt 9:22 [c]Mt 4:19
11:1 [d]Mt 21:17 [e]Mt 21:1
11:2 [f]Nu 19:2; Dt 21:3; 1Sa 6:7
11:4 [g]Mk 14:16
11:9 [h]Ps 118:25,26; Mt 23:39
11:10 [i]Lk 2:14
11:11 [j]Mt 21:12,17
11:13 [k]Lk 13:6-9

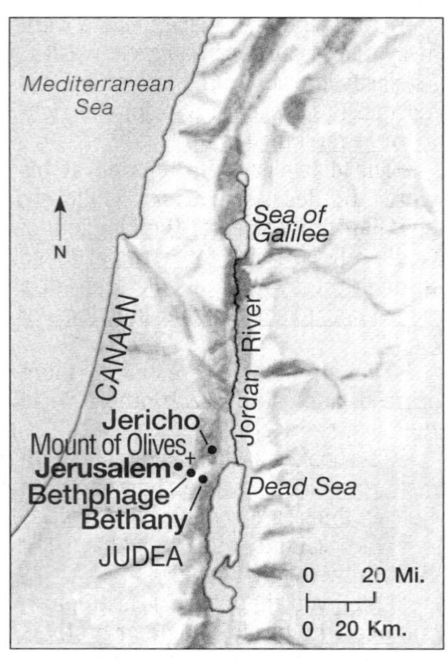

Jesus Nears Jerusalem

Leaving Jericho, Jesus headed toward acclaim then crucifixion, in Jerusalem. During his last week he stayed outside the city in Bethany, a village on the Mount of Olives, entering Jerusalem to teach, eat the Passover, and finally be crucified.

Jesus forces money changers from the temple.

11:12-14pp— Mt 21:18-22
11:15-18pp— Mt 21:12-16; Lk 19:45-47; Jn 2:13-16

12 The next day as they were leaving
Bethany, Jesus was hungry. 13 Seeing in
the distance a fig tree in leaf, he went
to find out if it had any fruit. When he
reached it, he found nothing but leaves,
because it was not the season for figs.[k]
14 Then he said to the tree, "May no one
ever eat fruit from you again." And his
disciples heard him say it.
15 On reaching Jerusalem, Jesus entered the temple area and began driving
out those who were buying and selling
there. He overturned the tables of the
money changers and the benches of
those selling doves, 16 and would not

o *9* A Hebrew expression meaning "Save!" which became an exclamation of praise; also in verse 10
p *9* Psalm 118:25,26

allow anyone to carry merchandise
through the temple courts. 17And as he
taught them, he said, "Is it not written:

"'My house will be called
a house of prayer for all nations'[q]?[a]

But you have made it 'a den of robbers.'[r]"[b]
18The chief priests and the teachers
of the law heard this and began looking
for a way to kill him, for they feared
him,[c] because the whole crowd was
amazed at his teaching.[d]
19When evening came, they[s] went out
of the city.[e]

The withered fig tree.

11:20-24pp— Mt 21:19-22

20In the morning, as they went along,
they saw the fig tree withered from the
roots. 21Peter remembered and said to
Jesus, "Rabbi,[f] look! The fig tree you
cursed has withered!"
22"Have[t] faith in God," Jesus answered. 23"I tell you the truth, if anyone says to this mountain, 'Go, throw
yourself into the sea,' and does not
doubt in his heart but believes that
what he says will happen, it will be done
for him.[g] 24Therefore I tell you, whatever you ask for in prayer, believe that
you have received it, and it will be
yours.[h] 25And when you stand praying,
if you hold anything against anyone, forgive him, so that your Father in heav-
en may forgive you your sins.[u]"[i]

Questioning of Jesus' authority.

11:27-33pp— Mt 21:23-27; Lk 20:1-8

27They arrived again in Jerusalem, and
while Jesus was walking in the temple
courts, the chief priests, the teachers of
the law and the elders came to him.
28"By what authority are you doing these
things?" they asked. "And who gave you
authority to do this?"
29Jesus replied, "I will ask you one
question. Answer me, and I will tell you
by what authority I am doing these
things. 30John's baptism—was it from
heaven, or from men? Tell me!"

11:17 [a]Isa 56:7 [b]Jer 7:11
11:18 [c]Mt 21:46; Mk 12:12; Lk 20:19 [d]Mt 7:28
11:19 [e]Lk 21:37
11:21 [f]Mt 23:7
11:23 [g]Mt 21:21
11:24 [h]Mt 7:7
11:25 [i]Mt 6:14
11:32 [j]Mt 11:9
12:1 [k]Isa 5:1-7
12:6 [l]Heb 1:1-3
12:10 [m]Ac 4:11
12:11 [n]Ps 118:22,23

31They discussed it among themselves
and said, "If we say, 'From heaven,' he
will ask, 'Then why didn't you believe
him?' 32But if we say, 'From men'. . . ."
(They feared the people, for everyone
held that John really was a prophet.)[j]
33So they answered Jesus, "We don't
know."
Jesus said, "Neither will I tell you by
what authority I am doing these things."

A parable: The wicked tenants.

12:1-12pp— Mt 21:33-46; Lk 20:9-19

12 He then began to speak to them
in parables: "A man planted a
vineyard.[k] He put a wall around it, dug
a pit for the winepress and built a watchtower. Then he rented the vineyard to
some farmers and went away on a journey. 2At harvest time he sent a servant
to the tenants to collect from them some
of the fruit of the vineyard. 3But they
seized him, beat him and sent him away
empty-handed. 4Then he sent another
servant to them; they struck this man on
the head and treated him shamefully.
5He sent still another, and that one they
killed. He sent many others; some of
them they beat, others they killed.
6"He had one left to send, a son,
whom he loved. He sent him last of all,[l]
saying, 'They will respect my son.'
7"But the tenants said to one another, 'This is the heir. Come, let's kill him,
and the inheritance will be ours.' 8So
they took him and killed him, and threw
him out of the vineyard.
9"What then will the owner of the
vineyard do? He will come and kill those
tenants and give the vineyard to others.
10Haven't you read this scripture:

"'The stone the builders rejected
has become the capstone[v];[m]
11the Lord has done this,
and it is marvelous in our eyes'[w]?"[n]

[q]*17* Isaiah 56:7 [r]*17* Jer. 7:11 [s]*19* Some early manuscripts *he* [t]*22* Some early manuscripts *If you have* [u]*25* Some manuscripts *sins.* *26But if you do not forgive, neither will your Father who is in heaven forgive your sins.* [v]*10* Or *cornerstone* [w]*11* Psalm 118:22,23

12Then they looked for a way to arrest
him because they knew he had spoken
the parable against them. But they were
afraid of the crowd;[a] so they left him
and went away.[b]

A question about taxes to Caesar.

12:13-17pp— Mt 22:15-22; Lk 20:20-26

13Later they sent some of the Pharisees and Herodians[c] to Jesus to catch
him[d] in his words. 14They came to him
and said, "Teacher, we know you are a
man of integrity. You aren't swayed by
men, because you pay no attention to
who they are; but you teach the way of
God in accordance with the truth. Is it
right to pay taxes to Caesar or not?
15Should we pay or shouldn't we?"
But Jesus knew their hypocrisy. "Why
are you trying to trap me?" he asked.
"Bring me a denarius and let me look
at it." 16They brought the coin, and he
asked them, "Whose portrait is this?
And whose inscription?"
"Caesar's," they replied.
17Then Jesus said to them, "Give to
Caesar what is Caesar's and to God what
is God's."[e]
And they were amazed at him.

Marriage at the resurrection.

12:18-27pp— Mt 22:23-33; Lk 20:27-38

18Then the Sadducees,[f] who say there
is no resurrection,[g] came to him with
a question. 19"Teacher," they said,
"Moses wrote for us that if a man's
brother dies and leaves a wife but no
children, the man must marry the widow and have children for his brother.[h]
20Now there were seven brothers. The
first one married and died without leaving any children. 21The second one married the widow, but he also died,
leaving no child. It was the same with
the third. 22In fact, none of the seven
left any children. Last of all, the woman died too. 23At the resurrection[x] whose
wife will she be, since the seven were
married to her?"
24Jesus replied, "Are you not in error
because you do not know the Scriptures[i]
or the power of God? 25When the dead
rise, they will neither marry nor be
given in marriage; they will be like the
angels in heaven.[j] 26Now about the
dead rising—have you not read in the
book of Moses, in the account of the bush,
how God said to him, 'I am the God of
Abraham, the God of Isaac, and the God
of Jacob'[y]?[k] 27He is not the God of the
dead, but of the living. You are badly
mistaken!"

The two greatest commandments.

12:28-34pp— Mt 22:34-40

28One of the teachers of the law[l] came
and heard them debating. Noticing that
Jesus had given them a good answer,
he asked him, "Of all the commandments, which is the most important?"
29"The most important one," answered Jesus, "is this: 'Hear, O Israel,
the Lord our God, the Lord is one.[z]
30Love the Lord your God with all your
heart and with all your soul and with
all your mind and with all your
strength.'[a][m] 31The second is this:
'Love your neighbor as yourself.'[b][n]
There is no commandment greater
than these."
32"Well said, teacher," the man replied. "You are right in saying that God
is one and there is no other but him.[o]
33To love him with all your heart, with
all your understanding and with all your
strength, and to love your neighbor as
yourself is more important than all burnt
offerings and sacrifices."[p]
34When Jesus saw that he had answered wisely, he said to him, "You are
not far from the kingdom of God."[q] And
from then on no one dared ask him any
more questions.[r]

A question about Jesus' sonship.

12:35-37pp— Mt 22:41-46; Lk 20:41-44
12:38-40pp— Mt 23:1-7; Lk 20:45-47

35While Jesus was teaching in the

12:12 [a]Mk 11:18 [b]Mt 22:22
12:13 [c]Mt 22:16; Mk 3:6 [d]Mt 12:10
12:17 [e]Ro 13:7
12:18 [f]Ac 4:1 [g]Ac 23:8; 1Co 15:12
12:19 [h]Dt 25:5
12:24 [i]2Ti 3:15-17
12:25 [j]1Co 15:42, 49,52
12:26 [k]Ex 3:6
12:28 [l]Lk 10:25-28; 20:39
12:30 [m]Dt 6:4,5
12:31 [n]Lev 19:18; Mt 5:43
12:32 [o]Dt 4:35,39; Isa 45:6,14; 46:9
12:33 [p]1Sa 15:22; Hos 6:6; Mic 6:6-8; Heb 10:8
12:34 [q]Mt 3:2 [r]Mt 22:46; Lk 20:40

[x]*23* Some manuscripts *resurrection, when men rise from the dead,* [y]*26* Exodus 3:6 [z]*29* Or *the Lord our God is one Lord* [a]*30* Deut. 6:4,5 [b]*31* Lev. 19:18

temple courts,[a] he asked, "How is it that
the teachers of the law say that the
Christ[c] is the son of David?[b] 36 David
himself, speaking by the Holy Spirit,[c]
declared:

"'The Lord said to my Lord:
"Sit at my right hand
until I put your enemies
under your feet."'[d][d]

37 David himself calls him 'Lord.' How
then can he be his son?"
The large crowd[e] listened to him with
delight.
38 As he taught, Jesus said, "Watch out
for the teachers of the law. They like to
walk around in flowing robes and be
greeted in the marketplaces, 39 and have
the most important seats in the synagogues and the places of honor at banquets.[f] 40 They devour widows' houses
and for a show make lengthy prayers.
Such men will be punished most
severely."

The poor widow's offering.

12:41-44pp— Lk 21:1-4

41 Jesus sat down opposite the place
where the offerings were put[g] and
watched the crowd putting their money into the temple treasury. Many rich
people threw in large amounts. 42 But a
poor widow came and put in two very
small copper coins,[e] worth only a frac-
tion of a penny.[f]
43 Calling his disciples to him, Jesus
said, "I tell you the truth, this poor widow has put more into the treasury than
all the others. 44 They all gave out of their
wealth; but she, out of her poverty, put
in everything—all she had to live on."[h]

Jesus foretells the destruction of the temple, and the signs of the last days.

13:1-37pp— Mt 24:1-51; Lk 21:5-36

13 As he was leaving the temple,
one of his disciples said to him,
"Look, Teacher! What massive stones!
What magnificent buildings!"
2 "Do you see all these great buildings?" replied Jesus. "Not one stone here
will be left on another; every one will
be thrown down."[i]
3 As Jesus was sitting on the Mount
of Olives[j] opposite the temple, Peter,
James, John[k] and Andrew asked him privately, 4 "Tell us, when will these things
happen? And what will be the sign
that they are all about to be fulfilled?"
5 Jesus said to them: "Watch out that
no one deceives you.[l] 6 Many will come
in my name, claiming, 'I am he,' and
will deceive many. 7 When you hear of
wars and rumors of wars, do not be
alarmed. Such things must happen, but
the end is still to come. 8 Nation will
rise against nation, and kingdom against
kingdom. There will be earthquakes in
various places, and famines. These are
the beginning of birth pains.
9 "You must be on your guard. You will
be handed over to the local councils and
flogged in the synagogues.[m] On account
of me you will stand before governors
and kings as witnesses to them. 10 And
the gospel must first be preached to all
nations. 11 Whenever you are arrested
and brought to trial, do not worry
beforehand about what to say. Just say
whatever is given you at the time, for
it is not you speaking, but the Holy
Spirit.[n]
12 "Brother will betray brother to
death, and a father his child. Children
will rebel against their parents and have
them put to death.[o] 13 All men will hate
you because of me,[p] but he who stands
firm to the end will be saved.[q]
14 "When you see 'the abomination
that causes desolation'[g][r] standing where
it[h] does not belong—let the reader
understand—then let those who are in
Judea flee to the mountains. 15 Let no
one on the roof of his house go down
or enter the house to take anything out.
16 Let no one in the field go back to get
his cloak. 17 How dreadful it will be in
those days for pregnant women and

12:35 [a] Mt 26:55 [b] Mt 9:27
12:36 [c] 2Sa 23:2 [d] Ps 110:1; Mt 22:44
12:37 [e] Jn 12:9
12:39 [f] Lk 11:43
12:41 [g] 2Ki 12:9; Jn 8:20
12:44 [h] 2Co 8:12
13:2 [i] Lk 19:44
13:3 [j] Mt 21:1 [k] Mt 4:21
13:5 [l] ver 22; Jer 29:8; Eph 5:6; 2Th 2:3,10-12; 1Ti 4:1; 2Ti 3:13; 1Jn 4:6
13:9 [m] Mt 10:17
13:11 [n] Mt 10:19,20; Lk 12:11,12
13:12 [o] Mic 7:6; Mt 10:21; Lk 12:51-53
13:13 [p] Jn 15:21 [q] Mt 10:22
13:14 [r] Da 9:27; 11:31; 12:11

[c] *35* Or *Messiah* [d] *36* Psalm 110:1 [e] *42* Greek *two lepta* [f] *42* Greek *kodrantes* [g] *14* Daniel 9:27; 11:31; 12:11 [h] *14* Or *he*; also in verse 29

nursing mothers![a] 18 Pray that this will
not take place in winter, 19 because those
will be days of distress unequaled from
the beginning, when God created the
world,[b] until now—and never to be
equaled again.[c] 20 If the Lord had not
cut short those days, no one would survive. But for the sake of the elect, whom
he has chosen, he has shortened them.
21 At that time if anyone says to you,
'Look, here is the Christ[i]!' or, 'Look,
there he is!' do not believe it.[d] 22 For
false Christs and false prophets[e] will
appear and perform signs and miracles[f]
to deceive the elect—if that were possible. 23 So be on your guard;[g] I have told
you everything ahead of time.

24 "But in those days, following that
distress,

" 'the sun will be darkened,
and the moon will not give its light;
25 the stars will fall from the sky,
and the heavenly bodies will be
shaken.'[j][h]

26 "At that time men will see the Son
of Man coming in clouds[i] with great
power and glory. 27 And he will send
his angels and gather his elect from the
four winds, from the ends of the earth
to the ends of the heavens.[j]

28 "Now learn this lesson from the fig
tree: As soon as its twigs get tender
and its leaves come out, you know that
summer is near. 29 Even so, when you
see these things happening, you know
that it is near, right at the door. 30 I tell
you the truth, this generation[k][k] will certainly not pass away until all these things
have happened.[l] 31 Heaven and earth will
pass away, but my words will never
pass away.[m]

32 "No one knows about that day or
hour, not even the angels in heaven,
nor the Son, but only the Father.[n] 33 Be
on guard! Be alert[l]![o] You do not know
when that time will come. 34 It's like a
man going away: He leaves his house
and puts his servants[p] in charge, each
with his assigned task, and tells the
one at the door to keep watch.

13:17 [a]Lk 23:29
13:19 [b]Mk 10:6 [c]Da 9:26; 12:1; Joel 2:2
13:21 [d]Lk 17:23; 21:8
13:22 [e]Mt 7:15 [f]Jn 4:48; 2Th 2:9,10
13:23 [g]2Pe 3:17
13:25 [h]Isa 13:10; 34:4; Mt 24:29
13:26 [i]Da 7:13; Mt 16:27; Rev 1:7
13:27 [j]Zec 2:6
13:30 [k]Lk 17:25 [l]Mk 9:1
13:31 [m]Mt 5:18
13:32 [n]Ac 1:7; 1Th 5:1,2
13:33 [o]1Th 5:6
13:34 [p]Mt 25:14
13:37 [q]Lk 12:35-40
14:1 [r]Jn 11:55; 13:1 [s]Mt 12:14
14:3 [t]Mt 21:17 [u]Lk 7:37-39
14:7 [v]Dt 15:11
14:8 [w]Jn 19:40
14:9 [x]Mt 24:14; Mk 16:15
14:10 [y]Mk 3:16-19 [z]Mt 10:4

35 "Therefore keep watch because you
do not know when the owner of the
house will come back—whether in the
evening, or at midnight, or when the
rooster crows, or at dawn. 36 If he comes
suddenly, do not let him find you sleeping. 37 What I say to you, I say to everyone: 'Watch!' "[q]

Jesus is anointed with perfume.

14:1-11pp— Mt 26:2-16
14:1,2,10,11pp— Lk 22:1-6
14:3-8Ref— Jn 12:1-8

14 Now the Passover[r] and the Feast
of Unleavened Bread were only
two days away, and the chief priests and
the teachers of the law were looking for
some sly way to arrest Jesus and kill
him.[s] 2 "But not during the Feast," they
said, "or the people may riot."

3 While he was in Bethany,[t] reclining
at the table in the home of a man known
as Simon the Leper, a woman came with
an alabaster jar of very expensive perfume, made of pure nard. She broke the
jar and poured the perfume on his
head.[u]

4 Some of those present were saying
indignantly to one another, "Why this
waste of perfume? 5 It could have been
sold for more than a year's wages[m] and
the money given to the poor." And they
rebuked her harshly.

6 "Leave her alone," said Jesus. "Why
are you bothering her? She has done a
beautiful thing to me. 7 The poor you will
always have with you, and you can help
them any time you want.[v] But you will
not always have me. 8 She did what she
could. She poured perfume on my body
beforehand to prepare for my burial.[w] 9 I
tell you the truth, wherever the gospel
is preached throughout the world,[x]
what she has done will also be told, in
memory of her."

10 Then Judas Iscariot, one of the
Twelve,[y] went to the chief priests to
betray Jesus to them.[z] 11 They were

[i] 21 Or *Messiah* [j] 25 Isaiah 13:10; 34:4 [k] 30 Or *race* [l] 33 Some manuscripts *alert and pray*
[m] 5 Greek *than three hundred denarii*

delighted to hear this and promised to
give him money. So he watched for an
opportunity to hand him over.

The Last Supper is prepared.

14:12-26pp— Mt 26:17-30; Lk 22:7-23
14:22-25pp— 1Co 11:23-25

12On the first day of the Feast of
Unleavened Bread, when it was customary to sacrifice the Passover lamb,[a] Jesus'
disciples asked him, "Where do you want
us to go and make preparations for you
to eat the Passover?"
13So he sent two of his disciples, telling them, "Go into the city, and a man
carrying a jar of water will meet you.
Follow him. 14Say to the owner of the
house he enters, 'The Teacher asks:
Where is my guest room, where I may
eat the Passover with my disciples?'
15He will show you a large upper room,[b]
furnished and ready. Make preparations
for us there."
16The disciples left, went into the city
and found things just as Jesus had told
them. So they prepared the Passover.
17When evening came, Jesus arrived
with the Twelve. 18While they were
reclining at the table eating, he said, "I
tell you the truth, one of you will betray
me—one who is eating with me."
19They were saddened, and one by
one they said to him, "Surely not I?"
20"It is one of the Twelve," he replied,
"one who dips bread into the bowl with
me.[c] 21The Son of Man[d] will go just as
it is written about him. But woe to that
man who betrays the Son of Man! It
would be better for him if he had not
been born."
22While they were eating, Jesus took
bread, gave thanks and broke it,[e] and
gave it to his disciples, saying, "Take it;
this is my body."
23Then he took the cup, gave thanks
and offered it to them, and they all drank
from it.[f]
24"This is my blood of the[n] covenant,[g]
which is poured out for many," he said
to them. 25"I tell you the truth, I will not
drink again of the fruit of the vine until

14:12 [a]Ex 12:1-11; Dt 16:1-4; 1Co 5:7
14:15 [b]Ac 1:13
14:20 [c]Jn 13:18-27
14:21 [d]Mt 8:20
14:22 [e]Mt 14:19
14:23 [f]1Co 10:16
14:24 [g]Mt 26:28
14:25 [h]Mt 3:2
14:26 [i]Mt 21:1
14:27 [j]Zec 13:7
14:28 [k]Mk 16:7
14:30 [l]ver 66-72; Lk 22:34; Jn 13:38
14:31 [m]Lk 22:33; Jn 13:37
14:33 [n]Mt 4:21
14:34 [o]Jn 12:27
14:35 [p]ver 41; Mt 26:18
14:36 [q]Ro 8:15; Gal 4:6 [r]Mt 20:22 [s]Mt 26:39

that day when I drink it anew in the
kingdom of God."[h]
26When they had sung a hymn, they
went out to the Mount of Olives.[i]

Peter's denial is predicted.

14:27-31pp— Mt 26:31-35

27"You will all fall away," Jesus told
them, "for it is written:

"'I will strike the shepherd,
and the sheep will be scattered.'[o][j]

28But after I have risen, I will go ahead
of you into Galilee."[k]
29Peter declared, "Even if all fall away,
I will not."
30"I tell you the truth," Jesus answered, "today—yes, tonight—before
the rooster crows twice[p] you yourself
will disown me three times."[l]
31But Peter insisted emphatically,
"Even if I have to die with you,[m] I will
never disown you." And all the others
said the same.

Jesus prays in the Garden of Gethsemane.

14:32-42pp— Mt 26:36-46; Lk 22:40-46

32They went to a place called Gethsemane, and Jesus said to his disciples,
"Sit here while I pray." 33He took Peter,
James and John[n] along with him, and
he began to be deeply distressed and
troubled. 34"My soul is overwhelmed
with sorrow to the point of death,"[o] he
said to them. "Stay here and keep
watch."
35Going a little farther, he fell to the
ground and prayed that if possible the
hour[p] might pass from him. 36"*Abba*,[q]
Father,"[q] he said, "everything is possible for you. Take this cup[r] from me. Yet
not what I will, but what you will."[s]
37Then he returned to his disciples
and found them sleeping. "Simon," he
said to Peter, "are you asleep? Could you
not keep watch for one hour? 38Watch

[n]24 Some manuscripts *the new* [o]27 Zech. 13:7
[p]30 Some early manuscripts do not have *twice.*
[q]36 Aramaic for *Father*

and pray so that you will not fall into temptation.[a] The spirit is willing, but the body is weak."[b]

39Once more he went away and prayed the same thing. 40When he came back, he again found them sleeping, because their eyes were heavy. They did not know what to say to him.

41Returning the third time, he said to them, "Are you still sleeping and resting? Enough! The hour[c] has come. Look, the Son of Man is betrayed into the hands of sinners. 42Rise! Let us go! Here comes my betrayer!"

Jesus is betrayed and arrested.

14:43-50pp— Mt 26:47-56; Lk 22:47-50; Jn 18:3-11

43Just as he was speaking, Judas,[d] one of the Twelve, appeared. With him was a crowd armed with swords and clubs, sent from the chief priests, the teachers of the law, and the elders.

44Now the betrayer had arranged a signal with them: "The one I kiss is the man; arrest him and lead him away under guard." 45Going at once to Jesus, Judas said, "Rabbi!"[e] and kissed him. 46The men seized Jesus and arrested him. 47Then one of those standing near drew his sword and struck the servant of the high priest, cutting off his ear.

48"Am I leading a rebellion," said Jesus, "that you have come out with swords and clubs to capture me? 49Every day I was with you, teaching in the temple courts,[f] and you did not arrest me. But the Scriptures must be fulfilled."[g] 50Then everyone deserted him and fled.[h]

51A young man, wearing nothing but a linen garment, was following Jesus. When they seized him, 52he fled naked, leaving his garment behind.

Jesus is tried before the Sanhedrin.

14:53-65pp— Mt 26:57-68; Jn 18:12,13,19-24
14:61-63pp— Lk 22:67-71

53They took Jesus to the high priest, and all the chief priests, elders and teachers of the law came together. 54Peter followed him at a distance, right into the courtyard of the high priest.[i] There he sat with the guards and warmed himself at the fire.[j]

55The chief priests and the whole Sanhedrin[k] were looking for evidence against Jesus so that they could put him to death, but they did not find any. 56Many testified falsely against him, but their statements did not agree.

57Then some stood up and gave this false testimony against him: 58"We heard him say, 'I will destroy this man-made temple and in three days will build another,[l] not made by man.'" 59Yet even then their testimony did not agree.

60Then the high priest stood up before them and asked Jesus, "Are you not going to answer? What is this testimony that these men are bringing against you?" 61But Jesus remained silent and gave no answer.[m]

Again the high priest asked him, "Are you the Christ,[r] the Son of the Blessed One?"[n]

62"I am," said Jesus. "And you will see the Son of Man sitting at the right hand of the Mighty One and coming on the clouds of heaven."[o]

63The high priest tore his clothes.[p] "Why do we need any more witnesses?" he asked. 64"You have heard the blasphemy. What do you think?"

They all condemned him as worthy of death.[q] 65Then some began to spit at him; they blindfolded him, struck him with their fists, and said, "Prophesy!" And the guards took him and beat him.[r]

Peter disowns Jesus.

14:66-72pp— Mt 26:69-75; Lk 22:56-62; Jn 18:16-18,25-27

66While Peter was below in the courtyard,[s] one of the servant girls of the high priest came by. 67When she saw Peter warming himself,[t] she looked closely at him.

"You also were with that Nazarene, Jesus,"[u] she said.

68But he denied it. "I don't know or understand what you're talking about,"[v]

14:38 [a]Mt 6:13 [b]Ro 7:22,23
14:41 [c]ver 35; Mt 26:18
14:43 [d]Mt 10:4
14:45 [e]Mt 23:7
14:49 [f]Mt 26:55 [g]Isa 53:7-12; Mt 1:22
14:50 [h]ver 27
14:54 [i]Mt 26:3 [j]Jn 18:18
14:55 [k]Mt 5:22
14:58 [l]Mk 15:29; Jn 2:19
14:61 [m]Isa 53:7; Mt 27:12,14; Mk 15:5; Lk 23:9; Jn 19:9 [n]Mt 16:16; Jn 4:25,26
14:62 [o]Rev 1:7
14:63 [p]Lev 10:6; 21:10; Nu 14:6; Ac 14:14
14:64 [q]Lev 24:16
14:65 [r]Mt 16:21
14:66 [s]ver 54
14:67 [t]ver 54 [u]Mk 1:24
14:68 [v]ver 30,72

[r]61 Or *Messiah*

he said, and went out into the entryway.[s]
69When the servant girl saw him there,
she said again to those standing around,
"This fellow is one of them." 70Again
he denied it.[a]
After a little while, those standing near
said to Peter, "Surely you are one of them,
for you are a Galilean."[b]
71He began to call down curses on himself, and he swore to them, "I don't know
this man you're talking about."[c]
72Immediately the rooster crowed the
second time.[t] Then Peter remembered
the word Jesus had spoken to him: "Before the rooster crows twice[u] you will
disown me three times."[d] And he broke
down and wept.

Jesus appears before Pilate, the Roman governor.

15:2-15pp— Mt 27:11-26; Lk 23:2,3,18-25; Jn 18:29-19:16

15 Very early in the morning, the
chief priests, with the elders, the
teachers of the law[e] and the whole Sanhedrin,[f] reached a decision. They bound
Jesus, led him away and handed him
over to Pilate.[g]
2"Are you the king of the Jews?"[h]
asked Pilate.
"Yes, it is as you say," Jesus replied.
3The chief priests accused him of many
things. 4So again Pilate asked him,
"Aren't you going to answer? See how
many things they are accusing you of."
5But Jesus still made no reply,[i] and
Pilate was amazed.
6Now it was the custom at the Feast
to release a prisoner whom the people
requested. 7A man called Barabbas was
in prison with the insurrectionists who
had committed murder in the uprising.
8The crowd came up and asked Pilate to
do for them what he usually did.
9"Do you want me to release to you
the king of the Jews?"[j] asked Pilate,
10knowing it was out of envy that the
chief priests had handed Jesus over to
him. 11But the chief priests stirred up the
crowd to have Pilate release Barabbas[k]
instead.

14:70 [a]ver 30,68,72 [b]Ac 2:7
14:71 [c]ver 30,72
14:72 [d]ver 30,68
15:1 [e]Mt 27:1; Lk 22:66 [f]Mt 5:22 [g]Mt 27:2
15:2 [h]ver 9,12,18, 26; Mt 2:2
15:5 [i]Mk 14:61
15:9 [j]ver 2
15:11 [k]Ac 3:14
15:15 [l]Isa 53:6
15:16 [m]Jn 18:28,33; 19:9
15:18 [n]ver 2
15:20 [o]Heb 13:12
15:21 [p]Mt 27:32 [q]Ro 16:13 [r]Mt 27:32; Lk 23:26
15:23 [s]ver 36; Ps 69:21; Pr 31:6
15:24 [t]Ps 22:18
15:26 [u]ver 2

12"What shall I do, then, with the one
you call the king of the Jews?" Pilate
asked them.
13"Crucify him!" they shouted.
14"Why? What crime has he committed?" asked Pilate.
But they shouted all the louder, "Crucify him!"
15Wanting to satisfy the crowd, Pilate
released Barabbas to them. He had Jesus
flogged,[l] and handed him over to be
crucified.

Soldiers mock Jesus.

15:16-20pp— Mt 27:27-31

16The soldiers led Jesus away into the
palace[m] (that is, the Praetorium) and
called together the whole company of
soldiers. 17They put a purple robe on
him, then twisted together a crown of
thorns and set it on him. 18And they
began to call out to him, "Hail, king of
the Jews!"[n] 19Again and again they struck
him on the head with a staff and spit
on him. Falling on their knees, they paid
homage to him. 20And when they had
mocked him, they took off the purple
robe and put his own clothes on him.
Then they led him out[o] to crucify him.

Jesus' crucifixion.

15:22-32pp— Mt 27:33-44; Lk 23:33-43; Jn 19:17-24

21A certain man from Cyrene,[p] Simon,
the father of Alexander and Rufus,[q] was
passing by on his way in from the country, and they forced him to carry the
cross.[r] 22They brought Jesus to the place
called Golgotha (which means The Place
of the Skull). 23Then they offered him
wine mixed with myrrh,[s] but he did not
take it. 24And they crucified him. Dividing up his clothes, they cast lots[t] to see
what each would get.
25It was the third hour when they
crucified him. 26The written notice
of the charge against him read: THE
KING OF THE JEWS.[u] 27They crucified two

[s]*68* Some early manuscripts *entryway and the rooster crowed* [t]*72* Some early manuscripts do not have *the second time.* [u]*72* Some early manuscripts do not have *twice.*

robbers with him, one on his right and one on his left.[v] 29 Those who passed by hurled insults at him, shaking their heads[a] and saying, "So! You who are going to destroy the temple and build it in three days,[b] 30 come down from the cross and save yourself!"

31 In the same way the chief priests and the teachers of the law mocked him[c] among themselves. "He saved others," they said, "but he can't save himself! 32 Let this Christ,[w][d] this King of Israel,[e] come down now from the cross, that we may see and believe." Those crucified with him also heaped insults on him.

Jesus' death.

15:33-41pp— Mt 27:45-56; Lk 23:44-49

33 At the sixth hour darkness came over the whole land until the ninth hour.[f] 34 And at the ninth hour Jesus cried out in a loud voice, *"Eloi, Eloi, lama sabachthani?"*—which means, "My God, my God, why have you forsaken me?"[x][g]

35 When some of those standing near heard this, they said, "Listen, he's calling Elijah."

36 One man ran, filled a sponge with wine vinegar,[h] put it on a stick, and offered it to Jesus to drink. "Now leave him alone. Let's see if Elijah comes to take him down," he said.

37 With a loud cry, Jesus breathed his last.[i]

38 The curtain of the temple was torn in two from top to bottom.[j] 39 And when the centurion,[k] who stood there in front of Jesus, heard his cry and[y] saw how he died, he said, "Surely this man was the Son[z] of God!"[l]

40 Some women were watching from a distance.[m] Among them were Mary Magdalene, Mary the mother of James the younger and of Joses, and Salome.[n] 41 In Galilee these women had followed him and cared for his needs. Many other women who had come up with him to Jerusalem were also there.[o]

15:29 [a]Ps 22:7; 109:25 [b]Mk 14:58; Jn 2:19
15:31 [c]Ps 22:7
15:32 [d]Mk 14:61 [e]ver 2
15:33 [f]Am 8:9
15:34 [g]Ps 22:1
15:36 [h]ver 23; Ps 69:21
15:37 [i]Jn 19:30
15:38 [j]Heb 10:19,20
15:39 [k]ver 45 [l]Mk 1:1,11; 9:7; Mt 4:3
15:40 [m]Ps 38:11 [n]Mk 16:1; Lk 24:10; Jn 19:25
15:41 [o]Mt 27:55,56; Lk 8:2,3
15:42 [p]Mt 27:62; Jn 19:31
15:43 [q]Mt 5:22 [r]Mt 3:2; Lk 2:25,38
15:45 [s]ver 39
15:46 [t]Mk 16:3
15:47 [u]ver 40
16:1 [v]Lk 23:56; Jn 19:39,40
16:3 [w]Mk 15:46
16:5 [x]Jn 20:12
16:6 [y]Mk 1:24

Jesus' burial.

15:42-47pp— Mt 27:57-61; Lk 23:50-56; Jn 19:38-42

42 It was Preparation Day (that is, the day before the Sabbath).[p] So as evening approached, 43 Joseph of Arimathea, a prominent member of the Council,[q] who was himself waiting for the kingdom of God,[r] went boldly to Pilate and asked for Jesus' body. 44 Pilate was surprised to hear that he was already dead. Summoning the centurion, he asked him if Jesus had already died. 45 When he learned from the centurion[s] that it was so, he gave the body to Joseph. 46 So Joseph bought some linen cloth, took down the body, wrapped it in the linen, and placed it in a tomb cut out of rock. Then he rolled a stone against the entrance of the tomb.[t] 47 Mary Magdalene and Mary the mother of Joses[u] saw where he was laid.

Jesus is victorious over the grave!

16:1-8pp— Mt 28:1-8; Lk 24:1-10

16 When the Sabbath was over, Mary Magdalene, Mary the mother of James, and Salome bought spices[v] so that they might go to anoint Jesus' body. 2 Very early on the first day of the week, just after sunrise, they were on their way to the tomb 3 and they asked each other, "Who will roll the stone away from the entrance of the tomb?"[w]

4 But when they looked up, they saw that the stone, which was very large, had been rolled away. 5 As they entered the tomb, they saw a young man dressed in a white robe[x] sitting on the right side, and they were alarmed.

6 "Don't be alarmed," he said. "You are looking for Jesus the Nazarene,[y] who was crucified. He has risen! He is not here. See the place where they laid him. 7 But go, tell his disciples and Peter, 'He

[v]27 Some manuscripts *left,* 28 *and the scripture was fulfilled which says, "He was counted with the lawless ones"* (Isaiah 53:12) [w]32 Or *Messiah* [x]34 Psalm 22:1 [y]39 Some manuscripts do not have *heard his cry and* [z]39 Or *a son*

is going ahead of you into Galilee. There
you will see him,[a] just as he told you.'"[b]
8 Trembling and bewildered, the wom-
en went out and fled from the tomb.
They said nothing to anyone, because
they were afraid.

[The earliest manuscripts and some
other ancient witnesses do not
have Mark 16:9-20.]

9 When Jesus rose early on the first day
of the week, he appeared first to Mary
Magdalene,[c] out of whom he had driv-
en seven demons. 10 She went and told
those who had been with him and who
were mourning and weeping. 11 When
they heard that Jesus was alive and that
she had seen him, they did not believe it.[d]
12 Afterward Jesus appeared in a different form to two of them while they
were walking in the country.[e] 13 These
returned and reported it to the rest;
but they did not believe them either.
14 Later Jesus appeared to the Eleven
as they were eating; he rebuked them for
their lack of faith and their stubborn
refusal to believe those who had seen
him after he had risen.[f]
15 He said to them, "Go into all the
world and preach the good news to all
creation.[g] 16 Whoever believes and is
baptized will be saved, but whoever
does not believe will be condemned.[h]
17 And these signs will accompany those
who believe: In my name they will drive
out demons;[i] they will speak in new
tongues;[j] 18 they will pick up snakes[k]
with their hands; and when they drink
deadly poison, it will not hurt them at
all; they will place their hands on[l] sick
people, and they will get well."
19 After the Lord Jesus had spoken to
them, he was taken up into heaven[m] and
he sat at the right hand of God.[n] 20 Then
the disciples went out and preached
everywhere, and the Lord worked with
them and confirmed his word by the
signs that accompanied it.

16:7 [a]Jn 21:1-23 [b]Mk 14:28
16:9 [c]Jn 20:11-18
16:11 [d]ver 13,14; Lk 24:11
16:12 [e]Lk 24:13-32
16:14 [f]Lk 24:36-43
16:15 [g]Mt 28:18-20; Lk 24:47,48
16:16 [h]Jn 3:16,18,36; Ac 16:31
16:17 [i]Mk 9:38; Lk 10:17; Ac 5:16; 8:7; 16:18; 19:13-16 [j]Ac 2:4; 10:46; 19:6; 1Co 12:10, 28,30
16:18 [k]Lk 10:19; Ac 28:3-5 [l]Ac 6:6
16:19 [m]Lk 24:50,51; Jn 6:62; Ac 1:9-11 1Ti 3:16 [n]Ps 110:1; Ro 8:34; Col 3:1; Heb 1:3; 12:2

LUKE

Author: Luke.

Date Written: Between A.D. 58 and 70.

Time Span: About 38 years (5 B.C.-A.D. 33).

Title: From the book's author: Luke.

Background: Luke's is the longest and most thorough of the 4 Gospels. Luke, a Gentile physician, writes both this Gospel and the book of Acts to aid a new Christian named Theophilus. As a missionary companion of the apostle Paul, Luke is able to present a detailed historical account of Jesus' life. Luke presents Jesus' humanity more than any of the other Gospels.

Where Written: Possibly at Caesarea or Rome.

To Whom: To Theophilus specifically; Greeks in particular; and to all Gentiles in general.

Content: Called "the most beautiful book ever written," Luke begins by telling us about Jesus' parents; the birth of his cousin, John the Baptist; Mary and Joseph's journey to Bethlehem, where Jesus is born in a manger; and the genealogy of Jesus through Joseph. Jesus' public ministry reveals his perfect compassion and forgiveness through the stories of the Good Samaritan (chapter 10); the lost (prodigal) son (chapter 15); and the rich man and Lazarus (chapter 16).

While many believe in Jesus' unprejudiced love that surpasses all human limits, many others challenge and oppose his claims. Jesus' followers are encouraged to count the cost of discipleship, while his enemies seek his death on the cross. Finally, Jesus is betrayed, tried, sentenced and crucified. But the grave cannot hold him! His resurrection assures the continuation of his ministry to seek and to save the lost (19:10). After appearing on a number of occasions to his disciples, his Holy Spirit is promised, and Christ ascends to the Father.

Key Words: "Jesus"; "Son of Man." As God incarnate, "Jesus" is often referred to as "the Son of Man." The genealogy of Jesus through Joseph is detailed, as are many other specifics of his human characteristics and life.

Themes: • Jesus understands our weaknesses, our temptations and our trials. • Jesus came to save both the Jews...and the Gentiles. • Jesus came to save both the outcasts...and the accepted. • Jesus came to save both the poor...and the rich. • Jesus came to save both adults...and children. • Jesus came to save both men...and women. • Jesus came to save both the free...and the oppressed. • Jesus came to save each and every one of us!

Outline:

1. Introduction. 1:1-1:4
2. The birth and childhood of John the Baptist and Jesus. 1:5-2:52
3. The ministry of John the Baptist. 3:1-3:20
4. Jesus' baptism, genealogy and temptation. 3:21-4:13
5. Jesus' teaching and healing ministry. 4:14-9:50
6. Jesus' journeys from Galilee to Jerusalem. 9:51-19:27
7. Jesus' suffering and crucifixion. 19:28-23:49
8. Jesus' burial, resurrection and ascension. 23:50-24:53

LUKE

Introduction to Luke's letter.

1:1-4Ref— Ac 1:1

1 Many have undertaken to draw up
an account of the things that have
been fulfilled[a] among us, 2just as they
were handed down to us by those who
from the first[a] were eyewitnesses[b] and
servants of the word.[c] 3Therefore, since
I myself have carefully investigated
everything from the beginning, it seemed
good also to me to write an orderly
account[d] for you, most excellent[e] Theophilus,[f] 4so that you may know the
certainty of the things you have been
taught.[g]

1:2
[a]Mk 1:1; Jn 15:27; Ac 1:21,22
[b]Heb 2:3; 1Pe 5:1; 2Pe 1:16; 1Jn 1:1
[c]Mk 4:14
1:3
[d]Ac 11:4
[e]Ac 24:3; 26:25
[f]Ac 1:1
1:4
[g]Jn 20:31
1:5
[h]Mt 2:1
[i]1Ch 24:10
1:6
[j]Ge 7:1; 1Ki 9:4

The angel Gabriel announces the coming birth of John the Baptist.

5In the time of Herod king of Judea[h]
there was a priest named Zechariah,
who belonged to the priestly division
of Abijah;[i] his wife Elizabeth was also
a descendant of Aaron. 6Both of them
were upright in the sight of God, observing all the Lord's commandments and
regulations blamelessly.[j] 7But they had
no children, because Elizabeth was barren; and they were both well along in
years.

a *1* Or *been surely believed*

KEY PLACES IN LUKE

Luke begins his account in the temple in Jerusalem, giving us the background for the birth of John the Baptist, then moves on to the town of Nazareth and the story of Mary, chosen to be Jesus' mother (1:26ff). As a result of Caesar's call for a census, Mary and Joseph had to travel to Bethlehem, where Jesus was born in fulfillment of prophecy (2:1ff). Jesus grew up in Nazareth and began his earthly ministry by being baptized by John (3:21,22) and tempted by Satan (4:1ff). Much of his ministry focused on Galilee—he set up his "home" in Capernaum (4:31ff) and from there he taught throughout the region (8:1ff). Later he visited the Gerasene region, where he healed a demon-possessed man (8:36ff). He fed more than 5,000 people with one lunch on the shores of the Sea of Galilee near Bethsaida (9:10ff). Jesus always traveled to Jerusalem for the major festivals, and he enjoyed visiting friends in nearby Bethany (10:38ff). He healed ten men with leprosy on the border between Galilee and Samaria (17:11), and helped a dishonest tax collector in Jericho turn his life around (19:1ff). The little villages of Bethphage and Bethany on the Mount of Olives were Jesus' resting places during his last days on earth. He was crucified outside Jerusalem's walls, but he would rise again. Two men on the road leading to Emmaus were among the first to see the resurrected Christ (24:13ff).

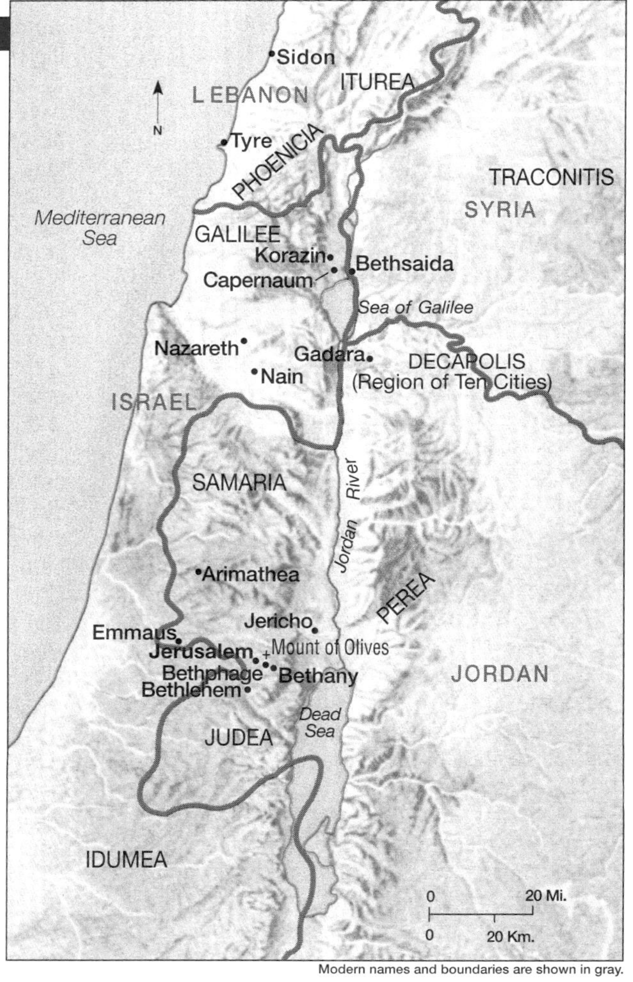

Modern names and boundaries are shown in gray.

8Once when Zechariah's division was
on duty and he was serving as priest
before God,[a] 9he was chosen by lot,
according to the custom of the priesthood, to go into the temple of the Lord
and burn incense.[b] 10And when the time
for the burning of incense came, all the
assembled worshipers were praying
outside.[c]

11Then an angel[d] of the Lord appeared
to him, standing at the right side of the
altar of incense.[e] 12When Zechariah saw
him, he was startled and was gripped
with fear.[f] 13But the angel said to him:
"Do not be afraid,[g] Zechariah; your
prayer has been heard. Your wife Elizabeth will bear you a son, and you are
to give him the name John.[h] 14He will
be a joy and delight to you, and many
will rejoice because of his birth,[i] 15for
he will be great in the sight of the Lord.
He is never to take wine or other fermented drink,[j] and he will be filled with
the Holy Spirit even from birth.[b][k] 16Many
of the people of Israel will he bring back
to the Lord their God. 17And he will go
on before the Lord,[l] in the spirit and
power of Elijah,[m] to turn the hearts of
the fathers to their children[n] and the
disobedient to the wisdom of the righteous—to make ready a people prepared for the Lord."

18Zechariah asked the angel, "How
can I be sure of this? I am an old man
and my wife is well along in years."[o]

19The angel answered, "I am Gabriel.[p]
I stand in the presence of God, and I
have been sent to speak to you and to
tell you this good news. 20And now you
will be silent and not able to speak[q]
until the day this happens, because you
did not believe my words, which will
come true at their proper time."

21Meanwhile, the people were waiting for Zechariah and wondering why
he stayed so long in the temple. 22When
he came out, he could not speak to
them. They realized he had seen a vision
in the temple, for he kept making signs[r]
to them but remained unable to speak.

23When his time of service was completed, he returned home. 24After this
his wife Elizabeth became pregnant and
for five months remained in seclusion.
25"The Lord has done this for me," she
said. "In these days he has shown his
favor and taken away my disgrace[s]
among the people."

The coming birth of Jesus to Mary is foretold.

26In the sixth month, God sent the
angel Gabriel[t] to Nazareth,[u] a town in
Galilee, 27to a virgin pledged to be mar-
ried to a man named Joseph,[v] a descen-
dant of David. The virgin's name was
Mary. 28The angel went to her and said,
"Greetings, you who are highly favored!
The Lord is with you."

29Mary was greatly troubled at his
words and wondered what kind of greeting this might be. 30But the angel said
to her, "Do not be afraid,[w] Mary, you
have found favor with God. 31You will
be with child and give birth to a son,
and you are to give him the name
Jesus.[x] 32He will be great and will be
called the Son of the Most High.[y] The
Lord God will give him the throne of
his father David, 33and he will reign over
the house of Jacob forever; his kingdom[z] will never end."[a]

34"How will this be," Mary asked the
angel, "since I am a virgin?"

35The angel answered, "The Holy Spirit will come upon you,[b] and the power
of the Most High[c] will overshadow you.
So the holy one[d] to be born will be
called[c] the Son of God.[e] 36Even Elizabeth your relative is going to have a
child in her old age, and she who was
said to be barren is in her sixth month.
37For nothing is impossible with God."[f]

38"I am the Lord's servant," Mary
answered. "May it be to me as you have
said." Then the angel left her.

39At that time Mary got ready and hurried to a town in the hill country of
Judea,[g] 40where she entered Zechariah's

1:8 [a] 1Ch 24:19; 2Ch 8:14 **1:9** [b] Ex 30:7,8; 1Ch 23:13; 2Ch 29:11 **1:10** [c] Lev 16:17 **1:11** [d] Ac 5:19 [e] Ex 30:1-10 **1:12** [f] Jdg 6:22,23; 13:22 **1:13** [g] ver 30; Mt 14:27 [h] ver 60,63 **1:14** [i] ver 58 **1:15** [j] Nu 6:3; Jdg 13:4; Lk 7:33 [k] Jer 1:5; Gal 1:15 **1:17** [l] ver 76 [m] Mt 11:14 [n] Mal 4:5,6 **1:18** [o] ver 34; Ge 17:17 **1:19** [p] ver 26; Mt 18:10; Da 8:16; 9:21 **1:20** [q] Eze 3:26 **1:22** [r] ver 62 **1:25** [s] Ge 30:23; Isa 4:1 **1:26** [t] ver 19 [u] Mt 2:23 **1:27** [v] Mt 1:16,18, 20; Lk 2:4 **1:30** [w] ver 13; Mt 14:27 **1:31** [x] Isa 7:14; Mt 1:21,25; Lk 2:21 **1:32** [y] ver 35,76; Mk 5:7 **1:33** [z] Mt 28:18 [a] Da 2:44; 7:14,27; Mic 4:7; Heb 1:8 **1:35** [b] Mt 1:18 [c] ver 32,76 [d] Mk 1:24 [e] Mt 4:3 **1:37** [f] Mt 19:26 **1:39** [g] ver 65

b *15* Or *from his mother's womb* c *35* Or *So the child to be born will be called holy,*

home and greeted Elizabeth. [41]When
Elizabeth heard Mary's greeting, the
baby leaped in her womb, and Elizabeth
was filled with the Holy Spirit. [42]In a
loud voice she exclaimed: "Blessed are
you among women,[a] and blessed is the
child you will bear! [43]But why am I so
favored, that the mother of my Lord
should come to me? [44]As soon as the
sound of your greeting reached my ears,
the baby in my womb leaped for joy.
[45]Blessed is she who has believed that
what the Lord has said to her will be
accomplished!"

Mary's song glorifies the Lord.

1:46-53pp— 1Sa 2:1-10

[46]And Mary said:

"My soul glorifies the Lord[b]
[47] and my spirit rejoices in God my Savior,[c]
[48]for he has been mindful
of the humble state of his servant.[d]
From now on all generations will call me blessed,[e]
[49] for the Mighty One has done great things[f] for me—
holy is his name.[g]
[50]His mercy extends to those who fear him,
from generation to generation.[h]
[51]He has performed mighty deeds with his arm;[i]
he has scattered those who are proud in their inmost thoughts.
[52]He has brought down rulers from their thrones
but has lifted up the humble.
[53]He has filled the hungry with good things[j]
but has sent the rich away empty.
[54]He has helped his servant Israel,
remembering to be merciful[k]
[55]to Abraham and his descendants[l] forever,
even as he said to our fathers."

[56]Mary stayed with Elizabeth for about
three months and then returned home.

John the Baptist is born.

[57]When it was time for Elizabeth to
have her baby, she gave birth to a son.
[58]Her neighbors and relatives heard that
the Lord had shown her great mercy,
and they shared her joy.

[59]On the eighth day they came to circumcise[m] the child, and they were going
to name him after his father Zechariah, [60]but his mother spoke up and said,
"No! He is to be called John."[n]

[61]They said to her, "There is no one
among your relatives who has that
name."

[62]Then they made signs[o] to his father,
to find out what he would like to name
the child. [63]He asked for a writing tablet,
and to everyone's astonishment he
wrote, "His name is John."[p] [64]Immedi-
ately his mouth was opened and his
tongue was loosed, and he began to
speak,[q] praising God. [65]The neighbors
were all filled with awe, and throughout the hill country of Judea[r] people
were talking about all these things.
[66]Everyone who heard this wondered
about it, asking, "What then is this child
going to be?" For the Lord's hand was
with him.[s]

Zechariah's song praises the Lord.

[67]His father Zechariah was filled with
the Holy Spirit and prophesied:[t]

[68]"Praise be to the Lord, the God of Israel,[u]
because he has come and has redeemed his people.[v]
[69]He has raised up a horn[d][w] of salvation for us
in the house of his servant David[x]
[70](as he said through his holy prophets of long ago),[y]
[71]salvation from our enemies
and from the hand of all who hate us—
[72]to show mercy to our fathers[z]
and to remember his holy covenant,[a]

1:42 [a]Jdg 5:24
1:46 [b]Ps 34:2,3
1:47 [c]1Ti 1:1; 2:3
1:48 [d]Ps 138:6 [e]Lk 11:27
1:49 [f]Ps 71:19 [g]Ps 111:9
1:50 [h]Ex 20:6; Ps 103:17
1:51 [i]Ps 98:1; Isa 40:10
1:53 [j]Ps 107:9
1:54 [k]Ps 98:3
1:55 [l]Ge 17:19; Ps 132:11; Gal 3:16
1:59 [m]Ge 17:12; Lev 12:3; Lk 2:21; Php 3:5
1:60 [n]ver 13,63
1:62 [o]ver 22
1:63 [p]ver 13,60
1:64 [q]ver 20
1:65 [r]ver 39
1:66 [s]Ge 39:2; Ac 11:21
1:67 [t]Joel 2:28
1:68 [u]Ps 72:18 [v]Ps 111:9; Lk 7:16
1:69 [w]1Sa 2:1,10; Ps 18:2; 89:17; 132:17; Eze 29:21 [x]Mt 1:1
1:70 [y]Jer 23:5
1:72 [z]Mic 7:20 [a]Ps 105:8,9; 106:45; Eze 16:60

d69 *Horn* here symbolizes strength.

73 the oath he swore to our father
Abraham:[a]
74 to rescue us from the hand of our
enemies,
and to enable us to serve him[b]
without fear
75 in holiness and righteousness[c]
before him all our days.

76 And you, my child, will be called a
prophet[d] of the Most High;[e]
for you will go on before the Lord
to prepare the way for him,[f]
77 to give his people the knowledge of
salvation
through the forgiveness of their
sins,[g]
78 because of the tender mercy of our
God,
by which the rising sun[h] will come
to us from heaven
79 to shine on those living in darkness
and in the shadow of death,[i]
to guide our feet into the path of
peace."

80 And the child grew and became
strong in spirit;[j] and he lived in the desert until he appeared publicly to Israel.

Jesus is born.

2 In those days Caesar Augustus[k] issued a decree that a census should
be taken of the entire Roman world.[l]
2 (This was the first census that took
place while Quirinius was governor of
Syria.)[m] 3 And everyone went to his own
town to register.
4 So Joseph also went up from the
town of Nazareth in Galilee to Judea,
to Bethlehem[n] the town of David, because he belonged to the house and
line of David. 5 He went there to register with Mary, who was pledged to be
married to him and was expecting a
child. 6 While they were there, the time
came for the baby to be born, 7 and she
gave birth to her firstborn, a son. She
wrapped him in cloths and placed him
in a manger, because there was no room
for them in the inn.
8 And there were shepherds living out

1:73 [a]Ge 22:16-18
1:74 [b]Heb 9:14
1:75 [c]Eph 4:24
1:76 [d]Mt 11:9 [e]ver 32,35 [f]ver 17; Mal 3:1
1:77 [g]Jer 31:34; Mk 1:4
1:78 [h]Mal 4:2
1:79 [i]Isa 9:2; 59:9; Mt 4:16; Ac 26:18
1:80 [j]Lk 2:40,52
2:1 [k]Lk 3:1; Mt 22:17 [l]Mt 24:14
2:2 [m]Mt 4:24
2:4 [n]Jn 7:42
2:9 [o]Lk 1:11; Ac 5:19
2:10 [p]Mt 14:27
2:11 [q]Mt 1:21; Jn 4:42; Ac 5:31 [r]Mt 1:16; 16:16,20; Jn 11:27; Ac 2:36
2:12 [s]1Sa 2:34; 2Ki 19:29; Isa 7:14
2:14 [t]Lk 1:79; Ro 5:1; Eph 2:14,17

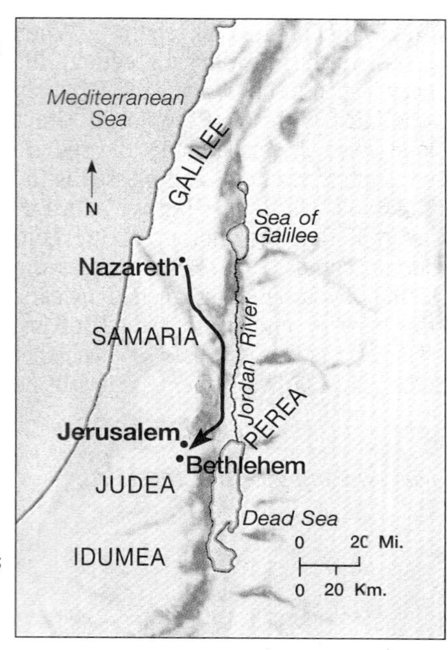

The Journey to Bethlehem

Caesar's decree for a census of the entire Roman empire made it necessary for Joseph and Mary to leave their hometown, Nazareth, and journey the 70 miles to the Judean village of Bethlehem.

in the fields nearby, keeping watch over
their flocks at night. 9 An angel[o] of the
Lord appeared to them, and the glory
of the Lord shone around them, and they
were terrified. 10 But the angel said to
them, "Do not be afraid.[p] I bring you
good news of great joy that will be for
all the people. 11 Today in the town of
David a Savior[q] has been born to you;
he is Christ[e][r] the Lord. 12 This will be a
sign[s] to you: You will find a baby
wrapped in cloths and lying in a
manger."
13 Suddenly a great company of the
heavenly host appeared with the angel,
praising God and saying,

14 "Glory to God in the highest,
and on earth peace[t] to men on
whom his favor rests."

15 When the angels had left them and
gone into heaven, the shepherds said

[e]11 Or *Messiah.* "The Christ" (Greek) and "the Messiah" (Hebrew) both mean "the Anointed One"; also in verse 26.

to one another, "Let's go to Bethlehem
and see this thing that has happened,
which the Lord has told us about."
16So they hurried off and found Mary
and Joseph, and the baby, who was lying
in the manger. 17When they had seen
him, they spread the word concerning
what had been told them about this
child, 18and all who heard it were
amazed at what the shepherds said to
them. 19But Mary treasured up all these
things and pondered them in her
heart.[a] 20The shepherds returned, glo-
rifying and praising God[b] for all the
things they had heard and seen, which
were just as they had been told.
21On the eighth day, when it was time
to circumcise him,[c] he was named Jesus,
the name the angel had given him
before he had been conceived.[d]
22When the time of their purification
according to the Law of Moses[e] had
been completed, Joseph and Mary took
him to Jerusalem to present him to the
Lord 23(as it is written in the Law of
the Lord, "Every firstborn male is to be
consecrated to the Lord"[f]),[f] 24and to
offer a sacrifice in keeping with what
is said in the Law of the Lord: "a pair
of doves or two young pigeons."[g][g]

Simeon praises God when he sees Jesus.

25Now there was a man in Jerusalem
called Simeon, who was righteous and
devout.[h] He was waiting for the consolation of Israel,[i] and the Holy Spirit was
upon him. 26It had been revealed to him
by the Holy Spirit that he would not die
before he had seen the Lord's Christ.
27Moved by the Spirit, he went into
the temple courts. When the parents
brought in the child Jesus to do for him
what the custom of the Law required,[j] 28Simeon took him in his arms
and praised God, saying:

29"Sovereign Lord, as you have
promised,[k]
you now dismiss[h] your servant in
peace.[l]

2:19 [a]ver 51
2:20 [b]Mt 9:8
2:21 [c]Lk 1:59 [d]Lk 1:31
2:22 [e]Lev 12:2-8
2:23 [f]Ex 13:2,12, 15; Nu 3:13
2:24 [g]Lev 12:8
2:25 [h]Lk 1:6 [i]ver 38; Isa 52:9; Lk 23:51
2:27 [j]ver 22
2:29 [k]ver 26 [l]Ac 2:24
2:30 [m]Isa 52:10; Lk 3:6
2:32 [n]Isa 42:6; 49:6; Ac 13:47; 26:23
2:34 [o]Mt 12:46 [p]Isa 8:14; Mt 21:44; 1Co 1:23; 2Co 2:16; 1Pe 2:7,8
2:36 [q]Ac 21:9
2:37 [r]1Ti 5:9 [s]Ac 13:3; 14:23; 1Ti 5:5
2:38 [t]ver 25; Isa 40:2; Lk 1:68; 24:21
2:39 [u]ver 51; Mt 2:23
2:40 [v]ver 52; Lk 1:80
2:41 [w]Ex 23:15; Dt 16:1-8

30For my eyes have seen your
salvation,[m]
31 which you have prepared in the
sight of all people,
32a light for revelation to the Gentiles
and for glory to your people Israel."[n]

33The child's father and mother marveled at what was said about him.
34Then Simeon blessed them and said
to Mary, his mother:[o] "This child is destined to cause the falling[p] and rising of
many in Israel, and to be a sign that will
be spoken against, 35so that the thoughts
of many hearts will be revealed. And a
sword will pierce your own soul too."

Anna testifies of Jesus.

36There was also a prophetess,[q] Anna,
the daughter of Phanuel, of the tribe of
Asher. She was very old; she had lived
with her husband seven years after her
marriage, 37and then was a widow until
she was eighty-four.[i][r] She never left the
temple but worshiped night and day, fasting and praying.[s] 38Coming up to them
at that very moment, she gave thanks to
God and spoke about the child to all who
were looking forward to the redemption of Jerusalem.[t]
39When Joseph and Mary had done
everything required by the Law of the
Lord, they returned to Galilee to their
own town of Nazareth.[u] 40And the child
grew and became strong; he was filled
with wisdom, and the grace of God was
upon him.[v]

Twelve-year-old Jesus amazes the teachers.

41Every year his parents went to Jerusalem for the Feast of the Passover.[w]
42When he was twelve years old, they
went up to the Feast, according to the
custom. 43After the Feast was over,
while his parents were returning home,
the boy Jesus stayed behind in Jerusalem, but they were unaware of it.
44Thinking he was in their company,

[f]*23* Exodus 13:2,12 [g]*24* Lev. 12:8 [h]*29* Or *promised, / now dismiss* [i]*37* Or *widow for eighty-four years*

they traveled on for a day. Then they began looking for him among their relatives and friends. 45When they did not find him, they went back to Jerusalem to look for him. 46After three days they found him in the temple courts, sitting among the teachers, listening to them and asking them questions. 47Everyone who heard him was amazed[a] at his understanding and his answers. 48When his parents saw him, they were astonished. His mother[b] said to him, "Son, why have you treated us like this? Your father[c] and I have been anxiously searching for you."

49"Why were you searching for me?" he asked. "Didn't you know I had to be in my Father's house?"[d] 50But they did not understand what he was saying to them.[e]

51Then he went down to Nazareth with them[f] and was obedient to them. But his mother treasured all these things in her heart.[g] 52And Jesus grew in wisdom and stature, and in favor with God and men.[h]

John the Baptist preaches repentance.

3:2-10pp— Mt 3:1-10; Mk 1:3-5
3:16,17pp— Mt 3:11,12; Mk 1:7,8

3 In the fifteenth year of the reign of Tiberius Caesar—when Pontius Pilate[i] was governor of Judea, Herod[j] tetrarch of Galilee, his brother Philip tetrarch of Iturea and Traconitis, and Lysanias tetrarch of Abilene— 2during the high priesthood of Annas and Caiaphas,[k] the word of God came to John[l] son of Zechariah[m] in the desert. 3He went into all the country around the Jordan, preaching a baptism of repentance for the forgiveness of sins.[n] 4As is written in the book of the words of Isaiah the prophet:

"A voice of one calling in the desert,
'Prepare the way for the Lord,
make straight paths for him.
5Every valley shall be filled in,
every mountain and hill made low.
The crooked roads shall become straight,
the rough ways smooth.
6And all mankind will see God's salvation.' "[j][o]

7John said to the crowds coming out to be baptized by him, "You brood of vipers![p] Who warned you to flee from the coming wrath?[q] 8Produce fruit in keeping with repentance. And do not begin to say to yourselves, 'We have Abraham as our father.'[r] For I tell you that out of these stones God can raise up children for Abraham. 9The ax is already at the root of the trees, and every tree that does not produce good fruit will be cut down and thrown into the fire."[s]

10"What should we do then?"[t] the crowd asked.

11John answered, "The man with two tunics should share with him who has none, and the one who has food should do the same."[u]

12Tax collectors also came to be baptized.[v] "Teacher," they asked, "what should we do?"

13"Don't collect any more than you are required to,"[w] he told them.

14Then some soldiers asked him, "And what should we do?"

He replied, "Don't extort money and don't accuse people falsely[x]—be content with your pay."

15The people were waiting expectantly and were all wondering in their hearts if John[y] might possibly be the Christ.[k][z] 16John answered them all, "I baptize you with[l] water.[a] But one more powerful than I will come, the thongs of whose sandals I am not worthy to untie. He will baptize you with the Holy Spirit and with fire.[b] 17His winnowing fork[c] is in his hand to clear his threshing floor and to gather the wheat into his barn, but he will burn up the chaff with unquenchable fire."[d] 18And with many other words John exhorted

2:47 [a]Mt 7:28
2:48 [b]Mt 12:46 [c]Lk 3:23; 4:22
2:49 [d]Jn 2:16
2:50 [e]Mk 9:32
2:51 [f]ver 39; Mt 2:23 [g]ver 19
2:52 [h]ver 40; 1Sa 2:26; Lk 1:80
3:1 [i]Mt 27:2 [j]Mt 14:1
3:2 [k]Mt 26:3; Jn 18:13; Ac 4:6 [l]Mt 3:1 [m]Lk 1:13
3:3 [n]ver 16; Mk 1:4
3:6 [o]Isa 40:3-5; Ps 98:2; Isa 42:16; 52:10; Lk 2:30
3:7 [p]Mt 12:34; 23:33 [q]Ro 1:18
3:8 [r]Isa 51:2; Lk 19:9; Jn 8:33,39; Ac 13:26; Ro 4:1,11,12, 16,17; Gal 3:7
3:9 [s]Mt 3:10
3:10 [t]ver 12,14; Ac 2:37; 16:30
3:11 [u]Isa 58:7
3:12 [v]Lk 7:29
3:13 [w]Lk 19:8
3:14 [x]Ex 23:1; Lev 19:11
3:15 [y]Mt 3:1 [z]Jn 1:19,20; Ac 13:25

3:16 [a]ver 3; Mk 1:4 [b]Jn 1:26,33; Ac 1:5; 11:16; 19:4 **3:17** [c]Isa 30:24 [d]Mt 13:30; 25:41

j*6* Isaiah 40:3-5 k*15* Or *Messiah* l*16* Or *in*

the people and preached the good news to them.

19But when John rebuked Herod[a] the tetrarch because of Herodias, his brother's wife, and all the other evil things he had done, 20Herod added this to them all: He locked John up in prison.[b]

Jesus' baptism and genealogy.

3:21,22pp— Mt 3:13-17; Mk 1:9-11
3:23-38pp— Mt 1:1-17

21When all the people were being baptized, Jesus was baptized too. And as he was praying,[c] heaven was opened 22and the Holy Spirit descended on him[d] in bodily form like a dove. And a voice came from heaven: "You are my Son,[e] whom I love; with you I am well pleased."[f]

23Now Jesus himself was about thirty years old when he began his ministry.[g] He was the son, so it was thought, of Joseph,[h]

the son of Heli, 24the son of Matthat,
the son of Levi, the son of Melki,
the son of Jannai, the son of Joseph,
25the son of Mattathias, the son of Amos,
the son of Nahum, the son of Esli,
the son of Naggai, 26the son of Maath,
the son of Mattathias, the son of Semein,
the son of Josech, the son of Joda,
27the son of Joanan, the son of Rhesa,
the son of Zerubbabel,[i] the son of Shealtiel,
the son of Neri, 28the son of Melki,
the son of Addi, the son of Cosam,
the son of Elmadam, the son of Er,
29the son of Joshua, the son of Eliezer,
the son of Jorim, the son of Matthat,
the son of Levi, 30the son of Simeon,
the son of Judah, the son of Joseph,
the son of Jonam, the son of Eliakim,
31the son of Melea, the son of Menna,
the son of Mattatha, the son of Nathan,[j]
the son of David, 32the son of Jesse,
the son of Obed, the son of Boaz,

3:19 [a]ver 1
3:20 [b]Mt 14:3,4; Mk 6:17-18
3:21 [c]Mt 14:23; Mk 1:35; 6:46; Lk 5:16; 6:12; 9:18,28; 11:1
3:22 [d]Isa 42:1; Jn 1:32,33; Ac 10:38 [e]Mt 3:17 [f]Mt 3:17
3:23 [g]Mt 4:17; Ac 1:1 [h]Lk 1:27
3:27 [i]Mt 1:12
3:31 [j]2Sa 5:14; 1Ch 3:5
3:33 [k]Ru 4:18-22; 1Ch 2:10-12
3:34 [l]Ge 11:24,26
3:36 [m]Ge 11:12 [n]Ge 5:28-32
3:38 [o]Ge 5:1,2,6-9
4:1 [p]ver 14,18 [q]Lk 3:3,21 [r]Lk 2:27
4:2 [s]Ex 34:28; 1Ki 19:8
4:4 [t]Dt 8:3
4:5 [u]Mt 24:14
4:6 [v]Jn 12:31; 14:30; 1Jn 5:19

the son of Salmon,[m] the son of Nahshon,
33the son of Amminadab, the son of Ram,[n]
the son of Hezron, the son of Perez,[k]
the son of Judah, 34the son of Jacob,
the son of Isaac, the son of Abraham,
the son of Terah, the son of Nahor,[l]
35the son of Serug, the son of Reu,
the son of Peleg, the son of Eber,
the son of Shelah, 36the son of Cainan,
the son of Arphaxad,[m] the son of Shem,
the son of Noah, the son of Lamech,[n]
37the son of Methuselah, the son of Enoch,
the son of Jared, the son of Mahalalel,
the son of Kenan, 38the son of Enosh,
the son of Seth, the son of Adam,
the son of God.[o]

The devil tempts Jesus.

4:1-13pp— Mt 4:1-11; Mk 1:12,13

4 Jesus, full of the Holy Spirit,[p] returned from the Jordan[q] and was led by the Spirit[r] in the desert, 2where for forty days[s] he was tempted by the devil. He ate nothing during those days, and at the end of them he was hungry.

3The devil said to him, "If you are the Son of God, tell this stone to become bread."

4Jesus answered, "It is written: 'Man does not live on bread alone.'[o]"[t]

5The devil led him up to a high place and showed him in an instant all the kingdoms of the world.[u] 6And he said to him, "I will give you all their authority and splendor, for it has been given to me,[v] and I can give it to anyone I want to. 7So if you worship me, it will all be yours."

[m]*32* Some early manuscripts *Sala* [n]*33* Some manuscripts *Amminadab, the son of Admin, the son of Arni*; other manuscripts vary widely. [o]*4* Deut. 8:3

8 Jesus answered, "It is written: 'Worship the Lord your God and serve him
only.'[p]"[a]
9 The devil led him to Jerusalem and
had him stand on the highest point of
the temple. "If you are the Son of God,"
he said, "throw yourself down from here.
10 For it is written:

"'He will command his angels
concerning you
to guard you carefully;
11 they will lift you up in their hands,
so that you will not strike your foot
against a stone.'[q]"[b]

12 Jesus answered, "It says: 'Do not
put the Lord your God to the test.'[r]"[c]
13 When the devil had finished all this
tempting,[d] he left him[e] until an opportune time.

Nazareth rejects Jesus.

14 Jesus returned to Galilee[f] in the
power of the Spirit, and news about him
spread through the whole countryside.[g]
15 He taught in their synagogues,[h] and
everyone praised him.
16 He went to Nazareth,[i] where he had
been brought up, and on the Sabbath day
he went into the synagogue,[j] as was his
custom. And he stood up to read. 17 The
scroll of the prophet Isaiah was handed
to him. Unrolling it, he found the place
where it is written:

18 "The Spirit of the Lord is on me,[k]
because he has anointed me
to preach good news to the poor.
He has sent me to proclaim freedom
for the prisoners
and recovery of sight for the blind,
to release the oppressed,
19 to proclaim the year of the Lord's
favor."[s][l]

20 Then he rolled up the scroll, gave it
back to the attendant and sat down.[m]
The eyes of everyone in the synagogue
were fastened on him, 21 and he began
by saying to them, "Today this scripture
is fulfilled in your hearing."
22 All spoke well of him and were
amazed at the gracious words that came
from his lips. "Isn't this Joseph's son?"
they asked.[n]
23 Jesus said to them, "Surely you will
quote this proverb to me: 'Physician,
heal yourself! Do here in your hometown[o] what we have heard that you
did in Capernaum.'"[p]
24 "I tell you the truth," he continued,
"no prophet is accepted in his hometown.[q] 25 I assure you that there were
many widows in Israel in Elijah's time,
when the sky was shut for three and a
half years and there was a severe famine
throughout the land.[r] 26 Yet Elijah was
not sent to any of them, but to a widow in Zarephath in the region of Sidon.[s]
27 And there were many in Israel with
leprosy[t] in the time of Elisha the
prophet, yet not one of them was
cleansed—only Naaman the Syrian."[t]
28 All the people in the synagogue
were furious when they heard this.
29 They got up, drove him out of the
town,[u] and took him to the brow of the
hill on which the town was built, in
order to throw him down the cliff. 30 But
he walked right through the crowd and
went on his way.[v]

Jesus drives demon from a man.

4:31-37pp— Mk 1:21-28

31 Then he went down to Capernaum,[w] a town in Galilee, and on the
Sabbath began to teach the people.
32 They were amazed at his teaching,[x]
because his message had authority.[y]
33 In the synagogue there was a man
possessed by a demon, an evil[u] spirit.
He cried out at the top of his voice,
34 "Ha! What do you want with us,[z]
Jesus of Nazareth?[a] Have you come to
destroy us? I know who you are[b]—the
Holy One of God!"[c]
35 "Be quiet!" Jesus said sternly.[d] "Come
out of him!" Then the demon threw the

4:8 [a]Dt 6:13
4:11 [b]Ps 91:11,12
4:12 [c]Dt 6:16
4:13 [d]Heb 4:15 [e]Jn 14:30
4:14 [f]Mt 4:12 [g]Mt 9:26
4:15 [h]Mt 4:23
4:16 [i]Mt 2:23 [j]Mt 13:54
4:18 [k]Jn 3:34
4:19 [l]Isa 61:1,2; Lev 25:10
4:20 [m]ver 17; Mt 26:55
4:22 [n]Mt 13:54,55; Jn 6:42; 7:15
4:23 [o]ver 16 [p]Mk 1:21-28; 2:1-12
4:24 [q]Mt 13:57; Jn 4:44
4:25 [r]1Ki 17:1; 18:1; Jas 5:17,18
4:26 [s]1Ki 17:8-16; Mt 11:21
4:27 [t]2Ki 5:1-14
4:29 [u]Nu 15:35; Ac 7:58; Heb 13:12
4:30 [v]Jn 8:59; 10:39
4:31 [w]ver 23; Mt 4:13
4:32 [x]Mt 7:28 [y]ver 36; Mt 7:29
4:34 [z]Mt 8:29 [a]Mk 1:24 [b]Jas 2:19 [c]ver 41; Mk 1:24
4:35 [d]ver 39,41; Mt 8:26; Lk 8:24

p*8* Deut. 6:13 q*11* Psalm 91:11,12
r*12* Deut. 6:16 s*19* Isaiah 61:1,2 t*27* The Greek word was used for various diseases affecting the skin—not necessarily leprosy. u*33* Greek *unclean*; also in verse 36

man down before them all and came out without injuring him.

36 All the people were amazed[a] and said to each other, "What is this teaching? With authority[b] and power he gives orders to evil spirits and they come out!" 37 And the news about him spread throughout the surrounding area.[c]

Jesus heals Peter's mother-in-law.

4:38-41pp— Mt 8:14-17
4:38-43pp— Mk 1:29-38

38 Jesus left the synagogue and went to the home of Simon. Now Simon's mother-in-law was suffering from a high fever, and they asked Jesus to help her. 39 So he bent over her and rebuked[d] the fever, and it left her. She got up at once and began to wait on them.

40 When the sun was setting, the people brought to Jesus all who had various kinds of sickness, and laying his hands on each one,[e] he healed them.[f] 41 Moreover, demons came out of many people, shouting, "You are the Son of God!"[g] But he rebuked[h] them and would not allow them to speak,[i] because they knew he was the Christ.[v]

42 At daybreak Jesus went out to a solitary place. The people were looking for him and when they came to where he was, they tried to keep him from leaving them. 43 But he said, "I must preach the good news of the kingdom of God[j] to the other towns also, because that is why I was sent." 44 And he kept on preaching in the synagogues of Judea.[w][k]

Jesus calls four fishermen to follow.

5:1-11pp— Mt 4:18-22; Mk 1:16-20; Jn 1:40-42

5 One day as Jesus was standing by the Lake of Gennesaret,[x] with the people crowding around him and listening to the word of God,[l] 2 he saw at the water's edge two boats, left there by the fishermen, who were washing their nets. 3 He got into one of the boats, the one belonging to Simon, and asked him to put out a little from shore. Then he sat down and taught the people from the boat.[m]

4 When he had finished speaking, he said to Simon, "Put out into deep water, and let down[y] the nets for a catch."[n]

5 Simon answered, "Master,[o] we've worked hard all night and haven't caught anything.[p] But because you say so, I will let down the nets."

6 When they had done so, they caught such a large number of fish that their nets began to break.[q] 7 So they signaled their partners in the other boat to come and help them, and they came and filled both boats so full that they began to sink.

8 When Simon Peter saw this, he fell at Jesus' knees and said, "Go away from me, Lord; I am a sinful man!"[r] 9 For he and all his companions were astonished at the catch of fish they had taken, 10 and so were James and John, the sons of Zebedee, Simon's partners.

Then Jesus said to Simon, "Don't be afraid;[s] from now on you will catch men." 11 So they pulled their boats up on shore, left everything and followed him.[t]

Jesus cleanses a man with leprosy.

5:12-14pp— Mt 8:2-4; Mk 1:40-44

12 While Jesus was in one of the towns, a man came along who was covered with leprosy.[z][u] When he saw Jesus, he fell with his face to the ground and begged him, "Lord, if you are willing, you can make me clean."

13 Jesus reached out his hand and touched the man. "I am willing," he said. "Be clean!" And immediately the leprosy left him.

14 Then Jesus ordered him, "Don't tell anyone,[v] but go, show yourself to the priest and offer the sacrifices that Moses commanded[w] for your cleansing, as a testimony to them."

15 Yet the news about him spread all the more,[x] so that crowds of people came to hear him and to be healed of their sicknesses. 16 But Jesus often withdrew to lonely places and prayed.[y]

4:36 [a]Mt 7:28 [b]ver 32; Mt 7:29; Mt 10:1
4:37 [c]ver 14; Mt 9:26
4:39 [d]ver 35,41
4:40 [e]Mk 5:23 [f]Mt 4:23
4:41 [g]Mt 4:3 [h]ver 35 [i]Mt 8:4
4:43 [j]Mt 3:2
4:44 [k]Mt 4:23
5:1 [l]Mk 4:14; Heb 4:12
5:3 [m]Mt 13:2
5:4 [n]Jn 21:6
5:5 [o]Lk 8:24,45; 9:33,49; 17:13 [p]Jn 21:3
5:6 [q]Jn 21:11
5:8 [r]Ge 18:27; Job 42:6; Isa 6:5
5:10 [s]Mt 14:27
5:11 [t]ver 28; Mt 4:19
5:12 [u]Mt 8:2
5:14 [v]Mt 8:4 [w]Lev 14:2-32
5:15 [x]Mt 9:26
5:16 [y]Mt 14:23; Lk 3:21

v*41* Or *Messiah* w*44* Or *the land of the Jews*; some manuscripts *Galilee* x*1* That is, Sea of Galilee y*4* The Greek verb is plural. z*12* The Greek word was used for various diseases affecting the skin—not necessarily leprosy.

Jesus heals a paralytic.

5:18-26pp— Mt 9:2-8; Mk 2:3-12

17One day as he was teaching, Pharisees and teachers of the law,[a] who had come from every village of Galilee and from Judea and Jerusalem, were sitting there. And the power of the Lord was present for him to heal the sick.[b] 18Some men came carrying a paralytic on a mat and tried to take him into the house to lay him before Jesus. 19When they could not find a way to do this because of the crowd, they went up on the roof and lowered him on his mat through the tiles into the middle of the crowd, right in front of Jesus.

20When Jesus saw their faith, he said, "Friend, your sins are forgiven."[c]

21The Pharisees and the teachers of the law began thinking to themselves, "Who is this fellow who speaks blasphemy? Who can forgive sins but God alone?"[d]

22Jesus knew what they were thinking and asked, "Why are you thinking these things in your hearts? 23Which is easier: to say, 'Your sins are forgiven,' or to say, 'Get up and walk'? 24But that you may know that the Son of Man[e] has authority on earth to forgive sins. . . ." He said to the paralyzed man, "I tell you, get up, take your mat and go home." 25Immediately he stood up in front of them, took what he had been lying on and went home praising God. 26Everyone was amazed and gave praise to God.[f] They were filled with awe and said, "We have seen remarkable things today."

Jesus calls Levi (Matthew).

5:27-32pp— Mt 9:9-13; Mk 2:14-17

27After this, Jesus went out and saw a tax collector by the name of Levi sitting at his tax booth. "Follow me,"[g] Jesus said to him, 28and Levi got up, left everything and followed him.[h]

29Then Levi held a great banquet for Jesus at his house, and a large crowd of tax collectors[i] and others were eating with them. 30But the Pharisees and the teachers of the law who belonged to their sect[j] complained to his disciples, "Why do you eat and drink with tax collectors and 'sinners'?"[k]

31Jesus answered them, "It is not the healthy who need a doctor, but the sick. 32I have not come to call the righteous, but sinners to repentance."[l]

Jesus is questioned about fasting.

5:33-39pp— Mt 9:14-17; Mk 2:18-22

33They said to him, "John's disciples[m] often fast and pray, and so do the disciples of the Pharisees, but yours go on eating and drinking."

34Jesus answered, "Can you make the guests of the bridegroom[n] fast while he is with them? 35But the time will come when the bridegroom will be taken from them;[o] in those days they will fast."

36He told them this parable: "No one tears a patch from a new garment and sews it on an old one. If he does, he will have torn the new garment, and the patch from the new will not match the old. 37And no one pours new wine into old wineskins. If he does, the new wine will burst the skins, the wine will run out and the wineskins will be ruined. 38No, new wine must be poured into new wineskins. 39And no one after drinking old wine wants the new, for he says, 'The old is better.'"

Sabbath teachings.

6:1-11pp— Mt 12:1-14; Mk 2:23–3:6

6 One Sabbath Jesus was going through the grainfields, and his disciples began to pick some heads of grain, rub them in their hands and eat the kernels.[p] 2Some of the Pharisees asked, "Why are you doing what is unlawful on the Sabbath?"[q]

3Jesus answered them, "Have you never read what David did when he and his companions were hungry?[r] 4He entered the house of God, and taking the consecrated bread, he ate what is lawful only for priests to eat.[s]

5:17 [a]Mt 15:1; Lk 2:46 [b]Mk 5:30; Lk 6:19
5:20 [c]Lk 7:48,49
5:21 [d]Isa 43:25
5:24 [e]Mt 8:20
5:26 [f]Mt 9:8
5:27 [g]Mt 4:19
5:28 [h]ver 11; Mt 4:19
5:29 [i]Lk 15:1
5:30 [j]Ac 23:9 [k]Mt 9:11
5:32 [l]Jn 3:17
5:33 [m]Lk 7:18; Jn 1:35; 3:25,26
5:34 [n]Jn 3:29
5:35 [o]Lk 9:22; 17:22; Jn 16:5-7
6:1 [p]Dt 23:25
6:2 [q]Mt 12:2
6:3 [r]1Sa 21:6
6:4 [s]Lev 24:5,9

And he also gave some to his companions." 5Then Jesus said to them, "The Son of Man[a] is Lord of the Sabbath."

6On another Sabbath[b] he went into the synagogue and was teaching, and a man was there whose right hand was shriveled. 7The Pharisees and the teachers of the law were looking for a reason to accuse Jesus, so they watched him closely[c] to see if he would heal on the Sabbath.[d] 8But Jesus knew what they were thinking[e] and said to the man with the shriveled hand, "Get up and stand in front of everyone." So he got up and stood there.

9Then Jesus said to them, "I ask you, which is lawful on the Sabbath: to do good or to do evil, to save life or to destroy it?"

10He looked around at them all, and then said to the man, "Stretch out your hand." He did so, and his hand was completely restored. 11But they were furious[f] and began to discuss with one another what they might do to Jesus.

Selection of the twelve apostles.

6:13-16pp— Mt 10:2-4; Mk 3:16-19; Ac 1:13

12One of those days Jesus went out to a mountainside to pray, and spent the night praying to God.[g] 13When morning came, he called his disciples to him and chose twelve of them, whom he also designated apostles:[h] 14Simon (whom he named Peter), his brother Andrew, James, John, Philip, Bartholomew, 15Matthew,[i] Thomas, James son of Alphaeus, Simon who was called the Zealot, 16Judas son of James, and Judas Iscariot, who became a traitor.

Healing and teaching the crowds.

6:20-23pp— Mt 5:3-12

17He went down with them and stood on a level place. A large crowd of his disciples was there and a great number of people from all over Judea, from Jerusalem, and from the coast of Tyre and Sidon,[j] 18who had come to hear him and to be healed of their diseases. Those troubled by evil[a] spirits were cured, 19and the people all tried to touch him,[k] because power was coming from him and healing them all.[l]

20Looking at his disciples, he said:

"Blessed are you who are poor,
for yours is the kingdom of God.[m]
21Blessed are you who hunger now,
for you will be satisfied.[n]
Blessed are you who weep now,
for you will laugh.[o]
22Blessed are you when men hate you,
when they exclude you[p] and insult you[q]
and reject your name as evil,
because of the Son of Man.[r]

23"Rejoice in that day and leap for joy,[s] because great is your reward in heaven. For that is how their fathers treated the prophets.[t]

24"But woe to you who are rich,[u]
for you have already received your comfort.[v]
25Woe to you who are well fed now,
for you will go hungry.[w]
Woe to you who laugh now,
for you will mourn and weep.[x]
26Woe to you when all men speak well of you,
for that is how their fathers treated the false prophets.[y]

Love for enemies.

6:29,30pp— Mt 5:39-42

27"But I tell you who hear me: Love your enemies, do good to those who hate you,[z] 28bless those who curse you, pray for those who mistreat you.[a] 29If someone strikes you on one cheek, turn to him the other also. If someone takes your cloak, do not stop him from taking your tunic. 30Give to everyone who asks you, and if anyone takes what belongs to you, do not demand it back.[b] 31Do to others as you would have them do to you.[c]

32"If you love those who love you, what credit is that to you?[d] Even 'sinners'

6:5 [a]Mt 8:20
6:6 [b]ver 1
6:7 [c]Mt 12:10 [d]Mt 12:2
6:8 [e]Mt 9:4
6:11 [f]Jn 5:18
6:12 [g]Lk 3:21
6:13 [h]Mk 6:30
6:15 [i]Mt 9:9
6:17 [j]Mt 4:25; Mt 11:21; Mk 3:7,8
6:19 [k]Mt 9:20 [l]Mt 14:36; Mk 5:30; Lk 5:17
6:20 [m]Mt 25:34
6:21 [n]Isa 55:1,2; Mt 5:6 [o]Isa 61:2,3; Mt 5:4; Rev 7:17
6:22 [p]Jn 9:22; 16:2 [q]Isa 51:7 [r]Jn 15:21
6:23 [s]Mt 5:12 [t]Mt 5:12
6:24 [u]Jas 5:1 [v]Lk 16:25
6:25 [w]Isa 65:13 [x]Pr 14:13
6:26 [y]Mt 7:15
6:27 [z]ver 35; Mt 5:44; Ro 12:20
6:28 [a]Mt 5:44
6:30 [b]Dt 15:7,8, 10; Pr 21:26
6:31 [c]Mt 7:12
6:32 [d]Mt 5:46

a *18* Greek *unclean*

love those who love them. 33And if you do good to those who are good to you, what credit is that to you? Even 'sinners' do that. 34And if you lend to those from whom you expect repayment, what credit is that to you?[a] Even 'sinners' lend to 'sinners,' expecting to be repaid in full. 35But love your enemies, do good to them,[b] and lend to them without expecting to get anything back. Then your reward will be great, and you will be sons[c] of the Most High,[d] because he is kind to the ungrateful and wicked. 36Be merciful,[e] just as your Father[f] is merciful.

Judging others.

6:37-42pp— Mt 7:1-5

37"Do not judge, and you will not be judged.[g] Do not condemn, and you will not be condemned. Forgive, and you will be forgiven.[h] 38Give, and it will be given to you. A good measure, pressed down, shaken together and running over, will be poured into your lap.[i] For with the measure you use, it will be measured to you."[j]

39He also told them this parable: "Can a blind man lead a blind man? Will they not both fall into a pit?[k] 40A student is not above his teacher, but everyone who is fully trained will be like his teacher.[l]

41"Why do you look at the speck of sawdust in your brother's eye and pay no attention to the plank in your own eye? 42How can you say to your brother, 'Brother, let me take the speck out of your eye,' when you yourself fail to see the plank in your own eye? You hypocrite, first take the plank out of your eye, and then you will see clearly to remove the speck from your brother's eye.

A tree and its fruit.

6:43,44pp— Mt 7:16,18,20

43"No good tree bears bad fruit, nor does a bad tree bear good fruit. 44Each tree is recognized by its own fruit.[m] People do not pick figs from thornbushes, or grapes from briers. 45The good man brings good things out of the good stored up in his heart, and the evil man brings evil things out of the evil stored up in his heart. For out of the overflow of his heart his mouth speaks.[n]

The wise and foolish builders.

6:47-49pp— Mt 7:24-27

46"Why do you call me, 'Lord, Lord,'[o] and do not do what I say?[p] 47I will show you what he is like who comes to me and hears my words and puts them into practice.[q] 48He is like a man building a house, who dug down deep and laid the foundation on rock. When a flood came, the torrent struck that house but could not shake it, because it was well built. 49But the one who hears my words and does not put them into practice is like a man who built a house on the ground without a foundation. The moment the torrent struck that house, it collapsed and its destruction was complete."

Jesus heals a centurion's servant.

7:1-10pp— Mt 8:5-13

7 When Jesus had finished saying all this[r] in the hearing of the people, he entered Capernaum. 2There a centurion's servant, whom his master valued highly, was sick and about to die. 3The centurion heard of Jesus and sent some elders of the Jews to him, asking him to come and heal his servant. 4When they came to Jesus, they pleaded earnestly with him, "This man deserves to have you do this, 5because he loves our nation and has built our synagogue." 6So Jesus went with them.

He was not far from the house when the centurion sent friends to say to him: "Lord, don't trouble yourself, for I do not deserve to have you come under my roof. 7That is why I did not even consider myself worthy to come to you. But say the word, and my servant will be healed.[s] 8For I myself am a man under authority, with soldiers under me. I tell this one, 'Go,' and he goes; and

6:34 [a]Mt 5:42
6:35 [b]ver 27 [c]Ro 8:14 [d]Mk 5:7
6:36 [e]Jas 2:13 [f]Mt 5:48; 6:1; Lk 11:2; 12:32; Ro 8:15; Eph 4:6; 1Pe 1:17; 1Jn 1:3; 3:1
6:37 [g]Mt 7:1 [h]Mt 6:14
6:38 [i]Ps 79:12; Isa 65:6,7 [j]Mt 7:2; Mk 4:24
6:39 [k]Mt 15:14
6:40 [l]Mt 10:24; Jn 13:16
6:44 [m]Mt 12:33
6:45 [n]Pr 4:23; Mt 12:34,35; Mk 7:20
6:46 [o]Jn 13:13 [p]Mal 1:6; Mt 7:21
6:47 [q]Lk 8:21; 11:28; Jas 1:22-25
7:1 [r]Mt 7:28
7:7 [s]Ps 107:20

that one, 'Come,' and he comes. I say to
my servant, 'Do this,' and he does it."
9When Jesus heard this, he was
amazed at him, and turning to the crowd
following him, he said, "I tell you, I
have not found such great faith even
in Israel." 10Then the men who had
been sent returned to the house and
found the servant well.

Jesus raises a widow's dead son.

7:11-16Ref— 1Ki 17:17-24; 2Ki 4:32-37; Mk 5:21-24,35-43; Jn 11:1-44

11Soon afterward, Jesus went to a
town called Nain, and his disciples and
a large crowd went along with him. 12As
he approached the town gate, a dead
person was being carried out—the only
son of his mother, and she was a widow. And a large crowd from the town
was with her. 13When the Lord[a] saw
her, his heart went out to her and he
said, "Don't cry."

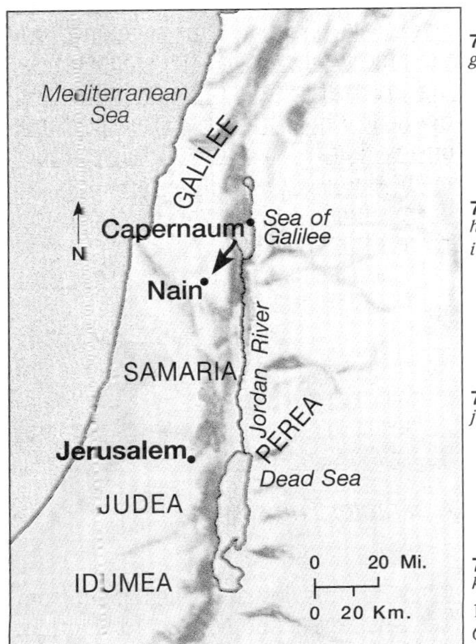

Jesus Raises a Widow's Son

Jesus traveled to Nain and met a funeral procession leaving the village. A widow's only son had died, leaving her virtually helpless, but Jesus brought the young man back to life. This miracle, recorded only in Luke, reveals Jesus' compassion for people's needs.

7:13 [a]ver 19; Lk 10:1; 13:15; 17:5; 22:61; 24:34; Jn 11:2
7:14 [b]Mt 9:25; Mk 1:31; Lk 8:54; Jn 11:43; Ac 9:40
7:16 [c]Lk 1:65 [d]Mt 9:8 [e]ver 39; Mt 21:11 [f]Lk 1:68
7:17 [g]Mt 9:26
7:18 [h]Mt 3:1 [i]Lk 5:33
7:21 [j]Mt 4:23
7:22 [k]Isa 29:18, 19; 35:5,6; 61:1,2; Lk 4:18
7:26 [l]Mt 11:9

14Then he went up and touched the
coffin, and those carrying it stood still.
He said, "Young man, I say to you, get
up!"[b] 15The dead man sat up and began
to talk, and Jesus gave him back to his
mother.
16They were all filled with awe[c] and
praised God.[d] "A great prophet[e] has
appeared among us," they said. "God has
come to help his people."[f] 17This news
about Jesus spread throughout Judea[b]
and the surrounding country.[g]

Jesus upholds John the Baptist's ministry.

7:18–35pp— Mt 11:2-19

18John's[h] disciples[i] told him about all
these things. Calling two of them, 19he
sent them to the Lord to ask, "Are you
the one who was to come, or should we
expect someone else?"
20When the men came to Jesus, they
said, "John the Baptist sent us to you to
ask, 'Are you the one who was to come,
or should we expect someone else?'"
21At that very time Jesus cured many
who had diseases, sicknesses[j] and evil
spirits, and gave sight to many who were
blind. 22So he replied to the messengers,
"Go back and report to John what you
have seen and heard: The blind receive
sight, the lame walk, those who have
leprosy[c] are cured, the deaf hear, the
dead are raised, and the good news is
preached to the poor.[k] 23Blessed is the
man who does not fall away on account
of me."
24After John's messengers left, Jesus
began to speak to the crowd about John:
"What did you go out into the desert
to see? A reed swayed by the wind? 25If
not, what did you go out to see? A man
dressed in fine clothes? No, those who
wear expensive clothes and indulge in
luxury are in palaces. 26But what did
you go out to see? A prophet?[l] Yes, I tell
you, and more than a prophet. 27This
is the one about whom it is written:

[b]17 Or *the land of the Jews* [c]22 The Greek word was used for various diseases affecting the skin—not necessarily leprosy.

> "'I will send my messenger ahead of you,
> who will prepare your way before you.'[d][a]

28I tell you, among those born of women there is no one greater than John; yet the one who is least in the kingdom of God[b] is greater than he."

29(All the people, even the tax collectors, when they heard Jesus' words, acknowledged that God's way was right, because they had been baptized by John.[c] 30But the Pharisees and experts in the law[d] rejected God's purpose for themselves, because they had not been baptized by John.)

31"To what, then, can I compare the people of this generation? What are they like? 32They are like children sitting in the marketplace and calling out to each other:

> "'We played the flute for you,
> and you did not dance;
> we sang a dirge,
> and you did not cry.'

33For John the Baptist came neither eating bread nor drinking wine,[e] and you say, 'He has a demon.' 34The Son of Man came eating and drinking, and you say, 'Here is a glutton and a drunkard, a friend of tax collectors and "sinners."'[f] 35But wisdom is proved right by all her children."

Jesus forgives a sinful woman.

7:37-39Ref— Mt 26:6-13; Mk 14:3-9; Jn 12:1-8
7:41,42Ref— Mt 18:23-34

36Now one of the Pharisees invited Jesus to have dinner with him, so he went to the Pharisee's house and reclined at the table. 37When a woman who had lived a sinful life in that town learned that Jesus was eating at the Pharisee's house, she brought an alabaster jar of perfume, 38and as she stood behind him at his feet weeping, she began to wet his feet with her tears. Then she wiped them with her hair, kissed them and poured perfume on them.

39When the Pharisee who had invited him saw this, he said to himself, "If this man were a prophet,[g] he would know who is touching him and what kind of woman she is—that she is a sinner."

40Jesus answered him, "Simon, I have something to tell you."

"Tell me, teacher," he said.

41"Two men owed money to a certain moneylender. One owed him five hundred denarii,[e] and the other fifty. 42Neither of them had the money to pay him back, so he canceled the debts of both. Now which of them will love him more?"

43Simon replied, "I suppose the one who had the bigger debt canceled."

"You have judged correctly," Jesus said.

44Then he turned toward the woman and said to Simon, "Do you see this woman? I came into your house. You did not give me any water for my feet,[h] but she wet my feet with her tears and wiped them with her hair. 45You did not give me a kiss,[i] but this woman, from the time I entered, has not stopped kissing my feet. 46You did not put oil on my head,[j] but she has poured perfume on my feet. 47Therefore, I tell you, her many sins have been forgiven—for she loved much. But he who has been forgiven little loves little."

48Then Jesus said to her, "Your sins are forgiven."[k]

49The other guests began to say among themselves, "Who is this who even forgives sins?"

50Jesus said to the woman, "Your faith has saved you;[l] go in peace."[m]

A parable: The sower.

8:4-15pp— Mt 13:2-23; Mk 4:1-20

8 After this, Jesus traveled about from one town and village to another, proclaiming the good news of the kingdom of God.[n] The Twelve were with him, 2and also some women who had been cured of evil spirits and dis-

7:27 [a]Mal 3:1; Mt 11:10; Mk 1:2
7:28 [b]Mt 3:2
7:29 [c]Mt 21:32; Mk 1:5; Lk 3:12
7:30 [d]Mt 22:35
7:33 [e]Lk 1:15
7:34 [f]Lk 5:29,30; 15:1,2
7:39 [g]ver 16; Mt 21:11
7:44 [h]Ge 18:4; 19:2; 43:24; Jdg 19:21; Jn 13:4-14; 1Ti 5:10
7:45 [i]Lk 22:47,48; Ro 16:16
7:46 [j]Ps 23:5; Ecc 9:8
7:48 [k]Mt 9:2
7:50 [l]Mt 9:22; Mk 5:34; Lk 8:48 [m]Ac 15:33
8:1 [n]Mt 4:23

d*27* Mal. 3:1 e*41* A denarius was a coin worth about a day's wages.

eases: Mary (called Magdalene)[a] from whom seven demons had come out; 3Joanna the wife of Cuza, the manager of Herod's[b] household; Susanna; and many others. These women were helping to support them out of their own means.

4While a large crowd was gathering and people were coming to Jesus from town after town, he told this parable: 5"A farmer went out to sow his seed. As he was scattering the seed, some fell along the path; it was trampled on, and the birds of the air ate it up. 6Some fell on rock, and when it came up, the plants withered because they had no moisture. 7Other seed fell among thorns, which grew up with it and choked the plants. 8Still other seed fell on good soil. It came up and yielded a crop, a hundred times more than was sown."

When he said this, he called out, "He who has ears to hear, let him hear."[c]

9His disciples asked him what this parable meant. 10He said, "The knowledge of the secrets of the kingdom of God has been given to you,[d] but to others I speak in parables, so that,

"'though seeing, they may not see;
though hearing, they may not
understand.'[f][e]

11"This is the meaning of the parable: The seed is the word of God.[f] 12Those along the path are the ones who hear, and then the devil comes and takes away the word from their hearts, so that they may not believe and be saved. 13Those on the rock are the ones who receive the word with joy when they hear it, but they have no root. They believe for a while, but in the time of testing they fall away.[g] 14The seed that fell among thorns stands for those who hear, but as they go on their way they are choked by life's worries, riches[h] and pleasures, and they do not mature. 15But the seed on good soil stands for those with a noble and good heart, who hear the word, retain it, and by persevering produce a crop.

8:2 [a]Mt 27:55,56
8:3 [b]Mt 14:1
8:8 [c]Mt 11:15
8:10 [d]Mt 13:11 [e]Isa 6:9; Mt 13:13,14
8:11 [f]Heb 4:12
8:13 [g]Mt 11:6
8:14 [h]Mt 19:23; 1Ti 6:9,10,17
8:16 [i]Mt 5:15; Mk 4:21; Lk 11:33
8:17 [j]Mt 10:26; Mk 4:22; Lk 12:2
8:18 [k]Mt 13:12; 25:29; Lk 19:26
8:20 [l]Jn 7:5
8:21 [m]Lk 6:47; 11:28; Jn 14:21
8:24 [n]Lk 5:5 [o]Lk 4:35, 39,41 [p]Ps 107:29; Jnh 1:15

16"No one lights a lamp and hides it in a jar or puts it under a bed. Instead, he puts it on a stand, so that those who come in can see the light.[i] 17For there is nothing hidden that will not be disclosed, and nothing concealed that will not be known or brought out into the open.[j] 18Therefore consider carefully how you listen. Whoever has will be given more; whoever does not have, even what he thinks he has will be taken from him."[k]

Jesus identifies his mother and brothers.

8:19-21pp— Mt 12:46-50; Mk 3:31-35

19Now Jesus' mother and brothers came to see him, but they were not able to get near him because of the crowd. 20Someone told him, "Your mother and brothers[l] are standing outside, wanting to see you."

21He replied, "My mother and brothers are those who hear God's word and put it into practice."[m]

Jesus calms a storm at sea.

8:22-25pp— Mt 8:23-27; Mk 4:36-41
8:22-25Ref— Mk 6:47-52; Jn 6:16-21

22One day Jesus said to his disciples, "Let's go over to the other side of the lake." So they got into a boat and set out. 23As they sailed, he fell asleep. A squall came down on the lake, so that the boat was being swamped, and they were in great danger.

24The disciples went and woke him, saying, "Master, Master,[n] we're going to drown!"

He got up and rebuked[o] the wind and the raging waters; the storm subsided, and all was calm.[p] 25"Where is your faith?" he asked his disciples.

In fear and amazement they asked one another, "Who is this? He commands even the winds and the water, and they obey him."

[f]*10* Isaiah 6:9

Demons sent into herd of pigs.

8:26-37pp— Mt 8:28-34
8:26-39pp— Mk 5:1-20

26They sailed to the region of the Gerasenes,[g] which is across the lake from Galilee. 27When Jesus stepped ashore, he was met by a demon-possessed man from the town. For a long time this man had not worn clothes or lived in a house, but had lived in the tombs. 28When he saw Jesus, he cried out and fell at his feet, shouting at the top of his voice, "What do you want with me,[a] Jesus, Son of the Most High God?[b] I beg you, don't torture me!" 29For Jesus had commanded the evil[h] spirit to come out of the man. Many times it had seized him, and though he was chained hand and foot and kept under guard, he had broken his chains and had been driven by the demon into solitary places.

30Jesus asked him, "What is your name?"

"Legion," he replied, because many demons had gone into him. 31And they begged him repeatedly not to order them to go into the Abyss.[c]

32A large herd of pigs was feeding there on the hillside. The demons begged Jesus to let them go into them, and he gave them permission. 33When the demons came out of the man, they went into the pigs, and the herd rushed down the steep bank into the lake[d] and was drowned.

34When those tending the pigs saw what had happened, they ran off and reported this in the town and countryside, 35and the people went out to see what had happened. When they came to Jesus, they found the man from whom the demons had gone out, sitting at Jesus' feet,[e] dressed and in his right mind; and they were afraid. 36Those who had seen it told the people how the demon-possessed[f] man had been cured. 37Then all the people of the region of the Gerasenes asked Jesus to leave them,[g] because they were overcome with fear. So he got into the boat and left.

38The man from whom the demons had gone out begged to go with him, but Jesus sent him away, saying, 39"Return home and tell how much God has done for you." So the man went away and told all over town how much Jesus had done for him.

Jairus's daughter raised, and woman healed.

8:40-56pp— Mt 9:18-26; Mk 5:22-43

40Now when Jesus returned, a crowd welcomed him, for they were all expecting him. 41Then a man named Jairus, a ruler of the synagogue,[h] came and fell at Jesus' feet, pleading with him to come to his house 42because his only daughter, a girl of about twelve, was dying.

As Jesus was on his way, the crowds almost crushed him. 43And a woman was there who had been subject to bleeding[i] for twelve years,[i] but no one could heal her. 44She came up behind him and touched the edge of his cloak,[j] and immediately her bleeding stopped.

45"Who touched me?" Jesus asked.

When they all denied it, Peter said, "Master,[k] the people are crowding and pressing against you."

46But Jesus said, "Someone touched me;[l] I know that power has gone out from me."[m]

47Then the woman, seeing that she could not go unnoticed, came trembling and fell at his feet. In the presence of all the people, she told why she had touched him and how she had been instantly healed. 48Then he said to her, "Daughter, your faith has healed you.[n] Go in peace."[o]

49While Jesus was still speaking, someone came from the house of Jairus, the synagogue ruler.[p] "Your daughter is dead," he said. "Don't bother the teacher any more."

50Hearing this, Jesus said to Jairus, "Don't be afraid; just believe, and she will be healed."

8:28 [a]Mt 8:29 [b]Mk 5:7
8:31 [c]Rev 9:1,2, 11; 11:7; 17:8; 20:1,3
8:33 [d]ver 22,23
8:35 [e]Lk 10:39
8:36 [f]Mt 4:24
8:37 [g]Ac 16:39
8:41 [h]ver 49; Mk 5:22
8:43 [i]Lev 15:25-30
8:44 [j]Mt 9:20
8:45 [k]Lk 5:5
8:46 [l]Mt 14:36; Mk 3:10 [m]Lk 5:17; 6:19
8:48 [n]Mt 9:22 [o]Ac 15:33
8:49 [p]ver 41

[g]26 Some manuscripts *Gadarenes*; other manuscripts *Gergesenes*; also in verse 37 [h]29 Greek *unclean* [i]43 Many manuscripts *years, and she had spent all she had on doctors*

51 When he arrived at the house of Jairus, he did not let anyone go in with him except Peter, John and James,[a] and the child's father and mother. 52 Meanwhile, all the people were wailing and mourning[b] for her. "Stop wailing," Jesus said. "She is not dead but asleep."[c]

53 They laughed at him, knowing that she was dead. 54 But he took her by the hand and said, "My child, get up!"[d] 55 Her spirit returned, and at once she stood up. Then Jesus told them to give her something to eat. 56 Her parents were astonished, but he ordered them not to tell anyone what had happened.[e]

Jesus sends the Twelve with power and authority.

9:3-5pp—Mt 10:9-15; Mk 6:8-11
9:7-9pp—Mt 14:1,2; Mk 6:14-16

9 When Jesus had called the Twelve together, he gave them power and authority to drive out all demons[f] and to cure diseases,[g] 2 and he sent them out to preach the kingdom of God[h] and to heal the sick. 3 He told them: "Take nothing for the journey—no staff, no bag, no bread, no money, no extra tunic.[i] 4 Whatever house you enter, stay there until you leave that town. 5 If people do not welcome you, shake the dust off your feet when you leave their town, as a testimony against them."[j] 6 So they set out and went from village to village, preaching the gospel and healing people everywhere.

7 Now Herod[k] the tetrarch heard about all that was going on. And he was perplexed, because some were saying that John[l] had been raised from the dead,[m] 8 others that Elijah had appeared,[n] and still others that one of the prophets of long ago had come back to life.[o] 9 But Herod said, "I beheaded John. Who, then, is this I hear such things about?" And he tried to see him.[p]

Jesus uses five loaves and two fish to feed 5,000 men.

9:10-17pp—Mt 14:13-21; Mk 6:32-44; Jn 6:5-13
9:13-17Ref— 2Ki 4:42-44

10 When the apostles[q] returned, they reported to Jesus what they had done. Then he took them with him and they withdrew by themselves to a town called Bethsaida,[r] 11 but the crowds learned about it and followed him. He welcomed them and spoke to them about the kingdom of God,[s] and healed those who needed healing.

12 Late in the afternoon the Twelve came to him and said, "Send the crowd away so they can go to the surrounding villages and countryside and find food and lodging, because we are in a remote place here."

13 He replied, "You give them something to eat."

They answered, "We have only five loaves of bread and two fish—unless we go and buy food for all this crowd." 14 (About five thousand men were there.)

But he said to his disciples, "Have them sit down in groups of about fifty each." 15 The disciples did so, and everybody sat down. 16 Taking the five loaves and the two fish and looking up to heaven, he gave thanks and broke them.[t] Then he gave them to the disciples to set before the people. 17 They all ate and were satisfied, and the disciples picked up twelve basketfuls of broken pieces that were left over.

Peter confesses Jesus to be the Christ.

9:18-20pp—Mt 16:13-16; Mk 8:27-29
9:22-27pp—Mt 16:21-28; Mk 8:31–9:1

18 Once when Jesus was praying[u] in private and his disciples were with him, he asked them, "Who do the crowds say I am?"

19 They replied, "Some say John the Baptist;[v] others say Elijah; and still others, that one of the prophets of long ago has come back to life."[w]

20 "But what about you?" he asked. "Who do you say I am?"

Peter answered, "The Christ[j] of God."[x]

21 Jesus strictly warned them not to tell this to anyone.[y] 22 And he said, "The

j20 Or *Messiah*

8:51 [a]Mt 4:21
8:52 [b]Lk 23:27 [c]Mt 9:24; Jn 11:11,13
8:54 [d]Lk 7:14
8:56 [e]Mt 8:4
9:1 [f]Mt 10:1 [g]Mt 4:23; Lk 5:17
9:2 [h]Mt 3:2
9:3 [i]Lk 10:4; 22:35
9:5 [j]Mt 10:14
9:7 [k]Mt 14:1 [l]Mt 3:1 [m]ver 19
9:8 [n]Mt 11:14 [o]ver 19; Jn 1:21
9:9 [p]Lk 23:8
9:10 [q]Mk 6:30 [r]Mt 11:21
9:11 [s]ver 2; Mt 3:2
9:16 [t]Mt 14:19
9:18 [u]Lk 3:21
9:19 [v]Mt 3:1 [w]ver 7,8
9:20 [x]Jn 1:49; 6:66-69; 11:27
9:21 [y]Mt 16:20; Mk 8:30

Son of Man[a] must suffer many things[b]
and be rejected by the elders, chief
priests and teachers of the law,[c] and he
must be killed[d] and on the third day[e] be
raised to life."[f]
23Then he said to them all: "If anyone
would come after me, he must deny
himself and take up his cross daily and
follow me.[g] 24For whoever wants to
save his life will lose it, but whoever loses his life for me will save it.[h] 25What
good is it for a man to gain the whole
world, and yet lose or forfeit his very
self? 26If anyone is ashamed of me and
my words, the Son of Man will be
ashamed of him[i] when he comes in his
glory and in the glory of the Father and
of the holy angels.[j] 27I tell you the truth,
some who are standing here will not
taste death before they see the kingdom
of God."

The transfiguration.

9:28-36pp— Mt 17:1-8; Mk 9:2-8

28About eight days after Jesus said
this, he took Peter, John and James[k]
with him and went up onto a mountain to pray.[l] 29As he was praying, the
appearance of his face changed, and his
clothes became as bright as a flash of
lightning. 30Two men, Moses and Elijah,
31appeared in glorious splendor, talking
with Jesus. They spoke about his departure,[m] which he was about to bring to
fulfillment at Jerusalem. 32Peter and his
companions were very sleepy,[n] but
when they became fully awake, they
saw his glory and the two men standing with him. 33As the men were leaving Jesus, Peter said to him, "Master,[o]
it is good for us to be here. Let us put
up three shelters—one for you, one for
Moses and one for Elijah." (He did not
know what he was saying.)
34While he was speaking, a cloud
appeared and enveloped them, and they
were afraid as they entered the cloud.
35A voice came from the cloud, saying,
"This is my Son, whom I have chosen;[p]
listen to him."[q] 36When the voice had
spoken, they found that Jesus was alone.

9:22 [a]Mt 8:20 [b]Mt 16:21 [c]Mt 27:1,2 [d]Ac 2:23; 3:13 [e]Mt 16:21 [f]Mt 16:21
9:23 [g]Mt 10:38; Lk 14:27
9:24 [h]Jn 12:25
9:26 [i]Mt 10:33; Lk 12:9; 2Ti 2:12 [j]Mt 16:27
9:28 [k]Mt 4:21 [l]Lk 3:21
9:31 [m]2Pe 1:15
9:32 [n]Mt 26:43
9:33 [o]Lk 5:5
9:35 [p]Isa 42:1 [q]Mt 3:17
9:36 [r]Mt 17:9
9:41 [s]Dt 32:5
9:44 [t]ver 22
9:45 [u]Mk 9:32
9:46 [v]Lk 22:24
9:47 [w]Mt 9:4

The disciples kept this to themselves,
and told no one at that time what they
had seen.[r]

Jesus rebukes demon in boy.

9:37-42,43-45pp— Mt 17:14-18, 22,23; Mk 9:14-27, 30-32

37The next day, when they came
down from the mountain, a large crowd
met him. 38A man in the crowd called
out, "Teacher, I beg you to look at my
son, for he is my only child. 39A spirit
seizes him and he suddenly screams; it
throws him into convulsions so that he
foams at the mouth. It scarcely ever
leaves him and is destroying him. 40I
begged your disciples to drive it out,
but they could not."
41"O unbelieving and perverse generation,"[s] Jesus replied, "how long shall
I stay with you and put up with you?
Bring your son here."
42Even while the boy was coming, the
demon threw him to the ground in a
convulsion. But Jesus rebuked the evil[k]
spirit, healed the boy and gave him back
to his father. 43And they were all amazed
at the greatness of God.
While everyone was marveling at all
that Jesus did, he said to his disciples,
44"Listen carefully to what I am about
to tell you: The Son of Man is going to
be betrayed into the hands of men."[t]
45But they did not understand what this
meant. It was hidden from them, so
that they did not grasp it,[u] and they
were afraid to ask him about it.

Who will be the greatest?

9:46-48pp— Mt 18:1-5
9:46-50pp— Mk 9:33-40

46An argument started among the
disciples as to which of them would
be the greatest.[v] 47Jesus, knowing their
thoughts,[w] took a little child and had
him stand beside him. 48Then he said
to them, "Whoever welcomes this little
child in my name welcomes me; and
whoever welcomes me welcomes the

[k]42 Greek *unclean*

one who sent me.[a] For he who is least
among you all—he is the greatest."[b]
49"Master,"[c] said John, "we saw a man
driving out demons in your name and
we tried to stop him, because he is not
one of us."
50"Do not stop him," Jesus said, "for
whoever is not against you is for you."[d]
51As the time approached for him to
be taken up to heaven,[e] Jesus resolutely
set out for Jerusalem.[f] 52And he sent
messengers on ahead, who went into a
Samaritan[g] village to get things ready
for him; 53but the people there did not
welcome him, because he was heading
for Jerusalem. 54When the disciples
James and John[h] saw this, they asked,
"Lord, do you want us to call fire down
from heaven to destroy them[l]?"[i] 55But
Jesus turned and rebuked them, 56and[m]
they went to another village.

Jesus lacks place to lay his head.

9:57-60pp— Mt 8:19-22

57As they were walking along the
road,[j] a man said to him, "I will follow
you wherever you go."
58Jesus replied, "Foxes have holes and
birds of the air have nests, but the Son
of Man[k] has no place to lay his head."
59He said to another man, "Follow me."[l]
But the man replied, "Lord, first let
me go and bury my father."
60Jesus said to him, "Let the dead bury
their own dead, but you go and proclaim the kingdom of God."[m]
61Still another said, "I will follow you,
Lord; but first let me go back and say
good-by to my family."[n]
62Jesus replied, "No one who puts his
hand to the plow and looks back is fit
for service in the kingdom of God."

Workers for God's harvest.

10:4-12pp— Lk 9:3-5
10:13-15,21,22pp— Mt 11:21-23,25-27
10:23,24pp— Mt 13:16,17

10 After this the Lord[o] appointed seventy-two[n] others[p] and sent them
two by two[q] ahead of him to every
town and place where he was about to
go.[r] 2He told them, "The harvest is plentiful, but the workers are few. Ask the
Lord of the harvest, therefore, to send
out workers into his harvest field.[s] 3Go!
I am sending you out like lambs among
wolves.[t] 4Do not take a purse or bag or
sandals; and do not greet anyone on the
road.
5"When you enter a house, first say,
'Peace to this house.' 6If a man of peace
is there, your peace will rest on him; if
not, it will return to you. 7Stay in that
house, eating and drinking whatever
they give you, for the worker deserves
his wages.[u] Do not move around from
house to house.
8"When you enter a town and are
welcomed, eat what is set before you.[v]
9Heal the sick who are there and tell
them, 'The kingdom of God[w] is near
you.' 10But when you enter a town and
are not welcomed, go into its streets
and say, 11'Even the dust of your town
that sticks to our feet we wipe off
against you.[x] Yet be sure of this: The
kingdom of God is near.'[y] 12I tell you,
it will be more bearable on that day for
Sodom[z] than for that town.[a]
13"Woe to you,[b] Korazin! Woe to you,
Bethsaida! For if the miracles that were
performed in you had been performed
in Tyre and Sidon, they would have
repented long ago, sitting in sackcloth[c]
and ashes. 14But it will be more bearable for Tyre and Sidon at the judgment
than for you. 15And you, Capernaum,[d]
will you be lifted up to the skies? No,
you will go down to the depths.[o]
16"He who listens to you listens to
me; he who rejects you rejects me; but
he who rejects me rejects him who
sent me."[e]
17The seventy-two[f] returned with joy
and said, "Lord, even the demons submit to us in your name."[g]

9:48 [a]Mt 10:40 [b]Mk 9:35
9:49 [c]Lk 5:5
9:50 [d]Mt 12:30; Lk 11:23
9:51 [e]Mk 16:19 [f]Lk 13:22; 17:11; 18:31; 19:28
9:52 [g]Mt 10:5
9:54 [h]Mt 4:21 [i]2Ki 1:10,12
9:57 [j]ver 51
9:58 [k]Mt 8:20
9:59 [l]Mt 4:19
9:60 [m]Mt 3:2
9:61 [n]1Ki 19:20
10:1 [o]Lk 7:13 [p]Lk 9:1,2,51, 52 [q]Mk 6:7 [r]Mt 10:1
10:2 [s]Mt 9:37,38; Jn 4:35
10:3 [t]Mt 10:16
10:7 [u]Mt 10:10; 1Co 9:14; 1Ti 5:18
10:8 [v]1Co 10:27
10:9 [w]Mt 3:2; 10:7
10:11 [x]Mt 10:14; Mk 6:11 [y]ver 9
10:12 [z]Mt 10:15 [a]Mt 11:24
10:13 [b]Lk 6:24-26 [c]Rev 11:3
10:15 [d]Mt 4:13
10:16 [e]Mt 10:40; Jn 13:20
10:17 [f]ver 1 [g]Mk 16:17

[l]54 Some manuscripts *them, even as Elijah did*
[m]55,56 Some manuscripts *them. And he said, "You do not know what kind of spirit you are of, for the Son of Man did not come to destroy men's lives, but to save them."* 56And [n]1 Some manuscripts *seventy;* also in verse 17 [o]15 Greek *Hades*

18He replied, "I saw Satan[a] fall like
lightning from heaven.[b] 19I have given
you authority to trample on snakes[c] and
scorpions and to overcome all the power
of the enemy; nothing will harm you.
20However, do not rejoice that the spirits submit to you, but rejoice that your
names are written in heaven."[d]
21At that time Jesus, full of joy through
the Holy Spirit, said, "I praise you,
Father, Lord of heaven and earth, because you have hidden these things
from the wise and learned, and revealed
them to little children.[e] Yes, Father, for
this was your good pleasure.
22"All things have been committed to
me by my Father.[f] No one knows who
the Son is except the Father, and no one
knows who the Father is except the Son
and those to whom the Son chooses to
reveal him."[g]
23Then he turned to his disciples and
said privately, "Blessed are the eyes that
see what you see. 24For I tell you that
many prophets and kings wanted to see
what you see but did not see it, and to
hear what you hear but did not hear it."[h]

A parable: The Good Samaritan.

10:25-28pp— Mt 22:34-40; Mk 12:28-31

25On one occasion an expert in the
law stood up to test Jesus. "Teacher," he
asked, "what must I do to inherit eternal life?"[i]
26"What is written in the Law?" he
replied. "How do you read it?"
27He answered: "'Love the Lord your
God with all your heart and with all
your soul and with all your strength and
with all your mind'[p];[j] and, 'Love your
neighbor as yourself.'[q]"[k]
28"You have answered correctly," Jesus
replied. "Do this and you will live."[l]
29But he wanted to justify himself,[m]
so he asked Jesus, "And who is my
neighbor?"
30In reply Jesus said: "A man was
going down from Jerusalem to Jericho,
when he fell into the hands of robbers.
They stripped him of his clothes, beat
him and went away, leaving him half
dead. 31A priest happened to be going
down the same road, and when he saw
the man, he passed by on the other
side.[n] 32So too, a Levite, when he came
to the place and saw him, passed by on
the other side. 33But a Samaritan,[o] as he
traveled, came where the man was;
and when he saw him, he took pity on
him. 34He went to him and bandaged
his wounds, pouring on oil and wine.
Then he put the man on his own donkey, took him to an inn and took care
of him. 35The next day he took out two
silver coins[r] and gave them to the innkeeper. 'Look after him,' he said, 'and
when I return, I will reimburse you for
any extra expense you may have.'
36"Which of these three do you think
was a neighbor to the man who fell
into the hands of robbers?"
37The expert in the law replied, "The
one who had mercy on him."
Jesus told him, "Go and do likewise."

Mary and Martha with Jesus.

38As Jesus and his disciples were on
their way, he came to a village where a
woman named Martha[p] opened her
home to him. 39She had a sister called
Mary,[q] who sat at the Lord's feet[r] listening to what he said. 40But Martha
was distracted by all the preparations
that had to be made. She came to him
and asked, "Lord, don't you care[s] that
my sister has left me to do the work by
myself? Tell her to help me!"
41"Martha, Martha," the Lord answered, "you are worried[t] and upset
about many things, 42but only one thing
is needed.[s][u] Mary has chosen what is
better, and it will not be taken away
from her."

The Lord's model prayer.

11:2-4pp— Mt 6:9-13

11 One day Jesus was praying[v] in a
certain place. When he finished,

10:18 [a]Mt 4:10 [b]Isa 14:12; Rev 9:1; 12:8,9
10:19 [c]Mk 16:18; Ac 28:3-5
10:20 [d]Ex 32:32; Ps 69:28; Da 12:1; Php 4:3; Heb 12:23; Rev 13:8; 20:12; 21:27
10:21 [e]1Co 1:26-29
10:22 [f]Mt 28:18 [g]Jn 1:18
10:24 [h]1Pe 1:10-12
10:25 [i]Mt 19:16; Lk 18:18
10:27 [j]Dt 6:5 [k]Lev 19:18; Mt 5:43
10:28 [l]Lev 18:5; Ro 7:10
10:29 [m]Lk 16:15
10:31 [n]Lev 21:1-3
10:33 [o]Mt 10:5
10:38 [p]Jn 11:1; 12:2
10:39 [q]Jn 11:1; 12:3 [r]Lk 8:35
10:40 [s]Mk 4:38
10:41 [t]Mt 6:25-34; Lk 12:11,22
10:42 [u]Ps 27:4
11:1 [v]Lk 3:21

p27 Deut. 6:5 q27 Lev. 19:18 r35 Greek *two denarii* s42 Some manuscripts *but few things are needed—or only one*

one of his disciples said to him, "Lord,[a] teach us to pray, just as John taught his disciples."

2He said to them, "When you pray, say:

"'Father,[t]
hallowed be your name,
your kingdom[b] come.[u]
3Give us each day our daily bread.
4Forgive us our sins,
for we also forgive everyone who
sins against us.[v][c]
And lead us not into temptation.[w]'"[d]

Reward for boldness.

11:9-13pp— Mt 7:7-11

5Then he said to them, "Suppose one of you has a friend, and he goes to him at midnight and says, 'Friend, lend me three loaves of bread, 6because a friend of mine on a journey has come to me, and I have nothing to set before him.'

7"Then the one inside answers, 'Don't bother me. The door is already locked, and my children are with me in bed. I can't get up and give you anything.' 8I tell you, though he will not get up and give him the bread because he is his friend, yet because of the man's boldness[x] he will get up and give him as much as he needs.[e]

9"So I say to you: Ask and it will be given to you;[f] seek and you will find; knock and the door will be opened to you. 10For everyone who asks receives; he who seeks finds; and to him who knocks, the door will be opened.

11"Which of you fathers, if your son asks for[y] a fish, will give him a snake instead? 12Or if he asks for an egg, will give him a scorpion? 13If you then, though you are evil, know how to give good gifts to your children, how much more will your Father in heaven give the Holy Spirit to those who ask him!"

Jesus and Beelzebub.

11:14,15, 17-22, 24-26pp— Mt 12:22,24-29, 43-45
11:17-22pp— Mk 3:23-27

14Jesus was driving out a demon that was mute. When the demon left, the man who had been mute spoke, and the crowd was amazed.[g] 15But some of them said, "By Beelzebub,[z][h] the prince of demons, he is driving out demons."[i] 16Others tested him by asking for a sign from heaven.[j]

17Jesus knew their thoughts[k] and said to them: "Any kingdom divided against itself will be ruined, and a house divided against itself will fall. 18If Satan[l] is divided against himself, how can his kingdom stand? I say this because you claim that I drive out demons by Beelzebub. 19Now if I drive out demons by Beelzebub, by whom do your followers drive them out? So then, they will be your judges. 20But if I drive out demons by the finger of God,[m] then the kingdom of God[n] has come to you.

21"When a strong man, fully armed, guards his own house, his possessions are safe. 22But when someone stronger attacks and overpowers him, he takes away the armor in which the man trusted and divides up the spoils.

23"He who is not with me is against me, and he who does not gather with me, scatters.[o]

24"When an evil[a] spirit comes out of a man, it goes through arid places seeking rest and does not find it. Then it says, 'I will return to the house I left.' 25When it arrives, it finds the house swept clean and put in order. 26Then it goes and takes seven other spirits more wicked than itself, and they go in and live there. And the final condition of that man is worse than the first."[p]

27As Jesus was saying these things, a woman in the crowd called out, "Blessed is the mother who gave you birth and nursed you."[q]

28He replied, "Blessed rather are those who hear the word of God[r] and obey it."[s]

11:1 [a]Jn 13:13
11:2 [b]Mt 3:2
11:4 [c]Mt 18:35; Mk 11:25 [d]Mt 26:41; Jas 1:13
11:8 [e]Lk 18:1-6
11:9 [f]Mt 7:7
11:14 [g]Mt 9:32,33
11:15 [h]Mk 3:22 [i]Mt 9:34
11:16 [j]Mt 12:38
11:17 [k]Mt 9:4
11:18 [l]Mt 4:10
11:20 [m]Ex 8:19 [n]Mt 3:2
11:23 [o]Mt 12:30; Mk 9:40; Lk 9:50
11:26 [p]2Pe 2:20
11:27 [q]Lk 23:29
11:28 [r]Heb 4:12 [s]Pr 8:32; Lk 6:47; 8:21; Jn 14:21

t*2* Some manuscripts *Our Father in heaven*
u*2* Some manuscripts *come. May your will be done on earth as it is in heaven.* v*4* Greek *everyone who is indebted to us* w*4* Some manuscripts *temptation but deliver us from the evil one* x*8* Or *persistence*
y*11* Some manuscripts *for bread, will give him a stone; or if he asks for* z*15* Greek *Beezeboul* or *Beelzeboul*; also in verses 18 and 19 a*24* Greek *unclean*

Request for a miraculous sign.

11:29-32pp— Mt 12:39-42

29 As the crowds increased, Jesus said,
"This is a wicked generation. It asks
for a miraculous sign,[a] but none will be
given it except the sign of Jonah.[b] 30 For
as Jonah was a sign to the Ninevites, so
also will the Son of Man be to this generation. 31 The Queen of the South will
rise at the judgment with the men of
this generation and condemn them; for
she came from the ends of the earth to
listen to Solomon's wisdom,[c] and now
one[b] greater than Solomon is here. 32 The
men of Nineveh will stand up at the
judgment with this generation and condemn it; for they repented at the preaching of Jonah,[d] and now one greater than
Jonah is here.

The lamp of the body.

11:34,35pp— Mt 6:22,23

33 "No one lights a lamp and puts it
in a place where it will be hidden, or
under a bowl. Instead he puts it on its
stand, so that those who come in may
see the light.[e] 34 Your eye is the lamp of
your body. When your eyes are good,
your whole body also is full of light.
But when they are bad, your body also
is full of darkness. 35 See to it, then, that
the light within you is not darkness.
36 Therefore, if your whole body is full
of light, and no part of it dark, it will be
completely lighted, as when the light of
a lamp shines on you."

Proclamation of six woes.

37 When Jesus had finished speaking, a
Pharisee invited him to eat with him;
so he went in and reclined at the table.[f]
38 But the Pharisee, noticing that Jesus
did not first wash before the meal,[g] was
surprised.

39 Then the Lord[h] said to him, "Now
then, you Pharisees clean the outside
of the cup and dish, but inside you are
full of greed and wickedness.[i] 40 You
foolish people![j] Did not the one who
made the outside make the inside also?
41 But give what is inside ⌊the dish⌋[c] to
the poor,[k] and everything will be clean
for you.[l]

42 "Woe to you Pharisees, because you
give God a tenth[m] of your mint, rue and
all other kinds of garden herbs, but you
neglect justice and the love of God.[n]
You should have practiced the latter
without leaving the former undone.[o]

43 "Woe to you Pharisees, because
you love the most important seats in
the synagogues and greetings in the
marketplaces.[p]

44 "Woe to you, because you are like
unmarked graves,[q] which men walk
over without knowing it."

45 One of the experts in the law[r] answered him, "Teacher, when you say
these things, you insult us also."

46 Jesus replied, "And you experts in
the law, woe to you, because you load
people down with burdens they can
hardly carry, and you yourselves will
not lift one finger to help them.[s]

47 "Woe to you, because you build
tombs for the prophets, and it was your
forefathers who killed them. 48 So you
testify that you approve of what your
forefathers did; they killed the prophets,
and you build their tombs.[t] 49 Because
of this, God in his wisdom[u] said, 'I
will send them prophets and apostles,
some of whom they will kill and others
they will persecute.'[v] 50 Therefore this
generation will be held responsible for
the blood of all the prophets that has
been shed since the beginning of the
world, 51 from the blood of Abel[w] to the
blood of Zechariah,[x] who was killed
between the altar and the sanctuary.
Yes, I tell you, this generation will be
held responsible for it all.[y]

52 "Woe to you experts in the law,
because you have taken away the key
to knowledge. You yourselves have not
entered, and you have hindered those
who were entering."[z]

53 When Jesus left there, the Pharisees and the teachers of the law began

11:29 [a]ver 16; Mt 12:38 [b]Jnh 1:17; Mt 16:4
11:31 [c]1Ki 10:1; 2Ch 9:1
11:32 [d]Jnh 3:5
11:33 [e]Mt 5:15; Mk 4:21; Lk 8:16
11:37 [f]Lk 7:36; 14:1
11:38 [g]Mk 7:3,4
11:39 [h]Lk 7:13 [i]Mt 23:25,26; Mk 7:20-23
11:40 [j]Lk 12:20; 1Co 15:36
11:41 [k]Lk 12:33 [l]Ac 10:15
11:42 [m]Lk 18:12 [n]Dt 6:5; Mic 6:8 [o]Mt 23:23
11:43 [p]Mt 23:6,7; Mk 12:38-39; Lk 14:7; 20:46
11:44 [q]Mt 23:27
11:45 [r]Mt 22:35
11:46 [s]Mt 23:4
11:48 [t]Mt 23:29-32; Ac 7:51-53
11:49 [u]1Co 1:24,30; Col 2:3 [v]Mt 23:34
11:51 [w]Ge 4:8 [x]2Ch 24:20,21 [y]Mt 23:35,36
11:52 [z]Mt 23:13

[b]*31* Or *something*; also in verse 32 [c]*41* Or *what you have*

to oppose him fiercely and to besiege
him with questions, 54waiting to catch
him in something he might say.[a]

Jesus' warning against hypocrisy.

12:2-9pp— Mt 10:26-33

12 Meanwhile, when a crowd of
many thousands had gathered,
so that they were trampling on one another, Jesus began to speak first to his
disciples, saying: "Be on your guard
against the yeast of the Pharisees, which
is hypocrisy.[b] 2There is nothing concealed that will not be disclosed, or
hidden that will not be made known.[c]
3What you have said in the dark will
be heard in the daylight, and what you
have whispered in the ear in the inner
rooms will be proclaimed from the
roofs.

4"I tell you, my friends,[d] do not be
afraid of those who kill the body and
after that can do no more. 5But I will
show you whom you should fear: Fear
him who, after the killing of the body,
has power to throw you into hell. Yes,
I tell you, fear him.[e] 6Are not five sparrows sold for two pennies[d]? Yet not one
of them is forgotten by God. 7Indeed,
the very hairs of your head are all numbered.[f] Don't be afraid; you are worth
more than many sparrows.[g]

8"I tell you, whoever acknowledges
me before men, the Son of Man will
also acknowledge him before the angels
of God.[h] 9But he who disowns me
before men will be disowned[i] before the
angels of God. 10And everyone who
speaks a word against the Son of Man[j]
will be forgiven, but anyone who blasphemes against the Holy Spirit will not
be forgiven.[k]

11"When you are brought before synagogues, rulers and authorities, do not
worry about how you will defend yourselves or what you will say,[l] 12for the
Holy Spirit will teach you at that time
what you should say."[m]

The rich fool.

13Someone in the crowd said to him,

11:54 [a]Mt 12:10; Mk 12:13
12:1 [b]Mt 16:6,11,12; Mk 8:15
12:2 [c]Mk 4:22; Lk 8:17
12:4 [d]Jn 15:14,15
12:5 [e]Heb 10:31
12:7 [f]Mt 10:30 [g]Mt 12:12
12:8 [h]Lk 15:10
12:9 [i]Mk 8:38; 2Ti 2:12
12:10 [j]Mt 8:20 [k]Mt 12:31,32; Mk 3:28-29; 1Jn 5:16
12:11 [l]Mt 10:17,19; Mk 13:11; Lk 21:12,14
12:12 [m]Ex 4:12; Mt 10:20; Mk 13:11; Lk 21:15
12:15 [n]Job 20:20; 31:24; Ps 62:10
12:20 [o]Jer 17:11; Lk 11:40 [p]Job 27:8 [q]Ps 39:6; 49:10
12:21 [r]ver 33
12:24 [s]Job 38:41; Ps 147:9
12:27 [t]1Ki 10:4-7

"Teacher, tell my brother to divide the
inheritance with me."

14Jesus replied, "Man, who appointed
me a judge or an arbiter between you?"
15Then he said to them, "Watch out! Be
on your guard against all kinds of greed;
a man's life does not consist in the abundance of his possessions."[n]

16And he told them this parable: "The
ground of a certain rich man produced
a good crop. 17He thought to himself,
'What shall I do? I have no place to store
my crops.'

18"Then he said, 'This is what I'll do.
I will tear down my barns and build
bigger ones, and there I will store all
my grain and my goods. 19And I'll say
to myself, "You have plenty of good
things laid up for many years. Take life
easy; eat, drink and be merry."'

20"But God said to him, 'You fool![o]
This very night your life will be demanded from you.[p] Then who will get what
you have prepared for yourself?'[q]

21"This is how it will be with anyone
who stores up things for himself but is
not rich toward God."[r]

Replacing worry with faith.

12:22-31pp— Mt 6:25-33

22Then Jesus said to his disciples:
"Therefore I tell you, do not worry about
your life, what you will eat; or about
your body, what you will wear. 23Life is
more than food, and the body more than
clothes. 24Consider the ravens: They do
not sow or reap, they have no storeroom or barn; yet God feeds them.[s] And
how much more valuable you are than
birds! 25Who of you by worrying can
add a single hour to his life[e]? 26Since
you cannot do this very little thing,
why do you worry about the rest?

27"Consider how the lilies grow. They
do not labor or spin. Yet I tell you, not
even Solomon in all his splendor[t] was
dressed like one of these. 28If that is
how God clothes the grass of the field,
which is here today, and tomorrow is

[d]6 Greek *two assaria* [e]25 Or *single cubit to his height*

thrown into the fire, how much more
will he clothe you, O you of little faith![a]
29And do not set your heart on what you
will eat or drink; do not worry about it.
30For the pagan world runs after all such
things, and your Father[b] knows that you
need them.[c] 31But seek his kingdom,[d]
and these things will be given to you as
well.[e]

32"Do not be afraid,[f] little flock, for
your Father has been pleased to give
you the kingdom.[g] 33Sell your possessions and give to the poor.[h] Provide
purses for yourselves that will not wear
out, a treasure in heaven[i] that will not
be exhausted, where no thief comes
near and no moth destroys.[j] 34For where
your treasure is, there your heart will
be also.[k]

Readiness for service.

12:35,36pp— Mt 25:1-13; Mk 13:33-37
12:39,40; 42-46pp— Mt 24:43-51

35"Be dressed ready for service and
keep your lamps burning, 36like men
waiting for their master to return from
a wedding banquet, so that when he
comes and knocks they can immediately
open the door for him. 37It will be good
for those servants whose master finds
them watching when he comes.[l] I tell
you the truth, he will dress himself to
serve, will have them recline at the
table and will come and wait on them.[m]
38It will be good for those servants
whose master finds them ready, even if
he comes in the second or third watch of
the night. 39But understand this: If the
owner of the house had known at what
hour the thief[n] was coming, he would
not have let his house be broken into.
40You also must be ready,[o] because the
Son of Man will come at an hour when
you do not expect him."

41Peter asked, "Lord, are you telling
this parable to us, or to everyone?"

42The Lord[p] answered, "Who then is
the faithful and wise manager, whom
the master puts in charge of his servants
to give them their food allowance at the
proper time? 43It will be good for that
servant whom the master finds doing so
when he returns. 44I tell you the truth,
he will put him in charge of all his possessions. 45But suppose the servant says
to himself, 'My master is taking a long
time in coming,' and he then begins to
beat the menservants and maidservants
and to eat and drink and get drunk.
46The master of that servant will come
on a day when he does not expect him
and at an hour he is not aware of.[q] He
will cut him to pieces and assign him a
place with the unbelievers.

47"That servant who knows his master's will and does not get ready or does
not do what his master wants will be
beaten with many blows.[r] 48But the one
who does not know and does things
deserving punishment will be beaten
with few blows.[s] From everyone who
has been given much, much will be
demanded; and from the one who has
been entrusted with much, much more
will be asked.

Not peace but division.

12:51-53pp— Mt 10:34-36

49"I have come to bring fire on the
earth, and how I wish it were already
kindled! 50But I have a baptism[t] to
undergo, and how distressed I am until
it is completed![u] 51Do you think I came
to bring peace on earth? No, I tell you,
but division. 52From now on there will
be five in one family divided against each
other, three against two and two against
three. 53They will be divided, father
against son and son against father, mother against daughter and daughter against
mother, mother-in-law against daughter-in-law and daughter-in-law against
mother-in-law."[v]

54He said to the crowd: "When you see
a cloud rising in the west, immediately
you say, 'It's going to rain,' and it does.[w]
55And when the south wind blows, you
say, 'It's going to be hot,' and it is.
56Hypocrites! You know how to interpret the appearance of the earth and
the sky. How is it that you don't know
how to interpret this present time?[x]

12:28 [a]Mt 6:30
12:30 [b]Lk 6:36 [c]Mt 6:8
12:31 [d]Mt 3:2 [e]Mt 19:29
12:32 [f]Mt 14:27 [g]Mt 25:34
12:33 [h]Mt 19:21; Ac 2:45 [i]Mt 6:20 [j]Jas 5:2
12:34 [k]Mt 6:21
12:37 [l]Mt 24:42,46; 25:13 [m]Mt 20:28
12:39 [n]Mt 6:19; 1Th 5:2; 2Pe 3:10; Rev 3:3; 16:15
12:40 [o]Mk 13:33; Lk 21:36
12:42 [p]Lk 7:13
12:46 [q]ver 40
12:47 [r]Dt 25:2
12:48 [s]Lev 5:17; Nu 15:27-30
12:50 [t]Mk 10:38 [u]Jn 19:30
12:53 [v]Mic 7:6; Mt 10:21
12:54 [w]Mt 16:2
12:56 [x]Mt 16:3

57“Why don’t you judge for yourselves
what is right? 58As you are going with
your adversary to the magistrate, try
hard to be reconciled to him on the way,
or he may drag you off to the judge, and
the judge turn you over to the officer,
and the officer throw you into prison.[a]
59I tell you, you will not get out until
you have paid the last penny.[f]”[b]

Jesus teaches repentance.

13 Now there were some present at
that time who told Jesus about the
Galileans whose blood Pilate[c] had mixed
with their sacrifices. 2Jesus answered,
“Do you think that these Galileans were
worse sinners than all the other Galileans because they suffered this way?[d] 3I
tell you, no! But unless you repent, you
too will all perish. 4Or those eighteen
who died when the tower in Siloam[e]
fell on them—do you think they were
more guilty than all the others living in
Jerusalem? 5I tell you, no! But unless
you repent,[f] you too will all perish.”
6Then he told this parable: “A man
had a fig tree, planted in his vineyard,
and he went to look for fruit on it, but
did not find any.[g] 7So he said to the man
who took care of the vineyard, ‘For
three years now I’ve been coming to
look for fruit on this fig tree and haven’t
found any. Cut it down![h] Why should it
use up the soil?’
8“ ‘Sir,’ the man replied, ‘leave it alone
for one more year, and I’ll dig around it
and fertilize it. 9If it bears fruit next
year, fine! If not, then cut it down.’ ”

A crippled woman is healed on the Sabbath.

10On a Sabbath Jesus was teaching in
one of the synagogues,[i] 11and a woman
was there who had been crippled by a
spirit for eighteen years.[j] She was bent
over and could not straighten up at all.
12When Jesus saw her, he called her forward and said to her, “Woman, you are
set free from your infirmity.” 13Then he
put his hands on her,[k] and immediately
she straightened up and praised God.

12:58 [a]Mt 5:25
12:59 [b]Mt 5:26; Mk 12:42
13:1 [c]Mt 27:2
13:2 [d]Jn 9:2,3
13:4 [e]Jn 9:7,11
13:5 [f]Mt 3:2; Ac 2:38
13:6 [g]Isa 5:2; Jer 8:13; Mt 21:19
13:7 [h]Mt 3:10
13:10 [i]Mt 4:23
13:11 [j]ver 16
13:13 [k]Mk 5:23
13:14 [l]Mt 12:2; Lk 14:3 [m]Mk 5:22 [n]Ex 20:9
13:15 [o]Lk 14:5
13:16 [p]Lk 3:8; 19:9 [q]Mt 4:10
13:17 [r]Isa 66:5
13:18 [s]Mt 3:2 [t]Mt 13:24
13:19 [u]Lk 17:6 [v]Mt 13:32
13:21 [w]1Co 5:6
13:22 [x]Lk 9:51
13:24 [y]Mt 7:13

14Indignant because Jesus had healed
on the Sabbath,[l] the synagogue ruler[m]
said to the people, “There are six days
for work.[n] So come and be healed on
those days, not on the Sabbath.”
15The Lord answered him, “You
hypocrites! Doesn’t each of you on the
Sabbath untie his ox or donkey from the
stall and lead it out to give it water?[o]
16Then should not this woman, a daughter of Abraham,[p] whom Satan[q] has kept
bound for eighteen long years, be set
free on the Sabbath day from what
bound her?”
17When he said this, all his opponents
were humiliated,[r] but the people were
delighted with all the wonderful things
he was doing.

Parables: The mustard seed, and the yeast.

13:18,19pp— Mk 4:30-32
13:18-21pp— Mt 13:31-33

18Then Jesus asked, “What is the kingdom of God[s] like?[t] What shall I compare it to? 19It is like a mustard seed,
which a man took and planted in his
garden. It grew and became a tree,[u]
and the birds of the air perched in its
branches.”[v]
20Again he asked, “What shall I compare the kingdom of God to? 21It is like
yeast that a woman took and mixed
into a large amount[g] of flour until it
worked all through the dough.”[w]

The narrow door.

22Then Jesus went through the towns
and villages, teaching as he made his
way to Jerusalem.[x] 23Someone asked
him, “Lord, are only a few people going
to be saved?”
He said to them, 24“Make every effort
to enter through the narrow door,[y]
because many, I tell you, will try to enter
and will not be able to. 25Once the owner of the house gets up and closes the
door, you will stand outside knocking
and pleading, ‘Sir, open the door for us.’

f*59* Greek *lepton* g*21* Greek *three satas* (probably about 1/2 bushel or 22 liters)

"But he will answer, 'I don't know
you or where you come from.'[a]
26"Then you will say, 'We ate and
drank with you, and you taught in our
streets.'
27"But he will reply, 'I don't know you
or where you come from. Away from
me, all you evildoers!'[b]
28"There will be weeping there, and
gnashing of teeth,[c] when you see Abraham, Isaac and Jacob and all the prophets in the kingdom of God, but you
yourselves thrown out. 29People will
come from east and west[d] and north
and south, and will take their places at
the feast in the kingdom of God.
30Indeed there are those who are last
who will be first, and first who will be
last."[e]

Jesus shows sorrow for Jerusalem.

13:34,35pp— Mt 23:37-39
13:34,35Ref— Lk 19:41

31At that time some Pharisees came
to Jesus and said to him, "Leave this
place and go somewhere else. Herod[f]
wants to kill you."
32He replied, "Go tell that fox, 'I will
drive out demons and heal people today
and tomorrow, and on the third day I
will reach my goal.'[g] 33In any case, I
must keep going today and tomorrow
and the next day—for surely no
prophet[h] can die outside Jerusalem!
34"O Jerusalem, Jerusalem, you who
kill the prophets and stone those sent to
you, how often I have longed to gather
your children together, as a hen gathers
her chicks under her wings,[i] but you
were not willing! 35Look, your house is
left to you desolate.[j] I tell you, you will
not see me again until you say, 'Blessed
is he who comes in the name of the
Lord.'[h]"[k]

A parable: A wedding feast.

14:8-10Ref— Pr 25:6,7

14 One Sabbath, when Jesus went to
eat in the house of a prominent
Pharisee,[l] he was being carefully
watched.[m] 2There in front of him was a
man suffering from dropsy. 3Jesus asked
the Pharisees and experts in the law,[n]
"Is it lawful to heal on the Sabbath or
not?"[o] 4But they remained silent. So
taking hold of the man, he healed him
and sent him away.
5Then he asked them, "If one of you
has a son[i] or an ox that falls into a well
on the Sabbath day, will you not immediately pull him out?"[p] 6And they had
nothing to say.
7When he noticed how the guests
picked the places of honor at the table,[q]
he told them this parable: 8"When someone invites you to a wedding feast, do
not take the place of honor, for a person more distinguished than you may
have been invited. 9If so, the host who
invited both of you will come and say
to you, 'Give this man your seat.' Then,
humiliated, you will have to take the
least important place. 10But when you
are invited, take the lowest place, so
that when your host comes, he will say
to you, 'Friend, move up to a better
place.' Then you will be honored in the
presence of all your fellow guests.
11For everyone who exalts himself will
be humbled, and he who humbles himself will be exalted."[r]
12Then Jesus said to his host, "When
you give a luncheon or dinner, do not
invite your friends, your brothers or
relatives, or your rich neighbors; if you
do, they may invite you back and so you
will be repaid. 13But when you give a
banquet, invite the poor, the crippled,
the lame, the blind,[s] 14and you will be
blessed. Although they cannot repay
you, you will be repaid at the resurrection of the righteous."[t]

A parable: A great banquet.

14:16-24Ref— Mt 22:2-14

15When one of those at the table with
him heard this, he said to Jesus, "Blessed
is the man who will eat at the feast[u] in
the kingdom of God."[v]
16Jesus replied: "A certain man was
preparing a great banquet and invited

13:25 [a]Mt 7:23; 25:10-12
13:27 [b]Mt 7:23; 25:41
13:28 [c]Mt 8:12
13:29 [d]Mt 8:11
13:30 [e]Mt 19:30
13:31 [f]Mt 14:1
13:32 [g]Heb 2:10
13:33 [h]Mt 21:11
13:34 [i]Mt 23:37
13:35 [j]Jer 12:17; 22:5 [k]Ps 118:26; Mt 21:9; Lk 19:38
14:1 [l]Lk 7:36; 11:37 [m]Mt 12:10
14:3 [n]Mt 22:35 [o]Mt 12:2
14:5 [p]Lk 13:15
14:7 [q]Lk 11:43
14:11 [r]Mt 23:12; Lk 18:14
14:13 [s]ver 21
14:14 [t]Ac 24:15
14:15 [u]Isa 25:6; Mt 26:29; Lk 13:29; Rev 19:9 [v]Mt 3:2

[h]*35* Psalm 118:26 [i]*5* Some manuscripts *donkey*

many guests. 17 At the time of the banquet he sent his servant to tell those
who had been invited, 'Come, for everything is now ready.'
18 "But they all alike began to make
excuses. The first said, 'I have just
bought a field, and I must go and see it.
Please excuse me.'
19 "Another said, 'I have just bought
five yoke of oxen, and I'm on my way to
try them out. Please excuse me.'
20 "Still another said, 'I just got married, so I can't come.'
21 "The servant came back and reported this to his master. Then the owner of
the house became angry and ordered his
servant, 'Go out quickly into the streets
and alleys of the town and bring in the
poor, the crippled, the blind and the
lame.'[a]
22 "'Sir,' the servant said, 'what you
ordered has been done, but there is still
room.'
23 "Then the master told his servant,
'Go out to the roads and country lanes
and make them come in, so that my
house will be full. 24 I tell you, not one
of those men who were invited will get
a taste of my banquet.'"[b]

The cost of following Jesus.

25 Large crowds were traveling with
Jesus, and turning to them he said: 26 "If
anyone comes to me and does not hate
his father and mother, his wife and
children, his brothers and sisters—yes,
even his own life—he cannot be my disciple.[c] 27 And anyone who does not carry
his cross and follow me cannot be my
disciple.[d]
28 "Suppose one of you wants to build
a tower. Will he not first sit down and
estimate the cost to see if he has enough
money to complete it? 29 For if he lays
the foundation and is not able to finish
it, everyone who sees it will ridicule
him, 30 saying, 'This fellow began to
build and was not able to finish.'
31 "Or suppose a king is about to go to
war against another king. Will he not
first sit down and consider whether he
is able with ten thousand men to oppose
the one coming against him with twenty
thousand? 32 If he is not able, he will
send a delegation while the other is still
a long way off and will ask for terms of
peace. 33 In the same way, any of you
who does not give up everything he has
cannot be my disciple.[e]
34 "Salt is good, but if it loses its saltiness, how can it be made salty again?[f]
35 It is fit neither for the soil nor for the
manure pile; it is thrown out.[g]
"He who has ears to hear, let him
hear."[h]

A parable: The lost sheep.

15:4-7pp— Mt 18:12-14

15 Now the tax collectors[i] and "sinners" were all gathering around
to hear him. 2 But the Pharisees and the
teachers of the law muttered, "This
man welcomes sinners and eats with
them."[j]
3 Then Jesus told them this parable:[k]
4 "Suppose one of you has a hundred
sheep and loses one of them. Does he
not leave the ninety-nine in the open
country and go after the lost sheep until
he finds it?[l] 5 And when he finds it, he
joyfully puts it on his shoulders 6 and
goes home. Then he calls his friends and
neighbors together and says, 'Rejoice
with me; I have found my lost sheep.'[m]
7 I tell you that in the same way there
will be more rejoicing in heaven over
one sinner who repents than over ninety-nine righteous persons who do not
need to repent.[n]

A parable: The lost coin.

8 "Or suppose a woman has ten silver
coins[j] and loses one. Does she not light
a lamp, sweep the house and search
carefully until she finds it? 9 And when
she finds it, she calls her friends and
neighbors together and says, 'Rejoice
with me; I have found my lost coin.'[o]
10 In the same way, I tell you, there is

14:21 [a]ver 13
14:24 [b]Mt 21:43; Ac 13:46
14:26 [c]Mt 10:37; Jn 12:25
14:27 [d]Mt 10:38; Lk 9:23
14:33 [e]Php 3:7,8
14:34 [f]Mk 9:50
14:35 [g]Mt 5:13 [h]Mt 11:15
15:1 [i]Lk 5:29
15:2 [j]Mt 9:11
15:3 [k]Mt 13:3
15:4 [l]Ps 23; 119:176; Jer 31:10; Eze 34:11-16; Lk 5:32; 19:10
15:6 [m]ver 9
15:7 [n]ver 10
15:9 [o]ver 6

j8 Greek *ten drachmas,* each worth about a day's wages

rejoicing in the presence of the angels of
God over one sinner who repents."[a]

A parable: The lost son and his loving father.

11 Jesus continued: "There was a man
who had two sons.[b] 12 The younger one
said to his father, 'Father, give me my
share of the estate.'[c] So he divided his
property[d] between them.
13 "Not long after that, the younger
son got together all he had, set off for a
distant country and there squandered
his wealth[e] in wild living. 14 After he had
spent everything, there was a severe
famine in that whole country, and he
began to be in need. 15 So he went and
hired himself out to a citizen of that
country, who sent him to his fields to
feed pigs.[f] 16 He longed to fill his stomach
with the pods that the pigs were eating,
but no one gave him anything.
17 "When he came to his senses, he
said, 'How many of my father's hired
men have food to spare, and here I am
starving to death! 18 I will set out and go
back to my father and say to him:
Father, I have sinned[g] against heaven
and against you. 19 I am no longer worthy
to be called your son; make me like one
of your hired men.' 20 So he got up and
went to his father.
"But while he was still a long way off,
his father saw him and was filled with
compassion for him; he ran to his son,
threw his arms around him and kissed
him.[h]
21 "The son said to him, 'Father, I have
sinned against heaven and against you.[i]
I am no longer worthy to be called your
son.[k]'
22 "But the father said to his servants,
'Quick! Bring the best robe[j] and put it
on him. Put a ring on his finger[k] and
sandals on his feet. 23 Bring the fattened
calf and kill it. Let's have a feast and celebrate. 24 For this son of mine was dead
and is alive again;[l] he was lost and is
found.' So they began to celebrate.[m]
25 "Meanwhile, the older son was in
the field. When he came near the house,
he heard music and dancing. 26 So he
called one of the servants and asked him
what was going on. 27 'Your brother has
come,' he replied, 'and your father has
killed the fattened calf because he has
him back safe and sound.'
28 "The older brother became angry[n]
and refused to go in. So his father went
out and pleaded with him. 29 But he
answered his father, 'Look! All these
years I've been slaving for you and never disobeyed your orders. Yet you never
gave me even a young goat so I could
celebrate with my friends. 30 But when
this son of yours who has squandered
your property[o] with prostitutes[p] comes
home, you kill the fattened calf for him!'
31 " 'My son,' the father said, 'you are
always with me, and everything I have is
yours. 32 But we had to celebrate and be
glad, because this brother of yours was
dead and is alive again; he was lost and
is found.' "[q]

A parable: The shrewd manager.

16 Jesus told his disciples: "There
was a rich man whose manager
was accused of wasting his possessions.[r]
2 So he called him in and asked him,
'What is this I hear about you? Give an
account of your management, because
you cannot be manager any longer.'
3 "The manager said to himself, 'What
shall I do now? My master is taking
away my job. I'm not strong enough to
dig, and I'm ashamed to beg— 4 I know
what I'll do so that, when I lose my job
here, people will welcome me into their
houses.'
5 "So he called in each one of his master's debtors. He asked the first, 'How
much do you owe my master?'
6 " 'Eight hundred gallons[l] of olive oil,'
he replied.
"The manager told him, 'Take your
bill, sit down quickly, and make it four
hundred.'

15:10 [a]ver 7
15:11 [b]Mt 21:28
15:12 [c]Dt 21:17 [d]ver 30
15:13 [e]ver 30; Lk 16:1
15:15 [f]Lev 11:7
15:18 [g]Lev 26:40; Mt 3:2
15:20 [h]Ge 45:14,15; 46:29; Ac 20:37
15:21 [i]Ps 51:4
15:22 [j]Zec 3:4; Rev 6:11 [k]Ge 41:42
15:24 [l]Eph 2:1,5; 5:14; 1Ti 5:6 [m]ver 32
15:28 [n]Jnh 4:1
15:30 [o]ver 12,13 [p]Pr 29:3
15:32 [q]ver 24; Mal 3:17
16:1 [r]Lk 15:13,30

k21 Some early manuscripts *son. Make me like one of your hired men.* l6 Greek *one hundred batous* (probably about 3 kiloliters)

[7]"Then he asked the second, 'And
how much do you owe?'
"'A thousand bushels[m] of wheat,' he
replied.
'He told him, 'Take your bill and
make it eight hundred.'
[8]"The master commended the dishonest manager because he had acted
shrewdly. For the people of this world[a]
are more shrewd[b] in dealing with their
own kind than are the people of the
light.[c] [9]I tell you, use worldly wealth[d] to
gain friends for yourselves, so that when
it is gone, you will be welcomed into
eternal dwellings.[e]
[10]"Whoever can be trusted with very
little can also be trusted with much,[f] and
whoever is dishonest with very little
will also be dishonest with much. [11]So if
you have not been trustworthy in han-
dling worldly wealth,[g] who will trust
you with true riches? [12]And if you have
not been trustworthy with someone
else's property, who will give you property of your own?
[13]"No servant can serve two masters.
Either he will hate the one and love the
other, or he will be devoted to the one
and despise the other. You cannot serve
both God and Money."[h]
[14]The Pharisees, who loved money,[i]
heard all this and were sneering at
Jesus.[j] [15]He said to them, "You are the
ones who justify yourselves[k] in the eyes
of men, but God knows your hearts.[l]
What is highly valued among men is
detestable in God's sight.
[16]"The Law and the Prophets were proclaimed until John.[m] Since that time, the
good news of the kingdom of God is being
preached,[n] and everyone is forcing his
way into it. [17]It is easier for heaven and
earth to disappear than for the least
stroke of a pen to drop out of the Law.[o]
[18]"Anyone who divorces his wife and
marries another woman commits adultery, and the man who marries a
divorced woman commits adultery.[p]

The rich man and Lazarus.

[19]"There was a rich man who was
dressed in purple and fine linen and
lived in luxury every day.[q] [20]At his gate
was laid a beggar[r] named Lazarus, covered with sores [21]and longing to eat
what fell from the rich man's table.[s] Even
the dogs came and licked his sores.
[22]"The time came when the beggar
died and the angels carried him to Abraham's side. The rich man also died and
was buried. [23]In hell,[n] where he was in
torment, he looked up and saw Abraham far away, with Lazarus by his side.
[24]So he called to him, 'Father Abraham,[t] have pity on me and send Lazarus
to dip the tip of his finger in water and
cool my tongue, because I am in agony
in this fire.'[u]
[25]"But Abraham replied, 'Son, remember that in your lifetime you received
your good things, while Lazarus received
bad things,[v] but now he is comforted
here and you are in agony.[w] [26]And besides all this, between us and you a great
chasm has been fixed, so that those who
want to go from here to you cannot, nor
can anyone cross over from there to us.'
[27]"He answered, 'Then I beg you,
father, send Lazarus to my father's house,
[28]for I have five brothers. Let him warn
them,[x] so that they will not also come to
this place of torment.'
[29]"Abraham replied, 'They have
Moses[y] and the Prophets;[z] let them listen to them.'
[30]"'No, father Abraham,'[a] he said, 'but
if someone from the dead goes to them,
they will repent.'
[31]"He said to him, 'If they do not listen to Moses and the Prophets, they will
not be convinced even if someone rises
from the dead.'"

Jesus gives instructions on forgiveness and faith.

17 Jesus said to his disciples: "Things
that cause people to sin[b] are
bound to come, but woe to that person
through whom they come.[c] [2]It would
be better for him to be thrown into

16:8 [a]Ps 17:14 [b]Ps 18:26 [c]Jn 12:36; Eph 5:8; 1Th 5:5
16:9 [d]ver 11,13 [e]Mt 19:21; Lk 12:33
16:10 [f]Mt 25:21,23; Lk 19:17
16:11 [g]ver 9,13
16:13 [h]ver 9,11; Mt 6:24
16:14 [i]1Ti 3:3 [j]Lk 23:35
16:15 [k]Lk 10:29 [l]1Sa 16:7; Rev 2:23
16:16 [m]Mt 11:12,13 [n]Mt 4:23
16:17 [o]Mt 5:18
16:18 [p]Mt 5:31,32; 19:9; Mk 10:11; Ro 7:2,3; 1Co 7:10,11
16:19 [q]Eze 16:49
16:20 [r]Ac 3:2
16:21 [s]Mt 15:27
16:24 [t]ver 30; Lk 3:8 [u]Mt 5:22
16:25 [v]Ps 17:14 [w]Lk 6:21,24,25
16:28 [x]Ac 2:40; 20:23; 1Th 4:6
16:29 [y]Lk 24:27,44; Jn 5:45-47; Ac 15:21 [z]Lk 4:17; Jn 1:45
16:30 [a]ver 24; Lk 3:8
17:1 [b]Mt 5:29 [c]Mt 18:7

m7 Greek *one hundred korous* (probably about 35 kiloliters) n23 Greek *Hades*

the sea with a millstone tied around his
neck than for him to cause one of these
little ones[a] to sin.[b] 3So watch yourselves.
"If your brother sins, rebuke him,[c]
and if he repents, forgive him.[d] 4If he sins
against you seven times in a day, and sev-
en times comes back to you and says, 'I
repent,' forgive him."[e]
5The apostles[f] said to the Lord,[g]
"Increase our faith!"
6He replied, "If you have faith as
small as a mustard seed,[h] you can say to
this mulberry tree, 'Be uprooted and
planted in the sea,' and it will obey you.[i]
7"Suppose one of you had a servant
plowing or looking after the sheep.
Would he say to the servant when he
comes in from the field, 'Come along
now and sit down to eat'? 8Would he not
rather say, 'Prepare my supper, get yourself ready and wait on me[j] while I eat
and drink; after that you may eat and
drink'? 9Would he thank the servant
because he did what he was told to do?
10So you also, when you have done
everything you were told to do, should
say, 'We are unworthy servants; we
have only done our duty.'"[k]

Jesus heals ten men of leprosy.

11Now on his way to Jerusalem,[l]
Jesus traveled along the border between
Samaria and Galilee.[m] 12As he was
going into a village, ten men who had
leprosy[o][n] met him. They stood at a distance[o] 13and called out in a loud voice,
"Jesus, Master,[p] have pity on us!"
14When he saw them, he said, "Go,
show yourselves to the priests."[q] And as
they went, they were cleansed.
15One of them, when he saw he was
healed, came back, praising God[r] in a
loud voice. 16He threw himself at Jesus'
feet and thanked him—and he was a
Samaritan.[s]
17Jesus asked, "Were not all ten
cleansed? Where are the other nine?
18Was no one found to return and give
praise to God except this foreigner?"
19Then he said to him, "Rise and go;
your faith has made you well."[t]

Jesus teaches about the second coming.

17:26,27pp— Mt 24:37-39

20Once, having been asked by the
Pharisees when the kingdom of God
would come,[u] Jesus replied, "The kingdom of God does not come with your
careful observation, 21nor will people
say, 'Here it is,' or 'There it is,'[v] because
the kingdom of God is within[p] you."
22Then he said to his disciples, "The
time is coming when you will long to see
one of the days of the Son of Man,[w] but
you will not see it.[x] 23Men will tell you,
'There he is!' or 'Here he is!' Do not go
running off after them.[y] 24For the Son of
Man in his day[q] will be like the lightning,[z] which flashes and lights up the
sky from one end to the other. 25But first
he must suffer many things[a] and be
rejected[b] by this generation.[c]
26"Just as it was in the days of Noah,[d]
so also will it be in the days of the Son of
Man. 27People were eating, drinking,
marrying and being given in marriage
up to the day Noah entered the ark. Then
the flood came and destroyed them all.
28"It was the same in the days of
Lot.[e] People were eating and drinking,
buying and selling, planting and building. 29But the day Lot left Sodom, fire
and sulfur rained down from heaven and
destroyed them all.
30"It will be just like this on the day
the Son of Man is revealed.[f] 31On that
day no one who is on the roof of his
house, with his goods inside, should
go down to get them. Likewise, no one
in the field should go back for anything.[g] 32Remember Lot's wife![h] 33Who-
ever tries to keep his life will lose it,
and whoever loses his life will preserve it.[i] 34I tell you, on that night two

17:2 [a]Mk 10:24; Lk 10:21 [b]Mt 5:29
17:3 [c]Mt 18:15 [d]Eph 4:32; Col 3:13
17:4 [e]Mt 18:21,22
17:5 [f]Mk 6:30 [g]Lk 7:13
17:6 [h]Mt 13:31; 17:20; Lk 13:19 [i]Mt 21:21; Mk 9:23
17:8 [j]Lk 12:37
17:10 [k]1Co 9:16
17:11 [l]Lk 9:51 [m]Lk 9:51,52; Jn 4:3,4
17:12 [n]Mt 8:2 [o]Lev 13:45, 46
17:13 [p]Lk 5:5
17:14 [q]Lev 14:2; Mt 8:4
17:15 [r]Mt 9:8
17:16 [s]Mt 10:5
17:19 [t]Mt 9:22
17:20 [u]Mt 3:2
17:21 [v]ver 23
17:22 [w]Mt 8:20 [x]Mt 9:15; Lk 5:35
17:23 [y]Mt 24:23; Mk 13:21; Lk 21:8
17:24 [z]Mt 24:27
17:25 [a]Mt 16:21 [b]Lk 9:22; 18:32 [c]Mk 13:30; Lk 21:32
17:26 [d]Ge 7:6-24
17:28 [e]Ge 19:1-28
17:30 [f]Mt 10:23; 16:27; 24:3,27,37,39; 25:31; 1Co 1:7; 1Th 2:19; 2Th 1:7; 2:8; 2Pe 3:4; Rev 1:7
17:31 [g]Mt 24:17,18; Mk 13:15-16
17:32 [h]Ge 19:26 **17:33** [i]Jn 12:25

o *12* The Greek word was used for various diseases affecting the skin—not necessarily leprosy. p *21* Or *among* q *24* Some manuscripts do not have *in his day.*

people will be in one bed; one will be taken and the other left. 35 Two women will be grinding grain together; one will be taken and the other left.[r]"[a]

37 "Where, Lord?" they asked.

He replied, "Where there is a dead body, there the vultures will gather."[b]

The unjust judge and the persistent widow.

18 Then Jesus told his disciples a parable to show them that they should always pray and not give up.[c] 2 He said: "In a certain town there was a judge who neither feared God nor cared about men. 3 And there was a widow in that town who kept coming to him with the plea, 'Grant me justice[d] against my adversary.'

4 "For some time he refused. But finally he said to himself, 'Even though I don't fear God or care about men, 5 yet because this widow keeps bothering me, I will see that she gets justice, so that she won't eventually wear me out with her coming!' "[e]

6 And the Lord[f] said, "Listen to what the unjust judge says. 7 And will not God bring about justice for his chosen ones, who cry out[g] to him day and night? Will he keep putting them off? 8 I tell you, he will see that they get justice, and quickly. However, when the Son of Man[h] comes,[i] will he find faith on the earth?"

Prayers of the Pharisee and the tax collector.

9 To some who were confident of their own righteousness[j] and looked down on everybody else,[k] Jesus told this parable: 10 "Two men went up to the temple to pray,[l] one a Pharisee and the other a tax collector. 11 The Pharisee stood up[m] and prayed about[s] himself: 'God, I thank you that I am not like other men—robbers, evildoers, adulterers—or even like this tax collector. 12 I fast[n] twice a week and give a tenth[o] of all I get.'

13 "But the tax collector stood at a distance. He would not even look up to heaven, but beat his breast[p] and said, 'God, have mercy on me, a sinner.'[q]

14 "I tell you that this man, rather than the other, went home justified before God. For everyone who exalts himself will be humbled, and he who humbles himself will be exalted."[r]

Jesus and the little children.

18:15-17pp— Mt 19:13-15; Mk 10:13-16

15 People were also bringing babies to Jesus to have him touch them. When the disciples saw this, they rebuked them. 16 But Jesus called the children to him and said, "Let the little children come to me, and do not hinder them, for the kingdom of God belongs to such as these. 17 I tell you the truth, anyone who will not receive the kingdom of God like a little child[s] will never enter it."

The rich ruler.

18:18-30pp— Mt 19:16-29; Mk 10:17-30

18 A certain ruler asked him, "Good teacher, what must I do to inherit eternal life?"[t]

19 "Why do you call me good?" Jesus answered. "No one is good—except God alone. 20 You know the commandments: 'Do not commit adultery, do not murder, do not steal, do not give false testimony, honor your father and mother.'[t]"[u]

21 "All these I have kept since I was a boy," he said.

22 When Jesus heard this, he said to him, "You still lack one thing. Sell everything you have and give to the poor,[v] and you will have treasure in heaven.[w] Then come, follow me."

23 When he heard this, he became very sad, because he was a man of great wealth. 24 Jesus looked at him and said, "How hard it is for the rich to enter the kingdom of God![x] 25 Indeed, it is easier for a camel to go through the eye of a needle than for a rich man to enter the kingdom of God."

17:35 [a]Mt 24:41
17:37 [b]Mt 24:28
18:1 [c]Isa 40:31; Lk 11:5-8; Ac 1:14; Ro 12:12; Eph 6:18; Col 4:2; 1Th 5:17
18:3 [d]Isa 1:17
18:5 [e]Lk 11:8
18:6 [f]Lk 7:13
18:7 [g]Ex 22:23; Ps 88:1; Rev 6:10
18:8 [h]Mt 8:20 [i]Mt 16:27
18:9 [j]Lk 16:15 [k]Isa 65:5
18:10 [l]Ac 3:1
18:11 [m]Mt 6:5; Mk 11:25
18:12 [n]Isa 58:3; Mt 9:14 [o]Mal 3:8; Lk 11:42
18:13 [p]Isa 66:2; Jer 31:19; Lk 23:48 [q]Lk 5:32; 1Ti 1:15
18:14 [r]Mt 23:12; Lk 14:11
18:17 [s]Mt 11:25; 18:3
18:18 [t]Lk 10:25
18:20 [u]Ex 20:12-16; Dt 5:16-20; Ro 13:9
18:22 [v]Ac 2:45 [w]Mt 6:20
18:24 [x]Pr 11:28

r *35* Some manuscripts *left.* [36] *Two men will be in the field; one will be taken and the other left.*
s *11* Or *to* t *20* Exodus 20:12-16; Deut. 5:16-20

26Those who heard this asked, "Who
then can be saved?"
27Jesus replied, "What is impossible
with men is possible with God."[a]
28Peter said to him, "We have left all
we had to follow you!"[b]
29"I tell you the truth," Jesus said to
them, "no one who has left home or wife
or brothers or parents or children for the
sake of the kingdom of God 30will fail to
receive many times as much in this age
and, in the age to come,[c] eternal life."[d]

Jesus' prediction of his death.

18:31-33pp— Mt 20:17-19; Mk 10:32-34

31Jesus took the Twelve aside and told
them, "We are going up to Jerusalem,[e]
and everything that is written by the
prophets[f] about the Son of Man[g] will be
fulfilled. 32He will be handed over to the
Gentiles.[h] They will mock him, insult
him, spit on him, flog him[i] and kill him.[j]
33On the third day[k] he will rise again."[l]
34The disciples did not understand any
of this. Its meaning was hidden from
them, and they did not know what he was
talking about.[m]

Healing of the blind man.

18:35-43pp— Mt 20:29-34; Mk 10:46-52

35As Jesus approached Jericho,[n] a blind
man was sitting by the roadside begging.
36When he heard the crowd going by, he
asked what was happening. 37They told
him, "Jesus of Nazareth is passing by."[o]
38He called out, "Jesus, Son of David,[p]
have mercy[q] on me!"
39Those who led the way rebuked him
and told him to be quiet, but he shouted
all the more, "Son of David, have mercy
on me!"[r]
40Jesus stopped and ordered the man
to be brought to him. When he came
near, Jesus asked him, 41"What do you
want me to do for you?"
"Lord, I want to see," he replied.
42Jesus said to him, "Receive your
sight; your faith has healed you."[s]
43Immediately he received his sight
and followed Jesus, praising God. When
all the people saw it, they also praised
God.[t]

Meeting of Jesus and Zacchaeus.

19 Jesus entered Jericho[u] and was
passing through. 2A man was
there by the name of Zacchaeus; he was
a chief tax collector and was wealthy.
3He wanted to see who Jesus was, but
being a short man he could not, because
of the crowd. 4So he ran ahead and
climbed a sycamore-fig[v] tree to see him,
since Jesus was coming that way.[w]
5When Jesus reached the spot, he
looked up and said to him, "Zacchaeus,
come down immediately. I must stay at
your house today." 6So he came down at
once and welcomed him gladly.
7All the people saw this and began to
mutter, "He has gone to be the guest of
a 'sinner.'"[x]
8But Zacchaeus stood up and said to
the Lord,[y] "Look, Lord! Here and now I
give half of my possessions to the poor,
and if I have cheated anybody out of
anything,[z] I will pay back four times the
amount."[a]
9Jesus said to him, "Today salvation
has come to this house, because this
man, too, is a son of Abraham.[b] 10For
the Son of Man came to seek and to save
what was lost."[c]

A parable: The ten minas.

19:12-27Ref— Mt 25:14-30

11While they were listening to this,
he went on to tell them a parable, because he was near Jerusalem and the
people thought that the kingdom of
God[d] was going to appear at once.[e]
12He said: "A man of noble birth went
to a distant country to have himself appointed king and then to return. 13So
he called ten of his servants[f] and gave
them ten minas.[u] 'Put this money to
work,' he said, 'until I come back.'
14"But his subjects hated him and
sent a delegation after him to say, 'We
don't want this man to be our king.'

18:27 [a]Mt 19:26
18:28 [b]Mt 4:19
18:30 [c]Mt 12:32 [d]Mt 25:46
18:31 [e]Lk 9:51 [f]Ps 22; Isa 53 [g]Mt 8:20
18:32 [h]Lk 23:1 [i]Mt 16:21 [j]Ac 2:23
18:33 [k]Mt 16:21 [l]Mt 16:21
18:34 [m]Mk 9:32; Lk 9:45
18:35 [n]Lk 19:1
18:37 [o]Lk 19:4
18:38 [p]ver 39; Mt 9:27 [q]Mt 17:15; Lk 18:13
18:39 [r]ver 38
18:42 [s]Mt 9:22
18:43 [t]Mt 9:8; Lk 13:17
19:1 [u]Lk 18:35
19:4 [v]1Ki 10:27; 1Ch 27:28; Isa 9:10 [w]Lk 18:37
19:7 [x]Mt 9:11
19:8 [y]Lk 7:13 [z]Lk 3:12,13 [a]Ex 22:1; Lev 6:4,5; Nu 5:7; 2Sa 12:6
19:9 [b]Lk 3:8; 13:16; Ro 4:16; Gal 3:7
19:10 [c]Eze 34:12, 16; Jn 3:17
19:11 [d]Mt 3:2 [e]Lk 17:20; Ac 1:6
19:13 [f]Mk 13:34

[u]13 A mina was about three months' wages.

15"He was made king, however, and
returned home. Then he sent for the
servants to whom he had given the
money, in order to find out what they
had gained with it.
16"The first one came and said, 'Sir,
your mina has earned ten more.'
17" 'Well done, my good servant!'[a] his
master replied. 'Because you have been
trustworthy in a very small matter, take
charge of ten cities.'[b]
18"The second came and said, 'Sir,
your mina has earned five more.'
19"His master answered, 'You take
charge of five cities.'
20"Then another servant came and
said, 'Sir, here is your mina; I have kept
it laid away in a piece of cloth. 21I was
afraid of you, because you are a hard
man. You take out what you did not put
in and reap what you did not sow.'[c]
22"His master replied, 'I will judge
you by your own words,[d] you wicked
servant! You knew, did you, that I am a
hard man, taking out what I did not put
in, and reaping what I did not sow?[e]
23Why then didn't you put my money
on deposit, so that when I came back,
I could have collected it with interest?'
24"Then he said to those standing by,
'Take his mina away from him and give
it to the one who has ten minas.'
25" 'Sir,' they said, 'he already has ten!'
26"He replied, 'I tell you that to everyone who has, more will be given, but as
for the one who has nothing, even what
he has will be taken away.[f] 27But those
enemies of mine who did not want me
to be king over them—bring them here
and kill them in front of me.' "

The Triumphal Entry.

19:29-38pp— Mt 21:1-9; Mk 11:1-10
19:35-38pp— Jn 12:12-15

28After Jesus had said this, he went
on ahead, going up to Jerusalem.[g] 29As
he approached Bethphage and Bethany[h]
at the hill called the Mount of Olives,[i] he
sent two of his disciples, saying to them,
30"Go to the village ahead of you, and as
you enter it, you will find a colt tied
there, which no one has ever ridden.
Untie it and bring it here. 31If anyone
asks you, 'Why are you untying it?' tell
him, 'The Lord needs it.' "
32Those who were sent ahead went
and found it just as he had told them.[j]
33As they were untying the colt, its owners asked them, "Why are you untying
the colt?"
34They replied, "The Lord needs it."
35They brought it to Jesus, threw their
cloaks on the colt and put Jesus on it.
36As he went along, people spread their
cloaks[k] on the road.
37When he came near the place where
the road goes down the Mount of
Olives,[l] the whole crowd of disciples
began joyfully to praise God in loud
voices for all the miracles they had seen:

38"Blessed is the king who comes in the
name of the Lord!"[v][m]

"Peace in heaven and glory in the
highest!"[n]

39Some of the Pharisees in the crowd
said to Jesus, "Teacher, rebuke your
disciples!"[o]
40"I tell you," he replied, "if they keep
quiet, the stones will cry out."[p]
41As he approached Jerusalem and
saw the city, he wept over it[q] 42and said,
"If you, even you, had only known on
this day what would bring you peace—
but now it is hidden from your eyes.
43The days will come upon you when
your enemies will build an embankment
against you and encircle you and hem
you in on every side.[r] 44They will dash
you to the ground, you and the children
within your walls.[s] They will not leave
one stone on another,[t] because you did
not recognize the time of God's coming[u]
to you."

Jesus' clearing of the temple.

19:45,46pp— Mt 21:12-16; Mk 11:15-18; Jn 2:13-16

45Then he entered the temple area
and began driving out those who
were selling. 46"It is written," he said

19:17 [a]Pr 27:18 [b]Lk 16:10
19:21 [c]Mt 25:24
19:22 [d]2Sa 1:16; Job 15:6 [e]Mt 25:26
19:26 [f]Mt 13:12; 25:29; Lk 8:18
19:28 [g]Mk 10:32; Lk 9:51
19:29 [h]Mt 21:17 [i]Mt 21:1
19:32 [j]Lk 22:13
19:36 [k]2Ki 9:13
19:37 [l]Mt 21:1
19:38 [m]Ps 118:26; Lk 13:35 [n]Lk 2:14
19:39 [o]Mt 21:15,16
19:40 [p]Hab 2:11
19:41 [q]Isa 22:4; Lk 13:34,35
19:43 [r]Isa 29:3; Jer 6:6; Eze 4:2; 26:8; Lk 21:20
19:44 [s]Ps 137:9 [t]Mt 24:2; Mk 13:2; Lk 21:6 [u]1Pe 2:12

v38 Psalm 118:26

to them, " 'My house will be a house of prayer'[w];[a] but you have made it 'a den of robbers.'[x]"[b]

47 Every day he was teaching at the temple.[c] But the chief priests, the teachers of the law and the leaders among the people were trying to kill him.[d] 48 Yet they could not find any way to do it, because all the people hung on his words.

Authority of Jesus.

20:1-8pp— Mt 21:23-27; Mk 11:27-33

20 One day as he was teaching the people in the temple courts[e] and preaching the gospel,[f] the chief priests and the teachers of the law, together with the elders, came up to him. 2 "Tell us by what authority you are doing these things," they said. "Who gave you this authority?"[g]

3 He replied, "I will also ask you a question. Tell me, 4 John's baptism[h]—was it from heaven, or from men?"

5 They discussed it among themselves and said, "If we say, 'From heaven,' he will ask, 'Why didn't you believe him?' 6 But if we say, 'From men,' all the people[i] will stone us, because they are persuaded that John was a prophet."[j]

7 So they answered, "We don't know where it was from."

8 Jesus said, "Neither will I tell you by what authority I am doing these things."

A parable: The vineyard and the wicked tenants.

20:9-19pp— Mt 21:33-46; Mk 12:1-12

9 He went on to tell the people this parable: "A man planted a vineyard,[k] rented it to some farmers and went away for a long time.[l] 10 At harvest time he sent a servant to the tenants so they would give him some of the fruit of the vineyard. But the tenants beat him and sent him away empty-handed. 11 He sent another servant, but that one also they beat and treated shamefully and sent away empty-handed. 12 He sent still a third, and they wounded him and threw him out.

13 "Then the owner of the vineyard said, 'What shall I do? I will send my son, whom I love;[m] perhaps they will respect him.'

14 "But when the tenants saw him, they talked the matter over. 'This is the heir,' they said. 'Let's kill him, and the inheritance will be ours.' 15 So they threw him out of the vineyard and killed him.

"What then will the owner of the vineyard do to them? 16 He will come and kill those tenants[n] and give the vineyard to others."

When the people heard this, they said, "May this never be!"

17 Jesus looked directly at them and asked, "Then what is the meaning of that which is written:

> " 'The stone the builders rejected
> has become the capstone'[y][z]?[o]

18 Everyone who falls on that stone will be broken to pieces, but he on whom it falls will be crushed."[p]

19 The teachers of the law and the chief priests looked for a way to arrest him[q] immediately, because they knew he had spoken this parable against them. But they were afraid of the people.[r]

Taxes to Caesar.

20:20-26pp— Mt 22:15-22; Mk 12:13-17

20 Keeping a close watch on him, they sent spies, who pretended to be honest. They hoped to catch Jesus in something he said[s] so that they might hand him over to the power and authority of the governor.[t] 21 So the spies questioned him: "Teacher, we know that you speak and teach what is right, and that you do not show partiality but teach the way of God in accordance with the truth.[u] 22 Is it right for us to pay taxes to Caesar or not?"

23 He saw through their duplicity and said to them, 24 "Show me a denarius. Whose portrait and inscription are on it?"

25 "Caesar's," they replied.

19:46 [a]Isa 56:7 [b]Jer 7:11
19:47 [c]Mt 26:55 [d]Mt 12:14; Mk 11:18
20:1 [e]Mt 26:55 [f]Lk 8:1
20:2 [g]Jn 2:18; Ac 4:7; 7:27
20:4 [h]Mk 1:4
20:6 [i]Lk 7:29 [j]Mt 11:9
20:9 [k]Isa 5:1-7 [l]Mt 25:14
20:13 [m]Mt 3:17
20:16 [n]Lk 19:27
20:17 [o]Ps 118:22; Ac 4:11
20:18 [p]Isa 8:14,15
20:19 [q]Lk 19:47 [r]Mk 11:18
20:20 [s]Mt 12:10 [t]Mt 27:2
20:21 [u]Jn 3:2

[w]*46* Isaiah 56:7 [x]*46* Jer. 7:11 [y]*17* Or *cornerstone* [z]*17* Psalm 118:22

He said to them, "Then give to Caesar what is Caesar's,[a] and to God what is God's."

26 They were unable to trap him in what he had said there in public. And astonished by his answer, they became silent.

Resurrection and marriage.

20:27-40pp— Mt 22:23-33; Mk 12:18-27

27 Some of the Sadducees,[b] who say there is no resurrection,[c] came to Jesus with a question. 28 "Teacher," they said, "Moses wrote for us that if a man's brother dies and leaves a wife but no children, the man must marry the widow and have children for his brother.[d] 29 Now there were seven brothers. The first one married a woman and died childless. 30 The second 31 and then the third married her, and in the same way the seven died, leaving no children. 32 Finally, the woman died too. 33 Now then, at the resurrection whose wife will she be, since the seven were married to her?"

34 Jesus replied, "The people of this age marry and are given in marriage. 35 But those who are considered worthy of taking part in that age[e] and in the resurrection from the dead will neither marry nor be given in marriage, 36 and they can no longer die; for they are like the angels. They are God's children,[f] since they are children of the resurrection. 37 But in the account of the bush, even Moses showed that the dead rise, for he calls the Lord 'the God of Abraham, and the God of Isaac, and the God of Jacob.'[a][g] 38 He is not the God of the dead, but of the living, for to him all are alive."

39 Some of the teachers of the law responded, "Well said, teacher!" 40 And no one dared to ask him any more questions.[h]

Questioning about Jesus' sonship.

20:41-47pp— Mt 22:41–23:7; Mk 12:35-40

41 Then Jesus said to them, "How is it that they say the Christ[b] is the Son of David?[i] 42 David himself declares in the Book of Psalms:

"'The Lord said to my Lord:
"Sit at my right hand
43 until I make your enemies
a footstool for your feet."'[c][j]

44 David calls him 'Lord.' How then can he be his son?"

45 While all the people were listening, Jesus said to his disciples, 46 "Beware of the teachers of the law. They like to walk around in flowing robes and love to be greeted in the marketplaces and have the most important seats in the synagogues and the places of honor at banquets.[k] 47 They devour widows' houses and for a show make lengthy prayers. Such men will be punished most severely."

The poor widow's offering.

21:1-4pp— Mk 12:41-44

21 As he looked up, Jesus saw the rich putting their gifts into the temple treasury.[l] 2 He also saw a poor widow put in two very small copper coins.[d] 3 "I tell you the truth," he said, "this poor widow has put in more than all the others. 4 All these people gave their gifts out of their wealth; but she out of her poverty put in all she had to live on."[m]

The destruction of the temple and Jerusalem, and the last days.

21:5-36pp— Mt 24; Mk 13
21:12-17pp— Mt 10:17-22

5 Some of his disciples were remarking about how the temple was adorned with beautiful stones and with gifts dedicated to God. But Jesus said, 6 "As for what you see here, the time will come when not one stone will be left on another;[n] every one of them will be thrown down."

7 "Teacher," they asked, "when will these things happen? And what will be

20:25 [a]Lk 23:2; Ro 13:7
20:27 [b]Ac 4:1 [c]Ac 23:8; 1Co 15:12
20:28 [d]Dt 25:5
20:35 [e]Mt 12:32
20:36 [f]Jn 1:12; 1Jn 3:1-2
20:37 [g]Ex 3:6
20:40 [h]Mt 22:46; Mk 12:34
20:41 [i]Mt 1:1
20:43 [j]Ps 110:1; Mt 22:44
20:46 [k]Lk 11:43
21:1 [l]Mt 27:6; Jn 8:20
21:4 [m]2Co 8:12
21:6 [n]Lk 19:44

a 37 Exodus 3:6 b 41 Or *Messiah*
c 43 Psalm 110:1 d 2 Greek *two lepta*

the sign that they are about to take
place?"
8He replied: "Watch out that you are
not deceived. For many will come in my
name, claiming, 'I am he,' and, 'The
time is near.' Do not follow them.[a]
9When you hear of wars and revolu-
tions, do not be frightened. These things
must happen first, but the end will not
come right away."

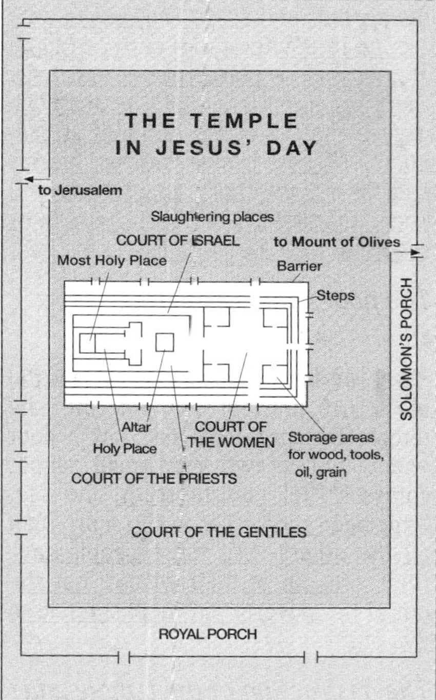

10Then he said to them: "Nation will
rise against nation, and kingdom against
kingdom.[b] 11There will be great earthquakes, famines and pestilences in various places, and fearful events and great
signs from heaven.[c]
12"But before all this, they will lay
hands on you and persecute you. They
will deliver you to synagogues and
prisons, and you will be brought before
kings and governors, and all on account
of my name. 13This will result in your
being witnesses to them.[d] 14But make
up your mind not to worry beforehand
how you will defend yourselves.[e] 15For
I will give you[f] words and wisdom that
none of your adversaries will be able
to resist or contradict. 16You will be
betrayed even by parents, brothers, relatives and friends,[g] and they will put
some of you to death. 17All men will
hate you because of me.[h] 18But not a
hair of your head will perish.[i] 19By
standing firm you will gain life.[j]
20"When you see Jerusalem being surrounded by armies,[k] you will know that
its desolation is near. 21Then let those
who are in Judea flee to the mountains,
let those in the city get out, and let
those in the country not enter the city.[l]
22For this is the time of punishment[m]
in fulfillment[n] of all that has been written. 23How dreadful it will be in those
days for pregnant women and nursing
mothers! There will be great distress in
the land and wrath against this people.
24They will fall by the sword and will
be taken as prisoners to all the nations.
Jerusalem will be trampled[o] on by the
Gentiles until the times of the Gentiles
are fulfilled.
25"There will be signs in the sun,
moon and stars. On the earth, nations
will be in anguish and perplexity at the
roaring and tossing of the sea.[p] 26Men
will faint from terror, apprehensive of
what is coming on the world, for the
heavenly bodies will be shaken.[q] 27At
that time they will see the Son of Man[r]
coming in a cloud[s] with power and great
glory. 28When these things begin to take
place, stand up and lift up your heads,
because your redemption is drawing
near."[t]
29He told them this parable: "Look at
the fig tree and all the trees. 30When
they sprout leaves, you can see for yourselves and know that summer is near.
31Even so, when you see these things
happening, you know that the kingdom
of God[u] is near.
32"I tell you the truth, this generation[e][v] will certainly not pass away until
all these things have happened. 33Heaven
and earth will pass away, but my words
will never pass away.[w]

21:8 [a]Lk 17:23
21:10 [b]2Ch 15:6; Isa 19:2
21:11 [c]Isa 29:6; Joel 2:30
21:13 [d]Php 1:12
21:14 [e]Lk 12:11
21:15 [f]Lk 12:12
21:16 [g]Lk 12:52,53
21:17 [h]Jn 15:21
21:18 [i]Mt 10:30
21:19 [j]Mt 10:22
21:20 [k]Lk 19:43
21:21 [l]Lk 17:31
21:22 [m]Isa 63:4; Da 9:24-27; Hos 9:7 [n]Mt 1:22
21:24 [o]Isa 5:5; 63:18; Da 8:13; Rev 11:2
21:25 [p]2Pe 3:10,12
21:26 [q]Mt 24:29
21:27 [r]Mt 8:20 [s]Rev 1:7
21:28 [t]Lk 18:7
21:31 [u]Mt 3:2
21:32 [v]Lk 11:50; 17:25
21:33 [w]Mt 5:18

e32 Or *race*

34"Be careful, or your hearts will be
weighed down with dissipation, drunkenness and the anxieties of life,[a] and
that day will close on you unexpectedly[b] like a trap. 35For it will come upon all
those who live on the face of the whole
earth. 36Be always on the watch, and
pray[c] that you may be able to escape all
that is about to happen, and that you
may be able to stand before the Son of
Man."

37Each day Jesus was teaching at the
temple,[d] and each evening he went out[e]
to spend the night on the hill called the
Mount of Olives,[f] 38and all the people
came early in the morning to hear him
at the temple.[g]

Conspiracy to kill Jesus.

22:1,2pp— Mt 26:2-5; Mk 14:1,2,10,11

22 Now the Feast of Unleavened
Bread, called the Passover, was
approaching,[h] 2and the chief priests and
the teachers of the law were looking for
some way to get rid of Jesus,[i] for they
were afraid of the people. 3Then Satan[j]
entered Judas, called Iscariot,[k] one of the
Twelve. 4And Judas went to the chief
priests and the officers of the temple
guard[l] and discussed with them how he
might betray Jesus. 5They were delighted and agreed to give him money.[m] 6He
consented, and watched for an opportunity to hand Jesus over to them when no
crowd was present.

The Last Supper.

22:7-13pp— Mt 26:17-19; Mk 14:12-16
22:17-20pp— Mt 26:26-29; Mk 14:22-25; 1Co 11:23-25
22:21-23pp— Mt 26:21-24; Mk 14:18-21; Jn 13:21-30
22:25-27pp— Mt 20:25-28; Mk 10:42-45
22:33,34pp— Mt 26:33-35; Mk 14:29-31; Jn 13:37,38

7Then came the day of Unleavened
Bread on which the Passover lamb had
to be sacrificed.[n] 8Jesus sent Peter and
John,[o] saying, "Go and make preparations for us to eat the Passover."

9"Where do you want us to prepare
for it?" they asked.

10He replied, "As you enter the city, a
man carrying a jar of water will meet
you. Follow him to the house that he
enters, 11and say to the owner of the
house, 'The Teacher asks: Where is the
guest room, where I may eat the
Passover with my disciples?' 12He will
show you a large upper room, all furnished. Make preparations there."

13They left and found things just as
Jesus had told them.[p] So they prepared
the Passover.

14When the hour came, Jesus and his
apostles[q] reclined at the table.[r] 15And
he said to them, "I have eagerly desired
to eat this Passover with you before I
suffer.[s] 16For I tell you, I will not eat it
again until it finds fulfillment in the
kingdom of God."[t]

17After taking the cup, he gave thanks
and said, "Take this and divide it among
you. 18For I tell you I will not drink again
of the fruit of the vine until the kingdom
of God comes."

19And he took bread, gave thanks and
broke it,[u] and gave it to them, saying,
"This is my body given for you; do this
in remembrance of me."

20In the same way, after the supper he
took the cup, saying, "This cup is the
new covenant[v] in my blood, which is
poured out for you. 21But the hand of
him who is going to betray me is with
mine on the table.[w] 22The Son of Man[x]
will go as it has been decreed,[y] but woe
to that man who betrays him." 23They
began to question among themselves
which of them it might be who would
do this.

24Also a dispute arose among them as
to which of them was considered to be
greatest.[z] 25Jesus said to them, "The
kings of the Gentiles lord it over them;
and those who exercise authority over
them call themselves Benefactors. 26But
you are not to be like that. Instead, the
greatest among you should be like the
youngest,[a] and the one who rules like the
one who serves.[b] 27For who is greater,
the one who is at the table or the one
who serves? Is it not the one who is at
the table? But I am among you as one
who serves.[c] 28You are those who have
stood by me in my trials. 29And I confer

21:34 [a]Mk 4:19 [b]Lk 12:40,46; 1Th 5:2-7
21:36 [c]Mt 26:41
21:37 [d]Mt 26:55 [e]Mk 11:19 [f]Mt 21:1
21:38 [g]Jn 8:2
22:1 [h]Jn 11:55
22:2 [i]Mt 12:14
22:3 [j]Mt 4:10; Jn 13:2 [k]Mt 10:4
22:4 [l]ver 52; Ac 4:1; 5:24
22:5 [m]Zec 11:12
22:7 [n]Ex 12:18-20; Dt 16:5-8; Mk 14:12
22:8 [o]Ac 3:1,11; 4:13,19; 8:14
22:13 [p]Lk 19:32
22:14 [q]Mk 6:30 [r]Mt 26:20; Mk 14:17,18
22:15 [s]Mt 16:21
22:16 [t]Lk 14:15; Rev 19:9
22:19 [u]Mt 14:19
22:20 [v]Ex 24:8; Isa 42:6; Jer 31:31-34; Zec 9:11; 2Co 3:6; Heb 8:6; 9:15
22:21 [w]Ps 41:9
22:22 [x]Mt 8:20 [y]Ac 2:23; 4:28
22:24 [z]Mk 9:34; Lk 9:46
22:26 [a]1Pe 5:5 [b]Mk 9:35; Lk 9:48
22:27 [c]Mt 20:28; Lk 12:37

on you a kingdom,[a] just as my Father
conferred one on me, 30so that you may
eat and drink at my table in my kingdom[b] and sit on thrones, judging the
twelve tribes of Israel.[c]
31"Simon, Simon, Satan has asked[d] to
sift you[f] as wheat.[e] 32But I have prayed
for you,[f] Simon, that your faith may not
fail. And when you have turned back,
strengthen your brothers."[g]
33But he replied, "Lord, I am ready to
go with you to prison and to death."[h]
34Jesus answered, "I tell you, Peter,
before the rooster crows today, you will
deny three times that you know me."
35Then Jesus asked them, "When I sent
you without purse, bag or sandals,[i] did
you lack anything?"
"Nothing," they answered.
36He said to them, "But now if you
have a purse, take it, and also a bag; and
if you don't have a sword, sell your cloak
and buy one. 37It is written: 'And he was
numbered with the transgressors'[g];[j] and
I tell you that this must be fulfilled in
me. Yes, what is written about me is
reaching its fulfillment."
38The disciples said, "See, Lord, here
are two swords."
"That is enough," he replied.

Jesus' torment on the Mount of Olives.

22:40-46pp— Mt 26:36-46; Mk 14:32-42

39Jesus went out as usual[k] to the
Mount of Olives,[l] and his disciples followed him. 40On reaching the place,
he said to them, "Pray that you will not
fall into temptation."[m] 41He withdrew
about a stone's throw beyond them,
knelt down[n] and prayed, 42"Father, if
you are willing, take this cup[o] from me;
yet not my will, but yours be done."[p]
43An angel from heaven appeared to him
and strengthened him.[q] 44And being
in anguish, he prayed more earnestly,
and his sweat was like drops of blood
falling to the ground.[h]
45When he rose from prayer and went
back to the disciples, he found them
asleep, exhausted from sorrow. 46"Why
are you sleeping?" he asked them. "Get
up and pray so that you will not fall into
temptation."[r]

22:29 [a]Mt 25:34; 2Ti 2:12
22:30 [b]Lk 14:15 [c]Mt 19:28
22:31 [d]Job 1:6-12 [e]Am 9:9
22:32 [f]Jn 17:9,15; Ro 8:34 [g]Jn 21:15-17
22:33 [h]Jn 11:16
22:35 [i]Mt 10:9,10; Lk 9:3; 10:4
22:37 [j]Isa 53:12
22:39 [k]Lk 21:37 [l]Mt 21:1
22:40 [m]Mt 6:13
22:41 [n]Lk 18:11
22:42 [o]Mt 20:22 [p]Mt 26:39
22:43 [q]Mt 4:11; Mk 1:13
22:46 [r]ver 40
22:49 [s]ver 38
22:52 [t]ver 4
22:53 [u]Mt 26:55 [v]Jn 12:27 [w]Mt 8:12; Jn 1:5; 3:20
22:54 [x]Mt 26:57; Mk 14:53 [y]Mt 26:58; Mk 14:54; Jn 18:15
22:59 [z]Lk 23:6

Jesus' betrayal and arrest.

22:47-53pp— Mt 26:47-56; Mk 14:43-50; Jn 18:3-11

47While he was still speaking a crowd
came up, and the man who was called
Judas, one of the Twelve, was leading
them. He approached Jesus to kiss him,
48but Jesus asked him, "Judas, are you
betraying the Son of Man with a kiss?"
49When Jesus' followers saw what was
going to happen, they said, "Lord, should
we strike with our swords?"[s] 50And
one of them struck the servant of the
high priest, cutting off his right ear.
51But Jesus answered, "No more of
this!" And he touched the man's ear and
healed him.
52Then Jesus said to the chief priests,
the officers of the temple guard,[t] and the
elders, who had come for him, "Am I
leading a rebellion, that you have come
with swords and clubs? 53Every day I was
with you in the temple courts,[u] and you
did not lay a hand on me. But this is
your hour[v]—when darkness reigns."[w]

Peter's great denial.

22:55-62pp — Mt 26:69-75; Mk 14:66-72; Jn 18:16-18,25-27

54Then seizing him, they led him away
and took him into the house of the high
priest.[x] Peter followed at a distance.[y]
55But when they had kindled a fire in the
middle of the courtyard and had sat
down together, Peter sat down with them.
56A servant girl saw him seated there in
the firelight. She looked closely at him
and said, "This man was with him."
57But he denied it. "Woman, I don't
know him," he said.
58A little later someone else saw him
and said, "You also are one of them."
"Man, I am not!" Peter replied.
59About an hour later another asserted,
"Certainly this fellow was with him,
for he is a Galilean."[z]

f31 The Greek is plural. g37 Isaiah 53:12
h44 Some early manuscripts do not have verses 43 and 44.

50Peter replied, "Man, I don't know
what you're talking about!" Just as he
was speaking, the rooster crowed. 61The
Lord[a] turned and looked straight at
Peter. Then Peter remembered the
word the Lord had spoken to him: "Before the rooster crows today, you will
disown me three times."[b] 62And he
went outside and wept bitterly.

The guards mock Jesus.

22:63-65pp— Mt 26:67,68; Mk 14:65; Jn 18:22,23

63The men who were guarding Jesus
began mocking and beating him. 64They
blindfolded him and demanded, "Prophesy! Who hit you?" 65And they said
many other insulting things to him.[c]

Jesus appears before Pilate and Herod.

22:67-71pp— Mt 26:63-66; Mk 14:61-63; Jn 18:19-21
23:2,3pp— Mt 27:11-14; Mk 15:2-5; Jn 18:29-37
23:18-25pp— Mt 27:15-26; Mk 15:6-15; Jn 18:39–19:16

66At daybreak the council[d] of the
elders of the people, both the chief
priests and teachers of the law, met
together,[e] and Jesus was led before
them. 67"If you are the Christ,[i]" they
said, "tell us."
Jesus answered, "If I tell you, you will
not believe me, 68and if I asked you,
you would not answer.[f] 69But from now
on, the Son of Man will be seated at
the right hand of the mighty God."[g]
70They all asked, "Are you then the
Son of God?"[h]
He replied, "You are right in saying
I am."[i]
71Then they said, "Why do we need
any more testimony? We have heard it
from his own lips."

23 Then the whole assembly rose
and led him off to Pilate.[j] 2And
they began to accuse him, saying, "We
have found this man subverting our
nation.[k] He opposes payment of taxes
to Caesar[l] and claims to be Christ,[j] a
king."[m]
3So Pilate asked Jesus, "Are you the
king of the Jews?"
"Yes, it is as you say," Jesus replied.

4Then Pilate announced to the chief
priests and the crowd, "I find no basis
for a charge against this man."[n]
5But they insisted, "He stirs up the
people all over Judea[k] by his teaching.
He started in Galilee[o] and has come all
the way here."
6On hearing this, Pilate asked if the
man was a Galilean.[p] 7When he learned
that Jesus was under Herod's jurisdic-
tion, he sent him to Herod,[q] who was
also in Jerusalem at that time.
8When Herod saw Jesus, he was
greatly pleased, because for a long time
he had been wanting to see him.[r] From
what he had heard about him, he hoped
to see him perform some miracle. 9He
plied him with many questions, but
Jesus gave him no answer.[s] 10The chief
priests and the teachers of the law were
standing there, vehemently accusing
him. 11Then Herod and his soldiers
ridiculed and mocked him. Dressing
him in an elegant robe,[t] they sent him
back to Pilate. 12That day Herod and
Pilate became friends[u]—before this they
had been enemies.
13Pilate called together the chief
priests, the rulers and the people, 14and
said to them, "You brought me this man
as one who was inciting the people
to rebellion. I have examined him in
your presence and have found no basis
for your charges against him.[v] 15Nei-
ther has Herod, for he sent him back to
us; as you can see, he has done nothing to deserve death. 16Therefore, I will
punish him[w] and then release him.[l]"
18With one voice they cried out,
"Away with this man! Release Barabbas
to us!"[x] 19(Barabbas had been thrown
into prison for an insurrection in the
city, and for murder.)
20Wanting to release Jesus, Pilate appealed to them again. 21But they kept
shouting, "Crucify him! Crucify him!"
22For the third time he spoke to
them: "Why? What crime has this man

22:61 [a]Lk 7:13 [b]ver 34
22:65 [c]Mt 16:21
22:66 [d]Mt 5:22 [e]Mt 27:1; Mk 15:1
22:68 [f]Lk 20:3-8
22:69 [g]Mk 16:19
22:70 [h]Mt 4:3 [i]Mt 27:11; Lk 23:3
23:1 [j]Mt 27:2; Mk 15:1; Jn 18:28
23:2 [k]ver 14 [l]Lk 20:22 [m]Jn 19:12
23:4 [n]ver 14,22,41; Mt 27:23; Jn 18:38; 1Ti 6:13; 2Co 5:21
23:5 [o]Mk 1:14
23:6 [p]Lk 22:59
23:7 [q]Mt 14:1; Lk 3:1
23:8 [r]Lk 9:9
23:9 [s]Mk 14:61
23:11 [t]Mk 15:17-19; Jn 19:2,3
23:12 [u]Ac 4:27
23:14 [v]ver 4
23:16 [w]ver 22; Mt 27:26; Jn 19:1; Ac 16:37; 2Co 11:23,24
23:18 [x]Ac 3:13,14

[i]67 Or *Messiah* [j]2 Or *Messiah*; also in verses 35 and 39 [k]5 Or *over the land of the Jews* [l]16 Some manuscripts *him." 17Now he was obliged to release one man to them at the Feast.*

committed? I have found in him no grounds for the death penalty. Therefore I will have him punished and then release him."[a]

23 But with loud shouts they insistently demanded that he be crucified, and their shouts prevailed. 24 So Pilate decided to grant their demand. 25 He released the man who had been thrown into prison for insurrection and murder, the one they asked for, and surrendered Jesus to their will.

Crucifixion of the King.

23:33-43pp— Mt 27:33-44; Mk 15:22-32; Jn 19:17-24

26 As they led him away, they seized Simon from Cyrene,[b] who was on his way in from the country, and put the cross on him and made him carry it behind Jesus.[c] 27 A large number of people followed him, including women who mourned and wailed[d] for him. 28 Jesus turned and said to them, "Daughters of Jerusalem, do not weep for me; weep for yourselves and for your children.[e] 29 For the time will come when you will say, 'Blessed are the barren women, the wombs that never bore and the breasts that never nursed!'[f] 30 Then

"'they will say to the mountains,
"Fall on us!"
and to the hills, "Cover us!"'[m][g]

31 For if men do these things when the tree is green, what will happen when it is dry?"[h]

32 Two other men, both criminals, were also led out with him to be executed.[i] 33 When they came to the place called the Skull, there they crucified him, along with the criminals—one on his right, the other on his left. 34 Jesus said, "Father,[j] forgive them, for they do not know what they are doing."[n][k] And they divided up his clothes by casting lots.[l]

35 The people stood watching, and the rulers even sneered at him.[m] They said, "He saved others; let him save himself if he is the Christ of God, the Chosen One."[n]

36 The soldiers also came up and mocked him.[o] They offered him wine vinegar[p] 37 and said, "If you are the king of the Jews,[q] save yourself."

38 There was a written notice above him, which read: THIS IS THE KING OF THE JEWS.[r]

39 One of the criminals who hung there hurled insults at him: "Aren't you the Christ? Save yourself and us!"[s]

40 But the other criminal rebuked him. "Don't you fear God," he said, "since you are under the same sentence? 41 We are punished justly, for we are getting what our deeds deserve. But this man has done nothing wrong."[t]

42 Then he said, "Jesus, remember me when you come into your kingdom.[o]"[u]

43 Jesus answered him, "I tell you the truth, today you will be with me in paradise."[v]

Jesus' death.

23:44-49pp— Mt 27:45-56; Mk 15:33-41

44 It was now about the sixth hour, and darkness came over the whole land until the ninth hour,[w] 45 for the sun stopped shining. And the curtain of the temple[x] was torn in two.[y] 46 Jesus called out with a loud voice,[z] "Father, into your hands I commit my spirit."[a] When he had said this, he breathed his last.[b]

47 The centurion, seeing what had happened, praised God[c] and said, "Surely this was a righteous man." 48 When all the people who had gathered to witness this sight saw what took place, they beat their breasts[d] and went away. 49 But all those who knew him, including the women who had followed him from Galilee,[e] stood at a distance,[f] watching these things.

Burial of Jesus by Joseph of Arimathea.

23:50-56pp— Mt 27:57-61; Mk 15:42-47; Jn 19:38-42

50 Now there was a man named Joseph,

23:22 [a]ver 16
23:26 [b]Mt 27:32 [c]Mk 15:21; Jn 19:17
23:27 [d]Lk 8:52
23:28 [e]Lk 19:41-44; 21:23,24
23:29 [f]Mt 24:19
23:30 [g]Hos 10:8; Isa 2:19; Rev 6:16
23:31 [h]Eze 20:47
23:32 [i]Isa 53:12; Mt 27:38; Mk 15:27; Jn 19:18
23:34 [j]Mt 11:25 [k]Mt 5:44 [l]Ps 22:18
23:35 [m]Ps 22:17 [n]Isa 42:1
23:36 [o]Ps 22:7 [p]Ps 69:21; Mt 27:48
23:37 [q]Lk 4:3,9
23:38 [r]Mt 2:2
23:39 [s]ver 35,37
23:41 [t]ver 4
23:42 [u]Mt 16:27
23:43 [v]2Co 12:3,4; Rev 2:7
23:44 [w]Am 8:9
23:45 [x]Ex 26:31-33; Heb 9:3,8 [y]Heb 10:19,20
23:46 [z]Mt 27:50 [a]Ps 31:5; 1Pe 2:23 [b]Jn 19:30
23:47 [c]Mt 9:8
23:48 [d]Lk 18:13
23:49 [e]Lk 8:2 [f]Ps 38:11

[m]*30* Hosea 10:8 [n]*34* Some early manuscripts do not have this sentence. [o]*42* Some manuscripts *come with your kingly power*

a member of the Council, a good and upright man, 51who had not consented to their decision and action. He came from the Judean town of Arimathea and he was waiting for the kingdom of God.[a] 52Going to Pilate, he asked for Jesus' body. 53Then he took it down, wrapped it in linen cloth and placed it in a tomb cut in the rock, one in which no one had yet been laid. 54It was Preparation Day,[b] and the Sabbath was about to begin.

55The women who had come with Jesus from Galilee[c] followed Joseph and saw the tomb and how his body was laid in it. 56Then they went home and prepared spices and perfumes.[d] But they rested on the Sabbath in obedience to the commandment.[e]

The victorious resurrection.

24:1-10pp— Mt 28:1-8; Mk 16:1-8; Jn 20:1-8

24 On the first day of the week, very early in the morning, the women took the spices they had prepared[f] and went to the tomb. 2They found the stone rolled away from the tomb, 3but when they entered, they did not find the body of the Lord Jesus.[g] 4While they were wondering about this, suddenly two men in clothes that gleamed like lightning[h] stood beside them. 5In their fright the women bowed down with their faces to the ground, but the men said to them, "Why do you look for the living among the dead? 6He is not here; he has risen! Remember how he told you, while he was still with you in Galilee:[i] 7'The Son of Man[j] must be delivered into the hands of sinful men, be crucified and on the third day be raised again.'"[k] 8Then they remembered his words.[l]

9When they came back from the tomb, they told all these things to the Eleven and to all the others. 10It was Mary Magdalene, Joanna, Mary the mother of James, and the others with them[m] who told this to the apostles.[n] 11But they did not believe[o] the women, because their words seemed to them like nonsense. 12Peter, however, got up and ran to the tomb. Bending over, he saw the strips of linen lying by themselves,[p] and he went away,[q] wondering to himself what had happened.

23:51 [a]Lk 2:25,38
23:54 [b]Mt 27:62
23:55 [c]ver 49
23:56 [d]Mk 16:1; Lk 24:1 [e]Ex 12:16; 20:10
24:1 [f]Lk 23:56
24:3 [g]ver 23,24
24:4 [h]Jn 20:12
24:6 [i]Mt 17:22,23; Mk 9:30-31; Lk 9:22; 24:44
24:7 [j]Mt 8:20 [k]Mt 16:21
24:8 [l]Jn 2:22
24:10 [m]Lk 8:1-3 [n]Mk 6:30
24:11 [o]Mk 16:11
24:12 [p]Jn 20:3-7 [q]Jn 20:10
24:13 [r]Mk 16:12
24:15 [s]ver 36
24:16 [t]Jn 20:14; 21:4
24:18 [u]Jn 19:25

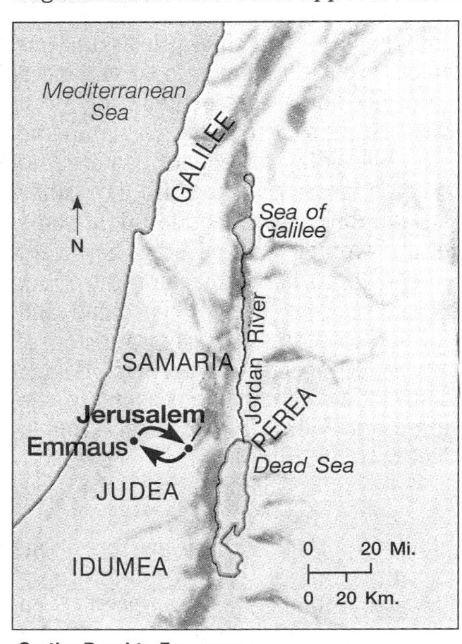

On the Road to Emmaus

After Jesus' death, two of his followers were walking from Jerusalem back toward Emmaus when a stranger joined them. After dinner in Emmaus, Jesus revealed himself to these men and then disappeared. They immediately returned to Jerusalem to tell the disciples the good news that Jesus was alive!

Encounter on the road to Emmaus.

13Now that same day two of them were going to a village called Emmaus, about seven miles[p] from Jerusalem.[r] 14They were talking with each other about everything that had happened. 15As they talked and discussed these things with each other, Jesus himself came up and walked along with them;[s] 16but they were kept from recognizing him.[t]

17He asked them, "What are you discussing together as you walk along?"

They stood still, their faces downcast. 18One of them, named Cleopas,[u] asked him, "Are you only a visitor to Jerusalem and do not know the things

[p]13 Greek *sixty stadia* (about 11 kilometers)

that have happened there in these days?”

19“What things?” he asked.

“About Jesus of Nazareth,”[a] they replied. “He was a prophet,[b] powerful in word and deed before God and all the people. 20The chief priests and our rulers[c] handed him over to be sentenced to death, and they crucified him; 21but we had hoped that he was the one who was going to redeem Israel.[d] And what is more, it is the third day[e] since all this took place. 22In addition, some of our women amazed us.[f] They went to the tomb early this morning 23but didn't find his body. They came and told us that they had seen a vision of angels, who said he was alive. 24Then some of our companions went to the tomb and found it just as the women had said, but him they did not see.”[g]

25He said to them, “How foolish you are, and how slow of heart to believe all that the prophets have spoken! 26Did not the Christ[q] have to suffer these things and then enter his glory?”[h] 27And beginning with Moses[i] and all the Prophets,[j] he explained to them what was said in all the Scriptures concerning himself.[k]

28As they approached the village to which they were going, Jesus acted as if he were going farther. 29But they urged him strongly, “Stay with us, for it is nearly evening; the day is almost over.” So he went in to stay with them.

30When he was at the table with them, he took bread, gave thanks, broke it[l] and began to give it to them. 31Then their eyes were opened and they recognized him,[m] and he disappeared from their sight. 32They asked each other, “Were not our hearts burning within us[n] while he talked with us on the road and opened the Scriptures[o] to us?”

33They got up and returned at once to Jerusalem. There they found the Eleven and those with them, assembled together 34and saying, “It is true! The Lord has risen and has appeared to Simon.”[p] 35Then the two told what had happened on the way, and how Jesus was recognized by them when he broke the bread.[q]

24:19 [a]Mk 1:24 [b]Mt 21:11
24:20 [c]Lk 23:13
24:21 [d]Lk 1:68; 2:38; 21:28 [e]Mt 16:21
24:22 [f]ver 1-10
24:24 [g]ver 12
24:26 [h]Heb 2:10; 1Pe 1:11
24:27 [i]Ge 3:15; Nu 21:9; Dt 18:15 [j]Isa 7:14; 9:6; 40:10,11; 53; Eze 34:23; Da 9:24; Mic 7:20; Mal 3:1 [k]Jn 1:45
24:30 [l]Mt 14:19
24:31 [m]ver 16
24:32 [n]Ps 39:3 [o]ver 27,45
24:34 [p]1Co 15:5
24:35 [q]ver 30,31
24:36 [r]Jn 20:19,21, 26; 14:27
24:37 [s]Mk 6:49
24:39 [t]Jn 20:27; 1Jn 1:1
24:43 [u]Ac 10:41
24:44 [v]Lk 9:45; 18:34 [w]Mt 16:21; Lk 9:22,44; 18:31-33; 22:37 [x]ver 27 [y]Ps 2; 16; 22; 69; 72; 110; 118
24:47 [z]Ac 5:31; 10:43; 13:38 [a]Mt 28:19
24:48 [b]Ac 1:8; 2:32; 5:32; 13:31; 1 Pe 5:1

36While they were still talking about this, Jesus himself stood among them and said to them, “Peace be with you.”[r]

37They were startled and frightened, thinking they saw a ghost.[s] 38He said to them, “Why are you troubled, and why do doubts rise in your minds? 39Look at my hands and my feet. It is I myself! Touch me and see;[t] a ghost does not have flesh and bones, as you see I have.”

40When he had said this, he showed them his hands and feet. 41And while they still did not believe it because of joy and amazement, he asked them, “Do you have anything here to eat?” 42They gave him a piece of broiled fish, 43and he took it and ate it in their presence.[u]

44He said to them, “This is what I told you while I was still with you:[v] Everything must be fulfilled[w] that is written about me in the Law of Moses,[x] the Prophets and the Psalms.”[y]

45Then he opened their minds so they could understand the Scriptures. 46He told them, “This is what is written: The Christ will suffer and rise from the dead on the third day, 47and repentance and forgiveness of sins will be preached in his name[z] to all nations,[a] beginning at Jerusalem. 48You are witnesses[b] of these things. 49I am going to send you what my Father has promised;[c] but stay in the city until you have been clothed with power from on high.”

Jesus' ascension.

50When he had led them out to the vicinity of Bethany,[d] he lifted up his hands and blessed them. 51While he was blessing them, he left them and was taken up into heaven.[e] 52Then they worshiped him and returned to Jerusalem with great joy. 53And they stayed continually at the temple,[f] praising God.

24:49 [c]Jn 14:16; Ac 1:4 **24:50** [d]Mt 28:17
24:51 [e]2Ki 2:11 **24:53** [f]Ac 2:46

q *26* Or *Messiah*; also in verse 46

JOHN

Author: John the Apostle.

Date Written: Between A.D. 85 and 96.

Time Span: About 3 1/2 years (A.D. 29-33).

Title: From the book's author: John.

Background: Although the Gospels of Matthew, Mark and Luke have different viewpoints, they are quite similar in content and, therefore, are called the "Synoptic Gospels." John is called the "Supplemental Gospel" because it stands uniquely in a class by itself. The book of John is different in many ways: style, structure, use of personal interviews, lack of parables, and spiritual explanations of events. John and his brother James follow John the Baptist until Jesus calls them to follow him. Jesus refers to these two as "Sons of Thunder," but later John is referred to as the disciple "whom Jesus loved." John, along with Peter and James, becomes especially close to Jesus. They alone are with Jesus at the transfiguration (Matthew 17:1-8) and at Gethsemane (Mark 14:32-41). John wrote this book for the specific purpose "...that you may believe that Jesus is the Christ, the Son of God, and that by believing you may have life in his name" (20:31). John also wrote 1, 2, 3 John and the book of Revelation.

Where Written: Probably at Ephesus.

To Whom: To the Gentiles and all Christians.

Content: While Luke presents Jesus as the "Son of Man," John presents Jesus in his deity as the "Son of God." Jesus' relationship to the Father is emphasized as he teaches, heals, prays and ministers. Miracles listed in John include: turning water to wine (2:1-11), feeding of the 5,000 (6:1-14), walking on water (6:16-21) and the raising of Lazarus (11:1-46). But in addition to being totally God, Jesus' humanity is shown by his being tired, hungry, thirsty and sorrowful. 7 times Jesus refers to himself in "I Am" passages which clearly show his claim to Godhood and the way to salvation. After Jesus' death and resurrection, great detail is given to appearances of the Lord before his ascension.

Key Words: "Word"; "Life"; "Believe." Jesus is the pre-existent, eternal "Word" who became a man. In order to gain eternal "life" one must "believe" upon the name of Jesus...Jesus, who always was with God and indeed is God.

Themes: • God loves each of us so much that he gave his Son so that anyone believing in Jesus shall not perish but shall have eternal life (3:16). • Miracles are given not only to heal, but also as signs pointing to Jesus. • God expects us to love not only him, but also our neighbors. • The blood of Christ covers our petitions and confessions to God. • Christ fully understands our hurts...he paid the supreme price to heal them. • The Holy Spirit gives us an eternal peace which the world cannot manufacture or purchase.

Outline:
1. The incarnation of the Son of God. 1:1-1:14
2. The introduction and public ministry of Jesus. 1:15-5:15
3. Opposition to Jesus' ministry. 5:16-12:50
4. Jesus' preparation of his disciples for his betrayal. 13:1-17:26
5. Jesus' arrest, trial and crucifixion. 18:1-19:37
6. Jesus' burial and resurrection. 19:38-21:25

JOHN

In the beginning was the Word.

1 In the beginning was the Word,[a] and
the Word was with God,[b] and the
Word was God.[c] 2He was with God in
the beginning.[d]
3Through him all things were made;
without him nothing was made that
has been made.[e] 4In him was life,[f] and
that life was the light[g] of men. 5The
light shines in the darkness, but the
darkness has not understood[a] it.[h]
6There came a man who was sent
from God; his name was John.[i] 7He
came as a witness to testify[j] concerning that light, so that through him all
men might believe.[k] 8He himself was
not the light; he came only as a witness to the light. 9The true light[l] that
gives light to every man[m] was coming
into the world.[b]
10He was in the world, and though
the world was made through him,[n] the
world did not recognize him. 11He
came to that which was his own, but
his own did not receive him. 12Yet to
all who received him, to those who

1:1 [a]Rev 19:13 [b]Jn 17:5; 1Jn 1:2 [c]Php 2:6
1:2 [d]Ge 1:1
1:3 [e]1Co 8:6; Col 1:16; Heb 1:2
1:4 [f]Jn 5:26; 11:25; 14:6 [g]Jn 8:12
1:5 [h]Jn 3:19
1:6 [i]Mt 3:1
1:7 [j]ver 15,19,32 [k]ver 12 **1:9** [l]1Jn 2:8 [m]Isa 49:6
1:10 [n]Heb 1:2

a5 Or *darkness, and the darkness has not overcome*
b9 Or *This was the true light that gives light to every man who comes into the world*

KEY PLACES IN JOHN

John's story begins as John the Baptist ministers near Bethany on the other side of the Jordan (1:28ff). Jesus also begins his ministry, talking to some of the men who would later become his 12 disciples. Jesus' ministry in Galilee began with a visit to a wedding in Cana (2:1ff). Then he went to Capernaum, which became his new home (2:12). He journeyed to Jerusalem for the special feasts (2:13) and there met with Nicodemus, a religious leader (3:1ff). When Jesus left Judea, he traveled through Samaria and ministered to the Samaritans (4:1ff). Jesus did miracles in Galilee (4:46ff) and in Judea and Jerusalem (5:1ff). We follow him as he fed 5,000 near Bethsaida beside the Sea of Galilee (Sea of Tiberias) (6:1ff), walked on the water to his frightened disciples (6:16ff), preached through Galilee (7:1), returned to Jerusalem (7:2ff), preached beyond the Jordan in Perea (10:40), raised Lazarus from the dead in Bethany (11:1ff), and finally entered Jerusalem for the last time to celebrate the Passover with his disciples and give them key teachings about what was to come and how they should act. His last hours before his crucifixion were spent in the city (13:1ff), in the Garden of Gethsemane (18:1ff), and finally in various buildings in Jerusalem during his trial (18:12ff). He would be crucified, but he would rise again as he had promised.

Modern names and boundaries are shown in gray.

believed[a] in his name,[b] he gave the
right to become children of God[c]—
13 children born not of natural descent,[c]
nor of human decision or a husband's
will, but born of God.[d]
14 The Word became flesh[e] and made
his dwelling among us. We have seen
his glory, the glory of the One and
Only,[d] who came from the Father, full
of grace and truth.[f]

John the Baptist points the way.

15 John testifies[g] concerning him. He
cries out, saying, "This was he of whom
I said, 'He who comes after me has
surpassed me because he was before
me.'"[h] 16 From the fullness[i] of his grace
we have all received one blessing after
another. 17 For the law was given
through Moses;[j] grace and truth came
through Jesus Christ.[k] 18 No one has
ever seen God,[l] but God the One and
Only,[d,e][m] who is at the Father's side,
has made him known.
19 Now this was John's testimony
when the Jews[n] of Jerusalem sent priests
and Levites to ask him who he was.
20 He did not fail to confess, but confessed freely, "I am not the Christ.[f]"[o]
21 They asked him, "Then who are
you? Are you Elijah?"[p]

He said, "I am not."

"Are you the Prophet?"[q]

He answered, "No."

22 Finally they said, "Who are you?
Give us an answer to take back to those
who sent us. What do you say about
yourself?"
23 John replied in the words of Isaiah
the prophet, "I am the voice of one calling in the desert,[r] 'Make straight the
way for the Lord.'"[g][s]
24 Now some Pharisees who had been
sent 25 questioned him, "Why then do
you baptize if you are not the Christ,
nor Elijah, nor the Prophet?"
26 "I baptize with[h] water," John replied,
"but among you stands one you do not
know. 27 He is the one who comes after
me,[t] the thongs of whose sandals I am
not worthy to untie."

1:12 *a* ver 7 *b* 1Jn 3:23 *c* Gal 3:26 **1:13** *d* Jn 3:6; Jas 1:18; 1Pe 1:23; 1Jn 3:9 **1:14** *e* Gal 4:4; Php 2:7,8; 1Ti 3:16; Heb 2:14 *f* Jn 14:6 **1:15** *g* ver 7 *h* ver 30; Mt 3:11 **1:16** *i* Eph 1:23; Col 1:19 **1:17** *j* Jn 7:19 *k* ver 14 **1:18** *l* Ex 33:20; Jn 6:46; Col 1:15; 1Ti 6:16 *m* Jn 3:16,18; 1Jn 4:9 **1:19** *n* Jn 2:18; 5:10,16; 6:41,52 **1:20** *o* Jn 3:28; Lk 3:15,16 **1:21** *p* Mt 11:14 *q* Dt 18:15 **1:23** *r* Mt 3:1 *s* Isa 40:3 **1:27** *t* ver 15,30 **1:28** *u* Jn 3:26; 10:40 **1:29** *v* ver 36; Isa 53:7; 1Pe 1:19; Rev 5:6 **1:30** *w* ver 15,27 **1:32** *x* Mt 3:16; Mk 1:10 **1:33** *y* Mk 1:4 *z* Mt 3:11; Mk 1:8 **1:34** *a* ver 49; Mt 4:3

28 This all happened at Bethany on
the other side of the Jordan,[u] where
John was baptizing.

Jesus is the Lamb of God.

29 The next day John saw Jesus coming toward him and said, "Look, the
Lamb of God,[v] who takes away the sin
of the world! 30 This is the one I meant
when I said, 'A man who comes after
me has surpassed me because he was
before me.'[w] 31 I myself did not know
him, but the reason I came baptizing
with water was that he might be
revealed to Israel."
32 Then John gave this testimony: "I
saw the Spirit come down from heav-
en as a dove and remain on him.[x] 33 I
would not have known him, except that
the one who sent me to baptize with
water[y] told me, 'The man on whom
you see the Spirit come down and
remain is he who will baptize with the
Holy Spirit.'[z] 34 I have seen and I testify
that this is the Son of God."[a]

Jesus calls the first disciples.

1:40-42pp— Mt 4:18-22; Mk 1:16-20; Lk 5:2-11

35 The next day John[b] was there again
with two of his disciples. 36 When he
saw Jesus passing by, he said, "Look,
the Lamb of God!"[c]
37 When the two disciples heard him
say this, they followed Jesus. 38 Turning
around, Jesus saw them following and
asked, "What do you want?"

They said, "Rabbi"[d] (which means
Teacher), "where are you staying?"
39 "Come," he replied, "and you will
see."

So they went and saw where he was
staying, and spent that day with him.
It was about the tenth hour.
40 Andrew, Simon Peter's brother, was

1:35 *b* Mt 3:1 **1:36** *c* ver 29 **1:38** *d* ver 49; Mt 23:7

c *13* Greek *of bloods* d *14,18* Or *the Only Begotten* e *18* Some manuscripts *but the only* (or *only begotten*) *Son* f *20* Or *Messiah*. "The Christ" (Greek) and "the Messiah" (Hebrew) both mean "the Anointed One"; also in verse 25. g *23* Isaiah 40:3 h *26* Or *in*; also in verses 31 and 33

one of the two who heard what John had said and who had followed Jesus. 41 The first thing Andrew did was to find his brother Simon and tell him, "We have found the Messiah" (that is, the Christ).[a] 42 And he brought him to Jesus.

Jesus looked at him and said, "You are Simon son of John. You will be called[b] Cephas" (which, when translated, is Peter[i]).[c]

43 The next day Jesus decided to leave for Galilee. Finding Philip,[d] he said to him, "Follow me."[e]

44 Philip, like Andrew and Peter, was from the town of Bethsaida.[f] 45 Philip found Nathanael[g] and told him, "We have found the one Moses wrote about in the Law,[h] and about whom the prophets also wrote[i]—Jesus of Nazareth,[j] the son of Joseph."[k]

46 "Nazareth! Can anything good come from there?"[l] Nathanael asked.

"Come and see," said Philip.

47 When Jesus saw Nathanael approaching, he said of him, "Here is a true Israelite,[m] in whom there is nothing false."[n]

48 "How do you know me?" Nathanael asked.

Jesus answered, "I saw you while you were still under the fig tree before Philip called you."

49 Then Nathanael declared, "Rabbi,[o] you are the Son of God;[p] you are the King of Israel."[q]

50 Jesus said, "You believe[j] because I told you I saw you under the fig tree. You shall see greater things than that." 51 He then added, "I tell you[k] the truth, you[k] shall see heaven open,[r] and the angels of God ascending and descending[s] on the Son of Man."[t]

Jesus' first miracle.

2 On the third day a wedding took place at Cana in Galilee.[u] Jesus' mother[v] was there, 2 and Jesus and his disciples had also been invited to the wedding. 3 When the wine was gone, Jesus' mother said to him, "They have no more wine."

4 "Dear woman,[w] why do you involve me?"[x] Jesus replied. "My time[y] has not yet come."

5 His mother said to the servants, "Do whatever he tells you."[z]

6 Nearby stood six stone water jars, the kind used by the Jews for ceremonial washing,[a] each holding from twenty to thirty gallons.[l]

7 Jesus said to the servants, "Fill the jars with water"; so they filled them to the brim.

8 Then he told them, "Now draw some out and take it to the master of the banquet."

They did so, 9 and the master of the banquet tasted the water that had been turned into wine.[b] He did not realize where it had come from, though the servants who had drawn the water knew. Then he called the bridegroom aside 10 and said, "Everyone brings out the choice wine first and then the cheaper wine after the guests have had too much to drink; but you have saved the best till now."

11 This, the first of his miraculous signs,[c] Jesus performed at Cana in Galilee. He thus revealed his glory,[d] and his disciples put their faith in him.[e]

Jesus drives money changers from the temple.

2:14-16pp— Mt 21:12,13; Mk 11:15-17; Lk 19:45,46

12 After this he went down to Capernaum[f] with his mother and brothers[g] and his disciples. There they stayed for a few days.

13 When it was almost time for the Jewish Passover,[h] Jesus went up to Jerusalem.[i] 14 In the temple courts he found men selling cattle, sheep and doves, and others sitting at tables exchanging money. 15 So he made a whip out of cords, and drove all from the temple area, both sheep and cattle;

1:41 [a]Jn 4:25
1:42 [b]Ge 17:5,15 [c]Mt 16:18
1:43 [d]Mt 10:3; Jn 6:5-7; 12:21,22; 14:8,9 [e]Mt 4:19
1:44 [f]Mt 11:21; Jn 12:21
1:45 [g]Jn 21:2 [h]Lk 24:27 [i]Lk 24:27 [j]Mt 2:23; Mk 1:24 [k]Lk 3:23
1:46 [l]Jn 7:41,42,52
1:47 [m]Ro 9:4,6 [n]Ps 32:2
1:49 [o]ver 38; Mt 23:7 [p]ver 34; Mt 4:3 [q]Mt 2:2; 27:42; Jn 12:13
1:51 [r]Mt 3:16 [s]Ge 28:12 [t]Mt 8:20
2:1 [u]Jn 4:46; 21:2 [v]Mt 12:46
2:4 [w]Jn 19:26 [x]Mt 8:29 [y]Mt 26:18; Jn 7:6
2:5 [z]Ge 41:55
2:6 [a]Mk 7:3,4; Jn 3:25
2:9 [b]Jn 4:46
2:11 [c]ver 23; Jn 3:2; 4:48; 6:2,14,26,30; 12:37; 20:30 [d]Jn 1:14 [e]Ex 14:31
2:12 [f]Mt 4:13 [g]Mt 12:46
2:13 [h]Jn 11:55 [i]Dt 16:1-6; Lk 2:41

[i]42 Both *Cephas* (Aramaic) and *Peter* (Greek) mean *rock.* [j]50 Or *Do you believe ...?* [k]51 The Greek is plural. [l]6 Greek *two to three metretes* (probably about 75 to 115 liters)

he scattered the coins of the money changers and overturned their tables. 16 To those who sold doves he said, "Get these out of here! How dare you turn my Father's house[a] into a market!"

17 His disciples remembered that it is written: "Zeal for your house will consume me."[m][b]

18 Then the Jews demanded of him, "What miraculous sign can you show us to prove your authority to do all this?"[c]

19 Jesus answered them, "Destroy this temple, and I will raise it again in three days."[d]

20 The Jews replied, "It has taken forty-six years to build this temple, and you are going to raise it in three days?" 21 But the temple he had spoken of was his body.[e] 22 After he was raised from the dead, his disciples recalled what he had said.[f] Then they believed the Scripture and the words that Jesus had spoken.

23 Now while he was in Jerusalem at the Passover Feast,[g] many people saw the miraculous signs he was doing and believed in his name.[n] 24 But Jesus would not entrust himself to them, for he knew all men. 25 He did not need man's testimony about man, for he knew what was in a man.[h]

Jesus tells Nicodemus: "You must be born again."

3 Now there was a man of the Pharisees named Nicodemus,[i] a member of the Jewish ruling council.[j] 2 He came to Jesus at night and said, "Rabbi, we know you are a teacher who has come from God. For no one could perform the miraculous signs[k] you are doing if God were not with him."[l]

3 In reply Jesus declared, "I tell you the truth, no one can see the kingdom of God unless he is born again.[o]"[m]

4 "How can a man be born when he is old?" Nicodemus asked. "Surely he cannot enter a second time into his mother's womb to be born!"

5 Jesus answered, "I tell you the truth, no one can enter the kingdom of God unless he is born of water and the Spirit.[n] 6 Flesh gives birth to flesh, but the Spirit[p] gives birth to spirit.[o] 7 You should not be surprised at my saying, 'You[q] must be born again.' 8 The wind blows wherever it pleases. You hear its sound, but you cannot tell where it comes from or where it is going. So it is with everyone born of the Spirit."

9 "How can this be?"[p] Nicodemus asked.

10 "You are Israel's teacher,"[q] said Jesus, "and do you not understand these things? 11 I tell you the truth, we speak of what we know,[r] and we testify to what we have seen, but still you people do not accept our testimony.[s] 12 I have spoken to you of earthly things and you do not believe; how then will you believe if I speak of heavenly things? 13 No one has ever gone into heaven[t] except the one who came from heaven[u]—the Son of Man.[r] 14 Just as Moses lifted up the snake in the desert,[v] so the Son of Man must be lifted up,[w] 15 that everyone who believes[x] in him may have eternal life.[s]

16 "For God so loved[y] the world that he gave his one and only Son,[t] that whoever believes in him shall not perish but have eternal life.[z] 17 For God did not send his Son into the world[a] to condemn the world, but to save the world through him.[b] 18 Whoever believes in him is not condemned,[c] but whoever does not believe stands condemned already because he has not believed in the name of God's one and only Son.[u][d] 19 This is the verdict: Light[e] has come into the world, but men loved darkness instead of light because their deeds were evil. 20 Everyone who does evil hates the light, and will not come into the light for fear that his deeds will be exposed.[f] 21 But whoever lives by the

2:16 [a]Lk 2:49 **2:17** [b]Ps 69:9 **2:18** [c]Mt 12:38 **2:19** [d]Mt 26:61; 27:40; Mk 14:58; 15:29 **2:21** [e]1Co 6:19 **2:22** [f]Lk 24:5-8; Jn 12:16; 14:26 **2:23** [g]ver 13 **2:25** [h]Mt 9:4; Jn 6:61,64; 13:11 **3:1** [i]Jn 7:50; 19:39 [j]Lk 23:13 **3:2** [k]Jn 9:16,33 [l]Ac 2:22; 10:38 **3:3** [m]Jn 1:13; 1Pe 1:23 **3:5** [n]Tit 3:5 **3:6** [o]Jn 1:13; 1Co 15:50 **3:9** [p]Jn 6:52,60 **3:10** [q]Lk 2:46 **3:11** [r]Jn 1:18; 7:16,17 [s]ver 32 **3:13** [t]Pr 30:4; Ac 2:34; Eph 4:8-10 [u]Jn 6:38,42 **3:14** [v]Nu 21:8,9 [w]Jn 8:28; 12:32 **3:15** [x]ver 16,36 **3:16** [y]Ro 5:8; Eph 2:4; 1Jn 4:9,10 [z]ver 36; Jn 6:29,40; 11:25,26 **3:17** [a]Jn 6:29,57; 10:36; 11:42; 17:8,21; 20:21 [b]Jn 12:47; 1Jn 4:14 **3:18** [c]Jn 5:24 [d]1Jn 4:9 **3:19** [e]Jn 1:4; 8:12 **3:20** [f]Eph 5:11,13

[m] *17* Psalm 69:9 [n] *23* Or *and believed in him* [o] *3* Or *born from above*; also in verse 7 [p] *6* Or *but spirit* [q] *7* The Greek is plural. [r] *13* Some manuscripts *Man, who is in heaven* [s] *15* Or *believes may have eternal life in him* [t] *16* Or *his only begotten Son* [u] *18* Or *God's only begotten Son*

truth comes into the light, so that it
may be seen plainly that what he has
done has been done through God."[v]

John the Baptist testifies of Jesus.

22After this, Jesus and his disciples
went out into the Judean countryside,
where he spent some time with them,
and baptized.[a] 23Now John also was
baptizing at Aenon near Salim, because
there was plenty of water, and people
were constantly coming to be baptized. 24(This was before John was put
in prison.)[b] 25An argument developed
between some of John's disciples and a
certain Jew[w] over the matter of ceremonial washing.[c] 26They came to John
and said to him, "Rabbi,[d] that man who
was with you on the other side of the
Jordan—the one you testified[e] about—
well, he is baptizing, and everyone is
going to him."
27To this John replied, "A man can
receive only what is given him from
heaven. 28You yourselves can testify that
I said, 'I am not the Christ[x] but am
sent ahead of him.'[f] 29The bride belongs
to the bridegroom.[g] The friend who
attends the bridegroom waits and listens for him, and is full of joy when
he hears the bridegroom's voice. That
joy is mine, and it is now complete.[h]
30He must become greater; I must
become less.
31"The one who comes from above[i]
is above all; the one who is from the
earth belongs to the earth, and speaks
as one from the earth.[j] The one who
comes from heaven is above all. 32He
testifies to what he has seen and heard,[k]
but no one accepts his testimony.[l] 33The
man who has accepted it has certified
that God is truthful. 34For the one whom
God has sent[m] speaks the words of
God, for God[y] gives the Spirit[n] without
limit. 35The Father loves the Son and
has placed everything in his hands.[o]
36Whoever believes in the Son has eternal life,[p] but whoever rejects the Son
will not see life, for God's wrath remains
on him."[z]

3:22 [a]Jn 4:2
3:24 [b]Mt 4:12; 14:3
3:25 [c]Jn 2:6
3:26 [d]Mt 23:7 [e]Jn 1:7
3:28 [f]Jn 1:20,23
3:29 [g]Mt 9:15 [h]Jn 16:24; 17:13; Php 2:2; 1Jn 1:4; 2Jn 12
3:31 [i]ver 13 [j]Jn 8:23; 1Jn 4:5
3:32 [k]Jn 8:26; 15:15 [l]ver 11
3:34 [m]ver 17 [n]Mt 12:18; Lk 4:18; Ac 10:38
3:35 [o]Mt 28:18; Jn 5:20,22; 17:2
3:36 [p]ver 15; Jn 5:24; 6:47
4:1 [q]Jn 3:22,26
4:3 [r]Jn 3:22
4:5 [s]Ge 33:19; 48:22; Jos 24:32

Jesus meets a Samaritan woman at the well.

4 The Pharisees heard that Jesus was
gaining and baptizing more disciples than John,[q] 2although in fact it was
not Jesus who baptized, but his disciples. 3When the Lord learned of this,
he left Judea[r] and went back once more
to Galilee.

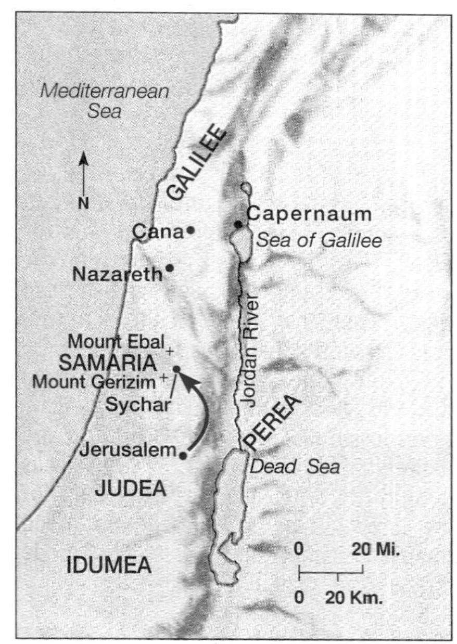

The Visit In Samaria
Jesus went to Jerusalem for the Passover, cleared the temple, and talked with Nicodemus, a religious leader, about eternal life. He then left Jerusalem and traveled in Judea. On his way to Galilee, he visited Sychar and other villages in Samaria. Unlike most Jews of the day, he did not try to avoid the region of Samaria.

4Now he had to go through Samaria.
5So he came to a town in Samaria
called Sychar, near the plot of ground
Jacob had given to his son Joseph.[s]
6Jacob's well was there, and Jesus, tired
as he was from the journey, sat down
by the well. It was about the sixth hour.
7When a Samaritan woman came to
draw water, Jesus said to her, "Will you

[v]*21* Some interpreters end the quotation after verse 15. [w]*25* Some manuscripts *and certain Jews* [x]*28* Or *Messiah* [y]*34* Greek *he* [z]*36* Some interpreters end the quotation after verse 30.

give me a drink?" 8(His disciples had
gone into the town[a] to buy food.)
9The Samaritan woman said to him,
"You are a Jew and I am a Samaritan[b]
woman. How can you ask me for a
drink?" (For Jews do not associate with
Samaritans.[a])
10Jesus answered her, "If you knew
the gift of God and who it is that asks
you for a drink, you would have asked
him and he would have given you living water."[c]
11"Sir," the woman said, "you have
nothing to draw with and the well is
deep. Where can you get this living
water? 12Are you greater than our father
Jacob, who gave us the well[d] and drank
from it himself, as did also his sons
and his flocks and herds?"
13Jesus answered, "Everyone who
drinks this water will be thirsty again,
14but whoever drinks the water I give
him will never thirst.[e] Indeed, the
water I give him will become in him a
spring of water[f] welling up to eternal
life."[g]
15The woman said to him, "Sir, give
me this water so that I won't get
thirsty[h] and have to keep coming here
to draw water."
16He told her, "Go, call your husband
and come back."
17"I have no husband," she replied.
Jesus said to her, "You are right when
you say you have no husband. 18The
fact is, you have had five husbands, and
the man you now have is not your husband. What you have just said is quite
true."
19"Sir," the woman said, "I can see
that you are a prophet.[i] 20Our fathers
worshiped on this mountain,[j] but you
Jews claim that the place where we
must worship is in Jerusalem."[k]
21Jesus declared, "Believe me, woman, a time is coming[l] when you will
worship the Father neither on this mountain nor in Jerusalem.[m] 22You Samaritans worship what you do not know;[n]
we worship what we do know, for salvation is from the Jews.[o] 23Yet a time
is coming and has now come[p] when
the true worshipers will worship the
Father in spirit[q] and truth, for they are
the kind of worshipers the Father seeks.
24God is spirit,[r] and his worshipers must
worship in spirit and in truth."
25The woman said, "I know that
Messiah" (called Christ)[s] "is coming.
When he comes, he will explain everything to us."
26Then Jesus declared, "I who speak
to you am he."[t]
27Just then his disciples returned[u]
and were surprised to find him talking
with a woman. But no one asked, "What
do you want?" or "Why are you talking
with her?"
28Then, leaving her water jar, the
woman went back to the town and
said to the people, 29"Come, see a man
who told me everything I ever did.[v]
Could this be the Christ[b]?"[w] 30They
came out of the town and made their
way toward him.
31Meanwhile his disciples urged him,
"Rabbi,[x] eat something."
32But he said to them, "I have food
to eat[y] that you know nothing about."
33Then his disciples said to each other, "Could someone have brought him
food?"
34"My food," said Jesus, "is to do the
will[z] of him who sent me and to finish
his work.[a] 35Do you not say, 'Four
months more and then the harvest'? I
tell you, open your eyes and look at
the fields! They are ripe for harvest.[b]
36Even now the reaper draws his wages,
even now he harvests[c] the crop for
eternal life,[d] so that the sower and the
reaper may be glad together. 37Thus
the saying 'One sows and another reaps'[e]
is true. 38I sent you to reap what you
have not worked for. Others have done
the hard work, and you have reaped
the benefits of their labor."
39Many of the Samaritans from that
town[f] believed in him because of the
woman's testimony, "He told me every-

4:8 [a]ver 5,39 **4:9** [b]Mt 10:5; Lk 9:52,53 **4:10** [c]Isa 44:3; Jer 2:13; Zec 14:8; Jn 7:37,38; Rev 21:6; 22:1,17 **4:12** [d]ver 6 **4:14** [e]Jn 6:35 [f]Jn 7:38 [g]Mt 25:46 **4:15** [h]Jn 6:34 **4:19** [i]Mt 21:11 **4:20** [j]Dt 11:29; Jos 8:33 [k]Lk 9:53 **4:21** [l]Jn 5:28; 16:2 [m]Mal 1:11; 1Ti 2:8 **4:22** [n]2Ki 17:28-41 [o]Isa 2:3; Ro 3:1,2; 9:4,5 **4:23** [p]Jn 5:25; 16:32 [q]Php 3:3 **4:24** [r]Php 3:3 **4:25** [s]Mt 1:16 **4:26** [t]Jn 8:24; 9:35-37 **4:27** [u]ver 8 **4:29** [v]ver 17,18 [w]Mt 12:23; Jn 7:26,31 **4:31** [x]Mt 23:7 **4:32** [y]Job 23:12; Mt 4:4; Jn 6:27 **4:34** [z]Mt 26:39; Jn 6:38; 17:4; 19:30 [a]Jn 19:30 **4:35** [b]Mt 9:37; Lk 10:2 **4:36** [c]Ro 1:13 [d]Mt 25:46

4:37 [e]Job 31:8; Mic 6:15 **4:39** [f]ver 5

a9 Or *do not use dishes Samaritans have used*
b29 Or *Messiah*

thing I ever did."[a] 40So when the Samaritans came to him, they urged him to
stay with them, and he stayed two days.
41And because of his words many more
became believers.
42They said to the woman, "We no
longer believe just because of what you
said; now we have heard for ourselves,
and we know that this man really is
the Savior of the world."[b]

Jesus heals the official's son.

43After the two days[c] he left for
Galilee. 44(Now Jesus himself had pointed out that a prophet has no honor in
his own country.)[d] 45When he arrived
in Galilee, the Galileans welcomed him.
They had seen all that he had done in
Jerusalem at the Passover Feast,[e] for
they also had been there.
46Once more he visited Cana in Galilee, where he had turned the water
into wine.[f] And there was a certain royal official whose son lay sick at Capernaum. 47When this man heard that
Jesus had arrived in Galilee from Judea,[g]
he went to him and begged him to
come and heal his son, who was close
to death.
48"Unless you people see miraculous
signs and wonders,"[h] Jesus told him,
"you will never believe."
49The royal official said, "Sir, come
down before my child dies."
50Jesus replied, "You may go. Your son
will live."
The man took Jesus at his word and
departed. 51While he was still on the
way, his servants met him with the
news that his boy was living. 52When
he inquired as to the time when his
son got better, they said to him, "The
fever left him yesterday at the seventh
hour."
53Then the father realized that this
was the exact time at which Jesus had
said to him, "Your son will live." So he
and all his household[i] believed.
54This was the second miraculous
sign[j] that Jesus performed, having come
from Judea to Galilee.

4:39 [a]ver 29
4:42 [b]Lk 2:11; 1Jn 4:14
4:43 [c]ver 40
4:44 [d]Mt 13:57; Lk 4:24
4:45 [e]Jn 2:23
4:46 [f]Jn 2:1-11
4:47 [g]ver 3,54
4:48 [h]Da 4:2,3; Jn 2:11; Ac 2:43; 14:3; Ro 15:19; 2Co 12:12; Heb 2:4
4:53 [i]Ac 11:14
4:54 [j]ver 48; Jn 2:11
5:2 [k]Ne 3:1; 12:39 [l]Jn 19:13, 17,20; 20:16; Ac 21:40; 22:2; 26:14
5:8 [m]Mt 9:5,6; Mk 2:11; Lk 5:24
5:9 [n]Jn 9:14
5:10 [o]ver 16 [p]Ne 13:15-22; Jer 17:21; Mt 12:2
5:14 [q]Mk 2:5; Jn 8:11
5:15 [r]Jn 1:19

Jesus heals a man at the Bethesda pool.

5 Some time later, Jesus went up to
Jerusalem for a feast of the Jews.
2Now there is in Jerusalem near the
Sheep Gate[k] a pool, which in Aramaic[l]
is called Bethesda[c] and which is surrounded by five covered colonnades.
3Here a great number of disabled people used to lie—the blind, the lame, the
paralyzed.[d] 5One who was there had
been an invalid for thirty-eight years.
6When Jesus saw him lying there and
learned that he had been in this condition for a long time, he asked him, "Do
you want to get well?"
7"Sir," the invalid replied, "I have no
one to help me into the pool when the
water is stirred. While I am trying to
get in, someone else goes down ahead
of me."
8Then Jesus said to him, "Get up! Pick
up your mat and walk."[m] 9At once the
man was cured; he picked up his mat
and walked.
The day on which this took place was
a Sabbath,[n] 10and so the Jews[o] said to
the man who had been healed, "It is the
Sabbath; the law forbids you to carry
your mat."[p]
11But he replied, "The man who made
me well said to me, 'Pick up your mat
and walk.'"
12So they asked him, "Who is this
fellow who told you to pick it up and
walk?"
13The man who was healed had no
idea who it was, for Jesus had slipped
away into the crowd that was there.
14Later Jesus found him at the temple and said to him, "See, you are well
again. Stop sinning[q] or something worse
may happen to you." 15The man went
away and told the Jews[r] that it was Jesus
who had made him well.

c2 Some manuscripts *Bethzatha*; other manuscripts *Bethsaida* d3 Some less important manuscripts *paralyzed—and they waited for the moving of the waters. 4From time to time an angel of the Lord would come down and stir up the waters. The first one into the pool after each such disturbance would be cured of whatever disease he had.*

Jesus is declared the Son of God.

16So, because Jesus was doing these
things on the Sabbath, the Jews persecuted him. 17Jesus said to them, "My
Father is always at his work[a] to this
very day, and I, too, am working." 18For
this reason the Jews tried all the harder to kill him;[b] not only was he breaking the Sabbath, but he was even calling
God his own Father, making himself
equal with God.[c]
19Jesus gave them this answer: "I tell
you the truth, the Son can do nothing
by himself;[d] he can do only what he
sees his Father doing, because whatever the Father does the Son also does.
20For the Father loves the Son[e] and shows
him all he does. Yes, to your amazement
he will show him even greater things
than these.[f] 21For just as the Father raises
the dead and gives them life,[g] even so
the Son gives life[h] to whom he is pleased
to give it. 22Moreover, the Father judges
no one, but has entrusted all judgment
to the Son,[i] 23that all may honor the Son
just as they honor the Father. He who
does not honor the Son does not honor
the Father, who sent him.[j]
24"I tell you the truth, whoever hears
my word and believes him who sent
me has eternal life and will not be condemned;[k] he has crossed over from
death to life.[l] 25I tell you the truth, a
time is coming and has now come[m]
when the dead will hear[n] the voice of
the Son of God and those who hear
will live. 26For as the Father has life in
himself, so he has granted the Son to
have life in himself. 27And he has giv-
en him authority to judge[o] because he
is the Son of Man.
28"Do not be amazed at this, for a
time is coming[p] when all who are in
their graves will hear his voice 29and
come out—those who have done good
will rise to live, and those who have
done evil will rise to be condemned.[q]
30By myself I can do nothing;[r] I judge
only as I hear, and my judgment is just,[s]
for I seek not to please myself but him
who sent me.[t]
31"If I testify about myself, my testimony is not valid.[u] 32There is another
who testifies in my favor,[v] and I know
that his testimony about me is valid.
33"You have sent to John and he has
testified[w] to the truth. 34Not that I accept
human testimony;[x] but I mention it that
you may be saved. 35John was a lamp
that burned and gave light,[y] and you
chose for a time to enjoy his light.
36"I have testimony weightier than
that of John.[z] For the very work that the
Father has given me to finish, and which
I am doing,[a] testifies that the Father has
sent me.[b] 37And the Father who sent me
has himself testified concerning me.[c]
You have never heard his voice nor seen
his form,[d] 38nor does his word dwell in
you,[e] for you do not believe the one he
sent.[f] 39You diligently study[e] the Scriptures[g] because you think that by them
you possess eternal life. These are the
Scriptures that testify about me,[h] 40yet
you refuse to come to me to have life.
41"I do not accept praise from men,[i]
42but I know you. I know that you do
not have the love of God in your hearts.
43I have come in my Father's name, and
you do not accept me; but if someone
else comes in his own name, you will
accept him. 44How can you believe if
you accept praise from one another, yet
make no effort to obtain the praise that
comes from the only God[f]?[j]
45"But do not think I will accuse you
before the Father. Your accuser is Moses,[k] on whom your hopes are set.[l] 46If
you believed Moses, you would believe
me, for he wrote about me.[m] 47But since
you do not believe what he wrote, how
are you going to believe what I say?"[n]

Jesus feeds 5,000 men.

6:1-13pp — Mt 14:13-21; Mk 6:32-44; Lk 9:10-17

6 Some time after this, Jesus crossed
to the far shore of the Sea of Galilee

5:17 [a]Jn 9:4; 14:10 **5:18** [b]Jn 7:1 [c]Jn 10:30,33; 19:7 **5:19** [d]ver 30; Jn 8:28 **5:20** [e]Jn 3:35 [f]Jn 14:12 **5:21** [g]Ro 4:17; 8:11 [h]Jn 11:25 **5:22** [i]ver 27; Jn 9:39; Ac 10:42; 17:31 **5:23** [j]Lk 10:16; 1Jn 2:23 **5:24** [k]Jn 3:18 [l]1Jn 3:14 **5:25** [m]Jn 4:23 [n]Jn 8:43,47 **5:27** [o]ver 22; Ac 10:42; 17:31 **5:28** [p]Jn 4:21 **5:29** [q]Da 12:2; Mt 25:46 **5:30** [r]ver 19 [s]Jn 8:16 [t]Mt 26:39; Jn 4:34; 6:38 **5:31** [u]Jn 8:14 **5:32** [v]ver 37; Jn 8:18 **5:33** [w]Jn 1:7 **5:34** [x]1Jn 5:9 **5:35** [y]2Pe 1:19 **5:36** [z]1Jn 5:9 [a]Jn 14:11; 15:24 [b]Jn 3:17; 10:25 **5:37** [c]Jn 8:18 [d]Dt 4:12; 1Ti 1:17; Jn 1:18 **5:38** [e]1Jn 2:14 [f]Jn 3:17

5:39 [g]Ro 2:17,18 [h]Lk 24:27,44; Ac 13:27 **5:41** [i]ver 44 **5:44** [j]Ro 2:29 **5:45** [k]Jn 9:28 [l]Ro 2:17 **5:46** [m]Ge 3:15; Lk 24:27,44; Ac 26:22 **5:47** [n]Lk 16:29,31

e39 Or *Study diligently* (the imperative) f44 Some early manuscripts *the Only One*

(that is, the Sea of Tiberias), 2and a great
crowd of people followed him because
they saw the miraculous signs[a] he had
performed on the sick. 3Then Jesus went
up on a mountainside[b] and sat down
with his disciples. 4The Jewish Passover
Feast[c] was near.
5When Jesus looked up and saw a
great crowd coming toward him, he said
to Philip,[d] "Where shall we buy bread
for these people to eat?" 6He asked this
only to test him, for he already had in
mind what he was going to do.
7Philip answered him, "Eight months'
wages[g] would not buy enough bread
for each one to have a bite!"
8Another of his disciples, Andrew,
Simon Peter's brother,[e] spoke up, 9"Here
is a boy with five small barley loaves
and two small fish, but how far will they
go among so many?"[f]
10Jesus said, "Have the people sit
down." There was plenty of grass in that
place, and the men sat down, about five
thousand of them. 11Jesus then took the
loaves, gave thanks,[g] and distributed to
those who were seated as much as they
wanted. He did the same with the fish.
12When they had all had enough to
eat, he said to his disciples, "Gather the
pieces that are left over. Let nothing be
wasted." 13So they gathered them and
filled twelve baskets with the pieces of
the five barley loaves left over by those
who had eaten.
14After the people saw the miraculous
sign[h] that Jesus did, they began to say,
"Surely this is the Prophet who is to
come into the world."[i] 15Jesus, knowing
that they intended to come and make
him king[j] by force, withdrew again to a
mountain by himself.[k]

Jesus walks on the water.

6:16-21pp— Mt 14:22-33; Mk 6:47-51

16When evening came, his disciples
went down to the lake, 17where they
got into a boat and set off across the
lake for Capernaum. By now it was dark,
and Jesus had not yet joined them. 18A
strong wind was blowing and the
waters grew rough. 19When they had
rowed three or three and a half miles,[h]
they saw Jesus approaching the boat,
walking on the water;[l] and they were
terrified. 20But he said to them, "It is I;
don't be afraid."[m] 21Then they were
willing to take him into the boat, and
immediately the boat reached the shore
where they were heading.

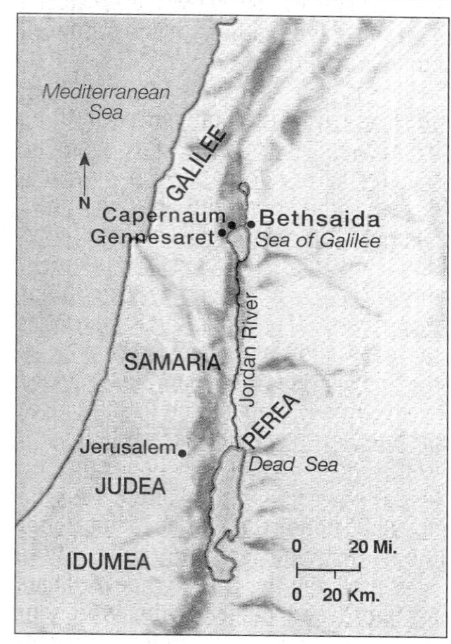

Jesus Walks on the Water
Jesus fed the 5,000 on a hill near the Sea of Galilee at Bethsaida. The disciples set out across the sea toward Capernaum. But they encountered a storm—and Jesus came walking to them on the water! The boat landed at Gennesaret (Mark 6:53); from there they went back to Capernaum.

22The next day the crowd that had
stayed on the opposite shore of the
lake[n] realized that only one boat had
been there, and that Jesus had not
entered it with his disciples, but that
they had gone away alone.[o] 23Then
some boats from Tiberias[p] landed near
the place where the people had eaten
the bread after the Lord had given
thanks.[q] 24Once the crowd realized that
neither Jesus nor his disciples were

6:2 [a]Jn 2:11
6:3 [b]ver 15
6:4 [c]Jn 2:13; 11:55
6:5 [d]Jn 1:43
6:8 [e]Jn 1:40
6:9 [f]2Ki 4:43
6:11 [g]ver 23; Mt 14:19
6:14 [h]Jn 2:11 [i]Dt 18:15,18; Mt 11:3; 21:11
6:15 [j]Jn 18:36 [k]Mt 14:23; Mk 6:46
6:19 [l]Job 9:8
6:20 [m]Mt 14:27
6:22 [n]ver 2 [o]ver 15-21
6:23 [p]ver 1 [q]ver 11

g7 Greek *two hundred denarii* h19 Greek *rowed twenty-five or thirty stadia* (about 5 or 6 kilometers)

there, they got into the boats and went
to Capernaum in search of Jesus.

Jesus is the bread of life.

25 When they found him on the other
side of the lake, they asked him, "Rabbi,[a] when did you get here?"
26 Jesus answered, "I tell you the truth,
you are looking for me,[b] not because
you saw miraculous signs[c] but because
you ate the loaves and had your fill.
27 Do not work for food that spoils, but
for food that endures[d] to eternal life,[e]
which the Son of Man[f] will give you.
On him God the Father has placed his
seal[g] of approval."
28 Then they asked him, "What must
we do to do the works God requires?"
29 Jesus answered, "The work of God
is this: to believe[h] in the one he has
sent."[i]
30 So they asked him, "What miraculous sign[j] then will you give that we may
see it and believe you?[k] What will you
do? 31 Our forefathers ate the manna[l]
in the desert; as it is written: 'He gave
them bread from heaven to eat.'[i]"[m]
32 Jesus said to them, "I tell you the
truth, it is not Moses who has given
you the bread from heaven, but it is
my Father who gives you the true bread
from heaven. 33 For the bread of God is
he who comes down from heaven[n] and
gives life to the world."
34 "Sir," they said, "from now on give
us this bread."[o]
35 Then Jesus declared, "I am the
bread of life.[p] He who comes to me will
never go hungry, and he who believes
in me will never be thirsty.[q] 36 But as I
told you, you have seen me and still
you do not believe. 37 All that the Father
gives me[r] will come to me, and whoever comes to me I will never drive
away. 38 For I have come down from
heaven not to do my will but to do the
will of him who sent me.[s] 39 And this is
the will of him who sent me, that I
shall lose none of all that he has given
me,[t] but raise them up at the last day.[u]
40 For my Father's will is that everyone
who looks to the Son and believes in
him shall have eternal life,[v] and I will
raise him up at the last day."
41 At this the Jews began to grumble
about him because he said, "I am the
bread that came down from heaven."
42 They said, "Is this not Jesus, the son
of Joseph,[w] whose father and mother
we know?[x] How can he now say, 'I
came down from heaven'?"[y]
43 "Stop grumbling among yourselves," Jesus answered. 44 "No one can
come to me unless the Father who sent
me draws him,[z] and I will raise him up
at the last day. 45 It is written in the
Prophets: 'They will all be taught by
God.'[j][a] Everyone who listens to the
Father and learns from him comes to
me. 46 No one has seen the Father except
the one who is from God;[b] only he has
seen the Father. 47 I tell you the truth,
he who believes has everlasting life.
48 I am the bread of life.[c] 49 Your forefathers ate the manna in the desert, yet
they died.[d] 50 But here is the bread that
comes down from heaven,[e] which a
man may eat and not die. 51 I am the
living bread that came down from heav-
en. If anyone eats of this bread, he will
live forever. This bread is my flesh,
which I will give for the life of the
world."[f]
52 Then the Jews began to argue
sharply among themselves,[g] "How can
this man give us his flesh to eat?"
53 Jesus said to them, "I tell you the
truth, unless you eat the flesh of the
Son of Man[h] and drink his blood, you
have no life in you. 54 Whoever eats my
flesh and drinks my blood has eternal
life, and I will raise him up at the last
day.[i] 55 For my flesh is real food and my
blood is real drink. 56 Whoever eats my
flesh and drinks my blood remains in
me, and I in him.[j] 57 Just as the living
Father sent me[k] and I live because of
the Father, so the one who feeds on me

6:25 [a]Mt 23:7
6:26 [b]ver 24 [c]ver 30; Jn 2:11
6:27 [d]Isa 55:2 [e]ver 54; Mt 25:46; Jn 4:14 [f]Mt 8:20 [g]Ro 4:11; 1Co 9:2; 2Co 1:22; Eph 1:13; 4:30; 2Ti 2:19; Rev 7:3
6:29 [h]1Jn 3:23 [i]Jn 3:17
6:30 [j]Jn 2:11 [k]Mt 12:38
6:31 [l]Nu 11:7-9 [m]Ex 16:4,15; Ne 9:15; Ps 78:24; 105:40
6:33 [n]ver 50
6:34 [o]Jn 4:15
6:35 [p]ver 48,51 [q]Jn 4:14
6:37 [r]ver 39; Jn 17:2,6,9,24
6:38 [s]Jn 4:34; 5:30
6:39 [t]Jn 10:28; 17:12; 18:9 [u]ver 40,44,54
6:40 [v]Jn 3:15,16
6:42 [w]Lk 4:22 [x]Jn 7:27,28 [y]ver 38,62
6:44 [z]ver 65; Jer 31:3; Jn 12:32
6:45 [a]Isa 54:13; Jer 31:33,34; Heb 8:10,11; 10:16
6:46 [b]Jn 1:18; 5:37; 7:29
6:48 [c]ver 35,51
6:49 [d]ver 31,58

6:50 [e]ver 33 **6:51** [f]Heb 10:10 **6:52** [g]Jn 7:43; 9:16; 10:19 **6:53** [h]Mt 8:20 **6:54** [i]ver 39 **6:56** [j]Jn 15:4-7; 1Jn 3:24; 4:15 **6:57** [k]Jn 3:17

i*31* Exodus 16:4; Neh. 9:15; Psalm 78:24,25
j*45* Isaiah 54:13

will live because of me. 58 This is the bread that came down from heaven. Your forefathers ate manna and died, but he who feeds on this bread will live forever."[a] 59 He said this while teaching in the synagogue in Capernaum.

Jesus is deserted by many of his disciples.

60 On hearing it, many of his disciples[b] said, "This is a hard teaching. Who can accept it?"

61 Aware that his disciples were grumbling about this, Jesus said to them, "Does this offend you?[c] 62 What if you see the Son of Man ascend to where he was before![d] 63 The Spirit gives life;[e] the flesh counts for nothing. The words I have spoken to you are spirit[k] and they are life. 64 Yet there are some of you who do not believe." For Jesus had known[f] from the beginning which of them did not believe and who would betray him. 65 He went on to say, "This is why I told you that no one can come to me unless the Father has enabled him."[g]

66 From this time many of his disciples[h] turned back and no longer followed him.

67 "You do not want to leave too, do you?" Jesus asked the Twelve.[i]

68 Simon Peter answered him,[j] "Lord, to whom shall we go? You have the words of eternal life. 69 We believe and know that you are the Holy One of God."[k]

70 Then Jesus replied, "Have I not chosen you,[l] the Twelve? Yet one of you is a devil!"[m] 71 (He meant Judas, the son of Simon Iscariot, who, though one of the Twelve, was later to betray him.)

Jesus teaches at the Feast of Tabernacles.

7 After this, Jesus went around in Galilee, purposely staying away from Judea because the Jews[n] there were waiting to take his life.[o] 2 But when the Jewish Feast of Tabernacles[p] was near, 3 Jesus' brothers[q] said to him, "You ought to leave here and go to Judea, so that your disciples may see the miracles you do. 4 No one who wants to become a public figure acts in secret. Since you are doing these things, show yourself to the world." 5 For even his own brothers did not believe in him.[r]

6 Therefore Jesus told them, "The right time[s] for me has not yet come; for you any time is right. 7 The world cannot hate you, but it hates me[t] because I testify that what it does is evil.[u] 8 You go to the Feast. I am not yet[l] going up to this Feast, because for me the right time[v] has not yet come." 9 Having said this, he stayed in Galilee.

10 However, after his brothers had left for the Feast, he went also, not publicly, but in secret. 11 Now at the Feast the Jews were watching for him[w] and asking, "Where is that man?"

12 Among the crowds there was widespread whispering about him. Some said, "He is a good man."

Others replied, "No, he deceives the people."[x] 13 But no one would say anything publicly about him for fear of the Jews.[y]

14 Not until halfway through the Feast did Jesus go up to the temple courts and begin to teach.[z] 15 The Jews[a] were amazed and asked, "How did this man get such learning[b] without having studied?"[c]

16 Jesus answered, "My teaching is not my own. It comes from him who sent me.[d] 17 If anyone chooses to do God's will, he will find out[e] whether my teaching comes from God or whether I speak on my own. 18 He who speaks on his own does so to gain honor for himself,[f] but he who works for the honor of the one who sent him is a man of truth; there is nothing false about him. 19 Has not Moses given you the law?[g] Yet not one of you keeps the law. Why are you trying to kill me?"[h]

6:58 [a]ver 49-51; Jn 3:36 **6:60** [b]ver 66 **6:61** [c]Mt 11:6 **6:62** [d]Mk 16:19; Jn 3:13; 17:5 **6:63** [e]2Co 3:6 **6:64** [f]Jn 2:25 **6:65** [g]ver 37,44 **6:66** [h]ver 60 **6:67** [i]Mt 10:2 **6:68** [j]Mt 16:16 **6:69** [k]Mk 8:29; Lk 9:20 **6:70** [l]Jn 15:16,19 [m]Jn 13:27 **7:1** [n]Jn 1:19 [o]Jn 5:18 **7:2** [p]Lev 23:34; Dt 16:16 **7:3** [q]Mt 12:46 **7:5** [r]Mk 3:21 **7:6** [s]Mt 26:18 **7:7** [t]Jn 15:18,19 [u]Jn 3:19,20 **7:8** [v]ver 6 **7:11** [w]Jn 11:56 **7:12** [x]ver 40,43 **7:13** [y]Jn 9:22; 12:42; 19:38 **7:14** [z]ver 28; Mt 26:55 **7:15** [a]Jn 1:19 [b]Ac 26:24 [c]Mt 13:54 **7:16** [d]Jn 3:11; 14:24 **7:17** [e]Ps 25:14; Jn 8:43 **7:18** [f]Jn 5:41; 8:50,54

7:19 [g]Jn 1:17 [h]ver 1; Mt 12:14

k63 Or *Spirit* l8 Some early manuscripts do not have *yet.*

20“You are demon-possessed,”[a] the
crowd answered. “Who is trying to kill
you?”
21Jesus said to them, “I did one miracle, and you are all astonished. 22Yet,
because Moses gave you circumcision[b] (though actually it did not come
from Moses, but from the patriarchs),[c]
you circumcise a child on the Sabbath. 23Now if a child can be circumcised on the Sabbath so that the law of
Moses may not be broken, why are
you angry with me for healing the
whole man on the Sabbath? 24Stop
judging by mere appearances, and make
a right judgment.”[d]
25At that point some of the people
of Jerusalem began to ask, “Isn’t this
the man they are trying to kill? 26Here
he is, speaking publicly, and they are
not saying a word to him. Have the
authorities[e] really concluded that he
is the Christ[m]? 27But we know where
this man is from;[f] when the Christ
comes, no one will know where he is
from.”
28Then Jesus, still teaching in the temple courts,[g] cried out, “Yes, you know
me, and you know where I am from.[h] I
am not here on my own, but he who
sent me is true.[i] You do not know him,
29but I know him[j] because I am from
him and he sent me.”
30At this they tried to seize him, but
no one laid a hand on him,[k] because
his time had not yet come. 31Still, many
in the crowd put their faith in him.[l]
They said, “When the Christ comes,
will he do more miraculous signs[m] than
this man?”
32The Pharisees heard the crowd
whispering such things about him.
Then the chief priests and the Pharisees sent temple guards to arrest him.
33Jesus said, “I am with you for only
a short time,[n] and then I go to the one
who sent me.[o] 34You will look for me,
but you will not find me; and where I
am, you cannot come.”[p]
35The Jews said to one another,
“Where does this man intend to go
that we cannot find him? Will he go
where our people live scattered[q] among
the Greeks,[r] and teach the Greeks?
36What did he mean when he said,
‘You will look for me, but you will not
find me,’ and ‘Where I am, you cannot
come’?”
37On the last and greatest day of the
Feast,[s] Jesus stood and said in a loud
voice, “If anyone is thirsty, let him come
to me and drink.[t] 38Whoever believes
in me, as[n] the Scripture has said,[u] streams
of living water[v] will flow from within
him.”[w] 39By this he meant the Spirit,[x]
whom those who believed in him were
later to receive.[y] Up to that time the
Spirit had not been given, since Jesus
had not yet been glorified.[z]
40On hearing his words, some of the
people said, “Surely this man is the
Prophet.”[a]
41Others said, “He is the Christ.”
Still others asked, “How can the Christ
come from Galilee?[b] 42Does not the
Scripture say that the Christ will come
from David’s family[o][c] and from Bethlehem,[d] the town where David lived?”
43Thus the people were divided[e] because
of Jesus. 44Some wanted to seize him,
but no one laid a hand on him.[f]

Temple guards fail to take Jesus captive.

45Finally the temple guards went
back to the chief priests and Pharisees,
who asked them, “Why didn’t you bring
him in?”
46“No one ever spoke the way this
man does,”[g] the guards declared.
47“You mean he has deceived you
also?”[h] the Pharisees retorted. 48“Has
any of the rulers or of the Pharisees
believed in him?[i] 49No! But this mob
that knows nothing of the law—there
is a curse on them.”
50Nicodemus,[j] who had gone to Jesus

7:20 [a]Jn 8:48; 10:20 **7:22** [b]Lev 12:3 [c]Ge 17:10-14 **7:24** [d]Isa 11:3,4; Jn 8:15 **7:26** [e]ver 48 **7:27** [f]Mt 13:55; Lk 4:22 **7:28** [g]ver 14 [h]Jn 8:14 [i]Jn 8:26,42 **7:29** [j]Mt 11:27 **7:30** [k]ver 32,44; Jn 10:39 **7:31** [l]Jn 8:30 [m]Jn 2:11 **7:33** [n]Jn 13:33; 16:16 **7:34** [o]Jn 16:5, 10,17,28 [p]Jn 8:21; 13:33 **7:35** [q]Jas 1:1 [r]Jn 12:20; 1Pe 1:1 **7:37** [s]Lev 23:36 [t]Isa 55:1; Rev 22:17 **7:38** [u]Isa 58:11 [v]Jn 4:10 [w]Jn 4:14 **7:39** [x]Joel 2:28; Ac 2:17,33 [y]Jn 20:22 [z]Jn 12:23; 13:31,32 **7:40** [a]Mt 21:11; Jn 1:21 **7:41** [b]ver 52; Jn 1:46 **7:42** [c]Mt 1:1 [d]Mic 5:2; Mt 2:5,6; Lk 2:4 **7:43** [e]Jn 9:16; 10:19 **7:44** [f]ver 30

7:46 [g]Mt 7:28 **7:47** [h]ver 12 **7:48** [i]Jn 12:42 **7:50** [j]Jn 3:1; 19:39

[m]*26* Or *Messiah*; also in verses 27, 31, 41 and 42
[n]*37,38* Or / *If anyone is thirsty, let him come to me. / And let him drink,* [38]*who believes in me. / As*
[o]*42* Greek *seed*

earlier and who was one of their own
number, asked, 51“Does our law condemn anyone without first hearing
him to find out what he is doing?”
52They replied, “Are you from Galilee,
too? Look into it, and you will find that
a prophet[p] does not come out of
Galilee.”[a]

[The earliest manuscripts and many
other ancient witnesses do not have
John 7:53–8:11.]

Jesus' forgiveness of the adulterous woman.

53Then each went to his own home.
8 But Jesus went to the Mount of
Olives.[b] 2At dawn he appeared
again in the temple courts, where all
the people gathered around him, and
he sat down to teach them.[c] 3The
teachers of the law and the Pharisees
brought in a woman caught in adultery. They made her stand before the
group 4and said to Jesus, “Teacher, this
woman was caught in the act of adultery. 5In the Law Moses commanded us
to stone such women.[d] Now what do
you say?” 6They were using this question as a trap,[e] in order to have a basis
for accusing him.[f]
But Jesus bent down and started to
write on the ground with his finger.
7When they kept on questioning him,
he straightened up and said to them, “If
any one of you is without sin, let him
be the first to throw a stone[g] at her.”[h]
8Again he stooped down and wrote on
the ground.
9At this, those who heard began to
go away one at a time, the older ones
first, until only Jesus was left, with the
woman still standing there. 10Jesus
straightened up and asked her, “Woman, where are they? Has no one condemned you?”
11“No one, sir,” she said.
“Then neither do I condemn you,”[i]
Jesus declared. “Go now and leave your
life of sin.”[j]

Jesus: The light of the world.

12When Jesus spoke again to the
people, he said, “I am[k] the light of the
world.[l] Whoever follows me will never
walk in darkness, but will have the
light of life.”[m]
13The Pharisees challenged him,
“Here you are, appearing as your own
witness; your testimony is not valid.”[n]
14Jesus answered, “Even if I testify
on my own behalf, my testimony is
valid, for I know where I came from
and where I am going.[o] But you have
no idea where I come from[p] or where
I am going. 15You judge by human
standards;[q] I pass judgment on no one.[r]
16But if I do judge, my decisions are
right, because I am not alone. I stand
with the Father, who sent me.[s] 17In
your own Law it is written that the
testimony of two men is valid.[t] 18I am
one who testifies for myself; my other
witness is the Father, who sent me.”[u]
19Then they asked him, “Where is
your father?”
“You do not know me or my Father,”[v]
Jesus replied. “If you knew me, you
would know my Father also.”[w] 20He
spoke these words while teaching[x] in
the temple area near the place where
the offerings were put.[y] Yet no one
seized him, because his time had not
yet come.[z]
21Once more Jesus said to them, “I
am going away, and you will look for
me, and you will die[a] in your sin. Where
I go, you cannot come.”[b]
22This made the Jews ask, “Will he
kill himself? Is that why he says, ‘Where
I go, you cannot come’?”
23But he continued, “You are from
below; I am from above. You are of this
world; I am not of this world.[c] 24I told
you that you would die in your sins; if

7:52 [a]ver 41
8:1 [b]Mt 21:1
8:2 [c]ver 20; Mt 26:55
8:5 [d]Lev 20:10; Dt 22:22
8:6 [e]Mt 22:15,18 [f]Mt 12:10
8:7 [g]Dt 17:7 [h]Ro 2:1,22
8:11 [i]Jn 3:17 [j]Jn 5:14
8:12 [k]Jn 6:35 [l]Jn 1:4; 12:35 [m]Pr 4:18; Mt 5:14
8:13 [n]Jn 5:31
8:14 [o]Jn 13:3; 16:28 [p]Jn 7:28; 9:29
8:15 [q]Jn 7:24 [r]Jn 3:17
8:16 [s]Jn 5:30
8:17 [t]Dt 17:6; Mt 18:16
8:18 [u]Jn 5:37
8:19 [v]Jn 16:3 [w]Jn 14:7; 1Jn 2:23
8:20 [x]Mt 26:55 [y]Mk 12:41 [z]Mt 26:18; Jn 7:30
8:21 [a]Eze 3:18 [b]Jn 7:34; 13:33
8:23 [c]Jn 3:31; 17:14

p52 Two early manuscripts *the Prophet*

you do not believe that I am ⌊the one I claim to be⌋,[q][a] you will indeed die in your sins."

25"Who are you?" they asked.

"Just what I have been claiming all along," Jesus replied. 26"I have much to say in judgment of you. But he who sent me is reliable,[b] and what I have heard from him I tell the world."[c]

27They did not understand that he was telling them about his Father. 28So Jesus said, "When you have lifted up the Son of Man,[d] then you will know that I am ⌊the one I claim to be⌋ and that I do nothing on my own but speak just what the Father has taught me. 29The one who sent me is with me; he has not left me alone,[e] for I always do what pleases him."[f] 30Even as he spoke, many put their faith in him.[g]

The true descendants of Abraham.

31To the Jews who had believed him, Jesus said, "If you hold to my teaching,[h] you are really my disciples. 32Then you will know the truth, and the truth will set you free."[i]

33They answered him, "We are Abraham's descendants[r][j] and have never been slaves of anyone. How can you say that we shall be set free?"

34Jesus replied, "I tell you the truth, everyone who sins is a slave to sin.[k] 35Now a slave has no permanent place in the family, but a son belongs to it forever.[l] 36So if the Son sets you free, you will be free indeed. 37I know you are Abraham's descendants. Yet you are ready to kill me,[m] because you have no room for my word. 38I am telling you what I have seen in the Father's presence,[n] and you do what you have heard from your father.[s]"

39"Abraham is our father," they answered.

"If you were Abraham's children,"[o] said Jesus, "then you would[t] do the things Abraham did. 40As it is, you are determined to kill me, a man who has told you the truth that I heard from God.[p] Abraham did not do such things. 41You are doing the things your own father does."[q]

"We are not illegitimate children," they protested. "The only Father we have is God himself."[r]

42Jesus said to them, "If God were your Father, you would love me,[s] for I came from God[t] and now am here. I have not come on my own;[u] but he sent me.[v] 43Why is my language not clear to you? Because you are unable to hear what I say. 44You belong to your father, the devil,[w] and you want to carry out your father's desire.[x] He was a murderer from the beginning, not holding to the truth, for there is no truth in him. When he lies, he speaks his native language, for he is a liar and the father of lies.[y] 45Yet because I tell the truth,[z] you do not believe me! 46Can any of you prove me guilty of sin? If I am telling the truth, why don't you believe me? 47He who belongs to God hears what God says.[a] The reason you do not hear is that you do not belong to God."

48The Jews answered him, "Aren't we right in saying that you are a Samaritan[b] and demon-possessed?"[c]

49"I am not possessed by a demon," said Jesus, "but I honor my Father and you dishonor me. 50I am not seeking glory for myself;[d] but there is one who seeks it, and he is the judge. 51I tell you the truth, if anyone keeps my word, he will never see death."[e]

52At this the Jews exclaimed, "Now we know that you are demon-possessed! Abraham died and so did the prophets, yet you say that if anyone keeps your word, he will never taste death. 53Are you greater than our father Abraham?[f] He died, and so did the prophets. Who do you think you are?"

54Jesus replied, "If I glorify myself,[g] my glory means nothing. My Father, whom you claim as your God, is the

8:24 [a]Jn 4:26; 13:19 **8:26** [b]Jn 7:28 [c]Jn 3:32; 15:15 **8:28** [d]Jn 3:14; 5:19; 12:32 **8:29** [e]ver 16; Jn 16:32 [f]Jn 4:34; 5:30; 6:38 **8:30** [g]Jn 7:31 **8:31** [h]Jn 15:7; 2Jn 9 **8:32** [i]Ro 8:2; Jas 2:12 **8:33** [j]ver 37,39; Mt 3:9 **8:34** [k]Ro 6:16; 2Pe 2:19 **8:35** [l]Gal 4:30 **8:37** [m]ver 39,40 **8:38** [n]Jn 5:19,30; 14:10,24 **8:39** [o]ver 37; Ro 9:7; Gal 3:7 **8:40** [p]ver 26 **8:41** [q]ver 38,44 [r]Isa 63:16; 64:8 **8:42** [s]1Jn 5:1 [t]Jn 16:27; 17:8 [u]Jn 7:28 [v]Jn 3:17 **8:44** [w]1Jn 3:8 [x]ver 38,41 [y]Ge 3:4 **8:45** [z]Jn 18:37 **8:47** [a]Jn 18:37; 1Jn 4:6 **8:48** [b]Mt 10:5 [c]ver 52; Jn 7:20 **8:50** [d]ver 54; Jn 5:41

8:51 [e]Jn 11:26 **8:53** [f]Jn 4:12 **8:54** [g]ver 50

q24 Or *I am he*; also in verse 28 r33 Greek *seed*; also in verse 37 s38 Or *presence. Therefore do what you have heard from the Father.* t39 Some early manuscripts *"If you are Abraham's children," said Jesus, "then*

one who glorifies me.[a] 55Though you do not know him,[b] I know him.[c] If I said I did not, I would be a liar like you, but I do know him and keep his word.[d] 56Your father Abraham[e] rejoiced at the thought of seeing my day; he saw it[f] and was glad."

57"You are not yet fifty years old," the Jews said to him, "and you have seen Abraham!"

58"I tell you the truth," Jesus answered, "before Abraham was born,[g] I am!"[h] 59At this, they picked up stones to stone him,[i] but Jesus hid himself,[j] slipping away from the temple grounds.

Jesus gives sight to a blind man.

9 As he went along, he saw a man blind from birth. 2His disciples asked him, "Rabbi,[k] who sinned,[l] this man[m] or his parents,[n] that he was born blind?"

3"Neither this man nor his parents sinned," said Jesus, "but this happened so that the work of God might be displayed in his life.[o] 4As long as it is day,[p] we must do the work of him who sent me. Night is coming, when no one can work. 5While I am in the world, I am the light of the world."[q]

6Having said this, he spit[r] on the ground, made some mud with the saliva, and put it on the man's eyes. 7"Go," he told him, "wash in the Pool of Siloam"[s] (this word means Sent). So the man went and washed, and came home seeing.[t]

8His neighbors and those who had formerly seen him begging asked, "Isn't this the same man who used to sit and beg?"[u] 9Some claimed that he was.

Others said, "No, he only looks like him."

But he himself insisted, "I am the man."

10"How then were your eyes opened?" they demanded.

11He replied, "The man they call Jesus made some mud and put it on my eyes. He told me to go to Siloam and wash. So I went and washed, and then I could see."[v]

12"Where is this man?" they asked him.

"I don't know," he said.

13They brought to the Pharisees the man who had been blind. 14Now the day on which Jesus had made the mud and opened the man's eyes was a Sabbath.[w] 15Therefore the Pharisees also asked him how he had received his sight.[x] "He put mud on my eyes," the man replied, "and I washed, and now I see."

16Some of the Pharisees said, "This man is not from God, for he does not keep the Sabbath."[y]

But others asked, "How can a sinner do such miraculous signs?" So they were divided.[z]

17Finally they turned again to the blind man, "What have you to say about him? It was your eyes he opened."

The man replied, "He is a prophet."[a]

18The Jews[b] still did not believe that he had been blind and had received his sight until they sent for the man's parents. 19"Is this your son?" they asked. "Is this the one you say was born blind? How is it that now he can see?"

20"We know he is our son," the parents answered, "and we know he was born blind. 21But how he can see now, or who opened his eyes, we don't know. Ask him. He is of age; he will speak for himself." 22His parents said this because they were afraid of the Jews,[c] for already the Jews had decided that anyone who acknowledged that Jesus was the Christ[u] would be put out[d] of the synagogue.[e] 23That was why his parents said, "He is of age; ask him."[f]

24A second time they summoned the man who had been blind. "Give glory to God,[v]"[g] they said. "We know this man is a sinner."[h]

25He replied, "Whether he is a sinner or not, I don't know. One thing I do know. I was blind but now I see!"

8:54 [a]Jn 16:14; 17:1,5 **8:55** [b]ver 19 [c]Jn 7:28,29 [d]Jn 15:10 **8:56** [e]ver 37,39 [f]Mt 13:17; Heb 11:13 **8:58** [g]Jn 1:2; 17:5,24 [h]Ex 3:14 **8:59** [i]Lev 24:16; Jn 10:31; 11:8 [j]Jn 12:36 **9:2** [k]Mt 23:7 [l]ver 34; Lk 13:2; Ac 28:4 [m]Eze 18:20 [n]Ex 20:5; Job 21:19 **9:3** [o]Jn 11:4 **9:4** [p]Jn 11:9; 12:35 **9:5** [q]Jn 1:4; 8:12; 12:46 **9:6** [r]Mk 7:33; 8:23 **9:7** [s]ver 11; 2Ki 5:10; Lk 13:4 [t]Isa 35:5; Jn 11:37 **9:8** [u]Ac 3:2,10 **9:11** [v]ver 7 **9:14** [w]Jn 5:9 **9:15** [x]ver 10 **9:16** [y]Mt 12:2 [z]Jn 6:52; 7:43; 10:19 **9:17** [a]Mt 21:11 **9:18** [b]Jn 1:19 **9:22** [c]Jn 7:13 [d]ver 34; Lk 6:22 [e]Jn 12:42; 16:2 **9:23** [f]ver 21

9:24 [g]Jos 7:19 [h]ver 16

[u]22 Or *Messiah* [v]24 A solemn charge to tell the truth (see Joshua 7:19)

26Then they asked him, "What did
he do to you? How did he open your
eyes?"
27He answered, "I have told you
already[a] and you did not listen. Why
do you want to hear it again? Do you
want to become his disciples, too?"
28Then they hurled insults at him and
said, "You are this fellow's disciple! We
are disciples of Moses![b] 29We know that
God spoke to Moses, but as for this fellow, we don't even know where he
comes from."[c]
30The man answered, "Now that is
remarkable! You don't know where he
comes from, yet he opened my eyes.
31We know that God does not listen to
sinners. He listens to the godly man
who does his will.[d] 32Nobody has ever
heard of opening the eyes of a man
born blind. 33If this man were not from
God,[e] he could do nothing."
34To this they replied, "You were
steeped in sin at birth;[f] how dare you
lecture us!" And they threw him out.[g]
35Jesus heard that they had thrown
him out, and when he found him, he
said, "Do you believe in the Son of
Man?"
36"Who is he, sir?" the man asked.
"Tell me so that I may believe in him."[h]
37Jesus said, "You have now seen
him; in fact, he is the one speaking with
you."[i]
38Then the man said, "Lord, I believe," and he worshiped him.[j]
39Jesus said, "For judgment[k] I have
come into this world,[l] so that the blind
will see[m] and those who see will become
blind."[n]
40Some Pharisees who were with
him heard him say this and asked,
"What? Are we blind too?"[o]
41Jesus said, "If you were blind, you
would not be guilty of sin; but now
that you claim you can see, your guilt
remains.[p]

Jesus: The Good Shepherd.

10 "I tell you the truth, the man
who does not enter the sheep
pen by the gate, but climbs in by some
other way, is a thief and a robber. 2The
man who enters by the gate is the
shepherd of his sheep.[q] 3The watchman opens the gate for him, and the
sheep listen to his voice.[r] He calls his
own sheep by name and leads them
out. 4When he has brought out all his
own, he goes on ahead of them, and
his sheep follow him because they
know his voice. 5But they will never
follow a stranger; in fact, they will run
away from him because they do not
recognize a stranger's voice." 6Jesus
used this figure of speech,[s] but they
did not understand what he was telling
them.
7Therefore Jesus said again, "I tell
you the truth, I am the gate for the
sheep. 8All who ever came before me[t]
were thieves and robbers, but the sheep
did not listen to them. 9I am the gate;
whoever enters through me will be
saved.[w] He will come in and go out,
and find pasture. 10The thief comes only
to steal and kill and destroy; I have
come that they may have life, and have
it to the full.
11"I am the good shepherd.[u] The good
shepherd lays down his life for the
sheep.[v] 12The hired hand is not the shepherd who owns the sheep. So when he
sees the wolf coming, he abandons the
sheep and runs away.[w] Then the wolf
attacks the flock and scatters it. 13The
man runs away because he is a hired
hand and cares nothing for the sheep.
14"I am the good shepherd;[x] I know
my sheep[y] and my sheep know me—
15just as the Father knows me and I
know the Father[z]—and I lay down my
life for the sheep. 16I have other
sheep[a] that are not of this sheep pen. I
must bring them also. They too will
listen to my voice, and there shall be
one flock[b] and one shepherd.[c] 17The
reason my Father loves me is that I lay
down my life[d]—only to take it up
again. 18No one takes it from me, but I

9:27 [a]ver 15 **9:28** [b]Jn 5:45 **9:29** [c]Jn 8:14 **9:31** [d]Ge 18:23-32; Ps 34:15,16; 66:18; 145:19,20; Pr 15:29; Isa 1:15; 59:1,2; Jn 15:7; Jas 5:16-18; 1Jn 5:14,15 **9:33** [e]ver 16; Jn 3:2 **9:34** [f]ver 2 [g]ver 22,35; Isa 66:5 **9:36** [h]Ro 10:14 **9:37** [i]Jn 4:26 **9:38** [j]Mt 28:9 **9:39** [k]Jn 5:22 [l]Jn 3:19 [m]Lk 4:18 [n]Mt 13:13 **9:40** [o]Ro 2:19 **9:41** [p]Jn 15:22,24 **10:2** [q]ver 11,14 **10:3** [r]ver 4,5,14, 16,27 **10:6** [s]Jn 16:25 **10:8** [t]Jer 23:1,2 **10:11** [u]ver 14; Isa 40:11; Eze 34:11-16, 23; Heb 13:20; 1Pe 5:4; Rev 7:17 [v]Jn 15:13; 1Jn 3:16 **10:12** [w]Zec 11:16,17 **10:14** [x]ver 11 [y]ver 27 **10:15** [z]Mt 11:27 **10:16** [a]Isa 56:8 [b]Jn 11:52; Eph 2:11-19 [c]Eze 37:24; 1Pe 2:25 **10:17** [d]ver 11,15,18

w9 Or *kept safe*

lay it down of my own accord.[a] I have authority to lay it down and authority to take it up again. This command I received from my Father."[b]

19At these words the Jews were again divided.[c] 20Many of them said, "He is demon-possessed[d] and raving mad.[e] Why listen to him?"

21But others said, "These are not the sayings of a man possessed by a demon.[f] Can a demon open the eyes of the blind?"[g]

The unbelief of the Jews.

22Then came the Feast of Dedication[x] at Jerusalem. It was winter, 23and Jesus was in the temple area walking in Solomon's Colonnade.[h] 24The Jews[i] gathered around him, saying, "How long will you keep us in suspense? If you are the Christ,[y] tell us plainly."[j]

25Jesus answered, "I did tell you,[k] but you do not believe. The miracles I do in my Father's name speak for me,[l] 26but you do not believe because you are not my sheep.[m] 27My sheep listen to my voice; I know them,[n] and they follow me.[o] 28I give them eternal life, and they shall never perish; no one can snatch them out of my hand.[p] 29My Father, who has given them to me,[q] is greater than all[z];[r] no one can snatch them out of my Father's hand. 30I and the Father are one."[s]

31Again the Jews picked up stones to stone him,[t] 32but Jesus said to them, "I have shown you many great miracles from the Father. For which of these do you stone me?"

33"We are not stoning you for any of these," replied the Jews, "but for blasphemy, because you, a mere man, claim to be God."[u]

34Jesus answered them, "Is it not written in your Law,[v] 'I have said you are gods'[a]?[w] 35If he called them 'gods,' to whom the word of God came—and the Scripture cannot be broken— 36what about the one whom the Father set apart[x] as his very own[y] and sent into the world?[z] Why then do you accuse me of blasphemy because I said, 'I am God's Son'?[a] 37Do not believe me unless I do what my Father does.[b] 38But if I do it, even though you do not believe me, believe the miracles, that you may know and understand that the Father is in me, and I in the Father."[c] 39Again they tried to seize him,[d] but he escaped their grasp.[e]

40Then Jesus went back across the Jordan[f] to the place where John had been baptizing in the early days. Here he stayed 41and many people came to him. They said, "Though John never performed a miraculous sign,[g] all that John said about this man was true."[h] 42And in that place many believed in Jesus.[i]

Jesus raises Lazarus from the dead.

11 Now a man named Lazarus was sick. He was from Bethany,[j] the village of Mary and her sister Martha.[k] 2This Mary, whose brother Lazarus now lay sick, was the same one who poured perfume on the Lord and wiped his feet with her hair.[l] 3So the sisters sent word to Jesus, "Lord, the one you love[m] is sick."

4When he heard this, Jesus said, "This sickness will not end in death. No, it is for God's glory[n] so that God's Son may be glorified through it." 5Jesus loved Martha and her sister and Lazarus. 6Yet when he heard that Lazarus was sick, he stayed where he was two more days.

7Then he said to his disciples, "Let us go back to Judea."[o]

8"But Rabbi,"[p] they said, "a short while ago the Jews tried to stone you,[q] and yet you are going back there?"

9Jesus answered, "Are there not twelve hours of daylight? A man who walks by day will not stumble, for he

10:18 [a]Mt 26:53 [b]Jn 15:10; Php 2:8; Heb 5:8 **10:19** [c]Jn 7:43; 9:16 **10:20** [d]Jn 7:20 [e]Mk 3:21 **10:21** [f]Mt 4:24 [g]Ex 4:11; Jn 9:32,33 **10:23** [h]Ac 3:11; 5:12 **10:24** [i]Jn 1:19 [j]Jn 16:25,29 **10:25** [k]Jn 8:58 [l]Jn 5:36 **10:26** [m]Jn 8:47 **10:27** [n]ver 14 [o]ver 4 **10:28** [p]Jn 6:39 **10:29** [q]Jn 17:2,6,24 [r]Jn 14:28 **10:30** [s]Jn 17:21-23 **10:31** [t]Jn 8:59 **10:33** [u]Lev 24:16; Jn 5:18 **10:34** [v]Jn 8:17; Ro 3:19 [w]Ps 82:6 **10:36** [x]Jer 1:5 [y]Jn 6:69 [z]Jn 3:17 [a]Jn 5:17,18 **10:37** [b]ver 25; Jn 15:24 **10:38** [c]Jn 14:10, 11,20; 17:21 **10:39** [d]Jn 7:30 [e]Lk 4:30; Jn 8:59 **10:40** [f]Jn 1:28 **10:41** [g]Jn 2:11; 3:30 [h]Jn 1:26,27, 30,34 **10:42** [i]Jn 7:31 **11:1** [j]Mt 21:17 [k]Lk 10:38 **11:2** [l]Mk 14:3; Lk 7:38; Jn 12:3 **11:3** [m]ver 5,36 **11:4** [n]ver 40; Jn 9:3 **11:7** [o]Jn 10:40 **11:8** [p]Mt 23:7 [q]Jn 8:59 10:31

[x]*22* That is, Hanukkah [y]*24* Or *Messiah* [z]*29* Many early manuscripts *What my Father has given me is greater than all* [a]*34* Psalm 82:6

sees by this world's light.[a] 10It is when he walks by night that he stumbles, for he has no light."

11After he had said this, he went on to tell them, "Our friend[b] Lazarus has fallen asleep;[c] but I am going there to wake him up."

12His disciples replied, "Lord, if he sleeps, he will get better." 13Jesus had been speaking of his death, but his disciples thought he meant natural sleep.[d]

14So then he told them plainly, "Lazarus is dead, 15and for your sake I am glad I was not there, so that you may believe. But let us go to him."

16Then Thomas[e] (called Didymus) said to the rest of the disciples, "Let us also go, that we may die with him."

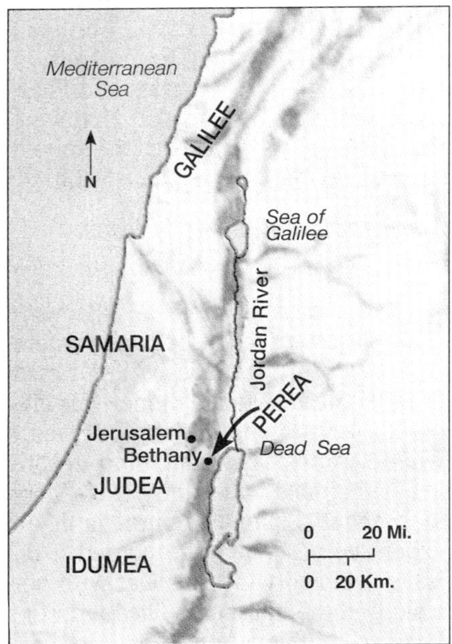

Jesus Raises Lazarus
Jesus had been preaching in the villages beyond the Jordan, probably in Perea, when he received the news of Lazarus's sickness. Jesus did not leave immediately, but waited two days before returning to Judea. He knew Lazarus would be dead when he arrived in Bethany, but he was going to do a great miracle.

17On his arrival, Jesus found that Lazarus had already been in the tomb for four days.[f] 18Bethany[g] was less than two miles[b] from Jerusalem, 19and many Jews had come to Martha and Mary to comfort them in the loss of their brother.[h] 20When Martha heard that Jesus was coming, she went out to meet him, but Mary stayed at home.[i]

21"Lord," Martha said to Jesus, "if you had been here, my brother would not have died.[j] 22But I know that even now God will give you whatever you ask."[k]

23Jesus said to her, "Your brother will rise again."

24Martha answered, "I know he will rise again in the resurrection[l] at the last day."

25Jesus said to her, "I am the resurrection and the life.[m] He who believes in me will live, even though he dies; 26and whoever lives and believes in me will never die. Do you believe this?"

27"Yes, Lord," she told him, "I believe that you are the Christ,[c][n] the Son of God,[o] who was to come into the world."[p]

28And after she had said this, she went back and called her sister Mary aside. "The Teacher[q] is here," she said, "and is asking for you." 29When Mary heard this, she got up quickly and went to him. 30Now Jesus had not yet entered the village, but was still at the place where Martha had met him.[r] 31When the Jews who had been with Mary in the house, comforting her,[s] noticed how quickly she got up and went out, they followed her, supposing she was going to the tomb to mourn there.

32When Mary reached the place where Jesus was and saw him, she fell at his feet and said, "Lord, if you had been here, my brother would not have died."[t]

33When Jesus saw her weeping, and the Jews who had come along with her also weeping, he was deeply moved[u] in spirit and troubled.[v] 34"Where have you laid him?" he asked.

"Come and see, Lord," they replied.

35Jesus wept.[w]

36Then the Jews said, "See how he loved him!"[x]

11:9 [a]Jn 9:4; 12:35
11:11 [b]ver 3 [c]Ac 7:60
11:13 [d]Mt 9:24
11:16 [e]Mt 10:3; Jn 14:5; 20:24-28; 21:2; Ac 1:13
11:17 [f]ver 6,39
11:18 [g]ver 1
11:19 [h]ver 31; Job 2:11
11:20 [i]Lk 10:38-42
11:21 [j]ver 32,37
11:22 [k]ver 41,42; Jn 9:31
11:24 [l]Da 12:2; Jn 5:28,29; Ac 24:15
11:25 [m]Jn 1:4
11:27 [n]Lk 2:11 [o]Mt 16:16 [p]Jn 6:14
11:28 [q]Mt 26:18; Jn 13:13
11:30 [r]ver 20
11:31 [s]ver 19
11:32 [t]ver 21
11:33 [u]ver 38 [v]Jn 12:27
11:35 [w]Lk 19:41
11:36 [x]ver 3

b*18* Greek *fifteen stadia* (about 3 kilometers)
c*27* Or *Messiah*

37But some of them said, "Could not he who opened the eyes of the blind man[a] have kept this man from dying?"[b]

38Jesus, once more deeply moved,[c] came to the tomb. It was a cave with a stone laid across the entrance.[d] 39"Take away the stone," he said.

"But, Lord," said Martha, the sister of the dead man, "by this time there is a bad odor, for he has been there four days."[e]

40Then Jesus said, "Did I not tell you that if you believed,[f] you would see the glory of God?"[g]

41So they took away the stone. Then Jesus looked up[h] and said, "Father,[i] I thank you that you have heard me. 42I knew that you always hear me, but I said this for the benefit of the people standing here,[j] that they may believe that you sent me."[k]

43When he had said this, Jesus called in a loud voice, "Lazarus, come out!"[l] 44The dead man came out, his hands and feet wrapped with strips of linen,[m] and a cloth around his face.[n]

Jesus said to them, "Take off the grave clothes and let him go."

The Jews plot to kill Jesus.

45Therefore many of the Jews who had come to visit Mary,[o] and had seen what Jesus did,[p] put their faith in him.[q] 46But some of them went to the Pharisees and told them what Jesus had done. 47Then the chief priests and the Pharisees[r] called a meeting[s] of the Sanhedrin.[t]

"What are we accomplishing?" they asked. "Here is this man performing many miraculous signs.[u] 48If we let him go on like this, everyone will believe in him, and then the Romans will come and take away both our place[d] and our nation."

49Then one of them, named Caiaphas,[v] who was high priest that year,[w] spoke up, "You know nothing at all! 50You do not realize that it is better for you that one man die for the people than that the whole nation perish."[x]

51He did not say this on his own, but as high priest that year he prophesied that Jesus would die for the Jewish nation, 52and not only for that nation but also for the scattered children of God, to bring them together and make them one.[y] 53So from that day on they plotted to take his life.[z]

54Therefore Jesus no longer moved about publicly among the Jews.[a] Instead he withdrew to a region near the desert, to a village called Ephraim, where he stayed with his disciples.

55When it was almost time for the Jewish Passover,[b] many went up from the country to Jerusalem for their ceremonial cleansing[c] before the Passover. 56They kept looking for Jesus,[d] and as they stood in the temple area they asked one another, "What do you think? Isn't he coming to the Feast at all?" 57But the chief priests and Pharisees had given orders that if anyone found out where Jesus was, he should report it so that they might arrest him.

Mary anoints the feet of Jesus.

12:1-8Ref— Mt 26:6-13; Mk 14:3-9; Lk 7:37-39

12 Six days before the Passover,[e] Jesus arrived at Bethany,[f] where Lazarus lived, whom Jesus had raised from the dead. 2Here a dinner was given in Jesus' honor. Martha served,[g] while Lazarus was among those reclining at the table with him. 3Then Mary took about a pint[e] of pure nard, an expensive perfume;[h] she poured it on Jesus' feet and wiped his feet with her hair.[i] And the house was filled with the fragrance of the perfume.

4But one of his disciples, Judas Iscariot, who was later to betray him,[j] objected, 5"Why wasn't this perfume sold and the money given to the poor? It was worth a year's wages.[f]" 6He did not say this because he cared about the poor but because he was a thief; as keeper of the money bag,[k] he used to help himself to what was put into it.

11:37 [a]Jn 9:6,7 [b]ver 21,32
11:38 [c]ver 33 [d]Mt 27:60; Lk 24:2; Jn 20:1
11:39 [e]ver 17
11:40 [f]ver 23-25 [g]ver 4
11:41 [h]Jn 17:1 [i]Mt 11:25
11:42 [j]Jn 12:30 [k]Jn 3:17
11:43 [l]Lk 7:14
11:44 [m]Jn 19:40 [n]Jn 20:7
11:45 [o]ver 19 [p]Jn 2:23 [q]Ex 14:31; Jn 7:31
11:47 [r]ver 57 [s]Mt 26:3 [t]Mt 5:22 [u]Jn 2:11
11:49 [v]Mt 26:3 [w]ver 51; Jn 18:13,14
11:50 [x]Jn 18:14
11:52 [y]Isa 49:6; Jn 10:16
11:53 [z]Mt 12:14
11:54 [a]Jn 7:1
11:55 [b]Ex 12:13,23,27; Mt 26:1,2; Mk 14:1; Jn 13:1 [c]2Ch 30:17,18
11:56 [d]Jn 7:11
12:1 [e]Jn 11:55 [f]Mt 21:17
12:2 [g]Lk 10:38-42
12:3 [h]Mk 14:3 [i]Jn 11:2
12:4 [j]Mt 10:4
12:6 [k]Jn 13:29

d*48* Or *temple* e*3* Greek *a litra* (probably about 0.5 liter) f*5* Greek *three hundred denarii*

7“Leave her alone,” Jesus replied. “⌞It was intended⌟ that she should save this perfume for the day of my burial.[a] 8You will always have the poor among you,[b] but you will not always have me.”

9Meanwhile a large crowd of Jews found out that Jesus was there and came, not only because of him but also to see Lazarus, whom he had raised from the dead.[c] 10So the chief priests made plans to kill Lazarus as well, 11for on account of him[d] many of the Jews were going over to Jesus and putting their faith in him.[e]

Jesus' Triumphal Entry.

12:12-15pp— Mt 21:4-9; Mk 11:7-10; Lk 19:35-38

12The next day the great crowd that had come for the Feast heard that Jesus was on his way to Jerusalem. 13They took palm branches and went out to meet him, shouting,

“Hosanna![g]”

“Blessed is he who comes in the
name of the Lord!”[h][f]

“Blessed is the King of Israel!”[g]

14Jesus found a young donkey and sat upon it, as it is written,

15“Do not be afraid, O Daughter of
Zion;
see, your king is coming,
seated on a donkey's colt.”[i][h]

16At first his disciples did not understand all this.[i] Only after Jesus was glorified[j] did they realize that these things had been written about him and that they had done these things to him.

17Now the crowd that was with him[k] when he called Lazarus from the tomb and raised him from the dead continued to spread the word. 18Many people, because they had heard that he had given this miraculous sign,[l] went out to meet him. 19So the Pharisees said to one another, “See, this is getting us nowhere. Look how the whole world has gone after him!”[m]

12:7 [a]Jn 19:40
12:8 [b]Dt 15:11
12:9 [c]Jn 11:43,44
12:11 [d]ver 17,18; Jn 11:45 [e]Jn 7:31
12:13 [f]Ps 118:25,26 [g]Jn 1:49
12:15 [h]Zec 9:9
12:16 [i]Mk 9:32 [j]Jn 2:22; 7:39; 14:26
12:17 [k]Jn 11:42
12:18 [l]ver 11
12:19 [m]Jn 11:47,48
12:20 [n]Jn 7:35; Ac 11:20
12:21 [o]Mt 11:21; Jn 1:44
12:23 [p]Jn 13:32; 17:1
12:24 [q]1Co 15:36
12:25 [r]Mt 10:39; Mk 8:35; Lk 14:26
12:26 [s]Jn 14:3; 17:24; 2Co 5:8; 1Th 4:17
12:27 [t]Mt 26:38,39; Jn 11:33,38; 13:21 [u]Mt 11:25 [v]ver 23
12:28 [w]Mt 3:17
12:30 [x]Jn 11:42
12:31 [y]Jn 16:11 [z]Jn 14:30; 16:11; 2Co 4:4; Eph 2:2; 1Jn 4:4
12:32 [a]ver 34; Jn 3:14; 8:28 [b]Jn 6:44
12:33 [c]Jn 18:32

Jesus predicts his death.

20Now there were some Greeks[n] among those who went up to worship at the Feast. 21They came to Philip, who was from Bethsaida[o] in Galilee, with a request. “Sir,” they said, “we would like to see Jesus.” 22Philip went to tell Andrew; Andrew and Philip in turn told Jesus.

23Jesus replied, “The hour has come for the Son of Man to be glorified.[p] 24I tell you the truth, unless a kernel of wheat falls to the ground and dies,[q] it remains only a single seed. But if it dies, it produces many seeds. 25The man who loves his life will lose it, while the man who hates his life in this world will keep it[r] for eternal life. 26Whoever serves me must follow me; and where I am, my servant also will be.[s] My Father will honor the one who serves me.

27“Now my heart is troubled,[t] and what shall I say? ‘Father,[u] save me from this hour’?[v] No, it was for this very reason I came to this hour. 28Father, glorify your name!”

Then a voice came from heaven,[w] “I have glorified it, and will glorify it again.” 29The crowd that was there and heard it said it had thundered; others said an angel had spoken to him.

30Jesus said, “This voice was for your benefit,[x] not mine. 31Now is the time for judgment on this world;[y] now the prince of this world[z] will be driven out. 32But I, when I am lifted up from the earth,[a] will draw all men to myself.”[b] 33He said this to show the kind of death he was going to die.[c]

34The crowd spoke up, “We have heard from the Law that the Christ[j] will remain forever,[d] so how can you say, ‘The Son of Man[e] must be lifted up’?[f] Who is this ‘Son of Man’?”

35Then Jesus told them, “You are

12:34 [d]Ps 110:4; Isa 9:7; Eze 37:25; Da 7:14 [e]Mt 8:20 [f]Jn 3:14

[g]*13* A Hebrew expression meaning “Save!” which became an exclamation of praise [h]*13* Psalm 118:25, 26 [i]*15* Zech. 9:9 [j]*34* Or *Messiah*

going to have the light[a] just a little while longer. Walk while you have the light,[b] before darkness overtakes you.[c] The man who walks in the dark does not know where he is going. 36Put your trust in the light while you have it, so that you may become sons of light."[d] When he had finished speaking, Jesus left and hid himself from them.[e]

The Jews continue in their unbelief.

37Even after Jesus had done all these miraculous signs[f] in their presence, they still would not believe in him. 38This was to fulfill the word of Isaiah the prophet:

"Lord, who has believed our
message
and to whom has the arm of the
Lord been revealed?"[k][g]

39For this reason they could not believe, because, as Isaiah says elsewhere:

40"He has blinded their eyes
and deadened their hearts,
so they can neither see with their
eyes,
nor understand with their hearts,
nor turn—and I would heal
them."[l][h]

41Isaiah said this because he saw Jesus' glory[i] and spoke about him.[j]

42Yet at the same time many even among the leaders believed in him.[k] But because of the Pharisees[l] they would not confess their faith for fear they would be put out of the synagogue;[m] 43for they loved praise from men more than praise from God.[n]

44Then Jesus cried out, "When a man believes in me, he does not believe in me only, but in the one who sent me.[o] 45When he looks at me, he sees the one who sent me.[p] 46I have come into the world as a light,[q] so that no one who believes in me should stay in darkness.

47"As for the person who hears my words but does not keep them, I do not judge him. For I did not come to judge the world, but to save it.[r] 48There is a judge for the one who rejects me and does not accept my words; that very word which I spoke will condemn him[s] at the last day. 49For I did not speak of my own accord, but the Father who sent me commanded me[t] what to say and how to say it. 50I know that his command leads to eternal life. So whatever I say is just what the Father has told me to say."

Jesus washes his disciples' feet.

13 It was just before the Passover Feast.[u] Jesus knew that the time had come[v] for him to leave this world and go to the Father.[w] Having loved his own who were in the world, he now showed them the full extent of his love.[m]

2The evening meal was being served, and the devil had already prompted Judas Iscariot, son of Simon, to betray Jesus. 3Jesus knew that the Father had put all things under his power,[x] and that he had come from God[y] and was returning to God; 4so he got up from the meal, took off his outer clothing, and wrapped a towel around his waist. 5After that, he poured water into a basin and began to wash his disciples' feet,[z] drying them with the towel that was wrapped around him.

6He came to Simon Peter, who said to him, "Lord, are you going to wash my feet?"

7Jesus replied, "You do not realize now what I am doing, but later you will understand."[a]

8"No," said Peter, "you shall never wash my feet."

Jesus answered, "Unless I wash you, you have no part with me."

9"Then, Lord," Simon Peter replied, "not just my feet but my hands and my head as well!"

10Jesus answered, "A person who has had a bath needs only to wash his feet; his whole body is clean. And you are

12:35 [a]ver 46 [b]Eph 5:8 [c]1Jn 2:11
12:36 [d]Lk 16:8 [e]Jn 8:59
12:37 [f]Jn 2:11
12:38 [g]Isa 53:1; Ro 10:16
12:40 [h]Isa 6:10; Mt 13:13,15
12:41 [i]Isa 6:1-4 [j]Lk 24:27
12:42 [k]ver 11; Jn 7:48 [l]Jn 7:13 [m]Jn 9:22
12:43 [n]Jn 5:44
12:44 [o]Mt 10:40; Jn 5:24
12:45 [p]Jn 14:9
12:46 [q]Jn 1:4; 3:19; 8:12; 9:5
12:47 [r]Jn 3:17
12:48 [s]Jn 5:45
12:49 [t]Jn 14:31
13:1 [u]Jn 11:55 [v]Jn 12:23 [w]Jn 16:28
13:3 [x]Mt 28:18 [y]Jn 8:42; 16:27,28,30
13:5 [z]Lk 7:44
13:7 [a]ver 12

k*38* Isaiah 53:1 l*40* Isaiah 6:10 m*1* Or *he loved them to the last*

clean,[a] though not every one of you." 11For he knew who was going to betray him, and that was why he said not every one was clean.

12When he had finished washing their feet, he put on his clothes and returned to his place. "Do you understand what I have done for you?" he asked them. 13"You call me 'Teacher'[b] and 'Lord,'[c] and rightly so, for that is what I am. 14Now that I, your Lord and Teacher, have washed your feet, you also should wash one another's feet.[d] 15I have set you an example that you should do as I have done for you.[e] 16I tell you the truth, no servant is greater than his master,[f] nor is a messenger greater than the one who sent him. 17Now that you know these things, you will be blessed if you do them.[g]

Jesus predicts his betrayal.

18"I am not referring to all of you;[h] I know those I have chosen.[i] But this is to fulfill the scripture: 'He who shares my bread[j] has lifted up his heel[k] against me.'[n][l]

19"I am telling you now before it happens, so that when it does happen you will believe[m] that I am He.[n] 20I tell you the truth, whoever accepts anyone I send accepts me; and whoever accepts me accepts the one who sent me."[o]

21After he had said this, Jesus was troubled in spirit[p] and testified, "I tell you the truth, one of you is going to betray me."[q]

22His disciples stared at one another, at a loss to know which of them he meant. 23One of them, the disciple whom Jesus loved,[r] was reclining next to him. 24Simon Peter motioned to this disciple and said, "Ask him which one he means."

25Leaning back against Jesus, he asked him, "Lord, who is it?"[s]

26Jesus answered, "It is the one to whom I will give this piece of bread when I have dipped it in the dish." Then, dipping the piece of bread, he gave it to Judas Iscariot, son of Simon. 27As soon as Judas took the bread, Satan entered into him.[t]

"What you are about to do, do quickly," Jesus told him, 28but no one at the meal understood why Jesus said this to him. 29Since Judas had charge of the money,[u] some thought Jesus was telling him to buy what was needed for the Feast, or to give something to the poor. 30As soon as Judas had taken the bread, he went out. And it was night.[v]

Jesus predicts Peter's denial.

13:37,38pp— Mt 26:33-35; Mk 14:29-31; Lk 22:33,34

31When he was gone, Jesus said, "Now is the Son of Man glorified[w] and God is glorified in him.[x] 32If God is glorified in him,[o] God will glorify the Son in himself,[y] and will glorify him at once.

33"My children, I will be with you only a little longer. You will look for me, and just as I told the Jews, so I tell you now: Where I am going, you cannot come.[z]

34"A new command[a] I give you: Love one another.[b] As I have loved you, so you must love one another.[c] 35By this all men will know that you are my disciples, if you love one another."[d]

36Simon Peter asked him, "Lord, where are you going?"

Jesus replied, "Where I am going, you cannot follow now,[e] but you will follow later."[f]

37Peter asked, "Lord, why can't I follow you now? I will lay down my life for you."

38Then Jesus answered, "Will you really lay down your life for me? I tell you the truth, before the rooster crows, you will disown me three times![g]

Jesus: The way, the truth and the life.

14 "Do not let your hearts be troubled.[h] Trust in God[p]; trust also

13:10 [a]Jn 15:3 **13:13** [b]Jn 11:28 [c]Lk 6:46; 1Co 12:3; Php 2:11 **13:14** [d]1Pe 5:5 **13:15** [e]Mt 11:29 **13:16** [f]Mt 10:24; Lk 6:40; Jn 15:20 **13:17** [g]Mt 7:24,25; Lk 11:28; Jas 1:25 **13:18** [h]ver 10 [i]Jn 15:16,19 [j]Mt 26:23 [k]Jn 6:70 [l]Ps 41:9 **13:19** [m]Jn 14:29; 16:4 [n]Jn 8:24 **13:20** [o]Mt 10:40; Lk 10:16 **13:21** [p]Jn 12:27 [q]Mt 26:21 **13:23** [r]Jn 19:26; 20:2; 21:7,20 **13:25** [s]Jn 21:20 **13:27** [t]Lk 22:3 **13:29** [u]Jn 12:6 **13:30** [v]Lk 22:53 **13:31** [w]Jn 7:39 [x]Jn 14:13; 17:4; 1Pe 4:11 **13:32** [y]Jn 17:1 **13:33** [z]Jn 7:33,34 **13:34** [a]1Jn 2:7-11; 3:11 [b]Lev 19:18; 1Th 4:9; 1Pe 1:22 [c]Jn 15:12; Eph 5:2; 1Jn 4:10,11 **13:35** [d]1Jn 3:14; 4:20 **13:36** [e]ver 33; Jn 14:2 [f]Jn 21:18,19; 2Pe 1:14 **13:38** [g]Jn 18:27 **14:1** [h]ver 27

n*18* Psalm 41:9 o*32* Many early manuscripts do not have *If God is glorified in him.* p*1* Or *You trust in God*

in me. 2In my Father's house are many
rooms; if it were not so, I would have
told you. I am going there[a] to prepare
a place for you. 3And if I go and prepare a place for you, I will come back
and take you to be with me that you
also may be where I am.[b] 4You know
the way to the place where I am going."
5Thomas[c] said to him, "Lord, we
don't know where you are going, so
how can we know the way?"
6Jesus answered, "I am the way[d] and
the truth and the life.[e] No one comes to
the Father except through me. 7If you
really knew me, you would know[q] my
Father as well.[f] From now on, you do
know him and have seen him."
8Philip said, "Lord, show us the Father
and that will be enough for us."
9Jesus answered: "Don't you know
me, Philip, even after I have been
among you such a long time? Anyone
who has seen me has seen the Father.[g]
How can you say, 'Show us the Father'?
10Don't you believe that I am in the
Father, and that the Father is in me?[h]
The words I say to you are not just my
own.[i] Rather, it is the Father, living in
me, who is doing his work. 11Believe
me when I say that I am in the Father
and the Father is in me; or at least
believe on the evidence of the miracles
themselves.[j] 12I tell you the truth, anyone who has faith[k] in me will do what
I have been doing.[l] He will do even
greater things than these, because I am
going to the Father. 13And I will do
whatever you ask[m] in my name, so that
the Son may bring glory to the Father.
14You may ask me for anything in my
name, and I will do it.

Promise of the Holy Spirit.

15"If you love me, you will obey what
I command.[n] 16And I will ask the Father,
and he will give you another Counselor[o] to be with you forever— 17the
Spirit of truth.[p] The world cannot accept
him,[q] because it neither sees him nor
knows him. But you know him, for he
lives with you and will be[r] in you.
18I will not leave you as orphans; I will
come to you.[r] 19Before long, the world
will not see me anymore, but you will
see me.[s] Because I live, you also will
live.[t] 20On that day you will realize
that I am in my Father,[u] and you are in
me, and I am in you. 21Whoever has my
commands and obeys them, he is the
one who loves me.[v] He who loves me
will be loved by my Father,[w] and I too
will love him and show myself to him."
22Then Judas[x] (not Judas Iscariot)
said, "But, Lord, why do you intend to
show yourself to us and not to the
world?"[y]
23Jesus replied, "If anyone loves me,
he will obey my teaching.[z] My Father
will love him, and we will come to
him and make our home with him.[a]
24He who does not love me will not
obey my teaching. These words you
hear are not my own; they belong to
the Father who sent me.[b]
25"All this I have spoken while still
with you. 26But the Counselor,[c] the Holy
Spirit, whom the Father will send in
my name,[d] will teach you all things[e]
and will remind you of everything I
have said to you.[f] 27Peace I leave with
you; my peace I give you.[g] I do not
give to you as the world gives. Do not
let your hearts be troubled and do not
be afraid.
28"You heard me say, 'I am going
away and I am coming back to you.'[h] If
you loved me, you would be glad that I
am going to the Father,[i] for the Father
is greater than I.[j] 29I have told you now
before it happens, so that when it does
happen you will believe.[k] 30I will not
speak with you much longer, for the
prince of this world[l] is coming. He has
no hold on me, 31but the world must
learn that I love the Father and that I
do exactly what my Father has commanded me.[m]
"Come now; let us leave.

14:2 [a]Jn 13:33,36
14:3 [b]Jn 12:26
14:5 [c]Jn 11:16
14:6 [d]Jn 10:9 [e]Jn 11:25
14:7 [f]Jn 8:19
14:9 [g]Jn 12:45; Col 1:15; Heb 1:3
14:10 [h]Jn 10:38 [i]Jn 5:19
14:11 [j]Jn 5:36; 10:38
14:12 [k]Mt 21:21 [l]Lk 10:17
14:13 [m]Mt 7:7
14:15 [n]ver 21,23; Jn 15:10; 1Jn 5:3
14:16 [o]Jn 15:26; 16:7
14:17 [p]Jn 15:26; 16:13; 1Jn 4:6 [q]1Co 2:14
14:18 [r]ver 3,28
14:19 [s]Jn 7:33,34; 16:16 [t]Jn 6:57
14:20 [u]Jn 10:38
14:21 [v]1Jn 5:3 [w]1Jn 2:5
14:22 [x]Lk 6:16; Ac 1:13 [y]Ac 10:41
14:23 [z]ver 15 [a]1Jn 2:24; Rev 3:20
14:24 [b]Jn 7:16
14:26 [c]Jn 15:26; 16:7 [d]Ac 2:33 [e]Jn 16:13; 1Jn 2:20,27 [f]Jn 2:22
14:27 [g]Jn 16:33; Php 4:7; Col 3:15
14:28 [h]ver 2-4,18 [i]Jn 5:18 [j]Jn 10:29 Php 2:6
14:29 [k]Jn 13:19; 16:4 **14:30** [l]Jn 12:31
14:31 [m]Jn 10:18; 12:49

q7 Some early manuscripts *If you really have known me, you will know* r17 Some early manuscripts *and is*

Jesus: The true vine.

15 “I am the true vine,[a] and my
Father is the gardener. 2He cuts
off every branch in me that bears no
fruit, while every branch that does
bear fruit he prunes[s] so that it will be
even more fruitful. 3You are already
clean because of the word I have spoken to you.[b] 4Remain in me, and I will
remain in you.[c] No branch can bear
fruit by itself; it must remain in the
vine. Neither can you bear fruit unless
you remain in me.
5“I am the vine; you are the branches. If a man remains in me and I in
him, he will bear much fruit;[d] apart
from me you can do nothing. 6If anyone does not remain in me, he is like a
branch that is thrown away and withers; such branches are picked up,
thrown into the fire and burned.[e] 7If
you remain in me and my words
remain in you, ask whatever you wish,
and it will be given you.[f] 8This is to
my Father's glory,[g] that you bear much
fruit, showing yourselves to be my disciples.[h]
9“As the Father has loved me,[i] so
have I loved you. Now remain in my
love. 10If you obey my commands,[j] you
will remain in my love, just as I have
obeyed my Father's commands and
remain in his love. 11I have told you
this so that my joy may be in you and
that your joy may be complete.[k] 12My
command is this: Love each other as I
have loved you.[l] 13Greater love has no
one than this, that he lay down his life
for his friends.[m] 14You are my friends[n]
if you do what I command.[o] 15I no
longer call you servants, because a servant does not know his master's business. Instead, I have called you friends,
for everything that I learned from my
Father I have made known to you.[p]
16You did not choose me, but I chose
you and appointed you[q] to go and bear
fruit—fruit that will last. Then the
Father will give you whatever you ask
in my name. 17This is my command:
Love each other.[r]

Jesus' disciples hated by the world.

18“If the world hates you,[s] keep in
mind that it hated me first. 19If you
belonged to the world, it would love
you as its own. As it is, you do not
belong to the world, but I have chosen
you[t] out of the world. That is why the
world hates you.[u] 20Remember the
words I spoke to you: 'No servant is
greater than his master.'[t][v] If they persecuted me, they will persecute you
also.[w] If they obeyed my teaching, they
will obey yours also. 21They will treat
you this way because of my name,[x] for
they do not know the One who sent
me.[y] 22If I had not come and spoken to
them, they would not be guilty of sin.
Now, however, they have no excuse
for their sin.[z] 23He who hates me hates
my Father as well. 24If I had not done
among them what no one else did,[a]
they would not be guilty of sin. But
now they have seen these miracles, and
yet they have hated both me and my
Father. 25But this is to fulfill what is
written in their Law: 'They hated me
without reason.'[u][b]
26“When the Counselor[c] comes,
whom I will send to you from the
Father,[d] the Spirit of truth[e] who goes
out from the Father, he will testify
about me.[f] 27And you also must testify,[g]
for you have been with me from the
beginning.[h]

The Holy Spirit will come as Counselor.

16 “All this[i] I have told you so that
you will not go astray.[j] 2They
will put you out of the synagogue;[k] in
fact, a time is coming when anyone
who kills you will think he is offering a
service to God.[l] 3They will do such
things because they have not known
the Father or me.[m] 4I have told you
this, so that when the time comes you

15:1 [a]Isa 5:1-7 **15:3** [b]Jn 13:10; 17:17; Eph 5:26 **15:4** [c]Jn 6:56; 1Jn 2:6 **15:5** [d]ver 16 **15:6** [e]ver 2 **15:7** [f]Mt 7:7 **15:8** [g]Mt 5:16 [h]Jn 8:31 **15:9** [i]Jn 17:23, 24,26 **15:10** [j]Jn 14:15 **15:11** [k]Jn 17:13 **15:12** [l]Jn 13:34 **15:13** [m]Jn 10:11; Ro 5:7,8 **15:14** [n]Lk 12:4 [o]Mt 12:50 **15:15** [p]Jn 8:26 **15:16** [q]Jn 6:70; 13:18 **15:17** [r]ver 12 **15:18** [s]1Jn 3:13 **15:19** [t]ver 16 [u]Jn 17:14 **15:20** [v]Jn 13:16 [w]2Ti 3:12 **15:21** [x]Mt 10:22 [y]Jn 16:3 **15:22** [z]Jn 9:41; Ro 1:20 **15:24** [a]Jn 5:36 **15:25** [b]Ps 35:19; 69:4 **15:26** [c]Jn 14:16 [d]Jn 14:26 [e]Jn 14:17 [f]1Jn 5:7 **15:27** [g]Lk 24:48; 1Jn 1:2; 4:14 [h]Lk 1:2

16:1 [i]Jn 15:18-27 [j]Mt 11:6 **16:2** [k]Jn 9:22 [l]Isa 66:5; Ac 26:9,10; Rev 6:9 **16:3** [m]Jn 15:21; 17:25; 1Jn 3:1

s*2* The Greek for *prunes* also means *cleans.*
t*20* John 13:16 u*25* Psalms 35:19; 69:4

will remember[a] that I warned you. I
did not tell you this at first because I
was with you.
5 "Now I am going to him who sent
me,[b] yet none of you asks me, 'Where
are you going?'[c] 6 Because I have said
these things, you are filled with grief.
7 But I tell you the truth: It is for your
good that I am going away. Unless I go
away, the Counselor[d] will not come to
you; but if I go, I will send him to you.[e]
8 When he comes, he will convict the
world of guilt[v] in regard to sin and
righteousness and judgment: 9 in regard
to sin,[f] because men do not believe in
me; 10 in regard to righteousness,[g]
because I am going to the Father, where
you can see me no longer; 11 and in
regard to judgment, because the prince
of this world[h] now stands condemned.
12 "I have much more to say to you,
more than you can now bear.[i] 13 But
when he, the Spirit of truth,[j] comes,
he will guide you into all truth.[k] He
will not speak on his own; he will
speak only what he hears, and he will
tell you what is yet to come. 14 He will
bring glory to me by taking from what
is mine and making it known to you.
15 All that belongs to the Father is
mine.[l] That is why I said the Spirit will
take from what is mine and make it
known to you.
16 "In a little while[m] you will see me
no more, and then after a little while
you will see me."[n]

Jesus will turn grief to joy.

17 Some of his disciples said to one
another, "What does he mean by saying, 'In a little while you will see me
no more, and then after a little while
you will see me,'[o] and 'Because I am
going to the Father'?"[p] 18 They kept asking, "What does he mean by 'a little
while'? We don't understand what he
is saying."
19 Jesus saw that they wanted to ask
him about this, so he said to them,
"Are you asking one another what I
meant when I said, 'In a little while you
will see me no more, and then after a
little while you will see me'? 20 I tell you
the truth, you will weep and mourn[q]
while the world rejoices. You will
grieve, but your grief will turn to joy.[r]
21 A woman giving birth to a child has
pain[s] because her time has come; but
when her baby is born she forgets the
anguish because of her joy that a child
is born into the world. 22 So with you:
Now is your time of grief,[t] but I will
see you again[u] and you will rejoice,
and no one will take away your joy.
23 In that day you will no longer ask me
anything. I tell you the truth, my
Father will give you whatever you ask
in my name.[v] 24 Until now you have
not asked for anything in my name.
Ask and you will receive, and your joy
will be complete.[w]
25 "Though I have been speaking figuratively,[x] a time is coming[y] when I
will no longer use this kind of language
but will tell you plainly about my
Father. 26 In that day you will ask in my
name.[z] I am not saying that I will ask
the Father on your behalf. 27 No, the
Father himself loves you because you
have loved me[a] and have believed that
I came from God. 28 I came from the
Father and entered the world; now I
am leaving the world and going back
to the Father."[b]
29 Then Jesus' disciples said, "Now
you are speaking clearly and without
figures of speech.[c] 30 Now we can see
that you know all things and that you
do not even need to have anyone ask
you questions. This makes us believe
that you came from God."
31 "You believe at last!"[w] Jesus
answered. 32 "But a time is coming,[d]
and has come, when you will be scattered,[e] each to his own home. You will
leave me all alone. Yet I am not alone,
for my Father is with me.[f]
33 "I have told you these things, so
that in me you may have peace.[g] In
this world you will have trouble.[h] But

16:4 [a]Jn 13:19
16:5 [b]Jn 7:33 [c]Jn 13:36; 14:5
16:7 [d]Jn 14:16,26; 15:26 [e]Jn 7:39
16:9 [f]Jn 15:22
16:10 [g]Ac 3:14; 7:52; 1Pe 3:18
16:11 [h]Jn 12:31
16:12 [i]Mk 4:33
16:13 [j]Jn 14:17 [k]Jn 14:26
16:15 [l]Jn 17:10
16:16 [m]Jn 7:33 [n]Jn 14:18-24
16:17 [o]ver 16 [p]ver 5
16:20 [q]Lk 23:27 [r]Jn 20:20
16:21 [s]Isa 26:17; 1Th 5:3
16:22 [t]ver 6 [u]ver 16
16:23 [v]Mt 7:7; Jn 15:16
16:24 [w]Jn 3:29; 15:11
16:25 [x]Mt 13:34; Jn 10:6 [y]ver 2
16:26 [z]ver 23,24
16:27 [a]Jn 14:21,23
16:28 [b]Jn 13:3
16:29 [c]ver 25
16:32 [d]ver 2,25 [e]Mt 26:31 [f]Jn 8:16,29
16:33 [g]Jn 14:27 [h]Jn 15:18-21

v8 Or *will expose the guilt of the world*   w31 Or *"Do you now believe?"*

take heart! I have overcome[a] the world."

Jesus prays for himself.

17 After Jesus said this, he looked toward heaven[b] and prayed:

"Father, the time has come. Glorify your Son, that your Son may glorify you.[c] **2**For you granted him authority over all people that he might give eternal life to all those you have given him.[d] **3**Now this is eternal life: that they may know you, the only true God, and Jesus Christ, whom you have sent.[e] **4**I have brought you glory[f] on earth by completing the work you gave me to do.[g] **5**And now, Father, glorify me in your presence with the glory I had with you[h] before the world began.[i]

Jesus prays for his disciples.

6"I have revealed you[x][j] to those whom you gave me[k] out of the world. They were yours; you gave them to me and they have obeyed your word. **7**Now they know that everything you have given me comes from you. **8**For I gave them the words you gave me[l] and they accepted them. They knew with certainty that I came from you,[m] and they believed that you sent me.[n] **9**I pray for them.[o] I am not praying for the world, but for those you have given me, for they are yours. **10**All I have is yours, and all you have is mine.[p] And glory has come to me through them. **11**I will remain in the world no longer, but they are still in the world,[q] and I am coming to you.[r] Holy Father, protect them by the power of your name—the name you gave me—so that they may be one[s] as we are one.[t] **12**While I was with them, I protected them and kept them safe by that name you gave me. None has been lost[u] except the one doomed to destruction[v] so that Scripture would be fulfilled.

13"I am coming to you now, but I say these things while I am still in the world, so that they may have the full measure of my joy[w] within them. **14**I have given them your word and the world has hated them,[x] for they are not of the world any more than I am of the world.[y] **15**My prayer is not that you take them out of the world but that you protect them from the evil one.[z] **16**They are not of the world, even as I am not of it.[a] **17**Sanctify[y] them by the truth; your word is truth.[b] **18**As you sent me into the world,[c] I have sent them into the world.[d] **19**For them I sanctify myself, that they too may be truly sanctified.

Jesus prays for all believers.

20"My prayer is not for them alone. I pray also for those who will believe in me through their message, **21**that all of them may be one, Father, just as you are in me and I am in you.[e] May they also be in us so that the world may believe that you have sent me.[f] **22**I have given them the glory that you gave me, that they may be one as we are one:[g] **23**I in them and you in me. May they be brought to complete unity to let the world know that you sent me[h] and have loved them[i] even as you have loved me.

24"Father, I want those you have given me to be with me where I am,[j] and to see my glory,[k] the glory you have given me because you loved me before the creation of the world.[l]

25"Righteous Father, though the world does not know you,[m] I know you, and they know that you have sent me.[n] **26**I have made you known

16:33 [a]Ro 8:37; 1Jn 4:4 **17:1** [b]Jn 11:41 [c]Jn 12:23; 13:31,32 **17:2** [d]ver 6,9,24; Da 7:14; Jn 6:37,39 **17:3** [e]ver 8,18,21, 23,25; Jn 3:17 **17:4** [f]Jn 13:31 [g]Jn 4:34 **17:5** [h]Php 2:6 [i]Jn 1:2 **17:6** [j]ver 26 [k]ver 2; Jn 6:37,39 **17:8** [l]ver 14,26 [m]Jn 16:27 [n]ver 3,18,21, 23,25; Jn 3:17 **17:9** [o]Lk 22:32 **17:10** [p]Jn 16:15 **17:11** [q]Jn 13:1 [r]Jn 7:33 [s]ver 21-23 [t]Jn 10:30 **17:12** [u]Jn 6:39 [v]Jn 6:70 **17:13** [w]Jn 3:29 **17:14** [x]Jn 15:19 [y]Jn 8:23 **17:15** [z]Mt 5:37 **17:16** [a]ver 14 **17:17** [b]Jn 15:3 **17:18** [c]ver 3,8,21, 23, 25 [d]Jn 20:21 **17:21** [e]Jn 10:38 [f]ver 3,8,18, 23,25; Jn 3:17 **17:22** [g]Jn 14:20 **17:23** [h]Jn 3:17 [i]Jn 16:27 **17:24** [j]Jn 12:26 [k]Jn 1:14 [l]ver 5; Mt 25:34 **17:25** [m]Jn 15:21; 16:3 [n]ver 3,8,18,21,23; Jn 3:17; 7:29; 16:27

x6 Greek *your name*; also in verse 26 y17 Greek *hagiazo (set apart for sacred use* or *make holy)*; also in verse 19

to them,[a] and will continue to make
you known in order that the love
you have for me may be in them[b]
and that I myself may be in them."

Jesus' betrayal and arrest.

18:3-11pp — Mt 26:47-56; Mk 14:43-50; Lk 22:47-53

18 When he had finished praying,
Jesus left with his disciples and
crossed the Kidron Valley.[c] On the other side there was an olive grove,[d] and
he and his disciples went into it.[e]
2Now Judas, who betrayed him, knew
the place, because Jesus had often met
there with his disciples.[f] 3So Judas came
to the grove, guiding[g] a detachment of
soldiers and some officials from the
chief priests and Pharisees.[h] They were
carrying torches, lanterns and weapons.
4Jesus, knowing all that was going
to happen to him,[i] went out and asked
them, "Who is it you want?"[j]
5"Jesus of Nazareth," they replied.
"I am he," Jesus said. (And Judas the
traitor was standing there with them.)
6When Jesus said, "I am he," they drew
back and fell to the ground.
7Again he asked them, "Who is it
you want?"[k]
And they said, "Jesus of Nazareth."
8"I told you that I am he," Jesus
answered. "If you are looking for me,
then let these men go." 9This happened
so that the words he had spoken would
be fulfilled: "I have not lost one of those
you gave me."[z] [l]
10Then Simon Peter, who had a
sword, drew it and struck the high
priest's servant, cutting off his right
ear. (The servant's name was Malchus.)
11Jesus commanded Peter, "Put your
sword away! Shall I not drink the
cup[m] the Father has given me?"

Jesus taken to Annas.

18:12,13pp — Mt 26:57

12Then the detachment of soldiers
with its commander and the Jewish officials[n] arrested Jesus. They bound him
13and brought him first to Annas, who

17:26 [a]ver 6 [b]Jn 15:9
18:1 [c]2Sa 15:23 [d]ver 26 [e]Mt 26:36
18:2 [f]Lk 21:37; 22:39
18:3 [g]Ac 1:16 [h]ver 12
18:4 [i]Jn 6:64; 13:1,11 [j]ver 7
18:7 [k]ver 4
18:9 [l]Jn 17:12
18:11 [m]Mt 20:22
18:12 [n]ver 3
18:13 [o]ver 24; Mt 26:3
18:14 [p]Jn 11:49-51
18:15 [q]Mt 26:3 [r]Mt 26:58; Mk 14:54; Lk 22:54
18:17 [s]ver 25
18:18 [t]Jn 21:9 [u]Mk 14:54,67
18:20 [v]Mt 4:23 [w]Mt 26:55 [x]Jn 7:26
18:22 [y]ver 3 [z]Mt 16:21; Jn 19:3
18:23 [a]Mt 5:39; Ac 23:2-5
18:24 [b]ver 13; Mt 26:3

was the father-in-law of Caiaphas,[o] the
high priest that year. 14Caiaphas was
the one who had advised the Jews that
it would be good if one man died for
the people.[p]

Peter's first denial of Jesus.

18:16-18pp — Mt 26:69,70; Mk 14:66-68; Lk 22:55-57

15Simon Peter and another disciple
were following Jesus. Because this disciple was known to the high priest,[q]
he went with Jesus into the high
priest's courtyard,[r] 16but Peter had to
wait outside at the door. The other
disciple, who was known to the high
priest, came back, spoke to the girl on
duty there and brought Peter in.
17"You are not one of his disciples, are
you?" the girl at the door asked Peter.
He replied, "I am not."[s]
18It was cold, and the servants and
officials stood around a fire[t] they had
made to keep warm. Peter also was
standing with them, warming himself.[u]

Questioning of Jesus by the high priest.

18:19-24pp — Mt 26:59-68; Mk 14:55-65; Lk 22:63-7

19Meanwhile, the high priest questioned Jesus about his disciples and his
teaching.
20"I have spoken openly to the
world," Jesus replied. "I always taught
in synagogues[v] or at the temple,[w] where
all the Jews come together. I said nothing in secret.[x] 21Why question me?
Ask those who heard me. Surely they
know what I said."
22When Jesus said this, one of the
officials[y] nearby struck him in the
face.[z] "Is this the way you answer the
high priest?" he demanded.
23"If I said something wrong," Jesus
replied, "testify as to what is wrong.
But if I spoke the truth, why did you
strike me?"[a] 24Then Annas sent him,
still bound, to Caiaphas[b] the high
priest.[a]

[z]9 John 6:39 [a]24 Or *(Now Annas had sent him, still bound, to Caiaphas the high priest.)*

Peter's second and third denials.

18:25-27pp— Mt 26:71-75; Mk 14:69-72; Lk 22:58-62

25As Simon Peter stood warming himself,[a] he was asked, "You are not one of
his disciples, are you?"

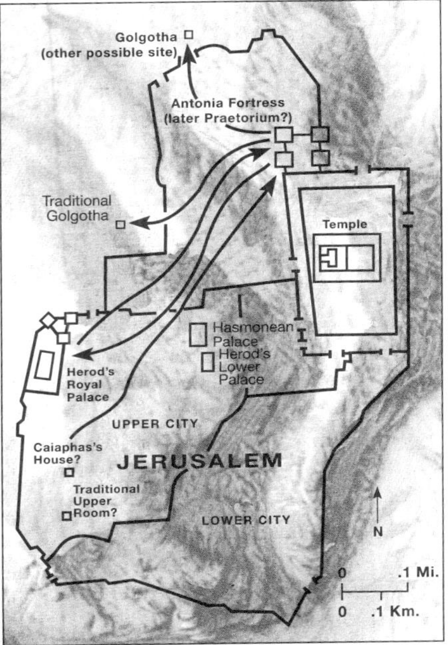

Jesus' Trial and Crucifixion
Jesus was taken from trial before the Jewish Sanhedrin to trial before the Roman governor, Pilate, in Pilate's palace. Pilate sent him to Herod (Luke 23:5-12), but Herod just returned Jesus to Pilate. Responding to threats from the mob, Pilate finally turned Jesus over to be crucified.

He denied it, saying, "I am not."[b]
26One of the high priest's servants, a
relative of the man whose ear Peter had
cut off,[c] challenged him, "Didn't I see
you with him in the olive grove?"[d]
27Again Peter denied it, and at that
moment a rooster began to crow.[e]

Jesus' arraignment before Pilate.

18:29-40pp— Mt 27:11-18,20-23; Mk 15:2-15; Lk 23:2,3,18-25

28Then the Jews led Jesus from Caiaphas to the palace of the Roman governor.[f] By now it was early morning, and
to avoid ceremonial uncleanness the
Jews did not enter the palace;[g] they
wanted to be able to eat the Passover.[h]

18:25 [a]ver 18 [b]ver 17
18:26 [c]ver 10 [d]ver 1
18:27 [e]Jn 13:38
18:28 [f]Mt 27:2; Mk 15:1; Lk 23:1 [g]ver 33; Jn 19:9 [h]Jn 11:55
18:32 [i]Mt 20:19; 26:2; Jn 3:14; 8:28; 12:32,33
18:33 [j]ver 28,29; Jn 19:9 [k]Lk 23:3; Mt 2:2
18:36 [l]Mt 3:2 [m]Mt 26:53 [n]Lk 17:21; Jn 6:15
18:37 [o]Jn 3:32 [p]Jn 8:47; 1Jn 4:6
18:38 [q]Lk 23:4; Jn 19:4,6
18:40 [r]Ac 3:14
19:1 [s]Dt 25:3; Isa 50:6; 53:5; Mt 27:26

29So Pilate came out to them and asked,
"What charges are you bringing against
this man?"
30"If he were not a criminal," they
replied, "we would not have handed
him over to you."
31Pilate said, "Take him yourselves
and judge him by your own law."
"But we have no right to execute anyone," the Jews objected. 32This happened so that the words Jesus had
spoken indicating the kind of death he
was going to die[i] would be fulfilled.
33Pilate then went back inside the
palace,[j] summoned Jesus and asked
him, "Are you the king of the Jews?"[k]
34"Is that your own idea," Jesus asked,
"or did others talk to you about me?"
35"Am I a Jew?" Pilate replied. "It
was your people and your chief priests
who handed you over to me. What is it
you have done?"
36Jesus said, "My kingdom[l] is not of
this world. If it were, my servants
would fight to prevent my arrest by the
Jews.[m] But now my kingdom is from
another place."[n]
37"You are a king, then!" said Pilate.
Jesus answered, "You are right in saying I am a king. In fact, for this reason I
was born, and for this I came into the
world, to testify to the truth.[o] Everyone
on the side of truth listens to me."[p]
38"What is truth?" Pilate asked. With
this he went out again to the Jews and
said, "I find no basis for a charge against
him.[q] 39But it is your custom for me to
release to you one prisoner at the time
of the Passover. Do you want me to
release 'the king of the Jews'?"
40They shouted back, "No, not him!
Give us Barabbas!" Now Barabbas had
taken part in a rebellion.[r]

Jesus' flogging and crowning with thorns.

19:1-16pp— Mt 27:27-31; Mk 15:16-20

19 Then Pilate took Jesus and had
him flogged.[s] 2The soldiers twisted together a crown of thorns and put
it on his head. They clothed him in a

purple robe 3and went up to him again and again, saying, "Hail, king of the Jews!"[a] And they struck him in the face.[b]

4Once more Pilate came out and said to the Jews, "Look, I am bringing him out[c] to you to let you know that I find no basis for a charge against him."[d] 5When Jesus came out wearing the crown of thorns and the purple robe,[e] Pilate said to them, "Here is the man!"

6As soon as the chief priests and their officials saw him, they shouted, "Crucify! Crucify!"

But Pilate answered, "You take him and crucify him.[f] As for me, I find no basis for a charge against him."[g]

7The Jews insisted, "We have a law, and according to that law he must die,[h] because he claimed to be the Son of God."[i]

8When Pilate heard this, he was even more afraid, 9and he went back inside the palace.[j] "Where do you come from?" he asked Jesus, but Jesus gave him no answer.[k] 10"Do you refuse to speak to me?" Pilate said. "Don't you realize I have power either to free you or to crucify you?"

11Jesus answered, "You would have no power over me if it were not given to you from above.[l] Therefore the one who handed me over to you[m] is guilty of a greater sin."

12From then on, Pilate tried to set Jesus free, but the Jews kept shouting, "If you let this man go, you are no friend of Caesar. Anyone who claims to be a king[n] opposes Caesar."

13When Pilate heard this, he brought Jesus out and sat down on the judge's seat[o] at a place known as the Stone Pavement (which in Aramaic[p] is Gabbatha). 14It was the day of Preparation[q] of Passover Week, about the sixth hour.[r]

"Here is your king,"[s] Pilate said to the Jews.

15But they shouted, "Take him away! Take him away! Crucify him!"

"Shall I crucify your king?" Pilate asked.

"We have no king but Caesar," the chief priests answered.

16Finally Pilate handed him over to them to be crucified.[t]

19:3 [a]Mt 27:29 [b]Jn 18:22
19:4 [c]Jn 18:38 [d]ver 6; Lk 23:4
19:5 [e]ver 2
19:6 [f]Ac 3:13 [g]ver 4; Lk 23:4
19:7 [h]Lev 24:16 [i]Mt 26:63-66; Jn 5:18; 10:33
19:9 [j]Jn 18:33 [k]Mk 14:61
19:11 [l]Ro 13:1 [m]Jn 18:28-30; Ac 3:13
19:12 [n]Lk 23:2
19:13 [o]Mt 27:19 [p]Jn 5:2
19:14 [q]Mt 27:62 [r]Mk 15:25 [s]ver 19,21
19:16 [t]Mt 27:26; Mk 15:15; Lk 23:25
19:17 [u]Ge 22:6; Lk 14:27; 23:26 [v]Lk 23:33 [w]Jn 5:2
19:18 [x]Lk 23:32
19:19 [y]Mk 1:24 [z]ver 14,21
19:20 [a]Heb 13:12
19:21 [b]ver 14
19:24 [c]ver 28,36,37; Mt 1:22 [d]Ps 22:18
19:25 [e]Mt 27:55,56; Mk 15:40,41; Lk 23:49 [f]Mt 12:46 [g]Lk 24:18
19:26 [h]Mt 12:46 [i]Jn 13:23

Jesus' crucifixion.

19:17-24pp — Mt 27:33-44; Mk 15:22-32; Lk 23:33-43

So the soldiers took charge of Jesus. 17Carrying his own cross,[u] he went out to the place of the Skull[v] (which in Aramaic[w] is called Golgotha). 18Here they crucified him, and with him two others[x]—one on each side and Jesus in the middle.

19Pilate had a notice prepared and fastened to the cross. It read: JESUS OF NAZARETH,[y] THE KING OF THE JEWS.[z] 20Many of the Jews read this sign, for the place where Jesus was crucified was near the city,[a] and the sign was written in Aramaic, Latin and Greek. 21The chief priests of the Jews protested to Pilate, "Do not write 'The King of the Jews,' but that this man claimed to be king of the Jews."[b]

22Pilate answered, "What I have written, I have written."

23When the soldiers crucified Jesus, they took his clothes, dividing them into four shares, one for each of them, with the undergarment remaining. This garment was seamless, woven in one piece from top to bottom.

24"Let's not tear it," they said to one another. "Let's decide by lot who will get it."

This happened that the scripture might be fulfilled[c] which said,

> "They divided my garments among
> them
> and cast lots for my clothing."[b][d]

So this is what the soldiers did.

25Near the cross[e] of Jesus stood his mother,[f] his mother's sister, Mary the wife of Clopas, and Mary Magdalene.[g] 26When Jesus saw his mother[h] there, and the disciple whom he loved[i] standing nearby, he said to his mother, "Dear woman, here is your son," 27and to the disciple, "Here is your mother." From

[b]24 Psalm 22:18

that time on, this disciple took her into his home.

Jesus' death.

19:29,30pp — Mt 27:48,50; Mk 15:36,37; Lk 23:36

28 Later, knowing that all was now completed,[a] and so that the Scripture would be fulfilled,[b] Jesus said, "I am thirsty." 29 A jar of wine vinegar[c] was there, so they soaked a sponge in it, put the sponge on a stalk of the hyssop plant, and lifted it to Jesus' lips. 30 When he had received the drink, Jesus said, "It is finished."[d] With that, he bowed his head and gave up his spirit.

31 Now it was the day of Preparation,[e] and the next day was to be a special Sabbath. Because the Jews did not want the bodies left on the crosses[f] during the Sabbath, they asked Pilate to have the legs broken and the bodies taken down. 32 The soldiers therefore came and broke the legs of the first man who had been crucified with Jesus, and then those of the other.[g] 33 But when they came to Jesus and found that he was already dead, they did not break his legs. 34 Instead, one of the soldiers pierced[h] Jesus' side with a spear, bringing a sudden flow of blood and water.[i] 35 The man who saw it[j] has given testimony, and his testimony is true.[k] He knows that he tells the truth, and he testifies so that you also may believe. 36 These things happened so that the scripture would be fulfilled:[l] "Not one of his bones will be broken,"[c m] 37 and, as another scripture says, "They will look on the one they have pierced."[d n]

Jesus' burial.

19:38-42pp — Mt 27:57-61; Mk 15:42-47; Lk 23:50-56

38 Later, Joseph of Arimathea asked Pilate for the body of Jesus. Now Joseph was a disciple of Jesus, but secretly because he feared the Jews. With Pilate's permission, he came and took the body away. 39 He was accompanied by Nicodemus,[o] the man who earlier had visited Jesus at night. Nicodemus brought a mixture of myrrh and aloes, about seventy-five pounds.[e] 40 Taking Jesus' body, the two of them wrapped it, with the spices, in strips of linen.[p] This was in accordance with Jewish burial customs.[q] 41 At the place where Jesus was crucified, there was a garden, and in the garden a new tomb, in which no one had ever been laid. 42 Because it was the Jewish day of Preparation[r] and since the tomb was nearby,[s] they laid Jesus there.

Jesus' resurrection.

20:1-8pp — Mt 28:1-8; Mk 16:1-8; Lk 24:1-10

20 Early on the first day of the week, while it was still dark, Mary Magdalene[t] went to the tomb and saw that the stone had been removed from the entrance.[u] 2 So she came running to Simon Peter and the other disciple, the one Jesus loved,[v] and said, "They have taken the Lord out of the tomb, and we don't know where they have put him!"[w]

3 So Peter and the other disciple started for the tomb.[x] 4 Both were running, but the other disciple outran Peter and reached the tomb first. 5 He bent over and looked in[y] at the strips of linen[z] lying there but did not go in. 6 Then Simon Peter, who was behind him, arrived and went into the tomb. He saw the strips of linen lying there, 7 as well as the burial cloth that had been around Jesus' head.[a] The cloth was folded up by itself, separate from the linen. 8 Finally the other disciple, who had reached the tomb first,[b] also went inside. He saw and believed. 9 (They still did not understand from Scripture[c] that Jesus had to rise from the dead.)[d]

The risen Lord appears to Mary Magdalene.

10 Then the disciples went back to their homes, 11 but Mary stood outside the tomb crying. As she wept, she bent

19:28 [a]ver 30; Jn 13:1 [b]ver 24,36,37
19:29 [c]Ps 69:21
19:30 [d]Lk 12:50; Jn 17:4
19:31 [e]ver 14,42 [f]Dt 21:23; Jos 8:29; 10:26,27
19:32 [g]ver 18
19:34 [h]Zec 12:10 [i]1Jn 5:6,8
19:35 [j]Lk 24:48 [k]Jn 15:27; 21:24
19:36 [l]ver 24,28,37; Mt 1:22 [m]Ex 12:46; Nu 9:12; Ps 34:20
19:37 [n]Zec 12:10; Rev 1:7
19:39 [o]Jn 3:1; 7:50
19:40 [p]Lk 24:12; Jn 11:44; 20:5,7 [q]Mt 26:12
19:42 [r]ver 14,31 [s]ver 20,41
20:1 [t]ver 18; Jn 19:25 [u]Mt 27:60,66
20:2 [v]Jn 13:23 [w]ver 13
20:3 [x]Lk 24:12
20:5 [y]ver 11 [z]Jn 19:40
20:7 [a]Jn 11:44
20:8 [b]ver 4
20:9 [c]Mt 22:29; Jn 2:22 [d]Lk 24:26,46

c*36* Exodus 12:46; Num. 9:12; Psalm 34:20
d*37* Zech. 12:10 e*39* Greek *a hundred litrai* (about 34 kilograms)

over to look into the tomb[a] 12 and saw
two angels in white,[b] seated where
Jesus' body had been, one at the head
and the other at the foot.
13 They asked her, "Woman, why are
you crying?"[c]
"They have taken my Lord away," she
said, "and I don't know where they have
put him."[d] 14 At this, she turned around
and saw Jesus standing there,[e] but she
did not realize that it was Jesus.[f]
15 "Woman," he said, "why are you
crying?[g] Who is it you are looking for?"
Thinking he was the gardener, she
said, "Sir, if you have carried him away,
tell me where you have put him, and I
will get him."
16 Jesus said to her, "Mary."
She turned toward him and cried out
in Aramaic,[h] "Rabboni!"[i] (which means
Teacher).
17 Jesus said, "Do not hold on to me,
for I have not yet returned to the Father.
Go instead to my brothers[j] and tell
them, 'I am returning to my Father[k] and
your Father, to my God and your God.'"
18 Mary Magdalene[l] went to the disciples[m] with the news: "I have seen the
Lord!" And she told them that he had
said these things to her.

Jesus appears to his disciples.

19 On the evening of that first day of
the week, when the disciples were
together, with the doors locked for fear
of the Jews,[n] Jesus came and stood
among them and said, "Peace[o] be with
you!"[p] 20 After he said this, he showed
them his hands and side.[q] The disciples
were overjoyed[r] when they saw the
Lord.
21 Again Jesus said, "Peace be with
you![s] As the Father has sent me,[t] I am
sending you."[u] 22 And with that he
breathed on them and said, "Receive the
Holy Spirit.[v] 23 If you forgive anyone his
sins, they are forgiven; if you do not
forgive them, they are not forgiven."[w]

Jesus appears to Thomas.

24 Now Thomas[x] (called Didymus), one
of the Twelve, was not with the disciples when Jesus came. 25 So the other
disciples told him, "We have seen the
Lord!"
But he said to them, "Unless I see
the nail marks in his hands and put my
finger where the nails were, and put
my hand into his side,[y] I will not
believe it."[z]
26 A week later his disciples were in
the house again, and Thomas was with
them. Though the doors were locked,
Jesus came and stood among them and
said, "Peace[a] be with you!"[b] 27 Then he
said to Thomas, "Put your finger here;
see my hands. Reach out your hand
and put it into my side. Stop doubting
and believe."[c]
28 Thomas said to him, "My Lord and
my God!"
29 Then Jesus told him, "Because you
have seen me, you have believed;[d]
blessed are those who have not seen
and yet have believed."[e]
30 Jesus did many other miraculous
signs[f] in the presence of his disciples,
which are not recorded in this book.[g]
31 But these are written that you may[f]
believe[h] that Jesus is the Christ, the
Son of God,[i] and that by believing you
may have life in his name.[j]

Jesus aids his disciples in a great catch of fish.

21 Afterward Jesus appeared again
to his disciples,[k] by the Sea of
Tiberias.[g][l] It happened this way:
2 Simon Peter, Thomas[m] (called Didymus), Nathanael[n] from Cana in Galilee,[o]
the sons of Zebedee,[p] and two other
disciples were together. 3 "I'm going
out to fish," Simon Peter told them,
and they said, "We'll go with you." So
they went out and got into the boat,
but that night they caught nothing.[q]
4 Early in the morning, Jesus stood

20:11 [a]ver 5
20:12 [b]Mt 28:2,3; Mk 16:5; Lk 24:4; Ac 5:19
20:13 [c]ver 15 [d]ver 2
20:14 [e]Mt 28:9; Mk 16:9 [f]Lk 24:16; Jn 21:4
20:15 [g]ver 13
20:16 [h]Jn 5:2 [i]Mt 23:7
20:17 [j]Mt 28:10 [k]Jn 7:33
20:18 [l]ver 1 [m]Lk 24:10, 22,23
20:19 [n]Jn 7:13 [o]Jn 14:27 [p]ver 21,26; Lk 24:36-39
20:20 [q]Lk 24:39,40; Jn 19:34 [r]Jn 16:20,22
20:21 [s]ver 19 [t]Jn 3:17 [u]Mt 28:19; Jn 17:18
20:22 [v]Jn 7:39; Ac 2:38; 8:15-17; 19:2; Gal 3:2
20:23 [w]Mt 16:19; 18:18
20:24 [x]Jn 11:16
20:25 [y]ver 20 [z]Mk 16:11
20:26 [a]Jn 14:27 [b]ver 21
20:27 [c]ver 25; Lk 24:40
20:29 [d]Jn 3:15 [e]1Pe 1:8
20:30 [f]Jn 2:11 [g]Jn 21:25
20:31 [h]Jn 3:15; 19:35

[i]Mt 4:3 [j]Mt 25:46 **21:1** [k]Jn 20:19,26 [l]Jn 6:1
21:2 [m]Jn 11:16 [n]Jn 1:45 [o]Jn 2:1 [p]Mt 4:21
21:3 [q]Lk 5:5

[f]31 Some manuscripts *may continue to* [g]1 That is, Sea of Galilee

on the shore, but the disciples did not
realize that it was Jesus.[a]
5 He called out to them, "Friends,
haven't you any fish?"
"No," they answered.
6 He said, "Throw your net on the
right side of the boat and you will find
some." When they did, they were
unable to haul the net in because of
the large number of fish.[b]
7 Then the disciple whom Jesus loved[c]
said to Peter, "It is the Lord!" As soon
as Simon Peter heard him say, "It is the
Lord," he wrapped his outer garment
around him (for he had taken it off) and
jumped into the water. 8 The other disciples followed in the boat, towing the
net full of fish, for they were not far
from shore, about a hundred yards.[h]
9 When they landed, they saw a fire[d] of
burning coals there with fish on it,[e]
and some bread.
10 Jesus said to them, "Bring some of
the fish you have just caught."
11 Simon Peter climbed aboard and
dragged the net ashore. It was full of
large fish, 153, but even with so many
the net was not torn. 12 Jesus said to
them, "Come and have breakfast." None
of the disciples dared ask him, "Who
are you?" They knew it was the Lord.
13 Jesus came, took the bread and gave
it to them, and did the same with the
fish.[f] 14 This was now the third time
Jesus appeared to his disciples[g] after
he was raised from the dead.

Peter's love for Jesus is affirmed.

15 When they had finished eating,
Jesus said to Simon Peter, "Simon son
of John, do you truly love me more than
these?"
"Yes, Lord," he said, "you know that
I love you."[h]
Jesus said, "Feed my lambs."[i]
16 Again Jesus said, "Simon son of
John, do you truly love me?"
He answered, "Yes, Lord, you know
that I love you."
Jesus said, "Take care of my sheep."[j]
17 The third time he said to him,
"Simon son of John, do you love me?"
Peter was hurt because Jesus asked
him the third time, "Do you love me?"[k]
He said, "Lord, you know all things;[l]
you know that I love you."
Jesus said, "Feed my sheep.[m] 18 I tell
you the truth, when you were younger
you dressed yourself and went where
you wanted; but when you are old you
will stretch out your hands, and someone else will dress you and lead you
where you do not want to go." 19 Jesus
said this to indicate the kind of death[n]
by which Peter would glorify God.[o]
Then he said to him, "Follow me!"
20 Peter turned and saw that the disciple whom Jesus loved[p] was following
them. (This was the one who had leaned
back against Jesus at the supper and
had said, "Lord, who is going to betray
you?")[q] 21 When Peter saw him, he
asked, "Lord, what about him?"
22 Jesus answered, "If I want him to
remain alive until I return,[r] what is
that to you? You must follow me."[s]
23 Because of this, the rumor spread
among the brothers[t] that this disciple
would not die. But Jesus did not say
that he would not die; he only said, "If
I want him to remain alive until I
return, what is that to you?"
24 This is the disciple who testifies
to these things[u] and who wrote them
down. We know that his testimony is
true.[v]
25 Jesus did many other things as
well.[w] If every one of them were written down, I suppose that even the
whole world would not have room for
the books that would be written.

21:4 [a]Lk 24:16; Jn 20:14
21:6 [b]Lk 5:4-7
21:7 [c]Jn 13:23
21:9 [d]Jn 18:18 [e]ver 10,13
21:13 [f]ver 9
21:14 [g]Jn 20:19,26
21:15 [h]Mt 26:33,35; Jn 13:37 [i]Lk 12:32
21:16 [j]Mt 2:6; Ac 20:28; 1Pe 5:2,3
21:17 [k]Jn 13:38 [l]Jn 16:30 [m]ver 16
21:19 [n]Jn 12:33; 18:32 [o]2Pe 1:14
21:20 [p]ver 7; Jn 13:23 [q]Jn 13:25
21:22 [r]Mt 16:27; 1Co 4:5; Rev 2:25 [s]ver 19
21:23 [t]Ac 1:16
21:24 [u]Jn 15:27 [v]Jn 19:35
21:25 [w]Jn 20:30

h8 Greek *about two hundred cubits* (about 90 meters)

ACTS

Author: Luke.

Date Written: Between A.D. 61 and 63.

Time Span: About 29 years (from the ascension of Christ, about A.D. 33, through the imprisonment of Paul in Rome, about A.D. 62).

Title: From the book's depiction of the deeds (acts) of the apostles as directed by the Holy Spirit of God.

Background: Luke begins the book of Acts where he left off in his Gospel. Both are written to aid a new Christian named Theophilus. Acts is the essential link connecting the 4 Gospels with all the other New Testament writings. Acts shows the ministry of the church carrying the Great Commission of Jesus to all the world. While mentioning most of the apostles, this book emphasizes the ministries of Peter (chapters 1-12) and of Paul (chapters 13-28).

Where Written: Possibly at Caesarea or Rome.

To Whom: To Theophilus and other Christian Gentiles.

Content: Acts carries out the story of the ministry of Christ through the lives of his disciples. The Holy Spirit comes at Pentecost giving power and boldness to aid Christians in witnessing to all the world of their risen Savior. Acts describes Peter's leadership of the Jewish church; the death of Stephen (chapter 7); intense persecution against Christianity led by Saul (chapter 8); and Saul's (Paul's) conversion on the road to Damascus (chapter 9). Paul leads 3 extensive missionary journeys teaching and preaching the gospel. The book ends with Paul's trip to Rome, where he is put into prison. But Christianity has spread like fire from Jerusalem throughout the entire Roman Empire. Nothing can stop the Good News now!

Key Words: "Holy Spirit"; "Growth." Acts mentions or refers to the "Holy Spirit" more than 30 times. He is the one who will guide, fill, sustain, convict and comfort the believer. The book also outlines the "growth" of the church: in number, strength and understanding.

Themes: • God will not ask us to do anything without also giving us the provision to do it well. • Church growth will be continuous and significant...with the Holy Spirit's leadership. • It is impossible to live successful Christian lives apart from the Holy Spirit. • Christians obedient to God's leading will have tremendous opportunities to share Christ.

Outline:

1. The ascension of Jesus. 1:1-1:11
2. Pentecost and the early church in Jerusalem. 1:12-8:3
3. The gospel's spread to Judea and Samaria. 8:4-12:25
4. Paul's first missionary journey. 13:1-14:28
5. The Jerusalem council. 15:1-15:35
6. Paul's second missionary journey. 15:36-18:22
7. Paul's third missionary journey. 18:23-21:14
8. Paul's journeys to Rome. 21:15-28:31

ACTS

Ascension of Jesus to heaven.

1 In my former book,[a] Theophilus, I
wrote about all that Jesus began to
do and to teach[b] 2until the day he was
taken up to heaven,[c] after giving instructions[d] through the Holy Spirit to the
apostles[e] he had chosen.[f] 3After his suffering, he showed himself to these men
and gave many convincing proofs that
he was alive. He appeared to them[g] over
a period of forty days and spoke about
the kingdom of God. 4On one occasion,
while he was eating with them, he gave
them this command: "Do not leave Jerusalem, but wait for the gift my Father
promised, which you have heard me
speak about.[h] 5For John baptized with[a]
water, but in a few days you will be baptized with the Holy Spirit."
6So when they met together, they
asked him, "Lord, are you at this time
going to restore[i] the kingdom to Israel?"
7He said to them: "It is not for you
to know the times or dates the Father
has set by his own authority.[j] 8But you
will receive power when the Holy Spirit
comes on you;[k] and you will be my witnesses[l] in Jerusalem, and in all Judea
and Samaria,[m] and to the ends of the
earth."[n]
9After he said this, he was taken up[o]
before their very eyes, and a cloud hid
him from their sight.
10They were looking intently up into
the sky as he was going, when suddenly
two men dressed in white[p] stood beside
them. 11"Men of Galilee,"[q] they said,
"why do you stand here looking into the
sky? This same Jesus, who has been tak-
en from you into heaven, will come
back[r] in the same way you have seen
him go into heaven."

Prayer meeting in upstairs room.

12Then they returned to Jerusalem[s]
from the hill called the Mount of Olives,[t]
a Sabbath day's walk[b] from the city.
13When they arrived, they went upstairs
to the room[u] where they were staying.
Those present were Peter, John, James
and Andrew; Philip and Thomas, Bartholomew and Matthew; James son of
Alphaeus and Simon the Zealot, and
Judas son of James.[v] 14They all joined
together constantly in prayer,[w] along
with the women[x] and Mary the mother of Jesus, and with his brothers.[y]

Selection of Matthias to replace Judas.

15In those days Peter stood up among
the believers[c] (a group numbering about
a hundred and twenty) 16and said,
"Brothers, the Scripture had to be fulfilled[z] which the Holy Spirit spoke long
ago through the mouth of David concerning Judas,[a] who served as guide for
those who arrested Jesus— 17he was
one of our number[b] and shared in this
ministry."[c]
18(With the reward[d] he got for his
wickedness, Judas bought a field;[e] there
he fell headlong, his body burst open
and all his intestines spilled out. 19Every-
one in Jerusalem heard about this, so
they called that field in their language
Akeldama, that is, Field of Blood.)
20"For," said Peter, "it is written in
the book of Psalms,

"'May his place be deserted;
let there be no one to dwell in it,'[d][f]

and,

"'May another take his place of
leadership.'[e][g]

21Therefore it is necessary to choose
one of the men who have been with us
the whole time the Lord Jesus went in
and out among us, 22beginning from
John's baptism[h] to the time when Jesus
was taken up from us. For one of these
must become a witness[i] with us of his
resurrection."
23So they proposed two men: Joseph
called Barsabbas (also known as Justus)

1:1 [a]Lk 1:1-4 [b]Lk 3:23
1:2 [c]ver 9,11; Mk 16:19 [d]Mt 28:19,20 [e]Mk 6:30 [f]Jn 13:18
1:3 [g]Mt 28:17; Lk 24:34,36; Jn 20:19,26; 21:1,14; 1Co 15:5-7
1:4 [h]Lk 24:49; Jn 14:16; Ac 2:33
1:6 [i]Mt 17:11
1:7 [j]Mt 24:36
1:8 [k]Ac 2:1-4 [l]Lk 24:48 [m]Ac 8:1-25 [n]Mt 28:19
1:9 [o]ver 2
1:10 [p]Lk 24:4; Jn 20:12
1:11 [q]Ac 2:7 [r]Mt 16:27
1:12 [s]Lk 24:52 [t]Mt 21:1
1:13 [u]Ac 9:37; 20:8 [v]Mt 10:2-4; Mk 3:16-19; Lk 6:14-16
1:14 [w]Ac 2:42; 6:4 [x]Lk 23:49,55 [y]Mt 12:46
1:16 [z]ver 20 [a]Jn 13:18
1:17 [b]Jn 6:70,71 [c]ver 25
1:18 [d]Mt 26:14,15 [e]Mt 27:3-10
1:20 [f]Ps 69:25 [g]Ps 109:8
1:22 [h]Mk 1:4 [i]ver 8

a*5* Or *in* b*12* That is, about 3/4 mile (about 1,100 meters) c*15* Greek *brothers* d*20* Psalm 69:25 e*20* Psalm 109:8

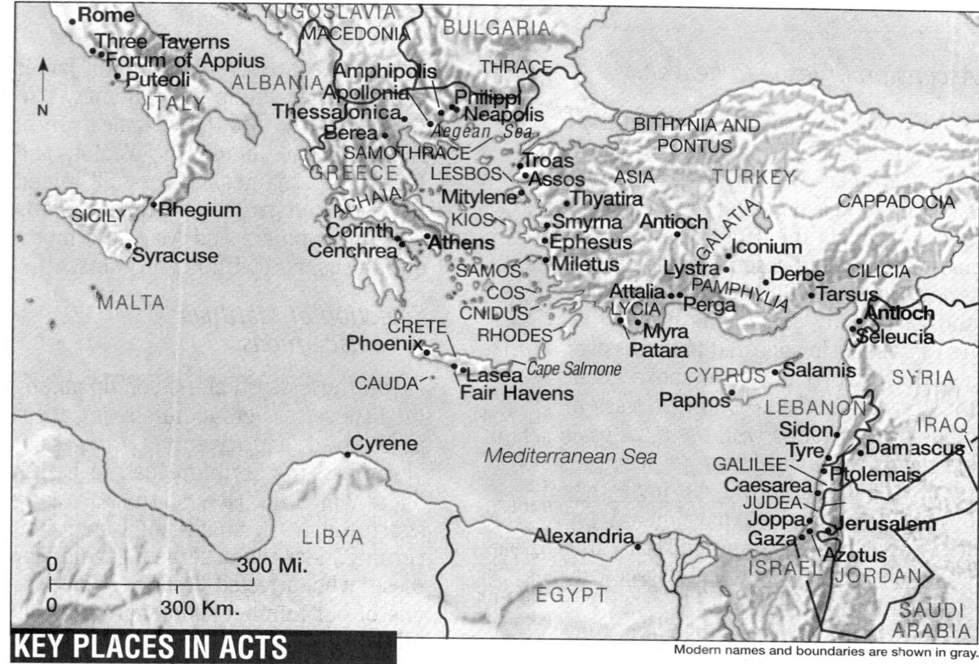

KEY PLACES IN ACTS

Modern names and boundaries are shown in gray.

The apostle Paul, whose missionary journeys fill much of this book, traveled tremendous distances as he tirelessly spread the gospel across much of the Roman empire. His combined trips, by land and ship, equal more than 13,000 airline miles.

Judea Jesus ascended to heaven from the Mount of Olives outside Jerusalem, and his followers returned to the city to await the infilling of the Holy Spirit, which occurred at Pentecost. Peter gave a powerful sermon that was heard by Jews from across the empire. The Jerusalem church grew, but Stephen was martyred for his faith by Jewish leaders who did not believe in Jesus (1:1-7:59).

Samaria After Stephen's death, persecution of Christians intensified, but it caused the believers to leave Jerusalem and spread the gospel to other cities in the empire. Philip took the gospel into Samaria, and even to a man from Ethiopia (8:1-40).

Syria Paul (Saul) began his story as a persecutor of Christians, only to be met by Jesus himself on the road to Damascus. He became a believer, but his new faith caused opposition, so he returned to Tarsus, his home, for safety. Barnabas sought out Paul in Tarsus and brought him to the church in Antioch in Syria, where they worked together. Meanwhile, Peter had received a vision that led him to Caesarea, where he presented the gospel to a Gentile family, who became believers (9:1-12:25).

Cyprus and Galatia Paul and Barnabas were dedicated by the church in Antioch in Syria for God's work of spreading the gospel to other cities. They set off on their first missionary journey through Cyprus and Galatia (13:1-14:28).

Jerusalem Controversy between Jewish Christians and Gentile Christians over the matter of keeping the law led to a special council, with delegates from the churches in Antioch and Jerusalem meeting in Jerusalem. Together, they resolved the conflict and the news was taken back to Antioch (15:1-35).

Macedonia Barnabas traveled to Cyprus while Paul took a second missionary journey. He revisited the churches in Galatia and headed toward Ephesus, but the Holy Spirit said no. He then turned north toward Bithynia and Pontus, but again was told not to go. He then received the "Macedonian call," and followed the Spirit's direction into the cities of Macedonia (15:36-17:14).

Achaia Paul traveled from Macedonia to Athens and Corinth in Achaia, then traveled by ship to Ephesus before returning to Caesarea, Jerusalem, and finally back to Antioch (17:15-18:22).

Ephesus Paul's third missionary journey took him back through Cilicia and Galatia, this time straight to Ephesus in Asia. He visited other cities in Asia before going back to Macedonia and Achaia. He returned to Jerusalem by ship, despite his knowledge that arrest awaited him there (18:23-23:30).

Caesarea Paul was arrested in Jerusalem and taken to Antipatris, then on to Caesarea under Roman guard. Paul always took advantage of any opportunity to share the gospel, and he did so before many Gentile leaders. Because Paul appealed to Caesar, he began the long journey to Rome (23:31-26:32).

Rome After storms, layovers in Crete, and a shipwreck on the island of Malta, Paul arrived in Sicily, and finally in Italy, where he traveled by land, under guard, to his long-awaited destination, Rome, the capital of the empire (27:1-28:31).

and Matthias. 24Then they prayed,[a]
"Lord, you know everyone's heart.[b]
Show us which of these two you have
chosen 25to take over this apostolic ministry, which Judas left to go where he
belongs." 26Then they cast lots, and the
lot fell to Matthias; so he was added to
the eleven apostles.[c]

Filling of the Holy Spirit at Pentecost.

2 When the day of Pentecost[d] came,
they were all together[e] in one place.
2Suddenly a sound like the blowing of
a violent wind came from heaven and
filled the whole house where they were
sitting.[f] 3They saw what seemed to be
tongues of fire that separated and came
to rest on each of them. 4All of them
were filled with the Holy Spirit and
began to speak in other tongues[f][g] as the
Spirit enabled them.

5Now there were staying in Jerusalem
God-fearing[h] Jews from every nation
under heaven. 6When they heard this
sound, a crowd came together in bewil-
derment, because each one heard them
speaking in his own language. 7Utterly
amazed,[i] they asked: "Are not all these
men who are speaking Galileans?[j] 8Then
how is it that each of us hears them in
his own native language? 9Parthians,
Medes and Elamites; residents of Mesopotamia, Judea and Cappadocia,[k] Pontus[l] and Asia,[m] 10Phrygia[n] and Pamphylia,[o] Egypt and the parts of Libya near
Cyrene;[p] visitors from Rome 11(both
Jews and converts to Judaism); Cretans
and Arabs—we hear them declaring
the wonders of God in our own tongues!"
12Amazed and perplexed, they asked
one another, "What does this mean?"

13Some, however, made fun of them
and said, "They have had too much
wine.[g]"[q]

Peter's explanation of Pentecost.

14Then Peter stood up with the
Eleven, raised his voice and addressed
the crowd: "Fellow Jews and all of you
who live in Jerusalem, let me explain
this to you; listen carefully to what I
say. 15These men are not drunk, as you
suppose. It's only nine in the morning![r] 16No, this is what was spoken by
the prophet Joel:

17" 'In the last days, God says,
I will pour out my Spirit on all
people.[s]
Your sons and daughters will
prophesy,[t]
your young men will see visions,
your old men will dream dreams.
18Even on my servants, both men and
women,
I will pour out my Spirit in those days,
and they will prophesy.[u]
19I will show wonders in the heaven
above
and signs on the earth below,
blood and fire and billows of smoke.
20The sun will be turned to darkness
and the moon to blood[v]
before the coming of the great and
glorious day of the Lord.
21And everyone who calls
on the name of the Lord will be
saved.'[h][w]

22"Men of Israel, listen to this: Jesus
of Nazareth was a man accredited by
God to you by miracles, wonders and
signs,[x] which God did among you
through him,[y] as you yourselves know.
23This man was handed over to you by
God's set purpose and foreknowledge;[z]
and you, with the help of wicked men,[i]
put him to death by nailing him to the
cross.[a] 24But God raised him from the
dead,[b] freeing him from the agony of
death, because it was impossible for
death to keep its hold on him.[c] 25David
said about him:

" 'I saw the Lord always before me.
Because he is at my right hand,
I will not be shaken.
26Therefore my heart is glad and my
tongue rejoices;
my body also will live in hope,

1:24 [a]Ac 6:6; 14:23 [b]1Sa 16:7; Jer 17:10; Ac 15:8; Rev 2:23 **1:26** [c]Ac 2:14 **2:1** [d]Lev 23:15, 16; Ac 20:16 [e]Ac 1:14 **2:2** [f]Ac 4:31 **2:4** [g]Mk 16:17; 1Co 12:10 **2:5** [h]Ac 8:2 **2:7** [i]ver 12 [j]Ac 1:11 **2:9** [k]1Pe 1:1 [l]Ac 18:2 [m]Ac 16:6; Ro 16:5; 1Co 16:19; 2Co 1:8 **2:10** [n]Ac 16:6; 18:23 [o]Ac 13:13; 15:38 [p]Mt 27:32 **2:13** [q]1Co 14:23 **2:15** [r]1Th 5:7 **2:17** [s]Isa 44:3; Jn 7:37-39; Ac 10:45 [t]Ac 21:9 **2:18** [u]Ac 21:9-12 **2:20** [v]Mt 24:29 **2:21** [w]Ro 10:13 **2:22** [x]Jn 4:48; Ac 10:38 [y]Jn 3:2 **2:23** [z]Lk 22:22; Ac 3:18; 4:28 [a]Lk 24:20; Ac 3:13 **2:24** [b]ver 32; 1Co 6:14; 2Co 4:14; Eph 1:20; Col 2:12; Heb 13:20; 1Pe 1:21 [c]Jn 20:9

[f]*4* Or *languages*; also in verse 11 [g]*13* Or *sweet wine* [h]*21* Joel 2:28-32 [i]*23* Or *of those not having the law* (that is, Gentiles)

27because you will not abandon me to
the grave,
nor will you let your Holy One see
decay.[a]
28You have made known to me the
paths of life;
you will fill me with joy in your
presence.'[j]

29"Brothers, I can tell you confidently that the patriarch[b] David died and was buried,[c] and his tomb is here[d] to this day. 30But he was a prophet and knew that God had promised him on oath that he would place one of his descendants on his throne.[e] 31Seeing what was ahead, he spoke of the resurrection of the Christ,[k] that he was not abandoned to the grave, nor did his body see decay.[f] 32God has raised this Jesus to life,[g] and we are all witnesses[h] of the fact. 33Exalted[i] to the right hand of God,[j] he has received from the Father[k] the promised Holy Spirit[l] and has poured out[m] what you now see and hear. 34For David did not ascend to heaven, and yet he said,

"'The Lord said to my Lord:
"Sit at my right hand
35until I make your enemies
a footstool for your feet."'[l][n]

36"Therefore let all Israel be assured of this: God has made this Jesus, whom you crucified, both Lord and Christ."[o]

Baptism of 3,000 believers.

37When the people heard this, they were cut to the heart and said to Peter and the other apostles, "Brothers, what shall we do?"[p]

38Peter replied, "Repent and be baptized,[q] every one of you, in the name of Jesus Christ for the forgiveness of your sins.[r] And you will receive the gift of the Holy Spirit. 39The promise is for you and your children[s] and for all who are far off[t]—for all whom the Lord our God will call."

40With many other words he warned them; and he pleaded with them, "Save yourselves from this corrupt generation."[u] 41Those who accepted his message were baptized, and about three thousand were added to their number that day.

42They devoted themselves to the apostles' teaching and to the fellowship, to the breaking of bread and to prayer.[v] 43Everyone was filled with awe, and many wonders and miraculous signs were done by the apostles.[w] 44All the believers were together and had everything in common.[x] 45Selling their possessions and goods, they gave to anyone as he had need.[y] 46Every day they continued to meet together in the temple courts.[z] They broke bread[a] in their homes and ate together with glad and sincere hearts, 47praising God and enjoying the favor of all the people.[b] And the Lord added to their number[c] daily those who were being saved.

Peter heals a man crippled from birth.

3 One day Peter and John[d] were going up to the temple[e] at the time of prayer—at three in the afternoon.[f] 2Now a man crippled from birth[g] was being carried to the temple gate[h] called Beautiful, where he was put every day to beg[i] from those going into the temple courts. 3When he saw Peter and John about to enter, he asked them for money. 4Peter looked straight at him, as did John. Then Peter said, "Look at us!" 5So the man gave them his attention, expecting to get something from them.

6Then Peter said, "Silver or gold I do not have, but what I have I give you. In the name of Jesus Christ of Nazareth,[j] walk." 7Taking him by the right hand, he helped him up, and instantly the man's feet and ankles became strong. 8He jumped to his feet and began to walk. Then he went with them into the temple courts, walking and jumping,[k]

2:27 [a]ver 31; Ac 13:35 **2:29** [b]Ac 7:8,9 [c]Ac 13:36; 1Ki 2:10 [d]Ne 3:16 **2:30** [e]2Sa 7:12; Ps 132:11 **2:31** [f]Ps 16:10 **2:32** [g]ver 24 [h]Ac 1:8 **2:33** [i]Php 2:9 [j]Mk 16:19 [k]Ac 1:4 [l]Jn 7:39; 14:26 [m]Ac 10:45 **2:35** [n]Ps 110:1; Mt 22:44 **2:36** [o]Lk 2:11 **2:37** [p]Lk 3:10, 12,14 **2:38** [q]Ac 8:12,16, 36,38; 22:16 [r]Lk 24:47; Ac 3:19 **2:39** [s]Isa 44:3 [t]Ac 10:45; Eph 2:13 **2:40** [u]Dt 32:5 **2:42** [v]Ac 1:14 **2:43** [w]Ac 5:12 **2:44** [x]Ac 4:32 **2:45** [y]Mt 19:21 **2:46** [z]Lk 24:53; Ac 5:21,42 [a]Ac 20:7 **2:47** [b]Ro 14:18 [c]ver 41; Ac 5:14 **3:1** [d]Lk 22:8 [e]Ac 2:46 [f]Ps 55:17 **3:2** [g]Ac 14:8 [h]Lk 16:20 [i]Jn 9:8 **3:6** [j]ver 16; Ac 4:10

3:8 [k]Ac 14:10

j*28* Psalm 16:8-11 k*31* Or *Messiah.* "The Christ" (Greek) and "the Messiah" (Hebrew) both mean "the Anointed One"; also in verse 36. l*35* Psalm 110:1

and praising God. 9 When all the people[a] saw him walking and praising God, 10 they recognized him as the same man who used to sit begging at the temple gate called Beautiful,[b] and they were filled with wonder and amazement at what had happened to him.

Peter uses this opportunity to preach about Jesus.

11 While the beggar held on to Peter and John,[c] all the people were astonished and came running to them in the place called Solomon's Colonnade.[d] 12 When Peter saw this, he said to them: "Men of Israel, why does this surprise you? Why do you stare at us as if by our own power or godliness we had made this man walk? 13 The God of Abraham, Isaac and Jacob, the God of our fathers,[e] has glorified his servant Jesus. You handed him over to be killed, and you disowned him before Pilate,[f] though he had decided to let him go.[g] 14 You disowned the Holy[h] and Righteous One[i] and asked that a murderer be released to you.[j] 15 You killed the author of life, but God raised him from the dead.[k] We are witnesses of this. 16 By faith in the name of Jesus, this man whom you see and know was made strong. It is Jesus' name and the faith that comes through him that has given this complete healing to him, as you can all see.

17 "Now, brothers, I know that you acted in ignorance,[l] as did your leaders.[m] 18 But this is how God fulfilled what he had foretold[n] through all the prophets,[o] saying that his Christ[m] would suffer.[p] 19 Repent, then, and turn to God, so that your sins may be wiped out,[q] that times of refreshing may come from the Lord, 20 and that he may send the Christ, who has been appointed for you—even Jesus. 21 He must remain in heaven[r] until the time comes for God to restore everything,[s] as he promised long ago through his holy prophets.[t] 22 For Moses said, 'The Lord your God will raise up for you a prophet like me from among your own people; you must listen to everything he tells you.[u] 23 Anyone who does not listen to him will be completely cut off from among his people.'[n][v]

24 "Indeed, all the prophets[w] from Samuel on, as many as have spoken, have foretold these days. 25 And you are heirs[x] of the prophets and of the covenant[y] God made with your fathers. He said to Abraham, 'Through your offspring all peoples on earth will be blessed.'[o][z] 26 When God raised up[a] his servant, he sent him first[b] to you to bless you by turning each of you from your wicked ways."

Peter and John are arrested.

4 The priests and the captain of the temple guard[c] and the Sadducees[d] came up to Peter and John while they were speaking to the people. 2 They were greatly disturbed because the apostles were teaching the people and proclaiming in Jesus the resurrection of the dead.[e] 3 They seized Peter and John, and because it was evening, they put them in jail[f] until the next day. 4 But many who heard the message believed, and the number of men grew[g] to about five thousand.

Peter preaches about Jesus to the Sanhedrin.

5 The next day the rulers,[h] elders and teachers of the law met in Jerusalem. 6 Annas the high priest was there, and so were Caiaphas,[i] John, Alexander and the other men of the high priest's family. 7 They had Peter and John brought before them and began to question them: "By what power or what name did you do this?"

8 Then Peter, filled with the Holy Spirit, said to them: "Rulers and elders of the people![j] 9 If we are being called to account today for an act of kindness shown to a cripple[k] and are asked how he was healed, 10 then know this, you and all the people of Israel: It is by the

3:9 [a]Ac 4:16,21
3:10 [b]ver 2
3:11 [c]Lk 22:8 [d]Jn 10:23; Ac 5:12
3:13 [e]Ac 5:30 [f]Mt 27:2 [g]Lk 23:4
3:14 [h]Mk 1:24; Ac 4:27 [i]Ac 7:52 [j]Mk 15:11; Lk 23:18-25
3:15 [k]Ac 2:24
3:17 [l]Lk 23:34 [m]Ac 13:27
3:18 [n]Ac 2:23 [o]Lk 24:27 [p]Ac 17:2,3; 26:22,23
3:19 [q]Ac 2:38
3:21 [r]Ac 1:11 [s]Mt 17:11 [t]Lk 1:70
3:22 [u]Dt 18:15,18; Ac 7:37
3:23 [v]Dt 18:19
3:24 [w]Lk 24:27
3:25 [x]Ac 2:39 [y]Ro 9:4,5 [z]Ge 12:3; 22:18; 26:4; 28:14
3:26 [a]ver 22; Ac 2:24 [b]Ac 13:46; Ro 1:16
4:1 [c]Lk 22:4 [d]Mt 3:7
4:2 [e]Ac 17:18
4:3 [f]Ac 5:18
4:4 [g]Ac 2:41
4:5 [h]Lk 23:13
4:6 [i]Mt 26:3; Lk 3:2
4:8 [j]ver 5; Lk 23:13
4:9 [k]Ac 3:6

[m] *18* Or *Messiah*; also in verse 20
[n] *23* Deut. 18:15,18,19 [o] *25* Gen. 22:18; 26:4

name of Jesus Christ of Nazareth, whom
you crucified but whom God raised from
the dead,[a] that this man stands before
you healed. 11 He is

"'the stone you builders rejected,
which has become the capstone.[p]'[q][b]

12 Salvation is found in no one else, for
there is no other name under heaven giv-
en to men by which we must be saved."[c]
13 When they saw the courage of
Peter and John[d] and realized that they
were unschooled, ordinary men,[e] they
were astonished and they took note that
these men had been with Jesus. 14 But
since they could see the man who had
been healed standing there with them,
there was nothing they could say. 15 So
they ordered them to withdraw from
the Sanhedrin[f] and then conferred together. 16 "What are we going to do
with these men?"[g] they asked. "Everybody living in Jerusalem knows they
have done an outstanding miracle,[h]
and we cannot deny it. 17 But to stop this
thing from spreading any further among
the people, we must warn these men to
speak no longer to anyone in this name."
18 Then they called them in again and
commanded them not to speak or teach
at all in the name of Jesus.[i] 19 But Peter
and John replied, "Judge for yourselves
whether it is right in God's sight to
obey you rather than God.[j] 20 For we
cannot help speaking about what we
have seen and heard."
21 After further threats they let them
go. They could not decide how to punish them, because all the people[k] were
praising God[l] for what had happened.
22 For the man who was miraculously
healed was over forty years old.

The disciples unite in prayer.

23 On their release, Peter and John
went back to their own people and
reported all that the chief priests and
elders had said to them. 24 When they
heard this, they raised their voices together in prayer to God. "Sovereign
Lord," they said, "you made the heaven
and the earth and the sea, and everything in them. 25 You spoke by the Holy
Spirit through the mouth of your servant, our father David:[m]

"'Why do the nations rage
and the peoples plot in vain?
26 The kings of the earth take their stand
and the rulers gather together
against the Lord
and against his Anointed One.[r]'[s][n]

27 Indeed Herod[o] and Pontius Pilate[p] met
together with the Gentiles and the
people[t] of Israel in this city to conspire
against your holy servant Jesus,[q] whom
you anointed. 28 They did what your power and will had decided beforehand
should happen.[r] 29 Now, Lord, consider
their threats and enable your servants to
speak your word with great boldness.[s]
30 Stretch out your hand to heal and perform miraculous signs and wonders[t]
through the name of your holy servant
Jesus."[u]
31 After they prayed, the place where
they were meeting was shaken.[v] And
they were all filled with the Holy Spirit
and spoke the word of God boldly.[w]

The believers share with others in need.

32 All the believers were one in heart
and mind. No one claimed that any of
his possessions was his own, but they
shared everything they had.[x] 33 With
great power the apostles continued to
testify[y] to the resurrection[z] of the Lord
Jesus, and much grace was upon them
all. 34 There were no needy persons
among them. For from time to time
those who owned lands or houses sold
them,[a] brought the money from the
sales 35 and put it at the apostles' feet,[b]
and it was distributed to anyone as he
had need.[c]
36 Joseph, a Levite from Cyprus, whom
the apostles called Barnabas[d] (which
means Son of Encouragement), 37 sold
a field he owned and brought the money and put it at the apostles' feet.[e]

4:10 [a]Ac 2:24
4:11 [b]Ps 118:22; Isa 28:16; Mt 21:42
4:12 [c]Mt 1:21; Ac 10:43; 1Ti 2:5
4:13 [d]Lk 22:8 [e]Mt 11:25
4:15 [f]Mt 5:22
4:16 [g]Jn 11:47 [h]Ac 3:6-10
4:18 [i]Ac 5:40
4:19 [j]Ac 5:29
4:21 [k]Ac 5:26 [l]Mt 9:8
4:25 [m]Ac 1:16
4:26 [n]Ps 2:1,2; Da 9:25; Lk 4:18; Ac 10:38; Heb 1:9
4:27 [o]Mt 14:1 [p]Mt 27:2; Lk 23:12 [q]ver 30
4:28 [r]Ac 2:23
4:29 [s]ver 13,31; Ac 9:27; 14:3; Php 1:14
4:30 [t]Jn 4:48 [u]ver 27
4:31 [v]Ac 2:2 [w]ver 29
4:32 [x]Ac 2:44
4:33 [y]Lk 24:48 [z]Ac 1:22
4:34 [a]Mt 19:21; Ac 2:45
4:35 [b]ver 37; Ac 5:2 [c]Ac 2:45; 6:1
4:36 [d]Ac 9:27; 1Co 9:6
4:37 [e]ver 35; Ac 5:2

[p] *11* Or *cornerstone* [q] *11* Psalm 118:22
[r] *26* That is, Christ or Messiah [s] *26* Psalm 2:1,2
[t] *27* The Greek is plural.

Ananias and Sapphira are judged for lying.

5 Now a man named Ananias, together with his wife Sapphira, also
sold a piece of property. 2With his wife's
full knowledge he kept back part of
the money for himself, but brought the
rest and put it at the apostles' feet.[a]
3Then Peter said, "Ananias, how is
it that Satan[b] has so filled your heart[c]
that you have lied to the Holy Spirit[d]
and have kept for yourself some of the
money you received for the land? 4Didn't
it belong to you before it was sold?
And after it was sold, wasn't the money at your disposal? What made you
think of doing such a thing? You have
not lied to men but to God."
5When Ananias heard this, he fell
down and died.[e] And great fear[f] seized
all who heard what had happened.
6Then the young men came forward,
wrapped up his body,[g] and carried him
out and buried him.
7About three hours later his wife came
in, not knowing what had happened.
8Peter asked her, "Tell me, is this the
price you and Ananias got for the land?"
"Yes," she said, "that is the price."[h]
9Peter said to her, "How could you
agree to test the Spirit of the Lord?[i]
Look! The feet of the men who buried
your husband are at the door, and they
will carry you out also."
10At that moment she fell down at
his feet and died.[j] Then the young men
came in and, finding her dead, carried
her out and buried her beside her husband. 11Great fear[k] seized the whole
church and all who heard about these
events.

The apostles do remarkable miracles.

12The apostles performed many miraculous signs and wonders[l] among the
people. And all the believers used to
meet together[m] in Solomon's Colonnade.[n] 13No one else dared join them,
even though they were highly regarded by the people.[o] 14Nevertheless, more
and more men and women believed in
the Lord and were added to their number. 15As a result, people brought the
sick into the streets and laid them on
beds and mats so that at least Peter's
shadow might fall on some of them as
he passed by.[p] 16Crowds gathered also
from the towns around Jerusalem, bringing their sick and those tormented by
evil[u] spirits, and all of them were
healed.[q]

An angel opens the doors of the jail.

17Then the high priest and all his
associates, who were members of the
party[r] of the Sadducees,[s] were filled
with jealousy. 18They arrested the apostles and put them in the public jail.[t]
19But during the night an angel[u] of the
Lord opened the doors of the jail[v] and
brought them out. 20"Go, stand in the
temple courts," he said, "and tell the
people the full message of this new
life."[w]
21At daybreak they entered the temple courts, as they had been told, and
began to teach the people.
When the high priest and his associates[x] arrived, they called together the
Sanhedrin[y]—the full assembly of the
elders of Israel—and sent to the jail for
the apostles. 22But on arriving at the
jail, the officers did not find them there.
So they went back and reported, 23"We
found the jail securely locked, with the
guards standing at the doors; but when
we opened them, we found no one
inside." 24On hearing this report, the
captain of the temple guard and the
chief priests[z] were puzzled, wondering
what would come of this.
25Then someone came and said,
"Look! The men you put in jail are
standing in the temple courts teaching
the people." 26At that, the captain went
with his officers and brought the apostles. They did not use force, because
they feared that the people[a] would
stone them.

5:2 [a]Ac 4:35,37
5:3 [b]Mt 4:10 [c]Jn 13:2,27 [d]ver 9
5:5 [e]ver 10 [f]ver 11
5:6 [g]Jn 19:40
5:8 [h]ver 2
5:9 [i]ver 3
5:10 [j]ver 5
5:11 [k]ver 5; Ac 19:17
5:12 [l]Ac 2:43 [m]Ac 4:32 [n]Ac 3:11
5:13 [o]Ac 2:47; 4:21
5:15 [p]Ac 19:12
5:16 [q]Mk 16:17
5:17 [r]Ac 15:5 [s]Ac 4:1
5:18 [t]Ac 4:3
5:19 [u]Mt 1:20; Lk 1:11; Ac 8:26; 27:23 [v]Ac 16:26
5:20 [w]Jn 6:63,68
5:21 [x]Ac 4:5,6 [y]ver 27, 34,41; Mt 5:22
5:24 [z]Ac 4:1
5:26 [a]Ac 4:21

[u]*16* Greek *unclean*

27Having brought the apostles, they made them appear before the Sanhedrin[a] to be questioned by the high priest. 28"We gave you strict orders not to teach in this name,"[b] he said. "Yet you have filled Jerusalem with your teaching and are determined to make us guilty of this man's blood."[c]

29Peter and the other apostles replied: "We must obey God rather than men![d] 30The God of our fathers[e] raised Jesus from the dead[f]—whom you had killed by hanging him on a tree.[g] 31God exalted him to his own right hand[h] as Prince and Savior[i] that he might give repentance and forgiveness of sins to Israel.[j] 32We are witnesses of these things,[k] and so is the Holy Spirit,[l] whom God has given to those who obey him."

Gamaliel addresses the men of Israel.

33When they heard this, they were furious[m] and wanted to put them to death. 34But a Pharisee named Gamaliel,[n] a teacher of the law,[o] who was honored by all the people, stood up in the Sanhedrin and ordered that the men be put outside for a little while. 35Then he addressed them: "Men of Israel, consider carefully what you intend to do to these men. 36Some time ago Theudas appeared, claiming to be somebody, and about four hundred men rallied to him. He was killed, all his followers were dispersed, and it all came to nothing. 37After him, Judas the Galilean appeared in the days of the census[p] and led a band of people in revolt. He too was killed, and all his followers were scattered. 38Therefore, in the present case I advise you: Leave these men alone! Let them go! For if their purpose or activity is of human origin, it will fail.[q] 39But if it is from God, you will not be able to stop these men; you will only find yourselves fighting against God."[r]

40His speech persuaded them. They called the apostles in and had them flogged.[s] Then they ordered them not to speak in the name of Jesus, and let them go.

41The apostles left the Sanhedrin, rejoicing[t] because they had been counted worthy of suffering disgrace for the Name.[u] 42Day after day, in the temple courts[v] and from house to house, they never stopped teaching and proclaiming the good news that Jesus is the Christ.[v]

Seven men are selected to administer care for widows.

6 In those days when the number of disciples was increasing,[w] the Grecian Jews[x] among them complained against the Hebraic Jews because their widows[y] were being overlooked in the daily distribution of food.[z] 2So the Twelve gathered all the disciples together and said, "It would not be right for us to neglect the ministry of the word of God in order to wait on tables. 3Brothers,[a] choose seven men from among you who are known to be full of the Spirit and wisdom. We will turn this responsibility over to them 4and will give our attention to prayer[b] and the ministry of the word."

5This proposal pleased the whole group. They chose Stephen,[c] a man full of faith and of the Holy Spirit;[d] also Philip,[e] Procorus, Nicanor, Timon, Parmenas, and Nicolas from Antioch, a convert to Judaism. 6They presented these men to the apostles, who prayed[f] and laid their hands on them.[g]

7So the word of God spread.[h] The number of disciples in Jerusalem increased rapidly, and a large number of priests became obedient to the faith.

Stephen is arrested due to false accusations.

8Now Stephen, a man full of God's grace and power, did great wonders and miraculous signs[i] among the people. 9Opposition arose, however, from mem-

5:27 [a]Mt 5:22
5:28 [b]Ac 4:18 [c]Mt 23:35; 27:25; Ac 2:23,36; 3:14,15; 7:52
5:29 [d]Ac 4:19
5:30 [e]Ac 3:13 [f]Ac 2:24 [g]Ac 10:39; 13:29; Gal 3:13; 1Pe 2:24
5:31 [h]Ac 2:33 [i]Lk 2:11 [j]Mt 1:21; Lk 24:47; Ac 2:38
5:32 [k]Lk 24:48 [l]Jn 15:26
5:33 [m]Ac 2:37; 7:54
5:34 [n]Ac 22:3 [o]Lk 2:46
5:37 [p]Lk 2:1,2
5:38 [q]Mt 15:13
5:39 [r]Pr 21:30; Ac 7:51; 11:17
5:40 [s]Mt 10:17
5:41 [t]Mt 5:12 [u]Jn 15:21
5:42 [v]Ac 2:46
6:1 [w]Ac 2:41 [x]Ac 9:29 [y]Ac 9:39,41 [z]Ac 4:35
6:3 [a]Ac 1:16
6:4 [b]Ac 1:14
6:5 [c]ver 8; Ac 11:19 [d]Ac 11:24 [e]Ac 8:5-40; 21:8
6:6 [f]Ac 1:24; 8:17; 13:3; 2Ti 1:6 [g]Nu 8:10; Ac 9:17; 1Ti 4:14

6:7 [h]Ac 12:24; 19:20 **6:8** [i]Jn 4:48

[v]*42* Or *Messiah*

bers of the Synagogue of the Freedmen
(as it was called)—Jews of Cyrene[a] and
Alexandria as well as the provinces of
Cilicia[b] and Asia.[c] These men began to
argue with Stephen, 10but they could not
stand up against his wisdom or the Spirit by whom he spoke.[d]

11Then they secretly[e] persuaded some
men to say, "We have heard Stephen
speak words of blasphemy against Moses
and against God."[f]

12So they stirred up the people and
the elders and the teachers of the law.
They seized Stephen and brought him
before the Sanhedrin.[g] 13They produced
false witnesses, who testified, "This fellow never stops speaking against this
holy place[h] and against the law. 14For
we have heard him say that this Jesus
of Nazareth will destroy this place
and change the customs Moses handed
down to us."[i]

15All who were sitting in the Sanhedrin[j] looked intently at Stephen, and
they saw that his face was like the face
of an angel.

Stephen preaches to the Sanhedrin.

7 Then the high priest asked him,
"Are these charges true?"

2To this he replied: "Brothers and
fathers[k] listen to me! The God of glory[l]
appeared to our father Abraham while
he was still in Mesopotamia, before he
lived in Haran.[m] 3'Leave your country
and your people,' God said, 'and go to
the land I will show you.'[w][n]

4"So he left the land of the Chaldeans
and settled in Haran. After the death
of his father, God sent him to this land
where you are now living.[o] 5He gave
him no inheritance here, not even a foot
of ground. But God promised him that
he and his descendants after him would
possess the land,[p] even though at that
time Abraham had no child. 6God spoke
to him in this way: 'Your descendants
will be strangers in a country not their
own, and they will be enslaved and mistreated four hundred years.[q] 7But I will
punish the nation they serve as slaves,'
God said, 'and afterward they will come
out of that country and worship me in
this place.'[x][r] 8Then he gave Abraham
the covenant of circumcision.[s] And
Abraham became the father of Isaac
and circumcised him eight days after his
birth.[t] Later Isaac became the father of
Jacob,[u] and Jacob became the father of
the twelve patriarchs.[v]

9"Because the patriarchs were jealous of Joseph,[w] they sold him as a slave
into Egypt.[x] But God was with him[y]
10and rescued him from all his troubles. He gave Joseph wisdom and
enabled him to gain the goodwill of
Pharaoh king of Egypt; so he made him
ruler over Egypt and all his palace.[z]

11"Then a famine struck all Egypt and
Canaan, bringing great suffering, and
our fathers could not find food.[a] 12When
Jacob heard that there was grain in
Egypt, he sent our fathers on their first
visit.[b] 13On their second visit, Joseph
told his brothers who he was,[c] and
Pharaoh learned about Joseph's family.
14After this, Joseph sent for his father
Jacob and his whole family,[d] seventy-
five in all.[e] 15Then Jacob went down to
Egypt, where he and our fathers died.[f]
16Their bodies were brought back to
Shechem and placed in the tomb that
Abraham had bought from the sons of
Hamor at Shechem for a certain sum
of money.[g]

17"As the time drew near for God to
fulfill his promise to Abraham, the number of our people in Egypt greatly increased.[h] 18Then another king, who
knew nothing about Joseph, became
ruler of Egypt.[i] 19He dealt treacherously with our people and oppressed our
forefathers by forcing them to throw
out their newborn babies so that they
would die.[j]

20"At that time Moses was born, and
he was no ordinary child.[y] For three

6:9 [a]Mt 27:32 [b]Ac 15:23,41; 22:3; 23:34 [c]Ac 2:9
6:10 [d]Lk 21:15
6:11 [e]1Ki 21:10 [f]Mt 26:59-61
6:12 [g]Mt 5:22
6:13 [h]Ac 21:28
6:14 [i]Ac 15:1; 21:21; 26:3; 28:17
6:15 [j]Mt 5:22
7:2 [k]Ac 22:1 [l]Ps 29:3 [m]Ge 11:31; 15:7
7:3 [n]Ge 12:1
7:4 [o]Ge 12:5
7:5 [p]Ge 12:7; 17:8; 26:3
7:6 [q]Ex 12:40
7:7 [r]Ex 3:12
7:8 [s]Ge 17:9-14 [t]Ge 21:2-4 [u]Ge 25:26 [v]Ge 29:31-35; 30:5-13,17-24; 35:16-18, 22-26
7:9 [w]Ge 37:4,11 [x]Ge 37:28; Ps 105:17 [y]Ge 39:2, 21,23
7:10 [z]Ge 41:37-43
7:11 [a]Ge 41:54
7:12 [b]Ge 42:1,2
7:13 [c]Ge 45:1-4
7:14 [d]Ge 45:9,10 [e]Ge 46:26, 27; Ex 1:5; Dt 10:22
7:15 [f]Ge 46:5-7; 49:33; Ex 1:6
7:16 [g]Ge 23:16-20; 33:18,19; 50:13; Jos 24:32
7:17 [h]Ex 1:7; Ps 105:24 **7:18** [i]Ex 1:8
7:19 [j]Ex 1:10-22

w*3* Gen. 12:1 x*7* Gen. 15:13,14 y*20* Or *was fair in the sight of God*

months he was cared for in his father's house.[a] 21 When he was placed outside, Pharaoh's daughter took him and brought him up as her own son.[b] 22 Moses was educated in all the wisdom of the Egyptians[c] and was powerful in speech and action.

23 "When Moses was forty years old, he decided to visit his fellow Israelites. 24 He saw one of them being mistreated by an Egyptian, so he went to his defense and avenged him by killing the Egyptian. 25 Moses thought that his own people would realize that God was using him to rescue them, but they did not. 26 The next day Moses came upon two Israelites who were fighting. He tried to reconcile them by saying, 'Men, you are brothers; why do you want to hurt each other?'

27 "But the man who was mistreating the other pushed Moses aside and said, 'Who made you ruler and judge over us? 28 Do you want to kill me as you killed the Egyptian yesterday?'[z] 29 When Moses heard this, he fled to Midian, where he settled as a foreigner and had two sons.[d]

30 "After forty years had passed, an angel appeared to Moses in the flames of a burning bush in the desert near Mount Sinai. 31 When he saw this, he was amazed at the sight. As he went over to look more closely, he heard the Lord's voice:[e] 32 'I am the God of your fathers, the God of Abraham, Isaac and Jacob.'[a] Moses trembled with fear and did not dare to look.[f]

33 "Then the Lord said to him, 'Take off your sandals; the place where you are standing is holy ground.[g] 34 I have indeed seen the oppression of my people in Egypt. I have heard their groaning and have come down to set them free. Now come, I will send you back to Egypt.'[b][h]

35 "This is the same Moses whom they had rejected with the words, 'Who made you ruler and judge?'[i] He was sent to be their ruler and deliverer by God himself, through the angel who appeared to him in the bush. 36 He led them out of Egypt[j] and did wonders and miraculous signs in Egypt, at the Red Sea[c][k] and for forty years in the desert.

37 "This is that Moses who told the Israelites, 'God will send you a prophet like me from your own people.'[d][l] 38 He was in the assembly in the desert, with the angel[m] who spoke to him on Mount Sinai, and with our fathers;[n] and he received living words[o] to pass on to us.[p]

39 "But our fathers refused to obey him. Instead, they rejected him and in their hearts turned back to Egypt.[q] 40 They told Aaron, 'Make us gods who will go before us. As for this fellow Moses who led us out of Egypt—we don't know what has happened to him!'[e][r] 41 That was the time they made an idol in the form of a calf. They brought sacrifices to it and held a celebration in honor of what their hands had made.[s] 42 But God turned away[t] and gave them over to the worship of the heavenly bodies.[u] This agrees with what is written in the book of the prophets:

"'Did you bring me sacrifices and
offerings
forty years in the desert, O house
of Israel?
43 You have lifted up the shrine of
Molech
and the star of your god Rephan,
the idols you made to worship.
Therefore I will send you into
exile'[f][v] beyond Babylon.

44 "Our forefathers had the tabernacle of the Testimony[w] with them in the desert. It had been made as God directed Moses, according to the pattern he had seen.[x] 45 Having received the tabernacle, our fathers under Joshua brought it with them when they took the land from the nations God drove out before them.[y] It remained in the land until the time of David, 46 who enjoyed God's favor and asked that he might provide a dwelling place for the God of Jacob.[g][z]

7:20 [a]Ex 2:2; Heb 11:23
7:21 [b]Ex 2:3-10
7:22 [c]1Ki 4:30; Isa 19:11
7:29 [d]Ex 2:11-15
7:31 [e]Ex 3:1-4
7:32 [f]Ex 3:6
7:33 [g]Ex 3:5; Jos 5:15
7:34 [h]Ex 3:7-10
7:35 [i]ver 27
7:36 [j]Ex 12:41; 33:1 [k]Ex 14:21
7:37 [l]Dt 18:15,18; Ac 3:22
7:38 [m]ver 53 [n]Ex 19:17 [o]Dt 32:45-47; Heb 4:12 [p]Ro 3:2
7:39 [q]Nu 14:3,4
7:40 [r]Ex 32:1,23
7:41 [s]Ex 32:4-6; Ps 106:19,20; Rev 9:20
7:42 [t]Jos 24:20; Isa 63:10 [u]Jer 19:13
7:43 [v]Am 5:25-27
7:44 [w]Ex 38:21 [x]Ex 25:8,9,40
7:45 [y]Jos 3:14-17; 18:1; 23:9; 24:18; Ps 44:2
7:46 [z]2Sa 7:8-16; Ps 132:1-5

z28 Exodus 2:14 a32 Exodus 3:6
b34 Exodus 3:5,7,8,10 c36 That is, Sea of Reeds
d37 Deut. 18:15 e40 Exodus 32:1
f43 Amos 5:25-27 g46 Some early manuscripts *the house of Jacob*

47But it was Solomon who built the
house for him.
48"However, the Most High does not
live in houses made by men.[a] As the
prophet says:

49"'Heaven is my throne,
and the earth is my footstool.[b]
What kind of house will you build
for me?
says the Lord.
Or where will my resting place be?
50Has not my hand made all these
things?'[hc]

51"You stiff-necked people,[d] with uncircumcised hearts[e] and ears! You are
just like your fathers: You always resist
the Holy Spirit! 52Was there ever a
prophet your fathers did not persecute?[f] They even killed those who predicted the coming of the Righteous
One. And now you have betrayed and
murdered him[g]— 53you who have received the law that was put into effect
through angels[h] but have not obeyed it."

Jewish leaders stone Stephen.

54When they heard this, they were
furious[i] and gnashed their teeth at him.
55But Stephen, full of the Holy Spirit,
looked up to heaven and saw the glory
of God, and Jesus standing at the right
hand of God.[j] 56"Look," he said, "I see
heaven open[k] and the Son of Man[l]
standing at the right hand of God."
57At this they covered their ears and,
yelling at the top of their voices, they
all rushed at him, 58dragged him out of
the city[m] and began to stone him.[n]
Meanwhile, the witnesses laid their
clothes[o] at the feet of a young man
named Saul.[p]
59While they were stoning him,
Stephen prayed, "Lord Jesus, receive
my spirit."[q] 60Then he fell on his
knees[r] and cried out, "Lord, do not
hold this sin against them."[s] When he
had said this, he fell asleep.

8 And Saul[t] was there, giving approval
to his death.

Saul persecutes the church.

On that day a great persecution broke
out against the church at Jerusalem, and
all except the apostles were scattered[u]
throughout Judea and Samaria.[v] 2Godly
men buried Stephen and mourned deeply
for him. 3But Saul[w] began to destroy the
church.[x] Going from house to house,
he dragged off men and women and put
them in prison.

Philip witnesses in Samaria.

4Those who had been scattered[y]
preached the word wherever they went.[z]
5Philip[a] went down to a city in Samaria and proclaimed the Christ[i] there.
6When the crowds heard Philip and
saw the miraculous signs he did, they
all paid close attention to what he said.
7With shrieks, evil[j] spirits came out of
many,[b] and many paralytics and crip-
ples were healed.[c] 8So there was great
joy in that city.

Simon the sorcerer is baptized.

9Now for some time a man named
Simon had practiced sorcery[d] in the city
and amazed all the people of Samaria.
He boasted that he was someone great,[e]
10and all the people, both high and low,
gave him their attention and exclaimed,
"This man is the divine power known
as the Great Power."[f] 11They followed
him because he had amazed them for
a long time with his magic. 12But when
they believed Philip as he preached the
good news of the kingdom of God[g] and
the name of Jesus Christ, they were baptized,[h] both men and women. 13Simon
himself believed and was baptized. And
he followed Philip everywhere, astonished by the great signs and miracles[i]
he saw.
14When the apostles in Jerusalem
heard that Samaria[j] had accepted the
word of God, they sent Peter and John[k]

7:48 [a]1Ki 8:27; 2Ch 2:6
7:49 [b]Mt 5:34,35
7:50 [c]Isa 66:1,2
7:51 [d]Ex 32:9; 33:3,5 [e]Lev 26:41; Dt 10:16; Jer 4:4; 9:26
7:52 [f]2Ch 36:16; Mt 5:12 [g]Ac 3:14; 1Th 2:15
7:53 [h]ver 38; Gal 3:19; Heb 2:2
7:54 [i]Ac 5:33
7:55 [j]Mk 16:19
7:56 [k]Mt 3:16 [l]Mt 8:20
7:58 [m]Lk 4:29 [n]Lev 24:14, 16; Dt 13:9 [o]Ac 22:20 [p]Ac 8:1
7:59 [q]Ps 31:5; Lk 23:46
7:60 [r]Ac 9:40 [s]Mt 5:44
8:1 [t]Ac 7:58 [u]Ac 11:19 [v]Ac 9:31
8:3 [w]Ac 7:58 [x]Ac 22:4,19; 26:10,11; 1Co 15:9; Gal 1:13,23; Php 3:6; 1Ti 1:13
8:4 [y]ver 1 [z]Ac 15:35
8:5 [a]Ac 6:5
8:7 [b]Mk 16:17 [c]Mt 4:24
8:9 [d]Ac 13:6 [e]Ac 5:36
8:10 [f]Ac 14:11; 28:6
8:12 [g]Ac 1:3 [h]Ac 2:38 **8:13** [i]ver 6; Ac 19:11
8:14 [j]ver 1 [k]Lk 22:8

[h]*50* Isaiah 66:1,2 [i]*5* Or *Messiah* [j]*7* Greek *unclean*

to them. 15When they arrived, they prayed for them that they might receive the Holy Spirit,[a] 16because the Holy Spirit had not yet come upon any of them;[b] they had simply been baptized into[k] the name of the Lord Jesus.[c] 17Then Peter and John placed their hands on them,[d] and they received the Holy Spirit.

18When Simon saw that the Spirit was given at the laying on of the apostles' hands, he offered them money 19and said, "Give me also this ability so that everyone on whom I lay my hands may receive the Holy Spirit."

20Peter answered: "May your money perish with you, because you thought you could buy the gift of God with money![e] 21You have no part or share in this ministry, because your heart is not right[f] before God. 22Repent of this wickedness and pray to the Lord. Perhaps he will forgive you for having such a thought in your heart. 23For I see that you are full of bitterness and captive to sin."

24Then Simon answered, "Pray to the Lord for me[g] so that nothing you have said may happen to me."

25When they had testified and proclaimed the word of the Lord, Peter and John returned to Jerusalem, preaching the gospel in many Samaritan villages.[h]

Philip encounters the Ethiopian eunuch.

26Now an angel[i] of the Lord said to Philip, "Go south to the road—the desert road—that goes down from Jerusalem to Gaza." 27So he started out, and on his way he met an Ethiopian[l][j] eunuch,[k] an important official in charge of all the treasury of Candace, queen of the Ethiopians. This man had gone to Jerusalem to worship,[l] 28and on his way home was sitting in his chariot reading the book of Isaiah the prophet. 29The Spirit told[m] Philip, "Go to that chariot and stay near it."

30Then Philip ran up to the chariot and heard the man reading Isaiah the prophet. "Do you understand what you are reading?" Philip asked.

8:15 [a]Ac 2:38
8:16 [b]Ac 19:2 [c]Mt 28:19; Ac 2:38
8:17 [d]Ac 6:6
8:20 [e]2Ki 5:16; Da 5:17; Mt 10:8; Ac 2:38
8:21 [f]Ps 78:37
8:24 [g]Ex 8:8; Nu 21:7; 1Ki 13:6
8:25 [h]ver 40
8:26 [i]Ac 5:19
8:27 [j]Ps 68:31; 87:4; Zep 3:10 [k]Isa 56:3-5 [l]1Ki 8:41-43; Jn 12:20
8:29 [m]Ac 10:19; 11:12; 13:2; 20:23; 21:11
8:33 [n]Isa 53:7,8
8:35 [o]Mt 5:2 [p]Lk 24:27; Ac 17:2; 18:28; 28:23
8:36 [q]Ac 10:47
8:39 [r]1Ki 18:12; 2Ki 2:16; Eze 3:12,14; 8:3; 11:1,24; 43:5; 2Co 12:2
8:40 [s]ver 25 [t]Ac 10:1,24; 12:19; 21:8,16; 23:23,33; 25:1,4,6,13
9:1 [u]Ac 8:3

31"How can I," he said, "unless someone explains it to me?" So he invited Philip to come up and sit with him.

32The eunuch was reading this passage of Scripture:

"He was led like a sheep to the
  slaughter,
and as a lamb before the shearer is
  silent,
so he did not open his mouth.
33In his humiliation he was deprived
  of justice.
Who can speak of his descendants?
For his life was taken from the
  earth."[m][n]

34The eunuch asked Philip, "Tell me, please, who is the prophet talking about, himself or someone else?" 35Then Philip began[o] with that very passage of Scripture[p] and told him the good news about Jesus.

36As they traveled along the road, they came to some water and the eunuch said, "Look, here is water. Why shouldn't I be baptized?"[n][q] 38And he gave orders to stop the chariot. Then both Philip and the eunuch went down into the water and Philip baptized him. 39When they came up out of the water, the Spirit of the Lord suddenly took Philip away,[r] and the eunuch did not see him again, but went on his way rejoicing. 40Philip, however, appeared at Azotus and traveled about, preaching the gospel in all the towns[s] until he reached Caesarea.[t]

Saul is converted on the road to Damascus.

9:1-19pp— Ac 22:3-16; 26:9-18

9 Meanwhile, Saul was still breathing out murderous threats against the Lord's disciples.[u] He went to the high priest 2and asked him for letters to the synagogues in Damascus, so that if he found any there who belonged to the

k *16* Or *in* l *27* That is, from the upper Nile region m *33* Isaiah 53:7,8 n *36* Some late manuscripts *baptized?" 37Philip said, "If you believe with all your heart, you may." The eunuch answered, "I believe that Jesus Christ is the Son of God."*

Way,[a] whether men or women, he might
take them as prisoners to Jerusalem.
3As he neared Damascus on his journey, suddenly a light from heaven
flashed around him.[b] 4He fell to the
ground and heard a voice say to him,
"Saul, Saul, why do you persecute me?"
5"Who are you, Lord?" Saul asked.
"I am Jesus, whom you are persecuting," he replied. 6"Now get up and go
into the city, and you will be told what
you must do."[c]
7The men traveling with Saul stood
there speechless; they heard the sound[d]
but did not see anyone.[e] 8Saul got up
from the ground, but when he opened
his eyes he could see nothing. So they
led him by the hand into Damascus.
9For three days he was blind, and did
not eat or drink anything.

Saul is baptized.

10In Damascus there was a disciple
named Ananias. The Lord called to him
in a vision,[f] "Ananias!"
"Yes, Lord," he answered.
11The Lord told him, "Go to the house
of Judas on Straight Street and ask for
a man from Tarsus[g] named Saul, for he
is praying. 12In a vision he has seen a
man named Ananias come and place
his hands on[h] him to restore his sight."
13"Lord," Ananias answered, "I have
heard many reports about this man and
all the harm he has done to your saints[i]
in Jerusalem.[j] 14And he has come here
with authority from the chief priests[k]
to arrest all who call on your name."
15But the Lord said to Ananias, "Go!
This man is my chosen instrument[l] to
carry my name before the Gentiles[m] and
their kings[n] and before the people of
Israel. 16I will show him how much he
must suffer for my name."[o]
17Then Ananias went to the house
and entered it. Placing his hands on[p]
Saul, he said, "Brother Saul, the Lord—
Jesus, who appeared to you on the road
as you were coming here—has sent me
so that you may see again and be filled
with the Holy Spirit." 18Immediately,
something like scales fell from Saul's
eyes, and he could see again. He got up
and was baptized, 19and after taking some
food, he regained his strength.

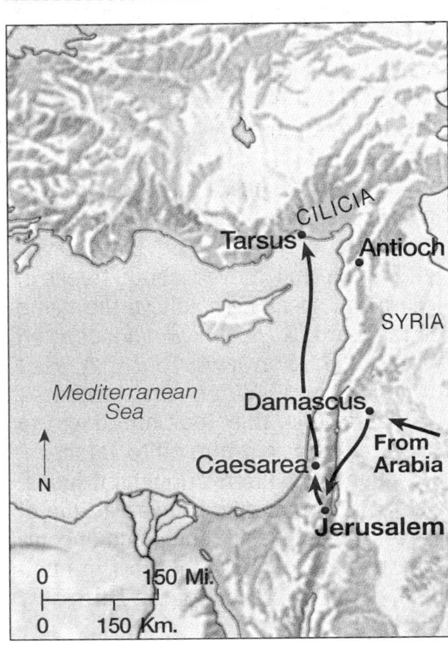

Saul's Return to Tarsus

At least three years elapsed between Acts 9:22 and 9:26. After time alone in Arabia (see Galatians 1:16-18), Saul (Paul) returned to Damascus and then to Jerusalem. The apostles were reluctant to believe that this former persecutor could have become one of them. He escaped to Caesarea, where he caught a ship and returned to Tarsus.

Saul spent several days with the disciples[q] in Damascus.[r] 20At once he began
to preach in the synagogues[s] that Jesus
is the Son of God.[t] 21All those who heard
him were astonished and asked, "Isn't
he the man who raised havoc in Jerusalem among those who call on this
name?[u] And hasn't he come here to
take them as prisoners to the chief
priests?"[v] 22Yet Saul grew more and
more powerful and baffled the Jews living in Damascus by proving that Jesus
is the Christ.[o][w]
23After many days had gone by, the
Jews conspired to kill him, 24but Saul
learned of their plan.[x] Day and night
they kept close watch on the city gates

[o]22 Or *Messiah*

9:2 [a]Ac 19:9, 23; 22:4; 24:14,22
9:3 [b]1Co 15:8
9:6 [c]ver 16
9:7 [d]Jn 12:29 [e]Da 10:7; Ac 22:9
9:10 [f]Ac 10:3, 17,19
9:11 [g]ver 30; Ac 21:39; 22:3
9:12 [h]Mk 5:23
9:13 [i]ver 32; Ro 1:7; 16:2,15 [j]Ac 8:3
9:14 [k]ver 2,21
9:15 [l]Ac 13:2; Ro 1:1; Gal 1:15 [m]Ro 11:13; 15:15,16; Gal 2:7,8; Eph 3:7,8 [n]Ac 25:22, 23; 26:1
9:16 [o]Ac 20:23; 21:11; 2Co 11:23-27
9:17 [p]Ac 6:6
9:19 [q]Ac 11:26 [r]Ac 26:20
9:20 [s]Ac 13:5,14 [t]Mt 4:3
9:21 [u]Ac 8:3 [v]Gal 1:13,23
9:22 [w]Ac 18:5,28
9:24 [x]Ac 20:3,19

in order to kill him. 25 But his followers
took him by night and lowered him in a
basket through an opening in the wall.[a]
26 When he came to Jerusalem,[b] he
tried to join the disciples, but they were
all afraid of him, not believing that he
really was a disciple. 27 But Barnabas[c]
took him and brought him to the apostles. He told them how Saul on his journey had seen the Lord and that the Lord
had spoken to him,[d] and how in Damascus he had preached fearlessly in
the name of Jesus.[e] 28 So Saul stayed
with them and moved about freely in
Jerusalem, speaking boldly in the name
of the Lord. 29 He talked and debated
with the Grecian Jews,[f] but they tried
to kill him.[g] 30 When the brothers[h]
learned of this, they took him down to
Caesarea[i] and sent him off to Tarsus.[j]
31 Then the church throughout Judea,
Galilee and Samaria[k] enjoyed a time of
peace. It was strengthened; and encouraged by the Holy Spirit, it grew in numbers, living in the fear of the Lord.

A paralytic, Aeneas, is healed at Lydda.

32 As Peter traveled about the country, he went to visit the saints[l] in Lydda.
33 There he found a man named Aeneas,
a paralytic who had been bedridden
for eight years. 34 "Aeneas," Peter said
to him, "Jesus Christ heals you.[m] Get
up and take care of your mat." Immediately Aeneas got up. 35 All those who
lived in Lydda and Sharon[n] saw him
and turned to the Lord.[o]

Dorcas is restored to life by Peter.

36 In Joppa[p] there was a disciple
named Tabitha (which, when translated, is Dorcas[p]), who was always doing
good[q] and helping the poor. 37 About that
time she became sick and died, and her
body was washed and placed in an
upstairs room.[r] 38 Lydda was near Joppa;
so when the disciples[s] heard that Peter
was in Lydda, they sent two men to him
and urged him, "Please come at once!"
39 Peter went with them, and when
he arrived he was taken upstairs to the
room. All the widows[t] stood around
him, crying and showing him the robes
and other clothing that Dorcas had made
while she was still with them.
40 Peter sent them all out of the room;[u]
then he got down on his knees[v] and
prayed. Turning toward the dead woman, he said, "Tabitha, get up." She
opened her eyes, and seeing Peter she
sat up. 41 He took her by the hand and
helped her to her feet. Then he called
the believers and the widows and presented her to them alive. 42 This became
known all over Joppa, and many people believed in the Lord. 43 Peter stayed
in Joppa for some time with a tanner
named Simon.[w]

Cornelius's call for Peter.

10 At Caesarea[x] there was a man
named Cornelius, a centurion in
what was known as the Italian Regiment. 2 He and all his family were
devout and God-fearing;[y] he gave generously to those in need and prayed to
God regularly. 3 One day at about three
in the afternoon[z] he had a vision.[a] He
distinctly saw an angel[b] of God, who
came to him and said, "Cornelius!"
4 Cornelius stared at him in fear. "What
is it, Lord?" he asked.
The angel answered, "Your prayers
and gifts to the poor have come up as
a memorial offering[c] before God.[d]
5 Now send men to Joppa[e] to bring back
a man named Simon who is called
Peter. 6 He is staying with Simon the
tanner,[f] whose house is by the sea."
7 When the angel who spoke to him
had gone, Cornelius called two of his
servants and a devout soldier who was
one of his attendants. 8 He told them
everything that had happened and sent
them to Joppa.[g]

Peter's vision.

10:9-32Ref— Ac 11:5-14

9 About noon the following day as they

9:25 [a] 1Sa 19:12; 2Co 11:32,33
9:26 [b] Ac 22:17; 26:20; Gal 1:17,18
9:27 [c] Ac 4:36 [d] ver 3-6 [e] ver 20,22
9:29 [f] Ac 6:1 [g] 2Co 11:26
9:30 [h] Ac 1:16 [i] Ac 8:40 [j] ver 11
9:31 [k] Ac 8:1
9:32 [l] ver 13
9:34 [m] Ac 3:6,16; 4:10
9:35 [n] 1Ch 5:16; 27:29; Isa 33:9; 35:2; 65:10 [o] Ac 11:21
9:36 [p] Jos 19:46; 2Ch 2:16; Ezr 3:7; Jnh 1:3; Ac 10:5 [q] 1Ti 2:10; Tit 3:8
9:37 [r] Ac 1:13
9:38 [s] Ac 11:26
9:39 [t] Ac 6:1
9:40 [u] Mt 9:25 [v] Lk 22:41; Ac 7:60
9:43 [w] Ac 10:6
10:1 [x] Ac 8:40
10:2 [y] ver 22,35; Ac 13:16,26
10:3 [z] Ac 3:1 [a] Ac 9:10 [b] Ac 5:19
10:4 [c] Mt 26:13 [d] Rev 8:4
10:5 [e] Ac 9:36
10:6 [f] Ac 9:43
10:8 [g] Ac 9:36

p36 Both *Tabitha* (Aramaic) and *Dorcas* (Greek) mean *gazelle*.

were on their journey and approaching the city, Peter went up on the roof[a] to pray. 10He became hungry and wanted something to eat, and while the meal was being prepared, he fell into a trance.[b] 11He saw heaven opened and something like a large sheet being let down to earth by its four corners. 12It contained all kinds of four-footed animals, as well as reptiles of the earth and birds of the air. 13Then a voice told him, "Get up, Peter. Kill and eat."

14"Surely not, Lord!"[c] Peter replied. "I have never eaten anything impure or unclean."[d]

15The voice spoke to him a second time, "Do not call anything impure that God has made clean."[e]

16This happened three times, and immediately the sheet was taken back to heaven.

17While Peter was wondering about the meaning of the vision, the men sent by Cornelius[f] found out where Simon's house was and stopped at the gate. 18They called out, asking if Simon who was known as Peter was staying there.

19While Peter was still thinking about the vision, the Spirit said[g] to him, "Simon, three[q] men are looking for you. 20So get up and go downstairs. Do not hesitate to go with them, for I have sent them."[h]

21Peter went down and said to the men, "I'm the one you're looking for. Why have you come?"

22The men replied, "We have come from Cornelius the centurion. He is a righteous and God-fearing man,[i] who is respected by all the Jewish people. A holy angel told him to have you come to his house so that he could hear what you have to say."[j] 23Then Peter invited the men into the house to be his guests.

The next day Peter started out with them, and some of the brothers[k] from Joppa went along.[l] 24The following day he arrived in Caesarea.[m] Cornelius was expecting them and had called together his relatives and close friends. 25As Peter entered the house, Cornelius met him and fell at his feet in reverence. 26But Peter made him get up. "Stand up," he said, "I am only a man myself."[n]

27Talking with him, Peter went inside and found a large gathering of people. 28He said to them: "You are well aware that it is against our law for a Jew to associate with a Gentile or visit him.[o] But God has shown me that I should not call any man impure or unclean.[p] 29So when I was sent for, I came without raising any objection. May I ask why you sent for me?"

30Cornelius answered: "Four days ago I was in my house praying at this hour, at three in the afternoon. Suddenly a man in shining clothes stood before me 31and said, 'Cornelius, God has heard your prayer and remembered your gifts to the poor. 32Send to Joppa for Simon who is called Peter. He is a guest in the home of Simon the tanner, who lives by the sea.' 33So I sent for you immediately, and it was good of you to come. Now we are all here in the presence of God to listen to everything the Lord has commanded you to tell us."

34Then Peter began to speak: "I now realize how true it is that God does not show favoritism[q] 35but accepts men from every nation who fear him and do what is right.[r] 36You know the message God sent to the people of Israel, telling the good news[s] of peace[t] through Jesus Christ, who is Lord of all.[u] 37You know what has happened throughout Judea, beginning in Galilee after the baptism that John preached— 38how God anointed[v] Jesus of Nazareth with the Holy Spirit and power, and how he went around doing good and healing[w] all who were under the power of the devil, because God was with him.[x]

39"We are witnesses[y] of everything he did in the country of the Jews and in Jerusalem. They killed him by hanging him on a tree,[z] 40but God raised him from the dead[a] on the third day and caused him to be seen. 41He was not seen by all the people,[b] but by witnesses whom God had already chosen—by

10:9 [a]Mt 24:17
10:10 [b]Ac 22:17
10:14 [c]Ac 9:5 [d]Lev 11:4-8, 13-20; 20:25; Dt 14:3-20; Eze 4:14
10:15 [e]Mt 15:11; Ro 14:14,17, 20; 1Co 10:25; 1Ti 4:3,4; Tit 1:15
10:17 [f]ver 7,8
10:19 [g]Ac 8:29
10:20 [h]Ac 15:7-9
10:22 [i]ver 2 [j]Ac 11:14
10:23 [k]Ac 1:16 [l]ver 45; Ac 11:12
10:24 [m]Ac 8:40
10:26 [n]Ac 14:15; Rev 19:10
10:28 [o]Jn 4:9; 18:28; Ac 11:3 [p]Ac 15:8,9
10:34 [q]Dt 10:17; 2Ch 19:7; Job 34:19; Ro 2:11; Gal 2:6; Eph 6:9; Col 3:25; 1Pe 1:17
10:35 [r]Ac 15:9
10:36 [s]Ac 13:32 [t]Lk 2:14 [u]Mt 28:18; Ro 10:12
10:38 [v]Ac 4:26 [w]Mt 4:23 [x]Jn 3:2
10:39 [y]Lk 24:48 [z]Ac 5:30
10:40 [a]Ac 2:24
10:41 [b]Jn 14:17,22

q *19* One early manuscript *two*; other manuscripts do not have the number.

us who ate[a] and drank with him after he rose from the dead. 42He commanded us to preach to the people[b] and to testify that he is the one whom God appointed as judge of the living and the dead.[c] 43All the prophets testify about him[d] that everyone[e] who believes in him receives forgiveness of sins through his name."

44While Peter was still speaking these words, the Holy Spirit came on[f] all who heard the message. 45The circumcised believers who had come with Peter[g] were astonished that the gift of the Holy Spirit had been poured out[h] even on the Gentiles.[i] 46For they heard them speaking in tongues[r] [j] and praising God.

Then Peter said, 47"Can anyone keep these people from being baptized with water?[k] They have received the Holy Spirit just as we have."[l] 48So he ordered that they be baptized in the name of Jesus Christ.[m] Then they asked Peter to stay with them for a few days.

Peter defends his ministry to Gentiles.

11 The apostles and the brothers[n] throughout Judea heard that the Gentiles also had received the word of God. 2So when Peter went up to Jerusalem, the circumcised believers[o] criticized him 3and said, "You went into the house of uncircumcised men and ate with them."[p]

4Peter began and explained everything to them precisely as it had happened: 5"I was in the city of Joppa praying, and in a trance I saw a vision.[q] I saw something like a large sheet being let down from heaven by its four corners, and it came down to where I was. 6I looked into it and saw four-footed animals of the earth, wild beasts, reptiles, and birds of the air. 7Then I heard a voice telling me, 'Get up, Peter. Kill and eat.'

8"I replied, 'Surely not, Lord! Nothing impure or unclean has ever entered my mouth.'

9"The voice spoke from heaven a second time, 'Do not call anything impure that God has made clean.'[r] 10This happened three times, and then it was all pulled up to heaven again.

11"Right then three men who had been sent to me from Caesarea stopped at the house where I was staying. 12The Spirit told[s] me to have no hesitation about going with them.[t] These six brothers also went with me, and we entered the man's house. 13He told us how he had seen an angel appear in his house and say, 'Send to Joppa for Simon who is called Peter. 14He will bring you a message through which you and all your household[u] will be saved.'

15"As I began to speak, the Holy Spirit came on[v] them as he had come on us at the beginning.[w] 16Then I remembered what the Lord had said: 'John baptized with[s] water, but you will be baptized with the Holy Spirit.'[x] 17So if God gave them the same gift as he gave us,[y] who believed in the Lord Jesus Christ, who was I to think that I could oppose God?"

18When they heard this, they had no further objections and praised God, saying, "So then, God has granted even the Gentiles repentance unto life."[z]

Antioch receives the Good News.

19Now those who had been scattered by the persecution in connection with Stephen[a] traveled as far as Phoenicia, Cyprus and Antioch,[b] telling the message only to Jews. 20Some of them, however, men from Cyprus[c] and Cyrene,[d] went to Antioch and began to speak to Greeks also, telling them the good news about the Lord Jesus. 21The Lord's hand was with them,[e] and a great number of people believed and turned to the Lord.[f]

22News of this reached the ears of the church at Jerusalem, and they sent Barnabas[g] to Antioch. 23When he arrived and saw the evidence of the grace of God,[h] he was glad and encouraged them all to remain true to the Lord with

10:41 [a]Lk 24:43; Jn 21:13
10:42 [b]Mt 28:19,20 [c]Jn 5:22; Ac 17:31; Ro 14:9; 2Co 5:10; 2Ti 4:1; 1Pe 4:5
10:43 [d]Isa 53:11 [e]Ac 15:9
10:44 [f]Ac 8:15,16; 11:15; 15:8
10:45 [g]ver 23 [h]Ac 2:33,38 [i]Ac 11:18
10:46 [j]Mk 16:17
10:47 [k]Ac 8:36 [l]Ac 11:17
10:48 [m]Ac 2:38; 8:16
11:1 [n]Ac 1:16
11:2 [o]Ac 10:45
11:3 [p]Ac 10:25,28; Gal 2:12
11:5 [q]Ac 10:9-32; 9:10
11:9 [r]Ac 10:15
11:12 [s]Ac 8:29 [t]Ac 15:9; Ro 3:22
11:14 [u]Jn 4:53; Ac 16:15, 31-34; 1Co 1:11,16
11:15 [v]Ac 10:44 [w]Ac 2:4
11:16 [x]Mk 1:8; Ac 1:5
11:17 [y]Ac 10:45,47
11:18 [z]Ro 10:12,13; 2Co 7:10
11:19 [a]Ac 8:1,4 [b]ver 26,27; Ac 13:1; 18:22; Gal 2:11
11:20 [c]Ac 4:36 [d]Mt 27:32 **11:21** [e]Lk 1:66 [f]Ac 2:47
11:22 [g]Ac 4:36 **11:23** [h]Ac 13:43; 14:26; 20:24

[r]*46* Or *other languages* [s]*16* Or *in*

all their hearts.[a] 24He was a good man,
full of the Holy Spirit and faith, and a
great number of people were brought
to the Lord.[b]
25Then Barnabas went to Tarsus[c] to
look for Saul, 26and when he found him,
he brought him to Antioch. So for a
whole year Barnabas and Saul met with
the church and taught great numbers
of people. The disciples[d] were called
Christians first[e] at Antioch.

Relief is sent to Judean Christians.

27During this time some prophets[f]
came down from Jerusalem to Antioch.
28One of them, named Agabus,[g] stood
up and through the Spirit predicted that
a severe famine would spread over the
entire Roman world.[h] (This happened
during the reign of Claudius.)[i] 29The
disciples,[j] each according to his ability,
decided to provide help[k] for the brothers[l] living in Judea. 30This they did,
sending their gift to the elders[m] by Barnabas and Saul.[n]

Herod directs James's execution and Peter's imprisonment.

12 It was about this time that King
Herod arrested some who belonged to the church, intending to persecute them. 2He had James, the brother
of John,[o] put to death with the sword.
3When he saw that this pleased the
Jews,[p] he proceeded to seize Peter also.
This happened during the Feast of Unleavened Bread.[q] 4After arresting him, he
put him in prison, handing him over to
be guarded by four squads of four soldiers each. Herod intended to bring him
out for public trial after the Passover.

An angel rescues Peter from prison.

5So Peter was kept in prison, but the
church was earnestly praying to God
for him.[r]
6The night before Herod was to bring
him to trial, Peter was sleeping between
two soldiers, bound with two chains,[s]
and sentries stood guard at the entrance.
7Suddenly an angel[t] of the Lord appeared
and a light shone in the cell. He struck
Peter on the side and woke him up.
"Quick, get up!" he said, and the chains
fell off Peter's wrists.[u]
8Then the angel said to him, "Put on
your clothes and sandals." And Peter did
so. "Wrap your cloak around you and
follow me," the angel told him. 9Peter
followed him out of the prison, but he
had no idea that what the angel was
doing was really happening; he thought
he was seeing a vision.[v] 10They passed
the first and second guards and came
to the iron gate leading to the city. It
opened for them by itself,[w] and they
went through it. When they had walked
the length of one street, suddenly the
angel left him.
11Then Peter came to himself[x] and
said, "Now I know without a doubt
that the Lord sent his angel and rescued
me[y] from Herod's clutches and from
everything the Jewish people were
anticipating."
12When this had dawned on him, he
went to the house of Mary the mother
of John, also called Mark,[z] where many
people had gathered and were praying.[a] 13Peter knocked at the outer
entrance, and a servant girl named Rho-
da came to answer the door.[b] 14When
she recognized Peter's voice, she was
so overjoyed[c] she ran back without
opening it and exclaimed, "Peter is at
the door!"
15"You're out of your mind," they told
her. When she kept insisting that it was
so, they said, "It must be his angel."[d]
16But Peter kept on knocking, and
when they opened the door and saw
him, they were astonished. 17Peter
motioned with his hand[e] for them to be
quiet and described how the Lord had
brought him out of prison. "Tell James[f]
and the brothers[g] about this," he said,
and then he left for another place.
18In the morning, there was no small
commotion among the soldiers as to
what had become of Peter. 19After Herod

11:23 [a]Ac 14:22
11:24 [b]ver 21; Ac 5:14
11:25 [c]Ac 9:11
11:26 [d]Ac 6:1,2; 13:52 [e]Ac 26:28; 1Pe 4:16
11:27 [f]Ac 13:1; 15:32; 1Co 12:28,29; Eph 4:11
11:28 [g]Ac 21:10 [h]Mt 24:14 [i]Ac 18:2
11:29 [j]ver 26 [k]Ro 15:26; 2Co 9:2 [l]Ac 1:16
11:30 [m]Ac 14:23 [n]Ac 12:25
12:2 [o]Mt 4:21
12:3 [p]Ac 24:27 [q]Ex 12:15; 23:15
12:5 [r]Eph 6:18
12:6 [s]Ac 21:33
12:7 [t]Ac 5:19 [u]Ac 16:26
12:9 [v]Ac 9:10
12:10 [w]Ac 5:19; 16:26
12:11 [x]Lk 15:17 [y]Ps 34:7; Da 3:28; 6:22; 2Co 1:10; 2Pe 2:9
12:12 [z]ver 25; Ac 15:37,39; Col 4:10; Phm 24; 1Pe 5:13 [a]ver 5
12:13 [b]Jn 18:16,17
12:14 [c]Lk 24:41
12:15 [d]Mt 18:10
12:17 [e]Ac 13:16; 19:33; 21:40 [f]Ac 15:13 [g]Ac 1:16

had a thorough search made for him and did not find him, he cross-examined the guards and ordered that they be executed.[a]

Herod's pride causes his violent death.

Then Herod went from Judea to Caesarea[b] and stayed there a while. 20 He had been quarreling with the people of Tyre and Sidon;[c] they now joined together and sought an audience with him. Having secured the support of Blastus, a trusted personal servant of the king, they asked for peace, because they depended on the king's country for their food supply.[d]

21 On the appointed day Herod, wearing his royal robes, sat on his throne and delivered a public address to the people. 22 They shouted, "This is the voice of a god, not of a man." 23 Immediately, because Herod did not give praise to God, an angel of the Lord struck him down,[e] and he was eaten by worms and died.

24 But the word of God continued to increase and spread.[f]

25 When Barnabas[g] and Saul had finished their mission,[h] they returned from[t] Jerusalem, taking with them John, also called Mark.[i]

The Holy Spirit calls Saul and Barnabas.

13 In the church at Antioch[j] there were prophets[k] and teachers: Barnabas,[l] Simeon called Niger, Lucius of Cyrene, Manaen (who had been brought up with Herod[m] the tetrarch) and Saul. 2 While they were worshiping the Lord and fasting, the Holy Spirit said,[n] "Set apart for me Barnabas and Saul for the work[o] to which I have called them."[p] 3 So after they had fasted and prayed, they placed their hands on them[q] and sent them off.[r]

Saul (Paul) and Barnabas proclaim the Word of God on Cyprus.

4 The two of them, sent on their way by the Holy Spirit,[s] went down to Seleucia and sailed from there to Cyprus.[t] 5 When they arrived at Salamis, they proclaimed the word of God in the Jewish synagogues.[u] John[v] was with them as their helper.

6 They traveled through the whole island until they came to Paphos. There they met a Jewish sorcerer[w] and false prophet[x] named Bar-Jesus, 7 who was an attendant of the proconsul,[y] Sergius Paulus. The proconsul, an intelligent man, sent for Barnabas and Saul because he wanted to hear the word of God. 8 But Elymas the sorcerer[z] (for that is what his name means) opposed them and tried to turn the proconsul[a] from the faith.[b] 9 Then Saul, who was also called Paul, filled with the Holy Spirit,[c] looked straight at Elymas and said, 10 "You are a child of the devil[d] and an enemy of everything that is right! You are full of all kinds of deceit and trickery. Will you never stop perverting the right ways of the Lord?[e] 11 Now the hand of the Lord is against you.[f] You are going to be blind, and for a time you will be unable to see the light of the sun."

Immediately mist and darkness came over him, and he groped about, seeking someone to lead him by the hand. 12 When the proconsul[g] saw what had happened, he believed, for he was amazed at the teaching about the Lord.

Paul and Barnabas minister in Pisidian Antioch.

13 From Paphos,[h] Paul and his companions sailed to Perga in Pamphylia, where John[i] left them to return to Jerusalem. 14 From Perga they went on to Pisidian Antioch.[j] On the Sabbath[k] they entered the synagogue[l] and sat down. 15 After the reading from the Law[m] and the Prophets, the synagogue rulers sent word to them, saying, "Brothers, if you have a message of encouragement for the people, please speak."

16 Standing up, Paul motioned with his hand[n] and said: "Men of Israel and you

12:19 [a] Ac 16:27 [b] Ac 8:40
12:20 [c] Mt 11:21 [d] 1Ki 5:9,11; Eze 27:17
12:23 [e] 1Sa 25:38; 2Sa 24:16,17
12:24 [f] Ac 6:7; 19:20
12:25 [g] Ac 4:36 [h] Ac 11:30 [i] ver 12
13:1 [j] Ac 11:19 [k] Ac 11:27 [l] Ac 4:36; 11:22-26 [m] Mt 14:1
13:2 [n] Ac 8:29 [o] Ac 14:26 [p] Ac 22:21
13:3 [q] Ac 6:6 [r] Ac 14:26
13:4 [s] ver 2,3 [t] Ac 4:36
13:5 [u] Ac 9:20 [v] Ac 12:12
13:6 [w] Ac 8:9 [x] Mt 7:15
13:7 [y] ver 8,12; Ac 19:38
13:8 [z] Ac 8:9 [a] ver 7 [b] Ac 6:7
13:9 [c] Ac 4:8
13:10 [d] Mt 13:38; Jn 8:44 [e] Hos 14:9
13:11 [f] Ex 9:3; 1Sa 5:6,7; Ps 32:4
13:12 [g] ver 7
13:13 [h] ver 6 [i] Ac 12:12
13:14 [j] Ac 14:19,21 [k] Ac 16:13 [l] Ac 9:20
13:15 [m] Ac 15:21
13:16 [n] Ac 12:17

[t] *25* Some manuscripts *to*

Gentiles who worship God, listen to me!
17 The God of the people of Israel chose
our fathers; he made the people prosper
during their stay in Egypt, with mighty
power he led them out of that country,[a]
18 he endured their conduct[ub] for about
forty years in the desert,[c] 19 he overthrew seven nations in Canaan[d] and gave
their land to his people[e] as their inheritance. 20 All this took about 450 years.
"After this, God gave them judges[f]
until the time of Samuel the prophet.[g]
21 Then the people asked for a king,[h] and
he gave them Saul[i] son of Kish, of the
tribe of Benjamin,[j] who ruled forty years.
22 After removing Saul,[k] he made David
their king.[l] He testified concerning him:
'I have found David son of Jesse a man
after my own heart;[m] he will do everything I want him to do.'
23 "From this man's descendants[n] God
has brought to Israel the Savior[o] Jesus,[p]
as he promised.[q] 24 Before the coming
of Jesus, John preached repentance and
baptism to all the people of Israel.[r] 25 As

13:17 [a]Ex 6:6,7; Dt 7:6-8 **13:18** [b]Dt 1:31 [c]Ac 7:36 **13:19** [d]Dt 7:1 [e]Jos 19:51 **13:20** [f]Jdg 2:16 [g]1Sa 3:19,20 **13:21** [h]1Sa 8:5,19 [i]1Sa 10:1 [j]1Sa 9:1,2

13:22 [k]1Sa 15:23,26 [l]1Sa 16:13;Ps 89:20 [m]1Sa 13:14 **13:23** [n]Mt 1:1 [o]Lk 2:11 [p]Mt 1:21 [q]ver 32 **13:24** [r]Mk 1:4

u *18* Some manuscripts *and cared for them*

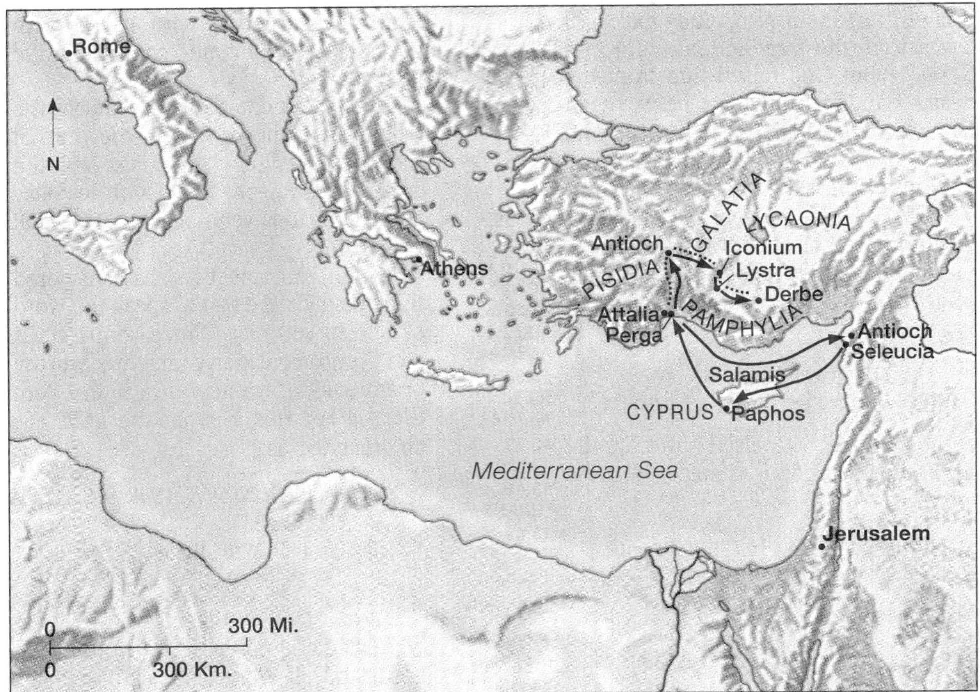

Paul's First Missionary Journey

The leaders of the church in Antioch chose Paul and Barnabas to take the gospel westward. Along with John Mark, they boarded a ship at Seleucia and set out across the Mediterranean for Cyprus. They preached in Salamis, the largest city, and went across the island to Paphos. Paul, Barnabas, and John Mark left Paphos and landed at Perga in the humid region of Pamphylia, a narrow strip of land between the sea and the Taurus Mountains. John Mark left them in Perga, but Paul and Barnabas traveled up the steep road into the higher elevation of Pisidia in Galatia. When the Jews rejected his message, Paul preached to Gentiles, and the Jews drove Paul and Barnabas out of the Pisidian city of Antioch. Paul and Barnabas then descended the mountains, going east into Lycaonia. They went first to Iconium, a commercial center on the road between Asia and Syria. After preaching there, they had to flee to Lystra, 25 miles south. Paul was stoned in Lystra, but he and Barnabas traveled the 50 miles to Derbe, a border town. The pair then boldly retraced their steps. From Antioch in Pisidia, Paul and Barnabas went down the mountains back to Pamphylia on the coast. Stopping first in Perga, where they had landed, they went west to Attalia, the main port that sent goods from Asia to Syria and Egypt. There they found a ship bound for Seleucia, the port of Antioch in Syria. This ended their first missionary journey.

John was completing his work,[a] he said: 'Who do you think I am? I am not that one.[b] No, but he is coming after me, whose sandals I am not worthy to untie.'[c]

26"Brothers, children of Abraham, and you God-fearing Gentiles, it is to us that this message of salvation[d] has been sent. 27The people of Jerusalem and their rulers did not recognize Jesus,[e] yet in condemning him they fulfilled the words of the prophets[f] that are read every Sabbath. 28Though they found no proper ground for a death sentence, they asked Pilate to have him executed.[g] 29When they had carried out all that was written about him,[h] they took him down from the tree[i] and laid him in a tomb.[j] 30But God raised him from the dead,[k] 31and for many days he was seen by those who had traveled with him from Galilee to Jerusalem.[l] They are now his witnesses[m] to our people.

32"We tell you the good news:[n] What God promised our fathers[o] 33he has fulfilled for us, their children, by raising up Jesus. As it is written in the second Psalm:

"'You are my Son;
today I have become your Father.[v]'[w][p]

34The fact that God raised him from the dead, never to decay, is stated in these words:

"'I will give you the holy and sure
blessings promised to David.'[x][q]

35So it is stated elsewhere:

"'You will not let your Holy One see
decay.'[y][r]

36"For when David had served God's purpose in his own generation, he fell asleep; he was buried with his fathers[s] and his body decayed. 37But the one whom God raised from the dead did not see decay.

38"Therefore, my brothers, I want you to know that through Jesus the forgiveness of sins is proclaimed to you.[t] 39Through him everyone who believes is justified from everything you could not be justified from by the law of Moses.[u] 40Take care that what the prophets have said does not happen to you:

41"'Look, you scoffers,
wonder and perish,
for I am going to do something in
your days
that you would never believe,
even if someone told you.'[z]"[v]

42As Paul and Barnabas were leaving the synagogue,[w] the people invited them to speak further about these things on the next Sabbath. 43When the congregation was dismissed, many of the Jews and devout converts to Judaism followed Paul and Barnabas, who talked with them and urged them to continue in the grace of God.[x]

44On the next Sabbath almost the whole city gathered to hear the word of the Lord. 45When the Jews saw the crowds, they were filled with jealousy and talked abusively[y] against what Paul was saying.[z]

46Then Paul and Barnabas answered them boldly: "We had to speak the word of God to you first.[a] Since you reject it and do not consider yourselves worthy of eternal life, we now turn to the Gentiles.[b] 47For this is what the Lord has commanded us:

"'I have made you[a] a light for the
Gentiles,[c]
that you[a] may bring salvation to
the ends of the earth.'[b]"[d]

48When the Gentiles heard this, they were glad and honored the word of the Lord; and all who were appointed for eternal life believed.

49The word of the Lord spread through the whole region. 50But the Jews incited the God-fearing women of high standing and the leading men of the city. They stirred up persecution against Paul and Barnabas, and expelled them from their region.[e] 51So they shook the dust from their feet[f] in protest against them

13:25 [a]Ac 20:24 [b]Jn 1:20 [c]Mt 3:11; Jn 1:27
13:26 [d]Ac 4:12
13:27 [e]Ac 3:17 [f]Lk 24:27
13:28 [g]Mt 27:20-25; Ac 3:14
13:29 [h]Lk 18:31 [i]Ac 5:30 [j]Lk 23:53
13:30 [k]Mt 28:6; Ac 2:24
13:31 [l]Mt 28:16 [m]Lk 24:48
13:32 [n]Ac 5:42 [o]Ac 26:6; Ro 4:13
13:33 [p]Ps 2:7
13:34 [q]Isa 55:3
13:35 [r]Ps 16:10; Ac 2:27
13:36 [s]1Ki 2:10; Ac 2:29
13:38 [t]Lk 24:47; Ac 2:38
13:39 [u]Ro 3:28
13:41 [v]Hab 1:5
13:42 [w]ver 14
13:43 [x]Ac 11:23; 14:22
13:45 [y]Ac 18:6; 1Pe 4:4; Jude 10 [z]1Th 2:16
13:46 [a]ver 26; Ac 3:26 [b]Ac 18:6; 22:21; 28:28
13:47 [c]Lk 2:32 [d]Isa 49:6
13:50 [e]1Th 2:16
13:51 [f]Mt 10:14; Ac 18:6

v33 Or *have begotten you* w33 Psalm 2:7
x34 Isaiah 55:3 y35 Psalm 16:10 z41 Hab. 1:5
a47 The Greek is singular. b47 Isaiah 49:6

and went to Iconium.[a] 52And the disciples were filled with joy and with the Holy Spirit.

Paul and Barnabas minister in Iconium, Lystra and Derbe.

14 At Iconium[b] Paul and Barnabas went as usual into the Jewish synagogue. There they spoke so effectively that a great number of Jews and Gentiles believed. 2But the Jews who refused to believe stirred up the Gentiles and poisoned their minds against the brothers. 3So Paul and Barnabas spent considerable time there, speaking boldly[c] for the Lord, who confirmed the message of his grace by enabling them to do miraculous signs and wonders.[d] 4The people of the city were divided; some sided with the Jews, others with the apostles.[e] 5There was a plot afoot among the Gentiles and Jews, together with their leaders, to mistreat them and stone them.[f] 6But they found out about it and fled[g] to the Lycaonian cities of Lystra and Derbe and to the surrounding country, 7where they continued to preach[h] the good news.[i]

A crippled man is healed.

8In Lystra there sat a man crippled in his feet, who was lame from birth[j] and had never walked. 9He listened to Paul as he was speaking. Paul looked directly at him, saw that he had faith to be healed[k] 10and called out, "Stand up on your feet!" At that, the man jumped up and began to walk.[l]

Paul and Barnabas are deified by the people.

11When the crowd saw what Paul had done, they shouted in the Lycaonian language, "The gods have come down to us in human form!"[m] 12Barnabas they called Zeus, and Paul they called Hermes because he was the chief speaker. 13The priest of Zeus, whose temple was just outside the city, brought bulls and wreaths to the city gates because he and the crowd wanted to offer sacrifices to them.

14But when the apostles Barnabas and Paul heard of this, they tore their clothes[n] and rushed out into the crowd, shouting: 15"Men, why are you doing this? We too are only men,[o] human like you. We are bringing you good news,[p] telling you to turn from these worthless things[q] to the living God,[r] who made heaven and earth[s] and sea and everything in them.[t] 16In the past, he let[u] all nations go their own way.[v] 17Yet he has not left himself without testimony:[w] He has shown kindness by giving you rain from heaven and crops in their seasons;[x] he provides you with plenty of food and fills your hearts with joy." 18Even with these words, they had difficulty keeping the crowd from sacrificing to them.

19Then some Jews[y] came from Antioch and Iconium[z] and won the crowd over. They stoned Paul[a] and dragged him outside the city, thinking he was dead. 20But after the disciples[b] had gathered around him, he got up and went back into the city. The next day he and Barnabas left for Derbe.

21They preached the good news in that city and won a large number of disciples. Then they returned to Lystra, Iconium[c] and Antioch, 22strengthening the disciples and encouraging them to remain true to the faith.[d] "We must go through many hardships[e] to enter the kingdom of God," they said. 23Paul and Barnabas appointed elders[c][f] for them in each church and, with prayer and fasting,[g] committed them to the Lord,[h] in whom they had put their trust. 24After going through Pisidia, they came into Pamphylia, 25and when they had preached the word in Perga, they went down to Attalia.

26From Attalia they sailed back to Antioch,[i] where they had been committed

13:51 [a]Ac 14:1,19,21; 2Ti 3:11 **14:1** [b]Ac 13:51 **14:3** [c]Ac 4:29 [d]Jn 4:48; Heb 2:4 **14:4** [e]Ac 17:4,5 **14:5** [f]ver 19 **14:6** [g]Mt 10:23 **14:7** [h]Ac 16:10 [i]ver 15,21 **14:8** [j]Ac 3:2 **14:9** [k]Mt 9:28,29 **14:10** [l]Ac 3:8 **14:11** [m]Ac 8:10; 28:6 **14:14** [n]Mk 14:63 **14:15** [o]Ac 10:26; Jas 5:17 [p]ver 7,21; Ac 13:32 [q]1Sa 12:21; 1Co 8:4; 1Th 1:9 [r]Mt 16:16 [s]Ge 1:1; Jer 14:22 [t]Ps 146:6; Rev 14:7 **14:16** [u]Ac 17:30 [v]Ps 81:12; Mic 4:5 **14:17** [w]Ac 17:27; Ro 1:20 [x]Dt 11:14; Job 5:10; Ps 65:10 **14:19** [y]Ac 13:45 [z]Ac 13:51 [a]2Co 11:25; 2Ti 3:11 **14:20** [b]ver 22,28; Ac 11:26 **14:21** [c]Ac 13:51 **14:22** [d]Ac 11:23; 13:43 [e]Jn 16:33; 1Th 3:3; 2Ti 3:12

14:23 [f]Ac 11:30; Tit 1:5 [g]Ac 13:3 [h]Ac 20:32
14:26 [i]Ac 11:19

c23 Or *Barnabas ordained elders*; or *Barnabas had elders elected*

to the grace of God[a] for the work they
had now completed.[b] **27**On arriving
there, they gathered the church together and reported all that God had done
through them[c] and how he had opened
the door[d] of faith to the Gentiles. **28**And
they stayed there a long time with the
disciples.

Dispute over circumcision of believers.

15 Some men[e] came down from
Judea to Antioch and were teaching the brothers: "Unless you are circumcised,[f] according to the custom
taught by Moses,[g] you cannot be saved."
2This brought Paul and Barnabas into
sharp dispute and debate with them. So
Paul and Barnabas were appointed, along
with some other believers, to go up to
Jerusalem[h] to see the apostles and
elders[i] about this question. **3**The church
sent them on their way, and as they
traveled through Phoenicia and Samaria, they told how the Gentiles had been
converted.[j] This news made all the
brothers very glad. **4**When they came
to Jerusalem, they were welcomed by
the church and the apostles and elders,
to whom they reported everything God
had done through them.[k]
5Then some of the believers who belonged to the party of the Pharisees
stood up and said, "The Gentiles must
be circumcised and required to obey the
law of Moses."

Meeting of the Jerusalem council.

6The apostles and elders met to consider this question. **7**After much discussion, Peter got up and addressed them:
"Brothers, you know that some time
ago God made a choice among you that
the Gentiles might hear from my lips
the message of the gospel and believe.
8God, who knows the heart,[l] showed
that he accepted them by giving the
Holy Spirit to them,[m] just as he did to
us. **9**He made no distinction between us
and them,[n] for he purified their hearts
by faith.[o] **10**Now then, why do you try
to test God by putting on the necks of
the disciples a yoke[p] that neither we
nor our fathers have been able to bear?
11No! We believe it is through the grace[q]
of our Lord Jesus that we are saved, just
as they are."
12The whole assembly became silent
as they listened to Barnabas and Paul
telling about the miraculous signs and
wonders[r] God had done among the Gentiles through them.[s] **13**When they finished, James[t] spoke up: "Brothers, listen
to me. **14**Simon[d] has described to us how
God at first showed his concern by taking from the Gentiles a people for himself. **15**The words of the prophets are
in agreement with this, as it is written:

16" 'After this I will return
and rebuild David's fallen tent.
Its ruins I will rebuild,
and I will restore it,
17that the remnant of men may seek
the Lord,
and all the Gentiles who bear my
name,
says the Lord, who does these things'[e][u]
18 that have been known for ages.[f]

19"It is my judgment, therefore, that
we should not make it difficult for the
Gentiles who are turning to God. **20**Instead we should write to them, telling
them to abstain from food polluted by
idols,[v] from sexual immorality,[w] from the
meat of strangled animals and from
blood.[x] **21**For Moses has been preached
in every city from the earliest times and
is read in the synagogues on every Sabbath."[y]

Decision of the Jerusalem council.

22Then the apostles and elders, with
the whole church, decided to choose
some of their own men and send them
to Antioch with Paul and Barnabas. They
chose Judas (called Barsabbas) and Silas,[z]
two men who were leaders among the
brothers. **23**With them they sent the following letter:

14:26 [a]Ac 15:40 [b]Ac 13:1,3
14:27 [c]Ac 15:4,12; 21:19 [d]1Co 16:9; 2Co 2:12; Col 4:3; Rev 3:8
15:1 [e]ver 24; Gal 2:12 [f]ver 5; Gal 5:2,3 [g]Ac 6:14
15:2 [h]Gal 2:2 [i]Ac 11:30
15:3 [j]Ac 14:27
15:4 [k]ver 12; Ac 14:27
15:8 [l]Ac 1:24 [m]Ac 10:44,47
15:9 [n]Ac 10:28,34; 11:12 [o]Ac 10:43
15:10 [p]Mt 23:4; Gal 5:1
15:11 [q]Ro 3:24; Eph 2:5-8
15:12 [r]Jn 4:48 [s]Ac 14:27
15:13 [t]Ac 12:17
15:17 [u]Am 9:11,12
15:20 [v]1Co 8:7-13; 10:14-28; Rev 2:14,20 [w]1Co 10:7,8 [x]ver 29; Ge 9:4; Lev 3:17; Dt 12:16,23
15:21 [y]Ac 13:15; 2Co 3:14,15
15:22 [z]ver 27,32,40

d *14* Greek *Simeon,* a variant of *Simon;* that is, Peter
e *17* Amos 9:11,12 f *17,18* Some manuscripts *things'— / 18known to the Lord for ages is his work*

The apostles and elders, your brothers,

To the Gentile believers in Antioch,[a] Syria and Cilicia:[b]

Greetings.[c]

24We have heard that some went
out from us without our authoriza-
tion and disturbed you, troubling
your minds by what they said.[d] 25So
we all agreed to choose some men
and send them to you with our dear
friends Barnabas and Paul— 26men
who have risked their lives[e] for the
name of our Lord Jesus Christ.
27Therefore we are sending Judas
and Silas to confirm by word of
mouth what we are writing. 28It
seemed good to the Holy Spirit[f]
and to us not to burden you with
anything beyond the following requirements: 29You are to abstain
from food sacrificed to idols, from
blood, from the meat of strangled
animals and from sexual immorality.[g] You will do well to avoid these
things.

Farewell.

30The men were sent off and went
down to Antioch, where they gathered
the church together and delivered the
letter. 31The people read it and were glad
for its encouraging message. 32Judas and
Silas, who themselves were prophets,
said much to encourage and strengthen
the brothers. 33After spending some
time there, they were sent off by the
brothers with the blessing of peace[h] to
return to those who had sent them.[g]
35But Paul and Barnabas remained in
Antioch, where they and many others
taught and preached[i] the word of the
Lord.

Division of Paul and Barnabas over John Mark.

36Some time later Paul said to Barnabas, "Let us go back and visit the brothers in all the towns[j] where we preached
the word of the Lord and see how they
are doing." 37Barnabas wanted to take
John, also called Mark,[k] with them, 38but
Paul did not think it wise to take him,
because he had deserted them[l] in Pamphylia and had not continued with them
in the work. 39They had such a sharp
disagreement that they parted company. Barnabas took Mark and sailed for
Cyprus, 40but Paul chose Silas[m] and
left, commended by the brothers to the
grace of the Lord.[n] 41He went through
Syria[o] and Cilicia,[p] strengthening the
churches.[q]

Enlistment of Timothy by Paul and Silas.

16 He came to Derbe and then to
Lystra,[r] where a disciple named
Timothy[s] lived, whose mother was a
Jewess and a believer, but whose
father was a Greek. 2The brothers[t] at
Lystra and Iconium[u] spoke well of him.
3Paul wanted to take him along on the
journey, so he circumcised him because
of the Jews who lived in that area, for
they all knew that his father was a
Greek.[v] 4As they traveled from town to
town, they delivered the decisions
reached by the apostles and elders[w] in
Jerusalem[x] for the people to obey.[y] 5So
the churches were strengthened[z] in
the faith and grew daily in numbers.

Paul's vision of a man from Macedonia.

6Paul and his companions traveled
throughout the region of Phrygia[a] and
Galatia,[b] having been kept by the Holy
Spirit from preaching the word in the
province of Asia.[c] 7When they came to
the border of Mysia, they tried to
enter Bithynia, but the Spirit of Jesus[d]
would not allow them to. 8So they passed
by Mysia and went down to Troas.[e]
9During the night Paul had a vision[f]
of a man of Macedonia[g] standing and

15:23 [a]ver 1 [b]ver 41 [c]Ac 23:25,26; Jas 1:1
15:24 [d]ver 1; Gal 1:7; 5:10
15:26 [e]Ac 9:23-25; 14:19
15:28 [f]Ac 5:32
15:29 [g]ver 20; Ac 21:25
15:33 [h]Mk 5:34; Ac 16:36; 1Co 16:11
15:35 [i]Ac 8:4
15:36 [j]Ac 13:4,13, 14,51; 14:1,6,24,25
15:37 [k]Ac 12:12
15:38 [l]Ac 13:13
15:40 [m]ver 22 [n]Ac 11:23
15:41 [o]ver 23 [p]Ac 6:9 [q]Ac 16:5
16:1 [r]Ac 14:6 [s]Ac 17:14; 18:5; 19:22; Ro 16:21; 1Co 4:17; 2Co 1:1,19; 1Th 3:2,6; 1Ti 1:2,18; 2Ti 1:2,5,6
16:2 [t]ver 40 [u]Ac 13:51
16:3 [v]Gal 2:3
16:4 [w]Ac 11:30 [x]Ac 15:2 [y]Ac 15:28,29
16:5 [z]Ac 9:31; 15:41
16:6 [a]Ac 18:23 [b]Ac 18:23; Gal 1:2; 3:1 [c]Ac 2:9
16:7 [d]Ro 8:9; Gal 4:6
16:8 [e]ver 11; 2Co 2:12; 2Ti 4:13 **16:9** [f]Ac 9:10 [g]Ac 20:1,3

g33 Some manuscripts *them,* 34*but Silas decided to remain there*

begging him, "Come over to Macedonia
and help us." 10After Paul had seen the
vision, we[a] got ready at once to leave for
Macedonia, concluding that God had
called us to preach the gospel[b] to them.

Lydia's conversion.

11From Troas[c] we put out to sea and
sailed straight for Samothrace, and the
next day on to Neapolis. 12From there
we traveled to Philippi,[d] a Roman colony
and the leading city of that district of
Macedonia.[e] And we stayed there several days.

16:10 [a]ver 10-17 [b]Ac 14:7
16:11 [c]ver 8
16:12 [d]Ac 20:6; Php 1:1; 1Th 2:2 [e]ver 9
16:13 [f]Ac 13:14
16:14 [g]Rev 1:11 [h]Lk 24:45
16:15 [i]Ac 11:14

13On the Sabbath[f] we went outside
the city gate to the river, where we expected to find a place of prayer. We sat
down and began to speak to the wom-
en who had gathered there. 14One of
those listening was a woman named
Lydia, a dealer in purple cloth from the
city of Thyatira,[g] who was a worshiper
of God. The Lord opened her heart[h] to
respond to Paul's message. 15When she
and the members of her household[i]
were baptized, she invited us to her
home. "If you consider me a believer
in the Lord," she said, "come and stay
at my house." And she persuaded us.

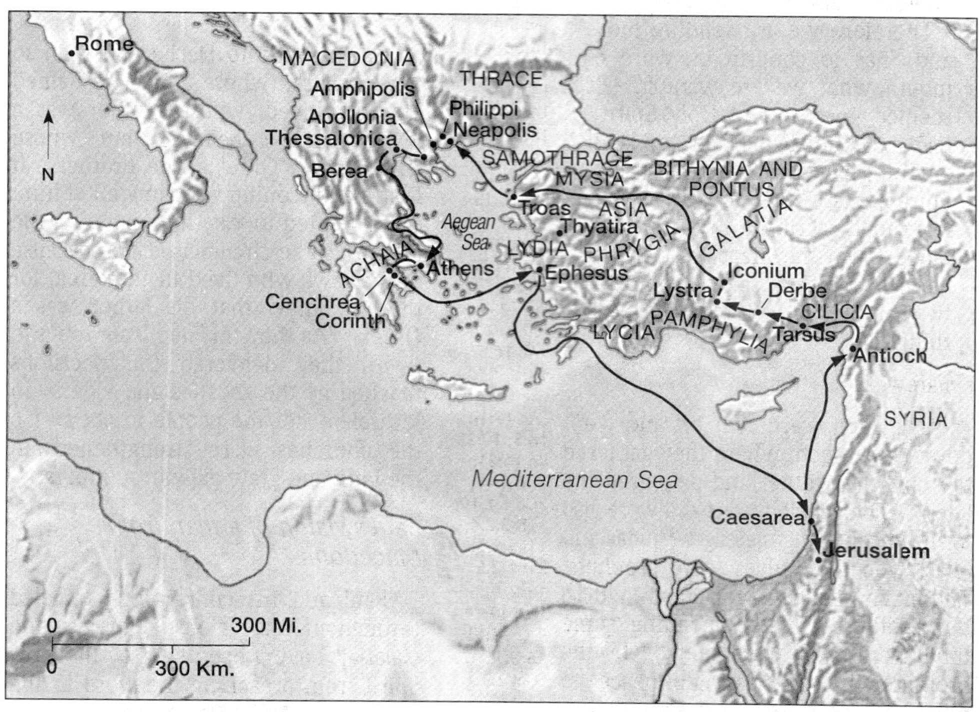

Paul's Second Missionary Journey

Paul and Silas set out on a second missionary journey to visit the cities Paul had preached in earlier. This time they set out by land rather than sea, traveling the Roman road through Cilicia and the Cilician Gates—a gorge through the Taurus Mountains—then northwest toward Derbe, Lystra, and Iconium. The Spirit told them not to go into Asia, so they turned northward toward Bithynia. Again the Spirit said no, so they turned west through Mysia to the harbor city of Troas. At Troas, Paul received the Macedonian call (16:9), and he, Silas, Timothy, and Luke boarded a ship. They sailed to the island of Samothrace, then on to Neapolis, the port for the city of Philippi. Philippi sat on the Egnatian Way, a main transportation artery connecting the eastern provinces with Italy. Luke stayed in Philippi while Paul, Silas, and Timothy continued on the Egnatian Way to Amphipolis, Apollonia, and Thessalonica. But trouble arose in Thessalonica, and they fled to Berea. When their enemies from Thessalonica pursued them, Paul set out by sea to Athens, leaving Silas and Timothy to encourage the believers. Paul left Athens and traveled on to Corinth, one of the greatest commercial centers of the empire, located on a narrow neck of land offering direct passage between the Aegean and Adriatic seas. When Paul left from the port of Corinth at Cenchrea, he visited Ephesus. He then traveled to Caesarea, from where he went on to Jerusalem to report on this trip before returning to Antioch.

Driving a demon from a slave girl.

16Once when we were going to the
place of prayer,[a] we were met by a slave
girl who had a spirit[b] by which she predicted the future. She earned a great
deal of money for her owners by for-
tune-telling. 17This girl followed Paul
and the rest of us, shouting, "These men
are servants of the Most High God,[c] who
are telling you the way to be saved."
18She kept this up for many days. Finally
Paul became so troubled that he turned
around and said to the spirit, "In the
name of Jesus Christ I command you
to come out of her!" At that moment
the spirit left her.[d]

Conversion of the Philippian jailer.

19When the owners of the slave girl
realized that their hope of making
money[e] was gone, they seized Paul and
Silas[f] and dragged[g] them into the marketplace to face the authorities. 20They
brought them before the magistrates and
said, "These men are Jews, and are
throwing our city into an uproar[h] 21by
advocating customs unlawful for us
Romans[i] to accept or practice."[j]
22The crowd joined in the attack
against Paul and Silas, and the magistrates ordered them to be stripped and
beaten.[k] 23After they had been severely flogged, they were thrown into prison,
and the jailer[l] was commanded to guard
them carefully. 24Upon receiving such
orders, he put them in the inner cell
and fastened their feet in the stocks.[m]
25About midnight Paul and Silas were
praying and singing hymns[n] to God,
and the other prisoners were listening
to them. 26Suddenly there was such a
violent earthquake that the foundations
of the prison were shaken.[o] At once all
the prison doors flew open,[p] and everybody's chains came loose.[q] 27The jailer
woke up, and when he saw the prison
doors open, he drew his sword and was
about to kill himself because he thought
the prisoners had escaped.[r] 28But Paul
shouted, "Don't harm yourself! We are
all here!"
29The jailer called for lights, rushed
in and fell trembling before Paul and
Silas. 30He then brought them out and
asked, "Sirs, what must I do to be
saved?"[s]
31They replied, "Believe in the Lord
Jesus, and you will be saved—you and
your household."[t] 32Then they spoke
the word of the Lord to him and to all
the others in his house. 33At that hour
of the night[u] the jailer took them and
washed their wounds; then immediately he and all his family were baptized. 34The jailer brought them into
his house and set a meal before them;
he[v] was filled with joy because he had
come to believe in God—he and his
whole family.
35When it was daylight, the magistrates sent their officers to the jailer with
the order: "Release those men." 36The
jailer[w] told Paul, "The magistrates have
ordered that you and Silas be released.
Now you can leave. Go in peace."[x]
37But Paul said to the officers: "They
beat us publicly without a trial, even
though we are Roman citizens,[y] and
threw us into prison. And now do they
want to get rid of us quietly? No! Let
them come themselves and escort us
out."
38The officers reported this to the
magistrates, and when they heard that
Paul and Silas were Roman citizens, they
were alarmed.[z] 39They came to appease
them and escorted them from the prison, requesting them to leave the city.[a]
40After Paul and Silas came out of the
prison, they went to Lydia's house,[b]
where they met with the brothers[c] and
encouraged them. Then they left.

Paul and Silas's ministry continues into Thessalonica, Berea and Athens.

17 When they had passed through
Amphipolis and Apollonia, they
came to Thessalonica,[d] where there was
a Jewish synagogue. 2As his custom was,
Paul went into the synagogue,[e] and on
three Sabbath[f] days he reasoned with

16:16 [a]ver 13 [b]Dt 18:11; 1Sa 28:3,7 **16:17** [c]Mk 5:7 **16:18** [d]Mk 16:17 **16:19** [e]ver 16; Ac 19:25,26 [f]Ac 15:22 [g]Ac 8:3; 17:6; 21:30; Jas 2:6 **16:20** [h]Ac 17:6 **16:21** [i]ver 12 [j]Est 3:8 **16:22** [k]2Co 11:25; 1Th 2:2 **16:23** [l]ver 27,36 **16:24** [m]Job 13:27; 33:11; Jer 20:2,3; 29:26 **16:25** [n]Eph 5:19 **16:26** [o]Ac 4:31 [p]Ac 12:10 [q]Ac 12:7 **16:27** [r]Ac 12:19 **16:30** [s]Ac 2:37 **16:31** [t]Ac 11:14 **16:33** [u]ver 25 **16:34** [v]Ac 11:14 **16:36** [w]ver 23,27 [x]Ac 15:33 **16:37** [y]Ac 22:25-29 **16:38** [z]Ac 22:29 **16:39** [a]Mt 8:34 **16:40** [b]ver 14 [c]ver 2; Ac 1:16 **17:1** [d]ver 11,13; Php 4:16; 1Th 1:1; 2Th 1:1; 2Ti 4:10 **17:2** [e]Ac 9:20 [f]Ac 13:14

them from the Scriptures,[a] 3explaining
and proving that the Christ[h] had to
suffer[b] and rise from the dead.[c] "This
Jesus I am proclaiming to you is the
Christ,[h]"[d] he said. 4Some of the Jews
were persuaded and joined Paul and
Silas,[e] as did a large number of God-fearing Greeks and not a few prominent
women.

5But the Jews were jealous; so they
rounded up some bad characters from
the marketplace, formed a mob and
started a riot in the city.[f] They rushed
to Jason's[g] house in search of Paul
and Silas in order to bring them out
to the crowd.[i] 6But when they did
not find them, they dragged[h] Jason and
some other brothers before the city
officials, shouting: "These men who
have caused trouble all over the world[i]
have now come here,[j] 7and Jason has
welcomed them into his house. They
are all defying Caesar's decrees, saying
that there is another king, one called
Jesus."[k] 8When they heard this, the
crowd and the city officials were
thrown into turmoil. 9Then they made
Jason[l] and the others post bond and let
them go.

10As soon as it was night, the brothers sent Paul and Silas away to Berea.[m]
On arriving there, they went to the
Jewish synagogue. 11Now the Bereans
were of more noble character than the
Thessalonians,[n] for they received the
message with great eagerness and examined the Scriptures[o] every day to see if
what Paul said was true. 12Many of the
Jews believed, as did also a number of
prominent Greek women and many
Greek men.

13When the Jews in Thessalonica
learned that Paul was preaching the
word of God at Berea, they went there
too, agitating the crowds and stirring
them up. 14The brothers immediately
sent Paul to the coast, but Silas[p] and
Timothy[q] stayed at Berea. 15The men
who escorted Paul brought him to
Athens[r] and then left with instructions
for Silas and Timothy to join him as soon
as possible.[s]

17:2 [a]Ac 8:35
17:3 [b]Lk 24:26; Ac 3:18 [c]Lk 24:46 [d]Ac 9:22; 18:28
17:4 [e]Ac 15:22
17:5 [f]ver 13; 1Th 2:16 [g]Ro 16:21
17:6 [h]Ac 16:19 [i]Mt 24:14 [j]Ac 16:20
17:7 [k]Lk 23:2; Jn 19:12
17:9 [l]ver 5
17:10 [m]ver 13; Ac 20:4
17:11 [n]ver 1 [o]Lk 16:29; Jn 5:39
17:14 [p]Ac 15:22 [q]Ac 16:1
17:15 [r]ver 16,21,22; Ac 18:1; 1Th 3:1 [s]Ac 18:5
17:17 [t]Ac 9:20
17:18 [u]ver 31,32; Ac 4:2
17:19 [v]ver 22 [w]Mk 1:27
17:23 [x]Jn 4:22
17:24 [y]Isa 42:5; Ac 14:15 [z]Dt 10:14; Mt 11:25 [a]Ac 7:48
17:25 [b]Ps 50:10-12; Isa 42:5
17:26 [c]Dt 32:8; Job 12:23

Paul gives a sermon to the Athenians.

16While Paul was waiting for them in
Athens, he was greatly distressed to see
that the city was full of idols. 17So he
reasoned in the synagogue[t] with the
Jews and the God-fearing Greeks, as well
as in the marketplace day by day with
those who happened to be there. 18A
group of Epicurean and Stoic philoso-
phers began to dispute with him. Some
of them asked, "What is this babbler
trying to say?" Others remarked, "He
seems to be advocating foreign gods."
They said this because Paul was preaching the good news about Jesus and the
resurrection.[u] 19Then they took him and
brought him to a meeting of the Areopagus,[v] where they said to him, "May
we know what this new teaching[w] is that
you are presenting? 20You are bringing
some strange ideas to our ears, and we
want to know what they mean." 21(All
the Athenians and the foreigners who
lived there spent their time doing nothing but talking about and listening to the
latest ideas.)

22Paul then stood up in the meeting
of the Areopagus and said: "Men of
Athens! I see that in every way you are
very religious. 23For as I walked around
and looked carefully at your objects of
worship, I even found an altar with
this inscription: TO AN UNKNOWN GOD.
Now what you worship as something
unknown[x] I am going to proclaim to
you.

24"The God who made the world and
everything in it[y] is the Lord of heaven
and earth[z] and does not live in temples
built by hands.[a] 25And he is not served
by human hands, as if he needed anything, because he himself gives all men
life and breath and everything else.[b]
26From one man he made every nation of
men, that they should inhabit the whole
earth; and he determined the times set
for them and the exact places where they
should live.[c] 27God did this so that men
would seek him and perhaps reach out

h3 Or *Messiah* i5 Or *the assembly of the people*

for him and find him, though he is not far from each one of us.[a] **28**‘For in him we live and move and have our being.’[b] As some of your own poets have said, ‘We are his offspring.’

29“Therefore since we are God’s offspring, we should not think that the divine being is like gold or silver or stone—an image made by man’s design and skill.[c] **30**In the past God overlooked[d] such ignorance,[e] but now he commands all people everywhere to repent.[f] **31**For he has set a day when he will judge[g] the world with justice[h] by the man he has appointed.[i] He has given proof of this to all men by raising him from the dead.”[j]

32When they heard about the resurrection of the dead,[k] some of them sneered, but others said, “We want to hear you again on this subject.” **33**At that, Paul left the Council. **34**A few men became followers of Paul and believed. Among them was Dionysius, a member of the Areopagus,[l] also a woman named Damaris, and a number of others.

Paul works with Aquila and Priscilla.

18 After this, Paul left Athens[m] and went to Corinth.[n] **2**There he met a Jew named Aquila, a native of Pontus, who had recently come from Italy with his wife Priscilla,[o] because Claudius[p] had ordered all the Jews to leave Rome. Paul went to see them, **3**and because he was a tentmaker as they were, he stayed and worked with them.[q] **4**Every Sabbath[r] he reasoned in the synagogue, trying to persuade Jews and Greeks.

5When Silas[s] and Timothy[t] came from Macedonia,[u] Paul devoted himself exclusively to preaching, testifying to the Jews that Jesus was the Christ.[j][v] **6**But when the Jews opposed Paul and became abusive,[w] he shook out his clothes in protest and said to them, “Your blood be on your own heads![x] I am clear of my responsibility.[y] From now on I will go to the Gentiles.”[z]

7Then Paul left the synagogue and went next door to the house of Titius Justus, a worshiper of God.[a] **8**Crispus,[b] the synagogue ruler,[c] and his entire household[d] believed in the Lord; and many of the Corinthians who heard him believed and were baptized.

9One night the Lord spoke to Paul in a vision: “Do not be afraid; keep on speaking, do not be silent. **10**For I am with you,[e] and no one is going to attack and harm you, because I have many people in this city.” **11**So Paul stayed for a year and a half, teaching them the word of God.

Gallio, the proconsul, releases Paul.

12While Gallio was proconsul of Achaia,[f] the Jews made a united attack on Paul and brought him into court. **13**“This man,” they charged, “is persuading the people to worship God in ways contrary to the law.”

14Just as Paul was about to speak, Gallio said to the Jews, “If you Jews were making a complaint about some misdemeanor or serious crime, it would be reasonable for me to listen to you. **15**But since it involves questions about words and names and your own law[g]—settle the matter yourselves. I will not be a judge of such things.” **16**So he had them ejected from the court. **17**Then they all turned on Sosthenes[h] the synagogue ruler and beat him in front of the court. But Gallio showed no concern whatever.

18Paul stayed on in Corinth for some time. Then he left the brothers[i] and sailed for Syria, accompanied by Priscilla and Aquila. Before he sailed, he had his hair cut off at Cenchrea[j] because of a vow he had taken.[k] **19**They arrived at Ephesus,[l] where Paul left Priscilla and Aquila. He himself went into the synagogue and reasoned with the Jews. **20**When they asked him to spend more time with them, he declined. **21**But as

17:27 [a]Dt 4:7; Jer 23:23,24; Ac 14:17
17:28 [b]Job 12:10; Da 5:23
17:29 [c]Isa 40:18-20; Ro 1:23
17:30 [d]Ac 14:16; Ro 3:25 [e]ver 23; 1Pe 1:14 [f]Lk 24:47; Tit 2:11,12
17:31 [g]Mt 10:15 [h]Ps 9:8; 96:13; 98:9 [i]Ac 10:42 [j]Ac 2:24
17:32 [k]ver 18,31
17:34 [l]ver 19,22
18:1 [m]Ac 17:15 [n]Ac 19:1; 1Co 1:2; 2Co 1:1,23; 2Ti 4:20
18:2 [o]Ro 16:3; 1Co 16:19; 2Ti 4:19 [p]Ac 11:28
18:3 [q]Ac 20:34; 1Co 4:12; 1Th 2:9; 2Th 3:8
18:4 [r]Ac 13:14
18:5 [s]Ac 15:22 [t]Ac 16:1 [u]Ac 16:9; 17:14,15 [v]ver 28; Ac 17:3
18:6 [w]Ac 13:45 [x]2Sa 1:16; Eze 18:13; 33:4 [y]Ac 20:26 [z]Ac 13:46
18:7 [a]Ac 16:14
18:8 [b]1Co 1:14 [c]Mk 5:22 [d]Ac 11:14
18:10 [e]Mt 28:20
18:12 [f]ver 27
18:15 [g]Ac 23:29; 25:11,19 **18:17** [h]1Co 1:1
18:18 [i]Ac 1:16 [j]Ro 16:1 [k]Nu 6:2,5,18; Ac 21:24
18:19 [l]ver 21,24; 1Co 15:32

j5 Or *Messiah;* also in verse 28

he left, he promised, "I will come back if it is God's will."[a] Then he set sail from Ephesus. 22When he landed at Caesarea,[b] he went up and greeted the church and then went down to Antioch.[c]

23After spending some time in Antioch, Paul set out from there and traveled from place to place throughout the region of Galatia[d] and Phrygia, strengthening all the disciples.[e]

Apollos ministers in Ephesus.

24Meanwhile a Jew named Apollos,[f] a native of Alexandria, came to Ephesus. He was a learned man, with a thorough knowledge of the Scriptures. 25He had been instructed in the way of the Lord, and he spoke with great fervor[k][g] and taught about Jesus accurately, though he knew only the baptism of John.[h] 26He began to speak boldly in the synagogue. When Priscilla and Aquila heard him, they invited him to their home and explained to him the way of God more adequately.

27When Apollos wanted to go to Achaia,[i] the brothers[j] encouraged him and wrote to the disciples there to welcome him. On arriving, he was a great help to those who by grace had believed. 28For he vigorously refuted the Jews in public debate, proving from the Scriptures[k] that Jesus was the Christ.[l]

Paul lays hands on disciples of John the Baptist.

19 While Apollos was at Corinth,[m] Paul took the road through the interior and arrived at Ephesus.[n] There he found some disciples 2and asked them, "Did you receive the Holy Spirit when[l] you believed?"

They answered, "No, we have not even heard that there is a Holy Spirit."

3So Paul asked, "Then what baptism did you receive?"

"John's baptism," they replied.

4Paul said, "John's baptism was a baptism of repentance. He told the people to believe in the one coming after him, that is, in Jesus."[o] 5On hearing this, they were baptized into[m] the name of the Lord Jesus. 6When Paul placed his hands on them,[p] the Holy Spirit came on them,[q] and they spoke in tongues[n][r] and prophesied. 7There were about twelve men in all.

8Paul entered the synagogue[s] and spoke boldly there for three months, arguing persuasively about the kingdom of God.[t] 9But some of them[u] became obstinate; they refused to believe and publicly maligned the Way.[v] So Paul left them. He took the disciples[w] with him and had discussions daily in the lecture hall of Tyrannus. 10This went on for two years,[x] so that all the Jews and Greeks who lived in the province of Asia[y] heard the word of the Lord.

God performs extraordinary miracles through Paul.

11God did extraordinary miracles[z] through Paul, 12so that even handkerchiefs and aprons that had touched him were taken to the sick, and their illnesses were cured[a] and the evil spirits left them.

13Some Jews who went around driving out evil spirits[b] tried to invoke the name of the Lord Jesus over those who were demon-possessed. They would say, "In the name of Jesus,[c] whom Paul preaches, I command you to come out." 14Seven sons of Sceva, a Jewish chief priest, were doing this. 15⌊One day⌋ the evil spirit answered them, "Jesus I know, and I know about Paul, but who are you?" 16Then the man who had the evil spirit jumped on them and overpowered them all. He gave them such a beating that they ran out of the house naked and bleeding.

17When this became known to the Jews and Greeks living in Ephesus,[d] they were all seized with fear,[e] and the name of the Lord Jesus was held in high honor. 18Many of those who believed now came and openly confessed their evil deeds. 19A number who had practiced sorcery brought their scrolls

18:21 [a]Ro 1:10; 1Co 4:19; Jas 4:15
18:22 [b]Ac 8:40 [c]Ac 11:19
18:23 [d]Ac 16:6 [e]Ac 14:22; 15:32,41
18:24 [f]Ac 19:1; 1Co 1:12; 3:5,6,22; 4:6; 16:12; Tit 3:13
18:25 [g]Ro 12:11 [h]Ac 19:3
18:27 [i]ver 12 [j]ver 18
18:28 [k]Ac 17:2 [l]ver 5; Ac 9:22
19:1 [m]Ac 18:1 [n]Ac 18:19
19:4 [o]Jn 1:7; Ac 13:24,25
19:6 [p]Ac 6:6; 8:17 [q]Ac 2:4 [r]Mk 16:17; Ac 10:46
19:8 [s]Ac 9:20 [t]Ac 1:3; 28:23
19:9 [u]Ac 14:4 [v]ver 23; Ac 9:2 [w]ver 30; Ac 11:26
19:10 [x]Ac 20:31 [y]ver 22,26,27
19:11 [z]Ac 8:13
19:12 [a]Ac 5:15
19:13 [b]Mt 12:27 [c]Mk 9:38
19:17 [d]Ac 18:19 [e]Ac 5:5,11

[k]25 Or *with fervor in the Spirit* [l]2 Or *after*
[m]5 Or *in* [n]6 Or *other languages*

together and burned them publicly.
When they calculated the value of the
scrolls, the total came to fifty thousand
drachmas.[o] 20In this way the word of the
Lord spread widely and grew in power.[a]

21After all this had happened, Paul
decided to go to Jerusalem,[b] passing
through Macedonia[c] and Achaia.[d] "After
I have been there," he said, "I must
visit Rome also."[e] 22He sent two of his
helpers,[f] Timothy[g] and Erastus,[h] to Macedonia, while he stayed in the province
of Asia[i] a little longer.

Demetrius, a silversmith, causes an uproar at Ephesus.

23About that time there arose a great
disturbance about the Way.[j] 24A silversmith named Demetrius, who made silver shrines of Artemis, brought in no
little business for the craftsmen. 25He
called them together, along with the
workmen in related trades, and said:
"Men, you know we receive a good income from this business.[k] 26And you see
and hear how this fellow Paul has convinced and led astray large numbers of
people here in Ephesus[l] and in practi-
cally the whole province of Asia. He says
that man-made gods are no gods at all.[m]
27There is danger not only that our trade

19:20 [a]Ac 6:7; 12:24
19:21 [b]Ac 20:16,22; Ro 15:25 [c]Ac 16:9 [d]Ac 18:12 [e]Ro 15:24,28
19:22 [f]Ac 13:5 [g]Ac 16:1 [h]Ro 16:23; 2Ti 4:20 [i]ver 10,26,27
19:23 [j]Ac 9:2
19:25 [k]Ac 16:16, 19,20
19:26 [l]Ac 18:19 [m]Dt 4:28; Ps 115:4; Isa 44:10-20; Jer 10:3-5; Ac 17:29; 1Co 8:4; Rev 9:20

[o]*19* A drachma was a silver coin worth about a day's wages.

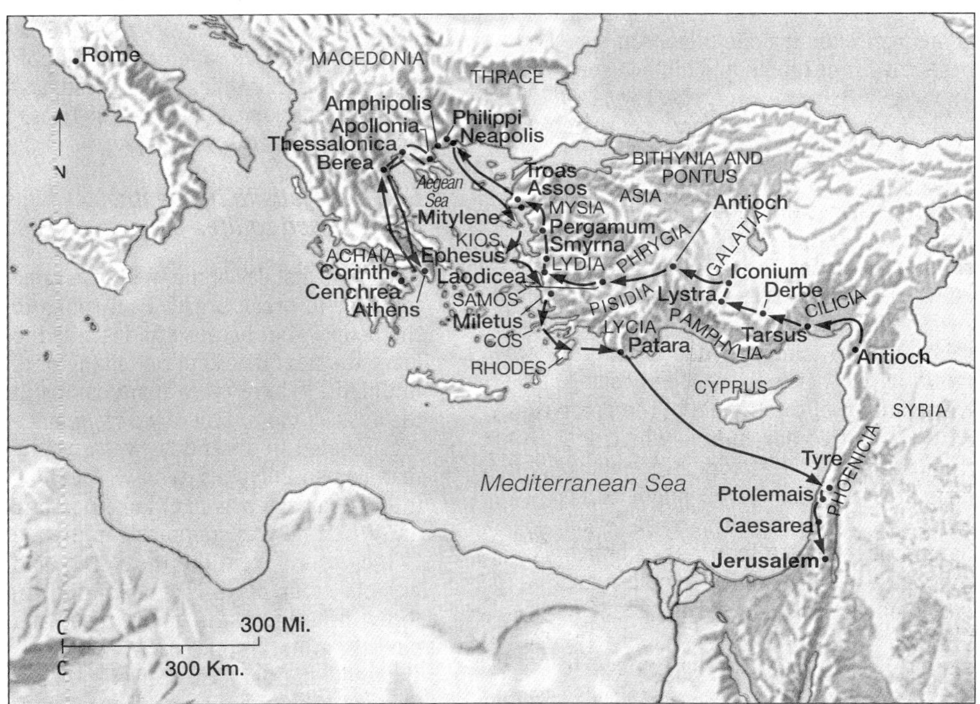

Paul's Third Missionary Journey

What prompted Paul's third journey may have been the need to correct any misunderstanding in the churches Paul had planted. So he hurried north, then west, returning to many of the cities he had previously visited. This time, however, he stayed on a more direct westward route toward Ephesus. A riot in Ephesus sent Paul to Troas, then through Macedonia to the region of Achaia. In Achaia he went to Corinth to deal with problems there. Paul had planned to sail from there straight to Antioch in Syria, but a plot against his life was discovered. So he retraced his steps through Macedonia. From Troas, Paul traveled overland to Assos, then boarded a ship to Mitylene and Samos on its way to Miletus. He summoned the elders of Ephesian church to say farewell to them, because he knew he would probably not see them again. The ship sailed from Miletus to Cos, Rhodes, and Patara. Paul and his companions then boarded a cargo ship bound for Phoenicia. They passed Cyprus and landed at Tyre, then Ptolemais, and finally Caesarea, where Paul disembarked and returned by land to Jerusalem.

will lose its good name, but also that
the temple of the great goddess Artemis
will be discredited, and the goddess
herself, who is worshiped throughout
the province of Asia and the world,
will be robbed of her divine majesty."
28When they heard this, they were
furious and began shouting: "Great is
Artemis of the Ephesians!"[a] 29Soon the
whole city was in an uproar. The people
seized Gaius[b] and Aristarchus,[c] Paul's traveling companions from Macedonia,[d] and
rushed as one man into the theater. 30Paul
wanted to appear before the crowd, but
the disciples would not let him. 31Even
some of the officials of the province,
friends of Paul, sent him a message begging him not to venture into the theater.
32The assembly was in confusion:
Some were shouting one thing, some another.[e] Most of the people did not even
know why they were there. 33The Jews
pushed Alexander to the front, and some
of the crowd shouted instructions to him.
He motioned[f] for silence in order to make
a defense before the people. 34But when
they realized he was a Jew, they all
shouted in unison for about two hours:
"Great is Artemis of the Ephesians!"
35The city clerk quieted the crowd and
said: "Men of Ephesus,[g] doesn't all the
world know that the city of Ephesus is
the guardian of the temple of the great
Artemis and of her image, which fell
from heaven? 36Therefore, since these
facts are undeniable, you ought to be
quiet and not do anything rash. 37You
have brought these men here, though
they have neither robbed temples[h] nor
blasphemed our goddess. 38If, then, Demetrius and his fellow craftsmen have
a grievance against anybody, the courts
are open and there are proconsuls.[i]
They can press charges. 39If there is anything further you want to bring up, it
must be settled in a legal assembly. 40As
it is, we are in danger of being charged
with rioting because of today's events.
In that case we would not be able to
account for this commotion, since there
is no reason for it." 41After he had said
this, he dismissed the assembly.

Paul ministers in Greece and Macedonia.

20 When the uproar had ended,
Paul sent for the disciples[j] and,
after encouraging them, said good-by
and set out for Macedonia.[k] 2He traveled
through that area, speaking many words
of encouragement to the people, and
finally arrived in Greece, 3where he
stayed three months. Because the Jews
made a plot against him[l] just as he was
about to sail for Syria, he decided to go
back through Macedonia.[m] 4He was accompanied by Sopater son of Pyrrhus
from Berea, Aristarchus[n] and Secundus
from Thessalonica,[o] Gaius[p] from Derbe,
Timothy[q] also, and Tychicus[r] and Trophimus[s] from the province of Asia. 5These
men went on ahead and waited for us[t]
at Troas.[u] 6But we sailed from Philippi[v]
after the Feast of Unleavened Bread, and
five days later joined the others at Troas,[w]
where we stayed seven days.

Eutychus falls to his death, but is raised to life.

7On the first day of the week[x] we came
together to break bread. Paul spoke to
the people and, because he intended to
leave the next day, kept on talking until
midnight. 8There were many lamps in
the upstairs room[y] where we were meeting. 9Seated in a window was a young
man named Eutychus, who was sinking
into a deep sleep as Paul talked on and
on. When he was sound asleep, he fell
to the ground from the third story and
was picked up dead. 10Paul went down,
threw himself on the young man[z] and
put his arms around him. "Don't be
alarmed," he said. "He's alive!"[a] 11Then
he went upstairs again and broke bread[b]
and ate. After talking until daylight, he
left. 12The people took the young man
home alive and were greatly comforted.

Paul gives a farewell message to the Ephesian elders.

13We went on ahead to the ship and
sailed for Assos, where we were going

19:28 [a]Ac 18:19
19:29 [b]Ac 20:4; Ro 16:23; 1Co 1:14 [c]Ac 20:4; 27:2; Col 4:10; Phm 24 [d]Ac 16:9
19:32 [e]Ac 21:34
19:33 [f]Ac 12:17
19:35 [g]Ac 18:19
19:37 [h]Ro 2:22
19:38 [i]Ac 13:7,8,12
20:1 [j]Ac 11:26 [k]Ac 16:9
20:3 [l]ver 19; Ac 9:23,24; 23:12,15, 30; 25:3; 2Co 11:26 [m]Ac 16:9
20:4 [n]Ac 19:29 [o]Ac 17:1 [p]Ac 19:29 [q]Ac 16:1 [r]Eph 6:21; Col 4:7; 2Ti 4:12; Tit 3:12 [s]Ac 21:29; 2Ti 4:20
20:5 [t]Ac 16:10 [u]Ac 16:8
20:6 [v]Ac 16:12 [w]Ac 16:8
20:7 [x]1Co 16:2; Rev 1:10
20:8 [y]Ac 1:13
20:10 [z]1Ki 17:21; 2Ki 4:34 [a]Mt 9:23,24
20:11 [b]ver 7

to take Paul aboard. He had made this
arrangement because he was going there
on foot. 14When he met us at Assos, we
took him aboard and went on to Mitylene. 15The next day we set sail from
there and arrived off Kios. The day after
that we crossed over to Samos, and on
the following day arrived at Miletus.[a]
16Paul had decided to sail past Ephesus[b]
to avoid spending time in the province
of Asia, for he was in a hurry to reach
Jerusalem,[c] if possible, by the day of
Pentecost.[d]

17From Miletus, Paul sent to Ephesus
for the elders[e] of the church. 18When
they arrived, he said to them: "You know
how I lived the whole time I was with
you,[f] from the first day I came into the
province of Asia. 19I served the Lord with
great humility and with tears, although
I was severely tested by the plots of the
Jews.[g] 20You know that I have not hesitated to preach anything[h] that would be
helpful to you but have taught you publicly and from house to house. 21I have
declared to both Jews[i] and Greeks that
they must turn to God in repentance[j]
and have faith in our Lord Jesus.[k]

22"And now, compelled by the Spirit, I am going to Jerusalem,[l] not knowing what will happen to me there. 23I
only know that in every city the Holy
Spirit warns me[m] that prison and hardships are facing me.[n] 24However, I consider my life worth nothing to me,[o] if
only I may finish the race and complete
the task[p] the Lord Jesus has given me[q]—
the task of testifying to the gospel of
God's grace.

25"Now I know that none of you
among whom I have gone about preaching the kingdom will ever see me again.[r]
26Therefore, I declare to you today that
I am innocent of the blood of all men.[s]
27For I have not hesitated to proclaim
to you the whole will of God.[t] 28Keep
watch over yourselves and all the flock
of which the Holy Spirit has made you
overseers.[p][u] Be shepherds of the church
of God,[q] which he bought with his own
blood. 29I know that after I leave, savage wolves[v] will come in among you and
will not spare the flock.[w] 30Even from
your own number men will arise and
distort the truth in order to draw away
disciples[x] after them. 31So be on your
guard! Remember that for three years[y]
I never stopped warning each of you
night and day with tears.[z]

32"Now I commit you to God[a] and to
the word of his grace, which can build
you up and give you an inheritance[b]
among all those who are sanctified.[c] 33I
have not coveted anyone's silver or gold
or clothing.[d] 34You yourselves know that
these hands of mine have supplied my
own needs and the needs of my companions.[e] 35In everything I did, I showed
you that by this kind of hard work we
must help the weak, remembering the
words the Lord Jesus himself said: 'It
is more blessed to give than to receive.'"

36When he had said this, he knelt
down with all of them and prayed.[f]
37They all wept as they embraced him
and kissed him.[g] 38What grieved them
most was his statement that they would
never see his face again.[h] Then they
accompanied him to the ship.

Paul is warned to avoid Jerusalem.

21 After we[i] had torn ourselves
away from them, we put out to
sea and sailed straight to Cos. The next
day we went to Rhodes and from there
to Patara. 2We found a ship crossing over
to Phoenicia,[j] went on board and set
sail. 3After sighting Cyprus and passing
to the south of it, we sailed on to Syria.
We landed at Tyre, where our ship was
to unload its cargo. 4Finding the disciples[k] there, we stayed with them sev-
en days. Through the Spirit[l] they urged
Paul not to go on to Jerusalem. 5But
when our time was up, we left and continued on our way. All the disciples and
their wives and children accompanied
us out of the city, and there on the beach
we knelt to pray.[m] 6After saying good-by

20:15 [a]ver 17; 2Ti 4:20 **20:16** [b]Ac 18:19 [c]Ac 19:21 [d]Ac 2:1; 1Co 16:8 **20:17** [e]Ac 11:30 **20:18** [f]Ac 18:19-21; 19:1-41 **20:19** [g]ver 3 **20:20** [h]ver 27 **20:21** [i]Ac 18:5 [j]Ac 2:38 [k]Ac 24:24; 26:18; Eph 1:15; Col 2:5; Phm 5 **20:22** [l]ver 16 **20:23** [m]Ac 21:4 [n]Ac 9:16 **20:24** [o]Ac 21:13 [p]2Co 4:1 [q]Gal 1:1; Tit 1:3 **20:25** [r]ver 38 **20:26** [s]Ac 18:6 **20:27** [t]ver 20 **20:28** [u]1Pe 5:2 **20:29** [v]Mt 7:15 [w]ver 28 **20:30** [x]Ac 11:26 **20:31** [y]Ac 19:10 [z]ver 19 **20:32** [a]Ac 14:23 [b]Eph 1:14; Col 1:12; 3:24; Heb 9:15; 1Pe 1:4 [c]Ac 26:18 **20:33** [d]1Sa 12:3; 1Co 9:12; 2Co 7:2; 11:9; 12:14-17 **20:34** [e]Ac 18:3 **20:36** [f]Lk 22:41; Ac 21:5

20:37 [g]Lk 15:20 **20:38** [h]ver 25 **21:1** [i]Ac 16:10 **21:2** [j]Ac 11:19 **21:4** [k]Ac 11:26 [l]ver 11; Ac 20:23 **21:5** [m]Ac 20:36

[p]*28* Traditionally *bishops* [q]*28* Many manuscripts *of the Lord*

to each other, we went aboard the ship,
and they returned home.
7We continued our voyage from Tyre[a]
and landed at Ptolemais, where we
greeted the brothers[b] and stayed with
them for a day. 8Leaving the next day,
we reached Caesarea[c] and stayed at the
house of Philip[d] the evangelist,[e] one of
the Seven. 9He had four unmarried
daughters who prophesied.[f]
10After we had been there a number
of days, a prophet named Agabus[g] came
down from Judea. 11Coming over to us,
he took Paul's belt, tied his own hands
and feet with it and said, "The Holy
Spirit says, 'In this way the Jews of Jerusalem
will bind[h] the owner of this
belt and will hand him over to the
Gentiles.'"[i]
12When we heard this, we and the
people there pleaded with Paul not to go
up to Jerusalem. 13Then Paul answered,
"Why are you weeping and breaking my
heart? I am ready not only to be bound,
but also to die[j] in Jerusalem for the
name of the Lord Jesus."[k] 14When he
would not be dissuaded, we gave up and
said, "The Lord's will be done."
15After this, we got ready and went
up to Jerusalem. 16Some of the disciples
from Caesarea[l] accompanied us and
brought us to the home of Mnason,
where we were to stay. He was a man
from Cyprus[m] and one of the early disciples.
17When we arrived at Jerusalem, the
brothers received us warmly.[n] 18The next
day Paul and the rest of us went to see
James,[o] and all the elders[p] were present.
19Paul greeted them and reported in
detail what God had done among the
Gentiles[q] through his ministry.[r]
20When they heard this, they praised
God. Then they said to Paul: "You see,
brother, how many thousands of Jews
have believed, and all of them are zealous[s]
for the law.[t] 21They have been informed
that you teach all the Jews who
live among the Gentiles to turn away
from Moses,[u] telling them not to circumcise
their children[v] or live according
to our customs.[w] 22What shall we do?
They will certainly hear that you have
come, 23so do what we tell you. There
are four men with us who have made a
vow.[x] 24Take these men, join in their
purification rites[y] and pay their expenses,
so that they can have their heads
shaved.[z] Then everybody will know
there is no truth in these reports about
you, but that you yourself are living in
obedience to the law. 25As for the Gentile
believers, we have written to them
our decision that they should abstain
from food sacrificed to idols, from
blood, from the meat of strangled animals
and from sexual immorality."[a]
26The next day Paul took the men and
purified himself along with them. Then
he went to the temple to give notice of
the date when the days of purification
would end and the offering would be
made for each of them.[b]

Paul is beaten by mob, then arrested.

27When the seven days were nearly
over, some Jews from the province of Asia
saw Paul at the temple. They stirred up
the whole crowd and seized him,[c]
28shouting, "Men of Israel, help us! This
is the man who teaches all men everywhere
against our people and our law
and this place. And besides, he has
brought Greeks into the temple area
and defiled this holy place."[d] 29(They
had previously seen Trophimus[e] the
Ephesian[f] in the city with Paul and
assumed that Paul had brought him into
the temple area.)
30The whole city was aroused, and the
people came running from all directions.
Seizing Paul,[g] they dragged him[h] from
the temple, and immediately the gates
were shut. 31While they were trying to
kill him, news reached the commander
of the Roman troops that the whole
city of Jerusalem was in an uproar. 32He
at once took some officers and soldiers
and ran down to the crowd. When the
rioters saw the commander and his soldiers,
they stopped beating Paul.[i]
33The commander came up and arrested
him and ordered him to be bound[j]

21:7 [a]Ac 12:20 [b]Ac 1:16
21:8 [c]Ac 8:40 [d]Ac 6:5; 8:5-40 [e]Eph 4:11; 2Ti 4:5
21:9 [f]Lk 2:36; Ac 2:17
21:10 [g]Ac 11:28
21:11 [h]ver 33 [i]1Ki 22:11
21:13 [j]Ac 20:24 [k]Ac 9:16
21:16 [l]Ac 8:40 [m]ver 3,4
21:17 [n]Ac 15:4
21:18 [o]Ac 15:13 [p]Ac 11:30
21:19 [q]Ac 14:27 [r]Ac 1:17
21:20 [s]Ac 22:3; Ro 10:2; Gal 1:14 [t]Ac 15:1,5
21:21 [u]ver 28 [v]Ac 15:19-21; 1Co 7:18,19 [w]Ac 6:14
21:23 [x]Ac 18:18
21:24 [y]ver 26; Ac 24:18 [z]Ac 18:18
21:25 [a]Ac 15:20,29
21:26 [b]Nu 6:13-20; Ac 24:18
21:27 [c]Ac 24:18; 26:21
21:28 [d]Mt 24:15; Ac 24:5,6
21:29 [e]Ac 20:4 [f]Ac 18:19
21:30 [g]Ac 26:21 [h]Ac 16:19
21:32 [i]Ac 23:27
21:33 [j]ver 11

with two[a] chains.[b] Then he asked who
he was and what he had done. 34Some
in the crowd shouted one thing and
some another,[c] and since the commander could not get at the truth because of
the uproar, he ordered that Paul be
taken into the barracks.[d] 35When Paul
reached the steps,[e] the violence of the
mob was so great he had to be carried
by the soldiers. 36The crowd that followed kept shouting, "Away with him!"[f]

Paul tells his conversion story.

22:3-16pp— Ac 9:1-22; 26:9-18

37As the soldiers were about to take
Paul into the barracks,[g] he asked the commander, "May I say something to you?"
"Do you speak Greek?" he replied.
38"Aren't you the Egyptian who started
a revolt and led four thousand terrorists
out into the desert[h] some time ago?"[i]
39Paul answered, "I am a Jew, from
Tarsus[j] in Cilicia,[k] a citizen of no ordinary
city. Please let me speak to the people."
40Having received the commander's
permission, Paul stood on the steps
and motioned[l] to the crowd. When they
were all silent, he said to them in Ara-
22 maic[r]:[m] 1"Brothers and fathers,[n]
listen now to my defense."
2When they heard him speak to them
in Aramaic,[o] they became very quiet.
Then Paul said: 3"I am a Jew,[p] born
in Tarsus[q] of Cilicia, but brought up in
this city. Under[r] Gamaliel[s] I was thoroughly trained in the law of our fathers[t]
and was just as zealous[u] for God as any
of you are today. 4I persecuted[v] the followers of this Way to their death, arresting both men and women and throwing
them into prison,[w] 5as also the high
priest and all the Council[x] can testify. I
even obtained letters from them to their
brothers[y] in Damascus,[z] and went there
to bring these people as prisoners to
Jerusalem to be punished.
6"About noon as I came near Damascus, suddenly a bright light from heav-
en flashed around me.[a] 7I fell to the
ground and heard a voice say to me,
'Saul! Saul! Why do you persecute me?'
8"'Who are you, Lord?' I asked.
"'I am Jesus of Nazareth, whom you
are persecuting,' he replied. 9My companions saw the light,[b] but they did not
understand the voice[c] of him who was
speaking to me.
10"'What shall I do, Lord?' I asked.
"'Get up,' the Lord said, 'and go into
Damascus. There you will be told all
that you have been assigned to do.'[d]
11My companions led me by the hand
into Damascus, because the brilliance
of the light had blinded me.[e]
12"A man named Ananias came to see
me.[f] He was a devout observer of the
law and highly respected by all the Jews
living there.[g] 13He stood beside me and
said, 'Brother Saul, receive your sight!'
And at that very moment I was able to
see him.
14"Then he said: 'The God of our fathers[h] has chosen you to know his will
and to see[i] the Righteous One[j] and to
hear words from his mouth. 15You will
be his witness[k] to all men of what you
have seen and heard. 16And now what
are you waiting for? Get up, be baptized[l] and wash your sins away,[m] calling
on his name.'[n]
17"When I returned to Jerusalem[o] and
was praying at the temple, I fell into a
trance[p] 18and saw the Lord speaking.
'Quick!' he said to me. 'Leave Jerusalem immediately, because they will not
accept your testimony about me.'
19"'Lord,' I replied, 'these men know
that I went from one synagogue to another to imprison[q] and beat[r] those who believe in you. 20And when the blood of
your martyr[s] Stephen was shed, I stood
there giving my approval and guarding
the clothes of those who were killing
him.'[s]
21"Then the Lord said to me, 'Go; I
will send you far away to the Gentiles.'"[t]

21:33 [a]Ac 12:6 [b]Ac 20:23; Eph 6:20; 2Ti 2:9 **21:34** [c]Ac 19:32 [d]ver 37; Ac 23:10, 16,32 **21:35** [e]ver 40 **21:36** [f]Lk 23:18; Jn 19:15; Ac 22:22 **21:37** [g]ver 34 **21:38** [h]Mt 24:26 [i]Ac 5:36 **21:39** [j]Ac 9:11 [k]Ac 22:3 **21:40** [l]Ac 12:17 [m]Jn 5:2 **22:1** [n]Ac 7:2 **22:2** [o]Ac 21:40 **22:3** [p]Ac 21:39 [q]Ac 9:11 [r]Lk 10:39 [s]Ac 5:34 [t]Ac 26:5 [u]Ac 21:20 **22:4** [v]Ac 8:3 [w]ver 19,20 **22:5** [x]Lk 22:66 [y]Ac 13:26 [z]Ac 9:2 **22:6** [a]Ac 9:3 **22:9** [b]Ac 26:13 [c]Ac 9:7 **22:10** [d]Ac 16:30 **22:11** [e]Ac 9:8 **22:12** [f]Ac 9:17 [g]Ac 10:22 **22:14** [h]Ac 3:13 [i]1Co 9:1; 15:8 [j]Ac 7:52 **22:15** [k]Ac 23:11; 26:16 **22:16** [l]Ac 2:38 [m]Heb 10:22 [n]Ro 10:13

22:17 [o]Ac 9:26 [p]Ac 10:10 **22:19** [q]ver 4; Ac 8:3 [r]Mt 10:17 **22:20** [s]Ac 7:57-60; 8:1 **22:21** [t]Ac 9:15; 13:46

[r]*40* Or possibly *Hebrew*; also in 22:2 [s]*20* Or *witness*

Paul announces his Roman citizenship.

22The crowd listened to Paul until he said this. Then they raised their voices and shouted, "Rid the earth of him![a] He's not fit to live!"[b]

23As they were shouting and throwing off their cloaks[c] and flinging dust into the air,[d] 24the commander ordered Paul to be taken into the barracks.[e] He directed[f] that he be flogged and questioned in order to find out why the people were shouting at him like this. 25As they stretched him out to flog him, Paul said to the centurion standing there, "Is it legal for you to flog a Roman citizen who hasn't even been found guilty?"[g]

26When the centurion heard this, he went to the commander and reported it. "What are you going to do?" he asked. "This man is a Roman citizen."

27The commander went to Paul and asked, "Tell me, are you a Roman citizen?"

"Yes, I am," he answered.

28Then the commander said, "I had to pay a big price for my citizenship."

"But I was born a citizen," Paul replied.

29Those who were about to question him withdrew immediately. The commander himself was alarmed when he realized that he had put Paul, a Roman citizen,[h] in chains.

Paul speaks to the Sanhedrin.

30The next day, since the commander wanted to find out exactly why Paul was being accused by the Jews,[i] he released him[j] and ordered the chief priests and all the Sanhedrin[k] to assemble. Then he brought Paul and had him stand before them.

23 Paul looked straight at the Sanhedrin[l] and said, "My brothers,[m] I have fulfilled my duty to God in all good conscience[n] to this day." 2At this the high priest Ananias[o] ordered those standing near Paul to strike him on the mouth.[p] 3Then Paul said to him, "God will strike you, you whitewashed wall![q] You sit there to judge me according to the law, yet you yourself violate the law by commanding that I be struck!"[r]

4Those who were standing near Paul said, "You dare to insult God's high priest?"

5Paul replied, "Brothers, I did not realize that he was the high priest; for it is written: 'Do not speak evil about the ruler of your people.'[t]"[s]

6Then Paul, knowing that some of them were Sadducees and the others Pharisees, called out in the Sanhedrin, "My brothers,[t] I am a Pharisee,[u] the son of a Pharisee. I stand on trial because of my hope in the resurrection of the dead."[v] 7When he said this, a dispute broke out between the Pharisees and the Sadducees, and the assembly was divided. 8(The Sadducees say that there is no resurrection,[w] and that there are neither angels nor spirits, but the Pharisees acknowledge them all.)

9There was a great uproar, and some of the teachers of the law who were Pharisees[x] stood up and argued vigorously. "We find nothing wrong with this man,"[y] they said. "What if a spirit or an angel has spoken to him?"[z] 10The dispute became so violent that the commander was afraid Paul would be torn to pieces by them. He ordered the troops to go down and take him away from them by force and bring him into the barracks.[a]

11The following night the Lord stood near Paul and said, "Take courage![b] As you have testified about me in Jerusalem, so you must also testify in Rome."[c]

The Jews conspire to kill Paul.

12The next morning the Jews formed a conspiracy and bound themselves with an oath not to eat or drink until they had killed Paul.[d] 13More than forty men were involved in this plot. 14They went to the chief priests and elders and said, "We have taken a solemn oath not to eat anything until we have killed Paul.[e]

22:22 [a]Ac 21:36 [b]Ac 25:24
22:23 [c]Ac 7:58 [d]2Sa 16:13
22:24 [e]Ac 21:34 [f]ver 29
22:25 [g]Ac 16:37
22:29 [h]ver 24,25; Ac 16:38
22:30 [i]Ac 23:28 [j]Ac 21:33 [k]Mt 5:22
23:1 [l]Ac 22:30 [m]Ac 22:5 [n]Ac 24:16; 1Co 4:4; 2Co 1:12; 2Ti 1:3; Heb 13:18
23:2 [o]Ac 24:1 [p]Jn 18:22
23:3 [q]Mt 23:27 [r]Lev 19:15; Dt 25:1,2; Jn 7:51
23:5 [s]Ex 22:28
23:6 [t]Ac 22:5 [u]Ac 26:5; Php 3:5 [v]Ac 24:15,21; 26:8
23:8 [w]Mt 22:23
23:9 [x]Mk 2:16 [y]ver 29; Ac 25:25; 26:31 [z]Ac 22:7, 17,18
23:10 [a]Ac 21:34
23:11 [b]Ac 18:9 [c]Ac 19:21; 28:23
23:12 [d]ver 14,21, 30; Ac 25:3
23:14 [e]ver 12

t5 Exodus 22:28

15 Now then, you and the Sanhedrin[a] petition the commander to bring him before you on the pretext of wanting more accurate information about his case. We are ready to kill him before he gets here."

16 But when the son of Paul's sister heard of this plot, he went into the barracks[b] and told Paul.

17 Then Paul called one of the centurions and said, "Take this young man to the commander; he has something to tell him." 18 So he took him to the commander.

The centurion said, "Paul, the prisoner,[c] sent for me and asked me to bring this young man to you because he has something to tell you."

19 The commander took the young man by the hand, drew him aside and asked, "What is it you want to tell me?"

20 He said: "The Jews have agreed to ask you to bring Paul before the Sanhedrin[d] tomorrow on the pretext of wanting more accurate information about him.[e] 21 Don't give in to them, because more than forty[f] of them are waiting in ambush for him. They have taken an oath not to eat or drink until they have killed him.[g] They are ready now, waiting for your consent to their request."

22 The commander dismissed the young man and cautioned him, "Don't tell anyone that you have reported this to me."

Paul is sent to Governor Felix.

23 Then he called two of his centurions and ordered them, "Get ready a detachment of two hundred soldiers, seventy horsemen and two hundred spearmen[u] to go to Caesarea[h] at nine tonight.[i] 24 Provide mounts for Paul so that he may be taken safely to Governor Felix."[j]

25 He wrote a letter as follows:

26 Claudius Lysias,

To His Excellency,[k] Governor Felix:

Greetings.[l]

23:15 [a]ver 1; Ac 22:30
23:16 [b]ver 10; Ac 21:34
23:18 [c]Eph 3:1
23:20 [d]ver 1 [e]ver 14,15
23:21 [f]ver 13 [g]ver 12,14
23:23 [h]Ac 8:40 [i]ver 33
23:24 [j]ver 26,33; Ac 24:1-3,10; 25:14
23:26 [k]Lk 1:3; Ac 24:3; 26:25 [l]Ac 15:23
23:27 [m]Ac 21:32 [n]Ac 21:33 [o]Ac 22:25-29
23:28 [p]Ac 22:30
23:29 [q]Ac 18:15; 25:19 [r]ver 9; Ac 26:31
23:30 [s]ver 20,21 [t]Ac 20:3 [u]ver 35; Ac 24:19; 25:16
23:32 [v]ver 23 [w]Ac 21:34
23:33 [x]ver 23,24 [y]Ac 8:40 [z]ver 26
23:34 [a]Ac 6:9; 21:39
23:35 [b]ver 30; Ac 24:19; 25:16 [c]Ac 24:27
24:1 [d]Ac 23:2 [e]Ac 23:30,35 [f]Ac 23:24
24:3 [g]Lk 1:3; Ac 23:26; 26:25

27 This man was seized by the Jews and they were about to kill him,[m] but I came with my troops and rescued him,[n] for I had learned that he is a Roman citizen.[o] 28 I wanted to know why they were accusing him, so I brought him to their Sanhedrin.[p] 29 I found that the accusation had to do with questions about their law,[q] but there was no charge against him[r] that deserved death or imprisonment. 30 When I was informed[s] of a plot[t] to be carried out against the man, I sent him to you at once. I also ordered his accusers[u] to present to you their case against him.

31 So the soldiers, carrying out their orders, took Paul with them during the night and brought him as far as Antipatris. 32 The next day they let the cavalry[v] go on with him, while they returned to the barracks.[w] 33 When the cavalry[x] arrived in Caesarea,[y] they delivered the letter to the governor[z] and handed Paul over to him. 34 The governor read the letter and asked what province he was from. Learning that he was from Cilicia,[a] 35 he said, "I will hear your case when your accusers[b] get here." Then he ordered that Paul be kept under guard[c] in Herod's palace.

Tertullus charges Paul.

24 Five days later the high priest Ananias[d] went down to Caesarea with some of the elders and a lawyer named Tertullus, and they brought their charges[e] against Paul before the governor.[f] 2 When Paul was called in, Tertullus presented his case before Felix: "We have enjoyed a long period of peace under you, and your foresight has brought about reforms in this nation. 3 Everywhere and in every way, most excellent[g] Felix, we acknowledge this with profound gratitude. 4 But in order not to weary you further, I

[u] *23* The meaning of the Greek for this word is uncertain.

would request that you be kind enough to hear us briefly.

5“We have found this man to be a troublemaker, stirring up riots[a] among the Jews[b] all over the world. He is a ringleader of the Nazarene[c] sect[d] 6and even tried to desecrate the temple;[e] so we seized him. 8By[v] examining him yourself you will be able to learn the truth about all these charges we are bringing against him.”

9The Jews joined in the accusation,[f] asserting that these things were true.

Paul preaches about Jesus while on trial before Felix and Drusilla.

10When the governor[g] motioned for him to speak, Paul replied: “I know that for a number of years you have been a judge over this nation; so I gladly make my defense. 11You can easily verify that no more than twelve days[h] ago I went up to Jerusalem to worship. 12My accusers did not find me arguing with anyone at the temple,[i] or stirring up a crowd[j] in the synagogues or anywhere else in the city. 13And they cannot prove to you the charges they are now making against me.[k] 14However, I admit that I worship the God of our fathers[l] as a follower of the Way,[m] which they call a sect.[n] I believe everything that agrees with the Law and that is written in the Prophets,[o] 15and I have the same hope in God as these men, that there will be a resurrection[p] of both the righteous and the wicked.[q] 16So I strive always to keep my conscience clear[r] before God and man.

17“After an absence of several years, I came to Jerusalem to bring my people gifts for the poor[s] and to present offerings. 18I was ceremonially clean[t] when they found me in the temple courts doing this. There was no crowd with me, nor was I involved in any disturbance.[u] 19But there are some Jews from the province of Asia, who ought to be here before you and bring charges if they have anything against me.[v] 20Or these who are here should state what crime they found in me when I stood before the Sanhedrin— 21unless it was this one thing I shouted as I stood in their presence: ‘It is concerning the resurrection of the dead that I am on trial before you today.’ ”[w]

22Then Felix, who was well acquainted with the Way, adjourned the proceedings. “When Lysias the commander comes,” he said, “I will decide your case.” 23He ordered the centurion to keep Paul under guard[x] but to give him some freedom[y] and permit his friends to take care of his needs.[z]

24Several days later Felix came with his wife Drusilla, who was a Jewess. He sent for Paul and listened to him as he spoke about faith in Christ Jesus.[a] 25As Paul discoursed on righteousness, self-control[b] and the judgment[c] to come, Felix was afraid and said, “That’s enough for now! You may leave. When I find it convenient, I will send for you.” 26At the same time he was hoping that Paul would offer him a bribe, so he sent for him frequently and talked with him.

27When two years had passed, Felix was succeeded by Porcius Festus,[d] but because Felix wanted to grant a favor to the Jews,[e] he left Paul in prison.[f]

Paul appears before Festus.

25 Three days after arriving in the province, Festus went up from Caesarea[g] to Jerusalem, 2where the chief priests and Jewish leaders appeared before him and presented the charges against Paul.[h] 3They urgently requested Festus, as a favor to them, to have Paul transferred to Jerusalem, for they were preparing an ambush to kill him along the way. 4Festus answered, “Paul is being held[i] at Caesarea, and I myself am going there soon. 5Let some of your leaders come with me and press charges against

24:5 [a]Ac 16:20; 17:6 [b]Ac 21:28 [c]Mk 1:24 [d]ver 14; Ac 26:5; 28:22 **24:6** [e]Ac 21:28 **24:9** [f]1Th 2:16 **24:10** [g]Ac 23:24 **24:11** [h]Ac 21:27; ver 1 **24:12** [i]Ac 25:8; 28:17 [j]ver 18 **24:13** [k]Ac 25:7 **24:14** [l]Ac 3:13 [m]Ac 9:2 [n]ver 5 [o]Ac 26:6,22; 28:23 **24:15** [p]Ac 23:6; 28:20 [q]Da 12:2; Jn 5:28,29 **24:16** [r]Ac 23:1 **24:17** [s]Ac 11:29,30; Ro 15:25-28, 31; 1Co 16:1-4,15; 2Co 8:1-4; Gal 2:10 **24:18** [t]Ac 21:26 [u]ver 12 **24:19** [v]Ac 23:30 **24:21** [w]Ac 23:6 **24:23** [x]Ac 23:35 [y]Ac 28:16 [z]Ac 23:16; 27:3 **24:24** [a]Ac 20:21 **24:25** [b]Gal 5:23; 2Pe 1:6 [c]Ac 10:42 **24:27** [d]Ac 25:1,4, 9,14 [e]Ac 12:3; 25:9 [f]Ac 23:35; 25:14 **25:1** [g]Ac 8:40 **25:2** [h]ver 15; Ac 24 1 **25:4** [i]Ac 24:23

[v]6-8 Some manuscripts *him and wanted to judge him according to our law. 7But the commander, Lysias, came and with the use of much force snatched him from our hands 8and ordered his accusers to come before you. By*

the man there, if he has done anything
wrong."
6After spending eight or ten days with
them, he went down to Caesarea, and
the next day he convened the court[a]
and ordered that Paul be brought before
him. 7When Paul appeared, the Jews
who had come down from Jerusalem
stood around him, bringing many serious
charges against him,[b] which they could
not prove.[c]
8Then Paul made his defense: "I have
done nothing wrong against the law of
the Jews or against the temple[d] or
against Caesar."

Paul appeals to Caesar.

9Festus, wishing to do the Jews a
favor,[e] said to Paul, "Are you willing to
go up to Jerusalem and stand trial before
me there on these charges?"[f]
10Paul answered: "I am now standing
before Caesar's court, where I ought to
be tried. I have not done any wrong to
the Jews, as you yourself know very
well. 11If, however, I am guilty of doing
anything deserving death, I do not refuse to die. But if the charges brought
against me by these Jews are not true,
no one has the right to hand me over to
them. I appeal to Caesar!"[g]
12After Festus had conferred with his
council, he declared: "You have appealed
to Caesar. To Caesar you will go!"
13A few days later King Agrippa and
Bernice arrived at Caesarea[h] to pay their
respects to Festus. 14Since they were
spending many days there, Festus discussed Paul's case with the king. He
said: "There is a man here whom Felix
left as a prisoner.[i] 15When I went to Jerusalem, the chief priests and elders of
the Jews brought charges against him[j]
and asked that he be condemned.
16"I told them that it is not the Roman
custom to hand over any man before he
has faced his accusers and has had an
opportunity to defend himself against
their charges.[k] 17When they came here
with me, I did not delay the case, but
convened the court the next day and
ordered the man to be brought in.[l]
18When his accusers got up to speak,
they did not charge him with any of the
crimes I had expected. 19Instead, they
had some points of dispute[m] with him
about their own religion[n] and about a
dead man named Jesus who Paul claimed
was alive. 20I was at a loss how to investigate such matters; so I asked if he
would be willing to go to Jerusalem and
stand trial there on these charges.[o]
21When Paul made his appeal to be held
over for the Emperor's decision, I
ordered him held until I could send him
to Caesar."[p]
22Then Agrippa said to Festus, "I
would like to hear this man myself."
He replied, "Tomorrow you will hear
him."[q]

Paul appears before Agrippa.

23The next day Agrippa and Bernice[r]
came with great pomp and entered the
audience room with the high ranking
officers and the leading men of the city.
At the command of Festus, Paul was
brought in. 24Festus said: "King Agrippa,
and all who are present with us, you see
this man! The whole Jewish community[s] has petitioned me about him in Jerusalem and here in Caesarea, shouting
that he ought not to live any longer.[t] 25I
found he had done nothing deserving of
death,[u] but because he made his appeal
to the Emperor[v] I decided to send him
to Rome. 26But I have nothing definite to
write to His Majesty about him. Therefore I have brought him before all of you,
and especially before you, King Agrippa,
so that as a result of this investigation I
may have something to write. 27For I
think it is unreasonable to send on a
prisoner without specifying the charges
against him."

Paul gives his testimony to Agrippa.

26:12-18pp— Ac 9:3-8; 22:6-11

26 Then Agrippa said to Paul, "You
have permission to speak for
yourself."[w]

25:6 [a]ver 17
25:7 [b]Mk 15:3; Lk 23:2,10; Ac 24:5,6 [c]Ac 24:13
25:8 [d]Ac 6:13; 24:12; 28:17
25:9 [e]Ac 24:27 [f]ver 20
25:11 [g]ver 21,25; Ac 26:32; 28:19
25:13 [h]Ac 8:40
25:14 [i]Ac 24:27
25:15 [j]ver 2; Ac 24:1
25:16 [k]ver 4,5; Ac 23:30
25:17 [l]ver 6,10
25:19 [m]Ac 18:15; 23:29 [n]Ac 17:22
25:20 [o]ver 9
25:21 [p]ver 11,12
25:22 [q]Ac 9:15
25:23 [r]ver 13; Ac 26:30
25:24 [s]ver 2,3,7 [t]Ac 22:22
25:25 [u]Ac 23:9 [v]ver 11
26:1 [w]Ac 9:15; 25:22

So Paul motioned with his hand and
began his defense: 2“King Agrippa, I
consider myself fortunate to stand before
you today as I make my defense against
all the accusations of the Jews, 3and
especially so because you are well acquainted with all the Jewish customs[a]
and controversies.[b] Therefore, I beg you
to listen to me patiently.

4“The Jews all know the way I have
lived ever since I was a child,[c] from the
beginning of my life in my own country,
and also in Jerusalem. 5They have
known me for a long time[d] and can testify, if they are willing, that according
to the strictest sect of our religion, I
lived as a Pharisee.[e] 6And now it is because of my hope[f] in what God has
promised our fathers[g] that I am on trial today. 7This is the promise our twelve
tribes[h] are hoping to see fulfilled as they
earnestly serve God day and night.[i] O
king, it is because of this hope that the
Jews are accusing me.[j] 8Why should any
of you consider it incredible that God
raises the dead?[k]

9“I too was convinced[l] that I ought to
do all that was possible to oppose[m] the
name of Jesus of Nazareth.[n] 10And that
is just what I did in Jerusalem. On the
authority of the chief priests I put many
of the saints[o] in prison,[p] and when they
were put to death, I cast my vote against
them.[q] 11Many a time I went from one
synagogue to another to have them
punished,[r] and I tried to force them to
blaspheme. In my obsession against
them, I even went to foreign cities to
persecute them.

12“On one of these journeys I was
going to Damascus with the authority
and commission of the chief priests.
13About noon, O king, as I was on the
road, I saw a light from heaven, brighter
than the sun, blazing around me and my
companions. 14We all fell to the ground,
and I heard a voice[s] saying to me in Aramaic,[w] ‘Saul, Saul, why do you persecute
me? It is hard for you to kick against the
goads.’

15“Then I asked, ‘Who are you, Lord?’

“ ‘I am Jesus, whom you are persecuting,’ the Lord replied. 16‘Now get up and
stand on your feet.[t] I have appeared to
you to appoint you as a servant and as a
witness of what you have seen of me and
what I will show you.[u] 17I will rescue
you[v] from your own people and from
the Gentiles.[w] I am sending you to them
18to open their eyes[x] and turn them from
darkness to light,[y] and from the power
of Satan to God, so that they may receive
forgiveness of sins[z] and a place among
those who are sanctified by faith in me.’[a]

19“So then, King Agrippa, I was not
disobedient to the vision from heaven.
20First to those in Damascus,[b] then to
those in Jerusalem[c] and in all Judea, and
to the Gentiles[d] also, I preached that
they should repent[e] and turn to God and
prove their repentance by their deeds.[f]
21That is why the Jews seized me[g] in
the temple courts and tried to kill me.[h]
22But I have had God’s help to this very
day, and so I stand here and testify to
small and great alike. I am saying nothing beyond what the prophets and
Moses said would happen[i]— 23that the
Christ[x] would suffer and, as the first to
rise from the dead,[j] would proclaim light
to his own people and to the Gentiles.”[k]

24At this point Festus interrupted
Paul’s defense. “You are out of your
mind,[l] Paul!” he shouted. “Your great
learning[m] is driving you insane.”

25“I am not insane, most excellent[n]
Festus,” Paul replied. “What I am saying
is true and reasonable. 26The king is
familiar with these things,[o] and I can
speak freely to him. I am convinced
that none of this has escaped his notice,
because it was not done in a corner.
27King Agrippa, do you believe the
prophets? I know you do.”

28Then Agrippa said to Paul, “Do you
think that in such a short time you can
persuade me to be a Christian?”[p]

29Paul replied, “Short time or long—
I pray God that not only you but all who

26:3 [a]ver 7; Ac 6:14 [b]Ac 25:19 **26:4** [c]Gal 1:13,14; Php 3:5 **26:5** [d]Ac 22:3 [e]Ac 23:6; Php 3:5 **26:6** [f]Ac 23:6; 24:15; 28:20 [g]Ac 13:32; Ro 15:8 **26:7** [h]Jas 1:1 [i]1Th 3:10; 1Ti 5:5 [j]ver 2 **26:8** [k]Ac 23:6 **26:9** [l]1Ti 1:13 [m]Jn 16:2 [n]Jn 15:21 **26:10** [o]Ac 9:13 [p]Ac 8:3; 9:2,14,21 [q]Ac 22:20 **26:11** [r]Mt 10:17 **26:14** [s]Ac 9:7 **26:16** [t]Eze 2:1; Da 10:11 [u]Ac 22:14,15 **26:17** [v]Jer 1:8,19 [w]Ac 9:15 **26:18** [x]Isa 35:5 [y]Isa 42:7,16; Eph 5:8; Col 1:13; 1Pe 2:9 [z]Lk 24:47; Ac 2:38 [a]Ac 20:21,32 **26:20** [b]Ac 9:19-25 [c]Ac 9:26-29; 22:17-20 [d]Ac 9:15; 13:46 [e]Ac 3:19 [f]Mt 3:8; Lk 3:8 **26:21** [g]Ac 21:27,30 [h]Ac 21:31 **26:22** [i]Lk 24:27,44; Ac 10:43; 24:14

26:23 [j]1Co 15:20,23; Col 1:18; Rev 1:5 [k]Lk 2:32 **26:24** [l]Jn 10:20; 1Co 4:10 [m]Jn 7:15 **26:25** [n]Ac 23:26 **26:26** [o]ver 3 **26:28** [p]Ac 11:26

[w]*14* Or *Hebrew* [x]*23* Or *Messiah*

are listening to me today may become
what I am, except for these chains."[a]
30The king rose, and with him the
governor and Bernice[b] and those sitting
with them. 31They left the room, and
while talking with one another, they
said, "This man is not doing anything
that deserves death or imprisonment."[c]
32Agrippa said to Festus, "This man
could have been set free[d] if he had not
appealed to Caesar."[e]

Agrippa sends Paul to Rome by ship.

27 When it was decided that we[f]
would sail for Italy,[g] Paul and
some other prisoners were handed over
to a centurion named Julius, who belonged to the Imperial Regiment.[h] 2We
boarded a ship from Adramyttium about
to sail for ports along the coast of the
province of Asia,[i] and we put out to sea.
Aristarchus,[j] a Macedonian[k] from Thessalonica,[l] was with us.
3The next day we landed at Sidon;[m]
and Julius, in kindness to Paul,[n] allowed
him to go to his friends so they might
provide for his needs.[o] 4From there we
put out to sea again and passed to the
lee of Cyprus because the winds were
against us.[p] 5When we had sailed across
the open sea off the coast of Cilicia[q] and
Pamphylia, we landed at Myra in Lycia.

26:29 [a] Ac 21:33 **26:30** [b] Ac 25:23 **26:31** [c] Ac 23:9 **26:32** [d] Ac 28:18 [e] Ac 25:11 **27:1** [f] Ac 16:10 [g] Ac 18:2; 25:12,25 [h] Ac 10:1 **27:2** [i] Ac 2:9 [j] Ac 19:29 [k] Ac 16:9 [l] Ac 17:1 **27:3** [m] Mt 11:21 [n] ver 43 [o] Ac 24:23; 28:16

27:4 [p] ver 7 **27:5** [q] Ac 6:9

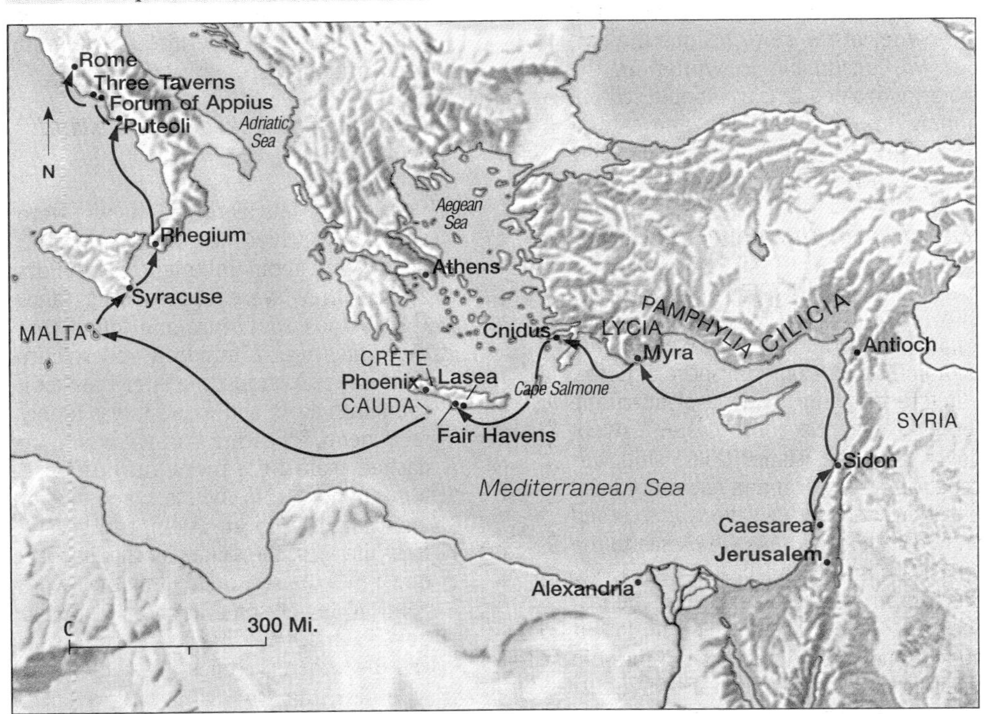

Paul's Journey to Rome

Paul began his 2,000-mile trip to Rome at Caesarea. To avoid the open seas, the ship followed the coastline. At Myra, Paul was put on a vessel bound for Italy. It arrived with difficulty at Cnidus, then went to Crete, landing at the port of Fair Havens. The next stop was Phoenix, but the ship was blown south around the island of Cauda, then drifted for two weeks until it was shipwrecked on the island of Malta, where the ship's company spent three months. Finally another ship gave them passage for the [illegible]00 miles to Syracuse, capital of Sicily, then on to Rhegium, finally dropping anchor at Puteoli. Paul was taken along the Appian Way to the Forum of Appius, and to the Three Taverns before arriving in Rome.

6There the centurion found an Alexandrian ship[a] sailing for Italy[b] and put us
on board. 7We made slow headway for
many days and had difficulty arriving off
Cnidus. When the wind did not allow us
to hold our course,[c] we sailed to the
lee of Crete,[d] opposite Salmone. 8We
moved along the coast with difficulty
and came to a place called Fair Havens,
near the town of Lasea.

9Much time had been lost, and sailing
had already become dangerous because
by now it was after the Fast.[y][e] So Paul
warned them, 10"Men, I can see that
our voyage is going to be disastrous and
bring great loss to ship and cargo, and to
our own lives also."[f] 11But the centurion, instead of listening to what Paul said,
followed the advice of the pilot and of
the owner of the ship. 12Since the harbor was unsuitable to winter in, the
majority decided that we should sail on,
hoping to reach Phoenix and winter
there. This was a harbor in Crete, facing
both southwest and northwest.

The voyage is threatened by storm.

13When a gentle south wind began to
blow, they thought they had obtained
what they wanted; so they weighed anchor and sailed along the shore of Crete.
14Before very long, a wind of hurricane
force,[g] called the "northeaster," swept
down from the island. 15The ship was
caught by the storm and could not head
into the wind; so we gave way to it and
were driven along. 16As we passed to the
lee of a small island called Cauda, we
were hardly able to make the lifeboat
secure. 17When the men had hoisted it
aboard, they passed ropes under the ship
itself to hold it together. Fearing that
they would run aground[h] on the sand-
bars of Syrtis, they lowered the sea
anchor and let the ship be driven along.
18We took such a violent battering from
the storm that the next day they began
to throw the cargo overboard.[i] 19On
the third day, they threw the ship's
tackle overboard with their own hands.
20When neither sun nor stars appeared
for many days and the storm continued
raging, we finally gave up all hope of
being saved.

21After the men had gone a long time
without food, Paul stood up before them
and said: "Men, you should have taken
my advice[j] not to sail from Crete;[k] then
you would have spared yourselves this
damage and loss. 22But now I urge you
to keep up your courage,[l] because not
one of you will be lost; only the ship will
be destroyed. 23Last night an angel[m] of
the God whose I am and whom I serve[n]
stood beside me[o] 24and said, 'Do not be
afraid, Paul. You must stand trial before
Caesar;[p] and God has graciously given
you the lives of all who sail with you.'[q]
25So keep up your courage,[r] men, for I
have faith in God that it will happen just
as he told me.[s] 26Nevertheless, we must
run aground[t] on some island."[u]

Paul is shipwrecked on the island of Malta.

27On the fourteenth night we were
still being driven across the Adriatic[z]
Sea, when about midnight the sailors
sensed they were approaching land.
28They took soundings and found that
the water was a hundred and twenty
feet[a] deep. A short time later they took
soundings again and found it was ninety
feet[b] deep. 29Fearing that we would be
dashed against the rocks, they dropped
four anchors from the stern and prayed
for daylight. 30In an attempt to escape
from the ship, the sailors let the lifeboat[v]
down into the sea, pretending they were
going to lower some anchors from the
bow. 31Then Paul said to the centurion
and the soldiers, "Unless these men stay
with the ship, you cannot be saved."[w]
32So the soldiers cut the ropes that held
the lifeboat and let it fall away.

33Just before dawn Paul urged them
all to eat. "For the last fourteen days," he

27:6 [a]Ac 28:11 [b]ver 1
27:7 [c]ver 4 [d]ver 12,13,21
27:9 [e]Lev 16:29-31; 23:27-29; Nu 29:7
27:10 [f]ver 21
27:14 [g]Mk 4:37
27:17 [h]ver 26,39
27:18 [i]ver 19,38; Jnh 1:5
27:21 [j]ver 10 [k]ver 7
27:22 [l]ver 25,36
27:23 [m]Ac 5:19 [n]Ro 1:9 [o]Ac 18:9; 23:11; 2Ti 4:17
27:24 [p]Ac 23:11 [q]ver 44
27:25 [r]ver 22,36 [s]Ro 4:20,21
27:26 [t]ver 17,39 [u]Ac 28:1
27:30 [v]ver 16
27:31 [w]ver 24

y*9* That is, the Day of Atonement (Yom Kippur)
z*27* In ancient times the name referred to an area extending well south of Italy. a*28* Greek *twenty orguias* (about 37 meters) b*28* Greek *fifteen orguias* (about 27 meters)

said, "you have been in constant suspense and have gone without food—you haven't eaten anything. 34Now I urge you to take some food. You need it to survive. Not one of you will lose a single hair from his head."[a] 35After he said this, he took some bread and gave thanks to God in front of them all. Then he broke it[b] and began to eat. 36They were all encouraged[c] and ate some food themselves. 37Altogether there were 276 of us on board. 38When they had eaten as much as they wanted, they lightened the ship by throwing the grain into the sea.[d]

39When daylight came, they did not recognize the land, but they saw a bay with a sandy beach,[e] where they decided to run the ship aground if they could. 40Cutting loose the anchors,[f] they left them in the sea and at the same time untied the ropes that held the rudders. Then they hoisted the foresail to the wind and made for the beach. 41But the ship struck a sandbar and ran aground. The bow stuck fast and would not move, and the stern was broken to pieces by the pounding of the surf.[g]

42The soldiers planned to kill the prisoners to prevent any of them from swimming away and escaping. 43But the centurion wanted to spare Paul's life[h] and kept them from carrying out their plan. He ordered those who could swim to jump overboard first and get to land. 44The rest were to get there on planks or on pieces of the ship. In this way everyone reached land in safety.[i]

The snake on Paul's hand does not harm him.

28 Once safely on shore, we[j] found out that the island[k] was called Malta. 2The islanders showed us unusual kindness. They built a fire and welcomed us all because it was raining and cold. 3Paul gathered a pile of brushwood and, as he put it on the fire, a viper, driven out by the heat, fastened itself on his hand. 4When the islanders saw the snake hanging from his hand,[l] they said to each other, "This man must be a murderer; for though he escaped from the sea, Justice has not allowed him to live."[m] 5But Paul shook the snake off into the fire and suffered no ill effects.[n] 6The people expected him to swell up or suddenly fall dead, but after waiting a long time and seeing nothing unusual happen to him, they changed their minds and said he was a god.[o]

7There was an estate nearby that belonged to Publius, the chief official of the island. He welcomed us to his home and for three days entertained us hospitably. 8His father was sick in bed, suffering from fever and dysentery. Paul went in to see him and, after prayer,[p] placed his hands on him and healed him.[q] 9When this had happened, the rest of the sick on the island came and were cured. 10They honored us in many ways and when we were ready to sail, they furnished us with the supplies we needed.

Paul is under guard while boldly preaching in Rome.

11After three months we put out to sea in a ship that had wintered in the island. It was an Alexandrian ship[r] with the figurehead of the twin gods Castor and Pollux. 12We put in at Syracuse and stayed there three days. 13From there we set sail and arrived at Rhegium. The next day the south wind came up, and on the following day we reached Puteoli. 14There we found some brothers[s] who invited us to spend a week with them. And so we came to Rome. 15The brothers[t] there had heard that we were coming, and they traveled as far as the Forum of Appius and the Three Taverns to meet us. At the sight of these men Paul thanked God and was encouraged. 16When we got to Rome, Paul was allowed to live by himself, with a soldier to guard him.[u]

17Three days later he called together the leaders of the Jews.[v] When they had assembled, Paul said to them: "My brothers,[w] although I have done nothing

27:34 [a]Mt 10:30
27:35 [b]Mt 14:19
27:36 [c]ver 22,25
27:38 [d]ver 18; Jnh 1:5
27:39 [e]Ac 28:1
27:40 [f]ver 29
27:41 [g]2Co 11:25
27:43 [h]ver 3
27:44 [i]ver 22,31
28:1 [j]Ac 16:10 [k]Ac 27:26,39
28:4 [l]Mk 16:18 [m]Lk 13:2,4
28:5 [n]Lk 10:19
28:6 [o]Ac 14:11
28:8 [p]Jas 5:14,15 [q]Ac 9:40
28:11 [r]Ac 27:6
28:14 [s]Ac 1:16
28:15 [t]Ac 1:16
28:16 [u]Ac 24:23; 27:3
28:17 [v]Ac 25:2 [w]Ac 22:5

against our people[a] or against the customs of our ancestors,[b] I was arrested in
Jerusalem and handed over to the Romans. 18They examined me[c] and wanted
to release me,[d] because I was not guilty
of any crime deserving death.[e] 19But
when the Jews objected, I was compelled
to appeal to Caesar[f]—not that I had any
charge to bring against my own people.
20For this reason I have asked to see you
and talk with you. It is because of the
hope of Israel[g] that I am bound with this
chain."[h]

21They replied, "We have not received
any letters from Judea concerning you,
and none of the brothers[i] who have
come from there has reported or said
anything bad about you. 22But we want
to hear what your views are, for we
know that people everywhere are talking against this sect."[j]

23They arranged to meet Paul on a
certain day, and came in even larger
numbers to the place where he was
staying. From morning till evening he
explained and declared to them the kingdom of God[k] and tried to convince them
about Jesus[l] from the Law of Moses and
from the Prophets.[m] 24Some were convinced by what he said, but others
would not believe.[n] 25They disagreed
among themselves and began to leave

28:17 [a]Ac 25:8 [b]Ac 6:14
28:18 [c]Ac 22:24 [d]Ac 26:31,32 [e]Ac 23:9
28:19 [f]Ac 25:11
28:20 [g]Ac 26:6,7 [h]Ac 21:33
28:21 [i]Ac 22:5
28:22 [j]Ac 24:5,14
28:23 [k]Ac 19:8 [l]Ac 17:3 [m]Ac 8:35
28:24 [n]Ac 14:4
28:27 [o]Ps 119:70 [p]Isa 6:9,10
28:28 [q]Lk 2:30 [r]Ac 13:46
28:31 [s]ver 23; Mt 4:23

after Paul had made this final statement:
"The Holy Spirit spoke the truth to your
forefathers when he said through Isaiah
the prophet:

26" 'Go to this people and say,
"You will be ever hearing but never
understanding;
you will be ever seeing but never
perceiving."
27For this people's heart has become
calloused;[o]
they hardly hear with their ears,
and they have closed their eyes.
Otherwise they might see with their
eyes,
hear with their ears,
understand with their hearts
and turn, and I would heal them.'[c][p]

28"Therefore I want you to know that
God's salvation[q] has been sent to the
Gentiles,[r] and they will listen!"[d]

30For two whole years Paul stayed
there in his own rented house and welcomed all who came to see him. 31Bold-
ly and without hindrance he preached
the kingdom of God[s] and taught about
the Lord Jesus Christ.

[c]*27* Isaiah 6:9,10 [d]*28* Some manuscripts *listen!" 29After he said this, the Jews left, arguing vigorously among themselves.*

ROMANS

Author: Paul the Apostle.

Date Written: Between A.D. 56 and 58.

Title: Refers to the addressee of this letter: the church at Rome.

Background: Paul is completing his third missionary journey and anticipating a visit to Jerusalem and, ultimately, his first trip to Rome. Paul writes this letter to introduce himself and to summarize his understanding of the gospel message.

Where Written: The city of Corinth in Greece.

To Whom: To the Christians in Rome, both Jewish and Gentile. (With over 1 million inhabitants, Rome was the center of one of the greatest empires the world has ever known.)

Content: The book of Romans, the longest of Paul's 13 New Testament letters, is an elaborate, theological discussion on salvation and the doctrine of justification by faith alone. Paul systematically reflects on his gratitude for God's salvation through grace, as law and grace are contrasted, and his determination to make Christ known to men everywhere. God's dealing with Israel and his purpose for the Jews are detailed. Righteousness apart from works is further illustrated through the example of Abraham's life (chapter 4). Finally, practical applications concerning Christian duties and ethics are given.

Key Words: "Sin"; "Salvation"; "Faith." Paul clearly explains that broken fellowship with God is a result of "sin" in our lives, and "salvation" is available only by "faith" in the Son of God, Jesus Christ.

Themes: • Everyone is born with a sinful nature, "for all have sinned and fall short of the glory of God" (3:23). • All of us, like Paul, have inner conflicts from the sinful tendencies of our natural man. • Salvation is a free gift...its essence is not S-I-N, but S-O-N (God's Son). • Absolutely nothing can separate us from the love of God. • Only through the perfect Jesus Christ can we become righteous. • Justification is by faith...not by good works. • Sanctification is through the indwelling Holy Spirit...not through keeping religious laws. • Everyone trusting in Jesus Christ will be saved and given the ability through the Spirit of God to live victoriously. • Divine power for holy living is imparted through the Holy Spirit.

Outline:

1. Introduction. 1:1-1:17
2. All men's guilt as sinners. 1:18-3:20
3. Salvation available to all by faith. 3:21-8:39
4. The plan of God for Israel. 9:1-11:36
5. Christian relationships and attitudes. 12:1-15:13
6. Final instructions and greetings. 15:14-16:27

ROMANS

Paul introduces himself and the gospel of Christ Jesus.

1 Paul, a servant of Christ Jesus, called
to be an apostle[a] and set apart[b]
for the gospel of God[c]— 2the gospel
he promised beforehand through his
prophets in the Holy Scriptures[d] 3re-
garding his Son, who as to his human
nature[e] was a descendant of David,
4and who through the Spirit[a] of holiness
was declared with power to be the Son
of God[b] by his resurrection from the
dead: Jesus Christ our Lord. 5Through
him and for his name's sake, we received grace and apostleship to call people from among all the Gentiles[f] to the
obedience that comes from faith.[g] 6And
you also are among those who are
called to belong to Jesus Christ.[h]

1:1 [a]1Co 1:1 [b]Ac 9:15 [c]2Co 11:7
1:2 [d]Gal 3:8
1:3 [e]Jn 1:14
1:5 [f]Ac 9:15 [g]Ac 6:7
1:6 [h]Rev 17:14
1:7 [i]Ro 8:39 [j]1Co 1:3
1:8 [k]1Co 1:4 [l]Ro 16:19
1:9 [m]2Ti 1:3 [n]Php 1:8
1:10 [o]Ro 15:32
1:11 [p]Ro 15:23

7To all in Rome who are loved by
God[i] and called to be saints:

Grace and peace to you from God our
Father and from the Lord Jesus Christ.[j]

8First, I thank my God through Jesus
Christ for all of you,[k] because your faith
is being reported all over the world.[l]
9God, whom I serve[m] with my whole
heart in preaching the gospel of his Son,
is my witness[n] how constantly I remember you 10in my prayers at all times;
and I pray that now at last by God's will
the way may be opened for me to come
to you.[o]

11I long to see you[p] so that I may
impart to you some spiritual gift to make
you strong— 12that is, that you and I

a4 Or *who as to his spirit* b4 Or *was appointed to be the Son of God with power*

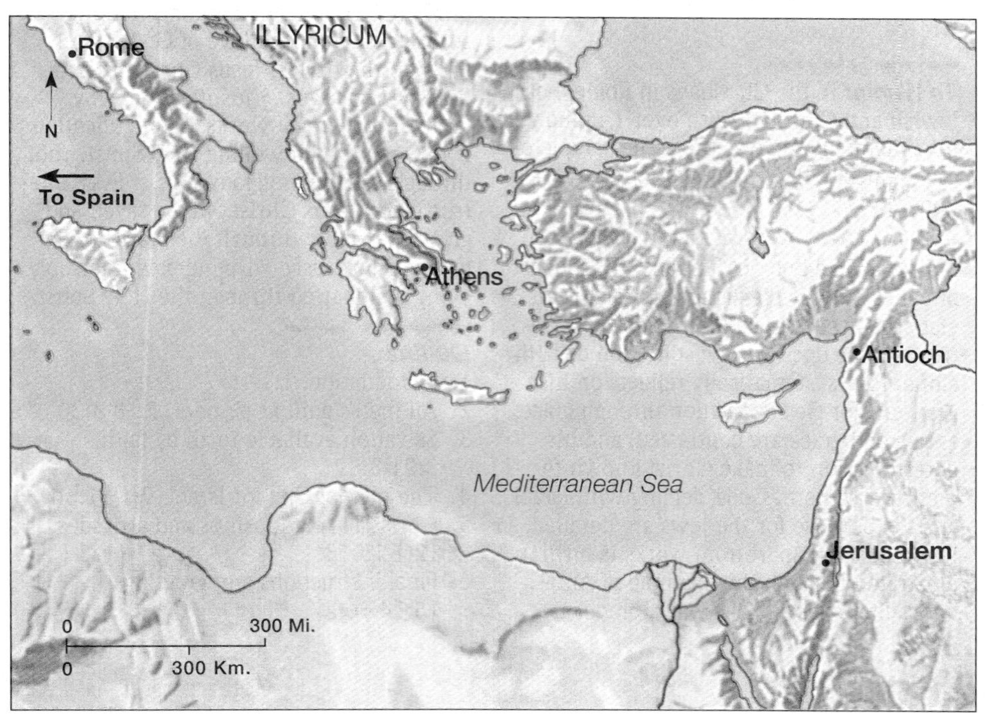

The Gospel Goes to Rome

When Paul wrote his letter to the church in Rome, he had not yet been there, but he had taken the gospel "from Jerusalem all the way around to Illyricum" (15:19). He planned to visit and preach in Rome one day, and hoped to continue to take the gospel farther west—even to Spain.

may be mutually encouraged by each
other's faith. **13**I do not want you to be
unaware, brothers, that I planned many
times to come to you (but have been
prevented from doing so until now)[a] in
order that I might have a harvest among
you, just as I have had among the other Gentiles.
14I am obligated[b] both to Greeks and
non-Greeks, both to the wise and the foolish. **15**That is why I am so eager to preach
the gospel also to you who are at Rome.[c]
16I am not ashamed of the gospel,[d]
because it is the power of God[e] for the
salvation of everyone who believes: first
for the Jew,[f] then for the Gentile.[g] **17**For
in the gospel a righteousness from God
is revealed,[h] a righteousness that is by
faith from first to last,[c] just as it is written: "The righteous will live by faith."[d][i]

God reveals himself in his creation.

18The wrath of God[j] is being revealed
from heaven against all the godlessness
and wickedness of men who suppress
the truth by their wickedness, **19**since
what may be known about God is plain
to them, because God has made it plain
to them.[k] **20**For since the creation of
the world God's invisible qualities—his
eternal power and divine nature—have
been clearly seen, being understood
from what has been made,[l] so that men
are without excuse.

God gives man over to his sin.

21For although they knew God, they
neither glorified him as God nor gave
thanks to him, but their thinking became futile and their foolish hearts were
darkened.[m] **22**Although they claimed to
be wise, they became fools[n] **23**and exchanged the glory of the immortal God
for images[o] made to look like mortal
man and birds and animals and reptiles.
24Therefore God gave them over[p] in
the sinful desires of their hearts to sexual impurity for the degrading of their
bodies with one another.[q] **25**They exchanged the truth of God for a lie,[r] and
worshiped and served created things[s]

1:13 [a]Ro 15:22,23
1:14 [b]1Co 9:16
1:15 [c]Ro 15:20
1:16 [d]2Ti 1:8 [e]1Co 1:18 [f]Ac 3:26 [g]Ro 2:9,10
1:17 [h]Ro 3:21 [i]Hab 2:4; Gal 3:11; Heb 10:38
1:18 [j]Eph 5:6; Col 3:6
1:19 [k]Ac 14:17
1:20 [l]Ps 19:1-6
1:21 [m]Jer 2:5; Eph 4:17,18
1:22 [n]1Co 1:20,27
1:23 [o]Ps 106:20; Jer 2:11; Ac 17:29
1:24 [p]Eph 4:19 [q]1Pe 4:3
1:25 [r]Isa 44:20 [s]Jer 10:14 [t]Ro 9:5
1:26 [u]ver 24,28 [v]1Th 4:5 [w]Lev 18:22,23
1:27 [x]Lev 18:22; 20:13
1:28 [y]ver 24,26
1:29 [z]2Co 12:20
1:30 [a]2Ti 3:2
1:31 [b]2Ti 3:3
1:32 [c]Ro 6:23 [d]Ps 50:18; Lk 11:48; Ac 8:1; 22:20
2:1 [e]Ro 1:20 [f]2Sa 12:5-7; Mt 7:1,2

rather than the Creator—who is forever
praised.[t] Amen.
26Because of this, God gave them
over[u] to shameful lusts.[v] Even their
women exchanged natural relations for
unnatural ones.[w] **27**In the same way the
men also abandoned natural relations
with women and were inflamed with
lust for one another. Men committed
indecent acts with other men, and received in themselves the due penalty
for their perversion.[x]
28Furthermore, since they did not
think it worthwhile to retain the knowledge of God, he gave them over[y] to a
depraved mind, to do what ought not
to be done. **29**They have become filled
with every kind of wickedness, evil,
greed and depravity. They are full of
envy, murder, strife, deceit and malice.
They are gossips,[z] **30**slanderers, God-
haters, insolent, arrogant and boastful;
they invent ways of doing evil; they
disobey their parents;[a] **31**they are senseless, faithless, heartless,[b] ruthless. **32**Although they know God's righteous de-
cree that those who do such things
deserve death,[c] they not only continue
to do these very things but also approve[d]
of those who practice them.

God judges sin impartially.

2 You, therefore, have no excuse,[e] you
who pass judgment on someone
else, for at whatever point you judge
the other, you are condemning yourself, because you who pass judgment
do the same things.[f] **2**Now we know
that God's judgment against those who
do such things is based on truth. **3**So
when you, a mere man, pass judgment
on them and yet do the same things,
do you think you will escape God's
judgment? **4**Or do you show contempt
for the riches[g] of his kindness,[h] toler-
ance[i] and patience,[j] not realizing that
God's kindness leads you toward repentance?[k]

2:4 [g]Ro 9:23; Eph 1:7,18; 2:7 [h]Ro 11:22 [i]Ro 3:25 [j]Ex 34:6 [k]2Pe 3:9

c *17* Or *is from faith to faith* d *17* Hab. 2:4

5But because of your stubbornness and your unrepentant heart, you are storing up wrath against yourself for the day of God's wrath, when his righteous judgment[a] will be revealed. 6God "will give to each person according to what he has done."[e][b] 7To those who by persistence in doing good seek glory, honor[c] and immortality,[d] he will give eternal life. 8But for those who are self-seeking and who reject the truth and follow evil,[e] there will be wrath and anger. 9There will be trouble and distress for every human being who does evil: first for the Jew, then for the Gentile;[f] 10but glory, honor and peace for everyone who does good: first for the Jew, then for the Gentile.[g] 11For God does not show favoritism.[h]

12All who sin apart from the law will also perish apart from the law, and all who sin under the law[i] will be judged by the law. 13For it is not those who hear the law who are righteous in God's sight, but it is those who obey[j] the law who will be declared righteous. 14(Indeed, when Gentiles, who do not have the law, do by nature things required by the law,[k] they are a law for themselves, even though they do not have the law, 15since they show that the requirements of the law are written on their hearts, their consciences also bearing witness, and their thoughts now accusing, now even defending them.) 16This will take place on the day when God will judge men's secrets[l] through Jesus Christ,[m] as my gospel[n] declares.

Jews are instructed on knowledge versus obedience of God's laws.

17Now you, if you call yourself a Jew; if you rely on the law and brag about your relationship to God;[o] 18if you know his will and approve of what is superior because you are instructed by the law; 19if you are convinced that you are a guide for the blind, a light for those who are in the dark, 20an instructor of the foolish, a teacher of infants, because you have in the law the embodiment of knowledge and truth— 21you, then, who teach others, do you not teach yourself? You who preach against stealing, do you steal?[p] 22You who say that people should not commit adultery, do you commit adultery? You who abhor idols, do you rob temples?[q] 23You who brag about the law,[r] do you dishonor God by breaking the law? 24As it is written: "God's name is blasphemed among the Gentiles because of you."[f][s]

25Circumcision has value if you observe the law,[t] but if you break the law, you have become as though you had not been circumcised.[u] 26If those who are not circumcised keep the law's requirements,[v] will they not be regarded as though they were circumcised?[w] 27The one who is not circumcised physically and yet obeys the law will condemn you[x] who, even though you have the[g] written code and circumcision, are a lawbreaker.

28A man is not a Jew if he is only one outwardly,[y] nor is circumcision merely outward and physical.[z] 29No, a man is a Jew if he is one inwardly; and circumcision is circumcision of the heart, by the Spirit,[a] not by the written code.[b] Such a man's praise is not from men, but from God.[c]

God can be depended on totally.

3 What advantage, then, is there in being a Jew, or what value is there in circumcision? 2Much in every way! First of all, they have been entrusted with the very words of God.[d]

3What if some did not have faith?[e] Will their lack of faith nullify God's faithfulness?[f] 4Not at all! Let God be true,[g] and every man a liar.[h] As it is written:

"So that you may be proved right
when you speak
and prevail when you judge."[h][i]

5But if our unrighteousness brings out

2:5 [a]Jude 6 **2:6** [b]Ps 62:12; Mt 16:27 **2:7** [c]ver 10 [d]1Co 15:53,54 **2:8** [e]2Th 2:12 **2:9** [f]1Pe 4:17 **2:10** [g]ver 9 **2:11** [h]Ac 10:34 **2:12** [i]Ro 3:19; 1Co 9:20,21 **2:13** [j]Jas 1:22,23,25 **2:14** [k]Ac 10:35 **2:16** [l]Ecc 12:14 [m]Ac 10:42 [n]Ro 16:25 **2:17** [o]ver 23; Mic 3:11; Ro 9:4 **2:21** [p]Mt 23:3,4 **2:22** [q]Ac 19:37 **2:23** [r]ver 17 **2:24** [s]Isa 52:5; Eze 36:22 **2:25** [t]Gal 5:3 [u]Jer 4:4 **2:26** [v]Ro 8:4 [w]1Co 7:19 **2:27** [x]Mt 12:41,42 **2:28** [y]Mt 3:9; Jn 8:39; Ro 9:6,7 [z]Gal 6:15 **2:29** [a]Php 3:3; Col 2:1 [b]Ro 7:6 [c]Jn 5:44; 1Co 4:5; 2Co 10:18; 1Th 2:4; 1Pe 3:4 **3:2** [d]Dt 4:8; Ps 147:19 **3:3** [e]Heb 4:2 [f]2Ti 2:13

3:4 [g]Jn 3:33 [h]Ps 116:11 [i]Ps 51:4

e *6* Psalm 62:12; Prov. 24:12 f *24* Isaiah 52:5; Ezek. 36:22 g *27* Or *who, by means of a* h *4* Psalm 51:4

God's righteousness more clearly, what shall we say? That God is unjust in bringing his wrath on us? (I am using a human argument.)[a] **6**Certainly not! If that were so, how could God judge the world?[b] **7**Someone might argue, "If my falsehood enhances God's truthfulness and so increases his glory,[c] why am I still condemned as a sinner?" **8**Why not say—as we are being slanderously reported as saying and as some claim that we say—"Let us do evil that good may result"?[d] Their condemnation is deserved.

Everyone is guilty of sin.

9What shall we conclude then? Are we any better[i]? Not at all! We have already made the charge that Jews and Gentiles alike are all under sin.[e] **10**As it is written:

"There is no one righteous, not even
one;
11 there is no one who understands,
no one who seeks God.
12All have turned away,
they have together become
worthless;
there is no one who does good,
not even one."[j][f]
13"Their throats are open graves;
their tongues practice deceit."[k][g]
"The poison of vipers is on their
lips."[l][h]
14 "Their mouths are full of cursing
and bitterness."[m][i]
15"Their feet are swift to shed blood;
16 ruin and misery mark their ways,
17and the way of peace they do not
know."[n]
18 "There is no fear of God before
their eyes."[o][j]

19Now we know that whatever the law says,[k] it says to those who are under the law,[l] so that every mouth may be silenced and the whole world held accountable to God. **20**Therefore no one will be declared righteous in his sight by observing the law;[m] rather, through the law we become conscious of sin.[n]

God's grace declares believers righteous through faith.

21But now a righteousness from God,[o] apart from law, has been made known, to which the Law and the Prophets testify.[p] **22**This righteousness from God comes through faith[q] in Jesus Christ to all who believe. There is no difference,[r] **23**for all have sinned and fall short of the glory of God, **24**and are justified freely by his grace[s] through the redemption[t] that came by Christ Jesus. **25**God presented him as a sacrifice of atonement,[p][u] through faith in his blood.[v] He did this to demonstrate his justice, because in his forbearance he had left the sins committed beforehand unpunished[w]— **26**he did it to demonstrate his justice at the present time, so as to be just and the one who justifies those who have faith in Jesus.

27Where, then, is boasting?[x] It is excluded. On what principle? On that of observing the law? No, but on that of faith. **28**For we maintain that a man is justified by faith apart from observing the law.[y] **29**Is God the God of Jews only? Is he not the God of Gentiles too? Yes, of Gentiles too,[z] **30**since there is only one God, who will justify the circumcised by faith and the uncircumcised through that same faith.[a] **31**Do we, then, nullify the law by this faith? Not at all! Rather, we uphold the law.

Abraham's justification by faith.

4 What then shall we say that Abraham, our forefather, discovered in this matter? **2**If, in fact, Abraham was justified by works, he had something to boast about—but not before God.[b] **3**What does the Scripture say? "Abraham believed God, and it was credited to him as righteousness."[q][c]

4Now when a man works, his wages are not credited to him as a gift,[d] but

3:5 [a]Ro 6:19; Gal 3:15
3:6 [b]Ge 18:25
3:7 [c]ver 4
3:8 [d]Ro 6:1
3:9 [e]ver 19,23; Gal 3:22
3:12 [f]Ps 14:1-3
3:13 [g]Ps 5:9 [h]Ps 140:3
3:14 [i]Ps 10:7
3:18 [j]Ps 36:1
3:19 [k]Jn 10:34 [l]Ro 2:12
3:20 [m]Ac 13:39; Gal 2:16 [n]Ro 7:7
3:21 [o]Ro 1:17; 9:30 [p]Ac 10:43
3:22 [q]Ro 9:30 [r]Ro 10:12; Gal 3:28; Col 3:11
3:24 [s]Ro 4:16; Eph 2:8 [t]Eph 1:7,14; Col 1:14; Heb 9:12
3:25 [u]1Jn 4:10 [v]Heb 9:12,14 [w]Ac 17:30
3:27 [x]Ro 2:17,23; 4:2; 1Co 1:29-31; Eph 2:9
3:28 [y]ver 20,21; Ac 13:39; Eph 2:9
3:29 [z]Ro 9:24
3:30 [a]Gal 3:8
4:2 [b]1Co 1:31
4:3 [c]ver 5,9,22; Ge 15:6; Gal 3:6; Jas 2:23
4:4 [d]Ro 11:6

i*9* Or *worse* j*12* Psalms 14:1-3;53:1-3; Eccles. 7:20 k*13* Psalm 5:9 l*13* Psalm 140:3 m*14* Psalm 10:7 n*17* Isaiah 59:7,8 o*18* Psalm 36:1 p*25* Or *as the one who would turn aside his wrath, taking away sin* q*3* Gen. 15:6; also in verse 22

as an obligation. 5However, to the man
who does not work but trusts God who
justifies the wicked, his faith is credited as righteousness. 6David says the
same thing when he speaks of the
blessedness of the man to whom God
credits righteousness apart from works:

7"Blessed are they
whose transgressions are forgiven,
whose sins are covered.
8Blessed is the man
whose sin the Lord will never
count against him."[r][a]

9Is this blessedness only for the circumcised, or also for the uncircumcised?[b] We have been saying that
Abraham's faith was credited to him as
righteousness.[c] 10Under what circumstances was it credited? Was it after he
was circumcised, or before? It was not
after, but before! 11And he received the
sign of circumcision, a seal of the righteousness that he had by faith while
he was still uncircumcised.[d] So then, he
is the father[e] of all who believe[f] but
have not been circumcised, in order that
righteousness might be credited to them.
12And he is also the father of the circumcised who not only are circumcised
but who also walk in the footsteps of
the faith that our father Abraham had
before he was circumcised.

13It was not through law that Abraham and his offspring received the
promise[g] that he would be heir of the
world,[h] but through the righteousness
that comes by faith. 14For if those who
live by law are heirs, faith has no value
and the promise is worthless,[i] 15because
law brings wrath.[j] And where there is
no law there is no transgression.[k]

16Therefore, the promise comes by
faith, so that it may be by grace[l] and
may be guaranteed[m] to all Abraham's
offspring—not only to those who are
of the law but also to those who are of
the faith of Abraham. He is the father
of us all. 17As it is written: "I have made
you a father of many nations."[s][n] He is
our father in the sight of God, in whom
he believed—the God who gives life[o]
to the dead and calls[p] things that are
not[q] as though they were.

18Against all hope, Abraham in hope
believed and so became the father of
many nations,[r] just as it had been said
to him, "So shall your offspring be."[t][s]
19Without weakening in his faith, he
faced the fact that his body was as good
as dead[t]—since he was about a hundred years old[u]—and that Sarah's womb
was also dead.[v] 20Yet he did not waver
through unbelief regarding the promise
of God, but was strengthened in his
faith and gave glory to God,[w] 21being
fully persuaded that God had power to
do what he had promised.[x] 22This is
why "it was credited to him as righteousness."[y] 23The words "it was credited to him" were written not for him
alone, 24but also for us,[z] to whom God
will credit righteousness—for us who
believe in him[a] who raised Jesus our
Lord from the dead.[b] 25He was delivered
over to death for our sins[c] and was raised
to life for our justification.

God forgives man through faith in Jesus Christ.

5 Therefore, since we have been justified through faith,[d] we[u] have peace
with God through our Lord Jesus Christ,
2through whom we have gained access[e]
by faith into this grace in which we now
stand.[f] And we[u] rejoice in the hope[g] of
the glory of God. 3Not only so, but we[u]
also rejoice in our sufferings,[h] because
we know that suffering produces perseverance;[i] 4perseverance, character;
and character, hope. 5And hope[j] does not
disappoint us, because God has poured
out his love into our hearts by the Holy
Spirit,[k] whom he has given us.

6You see, at just the right time,[l] when
we were still powerless, Christ died
for the ungodly.[m] 7Very rarely will anyone die for a righteous man, though for
a good man someone might possibly
dare to die. 8But God demonstrates his

4:8 [a]Ps 32:1,2; 2Co 5:19
4:9 [b]Ro 3:30 [c]ver 3
4:11 [d]Ge 17:10,11 [e]ver 16,17; Lk 19:9 [f]Ro 3:22
4:13 [g]Gal 3:16,29 [h]Ge 17:4-6
4:14 [i]Gal 3:18
4:15 [j]Ro 7:7-25; 1Co 15:56; 2Co 3:7; Gal 3:10; Ro 7:12 [k]Ro 3:20; 7:7
4:16 [l]Ro 3:24 [m]Ro 15:8
4:17 [n]Ge 17:5 [o]Jn 5:21 [p]Isa 48:13 [q]1Co 1:28
4:18 [r]ver 17 [s]Ge 15:5
4:19 [t]Heb 11:11,12 [u]Ge 17:17 [v]Ge 18:11
4:20 [w]Mt 9:8
4:21 [x]Ge 18:14; Heb 11:19
4:22 [y]ver 3
4:24 [z]Ro 15:4; 1Co 9:10; 10:11 [a]Ro 10:9 [b]Ac 2:24
4:25 [c]Isa 53:5,6; Ro 5:6,8
5:1 [d]Ro 3:28
5:2 [e]Eph 2:18 [f]1Co 15:1 [g]Heb 3:6
5:3 [h]Mt 5:12 [i]Jas 1:2,3
5:5 [j]Php 1:20 [k]Ac 2:33
5:6 [l]Gal 4:4 [m]Ro 4:25

[r]*8* Psalm 32:1,2 [s]*17* Gen. 17:5 [t]*18* Gen. 15:5
[u]*1,2,3* Or *let us*

own love for us in this: While we were still sinners, Christ died for us.[a] 9 Since we have now been justified by his blood,[b] how much more shall we be saved from God's wrath[c] through him! 10 For if, when we were God's enemies,[d] we were reconciled[e] to him through the death of his Son, how much more, having been reconciled, shall we be saved through his life![f] 11 Not only is this so, but we also rejoice in God through our Lord Jesus Christ, through whom we have now received reconciliation.

Adam brings death; Christ brings life.

12 Therefore, just as sin entered the world through one man,[g] and death through sin,[h] and in this way death came to all men, because all sinned— 13 for before the law was given, sin was in the world. But sin is not taken into account when there is no law.[i] 14 Nevertheless, death reigned from the time of Adam to the time of Moses, even over those who did not sin by breaking a command, as did Adam, who was a pattern of the one to come.[j]

15 But the gift is not like the trespass. For if the many died by the trespass of the one man,[k] how much more did God's grace and the gift that came by the grace of the one man, Jesus Christ,[l] overflow to the many! 16 Again, the gift of God is not like the result of the one man's sin: The judgment followed one sin and brought condemnation, but the gift followed many trespasses and brought justification. 17 For if, by the trespass of the one man, death[m] reigned through that one man, how much more will those who receive God's abundant provision of grace and of the gift of righteousness reign in life through the one man, Jesus Christ.

18 Consequently, just as the result of one trespass was condemnation for all men,[n] so also the result of one act of righteousness was justification[o] that brings life for all men. 19 For just as through the disobedience of the one man[p] the many were made sinners, so also through the obedience[q] of the one man the many will be made righteous.

20 The law was added so that the trespass might increase.[r] But where sin increased, grace increased all the more,[s] 21 so that, just as sin reigned in death,[t] so also grace might reign through righteousness to bring eternal life through Jesus Christ our Lord.

Be dead to sin and alive to Christ.

6 What shall we say, then? Shall we go on sinning so that grace may increase?[u] 2 By no means! We died to sin;[v] how can we live in it any longer? 3 Or don't you know that all of us who were baptized[w] into Christ Jesus were baptized into his death? 4 We were therefore buried with him through baptism into death in order that, just as Christ was raised from the dead[x] through the glory of the Father, we too may live a new life.[y]

5 If we have been united with him like this in his death, we will certainly also be united with him in his resurrection.[z] 6 For we know that our old self[a] was crucified with him[b] so that the body of sin[c] might be done away with,[v] that we should no longer be slaves to sin— 7 because anyone who has died has been freed from sin.

8 Now if we died with Christ, we believe that we will also live with him. 9 For we know that since Christ was raised from the dead,[d] he cannot die again; death no longer has mastery over him.[e] 10 The death he died, he died to sin[f] once for all; but the life he lives, he lives to God.

11 In the same way, count yourselves dead to sin[g] but alive to God in Christ Jesus. 12 Therefore do not let sin reign in your mortal body so that you obey its evil desires. 13 Do not offer the parts of your body to sin, as instruments of wickedness,[h] but rather offer yourselves to God, as those who have been brought

5:8 [a]Jn 15:13; 1Pe 3:18
5:9 [b]Ro 3:25 [c]Ro 1:18
5:10 [d]Ro 11:28; Col 1:21 [e]2Co 5:18,19; Col 1:20,22 [f]Ro 8:34
5:12 [g]ver 15,16,17; 1Co 15:21,22 [h]Ge 2:17; 3:19; Ro 6:23
5:13 [i]Ro 4:15
5:14 [j]1Co 15:22,45
5:15 [k]ver 12,18,19 [l]Ac 15:11
5:17 [m]ver 12
5:18 [n]ver 12 [o]Ro 4:25
5:19 [p]ver 12 [q]Php 2:8
5:20 [r]Ro 7:7,8; Gal 3:19 [s]1Ti 1:13,14
5:21 [t]ver 12,14
6:1 [u]ver 15; Ro 3:5,8
6:2 [v]Col 3:3,5; 1Pe 2:24
6:3 [w]Mt 28:19
6:4 [x]Col 2:12 [y]Ro 7:6; Gal 6:15; Eph 4:22-24; Col 3:10
6:5 [z]2Co 4:10; Php 3:10,11
6:6 [a]Eph 4:22; Col 3:9 [b]Gal 2:20; Col 2:12,20 [c]Ro 7:24
6:9 [d]Ac 2:24 [e]Rev 1:18
6:10 [f]ver 2
6:11 [g]ver 2
6:13 [h]ver 16,19; Ro 7:5

v6 Or *be rendered powerless*

from death to life; and offer the parts
of your body to him as instruments of
righteousness.[a] 14For sin shall not be
your master, because you are not under
law,[b] but under grace.[c]

Be victorious with God
over the slavery of sin.

15What then? Shall we sin because we
are not under law but under grace? By
no means! 16Don't you know that when
you offer yourselves to someone to obey
him as slaves, you are slaves to the
one whom you obey—whether you are
slaves to sin,[d] which leads to death,[e] or
to obedience, which leads to righteousness? 17But thanks be to God[f] that,
though you used to be slaves to sin, you
wholeheartedly obeyed the form of teaching[g] to which you were entrusted. 18You
have been set free from sin[h] and have
become slaves to righteousness.
19I put this in human terms[i] because
you are weak in your natural selves. Just
as you used to offer the parts of your
body in slavery to impurity and to ever-
increasing wickedness, so now offer
them in slavery to righteousness[j] leading to holiness. 20When you were slaves
to sin,[k] you were free from the control
of righteousness. 21What benefit did
you reap at that time from the things
you are now ashamed of? Those things
result in death![l] 22But now that you have
been set free from sin[m] and have become slaves to God,[n] the benefit you
reap leads to holiness, and the result is
eternal life. 23For the wages of sin is
death,[o] but the gift of God is eternal
life[p] in[w] Christ Jesus our Lord.

A better way to serve God
is explained.

7 Do you not know, brothers[q]—for I
am speaking to men who know the
law—that the law has authority over a
man only as long as he lives? 2For
example, by law a married woman is
bound to her husband as long as he is
alive, but if her husband dies, she is
released from the law of marriage.[r] 3So
then, if she marries another man while
her husband is still alive, she is called
an adulteress. But if her husband dies,
she is released from that law and is not
an adulteress, even though she marries
another man.
4So, my brothers, you also died to the
law[s] through the body of Christ,[t] that
you might belong to another, to him who
was raised from the dead, in order that
we might bear fruit to God. 5For when
we were controlled by the sinful nature,[x] the sinful passions aroused by
the law[u] were at work in our bodies,[v]
so that we bore fruit for death. 6But
now, by dying to what once bound us,
we have been released from the law so
that we serve in the new way of the
Spirit, and not in the old way of the
written code.[w]

The laws of God reveal our guilt.

7What shall we say, then? Is the law
sin? Certainly not! Indeed I would not
have known what sin was except
through the law.[x] For I would not have
known what coveting really was if the
law had not said, "Do not covet."[y][y]
8But sin, seizing the opportunity
afforded by the commandment,[z] produced in me every kind of covetous
desire. For apart from law, sin is
dead.[a] 9Once I was alive apart from
law; but when the commandment came,
sin sprang to life and I died. 10I found
that the very commandment that was
intended to bring life[b] actually brought
death. 11For sin, seizing the opportunity
afforded by the commandment, deceived me,[c] and through the commandment put me to death. 12So then, the
law is holy, and the commandment is
holy, righteous and good.[d]
13Did that which is good, then, become death to me? By no means! But in
order that sin might be recognized as sin,
it produced death in me through what
was good, so that through the commandment sin might become utterly sinful.

6:13 [a]Ro 12:1; 1Pe 2:24
6:14 [b]Gal 5:18 [c]Ro 3:24
6:16 [d]Jn 8:34; 2Pe 2:19 [e]ver 23
6:17 [f]Ro 1:8; 2Co 2:14 [g]2Ti 1:13
6:18 [h]ver 7,22; Ro 8:2
6:19 [i]Ro 3:5 [j]ver 13
6:20 [k]ver 16
6:21 [l]ver 23
6:22 [m]ver 18 [n]1Co 7:22; 1Pe 2:16
6:23 [o]Ge 2:17; Ro 5:12; Gal 6:7,8; Jas 1:15 [p]Mt 25:46
7:1 [q]Ro 1:13
7:2 [r]1Co 7:39
7:4 [s]Ro 8:2; Gal 2:19 [t]Col 1:22
7:5 [u]Ro 7:7-11 [v]Ro 6:13
7:6 [w]Ro 2:29; 2Co 3:6
7:7 [x]Ro 3:20; 4:15 [y]Ex 20:17; Dt 5:21
7:8 [z]ver 11 [a]Ro 4:15; 1Co 15:56
7:10 [b]Lev 18:5; Lk 10:26-28; Ro 10:5; Gal 3:12
7:11 [c]Ge 3:13
7:12 [d]1Ti 1:8

w*23* Or *through* x*5* Or *the flesh*; also in verse 25
y*7* Exodus 20:17; Deut. 5:21

14We know that the law is spiritual;
but I am unspiritual,[a] sold[b] as a slave to
sin. 15I do not understand what I do. For
what I want to do I do not do, but what
I hate I do.[c] 16And if I do what I do not
want to do, I agree that the law is good.[d]
17As it is, it is no longer I myself who do
it, but it is sin living in me.[e] 18I know
that nothing good lives in me, that is,
in my sinful nature.[z][f] For I have the
desire to do what is good, but I cannot
carry it out. 19For what I do is not the
good I want to do; no, the evil I do not
want to do—this I keep on doing.[g]
20Now if I do what I do not want to do,
it is no longer I who do it, but it is sin
living in me that does it.[h]

21So I find this law at work:[i] When I
want to do good, evil is right there with
me. 22For in my inner being[j] I delight in
God's law;[k] 23but I see another law at
work in the members of my body, waging war[l] against the law of my mind and
making me a prisoner of the law of sin
at work within my members. 24What a
wretched man I am! Who will rescue me
from this body of death?[m] 25Thanks be
to God—through Jesus Christ our Lord!

So then, I myself in my mind am a
slave to God's law, but in the sinful nature a slave to the law of sin.

Removal of condemnation through Jesus Christ.

8 Therefore, there is now no condemnation[n] for those who are in
Christ Jesus,[a][o] 2because through Christ
Jesus the law of the Spirit of life[p] set
me free[q] from the law of sin[r] and death.
3For what the law was powerless[s] to do
in that it was weakened by the sinful
nature,[b] God did by sending his own
Son in the likeness of sinful man[t] to be
a sin offering.[c][u] And so he condemned
sin in sinful man,[d] 4in order that the
righteous requirements of the law might
be fully met in us, who do not live according to the sinful nature but according to the Spirit.[v]

5Those who live according to the sinful nature have their minds set on what
that nature desires;[w] but those who
live in accordance with the Spirit have
their minds set on what the Spirit
desires.[x] 6The mind of sinful man[e] is
death, but the mind controlled by the
Spirit is life[y] and peace; 7the sinful
mind[f] is hostile to God.[z] It does not
submit to God's law, nor can it do so.
8Those controlled by the sinful nature
cannot please God.

9You, however, are controlled not by
the sinful nature but by the Spirit, if the
Spirit of God lives in you.[a] And if anyone does not have the Spirit of Christ,[b]
he does not belong to Christ. 10But if
Christ is in you,[c] your body is dead because of sin, yet your spirit is alive
because of righteousness. 11And if the
Spirit of him who raised Jesus from the
dead[d] is living in you, he who raised
Christ from the dead will also give life to
your mortal bodies[e] through his Spirit,
who lives in you.

Following the Spirit.

12Therefore, brothers, we have an obligation—but it is not to the sinful nature, to live according to it. 13For if you
live according to the sinful nature, you
will die; but if by the Spirit you put to
death the misdeeds of the body, you
will live,[f] 14because those who are led
by the Spirit of God[g] are sons of God.[h]
15For you did not receive a spirit that
makes you a slave again to fear,[i] but you
received the Spirit of sonship.[g] And by
him we cry, "*Abba*,[h] Father."[j] 16The
Spirit himself testifies with our spirit[k]
that we are God's children. 17Now if we
are children, then we are heirs[l]—heirs
of God and co-heirs with Christ, if indeed we share in his sufferings in order
that we may also share in his glory.[m]

7:14 [a]1Co 3:1 [b]1Ki 21:20, 25; 2Ki 17:17 **7:15** [c]ver 19; Gal 5:17 **7:16** [d]ver 12 **7:17** [e]ver 20 **7:18** [f]ver 25 **7:19** [g]ver 15 **7:20** [h]ver 17 **7:21** [i]ver 23,25 **7:22** [j]Eph 3:16 [k]Ps 1:2 **7:23** [l]Gal 5:17; Jas 4:1; 1Pe 2:11 **7:24** [m]Ro 6:6; 8:2 **8:1** [n]ver 34 [o]ver 39; Ro 16:3 **8:2** [p]1Co 15:45 [q]Ro 6:18 [r]Ro 7:4 **8:3** [s]Ac 13:39; Heb 7:18 [t]Php 2:7 [u]Heb 2:14,17 **8:4** [v]Gal 5:16 **8:5** [w]Gal 5:19-21 [x]Gal 5:22-25 **8:6** [y]Gal 6:8 **8:7** [z]Jas 4:4 **8:9** [a]1Co 6:19; Gal 4:6 [b]Jn 14:17; 1Jn 4:13 **8:10** [c]Gal 2:20; Eph 3:17; Col 1:27 **8:11** [d]Ac 2:24 [e]Jn 5:21 **8:13** [f]Gal 6:8 **8:14** [g]Gal 5:18 [h]Jn 1:12; Rev 21:7

8:15 [i]2Ti 1:7; Heb 2:15 [j]Mk 14:36; Gal 4:5,6 **8:16** [k]Eph 1:13 **8:17** [l]Ac 20:32; Gal 4:7 [m]1Pe 4:13

z *18* Or *my flesh* a *1* Some later manuscripts *Jesus, who do not live according to the sinful nature but according to the Spirit,* b *3* Or *the flesh*; also in verses 4, 5, 8, 9, 12 and 13 c *3* Or *man, for sin* d *3* Or *in the flesh* e *6* Or *mind set on the flesh* f *7* Or *the mind set on the flesh* g *15* Or *adoption* h *15* Aramaic for *Father*

Present suffering compared to future glory.

18I consider that our present sufferings are not worth comparing with the glory that will be revealed in us.[a] 19The creation waits in eager expectation for the sons of God to be revealed. 20For the creation was subjected to frustration, not by its own choice, but by the will of the one who subjected it,[b] in hope 21that[i] the creation itself will be liberated from its bondage to decay[c] and brought into the glorious freedom of the children of God.

22We know that the whole creation has been groaning[d] as in the pains of childbirth right up to the present time. 23Not only so, but we ourselves, who have the firstfruits of the Spirit,[e] groan[f] inwardly as we wait eagerly[g] for our adoption as sons, the redemption of our bodies. 24For in this hope we were saved.[h] But hope that is seen is no hope at all. Who hopes for what he already has? 25But if we hope for what we do not yet have, we wait for it patiently.

26In the same way, the Spirit helps us in our weakness. We do not know what we ought to pray for, but the Spirit himself intercedes for us[i] with groans that words cannot express. 27And he who searches our hearts[j] knows the mind of the Spirit, because the Spirit intercedes for the saints in accordance with God's will.

Power of God's love.

28And we know that in all things God works for the good of those who love him,[j] who[k] have been called[k] according to his purpose. 29For those God foreknew[l] he also predestined[m] to be conformed to the likeness of his Son,[n] that he might be the firstborn among many brothers. 30And those he predestined,[o] he also called; those he called, he also justified;[p] those he justified, he also glorified.[q]

31What, then, shall we say in response to this?[r] If God is for us, who can be against us?[s] 32He who did not spare his own Son,[t] but gave him up for us all—how will he not also, along with him, graciously give us all things? 33Who will bring any charge[u] against those whom God has chosen? It is God who justifies. 34Who is he that condemns? Christ Jesus, who died[v]—more than that, who was raised to life—is at the right hand of God[w] and is also interceding for us.[x] 35Who shall separate us from the love of Christ? Shall trouble or hardship or persecution or famine or nakedness or danger or sword?[y] 36As it is written:

> "For your sake we face death all day long;
> we are considered as sheep to be slaughtered."[l][z]

37No, in all these things we are more than conquerors[a] through him who loved us.[b] 38For I am convinced that neither death nor life, neither angels nor demons,[m] neither the present nor the future, nor any powers,[c] 39neither height nor depth, nor anything else in all creation, will be able to separate us from the love of God[d] that is in Christ Jesus our Lord.

Paul is sorrowful for Israel's unbelief.

9 I speak the truth in Christ—I am not lying,[e] my conscience confirms[f] it in the Holy Spirit— 2I have great sorrow and unceasing anguish in my heart. 3For I could wish that I myself[g] were cursed[h] and cut off from Christ for the sake of my brothers, those of my own race,[i] 4the people of Israel. Theirs is the adoption as sons;[j] theirs the divine glory, the covenants,[k] the receiving of the law,[l] the temple worship[m] and the promises.[n] 5Theirs are the patriarchs,

8:18 [a]2Co 4:17; 1Pe 4:13
8:20 [b]Ge 3:17-19
8:21 [c]Ac 3:21; 2Pe 3:13; Rev 21:1
8:22 [d]Jer 12:4
8:23 [e]2Co 5:5 [f]2Co 5:2,4 [g]Gal 5:5
8:24 [h]1Th 5:8
8:26 [i]Eph 6:18
8:27 [j]Rev 2:23
8:28 [k]1Co 1:9; 2Ti 1:9
8:29 [l]Ro 11:2 [m]Eph 1:5,11 [n]1Co 15:49; 2Co 3:18; Php 3:21; 1Jn 3:2
8:30 [o]Eph 1:5,11 [p]1Co 6:11 [q]Ro 9:23
8:31 [r]Ro 4:1 [s]Ps 118:6
8:32 [t]Jn 3:16; Ro 4:25; 5:8
8:33 [u]Isa 50:8,9
8:34 [v]Ro 5:6-8 [w]Mk 16:19 [x]Heb 7:25; 9:24; 1Jn 2:1
8:35 [y]1Co 4:11
8:36 [z]Ps 44:22; 2Co 4:11
8:37 [a]1Co 15:57 [b]Gal 2:20; Rev 1:5; 3:9
8:38 [c]Eph 1:21; 1Pe 3:22
8:39 [d]Ro 5:8
9:1 [e]2Co 11:10; Gal 1:20; 1Ti 2:7 [f]Ro 1:9

9:3 [g]Ex 32:32 [h]1Co 12:3; 16:22 [i]Ro 11:14
9:4 [j]Ex 4:22 [k]Ge 17:2; Ac 3:25; Eph 2:12 [l]Ps 147:19 [m]Heb 9:1 [n]Ac 13:32

[i]*20,21* Or *subjected it in hope.* [21]*For* [j]*28* Some manuscripts *And we know that all things work together for good to those who love God* [k]*28* Or *works together with those who love him to bring about what is good—with those who* [l]*36* Psalm 44:22 [m]*38* Or *nor heavenly rulers*

and from them is traced the human ancestry of Christ,[a] who is God over all,[b]
forever praised![n,c] Amen.

God makes promises to Israel.

6 It is not as though God's word had
failed. For not all who are descended
from Israel are Israel.[d] 7 Nor because
they are his descendants are they all
Abraham's children. On the contrary,
"It is through Isaac that your offspring
will be reckoned."[o,e] 8 In other words,
it is not the natural children who are
God's children,[f] but it is the children of
the promise who are regarded as Abraham's offspring. 9 For this was how the
promise was stated: "At the appointed
time I will return, and Sarah will have
a son."[p,g]
10 Not only that, but Rebekah's children had one and the same father, our
father Isaac.[h] 11 Yet, before the twins
were born or had done anything good
or bad—in order that God's purpose[i]
in election might stand: 12 not by works
but by him who calls—she was told,
"The older will serve the younger."[q,j]
13 Just as it is written: "Jacob I loved, but
Esau I hated."[r,k]
14 What then shall we say? Is God unjust? Not at all![l] 15 For he says to Moses,

"I will have mercy on whom I have
mercy,
and I will have compassion on
whom I have compassion."[s,m]

16 It does not, therefore, depend on man's
desire or effort, but on God's mercy.[n]
17 For the Scripture says to Pharaoh: "I
raised you up for this very purpose,
that I might display my power in you
and that my name might be proclaimed in all the earth."[t,o] 18 Therefore
God has mercy on whom he wants to
have mercy, and he hardens whom he
wants to harden.[p]
19 One of you will say to me:[q] "Then
why does God still blame us? For who
resists his will?"[r] 20 But who are you, O
man, to talk back to God? "Shall what is
formed say to him who formed it,[s]
'Why did you make me like this?'"[u,t]
21 Does not the potter have the right to
make out of the same lump of clay some
pottery for noble purposes and some
for common use?[u]
22 What if God, choosing to show his
wrath and make his power known, bore
with great patience[v] the objects of his
wrath—prepared for destruction? 23 What
if he did this to make the riches of his
glory[w] known to the objects of his mercy, whom he prepared in advance for
glory[x]— 24 even us, whom he also
called,[y] not only from the Jews but
also from the Gentiles?[z] 25 As he says
in Hosea:

"I will call them 'my people' who
are not my people;
and I will call her 'my loved one'
who is not my loved one,"[v,a]

26 and,

"It will happen that in the very place
where it was said to them,
'You are not my people,'
they will be called 'sons of the living
God.'"[w,b]

27 Isaiah cries out concerning Israel:

"Though the number of the Israelites
be like the sand by the sea,[c]
only the remnant will be saved.[d]
28 For the Lord will carry out
his sentence on earth with speed
and finality."[x,e]

29 It is just as Isaiah said previously:

"Unless the Lord Almighty[f]
had left us descendants,
we would have become like Sodom,
we would have been like
Gomorrah."[y,g]

9:5 [a]Mt 1:1-16 [b]Jn 1:1 [c]Ro 1:25
9:6 [d]Ro 2:28,29; Gal 6:16
9:7 [e]Ge 21:12; Heb 11:18
9:8 [f]Ro 8:14
9:9 [g]Ge 18:10,14
9:10 [h]Ge 25:21
9:11 [i]Ro 8:28
9:12 [j]Ge 25:23
9:13 [k]Mal 1:2,3
9:14 [l]2Ch 19:7
9:15 [m]Ex 33:19
9:16 [n]Eph 2:8
9:17 [o]Ex 9:16
9:18 [p]Ex 4:21
9:19 [q]Ro 11:19 [r]2Ch 20:6; Da 4:35
9:20 [s]Isa 64:8 [t]Isa 29:16
9:21 [u]2Ti 2:20
9:22 [v]Ro 2:4
9:23 [w]Ro 2:4 [x]Ro 8:30
9:24 [y]Ro 8:28 [z]Ro 3:29
9:25 [a]Hos 2:23; 1Pe 2:10
9:26 [b]Hos 1:10
9:27 [c]Ge 22:17; Hos 1:10 [d]Ro 11:5
9:28 [e]Isa 10:22,23
9:29 [f]Jas 5:4 [g]Isa 1:9; Dt 29:23; Isa 13:19; Jer 50:40

[n] *5* Or *Christ, who is over all. God be forever praised!* Or *Christ. God who is over all be forever praised!*
[o] *7* Gen. 21:12 [p] *9* Gen. 18:10,14
[q] *12* Gen. 25:23 [r] *13* Mal. 1:2,3
[s] *15* Exodus 33:19 [t] *17* Exodus 9:16
[u] *20* Isaiah 29:16; 45:9 [v] *25* Hosea 2:23
[w] *26* Hosea 1:10 [x] *28* Isaiah 10:22,23
[y] *29* Isaiah 1:9

Gentiles are called to faith.

30 What then shall we say? That the Gentiles, who did not pursue righteousness, have obtained it, a righteousness that is by faith;[a] 31 but Israel, who pursued a law of righteousness,[b] has not attained it.[c] 32 Why not? Because they pursued it not by faith but as if it were by works. They stumbled over the "stumbling stone."[d] 33 As it is written:

> "See, I lay in Zion a stone that
> causes men to stumble
> and a rock that makes them fall,
> and the one who trusts in him will
> never be put to shame."[z][e]

Paul reminds Israel of the necessity of believing in Jesus Christ.

10 Brothers, my heart's desire and prayer to God for the Israelites is that they may be saved. 2 For I can testify about them that they are zealous[f] for God, but their zeal is not based on knowledge. 3 Since they did not know the righteousness that comes from God and sought to establish their own, they did not submit to God's righteousness.[g] 4 Christ is the end of the law[h] so that there may be righteousness for everyone who believes.[i]

5 Moses describes in this way the righteousness that is by the law: "The man who does these things will live by them."[a][j] 6 But the righteousness that is by faith[k] says: "Do not say in your heart, 'Who will ascend into heaven?'[b]"[l] (that is, to bring Christ down) 7 "or 'Who will descend into the deep?'[c]" (that is, to bring Christ up from the dead). 8 But what does it say? "The word is near you; it is in your mouth and in your heart,"[d][m] that is, the word of faith we are proclaiming: 9 That if you confess[n] with your mouth, "Jesus is Lord," and believe in your heart that God raised him from the dead,[o] you will be saved. 10 For it is with your heart that you believe and are justified, and it is with your mouth that you confess and are saved. 11 As the Scripture says, "Anyone who trusts in him will never be put to shame."[e][p] 12 For there is no difference between Jew and Gentile[q]—the same Lord is Lord of all[r] and richly blesses all who call on him, 13 for, "Everyone who calls on the name of the Lord[s] will be saved."[f][t]

14 How, then, can they call on the one they have not believed in? And how can they believe in the one of whom they have not heard? And how can they hear without someone preaching to them? 15 And how can they preach unless they are sent? As it is written, "How beautiful are the feet of those who bring good news!"[g][u]

16 But not all the Israelites accepted the good news. For Isaiah says, "Lord, who has believed our message?"[h][v] 17 Consequently, faith comes from hearing the message,[w] and the message is heard through the word of Christ.[x] 18 But I ask: Did they not hear? Of course they did:

> "Their voice has gone out into all
> the earth,
> their words to the ends of the
> world."[i][y]

19 Again I ask: Did Israel not understand? First, Moses says,

> "I will make you envious[z] by those
> who are not a nation;
> I will make you angry by a nation
> that has no understanding."[j][a]

20 And Isaiah boldly says,

> "I was found by those who did not
> seek me;
> I revealed myself to those who did
> not ask for me."[k][b]

21 But concerning Israel he says,

> "All day long I have held out my
> hands
> to a disobedient and obstinate
> people."[l][c]

9:30 [a] Ro 1:17; 10:6; Gal 2:16; Php 3:9; Heb 11:7
9:31 [b] Isa 51:1; Ro 10:2,3 [c] Gal 5:4
9:32 [d] 1Pe 2:8
9:33 [e] Isa 28:16; Ro 10:11
10:2 [f] Ac 21:20
10:3 [g] Ro 1:17
10:4 [h] Gal 3:24; Ro 7:1-4 [i] Ro 3:22
10:5 [j] Lev 18:5; Ne 9:29; Eze 20:11,13, 21; Ro 7:10
10:6 [k] Ro 9:30 [l] Dt 30:12
10:8 [m] Dt 30:14
10:9 [n] Mt 10:32; Lk 12:8 [o] Ac 2:24
10:11 [p] Isa 28:16; Ro 9:33
10:12 [q] Ro 3:22,29 [r] Ac 10:36
10:13 [s] Ac 2:21 [t] Joel 2:32
10:15 [u] Isa 52:7; Na 1:15
10:16 [v] Isa 53:1; Jn 12:38
10:17 [w] Gal 3:2,5 [x] Col 3:16
10:18 [y] Ps 19:4; Mt 24:14; Col 1:6,23; 1Th 1:8
10:19 [z] Ro 11:11,14 [a] Dt 32:21
10:20 [b] Isa 65:1; Ro 9:30
10:21 [c] Isa 65:2

z *33* Isaiah 8:14; 28:16 a *5* Lev. 18:5
b *6* Deut. 30:12 c *7* Deut. 30:13 d *8* Deut. 30:14
e *11* Isaiah 28:16 f *13* Joel 2:32 g *15* Isaiah 52:7
h *16* Isaiah 53:1 i *18* Psalm 19:4 j *19* Deut. 32:21
k *20* Isaiah 65:1 l *21* Isaiah 65:2

A remnant of Israel remains faithful.

11 I ask then: Did God reject his people? By no means![a] I am an Israelite myself, a descendant of Abraham,[b] from the tribe of Benjamin.[c] 2God did not reject his people, whom he foreknew.[d] Don't you know what the Scripture says in the passage about Elijah—how he appealed to God against Israel: 3"Lord, they have killed your prophets and torn down your altars; I am the only one left, and they are trying to kill me"[m]?[e] 4And what was God's answer to him? "I have reserved for myself seven thousand who have not bowed the knee to Baal."[n][f] 5So too, at the present time there is a remnant[g] chosen by grace. 6And if by grace, then it is no longer by works;[h] if it were, grace would no longer be grace.[o]

7What then? What Israel sought so earnestly it did not obtain,[i] but the elect did. The others were hardened,[j] 8as it is written:

> "God gave them a spirit of stupor,
> eyes so that they could not see
> and ears so that they could not hear,[k]
> to this very day."[p][l]

9And David says:

> "May their table become a snare and a trap,
> a stumbling block and a retribution for them.
> 10May their eyes be darkened so they cannot see,
> and their backs be bent forever."[q][m]

The Gentiles are grafted into God's tree.

11Again I ask: Did they stumble so as to fall beyond recovery? Not at all![n] Rather, because of their transgression, salvation has come to the Gentiles[o] to make Israel envious.[p] 12But if their transgression means riches for the world, and their loss means riches for the Gentiles,[q] how much greater riches will their fullness bring!

13I am talking to you Gentiles. Inasmuch as I am the apostle to the Gentiles,[r] I make much of my ministry 14in the hope that I may somehow arouse my own people to envy[s] and save[t] some of them. 15For if their rejection is the reconciliation[u] of the world, what will their acceptance be but life from the dead?[v] 16If the part of the dough offered as firstfruits[w] is holy, then the whole batch is holy; if the root is holy, so are the branches.

17If some of the branches have been broken off,[x] and you, though a wild olive shoot, have been grafted in among the others[y] and now share in the nourishing sap from the olive root, 18do not boast over those branches. If you do, consider this: You do not support the root, but the root supports you.[z] 19You will say then, "Branches were broken off so that I could be grafted in." 20Granted. But they were broken off because of unbelief, and you stand by faith.[a] Do not be arrogant,[b] but be afraid.[c] 21For if God did not spare the natural branches, he will not spare you either.

22Consider therefore the kindness[d] and sternness of God: sternness to those who fell, but kindness to you, provided that you continue[e] in his kindness. Otherwise, you also will be cut off.[f] 23And if they do not persist in unbelief, they will be grafted in, for God is able to graft them in again.[g] 24After all, if you were cut out of an olive tree that is wild by nature, and contrary to nature were grafted into a cultivated olive tree, how much more readily will these, the natural branches, be grafted into their own olive tree!

A restoration of Israel is promised.

25I do not want you to be ignorant[h] of this mystery,[i] brothers, so that you

11:1 [a] 1Sa 12:22; Jer 31:37 [b] 2Co 11:22 [c] Php 3:5
11:2 [d] Ro 8:29
11:3 [e] 1Ki 19:10,14
11:4 [f] 1Ki 19:18
11:5 [g] Ro 9:27
11:6 [h] Ro 4:4
11:7 [i] Ro 9:31 [j] ver 25; Ro 9:18
11:8 [k] Mt 13:13-15 [l] Dt 29:4; Isa 29:10
11:10 [m] Ps 69:22,23
11:11 [n] ver 1 [o] Ac 13:46 [p] Ro 10:19
11:12 [q] ver 25
11:13 [r] Ac 9:15
11:14 [s] ver 11; Ro 10:19 [t] 1Co 1:21; 1Ti 2:4; Tit 3:5
11:15 [u] Ro 5:10 [v] Lk 15:24,32
11:16 [w] Lev 23:10,17; Nu 15:18-21
11:17 [x] Jer 11:16; Jn 15:2 [y] Ac 2:39; Eph 2:11-13
11:18 [z] Jn 4:22
11:20 [a] 1Co 10:12; 2Co 1:24 [b] Ro 12:16; 1Ti 6:17 [c] 1Pe 1:17
11:22 [d] Ro 2:4 [e] 1Co 15:2; Heb 3:6 [f] Jn 15:2
11:23 [g] 2Co 3:16
11:25 [h] Ro 1:13 [i] Ro 16:25

[m] *3* 1 Kings 19:10,14 [n] *4* 1 Kings 19:18 [o] *6* Some manuscripts *by grace. But if by works, then it is no longer grace; if it were, work would no longer be work.* [p] *8* Deut. 29:4; Isaiah 29:10
[q] *10* Psalm 69:22,23

may not be conceited:[a] Israel has experienced a hardening[b] in part until the
full number of the Gentiles has come
in.[c] 26And so all Israel will be saved, as
it is written:

"The deliverer will come from Zion;
he will turn godlessness away from
Jacob.
27And this is[r] my covenant with them
when I take away their sins."[s][d]

28As far as the gospel is concerned,
they are enemies[e] on your account; but
as far as election is concerned, they are
loved on account of the patriarchs,[f] 29for
God's gifts and his call[g] are irrevocable.[h]
30Just as you who were at one time disobedient[i] to God have now received
mercy as a result of their disobedience,
31so they too have now become disobedient in order that they too may now[t]
receive mercy as a result of God's mercy to you. 32For God has bound all men
over to disobedience[j] so that he may
have mercy on them all.

33Oh, the depth of the riches[k] of the
wisdom and[u] knowledge of
God![l]
How unsearchable his judgments,
and his paths beyond tracing out![m]
34"Who has known the mind of the
Lord?
Or who has been his counselor?"[v][n]
35"Who has ever given to God,
that God should repay him?"[w][o]
36For from him and through him and
to him are all things.[p]
To him be the glory forever! Amen.[q]

Living sacrifices to God.

12 Therefore, I urge you,[r] brothers,
in view of God's mercy, to offer
your bodies as living sacrifices,[s] holy
and pleasing to God—this is your spiritual[x] act of worship. 2Do not conform[t]
any longer to the pattern of this world,[u]
but be transformed by the renewing of
your mind.[v] Then you will be able to
test and approve what God's will is[w]—
his good, pleasing and perfect will.

Gifts in the body of Christ.

3For by the grace given me[x] I say to
every one of you: Do not think of yourself more highly than you ought, but
rather think of yourself with sober judgment, in accordance with the measure
of faith God has given you. 4Just as each
of us has one body with many members,
and these members do not all have the
same function,[y] 5so in Christ we who
are many form one body,[z] and each
member belongs to all the others. 6We
have different gifts,[a] according to the
grace given us. If a man's gift is prophesying, let him use it in proportion to
his[y] faith.[b] 7If it is serving, let him serve;
if it is teaching, let him teach;[c] 8if it is
encouraging, let him encourage;[d] if it is
contributing to the needs of others, let
him give generously;[e] if it is leadership,
let him govern diligently; if it is showing mercy, let him do it cheerfully.

Love and respect for others.

9Love must be sincere.[f] Hate what is
evil; cling to what is good. 10Be devoted
to one another in brotherly love.[g] Honor
one another above yourselves.[h] 11Never
be lacking in zeal, but keep your spiritual fervor,[i] serving the Lord. 12Be joyful in hope,[j] patient in affliction,[k] faithful
in prayer. 13Share with God's people who
are in need. Practice hospitality.[l]
14Bless those who persecute you;[m]
bless and do not curse. 15Rejoice with
those who rejoice; mourn with those
who mourn.[n] 16Live in harmony with
one another.[o] Do not be proud, but be
willing to associate with people of low
position.[z] Do not be conceited.[p]
17Do not repay anyone evil for evil.[q]
Be careful to do what is right in the eyes
of everybody.[r] 18If it is possible, as far as

11:25 [a]Ro 12:16 [b]ver 7; Ro 9:18 [c]Lk 21:24 **11:27** [d]Isa 27:9; Heb 8:10,12 **11:28** [e]Ro 5:10 [f]Dt 7:8; 10:15; Ro 9:5 **11:29** [g]Ro 8:28 [h]Heb 7:21 **11:30** [i]Eph 2:2 **11:32** [j]Ro 3:9 **11:33** [k]Ro 2:4 [l]Ps 92:5 [m]Job 11:7 **11:34** [n]Isa 40:13,14; Job 15:8; 36:22; 1Co 2:16 **11:35** [o]Job 35:7 **11:36** [p]1Co 8:6; Col 1:16; Heb 2:10 [q]Ro 16:27 **12:1** [r]Eph 4:1 [s]Ro 6:13,16, 19; 1Pe 2:5 **12:2** [t]1Pe 1:14 [u]1Jn 2:15 [v]Eph 4:23 [w]Eph 5:17 **12:3** [x]Ro 15:15; Gal 2:9; Eph 4:7 **12:4** [y]1Co 12:12-14; Eph 4:16 **12:5** [z]1Co 10:17 **12:6** [a]1Co 7:7; 12:4,8-10 [b]1Pe 4:10,11 **12:7** [c]Eph 4:11 **12:8** [d]Ac 15:32 [e]2Co 9:5-13 **12:9** [f]1Ti 1:5 **12:10** [g]Heb 13:1 [h]Php 2:3 **12:11** [i]Ac 18:25

12:12 [j]Ro 5:2 [k]Heb 10:32,36 **12:13** [l]1Ti 3:2 **12:14** [m]Mt 5:44 **12:15** [n]Job 30:25 **12:16** [o]Ro 15:5 [p]Jer 45:5; Ro 11:25 **12:17** [q]Pr 20:22 [r]2Co 8:21

r27 Or *will be* s27 Isaiah 59:20,21; 27:9; Jer. 31:33,34 t31 Some manuscripts do not have *now.* u33 Or *riches and the wisdom and the* v34 Isaiah 40:13 w35 Job 41:11 x1 Or *reasonable* y6 Or *in agreement with the* z16 Or *willing to do menial work*

it depends on you, live at peace with everyone.[a] 19 Do not take revenge,[b] my friends, but leave room for God's wrath, for it is written: "It is mine to avenge; I will repay,"[a][c] says the Lord. 20 On the contrary:

"If your enemy is hungry, feed him;
if he is thirsty, give him something to drink.
In doing this, you will heap burning coals on his head."[b][d]

21 Do not be overcome by evil, but overcome evil with good.

Christians' obedience to the government.

13 Everyone must submit himself to the governing authorities,[e] for there is no authority except that which God has established.[f] The authorities that exist have been established by God. 2 Consequently, he who rebels against the authority is rebelling against what God has instituted, and those who do so will bring judgment on themselves. 3 For rulers hold no terror for those who do right, but for those who do wrong. Do you want to be free from fear of the one in authority? Then do what is right and he will commend you.[g] 4 For he is God's servant to do you good. But if you do wrong, be afraid, for he does not bear the sword for nothing. He is God's servant, an agent of wrath to bring punishment on the wrongdoer.[h] 5 Therefore, it is necessary to submit to the authorities, not only because of possible punishment but also because of conscience.

6 This is also why you pay taxes, for the authorities are God's servants, who give their full time to governing. 7 Give everyone what you owe him: If you owe taxes, pay taxes;[i] if revenue, then revenue; if respect, then respect; if honor, then honor.

Debt of love.

8 Let no debt remain outstanding, except the continuing debt to love one another, for he who loves his fellowman has fulfilled the law.[j] 9 The commandments, "Do not commit adultery," "Do not murder," "Do not steal," "Do not covet,"[c][k] and whatever other commandment there may be, are summed up in this one rule: "Love your neighbor as yourself."[d][l] 10 Love does no harm to its neighbor. Therefore love is the fulfillment of the law.[m]

11 And do this, understanding the present time. The hour has come[n] for you to wake up from your slumber,[o] because our salvation is nearer now than when we first believed. 12 The night is nearly over; the day is almost here.[p] So let us put aside the deeds of darkness[q] and put on the armor[r] of light. 13 Let us behave decently, as in the daytime, not in orgies and drunkenness, not in sexual immorality and debauchery, not in dissension and jealousy.[s] 14 Rather, clothe yourselves with the Lord Jesus Christ,[t] and do not think about how to gratify the desires of the sinful nature.[e]

Do not be critical of weaker brothers.

14 Accept him whose faith is weak,[u] without passing judgment on disputable matters. 2 One man's faith allows him to eat everything, but another man, whose faith is weak, eats only vegetables. 3 The man who eats everything must not look down on[v] him who does not, and the man who does not eat everything must not condemn[w] the man who does, for God has accepted him. 4 Who are you to judge someone else's servant?[x] To his own master he stands or falls. And he will stand, for the Lord is able to make him stand.

5 One man considers one day more sacred than another;[y] another man considers every day alike. Each one should be fully convinced in his own mind. 6 He who regards one day as special, does so to the Lord. He who eats meat, eats to the Lord, for he gives thanks to God;[z] and he who abstains, does so to the Lord

12:18 [a] Mk 9:50; Ro 14:19
12:19 [b] Lev 19:18; Pr 20:22; 24:29 [c] Dt 32:35
12:20 [d] Pr 25:21,22; Mt 5:44; Lk 6:27
13:1 [e] Tit 3:1; 1Pe 2:13,14 [f] Da 2:21; Jn 19:11
13:3 [g] 1Pe 2:14
13:4 [h] 1Th 4:6
13:7 [i] Mt 17:25; 22:17,21; Lk 23:2
13:8 [j] ver 10; Jn 13:34; Gal 5:14; Col 3:14
13:9 [k] Ex 20:13-15, 17; Dt 5:17-19,21 [l] Lev 19:18; Mt 19:19
13:10 [m] ver 8; Mt 22:39,40
13:11 [n] 1Co 7:29-31; 10:11 [o] Eph 5:14; 1Th 5:5,6
13:12 [p] 1Jn 2:8 [q] Eph 5:11 [r] Eph 6:11,13
13:13 [s] Gal 5:20,21
13:14 [t] Gal 3:27; 5:16; Eph 4:24
14:1 [u] Ro 15:1; 1Co 8:9-12
14:3 [v] Lk 18:9 [w] Col 2:16
14:4 [x] Jas 4:12
14:5 [y] Gal 4:10
14:6 [z] Mt 14:19; 1Co 10:30,31; 1Ti 4:3,4

a *19* Deut. 32:35 b *20* Prov. 25:21,22
c *9* Exodus 20:13-15,17; Deut. 5:17-19,21
d *9* Lev. 19:18 e *14* Or *the flesh*

and gives thanks to God. 7For none of us
lives to himself alone[a] and none of us
dies to himself alone. 8If we live, we live
to the Lord; and if we die, we die to the
Lord. So, whether we live or die, we
belong to the Lord.[b]
9For this very reason, Christ died and
returned to life[c] so that he might be the
Lord of both the dead and the living.[d]
10You, then, why do you judge your brother? Or why do you look down on your
brother? For we will all stand before
God's judgment seat.[e] 11It is written:

"'As surely as I live,' says the Lord,
'every knee will bow before me;
every tongue will confess to
God.'"[f][f]

12So then, each of us will give an account of himself to God.[g]

Do not be a stumbling block for weaker brothers.

13Therefore let us stop passing judgment[h] on one another. Instead, make up
your mind not to put any stumbling block
or obstacle in your brother's way. 14As
one who is in the Lord Jesus, I am fully
convinced that no food[g] is unclean in
itself.[i] But if anyone regards something
as unclean, then for him it is unclean.[j]
15If your brother is distressed because
of what you eat, you are no longer acting in love.[k] Do not by your eating
destroy your brother for whom Christ
died.[l] 16Do not allow what you consider good to be spoken of as evil.[m] 17For
the kingdom of God is not a matter of
eating and drinking,[n] but of righteousness, peace and joy in the Holy Spirit,[o]
18because anyone who serves Christ in
this way is pleasing to God and approved by men.[p]
19Let us therefore make every effort
to do what leads to peace[q] and to mutual
edification.[r] 20Do not destroy the work
of God for the sake of food.[s] All food is
clean, but it is wrong for a man to eat
anything that causes someone else to
stumble.[t] 21It is better not to eat meat
or drink wine or to do anything else
that will cause your brother to fall.[u]
22So whatever you believe about these
things keep between yourself and God.
Blessed is the man who does not condemn[v] himself by what he approves.
23But the man who has doubts[w] is condemned if he eats, because his eating is
not from faith; and everything that does
not come from faith is sin.

Building up others in the Lord.

15 We who are strong ought to bear
with the failings of the weak[x]
and not to please ourselves. 2Each of
us should please his neighbor for his
good,[y] to build him up.[z] 3For even Christ
did not please himself[a] but, as it is written: "The insults of those who insult
you have fallen on me."[h][b] 4For everything that was written in the past was
written to teach us,[c] so that through
endurance and the encouragement of
the Scriptures we might have hope.
5May the God who gives endurance
and encouragement give you a spirit of
unity[d] among yourselves as you follow
Christ Jesus, 6so that with one heart and
mouth you may glorify the God and
Father[e] of our Lord Jesus Christ.

Accepting others as Christ has accepted us.

7Accept one another,[f] then, just as
Christ accepted you, in order to bring
praise to God. 8For I tell you that Christ
has become a servant of the Jews[i][g] on
behalf of God's truth, to confirm the
promises[h] made to the patriarchs 9so
that the Gentiles[i] may glorify God[j] for
his mercy, as it is written:

"Therefore I will praise you among
the Gentiles;
I will sing hymns to your name."[j][k]

10Again, it says,

14:7 [a]2Co 5:15; Gal 2:20 **14:8** [b]Php 1:20 **14:9** [c]Rev 1:18 [d]2Co 5:15 **14:10** [e]2Co 5:10 **14:11** [f]Isa 45:23; Php 2:10,11 **14:12** [g]Mt 12:36; 1Pe 4:5 **14:13** [h]Mt 7:1 **14:14** [i]Ac 10:15 [j]1Co 8:7 **14:15** [k]Eph 5:2 [l]1Co 8:11 **14:16** [m]1Co 10:30 **14:17** [n]1Co 8:8 [o]Ro 15:13 **14:18** [p]2Co 8:21 **14:19** [q]Ps 34:14; Ro 12:18; Heb 12:14 [r]Ro 15:2; 2Co 12:19 **14:20** [s]ver 15 [t]1Co 8:9-12 **14:21** [u]1Co 8:13 **14:22** [v]1Jn 3:21 **14:23** [w]ver 5 **15:1** [x]Ro 14:1; Gal 6:1,2; 1Th 5:14 **15:2** [y]1Co 10:33 [z]Ro 14:19 **15:3** [a]2Co 8:9 [b]Ps 69:9 **15:4** [c]Ro 4:23,24 **15:5** [d]Ro 12:16; 1Co 1:10 **15:6** [e]Rev 1:6 **15:7** [f]Ro 14:1 **15:8** [g]Mt 15:24; Ac 3:25,26 [h]2Co 1:20 **15:9** [i]Ro 3:29 [j]Mt 9:8 [k]2Sa 22:50; Ps 18:49

f *11* Isaiah 45:23 g *14* Or *that nothing*
h *3* Psalm 69:9 i *8* Greek *circumcision*
j *9* 2 Samuel 22:50; Psalm 18:49

"Rejoice, O Gentiles, with his
people."[k][a]

11And again,

"Praise the Lord, all you Gentiles,
and sing praises to him, all you
peoples."[l][b]

12And again, Isaiah says,

"The Root of Jesse[c] will spring up,
one who will arise to rule over the
nations;
the Gentiles will hope in him."[m][d]

13May the God of hope fill you with
all joy and peace[e] as you trust in him,
so that you may overflow with hope by
the power of the Holy Spirit.[f]

Reviewing Paul's past ministries and future plans.

14I myself am convinced, my brothers,
that you yourselves are full of goodness,[g]
complete in knowledge[h] and competent
to instruct one another. 15I have written
you quite boldly on some points, as if to
remind you of them again, because of
the grace God gave me[i] 16to be a minister of Christ Jesus to the Gentiles[j] with
the priestly duty of proclaiming the gospel of God,[k] so that the Gentiles might
become an offering[l] acceptable to God,
sanctified by the Holy Spirit.
17Therefore I glory in Christ Jesus[m]
in my service to God.[n] 18I will not venture to speak of anything except what
Christ has accomplished through me
in leading the Gentiles[o] to obey God[p]
by what I have said and done— 19by the
power of signs and miracles,[q] through the
power of the Spirit.[r] So from Jerusalem[s] all the way around to Illyricum, I
have fully proclaimed the gospel of
Christ. 20It has always been my ambition to preach the gospel where Christ
was not known, so that I would not be
building on someone else's foundation.[t]
21Rather, as it is written:

"Those who were not told about him
will see,
and those who have not heard will
understand."[n][u]

22This is why I have often been hindered from coming to you.[v]
23But now that there is no more place
for me to work in these regions, and
since I have been longing for many years
to see you,[w] 24I plan to do so when I
go to Spain.[x] I hope to visit you while
passing through and to have you assist
me on my journey there, after I have
enjoyed your company for a while.
25Now, however, I am on my way to
Jerusalem[y] in the service[z] of the saints
there. 26For Macedonia[a] and Achaia[b]
were pleased to make a contribution for
the poor among the saints in Jerusalem. 27They were pleased to do it, and
indeed they owe it to them. For if the
Gentiles have shared in the Jews' spiritual blessings, they owe it to the Jews
to share with them their material blessings.[c] 28So after I have completed this
task and have made sure that they have
received this fruit, I will go to Spain
and visit you on the way. 29I know that
when I come to you,[d] I will come in the
full measure of the blessing of Christ.
30I urge you, brothers, by our Lord
Jesus Christ and by the love of the Spirit,[e] to join me in my struggle by praying to God for me.[f] 31Pray that I may be
rescued[g] from the unbelievers in Judea
and that my service in Jerusalem may be
acceptable to the saints there, 32so that
by God's will[h] I may come to you[i] with
joy and together with you be refreshed.[j]
33The God of peace[k] be with you all.
Amen.

Paul's commendation of Phoebe.

16 I commend[l] to you our sister
Phoebe, a servant[o] of the church
in Cenchrea.[m] 2I ask you to receive her
in the Lord[n] in a way worthy of the
saints and to give her any help she may
need from you, for she has been a great
help to many people, including me.

15:10 [a]Dt 32:43
15:11 [b]Ps 117:1
15:12 [c]Rev 5:5 [d]Isa 11:10; Mt 12:21
15:13 [e]Ro 14:17 [f]ver 19; 1Co 2:4; 1Th 1:5
15:14 [g]Eph 5:9 [h]2Pe 1:12
15:15 [i]Ro 12:3
15:16 [j]Ac 9:15; Ro 11:13 [k]Ro 1:1 [l]Isa 66:20
15:17 [m]Php 3:3 [n]Heb 2:17
15:18 [o]Ac 15:12; 21:19; Ro 1:5 [p]Ro 16:26
15:19 [q]Jn 4:48; Ac 19:11 [r]ver 13 [s]Ac 22:17-21
15:20 [t]2Co 10:15,16
15:21 [u]Isa 52:15
15:22 [v]Ro 1:13
15:23 [w]Ac 19:21; Ro 1:10,11
15:24 [x]ver 28
15:25 [y]Ac 19:21 [z]Ac 24:17
15:26 [a]Ac 16:9; 2Co 8:1 [b]Ac 18:12
15:27 [c]1Co 9:11
15:29 [d]Ro 1:10,11
15:30 [e]Gal 5:22 [f]2Co 1:11; Col 4:12
15:31 [g]2Th 3:2
15:32 [h]Ac 18:21 [i]Ro 1:10,13 [j]1Co 16:18
15:33 [k]Ro 16:20; 2Co 13:11; Php 4:9; 1Th 5:23; Heb 13:20 **16:1** [l]2Co 3:1 [m]Ac 18:18
16:2 [n]Php 2:29

k *10* Deut. 32:43 l *11* Psalm 117:1 m *12* Isaiah 11:10
n *21* Isaiah 52:15 o *1* Or *deaconess*

Paul's praise and greetings to the saints at Rome.

3 Greet Priscilla[p] and Aquila,[a] my fellow
workers in Christ Jesus.[b] 4 They
risked their lives for me. Not only
I but all the churches of the Gentiles are grateful to them.
5 Greet also the church that meets at
their house.[c]
Greet my dear friend Epenetus, who
was the first convert[d] to Christ in
the province of Asia.
6 Greet Mary, who worked very hard
for you.
7 Greet Andronicus and Junias, my relatives[e] who have been in prison with
me. They are outstanding among the
apostles, and they were in Christ
before I was.
8 Greet Ampliatus, whom I love in the
Lord.
9 Greet Urbanus, our fellow worker in
Christ,[f] and my dear friend Stachys.
10 Greet Apelles, tested and approved in
Christ.
Greet those who belong to the household of Aristobulus.
11 Greet Herodion, my relative.[g]
Greet those in the household of Nar-
cissus who are in the Lord.
12 Greet Tryphena and Tryphosa, those
women who work hard in the Lord.
Greet my dear friend Persis, another
woman who has worked very hard
in the Lord.
13 Greet Rufus, chosen in the Lord, and
his mother, who has been a mother
to me, too.
14 Greet Asyncritus, Phlegon, Hermes,
Patrobas, Hermas and the brothers
with them.
15 Greet Philologus, Julia, Nereus and
his sister, and Olympas and all the
saints[h] with them.[i]
16 Greet one another with a holy kiss.[j]

16:3 [a]Ac 18:2 [b]ver 7,9,10
16:5 [c]1Co 16:19; Col 4:15; Phm 2 [d]1Co 16:15
16:7 [e]ver 11,21
16:9 [f]ver 3
16:11 [g]ver 7,21
16:15 [h]ver 2 [i]ver 14
16:16 [j]1Co 16:20; 2Co 13:12; 1Th 5:26
16:17 [k]Gal 1:8,9; 1Ti 1:3; 6:3 [l]2Th 3:6,14; 2Jn 10
16:18 [m]Php 3:19 [n]Col 2:4
16:19 [o]Ro 1:8 [p]Mt 10:16; 1Co 14:20
16:20 [q]Ro 15:33 [r]Ge 3:15 [s]1Th 5:28
16:21 [t]Ac 16:1 [u]Ac 13:1 [v]Ac 17:5 [w]ver 7,11
16:23 [x]Ac 19:22
16:25 [y]Eph 3:20 [z]Ro 2:16 [a]Eph 1:9; Col 1:26,27
16:27 [b]Ro 11:36

All the churches of Christ send greetings.

Paul's exhortation to avoid divisive people.

17 I urge you, brothers, to watch out
for those who cause divisions and put
obstacles in your way that are contrary
to the teaching you have learned.[k] Keep
away from them.[l] 18 For such people are
not serving our Lord Christ, but their
own appetites.[m] By smooth talk and flattery they deceive[n] the minds of naive
people. 19 Everyone has heard[o] about
your obedience, so I am full of joy over
you; but I want you to be wise about
what is good, and innocent about what
is evil.[p]
20 The God of peace[q] will soon crush[r]
Satan under your feet.
The grace of our Lord Jesus be with
you.[s]
21 Timothy,[t] my fellow worker, sends
his greetings to you, as do Lucius,[u]
Jason[v] and Sosipater, my relatives.[w]
22 I, Tertius, who wrote down this letter, greet you in the Lord.
23 Gaius, whose hospitality I and the
whole church here enjoy, sends you his
greetings.
Erastus,[x] who is the city's director of
public works, and our brother Quartus
send you their greetings.[q]
25 Now to him who is able[y] to establish
you by my gospel[z] and the proclamation
of Jesus Christ, according to the revelation of the mystery[a] hidden for long ages
past, 26 but now revealed and made
known through the prophetic writings
by the command of the eternal God, so
that all nations might believe and obey
him— 27 to the only wise God be glory
forever through Jesus Christ! Amen.[b]

p3 Greek *Prisca*, a variant of *Priscilla* q23 Some manuscripts *their greetings.* [24]*May the grace of our Lord Jesus Christ be with all of you. Amen.*

1 CORINTHIANS

Author: Paul the Apostle.

Date Written: Between A.D. 55 and 57.

Title: From Paul's first recorded letter to the church at Corinth.

Background: The Roman general Mummius destroys the Greek city of Corinth in the second century B.C., but Julius Caesar restores the city in about 46 B.C. Corinth, located on the Mediterranean, becomes the commercial and economic hub of Greece. This wealthy cosmopolitan center of about 700,000 people soon sets the standard for immorality and licentiousness. It is in this perverse environment that Paul establishes the church at Corinth while there for over a year-and-a-half on his second missionary journey. Priscilla, Aquila, Silas and Timothy are instrumental in aiding Paul's efforts. But soon after Paul's departure, severe evils and factions threaten the stability and very existence of the church.

Where Written: Ephesus.

To Whom: To the church at Corinth.

Content: The household of Chloe has reported to Paul strife in the church at Corinth. The church sends a delegation of 3 men with a letter to Paul that seeks his wisdom on several concerns and questions the church has. This letter from Paul to the Corinthians systematically answers these issues: divisions in the church, immorality, lawsuits, challenges to Paul's apostleship, meat sacrificed to idols, marriage, divorce and the Lord's Supper. Classic teaching is offered on spiritual gifts (chapter 12), Christian love (chapter 13) and the resurrection (chapter 15). In addition to Paul's words of discipline, he gives practical suggestions to the people while proclaiming the gospel as the power and wisdom of God.

Key Words: "Correction"; "Unity." Paul offers words of "correction" with both love and firmness. The only hope available to the Corinthians is "unity" in Jesus Christ. Bound together they can love, serve, minister and overcome evil by drawing their strength from the same Spirit of God within each of them.

Themes: • Christ alone is able to cleanse us of our sins and give us right standing before God. • Only Christians are able to give true love. • True love is a decision, an action and a commitment. • God will never let us be tempted beyond our limits to endure. • Brothers and sisters in Christ share a oneness and unity not made available to the world. • Mature Christians sometimes need to limit their personal liberties for the benefit of those weaker. • Believers receive gifts in order to glorify God and build up the body in love. • Jesus Christ is interested in all areas of our lives and is the answer to all our problems.

Outline:
1. Introduction. 1:1-1:9
2. Problems in the Corinthian church. 1:10-4:21
3. Discipline for the church. 5:1-6:20
4. Concerning marriage. 7:1-7:40
5. Principles of Christian rights and liberty. 8:1-11:1
6. Concerning public worship and spiritual gifts. 11:2-14:40
7. Concerning the resurrection. 15:1-15:58
8. Paul's plans and final instructions. 16:1-16:24

1 CORINTHIANS

Blessings for the Christians.

1 Paul, called to be an apostle[a] of Christ
Jesus by the will of God,[b] and our
brother Sosthenes,[c]

2 To the church of God in Corinth,[d] to
those sanctified in Christ Jesus and
called[e] to be holy, together with all those
everywhere who call on the name of our
Lord Jesus Christ—their Lord and ours:

3 Grace and peace to you from God
our Father and the Lord Jesus Christ.[f]

4 I always thank God for you[g] because
of his grace given you in Christ Jesus.
5 For in him you have been enriched[h] in
every way—in all your speaking and in
all your knowledge[i]— 6 because our testimony[j] about Christ was confirmed in
you. 7 Therefore you do not lack any spiritual gift as you eagerly wait for our Lord
Jesus Christ to be revealed.[k] 8 He will
keep you strong to the end, so that you
will be blameless[l] on the day of our Lord
Jesus Christ. 9 God, who has called you
into fellowship with his Son Jesus Christ
our Lord,[m] is faithful.[n]

The church's division
over leadership.

10 I appeal to you, brothers, in the name
of our Lord Jesus Christ, that all of you
agree with one another so that there
may be no divisions among you and that
you may be perfectly united in mind and
thought. 11 My brothers, some from
Chloe's household have informed me
that there are quarrels among you. 12 What
I mean is this: One of you says, "I follow

1:1 [a]Ro 1:1; Eph 1:1 [b]2Co 1:1 [c]Ac 18:17
1:2 [d]Ac 18:1 [e]Ro 1:7
1:3 [f]Ro 1:7
1:4 [g]Ro 1:8
1:5 [h]2Co 9:11 [i]2Co 8:7
1:6 [j]Rev 1:2
1:7 [k]Php 3:20; Tit 2:13; 2Pe 3:12
1:8 [l]1Th 3:13
1:9 [m]1Jn 1:3 [n]Isa 49:7; 1Th 5:24

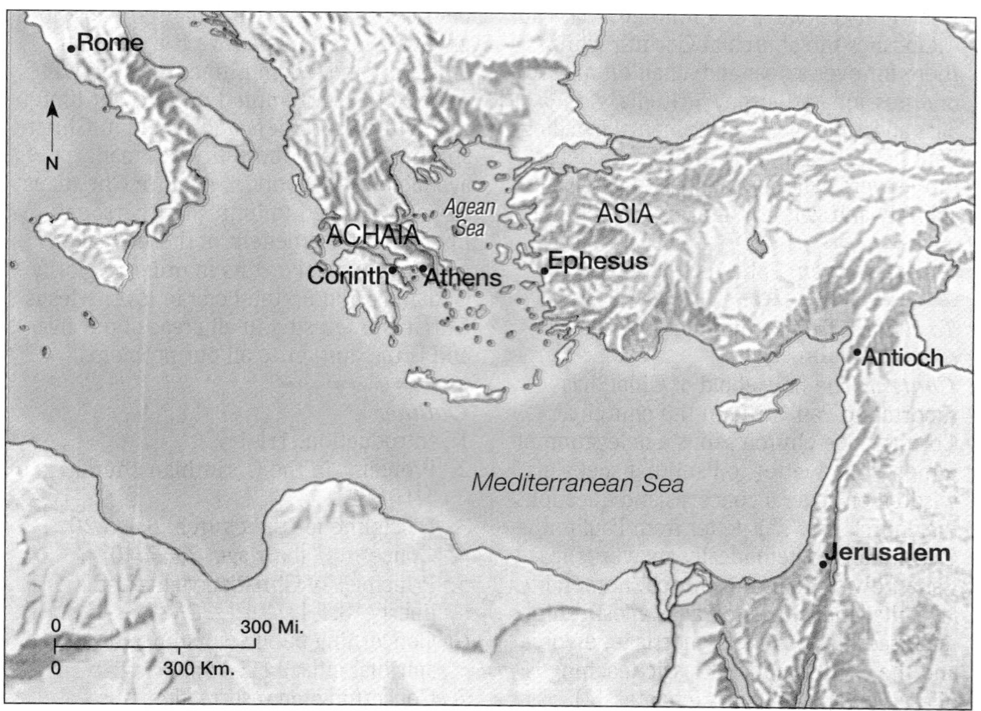

Corinth and Ephesus

Paul wrote this letter to Corinth during his three-year visit in Ephesus on his third missionary journey. The two cities sat across from each other on the Aegean Sea—both were busy and important ports. Titus may have carried this letter from Ephesus to Corinth (2 Corinthians 12:18).

Paul";[a] another, "I follow Apollos";[b] another, "I follow Cephas[a]";[c] still another, "I follow Christ."

13 Is Christ divided? Was Paul crucified for you? Were you baptized into[b] the name of Paul?[d] 14 I am thankful that I did not baptize any of you except Crispus[e] and Gaius,[f] 15 so no one can say that you were baptized into my name. 16 (Yes, I also baptized the household of Stephanas;[g] beyond that, I don't remember if I baptized anyone else.) 17 For Christ did not send me to baptize,[h] but to preach the gospel—not with words of human wisdom,[i] lest the cross of Christ be emptied of its power.

God's wisdom versus humanity's foolishness.

18 For the message of the cross is foolishness to those who are perishing,[j] but to us who are being saved it is the power of God.[k] 19 For it is written:

> "I will destroy the wisdom of the wise;
> the intelligence of the intelligent I will frustrate."[c][l]

20 Where is the wise man?[m] Where is the scholar? Where is the philosopher of this age? Has not God made foolish[n] the wisdom of the world? 21 For since in the wisdom of God the world through its wisdom did not know him, God was pleased through the foolishness of what was preached to save those who believe. 22 Jews demand miraculous signs[o] and Greeks look for wisdom, 23 but we preach Christ crucified: a stumbling block[p] to Jews and foolishness[q] to Gentiles, 24 but to those whom God has called,[r] both Jews and Greeks, Christ the power of God and the wisdom of God.[s] 25 For the foolishness[t] of God is wiser than man's wisdom, and the weakness[u] of God is stronger than man's strength.

26 Brothers, think of what you were when you were called. Not many of you were wise by human standards; not many were influential; not many were of noble birth. 27 But God chose[v] the foolish[w] things of the world to shame the wise; God chose the weak things of the world to shame the strong. 28 He chose the lowly things of this world and the despised things—and the things that are not[x]—to nullify the things that are, 29 so that no one may boast before him.[y] 30 It is because of him that you are in Christ Jesus, who has become for us wisdom from God—that is, our righteousness,[z] holiness and redemption.[a] 31 Therefore, as it is written: "Let him who boasts boast in the Lord."[d][b]

Paul's preaching is simple, yet powerful.

2 When I came to you, brothers, I did not come with eloquence or superior wisdom[c] as I proclaimed to you the testimony about God.[e] 2 For I resolved to know nothing while I was with you except Jesus Christ and him crucified.[d] 3 I came to you[e] in weakness and fear, and with much trembling. 4 My message and my preaching were not with wise and persuasive words, but with a demonstration of the Spirit's power,[f] 5 so that your faith might not rest on men's wisdom, but on God's power.[g]

The Holy Spirit teaches believers about God.

6 We do, however, speak a message of wisdom among the mature,[h] but not the wisdom of this age[i] or of the rulers of this age, who are coming to nothing. 7 No, we speak of God's secret wisdom, a wisdom that has been hidden and that God destined for our glory before time began. 8 None of the rulers of this age understood it, for if they had, they would not have crucified the Lord of glory.[j] 9 However, as it is written:

> "No eye has seen,
> no ear has heard,
> no mind has conceived

1:12 [a] 1Co 3:4,22 [b] Ac 18:24 [c] Jn 1:42
1:13 [d] Mt 28:19
1:14 [e] Ac 18:8; Ro 16:23 [f] Ac 19:29
1:16 [g] 1Co 16:15
1:17 [h] Jn 4:2 [i] 1Co 2:1, 4,13
1:18 [j] 2Co 2:15 [k] Ro 1:16
1:19 [l] Isa 29:14
1:20 [m] Isa 19:11, 12 [n] Job 12:17; Ro 1:22
1:22 [o] Mt 12:38
1:23 [p] Lk 2:34; Gal 5:11 [q] 1Co 2:14
1:24 [r] Ro 8:28 [s] ver 30; Col 2:3
1:25 [t] ver 18 [u] 2Co 13:4
1:27 [v] Jas 2:5 [w] ver 20
1:28 [x] Ro 4:17
1:29 [y] Eph 2:9
1:30 [z] Jer 23:5,6; 2Co 5:21 [a] Ro 3:24; Eph 1:7,14
1:31 [b] Jer 9:23,24; 2Co 10:17
2:1 [c] 1Co 1:17
2:2 [d] Gal 6:14; 1Co 1:23
2:3 [e] Ac 18:1-18
2:4 [f] Ro 15:19
2:5 [g] 2Co 4:7; 6:7
2:6 [h] Eph 4:13; Php 3:15; Heb 5:14 [i] 1Co 1:20
2:8 [j] Ac 7:2; Jas 2:1

a *12* That is, Peter b *13* Or *in*; also in verse 15 c *19* Isaiah 29:14 d *31* Jer. 9:24 e *1* Some manuscripts *as I proclaimed to you God's mystery*

what God has prepared for those
who love him"[f][a]—

10but God has revealed[b] it to us by his
Spirit.[c]
The Spirit searches all things, even the
deep things of God. 11For who among
men knows the thoughts of a man[d] except the man's spirit[e] within him? In the
same way no one knows the thoughts of
God except the Spirit of God. 12We
have not received the spirit[f] of the
world[g] but the Spirit who is from God,
that we may understand what God has
freely given us. 13This is what we
speak, not in words taught us by human
wisdom[h] but in words taught by the
Spirit, expressing spiritual truths in
spiritual words.[g] 14The man without
the Spirit does not accept the things that
come from the Spirit of God, for they
are foolishness[i] to him, and he cannot
understand them, because they are spiritually discerned. 15The spiritual man
makes judgments about all things, but
he himself is not subject to any man's
judgment:

16"For who has known the mind of the
Lord
that he may instruct him?"[h][j]

But we have the mind of Christ.[k]

Infant Christians are fed milk.

3 Brothers, I could not address you as
spiritual[l] but as worldly[m]—mere
infants[n] in Christ. 2I gave you milk, not
solid food,[o] for you were not yet ready
for it.[p] Indeed, you are still not ready.
3You are still worldly. For since there is
jealousy and quarreling[q] among you, are
you not worldly? Are you not acting like
mere men? 4For when one says, "I follow Paul," and another, "I follow Apollos,"[r] are you not mere men?

Paul plants and Apollos waters God's field.

5What, after all, is Apollos? And what
is Paul? Only servants, through whom
you came to believe—as the Lord has
assigned to each his task. 6I planted the
seed,[s] Apollos watered it, but God made
it grow. 7So neither he who plants nor
he who waters is anything, but only
God, who makes things grow. 8The man
who plants and the man who waters
have one purpose, and each will be rewarded according to his own labor.[t] 9For
we are God's fellow workers;[u] you are
God's field,[v] God's building.[w]
10By the grace God has given me,[x] I
laid a foundation[y] as an expert builder,
and someone else is building on it. But
each one should be careful how he
builds. 11For no one can lay any foundation other than the one already laid,
which is Jesus Christ.[z] 12If any man
builds on this foundation using gold, silver, costly stones, wood, hay or straw,
13his work will be shown for what it
is,[a] because the Day[b] will bring it to
light. It will be revealed with fire, and
the fire will test the quality of each man's
work. 14If what he has built survives, he
will receive his reward. 15If it is burned
up, he will suffer loss; he himself will be
saved, but only as one escaping through
the flames.[c]
16Don't you know that you yourselves
are God's temple[d] and that God's Spirit
lives in you? 17If anyone destroys God's
temple, God will destroy him; for God's
temple is sacred, and you are that temple.

This world's wisdom is foolishness.

18Do not deceive yourselves. If any
one of you thinks he is wise[e] by the standards of this age, he should become a
"fool" so that he may become wise.
19For the wisdom of this world is foolishness[f] in God's sight. As it is written: "He
catches the wise in their craftiness"[i];[g]
20and again, "The Lord knows that the
thoughts of the wise are futile."[j][h] 21So
then, no more boasting about men![i]
All things are yours,[j] 22whether Paul or

2:9 [a]Isa 64:4; 65:17
2:10 [b]Mt 13:11; Eph 3:3,5 [c]Jn 14:26
2:11 [d]Jer 17:9 [e]Pr 20:27
2:12 [f]Ro 8:15 [g]1Co 1:20,27
2:13 [h]1Co 1:17
2:14 [i]1Co 1:18
2:16 [j]Isa 40:13 [k]Jn 15:15
3:1 [l]1Co 2:15 [m]Ro 7:14; 1Co 2:14 [n]Heb 5:13
3:2 [o]Heb 5:12-14; 1Pe 2:2 [p]Jn 16:12
3:3 [q]1Co 1:11; Gal 5:20
3:4 [r]1Co 1:12
3:6 [s]Ac 18:4-11
3:8 [t]Ps 62:12
3:9 [u]2Co 6:1 [v]Isa 61:3 [w]Eph 2:20-22; 1Pe 2:5
3:10 [x]Ro 12:3 [y]Ro 15:20
3:11 [z]Isa 28:16; Eph 2:20
3:13 [a]1Co 4:5 [b]2Th 1:7-10
3:15 [c]Jude 23
3:16 [d]1Co 6:19; 2Co 6:16
3:18 [e]Isa 5:21; 1Co 8:2
3:19 [f]1Co 1:20,27 [g]Job 5:13
3:20 [h]Ps 94:11
3:21 [i]1Co 4:6 [j]Ro 8:32

f9 Isaiah 64:4 g13 Or *Spirit, interpreting spiritual truths to spiritual men* h16 Isaiah 40:13
i19 Job 5:13 j20 Psalm 94:11

Apollos or Cephas[k][a] or the world or life
or death or the present or the future[b]—all
are yours, 23and you are of Christ,[c] and
Christ is of God.

Apostles directed to be good servants.

4 So then, men ought to regard us as
servants of Christ and as those entrusted[d] with the secret things[e] of God.
2Now it is required that those who have
been given a trust must prove faithful.
3I care very little if I am judged by you
or by any human court; indeed, I do not
even judge myself. 4My conscience is
clear, but that does not make me innocent.[f] It is the Lord who judges me.
5Therefore judge nothing[g] before the appointed time; wait till the Lord comes. He
will bring to light what is hidden in
darkness and will expose the motives of
men's hearts. At that time each will
receive his praise from God.[h]

6Now, brothers, I have applied these
things to myself and Apollos for your
benefit, so that you may learn from us
the meaning of the saying, "Do not go
beyond what is written."[i] Then you will
not take pride in one man over against
another.[j] 7For who makes you different
from anyone else? What do you have
that you did not receive?[k] And if you did
receive it, why do you boast as though
you did not?

8Already you have all you want! Already you have become rich![l] You have
become kings—and that without us!
How I wish that you really had become
kings so that we might be kings with
you! 9For it seems to me that God has
put us apostles on display at the end of
the procession, like men condemned to
die[m] in the arena. We have been made
a spectacle[n] to the whole universe, to
angels as well as to men. 10We are fools
for Christ,[o] but you are so wise in
Christ![p] We are weak, but you are
strong![q] You are honored, we are dishonored! 11To this very hour we go hungry and thirsty, we are in rags, we are
brutally treated, we are homeless.[r] 12We
work hard with our own hands.[s] When

3:22 [a]1Co 1:12 [b]Ro 8:38
3:23 [c]1Co 15:23; 2Co 10:7; Gal 3:29
4:1 [d]1Co 9:17; Tit 1:7 [e]Ro 16:25
4:4 [f]Ro 2:13
4:5 [g]Mt 7:1,2; Ro 2:1 [h]Ro 2:29
4:6 [i]1Co 1:19,31; 3:19,20 [j]1Co 1:12
4:7 [k]Jn 3:27; Ro 12:3,6
4:8 [l]Rev 3:17,18
4:9 [m]Ro 8:36 [n]Heb 10:33
4:10 [o]1Co 1:18; Ac 17:18 [p]1Co 3:18 [q]1Co 2:3
4:11 [r]Ro 8:35; 2Co 11:23-27
4:12 [s]Ac 18:3 [t]1Pe 3:9
4:13 [u]La 3:45
4:14 [v]1Th 2:11
4:15 [w]1Co 9:12,14, 18,23
4:16 [x]1Co 11:1; Php 3:17; 1Th 1:6; 2Th 3:7,9
4:17 [y]1Ti 1:2 [z]1Co 7:17
4:19 [a]2Co 1:15,16 [b]Ac 18:21
4:21 [c]2Co 1:23; 13:2,10
5:1 [d]Lev 18:8; Dt 22:30
5:2 [e]2Co 7:7-11
5:3 [f]Col 2:5

we are cursed, we bless;[t] when we are
persecuted, we endure it; 13when we
are slandered, we answer kindly. Up to
this moment we have become the scum
of the earth, the refuse[u] of the world.

People exhorted to imitate Paul.

14I am not writing this to shame you,
but to warn you, as my dear children.[v]
15Even though you have ten thousand
guardians in Christ, you do not have
many fathers, for in Christ Jesus I became your father through the gospel.[w]
16Therefore I urge you to imitate me.[x]
17For this reason I am sending to you
Timothy, my son[y] whom I love, who is
faithful in the Lord. He will remind you
of my way of life in Christ Jesus, which
agrees with what I teach everywhere
in every church.[z]

18Some of you have become arrogant,
as if I were not coming to you. 19But I
will come to you very soon,[a] if the Lord
is willing,[b] and then I will find out not
only how these arrogant people are talking, but what power they have. 20For
the kingdom of God is not a matter of
talk but of power. 21What do you prefer?
Shall I come to you with a whip,[c] or in
love and with a gentle spirit?

Condemnation of incest within the church.

5 It is actually reported that there is
sexual immorality among you, and
of a kind that does not occur even
among pagans: A man has his father's
wife.[d] 2And you are proud! Shouldn't
you rather have been filled with grief[e]
and have put out of your fellowship the
man who did this? 3Even though I am
not physically present, I am with you in
spirit.[f] And I have already passed
judgment on the one who did this, just
as if I were present. 4When you are assembled in the name of our Lord Jesus[g]
and I am with you in spirit, and the
power of our Lord Jesus is present,
5hand this man over[h] to Satan, so that

5:4 [g]2Th 3:6 **5:5** [h]1Ti 1:20

[k]*22* That is, Peter

the sinful nature[l] may be destroyed and his spirit saved on the day of the Lord.

6Your boasting is not good.[a] Don't you know that a little yeast[b] works through the whole batch of dough?[c] 7Get rid of the old yeast that you may be a new batch without yeast—as you really are. For Christ, our Passover lamb, has been sacrificed.[d] 8Therefore let us keep the Festival, not with the old yeast, the yeast of malice and wickedness, but with bread without yeast,[e] the bread of sincerity and truth.

Exhortation against associating with evil people claiming to be Christians.

9I have written you in my letter not to associate[f] with sexually immoral people—10not at all meaning the people of this world[g] who are immoral, or the greedy and swindlers, or idolaters. In that case you would have to leave this world. 11But now I am writing you that you must not associate with anyone who calls himself a brother but is sexually immoral or greedy, an idolater[h] or a slanderer, a drunkard or a swindler. With such a man do not even eat.

12What business is it of mine to judge those outside[i] the church? Are you not to judge those inside?[j] 13God will judge those outside. "Expel the wicked man from among you."[m][k]

Appeal against lawsuits between Christians.

6 If any of you has a dispute with another, dare he take it before the ungodly for judgment instead of before the saints?[l] 2Do you not know that the saints will judge the world?[m] And if you are to judge the world, are you not competent to judge trivial cases? 3Do you not know that we will judge angels? How much more the things of this life! 4Therefore, if you have disputes about such matters, appoint as judges even men of little account in the church![n] 5I say this to shame you.[n] Is it possible that there is nobody among you wise enough to judge a dispute between

5:6 [a]Jas 4:16 [b]Mt 16:6,12 [c]Gal 5:9
5:7 [d]Mk 14:12; 1Pe 1:19
5:8 [e]Ex 12:14,15; Dt 16:3
5:9 [f]Eph 5:11; 2Th 3:6,14
5:10 [g]1Co 10:27
5:11 [h]1Co 10:7,14
5:12 [i]Mk 4:11 [j]ver 3-5; 1Co 6:1-4
5:13 [k]Dt 13:5
6:1 [l]Mt 18:17
6:2 [m]Mt 19:28; Lk 22:30
6:5 [n]1Co 4:14 [o]Ac 1:15
6:6 [p]2Co 6:14,15
6:7 [q]Mt 5:39,40
6:8 [r]1Th 4:6
6:9 [s]Gal 5:21 [t]1Co 15:33; Jas 1:16
6:11 [u]Eph 2:2 [v]Ac 22:16 [w]1Co 1:2
6:12 [x]1Co 10:23
6:13 [y]Col 2:22
6:14 [z]Ro 6:5; Eph 1:19,20
6:15 [a]Ro 12:5
6:16 [b]Ge 2:24; Mt 19:5; Eph 5:31
6:17 [c]Jn 17:21-23; Gal 2:20

believers?[o] 6But instead, one brother goes to law against another—and this in front of unbelievers![p]

7The very fact that you have lawsuits among you means you have been completely defeated already. Why not rather be wronged? Why not rather be cheated?[q] 8Instead, you yourselves cheat and do wrong, and you do this to your brothers.[r]

9Do you not know that the wicked will not inherit the kingdom of God?[s] Do not be deceived:[t] Neither the sexually immoral nor idolaters nor adulterers nor male prostitutes nor homosexual offenders 10nor thieves nor the greedy nor drunkards nor slanderers nor swindlers will inherit the kingdom of God. 11And that is what some of you were.[u] But you were washed,[v] you were sanctified,[w] you were justified in the name of the Lord Jesus Christ and by the Spirit of our God.

Avoiding sexual immorality.

12"Everything is permissible for me"—but not everything is beneficial.[x] "Everything is permissible for me"—but I will not be mastered by anything. 13"Food for the stomach and the stomach for food"—but God will destroy them both.[y] The body is not meant for sexual immorality, but for the Lord, and the Lord for the body. 14By his power God raised the Lord from the dead, and he will raise us also.[z] 15Do you not know that your bodies are members of Christ himself?[a] Shall I then take the members of Christ and unite them with a prostitute? Never! 16Do you not know that he who unites himself with a prostitute is one with her in body? For it is said, "The two will become one flesh."[o][b] 17But he who unites himself with the Lord is one with him in spirit.[c]

18Flee from sexual immorality.[d] All

6:18 [d]2Co 12:21; 1Th 4:3,4; Heb 13:4

[l]*5* Or *that his body*; or *that the flesh*
[m]*13* Deut. 17:7; 19:19; 21:21; 22:21,24; 24:7
[n]*4* Or *matters, do you appoint as judges men of little account in the church?*
[o]*16* Gen. 2:24

other sins a man commits are outside his body, but he who sins sexually sins against his own body.[a] 19 Do you not know that your body is a temple[b] of the Holy Spirit, who is in you, whom you have received from God? You are not your own;[c] 20 you were bought at a price.[d] Therefore honor God with your body.

Reasons to marry or to remain single.

7 Now for the matters you wrote about: It is good for a man not to marry.[p][e] 2 But since there is so much immorality, each man should have his own wife, and each woman her own husband. 3 The husband should fulfill his marital duty to his wife,[f] and likewise the wife to her husband. 4 The wife's body does not belong to her alone but also to her husband. In the same way, the husband's body does not belong to him alone but also to his wife. 5 Do not deprive each other except by mutual consent and for a time,[g] so that you may devote yourselves to prayer. Then come together again so that Satan[h] will not tempt you[i] because of your lack of self-control. 6 I say this as a concession, not as a command.[j] 7 I wish that all men were as I am.[k] But each man has his own gift from God; one has this gift, another has that.[l]

8 Now to the unmarried and the widows I say: It is good for them to stay unmarried, as I am.[m] 9 But if they cannot control themselves, they should marry,[n] for it is better to marry than to burn with passion.

10 To the married I give this command (not I, but the Lord): A wife must not separate from her husband.[o] 11 But if she does, she must remain unmarried or else be reconciled to her husband. And a husband must not divorce his wife.

12 To the rest I say this (I, not the Lord):[p] If any brother has a wife who is not a believer and she is willing to live with him, he must not divorce her. 13 And if a woman has a husband who is not a believer and he is willing to live with her, she must not divorce him. 14 For the unbelieving husband has been sanctified through his wife, and the unbelieving wife has been sanctified through her believing husband. Otherwise your children would be unclean, but as it is, they are holy.[q]

15 But if the unbeliever leaves, let him do so. A believing man or woman is not bound in such circumstances; God has called us to live in peace.[r] 16 How do you know, wife, whether you will save[s] your husband?[t] Or, how do you know, husband, whether you will save your wife?

17 Nevertheless, each one should retain the place in life that the Lord assigned to him and to which God has called him.[u] This is the rule I lay down in all the churches.[v] 18 Was a man already circumcised when he was called? He should not become uncircumcised. Was a man uncircumcised when he was called? He should not be circumcised.[w] 19 Circumcision is nothing and uncircumcision is nothing.[x] Keeping God's commands is what counts. 20 Each one should remain in the situation which he was in when God called him.[y] 21 Were you a slave when you were called? Don't let it trouble you—although if you can gain your freedom, do so. 22 For he who was a slave when he was called by the Lord is the Lord's freedman;[z] similarly, he who was a free man when he was called is Christ's slave.[a] 23 You were bought at a price;[b] do not become slaves of men. 24 Brothers, each man, as responsible to God, should remain in the situation God called him to.[c]

25 Now about virgins: I have no command from the Lord,[d] but I give a judgment as one who by the Lord's mercy[e] is trustworthy. 26 Because of the present crisis, I think that it is good for you to remain as you are.[f] 27 Are you married? Do not seek a divorce. Are

6:18 [a]Ro 6:12 **6:19** [b]Jn 2:21 [c]Ro 14:7,8 **6:20** [d]Ac 20:28; 1Co 7:23; 1Pe 1:18,19; Rev 5:9 **7:1** [e]ver 8,26 **7:3** [f]Ex 21:10; 1Pe 3:7 **7:5** [g]Ex 19:15; 1Sa 21:4,5 [h]Mt 4:10 [i]1Th 3:5 **7:6** [j]2Co 8:8 **7:7** [k]ver 8; 1Co 9:5 [l]Mt 19:11,12; Ro 12:6; 1Co 12:4,11 **7:8** [m]ver 1,26 **7:9** [n]1Ti 5:14 **7:10** [o]Mal 2:14-16; Mt 5:32; 19:3-9; Mk 10:11; Lk 16:18 **7:12** [p]ver 6,10; 2Co 11:17 **7:14** [q]Mal 2:15 **7:15** [r]Ro 14:19; 1Co 14:33 **7:16** [s]Ro 11:14 [t]1Pe 3:1 **7:17** [u]Ro 12:3 [v]1Co 4:17; 14:33; 2Co 8:18; 11:28 **7:18** [w]Ac 15:1,2 **7:19** [x]Ro 2:25-27; Gal 5:6; 6:15; Col 3:11 **7:20** [y]ver 24 **7:22** [z]Jn 8:32,36; Phm 16 [a]Eph 6:6

7:23 [b]1Co 6:20 **7:24** [c]ver 20 **7:25** [d]ver 6; 2Co 8:8 [e]2Co 4:1; 1Ti 1:13,16 **7:26** [f]ver 1,8

p 1 Or *"It is good for a man not to have sexual relations with a woman."*

you unmarried? Do not look for a wife.
28But if you do marry, you have not
sinned; and if a virgin marries, she has
not sinned. But those who marry will
face many troubles in this life, and I
want to spare you this.
29What I mean, brothers, is that the
time is short.[a] From now on those who
have wives should live as if they had
none; 30those who mourn, as if they did
not; those who are happy, as if they
were not; those who buy something,
as if it were not theirs to keep; 31those
who use the things of the world, as if
not engrossed in them. For this world
in its present form is passing away.[b]
32I would like you to be free from concern. An unmarried man is concerned
about the Lord's affairs[c]—how he can
please the Lord. 33But a married man is
concerned about the affairs of this
world—how he can please his wife—
34and his interests are divided. An unmarried woman or virgin is concerned
about the Lord's affairs: Her aim is to
be devoted to the Lord in both body and
spirit.[d] But a married woman is concerned about the affairs of this world—
how she can please her husband. 35I
am saying this for your own good, not to
restrict you, but that you may live in a
right way in undivided[e] devotion to
the Lord.
36If anyone thinks he is acting improp-
erly toward the virgin he is engaged to,
and if she is getting along in years and
he feels he ought to marry, he should do
as he wants. He is not sinning.[f] They
should get married. 37But the man who
has settled the matter in his own mind,
who is under no compulsion but has
control over his own will, and who has
made up his mind not to marry the virgin—this man also does the right thing.
38So then, he who marries the virgin does
right,[g] but he who does not marry her
does even better.[q]
39A woman is bound to her husband
as long as he lives.[h] But if her husband
dies, she is free to marry anyone she
wishes, but he must belong to the
Lord.[i] 40In my judgment,[j] she is happier
if she stays as she is—and I think that I
too have the Spirit of God.

Paul discusses eating food sacrificed to idols and the need to be sensitive to others.

8 Now about food sacrificed to idols:[k]
We know that we all possess knowledge.[r][l] Knowledge puffs up, but love
builds up. 2The man who thinks he
knows something[m] does not yet know
as he ought to know.[n] 3But the man
who loves God is known by God.[o]
4So then, about eating food sacrificed
to idols:[p] We know that an idol is nothing at all in the world[q] and that there
is no God but one.[r] 5For even if there
are so-called gods,[s] whether in heaven
or on earth (as indeed there are many
"gods" and many "lords"), 6yet for us
there is but one God, the Father,[t] from
whom all things came[u] and for whom
we live; and there is but one Lord,[v]
Jesus Christ, through whom all things
came[w] and through whom we live.
7But not everyone knows this. Some
people are still so accustomed to idols
that when they eat such food they think
of it as having been sacrificed to an idol,
and since their conscience is weak,[x] it
is defiled. 8But food does not bring us
near to God;[y] we are no worse if we do
not eat, and no better if we do.
9Be careful, however, that the exercise of your freedom does not become
a stumbling block[z] to the weak.[a] 10For
if anyone with a weak conscience sees
you who have this knowledge eating
in an idol's temple, won't he be em-
boldened to eat what has been sacrificed to idols? 11So this weak brother,
for whom Christ died, is destroyed[b] by

7:29 [a]ver 31; Ro 13:11,12
7:31 [b]1Jn 2:17
7:32 [c]1Ti 5:5
7:34 [d]Lk 2:37
7:35 [e]Ps 86:11
7:36 [f]ver 28
7:38 [g]Heb 13:4
7:39 [h]Ro 7:2,3 [i]2Co 6:14
7:40 [j]ver 25
8:1 [k]Ac 15:20 [l]Ro 15:14
8:2 [m]1Co 3:18 [n]1Co 13:8,9, 12; 1Ti 6:4
8:3 [o]Ro 8:29; Gal 4:9
8:4 [p]ver 1,7,10 [q]1Co 10:19 [r]Dt 6:4; Eph 4:6
8:5 [s]2Th 2:4
8:6 [t]Mal 2:10 [u]Ro 11:36 [v]Eph 4:5 [w]Jn 1:3
8:7 [x]Ro 14:14; 1Co 10:28
8:8 [y]Ro 14:17
8:9 [z]Gal 5:13 [a]Ro 14:1
8:11 [b]Ro 14:15,20

[q] *36-38* Or *36If anyone thinks he is not treating his daughter properly, and if she is getting along in years, and he feels she ought to marry, he should do as he wants. He is not sinning. He should let her get married. 37But the man who has settled the matter in his own mind, who is under no compulsion but has control over his own will, and who has made up his mind to keep the virgin unmarried— this man also does the right thing. 38So then, he who gives his virgin in marriage does right, but he who does not give her in marriage does even better.* [r] *1* Or *"We all possess knowledge," as you say*

your knowledge. 12When you sin against your brothers[a] in this way and wound their weak conscience, you sin against Christ. 13Therefore, if what I eat causes my brother to fall into sin, I will never eat meat again, so that I will not cause him to fall.[b]

Rights of apostles.

9 Am I not free? Am I not an apostle?[c] Have I not seen Jesus our Lord?[d] Are you not the result of my work in the Lord?[e] 2Even though I may not be an apostle to others, surely I am to you! For you are the seal[f] of my apostleship in the Lord.

3This is my defense to those who sit in judgment on me. 4Don't we have the right to food and drink?[g] 5Don't we have the right to take a believing wife[h] along with us, as do the other apostles and the Lord's brothers[i] and Cephas[s]? 6Or is it only I and Barnabas[j] who must work for a living?

7Who serves as a soldier at his own expense? Who plants a vineyard[k] and does not eat of its grapes? Who tends a flock and does not drink of the milk? 8Do I say this merely from a human point of view? Doesn't the Law say the same thing? 9For it is written in the Law of Moses: "Do not muzzle an ox while it is treading out the grain."[t][l] Is it about oxen that God is concerned?[m] 10Surely he says this for us, doesn't he? Yes, this was written for us,[n] because when the plowman plows and the thresher threshes, they ought to do so in the hope of sharing in the harvest.[o] 11If we have sown spiritual seed among you, is it too much if we reap a material harvest from you?[p] 12If others have this right of support from you, shouldn't we have it all the more?

But we did not use this right.[q] On the contrary, we put up with anything rather than hinder[r] the gospel of Christ. 13Don't you know that those who work in the temple get their food from the temple, and those who serve at the altar share in what is offered on the altar?[s] 14In the same way, the Lord has commanded that those who preach the gospel should receive their living from the gospel.[t]

15But I have not used any of these rights.[u] And I am not writing this in the hope that you will do such things for me. I would rather die than have anyone deprive me of this boast.[v] 16Yet when I preach the gospel, I cannot boast, for I am compelled to preach.[w] Woe to me if I do not preach the gospel! 17If I preach voluntarily, I have a reward;[x] if not voluntarily, I am simply discharging the trust committed to me.[y] 18What then is my reward? Just this: that in preaching the gospel I may offer it free of charge,[z] and so not make use of my rights in preaching it.

19Though I am free[a] and belong to no man, I make myself a slave to everyone,[b] to win as many as possible.[c] 20To the Jews I became like a Jew, to win the Jews.[d] To those under the law I became like one under the law (though I myself am not under the law), so as to win those under the law. 21To those not having the law I became like one not having the law[e] (though I am not free from God's law but am under Christ's law), so as to win those not having the law. 22To the weak I became weak, to win the weak. I have become all things to all men[f] so that by all possible means I might save some.[g] 23I do all this for the sake of the gospel, that I may share in its blessings.

Running the race for the prize.

24Do you not know that in a race all the runners run, but only one gets the prize? Run[h] in such a way as to get the prize. 25Everyone who competes in the games goes into strict training. They do it to get a crown that will not last; but we do it to get a crown that will last forever.[i] 26Therefore I do not run like a

8:12 [a]Mt 18:6
8:13 [b]Ro 14:21
9:1 [c]2Co 12:12 [d]1Co 15:8 [e]1Co 3:6; 4:15
9:2 [f]2Co 3:2,3
9:4 [g]1Th 2:6
9:5 [h]1Co 7:7,8 [i]Mt 12:46
9:6 [j]Ac 4:36
9:7 [k]Dt 20:6; Pr 27:18
9:9 [l]Dt 25:4; 1Ti 5:18 [m]Dt 22:1-4
9:10 [n]Ro 4:23,24 [o]2Ti 2:6
9:11 [p]Ro 15:27
9:12 [q]Ac 18:3 [r]2Co 11:7-12
9:13 [s]Lev 6:16,26; Dt 18:1
9:14 [t]Mt 10:10; 1Ti 5:18
9:15 [u]Ac 18:3 [v]2Co 11:9,10
9:16 [w]Ro 1:14; Ac 9:15
9:17 [x]1Co 3:8,14 [y]Gal 2:7; Col 1:25
9:18 [z]2Co 11:7; 12:13
9:19 [a]ver 1 [b]Gal 5:13 [c]Mt 18:15; 1Pe 3:1
9:20 [d]Ac 16:3; 21:20-26; Ro 11:14
9:21 [e]Ro 2:12,14
9:22 [f]1Co 10:33 [g]Ro 11:14
9:24 [h]Gal 2:2; 2Ti 4:7; Heb 12:1
9:25 [i]Jas 1:12; Rev 2:10

s *5* That is, Peter   t *9* Deut. 25:4

man running aimlessly; I do not fight
like a man beating the air. 27No, I beat
my body[a] and make it my slave so that
after I have preached to others, I myself
will not be disqualified for the prize.

Old Testament lessons from Israel's sins.

10 For I do not want you to be ignorant of the fact, brothers, that our
forefathers were all under the cloud[b]
and that they all passed through the
sea.[c] 2They were all baptized into Moses
in the cloud and in the sea. 3They all
ate the same spiritual food 4and drank
the same spiritual drink; for they drank
from the spiritual rock[d] that accompanied them, and that rock was Christ.
5Nevertheless, God was not pleased
with most of them; their bodies were
scattered over the desert.[e]
6Now these things occurred as examples[u] to keep us from setting our hearts
on evil things as they did. 7Do not be
idolaters,[f] as some of them were; as it
is written: "The people sat down to eat
and drink and got up to indulge in
pagan revelry."[v][g] 8We should not commit sexual immorality, as some of them
did—and in one day twenty-three thousand of them died.[h] 9We should not test
the Lord, as some of them did—and were
killed by snakes.[i] 10And do not grumble, as some of them did[j]—and were
killed[k] by the destroying angel.[l]
11These things happened to them as
examples and were written down as
warnings for us, on whom the fulfillment of the ages has come.[m] 12So, if
you think you are standing firm,[n] be
careful that you don't fall! 13No temptation has seized you except what is common to man. And God is faithful;[o] he
will not let you be tempted beyond
what you can bear.[p] But when you are
tempted, he will also provide a way
out so that you can stand up under it.

Avoiding any association with idolatry.

14Therefore, my dear friends, flee from
idolatry. 15I speak to sensible people;
judge for yourselves what I say. 16Is not
the cup of thanksgiving for which we
give thanks a participation in the blood
of Christ? And is not the bread that we
break a participation in the body of
Christ?[q] 17Because there is one loaf,
we, who are many, are one body,[r] for
we all partake of the one loaf.
18Consider the people of Israel: Do
not those who eat the sacrifices[s] participate in the altar? 19Do I mean then that
a sacrifice offered to an idol is anything,
or that an idol is anything?[t] 20No, but
the sacrifices of pagans are offered to
demons,[u] not to God, and I do not want
you to be participants with demons.
21You cannot drink the cup of the Lord
and the cup of demons too; you cannot
have a part in both the Lord's table and
the table of demons.[v] 22Are we trying
to arouse the Lord's jealousy?[w] Are we
stronger than he?[x]

Freedom concerning food offered to idols.

23"Everything is permissible"—but
not everything is beneficial.[y] "Everything is permissible"—but not everything is constructive. 24Nobody should
seek his own good, but the good of
others.[z]
25Eat anything sold in the meat market without raising questions of conscience,[a] 26for, "The earth is the Lord's,
and everything in it."[w][b]
27If some unbeliever invites you to a
meal and you want to go, eat whatever
is put before you[c] without raising questions of conscience. 28But if anyone says
to you, "This has been offered in sacrifice," then do not eat it, both for the
sake of the man who told you and for
conscience' sake[x][d]— 29the other man's
conscience, I mean, not yours. For why
should my freedom[e] be judged by
another's conscience? 30If I take part
in the meal with thankfulness, why

9:27 [a]Ro 8:13
10:1 [b]Ex 13:21 [c]Ex 14:22,29
10:4 [d]Ex 17:6; Nu 20:11; Ps 78:15
10:5 [e]Nu 14:29; Heb 3:17
10:7 [f]ver 14 [g]Ex 32:4,6,19
10:8 [h]Nu 25:1-9
10:9 [i]Nu 21:5,6
10:10 [j]Nu 16:41 [k]Nu 16:49 [l]Ex 12:23
10:11 [m]Ro 13:11
10:12 [n]Ro 11:20
10:13 [o]1Co 1:9 [p]2Pe 2:9
10:16 [q]Mt 26:26-28
10:17 [r]Ro 12:5; 1Co 12:27
10:18 [s]Lev 7:6,14,15
10:19 [t]1Co 8:4
10:20 [u]Dt 32:17; Ps 106:37; Rev 9:20
10:21 [v]2Co 6:15,16
10:22 [w]Dt 32:16,21 [x]Ecc 6:10; Isa 45:9
10:23 [y]1Co 6:12
10:24 [z]ver 33; Ro 15:1,2; 1Co 13:5; Php 2:4,21
10:25 [a]Ac 10:15; 1Co 8:7
10:26 [b]Ps 24:1
10:27 [c]Lk 10:7
10:28 [d]1Co 8:7,10-12
10:29 [e]Ro 14:16; 1Co 9:1,19

[u]*6* Or *types*; also in verse 11 [v]*7* Exodus 32:6
[w]*26* Psalm 24:1 [x]*28* Some manuscripts *conscience' sake, for "the earth is the Lord's and everything in it"*

am I denounced because of something
I thank God for?[a]
31So whether you eat or drink or
whatever you do, do it all for the glory
of God.[b] 32Do not cause anyone to stumble,[c] whether Jews, Greeks or the
church of God[d]— 33even as I try to
please everybody in every way.[e] For
I am not seeking my own good but
the good of many, so that they may be
11 saved.[f] 1Follow my example,[g] as I
follow the example of Christ.

Head coverings for women.

2I praise you[h] for remembering me in
everything[i] and for holding to the teachings,[y] just as I passed them on to you.[j]
3Now I want you to realize that the
head of every man is Christ,[k] and the
head of the woman is man,[l] and the head
of Christ is God.[m] 4Every man who prays
or prophesies with his head covered
dishonors his head. 5And every woman who prays or prophesies[n] with her
head uncovered dishonors her head—
it is just as though her head were
shaved.[o] 6If a woman does not cover her
head, she should have her hair cut off;
and if it is a disgrace for a woman to
have her hair cut or shaved off, she
should cover her head. 7A man ought
not to cover his head,[z] since he is the
image[p] and glory of God; but the woman is the glory of man. 8For man did not
come from woman, but woman from
man;[q] 9neither was man created for
woman, but woman for man.[r] 10For this
reason, and because of the angels, the
woman ought to have a sign of authority
on her head.
11In the Lord, however, woman is
not independent of man, nor is man
independent of woman. 12For as woman came from man, so also man is born
of woman. But everything comes from
God.[s] 13Judge for yourselves: Is it proper for a woman to pray to God with
her head uncovered? 14Does not the
very nature of things teach you that if
a man has long hair, it is a disgrace to
him, 15but that if a woman has long
hair, it is her glory? For long hair is giv-
en to her as a covering. 16If anyone wants
to be contentious about this, we have
no other practice—nor do the churches
of God.[t]

Proper conduct for observing the Lord's Supper.

11:23-25pp— Mt 26:26-28; Mk 14:22-24; Lk 22:17-20

17In the following directives I have no
praise for you,[u] for your meetings do
more harm than good. 18In the first place,
I hear that when you come together as a
church, there are divisions[v] among you,
and to some extent I believe it. 19No
doubt there have to be differences among
you to show which of you have God's
approval.[w] 20When you come together,
it is not the Lord's Supper you eat, 21for
as you eat, each of you goes ahead without waiting for anybody else.[x] One
remains hungry, another gets drunk.
22Don't you have homes to eat and
drink in? Or do you despise the church
of God[y] and humiliate those who have
nothing?[z] What shall I say to you? Shall
I praise you[a] for this? Certainly not!
23For I received from the Lord[b] what
I also passed on to you:[c] The Lord Jesus,
on the night he was betrayed, took
bread, 24and when he had given thanks,
he broke it and said, "This is my body,
which is for you; do this in remembrance of me." 25In the same way, after
supper he took the cup, saying, "This
cup is the new covenant[d] in my blood;[e]
do this, whenever you drink it, in remembrance of me." 26For whenever you
eat this bread and drink this cup, you
proclaim the Lord's death until he comes.
27Therefore, whoever eats the bread
or drinks the cup of the Lord in an unworthy manner will be guilty of sinning

10:30 [a]Ro 14:6
10:31 [b]Col 3:17; 1Pe 4:11
10:32 [c]Ac 24:16 [d]Ac 20:28
10:33 [e]Ro 15:2; 1Co 9:22 [f]Ro 11:14
11:1 [g]1Co 4:16
11:2 [h]ver 17,22 [i]1Co 4:17 [j]1Co 15:2,3; 2Th 2:15
11:3 [k]Eph 1:22 [l]Ge 3:16; Eph 5:23 [m]1Co 3:23
11:5 [n]Ac 21:9 [o]Dt 21:12
11:7 [p]Ge 1:26; Jas 3:9
11:8 [q]Ge 2:21-23; 1Ti 2:13
11:9 [r]Ge 2:18
11:12 [s]Ro 11:36
11:16 [t]1Co 7:17
11:17 [u]ver 2,22
11:18 [v]1Co 1:10-12; 3:3
11:19 [w]1Jn 2:19
11:21 [x]2Pe 2:13; Jude 12
11:22 [y]1Co 10:32 [z]Jas 2:6 [a]ver 2,17
11:23 [b]Gal 1:12 [c]1Co 15:3
11:25 [d]Lk 22:20 [e]1Co 10:16

y2 Or *traditions* z4-7 Or *4Every man who prays or prophesies with long hair dishonors his head. 5And every woman who prays or prophesies with no covering ⌊of hair⌋ on her head dishonors her head—she is just like one of the "shorn women." 6If a woman has no covering, let her be for now with short hair, but since it is a disgrace for a woman to have her hair shorn or shaved, she should grow it again. 7A man ought not to have long hair*

against the body and blood of the Lord.[a] 28 A man ought to examine himself[b] before he eats of the bread and drinks of the cup. 29 For anyone who eats and drinks without recognizing the body of the Lord eats and drinks judgment on himself. 30 That is why many among you are weak and sick, and a number of you have fallen asleep. 31 But if we judged ourselves, we would not come under judgment.[c] 32 When we are judged by the Lord, we are being disciplined[d] so that we will not be condemned with the world.

33 So then, my brothers, when you come together to eat, wait for each other. 34 If anyone is hungry,[e] he should eat at home,[f] so that when you meet together it may not result in judgment.

And when I come[g] I will give further directions.

Spiritual gifts from the Holy Spirit.

12 Now about spiritual gifts,[h] brothers, I do not want you to be ignorant. 2 You know that when you were pagans,[i] somehow or other you were influenced and led astray to mute idols.[j] 3 Therefore I tell you that no one who is speaking by the Spirit of God says, "Jesus be cursed,"[k] and no one can say, "Jesus is Lord,"[l] except by the Holy Spirit.[m]

4 There are different kinds of gifts, but the same Spirit.[n] 5 There are different kinds of service, but the same Lord. 6 There are different kinds of working, but the same God[o] works all of them in all men.

7 Now to each one the manifestation of the Spirit is given for the common good.[p] 8 To one there is given through the Spirit the message of wisdom,[q] to another the message of knowledge[r] by means of the same Spirit, 9 to another faith[s] by the same Spirit, to another gifts of healing[t] by that one Spirit, 10 to another miraculous powers,[u] to another prophecy, to another distinguishing between spirits,[v] to another speaking in different kinds of tongues,[a][w] and to still another the interpretation of tongues.[a] 11 All these are the work of one and the same Spirit,[x] and he gives them to each one, just as he determines.

Functions of spiritual gifts in the body of Christ.

12 The body is a unit, though it is made up of many parts; and though all its parts are many, they form one body.[y] So it is with Christ.[z] 13 For we were all baptized by[b] one Spirit[a] into one body—whether Jews or Greeks, slave or free[b]—and we were all given the one Spirit to drink.[c]

14 Now the body is not made up of one part but of many. 15 If the foot should say, "Because I am not a hand, I do not belong to the body," it would not for that reason cease to be part of the body. 16 And if the ear should say, "Because I am not an eye, I do not belong to the body," it would not for that reason cease to be part of the body. 17 If the whole body were an eye, where would the sense of hearing be? If the whole body were an ear, where would the sense of smell be? 18 But in fact God has arranged[d] the parts in the body, every one of them, just as he wanted them to be.[e] 19 If they were all one part, where would the body be? 20 As it is, there are many parts, but one body.[f]

21 The eye cannot say to the hand, "I don't need you!" And the head cannot say to the feet, "I don't need you!" 22 On the contrary, those parts of the body that seem to be weaker are indispensable, 23 and the parts that we think are less honorable we treat with special honor. And the parts that are unpresentable are treated with special modesty, 24 while our presentable parts need no special treatment. But God has combined the members of the body and has given greater honor to the parts that lacked it, 25 so that there should be no division in the body, but that its parts should have equal concern for each other. 26 If one

11:27 [a]Heb 10:29
11:28 [b]2Co 13:5
11:31 [c]Ps 32:5; 1Jn 1:9
11:32 [d]Ps 94:12; Heb 12:7-10; Rev 3:19
11:34 [e]ver 21 [f]ver 22 [g]1Co 4:19
12:1 [h]Ro 1:11; 1Co 14:1,37
12:2 [i]Eph 2:11,12; 1Pe 4:3 [j]Ps 115:5; Jer 10:5; Hab 2:18,19; 1Th 1:9
12:3 [k]Ro 9:3 [l]Jn 13:13 [m]1Jn 4:2,3
12:4 [n]Ro 12:4-8; Eph 4:11; Heb 2:4
12:6 [o]Eph 4:6
12:7 [p]Eph 4:12
12:8 [q]1Co 2:6 [r]2Co 8:7
12:9 [s]Mt 17:19,20; 2Co 4:13 [t]ver 28,30
12:10 [u]Gal 3:5 [v]1Jn 4:1 [w]Mk 16:17
12:11 [x]ver 4
12:12 [y]Ro 12:5 [z]ver 27
12:13 [a]Eph 2:18 [b]Gal 3:28; Col 3:11 [c]Jn 7:37-39
12:18 [d]ver 28 [e]ver 11
12:20 [f]ver 12,14

a *10* Or *languages*; also in verse 28 b *13* Or *with*; or *in* part suffers, every part suffers with it; if one part is honored, every part rejoices with it.

27 Now you are the body of Christ,[a] and each one of you is a part of it.[b] 28 And in the church[c] God has appointed first of all apostles,[d] second prophets, third teachers, then workers of miracles, also those having gifts of healing,[e] those able to help others, those with gifts of administration,[f] and those speaking in different kinds of tongues.[g] 29 Are all apostles? Are all prophets? Are all teachers? Do all work miracles? 30 Do all have gifts of healing? Do all speak in tongues[c]?[h] Do all interpret? 31 But eagerly desire[d] [i] the greater gifts.

Faith, hope, and love—
but the greatest of these is love.

And now I will show you the most excellent way.

13 If I speak in the tongues[e] [j] of men and of angels, but have not love, I am only a resounding gong or a clanging cymbal. 2 If I have the gift of prophecy and can fathom all mysteries[k] and all knowledge, and if I have a faith[l] that can move mountains,[m] but have not love, I am nothing. 3 If I give all I possess to the poor[n] and surrender my body to the flames,[f] [o] but have not love, I gain nothing.

4 Love is patient,[p] love is kind. It does not envy, it does not boast, it is not proud. 5 It is not rude, it is not self-seeking,[q] it is not easily angered, it keeps no record of wrongs. 6 Love does not delight in evil[r] but rejoices with the truth.[s] 7 It always protects, always trusts, always hopes, always perseveres.

8 Love never fails. But where there are prophecies,[t] they will cease; where there are tongues,[u] they will be stilled; where there is knowledge, it will pass away. 9 For we know in part[v] and we prophesy in part, 10 but when perfection comes,[w] the imperfect disappears. 11 When I was a child, I talked like a child, I thought like a child, I reasoned like a child. When I became a man, I put childish ways behind me. 12 Now we see but a poor reflection as in a mirror; then we shall see face to face.[x] Now I know in part; then I shall know fully, even as I am fully known.[y]

13 And now these three remain: faith, hope and love.[z] But the greatest of these is love.[a]

Gifts of prophecy and tongues.

14 Follow the way of love[b] and eagerly desire[c] spiritual gifts,[d] especially the gift of prophecy. 2 For anyone who speaks in a tongue[g] [e] does not speak to men but to God. Indeed, no one understands him; he utters mysteries[f] with his spirit.[h] 3 But everyone who prophesies speaks to men for their strengthening,[g] encouragement and comfort. 4 He who speaks in a tongue[h] edifies himself, but he who prophesies[i] edifies the church. 5 I would like every one of you to speak in tongues,[i] but I would rather have you prophesy.[j] He who prophesies is greater than one who speaks in tongues,[i] unless he interprets, so that the church may be edified.

6 Now, brothers, if I come to you and speak in tongues, what good will I be to you, unless I bring you some revelation[k] or knowledge or prophecy or word of instruction?[l] 7 Even in the case of lifeless things that make sounds, such as the flute or harp, how will anyone know what tune is being played unless there is a distinction in the notes? 8 Again, if the trumpet does not sound a clear call, who will get ready for battle?[m] 9 So it is with you. Unless you speak intelligible words with your tongue, how will anyone know what you are saying? You will just be speaking into the air. 10 Undoubtedly there are all sorts of languages in the world, yet none of them is without meaning. 11 If then I do not grasp the meaning of what someone is saying, I am a foreigner to the speaker, and he is

12:27 [a]Eph 1:23; 4:12; Col 1:18,24 [b]Ro 12:5
12:28 [c]1Co 10:32 [d]Eph 4:11 [e]ver 9 [f]Ro 12:6-8 [g]ver 10
12:30 [h]ver 10
12:31 [i]1Co 14:1,39
13:1 [j]ver 8
13:2 [k]1Co 14:2 [l]1Co 12:9 [m]Mt 17:20; 21:21
13:3 [n]Mt 6:2 [o]Da 3:28
13:4 [p]1Th 5:14
13:5 [q]1Co 10:24
13:6 [r]2Th 2:12 [s]2Jn 4; 3Jn 3,4
13:8 [t]ver 2 [u]ver 1
13:9 [v]ver 12; 1Co 8:2
13:10 [w]Php 3:12
13:12 [x]Ge 32:30; 2Co 5:7; 1Jn 3:2 [y]1Co 8:3
13:13 [z]Gal 5:5,6 [a]1Co 16:14
14:1 [b]1Co 16:14 [c]ver 39; 1Co 12:31 [d]1Co 12:1
14:2 [e]Mk 16:17 [f]1Co 13:2
14:3 [g]ver 4,5,12,17, 26; Ro 14:19
14:4 [h]Mk 16:17 [i]1Co 13:2
14:5 [j]Nu 11:29
14:6 [k]ver 26; Eph 1:17 [l]Ro 6:17
14:8 [m]Nu 10:9; Jer 4:19

c *30* Or *other languages* d *31* Or *But you are eagerly desiring* e *1* Or *languages* f *3* Some early manuscripts *body that I may boast* g *2* Or *another language*; also in verses 4, 13, 14, 19, 26 and 27 h *2* Or *by the Spirit* i *5* Or *other languages*; also in verses 6, 18, 22, 23 and 39

a foreigner to me. 12So it is with you.
Since you are eager to have spiritual gifts,
try to excel in gifts that build up the
church.
13For this reason anyone who speaks
in a tongue should pray that he may
interpret what he says. 14For if I pray in
a tongue, my spirit prays, but my mind is
unfruitful. 15So what shall I do? I will
pray with my spirit, but I will also pray
with my mind; I will sing[a] with my spirit, but I will also sing with my mind.
16If you are praising God with your
spirit, how can one who finds himself
among those who do not understand[j]
say "Amen"[b] to your thanksgiving,[c] since
he does not know what you are saying?
17You may be giving thanks well enough,
but the other man is not edified.
18I thank God that I speak in tongues
more than all of you. 19But in the church
I would rather speak five intelligible
words to instruct others than ten thousand words in a tongue.
20Brothers, stop thinking like children.[d] In regard to evil be infants,[e] but
in your thinking be adults. 21In the Law[f]
it is written:

"Through men of strange tongues
and through the lips of foreigners
I will speak to this people,
but even then they will not listen
to me,"[k][g]
says the Lord.

22Tongues, then, are a sign, not for
believers but for unbelievers; prophecy,[h] however, is for believers, not for
unbelievers. 23So if the whole church
comes together and everyone speaks in
tongues, and some who do not understand[l] or some unbelievers come in, will
they not say that you are out of your
mind?[i] 24But if an unbeliever or someone who does not understand[m] comes
in while everybody is prophesying, he
will be convinced by all that he is a
sinner and will be judged by all, 25and
the secrets of his heart will be laid
bare. So he will fall down and worship
God, exclaiming, "God is really among
you!"[j]

14:15 [a]Eph 5:19; Col 3:16
14:16 [b]Dt 27:15-26; 1Ch 16:36; Ne 8:6; Ps 106:48; Rev 5:14; 7:12 [c]1Co 11:24
14:20 [d]Eph 4:14; Heb 5:12,13; 1Pe 2:2 [e]Ro 16:19
14:21 [f]Jn 10:34 [g]Isa 28:11,12
14:22 [h]ver 1
14:23 [i]Ac 2:13
14:25 [j]Isa 45:14; Zec 8:23
14:26 [k]1Co 12:7-10 [l]Eph 5:19 [m]ver 6 [n]Ro 14:19
14:29 [o]1Co 12:10
14:32 [p]1Jn 4:1
14:33 [q]ver 40 [r]Ac 9:13
14:34 [s]1Ti 2:11,12 [t]Ge 3:16
14:37 [u]2Co 10:7 [v]1Jn 4:6
14:39 [w]1Co 12:31
14:40 [x]ver 33
15:1 [y]Ro 2:16

Gifts should not interfere with orderly worship.

26What then shall we say, brothers?
When you come together, everyone[k] has
a hymn,[l] or a word of instruction,[m] a
revelation, a tongue or an interpretation. All of these must be done for
the strengthening[n] of the church. 27If
anyone speaks in a tongue, two—or at
the most three—should speak, one at
a time, and someone must interpret.
28If there is no interpreter, the speaker
should keep quiet in the church and
speak to himself and God.
29Two or three prophets should speak,
and the others should weigh carefully
what is said.[o] 30And if a revelation
comes to someone who is sitting down,
the first speaker should stop. 31For you
can all prophesy in turn so that everyone may be instructed and encouraged.
32The spirits of prophets are subject to
the control of prophets.[p] 33For God is
not a God of disorder[q] but of peace.
As in all the congregations of the
saints,[r] 34women should remain silent
in the churches. They are not allowed
to speak, but must be in submission,[s]
as the Law[t] says. 35If they want to inquire
about something, they should ask their
own husbands at home; for it is disgraceful for a woman to speak in the church.
36Did the word of God originate with
you? Or are you the only people it has
reached? 37If anybody thinks he is a
prophet[u] or spiritually gifted, let him
acknowledge that what I am writing to
you is the Lord's command.[v] 38If he ignores this, he himself will be ignored.[n]
39Therefore, my brothers, be eager[w]
to prophesy, and do not forbid speaking
in tongues. 40But everything should be
done in a fitting and orderly[x] way.

Eyewitnesses to the resurrected Christ.

15 Now, brothers, I want to remind
you of the gospel[y] I preached to

j*16* Or *among the inquirers* k*21* Isaiah 28:11,12 l*23* Or *some inquirers* m*24* Or *or some inquirer* n*38* Some manuscripts *If he is ignorant of this, let him be ignorant*

you, which you received and on which
you have taken your stand. **2**By this gospel you are saved,[a] if you hold firmly[b]
to the word I preached to you. Otherwise, you have believed in vain.
3For what I received[c] I passed on to
you[d] as of first importance[o]: that Christ
died for our sins[e] according to the Scriptures,[f] **4**that he was buried, that he was
raised[g] on the third day[h] according to
the Scriptures,[i] **5**and that he appeared to
Peter,[p][j] and then to the Twelve.[k] **6**After
that, he appeared to more than five hundred of the brothers at the same time,
most of whom are still living, though
some have fallen asleep. **7**Then he appeared to James, then to all the apostles,[l] **8**and last of all he appeared to me
also,[m] as to one abnormally born.
9For I am the least of the apostles[n]
and do not even deserve to be called
an apostle, because I persecuted[o] the
church of God. **10**But by the grace of
God I am what I am, and his grace to
me[p] was not without effect. No, I
worked harder than all of them[q]—yet
not I, but the grace of God that was
with me.[r] **11**Whether, then, it was I or
they, this is what we preach, and this
is what you believed.

Absolute necessity of Christ's resurrection.

12But if it is preached that Christ has
been raised from the dead, how can
some of you say that there is no resurrection of the dead?[s] **13**If there is no
resurrection of the dead, then not even
Christ has been raised. **14**And if Christ
has not been raised,[t] our preaching is
useless and so is your faith. **15**More
than that, we are then found to be false
witnesses about God, for we have testified about God that he raised Christ
from the dead.[u] But he did not raise him
if in fact the dead are not raised. **16**For
if the dead are not raised, then Christ
has not been raised either. **17**And if Christ
has not been raised, your faith is futile;
you are still in your sins.[v] **18**Then those
also who have fallen asleep in Christ
are lost. **19**If only for this life we have
hope in Christ, we are to be pitied more
than all men.[w]
20But Christ has indeed been raised
from the dead,[x] the firstfruits[y] of those
who have fallen asleep.[z] **21**For since death
came through a man,[a] the resurrection
of the dead comes also through a man.
22For as in Adam all die, so in Christ all
will be made alive.[b] **23**But each in his
own turn: Christ, the firstfruits;[c] then,
when he comes,[d] those who belong to
him. **24**Then the end will come, when
he hands over the kingdom[e] to God the
Father after he has destroyed all dominion, authority and power.[f] **25**For he must
reign until he has put all his enemies
under his feet.[g] **26**The last enemy to be
destroyed is death.[h] **27**For he "has put
everything under his feet."[q][i] Now when
it says that "everything" has been put
under him, it is clear that this does not
include God himself, who put everything under Christ.[j] **28**When he has
done this, then the Son himself will be
made subject to him who put everything under him,[k] so that God may be
all in all.[l]
29Now if there is no resurrection,
what will those do who are baptized
for the dead? If the dead are not raised
at all, why are people baptized for
them? **30**And as for us, why do we
endanger ourselves every hour?[m] **31**I
die every day[n]—I mean that, brothers—
just as surely as I glory over you in
Christ Jesus our Lord. **32**If I fought wild
beasts[o] in Ephesus[p] for merely human
reasons, what have I gained? If the
dead are not raised,

"Let us eat and drink,
for tomorrow we die."[r][q]

33Do not be misled: "Bad company
corrupts good character." **34**Come back
to your senses as you ought, and stop

15:2 [a]Ro 1:16 [b]Ro 11:22 **15:3** [c]Gal 1:12 [d]1Co 11:23 [e]Isa 53:5; 1Pe 2:24 [f]Lk 24:27; Ac 26:22,23 **15:4** [g]Ac 2:24 [h]Mt 16:21 [i]Ac 2:25,30,31 **15:5** [j]Lk 24:34 [k]Mk 16:14 **15:7** [l]Lk 24:33,36, 37; Ac 1:3,4 **15:8** [m]Ac 9:3-6,17; 1Co 9:1 **15:9** [n]Eph 3:8; 1Ti 1:15 [o]Ac 8:3 **15:10** [p]Ro 12:3 [q]2Co 11:23 [r]Php 2:13 **15:12** [s]Ac 17:32; 23:8; 2Ti 2:18 **15:14** [t]1Th 4:14 **15:15** [u]Ac 2:24 **15:17** [v]Ro 4:25 **15:19** [w]1Co 4:9 **15:20** [x]1Pe 1:3 [y]ver 23; Ac 26:23; Rev 1:5 [z]ver 6,18 **15:21** [a]Ro 5:12 **15:22** [b]Ro 5:14-18 **15:23** [c]ver 20 [d]ver 52 **15:24** [e]Da 7:14,27 [f]Ro 8:38 **15:25** [g]Ps 110:1; Mt 22:44 **15:26** [h]2Ti 1:10; Rev 20:14; 21:4 **15:27** [i]Ps 8:6 [j]Mt 28:18

15:28 [k]Php 3:21 [l]1Co 3:23 **15:30** [m]2Co 11:26 **15:31** [n]Ro 8:36 **15:32** [o]2Co 1:8 [p]Ac 18:19 [q]Isa 22:13; Lk 12:19

[o]*3* Or *you at the first* [p]*5* Greek *Cephas*
[q]*27* Psalm 8:6 [r]*32* Isaiah 22:13

sinning; for there are some who are ignorant of God—I say this to your shame.

A new heavenly body.

35But someone may ask,[a] "How are the dead raised? With what kind of body will they come?"[b] 36How foolish![c] What you sow does not come to life unless it dies.[d] 37When you sow, you do not plant the body that will be, but just a seed, perhaps of wheat or of something else. 38But God gives it a body as he has determined, and to each kind of seed he gives its own body.[e] 39All flesh is not the same: Men have one kind of flesh, animals have another, birds another and fish another. 40There are also heavenly bodies and there are earthly bodies; but the splendor of the heavenly bodies is one kind, and the splendor of the earthly bodies is another. 41The sun has one kind of splendor, the moon another and the stars another; and star differs from star in splendor.

42So will it be[f] with the resurrection of the dead. The body that is sown is perishable, it is raised imperishable; 43it is sown in dishonor, it is raised in glory;[g] it is sown in weakness, it is raised in power; 44it is sown a natural body, it is raised a spiritual body.[h]

If there is a natural body, there is also a spiritual body. 45So it is written: "The first man Adam became a living being"[s];[i] the last Adam,[j] a life-giving spirit.[k] 46The spiritual did not come first, but the natural, and after that the spiritual. 47The first man was of the dust of the earth,[l] the second man from heaven.[m] 48As was the earthly man, so are those who are of the earth; and as is the man from heaven, so also are those who are of heaven.[n] 49And just as we have borne the likeness of the earthly man,[o] so shall we[t] bear the likeness of the man from heaven.[p]

Final victory over death.

50I declare to you, brothers, that flesh and blood[q] cannot inherit the kingdom of God, nor does the perishable inherit the imperishable. 51Listen, I tell you a mystery:[r] We will not all sleep, but we will all be changed[s]— 52in a flash, in the twinkling of an eye, at the last trumpet. For the trumpet will sound,[t] the dead[u] will be raised imperishable, and we will be changed. 53For the perishable must clothe itself with the imperishable,[v] and the mortal with immortality. 54When the perishable has been clothed with the imperishable, and the mortal with immortality, then the saying that is written will come true: "Death has been swallowed up in victory."[u][w]

55"Where, O death, is your victory?
Where, O death, is your sting?"[v][x]

56The sting of death is sin,[y] and the power of sin is the law.[z] 57But thanks be to God![a] He gives us the victory through our Lord Jesus Christ.[b]

58Therefore, my dear brothers, stand firm. Let nothing move you. Always give yourselves fully to the work of the Lord,[c] because you know that your labor in the Lord is not in vain.

Directions concerning the collection for God's people in Jerusalem.

16 Now about the collection[d] for God's people:[e] Do what I told the Galatian[f] churches to do. 2On the first day of every week,[g] each one of you should set aside a sum of money in keeping with his income, saving it up, so that when I come no collections will have to be made.[h] 3Then, when I arrive, I will give letters of introduction to the men you approve[i] and send them with your gift to Jerusalem. 4If it seems advisable for me to go also, they will accompany me.

Paul's plan to visit Corinth.

5After I go through Macedonia, I will come to you[j]—for I will be going through Macedonia.[k] 6Perhaps I will stay with you awhile, or even spend the winter,

15:35 [a]Ro 9:19 [b]Eze 37:3
15:36 [c]Lk 11:40 [d]Jn 12:24
15:38 [e]Ge 1:11
15:42 [f]Da 12:3; Mt 13:43
15:43 [g]Php 3:21; Col 3:4
15:44 [h]ver 50
15:45 [i]Ge 2:7 [j]Ro 5:14 [k]Jn 5:21; Ro 8:2
15:47 [l]Ge 2:7; 3:19 [m]Jn 3:13,31
15:48 [n]Php 3:20,21
15:49 [o]Ge 5:3 [p]Ro 8:29
15:50 [q]Jn 3:3,5
15:51 [r]1Co 13:2 [s]Php 3:21
15:52 [t]Mt 24:31 [u]Jn 5:25
15:53 [v]2Co 5:2,4
15:54 [w]Isa 25:8; Rev 20:14
15:55 [x]Hos 13:14
15:56 [y]Ro 5:12 [z]Ro 4:15
15:57 [a]2Co 2:14 [b]Ro 8:37
15:58 [c]1Co 16:10
16:1 [d]Ac 24:17 [e]Ac 9:13 [f]Ac 16:6
16:2 [g]Ac 20:7 [h]2Co 9:4,5
16:3 [i]2Co 8:18,19
16:5 [j]1Co 4:19 [k]Ac 19:21

s*45* Gen. 2:7 t*49* Some early manuscripts *so let us*
u*54* Isaiah 25:8 v*55* Hosea 13:14

so that you can help me on my journey,[a] wherever I go. **7**I do not want to see you now and make only a passing visit; I hope to spend some time with you, if the Lord permits.[b] **8**But I will stay on at Ephesus[c] until Pentecost,[d] **9**because a great door for effective work has opened to me,[e] and there are many who oppose me.

Final instructions and greetings.

10If Timothy[f] comes, see to it that he has nothing to fear while he is with you, for he is carrying on the work of the Lord,[g] just as I am. **11**No one, then, should refuse to accept him.[h] Send him on his way in peace[i] so that he may return to me. I am expecting him along with the brothers.

12Now about our brother Apollos:[j] I strongly urged him to go to you with the brothers. He was quite unwilling to go now, but he will go when he has the opportunity.

13Be on your guard; stand firm[k] in the faith; be men of courage; be strong.[l] **14**Do everything in love.[m]

15You know that the household of Stephanas[n] were the first converts[o] in Achaia,[p] and they have devoted themselves to the service of the saints. I urge you, brothers, **16**to submit[q] to such as these and to everyone who joins in the work, and labors at it. **17**I was glad when Stephanas, Fortunatus and Achaicus arrived, because they have supplied what was lacking from you.[r] **18**For they refreshed[s] my spirit and yours also. Such men deserve recognition.[t]

19The churches in the province of Asia send you greetings. Aquila and Priscilla[w][u] greet you warmly in the Lord, and so does the church that meets at their house.[v] **20**All the brothers here send you greetings. Greet one another with a holy kiss.[w]

21I, Paul, write this greeting in my own hand.[x]

22If anyone does not love the Lord[y]—a curse[z] be on him. Come, O Lord[x]![a]

23The grace of the Lord Jesus be with you.[b]

24My love to all of you in Christ Jesus. Amen.[y]

16:6 [a]Ro 15:24 **16:7** [b]Ac 18:21 **16:8** [c]Ac 18:19 [d]Ac 2:1 **16:9** [e]Ac 14:27 **16:10** [f]Ac 16:1 [g]1Co 15:58 **16:11** [h]1Ti 4:12 [i]Ac 15:33 **16:12** [j]Ac 18:24; 1Co 1:12 **16:13** [k]Gal 5:1; Php 1:27; 1Th 3:8; 2Th 2:15 [l]Eph 6:10 **16:14** [m]1Co 14:1 **16:15** [n]1Co 1:16 [o]Ro 16:5 [p]Ac 18:12 **16:16** [q]Heb 13:17 **16:17** [r]2Co 11:9; Php 2:30 **16:18** [s]Phm 7 [t]Php 2:29

16:19 [u]Ac 18:2 [v]Ro 16:5 **16:20** [w]Ro 16:16 **16:21** [x]Gal 6:11; Col 4:18 **16:22** [y]Eph 6:24 [z]Ro 9:3 [a]Rev 22:20 **16:23** [b]Ro 16:20

w *19* Greek *Prisca,* a variant of *Priscilla* x *22* In Aramaic the expression *Come, O Lord* is *Marana tha.* y *24* Some manuscripts do not have *Amen.*

2 CORINTHIANS

Author: Paul the Apostle.

Date Written: Between A.D. 55 and 57, a few months after 1 Corinthians.

Title: From Paul's second recorded letter to the church at Corinth.

Background: Titus returns to Paul at Macedonia to report on the Corinthians' reactions to Paul's previous letter (what we know as 1 Corinthians)—that most of the church at Corinth has repented. Nevertheless, some false teachers, leaders of a rebellious minority, seek to belittle Paul's authority and to sway the people away from the message he has shared with them. These false prophets accuse Paul of being proud, dishonest, lacking in speech and stature, and unqualified as an apostle of Jesus Christ.

Where Written: Possibly the Macedonian city of Philippi.

To Whom: To the church at Corinth.

Content: This intensely personal letter from Paul uncovers his heartfelt emotions, ambitions and love for the church. Paul explains in detail his career and some of the trials he endures in the service of Christ, including a thorn in the flesh to keep him humble. He then recounts the need for a collection to be made ready for Macedonian churches. The joy of generous giving is emphasized. Finally, Paul defends the validity of his apostolic ministry and calling from God.

Key Words: "Authority"; "Reconciliation"; "Sharing." The "authority" which Paul declares over the Corinthians as their spiritual father is granted to him by God, and he challenges every Christian with the responsibility of seeking "reconciliation" of divisions within his church, his family and with others. Once Christians understand the principles of total "sharing," they can begin to stand upon the other promises of God.

Themes: • God's goodness is more powerful than Satan's evil. • Being granted the ability and privilege to give to God's work is a blessing in itself. • Not all religious teachers are of the Lord. • Not all religious teachers have our best interests in mind. • Words from the righteous are sometimes misunderstood and condemned by the world. • It is okay to boast...about Jesus Christ and what he has done.

Outline:

1. Introduction. 1:1-1:11
2. Paul's ministry and philosophy expounded. 1:12-7:16
3. Stewardship encouraged. 8:1-9:15
4. Paul's authority as an apostle examined. 10:1-13:10
5. Final exhortations. 13:11-13:14

2 CORINTHIANS

1 Paul, an apostle of Christ Jesus by the
will of God,[a] and Timothy our brother,

To the church of God[b] in Corinth, together with all the saints throughout
Achaia:[c]

2Grace and peace to you from God
our Father and the Lord Jesus Christ.[d]

Those in Christ will be comforted.

3Praise be to the God and Father of
our Lord Jesus Christ,[e] the Father of
compassion and the God of all comfort,
4who comforts us[f] in all our troubles, so
that we can comfort those in any trouble with the comfort we ourselves have
received from God. 5For just as the sufferings of Christ flow over into our
lives,[g] so also through Christ our comfort overflows. 6If we are distressed, it
is for your comfort and salvation;[h] if we
are comforted, it is for your comfort,
which produces in you patient endurance
of the same sufferings we suffer. 7And
our hope for you is firm, because we
know that just as you share in our sufferings,[i] so also you share in our comfort.

8We do not want you to be unin-
formed, brothers, about the hardships
we suffered[j] in the province of Asia. We
were under great pressure, far beyond
our ability to endure, so that we de-
spaired even of life. 9Indeed, in our
hearts we felt the sentence of death. But
this happened that we might not rely on
ourselves but on God,[k] who raises the
dead. 10He has delivered us from such
a deadly peril,[l] and he will deliver us.
On him we have set our hope that he
will continue to deliver us, 11as you help
us by your prayers.[m] Then many will
give thanks[n] on our[a] behalf for the gracious favor granted us in answer to the
prayers of many.

Paul's sincerity is reported.

12Now this is our boast: Our conscience[o] testifies that we have conducted ourselves in the world, and especially in our relations with you, in the
holiness and sincerity[p] that are from
God. We have done so not according to
worldly wisdom[q] but according to God's
grace. 13For we do not write you anything you cannot read or understand.
And I hope that, 14as you have understood us in part, you will come to understand fully that you can boast of us just
as we will boast of you in the day of the
Lord Jesus.[r]

Paul's visit is delayed.

15Because I was confident of this, I
planned to visit you[s] first so that you
might benefit twice.[t] 16I planned to visit you on my way[u] to Macedonia and to
come back to you from Macedonia, and
then to have you send me on my way
to Judea. 17When I planned this, did I
do it lightly? Or do I make my plans in
a worldly manner[v] so that in the same
breath I say, "Yes, yes" and "No, no"?

18But as surely as God is faithful,[w]
our message to you is not "Yes" and
"No." 19For the Son of God, Jesus Christ,
who was preached among you by me
and Silas[b] and Timothy, was not "Yes"
and "No," but in him it has always[x]
been "Yes." 20For no matter how many
promises[y] God has made, they are "Yes"
in Christ. And so through him the
"Amen"[z] is spoken by us to the glory of
God. 21Now it is God who makes both
us and you stand firm in Christ. He
anointed[a] us, 22set his seal of ownership on us, and put his Spirit in our
hearts as a deposit, guaranteeing what
is to come.[b]

Paul encourages forgiveness of an offender.

23I call God as my witness[c] that it was
in order to spare you[d] that I did not return to Corinth. 24Not that we lord it
over[e] your faith, but we work with

1:1 [a] 1Co 1:1; Eph 1:1; Col 1:1; 2Ti 1:1 [b] 1Co 10:32 [c] Ac 18:12
1:2 [d] Ro 1:7
1:3 [e] Eph 1:3; 1Pe 1:3
1:4 [f] 2Co 7:6,7,13
1:5 [g] 2Co 4:10; Col 1:24
1:6 [h] 2Co 4:15
1:7 [i] Ro 8:17
1:8 [j] 1Co 15:32
1:9 [k] Jer 17:5,7
1:10 [l] Ro 15:31
1:11 [m] Ro 15:30; Php 1:19 [n] 2Co 4:15
1:12 [o] Ac 23:1 [p] 2Co 2:17 [q] 1Co 2:1, 4,13
1:14 [r] 1Co 1:8
1:15 [s] 1Co 4:19 [t] Ro 1:11,13; 15:29
1:16 [u] 1Co 16:5-7
1:17 [v] 2Co 10:2,3
1:18 [w] 1Co 1:9
1:19 [x] Heb 13:8
1:20 [y] Ro 15:8 [z] 1Co 14:16
1:21 [a] 1Jn 2:20,27
1:22 [b] 2Co 5:5
1:23 [c] Ro 1:9; Gal 1:20 [d] 1Co 4:21; 2Co 2:1,3; 13:2,10
1:24 [e] 1Pe 5:3

a *11* Many manuscripts *your*   b *19* Greek *Silvanus*, a variant of *Silas*

you for your joy, because it is by faith
you stand firm.[a]

2 1So I made up my
mind that I would not make anoth-
er painful visit to you.[b] 2For if I grieve
you,[c] who is left to make me glad but
you whom I have grieved? 3I wrote as
I did[d] so that when I came I should
not be distressed[e] by those who ought
to make me rejoice. I had confidence[f]
in all of you, that you would all share
my joy. 4For I wrote you[g] out of great
distress and anguish of heart and with
many tears, not to grieve you but to let
you know the depth of my love for
you.
5If anyone has caused grief,[h] he has
not so much grieved me as he has
grieved all of you, to some extent—
not to put it too severely. 6The punishment[i] inflicted on him by the majority
is sufficient for him. 7Now instead, you
ought to forgive and comfort him,[j] so
that he will not be overwhelmed by excessive sorrow. 8I urge you, therefore,
to reaffirm your love for him. 9The
reason I wrote you was to see if you
would stand the test and be obedient
in everything.[k] 10If you forgive anyone,
I also forgive him. And what I have
forgiven—if there was anything to forgive—I have forgiven in the sight of
Christ for your sake, 11in order that
Satan[l] might not outwit us. For we are
not unaware of his schemes.[m]

Christ's triumph in the lives of the apostles.

12Now when I went to Troas[n] to
preach the gospel of Christ[o] and found
that the Lord had opened a door[p] for
me, 13I still had no peace of mind,[q] because I did not find my brother Titus[r]
there. So I said good-by to them and
went on to Macedonia.
14But thanks be to God,[s] who always
leads us in triumphal procession in
Christ and through us spreads everywhere the fragrance[t] of the knowledge
of him. 15For we are to God the aroma
of Christ among those who are being
saved and those who are perishing.[u]
16To the one we are the smell of death;[v]
to the other, the fragrance of life. And
who is equal to such a task?[w] 17Unlike
so many, we do not peddle the word of
God for profit.[x] On the contrary, in
Christ we speak before God with sincerity,[y] like men sent from God.[z]

All power and success come from God.

3 Are we beginning to commend ourselves[a] again? Or do we need, like
some people, letters of recommenda-
tion[b] to you or from you? 2You yourselves are our letter, written on our
hearts, known and read by everybody.[c]
3You show that you are a letter from
Christ, the result of our ministry, written not with ink but with the Spirit of
the living God, not on tablets of stone[d]
but on tablets of human hearts.[e]
4Such confidence[f] as this is ours
through Christ before God. 5Not that
we are competent in ourselves to claim
anything for ourselves, but our competence comes from God.[g] 6He has made
us competent as ministers of a new
covenant[h]—not of the letter but of the
Spirit; for the letter kills, but the Spirit
gives life.[i]

Greater is the glory which lasts.

7Now if the ministry that brought
death, which was engraved in letters on
stone, came with glory, so that the Israelites could not look steadily at the face
of Moses because of its glory,[j] fading
though it was, 8will not the ministry of
the Spirit be even more glorious? 9If the
ministry that condemns men[k] is glorious, how much more glorious is the
ministry that brings righteousness![l]
10For what was glorious has no glory
now in comparison with the surpassing
glory. 11And if what was fading away
came with glory, how much greater is
the glory of that which lasts!
12Therefore, since we have such a
hope, we are very bold.[m] 13We are not
like Moses, who would put a veil over

1:24 [a]Ro 11:20; 1Co 15:1 **2:1** [b]2Co 1:23 **2:2** [c]2Co 7:8 **2:3** [d]2Co 7:8,12 [e]2Co 12:21 [f]2Co 8:22; Gal 5:10 **2:4** [g]2Co 7:8,12 **2:5** [h]1Co 5:1,2 **2:6** [i]1Co 5:4,5 **2:7** [j]Gal 6:1; Eph 4:32 **2:9** [k]2Co 10:6 **2:11** [l]Mt 4:10 [m]Lk 22:31; 2Co 4:4; 1Pe 5:8,9 **2:12** [n]Ac 16:8 [o]Ro 1:1 [p]Ac 14:27 **2:13** [q]2Co 7:5 [r]2Co 7:6,13; 12:18 **2:14** [s]Ro 6:17 [t]Eph 5:2; Php 4:18 **2:15** [u]1Co 1:18 **2:16** [v]Lk 2:34 [w]2Co 3:5,6 **2:17** [x]2Co 4:2 [y]1Co 5:8 [z]2Co 1:12 **3:1** [a]2Co 5:12; 12:11 [b]Ac 18:27 **3:2** [c]1Co 9:2 **3:3** [d]Ex 24:12 [e]Pr 3:3; Jer 31:33; Eze 11:19 **3:4** [f]Eph 3:12 **3:5** [g]1Co 15:10 **3:6** [h]Lk 22:20 [i]Jn 6:63 **3:7** [j]Ex 34:29-35

3:9 [k]ver 7 [l]Ro 1:17; 3:21,22 **3:12** [m]Eph 6:19

his face[a] to keep the Israelites from gazing at it while the radiance was fading away. 14But their minds were made dull,[b] for to this day the same veil remains when the old covenant[c] is read.[d] It has not been removed, because only in Christ is it taken away. 15Even to this day when Moses is read, a veil covers their hearts. 16But whenever anyone turns to the Lord,[e] the veil is taken away.[f] 17Now the Lord is the Spirit,[g] and where the Spirit of the Lord is, there is freedom.[h] 18And we, who with unveiled faces all reflect[c][i] the Lord's glory,[j] are being transformed into his likeness[k] with ever-increasing glory, which comes from the Lord, who is the Spirit.

Jesus is the essence of Paul's preaching.

4 Therefore, since through God's mercy[l] we have this ministry, we do not lose heart. 2Rather, we have renounced secret and shameful ways;[m] we do not use deception, nor do we distort the word of God.[n] On the contrary, by setting forth the truth plainly we commend ourselves to every man's conscience[o] in the sight of God. 3And even if our gospel[p] is veiled,[q] it is veiled to those who are perishing.[r] 4The god[s] of this age has blinded[t] the minds of unbelievers, so that they cannot see the light of the gospel of the glory of Christ, who is the image of God. 5For we do not preach ourselves,[u] but Jesus Christ as Lord, and ourselves as your servants[v] for Jesus' sake. 6For God, who said, "Let light shine out of darkness,"[d][w] made his light shine in our hearts[x] to give us the light of the knowledge of the glory of God in the face of Christ.

Trials and persecutions abound.

7But we have this treasure in jars of clay[y] to show that this all-surpassing power is from God[z] and not from us. 8We are hard pressed on every side,[a] but not crushed; perplexed, but not in despair; 9persecuted,[b] but not abandoned;[c] struck down, but not destroyed.[d] 10We always carry around in our body the death of Jesus, so that the life of Jesus may also be revealed in our body.[e] 11For we who are alive are always being given over to death for Jesus' sake,[f] so that his life may be revealed in our mortal body. 12So then, death is at work in us, but life is at work in you.[g]

13It is written: "I believed; therefore I have spoken."[e][h] With that same spirit of faith we also believe and therefore speak, 14because we know that the one who raised the Lord Jesus from the dead will also raise us with Jesus[i] and present us with you in his presence.[j] 15All this is for your benefit, so that the grace that is reaching more and more people may cause thanksgiving[k] to overflow to the glory of God.

What is unseen is eternal.

16Therefore we do not lose heart. Though outwardly we are wasting away, yet inwardly[l] we are being renewed[m] day by day. 17For our light and momentary troubles are achieving for us an eternal glory that far outweighs them all.[n] 18So we fix our eyes not on what is seen, but on what is unseen.[o] For what is seen is temporary, but what is unseen is eternal.

Heavenly bodies for believers.

5 Now we know that if the earthly[p] tent[q] we live in is destroyed, we have a building from God, an eternal house in heaven, not built by human hands. 2Meanwhile we groan,[r] longing to be clothed with our heavenly dwelling,[s] 3because when we are clothed, we will not be found naked. 4For while we are in this tent, we groan and are burdened, because we do not wish to be unclothed but to be clothed with our heavenly dwelling,[t] so that what is mortal may be swallowed up by life. 5Now it is God who has made us for this very purpose and has given us the

3:13 [a]ver 7; Ex 34:33
3:14 [b]Ro 11:7,8 [c]Ac 13:15 [d]ver 6
3:16 [e]Ro 11:23 [f]Ex 34:34
3:17 [g]Isa 61:1,2 [h]Jn 8:32
3:18 [i]1Co 13:12 [j]2Co 4:4,6 [k]Ro 8:29
4:1 [l]1Co 7:25
4:2 [m]1Co 4:5 [n]2Co 2:17 [o]2Co 5:11
4:3 [p]2Co 2:12 [q]2Co 3:14 [r]1Co 1:18
4:4 [s]Jn 12:31 [t]2Co 3:14
4:5 [u]1Co 1:13 [v]1Co 9:19
4:6 [w]Ge 1:3 [x]2Pe 1:19
4:7 [y]Job 4:19; 2Co 5:1 [z]1Co 2:5
4:8 [a]2Co 7:5
4:9 [b]Jn 15:20 [c]Heb 13:5 [d]Ps 37:24
4:10 [e]Ro 6:5
4:11 [f]Ro 8:36
4:12 [g]2Co 13:9
4:13 [h]Ps 116:10
4:14 [i]1Th 4:14 [j]Eph 5:27
4:15 [k]2Co 1:11
4:16 [l]Ro 7:22 [m]Col 3:10
4:17 [n]Ro 8:18; 1Pe 1:6,7
4:18 [o]Ro 8:24; Heb 11:1

5:1 [p]1Co 15:47 [q]2Pe 1:13,14 **5:2** [r]ver 4; Ro 8:23 [s]1Co 15:53,54 **5:4** [t]1Co 15:53,54

c *18* Or *contemplate* d *6* Gen. 1:3 e *13* Psalm 116:10

Spirit as a deposit, guaranteeing what is to come.[a]

6 Therefore we are always confident and know that as long as we are at home in the body we are away from the Lord. 7 We live by faith, not by sight.[b] 8 We are confident, I say, and would prefer to be away from the body and at home with the Lord.[c] 9 So we make it our goal to please him,[d] whether we are at home in the body or away from it. 10 For we must all appear before the judgment seat of Christ, that each one may receive what is due him[e] for the things done while in the body, whether good or bad.

Ambassadors of God's love.

11 Since, then, we know what it is to fear the Lord,[f] we try to persuade men. What we are is plain to God, and I hope it is also plain to your conscience.[g] 12 We are not trying to commend ourselves to you again,[h] but are giving you an opportunity to take pride in us,[i] so that you can answer those who take pride in what is seen rather than in what is in the heart. 13 If we are out of our mind,[j] it is for the sake of God; if we are in our right mind, it is for you. 14 For Christ's love compels us, because we are convinced that one died for all, and therefore all died.[k] 15 And he died for all, that those who live should no longer live for themselves[l] but for him who died for them and was raised again.

16 So from now on we regard no one from a worldly[m] point of view. Though we once regarded Christ in this way, we do so no longer. 17 Therefore, if anyone is in Christ, he is a new creation;[n] the old has gone, the new has come![o] 18 All this is from God, who reconciled us to himself through Christ[p] and gave us the ministry of reconciliation: 19 that God was reconciling the world to himself in Christ, not counting men's sins against them.[q] And he has committed to us the message of reconciliation. 20 We are therefore Christ's ambassadors,[r] as though God were making his appeal through us. We implore you on Christ's behalf: Be reconciled to God. 21 God made him who had no sin[s] to be sin[f] for us, so that in him we might become the righteousness of God.[t]

6 As God's fellow workers[u] we urge you not to receive God's grace in vain. 2 For he says,

> "In the time of my favor I heard you,
> and in the day of salvation I helped you."[g][v]

I tell you, now is the time of God's favor, now is the day of salvation.

Paul is diligent in his ministry.

3 We put no stumbling block in anyone's path,[w] so that our ministry will not be discredited. 4 Rather, as servants of God we commend ourselves in every way: in great endurance; in troubles, hardships and distresses; 5 in beatings, imprisonments[x] and riots; in hard work, sleepless nights and hunger;[y] 6 in purity, understanding, patience and kindness; in the Holy Spirit[z] and in sincere love; 7 in truthful speech[a] and in the power of God; with weapons of righteousness[b] in the right hand and in the left; 8 through glory and dishonor,[c] bad report and good report; genuine, yet regarded as impostors;[d] 9 known, yet regarded as unknown; dying,[e] and yet we live on;[f] beaten, and yet not killed; 10 sorrowful, yet always rejoicing;[g] poor, yet making many rich;[h] having nothing, and yet possessing everything.[i]

11 We have spoken freely to you, Corinthians, and opened wide our hearts to you.[j] 12 We are not withholding our affection from you, but you are withholding yours from us. 13 As a fair exchange—I speak as to my children[k]—open wide your hearts also.

5:5 [a]Ro 8:23; 2Co 1:22
5:7 [b]1Co 13:12
5:8 [c]Php 1:23
5:9 [d]Ro 14:18
5:10 [e]Mt 16:27; Ro 14:10; Eph 6:8
5:11 [f]Heb 10:31; Jude 23 [g]2Co 4:2
5:12 [h]2Co 3:1 [i]2Co 1:14
5:13 [j]2Co 11:1, 16,17
5:14 [k]Gal 2:20
5:15 [l]Ro 14:7-9
5:16 [m]2Co 11:18
5:17 [n]Gal 6:15 [o]Isa 65:17; Rev 21:4,5
5:18 [p]Ro 5:10; Col 1:20
5:19 [q]Ro 4:8
5:20 [r]2Co 6:1; Eph 6:20
5:21 [s]Heb 4:15; 1Pe 2:22,24; 1Jn 3:5 [t]Ro 1:17
6:1 [u]1Co 3:9; 2Co 5:20
6:2 [v]Isa 49:8
6:3 [w]Ro 14:13,20; 1Co 9:12; 10:32
6:5 [x]2Co 11:23-25 [y]1Co 4:11
6:6 [z]1Th 1:5
6:7 [a]2Co 4:2 [b]2Co 10:4; Eph 6:10-18
6:8 [c]1Co 4:10 [d]Mt 27:63 **6:9** [e]Ro 8:36 [f]2Co 1:8-10; 4:10,11 **6:10** [g]2Co 7:4 [h]2Co 8:9 [i]Ro 8:32; 1Co 3:21 **6:11** [j]2Co 7:3
6:13 [k]1Co 4:14

[f]*21* Or *be a sin offering* [g]*2* Isaiah 49:8

Believers are exhorted to be separate from unbelievers.

[14]Do not be yoked together[a] with unbelievers. For what do righteousness
and wickedness have in common? Or
what fellowship can light have with
darkness?[b] [15]What harmony is there between Christ and Belial[h]? What does a
believer[c] have in common with an
unbeliever? [16]What agreement is there
between the temple of God and idols?
For we are the temple[d] of the living God.
As God has said: "I will live with them
and walk among them, and I will be
their God, and they will be my
people."[ie]

[17]"Therefore come out from them[f]
and be separate,
says the Lord.
Touch no unclean thing,
and I will receive you."[jg]
[18]"I will be a Father to you,
and you will be my sons and
daughters,[h]
says the Lord
Almighty."[k]

7 Since we have these promises,[i]
dear friends, let us purify ourselves
from everything that contaminates body
and spirit, perfecting holiness out of
reverence for God.

Paul is joyfully encouraged by the Corinthians' repentance.

[2]Make room for us in your hearts.[j] We
have wronged no one, we have corrupted no one, we have exploited no one. [3]I
do not say this to condemn you; I have
said before that you have such a place
in our hearts[k] that we would live or
die with you. [4]I have great confidence in
you; I take great pride in you. I am
greatly encouraged; in all our troubles
my joy knows no bounds.[l]
[5]For when we came into Macedonia,[m]
this body of ours had no rest, but we
were harassed at every turn[n]—conflicts
on the outside, fears within.[o] [6]But God,
who comforts the downcast,[p] comforted us by the coming of Titus,[q] [7]and not
only by his coming but also by the
comfort you had given him. He told us
about your longing for me, your deep
sorrow, your ardent concern for me, so
that my joy was greater than ever.
[8]Even if I caused you sorrow by my
letter,[r] I do not regret it. Though I did
regret it—I see that my letter hurt
you, but only for a little while— [9]yet
now I am happy, not because you were
made sorry, but because your sorrow
led you to repentance. For you became
sorrowful as God intended and so were
not harmed in any way by us. [10]Godly
sorrow brings repentance that leads to
salvation[s] and leaves no regret, but
worldly sorrow brings death. [11]See what
this godly sorrow has produced in you:
what earnestness, what eagerness to
clear yourselves, what indignation, what
alarm, what longing, what concern,[t]
what readiness to see justice done. At
every point you have proved yourselves
to be innocent in this matter. [12]So even
though I wrote to you,[u] it was not on
account of the one who did the wrong[v]
or of the injured party, but rather that
before God you could see for yourselves
how devoted to us you are. [13]By all this
we are encouraged.
In addition to our own encouragement, we were especially delighted to
see how happy Titus[w] was, because
his spirit has been refreshed by all of
you. [14]I had boasted to him about you,[x]
and you have not embarrassed me. But
just as everything we said to you was
true, so our boasting about you to Titus[y]
has proved to be true as well. [15]And
his affection for you is all the greater
when he remembers that you were all
obedient,[z] receiving him with fear and
trembling.[a] [16]I am glad I can have complete confidence in you.[b]

6:14 [a]1Co 5:9,10 [b]Eph 5:7,11; 1Jn 1:6
6:15 [c]Ac 5:14
6:16 [d]1Co 3:16 [e]Lev 26:12; Jer 32:38; Eze 37:27
6:17 [f]Rev 18:4 [g]Isa 52:11
6:18 [h]Isa 43:6
7:1 [i]2Co 6:17,18
7:2 [j]2Co 6:12,13
7:3 [k]2Co 6:11,12
7:4 [l]2Co 6:10
7:5 [m]2Co 2:13 [n]2Co 4:8 [o]Dt 32:25
7:6 [p]2Co 1:3,4 [q]ver 13; 2Co 2:13
7:8 [r]2Co 2:2,4
7:10 [s]Ac 11:18
7:11 [t]ver 7
7:12 [u]ver 8; 2Co 2:3,9 [v]1Co 5:1,2
7:13 [w]ver 6; 2Co 2:13
7:14 [x]ver 4 [y]ver 6
7:15 [z]2Co 2:9 [a]Php 2:12
7:16 [b]2Co 2:3

h *15* Greek *Beliar,* a variant of *Belial*
i *16* Lev. 26:12; Jer. 32:38; Ezek. 37:27
j *17* Isaiah 52:11; Ezek. 20:34,41
k *18* 2 Samuel 7:14; 7:8

The Macedonian churches give abundantly to the saints in Jerusalem.

8 And now, brothers, we want you
to know about the grace that God
has given the Macedonian[a] churches.
2Out of the most severe trial, their overflowing joy and their extreme poverty
welled up in rich generosity. 3For I testify that they gave as much as they were
able,[b] and even beyond their ability.
Entirely on their own, 4they urgently
pleaded with us for the privilege of sharing in this service[c] to the saints.[d] 5And
they did not do as we expected, but
they gave themselves first to the Lord
and then to us in keeping with God's
will. 6So we urged[e] Titus,[f] since he had
earlier made a beginning, to bring also
to completion[g] this act of grace on
your part. 7But just as you excel in
everything[h]—in faith, in speech, in
knowledge,[i] in complete earnestness
and in your love for us[l]—see that you
also excel in this grace of giving.

The Corinthians are encouraged to be generous givers.

8I am not commanding you,[j] but I
want to test the sincerity of your love
by comparing it with the earnestness of
others. 9For you know the grace of our
Lord Jesus Christ,[k] that though he was
rich, yet for your sakes he became
poor,[l] so that you through his poverty
might become rich.
10And here is my advice[m] about
what is best for you in this matter:
Last year you were the first not only to
give but also to have the desire to do
so.[n] 11Now finish the work, so that
your eager willingness[o] to do it may be
matched by your completion of it,
according to your means. 12For if the
willingness is there, the gift is acceptable according to what one has,[p] not
according to what he does not have.
13Our desire is not that others might
be relieved while you are hard pressed,
but that there might be equality. 14At
the present time your plenty will supply what they need,[q] so that in turn
their plenty will supply what you need.
Then there will be equality, 15as it is
written: "He who gathered much did
not have too much, and he who gathered little did not have too little."[m] [r]

The offering is safeguarded.

16I thank God,[s] who put into the
heart[t] of Titus[u] the same concern I have
for you. 17For Titus not only welcomed
our appeal, but he is coming to you
with much enthusiasm and on his own
initiative.[v] 18And we are sending along
with him the brother[w] who is praised
by all the churches[x] for his service to
the gospel.[y] 19What is more, he was
chosen by the churches to accompany
us[z] as we carry the offering, which we
administer in order to honor the Lord
himself and to show our eagerness to
help.[a] 20We want to avoid any criticism
of the way we administer this liberal
gift. 21For we are taking pains to do what
is right, not only in the eyes of the
Lord but also in the eyes of men.[b]
22In addition, we are sending with
them our brother who has often proved
to us in many ways that he is zealous,
and now even more so because of his
great confidence in you. 23As for Titus,
he is my partner[c] and fellow worker[d]
among you; as for our brothers,[e] they
are representatives of the churches and
an honor to Christ. 24Therefore show
these men the proof of your love and
the reason for our pride in you,[f] so
that the churches can see it.

Timely giving.

9 There is no need[g] for me to write
to you about this service to the
saints.[h] 2For I know your eagerness to
help, and I have been boasting[i] about
it to the Macedonians, telling them that
since last year[j] you in Achaia[k] were
ready to give; and your enthusiasm has
stirred most of them to action. 3But I
am sending the brothers in order that
our boasting about you in this matter

8:1 [a]Ac 16:9
8:3 [b]1Co 16:2
8:4 [c]Ac 24:17 [d]Ro 15:25; 2Co 9:1
8:6 [e]ver 17; 2Co 12:18 [f]ver 16,23 [g]ver 10,11
8:7 [h]2Co 9:8 [i]1Co 1:5
8:8 [j]1Co 7:6
8:9 [k]2Co 13:14 [l]Mt 20:28; Php 2:6-8
8:10 [m]1Co 7:25,40 [n]1Co 16:2,3; 2Co 9:2
8:11 [o]2Co 9:2
8:12 [p]Mk 12:43,44; Lk 21:3
8:14 [q]2Co 9:12
8:15 [r]Ex 16:18
8:16 [s]2Co 2:14 [t]Rev 17:17 [u]2Co 2:13
8:17 [v]ver 6
8:18 [w]2Co 12:18 [x]1Co 7:17 [y]2Co 2:12
8:19 [z]1Co 16:3,4 [a]ver 11,12
8:21 [b]Ro 12:17; 14:18
8:23 [c]Phm 17 [d]Php 2:25 [e]ver 18,22
8:24 [f]2Co 7:4,14; 9:2
9:1 [g]1Th 4:9 [h]2Co 8:4
9:2 [i]2Co 7:4,14 [j]2Co 8:10 [k]Ac 18:12

l7 Some manuscripts *in our love for you*
m15 Exodus 16:18

should not prove hollow, but that you
may be ready, as I said you would be.[a]
4For if any Macedonians[b] come with me
and find you unprepared, we—not to
say anything about you—would be
ashamed of having been so confident.
5So I thought it necessary to urge the
brothers to visit you in advance and
finish the arrangements for the generous gift you had promised. Then it will
be ready as a generous gift,[c] not as one
grudgingly given.[d]

The cheerful giver.

6Remember this: Whoever sows sparingly will also reap sparingly, and whoever sows generously will also reap
generously.[e] 7Each man should give
what he has decided in his heart to
give,[f] not reluctantly or under compulsion,[g] for God loves a cheerful giver.[h]
8And God is able[i] to make all grace
abound to you, so that in all things at
all times, having all that you need,[j] you
will abound in every good work. 9As it
is written:

> "He has scattered abroad his gifts to
> the poor;
> his righteousness endures
> forever."[n][k]

10Now he who supplies seed to the
sower and bread for food[l] will also supply and increase your store of seed and
will enlarge the harvest of your righteousness.[m] 11You will be made rich[n]
in every way so that you can be generous on every occasion, and through us
your generosity will result in thanksgiving to God.[o]
12This service that you perform is
not only supplying the needs[p] of God's
people but is also overflowing in many
expressions of thanks to God.[q] 13Be-
cause of the service[r] by which you
have proved yourselves, men will praise
God[s] for the obedience that accompanies your confession of the gospel of
Christ,[t] and for your generosity in sharing with them and with everyone else.
14And in their prayers for you their

9:3 [a]1Co 16:2
9:4 [b]Ro 15:26
9:5 [c]Php 4:17 [d]2Co 12:17,18
9:6 [e]Pr 11:24,25; 22:9; Gal 6:7,9
9:7 [f]Ex 25:2; 2Co 8:12 [g]Dt 15:10 [h]Ro 12:8
9:8 [i]Eph 3:20 [j]Php 4:19
9:9 [k]Ps 112:9
9:10 [l]Isa 55:10 [m]Hos 10:12
9:11 [n]1Co 1:5 [o]2Co 1:11
9:12 [p]2Co 8:14 [q]2Co 1:11
9:13 [r]2Co 8:4 [s]Mt 9:8 [t]2Co 2:12
9:15 [u]2Co 2:14 [v]Ro 5:15,16
10:1 [w]Mt 11:29 [x]Gal 5:2
10:2 [y]1Co 4:21; 2Co 13:2,10
10:4 [z]2Co 6:7 [a]1Co 2:5 [b]Jer 1:10; 2Co 13:10
10:5 [c]Isa 2:11,12; 1Co 1:19 [d]2Co 9:13
10:6 [e]2Co 2:9; 7:15
10:7 [f]Jn 7:24 [g]1Co 1:12; 3:23; 14:37 [h]2Co 11:23
10:8 [i]2Co 13:10
10:10 [j]1Co 2:3; Gal 4:13,14 [k]1Co 1:17

hearts will go out to you, because of
the surpassing grace God has given you.
15Thanks be to God[u] for his indescribable gift![v]

Paul's strength is in the power of God.

10 By the meekness and gentleness[w]
of Christ, I appeal to you—I,
Paul,[x] who am "timid" when face to
face with you, but "bold" when away!
2I beg you that when I come I may not
have to be as bold[y] as I expect to be
toward some people who think that
we live by the standards of this world.
3For though we live in the world, we
do not wage war as the world does.
4The weapons we fight with[z] are not
the weapons of the world. On the contrary, they have divine power[a] to demolish strongholds.[b] 5We demolish arguments and every pretension that sets
itself up against the knowledge of God,[c]
and we take captive every thought to
make it obedient[d] to Christ. 6And we
will be ready to punish every act of
disobedience, once your obedience is
complete.[e]
7You are looking only on the surface
of things.[o][f] If anyone is confident that
he belongs to Christ,[g] he should consider again that we belong to Christ just
as much as he.[h] 8For even if I boast
somewhat freely about the authority
the Lord gave us for building you up
rather than pulling you down,[i] I will
not be ashamed of it. 9I do not want to
seem to be trying to frighten you with
my letters. 10For some say, "His letters
are weighty and forceful, but in person
he is unimpressive[j] and his speaking
amounts to nothing."[k] 11Such people
should realize that what we are in our
letters when we are absent, we will be
in our actions when we are present.

Limits of Paul's authority are set by God.

12We do not dare to classify or compare ourselves with some who com-

[n]9 Psalm 112:9 [o]7 Or *Look at the obvious facts*

mend themselves.[a] When they measure
themselves by themselves and compare
themselves with themselves, they are
not wise. 13We, however, will not boast
beyond proper limits, but will confine
our boasting to the field God has assigned to us,[b] a field that reaches even
to you. 14We are not going too far in our
boasting, as would be the case if we had
not come to you, for we did get as far
as you[c] with the gospel of Christ.[d]
15Neither do we go beyond our limits
by boasting of work done by others.[p][e]
Our hope is that, as your faith continues to grow,[f] our area of activity among
you will greatly expand, 16so that we
can preach the gospel in the regions
beyond you.[g] For we do not want to
boast about work already done in another man's territory. 17But, "Let him who
boasts boast in the Lord."[q][h] 18For it is
not the one who commends himself[i]
who is approved, but the one whom
the Lord commends.[j]

Paul commends his ministry and condemns all false ministries.

11 I hope you will put up with[k] a little of my foolishness;[l] but you are
already doing that. 2I am jealous for
you with a godly jealousy. I promised
you to one husband,[m] to Christ, so that
I might present you[n] as a pure virgin
to him. 3But I am afraid that just as Eve
was deceived by the serpent's cunning,[o]
your minds may somehow be led astray
from your sincere and pure devotion
to Christ. 4For if someone comes to you
and preaches a Jesus other than the
Jesus we preached,[p] or if you receive a
different spirit[q] from the one you received, or a different gospel[r] from the
one you accepted, you put up with it
easily enough. 5But I do not think I am
in the least inferior to those "super-
apostles."[s] 6I may not be a trained speaker,[t] but I do have knowledge.[u] We have
made this perfectly clear to you in
every way.

7Was it a sin[v] for me to lower myself
in order to elevate you by preaching the
gospel of God to you free of charge?[w]
8I robbed other churches by receiving support from them[x] so as to serve
you. 9And when I was with you and
needed something, I was not a burden
to anyone, for the brothers who came
from Macedonia supplied what I needed. I have kept myself from being a
burden to you[y] in any way, and will
continue to do so. 10As surely as the
truth of Christ is in me,[z] nobody in the
regions of Achaia[a] will stop this boasting[b] of mine. 11Why? Because I do not
love you? God knows I do![c] 12And I will
keep on doing what I am doing in order
to cut the ground from under those who
want an opportunity to be considered
equal with us in the things they boast
about.

13For such men are false apostles,[d]
deceitful[e] workmen, masquerading as
apostles of Christ.[f] 14And no wonder, for
Satan himself masquerades as an angel
of light. 15It is not surprising, then, if
his servants masquerade as servants of
righteousness. Their end will be what
their actions deserve.[g]

Paul's sufferings support his reluctant boasts.

16I repeat: Let no one take me for a
fool.[h] But if you do, then receive me
just as you would a fool, so that I may
do a little boasting. 17In this self-confi-
dent boasting I am not talking as the
Lord would,[i] but as a fool. 18Since many
are boasting in the way the world does,
I too will boast.[j] 19You gladly put up
with fools since you are so wise![k] 20In
fact, you even put up with anyone who
enslaves you[l] or exploits you or takes
advantage of you or pushes himself forward or slaps you in the face. 21To my
shame I admit that we were too weak[m]
for that!

10:12 [a]2Co 3:1
10:13 [b]ver 15,16
10:14 [c]1Co 3:6 [d]2Co 2:12
10:15 [e]Ro 15:20 [f]2Th 1:3
10:16 [g]Ac 19:21
10:17 [h]Jer 9:24; 1Co 1:31
10:18 [i]ver 12 [j]Ro 2:29; 1Co 4:5
11:1 [k]ver 4,19,20; Mt 17:17 [l]ver 16,17,21; 2Co 5:13
11:2 [m]Hos 2:19; Eph 5:26,27 [n]2Co 4:14
11:3 [o]Ge 3:1-6,13; Jn 8:44; 1Ti 2:14; Rev 12:9
11:4 [p]1Co 3:11 [q]Ro 8:15 [r]Gal 1:6-9
11:5 [s]2Co 12:11; Gal 2:6
11:6 [t]1Co 1:17 [u]Eph 3:4
11:7 [v]2Co 12:13 [w]1Co 9:18
11:8 [x]Php 4:15,18
11:9 [y]2Co 12:13, 14,16
11:10 [z]Ro 9:1 [a]Ac 18:12 [b]1Co 9:15
11:11 [c]2Co 12:15
11:13 [d]2Pe 2:1 [e]Tit 1:10 [f]Rev 2:2
11:15 [g]Php 3:19
11:16 [h]ver 1
11:17 [i]1Co 7:12,25
11:18 [j]Php 3:3,4
11:19 [k]1Co 4:10 **11:20** [l]Gal 2:4 **11:21** [m]2Co 10:1,10

[p]*13-15* Or *13We, however, will not boast about things that cannot be measured, but we will boast according to the standard of measurement that the God of measure has assigned us—a measurement that relates even to you. 14.... 15Neither do we boast about things that cannot be measured in regard to the work done by others.* [q]*17* Jer. 9:24

What anyone else dares to boast about—I am speaking as a fool—I also dare to boast about.[a] 22Are they Hebrews? So am I.[b] Are they Israelites? So am I.[c] Are they Abraham's descendants? So am I. 23Are they servants of Christ? (I am out of my mind to talk like this.) I am more. I have worked much harder,[d] been in prison more frequently,[e] been flogged more severely, and been exposed to death again and again. 24Five times I received from the Jews the forty lashes[f] minus one. 25Three times I was beaten with rods,[g] once I was stoned,[h] three times I was shipwrecked, I spent a night and a day in the open sea, 26I have been constantly on the move. I have been in danger from rivers, in danger from bandits, in danger from my own countrymen,[i] in danger from Gentiles; in danger in the city,[j] in danger in the country, in danger at sea; and in danger from false brothers.[k] 27I have labored and toiled and have often gone without sleep; I have known hunger and thirst and have often gone without food;[l] I have been cold and naked. 28Besides everything else, I face daily the pressure of my concern for all the churches. 29Who is weak, and I do not feel weak? Who is led into sin, and I do not inwardly burn?

30If I must boast, I will boast of the things that show my weakness.[m] 31The God and Father of the Lord Jesus, who is to be praised forever,[n] knows that I am not lying. 32In Damascus the governor under King Aretas had the city of the Damascenes guarded in order to arrest me.[o] 33But I was lowered in a basket from a window in the wall and slipped through his hands.[p]

Paul's vision of paradise.

12 I must go on boasting.[q] Although there is nothing to be gained, I will go on to visions and revelations[r] from the Lord. 2I know a man in Christ who fourteen years ago was caught up[s] to the third heaven.[t] Whether it was in the body or out of the body I do not know—God knows.[u] 3And I know that this man—whether in the body or apart from the body I do not know, but God knows— 4was caught up to paradise.[v] He heard inexpressible things, things that man is not permitted to tell. 5I will boast about a man like that, but I will not boast about myself, except about my weaknesses. 6Even if I should choose to boast, I would not be a fool,[w] because I would be speaking the truth. But I refrain, so no one will think more of me than is warranted by what I do or say.

Paul's thorn in his flesh.

7To keep me from becoming conceited because of these surpassingly great revelations, there was given me a thorn in my flesh,[x] a messenger of Satan, to torment me. 8Three times I pleaded with the Lord to take it away from me.[y] 9But he said to me, "My grace is sufficient for you, for my power[z] is made perfect in weakness." Therefore I will boast all the more gladly about my weaknesses, so that Christ's power may rest on me. 10That is why, for Christ's sake, I delight in weaknesses, in insults, in hardships,[a] in persecutions,[b] in difficulties. For when I am weak, then I am strong.[c]

Paul's proof of apostleship.

11I have made a fool of myself,[d] but you drove me to it. I ought to have been commended by you, for I am not in the least inferior to the "super-apostles,"[e] even though I am nothing.[f] 12The things that mark an apostle—signs, wonders and miracles[g]—were done among you with great perseverance. 13How were you inferior to the other churches, except that I was never a burden to you?[h] Forgive me this wrong![i]

Paul's concern for the Corinthians' spiritual welfare.

14Now I am ready to visit you for the

11:21 [a]Php 3:4
11:22 [b]Php 3:5 [c]Ro 9:4
11:23 [d]1Co 15:10 [e]Ac 16:23; 2Co 6:4,5
11:24 [f]Dt 25:3
11:25 [g]Ac 16:22 [h]Ac 14:19
11:26 [i]Ac 9:23; 14:5 [j]Ac 21:31 [k]Gal 2:4
11:27 [l]1Co 4:11,12; 2Co 6:5
11:30 [m]1Co 2:3
11:31 [n]Ro 9:5
11:32 [o]Ac 9:24
11:33 [p]Ac 9:25
12:1 [q]2Co 11:16,30 [r]ver 7
12:2 [s]Ac 8:39 [t]Eph 4:10 [u]2Co 11:11
12:4 [v]Lk 23:43; Rev 2:7
12:6 [w]2Co 11:16
12:7 [x]Nu 33:55
12:8 [y]Mt 26:39,44
12:9 [z]Php 4:13
12:10 [a]2Co 6:4 [b]Ro 5:3; 2Th 1:4 [c]2Co 13:4
12:11 [d]2Co 11:1 [e]2Co 11:5 [f]1Co 15:9,10
12:12 [g]Jn 4:48
12:13 [h]1Co 9:12,18 [i]2Co 11:7

third time,[a] and I will not be a burden
to you, because what I want is not your
possessions but you. After all, children
should not have to save up for their
parents,[b] but parents for their children.[c] 15So I will very gladly spend for
you everything I have and expend
myself as well.[d] If I love you more, will
you love me less? 16Be that as it may, I
have not been a burden to you.[e] Yet,
crafty fellow that I am, I caught you by
trickery! 17Did I exploit you through
any of the men I sent you? 18I urged[f]
Titus to go to you and I sent our brother[g] with him. Titus did not exploit you,
did he? Did we not act in the same
spirit and follow the same course?
19Have you been thinking all along
that we have been defending ourselves
to you? We have been speaking in the
sight of God[h] as those in Christ; and
everything we do, dear friends, is for
your strengthening.[i] 20For I am afraid
that when I come[j] I may not find you as
I want you to be, and you may not find
me as you want me to be.[k] I fear that
there may be quarreling,[l] jealousy, out-
bursts of anger, factions,[m] slander, gossip,[n] arrogance and disorder.[o] 21I am
afraid that when I come again my God
will humble me before you, and I will
be grieved[p] over many who have sinned
earlier[q] and have not repented of the
impurity, sexual sin and debauchery in
which they have indulged.

Paul's warning for sinners.

13 This will be my third visit to
you.[r] "Every matter must be established by the testimony of two or
three witnesses."[r][s] 2I already gave you
a warning when I was with you the
second time. I now repeat it while
absent: On my return I will not spare[t]
those who sinned earlier[u] or any of
the others, 3since you are demanding
proof that Christ is speaking through
me.[v] He is not weak in dealing with
you, but is powerful among you. 4For
to be sure, he was crucified in weakness,[w] yet he lives by God's power.[x]
Likewise, we are weak[y] in him, yet by
God's power we will live with him to
serve you.
5Examine yourselves[z] to see whether
you are in the faith; test yourselves.[a]
Do you not realize that Christ Jesus is
in you[b]—unless, of course, you fail
the test? 6And I trust that you will discover that we have not failed the test.
7Now we pray to God that you will not
do anything wrong. Not that people
will see that we have stood the test
but that you will do what is right even
though we may seem to have failed.
8For we cannot do anything against the
truth, but only for the truth. 9We are
glad whenever we are weak but you are
strong; and our prayer is for your perfection.[c] 10This is why I write these
things when I am absent, that when I
come I may not have to be harsh in
my use of authority—the authority the
Lord gave me for building you up, not
for tearing you down.[d]

Final exhortations and greetings.

11Finally, brothers,[e] good-by. Aim for
perfection, listen to my appeal, be of
one mind, live in peace.[f] And the God
of love and peace[g] will be with you.
12Greet one another with a holy kiss.[h]
13All the saints send their greetings.[i]
14May the grace of the Lord Jesus
Christ,[j] and the love of God,[k] and the
fellowship of the Holy Spirit[l] be with
you all.

12:14 [a]2Co 13:1 [b]1Co 4:14,15 [c]Pr 19:14
12:15 [d]Php 2:17; 1Th 2:8
12:16 [e]2Co 11:9
12:18 [f]2Co 8:6,16 [g]2Co 8:18
12:19 [h]Ro 9:1 [i]2Co 10:8
12:20 [j]2Co 2:1-4 [k]1Co 4:21 [l]1Co 1:11; 3:3 [m]Gal 5:20 [n]Ro 1:29 [o]1Co 14:33
12:21 [p]2Co 2:1,4 [q]2Co 13:2
13:1 [r]2Co 12:14 [s]Dt 19:15; Mt 18:16
13:2 [t]2Co 1:23 [u]2Co 12:21
13:3 [v]Mt 10:20; 1Co 5:4
13:4 [w]Php 2:7,8; 1Pe 3:18 [x]Ro 1:4; 6:4 [y]ver 9
13:5 [z]1Co 11:28 [a]Jn 6:6 [b]Ro 8:10
13:9 [c]ver 11
13:10 [d]2Co 10:8
13:11 [e]1Th 4:1; 2Th 3:1 [f]Mk 9:50 [g]Ro 15:33; Eph 6:23
13:12 [h]Ro 16:16
13:13 [i]Php 4:22 **13:14** [j]Ro 16:20; 2Co 8:9 [k]Ro 5:5; Jude 21 [l]Php 2:1

[r]1 Deut. 19:15

GALATIANS

Author: Paul the Apostle.

Date Written: Between A.D. 49 and 55.

Title: Named after the addressee of this letter: the church at Galatia.

Background: Jews greatly outnumber Gentiles in the early churches, such as the one at Galatia; thus, many questions and issues arise when non-Jews come into the church. The Judaizers, a group of Jewish believers, follow Paul as he evangelizes. They insist that the Gentile believers must submit to circumcision and the laws of Moses in order to be saved. The book of Galatians is Paul's response to this erroneous teaching. Salvation is a gift of grace, wholly dependent upon faith in Jesus Christ. Galatians has been called the "Magna Charta" of the church.

Where Written: Possibly Antioch or Ephesus.

To Whom: To the Christians at Galatia.

Content: Paul uses this letter to remind Christians that they are heirs of God as his own children. This inheritance is not available by works, but only by faith in Jesus Christ. Paul, a Jew himself, refutes the false teaching that each Gentile Christian must be converted to Judaism and follow strict observance of every Mosaic law. He summarizes the gospel and then declares how Abraham was saved by faith about 400 years before the law was revealed through Moses. After defending his credentials as an apostle, Paul concludes with discussions on walking in the Spirit and the fruit of the Spirit.

Key Words: "Grace"; "Liberty." Not by our own good works, but only by the "grace" of God are we justified and brought into a right relationship with God. This "liberty" God has granted us is made possible by Christ's payment for our sins and the Holy Spirit's leading us from sin's bondage.

Themes: • The law was given to reveal man's sinfulness and guilt. • To live under the law is bondage...to live by faith is freedom. • Christians are not bound by the law...Christ has set us free. • Liberty is not license to continue in sin. • The Christian's power to live victoriously over sin comes from the Holy Spirit.

Outline:

1. The only gospel. 1:1-1:10
2. Paul's calling by God and acceptance by the apostles. 1:11-2:10
3. Explanation of grace by faith. 2:11-4:31
4. Freedom in Christ. 5:1-6:10
5. Final blessings. 6:11-6:18

GALATIANS

1 Paul, an apostle—sent not from men
nor by man, but by Jesus Christ[a]
and God the Father, who raised him
from the dead[b]— **2**and all the brothers
with me,[c]

To the churches in Galatia:[d]

3Grace and peace to you from God
our Father and the Lord Jesus Christ,[e]
4who gave himself for our sins[f] to rescue
us from the present evil age, according
to the will of our God and Father,[g] **5**to
whom be glory for ever and ever. Amen.[h]

The gospel of Christ, the only gospel.

6I am astonished that you are so quickly deserting the one who called[i] you by
the grace of Christ and are turning to a
different gospel[j]— **7**which is really no
gospel at all. Evidently some people are
throwing you into confusion[k] and are
trying to pervert the gospel of Christ.
8But even if we or an angel from heaven
should preach a gospel other than the
one we preached to you,[l] let him be eternally condemned![m] **9**As we have already
said, so now I say again: If anybody is
preaching to you a gospel other than
what you accepted,[n] let him be eternally
condemned!
10Am I now trying to win the approval
of men, or of God? Or am I trying to
please men?[o] If I were still trying to
please men, I would not be a servant of
Christ.

Paul's message is from Jesus Christ.

11I want you to know, brothers,[p] that
the gospel I preached is not something
that man made up. **12**I did not receive it
from any man,[q] nor was I taught it;
rather, I received it by revelation[r] from
Jesus Christ.
13For you have heard of my previous
way of life in Judaism,[s] how intensely I
persecuted the church of God and tried
to destroy it.[t] **14**I was advancing in
Judaism beyond many Jews of my own
age and was extremely zealous for the
traditions of my fathers.[u] **15**But when
God, who set me apart from birth[a][v] and
called me[w] by his grace, was pleased
16to reveal his Son in me so that I might
preach him among the Gentiles,[x] I did
not consult any man,[y] **17**nor did I go up
to Jerusalem to see those who were
apostles before I was, but I went immediately into Arabia and later returned to
Damascus.
18Then after three years,[z] I went up to
Jerusalem[a] to get acquainted with Peter[b]
and stayed with him fifteen days. **19**I saw
none of the other apostles—only James,[b]
the Lord's brother. **20**I assure you before
God that what I am writing you is no
lie.[c] **21**Later I went to Syria and Cilicia.[d]
22I was personally unknown to the
churches of Judea[e] that are in Christ.
23They only heard the report: "The man
who formerly persecuted us is now
preaching the faith[f] he once tried to destroy." **24**And they praised God[g] because of me.

The Jerusalem church accepts Paul.

2 Fourteen years later I went up again
to Jerusalem,[h] this time with Barnabas. I took Titus along also. **2**I went in
response to a revelation and set before
them the gospel that I preach among the
Gentiles.[i] But I did this privately to
those who seemed to be leaders, for fear
that I was running or had run my race[j]
in vain. **3**Yet not even Titus,[k] who was
with me, was compelled to be circumcised, even though he was a Greek.[l]
4⌊This matter arose⌋ because some false
brothers[m] had infiltrated our ranks to
spy on[n] the freedom[o] we have in Christ
Jesus and to make us slaves. **5**We did not
give in to them for a moment, so that

1:1 [a]Ac 9:15 [b]Ac 2:24
1:2 [c]Php 4:21 [d]Ac 16:6; 1Co 16:1
1:3 [e]Ro 1:7
1:4 [f]Mt 20:28; Ro 4:25; Gal 2:20 [g]Php 4:20
1:5 [h]Ro 11:36
1:6 [i]Gal 5:8 [j]2Co 11:4
1:7 [k]Ac 15:24; Gal 5:10
1:8 [l]2Co 11:4 [m]Ro 9:3
1:9 [n]Ro 16:17
1:10 [o]Ro 2:29; 1Th 2:4
1:11 [p]1Co 15:1
1:12 [q]ver 1 [r]ver 16
1:13 [s]Ac 26:4,5 [t]Ac 8:3
1:14 [u]Mt 15:2
1:15 [v]Isa 49:1,5; Jer 1:5 [w]Ac 9:15
1:16 [x]Gal 2:9 [y]Mt 16:17
1:18 [z]Ac 9:22,23 [a]Ac 9:26,27
1:19 [b]Mt 13:55
1:20 [c]Ro 9:1
1:21 [d]Ac 6:9
1:22 [e]1Th 2:14
1:23 [f]Ac 6:7
1:24 [g]Mt 9:8
2:1 [h]Ac 15:2

2:2 [i]Ac 15:4,12 [j]1Co 9:24; Php 2:16
2:3 [k]2Co 2:13 [l]Ac 16:3; 1Co 9:21
2:4 [m]2Co 11:26 [n]Jude 4 [o]Ac 15:1; Gal 5:1,13

a *15* Or *from my mother's womb* b *18* Greek *Cephas*

the truth of the gospel[a] might remain
with you.
6As for those who seemed to be
important[b]—whatever they were makes
no difference to me; God does not judge
by external appearance[c]—those men
added nothing to my message. 7On the
contrary, they saw that I had been entrusted with the task[d] of preaching the
gospel to the Gentiles,[c][e] just as Peter[f]
had been to the Jews.[d] 8For God, who
was at work in the ministry of Peter as
an apostle[g] to the Jews, was also at work
in my ministry as an apostle to the Gentiles. 9James, Peter[e][h] and John, those
reputed to be pillars,[i] gave me and Barnabas[j] the right hand of fellowship
when they recognized the grace given to
me.[k] They agreed that we should go to
the Gentiles, and they to the Jews. 10All
they asked was that we should continue
to remember the poor,[l] the very thing I
was eager to do.

Paul opposes Peter on the circumcision issue.

11When Peter[m] came to Antioch,[n] I
opposed him to his face, because he was
clearly in the wrong. 12Before certain
men came from James, he used to eat
with the Gentiles.[o] But when they
arrived, he began to draw back and separate himself from the Gentiles because
he was afraid of those who belonged to
the circumcision group.[p] 13The other
Jews joined him in his hypocrisy, so that
by their hypocrisy even Barnabas[q] was
led astray.
14When I saw that they were not acting in line with the truth of the gospel,[r]
I said to Peter[s] in front of them all,
"You are a Jew, yet you live like a Gentile and not like a Jew.[t] How is it, then,
that you force Gentiles to follow Jewish
customs?
15"We who are Jews by birth[u] and not
'Gentile sinners'[v] 16know that a man is
not justified by observing the law, but by
faith in Jesus Christ.[w] So we, too, have
put our faith in Christ Jesus that we may
be justified by faith in Christ and not by
observing the law, because by observing
the law no one will be justified.
17"If, while we seek to be justified in
Christ, it becomes evident that we ourselves are sinners,[x] does that mean that
Christ promotes sin? Absolutely not![y]
18If I rebuild what I destroyed, I prove
that I am a lawbreaker. 19For through
the law I died to the law[z] so that I might
live for God.[a] 20I have been crucified
with Christ[b] and I no longer live, but
Christ lives in me.[c] The life I live in the
body, I live by faith in the Son of God,[d]
who loved me[e] and gave himself for
me.[f] 21I do not set aside the grace of
God, for if righteousness could be
gained through the law,[g] Christ died for
nothing!"[f]

God gives his Spirit to those who believe.

3 You foolish Galatians! Who has be-
witched you?[h] Before your very
eyes Jesus Christ was clearly portrayed
as crucified.[i] 2I would like to learn just
one thing from you: Did you receive the
Spirit by observing the law, or by believing what you heard?[j] 3Are you so foolish? After beginning with the Spirit, are
you now trying to attain your goal by
human effort? 4Have you suffered so
much for nothing—if it really was for
nothing? 5Does God give you his Spirit
and work miracles[k] among you because
you observe the law, or because you
believe what you heard?

Abraham was justified by faith.

6Consider Abraham: "He believed
God, and it was credited to him as righteousness."[g][l] 7Understand, then, that
those who believe[m] are children of Abraham. 8The Scripture foresaw that God
would justify the Gentiles by faith, and
announced the gospel in advance to
Abraham: "All nations will be blessed
through you."[h][n] 9So those who have

2:5 *a*ver 14
2:6 *b*Gal 6:3 *c*Ac 10:34
2:7 *d*1Th 2:4; 1Ti 1:11 *e*Ac 9:15 *f*ver 9,11,14
2:8 *g*Ac 1:25
2:9 *h*ver 7,11,14 *i*1Ti 3:15 *j*Ac 4:36 *k*Ro 12:3
2:10 *l*Ac 24:17
2:11 *m*ver 7,9,14 *n*Ac 11:19
2:12 *o*Ac 11:3 *p*Ac 11:2
2:13 *q*ver 1; Ac 4:36
2:14 *r*ver 5 *s*ver 7,9,11 *t*Ac 10:28
2:15 *u*Php 3:4,5 *v*1Sa 15:18
2:16 *w*Ac 13:39; Ro 9:30
2:17 *x*ver 15 *y*Gal 3:21
2:19 *z*Ro 7:4 *a*Ro 6:10,11, 14; 2Co 5:15
2:20 *b*Ro 6:6 *c*1Pe 4:2 *d*Mt 4:3 *e*Ro 8:37 *f*Gal 1:4
2:21 *g*Gal 3:21
3:1 *h*Gal 5:7 *i*1Co 1:23
3:2 *j*Ro 10:17
3:5 *k*1Co 12:10
3:6 *l*Ge 15:6; Ro 4:3
3:7 *m*ver 9
3:8 *n*Ge 12:3; Ac 3:25

c *7* Greek *uncircumcised* d *7* Greek *circumcised*; also in verses 8 and 9 e *9* Greek *Cephas*; also in verses 11 and 14 f *21* Some interpreters end the quotation after verse 14. g *6* Gen. 15:6
h *8* Gen. 12:3; 18:18; 22:18

faith[a] are blessed along with Abraham, the man of faith.

10All who rely on observing the law are under a curse, for it is written: "Cursed is everyone who does not continue to do everything written in the Book of the Law."[i][b] 11Clearly no one is justified before God by the law, because, "The righteous will live by faith."[j][c] 12The law is not based on faith; on the contrary, "The man who does these things will live by them."[k][d] 13Christ redeemed us from the curse of the law[e] by becoming a curse for us, for it is written: "Cursed is everyone who is hung on a tree."[l][f] 14He redeemed us in order that the blessing given to Abraham might come to the Gentiles through Christ Jesus,[g] so that by faith we might receive the promise of the Spirit.[h]

15Brothers, let me take an example from everyday life. Just as no one can set aside or add to a human covenant that has been duly established, so it is in this case. 16The promises were spoken to Abraham and to his seed.[i] The Scripture does not say "and to seeds," meaning many people, but "and to your seed,"[m] meaning one person, who is Christ. 17What I mean is this: The law, introduced 430 years[j] later, does not set aside the covenant previously established by God and thus do away with the promise. 18For if the inheritance depends on the law, then it no longer depends on a promise;[k] but God in his grace gave it to Abraham through a promise.

The law was given to lead us to Christ.

19What, then, was the purpose of the law? It was added because of transgressions[l] until the Seed[m] to whom the promise referred had come. The law was put into effect through angels[n] by a mediator.[o] 20A mediator,[p] however, does not represent just one party; but God is one.

21Is the law, therefore, opposed to the promises of God? Absolutely not![q] For if a law had been given that could impart life, then righteousness would certainly have come by the law.[r] 22But the Scripture declares that the whole world is a prisoner of sin,[s] so that what was promised, being given through faith in Jesus Christ, might be given to those who believe.

23Before this faith came, we were held prisoners[t] by the law, locked up until faith should be revealed. 24So the law was put in charge to lead us to Christ[n][u] that we might be justified by faith.[v] 25Now that faith has come, we are no longer under the supervision of the law.

Privileges are given to children of God.

26You are all sons of God[w] through faith in Christ Jesus, 27for all of you who were baptized into Christ[x] have clothed yourselves with Christ.[y] 28There is neither Jew nor Greek, slave nor free,[z] male nor female, for you are all one in Christ Jesus.[a] 29If you belong to Christ,[b] then you are Abraham's seed, and heirs according to the promise.[c]

4 What I am saying is that as long as the heir is a child, he is no different from a slave, although he owns the whole estate. 2He is subject to guardians and trustees until the time set by his father. 3So also, when we were children, we were in slavery[d] under the basic principles of the world.[e] 4But when the time had fully come,[f] God sent his Son, born of a woman,[g] born under law,[h] 5to redeem those under law, that we might receive the full rights[i] of sons. 6Because you are sons, God sent the Spirit of his Son into our hearts,[j] the Spirit who calls out, "*Abba*,[o] Father."[k] 7So you are no longer a slave, but a son; and since you

3:9 [a]ver 7; Ro 4:16 **3:10** [b]Dt 27:26; Jer 11:3 **3:11** [c]Hab 2:4; Gal 2:16; Heb 10:38 **3:12** [d]Lev 18:5; Ro 10:5 **3:13** [e]Gal 4:5 [f]Dt 21:23; Ac 5:30 **3:14** [g]Ro 4:9,16 [h]ver 2; Joel 2:28; Ac 2:33 **3:16** [i]Lk 1:55; Ro 4:13,16 **3:17** [j]Ge 15:13,14; Ex 12:40 **3:18** [k]Ro 4:14 **3:19** [l]Ro 5:20 [m]ver 16 [n]Ac 7:53 [o]Ex 20:19 **3:20** [p]Heb 8:6; 9:15; 12:24 **3:21** [q]Gal 2:17 [r]Gal 2:21 **3:22** [s]Ro 3:9-19; 11:32 **3:23** [t]Ro 11:32 **3:24** [u]Ro 10:4 [v]Gal 2:16 **3:26** [w]Ro 8:14 **3:27** [x]Mt 28:19; Ro 6:3 [y]Ro 13:14 **3:28** [z]Col 3:11 [a]Jn 10:16; 17:11; Eph 2:14,15 **3:29** [b]1Co 3:23 [c]ver 16 **4:3** [d]Gal 2:4 [e]Col 2:8,20

4:4 [f]Mk 1:15; Eph 1:10 [g]Jn 1:14 [h]Lk 2:27 **4:5** [i]Jn 1:12 **4:6** [j]Ro 5:5 [k]Ro 8:15,16

[i]*10* Deut. 27:26 [j]*11* Hab. 2:4 [k]*12* Lev. 18:5 [l]*13* Deut. 21:23 [m]*16* Gen. 12:7; 13:15; 24:7 [n]*24* Or *charge until Christ came* [o]*6* Aramaic for *Father*

are a son, God has made you also an heir.[a]

Legalism in the church.

8Formerly, when you did not know God,[b] you were slaves to those who by nature are not gods.[c] 9But now that you know God—or rather are known by God[d]—how is it that you are turning back to those weak and miserable principles? Do you wish to be enslaved[e] by them all over again?[f] 10You are observing special days and months and seasons and years![g] 11I fear for you, that somehow I have wasted my efforts on you.[h]

12I plead with you, brothers,[i] become like me, for I became like you. You have done me no wrong. 13As you know, it was because of an illness[j] that I first preached the gospel to you. 14Even though my illness was a trial to you, you did not treat me with contempt or scorn. Instead, you welcomed me as if I were an angel of God, as if I were Christ Jesus himself.[k] 15What has happened to all your joy? I can testify that, if you could have done so, you would have torn out your eyes and given them to me. 16Have I now become your enemy by telling you the truth?[l]

17Those people are zealous to win you over, but for no good. What they want is to alienate you ⌊from us⌋, so that you may be zealous for them. 18It is fine to be zealous, provided the purpose is good, and to be so always and not just when I am with you.[m] 19My dear children,[n] for whom I am again in the pains of childbirth until Christ is formed in you,[o] 20how I wish I could be with you now and change my tone, because I am perplexed about you!

Illustration of God's two covenants through Abraham's two sons.

21Tell me, you who want to be under the law, are you not aware of what the law says? 22For it is written that Abraham had two sons, one by the slave woman[p] and the other by the free woman.[q] 23His son by the slave woman was born in the ordinary way;[r] but his son by the free woman was born as the result of a promise.[s]

24These things may be taken figuratively, for the women represent two covenants. One covenant is from Mount Sinai and bears children who are to be slaves: This is Hagar. 25Now Hagar stands for Mount Sinai in Arabia and corresponds to the present city of Jerusalem, because she is in slavery with her children. 26But the Jerusalem that is above[t] is free, and she is our mother. 27For it is written:

"Be glad, O barren woman,
  who bears no children;
break forth and cry aloud,
  you who have no labor pains;
because more are the children of the
    desolate woman
  than of her who has a husband."[p][u]

28Now you, brothers, like Isaac, are children of promise. 29At that time the son born in the ordinary way[v] persecuted the son born by the power of the Spirit.[w] It is the same now. 30But what does the Scripture say? "Get rid of the slave woman and her son, for the slave woman's son will never share in the inheritance with the free woman's son."[q][x] 31Therefore, brothers, we are not children of the slave woman, but of the free woman.

Freedom in Christ.

5 It is for freedom that Christ has set us free.[y] Stand firm,[z] then, and do not let yourselves be burdened again by a yoke of slavery.[a]

2Mark my words! I, Paul, tell you that if you let yourselves be circumcised,[b] Christ will be of no value to you at all. 3Again I declare to every man who lets himself be circumcised that he is obligated to obey the whole law.[c] 4You who are trying to be justified by law have been alienated from Christ; you have fallen away from grace.[d] 5But by faith

4:7 [a]Ro 8:17
4:8 [b]1Co 1:21; Eph 2:12; 1Th 4:5 [c]2Ch 13:9; Isa 37:19
4:9 [d]1Co 8:3 [e]ver 3 [f]Col 2:20
4:10 [g]Ro 14:5
4:11 [h]1Th 3:5
4:12 [i]Gal 6:18
4:13 [j]1Co 2:3
4:14 [k]Mt 10:40
4:16 [l]Am 5:10
4:18 [m]ver 13,14
4:19 [n]1Co 4:15 [o]Eph 4:13
4:22 [p]Ge 16:15 [q]Ge 21:2
4:23 [r]Ro 9:7,8 [s]Ge 18:10-14; Heb 11:11
4:26 [t]Heb 12:22; Rev 3:12
4:27 [u]Isa 54:1
4:29 [v]ver 23 [w]Ge 21:9
4:30 [x]Ge 21:10
5:1 [y]Jn 8:32 [z]1Co 16:13 [a]Ac 15:10; Gal 2:4
5:2 [b]Ac 15:1
5:3 [c]Gal 3:10
5:4 [d]Heb 12:15; 2Pe 3:17

p27 Isaiah 54:1   q30 Gen. 21:10

we eagerly await through the Spirit the righteousness for which we hope.[a] **6**For in Christ Jesus neither circumcision nor uncircumcision has any value.[b] The only thing that counts is faith expressing itself through love.[c]

7You were running a good race.[d] Who cut in on you[e] and kept you from obeying the truth? **8**That kind of persuasion does not come from the one who calls you.[f] **9**"A little yeast works through the whole batch of dough."[g] **10**I am confident[h] in the Lord that you will take no other view.[i] The one who is throwing you into confusion[j] will pay the penalty, whoever he may be. **11**Brothers, if I am still preaching circumcision, why am I still being persecuted?[k] In that case the offense[l] of the cross has been abolished. **12**As for those agitators,[m] I wish they would go the whole way and emasculate themselves!

13You, my brothers, were called to be free. But do not use your freedom to indulge the sinful nature[r];[n] rather, serve one another[o] in love. **14**The entire law is summed up in a single command: "Love your neighbor as yourself."[s][p] **15**If you keep on biting and devouring each other, watch out or you will be destroyed by each other.

Spirit and sinful nature in constant battle.

16So I say, live by the Spirit,[q] and you will not gratify the desires of the sinful nature.[r] **17**For the sinful nature desires what is contrary to the Spirit, and the Spirit what is contrary to the sinful nature.[s] They are in conflict with each other, so that you do not do what you want.[t] **18**But if you are led by the Spirit, you are not under law.[u]

Acts of the sinful nature.

19The acts of the sinful nature are obvious: sexual immorality,[v] impurity and debauchery; **20**idolatry and witchcraft; hatred, discord, jealousy, fits of rage, selfish ambition, dissensions, factions **21**and envy; drunkenness, orgies, and the like.[w] I warn you, as I did before, that those who live like this will not inherit the kingdom of God.

Fruit of the Spirit.

22But the fruit[x] of the Spirit is love,[y] joy, peace, patience, kindness, goodness, faithfulness, **23**gentleness and self-control.[z] Against such things there is no law. **24**Those who belong to Christ Jesus have crucified the sinful nature[a] with its passions and desires.[b] **25**Since we live by the Spirit, let us keep in step with the Spirit. **26**Let us not become conceited,[c] provoking and envying each other.

Carrying others' burdens.

6 Brothers, if someone is caught in a sin, you who are spiritual[d] should restore him gently. But watch yourself, or you also may be tempted. **2**Carry each other's burdens, and in this way you will fulfill the law of Christ.[e] **3**If anyone thinks he is something[f] when he is nothing, he deceives himself. **4**Each one should test his own actions. Then he can take pride in himself, without comparing himself to somebody else, **5**for each one should carry his own load.

Reaping what is sown.

6Anyone who receives instruction in the word must share all good things with his instructor.[g]

7Do not be deceived:[h] God cannot be mocked. A man reaps what he sows.[i] **8**The one who sows to please his sinful nature, from that nature[t] will reap destruction;[j] the one who sows to please the Spirit, from the Spirit will reap eternal life.[k] **9**Let us not become weary in doing good,[l] for at the proper time we will reap a harvest if we do not give up.[m] **10**Therefore, as we have opportunity, let us do good[n] to all people, espe-

5:5 [a]Ro 8:23,24 **5:6** [b]1Co 7:19 [c]1Th 1:3 **5:7** [d]1Co 9:24 [e]Gal 3:1 **5:8** [f]Ro 8:28; Gal 1:6 **5:9** [g]1Co 5:6 **5:10** [h]2Co 2:3 [i]Php 3:15 [j]Gal 1:7 **5:11** [k]Gal 4:29; 6:12 [l]1Co 1:23 **5:12** [m]ver 10 **5:13** [n]1Co 8:9; 1Pe 2:16 [o]1Co 9:19; Eph 5:21 **5:14** [p]Lev 19:18; Mt 22:39 **5:16** [q]Ro 8:2, 4-6 ,9,14 [r]ver 24 **5:17** [s]Ro 8:5-8 [t]Ro 7:15-23 **5:18** [u]Ro 6:14; 1Ti 1:9 **5:19** [v]1Co 6:18 **5:21** [w]Ro 13:13 **5:22** [x]Mt 7:16-20; Eph 5:9 [y]Col 3:12-15 **5:23** [z]Ac 24:25 **5:24** [a]Ro 6:6 [b]ver 16,17 **5:26** [c]Php 2:3 **6:1** [d]1Co 2:15 **6:2** [e]Ro 15:1; Jas 2:8 **6:3** [f]Ro 12:3; 1Co 8:2 **6:6** [g]1Co 9:11,14

6:7 [h]1Co 6:9 [i]2Co 9:6 **6:8** [j]Job 4:8; Hos 8:7 [k]Jas 3:18 **6:9** [l]1Co 15:58 [m]Rev 2:10 **6:10** [n]Pr 3:27

[r]*13* Or *the flesh*; also in verses 16, 17, 19 and 24
[s]*14* Lev. 19:18 [t]*8* Or *his flesh, from the flesh*

cially to those who belong to the family[a] of believers.

Boasting only in the cross of Jesus.

11See what large letters I use as I
write to you with my own hand![b]
12Those who want to make a good
impression outwardly are trying to com-
pel you to be circumcised.[c] The only
reason they do this is to avoid being persecuted[d] for the cross of Christ. 13Not
even those who are circumcised obey
the law,[e] yet they want you to be circumcised that they may boast about
your flesh.[f] 14May I never boast except
in the cross of our Lord Jesus Christ,
through which[u] the world has been crucified to me, and I to the world.[g] 15Nei-
ther circumcision nor uncircumcision
means anything;[h] what counts is a
new creation.[i] 16Peace and mercy to
all who follow this rule, even to the
Israel of God.

Final blessings and exhortations.

17Finally, let no one cause me trouble,
for I bear on my body the marks[j] of
Jesus.
18The grace of our Lord Jesus Christ[k]
be with your spirit,[l] brothers. Amen.

6:10 [a]Eph 2:19
6:11 [b]1Co 16:21
6:12 [c]Ac 15:1 [d]Gal 5:11
6:13 [e]Ro 2:25 [f]Php 3:3
6:14 [g]Ro 6:2,6
6:15 [h]1Co 7:19 [i]2Co 5:17
6:17 [j]Isa 44:5; 2Co 1:5
6:18 [k]Ro 16:20 [l]2Ti 4:22

[u]*14* Or *whom*

EPHESIANS

Author: Paul the Apostle.

Date Written: Between A.D. 60 and 61.

Title: Named after the addressee of this letter: the church at Ephesus. However, this letter to the Ephesians is passed along to other Roman cities as well.

Background: Jewish converts in the early churches are often separating themselves and excluding their Gentile brothers. Paul uses this occasion to stress the unity of believers. Along with Colossians, Philippians and Philemon, Ephesians is considered one of the 4 "Prison Epistles" because it is written during Paul's two-year imprisonment in Rome; therefore, he sends the letter to Asia by his friend Tychicus. Paul has visited Ephesus before, and on his third missionary journey he stays there for about 3 years preaching Christ. It is during this time Paul develops a special concern for the people, as revealed in his letter.

Where Written: From a Roman prison.

To Whom: To the Christians at Ephesus.

Content: Ephesians does not address specific problems or situations in the church. Instead, it is written to encourage the body of Christ to maturity in him. Paul presents an overview of the plan and purposes of God from the beginning of time. The privileges and unity which Christ gives believers prepare them daily for spiritual warfare. Practical guidance is given for relationships between husbands and wives (chapter 5); parents and children, and masters and slaves (chapter 6). Paul shares that for a Christian to be successful, he must first realize the wealth of his position in Christ and the power found if he will "put on the full armor of God" (6:11).

Key Words: "Riches"; "One." All believers in Christ are heirs of the "riches" of Christ and of his grace and glory. Ephesians seeks to unify the body by emphasizing that there is "one" Lord, "one" faith and "one" baptism (4:5).

Themes: • The Holy Spirit seals believers as belonging to God. • The body of Christ is the church...through which his eternal plan is fulfilled. • God has given every believer all the provisions necessary to have victory over attacks from Satan. • We are helpless against Satan's onslaughts in our own might...our strength is obtained from the armor of God. • If Christians will understand their calling in Christ, proper conduct in him will follow.

Outline:
1. Salutation. 1:1-1:2
2. Christians' position in Christ. 1:3-3:21
3. Unity and holiness for the Ephesian church. 4:1-5:21
4. Relationships based on Christ. 5:22-6:9
5. Spiritual warfare. 6:10-6:20
6. Final words. 6:21-6:24

EPHESIANS

1 Paul, an apostle[a] of Christ Jesus by
the will of God,[b]

To the saints in Ephesus,[a] the faithful[b][c] in Christ Jesus:

2Grace and peace to you from God
our Father and the Lord Jesus Christ.[d]

God lovingly adopts us.

3Praise be to the God and Father of
our Lord Jesus Christ,[e] who has blessed
us in the heavenly realms[f] with every
spiritual blessing in Christ. 4For he
chose us in him before the creation of
the world to be holy and blameless[g] in
his sight. In love[h] 5he[c] predestined[i] us
to be adopted as his sons through Jesus
Christ, in accordance with his pleasure[j]
and will— 6to the praise of his glorious
grace, which he has freely given us in

1:1 [a]1Co 1:1 [b]2Co 1:1 [c]Col 1:2
1:2 [d]Ro 1:7
1:3 [e]2Co 1:3 [f]Eph 2:6; 3:10; 6:12
1:4 [g]Eph 5:27; Col 1:22 [h]Eph 4:2,15, 16
1:5 [i]Ro 8:29,30 [j]1Co 1:21
1:6 [k]Mt 3:17
1:7 [l]Ro 3:24
1:9 [m]Ro 16:25
1:10 [n]Gal 4:4 [o]Col 1:20

the One he loves.[k] 7In him we have redemption[l] through his blood, the forgiveness of sins, in accordance with the
riches of God's grace 8that he lavished
on us with all wisdom and understanding. 9And he[d] made known to us the
mystery[m] of his will according to his
good pleasure, which he purposed in
Christ, 10to be put into effect when the
times will have reached their fulfillment[n]—to bring all things in heaven
and on earth together under one head,
even Christ.[o]

11In him we were also chosen,[e] having been predestined according to the
plan of him who works out everything

a *1* Some early manuscripts do not have *in Ephesus.*
b *1* Or *believers who are* c *4,5* Or *sight in love. 5He*
d *8,9* Or *us. With all wisdom and understanding, 9he*
e *11* Or *were made heirs*

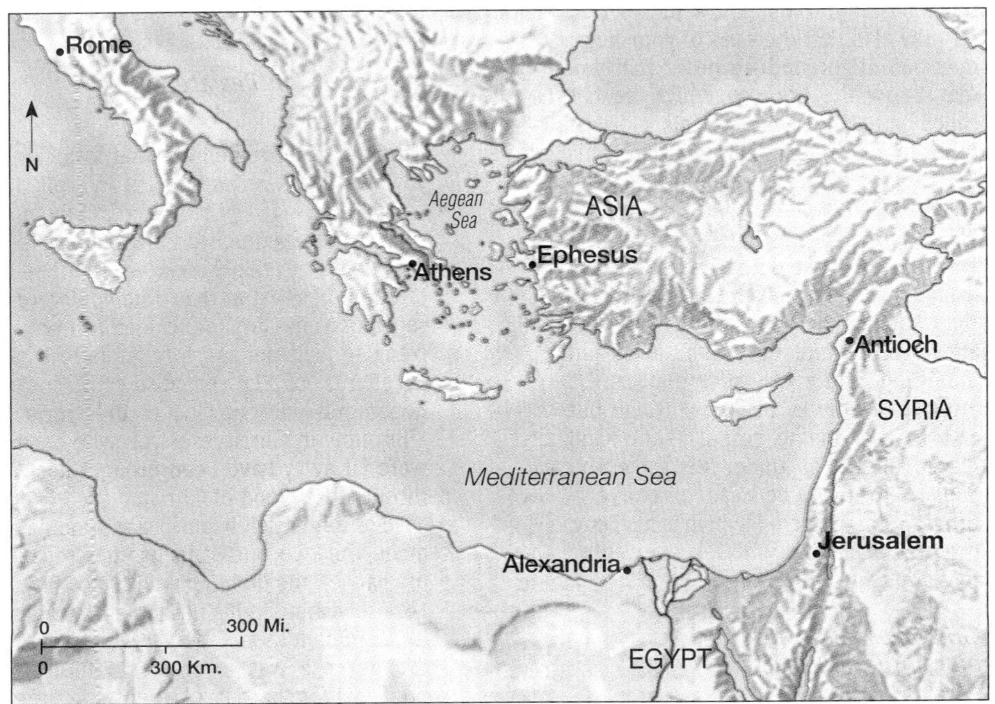

Location of Ephesus

Ephesus was a strategic city, ranking in importance with Alexandria in Egypt and Antioch in Syria as a port. It lay on the most western edge of Asia Minor (modern-day Turkey), the most important port on the Aegean Sea on the main route from Rome to the east.

in conformity with the purpose[a] of his will, 12in order that we, who were the first to hope in Christ, might be for the praise of his glory.[b] 13And you also were included in Christ when you heard the word of truth,[c] the gospel of your salvation. Having believed, you were marked in him with a seal,[d] the promised Holy Spirit, 14who is a deposit guaranteeing our inheritance[e] until the redemption of those who are God's possession—to the praise of his glory.

Paul gives thanks for the Ephesians.

15For this reason, ever since I heard about your faith in the Lord Jesus and your love for all the saints,[f] 16I have not stopped giving thanks for you,[g] remembering you in my prayers. 17I keep asking that the God of our Lord Jesus Christ, the glorious Father,[h] may give you the Spirit[f] of wisdom[i] and revelation, so that you may know him better. 18I pray also that the eyes of your heart may be enlightened[j] in order that you may know the hope to which he has called you, the riches of his glorious inheritance in the saints, 19and his incomparably great power for us who believe. That power[k] is like the working of his mighty strength,[l] 20which he exerted in Christ when he raised him from the dead[m] and seated him at his right hand in the heavenly realms, 21far above all rule and authority, power and dominion, and every title[n] that can be given, not only in the present age but also in the one to come. 22And God placed all things under his feet[o] and appointed him to be head[p] over everything for the church, 23which is his body, the fullness of him who fills everything in every way.

God loves us despite our sinful nature.

2 As for you, you were dead in your transgressions and sins,[q] 2in which you used to live[r] when you followed the ways of this world and of the ruler of the kingdom of the air,[s] the spirit who is now at work in those who are disobedient.[t] 3All of us also lived among them at one time, gratifying the cravings of our sinful nature[g][u] and following its desires and thoughts. Like the rest, we were by nature objects of wrath. 4But because of his great love for us, God, who is rich in mercy, 5made us alive with Christ even when we were dead in transgressions[v]—it is by grace you have been saved.[w] 6And God raised us up with Christ and seated us with him[x] in the heavenly realms[y] in Christ Jesus, 7in order that in the coming ages he might show the incomparable riches of his grace, expressed in his kindness[z] to us in Christ Jesus. 8For it is by grace you have been saved,[a] through faith—and this not from yourselves, it is the gift of God— 9not by works,[b] so that no one can boast.[c] 10For we are God's workmanship, created[d] in Christ Jesus to do good works,[e] which God prepared in advance for us to do.

Jews and Gentiles are united at the cross.

11Therefore, remember that formerly you who are Gentiles by birth and called "uncircumcised" by those who call themselves "the circumcision" (that done in the body by the hands of men)[f]— 12remember that at that time you were separate from Christ, excluded from citizenship in Israel and foreigners to the covenants of the promise,[g] without hope[h] and without God in the world. 13But now in Christ Jesus you who once were far away have been brought near[i] through the blood of Christ.[j]

14For he himself is our peace, who has made the two one[k] and has destroyed the barrier, the dividing wall of hostility, 15by abolishing in his flesh[l] the law with its commandments and regulations.[m] His purpose was to create in himself one[n] new man out of the two, thus making peace, 16and in this one body

1:11 [a]Eph 3:11; Heb 6:17 **1:12** [b]ver 6,14 **1:13** [c]Col 1:5 [d]Eph 4:30 **1:14** [e]Ac 20:32 **1:15** [f]Col 1:4 **1:16** [g]Ro 1:8 **1:17** [h]Jn 20:17 [i]Col 1:9 **1:18** [j]Ac 26:18; 2Co 4:6 **1:19** [k]Col 1:29 [l]Eph 6:10 **1:20** [m]Ac 2:24 **1:21** [n]Php 2:9,10 **1:22** [o]Mt 28:18 [p]Eph 4:15; 5:23 **2:1** [q]ver 5; Col 2:13 **2:2** [r]Col 3:7 [s]Jn 12:31; Eph 6:12 [t]Eph 5:6 **2:3** [u]Gal 5:16 **2:5** [v]ver 1 [w]ver 8; Ac 15:11 **2:6** [x]Eph 1:20 [y]Eph 1:3 **2:7** [z]Tit 3:4 **2:8** [a]ver 5 **2:9** [b]2Ti 1:9 [c]1Co 1:29 **2:10** [d]Eph 4:24 [e]Tit 2:14 **2:11** [f]Col 2:11 **2:12** [g]Gal 3:17 [h]1Th 4:13 **2:13** [i]ver 17; Ac 2:39 [j]Col 1:20

2:14 [k]1Co 12:13 **2:15** [l]Col 1:21,22 [m]Col 2:14 [n]Gal 3:28

[f]17 Or *a spirit* [g]3 Or *our flesh*

to reconcile both of them to God through the cross,[a] by which he put to death their hostility. 17He came and preached peace to you who were far away and peace to those who were near.[b] 18For through him we both have access[c] to the Father[d] by one Spirit.[e]

19Consequently, you are no longer foreigners and aliens,[f] but fellow citizens[g] with God's people and members of God's household,[h] 20built on the foundation[i] of the apostles and prophets, with Christ Jesus himself as the chief cornerstone.[j] 21In him the whole building is joined together and rises to become a holy temple[k] in the Lord. 22And in him you too are being built together to become a dwelling in which God lives by his Spirit.

Paul's special mission of preaching Christ to the Gentiles.

3 For this reason I, Paul, the prisoner[l] of Christ Jesus for the sake of you Gentiles—

2Surely you have heard about the administration of God's grace that was given to me[m] for you, 3that is, the mystery[n] made known to me by revelation,[o] as I have already written briefly. 4In reading this, then, you will be able to understand my insight[p] into the mystery of Christ, 5which was not made known to men in other generations as it has now been revealed by the Spirit to God's holy apostles and prophets.[q] 6This mystery is that through the gospel the Gentiles are heirs[r] together with Israel, members together of one body,[s] and sharers together in the promise in Christ Jesus.

7I became a servant of this gospel[t] by the gift of God's grace given me through the working of his power.[u] 8Although I am less than the least of all God's people,[v] this grace was given me: to preach to the Gentiles the unsearchable riches of Christ, 9and to make plain to everyone the administration of this mystery,[w] which for ages past was kept hidden in God, who created all things. 10His intent was that now, through the church, the manifold wisdom of God[x] should be made known[y] to the rulers and authorities[z] in the heavenly realms, 11according to his eternal purpose which he accomplished in Christ Jesus our Lord. 12In him and through faith in him we may approach God[a] with freedom and confidence.[b] 13I ask you, therefore, not to be discouraged because of my sufferings for you, which are your glory.

Paul's prayer that the love of God be appreciated.

14For this reason I kneel[c] before the Father, 15from whom his whole family[h] in heaven and on earth derives its name. 16I pray that out of his glorious riches he may strengthen you with power[d] through his Spirit in your inner being,[e] 17so that Christ may dwell in your hearts[f] through faith. And I pray that you, being rooted[g] and established in love, 18may have power, together with all the saints, to grasp how wide and long and high and deep[h] is the love of Christ, 19and to know this love that surpasses knowledge—that you may be filled[i] to the measure of all the fullness of God.[j]

20Now to him who is able[k] to do immeasurably more than all we ask or imagine, according to his power that is at work within us, 21to him be glory in the church and in Christ Jesus throughout all generations, for ever and ever! Amen.[l]

One Lord, one faith, one baptism.

4 As a prisoner[m] for the Lord, then, I urge you to live a life worthy[n] of the calling you have received. 2Be completely humble and gentle; be patient, bearing with one another[o] in love.[p] 3Make every effort to keep the unity[q] of the Spirit through the bond of peace. 4There is one body and one Spirit[r]—

2:16 [a]Col 1:20,22
2:17 [b]Ps 148:14; Isa 57:19
2:18 [c]Eph 3:12 [d]Col 1:12 [e]1Co 12:13
2:19 [f]ver 12 [g]Php 3:20 [h]Gal 6:10
2:20 [i]Mt 16:18; Rev 21:14 [j]1Pe 2:4-8
2:21 [k]1Co 3:16,17
3:1 [l]Ac 23:18; Eph 4:1
3:2 [m]Col 1:25
3:3 [n]Ro 16:25 [o]1Co 2:10
3:4 [p]2Co 11:6
3:5 [q]Ro 16:26
3:6 [r]Gal 3:29 [s]Eph 2:15,16
3:7 [t]1Co 3:5 [u]Eph 1:19
3:8 [v]1Co 15:9
3:9 [w]Ro 16:25
3:10 [x]1Co 2:7 [y]1Pe 1:12 [z]Eph 1:21
3:12 [a]Eph 2:18 [b]Heb 4:16
3:14 [c]Php 2:10
3:16 [d]Col 1:11 [e]Ro 7:22
3:17 [f]Jn 14:23 [g]Col 1:23
3:18 [h]Job 11:8,9
3:19 [i]Col 2:10 [j]Eph 1:23
3:20 [k]Ro 16:25
3:21 [l]Ro 11:36

4:1 [m]Eph 3:1 [n]Php 1:27; Col 1:10
4:2 [o]Col 3:12,13 [p]Eph 1:4 **4:3** [q]Col 3:14
4:4 [r]1Co 12:13

h *15* Or *whom all fatherhood*

just as you were called to one hope
when you were called— 5one Lord, one
faith, one baptism; 6one God and Father
of all, who is over all and through all
and in all.[a]

7But to each one of us[b] grace has been
given[c] as Christ apportioned it. 8This is
why it[i] says:

> "When he ascended on high,
> he led captives[d] in his train
> and gave gifts to men."[j][e]

9(What does "he ascended" mean except
that he also descended to the lower,
earthly regions[k]? 10He who descended is
the very one who ascended higher than
all the heavens, in order to fill the whole
universe.) 11It was he who gave some
to be apostles,[f] some to be prophets,
some to be evangelists,[g] and some to be
pastors and teachers, 12to prepare God's
people for works of service, so that the
body of Christ[h] may be built up 13until
we all reach unity[i] in the faith and in
the knowledge of the Son of God and
become mature,[j] attaining to the whole
measure of the fullness of Christ.

14Then we will no longer be infants,[k]
tossed back and forth by the waves,[l] and
blown here and there by every wind of
teaching and by the cunning and craftiness of men in their deceitful scheming.[m] 15Instead, speaking the truth in
love, we will in all things grow up into
him who is the Head,[n] that is, Christ.
16From him the whole body, joined and
held together by every supporting liga-
ment, grows[o] and builds itself up in
love, as each part does its work.

Put off your old self; put on the new self.

17So I tell you this, and insist on it in
the Lord, that you must no longer live as
the Gentiles do, in the futility of their
thinking.[p] 18They are darkened in their
understanding[q] and separated from the
life of God[r] because of the ignorance
that is in them due to the hardening of
their hearts.[s] 19Having lost all sensitivity,[t] they have given themselves over[u]
to sensuality[v] so as to indulge in every
kind of impurity, with a continual lust
for more.

20You, however, did not come to know
Christ that way. 21Surely you heard of
him and were taught in him in accordance with the truth that is in Jesus.
22You were taught, with regard to your
former way of life, to put off[w] your old
self,[x] which is being corrupted by its
deceitful desires; 23to be made new in
the attitude of your minds;[y] 24and to put
on the new self,[z] created to be like God
in true righteousness and holiness.[a]

25Therefore each of you must put off
falsehood and speak truthfully[b] to his
neighbor, for we are all members of one
body.[c] 26"In your anger do not sin"[l]: Do
not let the sun go down while you are
still angry, 27and do not give the devil a
foothold. 28He who has been stealing
must steal no longer, but must work,[d]
doing something useful with his own
hands,[e] that he may have something to
share with those in need.[f]

29Do not let any unwholesome talk
come out of your mouths,[g] but only
what is helpful for building others up
according to their needs, that it may
benefit those who listen. 30And do not
grieve the Holy Spirit of God,[h] with
whom you were sealed for the day of
redemption.[i] 31Get rid of all bitterness,
rage and anger, brawling and slander,
along with every form of malice.[j] 32Be
kind and compassionate to one another,
forgiving each other, just as in Christ
God forgave you.[k]

Imitators of God should walk as children of light.

5 Be imitators of God,[l] therefore, as
dearly loved children 2and live a life
of love, just as Christ loved us and gave
himself up for us[m] as a fragrant offering
and sacrifice to God.[n]

3But among you there must not be
even a hint of sexual immorality, or of
any kind of impurity, or of greed,[o]

4:6 [a]Ro 11:36
4:7 [b]1Co 12:7,11 [c]Ro 12:3
4:8 [d]Col 2:15 [e]Ps 68:18
4:11 [f]1Co 12:28 [g]Ac 21:8
4:12 [h]1Co 12:27
4:13 [i]ver 3,5 [j]Col 1:28
4:14 [k]1Co 14:20 [l]Jas 1:6 [m]Eph 6:11
4:15 [n]Eph 1:22
4:16 [o]Col 2:19
4:17 [p]Ro 1:21
4:18 [q]Ro 1:21 [r]Eph 2:12 [s]2Co 3:14
4:19 [t]1Ti 4:2 [u]Ro 1:24 [v]Col 3:5
4:22 [w]1Pe 2:1 [x]Ro 6:6
4:23 [y]Col 3:10
4:24 [z]Ro 6:4 [a]Eph 2:10
4:25 [b]Zec 8:16 [c]Ro 12:5
4:28 [d]Ac 20:35 [e]1Th 4:11 [f]Lk 3:11
4:29 [g]Col 3:8
4:30 [h]1Th 5:19 [i]Ro 8:23
4:31 [j]Col 3:8
4:32 [k]Mt 6:14,15
5:1 [l]Lk 6:36
5:2 [m]Gal 1:4 [n]2Co 2:15; Heb 7:27
5:3 [o]Col 3:5

[i]8 Or *God* [j]8 Psalm 68:18 [k]9 Or *the depths of the earth* [l]26 Psalm 4:4

because these are improper for God's holy people. 4 Nor should there be obscenity, foolish talk or coarse joking, which are out of place, but rather thanksgiving.[a] 5 For of this you can be sure: No immoral, impure or greedy person—such a man is an idolater[b]—has any inheritance in the kingdom of Christ and of God.[m][c] 6 Let no one deceive you with empty words, for because of such things God's wrath[d] comes on those who are disobedient. 7 Therefore do not be partners with them.

8 For you were once[e] darkness, but now you are light in the Lord. Live as children of light[f] 9 (for the fruit[g] of the light consists in all goodness, righteousness and truth) 10 and find out what pleases the Lord. 11 Have nothing to do with the fruitless deeds of darkness, but rather expose them. 12 For it is shameful even to mention what the disobedient do in secret. 13 But everything exposed by the light[h] becomes visible, 14 for it is light that makes everything visible. This is why it is said:

"Wake up, O sleeper,[i]
rise from the dead,[j]
and Christ will shine on you."[k]

15 Be very careful, then, how you live—not as unwise but as wise, 16 making the most of every opportunity,[l] because the days are evil.[m] 17 Therefore do not be foolish, but understand what the Lord's will is.[n] 18 Do not get drunk on wine,[o] which leads to debauchery. Instead, be filled with the Spirit.[p] 19 Speak to one another with psalms, hymns and spiritual songs.[q] Sing and make music in your heart to the Lord, 20 always giving thanks[r] to God the Father for everything, in the name of our Lord Jesus Christ.

21 Submit to one another[s] out of reverence for Christ.

Wives submit; husbands love.

5:22–6:9pp— Col 3:18–4:1

22 Wives, submit to your husbands[t] as to the Lord.[u] 23 For the husband is the head of the wife as Christ is the head of the church,[v] his body, of which he is the Savior. 24 Now as the church submits to Christ, so also wives should submit to their husbands in everything.

25 Husbands, love your wives,[w] just as Christ loved the church and gave himself up for her[x] 26 to make her holy, cleansing[n] her by the washing[y] with water through the word, 27 and to present her to himself as a radiant church, without stain or wrinkle or any other blemish, but holy and blameless.[z] 28 In this same way, husbands ought to love their wives[a] as their own bodies. He who loves his wife loves himself. 29 After all, no one ever hated his own body, but he feeds and cares for it, just as Christ does the church— 30 for we are members of his body.[b] 31 "For this reason a man will leave his father and mother and be united to his wife, and the two will become one flesh."[o][c] 32 This is a profound mystery—but I am talking about Christ and the church. 33 However, each one of you also must love his wife[d] as he loves himself, and the wife must respect her husband.

Proper behavior for children and parents.

6 Children, obey your parents in the Lord, for this is right.[e] 2 "Honor your father and mother"—which is the first commandment with a promise— 3 "that it may go well with you and that you may enjoy long life on the earth."[p][f]

4 Fathers, do not exasperate your children;[g] instead, bring them up in the training and instruction of the Lord.[h]

Proper behavior for slaves and masters.

5 Slaves, obey your earthly masters with respect[i] and fear, and with sincerity of heart,[j] just as you would obey Christ.[k] 6 Obey them not only to win

5:4 [a]ver 20
5:5 [b]Col 3:5 [c]1Co 6:9
5:6 [d]Ro 1:18
5:8 [e]Eph 2:2 [f]Lk 16:8
5:9 [g]Gal 5:22
5:13 [h]Jn 3:20,21
5:14 [i]Ro 13:11 [j]Jn 5:25 [k]Isa 60:1
5:16 [l]Col 4:5 [m]Eph 6:13
5:17 [n]Ro 12:2; 1Th 4:3
5:18 [o]Pr 20:1 [p]Lk 1:15
5:19 [q]Ac 16:25; Col 3:16
5:20 [r]Ps 34:1
5:21 [s]Gal 5:13
5:22 [t]Ge 3:16; 1Pe 3:1,5,6 [u]Eph 6:5
5:23 [v]1Co 11:3; Eph 1:22
5:25 [w]Col 3:19 [x]ver 2
5:26 [y]Ac 22:16
5:27 [z]Eph 1:4; Col 1:22
5:28 [a]ver 25
5:30 [b]1Co 12:27
5:31 [c]Ge 2:24; Mt 19:5; 1Co 6:16
5:33 [d]ver 25
6:1 [e]Col 3:20
6:3 [f]Ex 20:12
6:4 [g]Col 3:21 [h]Ge 18:19; Dt 6:7

6:5 [i]1Ti 6:1 [j]Col 3:22 [k]Eph 5:22

[m]5 Or *kingdom of the Christ and God* [n]26 Or *having cleansed* [o]31 Gen. 2:24 [p]3 Deut. 5:16

their favor when their eye is on you,
but like slaves of Christ, doing the will
of God from your heart. 7Serve wholeheartedly, as if you were serving the
Lord, not men,[a] 8because you know that
the Lord will reward everyone for whatever good he does,[b] whether he is slave
or free.

9And masters, treat your slaves in the
same way. Do not threaten them, since
you know that he who is both their
Master and yours[c] is in heaven, and
there is no favoritism with him.

Armor of God.

10Finally, be strong in the Lord[d] and
in his mighty power.[e] 11Put on the full
armor of God[f] so that you can take your
stand against the devil's schemes. 12For
our struggle is not against flesh and
blood, but against the rulers, against the
authorities,[g] against the powers[h] of this
dark world and against the spiritual
forces of evil in the heavenly realms.[i]
13Therefore put on the full armor of
God, so that when the day of evil comes,
you may be able to stand your ground,
and after you have done everything, to
stand. 14Stand firm then, with the belt
of truth buckled around your waist,[j]
with the breastplate of righteousness in
place,[k] 15and with your feet fitted with
the readiness that comes from the gospel
of peace.[l] 16In addition to all this, take
up the shield of faith,[m] with which you
can extinguish all the flaming arrows of
the evil one. 17Take the helmet of salvation[n] and the sword of the Spirit, which
is the word of God.[o] 18And pray in the
Spirit on all occasions[p] with all kinds of
prayers and requests.[q] With this in mind,
be alert and always keep on praying for
all the saints.

19Pray also for me,[r] that whenever I
open my mouth, words may be given me
so that I will fearlessly[s] make known the
mystery of the gospel, 20for which I am
an ambassador[t] in chains.[u] Pray that I
may declare it fearlessly, as I should.

Final words and blessings.

21Tychicus,[v] the dear brother and
faithful servant in the Lord, will tell you
everything, so that you also may know
how I am and what I am doing. 22I am
sending him to you for this very purpose, that you may know how we are,[w]
and that he may encourage you.

23Peace[x] to the brothers, and love
with faith from God the Father and the
Lord Jesus Christ. 24Grace to all who
love our Lord Jesus Christ with an undying love.

6:7 [a]Col 3:23
6:8 [b]Col 3:24
6:9 [c]Job 31:13,14
6:10 [d]1Co 16:13 [e]Eph 1:19
6:11 [f]Ro 13:12
6:12 [g]Eph 1:21 [h]Ro 8:38 [i]Eph 1:3
6:14 [j]Isa 11:5 [k]Isa 59:17
6:15 [l]Isa 52:7
6:16 [m]1Jn 5:4
6:17 [n]Isa 59:17 [o]Heb 4:12
6:18 [p]Lk 18:1 [q]Mt 26:41; Php 1:4
6:19 [r]1Th 5:25 [s]Ac 4:29; 2Co 3:12
6:20 [t]2Co 5:20 [u]Ac 21:33
6:21 [v]Ac 20:4
6:22 [w]Col 4:7-9
6:23 [x]Gal 6:16; 1Pe 5:14

PHILIPPIANS

Author: Paul the Apostle.

Date Written: Between A.D. 60 and 62.

Title: Named after the addressee of this letter: the church at Philippi.

Background: There are not enough Jews for a synagogue in the Macedonian city of Philippi when Paul arrives on his second missionary journey, so he establishes a church that is predominantly Gentile. These believers hold a special place in Paul's heart because of their unsolicited financial aid to his ministry of the gospel on several occasions. Epaphroditus becomes deathly ill after bringing the most recent gift from the church at Philippi to Paul. After his recovery, Paul sends this letter with Epaphroditus to the Philippians as a personal "thank you" note and to strengthen their roots in Christ. Philippians, along with Ephesians, Colossians and Philemon, is one of Paul's "Prison Epistles."

Where Written: From a prison in Rome.

To Whom: To the church at Philippi.

Content: This warmly affectionate letter from Paul commends the Philippians for their faith and support. He exhorts them to center their lives in Christ and to be content in all situations. Paul has very little occasion to acknowledge any problems in the church although 2 quarreling women, Euodia and Syntyche, are admonished to settle their differences (chapter 4). Paul sets most worthy goals before the people: to live in godly unity and love, to be strong in prayer and to joyfully imitate the example of their Savior, Jesus Christ.

Key Words: "Gospel"; "Joy." Paul shares the significance of the "gospel" in his relationship with God, as well as with other people. The overwhelming "joy" which Paul has is shown to be available to all Christians, regardless of their circumstances, through an intimate walk with the Lord and by living under the loving care of his church.

Themes: • A quitter never wins...a winner never quits. • What goes into our minds, comes out in our actions. • God never fails. • Lasting joy comes only through a relationship with Jesus Christ. • Christians also have problems, but Christ is the power to overcome. • We have no basis for pride except in our perfect example, Jesus Christ.

Outline:

1. Paul prays for the Philippians. 1:1-1:11
2. Paul's chains advance the gospel. 1:12-1:26
3. Christ is Paul's model for humility. 1:27-2:18
4. Paul commends Timothy and Epaphroditus. 2:19-2:30
5. Knowledge and peace of Christ are exhorted. 3:1-4:20
6. Final greetings. 4:21-4:23

PHILIPPIANS

1 Paul and Timothy,[a] servants of Christ Jesus,

To all the saints[b] in Christ Jesus at Philippi,[c] together with the overseers[a][d] and deacons:[e]

2Grace and peace to you from God our Father and the Lord Jesus Christ.[f]

Paul joyfully prays for the Philippians.

3I thank my God every time I remember you.[g] 4In all my prayers for all of you, I always pray[h] with joy 5because of your partnership[i] in the gospel from the first day[j] until now, 6being confident of this, that he who began a good work in you will carry it on to completion until the day of Christ Jesus.[k]

7It is right[l] for me to feel this way about all of you, since I have you in my heart;[m] for whether I am in chains[n] or defending[o] and confirming the gospel, all of you share in God's grace with me. 8God can testify[p] how I long for all of you with the affection of Christ Jesus.

9And this is my prayer: that your love[q] may abound more and more in knowledge and depth of insight, 10so that you may be able to discern what is best and may be pure and blameless until the day of Christ,[r] 11filled with the fruit of righteousness[s] that comes through Jesus Christ—to the glory and praise of God.

The gospel is advanced by Paul's chains.

12Now I want you to know, brothers, that what has happened to me has really

1:1 [a]Ac 16:1; 2Co 1:1 [b]Ac 9:13 [c]Ac 16:12 [d]1Ti 3:1 [e]1Ti 3:8
1:2 [f]Ro 1:7
1:3 [g]Ro 1:8
1:4 [h]Ro 1:10
1:5 [i]Ac 2:42; Php 4:15 [j]Ac 16:12-40
1:6 [k]ver 10; 1Co 1:8
1:7 [l]2Pe 1:13 [m]2Co 7:3 [n]ver 13,14,17; Ac 21:33 [o]ver 16
1:8 [p]Ro 1:9

1:9 [q]1Th 3:12 **1:10** [r]ver 6; 1Co 1:8 **1:11** [s]Jas 3:18

a *1* Traditionally *bishops*

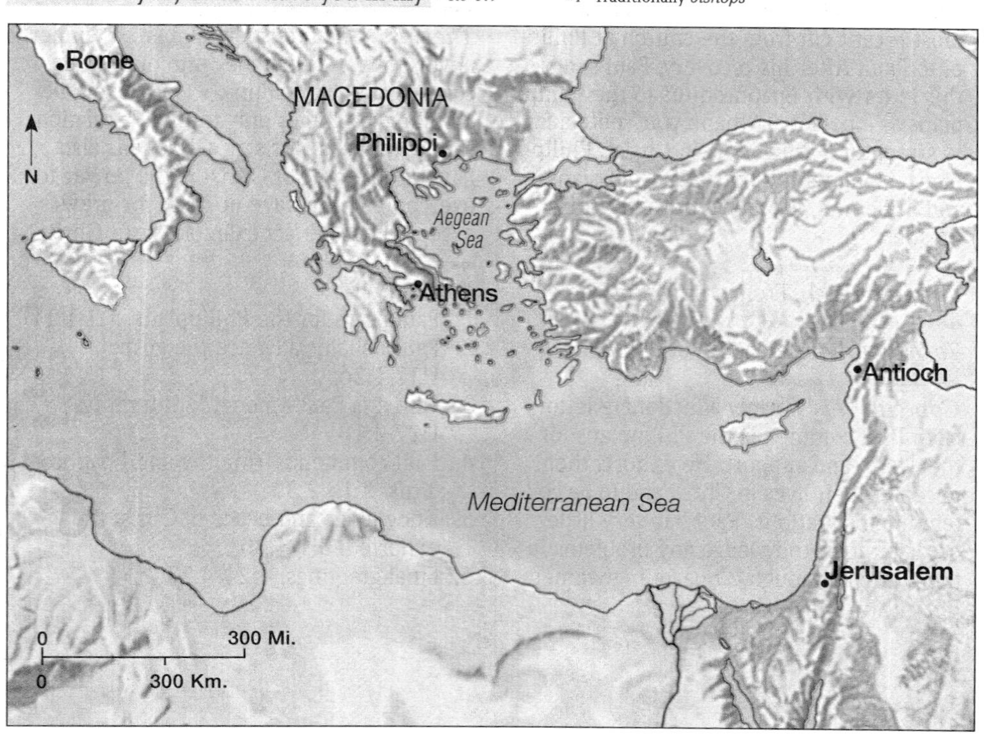

Location of Philippi

Philippi sat on the Egnatian Way, the main transportation route in Macedonia, an extension of the Appian Way, which joined the eastern empire with Italy.

served to advance the gospel. [13]As a
result, it has become clear throughout
the whole palace guard[b] and to everyone else that I am in chains[a] for Christ.
[14]Because of my chains,[b] most of the
brothers in the Lord have been encouraged to speak the word of God more
courageously and fearlessly.

[15]It is true that some preach Christ
out of envy and rivalry, but others out
of goodwill. [16]The latter do so in love,
knowing that I am put here for the
defense of the gospel.[c] [17]The former
preach Christ out of selfish ambition,[d]
not sincerely, supposing that they can
stir up trouble for me while I am in
chains.[c][e] [18]But what does it matter? The
important thing is that in every way,
whether from false motives or true,
Christ is preached. And because of this
I rejoice.

Yes, and I will continue to rejoice,
[19]for I know that through your prayers[f]
and the help given by the Spirit of Jesus
Christ,[g] what has happened to me will
turn out for my deliverance.[d] [20]I eagerly
expect[h] and hope that I will in no way
be ashamed, but will have sufficient
courage[i] so that now as always Christ
will be exalted in my body,[j] whether by
life or by death.[k] [21]For to me, to live is
Christ[l] and to die is gain. [22]If I am to go
on living in the body, this will mean
fruitful labor for me. Yet what shall I
choose? I do not know! [23]I am torn
between the two: I desire to depart[m]
and be with Christ,[n] which is better by
far; [24]but it is more necessary for you
that I remain in the body. [25]Convinced
of this, I know that I will remain, and I
will continue with all of you for your
progress and joy in the faith, [26]so that
through my being with you again your
joy in Christ Jesus will overflow on
account of me.

It is a privilege to suffer for Christ.

[27]Whatever happens, conduct yourselves in a manner worthy[o] of the gospel
of Christ. Then, whether I come and
see you or only hear about you in my
absence, I will know that you stand
firm[p] in one spirit, contending[q] as one
man for the faith of the gospel [28]without
being frightened in any way by those
who oppose you. This is a sign to them
that they will be destroyed, but that
you will be saved—and that by God.
[29]For it has been granted to you[r] on
behalf of Christ not only to believe on
him, but also to suffer[s] for him, [30]since
you are going through the same struggle[t] you saw[u] I had, and now hear[v] that
I still have.

Christ is the model for humility.

2 If you have any encouragement
from being united with Christ, if
any comfort from his love, if any fellowship with the Spirit,[w] if any tenderness and compassion,[x] [2]then make my
joy complete[y] by being like-minded,[z]
having the same love, being one[a] in
spirit and purpose. [3]Do nothing out of
selfish ambition or vain conceit,[b] but
in humility consider others better than
yourselves.[c] [4]Each of you should look
not only to your own interests, but
also to the interests of others.

[5]Your attitude should be the same as
that of Christ Jesus:[d]

[6]Who, being in very nature[e] God,[e]
did not consider equality with
God[f] something to be grasped,
[7]but made himself nothing,
taking the very nature[f] of a
servant,[g]
being made in human likeness.[h]
[8]And being found in appearance as a
man,
he humbled himself
and became obedient to death[i]—
even death on a cross!
[9]Therefore God exalted him[j] to the
highest place
and gave him the name that is
above every name,[k]

1:13 [a]ver 7,14,17
1:14 [b]ver 7,13,17
1:16 [c]ver 7,12
1:17 [d]Php 2:3 [e]ver 7,13,14
1:19 [f]2Co 1:11 [g]Ac 16:7
1:20 [h]Ro 8:19 [i]ver 14 [j]1Co 6:20 [k]Ro 14:8
1:21 [l]Gal 2:20
1:23 [m]2Ti 4:6 [n]Jn 12:26; 2Co 5:8
1:27 [o]Eph 4:1 [p]1Co 16:13 [q]Jude 3
1:29 [r]Mt 5:11,12 [s]Ac 14:22
1:30 [t]Col 2:1; 1Th 2:2 [u]Ac 16:19-40 [v]ver 13
2:1 [w]2Co 13:14 [x]Col 3:12
2:2 [y]Jn 3:29 [z]Php 4:2 [a]Ro 12:16
2:3 [b]Gal 5:26 [c]Ro 12:10; 1Pe 5:5
2:5 [d]Mt 11:29
2:6 [e]Jn 1:1 [f]Jn 5:18
2:7 [g]Mt 20:28 [h]Jn 1:14; Heb 2:17
2:8 [i]Mt 26:39; Jn 10:18; Heb 5:8
2:9 [j]Ac 2:33; Heb 2:9 [k]Eph 1:20,21

[b] *13* Or *whole palace* [c] *16,17* Some late manuscripts have verses 16 and 17 in reverse order.
[d] *19* Or *salvation* [e] *6* Or *in the form of*
[f] *7* Or *the form*

10that at the name of Jesus every knee
should bow,[a]
in heaven and on earth and under
the earth,[b]
11and every tongue confess that Jesus
Christ is Lord,[c]
to the glory of God the Father.

Children of God should shine like stars.

12Therefore, my dear friends, as you have always obeyed—not only in my presence, but now much more in my absence—continue to work out your salvation with fear and trembling,[d] **13**for it is God who works in you[e] to will and to act according to his good purpose.

14Do everything without complaining[f] or arguing, **15**so that you may become blameless and pure, children of God[g] without fault in a crooked and depraved generation,[h] in which you shine like stars in the universe **16**as you hold out[g] the word of life—in order that I may boast on the day of Christ that I did not run or labor for nothing.[i] **17**But even if I am being poured out like a drink offering[j] on the sacrifice[k] and service coming from your faith, I am glad and rejoice with all of you. **18**So you too should be glad and rejoice with me.

Plans are made to send Timothy and Epaphroditus to the Philippians.

19I hope in the Lord Jesus to send Timothy to you soon,[l] that I also may be cheered when I receive news about you. **20**I have no one else like him,[m] who takes a genuine interest in your welfare. **21**For everyone looks out for his own interests,[n] not those of Jesus Christ. **22**But you know that Timothy has proved himself, because as a son with his father[o] he has served with me in the work of the gospel. **23**I hope, therefore, to send him as soon as I see how things go with me.[p] **24**And I am confident[q] in the Lord that I myself will come soon.

25But I think it is necessary to send back to you Epaphroditus, my brother, fellow worker[r] and fellow soldier,[s] who is also your messenger, whom you sent to take care of my needs.[t] **26**For he longs for all of you[u] and is distressed because you heard he was ill. **27**Indeed he was ill, and almost died. But God had mercy on him, and not on him only but also on me, to spare me sorrow upon sorrow. **28**Therefore I am all the more eager to send him, so that when you see him again you may be glad and I may have less anxiety. **29**Welcome him in the Lord with great joy, and honor men like him,[v] **30**because he almost died for the work of Christ, risking his life to make up for the help you could not give me.[w]

True circumcision.

3 Finally, my brothers, rejoice in the Lord! It is no trouble for me to write the same things to you again, and it is a safeguard for you.

2Watch out for those dogs,[x] those men who do evil, those mutilators of the flesh. **3**For it is we who are the circumcision,[y] we who worship by the Spirit of God, who glory in Christ Jesus, and who put no confidence in the flesh— **4**though I myself have reasons for such confidence.

If anyone else thinks he has reasons to put confidence in the flesh, I have more: **5**circumcised[z] on the eighth day, of the people of Israel,[a] of the tribe of Benjamin,[b] a Hebrew of Hebrews; in regard to the law, a Pharisee;[c] **6**as for zeal, persecuting the church;[d] as for legalistic righteousness,[e] faultless.

7But whatever was to my profit I now consider loss[f] for the sake of Christ. **8**What is more, I consider everything a loss compared to the surpassing greatness of knowing[g] Christ Jesus my Lord, for whose sake I have lost all things. I consider them rubbish, that I may gain Christ **9**and be found in him, not having a righteousness of my own that comes from the law,[h] but that which is through faith in Christ—the righteousness that

2:10 [a]Ro 14:11 [b]Mt 28:18
2:11 [c]Jn 13:13
2:12 [d]2Co 7:15
2:13 [e]Ezr 1:5
2:14 [f]1Co 10:10; 1Pe 4:9
2:15 [g]Mt 5:45,48; Eph 5:1 [h]Ac 2:40
2:16 [i]1Th 2:19
2:17 [j]2Ti 4:6 [k]Ro 15:16
2:19 [l]ver 23
2:20 [m]1Co 16:10
2:21 [n]1Co 10:24; 13:5
2:22 [o]1Co 4:17; 1Ti 1:2
2:23 [p]ver 19
2:24 [q]Php 1:25
2:25 [r]Php 4:3 [s]Phm 2 [t]Php 4:18
2:26 [u]Php 1:8
2:29 [v]1Co 16:18; 1Ti 5:17
2:30 [w]1Co 16:17
3:2 [x]Ps 22:16,20
3:3 [y]Ro 2:28,29; Gal 6:15; Col 2:11
3:5 [z]Lk 1:59 [a]2Co 11:22 [b]Ro 11:1 [c]Ac 23:6
3:6 [d]Ac 8:3 [e]Ro 10:5
3:7 [f]Mt 13:44; Lk 14:33
3:8 [g]Eph 4:13; 2Pe 1:2
3:9 [h]Ro 10:5

g16 Or *hold on to*

comes from God and is by faith.[a] 10I want to know Christ and the power of his resurrection and the fellowship of sharing in his sufferings,[b] becoming like him in his death,[c] 11and so, somehow, to attain to the resurrection[d] from the dead.

Pressing toward the goal.

12Not that I have already obtained all this, or have already been made perfect,[e] but I press on to take hold[f] of that for which Christ Jesus took hold of me.[g] 13Brothers, I do not consider myself yet to have taken hold of it. But one thing I do: Forgetting what is behind[h] and straining toward what is ahead, 14I press on[i] toward the goal to win the prize for which God has called[j] me heavenward in Christ Jesus.

15All of us who are mature[k] should take such a view of things.[l] And if on some point you think differently, that too God will make clear to you. 16Only let us live up to what we have already attained.

17Join with others in following my example,[m] brothers, and take note of those who live according to the pattern we gave you. 18For, as I have often told you before and now say again even with tears,[n] many live as enemies of the cross of Christ.[o] 19Their destiny is destruction, their god is their stomach,[p] and their glory is in their shame.[q] Their mind is on earthly things.[r] 20But our citizenship[s] is in heaven.[t] And we eagerly await a Savior from there, the Lord Jesus Christ,[u] 21who, by the power[v] that enables him to bring everything under his control, will transform our lowly bodies[w] so that they will be like his glorious body.[x]

4 Therefore, my brothers, you whom I love and long for,[y] my joy and crown, that is how you should stand firm[z] in the Lord, dear friends!

Paul pleads for contention to end between Euodia and Syntyche.

2I plead with Euodia and I plead with Syntyche to agree with each other[a] in the Lord. 3Yes, and I ask you, loyal yokefellow,[h] help these women who have contended at my side in the cause of the gospel, along with Clement and the rest of my fellow workers, whose names are in the book of life.

The peace of God transcends all understanding.

4Rejoice in the Lord always. I will say it again: Rejoice![b] 5Let your gentleness be evident to all. The Lord is near.[c] 6Do not be anxious about anything,[d] but in everything, by prayer and petition, with thanksgiving, present your requests to God.[e] 7And the peace of God,[f] which transcends all understanding, will guard your hearts and your minds in Christ Jesus.

8Finally, brothers, whatever is true, whatever is noble, whatever is right, whatever is pure, whatever is lovely, whatever is admirable—if anything is excellent or praiseworthy—think about such things. 9Whatever you have learned or received or heard from me, or seen in me—put it into practice.[g] And the God of peace[h] will be with you.

Paul gives thanks to the Philippians for their generosity.

10I rejoice greatly in the Lord that at last you have renewed your concern for me.[i] Indeed, you have been concerned, but you had no opportunity to show it. 11I am not saying this because I am in need, for I have learned to be content[j] whatever the circumstances. 12I know what it is to be in need, and I know what it is to have plenty. I have learned the secret of being content in any and every situation, whether well fed or hungry,[k] whether living in plenty or in want.[l] 13I can do everything through him who gives me strength.[m]

14Yet it was good of you to share[n] in my troubles. 15Moreover, as you Philip-

3:9 [a]Ro 9:30
3:10 [b]Ro 8:17 [c]Ro 6:3-5
3:11 [d]Rev 20:5,6
3:12 [e]1Co 13:10 [f]1Ti 6:12 [g]Ac 9:5,6
3:13 [h]Lk 9:62
3:14 [i]Heb 6:1 [j]Ro 8:28
3:15 [k]1Co 2:6 [l]Gal 5:10
3:17 [m]1Co 4:16; 1Pe 5:3
3:18 [n]Ac 20:31 [o]Gal 6:12
3:19 [p]Ro 16:18 [q]Ro 6:21 [r]Ro 8:5,6
3:20 [s]Eph 2:19 [t]Col 3:1 [u]1Co 1:7
3:21 [v]Eph 1:19 [w]1Co 15:43-53 [x]Col 3:4
4:1 [y]Php 1:8 [z]1Co 16:13; Php 1:27
4:2 [a]Php 2:2
4:4 [b]Ro 12:12; Php 3:1
4:5 [c]Heb 10:37; Jas 5:8,9
4:6 [d]Mt 6:25-34 [e]Eph 6:18
4:7 [f]Isa 26:3; Jn 14:27; Col 3:15
4:9 [g]Php 3:17 [h]Ro 15:33
4:10 [i]2Co 11:9
4:11 [j]1Ti 6:6,8
4:12 [k]1Co 4:11 [l]2Co 11:9
4:13 [m]2Co 12:9
4:14 [n]Php 1:7

[h]3 Or *loyal Syzygus*

pians know, in the early days[a] of your
acquaintance with the gospel, when I
set out from Macedonia, not one church
shared with me in the matter of giving
and receiving, except you only;[b] 16for
even when I was in Thessalonica,[c] you
sent me aid again and again when I was
in need.[d] 17Not that I am looking for a
gift, but I am looking for what may be
credited to your account.[e] 18I have
received full payment and even more;
I am amply supplied, now that I have
received from Epaphroditus[f] the gifts
you sent. They are a fragrant[g] offering,
an acceptable sacrifice, pleasing to God.
19And my God will meet all your needs[h]
according to his glorious riches[i] in
Christ Jesus.
20To our God and Father[j] be glory
for ever and ever. Amen.[k]

4:15 [a]Php 1:5 [b]2Co 11:8,9 4:16 [c]Ac 17:1 [d]1Th 2:9 4:17 [e]1Co 9:11,12 4:18 [f]Php 2:25 [g]2Co 2:14 4:19 [h]Ps 23:1; 2Co 9:8 [i]Ro 2:4 4:20 [j]Gal 1:4 [k]Ro 11:36 4:21 [l]Gal 1:2

Final greetings and blessings.

21Greet all the saints in Christ Jesus.
The brothers who are with me[l] send
greetings. 22All the saints[m] send you
greetings, especially those who belong
to Caesar's household.
23The grace of the Lord Jesus Christ[n]
be with your spirit. Amen.[i]

4:22 [m]Ac 9:13 **4:23** [n]Ro 16:20

[i]23 Some manuscripts do not have *Amen*.

COLOSSIANS

Author: Paul the Apostle.

Date Written: Between A.D. 60 and 61.

Title: Named after the addressee of this letter: the church at Colosse.

Background: Paul establishes the church at Ephesus on his second missionary journey. While at Ephesus he develops a special concern for the church at Colosse, even though he has never visited there. Colosse, once similar to the thriving commercial cities of her neighbors, Laodicea and Hierapolis, is declining. The city is infiltrated with false teachings from the Jews, Greeks and Orientals. Paul responds to these false teachings, especially that of Gnosticism—which claims secret knowledge and powers and denies Christ's true humanity. Paul sends this letter by way of Tychicus and the converted slave Onesimus to the church at Colosse after Epaphras's visit and report on the conditions there. Colossians, Ephesians, Philippians and Philemon comprise Paul's "Prison Epistles."

Where Written: From a Roman prison.

To Whom: To the church at Colosse.

Content: The first portion of Colossians is doctrinal in nature, and the last is practical application. Paul combats the false teachings of legalism, angel worship and ceremonialism. His defense against such heresy is coupled with his urging commitment to the lordship of Christ. Believers are encouraged to take off the old self and put on the new self (3:9,10) by living righteous lives before God. These rules for holy living give them freedom from human regulations as they follow Christ's example.

Key Words: "Supremacy"; "Head." The book of Colossians is written to a church being diluted with vain, worldly philosophies. The "supremacy" of Christ in every area of life is emphasized as Christ is presented as "head" of the body, his church.

Themes: • Jesus alone is sufficient to meet every need of our lives. • The perfect reflection of invisible God is the perfect Jesus Christ. • Philosophies which do not exalt Christ are not from God. • Our relationship with God is reflected through our relationship with others.

Outline:
1. Paul's prayer for the Colossians. 1:1-1:14
2. Supremacy of Christ. 1:15-2:5
3. Deceptive philosophies. 2:6-2:23
4. Exhortation for holy living. 3:1-3:17
5. Guidelines for Christian relationships. 3:18-4:1
6. Final instructions. 4:2-4:18

COLOSSIANS

1 Paul, an apostle[a] of Christ Jesus by the
will of God,[b] and Timothy our brother,

2To the holy and faithful[a] brothers in
Christ at Colosse:

Grace[c] and peace to you from God
our Father.[b][d]

Paul's thanks to God for the Colossians' faithfulness.

3We always thank God,[e] the Father of
our Lord Jesus Christ, when we pray for
you, 4because we have heard of your
faith in Christ Jesus and of the love[f] you
have for all the saints[g]— 5the faith and
love that spring from the hope[h] that is
stored up for you in heaven[i] and that
you have already heard about in the
word of truth, the gospel 6that has come
to you. All over the world[j] this gospel
is bearing fruit[k] and growing, just as it
has been doing among you since the
day you heard it and understood God's
grace in all its truth. 7You learned it
from Epaphras,[l] our dear fellow servant,
who is a faithful minister[m] of Christ on
our[c] behalf, 8and who also told us of
your love in the Spirit.[n]
9For this reason, since the day we
heard about you,[o] we have not stopped
praying for you and asking God to fill you
with the knowledge of his will[p] through
all spiritual wisdom and understanding.[q]
10And we pray this in order that you
may live a life worthy[r] of the Lord and
may please him in every way: bearing
fruit in every good work, growing in the

1:1 [a]1Co 1:1 [b]2Co 1:1
1:2 [c]Col 4:18 [d]Ro 1:7
1:3 [e]Ro 1:8
1:4 [f]Gal 5:6 [g]Eph 1:15
1:5 [h]1Th 5:8; Tit 1:2 [i]1Pe 1:4
1:6 [j]Ro 10:18 [k]Jn 15:16
1:7 [l]Phm 23 [m]Col 4:7
1:8 [n]Ro 15:30
1:9 [o]Eph 1:15 [p]Eph 5:17 [q]Eph 1:17
1:10 [r]Eph 4:1

a2 Or *believing* b2 Some manuscripts *Father and the Lord Jesus Christ* c7 Some manuscripts *your*

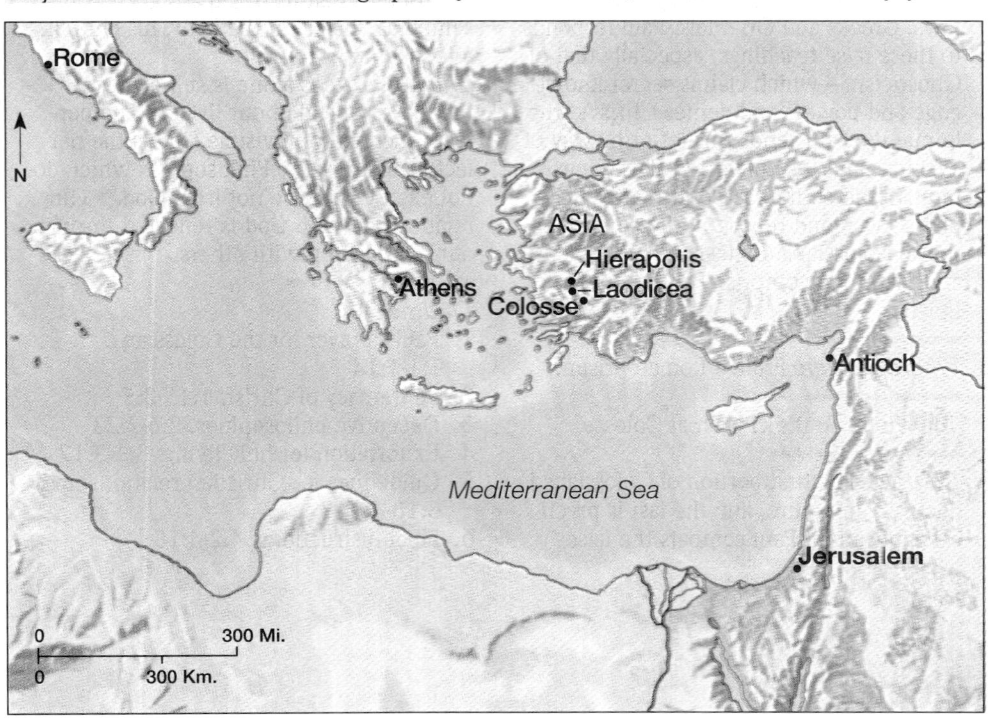

Location of Colosse

Paul had no doubt been through Laodicea on his third missionary journey, as it lay on the main route to Ephesus, but he had never been to Colosse. Though a large city with a significant population, Colosse was smaller and less important than the nearby cities of Laodicea and Hierapolis.

knowledge of God, 11being strengthened
with all power[a] according to his glorious might so that you may have great
endurance and patience,[b] and joyfully
12giving thanks to the Father,[c] who has
qualified you[d] to share in the inheritance[d] of the saints in the kingdom of
light. 13For he has rescued us from the
dominion of darkness[e] and brought us
into the kingdom[f] of the Son he loves,[g]
14in whom we have redemption,[eh] the
forgiveness of sins.[i]

The nature of Jesus Christ.

15He is the image[j] of the invisible
God,[k] the firstborn over all creation.
16For by him all things were created:[l]
things in heaven and on earth, visible
and invisible, whether thrones or powers or rulers or authorities;[m] all things
were created by him and for him.[n] 17He
is before all things,[o] and in him all things
hold together. 18And he is the head[p] of
the body, the church; he is the beginning and the firstborn from among the
dead,[q] so that in everything he might
have the supremacy. 19For God was
pleased[r] to have all his fullness[s] dwell in
him, 20and through him to reconcile[t] to
himself all things, whether things on
earth or things in heaven,[u] by making
peace through his blood,[v] shed on the
cross.
21Once you were alienated from God
and were enemies[w] in your minds[x] because of[f] your evil behavior. 22But now
he has reconciled you by Christ's physical body[y] through death to present you
holy in his sight, without blemish and
free from accusation[z]— 23if you continue in your faith, established[a] and firm,
not moved from the hope[b] held out in
the gospel. This is the gospel that you
heard and that has been proclaimed to
every creature under heaven,[c] and of
which I, Paul, have become a servant.[d]

Paul's ministry to the Gentiles.

24Now I rejoice in what was suffered
for you, and I fill up in my flesh what is
still lacking in regard to Christ's afflictions,[e] for the sake of his body, which is
the church. 25I have become its servant[f] by the commission God gave me[g]
to present to you the word of God in
its fullness— 26the mystery[h] that has
been kept hidden for ages and generations, but is now disclosed to the saints.
27To them God has chosen to make
known[i] among the Gentiles the glorious
riches of this mystery, which is Christ in
you, the hope of glory.
28We proclaim him, admonishing[j] and
teaching everyone with all wisdom,[k] so
that we may present everyone perfect[l]
in Christ. 29To this end I labor,[m] struggling[n] with all his energy, which so
powerfully works in me.[o]

Growth in the knowledge of Jesus Christ.

2 I want you to know how much I
am struggling[p] for you and for those
at Laodicea,[q] and for all who have not
met me personally. 2My purpose is that
they may be encouraged in heart[r] and
united in love, so that they may have
the full riches of complete understanding, in order that they may know the
mystery of God, namely, Christ, 3in
whom are hidden all the treasures of
wisdom and knowledge.[s] 4I tell you this
so that no one may deceive you by fine-
sounding arguments.[t] 5For though I am
absent from you in body, I am present
with you in spirit[u] and delight to see
how orderly[v] you are and how firm[w]
your faith in Christ is.

Freedom from deceptive philosophies.

6So then, just as you received Christ
Jesus as Lord,[x] continue to live in him,
7rooted[y] and built up in him, strengthened in the faith as you were taught,
and overflowing with thankfulness.

1:11 [a]Eph 3:16 [b]Eph 4:2 **1:12** [c]Eph 5:20 [d]Ac 20:32 **1:13** [e]Ac 26:18 [f]Eph 6:12; 2Pe 1:11 [g]Mt 3:17 **1:14** [h]Ro 3:24 [i]Eph 1:7 **1:15** [j]2Co 4:4 [k]Jn 1:18 **1:16** [l]Jn 1:3 [m]Eph 1:20,21 [n]Ro 11:36 **1:17** [o]Jn 1:2 **1:18** [p]Eph 1:22 [q]Ac 26:23; Rev 1:5 **1:19** [r]Eph 1:5 [s]Jn 1:16 **1:20** [t]2Co 5:18 [u]Eph 1:10 [v]Eph 2:13 **1:21** [w]Ro 5:10 [x]Eph 2:3 **1:22** [y]Ro 7:4 [z]Eph 5:27 **1:23** [a]Eph 3:17 [b]ver 5 [c]Ro 10:18 [d]ver 25; 1Co 3:5 **1:24** [e]2Co 1:5 **1:25** [f]ver 23 [g]Eph 3:2 **1:26** [h]Ro 16:25 **1:27** [i]Mt 13:11 **1:28** [j]Col 3:16 [k]1Co 2:6,7 [l]Eph 5:27 **1:29** [m]1Co 15:10 [n]Col 2:1 [o]Eph 1:19 **2:1** [p]Col 1:29; 4:12 [q]Rev 1:11 **2:2** [r]Col 4:8

2:3 [s]Ro 11:33; 1Co 1:24,30 **2:4** [t]Ro 16:18 **2:5** [u]1Th 2:17 [v]1Co 14:40 [w]1Pe 5:9 **2:6** [x]Col 1:10 **2:7** [y]Eph 3:17

d *12* Some manuscripts *us* e *14* A few late manuscripts *redemption through his blood* f *21* Or *minds, as shown by*

8 See to it that no one takes you captive through hollow and deceptive philosophy,[a] which depends on human tradition and the basic principles of this world[b] rather than on Christ.

9 For in Christ all the fullness of the Deity lives in bodily form, 10 and you have been given fullness in Christ, who is the head[c] over every power and authority. 11 In him you were also circumcised,[d] in the putting off of the sinful nature,[g][e] not with a circumcision done by the hands of men but with the circumcision done by Christ, 12 having been buried with him in baptism and raised with him[f] through your faith in the power of God, who raised him from the dead.[g]

13 When you were dead in your sins[h] and in the uncircumcision of your sinful nature,[h] God made you[i] alive with Christ. He forgave us all our sins, 14 having canceled the written code, with its regulations,[i] that was against us and that stood opposed to us; he took it away, nailing it to the cross.[j] 15 And having disarmed the powers and authorities,[k] he made a public spectacle of them, triumphing over them[l] by the cross.[j]

16 Therefore do not let anyone judge you[m] by what you eat or drink,[n] or with regard to a religious festival,[o] a New Moon celebration[p] or a Sabbath day.[q] 17 These are a shadow of the things that were to come;[r] the reality, however, is found in Christ. 18 Do not let anyone who delights in false humility[s] and the worship of angels disqualify you for the prize.[t] Such a person goes into great detail about what he has seen, and his unspiritual mind puffs him up with idle notions. 19 He has lost connection with the Head,[u] from whom the whole body, supported and held together by its ligaments and sinews, grows as God causes it to grow.[v]

20 Since you died with Christ to the basic principles of this world,[w] why, as though you still belonged to it, do you submit to its rules:[x] 21 "Do not handle! Do not taste! Do not touch!"? 22 These are all destined to perish[y] with use, because they are based on human commands and teachings.[z] 23 Such regulations indeed have an appearance of wisdom, with their self-imposed worship, their false humility and their harsh treatment of the body, but they lack any value in restraining sensual indulgence.

2:8 [a] 1Ti 6:20 [b] Gal 4:3 **2:10** [c] Eph 1:22 **2:11** [d] Ro 2:29; Php 3:3 [e] Gal 5:24 **2:12** [f] Ro 6:5 [g] Ac 2:24 **2:13** [h] Eph 2:1,5 **2:14** [i] Eph 2:15 [j] 1Pe 2:24 **2:15** [k] Eph 6:12 [l] Lk 10:18 **2:16** [m] Ro 14:3,4 [n] Ro 14:17 [o] Ro 14:5 [p] 1Ch 23:31 [q] Gal 4:10 **2:17** [r] Heb 8:5 **2:18** [s] ver 23 [t] Php 3:14 **2:19** [u] Eph 1:22 [v] Eph 4:16 **2:20** [w] Gal 4:3,9 [x] ver 14,16 **2:22** [y] 1Co 6:13 [z] Isa 29:13; Mt 15:9; Tit 1:14 **3:2** [a] Php 3:19,20 **3:3** [b] Ro 6:2; 2Co 5:14 **3:4** [c] 1Co 1:7 [d] 1Pe 1:13; 1Jn 3:2 **3:5** [e] Eph 5:3 [f] Eph 5:5 **3:6** [g] Ro 1:18 **3:7** [h] Eph 2:2 **3:8** [i] Eph 4:22 [j] Eph 4:31 [k] Eph 4:29 **3:9** [l] Eph 4:22,25 **3:10** [m] Ro 12:2; Eph 4:23 [n] Eph 2:10

Have heavenly thoughts and desires.

3 Since, then, you have been raised with Christ, set your hearts on things above, where Christ is seated at the right hand of God. 2 Set your minds on things above, not on earthly things.[a] 3 For you died,[b] and your life is now hidden with Christ in God. 4 When Christ, who is your[k] life, appears,[c] then you also will appear with him in glory.[d]

Put to death the earthly nature and put on love.

5 Put to death, therefore, whatever belongs to your earthly nature: sexual immorality, impurity, lust, evil desires and greed,[e] which is idolatry.[f] 6 Because of these, the wrath of God[g] is coming.[l] 7 You used to walk in these ways, in the life you once lived.[h] 8 But now you must rid yourselves[i] of all such things as these: anger, rage, malice, slander,[j] and filthy language from your lips.[k] 9 Do not lie to each other,[l] since you have taken off your old self with its practices 10 and have put on the new self, which is being renewed[m] in knowledge in the image of its Creator.[n] 11 Here there is no Greek or Jew,[o] circumcised or uncircumcised,[p] barbarian, Scythian, slave or free,[q] but Christ is all,[r] and is in all.

12 Therefore, as God's chosen people, holy and dearly loved, clothe yourselves with compassion, kindness, humility,[s] gentleness and patience.[t] 13 Bear with each other[u] and forgive whatever grievances

3:11 [o] Ro 10:12 [p] 1Co 7:19 [q] Gal 3:28 [r] Eph 1:23
3:12 [s] Php 2:3 [t] 2Co 6:6; Gal 5:22,23
3:13 [u] Eph 4:2

[g] *11* Or *the flesh* [h] *13* Or *your flesh* [i] *13* Some manuscripts *us* [j] *15* Or *them in him* [k] *4* Some manuscripts *our* [l] *6* Some early manuscripts *coming on those who are disobedient*

you may have against one another. Forgive as the Lord forgave you.[a] 14And over all these virtues put on love,[b] which binds them all together in perfect unity.[c]

15Let the peace of Christ[d] rule in your hearts, since as members of one body you were called to peace. And be thankful. 16Let the word of Christ[e] dwell in you richly as you teach and admonish one another with all wisdom,[f] and as you sing psalms, hymns and spiritual songs with gratitude in your hearts to God.[g] 17And whatever you do,[h] whether in word or deed, do it all in the name of the Lord Jesus, giving thanks[i] to God the Father through him.

Follow guidelines for the Christian family.

3:18–4:1pp— Eph 5:22–6:9

18Wives, submit to your husbands,[j] as is fitting in the Lord.

19Husbands, love your wives and do not be harsh with them.

20Children, obey your parents in everything, for this pleases the Lord.

21Fathers, do not embitter your children, or they will become discouraged.

22Slaves, obey your earthly masters in everything; and do it, not only when their eye is on you and to win their favor, but with sincerity of heart and reverence for the Lord. 23Whatever you do, work at it with all your heart, as working for the Lord, not for men, 24since you know that you will receive an inheritance[k] from the Lord as a reward. It is the Lord Christ you are serving. 25Anyone who does wrong will be repaid for his wrong, and there is no favoritism.[l]

4 Masters, provide your slaves with what is right and fair, because you know that you also have a Master in heaven.

Paul's appeal for prayer and witnessing.

2Devote yourselves to prayer,[m] being watchful and thankful. 3And pray for us, too, that God may open a door[n] for our message, so that we may proclaim the mystery of Christ, for which I am in chains.[o] 4Pray that I may proclaim it clearly, as I should. 5Be wise[p] in the way you act toward outsiders;[q] make the most of every opportunity.[r] 6Let your conversation be always full of grace,[s] seasoned with salt,[t] so that you may know how to answer everyone.[u]

Introduction of Tychicus and Onesimus.

7Tychicus[v] will tell you all the news about me. He is a dear brother, a faithful minister and fellow servant[w] in the Lord. 8I am sending him to you for the express purpose that you may know about our[m] circumstances and that he may encourage your hearts.[x] 9He is coming with Onesimus,[y] our faithful and dear brother, who is one of you. They will tell you everything that is happening here.

Final greetings and instructions.

10My fellow prisoner Aristarchus[z] sends you his greetings, as does Mark, the cousin of Barnabas.[a] (You have received instructions about him; if he comes to you, welcome him.) 11Jesus, who is called Justus, also sends greetings. These are the only Jews among my fellow workers for the kingdom of God, and they have proved a comfort to me. 12Epaphras,[b] who is one of you and a servant of Christ Jesus, sends greetings. He is always wrestling in prayer for you,[c] that you may stand firm in all the will of God, mature[d] and fully assured. 13I vouch for him that he is working hard for you and for those at Laodicea[e] and Hierapolis. 14Our dear friend Luke,[f] the doctor, and Demas[g] send greetings. 15Give my greetings to the brothers at Laodicea, and to Nympha and the church in her house.[h]

16After this letter has been read to you, see that it is also read[i] in the church

3:13 [a]Eph 4:32
3:14 [b]1Co 13:1-13 [c]Eph 4:3
3:15 [d]Jn 14:27
3:16 [e]Ro 10:17 [f]Col 1:28 [g]Eph 5:19
3:17 [h]1Co 10:31 [i]Eph 5:20
3:18 [j]Eph 5:22
3:24 [k]Ac 20:32
3:25 [l]Ac 10:34
4:2 [m]Lk 18:1
4:3 [n]Ac 14:27 [o]Eph 6:19,20
4:5 [p]Eph 5:15 [q]Mk 4:11 [r]Eph 5:16
4:6 [s]Eph 4:29 [t]Mk 9:50 [u]1Pe 3:15
4:7 [v]Ac 20:4 [w]Eph 6:21,22
4:8 [x]Eph 6:21,22
4:9 [y]Phm 10
4:10 [z]Ac 19:29 [a]Ac 4:36
4:12 [b]Col 1:7; Phm 23 [c]Ro 15:30 [d]1Co 2:6
4:13 [e]Col 2:1
4:14 [f]2Ti 4:11; Phm 24 [g]2Ti 4:10
4:15 [h]Ro 16:5
4:16 [i]2Th 3:14

[m]*8* Some manuscripts *that he may know about your*

of the Laodiceans and that you in turn
read the letter from Laodicea.
17 Tell Archippus:[a] "See to it that you
complete the work you have received
in the Lord."[b]

4:17
[a] Phm 2
[b] 2Ti 4:5

4:18
[c] 1Co 16:21
[d] Heb 13:3

18 I, Paul, write this greeting in my
own hand.[c] Remember[d] my chains.
Grace be with you.[e]

[e] 1Ti 6:21; 2Ti 4:22; Tit 3:15; Heb 13:25

1 THESSALONIANS

Author: Paul the Apostle.

Date Written: Between A.D. 50 and 51.

Title: From Paul's first recorded letter to the church at Thessalonica.

Background: Thessalonica is the capital city of Macedonia, a Roman province. When Paul arrives there on his second missionary journey, it is a thriving trade center and seaport of some 200,000 people. Paul's preaching brings many to faith in Jesus Christ, but intense persecution by the unbelievers forces him to flee the city. Paul goes to Berea where he leaves his companions, Timothy and Silas, to carry on the ministry. But the dissenting Jews from Thessalonica follow him there to incite a riot. Paul goes to Athens and then to Corinth where he receives an updated report from Timothy on the Thessalonian Christians. This letter is Paul's response.

Where Written: Corinth.

To Whom: To the church at Thessalonica.

Content: Among the first of Paul's letters, Thessalonians is written to encourage the young church at Thessalonica and to commend them for their diligent faith. Paul instructs the believers to live lives of holiness and orderliness and includes a plea against sexual immorality. This dynamic fellowship is a constant source of joy for Paul. But some in the church misunderstand the second coming of Christ, thinking the believers who die before Christ's return will miss out on the resurrection. Paul assures them that the dead in Christ will indeed be the first to rise, and they then will be caught up together with those alive to meet the Lord in the air. This letter from Paul closes with various exhortations and blessings.

Key Words: "Steadfastness"; "Second Coming." Paul commends the Thessalonian believers for their "steadfastness" in faith despite their background of Greek paganism. At a time when the "second coming" of Christ is expected soon, Paul writes on the comfort, necessity and certainty of Christ's return.

Themes: • God expects believers to be examples for unbelievers. • Persecution is never a reason to leave God. • Our ultimate victory is in Christ. • The return of Jesus Christ is certain. • Christians should pray for their church and their leaders. • Living a sanctified life is God's will for every believer.

Outline:

1. Salutation. 1:1
2. Thanksgiving for the Thessalonians' faith. 1:2-1:10
3. Paul's ministry in Thessalonica. 2:1-4:12
4. Preparations for the coming of the Lord. 4:13-5:11
5. Final admonitions. 5:12-5:28

1 THESSALONIANS

1 Paul, Silas[a] and Timothy,[a]

To the church of the Thessalonians[b] in
God the Father and the Lord Jesus
Christ:

Grace and peace to you.[b][c]

Paul thanks God for the faithfulness of the Thessalonian believers.

2 We always thank God for all of you,[d]
mentioning you in our prayers. 3 We
continually remember before our God
and Father your work produced by
faith,[e] your labor prompted by love, and
your endurance inspired by hope in our
Lord Jesus Christ.
4 For we know, brothers loved by God,
that he has chosen you, 5 because our
gospel[f] came to you not simply with
words, but also with power, with the
Holy Spirit and with deep conviction.
You know how we lived among you
for your sake. 6 You became imitators of
us[g] and of the Lord; in spite of severe
suffering,[h] you welcomed the message
with the joy given by the Holy Spirit.[i]
7 And so you became a model to all the
believers in Macedonia and Achaia. 8 The
Lord's message rang out from you not
only in Macedonia and Achaia—your
faith in God has become known everywhere.[j] Therefore we do not need to
say anything about it, 9 for they themselves report what kind of reception you
gave us. They tell how you turned to
God from idols[k] to serve the living and
true God, 10 and to wait for his Son
from heaven, whom he raised from the

1:1 [a] Ac 16:1; 2Th 1:1 [b] Ac 17:1 [c] Ro 1:7
1:2 [d] Ro 1:8
1:3 [e] 2Th 1:11
1:5 [f] 2Th 2:14
1:6 [g] 1Co 4:16 [h] Ac 17:5-10 [i] Ac 13:52
1:8 [j] Ro 1:8; 10:18
1:9 [k] 1Co 12:2; Gal 4:8

a *1* Greek *Silvanus,* a variant of *Silas* b *1* Some early manuscripts *you from God our Father and the Lord Jesus Christ*

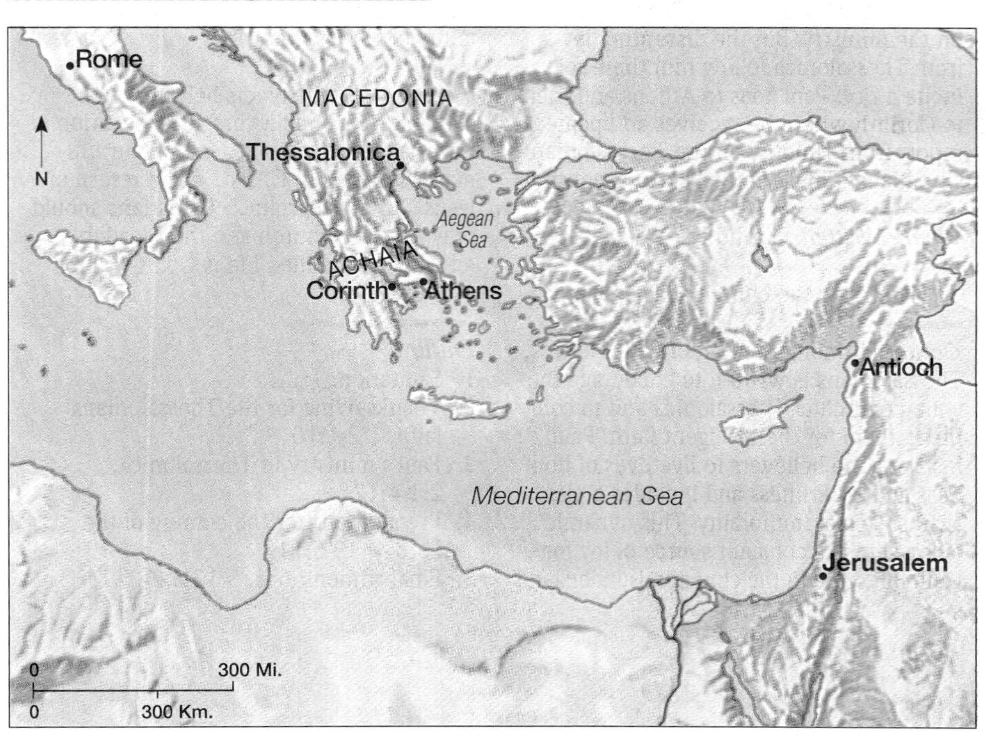

Location of Thessalonica

Paul visited Thessalonica on his second and third missionary journeys. It was a seaport and trade center located on the Egnatian Way, a busy international highway. Paul probably wrote his two letters to the Thessalonians from Corinth.

dead[a]—Jesus, who rescues us from the coming wrath.[b]

Paul's motives for preaching.

2 You know, brothers, that our visit to you[c] was not a failure. 2We had previously suffered[d] and been insulted in Philippi, as you know, but with the help of our God we dared to tell you his gospel in spite of strong opposition. 3For the appeal we make does not spring from error or impure motives,[e] nor are we trying to trick you. 4On the contrary, we speak as men approved by God to be entrusted with the gospel.[f] We are not trying to please men[g] but God, who tests our hearts. 5You know we never used flattery, nor did we put on a mask to cover up greed[h]—God is our witness.[i] 6We were not looking for praise from men, not from you or anyone else.

As apostles[j] of Christ we could have been a burden to you, 7but we were gentle among you, like a mother caring for her little children.[k] 8We loved you so much that we were delighted to share with you not only the gospel of God but our lives as well,[l] because you had become so dear to us. 9Surely you remember, brothers, our toil and hardship; we worked[m] night and day in order not to be a burden to anyone[n] while we preached the gospel of God to you.

10You are witnesses,[o] and so is God, of how holy,[p] righteous and blameless we were among you who believed. 11For you know that we dealt with each of you as a father deals with his own children,[q] 12encouraging, comforting and urging you to live lives worthy[r] of God, who calls you into his kingdom and glory.

13And we also thank God continually[s] because, when you received the word of God,[t] which you heard from us, you accepted it not as the word of men, but as it actually is, the word of God, which is at work in you who believe. 14For you, brothers, became imitators of God's churches in Judea,[u] which are in Christ Jesus: You suffered from your own countrymen[v] the same things those churches suffered from the Jews, 15who killed the Lord Jesus[w] and the prophets[x] and also drove us out. They displease God and are hostile to all men 16in their effort to keep us from speaking to the Gentiles[y] so that they may be saved. In this way they always heap up their sins to the limit.[z] The wrath of God has come upon them at last.[c]

Satan's hindrance of Paul.

17But, brothers, when we were torn away from you for a short time (in person, not in thought),[a] out of our intense longing we made every effort to see you.[b] 18For we wanted to come to you—certainly I, Paul, did, again and again—but Satan[c] stopped us.[d] 19For what is our hope, our joy, or the crown[e] in which we will glory[f] in the presence of our Lord Jesus when he comes?[g] Is it not you? 20Indeed, you are our glory[h] and joy.

Paul sends Timothy to encourage the Thessalonians.

3 So when we could stand it no longer,[i] we thought it best to be left by ourselves in Athens.[j] 2We sent Timothy, who is our brother and God's fellow worker[d] in spreading the gospel of Christ, to strengthen and encourage you in your faith, 3so that no one would be unsettled by these trials. You know quite well that we were destined for them.[k] 4In fact, when we were with you, we kept telling you that we would be persecuted. And it turned out that way, as you well know.[l] 5For this reason, when I could stand it no longer,[m] I sent to find out about your faith. I was afraid that in some way the tempter[n] might have tempted you and our efforts might have been useless.[o]

6But Timothy has just now come to

1:10 [a]Ac 2:24 [b]Ro 5:9
2:1 [c]1Th 1:5,9
2:2 [d]Ac 16:22; Php 1:30
2:3 [e]2Co 2:17
2:4 [f]Gal 2:7 [g]Gal 1:10
2:5 [h]Ac 20:33 [i]Ro 1:9
2:6 [j]1Co 9:1,2
2:7 [k]ver 11
2:8 [l]2Co 12:15; 1Jn 3:16
2:9 [m]Ac 18:3 [n]2Th 3:8
2:10 [o]1Th 1:5 [p]2Co 1:12
2:11 [q]ver 7; 1Co 4:14
2:12 [r]Eph 4:1
2:13 [s]1Th 1:2 [t]Heb 4:12
2:14 [u]Gal 1:22 [v]Ac 17:5; 2Th 1:4
2:15 [w]Ac 2:23 [x]Mt 5:12
2:16 [y]Ac 13:45,50 [z]Mt 23:32
2:17 [a]1Co 5:3; Col 2:5 [b]1Th 3:10
2:18 [c]Mt 4:10 [d]Ro 1:13; 15:22
2:19 [e]Php 4:1 [f]2Co 1:14 [g]Mt 16:27; 1Th 3:13
2:20 [h]2Co 1:14
3:1 [i]ver 5 [j]Ac 17:15
3:3 [k]Ac 9:16; 14:22
3:4 [l]1Th 2:14 **3:5** [m]ver 1 [n]Mt 4:3 [o]Gal 2:2; Php 2:16

c *16* Or *them fully* d *2* Some manuscripts *brother and fellow worker*; other manuscripts *brother and God's servant*

us from you[a] and has brought good news
about your faith and love.[b] He has told
us that you always have pleasant memories of us and that you long to see us,
just as we also long to see you. 7There-
fore, brothers, in all our distress and
persecution we were encouraged about
you because of your faith. 8For now we
really live, since you are standing firm[c]
in the Lord. 9How can we thank God
enough for you[d] in return for all the joy
we have in the presence of our God
because of you? 10Night and day we
pray[e] most earnestly that we may see
you again[f] and supply what is lacking
in your faith.

Paul prays for the believers' growth in the Lord.

11Now may our God and Father himself and our Lord Jesus clear the way for
us to come to you. 12May the Lord make
your love increase and overflow for each
other[g] and for everyone else, just as
ours does for you. 13May he strengthen
your hearts so that you will be blameless[h] and holy in the presence of our
God and Father when our Lord Jesus
comes[i] with all his holy ones.

Plea for sexual purity.

4 Finally, brothers,[j] we instructed you
how to live in order to please God,[k]
as in fact you are living. Now we ask
you and urge you in the Lord Jesus to do
this more and more. 2For you know
what instructions we gave you by the
authority of the Lord Jesus.
3It is God's will that you should be
sanctified: that you should avoid sexual
immorality;[l] 4that each of you should
learn to control his own body[e][m] in a way
that is holy and honorable, 5not in passionate lust[n] like the heathen,[o] who do
not know God; 6and that in this matter
no one should wrong his brother or take
advantage of him.[p] The Lord will punish
men for all such sins,[q] as we have already told you and warned you. 7For
God did not call us to be impure, but to
live a holy life.[r] 8Therefore, he who
rejects this instruction does not reject
man but God, who gives you his Holy
Spirit.[s]

Brotherly love.

9Now about brotherly love[t] we do not
need to write to you,[u] for you yourselves have been taught by God to love
each other.[v] 10And in fact, you do love
all the brothers throughout Macedonia.[w] Yet we urge you, brothers, to do
so more and more.[x]
11Make it your ambition to lead a quiet life, to mind your own business and
to work with your hands,[y] just as we
told you, 12so that your daily life may
win the respect of outsiders[z] and so that
you will not be dependent on anybody.

Sequence of the resurrection and the second coming of Christ.

13Brothers, we do not want you to be
ignorant about those who fall asleep,
or to grieve like the rest of men, who
have no hope.[a] 14We believe that Jesus
died and rose again and so we believe
that God will bring with Jesus those who
have fallen asleep in him.[b] 15According
to the Lord's own word, we tell you that
we who are still alive, who are left till
the coming of the Lord, will certainly
not precede those who have fallen
asleep.[c] 16For the Lord himself will come
down from heaven, with a loud command, with the voice of the archangel
and with the trumpet call of God,[d] and
the dead in Christ will rise first.[e] 17After
that, we who are still alive and are left[f]
will be caught up together with them
in the clouds[g] to meet the Lord in the
air. And so we will be with the Lord[h]
forever. 18Therefore encourage each other with these words.

The day of the Lord will come like a thief in the night.

5 Now, brothers, about times and
dates[i] we do not need to write to

3:6 [a]Ac 18:5 [b]1Th 1:3
3:8 [c]1Co 16:13
3:9 [d]1Th 1:2
3:10 [e]2Ti 1:3 [f]1Th 2:17
3:12 [g]1Th 4:9,10
3:13 [h]1Co 1:8 [i]1Th 2:19
4:1 [j]2Co 13:11 [k]2Co 5:9
4:3 [l]1Co 6:18
4:4 [m]1Co 7:2,9
4:5 [n]Ro 1:26 [o]Eph 4:17
4:6 [p]1Co 6:8 [q]Heb 13:4
4:7 [r]Lev 11:44; 1Pe 1:15
4:8 [s]Ro 5:5; Gal 4:6
4:9 [t]Ro 12:10 [u]1Th 5:1 [v]Jn 13:34
4:10 [w]1Th 1:7 [x]1Th 3:12
4:11 [y]Eph 4:28; 2Th 3:10-12
4:12 [z]Mk 4:11
4:13 [a]Eph 2:12
4:14 [b]1Co 15:18
4:15 [c]1Co 15:52
4:16 [d]Mt 24:31 [e]1Co 15:23; 2Th 2:1
4:17 [f]1Co 15:52 [g]Ac 1:9; Rev 11:12 [h]Jn 12:26
5:1 [i]Ac 1:7

e4 Or *learn to live with his own wife*; or *learn to acquire a wife*

you,[a] 2for you know very well that the day of the Lord[b] will come like a thief in the night.[c] 3While people are saying, "Peace and safety," destruction will come on them suddenly, as labor pains on a pregnant woman, and they will not escape.

4But you, brothers, are not in darkness[d] so that this day should surprise you like a thief. 5You are all sons of the light and sons of the day. We do not belong to the night or to the darkness. 6So then, let us not be like others, who are asleep,[e] but let us be alert and self-controlled. 7For those who sleep, sleep at night, and those who get drunk, get drunk at night.[f] 8But since we belong to the day, let us be self-controlled, putting on faith and love as a breastplate,[g] and the hope of salvation[h] as a helmet.[i] 9For God did not appoint us to suffer wrath but to receive salvation through our Lord Jesus Christ.[j] 10He died for us so that, whether we are awake or asleep, we may live together with him.[k] 11Therefore encourage one another and build each other up, just as in fact you are doing.

Final admonitions for holy living.

12Now we ask you, brothers, to respect those who work hard among you, who are over you in the Lord[l] and who admonish you. 13Hold them in the highest regard in love because of their work. Live in peace with each other.[m] 14And we urge you, brothers, warn those who are idle,[n] encourage the timid, help the weak,[o] be patient with everyone. 15Make sure that nobody pays back wrong for wrong,[p] but always try to be kind to each other[q] and to everyone else.

16Be joyful always;[r] 17pray continually; 18give thanks in all circumstances, for this is God's will for you in Christ Jesus.

19Do not put out the Spirit's fire;[s] 20do not treat prophecies[t] with contempt. 21Test everything.[u] Hold on to the good. 22Avoid every kind of evil.

23May God himself, the God of peace,[v] sanctify you through and through. May your whole spirit, soul and body be kept blameless at the coming of our Lord Jesus Christ. 24The one who calls you is faithful[w] and he will do it.

25Brothers, pray for us.[x] 26Greet all the brothers with a holy kiss.[y] 27I charge you before the Lord to have this letter read to all the brothers.[z]

28The grace of our Lord Jesus Christ be with you.[a]

5:1 [a]1Th 4:9 **5:2** [b]1Co 1:8 [c]2Pe 3:10 **5:4** [d]Ac 26:18; 1Jn 2:8 **5:6** [e]Ro 13:11 **5:7** [f]Ac 2:15; 2Pe 2:13 **5:8** [g]Eph 6:14 [h]Ro 8:24 [i]Eph 6:17 **5:9** [j]2Th 2:13,14 **5:10** [k]2Co 5:15 **5:12** [l]1Ti 5:17; Heb 13:17 **5:13** [m]Mk 9:50 **5:14** [n]2Th 3:6, 7,11 [o]Ro 14:1 **5:15** [p]1Pe 3:9 [q]Gal 6:10; Eph 4:32 **5:16** [r]Php 4:4 **5:19** [s]Eph 4:30 **5:20** [t]1Co 14:1-40 **5:21** [u]1Co 14:29; 1Jn 4:1 **5:23** [v]Ro 15:33

5:24 [w]1Co 1:9 **5:25** [x]Eph 6:19 **5:26** [y]Ro 16:16 **5:27** [z]Col 4:16 **5:28** [a]Ro 16:20

2 THESSALONIANS

Author: Paul the Apostle.

Date Written: About A.D. 51, a few months after the first letter to the Thessalonians.

Title: From Paul's second recorded letter to the church at Thessalonica.

Background: The Thessalonian church is confused concerning the second coming of Christ. Either they have misinterpreted Paul's first letter, or they have fallen victim to the deceit of a forged letter claiming to be from the hand of Paul. The church believes Christ's return is about to take place; therefore, many are neglecting their responsibilities and work. They are letting others take care of them while they do nothing more than wait for the Lord's return.

Where Written: Corinth.

To Whom: To the believers at Thessalonica.

Content: In this letter to the Thessalonians, Paul stresses the importance of Christians using their time wisely. They are commended for their spiritual growth and promised judgment of those persecuting them. The conditions that will prevail at the time of Christ's return are outlined, including the great apostasy which will take place. Paul exhorts the Thessalonian church to remain steadfast in their service as the time of Christ's return is not known. But the absolute surety of his coming is known and is the essence of these words from Paul.

Key Words: "Persecution"; "Work." The "persecution" of these new Christians continues from legalistic Jews who will not submit to the Word of God. It is against this background that Paul implores the church not to be idle, but to "work" with patience and diligence.

Themes: • God's presence gives peace in every circumstance. • Do not put off until tomorrow what you can do for God today. • Condemnation awaits those who take pleasure in unrighteousness. • The ministry of the Lord is active, not idle. • Christians should never grow tired of doing good works.

Outline:
1. Salutation. 1:1-1:2
2. Paul's thanksgiving and prayer. 1:3-1:12
3. Concerning the coming of the Lord. 2:1-2:17
4. Exhortation against idleness. 3:1-3:15
5. Final greetings. 3:16-3:18

2 THESSALONIANS

1 Paul, Silas[a] and Timothy,[a]
To the church of the Thessalonians
in God our Father and the Lord Jesus
Christ:
2Grace and peace to you from God the
Father and the Lord Jesus Christ.[b]

Paul commends the Thessalonians for their faith, love and perseverance.

3We ought always to thank God for
you, brothers, and rightly so, because
your faith is growing more and more,
and the love every one of you has for each
other is increasing.[c] 4Therefore, among
God's churches we boast[d] about your
perseverance and faith[e] in all the persecutions and trials you are enduring.[f]

Suffering for God will be rewarded.

5All this is evidence[g] that God's
judgment is right, and as a result you
will be counted worthy of the kingdom
of God, for which you are suffering.
6God is just: He will pay back trouble
to those who trouble you[h] 7and give
relief to you who are troubled, and to
us as well. This will happen when the
Lord Jesus is revealed from heaven in
blazing fire with his powerful angels.[i]
8He will punish those who do not
know God[j] and do not obey the gospel
of our Lord Jesus.[k] 9They will be punished with everlasting destruction[l] and
shut out from the presence of the Lord
and from the majesty of his power[m]
10on the day[n] he comes to be glorified[o]
in his holy people and to be marveled
at among all those who have believed.
This includes you, because you believed
our testimony to you.[p]
11With this in mind, we constantly
pray for you, that our God may count
you worthy[q] of his calling, and that by
his power he may fulfill every good purpose of yours and every act prompted
by your faith.[r] 12We pray this so that the
name of our Lord Jesus may be glorified
in you,[s] and you in him, according to
the grace of our God and the Lord Jesus
Christ.[b]

The man of lawlessness and his deceitful works.

2 Concerning the coming of our Lord
Jesus Christ and our being gathered to him,[t] we ask you, brothers, 2not
to become easily unsettled or alarmed
by some prophecy, report or letter[u] sup-
posed to have come from us, saying that
the day of the Lord[v] has already come.
3Don't let anyone deceive you[w] in any
way, for ⌊that day will not come⌋ until
the rebellion occurs and the man of lawlessness[c] is revealed,[x] the man doomed
to destruction. 4He will oppose and will
exalt himself over everything that is
called God[y] or is worshiped, so that he
sets himself up in God's temple, proclaiming himself to be God.[z]
5Don't you remember that when I
was with you I used to tell you these
things? 6And now you know what is
holding him back, so that he may be
revealed at the proper time. 7For the
secret power of lawlessness is already
at work; but the one who now holds it
back will continue to do so till he is
taken out of the way. 8And then the
lawless one will be revealed, whom
the Lord Jesus will overthrow with the
breath of his mouth[a] and destroy by
the splendor of his coming. 9The coming of the lawless one will be in accordance with the work of Satan displayed
in all kinds of counterfeit miracles, signs
and wonders,[b] 10and in every sort of evil
that deceives those who are perishing.[c]
They perish because they refused to love
the truth and so be saved. 11For this reason God sends them[d] a powerful delusion so that they will believe the lie
12and so that all will be condemned who
have not believed the truth but have
delighted in wickedness.[e]

1:1 [a]Ac 16:1; 1Th 1:1
1:2 [b]Ro 1:7
1:3 [c]1Th 3:12
1:4 [d]2Co 7:14 [e]1Th 1:3 [f]1Th 2:14
1:5 [g]Php 1:28
1:6 [h]Col 3:25; Rev 6:10
1:7 [i]1Th 4:16; Jude 14
1:8 [j]Gal 4:8 [k]Ro 2:8
1:9 [l]Php 3:19; 2Pe 3:7 [m]2Th 2:8
1:10 [n]1Co 3:13 [o]Jn 17:10 [p]1Co 1:6
1:11 [q]ver 5 [r]1Th 1:3
1:12 [s]Php 2:9-11
2:1 [t]Mk 13:27; 1Th 4:15-17
2:2 [u]2Th 3:17 [v]1Co 1:8
2:3 [w]Eph 5:6-8 [x]Da 7:25; 8:25; 11:36; Rev 13:5,6
2:4 [y]1Co 8:5 [z]Isa 14:13,14; Eze 28:2
2:8 [a]Isa 11:4; Rev 19:15
2:9 [b]Mt 24:24; Jn 4:48
2:10 [c]1Co 1:18
2:11 [d]Ro 1:28
2:12 [e]Ro 1:32

a*1* Greek *Silvanus*, a variant of *Silas* b*12* Or *God and Lord, Jesus Christ* c*3* Some manuscripts *sin*

Standing firm in the truth.

13 But we ought always to thank God
for you, brothers loved by the Lord,
because from the beginning God chose
you[d][a] to be saved[b] through the sanctifying work of the Spirit[c] and through
belief in the truth. 14 He called you to
this through our gospel, that you might
share in the glory of our Lord Jesus
Christ. 15 So then, brothers, stand firm[d]
and hold to the teachings[e] we passed on
to you,[e] whether by word of mouth or
by letter.
16 May our Lord Jesus Christ himself
and God our Father, who loved us[f] and
by his grace gave us eternal encouragement and good hope, 17 encourage[g] your
hearts and strengthen[h] you in every
good deed and word.

Paul asks for prayers.

3 Finally, brothers,[i] pray for us[j] that
the message of the Lord[k] may
spread rapidly and be honored, just as
it was with you. 2 And pray that we may
be delivered from wicked and evil men,[l]
for not everyone has faith. 3 But the Lord
is faithful,[m] and he will strengthen and
protect you from the evil one.[n] 4 We have
confidence[o] in the Lord that you are
doing and will continue to do the things
we command. 5 May the Lord direct your
hearts[p] into God's love and Christ's perseverance.

Paul warns against idleness.

6 In the name of the Lord Jesus
Christ,[q] we command you, brothers, to
keep away from[r] every brother who is
idle[s] and does not live according to the
teaching[f] you received from us.[t] 7 For
you yourselves know how you ought to
follow our example.[u] We were not idle
when we were with you, 8 nor did we
eat anyone's food without paying for it.
On the contrary, we worked[v] night and
day, laboring and toiling so that we
would not be a burden to any of you.
9 We did this, not because we do not
have the right to such help,[w] but in
order to make ourselves a model for you
to follow.[x] 10 For even when we were
with you,[y] we gave you this rule: "If a
man will not work,[z] he shall not eat."
11 We hear that some among you are
idle. They are not busy; they are busybodies.[a] 12 Such people we command
and urge in the Lord Jesus Christ[b] to
settle down and earn the bread they
eat.[c] 13 And as for you, brothers, never
tire of doing what is right.[d]
14 If anyone does not obey our instruction in this letter, take special note of
him. Do not associate with him,[e] in
order that he may feel ashamed. 15 Yet
do not regard him as an enemy, but
warn him as a brother.[f]

Final greetings.

16 Now may the Lord of peace[g] himself
give you peace at all times and in every
way. The Lord be with all of you.[h]
17 I, Paul, write this greeting in my own
hand,[i] which is the distinguishing mark
in all my letters. This is how I write.
18 The grace of our Lord Jesus Christ
be with you all.[j]

2:13 [a] Eph 1:4 [b] 1Th 5:9 [c] 1Pe 1:2
2:15 [d] 1Co 16:13 [e] 1Co 11:2
2:16 [f] Jn 3:16
2:17 [g] 1Th 3:2 [h] 2Th 3:3
3:1 [i] 1Th 4:1 [j] 1Th 5:25 [k] 1Th 1:8
3:2 [l] Ro 15:31
3:3 [m] 1Co 1:9 [n] Mt 5:37
3:4 [o] 2Co 2:3
3:5 [p] 1Ch 29:18
3:6 [q] 1Co 5:4 [r] Ro 16:17 [s] ver 7,11 [t] 1Co 11:2
3:7 [u] 1Co 4:16
3:8 [v] Ac 18:3; Eph 4:28
3:9 [w] 1Co 9:4-14 [x] ver 7
3:10 [y] 1Th 3:4 [z] 1Th 4:11
3:11 [a] ver 6,7; 1Ti 5:13
3:12 [b] 1Th 4:1 [c] 1Th 4:11; Eph 4:28
3:13 [d] Gal 6:9
3:14 [e] ver 6
3:15 [f] Gal 6:1; 1Th 5:14
3:16 [g] Ro 15:33 [h] Ru 2:4 **3:17** [i] 1Co 16:21
3:18 [j] Ro 16:20

d *13* Some manuscripts *because God chose you as his firstfruits* e *15* Or *traditions* f *6* Or *tradition*

1 TIMOTHY

Author: Paul the Apostle.

Date Written: Between A.D. 62 and 64.

Title: From Paul's first recorded letter to his associate: Timothy.

Background: Timothy, born in Lystra, is the son of a devout Jewish woman named Eunice. His spiritual strength and physical weakness, characteristics much like Paul's, make him an ideal co-laborer with Paul. Paul leaves Timothy in Ephesus to give guidance to the church there, which is experiencing some problems. The young and timid Timothy is inexperienced in such pastoral concerns, however, so Paul writes this letter to encourage Timothy and to give his "true son" advice on spiritual leadership and development of a godly church.

Where Written: Possibly the Macedonian city of Philippi.

To Whom: To Timothy.

Content: This personal letter from Paul to his close ally Timothy serves several purposes. It offers hope and comfort to keep young Timothy on the right path and is a sign for the church that Timothy has the express backing and support of the apostle Paul. Paul offers Timothy advice for his congregation on these concerns: proper worship; qualifications for church officers; relationships with widows, elders and slaves; and the danger of loving money. Admonitions permeate the letter with counsel to help the Christians live godly lives in a healthy church committed to following good and fleeing evil.

Key Words: "Doctrine"; "Qualifications." Paul exhorts Timothy to remain true to God's ways and to follow no other "doctrine." Specific examples of God's ways include a list of the "qualifications" which the Lord has given for the church's leadership.

Themes: • There is only one true doctrine, and only committed Christians are capable of living within it. • What we really believe as doctrine will be exhibited by our attitudes and actions. • Age is no barrier to being used mightily by God. • True leadership is God-given, not man-made. • As an athlete must train, so a Christian must exercise and discipline his faith.

Outline:

1. Law versus faith. 1:1-2:15
2. Instructions on church offices. 3:1-3:16
3. Advice to Timothy concerning false teachings. 4:1-4:16
4. Advice to Timothy concerning church discipline. 5:1-6:2
5. Dangers of loving money. 6:3-6:21

1 TIMOTHY

1 Paul, an apostle of Christ Jesus by
the command of God[a] our Savior and
of Christ Jesus our hope,[b]

2To Timothy[c] my true son[d] in the
faith:

Grace, mercy and peace from God the
Father and Christ Jesus our Lord.

Timothy is warned against false teachers.

3As I urged you when I went into
Macedonia, stay there in Ephesus[e] so
that you may command certain men not
to teach false doctrines[f] any longer **4**nor
to devote themselves to myths[g] and
endless genealogies. These promote
controversies[h] rather than God's work—
which is by faith. **5**The goal of this command is love, which comes from a pure
heart[i] and a good conscience and a sincere faith.[j] **6**Some have wandered
away from these and turned to meaningless talk. **7**They want to be teachers
of the law, but they do not know what
they are talking about or what they so
confidently affirm.

8We know that the law is good[k] if one
uses it properly. **9**We also know that
law[a] is made not for the righteous but
for lawbreakers and rebels,[l] the ungodly and sinful, the unholy and irreligious;
for those who kill their fathers or mothers, for murderers, **10**for adulterers and
perverts, for slave traders and liars
and perjurers—and for whatever else
is contrary to the sound doctrine[m]
11that conforms to the glorious gospel
of the blessed God, which he entrusted to me.[n]

Paul is grateful for his salvation.

12I thank Christ Jesus our Lord, who
has given me strength,[o] that he considered me faithful, appointing me to his
service. **13**Even though I was once a blasphemer and a persecutor[p] and a violent man, I was shown mercy because
I acted in ignorance and unbelief.[q]
14The grace of our Lord was poured out
on me abundantly,[r] along with the faith
and love that are in Christ Jesus.[s]

15Here is a trustworthy saying[t] that
deserves full acceptance: Christ Jesus
came into the world to save sinners—
of whom I am the worst. **16**But for that
very reason I was shown mercy[u] so that
in me, the worst of sinners, Christ Jesus
might display his unlimited patience as
an example for those who would believe
on him and receive eternal life. **17**Now
to the King[v] eternal, immortal, invisible,[w] the only God, be honor and glory
for ever and ever. Amen.[x]

18Timothy, my son, I give you this
instruction in keeping with the prophecies once made about you,[y] so that by
following them you may fight the good
fight,[z] **19**holding on to faith and a good
conscience. Some have rejected these
and so have shipwrecked their faith.[a]
20Among them are Hymenaeus[b] and
Alexander,[c] whom I have handed over
to Satan[d] to be taught not to blaspheme.

Prayer is encouraged.

2 I urge, then, first of all, that
requests, prayers, intercession and
thanksgiving be made for everyone—
2for kings and all those in authority,[e]
that we may live peaceful and quiet
lives in all godliness and holiness. **3**This
is good, and pleases God our Savior,
4who wants[f] all men[g] to be saved and
to come to a knowledge of the truth.[h]
5For there is one God[i] and one mediator[j] between God and men, the man
Christ Jesus, **6**who gave himself as a
ransom for all men—the testimony[k] giv-
en in its proper time.[l] **7**And for this
purpose I was appointed a herald and an
apostle—I am telling the truth, I am not
lying—and a teacher[m] of the true faith
to the Gentiles.[n]

8I want men everywhere to lift up

1:1 [a]Tit 1:3 [b]Col 1:27 **1:2** [c]Ac 16:1 [d]2Ti 1:2; Tit 1:4 **1:3** [e]Ac 18:19 [f]Gal 1:6,7 **1:4** [g]1Ti 4:7; Tit 1:14 [h]1Ti 6:4 **1:5** [i]2Ti 2:22 [j]2Ti 1:5 **1:8** [k]Ro 7:12 **1:9** [l]Gal 3:19 **1:10** [m]2Ti 4:3; Tit 1:9 **1:11** [n]Gal 2:7 **1:12** [o]Php 4:13 **1:13** [p]Ac 8:3 [q]Ac 26:9 **1:14** [r]Ro 5:20 [s]2Ti 1:13 **1:15** [t]1Ti 3:1; 2Ti 2:11; Tit 3:8 **1:16** [u]ver 13 **1:17** [v]Rev 15:3 [w]Col 1:15 [x]Ro 11:36 **1:18** [y]1Ti 4:14 [z]2Ti 2:3 **1:19** [a]1Ti 6:21 **1:20** [b]2Ti 2:17 [c]2Ti 4:14 [d]1Co 5:5 **2:2** [e]Ezr 6:10; Ro 13:1 **2:4** [f]Eze 18:23,32 [g]Tit 2:11 [h]2Ti 2:25 **2:5** [i]Ro 3:29,30 [j]Gal 3:20 **2:6** [k]1Co 1:6 [l]1Ti 6:15

2:7 [m]2Ti 1:11 [n]Ac 9:15; Eph 3:7,8

[a]9 Or *that the law*

holy hands[a] in prayer, without anger or disputing.

Instructions are given on proper dress and conduct for women in the church.

9I also want women to dress modestly, with decency and propriety, not with braided hair or gold or pearls or expensive clothes,[b] 10but with good deeds, appropriate for women who profess to worship God.

11A woman should learn in quietness and full submission.[c] 12I do not permit a woman to teach or to have authority over a man; she must be silent. 13For Adam was formed first, then Eve.[d] 14And Adam was not the one deceived; it was the woman who was deceived and became a sinner.[e] 15But women[b] will be saved[c] through childbearing—if they continue in faith, love[f] and holiness with propriety.

Guidelines for the church's leadership.

3 Here is a trustworthy saying:[g] If anyone sets his heart on being an overseer,[d][h] he desires a noble task. 2Now the overseer must be above reproach,[i] the husband of but one wife, temperate, self-controlled, respectable, hospitable,[j] able to teach,[k] 3not given to drunkenness, not violent but gentle, not quarrelsome,[l] not a lover of money.[m] 4He must manage his own family well and see that his children obey him with proper respect.[n] 5(If anyone does not know how to manage his own family, how can he take care of God's church?)[o] 6He must not be a recent convert, or he may become conceited[p] and fall under the same judgment as the devil. 7He must also have a good reputation with outsiders, so that he will not fall into disgrace and into the devil's trap.[q]

8Deacons,[r] likewise, are to be men worthy of respect, sincere, not indulging in much wine,[s] and not pursuing dishonest gain. 9They must keep hold of the deep truths of the faith with a clear conscience.[t] 10They must first be tested; and then if there is nothing against them, let them serve as deacons.

11In the same way, their wives[e] are to be women worthy of respect, not malicious talkers[u] but temperate and trustworthy in everything.

12A deacon must be the husband of but one wife and must manage his children and his household well.[v] 13Those who have served well gain an excellent standing and great assurance in their faith in Christ Jesus.

14Although I hope to come to you soon, I am writing you these instructions so that, 15if I am delayed, you will know how people ought to conduct themselves in God's household, which is the church[w] of the living God, the pillar and foundation of the truth. 16Beyond all question, the mystery[x] of godliness is great:

He[f] appeared in a body,[g][y]
 was vindicated by the Spirit,
was seen by angels,
 was preached among the nations,[z]
was believed on in the world,
 was taken up in glory.[a]

Paul predicts the coming of false teachers.

4 The Spirit[b] clearly says that in later times[c] some will abandon the faith and follow deceiving spirits[d] and things taught by demons. 2Such teachings come through hypocritical liars, whose consciences have been seared as with a hot iron.[e] 3They forbid people to marry[f] and order them to abstain from certain foods,[g] which God created[h] to be received with thanksgiving[i] by those who believe and who know the truth. 4For everything God created is good,[j] and nothing is to be rejected if it is received with thanksgiving, 5because it is consecrated by the word of God and prayer.

2:8 [a]Ps 134:2; Lk 24:50
2:9 [b]1Pe 3:3
2:11 [c]1Co 14:34
2:13 [d]Ge 2:7,22; 1Co 11:8
2:14 [e]Ge 3:1-6,13; 2Co 11:3
2:15 [f]1Ti 1:14
3:1 [g]1Ti 1:15 [h]Ac 20:28
3:2 [i]Tit 1:6-8 [j]Ro 12:13 [k]2Ti 2:24
3:3 [l]2Ti 2:24 [m]Heb 13:5; 1Pe 5:2
3:4 [n]Tit 1:6
3:5 [o]1Co 10:32
3:6 [p]1Ti 6:4
3:7 [q]2Ti 2:26
3:8 [r]Php 1:1 [s]Tit 2:3
3:9 [t]1Ti 1:19
3:11 [u]2Ti 3:3; Tit 2:3
3:12 [v]ver 4
3:15 [w]ver 5; Eph 2:21
3:16 [x]Ro 16:25 [y]Jn 1:14 [z]Col 1:23 [a]Mk 16:19
4:1 [b]Jn 16:13 [c]2Ti 3:1 [d]2Th 2:3
4:2 [e]Eph 4:19
4:3 [f]Heb 13:4 [g]Col 2:16 [h]Ge 1:29 [i]Ro 14:6
4:4 [j]Ro 14:14-18

[b] *15* Greek *she* [c] *15* Or *restored* [d] *1* Traditionally *bishop*; also in verse 2 [e] *11* Or *way, deaconesses* [f] *16* Some manuscripts *God* [g] *16* Or *in the flesh*

Paul charges Timothy to promote the truth of God's Word.

6If you point these things out to the
brothers, you will be a good minister
of Christ Jesus, brought up in the truths
of the faith[a] and of the good teaching
that you have followed. 7Have nothing
to do with godless myths and old wives'
tales;[b] rather, train yourself to be godly.
8For physical training is of some value,
but godliness has value for all things,[c]
holding promise for both the present
life[d] and the life to come.
9This is a trustworthy saying[e] that
deserves full acceptance 10(and for this
we labor and strive), that we have put
our hope in the living God, who is the
Savior of all men, and especially of those
who believe.
11Command and teach these things.[f]
12Don't let anyone look down on you
because you are young, but set an
example[g] for the believers in speech,
in life, in love, in faith[h] and in purity.
13Until I come, devote yourself to the
public reading of Scripture, to preaching
and to teaching. 14Do not neglect your
gift, which was given you through a
prophetic message[i] when the body of
elders laid their hands on you.[j]
15Be diligent in these matters; give
yourself wholly to them, so that everyone may see your progress. 16Watch
your life and doctrine closely. Persevere
in them, because if you do, you will save
both yourself and your hearers.

The church's proper treatment of widows.

5 Do not rebuke an older man[k] harshly,[l] but exhort him as if he were
your father. Treat younger men[m] as
brothers, 2older women as mothers, and
younger women as sisters, with absolute purity.
3Give proper recognition to those
widows who are really in need.[n] 4But if
a widow has children or grandchildren,
these should learn first of all to put
their religion into practice by caring for
their own family and so repaying their
parents and grandparents,[o] for this is
pleasing to God.[p] 5The widow who is
really in need[q] and left all alone puts
her hope in God[r] and continues night
and day to pray[s] and to ask God for
help. 6But the widow who lives for
pleasure is dead even while she lives.[t]
7Give the people these instructions,[u]
too, so that no one may be open to
blame. 8If anyone does not provide for
his relatives, and especially for his
immediate family, he has denied[v] the
faith and is worse than an unbeliever.
9No widow may be put on the list of
widows unless she is over sixty, has
been faithful to her husband,[h] 10and is
well known for her good deeds,[w] such
as bringing up children, showing hospitality, washing the feet[x] of the saints,
helping those in trouble[y] and devoting
herself to all kinds of good deeds.
11As for younger widows, do not put
them on such a list. For when their sensual desires overcome their dedication
to Christ, they want to marry. 12Thus
they bring judgment on themselves,
because they have broken their first
pledge. 13Besides, they get into the habit
of being idle and going about from
house to house. And not only do they
become idlers, but also gossips and
busybodies,[z] saying things they ought
not to. 14So I counsel younger widows
to marry,[a] to have children, to manage
their homes and to give the enemy no
opportunity for slander.[b] 15Some have in
fact already turned away to follow
Satan.[c]
16If any woman who is a believer
has widows in her family, she should
help them and not let the church be
burdened with them, so that the church
can help those widows who are really
in need.[d]

The church's proper treatment of elders.

17The elders[e] who direct the affairs
of the church well are worthy of double
honor,[f] especially those whose work is

4:6 [a]1Ti 1:10
4:7 [b]2Ti 2:16
4:8 [c]1Ti 6:6 [d]Ps 37:9,11; Mk 10:29,30
4:9 [e]1Ti 1:15
4:11 [f]1Ti 5:7; 6:2
4:12 [g]Tit 2:7; 1Pe 5:3 [h]1Ti 1:14
4:14 [i]1Ti 1:18 [j]Ac 6:6; 2Ti 1:6
5:1 [k]Tit 2:2 [l]Lev 19:32 [m]Tit 2:6
5:3 [n]ver 5,16
5:4 [o]Eph 6:1,2 [p]1Ti 2:3
5:5 [q]ver 3,16 [r]1Co 7:34; 1Pe 3:5 [s]Lk 2:37
5:6 [t]Lk 15:24
5:7 [u]1Ti 4:11
5:8 [v]2Pe 2:1; Jude 4; Tit 1:16
5:10 [w]Ac 9:36; 1Ti 6:18; 1Pe 2:12 [x]Lk 7:44 [y]ver 16
5:13 [z]2Th 3:11
5:14 [a]1Co 7:9 [b]1Ti 6:1
5:15 [c]Mt 4:10
5:16 [d]ver 3-5
5:17 [e]Ac 11:30 [f]Php 2:29; 1Th 5:12

h 9 Or *has had but one husband*

preaching and teaching. 18For the Scripture says, "Do not muzzle the ox while it is treading out the grain,"[i][a] and "The worker deserves his wages."[j][b] 19Do not entertain an accusation against an elder[c] unless it is brought by two or three witnesses.[d] 20Those who sin are to be rebuked[e] publicly, so that the others may take warning.[f]

21I charge you, in the sight of God and Christ Jesus[g] and the elect angels, to keep these instructions without partiality, and to do nothing out of favoritism.

22Do not be hasty in the laying on of hands,[h] and do not share in the sins of others.[i] Keep yourself pure.

23Stop drinking only water, and use a little wine[j] because of your stomach and your frequent illnesses.

24The sins of some men are obvious, reaching the place of judgment ahead of them; the sins of others trail behind them. 25In the same way, good deeds are obvious, and even those that are not cannot be hidden.

Proper attitude of the slave.

6 All who are under the yoke of slavery should consider their masters worthy of full respect,[k] so that God's name and our teaching may not be slandered.[l] 2Those who have believing masters are not to show less respect for them because they are brothers.[m] Instead, they are to serve them even better, because those who benefit from their service are believers, and dear to them. These are the things you are to teach and urge on them.[n]

Danger of loving money.

3If anyone teaches false doctrines[o] and does not agree to the sound instruction[p] of our Lord Jesus Christ and to godly teaching, 4he is conceited and understands nothing. He has an unhealthy interest in controversies and quarrels about words[q] that result in envy, strife, malicious talk, evil suspicions 5and constant friction between men of corrupt mind, who have been robbed of the truth[r] and who think that godliness is a means to financial gain.

6But godliness with contentment[s] is great gain.[t] 7For we brought nothing into the world, and we can take nothing out of it.[u] 8But if we have food and clothing, we will be content with that.[v] 9People who want to get rich[w] fall into temptation and a trap[x] and into many foolish and harmful desires that plunge men into ruin and destruction. 10For the love of money[y] is a root of all kinds of evil. Some people, eager for money, have wandered from the faith[z] and pierced themselves with many griefs.

Paul's charge to Timothy.

11But you, man of God,[a] flee from all this, and pursue righteousness, godliness, faith, love,[b] endurance and gentleness. 12Fight the good fight[c] of the faith. Take hold of[d] the eternal life to which you were called when you made your good confession in the presence of many witnesses. 13In the sight of God, who gives life to everything, and of Christ Jesus, who while testifying before Pontius Pilate[e] made the good confession, I charge you[f] 14to keep this command without spot or blame until the appearing of our Lord Jesus Christ, 15which God will bring about in his own time—God, the blessed[g] and only Ruler,[h] the King of kings and Lord of lords,[i] 16who alone is immortal[j] and who lives in unapproachable light, whom no one has seen or can see.[k] To him be honor and might forever. Amen.

Proper use of riches.

17Command those who are rich in this present world not to be arrogant nor to put their hope in wealth,[l] which is so uncertain, but to put their hope in God,[m] who richly provides us with everything for our enjoyment.[n] 18Command them to do good, to be rich in

5:18 [a]Dt 25:4; 1Co 9:7-9 [b]Lk 10:7; Lev 19:13; Dt 24:14,15; Mt 10:10; 1Co 9:14
5:19 [c]Ac 11:30 [d]Mt 18:16
5:20 [e]2Ti 4:2; Tit 1:13 [f]Dt 13:11
5:21 [g]1Ti 6:13; 2Ti 4:1
5:22 [h]Ac 6:6 [i]Eph 5:11
5:23 [j]1Ti 3:8
6:1 [k]Eph 6:5; Tit 2:9; 1Pe 2:18 [l]Tit 2:5,8
6:2 [m]Phm 16 [n]1Ti 4:11
6:3 [o]1Ti 1:3 [p]1Ti 1:10
6:4 [q]2Ti 2:14
6:5 [r]Tit 1:15
6:6 [s]Php 4:11; Heb 13:5 [t]1Ti 4:8
6:7 [u]Job 1:21; Ecc 5:15
6:8 [v]Heb 13:5
6:9 [w]Pr 15:27 [x]1Ti 3:7
6:10 [y]1Ti 3:3 [z]Jas 5:19
6:11 [a]2Ti 3:17 [b]2Ti 2:22
6:12 [c]1Co 9:25,26; 1Ti 1:18 [d]Php 3:12
6:13 [e]Jn 18:33-37 [f]1Ti 5:21
6:15 [g]1Ti 1:11 [h]1Ti 1:17 [i]Rev 17:14; 19:16
6:16 [j]1Ti 1:17 [k]Jn 1:18 **6:17** [l]Lk 12:20,21 [m]1Ti 4:10 [n]Ac 14:17

[i]*18* Deut. 25:4 [j]*18* Luke 10:7

good deeds,[a] and to be generous and
willing to share.[b] 19In this way they will
lay up treasure for themselves[c] as a firm
foundation for the coming age, so that
they may take hold of the life that is
truly life.

20Timothy, guard what has been
entrusted[d] to your care. Turn away
from godless chatter[e] and the opposing
ideas of what is falsely called knowledge, 21which some have professed and
in so doing have wandered from the
faith.[f]

Grace be with you.[g]

6:18 [a]1Ti 5:10 [b]Ro 12:8,13
6:19 [c]Mt 6:20
6:20 [d]2Ti 1:12,14 [e]2Ti 2:16
6:21 [f]2Ti 2:18 [g]Col 4:18

2 TIMOTHY

Author: Paul the Apostle.

Date Written: Between A.D. 66 and 67.

Title: From Paul's second recorded letter to his associate: Timothy.

Background: During Paul's first missionary journey John Mark leaves, but Timothy is his able replacement. Through the years Paul and Timothy become like father and son as they co-labor to bring the gospel to the world. But now Paul is alone in a cold, hard Roman prison, and only Luke is with him. As Paul awaits his execution, he uses this occasion to write what is probably his last recorded letter. Paul, longing for Christian fellowship, is anxious for Timothy to come see him at Rome before winter sets in.

Where Written: Probably from a Roman prison.

To Whom: To Timothy.

Content: In spite of Paul's dismal circumstances, his primary concern is for Timothy and his ministry since Paul is certain that when his own death comes, God will have an eternal home waiting for him in heaven. Paul admonishes Timothy to never be ashamed of the gospel, but to persevere in faith and obedience. He then instructs that in the last days there will be a devastating turn away from God as men glorify sin, and that those who harm the ministry of Christ should be avoided. The Word of God is presented as the power and inspiration of God to complete and equip the believer for service. Paul concludes by asking Timothy to come see him soon.

Key Words: "Endure"; "Teach." Even as Paul has remained strong while in prison, he encourages Timothy to "endure" his trials as a good soldier of Jesus Christ. Timothy is admonished to flee youthful lusts and to follow faith and righteousness. Then he can "teach" the things of God to reliable men who will be qualified to "teach" others (2:2).

Themes: • The Spirit God gives his children is not one of timidity...it is one of power, love and self-discipline (1:7). • Persecution is a certainty for those committed to living for Jesus. • "All Scripture is God-breathed..." (3:16). • Christians should avoid disputes and quarrels. • Though all may forsake us, God will always remain true.

Outline:

1. Salutation. 1:1-1:2
2. Encouragement to be faithful. 1:3-2:26
3. Apostasy in the last days. 3:1-3:17
4. Charge to preach the Word. 4:1-4:5
5. Approach of Paul's death. 4:6-4:18
6. Paul's final greetings. 4:19-4:22

2 TIMOTHY

1 Paul, an apostle of Christ Jesus by the will of God,[a] according to the promise of life that is in Christ Jesus,[b]

2To Timothy,[c] my dear son:[d]

Grace, mercy and peace from God the Father and Christ Jesus our Lord.

Paul charges Timothy to be bold for Christ.

3I thank God,[e] whom I serve, as my forefathers did, with a clear conscience, as night and day I constantly remember you in my prayers.[f] 4Recalling your tears,[g] I long to see you,[h] so that I may be filled with joy. 5I have been reminded of your sincere faith,[i] which first lived in your grandmother Lois and in your mother Eunice[j] and, I am persuaded, now lives in you also. 6For this reason I remind you to fan into flame the gift of God, which is in you through the laying on of my hands.[k] 7For God did not give us a spirit of timidity,[l] but a spirit of power, of love and of self-discipline.

8So do not be ashamed[m] to testify about our Lord, or ashamed of me his prisoner.[n] But join with me in suffering for the gospel,[o] by the power of God, 9who has saved us and called[p] us to a holy life—not because of anything we have done but because of his own purpose and grace. This grace was given us in Christ Jesus before the beginning of time, 10but it has now been revealed[q] through the appearing of our Savior, Christ Jesus, who has destroyed death[r] and has brought life and immortality to light through the gospel. 11And of this gospel I was appointed a herald and an apostle and a teacher.[s] 12That is why I am suffering as I am. Yet I am not ashamed, because I know whom I have believed, and am convinced that he is able to guard[t] what I have entrusted to him for that day.[u]

13What you heard from me, keep[v] as the pattern of sound teaching, with faith and love in Christ Jesus.[w] 14Guard the good deposit that was entrusted to you—guard it with the help of the Holy Spirit who lives in us.[x]

15You know that everyone in the province of Asia has deserted me,[y] including Phygelus and Hermogenes.

16May the Lord show mercy to the household of Onesiphorus,[z] because he often refreshed me and was not ashamed of my chains. 17On the contrary, when he was in Rome, he searched hard for me until he found me. 18May the Lord grant that he will find mercy from the Lord on that day! You know very well in how many ways he helped me[a] in Ephesus.

Serving Christ is illustrated by a soldier, an athlete and a farmer.

2 You then, my son, be strong[b] in the grace that is in Christ Jesus. 2And the things you have heard me say[c] in the presence of many witnesses[d] entrust to reliable men who will also be qualified to teach others. 3Endure hardship with us like a good soldier[e] of Christ Jesus. 4No one serving as a soldier gets involved in civilian affairs—he wants to please his commanding officer. 5Similarly, if anyone competes as an athlete, he does not receive the victor's crown[f] unless he competes according to the rules. 6The hardworking farmer should be the first to receive a share of the crops. 7Reflect on what I am saying, for the Lord will give you insight into all this.

8Remember Jesus Christ, raised from the dead,[g] descended from David.[h] This is my gospel,[i] 9for which I am suffering[j] even to the point of being chained like a criminal. But God's word is not chained. 10Therefore I endure everything[k] for the sake of the elect, that they too may obtain the salvation that is in Christ Jesus, with eternal glory.[l]

11Here is a trustworthy saying:

If we died with him,
we will also live with him;[m]

1:1 [a]2Co 1:1 [b]Eph 3:6; 1Ti 6:19
1:2 [c]Ac 16:1 [d]1Ti 1:2
1:3 [e]Ro 1:8 [f]Ro 1:10
1:4 [g]Ac 20:37 [h]2Ti 4:9
1:5 [i]1Ti 1:5 [j]Ac 16:1
1:6 [k]1Ti 4:14
1:7 [l]Ro 8:15
1:8 [m]Mk 8:38; Ro 1:16 [n]Eph 3:1 [o]2Ti 2:3,9; 4:5
1:9 [p]Ro 8:28
1:10 [q]Eph 1:9 [r]1Co 15:26, 54
1:11 [s]1Ti 2:7
1:12 [t]1Ti 6:20 [u]ver 18
1:13 [v]Tit 1:9 [w]1Ti 1:14
1:14 [x]Ro 8:9
1:15 [y]2Ti 4:10,11, 16
1:16 [z]2Ti 4:19
1:18 [a]Heb 6:10
2:1 [b]Eph 6:10
2:2 [c]2Ti 1:13 [d]1Ti 6:12
2:3 [e]1Ti 1:18
2:5 [f]1Co 9:25
2:8 [g]Ac 2:24 [h]Mt 1:1 [i]Ro 2:16
2:9 [j]Ac 9:16
2:10 [k]Col 1:24 [l]2Co 4:17

2:11 [m]Ro 6:2-11

12if we endure,
we will also reign with him.[a]
If we disown him,
he will also disown us;[b]
13if we are faithless,
he will remain faithful,[c]
for he cannot disown himself.

Know the Word of God and avoid arguments.

14Keep reminding them of these
things. Warn them before God against
quarreling about words;[d] it is of no value, and only ruins those who listen.
15Do your best to present yourself to
God as one approved, a workman who
does not need to be ashamed and who
correctly handles the word of truth.[e]
16Avoid godless chatter,[f] because those
who indulge in it will become more and
more ungodly. 17Their teaching will
spread like gangrene. Among them are
Hymenaeus[g] and Philetus, 18who have
wandered away from the truth. They
say that the resurrection has already tak-
en place, and they destroy the faith of
some.[h] 19Nevertheless, God's solid foundation stands firm,[i] sealed with this
inscription: "The Lord knows those who
are his,"[a][j] and, "Everyone who confesses the name of the Lord[k] must turn
away from wickedness."

20In a large house there are articles
not only of gold and silver, but also of
wood and clay; some are for noble purposes and some for ignoble.[l] 21If a man
cleanses himself from the latter, he will
be an instrument for noble purposes,
made holy, useful to the Master and prepared to do any good work.[m]

22Flee the evil desires of youth, and
pursue righteousness, faith, love[n] and
peace, along with those who call on the
Lord out of a pure heart.[o] 23Don't have
anything to do with foolish and stupid
arguments, because you know they produce quarrels. 24And the Lord's servant
must not quarrel; instead, he must be
kind to everyone, able to teach, not
resentful.[p] 25Those who oppose him he
must gently instruct, in the hope that
God will grant them repentance leading
them to a knowledge of the truth,[q]
26and that they will come to their senses
and escape from the trap of the devil,[r]
who has taken them captive to do his
will.

Rampant sin in the last days.

3 But mark this: There will be terrible times in the last days.[s] 2People
will be lovers of themselves, lovers of
money,[t] boastful, proud,[u] abusive, disobedient to their parents,[v] ungrateful,
unholy, 3without love, unforgiving, slanderous, without self-control, brutal, not
lovers of the good, 4treacherous, rash,
conceited,[w] lovers of pleasure rather
than lovers of God— 5having a form of
godliness but denying its power. Have
nothing to do with them.

6They are the kind who worm their
way[x] into homes and gain control over
weak-willed women, who are loaded
down with sins and are swayed by all
kinds of evil desires, 7always learning
but never able to acknowledge the truth.
8Just as Jannes and Jambres opposed
Moses,[y] so also these men oppose[z] the
truth—men of depraved minds,[a] who,
as far as the faith is concerned, are
rejected. 9But they will not get very far
because, as in the case of those men,[b]
their folly will be clear to everyone.

Paul's example and teaching on Scripture.

10You, however, know all about my
teaching,[c] my way of life, my purpose,
faith, patience, love, endurance, 11per-
secutions, sufferings—what kinds of
things happened to me in Antioch,[d] Iconium and Lystra, the persecutions I
endured.[e] Yet the Lord rescued me from
all of them.[f] 12In fact, everyone who
wants to live a godly life in Christ Jesus
will be persecuted,[g] 13while evil men
and impostors will go from bad to
worse,[h] deceiving and being deceived.
14But as for you, continue in what you

2:12 [a]Ro 8:17; 1Pe 4:13 [b]Mt 10:33
2:13 [c]Nu 23:19; Ro 3:3
2:14 [d]1Ti 6:4
2:15 [e]Eph 1:13; Jas 1:18
2:16 [f]Tit 3:9
2:17 [g]1Ti 1:20
2:18 [h]1Ti 1:19
2:19 [i]Isa 28:16 [j]Jn 10:14 [k]1Co 1:2
2:20 [l]Ro 9:21
2:21 [m]2Ti 3:17
2:22 [n]1Ti 1:14; 6:11 [o]1Ti 1:5
2:24 [p]1Ti 3:2,3
2:25 [q]1Ti 2:4
2:26 [r]1Ti 3:7
3:1 [s]1Ti 4:1
3:2 [t]1Ti 3:3 [u]Ro 1:30 [v]Ro 1:30
3:4 [w]1Ti 3:6
3:6 [x]Jude 4
3:8 [y]Ex 7:11 [z]Ac 13:8 [a]1Ti 6:5
3:9 [b]Ex 7:12
3:10 [c]1Ti 4:6
3:11 [d]Ac 13:14,50 [e]2Co 11:23-27 [f]Ps 34:19
3:12 [g]Ac 14:22
3:13 [h]2Ti 2:16

a *19* Num. 16:5 (see Septuagint)

have learned and have become convinced of, because you know those from whom you learned it,[a] 15 and how from infancy[b] you have known the holy Scriptures,[c] which are able to make you wise[d] for salvation through faith in Christ Jesus. 16 All Scripture is God-breathed[e] and is useful for teaching,[f] rebuking, correcting and training in righteousness, 17 so that the man of God[g] may be thoroughly equipped for every good work.[h]

Timothy is exhorted to preach the Word of God.

4 In the presence of God and of Christ Jesus, who will judge the living and the dead,[i] and in view of his appearing and his kingdom, I give you this charge:[j] 2 Preach[k] the Word;[l] be prepared in season and out of season; correct, rebuke[m] and encourage—with great patience and careful instruction. 3 For the time will come when men will not put up with sound doctrine.[n] Instead, to suit their own desires, they will gather around them a great number of teachers to say what their itching ears want to hear. 4 They will turn their ears away from the truth and turn aside to myths.[o] 5 But you, keep your head in all situations, endure hardship,[p] do the work of an evangelist,[q] discharge all the duties of your ministry.

Paul's death draws near.

6 For I am already being poured out like a drink offering,[r] and the time has come for my departure.[s] 7 I have fought the good fight,[t] I have finished the race,[u] I have kept the faith. 8 Now there is in store for me[v] the crown of righteousness, which the Lord, the righteous Judge, will award to me on that day[w]—and not only to me, but also to all who have longed for his appearing.

3:14 [a]2Ti 1:13
3:15 [b]2Ti 1:5 [c]Jn 5:39 [d]Ps 119:98, 99
3:16 [e]2Pe 1:20,21 [f]Ro 4:23,24
3:17 [g]1Ti 6:11 [h]2Ti 2:21
4:1 [i]Ac 10:42 [j]1Ti 5:21
4:2 [k]1Ti 4:13 [l]Gal 6:6 [m]1Ti 5:20; Tit 1:13; 2:15
4:3 [n]1Ti 1:10
4:4 [o]1Ti 1:4
4:5 [p]2Ti 1:8 [q]Ac 21:8
4:6 [r]Php 2:17 [s]Php 1:23
4:7 [t]1Ti 1:18 [u]1Co 9:24
4:8 [v]Col 1:5 [w]2Ti 1:12
4:10 [x]Col 4:14 [y]1Jn 2:15 [z]Ac 16:6
4:11 [a]Col 4:14 [b]2Ti 1:15 [c]Ac 12:12
4:12 [d]Ac 20:4
4:14 [e]Ac 19:33 [f]Ro 12:19
4:16 [g]Ac 7:60
4:17 [h]Ac 23:11 [i]Ac 9:15
4:18 [j]Ps 121:7 [k]Ro 11:36
4:19 [l]Ac 18:2

Only Luke is with Paul.

9 Do your best to come to me quickly, 10 for Demas,[x] because he loved this world,[y] has deserted me and has gone to Thessalonica. Crescens has gone to Galatia,[z] and Titus to Dalmatia. 11 Only Luke[a] is with me.[b] Get Mark[c] and bring him with you, because he is helpful to me in my ministry. 12 I sent Tychicus[d] to Ephesus. 13 When you come, bring the cloak that I left with Carpus at Troas, and my scrolls, especially the parchments.

14 Alexander[e] the metalworker did me a great deal of harm. The Lord will repay him for what he has done.[f] 15 You too should be on your guard against him, because he strongly opposed our message.

16 At my first defense, no one came to my support, but everyone deserted me. May it not be held against them.[g] 17 But the Lord stood at my side[h] and gave me strength, so that through me the message might be fully proclaimed and all the Gentiles might hear it.[i] And I was delivered from the lion's mouth. 18 The Lord will rescue me from every evil attack[j] and will bring me safely to his heavenly kingdom. To him be glory for ever and ever. Amen.[k]

Final greetings.

19 Greet Priscilla[b] and Aquila[l] and the household of Onesiphorus. 20 Erastus[m] stayed in Corinth, and I left Trophimus[n] sick in Miletus. 21 Do your best to get here before winter.[o] Eubulus greets you, and so do Pudens, Linus, Claudia and all the brothers.

22 The Lord be with your spirit.[p] Grace be with you.[q]

4:20 [m]Ac 19:22 [n]Ac 20:4 **4:21** [o]ver 9
4:22 [p]Gal 6:18; Phm 25 [q]Col 4:18

[b]*19* Greek *Prisca*, a variant of *Priscilla*

TITUS

Author: Paul the Apostle.

Date Written: Between A.D. 63 and 65.

Title: Refers to the addressee of this letter: Titus.

Background: Titus is a Greek Gentile convert from Antioch who ministers for a number of years alongside Paul, taking on several notable assignments. One of these is at the Corinthian church where he gives guidance to prepare the people in their offering for the Jerusalem saints. He also accompanies Paul and Barnabas to the Jerusalem council. One of Paul's own converts, Titus is not circumcised since it would be assumed a concession to Jewish legalism. Paul leaves the young but mature Titus on the Mediterranean island of Crete (which is 152 miles long and up to 35 miles wide) to organize the believers into churches. His mission there is complicated by false teachings, immaturity and immorality.

Where Written: Uncertain (possibly from Greece or Macedonia).

To Whom: To Titus.

Content: Paul's request in this letter is that Titus appoint qualified elders in every city to guide the believers of Crete. Special exhortations are given to the young and the old of both sexes to live righteously as they hope in the return of Jesus Christ. Believers are encouraged in good works, but admonished to remember that their justification is a product of God's grace and mercy. False teachers are rebuked by Paul as he emphasizes how sound doctrine should be the focus of every believer. Paul uses this letter to give Titus the spiritual wisdom he needs to effectively lead the church.

Key Words: "Pure"; "Heir." Christians are exhorted not only to live "pure" lives, but to have "pure" motives as well. Every believer is justified before God to be an eternal "heir" to all that God has made available.

Themes: • Good works are not to bring us salvation, but to reflect our salvation. • Christians should not speak evil of anyone. • Believers should say "No" to worldly passions (2:12). • We should never let our speech be such that we could be condemned or bring disgrace to the ways of the Lord.

Outline:

1. Introduction. 1:1-1:4
2. Appoint church elders. 1:5-1:9
3. Rebuke false teachers. 1:10-1:16
4. Teach sound doctrine. 2:1-2:15
5. Live obedient and upright lives. 3:1-3:11
6. Concluding instructions. 3:12-3:15

TITUS

1 Paul, a servant of God[a] and an apostle of Jesus Christ for the faith of
God's elect and the knowledge of the
truth[b] that leads to godliness— 2a faith
and knowledge resting on the hope of
eternal life,[c] which God, who does not
lie, promised before the beginning of
time,[d] 3and at his appointed season[e] he
brought his word to light[f] through the
preaching entrusted to me[g] by the
command of God our Savior,[h]

4To Titus,[i] my true son in our common faith:

Grace and peace from God the Father
and Christ Jesus our Savior.

1:1 [a]Ro 1:1 [b]1Ti 2:4
1:2 [c]2Ti 1:1 [d]2Ti 1:9
1:3 [e]1Ti 2:6 [f]2Ti 1:10 [g]1Ti 1:11 [h]Lk 1:47
1:4 [i]2Co 2:13
1:5 [j]Ac 27:7 [k]Ac 11:30
1:6 [l]1Ti 3:2
1:7 [m]1Ti 3:1 [n]1Co 4:1

Titus is charged to appoint qualified elders in every town.

1:6-8Ref— 1Ti 3:2-4

5The reason I left you in Crete[j] was
that you might straighten out what was
left unfinished and appoint[a] elders[k] in
every town, as I directed you. 6An elder
must be blameless,[l] the husband of but
one wife, a man whose children believe
and are not open to the charge of being
wild and disobedient. 7Since an overseer[b][m] is entrusted with God's work,[n]
he must be blameless—not overbear-
ing, not quick-tempered, not given to

a5 Or *ordain* b7 Traditionally *bishop*

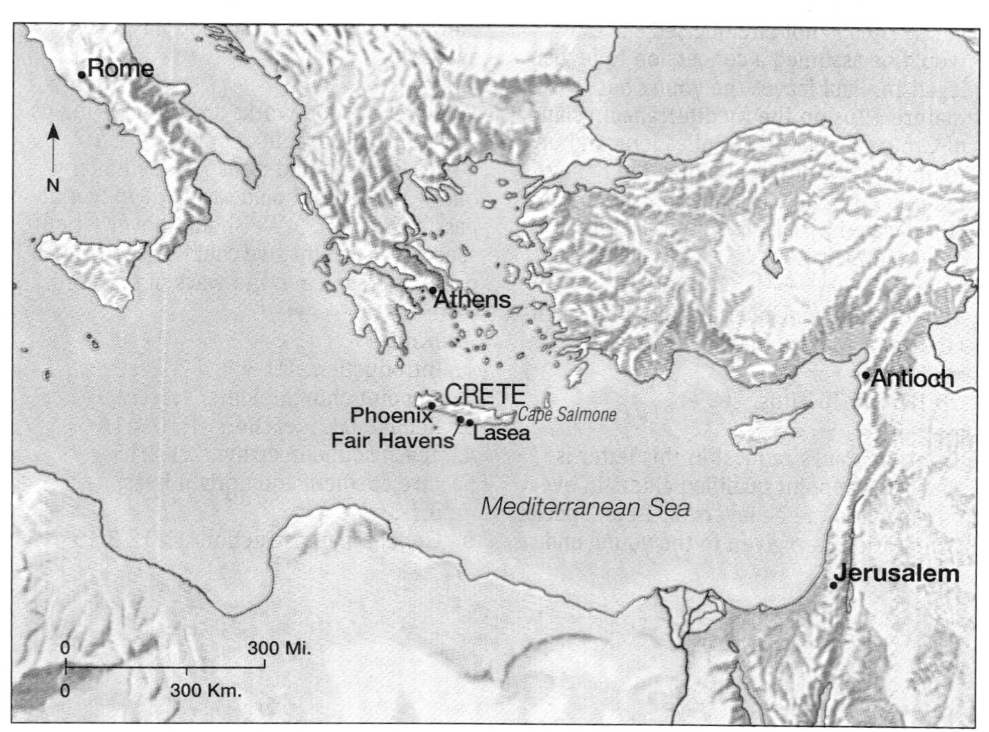

Titus Goes to Crete

Tradition says that after Paul was released from prison in Rome (before his second and final Roman imprisonment), he and Titus traveled together for a while. They stopped in Crete, and when it was time for Paul to go, he left Titus behind to help the churches there.

drunkenness, not violent, not pursuing dishonest gain.[a] 8Rather he must be hospitable,[b] one who loves what is good,[c] who is self-controlled, upright, holy and disciplined. 9He must hold firmly[d] to the trustworthy message as it has been taught, so that he can encourage others by sound doctrine[e] and refute those who oppose it.

Paul instructs Titus to rebuke false teachers.

10For there are many rebellious people, mere talkers[f] and deceivers, especially those of the circumcision group.[g] 11They must be silenced, because they are ruining whole households[h] by teaching things they ought not to teach—and that for the sake of dishonest gain. 12Even one of their own prophets[i] has said, "Cretans[j] are always liars, evil brutes, lazy gluttons." 13This testimony is true. Therefore, rebuke[k] them sharply, so that they will be sound in the faith[l] 14and will pay no attention to Jewish myths[m] or to the commands[n] of those who reject the truth. 15To the pure, all things are pure, but to those who are corrupted and do not believe, nothing is pure.[o] In fact, both their minds and consciences are corrupted. 16They claim to know God, but by their actions they deny him.[p] They are detestable, disobedient and unfit for doing anything good.

Proper conduct defined for various groups in the church.

2 You must teach what is in accord with sound doctrine.[q] 2Teach the older men to be temperate, worthy of respect, self-controlled, and sound in faith,[r] in love and in endurance.

3Likewise, teach the older women to be reverent in the way they live, not to be slanderers or addicted to much wine,[s] but to teach what is good. 4Then they can train the younger women to love their husbands and children, 5to be self-controlled and pure, to be busy at home, to be kind, and to be subject to their husbands,[t] so that no one will malign the word of God.[u]

6Similarly, encourage the young men[v] to be self-controlled. 7In everything set them an example[w] by doing what is good. In your teaching show integrity, seriousness 8and soundness of speech that cannot be condemned, so that those who oppose you may be ashamed because they have nothing bad to say about us.[x]

9Teach slaves to be subject to their masters in everything,[y] to try to please them, not to talk back to them, 10and not to steal from them, but to show that they can be fully trusted, so that in every way they will make the teaching about God our Savior attractive.[z]

Titus exhorted to teach of redemption through Jesus Christ.

11For the grace of God that brings salvation has appeared to all men.[a] 12It teaches us to say "No" to ungodliness and worldly passions,[b] and to live self-controlled, upright and godly lives[c] in this present age, 13while we wait for the blessed hope—the glorious appearing of our great God and Savior, Jesus Christ,[d] 14who gave himself for us to redeem us from all wickedness and to purify for himself a people that are his very own,[e] eager to do what is good.[f]

15These, then, are the things you should teach. Encourage and rebuke with all authority. Do not let anyone despise you.

Justified by grace.

3 Remind the people to be subject to rulers and authorities,[g] to be obedient, to be ready to do whatever is good,[h] 2to slander no one,[i] to be peaceable and considerate, and to show true humility toward all men.

3At one time we too were foolish, disobedient, deceived and enslaved by all kinds of passions and pleasures. We lived in malice and envy, being hated and hating one another. 4But when the

1:7 [a]1Ti 3:3,8
1:8 [b]1Ti 3:2 [c]2Ti 3:3
1:9 [d]1Ti 1:19 [e]1Ti 1:10
1:10 [f]1Ti 1:6 [g]11:2
1:11 [h]2Ti 3:6
1:12 [i]Ac 17:28 [j]Ac 2:11
1:13 [k]2Co 13:10 [l]Tit 2:2
1:14 [m]1Ti 1:4 [n]Col 2:22
1:15 [o]Ro 14:14,23
1:16 [p]1Jn 2:4
2:1 [q]1Ti 1:10
2:2 [r]Tit 1:13
2:3 [s]1Ti 3:8
2:5 [t]Eph 5:22 [u]1Ti 6:1
2:6 [v]1Ti 5:1
2:7 [w]1Ti 4:12
2:8 [x]1Pe 2:12
2:9 [y]Eph 6:5
2:10 [z]Mt 5:16
2:11 [a]1Ti 2:4
2:12 [b]Tit 3:3 [c]2Ti 3:12
2:13 [d]2Pe 1:1
2:14 [e]Ex 19:5 [f]Eph 2:10
3:1 [g]Ro 13:1 [h]2Ti 2:21
3:2 [i]Eph 4:31; 2Ti 2:24

kindness[a] and love of God our Savior
appeared,[b] 5he saved us, not because
of righteous things we had done,[c] but
because of his mercy. He saved us
through the washing of rebirth and
renewal[d] by the Holy Spirit, 6whom he
poured out on us[e] generously through
Jesus Christ our Savior, 7so that, having
been justified by his grace,[f] we might
become heirs[g] having the hope[h] of
eternal life.[i] 8This is a trustworthy saying.[j] And I want you to stress these
things, so that those who have trusted
in God may be careful to devote themselves to doing what is good.[k] These
things are excellent and profitable for
everyone.

Avoiding foolish controversies.

9But avoid foolish controversies and
genealogies and arguments and quarrels[l] about the law, because these are
unprofitable and useless. 10Warn a divisive person once, and then warn him a
second time. After that, have nothing
to do with him.[m] 11You may be sure
that such a man is warped and sinful;
he is self-condemned.

Concluding instructions
and greetings.

12As soon as I send Artemas or Tychicus[n] to you, do your best to come to me
at Nicopolis, because I have decided to
winter there.[o] 13Do everything you can
to help Zenas the lawyer and Apollos[p]
on their way and see that they have
everything they need. 14Our people
must learn to devote themselves to
doing what is good,[q] in order that they
may provide for daily necessities and
not live unproductive lives.
15Everyone with me sends you greetings. Greet those who love us in the
faith.[r]
Grace be with you all.[s]

3:4
[a]Eph 2:7
[b]Tit 2:11
3:5
[c]Eph 2:9
[d]Ro 12:2
3:6
[e]Ro 5:5
3:7
[f]Ro 3:24
[g]Ro 8:17
[h]Ro 8:24
[i]Tit 1:2
3:8
[j]1Ti 1:15
[k]Tit 2:14
3:9
[l]1Ti 1:4; 2Ti 2:14
3:10
[m]Ro 16:17
3:12
[n]Ac 20:4
[o]2Ti 4:9,21
3:13
[p]Ac 18:24
3:14
[q]ver 8
3:15
[r]1Ti 1:2
[s]Col 4:18

PHILEMON

Author: Paul the Apostle.

Date Written: Between A.D. 60 and 61.

Title: Refers to the addressee of this letter: Philemon.

Background: Philemon is a well-to-do Christian from Colosse who owns slaves. One of these slaves, Onesimus, steals some of his master's property and runs away to Rome. While in Rome, Onesimus becomes a believer after hearing the gospel from Paul. (Paul had also been instrumental in leading Philemon to saving faith in Christ.) Paul enjoys having Onesimus with him, but he knows the right thing to do is to send Onesimus home to his lawful owner, Philemon. Paul sends Onesimus home with this letter, accompanied by Tychicus, to petition Philemon to restore Onesimus's freedom. The book of Philemon, along with Philippians, Colossians and Ephesians, is one of Paul's "Prison Epistles."

Where Written: Rome, while Paul is under house arrest.

To Whom: To Philemon. Also to Apphia and Archippus (probably Philemon's wife and son), and to the church at Colosse, which meets at Philemon's home.

Content: The shortest of Paul's letters, the book of Philemon is a striking analogy to the redemption story of the gospel. Paul pleads with Philemon to forgive Onesimus and to restore him beyond his original position as a slave. Now he can be a Christian brother, useful to all members of the church. Philemon is reminded of his debt to Paul, but Paul still offers to repay for any loss of Philemon's. Tradition reveals that Philemon uses this opportunity to free Onesimus.

Key Words: "Slave"; "Useful." Paul is spiritually a prisoner of Jesus Christ and physically in the bondage of a Roman prison, so he understands Onesimus's debt as a "slave" to Philemon. Paul plays upon the word "useful" (verse 11), which is the meaning of *Onesimus* and which, indeed, all Christians are.

Themes: • All sins against people are also sins against God. • The laws of the land are for both Christians and non-Christians alike. • A right relationship with Jesus Christ will break down social and economic barriers. • Reconciliation requires action from both the wrong and the wronged. • Christ will forgive our sins and give us a fresh beginning.

Outline:
1. Greeting. 1-3
2. Thanksgiving and prayer for Philemon. 4-7
3. Paul's plea for Onesimus. 8-21
4. Farewell. 22-25

PHILEMON

1Paul, a prisoner[a] of Christ Jesus, and
Timothy our brother,[b]

To Philemon our dear friend and fellow worker,[c] 2to Apphia our sister, to
Archippus[d] our fellow soldier[e] and to
the church that meets in your home:[f]

3Grace to you and peace from God
our Father and the Lord Jesus Christ.

Paul commends Philemon for his love.

4I always thank my God[g] as I remember you in my prayers, 5because I hear
about your faith in the Lord Jesus and
your love for all the saints.[h] 6I pray
that you may be active in sharing your
faith, so that you will have a full understanding of every good thing we have
in Christ. 7Your love has given me great
joy and encouragement,[i] because you,
brother, have refreshed[j] the hearts of
the saints.

Paul pleads for Onesimus to be forgiven.

8Therefore, although in Christ I could
be bold and order you to do what you
ought to do, 9yet I appeal to you on the
basis of love. I then, as Paul—an old
man and now also a prisoner[k] of Christ
Jesus— 10I appeal to you for my son[l]
Onesimus,[a][m] who became my son while
I was in chains. 11Formerly he was useless to you, but now he has become
useful both to you and to me.
12I am sending him—who is my very
heart—back to you. 13I would have liked
to keep him with me so that he could
take your place in helping me while I
am in chains for the gospel. 14But I did
not want to do anything without your
consent, so that any favor you do will
be spontaneous and not forced.[n] 15Per-
haps the reason he was separated from
you for a little while was that you might
have him back for good— 16no longer
as a slave, but better than a slave, as a
dear brother.[o] He is very dear to me but
even dearer to you, both as a man and
as a brother in the Lord.

Paul gives Philemon his guarantee.

17So if you consider me a partner,[p]
welcome him as you would welcome
me. 18If he has done you any wrong or
owes you anything, charge it to me. 19I,
Paul, am writing this with my own hand.
I will pay it back—not to mention that
you owe me your very self. 20I do wish,
brother, that I may have some benefit
from you in the Lord; refresh[q] my heart
in Christ. 21Confident[r] of your obedience, I write to you, knowing that you
will do even more than I ask.
22And one thing more: Prepare a
guest room for me, because I hope to
be[s] restored to you in answer to your
prayers.[t]

23Epaphras,[u] my fellow prisoner in
Christ Jesus, sends you greetings. 24And
so do Mark,[v] Aristarchus,[w] Demas[x] and
Luke, my fellow workers.
25The grace of the Lord Jesus Christ
be with your spirit.[y]

1:1 [a]ver 9,23; Eph 3:1 [b]2Co 1:1 [c]Php 2:25
1:2 [d]Col 4:17 [e]Php 2:25 [f]Ro 16:5
1:4 [g]Ro 1:8
1:5 [h]Eph 1:15; Col 1:4
1:7 [i]2Co 7:4,13 [j]ver 20
1:9 [k]ver 1,23
1:10 [l]1Co 4:15 [m]Col 4:9
1:14 [n]2Co 9:7; 1Pe 5:2
1:16 [o]Mt 23:8; 1Ti 6:2
1:17 [p]2Co 8:23
1:20 [q]ver 7
1:21 [r]2Co 2:3
1:22 [s]Php 1:25; 2:24 [t]2Co 1:11
1:23 [u]Col 1:7
1:24 [v]Ac 12:12 [w]Ac 19:29 [x]Col 4:14
1:25 [y]2Ti 4:22

a *10 Onesimus* means *useful.*

HEBREWS

Author: Uncertain. (Suggestions include: Apollos, Barnabas, Clement, Luke, Paul, Philip, Priscilla or Silas.)

Date Written: Between A.D. 64 and 70.

Title: Refers to the addressee of this letter: a congregation of Hebrew believers probably located in Rome.

Background: Persecution is a real threat to the church at Rome. This persecution causes many Jewish believers, who have died to their legalistic, Judaic ways, to take some steps backward. The author uses this occasion to express the freedom that Christ has given to all believers, and asserts that with Christ there is no need for any of the rituals offered by Judaism. Appealing to their knowledge of the Old Testament, the author especially comments on parallels from the Pentateuch (Genesis, Exodus, Leviticus, Numbers and Deuteronomy).

Where Written: Uncertain (possibly Rome).

To Whom: To the Jewish Christians.

Content: The writer of Hebrews exhorts the Hebrew Christians to maturity by showing them that present suffering for Christ is followed by eternal glory with him that Judaism or no other religion can offer. The entire Old Testament pointed to the ministry of Christ, for the offerings, feasts, tabernacles and priests were all used to show the better way of Jesus. Faith is defined and encouragement is given to all believers by detailing the faith of such men and women as Abel, Enoch, Noah, Abraham, Sarah, Isaac, Jacob, Joseph and Moses (chapter 11). The author of Hebrews reveals that the new, eternal covenant has replaced a temporal one, and its price has been paid-in-full by the blood of Christ.

Key Words: "Sacrifice"; "Better." The "sacrifice" of Christ is presented as being superior to anything offered by the Judaic system: Christ is "better" than the angels, since he is worshiped by them; he is "better" than Moses, since he created him; he is "better" than Aaron's priesthood, since his atonement is eternal; and he is "better" than the law, since he mediates a superior covenant.

Themes: • Christianity is more than a religion...it is a relationship with Jesus Christ. • To be victorious, we must run the race with our eyes on Jesus. • We can give our temptations to Jesus...he has already faced all of them and won the victory. • God desires his children to give strength of testimony to each other. • Only the blood of Christ can cleanse us of our sins.

Outline:

1. Jesus Christ's superiority over the prophets and angels. 1:1-2:18
2. Jesus Christ's superiority over Moses. 3:1-4:13
3. Jesus Christ, the superior priest. 4:14-7:28
4. Jesus Christ's superior covenant and sacrifice. 8:1-10:18
5. Obedience through faith. 10:19-12:29
6. Concluding instructions. 13:1-13:25

HEBREWS

God's Son is superior to the angels.

1 In the past God spoke[a] to our forefathers through the prophets[b] at many times and in various ways,[c] 2 but in these last days he has spoken to us by his Son, whom he appointed heir[d] of all things, and through whom[e] he made the universe. 3 The Son is the radiance of God's glory[f] and the exact representation of his being, sustaining all things[g] by his powerful word. After he had provided purification for sins,[h] he sat down at the right hand of the Majesty in heaven.[i] 4 So he became as much superior to the angels as the name he has inherited is superior to theirs.[j]

5 For to which of the angels did God ever say,

"You are my Son;
today I have become your
Father[a]"[b]?[k]

Or again,

"I will be his Father,
and he will be my Son"[c]?[l]

6 And again, when God brings his firstborn into the world,[m] he says,

"Let all God's angels worship him."[d][n]

7 In speaking of the angels he says,

"He makes his angels winds,
his servants flames of fire."[e][o]

8 But about the Son he says,

"Your throne, O God, will last for
ever and ever,
and righteousness will be the
scepter of your kingdom.
9 You have loved righteousness and
hated wickedness;
therefore God, your God, has set
you above your companions[p]
by anointing you with the oil[q] of
joy."[f]

10 He also says,

"In the beginning, O Lord, you laid
the foundations of the earth,
and the heavens are the work of
your hands.
11 They will perish, but you remain;
they will all wear out like a
garment.[r]
12 You will roll them up like a robe;
like a garment they will be
changed.
But you remain the same,[s]
and your years will never end."[g][t]

13 To which of the angels did God ever say,

"Sit at my right hand
until I make your enemies
a footstool[u] for your feet"[h]?[v]

14 Are not all angels ministering spirits[w] sent to serve those who will inherit salvation?[x]

No escape for those ignoring the Lord's salvation.

2 We must pay more careful attention, therefore, to what we have heard, so that we do not drift away. 2 For if the message spoken[y] by angels[z] was binding, and every violation and disobedience received its just punishment,[a] 3 how shall we escape if we ignore such a great salvation?[b] This salvation, which was first announced by the Lord,[c] was confirmed to us by those who heard him.[d] 4 God also testified to it by signs, wonders and various miracles,[e] and gifts of the Holy Spirit[f] distributed according to his will.[g]

Jesus' death brought salvation.

5 It is not to angels that he has subjected the world to come, about which we are speaking. 6 But there is a place where someone has testified:

1:1 [a]Jn 9:29; Heb 2:2,3 [b]Ac 2:30 [c]Nu 12:6,8
1:2 [d]Ps 2:8 [e]Jn 1:3
1:3 [f]Jn 1:14 [g]Col 1:17 [h]Heb 7:27 [i]Mk 16:19
1:4 [j]Eph 1:21; Php 2:9,10
1:5 [k]Ps 2:7 [l]2Sa 7:14
1:6 [m]Heb 10:5 [n]Dt 32:43 (LXX and DSS) Ps 97:7
1:7 [o]Ps 104:4
1:9 [p]Php 2:9 [q]Isa 61:1,3
1:11 [r]Isa 34:4
1:12 [s]Heb 13:8 [t]Ps 102:25-27
1:13 [u]Jos 10:24; Heb 10:13 [v]Ps 110:1
1:14 [w]Ps 103:20 [x]Heb 5:9
2:2 [y]Heb 1:1 [z]Dt 33:2; Ac 7:53 [a]Heb 10:28
2:3 [b]Heb 10:29 [c]Heb 1:2 [d]Lk 1:2
2:4 [e]Jn 4:48 [f]1Co 12:4 [g]Eph 1:5

a *5* Or *have begotten you* b *5* Psalm 2:7
c *5* 2 Samuel 7:14; 1 Chron. 17:13 d *6* Deut. 32:43 (see Dead Sea Scrolls and Septuagint)
e *7* Psalm 104:4 f *9* Psalm 45:6,7
g *12* Psalm 102:25-27 h *13* Psalm 110:1

"What is man that you are mindful of
him,
the son of man that you care for
him?[a]
7You made him a little[i] lower than the
angels;
you crowned him with glory and
honor
8 and put everything under his
feet."[j][b]

In putting everything under him, God
left nothing that is not subject to him.
Yet at present we do not see everything
subject to him. 9But we see Jesus, who
was made a little lower than the angels,
now crowned with glory and honor[c]
because he suffered death,[d] so that by
the grace of God he might taste death
for everyone.[e]
10In bringing many sons to glory, it
was fitting that God, for whom and
through whom everything exists,[f]
should make the author of their salvation perfect through suffering.[g] 11Both
the one who makes men holy and those
who are made holy[h] are of the same
family. So Jesus is not ashamed to call
them brothers.[i] 12He says,

"I will declare your name to my
brothers;
in the presence of the congregation
I will sing your praises."[k][j]

13And again,

"I will put my trust in him."[l][k]

And again he says,

"Here am I, and the children God
has given me."[m][l]

14Since the children have flesh and
blood, he too shared in their humanity[m]
so that by his death he might destroy[n]
him who holds the power of death—
that is, the devil[o]— 15and free those
who all their lives were held in slavery
by their fear[p] of death. 16For surely it is
not angels he helps, but Abraham's
descendants. 17For this reason he had to
be made like his brothers[q] in every way,

2:6 [a]Job 7:17
2:8 [b]Ps 8:4-6; 1Co 15:25
2:9 [c]Ac 2:33; 3:13; Php 2:9 [d]Php 2:7-9 [e]Jn 3:16; 2Co 5:15
2:10 [f]Ro 11:36 [g]Lk 24:26; Heb 7:28
2:11 [h]Heb 10:10 [i]Mt 28:10; Jn 20:17
2:12 [j]Ps 22:22
2:13 [k]Isa 8:17 [l]Isa 8:18; Jn 10:29
2:14 [m]Jn 1:14 [n]1Co 15:54-57; 2Ti 1:10 [o]1Jn 3:8
2:15 [p]2Ti 1:7
2:17 [q]Php 2:7 [r]Heb 5:2 [s]Heb 4:14,15; 7:26,28 [t]Heb 5:1
2:18 [u]Heb 4:15
3:1 [v]Heb 2:11 [w]Heb 2:17 [x]Heb 4:14
3:2 [y]Nu 12:7
3:5 [z]Ex 14:31 [a]ver 2; Nu 12:7
3:6 [b]Heb 1:2 [c]1Co 3:16 [d]Ro 11:22 [e]Ro 5:2
3:7 [f]Heb 9:8
3:9 [g]Ac 7:36

in order that he might become a merciful[r] and faithful high priest[s] in service to
God,[t] and that he might make atonement for[n] the sins of the people. 18Be-
cause he himself suffered when he was
tempted, he is able to help those who
are being tempted.[u]

Jesus is greater than Moses.

3 Therefore, holy brothers,[v] who
share in the heavenly calling, fix
your thoughts on Jesus, the apostle and
high priest[w] whom we confess.[x] 2He
was faithful to the one who appointed
him, just as Moses was faithful in all
God's house.[y] 3Jesus has been found
worthy of greater honor than Moses,
just as the builder of a house has greater
honor than the house itself. 4For every
house is built by someone, but God is
the builder of everything. 5Moses was
faithful as a servant[z] in all God's house,[a]
testifying to what would be said in the
future. 6But Christ is faithful as a son[b]
over God's house. And we are his
house,[c] if we hold on[d] to our courage
and the hope[e] of which we boast.

The call of the Holy Spirit should be obeyed today.

7So, as the Holy Spirit says:[f]

"Today, if you hear his voice,
8 do not harden your hearts
as you did in the rebellion,
during the time of testing in the
desert,
9where your fathers tested and tried
me
and for forty years saw what I
did.[g]
10That is why I was angry with that
generation,
and I said, 'Their hearts are always
going astray,
and they have not known my
ways.'

[i]7 Or *him for a little while*; also in verse 9
[j]8 Psalm 8:4-6 [k]12 Psalm 22:22 [l]13 Isaiah 8:17
[m]13 Isaiah 8:18 [n]17 Or *and that he might turn aside God's wrath, taking away*

11So I declared on oath in my anger,
'They shall never enter my
rest.'[a]"[o][b]

12See to it, brothers, that none of you has a sinful, unbelieving heart that turns away from the living God. 13But encourage one another daily,[c] as long as it is called Today, so that none of you may be hardened by sin's deceitfulness.[d] 14We have come to share in Christ if we hold firmly[e] till the end the confidence we had at first. 15As has just been said:

"Today, if you hear his voice,
do not harden your hearts
as you did in the rebellion."[p][f]

16Who were they who heard and rebelled? Were they not all those Moses led out of Egypt?[g] 17And with whom was he angry for forty years? Was it not with those who sinned, whose bodies fell in the desert?[h] 18And to whom did God swear that they would never enter his rest[i] if not to those who disobeyed[q]?[j] 19So we see that they were not able to enter, because of their unbelief.[k]

Christ's rest is promised to all who believe.

4 Therefore, since the promise of entering his rest still stands, let us be careful that none of you be found to have fallen short of it.[l] 2For we also have had the gospel preached to us, just as they did; but the message they heard was of no value to them, because those who heard did not combine it with faith.[r][m] 3Now we who have believed enter that rest, just as God has said,

"So I declared on oath in my anger,
'They shall never enter my rest.'"[s][n]

And yet his work has been finished since the creation of the world. 4For somewhere he has spoken about the seventh day in these words: "And on the seventh day God rested from all his work."[t][o] 5And again in the passage above he says, "They shall never enter my rest."[p]

6It still remains that some will enter that rest, and those who formerly had the gospel preached to them did not go in, because of their disobedience.[q] 7Therefore God again set a certain day, calling it Today, when a long time later he spoke through David, as was said before:

"Today, if you hear his voice,
do not harden your hearts."[u][r]

8For if Joshua had given them rest,[s] God would not have spoken[t] later about another day. 9There remains, then, a Sabbath-rest for the people of God; 10for anyone who enters God's rest also rests from his own work, just as God did from his.[u] 11Let us, therefore, make every effort to enter that rest, so that no one will fall by following their example of disobedience.[v]

The Word of God is sharper than a double-edged sword.

12For the word of God[w] is living and active.[x] Sharper than any double-edged sword,[y] it penetrates even to dividing soul and spirit, joints and marrow; it judges the thoughts and attitudes of the heart.[z] 13Nothing in all creation is hidden from God's sight.[a] Everything is uncovered and laid bare before the eyes of him to whom we must give account.

Mercy is found at the throne of God.

14Therefore, since we have a great high priest who has gone through the heavens,[v][b] Jesus the Son of God, let us hold firmly to the faith we profess.[c] 15For we do not have a high priest who is unable to sympathize with our weaknesses, but we have one who has been tempted in every way, just as we are[d]—yet was without sin.[e] 16Let us then approach the throne of grace with confidence, so that we may receive

3:11 [a]Heb 4:3,5 [b]Ps 95:7-11
3:13 [c]Heb 10:24, 25 [d]Eph 4:22
3:14 [e]ver 6
3:15 [f]ver 7,8; Ps 95:7,8
3:16 [g]Nu 14:2
3:17 [h]Nu 14:29; Ps 106:26
3:18 [i]Nu 14:20-23 [j]Heb 4:6
3:19 [k]Jn 3:36
4:1 [l]Heb 12:15
4:2 [m]1Th 2:13
4:3 [n]Ps 95:11; Heb 3:11
4:4 [o]Ge 2:2,3; Ex 20:11
4:5 [p]Ps 95:11
4:6 [q]Heb 3:18
4:7 [r]Ps 95:7,8; Heb 3:7,8,15
4:8 [s]Jos 22:4 [t]Heb 1:1
4:10 [u]ver 4
4:11 [v]Heb 3:18
4:12 [w]1Pe 1:23 [x]Jer 23:29 [y]Eph 6:17; Rev 1:16 [z]1Co 14:24, 25
4:13 [a]Ps 33:13-15
4:14 [b]Heb 6:20 [c]Heb 3:1
4:15 [d]Heb 2:18 [e]2Co 5:21

o *11* Psalm 95:7-11 p *15* Psalm 95:7,8
q *18* Or *disbelieved* r *2* Many manuscripts *because they did not share in the faith of those who obeyed*
s *3* Psalm 95:11; also in verse 5 t *4* Gen. 2:2
u *7* Psalm 95:7,8 v *14* Or *gone into heaven*

mercy and find grace to help us in our
time of need.

5 Every high priest is selected from
among men and is appointed to
represent them in matters related to
God, to offer gifts and sacrifices[a] for
sins.[b] 2He is able to deal gently with
those who are ignorant and are going
astray,[c] since he himself is subject to
weakness.[d] 3This is why he has to offer
sacrifices for his own sins, as well as
for the sins of the people.[e]

4No one takes this honor upon himself; he must be called by God, just as
Aaron was.[f] 5So Christ also did not take
upon himself the glory[g] of becoming a
high priest. But God said[h] to him,

"You are my Son;
today I have become your
Father.[w]"[x][i]

6And he says in another place,

"You are a priest forever,
in the order of Melchizedek."[y][j]

7During the days of Jesus' life on
earth, he offered up prayers and petitions with loud cries and tears[k] to the
one who could save him from death,
and he was heard because of his reverent submission.[l] 8Although he was a
son, he learned obedience from what he
suffered[m] 9and, once made perfect,[n] he
became the source of eternal salvation
for all who obey him 10and was designated by God to be high priest[o] in the
order of Melchizedek.[p]

Maturity in Christ is stressed.

6:4-6Ref— Heb 10:26-31

11We have much to say about this, but
it is hard to explain because you are
slow to learn. 12In fact, though by this
time you ought to be teachers, you need
someone to teach you the elementary
truths[q] of God's word all over again. You
need milk, not solid food![r] 13Anyone
who lives on milk, being still an infant,[s]
is not acquainted with the teaching
about righteousness. 14But solid food is
for the mature,[t] who by constant use
have trained themselves to distinguish
good from evil.[u]

6 Therefore let us leave[v] the elementary teachings[w] about Christ and
go on to maturity, not laying again the
foundation of repentance from acts that
lead to death,[z][x] and of faith in God,
2instruction about baptisms,[y] the laying on of hands,[z] the resurrection of
the dead,[a] and eternal judgment. 3And
God permitting,[b] we will do so.

4It is impossible for those who have
once been enlightened,[c] who have tasted the heavenly gift,[d] who have shared
in the Holy Spirit,[e] 5who have tasted the
goodness of the word of God and the
powers of the coming age, 6if they fall
away, to be brought back to repentance,[f]
because[a] to their loss they are crucifying
the Son of God all over again and sub-
jecting him to public disgrace.

7Land that drinks in the rain often
falling on it and that produces a crop
useful to those for whom it is farmed
receives the blessing of God. 8But land
that produces thorns and thistles is
worthless and is in danger of being
cursed.[g] In the end it will be burned.

9Even though we speak like this, dear
friends,[h] we are confident of better
things in your case—things that accompany salvation. 10God is not unjust; he
will not forget your work and the love
you have shown him as you have helped
his people and continue to help them.[i]
11We want each of you to show this
same diligence to the very end, in order
to make your hope[j] sure. 12We do not
want you to become lazy, but to imitate[k]
those who through faith and patience[l]
inherit what has been promised.[m]

God's promise of salvation is assured.

13When God made his promise to
Abraham, since there was no one greater

5:1 [a]Heb 8:3 [b]Heb 7:27
5:2 [c]Heb 2:18 [d]Heb 7:28
5:3 [e]Heb 7:27; 9:7
5:4 [f]Ex 28:1
5:5 [g]Jn 8:54 [h]Heb 1:1 [i]Ps 2:7
5:6 [j]Ps 110:4; Heb 7:17,21
5:7 [k]Mt 27:46,50 [l]Mk 14:36
5:8 [m]Php 2:8
5:9 [n]Heb 2:10
5:10 [o]ver 5 [p]ver 6
5:12 [q]Heb 6:1 [r]1Co 3:2; 1Pe 2:2
5:13 [s]1Co 14:20
5:14 [t]1Co 2:6 [u]Isa 7:15
6:1 [v]Php 3:12-14 [w]Heb 5:12 [x]Heb 9:14
6:2 [y]Jn 3:25 [z]Ac 6:6 [a]Ac 17:18,32
6:3 [b]Ac 18:21
6:4 [c]Heb 10:32 [d]Eph 2:8 [e]Gal 3:2
6:6 [f]2Pe 2:21; 1Jn 5:16
6:8 [g]Ge 3:17,18; Isa 5:6
6:9 [h]1Co 10:14
6:10 [i]Mt 10:40,42; 25:40; 1Th 1:3
6:11 [j]Heb 3:6
6:12 [k]Heb 13:7 [l]2Th 1:4; Jas 1:3; Rev 13:10 [m]Heb 10:36

[w]5 Or *have begotten you* [x]5 Psalm 2:7
[y]6 Psalm 110:4 [z]1 Or *from useless rituals*
[a]6 Or *repentance while*

for him to swear by, he swore by himself,[a] 14saying, "I will surely bless you and give you many descendants."[b][b] 15And so after waiting patiently, Abraham received what was promised.[c]

16Men swear by someone greater than themselves, and the oath confirms what is said and puts an end to all argument.[d] 17Because God wanted to make the unchanging[e] nature of his purpose very clear to the heirs of what was promised,[f] he confirmed it with an oath. 18God did this so that, by two unchangeable things in which it is impossible for God to lie,[g] we who have fled to take hold of the hope[h] offered to us may be greatly encouraged. 19We have this hope as an anchor for the soul, firm and secure. It enters the inner sanctuary behind the curtain,[i] 20where Jesus, who went before us, has entered on our behalf.[j] He has become a high priest[k] forever, in the order of Melchizedek.[l]

Priesthood of Melchizedek.

7 This Melchizedek was king of Salem and priest of God Most High.[m] He met Abraham returning from the defeat of the kings and blessed him,[n] 2and Abraham gave him a tenth of everything. First, his name means "king of righteousness"; then also, "king of Salem" means "king of peace." 3Without father or mother, without genealogy,[o] without beginning of days or end of life, like the Son of God[p] he remains a priest forever.

4Just think how great he was: Even the patriarch[q] Abraham gave him a tenth of the plunder![r] 5Now the law requires the descendants of Levi who become priests to collect a tenth from the people[s]—that is, their brothers—even though their brothers are descended from Abraham. 6This man, however, did not trace his descent from Levi, yet he collected a tenth from Abraham and blessed[t] him who had the promises.[u] 7And without doubt the lesser person is blessed by the greater. 8In the one case, the tenth is collected by men who die; but in the other case, by him who is declared to be living.[v] 9One might even say that Levi, who collects the tenth, paid the tenth through Abraham, 10because when Melchizedek met Abraham, Levi was still in the body of his ancestor.

Superiority of Jesus' priesthood.

11If perfection could have been attained through the Levitical priesthood (for on the basis of it the law was given to the people),[w] why was there still need for another priest to come[x]—one in the order of Melchizedek,[y] not in the order of Aaron? 12For when there is a change of the priesthood, there must also be a change of the law. 13He of whom these things are said belonged to a different tribe,[z] and no one from that tribe has ever served at the altar.[a] 14For it is clear that our Lord descended from Judah,[b] and in regard to that tribe Moses said nothing about priests. 15And what we have said is even more clear if another priest like Melchizedek appears, 16one who has become a priest not on the basis of a regulation as to his ancestry but on the basis of the power of an indestructible life. 17For it is declared:

"You are a priest forever,
in the order of Melchizedek."[c][c]

18The former regulation is set aside because it was weak and useless[d] 19(for the law made nothing perfect),[e] and a better hope is introduced, by which we draw near to God.[f]

20And it was not without an oath! Others became priests without any oath, 21but he became a priest with an oath when God said to him:

"The Lord has sworn
and will not change his mind:[g]
'You are a priest forever.'"[c][h]

22Because of this oath, Jesus has become the guarantee of a better covenant.[i]

23Now there have been many of those

6:13 [a]Ge 22:16; Lk 1:73
6:14 [b]Ge 22:17
6:15 [c]Ge 21:5
6:16 [d]Ex 22:11
6:17 [e]Ps 110:4 [f]Heb 11:9
6:18 [g]Nu 23:19; Tit 1:2 [h]Heb 3:6
6:19 [i]Lev 16:2; Heb 9:2,3,7
6:20 [j]Heb 4:14 [k]Heb 2:17 [l]Heb 5:6
7:1 [m]Mk 5:7 [n]Ge 14:18-20
7:3 [o]ver 6 [p]Mt 4:3
7:4 [q]Ac 2:29 [r]Ge 14:20
7:5 [s]Nu 18:21,26
7:6 [t]Ge 14:19,20 [u]Ro 4:13
7:8 [v]Heb 5:6; 6:20
7:11 [w]ver 18,19; Heb 8:7 [x]Heb 10:1 [y]ver 17
7:13 [z]ver 11 [a]ver 14
7:14 [b]Isa 11:1; Mt 1:3; Lk 3:33
7:17 [c]Ps 110:4; ver 21; Heb 5:6
7:18 [d]Ro 8:3
7:19 [e]Ac 13:39; Ro 3:20; Heb 9:9 [f]Heb 4:16
7:21 [g]1Sa 15:29 [h]Ps 110:4
7:22 [i]Heb 8:6

b *14* Gen. 22:17 c *17,21* Psalm 110:4

priests, since death prevented them
from continuing in office; 24 but because
Jesus lives forever, he has a permanent
priesthood.[a] 25 Therefore he is able to
save completely[d] those who come to
God[b] through him, because he always
lives to intercede for them.[c]

26 Such a high priest meets our need—
one who is holy, blameless, pure, set
apart from sinners,[d] exalted above the
heavens.[e] 27 Unlike the other high priests,
he does not need to offer sacrifices[f]
day after day, first for his own sins,[g] and
then for the sins of the people. He sacrificed for their sins once for all[h] when he
offered himself.[i] 28 For the law appoints
as high priests men who are weak;[j] but
the oath, which came after the law,
appointed the Son,[k] who has been made
perfect[l] forever.

Jesus' priesthood presents a new and better covenant.

8 The point of what we are saying is
this: We do have such a high
priest,[m] who sat down at the right hand
of the throne of the Majesty in heaven,
2 and who serves in the sanctuary, the
true tabernacle[n] set up by the Lord, not
by man.

3 Every high priest is appointed to
offer both gifts and sacrifices,[o] and so it
was necessary for this one also to have
something to offer.[p] 4 If he were on
earth, he would not be a priest, for
there are already men who offer the
gifts prescribed by the law.[q] 5 They serve
at a sanctuary that is a copy[r] and shadows[s] of what is in heaven. This is why
Moses was warned[t] when he was about
to build the tabernacle: "See to it that you
make everything according to the pattern shown you on the mountain."[e][u] 6 But
the ministry Jesus has received is as superior to theirs as the covenant[v] of which
he is mediator[w] is superior to the old
one, and it is founded on better promises.

7 For if there had been nothing wrong
with that first covenant, no place would
have been sought for another.[x] 8 But God
found fault with the people and said[f]:

"The time is coming, declares the
Lord,
when I will make a new covenant[y]
with the house of Israel
and with the house of Judah.
9 It will not be like the covenant
I made with their forefathers[z]
when I took them by the hand
to lead them out of Egypt,
because they did not remain faithful
to my covenant,
and I turned away from them,
declares the Lord.
10 This is the covenant I will make
with the house of Israel
after that time, declares the Lord.
I will put my laws in their minds
and write them on their hearts.[a]
I will be their God,
and they will be my people.[b]
11 No longer will a man teach his
neighbor,
or a man his brother, saying,
'Know the Lord,'
because they will all know me,[c]
from the least of them to the
greatest.
12 For I will forgive their wickedness
and will remember their sins no
more."[d][g][e]

13 By calling this covenant "new," he
has made the first one obsolete;[f] and
what is obsolete and aging will soon
disappear.

Sacrifice in the earthly tabernacle.

9 Now the first covenant had regulations for worship and also an earthly sanctuary.[g] 2 A tabernacle[h] was set up.
In its first room were the lampstand,[i]
the table[j] and the consecrated bread;[k]
this was called the Holy Place. 3 Behind
the second curtain was a room called
the Most Holy Place,[l] 4 which had the
golden altar of incense[m] and the gold-
covered ark of the covenant.[n] This ark
contained the gold jar of manna,[o]

7:24 [a]ver 28
7:25 [b]ver 19 [c]Ro 8:34
7:26 [d]2Co 5:21 [e]Heb 4:14
7:27 [f]Heb 5:1 [g]Heb 5:3 [h]Heb 9:12, 26,28 [i]Eph 5:2; Heb 9:14,28
7:28 [j]Heb 5:2 [k]Heb 1:2 [l]Heb 2:10
8:1 [m]Heb 2:17
8:2 [n]Heb 9:11,24
8:3 [o]Heb 5:1 [p]Heb 9:14
8:4 [q]Heb 5:1
8:5 [r]Heb 9:23 [s]Col 2:17; Heb 10:1 [t]Heb 11:7; 12:25 [u]Ex 25:40
8:6 [v]Lk 22:20 [w]Heb 7:22
8:7 [x]Heb 7:11,18
8:8 [y]Jer 31:31
8:9 [z]Ex 19:5,6
8:10 [a]2Co 3:3; Heb 10:16 [b]Zec 8:8
8:11 [c]Isa 54:13; Jn 6:45
8:12 [d]Heb 10:17 [e]Jer 31:31-34
8:13 [f]2Co 5:17
9:1 [g]Ex 25:8
9:2 [h]Ex 25:8,9 [i]Ex 25:31-39 [j]Ex 25:23-29 [k]Lev 24:5-8
9:3 [l]Ex 26:31-33
9:4 [m]Ex 30:1-5 [n]Ex 25:10-22 [o]Ex 16:32,33

d *25* Or *forever* e *5* Exodus 25:40
f *8* Some manuscripts may be translated *fault and said to the people.* g *12* Jer. 31:31-34

Aaron's staff that had budded,[a] and the stone tablets of the covenant. **5**Above the ark were the cherubim of the Glory,[b] overshadowing the atonement cover.[h] But we cannot discuss these things in detail now.

6When everything had been arranged like this, the priests entered regularly[c] into the outer room to carry on their ministry. **7**But only the high priest entered[d] the inner room, and that only once a year,[e] and never without blood, which he offered for himself[f] and for the sins the people had committed in ignorance. **8**The Holy Spirit was showing[g] by this that the way[h] into the Most Holy Place had not yet been disclosed as long as the first tabernacle was still standing. **9**This is an illustration for the present time, indicating that the gifts and sacrifices being offered[i] were not able to clear the conscience of the worshiper. **10**They are only a matter of food[j] and drink[k] and various ceremonial washings—external regulations[l] applying until the time of the new order.

The new covenant and the sacrifice of Christ's blood.

11When Christ came as high priest[m] of the good things that are already here,[i][n] he went through the greater and more perfect tabernacle[o] that is not man-made, that is to say, not a part of this creation. **12**He did not enter by means of the blood of goats and calves;[p] but he entered the Most Holy Place[q] once for all[r] by his own blood, having obtained eternal redemption. **13**The blood of goats and bulls and the ashes of a heifer[s] sprinkled on those who are ceremonially unclean sanctify them so that they are outwardly clean. **14**How much more, then, will the blood of Christ, who through the eternal Spirit[t] offered himself unblemished to God, cleanse our consciences[u] from acts that lead to death,[j][v] so that we may serve the living God!

15For this reason Christ is the mediator[w] of a new covenant, that those who are called may receive the promised eternal inheritance—now that he has died as a ransom to set them free from the sins committed under the first covenant.[x]

16In the case of a will,[k] it is necessary to prove the death of the one who made it, **17**because a will is in force only when somebody has died; it never takes effect while the one who made it is living. **18**This is why even the first covenant was not put into effect without blood.[y] **19**When Moses had proclaimed every commandment of the law to all the people, he took the blood of calves, together with water, scarlet wool and branches of hyssop, and sprinkled the scroll and all the people.[z] **20**He said, "This is the blood of the covenant, which God has commanded you to keep."[l][a] **21**In the same way, he sprinkled with the blood both the tabernacle and everything used in its ceremonies. **22**In fact, the law requires that nearly everything be cleansed with blood,[b] and without the shedding of blood there is no forgiveness.[c]

23It was necessary, then, for the copies[d] of the heavenly things to be purified with these sacrifices, but the heavenly things themselves with better sacrifices than these. **24**For Christ did not enter a man-made sanctuary that was only a copy of the true one;[e] he entered heaven itself, now to appear for us in God's presence. **25**Nor did he enter heaven to offer himself again and again, the way the high priest enters the Most Holy Place[f] every year with blood that is not his own.[g] **26**Then Christ would have had to suffer many times since the creation of the world.[h] But now he has appeared once for all[i] at the end of the ages to do away with sin by the sacrifice of himself. **27**Just as man is destined to die once,[j] and after that to face judgment,[k] **28**so Christ was sacrificed once to take away the sins of many people; and he will appear a second time,[l] not to bear sin,[m] but to bring

9:4 [a]Nu 17:10
9:5 [b]Ex 25:17-19
9:6 [c]Nu 28:3
9:7 [d]Lev 16:11-19 [e]Lev 16:34 [f]Heb 5:2,3
9:8 [g]Heb 3:7 [h]Jn 14:6; Heb 10:19,20
9:9 [i]Heb 5:1
9:10 [j]Lev 11:2-23 [k]Col 2:16 [l]Heb 7:16
9:11 [m]Heb 2:17 [n]Heb 10:1 [o]Heb 8:2
9:12 [p]Heb 10:4 [q]ver 24 [r]Heb 7:27
9:13 [s]Nu 19:9,17, 18
9:14 [t]1Pe 3:18 [u]Tit 2:14; Heb 10:2,22 [v]Heb 6:1
9:15 [w]1Ti 2:5 [x]Heb 7:22
9:18 [y]Ex 24:6-8
9:19 [z]Ex 24:6-8
9:20 [a]Ex 24:8; Mt 26:28
9:22 [b]Lev 8:15 [c]Lev 17:11
9:23 [d]Heb 8:5
9:24 [e]Heb 8:2
9:25 [f]Heb 10:19 [g]ver 7,8
9:26 [h]Heb 4:3 [i]Heb 7:27
9:27 [j]Ge 3:19 [k]2Co 5:10
9:28 [l]Tit 2:13 [m]1Pe 2:24

h *5* Traditionally *the mercy seat* i *11* Some early manuscripts *are to come* j *14* Or *from useless rituals* k *16* Same Greek word as *covenant*; also in verse 17 l *20* Exodus 24:8

salvation to those who are waiting for
him.[a]

Christ's perfect sacrifice, once for all.

10 The law is only a shadow[b] of the
good things[c] that are coming—
not the realities themselves.[d] For this
reason it can never, by the same sacrifices repeated endlessly year after year,
make perfect[e] those who draw near to
worship. 2If it could, would they not
have stopped being offered? For the
worshipers would have been cleansed
once for all, and would no longer have
felt guilty for their sins. 3But those sacrifices are an annual reminder of sins,[f]
4because it is impossible for the blood
of bulls and goats[g] to take away sins.
5Therefore, when Christ came into
the world,[h] he said:

"Sacrifice and offering you did not
desire,
but a body you prepared for me;[i]
6with burnt offerings and sin
offerings
you were not pleased.
7Then I said, 'Here I am—it is
written about me in the
scroll[j]—
I have come to do your will,
O God.'"[m][k]

8First he said, "Sacrifices and offerings,
burnt offerings and sin offerings you did
not desire, nor were you pleased with
them"[l] (although the law required them
to be made). 9Then he said, "Here I am,
I have come to do your will."[m] He sets
aside the first to establish the second.
10And by that will, we have been made
holy[n] through the sacrifice of the body[o]
of Jesus Christ once for all.[p]
11Day after day every priest stands
and performs his religious duties; again
and again he offers the same sacrifices,[q]
which can never take away sins.[r] 12But
when this priest had offered for all time
one sacrifice for sins, he sat down at the
right hand of God. 13Since that time he
waits for his enemies to be made his
footstool,[s] 14because by one sacrifice he
has made perfect[t] forever those who are
being made holy.
15The Holy Spirit also testifies[u] to us
about this. First he says:

16"This is the covenant I will make
with them
after that time, says the Lord.
I will put my laws in their hearts,
and I will write them on their
minds."[n][v]

17Then he adds:

"Their sins and lawless acts
I will remember no more."[o][w]

18And where these have been forgiven,
there is no longer any sacrifice for sin.

Perseverance in faithful obedience.

19Therefore, brothers, since we have
confidence to enter the Most Holy
Place[x] by the blood of Jesus, 20by a new
and living way[y] opened for us through
the curtain,[z] that is, his body, 21and since
we have a great priest[a] over the house
of God, 22let us draw near to God[b] with
a sincere heart in full assurance of faith,
having our hearts sprinkled to cleanse
us from a guilty conscience[c] and having
our bodies washed with pure water.
23Let us hold unswervingly to the
hope[d] we profess, for he who promised
is faithful.[e] 24And let us consider how
we may spur one another on toward
love and good deeds. 25Let us not give
up meeting together,[f] as some are in
the habit of doing, but let us encourage
one another[g]—and all the more as you
see the Day approaching.
26If we deliberately keep on sinning[h] after we have received the knowledge of the truth, no sacrifice for sins
is left, 27but only a fearful expectation
of judgment and of raging fire[i] that will
consume the enemies of God. 28Any-
one who rejected the law of Moses
died without mercy on the testimony

9:28 [a]1Co 1:7
10:1 [b]Heb 8:5 [c]Heb 9:11 [d]Heb 9:23 [e]Heb 7:19
10:3 [f]Heb 9:7
10:4 [g]Heb 9:12,13
10:5 [h]Heb 1:6 [i]1Pe 2:24
10:7 [j]Jer 36:2 [k]Ps 40:6-8
10:8 [l]ver 5,6; Mk 12:33
10:9 [m]ver 7
10:10 [n]Jn 17:19 [o]Heb 2:14; 1Pe 2:24 [p]Heb 7:27
10:11 [q]Heb 5:1 [r]ver 1,4
10:13 [s]Heb 1:13
10:14 [t]ver 1
10:15 [u]Heb 3:7
10:16 [v]Jer 31:33; Heb 8:10
10:17 [w]Heb 8:12
10:19 [x]Eph 2:18; Heb 9:8,12, 25
10:20 [y]Heb 9:8 [z]Heb 9:3
10:21 [a]Heb 2:17
10:22 [b]Heb 7:19 [c]Eze 36:25; Heb 9:14
10:23 [d]Heb 3:6 [e]1Co 1:9
10:25 [f]Ac 2:42 [g]Heb 3:13
10:26 [h]Nu 15:30; 2Pe 2:20
10:27 [i]Isa 26:11; 2Th 1:7; Heb 9:27

m *7* Psalm 40:6-8 (see Septuagint) n *16* Jer. 31:33
o *17* Jer. 31:34

of two or three witnesses.[a] 29 How much more severely do you think a man deserves to be punished who has trampled the Son of God under foot,[b] who has treated as an unholy thing the blood of the covenant[c] that sanctified him, and who has insulted the Spirit[d] of grace?[e] 30 For we know him who said, "It is mine to avenge; I will repay,"[p][f] and again, "The Lord will judge his people."[q][g] 31 It is a dreadful thing to fall into the hands of the living God.[h]

32 Remember those earlier days after you had received the light,[i] when you stood your ground in a great contest in the face of suffering.[j] 33 Sometimes you were publicly exposed to insult and persecution;[k] at other times you stood side by side with those who were so treated.[l] 34 You sympathized with those in prison[m] and joyfully accepted the confiscation of your property, because you knew that you yourselves had better and lasting possessions.[n]

35 So do not throw away your confidence; it will be richly rewarded. 36 You need to persevere[o] so that when you have done the will of God, you will receive what he has promised. 37 For in just a very little while,

"He who is coming[p] will come and
will not delay.[q]
38 But my righteous one[r] will live by
faith.[r]
And if he shrinks back,
I will not be pleased with him."[s]

39 But we are not of those who shrink back and are destroyed, but of those who believe and are saved.

Faith is defined and illustrated through the lives of Old Testament heroes.

11 Now faith is being sure of what we hope for and certain of what we do not see.[s] 2 This is what the ancients were commended for.[t]

3 By faith we understand that the universe was formed at God's command,[u] so that what is seen was not made out of what was visible.

4 By faith Abel offered God a better sacrifice than Cain did. By faith he was commended as a righteous man, when God spoke well of his offerings.[v] And by faith he still speaks, even though he is dead.[w]

5 By faith Enoch was taken from this life, so that he did not experience death; he could not be found, because God had taken him away.[x] For before he was taken, he was commended as one who pleased God. 6 And without faith it is impossible to please God, because anyone who comes to him[y] must believe that he exists and that he rewards those who earnestly seek him.

7 By faith Noah, when warned about things not yet seen, in holy fear built an ark[z] to save his family.[a] By his faith he condemned the world and became heir of the righteousness that comes by faith.

8 By faith Abraham, when called to go to a place he would later receive as his inheritance,[b] obeyed and went,[c] even though he did not know where he was going. 9 By faith he made his home in the promised land[d] like a stranger in a foreign country; he lived in tents,[e] as did Isaac and Jacob, who were heirs with him of the same promise.[f] 10 For he was looking forward to the city[g] with foundations,[h] whose architect and builder is God.

11 By faith Abraham, even though he was past age—and Sarah herself was barren[i]—was enabled to become a father[j] because he[t] considered him faithful who had made the promise. 12 And so from this one man, and he as good as dead,[k] came descendants as numerous as the stars in the sky and as countless as the sand on the seashore.[l]

13 All these people were still living by faith when they died. They did not receive the things promised;[m] they only saw them and welcomed them from a

10:28 [a]Dt 17:6,7; Heb 2:2
10:29 [b]Heb 6:6 [c]Mt 26:28 [d]Eph 4:30; Heb 6:4 [e]Heb 2:3
10:30 [f]Dt 32:35; Ro 12:19 [g]Dt 32:36
10:31 [h]Mt 16:16
10:32 [i]Heb 6:4 [j]Php 1:29,30
10:33 [k]1Co 4:9 [l]Php 4:14; 1Th 2:14
10:34 [m]Heb 13:3 [n]Heb 11:16
10:36 [o]Lk 21:19; Heb 12:1
10:37 [p]Mt 11:3 [q]Rev 22:20
10:38 [r]Ro 1:17; Gal 3:11
11:1 [s]Ro 8:24; 2Co 4:18
11:2 [t]ver 4,39
11:3 [u]Ge 1; Jn 1:3; 2Pe 3:5
11:4 [v]Ge 4:4; 1Jn 3:12 [w]Heb 12:24
11:5 [x]Ge 5:21-24
11:6 [y]Heb 7:19
11:7 [z]Ge 6:13-22 [a]1Pe 3:20
11:8 [b]Ge 12:7 [c]Ge 12:1-4; Ac 7:2-4
11:9 [d]Ac 7:5 [e]Ge 12:8; 18:1,9 [f]Heb 6:17
11:10 [g]Heb 12:22; 13:14 [h]Rev 21:2,14
11:11 [i]Ge 17:17-19; 18:11-14 [j]Ge 21:2
11:12 [k]Ro 4:19 [l]Ge 22:17 **11:13** [m]ver 39

p *30* Deut. 32:35 q *30* Deut. 32:36; Psalm 135:14
r *38* One early manuscript *But the righteous*
s *38* Hab. 2:3,4 t *11* Or *By faith even Sarah, who was past age, was enabled to bear children because she*

distance.[a] And they admitted that they
were aliens and strangers on earth.[b]
14People who say such things show that
they are looking for a country of their
own. 15If they had been thinking of the
country they had left, they would have
had opportunity to return.[c] 16Instead,
they were longing for a better country—
a heavenly one.[d] Therefore God is not
ashamed[e] to be called their God,[f] for he
has prepared a city[g] for them.
17By faith Abraham, when God tested
him, offered Isaac as a sacrifice.[h] He who
had received the promises was about to
sacrifice his one and only son, 18even
though God had said to him, "It is
through Isaac that your offspring[u] will
be reckoned."[v][i] 19Abraham reasoned
that God could raise the dead,[j] and figuratively speaking, he did receive Isaac
back from death.
20By faith Isaac blessed Jacob and
Esau in regard to their future.[k]
21By faith Jacob, when he was dying,
blessed each of Joseph's sons,[l] and worshiped as he leaned on the top of his
staff.
22By faith Joseph, when his end was
near, spoke about the exodus of the
Israelites from Egypt and gave instructions about his bones.[m]
23By faith Moses' parents hid him for
three months after he was born,[n] because
they saw he was no ordinary child, and
they were not afraid of the king's edict.[o]
24By faith Moses, when he had grown
up, refused to be known as the son of
Pharaoh's daughter.[p] 25He chose to be
mistreated[q] along with the people of
God rather than to enjoy the pleasures
of sin for a short time. 26He regarded
disgrace[r] for the sake of Christ as of
greater value than the treasures of Egypt,
because he was looking ahead to his
reward.[s] 27By faith he left Egypt,[t] not
fearing the king's anger; he persevered
because he saw him who is invisible.
28By faith he kept the Passover and the
sprinkling of blood, so that the destroyer
of the firstborn would not touch the
firstborn of Israel.[u]
29By faith the people passed through

11:13 [a]Mt 13:17 [b]Ge 23:4; Ps 39:12; 1Pe 1:17 **11:15** [c]Ge 24:6-8 **11:16** [d]2Ti 4:18 [e]Mk 8:38 [f]Ex 3:6,15 [g]Heb 13:14 **11:17** [h]Ge 22:1-10; Jas 2:21 **11:18** [i]Ge 21:12; Ro 9:7 **11:19** [j]Ro 4:21 **11:20** [k]Ge 27:27-29, 39,40 **11:21** [l]Ge 48:1, 8-22 **11:22** [m]Ge 50:24, 25; Ex 13:19 **11:23** [n]Ex 2:2 [o]Ex 1:16,22 **11:24** [p]Ex 2:10,11 **11:25** [q]ver 37 **11:26** [r]Heb 13:13 [s]Heb 10:35 **11:27** [t]Ex 12:50,51 **11:28** [u]Ex 12:21-23 **11:29** [v]Ex 14:21-31 **11:30** [w]Jos 6:12-20 **11:31** [x]Jos 2:1,9-14; 6:22-25; Jas 2:25 **11:32** [y]Jdg 4–5 [z]1Sa 16:1,13 [a]1Sa 1:20 **11:33** [b]2Sa 7:11; 8:1-3 [c]Da 6:22 **11:34** [d]2Ki 20:7 [e]Jdg 15:8 **11:35** [f]1Ki 17:22,23 **11:36** [g]Jer 20:2 [h]Ge 39:20

the Red Sea[w] as on dry land; but when
the Egyptians tried to do so, they were
drowned.[v]
30By faith the walls of Jericho fell, after
the people had marched around them
for seven days.[w]
31By faith the prostitute Rahab, because she welcomed the spies, was
not killed with those who were disobedient.[x][x]
32And what more shall I say? I do not
have time to tell about Gideon, Barak,[y]
Samson, Jephthah, David,[z] Samuel[a] and
the prophets, 33who through faith conquered kingdoms,[b] administered justice,
and gained what was promised; who
shut the mouths of lions,[c] 34quenched
the fury of the flames, and escaped the
edge of the sword; whose weakness was
turned to strength;[d] and who became
powerful in battle and routed foreign
armies.[e] 35Women received back their
dead, raised to life again.[f] Others were
tortured and refused to be released, so
that they might gain a better resurrection. 36Some faced jeers and flogging,[g]
while still others were chained and put
in prison.[h] 37They were stoned[y];[i] they
were sawed in two; they were put to
death by the sword.[j] They went about
in sheepskins and goatskins,[k] destitute, persecuted and mistreated— 38the
world was not worthy of them. They
wandered in deserts and mountains,
and in caves[l] and holes in the ground.
39These were all commended[m] for
their faith, yet none of them received
what had been promised.[n] 40God had
planned something better for us so that
only together with us would they be
made perfect.

God's loving discipline.

12 Therefore, since we are surrounded by such a great cloud of
witnesses, let us throw off everything

11:37 [i]2Ch 24:21 [j]1Ki 19:10 [k]2Ki 1:8 **11:38** [l]1Ki 18:4 **11:39** [m]ver 2,4 [n]ver 13

[u] *18* Greek *seed* [v] *18* Gen. 21:12 [w] *29* That is, Sea of Reeds [x] *31* Or *unbelieving* [y] *37* Some early manuscripts *stoned; they were put to the test;*

that hinders and the sin that so easily
entangles, and let us run[a] with perseverance[b] the race marked out for us.
2Let us fix our eyes on Jesus, the author
and perfecter of our faith, who for the
joy set before him endured the cross,[c]
scorning its shame,[d] and sat down at the
right hand of the throne of God. 3Con-
sider him who endured such opposition
from sinful men, so that you will not
grow weary[e] and lose heart.

4In your struggle against sin, you
have not yet resisted to the point of
shedding your blood.[f] 5And you have
forgotten that word of encouragement
that addresses you as sons:

"My son, do not make light of the
Lord's discipline,
and do not lose heart when he
rebukes you,
6because the Lord disciplines those
he loves,[g]
and he punishes everyone he
accepts as a son."[z][h]

7Endure hardship as discipline; God
is treating you as sons.[i] For what son is
not disciplined by his father? 8If you
are not disciplined (and everyone under-
goes discipline),[j] then you are illegitimate children and not true sons.
9Moreover, we have all had human
fathers who disciplined us and we respected them for it. How much more
should we submit to the Father of our
spirits[k] and live![l] 10Our fathers disciplined us for a little while as they
thought best; but God disciplines us for
our good, that we may share in his holiness.[m] 11No discipline seems pleasant
at the time, but painful. Later on, however, it produces a harvest of righteousness and peace[n] for those who have
been trained by it.

12Therefore, strengthen your feeble
arms and weak knees.[o] 13"Make level
paths for your feet,"[a][p] so that the lame
may not be disabled, but rather healed.[q]

Warnings of the dangers of disobedience.

14Make every effort to live in peace
with all men[r] and to be holy;[s] without
holiness no one will see the Lord.[t] 15See
to it that no one misses the grace of
God[u] and that no bitter root grows up
to cause trouble and defile many. 16See
that no one is sexually immoral, or is
godless like Esau, who for a single meal
sold his inheritance rights as the oldest
son.[v] 17Afterward, as you know, when
he wanted to inherit this blessing, he
was rejected. He could bring about no
change of mind, though he sought the
blessing with tears.[w]

18You have not come to a mountain
that can be touched and that is burning with fire; to darkness, gloom and
storm;[x] 19to a trumpet blast[y] or to such
a voice speaking words that those who
heard it begged that no further word
be spoken to them,[z] 20because they
could not bear what was commanded:
"If even an animal touches the mountain, it must be stoned."[b][a] 21The sight
was so terrifying that Moses said, "I am
trembling with fear."[c]

22But you have come to Mount Zion,
to the heavenly Jerusalem,[b] the city[c] of
the living God. You have come to thousands upon thousands of angels in joyful
assembly, 23to the church of the firstborn, whose names are written in heav-
en.[d] You have come to God, the judge
of all men,[e] to the spirits of righteous
men made perfect,[f] 24to Jesus the mediator of a new covenant, and to the sprinkled blood that speaks a better word
than the blood of Abel.[g]

25See to it that you do not refuse him
who speaks. If they did not escape when
they refused him who warned[h] them on
earth, how much less will we, if we
turn away from him who warns us from
heaven?[i] 26At that time his voice shook
the earth,[j] but now he has promised,
"Once more I will shake not only the
earth but also the heavens."[d][k] 27The
words "once more" indicate the removing of what can be shaken[l]—that is,

12:1 [a]1Co 9:24 [b]Heb 10:36 **12:2** [c]Php 2:8,9 [d]Heb 13:13 **12:3** [e]Gal 6:9 **12:4** [f]Heb 10:32-34 **12:6** [g]Ps 94:12; Rev 3:19 [h]Pr 3:11,12 **12:7** [i]Dt 8:5 **12:8** [j]1Pe 5:9 **12:9** [k]Nu 16:22 [l]Isa 38:16 **12:10** [m]2Pe 1:4 **12:11** [n]Isa 32:17; Jas 3:17,18 **12:12** [o]Isa 35:3 **12:13** [p]Pr 4:26 [q]Gal 6:1 **12:14** [r]Ro 14:19 [s]Ro 6:22 [t]Mt 5:8 **12:15** [u]Gal 5:4; Heb 3:12 **12:16** [v]Ge 25:29-34 **12:17** [w]Ge 27:30-40 **12:18** [x]Ex 19:12-22; Dt 4:11 **12:19** [y]Ex 20:18 [z]Ex 20:19; Dt 5:5,25 **12:20** [a]Ex 19:12,13 **12:22** [b]Gal 4:26 [c]Heb 11:10 **12:23** [d]Lk 10:20 [e]Ps 94:2 [f]Php 3:12 **12:24** [g]Ge 4:10; Heb 11:4 **12:25** [h]Heb 8:5; 11:7 [i]Heb 2:2,3 **12:26** [j]Ex 19:18 [k]Hag 2:6

12:27 [l]1Co 7:31; 2Pe 3:10

z*6* Prov. 3:11,12 a*13* Prov. 4:26
b*20* Exodus 19:12,13 c*21* Deut. 9:19
d*26* Haggai 2:6

created things—so that what cannot be shaken may remain.

28Therefore, since we are receiving a kingdom that cannot be shaken,[a] let us be thankful, and so worship God acceptably with reverence and awe,[b] 29for our "God is a consuming fire."[e][c]

Instructions on hospitality, marriage and sacrificial giving.

13 Keep on loving each other as brothers.[d] 2Do not forget to entertain strangers,[e] for by so doing some people have entertained angels without knowing it.[f] 3Remember those in prison[g] as if you were their fellow prisoners, and those who are mistreated as if you yourselves were suffering.

4Marriage should be honored by all, and the marriage bed kept pure, for God will judge the adulterer and all the sexually immoral.[h] 5Keep your lives free from the love of money and be content with what you have,[i] because God has said,

> "Never will I leave you;
> never will I forsake you."[f][j]

6So we say with confidence,

> "The Lord is my helper; I will not be afraid.
> What can man do to me?"[g]

7Remember your leaders,[k] who spoke the word of God to you. Consider the outcome of their way of life and imitate[l] their faith. 8Jesus Christ is the same yesterday and today and forever.[m]

9Do not be carried away by all kinds of strange teachings.[n] It is good for our hearts to be strengthened[o] by grace, not by ceremonial foods,[p] which are of no value to those who eat them. 10We have an altar from which those who minister at the tabernacle have no right to eat.[q]

11The high priest carries the blood of animals into the Most Holy Place as a sin offering, but the bodies are burned outside the camp.[r] 12And so Jesus also suffered outside the city gate[s] to make the people holy through his own blood. 13Let us, then, go to him outside the camp, bearing the disgrace he bore.[t] 14For here we do not have an enduring city, but we are looking for the city that is to come.[u]

15Through Jesus, therefore, let us continually offer to God a sacrifice[v] of praise—the fruit of lips[w] that confess his name. 16And do not forget to do good and to share with others,[x] for with such sacrifices[y] God is pleased.

17Obey your leaders and submit to their authority. They keep watch over you[z] as men who must give an account. Obey them so that their work will be a joy, not a burden, for that would be of no advantage to you.

Concluding requests and greetings.

18Pray for us.[a] We are sure that we have a clear conscience[b] and desire to live honorably in every way. 19I particularly urge you to pray so that I may be restored to you soon.[c]

20May the God of peace,[d] who through the blood of the eternal covenant[e] brought back from the dead[f] our Lord Jesus, that great Shepherd of the sheep,[g] 21equip you with everything good for doing his will, and may he work in us[h] what is pleasing to him,[i] through Jesus Christ, to whom be glory for ever and ever. Amen.[j]

22Brothers, I urge you to bear with my word of exhortation, for I have written you only a short letter.[k]

23I want you to know that our brother Timothy[l] has been released. If he arrives soon, I will come with him to see you.

24Greet all your leaders[m] and all God's people. Those from Italy[n] send you their greetings.

25Grace be with you all.[o]

12:28 [a]Da 2:44 [b]Heb 13:15
12:29 [c]Dt 4:24
13:1 [d]Ro 12:10; 1Pe 1:22
13:2 [e]Mt 25:35 [f]Ge 18:1-33
13:3 [g]Mt 25:36; Col 4:18
13:4 [h]1Co 6:9
13:5 [i]Php 4:11 [j]Dt 31:6,8; Jos 1:5
13:7 [k]ver 17,24 [l]Heb 6:12
13:8 [m]Heb 1:12
13:9 [n]Eph 4:14 [o]Col 2:7 [p]Col 2:16
13:10 [q]1Co 9:13; 10:18
13:11 [r]Ex 29:14; Lev 16:27
13:12 [s]Jn 19:17
13:13 [t]Heb 11:26
13:14 [u]Php 3:20; Heb 12:22
13:15 [v]1Pe 2:5 [w]Hos 14:2
13:16 [x]Ro 12:13 [y]Php 4:18
13:17 [z]Isa 62:6; Ac 20:28
13:18 [a]1Th 5:25 [b]Ac 23:1
13:19 [c]Phm 22
13:20 [d]Ro 15:33 [e]Isa 55:3; Eze 37:26; Zec 9:11 [f]Ac 2:24 [g]Jn 10:11
13:21 [h]Php 2:13 [i]1Jn 3:22 [j]Ro 11:36
13:22 [k]1Pe 5:12 **13:23** [l]Ac 16:1 **13:24** [m]ver 7,17 [n]Ac 18:2 **13:25** [o]Col 4:18

[e]29 Deut. 4:24 [f]5 Deut. 31:6 [g]6 Psalm 118:6,7

JAMES

Author: James (the son of Mary and Joseph, and the half-brother of Jesus).

Date Written: Between A.D. 45 and 49.

Title: From the book's author: James.

Background: James does not become a believer until after the resurrection of the Lord Jesus. He later becomes the leader of the church in Jerusalem, presides at the Jerusalem council, and is among those awaiting the Holy Spirit on the day of Pentecost. These teachings of James can be likened to the book of Proverbs and to the teachings of Jesus, especially to his Sermon on the Mount. The emphasis of James's letter is to stress the importance of good deeds in the life of every believer.

Where Written: Possibly Jerusalem.

To Whom: To the twelve tribes scattered among the nations (Jewish Christians).

Content: To merely say we have faith is insufficient. James stresses that we must have faith that manifests itself in the action of good deeds. His letter covers a wide range of sins: pride, prejudice, hypocrisy, worldliness, the untamed tongue and apathy. This practical treatise gives the scattered Jewish Christians a strong understanding of their union in Christ. Their trials, desires, relationships, prayers, compassion, patience and faith are all shown to have a place in their worship of God and in their ministry to others. The letter closes with a dramatic account of the faith of Elijah.

Key Words: "Patience"; "Pure Religion." James emphasizes "patience" as a godly virtue each believer needs in order to become perfect and complete in Christ. "Pure religion" is living righteously before God and as an example before the world. This includes a proper relationship with orphans, widows and others.

Themes: • We are saved by faith alone, but saving faith never stands alone...it reveals itself through obedience and fruit of the believer. • We cannot be saved by any number of good deeds. • Faith without good deeds is not real faith. • We must be doers of the Word, not just hearers. • Our human strength is unable to tame the tongue...but through God's strength it can be done. • There is no place for discrimination or greed in the life of a committed believer.

Outline:

1. Introduction. 1:1
2. Concerning trials and temptations. 1:2-1:18
3. Characteristics of true faith. 1:19-2:26
4. Stumbling blocks. 3:1-5:6
5. Faith that triumphs. 5:7-5:20

JAMES

1 James,[a] a servant of God[b] and of the Lord Jesus Christ,

To the twelve tribes[c] scattered[d] among the nations:

Greetings.

Trials bring maturity.

2 Consider it pure joy, my brothers, whenever you face trials of many kinds,[e] 3 because you know that the testing of your faith develops perseverance. 4 Perseverance must finish its work so that you may be mature and complete, not lacking anything. 5 If any of you lacks wisdom, he should ask God,[f] who gives generously to all without finding fault, and it will be given to him.[g] 6 But when he asks, he must believe and not doubt,[h] because he who doubts is like a wave of the sea, blown and tossed by the wind. 7 That man should not think he will receive anything from the Lord; 8 he is a double-minded man,[i] unstable in all he does.

9 The brother in humble circumstances ought to take pride in his high position. 10 But the one who is rich should take pride in his low position, because he will pass away like a wild flower.[j] 11 For the sun rises with scorching heat and withers[k] the plant; its blossom falls and its beauty is destroyed.[l] In the same way, the rich man will fade away even while he goes about his business.

Temptations are not from God.

12 Blessed is the man who perseveres under trial, because when he has stood the test, he will receive the crown of life[m] that God has promised to those who love him.[n]

13 When tempted, no one should say, "God is tempting me." For God cannot be tempted by evil, nor does he tempt anyone; 14 but each one is tempted when, by his own evil desire, he is dragged away and enticed. 15 Then, after desire has conceived, it gives birth to sin;[o] and sin, when it is full-grown, gives birth to death.[p]

16 Don't be deceived,[q] my dear brothers.[r] 17 Every good and perfect gift is from above,[s] coming down from the Father of the heavenly lights, who does not change[t] like shifting shadows. 18 He chose to give us birth[u] through the word of truth, that we might be a kind of firstfruits[v] of all he created.

Believers must obey God's Word, not just listen to it.

19 My dear brothers, take note of this: Everyone should be quick to listen, slow to speak[w] and slow to become angry, 20 for man's anger does not bring about the righteous life that God desires. 21 Therefore, get rid of[x] all moral filth and the evil that is so prevalent and humbly accept the word planted in you,[y] which can save you.

22 Do not merely listen to the word, and so deceive yourselves. Do what it says. 23 Anyone who listens to the word but does not do what it says is like a man who looks at his face in a mirror 24 and, after looking at himself, goes away and immediately forgets what he looks like. 25 But the man who looks intently into the perfect law that gives freedom,[z] and continues to do this, not forgetting what he has heard, but doing it—he will be blessed in what he does.[a]

26 If anyone considers himself religious and yet does not keep a tight rein on his tongue,[b] he deceives himself and his religion is worthless. 27 Religion that God our Father accepts as pure and faultless is this: to look after[c] orphans and widows[d] in their distress and to keep oneself from being polluted by the world.[e]

Favoritism should not be shown.

2 My brothers, as believers in our glorious[f] Lord Jesus Christ, don't show favoritism.[g] 2 Suppose a man comes into your meeting wearing a gold ring and fine clothes, and a poor man in

1:1 [a] Ac 15:13 [b] Tit 1:1 [c] Ac 26:7 [d] Dt 32:26; Jn 7:35; 1Pe 1:1
1:2 [e] Mt 5:12; 1Pe 1:6
1:5 [f] 1Ki 3:9,10; Pr 2:3-6 [g] Mt 7:7
1:6 [h] Mk 11:24
1:8 [i] Jas 4:8
1:10 [j] 1Co 7:31; 1Pe 1:24
1:11 [k] Ps 102:4,11 [l] Isa 40:6-8
1:12 [m] 1Co 9:25 [n] Jas 2:5
1:15 [o] Job 15:35; Ps 7:14 [p] Ro 6:23
1:16 [q] 1Co 6:9 [r] ver 19
1:17 [s] Jn 3:27 [t] Nu 23:19; Mal 3:6
1:18 [u] Jn 1:13 [v] Eph 1:12; Rev 14:4
1:19 [w] Pr 10:19
1:21 [x] Eph 4:22 [y] Eph 1:13
1:25 [z] Jas 2:12 [a] Jn 13:17
1:26 [b] Ps 34:13; 1Pe 3:10
1:27 [c] Mt 25:36 [d] Isa 1:17,23 [e] Ro 12:2
2:1 [f] 1Co 2:8 [g] Lev 19:15

shabby clothes also comes in. 3If you show special attention to the man wearing fine clothes and say, "Here's a good seat for you," but say to the poor man, "You stand there" or "Sit on the floor by my feet," 4have you not discriminated among yourselves and become judges[a] with evil thoughts?

5Listen, my dear brothers:[b] Has not God chosen those who are poor in the eyes of the world[c] to be rich in faith[d] and to inherit the kingdom he promised those who love him?[e] 6But you have insulted the poor.[f] Is it not the rich who are exploiting you? Are they not the ones who are dragging you into court?[g] 7Are they not the ones who are slandering the noble name of him to whom you belong?

8If you really keep the royal law found in Scripture, "Love your neighbor as yourself,"[a][h] you are doing right. 9But if you show favoritism,[i] you sin and are convicted by the law as lawbreakers.[j] 10For whoever keeps the whole law and yet stumbles at just one point is guilty of breaking all of it.[k] 11For he who said, "Do not commit adultery,"[b][l] also said, "Do not murder."[c][m] If you do not commit adultery but do commit murder, you have become a lawbreaker.

12Speak and act as those who are going to be judged by the law that gives freedom,[n] 13because judgment without mercy will be shown to anyone who has not been merciful.[o] Mercy triumphs over judgment!

Real faith shows itself by deeds.

14What good is it, my brothers, if a man claims to have faith but has no deeds?[p] Can such faith save him? 15Suppose a brother or sister is without clothes and daily food.[q] 16If one of you says to him, "Go, I wish you well; keep warm and well fed," but does nothing about his physical needs, what good is it?[r] 17In the same way, faith by itself, if it is not accompanied by action, is dead.

18But someone will say, "You have faith; I have deeds."

Show me your faith without deeds,[s] and I will show you my faith by what I do.[t] 19You believe that there is one God.[u] Good! Even the demons believe that[v]—and shudder.

20You foolish man, do you want evidence that faith without deeds is useless[d]?[w] 21Was not our ancestor Abraham considered righteous for what he did when he offered his son Isaac on the altar?[x] 22You see that his faith and his actions were working together,[y] and his faith was made complete by what he did.[z] 23And the scripture was fulfilled that says, "Abraham believed God, and it was credited to him as righteousness,"[e][a] and he was called God's friend.[b] 24You see that a person is justified by what he does and not by faith alone.

25In the same way, was not even Rahab the prostitute considered righteous for what she did when she gave lodging to the spies and sent them off in a different direction?[c] 26As the body without the spirit is dead, so faith without deeds is dead.[d]

Importance of controlling the tongue.

3 Not many of you should presume to be teachers, my brothers, because you know that we who teach will be judged more strictly. 2We all stumble[e] in many ways. If anyone is never at fault in what he says,[f] he is a perfect man,[g] able to keep his whole body in check.[h]

3When we put bits into the mouths of horses to make them obey us, we can turn the whole animal.[i] 4Or take ships as an example. Although they are so large and are driven by strong winds, they are steered by a very small rudder wherever the pilot wants to go. 5Likewise the tongue is a small part of the body, but it makes great boasts.[j] Con-

2:4 [a]Jn 7:24
2:5 [b]Jas 1:16,19 [c]1Co 1:26-28 [d]Lk 12:21 [e]Jas 1:12
2:6 [f]1Co 11:22 [g]Ac 8:3
2:8 [h]Lev 19:18
2:9 [i]ver 1 [j]Dt 1:17
2:10 [k]Mt 5:19; Gal 3:10
2:11 [l]Ex 20:14; Dt 5:18 [m]Ex 20:13; Dt 5:17
2:12 [n]Jas 1:25
2:13 [o]Mt 5:7; 18:32-35
2:14 [p]Mt 7:26; Jas 1:22-25
2:15 [q]Mt 25:35,36
2:16 [r]1Jn 3:17,18
2:18 [s]Ro 3:28 [t]Jas 3:13
2:19 [u]Dt 6:4 [v]Mt 8:29; Lk 4:34
2:20 [w]ver 17,26
2:21 [x]Ge 22:9,12
2:22 [y]Heb 11:17 [z]1Th 1:3
2:23 [a]Ge 15:6; Ro 4:3 [b]2Ch 20:7; Isa 41:8
2:25 [c]Heb 11:31
2:26 [d]ver 17,20
3:2 [e]1Ki 8:46; Jas 2:10 [f]1Pe 3:10 [g]Mt 12:37 [h]Jas 1:26
3:3 [i]Ps 32:9
3:5 [j]Ps 12:3,4

a *8* Lev. 19:18 b *11* Exodus 20:14; Deut. 5:18 c *11* Exodus 20:13; Deut. 5:17 d *20* Some early manuscripts *dead* e *23* Gen. 15:6

sider what a great forest is set on fire by a small spark. 6The tongue also is a fire,[a] a world of evil among the parts of the body. It corrupts the whole person,[b] sets the whole course of his life on fire, and is itself set on fire by hell.

7All kinds of animals, birds, reptiles and creatures of the sea are being tamed and have been tamed by man, 8but no man can tame the tongue. It is a restless evil, full of deadly poison.[c]

9With the tongue we praise our Lord and Father, and with it we curse men, who have been made in God's likeness.[d] 10Out of the same mouth come praise and cursing. My brothers, this should not be. 11Can both fresh water and salt[f] water flow from the same spring? 12My brothers, can a fig tree bear olives, or a grapevine bear figs?[e] Neither can a salt spring produce fresh water.

Earthly wisdom versus heavenly wisdom.

13Who is wise and understanding among you? Let him show it[f] by his good life, by deeds done in the humility that comes from wisdom. 14But if you harbor bitter envy and selfish ambition[g] in your hearts, do not boast about it or deny the truth.[h] 15Such "wisdom" does not come down from heaven[i] but is earthly, unspiritual, of the devil.[j] 16For where you have envy and selfish ambition, there you find disorder and every evil practice.

17But the wisdom that comes from heaven[k] is first of all pure; then peace-loving, considerate, submissive, full of mercy[l] and good fruit, impartial and sincere.[m] 18Peacemakers who sow in peace raise a harvest of righteousness.[n]

Friendship with the world is hatred toward God.

4 What causes fights and quarrels[o] among you? Don't they come from your desires that battle[p] within you? 2You want something but don't get it. You kill and covet, but you cannot have what you want. You quarrel and fight. You do not have, because you do not ask God. 3When you ask, you do not receive,[q] because you ask with wrong motives,[r] that you may spend what you get on your pleasures.

4You adulterous people, don't you know that friendship with the world[s] is hatred toward God?[t] Anyone who chooses to be a friend of the world becomes an enemy of God.[u] 5Or do you think Scripture says without reason that the spirit he caused to live in us envies intensely?[g] 6But he gives us more grace. That is why Scripture says:

> "God opposes the proud
> but gives grace to the humble."[h][v]

7Submit yourselves, then, to God. Resist the devil,[w] and he will flee from you. 8Come near to God and he will come near to you.[x] Wash your hands,[y] you sinners, and purify your hearts, you double-minded.[z] 9Grieve, mourn and wail. Change your laughter to mourning and your joy to gloom.[a] 10Humble yourselves before the Lord, and he will lift you up.

11Brothers, do not slander one another.[b] Anyone who speaks against his brother or judges him[c] speaks against the law and judges it. When you judge the law, you are not keeping it,[d] but sitting in judgment on it. 12There is only one Lawgiver and Judge, the one who is able to save and destroy.[e] But you—who are you to judge your neighbor?[f]

Boasting about tomorrow is evil.

13Now listen, you who say, "Today or tomorrow we will go to this or that city, spend a year there, carry on business and make money."[g] 14Why, you do not even know what will happen tomorrow. What is your life? You are a mist that appears for a little while and then vanishes.[h] 15Instead, you ought to say, "If it is the Lord's will,[i] we will live and do

3:6 [a]Pr 16:27 [b]Mt 15:11, 18,19
3:8 [c]Ps 140:3; Ro 3:13
3:9 [d]Ge 1:26,27; 1Co 11:7
3:12 [e]Mt 7:16
3:13 [f]Jas 2:18
3:14 [g]ver 16 [h]Jas 5:19
3:15 [i]Jas 1:17 [j]1Ti 4:1
3:17 [k]1Co 2:6 [l]Lk 6:36 [m]Ro 12:9
3:18 [n]Pr 11:18; Isa 32:17
4:1 [o]Tit 3:9 [p]Ro 7:23
4:3 [q]Ps 18:41 [r]1Jn 3:22; 5:14
4:4 [s]Jas 1:27 [t]1Jn 2:15 [u]Jn 15:19
4:6 [v]Ps 138:6; Pr 3:34; Mt 23:12
4:7 [w]Eph 4:27; 1Pe 5:6-9
4:8 [x]2Ch 15:2 [y]Isa 1:16 [z]Jas 1:8
4:9 [a]Lk 6:25
4:11 [b]1Pe 2:1 [c]Mt 7:1 [d]Jas 1:22
4:12 [e]Mt 10:28 [f]Ro 14:4
4:13 [g]Pr 27:1
4:14 [h]Job 7:7; Ps 102:3
4:15 [i]Ac 18:21

[f] *11* Greek *bitter* (see also verse 14) [g] *5* Or *that God jealously longs for the spirit that he made to live in us*; or *that the Spirit he caused to live in us longs jealously* [h] *6* Prov. 3:34

this or that." 16As it is, you boast and brag. All such boasting is evil.[a] 17Anyone, then, who knows the good he ought to do and doesn't do it, sins.[b]

Rebuke for wealthy oppressors.

5 Now listen, you rich people,[c] weep and wail because of the misery that is coming upon you. 2Your wealth has rotted, and moths have eaten your clothes.[d] 3Your gold and silver are corroded. Their corrosion will testify against you and eat your flesh like fire. You have hoarded wealth in the last days.[e] 4Look! The wages you failed to pay the workmen[f] who mowed your fields are crying out against you. The cries[g] of the harvesters have reached the ears of the Lord Almighty.[h] 5You have lived on earth in luxury and self-indulgence. You have fattened yourselves[i] in the day of slaughter.[i][j] 6You have condemned and murdered innocent men,[k] who were not opposing you.

Patience until the Lord returns.

7Be patient, then, brothers, until the Lord's coming. See how the farmer waits for the land to yield its valuable crop and how patient he is for the autumn and spring rains.[l] 8You too, be patient and stand firm, because the Lord's coming is near.[m] 9Don't grumble against each other, brothers,[n] or you will be judged. The Judge[o] is standing at the door![p]

10Brothers, as an example of patience in the face of suffering, take the prophets[q] who spoke in the name of the Lord. 11As you know, we consider blessed[r] those who have persevered. You have heard of Job's perseverance[s] and have seen what the Lord finally brought about.[t] The Lord is full of compassion and mercy.[u]

12Above all, my brothers, do not swear—not by heaven or by earth or by anything else. Let your "Yes" be yes, and your "No," no, or you will be condemned.[v]

Healing power of prayer.

13Is any one of you in trouble? He should pray.[w] Is anyone happy? Let him sing songs of praise.[x] 14Is any one of you sick? He should call the elders of the church to pray over him and anoint him with oil[y] in the name of the Lord. 15And the prayer offered in faith will make the sick person well; the Lord will raise him up. If he has sinned, he will be forgiven. 16Therefore confess your sins[z] to each other and pray for each other so that you may be healed.[a] The prayer of a righteous man is powerful and effective.[b]

17Elijah was a man just like us.[c] He prayed earnestly that it would not rain, and it did not rain on the land for three and a half years.[d] 18Again he prayed, and the heavens gave rain, and the earth produced its crops.[e]

Turning a sinner from the error of his way.

19My brothers, if one of you should wander from the truth[f] and someone should bring him back,[g] 20remember this: Whoever turns a sinner from the error of his way will save[h] him from death and cover over a multitude of sins.[i]

4:16 [a]1Co 5:6 **4:17** [b]Lk 12:47; Jn 9:41 **5:1** [c]Lk 6:24 **5:2** [d]Job 13:28; Mt 6:19,20 **5:3** [e]ver 7,8 **5:4** [f]Lev 19:13 [g]Dt 24:15 [h]Ro 9:29 **5:5** [i]Am 6:1 [j]Jer 12:3; 25:34 **5:6** [k]Heb 10:38 **5:7** [l]Dt 11:14; Jer 5:24 **5:8** [m]Ro 13:11; 1Pe 4:7 **5:9** [n]Jas 4:11 [o]1Co 4:5; 1Pe 4:5 [p]Mt 24:33 **5:10** [q]Mt 5:12 **5:11** [r]Mt 5:10 [s]Job 1:21,22; 2:10 [t]Job 42:10, 12-17 [u]Nu 14:18 **5:12** [v]Mt 5:34-37 **5:13** [w]Ps 50:15 [x]Col 3:16 **5:14** [y]Mk 6:13 **5:16** [z]Mt 3:6 [a]1Pe 2:24 [b]Jn 9:31 **5:17** [c]Ac 14:15 [d]1Ki 17:1; Lk 4:25

5:18 [e]1Ki 18:41-45 **5:19** [f]Jas 3:14 [g]Mt 18:15 **5:20** [h]Ro 11:14 [i]1Pe 4:8

[i]5 Or *yourselves as in a day of feasting*

1 PETER

Author: Peter the Apostle.

Date Written: Between A.D. 63 and 64.

Title: From the book's author: Peter.

Background: Though persecution has been an undesirable fixture of the church since the time of Christ, the evil reign of Nero in Rome is destined to make matters even worse. This letter is the apostle Peter's attempt to prepare, comfort and urge the believers in Asia Minor to remain strong despite their suffering.

Where Written: Rome (symbolically referred to as Babylon).

To Whom: To the scattered Christians in Asia Minor.

Content: To many this time of persecution is one of despair, but Peter reveals that this is actually a time to rejoice. He encourages the believers to count it a privilege to suffer for the sake of Christ, for even as their Savior was persecuted, so will all followers of Christ be persecuted as they identify with him. This letter from Peter makes reference to his sermons from the book of Acts and also to his personal experiences with Jesus. To further identify with Christ, all believers are called to holiness, purity and brotherly love. The Christian's wealth in Christ enables him to live with the mind of Christ in all of life's associations. Peter concludes his practical advice by confirming Satan as the great enemy of every Christian (5:8). But the assurance of Christ's future return gives the incentive of hope.

Key Words: "Suffering"; "Glory"; "Rejoice." The trials and "suffering" which believers face because of their commitment to Jesus Christ will bring them spiritual "glory." For this reason Christians have occasion to "rejoice" even when Satan and the world aim to hurt them.

Themes: • The assurance of eternal life is given to all Christians. • "The word of the Lord stands forever" (1:25). • God desires for us to cast all our cares upon him. • One way to identify with Christ is to share in his suffering. • Suffering for righteous living brings glory...suffering for sinful living brings shame. • Satan hates us and seeks our defeat. • Happiness comes to those who are obedient and submissive to Christ.

Outline:
1. Salutation. 1:1-1:2
2. Praises to God. 1:3-1:12
3. Exhortation to holiness. 1:13-2:12
4. Submission of the believer. 2:13-3:7
5. Suffering of the believer. 3:8-5:11
6. Final greetings. 5:12-5:14

1 PETER

1 Peter, an apostle of Jesus Christ,[a]
To God's elect,[b] strangers in the world,
scattered throughout Pontus, Galatia,
Cappadocia, Asia and Bithynia,[c] 2who
have been chosen according to the foreknowledge[d] of God the Father, through
the sanctifying work of the Spirit,[e] for
obedience to Jesus Christ and sprinkling by his blood:[f]

Grace and peace be yours in abundance.

An inheritance kept in heaven.

3Praise be to the God and Father of our
Lord Jesus Christ![g] In his great mercy[h]
he has given us new birth into a living
hope through the resurrection of Jesus
Christ from the dead,[i] 4and into an

1:1 [a]2Pe 1:1 [b]Mt 24:22 [c]Ac 16:7
1:2 [d]Ro 8:29 [e]2Th 2:13 [f]Heb 10:22; 12:24
1:3 [g]2Co 1:3; Eph 1:3 [h]Tit 3:5; Jas 1:18 [i]1Co 15:20
1:4 [j]Col 1:5
1:5 [k]Jn 10:28
1:6 [l]Ro 5:2 [m]1Pe 5:10 [n]Jas 1:2

inheritance that can never perish, spoil
or fade—kept in heaven for you,[j] 5who
through faith are shielded by God's
power[k] until the coming of the salvation that is ready to be revealed in the
last time. 6In this you greatly rejoice,[l]
though now for a little while[m] you may
have had to suffer grief in all kinds of
trials.[n] 7These have come so that your
faith—of greater worth than gold,
which perishes even though refined by
fire[o]—may be proved genuine[p] and
may result in praise, glory and honor
when Jesus Christ is revealed.[q] 8Though
you have not seen him, you love him;
and even though you do not see him
now, you believe in him[r] and are filled
with an inexpressible and glorious joy,

1:7 [o]Job 23:10; Ps 66:10; Pr 17:3 [p]Jas 1:3 [q]Ro 2:7
1:8 [r]Jn 20:29

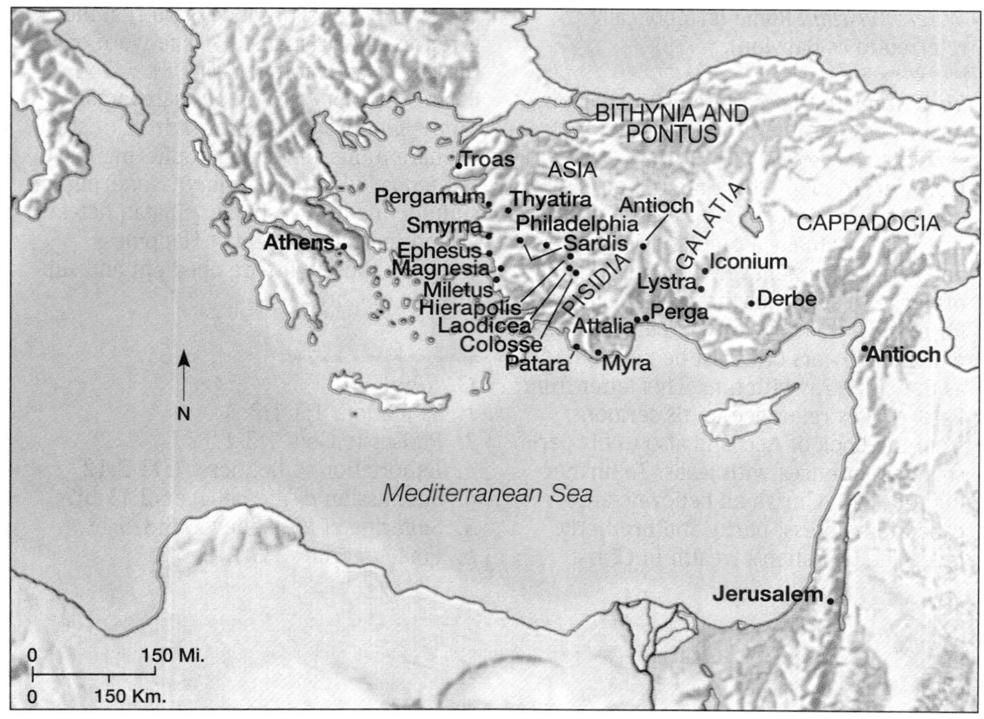

The Churches of Peter's Letter

Peter addressed his letter to the churches located through Bithynia, Pontus, Asia, Galatia, and Cappadocia. Paul had evangelized many of the areas; other areas had churches that were begun by the Jews who were in Jerusalem on the day of Pentecost and heard Peter's powerful sermon (see Acts 2:9-11).

9for you are receiving the goal of your
faith, the salvation of your souls.[a]
10Concerning this salvation, the prophets, who spoke[b] of the grace that was
to come to you, searched intently and
with the greatest care,[c] 11trying to find
out the time and circumstances to
which the Spirit of Christ[d] in them was
pointing when he predicted the sufferings of Christ and the glories that
would follow. 12It was revealed to them
that they were not serving themselves
but you, when they spoke of the things
that have now been told you by those
who have preached the gospel to you[e]
by the Holy Spirit sent from heaven.
Even angels long to look into these
things.

Holiness commanded.

13Therefore, prepare your minds for
action; be self-controlled; set your hope
fully on the grace to be given you when
Jesus Christ is revealed. 14As obedient
children, do not conform[f] to the evil
desires you had when you lived in ignorance.[g] 15But just as he who called you
is holy, so be holy in all you do;[h] 16for
it is written: "Be holy, because I am
holy."[a][i]
17Since you call on a Father who
judges each man's work impartially,[j]
live your lives as strangers here in reverent fear.[k] 18For you know that it was
not with perishable things such as silver
or gold that you were redeemed[l] from
the empty way of life handed down to
you from your forefathers, 19but with
the precious blood of Christ, a lamb[m]
without blemish or defect.[n] 20He was
chosen before the creation of the world[o]
but was revealed in these last times[p]
for your sake. 21Through him you
believe in God,[q] who raised him from
the dead and glorified him, and so
your faith and hope are in God.
22Now that you have purified[r] yourselves by obeying the truth so that you
have sincere love for your brothers, love
one another deeply,[s] from the heart.[b]
23For you have been born again,[t] not
of perishable seed, but of imperishable,
through the living and enduring word
of God.[u] 24For,

"All men are like grass,
and all their glory is like the
flowers of the field;
the grass withers and the flowers fall,
25 but the word of the Lord stands
forever."[c][v]

And this is the word that was preached
to you.

2 Therefore, rid yourselves[w] of all
malice and all deceit, hypocrisy,
envy, and slander[x] of every kind. 2Like
newborn babies, crave pure spiritual
milk,[y] so that by it you may grow up[z]
in your salvation, 3now that you have
tasted that the Lord is good.[a]

Believers are like living stones.

4As you come to him, the living
Stone[b]—rejected by men but chosen by
God and precious to him— 5you also,
like living stones, are being built[c] into
a spiritual house[d] to be a holy priesthood,[e] offering spiritual sacrifices acceptable to God through Jesus Christ.[f] 6For
in Scripture it says:

"See, I lay a stone in Zion,
a chosen and precious
cornerstone,[g]
and the one who trusts in him
will never be put to shame."[d][h]

7Now to you who believe, this stone is
precious. But to those who do not
believe,[i]

"The stone the builders rejected
has become the capstone,[e]"[f][j]

8and,

"A stone that causes men to stumble
and a rock that makes them fall."[g][k]

They stumble because they disobey the
message—which is also what they were
destined for.[l]

1:9 [a]Ro 6:22
1:10 [b]Mt 26:24 [c]Mt 13:17
1:11 [d]2Pe 1:21
1:12 [e]ver 25
1:14 [f]Ro 12:2 [g]Eph 4:18
1:15 [h]2Co 7:1; 1Th 4:7
1:16 [i]Lev 11:44,45
1:17 [j]Ac 10:34 [k]Heb 12:28
1:18 [l]Mt 20:28; 1Co 6:20
1:19 [m]Jn 1:29 [n]Ex 12:5
1:20 [o]Eph 1:4 [p]Heb 9:26
1:21 [q]Ro 4:24
1:22 [r]Jas 4:8 [s]Jn 13:34; Heb 13:1
1:23 [t]Jn 1:13 [u]Heb 4:12
1:25 [v]Isa 40:6-8
2:1 [w]Eph 4:22 [x]Jas 4:11
2:2 [y]1Co 3:2 [z]Eph 4:15,16
2:3 [a]Heb 6:5
2:4 [b]ver 7
2:5 [c]1Co 3:9 [d]1Ti 3:15 [e]Isa 61:6 [f]Php 4:18; Heb 13:15
2:6 [g]Eph 2:20 [h]Isa 28:16
2:7 [i]2Co 2:16 [j]Ps 118:22
2:8 [k]Isa 8:14; 1Co 1:23 [l]Ro 9:22

a*16* Lev. 11:44,45; 19:2; 20:7 b*22* Some early manuscripts *from a pure heart* c*25* Isaiah 40:6-8
d*6* Isaiah 28:16 e*7* Or *cornerstone*
f*7* Psalm 118:22 g*8* Isaiah 8:14

9But you are a chosen people,[a] a royal priesthood, a holy nation,[b] a people belonging to God, that you may declare the praises of him who called you out of darkness into his wonderful light.[c] 10Once you were not a people, but now you are the people of God;[d] once you had not received mercy, but now you have received mercy.

Live lives that glorify God.

11Dear friends, I urge you, as aliens and strangers in the world, to abstain from sinful desires,[e] which war against your soul.[f] 12Live such good lives among the pagans that, though they accuse you of doing wrong, they may see your good deeds[g] and glorify God[h] on the day he visits us.

13Submit yourselves for the Lord's sake to every authority[i] instituted among men: whether to the king, as the supreme authority, 14or to governors, who are sent by him to punish those who do wrong[j] and to commend those who do right.[k] 15For it is God's will[l] that by doing good you should silence the ignorant talk of foolish men.[m] 16Live as free men,[n] but do not use your freedom as a cover-up for evil; live as servants of God.[o] 17Show proper respect to everyone: Love the brotherhood of believers,[p] fear God, honor the king.[q]

18Slaves, submit yourselves to your masters with all respect,[r] not only to those who are good and considerate,[s] but also to those who are harsh. 19For it is commendable if a man bears up under the pain of unjust suffering because he is conscious of God.[t] 20But how is it to your credit if you receive a beating for doing wrong and endure it? But if you suffer for doing good and you endure it, this is commendable before God.[u] 21To this[v] you were called, because Christ suffered for you, leaving you an example,[w] that you should follow in his steps.

22"He committed no sin,
and no deceit was found in his
mouth."[h][x]

23When they hurled their insults at him, he did not retaliate; when he suffered, he made no threats.[y] Instead, he entrusted himself[z] to him who judges justly. 24He himself bore our sins[a] in his body on the tree, so that we might die to sins[b] and live for righteousness; by his wounds you have been healed.[c] 25For you were like sheep going astray,[d] but now you have returned to the Shepherd[e] and Overseer of your souls.

Godly relationships in marriage.

3 Wives, in the same way be submissive[f] to your husbands[g] so that, if any of them do not believe the word, they may be won over[h] without words by the behavior of their wives, 2when they see the purity and reverence of your lives. 3Your beauty should not come from outward adornment, such as braided hair and the wearing of gold jewelry and fine clothes.[i] 4Instead, it should be that of your inner self,[j] the unfading beauty of a gentle and quiet spirit, which is of great worth in God's sight. 5For this is the way the holy women of the past who put their hope in God[k] used to make themselves beautiful. They were submissive to their own husbands, 6like Sarah, who obeyed Abraham and called him her master.[l] You are her daughters if you do what is right and do not give way to fear.

7Husbands,[m] in the same way be considerate as you live with your wives, and treat them with respect as the weaker partner and as heirs with you of the gracious gift of life, so that nothing will hinder your prayers.

Suffering for doing good.

8Finally, all of you, live in harmony with one another; be sympathetic, love as brothers,[n] be compassionate and humble.[o] 9Do not repay evil with evil[p] or insult with insult,[q] but with blessing, because to this[r] you were called so that

2:9 [a]Dt 10:15 [b]Isa 62:12 [c]Ac 26:18
2:10 [d]Hos 1:9,10
2:11 [e]Gal 5:16 [f]Jas 4:1
2:12 [g]Php 2:15; 1Pe 3:16 [h]Mt 5:16; 9:8
2:13 [i]Ro 13:1
2:14 [j]Ro 13:4 [k]Ro 13:3
2:15 [l]1Pe 3:17 [m]ver 12
2:16 [n]Jn 8:32 [o]Ro 6:22
2:17 [p]Ro 12:10 [q]Ro 13:7
2:18 [r]Eph 6:5 [s]Jas 3:17
2:19 [t]1Pe 3:14,17
2:20 [u]1Pe 3:17
2:21 [v]Ac 14:22 [w]Mt 16:24
2:22 [x]Isa 53:9
2:23 [y]Isa 53:7 [z]Lk 23:46
2:24 [a]Heb 9:28 [b]Ro 6:2 [c]Isa 53:5; Heb 12:13; Jas 5:16
2:25 [d]Isa 53:6 [e]Jn 10:11
3:1 [f]1Pe 2:18 [g]Eph 5:22 [h]1Co 7:16; 9:19
3:3 [i]Isa 3:18-23; 1Ti 2:9
3:4 [j]Ro 7:22
3:5 [k]1Ti 5:5
3:6 [l]Ge 18:12
3:7 [m]Eph 5:25-33

3:8 [n]Ro 12:10 [o]1Pe 5:5 **3:9** [p]Ro 12:17 [q]1Pe 2:23 [r]1Pe 2:21

h*22* Isaiah 53:9

you may inherit a blessing.[a] **10**For,

"Whoever would love life
and see good days
must keep his tongue from evil
and his lips from deceitful speech.
11He must turn from evil and do good;
he must seek peace and pursue it.
12For the eyes of the Lord are on the
righteous
and his ears are attentive to their
prayer,
but the face of the Lord is against
those who do evil."[i][b]

13Who is going to harm you if you are eager to do good?[c] **14**But even if you should suffer for what is right, you are blessed.[d] "Do not fear what they fear[j]; do not be frightened."[k][e] **15**But in your hearts set apart Christ as Lord. Always be prepared to give an answer[f] to everyone who asks you to give the reason for the hope that you have. But do this with gentleness and respect, **16**keeping a clear conscience,[g] so that those who speak maliciously against your good behavior in Christ may be ashamed of their slander.[h] **17**It is better, if it is God's will,[i] to suffer for doing good[j] than for doing evil. **18**For Christ died for sins[k] once for all, the righteous for the unrighteous, to bring you to God. He was put to death in the body[l] but made alive by the Spirit,[m] **19**through whom[l] also he went and preached to the spirits in prison[n] **20**who disobeyed long ago when God waited patiently in the days of Noah while the ark was being built.[o] In it only a few people, eight in all, were saved[p] through water, **21**and this water symbolizes baptism that now saves you[q] also—not the removal of dirt from the body but the pledge[m] of a good conscience toward God. It saves you by the resurrection of Jesus Christ,[r] **22**who has gone into heaven and is at God's right hand[s]—with angels, authorities and powers in submission to him.[t]

Exhortation to pray, love and serve.

4 Therefore, since Christ suffered in his body, arm yourselves also with the same attitude, because he who has suffered in his body is done with sin. **2**As a result, he does not live the rest of his earthly life for evil human desires,[u] but rather for the will of God. **3**For you have spent enough time in the past[v] doing what pagans choose to do—living in debauchery, lust, drunkenness, orgies, carousing and detestable idolatry. **4**They think it strange that you do not plunge with them into the same flood of dissipation, and they heap abuse on you.[w] **5**But they will have to give account to him who is ready to judge the living and the dead.[x] **6**For this is the reason the gospel was preached even to those who are now dead,[y] so that they might be judged according to men in regard to the body, but live according to God in regard to the spirit.

7The end of all things is near.[z] Therefore be clear minded and self-controlled so that you can pray. **8**Above all, love each other deeply,[a] because love covers over a multitude of sins.[b] **9**Offer hospitality to one another without grumbling.[c] **10**Each one should use whatever gift he has received to serve others,[d] faithfully[e] administering God's grace in its various forms. **11**If anyone speaks, he should do it as one speaking the very words of God. If anyone serves, he should do it with the strength God provides,[f] so that in all things God may be praised[g] through Jesus Christ. To him be the glory and the power for ever and ever. Amen.

Participation in Christ's suffering.

12Dear friends, do not be surprised at the painful trial you are suffering,[h] as though something strange were happening to you. **13**But rejoice that you participate in the sufferings of Christ, so that you may be overjoyed when his glory is revealed.[i] **14**If you are insulted because of the name of Christ, you are blessed,[j] for the Spirit of glory and of God rests

3:9 [a]Heb 6:14
3:12 [b]Ps 34:12-16
3:13 [c]Pr 16:7
3:14 [d]1Pe 2:19,20; 4:15,16 [e]Isa 8:12,13
3:15 [f]Col 4:6
3:16 [g]Heb 13:18 [h]1Pe 2:12,15
3:17 [i]1Pe 2:15 [j]1Pe 2:20
3:18 [k]1Pe 2:21 [l]Col 1:22; 1Pe 4:1 [m]1Pe 4:6
3:19 [n]1Pe 4:6
3:20 [o]Ge 6:3,5, 13,14 [p]Heb 11:7
3:21 [q]Tit 3:5 [r]1Pe 1:3
3:22 [s]Mk 16:19 [t]Ro 8:38
4:2 [u]Ro 6:2
4:3 [v]Eph 2:2
4:4 [w]1Pe 3:16
4:5 [x]Ac 10:42; 2Ti 4:1
4:6 [y]1Pe 3:19
4:7 [z]Ro 13:11
4:8 [a]1Pe 1:22 [b]Pr 10:12
4:9 [c]Php 2:14
4:10 [d]Ro 12:6,7 [e]1Co 4:2
4:11 [f]Eph 6:10 [g]1Co 10:31
4:12 [h]1Pe 1:6,7
4:13 [i]Ro 8:17
4:14 [j]Mt 5:11

[i]*12* Psalm 34:12-16 [j]*14* Or *not fear their threats* [k]*14* Isaiah 8:12 [l]*18,19* Or *alive in the spirit, 19 through which* [m]*21* Or *response*

on you. 15If you suffer, it should not be
as a murderer or thief or any other kind
of criminal, or even as a meddler. 16How-
ever, if you suffer as a Christian, do not
be ashamed, but praise God that you
bear that name.[a] 17For it is time for
judgment to begin with the family of
God;[b] and if it begins with us, what will
the outcome be for those who do not
obey the gospel of God?[c] 18And,

> "If it is hard for the righteous to be
> saved,
> what will become of the ungodly
> and the sinner?"[n][d]

19So then, those who suffer according
to God's will should commit themselves
to their faithful Creator and continue to
do good.

Instructions for elders to shepherd God's flock.

5 To the elders among you, I appeal as
a fellow elder,[e] a witness[f] of Christ's
sufferings and one who also will share
in the glory to be revealed:[g] 2Be shepherds of God's flock[h] that is under your
care, serving as overseers—not because
you must, but because you are willing,
as God wants you to be; not greedy for
money,[i] but eager to serve; 3not lording it over[j] those entrusted to you, but
being examples[k] to the flock. 4And when
the Chief Shepherd appears, you will
receive the crown of glory[l] that will
never fade away.
5Young men, in the same way be
submissive[m] to those who are older. All
of you, clothe yourselves with humility

4:16 [a]Ac 5:41
4:17 [b]Jer 25:29 [c]2Th 1:8
4:18 [d]Pr 11:31; Lk 23:31
5:1 [e]Ac 11:30 [f]Lk 24:48 [g]1Pe 1:5,7; Rev 1:9
5:2 [h]Jn 21:16 [i]1Ti 3:3
5:3 [j]Eze 34:4 [k]Php 3:17
5:4 [l]1Co 9:25
5:5 [m]Eph 5:21 [n]Pr 3:34; Jas 4:6
5:6 [o]Jas 4:10
5:7 [p]Ps 37:5; Mt 6:25 [q]Heb 13:5
5:8 [r]Job 1:7
5:9 [s]Jas 4:7 [t]Col 2:5 [u]Ac 14:22
5:10 [v]2Co 4:17 [w]2Th 2:17
5:11 [x]Ro 11:36
5:12 [y]2Co 1:19 [z]Heb 13:22
5:13 [a]Ac 12:12
5:14 [b]Ro 16:16 [c]Eph 6:23

toward one another, because,

> "God opposes the proud
> but gives grace to the humble."[o][n]

6Humble yourselves, therefore, under
God's mighty hand, that he may lift you
up in due time.[o] 7Cast all your anxiety
on him[p] because he cares for you.[q]

The devil, your enemy.

8Be self-controlled and alert. Your enemy the devil prowls around[r] like a roaring lion looking for someone to devour.
9Resist him,[s] standing firm in the faith,[t]
because you know that your brothers
throughout the world are undergoing
the same kind of sufferings.[u]
10And the God of all grace, who called
you to his eternal glory[v] in Christ, after
you have suffered a little while, will himself restore you and make you strong,[w]
firm and steadfast. 11To him be the
power for ever and ever. Amen.[x]

Closing remarks and greetings.

12With the help of Silas,[p][y] whom I
regard as a faithful brother, I have written to you briefly,[z] encouraging you and
testifying that this is the true grace of
God. Stand fast in it.
13She who is in Babylon, chosen
together with you, sends you her
greetings, and so does my son Mark.[a]
14Greet one another with a kiss of
love.[b]
Peace[c] to all of you who are in Christ.

[n] *18* Prov. 11:31 [o] *5* Prov. 3:34 [p] *12* Greek *Silvanus*, a variant of *Silas*

2 PETER

Author: Peter the Apostle.

Date Written: Between A.D. 64 and 66.

Title: From the book's author: Peter.

Background: This second letter of Peter is written not long before his death. Whereas his first letter to the believers combated persecution from the outside, this time Peter is addressing the second major threat—false teaching from the inside. Such false teaching has greatly contributed to the apostasy of the Christians in Asia Minor to whom Peter is writing. The mission of Peter's words is to expose these false teachers and to encourage the believers to mature in the truth of God. Tradition has it that Peter was crucified upside down in the city of Rome.

Where Written: Probably Rome.

To Whom: To all Christians.

Content: This letter from Peter encourages believers to grow in Christ, which is made possible by a proper knowledge of the gospel. God's Word gives the promises necessary for obedience and can be totally relied upon as revealing all truth and prophecy. Peter discusses in detail the danger and destructiveness of the evil ministry of false teachers, whose interests are not in God, but in self-glorification and worldly lusts. But God's righteousness shall prevail when, at the day of the Lord, the old earth will be laid bare and a new heaven and a new earth will replace it (chapter 3).

Key Words: "Knowledge"; "Last Days." Peter's method of refuting the false "knowledge" being propagated is to remind the believers of the true "knowledge," which is based on a personal experience with Christ. This growth in the grace of God is aided by a better understanding of the "last days," when the ungodly will receive their judgment.

Themes: • Deceit comes in many forms, but truth comes in one form (the form of God). • God has delayed his judgment so that more may come to repentence (3:9). • Destruction comes to those who scoff at the Word of God. • Maturity in God will come as we develop an intense and personal relationship with God's Son, God's Spirit and God's Word. • Righteousness shall prevail over wickedness in the end.

Outline:
1. Salutation. 1:1-1:2
2. Growth and knowledge in Christ. 1:3-1:21
3. False teachers and their condemnation. 2:1-2:22
4. The day of the Lord. 3:1-3:18

2 PETER

1

Simon Peter, a servant[a] and apostle
of Jesus Christ,[b]

To those who through the righteousness[c] of our God and Savior Jesus
Christ[d] have received a faith as precious as ours:

2Grace and peace be yours in abundance through the knowledge of God
and of Jesus our Lord.[e]

Making one's calling and election sure.

3His divine power[f] has given us everything we need for life and godliness
through our knowledge of him who
called us[g] by his own glory and goodness. **4**Through these he has given us
his very great and precious promises,[h]
so that through them you may participate in the divine nature[i] and escape
the corruption in the world caused by
evil desires.[j]

5For this very reason, make every
effort to add to your faith goodness;
and to goodness, knowledge;[k] **6**and to
knowledge, self-control;[l] and to self-
control, perseverance; and to perseverance, godliness;[m] **7**and to godliness,
brotherly kindness; and to brotherly
kindness, love.[n] **8**For if you possess
these qualities in increasing measure,
they will keep you from being ineffective and unproductive[o] in your knowledge of our Lord Jesus Christ. **9**But if
anyone does not have them, he is
nearsighted and blind,[p] and has forgotten that he has been cleansed from his
past sins.[q]

10Therefore, my brothers, be all the
more eager to make your calling and
election sure. For if you do these things,
you will never fall,[r] **11**and you will
receive a rich welcome into the eternal
kingdom of our Lord and Savior Jesus
Christ.

Peter's approaching death.

12So I will always remind you of these
things,[s] even though you know them
and are firmly established in the truth
you now have. **13**I think it is right to
refresh your memory as long as I live
in the tent of this body,[t] **14**because I
know that I will soon put it aside,[u] as
our Lord Jesus Christ has made clear
to me.[v] **15**And I will make every effort
to see that after my departure[w] you will
always be able to remember these
things.

The Holy Spirit's inspiration of Scripture.

16We did not follow cleverly invented stories when we told you about the
power and coming of our Lord Jesus
Christ, but we were eyewitnesses of his
majesty.[x] **17**For he received honor and
glory from God the Father when the
voice came to him from the Majestic
Glory, saying, "This is my Son, whom I
love; with him I am well pleased."[a][y]
18We ourselves heard this voice that
came from heaven when we were with
him on the sacred mountain.[z]

19And we have the word of the
prophets made more certain, and you
will do well to pay attention to it, as to
a light[a] shining in a dark place, until
the day dawns and the morning star[b]
rises in your hearts. **20**Above all, you
must understand that no prophecy of
Scripture came about by the prophet's
own interpretation. **21**For prophecy never had its origin in the will of man, but
men spoke from God[c] as they were
carried along by the Holy Spirit.[d]

Destruction of false teachers.

2

But there were also false prophets[e]
among the people, just as there
will be false teachers among you.[f] They
will secretly introduce destructive heresies, even denying the sovereign Lord[g]
who bought them[h]—bringing swift
destruction on themselves. **2**Many will
follow their shameful ways and will
bring the way of truth into disrepute.

1:1 [a]Ro 1:1 [b]1Pe 1:1 [c]Ro 3:21-26 [d]Tit 2:13
1:2 [e]Php 3:8
1:3 [f]1Pe 1:5 [g]1Th 2:12
1:4 [h]2Co 7:1 [i]Eph 4:24; Heb 12:10; 1Jn 3:2 [j]2Pe 2:18-20
1:5 [k]Col 2:3
1:6 [l]Ac 24:25 [m]ver 3
1:7 [n]1Th 3:12
1:8 [o]Jn 15:2; Tit 3:14
1:9 [p]1Jn 2:11 [q]Eph 5:26
1:10 [r]2Pe 3:17
1:12 [s]Php 3:1; 1Jn 2:21
1:13 [t]2Co 5:1,4
1:14 [u]2Ti 4:6 [v]Jn 21:18,19
1:15 [w]Lk 9:31
1:16 [x]Mt 17:1-8
1:17 [y]Mt 3:17
1:18 [z]Mt 17:6
1:19 [a]Ps 119:105 [b]Rev 22:16
1:21 [c]2Ti 3:16 [d]2Sa 23:2; Ac 1:16; 1Pe 1:11
2:1 [e]Dt 13:1-3 [f]1Ti 4:1 [g]Jude 4 [h]1Co 6:20

a *17* Matt. 17:5; Mark 9:7; Luke 9:35

3In their greed these teachers will exploit you[a] with stories they have made up. Their condemnation has long been hanging over them, and their destruction has not been sleeping.

4For if God did not spare angels when they sinned, but sent them to hell,[b] putting them into gloomy dungeons[c] to be held for judgment;[b] 5if he did not spare the ancient world[c] when he brought the flood on its ungodly people, but protected Noah, a preacher of righteousness, and seven others;[d] 6if he condemned the cities of Sodom and Gomorrah by burning them to ashes,[e] and made them an example[f] of what is going to happen to the ungodly; 7and if he rescued Lot,[g] a righteous man, who was distressed by the filthy lives of lawless men[h] 8(for that righteous man, living among them day after day, was tormented in his righteous soul by the lawless deeds he saw and heard)— 9if this is so, then the Lord knows how to rescue godly men from trials[i] and to hold the unrighteous for the day of judgment, while continuing their punishment.[d] 10This is especially true of those who follow the corrupt desire[j] of the sinful nature[e] and despise authority.

Bold and arrogant, these men are not afraid to slander celestial beings;[k] 11yet even angels, although they are stronger and more powerful, do not bring slanderous accusations against such beings in the presence of the Lord.[l] 12But these men blaspheme in matters they do not understand. They are like brute beasts, creatures of instinct, born only to be caught and destroyed, and like beasts they too will perish.[m]

13They will be paid back with harm for the harm they have done. Their idea of pleasure is to carouse in broad daylight.[n] They are blots and blemishes, reveling in their pleasures while they feast with you.[f][o] 14With eyes full of adultery, they never stop sinning; they seduce[p] the unstable; they are experts in greed[q]—an accursed brood![r] 15They have left the straight way and wandered off to follow the way of Balaam[s] son of Beor, who loved the wages of wickedness. 16But he was rebuked for his wrongdoing by a donkey—a beast without speech—who spoke with a man's voice and restrained the prophet's madness.[t]

17These men are springs without water[u] and mists driven by a storm. Blackest darkness is reserved for them.[v] 18For they mouth empty, boastful words[w] and, by appealing to the lustful desires of sinful human nature, they entice people who are just escaping from those who live in error. 19They promise them freedom, while they themselves are slaves of depravity—for a man is a slave to whatever has mastered him.[x] 20If they have escaped the corruption of the world by knowing[y] our Lord and Savior Jesus Christ and are again entangled in it and overcome, they are worse off at the end than they were at the beginning.[z] 21It would have been better for them not to have known the way of righteousness, than to have known it and then to turn their backs on the sacred command that was passed on to them.[a] 22Of them the proverbs are true: "A dog returns to its vomit,"[g][b] and, "A sow that is washed goes back to her wallowing in the mud."

The coming day of the Lord.

3 Dear friends, this is now my second letter to you. I have written both of them as reminders[c] to stimulate you to wholesome thinking. 2I want you to recall the words spoken in the past by the holy prophets and the command given by our Lord and Savior through your apostles.

3First of all, you must understand that in the last days[d] scoffers will come, scoffing and following their own evil desires.[e] 4They will say, "Where is this 'coming' he promised?[f] Ever since our fathers died, everything goes on as it

2:3 [a] 2Co 2:17; 1Th 2:5
2:4 [b] Jude 6; Rev 20:1,2
2:5 [c] 2Pe 3:6 [d] Heb 11:7; 1Pe 3:20
2:6 [e] Ge 19:24,25 [f] Nu 26:10; Jude 7
2:7 [g] Ge 19:16 [h] 2Pe 3:17
2:9 [i] 1Co 10:13
2:10 [j] 2Pe 3:3 [k] Jude 8
2:11 [l] Jude 9
2:12 [m] Jude 10
2:13 [n] Ro 13:13 [o] 1Co 11:20, 21; Jude 12
2:14 [p] ver 18 [q] ver 3 [r] Eph 2:3
2:15 [s] Nu 22:4-20; Jude 11
2:16 [t] Nu 22:21-30
2:17 [u] Jude 12 [v] Jude 13
2:18 [w] Jude 16
2:19 [x] Jn 8:34; Ro 6:16
2:20 [y] 2Pe 1:2 [z] Mt 12:45
2:21 [a] Heb 6:4-6
2:22 [b] Pr 26:11
3:1 [c] 2Pe 1:13
3:3 [d] 1Ti 4:1 [e] 2Pe 2:10; Jude 18
3:4 [f] Isa 5:19; Eze 12:22; Mt 24:48

b *4* Greek *Tartarus* c *4* Some manuscripts *into chains of darkness* d *9* Or *unrighteous for punishment until the day of judgment* e *10* Or *the flesh* f *13* Some manuscripts *in their love feasts* g *22* Prov. 26:11

has since the beginning of creation."[a]
5But they deliberately forget that long
ago by God's word[b] the heavens existed
and the earth was formed out of water
and by water.[c] 6By these waters also the
world of that time was deluged and
destroyed.[d] 7By the same word the present heavens and earth are reserved
for fire,[e] being kept for the day of judgment and destruction of ungodly men.
8But do not forget this one thing, dear
friends: With the Lord a day is like a
thousand years, and a thousand years
are like a day.[f] 9The Lord is not slow in
keeping his promise,[g] as some understand slowness. He is patient[h] with
you, not wanting anyone to perish, but
everyone to come to repentance.[i]
10But the day of the Lord will come
like a thief.[j] The heavens will disappear
with a roar; the elements will be destroyed by fire, and the earth and everything in it will be laid bare.[h][k]
11Since everything will be destroyed
in this way, what kind of people ought
you to be? You ought to live holy and
godly lives 12as you look forward[l] to
the day of God and speed its coming.[i][m]
That day will bring about the destruction of the heavens by fire, and
the elements will melt in the heat.[n]

3:4 [a]Mk 10:6
3:5 [b]Ge 1:6,9; Heb 11:3 [c]Ps 24:2
3:6 [d]Ge 7:21,22
3:7 [e]ver 10,12; 2Th 1:7
3:8 [f]Ps 90:4
3:9 [g]Hab 2:3; Heb 10:37 [h]Ro 2:4 [i]1Ti 2:4
3:10 [j]Lk 12:39; 1Th 5:2 [k]Mt 24:35; Rev 21:1
3:12 [l]1Co 1:7 [m]Ps 50:3 [n]ver 10
3:13 [o]Isa 65:17; 66:22; Rev 21:1
3:14 [p]1Th 3:13
3:15 [q]Ro 2:4 [r]ver 9 [s]Eph 3:3

13But in keeping with his promise we
are looking forward to a new heaven
and a new earth,[o] the home of righteousness.
14So then, dear friends, since you are
looking forward to this, make every
effort to be found spotless, blameless[p]
and at peace with him. 15Bear in mind
that our Lord's patience[q] means salvation,[r] just as our dear brother Paul also
wrote you with the wisdom that God
gave him.[s] 16He writes the same way in
all his letters, speaking in them of these
matters. His letters contain some things
that are hard to understand, which
ignorant and unstable[t] people distort,
as they do the other Scriptures,[u] to their
own destruction.
17Therefore, dear friends, since you
already know this, be on your guard[v] so
that you may not be carried away by the
error[w] of lawless men and fall from your
secure position.[x] 18But grow in the grace
and knowledge of our Lord and Savior
Jesus Christ.[y] To him be glory both now
and forever! Amen.

3:16 [t]2Pe 2:14 [u]ver 2 **3:17** [v]1Co 10:12 [w]2Pe 2:18 [x]Rev 2:5 **3:18** [y]2Pe 1:11

h *10* Some manuscripts *be burned up* i *12* Or *as you wait eagerly for the day of God to come*

1 JOHN

Author: John the Apostle.

Date Written: Between A.D. 85 and 96.

Title: From the book's author: John.

Background: In addition to the 3 letters bearing his name, John is also the author of the fourth Gospel and the book of Revelation. This letter of John is written to Christian congregations founded in truth and faith, but receiving serious challenges from false teachers. The particular error being propagated is a philosophy of religion called Gnosticism. It is built on the premise that all matter is totally evil, spirit is totally good, and that man will progress spiritually as he increases in this knowledge. This leads to further false teachings about Christ, stating that he could not have been born in the flesh since all flesh is evil. The Gnostic theories are that Jesus Christ is either a ghost that only seems to have a human body, or that he has a dual personality, sometimes divine and sometimes human. John's mission here is to combat these errors.

Where Written: Probably Ephesus.

To Whom: To all Christians.

Content: This message of John is a warning to the believers not to be deceived by the false doctrines being spread. He addresses them as his "dear children" and "dear friends" marking his closeness to them. The union between the Father and the Son is boldly proclaimed, for only as one comes to know Jesus Christ can he know the Father. John urges the believers to find full joy in God and in the knowledge of his forgiveness and grace. John's practical instructions include admonitions for the believer to walk in the light of righteousness, to live a spiritual life marked by a spiritual birth and to show brotherly love for others. The Christians are encouraged not to love the things of this world, to beware of antichrists and to test the spirits to see whether they are from God or Satan. John concludes his letter of happiness and hope for the believers by reassuring them of the power of prayer and their protection in God from the evil one.

Key Words: "Fellowship"; "Love." The emphasis of 1 John is to stress that in order for a believer to have a proper "fellowship" with God, he must walk in obedience and truth. Proper "fellowship" with others is manifested by having "love" for one another. This "love" for others is made possible by the fact that Christ first loved us enough to lay down his life.

Themes: • God is life...God is light... God is love. • A believer's birthmark is righteousness. • True love will manifest itself in actions, not just in words. • Perfect love drives out all fears (4:18). • The love God has for us is totally unconditional. • Only the blood of Christ can cleanse us of all our sins.

Outline:
1. Walking in the light. 1:1-2:14
2. Hindrances to fellowship. 2:15-2:27
3. Abiding in Christ's love. 2:28-5:5
4. Victory and assurance through faith. 5:6-5:21

1 JOHN

The light of God is without darkness.

1 That which was from the beginning,[a] which we have heard, which
we have seen with our eyes,[b] which we
have looked at and our hands have
touched[c]—this we proclaim concerning
the Word of life. 2The life appeared;[d] we
have seen it and testify to it, and we
proclaim to you the eternal life, which
was with the Father and has appeared to
us. 3We proclaim to you what we have
seen and heard, so that you also may
have fellowship with us. And our fellowship is with the Father and with his
Son, Jesus Christ.[e] 4We write this[f] to
make our[a] joy complete.[g]

5This is the message we have heard[h]
from him and declare to you: God is
light; in him there is no darkness at all.
6If we claim to have fellowship with
him yet walk in the darkness,[i] we lie
and do not live by the truth.[j] 7But if we
walk in the light, as he is in the light,
we have fellowship with one another,
and the blood of Jesus, his Son, purifies
us from all[b] sin.[k]

Confession brings forgiveness and purification.

8If we claim to be without sin,[l] we
deceive ourselves and the truth is not in
us.[m] 9If we confess our sins, he is faithful
and just and will forgive us our sins[n]
and purify us from all unrighteousness.
10If we claim we have not sinned, we
make him out to be a liar[o] and his word
has no place in our lives.[p]

Christians show themselves by love and obedience.

2 My dear children,[q] I write this to
you so that you will not sin. But if
anybody does sin, we have one who
speaks to the Father in our defense[r]—
Jesus Christ, the Righteous One. 2He is
the atoning sacrifice for our sins,[s] and
not only for ours but also for[c] the sins
of the whole world.

3We know that we have come to
know him if we obey his commands.[t]
4The man who says, "I know him," but
does not do what he commands is a
liar, and the truth is not in him.[u] 5But if
anyone obeys his word,[v] God's love[d] is
truly made complete in him.[w] This is
how we know we are in him: 6Whoev-
er claims to live in him must walk as
Jesus did.[x]

7Dear friends, I am not writing you a
new command but an old one, which
you have had since the beginning.[y]
This old command is the message you
have heard. 8Yet I am writing you a new
command;[z] its truth is seen in him and
you, because the darkness is passing[a]
and the true light[b] is already shining.[c]

9Anyone who claims to be in the light
but hates his brother is still in the
darkness. 10Whoever loves his brother
lives in the light,[d] and there is nothing
in him[e] to make him stumble. 11But
whoever hates his brother is in the
darkness and walks around in the darkness; he does not know where he is
going, because the darkness has blinded him.[e]

12I write to you, dear children,
  because your sins have been
    forgiven on account of his
    name.
13I write to you, fathers,
  because you have known him who
    is from the beginning.
I write to you, young men,
  because you have overcome the
    evil one.[f]
I write to you, dear children,
  because you have known the
    Father.
14I write to you, fathers,
  because you have known him who
    is from the beginning.

1:1 [a]Jn 1:2 [b]Jn 1:14; 2Pe 1:16 [c]Jn 20:27
1:2 [d]Jn 1:1-4; 1Ti 3:16
1:3 [e]1Co 1:9
1:4 [f]1Jn 2:1 [g]Jn 3:29
1:5 [h]1Jn 3:11
1:6 [i]2Co 6:14 [j]Jn 3:19-21
1:7 [k]Heb 9:14; Rev 1:5
1:8 [l]Pr 20:9; Jas 3:2 [m]1Jn 2:4
1:9 [n]Ps 32:5; 51:2
1:10 [o]1Jn 5:10 [p]1Jn 2:14
2:1 [q]ver 12,13,28 [r]Ro 8:34; Heb 7:25
2:2 [s]Ro 3:25
2:3 [t]Jn 14:15
2:4 [u]1Jn 1:6,8
2:5 [v]Jn 14:21,23 [w]1Jn 4:12
2:6 [x]Mt 11:29; 1Pe 2:21
2:7 [y]1Jn 3:11,23; 2Jn 5,6
2:8 [z]Jn 13:34 [a]Ro 13:12 [b]Jn 1:9 [c]Eph 5:8; 1Th 5:5
2:10 [d]1Jn 3:14
2:11 [e]Jn 12:35
2:13 [f]ver 14

a4 Some manuscripts *your* b7 Or *every*
c2 Or *He is the one who turns aside God's wrath, taking away our sins, and not only ours but also*
d5 Or *word, love for God* e10 Or *it*

I write to you, young men,
because you are strong,[a]
and the word of God lives in you,[b]
and you have overcome the evil
one.[c]

Christians should not love the world.

15Do not love the world or anything
in the world.[d] If anyone loves the world,
the love of the Father is not in him.[e]
16For everything in the world—the cravings of sinful man,[f] the lust of his eyes[g]
and the boasting of what he has and
does—comes not from the Father but
from the world. 17The world and its
desires pass away,[h] but the man who
does the will of God lives forever.

The antichrist is a liar.

18Dear children, this is the last hour;
and as you have heard that the antichrist is coming,[i] even now many antichrists have come.[j] This is how we
know it is the last hour. 19They went
out from us,[k] but they did not really
belong to us. For if they had belonged
to us, they would have remained with
us; but their going showed that none of
them belonged to us.[l]

20But you have an anointing[m] from
the Holy One,[n] and all of you know the
truth.[f][o] 21I do not write to you because
you do not know the truth, but because
you do know it[p] and because no lie
comes from the truth. 22Who is the
liar? It is the man who denies that
Jesus is the Christ. Such a man is the
antichrist—he denies the Father and
the Son.[q] 23No one who denies the
Son has the Father; whoever acknowledges the Son has the Father also.[r]

24See that what you have heard from
the beginning remains in you. If it does,
you also will remain in the Son and in
the Father.[s] 25And this is what he
promised us—even eternal life.

26I am writing these things to you
about those who are trying to lead you
astray.[t] 27As for you, the anointing[u]
you received from him remains in you,
and you do not need anyone to teach
you. But as his anointing teaches you
about all things and as that anointing
is real, not counterfeit—just as it has
taught you, remain in him.

Children of God do not keep on sinning.

28And now, dear children,[v] continue
in him, so that when he appears[w] we
may be confident[x] and unashamed before him at his coming.[y]

29If you know that he is righteous,[z]
you know that everyone who does what
is right has been born of him.

3 How great is the love[a] the Father
has lavished on us, that we should
be called children of God![b] And that is
what we are! The reason the world does
not know us is that it did not know
him.[c] 2Dear friends, now we are children of God, and what we will be has
not yet been made known. But we
know that when he appears,[g] we shall
be like him,[d] for we shall see him as
he is.[e] 3Everyone who has this hope in
him purifies himself,[f] just as he is pure.

4Everyone who sins breaks the law; in
fact, sin is lawlessness.[g] 5But you know
that he appeared so that he might take
away our sins. And in him is no sin.[h]
6No one who lives in him keeps on sinning.[i] No one who continues to sin has
either seen him[j] or known him.[k]

7Dear children,[l] do not let anyone
lead you astray.[m] He who does what is
right is righteous, just as he is righteous.[n] 8He who does what is sinful is
of the devil,[o] because the devil has been
sinning from the beginning. The reason
the Son of God appeared was to destroy
the devil's work. 9No one who is born
of God[p] will continue to sin,[q] because
God's seed[r] remains in him; he cannot
go on sinning, because he has been
born of God. 10This is how we know
who the children of God are and who
the children of the devil are: Anyone

2:14 [a]Eph 6:10 [b]Jn 5:38; 1Jn 1:10 [c]ver 13
2:15 [d]Ro 12:2 [e]Jas 4:4
2:16 [f]Ro 13:14 [g]Pr 27:20
2:17 [h]1Co 7:31
2:18 [i]ver 22; 1Jn 4:3; 2Jn 7 [j]1Jn 4:1
2:19 [k]Ac 20:30 [l]1Co 11:19
2:20 [m]2Co 1:21 [n]Mk 1:24 [o]Jn 14:26
2:21 [p]2Pe 1:12; Jude 5
2:22 [q]2Jn 7
2:23 [r]Jn 8:19; 1Jn 4:15
2:24 [s]Jn 14:23
2:26 [t]2Jn 7
2:27 [u]ver 20
2:28 [v]ver 1 [w]1Jn 3:2 [x]1Jn 4:17 [y]1Th 2:19
2:29 [z]1Jn 3:7
3:1 [a]Jn 3:16 [b]Jn 1:12 [c]Jn 16:3
3:2 [d]Ro 8:29; 2Pe 1:4 [e]2Co 3:18
3:3 [f]2Co 7:1; 2Pe 3:13,14
3:4 [g]1Jn 5:17
3:5 [h]2Co 5:21
3:6 [i]ver 9 [j]3Jn 11 [k]1Jn 2:4
3:7 [l]1Jn 2:1 [m]1Jn 2:26 [n]1Jn 2:29
3:8 [o]Jn 8:44 **3:9** [p]Jn 1:13 [q]1Jn 5:18 [r]1Pe 1:23

[f]20 Some manuscripts *and you know all things*
[g]2 Or *when it is made known*

who does not do what is right is not a
child of God; nor is anyone who does
not love[a] his brother.

Love one another.

11This is the message you heard[b]
from the beginning: We should love one
another.[c] 12Do not be like Cain, who
belonged to the evil one and murdered
his brother.[d] And why did he murder
him? Because his own actions were
evil and his brother's were righteous.
13Do not be surprised, my brothers, if
the world hates you.[e] 14We know that
we have passed from death to life,[f]
because we love our brothers. Anyone
who does not love remains in death.[g]
15Anyone who hates his brother is a
murderer,[h] and you know that no murderer has eternal life in him.[i]
16This is how we know what love is:
Jesus Christ laid down his life for us.
And we ought to lay down our lives for
our brothers.[j] 17If anyone has material
possessions and sees his brother in need
but has no pity on him,[k] how can the
love of God be in him?[l] 18Dear children,[m] let us not love with words or
tongue but with actions and in truth.[n]
19This then is how we know that we
belong to the truth, and how we set our
hearts at rest in his presence 20when-
ever our hearts condemn us. For God
is greater than our hearts, and he knows
everything.
21Dear friends, if our hearts do not
condemn us, we have confidence before
God[o] 22and receive from him anything
we ask,[p] because we obey his commands
and do what pleases him.[q] 23And this is
his command: to believe[r] in the name of
his Son, Jesus Christ, and to love one
another as he commanded us.[s] 24Those
who obey his commands live in him,[t]
and he in them. And this is how we
know that he lives in us: We know it by
the Spirit he gave us.[u]

Test the spirits.

4 Dear friends, do not believe every
spirit, but test the spirits to see

3:10 [a]1Jn 4:8
3:11 [b]1Jn 1:5 [c]Jn 13:34,35; 2Jn 5
3:12 [d]Ge 4:8
3:13 [e]Jn 15:18,19; 17:14
3:14 [f]Jn 5:24 [g]1Jn 2:9
3:15 [h]Mt 5:21,22; Jn 8:44 [i]Gal 5:20,21
3:16 [j]Jn 15:13
3:17 [k]Dt 15:7,8 [l]1Jn 4:20
3:18 [m]1Jn 2:1 [n]Eze 33:31; Ro 12:9
3:21 [o]1Jn 5:14
3:22 [p]Mt 7:7 [q]Jn 8:29
3:23 [r]Jn 6:29 [s]Jn 13:34
3:24 [t]1Jn 2:6 [u]1Jn 4:13
4:1 [v]2Pe 2:1; 1Jn 2:18
4:2 [w]Jn 1:14; 1Jn 2:23 [x]1Co 12:3
4:3 [y]1Jn 2:22; 2Jn 7
4:4 [z]Ro 8:31 [a]Jn 12:31
4:5 [b]Jn 15:19
4:6 [c]Jn 8:47 [d]Jn 14:17
4:7 [e]1Jn 3:11 [f]1Jn 2:4
4:8 [g]ver 7,16
4:9 [h]Jn 3:16,17; 1Jn 5:11
4:10 [i]Ro 5:8,10 [j]1Jn 2:2

whether they are from God, because
many false prophets have gone out into
the world.[v] 2This is how you can recognize the Spirit of God: Every spirit that
acknowledges that Jesus Christ has
come in the flesh[w] is from God,[x] 3but
every spirit that does not acknowledge
Jesus is not from God. This is the spirit
of the antichrist,[y] which you have heard
is coming and even now is already in
the world.
4You, dear children, are from God
and have overcome them, because the
one who is in you[z] is greater than the
one who is in the world.[a] 5They are
from the world[b] and therefore speak
from the viewpoint of the world, and
the world listens to them. 6We are
from God, and whoever knows God
listens to us; but whoever is not from
God does not listen to us.[c] This is how
we recognize the Spirit[h] of truth[d] and
the spirit of falsehood.

God is love.

7Dear friends, let us love one another,[e] for love comes from God. Everyone who loves has been born of God
and knows God.[f] 8Whoever does not
love does not know God, because God
is love.[g] 9This is how God showed his
love among us: He sent his one and
only Son[i] into the world that we might
live through him.[h] 10This is love: not
that we loved God, but that he loved
us[i] and sent his Son as an atoning sacrifice for[j] our sins.[j] 11Dear friends,
since God so loved us,[k] we also ought
to love one another. 12No one has ever
seen God;[l] but if we love one another,
God lives in us and his love is made
complete in us.[m]
13We know that we live in him and
he in us, because he has given us of his
Spirit.[n] 14And we have seen and testify[o] that the Father has sent his Son to

4:11 [k]Jn 3:16 **4:12** [l]Jn 1:18; 1Ti 6:16 [m]1Jn 2:5
4:13 [n]1Jn 3:24 **4:14** [o]Jn 15:27

[h]6 Or *spirit* [i]9 Or *his only begotten Son* [j]10 Or *as the one who would turn aside his wrath, taking away*

be the Savior of the world.[a] 15If anyone
acknowledges that Jesus is the Son of
God,[b] God lives in him and he in God.
16And so we know and rely on the love
God has for us.
God is love.[c] Whoever lives in love
lives in God, and God in him.[d] 17In this
way, love is made complete[e] among us
so that we will have confidence on the
day of judgment, because in this world
we are like him. 18There is no fear in
love. But perfect love drives out fear,[f]
because fear has to do with punishment.
The one who fears is not made perfect
in love.
19We love because he first loved us.[g]
20If anyone says, "I love God," yet hates
his brother,[h] he is a liar.[i] For anyone
who does not love his brother, whom
he has seen,[j] cannot love God, whom he
has not seen.[k] 21And he has given us
this command: Whoever loves God
must also love his brother.[l]

Loving God requires obedience.

5 Everyone who believes that Jesus
is the Christ[m] is born of God,[n] and
everyone who loves the father loves his
child as well.[o] 2This is how we know
that we love the children of God: by
loving God and carrying out his commands. 3This is love for God: to obey
his commands.[p] And his commands are
not burdensome,[q] 4for everyone born of
God overcomes[r] the world. This is the
victory that has overcome the world,
even our faith. 5Who is it that overcomes
the world? Only he who believes that
Jesus is the Son of God.

Three testify that Jesus is the Son of God.

6This is the one who came by water
and blood[s]—Jesus Christ. He did not
come by water only, but by water and
blood. And it is the Spirit who testifies,
because the Spirit is the truth.[t] 7For
there are three[u] that testify: 8the[k] Spirit,
the water and the blood; and the three
are in agreement. 9We accept man's testimony,[v] but God's testimony is greater
because it is the testimony of God,[w]
which he has given about his Son.
10Anyone who believes in the Son of
God has this testimony in his heart.[x]
Anyone who does not believe God has
made him out to be a liar,[y] because he
has not believed the testimony God
has given about his Son. 11And this is
the testimony: God has given us eternal life, and this life is in his Son.[z]
12He who has the Son has life; he who
does not have the Son of God does not
have life.[a]

God hears and answers prayer.

13I write these things to you who believe in the name of the Son of God[b] so
that you may know that you have
eternal life.[c] 14This is the confidence[d]
we have in approaching God: that if we
ask anything according to his will, he
hears us.[e] 15And if we know that he
hears us—whatever we ask—we know[f]
that we have what we asked of him.
16If anyone sees his brother commit
a sin that does not lead to death, he
should pray and God will give him life.[g]
I refer to those whose sin does not lead
to death. There is a sin that leads to
death.[h] I am not saying that he should
pray about that.[i] 17All wrongdoing is
sin,[j] and there is sin that does not lead
to death.[k]

Sin is contrary to the children of God.

18We know that anyone born of God
does not continue to sin; the one who
was born of God keeps him safe, and
the evil one cannot harm him.[l] 19We
know that we are children of God,[m] and
that the whole world is under the con-

4:14 [a]Jn 3:17 **4:15** [b]Ro 10:9 **4:16** [c]ver 8 [d]1Jn 3:24 **4:17** [e]1Jn 2:5 **4:18** [f]Ro 8:15 **4:19** [g]ver 10 **4:20** [h]1Jn 2:9 [i]1Jn 2:4 [j]1Jn 3:17 [k]ver 12 **4:21** [l]Mt 5:43 **5:1** [m]1Jn 2:22 [n]Jn 1:13; 1Jn 2:23 [o]Jn 8:42 **5:3** [p]Jn 14:15; 2Jn 6 [q]Mt 11:30 **5:4** [r]Jn 16:33 **5:6** [s]Jn 19:34 [t]Jn 14:17 **5:7** [u]Mt 18:16 **5:9** [v]Jn 5:34 [w]Mt 3:16,17; Jn 8:17,18 **5:10** [x]Ro 8:16; Gal 4:6 [y]Jn 3:33 **5:11** [z]Jn 1:4; 1Jn 2:25 **5:12** [a]Jn 3:15,16, 36 **5:13** [b]1Jn 3:23 [c]Jn 20:31; 1Jn 1:1,2 **5:14** [d]1Jn 3:21 [e]Mt 7:7 **5:15** [f]ver 18,19,20 **5:16** [g]Jas 5:15 [h]Heb 6:4-6; 10:26 [i]Jer 7:16 **5:17** [j]1Jn 3:4 [k]1Jn 2:1

5:18 [l]Jn 14:30 **5:19** [m]1Jn 4:6

[k] *7,8* Late manuscripts of the Vulgate *testify in heaven: the Father, the Word and the Holy Spirit, and these three are one. 8And there are three that testify on earth: the* (not found in any Greek manuscript before the sixteenth century)

trol of the evil one.[a] 20 We know also
that the Son of God has come and has
given us understanding,[b] so that we may
know him who is true.[c] And we are in
him who is true—even in his Son Jesus
Christ. He is the true God and eternal
life.[d]
21 Dear children, keep yourselves from
idols.[e]

5:19 [a]Gal 1:4
5:20 [b]Lk 24:45 [c]Jn 17:3 [d]ver 11
5:21 [e]1Co 10:14; 1Th 1:9

2 JOHN

Author: John the Apostle.

Date Written: Between A.D. 85 and 96.

Title: From the book's author: John.

Background: John reveals in his first letter how a number of false teachers have broken from the church. 2 John addresses some of the problems associated with these erroneous teachers, who travel through the area at the expense of both the church's material and spiritual welfare. At the heart of these heresies is a false belief called Gnosticism, which claims a hidden knowledge for its adherents. The Gnostics profess they are a special, spiritual elite, which keeps them from being accountable for right or wrong behavior. This letter is John's effort to combat the ungodly conduct which results and to encourage true believers to withdraw all fellowship from these false teachers. John, "the beloved disciple," probably wrote his 3 letters during the final years of his life.

Where Written: Probably Ephesus.

To Whom: To the chosen lady and her children. (This could either be a Christian woman and her children, or it could refer figuratively to a local church and the believers in it.)

Content: John continues showing his concern for others by warning of those who do not teach the truth about Jesus Christ. But John does have joy for those walking according to the commands of God. Jesus Christ is indeed the Son of God, and those trusting him for salvation should live in truth, love and obedience. The relationship believers have with those of the world must be discerning; false teachers should not be encouraged in any way (10,11). The apostle John concludes this small letter by stating his desire to return for a personal visit with the Christians.

Key Words: "Truth"; "Walk." The theme of "truth" transcends 2 John. This "truth" advocates love, knowledge and joy for believers who "walk" in these virtues. John uses his apostolic authority to command this "walk" of obedience and to warn believers of false teachers who do not follow Christ's teachings.

Themes: • Antichrists are in the world, and they seek to deceive us. • Obedience and love are inseparable. • A Christian's support for heathen activities is being a partaker in that evil. • Great joy comes to those who help others grow in truth.

Outline:
1. Salutation. 1-3
2. Walk in obedient love. 4-6
3. Avoid false teachers. 7-11
4. Concluding remarks. 12,13

2 JOHN

Do not accept any teaching
contrary to that of Christ.

1 The elder,[a]

To the chosen[b] lady and her children,
whom I love in the truth—and not I
only, but also all who know the truth[c]—
2 because of the truth,[d] which lives in
us[e] and will be with us forever:

3 Grace, mercy and peace from God
the Father and from Jesus Christ,[f] the
Father's Son, will be with us in truth
and love.

4 It has given me great joy to find some
of your children walking in the truth,[g]
just as the Father commanded us. 5 And
now, dear lady, I am not writing you a
new command but one we have had
from the beginning.[h] I ask that we love
one another. 6 And this is love:[i] that we
walk in obedience to his commands. As
you have heard from the beginning, his
command is that you walk in love.

7 Many deceivers, who do not
acknowledge Jesus Christ[j] as coming
in the flesh, have gone out into the
world.[k] Any such person is the deceiver and the antichrist.[l] 8 Watch out that
you do not lose what you have worked
for, but that you may be rewarded fully.[m] 9 Anyone who runs ahead and does
not continue in the teaching of Christ
does not have God; whoever continues
in the teaching has both the Father
and the Son.[n] 10 If anyone comes to you
and does not bring this teaching, do
not take him into your house or welcome him.[o] 11 Anyone who welcomes
him shares[p] in his wicked work.

12 I have much to write to you, but I
do not want to use paper and ink. Instead, I hope to visit you and talk with
you face to face,[q] so that our joy may
be complete.

13 The children of your chosen[r] sister
send their greetings.

1:1 [a] 3Jn 1 [b] Ro 16:13 [c] Jn 8:32
1:2 [d] 2Pe 1:12 [e] 1Jn 1:8
1:3 [f] Ro 1:7
1:4 [g] 3Jn 3,4
1:5 [h] 1Jn 2:7; 3:11
1:6 [i] 1Jn 2:5
1:7 [j] 1Jn 2:22; 4:2,3 [k] 1Jn 4:1 [l] 1Jn 2:18
1:8 [m] 1Co 3:8
1:9 [n] 1Jn 2:23
1:10 [o] Ro 16:17
1:11 [p] 1Ti 5:22
1:12 [q] 3Jn 13,14
1:13 [r] ver 1

3 JOHN

Author: John the Apostle.

Date Written: Between A.D. 85 and 96.

Title: From the book's author: John.

Background: 3 John, a book of only 14 verses, centers around 3 characters. Gaius is either a pastor or a church leader who consistently walks in the truth; Diotrephes is a disruptive and prideful leading man in the church; and Demetrius is the reputable layman who probably took this letter from John to Gaius. At this time there are a number of traveling missionaries who spread the gospel from church to church and are supported by church members taking them into their homes. John uses this occasion to encourage such generosity. John was a leader in the church at Ephesus for many years, having moved there from Jerusalem where he cared for Jesus' mother after the crucifixion.

Where Written: Probably Ephesus.

To Whom: To Gaius.

Content: Having traveled with Jesus, John understands the need for itinerant ministers to be aided in their efforts. John writes this letter to his friend Gaius commending him and encouraging him to continue his support for the evangelists who travel throughout Asia Minor. Gaius is further warned not to be like Diotrephes, who refuses to help the missionaries, undermines the authority of John and even banishes from the church all who desire to give aid to these traveling bearers of truth. In contrast, Demetrius is highly commended as a model church member. John closes this third letter with his hope to visit soon.

Key Words: "Joy"; "Hospitality." The abundant "joy" which John expresses is for the faithfulness of Gaius and other believers who continue to walk in truth. The "hospitality" which they show to the itinerant preachers and other Christian brothers is a trait which the entire church is commissioned to develop.

Themes: • The family of God should support other members of the family who proclaim the gospel. • When we support a ministry, we become a partner of that ministry. • A good reputation will follow a conscientious walk with God. • Believers should stand firm against hypocrites diluting the mission of the church.

Outline:
1. Salutation. 1
2. Gaius's love and faith commended. 2-8
3. Diotrephes's actions rebuked. 9,10
4. Demetrius's actions praised. 11,12
5. Final greetings. 13,14

3 JOHN

Faithfulness of Gaius commended.

1 The elder,[a]

To my dear friend Gaius, whom I love
in the truth.

2 Dear friend, I pray that you may
enjoy good health and that all may go
well with you, even as your soul is getting along well. 3 It gave me great joy to
have some brothers[b] come and tell about
your faithfulness to the truth and how
you continue to walk in the truth.[c] 4 I
have no greater joy than to hear that
my children[d] are walking in the truth.
5 Dear friend, you are faithful in what
you are doing for the brothers, even
though they are strangers to you.[e] 6 They
have told the church about your love.
You will do well to send them on their
way in a manner worthy of God. 7 It was
for the sake of the Name[f] that they went
out, receiving no help from the pagans.[g]
8 We ought therefore to show hospitality
to such men so that we may work together for the truth.

Pride of Diotrephes rebuked.

9 I wrote to the church, but Diotrephes, who loves to be first, will have
nothing to do with us. 10 So if I come,[h] I
will call attention to what he is doing,
gossiping maliciously about us. Not satisfied with that, he refuses to welcome
the brothers.[i] He also stops those who
want to do so and puts them out of the
church.[j]

Praise for Demetrius and final greetings.

11 Dear friend, do not imitate what
is evil but what is good.[k] Anyone who
does what is good is from God.[l] Anyone who does what is evil has not
seen God.[m] 12 Demetrius is well spoken
of by everyone[n]—and even by the
truth itself. We also speak well of him,
and you know that our testimony is
true.[o]
13 I have much to write you, but I do
not want to do so with pen and ink. 14 I
hope to see you soon, and we will talk
face to face.[p]

Peace to you. The friends here send their greetings. Greet the friends there by name.[q]

1:1 [a]2Jn 1
1:3 [b]ver 5,10 [c]2Jn 4
1:4 [d]1Co 4:15; 1Jn 2:1
1:5 [e]Ro 12:13; Heb 13:2
1:7 [f]Jn 15:21 [g]Ac 20:33,35
1:10 [h]2Jn 12 [i]ver 5 [j]Jn 9:22,34
1:11 [k]Ps 37:27 [l]1Jn 2:29 [m]1Jn 3:6,9,10
1:12 [n]1Ti 3:7 [o]Jn 21:24
1:14 [p]2Jn 12 [q]Jn 10:3

JUDE

Author: Jude (the brother of James, and the half-brother of Jesus Christ).

Date Written: Between A.D. 65 and 80.

Title: From the book's author: Jude.

Background: Jude writes this letter to combat a false teaching in the church which is a form of Gnosticism. This erroneous doctrine teaches that the sins of the body do not affect the purity of the soul and, thus, opens the door for people to engage in all kinds of immoral and perverted evils. Jude, like his brother James, did not believe that his half-brother Jesus was the Son of God until after the resurrection. This may account for why he refers to himself only as a servant of Jesus Christ.

Where Written: Uncertain (possibly outside of Palestine).

To Whom: To believers in Jesus Christ.

Content: Jude writes this letter to warn believers that godless men bearing false doctrines about Jesus and the Christian walk are polluting the churches. Jude reminds the people of God's previous judgments against Israel's unbelief, angels' disobedience and Sodom and Gomorrah's corruption. These 3 Old Testament judgments are followed by 3 declarations of woe to godless men who have taken the way of Cain, Balaam and Korah. Jude refers to Jewish tradition regarding Enoch's prophecy of the doom of the ungodly and makes reference to the apostles' predictions of evil, divisions and apostasy. But still Jude encourages the faithful to remain strong and true and to show mercy to those who doubt. The power and authority of Jesus Christ is proclaimed with great joy.

Key Words: "Contend"; "Godless." The mission of this letter from Jude is to urge the believers to "contend" for the faith which has been entrusted to them (verse 3). It painstakingly details the sin and the assured judgment of all "godless" people.

Themes: • Christians need to beware of false teachers infiltrating their churches. • Godless people can be detected by their beliefs, their acts and their words. • Believers should be merciful to unbelievers. • Jesus Christ will cleanse all believers and present them without fault to God. • The judgment of God on unbelievers is certain.

Outline:

1. Introduction. 1,2
2. Condemnation of false teachers. 3-16
3. A call to persevere. 17-23
4. Doxology of Jude. 24,25

JUDE

1Jude,[a] a servant of Jesus Christ and a brother of James,

To those who have been called,[b] who are loved by God the Father and kept by[a] Jesus Christ:[c]

2Mercy, peace and love be yours in abundance.[d]

Defend the truth of God against false teachers.

3Dear friends, although I was very eager to write to you about the salvation we share,[e] I felt I had to write and urge you to contend[f] for the faith that was once for all entrusted to the saints. **4**For certain men whose condemnation was written about[b] long ago have secretly slipped in among you.[g] They are godless men, who change the grace of our God into a license for immorality and deny Jesus Christ our only Sovereign and Lord.[h]

5Though you already know all this, I want to remind you that the Lord[c] delivered his people out of Egypt, but later destroyed those who did not believe.[i] **6**And the angels who did not keep their positions of authority but abandoned their own home—these he has kept in darkness, bound with everlasting chains for judgment on the great Day.[j] **7**In a similar way, Sodom and Gomorrah and the surrounding towns[k] gave themselves up to sexual immorality and perversion. They serve as an example of those who suffer the punishment of eternal fire.[l]

8In the very same way, these dreamers pollute their own bodies, reject authority and slander celestial beings.[m] **9**But even the archangel Michael,[n] when he was disputing with the devil about the body of Moses, did not dare to bring a slanderous accusation against him, but said, "The Lord rebuke you!"[o] **10**Yet these men speak abusively against whatever they do not understand; and what things they do understand by instinct, like unreasoning animals—these are the very things that destroy them.[p]

11Woe to them! They have taken the way of Cain;[q] they have rushed for profit into Balaam's error;[r] they have been destroyed in Korah's rebellion.[s]

12These men are blemishes at your love feasts,[t] eating with you without the slightest qualm—shepherds who feed only themselves. They are clouds without rain,[u] blown along by the wind;[v] autumn trees, without fruit and uprooted[w]— twice dead. **13**They are wild waves of the sea,[x] foaming up their shame;[y] wandering stars, for whom blackest darkness has been reserved forever.[z]

The Lord is coming to judge ungodly men.

14Enoch,[a] the seventh from Adam, prophesied about these men: "See, the Lord is coming with thousands upon thousands of his holy ones[b] **15**to judge[c] everyone, and to convict all the ungodly of all the ungodly acts they have done in the ungodly way, and of all the harsh words ungodly sinners have spoken against him."[d] **16**These men are grumblers and faultfinders; they follow their own evil desires; they boast[e] about themselves and flatter others for their own advantage.

A call to persevere.

17But, dear friends, remember what the apostles of our Lord Jesus Christ foretold.[f] **18**They said to you, "In the last times[g] there will be scoffers who will follow their own ungodly desires."[h] **19**These are the men who divide you, who follow mere natural instincts and do not have the Spirit.[i]

20But you, dear friends, build yourselves up[j] in your most holy faith and pray in the Holy Spirit.[k] **21**Keep yourselves in God's love as you wait[l] for the mercy of our Lord Jesus Christ to bring you to eternal life.

1:1 [a]Mt 13:55; Ac 1:13 [b]Ro 1:6,7 [c]Jn 17:12
1:2 [d]2Pe 1:2
1:3 [e]Tit 1:4 [f]1Ti 6:12
1:4 [g]Gal 2:4 [h]Tit 1:16; 2Pe 2:1
1:5 [i]Nu 14:29; Ps 106:26
1:6 [j]2Pe 2:4,9
1:7 [k]Dt 29:23 [l]2Pe 2:6
1:8 [m]2Pe 2:10
1:9 [n]Da 10:13,21 [o]Zec 3:2
1:10 [p]2Pe 2:12
1:11 [q]Ge 4:3-8; 1Jn 3:12 [r]2Pe 2:15 [s]Nu 16:1-3, 31-35
1:12 [t]2Pe 2:13; 1Co 11:20-22 [u]Pr 25:14; 2Pe 2:17 [v]Eph 4:14 [w]Mt 15:13
1:13 [x]Isa 57:20 [y]Php 3:19 [z]2Pe 2:17
1:14 [a]Ge 5:18, 21-24 [b]Dt 33:2; Da 7:10
1:15 [c]2Pe 2:6-9 [d]1Ti 1:9
1:16 [e]2Pe 2:18
1:17 [f]2Pe 3:2
1:18 [g]1Ti 4:1 [h]2Pe 2:1
1:19 [i]1Co 2:14,15
1:20 [j]Col 2:7 [k]Eph 6:18
1:21 [l]Tit 2:13; 2Pe 3:12

a *1* Or *for;* or *in*   b *4* Or *men who were marked out for condemnation*   c *5* Some early manuscripts *Jesus*

22 Be merciful to those who doubt;
23 snatch others from the fire and save
them;[a] to others show mercy, mixed
with fear—hating even the clothing
stained by corrupted flesh.[b]
24 To him who is able[c] to keep you
from falling and to present you before
his glorious presence[d] without fault[e]
and with great joy— 25 to the only God[f]
our Savior be glory, majesty, power and
authority, through Jesus Christ our
Lord, before all ages, now and forevermore![g] Amen.[h]

1:23 [a] Am 4:11; Zec 3:2-5 [b] Rev 3:4
1:24 [c] Ro 16:25 [d] 2Co 4:14 [e] Col 1:22
1:25 [f] Jn 5:44; 1Ti 1:17 [g] Heb 13:8 [h] Ro 11:36

REVELATION

Author: John the Apostle.

Date Written: Between A.D. 90 and 96.

Title: This book is so named because it is the "revelation" of Jesus Christ as given to the apostle John. It is also called the "Apocalypse," which means "revelation" or "unveiling."

Background: John is exiled by the Roman government to Patmos, a small island off the coast of Greece, for preaching the Word of God. His exile is only part of an intense period of persecution against the church, which follows the Roman emperor Domitian's proclamation that he should be worshiped as deity. While on Patmos, John receives this revelation about Jesus Christ from God the Father. An angel helps John to understand the vision. Whereas the first book of the Bible— Genesis— tells of the beginning of sin and Satan's triumph, the last book of the Bible—Revelation— tells of sin's end and Satan's defeat. A special blessing is promised to all who read, hear and obey this book. But also a special curse is promised to those who add to or take away from these words. John also wrote the fourth Gospel and the 3 letters which bear his name.

Where Written: On the island of Patmos, in the Aegean Sea.

To Whom: To 7 churches in Asia Minor (modern Turkey).

Content: Revelation is lavish in colorful descriptions of the visions which proclaim for us the last days before Christ's return and the ushering in of the new heaven and new earth. The fact that it may at first seem too complex is no reason to avoid this book, for it is a full disclosure of the prophetic events which await every person, whether dead or alive. Revelation makes known what is to come: the series of devastations to be poured out upon the earth; the mark of the beast, "666" (13:18); the climactic battle of Armageddon; the binding of Satan; the reign of the Lord; the great white throne judgment; and the nature of the eternal city of God. Prophecies concerning Jesus Christ are fulfilled, and a concluding call to his lordship assures us that he will soon return.

Key Words: "Revelation"; "Jesus Christ"; "Seven." This book is a thorough "revelation" of the total person of "Jesus Christ": his glory, power and wisdom; his judgment, kingdom and grace; and the Lamb of God from Alpha to Omega. Several numbers have significant symbolism in Revelation, but the number "seven" is dominant throughout with 7 letters, 7 seals, 7 trumpets, 7 signs, 7 plagues, 7 dooms and 7 new things.

Themes: • The end of earthly life is only the beginning of eternal life. • Christians shall spend eternity with God in the new Jerusalem. • Unbelievers shall spend eternity with Satan in the lake of fire. • God desires that everyone trust in his Son for redemption...today!

Outline:

1. Introduction. 1:1-1:7
2. Christ's revelation of himself to John. 1:8-1:20
3. Letters to the 7 churches. 2:1-3:22
4. The throne in heaven. 4:1-5:14
5. The 7 seals. 6:1-8:5
6. The 7 trumpets. 8:6-11:19
7. The 7 explanatory prophecies. 12:1-14:20
8. The 7 bowls of wrath. 15:1-16:21
9. The overthrow of Babylon. 17:1-19:5
10. Prophecies concerning the second coming of Christ. 19:6-19:21
11. Prophecies concerning the Millennium. 20:1-20:6
12. The rebellion and Satan's final doom. 20:7-20:15
13. The new heaven, new earth and new Jerusalem. 21:1-22:6
14. The coming of the Lord Jesus Christ. 22:7-22:21

REVELATION

Introduction to the revelation given to John.

1 The revelation of Jesus Christ, which God gave him to show his servants
what must soon take place. He made it
known by sending his angel[a] to his servant John, 2who testifies to everything
he saw—that is, the word of God and
the testimony of Jesus Christ.[b] 3Blessed
is the one who reads the words of this
prophecy, and blessed are those who
hear it and take to heart what is written in it,[c] because the time is near.

4John,

To the seven churches in the province of Asia:

Grace and peace to you from him who is, and who was, and who is to come, and from the seven spirits[a][d] before his
throne, 5and from Jesus Christ, who is
the faithful witness,[e] the firstborn from the dead,[f] and the ruler of the kings of the earth.[g]

To him who loves us and has freed
us from our sins by his blood, 6and has
made us to be a kingdom and priests[h] to serve his God and Father—to him be glory and power for ever and ever! Amen.[i]

7Look, he is coming with the clouds,[j]
and every eye will see him,

1:1 [a]Rev 22:16
1:2 [b]1Co 1:6; Rev 12:17
1:3 [c]Lk 11:28
1:4 [d]Rev 3:1; 4:5
1:5 [e]Rev 3:14 [f]Col 1:18 [g]Rev 17:14
1:6 [h]1Pe 2:5 [i]Ro 11:36
1:7 [j]Da 7:13

a4 Or *the sevenfold Spirit*

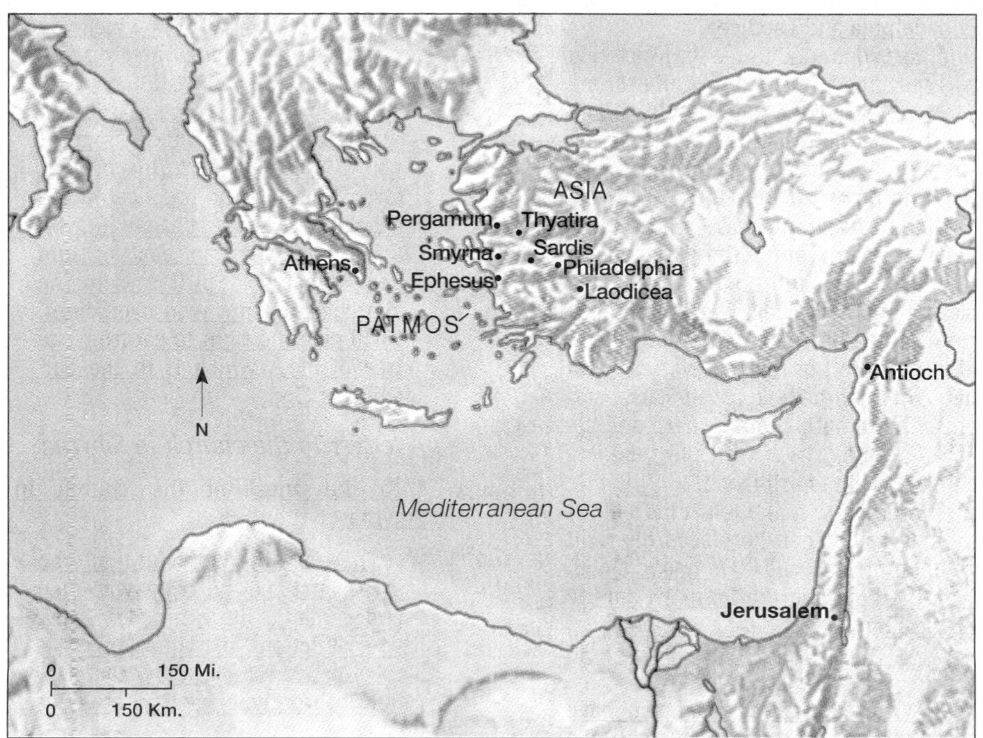

The Seven Churches

The seven churches were located on a major Roman road. A letter carrier would leave the island of Patmos (where John was exiled), arriving first at Ephesus. He would travel north to Smyrna and Pergamum, turn southeast to Thyatira, and continue on to Sardis, Philadelphia, and Laodicea—in the exact order in which the letters were dictated.

even those who pierced him;
and all the peoples of the earth will
mourn[a] because of him.
So shall it be! Amen.

The Alpha and the Omega revealed at Patmos.

8“I am the Alpha and the Omega,”[b]
says the Lord God, “who is, and who
was, and who is to come, the Almighty.”[c]
9I, John, your brother and companion
in the suffering[d] and kingdom and patient endurance[e] that are ours in Jesus,
was on the island of Patmos because of
the word of God and the testimony of
Jesus. 10On the Lord's Day I was in the
Spirit,[f] and I heard behind me a loud
voice like a trumpet,[g] 11which said:
“Write on a scroll what you see and send
it to the seven churches:[h] to Ephesus,
Smyrna, Pergamum, Thyatira, Sardis,[i]
Philadelphia and Laodicea.”
12I turned around to see the voice that
was speaking to me. And when I turned
I saw seven golden lampstands,[j] 13and
among the lampstands was someone
“like a son of man,”[b][k] dressed in a robe
reaching down to his feet and with a
golden sash around his chest.[l] 14His
head and hair were white like wool, as
white as snow, and his eyes were like
blazing fire.[m] 15His feet were like bronze
glowing in a furnace,[n] and his voice was
like the sound of rushing waters.[o] 16In
his right hand he held seven stars,[p] and
out of his mouth came a sharp double-
edged sword.[q] His face was like the sun
shining in all its brilliance.
17When I saw him, I fell at his feet[r] as
though dead. Then he placed his right
hand on me and said: “Do not be afraid.
I am the First and the Last.[s] 18I am the
Living One; I was dead,[t] and behold I
am alive for ever and ever![u] And I hold
the keys of death and Hades.[v]
19“Write, therefore, what you have
seen, what is now and what will take
place later. 20The mystery of the seven
stars that you saw in my right hand and
of the seven golden lampstands[w] is
this: The seven stars are the angels[c] of
the seven churches,[x] and the seven
lampstands are the seven churches.[y]

1:7 [a]Zec 12:10 **1:8** [b]Rev 21:6 [c]Rev 4:8 **1:9** [d]Php 4:14 [e]2Ti 2:12 **1:10** [f]Rev 4:2 [g]Rev 4:1 **1:11** [h]ver 4,20 [i]Rev 3:1 **1:12** [j]Ex 25:31-40; Zec 4:2 **1:13** [k]Eze 1:26; Da 7:13; 10:16 [l]Da 10:5; Rev 15:6 **1:14** [m]Da 7:9; 10:6; Rev 19:12 **1:15** [n]Da 10:6 [o]Eze 43:2; Rev 14:2 **1:16** [p]Rev 2:1; 3:1 [q]Isa 49:2; Heb 4:12; Rev 2:12,16 **1:17** [r]Eze 1:28; Da 8:17,18 [s]Isa 41:4; 44:6; 48:12; Rev 22:13 **1:18** [t]Ro 6:9 [u]Rev 4:9,10 [v]Rev 20:1 **1:20** [w]Zec 4:2 [x]ver 4,11 [y]Mt 5:14,15 **2:1** [z]Rev 1:16 [a]Rev 1:12,13 **2:2** [b]Rev 3:1,8,15 [c]1Jn 4:1 [d]2Co 11:13 **2:3** [e]Jn 15:21 **2:4** [f]Mt 24:12 **2:5** [g]ver 16,22 [h]Rev 1:20 **2:6** [i]ver 15

A letter: To the church in Ephesus.

2 “To the angel[d] of the church in
Ephesus write:
These are the words of him who
holds the seven stars in his right
hand[z] and walks among the seven
golden lampstands:[a] 2I know your
deeds,[b] your hard work and your
perseverance. I know that you cannot tolerate wicked men, that you
have tested[c] those who claim to
be apostles but are not, and have
found them false.[d] 3You have persevered and have endured hardships for my name,[e] and have not
grown weary.
4Yet I hold this against you: You
have forsaken your first love.[f] 5Re-
member the height from which you
have fallen! Repent[g] and do the
things you did at first. If you do
not repent, I will come to you and
remove your lampstand[h] from its
place. 6But you have this in your
favor: You hate the practices of the
Nicolaitans,[i] which I also hate.
7He who has an ear, let him
hear[j] what the Spirit says to the
churches. To him who overcomes,
I will give the right to eat from the
tree of life,[k] which is in the paradise[l] of God.

A letter: To the church in Smyrna.

8“To the angel of the church in
Smyrna[m] write:
These are the words of him who
is the First and the Last,[n] who died
and came to life again.[o] 9I know
your afflictions and your poverty—
yet you are rich![p] I know the slander of those who say they are Jews

2:7 [j]Mt 11:15; Rev 3:6,13,22 [k]Ge 2:9; Rev 22:2, 14,19 [l]Lk 23:43 **2:8** [m]Rev 1:11 [n]Rev 1:17 [o]Rev 1:18 **2:9** [p]Jas 2:5

b *13* Daniel 7:13 c *20* Or *messengers* d *1* Or *messenger*; also in verses 8, 12 and 18

and are not,[a] but are a synagogue
of Satan.[b] 10 Do not be afraid of what
you are about to suffer. I tell you,
the devil will put some of you in
prison to test you,[c] and you will
suffer persecution for ten days.[d] Be
faithful,[e] even to the point of death,
and I will give you the crown of life.
11 He who has an ear, let him hear
what the Spirit says to the churches. He who overcomes will not be
hurt at all by the second death.[f]

A letter: To the church in Pergamum.

12 "To the angel of the church in Pergamum[g] write:

These are the words of him who
has the sharp, double-edged sword.[h]
13 I know where you live—where
Satan has his throne. Yet you remain true to my name. You did not
renounce your faith in me,[i] even
in the days of Antipas, my faithful
witness, who was put to death in
your city—where Satan lives.[j]
14 Nevertheless, I have a few things
against you:[k] You have people there
who hold to the teaching of Balaam,[l] who taught Balak to entice
the Israelites to sin by eating food
sacrificed to idols and by committing sexual immorality.[m] 15 Likewise
you also have those who hold to
the teaching of the Nicolaitans.[n]
16 Repent therefore! Otherwise, I
will soon come to you and will
fight against them with the sword
of my mouth.[o]
17 He who has an ear, let him
hear what the Spirit says to the
churches. To him who overcomes,
I will give some of the hidden
manna.[p] I will also give him a
white stone with a new name[q]
written on it, known only to him
who receives it.[r]

A letter: To the church in Thyatira.

18 "To the angel of the church in Thyatira[s] write:

These are the words of the Son
of God, whose eyes are like blazing
fire and whose feet are like burnished bronze.[t] 19 I know your
deeds,[u] your love and faith, your
service and perseverance, and that
you are now doing more than you
did at first.
20 Nevertheless, I have this against
you: You tolerate that woman Jezebel,[v] who calls herself a prophetess. By her teaching she misleads
my servants into sexual immorality
and the eating of food sacrificed to
idols. 21 I have given her time[w] to
repent of her immorality, but she
is unwilling.[x] 22 So I will cast her on
a bed of suffering, and I will make
those who commit adultery[y] with
her suffer intensely, unless they repent of her ways. 23 I will strike her
children dead. Then all the churches will know that I am he who
searches hearts and minds,[z] and I
will repay each of you according to
your deeds. 24 Now I say to the rest
of you in Thyatira, to you who do
not hold to her teaching and have
not learned Satan's so-called deep
secrets (I will not impose any other
burden on you):[a] 25 Only hold on to
what you have[b] until I come.
26 To him who overcomes and
does my will to the end, I will give
authority over the nations[c]—

27 'He will rule them with an iron
scepter;[d]
he will dash them to pieces
like pottery'[e][e]—

just as I have received authority
from my Father. 28 I will also give
him the morning star.[f] 29 He who
has an ear, let him hear[g] what the
Spirit says to the churches.

A letter: To the church in Sardis.

3 "To the angel[f] of the church in
Sardis write:

2:9 [a] Rev 3:9 [b] Mt 4:10
2:10 [c] Rev 3:10 [d] Da 1:12,14 [e] ver 13
2:11 [f] Rev 20:6,14; 21:8
2:12 [g] Rev 1:11 [h] Rev 1:16
2:13 [i] Rev 14:12 [j] ver 9,24
2:14 [k] ver 20 [l] 2Pe 2:15 [m] 1Co 6:13
2:15 [n] ver 6
2:16 [o] 2Th 2:8; Rev 1:16
2:17 [p] Jn 6:49,50 [q] Isa 62:2 [r] Rev 19:12
2:18 [s] Rev 1:11 [t] Rev 1:14,15
2:19 [u] ver 2
2:20 [v] 1Ki 16:31; 21:25; 2Ki 9:7
2:21 [w] Ro 2:4 [x] Rev 9:20
2:22 [y] Rev 17:2; 18:9
2:23 [z] 1Sa 16:7; Jer 11:20; Ac 1:24; Ro 8:27
2:24 [a] Ac 15:28
2:25 [b] Rev 3:11
2:26 [c] Ps 2:8; Rev 3:21
2:27 [d] Rev 12:5 [e] Isa 30:14; Jer 19:11
2:28 [f] Rev 22:16
2:29 [g] ver 7

[e] 27 Psalm 2:9 [f] 1 Or *messenger*; also in verses 7 and 14

These are the words of him who
holds the seven spirits[g][a] of God
and the seven stars.[b] I know your
deeds;[c] you have a reputation of
being alive, but you are dead.[d]
2Wake up! Strengthen what remains
and is about to die, for I have not
found your deeds complete in the
sight of my God. 3Remember, therefore, what you have received and
heard; obey it, and repent.[e] But if
you do not wake up, I will come like
a thief,[f] and you will not know at
what time I will come to you.

4Yet you have a few people in
Sardis who have not soiled their
clothes.[g] They will walk with me,
dressed in white,[h] for they are worthy. 5He who overcomes will, like
them, be dressed in white. I will
never blot out his name from the
book of life,[i] but will acknowledge
his name before my Father[j] and his
angels. 6He who has an ear, let him
hear[k] what the Spirit says to the
churches.

A letter: To the church in Philadelphia.

7"To the angel of the church in Philadelphia[l] write:

These are the words of him who
is holy and true,[m] who holds the key
of David.[n] What he opens no one
can shut, and what he shuts no one
can open. 8I know your deeds. See,
I have placed before you an open
door[o] that no one can shut. I know
that you have little strength, yet
you have kept my word and have
not denied my name.[p] 9I will make
those who are of the synagogue of
Satan,[q] who claim to be Jews though
they are not, but are liars—I will
make them come and fall down at
your feet[r] and acknowledge that I
have loved you.[s] 10Since you have
kept my command to endure patiently, I will also keep you[t] from
the hour of trial that is going to
come upon the whole world to
test[u] those who live on the earth.[v]
11I am coming soon. Hold on to
what you have,[w] so that no one
will take your crown.[x] 12Him who
overcomes I will make a pillar[y] in
the temple of my God. Never
again will he leave it. I will write
on him the name of my God[z] and
the name of the city of my God, the
new Jerusalem,[a] which is coming
down out of heaven from my God;
and I will also write on him my
new name. 13He who has an ear,
let him hear what the Spirit says
to the churches.

A letter: To the church in Laodicea.

14"To the angel of the church in Laodicea write:

These are the words of the Amen,
the faithful and true witness, the
ruler of God's creation.[b] 15I know
your deeds, that you are neither cold
nor hot.[c] I wish you were either
one or the other! 16So, because you
are lukewarm—neither hot nor
cold—I am about to spit you out
of my mouth. 17You say, 'I am rich;
I have acquired wealth and do not
need a thing.'[d] But you do not realize that you are wretched, pitiful,
poor, blind and naked. 18I counsel
you to buy from me gold refined in
the fire, so you can become rich;
and white clothes to wear, so you
can cover your shameful nakedness;[e] and salve to put on your
eyes, so you can see.

19Those whom I love I rebuke
and discipline.[f] So be earnest, and
repent.[g] 20Here I am! I stand at the
door[h] and knock. If anyone hears
my voice and opens the door,[i] I will
come in[j] and eat with him, and he
with me.

21To him who overcomes, I will
give the right to sit with me on my
throne,[k] just as I overcame[l] and sat

3:1 [a]Rev 1:4 [b]Rev 1:16 [c]Rev 2:2 [d]1Ti 5:6
3:3 [e]Rev 2:5 [f]2Pe 3:10
3:4 [g]Jude 23 [h]Rev 4:4; 6:11; 7:9,13,14
3:5 [i]Rev 20:12 [j]Mt 10:32
3:6 [k]Rev 2:7
3:7 [l]Rev 1:11 [m]1Jn 5:20 [n]Isa 22:22; Mt 16:19
3:8 [o]Ac 14:27 [p]Rev 2:13
3:9 [q]Rev 2:9 [r]Isa 49:23 [s]Isa 43:4
3:10 [t]2Pe 2:9 [u]Rev 2:10 [v]Rev 6:10; 17:8
3:11 [w]Rev 2:25 [x]Rev 2:10
3:12 [y]Gal 2:9 [z]Rev 14:1; 22:4 [a]Rev 21:2,10
3:14 [b]Col 1:16,18
3:15 [c]Ro 12:11
3:17 [d]Hos 12:8; 1Co 4:8
3:18 [e]Rev 16:15
3:19 [f]Pr 3:12; Heb 12:5,6 [g]Rev 2:5
3:20 [h]Mt 24:33 [i]Lk 12:36 [j]Jn 14:23
3:21 [k]Mt 19:28 [l]Rev 5:5

g *1* Or *the sevenfold Spirit*

down with my Father on his
throne. 22He who has an ear, let
him hear[a] what the Spirit says to
the churches."

The throne of God in heaven.

4 After this I looked, and there before
me was a door standing open in
heaven. And the voice I had first heard
speaking to me like a trumpet[b] said,
"Come up here,[c] and I will show you
what must take place after this."[d] 2At
once I was in the Spirit,[e] and there before me was a throne in heaven[f] with
someone sitting on it. 3And the one
who sat there had the appearance of
jasper and carnelian. A rainbow,[g] resem-
bling an emerald, encircled the throne.
4Surrounding the throne were twenty-
four other thrones, and seated on them
were twenty-four elders.[h] They were
dressed in white[i] and had crowns of
gold on their heads. 5From the throne
came flashes of lightning, rumblings and
peals of thunder.[j] Before the throne,
seven lamps[k] were blazing. These are
the seven spirits[h][l] of God. 6Also before
the throne there was what looked like
a sea of glass,[m] clear as crystal.
In the center, around the throne, were
four living creatures,[n] and they were
covered with eyes, in front and in
back. 7The first living creature was like
a lion, the second was like an ox, the
third had a face like a man, the fourth
was like a flying eagle.[o] 8Each of the
four living creatures had six wings[p] and
was covered with eyes all around, even
under his wings. Day and night they
never stop saying:

"Holy, holy, holy
is the Lord God Almighty,[q]
who was, and is, and is to come."[r]

9Whenever the living creatures give glory, honor and thanks to him who sits
on the throne[s] and who lives for ever
and ever, 10the twenty-four elders[t] fall
down before him[u] who sits on the
throne,[v] and worship him who lives for
ever and ever. They lay their crowns
before the throne and say:

11"You are worthy, our Lord and God,
to receive glory and honor and
power,[w]
for you created all things,
and by your will they were created
and have their being."[x]

Only the Lamb is worthy to open the scroll with seven seals.

5 Then I saw in the right hand of him
who sat on the throne[y] a scroll with
writing on both sides[z] and sealed[a] with
seven seals. 2And I saw a mighty angel
proclaiming in a loud voice, "Who is
worthy to break the seals and open the
scroll?" 3But no one in heaven or on
earth or under the earth could open the
scroll or even look inside it. 4I wept and
wept because no one was found who
was worthy to open the scroll or look
inside. 5Then one of the elders said to
me, "Do not weep! See, the Lion[b] of the
tribe of Judah, the Root of David,[c] has
triumphed. He is able to open the scroll
and its seven seals."
6Then I saw a Lamb,[d] looking as if it
had been slain, standing in the center
of the throne, encircled by the four living creatures and the elders. He had
seven horns and seven eyes,[e] which
are the seven spirits[h] of God sent out
into all the earth. 7He came and took
the scroll from the right hand of him
who sat on the throne.[f] 8And when he
had taken it, the four living creatures
and the twenty-four elders fell down before the Lamb. Each one had a harp[g]
and they were holding golden bowls full
of incense, which are the prayers[h] of the
saints. 9And they sang a new song:[i]

"You are worthy[j] to take the scroll
and to open its seals,
because you were slain,
and with your blood[k] you
purchased[l] men for God
from every tribe and language and
people and nation.

3:22 [a]Rev 2:7
4:1 [b]Rev 1:10 [c]Rev 11:12 [d]Rev 1:19
4:2 [e]Rev 1:10 [f]Isa 6:1; Eze 1:26-28; Da 7:9
4:3 [g]Eze 1:28
4:4 [h]Rev 11:16 [i]Rev 3:4,5
4:5 [j]Rev 8:5; 16:18 [k]Zec 4:2 [l]Rev 1:4
4:6 [m]Rev 15:2 [n]Eze 1:5
4:7 [o]Eze 1:10; 10:14
4:8 [p]Isa 6:2 [q]Isa 6:3; Rev 1:8 [r]Rev 1:4
4:9 [s]Ps 47:8
4:10 [t]ver 4 [u]Rev 5:8,14 [v]ver 2
4:11 [w]Rev 5:12 [x]Rev 10:6
5:1 [y]ver 7,13 [z]Eze 2:9,10 [a]Isa 29:11; Da 12:4
5:5 [b]Ge 49:9 [c]Isa 11:1,10; Ro 15:12; Rev 22:16
5:6 [d]Jn 1:29 [e]Zec 4:10
5:7 [f]ver 1
5:8 [g]Rev 14:2 [h]Ps 141:2
5:9 [i]Ps 40:3 [j]Rev 4:11 [k]Heb 9:12 [l]1Co 6:20

h 5,6 Or *the sevenfold Spirit*

10You have made them to be a
kingdom and priests[a] to
serve our God,
and they will reign on the earth."

11Then I looked and heard the voice
of many angels, numbering thousands
upon thousands, and ten thousand times
ten thousand.[b] They encircled the throne
and the living creatures and the elders.
12In a loud voice they sang:

"Worthy is the Lamb, who was slain,
to receive power and wealth and
wisdom and strength
and honor and glory and praise!"[c]

13Then I heard every creature in
heaven and on earth and under the
earth[d] and on the sea, and all that is in
them, singing:

"To him who sits on the throne and
to the Lamb[e]
be praise and honor and glory and
power,
for ever and ever!"[f]

14The four living creatures said,
"Amen,"[g] and the elders fell down and
worshiped.[h]

The Lamb opens the first six seals.

6 I watched as the Lamb[i] opened the
first of the seven seals.[j] Then I
heard one of the four living creatures[k]
say in a voice like thunder,[l] "Come!" 2I
looked, and there before me was a
white horse![m] Its rider held a bow, and
he was given a crown,[n] and he rode
out as a conqueror bent on conquest.[o]
3When the Lamb opened the second
seal, I heard the second living creature[p]
say, "Come!" 4Then another horse came
out, a fiery red one.[q] Its rider was given
power to take peace from the earth[r]
and to make men slay each other. To
him was given a large sword.
5When the Lamb opened the third
seal, I heard the third living creature[s]
say, "Come!" I looked, and there before
me was a black horse![t] Its rider was
holding a pair of scales in his hand.

5:10 [a]1Pe 2:5
5:11 [b]Da 7:10; Heb 12:22
5:12 [c]Rev 4:11
5:13 [d]ver 3; Php 2:10 [e]Rev 6:16 [f]1Ch 29:11
5:14 [g]Rev 4:9 [h]Rev 4:10; 19:4
6:1 [i]Rev 5:6 [j]Rev 5:1 [k]Rev 4:6,7 [l]Rev 14:2; 19:6
6:2 [m]Zec 6:3; Rev 19:11 [n]Zec 6:11; Rev 14:14 [o]Ps 45:4
6:3 [p]Rev 4:7
6:4 [q]Zec 6:2 [r]Mt 10:34
6:5 [s]Rev 4:7 [t]Zec 6:2
6:6 [u]Rev 4:6,7 [v]Rev 9:4
6:7 [w]Rev 4:7
6:8 [x]Zec 6:3 [y]Hos 13:14 [z]Jer 15:2,3; Eze 5:12,17
6:9 [a]Rev 14:18; 16:7 [b]Rev 20:4
6:10 [c]Zec 1:12 [d]Rev 3:7 [e]Rev 19:2
6:11 [f]Rev 3:4 [g]Heb 11:40
6:12 [h]Rev 16:18 [i]Mt 24:29
6:13 [j]Mt 24:29; Rev 8:10; 9:1 [k]Isa 34:4
6:14 [l]Jer 4:24; Rev 16:20

6Then I heard what sounded like a voice
among the four living creatures,[u] saying, "A quart[i] of wheat for a day's
wages,[j] and three quarts of barley for a
day's wages,[j] and do not damage[v] the
oil and the wine!"
7When the Lamb opened the fourth
seal, I heard the voice of the fourth living creature[w] say, "Come!" 8I looked,
and there before me was a pale horse![x]
Its rider was named Death, and Hades[y]
was following close behind him. They
were given power over a fourth of the
earth to kill by sword, famine and
plague, and by the wild beasts of the
earth.[z]
9When he opened the fifth seal, I saw
under the altar[a] the souls of those who
had been slain[b] because of the word of
God and the testimony they had maintained. 10They called out in a loud
voice, "How long,[c] Sovereign Lord, holy
and true,[d] until you judge the inhabitants of the earth and avenge our
blood?"[e] 11Then each of them was given
a white robe,[f] and they were told to
wait a little longer, until the number of
their fellow servants and brothers who
were to be killed as they had been was
completed.[g]
12I watched as he opened the sixth
seal. There was a great earthquake.[h]
The sun turned black[i] like sackcloth
made of goat hair, the whole moon
turned blood red, 13and the stars in the
sky fell to earth,[j] as late figs drop from
a fig tree[k] when shaken by a strong
wind. 14The sky receded like a scroll,
rolling up, and every mountain and
island was removed from its place.[l]
15Then the kings of the earth, the
princes, the generals, the rich, the
mighty, and every slave and every free
man hid in caves and among the rocks
of the mountains.[m] 16They called to
the mountains and the rocks, "Fall on
us[n] and hide us from the face of him
who sits on the throne and from the

6:15 [m]Isa 2:10,19,21 **6:16** [n]Hos 10:8; Lk 23:30

[i]6 Greek *a choinix* (probably about a liter)
[j]6 Greek *a denarius*

wrath of the Lamb! 17For the great day[a]
of their wrath has come, and who can
stand?"[b]

Seal of God on 144,000 from the twelve tribes of Israel.

7 After this I saw four angels standing at the four corners of the earth,
holding back the four winds[c] of the
earth to prevent any wind from blowing on the land or on the sea or on any
tree. 2Then I saw another angel coming
up from the east, having the seal of the
living God. He called out in a loud voice
to the four angels who had been given
power to harm the land and the sea:
3"Do not harm[d] the land or the sea or
the trees until we put a seal on the
foreheads[e] of the servants of our God."
4Then I heard the number[f] of those
who were sealed: 144,000[g] from all
the tribes of Israel.

5From the tribe of Judah 12,000
were sealed,
from the tribe of Reuben 12,000,
from the tribe of Gad 12,000,
6from the tribe of Asher 12,000,
from the tribe of Naphtali 12,000,
from the tribe of Manasseh 12,000,
7from the tribe of Simeon 12,000,
from the tribe of Levi 12,000,
from the tribe of Issachar 12,000,
8from the tribe of Zebulun 12,000,
from the tribe of Joseph 12,000,
from the tribe of Benjamin 12,000.

Great multitude wearing white robes.

9After this I looked and there before
me was a great multitude that no one
could count, from every nation, tribe,
people and language,[h] standing before
the throne[i] and in front of the Lamb.
They were wearing white robes and
were holding palm branches in their
hands. 10And they cried out in a loud
voice:

"Salvation belongs to our God,[j]
who sits on the throne,
and to the Lamb."

11All the angels were standing around
the throne and around the elders[k] and
the four living creatures.[l] They fell down
on their faces[m] before the throne and
worshiped God, 12saying:

"Amen!
Praise and glory
and wisdom and thanks and honor
and power and strength
be to our God for ever and ever.
Amen!"[n]

13Then one of the elders asked me,
"These in white robes—who are they,
and where did they come from?"
14I answered, "Sir, you know."
And he said, "These are they who
have come out of the great tribulation;
they have washed their robes[o] and made
them white in the blood of the Lamb.[p]
15Therefore,

"they are before the throne of God[q]
and serve him[r] day and night in his
temple;[s]
and he who sits on the throne will
spread his tent over them.[t]
16Never again will they hunger;
never again will they thirst.
The sun will not beat upon them,
nor any scorching heat.[u]
17For the Lamb at the center of the
throne will be their
shepherd;[v]
he will lead them to springs of
living water.
And God will wipe away every tear
from their eyes."[w]

The Lamb opens the seventh seal.

8 When he opened the seventh seal,[x]
there was silence in heaven for
about half an hour.
2And I saw the seven angels[y] who
stand before God, and to them were
given seven trumpets.
3Another angel,[z] who had a golden
censer, came and stood at the altar. He
was given much incense to offer, with
the prayers of all the saints,[a] on the
golden altar[b] before the throne. 4The
smoke of the incense, together with the

6:17 [a]Zep 1:14,15; Rev 16:14 [b]Ps 76:7
7:1 [c]Da 7:2
7:3 [d]Rev 6:6 [e]Eze 9:4; Rev 22:4
7:4 [f]Rev 9:16 [g]Rev 14:1,3
7:9 [h]Rev 5:9 [i]ver 15
7:10 [j]Ps 3:8; Rev 12:10; 19:1
7:11 [k]Rev 4:4 [l]Rev 4:6 [m]Rev 4:10
7:12 [n]Rev 5:12-14
7:14 [o]Rev 22:14 [p]Heb 9:14; 1Jn 1:7
7:15 [q]ver 9 [r]Rev 22:3 [s]Rev 11:19 [t]Isa 4:5,6; Rev 21:3
7:16 [u]Isa 49:10
7:17 [v]Ps 23:1; Jn 10:11 [w]Isa 25:8; Rev 21:4
8:1 [x]Rev 6:1
8:2 [y]ver 6-13; Rev 9:1,13; 11:15
8:3 [z]Rev 7:2 [a]Rev 5:8 [b]Ex 30:1-6; Heb 9:4; Rev 9:13

prayers of the saints, went up before
God[a] from the angel's hand. 5 Then the
angel took the censer, filled it with fire
from the altar,[b] and hurled it on the
earth; and there came peals of thunder,[c]
rumblings, flashes of lightning and an
earthquake.[d]

The first six angels sound their trumpets.

6 Then the seven angels who had the
seven trumpets[e] prepared to sound
them.
7 The first angel sounded his trumpet,
and there came hail and fire[f] mixed
with blood, and it was hurled down
upon the earth. A third[g] of the earth
was burned up, a third of the trees were
burned up, and all the green grass was
burned up.[h]
8 The second angel sounded his trumpet, and something like a huge mountain,[i] all ablaze, was thrown into the
sea. A third[j] of the sea turned into
blood,[k] 9 a third[l] of the living creatures
in the sea died, and a third of the ships
were destroyed.
10 The third angel sounded his trumpet, and a great star, blazing like a
torch, fell from the sky[m] on a third of
the rivers and on the springs of water[n]—
11 the name of the star is Wormwood.[k]
A third[o] of the waters turned bitter,
and many people died from the waters
that had become bitter.[p]
12 The fourth angel sounded his trumpet, and a third of the sun was struck,
a third of the moon, and a third of the
stars, so that a third[q] of them turned
dark.[r] A third of the day was without
light, and also a third of the night.
13 As I watched, I heard an eagle that
was flying in midair[s] call out in a loud
voice: "Woe! Woe! Woe[t] to the inhabitants of the earth, because of the
trumpet blasts about to be sounded by
the other three angels!"

9 The fifth angel sounded his trumpet, and I saw a star that had fallen
from the sky to the earth.[u] The star was
given the key to the shaft of the Abyss.[v]
2 When he opened the Abyss, smoke
rose from it like the smoke from a
gigantic furnace.[w] The sun and sky were
darkened[x] by the smoke from the Abyss.
3 And out of the smoke locusts[y] came
down upon the earth and were given
power like that of scorpions[z] of the
earth. 4 They were told not to harm[a] the
grass of the earth or any plant or
tree,[b] but only those people who did
not have the seal of God on their foreheads.[c] 5 They were not given power to
kill them, but only to torture them for
five months.[d] And the agony they suffered was like that of the sting of a
scorpion[e] when it strikes a man. 6 During those days men will seek death, but
will not find it; they will long to die,
but death will elude them.[f]
7 The locusts looked like horses prepared for battle.[g] On their heads they
wore something like crowns of gold, and
their faces resembled human faces.[h]
8 Their hair was like women's hair, and
their teeth were like lions' teeth.[i] 9 They
had breastplates like breastplates of
iron, and the sound of their wings was
like the thundering of many horses and
chariots rushing into battle.[j] 10 They
had tails and stings like scorpions, and
in their tails they had power to torment
people for five months.[k] 11 They had as
king over them the angel of the Abyss,[l]
whose name in Hebrew is Abaddon,
and in Greek, Apollyon.[l]
12 The first woe is past; two other
woes are yet to come.[m]
13 The sixth angel sounded his trumpet, and I heard a voice coming from
the horns[m][n] of the golden altar that
is before God.[o] 14 It said to the sixth
angel who had the trumpet, "Release
the four angels who are bound at the
great river Euphrates."[p] 15 And the four
angels who had been kept ready for
this very hour and day and month and

8:4 [a]Ps 141:2
8:5 [b]Lev 16:12,13 [c]Rev 4:5 [d]Rev 6:12
8:6 [e]ver 2
8:7 [f]Eze 38:22 [g]ver 7-12; Rev 9:15,18; 12:4 [h]Rev 9:4
8:8 [i]Jer 51:25 [j]ver 7 [k]Rev 16:3
8:9 [l]ver 7
8:10 [m]Isa 14:12; Rev 6:13; 9:1 [n]Rev 14:7; 16:4
8:11 [o]ver 7 [p]Jer 9:15; 23:15
8:12 [q]ver 7 [r]Ex 10:21-23; Rev 6:12,13
8:13 [s]Rev 14:6; 19:17 [t]Rev 9:12; 11:14
9:1 [u]Rev 8:10 [v]ver 2,11; Lk 8:31
9:2 [w]Ge 19:28; Ex 19:18 [x]Joel 2:2,10
9:3 [y]Ex 10:12-15 [z]ver 5,10
9:4 [a]Rev 6:6 [b]Rev 8:7 [c]Rev 7:2,3
9:5 [d]ver 10 [e]ver 3
9:6 [f]Job 3:21; Jer 8:3; Rev 6:16
9:7 [g]Joel 2:4 [h]Da 7:8
9:8 [i]Joel 1:6
9:9 [j]Joel 2:5
9:10 [k]ver 3,5,19 **9:11** [l]ver 1,2
9:12 [m]Rev 8:13 **9:13** [n]Ex 30:1-3 [o]Rev 8:3
9:14 [p]Rev 16:12

k *11* That is, Bitterness l *11* *Abaddon* and *Apollyon* mean *Destroyer.* m *13* That is, projections

year were released to kill a third of
mankind.[a] 16The number of the mounted troops was two hundred million. I
heard their number.[b]
17The horses and riders I saw in my
vision looked like this: Their breastplates were fiery red, dark blue, and
yellow as sulfur. The heads of the horses
resembled the heads of lions, and out of
their mouths[c] came fire, smoke and
sulfur.[d] 18A third of mankind was killed[e]
by the three plagues of fire, smoke and
sulfur[f] that came out of their mouths.
19The power of the horses was in their
mouths and in their tails; for their tails
were like snakes, having heads with
which they inflict injury.
20The rest of mankind that were not
killed by these plagues still did not repent of the work of their hands;[g] they
did not stop worshiping demons,[h] and
idols of gold, silver, bronze, stone and
wood—idols that cannot see or hear or
walk.[i] 21Nor did they repent[j] of their
murders, their magic arts,[k] their sexual
immorality[l] or their thefts.

The mighty angel with the little scroll.

10 Then I saw another mighty
angel[m] coming down from heav-
en. He was robed in a cloud, with a
rainbow above his head; his face was
like the sun,[n] and his legs were like
fiery pillars.[o] 2He was holding a little
scroll, which lay open in his hand. He
planted his right foot on the sea and
his left foot on the land, 3and he gave a
loud shout like the roar of a lion. When
he shouted, the voices of the seven
thunders[p] spoke. 4And when the sev-
en thunders spoke, I was about to
write; but I heard a voice from heaven
say, "Seal up what the seven thunders
have said and do not write it down."[q]
5Then the angel I had seen standing
on the sea and on the land raised his
right hand to heaven.[r] 6And he swore
by him who lives for ever and ever, who
created the heavens and all that is in
them, the earth and all that is in it, and
the sea and all that is in it,[s] and said,
"There will be no more delay![t] 7But in
the days when the seventh angel is
about to sound his trumpet, the
mystery[u] of God will be accomplished,
just as he announced to his servants
the prophets."

John instructed to eat the little scroll.

8Then the voice that I had heard from
heaven[v] spoke to me once more: "Go,
take the scroll that lies open in the hand
of the angel who is standing on the sea
and on the land."
9So I went to the angel and asked him
to give me the little scroll. He said to
me, "Take it and eat it. It will turn your
stomach sour, but in your mouth it will
be as sweet as honey."[w] 10I took the little scroll from the angel's hand and ate
it. It tasted as sweet as honey in my
mouth, but when I had eaten it, my
stomach turned sour. 11Then I was told,
"You must prophesy[x] again about many
peoples, nations, languages and kings."

Two witnesses will prophesy.

11 I was given a reed like a measuring rod[y] and was told, "Go and
measure the temple of God and the
altar, and count the worshipers there.
2But exclude the outer court;[z] do not
measure it, because it has been given
to the Gentiles.[a] They will trample on
the holy city[b] for 42 months.[c] 3And I
will give power to my two witnesses,[d]
and they will prophesy for 1,260 days,
clothed in sackcloth."[e] 4These are the
two olive trees[f] and the two lampstands
that stand before the Lord of the earth.[g]
5If anyone tries to harm them, fire
comes from their mouths and devours
their enemies.[h] This is how anyone who
wants to harm them must die.[i] 6These
men have power to shut up the sky so
that it will not rain during the time they
are prophesying; and they have power
to turn the waters into blood[j] and to

9:15 [a]ver 18
9:16 [b]Rev 5:11; 7:4
9:17 [c]Rev 11:5 [d]ver 18
9:18 [e]ver 15 [f]ver 17
9:20 [g]Dt 31:29 [h]1Co 10:20 [i]Ps 115:4-7; 135:15-17; Da 5:23
9:21 [j]Rev 2:21 [k]Rev 18:23 [l]Rev 17:2,5
10:1 [m]Rev 5:2 [n]Mt 17:2; Rev 1:16 [o]Rev 1:15
10:3 [p]Rev 4:5
10:4 [q]Da 8:26; 12:4,9; Rev 22:10
10:5 [r]Da 12:7
10:6 [s]Rev 4:11; 14:7 [t]Rev 16:17
10:7 [u]Ro 16:25
10:8 [v]ver 4
10:9 [w]Jer 15:16; Eze 2:8–3:3
10:11 [x]Eze 37:4,9
11:1 [y]Eze 40:3; Rev 21:15
11:2 [z]Eze 40:17,20 [a]Lk 21:24 [b]Rev 21:2 [c]Da 7:25; Rev 13:5
11:3 [d]Rev 1:5 [e]Ge 37:34
11:4 [f]Ps 52:8; Jer 11:16; Zec 4:3,11 [g]Zec 4:14
11:5 [h]2Ki 1:10; Jer 5:14 [i]Nu 16:29,35
11:6 [j]Ex 7:17,19

strike the earth with every kind of
plague as often as they want.
7Now when they have finished their
testimony, the beast[a] that comes up
from the Abyss will attack them,[b] and
overpower and kill them. 8Their bodies will lie in the street of the great city,
which is figuratively called Sodom[c] and
Egypt, where also their Lord was crucified.[d] 9For three and a half days men
from every people, tribe, language and
nation will gaze on their bodies and
refuse them burial.[e] 10The inhabitants of
the earth[f] will gloat over them and will
celebrate by sending each other gifts,[g]
because these two prophets had tormented those who live on the earth.
11But after the three and a half days
a breath of life from God entered them,[h]
and they stood on their feet, and terror
struck those who saw them. 12Then
they heard a loud voice from heaven
saying to them, "Come up here."[i] And
they went up to heaven in a cloud,[j]
while their enemies looked on.
13At that very hour there was a severe
earthquake[k] and a tenth of the city collapsed. Seven thousand people were
killed in the earthquake, and the survivors were terrified and gave glory[l] to
the God of heaven.[m]
14The second woe has passed; the
third woe is coming soon.[n]

The seventh angel sounds his trumpet.

15The seventh angel sounded his
trumpet,[o] and there were loud voices[p]
in heaven, which said:

"The kingdom of the world has
become the kingdom of our
Lord and of his Christ,[q]
and he will reign for ever and ever."[r]

16And the twenty-four elders,[s] who were
seated on their thrones before God, fell
on their faces and worshiped God,
17saying:

"We give thanks to you, Lord God
Almighty,[t]
the One who is and who was,
because you have taken your great
power
and have begun to reign.[u]
18The nations were angry;[v]
and your wrath has come.
The time has come for judging the
dead,
and for rewarding your servants
the prophets[w]
and your saints and those who
reverence your name,
both small and great[x]—
and for destroying those who destroy
the earth."

19Then God's temple[y] in heaven was
opened, and within his temple was seen
the ark of his covenant. And there came
flashes of lightning, rumblings, peals of
thunder, an earthquake and a great
hailstorm.[z]

A woman, a child and a dragon.

12 A great and wondrous sign appeared in heaven: a woman
clothed with the sun, with the moon
under her feet and a crown of twelve
stars on her head. 2She was pregnant
and cried out in pain[a] as she was about
to give birth. 3Then another sign appeared in heaven: an enormous red
dragon with seven heads and ten horns[b]
and seven crowns[c] on his heads. 4His
tail swept a third[d] of the stars out of the
sky and flung them to the earth.[e] The
dragon stood in front of the woman who
was about to give birth, so that he
might devour her child[f] the moment it
was born. 5She gave birth to a son, a
male child, who will rule all the nations
with an iron scepter.[g] And her child was
snatched up to God and to his throne.
6The woman fled into the desert to a
place prepared for her by God, where
she might be taken care of for 1,260
days.[h]

Satan is cast out of heaven in war with Michael.

7And there was war in heaven.
Michael and his angels fought against

11:7 [a]Rev 13:1-4 [b]Da 7:21
11:8 [c]Isa 1:9 [d]Heb 13:12
11:9 [e]Ps 79:2,3
11:10 [f]Rev 3:10 [g]Est 9:19,22
11:11 [h]Eze 37:5,9, 10,14
11:12 [i]Rev 4:1 [j]2Ki 2:11; Ac 1:9
11:13 [k]Rev 6:12 [l]Rev 14:7 [m]Rev 16:11
11:14 [n]Rev 8:13
11:15 [o]Rev 10:7 [p]Rev 16:17; 19:1 [q]Rev 12:10 [r]Da 2:44; 7:14,27
11:16 [s]Rev 4:4
11:17 [t]Rev 1:8 [u]Rev 19:6
11:18 [v]Ps 2:1 [w]Rev 10:7 [x]Rev 19:5
11:19 [y]Rev 15:5,8 [z]Rev 16:21
12:2 [a]Gal 4:19
12:3 [b]Da 7:7,20; Rev 13:1 [c]Rev 19:12
12:4 [d]Rev 8:7 [e]Da 8:10 [f]Mt 2:16
12:5 [g]Ps 2:9; Rev 2:27
12:6 [h]Rev 11:2

the dragon,[a] and the dragon and his
angels fought back. 8But he was not
strong enough, and they lost their place
in heaven. 9The great dragon was hurled
down—that ancient serpent[b] called the
devil,[c] or Satan, who leads the whole
world astray.[d] He was hurled to the
earth,[e] and his angels with him.

10Then I heard a loud voice in
heaven[f] say:

"Now have come the salvation and
the power and the kingdom
of our God,
and the authority of his Christ.
For the accuser of our brothers,[g]
who accuses them before our God
day and night,
has been hurled down.
11They overcame him
by the blood of the Lamb[h]
and by the word of their
testimony;[i]
they did not love their lives so much
as to shrink from death.[j]
12Therefore rejoice, you heavens[k]
and you who dwell in them!
But woe[l] to the earth and the sea,[m]
because the devil has gone down
to you!
He is filled with fury,
because he knows that his time is
short."

The dragon pursues the woman on earth.

13When the dragon[n] saw that he had
been hurled to the earth, he pursued
the woman who had given birth to the
male child.[o] 14The woman was given
the two wings of a great eagle,[p] so that
she might fly to the place prepared for
her in the desert, where she would be
taken care of for a time, times and half
a time,[q] out of the serpent's reach.
15Then from his mouth the serpent
spewed water like a river, to overtake
the woman and sweep her away with
the torrent. 16But the earth helped the
woman by opening its mouth and swal-
lowing the river that the dragon had
spewed out of his mouth. 17Then the
dragon was enraged at the woman and
went off to make war[r] against the rest
of her offspring[s]—those who obey God's
commandments[t] and hold to the testimony of Jesus.[u]

13 1And the dragon[n]
stood on the shore of the sea.

A beast comes out of the sea.

And I saw a beast coming out of the
sea.[v] He had ten horns and seven
heads,[w] with ten crowns on his horns,
and on each head a blasphemous
name.[x] 2The beast I saw resembled a
leopard,[y] but had feet like those of a
bear[z] and a mouth like that of a lion.[a]
The dragon gave the beast his power
and his throne and great authority.[b]
3One of the heads of the beast seemed
to have had a fatal wound, but the fatal
wound had been healed.[c] The whole
world was astonished[d] and followed
the beast. 4Men worshiped the dragon
because he had given authority to the
beast, and they also worshiped the beast
and asked, "Who is like[e] the beast? Who
can make war against him?"

5The beast was given a mouth to utter
proud words and blasphemies[f] and to
exercise his authority for forty-two
months.[g] 6He opened his mouth to
blaspheme God, and to slander his
name and his dwelling place and those
who live in heaven.[h] 7He was given
power to make war[i] against the saints
and to conquer them. And he was given
authority over every tribe, people, language and nation.[j] 8All inhabitants of
the earth[k] will worship the beast—all
whose names have not been written in
the book of life[l] belonging to the Lamb
that was slain from the creation of the
world.[o][m]

9He who has an ear, let him hear.[n]

10If anyone is to go into captivity,
into captivity he will go.

12:7 [a]ver 3
12:9 [b]Ge 3:1-7 [c]Mt 25:41 [d]Rev 20:3, 8,10 [e]Lk 10:18; Jn 12:31
12:10 [f]Rev 11:15 [g]Job 1:9-11; Zec 3:1
12:11 [h]Rev 7:14 [i]Rev 6:9 [j]Lk 14:26
12:12 [k]Ps 96:11; Isa 49:13; Rev 18:20 [l]Rev 8:13 [m]Rev 10:6
12:13 [n]ver 3 [o]ver 5
12:14 [p]Ex 19:4 [q]Da 7:25
12:17 [r]Rev 11:7 [s]Ge 3:15 [t]Rev 14:12 [u]Rev 1:2
13:1 [v]Da 7:1-6; Rev 15:2 [w]Rev 12:3 [x]Da 11:36; Rev 17:3
13:2 [y]Da 7:6 [z]Da 7:5 [a]Da 7:4 [b]Rev 16:10
13:3 [c]ver 12,14 [d]Rev 17:8
13:4 [e]Ex 15:11
13:5 [f]Da 7:8,11, 20,25; 11:36; 2Th 2:4 [g]Rev 11:2
13:6 [h]Rev 12:12
13:7 [i]Da 7:21; Rev 11:7 [j]Rev 5:9
13:8 [k]Rev 3:10 [l]Rev 3:5; 20:12 [m]Mt 25:34
13:9 [n]Rev 2:7

[n]*1* Some late manuscripts *And I* [o]*8* Or *written from the creation of the world in the book of life belonging to the Lamb that was slain*

If anyone is to be killed[p] with the
sword,
with the sword he will be killed.[a]

This calls for patient endurance and
faithfulness[b] on the part of the saints.[c]

A beast comes out of the earth.

11Then I saw another beast, coming
out of the earth. He had two horns like
a lamb, but he spoke like a dragon.
12He exercised all the authority[d] of the
first beast on his behalf,[e] and made the
earth and its inhabitants worship the
first beast,[f] whose fatal wound had been
healed.[g] 13And he performed great and
miraculous signs,[h] even causing fire to
come down from heaven[i] to earth in
full view of men. 14Because of the signs[j]
he was given power to do on behalf of
the first beast, he deceived[k] the inhabitants of the earth. He ordered them to
set up an image in honor of the beast
who was wounded by the sword and yet
lived. 15He was given power to give
breath to the image of the first beast,
so that it could speak and cause all who
refused to worship the image to be
killed.[l] 16He also forced everyone, small
and great,[m] rich and poor, free and
slave, to receive a mark on his right
hand or on his forehead,[n] 17so that no
one could buy or sell unless he had the
mark,[o] which is the name of the beast
or the number of his name.[p]
18This calls for wisdom.[q] If anyone has
insight, let him calculate the number
of the beast, for it is man's number.[r] His
number is 666.

The Lamb with the 144,000 who were redeemed.

14 Then I looked, and there before
me was the Lamb,[s] standing on
Mount Zion,[t] and with him 144,000[u]
who had his name and his Father's
name[v] written on their foreheads. 2And
I heard a sound from heaven like the
roar of rushing waters[w] and like a loud
peal of thunder. The sound I heard was
like that of harpists playing their harps.[x]
3And they sang a new song[y] before the
throne and before the four living creatures and the elders. No one could learn
the song except the 144,000[z] who had
been redeemed from the earth. 4These
are those who did not defile themselves
with women, for they kept themselves
pure.[a] They follow the Lamb wherever
he goes. They were purchased from
among men[b] and offered as firstfruits[c]
to God and the Lamb. 5No lie was found
in their mouths;[d] they are blameless.[e]

Proclamations of three angels.

6Then I saw another angel flying in
midair,[f] and he had the eternal gospel
to proclaim to those who live on the
earth[g]—to every nation, tribe, language
and people.[h] 7He said in a loud voice,
"Fear God[i] and give him glory,[j] because
the hour of his judgment has come.
Worship him who made the heavens,
the earth, the sea and the springs of
water."[k]
8A second angel followed and said,
"Fallen! Fallen is Babylon the Great,[l]
which made all the nations drink the
maddening wine of her adulteries."[m]
9A third angel followed them and said
in a loud voice: "If anyone worships the
beast and his image[n] and receives his
mark on the forehead or on the hand,
10he, too, will drink of the wine of God's
fury,[o] which has been poured full
strength into the cup of his wrath.[p] He
will be tormented with burning sulfur
in the presence of the holy angels and
of the Lamb. 11And the smoke of their
torment rises for ever and ever.[q] There
is no rest day or night for those who
worship the beast and his image, or
for anyone who receives the mark of
his name." 12This calls for patient endurance on the part of the saints[r] who
obey God's commandments and remain
faithful to Jesus.

13:10 [a]Jer 15:2; 43:11 [b]Heb 6:12 [c]Rev 14:12
13:12 [d]ver 4 [e]ver 14 [f]Rev 14:9,11 [g]ver 3
13:13 [h]Mt 24:24 [i]1Ki 18:38; Rev 20:9
13:14 [j]2Th 2:9,10 [k]Rev 12:9
13:15 [l]Da 3:3-6
13:16 [m]Rev 19:5 [n]Rev 14:9
13:17 [o]Rev 14:9 [p]Rev 14:11; 15:2
13:18 [q]Rev 17:9 [r]Rev 15:2; 21:17
14:1 [s]Rev 5:6 [t]Ps 2:6 [u]Rev 7:4 [v]Rev 3:12
14:2 [w]Rev 1:15 [x]Rev 5:8
14:3 [y]Rev 5:9 [z]ver 1
14:4 [a]2Co 11:2; Rev 3:4 [b]Rev 5:9 [c]Jas 1:18
14:5 [d]Ps 32:2; Zep 3:13 [e]Eph 5:27
14:6 [f]Rev 8:13 [g]Rev 3:10 [h]Rev 13:7
14:7 [i]Rev 15:4 [j]Rev 11:13 [k]Rev 8:10
14:8 [l]Isa 21:9; Jer 51:8 [m]Rev 17:2,4 18:3,9
14:9 [n]Rev 13:14
14:10 [o]Isa 51:17; Jer 25:15 [p]Rev 18:6
14:11 [q]Isa 34:10; Rev 19:3 **14:12** [r]Rev 13:10

[p]*10* Some manuscripts *anyone kills*

13Then I heard a voice from heaven
say, "Write: Blessed are the dead who
die in the Lord[a] from now on."
"Yes," says the Spirit, "they will rest
from their labor, for their deeds will
follow them."

Harvest of the earth.

14I looked, and there before me was
a white cloud, and seated on the cloud
was one "like a son of man"[q][b] with a
crown[c] of gold on his head and a sharp
sickle in his hand. 15Then another angel
came out of the temple and called in a
loud voice to him who was sitting on
the cloud, "Take your sickle[d] and reap,
because the time to reap has come, for
the harvest[e] of the earth is ripe." 16So
he who was seated on the cloud swung
his sickle over the earth, and the earth
was harvested.
17Another angel came out of the temple in heaven, and he too had a sharp
sickle. 18Still another angel, who had
charge of the fire, came from the altar
and called in a loud voice to him who
had the sharp sickle, "Take your sharp
sickle and gather the clusters of grapes
from the earth's vine, because its grapes
are ripe." 19The angel swung his sickle
on the earth, gathered its grapes and
threw them into the great winepress
of God's wrath.[f] 20They were trampled
in the winepress[g] outside the city,[h] and
blood flowed out of the press, rising as
high as the horses' bridles for a distance of 1,600 stadia.[r]

The seven angels with the last seven plagues.

15 I saw in heaven another great
and marvelous sign:[i] seven angels[j] with the seven last plagues[k]—
last, because with them God's wrath is
completed. 2And I saw what looked
like a sea of glass[l] mixed with fire and,
standing beside the sea, those who
had been victorious over the beast and
his image[m] and over the number of his
name. They held harps given them by
God 3and sang the song of Moses[n] the

14:13 [a]1Co 15:18; 1Th 4:16
14:14 [b]Da 7:13; Rev 1:13 [c]Rev 6:2
14:15 [d]Joel 3:13 [e]Jer 51:33
14:19 [f]Rev 19:15
14:20 [g]Isa 63:3 [h]Heb 13:12; Rev 11:8
15:1 [i]Rev 12:1,3 [j]Rev 16:1 [k]Lev 26:21
15:2 [l]Rev 4:6 [m]Rev 13:14
15:3 [n]Ex 15:1; Dt 32:4 [o]Ps 111:2 [p]Ps 145:17
15:4 [q]Jer 10:7 [r]Isa 66:23
15:5 [s]Rev 11:19 [t]Nu 1:50
15:6 [u]Rev 14:15 [v]ver 1 [w]Rev 1:13
15:7 [x]Rev 4:6
15:8 [y]Isa 6:4 [z]Ex 40:34,35; 1Ki 8:10,11; 2Ch 5:13,14
16:1 [a]Rev 15:1
16:2 [b]Rev 8:7 [c]Ex 9:9-11 [d]Rev 13:15-17
16:3 [e]Ex 7:17-21; Rev 8:8,9
16:4 [f]Rev 8:10

servant of God and the song of the
Lamb:

"Great and marvelous are your
deeds,[o]
Lord God Almighty.
Just and true are your ways,[p]
King of the ages.
4Who will not fear you, O Lord,[q]
and bring glory to your name?
For you alone are holy.
All nations will come
and worship before you,[r]
for your righteous acts have been
revealed."

5After this I looked and in heaven
the temple,[s] that is, the tabernacle of
the Testimony,[t] was opened. 6Out of the
temple[u] came the seven angels with
the seven plagues.[v] They were dressed
in clean, shining linen and wore golden
sashes around their chests.[w] 7Then one
of the four living creatures[x] gave to the
seven angels seven golden bowls filled
with the wrath of God, who lives for
ever and ever. 8And the temple was
filled with smoke[y] from the glory of
God and from his power, and no one
could enter the temple[z] until the sev-
en plagues of the seven angels were
completed.

The seven angels pour out the seven bowls of God's wrath.

16 Then I heard a loud voice from
the temple saying to the seven
angels,[a] "Go, pour out the seven bowls
of God's wrath on the earth."
2The first angel went and poured out
his bowl on the land,[b] and ugly and
painful sores[c] broke out on the people
who had the mark of the beast and
worshiped his image.[d]
3The second angel poured out his
bowl on the sea, and it turned into
blood like that of a dead man, and every
living thing in the sea died.[e]
4The third angel poured out his bowl
on the rivers and springs of water,[f] and

[q] *14* Daniel 7:13 [r] *20* That is, about 180 miles (about 300 kilometers)

they became blood.[a] 5Then I heard the
angel in charge of the waters say:

"You are just in these judgments,[b]
you who are and who were,[c] the
Holy One,[d]
because you have so judged;
6for they have shed the blood of your
saints and prophets,
and you have given them blood to
drink[e] as they deserve."

7And I heard the altar[f] respond:

"Yes, Lord God Almighty,
true and just are your judgments."[g]

8The fourth angel[h] poured out his
bowl on the sun, and the sun was giv-
en power to scorch people with fire.[i]
9They were seared by the intense heat
and they cursed the name of God,[j]
who had control over these plagues,
but they refused to repent[k] and glorify
him.[l]
10The fifth angel poured out his bowl
on the throne of the beast,[m] and his kingdom was plunged into darkness.[n] Men
gnawed their tongues in agony 11and
cursed[o] the God of heaven[p] because of
their pains and their sores,[q] but they
refused to repent of what they had
done.[r]
12The sixth angel poured out his bowl
on the great river Euphrates,[s] and its
water was dried up to prepare the way
for the kings from the East.[t] 13Then I
saw three evil[s] spirits that looked like
frogs; they came out of the mouth of
the dragon,[u] out of the mouth of the
beast[v] and out of the mouth of the false
prophet.[w] 14They are spirits of demons[x]
performing miraculous signs, and they
go out to the kings of the whole world,
to gather them for the battle[y] on the
great day of God Almighty.
15"Behold, I come like a thief! Blessed
is he who stays awake[z] and keeps his
clothes with him, so that he may not
go naked and be shamefully exposed."
16Then they gathered the kings together to the place that in Hebrew[a] is called
Armageddon.[b]

16:4 [a]Ex 7:17-21
16:5 [b]Rev 15:3 [c]Rev 1:4 [d]Rev 15:4
16:6 [e]Isa 49:26; Rev 17:6
16:7 [f]Rev 6:9 [g]Rev 15:3; 19:2
16:8 [h]Rev 8:12 [i]Rev 14:18
16:9 [j]ver 11,21 [k]Rev 2:21 [l]Rev 11:13
16:10 [m]Rev 13:2 [n]Rev 9:2
16:11 [o]ver 9,21 [p]Rev 11:13 [q]ver 2 [r]Rev 2:21
16:12 [s]Rev 9:14 [t]Isa 41:2
16:13 [u]Rev 12:3 [v]Rev 13:1 [w]Rev 19:20
16:14 [x]1Ti 4:1 [y]Rev 17:14
16:15 [z]Lk 12:37
16:16 [a]Rev 9:11 [b]2Ki 23:29, 30
16:17 [c]Eph 2:2 [d]Rev 14:15 [e]Rev 11:15 [f]Rev 21:6
16:18 [g]Rev 4:5 [h]Rev 6:12 [i]Da 12:1
16:19 [j]Rev 17:18 [k]Rev 18:5 [l]Rev 14:8 [m]Rev 14:10
16:20 [n]Rev 6:14
16:21 [o]Rev 11:19 [p]Ex 9:23-25

17The seventh angel poured out his
bowl into the air,[c] and out of the temple[d] came a loud voice[e] from the throne,
saying, "It is done!"[f] 18Then there came
flashes of lightning, rumblings, peals of
thunder[g] and a severe earthquake.[h] No
earthquake like it has ever occurred
since man has been on earth,[i] so tremendous was the quake. 19The great
city[j] split into three parts, and the cities
of the nations collapsed. God remembered[k] Babylon the Great[l] and gave her
the cup filled with the wine of the fury
of his wrath.[m] 20Every island fled away
and the mountains could not be found.[n]
21From the sky huge hailstones[o] of
about a hundred pounds each fell upon
men. And they cursed God on account
of the plague of hail,[p] because the plague
was so terrible.

Woman dressed in purple and scarlet sitting on the beast.

17 One of the seven angels[q] who
had the seven bowls[r] came and
said to me, "Come, I will show you the
punishment[s] of the great prostitute,[t]
who sits on many waters.[u] 2With her
the kings of the earth committed adultery and the inhabitants of the earth
were intoxicated with the wine of her
adulteries."[v]
3Then the angel carried me away in
the Spirit into a desert.[w] There I saw a
woman sitting on a scarlet beast that
was covered with blasphemous names[x]
and had seven heads and ten horns.[y]
4The woman was dressed in purple and
scarlet, and was glittering with gold,
precious stones and pearls.[z] She held a
golden cup[a] in her hand, filled with
abominable things and the filth of her
adulteries. 5This title was written on
her forehead:

17:1 [q]Rev 15:1 [r]Rev 21:9 [s]Rev 16:19 [t]Rev 19:2 [u]Jer 51:13 **17:2** [v]Rev 14:8; 18:3
17:3 [w]Rev 12:6,14 [x]Rev 13:1 [y]Rev 12:3
17:4 [z]Rev 18:16 [a]Jer 51:7; Rev 18:6

s13 Greek *unclean*

MYSTERY
BABYLON THE GREAT[a]
THE MOTHER OF PROSTITUTES
AND OF THE ABOMINATIONS OF THE EARTH.

6I saw that the woman was drunk with
the blood of the saints,[b] the blood of
those who bore testimony to Jesus.

Mystery of the woman and the beast explained.

When I saw her, I was greatly astonished. 7Then the angel said to me: "Why
are you astonished? I will explain to
you the mystery[c] of the woman and of
the beast she rides, which has the sev-
en heads and ten horns.[d] 8The beast,
which you saw, once was, now is not,
and will come up out of the Abyss and
go to his destruction.[e] The inhabitants
of the earth[f] whose names have not
been written in the book of life[g] from
the creation of the world will be astonished[h] when they see the beast, because
he once was, now is not, and yet will
come.

9"This calls for a mind with wisdom.[i]
The seven heads are seven hills on
which the woman sits. 10They are also
seven kings. Five have fallen, one is,
the other has not yet come; but when
he does come, he must remain for a little while. 11The beast who once was,
and now is not,[j] is an eighth king. He
belongs to the seven and is going to his
destruction.

12"The ten horns[k] you saw are ten
kings who have not yet received a
kingdom, but who for one hour[l] will
receive authority as kings along with
the beast. 13They have one purpose
and will give their power and authority
to the beast.[m] 14They will make war[n]
against the Lamb, but the Lamb will
overcome them because he is Lord of
lords and King of kings[o]—and with him
will be his called, chosen[p] and faithful
followers."

15Then the angel said to me, "The
waters[q] you saw, where the prostitute
sits, are peoples, multitudes, nations
and languages.[r] 16The beast and the ten
horns you saw will hate the prostitute.
They will bring her to ruin[s] and leave
her naked;[t] they will eat her flesh[u] and
burn her with fire.[v] 17For God has put
it into their hearts to accomplish his
purpose by agreeing to give the beast
their power to rule, until God's words
are fulfilled.[w] 18The woman you saw is
the great city[x] that rules over the kings
of the earth."

Fall of Babylon.

18 After this I saw another angel[y]
coming down from heaven.[z] He
had great authority, and the earth was
illuminated by his splendor.[a] 2With a
mighty voice he shouted:

"Fallen! Fallen is Babylon the Great![b]
She has become a home for
demons
and a haunt for every evil[†] spirit,
a haunt for every unclean and
detestable bird.[c]
3For all the nations have drunk
the maddening wine of her
adulteries.[d]
The kings of the earth committed
adultery with her,[e]
and the merchants of the earth
grew rich[f] from her excessive
luxuries."[g]

4Then I heard another voice from
heaven say:

"Come out of her, my people,[h]
so that you will not share in her
sins,
so that you will not receive any of
her plagues;
5for her sins are piled up to heaven,[i]
and God has remembered[j] her
crimes.
6Give back to her as she has given;
pay her back[k] double for what she
has done.
Mix her a double portion from her
own cup.[l]

17:5 [a]Rev 14:8
17:6 [b]Rev 18:24
17:7 [c]ver 5 [d]ver 3
17:8 [e]Rev 13:10 [f]Rev 3:10 [g]Rev 13:8 [h]Rev 13:3
17:9 [i]Rev 13:18
17:11 [j]ver 8
17:12 [k]Rev 12:3 [l]Rev 18:10, 17,19
17:13 [m]ver 17
17:14 [n]Rev 16:14 [o]1Ti 6:15; Rev 19:16 [p]Mt 22:14
17:15 [q]Isa 8:7 [r]Rev 13:7
17:16 [s]Rev 18:17,19 [t]Eze 16:37,39 [u]Rev 19:18 [v]Rev 18:8
17:17 [w]Rev 10:7
17:18 [x]Rev 16:19
18:1 [y]Rev 17:1 [z]Rev 10:1 [a]Eze 43:2
18:2 [b]Rev 14:8 [c]Isa 13:21,22; Jer 50:39
18:3 [d]Rev 14:8 [e]Rev 17:2 [f]Eze 27:9-25 [g]ver 7,9
18:4 [h]Isa 48:20; Jer 50:8; 2Co 6:17
18:5 [i]Jer 51:9 [j]Rev 16:19
18:6 [k]Ps 137:8; Jer 50:15,29 [l]Rev 14:10; 16:19

†2 Greek *unclean*

7 Give her as much torture and grief
as the glory and luxury she gave
herself.[a]
In her heart she boasts,
'I sit as queen; I am not a widow,
and I will never mourn.'[b]
8 Therefore in one day[c] her plagues
will overtake her:
death, mourning and famine.
She will be consumed by fire,[d]
for mighty is the Lord God who
judges her.

Mourning from the earth for Babylon's destruction.

9 "When the kings of the earth who
committed adultery with her[e] and shared
her luxury see the smoke of her burning,[f] they will weep and mourn over
her.[g] 10 Terrified at her torment, they
will stand far off[h] and cry:

"'Woe! Woe, O great city,[i]
O Babylon, city of power!
In one hour[j] your doom has come!'

11 "The merchants[k] of the earth will
weep and mourn over her because no
one buys their cargoes any more[l]—
12 cargoes of gold, silver, precious stones
and pearls; fine linen, purple, silk and
scarlet cloth; every sort of citron wood,
and articles of every kind made of ivory,
costly wood, bronze, iron and marble;[m] 13 cargoes of cinnamon and spice,
of incense, myrrh and frankincense, of
wine and olive oil, of fine flour and
wheat; cattle and sheep; horses and
carriages; and bodies and souls of men.[n]
14 "They will say, 'The fruit you longed
for is gone from you. All your riches
and splendor have vanished, never to
be recovered.' 15 The merchants who
sold these things and gained their wealth
from her[o] will stand far off, terrified
at her torment. They will weep and
mourn[p] 16 and cry out:

"'Woe! Woe, O great city,
dressed in fine linen, purple and
scarlet,
and glittering with gold, precious
stones and pearls![q]
17 In one hour[r] such great wealth has
been brought to ruin!'[s]

"Every sea captain, and all who travel
by ship, the sailors, and all who earn
their living from the sea,[t] will stand far
off. 18 When they see the smoke of her
burning, they will exclaim, 'Was there
ever a city like this great city?'[u] 19 They
will throw dust on their heads,[v] and
with weeping and mourning cry out:

"'Woe! Woe, O great city,
where all who had ships on the sea
became rich through her wealth!
In one hour she has been brought to
ruin![w]

Rejoicing from heaven for Babylon's destruction.

20 Rejoice over her, O heaven![x]
Rejoice, saints and apostles and
prophets!
God has judged her for the way she
treated you.'"[y]

21 Then a mighty angel[z] picked up a
boulder the size of a large millstone and
threw it into the sea,[a] and said:

"With such violence
the great city of Babylon will be
thrown down,
never to be found again.
22 The music of harpists and musicians,
flute players and trumpeters,
will never be heard in you again.[b]
No workman of any trade
will ever be found in you again.
The sound of a millstone
will never be heard in you again.[c]
23 The light of a lamp
will never shine in you again.
The voice of bridegroom and bride
will never be heard in you again.[d]
Your merchants were the world's
great men.[e]
By your magic spell[f] all the nations
were led astray.
24 In her was found the blood of
prophets and of the saints,[g]
and of all who have been killed on
the earth."[h]

18:7 [a]Eze 28:2-8 [b]Isa 47:7,8; Zep 2:15
18:8 [c]ver 10; Isa 47:9; Jer 50:31,32 [d]Rev 17:16
18:9 [e]Rev 17:2,4 [f]ver 18; Rev 19:3 [g]Eze 26:17, 18
18:10 [h]ver 15,17 [i]ver 16,19 [j]Rev 17:12
18:11 [k]Eze 27:27 [l]ver 3
18:12 [m]Rev 17:4
18:13 [n]Eze 27:13; 1Ti 1:10
18:15 [o]ver 3 [p]Eze 27:31
18:16 [q]Rev 17:4
18:17 [r]ver 10 [s]Rev 17:16 [t]Eze 27:28-30
18:18 [u]Eze 27:32; Rev 13:4
18:19 [v]Jos 7:6; Eze 27:30 [w]Rev 17:16
18:20 [x]Jer 51:48; Rev 12:12 [y]Rev 19:2
18:21 [z]Rev 5:2 [a]Jer 51:63
18:22 [b]Isa 24:8; Eze 26:13 [c]Jer 25:10
18:23 [d]Jer 7:34; 16:9; 25:10 [e]Isa 23:8 [f]Na 3:4
18:24 [g]Rev 16:6; 17:6 [h]Jer 51:49

19 After this I heard what sounded
like the roar of a great multitude[a]
in heaven shouting:

"Hallelujah!
Salvation[b] and glory and power[c]
belong to our God,
2 for true and just are his judgments.
He has condemned the great
prostitute
who corrupted the earth by her
adulteries.
He has avenged on her the blood of
his servants."[d]

3And again they shouted:

"Hallelujah!
The smoke from her goes up for ever
and ever."[e]

4The twenty-four elders[f] and the four
living creatures[g] fell down[h] and worshiped God, who was seated on the
throne. And they cried:

"Amen, Hallelujah!"

5Then a voice came from the throne,
saying:

"Praise our God,
all you his servants,[i]
you who fear him,
both small and great!"[j]

Wedding supper of the Lamb.

6Then I heard what sounded like a
great multitude,[k] like the roar of rushing
waters and like loud peals of thunder,
shouting:

"Hallelujah!
For our Lord God Almighty reigns.
7Let us rejoice and be glad
and give him glory!
For the wedding of the Lamb[l] has
come,
and his bride[m] has made herself
ready.
8Fine linen, bright and clean,
was given her to wear."
(Fine linen stands for the righteous
acts[n] of the saints.)

9Then the angel said to me,[o] "Write:[p]
'Blessed are those who are invited to
the wedding supper of the Lamb!'"[q] And
he added, "These are the true words
of God."[r]
10At this I fell at his feet to worship
him.[s] But he said to me, "Do not do it!
I am a fellow servant with you and
with your brothers who hold to the
testimony of Jesus. Worship God![t] For
the testimony of Jesus[u] is the spirit of
prophecy."

The rider coming on a white horse.

11I saw heaven standing open and
there before me was a white horse,
whose rider[v] is called Faithful and
True.[w] With justice he judges and makes
war.[x] 12His eyes are like blazing fire,[y]
and on his head are many crowns.[z] He
has a name written on him that no one
knows but he himself.[a] 13He is dressed
in a robe dipped in blood,[b] and his name
is the Word of God.[c] 14The armies of
heaven were following him, riding on
white horses and dressed in fine linen,[d]
white and clean. 15Out of his mouth
comes a sharp sword[e] with which to
strike down[f] the nations. "He will rule
them with an iron scepter."[u][g] He treads
the winepress[h] of the fury of the wrath
of God Almighty. 16On his robe and on
his thigh he has this name written:[i]

KING OF KINGS AND LORD OF LORDS.[j]

17And I saw an angel standing in the
sun, who cried in a loud voice to all
the birds[k] flying in midair,[l] "Come,[m]
gather together for the great supper of
God, 18so that you may eat the flesh of
kings, generals, and mighty men, of
horses and their riders, and the flesh
of all people,[n] free and slave, small and
great."

Beast and false prophet thrown alive into the lake of fire.

19Then I saw the beast and the kings

19:1 [a]Rev 11:15 [b]Rev 7:10 [c]Rev 4:11
19:2 [d]Dt 32:43; Rev 6:10
19:3 [e]Isa 34:10; Rev 14:11
19:4 [f]Rev 4:4 [g]Rev 4:6 [h]Rev 5:14
19:5 [i]Ps 134:1 [j]Rev 11:18; 20:12
19:6 [k]Rev 11:15
19:7 [l]Mt 22:2; 25:10; Eph 5:32 [m]Rev 21:2,9
19:8 [n]Rev 15:4
19:9 [o]ver 10 [p]Rev 1:19 [q]Lk 14:15 [r]Rev 21:5; 22:6
19:10 [s]Rev 22:8 [t]Ac 10:25,26; Rev 22:9 [u]Rev 12:17
19:11 [v]Rev 6:2 [w]Rev 3:14 [x]Isa 11:4
19:12 [y]Rev 1:14 [z]Rev 6:2 [a]Rev 2:17
19:13 [b]Isa 63:2,3 [c]Jn 1:1
19:14 [d]ver 8
19:15 [e]Rev 1:16 [f]Isa 11:4; 2Th 2:8 [g]Ps 2:9; Rev 2:27 [h]Rev 14:20
19:16 [i]ver 12 [j]Rev 17:14
19:17 [k]ver 21 [l]Rev 8:13 [m]Eze 39:17
19:18 [n]Eze 39:18-20

u *15* Psalm 2:9

of the earth[a] and their armies gathered together to make war against the rider on the horse and his army. 20But the beast was captured, and with him the false prophet[b] who had performed the miraculous signs on his behalf.[c] With these signs he had deluded those who had received the mark of the beast and worshiped his image. The two of them were thrown alive into the fiery lake[d] of burning sulfur.[e] 21The rest of them were killed with the sword[f] that came out of the mouth of the rider on the horse,[g] and all the birds[h] gorged themselves on their flesh.

Satan bound for 1,000 years.

20 And I saw an angel coming down out of heaven,[i] having the key[j] to the Abyss and holding in his hand a great chain. 2He seized the dragon, that ancient serpent, who is the devil, or Satan,[k] and bound him for a thousand years.[l] 3He threw him into the Abyss, and locked and sealed[m] it over him, to keep him from deceiving the nations[n] anymore until the thousand years were ended. After that, he must be set free for a short time.

Christian martyrs reign with Christ for 1,000 years.

4I saw thrones[o] on which were seated those who had been given authority to judge. And I saw the souls of those who had been beheaded[p] because of their testimony for Jesus and because of the word of God. They had not worshiped the beast[q] or his image and had not received his mark on their foreheads or their hands.[r] They came to life and reigned with Christ a thousand years. 5(The rest of the dead did not come to life until the thousand years were ended.) This is the first resurrection.[s] 6Blessed[t] and holy are those who have part in the first resurrection. The second death[u] has no power over them, but they will be priests[v] of God and of Christ and will reign with him[w] for a thousand years.

Final revolt of Satan after his release.

7When the thousand years are over,[x] Satan will be released from his prison 8and will go out to deceive the nations[y] in the four corners of the earth—Gog and Magog[z]—to gather them for battle.[a] In number they are like the sand on the seashore.[b] 9They marched across the breadth of the earth and surrounded[c] the camp of God's people, the city he loves. But fire came down from heaven[d] and devoured them. 10And the devil, who deceived them,[e] was thrown into the lake of burning sulfur, where the beast and the false prophet had been thrown. They will be tormented day and night for ever and ever.[f]

Judgment at the great white throne.

11Then I saw a great white throne[g] and him who was seated on it. Earth and sky fled from his presence, and there was no place for them. 12And I saw the dead, great and small, standing before the throne, and books were opened.[h] Another book was opened, which is the book of life.[i] The dead were judged according to what they had done[j] as recorded in the books. 13The sea gave up the dead that were in it, and death and Hades[k] gave up the dead[l] that were in them, and each person was judged according to what he had done. 14Then death[m] and Hades were thrown into the lake of fire. The lake of fire is the second death. 15If anyone's name was not found written in the book of life,[n] he was thrown into the lake of fire.

A new heaven, a new earth and the new Jerusalem.

21 Then I saw a new heaven and a new earth,[o] for the first heaven and the first earth had passed away, and there was no longer any sea. 2I saw the Holy City, the new Jerusalem, coming

19:19 [a]Rev 16:14,16
19:20 [b]Rev 16:13 [c]Rev 13:12 [d]Da 7:11; Rev 20:10,14,15; 21:8 [e]Rev 14:10
19:21 [f]ver 15 [g]ver 11,19 [h]ver 17
20:1 [i]Rev 10:1 [j]Rev 1:18
20:2 [k]Rev 12:9 [l]2Pe 2:4
20:3 [m]Da 6:17 [n]Rev 12:9
20:4 [o]Da 7:9 [p]Rev 6:9 [q]Rev 13:12 [r]Rev 13:16
20:5 [s]Lk 14:14; Php 3:11
20:6 [t]Rev 14:13 [u]Rev 2:11 [v]Rev 1:6 [w]ver 4
20:7 [x]ver 2
20:8 [y]ver 3,10 [z]Eze 38:2; 39:1 [a]Rev 16:14 [b]Heb 11:12
20:9 [c]Eze 38:9,16 [d]Eze 38:22; 39:6
20:10 [e]Rev 19:20 [f]Rev 14:10,11
20:11 [g]Rev 4:2
20:12 [h]Da 7:10 [i]Rev 3:5 [j]Jer 17:10; Mt 16:27; Rev 2:23
20:13 [k]Rev 6:8 [l]Isa 26:19
20:14 [m]1Co 15:26
20:15 [n]ver 12

21:1 [o]Isa 65:17; 2Pe 3:13

down out of heaven from God,[a] prepared as a bride beautifully dressed for her husband. 3And I heard a loud voice from the throne saying, "Now the dwelling of God is with men, and he will live with them. They will be his people, and God himself will be with them and be their God.[b] 4He will wipe every tear from their eyes.[c] There will be no more death[d] or mourning or crying or pain,[e] for the old order of things has passed away."

5He who was seated on the throne[f] said, "I am making everything new!" Then he said, "Write this down, for these words are trustworthy and true."[g]

6He said to me: "It is done.[h] I am the Alpha and the Omega,[i] the Beginning and the End. To him who is thirsty I will give to drink without cost from the spring of the water of life.[j] 7He who overcomes will inherit all this, and I will be his God and he will be my son. 8But the cowardly, the unbelieving, the vile, the murderers, the sexually immoral, those who practice magic arts, the idolaters and all liars[k]—their place will be in the fiery lake of burning sulfur. This is the second death."[l]

9One of the seven angels who had the seven bowls full of the seven last plagues[m] came and said to me, "Come, I will show you the bride,[n] the wife of the Lamb." 10And he carried me away[o] in the Spirit[p] to a mountain great and high, and showed me the Holy City, Jerusalem, coming down out of heaven from God. 11It shone with the glory of God,[q] and its brilliance was like that of a very precious jewel, like a jasper, clear as crystal.[r] 12It had a great, high wall with twelve gates, and with twelve angels at the gates. On the gates were written the names of the twelve tribes of Israel.[s] 13There were three gates on the east, three on the north, three on the south and three on the west. 14The wall of the city had twelve foundations, and on them were the names of the twelve apostles of the Lamb.

15The angel who talked with me had a measuring rod[t] of gold to measure the city, its gates and its walls. 16The city was laid out like a square, as long as it was wide. He measured the city with the rod and found it to be 12,000 stadia[v] in length, and as wide and high as it is long. 17He measured its wall and it was 144 cubits[w] thick,[x] by man's measurement, which the angel was using. 18The wall was made of jasper,[u] and the city of pure gold, as pure as glass.[v] 19The foundations of the city walls were decorated with every kind of precious stone.[w] The first foundation was jasper, the second sapphire, the third chalcedony, the fourth emerald, 20the fifth sardonyx, the sixth carnelian,[x] the seventh chrysolite, the eighth beryl, the ninth topaz, the tenth chrysoprase, the eleventh jacinth, and the twelfth amethyst.[y] 21The twelve gates were twelve pearls, each gate made of a single pearl. The great street of the city was of pure gold, like transparent glass.[y]

22I did not see a temple[z] in the city, because the Lord God Almighty[a] and the Lamb[b] are its temple. 23The city does not need the sun or the moon to shine on it, for the glory of God gives it light,[c] and the Lamb is its lamp. 24The nations will walk by its light, and the kings of the earth will bring their splendor into it.[d] 25On no day will its gates ever be shut,[e] for there will be no night there.[f] 26The glory and honor of the nations will be brought into it. 27Nothing impure will ever enter it, nor will anyone who does what is shameful or deceitful,[g] but only those whose names are written in the Lamb's book of life.

The river of life and the tree of life.

22 Then the angel showed me the river of the water of life, as clear as crystal,[h] flowing[i] from the throne of

21:2 [a]Heb 11:10; 12:22; Rev 3:12
21:3 [b]2Co 6:16
21:4 [c]Rev 7:17 [d]1Co 15:26; Rev 20:14 [e]Isa 35:10; 65:19
21:5 [f]Rev 4:9; 20:11 [g]Rev 19:9
21:6 [h]Rev 16:17 [i]Rev 1:8; 22:13 [j]Jn 4:10
21:8 [k]1Co 6:9 [l]Rev 2:11
21:9 [m]Rev 15:1, 6,7 [n]Rev 19:7
21:10 [o]Rev 17:3 [p]Rev 1:10
21:11 [q]Rev 15:8; 22:5 [r]Rev 4:6
21:12 [s]Eze 48:30-34
21:15 [t]Rev 11:1
21:18 [u]ver 11 [v]ver 21
21:19 [w]Isa 54:11,12
21:20 [x]Rev 4:3
21:21 [y]ver 18
21:22 [z]Jn 4:21,23 [a]Rev 1:8 [b]Rev 5:6
21:23 [c]Isa 24:23; 60:19,20; Rev 22:5
21:24 [d]Isa 60:3,5
21:25 [e]Isa 60:11 [f]Zec 14:7; Rev 22:5
21:27 [g]Isa 52:1; Joel 3:17; Rev 22:14,15

22:1 [h]Rev 4:6 [i]Eze 47:1; Zec 14:8

v *16* That is, about 1,400 miles (about 2,200 kilometers) w *17* That is, about 200 feet (about 65 meters) x *17* Or *high* y *20* The precise identification of some of these precious stones is uncertain.

God and of the Lamb 2down the middle
of the great street of the city. On each
side of the river stood the tree of life,[a]
bearing twelve crops of fruit, yielding
its fruit every month. And the leaves
of the tree are for the healing of the
nations.[b] 3No longer will there be any
curse.[c] The throne of God and of the
Lamb will be in the city, and his servants will serve him.[d] 4They will see
his face,[e] and his name will be on their
foreheads.[f] 5There will be no more
night.[g] They will not need the light of
a lamp or the light of the sun, for the
Lord God will give them light.[h] And
they will reign for ever and ever.[i]

6The angel said to me,[j] "These words
are trustworthy and true.[k] The Lord,
the God of the spirits of the prophets,[l]
sent his angel[m] to show his servants the
things that must soon take place."

The return of our Lord Jesus Christ!

7"Behold, I am coming soon![n] Blessed[o]
is he who keeps the words of the prophecy in this book."

8I, John, am the one who heard and
saw these things.[p] And when I had
heard and seen them, I fell down to
worship at the feet[q] of the angel who
had been showing them to me. 9But
he said to me, "Do not do it! I am a
fellow servant with you and with your
brothers the prophets and of all who
keep the words of this book.[r] Worship
God!"[s]

10Then he told me, "Do not seal up[t]
the words of the prophecy of this book,
because the time is near.[u] 11Let him
who does wrong continue to do wrong;
let him who is vile continue to be vile;
let him who does right continue to do

22:2 [a]Rev 2:7 [b]Eze 47:12
22:3 [c]Zec 14:11 [d]Rev 7:15
22:4 [e]Mt 5:8 [f]Rev 14:1
22:5 [g]Rev 21:25 [h]Rev 21:23 [i]Da 7:27; Rev 20:4
22:6 [j]Rev 1:1 [k]Rev 19:9; 21:5 [l]Heb 12:9 [m]ver 16
22:7 [n]Rev 3:11 [o]Rev 1:3
22:8 [p]Rev 1:1 [q]Rev 19:10
22:9 [r]ver 10,18,19 [s]Rev 19:10
22:10 [t]Da 8:26; Rev 10:4 [u]Rev 1:3
22:11 [v]Eze 3:27; Da 12:10
22:12 [w]ver 7,20 [x]Isa 40:10
22:13 [y]Rev 1:8 [z]Rev 1:17 [a]Rev 21:6
22:14 [b]Rev 2:7 [c]Rev 21:12 [d]Rev 21:27
22:15 [e]1Co 6:9,10; Gal 5:19-21; Col 3:5,6 [f]Php 3:2
22:16 [g]Rev 1:1 [h]Rev 1:4 [i]Rev 5:5 [j]2Pe 1:19; Rev 2:28

right; and let him who is holy continue
to be holy."[v]

12"Behold, I am coming soon![w] My
reward is with me,[x] and I will give to
everyone according to what he has done.
13I am the Alpha and the Omega,[y] the
First and the Last,[z] the Beginning and
the End.[a]

14"Blessed are those who wash their
robes, that they may have the right to
the tree of life[b] and may go through the
gates[c] into the city.[d] 15Outside[e] are the
dogs,[f] those who practice magic arts,
the sexually immoral, the murderers, the
idolaters and everyone who loves and
practices falsehood.

16"I, Jesus,[g] have sent my angel to
give you[z] this testimony for the churches.[h] I am the Root[i] and the Offspring of
David, and the bright Morning Star."[j]

17The Spirit[k] and the bride say,
"Come!" And let him who hears say,
"Come!" Whoever is thirsty, let him
come; and whoever wishes, let him
take the free gift of the water of life.

18I warn everyone who hears the
words of the prophecy of this book: If
anyone adds anything to them,[l] God
will add to him the plagues described
in this book.[m] 19And if anyone takes
words away[n] from this book of prophecy, God will take away from him his
share in the tree of life and in the holy
city, which are described in this book.

20He who testifies to these things[o]
says, "Yes, I am coming soon."

Amen. Come, Lord Jesus.[p]

21The grace of the Lord Jesus be with
God's people.[q] Amen.

22:17 [k]Rev 2:7 **22:18** [l]Dt 4:2; Pr 30:6 [m]Rev 15:6–16:21 **22:19** [n]Dt 4:2 **22:20** [o]Rev 1:2 [p]1Co 16:22 **22:21** [q]Ro 16:20

[z]*16* The Greek is plural.

SUPPLEMENTAL STUDY AIDS

TABLE OF WEIGHTS AND MEASURES

KNOW WHAT GOD SAYS...

100 POPULAR BIBLE PASSAGES

365 POPULAR BIBLE QUOTATIONS
FOR MEMORIZATION AND MEDITATION

ONE-YEAR DAILY BIBLE READING CALENDAR

PERSONAL DAILY BIBLE READING CALENDAR

SUBJECT GUIDE

WHERE TO FIND IT

OUTLINE OF OLD TESTAMENT HISTORY

CONCORDANCE

BIBLE MAPS AND INDEX

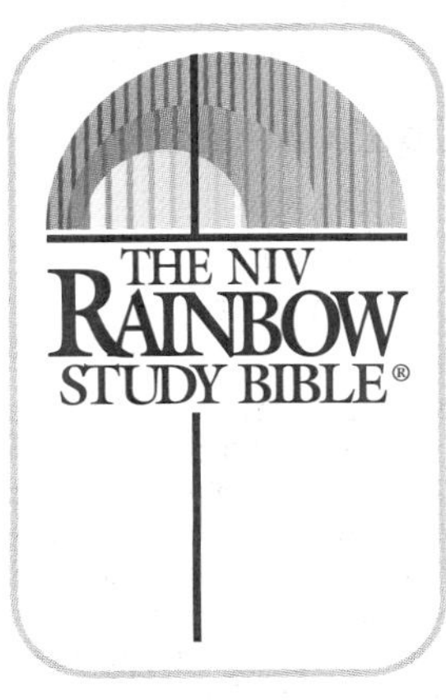

TABLE OF WEIGHTS AND MEASURES

BIBLICAL UNIT		APPROXIMATE AMERICAN EQUIVALENT	APPROXIMATE METRIC EQUIVALENT
		WEIGHTS	
talent	*(60 minas)*	75 pounds	34 kilograms
mina	*(50 shekels)*	1 1/4 pounds	0.6 kilogram
shekel	*(2 bekas)*	2/5 ounce	11.5 grams
pim	*(2/3 shekel)*	1/3 ounce	7.6 grams
beka	*(10 gerahs)*	1/5 ounce	5.5 grams
gerah		1/50 ounce	0.6 gram
		LENGTH	
cubit		18 inches	0.5 meter
span		9 inches	23 centimeters
handbreadth		3 inches	8 centimeters
		CAPACITY	
		Dry Measure	
cor [homer]	*(10 ephahs)*	6 bushels	220 liters
lethek	*(5 ephahs)*	3 bushels	110 liters
ephah	*(10 omers)*	3/5 bushel	22 liters
seah	*(1/3 ephah)*	7 quarts	7.3 liters
omer	*(1/10 ephah)*	2 quarts	2 liters
cab	*(1/18 ephah)*	1 quart	1 liter
		Liquid Measure	
bath	*(1 ephah)*	6 gallons	22 liters
hin	*(1/6 bath)*	4 quarts	4 liters
log	*(1/72 bath)*	1/3 quart	0.3 liter

The figures of the table are calculated on the basis of a shekel equaling 11.5 grams, a cubit equaling 18 inches and an ephah equaling 22 liters. The quart referred to is either a dry quart (slightly larger than a liter) or a liquid quart (slightly smaller than a liter), whichever is applicable. The ton referred to in the footnotes is the American ton of 2,000 pounds.

This table is based upon the best available information, but it is not intended to be mathematically precise; like the measurement equivalents in the footnotes, it merely gives approximate amounts and distances. Weights and measures differed somewhat at various times and places in the ancient world. There is uncertainty particularly about the ephah and the bath; further discoveries may give more light on these units of capacity.

KNOW WHAT GOD SAYS...

Who is God?	Read all the ***purple*** verses about God. "Great is the LORD and most worthy of praise; his greatness no one can fathom." Ps. 145:3
Does God really love ME?	Read all the ***green*** verses about love. "Neither height nor depth, nor anything else in all creation, will be able to separate us from the love of God..." Rom. 8:39
*How do I get to Heaven?**	Read all the ***blue*** verses about salvation. "For, 'Everyone who calls on the name of the Lord will be saved.'" Rom. 10:13
*Where do I get more faith?***	Read all the ***orange*** verses about faith. "...faith comes from hearing the message, and the message is heard through the word of Christ." Rom. 10:17
What are Satan's tactics?	Read all the ***brown*** verses about Satan. "...take your stand against the devil's schemes. For our struggle is not against flesh and blood, but against the rulers, against the authorities, against the powers of this dark world..." Eph. 6:11,12
Why is my marriage important?	Read all the ***yellow*** verses about the family. "For this reason a man will leave his father and mother and be united to his wife, and they will become one flesh." Gen. 2:24
When should I tell others?	Read all the ***pink*** verses about witnessing. "...Always be prepared to give an answer to everyone who asks you to give the reason for the hope that you have." 1 Peter 3:15

Know also what God says about discipleship, sin, commandments, history and prophecy in ***The NIV Rainbow Study Bible®.***

*It takes less than 6 minutes to read all the ***blue*** verses (Salvation) in the Gospel of John. AN IDEAL WAY TO EVANGELIZE.

It takes 10 minutes to read all the ***orange* verses (Faith) in the Gospel of John. AN IDEAL WAY TO BUILD FAITH.

100 Popular Bible Passages

50 Old Testament and 50 New Testament

Old Testament

1	God's Creation of the World	Genesis 1:1–2:7
2	Adam and Eve's Fall	Genesis 3
3	Cain's Murder of Abel	Genesis 4
4	Noah's Ark	Genesis 6-8
5	The RAINBOW Covenant	Genesis 9:1-17
6	The Tower of Babel	Genesis 11:1-9
7	God's Call of Abraham	Genesis 12
8	Abraham's Offering of Isaac	Genesis 22
9	Marriage of Isaac and Rebekah	Genesis 24
10	Jacob and Esau	Genesis 27
11	Jacob's Stairway	Genesis 28
12	The Story of Joseph	Genesis 37-50
13	Moses' Birth	Exodus 2
14	The Burning Bush	Exodus 3-4
15	Plagues on Egypt	Exodus 7-11
16	The Passover and Exodus	Exodus 12
17	Israel's Crossing of the Red Sea	Exodus 14
18	Manna for Food	Exodus 16
19	The Ten Commandments	Exodus 20:1-17
20	The Golden Calf	Exodus 32
21	Exploring the Land of Canaan	Numbers 13
22	Rahab's Hiding of the Spies	Joshua 2
23	The Walls of Jericho	Joshua 6
24	The Story of Gideon	Judges 6-8
25	The Story of Samson and Delilah	Judges 13-16
26	The Story of Ruth and Naomi	Ruth 1-4
27	Samuel's Birth	1 Samuel 1
28	Anointing of Saul as King	1 Samuel 8–10
29	Anointing of David as King	1 Samuel 16
30	David and Goliath	1 Samuel 17
31	David and His Friend Jonathan	1 Samuel 18-20
32	David and Bathsheba	2 Samuel 11
33	Solomon's Request for Wisdom	1 Kings 3
34	Solomon's Building of the Temple	1 Kings 6
35	The Queen of Sheba's Visit	1 Kings 10
36	Elijah's Defeat of the Prophets of Baal	1 Kings 18
37	Healing of Naaman's Leprosy	2 Kings 5
38	Satan's Attack on Job	Job 1:1-2:10
39	The Shepherd's Psalm	Psalm 23
40	Psalm of Repentance	Psalm 51
41	Psalm of Praise for God's Word	Psalm 119
42	The Virtue of Wisdom	Proverbs 8
43	The Virtuous Wife	Proverbs 31
44	A Time for Everything	Ecclesiastes 3
45	The Suffering Servant	Isaiah 52:13-53:12
46	The Valley of Dry Bones	Ezekiel 37
47	Daniel's Friends in the Blazing Furnace	Daniel 3
48	The Writing on the Wall	Daniel 5
49	Daniel in the Lions' Den	Daniel 6
50	Jonah and the Great Fish	Jonah 1-4

100 Popular Bible Passages

50 Old Testament and 50 New Testament

New Testament

51	The Magi (Wise Men)	Matthew 2:1-12
52	John the Baptist	Matthew 3
53	The Devil's Temptation of Jesus	Matthew 4:1-11
54	The Beatitudes	Matthew 5:3-12
55	The Sermon on the Mount	Matthew 5-7
56	The Lord's Prayer	Matthew 6:5-15
57	No Worry about Tomorrow	Matthew 6:25-34
58	The Parable of the Sower	Matthew 13:1-23
59	Jesus' Walking on Water	Matthew 14:22-33
60	Forgiveness: Seventy-Seven Times	Matthew 18:21-35
61	The Triumphal Entry into Jerusalem	Matthew 21:1-11
62	The Parable of the Talents	Matthew 25:14-30
63	The Least of My Brothers	Matthew 25:31-46
64	The Garden of Gethsemane	Matthew 26:36-46
65	Jesus' Trial by Pilate	Matthew 27:1-26
66	The Great Commission	Matthew 28:16-20
67	Jesus' Calming of the Storm	Mark 4:35-41
68	The Transfiguration	Mark 9:2-13
69	The Rich Young Man	Mark 10:17-31
70	Jesus' Clearing of the Temple	Mark 11:12-19
71	The Poor Widow's Offering	Mark 12:41-44
72	Mary's Anointing of Jesus	Mark 14:3-9
73	The Last Supper	Mark 14:12-26
74	The Story of Jesus' Birth	Luke 1:26-2:40
75	Jesus at Twelve	Luke 2:41-52
76	The Good Samaritan	Luke 10:25-37
77	Mary and Martha	Luke 10:38-42
78	The Lost (Prodigal) Son	Luke 15:11-32
79	The Rich Man and Lazarus	Luke 16:19-31
80	Prayers of the Pharisee and the Tax Collector	Luke 18:9-14
81	The Story of Zacchaeus	Luke 19:1-10
82	The Burial and Resurrection of Jesus	Luke 23:50-24:49
83	Miracle of Water to Wine	John 2:1-11
84	Jesus and Nicodemus	John 3:1-21
85	The Woman at the Well	John 4:1-42
86	The Feeding of 5,000	John 6:1-14
87	Jesus, the Good Shepherd	John 10:1-30
88	The Resurrection of Lazarus	John 11:1-44
89	The True Vine	John 15
90	Jesus' Crucifixion	John 19:17-37
91	Doubting Thomas	John 20:19-29
92	The Ascension of Jesus	Acts 1:1-11
93	The Day of Pentecost	Acts 2
94	The Story of Stephen	Acts 6-7
95	Philip and the Ethiopian	Acts 8:26-40
96	The Conversion of Saul	Acts 9:1-31
97	The Love Chapter	1 Corinthians 13
98	The Armor of God	Ephesians 6:10-20
99	The Faith Chapter	Hebrews 11
100	A New Heaven and a New Earth	Revelation 21:1–22:6

365 POPULAR BIBLE QUOTATIONS FOR MEMORIZATION AND MEDITATION

Selections From Every Book of the Old and New Testaments

DATE MEMORIZED

(1) *January 1* So God created man in his own image, in the image of God he created him; male and female he created them. *Genesis 1:27*

(2) *January 2* By the sweat of your brow you will eat your food until you return to the ground, since from it you were taken; for dust you are and to dust you will return. *Genesis 3:19*

(3) *January 3* The LORD will fight for you; you need only to be still. *Exodus 14:14*

(4) *January 4* Remember the Sabbath day by keeping it holy. Six days you shall labor and do all your work, but the seventh day is a Sabbath to the LORD your God. On it you shall not do any work. *Exodus 20:8-10*

(5) *January 5* See, I am sending an angel ahead of you to guard you along the way and to bring you to the place I have prepared. *Exodus 23:20*

(6) *January 6* For the life of a creature is in the blood, and I have given it to you to make atonement for yourselves on the altar; it is the blood that makes atonement for one's life. *Leviticus 17:11*

(7) *January 7* God is not a man, that he should lie, nor a son of man, that he should change his mind. Does he speak and then not act? Does he promise and not fulfill? *Numbers 23:19*

(8) *January 8* But if you fail to do this, you will be sinning against the LORD; and you may be sure that your sin will find you out. *Numbers 32:23*

(9) *January 9* Love the LORD your God with all your heart and with all your soul and with all your strength. These commandments that I give you today are to be upon your hearts. Impress them on your children. Talk about them when you sit at home and when you walk along the road, when you lie down and when you get up. *Deuteronomy 6:5-7*

(10) *January 10* He humbled you, causing you to hunger and then feeding you with manna, which neither you nor your fathers had known, to teach you that man does not live on bread alone but on every word that comes from the mouth of the LORD. *Deuteronomy 8:3*

(11) *January 11* And now, O Israel, what does the LORD your God ask of you but to fear the LORD your God, to walk in all his ways, to love him, to serve the LORD your God with all your heart and with all your soul, and to observe the LORD's commands and decrees that I am giving you today for your own good? *Deuteronomy 10:12,13*

(12) *January 12* See, I am setting before you today a blessing and a curse—the blessing if you obey the commands of the LORD your God that I am giving you today; the curse if you disobey the commands of the LORD your God and turn from the way that I command you today by following other gods, which you have not known. *Deuteronomy 11:26-28*

(13) *January 13* The secret things belong to the LORD our God, but the things revealed belong to us and to our children forever, that we may follow all the words of this law. *Deuteronomy 29:29*

(14) *January 14* Be strong and courageous. Do not be afraid or terrified because of them, for the LORD your God goes with you; he will never leave you nor forsake you. *Deuteronomy 31:6*

(15) *January 15* Do not let this Book of the Law depart from your mouth; meditate on it day and night, so that you may be careful to do everything written in it. Then you will be prosperous and successful. *Joshua 1:8*

(16) *January 16* But if serving the LORD seems undesirable to you, then choose for yourselves this day whom you will serve, whether the gods your forefathers served beyond the River, or the gods of the Amorites, in whose land you are living. But as for me and my household, we will serve the LORD. *Joshua 24:15*

(17) *January 17* In those days Israel

DATE MEMORIZED

had no king; everyone did as he saw fit. *Judges 21:25*

(18) *January 18* Ruth replied, "Don't urge me to leave you or to turn back from you. Where you go I will go, and where you stay I will stay. Your people will be my people and your God my God." *Ruth 1:16*

(19) *January 19* Samuel replied: "Does the LORD delight in burnt offerings and sacrifices as much as in obeying the voice of the LORD? To obey is better than sacrifice, and to heed is better than the fat of rams." *1 Samuel 15:22*

(20) *January 20* The LORD said to Samuel, "Do not consider his appearance or his height, for I have rejected him. The LORD does not look at the things man looks at. Man looks at the outward appearance, but the LORD looks at the heart." *1 Samuel 16:7*

(21) *January 21* A champion named Goliath, who was from Gath, came out of the Philistine camp. He was over nine feet tall. *1 Samuel 17:4*

(22) *January 22* As for God, his way is perfect; the word of the LORD is flawless. He is a shield for all who take refuge in him. *2 Samuel 22:31*

(23) *January 23* Observe what the LORD your God requires: Walk in his ways, and keep his decrees and commands, his laws and requirements, as written in the Law of Moses, so that you may prosper in all you do and wherever you go. *1 Kings 2:3*

(24) *January 24* Elijah went before the people and said, "How long will you waver between two opinions? If the LORD is God, follow him; but if Baal is God, follow him." *1 Kings 18:21*

(25) *January 25* Worship the LORD your God; it is he who will deliver you from the hand of all your enemies. *2 Kings 17:39*

(26) *January 26* But I know where you stay and when you come and go and how you rage against me. *2 Kings 19:27*

(27) *January 27* Look to the LORD and his strength; seek his face always. *1 Chronicles 16:11*

(28) *January 28* Yours, O LORD, is the greatness and the power and the glory and the majesty and the splendor, for everything in heaven and earth is yours. *1 Chronicles 29:11*

(29) *January 29* If my people, who are called by my name, will humble themselves and pray and seek my face and turn from their wicked ways, then will I hear from heaven and will forgive their sin and will heal their land. *2 Chronicles 7:14*

(30) *January 30* For the eyes of the LORD range throughout the earth to strengthen those whose hearts are fully committed to him. *2 Chronicles 16:9*

(31) *January 31* So we fasted and petitioned our God about this, and he answered our prayer. *Ezra 8:23*

(32) *February 1* You alone are the LORD. You made the heavens, even the highest heavens, and all their starry host, the earth and all that is on it, the seas and all that is in them. You give life to everything, and the multitudes of heaven worship you. *Nehemiah 9:6*

(33) *February 2* For if you remain silent at this time, relief and deliverance for the Jews will arise from another place, but you and your father's family will perish. And who knows but that you have come to royal position for such a time as this? *Esther 4:14*

(34) *February 3* His wisdom is profound, his power is vast. Who has resisted him and come out unscathed? *Job 9:4*

(35) *February 4* You gave me life and showed me kindness, and in your providence watched over my spirit. *Job 10:12*

(36) *February 5* To God belong wisdom and power; counsel and understanding are his. *Job 12:13*

(37) *February 6* Is not God in the heights of heaven? And see how lofty are the highest stars! *Job 22:12*

(38) *February 7* Submit to God and be at peace with him; in this way prosperity will come to you. Accept instruction from his mouth and lay up his words in your heart. *Job 22:21,22*

(39) *February 8* But he knows the way that I take; when he has tested me, I will come forth as gold. *Job 23:10*

(40) *February 9* And he said to man, "The fear of the Lord—that is wisdom, and to shun evil is understanding." *Job 28:28*

(41) *February 10* His eyes are on the ways of men; he sees their every step. *Job 34:21*

(42) *February 11* Blessed is the man who does not walk in the counsel of the wicked or stand in the way of sinners or sit in the seat of mockers. *Psalm 1:1*

DATE MEMORIZED

(43) *February 12* When I consider your heavens, the work of your fingers, the moon and the stars, which you have set in place, what is man that you are mindful of him, the son of man that you care for him? *Psalm 8:3,4*

(44) *February 13* The words of the LORD are flawless, like silver refined in a furnace of clay, purified seven times. *Psalm 12:6*

(45) *February 14* The law of the LORD is perfect, reviving the soul. The statutes of the LORD are trustworthy, making wise the simple. The precepts of the LORD are right, giving joy to the heart. The commands of the LORD are radiant, giving light to the eyes. The fear of the LORD is pure, enduring forever. The ordinances of the LORD are sure and altogether righteous. They are more precious than gold, than much pure gold; they are sweeter than honey, than honey from the comb. By them is your servant warned; in keeping them there is great reward. *Psalm 19:7-11*

(46) *February 15* May the words of my mouth and the meditation of my heart be pleasing in your sight, O LORD, my Rock and my Redeemer. *Psalm 19:14*

(47) *February 16* The earth is the LORD's, and everything in it, the world, and all who live in it. *Psalm 24:1*

(48) *February 17* The LORD is my light and my salvation—whom shall I fear? The LORD is the stronghold of my life—of whom shall I be afraid? *Psalm 27:1*

(49) *February 18* His anger lasts only a moment, but his favor lasts a lifetime; weeping may remain for a night, but rejoicing comes in the morning. *Psalm 30:5*

(50) *February 19* The lions may grow weak and hungry, but those who seek the LORD lack no good thing. *Psalm 34:10*

(51) *February 20* A righteous man may have many troubles, but the LORD delivers him from them all. *Psalm 34:19*

(52) *February 21* Delight yourself in the LORD and he will give you the desires of your heart. *Psalm 37:4*

(53) *February 22* Be still before the LORD and wait patiently for him; do not fret when men succeed in their ways, when they carry out their wicked schemes. *Psalm 37:7*

(54) *February 23* Why are you downcast, O my soul? Why so disturbed within me? Put your hope in God, for I will yet praise him, my Savior and my God. *Psalm 42:11*

(55) *February 24* I will perpetuate your memory through all generations; therefore the nations will praise you for ever and ever. *Psalm 45:17*

(56) *February 25* Be still, and know that I am God; I will be exalted among the nations, I will be exalted in the earth. *Psalm 46:10*

(57) *February 26* How awesome is the LORD Most High, the great King over all the earth! *Psalm 47:2*

(58) *February 27* Do not be overawed when a man grows rich, when the splendor of his house increases; for he will take nothing with him when he dies, his splendor will not descend with him. *Psalm 49:16,17*

(59) *February 28/29* I have no need of a bull from your stall or of goats from your pens, for every animal of the forest is mine, and the cattle on a thousand hills. I know every bird in the mountains, and the creatures of the field are mine. *Psalm 50:9-11*

(60) *March 1* Create in me a pure heart, O God, and renew a steadfast spirit within me. Restore to me the joy of your salvation and grant me a willing spirit, to sustain me. *Psalm 51:10,12*

(61) *March 2* Evening, morning and noon I cry out in distress, and he hears my voice. *Psalm 55:17*

(62) *March 3* No one from the east or the west or from the desert can exalt a man. But it is God who judges: He brings one down, he exalts another. *Psalm 75:6,7*

(63) *March 4* For the LORD God is a sun and shield; the LORD bestows favor and honor; no good thing does he withhold from those whose walk is blameless. *Psalm 84:11*

(64) *March 5* For the LORD is the great God, the great King above all gods. *Psalm 95:3*

(65) *March 6* As far as the east is from the west, so far has he removed our transgressions from us. *Psalm 103:12*

(66) *March 7* This is the day the LORD has made; let us rejoice and be glad in it. *Psalm 118:24*

(67) *March 8* How can a young man keep his way pure? By living according to your word. *Psalm 119:9*

(68) *March 9* Praise be to you, O LORD; teach me your decrees. With my lips I recount all the laws that come from your mouth. I rejoice in following your statutes as

DATE MEMORIZED

one rejoices in great riches. I meditate on your precepts and consider your ways. I delight in your decrees; I will not neglect your word. *Psalm 119:12-16*

(69) *March 10* To all perfection I see a limit; but your commands are boundless. Oh, how I love your law! I meditate on it all day long. Your commands make me wiser than my enemies, for they are ever with me. I have more insight than all my teachers, for I meditate on your statutes. I have more understanding than the elders, for I obey your precepts. *Psalm 119:96-100*

(70) *March 11* Your word is a lamp to my feet and a light for my path. *Psalm 119:105*

(71) *March 12* Unless the LORD builds the house, its builders labor in vain. Unless the LORD watches over the city, the watchmen stand guard in vain. In vain you rise early and stay up late, toiling for food to eat—for he grants sleep to those he loves. *Psalm 127:1,2*

(72) *March 13* Sons are a heritage from the LORD, children a reward from him. *Psalm 127:3*

(73) *March 14* How precious to me are your thoughts, O God! How vast is the sum of them! Were I to count them, they would outnumber the grains of sand. When I awake, I am still with you. *Psalm 139:17,18*

(74) *March 15* Search me, O God, and know my heart; test me and know my anxious thoughts. See if there is any offensive way in me, and lead me in the way everlasting. *Psalm 139:23,24*

(75) *March 16* Trust in the LORD with all your heart and lean not on your own understanding; in all your ways acknowledge him, and he will make your paths straight. *Proverbs 3:5,6*

(76) *March 17* There are six things the LORD hates, seven that are detestable to him: haughty eyes, a lying tongue, hands that shed innocent blood, a heart that devises wicked schemes, feet that are quick to rush into evil, a false witness who pours out lies and a man who stirs up dissension among brothers. *Proverbs 6:16-19*

(77) *March 18* The fear of the LORD is the beginning of wisdom, and knowledge of the Holy One is understanding. *Proverbs 9:10*

(78) *March 19* He who walks with the wise grows wise, but a companion of fools suffers harm. *Proverbs 13:20*

(79) *March 20* There is a way that seems right to a man, but in the end it leads to death. *Proverbs 14:12*

(80) *March 21* A truthful witness saves lives, but a false witness is deceitful. *Proverbs 14:25*

(81) *March 22* Pride goes before destruction, a haughty spirit before a fall. *Proverbs 16:18*

(82) *March 23* He who finds a wife finds what is good and receives favor from the LORD. *Proverbs 18:22*

(83) *March 24* A man of many companions may come to ruin, but there is a friend who sticks closer than a brother. *Proverbs 18:24*

(84) *March 25* He who is kind to the poor lends to the LORD, and he will reward him for what he has done. *Proverbs 19:17*

(85) *March 26* Discipline your son, for in that there is hope; do not be a willing party to his death. *Proverbs 19:18*

(86) *March 27* All a man's ways seem right to him, but the LORD weighs the heart. *Proverbs 21:2*

(87) *March 28* Train a child in the way he should go, and when he is old he will not turn from it. *Proverbs 22:6*

(88) *March 29* Do not boast about tomorrow, for you do not know what a day may bring forth. *Proverbs 27:1*

(89) *March 30* As water reflects a face, so a man's heart reflects the man. *Proverbs 27:19*

(90) *March 31* Two things I ask of you, O LORD; do not refuse me before I die: Keep falsehood and lies far from me; give me neither poverty nor riches, but give me only my daily bread. *Proverbs 30:7,8*

(91) *April 1* There is a time for everything, and a season for every activity under heaven. *Ecclesiastes 3:1*

(92) *April 2* Two are better than one, because they have a good return for their work: If one falls down, his friend can help him up. But pity the man who falls and has no one to help him up! *Ecclesiastes 4:9,10*

(93) *April 3* Whoever loves money never has money enough; whoever loves wealth is never satisfied with his income. This too is meaningless. *Ecclesiastes 5:10*

DATE MEMORIZED

(94) *April 4* There is not a righteous man on earth who does what is right and never sins. *Ecclesiastes 7:20*

(95) *April 5* Be happy, young man, while you are young, and let your heart give you joy in the days of your youth. Follow the ways of your heart and whatever your eyes see, but know that for all these things God will bring you to judgment. *Ecclesiastes 11:9*

(96) *April 6* Many waters cannot quench love; rivers cannot wash it away. If one were to give all the wealth of his house for love, it would be utterly scorned. *Song of Songs 8:7*

(97) *April 7* "Come now, let us reason together," says the LORD. "Though your sins are like scarlet, they shall be as white as snow; though they are red as crimson, they shall be like wool." *Isaiah 1:18*

(98) *April 8* Woe to those who draw sin along with cords of deceit, and wickedness as with cart ropes. *Isaiah 5:18*

(99) *April 9* Then I heard the voice of the Lord saying, "Whom shall I send? And who will go for us?" And I said, "Here am I. Send me!" *Isaiah 6:8*

(100) *April 10* For to us a child is born, to us a son is given, and the government will be on his shoulders. And he will be called Wonderful Counselor, Mighty God, Everlasting Father, Prince of Peace. *Isaiah 9:6*

(101) *April 11* You will keep in perfect peace him whose mind is steadfast, because he trusts in you. Trust in the LORD forever, for the LORD, the LORD, is the Rock eternal. *Isaiah 26:3,4*

(102) *April 12* Yes, LORD, walking in the way of your laws, we wait for you; your name and renown are the desire of our hearts. *Isaiah 26:8*

(103) *April 13* Whether you turn to the right or to the left, your ears will hear a voice behind you, saying, "This is the way; walk in it." *Isaiah 30:21*

(104) *April 14* The grass withers and the flowers fall, but the word of our God stands forever. *Isaiah 40:8*

(105) *April 15* Do you not know? Have you not heard? The LORD is the everlasting God, the Creator of the ends of the earth. He will not grow tired or weary, and his understanding no one can fathom. He gives strength to the weary and increases the power of the weak. *Isaiah 40:28,29*

(106) *April 16* Those who hope in the LORD will renew their strength. They will soar on wings like eagles; they will run and not grow weary, they will walk and not be faint. *Isaiah 40:31*

(107) *April 17* Who has done this and carried it through, calling forth the generations from the beginning? I, the LORD—with the first of them and with the last—I am he. *Isaiah 41:4*

(108) *April 18* So do not fear, for I am with you; do not be dismayed, for I am your God. I will strengthen you and help you; I will uphold you with my righteous right hand. *Isaiah 41:10*

(109) *April 19* When you pass through the waters, I will be with you; and when you pass through the rivers, they will not sweep over you. When you walk through the fire, you will not be burned; the flames will not set you ablaze. *Isaiah 43:2*

(110) *April 20* I, even I, am he who blots out your transgressions, for my own sake, and remembers your sins no more. *Isaiah 43:25*

(111) *April 21* This is what the LORD says—your Redeemer, who formed you in the womb: I am the LORD, who has made all things, who alone stretched out the heavens, who spread out the earth by myself. *Isaiah 44:24*

(112) *April 22* Truly you are a God who hides himself, O God and Savior of Israel. *Isaiah 45:15*

(113) *April 23* But he was pierced for our transgressions, he was crushed for our iniquities; the punishment that brought us peace was upon him, and by his wounds we are healed. We all, like sheep, have gone astray, each of us has turned to his own way; and the LORD has laid on him the iniquity of us all. *Isaiah 53:5,6*

(114) *April 24* Seek the LORD while he may be found; call on him while he is near. Let the wicked forsake his way and the evil man his thoughts. Let him turn to the LORD, and he will have mercy on him, and to our God, for he will freely pardon. *Isaiah 55:6,7*

(115) *April 25* As the rain and the snow come down from heaven, and do not return to it without watering the earth and making it bud and flourish, so that it yields seed for the sower and bread for the eater, so is my word that goes out from my mouth:

DATE MEMORIZED

It will not return to me empty, but will accomplish what I desire and achieve the purpose for which I sent it. *Isaiah 55:10,11*

(116) *April 26* Your iniquities have separated you from your God; your sins have hidden his face from you, so that he will not hear. *Isaiah 59:2*

(117) *April 27* The Spirit of the Sovereign LORD is on me, because the LORD has anointed me to preach good news to the poor. He has sent me to bind up the brokenhearted, to proclaim freedom for the captives and release from darkness for the prisoners. *Isaiah 61:1*

(118) *April 28* Before they call I will answer; while they are still speaking I will hear. *Isaiah 65:24*

(119) *April 29* This is what the LORD says: "Let not the wise man boast of his wisdom or the strong man boast of his strength or the rich man boast of his riches, but let him who boasts boast about this: that he understands and knows me, that I am the LORD, who exercises kindness, justice and righteousness on earth, for in these I delight," declares the LORD. *Jeremiah 9:23,24*

(120) *April 30* Blessed is the man who trusts in the LORD, whose confidence is in him. He will be like a tree planted by the water that sends out its roots by the stream. It does not fear when heat comes; its leaves are always green. It has no worries in a year of drought and never fails to bear fruit. *Jeremiah 17:7,8*

(121) *May 1* "For I know the plans I have for you," declares the LORD, "plans to prosper you and not to harm you, plans to give you hope and a future. Then you will call upon me and come and pray to me, and I will listen to you. You will seek me and find me when you seek me with all your heart." *Jeremiah 29:11-13*

(122) *May 2* I am the LORD, the God of all mankind. Is anything too hard for me? *Jeremiah 32:27*

(123) *May 3* Because of the LORD's great love we are not consumed, for his compassions never fail. *Lamentations 3:22*

(124) *May 4* I will search for the lost and bring back the strays. I will bind up the injured and strengthen the weak, but the sleek and the strong I will destroy. I will shepherd the flock with justice. *Ezekiel 34:16*

(125) *May 5* He changes times and seasons; he sets up kings and deposes them. He gives wisdom to the wise and knowledge to the discerning. He reveals deep and hidden things; he knows what lies in darkness, and light dwells with him. *Daniel 2:21,22*

(126) *May 6* Shadrach, Meshach and Abednego replied to the king, "O Nebuchadnezzar, we do not need to defend ourselves before you in this matter. If we are thrown into the blazing furnace, the God we serve is able to save us from it, and he will rescue us from your hand, O king. But even if he does not, we want you to know, O king, that we will not serve your gods or worship the image of gold you have set up." *Daniel 3:16-18*

(127) *May 7* Those who are wise will shine like the brightness of the heavens, and those who lead many to righteousness, like the stars for ever and ever. *Daniel 12:3*

(128) *May 8* Let us acknowledge the LORD; let us press on to acknowledge him. As surely as the sun rises, he will appear; he will come to us like the winter rains, like the spring rains that water the earth. *Hosea 6:3*

(129) *May 9* Who is wise? He will realize these things. Who is discerning? He will understand them. The ways of the LORD are right; the righteous walk in them, but the rebellious stumble in them. *Hosea 14:9*

(130) *May 10* I will pour out my Spirit on all people. Your sons and daughters will prophesy, your old men will dream dreams, your young men will see visions. *Joel 2:28*

(131) *May 11* "The days are coming," declares the Sovereign LORD, "when I will send a famine through the land—not a famine of food or a thirst for water, but a famine of hearing the words of the LORD." *Amos 8:11*

(132) *May 12* "Though you soar like the eagle and make your nest among the stars, from there I will bring you down," declares the LORD. *Obadiah 4*

(133) *May 13* In my distress I called to the LORD, and he answered me. From the depths of the grave I called for help, and you listened to my cry. *Jonah 2:2*

(134) *May 14* He has showed you, O man, what is good. And what does the

DATE MEMORIZED

LORD require of you? To act justly and to love mercy and to walk humbly with your God. *Micah 6:8*

(135) *May 15* The LORD is good, a refuge in times of trouble. He cares for those who trust in him. *Nahum 1:7*

(136) *May 16* Though the fig tree does not bud and there are no grapes on the vines, though the olive crop fails and the fields produce no food, though there are no sheep in the pen and no cattle in the stalls, yet I will rejoice in the LORD, I will be joyful in God my Savior. *Habakkuk 3:17,18*

(137) *May 17* The Lord your God is with you, he is mighty to save. He will take great delight in you, he will quiet you with his love, he will rejoice over you with singing. *Zephaniah 3:17*

(138) *May 18* Now this is what the LORD Almighty says: "Give careful thought to your ways. You have planted much, but have harvested little. You eat, but never have enough. You drink, but never have your fill. You put on clothes, but are not warm. You earn wages, only to put them in a purse with holes in it." *Haggai 1:5,6*

(139) *May 19* "Not by might nor by power, but by my Spirit," says the LORD Almighty. *Zechariah 4:6*

(140) *May 20* Has not ⌊the LORD⌋ made them one? In flesh and spirit they are his. And why one? Because he was seeking godly offspring. So guard yourself in your spirit, and do not break faith with the wife of your youth. *Malachi 2:15*

(141) *May 21* "Bring the whole tithe into the storehouse, that there may be food in my house. Test me in this," says the LORD Almighty, "and see if I will not throw open the floodgates of heaven and pour out so much blessing that you will not have room enough for it." *Malachi 3:10*

(142) *May 22* In the same way, let your light shine before men, that they may see your good deeds and praise your Father in heaven. *Matthew 5:16*

(143) *May 23* I tell you that anyone who looks at a woman lustfully has already committed adultery with her in his heart. *Matthew 5:28*

(144) *May 24* You have heard that it was said, "Love your neighbor and hate your enemy." But I tell you: Love your enemies and pray for those who persecute you, that you may be sons of your Father in heaven. He causes his sun to rise on the evil and the good, and sends rain on the righteous and the unrighteous. *Matthew 5:43-45*

(145) *May 25* And when you pray, do not be like the hypocrites, for they love to pray standing in the synagogues and on the street corners to be seen by men. I tell you the truth, they have received their reward in full. But when you pray, go into your room, close the door and pray to your Father, who is unseen. Then your Father, who sees what is done in secret, will reward you. *Matthew 6:5,6*

(146) *May 26* For if you forgive men when they sin against you, your heavenly Father will also forgive you. *Matthew 6:14*

(147) *May 27* For where your treasure is, there your heart will be also. *Matthew 6:21*

(148) *May 28* No one can serve two masters. Either he will hate the one and love the other, or he will be devoted to the one and despise the other. You cannot serve both God and Money. *Matthew 6:24*

(149) *May 29* So do not worry, saying, "What shall we eat?" or "What shall we drink?" or "What shall we wear?" For the pagans run after all these things, and your heavenly Father knows that you need them. But seek first his kingdom and his righteousness, and all these things will be given to you as well. *Matthew 6:31-33*

(150) *May 30* Ask and it will be given to you; seek and you will find; knock and the door will be opened to you. For everyone who asks receives; he who seeks finds; and to him who knocks, the door will be opened. *Matthew 7:7,8*

(151) *May 31* So in everything, do to others what you would have them do to you, for this sums up the Law and the Prophets. *Matthew 7:12*

(152) *June 1* Enter through the narrow gate. For wide is the gate and broad is the road that leads to destruction, and many enter through it. But small is the gate and narrow the road that leads to life, and only a few find it. *Matthew 7:13,14*

(153) *June 2* Not everyone who says to me, "Lord, Lord," will enter the kingdom of heaven, but only he who does the will of my Father who is in heaven. *Matthew 7:21*

(154) *June 3* Whoever acknowledges me before men, I will also acknowledge

DATE MEMORIZED

him before my Father in heaven. But whoever disowns me before men, I will disown him before my Father in heaven. *Matthew 10:32,33*

(155) *June 4* Come to me, all you who are weary and burdened, and I will give you rest. *Matthew 11:28*

(156) *June 5* Take my yoke upon you and learn from me, for I am gentle and humble in heart, and you will find rest for your souls. For my yoke is easy and my burden is light. *Matthew 11:29,30*

(157) *June 6* But I tell you that men will have to give account on the day of judgment for every careless word they have spoken. *Matthew 12:36*

(158) *June 7* Then Jesus said to his disciples, "If anyone would come after me, he must deny himself and take up his cross and follow me. For whoever wants to save his life will lose it, but whoever loses his life for me will find it." *Matthew 16:24,25*

(159) *June 8* He called a little child and had him stand among them. And he said: "I tell you the truth, unless you change and become like little children, you will never enter the kingdom of heaven. *Matthew 18:2,3*

(160) *June 9* I tell you the truth, whatever you bind on earth will be bound in heaven, and whatever you loose on earth will be loosed in heaven. Again, I tell you that if two of you on earth agree about anything you ask for, it will be done for you by my Father in heaven. For where two or three come together in my name, there am I with them. *Matthew 18:18-20*

(161) *June 10* So the last will be first, and the first will be last. *Matthew 20:16*

(162) *June 11* The Son of Man did not come to be served, but to serve, and to give his life as a ransom for many. *Matthew 20:28*

(163) *June 12* If you believe, you will receive whatever you ask for in prayer. *Matthew 21:22*

(164) *June 13* Many are invited, but few are chosen. *Matthew 22:14*

(165) *June 14* Jesus replied: "'Love the Lord your God with all your heart and with all your soul and with all your mind.' This is the first and greatest commandment. And the second is like it: 'Love your neighbor as yourself.' " *Matthew 22:37-39*

(166) *June 15* Heaven and earth will pass away, but my words will never pass away. *Matthew 24:35*

(167) *June 16* Therefore go and make disciples of all nations, baptizing them in the name of the Father and of the Son and of the Holy Spirit, and teaching them to obey everything I have commanded you. And surely I am with you always, to the very end of the age. *Matthew 28:19,20*

(168) *June 17* Then he called the crowd to him along with his disciples and said: "If anyone would come after me, he must deny himself and take up his cross and follow me. For whoever wants to save his life will lose it, but whoever loses his life for me and for the gospel will save it. What good is it for a man to gain the whole world, yet forfeit his soul?" *Mark 8:34-36*

(169) *June 18* "If you can?" said Jesus. "Everything is possible for him who believes." *Mark 9:23*

(170) *June 19* Whoever wants to be first must be slave of all. For even the Son of Man did not come to be served, but to serve, and to give his life as a ransom for many. *Mark 10:44,45*

(171) *June 20* "Have faith in God," Jesus answered. "I tell you the truth, if anyone says to this mountain, 'Go, throw yourself into the sea,' and does not doubt in his heart but believes that what he says will happen, it will be done for him." *Mark 11:22,23*

(172) *June 21* Therefore I tell you, whatever you ask for in prayer, believe that you have received it, and it will be yours. *Mark 11:24*

(173) *June 22* He said to them, "Go into all the world and preach the good news to all creation." *Mark 16:15*

(174) *June 23* The Spirit of the Lord is on me, because he has anointed me to preach good news to the poor. He has sent me to proclaim freedom for the prisoners and recovery of sight for the blind, to release the oppressed, to proclaim the year of the Lord's favor. *Luke 4:18,19*

(175) *June 24* Which is easier: to say, "Your sins are forgiven," or to say, "Get up and walk"? *Luke 5:23*

(176) *June 25* Do to others as you would have them do to you. *Luke 6:31*

(177) *June 26* Give, and it will be given to you. A good measure, pressed down, shaken together and running over,

DATE MEMORIZED

will be poured into your lap. For with the measure you use, it will be measured to you. *Luke 6:38*

(178) *June 27* The good man brings good things out of the good stored up in his heart, and the evil man brings evil things out of the evil stored up in his heart. For out of the overflow of his heart his mouth speaks. *Luke 6:45*

(179) *June 28* He told them, "The harvest is plentiful, but the workers are few. Ask the Lord of the harvest, therefore, to send out workers into his harvest field." *Luke 10:2*

(180) *June 29* Then he said to them, "Watch out! Be on your guard against all kinds of greed; a man's life does not consist in the abundance of his possessions." *Luke 12:15*

(181) *June 30* Then Jesus said to his disciples: "Therefore I tell you, do not worry about your life, what you will eat; or about your body, what you will wear. Life is more than food, and the body more than clothes." *Luke 12:22,23*

(182) *July 1* But seek his kingdom, and these things will be given to you as well. *Luke 12:31*

(183) *July 2* In the same way, any of you who does not give up everything he has cannot be my disciple. *Luke 14:33*

(184) *July 3* In the beginning was the Word, and the Word was with God, and the Word was God. *John 1:1*

(185) *July 4* Yet to all who received him, to those who believed in his name, he gave the right to become children of God. *John 1:12*

(186) *July 5* In reply Jesus declared, "I tell you the truth, no one can see the kingdom of God unless he is born again." *John 3:3*

(187) *July 6* For God so loved the world that he gave his one and only Son, that whoever believes in him shall not perish but have eternal life. For God did not send his Son into the world to condemn the world, but to save the world through him. *John 3:16,17*

(188) *July 7* I tell you the truth, whoever hears my word and believes him who sent me has eternal life and will not be condemned; he has crossed over from death to life. *John 5:24*

(189) *July 8* Then Jesus declared, "I am the bread of life. He who comes to me will never go hungry, and he who believes in me will never be thirsty." *John 6:35*

(190) *July 9* Then you will know the truth, and the truth will set you free. *John 8:32*

(191) *July 10* So if the Son sets you free, you will be free indeed. *John 8:36*

(192) *July 11* The thief comes only to steal and kill and destroy; I have come that they may have life, and have it to the full. *John 10:10*

(193) *July 12* I give them eternal life, and they shall never perish; no one can snatch them out of my hand. My Father, who has given them to me, is greater than all; no one can snatch them out of my Father's hand. I and the Father are one. *John 10:28-30*

(194) *July 13* Jesus said to her, "I am the resurrection and the life. He who believes in me will live, even though he dies; and whoever lives and believes in me will never die. Do you believe this?" *John 11:25,26*

(195) *July 14* Whoever serves me must follow me; and where I am, my servant also will be. My Father will honor the one who serves me. *John 12:26*

(196) *July 15* By this all men will know that you are my disciples, if you love one another. *John 13:35*

(197) *July 16* Do not let your hearts be troubled. Trust in God; trust also in me. In my Father's house are many rooms; if it were not so, I would have told you. I am going there to prepare a place for you. And if I go and prepare a place for you, I will come back and take you to be with me that you also may be where I am. *John 14:1-3*

(198) *July 17* Jesus answered, "I am the way and the truth and the life. No one comes to the Father except through me." *John 14:6*

(199) *July 18* I tell you the truth, anyone who has faith in me will do what I have been doing. He will do even greater things than these, because I am going to the Father. *John 14:12*

(200) *July 19* If you love me, you will obey what I command. And I will ask the Father, and he will give you another Counselor to be with you forever. *John 14:15,16*

DATE MEMORIZED

(201) *July 20* Whoever has my commands and obeys them, he is the one who loves me. He who loves me will be loved by my Father, and I too will love him and show myself to him. *John 14:21*

(202) *July 21* Peace I leave with you; my peace I give you. I do not give to you as the world gives. Do not let your hearts be troubled and do not be afraid. *John 14:27*

(203) *July 22* I am the vine; you are the branches. If a man remains in me and I in him, he will bear much fruit; apart from me you can do nothing. If anyone does not remain in me, he is like a branch that is thrown away and withers; such branches are picked up, thrown into the fire and burned. If you remain in me and my words remain in you, ask whatever you wish, and it will be given you. This is to my Father's glory, that you bear much fruit, showing yourselves to be my disciples. *John 15:5-8*

(204) *July 23* My command is this: Love each other as I have loved you. Greater love has no one than this, that he lay down his life for his friends. You are my friends if you do what I command. *John 15:12-14*

(205) *July 24* You did not choose me, but I chose you and appointed you to go and bear fruit—fruit that will last. Then the Father will give you whatever you ask in my name. *John 15:16*

(206) *July 25* But when he, the Spirit of truth, comes, he will guide you into all truth. He will not speak on his own; he will speak only what he hears, and he will tell you what is yet to come. *John 16:13*

(207) *July 26* I have told you these things, so that in me you may have peace. In this world you will have trouble. But take heart! I have overcome the world. *John 16:33*

(208) *July 27* But you will receive power when the Holy Spirit comes on you; and you will be my witnesses in Jerusalem, and in all Judea and Samaria, and to the ends of the earth. *Acts 1:8*

(209) *July 28* Repent, then, and turn to God, so that your sins may be wiped out, that times of refreshing may come from the Lord. *Acts 3:19*

(210) *July 29* Salvation is found in no one else, for there is no other name under heaven given to men by which we must be saved. *Acts 4:12*

(211) *July 30* Now the Bereans were of more noble character than the Thessalonians, for they received the message with great eagerness and examined the Scriptures every day to see if what Paul said was true. *Acts 17:11*

(212) *July 31* The God who made the world and everything in it is the Lord of heaven and earth and does not live in temples built by hands. And he is not served by human hands, as if he needed anything, because he himself gives all men life and breath and everything else. *Acts 17:24,25*

(213) *August 1* God did this so that men would seek him and perhaps reach out for him and find him, though he is not far from each one of us. "For in him we live and move and have our being." As some of your own poets have said, "We are his offspring." *Acts 17:27,28*

(214) *August 2* I am not ashamed of the gospel, because it is the power of God for the salvation of everyone who believes: first for the Jew, then for the Gentile. *Romans 1:16*

(215) *August 3* Although they claimed to be wise, they became fools. *Romans 1:22*

(216) *August 4* As it is written: "There is no one righteous, not even one." *Romans 3:10*

(217) *August 5* For all have sinned and fall short of the glory of God. *Romans 3:23*

(218) *August 6* We also rejoice in our sufferings, because we know that suffering produces perseverance; perseverance, character; and character, hope. *Romans 5:3,4*

(219) *August 7* But God demonstrates his own love for us in this: While we were still sinners, Christ died for us. *Romans 5:8*

(220) *August 8* For if, by the trespass of the one man, death reigned through that one man, how much more will those who receive God's abundant provision of grace and of the gift of righteousness reign in life through the one man, Jesus Christ. *Romans 5:17*

(221) *August 9* The law was added so that the trespass might increase. But where sin increased, grace increased all the more. *Romans 5:20*

(222) *August 10* For sin shall not be your master, because you are not under law, but under grace. *Romans 6:14*

DATE MEMORIZED

(223) *August 11* For the wages of sin is death, but the gift of God is eternal life in Christ Jesus our Lord. *Romans 6:23*

(224) *August 12* Therefore, there is now no condemnation for those who are in Christ Jesus. *Romans 8:1*

(225) *August 13* Those who are led by the Spirit of God are sons of God. For you did not receive a spirit that makes you a slave again to fear, but you received the Spirit of sonship. And by him we cry, *"Abba,* Father." The Spirit himself testifies with our spirit that we are God's children. *Romans 8:14,16*

(226) *August 14* Now if we are children, then we are heirs—heirs of God and co-heirs with Christ, if indeed we share in his sufferings in order that we may also share in his glory. I consider that our present sufferings are not worth comparing with the glory that will be revealed in us. *Romans 8:17,18*

(227) *August 15* In the same way, the Spirit helps us in our weakness. We do not know what we ought to pray for, but the Spirit himself intercedes for us with groans that words cannot express. And he who searches our hearts knows the mind of the Spirit, because the Spirit intercedes for the saints in accordance with God's will. *Romans 8:26,27*

(228) *August 16* And we know that in all things God works for the good of those who love him, who have been called according to his purpose. *Romans 8:28*

(229) *August 17* What, then, shall we say in response to this? If God is for us, who can be against us? He who did not spare his own Son, but gave him up for us all—how will he not also, along with him, graciously give us all things? *Romans 8:31,32*

(230) *August 18* No, in all these things we are more than conquerors through him who loved us. For I am convinced that neither death nor life, neither angels nor demons, neither the present nor the future, nor any powers, neither height nor depth, nor anything else in all creation, will be able to separate us from the love of God that is in Christ Jesus our Lord. *Romans 8:37-39*

(231) *August 19* If you confess with your mouth, "Jesus is Lord," and believe in your heart that God raised him from the dead, you will be saved. For it is with your heart that you believe and are justified, and it is with your mouth that you confess and are saved. *Romans 10:9,10*

(232) *August 20* Consequently, faith comes from hearing the message, and the message is heard through the word of Christ. *Romans 10:17*

(233) *August 21* Therefore, I urge you, brothers, in view of God's mercy, to offer your bodies as living sacrifices, holy and pleasing to God—this is your spiritual act of worship. Do not conform any longer to the pattern of this world, but be transformed by the renewing of your mind. Then you will be able to test and approve what God's will is—his good, pleasing and perfect will. *Romans 12:1,2*

(234) *August 22* For by the grace given me I say to every one of you: Do not think of yourself more highly than you ought, but rather think of yourself with sober judgment, in accordance with the measure of faith God has given you. Just as each of us has one body with many members, and these members do not all have the same function, so in Christ we who are many form one body, and each member belongs to all the others. *Romans 12:3-5*

(235) *August 23* Let no debt remain outstanding, except the continuing debt to love one another, for he who loves his fellowman has fulfilled the law. *Romans 13:8*

(236) *August 24* It is written: "As surely as I live," says the Lord, "every knee will bow before me; every tongue will confess to God." So then, each of us will give an account of himself to God. Therefore let us stop passing judgment on one another. Instead, make up your mind not to put any stumbling block or obstacle in your brother's way. *Romans 14:11-13*

(237) *August 25* For everything that was written in the past was written to teach us, so that through endurance and the encouragement of the Scriptures we might have hope. *Romans 15:4*

(238) *August 26* For the message of the cross is foolishness to those who are perishing, but to us who are being saved it is the power of God. *1 Corinthians 1:18*

(239) *August 27* For the foolishness of God is wiser than man's wisdom, and the weakness of God is stronger than man's strength. *1 Corinthians 1:25*

(240) *August 28* However, as it is written: "No eye has seen, no ear has heard, no mind has conceived what God has prepared for those who love him." *1 Corinthians 2:9*

DATE MEMORIZED

(241) *August 29* Don't you know that you yourselves are God's temple and that God's Spirit lives in you? *1 Corinthians 3:16*

(242) *August 30* Do you not know that the wicked will not inherit the kingdom of God? Do not be deceived: Neither the sexually immoral nor idolaters nor adulterers nor male prostitutes nor homosexual offenders nor thieves nor the greedy nor drunkards nor slanderers nor swindlers will inherit the kingdom of God. *1 Corinthians 6:9,10*

(243) *August 31* No temptation has seized you except what is common to man. And God is faithful; he will not let you be tempted beyond what you can bear. But when you are tempted, he will also provide a way out so that you can stand up under it. *1 Corinthians 10:13*

(244) *September 1* Love is patient, love is kind. It does not envy, it does not boast, it is not proud. It is not rude, it is not self-seeking, it is not easily angered, it keeps no record of wrongs. Love does not delight in evil but rejoices with the truth. It always protects, always trusts, always hopes, always perseveres. *1 Corinthians 13:4-7*

(245) *September 2* Now we see but a poor reflection as in a mirror; then we shall see face to face. Now I know in part; then I shall know fully, even as I am fully known. And now these three remain: faith, hope and love. But the greatest of these is love. *1 Corinthians 13:12,13*

(246) *September 3* And just as we have borne the likeness of the earthly man, so shall we bear the likeness of the man from heaven. *1 Corinthians 15:49*

(247) *September 4* "Where, O death, is your victory? Where, O death, is your sting?" The sting of death is sin, and the power of sin is the law. But thanks be to God! He gives us the victory through our Lord Jesus Christ. Therefore, my dear brothers, stand firm. Let nothing move you. Always give yourselves fully to the work of the Lord, because you know that your labor in the Lord is not in vain. *1 Corinthians 15:55-58*

(248) *September 5* Praise be to the God and Father of our Lord Jesus Christ, the Father of compassion and the God of all comfort, who comforts us in all our troubles, so that we can comfort those in any trouble with the comfort we ourselves have received from God. For just as the sufferings of Christ flow over into our lives, so also through Christ our comfort overflows. *2 Corinthians 1:3-5*

(249) *September 6* He anointed us, set his seal of ownership on us, and put his Spirit in our hearts as a deposit, guaranteeing what is to come. *2 Corinthians 1:21,22*

(250) *September 7* We are hard pressed on every side, but not crushed; perplexed, but not in despair; persecuted, but not abandoned; struck down, but not destroyed. *2 Corinthians 4:8,9*

(251) *September 8* For our light and momentary troubles are achieving for us an eternal glory that far outweighs them all. *2 Corinthians 4:17*

(252) *September 9* So we fix our eyes not on what is seen, but on what is unseen. For what is seen is temporary, but what is unseen is eternal. *2 Corinthians 4:18*

(253) *September 10* For we must all appear before the judgment seat of Christ, that each one may receive what is due him for the things done while in the body, whether good or bad. *2 Corinthians 5:10*

(254) *September 11* Therefore, if anyone is in Christ, he is a new creation; the old has gone, the new has come! *2 Corinthians 5:17*

(255) *September 12* God made him who had no sin to be sin for us, so that in him we might become the righteousness of God. *2 Corinthians 5:21*

(256) *September 13* Do not be yoked together with unbelievers. For what do righteousness and wickedness have in common? Or what fellowship can light have with darkness? *2 Corinthians 6:14*

(257) *September 14* Each man should give what he has decided in his heart to give, not reluctantly or under compulsion, for God loves a cheerful giver. *2 Corinthians 9:7*

(258) *September 15* For though we live in the world, we do not wage war as the world does. The weapons we fight with are not the weapons of the world. On the contrary, they have divine power to demolish strongholds. We demolish arguments and every pretension that sets itself up against the knowledge of God, and we take captive every thought to make it obedient to Christ. *2 Corinthians 10:3-5*

(259) *September 16* To keep me from becoming conceited because of these surpassingly great revelations, there was given me a thorn in my flesh, a messenger of Satan, to torment me. Three times I pleaded with the Lord to take it away from me. But he said to me, "My grace is sufficient for you,

DATE MEMORIZED

for my power is made perfect in weakness." Therefore I will boast all the more gladly about my weaknesses, so that Christ's power may rest on me. That is why, for Christ's sake, I delight in weaknesses, in insults, in hardships, in persecutions, in difficulties. For when I am weak, then I am strong. *2 Corinthians 12:7-10*

(260) *September 17* I have been crucified with Christ and I no longer live, but Christ lives in me. The life I live in the body, I live by faith in the Son of God, who loved me and gave himself for me. *Galatians 2:20*

(261) *September 18* So also, when we were children, we were in slavery under the basic principles of the world. But when the time had fully come, God sent his Son, born of a woman, born under law, to redeem those under law, that we might receive the full rights of sons. Because you are sons, God sent the Spirit of his Son into our hearts, the Spirit who calls out, *"Abba, Father."* So you are no longer a slave, but a son; and since you are a son, God has made you also an heir. *Galatians 4:3-7*

(262) *September 19* It is for freedom that Christ has set us free. Stand firm, then, and do not let yourselves be burdened again by a yoke of slavery. *Galatians 5:1*

(263) *September 20* So I say, live by the Spirit, and you will not gratify the desires of the sinful nature. For the sinful nature desires what is contrary to the Spirit, and the Spirit what is contrary to the sinful nature. They are in conflict with each other, so that you do not do what you want. *Galatians 5:16,17*

(264) *September 21* But the fruit of the Spirit is love, joy, peace, patience, kindness, goodness, faithfulness, gentleness and self-control. Against such things there is no law. *Galatians 5:22,23*

(265) *September 22* Do not be deceived: God cannot be mocked. A man reaps what he sows. The one who sows to please his sinful nature, from that nature will reap destruction; the one who sows to please the Spirit, from the Spirit will reap eternal life. Let us not become weary in doing good, for at the proper time we will reap a harvest if we do not give up. *Galatians 6:7-9*

(266) *September 23* For it is by grace you have been saved, through faith—and this not from yourselves, it is the gift of God—not by works, so that no one can boast. *Ephesians 2:8,9*

(267) *September 24* Be completely humble and gentle; be patient, bearing with one another in love. Make every effort to keep the unity of the Spirit through the bond of peace. *Ephesians 4:2,3*

(268) *September 25* One Lord, one faith, one baptism. *Ephesians 4:5*

(269) *September 26* Prepare God's people for works of service, so that the body of Christ may be built up. *Ephesians 4:12*

(270) *September 27* Put on the new self, created to be like God in true righteousness and holiness. *Ephesians 4:24*

(271) *September 28* In your anger do not sin: Do not let the sun go down while you are still angry, and do not give the devil a foothold. *Ephesians 4:26,27*

(272) *September 29* Be kind and compassionate to one another, forgiving each other, just as in Christ God forgave you. *Ephesians 4:32*

(273) *September 30* Do not get drunk on wine, which leads to debauchery. Instead, be filled with the Spirit. *Ephesians 5:18*

(274) *October 1* Wives, submit to your husbands as to the Lord. *Ephesians 5:22*

(275) *October 2* Husbands, love your wives, just as Christ loved the church and gave himself up for her. *Ephesians 5:25*

(276) *October 3* For this reason a man will leave his father and mother and be united to his wife, and the two will become one flesh. *Ephesians 5:31*

(277) *October 4* Children, obey your parents in the Lord, for this is right. "Honor your father and mother"—which is the first commandment with a promise—"that it may go well with you and that you may enjoy long life on the earth." *Ephesians 6:1-3*

(278) *October 5* Fathers, do not exasperate your children; instead, bring them up in the training and instruction of the Lord. *Ephesians 6:4*

(279) *October 6* Finally, be strong in the Lord and in his mighty power. Put on the full armor of God so that you can take your stand against the devil's schemes. For our struggle is not against flesh and blood, but against the rulers, against the authorities, against the powers of this dark world and against the spiritual forces of evil in the heavenly realms. Therefore put on the full armor of God, so that when the day of evil comes,

DATE MEMORIZED

you may be able to stand your ground, and after you have done everything, to stand. *Ephesians 6:10-13*

(280) *October 7* For to me, to live is Christ and to die is gain. *Philippians 1:21*

(281) *October 8* Do nothing out of selfish ambition or vain conceit, but in humility consider others better than yourselves. Each of you should look not only to your own interests, but also to the interests of others. *Philippians 2:3,4*

(282) *October 9* Your attitude should be the same as that of Christ Jesus: Who, being in very nature God, did not consider equality with God something to be grasped, but made himself nothing, taking the very nature of a servant, being made in human likeness. And being found in appearance as a man, he humbled himself and became obedient to death—even death on a cross! *Philippians 2:5-8*

(283) *October 10* Therefore God exalted him to the highest place and gave him the name that is above every name, that at the name of Jesus every knee should bow, in heaven and on earth and under the earth, and every tongue confess that Jesus Christ is Lord, to the glory of God the Father. *Philippians 2:9-11*

(284) *October 11* Brothers, I do not consider myself yet to have taken hold of it. But one thing I do: Forgetting what is behind and straining toward what is ahead, I press on toward the goal to win the prize for which God has called me heavenward in Christ Jesus. *Philippians 3:13,14*

(285) *October 12* Do not be anxious about anything, but in everything, by prayer and petition, with thanksgiving, present your requests to God. And the peace of God, which transcends all understanding, will guard your hearts and your minds in Christ Jesus. *Philippians 4:6,7*

(286) *October 13* I am not saying this because I am in need, for I have learned to be content whatever the circumstances. I know what it is to be in need, and I know what it is to have plenty. I have learned the secret of being content in any and every situation, whether well fed or hungry, whether living in plenty or in want. I can do everything through him who gives me strength. *Philippians 4:11-13*

(287) *October 14* And my God will meet all your needs according to his glorious riches in Christ Jesus. *Philippians 4:19*

(288) *October 15* He is the image of the invisible God, the firstborn over all creation. For by him all things were created: things in heaven and on earth, visible and invisible, whether thrones or powers or rulers or authorities; all things were created by him and for him. He is before all things, and in him all things hold together. And he is the head of the body, the church; he is the beginning and the firstborn from among the dead, so that in everything he might have the supremacy. For God was pleased to have all his fullness dwell in him. *Colossians 1:15-19*

(289) *October 16* See to it that no one takes you captive through hollow and deceptive philosophy, which depends on human tradition and the basic principles of this world rather than on Christ. *Colossians 2:8*

(290) *October 17* Let the word of Christ dwell in you richly as you teach and admonish one another with all wisdom, and as you sing psalms, hymns and spiritual songs with gratitude in your hearts to God. *Colossians 3:16*

(291) *October 18* Children, obey your parents in everything, for this pleases the Lord. *Colossians 3:20*

(292) *October 19* Whatever you do, work at it with all your heart, as working for the Lord, not for men. *Colossians 3:23*

(293) *October 20* Brothers, we do not want you to be ignorant about those who fall asleep, or to grieve like the rest of men, who have no hope. We believe that Jesus died and rose again and so we believe that God will bring with Jesus those who have fallen asleep in him. *1 Thessalonians 4:13,14*

(294) *October 21* For the Lord himself will come down from heaven, with a loud command, with the voice of the archangel and with the trumpet call of God, and the dead in Christ will rise first. After that, we who are still alive and are left will be caught up together with them in the clouds to meet the Lord in the air. And so we will be with the Lord forever. *1 Thessalonians 4:16,17*

(295) *October 22* Be joyful always; pray continually; give thanks in all circumstances, for this is God's will for you in Christ Jesus. *1 Thessalonians 5:16-18*

(296) *October 23* But the Lord is faithful, and he will strengthen and protect you from the evil one. *2 Thessalonians 3:3*

(297) *October 24* For even when we were with you, we gave you this rule: "If a

DATE MEMORIZED

man will not work, he shall not eat." *2 Thessalonians 3:10*

(298) *October 25* For there is one God and one mediator between God and men, the man Christ Jesus. *1 Timothy 2:5*

(299) *October 26* Beyond all question, the mystery of godliness is great: He appeared in a body, was vindicated by the Spirit, was seen by angels, was preached among the nations, was believed on in the world, was taken up in glory. *1 Timothy 3:16*

(300) *October 27* For physical training is of some value, but godliness has value for all things, holding promise for both the present life and the life to come. *1 Timothy 4:8*

(301) *October 28* Don't let anyone look down on you because you are young, but set an example for the believers in speech, in life, in love, in faith and in purity. *1 Timothy 4:12*

(302) *October 29* But godliness with contentment is great gain. For we brought nothing into the world, and we can take nothing out of it. *1 Timothy 6:6,7*

(303) *October 30* For the love of money is a root of all kinds of evil. Some people, eager for money, have wandered from the faith and pierced themselves with many griefs. *1 Timothy 6:10*

(304) *October 31* For God did not give us a spirit of timidity, but a spirit of power, of love and of self-discipline. *2 Timothy 1:7*

(305) *November 1* That is why I am suffering as I am. Yet I am not ashamed, because I know whom I have believed, and am convinced that he is able to guard what I have entrusted to him for that day. *2 Timothy 1:12*

(306) *November 2* And the things you have heard me say in the presence of many witnesses entrust to reliable men who will also be qualified to teach others. Endure hardship with us like a good soldier of Christ Jesus. No one serving as a soldier gets involved in civilian affairs—he wants to please his commanding officer. *2 Timothy 2:2-4*

(307) *November 3* Do your best to present yourself to God as one approved, a workman who does not need to be ashamed and who correctly handles the word of truth. *2 Timothy 2:15*

(308) *November 4* Nevertheless, God's solid foundation stands firm, sealed with this inscription: "The Lord knows those who are his," and, "Everyone who confesses the name of the Lord must turn away from wickedness." *2 Timothy 2:19*

(309) *November 5* All Scripture is God-breathed and is useful for teaching, rebuking, correcting and training in righteousness, so that the man of God may be thoroughly equipped for every good work. *2 Timothy 3:16,17*

(310) *November 6* Preach the Word; be prepared in season and out of season; correct, rebuke and encourage—with great patience and careful instruction. *2 Timothy 4:2*

(311) *November 7* He saved us, not because of righteous things we had done, but because of his mercy. He saved us through the washing of rebirth and renewal by the Holy Spirit. *Titus 3:5*

(312) *November 8* I pray that you may be active in sharing your faith, so that you will have a full understanding of every good thing we have in Christ. *Philemon 6*

(313) *November 9* Because he himself suffered when he was tempted, he is able to help those who are being tempted. *Hebrews 2:18*

(314) *November 10* For the word of God is living and active. Sharper than any double-edged sword, it penetrates even to dividing soul and spirit, joints and marrow; it judges the thoughts and attitudes of the heart. Nothing in all creation is hidden from God's sight. Everything is uncovered and laid bare before the eyes of him to whom we must give account. *Hebrews 4:12,13*

(315) *November 11* Let us then approach the throne of grace with confidence, so that we may receive mercy and find grace to help us in our time of need. *Hebrews 4:16*

(316) *November 12* In fact, the law requires that nearly everything be cleansed with blood, and without the shedding of blood there is no forgiveness. *Hebrews 9:22*

(317) *November 13* Just as man is destined to die once, and after that to face judgment, so Christ was sacrificed once to take away the sins of many people; and he will appear a second time, not to bear sin, but to bring salvation to those who are waiting for him. *Hebrews 9:27,28*

(318) *November 14* Let us not give up meeting together, as some are in the habit of doing, but let us encourage one another—and all the more as you see the Day approaching. *Hebrews 10:25*

DATE MEMORIZED

(319) *November 15* Now faith is being sure of what we hope for and certain of what we do not see. *Hebrews 11:1*

(320) *November 16* And without faith it is impossible to please God, because anyone who comes to him must believe that he exists and that he rewards those who earnestly seek him. *Hebrews 11:6*

(321) *November 17* In your struggle against sin, you have not yet resisted to the point of shedding your blood. *Hebrews 12:4*

(322) *November 18* And you have forgotten that word of encouragement that addresses you as sons: "My son, do not make light of the Lord's discipline, and do not lose heart when he rebukes you, because the Lord disciplines those he loves, and he punishes everyone he accepts as a son." *Hebrews 12:5,6*

(323) *November 19* Our fathers disciplined us for a little while as they thought best; but God disciplines us for our good, that we may share in his holiness. No discipline seems pleasant at the time, but painful. Later on, however, it produces a harvest of righteousness and peace for those who have been trained by it. *Hebrews 12:10,11*

(324) *November 20* Keep your lives free from the love of money and be content with what you have, because God has said, "Never will I leave you; never will I forsake you." *Hebrews 13:5*

(325) *November 21* So we say with confidence, "The Lord is my helper; I will not be afraid. What can man do to me?" *Hebrews 13:6*

(326) *November 22* Jesus Christ is the same yesterday and today and forever. *Hebrews 13:8*

(327) *November 23* Consider it pure joy, my brothers, whenever you face trials of many kinds, because you know that the testing of your faith develops perseverance. Perseverance must finish its work so that you may be mature and complete, not lacking anything. *James 1:2-4*

(328) *November 24* If any of you lacks wisdom, he should ask God, who gives generously to all without finding fault, and it will be given to him. But when he asks, he must believe and not doubt, because he who doubts is like a wave of the sea, blown and tossed by the wind. *James 1:5,6*

(329) *November 25* Blessed is the man who perseveres under trial, because when he has stood the test, he will receive the crown of life that God has promised to those who love him. When tempted, no one should say, "God is tempting me." For God cannot be tempted by evil, nor does he tempt anyone; but each one is tempted when, by his own evil desire, he is dragged away and enticed. Then, after desire has conceived, it gives birth to sin; and sin, when it is full-grown, gives birth to death. *James 1:12-15*

(330) *November 26* Every good and perfect gift is from above, coming down from the Father of the heavenly lights, who does not change like shifting shadows. *James 1:17*

(331) *November 27* My dear brothers, take note of this: Everyone should be quick to listen, slow to speak and slow to become angry, for man's anger does not bring about the righteous life that God desires. *James 1:19,20*

(332) *November 28* But if you harbor bitter envy and selfish ambition in your hearts, do not boast about it or deny the truth. Such "wisdom" does not come down from heaven but is earthly, unspiritual, of the devil. For where you have envy and selfish ambition, there you find disorder and every evil practice. *James 3:14-16*

(333) *November 29* Submit yourselves, then, to God. Resist the devil, and he will flee from you. Come near to God and he will come near to you. *James 4:7,8*

(334) *November 30* Anyone, then, who knows the good he ought to do and doesn't do it, sins. *James 4:17*

(335) *December 1* Be patient, then, brothers, until the Lord's coming. See how the farmer waits for the land to yield its valuable crop and how patient he is for the autumn and spring rains. You too, be patient and stand firm, because the Lord's coming is near. *James 5:7,8*

(336) *December 2* Therefore confess your sins to each other and pray for each other so that you may be healed. The prayer of a righteous man is powerful and effective. *James 5:16*

(337) *December 3* But you are a chosen people, a royal priesthood, a holy nation, a people belonging to God, that you may declare the praises of him who called you out of darkness into his wonderful light. *1 Peter 2:9*

(338) *December 4* Wives, in the same way be submissive to your husbands so that, if any of them do not believe the word, they

DATE MEMORIZED

may be won over without words by the behavior of their wives, when they see the purity and reverence of your lives. Your beauty should not come from outward adornment, such as braided hair and the wearing of gold jewelry and fine clothes. Instead, it should be that of your inner self, the unfading beauty of a gentle and quiet spirit, which is of great worth in God's sight. For this is the way the holy women of the past who put their hope in God used to make themselves beautiful. They were submissive to their own husbands. *1 Peter 3:1-5*

(339) *December 5* Husbands, in the same way be considerate as you live with your wives, and treat them with respect as the weaker partner and as heirs with you of the gracious gift of life, so that nothing will hinder your prayers. *1 Peter 3:7*

(340) *December 6* But in your hearts set apart Christ as Lord. Always be prepared to give an answer to everyone who asks you to give the reason for the hope that you have. But do this with gentleness and respect. *1 Peter 3:15*

(341) *December 7* It is better, if it is God's will, to suffer for doing good than for doing evil. For Christ died for sins once for all, the righteous for the unrighteous, to bring you to God. He was put to death in the body but made alive by the Spirit. *1 Peter 3:17,18*

(342) *December 8* Above all, love each other deeply, because love covers over a multitude of sins. *1 Peter 4:8*

(343) *December 9* Dear friends, do not be surprised at the painful trial you are suffering, as though something strange were happening to you. But rejoice that you participate in the sufferings of Christ, so that you may be overjoyed when his glory is revealed. *1 Peter 4:12,13*

(344) *December 10* Cast all your anxiety on him because he cares for you. Be self-controlled and alert. Your enemy the devil prowls around like a roaring lion looking for someone to devour. Resist him, standing firm in the faith, because you know that your brothers throughout the world are undergoing the same kind of sufferings. *1 Peter 5:7-9*

(345) *December 11* For prophecy never had its origin in the will of man, but men spoke from God as they were carried along by the Holy Spirit. *2 Peter 1:21*

(346) *December 12* The Lord is not slow in keeping his promise, as some understand slowness. He is patient with you, not wanting anyone to perish, but everyone to come to repentance. *2 Peter 3:9*

(347) *December 13* If we confess our sins, he is faithful and just and will forgive us our sins and purify us from all unrighteousness. *1 John 1:9*

(348) *December 14* My dear children, I write this to you so that you will not sin. But if anybody does sin, we have one who speaks to the Father in our defense—Jesus Christ, the Righteous One. *1 John 2:1*

(349) *December 15* Do not love the world or anything in the world. If anyone loves the world, the love of the Father is not in him. For everything in the world—the cravings of sinful man, the lust of his eyes and the boasting of what he has and does—comes not from the Father but from the world. *1 John 2:15,16*

(350) *December 16* No one who is born of God will continue to sin, because God's seed remains in him; he cannot go on sinning, because he has been born of God. *1 John 3:9*

(351) *December 17* You, dear children, are from God and have overcome them, because the one who is in you is greater than the one who is in the world. *1 John 4:4*

(352) *December 18* Dear friends, let us love one another, for love comes from God. Everyone who loves has been born of God and knows God. *1 John 4:7*

(353) *December 19* Dear friends, since God so loved us, we also ought to love one another. No one has ever seen God; but if we love one another, God lives in us and his love is made complete in us. We know that we live in him and he in us, because he has given us of his Spirit. *1 John 4:11-13*

(354) *December 20* There is no fear in love. But perfect love drives out fear, because fear has to do with punishment. The one who fears is not made perfect in love. We love because he first loved us. *1 John 4:18,19*

(355) *December 21* If anyone says, "I love God," yet hates his brother, he is a liar. For anyone who does not love his brother, whom he has seen, cannot love God, whom he has not seen. And he has given us this command: Whoever loves God must also love his brother. *1 John 4:20,21*

(356) *December 22* I write these things to you who believe in the name of the Son of

DATE MEMORIZED

God so that you may know that you have eternal life. *1 John 5:13*

(357) *December 23* This is the confidence we have in approaching God: that if we ask anything according to his will, he hears us. And if we know that he hears us—whatever we ask—we know that we have what we asked of him. *1 John 5:14,15*

(358) *December 24* We know that anyone born of God does not continue to sin; the one who was born of God keeps him safe, and the evil one cannot harm him. *1 John 5:18*

(359) *December 25* Anyone who runs ahead and does not continue in the teaching of Christ does not have God; whoever continues in the teaching has both the Father and the Son. *2 John 9*

(360) *December 26* Dear friend, I pray that you may enjoy good health and that all may go well with you, even as your soul is getting along well. *3 John 2*

(361) *December 27* Keep yourselves in God's love as you wait for the mercy of our Lord Jesus Christ to bring you to eternal life. *Jude 21*

(362) *December 28* To him who is able to keep you from falling and to present you before his glorious presence without fault and with great joy—to the only God our Savior be glory, majesty, power and authority, through Jesus Christ our Lord, before all ages, now and forevermore! Amen. *Jude 24,25*

(363) *December 29* Here I am! I stand at the door and knock. If anyone hears my voice and opens the door, I will come in and eat with him, and he with me. *Revelation 3:20*

(364) *December 30* You are worthy, our Lord and God, to receive glory and honor and power, for you created all things, and by your will they were created and have their being. *Revelation 4:11*

(365) *December 31* He will wipe every tear from their eyes. There will be no more death or mourning or crying or pain, for the old order of things has passed away. *Revelation 21:4*

One-Year Daily Bible Reading Calendar

To completely guide the reader each year—once through the Old Testament and twice through the New Testament

JANUARY

Date	O.T.	N.T.
1	Genesis 1-2	Matthew 1
2	3-5	2
3	6-9	3
4	10-11	4
5	12-14	5
6	15-17	6
7	18-19	7
8	20-22	8
9	23-24	9
10	25-26	10
11	27-28	11
12	29-30	12
13	31-32	13:1-30
14	33-36	13:31-58
15	37-38	14
16	39-41	15
17	42-44	16
18	45-47	17
19	48-50	18
20	Exodus 1-2	19
21	3-4	20
22	5-7	21
23	8-10	22
24	11-13	23
25	14-15	24
26	16-18	25
27	19-21	26:1-35
28	22-24	26:36-75
29	25-28	27:1-31
30	29-31	27:32-66
31	32-34	28

FEBRUARY

Date	O.T.	N.T.
1	Exodus 35-37	Mark 1
2	38-40	2
3	Leviticus 1-3	3
4	4-6	4
5	7-9	5
6	10-12	6:1-29
7	13-14	6:30-56
8	15-18	7
9	19-21	8
10	22-24	9
11	25-27	10
12	Numbers 1-2	11
13	3-4	12
14	5-6	13
15	7-8	14:1-31
16	9-10	14:32-72
17	11-13	15
18	14-15	16
19	16-18	Luke 1:1-45
20	19-21	1:46-80
21	22-23	2
22	24-25	3
23	26-27	4
24	28-30	5
25	31-32	6
26	33-36	7
27	Deut. 1-2	8:1-25
28	3-4	8:26-56

MARCH

Date	O.T.	N.T.
1	Deut. 5-7	Luke 9:1-27
2	8-11	9:28-62
3	12-16	10
4	17-20	11
5	21-23	12:1-34
6	24-26	12:35-59
7	27-28	13
8	29-30	14
9	31-32	15
10	33-34	16
11	Joshua 1-2	17
12	3-5	18
13	6-8	19
14	9-10	20
15	11-14	21
16	15-17	22:1-38
17	18-21	22:39-71
18	22-24	23:1-25
19	Judges 1-2	23:26-56
20	3-5	24
21	6-8	John 1
22	9-11	2
23	12-15	3
24	16-18	4
25	19-21	5
26	Ruth 1-4	6
27	1 Samuel 1-3	7
28	4-7	8:1-30
29	8-10	8:31-59
30	11-13	9
31	14-15	10

APRIL

Date	O.T.	N.T.
1	1 Samuel 16-17	John 11:1-27
2	18-19	11:28-57
3	20-21	12
4	22-23	13
5	24-25	14
6	26-27	15
7	28-29	16
8	30-31	17
9	2 Samuel 1-2	18
10	3-5	19
11	6-8	20
12	9-12	21
13	13-14	Acts 1
14	15-17	2
15	18-20	3
16	21-22	4
17	23-24	5
18	1 Kings 1-2	6
19	3-6	7
20	7-8	8
21	9-11	9
22	12-13	10
23	14-15	11
24	16-18	12
25	19-20	13
26	21-22	14
27	2 Kings 1-3	15
28	4-5	16
29	6-8	17
30	9-10	18

MAY

Date	O.T.	N.T.
1	2 Kings 11-12	Acts 19
2	13-15	20
3	16-17	21
4	18-20	22
5	21-23	23
6	24-25	24
7	1 Chron. 1-2	25
8	3-5	26
9	6-7	27
10	8-10	28
11	11-12	Romans 1
12	13-16	2
13	17-20	3
14	21-23	4
15	24-25	5
16	26-27	6
17	28-29	7
18	2 Chron. 1-5	8
19	6-7	9
20	8-10	10
21	11-14	11
22	15-18	12
23	19-20	13
24	21-23	14
25	24-25	15
26	26-28	16
27	29-30	1 Cor. 1
28	31-33	2
29	34-36	3
30	Ezra 1-3	4
31	4-6	5

JUNE

Date	O.T.	N.T.
1	Ezra 7-8	1 Cor. 6
2	9-10	7
3	Nehemiah 1-3	8
4	4-6	9
5	7-8	10
6	9-11	11
7	12-13	12
8	Esther 1-2	13
9	3-5	14
10	6-8	15
11	9-10	16
12	Job 1-2	2 Cor. 1
13	3-7	2
14	8-10	3
15	11-14	4
16	15-17	5
17	18-21	6
18	22-24	7
19	25-28	8
20	29-31	9
21	32-34	10
22	35-37	11
23	38-39	12
24	40-42	13
25	Psalms 1-9	Galatians 1
26	10-18	2
27	19-24	3
28	25-30	4
29	31-35	5
30	36-41	6

One-Year Daily Bible Reading Calendar

To completely guide the reader each year—once through the Old Testament and twice through the New Testament

JULY

Date	O.T.	N.T.
1	Psalms 42-49	Ephesians 1
2	50-57	2
3	58-66	3
4	67-72	4
5	73-77	5
6	78-83	6
7	84-91	Philippians 1
8	92-102	2
9	103-106	3
10	107-110	4
11	111-118	Colossians 1
12	119	2
13	120-131	3
14	132-139	4
15	140-150	1 Thess. 1
16	Proverbs 1-4	2
17	5-9	3
18	10-12	4
19	13-15	5
20	16-19	2 Thess. 1
21	20-22	2
22	23-25	3
23	26-29	1 Timothy 1
24	30-31	2
25	Eccl. 1-4	3
26	5-8	4
27	9-12	5
28	Song 1-8	6
29	Isaiah 1-4	2 Timothy 1
30	5-7	2
31	8-12	3

AUGUST

Date	O.T.	N.T.
1	Isaiah 13-17	2 Timothy 4
2	18-21	Titus 1
3	22-24	2
4	25-27	3
5	28-31	Philemon 1
6	32-35	Hebrews 1
7	36-39	2
8	40-43	3
9	44-48	4
10	49-51	5
11	52-57	6
12	58-62	7
13	63-66	8
14	Jeremiah 1-3	9
15	4-6	10
16	7-10	11
17	11-15	12
18	16-20	13
19	21-24	James 1
20	25-28	2
21	29-31	3
22	32-35	4
23	36-39	5
24	40-45	1 Peter 1
25	46-49	2
26	50-52	3
27	Lam. 1-5	4
28	Ezekiel 1-6	5
29	7-10	2 Peter 1
30	11-15	2
31	16-19	3

SEPTEMBER

Date	O.T.	N.T.
1	Ezekiel 20-22	1 John 1
2	23-24	2
3	25-28	3
4	29-32	4
5	33-36	5
6	37-39	2 John 1
7	40-42	3 John 1
8	43-45	Jude 1
9	46-48	Revelation 1
10	Daniel 1-3	2
11	4-6	3
12	7-9	4
13	10-12	5
14	Hosea 1-6	6
15	7-14	7
16	Joel 1-3	8
17	Amos 1-5	9
18	6-9	10
19	Obadiah 1	11
20	Jonah 1-4	12
21	Micah 1-7	13
22	Nahum 1-3	14
23	Habakkuk 1-3	15
24	Zephaniah 1-3	16
25	Haggai 1-2	17
26	Zechariah 1-4	18
27	5-8	19
28	9-11	20
29	12-14	21
30	Malachi 1-4	22

OCTOBER

Date	N.T.
1	Matthew 1-4
2	5-7
3	8-11
4	12-13
5	14-16
6	17-20
7	21-22
8	23-25
9	26-28
10	Mark 1-3
11	4-5
12	6-7
13	8-9
14	10-11
15	12-13
16	14-16
17	Luke 1-2
18	3-4
19	5-7
20	8-9
21	10-11
22	12-13
23	14-16
24	17-18
25	19-20
26	21-22
27	23-24
28	John 1-2
29	3-5
30	6-7
31	8-10

NOVEMBER

Date	N.T.
1	John 11-12
2	13-14
3	15-17
4	18-19
5	20-21
6	Acts 1-3
7	4-5
8	6-7
9	8-9
10	10-12
11	13-15
12	16-18
13	19-20
14	21-23
15	24-26
16	27-28
17	Romans 1-3
18	4-5
19	6-8
20	9-11
21	12-14
22	15-16
23	1 Cor. 1-3
24	4-6
25	7-8
26	9-11
27	12-14
28	15-16
29	2 Cor. 1-4
30	5-9

DECEMBER

Date	N.T.
1	2 Cor. 10-13
2	Galatians 1-6
3	Ephesians 1-6
4	Philippians 1-4
5	Colossians 1-4
6	1 Thess. 1-5
7	2 Thess. 1-3
8	1 Timothy 1-6
9	2 Timothy 1-4
10	Titus 1-3
11	Philemon 1
12	Hebrews 1-2
13	3-4
14	5-7
15	8-10
16	11-13
17	James 1-5
18	1 Peter 1-5
19	2 Peter 1-3
20	1 John 1-5
21	2 John 1
22	3 John 1
23	Jude 1
24	Revelation 1-3
25	4-5
26	6-8
27	9-11
28	12-14
29	15-16
30	17-19
31	20-22

Personal Daily Bible Reading Calendar

Set your own pace. Just mark once diagonally through each box until you have read the entire Bible. For the second time through, mark diagonally the other way.

THE OLD TESTAMENT																				
Genesis	1	2	3	4	5	6	7	8	9	10	11	12	13	14	15	16	17	18	19	20
	21	22	23	24	25	26	27	28	29	30	31	32	33	34	35	36	37	38	39	40
	41	42	43	44	45	46	47	48	49	50										
Exodus	1	2	3	4	5	6	7	8	9	10	11	12	13	14	15	16	17	18	19	20
	21	22	23	24	25	26	27	28	29	30	31	32	33	34	35	36	37	38	39	40
Leviticus	1	2	3	4	5	6	7	8	9	10	11	12	13	14	15	16	17	18	19	20
	21	22	23	24	25	26	27													
Numbers	1	2	3	4	5	6	7	8	9	10	11	12	13	14	15	16	17	18	19	20
	21	22	23	24	25	26	27	28	29	30	31	32	33	34	35	36				
Deuteronomy	1	2	3	4	5	6	7	8	9	10	11	12	13	14	15	16	17	18	19	20
	21	22	23	24	25	26	27	28	29	30	31	32	33	34						
Joshua	1	2	3	4	5	6	7	8	9	10	11	12	13	14	15	16	17	18	19	20
	21	22	23	24																
Judges	1	2	3	4	5	6	7	8	9	10	11	12	13	14	15	16	17	18	19	20
	21																			
Ruth	1	2	3	4																
1 Samuel	1	2	3	4	5	6	7	8	9	10	11	12	13	14	15	16	17	18	19	20
	21	22	23	24	25	26	27	28	29	30	31									
2 Samuel	1	2	3	4	5	6	7	8	9	10	11	12	13	14	15	16	17	18	19	20
	21	22	23	24																
1 Kings	1	2	3	4	5	6	7	8	9	10	11	12	13	14	15	16	17	18	19	20
	21	22																		
2 Kings	1	2	3	4	5	6	7	8	9	10	11	12	13	14	15	16	17	18	19	20
	21	22	23	24	25															
1 Chronicles	1	2	3	4	5	6	7	8	9	10	11	12	13	14	15	16	17	18	19	20
	21	22	23	24	25	26	27	28	29											
2 Chronicles	1	2	3	4	5	6	7	8	9	10	11	12	13	14	15	16	17	18	19	20
	21	22	23	24	25	26	27	28	29	30	31	32	33	34	35	36				
Ezra	1	2	3	4	5	6	7	8	9	10										
Nehemiah	1	2	3	4	5	6	7	8	9	10	11	12	13							

Personal Daily Bible Reading Calendar

Esther	1	2	3	4	5	6	7	8	9	10										
Job	1	2	3	4	5	6	7	8	9	10	11	12	13	14	15	16	17	18	19	20
	21	22	23	24	25	26	27	28	29	30	31	32	33	34	35	36	37	38	39	40
	41	42																		
Psalms	1	2	3	4	5	6	7	8	9	10	11	12	13	14	15	16	17	18	19	20
	21	22	23	24	25	26	27	28	29	30	31	32	33	34	35	36	37	38	39	40
	41	42	43	44	45	46	47	48	49	50	51	52	53	54	55	56	57	58	59	60
	61	62	63	64	65	66	67	68	69	70	71	72	73	74	75	76	77	78	79	80
	81	82	83	84	85	86	87	88	89	90	91	92	93	94	95	96	97	98	99	100
	101	102	103	104	105	106	107	108	109	110	111	112	113	114	115	116	117	118	119	120
	121	122	123	124	125	126	127	128	129	130	131	132	133	134	135	136	137	138	139	140
	141	142	143	144	145	146	147	148	149	150										
Proverbs	1	2	3	4	5	6	7	8	9	10	11	12	13	14	15	16	17	18	19	20
	21	22	23	24	25	26	27	28	29	30	31									
Ecclesiastes	1	2	3	4	5	6	7	8	9	10	11	12								
Song of Songs	1	2	3	4	5	6	7	8												
Isaiah	1	2	3	4	5	6	7	8	9	10	11	12	13	14	15	16	17	18	19	20
	21	22	23	24	25	26	27	28	29	30	31	32	33	34	35	36	37	38	39	40
	41	42	43	44	45	46	47	48	49	50	51	52	53	54	55	56	57	58	59	60
	61	62	63	64	65	66														
Jeremiah	1	2	3	4	5	6	7	8	9	10	11	12	13	14	15	16	17	18	19	20
	21	22	23	24	25	26	27	28	29	30	31	32	33	34	35	36	37	38	39	40
	41	42	43	44	45	46	47	48	49	50	51	52								
Lamentations	1	2	3	4	5															
Ezekiel	1	2	3	4	5	6	7	8	9	10	11	12	13	14	15	16	17	18	19	20
	21	22	23	24	25	26	27	28	29	30	31	32	33	34	35	36	37	38	39	40
	41	42	43	44	45	46	47	48												
Daniel	1	2	3	4	5	6	7	8	9	10	11	12								
Hosea	1	2	3	4	5	6	7	8	9	10	11	12	13	14						
Joel	1	2	3																	
Amos	1	2	3	4	5	6	7	8	9											

Personal Daily Bible Reading Calendar

Obadiah	1													
Jonah	1	2	3	4										
Micah	1	2	3	4	5	6	7							
Nahum	1	2	3											
Habakkuk	1	2	3											
Zephaniah	1	2	3											
Haggai	1	2												
Zechariah	1	2	3	4	5	6	7	8	9	10	11	12	13	14
Malachi	1	2	3	4										

Personal Daily Bible Reading Calendar

THE NEW TESTAMENT

Matthew	1	2	3	4	5	6	7	8	9	10	11	12	13	14	15	16	17	18	19	20
	21	22	23	24	25	26	27	28												
Mark	1	2	3	4	5	6	7	8	9	10	11	12	13	14	15	16				
Luke	1	2	3	4	5	6	7	8	9	10	11	12	13	14	15	16	17	18	19	20
	21	22	23	24																
John	1	2	3	4	5	6	7	8	9	10	11	12	13	14	15	16	17	18	19	20
	21																			
Acts	1	2	3	4	5	6	7	8	9	10	11	12	13	14	15	16	17	18	19	20
	21	22	23	24	25	26	27	28												
Romans	1	2	3	4	5	6	7	8	9	10	11	12	13	14	15	16				
1 Corinthians	1	2	3	4	5	6	7	8	9	10	11	12	13	14	15	16				
2 Corinthians	1	2	3	4	5	6	7	8	9	10	11	12	13							
Galatians	1	2	3	4	5	6														
Ephesians	1	2	3	4	5	6														
Philippians	1	2	3	4																
Colossians	1	2	3	4																
1 Thessalonians	1	2	3	4	5															
2 Thessalonians	1	2	3																	
1 Timothy	1	2	3	4	5	6														
2 Timothy	1	2	3	4																
Titus	1	2	3																	
Philemon	1																			
Hebrews	1	2	3	4	5	6	7	8	9	10	11	12	13							
James	1	2	3	4	5															
1 Peter	1	2	3	4	5															
2 Peter	1	2	3																	
1 John	1	2	3	4	5															
2 John	1																			
3 John	1																			
Jude	1																			
Revelation	1	2	3	4	5	6	7	8	9	10	11	12	13	14	15	16	17	18	19	20
	21	22																		

SUBJECT GUIDE

The Subject Guide is not a "concordance" that shows where the Bible uses a certain word. Rather, it lists major subjects that may be of interest, along with the Bible *passages* (not single verses, usually) that speak to these subjects. Although we have tried to be comprehensive, any list of subjects must necessarily be restrictive. Page numbers are given in boldface type.

A

AARON — brother of and spokesman for Moses; became the first high priest
with Moses, Exodus 4:10—12:50—**p. 69**
made priest, Exodus 28—29—**p. 95**
his role with golden calf, Exodus 32—**p. 100**
budding of his staff, Numbers 17—**p. 171**
his death, Numbers 20:23-29—**p. 174**
ABEL — Adam's second son; murdered by his brother Cain
his life, Genesis 4:1-9—**p. 8**
example of faith, Hebrews 11:1-4—**p. 1356**
relationship to Christ, Hebrews 12:22-24—**p. 1358**
ABORTION — death of a fetus through a medical procedure
penalty for harming fetus, Exodus 21:22-25—**p. 88**
unborn life important to God, Psalm 139—**p. 699**
ABRAHAM — founder of the Jewish nation
called by God, Genesis 11:26—12:20—**p. 15**
his life, Genesis 11:26—25:11—**p. 15**
and Melchizedek, Genesis 14:18-24—**p. 18**
covenant with, Genesis 15,17—**p. 19**
and Hagar, Genesis 16—**p. 19**
prayed for Sodom and Gomorrah, Genesis 18:16-33—**p. 21**
asked to sacrifice his son, Genesis 22—**p. 25**
his death, Genesis 25:1-11—**p. 29**
his true offspring are believers, Romans 4—**p. 1255**; Galatians 3:6-29—**p. 1299**
faith demonstrated by deeds, James 2:20-24—**p. 1362**
ABSALOM — third son of David, by Maacah
his revenge on Amnon, 2 Samuel 13–14—**p. 354**
rebellion against David, 2 Samuel 15:1—19:8—**p. 357**
ADAM— the first man
his creation and life, Genesis 1:26—5:5—**p. 4**
his fall into sin, Genesis 3—**p. 7**
Jesus and the line of Adam, Luke 3:23-38—**p. 1139**
Jesus as second Adam, Romans 5:12-21—**p. 1257**; 1 Corinthians 15:21-22, 42-57—**p. 1283**
ADOPTION — becoming a child of one who is not your biological parent
Abraham and adoption of an heir, Genesis 15:1-6—**p. 18**; Genesis 16—**p. 19**
Israel as God's adopted son, Exodus 4:21-23—**p. 69**; Jeremiah 31:9, 16-20—**p. 872**
Believers as God's adopted children, John 1:12-13—**p. 1176**; Romans 8:12-25—**p. 1259**; Galatians 3:26—4:7—**p. 1300**; Ephesians 1:3-8—**p. 1305**
ADULTERY— sexual unfaithfulness of a married person
laws against, Numbers 5:12-31—**p. 154**
David and Bathsheba, 2 Samuel 11—12—**p. 352**
warnings against, Proverbs 5—**p. 711**; Proverbs 6:20-35—**p. 712**
Jesus' views on, Matthew 5:27-32—**p. 1069**
effect on the church, 1 Corinthians 5—**p. 1273**
AFTERLIFE — *see* ETERNAL LIFE, HEAVEN, HELL, RESURRECTION
AHAB — Israel's most wicked king
ascended throne, 1 Kings 16:29-33—**p. 402**
contest with Elijah, 1 Kings 18—**p. 403**
and Naboth's vineyard, 1 Kings 21—**p. 408**
his death, 1 Kings 22:34-38—**p. 410**
ALCOHOL — *see* DRINKING ALCOHOL, WINE
— strong desire for success, honor, or power (*see also* PRIDE, SERVANT)
at the tower of Babel, Genesis 11:1-11—**p. 14**
results of, Matthew 16:21-27—**p. 1085**
of disciples, Mark 9:33-37; 10:35-45—**p. 1119**
the antichrist, 2 Thessalonians 2:1-4—**p. 1329**
ANGELS — heavenly beings created by God
assist people, Genesis 24—**p. 27**
protect people, Psalm 91:11-13—**p. 670**
deliver messages, Luke 1:26-38—**p. 1134**; 2:8-15—**p. 1136**
execute judgment, Matthew 13:24-50—**p. 1080**; Revelation 14:17—16:21—**p. 1401**
Christ greater than, Hebrews 1:5-14—**p. 1348**
serve in heaven, Revelation 8—9—**p. 1395**
spiritual warriors, Revelation 12:7-12—**p. 1398**
ANGER
of God:
toward sin, Numbers 11:1-35—**p. 162**; Romans 1:18-32—**p. 1253**
tempered with mercy, Psalm 103—**p. 676**; Hosea 11:8-11—**p. 995**
averted through Christ, Romans 5—**p. 1256**
of human beings:
Moses', Exodus 32:15-35—**p. 101**
Jonah's, Jonah 3—4—**p. 1020**
"In your anger do not sin", Ephesians 4:26—**p. 1308**
be slow to anger, James 1:19-20—**p. 1361**
ANTICHRIST — an evil person or power; a false Christ, expected in the end times
prophesied by Daniel, Daniel 11:36-45—**p. 985**
Jesus' teaching on, Mark 13:1-37—**p. 1125**
will be destroyed, 2 Thessalonians 2:1-12—**p. 1329**
qualities of, 1 John 2:18-23—**p. 1377**; 4:1-6—**p. 1378**
visions of, Revelation 11—13—**p. 1397**
destruction of, Revelation 19:19-21—**p. 1405**
ANXIETY
overcome by trust in God, Matthew 6:25-34—**p. 1071**; Luke 12:22-34—**p. 1155**
subdued through prayer, Philippians 4:4-9—**p. 1315**
APOLLOS — an Alexandrian Jew who preached in Corinth

with Priscilla and Aquila, Acts 18:24-28—**p. 1236**
followers of, 1 Corinthians 3:1-9—**p. 1272**
partners with Paul, 1 Corinthians 4:1-7—**p. 1273**
APOSTLES — title given to the followers of Christ who founded the early church, especially the 12 disciples and Paul
commissioned, Matthew 28:16-20—**p. 1104**
disciples called, Luke 5:1-11—**p. 1141**; 6:12-16—**p. 1143**
replacement for Judas, Acts 1:12-26—**p. 1209**
received Holy Spirit, Acts 2—**p. 1211**
Paul as, 1 Corinthians 9—**p. 1277**; Galatians 1:1—2:10—**p. 1298**
foundation of the church, Ephesians 2:19-22—**p. 1307**; Revelation 21:14—**p. 1407**
ARK OF THE COVENANT — the Israelites' sacred chest containing the tablets of the law
description of, Exodus 25:10-22—**p. 92**
and crossing the Jordan, Joshua 3—**p. 239**
represented God's power, 1 Samuel 4—5—**p. 306**
David returns it to Jerusalem, 2 Samuel 6:1-15—**p. 347**; 1 Chronicles 13:1-14—**p. 469**; 15:1—16:6—**p. 470**
ART — creative expression such as music, dance, painting, sculpture, writing, architecture
ordained by God, Exodus 31:1-11—**p. 100**; 35:30—36:2—**p. 105**
excellence needed, Psalm 33:1-3—**p. 629**
ASCENSION — Christ's rising into heaven after the resurrection
prophesied, Psalm 27—**p. 625**
described, Luke 24:36-53—**p. 1174**; Acts 1:1-11—**p. 1209**
related to Pentecost, John 16:5-16—**p. 1200**; Ephesians 4:7-13—**p. 1308**
ASSURANCE OF SALVATION — certainty of God's forgiveness and love
built on trust, Psalm 37—**p. 632**
through Christ, Romans 8—**p. 1259**
produced by faith, 2 Timothy 1:8-12—**p. 1338**
achieved by obeying God, 1 John 2:28—3:24—**p. 1377**
achieved by believing God's word, 1 John 5:9-13—**p. 1379**
ASTROLOGY — seeking information about human events from the stars (*see also* WITCHCRAFT)
powerless, Isaiah 47:12-15—**p. 811**
Daniel discredits, Daniel 2—**p. 971**
ATHLETICS
Christianity compared to running, 1 Corinthians 9:24-27—**p. 1277**; Hebrews 12:1-2—**p. 1357**
Christianity compared to wrestling, Ephesians 6:10-18—**p. 1310**
competing according to rules, 2 Timothy 2:5—**p. 1338**
ATONEMENT — payment for sin; associated with the Israelites' Day of Atonement, when a blood sacrifice was made for the sins of the nation (*see also* JUSTIFICATION, SALVATION)
Hebrew ritual of, Leviticus 16—**p. 130**
Christ as our, Romans 3:21-26—**p. 1255**; 2 Corinthians 5:14-21—**p. 1290**; Hebrews 9—**p. 1353**; 1 Peter 2:22-25—**p. 1368**; 1 John 1:8—2:2—**p. 1376**

B

BAAL — god of the Phoenicians and Canaanites
worshiped in Israel, 1 Kings 16:29-34—**p. 402**; 2 Kings 17:7-23—**p. 435**; 21:1-9—**p. 441**
defeated by Elijah, 1 Kings 18—**p. 403**
BABYLON
prophecies against, Isaiah 13:1—14:23—**p. 773**; 21:1-10—**p. 780**; 47:1-15—**p. 811**; Jeremiah 50:1—51:58—**p. 895**
BACKSLIDING — departure from a life of faith in and obedience to God
displeases God, Psalm 78—**p. 659**
a serious sin, Hebrews 6:4-6—**p. 1351**; 10:26-31—**p. 1355**
forgiveness for, Revelation 2:4-5—**p. 1390**; 3:2-3,15-21—**p. 1392**
examples of:
Israel at Mount Sinai, Exodus 32—**p. 100**
Solomon, 1 Kings 11—**p. 392**
Hymenaeus and Alexander, 1 Timothy 1:19-20—**p. 1332**
in the end times, 2 Timothy 3:1-10—**p. 1339**
BALAAM — man employed by the Moabites to curse the Israelites
stopped by God, Numbers 22—24—**p. 176**
death of, Numbers 31:1-24—**p. 188**
BAPTISM — a water ritual, used as a spiritual symbol (*see also* HOLY SPIRIT, JOHN THE BAPTIST)
Jesus' baptism, Matthew 3:13-15—**p. 1067**
as sign of repentance, Matthew 3:1-12—**p. 1067**
as sign of conversion, Matthew 28:16-20—**p. 1104**
in the early church, Acts 2:37-41—**p. 1212**; 8:26-39—**p. 1220**
and the believer's death and resurrection in Christ, Romans 6—**p. 1257**; Colossians 2:11-12—**p. 1320**
of the Holy Spirit, Acts 1:1-8—**p. 1209**; 1 Corinthians 12:12-13—**p. 1280**
BARABBAS — criminal released by Pilate instead of Jesus
set free, Matthew 27:11-26—**p. 1101**
BATHSHEBA — committed adultery with David and later married him (*see also* DAVID, SOLOMON)
life of, 2 Samuel 11:1—12:25—**p. 352**
helped Solomon become king, 1 Kings 1:11-31—**p. 374**
BEAUTY
inner, 1 Samuel 16:1-13—**p. 320**; 1 Timothy 2:9—**p. 1333**; 1 Peter 3:1-7—**p. 1368**
of Bathsheba, 2 Samuel 11—**p. 352**
of Esther, Esther 2:1-18—**p. 564**
BEGGARS — *see* POOR
BETRAYAL
of Jesus by Judas, Matthew 26:14-16,47-49—**p. 1098**
BIBLE
in praise of, Psalm 19:7-11—**p. 621**; 119:1-176—**p. 688**
importance of, 2 Timothy 3:14-17—**p. 1339**
inspired by God, 2 Peter 1:19-21—**p. 1372**
act on, James 1:19-27—**p. 1361**
BITTERNESS — lingering resentment or anger
avoid, Ephesians 4:29-32—**p. 1308**
as sin, James 3:13-18—**p. 1363**
BLASPHEMY — bringing reproach against God and his name

a sin against God, Exodus 20:7—**p. 87**; Leviticus 24:13-23—**p. 140**
Jesus charged with, Matthew 9:1-8—**p. 1073**; Matthew 26:57-67—**p. 1100**
against the Holy Spirit, Mark 3:20-30—**p. 1110**

BLESSINGS
material blessings, Deuteronomy 7:12-16—**p. 206**; Psalm 67—**p. 651**
spiritual blessings, Psalm 32—**p. 628**; John 1:14-17—**p. 1177**; Ephesians 1:3-14—**p. 1305**
showers of blessings, Ezekiel 34:26-30—**p. 951**
the Beatitudes, Matthew 5:1-11—**p. 1068**; Luke 6:20-22—**p. 1143**

BLOOD — used to represent the life of a creature, often in sacrifices or rituals of cleansing
instructions to Noah about shedding, Genesis 9:1-6—**p. 12**
for purification of priests, Exodus 29—**p. 97**
in offerings to God, especially for sin, Leviticus 1,3,4—**p. 113**
the Day of Atonement, Leviticus 16—**p. 130**

BLOOD OF CHRIST — shed on the cross as Jesus died
wine as sign of, in the Lord's Supper, Matthew 26:27-29—**p. 1099**; 1 Corinthians 11:23-32—**p. 1279**
as payment for sin, Hebrews 9:11-28—**p. 1354**
redemption through, Ephesians 1:7-8—**p. 1305**; 1 Peter 1:18-19—**p. 1367**
reconciliation through, Ephesians 2:11-18—**p. 1306**
cleansing through, 1 John 1:7-10—**p. 1376**

BODY OF CHRIST
signified by bread in the Lord's Supper, Mark 14:22-24—**p. 1127**
as metaphor for church, Romans 12:3-8—**p. 1264;** 1 Corinthians 12:12-31—**p. 1280**
Jesus as the head, Ephesians 1:22-23—**p. 1306**; Colossians 1:18-24—**p. 1319**
completely human, Hebrews 2:14-18—**p. 1349**
now a glorious body, 1 Corinthians 15:35-49—**p. 1284**; Philippians 3:20-21—**p. 1315**

BORN AGAIN — spiritual rebirth or conversion (*see also* CONVERSION, SALVATION)
necessity of, John 3:1-21—**p. 1179**
marked by holiness, Titus 3:4-8—**p. 1343**; 1 Peter 1:13-23—**p. 1367**

C

CAIN — first son of Adam and Eve; murdered his brother Abel
life of, Genesis 4:1-26—**p. 8**
a warning to believers, 1 John 3:11-13—**p. 1378**

CALEB — one of 12 spies sent by Moses into promised land
report of, Numbers 13:1—14:38—**p. 165**
receives Hebron, Joshua 14:1-15—**p. 252**

CALVARY — *see* GOLGOTHA

CANAAN — land God promised to the Israelites; later called Palestine
promised to Abraham, Genesis 13:14-17—**p. 17**; Genesis 15:12-21—**p. 18**
promised to Isaac, Genesis 26:1-6—**p. 31**
promised to Jacob, Genesis 28:10-22—**p. 34**
Moses can't go in, Deuteronomy 34:1-12—**p. 235**
Joshua conquers, Joshua 1—12—**p. 237**

CELIBACY — abstaining from marriage
calling to, Matthew 19:4-12—**p. 1088**
advantages of, 1 Corinthians 7:32-40—**p. 1276**
not required, 1 Timothy 4:1-5—**p. 1333**

CHILDREN
should honor parents, Exodus 20:12—**p. 87**; Ephesians 6:1-4—**p. 1309**
a gift from God, Psalm 127—**p. 695**
formed by God in the womb, Psalm 139:13-16—**p. 700**
should listen to instruction, Proverbs 1—**p. 707**
used as an example of humility, Matthew 18:1-4—**p. 1086**
blessed by Jesus, Mark 10:13-16—**p. 1120**
of God through Christ, John 1:12-13—**p. 1176**; Romans 8:12-17—**p. 1259**; Galatians 3:26—4:7—**p. 1300**

CHRIST — *see* MESSIAH

CHRISTIANS — name given to followers of Christ
first called, Acts 11:26—**p. 1225**
how to become, Romans 10:9-13—**p. 1262**
marks of, Galatians 5:22-26—**p. 1302**

CHURCH — both the local assemblies of Christians and the worldwide community of believers
promised by Christ, Matthew 16:13-20—**p. 1085**
unity of, Romans 12:3-8—**p. 1264**; Ephesians 4:1-14—**p. 1307**
founded on Christ and the apostles, 1 Corinthians 3:1-15—**p. 1272**; Ephesians 2:19-22—**p. 1307**
as body of Christ, 1 Corinthians 12:12-28—**p. 1280**
Christ's relationship to, Ephesians 4:7-16—**p. 1308**
Christ's message to seven churches, Revelation 2—3—**p. 1390**

CIRCUMCISION — removal of the foreskin in males; established by God to signify his relationship with the Israelites
sign of covenant, Genesis 17:9-14—**p. 20**
no longer necessary, Romans 4:4-12—**p. 1255**; Galatians 5:1-12—**p. 1301**
linked with baptism, Colossians 2:11-12—**p. 1320**

CLEANNESS
laws of clean and unclean, Leviticus 11—15—**p. 123**
cleansing from sin, Psalm 51:1-9—**p. 642**; Hebrews 10:19-22—**p. 1355**; 1 John 1:5-10—**p. 1376**

COLOSSE — city in Asia to which Paul wrote the letter "Colossians"

COMFORT
in grief, Job 2:11-13—**p. 574**; Psalm 23—**p. 623**
in trouble, Psalm 46—**p. 639**; Romans 8:18-39—**p. 1260**
when we sin, Psalm 103—**p. 676**
when afraid, Isaiah 41:8-20—**p. 803**
from God, Isaiah 40:1-11—**p. 801**
from Holy Spirit, John 14:1-4,15-27—**p. 1197**
share with others, 2 Corinthians 1:3-7—**p. 1287**

COMMUNION — *see* LORD'S SUPPER

COMPASSION — to have pity for and show kindness to another
of God, Exodus 34:4-7—**p. 103**; Psalm 103:8-12—**p. 676**; Jonah 3—**p. 1020**
commanded by God, Micah 6:6-8—**p. 1027**; Galatians 6:1-10—**p. 1302**

of Jesus, Matthew 9:35-38—**p. 1075**; 14:13-14—**p. 1082**; 15:29-39—**p. 1084**; John 11:17-44—**p. 1193**
sign of faith, 1 John 3:11-24—**p. 1378**

CONFESSION — an acknowledgment of the truth
of Christ:
Peter's, Matthew 16:13-20—**p. 1085**
Thomas's, John 20:24-31—**p. 1206**
as Lord, Romans 10:9-13—**p. 1262**; Philippians 2:9-11—**p. 1313**
as Son of God, 1 John 4:2-3,13-16—**p. 1378**
of sin:
Ezra's, Ezra 9—**p. 540**
David's, Psalm 51—**p. 642**
Isaiah's, Isaiah 6—**p. 766**
Daniel's, Daniel 9—**p. 981**
lost son's, Luke 15:11-32—**p. 1160**
tax collector's, Luke 18:9-14—**p. 1163**
to one another, James 5:16—**p. 1364**
to God, 1 John 1:5—2:2—**p. 1376**

CONFORMITY — to adopt the values and practices of a group
to evildoers, Proverbs 4:10-19—**p. 710**
to the world, James 4:1-10,17—**p. 1363**

CONSCIENCE — awareness of one's actions as either right or wrong (*see also* CONFESSION, FORGIVENESS)
guilty, Psalm 38—**p. 633**
accuses us of sin, Romans 2:12-16—**p. 1254**
be sensitive to others', Romans 14—**p. 1265**; 1 Corinthians 8—**p. 1276**; 10:23—11:1—**p. 1278**
cleansed by Christ, Hebrews 10:19-22—**p. 1355**

CONVERSION — to turn away from sin and to God through repentance and faith (*see also* BORN AGAIN, PAUL, SALVATION)
result of God's love, Jeremiah 31:3-14—**p. 872**
of Samaritan woman, John 4:1-30,39-42—**p. 1180**
of an Ethiopian eunuch, Acts 8:26-40—**p. 1220**
of Paul, Acts 9:1-25—**p. 1220**
of Lydia, Acts 16:11-15—**p. 1232**
of a jailer, Acts 16:22-34—**p. 1233**
become new through, 2 Corinthians 5:17-19—**p. 1290**
by grace, Ephesians 2:1-10—**p. 1306**

CORINTH
church started, Acts 18:1-17—**p. 1235**

COURAGE
the call to be courageous, Joshua 1—**p. 237**
David's, 1 Samuel 17:26-50—**p. 322**
Daniel's three friends, Daniel 3—**p. 973**
the apostles', Acts 4—**p. 1213**; 5:17-42—**p. 1215**

COVENANT — an agreement between two parties; a solemn promise or vow, especially between God and people
with Noah, Genesis 9:1-17—**p. 12**
with Abraham, Genesis 15; 17:1-14—**p. 18**
with Israelites in Old Testament, Exodus 19:3-8,24—**p. 86**; Deuteronomy 29—**p. 228**
with David, 2 Samuel 7:1-17—**p. 348**
new, 2 Corinthians 2:12—3:18—**p. 1288**; Hebrews 8:7-13—**p. 1353**; 10:1-18—**p. 1355**

COVETING — envious desire for something that belongs to another (*see also* ENVY, GREED)
commandment on, Exodus 20:17—**p. 87**
Achan's, Joshua 7—**p. 243**
Ahab's, 1 Kings 21:1-14—**p. 408**
result of, James 4:1-10—**p. 1363**

CREATION
account of, Genesis 1—2—**p. 4**
God revealed through, Job 38—**p. 605**; Psalm 19:1-6—**p. 620**; Romans 1:18-23—**p. 1253**
God's delight in, Psalm 104—**p. 676**
God's wisdom in, Proverbs 8:12-36—**p. 714**
Christ's work in, John 1:1-14—**p. 1176**; Colossians 1:15-17—**p. 1319**
renewal of, Romans 8:18-25—**p. 1260**

CROSS — means by which Jesus died; also used as a metaphor for self-sacrifice
take up your, Mark 8:31—9:1—**p. 1118**
Jesus' crucifixion on, Luke 23:26-49—**p. 1172**
center of preaching, 1 Corinthians 1:18—2:5—**p. 1271**
removed God's curse, Galatians 3:1-14—**p. 1299**
created peace and unity, Ephesians 2:11-18—**p. 1306**

CURSING — *see* PROFANITY

D

DANCING
David before the ark, 2 Samuel 6:12-23—**p. 347**
in worship, Exodus 15—**p. 81**; Psalm 150—**p. 705**
in celebration, Luke 15:22-27—**p. 1160**
provocative, Matthew 14:1-12—**p. 1081**

DANIEL
interpreted dreams, Daniel 2—**p. 971**; Daniel 4—**p. 974**
in the lions' den, Daniel 6—**p. 977**

DARKNESS
dispelled by God, Genesis 1:1-5—**p. 4**
picture of God's judgment, Joel 2:1-2—**p. 1001**; Jude 8-13—**p. 1386**
Jesus came to dispel, John 1:1-9—**p. 1176**
symbol of evil, Romans 13:11-14—**p. 1265**; Ephesians 5:1-14—**p. 1308**; 1 Thessalonians 5:1-10—**p. 1326**
not in heaven, Revelation 22:1-5—**p. 1407**

DAVID — Israel's greatest king; associated with many of the psalms (*see also* JONATHAN, SAUL)
chosen king, 1 Samuel 16—**p. 320**
and Goliath, 1 Samuel 17—**p. 321**
God's promise to, 2 Samuel 7—**p. 348**
and Bathsheba, 2 Samuel 11—12—**p. 352**
confession of sin, Psalm 51—**p. 642**
Jesus as son of, Matthew 1:1-18—**p. 1064**; Luke 1:26-33—**p. 1134**
Jesus of Lord of, Matthew 21:41-45—**p. 1092**

DAY OF ATONEMENT (Yom Kippur)
described and reinterpreted, Leviticus 16—**p. 130**

DAY OF THE LORD — a common Old Testament phrase for God's final victory over evil
as punishment for Israelites, Zephaniah 1:14—2:7—**p. 1039**
as cleansing the world, Isaiah 24—**p. 783**

DEACON — an official in the early church who served the needs of people
established, Acts 6:1-4—**p. 1216**
requirements for, 1 Timothy 3:8-13—**p. 1333**

DEATH
physical:
result of sin, Genesis 3—**p. 7**; Romans 5:12-21—**p. 1257**

being unprepared for, Luke 12:13-21—**p. 1155**
victory over, 1 Corinthians 15—**p. 1282**
spiritual:
by nature true of everyone, Ephesians 2:1-10—**p. 1306**
to self, John 12:23-26—**p. 1195**
to sin, Romans 6:1-23—**p. 1257**
of Jesus (*see* BLOOD OF CHRIST, CROSS)
of Stephen, Acts 7—**p. 1217**
DEBORAH — one of Israel's greatest judges and a prophetess
delivers Israel, Judges 4—**p. 272**
song of, Judges 5—**p. 273**
DEBTS (*see also* FORGIVENESS, LORD'S PRAYER)
compassion to debtors, Exodus 22:25-27—**p. 90**
pay promptly, Romans 13:8-10—**p. 1265**
DEEDS — actions or accomplishments, often in the sense of attempts to please God through moral living (*see also* FAITH)
do not gain salvation, Ephesians 2:1-10—**p. 1306**
outgrowth of faith, James 2:14-26—**p. 1362**
DELILAH — *see* SAMSON
DEMONS — powerful evil spirits that can possess a person (*see also* EVIL)
driven out, Matthew 8:28-34—**p. 1073**; Mark 5:1-10—**p. 1112**; Acts 16:16-19—**p. 1233**
ignore teaching of, 1 Timothy 4:1-10—**p. 1333**
DEVIL — *see* SATAN
DISCIPLES
make them of all nations, Matthew 28:6-20—**p. 1103**
called Christians, Acts 11:26—**p. 1225**
DISCIPLESHIP — the act of following and learning from a teacher, especially Jesus
cost of, Luke 14:25-34—**p. 1159**
evidence of, John 15:1-17—**p. 1199**
result of love, John 21:15-19—**p. 1207**
DISCIPLINE — training that molds, instructs, corrects
by parents, Proverbs 23:13-23—**p. 730**
by God, Hebrews 12:1-13—**p. 1357**
by the church, 1 Corinthians 5—**p. 1273**
by God's Word, 2 Timothy 3:14-17—**p. 1339**
DISCOURAGEMENT (*see also* COMFORT)
overcoming, Joshua 1:1-9—**p. 237**; Psalm 42—**p. 636**; Psalm 77:1-15—**p. 658**; John 14:1-27—**p. 1197**; 2 Corinthians 4:7-12,16-18—**p. 1289**
DISCRIMINATION (*see also* RACISM)
eliminated in Christ, Ephesians 2:11-18—**p. 1306**
DISEASE — *see* HEALING
DISOBEDIENCE — *see* OBEDIENCE
DIVORCE
Mosaic law on, Deuteronomy 24:1-4—**p. 222**
Jesus' teaching on, Matthew 19:1-12—**p. 1088**; Mark 10:2-12—**p. 1120**
a pardonable sin, John 4:4-42—**p. 1180**
Paul's teaching on, 1 Corinthians 7:10-16—**p. 1275**
DOUBT (*see also* FAITH)
of Abraham, Genesis 12:10-20—**p. 16**
of Sarah, Genesis 18:1-15—**p. 20**
of Moses, Exodus 4:1-17—**p. 68**
of Gideon, Judges 6—**p. 274**
of Peter, Matthew 14:22-32—**p. 1082**
overcoming, Mark 9:14-29—**p. 1118**; 11:22-25—**p. 1123**; James 1:2-7—**p. 1361**
of John the Baptist, Luke 7:18-23—**p. 1145**
of Thomas, John 20:24-31—**p. 1206**
DREAMS (*see also* VISIONS)
of Jacob, Genesis 28:10-22—**p. 34**
interpreted by Joseph, Genesis 37—**p. 46**; 41—**p. 50**
false prophecy through, Jeremiah 23:25-32—**p. 863**; Ezekiel 13:1-9—**p. 923**
interpreted by Daniel, Daniel 2—**p. 971**; 4—**p. 974**
at the birth of Jesus, Matthew 2—**p. 1065**
of Pilate's wife, Matthew 27:19—**p. 1102**
in the last days, Acts 2:14-21—**p. 1211**
DRINKING ALCOHOL (*see also* WINE)
warnings about, Proverbs 20:1—**p. 727**; 23:29-35—**p. 731**; Isaiah 5:11-12—**p. 765**; Ephesians 5:18—**p. 1309**
examples of overindulgence
of Noah, Genesis 9:20—**p. 13**
of Lot, Genesis 19:32-35—**p. 23**
of Xerxes, Esther 1:10—**p. 564**
at the Lord's Supper, 1 Corinthians 11:21—**p. 1279**

E

EARTH
created by God, Genesis 1:1-25—**p. 4**
care for, Genesis 1:26-31—**p. 4**
exhibits God's love, Psalm 33:1-11—**p. 629**
waits for redemption, Romans 8:18-25—**p. 1260**
new, 2 Peter 3:3-13—**p. 1373**; Revelation 21:1—22:5—**p. 1406**
EDOM — *see* ESAU
EGYPT
Joseph taken there, Genesis 37—**p. 46**
Israelites moved there, Genesis 39—50—**p. 48**
exodus from, Exodus 1—13—**p. 65**
judgment of, Isaiah 19—**p. 778**; Jeremiah 42—**p. 885**; Ezekiel 29—30—**p. 944**
Jesus taken there, Matthew 2:13-20—**p. 1066**
ELDER — a designated leader of the Jewish people and of the church
leaders of the Jewish council, Acts 5:17-42—**p. 1215**
leaders appointed in churches, Acts 14:21-25—**p. 1229**; Titus 1:5-9—**p. 1342**
Paul's farewell speech to, Acts 20:13-38—**p. 1238**
qualifications for, 1 Timothy 3:1-7—**p. 1333**
ELECTION — God's choosing a people for himself
of Abraham, Genesis 12:1-9—**p. 16**
of Israel, Exodus 19:1-6—**p. 86**; Deuteronomy 10:12-22—**p. 209**; Isaiah 41:8-16—**p. 803**
of Jesus' disciples, John 15:9-17—**p. 1199**
of Jacob, Romans 9:6-13—**p. 1261**
of the church, Ephesians 1:3-14—**p. 1305**; 1 Peter 2:1-10—**p. 1367**
make it sure, 2 Peter 1:3-10—**p. 1372**
ELI — a priest and judge of Israel
life of, 1 Samuel 1—4—**p. 302**
ELIJAH — Israelite prophet well known for his confrontation with the priests of Baal (*see also* BAAL, ELISHA)
life of, 1 Kings 17—19—**p. 402**; 21—**p. 408**
and Baal, 1 Kings 18:16-46—**p. 403**
death of, 2 Kings 2—**p. 413**
at transfiguration, Luke 9:28-36—**p. 1150**

ELISHA — prophet who succeeded Elijah
chosen by Elijah, 1 Kings 19:16-21—**p. 405**
life of, 2 Kings 2—13—**p. 413**
heals Naaman, 2 Kings 5:1-27—**p. 419**
ENEMY
treat with kindness, Proverbs 25:21-22—**p. 733**; Romans 12:19-21—**p. 1265**
love for, Luke 6:27-36—**p. 1143**
ENVY (*see also* JEALOUSY, GREED)
of Joseph by brothers, Genesis 37—**p. 46**
comes from inside, Mark 7:20-23—**p. 1116**
trouble from, James 3:13—4:10—**p. 1363**
EPHESUS
Paul's farewell to, Acts 20:13-38—**p. 1238**
ESAU — son of Isaac and Rebekah; older brother of Jacob
cheated by Jacob, Genesis 25:19-34—**p. 30**; Genesis 27:1—28:9—**p. 32**
forgives Jacob, Genesis 33—**p. 41**
ESTHER
made queen, Esther 2—**p. 564**
ETERNAL LIFE — life everlasting with God, which begins at conversion (*see also* BORN AGAIN, CONVERSION, SALVATION, HEAVEN)
to inherit, Matthew 19:16-30—**p. 1088**
through rebirth, John 3:1-21—**p. 1179**
gift of God, Romans 6:15-23—**p. 1258**
assurance of, 1 John 5:1-15—**p. 1379**
EVANGELISM — telling and living the good news of Christ's salvation (*see also* MISSIONS)
call to, Matthew 28:16-20—**p. 1104**; Luke 24:45-52—**p. 1174**; Acts 1:1-11—**p. 1209**
gift of, Ephesians 4:1-16—**p. 1307**; 2 Timothy 4:1-5—**p. 1340**
EVE — the first woman
life of, Genesis 1:26—5:2—**p. 4**
temptation of, Genesis 3—**p. 7**
mentioned in the New Testament, 1 Corinthians 11:2-16—**p. 1279**; 1 Timothy 2:8-15—**p. 1332**
EVIL (*see also* SATAN, SIN)
introduction of, Genesis 3:1-24—**p. 7**
repent of, Jeremiah 18:1-12—**p. 857**
problem of, Job 1—42—**p. 573**
EVOLUTION — theory of the development of species (*see* CREATION)
EXCOMMUNICATION
for purpose of teaching, 1 Corinthians 5—**p. 1273**; 1 Timothy 1:20—**p. 1332**
EXAMPLE
Christ as, John 13:1-17—**p. 1196**; Philippians 2:1-11—**p. 1313**
Old Testament stories as, 1 Corinthians 10:1-13—**p. 1278**; Hebrews 11:4-40—**p. 1356**
Christians as, Philippians 2:14-15—**p. 1314**; 1 Thessalonians 1—**p. 1324**; 1 Peter 2:11-12—**p. 1368**
Job, of patience, James 5:10-11—**p. 1364**
Elijah, of prayer, James 5:16-18—**p. 1364**
EXILE
northern kingdom to Assyria, 2 Kings 17—**p. 435**
southern kingdom to Babylon, 2 Kings 25—**p. 446**; 2 Chronicles 36—**p. 528**
EZRA — a leader of the Jews who returned from exile
life of, Ezra 7—10—**p. 537**; Nehemiah 8—**p. 552**; 12—**p. 558**

F

FAITH — trust in and reliance on God
of Abraham, Genesis 15:6—**p. 18**
living by, Matthew 6:25-34—**p. 1071**
necessary for salvation, Romans 3:21—5:11—**p. 1255**; Galatians 2—3—**p. 1298**; Ephesians 2:1-10—**p. 1306**
heroes of, Hebrews 11—**p. 1356**
shown by deeds, James 2:14-26—**p. 1362**
FAITHFULNESS
of God, Psalm 78—**p. 659**; Psalm 111—**p. 684**; Lamentations 3:22-32—**p. 909**
an aspect of the Spirit's fruit, Galatians 5:16-26—**p. 1302**
of Moses, Hebrews 3—**p. 1349**
expected of Christians, Revelation 2:8-11—**p. 1390**
FAME
transience of, Isaiah 14:9-20—**p. 774**
unreliability of, Ezekiel 33:30-32—**p. 950**
unimportant, 1 Corinthians 3:1-23—**p. 1272**
FAMILY
established in Garden of Eden, Genesis 2:18-24—**p. 6**
built by God, Psalm 127—128—**p. 695**
of God, Ephesians 2:19-22—**p. 1307**
family relations, Ephesians 5:21—6:4—**p. 1309**; Colossians 3:18-21—**p. 1321**
FAMINE
in Israel, Ruth 1:1—**p. 296**; 1 Kings 17—**p. 402**; 2 Kings 6:25—8:2—**p. 421**
FASTING — abstinence from food or drink for a period of time, especially for spiritual reasons
at a time of national crisis, 2 Chronicles 20:1-13—**p. 508**; Esther 4—**p. 566**; Joel 2:15-17—**p. 1001**
true, Isaiah 58—**p. 822**
Jesus' teaching on, Matthew 6:16-18—**p. 1070**
disciples', Acts 13:1-3—**p. 1226**; 14:23—**p. 1229**
FEAR — reverence and awe for God
commanded, Deuteronomy 6:10-25—**p. 205**; Ecclesiastes 12:8-14—**p. 751**
good, Psalm 33—**p. 629**
the beginning of wisdom, Proverbs 9:10-12—**p. 715**
FEAR — fright or alarm
combating, Psalm 23—**p. 623**; 56—**p. 645**; 91—**p. 670**; Jeremiah 1:4-19—**p. 834**; Luke 12:4-12—**p. 1155**
comfort in, John 14—**p. 1197**
FELLOWSHIP
expressed in sharing, Acts 2:42-47—**p. 1212**; 4:24-35—**p. 1214**
with the Holy Spirit, 2 Corinthians 13:14—**p. 1296**
in church, Ephesians 4:17—5:21—**p. 1308**
with God, 1 John 1—**p. 1376**
FESTIVALS — *see* JEWISH HOLY DAYS
FLATTERY
displeases God, Psalm 12—**p. 616**
FOOD
provided by Christ, Matthew 14:13-21—**p. 1082**; John 6—**p. 1183**
glorify God through, 1 Corinthians 10:23—11:1—**p. 1278**
as god, Philippians 3:19—**p. 1315**

by Jesus, Matthew 8:1-17—**p. 1072**;
Mark 5—**p. 1112**; Luke 4:38-41—**p. 1141**
by disciples, Acts 3:1-10—**p. 1212**;
5:12-16—**p. 1215**; 14:8-10—**p. 1229**;
28:7-10—**p. 1249**
encouraged, James 5:13-18—**p. 1364**
HEART — figuratively, the center of a person; that which gives direction to a person
God knows, 1 Samuel 16:1-13—**p. 320**
cleansing of, Psalm 51—**p. 642**
life flows from, Proverbs 4:23—**p. 710**
deceitful, Jeremiah 17:9-10—**p. 856**
leads to action, Matthew 12:33-37—**p. 1078**
HEAVEN — a place of perfect happiness and eternal communion with God
God rules from, Psalm 99—**p. 674**;
Isaiah 66:1-2—**p. 831**
new, Isaiah 65:17-25—**p. 830**;
Revelation 21—22—**p. 1406**
treasures in, Matthew 6:19-24—**p. 1070**
for righteous, Matthew 25:31-46—**p. 1097**
citizenship in, Philippians 3:12—4:1—**p. 1315**
inhabitants of, Hebrews 11—**p. 1356**
visions of, Revelation 4—5—**p. 1393**;
Revelation 7—**p. 1395**
HELL — a place of eternal punishment and sorrow
hints of in Old Testament, Job 24:21-26—**p. 593**;
Psalm 49:10-15—**p. 640**; Daniel 12—**p. 986**
to avoid, Matthew 5:21-30—**p. 1069**;
Romans 8:1-16—**p. 1259**
for evildoers, Matthew 13:24-30,36-43—**p. 1080**
punishment in, 2 Thessalonians 1:3-12—**p. 1329**;
Jude 5-13—**p. 1386**;
Revelation 20:11-14—**p. 1406**
keep others from, Jude 17-23—**p. 1386**
HEROD — name of a line of rulers of Palestine
the Great, Matthew 2—**p. 1065**
Antipas, Matthew 14:1-12—**p. 1081**
Agrippa I, Acts 12:1-23—**p. 1225**
HEZEKIAH — king of Judah for 29 years; reopened the temple his father had closed
life of, 2 Kings 18—20—**p. 437**
restores worship, 2 Chronicles 29—31—**p. 518**
crisis with Isaiah, Isaiah 36—39—**p. 796**
HOLY — separated or set apart for God
called to be, Exodus 19:1-5—**p. 86**;
Leviticus 11:44-45—**p. 124**;
1 Peter 1:13-16—**p. 1367**; 2:9-10—**p. 1368**
God's character, Psalm 99—**p. 674**;
Isaiah 6—**p. 766**
imitate God's holiness,
Ephesians 4:17—5:21—**p. 1308**
HOLY SPIRIT — the third person of the Trinity; also known as the Counselor who is active in the lives of believers (*see also* FRUIT OF THE SPIRIT)
in the Old Testament, Psalm 51:11—**p. 642**;
Isaiah 11:1-5—**p. 772**; 61:1-3—**p. 826**
anointed Jesus, Luke 3:21-22—**p. 1139**;
4:1-27—**p. 1139**
comfort from, John 14:15-31—**p. 1198**
work of, John 16:5-16—**p. 1200**
coming to the disciples, Acts 2—**p. 1211**
directs the church, Acts 13:1-4—**p. 1226**;
16:6-7—**p. 1231**
filled with, Acts 19:1-7—**p. 1236**;
Ephesians 5:18—**p. 1309**
life through, Romans 8:1-17—**p. 1259**
in Christians, 1 Corinthians 2:6-16—**p. 1271**;
3:16-17—**p. 1272**
HOMOSEXUALITY
result of sin, Romans 1:18-32—**p. 1253**
listed as sin, 1 Corinthians 6:9-11—**p. 1274**;
1 Timothy 1:9-11—**p. 1332**
HONESTY
God desires, Psalm 15—**p. 617**
HOPE
in the Lord, Psalm 42—43—**p. 636**;
1 Timothy 6:17-19—**p. 1335**
does not disappoint, Romans 5:1-11—**p. 1256**
for resurrection, 1 Corinthians 15—**p. 1282**
in Christ, Colossians 1:3-27—**p. 1318**;
1 Peter 1:13-16—**p. 1367**
HOSPITALITY
Jesus' words on, Luke 14:12-14—**p. 1158**
responsibility of, Romans 12:13—**p. 1264**;
1 Peter 4:9—**p. 1369**
entertaining angels, Hebrews 13:1-3—**p. 1359**
HUMAN BEINGS
created in God's image, Genesis 1:26-31—**p. 4**
glory of, Psalm 8—**p. 614**
intricately made, Psalm 139:13-16—**p. 700**
HUMILITY
living in, Micah 6:6-8—**p. 1027**;
Colossians 3:12-17—**p. 1320**;
1 Peter 5:5-7—**p. 1370**
like children, Matthew 18:1-4—**p. 1086**
encouraged, Romans 12:1-21—**p. 1264**;
1 Peter 5:5-7—**p. 1370**
of Christ, 2 Corinthians 8:8-9—**p. 1292**;
Philippians 2:1-11—**p. 1313**
HUSBAND
duty to wife, 1 Corinthians 7:1-5—**p. 1275**
love for wife, Ephesians 5:25-33—**p. 1309**;
Colossians 3:19—**p. 1321**
HYPOCRISY
avoid, Matthew 6:1-24—**p. 1070**
described, Matthew 23—**p. 1094**
condemned, James 1:19—2:13—**p. 1361**;
1 John 3:17-19—**p. 1378**

I

IDOLATRY — the worship of idols; putting something before God
commandment against, Exodus 20:3-6—**p. 87**
emptiness of, Isaiah 44:6-23—**p. 807**
greed is, Colossians 3:5—**p. 1320**
IMAGE OF GOD — *see HUMAN BEING*
INCARNATION — God taking human flesh; birth of Jesus
taught, Matthew 1:18-25—**p. 1065**;
Luke 1—2—**p. 1133**; John 1:1-18—**p. 1176**
INCEST — sexual relations with a family member
forbidden, Leviticus 18:1-18—**p. 132**
INFERTILITY
Sarah's, Genesis 18:1-15—**p. 20**
Hannah's prayer concerning,
1 Samuel 1:1—2:11—**p. 302**
Elizabeth's, Luke 1:7-25—**p. 1133**
INSPIRATION — the Bible as inspired by the Holy Spirit (*see* BIBLE)
INTERCESSION — the prayer of one person for another
examples of, Genesis 18:23-32—**p. 21**;
1 Kings 8:33-51—**p. 388**;

Ezra 9:5-15—**p. 540**; Daniel 9:3-19—**p. 981**
of Jesus for us, John 17—**p. 1201**;
Romans 8:31-34—**p. 1260**;
Hebrews 7:24-25—**p. 1353**;
1 John 2:1—**p. 1376**
of the Holy Spirit, Romans 8:26-27—**p. 1260**
commanded, 1 Timothy 2:1-2—**p. 1332**;
James 5:16—**p. 1364**

ISAAC — only son of Abraham by Sarah; born miraculously in their old age
birth predicted, Genesis 18:1-15—**p. 20**
as sacrifice, Genesis 22:1-19—**p. 25**
marries Rebekah, Genesis 24—**p. 27**
blesses sons, Genesis 27—**p. 32**
death of, Genesis 35:16-29—**p. 43**
chosen by God, Romans 9:6-9—**p. 1261**;
Galatians 4:21-31—**p. 1301**

ISAIAH
his call as prophet, Isaiah 6—**p. 766**

ISRAEL — name God gave to Jacob, the father of the Israelite nation (*see also* JACOB)
given name, Genesis 32:22-32—**p. 41**
twelve sons of, Genesis 49—**p. 61**

ISRAEL — nation of God's chosen people, composed of 12 tribes; its history makes up much of the Old Testament (*see also* JUDAH)

ISRAEL — Northern Kingdom; the nation of the northern 10 tribes after rebelling against Rehoboam

J

JACOB — son of Isaac and Rebekah; younger brother of Esau (*see also* ISRAEL)
life of, Genesis 25—49—**p. 29**
steals birthright, Genesis 25:19-34—**p. 30**
steals blessing, Genesis 27—**p. 32**
dream of, Genesis 28:10-22—**p. 34**
his marriages, Genesis 29—30—**p. 35**
wrestles with God, Genesis 32—**p. 40**

JAMES — son of Zebedee; an apostle and brother of apostle John
call of, Matthew 4:18-22—**p. 1068**
at transfiguration, Matthew 17:1-13—**p. 1085**
sought top place in kingdom,
Mark 10:35-45—**p. 1121**
death of, Acts 12:1-2—**p. 1225**

JEALOUSY
of God, Exodus 34:14—**p. 103**;
Deuteronomy 32:15-22—**p. 232**
command against, Romans 13:13—**p. 1265**;
2 Corinthians 12:19-21—**p. 1296**
between people, 1 Corinthians 3:1-23—**p. 1272**

JEHOSHAPHAT — king of Judah
life of, 1 Kings 22—**p. 409**;
2 Chronicles 17—22—**p. 505**

JEPHTHAH — judge of Israel, known for his foolish vow

JERICHO — city near the Dead Sea, destroyed by Joshua and later rebuilt
fall of, Joshua 5:13—6:27—**p. 241**
Jesus' healings there, Matthew 20:29-34—**p. 1090**

JEROBOAM I — first king of northern kingdom after split
life of, 1 Kings 11—14—**p. 392**

JERUSALEM — capital of Israel and a symbol for a spiritual home as well; often called Zion or the city of God
David captures, 2 Samuel 5—6—**p. 346**
temple built there, 2 Chronicles 3—7—**p. 492**
fall to Babylonians, 2 Chronicles 36:15-23—**p. 529**
rebuilding of temple, Ezra 3—**p. 533**
new, Revelation 21—22—**p. 1406**
Jesus weeps over, Luke 19:28-44—**p. 1165**
birthplace of Christian church, Acts 2—**p. 1211**

JEWISH HOLY DAYS
described, Exodus 12—**p. 77**;
Leviticus 16—**p. 130**; 23:4-43—**p. 138**;
Deuteronomy 16—**p. 214**

JEWS — (*see also* ISRAEL)
Paul's concern for, Romans 9—11—**p. 1260**

JEZEBEL — wicked queen of Israel, married to King Ahab

JOB
his story, Job 1—2—**p. 573**; Job 42—**p. 609**

JOHN THE APOSTLE — one of three disciples closest to Jesus; author of the fourth Gospel, three letters, and the book of Revelation
his call, Matthew 4:18-22—**p. 1068**
at transfiguration, Matthew 17:1-13—**p. 1085**
his desire to be first in the kingdom,
Mark 10:35-45—**p. 1121**
exiled on Patmos, Revelation 1—**p. 1389**

JOHN THE BAPTIST — forerunner of Jesus; preached repentance to prepare the way for the Messiah
praised by Jesus, Matthew 11:1-19—**p. 1076**
death of, Mark 6:14-29—**p. 1114**
birth of, Luke 1:5-25,57-80—**p. 1133**
baptizing, Luke 3:1-20—**p. 1138**
testimony of, John 1:19-34—**p. 1177**;
3:22-36—**p. 1180**

JONAH
prophet during Jeroboam II, 2 Kings 14:25—**p. 432**
his story, Jonah 1—4—**p. 1019**

JONATHAN — oldest son of King Saul; loyal friend to David
a mighty warrior, 1 Samuel 14—**p. 316**
helps David, 1 Samuel 19—20—**p. 324**
encourages David, 1 Samuel 23:7-18—**p. 329**
death of, 1 Samuel 31—2 Samuel 1—**p. 337**
mourned by David, 2 Samuel 1—**p. 340**

JORDAN RIVER
Naaman washed in, 2 Kings 5:1-14—**p. 419**
Jesus baptized in, Matthew 3:13—**p. 1067**

JOSEPH — son of Rachel and Jacob; Jacob's favorite son
life of, Genesis 37—50—**p. 46**
sold as slave, Genesis 37—**p. 46**
and Potiphar's wife, Genesis 39—**p. 48**
forgives brothers, Genesis 45—**p. 56**;
Genesis 50—**p. 62**

JOSEPH — earthly adoptive father of Jesus
visited by angel, Matthew 1:18-25—**p. 1065**
went to Egypt, Matthew 2—**p. 1065**
went to Bethlehem, Luke 2—**p. 1136**

JOSHUA — successor to Moses who led the Israelites into Canaan
spied out Canaan, Numbers 13—14—**p. 165**
commissioned, Numbers 27:12-23—**p. 184**

JOY
in salvation, Isaiah 12—**p. 773**; 35—**p. 795**;
1 Peter 1:1-9—**p. 1366**
Jesus' teaching on, Matthew 5:1-12—**p. 1068**
for repentance, Luke 15—**p. 1159**
through servanthood, John 13:1-17—**p. 1196**

an aspect of the Spirit's fruit,
Galatians 5:16-26—**p. 1302**
always, Philippians 4:4-9—**p. 1315**
in suffering, Colossians 1:24—**p. 1319**;
James 1:2-18—**p. 1361**;
1 Peter 4:12-19 —**p. 1369**
JUDAH — Southern Kingdom; nation of the southern tribes of Benjamin and Judah that remained loyal to Rehoboam
JUDAS ISCARIOT — the disciple who betrayed Jesus
as betrayer, Matthew 26:47-56—**p. 1100**
death of, Matthew 27:1-10—**p. 1101**;
Acts 1:18-19—**p. 1209**
as treasurer, John 12:1-8—**p. 1194**
JUDGING OTHERS
not to be done, Romans 14:1-13—**p. 1265**;
James 4:9-12—**p. 1363**
Jesus' words on, Matthew 7:1-5 —**p. 1071**
with mercy, James 2:1-13—**p. 1361**
JUDGMENT
God as judge, Psalm 94—**p. 671**
Jesus as judge, Acts 10:34-43—**p. 1223**
final, Matthew 24:36—25:46—**p. 1096**;
2 Thessalonians 1—2—**p. 1329**;
Revelation 18—20—**p. 1403**
JUSTICE
God executes, Psalm 146—**p. 703**
as true worship, Isaiah 58—**p. 822**
injustice condemned, Amos 5—**p. 1009**;
Micah 6—**p. 1027**
JUSTIFICATION — to be freed from guilt or blame
by faith, Romans 3:21-31—**p. 1255**;
4:1—5:11—**p. 1255**;
Galatians 2:15-21—**p. 1299**

K

KINDNESS — a hospitable, friendly attitude toward others (*see also* HOSPITALITY)
an aspect of the Spirit's fruit,
Galatians 5:16-26—**p. 1302**
KING
Israel asks for, 1 Samuel 8—**p. 310**
Samuel's comments on, 1 Samuel 12—**p. 314**
God as, Psalm 47—**p. 639**; 99—**p. 674**;
1 Timothy 1:15-17—**p. 1332**
Jesus on David's throne, Luke 1:26-38—**p. 1134**
Jesus now ruling at God's right hand,
Ephesians 1:15-34—**p. 1306**;
Hebrews 1:1-12—**p. 1348**
KINGDOM OF GOD (*or* KINGDOM OF HEAVEN) — wherever God is reigning; also, the people experiencing God's reign
parables of, Matthew 13:1-52—**p. 1079**;
18:10-14, 21-35—**p. 1087**;
20:1-16—**p. 1089**; 21:28-46—**p. 1091**;
22:1-14—**p. 1092**; 25:1-46—**p. 1096**
has come in Jesus, Mark 1:14-15—**p. 1107**;
Luke 7:18-22—**p. 1145**; 11:14-20—**p. 1153**
to be handed over to God,
1 Corinthians 15:20-28—**p. 1283**

L

LAMB OF GOD — a title John the Baptist gave to Jesus
removes sin, John 1:29-42—**p. 1177**
receives praise, Revelation 5—**p. 1393**
LAUGHTER
of Sarah, Genesis 18:1-15—**p. 20**; 21:1-7—**p. 24**
God's, Psalm 2—**p. 611**
time for, Ecclesiastes 3:1-8—**p. 743**
LAW — a set of commandments given by God
given to Moses, Exodus 19:1—24:8—**p. 86**
fulfillment of, Matthew 5:17-48—**p. 1069**
in hearts, Jeremiah 31:33—**p. 873**;
Hebrews 8—**p. 1353**
LAZARUS — brother of Mary and Martha; close friend of Jesus
Jesus raises from the dead, John 11:1-44—**p. 1192**
LAZARUS — character in story Jesus told
carried to Abraham's side, Luke 16:19-31—**p. 1161**
LAZINESS
warnings against, 2 Thessalonians 3:6-15—**p. 1330**
LEADERSHIP
following, Hebrews 13:7-17 —**p. 1359**
qualities of, 1 Timothy 3:1-10—**p. 1333**
LEGALISM — *see* LAW
LEPROSY — *see* HEALING
LEVITE — a descendant of Levi who served God and worked in the temple. (Priests were Levites, but not all Levites were priests; some had lesser duties.)
duties established for, Numbers 3—**p. 151**;
1 Chronicles 23—24—**p. 478**
received cities, Numbers 35—**p. 193**
LIFE (*see also* ETERNAL LIFE)
shortness of, Psalm 39—**p. 634**
saving your, Matthew 16:24-28—**p. 1085**
eternal, John 3:16-21—**p. 1179**;
John 6:25-69—**p. 1185**;
Colossians 3:1-4—**p. 1320**
living water, John 4:1-26—**p. 1180**
Jesus brings it to the full, John 10:1-18—**p. 1191**
a gift of God, Acts 17:24-28—**p. 1234**
LIGHT
created first by God, Genesis 1:1-5—**p. 4**
God's Word as, Psalm 119:105—**p. 691**
of the world, Matthew 5:14-16—**p. 1069**
Jesus as, John 1:1-18—**p. 1176**; 8:12—**p. 1188**
believers as children of,
Ephesians 5:8-14—**p. 1309**;
1 John 1—**p. 1376**
LION
killed by Samson, Judges 14—**p. 284**
killed by David, 1 Samuel 17:34-35—**p. 322**
and lamb together, Isaiah 11:6-9—**p. 772**;
65:25—**p. 831**
Daniel in den of, Daniel 6—**p. 977**
Christ as, Revelation 5:1-5—**p. 1393**
LONELINESS
cry of, Psalm 22—**p. 622**
Jesus', Matthew 26:36-46—**p. 1100**
Paul's, 2 Timothy 4:16-18—**p. 1340**
LORD
revealed to Moses, Exodus 3—**p. 67**
of lords, Deuteronomy 10:17—**p. 209**;
1 Timothy 6:13-16—**p. 1335**;
Revelation 19:13-16—**p. 1405**
Jesus as, Acts 2:14-36—**p. 1211**;
Romans 10:9-10—**p. 1262**;
Philippians 2:5-11—**p. 1313**
LORD'S PRAYER
taught, Matthew 6:5-15—**p. 1070**
LORD'S SUPPER — a ritual sharing bread and wine; also called Communion and Eucharist

Jesus began, Luke 22:7-23—**p. 1169**
instructions concerning,
1 Corinthians 11:17-34—**p. 1279**
LOT — nephew of Abraham who settled in the land near Sodom
separates from Abram, Genesis 13—**p. 16**
in Sodom, Genesis 18:16—19:38—**p. 21**
LOVE
shown to an enemy, Romans 12:18-21—**p. 1264**
of God for his people, Jeremiah 31:1-6—**p. 871**
commanded, Mark 12:28-34—**p. 1124**;
John 13:34-35—**p. 1197**;
Romans 12:9-21—**p. 1264**
described, 1 Corinthians 13—**p. 1281**
an aspect of the Spirit's fruit,
Galatians 5:13-26—**p. 1302**
of the world, 1 John 2:15-17—**p. 1377**
God is, 1 John 4:7-21—**p. 1378**
LUKE — author of the third Gospel; physician who traveled with Paul
travel companion of Paul, Acts 16:10-17—**p. 1232**;
20:5—21:18—**p. 1238**;
27:1—28:16—**p. 1247**
LUST — intense desire (*see* SEX)
LYING
law against, Exodus 20:16—**p. 87**
penalty for, Leviticus 6:1-7—**p. 117**
by Peter, Matthew 26:69-74—**p. 1101**
Satan the father of, John 8:44—**p. 1189**
mark of old nature,
Ephesians 4:17—5:21—**p. 1308**

M

MAGIC — *see* ASTROLOGY, WITCHCRAFT
MARK — author of the second Gospel and missionary helper to Paul and Barnabas
MARRIAGE (*see also* DIVORCE, HUSBAND, LOVE, WIFE)
God ordained, Genesis 2:18-25—**p. 6**
importance of, Matthew 19:1-12—**p. 1088**
relationship, Ephesians 5:22-33—**p. 1309**;
Colossians 3:18-19—**p. 1321**;
1 Peter 3:1-7—**p. 1368**
Paul's advice on, 1 Corinthians 7—**p. 1275**
MARTHA AND MARY — sisters of Lazarus; friends of Jesus
Jesus at home of, Luke 10:38-42—**p. 1152**
at Lazarus's death, John 11—**p. 1192**
washed Jesus' feet, John 12:1-8—**p. 1194**
MARTYR — one who gives up life for the faith
Stephen as, Acts 7—**p. 1217**
many examples of, Hebrews 11:35-40—**p. 1357**;
Revelation 6:9-11—**p. 1394**
MARY — mother of Jesus; wife of Joseph
Jesus born to, Matthew 1:18—2:23—**p. 1065**;
Luke 1:26-56—**p. 1134**; Luke 2—**p. 1136**
concerned for Jesus, Mark 3:20-35—**p. 1110**;
Luke 2:41-52—**p. 1137**
requests Jesus' first miracle, John 2:1-11—**p. 1178**
at crucifixion, John 19:16-27—**p. 1204**
MARY MAGDALENE — a close friend of Jesus
present at crucifixion, Mark 15:33-41—**p. 1130**
had been demon-possessed, Luke 8:1-3—**p. 1146**
first one at empty tomb, John 20:1-18—**p. 1205**
MATTHEW — author of the first Gospel; left his work to follow Jesus; also called Levi
hosted a dinner for Jesus, Mark 2:13-17—**p. 1109**
MEDIATOR — someone who helps bring harmony between two parties
Jesus as, 1 Timothy 2:1-6—**p. 1332**;
Hebrews 9:11-28—**p. 1354**
MEDITATION — *see* QUIET TIME
MELCHIZEDEK — priest and king
blessed Abram, Genesis 14:17-20—**p. 18**
pointed to Christ, Psalm 110—**p. 684**;
Hebrews 5:1-10—**p. 1351**;
Hebrews 7—**p. 1352**
MERCY
pleading for, Psalm 4—**p. 612**;
Luke 18:9-14—**p. 1163**
of God, Psalm 108:8-12—**p. 682**;
Psalm 123—**p. 694**; Luke 1:46-79—**p. 1135**;
Romans 9:15-18—**p. 1261**
for the merciful, James 2:12-13—**p. 1362**
MESSIAH — a king and deliverer expected by the Jewish people; Christ
prophecies concerning, Psalm 2—**p. 611**;
110—**p. 684**; Isaiah 9:1-7—**p. 769**;
11:1-12—**p. 772**; 53:1-12—**p. 818**;
61:1-3—**p. 826**; Daniel 7:13-14—**p. 979**
Jesus as, Matthew 11:1-6—**p. 1076**;
Luke 4:14-21—**p. 1140**
MICHAEL — the archangel appointed to guard the Jewish people
with Daniel, Daniel 10—**p. 983**; 12:1-13—**p. 986**
and war in heaven, Revelation 12—**p. 1398**
MILITARY — *see* WAR
MILLENNIUM — Latin word for "thousand years"; used in connection with a period in the last days
described, Revelation 20:1-15—**p. 1406**
MINISTER — *see* PASTOR
MIRACLES — extraordinary events done through God's power
lead to belief, John 4:43-54—**p. 1182**;
20:30-31—**p. 1206**
done to glorify God, John 11:1-44—**p. 1192**
MIRIAM — prophetess, sister of Moses and Aaron
led singing/dancing, Exodus 15:19-21—**p. 82**
disagreed with Moses, Numbers 12—**p. 164**
MISSIONS (*see also* EVANGELISM)
highly praised, Isaiah 52:7-10—**p. 817**;
Romans 10:14-15—**p. 1262**
command to, Matthew 28:16-20—**p. 1104**;
Luke 24:45-52—**p. 1174**;
Acts 1:1-11—**p. 1209**
responsibility of every Christian,
Acts 8:1-6—**p. 1219**;
1 Peter 3:15-16—**p. 1369**
Barnabas and Saul (Paul) sent,
Acts 13:1-3—**p. 1226**
Paul's journeys, Acts 13—28—**p. 1226**
MONEY
God owns everything, Deuteronomy 8—**p. 206**;
Psalm 24—**p. 624**
serving, Matthew 6:19-34—**p. 1070**
trusting, Psalm 62:10—**p. 648**
love of, 1 Timothy 6:3-19—**p. 1335**;
James 5:1-5—**p. 1364**
MOSES — used by God to deliver Israelites from slavery in Egypt; God gave him the Ten Commandments
life of, Exodus 2—40—**p. 65**; Numbers 1—36—**p. 147**; Deuteronomy 1—34—**p. 197**

Q

R

pure, James 1:26-27—**p. 1361**
REPENTANCE — to feel sorry for and turn from sins; a common theme of Old Testament prophets
preached by Jesus, Matthew 4:12-17—**p. 1068**; Luke 13:1-5—**p. 1157**
parable concerning, Luke 18:9-14—**p. 1163**
preached by Peter, Acts 2:38-41—**p. 1212**
preached by Paul, Acts 17:22-31—**p. 1234**
described by Paul, 2 Corinthians 7:9-10—**p. 1291**
RESPONSIBILITY
for sin, Ezekiel 18—**p. 929**
to love others, 1 John 3:11-24—**p. 1378**
REST
day of, Genesis 2:1-3—**p. 6**; Exodus 20:8—**p. 87**
in God, Psalm 23—**p. 623**; 62—**p. 648**
for weary, Matthew 11:25-30—**p. 1077**
RESURRECTION
hinted in Old Testament, Job 19:23-27—**p. 588**; Ezekiel 37:1-14—**p. 953**; Daniel 12:1-2—**p. 986**
of Jesus, Matthew 27:57—28:20—**p. 1103**
Jesus predicts his own, Mark 8:31—**p. 1118**; 9:31—**p. 1119**; 10:33-34—**p. 1121**
of the dead, 1 Corinthians 15—**p. 1282**; 1 Thessalonians 4:13-18—**p. 1326**
Ephesians 1:15-23—**p. 1306**
spiritual in Christ, Romans 6:1-14—**p. 1257**; Colossians 2:9-15—**p. 1320**; 3:1-17—**p. 1320**
REVENGE
on enemies, do not take, Matthew 5:38-47—**p. 1069**; Romans 12:17-21—**p. 1265**
REVERENCE — *see* FEAR
REVELATION — God's disclosure of himself and his truth
in nature, Psalm 19:1-6—**p. 620**; Acts 14:14-17—**p. 1229**; Romans 1:18-23—**p. 1253**
in Jesus Christ, John 1:1-18—**p. 1176**; Hebrews 1—**p. 1348**
in the Bible, 2 Timothy 3:14-17—**p. 1339**; 2 Peter 1:19-21—**p. 1372**
REWARD
everyone according to deeds, Leviticus 26—**p. 142**; Psalm 62:11-12—**p. 648**; Jeremiah 17:10—**p. 856**; 2 Corinthians 5:1-10—**p. 1289**
in heaven, Matthew 5:3-12—**p. 1068**; Mark 10:29-31—**p. 1121**; 1 Corinthians 3:10-15—**p. 1272**
RICHES — *see* MONEY, POOR, WEALTH
RIGHTEOUSNESS — the state of being perfect, without sin
attribute of God, Psalm 7—**p. 613**; Jeremiah 23:1-6—**p. 862**
by faith, Romans 4:6-8—**p. 1256**; Galatians 2:15-21—**p. 1299**; Philippians 3:7-11—**p. 1314**
goal of Christian life, Matthew 6:25-34—**p. 1071**; 1 Timothy 6:11-16—**p. 1335**; 1 Peter 2:24-25—**p. 1368**
ROCK
God as, Deuteronomy 32:1-4—**p. 231**; Psalm 18—**p. 619**; Isaiah 26—**p. 785**
Peter as, Matthew 16:16-20—**p. 1085**; John 1:35-42—**p. 1177**
Christ as, 1 Corinthians 10:1-4—**p. 1278**; 1 Peter 2:1-10—**p. 1367**
ROME — capital of the Roman empire; ruled Palestine during the time of Christ; a church was started here
Paul travels to, Acts 27:1—28:31—**p. 1247**
RUTH — Moabite woman who married Boaz and became an ancestor of Jesus
in Jesus' genealogy, Matthew 1:5—**p. 1064**

S

SABBATH — a day of worship and rest; traditionally Saturday for Jews
to be kept holy, Exodus 20:8-11—**p. 87**; Ezekiel 20:1-29—**p. 931**
laws concerning, Exodus 31:14-15—**p. 100**; Leviticus 23:1-3—**p. 138**
made for people, Mark 2:23—3:6—**p. 1109**
symbol of eternal rest, Hebrews 4:1-11—**p. 1350**
SACRIFICE — offering of something valuable to God
Cain's and Abel's, Genesis 4:1-5—**p. 8**
Noah's, Genesis 8:20-22—**p. 12**
Abraham's, Genesis 12:1-11—**p. 16**; 22:1-19—**p. 25**
prescribed, Leviticus 1—7—**p. 113**
Christ as, Isaiah 53—**p. 818**; Hebrews 10—**p. 1355**
our lives as, Romans 12:1-2—**p. 1264**
SADDUCEES — a small but powerful Jewish sect in Christ's time; denied life after death
Jesus warns against, Matthew 16:1-12—**p. 1084**
Jesus confronts, Mark 12:18-23—**p. 1124**
opposed early church, Acts 4:1-22—**p. 1213**; Acts 5:17-42—**p. 1215**
opposed Paul, Acts 23:1-11—**p. 1242**
SALVATION — deliverance from danger or evil; especially deliverance from all that separates people from God (*see also* CONVERSION, JUSTIFICATION, REPENTANCE)
available to all, Romans 10:1-13—**p. 1262**
Jesus' mission of, Luke 19:1-10—**p. 1164**
through faith, Acts 16:16-34—**p. 1233**
to be completed at end of time, Romans 5:6-11—**p. 1256**
by grace, Ephesians 2:1-10—**p. 1306**; Titus 3:3-8—**p. 1343**
SAMARITAN — an inhabitant of Samaria; a people held in contempt by the Jews
conflict with returned exiles, Ezra 4—5—**p. 533**; Nehemiah 4—6—**p. 548**
parable of the good, Luke 10:25-37 —**p. 1152**
woman with Jesus, John 4:1-42—**p. 1180**
SAMSON — one of the last judges of Israel; a Nazirite known for his physical strength
life of, Judges 13—16—**p. 283**
and Delilah, Judges 16—**p. 286**
SAMUEL — last of the judges of Israel
his early years, 1 Samuel 1:1—3:21—**p. 302**
leads Israel, 1 Samuel 5:1—8:22—**p. 307**
with Saul, 1 Samuel 9:1—15:35—**p. 311**
anoints David, 1 Samuel 16:1-13—**p. 320**
his death, 1 Samuel 25:1—**p. 331**
man of faith, Hebrews 11:32—**p. 1357**
SANCTIFICATION — act of God by which a believer conforms more and more to the image of Christ (*see also* HOLY)
Jesus' prayer for, John 17:17-19—**p. 1201**
possible only in Christ,

WHERE TO FIND IT

WELL-KNOWN EVENTS
(in approximate order of occurrence)

Creation, Genesis 1-2
The first sin, or fall, Genesis 3
Cain kills Abel, Genesis 4
Noah and the ark, Genesis 6-9
Sodom and Gomorrah, Genesis 18-19
Abraham sacrifices Isaac, Genesis 22
Jacob's ladder, Genesis 28:10-22
Joseph and the coat, Genesis 37
Moses' birth, Exodus 2
Moses and the burning bush, Exodus 3
Plagues on Egypt, Exodus 7-11
The exodus, Exodus 12-13
The Ten Commandments, Exodus 20
The battle of Jericho, Joshua 6
Gideon and the fleece, Judges 6-7
Samson and Delilah, Judges 13-16
God calls the boy Samuel, 1 Samuel 1-3
David and Goliath, 1 Samuel 17
David and Bathsheba, 2 Samuel 11
Elijah versus the priests of Baal, 1 Kings 18
The miracles of Elisha, 2 Kings 4-5
Jonah and the fish, Jonah 1
Hosea and his adulterous wife, Hosea 1-3
Ezekiel and the dry bones, Ezekiel 37
Daniel in the lions' den, Daniel 6
Birth of Jesus, Luke 1-2
Baptism of Jesus, Mark 1:9-11
Temptation of Jesus, Luke 4:1-13
Jesus clears the temple, John 2:12-25
The transfiguration of Jesus, Matthew 17:1-13
Jesus raises Lazarus from the dead, John 11:1-46
Jesus' Triumphal Entry into Jerusalem, Mark 11:1-11
Jesus and the widow's offering, Mark 12:41-44
The Last Supper, Luke 22:7-38
Jesus washes his disciples' feet, John 13:1-17
Jesus at Gethsemane, Matthew 26:36-56
Judas betrays Jesus, Luke 22:1-53
Peter denies Christ, Luke 22:54-62
The crucifixion, Matthew 26:57-27:66
Resurrection and ascension, Luke 24
Holy Spirit at Pentecost, Acts 2
Stephen stoned, Acts 6-7
Paul's conversion, Acts 9:1-31
Peter's escape from prison, Acts 12:1-19
Paul and Silas in prison, Acts 16:16-40

MIRACLES OF JESUS
(in biblical order)

Healing of individuals
Man with leprosy, Matthew 8:1-4; Mark 1:40-44; Luke 5:12-14
Roman centurion's servant, Matthew 8:5-13; Luke 7:1-10
Peter's mother-in-law, Matthew 8:14-17; Mark 1:29-31; Luke 4:38-39
Two demon-possessed men from Gadara, Matthew 8:28-34
Paralyzed man, Matthew 9:1-8; Mark 2:1-12; Luke 5:17-26
Two blind men, Matthew 9:27-31
Man mute and possessed, Matthew 9:32-33
Man blind, mute, and possessed, Matthew 12:22
Canaanite woman's daughter, Matthew 15:21-28
Boy with epilepsy, Matthew 17:14-18
Two blind men, Matthew 20:29-34
Man with a shriveled hand, Matthew 12:9-13; Mark 3:1-5; Luke 6:6-11
Man with an evil spirit, Mark 1:23-26; Luke 4:33-36
Deaf mute, Mark 7:31-37
Blind man, Mark 8:22-26
Bartimaeus, or one blind man, Mark 10:46-52; Luke 18:35-43
Woman with bleeding, Luke 8:43-48
Crippled woman, Luke 13:11-13
Man with dropsy, Luke 14:1-4

Ten men with leprosy, Luke 17:11-19
The high priest's servant, Luke 22:50-51
Royal official's son, John 4:46-54
Man at the pool of Bethesda, John 5:1-9

Control of nature
Calming of storm, Matthew 8:23-27; Mark 4:35-41; Luke 8:22-25
Feeding of 5,000, Matthew 14:1-21; Mark 6:35-44; Luke 9:12-17; John 6:5-15
Walking on water, Matthew 14:22-23; Mark 6:45-52; John 6:16-21
Feeding of 4,000, Matthew 15:29-39; Mark 8:1-9
Fish with coin, Matthew 17:24-27
Fig tree withers, Matthew 21:18-22; Mark 11:12-14,20-25
Huge catch of fish, Luke 5:1-11; John 21:1-11
Water into wine, John 2:1-11

Raising the dead
Jairus's daughter, Mark 5:22-42
Widow's son at Nain, Luke 7:11-15
Lazarus, John 11:1-44

PARABLES OF JESUS
(*in alphabetical order*)

Canceled debts, Luke 7:41-43
Cost of discipleship, Luke 14:28-33
Faithful servant, Luke 12:42-48
Fig tree, Matthew 24:32-35; Mark 13:28-29; Luke 21:29-31
Good Samaritan, Luke 10:30-37
The great banquet, Luke 14:16-24
Growing seed, Mark 4:26-29
Hidden treasure and pearl, Matthew 13:44-46
Honor at a banquet, Luke 14:7-14
Light of the world, Matthew 5:14-15
Lost coin, Luke 15:8-10
Lost sheep, Matthew 18:12-14; Luke 15:3-7
Mustard seed, Matthew 13:31-32
New wine in old wineskins, Matthew 9:16-17; Mark 2:21-22; Luke 5:36-39
Net, Matthew 13:47-50
Obedient servants, Luke 17:7-10
Persistent friend, Luke 11:5-8
Persistent widow (unjust judge), Luke 18:2-8
Pharisee and the tax collector (publican), Luke 18:10-14
Prodigal (or lost) son, Luke 15:11-32
Rich fool, Luke 12:16-21
Rich man and Lazarus, Luke 16:19-31
Sheep and the goats, Matthew 25:31-46
Shrewd manager (unjust steward), Luke 16:1-8
Sower, Matthew 13:1-8,18-23; Mark 4:3-8, 14-20; Luke 8:5-8, 11-15
Talents, Matthew 25:14-30
Tenants, Matthew 21:33-44; Mark 12:1-12; Luke 20:9-18
Ten minas (pounds), Luke 19:11-27
Ten virgins, Matthew 25:1-13
Two sons, Matthew 21:28-31
Unfruitful fig tree, Luke 13:6-9
Unmerciful servant, Matthew 18:23-34
Watchful servants, Luke 12:35-40
Wedding banquet, Matthew 22:2-14
Weeds, Matthew 13:24-30,36-43
Wise and foolish builders, Matthew 7:24-27; Luke 6:47-49
Workers in the vineyard, Matthew 20:1-16
Yeast (leaven), Matthew 13:33; Luke 13:20-21

TEACHINGS OF JESUS
(*in alphabetical order*)

Beatitudes, Matthew 5:1-12
Bread of life, John 6:25-59
Born again, John 3:1-21
Discipleship, Luke 14:25-35
Give to Caesar, Mark 12:13-17
Good shepherd, John 10:1-21
Golden rule, Luke 6:31
Greatest commandment, Matthew 22:34-40
Living water, John 4:1-26
Lord's prayer, Matthew 6:5-15
Sending out the Twelve, Matthew 10
Sermon on the Mount, Matthew 5-7
Vine and branches, John 15:1-17
The way, the truth, and the life, John 14:5-14
Wealth, Matthew 19:16-30
Worry, Luke 12:22-34

OUTLINE OF OLD TESTAMENT HISTORY

This outline emphasizes broad historical periods rather than specific events. Dates, which often depend on scholarly interpretation, are approximate.

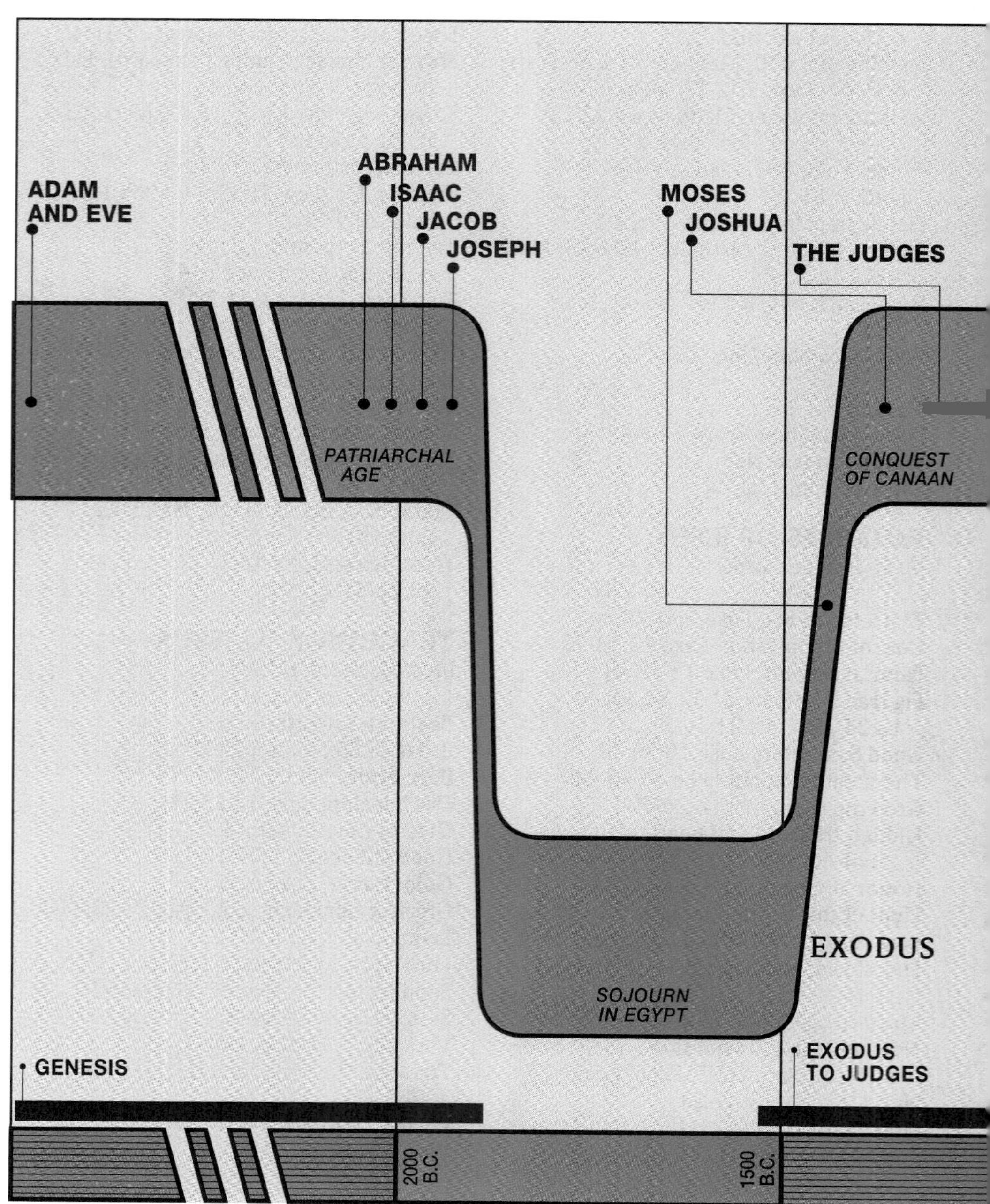

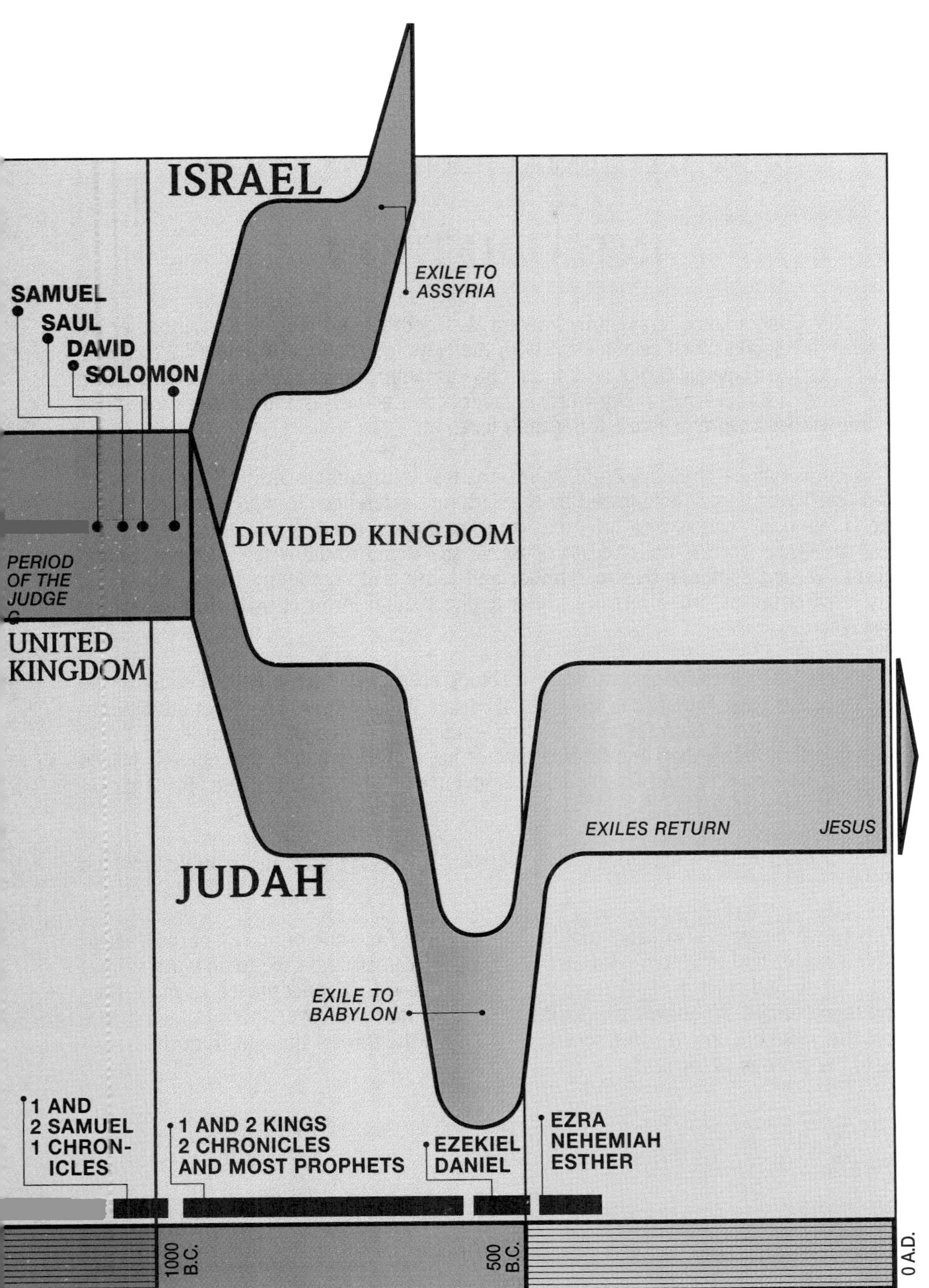
ISRAEL
EXILE TO
ASSYRIA
SAMUEL
SAUL
DAVID
SOLOMON
DIVIDED KINGDOM
PERIOD
OF THE
JUDGE
S
UNITED
KINGDOM
EXILES RETURN
JESUS
JUDAH
EXILE TO
BABYLON
1 AND
2 SAMUEL
1 CHRON-
ICLES
1 AND 2 KINGS
2 CHRONICLES
AND MOST PROPHETS
EZEKIEL
DANIEL
EZRA
NEHEMIAH
ESTHER
1000
B.C.
500
B.C.
0 A.D.

A CONCORDANCE
to the
NEW INTERNATIONAL VERSION

INTRODUCTION

The NIV Concordance, created by Edward W. Goodrick and John R. Kohlenberger III, has been developed specifically for use with the New International Version. Like all concordances, it is a special index which contains an alphabetical listing of words used in the Bible text. By looking up key words, readers can find verses and passages for which they remember a word or two but not their location.

This concordance contains 2,000 word entries, with some 13,000 Scripture references. Each word entry is followed by the Scripture references in which that particular word is found, as well as by a brief excerpt from the surrounding context. The first letter of the entry word is italicized to conserve space and to allow for a longer context excerpt. Variant spellings due to number and tense and compound forms follow the entry in parentheses, and direct the reader to check other forms of that word in locating a passage.

This concordance contains a number of "block entries," which highlight some of the key events and characteristics in the lives of certain Bible figures. The descriptive phrases replace the brief context surrounding each occurrence of the name. In those instances where more than one Bible character has the same name, that name is placed under one block entry, and each person is given a number (1), (2), etc. Insignificant names are not included.

Word or block entries marked with an asterisk (*) list every verse in the Bible in which the word appears.

This concordance is a valuable tool for Bible study. While one of its key purposes is to help the reader find forgotten references to verses, it can also be used to do word studies and to locate and trace biblical themes. Be sure to use this concordance as more than just a verse finder. Whenever you look up a verse, aim to discover the intended meaning of the verse in context. Give special attention to the flow of thought from the beginning of the passage to the end.

AARON

Priesthood of (Ex 28:1; Nu 17; Heb 5:1-4; 7), garments (Ex 28; 39), consecration (Ex 29), ordination (Lev 8).

Spokesman for Moses (Ex 4:14-16, 27-31; 7:1-2). Supported Moses' hands in battle (Ex 17:8-13). Built golden calf (Ex 32; Dt 9:20). Talked against Moses (Nu 12). Priesthood opposed (Nu 16); staff budded (Nu 17). Forbidden to enter land (Nu 20:1-12). Death (Nu 20:22-29; 33:38-39).

ABANDON

Dt 4: 31 he will not *a* or destroy you
1Ti 4: 1 in later times some will *a* the faith

ABBA

Ro 8: 15 And by him we cry, *"A,* Father."
Gal 4: 6 the Spirit who calls out, *"A,* Father

ABEL

Second son of Adam (Ge 4:2). Offered proper sacrifice (Ge 4:4; Heb 11:4). Murdered by Cain (Ge 4:8; Mt 23:35; Lk 11:51; 1Jn 3:12).

ABHORS

Pr 11: 1 The LORD *a* dishonest scales,

ABIGAIL

Wife of Nabal (1Sa 25:30); pled for his life with David (1Sa 25:14-35). Became David's wife (1Sa 25:36-42).

ABIJAH

Son of Rehoboam; king of Judah (1Ki 14:31-15:8; 2Ch 12:16-14:1).

ABILITY (ABLE)

Ezr 2: 69 According to their *a* they gave
2Co 1: 8 far beyond our *a* to endure,
8: 3 were able, and even beyond their *a.*

ABIMELECH

1. King of Gerar who took Abraham's wife Sarah, believing her to be his sister (Ge 20). Later made a covenant with Abraham (Ge 21:22-33).

2. King of Gerar who took Isaac's wife Rebekah, believing her to be his sister (Ge 26:1-11). Later made a covenant with Isaac (Ge 26:12-31).

ABLE (ABILITY ENABLE ENABLED ENABLES)

Eze 7: 19 and gold will not be *a* to save them
Da 3: 17 the God we serve is *a* to save us
Ro 8: 39 will be *a* to separate us
14: 4 for the Lord is *a* to make him stand
16: 25 to him who is *a* to establish you
2Co 9: 8 God is *a* to make all grace abound
Eph 3: 20 him who is *a* to do immeasurably
2Ti 1: 12 and am convinced that he is *a*
3: 15 which are *a* to make you wise
Heb 7: 25 he is *a* to save completely
Jude : 24 To him who is *a* to keep you
Rev 5: 5 He is *a* to open the scroll

ABOLISH

Mt 5: 17 that I have come to *a* the Law

ABOMINATION

Da 11: 31 set up the *a* that causes desolation.

ABOUND (ABOUNDING)

2Co 9: 8 able to make all grace *a* to you,
Php 1: 9 that your love may *a* more

ABOUNDING (ABOUND)

Ex 34: 6 slow to anger, *a* in love
Ps 86: 5 *a* in love to all who call to you.

ABRAHAM

Covenant relation with the LORD (Ge 12:1-3; 13:14-17; 15; 17; 22:15-18; Ex 2:24; Ne 9:8; Ps 105; Mic 7:20; Lk 1:68-75; Ro 4; Heb 6:13-15).

Called from Ur, via Haran, to Canaan (Ge 12:1; Ac 7:2-4; Heb 11:8-10). Moved to Egypt, nearly lost Sarah to Pharoah (Ge 12:10-20). Divided the land with Lot (Ge 13). Saved Lot from four kings (Ge 14:1-16); blessed by Melchizedek (Ge 14:17-20; Heb 7:1-20). Declared righteous by faith (Ge 15:6; Ro 4:3; Gal 3:6-9). Fathered Ishmael by Hagar (Ge 16).

Name changed from Abram (Ge 17:5; Ne 9:7). Circumcised (Ge 17; Ro 4:9-12). Entertained three visitors (Ge 18); promised a son by Sarah (Ge 18:9-15; 17:16). Moved to Gerar; nearly lost Sarah to Abimelech (Ge 20). Fathered Isaac by Sarah (Ge 21:1-7; Ac 7:8; Heb 11:11-12); sent away Hagar and Ishmael (Ge 21:8-21; Gal 4:22-30). Tested by offering Isaac (Ge 22; Heb 11:17-19; Jas 2:21-24). Sarah died; bought field of Ephron for burial (Ge 23). Secured wife for Isaac (Ge 24). Death (Ge 25:7-11).

ABSALOM

Son of David by Maacah (2Sa 3:3; 1Ch 3:2). Killed Amnon for rape of his sister Tamar; banished by David (2Sa 13). Returned to Jerusalem; received by David (2Sa 14). Rebelled against David; seized kingdom (2Sa 15-17). Killed (2Sa 18).

ABSTAIN (ABSTAINS)

1Pe 2: 11 to *a* from sinful desires,

ABSTAINS* (ABSTAIN)

Ro 14: 6 thanks to God; and he who *a,*

ABUNDANCE (ABUNDANT)

Lk 12: 15 consist in the *a* of his possessions."
Jude : 2 peace and love be yours in *a.*

ABUNDANT (ABUNDANCE)

Dt 28: 11 will grant you *a* prosperity—
Ps 145: 7 will celebrate your *a* goodness
Pr 28: 19 works his land will have *a* food,
Ro 5: 17 who receive God's *a* provision

ACCEPT (ACCEPTED ACCEPTS)

Ex 23: 8 "Do not *a* a bribe,
Pr 10: 8 The wise in heart *a* commands,
19: 20 Listen to advice and *a* instruction,
Ro 15: 7 *A* one another, then, just
Jas 1: 21 humbly *a* the word planted in you,

ACCEPTED (ACCEPT)

Lk 4: 24 "no prophet is *a* in his hometown.

ACCEPTS (ACCEPT)

Ps 6: 9 the LORD *a* my prayer.
Jn 13: 20 whoever *a* anyone I send *a* me;

ACCOMPANY

Mk 16: 17 these signs will *a* those who believe
Heb 6: 9 your case—things that *a* salvation.

ACCOMPLISH

Isa 55: 11 but will *a* what I desire

ACCORD

Nu 24: 13 not do anything of my own *a,*
Jn 10: 18 but I lay it down of my own *a.*
12: 49 For I did not speak of my own *a,*

ACCOUNT (ACCOUNTABLE)

Mt 12: 36 to give *a* on the day of judgment
Ro 14: 12 each of us will give an *a* of himself
Heb 4: 13 of him to whom we must give *a.*

ACCOUNTABLE (ACCOUNT)

Eze 33: 6 but I will hold the watchman *a*
Ro 3: 19 and the whole world held *a* to God.

ACCUSATION (ACCUSE)

1Ti 5: 19 Do not entertain an *a*

ACCUSATIONS (ACCUSE)

2Pe 2: 11 do not bring slanderous *a*

ACCUSE (ACCUSATION ACCUSATIONS)

Pr 3: 30 Do not *a* a man for no reason—
Lk 3: 14 and don't *a* people falsely—

ACHAN*

Sin at Jericho caused defeat at Ai; stoned (Jos 7; 22:20; 1Ch 2:7).

ACHE*

Pr 14: 13 Even in laughter the heart may *a,*

ACKNOWLEDGE

Mt 10: 32 *a* him before my Father in heaven.
1Jn 4: 3 spirit that does not *a* Jesus is not

ACQUIT

Ex 23: 7 to death, for I will not *a* the guilty.

ACTION (ACTIONS ACTIVE ACTS)

Jas 2: 17 if it is not accompanied by *a,*
1Pe 1: 13 minds for *a;* be self-controlled;

ACTIONS (ACTION)

Mt 11: 19 wisdom is proved right by her *a."*
Gal 6: 4 Each one should test his own *a.*
Tit 1: 16 but by their *a* they deny him.

ACTIVE (ACTION)

Heb 4: 12 For the word of God is living and *a*

ACTS (ACTION)

Ps 145: 12 all men may know of your mighty *a*
150: 2 Praise him for his *a* of power;
Isa 64: 6 all our righteous *a* are like filthy
Mt 6: 1 not to do your '*a* of righteousness'

ADAM

First man (Ge 1:26-2:25; Ro 5:14; 1Ti 2:13). Sin of (Ge 3; Hos 6:7; Ro 5:12-21). Children of (Ge 4:1-5:5). Death of (Ge 5:5; Ro 5:12-21; 1Co 15:22).

ADD

Dt 12: 32 do not *a* to it or take away from it.
Pr 30: 6 Do not *a* to his words,
Lk 12: 25 by worrying can *a* a single hour

Rev 22: 18 God will *a* to him the plagues

ADMIRABLE*

Php 4: 8 whatever is lovely, whatever is *a*—

ADMONISH

Col 3: 16 and *a* one another with all wisdom,

ADOPTED (ADOPTION)

Eph 1: 5 In love he predestined us to be *a*

ADOPTION (ADOPTED)

Ro 8: 23 as we wait eagerly for our *a* as sons,

ADORE*

SS 1: 4 How right they are to *a* you!

ADORNMENT* (ADORNS)

1Pe 3: 3 should not come from outward *a*,

ADORNS (ADORNMENT)

Ps 93: 5 holiness *a* your house

ADULTERY

Ex 20: 14 "You shall not commit *a*.
Mt 5: 27 that it was said, 'Do not commit *a*.'
5: 28 lustfully has already committed *a*
5: 32 the divorced woman commits *a*.
15: 19 murder, *a*, sexual immorality, theft

ADULTS*

1Co 14: 20 but in your thinking be *a*.

ADVANCED

Job 32: 7 *a* years should teach wisdom.'

ADVANTAGE

Ex 22: 22 "Do not take *a* of a widow
Dt 24: 14 Do not take *a* of a hired man who is
1Th 4: 6 should wrong his brother or take *a*

ADVERSITY

Pr 17: 17 and a brother is born for *a*.

ADVICE

1Ki 12: 8 rejected the *a* the elders
12: 14 he followed the *a* of the young men
Pr 12: 5 but the *a* of the wicked is deceitful.
12: 15 but a wise man listens to *a*.
19: 20 Listen to *a* and accept instruction,
20: 18 Make plans by seeking *a*;

AFFLICTION

Ro 12: 12 patient in *a*, faithful in prayer.

AFRAID (FEAR)

Ge 26: 24 Do not be *a*, for I am with you;
Ex 3: 6 because he was *a* to look at God.
Ps 27: 1 of whom shall I be *a*?
56: 3 When I am *a*, / I will trust in you.
Pr 3: 24 lie down, you will not be *a*;
Jer 1: 8 Do not be *a* of them, for I am
Mt 8: 26 You of little faith, why are you so *a*
10: 28 be *a* of the One who can destroy
10: 31 So don't be *a*; you are worth more
Mk 5: 36 "Don't be *a*; just believe."
Jn 14: 27 hearts be troubled and do not be *a*.
Heb 13: 6 Lord is my helper; I will not be *a*.

AGED

Job 12: 12 Is not wisdom found among the *a*?
Pr 17: 6 children are a crown to the *a*,

AGREE

Mt 18: 19 on earth *a* about anything you ask
Ro 7: 16 want to do, I *a* that the law is good.
Php 4: 2 with Syntyche to *a* with each other

AHAB

Son of Omri; king of Israel (1Ki 16:28-22:40), husband of Jezebel (1Ki 16:31). Promoted Baal worship (1Ki 16:31-33); opposed by Elijah (1Ki 17:1; 18; 21), a prophet (1Ki 20:35-43), Micaiah (1Ki 22:1-28). Defeated Ben-Hadad (1Ki 20). Killed for failing to kill Ben-Hadad and for murder of Naboth (1Ki 20:35-21:40).

AHAZ

Son of Jotham; king of Judah, (2Ki 16; 2Ch 28; Isa 7).

AHAZIAH

1. Son of Ahab; king of Israel (1Ki 22:51-2Ki 1:18; 2Ch 20:35-37).
2. Son of Jehoram; king of Judah (2Ki 8:25-29; 9:14-29), also called Jehoahaz (2Ch 21:17-22:9; 25:23).

AIM

1Co 7: 34 Her *a* is to be devoted to the Lord
2Co 13: 11 *A* for perfection, listen

AIR

Mt 8: 20 and birds of the *a* have nests,
1Co 9: 26 not fight like a man beating the *a*.
Eph 2: 2 of the ruler of the kingdom of the *a*,
1Th 4: 17 clouds to meet the Lord in the *a*.

ALABASTER

Mt 26: 7 came to him with an *a* jar

ALERT

Jos 8: 4 All of you be on the *a*.
Mk 13: 33 Be *a*! You do not know
Eph 6: 18 be *a* and always keep on praying
1Th 5: 6 but let us be *a* and self-controlled.

ALIEN (ALIENATED)

Ex 22: 21 "Do not mistreat an *a*

ALIENATED (ALIEN)

Gal 5: 4 by law have been *a* from Christ;

ALIVE (LIVE)

Ac 1: 3 convincing proofs that he was *a*.
Ro 6: 11 but *a* to God in Christ Jesus.
1Co 15: 22 so in Christ all will be made *a*.

ALMIGHTY (MIGHT)

Ge 17: 1 "I am God *A*; walk before me
Job 11: 7 Can you probe the limits of the *A*?
33: 4 the breath of the *A* gives me life.
Ps 91: 1 will rest in the shadow of the *A*.
Isa 6: 3 "Holy, holy, holy is the LORD *A*;

ALTAR

Ge 22: 9 his son Isaac and laid him on the *a*,
Ex 27: 1 "Build an *a* of acacia wood,
1Ki 18: 30 and he repaired the *a* of the LORD
2Ch 4: 1 made a bronze *a* twenty cubits
4: 19 the golden *a*; the tables

ALWAYS

Ps 16: 8 I have set the LORD *a* before me.
51: 3 and my sin is *a* before me.
Mt 26: 11 The poor you will *a* have with you,
28: 20 And surely I will be with you *a*,
1Co 13: 7 *a* protects, *a* trusts, *a* hopes, *a*
Php 4: 4 Rejoice in the Lord *a*.
1Pe 3: 15 *A* be prepared to give an answer

AMAZIAH

Son of Joash; king of Judah (2Ki 14; 2Ch 25).

AMBASSADORS

2Co 5: 20 We are therefore Christ's *a*,

AMBITION

Ro 15: 20 It has always been my *a*
1Th 4: 11 Make it your *a* to lead a quiet life,

AMON

Son of Manasseh; king of Judah (2Ki 21:18-26; 1Ch 3:14; 2Ch 33:21-25).

ANANIAS

1. Husband of Sapphira; died for lying to God (Ac 5:1-11).
2. Disciple who baptized Saul (Ac 9:10-19).
3. High priest at Paul's arrest (Ac 22:30-24:1).

ANCHOR

Heb 6: 19 We have this hope as an *a*

ANCIENT

Da 7: 9 and the *A* of Days took his seat.

ANDREW*

Apostle; brother of Simon Peter (Mt 4:18; 10:2; Mk 1:16-18, 29; 3:18; 13:3; Lk 6:14; Jn 1:35-44; 6:8-9; 12:22; Ac 1:13).

ANGEL (ANGELS ARCHANGEL)

Ps 34: 7 The *a* of the LORD encamps
Ac 6: 15 his face was like the face of an *a*.
2Co 11: 14 Satan himself masquerades as an *a*
Gal 1: 8 or an *a* from heaven should preach

ANGELS (ANGEL)

Ps 91: 11 command his *a* concerning you
Mt 18: 10 For I tell you that their *a*
25: 41 prepared for the devil and his *a*.
Lk 20: 36 for they are like the *a*.
1Co 6: 3 you not know that we will judge *a*?
Heb 1: 4 as much superior to the *a*
1: 14 Are not all *a* ministering spirits
2: 7 made him a little lower than the *a*;
13: 2 some people have entertained *a*

1Pe 1: 12 Even *a* long to look
2Pe 2: 4 For if God did not spare *a*

ANGER (ANGERED ANGRY)

Ex 32: 10 alone so that my *a* may burn
34: 6 slow to *a,* abounding in love
Dt 29: 28 In furious *a* and in great wrath
2Ki 22: 13 Great is the LORD's *a* that burns
Ps 30: 5 For his *a* lasts only a moment,
Pr 15: 1 but a harsh word stirs up *a.*
29: 11 A fool gives full vent to his *a,*

ANGERED (ANGER)

Pr 22: 24 do not associate with one easily *a,*
1Co 13: 5 it is not easily *a,* it keeps no record

ANGRY (ANGER)

Ps 2: 12 Kiss the Son, lest he be *a*
Pr 29: 22 An *a* man stirs up dissension,
Jas 1: 19 slow to speak and slow to become *a*

ANGUISH

Ps 118: 5 In my *a* I cried to the LORD,

ANOINT

Ps 23: 5 You *a* my head with oil;
Jas 5: 14 and *a* him with oil in the name

ANT*

Pr 6: 6 Go to the *a,* you sluggard;

ANTICHRIST

1Jn 2: 18 have heard that the *a* is coming,
2Jn : 7 person is the deceiver and the *a.*

ANTIOCH

Ac 11: 26 were called Christians first at *A.*

ANXIETY (ANXIOUS)

1Pe 5: 7 Cast all your *a* on him

ANXIOUS (ANXIETY)

Pr 12: 25 An *a* heart weighs a man down,
Php 4: 6 Do not be *a* about anything,

APOLLOS*

Christian from Alexandria, learned in the Scriptures; instructed by Aquila and Priscilla (Ac 18:24-28). Ministered at Corinth (Ac 19:1; 1Co 1:12; 3; Tit 3:13).

APOSTLES

See also Andrew, Bartholomew, James, John, Judas, Matthew, Nathanael, Paul, Peter, Philip, Simon, Thaddaeus, Thomas.

Mk 3: 14 twelve—designating them *a*—
Ac 1: 26 so he was added to the eleven *a.*
2: 43 signs were done by the *a.*
1Co 12: 28 God has appointed first of all *a,*
15: 9 For I am the least of the *a*
2Co 11: 13 masquerading as *a* of Christ.
Eph 2: 20 built on the foundation of the *a*

APPEAR (APPEARANCE APPEARING)

Mk 13: 22 false prophets will *a* and perform
2Co 5: 10 we must all *a* before the judgment
Col 3: 4 also will *a* with him in glory.
Heb 9: 24 now to *a* for us in God's presence.
9: 28 and he will *a* a second time,

APPEARANCE (APPEAR)

1Sa 16: 7 Man looks at the outward *a,*
Gal 2: 6 God does not judge by external *a*—

APPEARING (APPEAR)

2Ti 4: 8 to all who have longed for his *a.*
Tit 2: 13 the glorious *a* of our great God

APPLY

Pr 22: 17 *a* your heart to what I teach,
23: 12 *A* your heart to instruction

APPROACH

Eph 3: 12 in him we may *a* God with freedom
Heb 4: 16 Let us then *a* the throne of grace

APPROVED

2Ti 2: 15 to present yourself to God as one *a,*

AQUILA*

Husband of Priscilla; co-worker with Paul, instructor of Apollos (Ac 18; Ro 16:3; 1Co 16:19; 2Ti 4:19).

ARARAT

Ge 8: 4 came to rest on the mountains of *A.*

ARCHANGEL* (ANGEL)

1Th 4: 16 with the voice of the *a*
Jude : 9 *a* Michael, when he was disputing

ARCHITECT*

Heb 11: 10 whose *a* and builder is God.

ARK

Ge 6: 14 So make yourself an *a*
Dt 10: 5 put the tablets in the *a* I had made,
2Ch 35: 3 "Put the sacred *a* in the temple that
Heb 9: 4 This *a* contained the gold jar

ARM (ARMY)

Nu 11: 23 "Is the LORD's *a* too short?
1Pe 4: 1 *a* yourselves also with the same

ARMAGEDDON*

Rev 16: 16 that in Hebrew is called *A.*

ARMOR (ARMY)

1Ki 20: 11 on his *a* should not boast like one
Eph 6: 11 Put on the full *a* of God
6: 13 Therefore put on the full *a* of God,

ARMS (ARMY)

Dt 33: 27 underneath are the everlasting *a.*
Ps 18: 32 It is God who *a* me with strength
Pr 31: 20 She opens her *a* to the poor
Isa 40: 11 He gathers the lambs in his *a*
Mk 10: 16 And he took the children in his *a,*

ARMY (ARM ARMOR ARMS)

Ps 33: 16 No king is saved by the size of his *a*
Rev 19: 19 the rider on the horse and his *a.*

AROMA

2Co 2: 15 For we are to God the *a* of Christ

ARRAYED*

Ps 110: 3 *A* in holy majesty,
Isa 61: 10 and *a* me in a robe of righteousness

ARROGANT

Ro 11: 20 Do not be *a,* but be afraid.

ARROWS

Eph 6: 16 you can extinguish all the flaming *a*

ASA

King of Judah (1Ki 15:8-24; 1Ch 3:10; 2Ch 14-16).

ASCENDED

Eph 4: 8 "When he *a* on high,

ASCRIBE

1Ch 16: 28 *a* to the LORD glory and strength,
Job 36: 3 I will *a* justice to my Maker.
Ps 29: 2 *A* to the LORD the glory due his

ASHAMED (SHAME)

Lk 9: 26 If anyone is *a* of me and my words,
Ro 1: 16 I am not *a* of the gospel,
2Ti 1: 8 So do not be *a* to testify about our
2: 15 who does not need to be *a*

ASSIGNED

Mk 13: 34 with his *a* task, and tells the one
1Co 3: 5 as the Lord has *a* to each his task.
7: 17 place in life that the Lord *a* to him

ASSOCIATE

Pr 22: 24 do not *a* with one easily angered,
Ro 12: 16 but be willing to *a* with people
1Co 5: 11 am writing you that you must not *a*
2Th 3: 14 Do not *a* with him,

ASSURANCE

Heb 10: 22 with a sincere heart in full *a* of faith

ASTRAY

Pr 10: 17 ignores correction leads others *a.*
Isa 53: 6 We all, like sheep, have gone *a,*
Jer 50: 6 their shepherds have led them *a*
Jn 16: 1 you so that you will not go *a.*
1Pe 2: 25 For you were like sheep going *a,*
1Jn 3: 7 do not let anyone lead you *a.*

ATHALIAH

Evil queen of Judah (2Ki 11; 2Ch 23).

ATHLETE*

2Ti 2: 5 if anyone competes as an *a,*

ATONEMENT

Ex 25: 17 "Make an *a* cover of pure gold—
30: 10 Once a year Aaron shall make *a*
Lev 17: 11 it is the blood that makes *a*
23: 27 this seventh month is the Day of *A.*
Nu 25: 13 and made *a* for the Israelites."
Ro 3: 25 presented him as a sacrifice of *a,*
Heb 2: 17 that he might make *a* for the sins

ATTENTION

Pr 4: 1 pay *a* and gain understanding.
5: 1 My son, pay *a* to my wisdom,
22: 17 Pay *a* and listen to the sayings
Tit 1: 14 and will pay no *a* to Jewish myths

ATTITUDE (ATTITUDES)

Eph 4: 23 new in the *a* of your minds;
Php 2: 5 Your *a* should be the same
1Pe 4: 1 yourselves also with the same *a,*

ATTITUDES (ATTITUDE)

Heb 4: 12 it judges the thoughts and *a*

ATTRACTIVE

Tit 2: 10 teaching about God our Savior *a.*

AUTHORITIES (AUTHORITY)

Ro 13: 5 it is necessary to submit to the *a,*
13: 6 for the *a* are God's servants,
Tit 3: 1 people to be subject to rulers and *a,*
1Pe 3: 22 *a* and powers in submission to him.

AUTHORITY (AUTHORITIES)

Mt 7: 29 because he taught as one who had *a*
9: 6 the Son of Man has *a* on earth
28: 18 "All *a* in heaven and on earth has
Ro 13: 1 for there is no *a* except that which
13: 2 rebels against the *a* is rebelling
1Co 11: 10 to have a sign of *a* on her head.
1Ti 2: 2 for kings and all those in *a,*
2: 12 to teach or to have *a* over a man;
Heb 13: 17 your leaders and submit to their *a.*

AVENGE (VENGEANCE)

Dt 32: 35 It is mine to *a;* I will repay.

AVOID

Pr 20: 3 It is to a man's honor to *a* strife,
20: 19 so *a* a man who talks too much.
1Th 4: 3 you should *a* sexual immorality;
5: 22 *A* every kind of evil.
2Ti 2: 16 *A* godless chatter, because those
Tit 3: 9 But *a* foolish controversies

AWAKE

Ps 17: 15 when I *a,* I will be satisfied

AWE (AWESOME)

Job 25: 2 "Dominion and *a* belong to God;
Ps 119:120 I stand in *a* of your laws.
Ecc 5: 7 Therefore stand in *a* of God.
Isa 29: 23 will stand in *a* of the God of Israel.
Jer 33: 9 they will be in *a* and will tremble
Hab 3: 2 I stand in *a* of your deeds,
Mal 2: 5 and stood in *a* of my name.
Mt 9: 8 they were filled with *a;*
Lk 7: 16 They were all filled with *a*
Ac 2: 43 Everyone was filled with *a,*
Heb 12: 28 acceptably with reverence and *a,*

AWESOME (AWE)

Ge 28: 17 and said, "How *a* is this place!
Ex 15: 11 *a* in glory,
Dt 7: 21 is among you, is a great and *a* God.
Dt 10: 17 the great God, mighty and *a,*
28: 58 revere this glorious and *a* name—
Jdg 13: 6 like an angel of God, very *a.*
Ne 1: 5 of heaven, the great and *a* God,
9: 32 the great, mighty and *a* God,
Job 10: 16 again display your *a* power
37: 22 God comes in *a* majesty.
Ps 45: 4 let your right hand display *a* deeds.
47: 2 How *a* is the LORD Most High,
66: 5 how *a* his works in man's behalf!
68: 35 You are *a,* O God,
89: 7 he is more *a* than all who surround
99: 3 praise your great and *a* name—
111: 9 holy and *a* is his name.
145: 6 of the power of your *a* works,
Da 9: 4 "O Lord, the great and *a* God,

BAAL

1Ki 18: 25 Elijah said to the prophets of *B,*

BAASHA

King of Israel (1Ki 15:16-16:7; 2Ch 16:1-6).

BABIES (BABY)

Lk 18: 15 also bringing *b* to Jesus
1Pe 2: 2 Like newborn *b,* crave pure

BABY (BABIES)

Isa 49: 15 "Can a mother forget the *b*
Lk 1: 44 the *b* in my womb leaped for joy.
2: 12 You will find a *b* wrapped in strips
Jn 16: 21 but when her *b* is born she forgets

BABYLON

Ps 137: 1 By the rivers of *B* we sat and wept

BACKSLIDING

Jer 3: 22 I will cure you of *b.*"
14: 7 For our *b* is great;
Eze 37: 23 them from all their sinful *b,*

BALAAM

Prophet who attempted to curse Israel (Nu 22-24; Dt 23:4-5; 2Pe 2:15; Jude 11). Killed (Nu 31:8; Jos 13:22).

BALM

Jer 8: 22 Is there no *b* in Gilead?

BANISH

Jer 25: 10 I will *b* from them the sounds of joy

BANQUET

SS 2: 4 He has taken me to the *b* hall,
Lk 14: 13 when you give a *b,* invite the poor,

BAPTIZE (BAPTIZED)

Mt 3: 11 He will *b* you with the Holy Spirit
Mk 1: 8 he will *b* you with the Holy Spirit."
1Co 1: 17 For Christ did not send me to *b,*

BAPTIZED (BAPTIZE)

Mt 3: 6 they were *b* by him in the Jordan
Mk 1: 9 and was *b* by John in the Jordan.
10: 38 or be *b* with the baptism I am
16: 16 believes and is *b* will be saved,
Jn 4: 2 in fact it was not Jesus who *b,*
Ac 1: 5 but in a few days you will be *b*

BARABBAS

Mt 27: 26 Then he released *B* to them.

BARBS*

Nu 33: 55 allow to remain will become *b*

BARE

Heb 4: 13 and laid *b* before the eyes of him

BARNABAS*

Disciple, originally Joseph (Ac 4:36), prophet (Ac 13:1), apostle (Ac 14:14). Brought Paul to apostles (Ac 9:27), Antioch (Ac 11:22-29; Gal 2:1-13), on the first missionary journey (Ac 13-14). Together at Jerusalem Council, they separated over John Mark (Ac 15). Later co-workers (1Co 9:6; Col 4:10).

BARREN

Ps 113: 9 He settles the *b* woman

BARTHOLOMEW*

Apostle (Mt 10:3; Mk 3:18; Lk 6:14; Ac 1:13). Possibly also known as Nathanael (Jn 1:45-49; 21:2).

BATH

Jn 13: 10 person who has had a *b* needs only

BATHSHEBA

Wife of Uriah who committed adultery with and became wife of David (2Sa 11), mother of Solomon (2Sa 12:24; 1Ki 1-2; 1Ch 3:5).

BATTLE

2Ch 20: 15 For the *b* is not yours, but God's.
Ps 24: 8 the LORD mighty in *b.*
Ecc 9: 11 or the *b* to the strong,

BEAR (BEARING BIRTH BIRTHRIGHT BORN FIRSTBORN NEWBORN)

Ge 4: 13 punishment is more than I can *b.*
Ps 38: 4 like a burden too heavy to *b.*
Isa 53: 11 and he will *b* their iniquities.
Da 7: 5 beast, which looked like a *b.*
Mt 7: 18 A good tree cannot *b* bad fruit,
Jn 15: 2 branch that does *b* fruit he prunes
15: 16 and appointed you to go and *b* fruit—
Ro 15: 1 ought to *b* with the failings
1Co 10: 13 tempted beyond what you can *b.*
Col 3: 13 *B* with each other and forgive

BEARING (BEAR)

Eph 4: 2 *b* with one another in love.
Col 1: 10 *b* fruit in every good work,

BEAST

Rev 13: 18 him calculate the number of the *b,*

BEAT (BEATING)

Isa 2: 4 They will *b* their swords
Joel 3: 10 *B* your plowshares into swords
1Co 9: 27 I *b* my body and make it my slave

BEATING (BEAT)

1Co 9: 26 I do not fight like a man *b* the air.
1Pe 2: 20 if you receive a *b* for doing wrong

BEAUTIFUL (BEAUTY)

Ge 6: 2 that the daughters of men were *b,*
12: 11 "I know what a *b* woman you are.
12: 14 saw that she was a very *b* woman.
24: 16 The girl was very *b,* a virgin;
26: 7 of Rebekah, because she is *b."*
29: 17 Rachel was lovely in form, and *b.*
Job 38: 31 "Can you bind the *b* Pleiades?
Pr 11: 22 is a *b* woman who shows no
Ecc 3: 11 He has made everything *b*
Isa 4: 2 of the LORD will be *b*
52: 7 How *b* on the mountains
Eze 20: 6 and honey, the most *b* of all lands.
Zec 9: 17 How attractive and *b* they will be!
Mt 23: 27 which look *b* on the outside
26: 10 She has done a *b* thing to me.
Ro 10: 15 "How *b* are the feet
1Pe 3: 5 in God used to make themselves *b.*

BEAUTY (BEAUTIFUL)

Ps 27: 4 to gaze upon the *b* of the LORD
45: 11 The king is enthralled by your *b;*
Pr 31: 30 is deceptive, and *b* is fleeting;
Isa 33: 17 Your eyes will see the king in his *b*
53: 2 He had no *b* or majesty
61: 3 to bestow on them a crown of *b*
Eze 28: 12 full of wisdom and perfect in *b.*
1Pe 3: 4 the unfading *b* of a gentle

BED

Heb 13: 4 and the marriage *b* kept pure,

BEELZEBUB

Lk 11: 15 "By *B,* the prince of demons,

BEER

Pr 20: 1 Wine is a mocker and *b* a brawler;

BEERSHEBA

Jdg 20: 1 all the Israelites from Dan to *B*

BEGINNING

Ge 1: 1 In the *b* God created the heavens
Ps 102: 25 In the *b* you laid the foundations
111: 10 of the LORD is the *b* of wisdom;
Pr 1: 7 of the LORD is the *b* of knowledge
Jn 1: 1 In the *b* was the Word,
1Jn 1: 1 That which was from the *b,*
Rev 21: 6 and the Omega, the *B* and the End.

BEHAVE

Ro 13: 13 Let us *b* decently, as in the daytime

BELIEVE (BELIEVED BELIEVER BELIEVERS BELIEVES BELIEVING)

Mt 18: 6 one of these little ones who *b* in me
21: 22 If you *b,* you will receive whatever
Mk 1: 15 Repent and *b* the good news!"
9: 24 "I do *b;* help me overcome my
16: 17 signs will accompany those who *b:*
Lk 8: 50 just *b,* and she will be healed."
Lk 24: 25 to *b* all that the prophets have
Jn 1: 7 that through him all men might *b.*
3: 18 does not *b* stands condemned
6: 29 to *b* in the one he has sent."
10: 38 you do not *b* me, *b* the miracles,
11: 27 "I *b* that you are the Christ,
14: 11 *B* me when I say that I am
16: 30 This makes us *b* that you came
16: 31 "You *b* at last!" Jesus answered.
17: 21 that the world may *b* that you have
20: 27 Stop doubting and *b."*
20: 31 written that you may *b* that Jesus is
Ac 16: 31 They replied, *"B* in the Lord Jesus,
24: 14 I *b* everything that agrees
Ro 3: 22 faith in Jesus Christ to all who *b.*
4: 11 he is the father of all who *b*
10: 9 *b* in your heart that God raised him
10: 14 And how can they *b* in the one
16: 26 so that all nations might *b*
1Th 4: 14 We *b* that Jesus died and rose again
2Th 2: 11 delusion so that they will *b* the lie
1Ti 4: 10 and especially of those who *b.*
Tit 1: 6 a man whose children *b*
Heb 11: 6 comes to him must *b* that he exists
Jas 2: 19 Even the demons *b* that—
1Jn 4: 1 Dear friends, do not *b* every spirit,

BELIEVED (BELIEVE)

Ge 15: 6 Abram *b* the LORD, and he
Jnh 3: 5 The Ninevites *b* God.
Jn 1: 12 to those who *b* in his name,
2: 22 Then they *b* the Scripture
3: 18 because he has not *b* in the name
20: 8 He saw and *b.*
20: 29 who have not seen and yet have *b."*
Ac 13: 48 were appointed for eternal life *b.*
Ro 4: 3 Scripture say? "Abraham *b* God,
10: 14 call on the one they have not *b* in?
1Co 15: 2 Otherwise, you have *b* in vain.
Gal 3: 6 Consider Abraham: "He *b* God,
2Ti 1: 12 because I know whom I have *b,*
Jas 2: 23 that says, "Abraham *b* God,

BELIEVER (BELIEVE)

1Co 7: 12 brother has a wife who is not a *b*
2Co 6: 15 What does a *b* have in common

BELIEVERS (BELIEVE)

Ac 4: 32 All the *b* were one in heart
5: 12 And all the *b* used to meet together
1Co 6: 5 to judge a dispute between *b?*
1Ti 4: 12 set an example for the *b* in speech,
1Pe 2: 17 Love the brotherhood of *b,*

BELIEVES (BELIEVE)

Pr 14: 15 A simple man *b* anything,
Mk 9: 23 is possible for him who *b."*
11: 23 *b* that what he says will happen,
16: 16 Whoever *b* and is baptized will be
Jn 3: 16 that whoever *b* in him shall not
3: 36 Whoever *b* in the Son has eternal
5: 24 *b* him who sent me has eternal life
6: 35 and he who *b* in me will never be
6: 40 and *b* in him shall have eternal life,
6: 47 he who *b* has everlasting life.
7: 38 Whoever *b* in me, as the Scripture
11: 26 and *b* in me will never die.
Ro 1: 16 for the salvation of everyone who *b*
10: 4 righteousness for everyone who *b.*
1Jn 5: 1 Everyone who *b* that Jesus is
5: 5 Only he who *b* that Jesus is the Son

BELIEVING (BELIEVE)

Jn 20: 31 and that by *b* you may have life

BELONG (BELONGS)

Dt 29: 29 The secret things *b*
Job 25: 2 "Dominion and awe *b* to God;
Ps 47: 9 for the kings of the earth *b* to God;
95: 4 and the mountain peaks *b* to him.
Jn 8: 44 You *b* to your father, the devil,
15: 19 As it is, you do not *b* to the world,
Ro 1: 6 called to *b* to Jesus Christ.
7: 4 that you might *b* to another,
14: 8 we live or die, we *b* to the Lord.
Gal 5: 24 Those who *b* to Christ Jesus have
1Th 5: 8 But since we *b* to the day, let us be

BELONGS (BELONG)

Job 41: 11 Everything under heaven *b* to me.
Ps 111: 10 To him *b* eternal praise.
Eze 18: 4 For every living soul *b* to me,
Jn 8: 47 He who *b* to God hears what God
Ro 12: 5 each member *b* to all the others.

BELOVED (LOVE)

Dt 33: 12 "Let the *b* of the LORD rest secure

BELT

Isa 11: 5 Righteousness will be his *b*
Eph 6: 14 with the *b* of truth buckled

BENEFIT (BENEFITS)

Ro 6: 22 the *b* you reap leads to holiness,
2Co 4: 15 All this is for your *b,*

BENEFITS (BENEFIT)

Ps 103: 2 and forget not all his *b.*
Jn 4: 38 you have reaped the *b* of their labor

BENJAMIN

Twelfth son of Jacob by Rachel (Ge 35:16-24; 46:19-21; 1Ch 2:2). Jacob refused to send him to Egypt, but relented (Ge 42-45).

BEREANS*

Ac 17: 11 the *B* were of more noble character

BESTOWS

Ps 84: 11 the LORD *b* favor and honor;

BETHLEHEM

Mt 2: 1 After Jesus was born in *B* in Judea,

BETRAY

Pr 25: 9 do not *b* another man's confidence,

BIND (BINDS)

Dt 6: 8 and *b* them on your foreheads.
Pr 6: 21 *B* them upon your heart forever;
Isa 61: 1 me to *b* up the brokenhearted,
Mt 16: 19 whatever you *b* on earth will be

BINDS (BIND)

Ps 147: 3 and *b* up their wounds.
Isa 30: 26 when the LORD *b* up the bruises

BIRDS

Mt 8: 20 and *b* of the air have nests,

BIRTH (BEAR)

Ps 58: 3 Even from *b* the wicked go astray;
Mt 1: 18 This is how the *b* of Jesus Christ
1Pe 1: 3 great mercy he has given us new *b*

BIRTHRIGHT (BEAR)

Ge 25: 34 So Esau despised his *b*.

BLAMELESS

Ge 17: 1 walk before me and be *b*.
Job 1: 1 This man was *b* and upright;
Ps 84: 11 from those whose walk is *b*.
119: 1 Blessed are they whose ways are *b*,
Pr 19: 1 Better a poor man whose walk is *b*
1Co 1: 8 so that you will be *b* on the day
Eph 5: 27 any other blemish, but holy and *b*.
Php 2: 15 so that you may become *b* and pure
1Th 3: 13 hearts so that you will be *b*
5: 23 and body be kept *b* at the coming
Tit 1: 6 An elder must be *b*, the husband of
Heb 7: 26 *b*, pure, set apart from sinners,
2Pe 3: 14 effort to be found spotless, *b*

BLASPHEMES

Mk 3: 29 whoever *b* against the Holy Spirit

BLEMISH

1Pe 1: 19 a lamb without *b* or defect.

BLESS (BLESSED BLESSING BLESSINGS)

Ge 12: 3 I will *b* those who *b* you,
Ro 12: 14 Bless those who persecute you; *b*

BLESSED (BLESS)

Ge 1: 22 God *b* them and said, "Be fruitful
2: 3 And God *b* the seventh day
22: 18 nations on earth will be *b*,
Ps 1: 1 *B* is the man
2: 12 *B* are all who take refuge in him.
33: 12 *B* is the nation whose God is
41: 1 *B* is he who has regard for the weak
Ps 84: 5 *B* are those whose strength is
106: 3 *B* are they who maintain justice,
112: 1 *B* is the man who fears the LORD,
118: 26 *B* is he who comes in the name
Pr 29: 18 but *b* is he who keeps the law.
31: 28 Her children arise and call her *b*;
Mt 5: 3 saying: "*B* are the poor in spirit,
5: 4 *B* are those who mourn,
5: 5 *B* are the meek,
5: 6 *B* are those who hunger
5: 7 *B* are the merciful,
5: 8 *B* are the pure in heart,
5: 9 *B* are the peacemakers,
5: 10 *B* are those who are persecuted
5: 11 "*B* are you when people insult you,
Lk 1: 48 on all generations will call me *b*,
Jn 12: 13 "*B* is he who comes in the name
Ac 20: 35 'It is more *b* to give than to receive
Tit 2: 13 while we wait for the *b* hope—
Jas 1: 12 *B* is the man who perseveres
Rev 1: 3 *B* is the one who reads the words
22: 14 "*B* are those who wash their robes,

BLESSING (BLESS)

Eze 34: 26 there will be showers of *b*.

BLESSINGS (BLESS)

Pr 10: 6 *B* crown the head of the righteous,

BLIND

Mt 15: 14 a *b* man leads a *b* man, both will fall
23: 16 "Woe to you, *b* guides! You say,
Jn 9: 25 I was *b* but now I see!"

BLOOD

Ge 9: 6 "Whoever sheds the *b* of man,
Ex 12: 13 and when I see the *b*, I will pass
24: 8 "This is the *b* of the covenant that
Lev 17: 11 For the life of a creature is in the *b*,
Ps 72: 14 for precious is their *b* in his sight.
Pr 6: 17 hands that shed innocent *b*,
Mt 26: 28 This is my *b* of the covenant,
Ro 3: 25 of atonement, through faith in his *b*
5: 9 have now been justified by his *b*,
1Co 11: 25 cup is the new covenant in my *b*;
Eph 1: 7 we have redemption through his *b*,
2: 13 near through the *b* of Christ.
Col 1: 20 by making peace through his *b*,
Heb 9: 12 once for all by his own *b*,
9: 22 of *b* there is no forgiveness.
1Pe 1: 19 but with the precious *b* of Christ,
1Jn 1: 7 and the *b* of Jesus, his Son,
Rev 1: 5 has freed us from our sins by his *b*,
5: 9 with your *b* you purchased men
7: 14 white in the *b* of the Lamb.
12: 11 him by the *b* of the Lamb

BLOT (BLOTS)

Ex 32: 32 then *b* me out of the book you have
Ps 51: 1 *b* out my transgressions.
Rev 3: 5 I will never *b* out his name

BLOTS (BLOT)

Isa 43: 25 "I, even I, am he who *b* out

BLOWN

Eph 4: 14 and *b* here and there by every wind
Jas 1: 6 doubts is like a wave of the sea, *b*

BOAST

1Ki 20: 11 armor should not *b* like one who
Ps 34: 2 My soul will *b* in the LORD;
44: 8 In God we make our *b* all day long,
Pr 27: 1 Do not *b* about tomorrow,
1Co 1: 31 Let him who boasts *b* in the Lord."
Gal 6: 14 May I never *b* except in the cross
Eph 2: 9 not by works, so that no one can *b*.

BOAZ

Wealthy Bethlehemite who showed favor to Ruth (Ru 2), married her (Ru 4). Ancestor of David (Ru 4:18-22; 1Ch 2:12-15), Jesus (Mt 1:5-16; Lk 3:23-32).

BODIES (BODY)

Ro 12: 1 to offer your *b* as living sacrifices,
1Co 6: 15 not know that your *b* are members
Eph 5: 28 to love their wives as their own *b*.

BODY (BODIES)

Zec 13: 6 What are these wounds on your *b*?'
Mt 10: 28 afraid of those who kill the *b*
26: 26 saying, "Take and eat; this is my *b*
26: 41 spirit is willing, but the *b* is weak."
Jn 13: 10 wash his feet; his whole *b* is clean.
Ro 6: 13 Do not offer the parts of your *b*
12: 4 us has one *b* with many members,
1Co 6: 19 not know that your *b* is a temple
11: 24 "This is my *b*, which is for you;
12: 12 The *b* is a unit, though it is made up
Eph 5: 30 for we are members of his *b*.

BOLD (BOLDNESS)

Ps 138: 3 you made me *b* and stouthearted.
Pr 21: 29 A wicked man puts up a *b* front,
28: 1 but the righteous are as *b* as a lion.

BOLDNESS* (BOLD)

Ac 4: 29 to speak your word with great *b*.

BONDAGE

Ezr 9: 9 God has not deserted us in our *b*.

BOOK (BOOKS)

Jos 1: 8 Do not let this *B* of the Law depart

Ne 8: 8 They read from the *B* of the Law
Jn 20: 30 which are not recorded in this *b.*
Php 4: 3 whose names are in the *b* of life.
Rev 21: 27 written in the Lamb's *b* of life.

BOOKS (BOOK)

Ecc 12: 12 Of making many *b* there is no end,

BORN (BEAR)

Isa 9: 6 For to us a child is *b,*
Jn 3: 7 at my saying, 'You must be *b* again
1Pe 1: 23 For you have been *b* again,
1Jn 4: 7 Everyone who loves has been *b*
5: 1 believes that Jesus is the Christ is *b*

BORROWER

Pr 22: 7 and the *b* is servant to the lender.

BOUGHT

Ac 20: 28 which he *b* with his own blood.
1Co 6: 20 You are not your own; you were *b*
7: 23 You were *b* at a price; do not
2Pe 2: 1 the sovereign Lord who *b* them—

BOW

Ps 95: 6 Come, let us *b* down in worship,
Isa 45: 23 Before me every knee will *b;*
Ro 14: 11 'every knee will *b* before me;
Php 2: 10 name of Jesus every knee should *b,*

BRANCH (BRANCHES)

Isa 4: 2 In that day the *B* of the LORD will
Jer 33: 15 I will make a righteous *B* sprout

BRANCHES (BRANCH)

Jn 15: 5 "I am the vine; you are the *b.*

BRAVE

2Sa 2: 7 Now then, be strong and *b,*

BREAD

Dt 8: 3 that man does not live on *b* alone
Pr 30: 8 but give me only my daily *b.*
Ecc 11: 1 Cast your *b* upon the waters,
Isa 55: 2 Why spend money on what is not *b*
Mt 4: 4 'Man does not live on *b* alone,
6: 11 Give us today our daily *b.*
Jn 6: 35 Jesus declared, "I am the *b* of life.
21: 13 took the *b* and gave it to them,
1Co 11: 23 took *b,* and when he had given

BREAK (BREAKING BROKEN)

Nu 30: 2 he must not *b* his word
Jdg 2: 1 'I will never *b* my covenant
Isa 42: 3 A bruised reed he will not *b,*
Mt 12: 20 A bruised reed he will not *b,*

BREAKING (BREAK)

Jas 2: 10 at just one point is guilty of *b* all

BREASTPIECE (BREASTPLATE)

Ex 28: 15 Fashion a *b* for making decisions—

BREASTPLATE* (BREASTPIECE)

Isa 59: 17 He put on righteousness as his *b,*
Eph 6: 14 with the *b* of righteousness in place
1Th 5: 8 putting on faith and love as a *b,*

BREATHED (GOD-BREATHED)

Ge 2: 7 *b* into his nostrils the breath of life,
Jn 20: 22 And with that he *b* on them

BREEDS*

Pr 13: 10 Pride only *b* quarrels,

BRIBE

Ex 23: 8 "Do not accept a *b,*
Pr 6: 35 will refuse the *b,* however great it

BRIDE

Rev 19: 7 and his *b* has made herself ready,

BRIGHTER (BRIGHTNESS)

Pr 4: 18 shining ever *b* till the full light

BRIGHTNESS (BRIGHTER)

2Sa 22: 13 Out of the *b* of his presence
Da 12: 3 who are wise will shine like the *b*

BROAD

Mt 7: 13 and *b* is the road that leads

BROKEN (BREAK)

Ps 51: 17 The sacrifices of God are a *b* spirit;
Ecc 4: 12 of three strands is not quickly *b.*
Jn 10: 35 and the Scripture cannot be *b*—

BROKENHEARTED* (HEART)

Ps 34: 18 The LORD is close to the *b*
109: 16 and the needy and the *b.*
147: 3 He heals the *b*
Isa 61: 1 He has sent me to bind up the *b,*

BROTHER (BROTHER'S BROTHERS)

Pr 17: 17 and a *b* is born for adversity.
18: 24 a friend who sticks closer than a *b.*
27: 10 neighbor nearby than a *b* far away.
Mt 5: 24 and be reconciled to your *b;*
18: 15 "If your *b* sins against you,
Mk 3: 35 Whoever does God's will is my *b*
Lk 17: 3 "If your *b* sins, rebuke him,
1Co 8: 13 if what I eat causes my *b* to fall
1Jn 2: 10 Whoever loves his *b* lives
4: 21 loves God must also love his *b.*

BROTHER'S (BROTHER)

Ge 4: 9 "Am I my *b* keeper?" The LORD

BROTHERS (BROTHER)

Ps 133: 1 is when *b* live together in unity!
Pr 6: 19 who stirs up dissension among *b.*
Mt 25: 40 one of the least of these *b* of mine,
Mk 10: 29 or *b* or sisters or mother or father
Heb 13: 1 Keep on loving each other as *b.*
1Pe 3: 8 be sympathetic, love as *b,*
1Jn 3: 14 death to life, because we love our *b.*

BUILD (BUILDING BUILDS BUILT)

Mt 16: 18 and on this rock I will *b* my church,
Ac 20: 32 which can *b* you up and give you
1Co 14: 12 excel in gifts that *b* up the church.
1Th 5: 11 one another and *b* each other up,

BUILDING (BUILD)

1Co 3: 9 you are God's field, God's *b.*
2Co 10: 8 us for *b* you up rather
Eph 4: 29 helpful for *b* others up according

BUILDS (BUILD)

Ps 127: 1 Unless the LORD *b* the house,
1Co 3: 10 one should be careful how he *b.*
8: 1 Knowledge puffs up, but love *b* up.

BUILT (BUILD)

Mt 7: 24 is like a wise man who *b* his house
Eph 2: 20 *b* on the foundation of the apostles
4: 12 the body of Christ may be *b* up

BURDEN (BURDENED BURDENS)

Ps 38: 4 like a *b* too heavy to bear.
Mt 11: 30 my yoke is easy and my *b* is light."

BURDENED (BURDEN)

Gal 5: 1 do not let yourselves be *b* again

BURDENS (BURDEN)

Ps 68: 19 who daily bears our *b.*
Gal 6: 2 Carry each other's *b,*

BURIED

Ro 6: 4 *b* with him through baptism
1Co 15: 4 that he was *b,* that he was raised

BURNING

Lev 6: 9 the fire must be kept *b* on the altar.
Ro 12: 20 you will heap *b* coals on his head."

BUSINESS

Da 8: 27 and went about the king's *b.*
1Th 4: 11 to mind your own *b* and to work

BUSY

1Ki 20: 40 While your servant was *b* here
2Th 3: 11 They are not *b;* they are
Tit 2: 5 to be *b* at home, to be kind,

CAESAR

Mt 22: 21 "Give to *C* what is Caesar's,

CAIN

Firstborn of Adam (Ge 4:1), murdered brother Abel (Ge 4:1-16; 1Jn 3:12).

CALEB

Judahite who spied out Canaan (Nu 13:6); allowed to enter land because of faith (Nu 13:30-14:38; Dt 1:36). Possessed Hebron (Jos 14:6-15:19).

CALF

Ex 32: 4 into an idol cast in the shape of a *c,*
Lk 15: 23 Bring the fattened *c* and kill it.

CALL (CALLED CALLING CALLS)

Ps 105: 1 to the LORD, *c* on his name;
145: 18 near to all who *c* on him,
Pr 31: 28 children arise and *c* her blessed;
Isa 5: 20 Woe to those who *c* evil good
55: 6 *c* on him while he is near.
65: 24 Before they *c* I will answer;
Jer 33: 3 '*C* to me and I will answer you
Mt 9: 13 come to *c* the righteous,
Ro 10: 12 and richly blesses all who *c* on him,
11: 29 gifts and his *c* are irrevocable.
1Th 4: 7 For God did not *c* us to be impure,

CALLED (CALL)

1Sa 3: 5 and said, "Here I am; you *c* me."
2Ch 7: 14 if my people, who are *c*
Ps 34: 6 This poor man *c*, and the LORD
Mt 21: 13 "'My house will be *c* a house
Ro 8: 30 And those he predestined, he also *c*
1Co 7: 15 God has *c* us to live in peace.
Gal 5: 13 You, my brothers, were *c* to be free
1Pe 2: 9 of him who *c* you out of darkness

CALLING (CALL)

Jn 1: 23 I am the voice of one *c* in the desert
Ac 22: 16 wash your sins away, *c* on his name
Eph 4: 1 worthy of the *c* you have received.
2Pe 1: 10 all the more eager to make your *c*

CALLS (CALL)

Joel 2: 32 And everyone who *c*
Jn 10: 3 He *c* his own sheep by name
Ro 10: 13 "Everyone who *c* on the name

CAMEL

Mt 19: 24 it is easier for a *c* to go
23: 24 strain out a gnat but swallow a *c*.

CANAAN

1Ch 16: 18 "To you I will give the land of *C*

CANCELED

Lk 7: 42 so he *c* the debts of both.
Col 2: 14 having *c* the written code,

CAPITAL

Dt 21: 22 guilty of a *c* offense is put to death

CAPSTONE (STONE)

Ps 118: 22 has become the *c*;
1Pe 2: 7 has become the *c*,"

CARE (CAREFUL CARES CARING)

Ps 8: 4 the son of man that you *c* for him?
Pr 29: 7 The righteous *c* about justice
Lk 10: 34 him to an inn and took *c* of him.
Jn 21: 16 Jesus said, "Take *c* of my sheep."
Heb 2: 6 the son of man that you *c* for him?
1Pe 5: 2 of God's flock that is under your *c*,

CAREFUL (CARE)

Ex 23: 13 "Be *c* to do everything I have said
Dt 6: 3 be *c* to obey so that it may go well
Jos 23: 6 be *c* to obey all that is written
23: 11 be very *c* to love the LORD your
Pr 13: 24 he who loves him is *c*
Mt 6: 1 "Be *c* not to do your 'acts
Ro 12: 17 Be *c* to do what is right in the eyes
1Co 3: 10 each one should be *c* how he builds
8: 9 Be *c*, however, that the exercise
Eph 5: 15 Be very *c*, then, how you live—

CARELESS

Mt 12: 36 for every *c* word they have spoken.

CARES (CARE)

Ps 55: 22 Cast your *c* on the LORD
Na 1: 7 He *c* for those who trust in him,
Eph 5: 29 but he feeds and *c* for it, just
1Pe 5: 7 on him because he *c* for you.

CARING* (CARE)

1Th 2: 7 like a mother *c* for her little
1Ti 5: 4 practice by *c* for their own family

CARRIED (CARRY)

Ex 19: 4 and how I *c* you on eagles' wings
Isa 53: 4 and *c* our sorrows,
Heb 13: 9 Do not be *c* away by all kinds
2Pe 1: 21 as they were *c* along by the Holy

CARRIES (CARRY)

Dt 32: 11 and *c* them on its pinions.
Isa 40: 11 and *c* them close to his heart;

CARRY (CARRIED CARRIES)

Lk 14: 27 anyone who does not *c* his cross
Gal 6: 2 *C* each other's burdens,
6: 5 for each one should *c* his own load.

CAST

Ps 22: 18 and *c* lots for my clothing.
55: 22 *C* your cares on the LORD
Ecc 11: 1 *C* your bread upon the waters,
Jn 19: 24 and *c* lots for my clothing."
1Pe 5: 7 *C* all your anxiety on him

CATCH (CAUGHT)

Lk 5: 10 from now on you will *c* men."

CATTLE

Ps 50: 10 and the *c* on a thousand hills.

CAUGHT (CATCH)

1Th 4: 17 and are left will be *c* up together

CAUSE (CAUSES)

Pr 24: 28 against your neighbor without *c*,
Ecc 8: 3 Do not stand up for a bad *c*,
Mt 18: 7 of the things that *c* people to sin!
Ro 14: 21 else that will *c* your brother
1Co 10: 32 Do not *c* anyone to stumble,

CAUSES (CAUSE)

Isa 8: 14 a stone that *c* men to stumble
Mt 18: 6 if anyone *c* one of these little ones

CAUTIOUS*

Pr 12: 26 A righteous man is *c* in friendship,

CEASE

Ps 46: 9 He makes wars *c* to the ends

CENSER

Lev 16: 12 is to take a *c* full of burning coals

CENTURION

Mt 8: 5 had entered Capernaum, a *c* came

CERTAIN (CERTAINTY)

2Pe 1: 19 word of the prophets made more *c*,

CERTAINTY* (CERTAIN)

Lk 1: 4 so that you may know the *c*
Jn 17: 8 They knew with *c* that I came

CHAFF

Ps 1: 4 They are like *c*

CHAINED

2Ti 2: 9 But God's word is not *c*.

CHAMPION

Ps 19: 5 like a *c* rejoicing to run his course.

CHANGE (CHANGED)

1Sa 15: 29 of Israel does not lie or *c* his mind;
Ps 110: 4 and will not *c* his mind:
Jer 7: 5 If you really *c* your ways
Mal 3: 6 "I the LORD do not *c*.
Mt 18: 3 unless you *c* and become like little
Heb 7: 21 and will not *c* his mind:
Jas 1: 17 who does not *c* like shifting

CHANGED (CHANGE)

1Co 15: 51 but we will all be *c* — in a flash,

CHARACTER

Ru 3: 11 that you are a woman of noble *c*.
Pr 31: 10 A wife of noble *c* who can find?
Ro 5: 4 perseverance, *c*; and *c*, hope.
1Co 15: 33 "Bad company corrupts good *c*."

CHARGE

Ro 8: 33 Who will bring any *c*
2Co 11: 7 the gospel of God to you free of *c*?
2Ti 4: 1 I give you this *c*: Preach the Word;

CHARIOTS

2Ki 6: 17 and *c* of fire all around Elisha.
Ps 20: 7 Some trust in *c* and some in horses,

CHARM

Pr 31: 30 *C* is deceptive, and beauty is

CHASES

Pr 12: 11 he who *c* fantasies lacks judgment.

CHATTER* (CHATTERING)

1Ti 6: 20 Turn away from godless *c*
2Ti 2: 16 Avoid godless *c*, because those

CHATTERING* (CHATTER)

Pr 10: 8 but a *c* fool comes to ruin.
10: 10 and a *c* fool comes to ruin.

CHEAT* (CHEATED)

Mal 1: 14 "Cursed is the *c* who has

1Co 6: 8 you yourselves *c* and do wrong,

CHEATED (CHEAT)

Lk 19: 8 if I have *c* anybody out of anything,
1Co 6: 7 Why not rather be *c?* Instead,

CHEEK

Mt 5: 39 someone strikes you on the right *c,*

CHEERFUL* (CHEERS)

Pr 15: 13 A happy heart makes the face *c,*
15: 15 but the *c* heart has a continual feast
15: 30 A *c* look brings joy to the heart,
17: 22 A *c* heart is good medicine,
2Co 9: 7 for God loves a *c* giver.

CHEERS (CHEERFUL)

Pr 12: 25 but a kind word *c* him up.

CHILD (CHILDISH CHILDREN)

Pr 20: 11 Even a *c* is known by his actions,
22: 6 Train a *c* in the way he should go,
22: 15 Folly is bound up in the heart of a *c*
23: 13 not withhold discipline from a *c;*
29: 15 *c* left to himself disgraces his mother.
Isa 7: 14 The virgin will be with *c*
9: 6 For to us a *c* is born,
11: 6 and a little *c* will lead them.
66: 13 As a mother comforts her *c,*
Mt 1: 23 "The virgin will be with *c*
18: 2 He called a little *c* and had him
Lk 1: 42 and blessed is the *c* you will bear!
1: 80 And the *c* grew and became strong
1Co 13: 11 When I was a *c,* I talked like a *c,*
1Jn 5: 1 who loves the father loves his *c*

CHILDISH* (CHILD)

1Co 13: 11 When I became a man, I put *c* ways

CHILDREN (CHILD)

Dt 4: 9 Teach them to your *c*
11: 19 them to your *c,* talking about them
Ps 8: 2 From the lips of *c* and infants
Pr 17: 6 Children's *c* are a crown
31: 28 Her *c* arise and call her blessed;
Mt 7: 11 how to give good gifts to your *c,*
11: 25 and revealed them to little *c.*
18: 3 you change and become like little *c*
19: 14 "Let the little *c* come to me,
21: 16 "'From the lips of *c* and infants
Mk 9: 37 one of these little *c* in my name
10: 14 "Let the little *c* come to me,
10: 16 And he took the *c* in his arms,
13: 12 *C* will rebel against their parents
Lk 10: 21 and revealed them to little *c.*
18: 16 "Let the little *c* come to me,
Ro 8: 16 with our spirit that we are God's *c.*
2Co 12: 14 parents, but parents for their *c.*
Eph 6: 1 *C,* obey your parents in the Lord,
Eph 6: 4 do not exasperate your *c;* instead,
Col 3: 20 *C,* obey your parents in everything,
3: 21 Fathers, do not embitter your *c,*
1Ti 3: 4 and see that his *c* obey him
3: 12 and must manage his *c* and his
5: 10 bringing up *c,* showing hospitality,
1Jn 3: 1 that we should be called *c* of God!

CHOOSE (CHOOSES CHOSE CHOSEN)

Dt 30: 19 Now *c* life, so that you
Jos 24: 15 then *c* for yourselves this day
Pr 8: 10 *C* my instruction instead of silver,
16: 16 to *c* understanding rather
Jn 15: 16 You did not *c* me, but I chose you

CHOOSES (CHOOSE)

Jn 7: 17 If anyone *c* to do God's will,

CHOSE (CHOOSE)

Ge 13: 11 So Lot *c* for himself the whole plain
Ps 33: 12 the people he *c* for his inheritance.
Jn 15: 16 but I *c* you and appointed you to go
1Co 1: 27 But God *c* the foolish things
Eph 1: 4 he *c* us in him before the creation
2Th 2: 13 from the beginning God *c* you

CHOSEN (CHOOSE)

Isa 41: 8 Jacob, whom I have *c,*
Mt 22: 14 For many are invited, but few are *c*
Lk 10: 42 Mary has *c* what is better,
23: 35 the Christ of God, the *C* One."
Jn 15: 19 but I have *c* you out of the world.
1Pe 1: 20 He was *c* before the creation
2: 9 But you are a *c* people, a royal

CHRIST (CHRIST'S CHRISTIAN CHRISTS)

Mt 1: 16 was born Jesus, who is called *C.*
16: 16 Peter answered, "You are the *C,*
22: 42 "What do you think about the *C?*
Jn 1: 41 found the Messiah" (that is, the *C).*
20: 31 you may believe that Jesus is the *C,*
Ac 2: 36 you crucified, both Lord and *C."*
5: 42 the good news that Jesus is the *C.*
9: 22 by proving that Jesus is the *C.*
17: 3 proving that the *C* had to suffer
18: 28 the Scriptures that Jesus was the *C.*
26: 23 that the *C* would suffer and,
Ro 3: 22 comes through faith in Jesus *C*
5: 6 we were still powerless, *C* died
5: 8 While we were still sinners, *C* died
5: 17 life through the one man, Jesus *C.*
6: 4 as *C* was raised from the dead
8: 1 for those who are in *C* Jesus,
8: 9 Spirit of *C,* he does not belong to *C.*
8: 35 us from the love of *C?*
Ro 10: 4 *C* is the end of the law
14: 9 *C* died and returned to life
15: 3 For even *C* did not please himself
1Co 1: 23 but we preach *C* crucified:
2: 2 except Jesus *C* and him crucified.
3: 11 one already laid, which is Jesus *C.*
5: 7 For *C,* our Passover lamb,
8: 6 and there is but one Lord, Jesus *C,*
10: 4 them, and that rock was *C.*
11: 1 as I follow the example of *C.*
11: 3 the head of every man is *C,*
12: 27 Now you are the body of *C,*
15: 3 that *C* died for our sins according
15: 14 And if *C* has not been raised,
15: 22 so in *C* all will be made alive.
15: 57 victory through our Lord Jesus *C.*
2Co 3: 3 show that you are a letter from *C,*
4: 5 not preach ourselves, but Jesus *C*
5: 10 before the judgment seat of *C,*
5: 17 Therefore, if anyone is in *C,*
11: 2 you to one husband, to *C,*
Gal 2: 20 I have been crucified with *C*
3: 13 *C* redeemed us from the curse
6: 14 in the cross of our Lord Jesus *C,*
Eph 1: 3 with every spiritual blessing in *C.*
3: 8 the unsearchable riches of *C,*
4: 13 measure of the fullness of *C.*
5: 2 as *C* loved us and gave himself up
5: 23 as *C* is the head of the church,
5: 25 just as *C* loved the church
Php 1: 21 to live is *C* and to die is gain.
1: 27 worthy of the gospel of *C.*
4: 19 to his glorious riches in *C* Jesus.
Col 1: 27 which is *C* in you, the hope of glory
1: 28 may present everyone perfect in *C.*
2: 6 as you received *C* Jesus as Lord,
2: 17 the reality, however, is found in *C.*
3: 15 Let the peace of *C* rule
2Th 2: 1 the coming of our Lord Jesus *C*
1Ti 1: 15 *C* Jesus came into the world
2: 5 the man *C* Jesus, who gave himself
2Ti 2: 3 us like a good soldier of *C* Jesus.
3: 15 salvation through faith in *C* Jesus.
Tit 2: 13 our great God and Savior, Jesus *C,*
Heb 3: 14 to share in *C* if we hold firmly
9: 14 more, then, will the blood of *C,*
9: 15 For this reason *C* is the mediator
9: 28 so *C* was sacrificed once
10: 10 of the body of Jesus *C* once for all.
13: 8 Jesus *C* is the same yesterday
1Pe 1: 19 but with the precious blood of *C,*
2: 21 because *C* suffered for you,
3: 18 For *C* died for sins once for all,
4: 14 insulted because of the name of *C,*
1Jn 2: 22 man who denies that Jesus is the *C.*
3: 16 Jesus *C* laid down his life for us.

1Jn 5: 1 believes that Jesus is the *C* is born
Rev 20: 4 reigned with *C* a thousand years.

CHRIST'S (CHRIST)
2Co 5: 14 For *C* love compels us,
5: 20 We are therefore *C* ambassadors,
12: 9 so that *C* power may rest on me.

CHRISTIAN (CHRIST)
1Pe 4: 16 as a *C,* do not be ashamed,

CHRISTS (CHRIST)
Mt 24: 24 For false *C* and false prophets will

CHURCH
Mt 16: 18 and on this rock I will build my *c,*
18: 17 if he refuses to listen even to the *c,*
Ac 20: 28 Be shepherds of the *c* of God,
1Co 5: 12 of mine to judge those outside the *c*
14: 4 but he who prophesies edifies the *c.*
14: 12 to excel in gifts that build up the *c.*
14: 26 done for the strengthening of the *c.*
Eph 5: 23 as Christ is the head of the *c,*
Col 1: 24 the sake of his body, which is the *c.*

CIRCUMCISED
Ge 17: 10 Every male among you shall be *c.*

CIRCUMSTANCES
Php 4: 11 to be content whatever the *c.*
1Th 5: 18 continually; give thanks in all *c,*

CITIZENS (CITIZENSHIP)
Eph 2: 19 but fellow *c* with God's people

CITIZENSHIP (CITIZENS)
Php 3: 20 But our *c* is in heaven.

CITY
Mt 5: 14 A *c* on a hill cannot be hidden.
Heb 13: 14 here we do not have an enduring *c,*

CIVILIAN*
2Ti 2: 4 a soldier gets involved in *c* affairs—

CLAIM (CLAIMS)
Pr 25: 6 do not *c* a place among great men;
1Jn 1: 6 If we *c* to have fellowship
1: 8 If we *c* to be without sin, we
1: 10 If we *c* we have not sinned,

CLAIMS (CLAIM)
Jas 2: 14 if a man *c* to have faith
1Jn 2: 6 Whoever *c* to live in him must walk
2: 9 Anyone who *c* to be in the light

CLAP
Ps 47: 1 *C* your hands, all you nations;
Isa 55: 12 will *c* their hands.

CLAY
Isa 45: 9 Does the *c* say to the potter,
64: 8 We are the *c,* you are the potter;
Jer 18: 6 "Like *c* in the hand of the potter,
La 4: 2 are now considered as pots of *c,*
Da 2: 33 partly of iron and partly of baked *c.*
Ro 9: 21 of the same lump of *c* some pottery
2Co 4: 7 we have this treasure in jars of *c*
2Ti 2: 20 and *c;* some are for noble purposes

CLEAN
Lev 16: 30 you will be *c* from all your sins.
Ps 24: 4 He who has *c* hands and a pure
Mt 12: 44 the house unoccupied, swept *c*
23: 25 You *c* the outside of the cup
Mk 7: 19 Jesus declared all foods *"c.")*
Jn 13: 10 to wash his feet; his whole body is *c*
15: 3 are already *c* because of the word
Ac 10: 15 impure that God has made *c."*
Ro 14: 20 All food is *c,* but it is wrong

CLING (CLINGS)
Ro 12: 9 Hate what is evil; *c* to what is good.

CLINGS (CLING)
Ps 63: 8 My soul *c* to you;

CLOAK
2Ki 4: 29 "Tuck your *c* into your belt,

CLOSE (CLOSER)
Ps 34: 18 LORD is *c* to the brokenhearted
Isa 40: 11 and carries them *c* to his heart;
Jer 30: 21 himself to be *c* to me?'

CLOSER (CLOSE)
Ex 3: 5 "Do not come any *c,"* God said.
Pr 18: 24 there is a friend who sticks *c*

CLOTHE (CLOTHED CLOTHES CLOTHING)
Ps 45: 3 *c* yourself with splendor
Isa 52: 1 *c* yourself with strength.
Ro 13: 14 *c* yourselves with the Lord Jesus
Col 3: 12 *c* yourselves with compassion,
1Pe 5: 5 *c* yourselves with humility

CLOTHED (CLOTHE)
Ps 30: 11 removed my sackcloth and *c* me
Pr 31: 25 She is *c* with strength and dignity;
Lk 24: 49 until you have been *c* with power

CLOTHES (CLOTHE)
Mt 6: 25 the body more important than *c?*
6: 28 "And why do you worry about *c?*
Jn 11: 44 Take off the grave *c* and let him go

CLOTHING (CLOTHE)
Dt 22: 5 A woman must not wear men's *c,*
Mt 7: 15 They come to you in sheep's *c,*

CLOUD (CLOUDS)
Ex 13: 21 them in a pillar of *c* to guide them
Isa 19: 1 See, the LORD rides on a swift *c*
Lk 21: 27 of Man coming in a *c* with power
Heb 12: 1 by such a great *c* of witnesses,

CLOUDS (CLOUD)
Ps 104: 3 He makes the *c* his chariot
Da 7: 13 coming with the *c* of heaven.
Mk 13: 26 coming in *c* with great power
1Th 4: 17 with them in the *c* to meet the Lord

CO-HEIRS* (INHERIT)
Ro 8: 17 heirs of God and *c* with Christ,

COALS
Pr 25: 22 you will heap burning *c* on his head
Ro 12: 20 you will heap burning *c* on his head

COLD
Pr 25: 25 Like *c* water to a weary soul
Mt 10: 42 if anyone gives even a cup of *c* water
24: 12 the love of most will grow *c,*

COMFORT (COMFORTED COMFORTS)
Ps 23: 4 rod and your staff, they *c* me.
119: 52 and I find *c* in them.
119: 76 May your unfailing love be my *c,*
Zec 1: 17 and the LORD will again *c* Zion
1Co 14: 3 encouragement and *c.*
2Co 1: 4 so that we can *c* those
2: 7 you ought to forgive and *c* him,

COMFORTED (COMFORT)
Mt 5: 4 for they will be *c.*

COMFORTS* (COMFORT)
Job 29: 25 I was like one who *c* mourners.
Isa 49: 13 For the LORD *c* his people
51: 12 "I, even I, am he who *c* you.
66: 13 As a mother *c* her child,
2Co 1: 4 who *c* us in all our troubles,
7: 6 But God, who *c* the downcast,

COMMAND (COMMANDED COMMANDING COMMANDMENT COMMANDMENTS COMMANDS)
Ex 7: 2 You are to say everything I *c* you,
Nu 24: 13 to go beyond the *c* of the LORD—
Dt 4: 2 Do not add to what I *c* you
30: 16 For I *c* you today to love
32: 46 so that you may *c* your children
Ps 91: 11 For he will *c* his angels concerning
Pr 13: 13 but he who respects a *c* is rewarded
Ecc 8: 2 Obey the king's *c,* I say,
Joel 2: 11 mighty are those who obey his *c.*
Jn 14: 15 love me, you will obey what I *c.*
15: 12 My *c* is this: Love each other
1Co 14: 37 writing to you is the Lord's *c.*
Gal 5: 14 law is summed up in a single *c:*
1Ti 1: 5 goal of this *c* is love, which comes
Heb 11: 3 universe was formed at God's *c,*
1Jn 3: 23 this is his *c:* to believe in the name
2Jn : 6 his *c* is that you walk in love.

COMMANDED (COMMAND)
Ps 33: 9 he *c,* and it stood firm.
Ps 148: 5 for he *c* and they were created.

Mt 28: 20 to obey everything I have *c* you.
1Co 9: 14 Lord has *c* that those who preach
1Jn 3: 23 and to love one another as he *c* us.

COMMANDING (COMMAND)
2Ti 2: 4 he wants to please his *c* officer.

COMMANDMENT (COMMAND)
Jos 22: 5 But be very careful to keep the *c*
Mt 22: 38 This is the first and greatest *c.*
Jn 13: 34 "A new *c* I give you: Love one
Ro 7: 12 and the *c* is holy, righteous
Eph 6: 2 which is the first *c* with a promise

COMMANDMENTS (COMMAND)
Ex 20: 6 who love me and keep my *c.*
34: 28 of the covenant—the Ten *C.*
Ecc 12: 13 Fear God and keep his *c,*
Mt 5: 19 one of the least of these *c*
22: 40 the Prophets hang on these two *c."*

COMMANDS (COMMAND)
Dt 7: 9 those who love him and keep his *c.*
11: 27 the blessing if you obey the *c*
Ps 112: 1 who finds great delight in his *c.*
119: 47 for I delight in your *c*
119: 86 All your *c* are trustworthy;
119: 98 Your *c* make me wiser
119:127 Because I love your *c*
119:143 but your *c* are my delight.
119:172 for all your *c* are righteous.
Pr 3: 1 but keep my *c* in your heart,
6: 23 For these *c* are a lamp,
10: 8 The wise in heart accept *c,*
Da 9: 4 all who love him and obey his *c,*
Mt 5: 19 teaches these *c* will be called great
Jn 14: 21 Whoever has my *c* and obeys them,
Ac 17: 30 but now he *c* all people everywhere
1Co 7: 19 Keeping God's *c* is what counts.
1Jn 5: 3 And his *c* are not burdensome,
5: 3 This is love for God: to obey his *c.*

COMMEND (COMMENDED COMMENDS)
Ecc 8: 15 So I *c* the enjoyment of life,
Ro 13: 3 do what is right and he will *c* you.
1Pe 2: 14 and to *c* those who do right.

COMMENDED (COMMEND)
Heb 11: 39 These were all *c* for their faith,

COMMENDS (COMMEND)
2Co 10: 18 not the one who *c* himself who is

COMMIT (COMMITS COMMITTED)
Ex 20: 14 "You shall not *c* adultery.
Ps 37: 5 *C* your way to the LORD;
Mt 5: 27 that it was said, 'Do not *c* adultery.'
Lk 23: 46 into your hands I *c* my spirit."
Ac 20: 32 I *c* you to God and to the word
1Co 10: 8 We should not *c* sexual immorality,
1Pe 4: 19 to God's will should *c* themselves

COMMITS (COMMIT)
Pr 6: 32 man who *c* adultery lacks
29: 22 a hot-tempered one *c* many sins.
Mt 19: 9 marries another woman *c* adultery

COMMITTED (COMMIT)
Nu 5: 7 and must confess the sin he has *c.*
1Ki 8: 61 But your hearts must be fully *c*
2Ch 16: 9 those whose hearts are fully *c*
Mt 5: 28 lustfully has already *c* adultery
2Co 5: 19 And he has *c* to us the message
1Pe 2: 22 "He *c* no sin,

COMMON
Pr 22: 2 Rich and poor have this in *c:*
1Co 10: 13 has seized you except what is *c*
2Co 6: 14 and wickedness have in *c?*

COMPANION (COMPANIONS)
Pr 13: 20 but a *c* of fools suffers harm.
28: 7 a *c* of gluttons disgraces his father.
29: 3 *c* of prostitutes squanders his

COMPANIONS (COMPANION)
Pr 18: 24 A man of many *c* may come to ruin

COMPANY
Pr 24: 1 do not desire their *c;*
Jer 15: 17 I never sat in the *c* of revelers,
1Co 15: 33 "Bad *c* corrupts good character."

COMPARED (COMPARING)
Eze 31: 2 Who can be *c* with you in majesty?
Php 3: 8 I consider everything a loss *c*

COMPARING* (COMPARED)
Ro 8: 18 present sufferings are not worth *c*
2Co 8: 8 the sincerity of your love by *c* it
Gal 6: 4 without *c* himself to somebody else

COMPASSION (COMPASSIONATE COMPASSIONS)
Ex 33: 19 I will have *c* on whom I will have *c.*
Ne 9: 19 of your great *c* you did not
9: 28 in your *c* you delivered them time
Ps 51: 1 according to your great *c*
103: 4 and crowns you with love and *c.*
103: 13 As a father has *c* on his children,
145: 9 he has *c* on all he has made.
Isa 49: 13 and will have *c* on his afflicted ones
49: 15 and have no *c* on the child she has
Hos 2: 19 in love and *c.*
11: 8 all my *c* is aroused.
Jnh 3: 9 with *c* turn from his fierce anger
Mt 9: 36 When he saw the crowds, he had *c*
Mk 8: 2 "I have *c* for these people;
Ro 9: 15 and I will have *c* on whom I have *c*
Col 3: 12 clothe yourselves with *c,* kindness,
Jas 5: 11 The Lord is full of *c* and mercy.

COMPASSIONATE (COMPASSION)
Ne 9: 17 gracious and *c,* slow to anger
Ps 103: 8 The LORD is *c* and gracious,
112: 4 the gracious and *c* and righteous
Eph 4: 32 Be kind and *c* to one another,
1Pe 3: 8 love as brothers, be *c* and humble.

COMPASSIONS* (COMPASSION)
La 3: 22 for his *c* never fail.

COMPELLED (COMPELS)
Ac 20: 22 "And now, *c* by the Spirit,
1Co 9: 16 I cannot boast, for I am *c* to preach.

COMPELS (COMPELLED)
2Co 5: 14 For Christ's love *c* us, because we

COMPETENCE* (COMPETENT)
2Co 3: 5 but our *c* comes from God.

COMPETENT* (COMPETENCE)
Ro 15: 14 and *c* to instruct one another.
1Co 6: 2 are you not *c* to judge trivial cases?
2Co 3: 5 Not that we are *c* in ourselves
3: 6 He has made us *c* as ministers

COMPETES*
1Co 9: 25 Everyone who *c* in the games goes
2Ti 2: 5 Similarly, if anyone *c* as an athlete,
2: 5 unless he *c* according to the rules.

COMPLACENT
Am 6: 1 Woe to you who are *c* in Zion,

COMPLAINING*
Php 2: 14 Do everything without *c* or arguing

COMPLETE
Jn 15: 11 and that your joy may be *c.*
16: 24 will receive, and your joy will be *c.*
17: 23 May they be brought to *c* unity
Ac 20: 24 *c* the task the Lord Jesus has given
Php 2: 2 then make my joy *c*
Col 4: 17 to it that you *c* the work you have
Jas 1: 4 so that you may be mature and *c,*
2: 22 his faith was made *c* by what he did

CONCEAL (CONCEALED CONCEALS)
Ps 40: 10 I do not *c* your love and your truth
Pr 25: 2 It is the glory of God to *c* a matter;

CONCEALED (CONCEAL)
Jer 16: 17 nor is their sin *c* from my eyes.
Mt 10: 26 There is nothing *c* that will not be
Mk 4: 22 and whatever is *c* is meant

CONCEALS (CONCEAL)
Pr 28: 13 He who *c* his sins does not prosper,

CONCEITED
Ro 12: 16 Do not be *c.*
Gal 5: 26 Let us not become *c,* provoking

1Ti 6: 4 he is *c* and understands nothing.

CONCEIVED

Mt 1: 20 what is *c* in her is from the Holy
1Co 2: 9 no mind has *c*

CONCERN (CONCERNED)

Eze 36: 21 I had *c* for my holy name, which
1Co 7: 32 I would like you to be free from *c*.
12: 25 that its parts should have equal *c*
2Co 11: 28 of my *c* for all the churches.

CONCERNED (CONCERN)

Jnh 4: 10 "You have been *c* about this vine,
1Co 7: 32 An unmarried man is *c* about

CONDEMN (CONDEMNATION CONDEMNED CONDEMNING CONDEMNS)

Job 40: 8 Would you *c* me to justify yourself?
Isa 50: 9 Who is he that will *c* me?
Lk 6: 37 Do not *c*, and you will not be
Jn 3: 17 Son into the world to *c* the world,
12: 48 very word which I spoke will *c* him
Ro 2: 27 yet obeys the law will *c* you who,
1Jn 3: 20 presence whenever our hearts *c* us.

CONDEMNATION (CONDEMN)

Ro 5: 18 of one trespass was *c* for all men,
8: 1 there is now no *c* for those who are

CONDEMNED (CONDEMN)

Ps 34: 22 no one will be *c* who takes refuge
Mt 12: 37 and by your words you will be *c*."
23: 33 How will you escape being *c* to hell
Jn 3: 18 Whoever believes in him is not *c*,
5: 24 has eternal life and will not be *c*;
16: 11 prince of this world now stands *c*.
Ro 14: 23 But the man who has doubts is *c*
1Co 11: 32 disciplined so that we will not be *c*
Heb 11: 7 By his faith he *c* the world

CONDEMNING (CONDEMN)

Pr 17: 15 the guilty and *c* the innocent—
Ro 2: 1 judge the other, you are *c* yourself,

CONDEMNS (CONDEMN)

Ro 8: 34 Who is he that *c*? Christ Jesus,
2Co 3: 9 the ministry that *c* men is glorious,

CONDUCT

Pr 10: 23 A fool finds pleasure in evil *c*,
20: 11 by whether his *c* is pure and right.
21: 8 but the *c* of the innocent is upright.
Ecc 6: 8 how to *c* himself before others?
Jer 4: 18 "Your own *c* and actions
17: 10 to reward a man according to his *c*,
Eze 7: 3 I will judge you according to your *c*
Php 1: 27 *c* yourselves in a manner worthy
1Ti 3: 15 to *c* themselves in God's household

CONFESS (CONFESSION)

Lev 16: 21 and *c* over it all the wickedness
26: 40 "'But if they will *c* their sins
Nu 5: 7 must *c* the sin he has committed.
Ps 38: 18 I *c* my iniquity;
Ro 10: 9 That if you *c* with your mouth,
Php 2: 11 every tongue *c* that Jesus Christ is
Jas 5: 16 Therefore *c* your sins to each other
1Jn 1: 9 If we *c* our sins, he is faithful

CONFESSION (CONFESS)

Ezr 10: 11 Now make *c* to the LORD,
2Co 9: 13 obedience that accompanies your *c*

CONFIDENCE

Ps 71: 5 my *c* since my youth.
Pr 3: 26 for the LORD will be your *c*
11: 13 A gossip betrays a *c*,
25: 9 do not betray another man's *c*,
31: 11 Her husband has full *c* in her
Isa 32: 17 will be quietness and *c* forever.
Jer 17: 7 whose *c* is in him.
Php 3: 3 and who put no *c* in the flesh—
Heb 3: 14 till the end the *c* we had at first.
4: 16 the throne of grace with *c*,
10: 19 since we have *c* to enter the Most
10: 35 So do not throw away your *c*;
1Jn 5: 14 This is the *c* we have

CONFORM* (CONFORMED)

Ro 12: 2 Do not *c* any longer to the pattern
1Pe 1: 14 do not *c* to the evil desires you had

CONFORMED (CONFORM)

Ro 8: 29 predestined to be *c* to the likeness

CONQUERORS

Ro 8: 37 than *c* through him who loved us.

CONSCIENCE (CONSCIENCES)

Ro 13: 5 punishment but also because of *c*.
1Co 8: 7 since their *c* is weak, it is defiled.
8: 12 in this way and wound their weak *c*
10: 25 without raising questions of *c*,
10: 29 freedom be judged by another's *c*?
Heb 10: 22 to cleanse us from a guilty *c*
1Pe 3: 16 and respect, keeping a clear *c*,

CONSCIENCES* (CONSCIENCE)

Ro 2: 15 their *c* also bearing witness,
1Ti 4: 2 whose *c* have been seared
Tit 1: 15 their minds and *c* are corrupted.
Heb 9: 14 cleanse our *c* from acts that lead

CONSCIOUS*

Ro 3: 20 through the law we become *c* of sin
1Pe 2: 19 of unjust suffering because he is *c*

CONSECRATE (CONSECRATED)

Ex 13: 2 "*C* to me every firstborn male.
Lev 20: 7 "'*C* yourselves and be holy,

CONSECRATED (CONSECRATE)

Ex 29: 43 and the place will be *c* by my glory.
1Ti 4: 5 because it is *c* by the word of God

CONSIDER (CONSIDERATE CONSIDERED CONSIDERS)

1Sa 12: 24 *c* what great things he has done
Job 37: 14 stop and *c* God's wonders.
Ps 8: 3 When I *c* your heavens
107: 43 and *c* the great love of the LORD.
143: 5 and *c* what your hands have done.
Lk 12: 24 *C* the ravens: They do not sow
12: 27 about the rest? "*C* how the lilies
Php 2: 3 but in humility *c* others better
3: 8 I *c* everything a loss compared
Heb 10: 24 And let us *c* how we may spur one
Jas 1: 2 *C* it pure joy, my brothers,

CONSIDERATE* (CONSIDER)

Tit 3: 2 to be peaceable and *c*,
Jas 3: 17 then peace-loving, *c*, submissive,
1Pe 2: 18 only to those who are good and *c*,
3: 7 in the same way be *c* as you live

CONSIDERED (CONSIDER)

Job 1: 8 "Have you *c* my servant Job?
2: 3 "Have you *c* my servant Job?
Ps 44: 22 we are *c* as sheep to be slaughtered.
Isa 53: 4 yet we *c* him stricken by God,
Ro 8: 36 we are *c* as sheep to be slaughtered

CONSIDERS (CONSIDER)

Pr 31: 16 She *c* a field and buys it;
Ro 14: 5 One man *c* one day more sacred
Jas 1: 26 If anyone *c* himself religious

CONSIST

Lk 12: 15 a man's life does not *c*

CONSOLATION

Ps 94: 19 your *c* brought joy to my soul.

CONSTRUCTIVE*

1Co 10: 23 but not everything is *c*.

CONSUME (CONSUMING)

Jn 2: 17 "Zeal for your house will *c* me."

CONSUMING (CONSUME)

Dt 4: 24 For the LORD your God is a *c* fire,
Heb 12: 29 and awe, for our "God is a *c* fire."

CONTAIN

1Ki 8: 27 the highest heaven, cannot *c* you.
2Pe 3: 16 His letters *c* some things that are

CONTAMINATES*

2Co 7: 1 from everything that *c* body

CONTEMPT

Pr 14: 31 He who oppresses the poor shows *c*
17: 5 He who mocks the poor shows *c*
18: 3 When wickedness comes, so does *c*
Da 12: 2 others to shame and everlasting *c*.
Ro 2: 4 Or do you show *c* for the riches
Gal 4: 14 you did not treat me with *c*
1Th 5: 20 do not treat prophecies with *c*.

CONTEND (CONTENDING)

Jude : 3 you to *c* for the faith that was once

CONTENDING* (CONTEND)

Php 1: 27 *c* as one man for the faith

CONTENT (CONTENTMENT)

Pr 13: 25 The righteous eat to their hearts' *c*,
Php 4: 11 to be *c* whatever the circumstances
4: 12 I have learned the secret of being *c*
1Ti 6: 8 and clothing, we will be *c* with that.
Heb 13: 5 and be *c* with what you have,

CONTENTMENT (CONTENT)

1Ti 6: 6 But godliness with *c* is great gain.

CONTINUAL (CONTINUE)

Pr 15: 15 but the cheerful heart has a *c* feast.

CONTINUE (CONTINUAL)

Php 2: 12 *c* to work out your salvation
2Ti 3: 14 *c* in what you have learned
1Jn 5: 18 born of God does not *c* to sin;
Rev 22: 11 and let him who is holy *c* to be holy
22: 11 let him who does right *c* to do right;

CONTRITE*

Ps 51: 17 a broken and *c* heart,
Isa 57: 15 also with him who is *c* and lowly
57: 15 and to revive the heart of the *c*.
66: 2 he who is humble and *c* in spirit,

CONTROL (CONTROLLED SELF CONTROL SELF-CONTROLLED)

Pr 29: 11 a wise man keeps himself under *c*.
1Co 7: 9 But if they cannot *c* themselves,
7: 37 but has *c* over his own will,
1Th 4: 4 you should learn to *c* his own body

CONTROLLED (CONTROL)

Ps 32: 9 but must be *c* by bit and bridle
Ro 8: 6 but the mind *c* by the Spirit is life
8: 8 Those *c* by the sinful nature cannot

CONTROVERSIES

Tit 3: 9 But avoid foolish *c* and genealogies

CONVERSATION

Col 4: 6 Let your *c* be always full of grace,

CONVERT

1Ti 3: 6 He must not be a recent *c*,

CONVICT

Jn 16: 8 he will *c* the world of guilt in regard

CONVINCED (CONVINCING)

Ro 8: 38 For I am *c* that neither death
2Ti 1: 12 and am *c* that he is able
3: 14 have learned and have become *c*

CONVINCING* (CONVINCED)

Ac 1: 3 and gave many *c* proofs that he was

CORNELIUS*

Roman to whom Peter preached; first Gentile Christian (Ac 10).

CORNERSTONE (STONE)

Isa 28: 16 a precious *c* for a sure foundation;
Eph 2: 20 Christ Jesus himself as the chief *c*.
1Pe 2: 6 a chosen and precious *c*,

CORRECT (CORRECTING CORRECTION CORRECTS)

2Ti 4: 2 *c*, rebuke and encourage—

CORRECTING* (CORRECT)

2Ti 3: 16 *c* and training in righteousness,

CORRECTION (CORRECT)

Pr 10: 17 whoever ignores *c* leads others
12: 1 but he who hates *c* is stupid.
15: 5 whoever heeds *c* shows prudence.
15: 10 he who hates *c* will die.
29: 15 The rod of *c* imparts wisdom,

CORRECTS* (CORRECT)

Job 5: 17 "Blessed is the man whom God *c*;
Pr 9: 7 Whoever *c* a mocker invites insult;

CORRUPT (CORRUPTS)

Ge 6: 11 Now the earth was *c* in God's sight

CORRUPTS* (CORRUPT)

Ecc 7: 7 and a bribe *c* the heart.
1Co 15: 33 "Bad company *c* good character."
Jas 3: 6 It *c* the whole person, sets

COST

Pr 4: 7 Though it *c* all you have, get
Isa 55: 1 milk without money and without *c*.
Rev 21: 6 to drink without *c* from the spring

COUNSEL (COUNSELOR)

1Ki 22: 5 "First seek the *c* of the LORD."
Pr 15: 22 Plans fail for lack of *c*,
Rev 3: 18 I *c* you to buy from me gold refined

COUNSELOR (COUNSEL)

Isa 9: 6 Wonderful *C*, Mighty God,
Jn 14: 16 he will give you another *C* to be
14: 26 But the *C*, the Holy Spirit,

COUNT (COUNTING COUNTS)

Ro 4: 8 whose sin the Lord will never *c*
6: 11 *c* yourselves dead to sin

COUNTING (COUNT)

2Co 5: 19 not *c* men's sins against them.

COUNTRY

Jn 4: 44 prophet has no honor in his own *c*.)

COUNTS (COUNT)

Jn 6: 63 The Spirit gives life; the flesh *c*
1Co 7: 19 God's commands is what *c*.
Gal 5: 6 only thing that *c* is faith expressing

COURAGE (COURAGEOUS)

Ac 23: 11 "Take *c*! As you have testified
1Co 16: 13 stand firm in the faith; be men of *c*;

COURAGEOUS (COURAGE)

Dt 31: 6 Be strong and *c*.
Jos 1: 6 and *c*, because you will lead these

COURSE

Ps 19: 5 a champion rejoicing to run his *c*.
Pr 15: 21 of understanding keeps a straight *c*.

COURTS

Ps 84: 10 Better is one day in your *c*
100: 4 and his *c* with praise;

COVENANT (COVENANTS)

Ge 9: 9 "I now establish my *c* with you
Ex 19: 5 if you obey me fully and keep my *c*,
1Ch 16: 15 He remembers his *c* forever,
Job 31: 1 "I made a *c* with my eyes
Jer 31: 31 "when I will make a new *c*
1Co 11: 25 "This cup is the new *c* in my blood;
Gal 4: 24 One *c* is from Mount Sinai
Heb 9: 15 Christ is the mediator of a new *c*,

COVENANTS (COVENANT)

Ro 9: 4 theirs the divine glory, the *c*,
Gal 4: 24 for the women represent two *c*.

COVER (COVER-UP COVERED COVERS)

Ps 91: 4 He will *c* you with his feathers,
Jas 5: 20 and *c* over a multitude of sins.

COVER-UP (COVER)

1Pe 2: 16 but do not use your freedom as a *c*

COVERED (COVER)

Ps 32: 1 whose sins are *c*.
Isa 6: 2 With two wings they *c* their faces,
Ro 4: 7 whose sins are *c*.
1Co 11: 4 with his head *c* dishonors his head.

COVERS (COVER)

Pr 10: 12 but love *c* over all wrongs.
1Pe 4: 8 love *c* over a multitude of sins.

COVET

Ex 20: 17 You shall not *c* your neighbor's
Ro 13: 9 "Do not steal," "Do not *c*,"

COWARDLY*

Rev 21: 8 But the *c*, the unbelieving, the vile,

CRAFTINESS (CRAFTY)

1Co 3: 19 "He catches the wise in their *c*";

CRAFTY (CRAFTINESS)

Ge 3: 1 the serpent was more *c* than any
2Co 12: 16 *c* fellow that I am, I caught you

CRAVE

Pr 23: 3 Do not *c* his delicacies,
1Pe 2: 2 newborn babies, *c* pure spiritual

CREATE (CREATED CREATION CREATOR)

Ps 51: 10 *C* in me a pure heart, O God,
Isa 45: 18 he did not *c* it to be empty,

CREATED (CREATE)

Ge 1: 1 In the beginning God *c* the heavens
1: 21 God *c* the great creatures of the sea
1: 27 So God *c* man in his own image,
Ps 148: 5 for he commanded and they were *c*
Isa 42: 5 he who *c* the heavens and stretched
Ro 1: 25 and served *c* things rather
1Co 11: 9 neither was man *c* for woman,
Col 1: 16 For by him all things were *c*:
1Ti 4: 4 For everything God *c* is good,
Rev 10: 6 who *c* the heavens and all that is

CREATION (CREATE)

Mk 16: 15 and preach the good news to all *c*.
Jn 17: 24 me before the *c* of the world.
Ro 8: 19 The *c* waits in eager expectation
8: 39 depth, nor anything else in all *c*,
2Co 5: 17 he is a new *c*; the old has gone,
Col 1: 15 God, the firstborn over all *c*.
1Pe 1: 20 chosen before the *c* of the world,
Rev 13: 8 slain from the *c* of the world.

CREATOR (CREATE)

Ge 14: 22 God Most High, *C* of heaven
Ro 1: 25 created things rather than the *C*—

CREATURE (CREATURES)

Lev 17: 11 For the life of a *c* is in the blood,

CREATURES (CREATURE)

Ge 6: 19 bring into the ark two of all living *c*,
Ps 104: 24 the earth is full of your *c*.

CREDIT (CREDITED)

Ro 4: 24 to whom God will *c* righteousness
1Pe 2: 20 it to your *c* if you receive a beating

CREDITED (CREDIT)

Ge 15: 6 and he *c* it to him as righteousness.
Ro 4: 5 his faith is *c* as righteousness.
Gal 3: 6 and it was *c* to him as righteousness
Jas 2: 23 and it was *c* to him as righteousness

CRIED (CRY)

Ps 18: 6 I *c* to my God for help.

CRIMSON

Isa 1: 18 though they are red as *c*,

CRIPPLED

Mk 9: 45 better for you to enter life *c*

CRITICISM

2Co 8: 20 We want to avoid any *c*

CROOKED

Pr 10: 9 he who takes *c* paths will be found
Php 2: 15 children of God without fault in a *c*

CROSS

Mt 10: 38 and anyone who does not take his *c*
Lk 9: 23 take up his *c* daily and follow me.
Ac 2: 23 to death by nailing him to the *c*.
1Co 1: 17 lest the *c* of Christ be emptied
Gal 6: 14 in the *c* of our Lord Jesus Christ,
Php 2: 8 even death on a *c*!
Col 1: 20 through his blood, shed on the *c*.
2: 14 he took it away, nailing it to the *c*.
2: 15 triumphing over them by the *c*.
Heb 12: 2 set before him endured the *c*,

CROWD

Ex 23: 2 Do not follow the *c* in doing wrong.

CROWN (CROWNED CROWNS)

Pr 4: 9 present you with a *c* of splendor."
10: 6 Blessings *c* the head
12: 4 noble character is her husband's *c*,
17: 6 Children's children are a *c*
Isa 61: 3 to bestow on them a *c* of beauty
Zec 9: 16 like jewels in a *c*.
Mt 27: 29 then twisted together a *c* of thorns
1Co 9: 25 it to get a *c* that will last forever.
2Ti 4: 8 store for me the *c* of righteousness,
Rev 2: 10 and I will give you the *c* of life.

CROWNED (CROWN)

Ps 8: 5 and *c* him with glory and honor.
Pr 14: 18 the prudent are *c* with knowledge.
Heb 2: 7 you *c* him with glory and honor

CROWNS (CROWN)

Rev 4: 10 They lay their *c* before the throne
19: 12 and on his head are many *c*.

CRUCIFIED (CRUCIFY)

Mt 20: 19 to be mocked and flogged and *c*.
27: 38 Two robbers were *c* with him,
Lk 24: 7 be *c* and on the third day be raised
Jn 19: 18 Here they *c* him, and with him two
Ac 2: 36 whom you *c*, both Lord and Christ
Ro 6: 6 For we know that our old self was *c*
1Co 1: 23 but we preach Christ *c*: a stumbling
2: 2 except Jesus Christ and him *c*.
Gal 2: 20 I have been *c* with Christ
5: 24 Christ Jesus have *c* the sinful

CRUCIFY (CRUCIFIED CRUCIFYING)

Mt 27: 22 They all answered, "*C* him!" "Why
27: 31 Then they led him away to *c* him.

CRUCIFYING* (CRUCIFY)

Heb 6: 6 to their loss they are *c* the Son

CRUSH (CRUSHED)

Ge 3: 15 he will *c* your head,
Isa 53: 10 it was the LORD's will to *c* him
Ro 16: 20 The God of peace will soon *c* Satan

CRUSHED (CRUSH)

Ps 34: 18 and saves those who are *c* in spirit.
Isa 53: 5 he was *c* for our iniquities;
2Co 4: 8 not *c*; perplexed, but not in despair;

CRY (CRIED)

Ps 34: 15 and his ears are attentive to their *c*;
40: 1 he turned to me and heard my *c*.
130: 1 Out of the depths I *c* to you,

CUP

Ps 23: 5 my *c* overflows.
Mt 10: 42 if anyone gives even a *c* of cold water
23: 25 You clean the outside of the *c*
26: 39 may this *c* be taken from me.
1Co 11: 25 after supper he took the *c*, saying,

CURSE (CURSED)

Dt 11: 26 before you today a blessing and a *c*
21: 23 hung on a tree is under God's *c*.
Lk 6: 28 bless those who *c* you, pray
Gal 3: 13 of the law by becoming a *c* for us,
Rev 22: 3 No longer will there be any *c*.

CURSED (CURSE)

Ge 3: 17 "*C* is the ground because of you;
Dt 27: 15 "*C* is the man who carves an image
27: 16 "*C* is the man who dishonors his
27: 17 "*C* is the man who moves his
27: 18 "*C* is the man who leads the blind
27: 19 *C* is the man who withholds justice
27: 20 "*C* is the man who sleeps
27: 21 "*C* is the man who has sexual
27: 22 "*C* is the man who sleeps
27: 23 "*C* is the man who sleeps
27: 24 "*C* is the man who kills his
27: 25 "*C* is the man who accepts a bribe
27: 26 "*C* is the man who does not uphold
Ro 9: 3 I could wish that I myself were *c*
Gal 3: 10 "*C* is everyone who does not

CURTAIN

Ex 26: 33 The *c* will separate the Holy Place
Lk 23: 45 the *c* of the temple was torn in two.
Heb 10: 20 opened for us through the *c*,

CYMBAL*
1Co 13: 1 a resounding gong or a clanging *c.*

DANCE (DANCING)
Ecc 3: 4 a time to mourn and a time to *d,*
Mt 11: 17 and you did not *d;*

DANCING (DANCE)
Ps 30: 11 You turned my wailing into *d;*
149: 3 Let them praise his name with *d*

DANGER
Pr 27: 12 The prudent see *d* and take refuge,
Ro 8: 35 famine or nakedness or *d* or sword?

DANIEL
Hebrew exile to Babylon, name changed to Belteshazzar (Da 1:6-7). Refused to eat unclean food (Da 1:8-21). Interpreted Nebuchadnezzar's dreams (Da 2; 4), writing on the wall (Da 5). Thrown into lion's den (Da 6). Visions of (Da 7-12).

DARK (DARKNESS)
Job 34: 22 There is no *d* place, no deep
Pr 31: 15 She gets up while it is still *d;*
Ro 2: 19 a light for those who are in the *d,*
2Pe 1: 19 as to a light shining in a *d* place,

DARKNESS (DARK)
Ge 1: 4 he separated the light from the *d.*
2Sa 22: 29 the LORD turns my *d* into light.
Jn 3: 19 but men loved *d* instead of light
2Co 6: 14 fellowship can light have with *d?*
Eph 5: 8 For you were once *d,* but now you
1Pe 2: 9 out of *d* into his wonderful light.
1Jn 1: 5 in him there is no *d* at all.
2: 9 but hates his brother is still in the *d.*

DAUGHTERS
Joel 2: 28 sons and *d* will prophesy,

DAVID
Son of Jesse (Ru 4:17-22; 1Ch 2:13-15), ancestor of Jesus (Mt 1:1-17; Lk 3:31).
Anointed king by Samuel (1Sa 16:1-13). Musician to Saul (1Sa 16:14-23; 18:10). Killed Goliath (1Sa 17). Relation with Jonathan (1Sa 18:1-4; 19-20; 23:16-18; 2Sa 1). Disfavor of Saul (1Sa 18:6-23:29). Spared Saul's life (1Sa 24; 26). Among Philistines (1Sa 21:10-14; 27-30). Lament for Saul and Jonathan (2Sa 1).
Anointed king of Judah (2Sa 2:1-11); of Israel (2Sa 5:1-4; 1Ch 11:1-3). Promised eternal dynasty (2Sa 7; 1Ch 17; Ps 132). Adultery with Bathsheba (2Sa 11-12). Absalom's revolt (2Sa 14-18). Last words (2Sa 23:1-7). Death (1Ki 2:10-12; 1Ch 29:28).

DAWN
Ps 37: 6 your righteousness shine like the *d,*
Pr 4: 18 is like the first gleam of *d,*

DAY (DAYS)
Ge 1: 5 God called the light *"d,"*
Ex 20: 8 "Remember the Sabbath *d*
Lev 23: 28 because it is the *D* of Atonement,
Nu 14: 14 before them in a pillar of cloud by *d*
Jos 1: 8 meditate on it *d* and night,
Ps 84: 10 Better is one *d* in your courts
96: 2 proclaim his salvation *d* after *d.*
118: 24 This is the *d* the LORD has made;
Pr 27: 1 not know what a *d* may bring forth.
Joel 2: 31 and dreadful *d* of the LORD.
Ob : 15 The *d* of the LORD is near
Lk 11: 3 Give us each *d* our daily bread.
Ac 17: 11 examined the Scriptures every *d*
2Co 4: 16 we are being renewed *d* by *d.*
1Th 5: 2 for you know very well that the *d*
2Pe 3: 8 With the Lord a *d* is like

DAYS (DAY)
Dt 17: 19 he is to read it all the *d,* of his life
Ps 23: 6 all the *d* of my life,
Ps 90: 10 The length of our *d* is seventy years
Ecc 12: 1 Creator in the *d* of your youth,
Joel 2: 29 I will pour out my Spirit in those *d.*
Mic 4: 1 In the last *d*
Heb 1: 2 in these last *d* he has spoken to us
2Pe 3: 3 that in the last *d* scoffers will come,

DEACONS
1Ti 3: 8 *D,* likewise, are to be men worthy

DEAD (DIE)
Dt 18: 11 or spiritist or who consults the *d.*
Mt 28: 7 'He has risen from the *d*
Ro 6: 11 count yourselves *d* to sin
Eph 2: 1 you were *d* in your transgressions
1Th 4: 16 and the *d* in Christ will rise first.
Jas 2: 17 is not accompanied by action, is *d.*
2: 26 so faith without deeds is *d.*

DEATH (DIE)
Nu 35: 16 the murderer shall be put to *d.*
Ps 23: 4 the valley of the shadow of *d,*
116: 15 is the *d* of his saints.
Pr 8: 36 all who hate me love *d."*
14: 12 but in the end it leads to *d.*
Ecc 7: 2 for *d* is the destiny of every man;
Isa 25: 8 he will swallow up *d* forever.
53: 12 he poured out his life unto *d,*
Jn 5: 24 he has crossed over from *d* to life.
Ro 5: 12 and in this way *d* came to all men,
6: 23 For the wages of sin is *d,*
8: 13 put to *d* the misdeeds of the body,
1Co 15: 21 For since *d* came through a man,
15: 55 Where, O *d,* is your sting?"
Rev 1: 18 And I hold the keys of *d* and Hades
20: 6 The second *d* has no power
20: 14 The lake of fire is the second *d.*
21: 4 There will be no more *d*

DEBAUCHERY
Ro 13: 13 not in sexual immorality and *d,*
Eph 5: 18 drunk on wine, which leads to *d.*

DEBORAH
Prophetess who led Israel to victory over Canaanites (Jdg 4-5).

DEBT (DEBTORS DEBTS)
Ro 13: 8 Let no *d* remain outstanding,
13: 8 continuing *d* to love one another,

DEBTORS (DEBT)
Mt 6: 12 as we also have forgiven our *d.*

DEBTS (DEBT)
Dt 15: 1 seven years you must cancel *d.*
Mt 6: 12 Forgive us our *d,*

DECAY
Ps 16: 10 will you let your Holy One see *d.*
Ac 2: 27 will you let your Holy One see *d.*

DECEIT (DECEIVE)
Mk 7: 22 greed, malice, *d,* lewdness, envy,
1Pe 2: 1 yourselves of all malice and all *d,*
2: 22 and no *d* was found in his mouth."

DECEITFUL (DECEIVE)
Jer 17: 9 The heart is *d* above all things
2Co 11: 13 men are false apostles, *d* workmen,

DECEITFULNESS (DECEIVE)
Mk 4: 19 the *d* of wealth and the desires
Heb 3: 13 of you may be hardened by sin's *d.*

DECEIVE (DECEIT DECEITFUL DECEITFULNESS DECEIVED DECEIVES DECEPTIVE)
Lev 19: 11 "'Do not *d* one another.
Pr 14: 5 A truthful witness does not *d,*
Mt 24: 5 'I am the Christ,' and will *d* many.
Ro 16: 18 and flattery they *d* the minds
1Co 3: 18 Do not *d* yourselves.
Eph 5: 6 Let no one *d* you with empty words
Jas 1: 22 to the word, and so *d* yourselves.
1Jn 1: 8 we *d* ourselves and the truth is not

DECEIVED (DECEIVE)
Ge 3: 13 "The serpent *d* me, and I ate."
Gal 6: 7 Do not be *d:* God cannot be
1Ti 2: 14 And Adam was not the one *d;*
2Ti 3: 13 to worse, deceiving and being *d.*
Jas 1: 16 Don't be *d,* my dear brothers.

DECEIVES (DECEIVE)
Gal 6: 3 when he is nothing, he *d* himself.
Jas 1: 26 he *d* himself and his religion is

DECENCY*
1Ti 2: 9 women to dress modestly, with *d*

DECEPTIVE (DECEIVE)
Pr 31: 30 Charm is *d,* and beauty is fleeting;
Col 2: 8 through hollow and *d* philosophy,

DECLARE (DECLARED DECLARING)
1Ch 16: 24 *D* his glory among the nations,
Ps 19: 1 The heavens *d* the glory of God;
96: 3 *D* his glory among the nations,
Isa 42: 9 and new things I *d;*

DECLARED (DECLARE)
Mk 7: 19 Jesus *d* all foods "clean.")
Ro 2: 13 the law who will be *d* righteous.
3: 20 no one will be *d* righteous

DECLARING (DECLARE)
Ps 71: 8 *d* your splendor all day long.
Ac 2: 11 we hear them *d* the wonders

DECREED (DECREES)
La 3: 37 happen if the Lord has not *d* it?
Lk 22: 22 Son of Man will go as it has been *d,*

DECREES (DECREED)
Lev 10: 11 Israelites all the *d* the LORD has
Ps 119:112 My heart is set on keeping your *d*

DEDICATE (DEDICATION)
Nu 6: 12 He must *d* himself to the LORD
Pr 20: 25 for a man to *d* something rashly

DEDICATION (DEDICATE)
1Ti 5: 11 sensual desires overcome their *d*

DEED (DEEDS)
Col 3: 17 you do, whether in word or *d,*

DEEDS (DEED)
1Sa 2: 3 and by him *d* are weighed.
Ps 65: 5 with awesome *d* of righteousness,
66: 3 "How awesome are your *d!*
78: 4 the praiseworthy *d* of the LORD,
86: 10 you are great and do marvelous *d;*
92: 4 For you make me glad by your *d,*
111: 3 Glorious and majestic are his *d,*
Hab 3: 2 I stand in awe of your *d,* O LORD.
Mt 5: 16 that they may see your good *d*
Ac 26: 20 prove their repentance by their *d.*
Jas 2: 14 claims to have faith but has no *d?*
2: 20 faith without *d* is useless?
1Pe 2: 12 they may see your good *d*

DEEP (DEPTH)
1Co 2: 10 all things, even the *d* things
1Ti 3: 9 hold of the *d* truths of the faith

DEER
Ps 42: 1 As the *d* pants for streams of water,

DEFEND (DEFENSE)
Ps 74: 22 Rise up, O God, and *d* your cause;
Pr 31: 9 *d* the rights of the poor and needy
Jer 50: 34 He will vigorously *d* their cause

DEFENSE (DEFEND)
Ps 35: 23 Awake, and rise to my *d!*
Php 1: 16 here for the *d* of the gospel.
1Jn 2: 1 speaks to the Father in our *d* —

DEFERRED*
Pr 13: 12 Hope *d* makes the heart sick,

DEFILE (DEFILED)
Da 1: 8 Daniel resolved not to *d* himself

DEFILED (DEFILE)
Isa 24: 5 The earth is *d* by its people;

DEFRAUD
Lev 19: 13 Do not *d* your neighbor or rob him.

DEITY*
Col 2: 9 of the *D* lives in bodily form,

DELIGHT (DELIGHTS)
1Sa 15: 22 "Does the LORD *d*
Ps 1: 2 But his *d* is in the law of the LORD
16: 3 in whom is all my *d.*
35: 9 and *d* in his salvation.
37: 4 *D* yourself in the LORD
43: 4 to God, my joy and my *d.*
51: 16 You do not *d* in sacrifice,
119: 77 for your law is my *d.*
Pr 29: 17 he will bring *d* to your soul.
Isa 42: 1 my chosen one in whom I *d;*
55: 2 and your soul will *d* in the richest
61: 10 I *d* greatly in the LORD;
Jer 9: 24 for in these I *d,"*
15: 16 they were my joy and my heart's *d,*
Mic 7: 18 but *d* to show mercy.
Zep 3: 17 He will take great *d* in you,
Mt 12: 18 the one I love, in whom I *d;*
1Co 13: 6 Love does not *d* in evil
2Co 12: 10 for Christ's sake, I *d* in weaknesses,

DELIGHTS (DELIGHT)
Ps 22: 8 since he *d* in him."
35: 27 who *d* in the well-being
36: 8 from your river of *d.*
37: 23 if the LORD *d* in a man's way,
Pr 3: 12 as a father the son he *d* in.
12: 22 but he *d* in men who are truthful.
23: 24 he who has a wise son *d* in him.

DELILAH*
Woman who betrayed Samson (Jdg 16:4-22).

DELIVER (DELIVERANCE DELIVERED DELIVERER DELIVERS)
Ps 72: 12 For he will *d* the needy who cry out
79: 9 *d* us and forgive our sins
Mt 6: 13 but *d* us from the evil one.'
2Co 1: 10 hope that he will continue to *d* us,

DELIVERANCE (DELIVER)
Ps 3: 8 From the LORD comes *d.*
32: 7 and surround me with songs of *d.*
33: 17 A horse is a vain hope for *d;*

DELIVERED (DELIVER)
Ps 34: 4 he *d* me from all my fears.
Ro 4: 25 He was *d* over to death for our sins

DELIVERER (DELIVER)
Ps 18: 2 is my rock, my fortress and my *d;*
40: 17 You are my help and my *d;*
140: 7 O Sovereign LORD, my strong *d,*
144: 2 my stronghold and my *d,*

DELIVERS (DELIVER)
Ps 34: 17 he *d* them from all their troubles.
34: 19 but the LORD *d* him from them all
37: 40 The LORD helps them and *d* them
37: 40 he *d* them from the wicked

DEMANDED
Lk 12: 20 This very night your life will be *d*
12: 48 been given much, much will be *d;*

DEMONS
Mt 12: 27 And if I drive out *d* by Beelzebub,
Mk 5: 15 possessed by the legion of *d,*
Ro 8: 38 neither angels nor *d,* neither
Jas 2: 19 Good! Even the *d* believe that—

DEMONSTRATE (DEMONSTRATES)
Ro 3: 26 he did it to *d* his justice

DEMONSTRATES* (DEMONSTRATE)
Ro 5: 8 God *d* his own love for us in this:

DEN
Da 6: 16 and threw him into the lions' *d.*
Mt 21: 13 you are making it a '*d* of robbers.'"

DENARIUS
Mk 12: 15 Bring me a *d* and let me look at it."

DENIED (DENY)
1Ti 5: 8 he has *d* the faith and is worse

DENIES (DENY)
1Jn 2: 23 No one who *d* the Son has

DENY (DENIED DENIES DENYING)
Ex 23: 6 "Do not *d* justice to your poor
Job 27: 5 till I die, I will not *d* my integrity.
La 3: 35 to *d* a man his rights
Lk 9: 23 he must *d* himself and take up his
Tit 1: 16 but by their actions they *d* him.

DENYING* (DENY)
Eze 22: 29 mistreat the alien, *d* them justice.
2Ti 3: 5 a form of godliness but *d* its power.
2Pe 2: 1 *d* the sovereign Lord who bought

DEPART (DEPARTED)
Ge 49: 10 The scepter will not *d* from Judah,
Job 1: 21 and naked I will *d.*
Mt 25: 41 '*D* from me, you who are cursed,
Php 1: 23 I desire to *d* and be with Christ,

DEPARTED (DEPART)
1Sa 4: 21 "The glory has *d* from Israel"—
Ps 119:102 I have not *d* from your laws,

DEPOSIT
2Co 1: 22 put his Spirit in our hearts as a *d,*

2Co 5: 5 and has given us the Spirit as a *d,*
Eph 1: 14 who is a *d* guaranteeing our
2Ti 1: 14 Guard the good *d* that was

DEPRAVED (DEPRAVITY)
Ro 1: 28 he gave them over to a *d* mind,
Php 2: 15 fault in a crooked and *d* generation,

DEPRAVITY (DEPRAVED)
Ro 1: 29 of wickedness, evil, greed and *d.*

DEPRIVE
Dt 24: 17 Do not *d* the alien or the fatherless
Pr 18: 5 or to *d* the innocent of justice.
Isa 10: 2 to *d* the poor of their rights
29: 21 with false testimony *d* the innocent
1Co 7: 5 Do not *d* each other

DEPTH (DEEP)
Ro 8: 39 any powers, neither height nor *d,*
11: 33 the *d* of the riches of the wisdom

DESERT
Nu 32: 13 wander in the *d* forty years,
Ne 9: 19 you did not abandon them in the *d.*
Ps 78: 19 "Can God spread a table in the *d?*
78: 52 led them like sheep through the *d.*
Mk 1: 13 and he was in the *d* forty days,

DESERTED (DESERTS)
Ezr 9: 9 our God has not *d* us
Mt 26: 56 all the disciples *d* him and fled.
2Ti 1: 15 in the province of Asia has *d* me,

DESERTING (DESERTS)
Gal 1: 6 are so quickly *d* the one who called

DESERTS (DESERTED DESERTING)
Zec 11: 17 who *d* the flock!

DESERVE (DESERVES)
Ps 103: 10 he does not treat us as our sins *d*
Jer 21: 14 I will punish you as your deeds *d,*
Mt 22: 8 those I invited did not *d* to come.
Ro 1: 32 those who do such things *d* death,

DESERVES (DESERVE)
2Sa 12: 5 the man who did this *d* to die!
Lk 10: 7 for the worker *d* his wages.
1Ti 5: 18 and "The worker *d* his wages."

DESIRABLE (DESIRE)
Pr 22: 1 A good name is more *d*

DESIRE (DESIRABLE DESIRES)
Ge 3: 16 Your *d* will be for your husband,
Dt 5: 21 You shall not set your *d*
1Ch 29: 18 keep this *d* in the hearts
Ps 40: 6 Sacrifice and offering you did not *d*
40: 8 I *d* to do your will, O my God;
73: 25 earth has nothing I *d* besides you
Pr 3: 15 nothing you *d* can compare
10: 24 what the righteous *d* will be
Pr 11: 23 The *d* of the righteous ends only
Isa 26: 8 are the *d* of our hearts.
53: 2 appearance that we should *d* him.
55: 11 but will accomplish what I *d*
Hos 6: 6 For I *d* mercy, not sacrifice,
Mt 9: 13 learn what this means: 'I *d* mercy,
Ro 7: 18 For I have the *d* to do what is good,
1Co 12: 31 But eagerly *d* the greater gifts.
14: 1 and eagerly *d* spiritual gifts,
Php 1: 23 I *d* to depart and be with Christ,
Heb 13: 18 *d* to live honorably in every way.
Jas 1: 15 Then, after *d* has conceived,

DESIRES (DESIRE)
Ge 4: 7 at your door; it *d* to have you,
Ps 34: 12 and *d* to see many good days,
37: 4 he will give you the *d* of your heart.
103: 5 satisfies your *d* with good things,
145: 19 He fulfills the *d* of those who fear
Pr 11: 6 the unfaithful are trapped by evil *d.*
19: 22 What a man *d* is unfailing love;
Mk 4: 19 and the *d* for other things come in
Ro 8: 5 set on what that nature *d;*
13: 14 to gratify the *d* of the sinful nature.
Gal 5: 16 and you will not gratify the *d*
5: 17 the sinful nature *d* what is contrary
1Ti 3: 1 an overseer, he *d* a noble task.
6: 9 and harmful *d* that plunge men
2Ti 2: 22 Flee the evil *d* of youth,
Jas 1: 20 about the righteous life that God *d.*
4: 1 from your *d* that battle within you?
1Pe 2: 11 to abstain from sinful *d,* which war
1Jn 2: 17 The world and its *d* pass away,

DESOLATE
Isa 54: 1 are the children of the *d* woman

DESPAIR
Isa 61: 3 instead of a spirit of *d.*
2Co 4: 8 perplexed, but not in *d;* persecuted,

DESPISE (DESPISED DESPISES)
Job 42: 6 Therefore I *d* myself
Pr 1: 7 but fools *d* wisdom and discipline.
3: 11 do not *d* the LORD's discipline
23: 22 do not *d* your mother
Lk 16: 13 devoted to the one and *d* the other.
Tit 2: 15 Do not let anyone *d* you.

DESPISED (DESPISE)
Ge 25: 34 So Esau *d* his birthright.
Isa 53: 3 He was *d* and rejected by men,
1Co 1: 28 of this world and the *d* things—

DESPISES (DESPISE)
Pr 14: 21 He who *d* his neighbor sins,
15: 20 but a foolish man *d* his mother.
15: 32 who ignores discipline *d* himself,
Zec 4: 10 "Who *d* the day of small things?

DESTINED (DESTINY)
Lk 2: 34 "This child is *d* to cause the falling

DESTINY (DESTINED PREDESTINED)
Ps 73: 17 then I understood their final *d.*
Ecc 7: 2 for death is the *d* of every man;

DESTITUTE
Pr 31: 8 for the rights of all who are *d.*
Heb 11: 37 *d,* persecuted and mistreated—

DESTROY (DESTROYED DESTROYS DESTRUCTION)
Pr 1: 32 complacency of fools will *d* them;
Mt 10: 28 of the One who can *d* both soul

DESTROYED (DESTROY)
Job 19: 26 And after my skin has been *d,*
Isa 55: 13 which will not be *d."*
1Co 8: 11 for whom Christ died, is *d*
15: 26 The last enemy to be *d* is death.
2Co 5: 1 if the earthly tent we live in is *d,*
Heb 10: 39 of those who shrink back and are *d,*
2Pe 3: 10 the elements will be *d* by fire,

DESTROYS (DESTROY)
Pr 6: 32 whoever does so *d* himself.
11: 9 mouth the godless *d* his neighbor,
18: 9 is brother to one who *d.*
28: 24 he is partner to him who *d.*
Ecc 9: 18 but one sinner *d* much good.
1Co 3: 17 If anyone *d* God's temple,

DESTRUCTION (DESTROY)
Pr 16: 18 Pride goes before *d,*
Hos 13: 14 Where, O grave, is your *d?*
Mt 7: 13 broad is the road that leads to *d,*
Gal 6: 8 from that nature will reap *d;*
2Th 1: 9 punished with everlasting *d*
1Ti 6: 9 that plunge men into ruin and *d.*
2Pe 2: 1 bringing swift *d* on themselves.
3: 16 other Scriptures, to their own *d.*

DETERMINED (DETERMINES)
Job 14: 5 Man's days are *d;*
Isa 14: 26 This is the plan *d* for the whole
Da 11: 36 for what has been *d* must take place
Ac 17: 26 and he *d* the times set for them

DETERMINES* (DETERMINED)
Ps 147: 4 He *d* the number of the stars
Pr 16: 9 but the LORD *d* his steps.
1Co 12: 11 them to each one, just as he *d.*

DETESTABLE (DETESTS)
Pr 21: 27 The sacrifice of the wicked is *d*—
28: 9 even his prayers are *d.*
Isa 1: 13 Your incense is *d* to me.
Lk 16: 15 among men is *d* in God's sight.
Tit 1: 16 They are *d,* disobedient

DETESTS (DETESTABLE)
Dt 22: 5 LORD your God *d* anyone who
23: 18 the LORD your God *d* them both.
25: 16 LORD your God *d* anyone who
Pr 12: 22 The LORD *d* lying lips,

Pr 15: 8 The LORD *d* the sacrifice
15: 9 The LORD *d* the way
15: 26 The LORD *d* the thoughts
16: 5 The LORD *d* all the proud of heart
17: 15 the LORD *d* them both.
20: 23 The LORD *d* differing weights,

DEVIL (DEVIL'S)

Mt 13: 39 the enemy who sows them is the *d.*
25: 41 the eternal fire prepared for the *d*
Lk 4: 2 forty days he was tempted by the *d.*
8: 12 then the *d* comes and takes away
Eph 4: 27 and do not give the *d* a foothold.
2Ti 2: 26 and escape from the trap of the *d,*
Jas 4: 7 Resist the *d,* and he will flee
1Pe 5: 8 Your enemy the *d* prowls
1Jn 3: 8 who does what is sinful is of the *d,*
Rev 12: 9 that ancient serpent called the *d*

DEVIL'S* (DEVIL)

Eph 6: 11 stand against the *d* schemes.
1Ti 3: 7 into disgrace and into the *d* trap.
1Jn 3: 8 was to destroy the *d* work.

DEVOTE (DEVOTED DEVOTING DEVOTION DEVOUT)

Job 11: 13 "Yet if you *d* your heart to him
Jer 30: 21 for who is he who will *d* himself
Col 4: 2 *D* yourselves to prayer, being
1Ti 4: 13 *d* yourself to the public reading
Tit 3: 8 may be careful to *d* themselves

DEVOTED (DEVOTE)

Ezr 7: 10 For Ezra had *d* himself to the study
Ac 2: 42 They *d* themselves
Ro 12: 10 Be *d* to one another
1Co 7: 34 Her aim is to be *d* to the Lord

DEVOTING (DEVOTE)

1Ti 5: 10 *d* herself to all kinds of good deeds.

DEVOTION (DEVOTE)

1Ch 28: 9 and serve him with wholehearted *d*
Eze 33: 31 With their mouths they express *d,*
1Co 7: 35 way in undivided *d* to the Lord.
2Co 11: 3 from your sincere and pure *d*

DEVOUR

2Sa 2: 26 "Must the sword *d* forever?
Mk 12: 40 They *d* widows' houses
1Pe 5: 8 lion looking for someone to *d.*

DEVOUT (DEVOTE)

Lk 2: 25 Simeon, who was righteous and *d.*

DIE (DEAD DEATH DIED DIES)

Ge 2: 17 when you eat of it you will surely *d*
Ex 11: 5 Every firstborn son in Egypt will *d,*
Ru 1: 17 Where you *d* I will *d,* and there I
2Ki 14: 6 each is to *d* for his own sins."
Pr 5: 23 He will *d* for lack of discipline,
10: 21 but fools *d* for lack of judgment.
Pr 15: 10 he who hates correction will *d.*
23: 13 with the rod, he will not *d.*
Ecc 3: 2 a time to be born and a time to *d,*
Isa 66: 24 their worm will not *d,* nor will their
Eze 3: 18 that wicked man will *d* for his sin,
18: 4 soul who sins is the one who will *d.*
33: 8 'O wicked man, you will surely *d,'*
Mt 26: 52 "for all who draw the sword will *d*
Jn 11: 26 and believes in me will never *d.*
Ro 5: 7 Very rarely will anyone *d*
14: 8 and if we *d,* we *d* to the Lord.
1Co 15: 22 in Adam all *d,* so in Christ all will
15: 31 I *d* every day—I mean that,
Php 1: 21 to live is Christ and to *d* is gain.
Heb 9: 27 Just as man is destined to *d* once,
Rev 14: 13 Blessed are the dead who *d*

DIED (DIE)

Ro 5: 6 we were still powerless, Christ *d*
6: 2 By no means! We *d* to sin;
6: 8 if we *d* with Christ, we believe that
14: 15 brother for whom Christ *d.*
1Co 8: 11 for whom Christ *d,* is destroyed
15: 3 that Christ *d* for our sins according
2Co 5: 14 *d* for all, and therefore all *d.*
Col 3: 3 For you *d,* and your life is now
1Th 5: 10 He *d* for us so that, whether we are
2Ti 2: 11 If we *d* with him,
Heb 9: 15 now that he has *d* as a ransom
1Pe 3: 18 For Christ *d* for sins once for all,
Rev 2: 8 who *d* and came to life again.

DIES (DIE)

Job 14: 14 If a man *d,* will he live again?
Pr 11: 7 a wicked man *d,* his hope perishes;
Jn 11: 25 in me will live, even though he *d;*
1Co 15: 36 does not come to life unless it *d.*

DIFFERENCE (DIFFERENT)

Ro 10: 12 For there is no *d* between Jew

DIFFERENT (DIFFERENCE)

1Co 12: 4 There are *d* kinds of gifts,
2Co 11: 4 or a *d* gospel from the one you

DIGNITY

Pr 31: 25 She is clothed with strength and *d;*

DIGS

Pr 26: 27 If a man *d* a pit, he will fall into it;

DILIGENCE (DILIGENT)

Heb 6: 11 to show this same *d* to the very end

DILIGENT (DILIGENCE)

Pr 21: 5 The plans of the *d* lead to profit
1Ti 4: 15 Be *d* in these matters; give yourself

DIRECT (DIRECTS)

Ps 119: 35 *D* me in the path of your
119:133 *D* my footsteps according
Jer 10: 23 it is not for man to *d* his steps.
2Th 3: 5 May the Lord *d* your hearts

DIRECTS (DIRECT)

Ps 42: 8 By day the LORD *d* his love,
Isa 48: 17 who *d* you in the way you should

DIRGE

Mt 11: 17 we sang a *d,*

DISAPPEAR

Mt 5: 18 will by any means *d* from the Law
Lk 16: 17 earth to *d* than for the least stroke

DISAPPOINT* (DISAPPOINTED)

Ro 5: 5 And hope does not *d* us,

DISAPPOINTED (DISAPPOINT)

Ps 22: 5 in you they trusted and were not *d.*

DISASTER

Ps 57: 1 wings until the *d* has passed.
Pr 3: 25 Have no fear of sudden *d*
17: 5 over *d* will not go unpunished.
Isa 45: 7 I bring prosperity and create *d;*
Eze 7: 5 An unheard-of *d* is coming.

DISCERN (DISCERNING DISCERNMENT)

Ps 19: 12 Who can *d* his errors?
139: 3 You *d* my going out and my lying
Php 1: 10 you may be able to *d* what is best

DISCERNING (DISCERN)

Pr 14: 6 knowledge comes easily to the *d.*
15: 14 The *d* heart seeks knowledge,
17: 24 A *d* man keeps wisdom in view,
17: 28 and *d* if he holds his tongue.
19: 25 rebuke a *d* man, and he will gain

DISCERNMENT (DISCERN)

Pr 17: 10 A rebuke impresses a man of *d*
28: 11 a poor man who has *d* sees

DISCIPLE (DISCIPLES)

Mt 10: 42 these little ones because he is my *d,*
Lk 14: 27 and follow me cannot be my *d.*

DISCIPLES (DISCIPLE)

Mt 28: 19 Therefore go and make *d*
Jn 8: 31 to my teaching, you are really my *d*
13: 35 men will know that you are my *d*
Ac 11: 26 The *d* were called Christians first

DISCIPLINE (DISCIPLINED DISCIPLINES)

Ps 38: 1 or *d* me in your wrath.
39: 11 You rebuke and *d* men for their sin;
94: 12 Blessed is the man you *d,* O LORD
Pr 1: 7 but fools despise wisdom and *d.*
3: 11 do not despise the LORD's *d*
5: 12 You will say, "How I hated *d!*
5: 23 He will die for lack of *d,*
6: 23 and the corrections of *d*

Pr 10: 17 He who heeds *d* shows the way
12: 1 Whoever loves *d* loves knowledge,
13: 18 He who ignores *d* comes to poverty
13: 24 who loves him is careful to *d* him.
15: 5 A fool spurns his father's *d,*
15: 32 He who ignores *d* despises himself,
19: 18 *D* your son, for in that there is hope
22: 15 the rod of *d* will drive it far
23: 13 Do not withhold *d* from a child;
29: 17 *D* your son, and he will give you
Heb 12: 5 do not make light of the Lord's *d,*
12: 7 as *d;* God is treating you
12: 11 No *d* seems pleasant at the time,
Rev 3: 19 Those whom I love I rebuke and *d.*

DISCIPLINED (DISCIPLINE)

Pr 1: 3 for acquiring a *d* and prudent life,
Jer 31: 18 'You *d* me like an unruly calf,
1Co 11: 32 we are being *d* so that we will not
Tit 1: 8 upright, holy and *d.*
Heb 12: 7 For what son is not *d* by his father?

DISCIPLINES (DISCIPLINE)

Dt 8: 5 your heart that as a man *d* his son,
Pr 3: 12 the LORD *d* those he loves,
Heb 12: 6 because the Lord *d* those he loves,
12: 10 but God *d* us for our good,

DISCLOSED

Lk 8: 17 is nothing hidden that will not be *d,*

DISCOURAGED

Jos 1: 9 Do not be terrified; do not be *d,*
Jos 10: 25 "Do not be afraid; do not be *d.*
1Ch 28: 20 or *d,* for the LORD God,
Isa 42: 4 he will not falter or be *d*
Col 3: 21 children, or they will become *d.*

DISCREDITED

2Co 6: 3 so that our ministry will not be *d.*

DISCRETION*

1Ch 22: 12 May the LORD give you *d*
Pr 1: 4 knowledge and *d* to the young—
2: 11 *D* will protect you,
5: 2 that you may maintain *d*
8: 12 I possess knowledge and *d.*
11: 22 a beautiful woman who shows no *d.*

DISCRIMINATED*

Jas 2: 4 have you not *d* among yourselves

DISFIGURED

Isa 52: 14 his appearance was so *d*

DISGRACE (DISGRACEFUL DISGRACES)

Pr 11: 2 When pride comes, then comes *d,*
14: 34 but sin is a *d* to any people.
19: 26 is a son who brings shame and *d.*
Ac 5: 41 of suffering *d* for the Name.
Heb 13: 13 the camp, bearing the *d* he bore.

DISGRACEFUL (DISGRACE)

Pr 10: 5 during harvest is a *d* son.
17: 2 wise servant will rule over a *d* son,

DISGRACES (DISGRACE)

Pr 28: 7 of gluttons *d* his father.
29: 15 but a child left to itself *d* his mother

DISHONEST

Pr 11: 1 The LORD abhors *d* scales,
29: 27 The righteous detest the *d;*
Lk 16: 10 whoever is *d* with very little will
1Ti 3: 8 wine, and not pursuing *d* gain.

DISHONOR (DISHONORS)

Lev 18: 7 "'Do not *d* your father
Pr 30: 9 and so *d* the name of my God.
1Co 15: 43 it is sown in *d,* it is raised in glory;

DISHONORS (DISHONOR)

Dt 27: 16 Cursed is the man who *d* his father

DISMAYED

Isa 28: 16 the one who trusts will never be *d.*
41: 10 do not be *d,* for I am your God.

DISOBEDIENCE (DISOBEY)

Ro 5: 19 as through the *d* of the one man
11: 32 to *d* so that he may have mercy
Heb 2: 2 and *d* received its just punishment,
4: 6 go in, because of their *d.*
4: 11 fall by following their example of *d.*

DISOBEDIENT (DISOBEY)

2Ti 3: 2 proud, abusive, *d* to their parents,
Tit 1: 6 to the charge of being wild and *d.*
1: 16 *d* and unfit for doing anything

DISOBEY (DISOBEDIENCE DISOBEDIENT)

Dt 11: 28 the curse if you *d* the commands
2Ch 24: 20 'Why do you *d* the LORD's
Ro 1: 30 they *d* their parents; they are

DISORDER

1Co 14: 33 For God is not a God of *d*
2Co 12: 20 slander, gossip, arrogance and *d.*
Jas 3: 16 there you find *d* and every evil

DISOWN

Pr 30: 9 I may have too much and *d* you
Mt 10: 33 I will *d* him before my Father
26: 35 to die with you, I will never *d* you."
2Ti 2: 12 If we *d* him,

DISPLAY (DISPLAYS)

Eze 39: 21 I will *d* my glory among the nations
1Ti 1: 16 Christ Jesus might *d* his unlimited

DISPLAYS (DISPLAY)

Isa 44: 23 he *d* his glory in Israel.

DISPUTE (DISPUTES)

Pr 17: 14 before a *d* breaks out.
1Co 6: 1 If any of you has a *d* with another,

DISPUTES (DISPUTE)

Pr 18: 18 Casting the lot settles *d*

DISQUALIFIED

1Co 9: 27 I myself will not be *d* for the prize.

DISREPUTE*

2Pe 2: 2 will bring the way of truth into *d.*

DISSENSION*

Pr 6: 14 he always stirs up *d.*
6: 19 and a man who stirs up *d*
10: 12 Hatred stirs up *d,*
15: 18 A hot-tempered man stirs up *d,*
16: 28 A perverse man stirs up *d,*
28: 25 A greedy man stirs up *d,*
29: 22 An angry man stirs up *d,*
Ro 13: 13 debauchery, not in *d* and jealousy.

DISSIPATION*

Lk 21: 34 will be weighed down with *d,*
1Pe 4: 4 with them into the same flood of *d,*

DISTINGUISH

1Ki 3: 9 and to *d* between right and wrong.
Heb 5: 14 themselves to *d* good from evil.

DISTORT

2Co 4: 2 nor do we *d* the word of God.
2Pe 3: 16 ignorant and unstable people *d,*

DISTRESS (DISTRESSED)

Ps 18: 6 In my *d* I called to the LORD;
Jnh 2: 2 "In my *d* I called to the LORD,
Jas 1: 27 after orphans and widows in their *d*

DISTRESSED (DISTRESS)

Ro 14: 15 If your brother is *d*

DIVIDED (DIVISION)

Mt 12: 25 household *d* against itself will not
Lk 23: 34 they *d* up his clothes by casting lots
1Co 1: 13 Is Christ *d?* Was Paul crucified

DIVINATION

Lev 19: 26 "'Do not practice *d* or sorcery.

DIVINE

Ro 1: 20 his eternal power and *d* nature—
2Co 10: 4 they have *d* power
2Pe 1: 4 you may participate in the *d* nature

DIVISION (DIVIDED DIVISIONS DIVISIVE)

Lk 12: 51 on earth? No, I tell you, but *d.*
1Co 12: 25 so that there should be no *d*

DIVISIONS (DIVISION)

Ro 16: 17 to watch out for those who cause *d*
1Co 1: 10 another so that there may be no *d*
11: 18 there are *d* among you,

DIVISIVE* (DIVISION)
Tit 3: 10 Warn a *d* person once,

DIVORCE
Mal 2: 16 "I hate *d,*" says the LORD God
Mt 19: 3 for a man to *d* his wife for any
1Co 7: 11 And a husband must not *d* his wife.
7: 27 Are you married? Do not seek a *d.*

DOCTOR
Mt 9: 12 "It is not the healthy who need a *d,*

DOCTRINE
1Ti 4: 16 Watch your life and *d* closely.
Tit 2: 1 is in accord with sound *d.*

DOMINION
Ps 22: 28 for *d* belongs to the LORD

DOOR
Ps 141: 3 keep watch over the *d* of my lips.
Mt 6: 6 close the *d* and pray to your Father
7: 7 and the *d* will be opened to you.
Rev 3: 20 I stand at the *d* and knock.

DOORKEEPER
Ps 84: 10 I would rather be a *d* in the house

DOUBLE-EDGED
Heb 4: 12 Sharper than any *d* sword,
Rev 1: 16 of his mouth came a sharp *d* sword.
2: 12 of him who has the sharp, *d* sword.

DOUBLE-MINDED (MIND)
Ps 119:113 I hate *d* men,
Jas 1: 8 he is a *d* man, unstable

DOUBT
Mt 14: 31 he said, "why did you *d?*"
21: 21 if you have faith and do not *d,*
Mk 11: 23 and does not *d* in his heart
Jas 1: 6 he must believe and not *d,*
Jude : 22 Be merciful to those who *d;*

DOWNCAST
Ps 42: 5 Why are you *d,* O my soul?
2Co 7: 6 But God, who comforts the *d,*

DRAW (DRAWING DRAWS)
Mt 26: 52 "for all who *d* the sword will die
Jn 12: 32 up from the earth, will *d* all men
Heb 10: 22 let us *d* near to God

DRAWING (DRAW)
Lk 21: 28 because your redemption is *d* near

DRAWS (DRAW)
Jn 6: 44 the Father who sent me *d* him,

DREADFUL
Heb 10: 31 It is a *d* thing to fall into the hands

DRESS
1Ti 2: 9 I also want women to *d* modestly,

DRINK (DRUNK DRUNKARDS DRUNKENNESS)
Pr 5: 15 *D* water from your own cistern,
Lk 12: 19 Take life easy; eat, *d* and be merry
Jn 7: 37 let him come to me and *d.*
1Co 12: 13 were all given the one Spirit to *d.*
Rev 21: 6 to *d* without cost from the spring

DRIVES
1Jn 4: 18 But perfect love *d* out fear,

DROP
Pr 17: 14 so *d* the matter before a dispute
Isa 40: 15 Surely the nations are like a *d*

DRUNK (DRINK)
Eph 5: 18 Do not get *d* on wine, which leads

DRUNKARDS (DRINK)
Pr 23: 21 for *d* and gluttons become poor,
1Co 6: 10 nor the greedy nor *d* nor slanderers

DRUNKENNESS (DRINK)
Lk 21: 34 weighed down with dissipation, *d*
Ro 13: 13 and *d,* not in sexual immorality
Gal 5: 21 factions and envy; *d,* orgies,
1Pe 4: 3 living in debauchery, lust, *d,* orgies,

DRY
Isa 53: 2 and like a root out of *d* ground.
Eze 37: 4 '*D* bones, hear the word

DUST
Ge 2: 7 man from the *d* of the ground
Ps 103: 14 he remembers that we are *d.*
Ecc 3: 20 all come from *d,* and to *d* all return.

DUTY
Ecc 12: 13 for this is the whole *d* of man.
Ac 23: 1 I have fulfilled my *d* to God
1Co 7: 3 husband should fulfill his marital *d*

DWELL (DWELLING)
1Ki 8: 27 "But will God really *d* on earth?
Ps 23: 6 I will *d* in the house of the LORD
Isa 43: 18 do not *d* on the past.
Eph 3: 17 so that Christ may *d* in your hearts
Col 1: 19 to have all his fullness *d* in him,
3: 16 the word of Christ *d* in you richly

DWELLING (DWELL)
Eph 2: 22 to become a *d* in which God lives

EAGER
Pr 31: 13 and works with *e* hands.
1Pe 5: 2 greedy for money, but *e* to serve;

EAGLE'S (EAGLES)
Ps 103: 5 your youth is renewed like the *e.*

EAGLES (EAGLE'S)
Isa 40: 31 They will soar on wings like *e;*

EAR (EARS)
1Co 2: 9 no *e* has heard,
1 12: 16 if the *e* should say, "Because I am

EARNED
Pr 31: 31 Give her the reward she has *e,*

EARS (EAR)
Job 42: 5 My *e* had heard of you
Ps 34: 15 and his *e* are attentive to their cry;
Pr 21: 13 If a man shuts his *e* to the cry
2Ti 4: 3 to say what their itching *e* want

EARTH (EARTHLY)
Ge 1: 1 God created the heavens and the *e.*
Ps 24: 1 *e* is the LORD's, and everything
108: 5 and let your glory be over all the *e.*
Isa 6: 3 the whole *e* is full of his glory."
51: 6 the *e* will wear out like a garment
55: 9 the heavens are higher than the *e,*
66: 1 and the *e* is my footstool.
Jer 23: 24 "Do not I fill heaven and *e?*"
Hab 2: 20 let all the *e* be silent before him."
Mt 6: 10 done on *e* as it is in heaven.
16: 19 bind on *e* will be bound
24: 35 Heaven and *e* will pass away,
28: 18 and on *e* has been given to me.
Lk 2: 14 on *e* peace to men
1Co 10: 26 The *e* is the Lord's, and everything
Php 2: 10 in heaven and on *e* and under the *e,*
2Pe 3: 13 to a new heaven and a new *e,*

EARTHLY (EARTH)
Php 3: 19 Their mind is on *e* things.
Col 3: 2 on things above, not on *e* things.

EAST
Ps 103: 12 as far as the *e* is from the west,

EASY
Mt 11: 30 For my yoke is *e* and my burden is

EAT (EATING)
Ge 2: 17 but you must not *e* from the tree
Isa 55: 1 come, buy and *e!*
65: 25 and the lion will *e* straw like the ox,
Mt 26: 26 "Take and *e;* this is my body."
Ro 14: 2 faith allows him to *e* everything,
1Co 8: 13 if what I *e* causes my brother to fall
10: 31 So whether you *e* or drink
2Th 3: 10 man will not work, he shall not *e.*"

EATING (EAT)
Ro 14: 17 kingdom of God is not a matter of *e*

EDICT
Heb 11: 23 they were not afraid of the king's *e.*

EDIFIES
1Co 14: 4 but he who prophesies *e* the church

EFFECT
Isa 32: 17 *e* of righteousness will be quietness
Heb 9: 18 put into *e* without blood.

EFFORT

Lk 13: 24 "Make every *e* to enter
Ro 9: 16 depend on man's desire or *e,*
14: 19 make every *e* to do what leads
Eph 4: 3 Make every *e* to keep the unity
Heb 4: 11 make every *e* to enter that rest,
12: 14 Make every *e* to live in peace
2Pe 1: 5 make every *e* to add
3: 14 make every *e* to be found spotless,

ELAH

Son of Baasha; king of Israel (1Ki 16:6-14).

ELDERLY* (ELDERS)

Lev 19: 32 show respect for the *e*

ELDERS (ELDERLY)

1Ti 5: 17 The *e* who direct the affairs

ELECTION

Ro 9: 11 God's purpose in *e* might stand:
2Pe 1: 10 to make your calling and *e* sure.

ELI

High priest in youth of Samuel (1Sa 1-4). Blessed Hannah (1Sa 1:12-18); raised Samuel (1Sa 2:11-26).

ELIJAH

Prophet; predicted famine in Israel (1Ki 17:1; Jas 5:17). Fed by ravens (1Ki 17:2-6). Raised Sidonian widow's son (1Ki 17:7-24). Defeated prophets of Baal at Carmel (1Ki 18:16-46). Ran from Jezebel (1Ki 19:1-9). Prophesied death of Azariah (2Ki 1). Succeeded by Elishah (1Ki 19:19-2 ; 2Ki 2:1-18). Taken to heaven in whirlwind (2Ki 2:11-12).

Return prophesied (Mal 4:5-6); equated with John the Baptist (Mt 17:9-13; Mk 9:9-13; Lk 1:17). Appeared with Moses in transfiguration of Jesus (Mt 17:1-8; Mk 9:1-8).

ELISHA

Prophet; successor of Elijah (1Ki 19:16-21); inherited his cloak (2Ki 2:1-18). Miracles of (2Ki 2-6).

ELIZABETH*

Mother of John the Baptist, relative of Mary (Lk 1:5-58).

EMBITTER*

Col 3: 21 Fathers, do not *e* your children,

EMPTY

Eph 5: 6 no one deceive you with *e* words,
1Pe 1: 18 from the *e* way of life handed

ENABLE (ABLE)

Lk 1: 74 to *e* us to serve him without fear
Ac 4: 29 *e* your servants to speak your word

ENABLED (ABLE)

Lev 26: 13 *e* you to walk with heads held high.
Jn 6: 65 unless the Father has *e* him."

ENABLES (ABLE)

Php 3: 21 by the power that *e* him

ENCAMPS*

Ps 34: 7 The angel of the LORD *e*

ENCOURAGE (ENCOURAGEMENT)

Ps 10: 17 you *e* them, and you listen
Isa 1: 17 *e* the oppressed.
Ac 15: 32 to *e* and strengthen the brothers.
Ro 12: 8 if it is encouraging, let him *e;*
1Th 4: 18 Therefore *e* each other
2Ti 4: 2 rebuke and *e*— with great patience
Tit 2: 6 *e* the young men to be
Heb 3: 13 But *e* one another daily, as long
10: 25 but let us *e* one another—

ENCOURAGEMENT (ENCOURAGE)

Ac 4: 36 Barnabas (which means Son of *E),*
Ro 15: 4 *e* of the Scriptures we might have
15: 5 and *e* give you a spirit of unity
1Co 14: 3 to men for their strengthening, *e*
Heb 12: 5 word of *e* that addresses you

END

Ps 119: 33 then I will keep them to the *e.*
Pr 14: 12 but in the *e* it leads to death.
19: 20 and in the *e* you will be wise.
23: 32 In the *e* it bites like a snake
Ecc 12: 12 making many books there is no *e,*
Mt 10: 22 firm to the *e* will be saved.
Lk 21: 9 but the *e* will not come right away
Ro 10: 4 Christ is the *e* of the law
1Co 15: 24 the *e* will come, when he hands

ENDURANCE (ENDURE)

Ro 15: 4 through *e* and the encouragement
15: 5 May the God who gives *e*
2Co 1: 6 which produces in you patient *e*
Col 1: 11 might so that you may have great *e*
1Ti 6: 11 faith, love, *e* and gentleness.
Tit 2: 2 and sound in faith, in love and in *e.*

ENDURE (ENDURANCE ENDURES)

Ps 72: 17 May his name *e* forever;
Pr 12: 19 Truthful lips *e* forever,
27: 24 for riches do not *e* forever,
Ecc 3: 14 everything God does will *e* forever;
Mal 3: 2 who can *e* the day of his coming?
2Ti 2: 3 *E* hardship with us like a good
2: 12 if we *e,* / we will also reign
Heb 12: 7 *E* hardship as discipline; God is
Rev 3: 10 kept my command to *e* patiently,

ENDURES (ENDURE)

Ps 112: 9 his righteousness *e* forever;
136: 1 *His love e forever.*
Da 9: 15 made for yourself a name that *e*

ENEMIES (ENEMY)

Ps 23: 5 in the presence of my *e.*
Mic 7: 6 a man's *e* are the members
Mt 5: 44 Love your *e* and pray
Lk 20: 43 hand until I make your *e*

ENEMY (ENEMIES ENMITY)

Pr 24: 17 Do not gloat when your *e* falls;
25: 21 If your *e* is hungry, give him food
27: 6 but an *e* multiplies kisses.
1Co 15: 26 The last *e* to be destroyed is death.
1Ti 5: 14 and to give the *e* no opportunity

ENJOY (JOY)

Dt 6: 2 and so that you may *e* long life.
Eph 6: 3 and that you may *e* long life
Heb 11: 25 rather than to *e* the pleasures of sin

ENJOYMENT (JOY)

Ecc 4: 8 and why am I depriving myself of *e*
1Ti 6: 17 us with everything for our *e.*

ENLIGHTENED* (LIGHT)

Eph 1: 18 that the eyes of your heart may be *e*
Heb 6: 4 for those who have once been *e,*

ENMITY* (ENEMY)

Ge 3: 15 And I will put *e*

ENOCH

Walked with God and taken by him (Ge 5: 18-24; Heb 11:5). Prophet (Jude 14).

ENTANGLED (ENTANGLES)

2Pe 2: 20 and are again *e* in it and overcome,

ENTANGLES* (ENTANGLED)

Heb 12: 1 and the sin that so easily *e,*

ENTER (ENTERED ENTERS ENTRANCE)

Ps 100: 4 *E* his gates with thanksgiving
Mt 5: 20 will certainly not *e* the kingdom
7: 13 "*E* through the narrow gate.
18: 8 It is better for you to *e* life maimed
Mk 10: 15 like a little child will never *e* it."
10: 23 is for the rich to *e* the kingdom

ENTERED (ENTER)

Ro 5: 12 as sin *e* the world through one man,
Heb 9: 12 but he *e* the Most Holy Place once

ENTERS (ENTER)

Mk 7: 18 you see that nothing that *e* a man
Jn 10: 2 The man who *e* by the gate is

ENTERTAIN

1Ti 5: 19 Do not *e* an accusation
Heb 13: 2 Do not forget to *e* strangers,

ENTHRALLED*

Ps 45: 11 The king is *e* by your beauty;

ENTHRONED (THRONE)

1Sa 4: 4 who is *e* between the cherubim.
Ps 2: 4 The One *e* in heaven laughs;
102: 12 But you, O LORD, sit *e* forever;
Isa 40: 22 He sits *e* above the circle

ENTICE

Pr 1: 10 My son, if sinners *e* you,
2Pe 2: 18 they *e* people who are just escaping

ENTIRE

Gal 5: 14 The *e* law is summed up

ENTRUSTED (TRUST)

1Ti 6: 20 guard what has been *e* to your care.

2Ti 1: 12 able to guard what I have *e* to him
1: 14 Guard the good deposit that was *e*
Jude : 3 once for all *e* to the saints.

ENVY

Pr 3: 31 Do not *e* a violent man
14: 30 but *e* rots the bones.
1Co 13: 4 It does not *e*, it does not boast,

EPHRAIM

1. Second son of Joseph (Ge 41:52; 46:20). Blessed as firstborn by Jacob (Ge 48).
2. Synonymous with Northern Kingdom (Isa 7:17; Hos 5).

EQUAL

Isa 40: 25 who is my *e?"* says the Holy One.
Jn 5: 18 making himself *e* with God.
1Co 12: 25 that its parts should have *e* concern

EQUIP* (EQUIPPED)

Heb 13: 21 *e* you with everything good

EQUIPPED (EQUIP)

2Ti 3: 17 man of God may be thoroughly *e*

ERROR

Jas 5: 20 Whoever turns a sinner from the *e*

ESAU

Firstborn of Isaac, twin of Jacob (Ge25:21-26). Also called Edom (Ge 25:30). Sold Jacob his birthright (Ge 25:29-34); lost blessing (Ge 27). Reconciled to Jacob (Gen 33).

ESCAPE (ESCAPING)

Ro 2: 3 think you will *e* God's judgment?
Heb 2: 3 how shall we *e* if we ignore such

ESCAPING (ESCAPE)

1Co 3: 15 only as one *e* through the flames.

ESTABLISH

Ge 6: 18 But I will *e* my covenant with you,
1Ch 28: 7 I will *e* his kingdom forever
Ro 10: 3 God and sought to *e* their own,

ESTEEMED

Pr 22: 1 to be *e* is better than silver or gold.
Isa 53: 3 he was despised, and we *e* him not.

ESTHER

Jewess who lived in Persia; cousin of Mordecai (Est 2:7). Chosen queen of Xerxes (Est 2:8-18). Foiled Haman's plan to exterminate the Jews (Est 3-4; 7-9).

ETERNAL (ETERNALLY ETERNITY)

Ps 16: 11 with *e* pleasures at your right hand.
111: 10 To him belongs *e* praise.
119: 89 Your word, O LORD, is *e;*
Isa 26: 4 LORD, the LORD, is the Rock *e.*
Mt 19: 16 good thing must I do to get *e* life?"
25: 41 into the *e* fire prepared for the devil
25: 46 they will go away to *e* punishment,
Jn 3: 15 believes in him may have *e* life.
3: 16 him shall not perish but have *e* life.
3: 36 believes in the Son has *e* life,
4: 14 spring of water welling up to *e* life."
5: 24 believes him who sent me has *e* life
6: 68 You have the words of *e* life.
10: 28 I give them *e* life, and they shall
17: 3 this is *e* life: that they may know
Ro 1: 20 his *e* power and divine nature—
6: 23 but the gift of God is *e* life
2Co 4: 17 for us an *e* glory that far outweighs
4: 18 temporary, but what is unseen is *e.*
1Ti 1: 16 believe on him and receive *e* life.
1: 17 Now to the King *e,* immortal,
Heb 9: 12 having obtained *e* redemption.
1Jn 5: 11 God has given us *e* life,
5: 13 you may know that you have *e* life.

ETERNALLY (ETERNAL)

Gal 1: 8 let him be *e* condemned! As we

ETERNITY (ETERNAL)

Ps 93: 2 you are from all *e.*
Ecc 3: 11 also set *e* in the hearts of men;

ETHIOPIAN

Jer 13: 23 Can the *E* change his skin

EUNUCHS

Mt 19: 12 For some are *e* because they were

EVANGELIST (EVANGELISTS)

2Ti 4: 5 hardship, do the work of an *e,*

EVANGELISTS* (EVANGELIST)

Eph 4: 11 some to be prophets, some to be *e,*

EVE

2Co 11: 3 as *E* was deceived by the serpent's
1Ti 2: 13 For Adam was formed first, then *E*

EVEN-TEMPERED*

Pr 17: 27 and a man of understanding is *e.*

EVER (EVERLASTING FOREVER)

Ex 15: 18 LORD will reign for *e* and *e."*
Dt 8: 19 If you *e* forget the LORD your
Ps 5: 11 let them *e* sing for joy.
10: 16 The LORD is King for *e* and *e;*
25: 3 will *e* be put to shame,
26: 3 for your love is *e* before me,
45: 6 O God, will last for *e* and *e;*
52: 8 God's unfailing love for *e* and *e.*
89: 33 nor will I *e* betray my faithfulness.
145: 1 I will praise your name for *e* and *e.*
Pr 4: 18 shining *e* brighter till the full light
5: 19 may you *e* be captivated
Isa 66: 8 Who has *e* heard of such a thing?
Jer 31: 36 the descendants of Israel *e* cease
Da 7: 18 it forever—yes, for *e* and *e.'*
12: 3 like the stars for *e* and *e.'*
Mk 4: 12 *e* hearing but never understanding;
Jn 1: 18 No one has *e* seen God,
Rev 1: 18 and behold I am alive for *e* and *e!*
22: 5 And they will reign for *e* and *e.*

EVER-INCREASING* (INCREASE)

Ro 6: 19 to impurity and to *e* wickedness,
2Co 3: 18 into his likeness with *e* glory,

EVERLASTING (EVER)

Dt 33: 27 and underneath are the *e* arms.
Ne 9: 5 your God, who is from *e* to *e."*
Ps 90: 2 from *e* to *e* you are God.
139: 24 and lead me in the way *e.*
Isa 9: 6 *E* Father, Prince of Peace.
33: 14 Who of us can dwell with *e* burning
35: 10 *e* joy will crown their heads.
45: 17 the LORD with an *e* salvation;
54: 8 but with *e* kindness
55: 3 I will make an *e* covenant with you,
63: 12 to gain for himself *e* renown,
Jer 31: 3 "I have loved you with an *e* love;
Da 9: 24 to bring in *e* righteousness,
12: 2 some to *e* life, others to shame
Jn 6: 47 the truth, he who believes has *e* life.
2Th 1: 9 punished with *e* destruction
Jude : 6 bound with *e* chains for judgment

EVER-PRESENT*

Ps 46: 1 an *e* help in trouble

EVIDENCE (EVIDENT)

Jn 14: 11 on the *e* of the miracles themselves.

EVIDENT (EVIDENCE)

Php 4: 5 Let your gentleness be *e* to all.

EVIL

Ge 2: 9 of the knowledge of good and *e.*
Job 1: 1 he feared God and shunned *e.*
1: 8 a man who fears God and shuns *e."*
34: 10 Far be it from God to do *e,*
Ps 23: 4 I will fear no *e,*
34: 14 Turn from *e* and do good;
51: 4 and done what is *e* in your sight,
97: 10 those who love the LORD hate *e,*
101: 4 I will have nothing to do with *e.*
Pr 8: 13 To fear the LORD is to hate *e;*
10: 23 A fool finds pleasure in *e* conduct,
11: 27 *e* comes to him who searches for it.
24: 19 Do not fret because of *e* men
24: 20 for the *e* man has no future hope,
Isa 5: 20 Woe to those who call *e* good
13: 11 I will punish the world for its *e,*
55: 7 and the *e* man his thoughts.
Hab 1: 13 Your eyes are too pure to look on *e;*
Mt 5: 45 He causes his sun to rise on the *e*
6: 13 but deliver us from the *e* one.'

Mt 7: 11 If you, then, though you are *e*,
12: 35 and the *e* man brings *e* things out
Jn 17: 15 you protect them from the *e* one.
Ro 2: 9 for every human being who does *e:*
12: 9 Hate what is *e;* cling
12: 17 Do not repay anyone *e* for *e.*
16: 19 and innocent about what is *e.*
1Co 13: 6 Love does not delight in *e*
14: 20 In regard to *e* be infants,
Eph 6: 16 all the flaming arrows of the *e* one.
1Th 5: 22 Avoid every kind of *e.*
1Ti 6: 10 of money is a root of all kinds of *e.*
2Ti 2: 22 Flee the *e* desires of youth,
Jas 1: 13 For God cannot be tempted by *e,*
1Pe 2: 16 your freedom as a cover-up for *e;*
3: 9 Do not repay *e* with *e* or insult

EXACT

Heb 1: 3 the *e* representation of his being,

EXALT (EXALTED EXALTS)

Ps 30: 1 I will *e* you, O LORD,
34: 3 let us *e* his name together.
118: 28 you are my God, and I will *e* you.
Isa 24: 15 *e* the name of the LORD, the God

EXALTED (EXALT)

2Sa 22: 47 *E* be God, the Rock, my Savior!
1Ch 29: 11 you are *e* as head over all.
Ne 9: 5 and may it be *e* above all blessing
Ps 21: 13 Be *e,* O LORD, in your strength;
46: 10 I will be *e* among the nations,
57: 5 Be *e,* O God, above the heavens;
97: 9 you are *e* far above all gods.
99: 2 he is *e* over all the nations.
108: 5 Be *e,* O God, above the heavens,
148: 13 for his name alone is *e;*
Isa 6: 1 *e,* and the train of his robe filled
12: 4 and proclaim that his name is *e.*
33: 5 The LORD is *e,* for he dwells
Eze 21: 26 The lowly will be *e* and the *e* will be
Mt 23: 12 whoever humbles himself will be *e.*
Php 1: 20 always Christ will be *e* in my body,
2: 9 Therefore God *e* him

EXALTS (EXALT)

Ps 75: 7 He brings one down, he *e* another.
Pr 14: 34 Righteousness *e* a nation,
Mt 23: 12 For whoever *e* himself will be

EXAMINE (EXAMINED)

Ps 26: 2 *e* my heart and my mind;
Jer 17: 10 and *e* the mind,
La 3: 40 Let us *e* our ways and test them,
1Co 11: 28 A man ought to *e* himself
2Co 13: 5 *E* yourselves to see whether you

EXAMINED (EXAMINE)

Ac 17: 11 *e* the Scriptures every day to see

EXAMPLE (EXAMPLES)

Jn 13: 15 have set you an *e* that you should
1Co 11: 1 Follow my *e,* as I follow
1Ti 4: 12 set an *e* for the believers in speech,
Tit 2: 7 In everything set them an *e*
1Pe 2: 21 leaving you an *e,* that you should

EXAMPLES* (EXAMPLE)

1Co 10: 6 Now these things occurred as *e*
10: 11 as *e* and were written down
1Pe 5: 3 to you, but being *e* to the flock.

EXASPERATE*

Eph 6: 4 Fathers, do not *e* your children;

EXCEL (EXCELLENT)

1Co 14: 12 to *e* in gifts that build up the church
2Co 8: 7 But just as you *e* in everything—

EXCELLENT (EXCEL)

1Co 12: 31 now I will show you the most *e* way
Php 4: 8 if anything is *e* or praiseworthy—
1Ti 3: 13 have served well gain an *e* standing
Tit 3: 8 These things are *e* and profitable

EXCHANGED

Ro 1: 23 *e* the glory of the immortal God
1: 25 They *e* the truth of God for a lie,

EXCUSE (EXCUSES)

Jn 15: 22 they have no *e* for their sin.
Ro 1: 20 so that men are without *e.*

EXCUSES* (EXCUSE)

Lk 14: 18 "But they all alike began to make *e.*

EXISTS

Heb 2: 10 and through whom everything *e,*
11: 6 to him must believe that he *e*

EXPECT (EXPECTATION)

Mt 24: 44 at an hour when you do not *e* him.

EXPECTATION (EXPECT)

Ro 8: 19 waits in eager *e* for the sons
Heb 10: 27 but only a fearful *e* of judgment

EXPEL*

1Co 5: 13 *E* the wicked man from among you

EXPENSIVE

1Ti 2: 9 or gold or pearls or *e* clothes,

EXPLOIT

Pr 22: 22 Do not *e* the poor because they are
2Co 12: 17 Did I *e* you through any

EXPOSE

1Co 4: 5 will *e* the motives of men's hearts.
Eph 5: 11 of darkness, but rather *e* them.

EXTENDS

Pr 31: 20 and *e* her hands to the needy.

Lk 1: 50 His mercy *e* to those who fear him,

EXTINGUISHED

2Sa 21: 17 the lamp of Israel will not be *e.*"

EXTOL*

Job 36: 24 Remember to *e* his work,
Ps 34: 1 I will *e* the LORD at all times;
68: 4 *e* him who rides on the clouds—
95: 2 and *e* him with music and song.
109: 30 mouth I will greatly *e* the LORD;
111: 1 I will *e* the LORD with all my heart
115: 18 it is we who *e* the LORD,
117: 1 *e* him, all you peoples.
145: 2 and *e* your name for ever and ever.
145: 10 your saints will *e* you.
147: 12 *E* the LORD, O Jerusalem;

EXTORT*

Lk 3: 14 "Don't *e* money and don't accuse

EYE (EYES)

Ex 21: 24 you are to take life for life, *e* for *e,*
Ps 94: 9 Does he who formed the *e* not see?
Mt 5: 29 If your right *e* causes you to sin,
5: 38 '*E* for *e,* and tooth for tooth.'
7: 3 of sawdust in your brother's *e*
1Co 2: 9 "No *e* has seen,
Col 3: 22 not only when their *e* is on you
Rev 1: 7 and every *e* will see him,

EYES (EYE)

Nu 33: 55 remain will become barbs in your *e*
Jos 23: 13 on your backs and thorns in your *e,*
2Ch 16: 9 For the *e* of the LORD range
Job 31: 1 "I made a covenant with my *e*
36: 7 He does not take his *e*
Ps 119: 18 Open my *e* that I may see
121: 1 I lift up my *e* to the hills—
141: 8 But my *e* are fixed on you,
Pr 3: 7 Do not be wise in your own *e;*
4: 25 Let your *e* look straight ahead,
15: 3 The *e* of the LORD are everywhere
Isa 6: 5 and my *e* have seen the King,
Hab 1: 13 Your *e* are too pure to look on evil;
Jn 4: 35 open your *e* and look at the fields!
2Co 4: 18 So we fix our *e* not on what is seen,
Heb 12: 2 Let us fix our *e* on Jesus, the author
Jas 2: 5 poor in the *e* of the world to be rich
1Pe 3: 12 For the *e* of the Lord are
Rev 7: 17 wipe away every tear from their *e.*"
Rev 21: 4 He will wipe every tear from their *e*

EZEKIEL

Priest called to be prophet to the exiles (Eze 1-3).

EZRA

Priest and teacher of the Law who led a return of exiles to Israel to reestablish temple and worship (Ezr 7-8). Corrected intermarriage of priests (Ezr 9-10). Read Law at celebration of Feast of Tabernacles (Neh 8).

FACE (FACES)

Ge 32: 30 “It is because I saw God *f* to *f*,
Ex 34: 29 was not aware that his *f* was radiant
Nu 6: 25 the LORD make his *f* shine
1Ch 16: 11 seek his *f* always.
2Ch 7: 14 and seek my *f* and turn
Ps 4: 6 Let the light of your *f* shine upon us
27: 8 Your *f*, LORD, I will seek.
31: 16 Let your *f* shine on your servant;
105: 4 seek his *f* always.
119:135 Make your *f* shine
Isa 50: 7 Therefore have I set my *f* like flint,
Mt 17: 2 His *f* shone like the sun,
1Co 13: 12 mirror; then we shall see *f* to *f*.
2Co 4: 6 the glory of God in the *f* of Christ.
1Pe 3: 12 but the *f* of the Lord is
Rev 1: 16 His *f* was like the sun shining

FACES (FACE)

2Co 3: 18 who with unveiled *f* all reflect

FACTIONS

Gal 5: 20 selfish ambition, dissensions, *f*

FADE

1Pe 5: 4 of glory that will never *f* away.

FAIL (FAILING FAILINGS FAILS)

1Ch 28: 20 He will not *f* you or forsake you
2Ch 34: 33 they did not *f* to follow the LORD,
Ps 89: 28 my covenant with him will never *f*.
Pr 15: 22 Plans *f* for lack of counsel,
Isa 51: 6 my righteousness will never *f*.
La 3: 22 for his compassions never *f*.
2Co 13: 5 unless, of course, you *f* the test?

FAILING (FAIL)

1Sa 12: 23 sin against the LORD by *f* to pray

FAILINGS (FAIL)

Ro 15: 1 ought to bear with the *f* of the weak

FAILS (FAIL)

1Co 13: 8 Love never *f*.

FAINT

Isa 40: 31 they will walk and not be *f*.

FAIR

Pr 1: 3 doing what is right and just and *f*;
Col 4: 1 slaves with what is right and *f*,

FAITH (FAITHFUL FAITHFULLY FAITHFULNESS FAITHLESS)

2Ch 20: 20 Have *f* in the LORD your God
Hab 2: 4 but the righteous will live by his *f*—
Mt 9: 29 According to your *f* will it be done
17: 20 if you have *f* as small as a mustard
24: 10 many will turn away from the *f*
Mk 11: 22 “Have *f* in God,” Jesus answered.
Lk 7: 9 I have not found such great *f*
12: 28 will he clothe you, O you of little *f*!
17: 5 “Increase our *f*!” He replied,
18: 8 will he find *f* on the earth?”
Ac 14: 9 saw that he had *f* to be healed
14: 27 the door of *f* to the Gentiles.
Ro 1: 12 encouraged by each other's *f*.
1: 17 is by *f* from first to last,
1: 17 “The righteous will live by *f*.”
3: 3 What if some did not have *f*?
3: 22 comes through *f* in Jesus Christ
3: 25 a sacrifice of atonement, through *f*
4: 5 his *f* is credited as righteousness.
5: 1 we have been justified through *f*,
10: 17 *f* comes from hearing the message,
14: 1 Accept him whose *f* is weak,
14: 23 that does not come from *f* is sin.
1Co 13: 2 and if I have a *f* that can move
13: 13 And now these three remain: *f*,
16: 13 stand firm in the *f*; be men
2Co 5: 7 We live by *f*, not by sight.
13: 5 to see whether you are in the *f*;
Gal 2: 16 Jesus that we may be justified by *f*
2: 20 I live by *f* in the Son of God,
3: 11 “The righteous will live by *f*.”
3: 24 that we might be justified by *f*.
Eph 2: 8 through *f*—and this not
4: 5 one Lord, one *f*, one baptism;
6: 16 to all this, take up the shield of *f*,
Col 1: 23 continue in your *f*, established
1Th 5: 8 on *f* and love as a breastplate,
1Ti 2: 15 if they continue in *f*, love
4: 1 later times some will abandon the *f*
5: 8 he has denied the *f* and is worse
6: 12 Fight the good fight of the *f*.
2Ti 3: 15 wise for salvation through *f*
4: 7 finished the race, I have kept the *f*.
Phm : 6 may be active in sharing your *f*,
Heb 10: 38 But my righteous one will live by *f*.
11: 1 *f* is being sure of what we hope for
11: 3 By *f* we understand that
11: 5 By *f* Enoch was taken from this life
11: 6 And without *f* it is impossible
11: 7 By *f* Noah, when warned about
11: 8 By *f* Abraham, when called to go
11: 17 By *f* Abraham, when God tested
11: 20 By *f* Isaac blessed Jacob
11: 21 By *f* Jacob, when he was dying,
11: 22 By *f* Joseph, when his end was near
11: 24 By *f* Moses, when he had grown up
11: 31 By *f* the prostitute Rahab,
12: 2 the author and perfecter of our *f*,
Jas 2: 14 if a man claims to have *f*
2: 17 In the same way, *f* by itself,
2: 26 so *f* without deeds is dead.
2Pe 1: 5 effort to add to your *f* goodness;
1Jn 5: 4 overcome the world, even our *f*.
Jude : 3 to contend for the *f* that was once

FAITHFUL (FAITH)

Nu 12: 7 he is *f* in all my house.
Dt 7: 9 your God is God; he is the *f* God,
32: 4 A *f* God who does no wrong,
2Sa 22: 26 “To the *f* you show yourself *f*,
Ps 25: 10 of the LORD are loving and *f*
31: 23 The LORD preserves the *f*,
33: 4 he is *f* in all he does.
37: 28 and will not forsake his *f* ones.
97: 10 for he guards the lives of his *f* ones
145: 13 The LORD is *f* to all his promises
146: 6 the LORD, who remains *f* forever.
Pr 31: 26 and *f* instruction is on her tongue.
Mt 25: 21 ‘Well done, good and *f* servant!
Ro 12: 12 patient in affliction, *f* in prayer.
1Co 4: 2 been given a trust must prove *f*.
10: 13 And God is *f*; he will not let you be
1Th 5: 24 The one who calls you is *f*
2Ti 2: 13 he will remain *f*,
Heb 3: 6 But Christ is *f* as a son
10: 23 for he who promised is *f*.
1Pe 4: 19 themselves to their *f* Creator
1Jn 1: 9 he is *f* and just and will forgive us
Rev 1: 5 who is the *f* witness, the firstborn
2: 10 Be *f*, even to the point of death,
19: 11 whose rider is called *F* and True.

FAITHFULLY (FAITH)

Dt 11: 13 if you *f* obey the commands I am
1Sa 12: 24 and serve him *f* with all your heart;
1Ki 2: 4 and if they walk *f* before me
1Pe 4: 10 *f* administering God's grace

FAITHFULNESS (FAITH)

Ps 57: 10 your *f* reaches to the skies.
85: 10 Love and *f* meet together;
86: 15 to anger, abounding in love and *f*.
89: 1 mouth I will make your *f* known
89: 14 love and *f* go before you.
91: 4 his *f* will be your shield
117: 2 the *f* of the LORD endures forever.
119: 75 and in *f* you have afflicted me.
Pr 3: 3 Let love and *f* never leave you;
Isa 11: 5 and *f* the sash around his waist.
La 3: 23 great is your *f*.
Ro 3: 3 lack of faith nullify God's *f*?
Gal 5: 22 patience, kindness, goodness, *f*,

FAITHLESS (FAITH)

Ps 119:158 I look on the *f* with loathing,
Jer 3: 22 “Return, *f* people;
Ro 1: 31 they are senseless, *f*, heartless,
2Ti 2: 13 if we are *f*,

FALL (FALLEN FALLING FALLS)

Ps 37: 24 though he stumble, he will not *f*,

Ps 55: 22 he will never let the righteous *f.*
69: 9 of those who insult you *f* on me.
Pr 11: 28 Whoever trusts in his riches will *f,*
Lk 11: 17 a house divided against itself will *f.*
Ro 3: 23 and *f* short of the glory of God,
Heb 6: 6 if they *f* away, to be brought back

FALLEN (FALL)

2Sa 1: 19 How the mighty have *f!*
Isa 14: 12 How you have *f* from heaven,
1Co 15: 20 of those who have *f* asleep.
Gal 5: 4 you have *f* away from grace.
1Th 4: 15 precede those who have *f* asleep.

FALLING (FALL)

Jude : 24 able to keep you from *f*

FALLS (FALL)

Pr 24: 17 Do not gloat when your enemy *f;*
Jn 12: 24 a kernel of wheat *f* to the ground
Ro 14: 4 To his own master he stands or *f.*

FALSE (FALSEHOOD FALSELY)

Ex 20: 16 "You shall not give *f* testimony
23: 1 "Do not spread *f* reports.
Pr 13: 5 The righteous hate what is *f,*
19: 5 A *f* witness will not go unpunished,
Mt 7: 15 "Watch out for *f* prophets.
19: 18 not steal, do not give *f* testimony,
24: 11 and many *f* prophets will appear
Php 1: 18 whether from *f* motives or true,
1Ti 1: 3 not to teach *f* doctrines any longer
2Pe 2: 1 there will be *f* teachers among you.

FALSEHOOD (FALSE)

Ps 119:163 I hate and abhor *f*
Pr 30: 8 Keep *f* and lies far from me;
Eph 4: 25 each of you must put off *f*

FALSELY (FALSE)

Lev 19: 12 "'Do not swear *f* by my name
Lk 3: 14 and don't accuse people *f*—
1Ti 6: 20 ideas of what is *f* called knowledge,

FALTER*

Pr 24: 10 If you *f* in times of trouble,
Isa 42: 4 he will not *f* or be discouraged

FAMILIES (FAMILY)

Ps 68: 6 God sets the lonely in *f,*

FAMILY (FAMILIES)

Pr 15: 27 greedy man brings trouble to his *f,*
31: 15 she provides food for her *f*
Lk 9: 61 go back and say good-by to my *f.*"
12: 52 in one *f* divided against each other,
1Ti 3: 4 He must manage his own *f* well
3: 5 how to manage his own *f,*
5: 4 practice by caring for their own *f*
5: 8 and especially for his immediate *f,*

FAMINE

Ge 41: 30 seven years of *f* will follow them.
Am 8: 11 but a *f* of hearing the words
Ro 8: 35 or persecution or *f* or nakedness

FAN*

2Ti 1: 6 you to *f* into flame the gift of God,

FAST

Dt 13: 4 serve him and hold *f* to him.
Jos 22: 5 to hold *f* to him and to serve him
23: 8 to hold *f* to the LORD your God,
Ps 119: 31 I hold *f* to your statutes, O LORD;
139: 10 your right hand will hold me *f.*
Mt 6: 16 "When you *f,* do not look somber
1Pe 5: 12 Stand *f* in it.

FATHER (FATHER'S FATHERLESS FATHERS FOREFATHERS)

Ge 2: 24 this reason a man will leave his *f*
17: 4 You will be the *f* of many nations.
Ex 20: 12 "Honor your *f* and your mother,
21: 15 "Anyone who attacks his *f*
21: 17 "Anyone who curses his *f*
Lev 18: 7 "'Do not dishonor your *f*
19: 3 you must respect his mother and *f,*
Dt 5: 16 "Honor your *f* and your mother,
21: 18 son who does not obey his *f*
Ps 27: 10 Though my *f* and mother forsake
68: 5 A *f* to the fatherless, a defender
Pr 10: 1 A wise son brings joy to his *f,*
17: 21 there is no joy for the *f* of a fool.
23: 22 Listen to your *f,* who gave you life,
23: 24 *f* of a righteous man has great joy;
28: 7 of gluttons disgraces his *f.*
29: 3 loves wisdom brings joy to his *f,*
Isa 9: 6 Everlasting *F,* Prince of Peace.
Mt 6: 9 "'Our *F* in heaven,
10: 37 "Anyone who loves his *f*
15: 4 'Honor your *f* and mother'
19: 5 this reason a man will leave his *f*
Lk 12: 53 *f* against son and son against *f,*
23: 34 Jesus said, "*F,* forgive them,
Jn 6: 44 the *F* who sent me draws him,
6: 46 No one has seen the *F*
8: 44 You belong to your *f,* the devil,
10: 30 I and the *F* are one."
14: 6 No one comes to the *F*
14: 9 who has seen me has seen the *F.*
Ro 4: 11 he is the *f* of all who believe
2Co 6: 18 "I will be a *F* to you,
Eph 6: 2 "Honor your *f* and mother"—
Heb 12: 7 what son is not disciplined by his *f?*

FATHER'S (FATHER)

Pr 13: 1 A wise son heeds his *f* instruction,
15: 5 A fool spurns his *f* discipline,
19: 13 A foolish son is his *f* ruin,
Lk 2: 49 had to be in my *F* house?"
Jn 2: 16 How dare you turn my *F* house
10: 29 can snatch them out of my *F* hand.
14: 2 In my *F* house are many rooms;

FATHERLESS (FATHER)

Dt 10: 18 He defends the cause of the *f*
24: 17 Do not deprive the alien or the *f*
24: 19 Leave it for the alien, the *f*
Ps 68: 5 A father to the *f,* a defender
Pr 23: 10 or encroach on the fields of the *f,*

FATHERS (FATHER)

Ex 20: 5 for the sin of the *f* to the third
Lk 11: 11 "Which of you *f,* if your son asks
Eph 6: 4 *F,* do not exasperate your children;
Col 3: 21 *F,* do not embitter your children,

FATHOM*

Job 11: 7 "Can you *f* the mysteries of God?
Ps 145: 3 his greatness no one can *f.*
Ecc 3: 11 yet they cannot *f* what God has
Isa 40: 28 and his understanding no one can *f*
1Co 13: 2 and can *f* all mysteries and all

FAULT (FAULTS)

Mt 18: 15 and show him his *f,* just
Php 2: 15 of God without *f* in a crooked
Jas 1: 5 generously to all without finding *f,*
Jude : 24 his glorious presence without *f*

FAULTFINDERS*

Jude : 16 These men are grumblers and *f;*

FAULTS (FAULT)

Ps 19: 12 Forgive my hidden *f.*

FAVORITISM*

Ex 23: 3 and do not show *f* to a poor man
Lev 19: 15 to the poor or *f* to the great,
Ac 10: 34 true it is that God does not show *f*
Ro 2: 11 For God does not show *f.*
Eph 6: 9 and there is no *f* with him.
Col 3: 25 for his wrong, and there is no *f.*
1Ti 5: 21 and to do nothing out of *f.*
Jas 2: 1 Lord Jesus Christ, don't show *f.*
2: 9 But if you show *f,* you sin

FEAR (AFRAID FEARS)

Dt 6: 13 *F* the LORD your God, serve him
10: 12 but to *f* the LORD your God,
31: 12 and learn to *f* the LORD your God
Ps 19: 9 The *f* of the LORD is pure,
23: 4 I will *f* no evil,
27: 1 whom shall I *f?*
91: 5 You will not *f* the terror of night,
111: 10 *f* of the LORD is the beginning
Pr 8: 13 To *f* the LORD is to hate evil;
9: 10 *f* of the LORD is the beginning
10: 27 The *f* of the LORD adds length
14: 27 The *f* of the LORD is a fountain
15: 33 *f* of the LORD teaches a man

Pr 16: 6 through the *f* of the LORD a man
19: 23 The *f* of the LORD leads to life:
29: 25 *F* of man will prove to be a snare,
Isa 11: 3 delight in the *f* of the LORD.
41: 10 So do not *f*, for I am with you;
Lk 12: 5 I will show you whom you should *f*:
Php 2: 12 to work out your salvation with *f*
1Jn 4: 18 But perfect love drives out *f*,

FEARS (FEAR)

Job 1: 8 a man who *f* God and shuns evil."
Ps 34: 4 he delivered me from all my *f*.
Pr 31: 30 a woman who *f* the LORD is
1Jn 4: 18 The one who *f* is not made perfect

FEED

Jn 21: 15 Jesus said, "*F* my lambs."
21: 17 Jesus said, "*F* my sheep.
Ro 12: 20 "If your enemy is hungry, *f* him;
Jude : 12 shepherds who *f* only themselves.

FEET (FOOT)

Ps 8: 6 you put everything under his *f*:
22: 16 have pierced my hands and my *f*.
40: 2 he set my *f* on a rock
110: 1 a footstool for your *f*."
119:105 Your word is a lamp to my *f*
Ro 10: 15 "How beautiful are the *f*
1Co 12: 21 And the head cannot say to the *f*,
15: 25 has put all his enemies under his *f*.
Heb 12: 13 "Make level paths for your *f*,"

FELLOWSHIP

2Co 6: 14 what *f* can light have with darkness
13: 14 and the *f* of the Holy Spirit be
Php 3: 10 the *f* of sharing in his sufferings,
1Jn 1: 6 claim to have *f* with him yet walk
1: 7 we have *f* with one another,

FEMALE

Ge 1: 27 male and *f* he created them.
Gal 3: 28 *f*, for you are all one in Christ Jesus

FERVOR

Ro 12: 11 but keep your spiritual *f*, serving

FIELD (FIELDS)

Mt 6: 28 See how the lilies of the *f* grow.
13: 38 *f* is the world, and the good seed
1Co 3: 9 you are God's *f*, God's building.

FIELDS (FIELD)

Lk 2: 8 were shepherds living out in the *f*
Jn 4: 35 open your eyes and look at the *f*!

FIG (FIGS)

Ge 3: 7 so they sewed *f* leaves together

FIGHT (FOUGHT)

Ex 14: 14 The LORD will *f* for you; you need
Dt 1: 30 going before you, will *f* for you,
3: 22 the LORD your God himself will *f*
Ne 4: 20 Our God will *f* for us!"
Ps 35: 1 *f* against those who *f* against me.
Jn 18: 36 my servants would *f*
1Co 9: 26 I do not *f* like a man beating the air.
2Co 10: 4 The weapons we *f*
1Ti 1: 18 them you may *f* the good *f*,
6: 12 Fight the good *f* of the faith.
2Ti 4: 7 fought the good *f*, I have finished

FIGS (FIG)

Lk 6: 44 People do not pick *f*

FILL (FILLED FILLS FULL FULLNESS FULLY)

Ge 1: 28 and increase in number; *f* the earth
Ps 16: 11 you will *f* me with joy
81: 10 wide your mouth and I will *f* it.
Pr 28: 19 who chases fantasies will have his *f*
Hag 2: 7 and I will *f* this house with glory,'
Jn 6: 26 you ate the loaves and had your *f*.
Ac 2: 28 you will *f* me with joy
Ro 15: 13 the God of hope *f* you with all joy

FILLED (FILL)

Ps 72: 19 may the whole earth be *f*
119: 64 The earth is *f* with your love,
Eze 43: 5 the glory of the LORD *f* the temple
Hab 2: 14 For the earth will be *f*
Lk 1: 15 and he will be *f* with the Holy Spirit
1: 41 and Elizabeth was *f* with the Holy
Jn 12: 3 the house was *f* with the fragrance
Ac 2: 4 All of them were *f*
4: 8 Then Peter, *f* with the Holy Spirit,
9: 17 and be *f* with the Holy Spirit."
13: 9 called Paul, *f* with the Holy Spirit,
Eph 5: 18 Instead, be *f* with the Spirit.
Php 1: 11 *f* with the fruit of righteousness

FILLS (FILL)

Nu 14: 21 of the LORD *f* the whole earth,
Ps 107: 9 and *f* the hungry with good things.
Eph 1: 23 fullness of him who *f* everything

FILTHY

Isa 64: 6 all our righteous acts are like *f* rags;
Col 3: 8 and *f* language from your lips.
2Pe 2: 7 by the *f* lives of lawless men

FIND (FINDS FOUND)

Nu 32: 23 be sure that your sin will *f* you out.
Dt 4: 29 you will *f* him if you look for him
1Sa 23: 16 and helped him *f* strength in God.
Ps 36: 7 *f* refuge in the shadow
91: 4 under his wings you will *f* refuge;
Pr 14: 22 those who plan what is good *f* love
31: 10 A wife of noble character who can *f*
Jer 6: 16 and you will *f* rest for your souls.
Mt 7: 7 seek and you will *f*; knock
11: 29 and you will *f* rest for your souls.
16: 25 loses his life for me will *f* it.
Lk 18: 8 will he *f* faith on the earth?"
Jn 10: 9 come in and go out, and *f* pasture.

FINDS (FIND)

Ps 62: 1 My soul *f* rest in God alone;
112: 1 who *f* great delight
119:162 like one who *f* great spoil.
Pr 18: 22 He who *f* a wife *f* what is good
Mt 7: 8 he who seeks *f*; and to him who
10: 39 Whoever *f* his life will lose it,
Lk 12: 37 whose master *f* them watching
15: 4 go after the lost sheep until he *f* it?

FINISH (FINISHED)

Jn 4: 34 him who sent me and to *f* his work.
5: 36 that the Father has given me to *f*,
Ac 20: 24 if only I may *f* the race
2Co 8: 11 Now *f* the work, so that your eager
Jas 1: 4 Perseverance must *f* its work

FINISHED (FINISH)

Ge 2: 2 seventh day God had *f* the work he
Jn 19: 30 the drink, Jesus said, "It is *f*."
2Ti 4: 7 I have *f* the race, I have kept

FIRE

Ex 13: 21 in a pillar of *f* to give them light,
Lev 6: 12 *f* on the altar must be kept burning;
Isa 30: 27 and his tongue is a consuming *f*.
Jer 23: 29 my word like *f*," declares
Mt 3: 11 you with the Holy Spirit and with *f*.
5: 22 will be in danger of the *f* of hell.
25: 41 into the eternal *f* prepared
Mk 9: 43 where the *f* never goes out.
Ac 2: 3 to be tongues of *f* that separated
1Co 3: 13 It will be revealed with *f*,
1Th 5: 19 Do not put out the Spirit's *f*;
Heb 12: 29 for our "God is a consuming *f*."
Jas 3: 5 set on *f* by a small spark.
2Pe 3: 10 the elements will be destroyed by *f*,
Jude : 23 snatch others from the *f*
Rev 20: 14 The lake of *f* is the second death.

FIRM

Ex 14: 13 Stand *f* and you will see
2Ch 20: 17 stand *f* and see the deliverance
Ps 33: 11 of the LORD stand *f* forever,
37: 23 he makes his steps *f*;
40: 2 and gave me a *f* place to stand.
89: 2 that your love stands *f* forever,
119: 89 it stands *f* in the heavens.
Pr 4: 26 and take only ways that are *f*.
Zec 8: 23 nations will take *f* hold of one Jew
Mk 13: 13 he who stands *f* to the end will be

1Co 16: 13 on your guard; stand *f* in the faith;
2Co 1: 24 because it is by faith you stand *f*.
Eph 6: 14 Stand *f* then, with the belt
Col 4: 12 that you may stand *f* in all the will
2Th 2: 15 stand *f* and hold to the teachings
2Ti 2: 19 God's solid foundation stands *f*,
Heb 6: 19 an anchor for the soul, *f* and secure
1Pe 5: 9 Resist him, standing *f* in the faith,

FIRST

Isa 44: 6 I am the *f* and I am the last;
48: 12 I am the *f* and I am the last.
Mt 5: 24 *F* go and be reconciled
6: 33 But seek *f* his kingdom
7: 5 *f* take the plank out
20: 27 wants to be *f* must be your slave—
22: 38 This is the *f* and greatest
23: 26 *F* clean the inside of the cup
Mk 13: 10 And the gospel must *f* be preached
Ac 11: 26 disciples were called Christians *f*
Ro 1: 16 *f* for the Jew, then for the Gentile.
1Co 12: 28 in the church God has appointed *f*
2Co 8: 5 they gave themselves *f* to the Lord
1Ti 2: 13 For Adam was formed *f*, then Eve.
Jas 3: 17 comes from heaven is *f* of all pure;
1Jn 4: 19 We love because he *f* loved us.
3Jn : 9 but Diotrephes, who loves to be *f*,
Rev 1: 17 I am the *F* and the Last.
2: 4 You have forsaken your *f* love.

FIRSTBORN (BEAR)

Ex 11: 5 Every *f* son in Egypt will die,

FIRSTFRUITS

Ex 23: 19 "Bring the best of the *f* of your soil

FISHERS

Mk 1: 17 "and I will make you *f* of men."

FITTING*

Ps 33: 1 it is *f* for the upright to praise him.
147: 1 how pleasant and *f* to praise him!
Pr 10: 32 of the righteous know what is *f*,
19: 10 It is not *f* for a fool to live in luxury
26: 1 honor is not *f* for a fool.
1Co 14: 40 everything should be done in a *f*
Col 3: 18 to your husbands, as is *f* in the Lord
Heb 2: 10 sons to glory, it was *f* that God,

FIX

Dt 11: 18 *F* these words of mine
Pr 4: 25 *f* your gaze directly before you.
2Co 4: 18 we *f* our eyes not on what is seen,
Heb 3: 1 heavenly calling, *f* your thoughts
12: 2 Let us *f* our eyes on Jesus,

FLAME (FLAMES FLAMING)

2Ti 1: 6 you to fan into *f* the gift of God,

FLAMES (FLAME)

1Co 3: 15 only as one escaping through the *f*.
13: 3 and surrender my body to the *f*,

FLAMING (FLAME)

Eph 6: 16 you can extinguish all the *f* arrows

FLASH

1Co 15: 52 in a *f*, in the twinkling of an eye,

FLATTER (FLATTERING FLATTERY)

Job 32: 21 nor will I *f* any man;
Jude : 16 *f* others for their own advantage.

FLATTERING (FLATTER)

Ps 12: 2 their *f* lips speak with deception.
12: 3 May the LORD cut off all *f* lips
Pr 26: 28 and a *f* mouth works ruin.

FLATTERY (FLATTER)

Ro 16: 18 and *f* they deceive the minds
1Th 2: 5 You know we never used *f*,

FLAWLESS*

2Sa 22: 31 the word of the LORD is *f*.
Job 11: 4 You say to God, 'My beliefs are *f*
Ps 12: 6 And the words of the LORD are *f*,
18: 30 the word of the LORD is *f*.
Pr 30: 5 "Every word of God is *f*;
SS 5: 2 my dove, my *f* one.

FLEE

Ps 139: 7 Where can I *f* from your presence?
1Co 6: 18 *F* from sexual immorality.
10: 14 my dear friends, *f* from idolatry.
1Ti 6: 11 But you, man of God, *f* from all this
2Ti 2: 22 *F* the evil desires of youth,
Jas 4: 7 Resist the devil, and he will *f*

FLEETING

Ps 89: 47 Remember how *f* is my life.
Pr 31: 30 Charm is deceptive, and beauty is *f*

FLESH

Ge 2: 23 and *f* of my *f*;
2: 24 and they will become one *f*.
Job 19: 26 yet in my *f* I will see God;
Eze 11: 19 of stone and give them a heart of *f*.
36: 26 of stone and give you a heart of *f*.
Mk 10: 8 and the two will become one *f*.'
Jn 1: 14 The Word became *f* and made his
6: 51 This bread is my *f*, which I will give
1Co 6: 16 "The two will become one *f*."
Eph 5: 31 and the two will become one *f*."
6: 12 For our struggle is not against *f*

FLOCK (FLOCKS)

Isa 40: 11 He tends his *f* like a shepherd:
Eze 34: 2 not shepherds take care of the *f*?
Zec 11: 17 who deserts the *f*!
Mt 26: 31 the sheep of the *f* will be scattered.'
Ac 20: 28 all the *f* of which the Holy Spirit
1Pe 5: 2 Be shepherds of God's *f* that is

FLOCKS (FLOCK)

Lk 2: 8 keeping watch over their *f* at night.

FLOG

Ac 22: 25 to *f* a Roman citizen who hasn't

FLOODGATES

Mal 3: 10 see if I will not throw open the *f*

FLOURISHING

Ps 52: 8 *f* in the house of God;

FLOW (FLOWING)

Nu 13: 27 and it does *f* with milk and honey!
Jn 7: 38 streams of living water will *f*

FLOWERS

Isa 40: 7 The grass withers and the *f* fall,

FLOWING (FLOW)

Ex 3: 8 a land *f* with milk and honey—

FOLDING

Pr 6: 10 a little *f* of the hands to rest—

FOLLOW (FOLLOWING FOLLOWS)

Ex 23: 2 Do not *f* the crowd in doing wrong.
Lev 18: 4 and be careful to *f* my decrees.
Dt 5: 1 Learn them and be sure to *f* them.
Ps 23: 6 Surely goodness and love will *f* me
Mt 16: 24 and take up his cross and *f* me.
Jn 10: 4 his sheep *f* him because they know
1Co 14: 1 *F* the way of love and eagerly
Rev 14: 4 They *f* the Lamb wherever he goes.

FOLLOWING (FOLLOW)

1Ti 1: 18 by *f* them you may fight the good

FOLLOWS (FOLLOW)

Jn 8: 12 Whoever *f* me will never walk

FOOD (FOODS)

Pr 20: 13 you will have *f* to spare.
22: 9 for he shares his *f* with the poor.
25: 21 If your enemy is hungry, give him *f*
31: 15 she provides *f* for her family
Da 1: 8 to defile himself with the royal *f*
Jn 6: 27 Do not work for *f* that spoils,
Ro 14: 14 fully convinced that no *f* is unclean
1Co 8: 8 But *f* does not bring us near to God
1Ti 6: 8 But if we have *f* and clothing,
Jas 2: 15 sister is without clothes and daily *f*.

FOODS (FOOD)
Mk 7: 19 Jesus declared all *f* "clean.")

FOOL (FOOLISH FOOLISHNESS FOOLS)
Ps 14: 1 The *f* says in his heart,
Pr 15: 5 A *f* spurns his father's discipline,
17: 28 Even a *f* is thought wise
18: 2 A *f* finds no pleasure
26: 5 Answer a *f* according to his folly,
28: 26 He who trusts in himself is a *f*,
Mt 5: 22 But anyone who says, 'You *f*!'

FOOLISH (FOOL)
Pr 10: 1 but a *f* son grief to his mother.
17: 25 A *f* son brings grief to his father
Mt 7: 26 practice is like a *f* man who built
25: 2 of them were *f* and five were wise.
1Co 1: 27 God chose the *f* things of the world

FOOLISHNESS (FOOL)
1Co 1: 18 of the cross is *f* to those who are
1: 25 For the *f* of God is wiser
2: 14 for they are *f* to him, and he cannot
3: 19 of this world is *f* in God's sight.

FOOLS (FOOL)
Pr 14: 9 *F* mock at making amends for sin,
1Co 4: 10 We are *f* for Christ, but you are

FOOT (FEET FOOTHOLD)
Jos 1: 3 every place where you set your *f*,
Isa 1: 6 From the sole of your *f* to the top
1Co 12: 15 If the *f* should say, "Because I am

FOOTHOLD (FOOT)
Eph 4: 27 and do not give the devil a *f*.

FORBEARANCE*
Ro 3: 25 because in his *f* he had left the sins

FORBID
1Co 14: 39 and do not *f* speaking in tongues.

FOREFATHERS (FATHER)
Heb 1: 1 spoke to our *f* through the prophets

FOREKNEW* (KNOW)
Ro 8: 29 For those God *f* he
11: 2 not reject his people, whom he *f*.

FOREVER (EVER)
1Ch 16: 15 He remembers his covenant *f*,
16: 34 his love endures *f*.
Ps 9: 7 The LORD reigns *f*;
23: 6 dwell in the house of the LORD *f*.
33: 11 the plans of the LORD stand firm *f*
86: 12 I will glorify your name *f*.
92: 8 But you, O LORD, are exalted *f*.
110: 4 "You are a priest *f*,
119:111 Your statutes are my heritage *f*;
Jn 6: 51 eats of this bread, he will live *f*.
14: 16 Counselor to be with you *f*—
1Co 9: 25 it to get a crown that will last *f*.
1Th 4: 17 And so we will be with the Lord *f*.
Heb 13: 8 same yesterday and today and *f*.
1Pe 1: 25 but the word of the Lord stands *f*."
1Jn 2: 17 who does the will of God lives *f*.

FORFEIT
Lk 9: 25 and yet lose or *f* his very self?

FORGAVE (FORGIVE)
Ps 32: 5 and you *f*
Eph 4: 32 just as in Christ God *f* you.
Col 2: 13 He *f* us all our sins, having
3: 13 Forgive as the Lord *f* you.

FORGET (FORGETS FORGETTING)
Dt 6: 12 that you do not *f* the LORD,
Ps 103: 2 and *f* not all his benefits.
137: 5 may my right hand *f* ⌞its skill⌟.
Isa 49: 15 "Can a mother *f* the baby
Heb 6: 10 he will not *f* your work

FORGETS (FORGET)
Jn 16: 21 her baby is born she *f* the anguish
Jas 1: 24 immediately *f* what he looks like.

FORGETTING (FORGET)
Php 3: 13 *F* what is behind and straining

FORGIVE (FORGAVE FORGIVENESS FORGIVING)
2Ch 7: 14 will *f* their sin and will heal their
Ps 19: 12 *F* my hidden faults.
Mt 6: 12 *F* us our debts,
6: 14 For if you *f* men when they sin
18: 21 many times shall I *f* my brother
Mk 11: 25 in heaven may *f* you your sins."
Lk 11: 4 *F* us our sins,
23: 34 Jesus said, "Father, *f* them,
Col 3: 13 *F* as the Lord forgave you.
1Jn 1: 9 and just and will *f* us our sins

FORGIVENESS (FORGIVE)
Ps 130: 4 But with you there is *f*;
Ac 10: 43 believes in him receives *f* of sins
Eph 1: 7 through his blood, the *f* of sins,
Col 1: 14 in whom we have redemption, the *f*
Heb 9: 22 the shedding of blood there is no *f*.

FORGIVING (FORGIVE)
Ne 9: 17 But you are a *f* God, gracious
Eph 4: 32 to one another, *f* each other,

FORMED
Ge 2: 7 And the LORD God *f* man
Ps 103: 14 for he knows how we are *f*,
Isa 45: 18 but *f* it to be inhabited—
Ro 9: 20 "Shall what is *f* say to him who *f* it,
1Ti 2: 13 For Adam was *f* first, then Eve.
Heb 11: 3 understand that the universe was *f*

FORSAKE (FORSAKEN)
Jos 1: 5 I will never leave you nor *f* you.
24: 16 "Far be it from us to *f* the LORD
2Ch 15: 2 but if you *f* him, he will *f* you.
Ps 27: 10 Though my father and mother *f* me
Isa 55: 7 Let the wicked *f* his way
Heb 13: 5 never will I *f* you."

FORSAKEN (FORSAKE)
Ps 22: 1 my God, why have you *f* me?
37: 25 I have never seen the righteous *f*
Mt 27: 46 my God, why have you *f* me?"
Rev 2: 4 You have *f* your first love.

FORTRESS
Ps 18: 2 The LORD is my rock, my *f*
71: 3 for you are my rock and my *f*.

FOUGHT (FIGHT)
2Ti 4: 7 I have *f* the good fight, I have

FOUND (FIND)
1Ch 28: 9 If you seek him, he will be *f* by you;
Isa 55: 6 Seek the LORD while he may be *f*;
Da 5: 27 on the scales and *f* wanting.
Lk 15: 6 with me; I have *f* my lost sheep.'
15: 9 with me; I have *f* my lost coin.'
Ac 4: 12 Salvation is *f* in no one else,

FOUNDATION
Isa 28: 16 a precious cornerstone for a sure *f*;
1Co 3: 11 For no one can lay any *f* other
Eph 2: 20 built on the *f* of the apostles
2Ti 2: 19 God's solid *f* stands firm,

FOXES
Mt 8: 20 "*F* have holes and birds

FRAGRANCE
2Co 2: 16 of death; to the other, the *f* of life.

FREE (FREED FREEDOM FREELY)
Ps 146: 7 The LORD sets prisoners *f*,
Jn 8: 32 and the truth will set you *f*."
Ro 6: 18 You have been set *f* from sin
Gal 3: 28 slave nor *f*, male nor female,
1Pe 2: 16 *f* men, but do not use your freedom

FREED (FREE)
Rev 1: 5 has *f* us from our sins by his blood,

FREEDOM (FREE)
Ro 8: 21 into the glorious *f* of the children
2Co 3: 17 the Spirit of the Lord is, there is *f*.
Gal 5: 13 But do not use your *f* to indulge
1Pe 2: 16 but do not use your *f* as a cover-up

FREELY (FREE)
Isa 55: 7 and to our God, for he will *f* pardon
Mt 10: 8 Freely you have received, *f* give.

Ro 3: 24 and are justified *f* by his grace
Eph 1: 6 which he has *f* given us

FRIEND (FRIENDS)

Ex 33: 11 as a man speaks with his *f.*
Pr 17: 17 A *f* loves at all times,
18: 24 there is a *f* who sticks closer
27: 6 Wounds from a *f* can be trusted,
27: 10 Do not forsake your *f* and the *f*
Jas 4: 4 Anyone who chooses to be a *f*

FRIENDS (FRIEND)

Pr 16: 28 and a gossip separates close *f.*
Zec 13: 6 given at the house of my *f.'*
Jn 15: 13 that he lay down his life for his *f.*

FRUIT (FRUITFUL)

Ps 1: 3 which yields its *f* in season
Pr 11: 30 The *f* of the righteous is a tree
Mt 7: 16 By their *f* you will recognize them.
Jn 15: 2 branch in me that bears no *f,*
Gal 5: 22 But the *f* of the Spirit is love, joy,
Rev 22: 2 of *f,* yielding its *f* every month.

FRUITFUL (FRUIT)

Ge 1: 22 "Be *f* and increase in number
Ps 128: 3 Your wife will be like a *f* vine
Jn 15: 2 prunes so that it will be even more *f.*

FULFILL (FULFILLED FULFILLMENT)

Ps 116: 14 I will *f* my vows to the LORD
Mt 5: 17 come to abolish them but to *f* them.
1Co 7: 3 husband should *f* his marital duty

FULFILLED (FULFILL)

Pr 13: 19 A longing *f* is sweet to the soul,
Mk 14: 49 But the Scriptures must be *f."*
Ro 13: 8 loves his fellowman has *f* the law.

FULFILLMENT (FULFILL)

Ro 13: 10 Therefore love is the *f* of the law.

FULL (FILL)

Ps 127: 5 whose quiver is *f* of them.
Pr 31: 11 Her husband has *f* confidence
Isa 6: 3 the whole earth is *f* of his glory."
11: 9 for the earth will be *f*
Jn 10: 10 may have life, and have it to the *f.*
Ac 6: 3 known to be *f* of the Spirit

FULLNESS (FILL)

Col 1: 19 to have all his *f* dwell in him,
2: 9 in Christ all the *f* of the Deity lives

FULLY (FILL)

1Ki 8: 61 your hearts must be *f* committed
2Ch 16: 9 whose hearts are *f* committed
Ps 119: 4 that are to be *f* obeyed.
119:138 they are *f* trustworthy.
1Co 15: 58 Always give yourselves *f*

FUTURE

Ps 37: 37 there is a *f* for the man of peace.
Pr 23: 18 There is surely a *f* hope for you,
Ro 8: 38 neither the present nor the *f,*

GABRIEL*

Angel who interpreted Daniel's visions (Da 8: 16-26; 9:20-27); announced births of John (Lk 1:11-20), Jesus (Lk 1:26-38).

GAIN (GAINED)

Ps 60: 12 With God we will *g* the victory,
Mk 8: 36 it for a man to *g* the whole world,
1Co 13: 3 but have not love, I *g* nothing.
Php 1: 21 to live is Christ and to die is *g.*
3: 8 that I may *g* Christ and be found
1Ti 6: 6 with contentment is great *g.*

GAINED (GAIN)

Ro 5: 2 through whom we have *g* access

GALILEE

Isa 9: 1 but in the future he will honor *G*

GALL

Mt 27: 34 mixed with *g;* but after tasting it,

GAP

Eze 22: 30 stand before me in the *g* on behalf

GARDENER

Jn 15: 1 true vine, and my Father is the *g.*

GARMENT (GARMENTS)

Ps 102: 26 they will all wear out like a *g.*
Mt 9: 16 of unshrunk cloth on an old *g,*
Jn 19: 23 This *g* was seamless, woven

GARMENTS (GARMENT)

Ge 3: 21 The LORD God made *g* of skin
Isa 61: 10 me with *g* of salvation
63: 1 with his *g* stained crimson?
Jn 19: 24 "They divided my *g* among them

GATE (GATES)

Mt 7: 13 For wide is the *g* and broad is
Jn 10: 9 I am the *g;* whoever enters

GATES (GATE)

Ps 100: 4 Enter his *g* with thanksgiving
Mt 16: 18 the *g* of Hades will not overcome it

GATHER (GATHERS)

Zec 14: 2 I will *g* all the nations to Jerusalem
Mt 12: 30 he who does not *g* with me scatters
23: 37 longed to *g* your children together,

GATHERS (GATHER)

Isa 40: 11 He *g* the lambs in his arms
Mt 23: 37 a hen *g* her chicks under her wings,

GAVE (GIVE)

Ezr 2: 69 According to their ability they *g*
Job 1: 21 LORD *g* and the LORD has taken
Jn 3: 16 so loved the world that he *g* his one
2Co 8: 5 they *g* themselves first to the Lord
Gal 2: 20 who loved me and *g* himself for me
1Ti 2: 6 who *g* himself as a ransom

GAZE

Ps 27: 4 to *g* upon the beauty of the LORD
Pr 4: 25 fix your *g* directly before you.

GENEALOGIES

1Ti 1: 4 themselves to myths and endless *g.*

GENERATIONS

Ps 22: 30 future *g* will be told about the Lord
102: 12 your renown endures through all *g.*
145: 13 dominion endures through all *g.*
Lk 1: 48 now on all *g* will call me blessed,
Eph 3: 5 not made known to men in other *g*

GENEROUS

Ps 112: 5 Good will come to him who is *g*
Pr 22: 9 A *g* man will himself be blessed,
2Co 9: 5 Then it will be ready as a *g* gift,
1Ti 6: 18 and to be *g* and willing to share.

GENTILE (GENTILES)

Ro 1: 16 first for the Jew, then for the *G.*
10: 12 difference between Jew and *G*—

GENTILES (GENTILE)

Isa 42: 6 and a light for the *G,*
Ro 3: 9 and *G* alike are all under sin.
11: 13 as I am the apostle to the *G,*
1Co 1: 23 block to Jews and foolishness to *G,*

GENTLE (GENTLENESS)

Pr 15: 1 A *g* answer turns away wrath,
Zec 9: 9 *g* and riding on a donkey,
Mt 11: 29 for I am *g* and humble in heart,
21: 5 *g* and riding on a donkey,
1Co 4: 21 or in love and with a *g* spirit?
1Pe 3: 4 the unfading beauty of a *g*

GENTLENESS* (GENTLE)

2Co 10: 1 By the meekness and *g* of Christ,
Gal 5: 23 faithfulness, *g* and self-control.
Php 4: 5 Let your *g* be evident to all.
Col 3: 12 kindness, humility, *g* and patience.
1Ti 6: 11 faith, love, endurance and *g.*
1Pe 3: 15 But do this with *g* and respect,

GETHSEMANE

Mt 26: 36 disciples to a place called *G,*

GIDEON*

Judge, also called Jerub-Baal; freed Israel from Midianites(Jdg 6-8; Heb 11:32). Given sign of fleece (Jdg 8:36-40).

GIFT (GIFTS)

Pr 21: 14 A *g* given in secret soothes anger,
Mt 5: 23 if you are offering your *g*
Ac 2: 38 And you will receive the *g*
Ro 6: 23 but the *g* of God is eternal life
1Co 7: 7 each man has his own *g* from God;

2Co 8: 12 the *g* is acceptable according
9: 15 be to God for his indescribable *g!*
Eph 2: 8 it is the *g* of God—not by works,
1Ti 4: 14 not neglect your *g,* which was
2Ti 1: 6 you to fan into flame the *g* of God,
Jas 1: 17 and perfect *g* is from above,
1Pe 4: 10 should use whatever *g* he has

GIFTS (GIFT)

Ro 11: 29 for God's *g* and his call are
12: 6 We have different *g,* according
1Co 12: 4 There are different kinds of *g,*
12: 31 But eagerly desire the greater *g.*
14: 1 and eagerly desire spiritual *g,*
14: 12 excel in *g* that build up the church.

GILEAD

Jer 8: 22 Is there no balm in *G?*

GIVE (GAVE GIVEN GIVER GIVES GIVING)

Nu 6: 26 and *g* you peace."'
1Sa 1: 11 then I will *g* him to the LORD
2Ch 15: 7 be strong and do not *g* up,
Pr 21: 26 but the righteous *g* without sparing
23: 26 My son, *g* me your heart
30: 8 but *g* me only my daily bread.
31: 31 *G* her the reward she has earned,
Isa 42: 8 I will not *g* my glory to another
Eze 36: 26 I will *g* you a new heart
Mt 6: 11 *G* us today our daily bread.
10: 8 Freely you have received, freely *g.*
22: 21 "*G* to Caesar what is Caesar's,
Mk 8: 37 Or what can a man *g* in exchange
Lk 6: 38 *G,* and it will be given to you.
11: 13 Father in heaven *g* the Holy Spirit
Jn 10: 28 I *g* them eternal life, and they shall
13: 34 "A new commandment I *g* you:
Ac 20: 35 blessed to *g* than to receive.'"
Ro 12: 8 let him *g* generously;
13: 7 *G* everyone what you owe him:
14: 12 each of us will *g* an account
2Co 9: 7 Each man should *g* what he has
Rev 14: 7 "Fear God and *g* him glory,

GIVEN (GIVE)

Nu 8: 16 are to be *g* wholly to me.
Ps 115: 16 but the earth he has *g* to man.
Isa 9: 6 to us a son is *g,*
Mt 6: 33 and all these things will be *g* to you
7: 7 "Ask and it will be *g* to you;
Lk 22: 19 saying, "This is my body *g* for you;
Jn 3: 27 man can receive only what is *g* him
Ro 5: 5 the Holy Spirit, whom he has *g* us.
1Co 4: 2 those who have been *g* a trust must
12: 13 we were all *g* the one Spirit to drink
Eph 4: 7 to each one of us grace has been *g*

GIVER* (GIVE)

Pr 18: 16 A gift opens the way for the *g*
2Co 9: 7 for God loves a cheerful *g.*

GIVES (GIVE)

Ps 119:130 The unfolding of your words *g* light;
Pr 14: 30 A heart at peace *g* life to the body,
15: 30 good news *g* health to the bones.
28: 27 He who *g* to the poor will lack
Isa 40: 29 He *g* strength to the weary
Mt 10: 42 if anyone *g* even a cup of cold water
Jn 6: 63 The Spirit *g* life; the flesh counts
1Co 15: 57 He *g* us the victory
2Co 3: 6 the letter kills, but the Spirit *g* life.

GIVING (GIVE)

Ne 8: 8 *g* the meaning so that the people
Ps 19: 8 *g* joy to the heart.
Mt 6: 4 so that your *g* may be in secret.
2Co 8: 7 also excel in this grace of *g.*

GLAD (GLADNESS)

Ps 31: 7 I will be *g* and rejoice in your love,
46: 4 whose streams make *g* the city
97: 1 LORD reigns, let the earth be *g;*
118: 24 let us rejoice and be *g* in it.
Pr 23: 25 May your father and mother be *g;*
Zec 2: 10 and be *g,* O Daughter of Zion.
Mt 5: 12 be *g,* because great is your reward

GLADNESS (GLAD)

Ps 45: 15 They are led in with joy and *g;*
51: 8 Let me hear joy and *g;*
100: 2 Serve the LORD with *g;*
Jer 31: 13 I will turn their mourning into *g;*

GLORIFIED (GLORY)

Jn 13: 31 Son of Man *g* and God is *g* in him.
Ro 8: 30 those he justified, he also *g.*
2Th 1: 10 comes to be *g* in his holy people

GLORIFY (GLORY)

Ps 34: 3 *G* the LORD with me;
86: 12 I will *g* your name forever.
Jn 13: 32 God will *g* the Son in himself,
17: 1 *G* your Son, that your Son may

GLORIOUS (GLORY)

Ps 45: 13 All *g* is the princess
111: 3 *G* and majestic are his deeds,
145: 5 of the *g* splendor of your majesty,
Isa 4: 2 the LORD will be beautiful and *g,*
12: 5 for he has done *g* things;
42: 21 to make his law great and *g.*
63: 15 from your lofty throne, holy and *g.*
Mt 19: 28 the Son of Man sits on his *g* throne,
Lk 9: 31 appeared in *g* splendor, talking
Ac 2: 20 of the great and *g* day of the Lord.
2Co 3: 8 of the Spirit be even more *g?*
Php 3: 21 so that they will be like his *g* body.
4: 19 to his *g* riches in Christ Jesus.
Tit 2: 13 the *g* appearing of our great God
Jude : 24 before his *g* presence without fault

GLORY (GLORIFIED GLORIFY GLORIOUS)

Ex 15: 11 awesome in *g,*
33: 18 Moses said, "Now show me your *g*
1Sa 4: 21 "The *g* has departed from Israel"—
1Ch 16: 24 Declare his *g* among the nations,
16: 28 ascribe to the LORD *g*
29: 11 and the *g* and the majesty
Ps 8: 5 and crowned him with *g* and honor
19: 1 The heavens declare the *g* of God;
24: 7 that the King of *g* may come in.
29: 1 ascribe to the LORD *g*
72: 19 the whole earth be filled with his *g.*
96: 3 Declare his *g* among the nations,
Pr 19: 11 it is to his *g* to overlook an offense.
25: 2 It is the *g* of God to conceal
Isa 6: 3 the whole earth is full of his *g.*"
48: 11 I will not yield my *g* to another.
Eze 43: 2 and the land was radiant with his *g.*
Mt 24: 30 of the sky, with power and great *g.*
25: 31 the Son of Man comes in his *g,*
Mk 8: 38 in his Father's *g* with the holy
13: 26 in clouds with great power and *g.*
Lk 2: 9 and the *g* of the Lord shone
2: 14 saying, "*G* to God in the highest,
Jn 1: 14 We have seen his *g,* the *g* of the One
17: 5 presence with the *g* I had with you
17: 24 to see my *g,* the *g* you have given
Ac 7: 2 The God of *g* appeared
Ro 1: 23 exchanged the *g* of the immortal
3: 23 and fall short of the *g* of God,
8: 18 with the *g* that will be revealed
9: 4 theirs the divine *g,* the covenants,
1Co 10: 31 whatever you do, do it all for the *g*
11: 7 but the woman is the *g* of man.
15: 43 it is raised in *g;* it is sown
2Co 3: 10 comparison with the surpassing *g.*
3: 18 faces all reflect the Lord's *g,*
4: 17 us an eternal *g* that far outweighs
Col 1: 27 Christ in you, the hope of *g.*
3: 4 also will appear with him in *g.*
1Ti 3: 16 was taken up in *g.*
Heb 1: 3 The Son is the radiance of God's *g*
2: 7 you crowned him with *g* and honor
1Pe 1: 24 and all their *g* is like the flowers
Rev 4: 11 to receive *g* and honor and power,
21: 23 for the *g* of God gives it light,

GLUTTONS

Tit 1: 12 always liars, evil brutes, lazy *g.*"

GNASHING

Mt 8: 12 where there will be weeping and *g*

GNAT*

Mt 23: 24 You strain out a *g* but swallow

GOAL

2Co 5: 9 So we make it our *g* to please him,
Gal 3: 3 to attain your *g* by human effort?
Php 3: 14 on toward the *g* to win the prize

GOAT (GOATS SCAPEGOAT)

Isa 11: 6 the leopard will lie down with the *g*

GOATS (GOAT)

Nu 7: 17 five male *g* and five male lambs

GOD (GOD'S GODLINESS GODLY GODS)

Ge 1: 1 In the beginning *G* created
1: 2 and the Spirit of *G* was hovering
1: 26 Then *G* said, "Let us make man
1: 27 So *G* created man in his own image
1: 31 *G* saw all that he had made,
2: 3 And *G* blessed the seventh day
2: 22 Then the LORD *G* made a woman
3: 21 The LORD *G* made garments
3: 23 So the LORD *G* banished him
5: 22 Enoch walked with *G* 300 years
6: 2 sons of *G* saw that the daughters
9: 16 everlasting covenant between *G*
17: 1 "I am *G* Almighty; walk before me
21: 33 name of the LORD, the Eternal *G*.
22: 8 "*G* himself will provide the lamb
28: 12 and the angels of *G* were ascending
32: 28 because you have struggled with *G*
32: 30 "It is because I saw *G* face to face,
35: 10 *G* said to him, "Your name is Jacob
41: 51 *G* has made me forget all my
50: 20 but *G* intended it for good
Ex 2: 24 *G* heard their groaning
3: 6 because he was afraid to look at *G*.
6: 7 own people, and I will be your *G*.
8: 10 is no one like the LORD our *G*.
13: 18 So *G* led the people
15: 2 He is my *G*, and I will praise him,
17: 9 with the staff of *G* in my hands."
19: 3 Then Moses went up to *G*,
20: 2 the LORD your *G*, who brought
20: 5 the LORD your *G*, am a jealous *G*,
20: 19 But do not have *G* speak to us
22: 28 "Do not blaspheme *G*
31: 18 inscribed by the finger of *G*.
34: 6 the compassionate and gracious *G*,
34: 14 name is Jealous, is a jealous *G*.
Lev 8: 21 not profane the name of your *G*.
Lev 19: 2 the LORD your *G*, am holy.
26: 12 walk among you and be your *G*,
Nu 22: 38 I must speak only what *G* puts
23: 19 *G* is not a man, that he should lie,
Dt 1: 17 for judgment belongs to *G*.
3: 22 LORD your *G* himself will fight
3: 24 For what *g* is there in heaven
4: 24 is a consuming fire, a jealous *G*.
4: 31 the LORD your *G* is a merciful *G*;
4: 39 heart this day that the LORD is *G*
5: 11 the name of the LORD your *G*,
5: 14 a Sabbath to the LORD your *G*.
5: 26 of the living *G* speaking out of fire,
6: 4 LORD our *G*, the LORD is one.
6: 5 Love the LORD your *G*
6: 13 the LORD your *G*, serve him only
6: 16 Do not test the LORD your *G*
7: 9 your *G* is *G*; he is the faithful *G*,
7: 12 the LORD your *G* will keep his
7: 21 is a great and awesome *G*.
8: 5 the LORD your *G* disciplines you.
10: 12 but to fear the LORD your *G*,
10: 14 the LORD your *G* belong
10: 17 For the LORD your *G* is *G* of gods
11: 13 to love the LORD your *G*
13: 3 The LORD your *G* is testing you
13: 4 the LORD your *G* you must
15: 6 the LORD your *G* will bless you
19: 9 to love the LORD your *G*
25: 16 the LORD your *G* detests anyone
29: 29 belong to the LORD our *G*,
30: 2 return to the LORD your *G*
30: 16 today to love the LORD your *G*,
30: 20 you may love the LORD your *G*,
31: 6 for the LORD your *G* goes
32: 3 Oh, praise the greatness of our *G*!
32: 4 A faithful *G* who does no wrong,
33: 27 The eternal *G* is your refuge,
Jos 1: 9 for the LORD your *G* will be
14: 8 the LORD my *G* wholeheartedly.
22: 5 to love the LORD your *G*,
22: 34 Between Us that the LORD is *G*.
23: 11 careful to love the LORD your *G*.
23: 14 the LORD your *G* gave you has
Jdg 16: 28 O *G*, please strengthen me just
Ru 1: 16 be my people and your *G* my *G*.
1Sa 2: 2 there is no Rock like our *G*.
2: 3 for the LORD is a *G* who knows,
2: 25 another man, *G* may mediate
10: 26 men whose hearts *G* had touched.
12: 12 the LORD your *G* was your king.
17: 26 defy the armies of the living *G*?"
17: 46 world will know that there is a *G*
30: 6 strength in the LORD his *G*.
2Sa 14: 14 But *G* does not take away life;
22: 3 my *G* is my rock, in whom I take
22: 31 "As for *G*, his way is perfect;
1Ki 4: 29 *G* gave Solomon wisdom
8: 23 there is no *G* like you in heaven
8: 27 "But will *G* really dwell on earth?
1Ki 8: 61 committed to the LORD our *G*,
18: 21 If the LORD is *G*, follow him;
18: 37 are *G*, and that you are turning
20: 28 a *g* of the hills and not a *g*
2Ki 19: 15 *G* of Israel, enthroned
1Ch 16: 35 Cry out, "Save us, O *G* our Savior;
28: 2 for the footstool of our *G*,
28: 9 acknowledge the *G* of your father,
29: 10 *G* of our father Israel,
29: 17 my *G*, that you test the heart
2Ch 2: 4 for the Name of the LORD my *G*
5: 14 of the LORD filled the temple of *G*
6: 18 "But will *G* really dwell on earth
18: 13 I can tell him only what my *G* says
20: 6 are you not the *G* who is in heaven?
25: 8 for *G* has the power to help
30: 9 for the LORD your *G* is gracious
33: 12 the favor of the LORD his *G*
Ezr 8: 22 "The good hand of our *G* is
9: 6 "O my *G*, I am too ashamed
9: 13 our *G*, you have punished us less
Ne 1: 5 the great and awesome *G*,
8: 8 from the Book of the Law of *G*,
9: 17 But you are a forgiving *G*,
9: 32 the great, mighty and awesome *G*,
Job 1: 1 he feared *G* and shunned evil.
2: 10 Shall we accept good from *G*,
4: 17 a mortal be more righteous than *G*?
5: 17 is the man whom *G* corrects;
11: 7 Can you fathom the mysteries of *G*
19: 26 yet in my flesh I will see *G*;
22: 13 Yet you say, 'What does *G* know?
25: 4 can a man be righteous before *G*?
33: 14 For *G* does speak—now one way,
34: 12 is unthinkable that *G* would do
36: 26 is *G*— beyond our understanding!
37: 22 *G* comes in awesome majesty.
Ps 18: 2 my *G* is my rock, in whom I take
18: 28 my *G* turns my darkness into light.
19: 1 The heavens declare the glory of *G*;
22: 1 *G*, my *G*, why have you forsaken
29: 3 the *G* of glory thunders,
31: 14 I say, "You are my *G*."
40: 3 a hymn of praise to our *G*.
40: 8 I desire to do your will, O my *G*;
42: 2 thirsts for *G*, for the living *G*.
42: 11 Put your hope in *G*,
45: 6 O *G*, will last for ever and ever;
46: 1 *G* is our refuge and strength,
46: 10 "Be still, and know that I am *G*;
47: 7 For *G* is the King of all the earth;
50: 3 Our *G* comes and will not be silent;
51: 1 Have mercy on me, O *G*,
51: 10 Create in me a pure heart, O *G*,
51: 17 O *G*, you will not despise.
62: 7 my honor depend on *G*;

Ps 65: 5 O *G* our Savior,
66: 1 Shout with joy to *G*, all the earth!
66: 16 listen, all you who fear *G*;
68: 6 *G* sets the lonely in families,
71: 17 my youth, O *G*, you have taught
71: 19 reaches to the skies, O *G*,
71: 22 harp for your faithfulness, O my *G*;
73: 26 but *G* is the strength of my heart
77: 13 What *g* is so great as our God?
78: 19 Can *G* spread a table in the desert?
81: 1 Sing for joy to *G* our strength;
84: 2 out for the living *G*.
84: 10 a doorkeeper in the house of my *G*
86: 12 O Lord my *G*, with all my heart;
89: 7 of the holy ones *G* is greatly feared;
90: 2 to everlasting you are *G*.
91: 2 my *G*, in whom I trust."
95: 7 for he is our *G*
100: 3 Know that the LORD is *G*.
108: 1 My heart is steadfast, O *G*;
113: 5 Who is like the LORD our *G*,
139: 23 Search me, O *G*, and know my
Pr 3: 4 in the sight of *G* and man.
25: 2 of *G* to conceal a matter;
30: 5 "Every word of *G* is flawless;
Ecc 3: 11 cannot fathom what *G* has done
11: 5 cannot understand the work of *G*,
12: 13 Fear *G* and keep his
Isa 9: 6 Wonderful Counselor, Mighty *G*,
37: 16 you alone are *G* over all
40: 3 a highway for our *G*.
40: 8 the word of our *G* stands forever."
40: 28 The LORD is the everlasting *G*,
41: 10 not be dismayed, for I am your *G*.
44: 6 apart from me there is no *G*.
52: 7 "Your *G* reigns!"
55: 7 to our *G*, for he will freely pardon.
57: 21 says my *G*, "for the wicked."
59: 2 you from your *G*;
61: 10 my soul rejoices in my *G*.
62: 5 so will your *G* rejoice over you.
Jer 23: 23 "Am I only a *G* nearby,"
31: 33 I will be their *G*,
32: 27 "I am the LORD, the *G*
Eze 28: 13 the garden of *G*;
Da 3: 17 the *G* we serve is able to save us
9: 4 O Lord, the great and awesome *G*,
Hos 12: 6 and wait for your *G* always.
Joel 2: 13 Return to the LORD your *G*,
Am 4: 12 prepare to meet your *G*, O Israel."
Mic 6: 8 and to walk humbly with your *G*.
Na 1: 2 LORD is a jealous and avenging *G*;
Zec 14: 5 Then the LORD my *G* will come,
Mal 3: 8 Will a man rob *G*? Yet you rob me.
Mt 1: 23 which means, "*G* with us."
5: 8 for they will see *G*.
6: 24 You cannot serve both *G*
19: 6 Therefore what *G* has joined
Mt 19: 26 but with *G* all things are possible."
22: 21 and to *G* what is God's."
22: 37 "'Love the Lord your *G*
27: 46 which means, "My *G*, my *G*,
Mk 12: 29 the Lord our *G*, the Lord is one.
16: 19 and he sat at the right hand of *G*.
Lk 1: 37 For nothing is impossible with *G*."
1: 47 my spirit rejoices in *G* my Savior,
10: 9 'The kingdom of *G* is near you.'
10: 27 "'Love the Lord your *G*
18: 19 "No one is good—except *G* alone.
Jn 1: 1 was with *G*, and the Word was *G*.
1: 18 seen *G*, but *G* the One and Only,
3: 16 "For *G* so loved the world that he
4: 24 *G* is spirit, and his worshipers must
14: 1 Trust in *G*; trust also in me.
20: 28 "My Lord and my *G*!"
Ac 2: 24 But *G* raised him from the dead,
5: 4 You have not lied to men but to *G*
5: 29 "We must obey *G* rather than men!
7: 55 to heaven and saw the glory of *G*,
17: 23 TO AN UNKNOWN *G*.
20: 27 to you the whole will of *G*.
20: 32 "Now I commit you to *G*
Ro 1: 17 a righteousness from *G* is revealed,
2: 11 For *G* does not show favoritism.
3: 4 Let *G* be true, and every man a liar.
3: 23 and fall short of the glory of *G*,
4: 24 to whom *G* will credit
5: 8 *G* demonstrates his own love for us
6: 23 but the gift of *G* is eternal life
8: 28 in all things *G* works for the good
11: 22 the kindness and sternness of *G*:
14: 12 give an account of himself to *G*.
1Co 1: 20 Has not *G* made foolish
2: 9 what *G* has prepared
3: 6 watered it, but *G* made it grow.
6: 20 Therefore honor *G* with your body.
7: 24 each man, as responsible to *G*,
8: 8 food does not bring us near to *G*;
10: 13 *G* is faithful; he will not let you be
10: 31 do it all for the glory of *G*.
14: 33 For *G* is not a *G* of disorder
15: 28 so that *G* may be all in all.
2Co 1: 9 rely on ourselves but on *G*,
2: 14 be to *G*, who always leads us
3: 5 but our competence comes from *G*.
4: 7 this all-surpassing power is from *G*
5: 19 that *G* was reconciling the world
5: 21 *G* made him who had no sin
6: 16 we are the temple of the living *G*.
9: 7 for *G* loves a cheerful giver.
2Co 9: 8 *G* is able to make all grace abound
Gal 2: 6 *G* does not judge by external
6: 7 not be deceived: *G* cannot be
Eph 2: 10 which *G* prepared in advance for us
4: 6 one baptism; one *G* and Father
5: 1 Be imitators of *G*, therefore,
Php 2: 6 Who, being in very nature *G*,
4: 19 And my *G* will meet all your needs
1Th 2: 4 trying to please men but *G*,
4: 7 For *G* did not call us to be impure,
4: 9 taught by *G* to love each other.
5: 9 For *G* did not appoint us
1Ti 2: 5 one mediator between *G* and men,
4: 4 For everything *G* created is good,
5: 4 for this is pleasing to *G*.
Tit 2: 13 glorious appearing of our great *G*
Heb 1: 1 In the past *G* spoke
4: 12 For the word of *G* is living
6: 10 *G* is not unjust; he will not forget
10: 31 to fall into the hands of the living *G*
11: 6 faith it is impossible to please *G*,
12: 10 but *G* disciplines us for our good,
12: 29 for our "*G* is a consuming fire."
13: 15 offer to *G* a sacrifice of praise—
Jas 1: 13 For *G* cannot be tempted by evil,
2: 19 You believe that there is one *G*.
2: 23 "Abraham believed *G*,
4: 4 the world becomes an enemy of *G*.
4: 8 Come near to *G* and he will come
1Pe 4: 11 it with the strength *G* provides,
2Pe 1: 21 but men spoke from *G*
1Jn 1: 5 *G* is light; in him there is no
3: 20 For *G* is greater than our hearts,
4: 7 for love comes from *G*.
4: 9 This is how *G* showed his love
4: 11 Dear friends, since *G* so loved us,
4: 12 No one has ever seen *G*;
4: 16 *G* is love.
Rev 4: 8 holy is the Lord *G* Almighty,
7: 17 *G* will wipe away every tear
19: 6 For our Lord *G* Almighty reigns.

GOD-BREATHED* (BREATHED)

2Ti 3: 16 All Scripture is *G* and is useful

GOD'S (GOD)

2Ch 20: 15 For the battle is not yours, but *G*.
Job 37: 14 stop and consider *G* wonders.
Ps 52: 8 I trust in *G* unfailing love
69: 30 I will praise *G* name in song
Mk 3: 35 Whoever does *G* will is my brother
Jn 7: 17 If anyone chooses to do *G* will,
10: 36 'I am *G* Son'? Do not believe me
Ro 2: 3 think you will escape *G* judgment?
2: 4 not realizing that *G* kindness leads
3: 3 lack of faith nullify *G* faithfulness?

Ro 7: 22 in my inner being I delight in *G* law
9: 16 or effort, but on *G* mercy.
11: 29 for *G* gifts and his call are
12: 2 and approve what *G* will is—
12: 13 Share with *G* people who are
13: 6 for the authorities are *G* servants,
1Co 7: 19 Keeping *G* commands is what
2Co 6: 2 now is the time of *G* favor,
Eph 1: 7 riches of *G* grace that he lavished
1Th 4: 3 It is *G* will that you should be
5: 18 for this is *G* will for you
1Ti 6: 1 so that *G* name and our teaching
2Ti 2: 19 *G* solid foundation stands firm,
Tit 1: 7 overseer is entrusted with *G* work,
Heb 1: 3 The Son is the radiance of *G* glory
9: 24 now to appear for us in *G* presence.
11: 3 was formed at *G* command,
1Pe 2: 15 For it is *G* will that
3: 4 which is of great worth in *G* sight.
1Jn 2: 5 *G* love is truly made complete

GODLINESS (GOD)

1Ti 2: 2 and quiet lives in all *g* and holiness.
4: 8 but *g* has value for all things,
6: 6 *g* with contentment is great gain.
6: 11 and pursue righteousness, *g,* faith,

GODLY (GOD)

Ps 4: 3 that the LORD has set apart the *g*
2Co 7: 10 *G* sorrow brings repentance that
11: 2 jealous for you with a *g* jealousy.
2Ti 3: 12 everyone who wants to live a *g* life
2Pe 3: 11 You ought to live holy and *g* lives

GODS (GOD)

Ex 20: 3 "You shall have no other *g*
Ac 19: 26 He says that man-made *g* are no *g*

GOLD

Job 23: 10 tested me, I will come forth as *g.*
Ps 19: 10 They are more precious than *g,*
119:127 more than *g,* more than pure *g,*
Pr 22: 1 esteemed is better than silver or *g.*

GOLGOTHA

Jn 19: 17 (which in Aramaic is called *G).*

GOLIATH

Philistine giant killed by David (1Sa 17; 21:9).

GOOD

Ge 1: 4 God saw that the light was *g,*
1: 31 he had made, and it was very *g.*
2: 18 "It is not *g* for the man to be alone.
50: 20 but God intended it for *g*
Job 2: 10 Shall we accept *g* from God,
Ps 14: 1 there is no one who does *g.*
34: 8 Taste and see that the LORD is *g;*
37: 3 Trust in the LORD and do *g;*
84: 11 no *g* thing does he withhold
86: 5 You are forgiving and *g,* O Lord
103: 5 satisfies your desires with *g* things,
119: 68 You are *g,* and what you do is *g;*
133: 1 How *g* and pleasant it is
147: 1 How *g* it is to sing praises
Pr 3: 4 you will win favor and a *g* name
11: 27 He who seeks *g* finds *g* will,
17: 22 A cheerful heart is *g* medicine,
18: 22 He who finds a wife finds what is *g*
22: 1 A *g* name is more desirable
31: 12 She brings him *g,* not harm,
Isa 5: 20 Woe to those who call evil *g*
52: 7 the feet of those who bring *g* news,
Jer 6: 16 ask where the *g* way is,
32: 39 the *g* of their children after them.
Mic 6: 8 has showed you, O man, what is *g.*
Mt 5: 45 sun to rise on the evil and the *g,*
7: 17 Likewise every *g* tree bears *g* fruit,
12: 35 The *g* man brings *g* things out
19: 17 "There is only One who is *g.*
25: 21 'Well done, *g* and faithful servant!
Mk 3: 4 lawful on the Sabbath: to do *g*
8: 36 What *g* is it for a man
Lk 6: 27 do *g* to those who hate you,
Jn 10: 11 "I am the *g* shepherd.
Ro 8: 28 for the *g* of those who love him,
10: 15 feet of those who bring *g* news!"
12: 9 Hate what is evil; cling to what is *g.*
1Co 10: 24 should seek his own *g,* but the *g*
15: 33 Bad company corrupts *g* character
2Co 9: 8 you will abound in every *g* work.
Gal 6: 9 us not become weary in doing *g,*
6: 10 as we have opportunity, let us do *g*
Eph 2: 10 in Christ Jesus to do *g* works,
Php 1: 6 that he who began a *g* work
1Th 5: 21 Hold on to the *g.*
1Ti 3: 7 have a *g* reputation with outsiders,
4: 4 For everything God created is *g,*
6: 12 Fight the *g* fight of the faith.
6: 18 them to do *g,* to be rich in *g* deeds,
2Ti 3: 17 equipped for every *g* work.
4: 7 I have fought the *g* fight, I have
Heb 12: 10 but God disciplines us for our *g,*
1Pe 2: 3 you have tasted that the Lord is *g.*
2: 12 Live such *g* lives among the pagans

GOSPEL

Ro 1: 16 I am not ashamed of the *g,*
15: 16 duty of proclaiming the *g* of God,
1Co 1: 17 to preach the *g* — not with words
9: 16 Woe to me if I do not preach the *g!*
15: 1 you of the *g* I preached to you,
Gal 1: 7 a different *g*— which is really no *g*
Php 1: 27 in a manner worthy of the *g*

GOSSIP

Pr 11: 13 A *g* betrays a confidence,
16: 28 and a *g* separates close friends.
18: 8 of a *g* are like choice morsels;
26: 20 without *g* a quarrel dies down.
2Co 12: 20 slander, *g,* arrogance and disorder.

GRACE (GRACIOUS)

Ps 45: 2 lips have been anointed with *g,*
Jn 1: 17 *g* and truth came through Jesus
Ac 20: 32 to God and to the word of his *g,*
Ro 3: 24 and are justified freely by his *g*
5: 15 came by the *g* of the one man,
5: 17 God's abundant provision of *g*
5: 20 where sin increased, *g* increased all
6: 14 you are not under law, but under *g.*
11: 6 if by *g,* then it is no longer by works
2Co 6: 1 not to receive God's *g* in vain.
8: 9 For you know the *g*
9: 8 able to make all *g* abound to you,
12: 9 "My *g* is sufficient for you,
Gal 2: 21 I do not set aside the *g* of God,
5: 4 you have fallen away from *g.*
Eph 1: 7 riches of God's *g* that he lavished
2: 5 it is by *g* you have been saved.
2: 7 the incomparable riches of his *g,*
2: 8 For it is by *g* you have been saved,
Php 1: 7 all of you share in God's *g* with me.
Col 4: 6 conversation be always full of *g,*
2Th 2: 16 and by his *g* gave us eternal
2Ti 2: 1 be strong in the *g* that is
Tit 2: 11 For the *g* of God that brings
3: 7 having been justified by his *g,*
Heb 2: 9 that by the *g* of God he might taste
4: 16 find *g* to help us in our time of need
4: 16 the throne of *g* with confidence,
Jas 4: 6 but gives *g* to the humble."
2Pe 3: 18 But grow in the *g* and knowledge

GRACIOUS (GRACE)

Nu 6: 25 and be *g* to you;
Pr 22: 11 a pure heart and whose speech is *g*
Isa 30: 18 Yet the LORD longs to be *g* to you

GRAIN

1Co 9: 9 ox while it is treading out the *g."*

GRANTED

Php 1: 29 For it has been *g* to you on behalf

GRASS

Ps 103: 15 As for man, his days are like *g*,
1Pe 1: 24 "All men are like *g*,

GRAVE (GRAVES)

Pr 7: 27 Her house is a highway to the *g*,
Hos 13: 14 Where, O *g*, is your destruction?

GRAVES (GRAVE)

Jn 5: 28 are in their *g* will hear his voice
Ro 3: 13 "Their throats are open *g*;

GREAT (GREATER GREATEST GREATNESS)

Ge 12: 2 "I will make you into a *g* nation
Dt 10: 17 the *g* God, mighty and awesome,
2Sa 22: 36 you stoop down to make me *g*.
Ps 19: 11 in keeping them there is *g* reward.
89: 1 of the LORD's *g* love forever;
103: 11 so *g* is his love for those who fear
107: 43 consider the *g* love of the LORD.
108: 4 For *g* is your love, higher
119:165 *G* peace have they who love your
145: 3 *G* is the LORD and most worthy
Pr 23: 24 of a righteous man has *g* joy;
Isa 42: 21 to make his law *g* and glorious.
La 3: 23 *g* is your faithfulness.
Mk 10: 43 whoever wants to become *g*
Lk 21: 27 in a cloud with power and *g* glory.
1Ti 6: 6 with contentment is *g* gain.
Tit 2: 13 glorious appearing of our *g* God
Heb 2: 3 if we ignore such a *g* salvation?
1Jn 3: 1 How *g* is the love the Father has

GREATER (GREAT)

Mk 12: 31 There is no commandment *g*
Jn 1: 50 You shall see *g* things than that."
15: 13 *G* love has no one than this,
1Co 12: 31 But eagerly desire the *g* gifts.
Heb 11: 26 as of *g* value than the treasures
1Jn 3: 20 For God is *g* than our hearts,
4: 4 is in you is *g* than the one who is

GREATEST (GREAT)

Mt 22: 38 is the first and *g* commandment.
Lk 9: 48 least among you all—he is the *g*."
1Co 13: 13 But the *g* of these is love.

GREATNESS (GREAT)

Ps 145: 3 his *g* no one can fathom.
150: 2 praise him for his surpassing *g*.
Isa 63: 1 forward in the *g* of his strength?
Php 3: 8 compared to the surpassing *g*

GREED (GREEDY)

Lk 12: 15 on your guard against all kinds of *g*
Ro 1: 29 kind of wickedness, evil, *g*
Eph 5: 3 or of any kind of impurity, or of *g*,
Col 3: 5 evil desires and *g*, which is idolatry
2Pe 2: 14 experts in *g*—an accursed brood!

GREEDY (GREED)

Pr 15: 27 A *g* man brings trouble
1Co 6: 10 nor thieves nor the *g* nor drunkards
Eph 5: 5 No immoral, impure or *g* person—
1Pe 5: 2 not *g* for money, but eager to serve;

GREEN

Ps 23: 2 makes me lie down in *g* pastures,

GREW (GROW)

Lk 2: 52 And Jesus *g* in wisdom and stature,
Ac 16: 5 in the faith and *g* daily in numbers.

GRIEF (GRIEVE)

Ps 10: 14 O God, do see trouble and *g*;
Pr 14: 13 and joy may end in *g*.
La 3: 32 Though he brings *g*, he will show
Jn 16: 20 but your *g* will turn to joy.
1Pe 1: 6 had to suffer *g* in all kinds of trials.

GRIEVE (GRIEF)

Eph 4: 30 do not *g* the Holy Spirit of God,
1Th 4: 13 or to *g* like the rest of men,

GROUND

Ge 3: 17 "Cursed is the *g* because of you;
Ex 3: 5 where you are standing is holy *g*."
Eph 6: 13 you may be able to stand your *g*,

GROW (GREW)

Pr 13: 11 by little makes it *g*.
1Co 3: 6 watered it, but God made it *g*.
2Pe 3: 18 But *g* in the grace and knowledge

GRUMBLE (GRUMBLING)

1Co 10: 10 And do not *g*, as some of them did
Jas 5: 9 Don't *g* against each other,

GRUMBLING (GRUMBLE)

Jn 6: 43 "Stop *g* among yourselves,"
1Pe 4: 9 to one another without *g*.

GUARANTEE (GUARANTEEING)

Heb 7: 22 Jesus has become the *g*

GUARANTEEING (GUARANTEE)

2Co 1: 22 as a deposit, *g* what is to come.
Eph 1: 14 who is a deposit *g* our inheritance

GUARD (GUARDS)

Ps 141: 3 Set a *g* over my mouth, O LORD;
Pr 4: 23 Above all else, *g* your heart,
Isa 52: 12 the God of Israel will be your rear *g*
Mk 13: 33 Be on *g*! Be alert! You do not know
1Co 16: 13 Be on your *g*; stand firm in the faith
Php 4: 7 will *g* your hearts and your minds
1Ti 6: 20 *g* what has been entrusted

GUARDS (GUARD)

Pr 13: 3 He who *g* his lips *g* his life,
19: 16 who obeys instructions *g* his life,
21: 23 He who *g* his mouth and his tongue
22: 5 he who *g* his soul stays far

GUIDE

Ex 13: 21 of cloud to *g* them on their way
15: 13 In your strength you will *g* them
Ne 9: 19 cease to *g* them on their path,
Ps 25: 5 *g* me in your truth and teach me,
43: 3 let them *g* me;
48: 14 he will be our *g* even to the end.
67: 4 and *g* the nations of the earth.
73: 24 You *g* me with your counsel,
139: 10 even there your hand will *g* me,
Pr 4: 11 I *g* you in the way of wisdom
6: 22 When you walk, they will *g* you;
Isa 58: 11 The LORD will *g* you always;
Jn 16: 13 comes, he will *g* you into all truth.

GUILTY

Ex 34: 7 does not leave the *g* unpunished;
Jn 8: 46 Can any of you prove me *g* of sin?
Heb 10: 22 to cleanse us from a *g* conscience
Jas 2: 10 at just one point is *g* of breaking all

HADES

Mt 16: 18 the gates of *H* will not overcome it.

HAGAR

Servant of Sarah, wife of Abraham, mother of Ishmael (Ge 16:1-6; 25:12). Driven away by Sarah while pregnant (Ge 16:5-16); after birth of Isaac (Ge 21:9-21; Gal 4:21-31).

HAGGAI*

Post-exilic prophet who encouraged rebuilding of the temple (Ezr 5:1; 6:14; Hag 1-2).

HAIR (HAIRS)

Lk 21: 18 But not a *h* of your head will perish
1Co 11: 6 for a woman to have her *h* cut

HAIRS (HAIR)

Mt 10: 30 even the very *h* of your head are all

HALLELUJAH*

Rev 19: 1 3, 4, 6.

HALLOWED (HOLY)

Mt 6: 9 *h* be your name,

HAND (HANDS)

Ps 16: 8 Because he is at my right *h*,
37: 24 the LORD upholds him with his *h*.
139: 10 even there your *h* will guide me,
Ecc 9: 10 Whatever your *h* finds to do,
Mt 6: 3 know what your right *h* is doing,
Jn 10: 28 one can snatch them out of my *h*.
1Co 12: 15 I am not a *h*, I do not belong

HANDS (HAND)

Ps 22: 16 they have pierced my *h*
24: 4 He who has clean *h* and a pure
31: 5 Into your *h* I commit my spirit;

Ps 31: 15 My times are in your *h;*
Pr 10: 4 Lazy *h* make a man poor,
31: 20 and extends her *h* to the needy.
Isa 55: 12 will clap their *h.*
65: 2 All day long I have held out my *h*
Lk 23: 46 into your *h* I commit my spirit."
1Th 4: 11 and to work with your *h,*
1Ti 2: 8 to lift up holy *h* in prayer,
5: 22 hasty in the laying on of *h,*

HANNAH*

Wife of Elkanah, mother of Samuel (1Sa 1). Prayer at dedication of Samuel (1Sa 2:1-10). Blessed (1Sa 2:18-21).

HAPPY

Ps 68: 3 may they be *h* and joyful.
Pr 15: 13 A *h* heart makes the face cheerful,
Ecc 3: 12 better for men than to be *h*
Jas 5: 13 Is anyone *h?* Let him sing songs

HARD (HARDEN HARDSHIP)

Ge 18: 14 Is anything too *h* for the LORD?
Mt 19: 23 it is *h* for a rich man
1Co 4: 12 We work *h* with our own hands.
1Th 5: 12 to respect those who work *h*

HARDEN (HARD)

Ro 9: 18 he hardens whom he wants to *h.*
Heb 3: 8 do not *h* your hearts

HARDHEARTED* (HEART)

Dt 15: 7 do not be *h* or tightfisted

HARDSHIP (HARD)

Ro 8: 35 Shall trouble or *h* or persecution
2Ti 2: 3 Endure *h* with us like a good
4: 5 endure *h,* do the work
Heb 12: 7 Endure *h* as discipline; God is

HARM

Ps 121: 6 the sun will not *h* you by day,
Pr 3: 29 not plot *h* against your neighbor,
31: 12 She brings him good, not *h,*
Ro 13: 10 Love does no *h* to its neighbor.
1Jn 5: 18 and the evil one cannot *h* him.

HARMONY

Ro 12: 16 Live in *h* with one another.
2Co 6: 15 What *h* is there between Christ
1Pe 3: 8 live in *h* with one another;

HARVEST

Mt 9: 37 *h* is plentiful but the workers are
Jn 4: 35 at the fields! They are ripe for *h.*
Gal 6: 9 at the proper time we will reap a *h*
Heb 12: 11 it produces a *h* of righteousness

HASTE (HASTY)

Pr 21: 5 as surely as *h* leads to poverty.
29: 20 Do you see a man who speaks in *h?*

HASTY* (HASTE)

Pr 19: 2 nor to be *h* and miss the way.
Ecc 5: 2 do not be *h* in your heart
1Ti 5: 22 Do not be *h* in the laying

HATE (HATED HATES HATRED)

Lev 19: 17 "'Do not *h* your brother
Ps 5: 5 you *h* all who do wrong.
45: 7 righteousness and *h* wickedness;
97: 10 those who love the LORD *h* evil,
139: 21 Do I not *h* those who *h* you,
Pr 8: 13 To fear the LORD is to *h* evil;
Am 5: 15 *H* evil, love good;
Mal 2: 16 "I *h* divorce," says the LORD God
Mt 5: 43 your neighbor and *h* your enemy.'
10: 22 All men will *h* you because of me,
Lk 6: 27 do good to those who *h* you,
Ro 12: 9 *H* what is evil; cling to what is good

HATED (HATE)

Ro 9: 13 "Jacob I loved, but Esau I *h.*"
Eph 5: 29 no one ever *h* his own body,
Heb 1: 9 righteousness and *h* wickedness;

HATES (HATE)

Pr 6: 16 There are six things the LORD *h,*
13: 24 He who spares the rod *h* his son,
Jn 3: 20 Everyone who does evil *h* the light,
1Jn 2: 9 *h* his brother is still in the darkness.

HATRED (HATE)

Pr 10: 12 *H* stirs up dissension,
Jas 4: 4 with the world is *h* toward God?

HAUGHTY

Pr 16: 18 a *h* spirit before a fall.

HAY

1Co 3: 12 costly stones, wood, *h* or straw,

HEAD (HEADS HOTHEADED)

Ge 3: 15 he will crush your *h,*
Ps 23: 5 You anoint my *h* with oil;
Pr 25: 22 will heap burning coals on his *h,*
Isa 59: 17 and the helmet of salvation on his *h*
Mt 8: 20 of Man has no place to lay his *h.*"
Ro 12: 20 will heap burning coals on his *h.*"
1Co 11: 3 and the *h* of Christ is God.
12: 21 And the *h* cannot say to the feet,
Eph 5: 23 For the husband is the *h* of the wife
2Ti 4: 5 keep your *h* in all situations,
Rev 19: 12 and on his *h* are many crowns.

HEADS (HEAD)

Lev 26: 13 you to walk with *h* held high.
Isa 35: 10 everlasting joy will crown their *h.*

HEAL (HEALED HEALING HEALS)

2Ch 7: 14 their sin and will *h* their land.
Ps 41: 4 *h* me, for I have sinned against you
Mt 10: 8 *H* the sick, raise the dead,
Lk 4: 23 to me: 'Physician, *h* yourself!
5: 17 present for him to *h* the sick.

HEALED (HEAL)

Isa 53: 5 and by his wounds we are *h.*
Mt 9: 22 he said, "your faith has *h* you."
14: 36 and all who touched him were *h.*
Ac 4: 10 this man stands before you *h.*
14: 9 saw that he had faith to be *h*
Jas 5: 16 for each other so that you may be *h*
1Pe 2: 24 by his wounds you have been *h.*

HEALING (HEAL)

Eze 47: 12 for food and their leaves for *h.*"
Mal 4: 2 rise with *h* in its wings.
1Co 12: 9 to another gifts of *h*
12: 30 Do all have gifts of *h?* Do all speak
Rev 22: 2 are for the *h* of the nations.

HEALS (HEAL)

Ex 15: 26 for I am the LORD, who *h* you."
Ps 103: 3 and *h* all your diseases;
147: 3 He *h* the brokenhearted

HEALTH (HEALTHY)

Pr 3: 8 This will bring *h* to your body
15: 30 and good news gives *h* to the bones

HEALTHY (HEALTH)

Mk 2: 17 "It is not the *h* who need a doctor,

HEAR (HEARD HEARING HEARS)

Dt 6: 4 *H,* O Israel: The LORD our God,
31: 13 must *h* it and learn
2Ch 7: 14 then will I *h* from heaven
Ps 94: 9 he who implanted the ear not *h?*
Isa 29: 18 that day the deaf will *h* the words
65: 24 while they are still speaking I will *h*
Mt 11: 15 He who has ears, let him *h.*
Jn 8: 47 reason you do not *h* is that you do
2Ti 4: 3 what their itching ears want to *h.*

HEARD (HEAR)

Job 42: 5 My ears had *h* of you
Isa 66: 8 Who has ever *h* of such a thing?
Mt 5: 21 "You have *h* that it was said
5: 27 "You have *h* that it was said,
5: 33 you have *h* that it was said
5: 38 "You have *h* that it was said,
5: 43 "You have *h* that it was said,
1Co 2: 9 no ear has *h,*
1Th 2: 13 word of God, which you *h* from us,
2Ti 1: 13 What you *h* from me, keep
Jas 1: 25 not forgetting what he has *h,*

HEARING (HEAR)

Ro 10: 17 faith comes from *h* the message,

HEARS (HEAR)

Jn 5: 24 whoever *h* my word and believes
1Jn 5: 14 according to his will, he *h* us.
Rev 3: 20 If anyone *h* my voice and opens

HEART (BROKENHEARTED HARD-HEARTED HEARTS WHOLEHEARTEDLY)

Ex 25: 2 each man whose *h* prompts him
Lev 19: 17 Do not hate your brother in your *h.*
Dt 4: 29 if you look for him with all your *h*

Dt 6: 5 LORD your God with all your *h*
10: 12 LORD your God with all your *h*
15: 10 and do so without a grudging *h;*
30: 6 you may love him with all your *h*
30: 10 LORD your God with all your *h*
Jos 22: 5 and to serve him with all your *h*
1Sa 13: 14 sought out a man after his own *h*
16: 7 but the LORD looks at the *h."*
2Ki 23: 3 with all his *h* and all his soul,
1Ch 28: 9 for the LORD searches every *h*
2Ch 7: 16 and my *h* will always be there.
Job 22: 22 and lay up his words in your *h.*
37: 1 "At this my *h* pounds
Ps 14: 1 The fool says in his *h,*
19: 14 and the meditation of my *h*
37: 4 will give you the desires of your *h.*
45: 1 My *h* is stirred by a noble theme
51: 10 Create in me a pure *h,* O God,
51: 17 a broken and contrite *h,*
66: 18 If I had cherished sin in my *h,*
86: 11 give me an undivided *h,*
119: 11 I have hidden your word in my *h*
119: 32 for you have set my *h* free.
139: 23 Search me, O God, and know my *h*
Pr 3: 5 Trust in the LORD with all your *h*
4: 21 keep them within your *h;*
4: 23 Above all else, guard your *h,*
7: 3 write them on the tablet of your *h.*
13: 12 Hope deferred makes the *h* sick,
14: 13 Even in laughter the *h* may ache,
15: 30 A cheerful look brings joy to the *h,*
17: 22 A cheerful *h* is good medicine,
24: 17 stumbles, do not let your *h* rejoice,
27: 19 so a man's *h* reflects the man.
Ecc 8: 5 wise *h* will know the proper time
SS 4: 9 You have stolen my *h,* my sister,
Isa 40: 11 and carries them close to his *h;*
57: 15 and to revive the *h* of the contrite.
Jer 17: 9 The *h* is deceitful above all things
29: 13 when you seek me with all your *h.*
Eze 36: 26 I will give you a new *h*
Mt 5: 8 Blessed are the pure in *h,*
6: 21 treasure is, there your *h* will be
12: 34 of the *h* the mouth speaks.
22: 37 the Lord your God with all your *h*
Lk 6: 45 overflow of his *h* his mouth speaks.
Ro 2: 29 is circumcision of the *h,*
10: 10 is with your *h* that you believe
1Co 14: 25 the secrets of his *h* will be laid bare.
Eph 5: 19 make music in your *h* to the Lord,
6: 6 doing the will of God from your *h.*
Col 3: 23 work at it with all your *h,*
1Pe 1: 22 one another deeply, from the *h.*

HEARTS (HEART)

Dt 11: 18 Fix these words of mine in your *h*
1Ki 8: 39 for you alone know the *h* of all men
8: 61 your *h* must be fully committed
Ps 62: 8 pour out your *h* to him,
Ecc 3: 11 also set eternity in the *h* of men;
Jer 31: 33 and write it on their *h.*
Lk 16: 15 of men, but God knows your *h.*
24: 32 "Were not our *h* burning within us
Jn 14: 1 "Do not let your *h* be troubled.
Ac 15: 9 for he purified their *h* by faith.
Ro 2: 15 of the law are written on their *h,*
2Co 3: 2 written on our *h,* known
3: 3 but on tablets of human *h.*
4: 6 shine in our *h* to give us the light
Eph 3: 17 dwell in your *h* through faith.
Col 3: 1 set your *h* on things above,
Heb 3: 8 do not harden your *h*
10: 16 I will put my laws in their *h,*
1Jn 3: 20 For God is greater than our *h,*

HEAT

2Pe 3: 12 and the elements will melt in the *h.*

HEAVEN (HEAVENLY HEAVENS)

Ge 14: 19 Creator of *h* and earth.
1Ki 8: 27 the highest *h,* cannot contain you.
2Ki 2: 1 up to *h* in a whirlwind,
2Ch 7: 14 then will I hear from *h*
Isa 14: 12 How you have fallen from *h,*
66: 1 *"H* is my throne,
Da 7: 13 coming with the clouds of *h.*
Mt 6: 9 "'Our Father in *h,*
6: 20 up for yourselves treasures in *h,*
16: 19 bind on earth will be bound in *h,*
19: 23 man to enter the kingdom of *h.*
24: 35 *H* and earth will pass away,
26: 64 and coming on the clouds of *h."*
28: 18 "All authority in *h*
Mk 16: 19 he was taken up into *h*
Lk 15: 7 in *h* over one sinner who repents
18: 22 and you will have treasure in *h.*
Ro 10: 6 'Who will ascend into *h?'"* (that is,
2Co 5: 1 an eternal house in *h,* not built
12: 2 ago was caught up to the third *h.*
Php 2: 10 *h* and on earth and under the earth,
3: 20 But our citizenship is in *h.*
1Th 1: 10 and to wait for his Son from *h,*
Heb 8: 5 and shadow of what is in *h.*
9: 24 he entered *h* itself, now to appear
2Pe 3: 13 we are looking forward to a new *h*
Rev 21: 1 Then I saw a new *h* and a new earth

HEAVENLY (HEAVEN)

Ps 8: 5 him a little lower than the *h* beings
2Co 5: 2 to be clothed with our *h* dwelling,
Eph 1: 3 in the *h* realms with every spiritual
1: 20 at his right hand in the *h* realms,
2Ti 4: 18 bring me safely to his *h* kingdom.
Heb 12: 22 to the *h* Jerusalem, the city

HEAVENS (HEAVEN)

Ge 1: 1 In the beginning God created the *h*
1Ki 8: 27 The *h,* even the highest heaven,
2Ch 2: 6 since the *h,* even the highest
Ps 8: 3 When I consider your *h,*
19: 1 The *h* declare the glory of God;
102: 25 the *h* are the work of your hands.
108: 4 is your love, higher than the *h;*
119: 89 it stands firm in the *h.*
139: 8 If I go up to the *h,* you are there;
Isa 51: 6 Lift up your eyes to the *h,*
55: 9 "As the *h* are higher than the earth,
65: 17 new *h* and a new earth.
Joel 2: 30 I will show wonders in the *h*
Eph 4: 10 who ascended higher than all the *h,*
2Pe 3: 10 The *h* will disappear with a roar;

HEBREW

Ge 14: 13 and reported this to Abram the *H.*

HEEDS

Pr 13: 1 wise son *h* his father's instruction,
13: 18 whoever *h* correction is honored.
15: 5 whoever *h* correction shows
15: 32 whoever *h* correction gains

HEEL

Ge 3: 15 and you will strike his *h."*

HEIRS (INHERIT)

Ro 8: 17 then we are *h*—*h* of God
Gal 3: 29 and *h* according to the promise.
Eph 3: 6 gospel the Gentiles are *h* together
1Pe 3: 7 as *h* with you of the gracious gift

HELL

Mt 5: 22 will be in danger of the fire of *h.*
Lk 16: 23 In *h,* where he was in torment,
2Pe 2: 4 but sent them to *h,* putting them

HELMET

Isa 59: 17 and the *h* of salvation on his head;
Eph 6: 17 Take the *h* of salvation
1Th 5: 8 and the hope of salvation as a *h.*

HELP (HELPED HELPER HELPING HELPS)

Ps 18: 6 I cried to my God for *h.*
30: 2 my God, I called to you for *h*
46: 1 an ever-present *h* in trouble.
79: 9 *H* us, O God our Savior,
121: 1 where does my *h* come from?

Isa 41:10 I will strengthen you and *h* you;
Jnh 2:2 depths of the grave I called for *h*,
Mk 9:24 *h* me overcome my unbelief!"
Ac 16:9 Come over to Macedonia and *h* us
1Co 12:28 those able to *h* others, those

HELPED (HELP)

1Sa 7:12 "Thus far has the LORD *h* us."

HELPER (HELP)

Ge 2:18 I will make a *h* suitable for him."
Ps 10:14 you are the *h* of the fatherless.
Heb 13:6 Lord is my *h;* I will not be afraid.

HELPING (HELP)

Ac 9:36 always doing good and *h* the poor.
1Ti 5:10 *h* those in trouble and devoting

HELPS (HELP)

Ro 8:26 the Spirit *h* us in our weakness.

HEN

Mt 23:37 as a *h* gathers her chicks

HERITAGE (INHERIT)

Ps 127:3 Sons are a *h* from the LORD,

HEROD

1. King of Judea who tried to kill Jesus (Mt 2; Lk 1:5).
2. Son of 1. Tetrarch of Galilee who arrested and beheaded John the Baptist (Mt 14:1-12; Mk 6:14-29; Lk 3:1, 19-20; 9:7-9); tried Jesus (Lk 23:6-15).
3. Grandson of 1. King of Judea who killed James (Ac 12:2); arrested Peter (Ac 12:3-19). Death (Ac 12:19-23).

HERODIAS

Wife of Herod the Tetrarch who persuaded her daughter to ask for John the Baptist's head (Mt 14:1-12; Mk 6:14-29).

HEZEKIAH

King of Judah. Restored the temple and worship (2Ch 29-31). Sought the LORD for help against Assyria (2Ki 18-19; 2Ch 32:1-23; Isa 36-37). Illness healed (2Ki 20:1-11; 2Ch 32:24-26; Isa 38). Judged for showing Babylonians his treasures (2Ki 20:12-21; 2Ch 32:31; Isa 39).

HID (HIDE)

Ge 3:8 and they *h* from the LORD God
Ex 2:2 she *h* him for three months.
Jos 6:17 because she *h* the spies we sent.
Heb 11:23 By faith Moses' parents *h* him

HIDDEN (HIDE)

Ps 19:12 Forgive my *h* faults.
119:11 I have *h* your word in my heart
Pr 2:4 and search for it as for *h* treasure,
Isa 59:2 your sins have *h* his face from you,
Mt 5:14 A city on a hill cannot be *h*.
13:44 of heaven is like treasure *h*
Col 1:26 the mystery that has been kept *h*
2:3 in whom are *h* all the treasures
3:3 and your life is now *h* with Christ

HIDE (HID HIDDEN)

Ps 17:8 *h* me in the shadow of your wings
143:9 for I *h* myself in you.

HILL (HILLS)

Mt 5:14 A city on a *h* cannot be hidden.

HILLS (HILL)

Ps 50:10 and the cattle on a thousand *h*.
121:1 I lift up my eyes to the *h*—

HINDER (HINDERS)

1Sa 14:6 Nothing can *h* the LORD
Mt 19:14 come to me, and do not *h* them,
1Co 9:12 anything rather than *h* the gospel
1Pe 3:7 so that nothing will *h* your prayers.

HINDERS (HINDER)

Heb 12:1 let us throw off everything that *h*

HINT*

Eph 5:3 even a *h* of sexual immorality,

HOLD

Ex 20:7 LORD will not *h* anyone guiltless
Lev 19:13 "'Do not *h* back the wages
Jos 22:5 to *h* fast to him and to serve him
Ps 73:23 you *h* me by my right hand.
Pr 4:4 "Lay *h* of my words
Isa 54:2 do not *h* back;
Mk 11:25 if you *h* anything against anyone,
Php 2:16 as you *h* out the word of life—
3:12 but I press on to take *h* of that
Col 1:17 and in him all things *h* together.
1Th 5:21 *H* on to the good.
1Ti 6:12 Take *h* of the eternal life
Heb 10:23 Let us *h* unswervingly

HOLINESS (HOLY)

Ex 15:11 majestic in *h*,
Ps 29:2 in the splendor of his *h*.
96:9 in the splendor of his *h;*
Ro 6:19 to righteousness leading to *h*.
2Co 7:1 perfecting *h* out of reverence
Eph 4:24 God in true righteousness and *h*.
Heb 12:10 that we may share in his *h*.
12:14 without *h* no one will see the Lord.

HOLY (HALLOWED HOLINESS)

Ex 19:6 kingdom of priests and a *h* nation.'
20:8 the Sabbath day by keeping it *h*.
Lev 11:44 and be *h*, because I am *h*.
20:7 "'Consecrate yourselves and be *h*,
20:26 You are to be *h* to me because I,
21:8 Consider them *h*, because I
22:32 Do not profane my *h* name.
Ps 16:10 will you let your *H* One see decay.
24:3 Who may stand in his *h* place?
77:13 Your ways, O God, are *h*.
99:3 he is *h*.
99:5 he is *h*.
99:9 for the LORD our God is *h*.
111:9 *h* and awesome is his name.
Isa 5:16 the *h* God will show himself *h*
6:3 *H, h, h* is the LORD Almighty;
Isa 40:25 who is my equal?" says the *H* One.
57:15 who lives forever, whose name is *h:*
Eze 28:25 I will show myself *h* among them
Da 9:24 prophecy and to anoint the most *h*.
Hab 2:20 But the LORD is in his *h* temple;
Ac 2:27 will you let your *H* One see decay.
Ro 7:12 and the commandment is *h*,
12:1 as living sacrifices, *h* and pleasing
Eph 5:3 improper for God's *h* people.
2Th 1:10 to be glorified in his *h* people
2Ti 1:9 saved us and called us to a *h* life—
3:15 you have known the *h* Scriptures,
Tit 1:8 upright, *h* and disciplined.
1Pe 1:15 But just as he who called you is *h*,
1:16 is written: "Be *h*, because I am *h*."
2:9 a royal priesthood, a *h* nation,
2Pe 3:11 You ought to live *h* and godly lives
Rev 4:8 "*H, h, h* is the Lord God

HOME (HOMES)

Dt 6:7 Talk about them when you sit at *h*
Ps 84:3 Even the sparrow has found a *h*,
Pr 3:33 but he blesses the *h* of the righteous
Mk 10:29 "no one who has left *h* or brothers
Jn 14:23 to him and make our *h* with him.
Tit 2:5 to be busy at *h*, to be kind,

HOMES (HOME)

Ne 4:14 daughters, your wives and your *h*."
1Ti 5:14 to manage their *h* and to give

HOMOSEXUAL*

1Co 6:9 male prostitutes nor *h* offenders

HONEST

Lev 19:36 Use *h* scales and *h* weights,
Dt 25:15 and *h* weights and measures,
Job 31:6 let God weigh me in *h* scales
Pr 12:17 truthful witness gives *h* testimony,

HONEY

Ex 3:8 a land flowing with milk and *h*—
Ps 19:10 than *h* from the comb.
119:103 sweeter than *h* to my mouth!

HONOR (HONORABLE HONORABLY HONORED HONORS)

Ex 20:12 "*H* your father and your mother,
Nu 25:13 he was zealous for the *h* of his God
Dt 5:16 "*H* your father and your mother,
1Sa 2:30 Those who *h* me I will *h*,
Ps 8:5 and crowned him with glory and *h*.
Pr 3:9 *H* the LORD with your wealth,
15:33 and humility comes before *h*.
20:3 It is to a man's *h* to avoid strife,
Mt 15:4 '*H* your father and mother'

Ro 12: 10 *H* one another above yourselves.
1Co 6: 20 Therefore *h* God with your body.
Eph 6: 2 "*H* your father and mother"—
1Ti 5: 17 well are worthy of double *h,*
Heb 2: 7 you crowned him with glory and *h*
Rev 4: 9 *h* and thanks to him who sits

HONORABLE (HONOR)

1Th 4: 4 body in a way that is holy and *h,*

HONORABLY (HONOR)

Heb 13: 18 and desire to live *h* in every way.

HONORED (HONOR)

Ps 12: 8 when what is vile is *h* among men.
Pr 13: 18 but whoever heeds correction is *h.*
1Co 12: 26 if one part is *h,* every part rejoices
Heb 13: 4 Marriage should be *h* by all,

HONORS (HONOR)

Ps 15: 4 but *h* those who fear the LORD,
Pr 14: 31 to the needy *h* God.

HOOKS

Isa 2: 4 and their spears into pruning *h.*
Joel 3: 10 and your pruning *h* into spears.

HOPE (HOPES)

Job 13: 15 Though he slay me, yet will I *h*
Ps 42: 5 Put your *h* in God,
62: 5 my *h* comes from him.
119: 74 for I have put my *h* in your word.
130: 7 O Israel, put your *h* in the LORD,
147: 11 who put their *h* in his unfailing love
Pr 13: 12 *H* deferred makes the heart sick,
Isa 40: 31 but those who *h* in the LORD
Ro 5: 4 character; and character, *h.*
8: 24 But *h* that is seen is no *h* at all.
12: 12 Be joyful in *h,* patient in affliction,
15: 4 of the Scriptures we might have *h.*
1Co 13: 13 now these three remain: faith, *h*
15: 19 for this life we have *h* in Christ,
Col 1: 27 Christ in you, the *h* of glory.
1Th 5: 8 and the *h* of salvation as a helmet.
1Ti 6: 17 but to put their *h* in God,
Tit 2: 13 while we wait for the blessed *h*—
Heb 6: 19 We have this *h* as an anchor
11: 1 faith is being sure of what we *h* for
1Jn 3: 3 Everyone who has this *h*

HOPES (HOPE)

1Co 13: 7 always *h,* always perseveres.

HORSE

Ps 147: 10 not in the strength of the *h,*
Pr 26: 3 A whip for the *h,* a halter
Zec 1: 8 before me was a man riding a red *h*
Rev 6: 2 and there before me was a white *h!*
6: 4 Come!" Then another *h* came out,
6: 5 and there before me was a black *h!*
6: 8 and there before me was a pale *h!*
19: 11 and there before me was a white *h,*

HOSANNA

Mt 21: 9 "*H* in the highest!"

HOSHEA

Last king of Israel (2Ki 15:30; 17:1-6).

HOSPITABLE* (HOSPITALITY)

1Ti 3: 2 self-controlled, respectable, *h,*
Tit 1: 8 Rather he must be *h,* one who loves

HOSPITALITY (HOSPITABLE)

Ro 12: 13 Practice *h.*
1Ti 5: 10 as bringing up children, showing *h,*
1Pe 4: 9 Offer *h* to one another

HOSTILE

Ro 8: 7 the sinful mind is *h* to God.

HOT

1Ti 4: 2 have been seared as with a *h* iron.
Rev 3: 15 that you are neither cold nor *h.*

HOT-TEMPERED

Pr 15: 18 A *h* man stirs up dissension,
19: 19 A *h* man must pay the penalty;
22: 24 Do not make friends with a *h* man,
29: 22 and a *h* one commits many sins.

HOTHEADED (HEAD)

Pr 14: 16 but a fool is *h* and reckless.

HOUR

Ecc 9: 12 knows when his *h* will come:
Mt 6: 27 you by worrying can add a single *h*
Lk 12: 40 the Son of Man will come at an *h*
Jn 12: 23 The *h* has come for the Son of Man
12: 27 for this very reason I came to this *h*

HOUSE (HOUSEHOLD STOREHOUSE)

Ex 20: 17 shall not covet your neighbor's *h.*
Ps 23: 6 I will dwell in the *h* of the LORD
84: 10 a doorkeeper in the *h* of my God
122: 1 "Let us go to the *h* of the LORD."
127: 1 Unless the LORD builds the *h,*
Pr 7: 27 Her *h* is a highway to the grave,
21: 9 than share a *h* with a quarrelsome
Isa 56: 7 a *h* of prayer for all nations."
Zec 13: 6 given at the *h* of my friends.'
Mt 7: 24 is like a wise man who built his *h*
12: 29 can anyone enter a strong man's *h*
21: 13 My *h* will be called a *h* of prayer,'
Mk 3: 25 If a *h* is divided against itself,
Lk 11: 17 a *h* divided against itself will fall.
Jn 2: 16 How dare you turn my Father's *h*
12: 3 the *h* was filled with the fragrance
14: 2 In my Father's *h* are many rooms;
Heb 3: 3 the builder of a *h* has greater honor

HOUSEHOLD (HOUSE)

Jos 24: 15 my *h,* we will serve the LORD."
Mic 7: 6 are the members of his own *h.*
Mt 10: 36 will be the members of his own *h.*'
12: 25 or *h* divided against itself will not
1Ti 3: 12 manage his children and his *h* well.
3: 15 to conduct themselves in God's *h,*

HUMAN (HUMANITY)

Gal 3: 3 to attain your goal by *h* effort?

HUMANITY* (HUMAN)

Heb 2: 14 he too shared in their *h* so that

HUMBLE (HUMBLED HUMBLES HUMILIATE HUMILITY)

2Ch 7: 14 will *h* themselves and pray
Ps 25: 9 He guides the *h* in what is right
Pr 3: 34 but gives grace to the *h.*
Isa 66: 2 he who is *h* and contrite in spirit,
Mt 11: 29 for I am gentle and *h* in heart,
Eph 4: 2 Be completely *h* and gentle;
Jas 4: 10 *H* yourselves before the Lord,
1Pe 5: 6 *H* yourselves,

HUMBLED (HUMBLE)

Mt 23: 12 whoever exalts himself will be *h,*
Php 2: 8 he *h* himself

HUMBLES (HUMBLE)

Mt 18: 4 whoever *h* himself like this child is
23: 12 whoever *h* himself will be exalted.

HUMILIATE* (HUMBLE)

Pr 25: 7 than for him to *h* you
1Co 11: 22 and *h* those who have nothing?

HUMILITY (HUMBLE)

Pr 11: 2 but with *h* comes wisdom.
15: 33 and *h* comes before honor.
Php 2: 3 but in *h* consider others better
Tit 3: 2 and to show true *h* toward all men.
1Pe 5: 5 clothe yourselves with *h*

HUNGRY

Ps 107: 9 and fills the *h* with good things.
146: 7 and gives food to the *h.*
Pr 25: 21 If your enemy is *h,* give him food
Eze 18: 7 but gives his food to the *h*
Mt 25: 35 For I was *h* and you gave me
Lk 1: 53 He has filled the *h* with good things
Jn 6: 35 comes to me will never go *h,*
Ro 12: 20 "If your enemy is *h,* feed him;

HURT (HURTS)

Ecc 8: 9 it over others to his own *h.*
Mk 16: 18 deadly poison, it will not *h* them
Rev 2: 11 He who overcomes will not be *h*

HURTS* (HURT)

Ps 15: 4 even when it *h,*
Pr 26: 28 A lying tongue hates those it *h,*

HUSBAND (HUSBAND'S HUSBANDS)

1Co 7: 3 The *h* should fulfill his marital duty
7: 10 wife must not separate from her *h.*
7: 11 And a *h* must not divorce his wife.
7: 13 And if a woman has a *h* who is not
7: 39 A woman is bound to her *h* as long
2Co 1: 2 I promised you to one *h,* to Christ,
Eph 5: 23 For the *h* is the head of the wife
5: 33 and the wife must respect her *h.*
1Ti 3: 2 the *h* of but one wife, temperate,

HUSBAND'S (HUSBAND)

Pr 2: 4 of noble character is her *h* crown,
1Co 7: 4 the *h* body does not belong

HUSBANDS (HUSBAND)

Eph 5: 22 submit to your *h* as to the Lord.
5: 25 *H,* love your wives, just
Tit 2: 4 the younger women to love their *h*
1Pe 3: 1 same way be submissive to your *h*
3: 7 *H,* in the same way be considerate

HYMN

1Co 14: 26 everyone has a *h,* or a word

HYPOCRISY (HYPOCRITE HYPOCRITES)

Mt 23: 28 but on the inside you are full of *h*
1Pe 2: 1 *h,* envy, and slander of every kind.

HYPOCRITE (HYPOCRISY)

Mt 7: 5 You *h,* first take the plank out

HYPOCRITES (HYPOCRISY)

Ps 26: 4 nor do I consort with *h;*
Mt 6: 5 when you pray, do not be like the *h*

HYSSOP

Ps 51: 7 with *h,* and I will be clean;

IDLE (IDLENESS)

1Th 5: 14 those who are *i,* encourage
2Th 3: 6 away from every brother who is *i*
1Ti 5: 13 they get into the habit of being *i*

IDLENESS* (IDLE)

Pr 31: 27 and does not eat the bread of *i.*

IDOL (IDOLATRY IDOLS)

Isa 44: 17 From the rest he makes a god, his *i;*
1Co 3: 4 We know that an *i* is nothing at all

IDOLATRY (IDOL)

Col 3: 5 evil desires and greed, which is *i.*

IDOLS (IDOL)

1Co 8: 1 Now about food sacrificed to *i:*

IGNORANT (IGNORE)

1Co 15: 34 for there are some who are *i* of God
Heb 5: 2 to deal gently with those who are *i*
1Pe 2: 15 good you should silence the *i* talk
2Pe 3: 16 which *i* and unstable people distort

IGNORE (IGNORANT IGNORES)

Dt 22: 1 do not *i* it but be sure
Ps 9: 12 he does not *i* the cry of the afflicted
Heb 2: 3 if we *i* such a great salvation?

IGNORES (IGNORE)

Pr 10: 17 whoever *i* correction leads others
15: 32 He who *i* discipline despises

ILLUMINATED*

Rev 18: 1 and the earth was *i* by his splendor.

IMAGE

Ge 1: 26 "Let us make man in our *i,*
1: 27 So God created man in his own *i,*
1Co 11: 7 since he is the *i* and glory of God;
Col 1: 15 He is the *i* of the invisible God,
3: 10 in knowledge in the *i* of its Creator.

IMAGINE

Eph 3: 20 more than all we ask or *i,*

IMITATE (IMITATORS)

1Co 4: 16 Therefore I urge you to *i* me.
Heb 6: 12 but to *i* those who through faith
13: 7 of their way of life and *i* their faith.
3Jn : 11 do not *i* what is evil but what is

IMITATORS* (IMITATE)

Eph 5: 1 Be *i* of God, therefore,
1Th 1: 6 You became *i* of us and of the Lord
2: 14 became *i* of God's churches

IMMANUEL

Isa 7: 14 birth to a son, and will call him *I.*
Mt 1: 23 and they will call him *I* "—

IMMORAL* (IMMORALITY)

Pr 6: 24 keeping you from the *i* woman,
1Co 5: 9 to associate with sexually *i* people
5: 10 the people of this world who are *i,*
5: 11 but is sexually *i* or greedy,
6: 9 Neither the sexually *i* nor idolaters
Eph 5: 5 No *i,* impure or greedy person—
Heb 12: 16 See that no one is sexually *i,*
13: 4 the adulterer and all the sexually *i.*
Rev 21: 8 the murderers, the sexually *i,*
22: 15 the sexually *i,* the murderers,

IMMORALITY (IMMORAL)

1Co 6: 13 The body is not meant for sexual *i,*
6: 18 Flee from sexual *i.*
10: 8 We should not commit sexual *i,*
Gal 5: 19 sexual *i,* impurity and debauchery;
Eph 5: 3 must not be even a hint of sexual *i,*
1Th 4: 3 that you should avoid sexual *i;*
Jude : 4 grace of our God into a license for *i*

IMMORTAL* (IMMORTALITY)

Ro 1: 23 glory of the *i* God for images made
1Ti 1: 17 Now to the King eternal, *i,*
6: 16 who alone is *i* and who lives

IMMORTALITY (IMMORTAL)

Ro 2: 7 honor and *i,* he will give eternal life
1Co 15: 53 and the mortal with *i.*
2Ti 1: 10 and *i* to light through the gospel.

IMPERISHABLE

1Pe 1: 23 not of perishable seed, but of *i,*

IMPORTANCE* (IMPORTANT)

1Co 15: 3 passed on to you as of first *i:*

IMPORTANT (IMPORTANCE)

Mt 6: 25 Is not life more *i* than food,
23: 23 have neglected the more *i* matters
Mk 12: 29 "The most *i* one," answered Jesus,
12: 33 as yourself is more *i* than all burnt
Php 1: 18 The *i* thing is that in every way,

IMPOSSIBLE

Mt 17: 20 Nothing will be *i* for you."
Lk 1: 37 For nothing is *i* with God."
18: 27 "What is *i* with men is possible
Heb 6: 18 things in which it is *i* for God to lie,
11: 6 without faith it is *i* to please God,

IMPROPER*

Eph 5: 3 these are *i* for God's holy people.

IMPURE (IMPURITY)

Ac 10: 15 not call anything *i* that God has
Eph 5: 5 No immoral, *i* or greedy person—
1Th 4: 7 For God did not call us to be *i,*
Rev 21: 27 Nothing *i* will ever enter it,

IMPURITY (IMPURE)

Ro 1: 24 hearts to sexual *i* for the degrading
Eph 5: 3 or of any kind of *i,* or of greed,

INCENSE

Ex 40: 5 Place the gold altar of *i* in front
Ps 141: 2 my prayer be set before you like *i;*
Mt 2: 11 him with gifts of gold and of *i*

INCOME

Ecc 5: 10 wealth is never satisfied with his *i.*
1Co 16: 2 sum of money in keeping with his *i,*

INCOMPARABLE*

Eph 2: 7 ages he might show the *i* riches

INCREASE (EVER-INCREASING INCREASED INCREASES INCREASING)

Ge 1: 22 "Be fruitful and *i* in number
Ps 62: 10 though your riches *i,*
Isa 9: 7 Of the *i* of his government
Lk 17: 5 said to the Lord, "*I* our faith!"
1Th 3: 12 May the Lord make your love *i*

INCREASED (INCREASE)

Ac 6: 7 of disciples in Jerusalem *i* rapidly,
Ro 5: 20 But where sin *i,* grace *i* all the more

INCREASES (INCREASE)

Pr 24: 5 and a man of knowledge *i* strength;

INCREASING (INCREASE)

Ac 6: 1 when the number of disciples was *i,*
2Th 1: 3 one of you has for eacn other is *i.*
2Pe 1: 8 these qualities in *i* measure,

INDEPENDENT*

1Co 11: 11 however, woman is not *i* of man,
11: 11 of man, nor is man *i* of woman.

INDESCRIBABLE*

2Co 9: 15 Thanks be to God for his *i* gift!

INDISPENSABLE*

1Co 12: 22 seem to be weaker are *i,*

INEFFECTIVE*

2Pe 1: 8 they will keep you from being *i*

INEXPRESSIBLE*

2Co 12: 4 He heard *i* things, things that man
1Pe 1: 8 are filled with an *i* and glorious joy,

INFANTS

Mt 21: 16 "'From the lips of children and *i*
1Co 14: 20 In regard to evil be *i,*

INFIRMITIES

Isa 53: 4 Surely he took up our *i*

INHERIT (CO-HEIRS HEIRS HERITAGE INHERITANCE)

Ps 37: 11 But the meek will *i* the land
37: 29 the righteous will *i* the land
Mt 5: 5 for they will *i* the earth.
Mk 10: 17 "what must I do to *i* eternal life?"
1Co 15: 50 blood cannot *i* the kingdom of God

INHERITANCE (INHERIT)

Dt 4: 20 to be the people of his *i,*
Pr 13: 22 A good man leaves an *i*
Eph 1: 14 who is a deposit guaranteeing our *i*
5: 5 has any *i* in the kingdom of Christ
Heb 9: 15 receive the promised eternal *i*—
1Pe 1: 4 and into an *i* that can never perish,

INIQUITIES (INIQUITY)

Ps 78: 38 he forgave their *i*
103: 10 or repay us according to our *i.*
Isa 59: 2 But your *i* have separated
Mic 7: 19 and hurl all our *i* into the depths

INIQUITY (INIQUITIES)

Ps 51: 2 Wash away all my *i*
Isa 53: 6 the *i* of us all.

INJUSTICE

2Ch 19: 7 the LORD our God there is no *i*

INNOCENT

Pr 17: 26 It is not good to punish an *i* man,
Mt 10: 16 shrewd as snakes and as *i* as doves.
27: 4 "for I have betrayed *i* blood."
1Co 4: 4 but that does not make me *i.*

INSCRIPTION

Mt 22: 20 And whose *i?*" "Caesar's,"

INSOLENT

Ro 1: 30 God-haters, *i,* arrogant

INSTITUTED

Ro 13: 2 rebelling against what God has *i,*
1Pe 2: 13 to every authority *i* among men:

INSTRUCT (INSTRUCTION)

Ps 32: 8 I will *i* you and teach you
Pr 9: 9 *I* a wise man and he will be wiser
Ro 15: 14 and competent to *i* one another.
2Ti 2: 25 who oppose him he must gently *i,*

INSTRUCTION (INSTRUCT)

Pr 1: 8 Listen, my son, to your father's *i*
4: 1 Listen, my sons, to a father's *i;*
4: 13 Hold on to *i,* do not let it go;
8: 10 Choose my *i* instead of silver,
8: 33 Listen to my *i* and be wise;
13: 1 A wise son heeds his father's *i,*
13: 13 He who scorns *i* will pay for it,
16: 20 Whoever gives heed to *i* prospers,
16: 21 and pleasant words promote *i.*
19: 20 Listen to advice and accept *i,*
23: 12 Apply your heart to *i*
1Co 14: 6 or prophecy or word of *i?*
14: 26 or a word of *i,* a revelation,
Eph 6: 4 up in the training and *i* of the Lord.
1Th 4: 8 he who rejects this *i* does not reject
2Th 3: 14 If anyone does not obey our *i*
1Ti 1: 18 I give you this *i* in keeping
6: 3 to the sound *i* of our Lord Jesus
2Ti 4: 2 with great patience and careful *i.*

INSULT

Pr 9: 7 corrects a mocker invites *i;*
12: 16 but a prudent man overlooks an *i.*
Mt 5: 11 Blessed are you when people *i* you,
Lk 6: 22 when they exclude you and *i* you
1Pe 3: 9 evil with evil or *i* with *i,*

INTEGRITY

1Ki 9: 4 if you walk before me in *i* of heart
Job 2: 3 And he still maintains his *i,*
27: 5 till I die, I will not deny my *i.*
Pr 10: 9 The man of *i* walks securely,
11: 3 The *i* of the upright guides them,
29: 10 Bloodthirsty men hate a man of *i*
Tit 2: 7 your teaching show *i,* seriousness

INTELLIGENCE

Isa 29: 14 the *i* of the intelligent will vanish."
1Co 1: 19 *i* of the intelligent I will frustrate."

INTELLIGIBLE

1Co 14: 19 I would rather speak five *i* words

INTERCEDE (INTERCEDES INTERCESSION)

Heb 7: 25 he always lives to *i* for them.

INTERCEDES (INTERCEDE)

Ro 8: 26 but the Spirit himself *i* for us

INTERCESSION* (INTERCEDE)

Isa 53: 12 and made *i* for the transgressors.
1Ti 2: 1 *i* and thanksgiving be made

INTERESTS

1Co 7: 34 his wife—and his *i* are divided.
Php 2: 4 only to your own *i,* but also to the *i*
2: 21 everyone looks out for his own *i,*

INTERMARRY (MARRY)

Dt 7: 3 Do not *i* with them.

INVENTED*

2Pe 1: 16 We did not follow cleverly *i* stories

INVESTIGATED

Lk 1: 3 I myself have carefully *i* everything

INVISIBLE

Ro 1: 20 of the world God's *i* qualities—
Col 1: 15 He is the image of the *i* God,
1Ti 1: 17 immortal, *i,* the only God,

INVITE (INVITED INVITES)

Lk 14: 13 you give a banquet, *i* the poor,

INVITED (INVITE)

Mt 22: 14 For many are *i,* but few are chosen
25: 35 I was a stranger and you *i* me in,

INVITES (INVITE)

1Co 10: 27 If some unbeliever *i* you to a meal

INVOLVED

2Ti 2: 4 a soldier gets *i* in civilian affairs—

IRON

1Ti 4: 2 have been seared as with a hot *i.*
Rev 2: 27 He will rule them with an *i* scepter;

IRREVOCABLE*

Ro 11: 29 for God's gifts and his call are *i.*

ISAAC

Son of Abraham by Sarah (Ge 17:19; 21:1-7; 1Ch 1:28). Offered up by Abraham (Ge 22; Heb 11:17-19). Rebekah taken as wife (Ge 24).

Fathered Esau and Jacob (Ge 25:19-26; 1Ch 1:34). Tricked into blessing Jacob (Ge 27). Father of Israel (Ex 3:6; Dt 29:13; Ro 9:10).

ISAIAH

Prophet to Judah (Isa 1:1). Called by the LORD (Isa 6).

ISHMAEL

Son of Abraham by Hagar (Ge 16; 1Ch 1:28). Blessed, but not son of covenant (Ge 17:18-21; Gal 4:21-31). Sent away by Sarah (Ge 21:8-21).

ISRAEL (ISRAELITES)

1. Name given to Jacob (see JACOB).
2. Corporate name of Jacob's descendants; often specifically Northern Kingdom.

Dt 6: 4 Hear, O *I:* The LORD our God,
1Sa 4: 21 "The glory has departed from *I*"—
Isa 27: 6 *I* will bud and blossom
Jer 31: 10 'He who scattered *I* will gather
Eze 39: 23 of *I* went into exile for their sin,
Mk 12: 29 'Hear, O *I,* the Lord our God,
Lk 22: 30 judging the twelve tribes of *I.*
Ro 9: 6 all who are descended from *I* are *I.*
11: 26 And so all *I* will be saved,
Eph 3: 6 Gentiles are heirs together with *I,*

ISRAELITES (ISRAEL)

Ex 14: 22 and the *I* went through the sea
16: 35 The *I* ate manna forty years,
Hos 1: 10 "Yet the *I* will be like the sand
Ro 9: 27 the number of the *I* be like the sand

ITCHING*

2Ti 4: 3 to say what their *i* ears want to hear

JACOB

Second son of Isaac, twin of Esau (Ge 26:21-26; 1Ch 1:34). Bought Esau's birthright (Ge 26:29-34); tricked Isaac into blessing him (Ge 27:1-37). Abrahamic covenant perpetuated through (Ge 28:13-15; Mal 1:2). Vision at Bethel (Ge 28:10-22). Wives and children (Ge 29:1-30:24; 35:16-26; 1Ch 2-9). Wrestled with God; name changed to Israel (Ge 32:22-32). Sent sons to Egypt during famine (Ge 42-43). Settled in Egypt (Ge 46). Blessed Ephraim and Manasseh (Ge 48) Blessed sons (Ge 49:1-28; Heb 11:21). Death (Ge 49:29-33). Burial (Ge 50:1-14).

JAMES

1. Apostle; brother of John (Mt 4:21-22; 10:2; Mk 3:17; Lk 5:1-10). At transfiguration (Mt 17:1-13; Mk 9:1-13; Lk 9:28-36). Killed by Herod (Ac 12:2).
2. Apostle; son of Alphaeus (Mt 10:3; Mk 3:18; Lk 6:15).
3. Brother of Jesus (Mt 13:55; Mk 6:3; Lk 24:10; Gal 1:19) and Judas (Jude 1). With believers before Pentecost (Ac 1:13). Leader of church at Jerusalem (Ac 12:17; 15; 21:18; Gal 2:9, 12). Author of epistle (Jas 1:1).

JAPHETH

Son of Noah (Ge 5:32; 1Ch 1:4-5). Blessed (Ge 9:18-28).

JARS

2Co 4: 7 we have this treasure in *j* of clay

JEALOUS (JEALOUSY)

Ex 20: 5 the LORD your God, am a *j* God,
34: 14 whose name is Jealous, is a *j* God.
Dt 4: 24 God is a consuming fire, a *j* God.
Joel 2: 18 the LORD will be *j* for his land
Zec 1: 14 I am very *j* for Jerusalem and Zion,
2Co 11: 2 I am *j* for you with a godly jealousy

JEALOUSY (JEALOUS)

1Co 3: 3 For since there is *j* and quarreling
2Co 11: 2 I am jealous for you with a godly *j.*
Gal 5: 20 hatred, discord, *j,* fits of rage,

JEHOAHAZ

1. Son of Jehu; king of Israel (2Ki 13:1-9).
2. Son of Josiah; king of Judah (2Ki 23:31-34; 2Ch 36:1-4).

JEHOASH

Son of Jehoahaz; king of Israel (2Ki 13-14; 2Ch 25).

JEHOIACHIN

Son of Jehoiakim; king of Judah exiled by Nebuchadnezzar (2Ki 24:8-17; 2Ch 36:8-10; Jer 22:24-30; 24:1). Raised from prisoner status (2Ki 25:27-30; Jer 52:31-34).

JEHOIAKIM

Son of Josiah; king of Judah (2Ki 23:34-24:6; 2Ch 36:4-8; Jer 22:18-23; 36).

JEHORAM

Son of Jehoshaphat; king of Judah (2Ki 8:16-24).

JEHOSHAPHAT

Son of Asa; king of Judah (1Ki 22:41-50; 2Ki 3; 2Ch 17-20).

JEHU

King of Israel (1Ki 19:16-19; 2Ki 9-10).

JEPHTHAH

Judge from Gilead who delivered Israel from Ammon (Jdg 10:6-12:7). Made rash vow concerning his daughter (Jdg 11:30-40).

JEREMIAH

Prophet to Judah (Jer 1:1-3). Called by the LORD (Jer 1). Put in stocks (Jer 20:1-3). Threatened for prophesying (Jer 11:18-23; 26). Opposed by Hananiah (Jer 28). Scroll burned (Jer 36).Imprisoned (Jer 37). Thrown into cistern (Jer 38). Forced to Egypt with those fleeing Babylonians (Jer 43).

JEROBOAM

1. Official of Solomon; rebelled to become first king of Israel (1Ki 11:26-40; 12:1-20; 2Ch 10). Idolatry (1Ki 12:25-33); judgment for (1Ki 13-14; 2Ch 13).
2. Son of Jehoash; king of Israel (1Ki 14:23-29).

JERUSALEM

2Ki 23: 27 and I will reject *J,* the city I chose,
2Ch 6: 6 now I have chosen *J* for my Name
Ne 2: 17 Come, let us rebuild the wall of *J,*
Ps 122: 6 Pray for the peace of *J:*
125: 2 As the mountains surround *J,*
137: 5 If I forget you, O *J,*
Isa 40: 9 You who bring good tidings to *J,*
65: 18 for I will create *J* to be a delight
Joel 3: 17 *J* will be holy;
Zep 3: 16 On that day they will say to *J,*
Zec 2: 4 '*J* will be a city without walls
8: 8 I will bring them back to live in *J;*
14: 8 living water will flow out from *J,*
Mt 23: 37 "O *J, J,* you who kill the prophets
Lk 13: 34 die outside *J!* "O *J, J,*
21: 24 *J* will be trampled
Jn 4: 20 where we must worship is in *J.*"
Ac 1: 8 and you will be my witnesses in *J,*
Gal 4: 25 corresponds to the present city of *J*
Rev 21: 2 I saw the Holy City, the new *J,*

JESUS

LIFE: Genealogy (Mt 1:1-17; Lk 3:21-37). Birth announced (Mt 1:18-25; Lk 1:26-45). Birth (Mt 2:1-12; Lk 2:1-40). Escape to Egypt (Mt 2:13-23). As a boy in the temple (Lk 2:41-52). Baptism (Mt 3:13-17; Mk 1:9-11; Lk 3:21-22; Jn 1:32-34). Temptation (Mt 4:1-11; Mk 1:12-13; Lk 4:1-13). Ministry in Galilee (Mt 4:12-18:35; Mk 1:14-9:50; Lk 4:14-13:9; Jn 1:35-2:11; 4; 6), Transfiguration (Mt 17:1-8; Mk 9:2-8; Lk 9:28-36), on the way to Jerusalem (Mt 19-20; Mk 10; Lk 13:10-19:27), in Jerusalem (Mt 21-25; Mk 11-13; Lk 19:28-21:38; Jn 2:12-3:36; 5; 7-12). Last supper (Mt 26:17-35; Mk 14:12-31; Lk 22:1-38; Jn 13-17). Arrest and trial (Mt 26:36-27:31; Mk 14:43-15:20; Lk 22:39-23:25; Jn 18:1-19:16). Crucifixion (Mt 27:32-66; Mk 15:21-47; Lk 23:26-55; Jn 19:28-42). Resurrection and appearances (Mt 28; Mk 16; Lk 24; Jn 20-21; Ac 1:1-11; 7:56; 9:3-6; 1Co 15:1-8; Rev 1:1-20).

MIRACLES. Healings: official's son (Jn 4:43-54), demoniac in Capernaum (Mk 1:23-26; Lk 4:33-35), Peter's mother-in-law (Mt 8:14-17; Mk 1:29-31; Lk 4:38-39), leper (Mt 8:2-4; Mk 1:40-45; Lk 5:12-16), paralytic (Mt 9:1-8; Mk 2:1-12; Lk 5:17-26), cripple (Jn 5:1-9), shriveled hand (Mt 12:10-13; Mk 3:1-5; Lk 6:6-11), centurion's servant (Mt 8:5-13; Lk 7:1-10), widow's son raised (Lk 7:11-17), demoniac (Mt 12:22-23; Lk 11:14), Gadarene demoniacs (Mt 8:28-34; Mk 5:1-20; Lk 8:26-39), woman's bleeding and Jairus' daughter (Mt 9:18-26; Mk 5:21-43; Lk 8:40-56), blind man (Mt 9:27-31), mute man (Mt 9:32-33), Canaanite woman's daughter (Mt 15:21-28; Mk 7:24-30), deaf man (Mk 7:31-37), blind man (Mk 8:22-26), demoniac boy (Mt 17:14-18; Mk 9:14-29; Lk 9:37-43), ten lepers (Lk 17:11-19), man born blind (Jn 9:1-7), Lazarus raised (Jn 11), crippled woman (Lk 13:11-17), man with dropsy (Lk 14:1-6), two blind men (Mt 20:29-34; Mk 10:46-52; Lk 18:35-43), Malchus' ear (Lk 22:50-51). Other Miracles: water to wine (Jn 2:1-11), catch of fish (Lk 5:1-11), storm stilled (Mt 8:23-27; Mk 4:37-41; Lk 8:22-25), 5,000 fed (Mt 14:15-21; Mk 6:35-44; Lk 9:10-17; Jn 6:1-14), walking on water (Mt 14:25-33; Mk 6:48-52; Jn 6:15-21), 4,000 fed (Mt 15:32-39; Mk 8:1-9), money from fish (Mt 17:24-27), fig tree cursed (Mt 21:18-22; Mk 11:12-14), catch of fish (Jn 21:1-14).

MAJOR TEACHING: Sermon on the Mount (Mt 5-7; Lk 6:17-49), to Nicodemus (Jn 3), to Samaritan woman (Jn 4), Bread of Life (Jn 6:22-59), at Feast of Tabernacles (Jn 7-8), woes to Pharisees (Mt 23; Lk 11:37-54), Good Shepherd (Jn 10:1-18), Olivet Discourse (Mt 24-25; Mk 13; Lk 21:5-36), Upper Room Discourse (Jn 13-16).

PARABLES: Sower (Mt 13:3-23; Mk 4:3-25; Lk 8:5-18), seed's growth (Mk 4:26-29), wheat and weeds (Mt 13:24-30, 36-43), mustard seed (Mt 13:31-32; Mk 4:30-32), yeast (Mt 13:33-35; Mk 4:33-34), hidden treasure (Mt 13:44), valuable pearl (Mt 13:45-46), net (Mt 13:47-51), house owner (Mt 13:52), good Samaritan (Lk 10:25-37), unmerciful servant (Mt 18:15-35), lost sheep (Mt 18:10-14; Lk 15:4-7), lost coin (Lk 15:8-10), prodigal son (Lk 15:11-32), dishonest manager (Lk 16:1-13), rich man and Lazarus (Lk 16:19-31), persistent widow (Lk 18:1-8), Pharisee and tax collector (Lk 18:9-14), payment of workers (Mt 20:1-16), tenants and the vineyard (Mt 21:28-46; Mt 12:1-12; Lk 20:9-19), wedding banquet (Mt 22:1-14), faithful servant (Mt 24:45-51), ten virgins (Mt 25:1-13), talents (Mt 25:1-30; Lk 19:12-27).

DISCIPLES see APOSTLES. Call of (Jn 1:35-51; Mt 4:18-22; 9:9; Mk 1:16-20; 2:13-14; Lk 5:1-11, 27-28). Named Apostles (Mk 3:13-19; Lk 6:12-16). Twelve sent out (Mt 10; Mk 6:7-11; Lk 9:1-5). Seventy sent out (Lk 10:1-24). Defection of (Jn 6:60-71; Mt 26:56; Mk 14:50-52). Final commission (Mt 28:16-20; Jn 21:15-23; Ac 1:3-8).

Ac 2: 32 God has raised this *J* to life,
9: 5 "I am *J*, whom you are persecuting
15: 11 of our Lord *J* that we are saved,
16: 31 "Believe in the Lord *J*,
Ro 3: 24 redemption that came by Christ *J*.
5: 17 life through the one man, *J* Christ.
8: 1 for those who are in Christ *J*,
1Co 2: 2 except *J* Christ and him crucified.
8: 6 and there is but one Lord, *J* Christ,
12: 3 and no one can say, "*J* is Lord,"
2Co 4: 5 not preach ourselves, but *J* Christ
Gal 2: 16 but by faith in *J* Christ.
3: 28 for you are all one in Christ *J*.
5: 6 in Christ *J* neither circumcision
Eph 2: 10 created in Christ *J*
2: 20 with Christ *J* himself as the chief
Php 1: 6 until the day of Christ *J*.
2: 5 be the same as that of Christ *J*:
2: 10 name of *J* every knee should bow,
Col 3: 17 do it all in the name of the Lord *J*,
2Th 2: 1 the coming of our Lord *J* Christ
1Ti 1: 15 Christ *J* came into the world
2Ti 3: 12 life in Christ *J* will be persecuted,
Tit 2: 13 our great God and Savior, *J* Christ,
Heb 2: 9 But we see *J*, who was made a little
3: 1 fix your thoughts on *J*, the apostle
4: 14 through the heavens, *J* the Son
7: 22 *J* has become the guarantee
7: 24 but because *J* lives forever,
12: 2 Let us fix our eyes on *J*, the author
2Pe 1: 16 and coming of our Lord *J* Christ,
1Jn 1: 7 and the blood of *J*, his Son,
2: 1 *J* Christ, the Righteous One.
2: 6 to live in him must walk as *J* did.
4: 15 anyone acknowledges that *J* is
Rev 22: 20 Come, Lord *J*.

JEW (JEWS JUDAISM)

Zec 8: 23 of one *J* by the edge of his robe
Ro 1: 16 first for the *J*, then for the Gentile.
10: 12 there is no difference between *J*
1Co 9: 20 To the Jews I became like a *J*,
Gal 3: 28 There is neither *J* nor Greek,

JEWELRY (JEWELS)

1Pe 3: 3 wearing of gold *j* and fine clothes.

JEWELS (JEWELRY)

Isa 61: 10 as a bride adorns herself with her *j*.
Zec 9: 16 like *j* in a crown.

JEWS (JEW)

Mt 2: 2 who has been born king of the *J*?
27: 11 "Are you the king of the *J*?" "Yes,
Jn 4: 22 for salvation is from the *J*.
Ro 3: 29 Is God the God of *J* only?
1Co 1: 22 *J* demand miraculous signs
9: 20 To the *J* I became like a Jew,
12: 13 whether *J* or Greeks, slave or free
Gal 2: 8 of Peter as an apostle to the *J*,
Rev 3: 9 claim to be *J* though they are not,

JEZEBEL

Sidonian wife of Ahab (1Ki 16:31). Promoted Baal worship (1Ki 16:32-33). Killed prophets of the LORD (1Ki 18:4, 13). Opposed Elijah (1Ki 19:1-2). Had Naboth killed (1Ki 21). Death prophesied (1Ki 21:17-24). Killed by Jehu (2Ki 9:30-37).

JOASH

Son of Ahaziah; king of Judah. Sheltered from Athaliah by Jehoiada (2Ki 11; 2Ch 22:10-23:21). Repaired temple (2Ki 12; 2Ch 24).

JOB

Wealthy man from Uz; feared God (Job 1:1-5). Righteousness tested by disaster (Job 1:6-22), personal affliction (Job 2). Maintained innocence in debate with three friends (Job 3-31), Elihu (Job 32-37). Rebuked by the LORD (Job 38-41). Vindicated and restored to greater stature by the LORD (Job 42). Example of righteousness (Eze 14:14, 20).

JOHN

1. Son of Zechariah and Elizabeth (Lk 1). Called the Baptist (Mt 3:1-12; Mk 1:2-8). Witness to Jesus (Mt 3:11-12; Mk 1:7-8; Lk 3:15-18; Jn 1:6-35; 3:27-30; 5:33-36). Doubts about Jesus (Mt 11:2-6; Lk 7:18-23). Arrest (Mt 4:12; Mk 1:14). Execution (Mt 14:1-12; Mk 6:14-29; Lk 9:7-9). Ministry compared to Elijah (Mt 11:7-19; Mk 9:11-13; Lk 7:24-35).

2. Apostle; brother of James (Mt 4:21-22; 10:2; Mk 3:17; Lk 5:1-10). At transfiguration (Mt 17:1-13; Mk 9:1-13; Lk 9:28-36). Desire to be greatest (Mk 10:35-45). Leader of church at Jerusalem (Ac 4:1-3; Gal 2:9). Elder who wrote epistles (2Jn 1; 3Jn 1). Prophet who wrote Revelation (Rev 1:1; 22:8).

3. Cousin of Barnabas, co-worker with Paul, (Ac 12:12-13:13; 15:37), see MARK.

JOIN (JOINED)

Pr 23: 20 Do not *j* those who drink too much
24: 21 and do not *j* with the rebellious,
Ro 15: 30 to *j* me in my struggle by praying
2Ti 1: 8 *j* with me in suffering for the gospel

JOINED (JOIN)

Mt 19: 6 Therefore what God has *j* together,
Mk 10: 9 Therefore what God has *j* together,
Eph 2: 21 him the whole building is *j* together
4: 16 *j* and held together

JOINTS

Heb 4: 12 even to dividing soul and spirit, *j*

JOKING

Eph 5: 4 or coarse *j*, which are out of place,

JONAH

Prophet in days of Jeroboam II (2Ki 14:25). Called to Nineveh; fled to Tarshish (Jnh 1:1-3). Cause of storm; thrown into sea (Jnh 1:4-16). Swallowed by fish (Jnh 1:17). Prayer (Jnh 2). Preached to Nineveh (Jnh 3). Attitude reproved by the LORD (Jnh 4). Sign of (Mt 12:39-41; Lk 11:29-32).

JONATHAN

Son of Saul (1Sa 13:16; 1Ch 8:33). Valiant warrior (1Sa 13-14). Relation to David (1Sa 18:1-4; 19-20; 23:16-18). Killed at Gilboa (1Sa 31). Mourned by David (2Sa 1).

JORAM

Son of Ahab; king of Israel (2Ki 3; 8-9; 2Ch 22).

JORDAN

Nu 34: 12 boundary will go down along the *J*
Jos 4: 22 Israel crossed the *J* on dry ground.'
Mt 3: 6 baptized by him in the *J* River.

JOSEPH

1. Son of Jacob by Rachel (Ge 30:24; 1Ch 2:2). Favored by Jacob, hated by brothers (Ge 37:3-4). Dreams (Ge 37:5-11). Sold by brothers (Ge 37:12-36). Served Potiphar; imprisoned by false accusation (Ge 39). Interpreted dreams of Pharaoh's servants (Ge 40), of Pharaoh (Ge 41:4-40). Made greatest in Egypt (Ge 41:41-57). Sold grain to brothers (Ge 42-45). Brought Jacob and sons to Egypt (Ge 46-47). Sons Ephraim and Manas-Zseh blessed (Ge 48). Blessed (Ge 49:22-26; Dt 33:13-17). Death (Ge 50:22-26; Ex 13:19; Heb 11:22). 12,000 from (Rev 7:8).

2. Husband of Mary, mother of Jesus (Mt 1:16-24; 2:13-19; Lk 1:27; 2; Jn 1:45).

3. Disciple from Arimathea, who gave his tomb for Jesus' burial (Mt 27:57-61; Mk 15:43-47; Lk 24:50-52).

4. Original name of Barnabas (Ac 4:36).

JOSHUA

1. Son of Nun; name changed from Hoshea (Nu 13:8, 16; 1Ch 7:27). Fought Amalekites under Moses (Ex 17:9-14). Servant of Moses on Sinai (Ex 24:13; 32:17). Spied Canaan (Nu 13). With Caleb, allowed to enter land (Nu 14:6, 30). Succeeded Moses (Dt 1:38; 31 1-8; 34:9).

Charged Israel to conquer Canaan (Jos 1). Crossed Jordan (Jos 3-4). Circumcised sons of wilderness wanderings (Jos 5). Conquered Jericho (Jos 6), Ai (Jos 7-8), five kings at Gibeon (Jos 10:1-28), southern Canaan (Jos 10:29-43), northern Canaan (Jos 11-12). Defeated at Ai (Jos 7. Deceived by Gibeonites (Jos 9). Renewed covenant (Jos 8:30-35; 24:1-27). Divided land among tribes (Jos 13-22). Last words (Jos 23). Death (Jos 24:28-31).

2. High priest during rebuilding of temple (Hag 1 2; Zec 3:1-9; 6:11).

JOSIAH

Son of Amon; king of Judah (2Ki 22-23; 2Ch 34-35).

JOTHAM

Son of Azariah (Uzziah); king of Judah (2Ki 15:32-38; 2Ch 26:21-27:9).

JOY (ENJOY ENJOYMENT JOYFUL OVERJOYED REJOICE REJOICES REJOICING)

Dt 16: 15 and your *j* will be complete.
1Ch 16: 27 strength and *j* in his dwelling place.
Ne 8: 10 for the *j* of the LORD is your
Est 9: 22 their sorrow was turned into *j*
Job 38: 7 and all the angels shouted for *j*?
Ps 4: 7 have filled my heart with greater *j*
21: 6 with the *j* of your presence.
30: 11 sackcloth and clothed me with *j*,
43: 4 to God, my *j* and my delight.
51: 12 to me the *j* of your salvation
66: 1 Shout with *j* to God, all the earth!
96: 12 the trees of the forest will sing for *j*;
107: 22 and tell of his works with songs of *j*
119:111 they are the *j* of my heart.
Pr 10: 1 A wise son brings *j* to his father,
10: 28 The prospect of the righteous is *j*,
12: 20 but *j* for those who promote peace.
Isa 35: 10 everlasting *j* will crown their heads
51: 11 Gladness and *j* will overtake them,
55: 12 You will go out in *j*
Lk 1: 44 the baby in my womb leaped for *j*.
2: 10 news of great *j* that will be
Jn 15: 11 and that your *j* may be complete.
16: 20 but your grief will turn to *j*.
2Co 8: 2 their overflowing *j* and their
Php 2: 2 then make my *j* complete
4: 1 and long for, my *j* and crown,
1Th 2: 19 For what is our hope, our *j*,
Phm : 7 Your love has given me great *j*
Heb 12: 2 for the *j* set before him endured
Jas 1: 2 Consider it pure *j*, my brothers,
1Pe 1: 8 with an inexpressible and glorious *j*
2Jn : 4 It has given me great *j* to find some
3Jn : 4 I have no greater *j*

JOYFUL (JOY)

Ps 100: 2 come before him with *j* songs.
Hab 3: 18 I will be *j* in God my Savior.
1Th 5: 16 Be *j* always; pray continually;

JUDAH

1. Son of Jacob by Leah (Ge 29:35; 35:23; 1Ch 2:1). Tribe of blessed as ruling tribe (Ge 49:8-12; Dt 33:7).

2. Name used for people and land of Southern Kingdom.

Jer 13: 19 All *J* will be carried into exile,
Zec 10: 4 From *J* will come the cornerstone,
Heb 7: 14 that our Lord descended from *J*,

JUDAISM (JEW)

Gal 1: 13 of my previous way of life in *J*,

JUDAS

1. Apostle (Lk 6:16; Jn 14:22; Ac 1:13). Probably also called Thaddaeus (Mt 10:3; Mk 3:18).

2. Brother of James and Jesus (Mt 13:55; Mk 6:3), also called Jude (Jude 1).

3. Apostle, also called Iscariot, who betrayed Jesus (Mt 10:4; 26:14-56; Mk 3:19; 14:10-50; Lk 6:16; 22:3-53; Jn 6:71; 12:4; 13:2-30; 18:2-11). Suicide of (Mt 27:3-5; Ac 1:16-25).

JUDGE (JUDGED JUDGES JUDGING JUDGMENT)

Ge 18: 25 Will not the *J* of all the earth do
1Ch 16: 33 for he comes to *j* the earth.
Ps 9: 8 He will *j* the world in righteousness
Joel 3: 12 sit to *j* all the nations on every side.
Mt 7: 1 Do not *j*, or you too will be judged.
Jn 12: 47 For I did not come to *j* the world,
Ac 17: 31 a day when he will *j* the world
Ro 2: 16 day when God will *j* men's secrets
1Co 4: 3 indeed, I do not even *j* myself.
6: 2 that the saints will *j* the world?
Gal 2: 6 not *j* by external appearance—
2Ti 4: 1 who will *j* the living and the dead,
4: 8 which the Lord, the righteous *J*,
Jas 4: 12 There is only one Lawgiver and *J*,
4: 12 who are you to *j* your neighbor?
Rev 20: 4 who had been given authority to *j*.

JUDGED (JUDGE)

Mt 7: 1 "Do not judge, or you too will be *j*.
1Co 11: 31 But if we *j* ourselves, we would not
Jas 3: 1 who teach will be *j* more strictly.
Rev 20: 12 The dead were *j* according

JUDGES (JUDGE)

Jdg 2: 16 Then the LORD raised up *j*,
Ps 58: 11 there is a God who *j* the earth."
Heb 4: 12 it *j* the thoughts and attitudes
Rev 19: 11 With justice he *j* and makes war.

JUDGING (JUDGE)

Mt 19: 28 *j* the twelve tribes of Israel.
Jn 7: 24 Stop *j* by mere appearances,

JUDGMENT (JUDGE)

Dt 1: 17 of any man, for *j* belongs to God.
Ps 1: 5 the wicked will not stand in the *j*,
119: 66 Teach me knowledge and good *j*,
Pr 6: 32 man who commits adultery lacks *j*;
12: 11 but he who chases fantasies lacks *j*.
Ecc 12: 14 God will bring every deed into *j*,
Isa 66: 16 the LORD will execute *j*
Mt 5: 21 who murders will be subject to *j*.'
10: 15 on the day of *j* than for that town.
Mt 12: 36 have to give account on the day of *j*
Jn 5: 22 but has entrusted all *j* to the Son,
7: 24 appearances, and make a right *j*."
16: 8 to sin and righteousness and *j*:
Ro 14: 10 stand before God's *j* seat.
14: 13 Therefore let us stop passing *j*
1Co 11: 29 body of the Lord eats and drinks *j*
2Co 5: 10 appear before the *j* seat of Christ,
Heb 9: 27 to die once, and after that to face *j*,
10: 27 but only a fearful expectation of *j*
1Pe 4: 17 For it is time for *j* to begin
Jude : 6 bound with everlasting chains for *j*

JUST (JUSTICE JUSTIFICATION JUSTIFIED JUSTIFY JUSTLY)

Dt 32: 4 and all his ways are *j*.
Ps 37: 28 For the LORD loves the *j*
111: 7 of his hands are faithful and *j*;
Pr 1: 3 doing what is right and *j* and fair;
2: 8 for he guards the course of the *j*
Da 4: 37 does is right and all his ways are *j*.
Ro 3: 26 as to be *j* and the one who justifies
Heb 2: 2 received its *j* punishment,
1Jn 1: 9 and *j* and will forgive us our sins
Rev 16: 7 true and *j* are your judgments."

JUSTICE (JUST)

Ex 23: 2 do not pervert *j* by siding
23: 6 "Do not deny *j* to your poor people
Job 37: 23 in his *j* and great righteousness,
Ps 9: 8 he will govern the peoples with *j*.
9: 16 The LORD is known by his *j*;
11: 7 he loves *j*;
45: 6 a scepter of *j* will be the scepter
101: 1 I will sing of your love and *j*;
106: 3 Blessed are they who maintain *j*,
Pr 21: 15 When *j* is done, it brings joy
28: 5 Evil men do not understand *j*,
29: 4 By *j* a king gives a country stability
29: 26 from the LORD that man gets *j*.
Isa 9: 7 it with *j* and righteousness
28: 17 I will make *j* the measuring line
30: 18 For the LORD is a God of *j*.
42: 1 and he will bring *j* to the nations.
42: 4 till he establishes *j* on earth.
56: 1 "Maintain *j*
61: 8 "For I, the LORD, love *j*;

Jer 30: 11 I will discipline you but only with *j;*
Eze 34: 16 I will shepherd the flock with *j.*
Am 5: 15 maintain *j* in the courts.
5: 24 But let *j* roll on like a river,
Zec 7: 9 'Administer true *j;* show mercy
Lk 11: 42 you neglect *j* and the love of God.
Ro 3: 25 He did this to demonstrate his *j,*

JUSTIFICATION (JUST)

Ro 4: 25 and was raised to life for our *j.*
5: 18 of righteousness was *j* that brings

JUSTIFIED (JUST)

Ac 13: 39 him everyone who believes is *j*
Ro 3: 24 and are *j* freely by his grace
3: 28 For we maintain that a man is *j*
5: 1 since we have been *j* through faith,
5: 9 Since we have now been *j*
8: 30 those he called, he also *j;* those he *j,*
1Co 6: 11 you were *j* in the name
Gal 2: 16 observing the law no one will be *j.*
3: 11 Clearly no one is *j* before God
3: 24 to Christ that we might be *j* by faith
Jas 2: 24 You see that a person is *j*

JUSTIFY (JUST)

Gal 3: 8 that God would *j* the Gentiles

JUSTLY (JUST)

Mic 6: 8 To act *j* and to love mercy

KEEP (KEEPER KEEPING KEEPS KEPT)

Ge 31: 49 "May the LORD *k* watch
Ex 20: 6 and *k* my commandments.
Nu 6: 24 and *k* you;
Ps 18: 28 You, O LORD, *k* my lamp burning
19: 13 *K* your servant also from willful
119: 9 can a young man *k* his way pure?
121: 7 The LORD will *k* you
141: 3 *k* watch over the door of my lips.
Pr 4: 24 *k* corrupt talk far from your lips.
Isa 26: 3 You will *k* in perfect peace
Mt 10: 10 for the worker is worth his *k.*
Lk 12: 35 and *k* your lamps burning,
Gal 5: 25 let us *k* in step with the Spirit.
Eph 4: 3 Make every effort to *k* the unity
1Ti 5: 22 *K* yourself pure.
2Ti 4: 5 *k* your head in all situations,
Heb 13: 5 *K* your lives free from the love
Jas 1: 26 and yet does not *k* a tight rein
2: 8 If you really *k* the royal law found
Jude : 24 able to *k* you from falling

KEEPER (KEEP)

Ge 4: 9 I my brother's *k?"* The LORD

KEEPING (KEEP)

Ex 20: 8 the Sabbath day by *k* it holy.
Ps 19: 11 in *k* them there is great reward.
Mt 3: 8 Produce fruit in *k* with repentance.
Lk 2: 8 *k* watch over their flocks at night.
1Co 7: 19 *K* God's commands is what counts.
2Pe 3: 9 Lord is not slow in *k* his promise,

KEEPS (KEEP)

Pr 17: 28 a fool is thought wise if he *k* silent,
Am 5: 13 Therefore the prudent man *k* quiet
1Co 13: 5 is not easily angered, it *k* no record
Jas 2: 10 For whoever *k* the whole law

KEPT (KEEP)

Ps 130: 3 If you, O LORD, *k* a record of sins,
2Ti 4: 7 finished the race, I have *k* the faith.
1Pe 1: 4 spoil or fade—*k* in heaven for you,

KEYS

Mt 16: 19 I will give you the *k* of the kingdom

KILL (KILLS)

Mt 17: 23 They will *k* him, and on the third

KILLS (KILL)

Lev 24: 21 but whoever *k* a man must be put
2Co 3: 6 for the letter *k,* but the Spirit gives

KIND (KINDNESS KINDS)

Ge 1: 24 animals, each according to its *k."*
2Ch 10: 7 "If you will be *k* to these people
Pr 11: 17 A *k* man benefits himself,
12: 25 but a *k* word cheers him up.
14: 21 blessed is he who is *k* to the needy.
14: 31 whoever is *k* to the needy honors
19: 17 He who is *k* to the poor lends
Da 4: 27 by being *k* to the oppressed.
Lk 6: 35 because he is *k* to the ungrateful
1Co 13: 4 Love is patient, love is *k.*
15: 35 With what *k* of body will they
Eph 4: 32 Be *k* and compassionate
1Th 5: 15 but always try to be *k* to each other
2Ti 2: 24 instead, he must be *k* to everyone,
Tit 2: 5 to be busy at home, to be *k,*

KINDNESS (KIND)

Ac 14: 17 He has shown *k* by giving you rain
Ro 11: 22 Consider therefore the *k*
Gal 5: 22 peace, patience, *k,* goodness,
Eph 2: 7 expressed in his *k* to us
2Pe 1: 7 brotherly *k;* and to brotherly *k,*

KINDS (KIND)

1Co 12: 4 There are different *k* of gifts,
1Ti 6: 10 of money is a root of all *k* of evil.

KING (KINGDOM KINGS)

1. Kings of Judah and Israel: see Saul, David, Solomon.

2. Kings of Judah: see Rehoboam, Abijah, Asa, Jehoshaphat, Jehoram, Ahaziah, Athaliah (Queen), Joash, Amaziah, Uzziah, Jotham, Ahaz, Hezekiah, Manasseh, Amon, Josiah, Jehoahaz, Jehoiakim, Jehoiachin, Zedekiah.

3. Kings of Israel: see Jeroboam I, Nadab, Basha, Elah, Zimri, Tibni, Omri, Ahab, Ahaziah, Joram, Jehu, Jehoahaz, Jehoash, Jeroboam II, Zechariah, Shallum, Menahem, Pekah, Pekahiah, Hoshea.

Jdg 17: 6 In those days Israel had no *k;*
1Sa 12: 12 the LORD your God was your *k.*
Ps 24: 7 that the *K* of glory may come in.
Isa 32: 1 See, a *k* will reign in righteousness
Zec 9: 9 See, your *k* comes to you,
1Ti 6: 15 the *K* of kings and Lord of lords,
1Pe 2: 17 of believers, fear God, honor the *k.*
Rev 19: 16 *K* OF KINGS AND LORD

KINGDOM (KING)

Ex 19: 6 you will be for me a *k* of priests
1Ch 29: 11 Yours, O LORD, is the *k;*
Ps 45: 6 justice will be the scepter of your *k.*
Da 4: 3 His *k* is an eternal *k;*
Mt 3: 2 Repent, for the *k* of heaven is near
5: 3 for theirs is the *k* of heaven.
6: 10 your *k* come,
6: 33 But seek first his *k* and his
7: 21 Lord,' will enter the *k* of heaven,
11: 11 least in the *k* of heaven is greater
13: 24 "The *k* of heaven is like a man who
13: 31 *k* of heaven is like a mustard seed,
13: 33 "The *k* of heaven is like yeast that
13: 44 *k* of heaven is like treasure hidden
13: 45 the *k* of heaven is like a merchant
13: 47 *k* of heaven is like a net that was let
16: 19 the keys of the *k* of heaven;
18: 23 the *k* of heaven is like a king who
19: 24 for a rich man to enter the *k* of God
24: 7 rise against nation, and *k* against *k.*
24: 14 gospel of the *k* will be preached
25: 34 the *k* prepared for you
Mk 9: 47 better for you to enter the *k* of God
10: 14 for the *k* of God belongs to such
10: 23 for the rich to enter the *k* of God!"
Lk 10: 9 'The *k* of God is near you.'
12: 31 seek his *k,* and these things will be
17: 21 because the *k* of God is within you
Jn 3: 5 no one can enter the *k* of God
18: 36 "My *k* is not of this world.
1Co 6: 9 the wicked will not inherit the *k*
15: 24 hands over the *k* to God the Father
Rev 1: 6 has made us to be a *k* and priests

Rev 11: 15 of the world has become the *k*

KINGS (KING)

Ps 2: 2 The *k* of the earth take their stand
72: 11 All *k* will bow down to him
Da 7: 24 ten horns are ten *k* who will come
1Ti 2: 2 for *k* and all those in authority,
Rev 1: 5 and the ruler of the *k* of the earth.

KINSMAN-REDEEMER (REDEEM)

Ru 3: 9 over me, since you are a *k.*"

KISS

Ps 2: 12 *K* the Son, lest he be angry
Pr 24: 26 is like a *k* on the lips.
Lk 22: 48 the Son of Man with a *k?*"

KNEE (KNEES)

Isa 45: 23 Before me every *k* will bow;
Ro 14: 11 every *k* will bow before me;
Php 2: 10 name of Jesus every *k* should bow,

KNEES (KNEE)

Isa 35: 3 steady the *k* that give way;
Heb 12: 12 your feeble arms and weak *k.*

KNEW (KNOW)

Job 23: 3 If only I *k* where to find him;
Jnh 4: 2 I *k* that you are a gracious
Mt 7: 23 tell them plainly,'I never *k* you.

KNOCK

Mt 7: 7 *k* and the door will be opened
Rev 3: 20 I am! I stand at the door and *k.*

KNOW (FOREKNEW KNEW KNOWING KNOWLEDGE KNOWN KNOWS)

Dt 18: 21 "How can we *k* when a message
Job 19: 25 I *k* that my Redeemer lives,
42: 3 things too wonderful for me to *k.*
Ps 46: 10 "Be still, and *k* that I am God;
139: 1 and you *k* me.
139: 23 Search me, O God, and *k* my heart;
Pr 27: 1 for you do not *k* what a day may
Jer 24: 7 I will give them a heart to *k* me,
31: 34 his brother, saying, '*K* the LORD,'
Mt 6: 3 let your left hand *k* what your right
24: 42 you do not *k* on what day your
Lk 1: 4 so that you may *k* the certainty
Jn 3: 11 we speak of what we *k,*
4: 22 we worship what we do *k,*
9: 25 One thing I do *k.*
10: 14 I *k* my sheep and my sheep *k* me—
17: 3 that they may *k* you, the only true
21: 24 We *k* that his testimony is true.
Ac 1: 7 "It is not for you to *k* the times
Ro 6: 6 For we *k* that our old self was
7: 18 I *k* that nothing good lives in me,
8: 28 we *k* that in all things God works
1Co 2: 2 For I resolved to *k* nothing
6: 15 Do you not *k* that your bodies are
6: 19 Do you not *k* that your body is
1Co 13: 12 Now I *k* in part; then I shall *k* fully,
15: 58 because you *k* that your labor
Php 3: 10 I want to *k* Christ and the power
2Ti 1: 12 because I *k* whom I have believed,
Jas 4: 14 *k* what will happen tomorrow.
1Jn 2: 4 The man who says, "I *k* him,"
3: 14 We *k* that we have passed
3: 16 This is how we *k* what love is:
5: 2 This is how we *k* that we love
5: 13 so that you may *k* that you have

KNOWING (KNOW)

Ge 3: 5 and you will be like God, *k* good
Php 3: 8 of *k* Christ Jesus my Lord,

KNOWLEDGE (KNOW)

Ge 2: 9 the tree of the *k* of good and evil.
Job 42: 3 obscures my counsel without *k?*'
Ps 19: 2 night after night they display *k.*
73: 11 Does the Most High have *k?*"
139: 6 Such *k* is too wonderful for me,
Pr 1: 7 of the LORD is the beginning of *k,*
10: 14 Wise men store up *k,*
12: 1 Whoever loves discipline loves *k,*
13: 16 Every prudent man acts out of *k,*
19: 2 to have zeal without *k,*
Isa 11: 9 full of the *k* of the LORD
Hab 2: 14 filled with the *k* of the glory
Ro 11: 33 riches of the wisdom and *k* of God!
1Co 8: 1 *K* puffs up, but love builds up.
8: 11 Christ died, is destroyed by your *k.*
13: 2 can fathom all mysteries and all *k,*
2Co 2: 14 everywhere the fragrance of the *k*
4: 6 light of the *k* of the glory of God
Eph 3: 19 to know this love that surpasses *k*
Col 2: 3 all the treasures of wisdom and *k.*
1Ti 6: 20 ideas of what is falsely called *k,*
2Pe 3: 18 grow in the grace and *k* of our Lord

KNOWN (KNOW)

Ps 16: 11 You have made *k* to me the path
105: 1 make *k* among the nations what he
Isa 46: 10 *k* the end from the beginning,
Mt 10: 26 or hidden that will not be made *k.*
Ro 1: 19 since what may be *k* about God is
11: 34 "Who has *k* the mind of the Lord?
15: 20 the gospel where Christ was not *k,*
2Co 3: 2 written on our hearts, *k*
2Pe 2: 21 than to have *k* it and then

KNOWS (KNOW)

1Sa 2: 3 for the LORD is a God who *k,*
Job 23: 10 But he *k* the way that I take;
Ps 44: 21 since he *k* the secrets of the heart?
94: 11 The LORD *k* the thoughts of man;
Ecc 8: 7 Since no man *k* the future,
Mt 6: 8 for your Father *k* what you need
24: 36 "No one *k* about that day or hour,
Ro 8: 27 who searches our hearts *k* the mind
1Co 8: 2 who thinks he *k* something does
2Ti 2: 19 The Lord *k* those who are his," and

LABAN

Brother of Rebekah (Ge 24:29-51), father of Rachel and Leah (Ge 29-31).

LABOR

Ex 20: 9 Six days you shall *l* and do all your
Isa 55: 2 and your *l* on what does not satisfy
Mt 6: 28 They do not *l* or spin.
1Co 3: 8 rewarded according to his own *l.*
15: 58 because you know that your *l*

LACK (LACKING LACKS)

Pr 15: 22 Plans fail for *l* of counsel,
Ro 3: 3 Will their *l* of faith nullify God's
Col 2: 23 *l* any value in restraining sensual

LACKING (LACK)

Ro 12: 11 Never be *l* in zeal, but keep your
Jas 1: 4 and complete, not *l* anything.

LACKS (LACK)

Pr 6: 32 who commits adultery *l* judgment;
12: 11 he who chases fantasies *l* judgment
Jas 1: 5 any of you *l* wisdom, he should ask

LAID (LAY)

Isa 53: 6 and the LORD has *l* on him
1Co 3: 11 other than the one already *l,*
1Jn 3: 16 Jesus Christ *l* down his life for us.

LAKE

Rev 19: 20 into the fiery *l* of burning sulfur.
20: 14 The *l* of fire is the second death.

LAMB (LAMB'S LAMBS)

Ge 22: 8 "God himself will provide the *l*
Ex 12: 21 and slaughter the Passover *l.*
Isa 11: 6 The wolf will live with the *l,*
53: 7 he was led like a *l* to the slaughter,
Jn 1: 29 *L* of God, who takes away the sin
1Co 5: 7 our Passover *l,* has been sacrificed.
1Pe 1: 19 a *l* without blemish or defect.
Rev 5: 6 Then I saw a *L,* looking
5: 12 "Worthy is the *L,* who was slain,
14: 4 They follow the *L* wherever he

LAMB'S (LAMB)

Rev 21: 27 written in the *L* book of life.

LAMBS (LAMB)

Lk 10: 3 I am sending you out like *l*
Jn 21: 15 Jesus said, "Feed my *l.*"

LAMENT
2Sa 1: 17 took up this *l* concerning Saul

LAMP (LAMPS)
2Sa 22: 29 You are my *l*, O LORD;
Ps 18: 28 You, O LORD, keep my *l* burning;
119:105 Your word is a *l* to my feet
Pr 31: 18 and her *l* does not go out at night.
Lk 8: 16 "No one lights a *l* and hides it
Rev 21: 23 gives it light, and the Lamb is its *l*.

LAMPS (LAMP)
Mt 25: 1 be like ten virgins who took their *l*
Lk 12: 35 for service and keep your *l* burning,

LAND
Ge 1: 10 God called the dry ground *"l,"*
1: 11 "Let the *l* produce vegetation:
12: 7 To your offspring I will give this *l*."
Ex 3: 8 a *l* flowing with milk and honey—
Nu 35: 33 Do not pollute the *l* where you are.
Dt 34: 1 LORD showed him the whole *l*—
Jos 13: 2 "This is the *l* that remains:
14: 4 Levites received no share of the *l*
2Ch 7: 14 their sin and will heal their *l*.
7: 20 then I will uproot Israel from my *l*,
Eze 36: 24 and bring you back into your own *l*.

LANGUAGE
Ge 11: 1 Now the whole world had one *l*
Ps 19: 3 There is no speech or *l*
Jn 8: 44 When he lies, he speaks his native *l*
Ac 2: 6 heard them speaking in his own *l*.
Col 3: 8 slander, and filthy *l* from your lips.
Rev 5: 9 from every tribe and *l* and people

LAST (LASTING LASTS LATTER)
2Sa 23: 1 These are the *l* words of David:
Isa 44: 6 I am the first and I am the *l*;
Mt 19: 30 But many who are first will be *l*,
Mk 10: 31 are first will be *l*, and the *l* first."
Jn 15: 16 and bear fruit—fruit that will *l*.
Ro 1: 17 is by faith from first to *l*,
2Ti 3: 1 will be terrible times in the *l* days.
2Pe 3: 3 in the *l* days scoffers will come,
Rev 1: 17 I am the First and the *L*.
22: 13 the First and the *L*, the Beginning

LASTING (LAST)
Ex 12: 14 to the LORD—a *l* ordinance.
Lev 24: 8 of the Israelites, as a *l* covenant.
Nu 25: 13 have a covenant of a *l* priesthood,
Heb 10: 34 had better and *l* possessions.

LASTS (LAST)
Ps 30: 5 For his anger *l* only a moment,
2Co 3: 11 greater is the glory of that which *l*!

LATTER (LAST)
Job 42: 12 The LORD blessed the *l* part

LAUGH (LAUGHS)
Ecc 3: 4 a time to weep and a time to *l*,

LAUGHS (LAUGH)
Ps 2: 4 The One enthroned in heaven *l*;
37: 13 but the Lord *l* at the wicked,

LAVISHED
Eph 1: 8 of God's grace that he *l* on us
1Jn 3: 1 great is the love the Father has *l*

LAW (LAWS)
Dt 31: 11 you shall read this *l* before them
31: 26 "Take this Book of the *L*
Jos 1: 8 of the *L* depart from your mouth;
Ne 8: 8 from the Book of the *L* of God,
Ps 1: 2 and on his *l* he meditates day
19: 7 The *l* of the LORD is perfect,
119: 18 wonderful things in your *l*.
119: 72 *l* from your mouth is more precious
119: 97 Oh, how I love your *l*!
119:165 peace have they who love your *l*,
Isa 8: 20 To the *l* and to the testimony!
Jer 31: 33 "I will put my *l* in their minds
Mt 5: 17 that I have come to abolish the *L*
7: 12 sums up the *L* and the Prophets.
22: 40 All the *L* and the Prophets hang
Lk 16: 17 stroke of a pen to drop out of the *L*.
Jn 1: 17 For the *l* was given through Moses;
Ro 2: 12 All who sin apart from the *l* will
2: 15 of the *l* are written on their hearts,
5: 13 for before the *l* was given,
5: 20 *l* was added so that the trespass
6: 14 because you are not under *l*,
7: 6 released from the *l* so that we serve
7: 12 *l* is holy, and the commandment is
8: 3 For what the *l* was powerless to do
10: 4 Christ is the end of the *l*
13: 10 love is the fulfillment of the *l*.
Gal 3: 13 curse of the *l* by becoming a curse
3: 24 So the *l* was put in charge to lead us
5: 3 obligated to obey the whole *l*.
5: 4 justified by *l* have been alienated
5: 14 The entire *l* is summed up
Heb 7: 19 (for the *l* made nothing perfect),
10: 1 The *l* is only a shadow
Jas 1: 25 intently into the perfect *l* that gives
2: 10 For whoever keeps the whole *l*

LAWLESSNESS*
2Th 2: 3 and the man of *l* is revealed,
2: 7 power of *l* is already at work;
1Jn 3: 4 sins breaks the law; in fact, sin is *l*.

LAWS (LAW)
Lev 25: 18 and be careful to obey my *l*,
Ps 119: 30 I have set my heart on your *l*.
119:120 I stand in awe of your *l*.
Heb 8: 10 I will put my *l* in their minds
10: 16 I will put my *l* in their hearts,

LAY (LAID LAYING)
Job 22: 22 and *l* up his words in your heart.
Isa 28: 16 "See, I *l* a stone in Zion,
Mt 8: 20 of Man has no place to *l* his head."
Jn 10: 15 and I *l* down my life for the sheep.
15: 13 that he *l* down his life
1Co 3: 11 no one can *l* any foundation other
1Jn 3: 16 And we ought to *l* down our lives
Rev 4: 10 They *l* their crowns

LAYING (LAY)
1Ti 5: 22 Do not be hasty in the *l* on of hands
Heb 6: 1 not *l* again the foundation

LAZARUS
1. Poor man in Jesus' parable (Lk 16:19-31).
2. Brother of Mary and Martha whom Jesus raised from the dead (Jn 11:1-12:19).

LAZY
Pr 10: 4 *L* hands make a man poor,
Heb 6: 12 We do not want you to become *l*,

LEAD (LEADERS LEADERSHIP LEADS LED)
Ex 15: 13 "In your unfailing love you will *l*
Ps 27: 11 *l* me in a straight path.
61: 2 *l* me to the rock that is higher
139: 24 and *l* me in the way everlasting.
143: 10 *l* me on level ground.
Ecc 5: 6 Do not let your mouth *l* you
Isa 11: 6 and a little child will *l* them.
Da 12: 3 those who *l* many to righteousness,
Mt 6: 13 And *l* us not into temptation,
1Jn 3: 7 do not let anyone *l* you astray.

LEADERS (LEAD)
Heb 13: 7 Remember your *l*, who spoke
13: 17 Obey your *l* and submit

LEADERSHIP (LEAD)
Ro 12: 8 if it is *l*, let him govern diligently;

LEADS (LEAD)
Ps 23: 2 he *l* me beside quiet waters,
Pr 19: 23 The fear of the LORD *l* to life:
Isa 40: 11 he gently *l* those that have young.
Mt 7: 13 and broad is the road that *l*
15: 14 If a blind man *l* a blind man,
Jn 10: 3 sheep by name and *l* them out.
Ro 14: 19 effort to do what *l* to peace
2Co 2: 14 always *l* us in triumphal procession

LEAH
Wife of Jacob (Ge 29:16-30); bore six sons and one daughter (Ge 29:31-30:21; 34:1; 35:23).

LEAN
Pr 3: 5 *l* not on your own understanding;

LEARN (LEARNED LEARNING)

Isa 1: 17 *l* to do right!
Mt 11: 29 yoke upon you and *l* from me,

LEARNED (LEARN)

Php 4: 11 for I have *l* to be content whatever
2Ti 3: 14 continue in what you have *l*

LEARNING (LEARN)

Pr 1: 5 let the wise listen and add to their *l*,
2Ti 3: 7 always *l* but never able

LED (LEAD)

Ps 68: 18 you *l* captives in your train;
Isa 53: 7 he was *l* like a lamb to the slaughter
Am 2: 10 and I *l* you forty years in the desert
Ro 8: 14 those who are *l* by the Spirit
Eph 4: 8 he *l* captives in his train

LEFT

Jos 1: 7 turn from it to the right or to the *l*,
Pr 4: 27 Do not swerve to the right or the *l*;
Mt 6: 3 do not let your *l* hand know what
25: 33 on his right and the goats on his *l*.

LEGION

Mk 5: 9 "My name is *L*," he replied,

LEND (LENDS)

Dt 15: 8 freely *l* him whatever he needs.
Ps 37: 26 are always generous and *l* freely;
Lk 6: 34 if you *l* to those from whom you

LENDS (LEND)

Pr 19: 17 to the poor *l* to the LORD,

LENGTH (LONG)

Ps 90: 10 The *l* of our days is seventy years—
Pr 10: 27 The fear of the LORD adds *l* to life

LEPROSY

2Ki 7: 3 men with *l* at the entrance

LETTER (LETTERS)

Mt 5: 18 not the smallest *l*, not the least
2Co 3: 2 You yourselves are our *l*, written
3: 6 for the *l* kills, but the Spirit gives
2Th 3: 14 not obey our instruction in this *l*,

LETTERS (LETTER)

2Co 3: 7 which was engraved in *l* on stone,
10: 10 "His *l* are weighty and forceful,
2Pe 3: 16 His *l* contain some things that are

LEVEL

Ps 143: 10 lead me on *l* ground.
Pr 4: 26 Make *l* paths for your feet
Isa 26: 7 The path of the righteous is *l*;
Heb 12: 13 "Make *l* paths for your feet,"

LEVI (LEVITES)

1. Son of Jacob by Leah (Ge 29:34; 46:11; 1Ch 2:1). Tribe of blessed (Ge 49:5-7; Dt 33: 8-11), chosen as priests (Nu 3-4), numbered (Nu 3:39; 26:62), allotted cities, but not land (Nu 18; 35; Dt 10:9; Jos 13:14; 21), land (Eze 48:8-22), 12,000 from (Rev 7:7).
2. See MATTHEW.

LEVITES (LEVI)

Nu 1: 53 The *L* are to be responsible
8: 6 "Take the *L* from among the other
18: 21 I give to the *L* all the tithes in Israel

LEWDNESS

Mk 7: 22 malice, deceit, *l*, envy, slander,

LIAR (LIE)

Pr 19: 22 better to be poor than a *l*.
Jn 8: 44 for he is a *l* and the father of lies.
Ro 3: 4 Let God be true, and every man a *l*.

LIBERATED*

Ro 8: 21 that the creation itself will be *l*

LIE (LIAR LIED LIES LYING)

Lev 19: 11 "'Do not *l*.
Nu 23: 19 God is not a man, that he should *l*,
Dt 6: 7 when you *l* down and when you get
Ps 23: 2 me *l* down in green pastures,
Isa 11: 6 leopard will *l* down with the goat,
Eze 34: 14 they will *l* down in good grazing
Ro 1: 25 exchanged the truth of God for a *l*,
Col 3: 9 Do not *l* to each other,
Heb 6: 18 which it is impossible for God to *l*,

LIED (LIE)

Ac 5: 4 You have not *l* to men but to God."

LIES (LIE)

Ps 34: 13 and your lips from speaking *l*.
Jn 8: 44 for he is a liar and the father of *l*.

LIFE (LIVE)

Ge 2: 7 into his nostrils the breath of *l*,
2: 9 of the garden were the tree of *l*
9: 11 Never again will all *l* be cut
Ex 21: 23 you are to take *l* for *l*, eye for eye,
Lev 17: 14 the *l* of every creature is its blood.
24: 18 must make restitution—*l* for *l*.
Dt 30: 19 Now choose *l*, so that you
Ps 16: 11 known to me the path of *l*;
23: 6 all the days of my *l*,
34: 12 Whoever of you loves *l*
39: 4 let me know how fleeting is my *l*.
49: 7 No man can redeem the *l*
104: 33 I will sing to the LORD all my *l*;
Pr 1: 3 a disciplined and prudent *l*,
6: 23 are the way to *l*,
7: 23 little knowing it will cost him his *l*.
8: 35 For whoever finds me finds *l*
11: 30 of the righteous is a tree of *l*,
21: 21 finds *l*, prosperity and honor.
Jer 10: 23 that a man's *l* is not his own;
Eze 37: 5 enter you, and you will come to *l*.
Da 12: 2 some to everlasting *l*, others
Mt 6: 25 Is not *l* more important than food,
7: 14 and narrow the road that leads to *l*,
10: 39 Whoever finds his *l* will lose it,
16: 25 wants to save his *l* will lose it,
20: 28 to give his *l* as a ransom for many."
Mk 10: 45 to give his *l* as a ransom for many."
Lk 12: 15 a man's *l* does not consist
12: 22 do not worry about your *l*,
14: 26 even his own *l*—he cannot be my
Jn 1: 4 In him was *l*, and that *l* was
3: 15 believes in him may have eternal *l*.
3: 36 believes in the Son has eternal *l*,
4: 14 of water welling up to eternal *l*."
5: 24 him who sent me has eternal *l*
6: 35 Jesus declared, "I am the bread of *l*
6: 47 he who believes has everlasting *l*.
6: 68 You have the words of eternal *l*.
10: 10 I have come that they may have *l*,
10: 15 and I lay down my *l* for the sheep.
10: 28 I give them eternal *l*, and they shall
11: 25 "I am the resurrection and the *l*.
14: 6 am the way and the truth and the *l*.
15: 13 lay down his *l* for his friends.
20: 31 that by believing you may have *l*
Ac 13: 48 appointed for eternal *l* believed.
Ro 4: 25 was raised to *l* for our justification.
6: 13 have been brought from death to *l*;
6: 23 but the gift of God is eternal *l*
8: 38 convinced that neither death nor *l*,
1Co 15: 19 If only for this *l* we have hope
2Co 3: 6 letter kills, but the Spirit gives *l*.
Gal 2: 20 The *l* I live in the body, I live
Eph 4: 1 I urge you to live a *l* worthy
Php 2: 16 as you hold out the word of *l*—
Col 1: 10 order that you may live a *l* worthy
1Th 4: 12 so that your daily *l* may win
1Ti 4: 8 for both the present *l* and the *l*
4: 16 Watch your *l* and doctrine closely.
6: 19 hold of the *l* that is truly *l*.
2Ti 3: 12 to live a godly *l* in Christ Jesus will
Jas 1: 12 crown of *l* that God has promised
3: 13 Let him show it by his good *l*,
1Pe 3: 10 "Whoever would love *l*
2Pe 1: 3 given us everything we need for *l*
1Jn 3: 14 we have passed from death to *l*,
5: 11 has given us eternal *l*, and this *l* is

Rev 13: 8 written in the book of *l* belonging
20: 12 was opened, which is the book of *l.*
21: 27 written in the Lamb's book of *l.*
22: 2 side of the river stood the tree of *l,*

LIFT (LIFTED)

Ps 121: 1 I *l* up my eyes to the hills—
134: 2 *L* up your hands in the sanctuary
La 3: 41 Let us *l* up our hearts and our
1Ti 2: 8 everywhere to *l* up holy hands

LIFTED (LIFT)

Ps 40: 2 He *l* me out of the slimy pit,
Jn 3: 14 Moses *l* up the snake in the desert,
12: 32 when I am *l* up from the earth,

LIGHT (ENLIGHTENED)

Ge 1: 3 "Let there be *l,*" and there was *l.*
2Sa 22: 29 LORD turns my darkness into *l.*
Job 38: 19 "What is the way to the abode of *l?*
Ps 4: 6 Let the *l* of your face shine upon us
19: 8 giving *l* to the eyes.
27: 1 LORD is my *l* and my salvation—
56: 13 God in the *l* of life.
76: 4 You are resplendent with *l,*
104: 2 He wraps himself in *l*
119:105 and a *l* for my path.
119:130 The unfolding of your words gives *l;*
Isa 2: 5 let us walk in the *l* of the LORD.
9: 2 have seen a great *l;*
49: 6 also make you a *l* for the Gentiles,
Mt 4: 16 have seen a great *l;*
5: 16 let your *l* shine before men,
11: 30 yoke is easy and my burden is *l.*"
Jn 3: 19 but men loved darkness instead of *l*
8: 12 he said, "I am the *l* of the world.
2Co 4: 6 made his *l* shine in our hearts
6: 14 Or what fellowship can *l* have
11: 14 masquerades as an angel of *l.*
1Ti 6: 16 and who lives in unapproachable *l,*
1Pe 2: 9 of darkness into his wonderful *l.*
1Jn 1: 5 God is *l;* in him there is no
1: 7 But if we walk in the *l,*
Rev 21: 23 for the glory of God gives it *l,*

LIGHTNING

Da 10: 6 his face like *l,* his eyes like flaming
Mt 24: 27 For as the *l* that comes from the east
28: 3 His appearance was like *l,*

LIKENESS

Ge 1: 26 man in our image, in our *l,*
Ps 17: 15 I will be satisfied with seeing your *l*
Isa 52: 14 his form marred beyond human *l*—
Ro 8: 3 Son in the *l* of sinful man
8: 29 to be conformed to the *l* of his Son,
2Co 3: 18 his *l* with ever-increasing glory,
Php 2: 7 being made in human *l.*
Jas 3: 9 who have been made in God's *l.*

LILIES

Lk 12: 27 "Consider how the *l* grow.

LION

Isa 11: 7 and the *l* will eat straw like the ox.
1Pe 5: 8 around like a roaring *l* looking
Rev 5: 5 See, the *L* of the tribe of Judah,

LIPS

Ps 8: 2 From the *l* of children and infants
34: 1 his praise will always be on my *l.*
119:171 May my *l* overflow with praise,
Pr 13: 3 He who guards his *l* guards his life,
27: 2 someone else, and not your own *l.*
Isa 6: 5 For I am a man of unclean *l,*
Mt 21: 16 "'From the *l* of children
Col 3: 8 and filthy language from your *l.*

LISTEN (LISTENING LISTENS)

Dt 30: 20 *l* to his voice, and hold fast to him.
Pr 1: 5 let the wise *l* and add
Jn 10: 27 My sheep *l* to my voice; I know
Jas 1: 19 Everyone should be quick to *l,*
1: 22 Do not merely *l* to the word,

LISTENING (LISTEN)

1Sa 3: 9 Speak, LORD, for your servant is *l*
Pr 18: 13 He who answers before *l*—

LISTENS (LISTEN)

Pr 12: 15 but a wise man *l* to advice.

LIVE (ALIVE LIFE LIVES LIVING)

Ex 20: 12 so that you may *l* long
33: 20 for no one may see me and *l.*"
Dt 8: 3 to teach you that man does not *l*
Job 14: 14 If a man dies, will he *l* again?
Ps 119:175 Let me *l* that I may praise you,
Isa 55: 3 hear me, that your soul may *l.*
Eze 37: 3 can these bones *l?*" I said,
Hab 2: 4 but the righteous will *l* by his faith
Mt 4: 4 'Man does not *l* on bread alone,
Ac 17: 24 does not *l* in temples built by hands
17: 28 'For in him we *l* and move
Ro 1: 17 "The righteous will *l* by faith."
2Co 5: 7 We *l* by faith, not by sight.
Gal 2: 20 The life I *l* in the body, I *l* by faith
5: 25 Since we *l* by the Spirit, let us keep
Php 1: 21 to *l* is Christ and to die is gain.
1Th 5: 13 *L* in peace with each other.
2Ti 3: 12 who wants to *l* a godly life
Heb 12: 14 Make every effort to *l* in peace
1Pe 1: 17 *l* your lives as strangers here

LIVES (LIVE)

Job 19: 25 I know that my Redeemer *l,*
Isa 57: 15 he who *l* forever, whose name is
Da 3: 28 to give up their *l* rather than serve
Jn 14: 17 for he *l* with you and will be in you.
Ro 7: 18 I know that nothing good *l* in me,
14: 7 For none of us *l* to himself alone
1Co 3: 16 and that God's Spirit *l* in you?
Gal 2: 20 I no longer live, but Christ *l* in me.
Heb 13: 5 Keep your *l* free from the love
2Pe 3: 11 You ought to live holy and godly *l*
1Jn 3: 16 to lay down our *l* for our brothers.
4: 16 Whoever *l* in love *l* in God,

LIVING (LIVE)

Ge 2: 7 and man became a *l* being.
Jer 2: 13 the spring of *l* water,
Mt 22: 32 the God of the dead but of the *l.*"
Jn 7: 38 streams of *l* water will flow
Ro 12: 1 to offer your bodies as *l* sacrifices,
Heb 4: 12 For the word of God is *l* and active.
10: 31 to fall into the hands of the *l* God.
Rev 1: 18 I am the *L* One; I was dead,

LOAD

Gal 6: 5 for each one should carry his own *l.*

LOCUSTS

Mt 3: 4 His food was *l* and wild honey.

LOFTY

Ps 139: 6 too *l* for me to attain.
Isa 57: 15 is what the high and *l* One says—

LONELY

Ps 68: 6 God sets the *l* in families,

LONG (LENGTH LONGED LONGING LONGS)

1Ki 18: 21 "How *l* will you waver
Jn 9: 4 As *l* as it is day, we must do
Eph 3: 18 to grasp how wide and *l* and high
1Pe 1: 12 Even angels *l* to look

LONGED (LONG)

Mt 13: 17 righteous men *l* to see what you see
23: 37 how often I have *l*
2Ti 4: 8 to all who have *l* for his appearing.

LONGING (LONG)

Pr 13: 19 A *l* fulfilled is sweet to the soul,
2Co 5: 2 *l* to be clothed with our heavenly

LONGS (LONG)

Isa 30: 18 Yet the LORD *l* to be gracious

LOOK (LOOKING LOOKS)

Dt 4: 29 you will find him if you *l* for him
Job 31: 1 not to *l* lustfully at a girl.
Ps 34: 5 Those who *l* to him are radiant;
Pr 4: 25 Let your eyes *l* straight ahead,
Isa 60: 5 Then you will *l* and be radiant,
Hab 1: 13 Your eyes are too pure to *l* on evil;
Zec 12: 10 They will *l* on me, the one they
Mk 13: 21 '*L,* here is the Christ!' or, '*L,*
Lk 24: 39 *L* at my hands and my feet.

Jn 1: 36 he said, "L, the Lamb of God!"
4: 35 open your eyes and *l* at the fields!
19: 37 "They will *l* on the one they have
Jas 1: 27 to *l* after orphans and widows
1Pe 1: 12 long to *l* into these things.

LOOKING (LOOK)

2Co 10: 7 You are *l* only on the surface
Rev 5: 6 I saw a Lamb, *l* as if it had been

LOOKS (LOOK)

1Sa 16: 7 Man *l* at the outward appearance,
Lk 9: 62 and *l* back is fit for service
Php 2: 21 For everyone *l* out

LORD⁻ (LORD'S† LORDING)

Ne 4: 14 Remember the *L*, who is great
Job 28: 28 'The fear of the *L*— that is wisdom,
Ps 54: 4 the *L* is the one who sustains me.
62: 12 and that you, O *L*, are loving.
86: 5 You are forgiving and good, O *L*,
110: 1 The LORD says to my *L*:
147: 5 Great is our *L* and mighty in power
Isa 6: 1 I saw the *L* seated on a throne,
Da 9: 4 "O *L*, the great and awesome God,
Mt 3: 3 'Prepare the way for the *L*,
4: 7 'Do not put the *L* your God
7: 21 "Not everyone who says to me, '*L*,
22: 37 "'Love the *L* your God
22: 44 For he says, "'The *L* said to my *L*:
Mk 12: 11 the *L* has done this,
12: 29 the *L* our God, the *L* is one.
Lk 2: 9 glory of the *L* shone around them,
6: 46 "Why do you call me, '*L*, *L*,'
10: 27 "'Love the *L* your God
Ac 2: 21 on the name of the *L* will be saved.'
16: 31 replied, "Believe in the *L* Jesus,
Ro 10: 9 with your mouth, "Jesus is *L*,"
10: 13 on the name of the *L* will be saved
12: 11 your spiritual fervor, serving the *L*.
14: 8 we live to the *L*; and if we die,
1Co 1: 31 Let him who boasts boast in the *L*."
3: 5 the *L* has assigned to each his task.
7: 34 to be devoted to the *L* in both body
10: 9 We should not test the *L*,
11: 23 For I received from the *L* what I
12: 3 "Jesus is *L*," except by the Holy
15: 57 victory through our *L* Jesus Christ.
16: 22 If anyone does not love the *L*—
2Co 3: 17 Now the *L* is the Spirit,
8: 5 they gave themselves first to the *L*
10: 17 Let him who boasts boast in the *L*."
Gal 6: 14 in the cross of our *L* Jesus Christ,
Eph 4: 5 one *L*, one faith, one baptism;
5: 10 and find out what pleases the *L*.
Eph 5: 19 make music in your heart to the *L*,
Php 2: 11 confess that Jesus Christ is *L*,
3: 1 my brothers, rejoice in the *L*!
4: 4 Rejoice in the *L* always.
Col 2: 6 as you received Christ Jesus as *L*,
3: 17 do it all in the name of the *L* Jesus,
3: 23 as working for the *L*, not for men,
4: 17 work you have received in the *L*."
1Th 3: 12 May the *L* make your love increase
5: 2 day of the *L* will come like a thief
5: 23 at the coming of our *L* Jesus Christ.
2Th 2: 1 the coming of our *L* Jesus Christ
2Ti 2: 19 "The *L* knows those who are his,"
Heb 12: 14 holiness no one will see the *L*.
13: 6 *L* is my helper; I will not be afraid.
Jas 4: 10 Humble yourselves before the *L*,
1Pe 1: 25 the word of the *L* stands forever."
2: 3 you have tasted that the *L* is good.
3: 15 in your hearts set apart Christ as *L*.
2Pe 1: 16 and coming of our *L* Jesus Christ,
2: 1 the sovereign *L* who bought
3: 9 The *L* is not slow in keeping his
Jude : 14 the *L* is coming with thousands
Rev 4: 8 holy, holy is the *L* God Almighty,
4: 11 "You are worthy, our *L* and God,
17: 14 he is *L* of lords and King of kings—
22: 20 Come, *L* Jesus.

LORD'S† (LORD†)

Ac 21: 14 and said, "The *L* will be done."
1Co 10: 26 "The earth is the *L*, and everything
11: 26 you proclaim the *L* death
2Co 3: 18 faces all reflect the *L* glory,
2Ti 2: 24 And the *L* servant must not quarrel
Jas 4: 15 you ought to say, "If it is the *L* will,

LORDING* (LORD†)

1Pe 5: 3 not *l* it over those entrusted to you,

LORD‡ (LORD'S‡)

Ge 2: 4 When the *L* God made the earth
2: 7 the *L* God formed the man
3: 21 The *L* God made garments of skin
7: 16 Then the *L* shut him in.
15: 6 Abram believed the *L*,
18: 14 Is anything too hard for the *L*?
31: 49 "May the *L* keep watch
Ex 3: 2 the angel of the *L* appeared to him
9: 12 the *L* hardened Pharaoh's heart
14: 30 That day the *L* saved Israel
20: 2 "I am the *L* your God, who
Ex 33: 11 The *L* would speak to Moses face
40: 34 glory of the *L* filled the tabernacle.
Lev 19: 2 'Be holy because I, the *L* your God,
Nu 8: 5 *L* said to Moses: "Take the Levites
14: 21 glory of the *L* fills the whole earth,
Dt 2: 7 forty years the *L* your God has
5: 9 the *L* your God, am a jealous God,
6: 4 The *L* our God, the *L* is one.
6: 5 Love the *L* your God
6: 16 Do not test the *L* your God
10: 14 To the *L* your God belong
10: 17 For the *L* your God is God of gods
11: 1 Love the *L* your God and keep his
28: 1 If you fully obey the *L* your God
30: 16 today to love the *L* your God,
30: 20 For the *L* is your life, and he will
31: 6 for the *L* your God goes with you;
Jos 22: 5 to love the *L* your God, to walk
24: 15 my household, we will serve the *L*
1Sa 1: 28 So now I give him to the *L*.
2: 2 "There is no one holy like the *L*;
7: 12 "Thus far has the *L* helped us."
12: 22 his great name the *L* will not reject
15: 22 "Does the *L* delight
2Sa 22: 2 "The *L* is my rock, my fortress
1Ki 2: 3 and observe what the *L* your God
8: 11 the glory of the *L* filled his temple.
8: 61 fully committed to the *L* our God,
18: 21 If the *L* is God, follow him;
2Ki 13: 23 But the *L* was gracious to them
1Ch 16: 8 Give thanks to the *L*, call
16: 23 Sing to the *L*, all the earth;
28: 9 for the *L* searches every heart
29: 11 O *L*, is the greatness and the power
2Ch 5: 14 the glory of the *L* filled the temple
16: 9 of the *L* range throughout the earth
19: 6 judging for man but for the *L*,
30: 9 for the *L* your God is gracious
Ne 1: 5 Then I said: "O *L*, God of heaven,
Job 1: 21 *L* gave and the *L* has taken away;
38: 1 the *L* answered Job out
42: 9 and the *L* accepted Job's prayer.
Ps 1: 2 But his delight is in the law of the *L*
9: 9 The *L* is a refuge for the oppressed,
12: 6 And the words of the *L* are flawless
16: 8 I have set the *L* always before me.
18: 30 the word of the *L* is flawless.
19: 7 The law of the *L* is perfect,
19: 14 O *L*, my Rock and my Redeemer.
23: 1 The *L* is my shepherd, I shall not be

‡ This entry represents the translation of the Hebrew name for God *Yahweh*, always indicated in the NIV by LORD. For Lord, see the concordance entries **LORD**† and **LORD'S**†.

Ps 23: 6 I will dwell in the house of the *L*
27: 1 The *L* is my light and my salvation
27: 4 to gaze upon the beauty of the *L*
29: 1 Ascribe to the *L,* O mighty ones,
32: 2 whose sin the *L* does not count
33: 12 is the nation whose God is the *L,*
33: 18 But the eyes of the *L* are
34: 3 Glorify the *L* with me;
34: 7 The angel of the *L* encamps
34: 8 Taste and see that the *L* is good;
34: 18 The *L* is close to the broken-hearted
37: 4 Delight yourself in the *L*
40: 1 I waited patiently for the *L;*
47: 2 How awesome is the *L* Most High,
48: 1 Great is the *L,* and most worthy
55: 22 Cast your cares on the *L*
75: 8 In the hand of the *L* is a cup
84: 11 For the *L* God is a sun and shield;
86: 11 Teach me your way, O *L,*
89: 5 heavens praise your wonders, O *L,*
91: 2 I will say of the *L,* "He is my refuge
95: 1 Come, let us sing for joy to the *L;*
96: 1 Sing to the *L* a new song;
98: 4 Shout for joy to the *L,* all the earth,
100: 1 Shout for joy to the *L,* all the earth.
103: 1 Praise the *L,* O my soul;
103: 8 The *L* is compassionate
104: 1 O *L* my God, you are very great;
107: 8 to the *L* for his unfailing love
110: 1 The *L* says to my Lord:
113: 4 *L* is exalted over all the nations,
115: 1 Not to us, O *L,* not to us
116: 15 Precious in the sight of the *L*
118: 1 Give thanks to the *L,* for he is good
118: 24 This is the day the *L* has made;
121: 2 My help comes from the *L,*
121: 5 The *L* watches over you—
125: 2 so the *L* surrounds his people
127: 1 Unless the *L* builds the house,
127: 3 Sons are a heritage from the *L,*
130: 3 If you, O *L,* kept a record of sins,
135: 6 The *L* does whatever pleases him,
136: 1 Give thanks to the *L,* for he is good
139: 1 O *L,* you have searched me
144: 3 O *L,* what is man that you care
145: 3 Great is the *L* and most worthy
145: 18 The *L* is near to all who call on him
Pr 1: 7 The fear of the *L* is the beginning
3: 5 Trust in the *L* with all your heart
3: 9 Honor the *L* with your wealth,
3: 12 the *L* disciplines those he loves,
3: 19 By wisdom the *L* laid the earth's
Pr 5: 21 are in full view of the *L,*
6: 16 There are six things the *L* hates,
10: 27 The fear of the *L* adds length to life
11: 1 The *L* abhors dishonest scales,
12: 22 The *L* detests lying lips,
14: 26 He who fears the *L* has a secure
15: 3 The eyes of the *L* are everywhere,
16: 2 but motives are weighed by the *L.*
16: 4 The *L* works out everything
16: 9 but the *L* determines his steps.
16: 33 but its every decision is from the *L.*
18: 10 The name of the *L* is a strong tower
18: 22 and receives favor from the *L.*
19: 14 but a prudent wife is from the *L.*
19: 17 to the poor lends to the *L,*
21: 3 to the *L* than sacrifice.
21: 30 that can succeed against the *L.*
21: 31 but victory rests with the *L.*
22: 2 The *L* is the Maker of them all.
24: 18 or the *L* will see and disapprove
31: 30 a woman who fears the *L* is
Isa 6: 3 holy, holy is the *L* Almighty;
11: 2 The Spirit of the *L* will rest on him
11: 9 full of the knowledge of the *L*
12: 2 The *L,* the *L,* is my strength
24: 1 the *L* is going to lay waste the earth
25: 8 The Sovereign *L* will wipe away
29: 15 to hide their plans from the *L,*
33: 6 the fear of the *L* is the key
35: 10 the ransomed of the *L* will return.
40: 5 the glory of the *L* will be revealed,
40: 7 the breath of the *L* blows on them.
40: 10 the Sovereign *L* comes with power,
40: 28 The *L* is the everlasting God,
40: 31 but those who hope in the *L*
42: 8 "I am the *L;* that is my name!
43: 11 I, even I, am the *L,*
44: 24 I am the *L,*
45: 5 I am the *L,* and there is no other;
45: 21 Was it not I, the *L?*
51: 11 The ransomed of the *L* will return.
53: 6 and the *L* has laid on him
53: 10 and the will of the *L* will prosper
55: 6 Seek the *L* while he may be found;
58: 8 of the *L* will be your rear guard.
58: 11 The *L* will guide you always;
59: 1 the arm of the *L* is not too short
61: 3 a planting of the *L*
61: 10 I delight greatly in the *L;*
Jer 1: 9 Then the *L* reached out his hand
9: 24 I am the *L,* who exercises kindness,
16: 19 O *L,* my strength and my fortress,
17: 7 is the man who trusts in the *L,*
La 3: 40 and let us return to the *L.*
Eze 1: 28 of the likeness of the glory of the *L.*
Hos 1: 7 horsemen, but by the *L* their God."
3: 5 They will come trembling to the *L*
6: 1 "Come, let us return to the *L.*
Joel 2: 1 for the day of the *L* is coming.
2: 11 The day of the *L* is great;
3: 14 For the day of the *L* is near
Am 5: 18 long for the day of the *L?*
Jnh 1: 3 But Jonah ran away from the *L*
Mic 4: 2 up to the mountain of the *L,*
6: 8 And what does the *L* require of you
Na 1: 2 The *L* takes vengeance on his foes
1: 3 The *L* is slow to anger
Hab 2: 14 knowledge of the glory of the *L,*
2: 20 But the *L* is in his holy temple;
Zep 3: 17 The *L* your God is with you,
Zec 1: 17 and the *L* will again comfort Zion
9: 16 The *L* their God will save them
14: 5 Then the *L* my God will come,
14: 9 The *L* will be king
Mal 4: 5 and dreadful day of the *L* comes.

LORD'S‡ (LORD‡)

Ex 34: 34 he entered the *L* presence
Nu 14: 41 you disobeying the *L* command?
Dt 6: 18 is right and good in the *L* sight,
32: 9 For the *L* portion is his people,
Jos 21: 45 Not one of all the *L* good promises
Ps 24: 1 The earth is the *L,* and everything
32: 10 but the *L* unfailing love
89: 1 of the *L* great love forever;
103: 17 *L* love is with those who fear him,
Pr 3: 11 do not despise the *L* discipline
Isa 24: 14 west they acclaim the *L* majesty.
62: 3 of splendor in the *L* hand,
Jer 48: 10 lax in doing the *L* work!
La 3: 22 of the *L* great love we are not
Mic 4: 1 of the *L* temple will be established

LOSE (LOSES LOSS LOST)

1Sa 17: 32 "Let no one *l* heart on account
Mt 10: 39 Whoever finds his life will *l* it,
Lk 9: 25 and yet *l* or forfeit his very self?
Jn 6: 39 that I shall *l* none of all that he has
Heb 12: 3 will not grow weary and *l* heart.
12: 5 do not *l* heart when he rebukes you

LOSES (LOSE)

Mt 5: 13 But if the salt *l* its saltiness,
Lk 15: 4 you has a hundred sheep and *l* one
15: 8 has ten silver coins and *l* one.

LOSS (LOSE)

Ro 11: 12 and their *l* means riches
1Co 3: 15 he will suffer *l;* he himself will be
Php 3: 8 I consider everything a *l* compared

LOST (LOSE)

Ps 73: 2 I had nearly *l* my foothold.

Jer 50: 6 “My people have been *l* sheep;
Eze 34: 4 the strays or searched for the *l*.
34: 16 for the *l* and bring back the strays.
Mt 18: 14 any of these little ones should be *l*.
Lk 15: 4 go after the *l* sheep until he finds it?
15: 6 with me; I have found my *l* sheep.’
15: 9 with me; I have found my *l* coin.’
15: 24 is alive again; he was *l* and is found
19: 10 to seek and to save what was *l*.”
Php 3: 8 for whose sake I have *l* all things.

LOT (LOTS)

Nephew of Abraham (Ge 11:27; 12:5). Chose to live in Sodom (Ge 13). Rescued from four kings (Ge 14). Rescued from Sodom (Ge 19:1-29; 2Pe 2:7). Fathered Moab and Ammon by his daughters (Ge 19:30-38).

Est 3: 7 the *l*) in the presence of Haman
9: 24 the *l*) for their ruin and destruction.
Pr 16: 33 The *l* is cast into the lap,
18: 18 Casting the *l* settles disputes
Ecc 3: 22 his work, because that is his *l*.
Ac 1: 26 Then they drew lots, and the *l* fell

LOTS (LOT)

Ps 22: 18 and cast *l* for my clothing.
Mt 27: 35 divided up his clothes by casting *l*.

LOVE (BELOVED LOVED LOVELY LOVER LOVERS LOVES LOVING)

Ge 22: 2 your only son, Isaac, whom you *l*,
Ex 15: 13 “In your unfailing *l* you will lead
20: 6 showing *l* to a thousand generations
20: 6 of those who *l* me
34: 6 abounding in *l* and faithfulness,
Lev 19: 18 but *l* your neighbor as yourself.
19: 34 *L* him as yourself,
Nu 14: 18 abounding in *l* and forgiving sin
Dt 5: 10 showing *l* to a thousand generations
5: 10 of those who *l* me
6: 5 *L* the LORD your God
7: 13 He will *l* you and bless you
10: 12 to walk in all his ways, to *l* him,
11: 13 to *l* the LORD your God
13: 6 wife you *l*, or your closest friend
30: 6 so that you may *l* him
Jos 22: 5 to *l* the LORD your God, to walk
1Ki 3: 3 Solomon showed his *l*
8: 23 you who keep your covenant of *l*
2Ch 5: 13 his *l* endures forever.”
Ne 1: 5 covenant of *l* with those who *l* him
Ps 8: 1 I *l* you, O LORD, my strength.
23: 6 Surely goodness and *l* will follow
25: 6 O LORD, your great mercy and *l*,
31: 16 save me in your unfailing *l*.
32: 10 but the LORD’s unfailing *l*

Ps 33: 5 the earth is full of his unfailing *l*.
33: 18 whose hope is in his unfailing *l*,
36: 5 Your *l*, O LORD, reaches
36: 7 How priceless is your unfailing *l*!
45: 7 You *l* righteousness and hate
51: 1 according to your unfailing *l*;
57: 10 For great is your *l*, reaching
63: 3 Because your *l* is better than life,
66: 20 or withheld his *l* from me!
70: 4 may those who *l* your salvation
77: 8 Has his unfailing *l* vanished forever
85: 7 Show us your unfailing *l*, O LORD
85: 10 *L* and faithfulness meet together;
86: 13 For great is your *l* toward me;
89: 1 of the LORD’s great *l* forever;
89: 33 but I will not take my *l* from him,
92: 2 to proclaim your *l* in the morning
94: 18 your *l*, O LORD, supported me.
100: 5 is good and his *l* endures forever;
101: 1 I will sing of your *l* and justice;
103: 4 crowns you with *l* and compassion.
103: 8 slow to anger, abounding in *l*.
103: 11 so great is his *l* for those who fear
107: 8 to the LORD for his unfailing *l*
108: 4 For great is your *l*, higher
116: 1 I *l* the LORD, for he heard my
118: 1 his *l* endures forever.
119: 47 because I *l* them.
119: 64 The earth is filled with your *l*,
119: 76 May your unfailing *l* be my
119: 97 Oh, how I *l* your law!
119:119 therefore I *l* your statutes.
119:124 your servant according to your *l*
119:132 to those who *l* your name.
119:159 O LORD, according to your *l*.
119:163 but I *l* your law.
119:165 peace have they who *l* your law,
122: 6 “May those who *l* you be secure.
130: 7 for with the LORD is unfailing *l*
136: 1 -26 *His l endures forever.*
143: 8 of your unfailing *l*,
145: 8 slow to anger and rich in *l*.
145: 20 over all who *l* him,
147: 11 who put their hope in his unfailing *l*
Pr 3: 3 Let *l* and faithfulness never leave
4: 6 *l* her, and she will watch over you.
5: 19 you ever be captivated by her *l*.
8: 17 I *l* those who *l* me,
9: 8 rebuke a wise man and he will *l* you
10: 12 but *l* covers over all wrongs.
14: 22 those who plan what is good find *l*
15: 17 of vegetables where there is *l*
17: 9 over an offense promotes *l*,
19: 22 What a man desires is unfailing *l*;
20: 6 claims to have unfailing *l*,
20: 13 Do not *l* sleep or you will grow
20: 28 through *l* his throne is made secure

Pr 21: 21 who pursues righteousness and *l*
27: 5 rebuke than hidden *l*.
Ecc 9: 6 Their *l*, their hate
9: 9 life with your wife, whom you *l*,
SS 2: 4 and his banner over me is *l*.
8: 6 for *l* is as strong as death,
8: 7 Many waters cannot quench *l*;
8: 7 all the wealth of his house for *l*,
Isa 5: 1 I will sing for the one I *l*
16: 5 In *l* a throne will be established;
38: 17 In your *l* you kept me
54: 10 yet my unfailing *l* for you will not
55: 3 my faithful *l* promised to David.
61: 8 “For I, the LORD, *l* justice;
63: 9 In his *l* and mercy he redeemed
Jer 5: 31 and my people *l* it this way.
31: 3 you with an everlasting *l*;
32: 18 You show *l* to thousands
33: 11 his *l* endures forever.”
La 3: 22 of the LORD’s great *l* we are not
3: 32 so great is his unfailing *l*.
Eze 33: 32 more than one who sings *l* songs
Da 9: 4 covenant of *l* with all who *l* him
Hos 2: 19 in *l* and compassion.
3: 1 Go, show your *l* to your wife again,
11: 4 with ties of *l*;
12: 6 maintain *l* and justice,
Joel 2: 13 slow to anger and abounding in *l*,
Am 5: 15 Hate evil, *l* good;
Mic 3: 2 you who hate good and *l* evil;
6: 8 To act justly and to *l* mercy
Zep 3: 17 he will quiet you with his *l*,
Zec 8: 19 Therefore *l* truth and peace.”
Mt 3: 17 “This is my Son, whom I *l*;
5: 44 *L* your enemies and pray
6: 24 he will hate the one and *l* the other,
17: 5 “This is my Son, whom I *l*;
19: 19 and *l* your neighbor as yourself.’ ”
22: 37 “‘*L* the Lord your God
Lk 6: 32 Even ‘sinners’ *l* those who *l* them.
7: 42 which of them will *l* him more?”
20: 13 whom I *l*; perhaps they will respect
Jn 13: 34 I give you: *L* one another.
13: 35 disciples, if you *l* one another.”
14: 15 “If you *l* me, you will obey what I
15: 13 Greater *l* has no one than this,
15: 17 This is my command: *L* each other.
21: 15 do you truly *l* me more than these
Ro 5: 5 because God has poured out his *l*
5: 8 God demonstrates his own *l* for us
8: 28 for the good of those who *l* him,
8: 35 us from the *l* of Christ?
8: 39 us from the *l* of God that is
12: 9 *L* must be sincere.
12: 10 to one another in brotherly *l*.
13: 8 continuing debt to *l* one another,

Ro 13: 9 *"L* your neighbor as yourself."
13: 10 Therefore *l* is the fulfillment
13: 10 *L* does no harm to its neighbor.
1Co 2: 9 prepared for those who *l* him"—
8: 1 Knowledge puffs up, but *l* builds up
13: 1 have not *l,* I am only a resounding
13: 2 but have not *l,* I am nothing.
13: 3 but have not *l,* I gain nothing.
13: 4 Love is patient, *l* is kind.
13: 4 *L* is patient, love is kind.
13: 6 *L* does not delight in evil
13: 8 *L* never fails.
13: 13 But the greatest of these is *l.*
13: 13 three remain: faith, hope and *l.*
14: 1 way of *l* and eagerly desire spiritual
16: 14 Do everything in *l.*
2Co 5: 14 For Christ's *l* compels us,
8: 8 sincerity of your *l* by comparing it
8: 24 show these men the proof of your *l*
Gal 5: 6 is faith expressing itself through *l.*
5: 13 rather, serve one another in *l.*
5: 22 But the fruit of the Spirit is *l,* joy,
Eph 1: 4 In *l* he predestined us
2: 4 But because of his great *l* for us,
3: 17 being rooted and established in *l,*
3: 18 and high and deep is the *l* of Christ,
3: 19 and to know this *l* that surpasses
4: 2 bearing with one another in *l.*
4: 15 Instead, speaking the truth in *l,*
5: 2 loved children and live a life of *l,*
5: 25 *l* your wives, just as Christ loved
5: 28 husbands ought to *l* their wives
5: 33 each one of you also must *l* his wife
Php 1: 9 that your *l* may abound more
2: 2 having the same *l,* being one
Col 1: 5 *l* that spring from the hope that is
2: 2 in heart and united in *l,*
3: 14 And over all these virtues put on *l,*
3: 19 *l* your wives and do not be harsh
1Th 1: 3 your labor prompted by *l,*
4: 9 taught by God to *l* each other.
5: 8 on faith and *l* as a breastplate,
2Th 3: 5 direct your hearts into God's *l*
1Ti 1: 5 The goal of this command is *l,*
2: 15 *l* and holiness with propriety.
4: 12 in life, in *l,* in faith and in purity.
6: 10 For the *l* of money is a root
6: 11 faith, *l,* endurance and gentleness.
2Ti 1: 7 of power, of *l* and of self-discipline.
2: 22 and pursue righteousness, faith, *l*
3: 10 faith, patience, *l,* endurance,
Tit 2: 4 women to *l* their husbands
Phm : 9 yet I appeal to you on the basis of *l.*
Heb 6: 10 and the *l* you have shown him
10: 24 may spur one another on toward *l*
Heb 13: 5 free from the *l* of money
Jas 1: 12 promised to those who *l* him.
2: 5 he promised those who *l* him?
2: 8 *"L* your neighbor as yourself,"
1Pe 1: 22 the truth so that you have sincere *l*
1: 22 *l* one another deeply,
2: 17 *L* the brotherhood of believers,
3: 8 be sympathetic, *l* as brothers,
3: 10 "Whoever would *l* life
4: 8 Above all, *l* each other deeply,
4: 8 *l* covers over a multitude of sins.
5: 14 Greet one another with a kiss of *l.*
2Pe 1: 7 and to brotherly kindness, *l.*
1: 17 "This is my Son, whom I *l;*
1Jn 2: 5 God's *l* is truly made complete
2: 15 Do not *l* the world or anything
3: 1 How great is the *l* the Father has
3: 10 anyone who does not *l* his brother.
3: 11 We should *l* one another.
3: 14 Anyone who does not *l* remains
3: 16 This is how we know what *l* is:
3: 18 let us not *l* with words or tongue
3: 23 to *l* one another as he commanded
4: 7 Dear friends, let us *l* one another,
4: 7 for *l* comes from God.
4: 8 Whoever does not *l* does not know
4: 9 This is how God showed his *l*
4: 10 This is *l:* not that we loved God,
4: 11 we also ought to *l* one another.
4: 12 and his *l* is made complete in us.
4: 16 God is *l.*
4: 16 Whoever lives in *l* lives in God,
4: 17 *l* is made complete among us
4: 18 But perfect *l* drives out fear,
4: 19 We *l* because he first loved us.
4: 20 If anyone says, "I *l* God,"
4: 21 loves God must also *l* his brother.
5: 2 we know that we *l* the children
5: 3 This is *l* for God: to obey his
2Jn : 5 I ask that we *l* one another.
: 6 his command is that you walk in *l.*
: 6 this is *l:* that we walk in obedience
Jude : 12 men are blemishes at your *l* feasts,
: 21 Keep yourselves in God's *l*
Rev 2: 4 You have forsaken your first *l.*
3: 19 Those whom I *l* I rebuke
12: 11 they did not *l* their lives so much

LOVED (LOVE)

Ge 24: 67 she became his wife, and he *l* her;
29: 30 and he *l* Rachel more than Leah.
37: 3 Now Israel *l* Joseph more than any
Dt 7: 8 But it was because the LORD *l* you
1Sa 1: 5 a double portion because he *l* her,
20: 17 because he *l* him as he *l* himself.
Ps 44: 3 light of your face, for you *l* them.
Jer 2: 2 how as a bride you *l* me
31: 3 "I have *l* you with an everlasting
Hos 2: 23 to the one I called 'Not my *l* one.'
3: 1 though she is *l* by another
9: 10 became as vile as the thing they *l.*
11: 1 "When Israel was a child, I *l* him,
Mal 1: 2 "But you ask, 'How have you *l* us?'
Mk 12: 6 left to send, a son, whom he *l.*
Jn 3: 16 so *l* the world that he gave his one
3: 19 but men *l* darkness instead of light
11: 5 Jesus *l* Martha and her sister
12: 43 for they *l* praise from men more
13: 1 Having *l* his own who were
13: 23 the disciple whom Jesus *l,*
13: 34 As I have *l* you, so you must love
14: 21 He who loves me will be *l*
15: 9 the Father has *l* me, so have I *l* you.
15: 12 Love each other as I have *l* you.
19: 26 the disciple whom he *l* standing
Ro 8: 37 conquerors through him who *l* us.
9: 13 "Jacob I *l,* but Esau I hated."
9: 25 her my '*l* one' who is not my *l* one,"
11: 28 they are *l* on account
Gal 2: 20 who *l* me and gave himself for me.
Eph 5: 2 as Christ *l* us and gave himself up
5: 25 just as Christ *l* the church
2Th 2: 16 who *l* us and by his grace gave us
2Ti 4: 10 for Demas, because he *l* this world,
Heb 1: 9 You have *l* righteousness
1Jn 4: 10 This is love: not that we *l* God,
4: 11 Dear friends, since God so *l* us,
1Jn 4: 19 We love because he first *l* us.

LOVELY (LOVE)

Ps 84: 1 How *l* is your dwelling place,
SS 2: 14 and your face is *l.*
5: 16 he is altogether *l.*
Php 4: 8 whatever is *l,* whatever is

LOVER (LOVE)

SS 2: 16 *Beloved* My *l* is mine and I am his;
7: 10 I belong to my *l,*
1Ti 3: 3 not quarrelsome, not a *l* of money.

LOVERS (LOVE)

2Ti 3: 2 People will be *l* of themselves,
3: 3 without self-control, brutal, not *l*
3: 4 *l* of pleasure rather than *l* of God—

LOVES (LOVE)

Ps 11: 7 he *l* justice;
33: 5 The LORD *l* righteousness
34: 12 Whoever of you *l* life
91: 14 Because he *l* me," says the LORD,

Ps 127: 2 for he grants sleep to those he *l*.
Pr 3: 12 the LORD disciplines those he *l*,
12: 1 Whoever *l* discipline *l* knowledge,
13: 24 he who *l* him is careful
17: 17 A friend *l* at all times,
17: 19 He who *l* a quarrel *l* sin;
22: 11 He who *l* a pure heart and whose
Ecc 5: 10 whoever *l* wealth is never satisfied
Mt 10: 37 anyone who *l* his son or daughter
Lk 7: 47 has been forgiven little *l* little."
Jn 3: 35 Father *l* the Son and has placed
10: 17 reason my Father *l* me is that I lay
12: 25 The man who *l* his life will lose it,
14: 21 obeys them, he is the one who *l* me.
14: 23 Jesus replied, "If anyone *l* me,
Ro 13: 8 for he who *l* his fellowman has
2Co 9: 7 for God *l* a cheerful giver.
Eph 5: 28 He who *l* his wife *l* himself.
5: 33 must love his wife as he *l* himself,
Heb 12: 6 the Lord disciplines those he *l*,
1Jn 2: 10 Whoever *l* his brother lives
2: 15 If anyone *l* the world, the love
4: 7 Everyone who *l* has been born
4: 21 Whoever *l* God must also love his
5: 1 who *l* the father *l* his child
3Jn : 9 but Diotrephes, who *l* to be first,
Rev 1: 5 To him who *l* us and has freed us

LOVING (LOVE)

Ps 25: 10 All the ways of the LORD are *l*
62: 12 and that you, O Lord, are *l*.
145: 17 and *l* toward all he has made.
Heb 13: 1 Keep on *l* each other as brothers.
1Jn 5: 2 by *l* God and carrying out his

LOWLY

Job 5: 11 The *l* he sets on high,
Pr 29: 23 but a man of *l* spirit gains honor.
Isa 57: 15 also with him who is contrite and *l*
Eze 21: 26 *l* will be exalted and the exalted
1Co 1: 28 He chose the *l* things of this world

LUKE*

Co-worker with Paul (Col 4:14; 2Ti 4:11; Phm 24).

LUKEWARM*

Rev 3: 16 So, because you are *l*—neither hot

LUST

Pr 6: 25 Do not *l* in your heart
Col 3: 5 sexual immorality, impurity, *l*,
1Th 4: 5 not in passionate *l* like the heathen,
1Jn 2: 16 the *l* of his eyes and the boasting

LYING (LIE)

Pr 6: 17 a *l* tongue,
26: 28 A *l* tongue hates those it hurts,

MACEDONIA

Ac 16: 9 "Come over to *M* and help us."

MADE (MAKE)

Ge 1: 16 He also *m* the stars.
1: 25 God *m* the wild animals according
2: 22 Then the LORD God *m* a woman
2Ki 19: 15 You have *m* heaven and earth.
Ps 95: 5 The sea is his, for he *m* it,
100: 3 It is he who *m* us, and we are his;
118: 24 This is the day the LORD has *m;*
139: 14 I am fearfully and wonderfully *m;*
Ecc 3: 11 He has *m* everything beautiful
Mk 2: 27 "The Sabbath was *m* for man,
Jn 1: 3 Through him all things were *m;*
Ac 17: 24 "The God who *m* the world
Heb 1: 2 through whom he *m* the universe.
Rev 14: 7 Worship him who *m* the heavens,

MAGI

Mt 2: 1 *M* from the east came to Jerusalem

MAGOG

Eze 38: 2 of the land of *M*, the chief prince
39: 6 I will send fire on *M*
Rev 20: 8 and *M*—to gather them for battle.

MAIDEN

Pr 30: 19 and the way of a man with a *m*.
Isa 62: 5 As a young man marries a *m*,
Jer 2: 32 Does a *m* forget her jewelry,

MAIMED

Mt 18: 8 It is better for you to enter life *m*

MAJESTIC (MAJESTY)

Ex 15: 6 was *m* in power.
15: 11 *m* in holiness,
Ps 8: 1 how *m* is your name in all the earth
29: 4 the voice of the LORD is *m*.
111: 3 Glorious and *m* are his deeds,
SS 6: 10 *m* as the stars in procession?
2Pe 1: 17 came to him from the *M* Glory,

MAJESTY (MAJESTIC)

Ex 15: 7 In the greatness of your *m*
Dt 33: 26 and on the clouds in his *m*.
1Ch 16: 27 Splendor and *m* are before him;
Est 1: 4 the splendor and glory of his *m*.
Job 37: 22 God comes in awesome *m*.
40: 10 and clothe yourself in honor and *m*
Ps 45: 4 In your *m* ride forth victoriously
93: 1 The LORD reigns, he is robed in *m*
110: 3 Arrayed in holy *m*,
145: 5 of the glorious splendor of your *m*,
Isa 53: 2 or *m* to attract us to him,
Eze 31: 2 can be compared with you in *m?*
2Pe 1: 16 but we were eyewitnesses of his *m*.
Jude : 25 only God our Savior be glory, *m*,

MAKE (MADE MAKER MAKES MAKING)

Ge 1: 26 "Let us *m* man in our image,
2: 18 I will *m* a helper suitable for him."
12: 2 "I will *m* you into a great nation
Ex 22: 3 thief must certainly *m* restitution,
Nu 6: 25 the LORD *m* his face shine
Ps 108: 1 *m* music with all my soul.
Isa 14: 14 I will *m* myself like the Most High
29: 16 "He did not *m* me"?
Jer 31: 31 "when I will *m* a new covenant
Mt 3: 3 *m* straight paths for him.'"
28: 19 and *m* disciples of all nations,
Mk 1: 17 "and I will *m* you fishers of men."
Lk 13: 24 "*M* every effort to enter
14: 23 country lanes and *m* them come in,
Ro 14: 19 *m* every effort to do what leads
2Co 5: 9 So we *m* it our goal to please him,
Eph 4: 3 *M* every effort to keep the unity
Col 4: 5 *m* the most of every opportunity.
1Th 4: 11 *M* it your ambition
Heb 4: 11 *m* every effort to enter that rest,
12: 14 *M* every effort to live in peace
2Pe 1: 5 *m* every effort to add
3: 14 *m* every effort to be found spotless,

MAKER (MAKE)

Job 4: 17 Can a man be more pure than his *M*
36: 3 I will ascribe justice to my *M*.
Ps 95: 6 kneel before the LORD our *M;*
Pr 22: 2 The LORD is the *M* of them all.
Isa 45: 9 to him who quarrels with his *M*,
54: 5 For your *M* is your husband—
Jer 10: 16 for he is the *M* of all things,

MAKES (MAKE)

1Co 3: 7 but only God, who *m* things grow.

MAKING (MAKE)

Ps 19: 7 *m* wise the simple.
Ecc 12: 12 Of *m* many books there is no end,
Jn 5: 18 *m* himself equal with God.
Eph 5: 16 *m* the most of every opportunity,

MALE

Ge 1: 27 *m* and female he created them.
Gal 3: 28 slave nor free, *m* nor female,

MALICE (MALICIOUS)

Ro 1: 29 murder, strife, deceit and *m*.
Col 3: 8 *m*, slander, and filthy language
1Pe 2: 1 rid yourselves of all *m*

MALICIOUS (MALICE)

Pr 26: 24 A *m* man disguises himself
1Ti 3: 11 not *m* talkers but temperate
6: 4 *m* talk, evil suspicions

MAN (MEN WOMAN WOMEN)

Ge 1: 26 "Let us make *m* in our image,
2: 7 God formed the *m* from the dust
2: 18 for the *m* to be alone

Ge 2: 23 she was taken out of *m.*
9: 6 Whoever sheds the blood of *m,*
Dt 8: 3 *m* does not live on bread
1Sa 13: 14 a *m* after his own heart
15: 29 he is not a *m* that he
Job 14: 1 *M* born of woman is of few
14: 14 If a *m* dies, will he live
Ps 1: 1 Blessed is the *m* who does
8: 4 what is *m* that you are
119: 9 can a young *m* keep his
127: 5 Blessed is the *m* whose quiver
Pr 14: 12 that seems right to a *m,*
30: 19 way of a *m* with a maiden.
Isa 53: 3 a *m* of sorrows,
Mt 19: 5 a *m* will leave his father
Mk 8: 36 What good is it for a *m*
Lk 4: 4 '*M* does not live on bread
Ro 5: 12 entered the world through one *m*
1Co 7: 2 each *m* should have his own
11: 3 head of every *m* is Christ,
11: 3 head of woman is *m*
13: 11 When I became a *m,*
Php 2: 8 found in appearance as a *m,*
1Ti 2: 5 the *m* Christ Jesus,
2: 11 have authority over a *m;*
Heb 9: 27 as *m* is destined to die

MANAGE

Jer 12: 5 how will you *m* in the thickets
1Ti 3: 4 He must *m* his own family well
3: 12 one wife and must *m* his children
5: 14 to *m* their homes and to give

MANASSEH

1. Firstborn of Joseph (Ge 41:51; 46:20). Blessed (Ge 48).
2. Son of Hezekiah; king of Judah (2Ki 21:1-18; 2Ch 33:1-20).

MANGER

Lk 2: 12 in strips of cloth and lying in a *m.*"

MANNA

Ex 16: 31 people of Israel called the bread *m.*
Dt 8: 16 He gave you *m* to eat in the desert,
Jn 6: 49 Your forefathers ate the *m*
Rev 2: 17 I will give some of the hidden *m.*

MANNER

1Co 11: 27 in an unworthy *m* will be guilty
Php 1: 27 conduct yourselves in a *m* worthy

MARITAL* (MARRY)

Ex 21: 10 of her food, clothing and *m* rights.
Mt 5: 32 except for *m* unfaithfulness,
19: 9 except for *m* unfaithfulness,
1Co 7: 3 husband should fulfill his *m* duty

MARK (MARKS)

Cousin of Barnabas (Col 4:10; 2Ti 4:11; Phm 24; 1Pe 5:13), see JOHN.
Ge 4: 15 Then the LORD put a *m* on Cain
Rev 13: 16 to receive a *m* on his right hand

MARKS (MARK)

Jn 20: 25 Unless I see the nail *m* in his hands
Gal 6: 17 bear on my body the *m* of Jesus.

MARRED

Isa 52: 14 his form *m* beyond human likeness

MARRIAGE (MARRY)

Mt 22: 30 neither marry nor be given in *m;*
24: 38 marrying and giving in *m,*
Ro 7: 2 she is released from the law of *m.*
Heb 13: 4 by all, and the *m* bed kept pure,

MARRIED (MARRY)

Ro 7: 2 by law a *m* woman is bound
1Co 7: 27 Are you *m?* Do not seek a divorce.
7: 33 But a *m* man is concerned about
7: 36 They should get *m.*

MARRIES (MARRY)

Mt 5: 32 and anyone who *m* the divorced
19: 9 and *m* another woman commits
Lk 16: 18 the man who *m* a divorced woman

MARRY (INTERMARRY MARITAL MARRIAGE MARRIED MARRIES)

Mt 22: 30 resurrection people will neither *m*
1Co 7: 1 It is good for a man not to *m.*
7: 9 control themselves, they should *m,*
1Ti 5: 14 So I counsel younger widows to *m,*

MARTHA*

Sister of Mary and Lazarus (Lk 10:38-42; Jn 11; 12:2).

MARVELED

Lk 2: 33 mother *m* at what was said about

MARY

1. Mother of Jesus (Mt 1:16-25; Lk 1:27-56; 2:1-40). With Jesus at temple (Lk 2:41-52), at the wedding in Cana (Jn 2:1-5), questioning his sanity (Mk 3:21), at the cross (Jn 19:25-27). Among disciples after Ascension (Ac 1:14).
2. Magdalene; former demoniac (Lk 8:2). Helped support Jesus' ministry (Lk 8:1-3). At the cross (Mt 27:56; Mk 15:40; Jn 19:25), burial (Mt 27:61; Mk 15:47). Saw angel after resurrection (Mt 28:1-10; Mk 16:1-9; Lk 24:1-12); also Jesus (Jn 20:1-18).
3. Sister of Martha and Lazarus (Jn 11). Washed Jesus' feet (Jn 12:1-8).

MASQUERADES*

2Co 11: 14 for Satan himself *m* as an angel

MASTER (MASTERED MASTERS)

Mt 10: 24 nor a servant above his *m.*
23: 8 for you have only one *M*
24: 46 that servant whose *m* finds him
25: 21 "His *m* replied, 'Well done,
Ro 6: 14 For sin shall not be your *m,*
14: 4 To his own *m* he stands or falls.
2Ti 2: 21 useful to the *M* and prepared

MASTERED* (MASTER)

1Co 6: 12 but I will not be *m* by any thing.
2Pe 2: 19 a slave to whatever has *m* him.

MASTERS (MASTER)

Mt 6: 24 "No one can serve two *m.*
Eph 6: 5 obey your earthly *m* with respect
6: 9 And *m,* treat your slaves
Tit 2: 9 subject to their *m* in everything,

MATTHEW*

Apostle; former tax collector (Mt 9:9-13; 10:3; Mk 3:18; Lk 6:15; Ac 1:13). Also called Levi (Mk 2:14-17; Lk 5:27-32).

MATURE (MATURITY)

Eph 4: 13 of the Son of God and become *m,*
Php 3: 15 of us who are *m* should take such
Heb 5: 14 But solid food is for the *m,*
Jas 1: 4 work so that you may be *m*

MATURITY* (MATURE)

Heb 6: 1 about Christ and go on to *m,*

MEAL

Pr 15: 17 Better a *m* of vegetables where
1Co 10: 27 some unbeliever invites you to a *m*
Heb 12: 16 for a single *m* sold his inheritance

MEANING

Ne 8: 8 and giving the *m* so that the people

MEANS

1Co 9: 22 by all possible *m* I might save some

MEAT

Ro 14: 6 He who eats *m,* eats to the Lord,
14: 21 It is better not to eat *m*

MEDIATOR

1Ti 2: 5 and one *m* between God and men,
Heb 8: 6 of which he is *m* is superior
9: 15 For this reason Christ is the *m*
12: 24 to Jesus the *m* of a new covenant,

MEDICINE*

Pr 17: 22 A cheerful heart is good *m,*

MEDITATE (MEDITATES MEDITATION)

Jos 1: 8 from your mouth; *m* on it day
Ps 119: 15 I *m* on your precepts
119: 78 but I will *m* on your precepts.
119: 97 I *m* on it all day long.
145: 5 I will *m* on your wonderful works.

MEDITATES* (MEDITATE)

Ps 1: 2 and on his law he *m* day and night.

MEDITATION* (MEDITATE)

Ps 19: 14 of my mouth and the *m* of my heart
104: 34 May my *m* be pleasing to him,

MEDIUM

Lev 20: 27 "'A man or woman who is a *m*

MEEK (MEEKNESS)

Ps 37: 11 But the *m* will inherit the land
Mt 5: 5 Blessed are the *m,*

MEEKNESS* (MEEK)

2Co 10: 1 By the *m* and gentleness of Christ,

MEET (MEETING)

Ps 85: 10 Love and faithfulness *m* together;
Am 4: 12 prepare to *m* your God, O Israel."
1Th 4: 17 them in the clouds to *m* the Lord

MEETING (MEET)

Heb 10: 25 Let us not give up *m* together,

MELCHIZEDEK

Ge 14: 18 *M* king of Salem brought out bread
Ps 110: 4 in the order of *M*."
Heb 7: 11 in the order of *M*, not in the order

MELT

2Pe 3: 12 and the elements will *m* in the heat.

MEMBERS

Mic 7: 6 a man's enemies are the *m*
Ro 7: 23 law at work in the *m* of my body,
12: 4 of us has one body with many *m*,
1Co 6: 15 not know that your bodies are *m*
12: 24 But God has combined the *m*
Eph 4: 25 for we are all *m* of one body.
Col 3: 15 as *m* of one body you were called

MEN (MAN)

Mt 4: 19 will make you fishers of *m*
5: 16 your light shine before *m*
12: 36 *m* will have to give account
Jn 12: 32 will draw all *m* to myself
Ac 5: 29 obey God rather than *m!*
Ro 1: 27 indecent acts with other *m*,
5: 12 death came to all *m*,
1Co 9: 22 all things to all *m*
2Co 5: 11 we try to persuade *m*.
1Ti 2: 4 wants all *m* to be saved
2Ti 2: 2 entrust to reliable *m*
2Pe 1: 21 but *m* spoke from God

MENAHEM

King of Israel (2Ki 15:17-22).

MERCIFUL (MERCY)

Dt 4: 31 the LORD your God is a *m* God;
Ne 9: 31 for you are a gracious and *m* God.
Mt 5: 7 Blessed are the *m*,
Lk 6: 36 Be *m*, just as your Father is *m*.
Heb 2: 17 in order that he might become a *m*
Jude : 22 Be *m* to those who doubt; snatch

MERCY (MERCIFUL)

Ex 33: 19 *m* on whom I will have *m*,
Ps 25: 6 O LORD, your great *m* and love,
Isa 63: 9 and *m* he redeemed them;
Hos 6: 6 For I desire *m*, not sacrifice,
Mic 6: 8 To act justly and to love *m*
Hab 3: 2 in wrath remember *m*.
Mt 12: 7 I desire *m*, not sacrifice,' you
23: 23 justice, *m* and faithfulness.
Ro 9: 15 "I will have *m* on whom I have *m*,
Eph 2: 4 who is rich in *m*, made us alive
Jas 2: 13 *M* triumphs over judgment!
1Pe 1: 3 In his great *m* he has given us new

MESSAGE

Isa 53: 1 Who has believed our *m*
Jn 12: 38 "Lord, who has believed our *m*
Ro 10: 17 faith comes from hearing the *m*,
1Co 1: 18 For the *m* of the cross is
2Co 5: 19 to us the *m* of reconciliation.

MESSIAH*

Jn 1: 41 "We have found the *M*" (that is,
4: 25 "I know that *M*" (called Christ) "is

METHUSELAH

Ge 5: 27 Altogether, *M* lived 969 years,

MICHAEL

Archangel (Jude 9); warrior in angelic realm, protector of Israel (Da 10:13, 21; 12:1; Rev 12:7).

MIDWIVES

Ex 1: 17 The *m*, however, feared God

MIGHT (ALMIGHTY MIGHTY)

Jdg 16: 30 Then he pushed with all his *m*,
2Sa 6: 14 before the LORD with all his *m*,
Ps 21: 13 we will sing and praise your *m*.
Zec 4: 6 'Not by *m* nor by power,
1Ti 6: 16 To him be honor and *m* for ever.

MIGHTY (MIGHT)

Ex 6: 1 of my *m* hand he will drive them
Dt 7: 8 he brought you out with a *m* hand
2Sa 1: 19 How the *m* have fallen!
23: 8 the names of David's *m* men:
Ps 24: 8 The LORD strong and *m*,
50: 1 The *M* One, God, the LORD,
89: 8 You are *m*, O LORD,
136: 12 with a *m* hand and outstretched
147: 5 Great is our Lord and *m* in power;
Isa 9: 6 Wonderful Counselor, *M* God,
Zep 3: 17 he is *m* to save.
Eph 6: 10 in the Lord and in his *m* power.

MILE*

Mt 5: 41 If someone forces you to go one *m*,

MILK

Ex 3: 8 a land flowing with *m* and honey—
Isa 55: 1 Come, buy wine and *m*
1Co 3: 2 I gave you *m*, not solid food,
Heb 5: 12 You need *m*, not solid food!
1Pe 2: 2 babies, crave pure spiritual *m*,

MILLSTONE (STONE)

Lk 17: 2 sea with a *m* tied around his neck

MIND (DOUBLE-MINDED MINDFUL MINDS)

1Sa 15: 29 Israel does not lie or change his *m*;
1Ch 28: 9 devotion and with a willing *m*,
Ps 26: 2 examine my heart and my *m*;
Isa 26: 3 him whose *m* is steadfast,
Mt 22: 37 all your soul and with all your *m*.'
Ac 4: 32 believers were one in heart and *m*.
Ro 7: 25 I myself in my *m* am a slave
8: 7 the sinful *m* is hostile to God.
12: 2 by the renewing of your *m*.
1Co 2: 9 no *m* has conceived
14: 14 spirit prays, but my *m* is unfruitful.
2Co 13: 11 be of one *m*, live in peace.
Php 3: 19 Their *m* is on earthly things.
1Th 4: 11 to *m* your own business
Heb 7: 21 and will not change his *m*:

MINDFUL* (MIND)

Ps 8: 4 what is man that you are *m* of him,
Lk 1: 48 God my Savior, for he has been *m*
Heb 2: 6 What is man that you are *m* of him,

MINDS (MIND)

Ps 7: 9 who searches *m* and hearts,
Jer 31: 33 "I will put my law in their *m*
Eph 4: 23 new in the attitude of your *m*;
Col 3: 2 Set your *m* on things above,
Heb 8: 10 I will put my laws in their *m*
Rev 2: 23 I am he who searches hearts and *m*,

MINISTERING (MINISTRY)

Heb 1: 14 Are not all angels *m* spirits sent

MINISTRY (MINISTERING)

Ac 6: 4 to prayer and the *m* of the word."
2Co 5: 18 gave us the *m* of reconciliation:
2Ti 4: 5 discharge all the duties of your *m*.

MIRACLES (MIRACULOUS)

1Ch 16: 12 his *m*, and the judgments he
Ps 77: 14 You are the God who performs *m*;
Mt 11: 20 most of his *m* had been performed,
11: 21 If the *m* that were performed
24: 24 and perform great signs and *m*
Mk 6: 2 does *m!* Isn't this the carpenter?
Jn 10: 32 "I have shown you many great *m*
14: 11 the evidence of the *m* themselves.
Ac 2: 22 accredited by God to you by *m*,
19: 11 God did extraordinary *m*
1Co 12: 28 third teachers, then workers of *m*,
Heb 2: 4 it by signs, wonders and various *m*,

MIRACULOUS (MIRACLES)

Jn 3: 2 could perform the *m* signs you are
9: 16 "How can a sinner do such *m* signs
20: 30 Jesus did many other *m* signs
1Co 1: 22 Jews demand *m* signs and Greeks

MIRE

Ps 40: 2 out of the mud and *m*;

Isa 57: 20 whose waves cast up *m* and mud.

MIRIAM

Sister of Moses and Aaron (Nu 26:59). Led dancing at Red Sea (Ex 15:20-21). Struck with leprosy for criticizing Moses (Nu 12). Death (Nu 20:1).

MIRROR

Jas 1: 23 a man who looks at his face in a *m*

MISERY

Ex 3: 7 "I have indeed seen the *m*
Jdg 10: 16 he could bear Israel's *m* no longer.
Hos 5: 15 in their *m* they will earnestly seek
Ro 3: 16 ruin and *m* mark their ways,
Jas 5: 1 of the *m* that is coming upon you.

MISLED

1Co 15: 33 Do not be *m:* "Bad company

MISS

Pr 19: 2 nor to be hasty and *m* the way.

MIST

Hos 6: 4 Your love is like the morning *m,*
Jas 4: 14 You are a *m* that appears for a little

MISUSE*

Ex 20: 7 "You shall not *m* the name
Dt 5: 11 "You shall not *m* the name
Ps 139: 20 your adversaries *m* your name.

MOCK (MOCKED MOCKER MOCKERS MOCKING)

Ps 22: 7 All who see me *m* me;
Pr 14: 9 Fools *m* at making amends for sin,
Mk 10: 34 who will *m* him and spit on him,

MOCKED (MOCK)

Mt 27: 29 knelt in front of him and *m* him.
27: 41 of the law and the elders *m* him.
Gal 6: 7 not be deceived: God cannot be *m.*

MOCKER (MOCK)

Pr 9: 7 corrects a *m* invites insult;
9: 12 if you are a *m,* you alone will suffer
20: 1 Wine is a *m* and beer a brawler;
22: 10 Drive out the *m,* and out goes strife

MOCKERS (MOCK)

Ps 1: 1 or sit in the seat of *m.*

MOCKING (MOCK)

Isa 50: 6 face from *m* and spitting.

MODEL*

Eze 28: 12 "'You were the *m* of perfection,
1Th 1: 7 And so you became a *m*
2Th 3: 9 to make ourselves a *m* for you

MOMENT

Job 20: 5 the joy of the godless lasts but a *m.*
Ps 30: 5 For his anger lasts only a *m,*
Isa 66: 8 or a nation be brought forth in a *m?*

Gal 2: 5 We did not give in to them for a *m,*

MONEY

Ecc 5: 10 Whoever loves *m* never has *m*
Isa 55: 1 and you who have no *m,*
Mt 6: 24 You cannot serve both God and *M.*
Lk 9: 3 no bread, no *m,* no extra tunic.
1Co 16: 2 set aside a sum of *m* in keeping
1Ti 3: 3 not quarrelsome, not a lover of *m.*
6: 10 For the love of *m* is a root
2Ti 3: 2 lovers of *m,* boastful, proud,
Heb 13: 5 free from the love of *m*
1Pe 5: 2 not greedy for *m,* but eager to serve

MOON

Ps 121: 6 nor the *m* by night.
Joel 2: 31 and the *m* to blood
1Co 15: 41 *m* another and the stars another;

MORNING

Ge 1: 5 and there was *m* —the first day.
Dt 28: 67 In the *m* you will say, "If only it
Ps 5: 3 In the *m,* O LORD,
2Pe 1: 19 and the *m* star rises in your hearts.
Rev 22: 16 of David, and the bright *M* Star."

MORTAL

1Co 15: 53 and the *m* with immortality.

MOSES

Levite; brother of Aaron (Ex 6:20; 1Ch 6:3). Put in basket into Nile; discovered and raised by Pharaoh's daughter (Ex 2:1-10). Fled to Midian after killing Egyptian (Ex 2:11-15). Married to Zipporah, fathered Gershom (Ex 2:16-22).

Called by the LORD to deliver Israel (Ex 3-4). Pharaoh's resistance (Ex 5). Ten plagues (Ex 7-11). Passover and Exodus (Ex 12-13). Led Israel through Red Sea (Ex 14). Song of deliverance (Ex 15:1-21). Brought water from rock (Ex 17:1-7). Raised hands to defeat Amalekites (Ex 17:8-16). Delegated judges (Ex 18; Dt 1:9-18).

Received Law at Sinai (Ex 19-23; 25-31; Jn 1:17). Announced Law to Israel (Ex 19:7-8; 24; 35). Broke tablets because of golden calf (Ex 32; Dt 9). Saw glory of the LORD (Ex 33-34). Supervised building of tabernacle (Ex 36-40). Set apart Aaron and priests (Lev 8-9). Numbered tribes (Nu 1-4; 26). Opposed by Aaron and Miriam (Nu 12). Sent spies into Canaan (Nu 13). Announced forty years of wandering for failure to enter land (Nu 14). Opposed by Korah (Nu 16). Forbidden to enter land for striking rock (Nu 20:1-13; Dt 1:37). Lifted bronze snake for healing (Nu 21:4-9; Jn 3:14). Final address to Israel (Dt 1-33). Succeeded by Joshua (Nu 27:12-23; Dt 34). Death (Dt 34:5-12).

"Law of Moses" (1Ki 2:3; Ezr 3:2; Mk 12:26; Lk 24:44). "Book of Moses" (2Ch 25:12; Ne 13:1). "Song of Moses" (Ex 15:1-21; Rev 15:3). "Prayer of Moses" (Ps 90).

MOTH

Mt 6: 19 where *m* and rust destroy,

MOTHER (MOTHER'S)

Ge 2: 24 and *m* and be united to his wife,
3: 20 because she would become the *m*
Ex 20: 12 "Honor your father and your *m,*
Lev 20: 9 "'If anyone curses his father or *m,*
Dt 5: 16 "Honor your father and your *m,*
21: 18 who does not obey his father and *m*
27: 16 who dishonors his father or his *m.*"
1Sa 2: 19 Each year his *m* made him a little
Ps 113: 9 as a happy *m* of children.
Pr 23: 25 May your father and *m* be glad;
29: 15 child left to himself disgraces his *m.*
31: 1 an oracle his *m* taught him:
Isa 49: 15 "Can a *m* forget the baby
66: 13 As a *m* comforts her child,
Mt 10: 37 or *m* more than me is not worthy
15: 4 'Honor your father and *m*'
19: 5 and *m* and be united to his wife,
Mk 7: 10 'Honor your father and your *m,*'
10: 19 honor your father and *m.*'"
Jn 19: 27 to the disciple, "Here is your *m.*"

MOTHER'S (MOTHER)

Job 1: 21 "Naked I came from my *m* womb,
Pr 1: 8 and do not forsake your *m* teaching

MOTIVES*

Pr 16: 2 but *m* are weighed by the LORD.
1Co 4: 5 will expose the *m* of men's hearts.
Php 1: 18 whether from false *m* or true,
1Th 2: 3 spring from error or impure *m,*
Jas 4: 3 because you ask with wrong *m,*

MOUNTAIN (MOUNTAINS)

Mic 4: 2 let us go up to the *m* of the LORD,
Mt 17: 20 say to this *m,* 'Move from here

MOUNTAINS (MOUNTAIN)

Isa 52: 7 How beautiful on the *m*
55: 12 the *m* and hills
1Co 13: 2 if I have a faith that can move *m,*

MOURN (MOURNING)

Ecc 3: 4 a time to *m* and a time to dance,
Isa 61: 2 to comfort all who *m,*
Mt 5: 4 Blessed are those who *m,*
Ro 12: 15 *m* with those who *m.*

MOURNING (MOURN)

Jer 31: 13 I will turn their *m* into gladness;
Rev 21: 4 There will be no more death or *m*

MOUTH

Jos 1: 8 of the Law depart from your *m;*
Ps 19: 14 May the words of my *m*
40: 3 He put a new song in my *m,*
119:103 sweeter than honey to my *m!*

Pr 16: 23 A wise man's heart guides his *m*,
27: 2 praise you, and not your own *m;*
Isa 51: 16 I have put my words in your *m*
Mt 12: 34 overflow of the heart the *m* speaks.
15: 11 into a man's *m* does not make him
Ro 10: 9 That if you confess with your *m*,

MUD

Ps 40: 2 out of the *m* and mire;
Isa 57: 20 whose waves cast up mire and *m.*
2Pe 2: 22 back to her wallowing in the *m.*"

MULTITUDE (MULTITUDES)

Isa 31: 1 who trust in the *m* of their chariots
1Pe 4: 8 love covers over a *m* of sins.
Rev 7: 9 me was a great *m* that no one could

MULTITUDES (MULTITUDE)

Joel 3: 14 *M, m* in the valley of decision!

MURDER (MURDERER MURDERERS)

Ex 20: 13 "You shall not *m.*
Mt 15: 19 *m,* adultery, sexual immorality,
Ro 13: 9 "Do not *m,*" "Do not steal,"
Jas 2: 11 adultery," also said, "Do not *m.*"

MURDERER (MURDER)

Nu 35: 16 he is a *m;* the *m* shall be put
Jn 8: 44 He was a *m* from the beginning,
1Jn 3: 15 who hates his brother is a *m,*

MURDERERS (MURDER)

1Ti 1: 9 for *m,* for adulterers and perverts,
Rev 21: 8 the *m,* the sexually immoral,

MUSIC

Jdg 5: 3 I will make *m* to the LORD,
Ps 27: 6 and make *m* to the LORD.
95: 2 and extol him with *m* and song.
98: 4 burst into jubilant song with *m;*
108: 1 make *m* with all my soul.
Eph 5: 19 make *m* in your heart to the Lord,

MUSTARD

Mt 13: 31 kingdom of heaven is like a *m* seed,
17: 20 you have faith as small as a *m* seed,

MUZZLE

Dt 25: 4 Do not *m* an ox while it is treading
Ps 39: 1 I will put a *m* on my mouth
1Co 9: 9 "Do not *m* an ox while it is

MYRRH

Mt 2: 11 of gold and of incense and of *m.*
Mk 15: 23 offered him wine mixed with *m,*

MYSTERY

Ro 16: 25 to the revelation of the *m* hidden
1Co 15: 51 I tell you a *m:* We will not all sleep,
Eph 5: 32 This is a profound *m* —
Col 1: 26 the *m* that has been kept hidden
1Ti 3: 16 the *m* of godliness is great:

MYTHS

1Ti 4: 7 Have nothing to do with godless *m*

NADAB

Son of Jeroboam I; king of Israel (1Ki 15:25-32).

NAIL* (NAILING)

Jn 20: 25 "Unless I see the *n* marks

NAILING* (NAIL)

Ac 2: 23 him to death by *n* him to the cross.
Col 2: 14 he took it away, *n* it to the cross.

NAKED

Ge 2: 25 The man and his wife were both *n,*
Job 1: 21 *N* I came from my mother's womb,
Isa 58: 7 when you see the *n,* to clothe him,
2Co 5: 3 are clothed, we will not be found *n.*

NAME

Ex 3: 15 This is my *n* forever, the *n*
20: 7 "You shall not misuse the *n*
Dt 5: 11 "You shall not misuse the *n*
28: 58 this glorious and awe-some *n* —
1Ki 5: 5 will build the temple for my *N.'*
2Ch 7: 14 my people, who are called by my *n,*
Ps 34: 3 let us exalt his *n* together.
103: 1 my inmost being, praise his holy *n.*
147: 4 and calls them each by *n.*
Pr 22: 1 A good *n* is more desirable
30: 4 What is his *n,* and the *n* of his son?
Isa 40: 26 and calls them each by *n.*
57: 15 who lives forever, whose *n* is holy:
Jer 14: 7 do something for the sake of your *n*
Da 12: 1 everyone whose *n* is found written
Joel 2: 32 on the *n* of the LORD will be saved
Zec 14: 9 one LORD, and his *n* the only *n.*
Mt 1: 21 and you are to give him the *n* Jesus,
6: 9 hallowed be your *n,*
18: 20 or three come together in my *n,*
Jn 10: 3 He calls his own sheep by *n*
16: 24 asked for anything in my *n.*
Ac 4: 12 for there is no other *n*
Ro 10: 13 "Everyone who calls on the *n*
Php 2: 9 him the *n* that is above every *n,*
Col 3: 17 do it all in the *n* of the Lord Jesus,
Heb 1: 4 as the *n* he has inherited is superior
Rev 20: 15 If anyone's *n* was not found written

NAOMI

Mother-in-law of Ruth (Ru 1). Advised Ruth to seek marriage with Boaz (Ru 2-4).

NARROW

Mt 7: 13 "Enter through the *n* gate.

NATHANAEL

Apostle (Jn 1:45-49; 21:2). Probably also called Bartholomew (Mt 10:3).

NATION (NATIONS)

Ge 12: 2 "I will make you into a great *n*
Ps 33: 12 Blessed is the *n* whose God is
Pr 14: 34 Righteousness exalts a *n,*
Isa 65: 1 To a *n* that did not call on my name
1Pe 2: 9 a royal priesthood, a holy *n,*
Rev 7: 9 from every *n,* tribe, people

NATIONS (NATION)

Ge 17: 4 You will be the father of many *n.*
18: 18 and all *n* on earth will be blessed
Ex 19: 5 of all *n* you will be my treasured
Ne 1: 8 I will scatter you among the *n,*
Ps 96: 3 Declare his glory among the *n,*
Isa 40: 15 Surely the *n* are like a drop
Eze 36: 23 *n* will know that I am the LORD,
Hag 2: 7 and the desired of all *n* will come,
Zec 8: 23 *n* will take firm hold of one Jew
14: 2 I will gather all the *n* to Jerusalem
Mt 28: 19 and make disciples of all *n,*
Rev 21: 24 The *n* will walk by its light,

NATURAL (NATURE)

Ro 6: 19 you are weak in your *n* selves.
1Co 15: 44 If there is a *n* body, there is

NATURE (NATURAL)

Ro 8: 4 do not live according to the sinful *n*
8: 8 by the sinful *n* cannot please God.
Gal 5: 19 The acts of the sinful *n* are obvious:
5: 24 Jesus have crucified the sinful *n*
Php 2: 6 Who, being in very *n* God,

NAZARENE

Mt 2: 23 prophets: "He will be called a *N.*"

NAZIRITE

Jdg 13: 7 because the boy will be a *N* of God

NECESSARY

Ro 13: 5 it is *n* to submit to the authorities,

NEED (NEEDS NEEDY)

Ps 116: 6 when I was in great *n,* he saved me.
Mt 6: 8 for your Father knows what you *n*
Ro 12: 13 with God's people who are in *n.*
1Co 12: 21 say to the hand, "I don't *n* you!"

1Jn 3: 17 sees his brother in *n* but has no pity

NEEDLE

Mt 19: 24 go through the eye of a *n*

NEEDS (NEED)

Isa 58: 11 he will satisfy your *n*
Php 4: 19 God will meet all your *n* according

NEEDY (NEED)

Pr 14: 21 blessed is he who is kind to the *n*.
14: 31 to the *n* honors God.
31: 20 and extends her hands to the *n*.
Mt 6: 2 "So when you give to the *n*,

NEGLECT (NEGLECTED)

Ne 10: 39 We will not *n* the house of our God
Ps 119: 16 I will not *n* your word.
Ac 6: 2 for us to *n* the ministry of the word
1Ti 4: 14 Do not *n* your gift, which was

NEGLECTED (NEGLECT)

Mt 23: 23 But you have *n* the more important

NEHEMIAH

Cupbearer of Artaxerxes (Ne 2:1); governor of Israel (Ne 8:9). Returned to Jerusalem to rebuild walls (Ne 2-6). With Ezra, reestablished worship (Ne 8). Prayer confessing nation's sin (Ne 9). Dedicated wall (Ne 12).

NEIGHBOR (NEIGHBOR'S)

Ex 20: 16 give false testimony against your *n*.
Lev 19: 13 Do not defraud your *n* or rob him.
19: 18 but love your *n* as yourself.
Pr 27: 10 better a *n* nearby than a brother far
Mt 19: 19 and 'love your *n* as yourself.'"
Lk 10: 29 who is my *n*?" In reply Jesus said:
Ro 13: 10 Love does no harm to its *n*.

NEIGHBOR'S (NEIGHBOR)

Ex 20: 17 You shall not covet your *n* wife,
Dt 5: 21 not set your desire on your *n* house
19: 14 not move your *n* boundary stone
Pr 25: 17 Seldom set foot in your *n* house—

NEW

Ps 40: 3 He put a *n* song in my mouth,
Ecc 1: 9 there is nothing *n* under the sun.
Isa 65: 17 *n* heavens and a *n* earth.
Jer 31: 31 "when I will make a *n* covenant
Eze 36: 26 give you a *n* heart and put a *n* spirit
Mt 9: 17 Neither do men pour *n* wine
Lk 22: 20 "This cup is the *n* covenant
2Co 5: 17 he is a *n* creation; the old has gone,
Eph 4: 24 and to put on the *n* self, created
2Pe 3: 13 to a *n* heaven and a *n* earth,
1Jn 2: 8 Yet I am writing you a *n* command;

NEWBORN (BEAR)

1Pe 2: 2 Like *n* babies, crave pure spiritual

NEWS

Isa 52: 7 the feet of those who bring good *n*,
Mk 1: 15 Repent and believe the good *n*!"
16: 15 preach the good *n* to all creation.
Lk 2: 10 I bring you good *n*
Ac 5: 42 proclaiming the good *n* that Jesus
17: 18 preaching the good *n* about Jesus
Ro 10: 15 feet of those who bring good *n*!"

NICODEMUS*

Pharisee who visted Jesus at night (Jn 3). Argued fair treatment of Jesus (Jn 7:50-52). With Joseph, prepared Jesus for burial (Jn 19:38-42).

NIGHT

Job 35: 10 who gives songs in the *n*,
Ps 1: 2 on his law he meditates day and *n*.
91: 5 You will not fear the terror of *n*,
Jn 3: 2 He came to Jesus at *n* and said,
1Th 5: 2 Lord will come like a thief in the *n*.
5: 5 We do not belong to the *n*
Rev 21: 25 for there will be no *n* there.

NOAH

Righteous man (Eze 14:14, 20) called to build ark (Ge 6-8; Heb 11:7; 1Pe 3:20; 2Pe 2:5). God's covenant with (Ge 9:1-17). Drunkenness of (Ge 9:18-23). Blessed sons, cursed Canaan (Ge 9:24-27).

NOBLE

Ru 3: 11 you are a woman of *n* character.
Ps 45: 1 My heart is stirred by a *n* theme
Pr 12: 4 of *n* character is her husband's
31: 10 A wife of *n* character who can find?
31: 29 "Many women do *n* things,
Isa 32: 8 But the *n* man makes *n* plans,
Lk 8: 15 good soil stands for those with a *n*
Ro 9: 21 of clay some pottery for *n* purposes
Php 4: 8 whatever is *n*, whatever is right,
2Ti 2: 20 some are for *n* purposes

NOTHING

Ne 9: 21 in the desert; they lacked *n*,
Jer 32: 17 *N* is too hard for you
Jn 15: 5 apart from me you can do *n*.

NULLIFY

Ro 3: 31 Do we, then, *n* the law by this faith

OATH

Dt 7: 8 and kept the *o* he swore

OBEDIENCE (OBEY)

2Ch 31: 21 in *o* to the law and the commands,
Pr 30: 17 that scorns *o* to a mother,
Ro 1: 5 to the *o* that comes from faith.
6: 16 to *o*, which leads to righteousness?
2Jn : 6 that we walk in *o* to his commands.

OBEDIENT (OBEY)

Lk 2: 51 with them and was *o* to them.
Php 2: 8 and became *o* to death—
1Pe 1: 14 As *o* children, do not conform

OBEY (OBEDIENCE OBEDIENT OBEYED)

Ex 12: 24 "*O* these instructions as a lasting
Dt 6: 3 careful to *o* so that it may go well
13: 4 Keep his commands and *o* him;
21: 18 son who does not *o* his father
30: 2 and *o* him with all your heart
32: 46 children to *o* carefully all the words
1Sa 15: 22 To *o* is better than sacrifice,
Ps 119: 34 and *o* it with all my heart.
Mt 28: 20 to *o* everything I have commanded
Jn 14: 23 loves me, he will *o* my teaching.
Ac 5: 29 "We must *o* God rather than men!
Ro 6: 16 slaves to the one whom you *o*—
Gal 5: 3 obligated to *o* the whole law.
Eph 6: 1 *o* your parents in the Lord,
6: 5 *o* your earthly masters with respect
Col 3: 20 *o* your parents in everything,
1Ti 3: 4 and see that his children *o* him
Heb 13: 17 *O* your leaders and submit
1Jn 5: 3 love for God: to *o* his commands.

OBEYED (OBEY)

Ps 119: 4 that are to be fully *o*.
Jnh 3: 3 Jonah *o* the word of the LORD
Jn 17: 6 and they have *o* your word.
Ro 6: 17 you wholeheartedly *o* the form
Heb 11: 8 *o* and went, even though he did not
1Pe 3: 6 who *o* Abraham and called him her

OBLIGATED

Ro 1: 14 I am *o* both to Greeks
Gal 5: 3 himself be circumcised that he is *o*

OBSCENITY

Eph 5: 4 Nor should there be *o*, foolish talk

OBSOLETE

Heb 8: 13 he has made the first one *o*;

OBTAINED

Ro 9: 30 not pursue righteousness, have *o* it,
Php 3: 12 Not that I have already *o* all this,
Heb 9: 12 having *o* eternal redemption.

OFFENDED (OFFENSE)

Pr 18: 19 An *o* brother is more unyielding

OFFENSE (OFFENDED OFFENSIVE)

Pr 17: 9 over an *o* promotes love,
19: 11 it is to his glory to overlook an *o*.

OFFENSIVE (OFFENSE)

Ps 139: 24 See if there is any *o* way in me,

OFFER (OFFERED OFFERING OFFERINGS)

Ro 12: 1 to *o* your bodies as living sacrifices,

Heb 13: 15 therefore, let us continually *o*

OFFERED (OFFER)

Heb 7: 27 once for all when he *o* himself.
11: 4 By faith Abel *o* God a better

OFFERING (OFFER)

Ge 22: 8 provide the lamb for the burnt *o*,
Ps 40: 6 Sacrifice and *o* you did not desire,
Isa 53: 10 the LORD makes his life a guilt *o*,
Mt 5: 23 if you are *o* your gift at the altar
Eph 5: 2 as a fragrant *o* and sacrifice to God.
Heb 10: 5 "Sacrifice and *o* you did not desire,

OFFERINGS (OFFER)

Mal 3: 8 do we rob you?' "In tithes and *o*.
Mk 12: 33 is more important than all burnt *o*

OFFICER

2Ti 2: 4 wants to please his commanding *o*.

OFFSPRING

Ge 3: 15 and between your *o* and hers;
12: 7 "To your *o* I will give this land."

OIL

Ps 23: 5 You anoint my head with *o*;
Isa 61: 3 the *o* of gladness
Heb 1: 9 by anointing you with the *o* of joy."

OLIVE (OLIVES)

Zec 4: 3 Also there are two *o* trees by it,
Ro 11: 17 and you, though a wild *o* shoot,
Rev 11: 4 These are the two *o* trees

OLIVES (OLIVE)

Jas 3: 12 a fig tree bear *o*, or a grape-vine bear

OMEGA

Rev 1: 8 "I am the Alpha and the *O*,"

OMRI

King of Israel (1Ki 16:21-26).

OPINIONS*

1Ki 18: 21 will you waver between two *o*?
Pr 18: 2 but delights in airing his own *o*.

OPPORTUNITY

Ro 7: 11 seizing the *o* afforded
Gal 6: 10 as we have *o*, let us do good
Eph 5: 16 making the most of every *o*,
Col 4: 5 make the most of every *o*.
1Ti 5: 14 to give the enemy no *o* for slander.

OPPOSES

Jas 4: 6 "God *o* the proud
1Pe 5: 5 because, "God *o* the proud

OPPRESS (OPPRESSED)

Ex 22: 21 "Do not mistreat an alien or *o* him,
Zec 7: 10 Do not *o* the widow

OPPRESSED (OPPRESS)

Ps 9: 9 The LORD is a refuge for the *o*,
Isa 53: 7 He was *o* and afflicted,
Zec 10: 2 *o* for lack of a shepherd.

ORDAINED

Ps 8: 2 you have *o* praise

ORDERLY

1Co 14: 40 done in a fitting and *o* way.
Col 2: 5 and delight to see how *o* you are

ORGIES*

Ro 13: 13 not in *o* and drunkenness,
Gal 5: 21 drunkenness, *o*, and the like.
1Pe 4: 3 *o*, carousing and detestable

ORIGIN

2Pe 1: 21 For prophecy never had its *o*

ORPHANS

Jn 14: 18 will not leave you as *o*; I will come
Jas 1: 27 to look after *o* and widows

OUTCOME

Heb 13: 7 Consider the *o* of their way of life
1Pe 4: 17 what will the *o* be for those who do

OUTSIDERS*

Col 4: 5 wise in the way you act toward *o*;
1Th 4: 12 daily life may win the respect of *o*
1Ti 3: 7 also have a good reputation with *o*,

OUTSTANDING

SS 5: 10 *o* among ten thousand.
Ro 13: 8 no debt remain *o*,

OUTSTRETCHED

Ex 6: 6 and will redeem you with an *o* arm
Jer 27: 5 and *o* arm I made the earth
Eze 20: 33 an *o* arm and with outpoured wrath

OUTWEIGHS

2Co 4: 17 an eternal glory that far *o* them all.

OVERCOME (OVERCOMES)

Mt 16: 18 and the gates of Hades will not *o* it.
Mk 9: 24 I do believe; help me *o* my unbelief
Jn 16: 33 But take heart! I have *o* the world."
Ro 12: 21 Do not be *o* by evil, but *o* evil
1Jn 5: 4 is the victory that has *o* the world,
Rev 17: 14 but the Lamb will *o* them

OVERCOMES* (OVERCOME)

1Jn 5: 4 born of God *o* the world.
5: 5 Who is it that *o* the world?
Rev 2: 7 To him who *o*, I will give the right
2: 11 He who *o* will not be hurt at all
2: 17 To him who *o*, I will give some
2: 26 To him who *o* and does my will
3: 5 He who *o* will, like them, be
3: 12 Him who *o* I will make a pillar
3: 21 To him who *o*, I will give the right
21: 7 He who *o* will inherit all this,

OVERFLOW (OVERFLOWS)

Ps 119:171 May my lips *o* with praise,
Lk 6: 45 out of the *o* of his heart his mouth
Ro 15: 13 so that you may *o* with hope
2Co 4: 15 to *o* to the glory of God.
1Th 3: 12 *o* for each other and for everyone

OVERFLOWS* (OVERFLOW)

Ps 23: 5 my cup *o*.
2Co 1: 5 also through Christ our comfort *o*.

OVERJOYED* (JOY)

Da 6: 23 The king was *o* and gave orders
Mt 2: 10 they saw the star, they were *o*.
Jn 20: 20 The disciples were *o*
Ac 12: 14 she was so *o* she ran back
1Pe 4: 13 so that you may be *o*

OVERSEER (OVERSEERS)

1Ti 3: 1 anyone sets his heart on being an *o*,
3: 2 Now the *o* must be above reproach,
Tit 1: 7 Since an *o* is entrusted

OVERSEERS* (OVERSEER)

Ac 20: 28 the Holy Spirit has made you *o*.
Php 1: 1 together with the *o* and deacons:
1Pe 5: 2 as *o* —not because you must,

OVERWHELMED

Ps 38: 4 My guilt has *o* me
65: 3 When we were *o* by sins,
Mt 26: 38 "My soul is *o* with sorrow
Mk 7: 37 People were *o* with amazement.

OWE

Ro 13: 7 If you *o* taxes, pay taxes; if revenue
Phm : 19 to mention that you *o* me your very

OX

Dt 25: 4 Do not muzzle an *o*
Isa 11: 7 and the lion will eat straw like the *o*
1Co 9: 9 "Do not muzzle an *o*

PAGANS

Mt 5: 47 Do not even *p* do that? Be perfect,
1Pe 2: 12 such good lives among the *p* that,

PAIN (PAINFUL)

Ge 3: 16 with *p* you will give birth
Job 33: 19 may be chastened on a bed of *p*
Jn 16: 21 woman giving birth to a child has *p*

PAINFUL (PAIN)

Ge 3: 17 through *p* toil you will eat of it
Heb 12: 11 seems pleasant at the time, but *p*.
1Pe 4: 12 at the *p* trial you are suffering,

PALMS

Isa 49: 16 you on the *p* of my hands;

PANTS

Ps 42: 1 As the deer *p* for streams of water,

PARADISE*
Lk 23: 43 today you will be with me in *p*."
2Co 12: 4 God knows—was caught up to *p*.
Rev 2: 7 of life, which is in the *p* of God.

PARALYTIC
Mk 2: 3 bringing to him a *p*, carried by four

PARDON (PARDONS)
Isa 55: 7 and to our God, for he will freely *p*.

PARDONS* (PARDON)
Mic 7: 18 who *p* sin and forgives

PARENTS
Pr 17: 6 and *p* are the pride of their children
Lk 18: 29 left home or wife or brothers or *p*
21: 16 You will be betrayed even by *p*,
Ro 1: 30 they disobey their *p*; they are
2Co 12: 14 for their *p*, but *p* for their children.
Eph 6: 1 Children, obey your *p* in the Lord,
Col 3: 20 obey your *p* in everything,
2Ti 3: 2 disobedient to their *p*, ungrateful,

PARTIALITY
Dt 10: 17 who shows no *p* and accepts no
2Ch 19: 7 our God there is no injustice or *p*
Lk 20: 21 and that you do not show *p*

PARTICIPATION
1Co 10: 16 is not the bread that we break a *p*

PASS
Ex 12: 13 and when I see the blood, I will *p*
La 1: 12 to you, all you who *p* by?
Lk 21: 33 Heaven and earth will *p* away,
1Co 13: 8 there is knowledge, it will *p* away.

PASSION (PASSIONS)
1Co 7: 9 better to marry than to burn with *p*.

PASSIONS (PASSION)
Gal 5: 24 crucified the sinful nature with its *p*
Tit 2: 12 to ungodliness and worldly *p*,

PASSOVER
Ex 12: 11 Eat it in haste; it is the LORD's *P*.
Dt 16: 1 celebrate the *P* of the LORD your
1Co 5: 7 our *P* lamb, has been sacrificed.

PAST
Isa 43: 18 do not dwell on the *p*.
Ro 15: 4 in the *p* was written to teach us,
Heb 1: 1 In the *p* God spoke

PASTORS*
Eph 4: 11 and some to be *p* and teachers,

PASTURE (PASTURES)
Ps 37: 3 dwell in the land and enjoy safe *p*.
Ps 100: 3 we are his people, the sheep of his *p*
Jer 50: 7 against the LORD, their true *p*,
Eze 34: 13 I will *p* them on the mountains
Jn 10: 9 come in and go out, and find *p*.

PASTURES (PASTURE)
Ps 23: 2 He makes me lie down in green *p*,

PATCH
Mt 9: 16 No one sews a *p* of unshrunk cloth

PATH (PATHS)
Ps 27: 11 lead me in a straight *p*
119:105 and a light for my *p*.
Pr 15: 19 the *p* of the upright is a highway.
15: 24 The *p* of life leads upward
Isa 26: 7 The *p* of the righteous is level;
Lk 1: 79 to guide our feet into the *p* of peace
2Co 6: 3 no stumbling block in anyone's *p*,

PATHS (PATH)
Ps 23: 3 He guides me in *p* of righteousness
25: 4 teach me your *p*;
Pr 3: 6 and he will make your *p* straight.
Ro 11: 33 and his *p* beyond tracing out!
Heb 12: 13 "Make level *p* for your feet,"

PATIENCE (PATIENT)
Pr 19: 11 A man's wisdom gives him *p*;
2Co 6: 6 understanding, *p* and kindness;
Gal 5: 22 joy, peace, *p*, kindness, goodness,
Col 1: 11 may have great endurance and *p*,
3: 12 humility, gentleness and *p*.

PATIENT (PATIENCE PATIENTLY)
Pr 15: 18 but a *p* man calms a quarrel.
Ro 12: 12 Be joyful in hope, *p* in affliction,
1Co 13: 4 Love is *p*, love is kind.
Eph 4: 2 humble and gentle; be *p*,
1Th 5: 14 help the weak, be *p* with everyone.

PATIENTLY (PATIENT)
Ps 40: 1 I waited *p* for the LORD;
Ro 8: 25 we do not yet have, we wait for it *p*.

PATTERN
Ro 5: 14 who was a *p* of the one to come.
12: 2 longer to the *p* of this world,
2Ti 1: 13 keep as the *p* of sound teaching,

PAUL

Also called Saul (Ac 13:9). Pharisee from Tarsus (Ac 9:11; Php 3:5). Apostle (Gal 1). At stoning of Stephen (Ac 8:1). Persecuted Church (Ac 9:1-2; Gal 1:13). Vision of Jesus on road to Damascus (Ac 9:4-9; 26:12-18). In Arabia (Gal 1:17). Preached in Damascus; escaped death through the wall in a basket (Ac 9:19-25). In Jerusalem; sent back to Tarsus (Ac 9:26-30).

Brought to Antioch by Barnabas (Ac 11:22-26). First missionary journey to Cyprus and Galatia (Ac 13-14). Stoned at Lystra (Ac 14:19-20). At Jerusalem council (Ac 15). Split with Barnabas over Mark (Ac 15:36-41).

Second missionary journey with Silas (Ac 16-20). Called to Macedonia (Ac 16:6-10). Freed from prison in Philippi (Ac 16:16-40). In Thessalonica (Ac 17:1-9). Speech in Athens (Ac 17:16-33). In Corinth (Ac 18). In Ephesus (Ac 19). Return to Jerusalem (Ac 20). Farewell to Ephesian elders (Ac 20:13-38). Arrival in Jerusalem (Ac 21:1-26). Arrested (Ac 21:27-36). Addressed crowds (Ac 22), Sanhedrin (Ac 23:1-11). Transferred to Caesarea (Ac 23:12-35). Trial before Felix (Ac 24), Festus (Ac 25:1-12). Before Agrippa (Ac 25:13-26:32). Voyage to Rome; shipwreck (Ac 27). Arrival in Rome (Ac 28).

PAY (REPAID REPAY)
Lev 26: 43 They will *p* for their sins
Pr 22: 17 *P* attention and listen
Mt 22: 17 Is it right to *p* taxes to Caesar
Ro 13: 6 This is also why you *p* taxes,
2Pe 1: 19 you will do well to *p* attention to it,

PEACE (PEACEMAKERS)
Nu 6: 26 and give you *p*."'
Ps 34: 14 seek *p* and pursue it.
85: 10 righteousness and *p* kiss each other
119:165 Great *p* have they who love your
122: 6 Pray for the *p* of Jerusalem:
Pr 14: 30 A heart at *p* gives life to the body,
17: 1 Better a dry crust with *p* and quiet
Isa 9: 6 Everlasting Father, Prince of *P*.
26: 3 You will keep in perfect *p*
48: 22 "There is no *p*," says the LORD,
Zec 9: 10 He will proclaim *p* to the nations.
Mt 10: 34 I did not come to bring *p*,
Lk 2: 14 on earth *p* to men on whom his
Jn 14: 27 *P* I leave with you; my *p*
16: 33 so that in me you may have *p*.
Ro 5: 1 we have *p* with God
1Co 7: 15 God has called us to live in *p*.
14: 33 a God of disorder but of *p*.
Gal 5: 22 joy, *p*, patience, kindness,
Eph 2: 14 he himself is our *p*, who has made
Php 4: 7 the *p* of God, which transcends all
Col 1: 20 by making *p* through his blood,
3: 15 Let the *p* of Christ rule
1Th 5: 3 While people are saying, "*P*
2Th 3: 16 the Lord of *p* himself give you *p*
2Ti 2: 22 righteousness, faith, love and *p*,
1Pe 3: 11 he must seek *p* and pursue it.
Rev 6: 4 power to take *p* from the earth

PEACEMAKERS* (PEACE)
Mt 5: 9 Blessed are the *p*,
Jas 3: 18 *P* who sow in peace raise a harvest

PEARL* (PEARLS)
Rev 21: 21 each gate made of a single *p*.

PEARLS (PEARL)
Mt 7: 6 do not throw your *p* to pigs.
13: 45 like a merchant looking for fine *p*.
1Ti 2: 9 or gold or *p* or expensive clothes,

Rev 21: 21 The twelve gates were twelve *p,*

PEKAH

King of Israel (2Ki 15:25-31; Isa 7:1).

PEKAHIAH*

Son of Menahem; king of Israel (2Ki 15:22-26).

PEN

Mt 5: 18 letter, not the least stroke of a *p,*

PENTECOST

Ac 2: 1 of *P* came, they were all together

PEOPLE (PEOPLES)

Dt 32: 9 the LORD's portion is his *p,*
Ru 1: 16 Your *p* will be my *p*
2Ch 7: 14 if my *p,* who are called
Jer 24: 7 They will be my *p,*
Zec 2: 11 and will become my *p.*
Lk 2: 10 joy that will be for all the *p.*
Ac 15: 14 from the Gentiles a *p.*
2Co 6: 16 and they will be my *p.*"
Tit 2: 14 a *p* that are his very own,
1Pe 2: 9 you are a chosen *p,*
Rev 21: 3 They will be his *p,*

PEOPLES (PEOPLE)

Da 7: 14 all *p,* nations and men
Mic 4: 1 and *p* will stream to it.

PERCEIVING

Isa 6: 9 be ever seeing, but never *p.*'

PERFECT (PERFECTER PERFECTION)

SS 6: 9 but my dove, my *p* one, is unique,
Isa 26: 3 You will keep in *p* peace
Mt 5: 48 as your heavenly Father is *p.*
Ro 12: 2 his good, pleasing and *p* will.
2Co 12: 9 for my power is made *p*
Col 1: 28 so that we may present everyone *p*
3: 14 binds them all together in *p* unity.
Heb 9: 11 and more *p* tabernacle that is not
10: 14 he has made *p* forever those who
Jas 1: 17 Every good and *p* gift is from above
1: 25 into the *p* law that gives freedom,
3: 2 he is a *p* man, able
1Jn 4: 18 But *p* love drives out fear,

PERFECTER* (PERFECT)

Heb 12: 2 the author and *p* of our faith,

PERFECTION (PERFECT)

Ps 119: 96 To all *p* I see a limit;
2Co 13: 11 Aim for *p,* listen to my appeal,
Heb 7: 11 If *p* could have been attained

PERFORMS

Ps 77: 14 You are the God who *p* miracles;

PERISH (PERISHABLE)

Ps 1: 6 but the way of the wicked will *p.*
102: 26 They will *p,* but you remain;
Lk 13: 3 unless you repent, you too will all *p*
Jn 10: 28 eternal life, and they shall never *p;*
Col 2: 22 These are all destined to *p* with use,
Heb 1: 11 They will *p,* but you remain;
2Pe 3: 9 not wanting anyone to *p,*

PERISHABLE (PERISH)

1Co 15: 42 The body that is sown is *p,*

PERJURERS

1Ti 1: 10 for slave traders and liars and *p*—

PERMISSIBLE (PERMIT)

1Co 10: 23 "Everything is *p*"—but not

PERMIT (PERMISSIBLE)

1Ti 2: 12 I do not *p* a woman to teach

PERSECUTE (PERSECUTED PERSECUTION)

Mt 5: 11 *p* you and falsely say all kinds
Jn 15: 20 they persecuted me, they will *p* you
Ac 9: 4 why do you *p* me?" "Who are you,
Ro 12: 14 Bless those who *p* you; bless

PERSECUTED (PERSECUTE)

1Co 4: 12 when we are *p,* we endure it;
2Ti 3: 12 life in Christ Jesus will be *p,*

PERSECUTION (PERSECUTE)

Ro 8: 35 or hardship or *p* or famine

PERSEVERANCE (PERSEVERE)

Ro 5: 3 we know that suffering produces *p;*
5: 4 *p,* character; and character, hope.
Heb 12: 1 run with *p* the race marked out
Jas 1: 3 the testing of your faith develops *p.*
2Pe 1: 6 *p;* and to *p,* godliness;

PERSEVERE* (PERSEVERANCE PERSEVERED PERSEVERES)

1Ti 4: 16 *P* in them, because if you do,
Heb 10: 36 You need to *p* so that

PERSEVERED* (PERSEVERE)

Heb 11: 27 he *p* because he saw him who is
Jas 5: 11 consider blessed those who have *p.*
Rev 2: 3 You have *p* and have endured

PERSEVERES* (PERSEVERE)

1Co 13: 7 trusts, always hopes, always *p.*
Jas 1: 12 Blessed is the man who *p*

PERSUADE

2Co 5: 11 is to fear the Lord, we try to *p* men.

PERVERSION (PERVERT)

Lev 18: 23 sexual relations with it; that is a *p.*
Jude : 7 up to sexual immorality and *p.*

PERVERT (PERVERSION PERVERTS)

Gal 1: 7 are trying to *p* the gospel of Christ.

PERVERTS* (PERVERT)

1Ti 1: 10 for murderers, for adulterers and *p,*

PESTILENCE

Ps 91: 6 nor the *p* that stalks in the darkness

PETER

Apostle, brother of Andrew, also called Simon (Mt 10:2; Mk 3:16; Lk 6:14; Ac 1:13), and Cephas (Jn 1:42). Confession of Christ (Mt 16:13-20; Mk 8:27-30; Lk 9:18-27). At transfiguration (Mt 17:1-8; Mk 9:2-8; Lk 9:28-36; 2Pe 1:16-18). Caught fish with coin (Mt 17:24-27). Denial of Jesus predicted (Mt 26:31-35; Mk 14:27-31; Lk 22:31-34; Jn 13:31-38). Denied Jesus (Mt 26:69-75; Mk 14:66-72; Lk 22:54-62; Jn 18:15-27). Commissioned by Jesus to shepherd his flock (Jn 21:15-23).

Speech at Pentecost (Ac 2). Healed beggar (Ac 3:1-10). Speech at temple (Ac 3:11-26), before Sanhedrin (Ac 4:1-22). In Samaria (Ac 8:14-25). Sent by vision to Cornelius (Ac 10). Announced salvation of Gentiles in Jerusalem (Ac 11;15). Freed from prison (Ac12). Inconsistency at Antioch (Gal 2:11-21). At Jerusalem Council (Ac15).

PHARISEES

Mt 5: 20 surpasses that of the *P*

PHILIP

1. Apostle (Mt 10:3; Mk 3:18; Lk 6:14; Jn 1:43-48; 14:8; Ac 1:13).

2. Deacon (Ac 6:1-7); evangelist in Samaria (Ac 8:4-25), to Ethiopian (Ac 8:26-40).

PHILOSOPHY*

Col 2: 8 through hollow and deceptive *p,*

PHYLACTERIES*

Mt 23: 5 They make their *p* wide

PHYSICAL

1Ti 4: 8 For *p* training is of some value,
Jas 2: 16 but does nothing about his *p* needs,

PIECES

Ge 15: 17 and passed between the *p.*
Jer 34: 18 and then walked between its *p.*

PIERCED

Ps 22: 16 they have *p* my hands and my feet.
Isa 53: 5 But he was *p* for our transgressions,
Zec 12: 10 look on me, the one they have *p,*
Jn 19: 37 look on the one they have *p.*"

PIGS

Mt 7: 6 do not throw your pearls to *p.*

PILATE

Governor of Judea. Questioned Jesus (Mt 27:1-26; Mk 15:15; Lk 22:66-23:25; Jn 18:28-19:16); sent him to Herod (Lk 23:6-12); consented to his crucifixion when crowds chose Barabbas (Mt 27:15-26; Mk 15:6-15; Lk 23:13-25; Jn 19:1-10).

PILLAR

Ge 19: 26 and she became a *p* of salt.
Ex 13: 21 ahead of them in a *p* of cloud
1Ti 3: 15 the *p* and foundation of the truth.

PIT

Ps 40: 2 He lifted me out of the slimy *p,*
103: 4 who redeems your life from the *p*
Mt 15: 14 a blind man, both will fall into a *p.*"

PITIED

1Co 15: 19 we are to be *p* more than all men.

PLAGUE

2Ch 6: 28 “When famine or *p* comes

PLAIN

Ro 1: 19 what may be known about God is *p*

PLAN (PLANNED PLANS)

Job 42: 2 no *p* of yours can be thwarted.
Pr 14: 22 those who *p* what is good find love
Eph 1: 11 predestined according to the *p*

PLANK

Mt 7: 3 attention to the *p* in your own eye?
Lk 6: 41 attention to the *p* in your own eye?

PLANNED (PLAN)

Ps 40: 5 The things you *p* for us
Isa 46: 11 what I have *p,* that will I do.
Heb 11: 40 God had *p* something better for us

PLANS (PLAN)

Ps 20: 4 and make all your *p* succeed.
33: 11 *p* of the LORD stand firm forever,
Pr 20: 18 Make *p* by seeking advice;
Isa 32: 8 But the noble man makes noble *p,*

PLANTED (PLANTS)

Ps 1: 3 He is like a tree *p* by streams
Mt 15: 13 Father has not *p* will be pulled
1Co 3: 6 I *p* the seed, Apollos watered it,

PLANTS (PLANTED)

1Co 3: 7 So neither he who *p* nor he who
9: 7 Who *p* a vineyard and does not eat

PLATTER

Mk 6: 25 head of John the Baptist on a *p.*”

PLAYED

Lk 7: 32 “‘We *p* the flute for you,
1Co 14: 7 anyone know what tune is being *p*

PLEADED

2Co 12: 8 Three times I *p* with the Lord

PLEASANT (PLEASE)

Ps 16: 6 for me in *p* places;
133: 1 How good and *p* it is
147: 1 how *p* and fitting to praise him!
Heb 12: 11 No discipline seems *p* at the time,

PLEASE (PLEASANT PLEASED PLEASES PLEASING PLEASURE PLEASURES)

Pr 20: 23 and dishonest scales do not *p* him.
Jer 6: 20 your sacrifices do not *p* me.”
Jn 5: 30 for I seek not to *p* myself
Ro 8: 8 by the sinful nature cannot *p* God.
15: 2 Each of us should *p* his neighbor
1Co 7: 32 affairs—how he can *p* the Lord.
10: 33 I try to *p* everybody in every way.
2Co 5: 9 So we make it our goal to *p* him,
Gal 1: 10 or of God? Or am I trying to *p* men
1Th 4: 1 how to live in order to *p* God,
2Ti 2: 4 wants to *p* his commanding officer.
Heb 11: 6 faith it is impossible to *p* God,

PLEASED (PLEASE)

Mt 3: 17 whom I love; with him I am well *p*
1Co 1: 21 God was *p* through the foolishness
Col 1: 19 For God was *p* to have all his
Heb 11: 5 commended as one who *p* God.
2Pe 1: 17 whom I love; with him I am well *p*

PLEASES (PLEASE)

Ps 135: 6 The LORD does whatever *p* him,
Pr 15: 8 but the prayer of the upright *p* him.
Jn 3: 8 The wind blows wherever it *p.*
8: 29 for I always do what *p* him.”
Col 3: 20 in everything, for this *p* the Lord.
1Ti 2: 3 This is good, and *p* God our Savior,
1Jn 3: 22 his commands and do what *p* him.

PLEASING (PLEASE)

Ps 104: 34 May my meditation be *p* to him,
Ro 12: 1 *p* to God—which is your spiritual
Php 4: 18 an acceptable sacrifice, *p* to God.
Heb 13: 21 may he work in us what is *p* to him,

PLEASURE (PLEASE)

Ps 5: 4 You are not a God who takes *p*
147: 10 His *p* is not in the strength
Pr 21: 17 He who loves *p* will become poor;
Eze 18: 32 For I take no *p* in the death
Eph 1: 5 in accordance with his *p* and will—
1: 9 of his will according to his good *p,*
2Ti 3: 4 lovers of *p* rather than lovers

PLEASURES (PLEASE)

Ps 16: 11 with eternal *p* at your right hand.
Heb 11: 25 rather than to enjoy the *p* of sin
2Pe 2: 13 reveling in their *p* while they feast

PLENTIFUL

Mt 9: 37 harvest is *p* but the workers are

PLOW (PLOWSHARES)

Lk 9: 62 “No one who puts his hand to the *p*

PLOWSHARES (PLOW)

Isa 2: 4 They will beat their swords into *p*
Joel 3: 10 Beat your *p* into swords

PLUNDER

Ex 3: 22 And so you will *p* the Egyptians.”

POINT

Jas 2: 10 yet stumbles at just one *p* is guilty

POISON

Mk 16: 18 and when they drink deadly *p,*
Jas 3: 8 It is a restless evil, full of deadly *p.*

POLLUTE* (POLLUTED)

Nu 35: 33 “‘Do not *p* the land where you are.
Jude : 8 these dreamers *p* their own bodies,

POLLUTED* (POLLUTE)

Ezr 9: 11 entering to possess is a land *p*
Pr 25: 26 Like a muddied spring or a *p* well
Ac 15: 20 to abstain from food *p* by idols,
Jas 1: 27 oneself from being *p* by the world.

PONDER

Ps 64: 9 and *p* what he has done
119: 95 but I will *p* your statutes.

POOR (POVERTY)

Dt 15: 4 there should be no *p* among you,
15: 11 There will always be *p* people
Ps 34: 6 This *p* man called, and the LORD
82: 3 maintain the rights of the *p*
112: 9 scattered abroad his gifts to the *p,*
Pr 10: 4 Lazy hands make a man *p,*
13: 7 to be *p,* yet has great wealth.
14: 31 oppresses the *p* shows contempt
19: 1 Better a *p* man whose walk is
19: 17 to the *p* lends to the LORD,
22: 2 Rich and *p* have this in common:
22: 9 for he shares his food with the *p.*
28: 6 Better a *p* man whose walk is
31: 20 She opens her arms to the *p*
Isa 61: 1 me to preach good news to the *p.*
Mt 5: 3 saying: “Blessed are the *p* in spirit,
11: 5 the good news is preached to the *p.*
19: 21 your possessions and give to the *p,*
26: 11 The *p* you will always have
Mk 12: 42 But a *p* widow came and put
Ac 10: 4 and gifts to the *p* have come up
1Co 13: 3 If I give all I possess to the *p*
2Co 8: 9 yet for your sakes he became *p,*
Jas 2: 2 and a *p* man in shabby clothes

PORTION

Dt 32: 9 For the LORD's *p* is his people,
2Ki 2: 9 “Let me inherit a double *p*
La 3: 24 to myself, “The LORD is my *p;*

POSSESS (POSSESSING POSSESSION POSSESSIONS)

Nu 33: 53 for I have given you the and to *p.*
Jn 5: 39 that by them you *p* eternal life.

POSSESSING* (POSSESS)

2Co 6: 10 nothing, and yet *p* everything.

POSSESSION (POSSESS)

Ge 15: 7 to give you this land to take *p* of it
Nu 13: 30 “We should go up and take *p*
Eph 1: 14 of those who are God's *p*—

POSSESSIONS (POSSESS)

Lk 12: 15 consist in the abundance of his *p*."
2Co 12: 14 what I want is not your *p* but you.
1Jn 3: 17 If anyone has material *p*

POSSIBLE

Mt 19: 26 but with God all things are *p*."
Mk 9: 23 "Everything is *p* for him who
10: 27 all things are *p* with God."
Ro 12: 18 If it is *p*, as far as it depends on you,
1Co 9: 22 by all *p* means I might save some.

POT (POTSHERD POTTER POTTERY)

2Ki 4: 40 there is death in the *p*!"
Jer 18: 4 But the *p* he was shaping

POTSHERD (POT)

Isa 45: 9 a *p* among the potsherds

POTTER (POT)

Isa 29: 16 Can the pot say of the *p*,
45: 9 Does the clay say to the *p*,
64: 8 We are the clay, you are the *p*;
Jer 18: 6 "Like clay in the hand of the *p*,
Ro 9: 21 Does not the *p* have the right

POTTERY (POT)

Ro 9: 21 of clay some *p* for noble purposes

POUR (POURED)

Ps 62: 8 *p* out your hearts to him,
Joel 2: 28 I will *p* out my Spirit on all people.
Mal 3: 10 *p* out so much blessing that you
Ac 2: 17 I will *p* out my Spirit on all people.

POURED (POUR)

Ac 10: 45 of the Holy Spirit had been *p* out
Ro 5: 5 because God has *p* out his love

POVERTY (POOR)

Pr 14: 23 but mere talk leads only to *p*.
21: 5 as surely as haste leads to *p*.
30: 8 give me neither *p* nor riches,
Mk 12: 44 out of her *p*, put in every-thing—
2Co 8: 2 and their extreme *p* welled up
8: 9 through his *p* might become rich.

POWER (POWERFUL POWERS)

1Ch 29: 11 LORD, is the greatness and the *p*
2Ch 32: 7 for there is a greater *p* with us
Job 36: 22 "God is exalted in his *p*.
Ps 63: 2 and beheld your *p* and your glory.
68: 34 Proclaim the *p* of God,
147: 5 Great is our Lord and mighty in *p*;
Pr 24: 5 A wise man has great *p*,
Isa 40: 10 the Sovereign LORD comes with *p*
Zec 4: 6 nor by *p*, but by my Spirit,'
Mt 22: 29 do not know the Scriptures or the *p*
24: 30 on the clouds of the sky, with *p*
Ac 1: 8 you will receive *p* when the Holy
Ac 4: 33 With great *p* the apostles
10: 38 with the Holy Spirit and *p*,
Ro 1: 16 it is the *p* of God for the salvation
1Co 1: 18 to us who are being saved it is the *p*
15: 56 of death is sin, and the *p*
2Co 12: 9 for my *p* is made perfect
Eph 1: 19 and his incomparably great *p*
Php 3: 10 and the *p* of his resurrection
Col 1: 11 strengthened with all *p* according
2Ti 1: 7 but a spirit of *p*, of love
Heb 7: 16 of the *p* of an indestructible life.
Rev 4: 11 to receive glory and honor and *p*,
19: 1 and glory and *p* belong to our God,
20: 6 The second death has no *p*

POWERFUL (POWER)

Ps 29: 4 The voice of the LORD is *p*;
Lk 24: 19 *p* in word and deed before God
2Th 1: 7 in blazing fire with his *p* angels.
Heb 1: 3 sustaining all things by his *p* word.
Jas 5: 16 The prayer of a righteous man is *p*

POWERLESS

Ro 5: 6 when we were still *p*, Christ died
8: 3 For what the law was *p* to do

POWERS (POWER)

Ro 8: 38 nor any *p*, neither height nor depth
1Co 12: 10 to another miraculous *p*,
Col 1: 16 whether thrones or *p* or rulers
2: 15 And having disarmed the *p*

PRACTICE

Lev 19: 26 "'Do not *p* divination or sorcery.
Mt 23: 3 for they do not *p* what they preach.
Lk 8: 21 hear God's word and put it into *p*."
Ro 12: 13 *P* hospitality.
1Ti 5: 4 to put their religion into *p* by caring

PRAISE (PRAISED PRAISES PRAISING)

Ex 15: 2 He is my God, and I will *p* him,
Dt 32: 3 Oh, *p* the greatness of our God!
Ru 4: 14 said to Naomi: "*P* be to the LORD,
2Sa 22: 47 The LORD lives! *P* be to my Rock
1Ch 16: 25 is the LORD and most worthy of *p*;
2Ch 20: 21 and to *p* him for the splendor
Ps 8: 2 you have ordained *p*
33: 1 it is fitting for the upright to *p* him.
34: 1 his *p* will always be on my lips.
40: 3 a hymn of *p* to our God.
48: 1 the LORD, and most worthy of *p*,
68: 19 *P* be to the Lord, to God our Savior
89: 5 The heavens *p* your wonders,
100: 4 and his courts with *p*;
105: 2 Sing to him, sing *p* to him;
Ps 106: 1 *P* the LORD.
119:175 Let me live that I may *p* you,
139: 14 I *p* you because I am fearfully
145: 21 Let every creature *p* his holy name
146: 1 *P* the LORD, O my soul.
150: 2 *p* him for his surpassing greatness.
150: 6 that has breath *p* the LORD.
Pr 27: 2 Let another *p* you, and not your
27: 21 man is tested by the *p* he receives.
31: 31 let her works bring her *p*
Mt 5: 16 and *p* your Father in heaven.
21: 16 you have ordained *p*'?"
Jn 12: 43 for they loved *p* from men more
Eph 1: 6 to the *p* of his glorious grace,
1: 12 might be for the *p* of his glory.
1: 14 to the *p* of his glory.
Heb 13: 15 offer to God a sacrifice of *p*—
Jas 5: 13 happy? Let him sing songs of *p*.

PRAISED (PRAISE)

1Ch 29: 10 David *p* the LORD in the presence
Ne 8: 6 Ezra *p* the LORD, the great God;
Da 2: 19 Then Daniel *p* the God of heaven
Ro 9: 5 who is God over all, forever *p*!
1Pe 4: 11 that in all things God may be *p*

PRAISES (PRAISE)

2Sa 22: 50 I will sing *p* to your name.
Ps 47: 6 Sing *p* to God, sing *p*;
147: 1 How good it is to sing *p* to our God,
Pr 31: 28 her husband also, and he *p* her:

PRAISING (PRAISE)

Ac 10: 46 speaking in tongues and *p* God.
1Co 14: 16 If you are *p* God with your spirit,

PRAY (PRAYED PRAYER PRAYERS PRAYING)

Dt 4: 7 is near us whenever we *p* to him?
1Sa 12: 23 the LORD by failing to *p* for you.
2Ch 7: 14 will humble themselves and *p*
Job 42: 8 My servant Job will *p* for you,
Ps 122: 6 *P* for the peace of Jerusalem:
Mt 5: 44 and *p* for those who persecute you,
6: 5 "And when you *p*, do not be like
6: 9 "This, then, is how you should *p*:
26: 36 Sit here while I go over there and *p*
Lk 6: 28 *p* for those who mistreat you.
18: 1 them that they should always *p*
22: 40 "*P* that you will not fall
Ro 8: 26 do not know what we ought to *p*,
1Co 14: 13 in a tongue should *p* that he may
1Th 5: 17 Be joyful always; *p* continually;
Jas 5: 13 one of you in trouble? He should *p*.
5: 16 *p* for each other so that you may be

PRAYED (PRAY)

1Sa 1: 27 I *p* for this child, and the LORD
Jnh 2: 1 From inside the fish Jonah *p*

Mk 14: 35 *p* that if possible the hour might

PRAYER (PRAY)

2Ch 30: 27 for their *p* reached heaven,
Ezr 8: 23 about this, and he answered our *p*.
Ps 6: 9 the LORD accepts my *p*.
86: 6 Hear my *p*, O LORD;
Pr 15: 8 but the *p* of the upright pleases him
Isa 56: 7 a house of *p* for all nations."
Mt 21: 13 house will be called a house of *p*,'
Mk 11: 24 whatever you ask for in *p*,
Jn 17: 15 My *p* is not that you take them out
Ac 6: 4 and will give our attention to *p*
Php 4: 6 but in everything, by *p* and petition
Jas 5: 15 *p* offered in faith will make the sick
1Pe 3: 12 and his ears are attentive to their *p*,

PRAYERS (PRAY)

1Ch 5: 20 He answered their *p*, because they
Mk 12: 40 and for a show make lengthy *p*.
1Pe 3: 7 so that nothing will hinder your *p*.
Rev 5: 8 which are the *p* of the saints.

PRAYING (PRAY)

Mk 11: 25 And when you stand *p*,
Jn 17: 9 I am not *p* for the world,
Ac 16: 25 and Silas were *p* and singing hymns
Eph 6: 18 always keep on *p* for all the saints.

PREACH (PREACHED PREACHING)

Mt 23: 3 they do not practice what they *p*.
Mk 16: 15 and *p* the good news to all creation.
Ac 9: 20 At once he began to *p*
Ro 10: 15 how can they *p* unless they are sent
15: 20 to *p* the gospel where Christ was
1Co 1: 17 to *p* the gospel—not with words
1: 23 wisdom, but we *p* Christ crucified:
9: 14 that those who *p* the gospel should
9: 16 Woe to me if I do not *p* the gospel!
2Co 10: 16 so that we can *p* the gospel
Gal 1: 8 from heaven should *p* a gospel
2Ti 4: 2 I give you this charge: *P* the Word;

PREACHED (PREACH)

Mk 13: 10 And the gospel must first be *p*
Ac 8: 4 had been scattered *p* the word
1Co 9: 27 so that after I have *p* to others,
15: 1 you of the gospel I *p* to you,
2Co 11: 4 other than the Jesus we *p*,
Gal 1: 8 other than the one we *p* to you,
Php 1: 18 false motives or true, Christ is *p*.
1Ti 3: 16 was *p* among the nations,

PREACHING (PREACH)

Ro 10: 14 hear without someone *p* to them?

1Co 9: 18 in *p* the gospel I may offer it free
1Ti 4: 13 the public reading of Scripture, to *p*
5: 17 especially those whose work is *p*

PRECEPTS

Ps 19: 8 The *p* of the LORD are right,
111: 7 all his *p* are trustworthy.
111: 10 who follow his *p* have good
119: 40 How I long for your *p*!
119: 69 I keep your *p* with all my heart.
119:104 I gain understanding from your *p*;
119:159 See how I love your *p*;

PRECIOUS

Ps 19: 10 They are more *p* than gold,
116: 15 *P* in the sight of the LORD
Pr 8: 11 for wisdom is more *p* than rubies,
Isa 28: 16 a *p* cornerstone for a sure
1Pe 1: 19 but with the *p* blood of Christ,
2: 6 a chosen and *p* cornerstone,
2Pe 1: 4 us his very great and *p* promises,

PREDESTINED* (DESTINY)

Ro 8: 29 *p* to be conformed to the likeness
8: 30 And those he *p*, he also called;
Eph 1: 5 In love he *p* us to be adopted
1: 11 having been *p* according

PREDICTION*

Jer 28: 9 only if his *p* comes true."

PREPARE (PREPARED)

Ps 23: 5 You *p* a table before me
Am 4: 12 *p* to meet your God, O Israel."
Jn 14: 2 there to *p* a place for you.
Eph 4: 12 to *p* God's people for works

PREPARED (PREPARE)

Mt 25: 34 the kingdom *p* for you
1Co 2: 9 what God has *p* for those who love
Eph 2: 10 which God *p* in advance for us
2Ti 4: 2 be *p* in season and out of season;
1Pe 3: 15 Always be *p* to give an answer

PRESENCE (PRESENT)

Ex 25: 30 Put the bread of the *P* on this table
Ezr 9: 15 one of us can stand in your *p*."
Ps 31: 20 the shelter of your *p* you hide them
89: 15 who walk in the light of your *p*,
90: 8 our secret sins in the light of your *p*
139: 7 Where can I flee from your *p*?
Jer 5: 22 "Should you not tremble in my *p*?
Heb 9: 24 now to appear for us in God's *p*.
Jude : 24 before his glorious *p* without fault

PRESENT (PRESENCE)

2Co 11: 2 so that I might *p* you as a pure
Eph 5: 27 and to *p* her to himself
2Ti 2: 15 Do your best to *p* yourself to God

PRESERVES

Ps 119: 50 Your promise *p* my life.

PRESS (PRESSED PRESSURE)

Php 3: 14 I *p* on toward the goal

PRESSED (PRESS)

Lk 6: 38 *p* down, shaken together

PRESSURE (PRESS)

2Co 1: 8 We were under great *p*, far
11: 28 I face daily the *p* of my concern

PREVAILS

1Sa 2: 9 "It is not by strength that one *p*;

PRICE

Job 28: 18 the *p* of wisdom is beyond rubies.
1Co 6: 20 your own; you were bought at a *p*.
7: 23 bought at a *p*; do not become slaves

PRIDE (PROUD)

Pr 8: 13 I hate *p* and arrogance,
16: 18 *P* goes before destruction,
Da 4: 37 And those who walk in *p* he is able
Gal 6: 4 Then he can take *p* in himself,
Jas 1: 9 ought to take *p* in his high position.

PRIEST (PRIESTHOOD PRIESTS)

Heb 4: 14 have a great high *p* who has gone
4: 15 do not have a high *p* who is unable
7: 26 Such a high *p* meets our need—
8: 1 We do have such a high *p*,

PRIESTHOOD (PRIEST)

Heb 7: 24 lives forever, he has a permanent *p*.
1Pe 2: 5 into a spiritual house to be a holy *p*,
2: 9 you are a chosen people, a royal *p*,

PRIESTS (PRIEST)

Ex 19: 6 you will be for me a kingdom of *p*
Rev 5: 10 to be a kingdom and *p*

PRINCE

Isa 9: 6 Everlasting Father, *P* of Peace.
Jn 12: 31 now the *p* of this world will be
Ac 5: 31 as *P* and Savior that he might give

PRISON (PRISONER)

Isa 42: 7 to free captives from *p*
Mt 25: 36 I was in *p* and you came to visit me
1Pe 3: 19 spirits in *p* who disobeyed long ago
Rev 20: 7 Satan will be released from his *p*

PRISONER (PRISON)

Ro 7: 23 and making me a *p* of the law of sin
Gal 3: 22 declares that the whole world is a *p*
Eph 3: 1 the *p* of Christ Jesus for the sake

PRIVILEGE*

2Co 8: 4 pleaded with us for the *p* of sharing

PRIZE
1Co 9: 24 Run in such a way as to get the *p*.
Php 3: 14 on toward the goal to win the *p*

PROCLAIM (PROCLAIMED PROCLAIMING)
1Ch 16: 23 *p* his salvation day after day.
Ps 19: 1 the skies *p* the work of his hands.
50: 6 the heavens *p* his righteousness,
68: 34 *P* the power of God,
118: 17 will *p* what the LORD has done.
Zec 9: 10 He will *p* peace to the nations.
Ac 20: 27 hesitated to *p* to you the whole will
1Co 11: 26 you *p* the Lord's death

PROCLAIMED (PROCLAIM)
Ro 15: 19 I have fully *p* the gospel of Christ.
Col 1: 23 that has been *p* to every creature

PROCLAIMING (PROCLAIM)
Ro 10: 8 the word of faith we are *p:*

PRODUCE (PRODUCES)
Mt 3: 8 *P* fruit in keeping with repentance.
3: 10 tree that does not *p* good fruit will

PRODUCES (PRODUCE)
Pr 30: 33 so stirring up anger *p* strife."
Ro 5: 3 that suffering *p* perseverance;
Heb 12: 11 it *p* a harvest of righteousness

PROFANE
Lev 22: 32 Do not *p* my holy name.

PROFESS*
1Ti 2: 10 for women who *p* to worship God.
Heb 4: 14 let us hold firmly to the faith we *p*.
10: 23 unswervingly to the hope we *p*,

PROMISE (PROMISED PROMISES)
1Ki 8: 20 The LORD has kept the *p* he made
Ac 2: 39 The *p* is for you and your children
Gal 3: 14 that by faith we might receive the *p*
1Ti 4: 8 holding *p* for both the present life
2Pe 3: 9 Lord is not slow in keeping his *p*,

PROMISED (PROMISE)
Ex 3: 17 And I have *p* to bring you up out
Dt 26: 18 his treasured possession as he *p*,
Ps 119: 57 I have *p* to obey your words.
Ro 4: 21 power to do what he had *p*.
Heb 10: 23 for he who *p* is faithful.
2Pe 3: 4 "Where is this 'coming' he *p?*

PROMISES (PROMISE)
Jos 21: 45 one of all the LORD's good *p*
Ro 9: 4 the temple worship and the *p*.
2Pe 1: 4 us his very great and precious *p*,

PROMPTED
1Th 1: 3 your labor *p* by love, and your
2Th 1: 11 and every act *p* by your faith.

PROPHECIES (PROPHESY)
1Co 13: 8 where there are *p*, they will cease;
1Th 5: 20 do not treat *p* with contempt.

PROPHECY (PROPHESY)
1Co 14: 1 gifts, especially the gift of *p*.
2Pe 1: 20 you must understand that no *p*

PROPHESY (PROPHECIES PROPHECY PROPHESYING PROPHET PROPHETS)
Joel 2: 28 Your sons and daughters will *p*,
Mt 7: 22 Lord, did we not *p* in your name,
1Co 14: 39 my brothers, be eager to *p*,

PROPHESYING (PROPHESY)
Ro 12: 6 If a man's gift is *p*, let him use it

PROPHET (PROPHESY)
Dt 18: 18 up for them a *p* like you
Am 7: 14 "I was neither a *p* nor a prophet's
Mt 10: 41 Anyone who receives a *p*
Lk 4: 24 "no *p* is accepted in his hometown.

PROPHETS (PROPHESY)
Ps 105: 15 do my *p* no harm."
Mt 5: 17 come to abolish the Law or the *P;*
7: 12 for this sums up the Law and the *P*.
24: 24 false Christs and false *p* will appear
Lk 24: 25 believe all that the *p* have spoken!
Ac 10: 43 All the *p* testify about him that
1Co 12: 28 second *p*, third teachers, then
14: 32 The spirits of *p* are subject
Eph 2: 20 foundation of the apostles and *p*,
Heb 1: 1 through the *p* at many times
1Pe 1: 10 Concerning this salvation, the *p*,
2Pe 1: 19 word of the *p* made more certain,

PROSPER (PROSPERITY PROSPERS)
Pr 28: 25 he who trusts in the LORD will *p*.

PROSPERITY (PROSPER)
Ps 73: 3 when I saw the *p* of the wicked.
Pr 13: 21 but *p* is the reward of the righteous.

PROSPERS (PROSPER)
Ps 1: 3 Whatever he does *p*.

PROSTITUTE (PROSTITUTES)
1Co 6: 15 of Christ and unite them with a *p?*

PROSTITUTES (PROSTITUTE)
Lk 15: 30 property with *p* comes home,
1Co 6: 9 male *p* nor homosexual offenders

PROSTRATE
Dt 9: 18 again I fell *p* before the LORD

PROTECT (PROTECTS)
Ps 32: 7 you will *p* me from trouble
Pr 2: 11 Discretion will *p* you,
Jn 17: 11 *p* them by the power of your name

PROTECTS (PROTECT)
1Co 13: 7 It always *p*, always trusts,

PROUD (PRIDE)
Pr 16: 5 The LORD detests all the *p*
Ro 12: 16 Do not be *p*, but be willing
1Co 13: 4 it does not boast, it is not *p*.

PROVE
Ac 26: 20 *p* their repentance by their deeds.
1Co 4: 2 been given a trust must *p* faithful.

PROVIDE (PROVIDED PROVIDES)
Ge 22: 8 "God himself will *p* the lamb
Isa 43: 20 because I *p* water in the desert
1Ti 5: 8 If anyone does not *p*

PROVIDED (PROVIDE)
Jnh 1: 17 But the LORD *p* a great fish
4: 6 Then the LORD God *p* a vine
4: 7 dawn the next day God *p* a worm,
4: 8 God *p* a scorching east wind,

PROVIDES (PROVIDE)
1Ti 6: 17 who richly *p* us with everything
1Pe 4: 11 it with the strength God *p*,

PROVOKED
Ecc 7: 9 Do not be quickly *p* in your spirit,

PRUDENT
Pr 14: 15 a *p* man gives thought to his steps.
19: 14 but a *p* wife is from the LORD.
Am 5: 13 Therefore the *p* man keeps quiet

PRUNING
Isa 2: 4 and their spears into *p* hooks.
Joel 3: 10 and your *p* hooks into spears.

PSALMS
Eph 5: 19 Speak to one another with *p*,
Col 3: 16 and as you sing *p*, hymns

PUBLICLY
Ac 20: 20 have taught you *p* and from house
1Ti 5: 20 Those who sin are to be rebuked *p*,

PUFFS
1Co 8: 1 Knowledge *p* up, but love builds up

PULLING
2Co 10: 8 building you up rather than *p* you

PUNISH (PUNISHED PUNISHES)
Ex 32: 34 I will *p* them for their sin."
Pr 23: 13 if you *p* him with the rod, he will
Isa 13: 11 I will *p* the world for its evil,
1Pe 2: 14 by him to *p* those who do wrong

PUNISHED (PUNISH)
La 3: 39 complain when *p* for his sins?
2Th 1: 9 be *p* with everlasting destruction
Heb 10: 29 to be *p* who has trampled the Son

PUNISHES (PUNISH)

Heb 12: 6 and he *p* everyone he accepts

PURE (PURIFIES PURIFY PURITY)

2Sa 22: 27 to the *p* you show yourself *p,*
Ps 24: 4 who has clean hands and a *p* heart,
51: 10 Create in me a *p* heart, O God,
119: 9 can a young man keep his way *p?*
Pr 20: 9 can say, "I have kept my heart *p;*
Isa 52: 11 Come out from it and be *p,*
Hab 1: 13 Your eyes are too *p* to look on evil;
Mt 5: 8 Blessed are the *p* in heart,
2Co 11: 2 I might present you as a *p* virgin
Php 4: 8 whatever is *p,* whatever is lovely,
1Ti 5: 22 Keep yourself *p.*
Tit 1: 15 To the *p,* all things are *p,*
2: 5 to be self-controlled and *p,*
Heb 13: 4 and the marriage bed kept *p,*
1Jn 3: 3 him purifies himself, just as he is *p.*

PURGE

Pr 20: 30 and beatings *p* the inmost being.

PURIFIES* (PURE)

1Jn 1: 7 of Jesus, his Son, *p* us from all sin.
3: 3 who has this hope in him *p* himself,

PURIFY (PURE)

Tit 2: 14 to *p* for himself a people that are
1Jn 1: 9 and *p* us from all unrighteousness.

PURITY (PURE)

2Co 6: 6 in *p,* understanding, patience
1Ti 4: 12 in life, in love, in faith and in *p.*

PURPOSE

Pr 19: 21 but it is the LORD's *p* that prevails
Isa 55: 11 and achieve the *p* for which I sent it
Ro 8: 28 have been called according to his *p.*
Php 2: 2 love, being one in spirit and *p.*

PURSES

Lk 12: 33 Provide *p* for yourselves that will

PURSUE

Ps 34: 14 seek peace and *p* it.
2Ti 2: 22 and *p* righteousness, faith,
1Pe 3: 11 he must seek peace and *p* it.

QUALITIES (QUALITY)

2Pe 1: 8 For if you possess these *q*

QUALITY (QUALITIES)

1Co 3: 13 and the fire will test the *q*

QUARREL (QUARRELSOME)

Pr 15: 18 but a patient man calms a *q.*
17: 14 Starting a *q* is like breaching a dam;
17: 19 He who loves a *q* loves sin;
2Ti 2: 24 And the Lord's servant must not *q;*

QUARRELSOME (QUARREL)

Pr 19: 13 a *q* wife is like a constant dripping.
1Ti 3: 3 not violent but gentle, not *q,*

QUICK-TEMPERED

Tit 1: 7 not *q,* not given to drunkenness,

QUIET (QUIETNESS)

Ps 23: 2 he leads me beside *q* waters,
Zep 3: 17 he will *q* you with his love,
Lk 19: 40 he replied, "if they keep *q,*
1Ti 2: 2 we may live peaceful and *q* lives
1Pe 3: 4 beauty of a gentle and *q* spirit,

QUIETNESS (QUIET)

Isa 30: 15 in *q* and trust is your strength,
32: 17 the effect of righteousness will be *q*
1Ti 2: 11 A woman should learn in *q*

QUIVER

Ps 127: 5 whose *q* is full of them.

RACE

Ecc 9: 11 The *r* is not to the swift
1Co 9: 24 that in a *r* all the runners run,
2Ti 4: 7 I have finished the *r,* I have kept
Heb 12: 1 perseverance the *r* marked out

RACHEL

Daughter of Laban (Ge 29:16); wife of Jacob (Ge 29:28); bore two sons (Ge 30:22-24; 35:16-24; 46:19).

RADIANCE (RADIANT)

Heb 1: 3 The Son is the *r* of God's glory

RADIANT (RADIANCE)

Ex 34: 29 he was not aware that his face was *r*
Ps 34: 5 Those who look to him are *r;*
SS 5: 10 *Beloved* My lover is *r* and ruddy,
Isa 60: 5 Then you will look and be *r,*
Eph 5: 27 her to himself as a *r* church,

RAIN (RAINBOW)

Mt 5: 45 and sends *r* on the righteous

RAINBOW (RAIN)

Ge 9: 13 I have set my *r* in the clouds,

RAISED (RISE)

Ro 4: 25 was *r* to life for our justification.
10: 9 in your heart that God *r* him
1Co 15: 4 that he was *r* on the third day

RAN (RUN)

Jnh 1: 3 But Jonah *r* away from the LORD

RANSOM

Mt 20: 28 and to give his life as a *r* for many."
Heb 9: 15 as a *r* to set them free

RAVENS

1Ki 17: 6 The *r* brought him bread
Lk 12: 24 Consider the *r:* They do not sow

READ (READS)

Jos 8: 34 Joshua *r* all the words of the law—
Ne 8: 8 They *r* from the Book of the Law
2Co 3: 2 known and *r* by everybody.

READS (READ)

Rev 1: 3 Blessed is the one who *r* the words

REAL (REALITY)

Jn 6: 55 is *r* food and my blood is *r* drink.

REALITY* (REAL)

Col 2: 17 the *r,* however, is found in Christ.

REAP (REAPS)

Job 4: 8 and those who sow trouble *r* it.
2Co 9: 6 generously will also *r* generously.

REAPS (REAP)

Gal 6: 7 A man *r* what he sows.

REASON

Isa 1: 18 "Come now, let us *r* together,"
1Pe 3: 15 to give the *r* for the hope that you

REBEKAH

Sister of Laban, secured as bride for Isaac (Ge 24). Mother of Esau and Jacob (Ge 25:19-26). Taken by Abimelech as sister of Isaac; returned (Ge 26:1-11). Encouraged Jacob to trick Isaac out of blessing (Ge 27:1-17).

REBEL

Mt 10: 21 children will *r* against their parents

REBUKE (REBUKED REBUKING)

Pr 9: 8 *r* a wise man and he will love you.
27: 5 Better is open *r*
Lk 17: 3 "If your brother sins, *r* him,
2Ti 4: 2 correct, *r* and encourage—
Rev 3: 19 Those whom I love I *r*

REBUKED (REBUKE)

1Ti 5: 20 Those who sin are to be *r* publicly,

REBUKING (REBUKE)

2Ti 3: 16 *r,* correcting and training

RECEIVE (RECEIVED RECEIVES)

Ac 1: 8 you will *r* power when the Holy
20: 35 'It is more blessed to give than to *r*
2Co 6: 17 and I will *r* you."
Rev 4: 11 to *r* glory and honor and power,

RECEIVED (RECEIVE)

Mt 6: 2 they have *r* their reward in full.
10: 8 Freely you have *r,* freely give.
1Co 11: 23 For I *r* from the Lord what I
Col 2: 6 just as you *r* Christ Jesus as Lord,
1Pe 4: 10 should use whatever gift he has *r*

RECEIVES (RECEIVE)

Mt 7: 8 everyone who asks *r;* he who seeks
10: 40 he who *r* me *r* the one who sent me.
Ac 10: 43 believes in him *r* forgiveness of sins

RECKONING

Isa 10: 3 What will you do on the day of *r,*

RECOGNIZE (RECOGNIZED)

Mt 7: 16 By their fruit you will *r* them.

RECOGNIZED (RECOGNIZE)

Mt 12: 33 for a tree is *r* by its fruit.
Ro 7: 13 in order that sin might be *r* as sin,

RECOMPENSE

Isa 40: 10 and his *r* accompanies him.

RECONCILE (RECONCILED RECONCILIATION)

Eph 2: 16 in this one body to *r* both of them

RECONCILED (RECONCILE)

Mt 5: 24 First go and be *r* to your brother;
Ro 5: 10 we were *r* to him through the death
2Co 5: 18 who *r* us to himself through Christ

RECONCILIATION* (RECONCILE)

Ro 5: 11 whom we have now received *r.*
11: 15 For if their rejection is the *r*
2Co 5: 18 and gave us the ministry of *r:*
5: 19 committed to us the message of *r.*

RECORD

Ps 130: 3 If you, O LORD, kept a *r* of sins,

RED

Isa 1: 18 though they are *r* as crimson,

REDEEM (KINSMAN-REDEEMER REDEEMED REDEEMER REDEMPTION)

2Sa 7: 23 on earth that God went out to *r*
Ps 49: 7 No man can *r* the life of another
Gal 4: 5 under law, to *r* those under law,

REDEEMED (REDEEM)

Gal 3: 13 Christ *r* us from the curse
1Pe 1: 18 or gold that you were *r*

REDEEMER (REDEEM)

Job 19: 25 I know that my *R* lives,

REDEMPTION (REDEEM)

Ps 130: 7 and with him is full *r.*
Lk 21: 28 because your *r* is drawing near."
Ro 8: 23 as sons, the *r* of our bodies.
Eph 1: 7 In him we have *r* through his blood
Col 1: 14 in whom we have *r,* the forgiveness
Heb 9: 12 having obtained eternal *r.*

REFLECT

2Co 3: 18 unveiled faces all *r* the Lord's

REFUGE

Nu 35: 11 towns to be your cities of *r,*
Dt 33: 27 The eternal God is your *r,*
Ru 2: 12 wings you have come to take *r.*"
Ps 46: 1 God is our *r* and strength,
91: 2 "He is my *r* and my fortress,

REHOBOAM

Son of Solomon (1Ki 11:43; 1Ch 3:10). Harsh treatment of subjects caused divided kingdom (1Ki 12:1-24; 14:21-31; 2Ch 10-12).

REIGN

Ex 15: 18 The LORD will *r*
Ro 6: 12 Therefore do not let sin *r*
1Co 15: 25 For he must *r* until he has put all
2Ti 2: 12 we will also *r* with him.
Rev 20: 6 will *r* with him for a thousand years

REJECTED (REJECTS)

Ps 118: 22 The stone the builders *r*
Isa 53: 3 He was despised and *r* by men,
1Ti 4: 4 nothing is to be *r* if it is received
1Pe 2: 4 *r* by men but chosen by God
2: 7 "The stone the builders *r*

REJECTS (REJECTED)

Lk 10: 16 but he who *r* me *r* him who sent me
Jn 3: 36 whoever *r* the Son will not see life,

REJOICE (JOY)

Ps 2: 11 and *r* with trembling.
66: 6 come, let us *r* in him.
118: 24 let us *r* and be glad in it.
Pr 5: 18 may you *r* in the wife of your youth
Lk 10: 20 but *r* that your names are written
15: 6 '*R* with me; I have found my lost
Ro 12: 15 Rejoice with those who *r;* mourn
Php 4: 4 *R* in the Lord always.

REJOICES (JOY)

Isa 61: 10 my soul *r* in my God.
Lk 1: 47 and my spirit *r* in God my Savior,
1Co 12: 26 if one part is honored, every part *r*
13: 6 delight in evil but *r* with the truth.

REJOICING (JOY)

Ps 30: 5 but *r* comes in the morning.
Lk 15: 7 in the same way there will be more *r*
Ac 5: 41 *r* because they had been counted

RELIABLE

2Ti 2: 2 witnesses entrust to *r* men who will

RELIGION

1Ti 5: 4 all to put their *r* into practice
Jas 1: 27 *R* that God our Father accepts

REMAIN (REMAINS)

Nu 33: 55 allow to *r* will become barbs
Jn 15: 7 If you *r* in me and my words
Ro 13: 8 Let no debt *r* outstanding,
1Co 13: 13 And now these three *r:* faith,
2Ti 2: 13 he will *r* faithful,

REMAINS (REMAIN)

Ps 146: 6 the LORD, who *r* faithful forever.
Heb 7: 3 Son of God he *r* a priest forever.

REMEMBER (REMEMBERS REMEMBRANCE)

Ex 20: 8 "*R* the Sabbath day
1Ch 16: 12 *R* the wonders he has done,
Ecc 12: 1 *R* your Creator
Jer 31: 34 and will *r* their sins no more."
Gal 2: 10 we should continue to *r* the poor,
Php 1: 3 I thank my God every time I *r* you.
Heb 8: 12 and will *r* their sins no more."

REMEMBERS (REMEMBER)

Ps 103: 14 he *r* that we are dust.
111: 5 he *r* his covenant forever.
Isa 43: 25 and *r* your sins no more.

REMEMBRANCE (REMEMBER)

1Co 11: 24 which is for you; do this in *r* of me

REMIND

Jn 14: 26 will *r* you of everything I have said

REMOVED

Ps 30: 11 you *r* my sackcloth and clothed me
103: 12 so far has he *r* our transgressions
Jn 20: 1 and saw that the stone had been *r*

RENEW (RENEWED RENEWING)

Ps 51: 10 and *r* a steadfast spirit within me.
Isa 40: 31 will *r* their strength.

RENEWED (RENEW)

Ps 103: 5 that your youth is *r* like the eagle's.
2Co 4: 16 yet inwardly we are being *r* day

RENEWING (RENEW)

Ro 12: 2 transformed by the *r* of your mind.

RENOUNCE (RENOUNCES)

Da 4: 27 *R* your sins by doing what is right,

RENOUNCES (RENOUNCE)

Pr 28: 13 confesses and *r* them finds

RENOWN

Isa 63: 12 to gain for himself everlasting *r,*
Jer 32: 20 have gained the *r* that is still yours.

REPAID (PAY)

Lk 14: 14 you will be *r* at the resurrection
Col 3: 25 Anyone who does wrong will be *r*

REPAY (PAY)

Dt 32: 35 It is mine to avenge; I will *r.*
Ru 2: 12 May the LORD *r* you
Ps 116: 12 How can I *r* the LORD
Ro 12: 19 "It is mine to avenge; I will *r,*"
1Pe 3: 9 Do not *r* evil with evil

REPENT (REPENTANCE REPENTS)

Job 42: 6 and *r* in dust and ashes."
Jer 15: 19 "If you *r,* I will restore you
Mt 4: 17 "*R,* for the kingdom of heaven is
Lk 13: 3 unless you *r,* you too will all perish.
Ac 2: 38 Peter replied, "*R* and be baptized,
17: 30 all people everywhere to *r.*

REPENTANCE (REPENT)

Lk 3: 8 Produce fruit in keeping with *r.*
5: 32 call the righteous, but sinners to *r.*"
Ac 26: 20 and prove their *r* by their deeds.

2Co 7: 10 Godly sorrow brings *r* that leads

REPENTS (REPENT)

Lk 15: 10 of God over one sinner who *r*."
17: 3 rebuke him, and if he *r*, forgive him

REPROACH

1Ti 3: 2 Now the overseer must be above *r*,

REPUTATION

1Ti 3: 7 also have a good *r* with outsiders,

REQUESTS

Ps 20: 5 May the LORD grant all your *r*.
Php 4: 6 with thanksgiving, present your *r*

REQUIRE

Mic 6: 8 And what does the LORD *r* of you

RESCUE (RESCUES)

Da 6: 20 been able to *r* you from the lions?"
2Pe 2: 9 how to *r* godly men from trials

RESCUES (RESCUE)

1Th 1: 10 who *r* us from the coming wrath.

RESIST

Jas 4: 7 *R* the devil, and he will flee
1Pe 5: 9 *R* him, standing firm in the faith,

RESOLVED

Ps 17: 3 I have *r* that my mouth will not sin.
Da 1: 8 But Daniel *r* not to defile himself
1Co 2: 2 For I *r* to know nothing while I was

RESPECT (RESPECTABLE)

Lev 19: 3 "'Each of you must *r* his mother
19: 32 show *r* for the elderly and revere
Pr 11: 16 A kindhearted woman gains *r*,
Mal 1: 6 where is the *r* due me?" says
1Th 4: 12 so that your daily life may win the *r*
5: 12 to *r* those who work hard
1Ti 3: 4 children obey him with proper *r*.
1Pe 2: 17 Show proper *r* to everyone:
3: 7 them with *r* as the weaker partner

RESPECTABLE* (RESPECT)

1Ti 3: 2 self-controlled, *r*, hospitable,

REST

Ex 31: 15 the seventh day is a Sabbath of *r*,
Ps 91: 1 will *r* in the shadow
Jer 6: 16 and you will find *r* for your souls.
Mt 11: 28 and burdened, and I will give you *r*.

RESTITUTION

Ex 22: 3 "A thief must certainly make *r*,
Lev 6: 5 He must make *r* in full, add a fifth

RESTORE (RESTORES)

Ps 51: 12 *R* to me the joy of your salvation
Gal 6: 1 are spiritual should *r* him gently.

RESTORES (RESTORE)

Ps 23: 3 he *r* my soul.

RESURRECTION

Mt 22: 30 At the *r* people will neither marry
Lk 14: 14 repaid at the *r* of the righteous."
Jn 11: 25 Jesus said to her, "I am the *r*
Ro 1: 4 Son of God by his *r* from the dead:
1Co 15: 12 some of you say that there is no *r*
Php 3: 10 power of his *r* and the fellowship
Rev 20: 5 This is the first *r*.

RETRIBUTION

Jer 51: 56 For the LORD is a God of *r*;

RETURN

2Ch 30: 9 If you *r* to the LORD, then your
Ne 1: 9 but if you *r* to me and obey my
Isa 55: 11 It will not *r* to me empty,
Hos 6: 1 "Come, let us *r* to the LORD.
Joel 2: 12 "*r* to me with all your heart,

REVEALED (REVELATION)

Dt 29: 29 but the things *r* belong to us
Isa 40: 5 the glory of the LORD will be *r*,
Mt 11: 25 and *r* them to little children.
Ro 1: 17 a righteousness from God is *r*,
8: 18 with the glory that will be *r* in us.

REVELATION (REVEALED)

Gal 1: 12 I received it by *r* from Jesus Christ.
Rev 1: 1 *r* of Jesus Christ, which God gave

REVENGE (VENGEANCE)

Lev 19: 18 "'Do not seek *r* or bear a grudge
Ro 12: 19 Do not take *r*, my friends,

REVERE (REVERENCE)

Ps 33: 8 let all the people of the world *r* him

REVERENCE (REVERE)

Lev 19: 30 and have *r* for my sanctuary.
Ps 5: 7 in *r* will I bow down
Col 3: 22 of heart and *r* for the Lord.
1Pe 3: 2 when they see the purity and *r*

REVIVE (REVIVING)

Ps 85: 6 Will you not *r* us again,
Isa 57: 15 to *r* the spirit of the lowly

REVIVING (REVIVE)

Ps 19: 7 *r* the soul.

REWARD (REWARDED)

Ps 19: 11 in keeping them there is great *r*.
127: 3 children a *r* from him.
Pr 19: 17 he will *r* him for what he has done.
25: 22 and the LORD will *r* you.
31: 31 Give her the *r* she has earned,
Jer 17: 10 to *r* a man according to his conduct
Mt 5: 12 because great is your *r* in heaven,
6: 5 they have received their *r* in full.
16: 27 and then he will *r* each person
1Co 3: 14 built survives, he will receive his *r*.
Rev 22: 12 I am coming soon! My *r* is with me

REWARDED (REWARD)

Ru 2: 12 May you be richly *r* by the LORD,
Ps 18: 24 The LORD has *r* me according
Pr 14: 14 and the good man *r* for his.
1Co 3: 8 and each will be *r* according

RICH (RICHES)

Pr 23: 4 Do not wear yourself out to get *r*;
Jer 9: 23 or the *r* man boast of his riches,
Mt 19: 23 it is hard for a *r* man
2Co 6: 10 yet making many *r*; having nothing
8: 9 he was *r*, yet for your sakes he
1Ti 6: 17 Command those who are *r*

RICHES (RICH)

Ps 119: 14 as one rejoices in great *r*.
Pr 30: 8 give me neither poverty nor *r*,
Isa 10: 3 Where will you leave your *r*?
Ro 9: 23 to make the *r* of his glory known
11: 33 the depth of the *r* of the wisdom
Eph 2: 7 he might show the incomparable *r*
3: 8 to the Gentiles the unsearchable *r*
Col 1: 27 among the Gentiles the glorious *r*

RID

Ge 21: 10 "Get *r* of that slave woman
1Co 5: 7 Get *r* of the old yeast that you may
Gal 4: 30 "Get *r* of the slave woman

RIGHT (RIGHTS)

Ge 18: 25 the Judge of all the earth do *r*?"
Ex 15: 26 and do what is *r* in his eyes,
Dt 5: 32 do not turn aside to the *r*
Ps 16: 8 Because he is at my *r* hand,
19: 8 The precepts of the LORD are *r*,
63: 8 your *r* hand upholds me.
110: 1 "Sit at my *r* hand
Pr 4: 27 Do not swerve to the *r* or the left;
14: 12 There is a way that seems *r*
Isa 1: 17 learn to do *r*!
Jer 23: 5 and do what is just and *r* in the land
Hos 14: 9 The ways of the LORD are *r*;
Mt 6: 3 know what your *r* hand is doing,
Jn 1: 12 he gave the *r* to become children
Ro 9: 21 Does not the potter have the *r*
12: 17 careful to do what is *r* in the eyes
Eph 1: 20 and seated him at his *r* hand
Php 4: 8 whatever is *r*, whatever is pure,
2Th 3: 13 never tire of doing what is *r*.

RIGHTEOUS (RIGHTEOUSNESS)

Ps 34: 15 The eyes of the LORD are on the *r*
37: 25 yet I have never seen the *r* forsaken

Ps 19:137 *R* are you, O LORD,
143: 2 for no one living is *r* before you.
Pr 3: 33 but he blesses the home of the *r*.
11: 30 The fruit of the *r* is a tree of life,
18: 10 the *r* run to it and are safe.
Isa 64: 6 and all our *r* acts are like filthy rags
Hab 2: 4 but the *r* will live by his faith—
Mt 5: 45 rain on the *r* and the unrighteous.
9: 13 For I have not come to call the *r*,
13: 49 and separate the wicked from the *r*
25: 46 to eternal punishment, but the *r*
Ro 1: 17 as it is written: "The *r* will live
3: 10 "There is no one *r*, not even one;
1Ti 1: 9 that law is made not for the *r*
1Pe 3: 18 the *r* for the unrighteous,
1Jn 3: 7 does what is right is *r*, just as he is *r*.
Rev 19: 8 stands for the *r* acts of the saints.)

RIGHTEOUSNESS (RIGHTEOUS)

Ge 15: 6 and he credited it to him as *r*.
1Sa 26: 23 LORD rewards every man for his *r*
Ps 9: 8 He will judge the world in *r*;
23: 3 He guides me in paths of *r*
45: 7 You love *r* and hate wickedness;
85: 10 *r* and peace kiss each other.
89: 14 *R* and justice are the foundation
111: 3 and his *r* endures forever.
Pr 14: 34 *R* exalts a nation,
21: 21 He who pursues *r* and love
Isa 5: 16 will show himself holy by his *r*.
59: 17 He put on *r* as his breastplate,
Eze 18: 20 The *r* of the righteous man will be
Da 9: 24 to bring in everlasting *r*,
12: 3 and those who lead many to *r*,
Mal 4: 2 the sun of *r* will rise with healing
Mt 5: 6 those who hunger and thirst for *r*,
5: 20 unless your *r* surpasses that
6: 33 But seek first his kingdom and his *r*
Ro 4: 3 and it was credited to him as *r*."
4: 9 faith was credited to him as *r*.
6: 13 body to him as instruments of *r*.
2Co 5: 21 that in him we might become the *r*
Gal 2: 21 for if *r* could be gained
3: 6 and it was credited to him as *r*."
Eph 6: 14 with the breastplate of *r* in place,
Php 3: 9 not having a *r* of my own that
2Ti 3: 16 correcting and training in *r*,
4: 8 is in store for me the crown of *r*,
Heb 11: 7 became heir of the *r* that comes
2Pe 2: 21 not to have known the way of *r*,

RIGHTS (RIGHT)

La 3: 35 to deny a man his *r*
Gal 4: 5 that we might receive the full *r*

RISE (RAISED)

Isa 26: 19 their bodies will *r*.
Mt 27: 63 'After three days I will *r* again.'
Jn 5: 29 those who have done good will *r*
1Th 4: 16 and the dead in Christ will *r* first.

ROAD

Mt 7: 13 and broad is the *r* that leads

ROBBERS

Jer 7: 11 become a den of *r* to you?
Mk 15: 27 They crucified two *r* with him,
Lk 19: 46 but you have made it 'a den of *r*.'"
Jn 10: 8 came before me were thieves and *r*,

ROCK

Ps 18: 2 The LORD is my *r*, my fortress
40: 2 he set my feet on a *r*
Mt 7: 24 man who built his house on the *r*.
16: 18 and on this *r* I will build my church
Ro 9: 33 and a *r* that makes them fall,
1Co 10: 4 the spiritual *r* that accompanied

ROD

Ps 23: 4 your *r* and your staff,
Pr 13: 24 He who spares the *r* hates his son,
23: 13 if you punish him with the *r*,

ROOM (ROOMS)

Mt 6: 6 But when you pray, go into your *r*,
Lk 2: 7 there was no *r* for them in the inn.
Jn 21: 25 the whole world would not have *r*

ROOMS (ROOM)

Jn 14: 2 In my Father's house are many *r*;

ROOT

Isa 53: 2 and like a *r* out of dry ground.
1Ti 6: 10 of money is a *r* of all kinds of evil.

ROYAL

Jas 2: 8 If you really keep the *r* law found
1Pe 2: 9 a *r* priesthood, a holy nation,

RUBBISH*

Php 3: 8 I consider them *r*, that I may gain

RUDE*

1Co 13: 5 It is not *r*, it is not self-seeking,

RUIN (RUINS)

Pr 18: 24 many companions may come to *r*,
1Ti 6: 9 desires that plunge men into *r*

RUINS (RUIN)

Pr 19: 3 A man's own folly *r* his life,
2Ti 2: 14 and only *r* those who listen.

RULE (RULER RULERS RULES)

1Sa 12: 12 'No, we want a king to *r* over us'—
Ps 2: 9 You will *r* them with an iron
119:133 let no sin *r* over me.
Zec 9: 10 His *r* will extend from sea to sea
Col 3: 15 the peace of Christ *r* in your hearts,
Rev 2: 27 He will *r* them with an iron scepter;

RULER (RULE)

Ps 8: 6 You made him *r* over the works
Eph 2: 2 of the *r* of the kingdom of the air,
1Ti 6: 15 God, the blessed and only *R*,

RULERS (RULE)

Ps 2: 2 and the *r* gather together
Col 1: 16 or powers or *r* or authorities;

RULES (RULE)

Ps 103: 19 and his kingdom *r* over all.
Lk 22: 26 one who *r* like the one who serves.
2Ti 2: 5 he competes according to the *r*.

RUMORS

Mt 24: 6 You will hear of wars and *r* of wars,

RUN (RAN)

Isa 40: 31 they will *r* and not grow weary,
1Co 9: 24 *R* in such a way as to get the prize.
Heb 12: 1 let us *r* with perseverance the race

RUST

Mt 6: 19 where moth and *r* destroy,

RUTH*

Moabitess; widow who went to Bethlehem with mother-in-law Naomi (Ru 1). Gleaned in field of Boaz; shown favor (Ru 2). Proposed marriage to Boaz (Ru 3). Married (Ru 4:1-12); bore Obed, ancestor of David (Ru 4:13-22), Jesus (Mt 1:5).

SABBATH

Ex 20: 8 "Remember the *S* day
Dt 5: 12 "Observe the *S* day
Col 2: 16 a New Moon celebration or a *S* day

SACKCLOTH

Mt 11: 21 would have repented long ago in *s*

SACRED

Mt 7: 6 "Do not give dogs what is *s*;
1Co 3: 17 for God's temple is *s*, and you are

SACRIFICE (SACRIFICED SACRIFICES)

Ge 22: 2 *S* him there as a burnt offering
Ex 12: 27 It is the Passover *s* to the LORD,
1Sa 15: 22 To obey is better than *s*,
Hos 6: 6 For I desire mercy, not *s*,
Mt 9: 13 this means: 'I desire mercy, not *s*.'
Heb 9: 26 away with sin by the *s* of himself.
13: 15 offer to God a *s* of praise—
1Jn 2: 2 He is the atoning *s* for our sins,

SACRIFICED (SACRIFICE)

1Co 5: 7 our Passover lamb, has been *s*.
8: 1 Now about food *s* to idols:

Heb 9: 28 so Christ was *s* once

SACRIFICES (SACRIFICE)

Ps 51: 17 The *s* of God are a broken spirit;
Ro 12: 1 to offer your bodies as living *s*,

SADDUCEES

Mk 12: 18 *S*, who say there is no resurrection,

SAFE (SAVE)

Ps 37: 3 in the land and enjoy *s* pasture.
Pr 18: 10 the righteous run to it and are *s*.

SAFETY (SAVE)

Ps 4: 8 make me dwell in *s*.
1Th 5: 3 people are saying, "Peace and *s*,"

SAINTS

Ps 116: 15 is the death of his *s*.
Ro 8: 27 intercedes for the *s* in accordance
Eph 1: 18 of his glorious inheritance in the *s*,
6: 18 always keep on praying for all the *s*
Rev 5: 8 which are the prayers of the *s*.
19: 8 for the righteous acts of the *s*.)

SAKE

Ps 44: 22 Yet for your *s* we face death all day
Php 3: 7 loss for the *s* of Christ.
Heb 11: 26 He regarded disgrace for the *s*

SALT

Ge 19: 26 and she became a pillar of *s*.
Mt 5: 13 "You are the *s* of the earth.

SALVATION (SAVE)

Ex 15: 2 he has become my *s*.
1Ch 16: 23 proclaim his *s* day after day.
Ps 27: 1 The LORD is my light and my *s*—
51: 12 Restore to me the joy of your *s*
62: 2 He alone is my rock and my *s*;
85: 9 Surely his *s* is near those who fear
96: 2 proclaim his *s* day after day.
Isa 25: 9 let us rejoice and be glad in his *s*."
45: 17 the LORD with an everlasting *s*;
51: 6 But my *s* will last forever,
59: 17 and the helmet of *s* on his head;
61: 10 me with garments of *s*
Jnh 2: 9 *S* comes from the LORD."
Zec 9: 9 righteous and having *s*,
Lk 2: 30 For my eyes have seen your *s*,
Jn 4: 22 for *s* is from the Jews.
Ac 4: 12 *S* is found in no one else,
13: 47 that you may bring *s* to the ends
Ro 11: 11 *s* has come to the Gentiles
2Co 7: 10 brings repentance that leads to *s*
Eph 6: 17 Take the helmet of *s* and the sword
Php 2: 12 to work out your *s* with fear
1Th 5: 8 and the hope of *s* as a helmet.
2Ti 3: 15 wise for *s* through faith
Heb 2: 3 escape if we ignore such a great *s*?
6: 9 case—things that accompany *s*.
1Pe 1: 10 Concerning this *s*, the prophets,
2: 2 by it you may grow up in your *s*,

SAMARITAN

Lk 10: 33 But a *S*, as he traveled, came where

SAMSON

Danite judge. Birth promised (Jdg 13). Married to Philistine (Jdg 14). Vengeance on Philistines (Jdg 15). Betrayed by Delilah (Jdg 16:1-22). Death (Jdg 16:23-31). Feats of strength: killed lion (Jdg 14:6), 30 Philistines (Jdg 14:19), 1,000 Philistines with jawbone (Jdg 15:13-17), carried off gates of Gaza (Jdg 16:3), pushed down temple of Dagon (Jdg 16:25-30).

SAMUEL

Ephraimite judge and prophet (Heb 11:32). Birth prayed for (1Sa 1:10-18). Dedicated to temple by Hannah (1Sa 1:21-28). Raised by Eli (1Sa 2:11,18-26).Called as prophet (1Sa 3). Led Israel to victory over Philistines (1Sa 7). Asked by Israel for a king (1Sa 8). Anointed Saul as king (1Sa 9-10). Farewell speech (1Sa 12). Rebuked Saul for sacrifice (1Sa 13). Announced rejection of Saul (1Sa 15). Anointed David as king (1Sa 16). Protected David from Saul (1Sa 19:18-24). Death (1Sa 25:1). Returned from dead to condemn Saul (1Sa 28).

SANCTIFIED (SANCTIFY)

Ac 20: 32 among all those who are *s*.
Ro 15: 16 to God, *s* by the Holy Spirit.
1Co 6: 11 But you were washed, you were *s*,
7: 14 and the unbelieving wife has been *s*
Heb 10: 29 blood of the covenant that *s* him,

SANCTIFY (SANCTIFIED SANCTIFYING)

1Th 5: 23 *s* you through and through.

SANCTIFYING (SANCTIFY)

2Th 2: 13 through the *s* work of the Spirit

SANCTUARY

Ex 25: 8 "Then have them make a *s* for me,

SAND

Ge 22: 17 and as the *s* on the seashore.
Mt 7: 26 man who built his house on *s*.

SANDALS

Ex 3: 5 off your *s*, for the place where you
Jos 5: 15 off your *s*, for the place where you

SANG (SING)

Job 38: 7 while the morning stars *s* together
Rev 5: 9 And they *s* a new song:

SARAH

Wife of Abraham, originally named Sarai; barren (Ge 11:29-31; 1Pe 3:6). Taken by Pharaoh as Abraham's sister; returned (Ge 12:10-20). Gave Hagar to Abraham; sent her away in pregnancy (Ge 16). Name changed; Isaac promised (Ge 17:15-21; 18:10-15; Heb 11:11). Taken by Abimelech as Abraham's sister; returned (Ge 20). Isaac born; Hagar and Ishmael sent away (Ge 21:1-21; Gal 4:21-31). Death (Ge 23).

SATAN

Job 1: 6 and *S* also came with them.
Zec 3: 2 said to *S*, "The LORD rebuke you,
Mk 4: 15 *S* comes and takes away the word
2Co 11: 14 for *S* himself masquerades
12: 7 a messenger of *S*, to torment me.
Rev 12: 9 serpent called the devil, or *S*,
20: 2 or *S*, and bound him for a thousand
20: 7 *S* will be released from his prison

SATISFIED (SATISFY)

Isa 53: 11 he will see the light ⌊of life⌋ and be *s*

SATISFIES (SATISFY)

Ps 103: 5 who *s* your desires with good things,

SATISFY (SATISFIED SATISFIES)

Isa 55: 2 and your labor on what does not *s*?

SAUL

1. Benjamite; anointed by Samuel as first king of Israel (1Sa 9-10). Defeated Ammonites (1Sa 11). Rebuked for offering sacrifice (1Sa 13:1-15). Defeated Philistines (1Sa 14). Rejected as king for failing to annihilate Amalekites (1Sa 15). Soothed from evil spirit by David (1Sa 16:14-23). Sent David against Goliath (1Sa 17). Jealousy and attempted murder of David (1Sa 18:1-11). Gave David Michal as wife (1Sa 18:12-30). Second attempt to kill David (1Sa 19). Anger at Jonathan (1Sa 20:26-34). Pursued David: killed priests at Nob (1Sa 22), went to Keilah and Ziph (1Sa 23), life spared by David at En Gedi (1Sa 24) and in his tent (1Sa 26). Rebuked by Samuel's spirit for consulting witch at Endor (1Sa 28). Wounded by Philistines; took his own life (1Sa 31; 1Ch 10).
2. See PAUL

SAVE (SAFE SAFETY SALVATION SAVED SAVIOR)

Isa 63: 1 mighty to *s*."
Da 3: 17 the God we serve is able to *s* us
Zep 3: 17 he is mighty to *s*.
Mt 1: 21 he will *s* his people from their sins
16: 25 wants to *s* his life will lose it,
Lk 19: 10 to seek and to *s* what was lost."
Jn 3: 17 but to *s* the world through him.
1Ti 1: 15 came into the world to *s* sinners—
Jas 5: 20 of his way will *s* him from death

SAVED (SAVE)

Ps 34: 6 he *s* him out of all his troubles.
Isa 45: 22 "Turn to me and be *s*,
Joel 2: 32 on the name of the LORD will be *s*;
Mk 13: 13 firm to the end will be *s*.
16: 16 believes and is baptized will be *s*,
Jn 10: 9 enters through me will be *s*.
Ac 4: 12 to men by which we must be *s*."
16: 30 do to be *s*?" They replied,
Ro 9: 27 only the remnant will be *s*.
10: 9 him from the dead, you will be *s*.

1Co 3: 15 will suffer loss; he himself will be *s,*
15: 2 By this gospel you are *s,*
Eph 2: 5 it is by grace you have been *s.*
2: 8 For it is by grace you have been *s,*
1Ti 2: 4 who wants all men to be *s*

SAVIOR (SAVE)
Ps 89: 26 my God, the Rock my *S.'*
Isa 43: 11 and apart from me there is no *s.*
Hos 13: 4 no *S* except me.
Lk 1: 47 and my spirit rejoices in God my *S,*
2: 11 of David a *S* has been born to you;
Jn 4: 42 know that this man really is the *S*
Eph 5: 23 his body, of which he is the *S.*
1Ti 4: 10 who is the *S* of all men,
Tit 2: 10 about God our *S* attractive.
2: 13 appearing of our great God and *S,*
3: 4 and love of God our *S* appeared,
1Jn 4: 14 Son to be the *S* of the world.
Jude : 25 to the only God our *S* be glory,

SCALES
Lev 19: 36 Use honest *s* and honest weights,
Da 5: 27 You have been weighed on the *s*

SCAPEGOAT (GOAT)
Lev 16: 10 by sending it into the desert as a *s.*

SCARLET
Isa 1: 18 "Though your sins are like *s,*

SCATTERED
Jer 31: 10 'He who *s* Israel will gather them
Ac 8: 4 who had been *s* preached the word

SCEPTER
Rev 19: 15 "He will rule them with an iron *s."*

SCHEMES
2Co 2: 11 For we are not unaware of his *s.*
Eph 6: 11 stand against the devil's *s.*

SCOFFERS
2Pe 3: 3 that in the last days *s* will come,

SCORPION
Rev 9: 5 sting of a *s* when it strikes a man.

SCRIPTURE (SCRIPTURES)
Jn 10: 35 and the *S* cannot be broken—
1Ti 4: 13 yourself to the public reading of *S,*
2Ti 3: 16 All *S* is God-breathed
2Pe 1: 20 that no prophecy of *S* came about

SCRIPTURES (SCRIPTURE)
Lk 24: 27 said in all the *S* concerning himself.
Jn 5: 39 These are the *S* that testify about
Ac 17: 11 examined the *S* every day to see

SCROLL
Eze 3: 1 eat what is before you, eat this *s;*

SEA
Ex 14: 16 go through the *s* on dry ground.
Isa 57: 20 the wicked are like the tossing *s,*
Mic 7: 19 iniquities into the depths of the *s.*
Jas 1: 6 who doubts is like a wave of the *s,*
Rev 13: 1 I saw a beast coming out of the *s.*

SEAL (SEALS)
Jn 6: 27 God the Father has placed his *s*
2Co 1: 22 set his *s* of ownership on us,
Eph 1: 13 you were marked in him with a *s,*

SEALS (SEAL)
Rev 5: 2 "Who is worthy to break the *s*
6: 1 opened the first of the seven *s.*

SEARCH (SEARCHED SEARCHES SEARCHING)
Ps 4: 4 *s* your hearts and be silent.
139: 23 *S* me, O God, and know my heart;
Pr 2: 4 and *s* for it as for hidden treasure,
Jer 17: 10 "I the LORD *s* the heart
Eze 34: 16 I will *s* for the lost and bring back
Lk 15: 8 and *s* carefully until she finds it?

SEARCHED (SEARCH)
Ps 139: 1 O LORD, you have *s* me

SEARCHES (SEARCH)
Ro 8: 27 And he who *s* our hearts knows
1Co 2: 10 The Spirit *s* all things,

SEARCHING (SEARCH)
Am 8: 12 *s* for the word of the LORD,

SEARED
1Ti 4: 2 whose consciences have been *s*

SEASON
2Ti 4: 2 be prepared in *s* and out of *s;*

SEAT (SEATED SEATS)
Ps 1: 1 or sit in the *s* of mockers.
Da 7: 9 and the Ancient of Days took his *s.*
2Co 5: 10 before the judgment *s* of Christ,

SEATED (SEAT)
Ps 47: 8 God is *s* on his holy throne.
Isa 6: 1 I saw the Lord *s* on a throne,
Col 3: 1 where Christ is *s* at the right hand

SEATS (SEAT)
Lk 11: 43 you love the most important *s*

SECRET (SECRETS)
Dt 29: 29 The *s* things belong
Jdg 16: 6 Tell me the *s* of your great strength
Ps 90: 8 our *s* sins in the light
Pr 11: 13 but a trustworthy man keeps a *s.*
Mt 6: 4 so that your giving may be in *s.*
2Co 4: 2 we have renounced *s* and shameful
Php 4: 12 I have learned the *s*

SECRETS (SECRET)
Ps 44: 21 since he knows the *s* of the heart?
1Co 14: 25 the *s* of his heart will be laid bare.

SECURE (SECURITY)
Ps 112: 8 His heart is *s,* he will have no fear;
Heb 6: 19 an anchor for the soul, firm and *s.*

SECURITY (SECURE)
Job 31: 24 or said to pure gold, 'You are my *s,'*

SEED (SEEDS)
Lk 8: 11 of the parable: The *s* is the word
1Co 3: 6 I planted the *s,* Apollos watered it,
2Co 9: 10 he who supplies *s* to the sower
Gal 3: 29 then you are Abraham's *s,*
1Pe 1: 23 not of perishable *s,*

SEEDS (SEED)
Jn 12: 24 But if it dies, it produces many *s.*
Gal 3: 16 Scripture does not say "and to *s,"*

SEEK (SEEKS SELF-SEEKING)
Dt 4: 29 if from there you *s* the LORD your
1Ch 28: 9 If you *s* him, he will be found
2Ch 7: 14 themselves and pray and *s* my face
Ps 119: 10 I *s* you with all my heart;
Isa 55: 6 *S* the LORD while he may be
65: 1 found by those who did not *s* me.
Mt 6: 33 But *s* first his kingdom
Lk 19: 10 For the Son of Man came to *s*
Ro 10: 20 found by those who did not *s* me;
1Co 7: 27 you married? Do not *s* a divorce.

SEEKS (SEEK)
Jn 4: 23 the kind of worshipers the Father *s.*

SEER
1Sa 9: 9 of today used to be called a *s.)*

SELF-CONTROL (CONTROL)
1Co 7: 5 you because of your lack of *s.*
Gal 5: 23 faithfulness, gentleness and *s.*
2Pe 1: 6 and to knowledge, *s;* and to *s,*

SELF-CONTROLLED* (CONTROL)
1Th 5: 6 are asleep, but let us be alert and *s.*
5: 8 let us be *s,* putting on faith and love
1Ti 3: 2 *s,* respectable, hospitable,
Tit 1: 8 who is *s,* upright, holy
2: 2 worthy of respect, *s,* and sound
2: 5 to be *s* and pure, to be busy at home
2: 6 encourage the young men to be *s.*
2: 12 to live *s,* upright and godly lives
1Pe 1: 13 prepare your minds for action; be *s;*

1Pe 4: 7 and *s* so that you can pray.
5: 8 Be *s* and alert.

SELF-INDULGENCE

Mt 23: 25 inside they are full of greed and *s*.

SELF-SEEKING (SEEK)

1Co 13: 5 it is not *s*, it is not easily angered,

SELFISH*

Ps 119: 36 and not toward *s* gain.
Pr 18: 1 An unfriendly man pursues *s* ends;
Gal 5: 20 fits of rage, *s* ambition, dissensions,
Php 1: 17 preach Christ out of *s* ambition,
2: 3 Do nothing out of *s* ambition
Jas 3: 14 and *s* ambition in your hearts,
3: 16 you have envy and *s* ambition,

SEND (SENDING SENT)

Isa 6: 8 *S* me!" He said, "Go and tell this
Mt 9: 38 to *s* out workers into his harvest
Jn 16: 7 but if I go, I will *s* him to you.

SENDING (SEND)

Jn 20: 21 Father has sent me, I am *s* you."

SENSES*

Lk 15: 17 "When he came to his *s*, he said,
1Co 15: 34 Come back to your *s* as you ought,
2Ti 2: 26 and that they will come to their *s*

SENSUAL

Col 2: 23 value in restraining *s* indulgence.

SENT (SEND)

Isa 55: 11 achieve the purpose for which I *s* it.
Mt 10: 40 me receives the one who *s* me.
Jn 4: 34 "is to do the will of him who *s* me
Ro 10: 15 can they preach unless they are *s*?
1Jn 4: 10 but that he loved us and *s* his Son

SEPARATE (SEPARATED SEPARATES)

Mt 19: 6 has joined together, let man not *s*."
Ro 8: 35 Who shall *s* us from the love
1Co 7: 10 wife must not *s* from her husband.
2Co 6: 17 and be *s*, says the Lord.

SEPARATED (SEPARATE)

Isa 59: 2 But your iniquities have *s*

SEPARATES (SEPARATE)

Pr 16: 28 and a gossip *s* close friends.

SERPENT

Ge 3: 1 the *s* was more crafty than any
Rev 12: 9 that ancient *s* called the devil

SERVANT (SERVANTS)

1Sa 3: 10 "Speak, for your *s* is listening."
Mt 20: 26 great among you must be your *s*,
25: 21 'Well done, good and faithful *s*!
Lk 16: 13 "No *s* can serve two masters.
Php 2: 7 taking the very nature of a *s*,
2Ti 2: 24 And the Lord's *s* must not quarrel;

SERVANTS (SERVANT)

Lk 17: 10 should say, 'We are unworthy *s*;
Jn 15: 15 longer call you *s*, because a servant

SERVE (SERVICE SERVING)

Dt 10: 12 to *s* the LORD your God
Jos 22: 5 and to *s* him with all your heart
24: 15 this day whom you will *s*,
Mt 4: 10 Lord your God, and *s* him only.'"
6: 24 "No one can *s* two masters.
20: 28 but to *s*, and to give his life
Eph 6: 7 *S* wholeheartedly,

SERVICE (SERVE)

1Co 12: 5 There are different kinds of *s*,
Eph 4: 12 God's people for works of *s*,

SERVING (SERVE)

Ro 12: 11 your spiritual fervor, *s* the Lord.
Eph 6: 7 as if you were *s* the Lord, not men,
Col 3: 24 It is the Lord Christ you are *s*.
2Ti 2: 4 No one *s* as a soldier gets involved

SEVEN (SEVENTH)

Ge 7: 2 Take with you *s* of every kind
Jos 6: 4 march around the city *s* times,
1Ki 19: 18 Yet I reserve *s* thousand in Israel—
Pr 6: 16 *s* that are detestable to him:
24: 16 a righteous man falls *s* times,
Isa 4: 1 In that day *s* women
Da 9: 25 comes, there will be *s* 'sevens,'
Mt 18: 21 Up to *s* times?" Jesus answered,
Lk 11: 26 takes *s* other spirits more wicked
Ro 11: 4 for myself *s* thousand who have not
Rev 1: 4 To the *s* churches in the province
6: 1 opened the first of the *s* seals.
8: 2 and to them were given *s* trumpets.
10: 4 And when the *s* thunders spoke,
15: 7 to the *s* angels *s* golden bowls filled

SEVENTH (SEVEN)

Ge 2: 2 By the *s* day God had finished
Ex 23: 12 but on the *s* day do not work,

SEXUAL (SEXUALLY)

1Co 6: 13 body is not meant for *s* immorality,
6: 18 Flee from *s* immorality.
10: 8 should not commit *s* immorality,
Eph 5: 3 even a hint of *s* immorality,
1Th 4: 3 that you should avoid *s* immorality

SEXUALLY (SEXUAL)

1Co 5: 9 to associate with *s* immoral people
6: 18 he who sins *s* sins against his own

SHADOW

Ps 23: 4 through the valley of the *s* of death,
36: 7 find refuge in the *s* of your wings.
Heb 10: 1 The law is only a *s*

SHALLUM

King of Israel (2Ki 15:10-16).

SHAME (ASHAMED)

Ps 34: 5 their faces are never covered with *s*.
Pr 13: 18 discipline comes to poverty and *s*,
Heb 12: 2 endured the cross, scorning its *s*,

SHARE (SHARED)

Ge 21: 10 that slave woman's son will never *s*
Lk 3: 11 "The man with two tunics should *s*
Gal 4: 30 the slave woman's son will never *s*
6: 6 in the word must *s* all good things
Eph 4: 28 something to *s* with those in need.
1Ti 6: 18 and to be generous and willing to *s*.
Heb 12: 10 that we may *s* in his holiness.
13: 16 to do good and to *s* with others,

SHARED (SHARE)

Heb 2: 14 he too *s* in their humanity so that

SHARON

SS 2: 1 I am a rose of *S*,

SHARPER*

Heb 4: 12 *S* than any double-edged sword,

SHED (SHEDDING)

Ge 9: 6 by man shall his blood be *s*;
Col 1: 20 through his blood, *s* on the cross.

SHEDDING (SHED)

Heb 9: 22 without the *s* of blood there is no

SHEEP

Ps 100: 3 we are his people, the *s*
119:176 I have strayed like a lost *s*
Isa 53: 6 We all, like *s*, have gone astray,
Jer 50: 6 "My people have been lost *s*;
Eze 34: 11 I myself will search for my *s*
Mt 9: 36 helpless, like *s* without a shepherd.
Jn 10: 3 He calls his own *s* by name
10: 15 and I lay down my life for the *s*.
10: 27 My *s* listen to my voice; I know
21: 17 Jesus said, "Feed my *s*.
1Pe 2: 25 For you were like *s* going astray,

SHELTER

Ps 61: 4 take refuge in the *s* of your wings.
91: 1 in the *s* of the Most High

SHEM

Son of Noah (Ge 5:32; 6:10). Blessed (Ge 9:26). Descendants (Ge 10:21-31; 11:10-32).

SHEPHERD (SHEPHERDS)

Ps 23: 1 LORD is my *s*, I shall not be in want.
Isa 40: 11 He tends his flock like a *s*:
Jer 31: 10 will watch over his flock like a *s*.'

Eze 34: 12 As a *s* looks after his scattered
Zec 11: 17 "Woe to the worthless *s*,
Mt 9: 36 and helpless, like sheep without a *s*.
Jn 10: 11 The good *s* lays down his life
10: 16 there shall be one flock and one *s*.
1Pe 5: 4 And when the Chief *S* appears,

SHEPHERDS (SHEPHERD)
Jer 23: 1 "Woe to the *s* who are destroying
Lk 2: 8 there were *s* living out in the fields
Ac 20: 28 Be *s* of the church of God,
1Pe 5: 2 Be *s* of God's flock that is

SHIELD
Ps 28: 7 LORD is my strength and my *s;*
Eph 6: 16 to all this, take up the *s* of faith,

SHINE (SHONE)
Ps 4: 6 Let the light of your face *s* upon us,
80: 1 between the cherubim, *s* forth
Isa 60: 1 "Arise, *s*, for your light has come,
Da 12: 3 are wise will *s* like the brightness
Mt 5: 16 let your light *s* before men,
13: 43 the righteous will *s* like the sun
2Co 4: 6 made his light *s* in our hearts
Eph 5: 14 and Christ will *s* on you."

SHIPWRECKED*
2Co 11: 25 I was stoned, three times I was *s*,
1Ti 1: 19 and so have *s* their faith.

SHONE (SHINE)
Mt 17: 2 His face *s* like the sun,
Lk 2: 9 glory of the Lord *s* around them,
Rev 21: 11 It *s* with the glory of God,

SHORT
Isa 59: 1 of the LORD is not too *s* to save,
Ro 3: 23 and fall *s* of the glory of God,

SHOULDERS
Isa 9: 6 and the government will be on his *s*
Lk 15: 5 he joyfully puts it on his *s*

SHOWED
1Jn 4: 9 This is how God *s* his love

SHREWD
Mt 10: 16 Therefore be as *s* as snakes and

SHUN*
Job 28: 28 and to *s* evil is understanding.'"
Pr 3: 7 fear the LORD and *s* evil.

SICK
Pr 13: 12 Hope deferred makes the heart *s*,
Mt 9: 12 who need a doctor, but the *s*.
25: 36 I was *s* and you looked after me,
Jas 5: 14 of you *s?* He should call the elders

SICKLE
Joel 3: 13 Swing the *s*,

SIDE
Ps 91: 7 A thousand may fall at your *s*,
124: 1 If the LORD had not been on our *s*
2Ti 4: 17 But the Lord stood at my *s*

SIGHT
Ps 90: 4 For a thousand years in your *s*
116: 15 Precious in the *s* of the LORD
2Co 5: 7 We live by faith, not by *s*.
1Pe 3: 4 which is of great worth in God's *s*.

SIGN (SIGNS)
Isa 7: 14 the Lord himself will give you a *s:*

SIGNS (SIGN)
Mk 16: 17 these *s* will accompany those who
Jn 20: 30 Jesus did many other miraculous *s*

SILENT
Pr 17: 28 a fool is thought wise if he keeps *s*,
Isa 53: 7 as a sheep before her shearers is *s*,
Hab 2: 20 let all the earth be *s* before him."
1Co 14: 34 women should remain *s*
1Ti 2: 12 over a man; she must be *s*.

SILVER
Pr 25: 11 is like apples of gold in settings of *s*.
Hag 2: 8 'The *s* is mine and the gold is mine,'
1Co 3: 12 *s*, costly stones, wood, hay or straw

SIMON
1. See PETER.
2. Apostle, called the Zealot (Mt 10:4; Mk 3:18; Lk 6:15; Ac 1:13).
3. Samaritan sorcerer (Ac 8:9-24).

SIN (SINFUL SINNED SINNER SINNERS SINNING SINS)
Nu 5: 7 and must confess the *s* he has
32: 23 be sure that your *s* will find you
Dt 24: 16 each is to die for his own *s*.
1Ki 8: 46 for there is no one who does not *s*
2Ch 7: 14 and will forgive their *s* and will heal
Ps 4: 4 In your anger do not *s;*
32: 2 whose *s* the LORD does not count
32: 5 Then I acknowledged my *s* to you
51: 2 and cleanse me from my *s*.
66: 18 If I had cherished *s* in my heart,
119: 11 that I might not *s* against you.
119:133 let no *s* rule over me.
Isa 6: 7 is taken away and your *s* atoned
Mic 7: 18 who pardons *s* and forgives
Mt 18: 6 little ones who believe in me to *s*,
Jn 1: 29 who takes away the *s* of the world!
8: 34 everyone who sins is a slave to *s*.
Ro 5: 12 as *s* entered the world
5: 20 where *s* increased, grace increased
6: 11 count yourselves dead to *s*
6: 23 For the wages of *s* is death,
14: 23 that does not come from faith is *s*.
2Co 5: 21 God made him who had no *s* to be *s*
Gal 6: 1 if someone is caught in a *s*,
Heb 9: 26 to do away with *s* by the sacrifice
11: 25 the pleasures of *s* for a short time.
12: 1 and the *s* that so easily entangles,
1Pe 2: 22 "He committed no *s*,
1Jn 1: 8 If we claim to be without *s*,
3: 4 in fact, *s* is lawlessness.
3: 5 And in him is no *s*.
3: 9 born of God will continue to *s*,
5: 18 born of God does not continue to *s;*

SINCERE
Ro 12: 9 Love must be *s*.
Heb 10: 22 near to God with a *s* heart

SINFUL (SIN)
Ps 51: 5 Surely I was *s* at birth
51: 5 *s* from the time my mother
Ro 7: 5 we were controlled by the *s* nature,
8: 4 not live according to the *s* nature
8: 9 are controlled not by the *s* nature
Gal 5: 19 The acts of the *s* nature are obvious
5: 24 Jesus have crucified the *s* nature
1Pe 2: 11 abstain from *s* desires, which war

SING (SANG SINGING SONG SONGS)
Ps 30: 4 *S* to the LORD, you saints of his;
47: 6 *S* praises to God, *s* praises;
59: 16 But I will *s* of your strength,
89: 1 I will *s* of the LORD's great love
101: 1 I will *s* of your love and justice;
Eph 5: 19 *S* and make music in your heart

SINGING (SING)
Ps 63: 5 with *s* lips my mouth will praise
Ac 16: 25 Silas were praying and *s* hymns

SINNED (SIN)
2Sa 12: 13 "I have *s* against the LORD."
Job 1: 5 "Perhaps my children have *s*
Ps 51: 4 Against you, you only, have I *s*
Da 9: 5 we have *s* and done wrong.
Mic 7: 9 Because I have *s* against him,
Lk 15: 18 I have *s* against heaven
Ro 3: 23 for all have *s* and fall short
1Jn 1: 10 claim we have not *s*, we make him

SINNER (SIN)
Ecc 9: 18 but one *s* destroys much good.
Lk 15: 7 in heaven over one *s* who repents
18: 13 'God, have mercy on me, a *s*.'
1Co 14: 24 convinced by all that he is a *s*
Jas 5: 20 Whoever turns a *s* from the error
1Pe 4: 18 become of the ungodly and the *s?"*

SINNERS (SIN)
Ps 1: 1 or stand in the way of *s*
Pr 23: 17 Do not let your heart envy *s*,
Mt 9: 13 come to call the righteous, but *s*."
Ro 5: 8 While we were still *s*, Christ died
1Ti 1: 15 came into the world to save *s*—

SINNING (SIN)
Ex 20: 20 be with you to keep you from *s*."

1Co 15: 34 stop *s;* for there are some who are
Heb 10: 26 If we deliberately keep on *s*
1Jn 3: 6 No one who lives in him keeps on *s*
3: 9 go on *s,* because he has been born

SINS (SIN)

2Ki 14: 6 each is to die for his own *s.*"
Ezr 9: 6 our *s* are higher than our heads
Ps 19: 13 your servant also from willful *s;*
32: 1 whose *s* are covered.
103: 3 who forgives all your *s*
130: 3 O LORD, kept a record of *s,*
Pr 28: 13 who conceals his *s* does not
Isa 1: 18 "Though your *s* are like scarlet,
43: 25 and remembers your *s* no more.
Isa 59: 2 your *s* have hidden his face
Eze 18: 4 soul who *s* is the one who will die.
Mt 1: 21 he will save his people from their *s*
18: 15 "If your brother *s* against you,
Lk 11: 4 Forgive us our *s,*
17: 3 "If your brother *s,* rebuke him,
Ac 22: 16 be baptized and wash your *s* away,
1Co 15: 3 died for our *s* according
Eph 2: 1 dead in your transgressions and *s,*
Col 2: 13 us all our *s,* having canceled
Heb 1: 3 he had provided purification for *s,*
7: 27 He sacrificed for their *s* once for all
8: 12 and will remember their *s* no more
10: 12 for all time one sacrifice for *s,*
Jas 4: 17 ought to do and doesn't do it,*s.*
5: 16 Therefore confess your *s*
5: 20 and cover over a multitude of *s.*
1Pe 2: 24 He himself bore our *s* in his body
3: 18 For Christ died for *s* once for all,
1Jn 1: 9 If we confess our *s,* he is faithful
Rev 1: 5 has freed us from our *s* by his blood

SITS

Ps 99: 1 *s* enthroned between the cherubim,
Isa 40: 22 He *s* enthroned above the circle
Mt 19: 28 of Man *s* on his glorious throne,
Rev 4: 9 thanks to him who *s* on the throne

SKIN

Job 19: 20 with only the *s* of my teeth.
19: 26 And after my *s* has been destroyed,
Jer 13: 23 Can the Ethiopian change his *s*

SLAIN (SLAY)

Rev 5: 12 "Worthy is the Lamb, who was *s,*

SLANDER (SLANDERED SLANDERERS)

Lev 19: 16 "'Do not go about spreading *s*
1Ti 5: 14 the enemy no opportunity for *s.*
Tit 3: 2 to *s* no one, to be peaceable

SLANDERED (SLANDER)

1Co 4: 13 when we are *s,* we answer kindly.

SLANDERERS (SLANDER)

Ro 1: 30 They are gossips, *s,* God-haters,
1Co 6: 10 nor the greedy nor drunkards nor *s*
Tit 2: 3 not to be *s* or addicted

SLAUGHTER

Isa 53: 7 he was led like a lamb to the *s,*

SLAVE (SLAVERY SLAVES)

Ge 21: 10 "Get rid of that *s* woman
Mt 20: 27 wants to be first must be your *s*—
Jn 8: 34 everyone who sins is a *s* to sin.
1Co 12: 13 whether Jews or Greeks, *s* or free
Gal 3: 28 *s* nor free, male nor female,
4: 30 Get rid of the *s* woman and her son
2Pe 2: 19 a man is a *s* to whatever has

SLAVERY (SLAVE)

Ro 6: 19 parts of your body in *s* to impurity
Gal 4: 3 were in *s* under the basic principles

SLAVES (SLAVE)

Ro 6: 6 that we should no longer be *s* to sin
6: 22 and have become *s* to God,

SLAY (SLAIN)

Job 13: 15 Though he *s* me, yet will I hope

SLEEP (SLEEPING)

Ps 121: 4 will neither slumber nor *s.*
1Co 15: 51 We will not all *s,* but we will all be

SLEEPING (SLEEP)

Mk 13: 36 suddenly, do not let him find you *s.*

SLOW

Ex 34: 6 and gracious God, *s* to anger,
Jas 1: 19 *s* to speak and *s* to become angry,
2Pe 3: 9 The Lord is not *s* in keeping his

SLUGGARD

Pr 6: 6 Go to the ant, you *s;*
20: 4 A *s* does not plow in season;

SLUMBER

Ps 121: 3 he who watches over you will not *s;*
Pr 6: 10 A little sleep, a little *s,*
Ro 13: 11 for you to wake up from your *s,*

SNAKE (SNAKES)

Nu 21: 8 "Make a *s* and put it up on a pole;
Pr 23: 32 In the end it bites like a *s*
Jn 3: 14 Moses lifted up the *s* in the desert,

SNAKES (SNAKE)

Mt 10: 16 as shrewd as *s* and as innocent
Mk 16: 18 they will pick up *s* with their hands;

SNATCH

Jn 10: 28 no one can *s* them out of my hand.
Jude : 23 *s* others from the fire and save

SNOW

Ps 51: 7 and I will be whiter than *s.*

SOAR

Isa 40: 31 They will *s* on wings like eagles;

SODOM

Ge 19: 24 rained down burning sulfur on *S*
Ro 9: 29 we would have become like *S,*

SOIL

Ge 4: 2 kept flocks, and Cain worked the *s.*
Mt 13: 23 on good *s* is the man who hears

SOLDIER

1Co 9: 7 as a *s* at his own expense?
2Ti 2: 3 with us like a good *s* of Christ Jesus

SOLE

Dt 28: 65 place for the *s* of your foot.
Isa 1: 6 From the *s* of your foot to the top

SOLID

2Ti 2: 19 God's *s* foundation stands firm,
Heb 5: 12 You need milk, not *s* food!

SOLOMON

Son of David by Bathsheba; king of Judah (2Sa 12:24; 1Ch 3:5, 10). Appointed king by David (1Ki 1); adversaries Adonijah, Joab, Shimei killed by Benaiah (1Ki 2). Asked for wisdom (1Ki 3; 2Ch 1). Judged between two prostitutes (1Ki 3:16-28). Built temple (1Ki 5-7; 2Ch 2-5); prayer of dedication (1Ki 8; 2Ch 6). Visited by Queen of Sheba (1Ki 10; 2Ch 9). Wives turned his heart from God (1Ki 11:1-13). Jeroboam rebelled against (1Ki 11:26-40). Death (1Ki 11:41-43; 2Ch 9:29-31).
Proverbs of (1Ki 4:32; Pr 1:1; 10:1; 25:1); psalms of (Ps 72; 127); song of (SS 1:1).

SON (SONS)

Ge 22: 2 "Take your *s,* your only *s,* Isaac,
Ex 11: 5 Every firstborn *s* in Egypt will die,
Dt 21: 18 rebellious *s* who does not obey his
Ps 2: 7 He said to me, "You are my *S;*
2: 12 Kiss the *S,* lest he be angry
Pr 10: 1 A wise *s* brings joy to his father,
13: 24 He who spares the rod hates his *s,*
29: 17 Discipline your *s,* and he will give
Isa 7: 14 with child and will give birth to a *s,*
Hos 11: 1 and out of Egypt I called my *s.*
Mt 2: 15 "Out of Egypt I called my *s.*"
3: 17 "This is my *S,* whom I love;
11: 27 one knows the *S* except the Father,
16: 16 "You are the Christ, the *S*
17: 5 "This is my *S,* whom I love;
20: 18 and the *S* of Man will be betrayed
24: 30 They will see the *S* of Man coming
24: 44 the *S* of Man will come at an hour
27: 54 "Surely he was the *S* of God!"
28: 19 and of the *S* and of the Holy Spirit,
Mk 10: 45 even the *S* of Man did not come
14: 62 you will see the *S* of Man sitting
Lk 9: 58 but the *S* of Man has no place
18: 8 when the *S* of Man comes,

Lk 19: 10 For the *S* of Man came to seek
Jn 3: 14 so the *S* of Man must be lifted up,
3: 16 that he gave his one and only *S*,
17: 1 Glorify your *S*, that your *S* may
Ro 8: 29 conformed to the likeness of his *S*,
8: 32 He who did not spare his own *S*,
1Co 15: 28 then the *S* himself will be made
Gal 4: 30 rid of the slave woman and her *s*,
1Th 1: 10 and to wait for his *S* from heaven,
Heb 1: 2 days he has spoken to us by his *S*,
10: 29 punished who has trampled the *S*
1Jn 1: 7 his *S*, purifies us from all sin.
4: 9 only *S* into the world that we might
5: 5 he who believes that Jesus is the *S*
5: 11 eternal life, and this life is in his *S*.

SONG (SING)

Ps 40: 3 He put a new *s* in my mouth,
96: 1 Sing to the LORD a new *s*;
149: 1 Sing to the LORD a new *s*,
Isa 49: 13 burst into *s*, O mountains!
55: 12 will burst into *s* before you,
Rev 5: 9 And they sang a new *s*:
15: 3 and sang the *s* of Moses the servant

SONGS (SING)

Job 35: 10 who gives *s* in the night,
Ps 100: 2 come before him with joyful *s*.
Eph 5: 19 with psalms, hymns and spiritual *s*.
Jas 5: 13 Is anyone happy? Let him sing *s*

SONS (SON)

Joel 2: 28 Your *s* and daughters will prophesy
Jn 12: 36 so that you may become *s* of light."
Ro 8: 14 by the Spirit of God are *s* of God.
2Co 6: 18 and you will be my *s* and daughters
Gal 4: 5 we might receive the full rights of *s*.
Heb 12: 7 discipline; God is treating you as *s*.

SORROW (SORROWS)

Jer 31: 12 and they will *s* no more.
Ro 9: 2 I have great *s* and unceasing
2Co 7: 10 Godly *s* brings repentance that

SORROWS (SORROW)

Isa 53: 3 a man of *s*, and familiar

SOUL (SOULS)

Dt 6: 5 with all your *s* and with all your
10: 12 all your heart and with all your *s*,
Jos 22: 5 with all your heart and all your *s*."
Ps 23: 3 he restores my *s*.
42: 1 so my *s* pants for you, O God.
42: 11 Why are you downcast, O my *s*?
103: 1 Praise the LORD, O my *s*;
Pr 13: 19 A longing fulfilled is sweet to the *s*,
Isa 55: 2 your *s* will delight in the richest
Mt 10: 28 kill the body but cannot kill the *s*.
16: 26 yet forfeits his *s*? Or what can
22: 37 with all your *s* and with all your
Heb 4: 12 even to dividing *s* and spirit,

SOULS (SOUL)

Pr 11: 30 and he who wins *s* is wise.
Jer 6: 16 and you will find rest for your *s*.
Mt 11: 29 and you will find rest for your *s*.

SOUND

1Co 14: 8 if the trumpet does not *s* a clear call
15: 52 the trumpet will *s*, the dead will
2Ti 4: 3 men will not put up with *s* doctrine.

SOVEREIGN

Da 4: 25 that the Most High is *s*

SOW (SOWS)

Job 4: 8 and those who *s* trouble reap it.
Mt 6: 26 they do not *s* or reap or store away
2Pe 2: 22 and, "A *s* that is washed goes back

SOWS (SOW)

Pr 11: 18 he who *s* righteousness reaps a sure
22: 8 He who *s* wickedness reaps trouble
2Co 9: 6 Whoever *s* sparingly will
Gal 6: 7 A man reaps what he *s*.

SPARE (SPARES)

Ro 8: 32 He who did not *s* his own Son,
11: 21 natural branches, he will not *s* you

SPARES (SPARE)

Pr 13: 24 He who *s* the rod hates his son,

SPEARS

Isa 2: 4 and their *s* into pruning hooks.
Joel 3: 10 and your pruning hooks into *s*.
Mic 4: 3 and their *s* into pruning hooks.

SPECTACLE

1Co 4: 9 We have been made a *s*
Col 2: 15 he made a public *s* of them,

SPIN

Mt 6: 28 They do not labor or *s*.

SPIRIT (SPIRIT'S SPIRITS SPIRITUAL SPIRITUALLY)

Ge 1: 2 and the *S* of God was hovering
6: 3 "My *S* will not contend
2Ki 2: 9 inherit a double portion of your *s*,"
Job 33: 4 The *S* of God has made me;
Ps 31: 5 Into your hands I commit my *s*;
51: 10 and renew a steadfast *s* within me.
51: 11 or take your Holy *S* from me.
51: 17 sacrifices of God are a broken *s*;
139: 7 Where can I go from your *S*?
Isa 57: 15 him who is contrite and lowly in *s*,
63: 10 and grieved his Holy *S*.
Eze 11: 19 an undivided heart and put a new *s*
36: 26 you a new heart and put a new *s*
Joel 2: 28 I will pour out my *S* on all people.
Zec 4: 6 but by my *S*,' says the LORD
Mt 1: 18 to be with child through the Holy *S*
3: 11 will baptize you with the Holy *S*
3: 16 he saw the *S* of God descending
4: 1 led by the *S* into the desert
5: 3 saying: "Blessed are the poor in *s*,
26: 41 *s* is willing, but the body is weak."
28: 19 and of the Son and of the Holy *S*,
Lk 1: 80 child grew and became strong in *s*;
11: 13 Father in heaven give the Holy *S*
Jn 4: 24 God is *s*, and his worshipers must
7: 39 Up to that time the *S* had not been
14: 26 But the Counselor, the Holy *S*,
16: 13 But when he, the *S* of truth, comes,
20: 22 and said, "Receive the Holy *S*.
Ac 1: 5 will be baptized with the Holy *S*."
2: 4 of them were filled with the Holy *S*
2: 38 will receive the gift of the Holy *S*.
6: 3 who are known to be full of the *S*
19: 2 "Did you receive the Holy *S*
Ro 8: 9 And if anyone does not have the *S*
8: 26 the *S* helps us in our weakness.
1Co 2: 10 God has revealed it to us by his *S*.
2: 14 man without the *S* does not accept
6: 19 body is a temple of the Holy *S*,
12: 13 baptized by one *S* into one body—
2Co 3: 6 the letter kills, but the *S* gives life.
5: 5 and has given us the *S* as a deposit,
Gal 5: 16 by the *S*, and you will not gratify
5: 22 But the fruit of the *S* is love, joy,
5: 25 let us keep in step with the *S*.
Eph 1: 13 with a seal, the promised Holy *S*,
4: 30 do not grieve the Holy *S* of God,
5: 18 Instead, be filled with the *S*.
6: 17 of salvation and the sword of the *S*,
2Th 2: 13 the sanctifying work of the *S*
Heb 4: 12 even to dividing soul and *s*,
1Pe 3: 4 beauty of a gentle and quiet *s*,
2Pe 1: 21 carried along by the Holy *S*.
1Jn 4: 1 Dear friends, do not believe every *s*

SPIRIT'S (SPIRIT)

1Th 5: 19 not put out the *S* fire; do not treat

SPIRITS (SPIRIT)

1Co 12: 10 to another distinguishing between *s*,

1Co 14: 32 The *s* of prophets are subject
1Jn 4: 1 test the *s* to see whether they are

SPIRITUAL (SPIRIT)

Ro 12: 1 this is your *s* act of worship.
12: 11 but keep your *s* fervor, serving
1Co 2: 13 expressing *s* truths in *s* words.
3: 1 I could not address you as *s* but
12: 1 Now about *s* gifts, brothers,
14: 1 of love and eagerly desire *s* gifts,
15: 44 a natural body, it is raised a *s* body.
Gal 6: 1 you who are *s* should restore him
Eph 1: 3 with every *s* blessing in Christ.
5: 19 with psalms, hymns and *s* songs.
6: 12 and against the *s* forces of evil
1Pe 2: 2 newborn babies, crave pure *s* milk,
2: 5 are being built into a *s* house

SPIRITUALLY (SPIRIT)

1Co 2: 14 because they are *s* discerned.

SPLENDOR

1Ch 16: 29 the LORD in the *s* of his holiness.
29: 11 the glory and the majesty and the *s*,
Job 37: 22 of the north he comes in golden *s*;
Ps 29: 2 in the *s* of his holiness.
45: 3 clothe yourself with *s* and majesty.
96: 6 *S* and majesty are before him;
96: 9 in the *s* of his holiness;
104: 1 you are clothed with *s* and majesty.
145: 5 of the glorious *s* of your majesty,
Isa 61: 3 the LORD for the display of his *s*.
63: 1 Who is this, robed in *s*,
Lk 9: 31 appeared in glorious *s*, talking
2Th 2: 8 and destroy by the *s* of his coming.

SPOIL

Ps 119:162 like one who finds great *s*.

SPOTLESS

2Pe 3: 14 make every effort to be found *s*,

SPREAD (SPREADING)

Ac 12: 24 of God continued to increase and *s*.
19: 20 the word of the Lord *s* widely

SPREADING (SPREAD)

1Th 3: 2 God's fellow worker in *s* the gospel

SPRING

Jer 2: 13 the *s* of living water,
Jn 4: 14 in him a *s* of water welling up
Jas 3: 12 can a salt *s* produce fresh water.

SPUR*

Heb 10: 24 how we may *s* one another

SPURNS*

Pr 15: 5 A fool *s* his father's discipline,

STAFF

Ps 23: 4 your rod and your *s*,

STAKES

Isa 54: 2 strengthen your *s*.

STAND (STANDING STANDS)

Ex 14: 13 *S* firm and you will see
2Ch 20: 17 *s* firm and see the deliverance
Ps 1: 5 Therefore the wicked will not *s*
40: 2 and gave me a firm place to *s*.
119:120 I *s* in awe of your laws.
Eze 22: 30 *s* before me in the gap on behalf
Zec 14: 4 On that day his feet will *s*
Mt 12: 25 divided against itself will not *s*.
Ro 14: 10 we will all *s* before God's judgment
1Co 10: 13 out so that you can *s* up under it.
15: 58 Therefore, my dear brothers, *s* firm
Eph 6: 14 *S* firm then, with the belt
2Th 2: 15 *s* firm and hold to the teachings we
Jas 5: 8 You too, be patient and *s* firm,
Rev 3: 20 Here I am! I *s* at the door

STANDING (STAND)

Ex 3: 5 where you are *s* is holy ground."
Jos 5: 15 the place where you are *s* is holy."
1Pe 5: 9 Resist him, *s* firm in the faith,

STANDS (STAND)

Ps 89: 2 that your love *s* firm forever,
119: 89 it *s* firm in the heavens.
Mt 10: 22 but he who *s* firm to the end will be
2Ti 2: 19 God's solid foundation *s* firm,
1Pe 1: 25 but the word of the Lord *s* forever

STAR (STARS)

Nu 24: 17 A *s* will come out of Jacob;
Rev 22: 16 and the bright Morning *S*."

STARS (STAR)

Da 12: 3 like the *s* for ever and ever.
Php 2: 15 in which you shine like *s*

STATURE

Lk 2: 52 And Jesus grew in wisdom and *s*,

STEADFAST

Ps 51: 10 and renew a *s* spirit within me.
Isa 26: 3 him whose mind is *s*,
1Pe 5: 10 and make you strong, firm and *s*.

STEAL

Ex 20: 15 "You shall not *s*.
Mt 19: 18 do not *s*, do not give false
Eph 4: 28 has been stealing must *s* no longer,

STEP (STEPS)

Gal 5: 25 let us keep in *s* with the Spirit.

STEPS (STEP)

Pr 16: 9 but the LORD determines his *s*.
Jer 10: 23 it is not for man to direct his *s*.
1Pe 2: 21 that you should follow in his *s*.

STICKS

Pr 18: 24 there is a friend who *s* closer

STIFF-NECKED

Ex 34: 9 Although this is a *s* people,

STILL

Ps 46: 10 "Be *s*, and know that I am God;
Zec 2: 13 Be *s* before the LORD, all mankind

STIRS

Pr 6: 19 and a man who *s* up dissension
10: 12 Hatred *s* up dissension,
15: 1 but a harsh word *s* up anger.
15: 18 hot-tempered man *s* up dissension,
16: 28 A perverse man *s* up dissension,
28: 25 A greedy man *s* up dissension,
29: 22 An angry man *s* up dissension,

STONE (CAPSTONE CORNERSTONE MILLSTONE)

1Sa 17: 50 the Philistine with a sling and a *s*;
Isa 8: 14 a *s* that causes men to stumble
Eze 11: 19 remove from them their heart of *s*
Mk 16: 3 "Who will roll the *s* away
Lk 4: 3 tell this *s* to become bread."
Jn 8: 7 the first to throw a *s* at her."
2Co 3: 3 not on tablets of *s* but on tablets

STOOP

2Sa 22: 36 you *s* down to make me great.

STORE

Pr 10: 14 Wise men *s* up knowledge
Mt 6: 19 not *s* up for yourselves treasures

STOREHOUSE (HOUSE)

Mal 3: 10 Bring the whole tithe into the *s*,

STRAIGHT

Pr 3: 6 and he will make your paths *s*.
4: 25 Let your eyes look *s* ahead,
15: 21 of understanding keeps a *s* course.
Jn 1: 23 'Make *s* the way for the Lord.'"

STRAIN

Mt 23: 24 You *s* out a gnat but swallow

STRANGER (STRANGERS)

Mt 25: 35 I was a *s* and you invited me in,
Jn 10: 5 But they will never follow a *s*;

STRANGERS (STRANGER)

1Pe 2: 11 as aliens and *s* in the world,

STREAMS

Ps 1: 3 He is like a tree planted by *s*
46: 4 is a river whose *s* make glad
Ecc 1: 7 All *s* flow into the sea,
Jn 7: 38 *s* of living water will flow

STRENGTH (STRONG)

Ex 15: 2 The LORD is my *s* and my song;
Dt 6: 5 all your soul and with all your *s*.
2Sa 22: 33 It is God who arms me with *s*
Ne 8: 10 for the joy of the LORD is your *s*."
Ps 28: 7 The LORD is my *s* and my shield;
46: 1 God is our refuge and *s*,
96: 7 ascribe to the LORD glory and *s*.
118: 14 The LORD is my *s* and my song;
147: 10 not in the *s* of the horse,
Isa 40: 31 will renew their *s*.
Mk 12: 30 all your mind and with all your *s*.'

1Co 1:25 of God is stronger than man's *s.*
Php 4:13 through him who gives me *s.*
1Pe 4:11 it with the *s* God provides,

STRENGTHEN (STRONG)
2Ch 16:9 to *s* those whose hearts are fully
Ps 119:28 *s* me according to your word.
Isa 35:3 *S* the feeble hands,
41:10 I will *s* you and help you;
Eph 3:16 of his glorious riches he may *s* you
2Th 2:17 and *s* you in every good deed
Heb 12:12 *s* your feeble arms and weak knees.

STRENGTHENING (STRONG)
1Co 14:26 done for the *s* of the church.

STRIFE
Pr 20:3 It is to a man's honor to avoid *s,*
22:10 out the mocker, and out goes *s;*

STRIKE (STRIKES)
Ge 3:15 and you will *s* his heel."
Zec 13:7 "*S* the shepherd,
Mt 26:31 "'I will *s* the shepherd,

STRIKES (STRIKE)
Mt 5:39 If someone *s* you on the right

STRONG (STRENGTH STRENGTHEN STRENGTHENING)
Dt 31:6 Be *s* and courageous.
1Ki 2:2 "So be *s,* show yourself a man,
Pr 18:10 The name of the LORD is a *s* tower
31:17 her arms are *s* for her tasks.
SS 8:6 for love is as *s* as death,
Lk 2:40 And the child grew and became *s;*
Ro 15:1 We who are *s* ought to bear
1Co 1:27 things of the world to shame the *s.*
16:13 in the faith; be men of courage; be *s*
2Co 12:10 For when I am weak, then I am *s.*
Eph 6:10 be *s* in the Lord and in his mighty

STRUGGLE
Ro 15:30 me in my *s* by praying to God
Eph 6:12 For our *s* is not against flesh
Heb 12:4 In your *s* against sin, you have not

STUDY
Ezr 7:10 Ezra had devoted himself to the *s*
Ecc 12:12 and much *s* wearies the body.
Jn 5:39 You diligently *s* the Scriptures

STUMBLE (STUMBLING)
Ps 37:24 though he *s,* he will not fall,
119:165 and nothing can make them *s.*
Isa 8:14 a stone that causes men to *s*
Jer 31:9 a level path where they will not *s,*
Eze 7:19 for it has made them *s* into sin.
1Co 10:32 Do not cause anyone to *s,*
1Pe 2:8 and, "A stone that causes men to *s*

STUMBLING (STUMBLE)
Ro 14:13 up your mind not to put any *s* block
1Co 8:9 freedom does not become a *s* block
2Co 6:3 We put no *s* block in anyone's path,

SUBDUE
Ge 1:28 in number; fill the earth and *s* it.

SUBJECT (SUBJECTED)
1Co 14:32 of prophets are *s* to the control
15:28 then the Son himself will be made *s*
Tit 2:5 and to be *s* to their husbands,
2:9 slaves to be *s* to their masters
3:1 Remind the people to be *s* to rulers

SUBJECTED (SUBJECT)
Ro 8:20 For the creation was *s*

SUBMISSION (SUBMIT)
1Co 14:34 but must be in *s,* as the Law says.
1Ti 2:11 learn in quietness and full *s.*

SUBMISSIVE (SUBMIT)
Jas 3:17 then peace-loving, considerate, *s,*
1Pe 3:1 in the same way be *s*
5:5 in the same way be *s*

SUBMIT (SUBMISSION SUBMISSIVE SUBMITS)
Ro 13:1 Everyone must *s* himself
13:5 necessary to *s* to the authorities,
1Co 16:16 to *s* to such as these
Eph 5:21 *S* to one another out of reverence
Col 3:18 Wives, *s* to your husbands,
Heb 12:9 How much more should we *s*
13:17 Obey your leaders and *s*
Jas 4:7 *S* yourselves, then, to God.
1Pe 2:18 *s* yourselves to your masters

SUBMITS* (SUBMIT)
Eph 5:24 Now as the church *s* to Christ,

SUCCESSFUL
Jos 1:7 that you may be *s* wherever you go.
2Ki 18:7 he was *s* in whatever he undertook.
2Ch 20:20 in his prophets and you will be *s.*"

SUFFER (SUFFERED SUFFERING SUFFERINGS SUFFERS)
Isa 53:10 to crush him and cause him to *s,*
Mk 8:31 the Son of Man must *s* many things
Lk 24:26 the Christ have to *s* these things
24:46 The Christ will *s* and rise
Php 1:29 to *s* for him, since you are going
1Pe 4:16 However, if you *s* as a Christian,

SUFFERED (SUFFER)
Heb 2:9 and honor because he *s* death,
2:18 Because he himself *s*
1Pe 2:21 Christ *s* for you, leaving you

SUFFERING (SUFFER)
Isa 53:3 of sorrows, and familiar with *s.*
Ac 5:41 worthy of *s* disgrace for the Name.
2Ti 1:8 But join with me in *s* for the gospel,
Heb 2:10 of their salvation perfect through *s.*

SUFFERINGS (SUFFER)
Ro 8:17 share in his *s* in order that we may
8:18 that our present *s* are not worth
2Co 1:5 as the *s* of Christ flow
Php 3:10 the fellowship of sharing in his *s,*

SUFFERS (SUFFER)
Pr 13:20 but a companion of fools *s* harm.
1Co 12:26 If one part *s,* every part *s* with it;

SUFFICIENT
2Co 12:9 said to me, "My grace is *s* for you,

SUITABLE
Ge 2:18 I will make a helper *s* for him."

SUN
Ecc 1:9 there is nothing new under the *s.*
Mal 4:2 the *s* of righteousness will rise
Mt 5:45 He causes his *s* to rise on the evil
17:2 His face shone like the *s,*
Rev 1:16 His face was like the *s* shining
21:23 The city does not need the *s*

SUPERIOR
Heb 1:4 he became as much *s* to the angels
8:6 ministry Jesus has received is as *s*

SUPERVISION
Gal 3:25 longer under the *s* of the law.

SUPREMACY* (SUPREME)
Col 1:18 in everything he might have the *s.*

SUPREME (SUPREMACY)
Pr 4:7 Wisdom is *s;* therefore get wisdom.

SURE
Nu 32:23 you may be *s* that your sin will find
Dt 6:17 Be *s* to keep the commands
14:22 Be *s* to set aside a tenth
Isa 28:16 cornerstone for a *s* foundation;
Heb 11:1 faith is being *s* of what we hope for
2Pe 1:10 to make your calling and election *s.*

SURPASS* (SURPASSES SURPASSING)
Pr 31:29 but you *s* them all."

SURPASSES (SURPASS)
Mt 5:20 unless your righteousness *s* that
Eph 3:19 to know this love that *s* knowledge

SURPASSING* (SURPASS)
Ps 150:2 praise him for his *s* greatness.
2Co 3:10 in comparison with the *s* glory.
9:14 of the *s* grace God has given you.
Php 3:8 the *s* greatness of knowing Christ

SURROUNDED

Heb 12: 1 since we are *s* by such a great cloud

SUSPENDS*

Job 26: 7 he *s* the earth over nothing.

SUSTAINING* (SUSTAINS)

Heb 1: 3 *s* all things by his powerful word.

SUSTAINS (SUSTAINING)

Ps 18: 35 and your right hand *s* me;
146: 9 and *s* the fatherless and the widow,
147: 6 The LORD *s* the humble
Isa 50: 4 to know the word that *s* the weary.

SWALLOWED

1Co 15: 54 "Death has been *s* up in victory."
2Co 5: 4 so that what is mortal may be *s* up

SWEAR

Mt 5: 34 Do not *s* at all: either by heaven,

SWORD (SWORDS)

Ps 45: 3 Gird your *s* upon your side,
Pr 12: 18 Reckless words pierce like a *s*,
Mt 10: 34 come to bring peace, but a *s*.
26: 52 all who draw the *s* will die by the *s*.
Lk 2: 35 a *s* will pierce your own soul too."
Ro 13: 4 for he does not bear the *s*
Eph 6: 17 of salvation and the *s* of the Spirit,
Heb 4: 12 Sharper than any double-edged *s*,
Rev 1: 16 came a sharp double-edged *s*.

SWORDS (SWORD)

Isa 2: 4 They will beat their *s*
Joel 3: 10 Beat your plowshares into *s*

SYMPATHETIC*

1Pe 3: 8 in harmony with one another; be *s*,

SYNAGOGUE

Lk 4: 16 the Sabbath day he went into the *s*,
Ac 17: 2 custom was, Paul went into the *s*,

TABERNACLE

Ex 40: 34 the glory of the LORD filled the *t*.

TABLE (TABLES)

Ps 23: 5 You prepare a *t* before me

TABLES (TABLE)

Ac 6: 2 word of God in order to wait on *t*.

TABLET (TABLETS)

Pr 3: 3 write them on the *t* of your heart.
7: 3 write them on the *t* of your heart.

TABLETS (TABLET)

Ex 31: 18 he gave him the two *t*
Dt 10: 5 and put the *t* in the ark I had made,
2Co 3: 3 not on *t* of stone but on *t*

TAKE (TAKEN TAKES TAKING TOOK)

Dt 12: 32 do not add to it or *t* away from it.
31: 26 "*T* this Book of the Law
Job 23: 10 But he knows the way that I *t*;
Ps 49: 17 for he will *t* nothing with him
51: 11 or *t* your Holy Spirit from me.
Mt 10: 38 anyone who does not *t* his cross
11: 29 *T* my yoke upon you and learn
16: 24 deny himself and *t* up his cross

TAKEN (TAKE)

Lev 6: 4 must return what he has stolen or *t*
Isa 6: 7 your guilt is *t* away and your sin
Mt 24: 40 one will be *t* and the other left.
Mk 16: 19 he was *t* up into heaven
1Ti 3: 16 was *t* up in glory.

TAKES (TAKE)

1Ki 20: 11 should not boast like one who *t* it
Ps 5: 4 You are not a God who *t* pleasure
Jn 1: 29 who *t* away the sin of the world!
Rev 22: 19 And if anyone *t* words away

TAKING (TAKE)

Ac 15: 14 by *t* from the Gentiles a people
Php 2: 7 *t* the very nature of a servant,

TALENT

Mt 25: 15 to another one *t*, each according

TAME*

Jas 3: 8 but no man can *t* the tongue.

TASK

Mk 13: 34 each with his assigned *t*,
Ac 20: 24 complete the *t* the Lord Jesus has
1Co 3: 5 the Lord has assigned to each his *t*.
2Co 2: 16 And who is equal to such a *t*?

TASTE (TASTED)

Ps 34: 8 *T* and see that the LORD is good;
Col 2: 21 Do not *t*! Do not touch!"?
Heb 2: 9 the grace of God he might *t* death

TASTED (TASTE)

1Pe 2: 3 now that you have *t* that the Lord

TAUGHT (TEACH)

Mt 7: 29 he *t* as one who had authority,
1Co 2: 13 but in words *t* by the Spirit,
Gal 1: 12 nor was I *t* it; rather, I received it

TAXES

Mt 22: 17 Is it right to pay *t* to Caesar or not
Ro 13: 7 If you owe *t*, pay *t*; if revenue,

TEACH (TAUGHT TEACHER TEACHERS TEACHES TEACHING)

Ex 33: 13 *t* me your ways so I may know you
Dt 4: 9 *T* them to your children
8: 3 to *t* you that man does not live
11: 19 *T* them to your children, talking
1Sa 12: 23 I will *t* you the way that is good
Ps 32: 8 *t* you in the way you should go;
51: 13 I will *t* transgressors your ways,
90: 12 *T* us to number our days aright,
143: 10 *T* me to do your will,
Jer 31: 34 No longer will a man *t* his neighbor
Lk 11: 1 said to him, "Lord, *t* us to pray,
Jn 14: 26 will *t* you all things and will remind
1Ti 2: 12 I do not permit a woman to *t*
3: 2 respectable, hospitable, able to *t*,
Tit 2: 1 You must *t* what is in accord
Heb 8: 11 No longer will a man *t* his neighbor
Jas 3: 1 know that we who *t* will be judged
1Jn 2: 27 you do not need anyone to *t* you.

TEACHER (TEACH)

Mt 10: 24 "A student is not above his *t*,
Jn 13: 14 and *T*, have washed your feet,

TEACHERS (TEACH)

1Co 12: 28 third *t*, then workers of miracles,
Eph 4: 11 and some to be pastors and *t*,
Heb 5: 12 by this time you ought to be *t*,

TEACHES (TEACH)

1Ti 6: 3 If anyone *t* false doctrines

TEACHING (TEACH)

Pr 1: 8 and do not forsake your mother's *t*.
Mt 28: 20 *t* them to obey everything I have
Jn 7: 17 whether my *t* comes from God or
14: 23 loves me, he will obey my *t*.
1Ti 4: 13 of Scripture, to preaching and to *t*.
2Ti 3: 16 is God-breathed and is useful for *t*,
Tit 2: 7 In your *t* show integrity,

TEAR (TEARS)

Rev 7: 17 God will wipe away every *t*

TEARS (TEAR)

Ps 126: 5 Those who sow in *t*
Php 3: 18 and now say again even with *t*,

TEETH (TOOTH)

Mt 8: 12 will be weeping and gnashing of *t*."

TEMPERATE*

1Ti 3: 2 *t*, self-controlled, respectable,
3: 11 not malicious talkers but *t*
Tit 2: 2 Teach the older men to be *t*,

TEMPEST

Ps 55: 8 far from the *t* and storm."

TEMPLE (TEMPLES)

1Ki 8: 27 How much less this *t* I have built!
Hab 2: 20 But the LORD is in his holy *t*;
1Co 3: 16 that you yourselves are God's *t*
6: 19 you not know that your body is a *t*
2Co 6: 16 For we are the *t* of the living God.

TEMPLES (TEMPLE)

Ac 17: 24 does not live in *t* built by hands.

TEMPT (TEMPTATION TEMPTED)

1Co 7: 5 again so that Satan will not *t* you

TEMPTATION (TEMPT)

Mt 6: 13 And lead us not into *t*,

Mt 26: 41 pray so that you will not fall into *t*.
1Co 10: 13 No *t* has seized you except what is

TEMPTED (TEMPT)
Mt 4: 1 into the desert to be *t* by the devil.
1Co 10: 13 he will not let you be *t*
Heb 2: 18 he himself suffered when he was *t*,
4: 15 but we have one who has been *t*
Jas 1: 13 For God cannot be *t* by evil,

TEN (TENTH TITHE TITHES)
Ex 34: 28 covenant—the *T* Commandments.
Ps 91: 7 *t* thousand at your right hand,
Mt 25: 28 it to the one who has the *t* talents.
Lk 15: 8 suppose a woman has *t* silver coins

TENTH (TEN)
Dt 14: 22 Be sure to set aside a *t*

TERRIBLE (TERROR)
2Ti 3: 1 There will be *t* times

TERROR (TERRIBLE)
Ps 91: 5 You will not fear the *t* of night,
Lk 21: 26 Men will faint from *t*, apprehensive
Ro 13: 3 For rulers hold no *t*

TEST (TESTED TESTS)
Dt 6: 16 Do not *t* the LORD your God
Ps 139: 23 *t* me and know my anxious
Ro 12: 2 Then you will be able to *t*
1Co 3: 13 and the fire will *t* the quality
1Jn 4: 1 *t* the spirits to see whether they are

TESTED (TEST)
Ge 22: 1 Some time later God *t* Abraham.
Job 23: 10 when he has *t* me, I will come forth
Pr 27: 21 man is *t* by the praise he receives.
1T 3: 10 They must first be *t;* and then

TESTIFY (TESTIMONY)
Jn 5: 39 are the Scriptures that *t* about me,
2Ti 1: 8 ashamed to *t* about our Lord,

TESTIMONY (TESTIFY)
Isa 8: 20 and to the *t!* If they do not speak
Lk 18: 20 not give false *t*, honor your father

TESTS (TEST)
Pr 17: 3 but the LORD *t* the heart.
1Th 2: 4 but God, who *t* our hearts.

THADDAEUS
Apostle (Mt 10:3; Mk 3:18); probably also known as Judas son of James (Lk 6:16; Ac 1:13).

THANKFUL (THANKS)
Heb 12: 28 let us be *t*, and so worship God

THANKS (THANKFUL THANKSGIVING)
1Ch 16: 8 Give *t* to the LORD, call
Ne 12: 31 assigned two large choirs to give *t*.
Ps 100: 4 give *t* to him and praise his name.
1Co 15: 57 *t* be to God! He gives us the victory
2Co 2: 14 *t* be to God, who always leads us
9: 15 *T* be to God for his indescribable
1Th 5: 18 give *t* in all circumstances,

THANKSGIVING (THANKS)
Ps 95: 2 Let us come before him with *t*
100: 4 Enter his gates with *t*
Php 4: 6 by prayer and petition, with *t*,
1Ti 4: 3 created to be received with *t*

THIEF (THIEVES)
Ex 22: 3 A *t* must certainly make restitution
1Th 5: 2 day of the Lord will come like a *t*
Rev 16: 15 I come like a *t!* Blessed is he who

THIEVES (THIEF)
1Co 6: 10 nor homosexual offenders nor *t*

THINK (THOUGHT THOUGHTS)
Ro 12: 3 Do not *t* of yourself more highly
Php 4: 8 praiseworthy —*t* about such things

THIRST (THIRSTY)
Ps 69: 21 and gave me vinegar for my *t*.
Mt 5: 6 Blessed are those who hunger and *t*
Jn 4: 14 the water I give him will never *t*.

THIRSTY (THIRST)
Isa 55: 1 "Come, all you who are *t*,
Jn 7: 37 "If anyone is *t*, let him come to me
Rev 22: 17 Whoever is *t*, let him come;

THOMAS
Apostle (Mt 10:3; Mk 3:18; Lk 6:15; Jn 11:16; 14:5; 21:2; Ac 1:13). Doubted resurrection (Jn 20:24-28).

THONGS
Mk 1: 7 *t* of whose sandals I am not worthy

THORN (THORNS)
2Co 12: 7 there was given me a *t* in my flesh,

THORNS (THORN)
Nu 33: 55 in your eyes and *t* in your sides.
Mt 27: 29 then twisted together a crown of *t*
Heb 6: 8 But land that produces *t*

THOUGHT (THINK)
Pr 14: 15 a prudent man gives *t* to his steps.
1Co 13: 11 I talked like a child, I *t* like a child,

THOUGHTS (THINK)
Ps 94: 11 The LORD knows the *t* of man;
139: 23 test me and know my anxious *t*.
Isa 55: 8 "For my *t* are not your *t*,
Heb 4: 12 it judges the *t* and attitudes

THREE
Ecc 4: 12 of *t* strands is not quickly broken.
Mt 12: 40 *t* nights in the belly of a huge fish,
Mt 18: 20 or *t* come together in my name,
27: 63 'After *t* days I will rise again.'
1Co 13: 13 And now these *t* remain: faith,
14: 27 or at the most *t*—should speak,
2Co 13: 1 testimony of two or *t* witnesses."

THRESHING
2Sa 24: 18 an altar to the LORD on the *t* floor

THRONE (ENTHRONED)
2Sa 7: 16 your *t* will be established forever
Ps 45: 6 Your *t*, O God, will last for ever
47: 8 God is seated on his holy *t*.
Isa 6: 1 I saw the Lord seated on a *t*,
66: 1 "Heaven is my *t*
Heb 4: 16 Let us then approach the *t* of grace
12: 2 at the right hand of the *t* of God.
Rev 4: 10 They lay their crowns before the *t*
20: 11 Then I saw a great white *t*
22: 3 *t* of God and of the Lamb will be

THROW
Jn 8: 7 the first to *t* a stone at her."
Heb 10: 35 So do not *t* away your confidence;
12: 1 let us *t* off everything that hinders

THWART*
Isa 14: 27 has purposed, and who can *t* him?

TIBNI
King of Israel (1Ki 16:21-22).

TIME (TIMES)
Est 4: 14 come to royal position for such a *t*
Da 7: 25 to him for a *t*, times and half a *t*.
Hos 10: 12 for it is *t* to seek the LORD,
Ro 9: 9 "At the appointed *t* I will return,
Heb 9: 28 and he will appear a second *t*,
10: 12 for all *t* one sacrifice for sins,
1Pe 4: 17 For it is *t* for judgment to begin

TIMES (TIME)
Ps 9: 9 a stronghold in *t* of trouble.
31: 15 My *t* are in your hands;
62: 8 Trust in him at all *t*, O people;
Pr 17: 17 A friend loves at all *t*,
Am 5: 13 for the *t* are evil.
Mt 18: 21 how many *t* shall I forgive my
Ac 1: 7 "It is not for you to know the *t*
Rev 12: 14 *t* and half a time, out

TIMIDITY*
2Ti 1: 7 For God did not give us a spirit of *t*

TIMOTHY
Believer from Lystra (Ac 16:1). Joined Paul on second missionary journey (Ac 16-20). Sent to settle problems at Corinth (1Co 4:17; 16:10). Led church at Ephesus (1Ti 1:3). Co-writer with Paul (1Th 1:1; 2Th 1:1; Phm 1).

TIRE (TIRED)
2Th 3: 13 never *t* of doing what is right.

TIRED (TIRE)
Ex 17: 12 When Moses' hands grew *t*,

Isa 40: 28 He will not grow *t* or weary,

TITHE (TEN)

Lev 27: 30 "A *t* of everything from the land,
Dt 12: 17 eat in your own towns the *t*
Mal 3: 10 the whole *t* into the storehouse,

TITHES (TEN)

Mal 3: 8 'How do we rob you?' "In *t*

TITUS

Gentile co-worker of Paul (Gal 2:1-3; 2Ti 4:10); sent to Corinth (2Co 2:13; 7-8; 12:18), Crete (Tit 1:4-5).

TODAY

Mt 6: 11 Give us *t* our daily bread.
Lk 23: 43 *t* you will be with me in paradise."
Heb 3: 13 daily, as long as it is called *T,*
13: 8 Christ is the same yesterday and *t*

TOIL

Ge 3: 17 through painful *t* you will eat of it

TOLERATE

Hab 1: 13 you cannot *t* wrong.
Rev 2: 2 that you cannot *t* wicked men,

TOMB

Mt 27: 65 make the *t* as secure as you know
Lk 24: 2 the stone rolled away from the *t,*

TOMORROW

Pr 27: 1 Do not boast about *t,*
Isa 22: 13 "for *t* we die!"
Mt 6: 34 Therefore do not worry about *t,*
Jas 4: 13 "Today or *t* we will go to this

TONGUE (TONGUES)

Ps 39: 1 and keep my *t* from sin;
Pr 12: 18 but the *t* of the wise brings healing.
1Co 14: 2 speaks in a *t* does not speak to men
14: 4 He who speaks in a *t* edifies himself
14: 13 in a *t* should pray that he may
14: 19 than ten thousand words in a *t.*
Php 2: 11 every *t* confess that Jesus Christ is
Jas 1: 26 does not keep a tight rein on his *t,*
3: 8 but no man can tame the *t.*

TONGUES (TONGUE)

Isa 28: 11 with foreign lips and strange *t*
66: 18 and gather all nations and *t,*
Mk 16: 17 in new *t;* they will pick up snakes
Ac 2: 4 and began to speak in other *t*
10: 46 For they heard them speaking in *t*
19: 6 and they spoke in *t* and prophesied
1Co 12: 30 Do all speak in *t?* Do all interpret?
14: 18 speak in *t* more than all of you.
14: 39 and do not forbid speaking in *t.*

TOOK (TAKE)

1Co 11: 23 the night he was betrayed, *t* bread,

Php 3: 12 for which Christ Jesus *t* hold of me.

TOOTH (TEETH)

Ex 21: 24 eye for eye, *t* for *t,* hand for hand,
Mt 5: 38 'Eye for eye, and *t* for *t.*'

TORMENTED

Rev 20: 10 They will be *t* day and night

TORN

Gal 4: 15 you would have *t* out your eyes
Php 1: 23 I do not know! I am *t*

TOUCH (TOUCHED)

Ps 105: 15 "Do not *t* my anointed ones;
Lk 24: 39 It is I myself! *T* me and see;
2Co 6: 17 *T* no unclean thing,
Col 2: 21 Do not taste! Do not *t!"?*

TOUCHED (TOUCH)

1Sa 10: 26 men whose hearts God had *t.*
Mt 14: 36 and all who *t* him were healed.

TOWER

Ge 11: 4 with a *t* that reaches to the heavens
Pr 18: 10 of the LORD is a strong *t;*

TOWNS

Nu 35: 2 to give the Levites *t* to live
35: 15 These six *t* will be a place of refuge

TRACING*

Ro 11: 33 and his paths beyond *t* out!

TRADITION

Mt 15: 6 word of God for the sake of your *t.*
Col 2: 8 which depends on human *t*

TRAIN (TRAINING)

Pr 22: 6 *T* a child in the way he should go,
Eph 4: 8 he led captives in his *t*

TRAINING (TRAIN)

1Co 9: 25 in the games goes into strict *t.*
2Ti 3: 16 correcting and *t* in righteousness,

TRAMPLED

Lk 21: 24 Jerusalem will be *t*
Heb 10: 29 to be punished who has *t* the Son

TRANCE

Ac 10: 10 was being prepared, he fell into a *t.*

TRANSCENDS*

Php 4: 7 which *t* all understanding,

TRANSFIGURED

Mt 17: 2 There he was *t* before them.

TRANSFORM* (TRANSFORMED)

Php 3: 21 will *t* our lowly bodies

TRANSFORMED (TRANSFORM)

Ro 12: 2 be *t* by the renewing of your mind.
2Co 3: 18 are being *t* into his likeness

TRANSGRESSION (TRANSGRESSIONS TRANSGRESSORS)

Isa 53: 8 for the *t* of my people he was
Ro 4: 15 where there is no law there is no *t.*

TRANSGRESSIONS (TRANSGRESSION)

Ps 32: 1 whose *t* are forgiven,
51: 1 blot out my *t.*
103: 12 so far has he removed our *t* from us
Isa 53: 5 But he was pierced for our *t,*
Eph 2: 1 you were dead in your *t* and sins,

TRANSGRESSORS (TRANSGRESSION)

Ps 51: 13 Then I will teach *t* your ways,
Isa 53: 12 and made intercession for the *t.*
53: 12 and was numbered with the *t.*

TREADING

Dt 25: 4 an ox while it is *t* out the grain.
1Co 9: 9 an ox while it is *t* out the grain."

TREASURE (TREASURED TREASURES)

Isa 33: 6 of the LORD is the key to this *t.*
Mt 6: 21 For where your *t* is, there your
2Co 4: 7 But we have this *t* in jars of clay

TREASURED (TREASURE)

Dt 7: 6 to be his people, his *t* possession.
Lk 2: 19 But Mary *t* up all these things

TREASURES (TREASURE)

Mt 6: 19 up for yourselves *t* on earth,
Col 2: 3 in whom are hidden all the *t*
Heb 11: 26 of greater value than the *t* of Egypt,

TREAT

Lev 22: 2 sons to *t* with respect the sacred
1Ti 5: 1 *T* younger men as brothers,
1Pe 3: 7 and *t* them with respect

TREATY

Dt 7: 2 Make no *t* with them, and show

TREE

Ge 2: 9 and the *t* of the knowledge of good
2: 9 of the garden were the *t* of life
Dt 21: 23 hung on a *t* is under God's curse.
Ps 1: 3 He is like a *t* planted by streams
Mt 3: 10 every *t* that does not produce good
12: 33 for a *t* is recognized by its fruit.
Gal 3: 13 is everyone who is hung on a *t.*"
Rev 22: 14 they may have the right to the *t*

TREMBLE (TREMBLING)

1Ch 16: 30 *T* before him, all the earth!
Ps 114: 7 *T,* O earth, at the presence

TREMBLING (TREMBLE)

Ps 2: 11 and rejoice with *t.*
Php 2: 12 out your salvation with fear and *t,*

TRESPASS

Ro 5: 17 For if, by the *t* of the one man,

TRIALS

1Th 3: 3 one would be unsettled by these *t.*
Jas 1: 2 whenever you face *t* of many kinds,
2Pe 2: 9 how to rescue godly men from *t*

TRIBES

Ge 49: 28 All these are the twelve *t* of Israel,
Mt 19: 28 judging the twelve *t* of Israel.

TRIBULATION*

Rev 7: 14 who have come out of the great *t;*

TRIUMPHAL* (TRIUMPHING)

Isa 60: 11 their kings led in *t* procession.
2Co 2: 14 us in *t* procession in Christ

TRIUMPHING* (TRIUMPHAL)

Col 2: 15 of them, *t* over them by the cross.

TROUBLE (TROUBLED TROUBLES)

Job 14: 1 is of few days and full of *t.*
Ps 46: 1 an ever-present help in *t.*
107: 13 they cried to the LORD in their *t,*
Pr 11: 29 He who brings *t* on his family will
24: 10 If you falter in times of *t,*
Mt 6: 34 Each day has enough *t* of its own.
Jn 16: 33 In this world you will have *t.*
Ro 8: 35 Shall *t* or hardship or persecution

TROUBLED (TROUBLE)

Jn 14: 1 "Do not let your hearts be *t.*
14: 27 Do not let your hearts be *t*

TROUBLES (TROUBLE)

1Co 7: 28 those who marry will face many *t*
2Co 1: 4 who comforts us in all our *t,*
4: 17 and momentary *t* are achieving

TRUE (TRUTH)

Dt 18: 22 does not take place or come *t,*
1Sa 9: 6 and everything he says comes *t.*
Ps 119:160 All your words are *t;*
Jn 17: 3 the only *t* God, and Jesus Christ,
Ro 3: 4 Let God be *t,* and every man a liar.
Php 4: 8 whatever is *t,* whatever is noble,
Rev 22: 6 These words are trustworthy and *t.*

TRUMPET

1Co 14: 8 if the *t* does not sound a clear call,
15: 52 For the *t* will sound, the dead will

TRUST (ENTRUSTED TRUSTED TRUSTS TRUSTWORTHY)

Ps 20: 7 we *t* in the name of the LORD our
37: 3 *T* in the LORD and do good;
56: 4 in God I *t;* I will not be afraid.
119: 42 for I *t* in your word.
Pr 3: 5 *T* in the LORD with all your heart
Isa 30: 15 in quietness and *t* is your strength,
Jn 14: 1 *T* in God; *t* also in me.
1Co 4: 2 been given a *t* must prove faithful.

TRUSTED (TRUST)

Ps 26: 1 I have *t* in the LORD
Isa 25: 9 we *t* in him, and he saved us.
Da 3: 28 They *t* in him and defied the king's
Lk 16: 10 *t* with very little can also be *t*

TRUSTS (TRUST)

Ps 32: 10 surrounds the man who *t* in him.
Pr 11: 28 Whoever *t* in his riches will fall,
28: 26 He who *t* in himself is a fool,
Ro 9: 33 one who *t* in him will never be put

TRUSTWORTHY (TRUST)

Ps 119:138 they are fully *t.*
Pr 11: 13 but a *t* man keeps a secret.
Rev 22: 6 "These words are *t* and true.

TRUTH (TRUE TRUTHFUL TRUTHS)

Ps 51: 6 Surely you desire *t*
Isa 45: 19 I, the LORD, speak the *t;*
Zec 8: 16 are to do: Speak the *t* to each other,
Jn 4: 23 worship the Father in spirit and *t,*
8: 32 Then you will know the *t,*
8: 32 and the *t* will set you free."
14: 6 I am the way and the *t* and the life.
16: 13 comes, he will guide you into all *t.*
18: 38 "What is *t?"* Pilate asked.
Ro 1: 25 They exchanged the *t* of God
1Co 13: 6 in evil but rejoices with the *t.*
2Co 13: 8 against the *t,* but only for the *t.*
Eph 4: 15 Instead, speaking the *t* in love,
6: 14 with the belt of *t* buckled
2Th 2: 10 because they refused to love the *t*
1Ti 2: 4 to come to a knowledge of the *t.*
3: 15 the pillar and foundation of the *t.*
2Ti 2: 15 correctly handles the word of *t.*
3: 7 never able to acknowledge the *t.*
Heb 10: 26 received the knowledge of the *t,*
1Pe 1: 22 by obeying the *t* so that you have
2Pe 2: 2 the way of *t* into disrepute.
1Jn 1: 6 we lie and do not live by the *t.*
1: 8 deceive ourselves and the *t* is not

TRUTHFUL (TRUTH)

Pr 12: 22 but he delights in men who are *t.*
Jn 3: 33 it has certified that God is *t.*

TRUTHS (TRUTH)

1Co 2: 13 expressing spiritual *t*
1Ti 3: 9 hold of the deep *t* of the faith
Heb 5: 12 to teach you the elementary *t*

TRY (TRYING)

Ps 26: 2 Test me, O LORD, and *t* me,
Isa 7: 13 enough to *t* the patience of men?
1Co 14: 12 *t* to excel in gifts that build up
2Co 5: 11 is to fear the Lord, we *t*
1Th 5: 15 always *t* to be kind to each other

TRYING (TRY)

2Co 5: 12 We are not *t* to commend ourselves
1Th 2: 4 We are not *t* to please men but God

TUNIC

Lk 6: 29 do not stop him from taking your *t.*

TURN (TURNED TURNS)

Ex 32: 12 *T* from your fierce anger; relent
Dt 5: 32 do not *t* aside to the right
28: 14 Do not *t* aside from any
Jos 1: 7 do not *t* from it to the right
2Ch 7: 14 and *t* from their wicked ways,
30: 9 He will not *t* his face from you
Ps 78: 6 they in *t* would tell their children.
Pr 22: 6 when he is old he will not *t* from it.
Isa 29: 16 You *t* things upside down,
30: 21 Whether you *t* to the right
45: 22 "*T* to me and be saved,
55: 7 Let him *t* to the LORD,
Eze 33: 11 *T! T* from your evil ways!
Mal 4: 6 He will *t* the hearts of the fathers
Mt 5: 39 you on the right cheek, *t*
10: 35 For I have come to *t*
Jn 12: 40 nor *t*—and I would heal them."
Ac 3: 19 Repent, then, and *t* to God,
26: 18 and *t* them from darkness to light,
1Ti 6: 20 *T* away from godless chatter
1Pe 3: 11 He must *t* from evil and do good;

TURNED (TURN)

Ps 30: 11 You *t* my wailing into dancing;
40: 1 he *t* to me and heard my cry.
Isa 53: 6 each of us has *t* to his own way;
Hos 7: 8 Ephraim is a flat cake not *t* over.
Joel 2: 31 The sun will be *t* to darkness
Ro 3: 12 All have *t* away,

TURNS (TURN)

2Sa 22: 29 the LORD *t* my darkness into light
Pr 15: 1 A gentle answer *t* away wrath,
Isa 44: 25 and *t* it into nonsense,
Jas 5: 20 Whoever *t* a sinner from the error

TWELVE

Ge 49: 28 All these are the *t* tribes of Israel,
Mt 10: 1 He called his *t* disciples to him

TWINKLING*

1Co 15: 52 in a flash, in the *t* of an eye,

UNAPPROACHABLE*

1Ti 6: 16 immortal and who lives in *u* light,

UNBELIEF (UNBELIEVER UNBELIEVERS UNBELIEVING)

Mk 9: 24 help me overcome my *u!*"
Ro 11: 20 they were broken off because of *u,*
Heb 3: 19 able to enter, because of their *u.*

UNBELIEVER* (UNBELIEF)

1Co 7: 15 But if the *u* leaves, let him do so.
10: 27 If some *u* invites you to a meal
14: 24 if an *u* or someone who does not
2Co 6: 15 have in common with an *u?*
1Ti 5: 8 the faith and is worse than an *u.*

UNBELIEVERS (UNBELIEF)

1Co 6: 6 another—and this in front of *u!*

2Co 6: 14 Do not be yoked together with *u*.

UNBELIEVING (UNBELIEF)

1Co 7: 14 For the *u* husband has been
Rev 21: 8 But the cowardly, the *u*, the vile,

UNCERTAIN*

1Ti 6: 17 which is so *u*, but to put their hope

UNCHANGEABLE*

Heb 6: 18 by two *u* things in which it is

UNCIRCUMCISED

1Sa 17: 26 Who is this *u* Philistine that he
Col 3: 11 circumcised or *u*, barbarian,

UNCIRCUMCISION

1Co 7: 19 is nothing and *u* is nothing.
Gal 5: 6 neither circumcision nor *u* has any

UNCLEAN

Isa 6: 5 ruined! For I am a man of *u* lips,
Ro 14: 14 fully convinced that no food is *u*
2Co 6: 17 Touch no *u* thing,

UNCONCERNED*

Eze 16: 49 were arrogant, overfed and *u;*

UNCOVERED

Heb 4: 13 Everything is *u* and laid bare

UNDERSTAND (UNDERSTANDING UNDERSTANDS)

Job 42: 3 Surely I spoke of things I did not *u*,
Ps 73: 16 When I tried to *u* all this,
119:125 that I may *u* your statutes.
Lk 24: 45 so they could *u* the Scriptures.
Ac 8: 30 "Do you *u* what you are reading?"
Ro 7: 15 I do not *u* what I do.
1Co 2: 14 and he cannot *u* them,
Eph 5: 17 but *u* what the Lord's will is.
2Pe 3: 16 some things that are hard to *u*,

UNDERSTANDING (UNDERSTAND)

Ps 119:104 I gain *u* from your precepts;
147: 5 his *u* has no limit.
Pr 3: 5 and lean not on your own *u;*
4: 7 Though it cost all you have, get *u*.
10: 23 but a man of *u* delights in wisdom.
11: 12 but a man of *u* holds his tongue.
15: 21 a man of *u* keeps a straight course.
15: 32 whoever heeds correction gains *u*.
23: 23 get wisdom, discipline and *u*.
Isa 40: 28 and his *u* no one can fathom.
Da 5: 12 a keen mind and knowledge and *u*,
Mk 4: 12 and ever hearing but never *u;*
12: 33 with all your *u* and with all your
Php 4: 7 of God, which transcends all *u*,

UNDERSTANDS (UNDERSTAND)

1Ch 28: 9 and *u* every motive
1Ti 6: 4 he is conceited and *u* nothing.

UNDIVIDED*

1Ch 12: 33 to help David with *u* loyalty—
Ps 86: 11 give me an *u* heart,
Eze 11: 19 I will give them an *u* heart
1Co 7: 35 way in *u* devotion to the Lord.

UNDOING

Pr 18: 7 A fool's mouth is his *u*,

UNDYING*

Eph 6: 24 Lord Jesus Christ with an *u* love.

UNFADING*

1Pe 3: 4 the *u* beauty of a gentle

UNFAILING

Ps 33: 5 the earth is full of his *u* love.
119: 76 May your *u* love be my comfort,
143: 8 bring me word of your *u* love,
Pr 19: 22 What a man desires is *u* love;
La 3: 32 so great is his *u* love.

UNFAITHFUL (UNFAITHFULNESS)

Lev 6: 2 is *u* to the LORD by deceiving his
1Ch 10: 13 because he was *u* to the LORD;
Pr 13: 15 but the way of the *u* is hard.

UNFAITHFULNESS (UNFAITHFUL)

Mt 5: 32 except for marital *u*, causes her
19: 9 for marital *u*, and marries another

UNFOLDING

Ps 119:130 the *u* of your words gives light;

UNGODLINESS

Tit 2: 12 It teaches us to say "No" to *u*

UNIT

1Co 12: 12 body is a *u*, though it is made up

UNITED (UNITY)

Ro 6: 5 If we have been *u* with him
Php 2: 1 from being *u* with Christ,
Col 2: 2 encouraged in heart and *u* in love,

UNITY (UNITED)

Ps 133: 1 is when brothers live together in *u!*
Ro 15: 5 a spirit of *u* among yourselves
Eph 4: 3 effort to keep the *u* of the Spirit
4: 13 up until we all reach *u* in the faith
Col 3: 14 them all together in perfect *u*.

UNIVERSE

Php 2: 15 which you shine like stars in the *u*
Heb 1: 2 and through whom he made the *u*.

UNKNOWN

Ac 17: 23 TO AN *U* GOD.

UNLEAVENED

Ex 12: 17 "Celebrate the Feast of *U* Bread,

UNPROFITABLE

Tit 3: 9 because these are *u* and useless.

UNPUNISHED

Ex 34: 7 Yet he does not leave the guilty *u;*
Pr 19: 5 A false witness will not go *u*,

UNREPENTANT*

Ro 2: 5 stubbornness and your *u* heart,

UNRIGHTEOUS*

Zep 3: 5 yet the *u* know no shame.
Mt 5: 45 rain on the righteous and the *u*.
1Pe 3: 18 the righteous for the *u*, to bring you
2Pe 2: 9 and to hold the *u* for the day

UNSEARCHABLE

Ro 11: 33 How *u* his judgments,
Eph 3: 8 preach to the Gentiles the *u* riches

UNSEEN

2Co 4: 18 on what is seen, but on what is *u*.
4: 18 temporary, but what is *u* is eternal.

UNSTABLE*

Jas 1: 8 he is a double-minded man, *u*
2Pe 2: 14 they seduce the *u;* they are experts
3: 16 ignorant and *u* people distort,

UNTHINKABLE*

Job 34: 12 It is *u* that God would do wrong,

UNVEILED*

2Co 3: 18 with *u* faces all reflect the Lord's

UNWORTHY

Job 40: 4 "I am *u*—how can I reply to you?
Lk 17: 10 should say, 'We are *u* servants;

UPRIGHT

Job 1: 1 This man was blameless and *u;*
Pr 2: 7 He holds victory in store for the *u*,
15: 8 but the prayer of the *u* pleases him.
Tit 1: 8 who is self-controlled, *u*, holy
2: 12 *u* and godly lives in this present

UPROOTED

Jude : 12 without fruit and *u*—twice dead.

USEFUL

2Ti 2: 21 *u* to the Master and prepared
3: 16 Scripture is God-breathed and is *u*

USELESS

1Co 15: 14 our preaching is *u*
Jas 2: 20 faith without deeds is *u?*

USURY

Ne 5: 10 But let the exacting of *u* stop!

UTTER

Ps 78: 2 I will *u* hidden things, things from of

UZZIAH

Son of Amaziah; king of Judah also known as Azariah (2Ki 15:1-7; 1Ch 6:24; 2Ch 26).

VAIN

Ps 33: 17 A horse is a *v* hope for deliverance;
Isa 65: 23 They will not toil in *v*

1Co 15: 2 Otherwise, you have believed in *v*.
15: 58 labor in the Lord is not in *v*.
2Co 6: 1 not to receive God's grace in *v*.

VALLEY

Ps 23: 4 walk through the *v* of the shadow
Isa 40: 4 Every *v* shall be raised up,
Joel 3: 14 multitudes in the *v* of decision!

VALUABLE (VALUE)

Lk 12: 24 And how much more *v* you are

VALUE (VALUABLE)

Mt 13: 46 When he found one of great *v*,
1Ti 4: 8 For physical training is of some *v*,
Heb 11: 26 as of greater *v* than the treasures

VEIL

Ex 34: 33 to them, he put a *v* over his face.
2Co 3: 14 for to this day the same *v* remains

VENGEANCE (AVENGE REVENGE)

Isa 34: 8 For the LORD has a day of *v*,

VICTORIES (VICTORY)

Ps 18: 50 He gives his king great *v*;
21: 1 great is his joy in the *v* you give!

VICTORIOUSLY* (VICTORY)

Ps 45: 4 In your majesty ride forth *v*

VICTORY (VICTORIES VICTORIOUSLY)

Ps 60: 12 With God we will gain the *v*,
1Co 15: 54 "Death has been swallowed up in *v*
15: 57 He gives us the *v* through our Lord
1Jn 5: 4 This is the *v* that has overcome

VINDICATED

1Ti 3: 16 was *v* by the Spirit,

VINE

Jn 15: 1 "I am the true *v*, and my Father is

VINEGAR

Mk 15: 36 filled a sponge with wine *v*,

VIOLATION

Heb 2: 2 every *v* and disobedience received

VIOLENCE

Isa 60: 18 No longer will *v* be heard
Eze 45: 9 Give up your *v* and oppression

VIPERS

Ro 3: 13 "The poison of *v* is on their lips."

VIRGIN

Isa 7: 14 The *v* will be with child
Mt 1: 23 "The *v* will be with child
2Co 11: 2 that I might present you as a pure *v*

VIRTUES*

Col 3: 14 And over all these *v* put on love,

VISION

Ac 26: 19 disobedient to the *v* from heaven.

VOICE

Ps 95: 7 Today, if you hear his *v*,
Isa 30: 21 your ears will hear a *v* behind you,
Jn 5: 28 are in their graves will hear his *v*
10: 3 and the sheep listen to his *v*.
Heb 3: 7 "Today, if you hear his *v*,
Rev 3: 20 If anyone hears my *v* and opens

VOMIT

Pr 26: 11 As a dog returns to its *v*,
2Pe 2: 22 "A dog returns to its *v*," and,

VOW

Nu 30: 2 When a man makes a *v*

WAGES

Lk 10: 7 for the worker deserves his *w*.
Ro 4: 4 his *w* are not credited to him
6: 23 For the *w* of sin is death,

WAILING

Ps 30: 11 You turned my *w* into dancing;

WAIST

2Ki 1: 8 with a leather belt around his *w*."
Mt 3: 4 he had a leather belt around his *w*.

WAIT (WAITED WAITS)

Ps 27: 14 *W* for the LORD;
130: 5 I *w* for the LORD, my soul waits,
Isa 30: 18 Blessed are all who *w* for him!
Ac 1: 4 *w* for the gift my Father promised,
Ro 8: 23 as we *w* eagerly for our adoption
1Th 1: 10 and to *w* for his Son from heaven,
Tit 2: 13 while we *w* for the blessed hope—

WAITED (WAIT)

Ps 40: 1 I *w* patiently for the LORD;

WAITS (WAIT)

Ro 8: 19 creation *w* in eager expectation

WALK (WALKED WALKS)

Dt 11: 19 and when you *w* along the road,
Ps 1: 1 who does not *w* in the counsel
23: 4 Even though I *w*
89: 15 who *w* in the light of your presence
Isa 2: 5 let us *w* in the light of the LORD.
30: 21 saying, "This is the way; *w* in it."
40: 31 they will *w* and not be faint.
Jer 6: 16 ask where the good way is, and *w*
Da 4: 37 And those who *w* in pride he is able
Am 3: 3 Do two *w* together
Mic 6: 8 and to *w* humbly with your God.
Mk 2: 9 'Get up, take your mat and *w*'?
Jn 8: 12 Whoever follows me will never *w*
1Jn 1: 7 But if we *w* in the light,
2Jn : 6 his command is that you *w* in love.

WALKED (WALK)

Ge 5: 24 Enoch *w* with God; then he was no

Jos 14: 9 which your feet have *w* will be your
Mt 14: 29 *w* on the water and came toward

WALKS (WALK)

Pr 13: 20 He who *w* with the wise grows wise

WALL

Jos 6: 20 *w* collapsed; so every man charged
Ne 2: 17 let us rebuild the *w* of Jerusalem,
Rev 21: 12 It had a great, high *w*

WALLOWING

2Pe 2: 22 back to her *w* in the mud."

WANT (WANTED WANTING WANTS)

1Sa 8: 19 "We *w* a king over us.
Ps 23: 1 is my shepherd, I shall not be in *w*.
Lk 19: 14 'We don't *w* this man to be our king
Ro 7: 15 For what I *w* to do I do not do,
Php 3: 10 I *w* to know Christ and the power

WANTED (WANT)

1Co 12: 18 of them, just as he *w* them to be.

WANTING (WANT)

Da 5: 27 weighed on the scales and found *w*.
2Pe 3: 9 with you, not *w* anyone to perish,

WANTS (WANT)

Mt 20: 26 whoever *w* to become great
Mk 8: 35 For whoever *w* to save his life will
Ro 9: 18 he hardens whom he *w* to harden.
1Ti 2: 4 who *w* all men to be saved

WAR (WARS)

Isa 2: 4 nor will they train for *w* anymore.
Da 9: 26 *W* will continue until the end,
2Co 10: 3 we do not wage *w* as the world does
Rev 19: 11 With justice he judges and makes *w*

WARN (WARNED WARNINGS)

Eze 3: 19 But if you do *w* the wicked man
33: 9 if you do *w* the wicked man to turn

WARNED (WARN)

Ps 19: 11 By them is your servant *w*;

WARNINGS (WARN)

1Co 10: 11 and were written down as *w* for us,

WARS (WAR)

Ps 46: 9 He makes *w* cease to the ends
Mt 24: 6 You will hear of *w* and rumors of *w*,

WASH (WASHED WASHING)

Ps 51: 7 *w* me, and I will be whiter
Jn 13: 5 and began to *w* his disciples' feet,
Ac 22: 16 be baptized and *w* your sins away,
Rev 22: 14 Blessed are those who *w* their robes

WASHED (WASH)

1Co 6: 11 you were *w,* you were sanctified,
Rev 7: 14 they have *w* their robes

WASHING (WASH)

Eph 5: 26 cleansing her by the *w* with water
Tit 3: 5 us through the *w* of rebirth

WATCH (WATCHES WATCHING WATCHMAN)

Ge 31: 49 "May the LORD keep *w*
Jer 31: 10 will *w* over his flock like a shepherd
Mt 24: 42 "Therefore keep *w,* because you do
26: 41 *W* and pray so that you will not fall
Lk 2: 8 keeping *w* over their flocks at night
1Ti 4: 16 *W* your life and doctrine closely.

WATCHES (WATCH)

Ps 1: 6 For the LORD *w* over the way
121: 3 he who *w* over you will not slumber

WATCHING (WATCH)

Lk 12: 37 whose master finds them *w*

WATCHMAN (WATCH)

Eze 3: 17 I have made you a *w* for the house

WATER (WATERED WATERS)

Ps 1: 3 like a tree planted by streams of *w,*
22: 14 I am poured out like *w,*
Pr 25: 21 if he is thirsty, give him *w* to drink.
Isa 49: 10 and lead them beside springs of *w.*
Jer 2: 13 broken cisterns that cannot hold *w.*
Zec 14: 8 On that day living *w* will flow out
Mk 9: 41 anyone who gives you a cup of *w*
Jn 4: 10 he would have given you living *w.*"
Jn 7: 38 streams of living *w* will flow
Eph 5: 26 washing with *w* through the word,
1Pe 3: 21 this *w* symbolizes baptism that now
Rev 21: 6 cost from the spring of the *w* of life.

WATERED (WATER)

1Co 3: 6 I planted the seed, Apollos *w* it,

WATERS (WATER)

Ps 23: 2 he leads me beside quiet *w,*
Ecc 11: 1 Cast your bread upon the *w,*
Isa 58: 11 like a spring whose *w* never fail.
1Co 3: 7 plants nor he who *w* is anything,

WAVE (WAVES)

Jas 1: 6 he who doubts is like a *w* of the sea,

WAVES (WAVE)

Isa 57: 20 whose *w* cast up mire and mud.
Mt 8: 27 Even the winds and the *w* obey him
Eph 4: 14 tossed back and forth by the *w,*

WAY (WAYS)

Dt 1: 33 to show you the *w* you should go.
2Sa 22: 31 "As for God, his *w* is perfect;
Job 23: 10 But he knows the *w* that I take;
Ps 1: 1 or stand in the *w* of sinners
37: 5 Commit your *w* to the LORD;
119: 9 can a young man keep his *w* pure?
139: 24 See if there is any offensive *w* in me
Pr 14: 12 There is a *w* that seems right
16: 17 he who guards his *w* guards his life.
22: 6 Train a child in the *w* he should go,
Isa 30: 21 saying, "This is the *w;* walk in it."
53: 6 each of us has turned to his own *w;*
Isa 55: 7 Let the wicked forsake his *w*
Mt 3: 3 Prepare the *w* for the Lord,
Jn 14: 6 "I am the *w* and the truth
1Co 10: 13 also provide a *w* out so that you can
12: 31 will show you the most excellent *w.*
Heb 4: 15 who has been tempted in every *w,*
9: 8 was showing by this that the *w*
10: 20 and living *w* opened for us

WAYS (WAY)

Ex 33: 13 teach me your *w* so I may know
Ps 25: 10 All the *w* of the LORD are loving
51: 13 I will teach transgressors your *w,*
Pr 3: 6 in all your *w* acknowledge him,
Isa 55: 8 neither are your *w* my *w,*"
Jas 3: 2 We all stumble in many *w.*

WEAK (WEAKER WEAKNESS)

Mt 26: 41 spirit is willing, but the body is *w.*"
Ro 14: 1 Accept him whose faith is *w,*
1Co 1: 27 God chose the *w* things
8: 9 become a stumbling block to the *w.*
9: 22 To the *w* I became *w,* to win the *w.*
2Co 12: 10 For when I am *w,* then I am strong.
Heb 12: 12 your feeble arms and *w* knees.

WEAKER (WEAK)

1Co 12: 22 seem to be *w* are indispensable,
1Pe 3: 7 them with respect as the *w* partner

WEAKNESS (WEAK)

Ro 8: 26 the Spirit helps us in our *w.*
1Co 1: 25 and the *w* of God is stronger
2Co 12: 9 for my power is made perfect in *w*
Heb 5: 2 since he himself is subject to *w.*

WEALTH

Pr 3: 9 Honor the LORD with your *w,*
Mk 10: 22 away sad, because he had great *w.*
Lk 15: 13 and there squandered his *w*

WEAPONS

2Co 10: 4 The *w* we fight with are not

WEARIES (WEARY)

Ecc 12: 12 and much study *w* the body.

WEARY (WEARIES)

Isa 40: 31 they will run and not grow *w,*
Mt 11: 28 all you who are *w* and burdened,
Gal 6: 9 Let us not become *w* in doing good,

WEDDING

Mt 22: 11 who was not wearing *w* clothes.
Rev 19: 7 For the *w* of the Lamb has come,

WEEP (WEEPING WEPT)

Ecc 3: 4 a time to *w* and a time to laugh,
Lk 6: 21 Blessed are you who *w* now,

WEEPING (WEEP)

Ps 30: 5 *w* may remain for a night,
126: 6 He who goes out *w,*
Mt 8: 12 where there will be *w* and gnashing

WELCOMES

Mt 18: 5 whoever *w* a little child like this
2Jn : 11 Anyone who *w* him shares

WELL

Lk 17: 19 your faith has made you *w.*"
Jas 5: 15 in faith will make the sick person *w*

WEPT (WEEP)

Ps 137: 1 of Babylon we sat and *w*
Jn 11: 35 Jesus *w.*

WEST

Ps 103: 12 as far as the east is from the *w,*

WHIRLWIND (WIND)

2Ki 2: 1 to take Elijah up to heaven in a *w,*
Hos 8: 7 and reap the *w.*
Na 1: 3 His way is in the *w* and the storm,

WHITE (WHITER)

Isa 1: 18 they shall be as *w* as snow;
Da 7: 9 His clothing was as *w* as snow;
Rev 1: 14 hair were *w* like wool, as *w* as snow,
3: 4 dressed in *w,* for they are worthy.
20: 11 Then I saw a great *w* throne

WHITER (WHITE)

Ps 51: 7 and I will be *w* than snow.

WHOLE

Mt 16: 26 for a man if he gains the *w* world,
24: 14 will be preached in the *w* world
Jn 13: 10 to wash his feet; his *w* body is clean
21: 25 the *w* world would not have room
Ac 20: 27 proclaim to you the *w* will of God.
Ro 3: 19 and the *w* world held accountable
8: 22 know that the *w* creation has been
Gal 3: 22 declares that the *w* world is
5: 3 obligated to obey the *w* law.

Eph 4: 13 attaining to the *w* measure
Jas 2: 10 For whoever keeps the *w* law
1Jn 2: 2 but also for the sins of the *w* world.

WHOLEHEARTEDLY (HEART)

Dt 1: 36 because he followed the LORD *w*
Eph 6: 7 Serve *w,* as if you were serving

WICKED (WICKEDNESS)

Ps 1: 1 walk in the counsel of the *w*
1: 5 Therefore the *w* will not stand
73: 3 when I saw the prosperity of the *w.*
Pr 10: 20 the heart of the *w* is of little value.
11: 21 The *w* will not go unpunished,
Isa 53: 9 He was assigned a grave with the *w*
55: 7 Let the *w* forsake his way
57: 20 But the *w* are like the tossing sea,
Eze 3: 18 that *w* man will die for his sin,
18: 23 pleasure in the death of the *w?*
33: 14 to the *w* man, 'You will surely die,'

WICKEDNESS (WICKED)

Eze 28: 15 created till *w* was found in you.

WIDE

Isa 54: 2 stretch your tent curtains *w,*
Mt 7: 13 For *w* is the gate and broad is
Eph 3: 18 to grasp how *w* and long and high

WIDOW (WIDOWS)

Dt 10: 18 cause of the fatherless and the *w,*
Lk 21: 2 saw a poor *w* put in two very small

WIDOWS (WIDOW)

Jas 1: 27 look after orphans and *w*

WIFE (WIVES)

Ge 2: 24 and mother and be united to his *w,*
24: 67 she became his *w,* and he loved her;
Ex 20: 17 shall not covet your neighbor's *w,*
Dt 5: 21 shall not covet your neighbor's *w.*
Pr 5: 18 in the *w* of your youth.
12: 4 *w* of noble character is her
18: 22 He who finds a *w* finds what is
19: 13 quarrelsome *w* is like a constant
31: 10 *w* of noble character who can find?
Mt 19: 3 for a man to divorce his *w* for any
1Co 7: 2 each man should have his own *w,*
7: 33 how he can please his *w*—
Eph 5: 23 the husband is the head of the *w*
5: 33 must love his *w* as he loves himself,
1Ti 3: 2 husband of but one *w,* temperate,
Rev 21: 9 I will show you the bride,the *w*

WILD

Lk 15: 13 squandered his wealth in *w* living.
Ro 11: 17 and you, though a *w* olive shoot,

WILL (WILLING WILLINGNESS)

Ps 40: 8 I desire to do your *w,* O my God;
143: 10 Teach me to do your *w,*
Isa 53: 10 Yet it was the LORD's *w*
Mt 6: 10 your *w* be done
26: 39 Yet not as I *w,* but as you *w.*"
Jn 7: 17 If anyone chooses to do God's *w,*
Ac 20: 27 to you the whole *w* of God.
Ro 12: 2 and approve what God's *w* is—
1Co 7: 37 but has control over his own *w,*
Eph 5: 17 understand what the Lord's *w* is.
Php 2: 13 for it is God who works in you to *w*
1Th 4: 3 God's *w* that you should be
5: 18 for this is God's *w* for you
Heb 9: 16 In the case of a *w,* it is necessary
10: 7 I have come to do your *w,* O God
Jas 4: 15 "If it is the Lord's *w,*
1Jn 5: 14 we ask anything according to his *w,*
Rev 4: 11 and by your *w* they were created

WILLING (WILL)

Ps 51: 12 grant me a *w* spirit, to sustain me.
Da 3: 28 were *w* to give up their lives rather
Mt 18: 14 Father in heaven is not *w* that any
23: 37 her wings, but you were not *w.*
26: 41 The spirit is *w,* but the body is weak

WILLINGNESS (WILL)

2Co 8: 12 For if the *w* is there, the gift is

WIN (WINS)

Php 3: 14 on toward the goal to *w* the prize
1Th 4: 12 your daily life may *w* the respect

WIND (WHIRLWIND)

Jas 1: 6 blown and tossed by the *w.*

WINE

Pr 20: 1 *W* is a mocker and beer a brawler;
Isa 55: 1 Come, buy *w* and milk
Mt 9: 17 Neither do men pour new *w*
Lk 23: 36 They offered him *w* vinegar
Ro 14: 21 not to eat meat or drink *w*
Eph 5: 18 on *w,* which leads to debauchery.

WINESKINS

Mt 9: 17 do men pour new wine into old *w.*

WINGS

Ru 2: 12 under whose *w* you have come
Ps 17: 8 hide me in the shadow of your *w*
Isa 40: 31 They will soar on *w* like eagles;
Mal 4: 2 rise with healing in its *w.*
Lk 13: 34 hen gathers her chicks under her *w,*

WINS (WIN)

Pr 11: 30 and he who *w* souls is wise.

WIPE

Rev 7: 17 God will *w* away every tear

WISDOM (WISE)

1Ki 4: 29 God gave Solomon *w* and very
Ps 111: 10 of the LORD is the beginning of *w;*
Pr 31: 26 She speaks with *w,*
Jer 10: 12 he founded the world by his *w*
Mt 11: 19 But *w* is proved right by her actions
Lk 2: 52 And Jesus grew in *w* and stature,
Ro 11: 33 the depth of the riches of the *w*
Col 2: 3 are hidden all the treasures of *w*
Jas 1: 5 of you lacks *w,* he should ask God,

WISE (WISDOM WISER)

1Ki 3: 12 give you a *w* and discerning heart,
Job 5: 13 He catches the *w* in their craftiness
Ps 19: 7 making *w* the simple.
Pr 3: 7 Do not be *w* in your own eyes;
9: 8 rebuke a *w* man and he will love
10: 1 A *w* son brings joy to his father,
11: 30 and he who wins souls is *w.*
13: 20 He who walks with the *w* grows *w,*
17: 28 Even a fool is thought *w*
Da 12: 3 Those who are *w* will shine like
Mt 11: 25 hidden these things from the *w*
1Co 1: 27 things of the world to shame the *w;*
2Ti 3: 15 able to make you *w* for salvation

WISER (WISE)

1Co 1: 25 of God is *w* than man's wisdom,

WITHER (WITHERS)

Ps 1: 3 and whose leaf does not *w.*

WITHERS (WITHER)

Isa 40: 7 The grass *w* and the flowers fall,
1Pe 1: 24 the grass *w* and the flowers fall,

WITHHOLD

Ps 84: 11 no good thing does he *w*
Pr 23: 13 Do not *w* discipline from a child;

WITNESS (WITNESSES)

Jn 1: 8 he came only as a *w* to the light.

WITNESSES (WITNESS)

Dt 19: 15 by the testimony of two or three *w.*
Ac 1: 8 and you will be my *w* in Jerusalem,

WIVES (WIFE)

Eph 5: 22 *W,* submit to your husbands
5: 25 love your *w,* just as Christ loved
1Pe 3: 1 words by the behavior of their *w,*

WOE

Isa 6: 5 "*W* to me!" I cried.

WOLF

Isa 65: 25 *w* and the lamb will feed together,

WOMAN (MAN)

Ge 2: 22 God made a *w* from
3: 15 between you and the *w*,
Lev 20: 13 as one lies with a *w*,
Dt 22: 5 *w* must not wear men's
Ru 3: 11 a *w* of noble character
Pr 31: 30 a *w* who fears the LORD
Mt 5: 28 looks at a *w* lustfully
Jn 8: 3 a *w* caught in adultery.
Ro 7: 2 a married *w* is bound to
1Co 11: 3 the head of the *w* is man,
11: 13 a *w* to pray to God with
1Ti 2: 11 A *w* should learn in

WOMEN (MAN)

Lk 1: 42 Blessed are you among *w*,
1Co 14: 34 *w* should remain silent in
1Ti 2: 9 want *w* to dress modestly
Tit 2: 3 teach the older *w* to be
1Pe 3: 5 the holy *w* of the past

WOMB

Job 1: 21 Naked I came from my mother's *w*,
Jer 1: 5 you in the *w* I knew you,
Lk 1: 44 the baby in my *w* leaped for joy.

WONDER (WONDERFUL WONDERS)

Ps 17: 7 Show the *w* of your great love,

WONDERFUL (WONDER)

Job 42: 3 things too *w* for me to know.
Ps 31: 21 for he showed his *w* love to me
119: 18 *w* things in your law.
119:129 Your statutes are *w*;
139: 6 Such knowledge is too *w* for me,
Isa 9: 6 *W* Counselor, Mighty God,
1Pe 2: 9 out of darkness into his *w* light.

WONDERS (WONDER)

Job 37: 14 stop and consider God's *w*.
Ps 119: 27 then I will meditate on your *w*.
Joel 2: 30 I will show *w* in the heavens
Ac 2: 19 I will show *w* in the heaven above

WOOD

Isa 44: 19 Shall I bow down to a block of *w*?"
1Co 3: 12 costly stones, *w*, hay or straw,

WORD (WORDS)

Dt 8: 3 but on every *w* that comes
2Sa 22: 31 the *w* of the LORD is flawless.
Ps 119: 9 By living according to your *w*.
119: 11 I have hidden your *w* in my heart
119:105 Your *w* is a lamp to my feet
Pr 12: 25 but a kind *w* cheers him up.
25: 11 A *w* aptly spoken
30: 5 "Every *w* of God is flawless;
Isa 55: 11 so is my *w* that goes out
Jn 1: 1 was the *W*, and the *W* was
1: 14 The *W* became flesh and made his
2Co 2: 17 we do not peddle the *w* of God
4: 2 nor do we distort the *w* of God.
Eph 6: 17 of the Spirit, which is the *w* of God.
Php 2: 16 as you hold out the *w* of life—
Col 3: 16 Let the *w* of Christ dwell
2Ti 2: 15 and who correctly handles the *w*
Heb 4: 12 For the *w* of God is living
Jas 1: 22 Do not merely listen to the *w*,
2Pe 1: 19 And we have the *w* of the prophets

WORDS (WORD)

Dt 11: 18 Fix these *w* of mine in your hearts
Ps 119:103 How sweet are your *w* to my taste
119:130 The unfolding of your *w* gives light;
119:160 All your *w* are true;
Pr 30: 6 Do not add to his *w*,
Jer 15: 16 When your *w* came, I ate them;
Mt 24: 35 but my *w* will never pass away.
Jn 6: 68 You have the *w* of eternal life.
15: 7 in me and my *w* remain in you,
1Co 14: 19 rather speak five intelligible *w*
Rev 22: 19 And if anyone takes *w* away

WORK (WORKER WORKERS WORKING WORKMAN WORKMANSHIP WORKS)

Ex 23: 12 "Six days do your *w*,
Nu 8: 11 ready to do the *w* of the LORD.
Dt 5: 14 On it you shall not do any *w*,
Ecc 5: 19 his lot and be happy in his *w*—
Jer 48: 10 lax in doing the LORD's *w*!
Jn 6: 27 Do not *w* for food that spoils,
9: 4 we must do the *w* of him who sent
1Co 3: 13 test the quality of each man's *w*.
Php 1: 6 that he who began a good *w*
2: 12 continue to *w* out your salvation
Col 3: 23 Whatever you do, *w* at it
1Th 5: 12 to respect those who *w* hard
2Th 3: 10 If a man will not *w*, he shall not eat
2Ti 3: 17 equipped for every good *w*.
Heb 6: 10 he will not forget your *w*

WORKER (WORK)

Lk 10: 7 for the *w* deserves his wages.
1Ti 5: 18 and "The *w* deserves his wages."

WORKERS (WORK)

Mt 9: 37 is plentiful but the *w* are few.
1Co 3: 9 For we are God's fellow *w*;

WORKING (WORK)

Col 3: 23 as *w* for the Lord, not for men,

WORKMAN (WORK)

2Ti 2: 15 a *w* who does not need

WORKMANSHIP* (WORK)

Eph 2: 10 For we are God's *w*, created

WORKS (WORK)

Pr 31: 31 let her *w* bring her praise
Ro 8: 28 in all things God *w* for the good
Eph 2: 9 not by *w*, so that no one can boast.
4: 12 to prepare God's people for *w*

WORLD (WORLDLY)

Ps 50: 12 for the *w* is mine, and all that is in it
Isa 13: 11 I will punish the *w* for its evil,
Mt 5: 14 "You are the light of the *w*.
Mt 16: 26 for a man if he gains the whole *w*,
Mk 16: 15 into all the *w* and preach the good
Jn 1: 29 who takes away the sin of the *w*!
3: 16 so loved the *w* that he gave his one
8: 12 he said, "I am the light of the *w*.
Jn 15: 19 As it is, you do not belong to the *w*,
16: 33 In this *w* you will have trouble.
18: 36 "My kingdom is not of this *w*.
Ro 3: 19 and the whole *w* held accountable
1Co 3: 19 the wisdom of this *w* is foolishness
2Co 5: 19 that God was reconciling the *w*
10: 3 For though we live in the *w*,
1Ti 6: 7 For we brought nothing into the *w*,
1Jn 2: 2 but also for the sins of the whole *w*.
2: 15 not love the *w* or anything in the *w*.
Rev 13: 8 slain from the creation of the *w*.

WORLDLY (WORLD)

Tit 2: 12 to ungodliness and *w* passions,

WORM

Mk 9: 48 "'their *w* does not die,

WORRY (WORRYING)

Mt 6: 25 I tell you, do not *w* about your life,
10: 19 do not *w* about what to say

WORRYING (WORRY)

Mt 6: 27 of you by *w* can add a single hour

WORSHIP

1Ch 16: 29 *w* the LORD in the splendor
Ps 95: 6 Come, let us bow down in *w*,
Mt 2: 2 and have come to *w* him."
Jn 4: 24 and his worshipers must *w* in spirit
Ro 12: 1 this is your spiritual act of *w*.

WORTH (WORTHY)

Job 28: 13 Man does not comprehend its *w*;
Pr 31: 10 She is *w* far more than rubies.
Mt 10: 31 are *w* more than many sparrows.
Ro 8: 18 sufferings are not *w* comparing
1Pe 1: 7 of greater *w* than gold,
3: 4 which is of great *w* in God's sight.

WORTHLESS

Pr 11: 4 Wealth is *w* in the day of wrath,
Jas 1: 26 himself and his religion is *w*.

WORTHY (WORTH)

1Ch 16: 25 For great is the LORD and most *w*
Eph 4: 1 to live a life *w* of the calling you
Php 1: 27 in a manner *w* of the gospel
3Jn : 6 on their way in a manner *w* of God.
Rev 5: 2 "Who is *w* to break the seals

WOUNDS

Pr 27: 6 *W* from a friend can be trusted,
Isa 53: 5 and by his *w* we are healed.
Zec 13: 6 'What are these *w* on your body?'
1Pe 2: 24 by his *w* you have been healed.

WRATH

2Ch 36: 16 scoffed at his prophets until the *w*
Ps 2: 5 and terrifies them in his *w*, saying,

Ps	76: 10	Surely your *w* against men brings
Pr	15: 1	A gentle answer turns away *w,*
Jer	25: 15	filled with the wine of my *w*
Ro	1: 18	The *w* of God is being revealed
	5: 9	saved from God's *w* through him!
1Th	5: 9	God did not appoint us to suffer *w*
Rev	6: 16	and from the *w* of the Lamb!

WRESTLED

Ge	32: 24	and a man *w* with him till daybreak

WRITE (WRITING WRITTEN)

Dt	6: 9	*W* them on the doorframes
Pr	7: 3	*w* them on the tablet of your heart.
Heb	8: 10	and *w* them on their hearts.

WRITING (WRITE)

1Co	14: 37	him acknowledge that what I am *w*

WRITTEN (WRITE)

Jos	1: 8	careful to do everything *w* in it.
Da	12: 1	everyone whose name is found *w*
Lk	10: 20	but rejoice that your names are *w*
Jn	20: 31	these are *w* that you may believe
1Co	4: 6	"Do not go beyond what is *w.*"
2Co	3: 3	*w* not with ink but with the Spirit
Col	2: 14	having canceled the *w* code,
Heb	12: 23	whose names are *w* in heaven.

WRONG (WRONGDOING WRONGED WRONGS)

Ex	23: 2	Do not follow the crowd in doing *w*
Nu	5: 7	must make full restitution for his *w,*
Job	34: 12	unthinkable that God would do *w,*
1Th	5: 15	that nobody pays back *w* for *w,*

WRONGDOING (WRONG)

Job	1: 22	sin by charging God with *w.*

WRONGED (WRONG)

1Co	6: 7	not rather be *w?* Why not rather

WRONGS (WRONG)

Pr	10: 12	but love covers over all *w.*
1Co	13: 5	angered, it keeps no record of *w.*

YEARS

Ps	90: 4	For a thousand *y* in your sight
	90: 10	The length of our days is seventy *y*
2Pe	3: 8	the Lord a day is like a thousand *y,*
Rev	20: 2	and bound him for a thousand *y.*

YESTERDAY

Heb	13: 8	Jesus Christ is the same *y*

YOKE (YOKED)

Mt	11: 29	Take my *y* upon you and learn

YOKED (YOKE)

2Co	6: 14	Do not be *y* together

YOUNG (YOUTH)

Ps	119: 9	How can a *y* man keep his way
1Ti	4: 12	down on you because you are *y,*

YOUTH (YOUNG)

Ps	103: 5	so that your *y* is renewed like
Ecc	12: 1	Creator in the days of your *y,*
2Ti	2: 22	Flee the evil desires of *y,*

ZEAL

Pr	19: 2	to have *z* without knowledge,
Ro	12: 11	Never be lacking in *z,*

ZECHARIAH

1. Son of Jeroboam II; king of Israel (2Ki 15:8-12).

2. Post-exilic prophet who encouraged rebuilding of temple (Ezr 5:1; 6:14; Zec 1:1).

ZEDEKIAH

Mattaniah, son of Josiah (1Ch 3:15), made king of Judah by Nebuchadnezzar (2Ki 24:17-25:7; 2Ch 36:10-14; Jer 37-39; 52:1-11).

ZERUBBABEL

Descendant of David (1Ch 3:19; Mt 1:3). Led return from exile (Ezr 2-3; Ne 7:7; Hag 1-2; Zec 4).

ZIMRI

King of Israel (1Ki 16:9-20).

ZION

Ps	137: 3	"Sing us one of the songs of *Z!*"
Jer	50: 5	They will ask the way to *Z*
Ro	9: 33	I lay in *Z* a stone that causes men
	11: 26	"The deliverer will come from *Z;*

INDEX TO COLOR MAPS

Each place name in the alphabetical index is followed by the number of the map on which it can be found, and then by the coordinates (letter/number) at which it is located.

EXAMPLE:	NAME	MAP NUMBER	COORDINATES
	GAD	4	C4

Map 1: **WORLD OF THE PATRIARCHS**

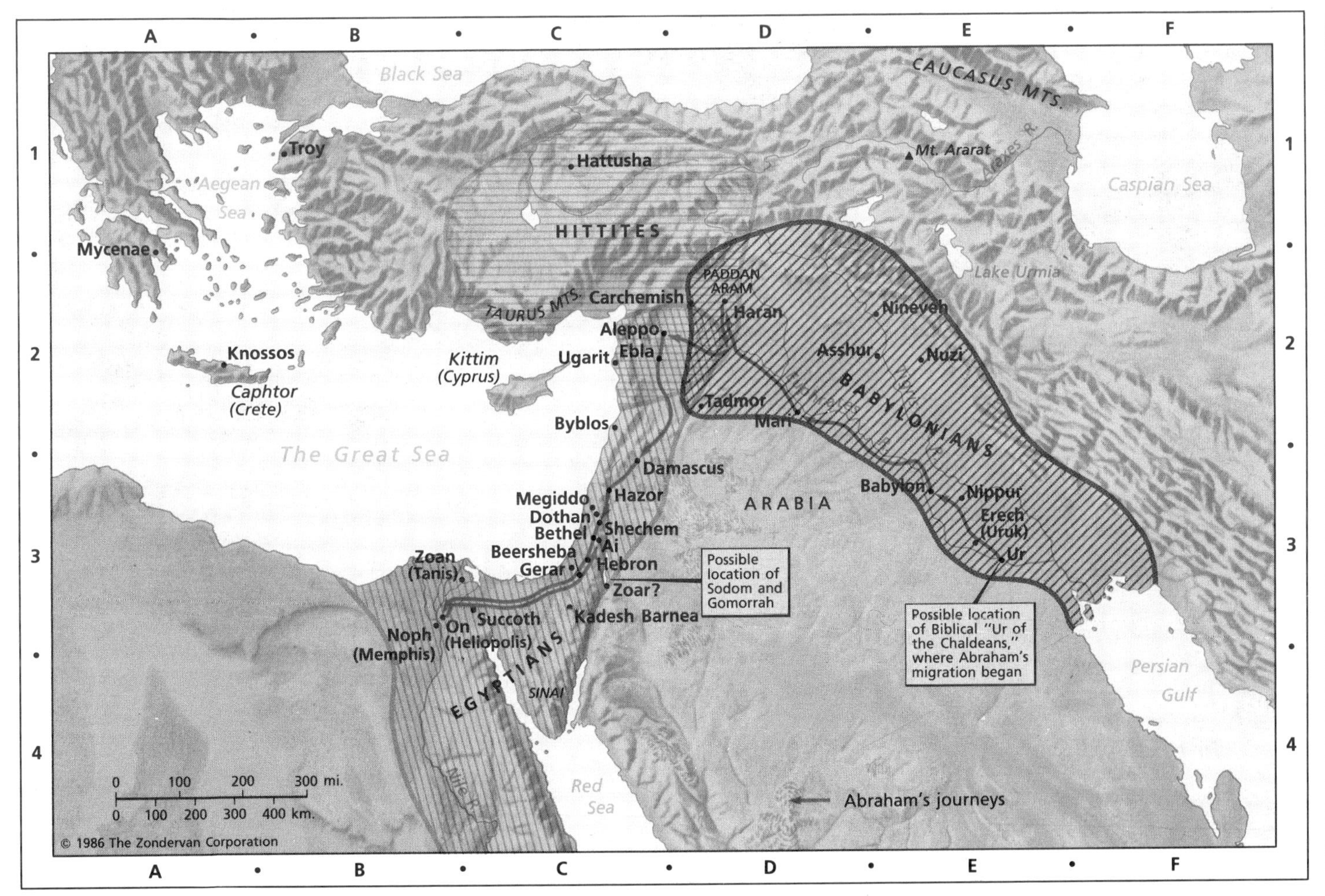

Map 2: **PALESTINE AND SINAI**

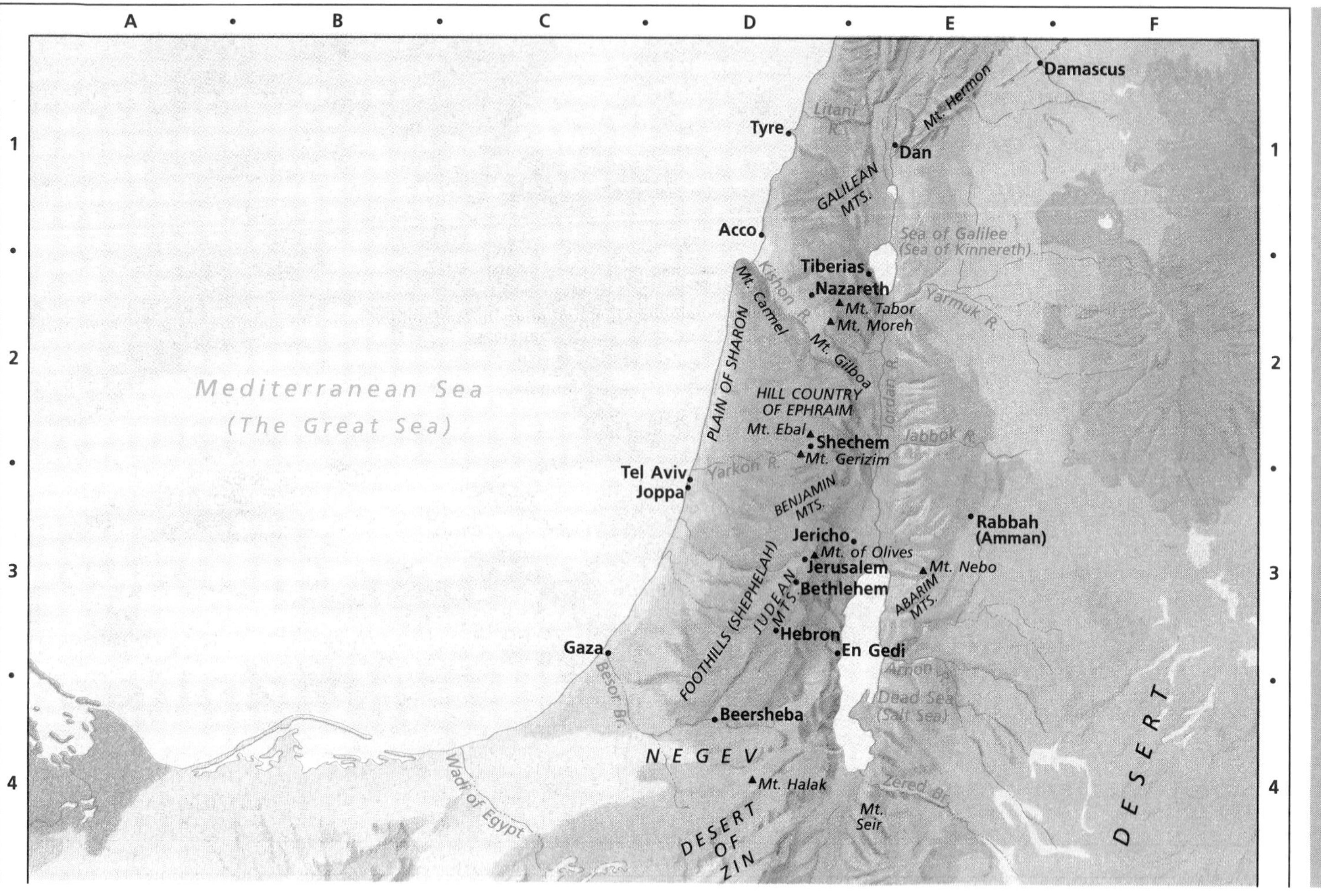

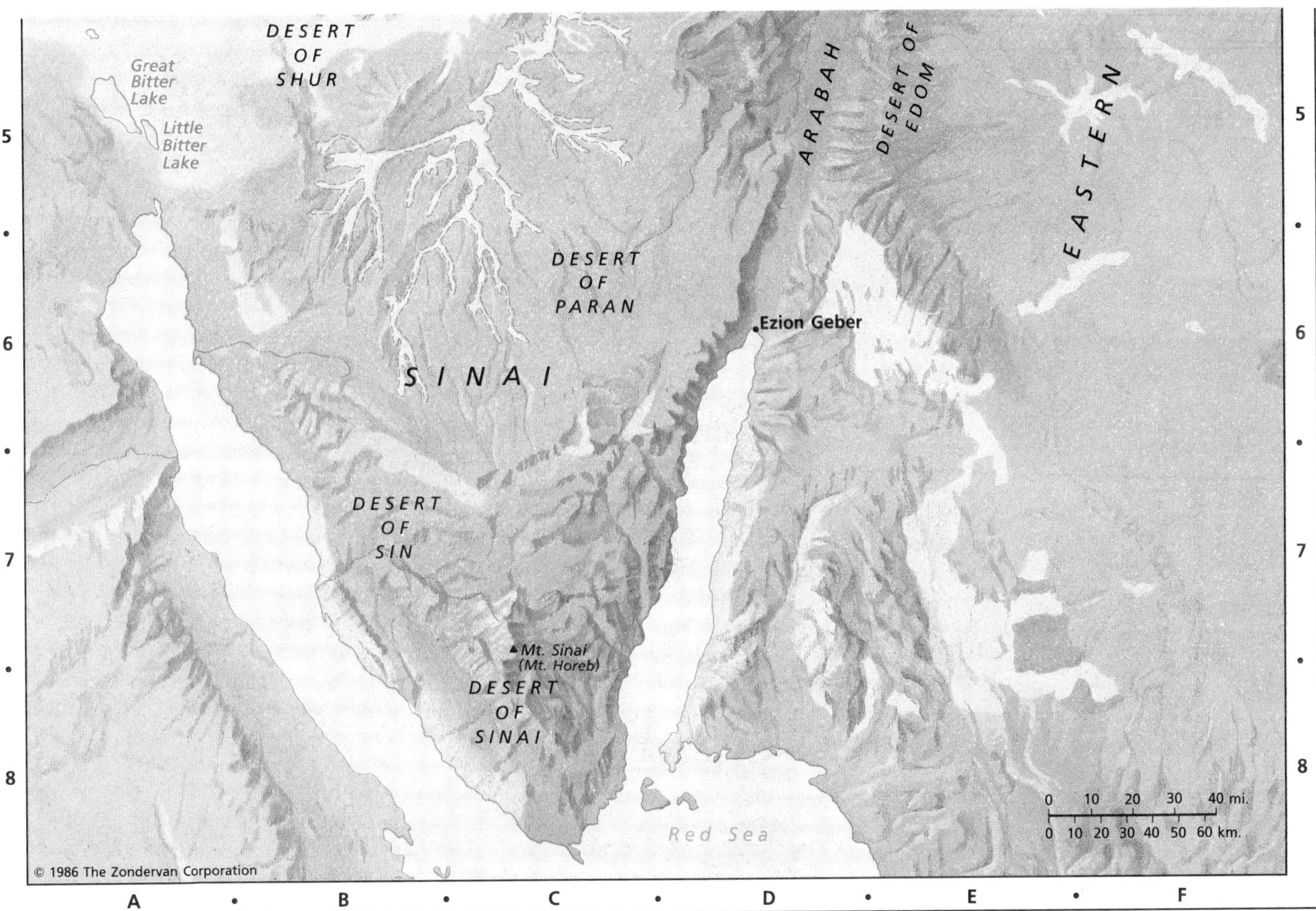
DESERT OF SHUR
Great Bitter Lake
Little Bitter Lake
DESERT OF PARAN
SINAI
ARABAH
DESERT OF EDOM
EASTERN
Ezion Geber
DESERT OF SIN
Mt. Sinai (Mt. Horeb)
DESERT OF SINAI
Red Sea
0 10 20 30 40 mi.
0 10 20 30 40 50 60 km.
© 1986 The Zondervan Corporation
A B C D E F
5 6 7 8

Map 3: EXODUS AND CONQUEST OF CANAAN

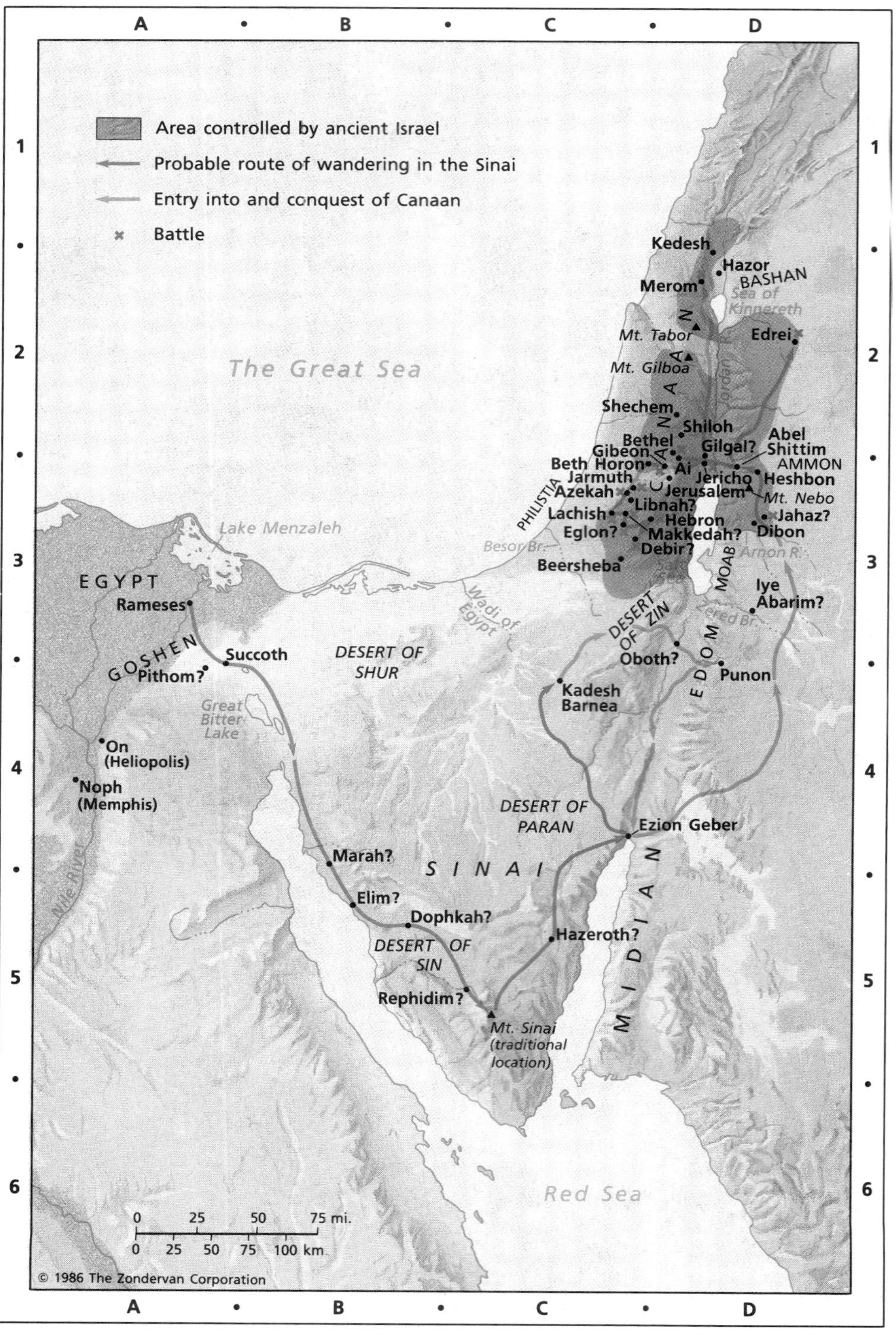

A
B
C
D
1
2
3
4
5
6
Area controlled by ancient Israel
Probable route of wandering in the Sinai
Entry into and conquest of Canaan
Battle
Kedesh
Hazor
BASHAN
Merom
Sea of Kinnereth
Mt. Tabor
Edrei
Mt. Gilboa
The Great Sea
Jordan
CANAAN
Shechem
Shiloh
Bethel
Abel Shittim
Gibeon
Gilgal?
AMMON
Beth Horon
Ai
Jericho
Heshbon
Jarmuth
Jerusalem
Mt. Nebo
PHILISTIA
Azekah
Libnah?
Jahaz?
Lachish
Hebron
Dibon
Eglon?
Makkedah?
Debir?
Arnon R.
Lake Menzaleh
Besor Br.
MOAB
Beersheba
Salt Sea
EGYPT
Rameses
Wadi of Egypt
DESERT OF ZIN
Zered Br.
Iye Abarim?
GOSHEN
Succoth
DESERT OF SHUR
Oboth?
Pithom?
EDOM
Punon
Kadesh Barnea
Great Bitter Lake
On (Heliopolis)
Noph (Memphis)
DESERT OF PARAN
Ezion Geber
Nile River
Marah?
SINAI
Elim?
Dophkah?
MIDIAN
DESERT OF SIN
Hazeroth?
Rephidim?
Mt. Sinai (traditional location)
Red Sea
0 25 50 75 mi.
0 25 50 75 100 km

Map 4: LAND OF THE TWELVE TRIBES

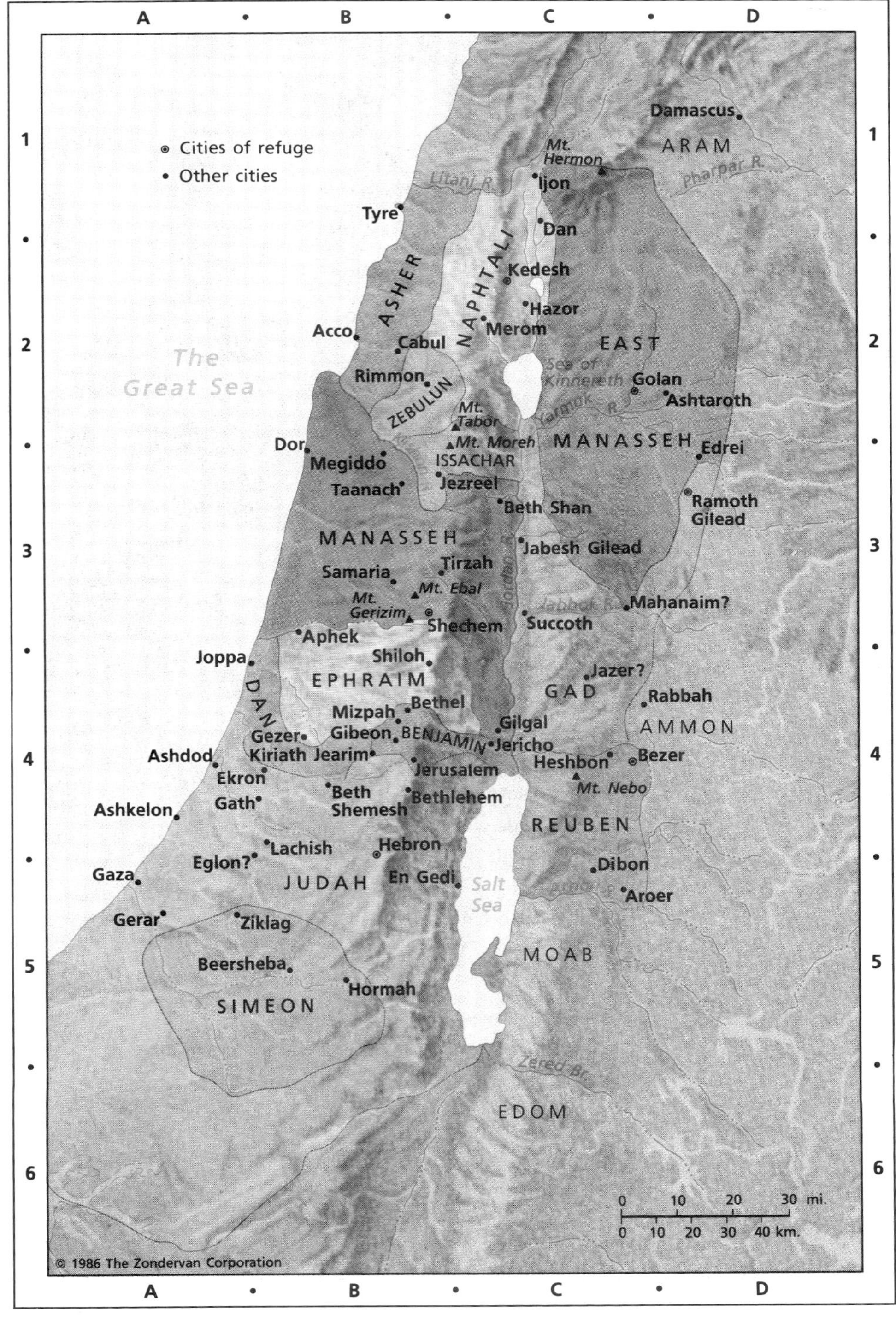

Map 5: **KINGDOM OF DAVID AND SOLOMON**

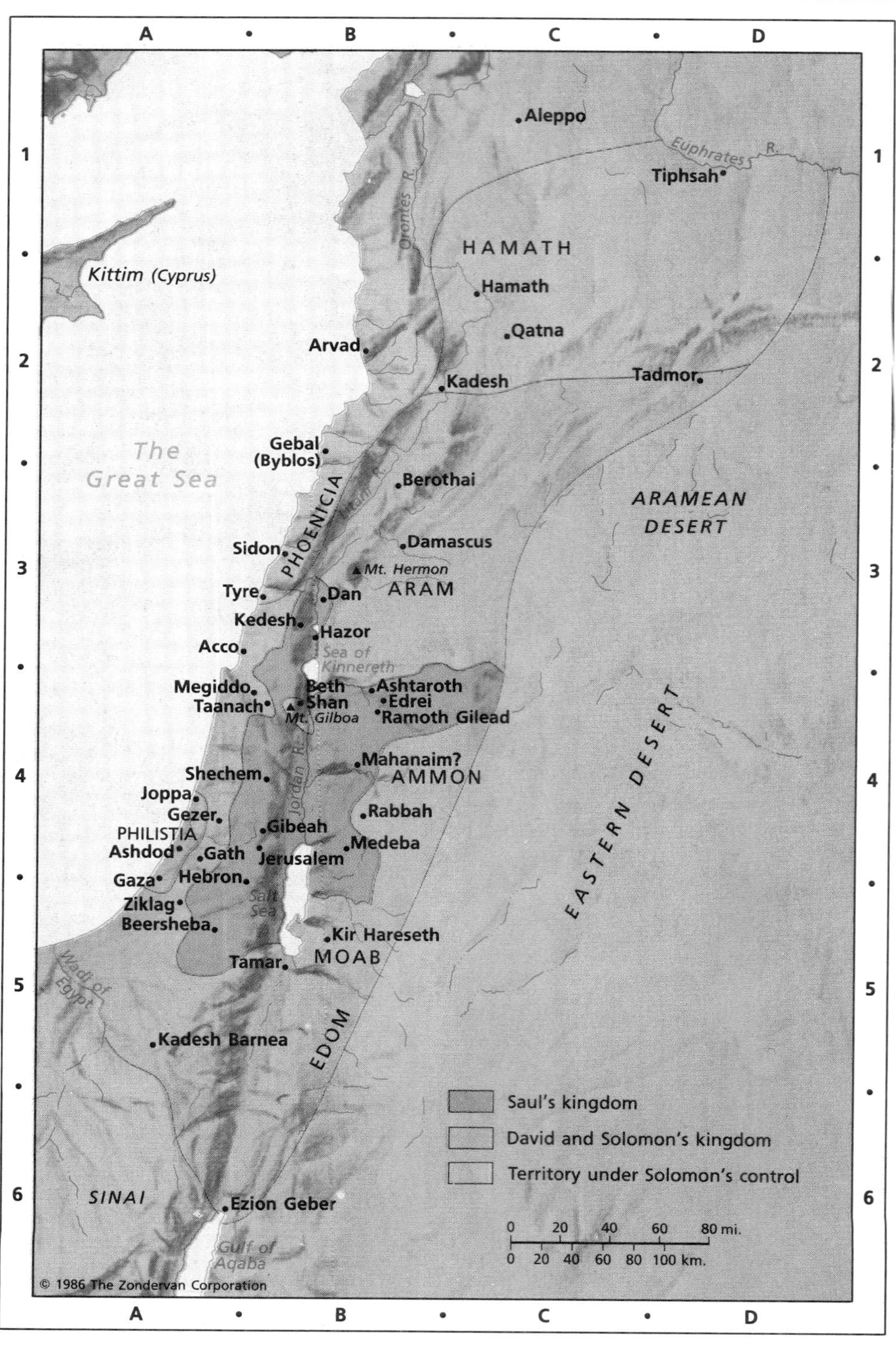

A • B • C • D
1 • 2 • 3 • 4 • 5 • 6
Aleppo
Euphrates R.
Tiphsah
Orontes R.
HAMATH
Hamath
Kittim (Cyprus)
Qatna
Arvad
Kadesh
Tadmor
The Great Sea
Gebal (Byblos)
Berothai
PHOENICIA
ARAMEAN DESERT
Sidon
Damascus
Mt. Hermon
ARAM
Tyre
Dan
Kedesh
Hazor
Acco
Sea of Kinnereth
Megiddo
Beth Shan
Ashtaroth
Edrei
Taanach
Mt. Gilboa
Ramoth Gilead
Mahanaim?
Shechem
AMMON
Jordan R.
Joppa
Gezer
Rabbah
PHILISTIA
Gibeah
Ashdod
Gath
Jerusalem
Medeba
Gaza
Hebron
Salt Sea
Ziklag
Beersheba
Kir Hareseth
MOAB
Tamar
EASTERN DESERT
Wadi of Egypt
EDOM
Kadesh Barnea
Saul's kingdom
David and Solomon's kingdom
Territory under Solomon's control
SINAI
Ezion Geber
0 20 40 60 80 mi.
0 20 40 60 80 100 km.
Gulf of Aqaba

Map 6: PROPHETS IN ISRAEL AND JUDAH

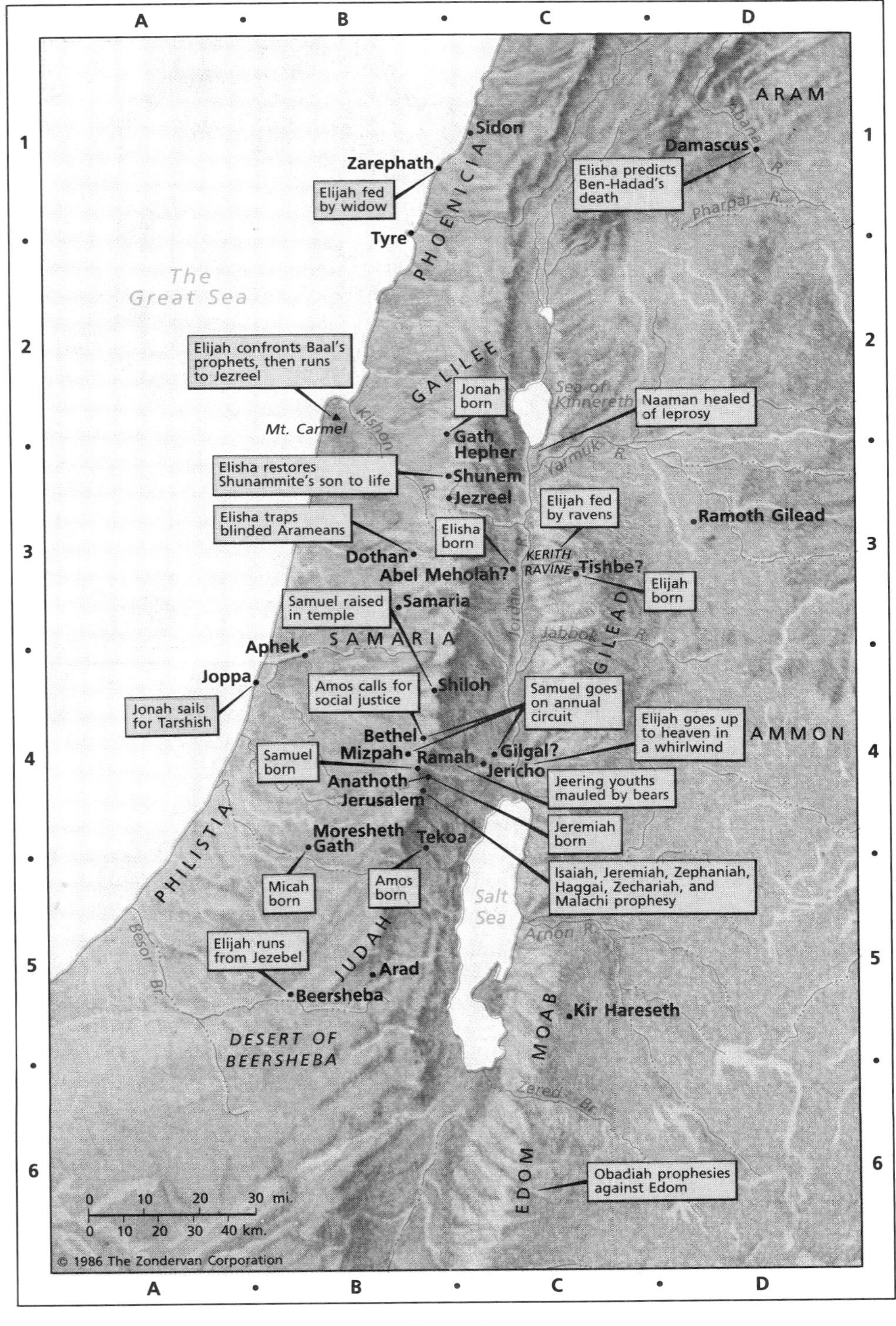

A
B
C
D
1
2
3
4
5
6
ARAM
Damascus
Abana R.
Pharpar R.
Elisha predicts Ben-Hadad's death
Sidon
Zarephath
Elijah fed by widow
Tyre
PHOENICIA
The Great Sea
Elijah confronts Baal's prophets, then runs to Jezreel
Mt. Carmel
Kishon R.
GALILEE
Jonah born
Gath Hepher
Sea of Kinnereth
Naaman healed of leprosy
Yarmuk R.
Elisha restores Shunammite's son to life
Shunem
Jezreel
Elijah fed by ravens
Ramoth Gilead
Elisha traps blinded Arameans
Elisha born
Dothan
Abel Meholah?
KERITH RAVINE
Tishbe?
Elijah born
Samuel raised in temple
Samaria
Jordan R.
SAMARIA
Jabbok R.
GILEAD
Aphek
Joppa
Jonah sails for Tarshish
Amos calls for social justice
Shiloh
Samuel goes on annual circuit
Elijah goes up to heaven in a whirlwind
AMMON
Bethel
Mizpah
Ramah
Gilgal?
Jericho
Samuel born
Anathoth
Jerusalem
Jeering youths mauled by bears
Jeremiah born
Isaiah, Jeremiah, Zephaniah, Haggai, Zechariah, and Malachi prophesy
PHILISTIA
Moresheth Gath
Tekoa
Micah born
Amos born
Salt Sea
Arnon R.
Besor Br.
Elijah runs from Jezebel
JUDAH
Arad
Beersheba
MOAB
Kir Hareseth
DESERT OF BEERSHEBA
Zered Br.
EDOM
Obadiah prophesies against Edom
0 10 20 30 mi.
0 10 20 30 40 km.

Map 7: ASSYRIAN AND BABYLONIAN EMPIRES

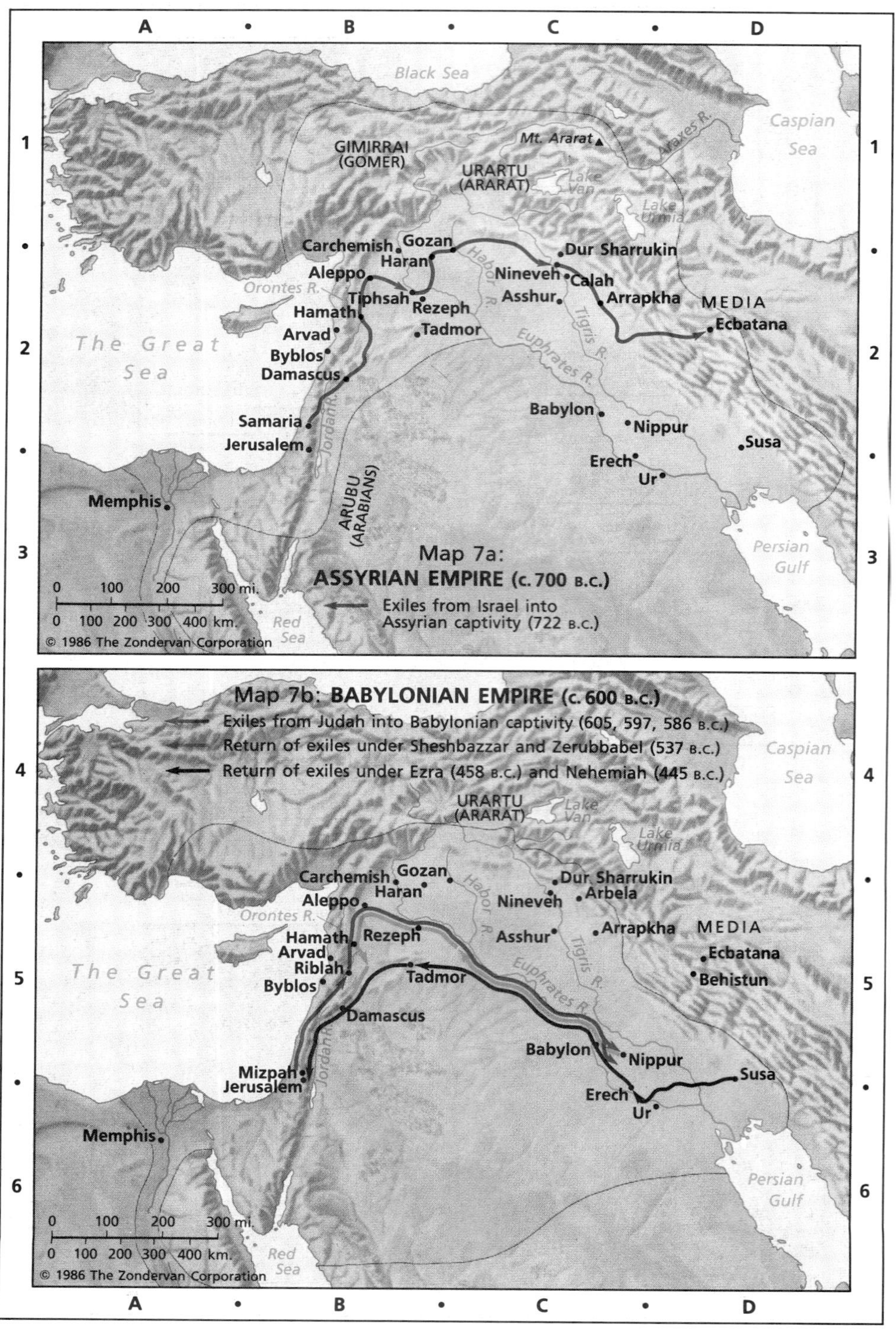

Map 8: JERUSALEM IN JESUS' TIME

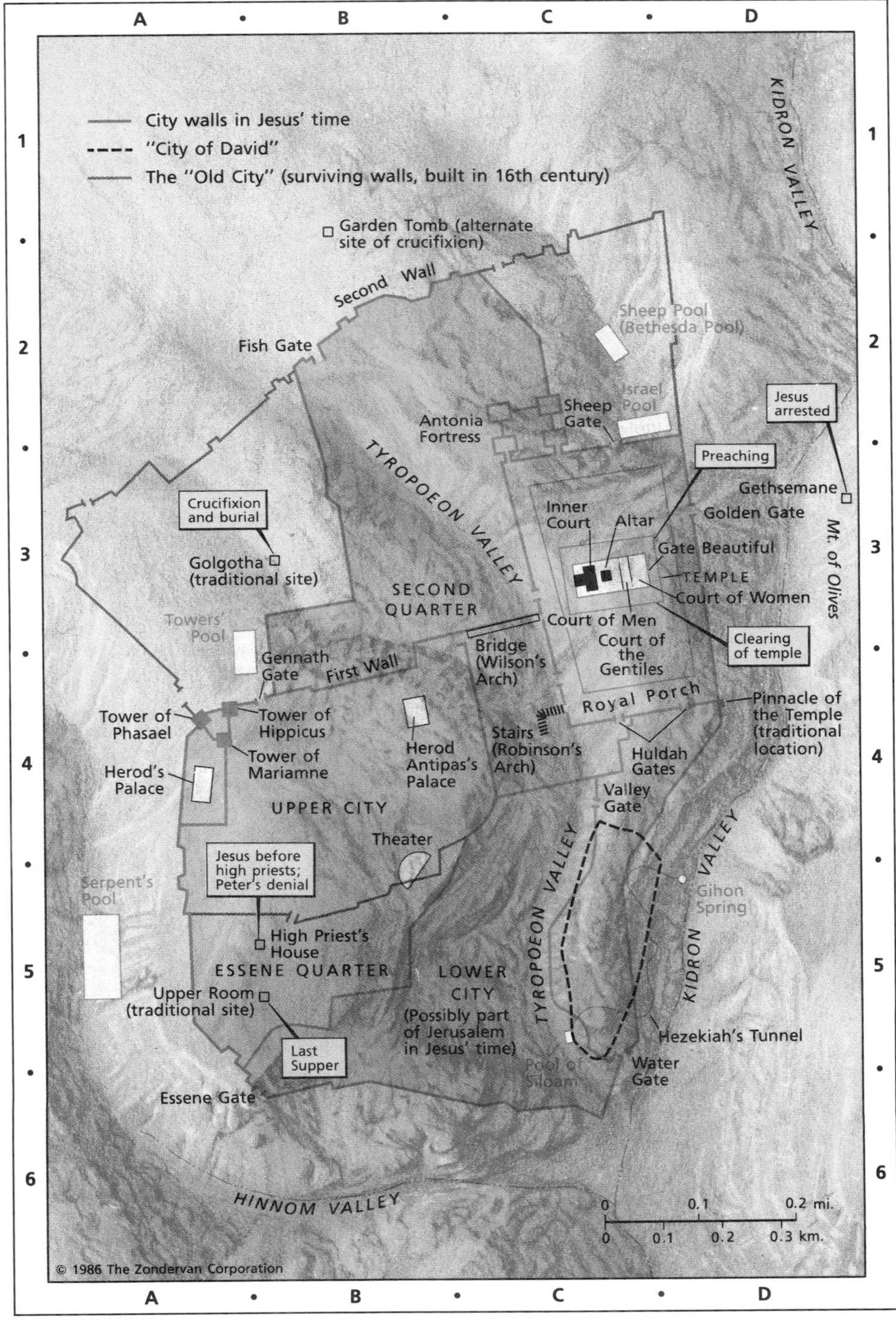

A
B
C
D
1
2
3
4
5
6
City walls in Jesus' time
"City of David"
The "Old City" (surviving walls, built in 16th century)
KIDRON VALLEY
Garden Tomb (alternate site of crucifixion)
Second Wall
Sheep Pool (Bethesda Pool)
Fish Gate
Israel Pool
Jesus arrested
Antonia Fortress
Sheep Gate
TYROPOEON VALLEY
Preaching
Gethsemane
Crucifixion and burial
Inner Court
Altar
Golden Gate
Mt. of Olives
Golgotha (traditional site)
Gate Beautiful
TEMPLE
Court of Women
SECOND QUARTER
Court of Men
Towers' Pool
Court of the Gentiles
Clearing of temple
Bridge (Wilson's Arch)
Gennath Gate
First Wall
Royal Porch
Pinnacle of the Temple (traditional location)
Tower of Phasael
Tower of Hippicus
Stairs (Robinson's Arch)
Tower of Mariamne
Herod Antipas's Palace
Huldah Gates
Herod's Palace
Valley Gate
UPPER CITY
Theater
Jesus before high priests; Peter's denial
Serpent's Pool
Gihon Spring
High Priest's House
ESSENE QUARTER
LOWER CITY
Upper Room (traditional site)
(Possibly part of Jerusalem in Jesus' time)
Hezekiah's Tunnel
Last Supper
Pool of Siloam
Water Gate
Essene Gate
HINNOM VALLEY
0 0.1 0.2 mi.
0 0.1 0.2 0.3 km.

Map 9: **JESUS' MINISTRY**

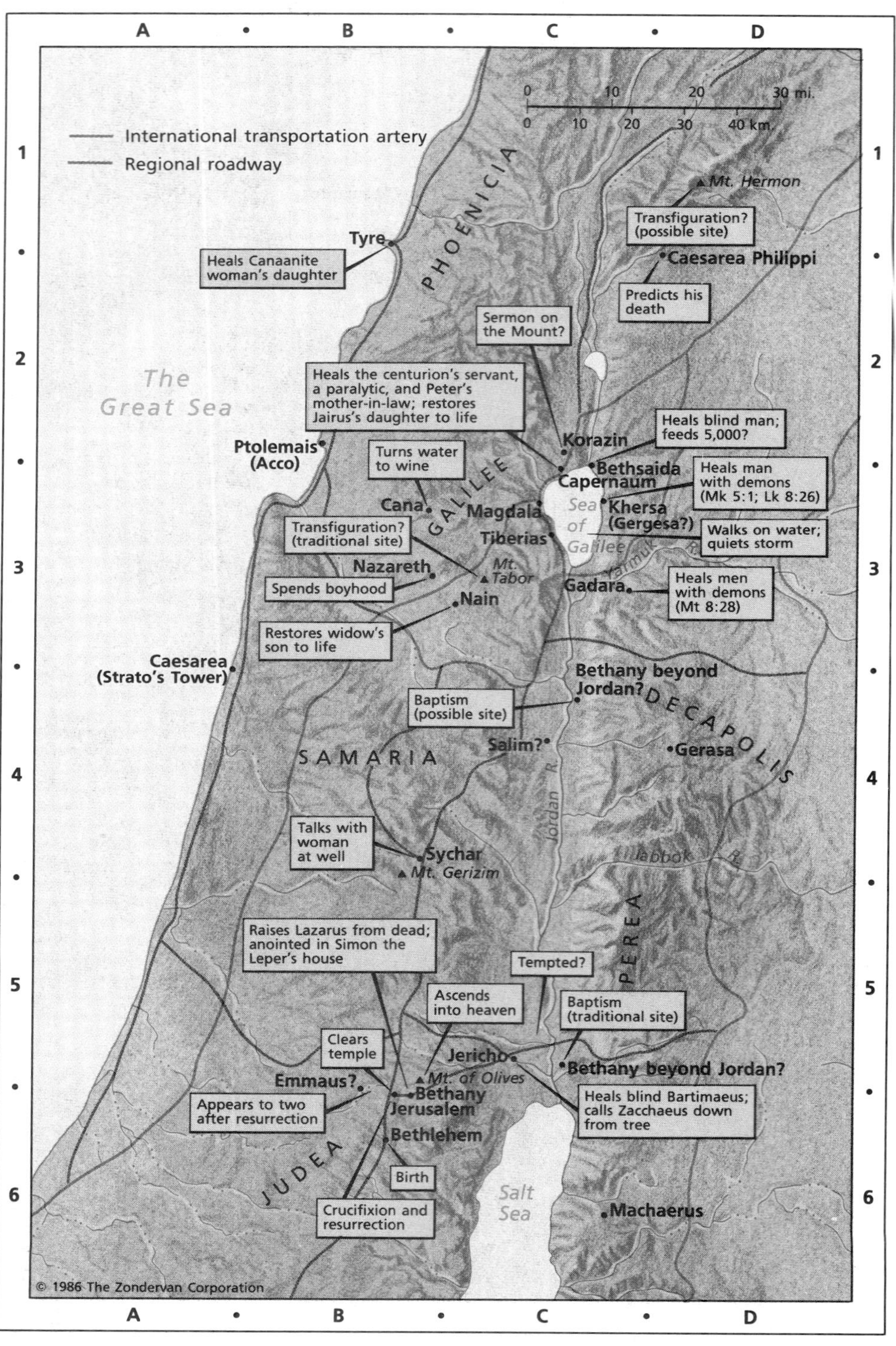

A
B
C
D
1
2
3
4
5
6
0
10
20
30 mi.
0
10
20
30
40 km.
International transportation artery
Regional roadway
PHOENICIA
Mt. Hermon
Transfiguration? (possible site)
Caesarea Philippi
Predicts his death
Tyre
Heals Canaanite woman's daughter
Sermon on the Mount?
The Great Sea
Heals the centurion's servant, a paralytic, and Peter's mother-in-law; restores Jairus's daughter to life
Korazin
Heals blind man; feeds 5,000?
Ptolemais (Acco)
Turns water to wine
Bethsaida
Capernaum
Heals man with demons (Mk 5:1; Lk 8:26)
Cana
GALILEE
Magdala
Sea of Galilee
Khersa (Gergesa?)
Walks on water; quiets storm
Transfiguration? (traditional site)
Tiberias
Yarmuk
Nazareth
Mt. Tabor
Gadara
Heals men with demons (Mt 8:28)
Spends boyhood
Nain
Restores widow's son to life
Caesarea (Strato's Tower)
Bethany beyond Jordan?
DECAPOLIS
Baptism (possible site)
Salim?
Gerasa
SAMARIA
Jordan R.
Talks with woman at well
Sychar
Mt. Gerizim
Jabbok R.
PEREA
Raises Lazarus from dead; anointed in Simon the Leper's house
Tempted?
Ascends into heaven
Baptism (traditional site)
Clears temple
Jericho
Bethany beyond Jordan?
Mt. of Olives
Emmaus?
Bethany
Appears to two after resurrection
Jerusalem
Heals blind Bartimaeus; calls Zacchaeus down from tree
Bethlehem
JUDEA
Birth
Salt Sea
Crucifixion and resurrection
Machaerus
© 1986 The Zondervan Corporation

Map 10: APOSTLES' EARLY TRAVELS

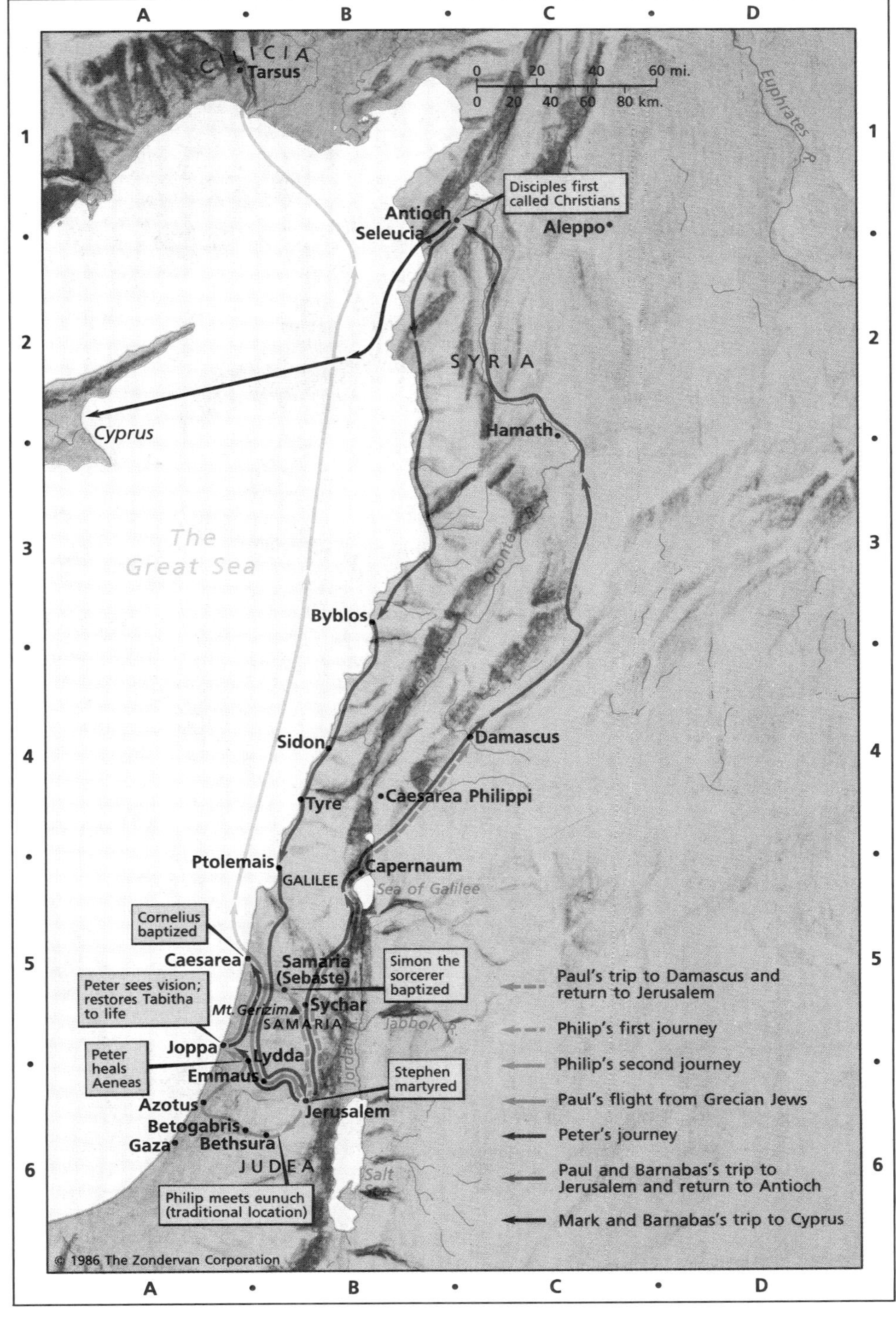

A
B
C
D
1
2
3
4
5
6
CILICIA
Tarsus
0 20 40 60 mi.
0 20 40 60 80 km.
Euphrates R.
Disciples first called Christians
Antioch
Seleucia
Aleppo
SYRIA
Cyprus
Hamath
The Great Sea
Orontes R.
Byblos
Sidon
Damascus
Tyre
Caesarea Philippi
Ptolemais
GALILEE
Capernaum
Sea of Galilee
Cornelius baptized
Caesarea
Samaria (Sebaste)
Simon the sorcerer baptized
Peter sees vision; restores Tabitha to life
Mt. Gerizim
Sychar
SAMARIA
Jabbok R.
Jordan
Joppa
Lydda
Peter heals Aeneas
Emmaus
Stephen martyred
Azotus
Jerusalem
Betogabris
Gaza
Bethsura
JUDEA
Salt Sea
Philip meets eunuch (traditional location)
Paul's trip to Damascus and return to Jerusalem
Philip's first journey
Philip's second journey
Paul's flight from Grecian Jews
Peter's journey
Paul and Barnabas's trip to Jerusalem and return to Antioch
Mark and Barnabas's trip to Cyprus

Map 11: **PAUL'S MISSIONARY JOURNEYS**

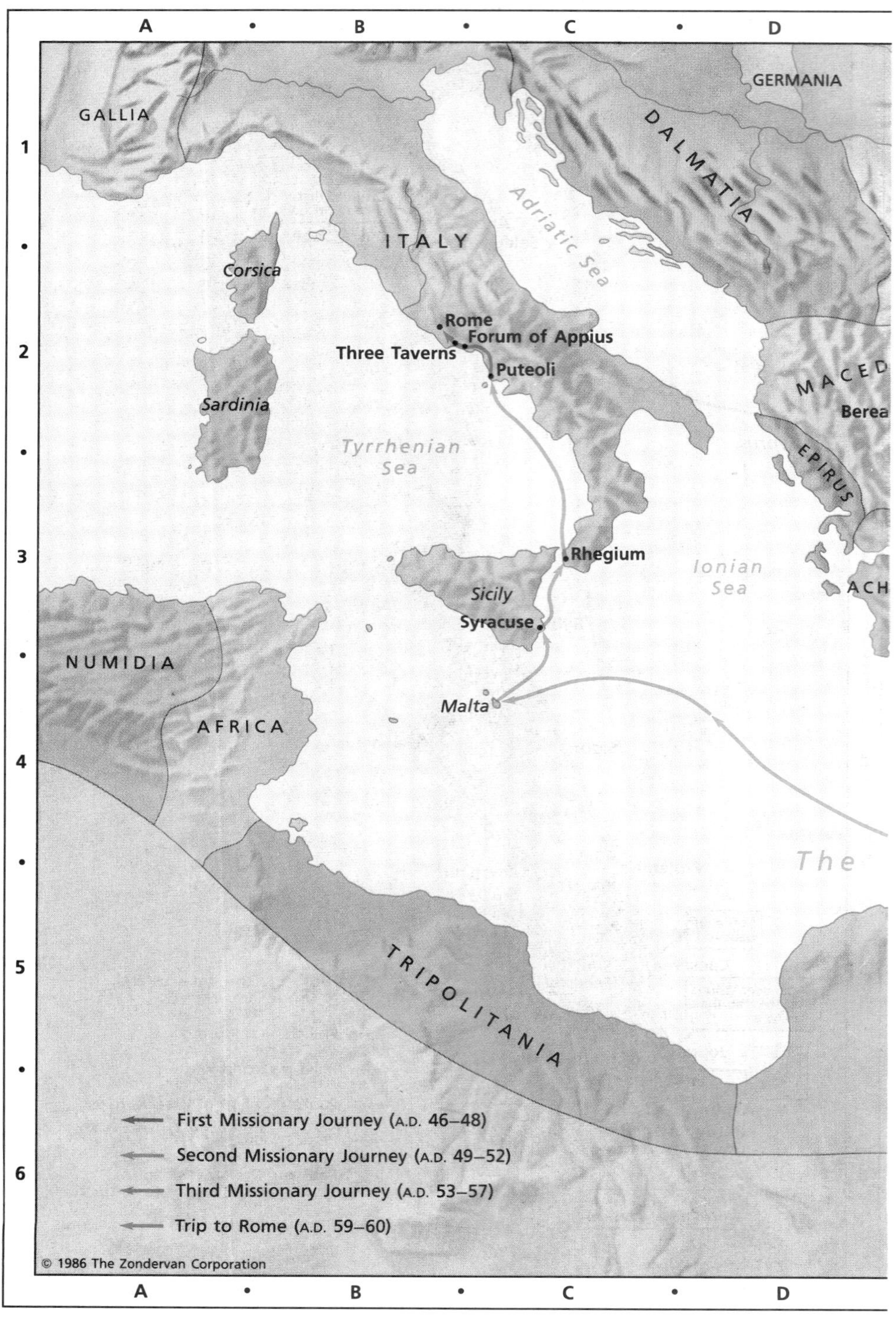
A
B
C
D
1
2
3
4
5
6
GERMANIA
GALLIA
DALMATIA
Adriatic Sea
ITALY
Corsica
Rome
Forum of Appius
Three Taverns
Puteoli
Sardinia
MACED
Berea
EPIRUS
Tyrrhenian Sea
Rhegium
Ionian Sea
ACH
Sicily
Syracuse
NUMIDIA
Malta
AFRICA
The
TRIPOLITANIA
First Missionary Journey (A.D. 46–48)
Second Missionary Journey (A.D. 49–52)
Third Missionary Journey (A.D. 53–57)
Trip to Rome (A.D. 59–60)
© 1986 The Zondervan Corporation

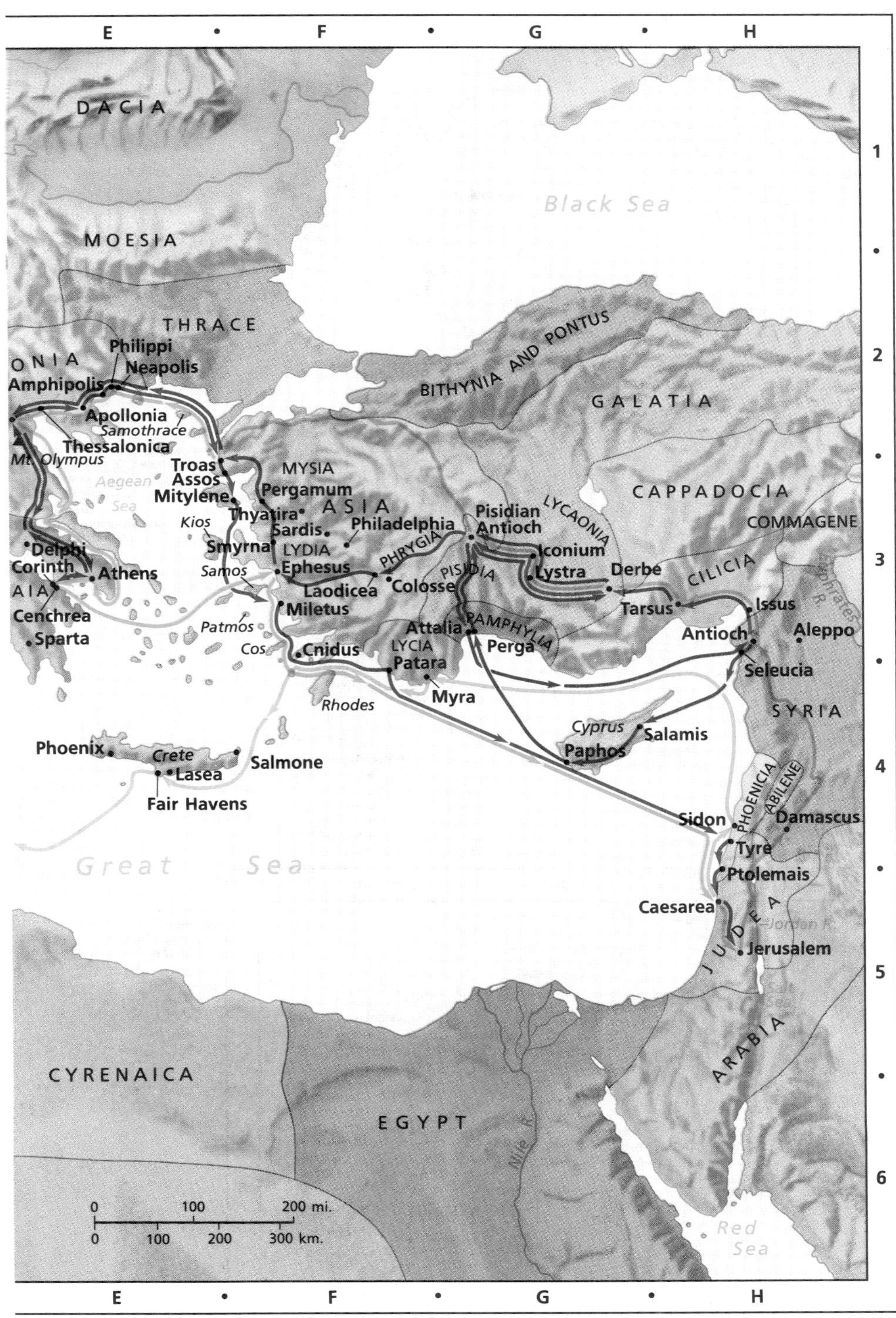
E
F
G
H
1
2
3
4
5
6
DACIA
MOESIA
THRACE
Black Sea
BITHYNIA AND PONTUS
GALATIA
CAPPADOCIA
COMMAGENE
LYCAONIA
CILICIA
Philippi
Neapolis
Amphipolis
Apollonia
Samothrace
Thessalonica
Mt. Olympus
Troas
Assos
Mitylene
Aegean Sea
MYSIA
Pergamum
ASIA
Thyatira
Sardis
LYDIA
Kios
Smyrna
Delphi
Corinth
Athens
Cenchrea
Sparta
Samos
Ephesus
Philadelphia
PHRYGIA
Laodicea
Colosse
Pisidian Antioch
Iconium
Lystra
Derbe
Tarsus
PISIDIA
Miletus
Patmos
Cos
Cnidus
LYCIA
Patara
Myra
Attalia
PAMPHYLIA
Perga
Issus
Antioch
Aleppo
Seleucia
SYRIA
Rhodes
Cyprus
Salamis
Paphos
Phoenix
Crete
Lasea
Salmone
Fair Havens
Sidon
PHOENICIA
ABILENE
Damascus
Tyre
Ptolemais
Caesarea
JUDEA
Jordan R.
Jerusalem
Salt Sea
ARABIA
Euphrates R.
Great Sea
CYRENAICA
EGYPT
Nile R.
Red Sea
0 100 200 mi.
0 100 200 300 km.

Map 12: THE WORLD TODAY

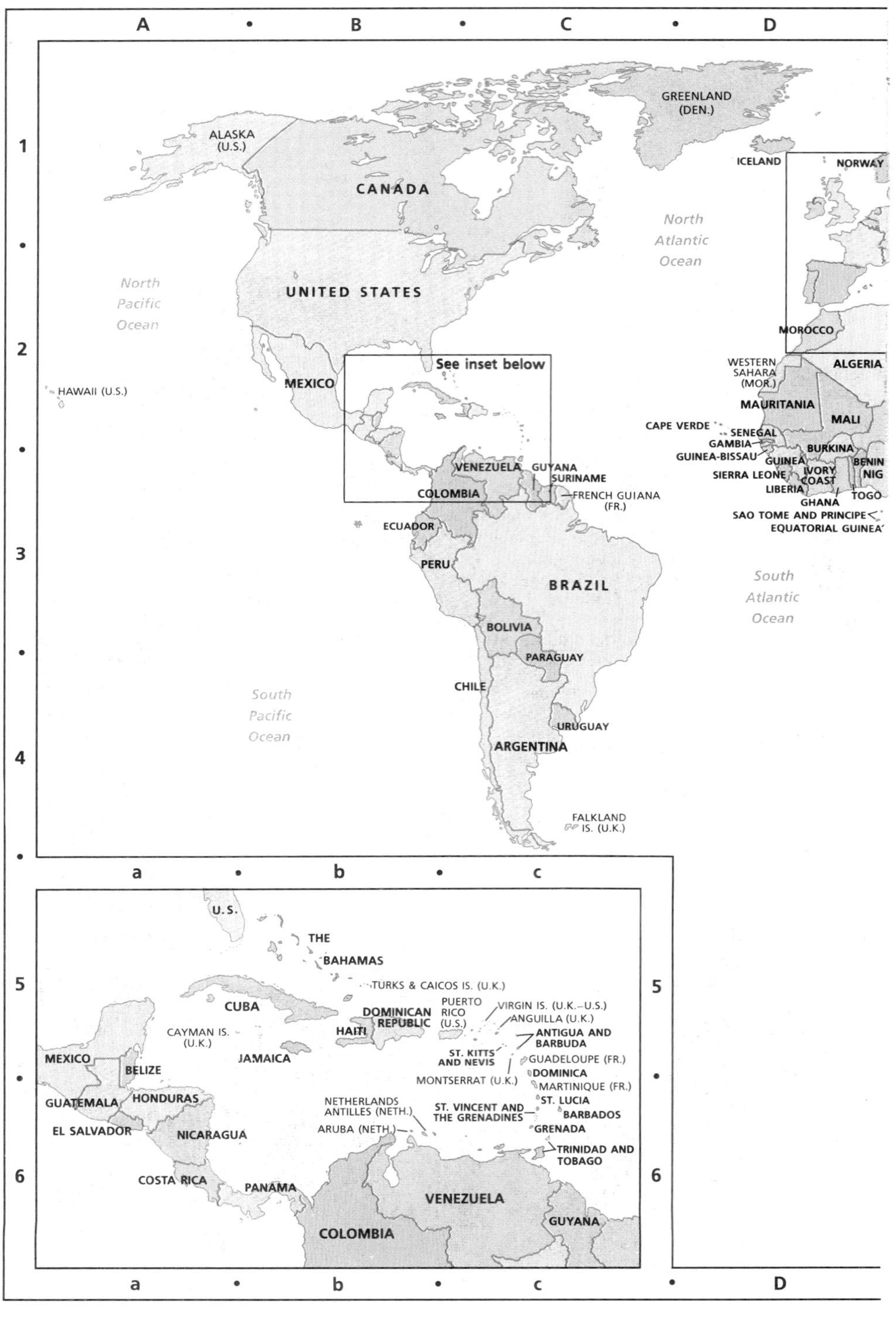

A
B
C
D
1
2
3
4
5
6
GREENLAND (DEN.)
ALASKA (U.S.)
ICELAND
NORWAY
CANADA
North Atlantic Ocean
North Pacific Ocean
UNITED STATES
MOROCCO
See inset below
WESTERN SAHARA (MOR.)
ALGERIA
MEXICO
HAWAII (U.S.)
MAURITANIA
MALI
CAPE VERDE
SENEGAL
GAMBIA
GUINEA-BISSAU
BURKINA
GUINEA
BENIN
SIERRA LEONE
IVORY COAST
NIG
LIBERIA
TOGO
GHANA
SAO TOME AND PRINCIPE
EQUATORIAL GUINEA
VENEZUELA
GUYANA
SURINAME
FRENCH GUIANA (FR.)
COLOMBIA
ECUADOR
PERU
BRAZIL
South Atlantic Ocean
BOLIVIA
PARAGUAY
CHILE
South Pacific Ocean
URUGUAY
ARGENTINA
FALKLAND IS. (U.K.)
a
b
c
U.S.
THE BAHAMAS
TURKS & CAICOS IS. (U.K.)
CUBA
DOMINICAN REPUBLIC
PUERTO RICO (U.S.)
VIRGIN IS. (U.K.–U.S.)
ANGUILLA (U.K.)
CAYMAN IS. (U.K.)
HAITI
ANTIGUA AND BARBUDA
JAMAICA
ST. KITTS AND NEVIS
GUADELOUPE (FR.)
MEXICO
BELIZE
DOMINICA
MONTSERRAT (U.K.)
MARTINIQUE (FR.)
GUATEMALA
HONDURAS
ST. LUCIA
NETHERLANDS ANTILLES (NETH.)
ST. VINCENT AND THE GRENADINES
BARBADOS
EL SALVADOR
NICARAGUA
ARUBA (NETH.)
GRENADA
TRINIDAD AND TOBAGO
COSTA RICA
PANAMA
VENEZUELA
GUYANA
COLOMBIA

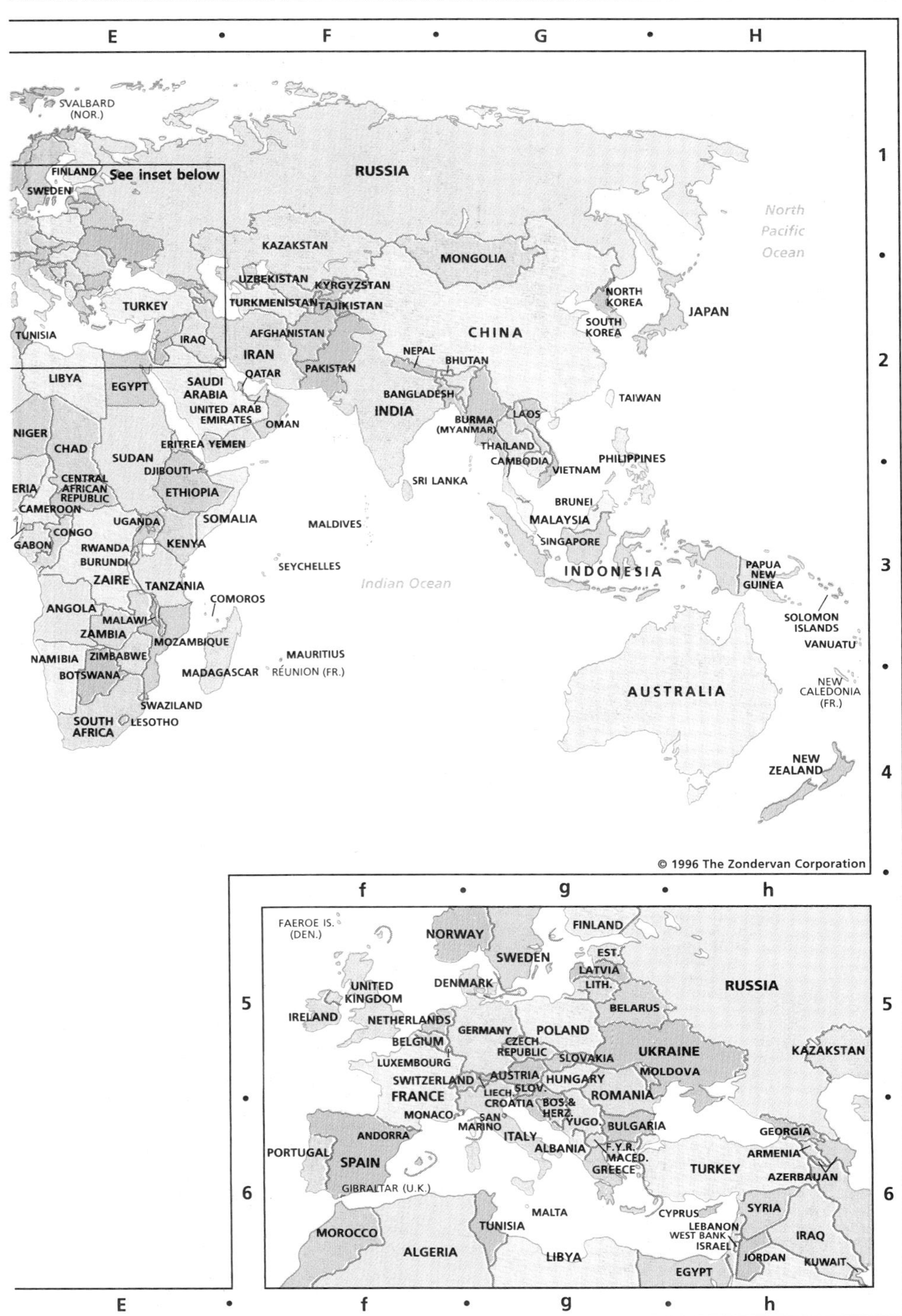

E
F
G
H
1
2
3
4
SVALBARD (NOR.)
FINLAND
See inset below
SWEDEN
RUSSIA
North Pacific Ocean
KAZAKSTAN
MONGOLIA
UZBEKISTAN
KYRGYZSTAN
TURKMENISTAN
TAJIKISTAN
TURKEY
NORTH KOREA
SOUTH KOREA
JAPAN
TUNISIA
IRAQ
AFGHANISTAN
CHINA
IRAN
NEPAL
BHUTAN
PAKISTAN
LIBYA
EGYPT
QATAR
SAUDI ARABIA
BANGLADESH
TAIWAN
UNITED ARAB EMIRATES
INDIA
OMAN
BURMA (MYANMAR)
LAOS
NIGER
CHAD
SUDAN
ERITREA
YEMEN
THAILAND
CAMBODIA
VIETNAM
PHILIPPINES
DJIBOUTI
CENTRAL AFRICAN REPUBLIC
ETHIOPIA
SRI LANKA
CAMEROON
BRUNEI
UGANDA
SOMALIA
MALAYSIA
CONGO
MALDIVES
GABON
RWANDA
KENYA
SINGAPORE
BURUNDI
SEYCHELLES
INDONESIA
PAPUA NEW GUINEA
ZAIRE
TANZANIA
Indian Ocean
COMOROS
ANGOLA
MALAWI
SOLOMON ISLANDS
ZAMBIA
MOZAMBIQUE
VANUATU
NAMIBIA
ZIMBABWE
MAURITIUS
BOTSWANA
MADAGASCAR
RÉUNION (FR.)
NEW CALEDONIA (FR.)
AUSTRALIA
SWAZILAND
SOUTH AFRICA
LESOTHO
NEW ZEALAND
© 1996 The Zondervan Corporation
f
g
h
5
6
FAEROE IS. (DEN.)
NORWAY
FINLAND
SWEDEN
EST.
LATVIA
LITH.
RUSSIA
UNITED KINGDOM
DENMARK
IRELAND
BELARUS
NETHERLANDS
GERMANY
POLAND
BELGIUM
CZECH REPUBLIC
UKRAINE
KAZAKSTAN
LUXEMBOURG
SLOVAKIA
MOLDOVA
SWITZERLAND
AUSTRIA
HUNGARY
FRANCE
LIECH.
SLOV.
ROMANIA
CROATIA
BOS.& HERZ.
MONACO
SAN MARINO
YUGO.
BULGARIA
ANDORRA
ITALY
GEORGIA
PORTUGAL
ALBANIA
F.Y.R. MACED.
ARMENIA
SPAIN
GREECE
TURKEY
AZERBAIJAN
GIBRALTAR (U.K.)
MALTA
CYPRUS
SYRIA
TUNISIA
LEBANON
WEST BANK
ISRAEL
IRAQ
MOROCCO
ALGERIA
LIBYA
JORDAN
KUWAIT
EGYPT

Map 13: ROMAN EMPIRE

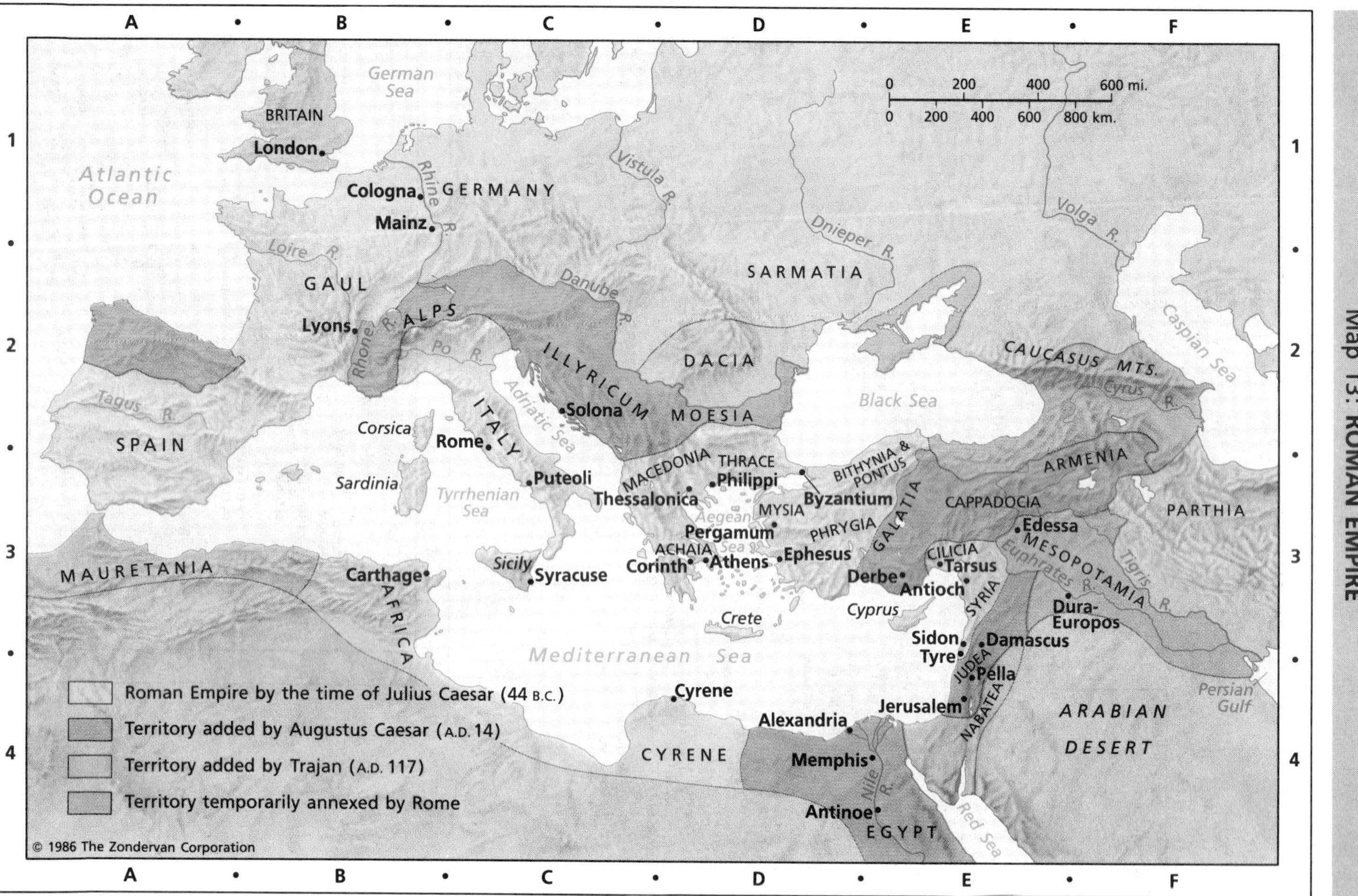

PERSONAL STUDY NOTES

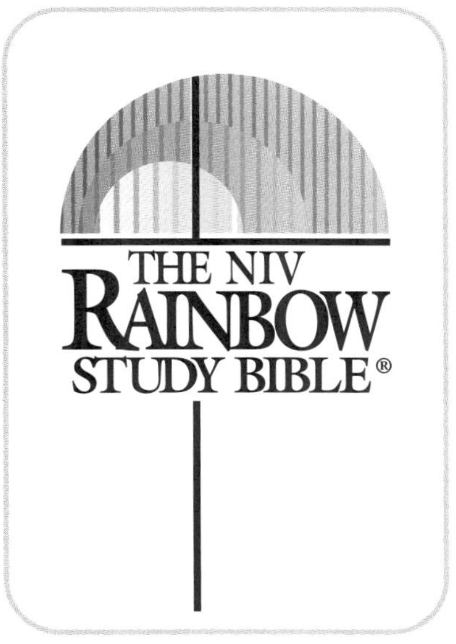

Personal Study Notes